VINTAGE 2020 ALMANAC

NUMBER 6

THE HOBBY'S MOST RELIABLE AND RELIED UPON SOURCE

Founder: Dr. James Beckett III
Edited by the staff of Beckett Media

BECKETT is a registered trademark of BECKETT MEDIA LLC, DALLAS, TEXAS
Manufactured in the United States of America | Published by Beckett Media LLC

Beckett Media LLC
4635 McEwen Dr.
Dallas, TX 75244
(972) 991-6657
www.beckett.com

First Printing
ISBN: 978-1-936681-42-6

CONTENTS

VINTAGE MINOR LEAGUES

Basketball

COLLEGE/DRAFT PICKS

Football

Hockey

HOW TO USE AND CONDITION GUIDE

Welcome to the sixth edition of the Vintage Almanac, a book created to bring together card checklists and pricing for the four core sports from our traditional single sport annuals. Beckett Price Guides have been successful where other attempts have failed because they are complete, current, and valid. The prices were added to the card lists just prior to printing and reflect the authors' valuations based upon analysis of real market sales data, and not opinions or desires. Data has been assembled from information obtained from memorabilia conventions and shows, sports card shops, online trading, auction results and other firsthand reports of realized sales.

What is the best price guide available on the market today? Of course sellers will prefer the price guide with the highest prices, while buyers will naturally prefer the one with the lower prices. Accuracy, however, is the true test. Compared to other price guides, this edition may not always have the highest or lowest values, but the accuracy of both our checklists and pricing – produced with the utmost integrity – have made our reference books the most widely used guides in the industry.

To facilitate your use of this book, please read the complete introductory section before going on to the pricing pages, paying special attention to the section on grading and card conditions, as the condition of the card greatly affects its value. We hope you find the book both interesting and useful in your collecting pursuits.

ADVERTISING

Within this Price Guide you will find advertisements for sports memorabilia material, mail order, and retail sports collectibles establishments. All advertisements were accepted in good faith based on the reputation of the advertiser. However, neither the author, publisher, the distributors, nor the other advertisers in this edition accept any responsibility for any particular advertiser not complying with the terms of his or her ad.

HOW TO COLLECT

Each collection is personal and reflects the individuality of its owner. There are no set rules on how to collect cards. Since card collecting is a hobby or leisure pastime, what you collect, how much you collect, and how much time and money you spend collecting are entirely up to you. The funds you have available for collecting and your own personal taste should determine how you collect.

It is impossible to collect every card ever produced. Therefore, beginners as well as intermediate and advanced collectors usually specialize in some way. One of the reasons this hobby is popular is that individual collectors can define and tailor their collecting methods to match their own tastes.

Many collectors select complete sets from particular years, acquire only certain players, some collectors are only interested in the first cards or Rookie Cards of certain players, and others collect cards by team.

Remember, this is a hobby, so pick a style of collecting that appeals to you.

GLOSSARY/LEGEND

Our glossary defines terms most frequently used in the card collecting hobby. Many of these terms are common to other types of sports memorabilia collecting. Some terms may have several meanings depending on the use and context.

Cabinet Card – Popular and highly valuable photographs on thick card stock produced in the 19th and early 20th century.

Checklist – A list of the cards contained in a particular set. The list is always in numerical order if the cards are numbered. Some unnumbered sets are artificially numbered in alphabetical order or by team.

CL – Checklist card. A card that lists, in order, the cards and players in the set or series.

CO – Coach.

Common Card – The typical card of any set. It has no premium value accruing from the

Continued on page 10

UNDERSTANDING CARD VALUES

Why are some cards more valuable than others? Obviously, the economic laws of supply and demand are applicable to card collecting just as they are to any other field where a commodity is bought, sold or traded in a free, unregulated market.

Supply (the number of cards available on the market) is less than the total number of cards originally produced since attrition diminishes that original quantity. Each year a percentage of cards is typically thrown away, destroyed or otherwise lost to collectors. This percentage is much, much smaller today than it was in the past because more and more people have become increasingly aware of the value of their cards.

For those who collect only Mint condition cards, the supply of older cards can be quite small indeed. In the early days of the hobby, collectors were not so conscious of the need to preserve the condition of their cards. For this reason, it is difficult to know exactly how many 1953 Topps are currently available, Mint or otherwise. It is generally accepted that there are fewer 1953 Topps available than 1963, 1973 or 1983 Topps cards. If demand were equal for each of these sets, the law of supply and demand would increase the price for the least available sets. Demand, however, is never equal for all sets, so price correlations can be complicated. The demand for a card is influenced by many factors. These include the age of the card, the number of cards printed, the player(s) portrayed on the card, the attractiveness and popularity of the set and the physical condition of the card.

In general, the older the card, the fewer the number of the cards printed, the more famous, popular and talented the player, the more attractive and popular the set, and the better the condition of the card, the higher the value of the card will be. There are exceptions to all but one of these factors: the condition of the card. Given two cards similar in all respects except condition, the one in the best condition will always be valued higher.

While those guidelines help to establish the value of a card, the countless exceptions and peculiarities make any simple, direct mathematical formula to determine card values impossible.

WHAT THE COLUMNS MEAN

The LO and HI columns reflect a range of current retail selling prices and are listed in U.S. dollars. The HI column represents the typical full retail selling price while the LO column represents the lowest price one could expect to find through extensive shopping. Both columns represent the same condition for the card listed. Keep in mind that market conditions can change quickly up and down based on extreme levels of demand.

PRICING PREMIUMS

Some cards can trade at premium price levels compared to values listed in this issue. Those include but are not limited to: cards of players who became hot since this book went to press, regional stars or fan favorites in high demand locally and memorabilia cards with unusually dramatic swatches or patches.

ONLY A REFERENCE

The data and pricing information contained within this publication is intended for reference only and is not to be used as an endorsement of any specific product(s) or as a recommendation to buy or sell any product(s). Beckett's goal is to provide the most accurate and

GLOSSARY/LEGEND

Continued from page 8

subject matter, numerical scarcity, popular demand, or anomaly.

COR – Corrected.

Die-cut – A card with part of its stock partially cut, allowing one or more parts to be folded or removed. After removal or appropriate folding, the remaining part of the card can frequently be made to stand up.

DP – Draft pick or double print. A double print is a card that was printed in double the quantity compared to other cards in the same series.

ERR – Error card. A card with erroneous information, spelling or depiction on either side of the card. Most errors are not corrected by the manufacturer.

High Number – The cards in the last series of a set in a year in which such high-numbered cards were printed or distributed in significantly less amounts than the lower numbered cards. Not all years have high numbers in terms of this definition.

Continued on page 12

verifiable information in the industry. However, Beckett cannot guarantee the accuracy of all data published. Typographical errors occasionally occur and unverifiable information may reach print from time to time. Buyers and sellers of sports collectibles should be aware of this and handle their personal transactions at their own risk. If you discover an error or misprint in this book, please notify us via email at customerservice@beckett.com

MULTIPLIERS

Some parallel sets are listed with multipliers to provide values of unlisted cards. Multiplier ranges (i.e. 10X to 20X HI) apply only to the HI column. Example: If basic-issue card A or the insert card in question lists for 20 to 50 cents, and the multiplier is "20X to 40X HI", then the parallel version of card A or the insert card in question is valued at $10 to $20. Please note that the term "basic card" used in the Price Guide refers to a player's standard regular-issue card. A "basic card" cannot be an insert or parallel card.

Condition Guide

Much of the value of your card is dependent on the condition or "grade" of your card. Prices in this issue reflect the highest raw condition (i.e. not professionally graded by a third party) of the card most commonly found at shows, shops, on the internet and right out of the pack for brand new releases. This generally means Near Mint-Mint condition for modern era cards. Use the chart below as a guide to estimate the value of your cards in a variety of condition using the prices found in this Annual. A complete condition guide follows.

The most widely used grades are defined on page 14. Obviously, many cards will not perfectly fit one of the definitions. Therefore, categories between the major grades known as in-between grades are used, such as Good to Very Good (G-Vg), Very Good to Excellent (VgEx), and Excellent-Mint to Near Mint (ExMt-NrMt). Such grades indicate a card with all qualities of the lower category but with at least a few qualities of the higher category.

Unopened packs, boxes and factory-collated sets are considered mint in their unknown (and presumed perfect) state. Once opened, however, each card can be graded (and valued) in its own right by taking into account any defects that may be present in spite of the fact that the card has never been handled.

GENERAL CARD FLAWS

Centering

Current centering terminology uses numbers representing the percentage of border on either side of the main design. Obviously, centering is diminished in importance for borderless cards.

Slightly Off-Center (60/40)

A slightly off-center card is one that upon close inspection is found to have one border bigger than the opposite border. This degree once was offensive to only purists, but now some hobbyists try to avoid cards that are anything other than perfectly centered.

Off-Center (70/30)

An off-center card has one border that is noticeably more than twice as wide as the opposite border.

Badly Off-Center (80/20 or worse)

A badly off-center card has virtually no border on one side of the card.

GLOSSARY/LEGEND

Continued from page 10

HOF – Hall of Fame or a card that pictures of Hall of Famer (HOFer).

HOR – Horizonal pose on a card as opposed to the standart vertical orientation found on most cards.

IA – In action.

Insert – A card or any other sports collectible contained and sold in the same package along with a card or cards from a major set. An insert card may or may not be numbered in the same sequence as the major set. Many times the inserts are randomly inserted in packs.

Mini – A small card; for example a 1975 Topps card of identical desing but smaller dimensions than the regular 1975 Topps issue.

NNO – Unnumbered.

Premium – A card that is obtained in conjunction with, or redemption for, another card or product. The premium is not packaged in the same unit as the primary item.

Continued on page 14

BECKETT LIVE PRESENTS

POWERED BY:

Pastime Marketplace
www.pastimemarketplace.com

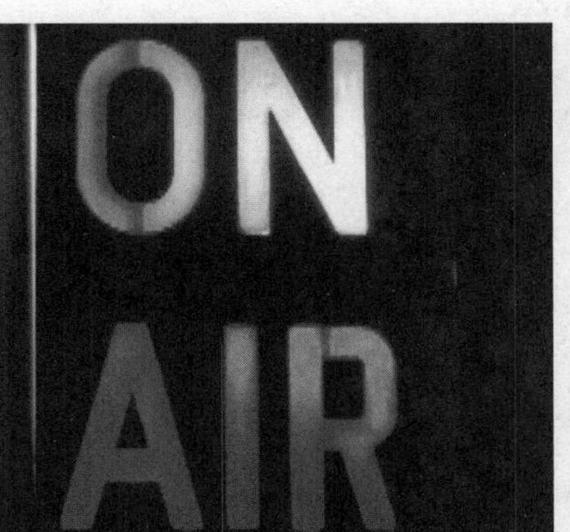

TUESDAY, WEDNESDAY AND THURSDAY AT 7 PM CST ON:

Miscut

A miscut card actually shows part of the adjacent card in its larger border and consequently a corresponding amount of its card is cut off.

Corner Wear

Corner wear is the most scrutinized grading criteria in the hobby.

Corner with a slight touch of wear

The corner still is sharp, but there is a slight touch of wear showing. On a dark-bordered card, this shows as a dot of white.

Fuzzy corner

The corner still comes to a point, but the point has just begun to fray. A slightly "dinged" corner is considered the same as a fuzzy corner.

Slightly rounded corner

The fraying of the corner has increased to where there is only a hint of a point. Mild layering may be evident. A "dinged" corner is considered the same as a slightly rounded corner.

Rounded corner

The point is completely gone. Some layering is noticeable.

Badly rounded corner

The corner is completely round and rough. Severe layering is evident.

Creases

A third common defect is the crease. The degree of creasing in a card is difficult to show in a drawing or picture. On giving the specific condition of an expensive card for sale, the seller should note any creases additionally. Creases can be categorized as to severity according to the following scale.

Light Crease

A light crease is a crease that is barely noticeable upon close inspection. In fact, when cards are in plastic sheets or holders, a light crease may not be seen (until the card is taken out of the holder). A light crease on the front is much more serious than a light crease on the card back only.

Medium Crease

A medium crease is noticeable when held and studied at arm's length by the naked eye, but does not overly detract from the appearance of the card. It is an obvious crease, but not one that breaks the picture surface of the card.

Heavy Crease: A heavy crease is one that has torn or broken through the card's surface, e.g., puts a tear in the photo surface.

ALTERATIONS

Deceptive Trimming

This occurs when someone alters the card in order to shave off edge wear, to improve the sharpness of the corners, or to improve centering — obviously their objective is to falsely increase the perceived value of the card to an unsuspecting buyer. The shrinkage usually is evident only if the trimmed card is compared to an adjacent full-sized card or if the trimmed card is itself measured.

Obvious Trimming

Trimming is noticeable. It is usually performed by non-collectors who give no thought to the present or future value of their cards.

Deceptively Retouched Borders

This occurs when the borders (especially on those cards with dark borders) are touched up on the edges and corners with magic marker or crayons of appropriate color in order to make the card appear to be Mint.

GLOSSARY/LEGEND

Continued from page 12

RC – Rookie Card. Typically the first card(s) of a player in a major mainstream base set from his rookie season or the first year in which he appeared on cards.

ROY – Rookie of the Year.

Series – The entire set of cards issued by a particular manufacturer in a particular year. Within a particular set, a series can refer to a group of consecutively numbered cards printed at the same time.

Set – One of each of the entire run of cards of the same type produced by a particular manufacturer during a single year.

Skip-numbered – A set that has many unissued card numbers between the lowest and highest number in the set. A major set in which only a few numbers were not printed is not considered to be skip-numbered.

SP – Single or Short Print. A short print is a card that was printed in less quantity compared to the other cards in the same series.

Continued on page 15

GLOSSARY/LEGEND

Continued from page 14

TC – Team card.

TP – Triple print. A card that was printed in triple the quantity compared to the other cards in the same series.

UER – Uncorrected error.

VAR – Variation card. One of two or more cards from the same series, with the same card number, that differ from one and other in some way. This sometimes occurs when the manufacture notices an error in one or more of the cards, corrects the mistake, and then resumes the printing process. In some cases, on of the variations may be relatively scarce.

Note: Nearly all other abbreviations signify various subsets (i.e. WS in the 1960s and 1970s Topps sets is short for World Series for example).

Miscellaneous Card Flaws

The following are common minor flaws that, depending on severity, lower a card's condition by one to four grades and often render it no better than Excellent-Mint: bubbles (lumps in surface), gum and wax stains, diamond cutting (slanted borders), notching, off-centered backs, paper wrinkles, scratched-off cartoons or puzzles on back, rubber band marks, scratches, surface impressions and warping.

The following are common serious flaws that, depending on severity, lower a card's condition at least four grades and often render it no better than Good: chemical or sun fading, erasure marks, mildew, miscutting (severe off-centering), holes, bleached or retouched borders, tape marks, tears, trimming, water or coffee stains and writing.

GRADES

Mint (Mt)

A card with no flaws or wear. The card has four perfect corners, 55/45 or better centering from top to bottom and from left to right, original gloss, smooth edges and original color borders. A Mint card does not have print spots, color or focus imperfections.

Near Mint-Mint (NrMt-Mt)

A card with one minor flaw. Any one of the following would lower a Mint card to Near Mint-Mint: one corner with a slight touch of wear, barely noticeable print spots, color or focus imperfections. The card must have 60/40 or better centering in both directions, original gloss, smooth edges and original color border.

Near Mint (NrMt)

A card with one minor flaw. Any one of the following would lower a Mint card to Near Mint: one fuzzy corner or two to four corners with slight touches of wear, 70/30 to 60/40 centering, slightly rough edges, minor print spots, color or focus imperfections. The card must have original gloss and original color borders.

Excellent-Mint (ExMt)

A card with two or three fuzzy, but not rounded, corners and centering no worse than 80/20. The card may have no more than two of the following: slightly rough edges, slightly discolored borders, minor print spots, color or focus imperfections. The card must have original gloss.

Excellent (Ex)

A card with four fuzzy but definitely not rounded corners and centering no worse than 70/30. The card may have a small amount of original gloss lost, rough edges, slightly discolored borders and minor print spots, color or focus imperfections.

Very Good (Vg)

A card that has been handled but not abused: slightly rounded corners with slight layering, slight notching on edges, a significant amount of gloss lost from the surface but no scuffing and moderate discoloration of borders. The card may have a few light creases.

Good (G), Fair (F), Poor (P)

A well-worn, mishandled or abused card: badly rounded and layered corners, scuffing, most or all original gloss missing, seriously discolored borders, moderate or heavy creases, and one or more serious flaws. The grade of Good, Fair or Poor depends on the severity of wear and flaws. Good, Fair and Poor cards generally are used only as fillers.

Baseball Card Price Guide

1906 A's Lincoln Publishing Postcards

These ornate postcards were issued by the Philadelphia A's to honor the pennant winning team of 1905. The fronts have the words "American League Champions" on the top along with the years 1905 and 1906. The backs are blank except for the words post card. These cards were issued by the Lincoln Publishing Co. The cards are unnumbered so we have sequenced them in alphabetical order.

COMPLETE SET (20)	5,000.00	10,000.00
1 Chief Bender	500.00	1,000.00
2 Andy Coakley	200.00	400.00
3 Lave Cross	200.00	400.00
4 Monte Cross	200.00	400.00
5 Harry Davis	200.00	400.00
6 Jimmy Dygert	200.00	400.00
7 Topsy Hartsel	200.00	400.00
8 Weldon Henley	200.00	400.00
9 Danny Hoffman	200.00	400.00
10 John Knight	200.00	400.00
11 Bris Lord	200.00	400.00
12 Connie Mack MG	800.00	1,500.00
13 Danny Murphy	200.00	400.00
14 Joe Myers	200.00	400.00
15 Rube Oldring	200.00	400.00
16 Eddie Plank	600.00	1,200.00
17 Mike Powers	200.00	400.00
18 Ossie Schreckengost	200.00	400.00
19 Ralph Seybold	200.00	400.00
20 Rube Waddell	600.00	1,200.00

1911 A's Fireside T208

The cards in this 18-card set of color lithographs measure 1 1/2" by 2 5/8"; the cards were marketed in 1911 by Fireside Cigarettes honoring the 1910 World Champion Philadelphia Athletics. This tobacco brand was a product of the Thomas Cullivan Company of Syracuse, New York. The same front designs were also used in the D359 set by Rochester Baking. The players have been alphabetized and numbered for reference in the checklist below since the cards are unnumbered.

COMPLETE SET (18)	12,500.00	25,000.00
1 Frank Baker	5,000.00	10,000.00
2 Jack Barry	1,250.00	2,500.00
3 Chief Bender	5,000.00	10,000.00
4 Eddie Collins	6,000.00	12,000.00
5 Harry Davis	1,250.00	2,500.00
6 Jimmy Dygert	1,250.00	2,500.00
7 Topsy Hartsel	1,250.00	2,500.00
8 Harry Krause	1,250.00	2,500.00
9 John Lapp	1,250.00	2,500.00
10 Paddy Livingston	1,250.00	2,500.00
11 Bris Lord	1,250.00	2,500.00
12 Connie Mack MG	5,000.00	10,000.00
13 Cy Morgan	1,250.00	2,500.00
14 Danny Murphy	1,250.00	2,500.00
15 Rube Oldring	1,250.00	2,500.00
16 Eddie Plank	6,000.00	12,000.00
17 Amos Strunk	1,250.00	2,500.00
18 Ira Thomas	1,250.00	2,500.00

1911 A's Monarch Typewriter

These postcards, which measure approximately 5 3/4" x 3 5/8" feature members of the Philadelphia Athletics. The front has a small advertisement for Monarch Typewriters along with the player's photo and his name on the bottom. The back has a message from Connie Mack along with results of all the World Series from 1903 to 1910. There may be more cards in this set.

COMPLETE SET (2)	600.00	1,200.00
1 Chief Bender	400.00	800.00
2 Eddie Plank	400.00	800.00

1911 A's Rochester/Williams Baking D359

This set measures approximately 1 1/2" by 2 5/8" and features members of the Philadelphia A's who had won the 1910 World Series. Over the player's photo is a "World Championship 1910" notation. Cards can be found with both Rochester and Williams backs.

1 Frank Baker	1,500.00	3,000.00
2 Jack Barry	1,000.00	2,000.00
3 Chief Bender	1,500.00	3,000.00
4 Eddie Collins	2,000.00	4,000.00
5 Harry Davis	1,500.00	3,000.00
6 Jimmy Dygert	750.00	1,500.00
7 Topsy Hartsel	750.00	1,500.00
8 Harry Krause	750.00	1,500.00
9 Jack Lapp	750.00	1,500.00
10 Paddy Livingston	750.00	1,500.00
11 Bristol Lord	750.00	1,500.00
12 Connie Mack MG	1,500.00	3,000.00
13 Cy Morgan	750.00	1,500.00
14 Danny Murphy	750.00	1,500.00
15 Rube Oldring	750.00	1,500.00
16 Eddie Plank	1,500.00	3,000.00
17 Amos Strunk	750.00	1,500.00
18 Ira Thomas 1910 above head	750.00	1,500.00
19 Ira Thomas 1910 on side	750.00	1,500.00

1911 A's Stevens Firearms

These blank-backed advertising blotters, which measure 6 1/8" by 3 1/2", feature members of the World Champion Philadelphia Athlethics. The front has a photo of the player on the left and then some advertising for Stevens Firearms on the right. Since these cards are unnumbered, we have sequenced them in alphabetical order.

COMPLETE SET (10)	2,500.00	5,000.00
1 Frank Baker	500.00	1,000.00
2 Jack Barry	250.00	500.00
3 Chief Bender	500.00	1,000.00
4 Eddie Collins	500.00	1,000.00
5 Harry Davis	250.00	500.00
6 Bris Lord	250.00	500.00
7 Connie Mack MG	500.00	1,000.00
8 Danny Murphy	250.00	500.00
9 Rube Oldring	250.00	500.00
10 Ira Thomas	250.00	500.00

1929 A's Villa

Little is known about these postcard size cards issued in the Philadelphia area around 1929. The cards feature a portrait of the player on the front with their name and position on the bottom right. The back mentions a free Saturday matinee on October 12th. The villa logo is on the bottom. This listing may be incomplete so all additions are appreciated.

COMPLETE SET (5)	600.00	1,200.00
1 Eddie Collins	300.00	600.00
2 Jimmy Dykes	100.00	200.00
3 Mule Haas	100.00	200.00
4 Bing Miller	100.00	200.00
5 Rube Walberg	100.00	200.00

1930 A's Becker

Similar to the 1929 A's Villa cards, these postcard size cards feature members of the Philadelphia A's. They were used to promote the local Becker Brothers Theatre. The front have a player photo while the back has a movie schedule. Since these cards are unnumbered we have sequenced them in alphabetical order.

COMPLETE SET (5)	500.00	1,000.00
1 Max Bishop	50.00	100.00
2 Mickey Cochrane	125.00	250.00
3 Sammy Hale	50.00	100.00
4 Jimmie Foxx	200.00	400.00
5 Al Simmons	125.00	250.00

1942 A's Team Issue

This 38-card set of the 1942 Athletics features black-and-white player posted photos with white borders. The backs are blank. The cards are unnumbered and checklisted below in alphabetical order.

COMPLETE SET (38)	200.00	400.00
1 Johnnie Babich	5.00	10.00
2 Bill Beckman	5.00	10.00
3 Herman Besse	5.00	10.00
4 Lena Blackburne CO	5.00	10.00
5 Buddy Blair	5.00	10.00
6 Al Brancato	5.00	10.00
7 Earle Brucker	5.00	10.00
8 Fred Caligiuri	5.00	10.00
9 Jim Castiglia	5.00	10.00
10 Russell Christopher	5.00	10.00
11 Eddie Collins Jr.	5.00	10.00
12 Lawrence Davis	5.00	10.00
13 Richard Fowler	5.00	10.00
14 Bob Harris	5.00	10.00
15 Lum Harris	6.00	12.00
16 Frank Hayes	5.00	10.00
17 Bob Johnson	7.50	15.00
18 Bill Knickerbocker	5.00	10.00
19 Jack Knott	5.00	10.00
20 Mike Kreevich	5.00	10.00
21 Connie Mack MG	12.50	25.00
22 Earle Mack	5.00	10.00
23 Felix Mackiewicz	5.00	10.00
24 Phil Marchildon	6.00	12.00
25 Benny McCoy	5.00	10.00
26 Dee Miles	5.00	10.00
27 Tex Shirley	5.00	10.00
28 Shibe Park	5.00	10.00
29 Dick Siebert	5.00	10.00
30 Al Simmons CO	12.50	25.00
31 Pete Suder	5.00	10.00
32 Bob Swift	5.00	10.00
33 Elmer Valo	5.00	10.00
34 Porter Vaughn	5.00	10.00
35 Harold Wagner	5.00	10.00
36 Jack Wallaesa	5.00	10.00
37 Roger Wolff	5.00	10.00
38 1942 Athletics Team	6.00	12.00

1943 A's Team Issue

This 28-card set of the Philadelphia Athletics was issued by the club and features 7" by 10" black-and-white player portraits in white borders and with blank backs. The cards are unnumbered and checklisted below in alphabetical order. The team picture (card number 1) measures 7 1/2" by 10 1/2". The two Connie Mack cards also measure differently than the other cards.

COMPLETE SET (28)	150.00	300.00
1 1943 Athletics Team	15.00	30.00
2 Tal Abernathy	5.00	10.00
3 Orie Arntzen	5.00	10.00
4 Herman Besse	5.00	10.00
5 Don Black	5.00	10.00
6 James Blackburne	5.00	10.00
7 Earle Brucker	5.00	10.00
8 Russ Christopher	5.00	10.00
9 Bobby Estalella	5.00	10.00
10 Everett Fagan	5.00	10.00
11 Jesse Flores	5.00	10.00
12 Irv Hall	5.00	10.00
13 Luman Harris	6.00	12.00
14 Sam Loury	5.00	10.00
15 Connie Mack No border; facsimile autograph	15.00	30.00
16 Connie Mack MG	15.00	30.00
17 Earle Mack CO	5.00	10.00
18 Eddie Mayo	5.00	10.00
19 Dick Siebert	5.00	10.00
20 Frank Skaff	5.00	10.00
21 Pete Suder	5.00	10.00
22 Bob Swift	5.00	10.00
23 Jim Tyack	5.00	10.00
24 Elmer Valo	6.00	12.00
25 Hal Wagner	5.00	10.00
26 Johnny Welaj	5.00	10.00
27 Jo-Jo White	5.00	10.00
28 Roger Wolff	5.00	10.00

1945 A's Team Issue

This 30-card set of the Philadelphia Athletics was issued by the club and features 7" by 10" black-and-white player portraits in white borders and with blank backs. The cards are unnumbered and checklisted below in alphabetical order.

COMPLETE SET (30)	150.00	300.00
1 1945 Athletics Team Photo	15.00	30.00
2 Charlie Berry CO	5.00	10.00
3 Don Black	5.00	10.00
4 Earle Brucker	5.00	10.00
5 Joe Burns	5.00	10.00
6 Ed Busch	5.00	10.00
7 Russ Christopher	5.00	10.00
8 Joseph Cicero	5.00	10.00
9 Larry Drake	5.00	10.00
10 Hal Epps	5.00	10.00
11 Bobby Estalella	5.00	10.00
12 Jesse Flores	5.00	10.00
13 Mike Garbark	5.00	10.00
14 Charles Gassaway	5.00	10.00
15 Steve Gerkin	5.00	10.00
16 Irv Hall	5.00	10.00
17 Frankie Hayes	5.00	10.00
18 Dave Keefe	5.00	10.00
19 George Kell	12.50	25.00
20 Lou Knerr	5.00	10.00
21 Bill McGhee	5.00	10.00
22 Charles Metro	5.00	10.00
23 Bobo Newsom	6.00	12.00
24 Earle Mack CO	5.00	10.00
25 Hal Peck	5.00	10.00
26 Jim Pruett	5.00	10.00
27 Reidy	5.00	10.00
28 Dick Siebert	5.00	10.00
29 Al Simmons CO	12.50	25.00
30 Bobby Wilkins	5.00	10.00

1946 A's Team Issue

This 15-card set of the Philadelphia Athletics was issued by the club and features 7" by 10" black-and-white player portraits in white borders and with blank backs. The cards are unnumbered and checklisted below in alphabetical order.

COMPLETE SET (15)	100.00	200.00
1 1946 Athletics Team Picture	15.00	30.00
2 Earle Brucker	4.00	8.00
3 Sam Chapman	4.00	8.00
4 Russ Christopher	4.00	8.00
5 Jess Flores	4.00	8.00
6 Richard Fowler	4.00	8.00
7 Luman Harris	5.00	10.00
8 Luther Kaear	4.00	8.00
9 Dave Keefe	4.00	8.00
10 Connie Mack MG	15.00	30.00
11 Phil Marchildon	4.00	8.00
12 Al Simmons	12.50	25.00
13 Pete Suder	4.00	8.00
14 Elmer Valo	6.00	12.00
15 Shibe Park	15.00	30.00

1947 A's Team Issue

This 30-card set of the Philadelphia Athletics measures approximately 7" by 10" and features black-and-white player photos with white borders. The backs are blank. The cards are unnumbered and checklisted below in alphabetical order. These sets were shipped in an team-issued envelope.

COMPLETE SET (30)	125.00	250.00
1 1947 Athletics Team Picture	15.00	30.00
2 Dick Adams	3.00	6.00
3 George Binks	3.00	6.00
4 Earle Brucker	3.00	6.00
5 Sam Chapman	3.00	6.00
6 Russ Christopher	3.00	6.00
7 Joe Coleman	3.00	6.00
8 Bill Dietrich	3.00	6.00
9 Everett Fagan	3.00	6.00
10 Ferris Fain	6.00	12.00
11 Jesse Flores	3.00	6.00
12 Dick Fowler	3.00	6.00
13 Mike Guerra	3.00	6.00
14 Gene Handley	3.00	6.00
15 Eddie Joost	5.00	10.00
16 Dave Keefe	3.00	6.00
17 Bill Knickerbocker	3.00	6.00
18 Connie Mack MG	12.50	25.00
19 Hank Majeski	3.00	6.00
20 Phil Marchildon	3.00	6.00
21 Bill McCahan	3.00	6.00
22 Barney McCosky	3.00	6.00
23 Ray Poole	3.00	6.00
24 Don Richmond	3.00	6.00
25 Buddy Rosar	3.00	6.00
26 Bob Savage	3.00	6.00
27 Carl Scheib	3.00	6.00
28 Al Simmons CO	12.50	25.00
29 Pete Suder	3.00	6.00
30 Elmer Valo	6.00	12.00

1948 A's Team Issue

This 27-card set of the Philadelphia Athletics measures approximately 7" by 10" and features black-and-white player photos with white borders. The backs are blank. The cards are unnumbered and checklisted below in alphabetical order.

COMPLETE SET (27)	100.00	200.00
1 1948 Athletics Team Picture	12.50	25.00
2 Leland Brissie	3.00	6.00
3 Earle Brucker	3.00	6.00
4 Sam Chapman	5.00	10.00
5 Joe Coleman	3.00	6.00
6 Billy DeMars	3.00	6.00
7 Ferris Fain	6.00	12.00
8 Dick Fowler	3.00	6.00
9 Herman Franks	4.00	8.00
10 Mike Guerra	3.00	6.00
11 Charles Harris	3.00	6.00
12 Eddie Joost	5.00	10.00
13 David Keefe	3.00	6.00
14 Connie Mack MG	12.50	25.00
15 Hank Majeski	3.00	6.00
16 Phil Marchildon	3.00	6.00
17 Bill McCahan	3.00	6.00
18 Barney McCosky	3.00	6.00
19 Buddy Rosar	3.00	6.00
20 Bob Savage	3.00	6.00
21 Carl Scheib	3.00	6.00
22 Al Simmons CO	12.50	25.00
23 Pete Suder	3.00	6.00
24 Elmer Valo	6.00	12.00
25 Skeeter Webb	3.00	6.00
26 Don White	3.00	6.00
27 Rudy York	4.00	8.00

1949 A's Team Issue

This 33-card set of the Philadelphia Athletics features black-and-white player photos with white borders. Card number 1 measures 8" by 10" and is an actual team photograph. The backs are blank. The cards are unnumbered and checklisted below in alphabetical order. The photos were available direct from the A's for either three cents each or $1 for the set at the time of issue.

COMPLETE SET (33)	150.00	300.00
1 1949 Athletics Team 8x10	15.00	30.00
2 1949 Athletics Team	15.00	30.00
3 Shibe Park	15.00	30.00
4 Joe Astroth	3.00	6.00
5 Henry Biasatti	3.00	6.00

Card	Low	High
6 Lou Brissie	4.00	8.00
7 Earle Brucker	3.00	6.00
8 Sam Chapman	5.00	10.00
9 Joe Coleman	3.00	6.00
10 Tom Davis	3.00	6.00
11 Jimmie Dykes CO	4.00	8.00
12 Ferris Fain	5.00	10.00
13 Dick Fowler	3.00	6.00
14 Nelson Fox	15.00	30.00
15 Mike Guerra	3.00	6.00
16 Charlie Harris	3.00	6.00
17 Eddie Joost	5.00	10.00
18 David Keefe	3.00	6.00
19 Alex Kellner	3.00	6.00
20 Connie Mack MG	12.50	25.00
21 Earl Mack	3.00	6.00
22 Hank Majeski	3.00	6.00
23 Phil Marchildon	3.00	6.00
24 Barney McCosky	3.00	6.00
25 Lester McCrabb	3.00	6.00
26 Wally Moses	4.00	8.00
27 Buddy Rosar	3.00	6.00
28 Carl Scheib	3.00	6.00
29 Bobby Shantz	6.00	12.00
30 Pete Suder	3.00	6.00
31 Elmer Valo	5.00	10.00
32 Don White	3.00	6.00
33 Taft Wright	3.00	6.00

1950 A's Team Issue

This 28-card set of the Philadelphia Athletics was issued by the club and features black-and-white player portraits that were used previously in the team sets. For a number of years, the A's did not issue new sets, but carried the same cards over several years. The backs are blank. The cards are unnumbered and checklisted below in alphabetical order.

Card	Low	High
COMPLETE SET (27)	75.00	150.00
1 Joseph Astroth	3.00	6.00
2 Leland Brissie	3.00	6.00
3 Lou Brissie	3.00	6.00
4 Samuel Chapman	4.00	8.00
5 Mickey Cochrane CO	12.50	25.00
6 Joseph Coleman	3.00	6.00
7 Bob Dillinger	3.00	6.00
8 Jimmy Dykes CO	4.00	8.00
9 Ferris Fain	4.00	8.00
10 Dick Fowler	3.00	6.00
11 Mike Guerra	3.00	6.00
12 William Hitchcock	3.00	6.00
13 Robert Hooper	3.00	6.00
14 Edwin Joost	4.00	8.00
15 Alex Kellner	3.00	6.00
16 Paul Lehner	3.00	6.00
17 Hank Majeski	3.00	6.00
18 Phil Marchildon	3.00	6.00
19 William McCoskey	3.00	6.00
20 Bing Miller CO	3.00	6.00
21 Wally Moses	4.00	8.00
22 Carl Scheib	3.00	6.00
23 Bobby Shantz	5.00	10.00
24 Pete Suder	3.00	6.00
25 Joe Tipton	3.00	6.00
26 Elmer Valo	4.00	8.00
27 Kermit Wahl	3.00	6.00
28 Henry Wyse	3.00	6.00

1951 A's Team Issue

This 35-card set of the Philadelphia Athletics was issued by the club and features the same photos as in the 1949 or 1950 Athletics team sets. The cards are unnumbered and checklisted below in alphabetical order.

Card	Low	High
COMPLETE SET (35)	125.00	250.00
1 1951 Athletics Team Photo	12.50	25.00
2 Joe Astroth	3.00	6.00
3 Chief Bender CO	6.00	12.00
4 Ed Burtaschy	3.00	6.00
5 Samuel Chapman	4.00	8.00
6 Allie Clark	3.00	6.00
7 Joe Coleman	3.00	6.00
8 Jimmy Dykes MG	4.00	8.00
9 Ferris Fain	4.00	8.00
10 Richard Fowler	3.00	6.00
11 Bill Hitchcock	3.00	6.00
12 Bob Hooper	3.00	6.00
13 Eddie Joost	4.00	8.00
14 Alex Kellner	3.00	6.00
15 Lou Klein	3.00	6.00
16 John Kucab	3.00	6.00
17 Paul Lehner	3.00	6.00
18 Lou Limmer	3.00	6.00
19 Connie Mack OWN	10.00	20.00
20 Earl Mack CO	3.00	6.00
21 Hank Majeski	3.00	6.00
22 Morris Martin	3.00	6.00
23 Bing Miller CO	4.00	8.00
24 Wallace Moses	4.00	8.00
25 Ray Murray	3.00	6.00
26 Tom Oliver CO	3.00	6.00
27 Dave Philley	4.00	8.00
28 Carl Scheib	3.00	6.00
29 Bobby Shantz	5.00	10.00
30 Pete Suder	3.00	6.00
31 Joe Tipton	3.00	6.00
32 Elmer Valo	4.00	8.00
33 Kermit Wahl	3.00	6.00
34 Gus Zernial	5.00	10.00
35 Sam Zoldack	3.00	6.00

1952 A's Team Issue

This 31-card set of the Philadelphia Athletics was issued by the club and features the same photos as in the 1949 and 1951 Athletics team sets. The cards are unnumbered and checklisted below in alphabetical order.

Card	Low	High
COMPLETE SET (31)	125.00	250.00
1 1952 Athletics Team Photo	12.50	25.00
2 Shibe Park	12.50	25.00
3 Joe Astroth	3.00	6.00
4 Hal Bevan	3.00	6.00
5 Harry Byrd	3.00	6.00
6 Allie Clark	3.00	6.00
7 Jimmy Dykes MG	4.00	8.00
8 Ferris Fain	5.00	10.00
9 Dick Fowler	3.00	6.00
10 Bill Hitchcock	3.00	6.00
11 Bob Hooper	3.00	6.00
12 Eddie Joost	4.00	8.00
13 Skeeter Kell	3.00	6.00
14 Alex Kellner	3.00	6.00
15 John Kucab	3.00	6.00
16 Connie Mack OWN	10.00	20.00
17 Morris Martin	3.00	6.00
18 Bing Miller CO	4.00	8.00
19 Wally Moses CO	4.00	8.00
20 Ray Murray	3.00	6.00
21 Bobo Newsom	4.00	8.00
22 Dave Philley	3.00	6.00
23 Sherry Robertson	3.00	6.00
24 Carl Scheib	3.00	6.00
25 Bobby Shantz	5.00	10.00
26 Pete Suder	3.00	6.00
27 Keith Thomas	3.00	6.00
28 Elmer Valo	4.00	8.00
29 Ed Wright	3.00	6.00
30 Gus Zernial	5.00	10.00
31 Sam Zoldak	3.00	6.00

1953 A's Team Issue

This 31-card set of the Philadelphia Athletics was issued by the club and features the same photos as in the 1951 and 1952 Athletics team sets. The cards are unnumbered and checklisted below in alphabetical order.

Card	Low	High
COMPLETE SET (31)	125.00	250.00
1 1953 Athletics Team Photo	12.50	25.00
2 Joe Astroth	3.00	6.00
3 Loren Babe	3.00	6.00
4 Chief Bender CO	6.00	12.00
5 Charlie Bishop	3.00	6.00
6 Harry Byrd	3.00	6.00
7 Joe Coleman	4.00	8.00
8 Joe DeMaestri	3.00	6.00
9 Jimmy Dykes MG	5.00	10.00
10 Frank Fanovich	3.00	6.00
11 Marion Fricano	3.00	6.00
12 Tom Hamilton	3.00	6.00
13 Eddie Joost	5.00	10.00
14 Alex Kellner	3.00	6.00
15 Morris Martin	3.00	6.00
16 Connie Mack OWN	10.00	20.00
17 Ed McGhee	3.00	6.00
18 Cass Michaels	3.00	6.00
19 Bing Miller CO	4.00	8.00
20 Ed Monahan	3.00	6.00
21 Wally Moses	4.00	8.00
22 Ray Murray	3.00	6.00
23 Bobo Newsom	4.00	8.00
24 Tom Oliver CO	3.00	6.00
25 Dave Philley	3.00	6.00
26 Ed Robinson	3.00	6.00
27 Carl Scheib	3.00	6.00
28 Bobby Shantz	5.00	10.00
29 Pete Suder	3.00	6.00
30 Elmer Valo	4.00	8.00
31 Gus Zernial	5.00	10.00

1954 A's Team Issue

This 30-card set of the Philadelphia Athletics was issued by the club and features the same photos as in the 1953 Athletics team set. The cards are unnumbered and checklisted below in alphabetical order.

Card	Low	High
COMPLETE SET (30)	100.00	200.00
1 1954 Athletics Team Photo	12.50	25.00
2 Joe Astroth	3.00	6.00
3 Charlie Bishop	3.00	6.00
4 Don Bollweg	3.00	6.00
5 Ed Burtchy	3.00	6.00
6 Joe DeMaestri	3.00	6.00
7 Art Dittmar	3.00	6.00
8 Jim Finigan	3.00	6.00
9 Marion Fricano	3.00	6.00
10 John Gray	3.00	6.00
11 Forest Jacobs	3.00	6.00
12 Eddie Joost	4.00	8.00
13 Alex Kellner	3.00	6.00
14 Lou Limmer	3.00	6.00
15 Wally Moses	4.00	8.00
16 Ray Murray	3.00	6.00
17 Dave Philley	3.00	6.00
18 Arnold Portocarrero	3.00	6.00
19 Vic Power	5.00	10.00
20 Bill Renna	3.00	6.00
21 Al Robertson	3.00	6.00
22 Carl Scheib	3.00	6.00
23 Bill Shantz	3.00	6.00
24 Bobby Shantz	5.00	10.00
25 Pete Suder	3.00	6.00
26 Bob Trice	3.00	6.00
27 Elmer Valo	4.00	8.00
28 Ozzie Van Brabant	3.00	6.00
29 Lee Wheat	3.00	6.00
30 Gus Zernial	5.00	10.00

1955 A's Rodeo Meats

The cards in this 47-card set measure 2 1/2" by 3 1/2". The 1955 Rodeo Meats set contains unnumbered, color cards of the first Kansas City A's team. There are many background color variations noted in the checklist, and the card reverses carry a scrapbook offer. The Grimes and Kryhoski cards listed in the scrapbook album were apparently never issued. The catalog number for this set is F152-1. The cards have been arranged in alphabetical order and assigned numbers for reference.

Card	Low	High
COMPLETE SET (47)	4,000.00	8,000.00
1 Joe Astroth	75.00	150.00
2 Harold Bevan	125.00	250.00
3 Charles Bishop	125.00	250.00
4 Don Bollweg	125.00	250.00
5 Lou Boudreau MG	225.00	450.00
6 Cloyd Boyer Salmon	75.00	150.00
7 Cloyd Boyer Light Blue	150.00	300.00
8 Ed Burtschy	150.00	300.00
9 Art Ceccarelli	125.00	250.00
10 Joe DeMaestri Yellow	75.00	150.00
11 Joe DeMaestri Green	75.00	150.00
12 Art Ditmar	75.00	150.00
13 John Dixon	125.00	250.00
14 Jim Finigan	75.00	150.00
15 Marion Fricano	125.00	250.00
16 Tom Gorman	75.00	150.00
17 John Gray	125.00	250.00
18 Ray Herbert	75.00	150.00
19 Forrest Jacobs	150.00	300.00
20 Alex Kellner	75.00	150.00
21 Harry Kraft CO UER	75.00	150.00
Last name misspelled		
22 Jack Littrell	75.00	150.00
23 Hector Lopez	100.00	200.00
24 Oscar Melillo CO	75.00	150.00
25 Arnold Portocarrero Purple	150.00	300.00
26 Arnold Portocarrero Gray	75.00	150.00
27 Vic Power Yellow	100.00	200.00
28 Vic Power Pink	150.00	300.00
29 Vic Raschi	150.00	300.00
30 Bill Renna Lavender	75.00	150.00
31 Bill Renna Dark Pink	150.00	300.00
32 Al Robertson	125.00	250.00
33 Johnny Sain	200.00	300.00
34 Bobby Schantz ERR	225.00	450.00
Name misspelled		
35 Bobby Shantz COR	150.00	300.00
36 Wilmer Shantz Orange	75.00	150.00
37 Wilmer Shantz Lavender	75.00	150.00
38 Harry Simpson	75.00	150.00
39 Enos Slaughter	225.00	450.00
40 Lou Sleater	75.00	150.00
41 George Susce CO	125.00	250.00
42 Bob Trice	125.00	250.00
43 Elmer Valo Yellow	150.00	300.00
44 Elmer Valo Green	100.00	200.00
45 Bill Wilson Yellow	150.00	300.00
46 Bill Wilson Lavender	75.00	150.00
47 Gus Zernial	125.00	250.00

1955 A's Team Issue

This 29-card set measuring approximately 6 1/4" by 9 1/4" features borderless sepia photos of the Kansas City Athletics. The backs are blank. The cards are unnumbered and checklisted below in alphabetical order.

Card	Low	High
COMPLETE SET (29)	50.00	100.00
1 Joe Asthroth	1.50	3.00
2 Lou Boudreau MG	5.00	10.00
3 Cloyd Boyer	2.50	5.00
4 Art Cecarelli	1.50	3.00
5 Harry Craft CO	1.50	3.00
6 Joe DeMaestri	1.50	3.00
7 Art Dittmar	1.50	3.00
8 Jim Finigan	1.50	3.00
9 Tom Gorman	1.50	3.00
10 Ray Herbert	1.50	3.00
11 Alex Kellner	1.50	3.00
12 Dick Kryhoski	1.50	3.00
13 Jack Littrell	1.50	3.00
14 Hector Lopez	2.00	4.00
15 Oscar Melillo CO	1.50	3.00
16 Arnold Portocarrero	1.50	3.00
17 Vic Power	2.50	5.00
18 Vic Raschi	2.50	5.00
19 Bill Renna	1.50	3.00
20 John Sain	3.00	6.00
21 Bill Shantz	1.50	3.00
22 Bobby Shantz	3.00	6.00
23 Harry Simpson	1.50	3.00
24 Enos Slaughter	4.00	8.00
25 Lou Sleator	1.50	3.00
26 George Susce	1.50	3.00
27 Elmer Valo	2.00	4.00
28 Bill Wilson	1.50	3.00
29 Gus Zernial	2.50	5.00

1956-60 A's Postcards

This multi-year postcard set of the Kansas City Athletics features borderless black-and-white player photos measuring approximately 3 1/4" by 5 1/2". The backs are blank. These set was issued by the club at no charge and issued over a series of years. The cards are unnumbered and checklisted below in alphabetical order.

Card	Low	High
COMPLETE SET (90)	300.00	600.00
1 Jim Archer	5.00	10.00
2 Hank Bauer	7.50	15.00
3 Mike Baxes	5.00	10.00
Fielding		
4 Mike Baxes	5.00	10.00
Portrait		
5 Zeke Bella	5.00	10.00
6 Lou Boudreau MG	10.00	20.00
7 Cletis Boyer	7.50	15.00
8 George Brunet	5.00	10.00
9 Wally Burnette	5.00	10.00
10 Ed Burtschy	5.00	10.00
11 Andy Carey	6.00	12.00
12 Chico Carrasquel	6.00	12.00
13 Robert Cerv	5.00	10.00
Portrait to letters		
14 Bob Cerv	5.00	10.00
Portrait to neck		
15 Harry Chiti	5.00	10.00
16 Rip Coleman	5.00	10.00
17 Walt Craddock	5.00	10.00
18 Harry Craft	5.00	10.00
19 Jack Crimian	5.00	10.00
20 Bud Daley	5.00	10.00
21 Pete Daley	5.00	10.00
22 Bob Davis	5.00	10.00
23 Joe DeMaestri	5.00	10.00
Fielding		
24 Joe DeMaestri	5.00	10.00
With bat		
25 Art Ditmar	5.00	10.00
26 Jim Ewell TR	5.00	10.00
27 Jim Finigan	5.00	10.00
28 Mark Freeman	5.00	10.00
29 Ned Garver	5.00	10.00
30 Bob Giggie	5.00	10.00
31 Joe Ginsberg	5.00	10.00
32 Tom Gorman	5.00	10.00
To hips		
33 Tom Gorman	5.00	10.00
Pitching		
34 Tom Gorman	5.00	10.00
Standing with glove		
35 Bob Grim	5.00	10.00
36 Johnny Groth	5.00	10.00
Portrait		
37 Johnny Groth	5.00	10.00
Standing with bat		
38 Kent Hadley	5.00	10.00
39 Dick Hall	5.00	10.00
40 Ken Hamlin	5.00	10.00
41 Ray Herbert	5.00	10.00
Dark background		
42 Ray Herbert	5.00	10.00
White background		
43 Troy Herriage	5.00	10.00
44 Whitey Herzog	7.50	15.00
45 Frank House	5.00	10.00
46 Spook Jacobs	5.00	10.00
47 Bob Johnson	5.00	10.00
48 Ken Johnson	5.00	10.00
49 Alex Kellner	5.00	10.00
50 Leo Kiely	5.00	10.00
51 Lou Kretlow	5.00	10.00
52 Johnny Kucks	5.00	10.00
53 Marty Kutyna	5.00	10.00
54 Don Larsen	7.50	15.00
55 Tom Lasorda	12.50	25.00
56 Hec Lopez	5.00	10.00
Batting		
57 Hector Lopez	5.00	10.00
Portrait		
58 Jerry Lumpe	5.00	10.00
59 Jack McMahan	5.00	10.00
60 Roger Maris	25.00	50.00
61 Oscar Melillo CO	5.00	10.00
62 Al Pilarcik	5.00	10.00
63 Rance Pless	5.00	10.00
64 Vic Power	7.50	15.00
65 Eddie Robinson	5.00	10.00
66 Jose Santiago	5.00	10.00
67 Bobby Shantz	7.50	15.00
68 Norm Siebern	5.00	10.00
69 Harry Simpson	5.00	10.00
Batting		
70 Harry Simpson	5.00	10.00
Portrait		
71 Harry Simpson	5.00	10.00
Fielding		
72 Lou Skizas	5.00	10.00
73 Enos Slaughter	10.00	20.00
Fielding		
74 Enos Slaughter	10.00	20.00
Batting		
75 Hal Smith	5.00	10.00
76 Russ Snyder	5.00	10.00
77 George Susce	5.00	10.00
78 Ralph Terry	5.00	10.00
79 Wayne Terwilliger	5.00	10.00
80 Charles Thompson	5.00	10.00
81 Dick Tomanek	5.00	10.00
82 John Tsitouris	5.00	10.00
83 Marv Throneberry	7.50	15.00
84 Bob Trowbridge	5.00	10.00
85 Bill Tuttle	5.00	10.00
86 Jack Urban	5.00	10.00
87 Preston Ward	5.00	10.00
88 Dick Williams	7.50	15.00
89 Gus Zernial	7.50	15.00
Batting		
90 Gus Zernial	7.50	15.00
Catching		

1956 A's Rodeo Meats

The cards in this 12-card set measure 2 1/2" by 3 1/2". The unnumbered, color cards of the 1956 Rodeo baseball series are easily distinguished from their 1955 counterparts by the absence of the scrapbook offer on the reverse. They were available only in packages of Rodeo All-Meat Wieners. The catalog designation for this set is F152-2, and the cards have been assigned numbers in alphabetical order in the checklist below.

COMPLETE SET (12)	750.00	1,500.00
1 Joe Astroth	75.00	150.00
2 Lou Boudreau MG	225.00	450.00
3 Joe DeMaestri	75.00	150.00
4 Art Ditmar	75.00	150.00
5 Jim Finigan	75.00	150.00
6 Hector Lopez	75.00	150.00
7 Vic Power	75.00	150.00
8 Bobby Shantz	125.00	250.00
9 Harry Simpson	75.00	150.00
10 Enos Slaughter	225.00	450.00
11 Elmer Valo	100.00	200.00
12 Gus Zernial	100.00	200.00

1957 A's Jay Publishing

This 12-card set of the Kansas City Athletics measures approximately 5" by 7" and features black-and-white player photos in a white border. These cards were packaged 12 to a packet. The backs are blank. The cards are unnumbered and checklisted below in alphabetical order. The cards have the player's name and Athletics on the bottom

COMPLETE SET (12)	20.00	50.00
1 Lou Boudreau MG	3.00	8.00
2 Bob Cerv	1.50	4.00
3 Tom Gorman	1.50	4.00
4 Milt Graff	1.50	4.00
5 Billy Hunter	1.50	4.00
6 Hector Lopez	1.50	4.00
7 Maury McDermott	1.50	4.00
8 Tom Morgan	1.50	4.00
9 Vic Power	1.50	4.00
10 Harry Simpson	1.50	4.00
11 Lou Skizas	1.50	4.00
12 Hal Smith	1.50	4.00

1958 A's Jay Publishing

This 12-card set of the Kansas City Athletics measures approximately 5" by 7" and features black-and-white player photos in a white border. These cards were packaged 12 to a packet. The backs are blank. The cards are unnumbered and checklisted below in alphabetical order.

COMPLETE SET (12)	25.00	50.00
1 Harry Craft MG	2.00	4.00
2 Joe DeMaestri	2.00	4.00
3 Ned Garver	2.00	4.00
4 Woody Held	2.00	4.00
5 Frank House	2.00	4.00
6 Hector Lopez	2.00	4.00
7 Vic Power	3.00	6.00
8 Hal Smith	2.00	4.00
9 Ralph Terry	2.50	5.00
10 Virgil Trucks	3.00	6.00
11 Bill Tuttle	2.00	4.00
12 Jack Urban	2.00	4.00

1959 A's Jay Publishing

This 12-card set of the Kansas City Athletics measures approximately 5" by 7" and features black-and-white player photos in a white border. The backs are blank. The cards are unnumbered and checklisted below in alphabetical order.

COMPLETE SET (12)	15.00	40.00
1 Bob Cerv	1.25	3.00
2 Harry Craft MG	1.25	3.00
3 Bud Daley	1.25	3.00
4 Ned Garver	1.25	3.00
5 Bob Grim	1.25	3.00
6 Ray Herbert	1.25	3.00
7 Frank House	1.25	3.00
8 Hector Lopez	1.25	3.00
9 Roger Maris	6.00	15.00
10 Hal Smith	1.25	3.00
11 Ralph Terry	1.50	4.00
12 Bill Tuttle	1.25	3.00

1960 A's Jay Publishing

This 12-card set of the Kansas City Athletics measures approximately 5" by 7" and features black-and-white player photos in a white border. The backs are blank. The cards are unnumbered and checklisted below in alphabetical order.

COMPLETE SET (11)	15.00	40.00
1 Hank Bauer	2.00	5.00
2 Bud Daley	1.25	3.00
3 Bob Elliott MG	1.25	3.00
4 Ned Garver	1.25	3.00
5 Ray Herbert	1.25	3.00
6 Johnny Kucks	1.25	3.00
7 Don Larsen	1.50	4.00
8 Jerry Lumpe	1.25	3.00
9 Norm Siebern	1.25	3.00
10 Marv Throneberry	2.00	5.00
11 Bill Tuttle	1.25	3.00
12 Dick Williams	2.00	5.00

1960 A's Team Issue

These 3 1/4" by 5 1/2" blank backed cards feature members of the 1960 A's. The fronts have fascimile autographs and we have sequenced the set in alphabetical order

COMPLETE SET (18)	20.00	50.00
1 Hank Bauer	2.00	5.00
2 Zeke Bella	1.00	2.50
3 Bob Cerv	1.00	2.50
4 Bud Daley	1.00	2.50
5 Jim Ewell	1.00	2.50
6 Ken Hamlin	1.00	2.50
7 Ray Herbert	1.00	2.50
8 Whitey Herzog	2.00	5.00
9 Bob Johnson	1.00	2.50
10 Ken Johnson	1.00	2.50
11 Johnny Kucks	1.00	2.50
12 Marty Kutyna	1.00	2.50
13 Jerry Lumpe	1.00	2.50
14 Norm Siebern	1.00	2.50
15 Russ Snyder	1.00	2.50
16 John Tsitouris	1.00	2.50
17 Bill Tuttle	1.00	2.50
18 Dick Williams	2.00	5.00

1961-62 A's Jay Publishing

This 24-card set of the Kansas City Athletics measures approximately 5" by 7". The fronts feature black-and-white posed player photos with the player's and team name printed below in the white border. These cards were packaged 12 to a packet and originally sold for 25 cents. The backs are blank. The cards are unnumbered and checklisted below in alphabetical order.

COMPLETE SET (24)	20.00	50.00
1 Jim Archer	.75	2.00
2 Norm Bass	.75	2.00
3 Hank Bauer 61	1.50	4.00
4 Bob Boyd 61	.75	2.00
5 Wayne Causey	.75	2.00
6 Frank Cipriani	.75	2.00
7 Bud Daley 61	.75	2.00
8 Joe Gordon MG 61	1.25	3.00
9 Ray Herbert 61	.75	2.00
10 Dick Howser	1.25	3.00
11 Manny Jimenez 62	.75	2.00
12 Jerry Lumpe Head photo	.75	2.00
13 Jerry Lumpe At bat	.75	2.00
14 Joe Nuxhall 61	.75	2.00
15 Joe Pignatano 61	.75	2.00
16 Leo Posada	.75	2.00
17 Ed Rakow	.75	2.00
18 Norm Siebern At bat	.75	2.00
19 Norm Siebern Head photo	.75	2.00
20 Haywood Sullivan Waist-up photo	.75	2.00
21 Haywood Sullivan Head photo	.75	2.00
22 Marv Throneberry 61	1.25	3.00
23 Bill Tuttle 61	.75	2.00
24 Jerry Walker	.75	2.00

1961 A's Team Issue

These cards measure 3 1/4" by 5 1/2" and are blank backs. The fronts have black and white borderless photos with fascimile autographs. We have sequenced this set in alphabetical order. Often, these cards are found with a red Kansas City A's envelope. It is believed that these cards were sold as a set at the ballpark.

COMPLETE SET	30.00	60.00
1 Jim Archer	.75	2.00
2 Norm Bass	.75	2.00
3 Hank Bauer	1.25	3.00
4 Bob Boyd	.75	2.00
5 Andy Carey	.75	2.00
6 Wayne Causey	.75	2.00
7 Clint Courtney	.75	2.00
8 Bud Daley	.75	2.00
9 Joe Gordon MG	1.25	3.00
10 Jay Hankins	.75	2.00
11 Ray Herbert	.75	2.00
12 Dick Howser	1.25	3.00
13 Ken Johnson	.75	2.00
14 Ed Keegan	.75	2.00
15 Lou Klimchock	.75	2.00
16 Bill Kunkel	.75	2.00
17 Frank Lane GM	.75	2.00
18 Don Larsen	1.50	4.00
19 Jerry Lumpe	.75	2.00
20 Joe Nuxhall	.75	2.00
21 Joe Pignatano	.75	2.00
22 Al Pilarcik	.75	2.00
23 Leo Posada	.75	2.00
24 Ed Rakow	.75	2.00
25 Norm Siebern	.75	2.00
26 Haywood Sullivan	.75	2.00
27 Marv Throneberry	1.25	3.00
28 Bill Tuttle	.75	2.00

1962 A's Team Issue

These 4" by 5" black and white cards were used by the Kansas City Athletics to deal with photo requests. These photos have the players name and position on the front surrounded by a white border. Since these cards are unnumbered, we have sequenced them in alphabetical order.

COMPLETE SET (32)	15.00	40.00
1 Jim Archer	.75	2.00
2 Joe Azcue	.75	2.00
3 Norm Bass	.75	2.00
4 Hank Bauer MG	1.00	2.50
5 Wayne Causey	.75	2.00
6 Ed Charles	1.00	2.50
7 Gino Cimoli	.75	2.00
8 Bob Del Greco	.75	2.00
9 Art Ditmar	.75	2.00
10 Bob Grim	.75	2.00
11 Dick Howser	1.00	2.50
12 Manny Jimenez	.75	2.00
13 Bill Kunkel	.75	2.00
14 Dario Lodigiani	.75	2.00
15 Ed Lopat CO	1.25	3.00
16 Jerry Lumpe	.75	2.00
17 Danny McDevitt	.75	2.00
18 Gus Niarhos CO	.75	2.00
19 Dan Osinski	.75	2.00
20 Dan Pfister	.75	2.00
21 Leo Posada	.75	2.00
22 Ed Rakow	.75	2.00
23 Diego Segui	.75	2.00
24 Norm Siebern	.75	2.00
25 Gene Stephens	.75	2.00
26 Haywood Sullivan	.75	2.00
27 Jose Tartabull	.75	2.00
28 Jerry Walker	.75	2.00
29 Jo-Jo White CO	.75	2.00
30 Dave Wickersham	.75	2.00
31 Gordon Windhorn	.75	2.00
32 John Wyatt	.75	2.00

1963 A's Jay Publishing

This 12-card set of the Kansas City Athletics measures approximately 5" by 7". The fronts feature black-and-white posed player photos with the player's and team name printed below in the white border. These cards were packaged 12 to a packet. The backs are blank. The cards are unnumbered and checklisted below in alphabetical order.

COMPLETE SET (12)	15.00	40.00
1 Jim Archer	.75	2.00
2 Norm Bass	.75	2.00
3 Wayne Causey	.75	2.00
4 Bill Fischer	.75	2.00
5 Dick Howser	1.25	3.00
6 Manny Jiminez	.75	2.00
7 Ed Lopat MG	1.25	3.00
8 Jerry Lumpe	1.25	3.00
9 Norm Siebern	.75	2.00
10 Haywood Sullivan	.75	2.00
11 Jose Tartabull	.75	2.00
12 Jerry Walker	.75	2.00

1964 A's Jay Publishing

This 12-card set of the Kansas City Athletics measures approximately 5" by 7". The fronts feature black-and-white posed player photos with the player's and team name printed below in the white border. These cards were packaged 12 to a packet. The backs are blank. The cards are unnumbered and checklisted below in alphabetical order.

COMPLETE SET (12)	12.50	30.00
1 Wayne Causey	1.25	3.00
2 Ed Charles	1.25	3.00
3 Moe Drabowsky	1.25	3.00
4 Doc Edwards	1.25	3.00
5 Jim Gentile	1.25	3.00
6 Ken Harrelson	2.00	5.00
7 Manny Jimenez	1.25	3.00
8 Charlie Lau	1.25	3.00
9 Ed Lopat MG	1.25	3.00
10 Orlando Pena	1.25	3.00
11 Diego Segui	1.25	3.00
12 Jose Tartabull	1.25	3.00

1965 A's Jay Publishing

This 12-card set of the Kansas City Athletics measures approximately 5" by 7". The fronts feature black-and-white posed player photos with the player's and team name printed below in the white border. These cards were packaged 12 to a packet. The backs are blank. The cards are unnumbered and checklisted below in alphabetical order.

COMPLETE SET (12)	10.00	25.00
1 Bill Bryan	.75	2.00
2 Wayne Causey	.75	2.00
3 Ed Charles	.75	2.00
4 Doc Edwards	.75	2.00
5 Jim Gentile	1.00	2.50
6 Dick Green	.75	2.00
7 Ken Harrelson	1.25	3.00
8 Mike Hershberger	.75	2.00
9 Jim Landis	.75	2.00
10 Mel McGaha MG	.75	2.00
11 Wes Stock	.75	2.00
12 Fred Talbot	.75	2.00

1969 A's Black and White

This 15-card set measures approximately 2 1/16" by 3 5/8" and features black-and-white close-up player photos on a white card face. The player's name and position appears below the picture along with the team name. The backs are blank. The cards are unnumbered and checklisted below in alphabetical order. This set features a card of Joe DiMaggio as an A's coach as well as a card from Reggie Jackson's Rookie Card year. The set is dated by the fact that 1969 was the only year Tom Reynolds played for the A's. It is believed that this is a collectors issue set produced by long time collector, Mike Andersen.

COMPLETE SET (15)	50.00	100.00
1 Sal Bando	1.50	4.00
2 Hank Bauer MG	1.25	3.00
3 Bert Campaneris	1.25	3.00
4 Danny Cater	.75	2.00
5 Joe DiMaggio CO	12.50	30.00
6 Chuck Dobson	.75	2.00
7 Dick Green	.75	2.00
8 Catfish Hunter	4.00	10.00
9 Reggie Jackson	40.00	80.00
10 Rick Monday	1.25	3.00
11 Jim Nash	.75	2.00
12 Blue Moon Odom	1.25	3.00
13 Tom Reynolds	.75	2.00
14 Phil Roof	.75	2.00
15 Ramon Webster	.75	2.00

1970 A's Black and White

Similar to the set which was issued in 1969 and some collectors call Jack in the Box, this set features members of the 1970 A's. The black and white photos take up most of the card with the players name and Oakland A logo on the bottom. The backs are blank so we have sequenced these cards in alphabetical order.

COMPLETE SET (24)	40.00	80.00
1 Felipe Alou	2.00	5.00
2 Sal Bando	1.50	4.00
3 Bert Campaneris	1.50	4.00
4 Chuck Dobson	.60	1.50
5 Al Downing	.60	1.50
6 Dave Duncan	.60	1.50
7 Frank Fernandez	.60	1.50
8 Tito Francona	.60	1.50
9 Rollie Fingers	4.00	10.00
10 Jim Mudcat Grant	.60	1.50
11 Dick Green	.60	1.50
12 Larry Haney	.60	1.50
13 Catfish Hunter	5.00	12.00
14 Reggie Jackson	10.00	25.00
15 Paul Lindblad	.60	1.50
16 John McNamara MG	.60	1.50
17 Don Mincher	.60	1.50
18 Rick Monday	.15	4.00
19 John Odom	.60	1.50
20 Roberto Pena	.60	1.50
21 Jim Roland	.60	1.50
22 Roberto Rodriguez	.60	1.50
23 Diego Segui	.60	1.50
24 Jose Tartabull	.60	1.50

1973 A's 1874 TCMA Postcards

These nine postcards issued feature members of the National Association Philadelphia Athletics of the 19th century. The fronts feature black and white posed photos while the backs mention these photos are reproduced from the July 25th 1874 Harpers Weekly. Interestingly, these players are from the National Association and this is one of the few sets which features players from that league which existed before the National League was formed.

COMPLETE SET (9)	4.00	10.00
1 Cap Anson	1.25	3.00
2 Joseph Battin	.40	1.00

3 John Clapp .40 1.00
4 Weston Fisler .40 1.00
5 Count Gedney .40 1.00
6 Dick McBride .40 1.00
7 Mike McGeary .40 1.00
8 John (Lefty) McMullen .40 1.00
9 Ezra Sutton .60 1.50

1974 A's 1910-14 TCMA Postcards

This 12-card set features photos of the 1910-1914 Philadelphia A's players printed on postcards. The cards are numbered on the front. This postcard set had two printings - one in black and white and the other in blue and white.

COMPLETE SET (12) 10.00 25.00
501 Chief Bender 2.50 6.00
502 John Coombs .40 1.00
503 Eddie Plank 2.50 6.00
504 Amos Strunk .40 1.00
506 Ira Thomas .40 1.00
508 Stuffy McInnis .40 1.00
510 Rube Oldring .40 1.00
511 Eddie Collins 3.00 8.00
512 Frank Baker 2.50 6.00
515 Jack Barry .40 1.00
516 Jack Lapp .40 1.00
518 Danny Murphy .40 1.00

1974 A's 1929-31 TCMA

This 28-card set features photos of the 1929-31 Philadelphia Athletics team and measure approximately 2 1/2" by 4". The cards are unnumbered and checklisted below in alphabetical order.

COMPLETE SET (28) 12.50 30.00
1 Max Bishop .40 1.00
2 Joe Boley .40 1.00
3 George Burns .40 1.00
4 Mickey Cochrane 1.50 4.00
5 Eddie Collins 1.25 3.00
Lew Krausse
6 Doc Cramer .60 1.50
7 Jimmy Dykes .75 2.00
8 George Earnshaw .60 1.50
9 Howard Ehmke .40 1.00
10 Lou Finney .40 1.00
John Heving
11 Jimmie Foxx 2.00 5.00
12 Walt French .60 1.50
Waite Hoyt
13 Lefty Grove 1.50 4.00
14 Mule Haas .40 1.00
15 Sammy Hale .40 1.00
16 Pinky Higgins .40 1.00
Phil Todt
17 Connie Mack .60 1.50
Earl Mack
18 Roy Mahaffey .40 1.00
19 Eric McNair .40 1.00
20 Bing Miller .40 1.00
21 Jack Quinn .75 2.00
22 Eddie Rommel .60 1.50
23 Wally Shang .60 1.50
24 Al Simmons 1.25 3.00
25 Homer Summa .40 1.00
26 Rube Walberg .40 1.00
27 Dib Williams .40 1.00
28 Jim Moore .40 1.00
Jim Peterson
29 A's Team Card 2.00 5.00
Large photo

1974 A's 1931 BraMac

This set, which measures 3 1/2" by 5" features members of the 1931 Philadelphia A's and was issued by the Bra-Mac collaboration.

COMPLETE SET (5) 6.00 15.00
1 Jimmy Moore .20 .50
2 Mule Haas .20 .50
3 Dib Williams .20 .50
4 Jimmie Foxx 1.50 4.00
5 Al Simmons 1.00 2.50
6 Bing Miller .20 .50
7 Jimmie Dykes .40 1.00
8 Eric McNair .20 .50
9 Joe Boley .20 .50
10 Mickey Cochrane 1.00 2.50
11 Max Bishop .20 .50
12 Joe Heving .20 .50
13 Doc Cramer .40 1.00
14 Lefty Grove 1.00 2.50
15 Ed Rommel .20 .50
16 Rube Walberg .20 .50
17 Roy Mahaffey .20 .50
18 Lew Krausse .20 .50
19 Hank McDonald .20 .50

1975 A's 1913 TCMA

These unnumbered black and white cards, which measure approximately 5 1/8" by 3 1/8", feature members of the 1913 Philadelphia A's. Since these cards are unnumbered, we have sequenced them in alphabetical order.

COMPLETE SET 6.00 15.00
1 Frank Baker .75 2.00
2 Jack Barry .20 .50
3 Chief Bender .75 2.00
4 Joe Bush .30 .75
5 Eddie Collins 1.25 3.00
6 Jack Coombs .20 .50
7 Connie Mack MG 1.00 2.50
8 Stuffy McInnis .20 .50
9 Danny Murphy .20 .50
10 Eddie Murphy .20 .50
11 Rube Oldring .20 .50
12 Bill Orr .20 .50
13 Eddie Plank .75 2.00
14 Wally Schang .30 .75
15 Amos Strunk .20 .50

1976 A's Rodeo Meat Commemorative

This 30-card standard-sized set commemorates the 1955 Rodeo Meat series. The cards feature posed black-and-white player photos with white borders. The player's name appears in the lower margin. The Rodeo Meat logo is superimposed at the lower left corner of the picture. The backs carry the player's name, biographical information and a player profile. The cards are arranged in alphabetical order and numbered on the back. These cards were also issued in uncut sheet form and the set was available from the producer for $6.50 for the card set or $10 for the uncut sheet. The biographies on the back of these cards did not appear on the originals; however, those biographies did appear in the albums of the 1950's cards which were available via mail.

COMPLETE SET (30) 6.00 15.00
1 Title Card .20 .50
2 Checklist .20 .50
3 Joe Astroth .20 .50
4 Lou Boudreau MG .60 1.50
5 Cloyd Boyer .40 1.00
6 Art Ceccarelli .20 .50
7 Harry Craft CO .20 .50
8 Joe DeMaestri .20 .50
9 Art Ditmar .40 1.00
10 Jim Finigan .20 .50
11 Tom Gorman .40 1.00
12 Ray Herbert .30 .75
13 Alex Kellner .20 .50
14 Jack Littrell .20 .50
15 Hector Lopez .40 1.00
16 Oscar Melillo CO .20 .50
17 Arnold Portocarrero .20 .50
18 Vic Power .30 .75
19 Vic Raschi .40 1.00
20 Bill Renna .20 .50
21 John Sain .40 1.00
22 Bobby Shantz .40 1.00
23 Wilmer Shantz .20 .50
24 Harry Simpson .20 .50
25 Enos Slaughter .75 2.00
26 Lou Sleator .20 .50
27 George Susce CO .20 .50
28 Elmer Valo .30 .75
29 Bill Wilson .20 .50
30 Gus Zernial .30 .75

1975 Aaron Magnavox

These promotional photos, which measures approximately 4" by 6 7/8" feature Hank Aaron in an Milwaukee Brewer uniform. The photos were issued in either black and white or in color are both types are surrounded by white borders and the bottom has the facsimile greeting "best wishes, Hank Aaron" on the bottom and the photo is courtesy of the Magnavox Company. In addition, a pin signifying membership into the Hank Aaron 715 Home Run Club was also issued by Magnavox as part of their promotional efforts

1 Hank Aaron B&W 4.00 10.00
2 Hank Aaron COL 4.00 10.00
3 Hank Aaron 4.00 10.00
Pin

1974 Aaron 715 Homer

These 12 black and white postcards, which measure approximately 3" by 5" features highlights from the game where Hank Aaron hit his 715th homer.

COMPLETE SET (12) 6.00 15.00
1 Hank Aaron .75 2.00
715
2 Hank Aaron .75 2.00
Picking the bat
3 Hank Aaron .75 2.00
Crack
4 Hank Aaron .75 2.00
Watching the ball
5 Hank Aaron .75 2.00
Going, going
6 Hank Aaron .75 2.00
Gone
7 Hank Aaron .75 2.00
Tom House
Catching the HR ball
8 Hank Aaron .75 2.00
With fans running bases
9 Hank Aaron .75 2.00
A hero's welcome
10 Hank Aaron .75 2.00
Tips his cap
11 Hank Aaron .75 2.00
Atlanta loves hank
12 Hank Aaron .75 2.00
Holding 715

1970-71 Action Cartridge

During the time period of 1970-71 a group of 8 mm cartridges featuring leading players with playing tips were issued. The yellow boxes which measured 2 5/8" by 6" featured the player photo as well as what the tips included. Each player photo includes a fascimile autograph. Since these are unnumbered, we have sequenced them in alphabetical order.

COMPLETE SET (12) 200.00 400.00
1 Hank Aaron 40.00 80.00
2 Glenn Beckert 6.00 15.00
Don Kessinger
3 Lou Brock 12.50 40.00
4 Rod Carew 20.00 50.00
5 Willie Davis 6.00 15.00
6 Bill Freehan 8.00 20.00
7 Reggie Jackson 20.00 50.00
8 Willie McCovey 12.50 40.00
9 Dave McNally 8.00 20.00
10 Brooks Robinson 12.50 40.00
11 Pete Rose 30.00 60.00
12 Tom Seaver 30.00 60.00

1956 Adventure R749

The Adventure series produced by Gum Products in 1956, contains a wide variety of subject matter. Cards in the set measure the standard size. The color drawings are printed on a heavy thickness of cardboard and have large white borders. The backs contain the card number, the caption, and a short text. The most expensive cards in the series of 100 are those associated with sports (Louis, Tunney, etc.). In addition, card number 86 (Schmelling) is notorious and sold at a premium price because of the Nazi symbol printed on the card. Although this set is considered by many to be a topical or non-sport set, several boxers are featured (cards 11, 22, 31-35, 41-44, 76-80, 86-90). One of the few cards of Boston-area legend Harry Agannis is in this set. The sports-related cards are in greater demand than the non-sport cards. These cards came in one-card penny packs where were packed 240 to a box.

COMPLETE SET (100) 225.00 450.00
55 Harry Agganis 10.00 20.00

1969 Ajman Hall of Fame Stamps

These six stamps, were issued by the little country of Ajman to commemorate the 100th anniversary of professional baseball. Six of the players who were on the all-time greatest teams were included in this set. Since these stamps were unnumbered, we have sequenced them in alphabetical order.

COMPLETE SET (6) 6.00 15.00
1 Joe DiMaggio 1.25 3.00
2 Babe Ruth 2.00 5.00
3 George Sisler .40 1.00
4 Stan Musial .75 2.00
5 Ty Cobb 1.25 3.00
6 Honus Wagner .75 2.00

1939-52 Albertype Hall of Fame PC754-2

The Albertype Company issued postcards of Hall of Fame inductees from 1936 through 1952. However, since the HOF was not offically opened until 1939, we are dating this set as 1939-52. This black and white postcard set, the cards being called plaques as they feature the Hall of Fame plaque of the player, was addended to each year by new Hall of Fame inductees. Sixty-two Albertype postcards are known and are listed in the checklist below. The set is sequenced in order of induction into the Hall of Fame.

COMPLETE SET (62) 425.00 850.00
1 Ty Cobb 25.00 50.00
2 Walter Johnson 20.00 40.00
3 Christy Mathewson 20.00 40.00
4 Babe Ruth 37.50 75.00
5 Honus Wagner 20.00 40.00
6 Morgan Bulkeley 5.00 10.00
7 Ban Johnson 5.00 10.00
8 Nap Lajoie 10.00 20.00
9 Connie Mack 10.00 20.00
10 John McGraw 10.00 20.00
11 Tris Speaker 10.00 20.00
12 George Wright 5.00 10.00
13 Cy Young 25.00 50.00
14 Grover Cleveland Alexander 10.00 20.00
15 Alexander Cartwright 7.50 15.00
16 Henry Chadwick 5.00 10.00
17 Cap Anson 12.50 25.00
18 Eddie Collins 10.00 20.00
19 Charlie Comiskey 5.00 10.00
20 Candy Cummings 5.00 10.00
21 Buck Ewing 5.00 10.00
22 Lou Gehrig 30.00 60.00
23 Willie Keeler 5.00 10.00
24 Ole Hoss Radbourne 5.00 10.00
25 George Sisler 7.50 15.00
26 Albert Spalding 5.00 10.00
27 Rogers Hornsby 12.50 25.00
28 Kenesaw Mountain Landis 5.00 10.00
29 Roger Bresnahan 5.00 10.00
30 Dan Brouthers 5.00 10.00
31 Fred Clarke 5.00 10.00
32 Jimmy Collins 5.00 10.00
33 Ed Delahanty 5.00 10.00
34 Hugh Duffy 5.00 10.00
35 Hugh Jennings 5.00 10.00
36 King Kelly 5.00 10.00
37 Jimmy O'Rourke 5.00 10.00
38 Wilbert Robinson 5.00 10.00
39 Jesse Burkett 5.00 10.00
40 Frank Chance 10.00 20.00
41 Jack Chesbro 5.00 10.00
42 Johnny Evers 10.00 20.00
43 Clark Griffith 7.50 15.00
44 Tom McCarthy 5.00 10.00
45 Joe McGinnity 5.00 10.00
46 Eddie Plank 10.00 20.00
47 Joe Tinker 10.00 20.00
48 Rube Waddell 5.00 10.00
49 Ed Walsh 7.50 15.00
50 Mickey Cochrane 10.00 20.00
51 Frankie Frisch 10.00 20.00
52 Lefty Grove 12.50 25.00
53 Carl Hubbell 12.50 25.00
54 Herb Pennock 7.50 15.00
55 Pie Traynor 10.00 20.00
56 Mordecai Brown 10.00 20.00
57 Charlie Gehringer 7.50 15.00
58 Kid Nichols 5.00 10.00
59 Jimmy Foxx 12.50 25.00
(Jimmie)
60 Mel Ott 10.00 20.00
61 Harry Heilmann 5.00 10.00
62 Paul Waner 7.50 15.00
63 Abner Doubleday 5.00 10.00
64 Christy Mathewson BUST 5.00 10.00
65 HOF Exterior 5.00 10.00
66 HOF Interior 5.00 10.00

1971 Aldana Yesterday Heroes

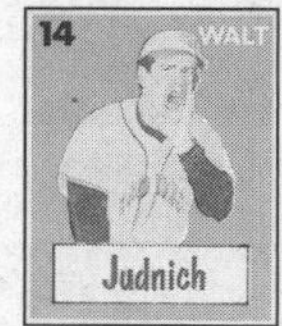

This crude 16 card blank-backed set was issued in the early 1970's and was presumebly issued by Carl Aldana as one of the many collector issue sets he produced around that time period. The fronts have small shots of the player with their first name on top and their last name on the bottom. The purpose of this set was to create cards for players who had never been on a card before.

COMPLETE SET (16) 125.00 250.00
1 Wally Hood 8.00 20.00
2 Jim Westlake 8.00 20.00
3 Stan McWilliams 8.00 20.00
4 Les Fleming 8.00 20.00
5 John Ritchey 8.00 20.00
6 Steve Nagy 8.00 20.00
7 Ken Gables 8.00 20.00
8 Maurice Fisher 8.00 20.00
9 Don Lang 8.00 20.00
10 Harry Malmberg 8.00 20.00
11 Jack Conway 8.00 20.00
12 Don White 8.00 20.00
13 Dick Lajeskie 8.00 20.00
14 Walt Judnich 8.00 20.00
15 Joe Kirrene 8.00 20.00
16 Ed Sauer 8.00 20.00

1908 All-American Ladies Baseball Club

This extremely rare set of printed postcards by an unknown publisher features stars of the All-American Ladies Base Ball Club which toured America early in the 20th century. Although no date is listed on the cards they were produced sometime after 1907 beacuse they have a divided back. Prior to 1907 all postcards backs were undivided and all messages had to be written on the front or picture side of the card. All cards show close up action views of the players on a white background. We have listed the known versions, all additions to this checklist are appreciated.

COMPLETE SET (5) 500.00 1,000.00
1 Bessie Barrett 100.00 200.00
2 May Fay 100.00 200.00
3 Harriett Murphy 100.00 200.00
4 Carrie Nation 100.00 200.00
5 Elizabeth Pull 100.00 200.00

1949 All-Star Photos

Sold as a group, these 21 photos which measure approximately 6 1/4" by 9", features players who for the most part had great seasons in either 1948 or 1949 and thus were among the leading players in the game. Since these photos are unnumbered, we have sequenced them in alphabetical order.

1 Luke Appling 12.50 25.00
2 Lou Boudreau P/MG 12.50 25.00
3 Dom DiMaggio 10.00 20.00
4 Joe DiMaggio 25.00 50.00
5 Bobby Doerr 12.00 25.00
6 Bob Feller 15.00 30.00
7 Joe Gordon 10.00 20.00
8 Tommy Henrich 10.00 20.00
9 George Kell 12.50 25.00
10 Bob Kennedy 5.00 12.00
11 Ralph Kiner 15.00 30.00
12 Bob Lemon 12.00 25.00
13 Marty Marion 6.00 15.00
14 Stan Musial 25.00 50.00

15 Don Newcombe	5.00	12.00
16 Pee Wee Reese	15.00	30.00
17 Phil Rizzuto	15.00	30.00
18 Jackie Robinson	50.00	100.00
19 Enos Slaughter	12.50	50.00
20 Vern Stephens	5.00	12.00
21 Ted Williams	50.00	100.00

1950 All-Star Pinups

These 10 pinups measure approximately 7" in diameter and feature the player photo along with a printed ID on the front. The back features instructions on how to pop out the pinup. These pinups are unnumbered and punched out from a book, which was issued with a 50 cent cover price. We have sequenced them in alphabetical order. Ted Williams is the featured player on the book cover.

COMPLETE SET (10)	700.00	1,400.00
1 Joe DiMaggio	125.00	250.00
2 Jim Hegan	10.00	20.00
3 Gil Hodges	40.00	80.00
4 George Kell	30.00	60.00
5 Ralph Kiner	40.00	80.00
6 Stan Musial	100.00	200.00
7 Mel Parnell	10.00	20.00
8 Phil Rizzuto	60.00	120.00
9 Jackie Robinson	200.00	400.00
10 Ted Williams	200.00	400.00

1971 All-Star Baseball Album

The 1971 All-Star Baseball Album contains two pages of 12 perforated player pictures for a total of 24 cards. Each page has three rows of four cards measuring approximately 7 1/2 by 8 3/4". The individual cards measure 1 7/8" by 2 7/8". The cards are printed on thin paper stock. The fronts feature a posed all star color player photo with the player's autograph facsimile across the bottom of the picture. The backs carry biography, team name, and player profile superimposed over a ghosted team logo. The cards are unnumbered and checklisted below in alphabetical order. On an additional page that follows each of the player picture pages, is a page listing the player's statitics. A 1971 American and National League team schedule appears on the back of the album. The album, titled Today's All-Stars was produced by Dell and originally sold for 39 cents.

COMPLETE SET (24)	10.00	25.00
1 Hank Aaron	.40	1.00
2 Luis Aparicio	.15	.40
3 Ernie Banks	.30	.75
4 Johnny Bench	.30	.75
5 Rico Carty	.08	.20
6 Roberto Clemente	1.25	3.00
7 Bob Gibson	.15	.40
8 Willie Horton	.08	.20
9 Frank Howard	.12	.30
10 Reggie Jackson	.30	.75
11 Ferguson Jenkins	.15	.40
12 Alex Johnson	.08	.20
13 Al Kaline	.15	.40
14 Harmon Killebrew	.15	.40
15 Willie Mays	.40	1.00
16 Sam McDowell	.08	.20
17 Denny McLain	.12	.30
18 Boog Powell	.12	.30
19 Brooks Robinson	.15	.40
20 Frank Robinson	.15	.40
21 Pete Rose	.30	.75
22 Tom Seaver	.30	.75
23 Rusty Staub	.12	.30
24 Carl Yastrzemski	.15	.40
NNO Album	2.00	5.00

1904 Allegheny Card Company

This set, which looks like playing cards, featured National League players only. The fronts of the cards feature the player's portrait in a circle with the team name on top and the player's name and position on the bottom. Since the cards are not numbered, we have sequenced them in alphabetical order. It is important to note that only one of these sets have been discovered so far.

COMPLETE SET

1887 Allen and Ginter N28

This 50-card set of The World's Champions was marketed by Allen and Ginter in 1887. The cards feature color lithographs of champion athletes from seven categories of sport, with baseball, rowing and boxing each having 10 individuals portrayed. Cards numbered 1 to 10 depict baseball players and cards numbered 11 to 20 depict popular boxers of the era. This set is called the first series although no such title appears on the cards. All 50 cards are checklisted on the reverse, and they are unnumbered. An album (catalog: A16) and an advertising banner (catalog: G20) were also issued in conjunction with this set.

COMPLETE SET (50)	5,000.00	10,000.00
1 Cap Anson Baseball	2,500.00	4,000.00
2 Charles Bennett Baseball	350.00	600.00
3 Robert L. Caruthers Baseball	350.00	600.00
4 John Clarkson Baseball	900.00	1,500.00
5 Charles Comiskey Baseball	1,200.00	2,000.00
6 Captain Jack Glasscock Baseball	500.00	800.00
7 Timothy Keefe Baseball	900.00	1,500.00
8 Mike Kelly Baseball	1,200.00	2,000.00
9 Joseph Mulvey Baseball	500.00	800.00
10 John M. Ward Baseball	900.00	1,500.00

1888 Allen and Ginter N29

The second series of The World's Champions was probably issued in 1888. Like the first series, the cards are backlisted and unnumbered. However, there are 17 distinct categories of sports represented in this set, with only six baseball players portrayed (as opposed to 10 in the first series). Each card has a color lithograph of the individual set against a white background. An album (catalog: A17) and an advertising banner (catalog: G21) were issued in conjunction with the set. The numbering below is alphabetical within sport, e.g., baseball players (1-6), boxers (7-14), and other sports (15-50).

COMPLETE SET (50)	5,000.00	10,000.00
1 Buck Ewing Baseball	800.00	1,500.00
2 James H. Fogarty Baseball	350.00	700.00
3 Charles H. Getzein Baseball	350.00	700.00
4 George F. Miller Baseball	350.00	700.00
5 John Morrell Baseball	350.00	700.00
6 James Ryan Baseball	375.00	750.00

1888 Allen and Ginter N43

The primary designs of this 50-card set are identical to those of N29, but these are placed on a much larger card with extraneous background detail. The set was produced in 1888 by Allen and Ginter as inserts for a larger tobacco package than those in which sets N28 and N29 were marketed. Cards of this set, which is backlisted, are considered to be much scarcer than their counterparts in N29.

COMPLETE SET (50)	9,000.00	18,000.00
1 Buck Ewing Baseball	1,500.00	3,000.00
2 James J. Fogarty Baseball	700.00	1,400.00
3 Charles H. Getzein Baseball	700.00	1,400.00
4 George F. Miller Baseball	700.00	1,400.00
5 John Morrell Baseball	700.00	1,400.00
6 James Ryan Baseball	750.00	1,500.00

1908-10 American Caramel E91

The cards in this 99-card set measure 1 1/2" by 2 3/4". E91 encompasses three separate sets of color cards issued in 1908 and 1910. The 33 ballplayer drawings of the 1908 set were also used in the two 1910 sets. Eleven players were dropped and 11 were added for set 3. There are only 75 different players, so that, for example, there are two cards of Bender with identical fronts, but a different player is "named" in the same pose in set 3. Likewise, there can be three different players assigned to the same pose -- one from each set. The set 1 checklist lists "Athletics" first; set 3 "Pittsburgh" first.

COMPLETE SET (99)	5,000.00	10,000.00
1 Chief Bender	150.00	300.00
2 Roger Bresnahan	150.00	300.00
3 Al Bridwell	75.00	150.00
4 Mordecai Brown	150.00	300.00
5 Frank Chance	100.00	200.00
6 James Collins	150.00	300.00
7 Harry Davis	75.00	150.00
8 Art Devlin	75.00	150.00
9 Mike Donlin	100.00	200.00
10 Johnny Evers	100.00	200.00
11 Topsy Hartsel	75.00	150.00
12 Johnny Kling	75.00	150.00
13 Christy Mathewson	150.00	300.00
14 Joe McGinnity	150.00	300.00
15 John McGraw	100.00	200.00
16 Danny Murphy	75.00	150.00
17 Simon Nichols	75.00	150.00
18 Rube Oldring	75.00	150.00
19 Orval Overall	75.00	150.00
20 Eddie Plank	100.00	200.00
21 Ed Reulbach	75.00	150.00
22 Jimmy Scheckard	75.00	150.00
23 Ossie Schreckengost	75.00	150.00
24 Frank Schulte	100.00	200.00
25 Ralph Seybold	75.00	150.00
26 J.B. Seymore	75.00	150.00
27 Daniel Shay	75.00	150.00
28 James Slagle	75.00	150.00
29 Harry Steinfeldt	100.00	200.00
30 Luther Taylor	75.00	150.00
31 Fred Tenney	75.00	150.00
32 Joe Tinker	200.00	400.00
33 Rube Waddell	150.00	300.00
34 Jimmy Archer	75.00	150.00
35 Frank Baker	150.00	300.00
36 Jack Barry	75.00	150.00
37 Chief Bender	150.00	300.00
38 Al Bridwell	75.00	150.00
39 Mordecai Brown	150.00	300.00
40 Frank Chance	200.00	400.00
41 Eddie Collins	200.00	400.00
42 Harry Davis	75.00	150.00
43 Art Devlin	75.00	150.00
44 Mike Donlin	100.00	200.00
45 Larry Doyle	100.00	200.00
46 Johnny Evers	200.00	400.00
47 Bob Ganley	75.00	150.00
48 Fred Hartzell	75.00	150.00
49 Solly Hoffman	75.00	150.00
50 Harry Krause	75.00	150.00
51 Rube Marquard	150.00	300.00
52 Christy Mathewson	300.00	600.00
53 John McGraw	150.00	300.00
54 Chief Meyers	100.00	200.00
55 Danny Murphy	75.00	150.00
56 Red Murray	75.00	150.00
57 Orval Overall	75.00	150.00
58 Eddie Plank	200.00	400.00
59 Ed Reulbach	75.00	150.00
60 Jimmy Scheckard	75.00	150.00
61 Frank Schulte	100.00	200.00
62 J.B. Seymore	75.00	150.00
63 Harry Steinfeldt	100.00	200.00
64 Fred Tenney	75.00	150.00
65 Ira Thomas	75.00	150.00
66 Joe Tinker	200.00	400.00
67 Jap Barbeau	75.00	150.00
68 George Browne	75.00	150.00
69 Ed Carger	75.00	150.00
70 Charlie Chech	75.00	150.00
71 Fred Clarke	150.00	300.00
72 Wid Conroy	75.00	150.00
73 Jim Delehanty	75.00	150.00
74 Jiggs Donahue	75.00	150.00
75 J.A. Donohue	75.00	150.00
76 George Gibson	75.00	150.00
77 Bob Groom	75.00	150.00
78 Harry Hooper	150.00	300.00
79 Tom Hughes	75.00	150.00
80 Walter Johnson	300.00	600.00
81 Tommy Leach	100.00	200.00
82 Sam Leever	75.00	150.00
83 Harry Lord	75.00	150.00
84 George McBride	75.00	150.00
85 Amby McConnell	75.00	150.00
86 Clyde Milan	100.00	200.00
87 J.B. Miller	75.00	150.00
88 Harry Niles	75.00	150.00
89 Deacon Phillippe	100.00	200.00
90 Tris Speaker	200.00	400.00
91 Jack Stahl	100.00	200.00
92 Allen Storke	75.00	150.00
93 Gabby Street	100.00	200.00
94 Bob Unglaub	75.00	150.00
95 Charlie Wagner	75.00	150.00
96 Honus Wagner	400.00	800.00
97 Vic Willis	150.00	300.00
98 Owen Wilson	75.00	150.00
99 Joe Wood	150.00	300.00

1909-11 American Caramel E90-1

The cards in this 120-card set measure 1 1/2" by 2 3/4". The E90-1 set contains in order, the Mitchell of Cincinnati, Sweeney of Boston, and Graham cards which are more difficult to obtain than other cards in the set. In fact, there are many differential levels of scarcity in this set which was issued from 1909 through 1911. Several players exist in more than one pose or color background; these cards are noted in the checklist below. Of note, pricing for raw cards is provided in VgEx condition due to the fact that most cards from this set are found in off-grade shape.

1 William Bailey	60.00	120.00
2 Frank Baker	200.00	400.00
3 Jack Barry	60.00	120.00
4 George Bell	60.00	120.00
5 Harry Bemis	150.00	300.00
6 Chief Bender	250.00	500.00
7 Bob Bescher	150.00	250.00
8 Cliff Blankenship	75.00	150.00
9 John Bliss	60.00	120.00
10 Bill Bradley	100.00	200.00
11 Kitty Bransfield P on Shirt	60.00	120.00
12 Kitty Bransfield No P on Shirt	75.00	150.00
13 Roger Bresnahan	200.00	400.00
14 Al Bridwell	60.00	120.00
15 Buster Brown	150.00	250.00
16 Mordecai Brown	400.00	800.00
17 Donie Bush	60.00	120.00
18 John Butler	60.00	120.00
19 Howie Camnitz	60.00	120.00
20 Frank Chance	200.00	400.00
21 Hal Chase	175.00	350.00
22 Fred Clarke Phil	200.00	400.00
23 Fred Clarke Pitt	600.00	1,000.00
24 Wallace O. Clement	75.00	150.00
25 Ty Cobb	2,000.00	3,000.00
26 Eddie Collins	200.00	400.00
27 Frank Corridon	60.00	120.00
28 Sam Crawford	200.00	400.00
29 Lou Criger	60.00	120.00
30 George Davis	250.00	500.00
31 Jasper Davis	60.00	120.00
32 Ray Demmitt	150.00	250.00
33 Mike Donlin	100.00	200.00
34 Wild Bill Donovan	75.00	150.00
35 Red Dooin	60.00	120.00
36 Patsy Dougherty	250.00	500.00
37 Hugh Duffy	1,500.00	2,000.00
38 Jimmy Dygert	60.00	120.00
39 Rube Ellis	60.00	120.00
40 Clyde Engle	100.00	200.00
41 Art Fromme	150.00	250.00
42 George Gibson Back	225.00	450.00
43 George Gibson Front	100.00	200.00
44 George Graham	1,500.00	2,000.00
45 Eddie Grant	75.00	150.00
46 Dolly Gray	75.00	150.00
47 Bob Groom	60.00	120.00
48 Charles Hall	75.00	150.00
49 Tippy Hartzell Green	60.00	120.00
50 Tippy Hartzell Pink	100.00	200.00
51 William Heitmuller	60.00	120.00
52 H.Howell Follow Through	60.00	120.00
53 H.Howell Wind Up	75.00	150.00
54 Tex Erwin	75.00	150.00
55 Frank Isbell	60.00	120.00
56 Joe Jackson	20,000.00	30,000.00
57 Hugh Jennings	100.00	200.00
58 Tim Jordan	60.00	120.00
59 Addie Joss Pitching	600.00	1,000.00
60 Addie Joss Portrait	400.00	800.00
61 Ed Karger	400.00	800.00
62 Willie Keeler Pink Port	300.00	600.00
63 Willie Keeler Red Port	1,000.00	1,500.00
64 Willie Keeler Throwing	1,000.00	1,500.00
65 John Knight	150.00	250.00
66 Harry Krause	75.00	150.00
67 Nap Lajoie	400.00	800.00
68 Tommy Leach Batting	75.00	150.00
69 Tommy Leach Throwing	75.00	150.00
70 Sam Leever	60.00	120.00
71 Hans Lobert	175.00	350.00
72 Harry Lumley	60.00	120.00
73 Rube Marquard	200.00	400.00
74 Christy Matthewson	1,000.00	1,500.00
75 Stuffy McInnes	75.00	150.00
76 Harry McIntyre	60.00	120.00
77 Larry McLean	225.00	450.00
78 George McQuillan	60.00	120.00
79 Dots Miller w/o sunset in background	60.00	120.00
80 Dots Miller Red sunset in background		
81 Mike Mitchell	3,000.00	5,000.00
82 Fred Mitchell	100.00	200.00
83 George Mullin	75.00	150.00
84 Rebel Oakes	200.00	400.00
85 Patrick O'Connor	75.00	150.00
86 Charley O'Leary	60.00	120.00
87 Orval Overall	200.00	400.00
88 Jim Pastorius	60.00	120.00
89 Ed Phelps	60.00	120.00
90 Eddie Plank	600.00	1,000.00
91 Lew Richie	60.00	120.00
92 Germany Schaefer	75.00	150.00
93 Victor Schlitzer	150.00	300.00
94 Johnny Siegle	150.00	250.00
95 Dave Shean	175.00	350.00
96 Jimmy Sheckard	75.00	150.00
97 Tris Speaker	3,000.00	4,000.00
98 Jake Stahl	800.00	1,200.00
99 Oscar Stanage	60.00	120.00
100 George Stone Left Hand	300.00	600.00
101 George Stone No Hands	60.00	120.00
102 George Stovall	60.00	120.00
103 Ed Summers	60.00	120.00
104 Bill Sweeney	1,000.00	1,500.00
105 Jeff Sweeney	60.00	120.00
106 Jesse Tannehill	60.00	120.00
107 Lee Tannehill	60.00	120.00
108 Fred Tenney	100.00	200.00
109 Ira Thomas	75.00	150.00
110 Roy Thomas	60.00	120.00
111 Joe Tinker	200.00	400.00
112 Bob Unglaub	60.00	120.00
113 Jerry Upp	300.00	600.00
114 Honus Wagner Batting	2,000.00	3,000.00
115 Honus Wagner Throwing	2,000.00	3,000.00
116 Bobby Wallace	150.00	300.00
117 Ed Walsh	1,500.00	2,500.00
118 Vic Willis	250.00	500.00
119 Hooks Wiltse	100.00	200.00
120 Cy Young Boston	1,500.00	2,000.00
121 Cy Young Cleveland	1,500.00	2,000.00

1910 American Caramel E90-3

The E90-3 American Caramels "All the Star Players" set contains 20 unnumbered cards (each measuring 1 1/2" by 2 3/4") featuring the Chicago White Sox and Chicago Cubs. The eleven Cubs are listed first in the checklist below in alphabetical order (1-11), followed by the White Sox (12-20). The backs are slightly different from E90-1 cards and the fronts differ in the use of the team nicknames.

COMPLETE SET (20)	5,000.00	10,000.00
1 Jimmy Archer	300.00	600.00
2 Mordecai Brown	1,000.00	2,000.00
3 Frank Chance	1,250.00	2,500.00

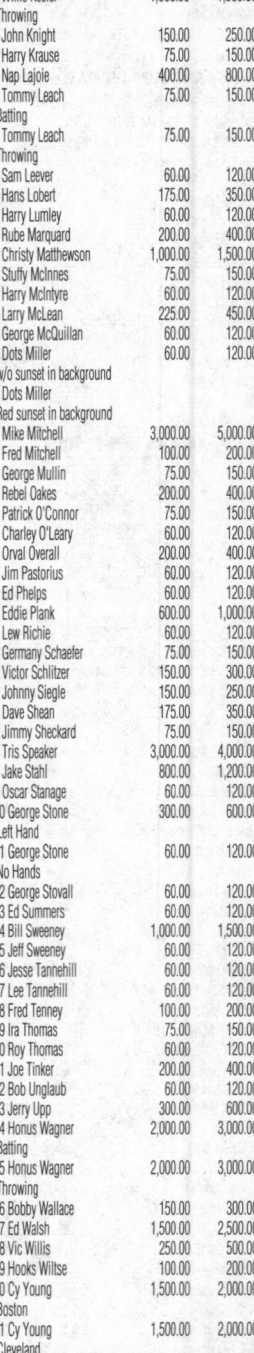

4 King Cole	300.00	600.00
5 Johnny Evers	1,000.00	2,000.00
6 Solly Hoffman	300.00	600.00
7 Orval Overall	300.00	600.00
8 Frank Schulte	400.00	800.00
9 Jimmy Scheckard	300.00	600.00
10 Harry Steinfeldt	400.00	800.00
11 Joe Tinker	1,000.00	2,000.00
12 Lena Blackburne	300.00	600.00
13 Patsy Dougherty	300.00	600.00
14 Chick Gandil	1,000.00	2,000.00
15 Ed Hahn	300.00	600.00
16 Fred Payne	300.00	600.00
17 Billy Purtell	300.00	600.00
18 Frank (Nig) Smith	300.00	600.00
19 Ed Walsh	1,000.00	2,000.00
20 Rollie Zeider	300.00	600.00

1915 American Caramel E106

The cards in this 48-card set measure 1 1/2" by 2 3/4". The color cards in this series of "leading Baseball players in the National, American and Federal Leagues" were produced by the American Caramel Company of York, PA. The obverse surfaces appear glazed, a process used in several other sets of this vintage (T213, T216), probably as protection against stain damage. The set was issued in 1915. The cards have been alphabetized and numbered in the checklist below. The complete set price includes all variation cards listed in the checklist below. Listed pricing references raw "VG" condition.

COMPLETE SET (48)	40,000.00	80,000.00
1 Jack Barry	150.00	250.00
2A Chief Bender Striped Hat	350.00	600.00
2B Chief Bender White Hat	350.00	600.00
3 Bob Bescher	150.00	250.00
4 Roger Bresnahan	300.00	500.00
5 Al Bridwell	150.00	250.00
6 Donie Bush	150.00	250.00
7A Hal Chase Portrait	250.00	400.00
7B Hal Chase Catching	250.00	400.00
8A Ty Cobb Batting Front	2,500.00	4,000.00
8B Ty Cobb Batting Side	2,500.00	4,000.00
9 Eddie Collins	300.00	500.00
10 Sam Crawford	300.00	500.00
11 Ray Demmitt	150.00	250.00
12 Bill Donovan	150.00	250.00
13 Red Dooin	150.00	250.00
14 Mickey Doolan	150.00	250.00
15 Larry Doyle	150.00	250.00
16 Clyde Engle	150.00	250.00
17 Johnny Evers	300.00	500.00
18 Art Fromme	150.00	250.00
19A George Gibson Back	150.00	250.00
19B George Gibson Front	150.00	250.00
20 Topsy Hartzell	150.00	250.00
21 Fred Jacklitsch	150.00	250.00
22 Hugh Jennings MG	300.00	500.00
23 Otto Knabe	150.00	250.00
24 Nap Lajoie	600.00	1,000.00
25 Hans Lobert	150.00	250.00
26 Rube Marquard	300.00	500.00
27 Christy Mathewson	1,500.00	2,500.00
28 John McGraw MG	300.00	500.00
29 George McQuillan	150.00	250.00
30 Dots Miller	150.00	250.00
31 Danny Murphy	150.00	250.00
32 Rebel Oakes	150.00	250.00
33 Eddie Plank	600.00	1,000.00
34 Germany Schaefer	150.00	250.00
35 Tris Speaker	700.00	1,200.00
36 Oscar Stanage	150.00	250.00
37 George Stovall	150.00	250.00
38 Jeff Sweeney	150.00	250.00
39A Joe Tinker Batting	350.00	600.00
39B Joe Tinker Portrait	350.00	600.00
40A Honus Wagner Batting	2,500.00	4,000.00
40B Honus Wagner Throwing	2,500.00	4,000.00
41 Hooks Wiltse	150.00	250.00
42 Heinie Zimmerman	150.00	250.00

1922 E122 American Caramel Series of 80

The cards in this 80-card set measure 2" by 3 1/2". The principal feature of this re-issue of the "80 series" of set E121 is the cross-hatch pattern or "screen" which covers the obverse of the card. The photos are black and white, and the player's name, position and team appear in a panel under his picture, all enclosed within the rectangular frame line. The set, which is unnumbered, was marketed in 1922 by the American Caramel Company. The cards have been alphabetized and numbered in the checklist below.

COMPLETE SET (80)	15,000.00	30,000.00
1 Grover C. Alexander	500.00	1,000.00
2 Jim Bagby	100.00	200.00
3 Frank Baker	250.00	500.00
4 Dave Bancroft	250.00	500.00
5 Ping Bodie	100.00	200.00
6 George H. Burns	100.00	200.00
7 George J. Burns	100.00	200.00
8 Owen Bush	100.00	200.00
9 Max Carey	250.00	500.00
10 Red Causey	100.00	200.00
11 Ty Cobb	1,250.00	2,500.00
12 Eddie Collins	500.00	1,000.00
13 Jake Daubert	150.00	300.00
14 Hooks Dauss	100.00	200.00
15 Charlie Deal	100.00	200.00
16 Bill Doak	100.00	200.00
17 Bill Donovan MG	100.00	200.00
18 Johnny Evers MG	250.00	500.00
19 Urban Faber	250.00	500.00
20 Eddie Foster	100.00	200.00
21 Larry Gardner	100.00	200.00
22 Kid Gleason MG	150.00	300.00
23 Hank Gowdy	150.00	300.00
24 John Graney	100.00	200.00
25 Tom Griffith	100.00	200.00
26 Harry Heilmann	250.00	500.00
27 Walter Holke	100.00	200.00
28 Charley Hollacher	100.00	200.00
29 Harry Hooper	250.00	500.00
30 Rogers Hornsby	600.00	1,200.00
31 Baby Doll Jacobson	100.00	200.00
32 Walter Johnson	750.00	1,500.00
33 James Johnston	100.00	200.00
34 Joe Judge	150.00	300.00
35 George Kelly	250.00	500.00
36 Dick Kerr	150.00	300.00
37 Pete Kilduff	100.00	200.00
38 Bill Killefer	100.00	200.00
39 John Lavan	100.00	200.00
40 Duffy Lewis	100.00	200.00
41 Al Mamaux	100.00	200.00
42 Rabbit Maranville	250.00	500.00
43 Carl Mays	150.00	300.00
44 John McGraw MG	250.00	500.00
45 Snuffy McInnis	150.00	300.00
46 Clyde Milan	150.00	300.00
47 Otto Miller	100.00	200.00
48 Guy Morton	100.00	200.00
49 Eddie Murphy	100.00	200.00
50 Hy Myers	100.00	200.00
51 Steve O'Neill	150.00	300.00
52 Roger Peckinpaugh	150.00	300.00
53 Jeff Pfeffer	100.00	200.00
54 Wally Pipp	150.00	300.00
55 Sam Rice	250.00	500.00
56 Eppa Rixey	250.00	500.00
57 Babe Ruth	2,500.00	5,000.00
58 Slim Sallee	100.00	200.00
59 Ray Schalk	250.00	500.00
60 Walter Schang	100.00	200.00
61 Ferd Schupp UER	100.00	200.00
62 Fred Schupp COR	100.00	200.00
63 Everett Scott	150.00	300.00
64 Hank Severeid	100.00	200.00
65 George Sisler Batting	500.00	1,000.00
66 George Sisler Throwing	500.00	1,000.00
67 Tris Speaker	500.00	1,000.00
68 Milton Stock	100.00	200.00
69 Amos Strunk	100.00	200.00
70 Chester Thomas	100.00	200.00
71 George Tyler	100.00	200.00
72 Jim Vaughn	100.00	200.00
73 Bob Veach	100.00	200.00
74 Oscar Vitt	100.00	200.00
75 Bill Wambsganss	150.00	300.00
76 Zach Wheat	250.00	500.00
77 Fred Williams	150.00	300.00
78 Ivy Wingo	100.00	200.00
79 Joe Wood	200.00	400.00
80 Pep Young	100.00	200.00

1910 American Caramel Die Cuts E125

These cards were first discovered in 1969. Cards from this set have been found from the following teams: Philadelphia A's; Boston Red Sox; New York Giants and Pittsburgh Pirates. The best supposition about this set places it being produced during the 1910 season. The cards are black and white and range as high as 7" and as much as 4" wide. Please not that this checklist may be incomplete.

COMPLETE SET (42)	60,000.00	120,000.00
1 Babe Adams	1,250.00	2,500.00
2 Red Ames	1,000.00	2,000.00
3 Frank Baker	3,000.00	6,000.00
4 Jack Barry	1,000.00	2,000.00
5 Chief Bender	3,000.00	6,000.00
6 Al Bridwell	1,000.00	2,000.00
7 Bobby Byrne	1,000.00	2,000.00
8 Bill Carrigan	1,000.00	2,000.00
9 Eddie Cicotte	3,000.00	6,000.00
10 Fred Clarke UER Name misspelled	3,000.00	6,000.00
11 Eddie Collins	4,000.00	8,000.00
12 Harry Davis	1,000.00	2,000.00
13 Art Devlin	1,000.00	2,000.00
14 Josh Devore	1,000.00	2,000.00
15 Larry Doyle	1,250.00	2,500.00
16 John Flynn	1,000.00	2,000.00
17 George Gibson	1,000.00	2,000.00
18 Topsy Hartsel UER Name misspelled	1,000.00	2,000.00
19 Harry Hooper	2,500.00	5,000.00
20 Harry Krause	1,000.00	2,000.00
21 Tommy Leach	1,000.00	2,000.00
22 Harry Lord	1,000.00	2,000.00
23 Christy Mathewson	7,500.00	15,000.00
24 Ambrose McConnell	1,000.00	2,000.00
25 Fred Merkle	1,250.00	2,500.00
26 Dots Miller	1,000.00	2,000.00
27 Danny Murphy	1,000.00	2,000.00
28 Red Murray	1,000.00	2,000.00
29 Harry Niles	1,000.00	2,000.00
30 Rube Oldring	1,000.00	2,000.00
31 Eddie Plank	4,000.00	8,000.00
32 Cy Seymour	1,000.00	2,000.00
33 Tris Speaker Batting	4,000.00	8,000.00
34 Tris Speaker Fielding	4,000.00	8,000.00
35 Jake Stahl	1,000.00	2,000.00
36 Ira Thomas	1,000.00	2,000.00
37 Heinie Wagner	1,000.00	2,000.00
38 Honus Wagner Batting	5,000.00	10,000.00
39 Honus Wagner Throwing	5,000.00	10,000.00
40 Art Wilson	1,000.00	2,000.00
41 Owen Wilson	1,250.00	2,500.00
42 Hooks Wiltse	1,000.00	2,000.00

1927 American Caramel E126

The cards in this 60-card set measure 1 5/8" by 3 1/4". The cards contain black and white pictures, with the individual's name centered underneath, and his team and position to either side below that. This is the only numbered series of baseball cards to be issued by American Caramel. The backs contain advertising for an album designed to hold the set.

COMPLETE SET (60)	7,500.00	15,000.00
1 John Gooch	100.00	200.00
2 Clyde Barnhart	100.00	200.00
3 Joe Bush	125.00	250.00
4 Lee Meadows	100.00	200.00
5 Dick Cox	100.00	200.00
6 Red Faber	200.00	400.00
7 Aaron Ward	100.00	200.00
8 Ray Schalk	200.00	400.00
9 Specs Toporcer	100.00	200.00
10 Billy Southworth	125.00	250.00
11 Allen Sothoron	100.00	200.00
12 Will Sherdel	100.00	200.00
13 Grover C. Alexander	250.00	500.00
14 Jack Quinn	125.00	250.00
15 Chick Galloway	100.00	200.00
16 Eddie Collins	250.00	500.00
17 Ty Cobb	1,000.00	2,000.00
18 Percy Jones	100.00	200.00
19 Charlie Grimm	125.00	250.00
20 Bennie Karr	100.00	200.00
21 Charlie Jamieson	100.00	200.00
22 Sherrod Smith	100.00	200.00
23 Vergil Cheeves	100.00	200.00
24 James Ring	100.00	200.00
25 Muddy Ruel	100.00	200.00
26 Joe Judge	125.00	250.00
27 Tris Speaker	300.00	600.00
28 Walter Johnson	500.00	1,000.00
29 Sam Rice	200.00	400.00
30 Hank DeBerry	100.00	200.00
31 Walter Henline	100.00	200.00
32 Max Carey	200.00	400.00
33 Arnold Statz	100.00	200.00
34 Irish Meusel	125.00	250.00
35 Pat Collins	100.00	200.00
36 Urban Shocker	125.00	250.00
37 Bob Shawkey	125.00	250.00
38 Babe Ruth	1,500.00	3,000.00
39 Bob Meusel	125.00	250.00
40 Alex Ferguson	100.00	200.00
41 Stuffy McInnis	125.00	250.00
42 Cy Williams	125.00	250.00
43 Russell Wrightstone	100.00	200.00
44 John Tobin UER photo is Ed Brown	125.00	250.00
45 Baby Doll Jacobson	100.00	200.00
46 Bryan Harris	100.00	200.00
47 Elam VanGilder	100.00	200.00
48 Ken Williams	125.00	250.00
49 George Sisler	250.00	500.00
50 Ed Brown UER photo is John Tobin	125.00	250.00
51 Jack Smith	100.00	200.00
52 Dave Bancroft	200.00	400.00
53 Larry Woodall	100.00	200.00
54 Lu Blue	100.00	200.00
55 Johnny Bassler	100.00	200.00
56 Jackie May	100.00	200.00
57 Horace Ford	100.00	200.00
58 Curt Walker	100.00	200.00
59 Art Nehf	100.00	200.00
60 George Kelly	200.00	400.00

1908 American League Publishing Co. PC770

This 1908-issued set features a large action shot or pose the player in uniform and also a small portrait of the player in street clothes in an oval at the top of the card. A short biography in a rectangular box is also featured at the base of the front, and the identifying line "American League Pub. Company, Cleveland, O." is located directly below the box.

COMPLETE SET (15)	4,000.00	8,000.00
1 Harry Bay	175.00	350.00
2 Charles Berger	175.00	350.00
3 Joe Birmingham	175.00	350.00
4 Bill Bradley	175.00	350.00
5 Walter Clarkson	175.00	350.00
6 Ty Cobb	900.00	1,800.00
7 Elmer Flick	300.00	600.00
8 Claude Hickman	175.00	350.00
9 William Hinchman	175.00	350.00
10 Addie Joss	400.00	800.00
11 Nap Lajoie	350.00	700.00
12 Glen Liebhardt	175.00	350.00
13 George Nill	175.00	350.00
14 George Perring	175.00	350.00
15 Honus Wagner	600.00	1,200.00

1968 American Oil Winners Circle

This set of 12 perforated game cards measures approximately 2 5/8" by 2 1/8". There are "left side" and "right side" game cards which had to be matched to win a car or a cash prize. The "right side" game cards have a color drawing of a sports personality in a circle on the left, surrounded by laurel leaf twigs, and a short career summary on the right. There is a color bar on the bottom of the game piece carrying a dollar amount and the words "right side". The "left side" game cards carry a rectangular drawing of a sports personality or a photo of a Camaro or a Corvette. A different color bar with a dollar amount and the words "left side" are under the picture. On a dark blue background, the "right side" backs carry the rules of the game, and the "left side" cards show a "Winners Circle". The cards are unnumbered and checklisted below in alphabetical order.

COMPLETE SET (12)	75.00	150.00
7 Mickey Mantle Left side	25.00	50.00
8 Willie Mays Right side	15.00	30.00
10 Babe Ruth Right side	25.00	50.00

1950 American Nut and Chocolate Co. Pennant

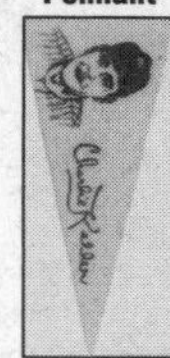

This 23-pennant set was distributed by the American Nut and Chocolate Co. and originally sold for 50 cents a set. The pennants measure approximately 1 7/8" by 4" and feature crude line-art drawings of the players with a facsimile autograph. The pennants are unnumbered and checklisted below in alphabetical order.

COMPLETE SET (23)	600.00	1,200.00
1 Ewell Blackwell	15.00	30.00
2 Harry Brecheen	15.00	30.00
3 Phil Cavarretta	20.00	40.00
4 Bobby Doerr	25.00	50.00
5 Bob Elliott	15.00	30.00
6 Boo Ferriss	15.00	30.00
7 Joe Gordon	20.00	40.00
8 Tommy Holmes	15.00	30.00
9 Charles Keller	20.00	40.00
10 Ken Keltner	15.00	30.00
11 Whitey Kurowski	15.00	30.00
12 Ralph Kiner	40.00	80.00
13 Johnny Pesky	20.00	40.00
14 Pee Wee Reese	40.00	80.00
15 Phil Rizzuto	40.00	80.00
16 Johnny Sain	20.00	40.00
17 Enos Slaughter	25.00	50.00
18 Warren Spahn	40.00	80.00
19 Vern Stephens	15.00	30.00
20 Earl Torgeson	15.00	30.00
21 Dizzy Trout	15.00	30.00
22 Ted Williams	100.00	200.00
23 Ted Williams CL	50.00	100.00

1961-66 American Tract Society

These cards are quite attractive and feature the "pure card" concept that is always popular with collectors, i.e., no borders or anything else on the card front to detract from the color photo. The cards are numbered on the back and the skip-numbering of the cards below is actually due to the fact that these cards are part of a much larger (sport and non-sport) set with a Christian theme. The set features Christian ballplayers giving first-person testimonies on the card backs telling how their belief in Jesus has changed their lives. These cards are sometimes referred to as "Tracards." The cards measure approximately 2 3/4" X 3 1/2". The set price below refers to only one of each player, not including any variations. These cards were issued throughout the 1960's, as one of the Felipe Alou cards features him in an Atlanta Braves cap (The Braves would not move to Atlanta until 1966)

COMPLETE SET (12)	60.00	120.00
43A Bobby Richardson Black print on back	8.00	20.00
43B Bobby Richardson Blue print on back	8.00	20.00
43C Bobby Richardson Black print on back with red Play Ball	8.00	20.00

43D Bobby Richardson	8.00	20.00
Black print on back		
with exclamation point		
51A Jerry Kindall	3.00	8.00
Portrait from chest up		
black print on back		
51B Jerry Kindall	3.00	8.00
On one knee		
blue print on back		
52A Felipe Alou	5.00	12.00
On one knee		
black print on back		
52B Felipe Alou	8.00	20.00
On one knee		
blue print on back		
52C Felipe Alou#Batting pose	5.00	12.00
52D Felipe Alou	3.00	8.00
66 Al Worthington	3.00	8.00
Black print on back		
XX Jim Kaat	8.00	20.00
Black and White		

1961 Angels Jay Publishing

This 12-card set of the Los Angeles Angels measures approximately 5" by 7". The fronts feature black-and-white posed player photos with the player's and team name printed below in the white border. These cards were packaged 12 to a packet. The backs are blank. The cards are unnumbered and checklisted below in alphabetical order.

COMPLETE SET (12)	6.00	15.00
1 Ken Aspromonte	.75	2.00
2 Julio Becquer	.75	2.00
3 Steve Bilko	.75	2.00
4 Fritz Brickell	.75	2.00
5 Bob Cerv	.75	2.00
6 Ned Garver	.75	2.00
7 Ted Kluszewski	3.00	8.00
8 Tom Morgan	.75	2.00
9 Albie Pearson	.75	2.00
10 Bill Rigney MG	.75	2.00
11 Faye Throneberry	.75	2.00
12 Ed Yost	.75	2.00

1962 Angels Jay Publishing

This 12-card set of the Los Angeles Angels measures approximately 5" by 7". The fronts feature black-and-white posed player photos with the player's and team name printed below in the white border. These cards were packaged 12 to a packet. The backs are blank. The cards are unnumbered and checklisted below in alphabetical order.

COMPLETE SET (12)	12.50	30.00
1 Earl Averill	.75	2.00
2 Steve Bilko	.75	2.00
3 Ryne Duren	1.25	3.00
4 Eli Grba	.75	2.00
5 Ken Hunt	.75	2.00
6 Ted Kluszewski	3.00	8.00
7 Tom Morgan	.75	2.00
8 Albie Pearson	.75	2.00
9 Bill Rigney MG	.75	2.00
10 Ed Sadowski	.75	2.00
11 Leon Wagner	.75	2.00
12 Eddie Yost	.75	2.00

1963-64 Angels Jay Publishing

This set of the Los Angeles Angels was issued over two years and measures approximately 5" by 7". The fronts feature black-and-white posed player photos with the player's and team name printed below in the white border. These cards were packaged 12 to a packet. The backs are blank. The cards are unnumbered and checklisted below in alphabetical order.

COMPLETE SET (19)	15.00	40.00
1 Bo Belinsky 64	1.25	3.00
2 Dean Chance	1.50	4.00
Head photo		
3 Dean Chance	1.50	4.00
Action pose		
4 Charlie Dees 64	.75	2.00
5 Jim Fregosi	1.50	4.00
6 Ken Hunt 63	.75	2.00
7 Don Lee	.75	2.00
8 Ken McBride 64	.75	2.00
9 Billy Moran	.75	2.00
10 Tom Morgan 63	.75	2.00
11 Dan Osinski 64	.75	2.00
12 Albie Pearson	.75	2.00
Action pose		
13 Albie Pearson	.75	2.00
Pose with bat		
14 Bill Rigney MG	.75	2.00
15 Bob Rodgers	.75	2.00
16 Ed Sadowski	.75	2.00
17 Lee Thomas	.75	2.00
Pose with bat		
18 Lee Thomas	.75	2.00
Closer pose with bat		
19 Leon Wagner 63	.75	2.00

1964 Angels Team Issue

This 10 card blank-backed set, which measures 5" by 7" was issued by the Angels as a package with a price of 25 cents. The fronts have white borders with the player's photo and the fascimile autograph on the bottom. Since the cards are unnumbered, we have sequenced them in alphabetical order.

COMPLETE SET (10)	20.00	40.00
1 Charlie Dees	2.00	5.00
2 Jim Fregosi	3.00	8.00
3 Ed Kirkpatrick	2.00	5.00
4 Joe Koppe	2.00	5.00
5 Barry Latman	2.00	5.00
6 Bob Lee	2.00	5.00
7 Albie Pearson	2.50	6.00
8 Jimmy Piersall	3.00	8.00
9 Bill Rigney MG	2.00	5.00
10 Bob Rodgers	2.00	5.00

1965 Angels Matchbooks County National

These matchbooks were issued by County National bank and feature members of the 1965 California Angels. The checklist is incomplete so any additions to finish the set are appreciated.

COMPLETE SET (8)	20.00	50.00
1 Jim Fregosi	4.00	10.00
2 Ed Kirkpatrick	2.50	6.00
3 Bobby Knoop	2.50	6.00
4 Barry Latman	2.50	6.00
5 Fred Newman	2.50	6.00
6 Bob Rodgers	2.50	6.00
7 Tom Satriano	2.50	6.00
8 Willie Smith	2.50	6.00

1965 Angels Matchbook Santa Ana

These matchbooks were issued by Santa Ana Savings bank and feature members of the 1965 California Angels. The checklist is incomplete so any additions to finish the set are appreciated.

COMPLETE SET (8)	20.00	50.00
1 Dean Chance	3.00	8.00
2 Jim Fregosi	4.00	10.00
3 Bobby Knoop	2.50	6.00
4 Ken McBride	2.50	6.00
5 Rick Reichardt	2.50	6.00
6 Bill Rigney MG	2.50	6.00
7 Bob Rodgers	2.50	6.00
8 Willie Smith	2.50	6.00

1966 Angels Dexter Press

Produced by Dexter Press, Inc. (West Nyack, New York), this sixteen-card set measures approximately 4" by 5 7/8". The fronts feature glossy posed color player photos with white borders. The player's autograph is inscribed in black across the top of the picture. In blue print, the back has the player's name, position, and biographical information. The cards are unnumbered and checklisted below in alphabetical order.

COMPLETE SET (16)	50.00	100.00
1 George Brunet	3.00	8.00
2 Jose Cardenal	3.00	8.00
3 Dean Chance	4.00	10.00
4 Jim Fregosi	5.00	12.00
5 Ed Kirkpatrick	3.00	8.00
6 Bob Knoop	3.00	8.00
7 Bob Lee	3.00	8.00
8 Marcelino Lopez	3.00	6.00
9 Fred Newman	3.00	8.00
10 Albie Pearson	3.00	8.00
11 Jimmy Piersall	5.00	12.00
12 Rick Reichardt	3.00	8.00
13 Bob Rodgers	3.00	8.00
14 Paul Schaal	3.00	8.00
15 Norm Siebern	3.00	8.00
16 Willie Smith	4.00	10.00

1966 Angels Matchbook

These matchbooks feature members of the 1966 California Angels and were produced for the County National Bank. This checklist may be incomplete so any additions are appreciated.

COMPLETE SET (8)	15.00	40.00
1 Dean Chance	2.50	6.00
2 Ed Kirkpatrick	2.00	5.00
3 Barry Latman	2.00	5.00
4 Bob Lee	2.00	5.00
5 Fred Newman	2.00	5.00
6 Bill Rigney MG	2.00	5.00
7 Bob Rodgers	2.00	5.00
8 Willie Smith	2.00	5.00

1969 Angels Jack in the Box

This 13-card set measures approximately 2 by 3 1/2" and features black-and-white player photos on a white card face. The cards are unnumbered and checklisted below in alphabetical order.

COMPLETE SET (13)	20.00	50.00
1 Sandy Alomar	1.25	3.00
2 Joe Azcue	1.00	2.50
3 Jim Fregosi	2.00	5.00
4 Lou Johnson	1.00	2.50
5 Jay Johnstone	1.25	3.00
6 Rudy May	1.00	2.50
7 Jim McGlothlin	1.00	2.50
8 Andy Messersmith	2.00	5.00
9 Tom Murphy	1.00	2.50
10 Rick Reichardt	1.00	2.50
11 Aurelio Rodriguez	1.00	2.50
12 Jim Spencer	1.00	2.50
13 Hoyt Wilhelm	4.00	10.00

1971 Angels Jack in the Box

This 10-card set measures approximately 4 by 2 1/2" and features yellowish tone player photos printed on tan paper stock. The cards are unnumbered and checklisted below in alphabetical order.

COMPLETE SET (10)	10.00	25.00
1 Sandy Alomar	1.00	2.50
2 Ken Berry	.75	2.00
3 Tony Conigliaro	2.50	6.00
4 Jim Fregosi	1.50	4.00
5 Alex Johnson	.75	2.00
6 Rudy May	.75	2.00
7 Andy Messersmith	1.25	3.00
8 Lefty Phillips MG	.75	2.00
9 Jim Spencer	.75	2.00
10 Clyde Wright	.75	2.00

1972 Angels Postcards

These 30 black and white 3 1/4" by 4 3/4" blank backed postcards feature members of the 1972 California Angels. A key card in the set is Nolan Ryan, during his first season as a member of the Angels.

COMPLETE SET (30)	8.00	20.00
1 Lloyd Allen	.20	.50
2 Sandy Alomar	.30	.75
3 Steve Barber	.20	.50
4 Ken Berry	.20	.50
5 Leo Cardenas	.20	.50
6 Rick Clark	.20	.50
7 Eddie Fisher	.20	.50
8 Art Kusnyer	.20	.50
9 Winston Llenas	.20	.50
10 Rudy May	.20	.50
11 Ken McMullen	.20	.50
12 Andy Messersmith	.20	.50
13 Bob Oliver	.20	.50
14 Vada Pinson	.40	1.00
15 Mel Queen	.20	.50
16 Mickey Rivers	.60	1.50
17 Don Rose	.20	.50
18 Nolan Ryan	4.00	10.00
19 Jim Spencer	.20	.50
20 Lee Stanton	.20	.50
21 John Stephenson	.20	.50
22 Jeff Torborg	.20	.50
23 Clyde Wright	.20	.50
24 Del Rice MG	.20	.50
25 Peanuts Lowrey CO	.20	.50
26 Tom Morgan CO	.20	.50
27 Jimmie Reese CO	.30	.75
28 John Roseboro CO	.20	.50
29 Bobby Winkles CO	.20	.50
30 Gene Autry OWN	.30	.75
Most of tie showing		

1973 Angels Postcards

These 40 3 1/4" by 4 3/4" blank-backed, black and white, postcards feature members of the 1973 California Angels.

COMPLETE SET (40)	10.00	25.00
1 Lloyd Allen	.20	.50
2 Sandy Alomar	.20	.50
3 Steve Barber	.20	.50
4 Ken Berry	.20	.50
5 Jerry DaVanon	.20	.50
6 Mike Epstein	.20	.50
7 Alan Gallagher	.20	.50
8 Bill Grabarkewitz	.20	.50
9 Rich Hand	.20	.50
10 Art Kusnyer	.20	.50
11 Dick Lange	.20	.50
12 Winston Llenas	.20	.50
13 Rudy May	.20	.50
14 Tom McCraw	.20	.50
15 Rudy Meoli	.20	.50
16 Aurelio Monteagudo	.20	.50
17 Tom Morgan CO	.20	.50
18 Bob Oliver	.20	.50
19 Bill Parker	.20	.50
20 Salty Parker CO	.20	.50
21 Ron Perranoski	.20	.50
22 Vada Pinson	.40	1.00
23 Jimmie Reese CO	.30	.75
24 Frank Robinson	1.50	4.00
25 John Roseboro CO	.20	.50
26 Nolan Ryan	3.00	8.00
27 Richie Scheinblum	.20	.50
28 Dave Sells	.20	.50
29 Bill Singer	.20	.50
30 Jim Spencer	.20	.50
31 Lee Stanton	.20	.50
32 John Stephenson	.20	.50
33 Jeff Torborg	.30	.75
34 Bobby Valentine	.30	.75
35 Bobby Winkles MG	.20	.50
36 Clyde Wright	.20	.50
37 Gene Autry OWN	.30	.75
Photo closely cropped		
38 Harry Dalton GM	.20	.50
39 Don Drysdale ANN	.60	1.50
40 Dick Enberg ANN	.30	.75

1974 Angels Postcards

These 39 black and white, blank-backed postcards feature members of the 1974 California Angels. They are unnumbered and we have sequenced them in alphabetical order. Dick Williams replaced Bobby Winkles as manager midway through the season which accounts for the two different manager cards in this set.

COMPLETE SET (39)	12.50	30.00
1 Sandy Alomar	.30	.75
2 Dave Chalk	.20	.50
3 John Doherty	.20	.50
4 Denny Doyle	.20	.50
5 Tom Egan	.20	.50
6 Ed Figueroa	.20	.50
7 Andy Hassler	.20	.50
8 Whitey Herzog CO	.30	.75
9 Doug Howard	.20	.50
10 Joe Lahoud	.20	.50
11 Dick Lange	.20	.50
12 Winston Llenas	.20	.50
13 Skip Lockwood	.20	.50
14 Rudy May	.20	.50
15 Tom McCraw	.20	.50
16 Tom Morgan CO	.20	.50
17 Bob Oliver	.20	.50
18 Salty Parker CO	.20	.50
19 Jimmie Reese CO	.30	.75
20 Mickey Rivers	.30	.75
21 Frank Robinson	1.50	4.00
22 Ellie Rodriguez	.20	.50
23 John Roseboro CO	.20	.50
24 Nolan Ryan	3.00	8.00
25 Charlie Sands	.20	.50
26 Paul Schaal	.20	.50
27 Dave Sells	.20	.50
28 Dick Selma	.20	.50
29 Bill Singer	.20	.50
30 Lee Stanton	.20	.50
31 Bill Stoneman	.30	.75
32 Frank Tanana	.40	1.00
33 Bobby Valentine	.30	.75
34 Dick Williams MG	.30	.75
35 Bob Winkles MG	.20	.50
36 Gene Autry OWN	.30	.75
37 Harry Dalton GM	.20	.50
38 Don Drysdale ANN	.60	1.50
39 Dick Enberg ANN	.30	.75

1975 Angels Postcards

This 48-card set of the California Angels features player photos on postcard-size cards. The cards are unnumbered and checklisted in alphabetical order.

COMPLETE SET (48)	12.50	30.00
1 Jerry Adair CO	.20	.50
2 Bob Allietta	.20	.50
3 Gene Autry OWN	.40	1.00
4 John Balaz	.20	.50
5 Steve Blateric	.20	.50
6 Bruce Bochte	.30	.75
7 Jim Brewer	.20	.50
8 Dave Chalk	.20	.50
9 Dave Collins	.20	.50
10 Harry Dalton GM	.20	.50
11 Chuck Dobson	.20	.50
12 John Doherty	.20	.50
13 Denny Doyle	.20	.50
14 Don Drysdale ANN	.75	2.00
15 Tom Egan	.20	.50
16 Dick Enberg ANN	.30	.75
17 Ed Figueroa	.20	.50
18 Ike Hampton	.20	.50
19 Tommy Harper	.20	.50
20 Andy Hassler	.20	.50
21 Whitey Herzog MG	.40	1.00
22 Chuck Hockenbery	.20	.50
23 Don Kirkwood	.20	.50
24 Joe Lahoud	.20	.50
25 Dick Lange	.20	.50
26 Winston Llenas	.20	.50
27 Rudy Meoli	.20	.50
28 Mike Miley	.20	.50
29 Billy Muffett CO	.20	.50
30 Morris Nettles	.20	.50
31 Orlando Pena	.20	.50
32 Orlando Ramirez	.20	.50
33 Jimmie Reese CO	.30	.75

34 Jerry Remy	.20	.50
35 Grover Resinger CO	.20	.50
36 Mickey Rivers	.30	.75
37 Ellie Rodriguez	.20	.50
38 Nolan Ryan	3.00	8.00
39 Mickey Scott	.20	.50
40 Dave Sells	.20	.50
41 Bill Singer	.20	.50
42 Billy Smith	.20	.50
43 Lee Stanton	.20	.50
44 Bill Sudakis	.20	.50
45 Frank Tahana	.40	1.00
46 Bob Valentine	.30	.75
47 Dick Williams MG	.30	.75
48 Anaheim Stadium	.20	.50

1976 Angels Postcards

These 39 blank-backed black and white postcards feature members of the 1976 California Angels. They measure 3 1/4" by 5 1/2" and we have sequenced them alphabetically.

COMPLETE SET (39)	10.00	25.00
1 Orlando Alvarez	.20	.50
2 Bruce Bochte	.20	.50
3 Bobby Bonds	.40	1.00
4 Jim Brewer	.20	.50
5 Dan Briggs	.20	.50
6 Dave Chalk	.20	.50
7 Bob Clear CO	.20	.50
8 Dave Collins	.20	.50
9 Paul Dade	.20	.50
10 Dick Drago	.20	.50
11 Andy Etchebarren	.20	.50
12 Adrian Garrett	.20	.50
13 Mario Guerrero	.20	.50
14 Ike Hampton	.20	.50
15 Paul Hartzell	.20	.50
16 Ed Herrmann	.20	.50
17 Vern Hoscheit CO	.20	.50
18 Terry Humphrey	.20	.50
19 Ron Jackson	.20	.50
20 Bob Jones	.20	.50
21 Bill Melton	.20	.50
22 Sid Monge	.20	.50
23 Billy Muffett CO	.20	.50
24 Mike Overy	.20	.50
25 Orlando Ramirez	.20	.50
26 Jimmie Reese CO	.30	.75
27 Jerry Remy Position listed as 2B	.20	.50
28 Jerry Remy Position listed as IF	.20	.50
29 Grover Resinger CO	.20	.50
30 Gary Ross	.20	.50
31 Nolan Ryan Entire collar on jersey	2.00	5.00
32 Nolan Ryan Collar cut off	2.00	5.00
33 Mickey Scott	.20	.50
34 Norm Sherry CO	.20	.50
35 Lee Stanton	.20	.50
36 Frank Tanana	.30	.75
37 Rusty Torres	.20	.50
38 John Verhoeven	.20	.50
39 Dick Williams MG	.30	.75

1977 Angels Postcards

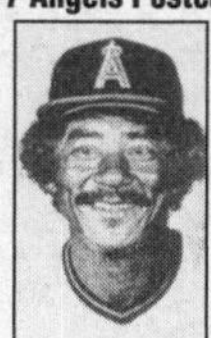

These 49 blank backed postcards measure 3 1/4" by 5 1/2" and feature members of the 1977 California Angels. These cards are unnumbered so we have sequenced them alphabetically.

COMPLETE SET (49)	12.50	30.00
1 Willie Aikens	.20	.50
2 Mike Barlow	.20	.50
3 Don Baylor	.60	1.50
4 Bruce Bochte	.20	.50
5 Bobby Bonds	.40	1.00
6 Thad Bosley	.20	.50
7 Ken Brett	.20	.50
8 Dan Briggs	.20	.50
9 John Caneira	.20	.50
10 Dave Chalk	.20	.50
11 Bob Clear CO	.20	.50
12 Del Crandall CO	.20	.50
13 Mike Cuellar	.30	.75
14 Dick Drago	.20	.50
15 Andy Etchebarren	.20	.50
16 Gil Flores	.20	.50
17 Dave Garcia MG	.20	.50
18 Dan Goodwin	.20	.50
19 Marv Grissom CO	.20	.50
20 Bobby Grich	.30	.75
21 Mario Guerrero	.20	.50
22 Ike Hampton	.20	.50
23 Paul Hartzell	.20	.50
24 Terry Humphrey	.20	.50
25 Ron Jackson	.20	.50
26 Bob Jones	.20	.50
27 Don Kirkwood	.20	.50
28 Fred Kuhaulua	.20	.50
29 Ken Landreaux	.30	.75
30 Dave LaRoche	.20	.50
31 Carlos May	.20	.50
32 Billy Muffett CO	.20	.50
33 Rance Mulliniks	.20	.50
34 Dyar Miller	.20	.50
35 Gary Nolan	.20	.50
36 Jimmie Reese CO	.30	.75
37 Jerry Remy	.20	.50
38 Frank Robinson CO	1.00	2.50
39 Gary Ross	.20	.50
40 Joe Rudi	.20	.50
41 Nolan Ryan	2.00	5.00
42 Mickey Scott	.20	.50
43 Norm Sherry MG	.20	.50
44 Wayne Simpson	.20	.50
45 Tony Soliata	.20	.50
46 Frank Tanana	.30	.75
47 Rusty Torres	.20	.50
48 John Verhoeven	.20	.50
49 Dick Enberg ANN	.30	.75

1978 Angels Family Fun Centers

This 37-card set features members of the 1978 California Angels. These large cards measure approximately 3 1/2" by 5 1/2" and display sepia tone player photos. The cards are unnumbered and checklisted below in alphabetical order. This set was also available in uncut sheet form.

COMPLETE SET (37)	20.00	50.00
1 Don Aase	.60	1.50
2 Mike Barlow	.60	1.50
3 Don Baylor	1.00	2.50
4 Lyman Bostock	2.00	5.00
5 Ken Brett	.75	2.00
6 Dave Chalk	.60	1.50
7 Bob Clear	.60	1.50
8 Brian Downing	1.00	2.50
9 Ron Fairly	.75	2.00
10 Gil Flores	.60	1.50
11 Dave Frost	.60	1.50
12 Dave Garcia	.60	1.50
13 Bobby Grich	1.00	2.50
14 Tom Griffin	.60	1.50
15 Marv Grissom CO	.60	1.50
16 Ike Hampton	.60	1.50
17 Paul Hartzell	.60	1.50
18 Terry Humphrey	.60	1.50
19 Ron Jackson	.60	1.50
20 Chris Knapp	.60	1.50
21 Ken Landreaux	.75	2.00
22 Carney Lansford	1.25	3.00
23 Dave LaRoche	.60	1.50
24 John McNamara MG	.75	2.00
25 Dyar Miller	.60	1.50
26 Rick Miller	.60	1.50
27 Balor Moore	.60	1.50
28 Rance Mulliniks	.75	2.00
29 Floyd Rayford	.60	1.50
30 Jimmie Reese CO	1.00	2.50
31 Merv Rettenmund	.60	1.50
32 Joe Rudi	.75	2.00
33 Nolan Ryan	6.00	15.00
34 Bob Skinner CO	.60	1.50
35 Tony Solaita	.60	1.50
36 Frank Tanana	1.00	2.50
37 Dickie Thon	.75	2.00

1979 Arizona Sports Collectors Show

COMPLETE SET (10)	7.50	15.00
1 Jim Colborn	.30	.75
2 Jocko Conlon	1.25	3.00
3 Gary Gentry	.30	.75
4 Charlie Grimm	.60	1.50
6 Ken Rudolph	.30	.75
7 Mike Sadek	.30	.75
10 George Zuverink	.30	.75

1953-63 Artvue Hall of Fame Postcards

This 91-card set features photos of the members of the Baseball Hall of Fame printed on postcard-size cards. The cards are unnumbered and checklisted below in alphabetical order.

COMPLETE SET (91)	300.00	600.00
1 Grover Alexander	5.00	12.00
2 Cap Anson	5.00	12.00
3 Frank Baker	4.00	10.00
4 Ed Barrow	2.00	5.00
5 Chief Bender	2.50	6.00
6 Roger Bresnahan	2.00	5.00
7 Modecai Brown	4.00	10.00
8 Morgan Bulkeley	2.00	5.00
9 Jesse Burkett	2.00	5.00
10 Max Carey	2.00	5.00
11 Alexander Cartwright	2.00	5.00
12 Henry Chadwick	2.00	5.00
13 Frank Chance	2.50	6.00
14 Jack Chesbro	2.00	5.00
15 Fred Clarke	2.00	5.00
16 John Clarkson	2.00	5.00
17 Ty Cobb	10.00	25.00
18 Mickey Cochrane	2.50	6.00
19 Eddie Collins	4.00	10.00
20 Jimmy Collins	2.00	5.00
21 Charlie Comiskey	2.00	5.00
22 Tom Connolly	2.00	5.00
23 Sam Crawford	3.00	8.00
24 Joe Cronin	2.50	6.00
25 Candy Cummings	2.00	5.00
26 Dizzy Dean	2.50	6.00
27 Ed Delehanty	2.00	5.00
28 Bill Dickey	2.50	6.00
29 Joe DiMaggio	15.00	40.00
30 Hugh Duffy	2.00	5.00
31 Johnny Evers	2.00	5.00
32 Buck Ewing	2.00	5.00
33 Bob Feller	40.00	80.00
34 Elmer Flick	2.00	5.00
35 Jimmy Foxx (Jimmie)	3.00	8.00
36 Frankie Frisch	2.50	6.00
37 Lou Gehrig	12.50	30.00
38 Charlie Gehringer	4.00	10.00
39 Hank Greenberg	4.00	10.00
40 Clark Griffith	2.50	6.00
41 Lefty Grove	6.00	15.00
42 Billy Hamilton	2.50	6.00
43 Gabby Hartnett	2.00	5.00
44 Harry Heilmann	2.00	5.00
45 Rogers Hornsby	6.00	12.00
46 Carl Hubbell	5.00	12.50
47 Hugh Jennings	2.00	5.00
48 Ban Johnson	2.00	5.00
49 Walter Johnson	7.50	20.00
50 Willie Keeler	2.50	6.00
51 King Kelly	2.50	6.00
52 Bill Klem	2.00	5.00
53 Nap Lajoie	7.50	20.00
54 Kenesaw Mountain Landis	2.00	5.00
55 Ted Lyons	2.00	5.00
56 Connie Mack	4.00	10.00
57 Rabbit Maranville	2.00	5.00
58 Christy Mathewson	6.00	15.00
59 Joe McCarthy	2.00	5.00
60 Tom McCarthy	2.00	5.00
61 Joe McGinnity	2.00	5.00
62 John McGraw	4.00	10.00
63 Bill McKechnie	2.00	5.00
64 Kid Nichols	2.00	5.00
65 Jimmy O'Rourke	2.00	5.00
66 Mel Ott	3.00	8.00
67 Herb Pennock	2.00	5.00
68 Eddie Plank	2.00	5.00
69 Sam Rice	2.00	5.00
70 Eppa Rixey	2.00	5.00
71 Jackie Robinson	10.00	25.00
72 Wilbert Robinson	2.00	5.00
73 Edd Roush	2.00	5.00
74 Babe Ruth	20.00	50.00
75 Ray Schalk	2.00	5.00
76 Al Simmons	2.50	6.00
77 George Sisler	4.00	10.00
78 Albert Spalding	2.50	6.00
79 Tris Speaker	4.00	10.00
80 Bill Terry	2.50	6.00
81 Joe Tinker	2.50	6.00
82 Dazzy Vance	2.00	5.00
83 Rube Waddell	3.00	8.00
84 Honus Wagner	8.00	20.00
85 Bobby Wallace	2.00	5.00
86 Ed Walsh	2.00	5.00
87 Paul Waner	2.50	6.00
88 Zach Wheat	2.00	5.00
89 George Wright	2.00	5.00
90 Harry Wright	2.00	5.00
91 Cy Young	8.00	20.00

1967 Ashland Oil

This 12 card set measures 2" by 7 1/2" and the cards are unnumbered. Therefore, we have sequenced the cards in alphabetical order. Jim Maloney is considered tougher and is notated as a SP in the listings below.

COMPLETE SET (9)	150.00	300.00
1 Jim Bunning	10.00	25.00
2 Elston Howard	6.00	15.00
3 Al Kaline	20.00	40.00
4 Harmon Killebrew	12.50	30.00
5 Ed Kranepool	4.00	10.00
6 Jim Maloney SP	30.00	60.00
7 Bill Mazeroski	10.00	25.00
8 Frank Robinson	10.00	25.00
9 Ron Santo	20.00	40.00
10 Joe Torre	8.00	20.00
11 Leon Wagner	4.00	10.00
12 Pete Ward	4.00	10.00

1965 Astros Jay Publishing

This 12-card set of the Houston Astros measures approximately 5" by 7". The fronts feature black-and-white posed player photos with the player's and team name printed below in the white border. These cards were packaged 12 to a packet. The backs are blank. The cards are unnumbered and checklisted below in alphabetical order. This was the debut season for Houston to be named the Astros.

COMPLETE SET (12)	20.00	50.00
1 Dave Adlesh	2.00	5.00
2 Bob Aspromonte	2.00	5.00
3 John Bateman	2.00	5.00
4 Walt Bond	2.00	5.00
5 Ron Brand	2.00	5.00
6 Nellie Fox	4.00	10.00
7 Jerry Grote	2.00	5.00
8 Sonny Jackson	2.00	5.00
9 Eddie Kasko	2.00	5.00
10 Bob Lillis	2.00	5.00
11 Mike White	2.00	5.00
12 Lum Harris MG	2.00	5.00

1965 Astros Team Issue

These blank-back black and white photos measure 3 1/4" by 5 1/2". The photos are facsimile autographs on the bottom and we have sequenced them in alphabetical order.

COMPLETE SET (25)	50.00	100.00
1 Jimmie Adair CO	1.25	3.00
2 Bob Aspromonte	1.50	4.00
3 John Bateman	1.25	3.00
4 Walt Bond	1.25	3.00
5 Bob Bruce	1.25	3.00
6 Jim Busby CO	1.25	3.00
7 Danny Coombs	1.25	3.00
8 Larry Dierker	2.50	6.00
9 Dick Farrell	1.25	3.00
10 Nellie Fox CO	6.00	15.00
11 Joe Gaines	1.25	3.00
12 Dave Giusti	1.50	4.00
13 Luman Harris MG	1.25	3.00
14 Eddie Kasko	1.25	3.00
15 Bob Lillis	1.25	3.00
16 Ken Mackenzie	1.25	3.00
17 Joe Morgan	4.00	10.00
18 Don Nottebart	1.25	3.00
19 Jim Owens	1.25	3.00
20 Howie Pollet CO	1.25	3.00
21 Gene Ratliff	1.25	3.00
22 Claude Raymond	1.25	3.00
23 Rusty Staub	3.00	8.00
24 Jim Wynn	2.50	6.00
25 Hal Woodeshick	1.25	3.00

1967 Astros

RUSTY STAUB
INFIELDER

These 30 blank-backed cards are irregularly cut, but most measure approximately 1 1/4" by 2". They feature white bordered black-and-white posed player photos and carry the player's name and position in black lettering within the lower white margin. The backs are blank. The cards are unnumbered and checklisted below in alphabetical order.

COMPLETE SET (30)	30.00	60.00
1 Dave Adlesh	.75	2.00
2 Bob Aspromonte	1.00	2.50
3 John Bateman	.75	2.00
4 Wade Blasingame	.75	2.00
5 John Buzhardt	.75	2.00
6 Danny Coombs	.75	2.00
7 Mike Cuellar	1.25	3.00
8 Ron Davis	.75	2.00
9 Larry Dierker	1.50	4.00
10 Dave Giusti	1.00	2.50
11 Fred Gladding	.75	2.00
12 Julio Gotay	.75	2.00
13 Buddy Hancken CO	.75	2.00
14 Grady Hatton MG	.75	2.00
15 Hal King	.75	2.00
16 Denny Lemaster	.75	2.00
17 Mel McGaha CO	.75	2.00
18 Denis Menke	.75	2.00
19 Norm Miller	.75	2.00
20 Joe Morgan	4.00	10.00
21 Ivan Murrell	.75	2.00
22 Jim Owens CO	.75	2.00
23 Salty Parker CO	.75	2.00
24 Doug Rader	1.25	3.00
25 Jim Ray	.75	2.00
26 Rusty Staub	2.50	6.00
27 Lee Thomas	.75	2.00
28 Hector Torres	.75	2.00
29 Don Wilson	1.25	3.00
30 Jimmy Wynn	1.50	4.00

1967 Astros Team Issue Postcards

These cards, which measure just slightly shorter than standard postcards, feature members of the 1967 Houston Astros. These cards have the player's name , position and Houston Astros (in all caps) at the bottom of the white borders. Since these cards are unnumbered, we have sequenced them in alphabetical order.

COMPLETE SET (27)	15.00	40.00
1 Bob Aspromonte	.60	1.50
2 Lee Bales	.40	1.00
3 John Bateman	.40	1.00
4 Ron Brand	.40	1.00
5 Bo Belinsky	.60	1.50
6 Mike Cuellar	.75	2.00
7 Ron Davis	.40	1.00
8 Larry Dierker	1.00	2.50
9 Dick Farrell	.40	1.00
10 Dave Giusti	.40	1.00
11 Chuck Harrison	.40	1.00
12 Grady Hatton MG	.40	1.00
13 Bill Heath	.40	1.00
14 Sonny Jackson	.40	1.00
15 Jim Landis	.40	1.00
16 Bob Lillis	.40	1.00
17 Barry Latman	.40	1.00
18 Ed Mathews	2.00	5.00
19 Joe Morgan	3.00	8.00
20 Aaron Pointer	.40	1.00
21 Claude Raymond	.40	1.00
22 Carroll Sembera	.40	1.00
23 Dan Schneider	.40	1.00
24 Rusty Staub	1.25	3.00
25 Don Wilson	.75	2.00
26 Jim Wynn	.60	1.50
27 Chris Zachary	.40	1.00

1967 Astros Team Issue

This 12-card team-issued set features the 1967 Houston Astros. The cards measure approximately 2 1/2" by 3" and show signs of perforation on their sides. The reason for the perforations were that the they were issued as a perforated sheet and sold at Astrodome souvenir stands. The posed color player photos have white borders and a facsimile autograph inscribed across them. The horizontally oriented backs have biography and career summary information on a yellow background, and complete statistics. The cards are unnumbered and checklisted below in alphabetical order. This set was available for $1 direct from the Astros.

COMPLETE SET (12) 50.00 100.00
1 Bob Aspromonte 2.00 5.00
2 John Bateman 1.25 3.00
3 Mike Cuellar 2.50 6.00
4 Larry Dierker 3.00 8.00
5 Dave Giusti 2.00 5.00
6 Grady Hatton MG 1.25 3.00
7 Bill Heath 1.25 3.00
8 Sonny Jackson 1.25 3.00
9 Eddie Mathews 10.00 25.00
10 Joe Morgan 10.00 25.00
11 Rusty Staub 3.00 8.00
12 Jim Wynn 3.00 8.00

1970 Astros Photos

These photos feature members of the 1970 Houston Astros. The photos are unnumbered and we have sequenced them in alphabetical order. A photo of Cesar Cedeno in his rookie season is included in this set.

COMPLETE SET 8.00 20.00
1 Jack Billingham .20 .50
2 Cesar Cedeno .60 1.50
3 Ron Cook .20 .50
4 George Culver .20 .50
5 Larry Dierker .40 1.00
6 Jack DiLauro .20 .50
7 John Edwards .20 .50
8 Ken Forsch .30 .75
9 Fred Gladding .20 .50
10 Larry Howard .20 .50
11 Keith Lampard .20 .50
12 Denny LeMaster .20 .50
13 Marty Martinez .20 .50
14 John Mayberry .30 .75
15 Denis Menke .20 .50
16 Roger Metzger .20 .50
17 Jesus Alou .30 .75
18 Norm Miller .20 .50
19 Joe Morgan 1.50 4.00
20 Doug Rader .40 1.00
21 Jim Ray .20 .50
22 Hector Torres .20 .50
23 Harry Walker MG .20 .50
24 Bob Watson .40 1.00
25 Bob Watson .40 1.00
26 Don Wilson .20 .50
27 Jim Wynn .40 1.00
28 Jim York .20 .50

1970 Astros Team Issue

This 12-card set of the Houston Astros measures approximately 4 1/4" by 7". The fronts display black-and-white player portraits bordered in white. The player's name and team are printed in the top margin. The backs are blank. The cards are unnumbered and checklisted below in alphabetical order.

COMPLETE SET (10) 8.00 20.00
1 Tommy Davis .75 2.00
2 Larry Dierker .75 2.00
3 John Edwards .40 1.00
4 Fred Gladding .40 1.00
5 Tom Griffin .40 1.00
6 Denny Lemaster .40 1.00
7 Denis Menke .40 1.00
8 Joe Morgan 2.00 5.00
9 Joe Pepitone .60 1.50
10 Doug Rader .60 1.50
11 Don Wilson .60 1.50
12 Jim Wynn .75 2.00

1971 Astros Coke

Sponsored by the Houston Coca-Cola Bottling Company, these twelve photos measure approximately 8" by 11" and feature artwork depicting Houston Astro players against stadium backgrounds. The pictures have white borders. A facsimile autograph is printed in black on the picture. The horizontal backs show a pale blue tinted photo of the Astrodome, with player biographical information, statistics and career highlights printed in darker blue over the photo. At the top are the Coca-Cola emblem and slogan. The photos are unnumbered and checklisted below in alphabetical order. Wade Blasingame and Jimmy Wynn are considered to be in shorter supply than the other cards and have been marked with SP in the checklist.

COMPLETE SET (12) 20.00 50.00
1 Jesus Alou 1.00 2.50
2 Wade Blasingame SP 4.00 10.00
3 Cesar Cedeno 1.50 4.00
4 Larry Dierker 1.25 3.00
5 John Edwards .75 2.00
6 Denis Menke .75 2.00
7 Roger Metzger .75 2.00
8 Joe Morgan 4.00 10.00
9 Doug Rader 1.00 2.50
10 Bob Watson 1.25 3.00
11 Don Wilson .75 2.00
12 Jim Wynn SP 6.00 15.00

1971 Astros Team Issue

This 24-card set measures approximately 3 1/2" by 5 3/8" and features black-and-white player portraits in a white border. A facsimile autograph is printed across the bottom of the picture. The backs are blank. The cards are unnumbered and checklisted below in alphabetical order.

COMPLETE SET (24) 6.00 15.00
1 Wade Blasingame .20 .50
2 Cesar Cedeno .60 1.50
3 Rich Chiles .20 .50
4 George Culver .20 .50
5 Larry Dierker .40 1.00
6 John Edwards .20 .50
7 Ken Forsch .30 .75
8 Fred Gladding .20 .50
9 Tom Griffin .20 .50
10 Buddy Harris .20 .50
11 Buddy Hancken CO .20 .50
12 Jack Hiatt .20 .50
13 Larry Howard .20 .50
14 Hub Kittle CO .20 .50
15 Roger Metzger .30 .75
16 Joe Morgan 1.25 3.00
17 Jim Owens CO .20 .50
18 Salty Parker CO .20 .50
19 Doug Rader .30 .75
20 Jim Ray .20 .50
21 Harry Walker MG .30 .75
22 Bob Watson .40 1.00
23 Don Wilson .30 .75
24 Jim Wynn .40 1.00

1972 Astros Team Issue

This 30-card set of the 1972 Houston Astros measures approximately 3 1/2" by 5" and features black-and-white player portraits with white borders. A facsimile autographed is printed across the bottom of the photo. The backs are blank. The cards are unnumbered and checklisted below in alphabetical order.

COMPLETE SET (30) 6.00 15.00
1 Jesus Alou .30 .75
2 Wade Blasingame .20 .50
3 Cesar Cedeno .60 1.50
4 George Culver .20 .50
5 Larry Dierker .40 1.00
6 John Edwards .20 .50
7 Robert Fenwick .20 .50
8 Ken Forsch .20 .50
9 Fred Gladding .20 .50
10 Tom Griffin .20 .50
11 Buddy Hancken CO .20 .50
12 Tommy Helms .20 .50
13 Jack Hiatt .20 .50
14 Hub Kittle CO .20 .50
15 Lee May .30 .75
16 Roger Metzger .20 .50
17 Norm Miller .20 .50
18 Jim Owens CO .20 .50
19 Salty Parker CO .20 .50
20 Doug Rader .30 .75
21 Jim Ray .20 .50
22 Jerry Reuss .40 1.00
23 Dave Roberts .20 .50
24 Jim Stewart .20 .50
25 Bob Stinson .20 .50
26 Harry Walker .20 .50
27 Bob Watson .40 1.00
28 Don Wilson .30 .75
29 Jim Wynn .40 1.00
30 Jim York .20 .50

1975 Astros Postcards

These photos were issued and featured members of the 1975 Houston Astros. They are unnumbered and we have sequenced them in alphabetical order.

COMPLETE SET (30) 6.00 15.00
1 Rob Andrews .20 .50
2 Rafael Batista .20 .50
3 Ken Boswell .20 .50
4 Enos Cabell .20 .50
5 Cesar Cedeno .60 1.50
6 Jose Cruz .30 .75
7 Larry Dierker .40 1.00
8 Mike Easler .30 .75
9 Ken Forsch .20 .50
10 Preston Gomez MG .20 .50
11 Wayne Granger .20 .50
12 Tom Griffin .20 .50
13 Greg Gross .20 .50
14 Tommy Helms .20 .50
15 Wilbur Howard .20 .50
16 Cliff Johnson .20 .50
17 Skip Jutze .20 .50
18 Hub Kittle CO .20 .50
19 Doug Konieczny .20 .50
20 Bob Lillis CO .20 .50
21 Milt May .20 .50
22 Roger Metzger .20 .50
23 Larry Milbourne .20 .50
24 Doug Rader .20 .50
25 J.R. Richard .40 1.00
26 Dave Roberts .20 .50
27 Fred Scherman .20 .50
28 Bob Watson .40 1.00
29 Jim Williams .20 .50
30 Jim York .20 .50

1976 Astros Postcards

This 32-card set of the Houston Astros features player photos on postcard-size cards. The cards are unnumbered and checklisted below in alphabetical order.

COMPLETE SET (32) 6.00 15.00
1 Joaquin Andujar .30 .75
2 Mike Barlow .20 .50
3 Ken Boswell .20 .50
4 Enos Cabell .20 .50
5 Cesar Cedeno .30 .75
6 Mike Cosgrove .20 .50
7 Jose Cruz .40 1.00
8 Larry Dierker .40 1.00
9 Jerry DaVanon .20 .50
10 Ken Forsch .20 .50
11 Tom Griffin .20 .50
12 Greg Gross .20 .50
13 Larry Hardy .20 .50
14 Wilbur Howard .20 .50
15 Art Howe .60 1.50
16 Cliff Johnson .30 .75
17 Deacon Jones CO .20 .50
18 Skip Jutze .20 .50
19 Bob Lillis CO .20 .50
20 Joe McIntosh .20 .50
21 Roger Metzger .20 .50
22 Larry Milbourne .20 .50
23 Joe Niekro .40 1.00
24 Tony Pacheco .20 .50
25 Gene Pentz .20 .50
26 J.R. Richard .40 1.00
27 Leon Roberts .20 .50
28 Gil Rondon .20 .50
29 Jose Sosa .20 .50
30 Bill Virdon MG .20 .50
31 Bob Watson .40 1.00
32 Mel Wright CO .20 .50

1978 Astros Burger King

The cards in this 23-card set measure 2 1/2" by 3 1/2". Released in local Houston Burger King outlets during the 1978 season, this Houston Astros series contains the standard 22 numbered player cards and one unnumbered checklist. The player poses found to differ from the regular Topps issue are marked with asterisks.

COMPLETE SET (23) 6.00 15.00
1 Bill Virdon MG .40 1.00
2 Joe Ferguson .20 .50
3 Ed Herrmann .20 .50
4 J.R. Richard .60 1.50
5 Joe Niekro .40 1.00
6 Floyd Bannister .30 .75
7 Joaquin Andujar .60 1.50
8 Ken Forsch .20 .50
9 Mark Lemongello .20 .50
10 Joe Sambito .20 .50
11 Gene Pentz .20 .50
12 Bob Watson .60 1.50
13 Julio Gonzalez .20 .50
14 Enos Cabell .30 .75
15 Roger Metzger .20 .50
16 Art Howe .40 1.00
17 Jose Cruz .60 1.50
18 Cesar Cedeno .60 1.50
19 Terry Puhl .30 .75
20 Wilbur Howard .20 .50
21 Dave Bergman * .30 .75
22 Jesus Alou * .30 .75
NNO Checklist Card TP .10 .25

1978 Astros Postcards

These postcards feature members of the 1978 Houston Astros. They are unnumbered and we have ordered them alphabetically.

COMPLETE SET (28) 6.00 15.00
1 Jesus Alou .20 .50
2 Joaquin Andujar .20 .50
3 Floyd Bannister .20 .50
4 Dave Bergman .20 .50
5 Enos Cabell .20 .50
6 Cesar Cedeno .40 1.00
7 Jose Cruz .30 .75
8 Tom Dixon .20 .50
9 Ken Forsch .20 .50
10 Julio Gonzalez .20 .50
11 Wilbur Howard .20 .50
12 Art Howe .40 1.00
13 Deacon Jones CO .20 .50
14 Rafael Landestoy .20 .50
15 Mark Lemongello .20 .50
16 Bob Lillis CO .20 .50
17 Tony Pacheco CO .20 .50
18 Terry Puhl .20 .50
19 Luis Pujois .20 .50
20 Joe Niekro .30 .75
21 J. R. Richard .40 1.00
22 Joe Sambito .30 .75
23 Jimmy Sexton .30 .75
24 Bill Virdon MG .20 .50
25 Dennis Walling .20 .50
26 Bob Watson .40 1.00
27 Rick Williams .20 .50
28 Mel Wright CO .20 .50

1979 Astros Postcards

These 4" by 5" postcards feature members of the 1979 Houston Astros. They are unnumbered and sequenced them in alphabetical order.

COMPLETE SET (28) 6.00 15.00
1 Jesus Alou .20 .50
2 Joaquin Andujar .20 .50
3 Alan Ashby .20 .50
4 Bruce Bochy .60 1.50
5 Enos Cabell .20 .50
6 Cedar Cedeno .30 .75
7 Jose Cruz .30 .75
8 Tom Dixon .20 .50
9 Ken Forsch .20 .50
10 Julio Gonzalez .20 .50
11 Art Howe .20 .50
12 Rafael Landestoy .20 .50
13 Jeff Leonard .20 .50
14 Bo McLaughlin .20 .50
15 Joe Niekro .30 .75
16 Randy Niemann .20 .50
17 Terry Puhl .20 .50
18 Craig Reynolds .20 .50
19 Frank Riccelli .20 .50
20 J.R. Richard .40 1.00
21 Bert Roberge .20 .50
22 Vern Ruhle .20 .50
23 Joe Sambito .20 .50
24 Jimmy Sexton .30 .75
25 Bill Virdon MG .20 .50
26 Denny Walling .20 .50
27 Bob Watson .40 1.00
28 Gary Wilson .20 .50

1980 Astros Team Issue

Measuring 4" by 5", these dull finish cards had a limited distribution. Since they are unnumbered we have sequenced them in alphabetical order.

COMPLETE SET (29) 8.00 20.00
1 Joaquin Andujar .20 .50
2 Alan Ashby .20 .50
3 Dave Bergman .20 .50
4 Bruce Bochy .30 .75
5 Enos Cabell .20 .50
6 Cesar Cedeno .40 1.00
7 Jose Cruz .30 .75
8 Ken Forsch .20 .50
9 Julio Gonzalez .20 .50
10 Danny Heep .20 .50
11 Art Howe .20 .50
12 Deacon Jones CO .20 .50
13 Frank LaCorte .20 .50
14 Rafael Landestoy .20 .50
15 Bob Lillis CO .20 .50
16 Don Leppert CO .20 .50
17 Joe Morgan .75 2.00
18 Joe Niekro .30 .75
19 Gordon Pladson .20 .50
20 Terry Puhl .20 .50
21 Craig Reynolds .20 .50
22 J.R. Richard .40 1.00
23 Bert Roberge .20 .50
24 Nolan Ryan 1.50 4.00
25 Joe Sambito .20 .50
26 Dave Smith .40 1.00
27 Bill Virdon MG .20 .50
28 Denny Walling .20 .50
29 Mel Wright CO .20 .50

1978 Atlanta Convention

This 24-card standard-size set features circular black-and-white player photos framed in light green and bordered in white. The player's name is printed in black across the top with his position, team name, and logo at the bottom. The white backs carry the player's name and career information. The cards are unnumbered and checklisted below in alphabetical order. Almost all of the players in this set played for the Braves at one time.

COMPLETE SET (24) 7.50 15.00
1 Hank Aaron 2.50 5.00
2 Joe Adcock .25 .50
3 Felipe Alou .50 1.00
4 Frank Bolling .13 .25
5 Orlando Cepeda .75 1.50
6 Ty Cline .13 .25
7 Tony Cloninger .13 .25
8 Del Crandall .13 .25
9 Fred Haney MG .13 .25
10 Pat Jarvis .13 .25
11 Ernie Johnson .25 .50
12 Ken Johnson .13 .25
13 Denver Lemaster .13 .25
14 Eddie Mathews .75 1.50
15 Lee Maye .13 .25
16 Denis Menke .13 .25
17 Felix Millan .13 .25
18 Johnny Mize .75 1.50
20 Gene Oliver .13 .25
21 Johnny Sain .25 .50
22 Warren Spahn .75 1.50
23 Joe Torre .50 1.00
24 Bob Turley .25 .50

1968 Atlantic Oil Play Ball Contest Cards

These fifty cards were issued in two-card panels which when split, become standard-size cards. For easier reference we have sequenced the set in alphabetical order and listed the player number and prize (when applicable) next to the player's name. Winning cards of more than $1 are not priced and not included in the complete set price. "Clean" cards - cards without glue underneath - may sell for a premium.

COMPLETE SET (50) 125.00 250.00
1 Hank Aaron-4 10.00 25.00
2 Tommy Agee-2 ($2500)
3 Felipe Alou-3 1.25 3.00
4 Max Alvis-2 .60 1.50
5 Bob Aspromonte-1 .60 1.50
6 Ernie Banks-5 ($100)
7 Lou Brock-1 6.00 15.00
8 Jim Bunning-9 1.50 4.00
9 Johnny Callison-1 .75 2.00
10 Bert Campaneris-2 .75 2.00
11 Norm Cash-5 1.25 3.00
12 Orlando Cepeda-4 1.50 4.00
13 Dean Chance-9 .60 1.50

14 Roberto Clemente-7 15.00 40.00
15 Tommy Davis-4 ($100)
16 Andy Etchebarren-8 ($5)
17 Ron Fairly-6 ($10)
18 Bill Freehan-3 ($2500)
19 Jim Fregosi-2 .75 2.00
20 Bob Gibson-9 6.00 15.00
21 Jim Hart-3 .60 1.50
22 Joe Horlen-9 .60 1.50
23 Al Kaline-2 8.00 20.00
24 Jim Lonborg-9 .75 2.00
25 Jim Maloney-9 .75 2.00
26 Roger Maris-7 6.00 15.00
27 Mike McCormick-9 .60 1.50
28 Willie McCovey-4 6.00 15.00
29 Sam McDowell-9 .75 2.00
30 Tug McGraw-7 ($10)
31 Tony Oliva-1 1.25 3.00
32 Claude Osteen-11 ($1) 1.50 4.00
33 Milt Pappas-10 .75 2.00
34 Joe Pepitone-6 .75 2.00
35 Vada Pinson-3 .75 2.00
36 Boog Powell-6 .75 2.00
37 Brooks Robinson-1 6.00 15.00
38 Frank Robinson-5 6.00 15.00
39 Pete Rose-1 15.00 40.00
40 Jose Santiago-11 .60 1.50
41 Ron Santo-4 1.25 3.00
42 George Scott-6 .60 1.50
43 Ron Swoboda-7 .60 1.50
44 Tom Tresh-2 .60 1.50
45 Fred Valentine-6 .60 1.50
46 Pete Ward-1 .60 1.50
47 Billy Williams-8 ($5)
48 Maury Wills-1 .75 2.00
49 Earl Wilson-10 ($1) 1.50 4.00
50 Carl Yastrzemski-5 6.00 15.00

1888 August Beck N403

The tobacco brand with the unusual name of Yum Yum was marketed by the August Beck Company of Chicago. The cards are blank-backed with sepia fronts and are not numbered. There are ballplayers known, and the series was released to the public in 1887 or 1888. We have sequenced this set in alphabetical order. There are new additions added to this checklist and more may be out there so any information would be greatly appreciated. The Cap Anson card actually features a photo of Ned Wiliamson which depresses its value slightly.

COMPLETE SET (51) 125,000.00 250,000.00
1 Cap Anson UER 6,000.00 12,000.00
Ned Williamson pictured
2 Lady Baldwin 2,500.00 5,000.00
3 Dan Brouthers 4,000.00 8,000.00
4 Bill Brown 2,500.00 5,000.00
5 Charlie Buffington 2,500.00 5,000.00
6A Tommy Burns 2,500.00 5,000.00
{Chicago Portrait
6B Tommy Burns 2,500.00 5,000.00
Chicago With bat
7A John Clarkson 4,000.00 8,000.00
Portrait
7B John Clarkson 4,000.00 8,000.00
Throwing
8 John Coleman 2,500.00 5,000.00
9 Roger Connor 4,000.00 8,000.00
10 Larry Corcoran 2,500.00 5,000.00
11 Tom Daly UER 2,500.00 5,000.00
Billy Sunday pictured
12 Tom Deasley 2,500.00 5,000.00
13 Mike Dorgan 2,500.00 5,000.00
14 Buck Ewing 4,000.00 8,000.00
15 Silver Flint 2,500.00 5,000.00
16 Pud Galvin 4,000.00 8,000.00
17 Joe Gerhardt 2,500.00 5,000.00
18 Charlie Getzien 2,500.00 5,000.00
19 Pete Gillespie 2,500.00 5,000.00
20 Jack Glasscock 2,500.00 5,000.00
21 George Gore 2,500.00 5,000.00
22 Ed Greer 2,500.00 5,000.00
23 Tim Keefe 4,000.00 8,000.00
24 Mike King Kelly 6,000.00 12,000.00
25 Gus Krock 2,500.00 5,000.00
26 Connie Mack 6,000.00 12,000.00
27 Kid Madden 2,500.00 5,000.00
28 George Miller 2,500.00 5,000.00
29 John Morrill 2,500.00 5,000.00
30 James Mutrie 5,000.00 10,000.00
31 Bill Nash: Boston 2,500.00 5,000.00
32A Jim O'Rourke 4,000.00 8,000.00
New York Portrait
32B Jim O'Rourke 4,000.00 8,000.00
No team; with bat
33 Danny Richardson 2,500.00 5,000.00
34 James (Chief) Roseman 2,500.00 5,000.00
35 Jimmy Ryan 3,000.00 6,000.00
36 Bill Sowders 2,500.00 5,000.00
37 Marty Sullivan 2,500.00 5,000.00
38A Billy Sunday 5,000.00 10,000.00
Fielding
38B Billy Sunday UER 4,000.00 8,000.00
Mark Baldwin pictured
39 Ezra Sutton 2,500.00 5,000.00
40 Mike Tiernan 2,500.00 5,000.00
41 George Van Haltren 2,500.00 5,000.00
42 John Montgomery Ward 5,000.00 10,000.00
43A Mickey Welch 4,000.00 8,000.00
New York Portrait
43B Mickey Welch 4,000.00 8,000.00
New York Pitching
43C Mickey Welch 4,000.00 8,000.00
New York Portrait
Righ arm extended
44 Jim Whitney 2,500.00 5,000.00
45 George Wood 2,500.00 5,000.00

1945 Autographs Playing Cards

Cards from this set are part of a playing card game released in 1945 by Leister Game Co. of Toledo Ohio. The cards feature a photo of a famous person, such as an actor or writer, or athlete on the top half of the card with his signature across the middle. A photo appears in the upper left hand corner along with some biographical information about him printed in orange in the center. The bottom half of the cardfront features a drawing along with information about a second personality in the same field or vocation. Those two characters are featured on another card with the positions reversed top and bottom. Note that a card number was also used in the upper left corner with each pair being featured on two of the same card number. We've listed the player who's photo appears on the card first, followed by the personality featured at the bottom of the card.

COMPLETE SET (55) 200.00 400.00
9A Joe DiMaggio 25.00 50.00
Babe Ruth
9A Babe Ruth 25.00 50.00
Joe DiMaggio

1914 B18 Blankets

This set of felt-type cloth squares was issued in 1914 with several brands of cigarettes. Each blanket is a 5 1/4" square. Each player exists with two different color combinations based on his team; however, only those variations reflecting price differentials are listed in the checklist below. Cleveland players have either yellow or purple bases; New York Yankees players have either blue or green infields; St. Louis Browns players have either red or purple paths; Washington players have either brown or green bases; Brooklyn players have either blue or green infields; New York Giants players have either brown or green paths; Pittsburgh players have either red or purple bases; and St. Louis Cardinals players have either purple or yellow paths. Some blankets are known to exist in a (third) different color scheme -- those with red infields. These blankets are quite scarce and are listed in the checklist below. The complete set price below reflects a set including all variations listed below. The blankets are unnumbered and are ordered below alphabetically within team, i.e., Cleveland Indians (1-9), Detroit Tigers (10-19), New York Yankees (20-28), St. Louis Browns (29-37), Washington Senators (38-46), Boston Bees NL (47-55), Brooklyn Dodgers (56-64), New York Giants (65-73), Pittsburgh Pirates (74-82) and St. Louis Cardinals (83-91).

1A Babe Adams 25.00 50.00
Purple bases
1B Babe Adams 25.00 50.00
Red bases
2A Sam Agnew 25.00 50.00
Purple paths
2B Sam Agnew 25.00 50.00
Red paths
3A Eddie Ainsmith 12.50 25.00
Brown bases
3B Eddie Ainsmith 12.50 25.00
Green bases
4A Jimmy Austin 25.00 50.00
Purple paths
4B Jimmy Austin 25.00 50.00
Red paths
5A Del Baker 30.00 60.00
Brown infield
5B Del Baker 1,500.00 3,000.00
Red infield
5C Del Baker 12.50 25.00
White infield
6A Johnny Bassler 20.00 40.00
Purple bases
6B Johnny Bassler 25.00 50.00
Yellow bases
7A Paddy Bauman UER 30.00 60.00
Name misspelled
Brown infield
7B Paddy Bauman UER 1,500.00 3,000.00
Name misspelled
Red infield
7C Paddy Bauman white infield 12.50 25.00
8A Luke Boone 12.50 25.00
Blue infield
8B Luke Boone 12.50 25.00
Green infield
9A George Burns 12.50 25.00
Brown infield
9B George Burns 1,500.00 3,000.00
Red infield
9C George Burns 12.50 25.00
White infield
10A George Burns 12.50 25.00
Brown infield
10B George Burns 30.00 60.00
White infield
11A Max Carey 75.00 150.00
Purple bases
11B Max Carey 75.00 150.00
Red bases
12A Marty Cavanaugh UER 30.00 60.00
Name misspelled
Brown infield
12B Marty Cavanaugh UER 1,500.00 3,000.00
Name misspelled
Red infield
12C Marty Cavanaugh UER 12.50 25.00
Name misspelled
White infield
12D Marty Kavanaugh UER 12.50 25.00
Name misspelled
White infield
13A Frank Chance 50.00 100.00
Brown pennants
13B Frank Chance 50.00 100.00
Green infield
13C Frank Chance 250.00 500.00
Yellow pennants
14A Ray Chapman 20.00 40.00
Purple bases
14B Ray Chapman 25.00 50.00
Yellow bases
15A Ty Cobb 300.00 600.00
Brown infield
15B Ty Cobb 7,000.00 14,000.00
Red infield
15C Ty Cobb 250.00 500.00
White infield
16A King Cole 12.50 25.00
Blue infield
16B King Cole 12.50 25.00
Green infield
17A Joe Connolly 30.00 60.00
Brown infield
17B Joe Connolly 1,500.00 3,000.00
Red infield
17C Joe Connolly 12.50 25.00
White infield
18A Harry Coveleski 30.00 60.00
Brown infield
18B Harry Coveleski 1,500.00 3,000.00
Red infield
18C Harry Coveleski 12.50 25.00
White infield
19A George Cutshaw 12.50 25.00
Blue infield
19B George Cutshaw 12.50 25.00
Green infield
20A Jake Daubert 15.00 30.00
Green infield
20B Jake Daubert#Blue infield 15.00 30.00
21A Ray Demmitt 30.00 60.00
Brown infield
21B Ray Demmitt 1,500.00 3,000.00
Red infield
21C Ray Demmitt 12.50 25.00
White infield
22A Bill Doak 20.00 40.00
Purple paths
22B Bill Doak 25.00 50.00
Yellow paths
23A Cozy Dolan 15.00 30.00
Purple paths
23B Cozy Dolan 25.00 50.00
Yellow paths
24A Larry Doyle 15.00 30.00
Brown paths
24B Larry Doyle 15.00 30.00
Geen paths
25A Art Fletcher 12.50 25.00
Brown paths
25B Art Fletcher 12.50 25.00
Green paths
26A Eddie Foster 12.50 25.00
Brown pennants
26B Eddie Foster 12.50 25.00
Green pennants
27A Del Gainor 30.00 60.00
Brown infield
27B Del Gainor 12.50 25.00
White infield
28A Chick Gandil 40.00 80.00
Green pennants
28B Chick Gandil#Brown pennants 40.00 80.00
29A George Gibson 25.00 50.00
Purple bases
29B George Gibson 25.00 50.00
Red bases
30A Hank Gowdy 30.00 60.00
Brown infield
30B Hank Gowdy 1,500.00 3,000.00
Red infield
30C Hank Gowdy 12.50 25.00
White infield
31A Jack Graney 20.00 40.00
Purple bases
31B Jack Graney 25.00 50.00
Yellow bases
32A Eddie Grant 15.00 30.00
Brown paths
32B Eddie Grant 15.00 30.00
Green paths
33A Tommy Griffith 30.00 60.00
Brown infield
33B Tommy Griffith 1,500.00 3,000.00
Red infield
33C Tommy Griffith 12.50 25.00
White infield
34A Earl Hamilton 25.00 50.00
Purple paths
34B Earl Hamilton 25.00 50.00
Red paths
35A Topsy Hartzell 12.50 25.00
Blue infield
35B Topsy Hartzell 12.50 25.00
Green infield
36A Miller Huggins 25.00 50.00
Purple paths
36B Miller Huggins 100.00 200.00
Yellow paths
37A John Hummel 12.50 25.00
Blue infield
37B John Hummel 12.50 25.00
Green infield
38A Ham Hyatt 25.00 50.00
Purple bases
38B Ham Hyatt 25.00 50.00
Red bases
39A Joe Jackson 400.00 800.00
Purple bases
39B Joe Jackson 600.00 1,200.00
Yellow bases
40A Bill James 30.00 60.00
Brown infield
40B Bill James 1,500.00 3,000.00
Red infield
40C Bill James 12.50 25.00
White infield
41A Walter Johnson 75.00 150.00
Brown pennants
41B Walter Johnson 75.00 150.00
Green pennants
42A Ray Keating 12.50 25.00
Blue infield
42B Ray Keating 12.50 25.00
Green infield
43A Joe Kelley UER 25.00 50.00
Name misspelled
Purple bases
43B Joe Kelley UER 25.00 50.00
Name misspelled
Red bases
44A Ed Konetchy 25.00 50.00
Purple bases
44B Ed Konetchy 25.00 50.00
Red bases
45A Nemo Leibold 20.00 40.00
Purple bases
45B Nemo Leibold 25.00 50.00
Yellow bases
46A Fritz Maisel 12.50 25.00
Blue infield
46B Fritz Maisel 12.50 25.00
Green infield
47A Les Mann 30.00 60.00
Brown infield
47B Les Mann 1,500.00 3,000.00
Red infield
47C Les Mann 12.50 25.00
White infield
48A Rabbit Maranville 50.00 100.00
Brown infield
48B Rabbit Maranville 1,500.00 3,000.00
Red infield
48C Rabbit Maranville 20.00 40.00
White infield
49A Bill McAllister UER 25.00 50.00
Name misspelled
Purple paths
49B Bill McAllister UER 25.00 50.00
Name misspelled
Red paths
50A George McBride 12.50 25.00
Brown pennants
50B George McBride 12.50 25.00
Green pennants
51A Chief Meyers 12.50 25.00
Brown paths
51B Chief Meyers 12.50 25.00
Green paths
52A Clyde Milan 15.00 30.00
Brown penannts
52B Clyde Milan 15.00 30.00
Green pennants
53A Dots Miller 20.00 40.00
Purple paths
53B Dots Miller 25.00 50.00
Yellow paths
54A Otto Miller 12.50 25.00
Brown infield
54B Otto Miller 12.50 25.00
Green infield
55A Willie Mitchell 25.00 50.00
Purple bases
55B Willie Mitchell 25.00 50.00
Yellow bases
56A Danney Moeller 12.50 25.00
Brown penannts
56B Danney Moeller 12.50 25.00
Green pennants
57A Ray Morgan 12.50 25.00
Brown penannts
57B Ray Morgan 12.50 25.00
Green pennants
58A George Moriarty 30.00 60.00
Brown infield
58B George Moriarty 1,500.00 3,000.00
Red infield
58C George Moriarty 12.50 25.00
White infield
59A Mike Mowrey 25.00 50.00
Purple bases
59B Mike Mowrey 25.00 50.00
Red bases
60A Red Murray 12.50 25.00
Brown paths
60B Red Murray 12.50 25.00
Green paths
61A Ivy Olson 20.00 40.00
Purple bases
61B Ivy Olson 25.00 50.00
Yellow bases
62A Steve O'Neil 20.00 40.00
Purple pennants
62B Steve O'Neil 25.00 50.00
Red pennants

Card	Low	High
62C Steve O'Neil Yellow bases	25.00	50.00
63A Marty O'Toole Purple bases	25.00	50.00
63B Marty O'Toole Red bases	25.00	50.00
64A Roger Peckinpaugh Blue infield	15.00	30.00
64B Roger Peckinpaugh Green infield	15.00	30.00
65A Hub Perdue Brown infield	30.00	60.00
65B Hub Perdue Red infield	1,500.00	3,000.00
65C Hub Perdue White infield	12.50	25.00
66A Del Pratt Purple paths	25.00	50.00
66B Del Pratt Red paths	25.00	50.00
67A Hank Robinson Purple paths	20.00	40.00
67B Hank Robinson Yellow paths	25.00	50.00
68A Nap Rucker Blue infield	15.00	30.00
68B Nap Rucker Green infield	15.00	30.00
69A Slim Sallee Purple paths	20.00	40.00
69B Slim Sallee Yellow paths	25.00	50.00
70A Howard Shanks Brown penannts	12.50	25.00
70B Howard Shanks Green pennants	12.50	25.00
70C Howard Shanks White infield	12.50	25.00
71A Burt Shotton Purple paths	25.00	50.00
71B Burt Shotton Red paths	25.00	50.00
72A Red Smith Blue infield	12.50	25.00
72B Red Smith Green infield	12.50	25.00
73A Fred Snodgrass Brown paths	12.50	25.00
73B Fred Snodgrass Green paths	12.50	25.00
74A Bill Steele Purple paths	20.00	40.00
74B Bill Steele Yellow paths	25.00	50.00
75A Casey Stengel Blue infield	50.00	100.00
75B Casey Stengel Green infield	50.00	100.00
76A Jeff Sweeney Blue infield	12.50	25.00
76B Jeff Sweeney Green infield	12.50	25.00
77A Jeff Tesreau Brown paths	12.50	25.00
77B Jeff Tesreau Green paths	12.50	25.00
78A Terry Turner Purple bases	20.00	40.00
78B Terry Turner Yellow bases	25.00	50.00
79A Lefty Tyler Brown infield	30.00	60.00
79B Lefty Tyler Red infield	1,500.00	3,000.00
79C Lefty Tyler White infield	12.50	25.00
80A Jim Viox Purple bases	25.00	50.00
80B Jim Viox Red bases	25.00	50.00
81A Bull Wagner Blue infield	12.50	25.00
81B Bull Wagner Green infield	12.50	25.00
82A Bobby Wallace Purple paths	30.00	60.00
82B Bobby Wallace Red paths	30.00	60.00
83A Dee Walsh Purple paths	12.50	25.00
83B Dee Walsh Red paths	12.50	25.00
84A Jimmy Walsh Purple paths	25.00	50.00
84B Jimmy Walsh Red paths	25.00	50.00
85A Bart Whaling Brown infield	30.00	60.00
85B Bart Whaling Red infield	1,500.00	3,000.00
85C Bart Whaling White infield	12.50	25.00
86A Zach Wheat Blue infield	20.00	40.00
86B Zach Wheat Green infield	20.00	40.00
87A Possum Whitted Purple paths	20.00	40.00
87B Possum Whitted Yellow paths	25.00	50.00
88A Gus Williams Purple paths	25.00	50.00
88B Gus Williams Red paths	25.00	50.00
89A Owen Wilson Purple paths	20.00	40.00
89B Owen Wilson Yellow paths	25.00	50.00
90A Hooks Wiltse Brown paths	12.50	25.00
90B Hooks Wiltse Green paths	12.50	25.00

1928 Babe Ruth Candy Company E-Unc.

This six-card set is one of the more obscure candy sets and features cards picturing Babe Ruth which measure approximately 1 7/8" by 4". The cards are sepia in color and depict scenes from either a movie, "Babe Comes Home" (numbers 1, 2 and 4), or scenes from the Yankee Post Season West Coast Exhibition Tour in 1924 (numbers 3 and 6). Each card has "Babe Ruth" below the photo followed by a caption. The backs contain instructions on how to exchange all six cards for a baseball with Babe Ruth's genuine signature on it. Compared to the others in the set, card number six seems to be considerably tougher to find.

Card	Low	High
COMPLETE SET (6)	1,250.00	2,500.00
1 Babe Ruth In uniform of Los Angeles	500.00	1,000.00
2 Babe Ruth Swinging, follow thru	500.00	1,000.00
3 Babe Ruth In uniform with a young boy	600.00	1,200.00
4 Babe Ruth In civilian dress with Anna Q. Nilsson	500.00	1,000.00
5 Babe Ruth In uniform kissing a small girl	500.00	1,000.00
6 Babe Ruth Autographing a ball	1,000.00	2,000.00

1948 Swell Babe Ruth Story

The 1948 Babe Ruth Story set of 28 black and white numbered cards (measuring approximately 2" by 2 1/2") was issued by the Philadelphia Chewing Gum Company to commemorate the 1949 movie of the same name starring William Bendix, Claire Trevor, and Charles Bickford. Babe Ruth himself appears on several cards. The last 12 cards (17 to 28) are more difficult to obtain than other cards in the set and are also more desirable in that most picture actual players as well as actors from the movie. Supposedly these last 12 cards were issued much later after the first 16 cards had already been released and distributed. The last seven cards (22-28) in the set are subtitled "The Babe Ruth Story in the Making" at the top of each reverse. The bottom of every card says "Swell Bubble Gum, Philadelphia Chewing Gum Corporation." The catalog designation for this set is R421.

Card	Low	High
COMPLETE SET (28)	750.00	1,500.00
1 The Babe Ruth Story In the Making Babe Ruth and William Bendix	75.00	150.00
2 Bat Boy Becomes the Babe Facsimile autograph by Bendix	12.50	25.00
3 Claire Hodgson played by Claire Trevor	10.00	20.00
4 Babe Ruth played by William Bendix Claire Hodgson played by Claire Trevor	10.00	20.00
5 Brother Matthias played by Charles Bickford	10.00	20.00
6 Phil Conrad played by Sam Levene	10.00	20.00
7 Night Club Singer played by Gertrude Niesen	10.00	20.00
8 Baseball's Famous Deal	10.00	20.00
9 Babe Ruth played by William Bendix Mrs.Babe Ruth played by Claire Trevor	10.00	20.00
10 Actors for Babe Ruth Mrs. Babe Ruth Brother Matthias	10.00	20.00
11 Babe Ruth played by William Bendix Miller Huggins played by Fred Lightner	10.00	20.00
12 Babe Ruth played by William Bendix Johnny Sylvester played by George Marshall	10.00	20.00
13 Actors for Mr. and Mrs. and Johnny Sylvester	10.00	20.00
14 When A Feller Needs A Friend	10.00	20.00
15 Dramatic Home Run	10.00	20.00
16 The Homer That Set the Record	10.00	20.00
17 The Slap That Started Baseball's Most Famous Career	25.00	50.00
18 The Babe Plays Santa Claus	25.00	50.00
19 Matt Briggs Fred Lightner Actors for Ed Barrow Jacob Ruppert Miller Huggins	25.00	50.00
20 Broken Window Paid Off	25.00	50.00
21 Regardless of the Generation Babe Ruth Bendix shown getting mobbed by crowd	25.00	50.00
22 Ted Lyons William Bendix	30.00	60.00
23 Charley Grimm William Bendix	25.00	50.00
24 Lefty Gomez William Bendix Bucky Harris	37.50	75.00
25 Babe Ruth William Bendix Babe Ruth pictured with ball	100.00	200.00
26 Babe Ruth William Bendix Babe Ruth pictured with bat	100.00	200.00
27 Babe Ruth Claire Trevor	100.00	200.00
28 William Bendix Babe Ruth Claire Trevor Babe Ruth pictured autographing ball	100.00	200.00

1948 Swell Babe Ruth Story Premium

This 8" by 9 1/2" sepia photo was given away at the movie theatre premiere of the "Babe Ruth Story" movie. The front shows long-time teammates Lou Gehrig and Ruth in a posed shot. The back has Babe Ruth's career information.

Card	Low	High
1 Babe Ruth Lou Gehrig	2,500.00	5,000.00

1911 Baseball Bats E-Unc.

This 44-card set was distributed on candy boxes with the player panel on one side and the name "Baseball Bats" printed on crossed bats and a ball on the opposite side. The two side panels indicate "All Leading Players" and an end flap displays "One Cent." The cards measure approximately 1 3/8" by 2 3/8" and feature a player picture surrounded by either a white or orange border and a thin black line.

Card	Low	High
COMPLETE SET (44)	2,500.00	5,000.00
1 Frank Baker	300.00	600.00
2 Jack Baker	125.00	250.00
3 Chief Bender	200.00	400.00
4 Al Bridwell	125.00	250.00
5 Mordecai Brown	200.00	400.00
6 Bill Corrigan UER Name misspelled	125.00	250.00
7 Frank Chance	250.00	500.00
8 Hal Chase	250.00	500.00
9 Eddie Cicotte	250.00	500.00
10 Fred Clarke UER Name misspelled	200.00	400.00
11 Ty Cobb	1,500.00	3,000.00
12 King Cole	125.00	250.00
13 Shano Collins	125.00	250.00
14 Sam Crawford	250.00	500.00
15 Lou Criger	125.00	250.00
16 Harry Davis	125.00	250.00
17 Jim Delehanty	125.00	250.00
18 Art Devlin	125.00	250.00
19 Josh Devore	125.00	250.00
20 Patsy Donovan	125.00	250.00
21 Larry Doyle	150.00	300.00
22 Johnny Evers	250.00	500.00
23 John Flynn	125.00	250.00
24 Solly Hofman	125.00	250.00
25 Walter Johnson	750.00	1,500.00
26 Johnny Kling	125.00	250.00
27 Nap Lajoie	400.00	800.00
28 Matthew McIntyre	125.00	250.00
29 Fred Merkle	150.00	300.00
30 Tom Needham	125.00	250.00
31 Rube Oldring	125.00	250.00
32 Frank Schulte	125.00	250.00
33 Cy Seymour	125.00	250.00
34 James Sheckard	125.00	250.00
35 Tris Speaker	250.00	500.00
36 Oscar Stanage Batting; side	125.00	250.00
37 Oscar Stanage Batting, front	125.00	250.00
38 Ira Thomas	125.00	250.00
39 Joe Tinker	250.00	500.00
40 Heinie Wagner	125.00	250.00
41 Honus Wagner	500.00	1,000.00
42 Ed Walsh	200.00	400.00
43 Chief Wilson	150.00	300.00
44 Art Wilson	125.00	250.00

1910 Baseball Comics T203

This 25-card set was issued by Winner Cut Plug and Mayo Cut Plug. Measuring 2 1/16" by 3 1/8", each card features a color comic picture relating to a baseball phrase or slogan. The back carries an advertisement inside a picture frame. The cards are unnumbered.

Card	Low	High
COMPLETE SET (25)	250.00	500.00
1 A Crack Outfielder	20.00	40.00
2 A Fancy Twirler	20.00	40.00
3 A Fine Slide	20.00	40.00
4 A Fowl Bawl	20.00	40.00
5 A Great Game	20.00	40.00
6 A Home Run	20.00	40.00
7 An All Star Battery	20.00	40.00
8 A Short Stop	20.00	40.00
9 A Star Catcher	20.00	40.00
10 A White Wash	20.00	40.00
11 A Tie Game	20.00	40.00
12 A Two Bagger	20.00	40.00
13 A Wild Pitch	20.00	40.00
14 Caught Napping	20.00	40.00
15 On to the Curves	20.00	40.00
16 Out	20.00	40.00
17 Put Out on 1st	20.00	40.00
18 Right over the Plate	20.00	40.00
19 Rooting for the Home Team	20.00	40.00
20 Stealing a Base	20.00	40.00
21 Stealing Home	20.00	40.00
22 Strike One	20.00	40.00
23 The Bleachers	20.00	40.00
24 The Naps	20.00	40.00
25 The Red Sox	20.00	40.00

1979 Baseball Greats

These 2 1/2" by 3 3/4" cards were issued in 1979 by Carl Berg. They have the same design as 53 Bowman Black and White and use photos from that era as well. The cards are numbered 65 through 80 as if they were a continuation of the 53 Bowman Black and White set.

Card	Low	High
COMPLETE SET (16)	10.00	25.00
65 Monte Irvin	.20	.50
66 Early Wynn	.20	.50
67 Robin Roberts	.20	.50
68 Stan Musial	1.25	3.00
69 Ernie Banks	.75	2.00
70 Willie Mays	2.00	5.00
71 Yogi Berra	.75	2.00
72 Mickey Mantle	3.00	8.00
73 Whitey Ford	.75	2.00
74 Bob Feller	.75	2.00
75 Ted Williams	2.00	5.00
76 Satchel Paige	1.25	3.00
77 Jackie Robinson	2.00	5.00
78 Ed Mathews	.20	.50
79 Warren Spahn	.20	.50
80 Ralph Kiner	.20	.50

1910 Baseball Fans

These four fans which measure 7 1/2" in diameter and 5 1/4" in length of handles features some of the leading players of the time. On the top of the fan is the expression "A fan for a fan:". The players photo and a fascimile signature is underneath that expression. Since these fans are unnumbered, we have sequenced them in alphabetical order.

Card	Low	High
COMPLETE SET (4)	3,000.00	6,000.00
1 Hal Chase	500.00	1,000.00
2 Ty Cobb	1,500.00	3,000.00
3 Larry Doyle	250.00	500.00
4 Christy Mathewson	1,000.00	2,000.00

1910 Baseball Magazine Premium Posters

Measuring approximately 11 1/2" by 19 1/2" this poster was probably an redemption issued by Baseball Magazine. Little is known about these posters and all future information and additions to our checklist would be appreciated.

Card	Low	High
1 Frank Chance	500.00	1,000.00
2 Ty Cobb	1,250.00	2,500.00
3 Walter Johnson	1,000.00	2,000.00
4 Honus Wagner	750.00	1,500.00

1963 Baseball Magazine M118

These 8 1/2" by 11" photos feature a player portrait surrounded by white borders. The backs are blank

Card	Low	High
COMPLETE SET (88)	400.00	800.00
1 Hank Aaron	8.00	20.00

2 Joe Adcock	2.50	6.00
3 Grover Alexander	4.00	10.00
4 Bob Allison	2.00	5.00
5 George Altman	2.00	5.00
6 Luis Aparicio	4.00	10.00
7 Richie Ashburn	4.00	10.00
8 Ernie Banks	5.00	12.00
9 Steve Barber	2.00	5.00
10 Earl Battey	2.00	5.00
11 Yogi Berra	6.00	15.00
12 Jim Bunning	4.00	10.00
13 Roy Campanella	6.00	15.00
14 Norm Cash	3.00	8.00
15 Orlando Cepeda	4.00	10.00
16 Ty Cobb	8.00	20.00
17 Rocky Colavito	3.00	8.00
18 Bennie Daniels	2.00	5.00
19 Dizzy Dean	4.00	10.00
20 Joe DiMaggio	12.50	30.00
21 Don Drysdale	4.00	10.00
22 Ryne Duren	2.00	5.00
23 Roy Face	2.50	6.00
24 Bob Feller	4.00	10.00
25 Whitey Ford	5.00	12.00
26 Nelson Fox	4.00	10.00
27 Tito Francona	2.00	5.00
28 Bob Friend	2.00	5.00
29 Lou Gehrig	10.00	25.00
30 Jim Gentile	2.00	5.00
31 Hank Greenberg	5.00	12.00
32 Dick Groat	2.50	6.00
33 Lefty Grove	4.00	10.00
34 Ron Hansen	2.00	5.00
35 Woody Held	2.00	5.00
36 Gil Hodges	4.00	10.00
37 Rogers Hornsby	4.00	10.00
38 Elston Howard	3.00	8.00
39 Dick Howser	2.00	5.00
40 Joe Jay	2.00	5.00
41 Jack Jensen	2.50	6.00
42 Walter Johnson	6.00	15.00
43 Al Kaline	4.00	10.00
44 Harmon Killebrew	4.00	10.00
45 Willie Kirkland	2.00	5.00
46 Sandy Koufax	8.00	20.00
47 Ted Kluszewski	3.00	8.00
48 Jim Landis	2.00	5.00
49 Dale Long	2.00	5.00
50 Jerry Lumpe	2.00	5.00
51 Connie Mack	4.00	10.00
52 Art Mahaffey	2.00	5.00
53 Frank Malzone	2.00	5.00
54 Mickey Mantle	12.50	30.00
55 Roger Maris	6.00	15.00
56 Eddie Mathews	4.00	10.00
57 Christy Mathewson	4.00	10.00
58 Willie Mays	8.00	20.00
59 Minnie Minoso	2.50	6.00
60 Wally Moon	2.00	5.00
61 Stan Musial	5.00	12.00
62 Charley Neal	2.00	5.00
63 Mel Ott	4.00	10.00
64 Camilo Pascual	2.00	5.00
65 Albie Pearson	2.00	5.00
66 Jim Piersall	2.50	6.00
67 Vada Pinson	2.50	6.00
68 Paul Richards	2.00	5.00
69 Robin Roberts		
70 Brooks Robinson	4.00	10.00
71 Frank Robinson	4.00	10.00
72 Jackie Robinson	8.00	20.00
73 Pete Runnels	2.00	5.00
74 Babe Ruth	12.50	30.00
75 Ron Santo	3.00	8.00
76 Norm Siebern	2.00	5.00
77 Roy Sievers	2.00	5.00
78 Duke Snider	5.00	12.00
79 Warren Spahn	4.00	10.00
80 Tris Speaker	4.00	10.00
81 Casey Stengel	4.00	10.00
82 Dick Stuart	2.00	5.00
83 Lee Thomas	2.00	5.00
84 Honus Wagner	4.00	10.00
85 Bill White	2.50	6.00
86 Ted Williams	10.00	25.00
87 Gene Woodling	2.00	5.00
88 Early Wynn	4.00	10.00
89 Cy Young	4.00	10.00

1975 Baseball Royalty

These eight cards were created for and given away to the 1st 500 attendees at the 1975 Mid-Atlantic Sports Collectors Association show. The fronts have the words "Baseball Royalty" on top with the players photo underneath and then the information about the show. These players were selected since each player had a "royal" nickname. Since these cards are unnumbered we have sequenced them in alphabetical order.

COMPLETE SET (5)	8.00	20.00
1 Paul Derringer	.40	1.00
2 Roy Face	.40	1.00
3 Rogers Hornsby	1.50	4.00
4 Carl Hubbell	1.00	2.50
5 Charlie Keller	.60	1.50
6 Babe Ruth	3.00	8.00
7 Hal Schumacher	.40	1.00
8 Duke Snider	1.25	3.00

1934-36 Batter-Up

The 1934-36 Batter-Up set, issued by National Chicle, contains 192 blank-backed die-cut cards. Numbers 1 to 80 are approximately 2 3/8" by 3 1/4" in size while 81 to 192 are 2 3/8" by 3". The latter are more difficult to find than the former. The pictures come in basic black and white or in tints of blue, brown, green, purple, red, or sepia. There are three combination cards (each featuring two players per card) in the high series (98, 111, and 115). Cards with the die-cut backing removed are graded fair at best.

COMPLETE SET (192)	10,000.00	20,000.00
WRAP.(1-CENT, CATCH)	150.00	200.00
WRAP.(1-CENT, BAT)	500.00	600.00
1 Wally Berger	60.00	120.00
2 Ed Brandt	25.00	50.00
3 Al Lopez XRC	60.00	120.00
4 Dick Bartell	30.00	60.00
5 Carl Hubbell	75.00	150.00
6 Bill Terry	100.00	175.00
7 Pepper Martin	40.00	80.00
8 Jim Bottomley	60.00	120.00
9 Tommy Bridges	30.00	60.00
10 Rick Ferrell	60.00	120.00
11 Ray Benge	25.00	50.00
12 Wes Ferrell	30.00	60.00
13 Chalmer Cissell	25.00	50.00
14 Pie Traynor	75.00	150.00
15 Leroy Mahaffey	25.00	50.00
16 Chick Hafey XRC	60.00	120.00
17 Lloyd Waner	60.00	120.00
18 Jack Burns	25.00	50.00
19 Buddy Myer	30.00	60.00
20 Bob Johnson XRC	30.00	60.00
21 Arky Vaughan	60.00	120.00
22 Red Rolfe XRC	30.00	60.00
23 Lefty Gomez	100.00	175.00
24 Earl Averill	75.00	150.00
25 Mickey Cochrane	100.00	175.00
26 Van Lingle Mungo XRC	40.00	80.00
27 Mel Ott	150.00	250.00
28 Jimmie Foxx	200.00	300.00
29 Jimmy Dykes	30.00	60.00
30 Bill Dickey	150.00	250.00
31 Lefty Grove	150.00	250.00
32 Joe Cronin	100.00	175.00
33 Frankie Frisch	75.00	150.00
34 Al Simmons	75.00	150.00
35 Rogers Hornsby	200.00	300.00
36 Ted Lyons	60.00	120.00
37 Rabbit Maranville	60.00	120.00
38 Jimmy Wilson	30.00	60.00
39 Willie Kamm	25.00	50.00
40 Bill Hallahan	25.00	50.00
41 Gus Suhr	25.00	50.00
42 Charley Gehringer	75.00	150.00
43 Joe Heving XRC	25.00	50.00
44 Adam Comorosky	25.00	50.00
45 Tony Lazzeri	125.00	200.00
46 Sam Leslie XRC	25.00	50.00
47 Bob Smith	25.00	50.00
48 Willis Hudlin	25.00	50.00
49 Carl Reynolds	25.00	50.00
50 Fred Schulte	25.00	50.00
51 Cookie Lavagetto XRC	40.00	80.00
52 Hal Schumacher	30.00	60.00
53 Roger Cramer XRC	30.00	60.00
54 Sylvester Johnson XRC	25.00	50.00
55 Ollie Bejma XRC	25.00	50.00
56 Sam Byrd	25.00	50.00
57 Hank Greenberg XRC	200.00	300.00
58 Bill Knickerbocker XRC	25.00	50.00
59 Bill Urbanski	25.00	50.00
60 Eddie Morgan	25.00	50.00
61 Rabbit McNair XRC	25.00	50.00
62 Ben Chapman	30.00	60.00
63 Roy Johnson	25.00	50.00
64 Dizzy Dean	300.00	450.00
65 Zeke Bonura XRC	25.00	50.00
66 Fred Marberry	25.00	50.00
67 Gus Mancuso	25.00	50.00
68 Joe Vosmik XRC	25.00	50.00
69 Earl Grace RC	25.00	50.00
70 Tony Piet	25.00	50.00
71 Rollie Hemsley XRC	25.00	50.00
72 Fred Fitzsimmons	30.00	60.00
73 Hack Wilson	100.00	175.00
74 Chick Fullis XRC	25.00	50.00
75 Fred Frankhouse	25.00	50.00
76 Ethan Allen	25.00	50.00
77 Heinie Manush	60.00	120.00
78 Rip Collins XRC	25.00	50.00
79 Tony Cuccinello	25.00	50.00
80 Joe Kuhel	25.00	50.00
81 Tommy Bridges	60.00	120.00
82 Clint Brown XRC	50.00	100.00
83 Albert Blanche XRC	50.00	100.00
84 Boze Berger XRC	50.00	100.00
85 Goose Goslin	125.00	200.00
86 Lefty Gomez	150.00	250.00
87 Joe Glenn XRC	50.00	100.00
88 Cy Blanton XRC	50.00	100.00
89 Tom Carey XRC	50.00	100.00
90 Ralph Birkofer XRC	50.00	100.00
91 Fred Gabler XRC	50.00	100.00
92 Dick Coffman	50.00	100.00
93 Ollie Bejma XRC	50.00	100.00
94 Leroy Parmelee	50.00	100.00
95 Carl Reynolds	50.00	100.00
96 Ben Cantwell	50.00	100.00
97 Curtis Davis XRC	50.00	100.00
98 E. Webb XRC/W. Moses XRC	75.00	150.00
99 Ray Benge	50.00	100.00
100 Pie Traynor	150.00	250.00
101 Phil Cavarretta XRC	60.00	120.00
102 Pep Young XRC	50.00	100.00
103 Willis Hudlin	50.00	100.00
104 Mickey Haslin XRC	50.00	100.00
105 Ossie Bluege	60.00	120.00
106 Paul Andrews XRC	50.00	100.00
107 Ed Brandt	50.00	100.00
108 Don Taylor XRC	50.00	100.00
109 Thornton Lee XRC	60.00	120.00
110 Hal Schumacher	60.00	120.00
111 F.Hayes XRC/T.Lyons	75.00	150.00
112 Odell Hale XRC	50.00	100.00
113 Earl Averill	125.00	200.00
114 Italo Chelini XRC	50.00	100.00
115 I.Andrews/J.Bottomley	75.00	150.00
116 Bill Walker	50.00	100.00
117 Bill Dickey	250.00	350.00
118 Gerald Walker XRC	50.00	100.00
119 Ted Lyons	125.00	200.00
120 Eldon Auker XRC	50.00	100.00
121 Bill Hallahan	60.00	120.00
122 Fred Lindstrom	125.00	200.00
123 Oral Hildebrand XRC	50.00	100.00
124 Luke Appling XRC	150.00	250.00
125 Pepper Martin	60.00	120.00
126 Rick Ferrell	125.00	200.00
127 Ival Goodman XRC	50.00	100.00
128 Joe Kuhel	50.00	100.00
129 Ernie Lombardi XRC	125.00	200.00
130 Charley Gehringer	150.00	250.00
131 Van Lingle Mungo XRC	60.00	120.00
132 Larry French XRC	50.00	100.00
133 Buddy Myer	60.00	120.00
134 Mel Harder XRC	60.00	120.00
135 Augie Galan XRC	50.00	100.00
136 Gabby Hartnett	125.00	200.00
137 Stan Hack XRC	60.00	120.00
138 Billy Herman	125.00	200.00
139 Bill Jurges	50.00	100.00
140 Bill Lee XRC	60.00	120.00
141 Zeke Bonura XRC	50.00	100.00
142 Tony Piet	50.00	100.00
143 Paul Dean XRC	60.00	120.00
144 Jimmie Foxx	300.00	450.00
145 Joe Medwick XRC	150.00	250.00
146 Rip Collins XRC	50.00	100.00
147 Mel Almada XRC	50.00	100.00
148 Allan Cooke XRC	50.00	100.00
149 Moe Berg	300.00	450.00
150 Dolph Camilli XRC	60.00	120.00
151 Oscar Melillo XRC	50.00	100.00
152 Bruce Campbell XRC	50.00	100.00
153 Lefty Grove	250.00	350.00
154 Johnny Murphy XRC	60.00	120.00
155 Luke Sewell	60.00	120.00
156 Leo Durocher	200.00	300.00
157 Lloyd Waner	125.00	200.00
158 Guy Bush	50.00	100.00
159 Jimmy Dykes	60.00	120.00
160 Steve O'Neill XRC	60.00	120.00
161 General Crowder	60.00	120.00
162 Joe Cascarella XRC	60.00	120.00
163 Daniel Hafey XRC	60.00	120.00
164 Gilly Campbell XRC	50.00	100.00
165 Ray Hayworth XRC	50.00	100.00
166 Frank Demaree	50.00	100.00
167 John Babich XRC	50.00	100.00
168 Marvin Owen XRC	50.00	100.00
169 Ralph Kress	50.00	100.00
170 Mule Haas	50.00	100.00
171 Frank Higgins XRC	60.00	120.00
172 Wally Berger	60.00	120.00
173 Frankie Frisch	200.00	300.00
174 Wes Ferrell	60.00	120.00
175 Pete Fox XRC	50.00	100.00
176 John Vergez	50.00	100.00
177 Billy Rogell	50.00	100.00
178 Don Brennan XRC	50.00	100.00
179 Jim Bottomley	125.00	200.00
180 Travis Jackson	125.00	200.00
181 Red Rolfe XRC	60.00	120.00
182 Frank Crosetti	75.00	150.00
183 Joe Cronin	125.00	200.00
184 Schoolboy Rowe XRC	60.00	120.00
185 Chuck Klein	150.00	250.00
186 Lon Warneke	60.00	120.00
187 Gus Suhr	50.00	100.00
188 Ben Chapman	60.00	120.00
189 Clint Brown XRC	50.00	100.00
190 Paul Derringer XRC	60.00	120.00
191 John Burns XRC	50.00	100.00
192 John Broaca XRC	75.00	150.00

1959 Bauer Hayes Company PC750

The 1959 Hayes Company postacrd consists of but one card. The Dexter Press printed Hank Bauer card is in full color and features a facsimile autograph of Bauer at the bottom of the card.

1 Hank Bauer	7.50	15.00

1959 Bazooka

The 23 full-color, unnumbered cards comprising the 1959 Bazooka set were cut from the bottom of the boxes of gum marketed nationally that year by Topps. Bazooka was the brand name which Topps had been using to sell its one cent bubblegum. This year, Topps decided to distribute 25 dual pieces of Bazooka gum in a box. The cards themselves measure 2 13/16" by 4 15/16". Only nine cards were originally issued; 14 more were added to the set at a later date (these are marked with SP in the checklist). The latter are less plentiful and hence more valuable than the original nine. All the cards are blank backed and the catalog designation is R414-15. The prices below are for the cards cut from the box; complete boxes intact would command a premium. Hank Aaron's card can be found with his name in either white or yellow print.

COMPLETE SET (23)	4,000.00	8,000.00
1 Hank Aaron White	250.00	500.00
1 Hank Aaron Yellow	250.00	500.00
2 Richie Ashburn SP	200.00	400.00
3 Ernie Banks SP	300.00	600.00
4 Ken Boyer SP	150.00	300.00
5 Orlando Cepeda	100.00	200.00
6 Bob Cerv SP	100.00	200.00
7 Rocky Colavito SP	200.00	400.00
8 Del Crandall	25.00	50.00
9 Jim Davenport	25.00	50.00
10 Don Drysdale SP	250.00	500.00
11 Nellie Fox SP	200.00	400.00
12 Jackie Jensen SP	150.00	300.00
13 Harvey Kuenn SP	125.00	250.00
14 Mickey Mantle	800.00	1,600.00
15 Willie Mays	300.00	600.00
16 Bill Mazeroski	100.00	200.00
17 Roy McMillan	25.00	50.00
18 Billy Pierce SP	125.00	250.00
19 Roy Sievers SP	100.00	200.00
20 Duke Snider SP	400.00	800.00
21 Gus Triandos SP	100.00	200.00
22 Bob Turley	50.00	100.00
23 Vic Wertz SP	100.00	200.00

1960 Bazooka

In 1960, Topps introduced a 36-card baseball player set in three card panels on the bottom of Bazooka gum boxes. The cards measure 1 13/16" by 2 3/4" and the panels measure 2 3/4" by 5 1/2". The cards carried full color pictures and were numbered at the bottom underneath the team position. The checklist below contains prices for individual cards. Complete panels or complete boxes would command a premium above these prices.

COMPLETE INDIV.SET (36)	600.00	1,200.00
1 Ernie Banks	20.00	50.00
2 Bud Daley	8.00	20.00
3 Wally Moon	8.00	20.00
4 Hank Aaron	50.00	100.00
5 Milt Pappas	8.00	20.00
6 Dick Stuart	8.00	20.00
7 Roberto Clemente	125.00	250.00
8 Yogi Berra	40.00	80.00
9 Ken Boyer	8.00	20.00
10 Orlando Cepeda	12.50	30.00
11 Gus Triandos	8.00	20.00
12 Frank Malzone	8.00	20.00
13 Willie Mays	60.00	120.00
14 Camilo Pascual	8.00	20.00
15 Bob Cerv	8.00	20.00
16 Vic Power	8.00	20.00
17 Larry Sherry	8.00	20.00
18 Al Kaline	20.00	50.00
19 Warren Spahn	20.00	50.00
20 Harmon Killebrew	20.00	50.00
21 Jackie Jensen	8.00	20.00
22 Luis Aparicio	12.50	30.00
23 Gil Hodges	12.50	30.00
24 Richie Ashburn	15.00	40.00
25 Nellie Fox	15.00	40.00
26 Robin Roberts	15.00	40.00
27 Joe Cunningham	8.00	20.00
28 Early Wynn	12.50	30.00
29 Frank Robinson	20.00	50.00
30 Rocky Colavito	12.50	30.00
31 Mickey Mantle	175.00	350.00
32 Glen Hobbie	8.00	20.00
33 Roy McMillan	8.00	20.00
34 Harvey Kuenn	8.00	20.00
35 Johnny Antonelli	8.00	20.00
36 Del Crandall	8.00	20.00

1961 Bazooka

The 36 card set issued by Bazooka in 1961 follows the format established in 1960; three full color, numbered cards to each panel found on a Bazooka gum box. The individual cards measure 1 13/16" by 2 3/4" whereas the panels measure 2 3/4" by 5 1/2". The cards of 1960 and 1961 are similar in design but are easily distinguished from one another by their numbers. Complete panels or complete boxes would command a premium above these prices.

COMPLETE INDIV. SET (36)	750.00	1,500.00
1 Art Mahaffey	8.00	20.00
2 Mickey Mantle	400.00	800.00
3 Ron Santo	10.00	25.00
4 Bud Daley	8.00	20.00
5 Roger Maris	50.00	100.00
6 Eddie Yost	8.00	20.00
7 Minnie Minoso	10.00	25.00
8 Dick Groat	8.00	20.00
9 Frank Malzone	8.00	20.00
10 Dick Donovan	8.00	20.00
11 Eddie Mathews	40.00	80.00
12 Jim Lemon	8.00	20.00
13 Chuck Estrada	8.00	20.00

14 Ken Boyer	10.00	25.00
15 Harvey Kuenn	8.00	20.00
16 Ernie Broglio	8.00	20.00
17 Rocky Colavito	20.00	50.00
18 Ted Kluszewski	20.00	50.00
19 Ernie Banks	40.00	80.00
20 Al Kaline	40.00	80.00
21 Ed Bailey	8.00	20.00
22 Jim Perry	8.00	20.00
23 Willie Mays	75.00	150.00
24 Bill Mazeroski	20.00	50.00
25 Gus Triandos	8.00	20.00
26 Don Drysdale	30.00	60.00
27 Frank Herrera	8.00	20.00
28 Earl Battey	8.00	20.00
29 Warren Spahn	40.00	80.00
30 Gene Woodling	8.00	20.00
31 Frank Robinson	40.00	80.00
32 Pete Runnels	8.00	20.00
33 Woodie Held	8.00	20.00
34 Norm Larker	8.00	20.00
35 Luis Aparicio	20.00	50.00
36 Bill Tuttle	8.00	20.00

1962 Bazooka

The 1962 Bazooka set of 45 full color, blank backed, unnumbered cards was issued in panels of three on Bazooka bubble gum. The individual cards measure 1 13/16" by 2 3/4" whereas the panels measure 2 3/4" by 5 1/2". The cards below are numbered by panel alphabetically based on the last name of the player pictured on the far left card of the panel. The cards with SP in the checklist below are more difficult to obtain. Complete panels or complete boxes would command a premium above these prices.

COMPLETE INDIV. SET (9)	1,700.00	3,400.00
1 Bob Allison SP	100.00	200.00
2 Eddie Mathews SP	250.00	500.00
3 Vada Pinson SP	125.00	250.00
4 Earl Battey	6.00	15.00
5 Warren Spahn	20.00	50.00
6 Lee Thomas	6.00	15.00
7 Orlando Cepeda	12.50	30.00
8 Woodie Held	6.00	15.00
9 Bob Aspromonte	6.00	15.00
10 Dick Howser	6.00	15.00
11 Roberto Clemente	125.00	250.00
12 Al Kaline	20.00	50.00
13 Joe Jay	6.00	15.00
14 Roger Maris	40.00	80.00
15 Frank Howard	8.00	20.00
16 Sandy Koufax	40.00	80.00
17 Jim Gentile	6.00	15.00
18 Johnny Callison	6.00	15.00
19 Jim Landis	6.00	15.00
20 Ken Boyer	8.00	20.00
21 Chuck Schilling	6.00	15.00
22 Art Mahaffey	6.00	15.00
23 Mickey Mantle	175.00	350.00
24 Dick Stuart	6.00	15.00
25 Ken McBride	6.00	15.00
26 Frank Robinson	20.00	50.00
27 Gil Hodges	15.00	40.00
28 Milt Pappas	6.00	15.00
29 Hank Aaron	50.00	100.00
30 Luis Aparicio	12.50	30.00
31 Johnny Romano SP	100.00	200.00
32 Ernie Banks SP	350.00	700.00
33 Norm Siebern SP	100.00	200.00
34 Ron Santo	10.00	25.00
35 Norm Cash	8.00	20.00
36 Jim Piersall	8.00	20.00
37 Don Schwall	6.00	15.00
38 Willie Mays	60.00	120.00
39 Norm Larker	6.00	15.00
40 Bill White	8.00	20.00
41 Whitey Ford	20.00	50.00
42 Rocky Colavito	12.50	30.00
43 Don Zimmer SP	50.00	100.00
44 Harmon Killebrew SP	350.00	700.00
45 Gene Woodling SP	100.00	200.00

1963 Bazooka

The 1963 Bazooka set of 36 full color, blank backed numbered cards was issued on Bazooka bubble gum boxes. This year marked a change in format from previous Bazooka issues with a smaller sized card being issued. The individual cards measure 1 9/16" by 2 1/2" whereas the panels measure 2 1/2" by 4 11/16". The card features a white strip with the player's name printed in black on the card. The number appears in the white border on the bottom of the card. Three cards were issued per panel. Complete panels or complete boxes would command a premium above these prices.

COMPLETE INDIV.SET (36)	400.00	800.00
1 Mickey Mantle	125.00	250.00
2 Bob Rodgers	3.00	8.00
3 Ernie Banks	20.00	50.00
4 Norm Siebern	3.00	8.00
5 Warren Spahn	15.00	40.00
6 Bill Mazeroski	8.00	20.00
7 Harmon Killebrew	15.00	40.00
8 Dick Farrell	3.00	8.00
9 Hank Aaron	40.00	80.00
10 Dick Donovan	3.00	8.00
11 Jim Gentile	3.00	8.00
12 Willie Mays	40.00	80.00
13 Camilo Pascual	3.00	8.00
14 Roberto Clemente	50.00	100.00
15 Johnny Callison	3.00	8.00
16 Carl Yastrzemski	20.00	50.00
17 Don Drysdale	12.50	30.00
18 Johnny Romano	3.00	8.00
19 Al Jackson	3.00	8.00
20 Ralph Terry	3.00	8.00
21 Bill Monbouquette	3.00	8.00
22 Orlando Cepeda	8.00	20.00
23 Stan Musial	20.00	50.00
24 Floyd Robinson	3.00	8.00
25 Chuck Hinton	3.00	8.00
26 Bob Purkey	3.00	8.00
27 Ken Hubbs	4.00	10.00
28 Bill White	4.00	10.00
29 Ray Herbert	3.00	8.00
30 Brooks Robinson	20.00	50.00
31 Frank Robinson	20.00	50.00
32 Lee Thomas	3.00	8.00
33 Rocky Colavito	8.00	20.00
34 Al Kaline	20.00	50.00
35 Art Mahaffey	3.00	8.00
36 Tommy Davis	3.00	8.00

1963 Bazooka ATG Silver

*SILVER: .75X TO 2X BASIC

1963 Bazooka ATG

The 1963 Bazooka All Time Greats set contains 41 black and white numbered cards issued as inserts in boxes of Bazooka Bubble gum. The cards feature bust shots with gold trim and measure 1 9/16" by 2 1/2". The backs are yellow with black print containing vital information and a biography of the player. Many of the players are pictured not as they looked during their playing careers but as they looked many years after their playing days were through. The cards also exist in a scarcer variety with silver trim instead of gold.

COMPLETE SET (41)	175.00	350.00
1 Joe Tinker	2.50	6.00
2 Harry Heilmann	2.50	6.00
3 Jack Chesbro	1.50	4.00
4 Christy Mathewson	6.00	15.00
5 Herb Pennock	2.50	6.00
6 Cy Young	4.00	10.00
7 Ed Walsh	2.50	6.00
8 Nap Lajoie	4.00	10.00
9 Eddie Plank	2.50	6.00
10 Honus Wagner	8.00	20.00
11 Chief Bender	2.50	6.00
12 Walter Johnson	6.00	15.00
13 Mordecai Brown	2.50	6.00
14 Rabbit Maranville	2.50	6.00
15 Lou Gehrig	20.00	50.00
16 Ban Johnson	1.50	4.00
17 Babe Ruth	40.00	80.00
18 Connie Mack	2.50	6.00
19 Hank Greenberg	2.50	6.00
20 John McGraw	2.50	6.00
21 Johnny Evers	2.50	6.00
22 Al Simmons	2.50	6.00
23 Jimmy Collins	2.50	6.00
24 Tris Speaker	3.00	8.00
25 Frank Chance	2.50	6.00
26 Fred Clarke	2.50	6.00
27 Wilbert Robinson	2.50	6.00
28 Dazzy Vance	2.50	6.00
29 Pete Alexander	3.00	8.00
30 Judge Landis	2.50	6.00
31 Willie Keeler	2.50	6.00
32 Rogers Hornsby	4.00	10.00
33 Hugh Duffy	2.50	6.00
34 Mickey Cochrane	2.50	6.00
35 Ty Cobb	20.00	50.00
36 Mel Ott	4.00	10.00
37 Clark Griffith	2.50	6.00
38 Ted Lyons	2.50	6.00
39 Cap Anson	2.50	6.00
40 Bill Dickey	2.50	6.00
41 Eddie Collins	2.50	6.00

1964 Bazooka

The 1964 Bazooka set of 36 full color, blank backed, numbered cards were issued in panels of three on the backs of Bazooka bubble gum boxes. The individual cards measure 1 9/16" by 2 1/2" whereas the panels measure 2 1/2" by 4 11/16". Many players who were in the 1963 set have the same number in this set; however, the pictures are different. Complete panels or complete boxes would command a premium above these prices.

COMPLETE INDIV. SET (36)	500.00	1,000.00
1 Mickey Mantle	125.00	250.00
2 Dick Groat	3.00	8.00
3 Steve Barber	3.00	8.00
4 Ken McBride	3.00	8.00
5 Warren Spahn	15.00	40.00
6 Bob Friend	3.00	8.00
7 Harmon Killebrew	15.00	40.00
8 Dick Farrell	3.00	8.00
9 Hank Aaron	40.00	80.00
10 Rich Rollins	3.00	8.00
11 Jim Gentile	3.00	8.00
12 Willie Mays	40.00	80.00
13 Camilo Pascual	3.00	8.00
14 Roberto Clemente	60.00	120.00
15 Johnny Callison	3.00	8.00
16 Carl Yastrzemski	30.00	60.00
17 Billy Williams	8.00	20.00
18 Johnny Romano	3.00	8.00
19 Jim Maloney	3.00	8.00
20 Norm Cash	4.00	10.00
21 Willie McCovey	8.00	20.00
22 Jim Fregosi	3.00	8.00
23 George Altman	3.00	8.00
24 Floyd Robinson	3.00	8.00
25 Chuck Hinton	3.00	8.00
26 Ron Hunt	3.00	8.00
27 Gary Peters	3.00	8.00
28 Dick Ellsworth	3.00	8.00
29 Elston Howard	4.00	10.00
30 Brooks Robinson	20.00	50.00
31 Frank Robinson	20.00	50.00
32 Sandy Koufax	40.00	80.00
33 Rocky Colavito	8.00	20.00
34 Al Kaline	20.00	50.00
35 Ken Boyer	4.00	10.00
36 Tommy Davis	3.00	8.00

1964 Bazooka Stamps

Each small stamp is 1" by 1 1/2". The subject's name, team and position are found in a colored rectangle beneath the picture area. Each sheet is numbered in the upper left hand corner outside the picture area. The sheet number is given after the player's name in the checklist below with the prefix S. The stamps were issued in sheets of 10 but an album to hold this particular set has not yet been seen.

COMPLETE SET (100)	400.00	800.00
1 Ed Charles	.75	2.00
2 Vada Pinson	1.25	3.00
3 Jimmy Hall	.75	2.00
4 Milt Pappas	1.00	2.50
5 Dick Ellsworth	.75	2.00
6 Frank Malzone	1.00	2.50
7 Max Alvis	.75	2.00
8 Pete Ward	.75	2.00
9 Tony Taylor	1.00	2.50
10 Bill White	1.50	4.00
11 Don Zimmer	1.25	3.00
12 Bobby Richardson	4.00	10.00
13 Larry Jackson	.75	2.00
14 Norm Siebern	.75	2.00
15 Frank Robinson	12.50	30.00
16 Bob Aspromonte	.75	2.00
17 Al McBean	.75	2.00
18 Floyd Robinson	.75	2.00
19 Bill Monbouquette	.75	2.00
20 Willie Mays	40.00	80.00
21 Brooks Robinson S3	10.00	25.00
22 Joe Pepitone S3	1.50	4.00
23 Carl Yastrzemski S3	12.50	30.00
24 Don Lock S3	.75	2.00
25 Ernie Banks S3	10.00	25.00
26 Dave Nicholson S3	.75	2.00
27 Roberto Clemente S3	60.00	120.00
28 Curt Flood S3	1.50	4.00
29 Woody Held S3	.75	2.00
30 Jesse Gonder S3	.75	2.00
31 Juan Pizarro	.75	2.00
32 Jim Maloney S4	1.00	2.50
33 Ron Santo	1.50	4.00
34 Harmon Killebrew	8.00	20.00
35 Ed Roebuck S4	.75	2.00
36 Boog Powell	1.50	4.00
37 Jim Grant S4	.75	2.00
38 Hank Aguirre S4	.75	2.00
39 Juan Marichal	8.00	20.00
40 Bill Mazeroski	2.50	6.00
41 Dick Radatz S5	.75	2.00
42 Albie Pearson S5	.75	2.00
43 Tommy Harper S5	1.00	2.50
44 Carl Willey S5	.75	2.00
45 Jim Bouton	1.50	4.00
46 Ron Perranoski S5	.75	2.00
47 Chuck Hinton S5	.75	2.00
48 John Romano S5	.75	2.00
49 Norm Cash	1.50	4.00
50 Orlando Cepeda	4.00	10.00
51 Dick Stuart S6	.75	2.00
52 Rich Rollins S6	.75	2.00
53 Mickey Mantle S6	100.00	200.00
54 Steve Barber S6	.75	2.00
55 Jim O'Toole S6	.75	2.00
56 Gary Peters S6	.75	2.00
57 Warren Spahn S6	10.00	25.00
58 Tony Gonzalez S6	.75	2.00
59 Joe Torre S6	1.50	4.00
60 Jim Fregosi S6	1.25	3.00
61 Ken Boyer	1.50	4.00
62 Felipe Alou	1.00	2.50
63 Jim Davenport S7	.75	2.00
64 Tommy Davis	1.25	3.00
65 Rocky Colavito	3.00	8.00
66 Bob Friend S7	1.00	2.50
67 Billy Moran S7	.75	2.00
68 Bill Freehan	1.25	3.00
69 George Altman S7	.75	2.00
70 Ken Johnson S7	.75	2.00
71 Earl Battey S8	.75	2.00
72 Elston Howard	1.50	4.00
73 Billy Williams	8.00	20.00
74 Claude Osteen	1.00	2.50
75 Jim Gentile	1.00	2.50
76 Donn Clendenon	1.00	2.50
77 Ernie Broglio	.75	2.00
78 Hal Woodeshick	.75	2.00
79 Don Drysdale	8.00	20.00
80 John Callison	1.00	2.50
81 Dick Groat	1.00	2.50
82 Moe Drabowsky	.75	2.00
83 Frank Howard	1.00	2.50
84 Hank Aaron	40.00	80.00
85 Al Jackson	.75	2.00
86 Jerry Lumpe	.75	2.00
87 Wayne Causey	.75	2.00
88 Rusty Staub	1.50	4.00
89 Ken McBride	.75	2.00
90 Jack Baldschun	.75	2.00
91 Sandy Koufax S10	20.00	50.00
92 Camilo Pascual S10	.75	2.00
93 Ron Hunt S10	.75	2.00
94 Willie McCovey S10	10.00	25.00
95 Al Kaline S10	12.50	30.00
96 Ray Culp S10	.75	2.00
97 Ed Mathews S10	10.00	25.00
98 Dick Farrell S10	.75	2.00
99 Lee Thomas S10	1.00	2.50
100 Vic Davalillo S10	.75	2.00

1965 Bazooka

The 1965 Bazooka set of 36 full color, blank backed, numbered cards was issued in panels of three on the backs of Bazooka bubble gum boxes. The individual cards measure 1 9/16" by 2 1/2" whereas the panels measure 2 1/2" by 4 11/16". As in the previous two years some of the players have the same numbers on their cards; however all pictures are different from the previous two years. Complete panels or complete boxes would command a premium above these prices.

COMPLETE INDIV. SET (36)	400.00	800.00
1 Mickey Mantle	125.00	250.00
2 Larry Jackson	3.00	8.00
3 Chuck Hinton	3.00	8.00
4 Tony Oliva	6.00	15.00
5 Dean Chance	3.00	8.00
6 Jim O'Toole	3.00	8.00
7 Harmon Killebrew	12.50	30.00
8 Pete Ward	3.00	8.00
9 Hank Aaron	40.00	80.00
10 Dick Radatz	3.00	8.00
11 Boog Powell	4.00	10.00
12 Willie Mays	40.00	80.00
13 Bob Veale	3.00	8.00
14 Roberto Clemente	60.00	120.00
15 Johnny Callison	3.00	8.00
16 Joe Torre	6.00	15.00
17 Billy Williams	10.00	25.00
18 Bob Chance	3.00	8.00
19 Bob Aspromonte	3.00	8.00
20 Joe Christopher	3.00	8.00
21 Jim Bunning	8.00	20.00
22 Jim Fregosi	3.00	8.00
23 Bob Gibson	12.50	30.00
24 Juan Marichal	12.50	30.00
25 Dave Wickersham	3.00	8.00
26 Ron Hunt	3.00	8.00
27 Gary Peters	3.00	8.00
28 Ron Santo	6.00	15.00
29 Elston Howard	4.00	10.00
30 Brooks Robinson	15.00	40.00
31 Frank Robinson	15.00	40.00
32 Sandy Koufax	20.00	50.00
33 Rocky Colavito	8.00	20.00
34 Al Kaline	15.00	40.00
35 Ken Boyer	4.00	10.00
36 Tommy Davis	3.00	8.00

1966 Bazooka

The 1966 Bazooka set of 48 full color, blank backed, numbered cards was issued in panels of three on the backs of Bazooka bubble gum boxes. The individual cardsd measure 1 9/16" by 2 1/2" whereas the complete panels measure 2 1/2" by 4 11/16". The set is distinguishable from the previous years by mention of "48 card set" at the bottom of the card. Complete panels or complete boxes would command a premium above these prices.

COMPLETE INDIV. SET (48)	500.00	1,000.00
1 Sandy Koufax	20.00	50.00
2 Willie Horton	3.00	8.00
3 Frank Howard	4.00	10.00
4 Richie Allen	4.00	10.00
5 Mel Stottlemyre	4.00	10.00
6 Tony Conigliaro	5.00	12.00
7 Mickey Mantle	125.00	250.00
8 Leon Wagner	3.00	8.00
9 Ed Kranepool	3.00	8.00
10 Juan Marichal	10.00	25.00
11 Harmon Killebrew	10.00	25.00
12 Johnny Callison	3.00	8.00
13 Roy McMillan	3.00	8.00
14 Willie McCovey	10.00	25.00
15 Rocky Colavito	6.00	15.00
16 Willie Mays	40.00	80.00
17 Sam McDowell	3.00	8.00
18 Vern Law	3.00	8.00
19 Jim Fregosi	3.00	8.00
20 Ron Fairly	3.00	8.00
21 Bob Gibson	10.00	25.00
22 Carl Yastrzemski	15.00	40.00
23 Bill White	4.00	10.00
24 Bob Aspromonte	3.00	8.00
25 Dean Chance	3.00	8.00
26 Roberto Clemente	60.00	120.00
27 Tony Cloninger	3.00	8.00
28 Curt Blefary	3.00	8.00
29 Milt Pappas	3.00	8.00
30 Hank Aaron	40.00	80.00
31 Jim Bunning	6.00	15.00
32 Frank Robinson	12.50	30.00
33 Bill Skowron	4.00	10.00
34 Brooks Robinson	12.50	30.00
35 Jim Wynn	3.00	8.00
36 Joe Torre	5.00	12.00
37 Jim Grant	3.00	8.00
38 Pete Rose	30.00	60.00
39 Ron Santo	5.00	12.00
40 Tom Tresh	4.00	10.00
41 Tony Oliva	5.00	12.00
42 Don Drysdale	10.00	25.00
43 Pete Richert	3.00	8.00
44 Bert Campaneris	3.00	8.00
45 Jim Maloney	3.00	8.00
46 Al Kaline	12.50	30.00
47 Eddie Fisher	3.00	8.00
48 Billy Williams	8.00	20.00

1967 Bazooka

The 1967 Bazooka set of 48 full color, blank backed, numbered cards was issued in panels of three on the backs of Bazooka bubble gum boxes. The individual cards measure 1 9/16" by 2 1/2" whereas the complete panels measure 2 1/2" by 4 11/16". This set is virtually identical to the 1966 set with the exception of ten new cards as replacements for ten 1966 cards. The remaining 38 cards are identical in pose and number. Complete panels or complete boxes would command a premium above these prices.

COMPLETE INDIV. SET (48)	500.00	1,000.00
1 Rick Reichardt	3.00	8.00
2 Tommie Agee	3.00	8.00
3 Frank Howard	4.00	10.00
4 Richie Allen	4.00	10.00
5 Mel Stottlemyre	4.00	10.00
6 Tony Conigliaro	5.00	12.00
7 Mickey Mantle	125.00	250.00
8 Leon Wagner	3.00	8.00
9 Gary Peters	3.00	8.00
10 Juan Marichal	10.00	25.00
11 Harmon Killebrew	10.00	25.00
12 Johnny Callison	3.00	8.00
13 Denny McLain	5.00	12.00
14 Willie McCovey	10.00	25.00
15 Rocky Colavito	6.00	15.00
16 Willie Mays	40.00	80.00
17 Sam McDowell	3.00	8.00
18 Jim Kaat	5.00	12.00
19 Jim Fregosi	3.00	8.00
20 Ron Fairly	3.00	8.00
21 Bob Gibson	10.00	25.00
22 Carl Yastrzemski	15.00	40.00
23 Bill White	4.00	10.00
24 Bob Aspromonte	3.00	8.00
25 Dean Chance	3.00	8.00
26 Roberto Clemente	60.00	120.00
27 Tony Cloninger	3.00	8.00
28 Curt Blefary	3.00	8.00
29 Phil Regan	3.00	8.00
30 Hank Aaron	40.00	80.00
31 Jim Bunning	6.00	15.00
32 Frank Robinson	12.50	30.00
33 Ken Boyer	4.00	10.00
34 Brooks Robinson	12.50	30.00
35 Jim Wynn	3.00	8.00
36 Joe Torre	5.00	12.00
37 Tommy Davis	3.00	8.00
38 Pete Rose	30.00	60.00
39 Ron Santo	5.00	12.00
40 Tom Tresh	4.00	10.00
41 Tony Oliva	5.00	12.00
42 Don Drysdale	10.00	25.00
43 Pete Richert	3.00	8.00
44 Bert Campaneris	3.00	8.00
45 Jim Maloney	3.00	8.00
46 Al Kaline	12.50	30.00
47 Matty Alou	3.00	8.00
48 Billy Williams	8.00	20.00

1968 Bazooka Panels

The 1968 Bazooka Tipps from the Topps is a set of 15 numbered boxes (measuring 5 1/2" by 6 1/4" when detached). each containing on the back panel (measuring 3" by 6 1/4") a baseball playing tip from a star, and on the side panels four mini cards, two per side, in full color, measuring 1 1/4" by 3 1/8". Although the set contains a total of 60 of these small cards, 4 are repeated; therefore there are only 56 different small cards. Some collectors cut the panels into individual card; however most collectors retain entire panels or boxes. The prices in the checklist therfore reflect only the values of the complete boxes.

COMPLETE BOX SET (15)	450.00	900.00
1 Maury Wills	60.00	120.00
Clete Boyer		
Paul Casanova		
Al Kaline		
Tom Seaver		
2 Carl Yastrzemski	50.00	100.00
Matty Alou		
Bill Freehan		
Jim Hunter		
Jim Lefebvre		
3 Bert Campaneris	20.00	50.00
Bobby Knoop		
Tim McCarver		
Frank Robinson		
Bob Veale		
4 Maury Wills	20.00	50.00
Jose Azcue		
Tony Conigliaro		
Ken Holtzman		
Bill White		
5 Julian Javier	60.00	120.00
Hank Aaron		
Juan Marichal		
Joe Pepitone		
Rico Petrocelli		
6 Orlando Cepeda	50.00	100.00
Tommie Agee		
Don Drysdale		
Pete Rose		
Ron Santo		
7 Bill Mazeroski	20.00	50.00
Jim Bunning		
Frank Howard		
John Roseboro		
George Scott		
8 Brooks Robinson	30.00	60.00
Tony Gonzalez		
Wille Horton		
Harmon Killebrew		
Jim McGlothlin		
9 Jim Fregosi	20.00	50.00
Max Alvis		
Bob Gibson		
Tony Oliva		
Vada Pinson		
10 Joe Torre	20.00	50.00
Dean Chance		
Tommy Davis		
Fergie Jenkins		
Rick Monday		
11 Jim Lonborg	125.00	250.00
Curt Flood		
Joel Horlen		
Mickey Mantle		
Jim Wynn		
12 Mike McCormick	30.00	60.00
Roberto Clemente		
Al Downing		
Don Mincher		
Tony Perez		
13 Frank Crosetti	20.00	50.00
Rod Carew		
Willie McCovey		
Ron Swoboda		
Don Wilson		
14 Willie Mays	60.00	120.00
Richie Allen		
Gary Peters		
Rusty Staub		
Billy Williams		
15 Lou Brock	75.00	150.00
Tommie Agee		
Don Drysdale		
Pete Rose		
Ron Santo		

1969-70 Bazooka Panels

The 1969-70 Bazooka Baseball Extra News set contains 12 complete panels, each comprising a large action shot of a significant event in baseball history and four small cards, comparable to those in the Tipps from the Topps set of 1968, of Hall of Famers. Although some collectors cut the panels into individual cards (measuring 3" by 6 1/4" or 1 1/4" by 3 1/8"), most collectors retain the entire panel, or box (measuring 5 1/2" by 6 1/4"). The prices in the checklist below reflect the value for the entire box, as these cards are more widely seen and collected as complete panels or boxes.

COMPLETE PANEL SET (12)	200.00	400.00
1 No Hit Duel - Brown/Cobb/Keeler/Plank	15.00	40.00
2 Alexander Conquers - Hornsby/Johnson/Johnson/Simmons	12.50	30.00
3 Yanks Lazzeri - Duffy Gehrig/Speaker/Tinker	12.50	30.00
4 Home Run Almost - Alexander Bender/Mathewson/Young	15.00	40.00
5 Four Consecutive - Chance Cochrane/McGraw/Ruth	50.00	100.00
6 No-Hit Game - Evers/Johnson McGraw/Young	12.50	30.00
7 Twelve RBIs - Cobb/Collins/Evers/Gehrig	20.00	50.00
8 Ty Ties Record - Cochrane Collins/Ott/Wagner	15.00	40.00
9 Babe Ruth Hits - Anson/Chesbro Simmons/Speaker	20.00	50.00
10 Calls Shot - Lajoie/Mack.Maranville Walsh	20.00	50.00
11 Ruth's 60th - Chance/Lajoie/Ott/Tinker	20.00	50.00
12 Double Shutout - Hornsby/Maranville/Mathewson/Wagner	12.50	30.00

1971 Bazooka Numbered Test

This was supposedly a test issue which was different from the more common unnumbered set and much more difficult to find. There are 48 cards (16 panels) in this numbered set whereas the unnumbered set had only 12 panels or 36 individual cards. Individual cards measure approximately 2" by 2 5/8" whereas the panels measure 2 5/8" by 5 15/16". Complete panels or complete boxes would command a premium above these prices. Cards #46-48 (Hundley,Mays and Hunter) are not priced due to scarcity.

COMPLETE SET (48)	900.00	1,800.00
1 Tim McCarver	8.00	20.00
2 Frank Robinson	40.00	80.00
3 Bill Mazeroski	30.00	60.00
4 Willie McCovey	30.00	60.00
5 Carl Yastrzemski	60.00	120.00
6 Clyde Wright	6.00	15.00
7 Jim Merritt	6.00	15.00
8 Luis Aparicio	30.00	60.00
9 Bobby Murcer	8.00	20.00
10 Rico Petrocelli	6.00	15.00
11 Sam McDowell	6.00	15.00
12 Clarence Gaston	6.00	15.00
13 Fergie Jenkins	30.00	60.00
14 Al Kaline	40.00	80.00
15 Ken Harrelson	6.00	15.00
16 Tommie Agee	6.00	15.00
17 Harmon Killebrew	30.00	60.00
18 Reggie Jackson	40.00	80.00
19 Juan Marichal	30.00	60.00
20 Frank Howard	8.00	20.00
21 Bill Melton	6.00	15.00
22 Brooks Robinson	40.00	80.00
23 Hank Aaron	50.00	100.00
24 Larry Dierker	6.00	15.00
25 Jim Fregosi	6.00	15.00
26 Billy Williams	30.00	60.00
27 Dave McNally	8.00	20.00
28 Rico Carty	6.00	15.00
29 Johnny Bench	75.00	150.00
30 Tommy Harper	6.00	15.00
31 Bert Campaneris	6.00	15.00
32 Pete Rose	125.00	250.00
33 Orlando Cepeda	30.00	60.00
34 Maury Wills	8.00	20.00
35 Tom Seaver	40.00	80.00
36 Tony Oliva	20.00	50.00
37 Bill Freehan	6.00	15.00
38 Roberto Clemente	200.00	400.00
39 Claude Osteen	6.00	15.00
40 Rusty Staub	8.00	20.00
41 Bob Gibson	30.00	60.00
42 Amos Otis	6.00	15.00
43 Jim Wynn	8.00	20.00
44 Rich Allen	20.00	50.00
45 Tony Conigliaro	20.00	50.00
46 Randy Hundley		
47 Willie Mays		
48 Jim Hunter		

1971 Bazooka Unnumbered

The 1971 Bazooka set of 36 full-color, unnumbered cards was issued in 12 panels of three cards each on the backs of boxes containing one cent Bazooka bubble gum. Individual cards measure approximately 2" by 2 5/8" whereas the panels measure 2 5/8" by 5 15/16". The panels are numbered in the checklist alphabetically by the player's last name on the left most card of the panel. Complete panels or complete boxes would command a premium above these prices

COMPLETE INDIV.SET (36)	200.00	400.00
1 Tommie Agee	1.25	3.00
2 Harmon Killebrew	6.00	15.00
3 Reggie Jackson	12.50	30.00
4 Bert Campaneris	1.25	3.00
5 Pete Rose	15.00	40.00
6 Orlando Cepeda	6.00	15.00
7 Rico Carty	1.25	3.00
8 Johnny Bench	10.00	25.00
9 Tommy Harper	1.25	3.00
10 Bill Freehan	1.25	3.00
11 Roberto Clemente	30.00	60.00
12 Claude Osteen	1.25	3.00
13 Jim Fregosi	1.25	3.00
14 Billy Williams	6.00	15.00
15 Dave McNally	1.25	3.00
16 Randy Hundley	1.25	3.00
17 Willie Mays	12.50	35.00
18 Jim Hunter	6.00	15.00
19 Juan Marichal	6.00	15.00
20 Frank Howard	2.00	5.00
21 Bill Melton	1.25	3.00
22 Willie McCovey	6.00	15.00
23 Carl Yastrzemski	10.00	25.00
24 Clyde Wright	1.25	3.00
25 Jim Merritt	1.25	3.00
26 Luis Aparicio	6.00	15.00
27 Bobby Murcer	2.00	5.00
28 Rico Petrocelli	1.25	3.00
29 Sam McDowell	1.25	3.00
30 Clarence Gaston	1.25	3.00
31 Brooks Robinson	8.00	20.00
32 Hank Aaron	12.50	30.00
33 Larry Dierker	1.25	3.00
34 Rusty Staub	2.00	5.00
35 Bob Gibson	6.00	15.00
36 Amos Otis	1.25	3.00

1976 Cool Papa Bell

This set features highlights in the career of Negro League great Cool Papa Bell. The set was issued soon after his induction into the Hall of Fame. We have received reports that this was actually a 20 card set. However, we have only 13 cards checklisted. Collectors with checklist additions are encouraged to contact Beckett. This set was available from the producer for $2.50 at the time of issue.

COMPLETE SET (13)	6.00	15.00
1 Cool Papa Bell	.60	1.50
Amazing Speed		
2 Cool Papa Bell	.40	1.00
Lou Brock		
Sets SB Record		
3 Cool Papa Bell	.60	1.50
4 Cool Papa Bell	.60	1.50
Cuba 1928		
5 Cool Papa Bell	.40	1.00
Great Fielder, Too		
6 Cool Papa Bell	.60	1.50
HOF, Cooperstown		
7 Cool Papa Bell	.60	1.50
HOF Favorite		
8 Cool Papa Bell	.40	1.00
Induction Day, 1974		
9 Cool Papa Bell	.40	1.00
The Mexican Leagues		
10 Cool Papa Bell	.60	1.50
On Deck in Cuba		
11 Cool Papa Bell	.40	1.00
On Deck In Cuba		
12 Cool Papa Bell	.60	1.50
Touring Havana		
13 Cool Papa Bell	.75	2.00
Josh Gibson		
NNO Header Card	.20	.50

1951 Berk Ross

The 1951 Berk Ross set consists of 72 cards (each measuring approximately 2 1/16" by 2 1/2") with tinted photographs, divided evenly into four series (designated in the checklist as 1, 2, 3 and 4). The cards were marketed in boxes containing two card panels, without gum, and the set includes stars of other sports as well as baseball players. The set is sometimes still found in the original packaging. Intact panels command a premium over the listed prices. The catalog designation for this set is W532-1. In every series the first ten cards are baseball players; the set has a heavy emphasis on Yankees and Phillies players as they were in the World Series the year before. The set includes the first card of Bob Cousy as well as a card of Whitey Ford in his Rookie Card year.

COMPLETE SET (72)	900.00	1,500.00
1-Jan Al Rosen	6.00	12.00
2-Jan Bob Lemon	12.50	25.00
3-Jan Phil Rizzuto	12.50	25.00
4-Jan Hank Bauer	10.00	20.00
5-Jan Billy Johnson	5.00	10.00
6-Jan Jerry Coleman	5.00	10.00
7-Jan Johnny Mize	12.50	25.00
8-Jan Dom DiMaggio	10.00	20.00
9-Jan Richie Ashburn	20.00	50.00
10-Jan Del Ennis	5.00	10.00
1-Feb Stan Musial	60.00	120.00
2-Feb Warren Spahn	15.00	30.00
3-Feb Tom Henrich	6.00	12.00
4-Feb Yogi Berra	40.00	80.00
5-Feb Joe DiMaggio	200.00	400.00
6-Feb Bobby Brown	6.00	12.00
7-Feb Granny Hamner	5.00	10.00

8-Feb Willie Jones	5.00	10.00
9-Feb Stan Lopata	5.00	10.00
10-Feb Mike Goliat	5.00	10.00
1-Mar Ralph Kiner	12.50	25.00
2-Mar Bill Goodman	5.00	10.00
3-Mar Allie Reynolds	10.00	20.00
4-Mar Vic Raschi	7.50	15.00
5-Mar Joe Page	7.50	15.00
6-Mar Eddie Lopat	10.00	20.00
7-Mar Andy Seminick	5.00	10.00
8-Mar Dick Sisler	5.00	10.00
9-Mar Eddie Waitkus	5.00	10.00
10-Mar Ken Heintzelman	5.00	10.00
1-Apr Gene Woodling	7.50	15.00
2-Apr Cliff Mapes	5.00	10.00
3-Apr Fred Sanford	5.00	10.00
4-Apr Tommy Byrne	5.00	10.00
5-Apr Whitey Ford	50.00	100.00
6-Apr Jim Konstanty	5.00	10.00
7-Apr Russ Meyer	6.00	12.00
8-Apr Robin Roberts	15.00	30.00
9-Apr Curt Simmons	6.00	12.00
10-Apr Sam Jethroe	6.00	12.00

1952 Berk Ross

The 1952 Berk Ross set of 72 unnumbered, tinted photocards, each measuring approximately 2" by 3", seems to have been patterned after the highly successful 1951 Bowman set. The reverses of Ewell Blackwell and Nellie Fox are transposed while Phil Rizzuto comes with two different poses. The complete set below includes both poses of Rizzuto. There is a card of Joe DiMaggio even though he retired after the 1951 season. The catalog designation for this set is W532-2, and the cards have been assigned numbers in the alphabetical checklist below.

COMPLETE SET (72)	2,500.00	5,000.00
WRAPPER	30.00	60.00
1 Richie Ashburn	25.00	50.00
2 Hank Bauer	7.50	15.00
3 Yogi Berra	60.00	120.00
4 Ewell Blackwell UER Nellie Fox pictured	10.00	20.00
5 Bobby Brown	7.50	15.00
6 Jim Busby	5.00	10.00
7 Roy Campanella	60.00	120.00
8 Chico Carrasquel	7.50	15.00
9 Jerry Coleman	7.50	15.00
10 Joe Collins	5.00	10.00
11 Alvin Dark	7.50	15.00
12 Dom DiMaggio	10.00	20.00
13 Joe DiMaggio	250.00	500.00
14 Larry Doby	12.50	25.00
15 Bobby Doerr	12.50	25.00
16 Bob Elliott	5.00	10.00
17 Del Ennis	5.00	10.00
18 Ferris Fain	5.00	10.00
19 Bob Feller	30.00	60.00
20 Nellie Fox UER Ewell Blackwell pictured	20.00	40.00
21 Ned Garver	5.00	10.00
22 Clint Hartung	5.00	10.00
23 Jim Hearn	5.00	10.00
24 Gil Hodges	25.00	50.00
25 Monte Irvin	12.50	25.00
26 Larry Jansen	5.00	10.00
27 Sheldon Jones	5.00	10.00
28 George Kell	12.50	25.00
29 Monte Kennedy	5.00	10.00
30 Ralph Kiner	25.00	50.00
31 Dave Koslo	5.00	10.00
32 Bob Kuzava	5.00	10.00
33 Bob Lemon	12.50	25.00
34 Whitey Lockman	5.00	10.00
35 Ed Lopat	7.50	15.00
36 Sal Maglie	7.50	15.00
37 Mickey Mantle	1,500.00	3,000.00
38 Billy Martin	25.00	50.00
39 Willie Mays	250.00	500.00
40 Gil McDougald	7.50	15.00
41 Minnie Minoso	10.00	20.00
42 Johnny Mize	25.00	50.00
43 Tom Morgan	5.00	10.00
44 Don Mueller	5.00	10.00
45 Stan Musial	125.00	250.00
46 Don Newcombe	10.00	20.00
47 Ray Noble	5.00	10.00
48 Joe Ostrowski	5.00	10.00
49 Mel Parnell	7.50	15.00
50 Vic Raschi	7.50	15.00
51 Pee Wee Reese	25.00	50.00
52 Allie Reynolds	7.50	15.00
53 Bill Rigney	5.00	10.00
54A Phil Rizzuto Bunting	25.00	50.00
54B Phil Rizzuto Swinging	25.00	50.00
55 Robin Roberts	20.00	40.00
56 Eddie Robinson UER White Cox on back	5.00	10.00
57 Jackie Robinson	300.00	600.00
58 Preacher Roe	7.50	15.00
59 Johnny Sain	7.50	15.00
60 Red Schoendienst	12.50	25.00
61 Duke Snider	60.00	120.00
62 George Spencer	5.00	10.00
63 Eddie Stanky	7.50	15.00
64 Hank Thompson	7.50	15.00
65 Bobby Thomson	10.00	20.00
66 Vic Wertz	5.00	10.00
67 Wally Westlake	5.00	10.00
68 Wes Westrum	5.00	10.00
69 Ted Williams	250.00	500.00
70 Gene Woodling	10.00	20.00
71 Gus Zernial	7.50	15.00

1916 Ferguson Bakery Felt Pennants BF2

These small triangular felt pennants were issued around 1916. The pennants themselves are 8 1/4" in length, whereas the unnumbered paper photos (glued on to the felt pennant) are 1 3/4" by 1 1/4". The photos are black and white and appear to have been taken from Sporting News issues of the same era. These unnumbered pennants are ordered below in alphabetical order within team. The teams themselves are ordered alphabetically within league beginning with the American League.

COMPLETE SET (97)	4,500.00	9,000.00
1 Jack Barry	50.00	100.00
2 Hick Cady	50.00	100.00
3 Del Gainer	50.00	100.00
4 Harry Hooper	100.00	200.00
5 Dutch Leonard	50.00	100.00
6 Duffy Lewis	50.00	100.00
7 Joe Wood	75.00	150.00
8 Joe Benz	50.00	100.00
9 Eddie Collins	100.00	200.00
10 Shano Collins	50.00	100.00
11 Charles Comiskey OWN	100.00	200.00
12 Red Faber	100.00	200.00
13 Joe Jackson	1,500.00	3,000.00
14 Jack Lapp	50.00	100.00
15 Eddie Murphy	50.00	100.00
16 Pants Rowland MG	50.00	100.00
17 Reb Russell	50.00	100.00
18 Ray Schalk	100.00	200.00
19 Jim Scott	50.00	100.00
20 Ed Walsh	100.00	200.00
21 Buck Weaver	150.00	300.00
22 Ray Chapman	60.00	120.00
23 Chick Gandil	75.00	150.00
24 Guy Morton	50.00	100.00
25 Donie Bush	50.00	100.00
26 Ty Cobb	1,250.00	2,500.00
27 Harry Coveleski	50.00	100.00
28 Sam Crawford	100.00	200.00
29 Jean Dubuc	50.00	100.00
30 Hugh Jennings MG	100.00	200.00
31 Oscar Stanage	50.00	100.00
32 Bobby Veach	50.00	100.00
33 Ralph Young	50.00	100.00
34 Frank Baker	100.00	200.00
35 Joe Gideon	50.00	100.00
36 Wally Pipp	60.00	120.00
37 Napoleon Lajoie	200.00	400.00
38 Connie Mack MG	200.00	400.00
39 Stuffy McInnis	60.00	120.00
40 Rube Oldring	50.00	100.00
41 Wally Schang	60.00	120.00
42 Earl Hamilton	50.00	100.00
43 Fielder Jones	50.00	100.00
44 Doc Lavan	50.00	100.00
45 George Sisler	100.00	200.00
46 Eddie Foster	50.00	100.00
47 Walter Johnson	400.00	800.00
48 Joe Judge	50.00	100.00
49 George McBride	50.00	100.00
50 Clyde Milan	60.00	120.00
51 Ray Morgan	50.00	100.00
52 Johnny Evers	100.00	200.00
53 Hank Gowdy	50.00	100.00
54 Bill James	50.00	100.00
55 Sherry Magee	60.00	120.00
56 Rabbit Maranville	100.00	200.00
57 Dick Rudolph	50.00	100.00
58 George Stallings MG	50.00	100.00
59 Lefty Tyler	50.00	100.00
60 Jake Daubert	50.00	100.00
61 Rube Marquard	100.00	200.00
62 Chief Meyers	60.00	120.00
63 Otto Miller	50.00	100.00
64 Nap Rucker	50.00	100.00
65 Jimmy Archer	50.00	100.00
66 Mordecai Brown	100.00	200.00
67 Claude Hendrix	50.00	100.00
68 Jimmy Lavender	50.00	100.00
69 Vic Saier	50.00	100.00
70 Wildfire Schulte	50.00	100.00
71 Joe Tinker	100.00	200.00
72 Hippo Vaughn	50.00	100.00
73 Heine Zimmerman	50.00	100.00
74 Buck Herzog	50.00	100.00
75 Ivy Wingo	50.00	100.00
76 George Burns	50.00	100.00
77 Red Dooin	50.00	100.00
78 Larry Doyle	60.00	120.00
79 Bennie Kauff	50.00	100.00
80 Hans Lobert	50.00	100.00
81 John McGraw MG	150.00	300.00
82 Fred Merkle	50.00	100.00
83 Jeff Tesreau	50.00	100.00
84 Grover C. Alexander	150.00	300.00
85 Dave Bancroft	100.00	200.00
86 Chief Bender	100.00	200.00
87 Gavvy Cravath	60.00	120.00
88 Josh Devore	50.00	100.00
89 Bill Killefer	50.00	100.00
90 Fred Luderus	50.00	100.00
91 Pat Moran	50.00	100.00
92 Dode Paskert	50.00	100.00
93 Max Carey	100.00	200.00
94 Al Mamaux	50.00	100.00
95 Honus Wagner	400.00	800.00
96 Miller Huggins	100.00	200.00
97 Slim Sallee	50.00	100.00

1937 BF104 Blanket

These blankets, which measure approximately 3 1/2" feature some of the leading players of the late 1930's. The fronts have the player's name on top with his team and league in separate "flags". The player's photo takes up the rest of the blanket. Since these are unnumbered, we have sequenced them in alphabetical order. It is possible this list is incomplete, so all additions are appreciated.

COMPLETE SET (23)	1,500.00	3,000.00
1 Luke Appling	125.00	250.00
2 Moe Berg	150.00	300.00
3 Cy Blanton	50.00	100.00
4 Mickey Cochrane	125.00	250.00
5 Joe Cronin	125.00	250.00
6 Tony Cuccinello	50.00	100.00
7 Dizzy Dean	200.00	400.00
8 Jimmie Dykes	60.00	120.00
9 Jimmie Foxx	200.00	400.00
10 Frankie Frisch	125.00	250.00
11 Woody Jensen	50.00	100.00
12 Harry Kelly	50.00	100.00
13 Thornton Lee	50.00	100.00
14 Connie Mack MG	150.00	300.00
16 Stu Martin	50.00	100.00
17 Joe Medwick	125.00	250.00
18 Ray Mueller	50.00	100.00
19 Bobo Newsome	60.00	120.00
20 Monty Stratton	75.00	150.00
21 Pie Traynor	125.00	250.00
22 Jim Turner	60.00	120.00
23 Bill Werber	60.00	120.00
24 Rudy York	60.00	120.00
15 Danny MacFayden	60.00	120.00

1916-20 Big Head Strip Cards W-UNC

These cards, which feature a player drawing with an enlarged head and the players name in an upper corner, were issued between 1916 and 1920. Since these cards are unnumbered, we have sequenced them in alphabetical order.

COMPLETE SET (20)	4,000.00	8,000.00
1 Jim Bagby	100.00	200.00
2 Frank Baker	300.00	600.00
3 Dave Bancroft	250.00	500.00
4 Ping Bodie	100.00	200.00
5 George Burns	100.00	200.00
6 Leon Cadore	125.00	250.00
7 Ty Cobb	1,000.00	2,000.00
8 Larry Doyle	125.00	250.00
9 Heinie Groh	100.00	200.00
10 Rogers Hornsby	800.00	1,600.00
11 Walter Johnson	800.00	1,600.00
12 Joe Judge	100.00	200.00
13 Ed Konetchy	100.00	200.00
14 Carl Mays	125.00	250.00
15 Clyde Milan	100.00	200.00
16 Sam Rice	250.00	500.00
17 Babe Ruth	1,200.00	2,400.00
18 Ray Schalk	250.00	500.00
19 Wally Schang	125.00	250.00
20 George Sisler	250.00	500.00

1975 Blankback Discs

This six-disc baseball-designed set measures approximately 3 3/8" in diameter. The fronts feature a black-and-white player head photo on a white background in the center with the player's name, position, and team name below. The blue and red sides contain biographical information. The backs are blank. The discs are unnumbered and checklisted below in alphabetical order. Bench and Seaver are available in lesser quantities than other players so they are labeled as SP's in the checklist below

COMPLETE SET (6)	250.00	500.00
1 Henry Aaron	12.50	30.00
2 Johnny Bench SP	75.00	150.00
3 Catfish Hunter	10.00	25.00
4 Fred Lynn	2.00	5.00
5 Pete Rose	40.00	80.00
6 Tom Seaver SP	125.00	250.00

1978 Blue Jays Postcards

1 Alan Ashby	2.50	6.00
2 Doug Ault	2.00	5.00
3 Bob Bailor	2.00	5.00
4 Rick Bosetti	2.00	5.00
5 Rico Carty	2.50	6.00
6 Rick Cerone	2.50	6.00
7 Jim Clancy	2.00	5.00
8 Joe Coleman	2.00	5.00
9 Hector Cruz	2.00	5.00
10 Sam Ewing	2.00	5.00
11 Ron Fairly	2.50	6.00
12 Jerry Garvin	2.00	5.00
13 Luis Gomez	2.00	5.00
14 Roy Hartsfield MG	2.00	5.00
15 Roy Howell	2.00	5.00
16 Jesse Jefferson	2.00	5.00
17 Tim Johnson	2.00	5.00
18 Don Kirkwood	2.00	5.00
19 Dave Lemanczyk	2.00	5.00
20 Don Leppert CO	2.00	5.00
21 John Mayberry	2.50	6.00
22 Dave McKay	2.00	5.00
23 Bob Miller CO	2.00	5.00
24 Brian Milner	2.00	5.00
25 Balor Moore	2.00	5.00
26 Jackie Moore	2.00	5.00
27 Tom Murphy	2.00	5.00
28 Phil Roof	2.00	5.00
29 Bill Singer	2.00	5.00
30 Hector Torres	2.00	5.00
31 Tom Underwood	2.00	5.00
32 Willie Upshaw	2.50	6.00
33 Otto Velez	2.00	5.00
34 Harry Warner CO	2.00	5.00
35 Mike Willis	2.00	5.00
36 Alvis Woods	2.00	5.00

1979 Blue Jays Bubble Yum

These 20 white-bordered posed black-and-white player photographs measure approximately 5 1/2" by 8 1/2". The player's name and position along with the Blue Jays logo and a picture of a pack of Bubble Yum, appear within the wide lower white margin. The white back carries the player's name and position at the top, followed below by his uniform number, biography and statistics. The photos are unnumbered and checklisted below in alphabetical order.

COMPLETE SET (20)	20.00	50.00
1 Bob Bailor	1.50	4.00
2 Rick Bosetti	1.00	2.50
3 Tom Buskey	1.00	2.50
4 Rico Carty	2.00	5.00
5 Rick Cerone	1.25	3.00
6 Jim Clancy	1.00	2.50
7 Bobby Doerr CO	2.50	6.00
8 Dave Freisleben	1.00	2.50
9 Luis Gomez	1.00	2.50
10 Alfredo Griffin	1.50	4.00
11 Roy Hartsfield MG	1.00	2.50
12 Roy Howell	1.00	2.50
13 Phil Huffman	1.00	2.50
14 Jesse Jefferson	1.00	2.50
15 Dave Lemanczyk	1.00	2.50
16 John Mayberry	2.00	5.00
17 Balor Moore	1.00	2.50
18 Tom Underwood	1.00	2.50
19 Otto Velez	1.25	3.00
20 Al Woods	1.00	2.50

1979 Blue Jays McCarthy Postcards

In the early days of the Blue Jays, they used postcards of sports photographer J.D. McCarthy as promotional team issues. These were the new photos issued in 1979, since they are unnumbered we have sequenced them in alphabetical order. The Dave Stieb postcard predates his Rookie Card by one year while the Danny Ainge predates his Rookie Card by two years.

COMPLETE SET (28)	10.00	25.00
1 Danny Ainge	2.50	6.00
2 Bob Bailor	.30	.75
3 Rick Bosetti	.30	.75
4 Bobby Brown	.30	.75
5 Tom Buskey	.30	.75
6 Joe Cannon	.30	.75
7 Rico Carty	.40	1.00
8 Rick Cerone	.40	1.00
9 Jim Clancy	.30	.75
10 Bob Davis	.30	.75
11 Dave Freisleben	.30	.75
12 Luis Gomez	.30	.75
13 Alfredo Griffin	.30	.75
14 Roy Lee Howell	.30	.75
15 Phil Huffman	.30	.75
16 Tim Johnson	.30	.75
17 Craig Kusick	.30	.75
18 Dave Lemancyzk	.30	.75
19 Mark Lemongello	.30	.75
20 Dave McKay	.30	.75
21 John Mayberry	.40	1.00
22 Balor Moore	.30	.75
23 Tom Murphy	.30	.75
24 Dave Stieb	2.50	6.00
25 Tom Underwood	.30	.75
26 Otto Velez	.30	.75
27 Ted Wilborn	.30	.75
28 Al Woods	.30	.75

1931 Blue Ribbon Malt

These photos were issued to promote both Blue Ribbon Malt as well as Hack Wilson. The fronts have posed action shots with the words "Compliments of Blue Ribbon Malt" on the bottom. This checklist may be incomplete and additional information would be greatly appreciated.

1 Lu Blue	40.00	80.00
2 Lew Fonseca	40.00	80.00
3 Vic Frasier	40.00	80.00
4 Johnny Kerr	40.00	80.00
5 Bobby Smith	40.00	80.00
6 Billy Sullivan	40.00	80.00
7 Hack Wilson	75.00	150.00

1948-49 Blue Tint R346

The cards in this 48-card set measure 2" by 2 5/8". The "Blue Tint" set derives its name from its distinctive coloration. Collector Ralph Triplette has pointed out in his research that the set was issued during 1948 and 1949, not in 1947 as had been previously commonly thought. The cards are blank-backed and unnumbered, and were issued in strips of six or eight. The set was probably produced in Brooklyn and hence has a heavy emphasis on New York teams, especially the Yankees. Known variations are No. 2, Durocher, listed with Brooklyn or New York Giants, and No. 18, Ott, listed with Giants or no team designation. The set was initially listed in the catalog as R346 as well as being listed as W518. Although the W categorization is undoubtedly the more correct, nevertheless, the R listing has become the popularly referenced designation for the set. The complete set price below includes all listed variations. Numbers 41 through 48 exist with or without numbers on the front.

COMPLETE SET	600.00	1,200.00
1 Bill Johnson	5.00	10.00
2A Leo Durocher	10.00	20.00
Brooklyn Dodgers		
2B Leo Durocher	10.00	20.00
New York Giants		
3 Marty Marion	6.00	12.00
4 Ewell Blackwell	6.00	12.00
5 John Lindell	5.00	10.00
6 Larry Jansen	5.00	10.00
7 Ralph Kiner	10.00	20.00
8 Chuck Dressen CO	6.00	12.00
9 Bobby Brown	6.00	12.00
10 Luke Appling	10.00	20.00
11 Bill Nicholson	6.00	12.00
12 Phil Masi	5.00	10.00
13 Frank Shea	5.00	10.00
14 Bob Dillinger	5.00	10.00
15 Pete Suder	5.00	10.00
16 Joe DiMaggio	100.00	200.00
17 John Corriden CO	5.00	10.00
18A Mel Ott MG	20.00	40.00
New York Giants		
18B Mel Ott MG	20.00	40.00
No team designation		
19 Buddy Rosar	5.00	10.00
20 Warren Spahn	12.50	25.00
21 Allie Reynolds	6.00	12.00
22 Lou Boudreau	10.00	20.00
23 Hank Majeski UER	5.00	10.00
Randy Gumpert pictured		
24 Frank Crosetti	7.50	15.00
25 Gus Niarhos	5.00	10.00
26 Bruce Edwards	5.00	10.00
27 Rudy York	5.00	10.00
28 Don Black	5.00	10.00
29 Lou Gehrig	100.00	200.00
30 Johnny Mize	10.00	20.00
31 Ed Stanky	6.00	12.00
32 Vic Raschi	6.00	12.00
33 Cliff Mapes	5.00	10.00
34 Enos Slaughter	10.00	20.00
35 Hank Greenberg	10.00	20.00
36 Jackie Robinson	60.00	120.00
37 Frank Hiller	5.00	10.00
38 Bob Elliott	6.00	12.00
39 Harry Walker	5.00	10.00
40 Ed Lopat	7.50	15.00
41 Bobby Thomson	7.50	15.00
42 Tommy Henrich	6.00	12.00
43 Bobby Feller	25.00	50.00
44 Ted Williams	75.00	150.00
45 Dixie Walker	6.00	12.00
46 Johnny Vander Meer	6.00	12.00
47 Clint Hartung	5.00	10.00
48 Charlie Keller	6.00	12.00

1933 Blum's Baseball Bulletin

These black-backed photos, which measure 9 1/2" by 13 5/8" or 11 1/2" by 13 3/4" feature leading players of the past and present. The player's photo is on the top with his name and a biography on the bottom. Since these are unnumbered, we have sequenced them in alphabetical order.

COMPLETE SET	3,000.00	6,000.00
1 Grover C. Alexander	300.00	600.00
2 Eddie Collins	300.00	600.00
3 Jake Daubert	100.00	200.00
4 Bill Donovan	100.00	200.00
5 John Evers	250.00	500.00
6 Lou Gehrig	600.00	1,200.00
7 Heinie Groh	100.00	200.00
8 Lefty Grove	400.00	800.00
9 Walter Johnson	500.00	1,000.00
10 Nap Lajoie	300.00	600.00
11 Rabbit Maranville	200.00	400.00
12 James McAvoy	100.00	200.00
13 Tris Speaker	300.00	600.00
14 George Toporcer	100.00	200.00

1973-06 Book Promotional Cards

This set features various cards used to promote baseball books. We have sequenced them in year order. Cards number two through number 13 all were used to promote "Who was Harry Steinfeldt? And other baseball trivia.". All of these cards measure the standard size. We are not using a complete set price for this set because of the wide variance in years and availability of how these cards were released. According to information at the time, four thousand copies of the Jim Bouton 1979 card was issued.

1 Bo Belinsky 1973	6.00	15.00
Pitching and Wooing		
2 Frank Baumholtz	1.25	3.00
3 Jim Bouton	2.00	5.00
4 Tony Conigliaro	2.00	5.00
5 Don Drysdale	4.00	10.00
6 Hank Greenberg	4.00	10.00
7 Walter Johnson	6.00	15.00
8 Billy Loes	1.25	3.00
9 Johnny Mize	4.00	10.00
10 Lefty O'Doul	2.00	5.00
11 Babe Ruth	10.00	25.00
12 Johnny Sain	2.00	5.00
13 Jim Thorpe	8.00	20.00
14 Jim Bouton 1979	1.25	3.00
Ball Four Plus Ball Five		
15 Billy Martin 1980	2.00	5.00
Number One		
16 Mickey Mantle 1986	4.00	10.00
The Mick		
17 Gary Carter 1987	1.50	4.00
A Dream Season		
17 Babe Ruth 1988	2.00	5.00
Babe Ruth's Book of Baseball Audio Cassette		
18 Nolan Ryan 1988	4.00	10.00
Throwing Heat		
19 Orel Hershiser 1989	1.25	3.00
Out of the Blue		
20 Gil Hodges 1992	2.00	5.00
The Quiet Man		
21 Joe Morgan 1993	1.25	3.00
A Life in Baseball		
22 Jim Bouton 1994	.75	2.00
Strike Zone		
23 Eliot Asinof 1994	.75	2.00
Strike Zone		
24 Charles Lupica 1997	.40	1.00
The Cleveland Indians Flagpole Sitter		
25 Joe Dittmar 1999	.75	2.00
Baseball Records Registry		
Postcard features Randy Johnson		
26 Sandy Koufax 2001	.40	1.00
Big Book of Jewish Baseball		
27 The Big Book of Jewish Baseball	4.00	10.00
Uncut Sheet		
Sandy Koufax		
Lipman Pike		
Moe Berg		
Jesse Levis		
Harry Shuman		
Hank Greenberg		
Harry Danning		
Cy Malis		
Hy Cohen		
28 Lou Gehrig 2002	.40	1.00
Breaking the Slump		
29 Babe Ruth 2002	.40	1.00
Breaking the Slump		
30 Hack Wilson	.40	1.00
Rogers Hornsby 2002		
Breaking the Slump		

1912 Boston Garter Color

These oversize gorgeous full color cards from the early part of the 20th century feature some of the leading players in the game. The front shows a drawing of the player along with a suitcase showing who they are. The Back lists details about how to use these cards to promote a storefront as well as a checklist on the back. According to advertising for these pieces, the cost of these photos from the manufacturer (George Frost Company in Boston) was 10 cents for a group of eight photos or 20 cents for all 16 photos.

COMPLETE SET (16)	100,000.00	200,000.00
1 Bob Bescher	7,500.00	15,000.00
2 Roger Breshnahan	12,500.00	25,000.00
3 Frank Chance	15,000.00	30,000.00
4 Hal Chase	10,000.00	20,000.00
5 Fred Clarke	15,000.00	30,000.00
6 Eddie Collins	20,000.00	40,000.00
7 Red Dooin	7,500.00	15,000.00
8 Hugh Jennings MG	12,500.00	25,000.00
9 Walter Johnson	25,000.00	50,000.00
10 Johnny Kling	7,500.00	15,000.00
11 Larry Lajoie	15,000.00	30,000.00
12 Frank LaPorte	7,500.00	15,000.00
13 Christy Mathewson	25,000.00	50,000.00
14 Nap Rucker	10,000.00	20,000.00
15 Tris Speaker	20,000.00	40,000.00
16 Ed Walsh	15,000.00	30,000.00

1914 Boston Garter Color

This 12 card oversize set features some of the leading players of the 1910's. These cards were issued free to retailers who sold the "Boston Garter" products. The front of the cards have a player photo in a "diamond" with the words "Boston Garter" written on baseballs located at the top. On the bottom are the words 25 and 50 cents as well as the design of the Boston Garter. The back gives career information about the player as well as has a checklist of the cards.

1 Tris Speaker
2 Ty Cobb
3 Burt Shotton UER
Name misspelled
4 Joe Tinker
5 Johnny Evers
6 Joe Jackson
7 Rabbit Maranville
8 Larry Doyle
9 Frank Baker
10 Ed Konetchy
11 Walter Johnson
12 Buck Herzog

1914 Boston Garter Sepia

This ten card white bordered set has a black and white portrait on the front with the players name and the Boston Garter logo in a baseball on the bottom. The back has information about the Boston Garter product along with a checklist and information on how to acquire these photos.

1 Christy Mathewson
2 Red Murray
3 Eddie Collins
4 Hugh Jennings MG
5 Hal Chase
6 Bob Bescher
7 Red Dooin
8 Nap Lajoie
9 Tris Speaker
10 Henie Zimmerman

1909 Boston Herald Supplements

These supplements, which feature only one player, and usually were cut from the newspaper at a 9" by 7" size, were issued in 1909 by the Boston Herald. Since these are unnumbered, we have sequenced them in alphabetical order by team.

COMPLETE SET (24)	2,500.00	5,000.00
1 Bill Carrigan	100.00	200.00
2 Charlie Chech	100.00	200.00
3 Ed Cicotte	300.00	600.00
4 Pat Donahue	100.00	200.00
5 Doc Gessler	100.00	200.00
6 Harry Hooper	200.00	400.00
7 Harry Lord	100.00	200.00
8 Ambrose McConnell	100.00	200.00
9 Harry Niles	100.00	200.00
10 Tris Speaker	400.00	800.00
11 Jake Stahl	100.00	200.00
12 Heinie Wagner	100.00	200.00
13 Chick Autry	100.00	200.00
14 Johnny Bates	100.00	200.00
15 Ginger Beaumont	100.00	200.00
16 Beals Becker	100.00	200.00
17 Frank Bowerman MG	100.00	200.00
18 Jack Coffey	100.00	200.00
19 Bill Dahlen	125.00	250.00
20 Peaches Graham	100.00	200.00
21 Al Mattern	100.00	200.00
22 Harry Smith	100.00	200.00
23 Bill Sweeney	100.00	200.00
24 Tom Tuckey	100.00	200.00

1909 Boston Herald Supplements Pairs

Issued in 1909, these double-sided newspaper supplements feature a member of the Boston Braves as well as the Boston Red Sox. Since these are not numbered, we have sequenced them in alphabetical order of the Red Sox player who appears. It is possible that there are more supplements to this set.

COMPLETE SET (9)	1,250.00	2,500.00
1 Eddie Cicotte	250.00	500.00
Tom Tuckey		
2 Pat Donahue	100.00	200.00
Harry Smith		
3 Doc Gessler	100.00	200.00
Frank Bowerman		
4 Harry Hooper	150.00	300.00
Johnny Bates		
5 Harry Lord	100.00	200.00
Unknown Player		
6 Amby McConnell	100.00	200.00
Jack Coffey		
7 Tris Speaker	250.00	500.00
Ginger Beaumont		
8 Jake Stahl	100.00	200.00
Chick Autry		
9 Heinie Wagner	100.00	200.00
Bill Dahlen		

1871 Boston Red Stockings Wright Cabinets

These cabinets, which measure approximately 4 1/4" by 6 1/2" feature members of the 1871 Boston Red Stockings. The fronts feature a posed portrait of the player in their uniforms while the back is an advertisment for the photo studio in which these photos were taken. Since these photos are unnumbered, we have sequenced them in alphabetical order.

1 Ross Barnes	7,500.00	15,000.00
2 David Birdsall	6,000.00	12,000.00
3 Andy Leonard	6,000.00	12,000.00
4 Cal McVey	12,500.00	25,000.00
5 John Ryan	6,000.00	12,000.00
6 Harry Schafer	6,000.00	12,000.00
7 Al Spalding	15,000.00	30,000.00
8 Harry Wright	12,500.00	25,000.00

1909 Boston Sunday Post Supplements

These supplements, each of which feature two players, were issued as supplements in the Sunday Papers in Boston in 1909.

COMPLETE SET (6)	750.00	1,500.00
1 Ambrose McConnell	100.00	200.00
2 Harry Lord	250.00	500.00
Tris Speaker		
3 Harry Wolter	150.00	300.00
Harry Hooper		
4 Jake Stahl	100.00	200.00
Bill Carrigan		
5 Ed Cicotte	200.00	400.00
Harry Niles		
6 Heinie Wagner	100.00	200.00
Frank Arellanes		

1948 Bowman

The 48-card Bowman set of 1948 was the first major set of the post-war period. Each 2 1/16" by 2 1/2" card had a black and white photo of a current player, with his biographical information printed in black ink on a gray back. Due to the printing process and the 36-card sheet size upon which Bowman was then printing, the 12 cards marked with an SP in the checklist are scarcer numerically, as they were removed from the printing sheet in order to make room for the 12 high numbers (37-48). Cards were issued in one-card penny packs. Many cards are found with over-printed, transposed, or blank backs. The set features the Rookie Cards of Hall of Famers Yogi Berra, Ralph Kiner, Stan Musial, Red Schoendienst, and Warren Spahn. Half of the cards in the set feature New York Yankees or Giants players.

COMPLETE SET (48)	3,000.00	5,000.00
WRAPPER (5-CENT)	600.00	700.00
CARDS PRICED IN NM CONDITION !		
1 Bob Elliott RC	75.00	125.00
2 Ewell Blackwell RC	35.00	60.00
3 Ralph Kiner RC	100.00	250.00
4 Johnny Mize RC	50.00	120.00
5 Bob Feller RC	125.00	250.00
6 Yogi Berra RC	500.00	1,000.00
7 Pete Reiser SP RC	75.00	125.00
8 Phil Rizzuto SP RC	150.00	300.00
9 Walker Cooper RC	10.00	20.00
10 Buddy Rosar RC	10.00	20.00
11 Johnny Lindell RC	12.50	25.00
12 Johnny Sain RC	20.00	50.00
13 Willard Marshall SP RC	20.00	40.00
14 Allie Reynolds RC	30.00	80.00
15 Eddie Joost	10.00	20.00
16 Jack Lohrke SP RC	20.00	40.00
17 Enos Slaughter RC	60.00	150.00
18 Warren Spahn RC	200.00	500.00
19 Tommy Henrich	20.00	50.00
20 Buddy Kerr SP RC	20.00	40.00
21 Ferris Fain RC	20.00	50.00
22 Floyd Bevens SP RC	30.00	50.00
23 Larry Jansen RC	12.50	25.00
24 Dutch Leonard SP	20.00	40.00
25 Barney McCosky	10.00	20.00
26 Frank Shea SP RC	30.00	50.00
27 Sid Gordon RC	20.00	50.00
28 Emil Verban SP RC	20.00	40.00
29 Joe Page SP RC	25.00	60.00
30 Whitey Lockman SP RC	30.00	50.00
31 Bill McCahan RC	10.00	20.00
32 Bill Rigney RC	10.00	20.00
33 Bill Johnson RC	12.50	25.00
34 Sheldon Jones SP RC	20.00	40.00
35 Snuffy Stirnweiss RC	20.00	40.00
36 Stan Musial RC	1,000.00	2,000.00
37 Clint Hartung RC	15.00	30.00
38 Red Schoendienst RC	150.00	400.00
39 Augie Galan RC	15.00	30.00
40 Marty Marion RC	50.00	80.00
41 Rex Barney RC	35.00	60.00
42 Ray Poat RC	15.00	30.00
43 Bruce Edwards RC	20.00	40.00
44 Johnny Wyrostek RC	15.00	30.00
45 Hank Sauer RC	35.00	60.00
46 Herman Wehmeier RC	15.00	30.00
47 Bobby Thomson RC	60.00	100.00
48 Dave Koslo RC	50.00	80.00

1949 Bowman

The cards in this 240-card set measure approximately 2 1/16" by 2 1/2". In 1949 Bowman took an intermediate step between black and white and full color with this set of tinted photos on colored backgrounds. Collectors should note the series price variations, which reflect some inconsistencies in the printing process. There are four major varieties in name printing, which are noted in the checklist below: NOF: name on front; NNOF: no name on front; PR: printed name on back; and SCR: script name on back. Cards were issued in five card nickel packs which came 24 packs to a box. These variations resulted when Bowman used twelve of the lower numbers to fill out the last press sheet of 36 cards, adding to numbers 217-240. Cards 1-3 and 5-73 can be found with either gray or white backs. Certain cards have been seen with a "gray" or "slate" background on the front. These cards are a result of a color printing error and are rarely seen on the secondary market so no value is established for them. Not all numbers are known to exist in this fashion. However, within the numbers between 75 and 107, slightly more of these cards have appeared on the market. Within the high numbers series (145-240), these cards have been seen but the appearance of these cards are very rare. Other cards are known to be extant with double printed backs. The set features the Rookie Cards of Hall of Famers Richie Ashburn, Roy Campanella, Bob Lemon, Robin Roberts, Duke Snider, and Early Wynn as well as Rookie Card of Gil Hodges.

COMP. MASTER SET (252)	10,000.00	16,000.00
COMPLETE SET (240)	10,000.00	15,000.00
WRAPPER (5-CENT, GR.)	200.00	250.00
WRAPPER (5-CENT, BL.)	150.00	200.00
CARDS PRICED IN NM CONDITION		
1 Vern Bickford RC	75.00	125.00
2 Whitey Lockman	20.00	40.00
3 Bob Porterfield RC	7.50	15.00
4A Jerry Priddy NNOF RC	7.50	15.00
4B Jerry Priddy NOF	30.00	50.00
5 Hank Sauer	20.00	40.00
6 Phil Cavarretta RC	20.00	40.00
7 Joe Dobson RC	7.50	15.00
8 Murry Dickson RC	7.50	15.00
9 Ferris Fain	20.00	40.00
10 Ted Gray RC	7.50	15.00
11 Lou Boudreau MG RC	25.00	60.00
12 Cass Michaels RC	7.50	15.00
13 Bob Chesnes RC	7.50	15.00
14 Curt Simmons RC	20.00	40.00
15 Ned Garver RC	7.50	15.00
16 Al Kozar RC	7.50	15.00
17 Earl Torgeson RC	7.50	15.00
18 Bobby Thomson	20.00	40.00
19 Bobby Brown RC	35.00	60.00
20 Gene Hermanski RC	7.50	15.00
21 Frank Baumholtz RC	12.50	25.00
22 Peanuts Lowrey RC	7.50	15.00
23 Bobby Doerr	50.00	80.00
24 Stan Musial	300.00	600.00
25 Carl Scheib RC	7.50	15.00
26 George Kell RC	50.00	80.00
27 Bob Feller	200.00	300.00
28 Don Kolloway RC	7.50	15.00
29 Ralph Kiner	75.00	125.00
30 Andy Seminick RC	20.00	40.00
31 Dick Kokos RC	7.50	15.00
32 Eddie Yost RC	35.00	60.00
33 Warren Spahn	100.00	250.00
34 Dave Koslo	7.50	15.00
35 Vic Raschi RC	35.00	60.00
36 Pee Wee Reese	125.00	200.00
37 Johnny Wyrostek	7.50	15.00
38 Emil Verban	7.50	15.00
39 Billy Goodman RC	12.50	25.00
40 George Munger RC	7.50	15.00
41 Lou Brissie RC	7.50	15.00
42 Hoot Evers RC	7.50	15.00
43 Dale Mitchell RC	20.00	40.00
44 Dave Philley RC	7.50	15.00
45 Wally Westlake RC	7.50	15.00
46 Robin Roberts RC	250.00	500.00
47 Johnny Sain	35.00	60.00
48 Willard Marshall	7.50	15.00
49 Frank Shea	12.50	25.00
50 Jackie Robinson RC	2,000.00	4,000.00
51 Herman Wehmeier	7.50	15.00
52 Johnny Schmitz RC	7.50	15.00
53 Jack Kramer RC	7.50	15.00
54 Marty Marion	35.00	60.00
55 Eddie Joost	7.50	15.00
56 Pat Mullin RC	7.50	15.00
57 Gene Bearden RC	20.00	40.00
58 Bob Elliott	20.00	40.00
59 Jack Lohrke	7.50	15.00
60 Yogi Berra	250.00	500.00
61 Rex Barney	20.00	40.00
62 Grady Hatton RC	7.50	15.00
63 Andy Pafko RC	20.00	40.00
64 Dom DiMaggio	40.00	100.00
65 Enos Slaughter	50.00	80.00
66 Elmer Valo RC	7.50	15.00
67 Alvin Dark RC	20.00	40.00
68 Sheldon Jones	7.50	15.00
69 Tommy Henrich	20.00	40.00
70 Carl Furillo RC	90.00	150.00
71 Vern Stephens RC	7.50	15.00
72 Tommy Holmes RC	20.00	40.00
73 Billy Cox RC	20.00	40.00
74 Tom McBride RC	7.50	15.00
75 Eddie Mayo RC	7.50	15.00
76 Bill Nicholson RC	12.50	25.00
77 Ernie Bonham RC	7.50	15.00
78A Sam Zoldak NNOF RC	7.50	15.00
78B Sam Zoldak NOF	30.00	50.00
79 Ron Northey RC	7.50	15.00
80 Bill McCahan	7.50	15.00
81 Virgil Stallcup RC	7.50	15.00
82 Joe Page	35.00	60.00
83A Bob Scheffing NNOF RC	7.50	15.00
83B Bob Scheffing NOF	30.00	50.00
84 Roy Campanella RC	400.00	1,000.00
85A Johnny Mize NNOF	60.00	100.00
85B Johnny Mize NOF	90.00	150.00
86 Johnny Pesky RC	35.00	60.00
87 Randy Gumpert RC	7.50	15.00
88A Bill Salkeld NNOF RC	7.50	15.00
88B Bill Salkeld NOF	30.00	50.00
89 Mizell Platt RC	7.50	15.00
90 Gil Coan RC	7.50	15.00
91 Dick Wakefield RC	7.50	15.00
92 Willie Jones RC	20.00	40.00
93 Ed Stevens RC	7.50	15.00
94 Mickey Vernon RC	20.00	40.00
95 Howie Pollet RC	7.50	15.00
96 Taft Wright	7.50	15.00
97 Danny Litwhiler RC	7.50	15.00
98A Phil Rizzuto NNOF	125.00	200.00
98B Phil Rizzuto NOF	150.00	250.00
99 Frank Gustine RC	7.50	15.00
100 Gil Hodges RC	150.00	250.00
101 Sid Gordon	7.50	15.00
102 Stan Spence RC	7.50	15.00
103 Joe Tipton RC	7.50	15.00
104 Eddie Stanky RC	20.00	40.00
105 Bill Kennedy RC	7.50	15.00
106 Jake Early RC	7.50	15.00
107 Eddie Lake RC	7.50	15.00
108 Ken Heintzelman RC	7.50	15.00
109A Ed Fitzgerald Script RC	7.50	15.00
109B Ed Fitzgerald Print	35.00	60.00
110 Early Wynn RC	100.00	250.00
111 Red Schoendienst	60.00	100.00
112 Sam Chapman	20.00	40.00
113 Ray LaManno RC	7.50	15.00
114 Allie Reynolds	35.00	60.00
115 Dutch Leonard	7.50	15.00
116 Joe Hatten RC	7.50	15.00
117 Walker Cooper	7.50	15.00
118 Sam Mele RC	7.50	15.00
119 Floyd Baker RC	7.50	15.00
120 Cliff Fannin RC	7.50	15.00
121 Mark Christman RC	7.50	15.00
122 George Vico RC	7.50	15.00
123 Johnny Blatnik UER Name misspelled	7.50	15.00
124A D.Murtaugh Script RC	20.00	40.00
124B D.Murtaugh Print	35.00	60.00
125 Ken Keltner RC	12.50	25.00
126A Al Brazle Script RC	7.50	15.00
126B Al Brazle Print	35.00	60.00
127A Hank Majeski Script RC	7.50	15.00
127B Hank Majeski Print	35.00	60.00
128 Johnny VanderMeer	35.00	60.00
129 Bill Johnson	20.00	40.00
130 Harry Walker RC	7.50	15.00
131 Paul Lehner RC	7.50	15.00
132A Al Evans Script RC	7.50	15.00
132B Al Evans Pint	35.00	60.00
133 Aaron Robinson RC	7.50	15.00
134 Hank Borowy RC	7.50	15.00
135 Stan Rojek RC	7.50	15.00
136 Hank Edwards RC	7.50	15.00
137 Ted Wilks RC	7.50	15.00
138 Buddy Rosar	7.50	15.00
139 Hank Arft RC	7.50	15.00
140 Ray Scarborough RC	7.50	15.00
141 Tony Lupien RC	7.50	15.00
142 Eddie Waitkus RC	20.00	40.00
143A Bob Dillinger Script RC	12.50	25.00
143B Bob Dillinger Print	35.00	60.00
144 Mickey Haefner RC	7.50	15.00
145 Sylvester Donnelly RC	30.00	50.00
146 Mike McCormick RC	30.00	50.00
147 Bert Singleton RC	30.00	50.00
148 Bob Swift RC	30.00	50.00
149 Roy Partee RC	30.00	50.00
150 Allie Clark RC	30.00	50.00
151 Mickey Harris RC	30.00	50.00
152 Clarence Maddern RC	30.00	50.00
153 Phil Masi RC	30.00	50.00
154 Clint Hartung	35.00	60.00
155 Mickey Guerra RC	30.00	50.00
156 Al Zarilla RC	30.00	50.00
157 Walt Masterson RC	30.00	50.00
158 Harry Brecheen RC	35.00	60.00
159 Glen Moulder RC	30.00	50.00
160 Jim Blackburn RC	30.00	50.00
161 Jocko Thompson RC	30.00	50.00
162 Preacher Roe RC	75.00	125.00
163 Clyde McCullough RC	30.00	50.00
164 Vic Wertz RC	50.00	80.00
165 Snuffy Stirnweiss	50.00	80.00
166 Mike Tresh RC	30.00	50.00
167 Babe Martin RC	30.00	50.00
168 Doyle Lade RC	30.00	50.00
169 Jeff Heath RC	35.00	60.00
170 Bill Rigney	35.00	60.00
171 Dick Fowler RC	30.00	50.00
172 Eddie Pellagrini RC	30.00	50.00
173 Eddie Stewart RC	30.00	50.00
174 Terry Moore RC	50.00	80.00
175 Luke Appling	75.00	200.00
176 Ken Raffensberger RC	30.00	50.00
177 Stan Lopata RC	35.00	60.00
178 Tom Brown RC	35.00	60.00
179 Hugh Casey	50.00	80.00
180 Connie Berry	30.00	50.00
181 Gus Niarhos RC	30.00	50.00
182 Hal Peck RC	30.00	50.00
183 Lou Stringer RC	30.00	50.00
184 Bob Chipman RC	30.00	50.00
185 Pete Reiser	50.00	80.00
186 Buddy Kerr	30.00	50.00
187 Phil Marchildon RC	30.00	50.00
188 Karl Drews RC	30.00	50.00
189 Earl Wooten RC	30.00	50.00
190 Jim Hearn RC	30.00	50.00
191 Joe Haynes RC	30.00	50.00
192 Harry Gumbert	30.00	50.00
193 Ken Trinkle RC	30.00	50.00
194 Ralph Branca RC	50.00	120.00
195 Eddie Bockman RC	30.00	50.00
196 Fred Hutchinson RC	35.00	60.00
197 Johnny Lindell	35.00	60.00
198 Steve Gromek RC	30.00	50.00
199 Tex Hughson RC	30.00	50.00
200 Jess Dobernic RC	30.00	50.00
201 Sibby Sisti RC	30.00	50.00
202 Larry Jansen	35.00	60.00
203 Barney McCosky	30.00	50.00
204 Bob Savage RC	30.00	50.00
205 Dick Sisler RC	35.00	60.00
206 Bruce Edwards	30.00	50.00
207 Johnny Hopp RC	30.00	50.00
208 Dizzy Trout	35.00	60.00
209 Charlie Keller	40.00	100.00
210 Joe Gordon RC	50.00	80.00
211 Boo Ferriss RC	30.00	50.00
212 Ralph Hamner RC	30.00	50.00
213 Red Barrett RC	30.00	50.00
214 Richie Ashburn RC	400.00	800.00
215 Kirby Higbe	30.00	50.00
216 Schoolboy Rowe	35.00	60.00
217 Marino Pieretti RC	30.00	50.00
218 Dick Kryhoski RC	30.00	50.00
219 Virgil Trucks RC	35.00	60.00
220 Johnny McCarthy	30.00	50.00
221 Bob Muncrief RC	30.00	50.00
222 Alex Kellner RC	30.00	50.00
223 Bobby Hofman RC	30.00	50.00
224 Satchel Paige RC	2,000.00	4,000.00
225 Jerry Coleman RC	50.00	80.00
226 Duke Snider RC	600.00	1,200.00
227 Fritz Ostermueller	30.00	50.00
228 Jackie Mayo RC	30.00	50.00
229 Ed Lopat RC	90.00	150.00
230 Augie Galan	35.00	60.00
231 Earl Johnson RC	30.00	50.00
232 George McQuinn	35.00	60.00
233 Larry Doby RC	400.00	800.00
234 Rip Sewell RC	30.00	50.00
235 Jim Russell RC	30.00	50.00
236 Fred Sanford RC	30.00	50.00
237 Monte Kennedy RC	30.00	50.00
238 Bob Lemon RC	250.00	500.00
239 Frank McCormick	30.00	50.00
240 Babe Young UER	60.00	100.00

1950 Bowman

The cards in this 252-card set measure approximately 2 1/16" by 2 1/2". This set, marketed in 1950 by Bowman, represented a major improvement in terms of quality over their previous efforts. Each card was a beautifully colored line drawing developed from a simple photograph. The first 72 cards are the scarcest in the set, while the final 72 cards may be found with or without the copyright line. This was the only Bowman sports set to carry the famous "5-Star" logo. Cards were issued in five-card nickel packs. Key rookies in this set are Hank Bauer, Don Newcombe, and Al Rosen.

COMPLETE SET (252)	6,000.00	8,500.00
COMMON CARD (1-72)	30.00	50.00
WRAPPER (1-CENT)	200.00	250.00
WRAPPER (5-CENT)	200.00	250.00
CARDS PRICED IN NM CONDITION		
1 Mel Parnell RC	90.00	150.00
2 Vern Stephens	35.00	60.00
3 Dom DiMaggio	50.00	80.00
4 Gus Zernial RC	20.00	50.00
5 Bob Kuzava RC	30.00	50.00
6 Bob Feller	100.00	250.00
7 Jim Hegan	35.00	60.00
8 George Kell	50.00	80.00
9 Vic Wertz	35.00	60.00
10 Tommy Henrich	40.00	100.00
11 Phil Rizzuto	125.00	300.00
12 Joe Page	20.00	50.00
13 Ferris Fain	35.00	60.00
14 Alex Kellner	20.00	50.00
15 Al Kozar	30.00	50.00
16 Roy Sievers RC	40.00	100.00
17 Sid Hudson	30.00	50.00
18 Eddie Robinson RC	30.00	50.00
19 Warren Spahn	100.00	250.00
20 Bob Elliott	35.00	60.00
21 Pee Wee Reese	100.00	250.00
22 Jackie Robinson	1,500.00	3,000.00
23 Don Newcombe RC	100.00	250.00
24 Johnny Schmitz	30.00	50.00
25 Hank Sauer	35.00	60.00
26 Grady Hatton	30.00	50.00
27 Herman Wehmeier	30.00	50.00
28 Bobby Thomson	50.00	80.00
29 Eddie Stanky	35.00	60.00
30 Eddie Waitkus	35.00	60.00
31 Del Ennis	50.00	80.00
32 Robin Roberts	75.00	200.00
33 Ralph Kiner	60.00	150.00
34 Murry Dickson	30.00	50.00
35 Enos Slaughter	30.00	80.00
36 Eddie Kazak RC	35.00	60.00
37 Luke Appling	40.00	100.00
38 Bill Wight RC	30.00	50.00
39 Larry Doby	60.00	150.00
40 Bob Lemon	50.00	80.00
41 Hoot Evers	30.00	50.00
42 Art Houtteman RC	30.00	50.00
43 Bobby Doerr	50.00	80.00
44 Joe Dobson	30.00	50.00
45 Al Zarilla	30.00	50.00
46 Yogi Berra	300.00	600.00
47 Jerry Coleman	20.00	50.00
48 Lou Brissie	30.00	50.00
49 Elmer Valo	15.00	40.00
50 Dick Kokos	30.00	50.00
51 Ned Garver	35.00	60.00
52 Sam Mele	30.00	50.00
53 Clyde Vollmer RC	30.00	50.00
54 Gil Coan	30.00	50.00
55 Buddy Kerr	30.00	50.00
56 Del Crandall RC	35.00	60.00
57 Vern Bickford	30.00	50.00
58 Carl Furillo	50.00	80.00
59 Ralph Branca	50.00	80.00
60 Andy Pafko	35.00	60.00
61 Bob Rush RC	30.00	50.00
62 Ted Kluszewski	30.00	80.00
63 Ewell Blackwell	35.00	60.00
64 Alvin Dark	20.00	50.00
65 Dave Koslo	30.00	50.00
66 Larry Jansen	35.00	60.00
67 Willie Jones	35.00	60.00
68 Curt Simmons	35.00	60.00
69 Wally Westlake	30.00	50.00
70 Bob Chesnes	30.00	50.00
71 Red Schoendienst	50.00	80.00
72 Howie Pollet	30.00	50.00
73 Willard Marshall	7.50	15.00
74 Johnny Antonelli RC	35.00	60.00
75 Roy Campanella	100.00	250.00
76 Rex Barney	20.00	40.00
77 Duke Snider	100.00	250.00
78 Mickey Owen	10.00	25.00
79 Johnny VanderMeer	20.00	50.00
80 Howard Fox RC	6.00	15.00
81 Ron Northey	6.00	15.00
82 Whitey Lockman	10.00	25.00
83 Sheldon Jones	6.00	15.00
84 Richie Ashburn	75.00	125.00
85 Ken Heintzelman	7.50	15.00
86 Stan Rojek	7.50	15.00
87 Bill Werle RC	7.50	15.00
88 Marty Marion	20.00	50.00
89 George Munger	7.50	15.00
90 Harry Brecheen	20.00	40.00
91 Cass Michaels	7.50	15.00
92 Hank Majeski	7.50	15.00
93 Gene Bearden	20.00	40.00
94 Lou Boudreau MG	35.00	60.00
95 Aaron Robinson	7.50	15.00
96 Virgil Trucks	12.50	25.00
97 Maurice McDermott RC	7.50	15.00
98 Ted Williams	400.00	800.00
99 Billy Goodman	12.50	25.00
100 Vic Raschi	35.00	60.00
101 Bobby Brown	15.00	40.00
102 Billy Johnson	12.50	25.00
103 Eddie Joost	7.50	15.00
104 Sam Chapman	7.50	15.00
105 Bob Dillinger	7.50	15.00
106 Cliff Fannin	7.50	15.00
107 Sam Dente RC	7.50	15.00
108 Ray Scarborough	10.00	25.00
109 Sid Gordon	7.50	15.00
110 Tommy Holmes	12.50	25.00
111 Walker Cooper	7.50	15.00
112 Gil Hodges	75.00	125.00
113 Gene Hermanski	7.50	15.00
114 Wayne Terwilliger RC	7.50	15.00
115 Roy Smalley	7.50	15.00
116 Virgil Stallcup	7.50	15.00
117 Bill Rigney	7.50	15.00
118 Clint Hartung	7.50	15.00
119 Dick Sisler	12.50	25.00
120 John Thompson	7.50	15.00
121 Andy Seminick	12.50	25.00
122 Johnny Hopp	12.50	25.00
123 Dino Restelli RC	7.50	15.00
124 Clyde McCullough	7.50	15.00
125 Del Rice RC	7.50	15.00
126 Al Brazle	7.50	15.00
127 Dave Philley	7.50	15.00
128 Phil Masi	7.50	15.00
129 Joe Gordon	20.00	50.00
130 Dale Mitchell	12.50	25.00
131 Steve Gromek	7.50	15.00
132 Mickey Vernon	12.50	25.00
133 Don Kolloway	7.50	15.00
134 Paul Trout	7.50	15.00
135 Pat Mullin	7.50	15.00
136 Buddy Rosar	7.50	15.00
137 Johnny Pesky	12.50	25.00
138 Allie Reynolds	20.00	50.00
139 Johnny Mize	25.00	60.00
140 Pete Suder RC	7.50	15.00
141 Joe Coleman RC	12.50	25.00
142 Sherman Lollar RC	20.00	40.00
143 Eddie Stewart	7.50	15.00
144 Al Evans	7.50	15.00
145 Jack Graham RC	7.50	15.00
146 Floyd Baker	7.50	15.00

147 Mike Garcia RC 20.00 40.00
148 Early Wynn 40.00 100.00
149 Bob Swift 7.50 15.00
150 George Vico 7.50 15.00
151 Fred Hutchinson 12.50 25.00
152 Ellis Kinder RC 7.50 15.00
153 Walt Masterson 10.00 25.00
154 Gus Niarhos 7.50 15.00
155 Frank Shea 12.50 25.00
156 Fred Sanford 12.50 25.00
157 Mike Guerra 7.50 15.00
158 Paul Lehner 7.50 15.00
159 Joe Tipton 7.50 15.00
160 Mickey Harris 7.50 15.00
161 Sherry Robertson RC 7.50 15.00
162 Eddie Yost 12.50 25.00
163 Earl Torgeson 7.50 15.00
164 Sibby Sisti 7.50 15.00
165 Bruce Edwards 7.50 15.00
166 Joe Hatten 7.50 15.00
167 Preacher Roe 15.00 40.00
168 Bob Scheffing 7.50 15.00
169 Hank Edwards 7.50 15.00
170 Dutch Leonard 7.50 15.00
171 Harry Gumbert 7.50 15.00
172 Peanuts Lowrey 7.50 15.00
173 Lloyd Merriman RC 7.50 15.00
174 Hank Thompson RC 20.00 40.00
175 Monte Kennedy 7.50 15.00
176 Sylvester Donnelly 7.50 15.00
177 Hank Borowy 7.50 15.00
178 Ed Fitzgerald 7.50 15.00
179 Chuck Diering RC 7.50 15.00
180 Harry Walker 12.50 25.00
181 Marino Pieretti 7.50 15.00
182 Sam Zoldak 7.50 15.00
183 Mickey Haefner 7.50 15.00
184 Randy Gumpert 7.50 15.00
185 Howie Judson RC 7.50 15.00
186 Ken Keltner 12.50 25.00
187 Lou Stringer 7.50 15.00
188 Earl Johnson 7.50 15.00
189 Owen Friend RC 12.00 30.00
190 Ken Wood RC 7.50 15.00
191 Dick Starr RC 7.50 15.00
192 Bob Chipman 7.50 15.00
193 Pete Reiser 20.00 40.00
194 Billy Cox 35.00 60.00
195 Phil Cavarretta 20.00 40.00
196 Doyle Lade 7.50 15.00
197 Johnny Wyrostek 7.50 15.00
198 Danny Litwhiler 7.50 15.00
199 Jack Kramer 7.50 15.00
200 Kirby Higbe 12.50 25.00
201 Pete Castiglione RC 7.50 15.00
202 Cliff Chambers RC 7.50 15.00
203 Danny Murtaugh 12.50 25.00
204 Granny Hamner RC 20.00 40.00
205 Mike Goliat RC 7.50 15.00
206 Stan Lopata 12.50 25.00
207 Max Lanier RC 7.50 15.00
208 Jim Hearn 7.50 15.00
209 Johnny Lindell 7.50 15.00
210 Ted Gray 7.50 15.00
211 Charlie Keller 20.00 40.00
212 Jerry Priddy 7.50 15.00
213 Carl Scheib 7.50 15.00
214 Dick Fowler 7.50 15.00
215 Ed Lopat 35.00 60.00
216 Bob Porterfield 12.50 25.00
217 Casey Stengel MG 40.00 100.00
218 Cliff Mapes RC 12.50 25.00
219 Hank Bauer RC 25.00 60.00
220 Leo Durocher MG 35.00 60.00
221 Don Mueller RC 20.00 40.00
222 Bobby Morgan RC 7.50 15.00
223 Jim Russell 7.50 15.00
224 Jack Banta RC 7.50 15.00
225 Eddie Sawyer MG RC 12.50 25.00
226 Jim Konstanty RC 35.00 60.00
227 Bob Miller RC 12.50 25.00
228 Bill Nicholson 12.50 30.00
229 Frankie Frisch MG 35.00 60.00
230 Bill Serena RC 7.50 15.00
231 Preston Ward RC 7.50 15.00
232 Al Rosen RC 35.00 60.00
233 Allie Clark 7.50 15.00
234 Bobby Shantz RC 35.00 60.00
235 Harold Gilbert RC 7.50 15.00
236 Bob Cain RC 7.50 15.00
237 Bill Salkeld 7.50 15.00
238 Nippy Jones RC 7.50 15.00
239 Bill Howerton RC 7.50 15.00
240 Eddie Lake 7.50 15.00
241 Neil Berry RC 7.50 15.00
242 Dick Kryhoski 7.50 15.00
243 Johnny Groth RC 7.50 15.00
244 Dale Coogan RC 7.50 15.00
245 Al Papai RC 7.50 15.00
246 Walt Dropo RC 20.00 40.00
247 Irv Noren RC 12.50 25.00
248 Sam Jethroe RC 20.00 50.00
249 Snuffy Stirnweiss 12.50 25.00
250 Ray Coleman RC 7.50 15.00
251 Les Moss RC 7.50 15.00
252 Billy DeMars RC 35.00 60.00

1951 Bowman

The cards in this 324-card set measure approximately 2 1/16" by 3 1/8". Many of the obverses of the cards appearing in the 1951 Bowman set are enlargements of those appearing in the previous year. The high number series (253-324) is highly valued and contains the true Rookie Cards of Mickey Mantle and Willie Mays. Card number 195 depicts Paul Richards in caricature. George Kell's card (number 46) incorrectly lists him as being in the "1941" Bowman series. Cards were issued either in one card penny packs which came 120 to a box or in six-card nickel packs which came 24 to a box. Player names are found printed in a panel on the front of the card. These cards were supposedly also sold in sheets in variety stores in the Philadelphia area.

COMPLETE SET (324) 15,000.00 20,000.00
COMMON CARD (1-252) 10.00 20.00
WRAPPER (1-CENT) 150.00 200.00
WRAPPER (5-CENT) 200.00 250.00
CARDS PRICED IN NM CONDITION
1 Whitey Ford RC 600.00 1,500.00
2 Yogi Berra 250.00 500.00
3 Robin Roberts 60.00 100.00
4 Del Ennis 20.00 50.00
5 Dale Mitchell 12.50 25.00
6 Don Newcombe 30.00 80.00
7 Gil Hodges 75.00 125.00
8 Paul Lehner 10.00 20.00
9 Sam Chapman 10.00 20.00
10 Red Schoendienst 35.00 60.00
11 George Munger 10.00 20.00
12 Hank Majeski 10.00 20.00
13 Eddie Stanky 12.50 25.00
14 Alvin Dark 20.00 40.00
15 Johnny Pesky 12.50 25.00
16 Maurice McDermott 10.00 20.00
17 Pete Castiglione 10.00 20.00
18 Gil Coan 10.00 20.00
19 Sid Gordon 10.00 20.00
20 Del Crandall UER 12.50 25.00
21 Snuffy Stirnweiss 12.50 25.00
22 Hank Sauer 12.50 25.00
23 Hoot Evers 10.00 20.00
24 Ewell Blackwell 20.00 40.00
25 Vic Raschi 35.00 60.00
26 Phil Rizzuto 90.00 150.00
27 Jim Konstanty 12.50 25.00
28 Eddie Waitkus 10.00 20.00
29 Allie Clark 10.00 20.00
30 Bob Feller 75.00 200.00
31 Roy Campanella 100.00 250.00
32 Duke Snider 150.00 250.00
33 Bob Hooper RC 10.00 20.00
34 Marty Marion MG 20.00 40.00
35 Al Zarilla 10.00 20.00
36 Joe Dobson 10.00 20.00
37 Whitey Lockman 20.00 40.00
38 Al Evans 10.00 20.00
39 Ray Scarborough 10.00 20.00
40 Gus Bell RC 35.00 60.00
41 Eddie Yost 12.50 25.00
42 Vern Bickford 10.00 25.00
43 Billy DeMars 10.00 20.00
44 Roy Smalley 10.00 20.00
45 Art Houtteman 10.00 20.00
46 George Kell UER 35.00 60.00
47 Grady Hatton 10.00 20.00
48 Ken Raffensberger 10.00 20.00
49 Jerry Coleman 12.50 25.00
50 Johnny Mize 50.00 80.00
51 Andy Seminick 10.00 20.00
52 Dick Sisler 20.00 40.00
53 Bob Lemon 35.00 60.00
54 Ray Boone RC 20.00 40.00
55 Gene Hermanski 10.00 20.00
56 Ralph Branca 35.00 60.00
57 Alex Kellner 10.00 20.00
58 Enos Slaughter 35.00 60.00
59 Randy Gumpert 10.00 25.00
60 Chico Carrasquel RC 35.00 60.00
61 Jim Hearn 12.50 25.00
62 Lou Boudreau MG 35.00 60.00
63 Bob Dillinger 10.00 20.00
64 Bill Werle 10.00 20.00
65 Mickey Vernon 20.00 40.00
66 Bob Elliott 12.50 25.00
67 Roy Sievers 12.00 30.00
68 Dick Kokos 10.00 20.00
69 Johnny Schmitz 10.00 20.00
70 Ron Northey 10.00 20.00
71 Jerry Priddy 10.00 20.00
72 Lloyd Merriman 10.00 20.00
73 Tommy Byrne RC 10.00 20.00
74 Billy Johnson 12.50 25.00
75 Russ Meyer RC 12.50 25.00
76 Stan Lopata 12.50 25.00
77 Mike Goliat 10.00 20.00
78 Early Wynn 35.00 60.00
79 Jim Hegan 12.50 25.00
80 Pee Wee Reese 50.00 120.00
81 Carl Furillo 35.00 60.00
82 Joe Tipton 10.00 20.00
83 Carl Scheib 10.00 20.00
84 Barney McCosky 10.00 20.00
85 Eddie Kazak 10.00 20.00
86 Harry Brecheen 12.50 25.00
87 Floyd Baker 10.00 20.00
88 Eddie Robinson 10.00 20.00
89 Hank Thompson 12.50 25.00
90 Dave Koslo 10.00 20.00
91 Clyde Vollmer 12.00 30.00
92 Vern Stephens 12.50 25.00
93 Danny O'Connell RC 10.00 25.00
94 Clyde McCullough 10.00 20.00
95 Sherry Robertson 10.00 20.00
96 Sandy Consuegra RC 10.00 20.00
97 Bob Kuzava 10.00 20.00
98 Willard Marshall 10.00 20.00
99 Earl Torgeson 10.00 20.00
100 Sherm Lollar 12.50 25.00
101 Owen Friend 10.00 20.00
102 Dutch Leonard 10.00 20.00
103 Andy Pafko 20.00 40.00
104 Virgil Trucks 12.50 25.00
105 Don Kolloway 10.00 20.00
106 Pat Mullin 10.00 20.00
107 Johnny Wyrostek 10.00 20.00
108 Virgil Stallcup 10.00 20.00
109 Allie Reynolds 35.00 60.00
110 Bobby Brown 20.00 40.00
111 Curt Simmons 12.50 25.00
112 Willie Jones 10.00 20.00
113 Bill Nicholson 10.00 20.00
114 Sam Zoldak 10.00 20.00
115 Steve Gromek 10.00 20.00
116 Bruce Edwards 10.00 20.00
117 Eddie Miksis RC 10.00 20.00
118 Preacher Roe 35.00 60.00
119 Eddie Joost 10.00 20.00
120 Joe Coleman 12.50 25.00
121 Gerry Staley RC 10.00 20.00
122 Joe Garagiola RC 30.00 80.00
123 Howie Judson 10.00 20.00
124 Gus Niarhos 10.00 20.00
125 Bill Rigney 12.50 25.00
126 Bobby Thomson 35.00 60.00
127 Sal Maglie RC 20.00 50.00
128 Ellis Kinder 10.00 20.00
129 Matt Batts 10.00 20.00
130 Tom Saffell RC 10.00 20.00
131 Cliff Chambers 10.00 20.00
132 Cass Michaels 10.00 20.00
133 Sam Dente 10.00 20.00
134 Warren Spahn 60.00 150.00
135 Walker Cooper 10.00 20.00
136 Ray Coleman 10.00 20.00
137 Dick Starr 10.00 20.00
138 Phil Cavarretta 12.50 25.00
139 Doyle Lade 10.00 20.00
140 Eddie Lake 10.00 20.00
141 Fred Hutchinson 12.50 25.00
142 Aaron Robinson 10.00 20.00
143 Ted Kluszewski 25.00 60.00
144 Herman Wehmeier 10.00 20.00
145 Fred Sanford 12.50 25.00
146 Johnny Hopp 12.50 25.00
147 Ken Heintzelman 10.00 20.00
148 Granny Hamner 10.00 20.00
149 Bubba Church RC 10.00 20.00
150 Mike Garcia 12.50 25.00
151 Larry Doby 40.00 100.00
152 Cal Abrams RC 10.00 20.00
153 Rex Barney 12.50 25.00
154 Pete Suder 10.00 20.00
155 Lou Brissie 10.00 20.00
156 Del Rice 10.00 20.00
157 Al Brazle 10.00 20.00
158 Chuck Diering 10.00 20.00
159 Eddie Stewart 10.00 20.00
160 Phil Masi 10.00 20.00
161 Wes Westrum RC 10.00 25.00
162 Larry Jansen 12.50 25.00
163 Monte Kennedy 10.00 20.00
164 Bill Wight 10.00 20.00
165 Ted Williams UER 300.00 600.00
166 Stan Rojek 10.00 20.00
167 Murry Dickson 10.00 20.00
168 Sam Mele 10.00 20.00
169 Sid Hudson 10.00 20.00
170 Sibby Sisti 10.00 20.00
171 Buddy Kerr 10.00 20.00
172 Ned Garver 10.00 20.00
173 Hank Arft 10.00 20.00
174 Mickey Owen 12.50 25.00
175 Wayne Terwilliger 10.00 20.00
176 Vic Wertz 20.00 40.00
177 Charlie Keller 12.50 25.00
178 Ted Gray 10.00 20.00
179 Danny Litwhiler 10.00 20.00
180 Howie Fox 10.00 20.00
181 Casey Stengel MG 40.00 100.00
182 Tom Ferrick RC 10.00 20.00
183 Hank Bauer 20.00 50.00
184 Eddie Sawyer MG 20.00 40.00
185 Jimmy Bloodworth 10.00 20.00
186 Richie Ashburn 60.00 100.00
187 Al Rosen 20.00 40.00
188 Bobby Avila RC 12.50 25.00
189 Erv Palica RC 10.00 20.00
190 Joe Hatten 10.00 20.00
191 Billy Hitchcock RC 10.00 20.00
192 Hank Wyse RC 10.00 20.00
193 Ted Wilks 10.00 20.00
194 Peanuts Lowrey 10.00 20.00
195 Paul Richards MG 12.50 25.00
196 Billy Pierce RC 20.00 50.00
197 Bob Cain 10.00 20.00
198 Monte Irvin RC 100.00 200.00
199 Sheldon Jones 10.00 20.00
200 Jack Kramer 10.00 20.00
201 Steve O'Neill MG RC 10.00 20.00
202 Mike Guerra 10.00 20.00
203 Vernon Law RC 35.00 60.00
204 Vic Lombardi RC 10.00 20.00
205 Mickey Grasso RC 10.00 20.00
206 Conrado Marrero RC 10.00 20.00
207 Billy Southworth MG RC 15.00 40.00
208 Blix Donnelly 10.00 20.00
209 Ken Wood 10.00 20.00
210 Les Moss 10.00 20.00
211 Hal Jeffcoat RC 10.00 20.00
212 Bob Rush 10.00 20.00
213 Neil Berry 10.00 25.00
214 Bob Swift 10.00 20.00
215 Ken Peterson 10.00 20.00
216 Connie Ryan RC 10.00 20.00
217 Joe Page 12.50 25.00
218 Ed Lopat 35.00 60.00
219 Gene Woodling RC 15.00 40.00
220 Bob Miller 10.00 20.00
221 Dick Whitman RC 10.00 20.00
222 Thurman Tucker RC 10.00 25.00
223 Johnny VanderMeer 20.00 40.00
224 Billy Cox 12.50 25.00
225 Dan Bankhead RC 20.00 40.00
226 Jimmy Dykes MG 10.00 20.00
227 Bobby Shantz UER 12.50 25.00
228 Cloyd Boyer RC 12.50 25.00
229 Bill Howerton 10.00 20.00
230 Max Lanier 10.00 20.00
231 Luis Aloma RC 10.00 20.00
232 Nellie Fox RC 100.00 250.00
233 Leo Durocher MG 20.00 50.00
234 Clint Hartung 12.50 25.00
235 Jack Lohrke 10.00 20.00
236 Buddy Rosar 10.00 20.00
237 Billy Goodman 12.50 25.00
238 Pete Reiser 20.00 40.00
239 Bill MacDonald RC 10.00 20.00
240 Joe Haynes 10.00 20.00
241 Irv Noren 12.50 25.00
242 Sam Jethroe 12.50 25.00
243 Johnny Antonelli 12.50 25.00
244 Cliff Fannin 10.00 20.00
245 John Berardino RC 8.00 20.00
246 Bill Serena 10.00 20.00
247 Bob Ramazzotti RC 10.00 20.00
248 Johnny Klippstein RC 10.00 20.00
249 Johnny Groth 10.00 20.00
250 Hank Borowy 10.00 20.00
251 Willard Ramsdell RC 12.00 30.00
252 Dixie Howell RC 10.00 20.00
253 Mickey Mantle RC 15,000.00 25,000.00
254 Jackie Jensen RC 60.00 100.00
255 Milo Candini RC 30.00 50.00
256 Ken Silvestri RC 30.00 50.00
257 Birdie Tebbetts RC 35.00 60.00
258 Luke Easter RC 35.00 60.00
259 Chuck Dressen MG 35.00 60.00
260 Carl Erskine RC 60.00 100.00
261 Wally Moses 35.00 60.00
262 Gus Zernial 35.00 60.00
263 Howie Pollet 20.00 50.00
264 Don Richmond RC 30.00 50.00
265 Steve Bilko RC 30.00 50.00
266 Harry Dorish RC 30.00 50.00
267 Ken Holcombe RC 30.00 50.00
268 Don Mueller 35.00 60.00
269 Ray Noble RC 30.00 50.00
270 Willard Nixon RC 15.00 40.00
271 Tommy Wright RC 30.00 50.00
272 Billy Meyer MG RC 30.00 50.00
273 Danny Murtaugh 35.00 60.00
274 George Metkovich RC 30.00 50.00
275 Bucky Harris MG 50.00 80.00
276 Frank Quinn RC 30.00 50.00
277 Roy Hartsfield RC 30.00 50.00
278 Norman Roy RC 30.00 50.00
279 Jim Delsing RC 30.00 50.00
280 Frank Overmire 30.00 50.00
281 Al Widmar RC 30.00 50.00
282 Frank Frisch MG 30.00 80.00
283 Walt Dubiel RC 30.00 50.00
284 Gene Bearden 35.00 60.00
285 Johnny Lipon RC 30.00 50.00
286 Bob Usher RC 30.00 50.00
287 Jim Blackburn 30.00 50.00
288 Bobby Adams 30.00 50.00
289 Cliff Mapes 35.00 60.00
290 Bill Dickey CO 50.00 120.00
291 Tommy Henrich CO 50.00 80.00
292 Eddie Pellagrini 30.00 50.00
293 Ken Johnson RC 30.00 50.00
294 Jocko Thompson 30.00 50.00
295 Al Lopez MG RC 75.00 125.00
296 Bob Kennedy RC 35.00 60.00
297 Dave Philley 30.00 50.00
298 Joe Astroth RC 12.00 30.00
299 Clyde King RC 30.00 50.00
300 Hal Rice RC 15.00 40.00
301 Tommy Glaviano RC 30.00 50.00
302 Jim Busby RC 30.00 50.00
303 Marv Rotblatt RC 30.00 50.00
304 Al Gettell RC 30.00 50.00
305 Willie Mays RC 6,000.00 12,000.00
306 Jim Piersall RC 75.00 125.00
307 Walt Masterson 30.00 50.00
308 Ted Beard RC 30.00 50.00
309 Mel Queen RC 30.00 50.00
310 Erv Dusak RC 30.00 50.00
311 Mickey Harris 30.00 50.00
312 Gene Mauch RC 35.00 60.00
313 Ray Mueller RC 30.00 50.00
314 Johnny Sain 25.00 60.00
315 Zack Taylor MG 30.00 50.00
316 Duane Pillette RC 30.00 50.00
317 Smoky Burgess RC 50.00 80.00
318 Warren Hacker RC 30.00 50.00
319 Red Rolfe MG 35.00 60.00
320 Hal White RC 30.00 50.00
321 Earl Johnson 30.00 50.00
322 Luke Sewell MG 35.00 60.00
323 Joe Adcock RC 50.00 80.00
324 Johnny Pramesa RC 75.00 125.00

1952 Bowman

The cards in this 252-card set measure approximately 2 1/16" by 3 1/8". While the Bowman set of 1952 retained the card size introduced in 1951, it employed a modification of color tones from the two preceding years. The cards also appeared with a facsimile autograph on the front and, for the first time since 1949, premium advertising on the back. The 1952 set was apparently sold in sheets as well as in gum packs. Artwork for 15 cards that were never issued was discovered in the early 1980s. Cards were issued in one card penny packs or five card nickel packs. The five cent packs came 24 to a box. Notable Rookie Cards in this set are Lew Burdette, Gil McDougald, and Minnie Minoso.

COMPLETE SET (252)	5,500.00	8,500.00
WRAPPER (1-CENT)	150.00	200.00
WRAPPER (5-CENT)	75.00	100.00
CARDS PRICED IN NM CONDITION		
1 Yogi Berra	300.00	600.00
2 Bobby Thomson	20.00	40.00
3 Fred Hutchinson	12.50	25.00
4 Robin Roberts	50.00	80.00
5 Minnie Minoso RC	75.00	125.00
6 Virgil Stallcup	7.50	15.00
7 Mike Garcia	12.50	25.00
8 Pee Wee Reese	50.00	120.00
9 Vern Stephens	12.50	25.00
10 Bob Hooper	7.50	15.00
11 Ralph Kiner	35.00	60.00
12 Max Surkont RC	7.50	15.00
13 Cliff Mapes	7.50	15.00
14 Cliff Chambers	7.50	15.00
15 Sam Mele	7.50	15.00
16 Turk Lown RC	7.50	15.00
17 Ed Lopat	20.00	40.00
18 Don Mueller	12.50	25.00
19 Bob Cain	7.50	15.00
20 Willie Jones	7.50	15.00
21 Nellie Fox	30.00	80.00
22 Willard Ramsdell	7.50	15.00
23 Bob Lemon	35.00	60.00
24 Carl Furillo	20.00	50.00
25 Mickey McDermott	7.50	15.00
26 Eddie Joost	7.50	15.00
27 Joe Garagiola	20.00	40.00
28 Roy Hartsfield	7.50	15.00
29 Ned Garver	7.50	15.00
30 Red Schoendienst	35.00	60.00
31 Eddie Yost	12.50	25.00
32 Eddie Miksis	7.50	15.00
33 Gil McDougald RC	50.00	80.00
34 Alvin Dark	12.50	25.00
35 Granny Hamner	7.50	15.00
36 Cass Michaels	7.50	15.00
37 Vic Raschi	12.50	25.00
38 Whitey Lockman	12.50	25.00
39 Vic Wertz	12.50	25.00
40 Bubba Church	7.50	15.00
41 Chico Carrasquel	12.50	25.00
42 Johnny Wyrostek	7.50	15.00
43 Bob Feller	90.00	150.00
44 Roy Campanella	100.00	200.00
45 Johnny Pesky	12.50	25.00
46 Carl Scheib	7.50	15.00
47 Pete Castiglione	7.50	15.00
48 Vern Bickford	7.50	15.00
49 Jim Hearn	7.50	15.00
50 Gerry Staley	7.50	15.00
51 Gil Coan	7.50	15.00
52 Phil Rizzuto	50.00	120.00
53 Richie Ashburn	30.00	80.00
54 Billy Pierce	12.50	25.00
55 Ken Raffensberger	7.50	15.00
56 Clyde King	12.50	25.00
57 Clyde Vollmer	7.50	15.00
58 Hank Majeski	7.50	15.00
59 Murry Dickson	7.50	15.00
60 Sid Gordon	7.50	15.00
61 Tommy Byrne	7.50	15.00
62 Joe Presko RC	7.50	15.00
63 Irv Noren	7.50	15.00
64 Roy Smalley	7.50	15.00
65 Hank Bauer	20.00	40.00
66 Sal Maglie	12.50	25.00
67 Johnny Groth	7.50	15.00
68 Jim Busby	7.50	15.00
69 Joe Adcock	12.50	25.00
70 Carl Erskine	20.00	40.00
71 Vern Law	12.50	25.00
72 Earl Torgeson	7.50	15.00
73 Jerry Coleman	12.50	25.00
74 Wes Westrum	12.50	25.00
75 George Kell	35.00	60.00
76 Del Ennis	12.50	25.00
77 Eddie Robinson	7.50	15.00
78 Lloyd Merriman	7.50	15.00
79 Lou Brissie	7.50	15.00
80 Gil Hodges	60.00	100.00
81 Billy Goodman	12.50	25.00
82 Gus Zernial	12.50	25.00
83 Howie Pollet	7.50	15.00
84 Sam Jethroe	12.50	25.00
85 Marty Marion CO	12.50	25.00
86 Cal Abrams	7.50	15.00
87 Mickey Vernon	12.50	25.00
88 Bruce Edwards	7.50	15.00
89 Billy Hitchcock	7.50	15.00
90 Larry Jansen	12.50	25.00
91 Don Kolloway	7.50	15.00
92 Eddie Waitkus	12.50	25.00
93 Paul Richards MG	12.50	25.00
94 Luke Sewell MG	12.50	25.00
95 Luke Easter	12.50	25.00
96 Ralph Branca	12.00	30.00
97 Willard Marshall	7.50	15.00
98 Jimmie Dykes MG	12.50	25.00
99 Clyde McCullough	7.50	15.00
100 Sibby Sisti	7.50	15.00
101 Mickey Mantle	2,500.00	5,000.00
102 Peanuts Lowrey	7.50	15.00
103 Joe Haynes	7.50	15.00
104 Hal Jeffcoat	7.50	15.00
105 Bobby Brown	12.50	25.00
106 Randy Gumpert	7.50	15.00
107 Del Rice	7.50	15.00
108 George Metkovich	7.50	15.00
109 Tom Morgan RC	15.00	40.00
110 Max Lanier	7.50	15.00
111 Hoot Evers	7.50	15.00
112 Smoky Burgess	12.50	25.00
113 Al Zarilla	7.50	15.00
114 Frank Hiller RC	7.50	15.00
115 Larry Doby	35.00	60.00
116 Duke Snider	125.00	200.00
117 Bill Wight	7.50	15.00
118 Ray Murray RC	7.50	15.00
119 Bill Howerton	7.50	15.00
120 Chet Nichols RC	7.50	15.00
121 Al Corwin RC	7.50	15.00
122 Billy Johnson	7.50	15.00
123 Sid Hudson	7.50	15.00
124 Birdie Tebbetts	7.50	15.00
125 Howie Fox	7.50	15.00
126 Phil Cavarretta	12.50	25.00
127 Dick Sisler	7.50	15.00
128 Don Newcombe	35.00	60.00
129 Gus Niarhos	7.50	15.00
130 Allie Clark	7.50	15.00
131 Bob Swift	7.50	15.00
132 Dave Cole RC	7.50	15.00
133 Dick Kryhoski	7.50	15.00
134 Al Brazle	7.50	15.00
135 Mickey Harris	7.50	15.00
136 Gene Hermanski	7.50	15.00
137 Stan Rojek	7.50	15.00
138 Ted Wilks	7.50	15.00
139 Jerry Priddy	7.50	15.00
140 Ray Scarborough	7.50	15.00
141 Hank Edwards	7.50	15.00
142 Early Wynn	20.00	50.00
143 Sandy Consuegra	7.50	15.00
144 Joe Hatten	7.50	15.00
145 Johnny Mize	35.00	60.00
146 Leo Durocher MG	20.00	50.00
147 Marlin Stuart RC	7.50	15.00
148 Ken Heintzelman	7.50	15.00
149 Howie Judson	7.50	15.00
150 Herman Wehmeier	7.50	15.00
151 Al Rosen	12.50	25.00
152 Billy Cox	7.50	15.00
153 Fred Hatfield RC	7.50	15.00
154 Ferris Fain	10.00	25.00
155 Billy Meyer MG	7.50	15.00
156 Warren Spahn	60.00	150.00
157 Jim Delsing	7.50	15.00
158 Bucky Harris MG	12.00	30.00
159 Dutch Leonard	10.00	25.00
160 Eddie Stanky	12.50	25.00
161 Jackie Jensen	20.00	50.00
162 Monte Irvin	30.00	80.00
163 Johnny Lipon	7.50	15.00
164 Connie Ryan	7.50	15.00
165 Saul Rogovin RC	7.50	15.00
166 Bobby Adams	7.50	15.00
167 Bobby Avila	12.50	25.00
168 Preacher Roe	12.50	25.00
169 Walt Dropo	12.50	25.00
170 Joe Astroth	7.50	15.00
171 Mel Queen	7.50	15.00
172 Ebba St.Claire RC	7.50	15.00
173 Gene Bearden	7.50	15.00
174 Mickey Grasso	7.50	15.00
175 Randy Jackson RC	7.50	15.00
176 Harry Brecheen	12.50	25.00
177 Gene Woodling	12.50	25.00
178 Dave Williams RC	12.50	25.00
179 Pete Suder	7.50	15.00
180 Ed Fitzgerald	7.50	15.00
181 Joe Collins RC	12.50	25.00
182 Dave Koslo	7.50	15.00
183 Pat Mullin	7.50	15.00
184 Curt Simmons	12.50	25.00
185 Eddie Stewart	7.50	15.00
186 Frank Smith RC	7.50	15.00
187 Jim Hegan	12.50	25.00
188 Chuck Dressen MG	12.50	25.00
189 Jimmy Piersall	15.00	40.00
190 Dick Fowler	7.50	15.00
191 Bob Friend RC	12.00	30.00
192 John Cusick RC	7.50	15.00
193 Bobby Young RC	7.50	15.00
194 Bob Porterfield	10.00	25.00
195 Frank Baumholtz	7.50	15.00
196 Stan Musial	200.00	500.00
197 Charlie Silvera RC	7.50	15.00
198 Chuck Diering	7.50	15.00
199 Ted Gray	7.50	15.00
200 Ken Silvestri	7.50	15.00
201 Ray Coleman	7.50	15.00
202 Harry Perkowski RC	7.50	15.00
203 Steve Gromek	7.50	15.00
204 Andy Pafko	15.00	40.00
205 Walt Masterson	7.50	15.00
206 Elmer Valo	7.50	15.00
207 George Strickland RC	7.50	15.00
208 Walker Cooper	7.50	15.00
209 Dick Littlefield RC	7.50	15.00
210 Archie Wilson RC	7.50	15.00
211 Paul Minner RC	7.50	15.00
212 Solly Hemus RC	7.50	15.00
213 Monte Kennedy	7.50	15.00
214 Ray Boone	7.50	15.00
215 Sheldon Jones	7.50	15.00
216 Matt Batts	7.50	15.00
217 Casey Stengel MG	50.00	120.00
218 Willie Mays	800.00	1,500.00
219 Neil Berry	35.00	60.00
220 Russ Meyer	35.00	60.00
221 Lou Kretlow RC	35.00	60.00
222 Dixie Howell	35.00	60.00
223 Harry Simpson RC	35.00	60.00
224 Johnny Schmitz	35.00	60.00
225 Del Wilber RC	35.00	60.00
226 Alex Kellner	35.00	60.00
227 Clyde Sukeforth CO RC	35.00	60.00
228 Bob Chipman	35.00	60.00
229 Hank Arft	35.00	60.00
230 Frank Shea	35.00	60.00
231 Dee Fondy RC	35.00	60.00
232 Enos Slaughter	60.00	100.00
233 Bob Kuzava	35.00	60.00
234 Fred Fitzsimmons CO	35.00	60.00
235 Steve Souchock RC	35.00	60.00
236 Tommy Brown	35.00	60.00
237 Sherm Lollar	35.00	60.00
238 Roy McMillan RC	35.00	60.00
239 Dale Mitchell	35.00	60.00
240 Billy Loes RC	35.00	60.00
241 Mel Parnell	35.00	60.00
242 Everett Kell RC	35.00	60.00
243 George Munger	35.00	60.00
244 Lew Burdette RC	40.00	100.00
245 George Schmees RC	35.00	60.00
246 Jerry Snyder RC	35.00	60.00
247 Johnny Pramesa	35.00	60.00
248 Bill Werle Full Name	35.00	60.00
248A Bill Werle No W	35.00	60.00
249 Hank Thompson	35.00	60.00
250 Ike Delock RC	35.00	60.00
251 Jack Lohrke	35.00	60.00
252 Frank Crosetti CO	60.00	150.00

1953 Bowman Black and White

The cards in this 64-card set measure approximately 2 1/2" by 3 3/4". Some collectors believe that the high cost of producing the 1953 color series forced Bowman to issue this set in black and white, since the two sets are identical in design except for the element of color. This set was also produced in fewer numbers than its color counterpart, and is popular among collectors for the challenge involved in completing it and the lack of short prints. Cards were issued in one-card penny packs which came 120 to a box and five-card nickel packs. There are no key Rookie Cards in this set. Card #43, Hal Bevan, exists with him being born in either 1930 or 1950. The 1950 version seems to be is much more difficult to find.

COMPLETE SET (64)	2,000.00	3,000.00
WRAPPER (1-CENT)	300.00	350.00
CARDS PRICED IN NM CONDITION !		
1 Gus Bell	75.00	125.00
2 Willard Nixon	25.00	40.00
3 Bill Rigney	25.00	40.00
4 Pat Mullin	25.00	40.00
5 Dee Fondy	25.00	40.00
6 Ray Murray	25.00	40.00
7 Andy Seminick	25.00	40.00
8 Pete Suder	25.00	40.00
9 Walt Masterson	25.00	40.00
10 Dick Sisler	35.00	60.00
11 Dick Gernert	25.00	40.00
12 Randy Jackson	25.00	40.00
13 Joe Tipton	25.00	40.00
14 Bill Nicholson	35.00	60.00
15 Johnny Mize	75.00	125.00
16 Stu Miller RC	35.00	60.00
17 Virgil Trucks	35.00	60.00
18 Billy Hoeft	25.00	40.00
19 Paul LaPalme	25.00	40.00
20 Eddie Robinson	25.00	40.00
21 Clarence Podbielan	25.00	40.00
22 Matt Batts	25.00	40.00
23 Wilmer Mizell	35.00	60.00
24 Del Wilber	25.00	40.00
25 Johnny Sain	50.00	80.00
26 Preacher Roe	50.00	80.00
27 Bob Lemon	100.00	175.00
28 Hoyt Wilhelm	75.00	125.00
29 Sid Hudson	25.00	40.00
30 Walker Cooper	25.00	40.00
31 Gene Woodling	50.00	80.00
32 Rocky Bridges	25.00	40.00
33 Bob Kuzava	25.00	40.00
34 Ebba St.Claire	25.00	40.00
35 Johnny Wyrostek	25.00	40.00
36 Jimmy Piersall	50.00	80.00
37 Hal Jeffcoat	25.00	40.00
38 Dave Cole	25.00	40.00
39 Casey Stengel MG	200.00	350.00
40 Larry Jansen	35.00	60.00
41 Bob Ramazzotti	25.00	40.00
42 Howie Judson	25.00	40.00
43 Hal Bevan ERR RC	25.00	40.00
43A Hal Bevan COR	25.00	40.00
44 Jim Delsing	25.00	40.00
45 Irv Noren	35.00	60.00
46 Bucky Harris MG	50.00	80.00
47 Jack Lohrke	25.00	40.00
48 Steve Ridzik RC	25.00	40.00
49 Floyd Baker	25.00	40.00
50 Dutch Leonard	25.00	40.00
51 Lou Burdette	50.00	80.00
52 Ralph Branca	50.00	80.00
53 Morrie Martin	25.00	40.00
54 Bill Miller	25.00	40.00
55 Don Johnson	25.00	40.00
56 Roy Smalley	25.00	40.00
57 Andy Pafko	35.00	60.00
58 Jim Konstanty	35.00	60.00
59 Duane Pillette	25.00	40.00
60 Billy Cox	50.00	80.00
61 Tom Gorman RC	25.00	40.00
62 Keith Thomas RC	25.00	40.00
63 Steve Gromek	25.00	40.00
64 Andy Hansen	50.00	80.00

1953 Bowman Color

The cards in this 160-card set measure approximately 2 1/2" by 3 3/4". The 1953 Bowman Color set features Kodachrome photographs with no names or facsimile autographs on the face. Cards were issued in five-card nickel packs in a 24 pack box with each pack having gum in it. The entire low number run were also printed in three card strips; it is believed that these three card strips in numerical order were box toppers to retailers. The box features an endorsement from Joe DiMaggio. Numbers 113 to 160 are somewhat more difficult to obtain, with numbers 113 to 128 being the most difficult. There are two cards of Al Corwin (126 and 149). There are no key Rookie Cards in this set.

COMPLETE SET (160)	9,000.00	15,000.00
WRAPPER (1-CENT)	300.00	400.00
WRAPPER (5-CENT)	250.00	300.00
CARDS PRICED IN NM CONDITION !		
1 Davey Williams	100.00	175.00
2 Vic Wertz	30.00	50.00
3 Sam Jethroe	30.00	50.00
4 Art Houtteman	20.00	40.00
5 Sid Gordon	20.00	40.00
6 Joe Ginsberg	20.00	40.00
7 Harry Chiti RC	20.00	40.00
8 Al Rosen	30.00	50.00
9 Phil Rizzuto	60.00	150.00
10 Richie Ashburn	40.00	100.00
11 Bobby Shantz	30.00	50.00
12 Carl Erskine	20.00	50.00
13 Gus Zernial	30.00	50.00
14 Billy Loes	12.00	30.00
15 Jim Busby	20.00	40.00
16 Bob Friend	30.00	50.00
17 Gerry Staley	20.00	40.00
18 Nellie Fox	40.00	100.00
19 Alvin Dark	30.00	50.00
20 Don Lenhardt	20.00	40.00
21 Joe Garagiola	15.00	40.00
22 Bob Porterfield	20.00	40.00
23 Herman Wehmeier	20.00	40.00
24 Jackie Jensen	15.00	40.00
25 Hoot Evers	20.00	40.00
26 Roy McMillan	30.00	50.00
27 Vic Raschi	35.00	60.00
28 Smoky Burgess	30.00	50.00
29 Bobby Avila	30.00	50.00
30 Phil Cavarretta	30.00	50.00
31 Jimmy Dykes MG	30.00	50.00
32 Stan Musial	200.00	500.00
33 Pee Wee Reese	300.00	600.00
34 Gil Coan	20.00	40.00
35 Maurice McDermott	20.00	40.00
36 Minnie Minoso	50.00	80.00
37 Jim Wilson	20.00	40.00
38 Harry Byrd RC	20.00	40.00
39 Paul Richards MG	30.00	50.00
40 Larry Doby	60.00	100.00
41 Sammy White	20.00	40.00
42 Tommy Brown	20.00	40.00
43 Mike Garcia	30.00	50.00
44 Bauer/Berra/Mantle	300.00	600.00
45 Walt Dropo	30.00	50.00
46 Roy Campanella	75.00	200.00
47 Ned Garver	20.00	40.00
48 Hank Sauer	30.00	50.00
49 Eddie Stanky MG	30.00	50.00
50 Lou Kretlow	20.00	40.00
51 Monte Irvin	50.00	80.00
52 Marty Marion MG	30.00	50.00
53 Del Rice	20.00	40.00
54 Chico Carrasquel	20.00	40.00
55 Leo Durocher MG	50.00	80.00
56 Bob Cain	20.00	40.00
57 Lou Boudreau MG	25.00	60.00
58 Willard Marshall	20.00	40.00
59 Mickey Mantle	1,500.00	2,500.00
60 Granny Hamner	20.00	40.00
61 George Kell	25.00	60.00
62 Ted Kluszewski	60.00	100.00
63 Gil McDougald	50.00	80.00
64 Curt Simmons	30.00	80.00
65 Robin Roberts	60.00	150.00
66 Mel Parnell	20.00	50.00
67 Mel Clark RC	20.00	40.00

68 Allie Reynolds	40.00	100.00
69 Charlie Grimm MG	30.00	50.00
70 Clint Courtney RC	20.00	40.00
71 Paul Minner	20.00	40.00
72 Ted Gray	20.00	40.00
73 Billy Pierce	30.00	50.00
74 Don Mueller	30.00	50.00
75 Saul Rogovin	20.00	40.00
76 Jim Hearn	20.00	40.00
77 Mickey Grasso	20.00	40.00
78 Carl Furillo	30.00	80.00
79 Ray Boone	30.00	50.00
80 Ralph Kiner	60.00	100.00
81 Enos Slaughter	40.00	100.00
82 Joe Astroth	20.00	40.00
83 Jack Daniels RC	20.00	40.00
84 Hank Bauer	35.00	60.00
85 Solly Hemus	20.00	40.00
86 Harry Simpson	20.00	40.00
87 Harry Perkowski	20.00	40.00
88 Joe Dobson	20.00	40.00
89 Sandy Consuegra	20.00	40.00
90 Joe Nuxhall	30.00	50.00
91 Steve Souchock	20.00	40.00
92 Gil Hodges	75.00	200.00
93 P.Rizzuto/B.Martin	100.00	250.00
94 Bob Addis	20.00	40.00
95 Wally Moses CO	30.00	50.00
96 Sal Maglie	30.00	50.00
97 Eddie Mathews	100.00	250.00
98 Hector Rodriguez RC	20.00	40.00
99 Warren Spahn	100.00	250.00
100 Bill Wight	20.00	40.00
101 Red Schoendienst	50.00	80.00
102 Jim Hegan	30.00	50.00
103 Del Ennis	25.00	60.00
104 Luke Easter	40.00	100.00
105 Eddie Joost	20.00	40.00
106 Ken Raffensberger	20.00	40.00
107 Alex Kellner	20.00	40.00
108 Bobby Adams	20.00	40.00
109 Ken Wood	20.00	40.00
110 Bob Rush	20.00	40.00
111 Jim Dyck RC	20.00	40.00
112 Toby Atwell	20.00	40.00
113 Karl Drews	40.00	100.00
114 Bob Feller	150.00	400.00
115 Cloyd Boyer	50.00	80.00
116 Eddie Yost	60.00	100.00
117 Duke Snider	250.00	500.00
118 Billy Martin	125.00	300.00
119 Dale Mitchell	60.00	100.00
120 Marlin Stuart	40.00	100.00
121 Yogi Berra	300.00	600.00
122 Bill Serena	50.00	80.00
123 Johnny Lipon	50.00	80.00
124 Charlie Dressen MG	60.00	100.00
125 Fred Hatfield	50.00	80.00
126 Al Corwin	50.00	80.00
127 Dick Kryhoski	50.00	80.00
128 Whitey Lockman	60.00	150.00
129 Russ Meyer	40.00	100.00
130 Cass Michaels	40.00	100.00
131 Connie Ryan	45.00	75.00
132 Fred Hutchinson	40.00	100.00
133 Willie Jones	45.00	75.00
134 Johnny Pesky	40.00	100.00
135 Bobby Morgan	40.00	100.00
136 Jim Brideweser RC	45.00	75.00
137 Sam Dente	20.00	50.00
138 Bubba Church	45.00	75.00
139 Pete Runnels	60.00	90.00
140 Al Brazle	25.00	60.00
141 Frank Shea	45.00	75.00
142 Larry Miggins RC	45.00	75.00
143 Al Lopez MG	50.00	120.00
144 Warren Hacker	45.00	75.00
145 George Shuba	40.00	100.00
146 Early Wynn	50.00	120.00
147 Clem Koshorek	45.00	75.00
148 Billy Goodman	60.00	90.00
149 Al Corwin	20.00	50.00
150 Carl Scheib	45.00	75.00
151 Joe Adcock	40.00	100.00
152 Clyde Vollmer	45.00	75.00
153 Whitey Ford	250.00	500.00
154 Turk Lown	30.00	80.00
155 Allie Clark	30.00	80.00
156 Max Surkont	45.00	75.00
157 Sherm Lollar	60.00	90.00
158 Howard Fox	25.00	80.00
159 Mickey Vernon UER	40.00	100.00
160 Cal Abrams	100.00	250.00

1954 Bowman

The cards in this 224-card set measure approximately 2 1/2" by 3 3/4". The set was distributed in two separate series: 1-128 in first series and 129-224 in second series. A contractual problem apparently resulted in the deletion of the number 66 Ted Williams card from this Bowman set, thereby creating a scarcity that is highly valued among collectors. The set price below does NOT include number 66 Williams but does include number 66 Jim Piersall, the apparent replacement for Williams in spite of the fact that Piersall was already number 210 to appear later in the set. Many errors in players' statistics exist (and some were corrected) while a few players' names were printed on the front, instead of appearing as a facsimile autograph. Most of these differences are so minor that there is no price differential for either card. The cards which changes were made on are numbers 12, 22,25,26,35,38,41,43,47,53,61,67,80,81,82,85,93,94,99,103,105,124,138,139, 140,145,153,156,174,179,185,212,216 and 217. The set was issued in seven-card nickel packs and one-card penny packs. The penny packs were issued 120 to a box while the nickel packs were issued 24 to a box. The notable Rookie Cards in this set are Harvey Kuenn and Don Larsen.

COMPLETE SET (224)	2,500.00	4,000.00
WRAP.(1-CENT, DATED)	100.00	150.00
WRAP.(1-CENT, UNDAT)	150.00	200.00
WRAP.(5-CENT, DATED)	100.00	150.00
WRAP.(5-CENT, UNDAT)	50.00	60.00
1 Phil Rizzuto	50.00	120.00
2 Jackie Jensen	15.00	30.00
3 Marion Fricano	6.00	12.00
4 Bob Hooper	6.00	12.00
5 Billy Hunter	6.00	12.00
6 Nellie Fox	50.00	80.00
7 Walt Dropo	10.00	20.00
8 Jim Busby	6.00	12.00
9 Dave Williams	6.00	12.00
10 Carl Erskine	12.00	30.00
11 Sid Gordon	6.00	12.00
12A Roy McMillan 551/1290 At Bat	10.00	20.00
12B Roy McMillan 557/1296 At Bat	10.00	20.00
13 Paul Minner	6.00	12.00
14 Gerry Staley	6.00	12.00
15 Richie Ashburn	25.00	60.00
16 Jim Wilson	6.00	12.00
17 Tom Gorman	6.00	12.00
18 Hoot Evers	6.00	12.00
19 Bobby Shantz	10.00	20.00
20 Art Houtteman	6.00	12.00
21 Vic Wertz	10.00	20.00
22A Sam Mele 213/1661 Putouts	6.00	12.00
22B Sam Mele 217/1665 Putouts	6.00	12.00
23 Harvey Kuenn RC	15.00	30.00
24 Bob Porterfield	6.00	12.00
25A Wes Westrum 1.000/.987 Fielding Avg.	10.00	20.00
25B Wes Westrum .982/.986 Fielding Avg.	10.00	20.00
26A Billy Cox 1.000/.960 Fielding Avg.	10.00	20.00
26B Billy Cox .972/.960 Fielding Avg.	10.00	20.00
27 Dick Cole RC	6.00	12.00
28A Jim Greengrass Birthplace Addison, NJ	6.00	12.00
28B Jim Greengrass Birthplace Addison, NY	6.00	12.00
29 Johnny Klippstein	6.00	12.00
30 Del Rice	6.00	12.00
31 Smoky Burgess	10.00	20.00
32 Del Crandall	10.00	20.00
33A Vic Raschi No Trade	10.00	20.00
33B Vic Raschi Traded to St.Louis	15.00	30.00
34 Sammy White	6.00	12.00
35A Eddie Joost Quiz Answer is 8	6.00	12.00
35B Eddie Joost Quiz Answer is 33	6.00	12.00
36 George Strickland	6.00	12.00
37 Dick Kokos	6.00	12.00
38A Minnie Minoso .895/.961 Fielding Avg.	15.00	30.00
38B Minnie Minoso .963/.963 Fielding Avg.	15.00	30.00
39 Ned Garver	6.00	12.00
40 Gil Coan	6.00	12.00
41A Alvin Dark .986/960 Fielding Avg.	10.00	20.00
41B Alvin Dark .968/.960 Fielding Avg.	10.00	20.00
42 Billy Loes	10.00	20.00
43A Bob Friend 20 Shutouts in Quiz	10.00	20.00
43B Bob Friend 16 Shutouts in Quiz	10.00	20.00
44 Harry Perkowski	6.00	12.00
45 Ralph Kiner	15.00	40.00
46 Rip Repulski	6.00	12.00
47A Granny Hamner .970/.953 Fielding Avg.	6.00	12.00
47B Granny Hamner .953/.951 Fielding Avg.	6.00	12.00
48 Jack Dittmer	6.00	12.00
49 Harry Byrd	6.00	12.00
50 George Kell	15.00	40.00
51 Alex Kellner	6.00	12.00
52 Joe Ginsberg	6.00	12.00
53A Don Lenhardt .969/.984 Fielding Avg.	6.00	12.00
53B Don Lenhardt .966/.983 Fielding Avg.	6.00	12.00
54 Chico Carrasquel	6.00	12.00
55 Jim Delsing	6.00	12.00
56 Maurice McDermott	6.00	12.00
57 Hoyt Wilhelm	15.00	40.00
58 Pee Wee Reese	40.00	100.00
59 Bob Schultz	6.00	12.00
60 Fred Baczewski RC	6.00	12.00
61A Eddie Miksis .954/.962 Fielding Avg.	6.00	12.00
61B Eddie Miksis .954/.961 Fielding Avg.	6.00	12.00
62 Enos Slaughter	20.00	50.00
63 Earl Torgeson	6.00	12.00
64 Eddie Mathews	40.00	100.00
65 Mickey Mantle	1,000.00	2,500.00
66A Ted Williams	1,800.00	3,000.00
66B Jimmy Piersall	50.00	80.00
67A Carl Scheib .306 Pct. Two Lines under Bio	6.00	12.00
67B Carl Scheib .306 Pct. One Line under Bio	6.00	12.00
67C Carl Scheib .300 Pct.	6.00	12.00
68 Bobby Avila	10.00	20.00
69 Clint Courtney	6.00	12.00
70 Willard Marshall	6.00	12.00
71 Ted Gray	6.00	12.00
72 Eddie Yost	10.00	20.00
73 Don Mueller	10.00	20.00
74 Jim Gilliam	15.00	30.00
75 Max Surkont	6.00	12.00
76 Joe Nuxhall	10.00	20.00
77 Bob Rush	6.00	12.00
78 Sal Yvars	6.00	12.00
79 Curt Simmons	10.00	20.00
80A Johnny Logan 106 Runs	6.00	12.00
80B Johnny Logan 100 Runs	6.00	12.00
81A Jerry Coleman 1.000/.975 Fielding Avg.	10.00	20.00
81B Jerry Coleman .952/.975 Fielding Avg.	10.00	20.00
82A Bill Goodman .965/.986 Fielding Avg.	10.00	20.00
82B Bill Goodman .972/.985 Fielding Avg.	10.00	20.00
83 Ray Murray	6.00	12.00
84 Larry Doby	25.00	50.00
85A Jim Dyck .926/.956 Fielding Avg.	6.00	12.00
85B Jim Dyck .947/.960 Fielding Avg.	6.00	12.00
86 Harry Dorish	6.00	12.00
87 Don Lund	6.00	12.00
88 Tom Umphlett RC	6.00	12.00
89 Willie Mays	250.00	600.00
90 Roy Campanella	50.00	120.00
91 Cal Abrams	6.00	12.00
92 Ken Raffensberger	6.00	12.00
93A Bill Serena .983/.966 Fielding Avg.	6.00	12.00
93B Bill Serena .977/.966 Fielding Avg.	6.00	12.00
94A Solly Hemus 476/1343 Assists	6.00	12.00
94B Solly Hemus 477/1343 Assists	6.00	12.00
95 Robin Roberts	25.00	50.00
96 Joe Adcock	10.00	20.00
97 Gil McDougald	10.00	20.00
98 Ellis Kinder	6.00	12.00
99A Peter Suder .985/.974 Fielding Avg.	6.00	12.00
99B Peter Suder .978/.974 Fielding Avg.	6.00	12.00
100 Mike Garcia	10.00	20.00
101 Don Larsen RC	25.00	60.00
102 Billy Pierce	10.00	20.00
103A Stephen Souchock 144/1192 Putouts	6.00	12.00
103B Stephen Souchock 147/1195 Putouts	6.00	12.00
104 Frank Shea	6.00	12.00
105A Sal Maglie Quiz Answer is 8	10.00	20.00
105B Sal Maglie Quiz Answer is 1904	10.00	20.00
106 Clem Labine	10.00	20.00
107 Paul LaPalme	6.00	12.00
108 Bobby Adams	6.00	12.00
109 Roy Smalley	6.00	12.00
110 Red Schoendienst	25.00	50.00
111 Murry Dickson	6.00	12.00
112 Andy Pafko	10.00	20.00
113 Allie Reynolds	10.00	20.00
114 Willard Nixon	6.00	12.00
115 Don Bollweg	6.00	12.00
116 Luke Easter	10.00	20.00
117 Dick Kryhoski	6.00	12.00
118 Bob Boyd	6.00	12.00
119 Fred Hatfield	6.00	12.00
120 Mel Hoderlein RC	6.00	12.00
121 Ray Katt RC	6.00	12.00
122 Carl Furillo	15.00	30.00
123 Toby Atwell	6.00	12.00
124A Gus Bell 15/27 Errors	10.00	20.00
124B Gus Bell 11/26 Errors	10.00	20.00
125 Warren Hacker	6.00	12.00
126 Cliff Chambers	6.00	12.00
127 Del Ennis	10.00	20.00
128 Ebba St.Claire	6.00	12.00
129 Hank Bauer	15.00	30.00
130 Milt Bolling	6.00	12.00
131 Joe Astroth	6.00	12.00
132 Bob Feller	40.00	100.00
133 Duane Pillette	6.00	12.00
134 Luis Aloma	6.00	12.00
135 Johnny Pesky	10.00	20.00
136 Clyde Vollmer	6.00	12.00
137 Al Corwin	6.00	12.00
138A Hodges .993/.991 Field.Avg.	50.00	80.00
138B Hodges .992/.991 Field.Avg.	50.00	80.00
139A Preston Ward .961/.992 Fielding Avg.	6.00	12.00
139B Preston Ward .990/.992 Fielding Avg.	6.00	12.00
140A Saul Rogovin 7-12 W-L 2 Strikeouts	6.00	12.00
140B Saul Rogovin 7-12 W-L 62 Strikeouts	6.00	12.00
140C Saul Rogovin 8-12 W-L	6.00	12.00
141 Joe Garagiola	15.00	30.00
142 Al Brazle	6.00	12.00
143 Willie Jones	6.00	12.00
144 Ernie Johnson RC	15.00	30.00
145A Martin .985/.983 Field.Avg.	50.00	80.00
145B Martin .983/.982 Field.Avg.	50.00	80.00
146 Dick Gernert	6.00	12.00
147 Joe DeMaestri	6.00	12.00
148 Dale Mitchell	10.00	20.00
149 Bob Young	6.00	12.00
150 Cass Michaels	6.00	12.00
151 Pat Mullin	6.00	12.00
152 Mickey Vernon	10.00	20.00
153A Whitey Lockman 100/331 Assists	10.00	20.00
153B Whitey Lockman 102/333 Assists	10.00	20.00
154 Don Newcombe	15.00	30.00
155 Frank Thomas RC	10.00	20.00
156A Rocky Bridges 320/467 Assists	6.00	12.00
156B Rocky Bridges 328/475 Assists	6.00	12.00
157 Turk Lown	6.00	12.00
158 Stu Miller	10.00	20.00
159 Johnny Lindell	6.00	12.00
160 Danny O'Connell	6.00	12.00
161 Yogi Berra	60.00	150.00
162 Ted Lepcio	6.00	12.00
163A Dave Philley No Trade 152 Games	10.00	20.00
163B Dave Philley Traded to Cleveland 152 Games	15.00	30.00
163C Dave Philley Traded to Cleveland 157 Games	15.00	30.00
164 Early Wynn	15.00	40.00
165 Johnny Groth	6.00	12.00
166 Sandy Consuegra	6.00	12.00
167 Billy Hoeft	6.00	12.00
168 Ed Fitzgerald	6.00	12.00
169 Larry Jansen	10.00	20.00
170 Duke Snider	50.00	120.00
171 Carlos Bernier	6.00	12.00
172 Andy Seminick	6.00	12.00
173 Dee Fondy	6.00	12.00
174A Pete Castiglione .966/.959 Fielding Avg.	6.00	12.00
174B Pete Castiglione .970/.959 Fielding Avg.	6.00	12.00
175 Mel Clark	6.00	12.00
176 Vern Bickford	6.00	12.00
177 Whitey Ford	60.00	100.00
178 Del Wilber	6.00	12.00
179A Morris Martin 44 ERA	6.00	12.00
179B Morris Martin 4.44 ERA	6.00	12.00
180 Joe Tipton	6.00	12.00
181 Les Moss	6.00	12.00
182 Sherm Lollar	10.00	20.00
183 Matt Batts	6.00	12.00
184 Mickey Grasso	6.00	12.00
185A Daryl Spencer .941/.944 Fielding Avg. RC	6.00	12.00
185B Daryl Spencer .933/.936 Fielding Avg.	6.00	12.00
186 Russ Meyer	6.00	12.00
187 Vern Law	10.00	20.00
188 Frank Smith	6.00	12.00
189 Randy Jackson	6.00	12.00
190 Joe Presko	6.00	12.00
191 Karl Drews	6.00	12.00
192 Lew Burdette	10.00	20.00
193 Eddie Robinson	6.00	12.00
194 Sid Hudson	6.00	12.00
195 Bob Cain	6.00	12.00
196 Bob Lemon	25.00	50.00
197 Lou Kretlow	6.00	12.00
198 Virgil Trucks	6.00	12.00
199 Steve Gromek	6.00	12.00
200 Conrado Marrero	6.00	12.00
201 Bobby Thomson	15.00	30.00
202 George Shuba	10.00	20.00
203 Vic Janowicz	10.00	20.00
204 Jack Collum RC	6.00	12.00
205 Hal Jeffcoat	6.00	12.00
206 Steve Bilko	6.00	12.00
207 Stan Lopata	6.00	12.00
208 Johnny Antonelli	10.00	20.00
209 Gene Woodling UER Reversed Photo	6.00	12.00
210 Jimmy Piersall	15.00	30.00
211 Al Robertson RC	6.00	12.00
212A Owen Friend .964/.957 Fielding Avg.	6.00	12.00
212B Owen Friend .967/.958 Fielding Avg.	6.00	12.00
213 Dick Littlefield	6.00	12.00
214 Ferris Fain	10.00	20.00
215 Johnny Bucha	6.00	12.00
216A Jerry Snyder .988/.988 Fielding Avg.	6.00	12.00
216B Jerry Snyder .968/.968 Fielding Avg.	6.00	12.00
217A Henry Thompson .956/.951 Fielding Avg.	10.00	20.00
217B Henry Thompson .958/.952 Fielding Avg.	10.00	20.00
218 Preacher Roe	10.00	20.00
219 Hal Rice	6.00	12.00
220 Hobie Landrith RC	6.00	12.00
221 Frank Baumholtz	6.00	12.00
222 Memo Luna RC	6.00	12.00
223 Steve Ridzik	6.00	12.00
224 Bill Bruton	25.00	50.00

1955 Bowman

The cards in this 320-card set measure approximately 2 1/2" by 3 3/4". The Bowman set of 1955 is known as the "TV set" because each player photograph is cleverly shown within a television set design. The set contains umpire cards, some transposed pictures (e.g., Johnsons and Bollings), an incorrect spelling for Harvey Kuenn, and a traded line for Palica (all of which are noted in the checklist below). Some three-card advertising strips exist, the backs of these panels contain advertising for Bowman products. Print advertisements for these cards featured Willie Mays along with publicizing the great value in nine cards for a nickel. Advertising panels seen include Nellie Fox/Carl Furillo/Carl Erskine; Hank Aaron/Johnny Logan/Eddie Miksis; Bob Rush/Ray Katt/Willie Mays; Steve Gromek/Milt Bolling/Vern Stephens, Russ Kemmemer/ Hal Jeffcoat/Dee Fondy and a Bob Darnell/Early Wynn/Pee Wee Reese. Cards were issued either in nine-card nickel packs or one card penny packs. Cello packs containing approximately 20 cards have also been seen, albeit on a very limited basis. The notable Rookie Cards in this set are Elston Howard and Don Zimmer. Hall of Fame umpires pictured in the set are Al Barlick, Jocko Conlon and Cal Hubbard. Undated five cent wrappers are also known to exist for this set.

COMPLETE SET (320)	3,500.00	6,000.00
COMMON CARD (1-96)	6.00	12.00
COM. CARD (97-224)	5.00	10.00
COM. CARD (225-320)	7.50	15.00
COM. UMPIRE (225-320)	18.00	30.00
WRAPPER (1-CENT)	50.00	60.00
WRAPPER (5-CENT)	50.00	60.00
1 Hoyt Wilhelm	60.00	100.00
2 Alvin Dark	7.50	15.00
3 Joe Coleman	7.50	15.00
4 Eddie Waitkus	7.50	15.00
5 Jim Robertson	6.00	12.00
6 Pete Suder	6.00	12.00
7 Gene Baker RC	6.00	12.00
8 Warren Hacker	6.00	12.00
9 Gil McDougald	10.00	20.00
10 Phil Rizzuto	30.00	80.00
11 Bill Bruton	7.50	15.00
12 Andy Pafko	7.50	15.00
13 Clyde Vollmer	6.00	12.00
14 Gus Keriazakos RC	6.00	12.00
15 Frank Sullivan RC	6.00	12.00
16 Jimmy Piersall	12.00	30.00
17 Del Ennis	7.50	15.00
18 Stan Lopata	6.00	12.00
19 Bobby Avila	7.50	15.00
20 Al Smith	7.50	15.00
21 Don Hoak	6.00	12.00
22 Roy Campanella	40.00	100.00
23 Al Kaline	40.00	100.00
24 Al Aber	6.00	12.00
25 Minnie Minoso	15.00	30.00
26 Virgil Trucks	7.50	15.00
27 Preston Ward	6.00	12.00
28 Dick Cole	6.00	12.00
29 Red Schoendienst	15.00	30.00
30 Bill Sarni	6.00	12.00
31 Johnny Temple RC	7.50	15.00
32 Wally Post	7.50	15.00
33 Nellie Fox	30.00	50.00
34 Clint Courtney	6.00	12.00
35 Bill Tuttle RC	6.00	12.00
36 Wayne Belardi RC	6.00	12.00
37 Pee Wee Reese	30.00	80.00
38 Early Wynn	15.00	30.00
39 Bob Darnell RC	7.50	15.00
40 Vic Wertz	7.50	15.00
41 Mel Clark	6.00	12.00
42 Bob Greenwood RC	6.00	12.00
43 Bob Buhl	7.50	15.00
44 Danny O'Connell	6.00	12.00
45 Tom Umphlett	6.00	12.00
46 Mickey Vernon	7.50	15.00
47 Sammy White	6.00	12.00
48A Milt Bolling ERR	10.00	20.00
48B Milt Bolling COR	10.00	20.00
49 Jim Greengrass	6.00	12.00
50 Hobie Landrith	6.00	12.00
51 Elvin Tappe RC	6.00	12.00
52 Hal Rice	6.00	12.00
53 Alex Kellner	6.00	12.00
54 Don Bollweg	6.00	12.00
55 Cal Abrams	6.00	12.00
56 Billy Cox	7.50	15.00
57 Bob Friend	7.50	15.00
58 Frank Thomas	7.50	15.00
59 Whitey Ford	40.00	100.00
60 Enos Slaughter	12.00	30.00
61 Paul LaPalme	6.00	12.00
62 Royce Lint RC	6.00	12.00
63 Irv Noren	7.50	15.00
64 Curt Simmons	7.50	15.00
65 Don Zimmer RC	20.00	50.00
66 George Shuba	10.00	20.00
67 Don Larsen	25.00	60.00
68 Elston Howard RC	50.00	80.00
69 Billy Hunter	6.00	12.00
70 Lew Burdette	10.00	20.00
71 Dave Jolly	6.00	12.00
72 Chet Nichols	6.00	12.00
73 Eddie Yost	7.50	15.00
74 Jerry Snyder	6.00	12.00
75 Brooks Lawrence RC	6.00	12.00
76 Tom Poholsky	6.00	12.00
77 Jim McDonald RC	6.00	12.00
78 Gil Coan	8.00	20.00
79 Willie Miranda	6.00	12.00
80 Lou Limmer	6.00	12.00
81 Bobby Morgan	6.00	12.00
82 Lee Walls RC	6.00	12.00
83 Max Surkont	6.00	12.00
84 George Freese RC	6.00	12.00
85 Cass Michaels	6.00	12.00
86 Ted Gray	6.00	12.00
87 Randy Jackson	6.00	12.00
88 Steve Bilko	6.00	12.00
89 Lou Boudreau MG	15.00	30.00
90 Art RC	6.00	12.00
91 Dick Marlowe RC	6.00	12.00
92 George Zuverink	6.00	12.00
93 Andy Seminick	6.00	12.00
94 Hank Thompson	7.50	15.00
95 Sal Maglie	7.50	15.00
96 Ray Narleski RC	6.00	12.00
97 Johnny Podres	15.00	30.00
98 Jim Gilliam	10.00	20.00
99 Jerry Coleman	7.50	15.00
100 Tom Morgan	5.00	10.00
101A Don Johnson ERR	10.00	20.00
101B Don Johnson COR	10.00	20.00
102 Bobby Thomson	7.50	15.00
103 Eddie Mathews	40.00	100.00
104 Bob Porterfield	5.00	10.00
105 Johnny Schmitz	5.00	10.00
106 Del Rice	5.00	10.00
107 Solly Hemus	5.00	10.00
108 Lou Kretlow	5.00	10.00
109 Vern Stephens	7.50	15.00
110 Bob Miller	5.00	10.00
111 Steve Ridzik	5.00	10.00
112 Granny Hamner	5.00	10.00
113 Bob Hall RC	5.00	10.00
114 Vic Janowicz	7.50	15.00
115 Roger Bowman RC	5.00	10.00
116 Sandy Consuegra	5.00	10.00
117 Johnny Groth	5.00	10.00
118 Bobby Adams	5.00	10.00
119 Joe Astroth	5.00	10.00
120 Ed Burtschy RC	5.00	10.00
121 Rufus Crawford RC	5.00	10.00
122 Al Corwin	5.00	10.00
123 Marv Grissom RC	5.00	10.00
124 Johnny Antonelli	12.00	30.00
125 Paul Giel RC	7.50	15.00
126 Billy Goodman	7.50	15.00
127 Hank Majeski	5.00	10.00
128 Mike Garcia	7.50	15.00
129 Hal Naragon RC	5.00	10.00
130 Richie Ashburn	25.00	60.00
131 Willard Marshall	6.00	15.00
132A Harvey Kueen ERR	30.00	50.00
132B Harvey Kuenn COR	15.00	30.00
133 Charles King RC	5.00	10.00
134 Bob Feller	40.00	100.00
135 Lloyd Merriman	5.00	10.00
136 Rocky Bridges	5.00	10.00
137 Bob Talbot	5.00	10.00
138 Davey Williams	7.50	15.00
139 W.Shantz/B.Shantz	7.50	15.00
140 Bobby Shantz	7.50	15.00
141 Wes Westrum	7.50	15.00
142 Rudy Regalado RC	5.00	10.00
143 Don Newcombe	20.00	50.00
144 Art Houtteman	5.00	10.00
145 Bob Nieman RC	5.00	10.00
146 Don Liddle	5.00	10.00
147 Sam Mele	5.00	10.00
148 Bob Chakales	5.00	10.00
149 Cloyd Boyer	5.00	10.00
150 Billy Klaus RC	5.00	10.00
151 Jim Brideweser	5.00	10.00
152 Johnny Klippstein	5.00	10.00
153 Eddie Robinson	5.00	10.00
154 Frank Lary RC	7.50	15.00
155 Gerry Staley	5.00	10.00
156 Jim Hughes	7.50	15.00
157A Ernie Johnson ERR	10.00	20.00
157B Ernie Johnson COR	10.00	20.00
158 Gil Hodges	30.00	50.00
159 Harry Byrd	5.00	10.00
160 Bill Skowron	10.00	20.00
161 Matt Batts	5.00	10.00
162 Charlie Maxwell	5.00	10.00
163 Sid Gordon	7.50	15.00
164 Toby Atwell	5.00	10.00
165 Maurice McDermott	5.00	10.00
166 Jim Busby	10.00	25.00
167 Bob Grim RC	10.00	20.00
168 Yogi Berra	60.00	150.00
169 Carl Furillo	15.00	40.00
170 Carl Erskine	15.00	40.00
171 Robin Roberts	30.00	50.00
172 Willie Jones	5.00	10.00
173 Chico Carrasquel	5.00	10.00
174 Sherm Lollar	7.50	15.00
175 Wilmer Shantz RC	5.00	10.00
176 Joe DeMaestri	5.00	10.00
177 Willard Nixon	5.00	10.00
178 Tom Brewer RC	5.00	10.00
179 Hank Aaron	150.00	400.00
180 Johnny Logan	7.50	15.00
181 Eddie Miksis	5.00	10.00
182 Bob Rush	5.00	10.00
183 Ray Katt	5.00	10.00
184 Willie Mays	200.00	500.00
185 Vic Raschi	5.00	10.00
186 Alex Grammas	5.00	10.00
187 Fred Hatfield	5.00	10.00
188 Ned Garver	5.00	10.00
189 Jack Collum	5.00	10.00
190 Fred Baczewski	5.00	10.00
191 Bob Lemon	15.00	30.00
192 George Strickland	5.00	10.00
193 Howie Judson	5.00	10.00
194 Joe Nuxhall	7.50	15.00
195A Erv Palica	7.50	15.00
195B Erv Palica TR	20.00	40.00
196 Russ Meyer	7.50	15.00
197 Ralph Kiner	20.00	50.00
198 Dave Pope RC	5.00	10.00
199 Vern Law	7.50	15.00
200 Dick Littlefield	8.00	20.00
201 Allie Reynolds	15.00	40.00
202 Mickey Mantle UER	600.00	1,500.00
203 Steve Gromek	5.00	10.00
204A Frank Bolling ERR RC	10.00	20.00
204B Frank Bolling COR	10.00	20.00
205 Rip Repulski	5.00	10.00
206 Ralph Beard RC	5.00	10.00
207 Frank Shea	5.00	10.00
208 Ed Fitzgerald	5.00	10.00
209 Smoky Burgess	7.50	15.00
210 Earl Torgeson	5.00	10.00
211 Sonny Dixon RC	5.00	10.00
212 Jack Dittmer	5.00	10.00
213 George Kell	15.00	30.00
214 Billy Pierce	7.50	15.00
215 Bob Kuzava	5.00	10.00
216 Preacher Roe	10.00	20.00
217 Del Crandall	7.50	15.00
218 Joe Adcock	7.50	15.00
219 Whitey Lockman	7.50	15.00
220 Jim Hearn	5.00	10.00
221 Hector Brown	5.00	10.00
222 Russ Kemmerer RC	5.00	10.00
223 Hal Jeffcoat	5.00	10.00
224 Dee Fondy	5.00	10.00
225 Paul Richards MG	7.50	15.00
226 Bill McKinley UMP	18.00	30.00
227 Frank Baumholtz	7.50	15.00
228 John Phillips RC	7.50	15.00
229 Jim Brosnan RC	10.00	20.00
230 Al Brazle	7.50	15.00
231 Jim Konstanty	10.00	20.00
232 Birdie Tebbetts MG	10.00	20.00
233 Bill Serena	7.50	15.00
234 Dick Bartell CO	10.00	20.00
235 Joe Paparella UMP	18.00	30.00
236 Murry Dickson	7.50	15.00
237 Johnny Wyrostek	7.50	15.00
238 Eddie Stanky MG	10.00	20.00
239 Edwin Rommel UMP	20.00	40.00
240 Billy Loes	10.00	20.00
241 Johnny Pesky	10.00	20.00
242 Ernie Banks	150.00	400.00
243 Gus Bell	10.00	20.00
244 Duane Pillette	7.50	15.00
245 Bill Miller	7.50	15.00
246 Hank Bauer	15.00	30.00
247 Dutch Leonard CO	7.50	15.00
248 Harry Dorish	7.50	15.00
249 Billy Gardner RC	10.00	20.00
250 Larry Napp UMP	18.00	30.00
251 Stan Jok	7.50	15.00
252 Roy Smalley	7.50	15.00
253 Jim Wilson	7.50	15.00
254 Bennett Flowers RC	7.50	15.00
255 Pete Runnels	10.00	20.00
256 Owen Friend	7.50	15.00
257 Tom Alston RC	7.50	15.00
258 John Stevens UMP	18.00	30.00
259 Don Mossi RC	15.00	30.00
260 Edwin Hurley UMP	18.00	30.00
261 Walt Moryn RC	10.00	20.00
262 Jim Lemon FBC	7.50	15.00
263 Eddie Joost	7.50	15.00
264 Bill Henry RC	7.50	15.00
265 Al Barlick UMP	50.00	80.00
266 Mike Fornieles	7.50	15.00
267 J.Honochick UMP	15.00	40.00
268 Roy Lee Hawes RC	7.50	15.00
269 Joe Amalfitano RC	10.00	20.00
270 Chico Fernandez RC	10.00	20.00
271 Bob Hooper	7.50	15.00
272 John Flaherty UMP	18.00	30.00
273 Bubba Church	7.50	15.00
274 Jim Delsing	7.50	15.00
275 William Grieve UMP	18.00	30.00
276 Ike Delock	7.50	15.00
277 Ed Runge UMP	18.00	30.00
278 Charlie Neal RC	20.00	40.00
279 Hank Soar UMP	20.00	40.00
280 Clyde McCullough	7.50	15.00
281 Charles Berry UMP	20.00	40.00
282 Phil Cavarretta MG	10.00	20.00
283 Nestor Chylak UMP	50.00	80.00
284 Bill Jackowski UMP	18.00	30.00
285 Walt Dropo	10.00	20.00
286 Frank Secory UMP	18.00	30.00
287 Ron Mrozinski RC	7.50	15.00
288 Dick Smith RC	7.50	15.00
289 Arthur Gore UMP	18.00	30.00
290 Hershell Freeman RC	7.50	15.00
291 Frank Dascoli UMP	18.00	30.00
292 Marv Blaylock RC	7.50	15.00
293 Thomas Gorman UMP	20.00	40.00
294 Wally Moses CO	7.50	15.00
295 Lee Ballanfant UMP	18.00	30.00
296 Bill Virdon RC	15.00	30.00
297 Dusty Boggess UMP	18.00	30.00
298 Charlie Grimm	10.00	20.00
299 Lon Warneke UMP	20.00	40.00
300 Tommy Byrne	10.00	20.00
301 William Engeln UMP	18.00	30.00
302 Frank Malzone RC	15.00	30.00
303 Jocko Conlan UMP	50.00	80.00
304 Harry Chiti	7.50	15.00
305 Frank Umont UMP	18.00	30.00
306 Bob Cerv	10.00	20.00
307 Babe Pinelli UMP	20.00	40.00
308 Al Lopez MG	30.00	50.00
309 Hal Dixon UMP	18.00	30.00
310 Ken Lehman RC	7.50	15.00
311 Lawrence Goetz UMP	18.00	30.00
312 Bill Wight	7.50	15.00
313 Augie Donatelli UMP	30.00	50.00
314 Dale Mitchell	10.00	20.00
315 Cal Hubbard UMP	25.00	60.00
316 Marion Fricano	7.50	15.00
317 William Summers UMP	10.00	20.00
318 Sid Hudson	7.50	15.00
319 Al Schroll RC	7.50	15.00
320 George Susce RC	30.00	50.00

1954 Bowman Advertising Strips

These strips were issued in four card salesman's sample and feature the actual card along with a diamond advertising in the back middle which notates these cards as 1954 Bowman's Advertising Samples.

COMPLETE SET	500.00	1,000.00
1 Martin Fricano	300.00	600.00
Bob Hooper		
Sid Gordon		
Roy McMillan		
2 Harvey Kuenn	300.00	600.00
Bob Porterfield		
Smoky Burgess		
Del Crandall		

1955 Bowman Advertising Strips

For Bowman's final set; these advertising panels have been seen. The fronts are standard 1955 Bowman cards while the backs have advertising information. More sheets have been recently discovered so please keep us informed on any additions to this list.

COMPLETE SET	6,000.00	12,000.00
1 Hank Aaron	750.00	1,500.00
Johnny Logan		
Eddie Miksis		
2 Don Bollweg	250.00	500.00
Cal Abrams		
Billy Cox		
3 Bob Darnell	600.00	1,200.00
Early Wynn		
Pee Wee Reese		
4 Del Ennis	250.00	500.00
Del Crandell		
Joe Adcock		
5 Whitey Ford	500.00	1,000.00
Enos Slaughter		
Paul LaPalme		
6 Nellie Fox	500.00	1,000.00
Carl Furillo		
Carl Erskine		
7 Bob Friend	250.00	500.00
Williard Nixon		
Tom Brewer		
8 Steve Gromek	250.00	500.00
Milt Bolling		
Vern Stephens		
9 Russ Kemmerer	250.00	500.00
Hal Jeffcoat		
Dee Fondy		
10 Paul LaPalme	250.00	500.00
Royce Lint		
Irv Noren		
11 Stan Lopata	250.00	500.00
Bobby Avila		
Al Smith		
12 Mickey Mantle	2,500.00	5,000.00
Steve Gromek		
Milt Bolling		
13 Bob Rush	750.00	1,500.00
Ray Katt		
Willie Mays		
14 Virgil Trucks	250.00	500.00
Preston Ward		
Dick Cole		

1974 Bramac 1933 National League All-Stars

This 18-card set features black-and-white photos of the 1933 All-Stars of the National League. The set measures approximately 2 1/2" by 3 1/4" and was originally available from the producers for $3.

COMPLETE SET (18)	12.50	30.00
1 Paul Waner	1.00	2.50
2 Woody English	.40	1.00
3 Dick Bartell	.40	1.00
4 Chuck Klein	1.00	2.50
5 Tony Cuccinello	.40	1.00
6 Lefty O'Doul	.60	1.50
7 Gabby Hartnett	1.00	2.50
8 Lon Warneke	.40	1.00
9 Walter Berger	.60	1.50
10 Chick Hafey	.75	2.00
11 Frank Frisch	1.00	2.50
12 Carl Hubbell	1.50	4.00
13 Bill Hallahan	.40	1.00
14 Hal Schumacher	.60	1.50
15 Pie Traynor	1.00	2.50
16 Bill Terry	1.00	2.50
17 Pepper Martin	.75	2.00
18 Jimmy Wilson	.60	1.50

1889 Braves Cabinets Smith

These three cabinets feature members of the 1889 Boston Beaneaters and were produced by the G. Walden Smith studio in Boston. Each of these cabinets measure approximately 4 1/4" by 6 1/2" and feature the player a posed shot in their uniforms. Since the cards are unnumbered, we have sequenced them in alphabetical order.vThere should be more to this set so any additions are greatly appreciated.

COMPLETE SET	2,000.00	4,000.00
1 Tom Brown	750.00	1,500.00
2 Charlie Ganzel	750.00	1,500.00
3 Charles Smith	750.00	1,500.00

1891 Braves Conly Cabinets

These Cabinets feature members of the 1891 Boston NL team. The players are all pictured in suit and tie. The back features an ad for Conly studios. This set is not numbered so we have sequenced them in alphabetical order.

1 Hugh Duffy	2,000.00	3,000.00
2 George Haddock	1,000.00	1,500.00
3 John Irwin	1,000.00	1,500.00

1899 Braves Chickering Cabinets

These cabinets, which measure approximately 8" by 9 1/2", feature members of the 1899 Boston team which was known as the Beaneaters at that time. The photographs were taken by the Elmer Chickering studio at that time, which was one of the leading photo studios of the time. Since these cabinets are unnumbered, we have sequenced them in alphabetical order. It is very possible that there are other cabinets so any further information is greatly appreciated.

COMPLETE SET	2,000.00	40,000.00
1 Harvey Bailey	1,000.00	2,000.00
2 Marty Bergen	1,000.00	2,000.00
3 William Clarke	1,000.00	2,000.00
4 Jimmy Collins	2,000.00	4,000.00
5 Hugh Duffy	2,000.00	4,000.00
6 Billy Hamilton	2,000.00	4,000.00
7 Charlie Hickman	1,000.00	2,000.00
8 Frank Killen	1,000.00	2,000.00
9 Edward Lewis	1,000.00	2,000.00
10 Herman Long	1,250.00	2,500.00
11 Robert Lowe	1,250.00	2,500.00
12 Jouett Meekin	1,000.00	2,000.00
13 Kid Nichols	2,000.00	4,000.00
14 Fred Tenney	1,250.00	2,500.00
15 Vic Willis	2,000.00	4,000.00

1932 Braves Team Issue

These blank-backed photos which measure 9" by 12" are a sepia color against cream borders. All photos are copyright 1932 by "Gowell Studios." Since they are unnumbered we have sequenced them in alphabetical order.

COMPLETE SET	75.00	150.00
1 Wally Berger	10.00	20.00
2 Huck Betts	5.00	10.00
3 Ed Brandt	5.00	10.00
4 Bobby Brown	5.00	10.00
5 Ben Cantwell	5.00	10.00
6 Pinky Hargrave	7.50	15.00
7 Fritz Knothe	5.00	10.00
8 Freddie Leach	5.00	10.00
9 Rabbit Maranville	12.50	25.00
10 Bill McKechnie MG	12.50	25.00
11 Randy Moore	5.00	10.00
12 Art Shires	7.50	15.00
13 Al Spohrer	5.00	10.00
14 Bill Urbanski	5.00	10.00
15 Red Worthington	5.00	10.00

1948 Braves Gentles Bread Label

These bread labels were issued one per loaf of Gentles bread. They feature a player photo with a fascimile signature on either the top or bottom with the "Gentles Bread" logo on the other end. These cards are unnumbered so we have sequenced them in alphabetical order. We suspect there might be more additions so any help is appreciated.

COMPLETE SET	600.00	1,200.00
1 Tommy Holmes	125.00	250.00
2 Phil Masi	100.00	200.00
3 John Sain	200.00	400.00
4 Warren Spahn	250.00	500.00

1953 Braves Johnston Cookies

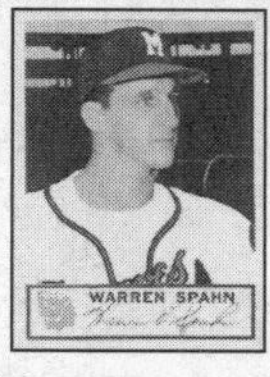

The cards in this 25-card set measure approximately 2 9/16" by 3 5/8". The 1953 Johnston's Cookies set of numbered cards features Milwaukee Braves players only. This set is the most plentiful of the three Johnston's Cookies sets and no known scarcities exist. The catalog designation for this set is D356-1.

COMPLETE SET (25)	250.00	500.00
1 Charlie Grimm MG	7.50	15.00
2 John Antonelli	7.50	15.00
3 Vern Bickford	6.00	12.00
4 Bob Buhl	10.00	20.00
5 Lew Burdette	12.50	25.00
6 Dave Cole	7.50	15.00
7 Ernie Johnson	10.00	20.00
8 Dave Jolly	7.50	15.00
9 Don Liddle	7.50	15.00
10 Warren Spahn	50.00	100.00
11 Max Surkont	7.50	15.00
12 Jim Wilson	7.50	15.00
13 Sibbi Sisti	7.50	15.00
14 Walker Cooper	7.50	15.00
15 Del Crandall	10.00	20.00
16 Ebba St.Claire	7.50	15.00
17 Joe Adcock	12.50	25.00
18 George Crowe	7.50	15.00
19 Jack Dittmer	7.50	15.00
20 Johnny Logan	10.00	20.00
21 Ed Mathews	50.00	100.00
22 Bill Bruton	10.00	20.00
23 Sid Gordon	7.50	15.00
24 Andy Pafko	10.00	20.00
25 Jim Pendleton	7.50	15.00

1953 Braves Merrell

This 17-card set features black-and-white art work of the Milwaukee Braves drawn by Marshall Merrell. The set measures 8" by 10" and was printed on heavy card stock. The prints originally were sold for 25 cents each. The cards are unnumbered and checklisted below in alphabetical order.

COMPLETE SET (17)	300.00	600.00
1 Joe Adcock	30.00	60.00
2 Johnny Antonelli	20.00	50.00
3 Billy Bruton	15.00	40.00
4 Bob Buhl	15.00	40.00
5 Lou Burdette	30.00	60.00
6 Del Crandall	20.00	50.00
7 Jack Dittmer	15.00	40.00
8 Sid Gordon	15.00	40.00
9 Charlie Grimm	20.00	50.00
10 Don Liddle	15.00	40.00
11 Johnny Logan	15.00	40.00
12 Ed Mathews	50.00	100.00
13 Andy Pafko	20.00	50.00
14 Jim Pendleton	15.00	40.00
15 Warren Spahn	75.00	150.00
16 Max Surkont	15.00	40.00
17 Jim Wilson	15.00	40.00

1953-54 Braves Spic and Span 3x5

This 27-card set features only members of the Milwaukee Braves. The cards are black and white and approximately 3 1/4" by 5 1/2". Some of the photos in the set are posed against blank backgrounds, but most are posed against seats and a chain link fence, hence the set is sometimes referred to as the "chain link fence" set. There is a facsimile autograph at the bottom of the card. The set was probably issued in 1953 and 1954 since Hank Aaron is not included in the set and Don Liddle, Ebba St.Claire, and Johnny Antonelli were traded from the Braves on February 1, 1954 for Bobby Thomson (who is also in the set). Cards can be found either blank back or with player's name, comment, and logo in blue on the back

COMPLETE SET (28)	600.00	1,200.00
1 Joe Adcock	17.50	35.00
2 Johnny Antonelli	15.00	30.00
3 Vern Bickford	12.50	25.00
4 Bill Bruton	15.00	30.00
5 Bob Buhl	15.00	30.00
6 Lew Burdette	17.50	35.00
7 Dick Cole	12.50	25.00
8 Walker Cooper	12.50	25.00
9 Del Crandall	15.00	30.00
10 George Crowe	12.50	25.00
11 Jack Dittmer	12.50	25.00
12 Sid Gordon	12.50	25.00
13 Ernie Johnson	15.00	30.00
14 Dave Jolly	12.50	25.00
15 Don Liddle	12.50	25.00
16 Johnny Logan	15.00	30.00
17 Ed Mathews	75.00	150.00
18 Danny O'Connell	12.50	25.00
19 Andy Pafko	15.00	30.00
20 Jim Pendleton	12.50	25.00
21 Ebba St.Claire	12.50	25.00
22 Warren Spahn	75.00	150.00
23 Max Surkont	12.50	25.00
24 Bobby Thomson	17.50	35.00
25 Bob Thorpe	12.50	25.00
26 Roberto Vargas	12.50	25.00
27 Jim Wilson	12.50	25.00
28 Hank Aaron	150.00	300.00

1953-56 Braves Spic and Span 7x10

This 13-card set features only members of the Milwaukee Braves. The set was issued beginning in 1953 but may have been issued for several years as they seem to be the most common of all the Spic and Span issues. In addition, Danny O'Connell and Bobby Thomson were not on the '53 Braves team. The front of each card shows the logo, "Spic and Span Dry Cleaners ... the Choice of Your Favorite Braves." There is a thick white border around the cards with facsimile autograph in black in the bottom border. The cards have blank backs and are approximately 7" by 10".

COMPLETE SET (13)	100.00	200.00
1 Joe Adcock	6.00	12.00
2 Billy Bruton	5.00	10.00
3 Bob Buhl	5.00	10.00
4 Lew Burdette	6.00	12.00
5 Del Crandall	5.00	10.00
6 Jack Dittmer	4.00	8.00
7 Johnny Logan	5.00	10.00
8 Eddie Mathews	25.00	50.00
9 Chet Nichols	4.00	8.00
10 Danny O'Connell	4.00	8.00
11 Andy Pafko	5.00	10.00
12 Warren Spahn	25.00	50.00
13 Bobby Thomson	6.00	12.00
14 Milwaukee County Stadium	3.00	8.00

1954 Braves Douglas Felts

These circular oversize felts feature members of the 1954 Milwaukee Braves. Against a white baseball background, the player's photo and fascimile signature is set. The backs are blank and since these are unnumbered, we have sequenced them in alphabetical order.

COMPLETE SET	250.00	500.00
1 Joe Adcock	40.00	80.00
2 Bill Bruton	30.00	60.00
3 Bob Buhl	20.00	50.00
4 Lew Burdette	30.00	60.00
5 Del Crandall	30.00	60.00
6 Johnny Logan	20.00	50.00
7 Eddie Mathews	50.00	100.00
8 Danny O'Connell	20.00	50.00
9 Andy Pafko	30.00	60.00
10 Jim Pendleton	20.00	50.00
11 Warren Spahn	60.00	120.00
12 Bobby Thomson	50.00	100.00

1954 Braves Douglas Portraits

These 8" by 10" portraits feature members of the 1954 Milwaukee Braves. The checklist is identical to the Douglas Felt checklist of the same year. The drawings are oin Sepia-toned paper and the backs are blank

COMPLETE SET	500.00	1,000.00
1 Joe Adcock	50.00	100.00
2 Bill Bruton	40.00	80.00
3 Bob Buhl	40.00	80.00
4 Lew Burdette	60.00	120.00
5 Del Crandall	40.00	80.00
6 Johnny Logan	40.00	80.00
7 Eddie Mathews	75.00	150.00
8 Danny O'Connell	30.00	60.00
9 Andy Pafko	50.00	100.00
10 Jim Pendleton	30.00	60.00
11 Warren Spahn	100.00	200.00
12 Bobby Thomson	50.00	100.00

1954 Braves Johnston Cookies

The cards in this 35-card set measure approximately 2" by 3 7/8". The 1954 Johnston's Cookies set of color cards of Milwaukee Braves are numbered according to the player's uniform number, except for the non-players, Lacks and Taylor, who are found at the end of the set. The Bobby Thomson card was withdrawn early in the year after his injury and is scarce. The catalog number for this set is D356-2. The Hank Aaron card shows him with uniform number 5, rather than the more familiar 44, that he switched to shortly thereafter.

COMPLETE SET (35)	600.00	1,200.00
COMMON SP	100.00	200.00
1 Del Crandall	10.00	20.00
3 Jim Pendleton	6.00	12.00
4 Danny O'Connell	6.00	12.00
5 Hank Aaron	600.00	1,200.00
6 Jack Dittmer	6.00	12.00
9 Joe Adcock	10.00	20.00
10 Bob Buhl	7.50	15.00
11 Phil Paine	6.00	12.00
12 Ben Johnson	6.00	12.00
13 Sibbi Sisti	6.00	12.00
15 Charles Gorin	6.00	12.00
16 Chet Nichols	6.00	12.00
17 Dave Jolly	6.00	12.00
19 Jim Wilson	6.00	12.00
20 Ray Crone	6.00	12.00
21 Warren Spahn	40.00	80.00
22 Gene Conley	7.50	15.00
23 Johnny Logan	10.00	20.00
24 Charlie White	6.00	12.00
27 George Metkovich	6.00	12.00
28 Johnny Cooney CO	6.00	12.00
29 Paul Burris	6.00	12.00
31 Bucky Walters CO	7.50	15.00
32 Ernie Johnson	7.50	15.00
33 Lou Burdette	10.00	20.00
34 Bobby Thomson SP	100.00	200.00
35 Bob Keely	6.00	12.00
38 Bill Bruton	7.50	15.00
40 Charlie Grimm MG	10.00	20.00
41 Eddie Mathews	40.00	80.00
42 Sam Calderone	6.00	12.00
47 Joey Jay	7.50	15.00
48 Andy Pafko	7.50	15.00
49 Dr. Charles Lacks/(Unnumbered)	6.00	12.00
50 Joseph F. Taylor/(Unnumbered)	6.00	12.00

1954 Braves Merrell

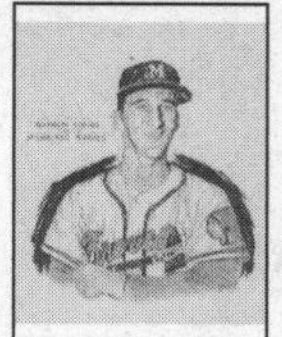

This set of the Milwaukee Braves measures approximately 8" by 10" and features black-and-white drawings of players by artist, Marshall Merrell. The cards are unnumbered and checklisted below in alphabetical order. This checklist may be incomplete and additions are welcome.

COMPLETE SET	450.00	900.00
1 Hank Aaron	125.00	250.00
2 Joe Adcock	40,00	80.00
3 Bob Buhl	20.00	50.00
4 Charlie Grimm MG	30.00	60.00
5 Johnny Logan	20.00	50.00
6 Ed Mathews	75.00	150.00
7 Danny O'Connell	20.00	50.00
8 Andy Pafko	30.00	60.00
9 Warren Spahn	75.00	150.00
10 Jim Wilson	20.00	50.00

1954 Braves Spic and Span Postcards

This black and white set features only members of the Milwaukee Braves. The cards have postcard backs and measure approximately 3 11/16" by 6". The postcards were issued beginning in 1954. There is a facsimile autograph on the front in black or white ink. The set apparently was also issued with white borders in a 5" by 7" size. The catalog designation for this set is PC756. The front of each card shows the logo, "Spic and Span Dry Cleaners ... the Choice of Your Favorite Braves."

COMPLETE SET (18)	300.00	600.00
1 Henry Aaron	125.00	250.00
2 Joe Adcock	12.50	25.00
3 Billy Bruton	10.00	20.00
4 Bob Buhl	10.00	20.00
5 Lew Burdette	12.50	25.00
6 Gene Conley	10.00	20.00
7 Del Crandall	12.50	25.00
8 Ray Crone	7.50	15.00
9 Jack Dittmer	7.50	15.00
10 Ernie Johnson	10.00	20.00
11 Dave Jolly	7.50	15.00
12 Johnny Logan	10.00	20.00
13 Eddie Mathews	40.00	80.00
14 Chet Nichols	7.50	15.00
15 Danny O'Connell	7.50	15.00
16 Andy Pafko	10.00	20.00
17 Warren Spahn	40.00	80.00
18 Bobby Thomson	12.50	25.00

1955 Braves Golden Stamps

This 32-stamp set features color photos of the Milwaukee Braves and measures approximately 1 15/16" by 2 5/8". The stamps are designed to be placed in a 32-page album which measures approximately 8 3/8" by 10 15/16". The album contains black-and-white drawings of players with their batting averages and life stories. The team's history and other information is also printed in the album. The stamps are unnumbered and listed below according to where they fall in the album.

COMPLETE SET (32)	75.00	150.00
1 1954 Team Photo	5.00	10.00
2 Charlie Grimm MG	5.00	10.00
3 Warren Spahn	7.50	15.00
4 Lew Burdette	4.00	8.00
5 Chet Nichols	1.00	2.00
6 Gene Conley	1.00	2.00
7 Bob Buhl	1.00	2.00
8 Jim Wilson	1.00	2.00

9 Dave Jolly	1.00	2.00
10 Ernie Johnson	1.50	3.00
11 Joey Jay	1.50	3.00
12 Dave Koslo	1.00	2.00
13 Charlie Gorin	1.00	2.00
14 Ray Crone	1.00	2.00
15 Del Crandall	1.50	3.00
16 Joe Adcock	2.00	4.00
17 Jack Dittmer	1.00	2.00
18 Eddie Mathews	10.00	20.00
19 Johnny Logan	1.50	3.00
20 Andy Pafko	1.50	3.00
21 Bill Bruton	1.00	2.00
22 Bobby Thomson	2.00	4.00
23 Charlie White	1.00	2.00
24 Danny O'Connell	1.00	2.00
25 Henry Aaron	12.50	25.00
26 Jim Pendleton	1.00	2.00
27 George Metkovich	1.00	2.00
28 Mel Roach	1.00	2.00
29 John Cooney CO	1.00	2.00
30 Bucky Walters CO	1.50	3.00
31 Charles Lacks TR	1.00	2.00
32 Milwaukee County Stadium	5.00	10.00
XX Album	2.50	5.00

1955 Braves Johnston Cookies

The cards in this 35-card set measure approximately 2 3/4" by 4". This set of Milwaukee Braves issued in 1955 by Johnston Cookies are numbered by the uniform number of the player depicted, except for non-players Lacks, Lewis and Taylor. The cards were issued in strips of six which accounts for the rouletted edges found on single cards. They are larger in size than the two previous sets but are printed on thinner cardboard. Each player in the checklist has been marked to show on which panel or strip he appeared (Pafko appears twice). A complete panel of six cards is worth 25 percent more than the sum of the individual players. The catalog designation for this set is D356-3.

COMPLETE SET (35)	500.00	1,000.00
1 Del Crandall P1	12.50	25.00
3 Jim Pendleton P3	7.50	15.00
4 Danny O'Connell P1	7.50	15.00
6 Jack Dittmer P6	7.50	15.00
9 Joe Adcock P2	12.50	25.00
10 Bob Buhl P6	10.00	20.00
11 Phil Paine P5	7.50	15.00
12 Ray Crone P5	7.50	15.00
15 Charlie Gorin P1	7.50	15.00
16 Dave Jolly P4	7.50	15.00
17 Chet Nichols P2	7.50	15.00
18 Chuck Tanner P5	15.00	30.00
19 Jim Wilson P6	7.50	15.00
20 Dave Koslo P4	7.50	15.00
21 Warren Spahn P3	40.00	80.00
22 Gene Conley P3	10.00	20.00
23 Johnny Logan P4	12.50	25.00
24 Charlie White P2	7.50	15.00
28 Johnny Cooney CO P4	7.50	15.00
30 Roy Smalley P3	7.50	15.00
31 Bucky Walters CO P6	10.00	20.00
32 Ernie Johnson P5	10.00	20.00
33 Lew Burdette P1	12.50	25.00
34 Bobby Thomson P6	12.50	25.00
35 Bob Keely P1	7.50	15.00
38 Bill Bruton P4	10.00	20.00
39 George Crowe P3	7.50	15.00
40 Charlie Grimm MG P6	10.00	20.00
41 Eddie Mathews P5	40.00	80.00
44 Hank Aaron P1	200.00	400.00
47 Joey Jay P2	10.00	20.00
48 Andy Pafko P2 P4	10.00	20.00
49 Dr. Charles Leaks P2/(Unnumbered)	7.50	15.00
50 Duffy Lewis P5 Trav.Sec./(Unnumbered)	10.00	20.00
51 Joe Taylor P3/(Unnumbered)	7.50	15.00

1955 Braves Spic and Span Die-Cut

This 18-card, die-cut, set features only members of the Milwaukee Braves. Each player measures differently according to the pose but they are, on average, approximately 8" by 8". The cards could be folded together to stand up. Each card contains a logo in the middle at the bottom and a copyright notice, "1955 Spic and Span Cleaners" in the lower right corner.

COMPLETE SET (18)	2,000.00	4,000.00
1 Hank Aaron	500.00	1,000.00
2 Joe Adcock	100.00	200.00
3 Billy Bruton	60.00	120.00
4 Bob Buhl	60.00	120.00
5 Lew Burdette	100.00	200.00
6 Gene Conley	60.00	120.00
7 Del Crandall	100.00	200.00
8 Jack Dittmer	60.00	120.00
9 Ernie Johnson	75.00	150.00
10 Dave Jolly	60.00	120.00
11 Johnny Logan	75.00	150.00
12 Eddie Mathews	200.00	400.00
13 Chet Nichols	60.00	120.00
14 Danny O'Connell	60.00	120.00
15 Andy Pafko	75.00	150.00
16 Warren Spahn	200.00	400.00
17 Bob Thomson	100.00	200.00
18 Jim Wilson	60.00	120.00

1956-60 Braves Bill and Bob Postcards PPC-741

The Bill and Bob postcards issued during the 1956-60 time period features only Milwaukee Braves. The cards are unnumbered, other than the K card number at the middle base on the reverse, and present some of the most attractive color postcards issued in the postwar period. Three poses of Adcock and two poses each of Bruton and Crandall exist. The Torre card has been seen with a Pepsi advertisment on the reverse. The complete set price includes only one of each player.

COMPLETE SET (15)	600.00	1,200.00
1 Hank Aaron	200.00	400.00
2 Joe Adcock (3)	25.00	50.00
3 Bill Bruton (2)	30.00	60.00
4 Bob Buhl	12.50	25.00
5 Lew Burdette	25.00	50.00
6 Gene Conley	20.00	40.00
7 Wes Covington	20.00	40.00
8 Del Crandall (2)	12.50	25.00
9 Chuck Dressen MG	20.00	40.00
10 Charlie Grimm MG	30.00	60.00
11 Fred Haney MG	25.00	50.00
12 Bobby Keely CO	12.50	25.00
13 Ed Mathews	75.00	150.00
14 Warren Spahn	75.00	150.00
15 Frank Torre	30.00	60.00

1957 Braves 8x10

This 12-card set features reddish sepia portraits of the Milwaukee Braves in a combination of photos and drawings printed on a yellowish card. The backs are blank. The cards are unnumbered and checklisted below in alphabetical order.

COMPLETE SET (12)	75.00	150.00
1 Joe Adcock	7.50	15.00
2 Bill Bruton	6.00	12.00
3 Bob Buhl	6.00	12.00
4 Lew Burdette	7.50	15.00
5 Del Crandall	6.00	12.00
6 Johnny Logan	6.00	12.00
7 Ed Mathews	12.50	25.00
8 Danny O'Connell	5.00	10.00
9 Andy Pafko	6.00	12.00
10 Jim Pendleton	5.00	10.00
11 Warren Spahn	15.00	30.00
12 Bob Thomson	7.50	15.00

1957 Braves Spic and Span 4x5

This set contains 20 black and white photos each with a blue-printed message such as "Stay in There and Pitch" and blue facsimile autograph The set features only members of the Milwaukee Braves. Red Schoendienst was traded to the Braves on June 15, 1957 in exchange for Danny O'Connell, Ray Crone, and Bobby Thomson. Wes Covington, Felix Mantilla, and Bob Trowbridge are also listed as shorter-printed (SP) cards as they were apparently mid-season call-ups. The cards are approximately 4 5/16" by 5" with a thick white border and are blank backed. Spic and Span appears in blue in the white border in the lower right corner of the card. Since the cards are unnumbered, they are numbered in alphabetical order in the checklist below.

COMPLETE SET (20)	250.00	500.00
COMMON CARD (1-20)	5.00	10.00
COMMON CARD SP	12.50	25.00
1 Henry Aaron	75.00	150.00
2 Joe Adcock	7.50	15.00
3 Billy Bruton	6.00	12.00
4 Bob Buhl	6.00	12.00
5 Lew Burdette	7.50	15.00
6 Gene Conley	6.00	12.00
7 Wes Covington SP	15.00	30.00
8 Del Crandall	7.50	15.00
9 Ray Crone	5.00	10.00
10 Fred Haney MG	5.00	10.00
11 Ernie Johnson	6.00	12.00
12 Johnny Logan	6.00	12.00
13 Felix Mantilla SP	12.50	25.00
14 Ed Mathews	25.00	50.00
15 Danny O'Connell	5.00	10.00
16 Andy Pafko	6.00	12.00
17 Red Schoendienst SP	30.00	60.00
18 Warren Spahn	25.00	50.00
19 Bobby Thomson	7.50	15.00
20 Bob Trowbridge SP	12.50	25.00

1958 Braves Jay Publishing

This 12-card set of the Milwaukee Braves measures approximately 5" by 7" and features black-and-white player photos in a white border. These cards were packaged 12 to a packet. The backs are blank. The cards are unnumbered and checklisted below in alphabetical order.

COMPLETE SET (12)	30.00	60.00
1 Hank Aaron	7.50	15.00
2 Joe Adcock	2.50	5.00
3 Lew Burdette	2.50	5.00
4 Wes Covington	2.00	4.00
5 Del Crandall	1.50	3.00
6 Robert Hazle	1.50	3.00
7 John Logan	1.50	3.00
8 Eddie Mathews	5.00	10.00
9 Donald McMahon	1.50	3.00
10 Andy Pafko	1.50	3.00
11 Red Schoendienst	4.00	8.00
12 Warren Spahn	5.00	10.00

1959 Braves Jay Publishing

This 12-card set of the Milwaukee Braves measures approximately 5" by 7" and features black-and-white player photos in a white border. These cards were packaged 12 to a packet. The backs are blank. The cards are unnumbered and checklisted below in alphabetical order.

COMPLETE SET		40
1 Joe Adcock	2.00	5.00
2 Billy Bruton	1.25	3.00
3 Wes Covington	1.25	3.00
4 Johnny Logan	1.50	4.00
5 Stan Lopata	1.25	3.00
6 Eddie Mathews	3.00	8.00
7 Don McMahon	1.25	3.00
8 Del Rice	1.25	3.00
9 Mel Roach	1.25	3.00
10 Bob Rush	1.25	3.00
11 Bob Trowbridge	1.25	3.00
12 Casey Wise	1.25	3.00

1960 Braves Davison's

These cards measure approximately 3" by 3 5/8" and features black-and-white player photos. The cards are unnumbered and checklisted below in alphabetical order. The checklist may be incomplete and additions are welcome.

COMPLETE SET	20.00	50.00
1 Hank Aaron	12.50	30.00
2 Eddie Mathews	8.00	20.00

1960 Braves Jay Publishing

This 12-card set of the Milwaukee Braves measures approximately 5" by 7" and features black-and-white player photos in a white border. These cards were packaged 12 to a packet. The backs are blank. The cards are unnumbered and checklisted below in alphabetical order.

COMPLETE SET (12)	15.00	40.00
1 Hank Aaron	4.00	10.00
2 Billy Bruton	1.25	3.00
3 Wes Covington	1.25	3.00
4 Charlie Dressen MG	1.25	3.00
5 Bob Giggie	.75	2.00
6 Joey Jay	1.25	3.00
7 Stan Lopata	.75	2.00
8 Felix Mantilla	.75	2.00
9 Bob Rush	.75	2.00
10 Red Schoendienst	1.50	4.00
11 Warren Spahn	3.00	8.00
12 Frank Torre	1.25	3.00

1960 Braves Lake to Lake

The cards in this 28-card set measure 2 1/2" by 3 1/4". The 1960 Lake to Lake set of unnumbered, blue tinted cards features Milwaukee Braves players only. For some reason, this set of Braves does not include Eddie Mathews. The cards were issued on milk cartons by Lake to Lake Dairy. Most cards have staple holes in the upper right corner. The backs are in red and give details and prizes associated with the card promotion. Cards with staple holes can be considered very good to excellent at best. The catalog designation for this set is F102-1.

COMPLETE SET (28)	600.00	1,200.00
1 Hank Aaron	200.00	400.00
2 Joe Adcock	10.00	25.00
3 Ray Boone	60.00	120.00
4 Bill Bruton	150.00	300.00
5 Bob Buhl	8.00	20.00
6 Lew Burdette	10.00	25.00
7 Chuck Cottier	6.00	15.00
8 Wes Covington	8.00	20.00
9 Del Crandall	10.00	25.00
10 Chuck Dressen MG	8.00	20.00
11 Bob Giggie	6.00	15.00
12 Joey Jay	8.00	20.00
13 Johnny Logan	8.00	20.00
14 Felix Mantilla	6.00	15.00
15 Lee Maye	6.00	15.00
16 Don McMahon	6.00	15.00
17 George Myatt CO	6.00	15.00
18 Andy Pafko CO	8.00	20.00
19 Juan Pizarro	6.00	15.00
20 Mel Roach	6.00	15.00
21 Bob Rush	6.00	15.00
22 Bob Scheffing CO	6.00	15.00
23 Red Schoendienst	15.00	40.00
24 Warren Spahn	40.00	80.00
25 Al Spangler	6.00	15.00
26 Frank Torre	8.00	20.00
27 Carlton Willey	6.00	15.00
28 Whit Wyatt CO	8.00	20.00

1960 Braves Spic and Span

This set features only members of the Milwaukee Braves. These small cards each measure approximately 2 13/16" by 3 1/16". The cards have a thin white border around a black and white photo with no other writing or words on the front. The card backs have the Spic and Span logo at the bottom along with "Photographed and Autographed Exclusively for Spic and Span". A message and facsimile autograph from the player is presented inside a square box all in blue on the card back.

COMPLETE SET (27)	250.00	500.00
1 Henry Aaron	75.00	150.00
2 Joe Adcock	6.00	15.00
3 Billy Bruton	5.00	12.00
4 Bob Buhl	5.00	12.00
5 Lew Burdette	6.00	15.00
6 Chuck Cottier	4.00	10.00
7A Del Crandall ERR/(Reversed negative)	20.00	50.00
7B Del Crandall COR	6.00	15.00
8 Charlie Dressen MG	5.00	12.00
9 Joey Jay	5.00	12.00
10 Johnny Logan	5.00	12.00
11 Felix Mantilla	4.00	10.00
12 Ed Mathews	20.00	50.00
13 Lee Maye	4.00	10.00
14 Don McMahon	4.00	10.00
15 George Myatt CO	4.00	10.00
16 Andy Pafko CO	5.00	12.00
17 Juan Pizarro	4.00	10.00
18 Mel Roach	4.00	10.00
19 Bob Rush	4.00	10.00
20 Bob Scheffing CO	4.00	10.00
21 Red Schoendienst	8.00	20.00
22 Warren Spahn	20.00	50.00
23 Al Spangler	4.00	10.00
24 Frank Torre	5.00	12.00
25 Carl Willey	4.00	10.00
26 Whit Wyatt CO	5.00	12.00

1962 Braves Jay Publishing

This 12-card set of the Milwaukee Braves measures approximately 5" by 7". The fronts feature black-and-white posed player photos with the player's and team name printed below in the white border. These cards were packaged 12 to a packet. The backs are blank. The cards are unnumbered and checklisted below in alphabetical order.

COMPLETE SET (12)	20.00	50.00
1 Hank Aaron	6.00	15.00
2 Joe Adcock	1.50	4.00
3 Frank Bolling	.75	2.00
4 Lou Burdette	1.50	4.00
5 Del Crandall	1.50	4.00
6 Eddie Mathews	3.00	8.00
7 Lee Maye	.75	2.00
8 Roy McMillan	1.25	3.00
9 Warren Spahn	3.00	8.00
10 George (Birdie) Tebbetts MG	.75	2.00
11 Joe Torre	2.00	5.00
12 Carl Willey	.75	2.00

1963 Braves Jay Publishing

This set of the Milwaukee Braves measures approximately 5" by 7". The fronts feature black-and-white posed player photos with the player's and team name printed below in the white border. These cards were packaged 12 to a packet. The backs are blank. The cards are unnumbered and checklisted below in alphabetical order. More than the standard 12 cards are listed as the Braves updated this set throughout the 1963 season.

COMPLETE SET	30.00	60.00
1 Hank Aaron	6.00	15.00
2 Tommie Aaron	1.25	3.00
3 Gus Bell	1.25	3.00
4 Frank Bolling	.75	2.00
5 Lew Burdette	1.50	4.00
6 Cecil Butler	.75	2.00
7 Tony Cloninger	1.25	3.00
8 Jim Constable	.75	2.00
9 Del Crandall	1.25	3.00
10 Frank Funk	.75	2.00
11 Bob Hendley	.75	2.00
12 Norm Larker	.75	2.00
13 Eddie Mathews	4.00	10.00
14 Roy McMillan	.75	2.00
15 Denis Menke	.75	2.00
16 Ron Piche	.75	2.00
17 Claude Raymond	.75	2.00
18 Amado Samuel	.75	2.00
19 Bob Shaw	.75	2.00
20 Warren Spahn	4.00	10.00
21 Joe Torre	2.50	6.00
22 Bob Uecker	2.00	5.00

1964 Braves Jay Publishing

This 12-card set of the Milwaukee Braves measures approximately 5" by 7". The fronts feature black-and-white posed player photos with the player's and team name printed below in the white border. These cards were packaged 12 to a packet. The backs are blank. The cards are unnumbered and checklisted below in alphabetical order.

COMPLETE SET (12)	20.00	50.00
1 Hank Aaron	6.00	15.00
2 Frank Bolling	.75	2.00
3 Bobby Bragan MG	.75	2.00
4 Tony Cloninger	.75	2.00
5 Denny Lemaster	.75	2.00
6 Eddie Mathews	4.00	10.00
7 Lee Maye	.75	2.00
8 Roy McMillan	1.25	3.00
9 Denis Menke	.75	2.00
10 Bob Sadowski	.75	2.00
11 Warren Spahn	4.00	10.00
12 Joe Torre	2.00	5.00

1965 Braves Jay Publishing

This 12-card set of the Milwaukee Braves measures approximately 5" by 7". The fronts feature black-and-white posed player photos with the player's and team name printed below in the white border. These cards were packaged 12 to a packet. The backs are blank. The cards are unnumbered and checklisted below in alphabetical order. 1965 would prove to be the Braves final season in Milwaukee.

COMPLETE SET (12)	20.00	50.00
1 Hank Aaron	6.00	15.00
2 Wade Blasingame	.75	2.00
3 Frank Bolling	.75	2.00
4 Bobby Bragan MG	.75	2.00
5 Hank Fischer	.75	2.00
6 Mack Jones	.75	2.00
7 Denny LeMaster	.75	2.00
8 Eddie Mathews	3.00	8.00
9 Phil Niekro	4.00	10.00
10 Billy O'Dell	.75	2.00
11 Dan Osinski	.75	2.00
12 Joe Torre	2.50	6.00

1965 Braves Team Issue

This 12-card set of the 1965 Milwaukee Braves measures approximately 4 7/8" by 7 1/8" and features black-and-white player photos with white borders. The backs are blank. The cards are unnumbered and checklisted below in alphabetical order.

COMPLETE SET (12)	8.00	20.00
1 Sandy Alomar	.75	2.00
2 Frank Bolling	.75	2.00
3 Ty Cline	.75	2.00
4 Mike De La Hoz	.75	2.00
5 Hank Fischer	.75	2.00
6 Mack Jones	.75	2.00
7 Gary Kolb	.75	2.00
8 Billy O'Dell	.75	2.00
9 Chi Chi Olivo	.75	2.00
10 Dan Osinski	.75	2.00
11 Bob Sadowski	.75	2.00
12 Bob Tiefenauer	.75	2.00

1966 Braves Postcards

This 27-card set of the Atlanta Braves features black-and-white player portraits in white borders and measures approximately 4" by 5". The backs are blank. The cards are unnumbered and checklisted below in alphabetical order.

COMPLETE SET (27)	100.00	200.00
1 Hank Aaron	12.50	30.00
2 Ted Abernathy	3.00	8.00
3 Felipe Alou	5.00	12.00
4 Wade Blasingame	3.00	8.00
5 Frank Bolling	3.00	8.00
6 Bobby Bragan MG	4.00	10.00
7 Clay Carroll	3.00	8.00
8 Rico Carty	4.00	10.00
9 Tony Cloninger	3.00	8.00
10 Mike de la Hoz	3.00	8.00
11 Gary Geiger	3.00	8.00
12 John Herrnstein	3.00	8.00
13 Billy Hitchcock CO	3.00	8.00
14 Ken Johnson	3.00	8.00
15 Mack Jones	3.00	8.00
16 Denver LeMaster	3.00	8.00
17 Eddie Mathews	10.00	25.00
18 Denis Menke	3.00	8.00
19 Felix Millan	4.00	10.00
20 Gene Oliver	3.00	8.00
21 Grover Resinger CO	3.00	8.00
22 Dan Schneider	3.00	8.00
23 Ken Silvestri	3.00	8.00
24 Joe Torre	8.00	20.00
25 Arnold Umbach	3.00	8.00
26 Jo Jo White CO	3.00	8.00
27 Whitlow Wyatt CO	4.00	10.00

1966 Braves Volpe

These 12 cards, which measure 8 1/2" by 11" feature members of the 1966 Atlanta Braves in their first year in Atlanta. These cards are unnumbered, so we have sequenced them in alphabetical order. The fronts feature drawings of the players while the back has biographical information, information blurbs and career statistics.

COMPLETE SET	60.00	120.00
1 Hank Aaron	12.50	30.00
2 Felipe Alou	5.00	12.00
3 Frank Bolling	3.00	8.00
4 Bobby Bragan MG	3.00	8.00
5 Rico Carty	4.00	10.00
6 Tony Cloninger	3.00	8.00
7 Mack Jones	3.00	8.00
8 Denny Lemaster	3.00	8.00
9 Eddie Mathews	8.00	20.00
10 Denis Menke	3.00	8.00
11 Lee Thomas	3.00	8.00
12 Joe Torre	5.00	12.00

1967 Braves Irvingdale Dairy

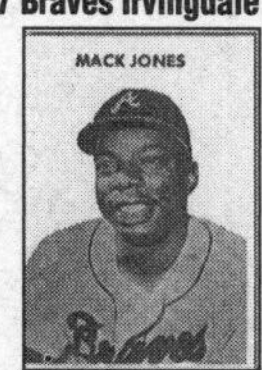

Four Atlanta Braves were featured on the back of one milk carton. If each player photo were cut, it would measure 1 3/4" by 2 5/8". The fronts feature a brown-tinted head-and-shoulders shot, with the player's name below. The backs are blank. The cards are unnumbered and checklisted below in alphabetical order.

COMPLETE SET (4)	150.00	300.00
1 Clete Boyer	50.00	100.00
2 Mack Jones	30.00	60.00
3 Denis Menke	30.00	60.00
4 Joe Torre	60.00	120.00

1967 Braves Photos

These photos were issued by the Atlanta Braves and features members of the 1967 Braves. The tops are black and white portrait photos with the players name on the bottom. The backs are blank so we have sequenced these cards in alphabetical order.

COMPLETE SET (29)	100.00	200.00
1 Hank Aaron	8.00	20.00
2 Felipe Alou	4.00	10.00
3 Wade Blasingame	2.00	5.00
4 Clete Boyer	3.00	8.00
5 Bob Bruce	2.00	5.00
6 Clay Carroll	2.00	5.00
7 Rico Carty	3.00	8.00
8 Ty Cline	2.00	5.00
9 Tony Cloninger	2.00	5.00
10 Mike de la Hoz	2.00	5.00
11 Gary Geiger	2.00	5.00
12 Ramon Hernandez	2.00	5.00
13 Billy Hitchcock MG	2.00	5.00
14 Pat Jarvis	2.00	5.00
15 Ken Johnson	2.00	5.00
16 Mack Jones	2.00	5.00
17 Dick Kelley	2.00	5.00
18 Bob Kennedy CO	2.00	5.00
19 Denver Lemaster	2.00	5.00
20 Orlando Martinez	2.00	5.00
21 Denis Menke	2.00	5.00
22 Felix Millan	2.00	5.00
23 Phil Niekro	8.00	20.00
24 Gene Oliver	2.00	5.00
25 Jay Ritchie	2.00	5.00
26 Joe Torre	8.00	20.00
27 Ken Silvestri CO	2.00	5.00
28 Woody Woodward	2.00	5.00
29 Whitlow Wyatt CO	3.00	8.00

1968 Braves Postcards

This 33-card set of the Atlanta Braves features black-and-white player portraits with white borders. The backs are blank. The cards are unnumbered and checklisted below in alphabetical order.

COMPLETE SET (33)	100.00	200.00
1 Hank Aaron	8.00	20.00
2 Tommie Aaron	2.50	6.00
3 Felipe Alou	3.00	8.00
4 Clete Boyer	2.50	6.00
5 Jim Britton	2.00	5.00
6 Jim Busby CO	2.00	5.00
7 Clay Carroll	2.00	5.00
8 Rico Carty	2.50	6.00
9 Tony Cloninger	2.00	5.00
10 Harry Dorish CO	2.00	5.00
11 Tito Francona	2.00	5.00
12 Billy Goodman CO	2.00	5.00
13 Luman Harris MG	2.00	5.00
14 Sonny Jackson	2.00	5.00
15 Pat Jarvis	2.00	5.00
16 Bob Johnson	2.00	5.00
17 Deron Johnson	2.00	5.00
18 Ken Johnson	2.00	5.00
19 Dick Kelley	2.00	5.00
20 Mike Lum	2.00	5.00
21 Marty Martinez	2.00	5.00
22 Felix Millan	2.50	6.00
23 Phil Niekro	6.00	15.00
24 Mike Page	2.00	5.00
25 Milt Pappas	2.50	6.00
26 Claude Raymond	2.00	5.00
27 Ron Reed	2.00	5.00
28 Ken Silvestri CO	2.00	5.00
29 George Stone	2.00	5.00
30 Bob Tillman	2.00	5.00
31 Joe Torre	5.00	12.00
32 Bob Uecker	3.00	8.00
33 Cecil Upshaw	2.00	5.00

1969 Braves Birthday Party Photo Stamps

This 25-stamp set was distributed as one sheet of postage-size stamps and features black-and-white portraits of the Atlanta Braves. The stamps are unnumbered and checklisted below in alphabetical order.

COMPLETE SET (25)	50.00	100.00
1 Hank Aaron/(dark photo)	8.00	20.00
2 Hank Aaron/(light photo)	8.00	20.00
3 Tommie Aaron	1.50	4.00
4 Clete Boyer	1.50	4.00
5 Rico Carty	1.50	4.00
6 Orlando Cepeda	3.00	8.00
7 Bob Didier	1.25	3.00
8 Ralph Garr	2.00	5.00
9 Gil Garrido	1.25	3.00
10 Tony Gonzalez	1.25	3.00
11 Luman Harris MG	1.25	3.00
12 Sonny Jackson	1.25	3.00
13 Pat Jarvis	1.25	3.00
14 Larry Jaster	1.25	3.00
15 Mike Lum	1.25	3.00
16 Felix Millan	1.50	4.00
17 Jim Nash	1.25	3.00
18 Phil Niekro	3.00	8.00
19 Milt Pappas	1.50	4.00
20 Ron Reed	1.25	3.00
21 George Stone	1.25	3.00
22 Bob Tillman	1.25	3.00
23 Cecil Upshaw	1.25	3.00
24 Hoyt Wilhelm	2.50	6.00
25 Title Stamp	1.25	3.00

1970 Braves Stamps

This eight-stamp set of the Atlanta Braves features black-and-white player portraits measuring approximately 1 1/4" by 1 3/4" with rounded corners. The stamps are unnumbered and checklisted below in alphabetical order.

COMPLETE SET (8)	10.00	25.00
1 Hank Aaron	4.00	10.00
2 Rico Carty	1.25	3.00
3 Orlando Cepeda	2.50	6.00
4 Luman Harris MG	.75	2.00
5 Pat Jarvis	.75	2.00
6 Felix Millan	1.25	3.00
7 Cecil Upshaw	.75	2.00
8 Hoyt Wilhelm	2.00	5.00

1974 Braves Photo Cards

This set of six photo cards was produced by the Atlanta Braves Sales Department. The photos were included in a special brochure promoting the 1974 season. The photo cards measure approximately 7" by 7 1/2" and feature full-bleed color portraits of the Braves' star players. A player autograph facsimile is superimposed on the photo in the upper left corner in white lettering. The backs have a ghosted baseball icon with the words "take 'em out to..." in bold black lettering in the upper left corner. Each card has promotional information regarding season tickets or player highlights from previous seasons. The cards are unnumbered and checklisted below alphabetically.

COMPLETE SET (6)	8.00	20.00
1 Hank Aaron	3.00	8.00
2 Dusty Baker	1.50	4.00
3 Darrell Evans	1.25	3.00
4 Eddie Mathews MG	2.00	5.00
5 Phil Niekro	2.50	6.00
6 Johnny Oates	.75	2.00

1974 Braves Team Issue

These 7" by 9" blank-backed full color photos feature members of the Atlanta Braves. The fronts have a full color photo with the players name and team on the bottom. There may be more players in this set so all additions are appreciated. Since these are unnumbered, we have sequenced these photos in alphabetical order.

COMPLETE SET	6.00	15.00
1 Dusty Baker	1.25	3.00
2 Darrell Evans	1.25	3.00
3 Ralph Garr	.75	2.00
4 Dave Johnson	1.25	3.00
5 Phil Niekro	2.00	5.00

1975 Braves Postcards

This 38-card set of the Atlanta Bravesw features player photos on postcard-size cards. The cards are unnumbered and checklisted below in alphabetical order.

COMPLETE SET (38)	8.00	20.00
1 Dusty Baker	.40	1.00
2 Larvell Blanks	.20	.50
3 Bob Beale	.20	.50
4 Mike Beard	.20	.50
5 Jim Busby CO	.20	.50
6 Buzz Capra	.20	.50
7 Vic Correll	.20	.50
8 Bruce Dal Canton	.20	.50
9 Jamie Easterly	.20	.50
10 Darrell Evans	.60	1.50
11 Ralph Garr	.30	.75
12 Clarence Gaston	.20	.50
13 Gary Gentry	.20	.50
14 Rod Gilbreath	.20	.50
15 Ed Goodson	.20	.50
16 Eddie Haas CO	.20	.50
17 Roric Harrison	.20	.50
18 Tom House	.20	.50
19 Clyde King	.20	.50
20 Dave Johnson	.60	1.50
21 Mike Lum	.20	.50
22 Dave May	.20	.50
23 Carl Morton	.20	.50
24 Phil Niekro	1.50	4.00
25 Johnny Oates	.20	.50
26 John Odom	.20	.50
27 Rowland Office	.20	.50
28 Marty Perez	.20	.50
29 Biff Pocoroba	.20	.50
30 Ron Reed	.20	.50
31 Craig Robinson	.20	.50
32 Ray Sadecki	.20	.50
33 Ken Silvestri CO	.20	.50
34 Elias Sosa	.20	.50
35 Herm Starrette CO	.20	.50
36 Frank Tepedino	.30	.75
37 Mike Thompson	.20	.50
38 Earl Williams	.20	.50

1976 Braves Postcards

This 34-card set of the Atlanta Braves features player photos on postcard-size cards. The cards are unnumbered and checklisted below in alphabetical order.

COMPLETE SET (34)	8.00	20.00
1 Mike Beard	.20	.50
2 Vern Benson CO	.20	.50
3 Dave Bristol CO	.20	.50
4 Chris Cannizzaro	.20	.50
5 Buzz Capra	.20	.50
6 Darrel Chaney	.20	.50
7 Vic Correll	.20	.50
8 Terry Crowley	.20	.50
9 Bruce Dal Canton	.20	.50
10 Adrian Devine	.20	.50
11 Darrell Evans	.60	1.50
12 Cito Gaston	.20	.50
13 Rod Gilbreath	.20	.50
14 Eddie Haas CO	.20	.50
15 Ken Henderson	.20	.50
16 Lee Lacy	.20	.50
17 Max Leon	.20	.50
18 Dave May	.20	.50
19 Andy Messersmith	.20	.50
20 Roger Moret	.20	.50
21 Carl Morton	.20	.50
22 Phil Niekro	1.50	4.00
23 Rowland Office	.20	.50
24 Marty Perez	.20	.50
25 Biff Pocoroba	.20	.50
26 Luis Quintana	.20	.50
27 Craig Robinson	.20	.50
28 Jerry Royster	.20	.50
29 Dick Ruthven	.20	.50
30 Elias Sosa	.20	.50
31 Herm Starrette CO	.20	.50
32 Pablo Torrealba	.20	.50
33 Earl Williams	.20	.50
34 Jim Wynn	.30	.75

1978 Braves Coke

This 14-card set of the Atlanta Braves measures approximately 3" by 4 1/4" and was sponsored by Coca-Cola and Atlanta Radio Station WPLO. The white fronts feature black-and-white drawings of player heads with the player's name and sponsor logos below. The backs carry the player's name, position, biography, and career information with the team and sponsor logos on a white background. The cards are unnumbered and checklisted below in alphabetical order. A poster was also made for this promotion, it has a value of $15.

COMPLETE SET (14)	8.00	20.00
1 Barry Bonnell	.40	1.00
2 Jeff Burroughs	.60	1.50
3 Rick Camp	.40	1.00
4 Gene Garber	.60	1.50
5 Rod Gilbreath	.40	1.00
6 Bob Horner	.75	2.00
7 Glenn Hubbard	.40	1.00
8 Gary Matthews	.75	2.00

9 Larry McWilliams	.40	1.00
10 Dale Murphy	2.00	5.00
11 Phil Niekro	1.50	4.00
12 Rowland Office	.40	1.00
13 Biff Pocoroba	.40	1.00
14 Jerry Royster	.40	1.00

1978 Braves TCC

These 16 standard-size cards feature past members of the Milwaukee Braves. Although the checklist mentions that uniform and card number are the same we have sequenced this set in alphabetical order.

COMPLETE SET (16)	3.00	8.00
1 Hank Aaron	.75	2.00
2 Joe Adcock	.30	.75
3 Billy Bruton	.10	.25
4 Bob Buhl	.10	.25
5 Lou Burdette	.20	.50
6 Wes Covington	.10	.25
7 Del Crandall	.20	.50
8 Johnny Logan	.10	.25
9 Eddie Mathews	.40	1.00
10 Andy Pafko	.10	.25
11 Red Schoendienst	.30	.75
12 Warren Spahn	.40	1.00
13 Joe Torre	.50	1.25
14 Bob Uecker	.40	1.00
15 Carl Willey	.10	.25
16 Checklist	.10	.25

1979 Braves Team Issue

These cards, issued on a light stock black and white, actually measure slightly smaller than a postcard. While many of the cards did have the players name printed on them, some did not. These cards are unnumbered so we have sequenced them in alphabetical order.

COMPLETE SET	10.00	25.00
1 Tommy Aaron CO	.20	.50
2 Barry Bonnell	.20	.50
3 Jeff Burroughs	.30	.75
4 Bobby Cox MG	.30	.75
Dark Background		
5 Bobby Cox MG	.30	.75
White Background		
6 Bobby Dews CO	.20	.50
7 Pepe Frias	.20	.50
8 Gene Garber	.20	.50
Portrait		
9 Gene Garber	.20	.50
Kneeling		
10 Cito Gaston	.20	.50
11 Alex Grammas CO	.20	.50
12 Bob Horner	.40	1.00
13 Glenn Hubbard	.20	.50
14 Mike Lum	.20	.50
Portrait		
15 Mike Lum	.20	.50
Ready to hit		
16 Gary Matthews	.30	.75
17 Gary Matthews	.30	.75
Close up		
18 Rick Matula	.20	.50
19 Joe McLaughlin	.20	.50
20 Larry McWilliams	.20	.50
21 Ed Miller	.20	.50
22 Dale Murphy	2.00	5.00
Name on Card		
23 Dale Murphy	2.00	5.00
No Name on Card		
24 Phil Niekro	1.25	3.00
Name on Card		
25 Phil Niekro	1.25	3.00
No Name on Card		
26 Rowland Office	.20	.50
27 Biff Pocoroba	.20	.50
28 Jerry Royster	.20	.50
29 Hank Small	.20	.50
30 Charlie Spikes	.20	.50

1980 Braves 1914 TCMA

This 33-card set features sepia tinted photos of the 1914 World Champion "Miracle Braves" with black-and-white designed borders. The backs carry player information and career statistics. We are missing cards number 31, we would appreciate any identification.

COMPLETE SET (32)	4.00	10.00
1 Joe Connolly	.08	.25
2 Lefty Tyler	.08	.25
3 Tom Hughes	.08	.25
4 Hank Gowdy	.20	.50
5 Gene Cocreham	.08	.25
6 Larry Gilbert	.08	.25
7 George Davis	.08	.25
8 Hub Perdue	.08	.25
9 Otto Hess		
10 Clarence Kraft	.08	.25
11 Tommy Griffith	.08	.25
12 Johnny Evers	.40	1.00
Ira Thomas		
Bill Klem		
Umpires		
13 Oscar Dugey	.08	.25
14 Josh Devore	.08	.25
15 George Stallings MG	.20	.50
16 Rabbit Maranville	.40	1.00
17 Paul Strand	.08	.25
18 Charlie Deal	.08	.25
19 Dick Rudolph	.20	.50
20 Butch Schmidt	.08	.25
21 Johnny Evers	.60	1.50
22 Dick Crutcher	.08	.25
23 Possum Whitted	.08	.25
24 Fred Mitchell CO	.08	.25
25 Herbie Moran	.08	.25
26 Bill James	.08	.25
27 Ted Cather	.08	.25
28 Red Smith	.08	.25
29 Less Mann	.08	.25
30 Herbie Moran	.08	.25
Wally Schang		
32 Johnny Evers MVP	.20	.50
Receives Gift of Car		
33 Jim Gafney	.08	.25
Owner		

1980 Braves 1957 TCMA

This 42-card set features photos of the 1957 Milwaukee Braves team with blue lettering. The backs carry player information.

COMPLETE SET (42)	10.00	25.00
1 Don McMahon	.08	.25
2 Joey Jay	.08	.25
3 Phil Paine	.08	.25
4 Bob Trowbridge	.08	.25
5 Bob Buhl	.08	.25
6 Lew Burdette	.30	.75
7 Ernie Johnson	.08	.25
8 Ray Crone	.08	.25
9 Taylor Phillips	.08	.25
10 Johnny Logan	.20	.50
11 Frank Torre	.20	.50
12 John DeMerit	.08	.25
13 Red Murff	.08	.25
14 Nippy Jones	.08	.25
15 Bobby Thomson	.30	.75
16 Chuck Tanner	.08	.25
17 Charlie Root	.20	.50
18 Juan Pizarro	.08	.25
19 Hawk Taylor	.08	.25
20 Mel Roach	.08	.25
21 Bob Hazle	.08	.25
22 Del Rice	.08	.25
23 Felix Mantilla	.08	.25
24 Andy Pafko	.20	.50
25 Del Crandall	.20	.50
26 Wes Covington	.08	.25
27 Eddie Mathews	.75	2.00
28 Joe Adcock	.40	1.00
29 Dick Cole	.08	.25
30 Carl Sawatski	.08	.25
31 Warren Spahn	.75	2.00
32 Hank Aaron	2.00	5.00
33 Bob Keely	.08	.25
34 Johnny Riddle CO	.08	.25
35 Connie Ryan	.08	.25
36 Harry Hanebrink	.08	.25
37 Danny O'Connell	.08	.25
38 Fred Haney MG	.08	.25
39 Dave Jolly	.08	.25
40 Red Schoendienst	.60	1.50
41 Gene Conley	.08	.25
42 Bill Bruton	.20	.50

1909 H.H. Bregstone PC743

The H.H. Bregstone postcards were issued during the 1909-11 time period. They feature St. Louis Browns and St. Louis Cardinals only. The cards are sepia and black in appearance and are of consistent quality in the printing. Each cards features the line "by H.H. Bregstone, St. Louis" at the bottom of the obverse. The player's last name, his position, and his team are enumerated. The reverses features the letters AZO in the stamp area. B. Gregory of the Trolley League is probably Howie Gregory who played for the Browns that year.

COMPLETE SET (53)	5,250.00	10,500.00
1 Bill Bailey	125.00	250.00
2 Jap Barbeau	125.00	250.00
3 Shad Barry	125.00	250.00
4 Fred Beebe	125.00	250.00
5 Frank Betcher	125.00	250.00
6 Jack Bliss	125.00	250.00
7 Roger Bresnahan	250.00	500.00
8 Bobby Byrne	125.00	250.00
9 Chappy Charles	125.00	250.00
10 Frank Corridon	125.00	250.00
11 Dade Criss	125.00	250.00
12 Lou Criger	125.00	250.00
13 Joe Delahanty	125.00	250.00
14 Bill Dineen	125.00	250.00
15 Rube Ellis	125.00	250.00
16 Steve Evans	125.00	250.00
17 Art Fromme	125.00	250.00
18 Rube Geyer	125.00	250.00
19 Billy Gilbert	125.00	250.00
20 Bert Graham	125.00	250.00
21 B. Gregory	125.00	250.00
Probably Howie Gregory		
22 Art Griggs	125.00	250.00
23 Bob Harmon	125.00	250.00
24 Roy Hartzell	125.00	250.00
25 Irv Higginbotham	125.00	250.00
26 Thomas Higgins	125.00	250.00
27 Danny Hoffman	125.00	250.00
28 Harry Howell	125.00	250.00
29 Miller Huggins	250.00	500.00
30 Rudy Hulswitt	125.00	250.00
31 Johnson	125.00	250.00
32 Tom Jones	125.00	250.00
33 Ed Konetchy	125.00	250.00
34 Johnny Lush	125.00	250.00
35 Lee Magee	125.00	250.00
36 Jimmy McAleer MG	125.00	250.00
37 Stoney McGlynn	125.00	250.00
38 Rebel Oakes	125.00	250.00
39 Tom O'Hara	125.00	250.00
40 Ham Patterson	125.00	250.00
41 Barney Pelty	125.00	250.00
42 Ed Phelps	125.00	250.00
43 Elmer Rieger	125.00	250.00
44 Charlie Rhodes	125.00	250.00
45 Slim Sallee	125.00	250.00
46 Schweitzer	125.00	250.00
47 Wib Smith	125.00	250.00
48 Jim Stephens	125.00	250.00
49 George Stone	125.00	250.00
50 Rube Waddell	250.00	500.00
51 Bobby Wallace	250.00	500.00
52 Jim Williams	125.00	250.00
53 Vic Willis	250.00	500.00

1903-04 Breisch-Williams E107

The cards in this 159-card set measure 1 1/4" by 2 1/2". The black and white cards of this series of "prominent baseball players" were marketed by the Breisch-Williams Company. Judging from the team changes for individual players, the set appears to have been issued in 1903-04. Cards have been found with smaller printing front and back and also with the company name hand stamped on back. There are several names misspelled. The cards have been alphabetized and numbered in the checklist below. A second type (sic Type II) of these cards is also known. These cards have thicker paper stock and more narrow borders. There is no definitive answer, however, as to how many players are available in Type II format. Any further information is greatly appreciated. A Deacon McGuire NY card was recently discovered, but due to market scarcity, no pricing is provided for this card. Due to the fact that most E107's are found in off-grade condition, our pricing references the technical grade of Good.

1 John Anderson/NY AL	900.00	1,500.00
2 John Anderson/St. Louis AL	900.00	1,500.00
3 Jimmy Barrett: Detroit/(sic, Barret)	900.00	1,500.00
4 Ginger Beaumont	1,200.00	2,000.00
5 Erve Beck	900.00	1,500.00
6 Jake Beckley	5,000.00	8,000.00
7 Harry Bemis: Cleve.	900.00	1,500.00
8 Chief Bender/Phila. AL	6,000.00	10,000.00
9 Bill Bernhard	900.00	1,500.00
10 Harry Bay/sic, Bey)	900.00	1,500.00
11 Bill Bradley	900.00	1,500.00
12 Fritz Buelow	900.00	1,500.00
13 Nixey Callahan	900.00	1,500.00
14 Scoops Carey	900.00	1,500.00
15 Charlie Carr	900.00	1,500.00
16 Bill Carrick	900.00	1,500.00
17 Doc Casey	900.00	1,500.00
18 Frank Chance	9,000.00	15,000.00
19 Jack Chesbro	6,000.00	10,000.00
20 Boileryard Clarke/sic, Clark	900.00	1,500.00
21 Fred Clarke	7,000.00	12,000.00
22 Jimmy Collins	5,000.00	8,000.00
23 Duff Cooley	900.00	1,500.00
24 Tommy Corcoran	900.00	1,500.00
25 Bill Coughlin/sic, Coughlan)	900.00	1,500.00
26 Lou Criger	900.00	1,500.00
27 Lave Cross	900.00	1,500.00
28 Monte Cross	900.00	1,500.00
29 Bill Dahlen/Brooklyn	1,200.00	2,000.00
30 Bill Dahlen/New York National	3,000.00	5,000.00
31 Tom Daly	900.00	1,500.00
32 George Davis	3,000.00	5,000.00
33 Harry Davis	900.00	1,500.00
34 Ed Delahanty	15,000.00	25,000.00
35 DeMont: Wash.	900.00	1,500.00
36 Pop Dillon/Brooklyn	900.00	1,500.00
37 Pop Dillon/Detroit	900.00	1,500.00
38 Bill Dinneen/(sic, Dineen)	900.00	1,500.00
39 Jiggs Donahue	900.00	1,500.00
40 Mike Donlin	1,200.00	2,000.00
41 Patsy Donovan	900.00	1,500.00
42 Patsy Dougherty	900.00	1,500.00
43 Klondike Douglass/sic, Douglas)	900.00	1,500.00
44 Jack Doyle/Brooklyn	900.00	1,500.00
45 Jack Doyle/Phila. NL	900.00	1,500.00
46 Lew Drill	900.00	1,500.00
47 Jack Dunn	900.00	1,500.00
48 Kid Elberfeld/sic, Elberfield	900.00	1,500.00
49 Kid Elberfeld/sic, Elberfield	900.00	1,500.00
50 Duke Farrell	900.00	1,500.00
51 Hobe Ferris	900.00	1,500.00
52 Elmer Flick	5,000.00	8,000.00
53 Buck Freeman	900.00	1,500.00
54 Bill Friel/sic, Freil	900.00	1,500.00
55 Dave Fultz	900.00	1,500.00
56 Ned Garvin	900.00	1,500.00
57 Billy Gilbert	900.00	1,500.00
58 Harry Gleason	900.00	1,500.00
59 Kid Gleason/NY NL	5,000.00	8,000.00
60 Kid Gleason/Phila. NL	3,500.00	6,000.00
61 John Gochnaur/Cleve./sic, Gochnauer	900.00	1,500.00
62 Danny Green	900.00	1,500.00
63 Noodles Hahn	1,200.00	2,000.00
64 Bill Hallman	900.00	1,500.00
65 Ned Hanlon MG	3,000.00	5,000.00
66 Dick Harley	900.00	1,500.00
67 Jack Harper	900.00	1,500.00
68 Topsy Hartsel/sic, Hartsell	900.00	1,500.00
69 Emmett Heidrick	900.00	1,500.00
70 Charlie Hemphill	900.00	1,500.00
71 Weldon Henley	900.00	1,500.00
72 Charlie Hickman	900.00	1,500.00
73 Harry Howell	900.00	1,500.00
74 Frank Isbell/sic, Isabel	900.00	1,500.00
75 Fred Jacklitsch/sic, Jacklitzch	900.00	1,500.00
76 Charlie Jones	900.00	1,500.00
77 Fielder Jones	900.00	1,500.00
78 Addie Joss	6,000.00	10,000.00
79 Mike Kahoe	900.00	1,500.00
80 Willie Keeler	9,000.00	15,000.00
81 Joe Kelley	5,000.00	8,000.00
82 Brickyard Kennedy	900.00	1,500.00
83 Frank Kitson	900.00	1,500.00
84 Malachi Kittredge/Boston NL	900.00	1,500.00
85 Malachi Kittredge/Wash.	900.00	1,500.00
86 Candy LaChance	900.00	1,500.00
87 Nap Lajoie	9,000.00	15,000.00
88 Thomas Leach	900.00	1,500.00
89 Watty Lee/Pittsburgh	900.00	1,500.00
90 Watty Lee/Washington	900.00	1,500.00
91 Sam Leever	900.00	1,500.00
92 Herman Long	1,200.00	2,000.00
93 Billy Lush/Cleveland	900.00	1,500.00
94 Billy Lush/Detroit	900.00	1,500.00
95 Christy Mathewson	30,000.00	50,000.00
96 Sport McAllister	900.00	1,500.00
97 Jack McCarthy	900.00	1,500.00
98 Barry McCormick	900.00	1,500.00
99 Ed McFarland	900.00	1,500.00
100 Herm McFarland	900.00	1,500.00
101 Joe McGinnity	5,000.00	8,000.00
102 John McGraw	7,000.00	12,000.00
103 Deacon McGuire/Brooklyn	3,000.00	5,000.00
104 Deacon McGuire/New York		
105 Jock Menefee	900.00	1,500.00
106 Sam Mertes	900.00	1,500.00
107 Roscoe Miller	900.00	1,500.00
108 Fred Mitchell	900.00	1,500.00
109 Earl Moore	900.00	1,500.00
110 Danny Murphy	900.00	1,500.00
111 Jack O'Connor	900.00	1,500.00
112 Al Orth	900.00	1,500.00
113 Dick Padden	900.00	1,500.00
114 Freddy Parent	900.00	1,500.00
115 Roy Patterson	900.00	1,500.00
116 Heinie Peitz	900.00	1,500.00
117 Deacon Phillipe/sic, Phillipi	1,200.00	2,000.00
118 Wiley Piatt	900.00	1,500.00
119 Ollie Pickering	900.00	1,500.00
120 Eddie Plank	9,000.00	15,000.00
121 Ed Poole/Brooklyn	900.00	1,500.00
122 Ed Poole/Cinc.	900.00	1,500.00
123 Jack Powell/New York AL	900.00	1,500.00
124 Jack Powell/StL AL	900.00	1,500.00
125 Doc Powers	900.00	1,500.00
126 Claude Ritchey/sic, Ritchie	900.00	1,500.00
127 Jimmy Ryan	1,200.00	2,000.00
128 Ossie Schreckengost	900.00	1,500.00
129 Kip Selbach	900.00	1,500.00
130 Socks Seybold	900.00	1,500.00
131 Jimmy Sheckard	900.00	1,500.00
132 Ed Siever	900.00	1,500.00
133 Harry Smith	900.00	1,500.00
134 Tully Sparks	900.00	1,500.00
135 Jake Stahl	1,200.00	2,000.00
136 Harry Steinfeldt	1,200.00	2,000.00
137 Sammy Strang	900.00	1,500.00
138 Willie Sudhoff	900.00	1,500.00
139 Joe Sugden	900.00	1,500.00
140 Billy Sullivan	1,200.00	2,000.00
141 Jack Taylor	900.00	1,500.00
142 Fred Tenney	900.00	1,500.00
143 Roy Thomas	1,250.00	1,500.00
144 Jack Thoney/Cleve.	900.00	1,500.00
145 Jack Thoney/NY AL	900.00	1,500.00
146 Happy Townsend	900.00	1,500.00
147 George Van Haltren	900.00	1,500.00
148 Rube Waddell	7,000.00	12,000.00
149 Honus Wagner	60,000.00	80,000.00
150 Bobby Wallace	5,000.00	8,000.00
151 John Warner	900.00	1,500.00
152 Jimmy Wiggs	900.00	1,500.00
153 Jimmy Williams	900.00	1,500.00
154 Vic Willis	5,000.00	8,000.00
155 Snake Wiltse	900.00	1,500.00
156 George Winter/sic, Winters	900.00	1,500.00
157 Bob Wood	900.00	1,500.00
158 Joe Yeager	900.00	1,500.00
159 Cy Young	15,000.00	30,000.00
160 Chief Zimmer	900.00	1,500.00

1970 Brewers McDonald's

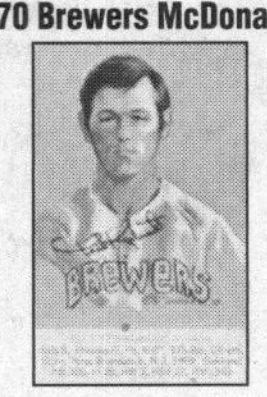

This 31-card set features cards measuring approximately 2 15/16" by 4 3/8" and was issued during the Brewers' first year in Milwaukee after moving from Seattle. The cards are drawings of the members of the 1970 Milwaukee Brewers and underneath the drawings there is information about the players. These cards are still often found in uncut sheet form and hence have no extra value in that form. The backs are blank. The set is checklisted alphabetically with the number of the sheet being listed next to the players name. There were six different sheets of six cards each although only one sheet contained six players; the other sheets depicted five players and a Brewers' logo.

COMPLETE SET (31)	3.00	8.00
1 Max Alvis 6	.10	.25
2 Bob Bolin 1	.10	.25
3 Gene Brabender 3	.10	.25
4 Dave Bristol 5 MG	.20	.50
5 Wayne Comer 2	.10	.25
6 Cal Ermer 3 CO	.10	.25
7 John Gelnar 4	.10	.25
8 Greg Goossen 5	.10	.25
9 Tommy Harper 5	.30	.75
10 Mike Hegan 3	.20	.50
11 Mike Hershberger 3	.10	.25
12 Steve Hovley 2	.10	.25
13 John Kennedy 2	.10	.25
14 Lew Krausse 4	.10	.25
15 Ted Kubiak 1	.10	.25
16 George Lauzerique 6	.10	.25
17 Bob Locker 5	.10	.25
18 Roy McMillan 4 CO	.20	.50
19 Jerry McNertney 4	.10	.25
20 Bob Meyer 2	.10	.25
21 Jackie Moore 6 CO	.20	.50
22 John Morris 1	.10	.25
23 John O'Donoghue 1	.10	.25
24 Marty Pattin 6	.10	.25
25 Rich Rollins 4	.20	.50
26 Phil Roof 5	.10	.25
27 Ted Savage 1	.10	.25
28 Russ Snyder 6	.10	.25
29 Wes Stock 2 CO	.20	.50
30 Sandy Valdespino 2	.10	.25
31 Danny Walton 3	.10	.25

1970 Brewers Milk

This 24-card set of the Milwaukee Brewers measures approximately 2 5/8" by 4 1/4" and features blue-and-white player photos. The players name is printed in blue in the white wide bottom border. The cards are unnumbered and checklisted below in alphabetical order.

COMPLETE SET (24)	4.00	10.00
1 Gene Brabender	.20	.50
2 Dave Bristol MG	.30	.75
3 Wayne Comer	.20	.50
4 Cal Ermer CO	.20	.50
5 Greg Goossen	.20	.50
6 Tom Harper	.40	1.00
7 Mike Hegan	.30	.75
8 Mike Hershberger	.20	.50
9 Steve Hovley	.20	.50
10 John Kennedy	.20	.50
11 Lew Krausse	.20	.50
12 Ted Kubiak	.20	.50
13 Bob Locker	.20	.50
14 Roy McMillan CO	.30	.75
15 Jerry McNertney	.20	.50
16 Bob Meyer	.20	.50
17 John Morris	.20	.50
18 John O'Donoghue	.20	.50
19 Marty Pattin	.20	.50
20 Rich Rollins	.30	.75
21 Phil Roof	.20	.50
22 Ted Savage	.20	.50
23 Russ Snyder	.20	.50
24 Dan Walton	.20	.50

1970 Brewers Team Issue

This 12-card set of the Milwaukee Brewers measures approximately 4 1/4" by 7". The fronts display black-and-white player portraits bordered in white. The player's name and team are printed in the top margin. The backs are blank. The cards are unnumbered and checklisted below in alphabetical order.

COMPLETE SET (12)	8.00	20.00
1 Max Alvis	.75	2.00
2 Dave Bristol	.75	2.00
3 Tommy Harper	1.00	2.50
4 Mike Hegan	.75	2.00
5 Mike Hershberger	.60	1.50
6 Lew Krausse	.60	1.50
7 Ted Kubiak	.60	1.50
8 Dave May	.60	1.50
9 Jerry McNertney	.60	1.50
10 Phil Roof	.60	1.50
11 Ted Savage	.60	1.50
12 Danny Walton	.60	1.50

1971 Brewers Team Issue

This 18-photo set features members of the Milwaukee Brewers. The photos are not dated, but can be identified as a 1971 issue since Bill Voss' card is included in the set and this was his first year with the team. Additionally, Tommy Harper's card is included and 1971 was his final year with the Brewers. The photos are printed on thin paper stock that has a pebbled texture. They measure approximately 4 1/4" by 7" and display black-and-white portraits edged in white. The player's name and team are printed in the top margin. The cards have blank backs and are numbered and checklisted alphabetically below.

COMMON PLAYER (1-18)	8.00	20.00
1 Max Alvis	.60	1.50
2 Dave Bristol MG	.60	1.50
3 Tommy Harper	.75	2.00
4 Mike Hegan	.75	2.00
5 Mike Hershberger	.60	1.50
6 Lew Krausse	.60	1.50
7 Ted Kubiak	.60	1.50
8 Dave May	.60	1.50
9 Jerry McNertney	.60	1.50
10 Bill Parsons	.60	1.50
11 Marty Pattin	.60	1.50
12 Roberto Pena	.60	1.50
13 Ellie Rodriguez	.60	1.50
14 Phil Roof	.60	1.50
15 Ken Sanders	.60	1.50
16 Ted Savage	.60	1.50
17 Bill Voss	.60	1.50
18 Danny Walton	.60	1.50

1975 Brewers Broadcasters

This seven-card standard-size set features four announcer cards and three schedule cards. The cards were issued as a seven-card pack with a piece of Topps gum included. All the cards have on the fronts black and white photos, with orange picture frame borders on a white card face. The backs are gray and present either comments on the announcers or broadcast schedules. The first four cards are numbered on the back.

COMMON PLAYER (1-4)	10.00	25.00
1 Jim Irwin ANN	1.25	3.00
2 Gary Bender ANN	1.50	4.00
3 Bob Uecker ANN	4.00	10.00
4 Merle Harmon ANN	2.00	5.00
x Television Schedule/(unnumbered)	1.25	3.00
x Radio Schedule Part 1/(unnumbered)	1.25	3.00
x Radio Schedule Part 2/(unnumbered)	1.25	3.00

1976 Brewers A and P

This 16-card set of the Milwaukee Brewers measures approximately 5 7/8" by 9". The white-bordered fronts feature color player head photos with a facsimile autograph below. The backs are blank. The cards are unnumbered and checklisted below in alphabetical order. They were issued four at a time over a four week period at participating A and P stores. These cards were made available to customers who bought specially marked items.

COMPLETE SET (16)	8.00	20.00
1 Hank Aaron	4.00	10.00
2 Pete Broberg	.20	.50
3 Jim Colborn	.20	.50
4 Mike Hegan	.20	.50
5 Von Joshua	.20	.50
6 Tim Johnson	.20	.50
7 Sixto Lezcano	.20	.50
8 Charlie Moore	.20	.50
9 Don Money	.20	.50
10 Darrell Porter	.60	1.50
11 George Scott	.60	1.50
12 Bill Sharp	.20	.50
13 Jim Slaton	.20	.50
14 Bill Travers	.20	.50
15 Robin Yount	3.00	8.00
16 County Stadium	.20	.50

1979 Brewers Team Issue

These cards, which measure 4" by 5 1/2" were issued either on light paper or on card stock. Some of these cards were issued both ways. All values are the same no matter what stock was used. These cards were not numbered so we have sequenced them alphabetically.

COMPLETE SET (29)	6.00	15.00
1 Jerry Augustine	.20	.50
2 George Bamberger MG	.20	.50
3 Sal Bando	.30	.75
4 Mike Caldwell	.20	.50
5 Bill Castro	.20	.50
6 Cecil Cooper	.40	1.00
7 Reggie Cleveland	.20	.50
8 Dick Davis	.20	.50
9 Ray Fosse	.20	.50
10 Bob Galasso	.20	.50
11 Jim Gantner	.20	.50
12 Moose Haas	.20	.50
13 Larry Haney CO	.20	.50
14 Larry Hisle	.20	.50
15 Frank Howard CO	.30	.75
16 Harvey Kuenn CO	.30	.75
17 Sixto Lezcano	.20	.50
18 Buck Martinez	.30	.75
19 Cal McLish CO	.20	.50
20 Bob McClure	.20	.50
21 Don Money	.20	.50
22 Ben Oglivie	.20	.50
23 Buck Rodgers CO	.20	.50
24 Jim Slaton	.20	.50
25 Lary Sorensen	.20	.50
26 Gorman Thomas	.30	.75
27 Bill Travers	.20	.50
28 Jim Wohlford	.20	.50
29 Robin Yount	2.00	5.00

1980 Brewers Team Issue

These 24 photos were issued by the team and feature members of the 1980 Milwaukee Brewers. The photos are unnumbered and sequenced in alphabetical order.

COMPLETE SET	6.00	15.00
1 Jerry Augustine	.20	.50
2 George Bamberger MG	.20	.50
3 Sal Bando	.30	.75
4 Mark Brouhard	.20	.50
5 Mike Caldwell	.20	.50
6 Bill Castro	.20	.50
7 Reggie Cleveland	.20	.50
8 Dick Davis	.20	.50
9 Jim Gantner	.30	.75
10 Moose Haas	.20	.50
11 Larry Haney CO	.20	.50
12 Ron Hansen CO	.20	.50
13 Larry Hisle	.20	.50
14 Frank Howard CO	.30	.75
15 Harvey Kuenn CO	.30	.75
16 Sixto Lezcano	.20	.50
17 Buck Martinez	.30	.75
18 Cal McLish CO	.20	.50
19 Don Money	.30	.75
20 Ben Oglivie	.30	.75
21 Buck Rodgers CO	.20	.50
22 Lary Sorenson	.20	.50
23 Gorman Thomas	.30	.75
24 Robin Yount	2.00	5.00

1909 Briggs E97

The cards in this 32-card set measure 1 1/2" by 2 3/4". The C.A. Briggs Company distributed this set in 1909, and it is one of the most highly prized of caramel issues. The cards come in two distinct varieties: one group in color with a brown print checklist on back; the other with identical player poses in black and white with blank backs. A comparison of team and name variations suggests that the black and white set pre-dates the color issue. The list below has been correctly alphabetized and hence does not exactly follow the checklist back order.

COMPLETE SET (32)	25,000.00	50,000.00
1 Jimmy Austin	500.00	1,000.00
2 Joe Birmingham	500.00	1,000.00
3 William J. Bradley	500.00	1,000.00
4 Kitty Bransfield	500.00	1,000.00
5 Howie Camnitz	500.00	1,000.00
6 Bill Carrigan	500.00	1,000.00
7 Harry Davis	500.00	1,000.00
8 Josh Devore	500.00	1,000.00
9 Mickey Doolan	500.00	1,000.00
10 Bull Durham	500.00	1,000.00
11 Jimmy Dygert	500.00	1,000.00
12A Topsy Hartsel	600.00	1,200.00
12B Topsy Hartsell (Hartsel)	500.00	1,000.00
13 Charlie Hemphill	500.00	1,000.00
14 Bill Heinchman (Hinchman)	500.00	1,000.00
15 Willie Keeler	2,500.00	5,000.00
16 Joseph J. Kelly (Kelley)	1,250.00	2,500.00
17 Red Kleinow	500.00	1,000.00
18 Rube Kroh	500.00	1,000.00
19 Amby McConnell	500.00	1,000.00
20 Matty McIntyre	500.00	1,000.00
21 Chief Meyers	600.00	1,200.00
22 Earl Moore	500.00	1,000.00
23 George Mullin	500.00	1,000.00
24 Red Murray	500.00	1,000.00
25 Simon Nichols (Nicholls)	500.00	1,000.00
26 Claude Rossman	500.00	1,000.00
27 Admiral Schlei	500.00	1,000.00
28A Harry Steinfeldt	600.00	1,200.00
28B Harry Steinfeldt/No T in Steinfeldt	1,500.00	3,000.00
29A Dennis Sullivan:/Boston	5,000.00	10,000.00
29B Dennis Sullivan:/Chicago	600.00	1,200.00
30A Cy Young/Boston Nat'l	2,000.00	4,000.00
30B Cy Young: Cleveland	1,500.00	3,000.00

1932 Briggs Chocolate

This set was issued by C.A. Briggs Chocolate company in 1932. The cards feature 31-different sports with each card including an artist's rendering of a sporting event. Although players are not named, it is thought that most were modeled after famous athletes of the time. The cardbacks include a written portion about the sport and an offer from Briggs for free baseball equipment for building a compete set of cards.

24 Baseball	800.00	1,500.00

1953-54 Briggs

The cards in this 37-card set measure 2 1/4" by 3 1/2". The 1953-54 Briggs Hot Dog set of color cards contains 25 Senators and 12 known players from the Dodgers, Yankees and Giants. They were issued in two card panels in the Washington, D.C. area as part of the hot dog package itself. The cards are unnumbered and are printed on waxed cardboard, and the style of the Senator cards differs from that of the New York players. The latter appear in poses which also exist in the Dan Dee and Stahl Meyer card sets. The catalog designation is F154. In the checklist below the Washington players are numbered 1-25 alphabetically by name and the New York players are numbered 26-40 similarly.

COMPLETE SET (40)	8,000.00	16,000.00
COMMON CARD	100.00	200.00
COMMON PLAYER (29-40)	150.00	300.00
1 Jim Busby	100.00	200.00
2 Tommy Byrne	100.00	200.00
3 Gilbert Coan	100.00	200.00
4 Sonny Dixon	100.00	200.00
5 Ed Fitzgerald	100.00	200.00
6 Mickey Grasso	100.00	200.00
7 Mel Hoderlein	100.00	200.00
8 Jackie Jensen	200.00	400.00
9 Connie Marrero	100.00	200.00
10 Carmen Mauro	100.00	200.00
11 Walt Masterson	100.00	200.00
12 Mickey McDermott	100.00	200.00
13 Julio Moreno	100.00	200.00
14 Bob Oldis	100.00	200.00
15 Erwin Porterfield	100.00	200.00
16 Pete Runnels	100.00	200.00
17 Johnny Schmitz	100.00	200.00
18 Angel Scull	100.00	200.00
19 Spec Shea	100.00	200.00
20 Albert Sima	100.00	200.00
21 Chuck Stobbs	100.00	200.00
22 Wayne Terwilliger	100.00	200.00
23 Joe Tipton	100.00	200.00
24 Tom Umphlett	100.00	200.00
25 Mickey Vernon	300.00	600.00
26 Clyde Vollmer	100.00	200.00
27 Gene Verble	100.00	200.00
28 Eddie Yost	100.00	200.00
29 Hank Bauer	300.00	600.00
30 Carl Erskine	300.00	600.00
31 Gil Hodges	500.00	1,000.00
32 Monte Irvin	500.00	1,000.00
33 Whitey Lockman	300.00	600.00
34 Mickey Mantle	4,000.00	8,000.00
35 Willie Mays	2,000.00	4,000.00
36 Gil McDougald	300.00	600.00
37 Don Mueller	300.00	600.00
38 Don Newcombe	300.00	600.00
39 Phil Rizzuto	500.00	1,000.00
40 Duke Snider	1,000.00	2,000.00

1941 Browns W753

The cards in this 29-card set measure approximately 2 1/8" by 2 5/8". The 1941 W753 set features unnumbered cards of the St. Louis Browns. The cards are numbered below alphabetically by player's name. Similar to the W711-2 set, it was issued in a box with a reverse side resembling a mailing label. These sets were also available via mail-order. This set is valued at an extra $100 when still in its original mailing box.

COMPLETE SET (30)	250.00	500.00
1 Johnny Allen	12.50	30.00
2 Elden Auker	12.50	30.00
3 Donald L. Barnes OWN	10.00	25.00
4 Johnny Berardino	20.00	50.00
5 George Caster	10.00	25.00
6 Harland Clift	12.50	30.00
7 Roy J. Cullenbine	10.00	25.00
8 William O. DeWitt GM	10.00	25.00
9 Robert Estalella	10.00	25.00
10 Rick Ferrell	50.00	100.00
11 Dennis W. Galehouse	12.50	30.00
12 Joseph L. Grace	10.00	25.00
13 Frank Grube	10.00	25.00
14 Robert A. Harris	10.00	25.00
15 Donald Heffner	10.00	25.00
16 Fred Hofmann	10.00	25.00
17 Walter F. Judnich	10.00	25.00
18 Jack Kramer	10.00	25.00
19 Chester(Chet) Laabs	10.00	25.00
20 John Lucadello	10.00	25.00
21 George H. McQuinn	10.00	25.00
22 Robert Muncrief Jr.	10.00	25.00
23 John Niggeling	10.00	25.00

24 Fritz Ostermueller	10.00	25.00
25 James(Luke) Sewell MG	12.50	30.00
26 Alan C. Strange	10.00	25.00
27 Bob Swift	10.00	25.00
28 James(Zack) Taylor CO	10.00	25.00
29 Bill Trotter	10.00	25.00
30 Title Card/(Order Coupon on back)	10.00	25.00

1952 Browns Postcards

The 12-card set has glossy black and white with PC backs. It appears that backs determine the year. The 1952 cards have "Post Card" in script block lettering over the top if you lay the card down horizontally. There is a line dividing the back on one side"Correspondence" and the other "Address". There is no postage box. The cards are unnumbered and listed alphabetically.

COMPLETE SET (12)	60.00	120.00
1 Tommy Byrne	8.00	20.00
2 Bob Cain	6.00	15.00
3 Clint Courtney	6.00	15.00
4 Jim Delsing	6.00	15.00
5 Jim Dyck	6.00	15.00
6 Marty Marion	12.50	30.00
7 Cass Michaels	6.00	15.00
8 Bob Nieman	6.00	15.00
9 Satchel Paige	20.00	50.00
10 Duane Pillette	6.00	15.00
11 Jim Rivera	6.00	15.00
12 Bobby Young	6.00	15.00

1953 Browns Postcards

All the 1953 cards have divided backs, but "Photo Post Card" in double block lettering and then "Address" under that in smaller lettering. The only variation known is one of Ned Garver where the "Photo Post Card" is in a different type of lettering. Everything else is the same. The set is unnumbered and listed below in alphabetical order. The Don Larsen card predates his Bowman Rookie Card.

COMPLETE SET (31)	200.00	400.00
1 Neil Berry	6.00	15.00
2 Mike Blyzka	6.00	15.00
3 Harry Breechen	8.00	20.00
4 Bob Cain	6.00	15.00
5 Clint Courtney	6.00	15.00
6 Jim Dyck	6.00	15.00
7 Hank Edwards	6.00	15.00
8 Ned Garver	8.00	20.00
9 Johnny Groth	6.00	15.00
10 Bobo Holloman	8.00	20.00
11 Bill Hunter	6.00	15.00
12 Dick Kokos	6.00	15.00
13 Dick Kryhoski	6.00	15.00
14 Max Lanier	6.00	15.00
15 Don Larsen	10.00	25.00
16 Don Lenhardt	6.00	15.00
17 Dick Littlefield	6.00	15.00
18 Marty Marion	12.50	30.00
19 Babe Martin	6.00	15.00
20 Willy Miranda	6.00	15.00
21 Les Moss	6.00	15.00
22 Bill Norman	6.00	15.00
23 Satchel Paige	30.00	60.00
24 Satchel Paige	30.00	60.00
25 Duane Pillette	6.00	15.00
26 Bob Sheffing	6.00	15.00
27 Roy Sievers	10.00	25.00
28 Marlin Stuart	6.00	15.00
29 Virgil Trucks	6.00	15.00
30 Bill Veeck	12.50	30.00
31 Vic Wertz	8.00	20.00

1887 Buchner Gold Coin N284

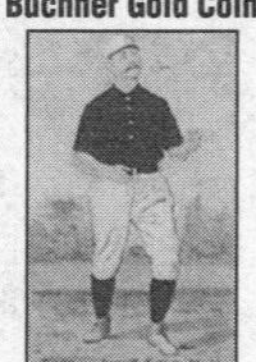

The baseball players found in this Buchner set are a part of a larger group of cards portraying policemen, jockeys and actors, all of which were issued with the tobacco brand "Gold Coin." The set is comprised of three major groupings or types. In the first type, nine players from eight teams, plus three Brooklyn players, are all portrayed in identical poses according to position. In the second type, St. Louis has 14 players depicted in poses which are not repeated. The last group contains 53 additional cards which vary according to pose, team change, spelling, etc. These third type cards are indicated in the checklist below by an asterisk. In all, there are 116 individuals portrayed on 142 cards. The existence of an additional player in the set, McClellan of Brooklyn, has never been verified and the card probably doesn't exist. The set was issued circa 1887. The cards are numbered below in alphabetical order within team with teams themselves listed in alphabetical order: Baltimore (1-4), Boston (5-13), Brooklyn (14-17), Chicago (18-26), Detroit (27-35), Indianapolis (36-47), LaCrosse (48-51), Milwaukee (52-55), New York Mets (56-63), New York (64-73), Philadelphia (74-83), Pittsburg (84-92), St. Louis (93-106), and Washington (107-117).

COMPLETE SET (152)	25,000.00	50,000.00
COMMON ST. LOUIS	200.00	400.00
COMMON CARD *	125.00	250.00
1 Tommy(Oyster) Burns *	250.00	500.00
2 Chris Fulmer *	250.00	500.00
3 Matt Kilroy	250.00	500.00
4 Blondie Purcell *	250.00	500.00
5 John Burdock	300.00	600.00
6 Bill Daley	300.00	600.00
7 Joe Hornung	300.00	600.00
8 Dick Johnston	300.00	600.00
9A King Kelly: Boston Right field	750.00	1,500.00
9B King Kelly: Boston Catcher *	1,250.00	2,500.00
10A John Morrell: Boston/(Both hands out- stretched	300.00	600.00
10B John Morrell: Boston */(Hands clasped near chin	250.00	500.00
11A Hoss Radbourn: Boston Sic, Radbourne	600.00	1,200.00
11B Hoss Radbourn: Boston */(Sic& Radbourne; hands	750.00	1,500.00
12 Ezra Sutton	300.00	600.00
13 Sam Wise	300.00	600.00
14 Bill McClellan: Brooklyn Never confirmed		
15 Jimmy Peoples	300.00	600.00
16 Bill Phillips	300.00	600.00
17 Henry Porter	300.00	600.00
18A Cap Anson Both hands out- stretche	1,500.00	3,000.00
18B Cap Anson Left hand on hip righ	3,000.00	6,000.00
19 Tom Burns	300.00	600.00
20A John Clarkson Chicago	750.00	1,500.00
20B John Clarkson: Chicago */(Right arm extended& l	1,000.00	2,000.00
21 Silver Flint	300.00	600.00
22 Fred Pfeffer	300.00	600.00
23 Jimmy Ryan	400.00	800.00
24 Billy Sullivan	400.00	800.00
25 Billy Sunday	750.00	1,500.00
26A Ned Williamson: Chicago Shortstop	300.00	600.00
26B Ned Williamson: Chicago Second base *	250.00	500.00
27 Charlie Bennett	400.00	800.00
28A Dan Brouthers: Detroit Fielding	750.00	1,500.00
28B Dan Brouthers: Detroit * Batting	1,000.00	2,000.00
29 Fred Dunlap	300.00	600.00
30 Charlie Getzien	300.00	600.00
31 Ned Hanlon	600.00	1,200.00
32 Jim Manning	300.00	600.00
33A Hardy Richardson: Detroit/(Hands together in fr	300.00	600.00
33B Hardy Richardson: Detroit */(Right hand holding#	250.00	500.00
34A Sam Thompson: Detroit Looking up with hands at	750.00	1,500.00
34B Sam Thompson: Detroit * Hands chest high	1,000.00	2,000.00
35 Deacon White	500.00	1,000.00
36 Tug Arundels	300.00	600.00
37 Charley Bassett	300.00	600.00
38 Henry Boyle *	250.00	500.00
39 John Cahill *	250.00	500.00
40A Jerry Denny: Indianapolis/(Hands on knees& legs	300.00	600.00
40B Jerry Denny: Indianapolis */(Hands on knees& le	250.00	500.00
41A Jack Glasscock: Indianapolis/(Crouching& catch-#	400.00	800.00
41B Jack Glasscock: Indianapolis * Hands on knees	300.00	600.00
42 John Healy	300.00	600.00
43 George Meyers *	250.00	500.00
44 Jack McGeachy	300.00	600.00
45 Mark Polhemus	300.00	600.00
46A Emmett Seery: Indianapolis/(Hands together in f	300.00	600.00
46B Emmett Seery: Indianapolis */(Hands outstretched	400.00	800.00
47 Shomberg	300.00	600.00
48 John Corbett *	250.00	500.00
49 Crowley *	250.00	500.00
50 Kennedy *	250.00	500.00
51 Rooks *	250.00	500.00
52 Forster *	250.00	500.00
53 Hart *	250.00	500.00
54 Morrissy *	250.00	500.00
55 Strauss *	250.00	500.00
56 Ed Cushmann *	250.00	500.00
57 Jim Donohue *	250.00	500.00
58 Dude Esterbrooke *	250.00	500.00
59 Joe Gerhardt *	250.00	500.00
60 Frank Hankinson *	250.00	500.00
61 Jack Nelson *	250.00	500.00
62 Dave Orr *	250.00	500.00
63 James Rosemann *	250.00	500.00
64A Roger Connor: New York/(Both hands out- stretch	750.00	1,500.00
64B Roger Connor: New York */(Hands outstretched& p	1,000.00	2,000.00
65 Pat Deasley *	250.00	500.00
66A Mike Dorgan Fielding	300.00	600.00
66B Mike Dorgan Batting *	250.00	500.00
67A Buck Ewing: New York (Ball in left hand& right a	750.00	1,500.00
67B Buck Ewing New York * Appears ready to clap	1,000.00	2,000.00
68A Pete Gillespie: New York Fielding	300.00	600.00
68B Pete Gillespie: New York Batting *	250.00	500.00
69 George Gore	300.00	600.00
70A Tim Keefe: New York	750.00	1,500.00
70B Tim Keefe: New York * Ball just released from	1,000.00	2,000.00
71A Jim O'Rourke: New York Hands cupped in front	750.00	1,500.00
71B Jim O'Rourke: New York */(Hands on knees& looki	1,000.00	2,000.00
72A Danny Richardson: New York Third base	300.00	600.00
72B Danny Richardson: New York Second base*	250.00	500.00
73A John M. Ward: New York/(Crouching& catch- ing a	750.00	1,500.00
73B John M. Ward: New York * Hands by left knee	1,000.00	2,000.00
73C John M. Ward: New York * Hands on knees	750.00	1,500.00
74A Ed Andrews: Philadelphia/(Hands together in fro	300.00	600.00
74B Ed Andrews: Philadelphia */(Catching& hands wai	250.00	500.00
75 Charlie Bastian	300.00	600.00
76 Dan Casey *	250.00	500.00
77 Jack Clements	300.00	600.00
78 Sid Farrar	400.00	800.00
79 Charlie Ferguson	300.00	600.00
80 Jim Fogarty	300.00	600.00
81 Arthur Irwin	300.00	600.00
82A Joel Mulvey: Philadelphia Hands on knees	300.00	600.00
82B Joel Mulvey: Philadelphia */(Hands together abo	250.00	500.00
83A Pete Wood Philadelphia Fielding	300.00	600.00
83B Pete Wood: Phila- delphia HOR (Stealing a Base)	400.00	800.00
84 Sam Barkley	300.00	600.00
85 Ed Beecher:	300.00	600.00
86 Tom Brown	300.00	600.00
87 Fred Carroll	300.00	600.00
88 John Coleman	300.00	600.00
89 Jim McCormick	300.00	600.00
90 Doggie Miller	300.00	600.00
91 Pop Smith	300.00	600.00
92 Art Whitney	300.00	600.00
93 Sam Barkley	400.00	800.00
94 Doc Bushong	400.00	800.00
95 Bob Carruthers	500.00	1,000.00
96 Charles Comiskey	1,250.00	2,500.00
97 Dave Foutz	400.00	800.00
98 William Gleason	500.00	1,000.00
99 Arlie Latham	600.00	1,200.00
100 Jumbo McGinnis	400.00	800.00
101 Hugh Nicol	400.00	800.00
102 James O'Neil	400.00	800.00
103 Yank Robinson	400.00	800.00
104 Sullivan	400.00	800.00
105 Chris Von Der Ahe OWN St. Louis/(Photo	1,500.00	3,000.00
106 Curt Welch	500.00	1,000.00
107 Cliff Carroll	300.00	600.00
108 Craig *	250.00	500.00
109 Sam Crane *	250.00	500.00
110 Ed Dailey	300.00	600.00
111 Jim Donnelly	300.00	600.00
112A Jack Farrell: Washington Ball in left hand, rig	300.00	600.00
112B Jack Farrell: Washington */(Ball in hands near	250.00	500.00
113 Barney Gilligan	300.00	600.00
114A Paul Hines: Washington Fielding	300.00	600.00
114B Paul Hines: Washington * Batting	250.00	500.00
115 Al Myers	300.00	600.00
116 Billy O'Brien	300.00	600.00
117 Jim Whitney	300.00	600.00

1932 Bulgaria Zigaretten Sport Photos

256 Babe Ruth Max Schmeling	40.00	80.00

1977 Burger Chef Discs

The individual discs measure approximately 2 1/2" in diameter and contain a burger-related caricature on the reverse. There were nine discs on each tray; five on the front and four on the back. Each tray contained one team and there were 24 different trays, obviously one for each team. On the tray the copyright notice indicates 1977. The player photos are shown without team logos on their caps. We have sequenced this set in the following order: Houston (1-9), St. Louis (10-18), Texas (19-27), Boston (28-36), Baltimore (37-45), Minnesota (46-54), Cleveland (55-63), Kansas City (64-72), Chicago White Sox (73-81), Milwaukee (82-90), Detroit (91-99), San Francisco (100-108), Oakland (109-117), California (118-126), San Diego (127-135), New York Mets (136-144), Los Angeles (145-153), Montreal (154-162), Philadelphia (163-171), New York Yankees (172-180), Pirates (181-189), Chicago Cubs (190-198), Cincinnati (199-207), Atlanta (208-216). No 1977 expansion teams were featured in this set. Complete Panels are worth twice the amount of the values for each team.

COMPLETE SET (216)	75.00	150.00
1 J.R. Richard	.20	.50
2 Enos Cabell	.10	.25
3 Leon Roberts	.10	.25
4 Ken Forsch	.10	.25
5 Roger Metzger	.10	.25
6 Bob Watson	.20	.50
7 Cesar Cedeno	.20	.50
8 Joe Ferguson	.10	.25
9 Jose Cruz	.20	.50
10 Al Hrabosky	.10	.25
11 Keith Hernandez	.60	1.50
12 Pete Falcone	.10	.25
13 Ken Reitz	.10	.25
14 John Denny	.10	.25
15 Lou Brock	1.50	4.00
16 Ted Simmons	.40	1.00
17 Bake McBride	.10	.25
18 Mike Tyson	.10	.25
19 Campy Campaneris	.20	.50
20 Gaylord Perry	1.25	3.00
21 Lenny Randle	.10	.25
22 Bert Blyleven	.40	1.00
23 Jim Sundberg	.20	.50
24 Mike Hargrove	.20	.50
25 Tom Grieve	.20	.50
26 Toby Harrah	.10	.25
27 Juan Beniquez	.10	.25
28 Rick Burleson	.10	.25
29 Jim Rice	.60	1.50
30 Dwight Evans	.40	1.00
31 Fergie Jenkins	1.25	3.00
32 Bill Lee	.10	.25
33 Carlton Fisk	2.50	6.00
34 Luis Tiant	.40	1.00
35 Fred Lynn	.20	.50
36 Carl Yastrzemski	1.50	4.00
37 Al Bumbry	.10	.25
38 Mark Belanger	.20	.50
39 Paul Blair	.10	.25
40 Ross Grimsley	.10	.25
41 Ken Singleton	.20	.50
42 Jim Palmer	1.50	4.00
43 Brooks Robinson	1.50	4.00
44 Doug DeCinces	.20	.50
45 Lee May	.20	.50
46 Tom Johnson	.10	.25
47 Dave Goltz	.10	.25
48 Dan Ford	.10	.25
49 Larry Hisle	.10	.25
50 Mike Cubbage	.10	.25
51 Rod Carew	1.50	4.00
52 Bobby Randall	.10	.25
53 Butch Wynegar	.10	.25
54 Lyman Bostock	.20	.50
55 Duane Kuiper	.10	.25
56 Rick Manning	.10	.25
57 Buddy Bell	.40	1.00
58 Dennis Eckersley	2.00	5.00
59 Wayne Garland	.10	.25
60 Dave LaRoche	.10	.25
61 Rick Waits	.10	.25
62 Ray Fosse	.10	.25
63 Frank Duffy	.10	.25
64 Paul Splittorff	.10	.25
65 Amos Otis	.20	.50
66 Tom Poquette	.10	.25
67 Fred Patek	.10	.25
68 Doug Bird	.10	.25
69 John Mayberry	.10	.25
70 Dennis Leonard	.10	.25
71 George Brett	10.00	25.00
72 Hal McRae	.40	1.00
73 Chet Lemon	.20	.50
74 Jorge Orta	.10	.25
75 Richie Zisk	.10	.25
76 Lamar Johnson	.10	.25
77 Bart Johnson	.10	.25
78 Jack Brohamer	.10	.25
79 Jim Spencer	.10	.25
80 Ralph Garr	.10	.25
81 Bucky Dent	.20	.50
82 Jerry Augustine	.10	.25
83 Jim Slaton	.10	.25
84 Charlie Moore	.10	.25
85 Von Joshua	.10	.25
86 Eduardo Rodriquez	.10	.25

87 Sal Bando	.20	.50
88 Robin Yount	2.50	6.00
89 Sixto Lezcano	.10	.25
90 Bill Travers	.10	.25
91 Ben Oglivie	.10	.25
92 Mark Fidrych	2.00	5.00
93 Aurelio Rodriguez	.10	.25
94 Bill Freehan	.40	1.00
95 John Hiller	.10	.25
96 Rusty Staub	.40	1.00
97 Willie Horton	.20	.50
98 Ron LeFlore	.20	.50
99 Jason Thompson	.20	.50
100 Marty Perez	.10	.25
101 Randy Moffitt	.10	.25
102 Gary Thomasson	.10	.25
103 Jim Barr	.10	.25
104 Larry Herndon	.10	.25
105 Bobby Murcer	.40	1.00
106 John Montefusco	.10	.25
107 Willie Crawford	.10	.25
108 Chris Speier	.10	.25
109 Phil Garner	.40	1.00
110 Mike Torrez	.10	.25
111 Manny Sanguillen	.10	.25
112 Stan Bahnsen	.10	.25
113 Mike Norris	.10	.25
114 Vida Blue	.40	1.00
115 Claudell Washington	.20	.50
116 Bill North	.10	.25
117 Paul Lindblad	.10	.25
118 Paul Hartzell	.10	.25
119 Dave Chalk	.10	.25
120 Ron Jackson	.10	.25
121 Jerry Remy	.10	.25
122 Frank Tanana	.40	1.00
123 Nolan Ryan	10.00	25.00
124 Bobby Bonds	.20	.50
125 Joe Rudi	.20	.50
126 Bobby Grich	.40	1.00
127 Butch Metzger	.10	.25
128 Doug Rader	.10	.25
129 George Hendrick	.20	.50
130 David Winfield	3.00	8.00
131 Gene Tenace	.40	1.00
132 Randy Jones	.10	.25
133 Rollie Fingers	1.25	3.00
134 Mike Ivie	.10	.25
135 Enzo Hernandez	.10	.25
136 Ed Kranepool	.10	.25
137 John Matlack	.10	.25
138 Felix Millan	.10	.25
139 Skip Lockwood	.10	.25
140 John Stearns	.10	.25
141 Dave Kingman	.60	1.50
142 Tom Seaver	2.50	6.00
143 Jerry Koosman	.40	1.00
144 Bud Harrelson	.10	.25
145 Davey Lopes	.20	.50
146 Rick Monday	.10	.25
147 Don Sutton	1.25	3.00
148 Rick Rhoden	.10	.25
149 Doug Rau	.10	.25
150 Steve Garvey	.75	2.00
151 Steve Yeager	.10	.25
152 Reggie Smith	.20	.50
153 Ron Cey	.40	1.00
154 Gary Carter	2.00	5.00
155 Del Unser	.10	.25
156 Tim Foli	.10	.25
157 Barry Foote	.10	.25
158 Ellis Valentine	.10	.25
159 Steve Rogers	.10	.25
160 Tony Perez	1.00	2.50
161 Larry Parrish	.20	.50
162 Dave Cash	.10	.25
163 Greg Luzinski	.40	1.00
164 Bob Boone	.40	1.00
165 Tug McGraw	.40	1.00
166 Jay Johnstone	.20	.50
167 Garry Maddox	.10	.25
168 Mike Schmidt	6.00	15.00
169 Jim Kaat	.60	1.50
170 Larry Bowa	.40	1.00
171 Steve Carlton	2.50	6.00
172 Don Gullett	.10	.25
173 Chris Chambliss	.10	.25
174 Graig Nettles	.40	1.00
175 Willie Randolph	.60	1.50
176 Reggie Jackson	2.50	6.00
177 Thurman Munson	1.00	2.50
178 Catfish Hunter	1.50	4.00
179 Roy White	.20	.50
180 Mickey Rivers	.10	.25
181 Jerry Reuss	.20	.50
182 Rennie Stennett	.10	.25
183 Bill Robinson	.10	.25
184 Frank Taveras	.10	.25
185 Duffy Dyer	.10	.25
186 Willie Stargell	1.50	4.00
187 Dave Parker	1.00	2.50
188 John Candelaria	.20	.50
189 Al Oliver	.40	1.00
190 Joe Wallis	.10	.25
191 Manny Trillo	.10	.25
192 Bill Bonham	.10	.25
193 Rich Reuschel	.20	.50
194 Ray Burris	.10	.25
195 Bill Buckner	.20	.50
196 Jerry Morales	.10	.25
197 Jose Cardenal	.10	.25
198 Bill Madlock	.40	1.00
199 Dan Driessen	.10	.25
200 Dave Concepcion	.40	1.00
201 George Foster	.40	1.00
202 Cesar Geronimo	.10	.25
203 Gary Nolan	.10	.25
204 Pete Rose	4.00	10.00
205 Johnny Bench	2.50	6.00
206 Ken Griffey	.40	1.00
207 Joe Morgan	1.50	4.00
208 Dick Ruthven	.10	.25
209 Phil Niekro	1.25	3.00
210 Gary Matthews	.20	.50
211 Willie Montanez	.10	.25
212 Jerry Royster	.10	.25
213 Andy Messersmith	.10	.25
214 Jeff Burroughs	.20	.50
215 Tom Paciorek	.20	.50
216 Darrel Chaney	.10	.25

1980 Burger King Pitch/Hit/Run

The cards in this 34-card set measure 2 1/2" by 3 1/2". The "Pitch, Hit, and Run" set was a promotion introduced by Burger King in 1980. The cards carry a Burger King logo on the front and those marked by an asterisk in the checklist contain a different photo from that found in the regularly issued Topps series. For example, Nolan Ryan was shown as a California Angel and Joe Morgan was a Cincinnati Red in the 1980 Topps regular set. Cards 1-11 are pitchers, 12-22 are hitters, and 23-33 are speedsters. Within each subgroup, the players are numbered corresponding to the alphabetical order of their names.

COMPLETE SET (34)	10.00	25.00
1 Vida Blue *	.20	.50
2 Steve Carlton	.75	2.00
3 Rollie Fingers	.40	1.00
4 Ron Guidry *	.20	.50
5 Jerry Koosman *	.08	.25
6 Phil Niekro	.50	1.25
7 Jim Palmer *	.75	2.00
8 J.R. Richard	.08	.25
9 Nolan Ryan *	7.50	15.00
Houston Astros		
10 Tom Seaver *	1.00	2.50
11 Bruce Sutter	.40	1.00
12 Don Baylor	.20	.50
13 George Brett	2.50	6.00
14 Rod Carew	.60	1.50
15 George Foster	.08	.25
16 Keith Hernandez *	.20	.50
17 Reggie Jackson *	1.50	4.00
18 Fred Lynn *	.20	.50
19 Dave Parker	.08	.25
20 Jim Rice	.08	.25
21 Pete Rose	1.50	4.00
22 Dave Winfield *	1.25	3.00
23 Bobby Bonds *	.20	.50
24 Enos Cabell	.02	.10
25 Cesar Cedeno	.08	.25
26 Julio Cruz	.02	.10
27 Ron LeFlore *	.08	.25
28 Dave Lopes *	.08	.25
29 Omar Moreno *	.08	.25
30 Joe Morgan *	1.00	2.50
Houston Astros		
31 Bill North	.02	.10
32 Frank Taveras	.02	.10
33 Willie Wilson	.08	.25
NNO Checklist Card TP	.01	.05

1938-59 George Burke PC744

The Burke postcards were issued by Chicago photographer George Burke during the period from 1938 through the 1950's. Because there are hundreds known and new ones are discovered frequently, a checklist has not been provided. The reverses feature the stamped name of "Geo. Burke, his address and the city "Chicago"

COMMON CARD (1938-48)	5.00	10.00
COMMON CARD (1948-on)	2.50	5.00

1978 Burlington Free Press

These newspaper inserts feature members of the Boston Red Sox and the Montreal Expos. Since each team was reasonably near Burlington, Vermont -- that is why the set consists of players from those teams. These cards are unnumbered, so we have sequenced them in alphabetical order. There are probably many additions to this set so any additional information is greatly appreciated.

COMPLETE SET	6.00	15.00
1 Bernie Carbo	.40	1.00
2 Dave Cash	.40	1.00
3 Dick Drago	.40	1.00
4 Pepe Frias	.40	1.00
5 Wayne Garrett	.40	1.00
6 Ross Grimsley	.40	1.00
7 Butch Hobson	.40	1.00
8 Bill Lee	.50	1.25
9 Rudy May	.40	1.00
10 Bob Montgomery	.40	1.00
11 Larry Parrish	.40	1.00
12 Jerry Remy	.40	1.00
13 Rodney Scott	.40	1.00
14 Chris Speier	.40	1.00
15 Wayne Twitchell	.40	1.00
16 Del Unser	.40	1.00
17 Ellis Valentine	.40	1.00
18 Dick Williams MG	.40	1.00

1933 Butter Cream R306

The small, elongated (measuring 1 1/4" by 3 1/2") cards of this 30 card set are unnumbered and contain many cut-down, blurry black and white photos. The producer's name is sometimes printed on the reverse. Despite their limitations, Butter Cream cards are highly prized by collectors. The cards have been alphabetized and numbered for reference in the checklist below. There are two varieties of the back for each card: One says "Your estimate of this year to Sept 1st; and "Your estimate of this year to Oct. 1st. The Babe Ruth card within this set is one of the more legendary rarities of the hobby. How rare is this Ruth card? Rare enough that through 1989 it was generally believed that the R306 set was complete at 29 cards. Two copies of the Ruth card, however, surfaced at the 1989 National Convention in Chicago, pushing the checklist up to 30 cards and establishing the R306 issue as perhaps Ruth's rarest card. Though a third (lower grade) copy was known to exist, according to the information provided in REA's 2008 catalog, it was lost in transit in 1990 in a deal involving hobby legends Lew Lipset and Barry Halper. To this date, the number of known copies remains at a mere two, one of which the whereabouts is unknown and the other – graded VgEx 4 by PSA – was offered for sale in REA's May, 2008 auction ultimately commanding $111,625. The Ruth is, understandably, unpriced due to scarcity and the set price references the collection of the 29 standard R306's. It's been theorized that the Ruth was intentionally short-printed perhaps as a stumbling block to send in all 30 cards for a special prize.

COMPLETE SET (29)	4,000.00	8,000.00
1 Earl Averill	300.00	600.00
2 Ed Brandt	200.00	400.00
3 Guy T. Bush	200.00	400.00
4 Mickey Cochrane	400.00	800.00
5 Joe Cronin	400.00	800.00
6 George Earnshaw	200.00	400.00
7 Wesley Ferrell	250.00	500.00
8 Jimmy Foxx	500.00	1,000.00
(Jimmie)		
9 Frank Frisch	400.00	800.00
10 Charles M. Gelbert	200.00	400.00
11 Lefty Grove	400.00	800.00
12 Gabby Hartnett	300.00	600.00
13 Babe Herman	300.00	600.00
14 Chuck Klein	300.00	600.00
15 Ray Kremer	200.00	400.00
16 Fred Lindstrom	300.00	600.00
17 Ted Lyons	300.00	600.00
18 Pepper Martin	250.00	500.00
19 Robert O'Farrell	200.00	400.00
20 Ed A. Rommell	200.00	400.00
21 Charles Root	200.00	400.00
22 Harold Ruel	200.00	400.00
23 Babe Ruth SP		
24 Al Simmons	400.00	800.00
25 Bill Terry	400.00	800.00
26 George Uhle	200.00	400.00
27 Lloyd Waner	300.00	600.00
28 Paul Waner	400.00	800.00
29 Hack Wilson	300.00	600.00
30 Glenn Wright	200.00	400.00

1933 Butterfinger Canadian V94

These large photos measure approximately 6 1/2" by 8 1/2" and are printed on thin paper stock. The fronts feature black-and-white posed action shots within white borders. A facsimile autograph is inscribed across the picture. The backs are blank.

COMPLETE SET	2,000.00	4,000.00
1 Earl Averill	40.00	80.00
2 Larry Benton	20.00	40.00
3 Jim Bottomley	40.00	80.00
4 Tom Bridges	25.00	50.00
5 Bob Brown	20.00	40.00
6 Owen T. Carroll	20.00	40.00
7 Mickey Cochrane	62.50	125.00
8 Roger Cramer	25.00	50.00
9 Joe Cronin	62.50	125.00
10 Alvin Crowder	25.00	50.00
11 Dizzy Dean	75.00	150.00
12 Edward Delker	20.00	40.00
13 Bill Dickey	62.50	125.00
14 Rick Ferrell	40.00	80.00
15 Lew Fonseca	25.00	50.00
16A Jimmy Foxx	75.00	150.00
Name spelled Fox		
(Jimmie)		
16B Jimmie Foxx	20.00	40.00
Name spelled correctly		
17 Chuck Fullis	20.00	40.00
18 Lou Gehrig	150.00	300.00
19 Charles Gehringer	62.50	125.00
20 Lefty Gomez	62.50	125.00
21 Lefty Grove	75.00	150.00
22 Mule Haas	20.00	40.00
23 Chick Hafey	40.00	80.00
24 Bucky Harris	40.00	80.00
25 Frank Higgins	20.00	40.00
26 J. Francis Hogan	20.00	40.00
27 Ed Holley	20.00	40.00
28 Waite Hoyt	40.00	80.00
29 Jim Jordan	20.00	40.00
30 Hal Lee	20.00	40.00
31 Gus Mancuso	25.00	50.00
32 Oscar Melillo	20.00	40.00
33 Austin Moore	20.00	40.00
34 Randy Moore	20.00	40.00
35 Joe Morrissey	20.00	40.00
36 Joe Mowry	20.00	40.00
37 Bobo Newsom	25.00	50.00
38 Ernest Orsatti	20.00	40.00
39 Carl Reynolds	20.00	40.00
40 Walter Roettger	20.00	40.00
41 Babe Ruth	200.00	400.00
42 Blondy Ryan	20.00	40.00
43 John Salveson	20.00	40.00
44 Al Simmons	62.50	125.00
45 Al Smith	20.00	40.00
46 Harold Smith	20.00	40.00
47 Allyn Stout	20.00	40.00
48 Fresco Thompson	25.00	50.00
49 Art Veltman	20.00	40.00
50 Johnny Vergez	20.00	40.00
51 Gerald Walker	20.00	40.00
52 Paul Waner	40.00	80.00
53 Burgess Whitehead	20.00	40.00
54 Earl Whitehill	20.00	40.00
55 Robert Weiland	20.00	40.00
56 Jimmy Wilson	25.00	50.00
57 Bob Worthington	20.00	40.00
58 Tom Zachary	25.00	50.00

1934 Butterfinger Premiums R310

This large-size premium set comes either in paper or on heavy cardboard stock with advertising for Butterfinger or other candy at the top. The heavy cardboard Butterfinger display advertising cards are valued at triple the prices in the list below. The cards are unnumbered and Foxx exists as Fox or Foxx. The cards measure approximately 7 3/4" by 9 3/4" and have a thick off-white border around the player photo.

COMPLETE SET (65)	2,500.00	5,000.00
1 Earl Averill	40.00	80.00
2 Dick Bartell	20.00	40.00
3 Lawrence Benton	20.00	40.00
4 Wally Berger	25.00	50.00
5 Jim Bottomley	40.00	80.00
6 Ralph Boyle	20.00	40.00
7 Tex Carleton	20.00	40.00
8 Owen T. Carroll	20.00	40.00
9 Ben Chapman	20.00	40.00
10 Mickey Cochrane	50.00	100.00
11 Jimmy Collins	20.00	40.00
12 Joe Cronin	50.00	100.00
13 Al Crowder	20.00	40.00
14 Dizzy Dean	100.00	200.00
15 Paul Derringer	25.00	50.00
16 Bill Dickey	50.00	100.00
17 Leo Durocher	50.00	100.00
18 George Earnshaw	20.00	40.00
19 Dick Ferrell	40.00	80.00
20 Lew Fonseca	25.00	50.00
21A Jimmie Fox/(sic& Foxx)	100.00	200.00
21B Jimmie Foxx	100.00	200.00
22 Benny Frey	20.00	40.00
23 Frankie Frisch	50.00	100.00
24 Lou Gehrig	250.00	500.00
25 Charley Gehringer	50.00	100.00
26 Lefty Gomez	50.00	100.00
27 Ray Grabowski	20.00	40.00
28 Lefty Grove	60.00	120.00
29 Mule Haas	20.00	40.00
30 Chick Hafey	40.00	80.00
31 Bucky Harris	40.00	80.00
32 J. Francis Hogan	20.00	40.00
33 Ed Holley	20.00	40.00
34 Rogers Hornsby	75.00	150.00
35 Waite Hoyt	40.00	80.00
36 Walter Johnson	150.00	300.00
37 Jim Jordan	20.00	40.00
38 Joe Kuhel	20.00	40.00
39 Hal Lee	20.00	40.00
40 Gus Mancuso	20.00	40.00
41 Heinie Manush	40.00	80.00
42 Fred Marberry	20.00	40.00
43 Pepper Martin	25.00	50.00
44 Oscar Melillo	20.00	40.00
45 Johnny Moore	20.00	40.00
46 Joe Morrisey	20.00	40.00
47 Joe Mowry	20.00	40.00
48 Bob O'Farrell	20.00	40.00
49 Mel Ott	60.00	120.00
50 Monte Pearson	25.00	50.00
51 Carl Reynolds	20.00	40.00
52 Red Ruffing	40.00	80.00
53 Babe Ruth	300.00	600.00
54 John Ryan	20.00	40.00
55 Al Simmons	40.00	80.00
56 Alfred Smith	40.00	80.00
57 Al Spohrer	20.00	40.00
58 Gus Suhr	20.00	40.00
59 Steve Swetonic	25.00	50.00
60 Dazzy Vance	40.00	80.00
61 Joe Vosmik	20.00	40.00
62 Lloyd Waner	40.00	80.00
63 Paul Waner	40.00	80.00
64 Sam West	20.00	40.00
65 Earl Whitehill	20.00	40.00
66 Jimmy Wilson	20.00	40.00

1950-56 Callahan HOF W576

The cards in this 82-card set measure approximately 1 3/4" by 2 1/2". The 1950-56 Callahan Hall of Fame set was issued over a number of years at the Baseball Hall of Fame museum in Cooperstown, New York. New cards were added to the set each year when new members were inducted into the Hall of Fame. The cards with (2) in the checklist exist with two different biographies. The year of each card's first inclusion in the set is also given in parentheses; those not listed parenthetically below were issued in 1950 as well as in all the succeeding years and are hence the most common. Naturally the supply of cards is directly related to how many years a player was included in the set; cards that were not issued until 1955 are much scarcer than those printed all the years between 1950 and 1956. The catalog designation is W576. One frequently finds "complete" sets in the original box; take care to investigate the year of issue, the set may be complete in the sense of all the cards issued up to a certain year, but not all 82 cards below. The box is priced below. For example, a "complete" 1950 set would obviously not include any of the cards marked below with ('52), ('54), or ('55) as none of those cards existed in 1950 since those respective players had not yet been inducted. The complete set price below refers to a set including all 83 cards below. Since the cards are unnumbered, they are numbered below for reference alphabetically by player's name.

COMPLETE SET (83)	400.00	800.00
COMMON CARD '50	2.00	5.00
COMMON CARD '52	3.00	8.00
COMMON CARD '54	4.00	10.00
COMMON CARD '55	5.00	12.00
1 Grover Alexander	3.00	8.00
2 Cap Anson	2.50	6.00
3 Frank Baker '55	5.00	12.00
4 Edward Barrow '54	4.00	10.00
5 Chief Bender (2) '54	4.00	10.00
6 Roger Bresnahan	2.00	5.00
7 Dan Brouthers	2.00	5.00
8 Mordecai Brown	2.00	5.00
9 Morgan Bulkeley	2.00	5.00
10 Jesse Burkett	2.00	5.00
11 Alexander Cartwright	2.00	5.00
12 Henry Chadwick	2.00	5.00
13 Frank Chance	2.00	5.00
14 Happy Chandler '52	50.00	100.00
15 Jack Chesbro	2.00	5.00
16 Fred Clarke	2.00	5.00
17 Ty Cobb	37.50	75.00
18A Mickey Cochrane ERR Name spelled Cochran	4.00	10.00
18B Mickey Cochrane COR	15.00	30.00
19 Eddie Collins (2)	2.00	5.00
20 Jimmie Collins	2.00	5.00
21 Charles Comiskey	2.00	5.00
22 Tom Connolly '54	4.00	10.00
23 Candy Cummings	2.00	5.00
24 Dizzy Dean '54	12.50	25.00
25 Ed Delahanty	2.00	5.00
26 Bill Dickey '54 (2)	8.00	20.00
27 Joe DiMaggio '55	125.00	250.00
28 Hugh Duffy	2.00	5.00
29 Johnny Evers	2.00	5.00
30 Buck Ewing	2.00	5.00
31 Jimmie Foxx	4.00	10.00
32 Frank Frisch	2.00	5.00
33 Lou Gehrig	40.00	80.00
34 Charles Gehringer	3.00	8.00
35 Clark Griffith	2.00	5.00
36 Lefty Grove	4.00	10.00
37 Gabby Hartnett '55	5.00	12.00
38 Harry Heilmann '52	3.00	8.00
39 Rogers Hornsby	4.00	10.00
40 Carl Hubbell	2.50	6.00
41 Hughie Jennings	2.00	5.00
42 Ban Johnson	2.00	5.00
43 Walter Johnson	8.00	20.00
44 Willie Keeler	2.00	5.00
45 Mike Kelly	2.00	5.00
46 Bill Klem '54	4.00	10.00
47 Napoleon Lajoie	3.00	8.00
48 Kenesaw Landis	2.00	5.00
49 Ted Lyons '55	5.00	12.00
50 Connie Mack	2.00	5.00
51 Rabbit Maranville '54	4.00	10.00
52 Christy Mathewson	8.00	20.00
53 Tommy McCarthy	2.00	5.00
54 Joe McGinnity	2.00	5.00
55 John McGraw	2.50	6.00
56 Kid Nichols	2.00	5.00
57 Jim O'Rourke	2.00	5.00
58 Mel Ott	3.00	8.00
59 Herb Pennock	2.00	5.00
60 Eddie Plank	2.00	5.00
61 Charles Radbourne	2.00	5.00
62 Wilbert Robinson	2.00	5.00
63 Babe Ruth	30.00	80.00
64 Ray Schalk '55	5.00	12.00
65 Al Simmons '54	4.00	10.00
66 George Sisler (2)	2.00	5.00
67 Albert G. Spalding	2.00	5.00
68 Tris Speaker	3.00	8.00
69 Bill Terry '54	5.00	12.00
70 Joe Tinker	2.00	5.00
71 Pie Traynor	2.00	5.00
72 Dazzy Vance '55	5.00	12.00
73 Rube Waddell	2.00	5.00
74 Hans Wagner	10.00	25.00
75 Bobby Wallace '54	4.00	10.00
76 Ed Walsh	2.00	5.00
77 Paul Waner '52	5.00	12.00
78 George Wright	2.00	5.00
79 Harry Wright '54	4.00	10.00
80 Cy Young	5.00	12.00
81 Museum Interior/'54 (2)	4.00	10.00
82 Museum Exterior/'54 (2)	4.00	10.00
XX Presentation Box	2.00	5.00

1974 Capital Publishing

This 110-card set was issued by Capital Publishing Company and features 4 1/8" by 5 1/4" black-and-white photos of great players. The fronts consist of nothing more than the picture of the player while the back has biographical information and statistics. It is believed that cards 106 through 110 are significantly tougher than the rest of the set.

COMPLETE SET (110)	50.00	100.00
COMMON CARD (106-110)	.40	1.00
1 Babe Ruth	2.00	5.00
2 Lou Gehrig	1.50	4.00
3 Ty Cobb	1.50	4.00
4 Jackie Robinson	1.50	4.00
5 Roger Connor	.40	1.00
6 Harry Heilmann	.40	1.00
7 Clark Griffith	.40	1.00
8 Ed Walsh	.40	1.00
9 Hugh Duffy	.40	1.00
10 Russ Christopher	.20	.50
11 Snuffy Stirnweiss	.20	.50
12 Willie Keller	.60	1.50
13 Buck Ewing	.40	1.00
14 Tony Lazzeri	.40	1.00
15 King Kelly	.60	1.50
16 Jimmy McAleer	.20	.50
17 Frank Chance	.75	2.00
18 Sam Zoldak	.20	.50
19 Christy Mathewson	.75	2.00
20 Eddie Collins	.75	2.00
21 Cap Anson	.75	2.00
22 Steve Evans	.20	.50
23 Mordecai Brown	.60	1.50
24 Don Black	.20	.50
25 Home Run Baker	.40	1.00
26 Jack Chesbro	.20	.50
27 Gil Hodges	.40	1.00
28 Dan Brouthers	.40	1.00
29 Don Hoak	.20	.50
30 Herb Pennock	.40	1.00
31 Vern Stephens	.20	.50
32 Cy Young	.75	2.00
33 Eddie Cicotte	.75	2.00
34 Sam Jones	.20	.50
35 Ed Waitkus	.20	.50
36 Roger Bresnahan	.40	1.00
37 Fred Merkle	.20	.50
38 Ed Delehanty	.75	2.00
39 Tris Speaker	.60	1.50
40 Fred Clarke	.40	1.00
41 Johnny Evers	.75	2.00
42 Mickey Cochrane	.60	1.50
43 Nap Lajoie	.75	2.00
44 Charles Comiskey	.40	1.00
45 Sam Crawford	.40	1.00
46 Ban Johnson	.40	1.00
47 Ray Schalk	.40	1.00
48 Pat Moran	.20	.50
49 Walt Judnich	.20	.50
50 Bill Killefer	.20	.50
51 Jimmie Foxx	.75	2.00
52 Red Rolfe	.20	.50
53 Howie Pollett	.20	.50
54 Wally Pipp	.20	.50
55 Chief Bender	.40	1.00
56 Connie Mack	.75	2.00
57 Bump Hadley	.20	.50
58 Al Simmons	.60	1.50
59 Hughie Jennings	.40	1.00
60 Johnny Allen	.20	.50
61 Fred Snodgrass	.20	.50
62 Heinie Manush	.40	1.00
63 Dazzy Vance	.40	1.00
64 George Sisler	.60	1.50
65 Jim Bottomley	.40	1.00
66 Roy Chapman	.20	.50
67 Hal Chase	.20	.50
68 Jack Barry	.20	.50
69 George Burns	.20	.50
70 Jim Barrett	.20	.50
71 Grover Alexander	.75	2.00
72 Elmer Flick	.20	.50
73 Jake Flowers	.20	.50
74 Al Orth	.20	.50
75 Cliff Aberson	.20	.50
76 Moe Berg	.75	2.00
77 Bill Bradley	.20	.50
78 Max Bishop	.20	.50
79 Jimmy Austin	.20	.50
80 Beals Becker	.20	.50
81 Jack Clements	.20	.50
82 Cy Blanton	.20	.50
83 Garland Braxton	.20	.50
84 Red Ames	.20	.50
85 Hippo Vaughn	.20	.50
86 Ray Caldwell	.20	.50
87 Clint Brown	.20	.50
88 Joe Jackson	1.25	3.00
89 Pete Appleton	.20	.50
90 Ed Brandt	.20	.50
91 Walter Johnson	.75	2.00
92 Dizzy Dean	.75	2.00
93 Nick Altrock	.20	.50
94 Buck Weaver	.75	2.00
95 George Blaeholder	.20	.50
96 Jim Bagby Sr.	.20	.50
97 Ted Blankenship	.20	.50
98 Babe Adams	.20	.50
99 Lefty Williams	.60	1.50
100 Tommy Bridges	.20	.50
101 Rube Benton	.20	.50
102 Jim Poole	.20	.50
103 Max Butcher	.20	.50
104 Larry Benton	.20	.50
105 Chick Gandil	.60	1.50
106 Lefty Grove	2.00	5.00
107 Roberto Clemente	4.00	10.00
108 Albert Spalding	2.00	5.00
109 Bill Barrett	.40	1.00
110 Bob O'Farrell	.40	1.00

1908 Cardinals Republic

Issued as a supplement in the St Louis Republic, these photos feature members of the 1908 St Louis Cardinals. There might be more of these so any additions to this checklist is appreciated. Since these are unnumbered, we have sequenced them in alphabetical order.

COMPLETE SET		400
1 Fred Beebe	50.00	100.00
2 Robert Byrne	50.00	100.00
3 Ed Konetchy	50.00	100.00
4 John Lush	50.00	100.00

1931 Cardinals Metropolitan

This 30-card set features white-bordered, sepia colored blank-backed photos of the 1931 St. Louis Cardinals and measures approximately 6 1/8" by 9 1/2". The cards are unnumbered and checklisted below in alphabetical order. The words "Metropolitan Studios St. Louis" are in the bottom right hand corner. These photos were sent to fans in an manila envelope. One could order another set from the team for 41 cents.

COMPLETE SET (30)	600.00	1,200.00
1 Earl Sparky Adams	15.00	30.00
2 Ray Blades	15.00	30.00
3 James Bottomly	30.00	60.00
4 Sam Breadon PRES	15.00	30.00
5 James Rip Collins	25.00	50.00
6 Dizzy Dean	75.00	150.00
7 Paul Derringer	15.00	30.00
8 Jake Flowers	15.00	30.00
9 Frank Frisch	60.00	120.00
10 Charles Gelbert	15.00	30.00
11 Miguel Gonzales	15.00	30.00
12 Burleigh Grimes	30.00	60.00
13 Charles Chick Hafey	30.00	60.00
14 Jesse Haines	30.00	60.00
15 William Hallahan	15.00	30.00
16 Andrew High	15.00	30.00
17 Sylvester Johnson	15.00	30.00
18 Tony Kaufmann	15.00	30.00
19 James Lindsey	15.00	30.00
20 Gus Mancuso	15.00	30.00
21 Pepper Martin	30.00	60.00
22 Ernest Orsatti	15.00	30.00
23 Charles Rhem	15.00	30.00
24 Branch Rickey VP	30.00	60.00
25 Walter Roettger	15.00	30.00
26 Allyn Stout	15.00	30.00
27 Gabby Street	15.00	30.00
28 Clyde Wares CO	15.00	30.00
29 George Watkins	15.00	30.00
30 James Wilson	15.00	30.00

1935 Cardinals Rice Stix

This two card set features the Dean brothers who won 49 games for the Cardinals in 1934. These cards measure approximately 2 1/4" by 3" and were issued as premiums when shirts were purchased from that St Louis firm.

COMPLETE SET	600.00	1,200.00
1 Paul Daffy Dean	250.00	500.00
2 Jay Dizzy Dean	400.00	800.00

1941 Cardinals W754

The cards in this 30-card set measure approximately 2 1/8" by 2 5/8". The 1941 W754 set of unnumbered cards features St. Louis Cardinals. The cards are numbered below alphabetically by player's name. This is another set issued in its own box with the other side being a mailing label. This set is worth about $100 more when still in the original box.

COMPLETE SET (30)	400.00	800.00
1 Sam Breadon OWN	12.50	30.00
2 Jimmy Brown	12.50	30.00
3 Mort Cooper	20.00	50.00
4 Walker Cooper	15.00	40.00
5 Estel Crabtree	12.50	30.00
6 Frank Crespi	12.50	30.00
7 Bill Crouch	12.50	30.00
8 Mike Gonzalez CO	15.00	40.00
9 Harry Gumpert	12.50	30.00
10 John Hopp	15.00	40.00
11 Ira Hutchinson	12.50	30.00
12 Howie Krist	12.50	30.00
13 Eddie Lake	12.50	30.00
14 Max Lanier	20.00	50.00
15 Gus Mancuso	12.50	30.00
16 Marty Marion	40.00	80.00
17 Steve Mesner	12.50	30.00
18 John Mize	75.00	150.00
19 Terry Moore	30.00	60.00
20 Sam Nahem	12.50	30.00
21 Don Padgett	12.50	30.00
22 Branch Rickey GM	60.00	120.00
23 Clyde Shoun	12.50	30.00
24 Enos Slaughter	75.00	150.00
25 Billy Southworth MG	15.00	40.00
26 Coaker Triplett	12.50	30.00
27 Buzzy Wares	12.50	30.00
28 Lon Warneke	15.00	40.00
29 Ernie White	12.50	30.00
30 Title Card/(Order Coupon on back)	12.50	30.00

1953 Cardinals Hunter's Wieners

The cards in this 26 card set measure 2 1/4" by 3 1/2". The 1953 Hunter's Wieners set of full color, blank backed unnumbered cards feature St. Louis Cardinal players only. The cards have red borders and were issued in panels of two on hot dog packages. The catalog designation is F 153-1. We have sequenced this set in alphabetical order.

COMPLETE SET	3,000.00	6,000.00
1 Steve Bilko	125.00	250.00
2 Alpha Brazle	125.00	250.00
3 Cloyd Boyer	150.00	300.00
4 Cliff Chambers	125.00	250.00
5 Mike Clark	125.00	250.00
6 Jack Crimian	125.00	250.00
7 Les Fusselman	125.00	250.00
8 Harvey Haddix	200.00	400.00
9 Solly Hemus	125.00	250.00
10 Ray Jablonski	125.00	250.00
11 Will Johnson	125.00	250.00
12 Harry Lowrey	125.00	250.00
13 Larry Miggins	125.00	250.00
14 Stuart Miller	125.00	250.00
15 Wilmer Mizell	125.00	250.00
16 Stan Musial	1,000.00	2,000.00
17 Joe Presko	125.00	250.00
18 Del Rice	125.00	250.00
19 Hal Rice	125.00	250.00
20 Willard Schmidt	125.00	250.00
21 Red Schoendienst	300.00	600.00
22 Dick Sisler	125.00	250.00
23 Enos Slaughter	300.00	600.00
24 Gerry Staley	125.00	250.00
25 Ed Stanky	200.00	400.00
26 Ed Yuhas	125.00	250.00

1954 Cardinals Hunter's Wieners

The cards in this 30 card set measure 2 1/4" by 3 1/2". The 1954 Hunter's Weiners set of full color, blank backed unnumbered cards features St. Louis Cardinals. They were issued in pairs on the backs of hot dog packages as in 1953; however one of the cards is a statistical record of the player's career. The poses are very similar to those used in the 1953 set; however, there are captions which read "What's My Name" and "What's My Record". The catalog designation is F153-2.

COMPLETE SET	3,000.00	6,000.00
1 Tom Alston	125.00	250.00
2 Steve Bilko	125.00	250.00
3 Alpha Brazle	125.00	250.00
4 Tom Burgess	125.00	250.00
5 Cot Deal	125.00	250.00
6 Alex Grammas	125.00	250.00
7 Harvey Haddix	150.00	300.00
8 Solly Hemus	125.00	250.00
9 Ray Jablonski	125.00	250.00
10 Royce Lint	125.00	250.00
11 Harry Lowrey	125.00	250.00
12 Memo Luna	125.00	250.00
13 Stu Miller	150.00	300.00
14 Stan Musial	750.00	1,500.00
15 Tom Poholsky	125.00	250.00
16 Bill Posedel CO	125.00	250.00
17 Joe Presko	125.00	250.00
18 Vic Raschi	200.00	400.00
19 Dick Rand	125.00	250.00
20 Rip Repulski	125.00	250.00
21 Del Rice	125.00	250.00
22 John Riddle CO	125.00	250.00
23 Mike Ryba CO	125.00	250.00
24 Red Schoendienst	200.00	500.00
25 Dick Schofield	150.00	300.00
26 Enos Slaughter	200.00	500.00
27 Gerry Staley	125.00	250.00
28 Ed Stanky MG	150.00	300.00
29 Ed Yuhas	125.00	250.00
30 Sal Yvars	125.00	250.00

1954-55 Cardinals Postcards

These postcards were issued over a two year period. The top of the card has a picture of the player on top and a message beginning "Dear Cardinal Fan". The backs are blank. Since these cards are unnumbered, we have sequenced them in alphabetical order.

COMPLETE SET	225.00	450.00
1 Luis Arroyo	10.00	25.00
2 Bill Baker	6.00	15.00
3 Ralph Beard	6.00	15.00
4 Ken Boyer	15.00	40.00
5 Al Brazle	6.00	15.00
6 Nelson Burbrink	6.00	15.00
7 Joe Cunningham	8.00	20.00
8 Cot Deal	6.00	15.00

9 Eddie Dyer	6.00	15.00
10 Joe Frazier	6.00	15.00
11 Ben Flowers	6.00	15.00
12 Al Gettel	6.00	15.00
13 Alex Grammas	6.00	15.00
14 Harvey Haddix	8.00	20.00
15 Solly Hemus	6.00	15.00
16 Ray Jablonski	6.00	15.00
17 Larry Jackson	8.00	20.00
18 Gordon Jones	6.00	15.00
19 Paul LaPalme	6.00	15.00
20 Brooks Lawrence	6.00	15.00
21 Royce Lint	6.00	15.00
22 Harry Lowrey	6.00	15.00
23 Wally Moon	8.00	20.00
24 Stan Musial	30.00	60.00
25 Bill Posedel	6.00	15.00
26 Tom Poholsky	6.00	15.00
27 Joe Presko	6.00	15.00
28 Vic Raschi	8.00	20.00
29 Del Rice	6.00	15.00
30 John Riddle	6.00	15.00
31 Rip Repulski	6.00	15.00
32 Mike Ryba	6.00	15.00
33 Bill Sarni	6.00	15.00
34 Will Schmidt	6.00	15.00
35 Red Schoendienst	15.00	40.00
36 Dick Schofield	6.00	15.00
37 Gerry Staley	6.00	15.00
38 Eddie Stanky	8.00	20.00
39 Bill Virdon	10.00	25.00
40 Ben Wade	6.00	15.00
41 Pete Whisenant	6.00	15.00
42 Sal Yvars	6.00	15.00

1955 Cardinals Hunter's Wieners

The cards in this 30 card set measure 2" by 4 3/4". The 1955 Hunter's Wieners set of full color, blank backed, unnumbered cards feature St. Louis Cardinals only. This year presented a different format from the previous two years in that there are two pictures on the front of each card, one full figure shot and a close up bust shot. The card was actually the side panel of the hot dog package rather than the back as in the previous two years. The catalog designation of this scarce regional issue is F153-3. Ken Boyer appears in his rookie season.

COMPLETE SET	3,000.00	6,000.00
1 Tom Alston	150.00	300.00
2 Ken Boyer	250.00	500.00
3 Harry Elliott	125.00	250.00
4 Jack Faszholz	125.00	250.00
5 Joe Frazier	125.00	250.00
6 Alex Grammas	125.00	250.00
7 Harvey Haddix	150.00	300.00
8 Solly Hemus	125.00	250.00
9 Larry Jackson	150.00	300.00
10 Tony Jacobs	125.00	250.00
11 Gordon Jones	125.00	250.00
12 Paul LaPalme	125.00	250.00
13 Brooks Lawrence	125.00	250.00
14 Wally Moon	150.00	300.00
15 Stan Musial	1,000.00	2,000.00
16 Tom Poholsky	125.00	250.00
17 Bill Posedel CO	125.00	250.00
18 Vic Raschi	200.00	400.00
19 Rip Repulski	125.00	250.00
20 Del Rice	125.00	250.00
21 John Riddle CO	125.00	250.00
22 Bill Sarni	125.00	250.00
23 Red Schoendienst	250.00	500.00
24 Dick Schofield	150.00	300.00
25 Frank Smith	125.00	250.00
26 Ed Stanky MG	150.00	300.00
27 Bob Tiefenauer	125.00	250.00
28 Bill Virdon	200.00	400.00
29 Fred Walker CO	125.00	250.00
30 Floyd Woolridge	125.00	250.00

1956 Cardinals Postcards

These cards were the first issued in the style the Cardinals would use for many years. The fronts have photos of players in the "Old" Cardinals uniform with Cardinals on it with a thick heavy line right under that word. The backs have postcard backs with a Busch Stadium address. Each card has a 1" border on the bottom which usually contained an fascimile autograph. Since these cards are unnumbered, we have sequenced them in alphabetical order.

COMPLETE SET	125.00	250.00
1 Tom Alston	6.00	15.00
2 Don Blasingame	5.00	12.00
3 Ken Boyer	8.00	20.00
4 Jack Brandt	5.00	12.00
5 Jackie Collum	5.00	12.00
6 Walker Cooper	5.00	12.00
7 Al Dark	6.00	15.00
8 Bob Del Greco	5.00	12.00
9 Murry Dickson	5.00	12.00
10 Chuck Harmon	5.00	12.00
11 Grady Hatton	5.00	12.00
12 Johnny Hopp CO	5.00	12.00
13 Fred Hutchinson MG	5.00	12.00
14 Ray Katt	5.00	12.00
15 Ellis Kinder	5.00	12.00
16 Jim Konstanty	6.00	15.00
17 Larry Jackson	5.00	12.00
18 Dick Littlefield	5.00	12.00
19 Lindy McDaniel	6.00	15.00
20 Vinegar Bend Mizell	5.00	12.00
21 Wally Moon	5.00	12.00
22 Terry Moore CO	6.00	15.00
23 Bobby Morgan	5.00	12.00
24 Stan Musial	15.00	40.00
25 Tom Poholsky	5.00	12.00
26 Bill Posedel CO	5.00	12.00
27 Rip Repulski	5.00	12.00
28 Hank Sauer	6.00	15.00
29 Hal Smith	5.00	12.00
30 Herm Wehmeier	5.00	12.00

1957-58 Cardinals Postcards

These postcards were issued by the St Louis Cardinals over a two year period and the players in the set are wearing the uniform that the Cards wore from 1957 through 1971. The only way a collector can tell the difference between the postcards is that the 1957 cards have a notation for a 2 cent stamp while the 1958 cards have a notation for a 3 cent stamp. Since these cards are unnumbered, we have sequenced them in alphabetical order.

COMPLETE SET	200.00	400.00
1 Ruben Amaro	5.00	12.00
2 Frank Barnes	5.00	12.00
3 Don Blasingame	5.00	12.00
4 Ken Boyer	10.00	25.00
5 Jim Brosnan	6.00	15.00
6 Tom Cheney	5.00	12.00
7 Nelson Chittum	5.00	12.00
8 Walker Cooper	5.00	12.00
9 Joe Cunningham	6.00	15.00
10 Al Dark	6.00	15.00
11 Jim Davis	5.00	12.00
12 Bing Devine GM	5.00	12.00
13 Murry Dickson	5.00	12.00
14 Del Ennis	6.00	15.00
15 Curt Flood	12.50	30.00
16 Gene Freese	5.00	12.00
17 Gene Green	5.00	12.00
18 Stan Hack CO	5.00	12.00
19 Al Hollingsworth	5.00	12.00
20 Fred Hutchinson MG	5.00	12.00
21 Larry Jackson	5.00	12.00
22 Sam Jones	5.00	12.00
23 Eddie Kasko	5.00	12.00
24 Ray Katt	5.00	12.00
25 Hobie Landrith	5.00	12.00
26 Bob Mabe	5.00	12.00
27 Sal Maglie	8.00	20.00
28 Morrie Martin	5.00	12.00
29 Lindy McDaniel	6.00	15.00
30 Von McDaniel	5.00	12.00
31 Lloyd Merritt	5.00	12.00
32 Eddie Miksis	5.00	12.00
33 Bob Miller	5.00	12.00
34 Vinegar Bend Mizell	5.00	12.00
35 Wally Moon	5.00	12.00
36 Terry Moore CO	5.00	12.00
37 Billy Muffett	5.00	12.00
38 Stan Musial	15.00	40.00
39 Irv Noren	5.00	12.00
40 Phil Paine	5.00	12.00
41 Will Schmidt	5.00	12.00
42 Dick Schofield	5.00	12.00
43 Bobby Gene Smith	5.00	12.00
44 Hal Smith	5.00	12.00
45 Chuck Stobbs	5.00	12.00
46 Joe Taylor	5.00	12.00
47 Herman Wehmeier	5.00	12.00
48 Bill Wight	5.00	12.00
49 Hoyt Wilhelm	12.50	30.00

1958 Cardinals Jay Publishing

This 14-card set of the St. Louis Cardinals measures approximately 5" by 7" and features black-and-white player photos in a white border. These cards were packaged 12 to a packet. The backs are blank. The cards are unnumbered and checklisted below in alphabetical order. Changes to the Cardinals roster during the season accounts for more than 12 cards in this set.

COMPLETE SET (14)	30.00	60.00
1 Don Blasingame	1.50	3.00
2 Ken Boyer	4.00	8.00
3 Joe Cunningham	2.00	4.00
4 Alvin Dark	3.00	6.00
5 Del Ennis	1.50	3.00
6 Larry Jackson	1.50	3.00
7 Sam Jones	1.50	3.00
8 Eddie Kasko	1.50	3.00
9 Lindy McDaniel	1.50	3.00
10 Von McDaniel	1.50	3.00
11 Wilmer Mizell	1.50	3.00
12 Wally Moon	1.50	3.00
13 Stan Musial	7.50	15.00
14 Hal Smith	1.50	3.00

1959 Cardinals Jay Publishing

This 12-card set of the St. Louis Cardinals measures approximately 5" by 7" and features black-and-white player photos in a white border. These cards were packaged 12 to a packet. The backs are blank. The cards are unnumbered and checklisted below in alphabetical order.

COMPLETE SET	20.00	50.00
1 Don Blasingame	1.25	3.00
2 Ken Boyer	2.50	6.00
3 Jim Brosnan	1.25	3.00
4 Gino Cimoli	1.25	3.00
5 Joe Cunningham	1.50	4.00
6 Curt Flood	2.50	6.00
7 Alex Grammas	1.25	3.00
8 Gene Green	1.25	3.00
9 Larry Jackson	1.25	3.00
10 Wilmer Mizell	1.25	3.00
11 Stan Musial	6.00	15.00
12 Hal R. Smith	1.25	3.00

1960 Cardinals Jay Publishing

This 12-card set of the St. Louis Cardinals measures approximately 5" by 7". The fronts feature black-and-white posed player photos with the player's and team name printed below in the white border. These cards were packaged 12 in a packet. The backs are blank. The cards are unnumbered and checklisted below in alphabetical order.

COMPLETE SET (12)	15.00	40.00
1 Ken Boyer	2.00	5.00
2 Joe Cunningham	1.25	3.00
3 Curt Flood	1.50	4.00
4 Larry Jackson	.75	2.00
5 Ronnie Kline	.75	2.00
6 Lindy McDaniel	.75	2.00
7 Wilmer Mizell	.75	2.00
8 Stan Musial	6.00	15.00
9 Bob Nieman	.75	2.00
10 Hal Smith	.75	2.00
11 Daryl Spencer	.75	2.00
12 Bill White	1.50	4.00

1961 Cardinals Jay Publishing

This 13-card set of the St. Louis Cardinals measures approximately 5" by 7". The fronts feature black-and-white posed player photos with the player's and team name printed below in the white border. These cards were packaged 12 in a packet. The backs are blank. The cards are unnumbered and checklisted below in alphabetical order. Thirteen cards are listed for this set as Walt Moryn is included this year. Since these sets were issued throughout the years, sometimes more than the 12 players listed are included. Additions to this or any other team issue set in the book is appreciated.

COMPLETE SET (13)	6.00	15.00
1 Ken Boyer	1.25	3.00
2 Ernie Broglio	.50	1.25
3 Joe Cunningham	.75	2.00
4 Curt Flood	1.25	3.00
5 Solly Hemus MG	.50	1.25
6 Larry Jackson	.50	1.25
7 Julian Javier	.75	2.00
8 Lindy McDaniel	.50	1.25
9 Walt Moryn	.50	1.25
10 Stan Musial	4.00	10.00
11 Hal Smith	.50	1.25
12 Daryl Spencer	.50	1.25
13 Bill White	1.25	3.00

1962 Cardinals Jay Publishing

The 1962 Jay Cardinals set consists of 14 cards produced by Jay Publishing. The Minoso card establishes the year of the set, since 1962 was Minoso's only year with the Cardinals. The cards measure approximately 4 3/4" by 7" and are printed on thin photographic paper stock. The white fronts feature a black-and-white player portrait with the player's name and the team name below. The backs are blank. The cards are packaged 12 to a packet and originally sold for 25 cents. The cards are unnumbered and checklisted below in alphabetical order. Updates during the season account for the additional cards.

COMPLETE SET (14)	30.00	60.00
1 Ken Boyer	2.00	5.00
2 Ernie Broglio	.75	2.00
3 Curt Flood	1.50	4.00
4 Bob Gibson	6.00	15.00
5 Julio Gotay	.75	2.00
6 Larry Jackson	.75	2.00
7 Julian Javier	1.25	3.00
8 Johnny Keane MG	.75	2.00
9 Lindy McDaniel	.75	2.00
10 Minnie Minoso	2.00	5.00
11 Stan Musial	6.00	15.00
12 Gene Oliver	.75	2.00
13 Curt Simmons	1.25	3.00
14 Bill White	1.50	4.00

1963-64 Cardinals Jay Publishing

This set of the St. Louis Cardinals measures approximately 5" by 7". The fronts feature black-and-white posed player photos with the player's and team name printed below in the white border. These cards were packaged 12 in a packet. The backs are blank. The cards are unnumbered and checklisted below in alphabetical order. These cards were issued over a two year period and where possible we have identified which year each card was issued.

COMPLETE SET (20)	40.00	80.00
1 Ken Boyer/(With glove)	2.00	5.00
2 Ken Boyer /(With bat)	2.00	5.00
3 Ernie Broglio/(Above waist pose)	.75	2.00
4 Ernie Broglio/(Action photo with glove)	.75	2.00
5 Curt Flood/(Smiling)	1.50	4.00
6 Curt Flood	1.50	4.00
7 Bob Gibson/(Head pose)	5.00	12.00
8 Bob Gibson/(Action pose)	5.00	12.00
9 Dick Groat 64	1.50	4.00
10 Julian Javier	1.25	3.00
11 John Keane MG/(Above waist pose)	.75	2.00
12 John Keane MG/(Full shot)	.75	2.00
13 Dal Maxvill 64	.75	2.00
14 Tim McCarver 64	2.00	5.00
15 Stan Musial 63	6.00	15.00
16 Ray Sadecki/(Without glasses)	.75	2.00
17 Ray Sadecki/(With glasses)	.75	2.00
18 Curt Simmons/(Close up head shot)	1.25	3.00
19 Curt Simmons/(With glove)	1.25	3.00
20 Bill White	1.50	4.00

1965 Cardinals Jay Publishing

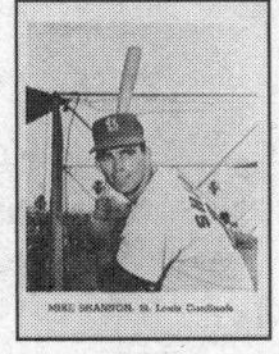

This 12-card set of the St. Louis Cardinals measures approximately 5" by 7". The fronts feature black-and-white posed player photos with the player's and team name printed below in the white border. These cards were packaged 12 in a packet. The backs are blank. The cards are unnumbered and checklisted below in alphabetical order.

COMPLETE SET (12)	15.00	40.00
1 Ken Boyer	2.00	5.00
2 Curt Flood	1.50	4.00
3 Bob Gibson	3.00	8.00
4 Dick Groat	1.25	3.00
5 Julian Javier	.75	2.00
6 Tim McCarver	2.00	5.00
7 Bob Purkey	.75	2.00
8 Red Schoendienst MG	2.00	5.00
9 Mike Shannon	1.50	4.00
10 Tracy Stallard	.75	2.00
11 Carl Warwick	.75	2.00
12 Bill White	1.50	4.00

1964 Cardinals Team Issue

This eight-card set measures approximately 4" by 5" and features black-and-white player portraits in a white border with the player's name and position in the bottom margin. The backs are blank. The cards are unnumbered and checklisted below in alphabetical order.

COMPLETE SET (8)	8.00	20.00
1 Ken Boyer	2.00	5.00
2 Curt Flood	1.50	4.00
3 Dick Groat	1.25	3.00
4 Charley James	.75	2.00
5 Julian Javier	1.25	3.00
6 Tim McCarver	2.00	5.00
7 Ray Sadecki	.75	2.00
8 Bill White	1.50	4.00

1965 Cardinals Team Issue

The 28-card set of the St. Louis Cardinals measures approximately 3 1/4" by 5 1/2" and features black-and-white player photos in a white border with a facsimile autograph in the wide bottom margin. The backs are blank. The cards are unnumbered and checklisted below in alphabetical order. Steve Carlton has a card in his Rookie Card year.

COMPLETE SET (28)	40.00	80.00
1 Dennis Aust	.75	2.00
2 Joe Becker CO	.75	2.00
3 Nellie Briles	.75	2.00
4 Lou Brock	3.00	8.00
5 Jerry Buchek	.75	2.00
6 Steve Carlton	6.00	15.00
7 Don Dennis	.75	2.00
8 Curt Flood	1.50	4.00
9 Bob Gibson	3.00	8.00
10 Tito Francona	.75	2.00
11 Phil Gagliano	.75	2.00
12 Larry Jaster	.75	2.00
13 Julian Javier	1.25	3.00
14 George Kernek	.75	2.00
15 Dal Maxvill	1.25	3.00
16 Tim McCarver	2.00	5.00

17 Bob Milliken .75 2.00
18 Bob Purkey .75 2.00
19 Ray Sadecki .75 2.00
20 Red Schoendienst MG 2.00 5.00
21 Joe Schultz .75 2.00
22 Mike Shannon 1.50 4.00
23 Curt Simmons 1.25 3.00
24 Bob Skinner .75 2.00
25 Tracy Stallard .75 2.00
26 Bob Tolan .75 2.00
27 Ray Washburn .75 2.00
28 Hal Woodeschick .75 2.00

1966 Cardinals Team Issue

These 12 black and white photos were available directly from Busch Stadium for twenty-five cents. The cards measure approximately 4 3/4" by 7 and have blank backs. We have dated this set as 1966 was Charlie Smith's last season and Alex Johnson's first season with the Cardinals.

COMPLETE SET (12) 15.00 40.00
1 Lou Brock 3.00 8.00
2 Jerry Buchek .75 2.00
3 Curt Flood 1.50 4.00
4 Phil Gagliano .75 2.00
5 Bob Gibson 3.00 8.00
6 Julian Javier 1.25 3.00
7 Alex Johnson .75 2.00
8 Tim McCarver 2.00 5.00
9 Red Schoendienst MG 2.00 5.00
10 Curt Simmons 1.25 3.00
11 Charlie Smith .75 2.00
12 Tracy Stallard .75 2.00

1969 Cardinals Team Issue

These photos, were issued by the St Louis Cardinals and featured members of the two-time defending NL Champions. These photos were designed to be sent out in response to fan requests. Since these photos are unnumbered, we have sequenced them in alphabetical order.

COMPLETE SET (12) 10.00 25.00
1 Nelson Briles .40 1.00
2 Lou Brock 2.50 6.00
3 Curt Flood 1.00 2.50
4 Bob Gibson 2.50 6.00
5 Julian Javier .40 1.00
6 Dal Maxvill .40 1.00
7 Tim McCarver 1.00 2.50
8 Vada Pinson .75 2.00
9 Red Schoendienst MGR 1.00 2.50
10 Mike Shannon .60 1.50
11 Joe Torre 1.00 2.50
12 Ray Washburn .40 1.00

1970 Cardinals Team Issue

This 33-card set of the St. Louis Cardinals measures approximately 4 1/4" by 7" and features black-and-white player photos in a white border. These cards were packaged 12 to a packet and some display facsimile autographs. The backs are blank. The cards are unnumbered and checklisted below in alphabetical order. Updates and changes during the year account for the odd number of cards. This set can be dated to 1970 as that was Richie (Dick) Allen's only season with the Cards.

COMPLETE SET (33) 40.00 80.00
1 Richie Allen Glasses 2.00 5.00
2 Richie Allen Uniform # showing 2.00 5.00
3 Jim Beauchamp .75 2.00
4 Lou Brock 3.00 8.00
5 Vern Benson CO .75 2.00
6 Sal Campisi .75 2.00
7 Jose Cardenal 1.25 3.00
8 Bob Chlupsa .75 2.00
9 Ed Crosby .75 2.00
10 George Culver .75 2.00
11 Vic Davilillo 1.25 3.00
12 Bob Gibson 3.00 8.00
13 Santiago Guzman .75 2.00
14 Joe Hague .75 2.00
15 Julian Javier 1.25 3.00
16 Al Hrabosky 1.25 3.00
17 Leron Lee Head and Shoulders .75 2.00
18 Leron Lee Uniform # Showing .75 2.00
19 Frank Linzy .75 2.00
20 Dal Maxvill .75 2.00
21 Milt Ramirez .75 2.00
22 Jerry Reuss 1.50 4.00
23 Cookie Rojas .75 2.00
24 Red Schoendienst 2.00 5.00
25 Mike Shannon 1.50 4.00
26 Ted Simmons 2.50 6.00
27 Dick Sisler CO .75 2.00
28 Carl Taylor Portrait .75 2.00
29 Carl Taylor Kneeling .75 2.00
30 Chuck Taylor .75 2.00
31 Joe Torre 2.00 5.00
32 Bart Zeller Portrait .75 2.00
33 Bart Zeller Batting .75 2.00

1971 Cardinals Team Issue

This 30-card set measures 3 1/4" by 5 1/2" and features black-and-white player portraits with white borders. A facsimile autograph appears in the wider white border area at the bottom. The backs are blank. The cards are unnumbered and checklisted below in alphabetical order.

COMPLETE SET (30) 40.00 80.00
1 Matty Alou 1.25 3.00
2 Jim Beauchamp .60 1.50
3 Vern Benson CO .60 1.50
4 Ken Boyer CO 1.50 4.00
5 Lou Brock 4.00 10.00
6 Bob Burda .60 1.50
7 Jose Cardenal .75 2.00
8 Steve Carlton 4.00 10.00
9 Reggie Cleveland .60 1.50
10 Moe Drabowsky .60 1.50
11 Bob Gibson 4.00 10.00
12 Joe Hague .60 1.50
13 Julian Javier .75 2.00
14 George Kissell CO .60 1.50
15 Frank Linzy .60 1.50
16 Dal Maxvill .75 2.00
17 Jerry McNertney .60 1.50
18 Luis Melendez .60 1.50
19 Jerry Reuss 1.25 3.00
20 Al Santorini .60 1.50
21 Red Schoendienst MG 1.50 4.00
22 Barney Schultz CO .60 1.50
23 Don Shaw .60 1.50
24 Ted Simmons 1.50 4.00
25 Ted Sizemore .60 1.50
26 Chuck Taylor .60 1.50
27 Lee Thomas CO .60 1.50
28 Joe Torre/(Profile) 1.50 4.00
29 Joe Torre/(Front View) 1.50 4.00
30 Chris Zachary .60 1.50

1972 Cardinals Team Issue

This 18-card set of the St. Louis Cardinals measures approximately 3 1/4" by 5 1/2" and features black-and-white player portraits with white borders. A facsimile autograph appears in the wide bottom margin. The backs are blank. The cards are unnumbered and checklisted below in alphabetical order.

COMPLETE SET (18) 30.00 60.00
1 Nelson Briles 1.25 3.00
2 Lou Brock 3.00 8.00
3 Steve Carlton 3.00 8.00
4 Donn Clendenon 1.25 3.00
5 Tony Cloninger 1.25 3.00
6 Ed Crosby 1.25 3.00
7 Jose Cruz 1.50 4.00
8 Moe Drabowsky 1.25 3.00
9 Bob Gibson 4.00 10.00
10 Joe Grzenda 1.25 3.00
11 George Kissell CO 1.25 3.00
12 Dal Maxvill 1.25 3.00
13 Billy Muffett CO 1.25 3.00
14 Ted Simmons 2.00 5.00
15 Ted Sizemore 1.25 3.00
16 Scipio Spinks 1.25 3.00
17 Mike Torrez 1.50 4.00
18 Rick Wise 1.50 4.00

1974 Cardinals 1931 Bra-Mac

This 20 card set, which measures 3 1/2" by 5" features members of the 1931 World Champion St Louis Cardinals.

COMPLETE SET 6.00 15.00
1 Burleigh Grimes .60 1.50
2 Sparky Adams .20 .50
3 Jesse Haines .60 1.50
4 Jimmie Wilson .30 .75
5 Ernie Orsatti .20 .50
6 Gus Mancuso .20 .50
7 Ray Blades .20 .50
8 Frank Frisch .75 2.00
9 Bill Hallahan .20 .50
10 George Watkins .20 .50
11 Pepper Martin .40 1.00
12 Charlie Gelbert .20 .50
13 Jake Flowers .20 .50
14 Jim Lindsey .20 .50
15 Rip Collins .20 .50
16 Flint Rhem .20 .50
17 Paul Derringer .20 .50
18 Syl Johnson .20 .50
19 Chick Hafey .40 1.00
20 Jim Bottomley .60 1.50

1974 Cardinals 1934 TCMA

This 31-card set of the 1934 World Champion St. Louis Cardinals measures approximately 2 1/4" by 3 5/8" and features black-and-white player photos. Each set includes four jumbo cards measuring approximately 3 5/8" by 4 1/2" and displaying action photos from the 1934 World Series Games with various information on the backs. The cards are unnumbered and checklisted below with the jumbo cards being the last four cards, numbers 28-31.

COMPLETE SET (31) 10.00 25.00
1 Tex Carleton .20 .50
2 Rip Collins .40 1.00
3 Cliff Crawford .20 .50
4 Spud Davis .20 .50
5 Daffy Dean Dizzy Dean .75 2.00
6 Paul Dean .40 1.00
7 Dizzy Dean 1.25 3.00
8 Bill DeLancey .20 .50
9 Leo Durocher 1.25 3.00
10 Frank Frisch P MG 1.00 2.50
11 Chick Fullis .20 .50
12 Mike Gonzalez CO .20 .50
13 Jesse Haines .75 2.00
14 Bill Hallahan .40 1.00
15 Francis Healy .20 .50
16 Jim Lindsey .20 .50
17 Pepper Martin .60 1.50
18 Joe Medwick 1.00 2.50
19 Jim Mooney .20 .50
20 Ernie Orsatti .20 .50
21 Flint Rhem .20 .50
22 John Rothrock .20 .50
23 Dazzy Vance .75 2.00
24 Bill Walker .20 .50
25 Buzzy Wares CO .20 .50
26 Whitey Whitehead .20 .50
27 Jim Winford .20 .50
28 Dizzy & Leo Celebrate .75 2.00
29 Durocher Scores 1.00 2.50
30 Medwick Out Cochrane Catcher .75 2.00
31 1934 St. Louis Cardinals World Champions .60 1.50

1974 Cardinals Postcards

These postcards, which were available directly from the Cardinals, feature members of the 1974 St Louis Cardinals. Some of the photos used in 1974 were used in previous years. Since these photos are not numbered, we have sequenced them alphabetically.

COMPLETE SET 8.00 20.00
1 Vern Benson CO .20 .50
2 Lou Brock 1.00 2.50
3 Jose Cruz .40 1.00
4 Joe Cunningham FO .20 .50
5 John Curtis .20 .50
6 Rich Folkers .20 .50
7 Bob Forsch .20 .50
8 Alan Foster .20 .50
9 Mike Garman .20 .50
10 Bob Gibson 1.25 3.00
11 Jim Hickman .20 .50
12 Marc Hill .20 .50
13 Al Hrabosky .20 .50
14 George Kissell CO .20 .50
15 Johnny Lewis CO .20 .50
16 Bake McBride .30 .75
17 Tim McCarver .60 1.50
18 Lynn McGlothen .20 .50
19 Luis Melendez .20 .50
20 Orlando Pena .20 .50
21 Ken Reitz .20 .50
22 Pete Richert .20 .50
23 Dave Ricketts .20 .50
24 Red Schoendienst MG .40 1.00
25 Barney Schultz .20 .50
26 Sonny Siebert .20 .50
27 Ted Simmons .40 1.00
28 Ted Sizemore .20 .50
29 Reggie Smith .30 .75
30 Joe Torre .60 1.50
31 Mike Tyson .20 .50

1975 Cardinals Postcards

This 30-card set of the St Louis Cardinals features player photos on postcard-size cards. The cards are unnumbered and checklisted below in alphabetical order.

COMPLETE SET (30) 8.00 20.00
1 Ed Brinkman .20 .50
2 Lou Brock 1.25 3.00
3 Ron Bryant .20 .50
4 Danny Cater .20 .50
5 John Curtis .20 .50
6 Willie Davis .30 .75
7 John Denny .20 .50
8 Jim Dwyer .20 .50
9 Ron Fairly .30 .75
10 Bob Forsch .20 .50
11 Mike Garman .20 .50
12 Bob Gibson 1.50 4.00
13 Mario Guerrero .20 .50
14 Keith Hernandez 2.00 5.00
15 Al Hrabosky .20 .50
16 Teddy Martinez .20 .50
17 Bake McBride .20 .50
18 Lynn McGlothen .20 .50
19 Luis Melendez .20 .50
20 Tommy Moore .20 .50
21 Ron Reed .20 .50
22 Ken Reitz .20 .50
23 Ken Rudolph .20 .50
24 Ray Sadecki .20 .50
25 Ted L. Simmons .60 1.50
26 Ted Sizemore .20 .50
27 Reggie Smith .30 .75
28 Elias Sosa .20 .50
29 Greg Terlecky .20 .50
30 Mike Tyson .20 .50

1975 Cardinals TCMA 1942-46

This 66-card set features the 1942-46 St. Louis Cardinals Team. The fronts display black-and-white player photos while the backs carry player statistics. The cards are unnumbered and checklisted below in alphabetical order with the jumbo cards listed last. The set concludes with several multi-player cards.

1 Buster Adams .20 .50
2 Red Barrett .20 .50
3 Johnny Beazley .20 .50
4 Augie Bergamo .20 .50
5 Buddy Blattner .20 .50
6 Al Brazle .20 .50
7 Harry Brecheen .40 1.00
8 Jimmy Brown .20 .50
9 Ken Burkhart .20 .50
10 Bud Byerly .20 .50
11 Mort Cooper .40 1.00
12 Walker Cooper .40 1.00
13 Estel Crabtree .20 .50
14 Frank Crespi .20 .50
15 Jeff Cross .20 .50
16 Frank Demaree .20 .50
17 Murry Dickson .30 .75
18 Blix Donnelly .20 .50
19 Erv Dusak .20 .50
20 Eddie Dyer MGR .20 .50
21 Bill Endicott .20 .50
22 George Fallon .20 .50
23 Joe Garagiola 1.00 2.50
24 Debs Garms .20 .50
25 Mike Gonzalez CO .20 .50
26 Johnny Grodzicki .20 .50
27 Harry Gumbert .20 .50
28 Johnny Hopp .20 .50
29 Nippy Jones .20 .50
30 Al Jurisich .20 .50
31 Lou Klein .20 .50
32 Clyde Klutz .20 .50
33 Howie Krist .20 .50
34 Whitey Kurowski .20 .50
35 Max Lanier .20 .50
36 Danny Litwhiler .20 .50
37 Bill Lohrman .20 .50
38 Marty Marion .75 2.00
39 Freddie Martin .20 .50
40 Pepper Martin .75 2.00
41 Terry Moore .40 1.00
42 George Munger .20 .50
43 Stan Musial 2.00 5.00
44 Sam Narron .20 .50
45 Ken O'Dea .20 .50
46 Howie Pollet .20 .50
47 Del Rice .20 .50
48 Ray Sanders .20 .50
49 Fred Schmidt .20 .50
50 Red Schoendienst 1.00 2.50
51 Walt Sessi .20 .50
52 Clyde Shoun .20 .50
53 Dick Sisler .20 .50
54 Enos Slaughter 1.00 2.50
55 Billy Southworth MGR .20 .50
56 Coaker Triplett .20 .50
57 Emil Verban .20 .50
58 Harry Walker .40 1.00
59 Buzzy Ware .20 .50
60 Lon Warneke .40 1.00
61 Ernie White .20 .50
62 Del Wilber .20 .50
63 Ted Wilks .20 .50
64 L.Durocher MGR/E.Dyer MGR .75 2.00
65 Musial/Southworth MGR/Hopp .75 2.00
66 Musial/Southworth MGR/Sanders .75 2.00
67 R.Ruffing/J.Beazley .40 1.00
68 1942 St. Louis Cardinals Team .40 1.00
69 Sportsman's Park .40 1.00

1976 Cardinals Postcards

This 35-card set of the St. Louis Cardinals features player photos on postcard-size cards. The cards are unnumbered and checklisted below in alphabetical order.

COMPLETE SET (35) 8.00 20.00
1 Mike Anderson .20 .50
2 Lou Brock 1.50 4.00
3 Willie Crawford .20 .50
4 John Curtis .20 .50
5 Hector Cruz .20 .50
6 John Denny .30 .75
7 Ron Fairly .30 .75
8 Pete Falcone .20 .50
9 Joe Ferguson .20 .50
10 Bob Forsch .20 .50
11 Danny Frisella .20 .50
12 Preston Gomez CO .20 .50
13 Bill Greif .20 .50
14 Vic Harris .20 .50
15 Keith Hernandez 1.25 3.00
16 Al Hrabosky .30 .75
17 Don Kessinger .20 .50
18 Fred Koenig CO .20 .50
19 Johnny Lewis .20 .50
20 Bake McBride .20 .50
21 Lynn McGlothen .20 .50
22 Luis Melendez .20 .50
23 Bob Milliken CO .20 .50
24 Jerry Mumphrey .20 .50
25 Mike Proly .20 .50
26 Harry Rasmussen .20 .50
27 Lee Richard .20 .50
28 Ken Rudolph .20 .50
29 Red Schoendienst MG .60 1.50
30 Ted Simmons .40 1.00
31 Reggie Smith .40 1.00
32 Eddie Solomon .20 .50
33 Mike Tyson .20 .50
34 Mike Wallace .20 .50
35 Tom Zimmer .20 .50

1977 Cardinals 5x7

This 30-card set features black-and-white player portraits in a white border with the player's name and position printed in the bottom margin. The backs are blank. The cards are unnumbered and checklisted below in alphabetical order.

COMPLETE SET (30)	6.00	15.00
1 Mike Anderson	.20	.50
2 Lou Brock	.75	2.00
3 Clay Carroll	.20	.50
4 Heity Cruz	.20	.50
5 John Denny	.20	.50
6 Larry Dierker	.20	.50
7 Rawly Eastwick	.20	.50
8 Pete Falcone	.20	.50
9 Bob Forsch	.20	.50
10 Roger Freed	.20	.50
11 Keith Hernandez	.60	1.50
12 Al Hrabosky	.30	.75
13 Jack Krol CO	.20	.50
14 Butch Metzger	.20	.50
15 Mo Mozzali CO	.20	.50
16 Jerry Mumphrey	.20	.50
17 Claude Osteen CO	.20	.50
18 Mike Phillips	.20	.50
19 Dave Rader	.20	.50
20 Vern Rapp	.20	.50
21 Eric Rasmussen	.20	.50
22 Ken Reitz	.20	.50
23 Sonny Ruberto CO	.20	.50
24 Bobby Schultz	.20	.50
25 Tony Scott	.20	.50
26 Ted Simmons	.60	1.50
27 Garry Templeton	.40	1.00
28 Mike Tyson	.20	.50
29 Tom Underwood	.20	.50
30 John Urrea	.20	.50

1977 Cardinals Team Issue

This 28-card set measures approximately 3 1/4" by 5 1/2" and features black-and-white player portraits in a white border. A facsimile autograph is printed in the wide bottom margin. The backs are blank. The cards are unnumbered and checklisted below in alphabetical order.

COMPLETE SET (28)	4.00	10.00
1 Mike Anderson	.10	.25
2 Lou Brock	1.00	2.50
3 Clay Carroll	.10	.25
4 Heity Cruz	.10	.25
5 John Denny	.20	.50
6 Larry Dierker	.10	.25
7 Pete Falcone	.10	.25
8 Bob Forsch	.10	.25
9 Roger Freed	.10	.25
10 Keith Hernandez	.40	1.00
11 Al Hrabosky	.20	.50
12 Don Kessinger	.10	.25
13 Jack Krol	.10	.25
14 Butch Metzger	.10	.25
15 Maurice Mo Mozzali	.10	.25
16 Jerry Mumphrey	.10	.25
17 Claude Osteen	.10	.25
18 Dave Rader	.10	.25
19 Vern Rapp MG	.10	.25
20 Eric Rasmussen	.10	.25
21 Ken Reitz	.10	.25
22 Sonny Ruberto	.10	.25
23 Buddy Schutz	.10	.25
24 Tony Scott	.10	.25
25 Ted Simmons	.40	1.00
26 Garry Templeton	.30	.75
27 Mike Tyson	.10	.25
28 John Urrea	.10	.25

1978 Cardinals Team Issue

This 37-card set measures approximately 3 1/4" by 5 1/2" and features black-and-white player portraits in a white border. A facsimile autograph is printed in the wide bottom margin. The backs are blank. The cards are unnumbered and checklisted below in alphabetical order.

COMPLETE SET (37)	6.00	15.00
1 Ken Boyer	.40	1.00
2 Lou Brock	1.00	2.50
3 Tom Bruno	.10	.25
4 John Denny	.10	.25
5 Jim Dwyer	.10	.25
6 Pete Falcone	.10	.25
7 Bob Forsch	.10	.25
8 Roger Freed	.10	.25
9 Dave Hamilton	1.00	2.50
10 George Hendrick	.10	.25
11 Keith Hernandez	.40	1.00
12 Dane Iorg	.10	.25
13 Jack Krol	.10	.25
14 Mark Littell	.10	.25
15 Aurelio Lopez	.10	.25
16 Silvio Martinez	.10	.25
17 Dal Maxvill	.10	.25
18 Jerry Morales	.10	.25
19 Maurice Mo Mozzali	.10	.25
20 Jerry Mumphrey	.10	.25
21 Ken Oberkfell	.10	.25
22 Claude Osteen	.10	.25
23 Mike Phillips	.10	.25
24 Eric Rasmussen	.10	.25
25 Ken Reitz	.10	.25
26 Dave Ricketts	.10	.25
27 Sonny Ruberto	.10	.25
28 Red Schoendienst MG	.40	1.00
29 Buddy Schultz	.10	.25
30 Tony Scott	.10	.25
31 Ted Simmons	.40	1.00
32 Gary Sutherland	1.00	2.50
33 Steve Swisher	.10	.25
34 Garry Templeton	.20	.50
35 Mike Tyson	.10	.25
36 Pete Vuckovich	.20	.50
37 John Urrea	.10	.25

1979 Cardinals 5x7

This set features black-and-white player portraits in a white border with the player's name and position printed in the bottom margin. The backs are blank. The cards are unnumbered and checklisted below in alphabetical order. According to published reports at the time, the Tom Grieve card was pulled very early in the season.

COMPLETE SET	8.00	20.00
COMMON CARD	.20	.50
COMMON SP		
1 Ken Boyer MG	.40	1.00
2 Lou Brock	1.00	2.50
3 Tom Bruno	.20	.50
4 Bernie Carbo	.20	.50
5 John Denny	.20	.50
6 Bob Forsch	.20	.50
7 George Frazier	.20	.50
8 Roger Freed	.20	.50
9 John Fulgham	.20	.50
10 Tom Grieve SP	.40	1.00
11 George Hendrick	.20	.50
12 Keith Hernandez	.60	1.50
13 Dane Iorg	.20	.50
14 Terry Kennedy	.30	.75
15 Darold Knowles	.20	.50
16 Jack Krol CO	.20	.50
17 Mark Littell	.20	.50
18 Silvio Martinez	.20	.50
19 Dal Maxvill CO	.20	.50
20 Will McEnaney	.20	.50
21 Jerry Mumphrey	.20	.50
22 Ken Oberkfell	.20	.50
23 Claude Osteen CO	.20	.50
24 Mike Phillips	.20	.50
25 Ken Reitz		
26 Dave Ricketts CO	.20	.50
27 Tony Scott	.20	.50
28 Ted Schoendienst CO	.60	1.50
29 Buddy Schultz	.20	.50
30 Ted Simmons	.40	1.00
31 Steve Swisher	.20	.50
number 9 on uniform		
32 Steve Swisher	.20	.50
No number on uniform		
33 Bob Sykes	.20	.50
34 Garry Templeton	.30	.75
35 Roy Thomas	.20	.50
36 Mike Tyson	.20	.50
37 Pete Vuckovich	.30	.75

1964 Challenge The Yankees

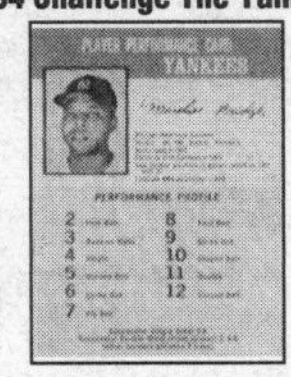

These cards were distributed as part of a baseball game produced in 1964. The cards each measure 4" by 5 3/8" and have square corners. The card fronts show a small black and white inset photo of the player, his name, position, vital statistics and the game outcomes associated with that particular player's card. The colors used on the front of the card are a blue border at the top and a yellow background for the game outcomes at the bottom. The game was played by rolling two dice. The outcomes (two through twelve) on the player's card related to the sum of the two dice. The game was noted for slightly inflated offensive production compared to real life. The cards are blank backed. Since the cards are unnumbered, they are listed below in alphabetical order within group. The first 25 cards are Yankees and the next 25 are All-Stars. Sets were put out in two different years, WG9 1964 and WG10 1965, which are difficult to distinguish. An empty box of either set, with the game pieces intact, is valued at approximately $75.

COMPLETE SET (50)	350.00	700.00
1 Yogi Berra	15.00	40.00
2 Johnny Blanchard	2.00	5.00
3 Jim Bouton	3.00	8.00
4 Clete Boyer	2.50	6.00
5 Marshall Bridges	2.00	5.00
6 Harry Bright	2.00	5.00
7 Al Downing	2.00	5.00
8 Whitey Ford	12.50	30.00
9 Jake Gibbs	2.00	5.00
10 Pedro Gonzalez	2.00	5.00
11 Steve Hamilton	2.00	5.00
12 Elston Howard	4.00	10.00
13 Tony Kubek	4.00	10.00
14 Phil Linz	2.00	5.00
15 Hector Lopez	2.00	5.00
16 Mickey Mantle	150.00	300.00
17 Roger Maris	30.00	60.00
18 Tom Metcalf	2.00	5.00
19 Joe Pepitone	2.50	6.00
20 Hal Reniff	2.00	5.00
21 Bobby Richardson	4.00	10.00
22 Bill Stafford	2.00	5.00
23 Ralph Terry	2.50	6.00
24 Tom Tresh	2.50	6.00
25 Stan Williams	2.00	5.00
26 Hank Aaron	20.00	50.00
27 Tom Cheney	2.50	6.00
28 Del Crandall	2.50	6.00
29 Tito Francona	2.50	6.00
30 Dick Groat	2.50	6.00
31 Al Kaline	12.50	30.00
32 Art Mahaffey	2.50	6.00
33 Frank Malzone	2.50	6.00
34 Juan Marichal	8.00	20.00
35 Eddie Mathews	8.00	20.00
36 Bill Mazeroski	8.00	20.00
37 Ken McBride	2.50	6.00
38 Willie McCovey	8.00	20.00
39 Jim O'Toole	2.50	6.00
40 Milt Pappas	3.00	8.00
41 Ron Perranoski	2.50	6.00
42 Johnny Podres	3.00	8.00
43 Dick Radatz	2.50	6.00
44 Rich Rollins	2.50	6.00
45 Ron Santo	5.00	12.00
46 Moose Skowron	3.00	8.00
47 Duke Snider	15.00	40.00
48 Pete Ward	2.50	6.00
49 Carl Warwick	2.50	6.00
50 Carl Yastrzemski	15.00	40.00

1965 Challenge The Yankees

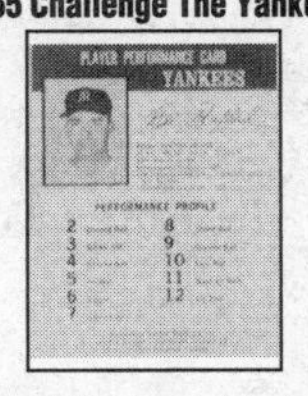

These cards were distributed as part of a baseball game produced in 1965. The cards each measure 4" by 5 3/8" and have square corners. The card fronts show a small black and white inset photo of the player, his name, position, vital statistics, and the game outcomes associated with that particular player's card. The colors used on the front of the card are a blue border at the top and a yellow background for the game outcomes at the bottom. The game was played by rolling two dice. The outcomes (two through twelve) on the player's card related to the sum of the two dice. The game was noted for slightly inflated offensive production compared to real life. The cards are blank backed. Since the cards are unnumbered, they are listed below in alphabetical order within group. The first 23 cards are Yankees and the next 25 are All-Stars. There were also 18 blank cards included in the set for extra players of your choice. These "Challenge The Yankees" sets were put out in two different years, WG9 1964 and WG10 1965, which are difficult to distinguish.

COMPLETE SET (48)	500.00	1,000.00
1 Johnny Blanchard	4.00	10.00
2 Jim Bouton	6.00	15.00
3 Clete Boyer	5.00	12.00
4 Leon Carmel	4.00	10.00
5 Al Downing	4.00	10.00
6 Whitey Ford	15.00	40.00
7 Jake Gibbs	4.00	10.00
8 Pedro Gonzalez	4.00	10.00
9 Steve Hamilton	4.00	10.00
10 Elston Howard	8.00	20.00
11 Tony Kubek	8.00	20.00
12 Phil Linz	4.00	10.00
13 Mickey Mantle	200.00	400.00
14 Roger Maris	50.00	100.00
15 Tom Metcalf	4.00	10.00
16 Pete Mikkelsen	4.00	10.00
17 Joe Pepitone	5.00	12.00
18 Pedro Ramos	4.00	10.00
19 Hal Reniff	4.00	10.00
20 Bobby Richardson	8.00	20.00
21 Bill Stafford	4.00	10.00
22 Mel Stottlemyre	5.00	12.00
23 Tom Tresh	5.00	12.00
24 Henry Aaron	40.00	80.00
25 Joe Christopher	4.00	10.00
26 Vic Davalillo	4.00	10.00
27 Bill Freehan	5.00	12.00
28 Jim Gentile	4.00	10.00
29 Dick Groat	5.00	12.00
30 Al Kaline	20.00	50.00
31 Don Lock	4.00	10.00
32 Art Mahaffey	4.00	10.00
33 Frank Malzone	4.00	10.00
34 Juan Marichal	12.50	30.00
35 Eddie Mathews	12.50	30.00
36 Bill Mazeroski	12.50	30.00
37 Ken McBride	4.00	10.00
38 Tim McCarver	8.00	20.00
39 Willie McCovey	12.50	30.00
40 Jim O'Toole	4.00	10.00
41 Milt Pappas	5.00	12.00
42 Ron Perranoski	4.00	10.00
43 Johnny Podres	5.00	12.00
44 Dick Radatz	4.00	10.00
45 Rich Rollins	4.00	10.00
46 Ron Santo	8.00	20.00
47 Pete Ward	4.00	10.00
48 Carl Yastrzemski	30.00	60.00

1961 Chemstrand Patches

This nine-card set features color star player portraits on 2 1/2" diameter cloth patches which were included with the purchase of a boy's sport shirt for a short period in 1961. The patches were issued one to a cello package with instructions for ironing the patch onto the shirt. The package also offered the opportunity to trade the player patch for a different star. The patches are unnumbered and checklisted below in alphabetical order. Values for unopened cello packs are slightly higher.

COMPLETE SET (9)	175.00	350.00
1 Ernie Banks	15.00	40.00
2 Yogi Berra	15.00	40.00
3 Nellie Fox	15.00	40.00
4 Dick Groat	8.00	20.00
5 Al Kaline	15.00	40.00
6 Harmon Killebrew	15.00	40.00
7 Frank Malzone	8.00	20.00
8 Willie Mays	40.00	80.00
9 Warren Spahn	15.00	40.00

1976 Chevy Prints

These four prints were drawn by Robert Thon, a noted historical illustrator and were commissioned by Chevrolet in honor of the 100th anniversary of the National League (and what is considered organized ball). The fronts feature four highlights from various times in baseball history and the backs have a description of these events.

COMPLETE SET (4)	4.00	10.00
1 The First Game	.40	1.00
2 Pepper Martin	.75	2.00
Bill Werber		
The Gashouse Gang		
3 Babe Ruth	2.00	5.00
The Mighty Babe		
4 Hank Aaron	2.00	5.00
The Record Breaker		

1976 Chicago Greats

This standard-size set features black-and-white action player photos with a red baseball and bat border design. A small, square close-up photo is superimposed on one of the upper corners of the picture. "Chicago's Greats" is printed in red at the bottom. The horizontal backs are white and carry the player's name, biographical information, statistics and career highlights. The cards are unnumbered and checklisted below in alphabetical order. The set was originally available for $2.50 from the producers.

COMPLETE SET (24)	5.00	12.00
1 Luke Appling	.30	.75
2 Ernie Banks	.60	1.50
3 Zeke Bonura	.10	.25
4 Phil Cavarretta	.20	.50
5 Jimmie Dykes	.20	.50
6 Nellie Fox	.40	1.00
7 Larry French	.10	.25
8 Charlie Grimm	.20	.50
9 Gabby Hartnett	.40	1.00
10 Billy Herman	.30	.75
11 Mike Kreevich	.10	.25
12 Sherm Lollar	.10	.25
13 Al Lopez	.30	.75
14 Ted Lyons	.20	.50
Red Faber		
15 Minnie Minoso	.30	.75
16 Wally Moses	.10	.25
17 Bill Nicholson	.10	.25
18 Claude Passeau	.10	.25
19 Billy Pierce	.20	.50
20 Ron Santo	.30	.75
21 Hank Sauer	.10	.25
22 Riggs Stephenson	.20	.50
23 Bill Veeck OWN	.30	.75
24 Philip K. Wrigley OWN	.20	.50
25 Checklist	.10	.25

1915 Chicago Tribune Supplements

These four newspaper supplements were issued by the Chicago Tribune. Based on the known date of the Eddie Collins card it is presumed that these supplements were supposed to increase interest in the upcoming baseball

season. Since these are unnumbered, we have sequenced these in alphabetical order.
1 Roger Bresnahan
2 Eddie Collins (April 18)
3 Vic Saier
4 Joe Tinker

1972 Classic Cards

This 120-card set was issued in four series and features sepia player photos printed on beige card stock. The backs carry a checklist of the series in which the player photo displayed on the front is found. The cards are checklisted below according to those checklists. Series 1 consists of cards numbered from 1-30; Series 2, cards numbered from 31-60; Series 3, cards numbered from 61-90; and Series 4, cards numbered from 91-120.

COMPLETE SET (120)	40.00	80.00
1 Clark Griffith	.75	2.00
2 Walter Johnson	1.25	3.00
3 Bob Ganley	.20	.50
4 Joe Tinker	.75	2.00
5 Frank Chance	.75	2.00
6 Wid Conroy	.20	.50
7 Roger Bresnahan	.40	1.00
8 Jack Powell	.20	.50
9 Jack Pfeister	.20	.50
10 Tom McCarthy	.40	1.00
11 Amby McConnell	.20	.50
12 Hugh Jennings	.40	1.00
13 Ed Lennox	.20	.50
14 Moose McCormick	.20	.50
15 Fred Merkle	.20	.50
16 Dick Hoblitzell	.20	.50
17 Bill Dahlen	.20	.50
18 Frank Chance	.75	2.00
19 George Ferguson	.20	.50
20 Howie Camnitz	.20	.50
21 Neal Ball	.20	.50
22 Charlie Hemphill	.20	.50
23 Frank Baker	.60	1.50
24 Christy Mathewson	.75	2.00
25 Al Burch	.20	.50
26 Eddie Grant	.40	1.00
27 Red Ames	.20	.50
28 Doc Newton	.20	.50
29 Pat Moran	.20	.50
30 Nap Lajoie	.75	2.00
31 Mordecai Brown	.60	1.50
32 Bill Abstein	.20	.50
33 Ty Cobb	2.00	5.00
34 Billy Campbell	.20	.50
35 Claude Rossman	.20	.50
36 Topsy Hartsel	.20	.50
37 Sam Crawford	.60	1.50
38 Red Dooin	.20	.50
39 Jack Dunn	.20	.50
40 Tom Downey	.20	.50
41 Bill Hinchman	.20	.50
42 John Titus	.20	.50
43 Patsy Dougherty	.20	.50
44 Art Devlin	.20	.50
45 Nap Lajoie	.75	2.00
46 Larry Doyle	.20	.50
47 Honus Wagner	1.25	3.00
48 Bull Durham	.40	1.00
49 Irv Higginbotham	.20	.50
50 George Gibson	.20	.50
51 Mike Mowrey	.20	.50
52 George Stone	.20	.50
53 George Perring	.20	.50
54 Orvie Overall	.20	.50
55 Hooks Wiltse	.20	.50
56 Jack Warhop	.20	.50
57 Harry Steinfeldt	.40	1.00
58 Bill O'Hara	.20	.50
59 Boss Schmidt	.20	.50
60 George Mullin	.20	.50
61 Buck Herzog	.20	.50
62 John Hummell	.20	.50
63 Art Fromme	.20	.50
64 Kid Elberfeld	.20	.50
65 Frank Bowerman	.20	.50
66 Roger Bresnahan	.40	1.00
67 Andy Coakley	.20	.50
68 Jim Pastorius	.20	.50
69 Tubby Spencer	.20	.50
70 Frank Schulte	.20	.50
71 Willie Keeler	.40	1.00
72 Joe McGinnity	.40	1.00
73 Harry McIntyre	.20	.50
74 Harry Lumley	.20	.50
75 Nick Maddox	.20	.50
76 Cy Barger	.20	.50
77 Bill Donovan	.20	.50
78 Tim Jordan	.20	.50
79 Johnnie Evers	.75	2.00
80 Zack Wheat	.40	1.00
81 Hippo Vaughn	.20	.50
82 Jimmy Sebring	.20	.50
83 Tom Tuckey	.20	.50
84 Tris Speaker	1.25	3.00
85 John McGraw	.75	2.00
86 Billy Purtell	.20	.50
87 George Moriarity	.20	.50
88 Charlie Smith	.20	.50
89 Bill Bergen	.20	.50
90 Kitty Bransfield	.20	.50
91 Joe Doyle	.20	.50
92 Amos Strunk	.20	.50
93 Bob Ewing	.20	.50
94 Tom Daley	.20	.50
95 Joe Delahanty	.20	.50
96 Ed Summers	.20	.50
97 Joe Lake	.20	.50
98 Dave Altizer	.20	.50
99 Roger Bresnahan	.40	1.00
100 Chief Bender	.60	1.50
101 Buck Herzog	.20	.50
102 Ira Thomas	.20	.50
103 Hal Chase	.75	2.00
104 Tom Needham	.20	.50
105 Ducky Pearce	.20	.50
106 Rube Ellis	.20	.50
107 Ed Konetchy	.20	.50
108 Harry Lord	.20	.50
109 Ossie Schreck	.20	.50
110 Heinie Wagner	.20	.50
111 Luther Taylor	.20	.50
112 Alan Storke	.20	.50
113 Bill Powell	.20	.50
114 Ham Hyatt	.20	.50
115 George Davis	.40	1.00
116 Bill Grahame	.20	.50
117 Larry McLean	.20	.50
118 Jiggs Donohue	.20	.50
119 Bill Chappelle	.20	.50
120 Billy Purtell	.20	.50

1910 Clement Brothers D380

This set, which measures approximately 1 1/2" by 2 3/4" was issued solely in the Rochester NY area. The set features a mix of established major leaguers and some local minor league players.

COMPLETE SET	100,000.00	200,000.00
1 Whitey Alperman	4,000.00	8,000.00
2 Bailey	4,000.00	8,000.00
3 Walter Blair	4,000.00	8,000.00
4 Ty Cobb	25,000.00	50,000.00
5 Eddie Collins	2,000.00	40,000.00
6 Roy Hartzell	4,000.00	8,000.00
7 Harry Howell	4,000.00	8,000.00
8 Addie Joss	12,500.00	25,000.00
9 George McConnell	4,000.00	8,000.00
10 Fred Osborn	4,000.00	8,000.00
11 Harry Pattee	4,000.00	8,000.00
12 Don Carlos Ragan	4,000.00	8,000.00
13 Oscar Stanage	4,000.00	8,000.00
14 George Stone	4,000.00	8,000.00
15 Ed Summers	4,000.00	8,000.00
16 Joe Tinker	12,500.00	25,000.00
17 Bert Tooley	4,000.00	8,000.00
18 Heinie Zimmerman	5,000.00	10,000.00

1972 Clemente Daily Juice

This slightly oversized card featured Pirate great Roberto Clemente. The borderless front has a full color photo of Clemente along with a fascimile signature. The horizontal back has information on how to join the Clemente fan club. These cards are still commonly found as part of uncut sheets.

1 Roberto Clemente	2.00	5.00

1973 Clemente Pictureform

The Roberto Clemente Pictureform set consists of 12 photos and originally sold for $2.00. The black-and-white action photos are in a circle format and measure approximately 8 3/16" in diameter. The photos are bordered by an orange or light blue 1 3/8" border and printed on medium weight paper stock. There are five scored lines surrounding the photo that indicate where to fold the picture to form the pictureform. Once assembled, the pictures form a twelve-sided sphere. No lettering is printed on the front and the backs are blank. The photos were packaged with a large folder which displayed a color posed photo of Clemente on the front. On the inside left side were Clemente's career highlights and quotes from his peers. The inside right contained instructions for assembling the pictureform with line drawn illustrations above and below.

COMPLETE SET (12)	50.00	100.00
COMMON PLAYER (1-12)	4.00	10.00
XX Album	4.00	10.00

1938 Clopay Foto-Fun R329

This set features sun-developed blue-tinted photos which are self-developed by the sun. They measure approximately 2 3/16" by 2 3/4". The backs are blank. The cards are unnumbered and checklisted below in alphabetical order. Holders in excellent condition are fairly rare and add a value of at least $25 to any individual clopay. It is believed that 100 subjects were issued for this set so any additions to this checklist are appreciated.

COMPLETE SET	2,000.00	4,000.00
1 Luke Appling	60.00	120.00
2 Morris Arnovich	30.00	60.00
3 Eldon Auker	30.00	60.00
4 Jim Bagby	30.00	60.00
5 Red Barrett	30.00	60.00
6 Roy Bell	30.00	60.00
7 Wally Berger	40.00	80.00
8 Oswald Bluege	30.00	60.00
9 Frenchy Bordagaray	30.00	60.00
10 Tom Bridges	40.00	80.00
11 Dolf Camilli	50.00	100.00
12 Ben Chapman	30.00	60.00
13 Harland Clift	40.00	80.00
14 Harry Craft	30.00	60.00
15 Roger Cramer	40.00	80.00
16 Joe Cronin MG	60.00	120.00
17 Kiki Cuyler	60.00	120.00
18 Babe Dahlgren	30.00	60.00
19 Harry Danning	40.00	80.00
20 Frank Demaree	30.00	60.00
21 Gene Desautels	30.00	60.00
22 Jim Deshong	30.00	60.00
23 Bill Dickey	60.00	120.00
24 Jim Dykes MG	40.00	80.00
25 Lou Fette	30.00	60.00
26 Louis Finney	30.00	60.00
27 Larry French	30.00	60.00
28 Linus Frey	30.00	60.00
29 Deb Garms	30.00	60.00
30 Charles Gehringer	60.00	120.00
31 Lefty Gomez	60.00	120.00
32 Ival Goodman	30.00	60.00
33 Lee Grissom	30.00	60.00
34 Stanley Hack	40.00	80.00
35 Irving Hadley	30.00	60.00
36 Mel Harder	40.00	80.00
37 Rollie Hemsley	30.00	60.00
38 Tommy Henrich	50.00	100.00
39 Billy Herman	40.00	80.00
40 Willard Hershberger	40.00	80.00
41 Michael Higgins	30.00	60.00
42 Oral Hildebrand	30.00	60.00
43 Carl Hubbell	60.00	120.00
44 Willis Hudlin	30.00	60.00
45 Mike Kreevich	30.00	60.00
46 Ralph Kress	30.00	60.00
47 John Lanning	30.00	60.00
48 Lyn Lary	30.00	60.00
49 Cookie Lavagetto	30.00	60.00
50 Thornton Lee	30.00	60.00
51 Ernie Lombardi	60.00	120.00
52 Al Lopez	60.00	120.00
53 Ted Lyons	60.00	120.00
54 Danny MacFayden	30.00	60.00
55 Max Macon	30.00	60.00
56 Pepper Martin	50.00	100.00
57 Joe Marty	30.00	60.00
58 Frank McCormick	30.00	60.00
59 Bill McKechnie MG	50.00	100.00
60 Joe Medwick	60.00	120.00
61 Cliff Melton	30.00	60.00
62 Charles Meyer	30.00	60.00
63 John Mize	60.00	120.00
64 Terry Moore	30.00	60.00
65 Whitey Moore	30.00	60.00
66 Emmett Mueller	30.00	60.00
67 Hugh Mulcahy	30.00	60.00
68 Van Mungo	40.00	80.00
69 John Murphy	40.00	80.00
70 Lynn Nelson	30.00	60.00
71 Mel Ott	60.00	120.00
72 Monte Pearson	30.00	60.00
73 Bill Rogell	30.00	60.00
74 George Selkirk	30.00	60.00
75 Milt Shoffner	30.00	60.00
76 Clyde Shoun	30.00	60.00
77 Al Simmons	60.00	120.00
78 Gus Suhr	30.00	60.00
79 Bill Sullivan	30.00	60.00
80 Cecil Travis	30.00	60.00
81 Pie Traynor MG	60.00	120.00
82 Harold Trosky	30.00	60.00
83 Jim Turner	30.00	60.00
84 Johnny VanderMeer	50.00	100.00
85 Oscar Vitt MG	30.00	60.00
86 Gerald Walker	30.00	60.00
87 Paul Waner	60.00	120.00
88 Lon Warneke	30.00	60.00
89 Rabbit Warstler	30.00	60.00
90 Bob Weiland	30.00	60.00
91 Burgess Whitehead	30.00	60.00
92 Earl Whitehill	30.00	60.00
93 Rudy York	40.00	80.00
94 Del Young	30.00	60.00

1975 Cobb McCallum

This 20-card set was produced to promote John McCallum's biography on Ty Cobb. The cards measure approximately 2 1/2" X 3 1/2" and feature on the fronts vintage black and white photos, with a hand-drawn artificial wood grain picture frame border. The title to each picture appears in a plaque below the picture. The back has a facsimile autograph and extended caption. The cards are numbered on the back in a baseball icon in the upper right corner. This set was issued at a price of $2.95 upon its release.

COMPLETE SET (20)	12.50	30.00
COMMON PLAYER (1-20)	.30	.75
6 Ty Cobb Walter Johnson	1.25	3.00
11 Ty Cobb Paul Cobb	.40	1.00
12 Ty Cobb Thomas Edison	1.00	2.50
13 Ty Cobb Tangles with John McGraw	1.00	2.50
14 Author McCallum with Cy Young	.60	1.50
15 Tris Speaker Joe DiMaggio and Ty Cobb	2.50	6.00
16 Ty Cobb Ted Williams	1.25	3.00

1952 Coke Tips

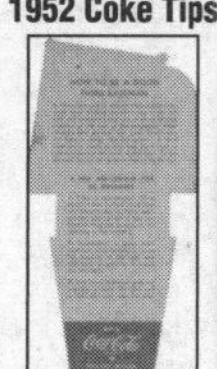

This 10-card set features artwork of various Yankees, Giants and Dodgers and was inserted into regional Coca-Cola bottle cartons. The fronts display the artwork depicting the players and team schedules. The backs carry tips on how to play the pictured player's position and other Big-League tips. The cards are unnumbered and checklisted below in alphabetical order. A Willie Mays card, considered a test for this series, is appended at the end of the checklist. It is possible that the Mays card was actually pulled from this series when he entered military service early during the 1952 season.

COMPLETE SET (10)	1,250.00	2,500.00
1 Hank Bauer	150.00	300.00
2 Carl Furillo	200.00	400.00
3 Gil Hodges	200.00	400.00
4 Ed Lopat	125.00	250.00
5 Gil McDougald	125.00	250.00
6 Don Mueller	100.00	200.00
7 Pee Wee Reese	200.00	400.00
8 Bobby Thomson/(Playing 3rd base)	150.00	300.00
9 Bobby Thomson/(Hitting)	150.00	300.00
10 Wes Westrum	100.00	200.00
T1 Willie Mays Test	750.00	1,500.00
T2 Phil Rizzuto Test	150.00	400.00

1980 Coke/7-11 NL MVPs

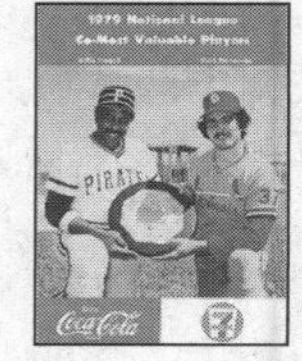

This one-card blank-backed set, sponsored by Coca-Cola and 7-11, features a color posed photo of the co-most valuable players of the 1979 National League.

1 Willie Stargell Keith Hernandez	2.00	5.00

1917 Collins-McCarthy E135

The cards in this 200-card set measure 2" by 3 1/4". Collins-McCarthy, the West Coast manufacturer of Zee Nuts (E137), issued the Baseball's Hall of Fame set of players in 1917. These black and white photos of current players were not only numbered but also listed alphabetically. The set is similar to D328, except that E135 is printed on thinner stock. The complete set price includes all variation cards listed in the checklist below. Recent research indicates that this set was issued in 1917, a good example of that is the Ping Bodie card. Bodie played the full 1916 season for San Francisco and his card indicates he is a member of the White Sox. At least four different back varieties are known: A card with a blank back, Collins-McCarthy, Boston Store and Standard Biscuit.

COMPLETE SET (200)	20,000.00	40,000.00
1 Sam Agnew	75.00	150.00
2 Grover C. Alexander	150.00	300.00
3 W.E. Alexander	75.00	150.00
4 Leon Ames	75.00	150.00
5 Fred Anderson	75.00	150.00
6 Ed Appleton	75.00	150.00
7 Jimmy Archer	75.00	150.00
8 Jimmy Austin	75.00	150.00
9 Jim Bagby	75.00	150.00
10 H.D. Baird	75.00	150.00
11 Frank Baker	150.00	300.00
12 Dave Bancroft	125.00	250.00
13 Jack Barry	75.00	150.00
14 Joe Benz	75.00	150.00
15 Al Betzel	75.00	150.00
16 Ping Bodie	75.00	150.00
17 Joe Boehling	75.00	150.00

Card	Low	High
18 Eddie Burns	75.00	150.00
19 George Burns Detroit	75.00	150.00
20 Geo. J. Burns NY	75.00	150.00
21 Joe Bush	100.00	200.00
22 Owen Bush	75.00	150.00
23 Bobbie Byrne	75.00	150.00
24 Forrest Cady	75.00	150.00
25 Max Carey	125.00	250.00
26 Ray Chapman	125.00	250.00
27 Larry Cheney	75.00	150.00
28 Eddie Cicotte	150.00	300.00
29 Tom Clarke	75.00	150.00
30 Ty Cobb	1,200.00	2,400.00
31 Eddie Collins	150.00	300.00
32 Shauno Collins	75.00	150.00
33 Fred Coumbe	75.00	150.00
34 Harry Coveleski	100.00	200.00
35 Gavvy Cravath	100.00	200.00
36 Sam Crawford	150.00	300.00
37 George Cutshaw	100.00	200.00
38 Jack Daubert	100.00	200.00
39 George Dauss	75.00	150.00
40 Charles Deal	75.00	150.00
41 Wheezer Dell	75.00	150.00
42 William Doak	75.00	150.00
43 Bill Donovan	75.00	150.00
44 Larry Doyle	100.00	200.00
45 Johnny Evers	150.00	300.00
46 Urban Faber	125.00	250.00
47 Happy Felsch	150.00	300.00
48 Bill Fischer	75.00	150.00
49 Ray Fisher	75.00	150.00
50 Art Fletcher	75.00	150.00
51 Eddie Foster	75.00	150.00
52 Jacques Fournier	75.00	150.00
53 Del Gainer	75.00	150.00
54 Bert Gallia	75.00	150.00
55 Chick Gandil	150.00	300.00
56 Larry Gardner	75.00	150.00
57 Joe Gedeon	75.00	150.00
58 Gus Getz	75.00	150.00
59 Frank Gilhooley	75.00	150.00
60 Kid Gleason MG	100.00	200.00
61 Mike Gonzales	75.00	150.00
62 Hank Gowdy	100.00	200.00
63 John Graney	75.00	150.00
64 Tom Griffith	75.00	150.00
65 Heinie Groh	100.00	200.00
66 Bob Groom	75.00	150.00
67 Louis Guisto	75.00	150.00
68 Earl Hamilton	75.00	150.00
69 Harry Harper	75.00	150.00
70 Grover Hartley	75.00	150.00
71 Harry Heilmann	125.00	250.00
72 Claude Hendrix	75.00	150.00
73 Olaf Henriksen	75.00	150.00
74 John Henry	75.00	150.00
75 Buck Herzog	75.00	150.00
76A Hugh High ERR photo actually Claude Williams white stockings	150.00	300.00
76B Hugh High COR black stockings	100.00	200.00
77 Dick Hoblitzell	75.00	150.00
78 Walter Holke	75.00	150.00
79 Harry Hooper	125.00	250.00
80 Rogers Hornsby	300.00	600.00
81 Ivan Howard	75.00	150.00
82 Joe Jackson	1,200.00	2,400.00
83 Harold Janvrin	75.00	150.00
84 William James	75.00	150.00
85 Charlie Jamieson	75.00	150.00
86 Hugh Jennings MG	125.00	250.00
87 Walter Johnson	350.00	700.00
88 James Johnston	75.00	150.00
89 Fielder Jones	75.00	150.00
90A Joe Judge ERR photo actually Ray Morgan bat right shoulder	150.00	300.00
90B Joe Judge COR/(bat left shoulder)	100.00	200.00
91 Hans Lobert	75.00	150.00
92 Benny Kauff	75.00	150.00
93 Wm. Killefer Jr.	75.00	150.00
94 Ed Konetchy	75.00	150.00
95 John Lavan	75.00	150.00
96 Jimmy Lavender	75.00	150.00
97 Nemo Leibold	75.00	150.00
98 Dutch Leonard	100.00	200.00
99 Duffy Lewis	75.00	150.00
100 Tom Long	75.00	150.00
101 Bill Louden	75.00	150.00
102 Fred Luderus	75.00	150.00
103 Lee Magee	75.00	150.00
104 Sherwood Magee	100.00	200.00
105 Al Mamaux	75.00	150.00
106 Leslie Mann	75.00	150.00
107 Rabbit Maranville	125.00	250.00
108 Rube Marquard	150.00	300.00
109 Armando Marsans	75.00	150.00
110 J. Erskine Mayer	75.00	150.00
111 George McBride	75.00	150.00
112 Lew McCarty	75.00	150.00
113 John J. McGraw MG	150.00	300.00
114 Jack McInnis	100.00	200.00
115 Lee Meadows	75.00	150.00
116 Fred Merkle	100.00	200.00
117 Chief Meyers	100.00	200.00
118 Clyde Milan	75.00	150.00
119 Otto Miller	75.00	150.00
120 Clarence Mitchell	75.00	150.00
121A Ray Morgan ERR photo actually Joe Judge bat left shoulder	150.00	300.00
121B Ray Morgan COR/(bat right shoulder)	100.00	200.00
122 Guy Morton	75.00	150.00
123 Mike Mowrey	75.00	150.00
124 Elmer Myers	75.00	150.00
125 Hy Myers	75.00	150.00
126 Greasy Neale	100.00	200.00
127 Art Nehf	75.00	150.00
128 J.A. Niehoff	75.00	150.00
129 Steve O'Neill	100.00	200.00
130 Dode Paskert	75.00	150.00
131 Roger Peckinpaugh	100.00	200.00
132 Pol Perritt	75.00	150.00
133 Jeff Pfeffer	75.00	150.00
134 Walter Pipp	125.00	250.00
135 Derril Pratt	75.00	150.00
136 Bill Rariden	75.00	150.00
137 Sam Rice	125.00	250.00
138 Hank Ritter	75.00	150.00
139 Eppa Rixey	125.00	250.00
140 Davey Robertson	75.00	150.00
141 Bob Roth	75.00	150.00
142 Ed Roush	125.00	250.00
143 Clarence Rowland MG	75.00	150.00
144 Dick Rudolph	75.00	150.00
145 William Rumler	75.00	150.00
146A Reb Russell ERR photo actually Mel Wolfgang pitching follow through	150.00	300.00
146B Reb Russell COR standing, hands at side	100.00	200.00
147 Babe Ruth	1,800.00	3,600.00
148 Vic Saier	75.00	150.00
149 Slim Sallee	75.00	150.00
150 Ray Schalk	125.00	250.00
151 Walter Schang	75.00	150.00
152 Frank Schulte	75.00	150.00
153 Ferd Schupp	75.00	150.00
154 Everett Scott	100.00	200.00
155 Hank Severeid	75.00	150.00
156 Howard Shanks	75.00	150.00
157 Bob Shawkey	100.00	200.00
158 Jimmy Sheckard CO	75.00	150.00
159 Ernie Shore	100.00	200.00
160 Chick Shorten	75.00	150.00
161 Burt Shotton	100.00	200.00
162 George Sisler	150.00	300.00
163 Elmer Smith	75.00	150.00
164 J. Carlisle Smith	75.00	150.00
165 Fred Snodgrass	100.00	200.00
166 Tris Speaker	150.00	300.00
167 Oscar Stanage	75.00	150.00
168 Casey Stengel	500.00	1,000.00
169 Milton Stock	75.00	150.00
170 Amos Strunk	75.00	150.00
171 Zeb Terry	75.00	150.00
172 Jeff Tesreau	75.00	150.00
173 Chester Thomas	75.00	150.00
174 Fred Toney	100.00	200.00
175 Terry Turner	75.00	150.00
176 George Tyler	75.00	150.00
177 Jim Vaughn	75.00	150.00
178 Bob Veach	75.00	150.00
179 Oscar Vitt	100.00	200.00
180 Honus Wagner	750.00	1,500.00
181 Clarence Walker	75.00	150.00
182 Jim Walsh	75.00	150.00
183 Al Walters	75.00	150.00
184 Bill Wambsganss	75.00	150.00
185 Buck Weaver	150.00	300.00
186 Carl Weilman	75.00	150.00
187 Zack Wheat	150.00	300.00
188 Geo. Whitted	75.00	150.00
189 Joe Wilhoit	75.00	150.00
190A Claude Williams ERR photo actually Hugh High black stockings	150.00	300.00
190B Claude Williams COR/(photo correct)	125.00	250.00
191 Fred Williams	100.00	200.00
192 Art Wilson	75.00	150.00
193 Lawton Witt	75.00	150.00
194 Joe Wood	125.00	250.00
195 William Wortman	75.00	150.00
196 Steve Yerkes	75.00	150.00
197 Earl Yingling	75.00	150.00
198 Pep Young/(2ndB. Detroit)	75.00	150.00
199 Rollie Zeider	75.00	150.00
200 Heine Zimmerman	75.00	150.00

1962 Colt .45's Booklets

These booklets feature members of the inagural Houston Colt 45's. They were issued and released at various retail outlets. Each booklet is 16 pages and has personal and career information on the players in the set. The following booklets are believed to be in shorter supply: Jim Campbell; J.C. Hartman, Roman Mejias, Jim Pendleton, Paul Richards, Bobby Shantz, Jim Umbricht, Hal Woodeshick, Coaches, Announcers. Umbricht is believed to be by far the hardest booklet to acquire. Three different versions of each booklet exist: they were sponsored by American Tobacco, Pearl Beer and Phillips 66 respectively. All sponsors are valued the same.

Card	Low	High
COMPLETE SET	125.00	250.00
COMMON PLAYER	2.50	6.00
COMMON SP'S	6.00	15.00
1 Joe Amalfitano	2.50	6.00
2 Bob Aspromonte	3.00	8.00
3 Bob Bruce	2.50	6.00
4 Jim Campbell SP	6.00	15.00
5 Harry Craft MG	2.50	6.00
6 Dick Farrell	2.50	6.00
7 Dave Giusti	2.50	6.00
8 Jim Golden	2.50	6.00
9 J.C. Hartman SP	6.00	15.00
10 Ken Johnson	2.50	6.00
11 Norm Larker	2.50	6.00
12 Bob Lillis	3.00	8.00
13 Don McMahon	2.50	6.00
14 Roman Mejias SP	6.00	15.00
15 Jim Pendleton SP	6.00	15.00
16 Paul Richards GM SP	8.00	20.00
17 Bobby Shantz SP	8.00	20.00
18 Hal Smith	2.50	6.00
19 Al Spangler	2.50	6.00
20 Jim Umbricht SP	20.00	50.00
21 Carl Warwick	2.50	6.00
22 Hal Woodeshick SP	8.00	20.00
23 The Coaches SP	8.00	20.00
24 The Announcers SP	6.00	15.00

1962 Colt .45's Houston Chronicle

This 20-card set features sketches of the Houston Colt .45's team as drawn by Tony Couch and appeared in the Houston Chronicle newspaper. The cards are unnumbered and checklisted below in alphabetical order.

Card	Low	High
COMPLETE SET (20)	12.50	30.00
1 Joe Amalfitano	.60	1.50
2 Bob Aspromonte	.75	2.00
3 Don Buddin	.60	1.50
4 Al Cicotte	.60	1.50
5 Dick Ferrell(Sic)	.60	1.50
6 Dick Gernert	.60	1.50
7 Jim Golden	.60	1.50
8 Al Heist	.60	1.50
9 Ken Johnson	.60	1.50
10 Norm Larker	.60	1.50
11 Roman Mejias	.60	1.50
12 Ed Olivares	.60	1.50
13 Jim Pendleton	.60	1.50
14 Bobby Shantz	.75	2.00
15 Hal W. Smith	.60	1.50
16 Al Spangler	.60	1.50
17 Don Taussig	.60	1.50
18 Bobby Tiefenauer	.60	1.50
19 Jim Umbricht	.60	1.50
20 Hal Woodeshick	.60	1.50

1962 Colt .45's Jay Publishing

This 12-card set of the Houston Colt .45's measures approximately 5" by 7". The fronts feature black-and-white posed player photos with the player's and team name printed below in the white border. These cards were packaged 12 in a packet. The backs are blank. The cards are unnumbered and checklisted below in alphabetical order. A complete set in the original envelope is valued at fifty percent higher.

Card	Low	High
COMPLETE SET (12)	50.00	100.00
1 Joe Amalfitano	4.00	10.00
2 Bob Aspromonte	5.00	12.00
3 Bob Bruce	3.00	8.00
4 Don Buddin	3.00	8.00
5 Harry Craft MG	3.00	8.00
6 Dick Farrell	3.00	8.00
7 Ken Johnson	3.00	8.00
8 Norm Larker	3.00	8.00
9 Roman Mejias	4.00	10.00
10 Paul Richards GM	5.00	12.00
11 Hal Smith	4.00	10.00
12 Al Spangler	3.00	8.00

1963 Colt .45's Jay Publishing

This 12-card set of the Houston Colt .45's measures approximately 5" by 7". The fronts feature black-and-white posed player photos with the player's and team name printed below in the white border. These cards were packaged 12 in a packet. The backs are blank. The cards are unnumbered and checklisted below in alphabetical order.

Card	Low	High
COMPLETE SET (12)	40.00	80.00
1 Bob Aspromonte	4.00	10.00
2 Bob Bruce	2.50	6.00
3 Harry Craft MG	3.00	8.00
4 Dick Farrell	2.50	6.00
5 Bob Lillis	3.00	8.00
6 Don McMahon	2.50	6.00
7 Jim Pendleton	2.50	6.00
8 Merritt Ranew	2.50	6.00
9 Pete Runnels	2.50	6.00
10 Hal Smith	2.50	6.00
11 Al Spangler	2.50	6.00
12 Carl Warwick	2.50	6.00

1963 Colt .45's Pepsi-Cola

The 1963 Pepsi carton insert set consists of 16 black and white cards portraying Houston Colt 45 players. Cards are often found with the tabs, which contain a schedule and ads. Lillis and Temple are the scarcest commons while Bateman and Warwick were never publicly distributed. The set has a catalog description of F230-3. Rusty Staub appears in his Rookie Card year.

Card	Low	High
COMPLETE SET	1,500.00	3,000.00
COMMON CARD	.75	2.00
COMMON SP'S	10.00	25.00
COMMON 4 BY 6	4.00	10.00
1 Bob Aspromonte	1.25	3.00
2 John Bateman SP	1,250.00	2,500.00
3 Bob Bruce	6.00	15.00
4 Jim Campbell	.75	2.00
5 Dick Farrell	.75	2.00
6 Ernie Fazio	.75	2.00
7 Carroll Hardy	.75	2.00
8 J.C. Hartman	.75	2.00
9 Ken Johnson	.75	2.00
10 Bob Lillis SP	10.00	25.00
11 Don McMahon	.75	2.00
12 Pete Runnels	.75	2.00
13 Al Spangler	.75	2.00
14 Rusty Staub	6.00	15.00
15 Johnny Temple SP	10.00	25.00
16 Carl Warwick SP	300.00	600.00
17 Ernie Fazio (4-in x 6-in)	4.00	10.00
18 Pete Runnels (4-in x 6-in)	6.00	15.00
19 Al Spangler (4-in x 6-in)	4.00	10.00
20 Rusty Staub (4-in x 6-in)	10.00	25.00

1964 Colt .45's Jay Publishing

This 12-card set of the Houston Colt .45's measures approximately 5" by 7". The fronts feature black-and-white posed player photos with the player's and team name printed below in the white border. These cards were packaged 12 in a packet. The backs are blank. The cards are unnumbered and checklisted below in alphabetical order.

Card	Low	High
COMPLETE SET (12)	40.00	80.00
1 Bob Aspromonte	3.00	8.00
2 Bob Bruce	2.50	6.00
3 Harry Craft MG	2.50	6.00
4 Dick Farrell	2.50	6.00
5 Ken Johnson	2.50	6.00
6 Pete Runnels	2.50	6.00
7 Al Spangler	2.50	6.00
8 Rusty Staub	6.00	15.00
9 Johnny Temple	3.00	8.00
10 Carl Warwick	2.50	6.00
11 Hal Woodeschick	2.50	6.00
12 Jim Wynn	5.00	12.00

1939 Coombs Mobil Booklets

This six-booklet set features tips by Jack Coombs, one of the greatest of all pitchers, on how the stars play the national game. Each pamphlet consists of eight fold-out pages and displays black-and-white photos of players demonstrating the instructions written by Jack Coombs on the various aspects of playing the game. When all six pamphlets were collected, the coupons on the back page of each were to be mailed in with the official contest entry blank printed in booklet No. 6 for a chance to win a trip to two World Series games for that season.

Card	Low	High
COMPLETE SET (6)	15.00	30.00
COMMON CARD (1-6)	2.50	5.00

1979-83 Coral-Lee Postcards

Little is known about this set. Seven of these postcards usually come together as a group and feature players in both game and non-game situations in photos taken by famous photographers such as Annie Leibovitz. Any additional information on these is greatly appreciated. We have sequenced these in alphabetical order. In addition, there have been several recently discovered Coral-Lee Postcards issued after 1981, any further information on those is appreciated as well. The Rose card was apparently issued a couple of years earlier.

Card	Low	High
COMPLETE SET	15.00	40.00
1 Dave Lopes	.60	1.50
2 Billy Martin MG	.75	2.00
3 Willie Mays Ronald Reagan PRES Ed Stack	2.00	5.00
4 Pete Rose Issued in 1979	2.50	6.00
5 George Steinbrenner OWN Billy Martin MG Reggie J	3.00	8.00

6 Fernando Valenzuela 1.25 3.00
Jose Lopez Portillo PRES
Nan
7 Dave Winfield UER 2.00 5.00
Name spelled Windfield
8 Carl Yastrzemski 1.50 4.00
Jimmy Carter PRES
9 Bobby Grich .60 1.50
Card numbered as number 8 on back
10 Reggie Jackson 2.00 5.00
Angels
11 Joe Morgan 1.25 3.00
Phillies
12 Rod Carew 1.25 3.00
Angels
17 Lou Piniella .75 2.00
Batting

1910-19 Coupon T213

The catalog designation T213, like its predecessor T212, actually contains three separate sets. Set 1 was issued about 1910 and consists of brown-captioned designs taken directly from the T206 set. Set 2 cards are also T206 designs, but with pale blue captions. They were produced in 1914-1915 and contain many team changes and Federal League affiliations. Set 3 cards were produced in 1919 and are physically slightly smaller than the the other two sets. Set 1 cards are printed on heavy paper; set 2 cards are printed on cardboard and have a glossy surface, which has resulted in a distinctive type of surface cracking. Each card in Set 1 and 2 measures 1 1/2" by 2 5/8" whereas Set 3 cards are only 1 3/8" by 2 9/16". The "Coupon" brand of cigarettes was manufactured by a branch of the American Tobacco Company located in New Orleans. The different sets can also be distinguished by their back titles, Set 1 (Coupon Mild Cigarettes), Set 2 (Mild and Sweet Coupon Cigarettes 20 for 5 cents), and Set 3 (Coupon Cigarettes 16 for 10 cts.).

COMMON TYPE 1 (1-68) 400.00 800.00
COMMON TYPE 2 (69-255) 400.00 800.00
COMMON TYPE 3 (256-325) 250.00 500.00
1 Harry Bay/Nashville 500.00 1,000.00
2 Beals Becker 400.00 800.00
3 Chief Bender 600.00 1,200.00
4 William H. Bernhard/Nashville 500.00 1,000.00
5 Ted Breitenstein/New Orleans 500.00 1,000.00
6 Bobby Byrne 400.00 800.00
7 William J. Campbell 400.00 800.00
8 Max Carey/Memphis 600.00 1,200.00
9 Frank Chance 750.00 1,500.00
10 Chappy Charles 400.00 800.00
11 Hal Chase (portrait) 500.00 1,000.00
12 Hal Chase (throwing) 500.00 1,000.00
13 Ty Cobb 4,000.00 8,000.00
14 Cranston/Memphis 400.00 800.00
15 Birdie Cree 400.00 800.00
16 Bill Donovan 400.00 800.00
17 Mickey Doolan 400.00 800.00
18 Jean Dubuc 400.00 800.00
19 Joe Dunn 400.00 800.00
20 Roy Ellam/Nashville 500.00 1,000.00
21 Clyde Engle 400.00 800.00
22 Johnny Evers 750.00 1,500.00
23 Art Fletcher 400.00 800.00
24 Charles Fritz/New Orleans 500.00 1,000.00
25 Edward Greminger/Montgomery 500.00 1,000.00
26 Hart/Little Rock 500.00 1,000.00
27 Hart/Montgomery 500.00 1,000.00
28 Topsy Hartsel 400.00 800.00
29 Charles Hickman/Mobile 500.00 1,000.00
30 Danny Hoffman 400.00 800.00
31 Harry Howell 400.00 800.00
32 Miller Huggins/portrait 600.00 1,200.00
33 Miller Huggins/yelling 600.00 1,200.00
34 George Hunter 400.00 800.00
35 Dutch Jordan/Atlanta 500.00 1,000.00
36 Ed Killian 400.00 800.00
37 Otto Knabe 400.00 800.00
38 Frank LaPorte 400.00 800.00
39 Ed Lennox 400.00 800.00
40 Harry Lentz/Little Rock 500.00 1,000.00
41 Rube Marquard 600.00 1,200.00
42 Doc Marshall 400.00 800.00
43 Christy Mathewson 1,500.00 3,000.00
44 George McBride 400.00 800.00
45 Pryor McElveen 400.00 800.00
46 Matty McIntyre 400.00 800.00
47 Michael Mitchell 400.00 800.00
48 Carlton Molesworth/Birmingham 500.00 1,000.00
49 Mike Mowrey 400.00 800.00
50 Hy Myers/batting 400.00 800.00
51 Hy Myers/fielding 400.00 800.00
52 Dode Paskert 400.00 800.00
53 Hub Perdue/Nashville 500.00 1,000.00
54 Archie Persons/Montgomery 500.00 1,000.00
55 Edward Reagan/New Orleans 500.00 1,000.00
56 Robert Rhoades 400.00 800.00
57 Isaac Rockenfeld/New Orleans 500.00 1,000.00
58 Claude Rossman 400.00 800.00
59 Boss Schmidt 400.00 800.00
60 Sid Smith/Atlanta 500.00 1,000.00
61 Charles Starr 400.00 800.00
62 Gabby Street 400.00 800.00
63 Ed Summers 400.00 800.00
64 William Sweeney 400.00 800.00
65 Chester Thomas 400.00 800.00
66 Woodie Thornton/Mobile 500.00 1,000.00
67 Ed Willett 400.00 800.00
68 Owen Wilson 400.00 800.00
69 Red Ames/Cincinnati 500.00 1,000.00
70 Red Ames/St. Louis 500.00 1,000.00
71 Frank Baker/New York Amer. 750.00 1,500.00
72 Frank Baker/Philadelphia 750.00 1,500.00
73 Frank Baker/Phila. 750.00 1,500.00
74 Cy Barger 400.00 800.00
75 Chief Bender/trees/Baltimore Fed. 750.00 1,500.00
76 Chief Bender/no trees/Baltimore Fed. 750.00 1,500.00
77 Chief Bender/trees/Philadelphia Amer. 750.00 1,500.00
78 Chief Bender/no trees
Philadelphia Amer. 750.00 1,500.00
79 Chief Bender/trees/Philadelphia Nat. 750.00 1,500.00
80 Chief Bender/no trees
Philadelphia Nat. 750.00 1,500.00
81 Bill Bradley 400.00 800.00
82 Roger Bresnahan/Chicago 750.00 1,500.00
83 Roger Bresnahan/Toledo 750.00 1,500.00
84 Al Bridwell/St. Louis 400.00 800.00
85 Al Bridwell/Nashville 400.00 800.00
86 Mordecai Brown/Chicago 750.00 1,500.00
87 Mordecai Brown/St. Louis Fed. 750.00 1,500.00
88 Bobby Byrne 400.00 800.00
89 Howie Camnitz/hands over
Pittsburgh Fed. 400.00 800.00
90 Howie Camnitz/arm at side
Pittsburgh Fed. 400.00 800.00
91 Howie Camnitz/Savannah 400.00 800.00
92 William J. Campbell 400.00 800.00
93 Frank Chance/Los Angeles/batting 750.00 1,500.00
94 Frank Chance/Los Angeles/portrait 750.00 1,500.00
95 Frank Chance/New York Amer./batting 750.00 1,500.00
96 Frank Chance/New York Amer./portrait 750.00 1,500.00
97 William Chappelle/Brooklyn 400.00 800.00
98 William Chappelle/Cleveland 400.00 800.00
99 Hal Chase/Buffalo Fed./portrait 600.00 1,200.00
100 Hal Chase/Buffalo Fed./holding cup 600.00 1,200.00
101 Hal Chase/Buffalo Fed./throwing 600.00 1,200.00
102 Hal Chase/Chicago Amer./portrait 600.00 1,200.00
103 Hal Chase/Chicago Amer./holding cup) 600.00 1,200.00
104 Hal Chase/Chicago Amer./throwing 600.00 1,200.00
105 Ty Cobb Batting 10,000.00 20,000.00
106 Ty Cobb Portrait 10,000.00 20,000.00
107 Eddie Collins/Chicago Amer./with A 750.00 1,500.00
108 Eddie Collins/Chicago Amer./without A 750.00 1,500.00
109 Eddie Collins/Philadelphia/with A 750.00 1,500.00
110 Doc Crandall/St. Louis Amer. 400.00 800.00
111 Doc Crandall/St. Louis Fed. 400.00 800.00
112 Sam Crawford 750.00 1,500.00
113 Birdie Cree 400.00 800.00
114 Harry Davis/Philadelphia 400.00 800.00
115 Harry Davis/Phila. 400.00 800.00
116 Ray Demmitt 400.00 800.00
117 Josh Devore/Philadelphia 400.00 800.00
118 Josh Devore/Chillicothe 400.00 800.00
119 Mike Donlin/New York Nat. 500.00 1,000.00
120 Mike Donlin/.300 Batter/7 Years 750.00 1,500.00
121 Mike Donlin/Name spelled
Dohlin on card 750.00 1,500.00
122 Bill Donovan 400.00 800.00
123 Mickey Doolan (batting)/Baltimore Fed. 400.00 800.00
124 Mickey Doolan (fielding)/Chicago Nat. 400.00 800.00
125 Mickey Doolan (batting)/Baltimore Fed. 400.00 800.00
126 Mickey Doolan (fielding)/Chicago Nat. 400.00 800.00
127 Tom Downey 400.00 800.00
128 Larry Doyle/batting 500.00 1,000.00
129 Larry Doyle/portrait 500.00 1,000.00
130 Jean Dubuc 400.00 800.00
131 Jack Dunn 400.00 800.00
132 Kid Elberfeld/Brooklyn 750.00 1,500.00
133 Kid Elberfeld/Chattanooga 750.00 1,500.00
134 Steve Evans 400.00 800.00
135 Johnny Evers 750.00 1,500.00
136 Russ Ford 400.00 800.00
137 Art Fromme 400.00 800.00
138 Chick Gandil/Cleveland 750.00 1,500.00
139 Chick Gandil/Washington 750.00 1,500.00
140 Rube Geyer 400.00 800.00
141 Clark Griffith 750.00 1,500.00
142 Bob Groom 400.00 800.00
143 Buck Herzog/with B 400.00 800.00
144 Buck Herzog/without B 400.00 800.00
145 Doc Hoblitzell/Boston Amer. 400.00 800.00
146 Doc Hoblitzell/Boston Fed. 400.00 800.00
147 Doc Hoblitzell/Cincinnati 400.00 800.00
148 Solly Hofman 400.00 800.00
149 Danny Hofmann 400.00 800.00
150 Miller Huggins/portrait 750.00 1,500.00
151 Miller Huggins/yelling 750.00 1,500.00
152 John Hummel/Brooklyn 400.00 800.00
153 John Hummel/Brooklyn Nat. 400.00 800.00
154 Hugh Jennings/yelling 750.00 1,500.00
155 Hugh Jennings/dancing 750.00 1,500.00
156 Walter Johnson 2,500.00 5,000.00
157 Tim Jordan/Ft. Worth 400.00 800.00
158 Tim Jordan/Toronto 400.00 800.00
159 Joe Kelley/New York Amer. 750.00 1,500.00
160 Joe Kelley/Toronto 750.00 1,500.00
161 Otto Knabe 400.00 800.00
162 Ed Konetchy/Boston Nat. 400.00 800.00
163 Ed Konetchy/Pittsburgh Fed. 400.00 800.00
164 Ed Konetchy/Pittsburgh Nat. 400.00 800.00
165 Harry Krause 400.00 800.00
166 Nap Lajoie/Cleveland 1,250.00 2,500.00
167 Nap Lajoie/Philadelphia 1,250.00 2,500.00
168 Nap Lajoie/Phila. 1,250.00 2,500.00
169 Tommy Leach/Chicago 400.00 800.00
170 Tommy Leach/Cincinnati 400.00 800.00
171 Tommy Leach/Rochester 400.00 800.00
172 Ed Lennox 400.00 800.00
173 Sherry Magee/Boston 500.00 1,000.00
174 Sherry Magee/Philadelphia 500.00 1,000.00
175 Sherry Magee/Phila. 500.00 1,000.00
176 Rube Marquard/Brooklyn/pitching 750.00 1,500.00
177 Rube Marquard/Brooklyn/portrait 750.00 1,500.00
178 Rube Marquard/New York/pitching 750.00 1,500.00
179 Rube Marquard/New York/portrait 750.00 1,500.00
180 Christy Mathewson Dark Cap 2,500.00 5,000.00
181 John McGraw/portrait 750.00 1,500.00
182 John McGraw/glove on hip 750.00 1,500.00
183 Larry McLean 400.00 800.00
184 George McQuillan/Philadelphia 400.00 800.00
185 George McQuillan/Phila. 400.00 800.00
186 George McQuillan/Pittsburgh 400.00 800.00
187 Fred Merkle 500.00 1,000.00
188 Chief Meyers/Brooklyn/T206-249 pose 500.00 1,000.00
189 Chief Meyers/Brooklyn/fielding 500.00 1,000.00
190 Chief Meyers/New York/T206-249 pose 500.00 1,000.00
191 Chief Meyers/New York/fielding 500.00 1,000.00
192 Dots Miller 400.00 800.00
193 Michael Mitchell 400.00 800.00
194 Mike Mowrey/Brooklyn 400.00 800.00
195 Mike Mowrey/Pittsburgh Fed. 400.00 800.00
196 Mike Mowrey/Pittsburgh Nat. 400.00 800.00
197 George Mullin/Indianapolis 400.00 800.00
198 George Mullin/Newark 400.00 800.00
199 Danny Murphy 400.00 800.00
200 Red Murray/Chicago 400.00 800.00
201 Red Murray/Kansas City 400.00 800.00
202 Red Murray/New York 400.00 800.00
203 Tom Needham 400.00 800.00
204 Rebel Oakes 400.00 800.00
205 Rube Oldring/Philadelphia 500.00 1,000.00
206 Rube Oldring/Phila. 500.00 1,000.00
207 Dode Paskert/Philadelphia 400.00 800.00
208 Dode Paskert/Phila. 400.00 800.00
209 William Purtell 400.00 800.00
210 Jack Quinn/Baltimore 500.00 1,000.00
211 Jack Quinn/Vernon 500.00 1,000.00
212 Ed Reulbach/Brooklyn Fed. 500.00 1,000.00
213 Ed Reulbach/Pittsburgh 500.00 1,000.00
214 Ed Reulbach/Brooklyn Nat. 500.00 1,000.00
215 Nap Rucker/Brooklyn 500.00 1,000.00
216 Nap Rucker/Brooklyn Nat. 500.00 1,000.00
217 Dick Rudolph 400.00 800.00
218 Germany Schaefer/Kansas City 500.00 1,000.00
219 Germany Schaefer/New York 500.00 1,000.00
220 Germany Schaefer/Washington 500.00 1,000.00
221 Admiral Schlei/portrait 400.00 800.00
222 Admiral Schlei/batting 400.00 800.00
223 Boss Schmidt 400.00 800.00
224 Frank Schulte 500.00 1,000.00
225 Nig Smith 400.00 800.00
226 Tris Speaker 750.00 1,500.00
227 George Stovall 400.00 800.00
228 Gabby Street/catching 400.00 800.00
229 Gabby Street/portrait 400.00 800.00
230 Ed Summers 400.00 800.00
231 Ed Sweeney/Boston 500.00 1,000.00
232 Ed Sweeney/Chicago 500.00 1,000.00
233 Ed Sweeney/New York 500.00 1,000.00
234 Ed Sweeney/Richmond 500.00 1,000.00
235 Chester Thomas/Philadelphia 400.00 800.00
236 Chester Thomas/Phila. 400.00 800.00
237 Joe Tinker/Chicago Fed.
bat on shoulder 750.00 1,500.00
238 Joe Tinker/Chicago Fed./swinging 750.00 1,500.00
239 Joe Tinker/Chicago Nat.
bat on shoulder 750.00 1,500.00
240 Joe Tinker/Chicago Nat./swinging 750.00 1,500.00
241 Honus Wagner 400.00 800.00
242 Jack Warhop/New York 400.00 800.00
243 Jack Warhop/St. Louis 400.00 800.00
244 Zack Wheat/Brooklyn 750.00 1,500.00
245 Zack Wheat/Brooklyn Nat. 750.00 1,500.00
246 Kaiser Wilhelm 400.00 800.00
247 Ed Willett/Memphis 400.00 800.00
248 Ed Willett/St. Louis 400.00 800.00
249 Owen Wilson/St. Louis 400.00 800.00
250 Hooks Wiltse/Brooklyn Fed./pitching 400.00 800.00
251 Hooks Wiltse/Brooklyn Fed./portrait 400.00 800.00
252 Hooks Wiltse/Jersey City/pitching 400.00 800.00
253 Hooks Wiltse/Jersey City/portrait 400.00 800.00
254 Hooks Wiltse/New York/pitching 400.00 800.00
255 Hooks Wiltse/New York/portrait 400.00 800.00
256 Heinie Zimmerman 400.00 800.00
257 Red Ames 250.00 500.00
258 Frank Baker/New York Amer. 500.00 1,000.00
259 Chief Bender 500.00 1,000.00
260 Chief Bender 500.00 1,000.00
261 Roger Bresnahan/Toledo 500.00 1,000.00
262 Al Bridwell 250.00 500.00
263 Mordecai Brown 500.00 1,000.00
264 Bobby Byrne/St.Louis Nat. 250.00 500.00
265 Frank Chance 500.00 1,000.00
266 Frank Chance 500.00 1,000.00
267 Hal Chase/N.Y. Nat. 400.00 800.00
268 Hal Chase/N.Y. Nat. 400.00 800.00
269 Hal Chase/N.Y. Nat. 400.00 800.00
270 Ty Cobb Detroit 7,500.00 15,000.00
271 Ty Cobb Detroit 7,500.00 15,000.00
272 Eddie Collins/Chicago Amer. 500.00 1,000.00
273 Sam Crawford 500.00 1,000.00
274 Harry Davis/Philadelphia Amer. 250.00 500.00
275 Mike Donlin 300.00 600.00
276 Bill Donovan/Jersey City 250.00 500.00
277 Mickey Doolan/Reading 250.00 500.00
278 Mickey Doolan/Reading 250.00 500.00
279 Larry Doyle/N.Y. Nat. 300.00 600.00
280 Larry Doyle/N.Y. Nat. 300.00 600.00
281 Jean Dubuc/N.Y. Nat. 250.00 500.00
282 Jack Dunn/Baltimore 300.00 600.00
283 Kid Elberfeld 250.00 500.00
284 Johnny Evers 500.00 1,000.00
285 Chick Gandil/Chicago Amer. 500.00 1,000.00
286 Clark Griffith/Washington 500.00 1,000.00
287 Buck Herzog/Boston Nat. 250.00 500.00
288 Doc Hoblitzell/Boston Amer. 250.00 500.00
289 Miller Huggins/N.Y. Amer. 500.00 1,000.00
290 Miller Huggins/N.Y. Amer. 500.00 1,000.00
291 John Hummel 250.00 500.00
292 Hugh Jennings MG/Detroit 500.00 1,000.00
293 Hugh Jennings MG/Detroit 500.00 1,000.00
294 Walter Johnson/Washington 1,500.00 3,000.00
295 Tim Jordan 250.00 500.00
296 Kelley/N.Y. Amer. 500.00 1,000.00
297 Ed Konetchy/Brooklyn 250.00 500.00
298 Nap Lajoie 750.00 1,500.00
299 Sherry Magee/Cincinnati 300.00 600.00
300 Rube Marquard/Brooklyn 500.00 1,000.00
301 Rube Marquard/Brooklyn 500.00 1,000.00
302 Christy Mathewson/New York Nat. 1,000.00 2,000.00
303 John McGraw MG/New York Nat. 500.00 1,000.00
304 John McGraw MG/New York Nat. 500.00 1,000.00
305 George McQuillan/Boston Nat. 250.00 500.00
306 Fred Merkle/Chicago Nat. 300.00 600.00
307 Dots Miller/St. Louis Nat. 250.00 500.00
308 Mike Mowrey/Brooklyn 250.00 500.00
309 Hy Myers/New Haven 250.00 500.00
310 Hy Myers/Brooklyn 250.00 500.00
311 Dode Paskert/Chicago Nat. 250.00 500.00
312 Jack Quinn/N.Y. Nat. 300.00 600.00
313 Ed Reulbach 300.00 600.00
314 Nap Rucker 300.00 600.00
315 Dick Rudolph/Boston Nat. 250.00 500.00
316 Germany Schaeffer 250.00 500.00
317 Frank Schulte/Binghamton 300.00 600.00
318 Tris Speaker/Cleveland 750.00 1,500.00
319 Gabby Street/Nashville 250.00 500.00
320 Gabby Street/Nashville 250.00 500.00
321 Ed Sweeney/Pittsburg 300.00 600.00
322 Ira Thomas 250.00 500.00
323 Joe Tinker 500.00 1,000.00
324 Zack Wheat/Brooklyn 500.00 1,000.00
325 Hooks Wiltse 250.00 500.00
326 Heinie Zimmerman/N.Y. Nat. 250.00 500.00

1914 Cracker Jack

The cards in this 144-card set measure approximately 2 1/4" by 3". This "Series of colored pictures of Famous Ball Players and Managers" was issued in packages of Cracker Jack in 1914. The cards have tinted photos set against red backgrounds and many are commonly found with caramel stains. The set contains American, National, and Federal League players. The company claims to have printed 15 million cards as noted on the backs. Most of the cards were issued in both 1914 and 1915, but each year can easily be distinguished from the other by the notation of the number of cards in the series as printed on the back (144 for 1914 and 176 for 1915) and by the orientation of the text on the back of the cards. For 1914, the cardback text is right side up when the card is turned over but will be upside down for the 1915 release. Team names are included below for some players to show more specific differences between the 1914 and 1915 issues on those cards.

COMPLETE SET (144) 70,000.00 140,000.00
1 Otto Knabe 300.00 600.00
2 Frank Baker 750.00 1,500.00
3 Joe Tinker 1,000.00 2,000.00
4 Larry Doyle 200.00 400.00
5 Ward Miller 200.00 400.00
6 Eddie Plank 750.00 1,500.00
7 Eddie Collins 750.00 1,500.00
8 Rube Oldring 200.00 400.00
9 Artie Hoffman 200.00 400.00
10 John McInnis 200.00 400.00
11 George Stovall 200.00 400.00
12 Connie Mack MG 750.00 1,500.00
13 Art Wilson 200.00 400.00
14 Sam Crawford 750.00 1,500.00
15 Reb Russell 200.00 400.00
16 Howie Camnitz 200.00 400.00
17 Roger Bresnahan 750.00 1,500.00
17B Roger Bresnahan NNO 2,000.00 4,000.00
18 Johnny Evers 750.00 1,500.00
19 Chief Bender 750.00 1,500.00
20 Cy Falkenberg 200.00 400.00
21 Heinie Zimmerman 200.00 400.00
22 Joe Wood 1,250.00 2,500.00
23 Charles Comiskey 750.00 1,500.00
24 George Mullen 200.00 400.00
25 Michael Simon 200.00 400.00
26 James Scott 200.00 400.00
27 Bill Carrigan 200.00 400.00
28 Jack Barry 200.00 400.00
29 Vean Gregg 200.00 400.00
30 Ty Cobb 5,000.00 10,000.00
31 Heinie Wagner 200.00 400.00
32 Mordecai Brown 750.00 1,500.00
33 Amos Strunk 200.00 400.00
34 Ira Thomas 300.00 600.00
35 Harry Hooper 750.00 1,500.00
36 Ed Walsh 750.00 1,500.00
37 Grover C. Alexander 2,000.00 4,000.00
38 Red Dooin 200.00 400.00
39 Chick Gandil 750.00 1,500.00
40 Jimmy Austin 200.00 400.00
41 Tommy Leach 200.00 400.00
42 Al Bridwell 200.00 400.00
43 Rube Marquard 750.00 1,500.00
44 Jeff (Charles) Tesreau 200.00 400.00
45 Fred Luderus 200.00 400.00
46 Bob Groom 200.00 400.00
47 Josh Devore 200.00 400.00
48 Harry Lord 300.00 600.00
49 John Miller 200.00 400.00
50 John Hummell 200.00 400.00
51 Nap Rucker 200.00 400.00
52 Zach Wheat 750.00 1,500.00
53 Otto Miller 200.00 400.00
54 Marty O'Toole 200.00 400.00
55 Dick Hoblitzel 200.00 400.00

56 Clyde Milan	200.00	400.00
57 Walter Johnson	2,000.00	4,000.00
58 Wally Schang	200.00	400.00
59 Harry Gessler	200.00	400.00
60 Rollie Zeider	300.00	600.00
61 Ray Schalk	1,000.00	2,000.00
62 Jay Cashion	300.00	600.00
63 Babe Adams	200.00	400.00
64 Jimmy Archer	200.00	400.00
65 Tris Speaker	750.00	1,500.00
66 Napoleon Lajoie	1,250.00	2,500.00
67 Otis Crandall	200.00	400.00
68 Honus Wagner	4,000.00	8,000.00
69 John McGraw	750.00	1,500.00
70 Fred Clarke	600.00	1,200.00
71 Chief Meyers	200.00	400.00
72 John Boehling	200.00	400.00
73 Max Carey	750.00	1,500.00
74 Frank Owens	200.00	400.00
75 Miller Huggins	600.00	1,200.00
76 Claude Hendrix	200.00	400.00
77 Hughie Jennings MG	750.00	1,500.00
78 Fred Merkle	200.00	400.00
79 Ping Bodie	200.00	400.00
80 Ed Ruelbach	200.00	400.00
81 Jim Delahanty	200.00	400.00
82 Gavvy Cravath	200.00	400.00
83 Russ Ford	200.00	400.00
84 Elmer E. Knetzer	200.00	400.00
85 Buck Herzog	200.00	400.00
86 Burt Shotton	200.00	400.00
87 Forrest Cady	200.00	400.00
88 Christy Mathewson	20,000.00	50,000.00
89 Lawrence Cheney	200.00	400.00
90 Frank Smith	200.00	400.00
91 Roger Peckinpaugh	200.00	400.00
92 Al Demaree	200.00	400.00
93 Del Pratt	200.00	400.00
94 Eddie Cicotte	750.00	1,500.00
95 Ray Keating	200.00	400.00
96 Beals Becker	200.00	400.00
97 John (Rube) Benton	200.00	400.00
98 Frank LaPorte	200.00	400.00
99 Frank Chance	2,000.00	4,000.00
100 Thomas Seaton	200.00	400.00
101 Frank Schulte	200.00	400.00
102 Ray Fisher	200.00	400.00
103 Joe Jackson	10,000.00	20,000.00
104 Vic Saier	200.00	400.00
105 James Lavender	200.00	400.00
106 Joe Birmingham	200.00	400.00
107 Tom Downey	200.00	400.00
108 Sherry Magee	200.00	400.00
109 Fred Blanding	200.00	400.00
110 Bob Bescher	200.00	400.00
111 Jim Callahan	200.00	400.00
112 Ed Sweeney	200.00	400.00
113 George Suggs	200.00	400.00
114 George Moriarity	200.00	400.00
115 Addison Brennan	200.00	400.00
116 Rollie Zeider	200.00	400.00
117 Ted Easterly	200.00	400.00
118 Ed Konetchy	200.00	400.00
119 George Perring	200.00	400.00
120 Mike Doolan	200.00	400.00
121 Hub Perdue	200.00	400.00
122 Owen Bush	200.00	400.00
123 Slim Sallee	200.00	400.00
124 Earl Moore	200.00	400.00
125 Bert Niehoff	200.00	400.00
126 Walter Blair	200.00	400.00
127 Butch Schmidt	200.00	400.00
128 Steve Evans	200.00	400.00
129 Ray Caldwell	200.00	400.00
130 Ivy Wingo	200.00	400.00
131 George Baumgardner	200.00	400.00
132 Les Nunamaker	200.00	400.00
133 Branch Rickey MG	1,000.00	2,000.00
134 Armando Marsans	200.00	400.00
135 Bill Killefer	200.00	400.00
136 Rabbit Maranville	750.00	1,500.00
137 William Rariden	200.00	400.00
138 Hank Gowdy	200.00	400.00
139 Rebel Oakes	200.00	400.00
140 Danny Murphy	200.00	400.00
141 Cy Barger	200.00	400.00
142 Eugene Packard	200.00	400.00
143 Jake Daubert	200.00	400.00
144 James C. Walsh	400.00	800.00

1915 Cracker Jack

The cards in this 176-card set measure approximately 2 1/4" by 3". The cards were available in boxes of Cracker Jack or from the company for "100 Cracker Jack coupons, or one coupon and 25 cents." An album was available for "50 coupons or one coupon and 10 cents." Most of the cards were issued in both 1914 and 1915, but each year can easily be distinguished from the other by the notation of the number of cards in the series as printed on the back (144 for 1914 and 176 for 1915) and by the orientation of the text on the back of the cards. For 1914, the cardback text is right side up when the card is turned over but will be upside down for the 1915 release. The 1915 Cracker Jack cards are noticeably easier to find than the 1914 Cracker Jack cards due to the mail-in offer, although neither set is plentiful. The set essentially duplicates E145-1 (1914 Cracker Jack) except for some additional cards and new poses. Players in the Federal League are indicated by FED in the checklist below.

COMPLETE SET (176)	35,000.00	70,000.00
COMMON CARD (1-144)	100.00	200.00
COMMON CARD(145-176)	125.00	250.00
1 Otto Knabe	300.00	600.00
2 Frank Baker	500.00	1,000.00
3 Joe Tinker	400.00	800.00
4 Larry Doyle	125.00	250.00
5 Ward Miller	100.00	200.00
6 Eddie Plank	750.00	1,500.00
7 Eddie Collins	400.00	800.00
8 Rube Oldring	100.00	200.00
9 Artie Hoffman	100.00	200.00
10 John McInnis	100.00	200.00
11 George Stovall	100.00	200.00
12 Connie Mack MG	400.00	800.00
13 Art Wilson	100.00	200.00
14 Sam Crawford	400.00	800.00
15 Reb Russell	100.00	200.00
16 Howie Camnitz	100.00	200.00
17 Roger Bresnahan	300.00	600.00
18 Johnny Evers	400.00	800.00
19 Chief Bender	400.00	800.00
20 Cy Falkenberg	100.00	200.00
21 Heinie Zimmerman	100.00	200.00
22 Joe Wood	500.00	1,000.00
23 Charles Comiskey	500.00	1,000.00
24 George Mullen	100.00	200.00
25 Michael Simon	100.00	200.00
26 James Scott	100.00	200.00
27 Bill Carrigan	100.00	200.00
28 Jack Barry	125.00	250.00
29 Vean Gregg	100.00	200.00
30 Ty Cobb	3,000.00	6,000.00
31 Heinie Wagner	100.00	200.00
32 Mordecai Brown	500.00	1,000.00
33 Amos Strunk	100.00	200.00
34 Ira Thomas	100.00	200.00
35 Harry Hooper	300.00	600.00
36 Ed Walsh	400.00	800.00
37 Grover C. Alexander	1,000.00	2,000.00
38 Red Dooin	100.00	200.00
39 Chick Gandil	400.00	800.00
40 Jimmy Austin	125.00	250.00
41 Tommy Leach	100.00	200.00
42 Al Bridwell	100.00	200.00
43 Rube Marquard	300.00	600.00
44 Jeff (Charles) Tesreau	100.00	200.00
45 Fred Luderus	100.00	200.00
46 Bob Groom	100.00	200.00
47 Josh Devore	100.00	200.00
48 Steve O'Neill	100.00	200.00
49 John Miller	100.00	200.00
50 John Hummell	100.00	200.00
51 Nap Rucker	100.00	200.00
52 Zach Wheat	300.00	600.00
53 Otto Miller	100.00	200.00
54 Marty O'Toole	100.00	200.00
55 Dick Hoblitzel	100.00	200.00
56 Clyde Milan	100.00	200.00
57 Walter Johnson	1,500.00	3,000.00
58 Wally Schang	100.00	200.00
59 Harry Gessler	100.00	200.00
60 Oscar Dugey	100.00	200.00
61 Ray Schalk	400.00	800.00
62 Willie Mitchell	100.00	200.00
63 Babe Adams	100.00	200.00
64 Jimmy Archer	100.00	200.00
65 Tris Speaker	750.00	1,500.00
66 Napoleon Lajoie	600.00	1,200.00
67 Otis Crandall	100.00	200.00
68 Honus Wagner	3,000.00	6,000.00
69 John McGraw MG	400.00	800.00
70 Fred Clarke	300.00	600.00
71 Chief Meyers	125.00	250.00
72 John Boehling	100.00	200.00
73 Max Carey	400.00	800.00
74 Frank Owens	100.00	200.00
75 Miller Huggins	300.00	600.00
76 Claude Hendrix	100.00	200.00
77 Hughie Jennings MG	300.00	600.00
78 Fred Merkle	100.00	200.00
79 Ping Bodie	100.00	200.00
80 Ed Ruelbach	100.00	200.00
81 Jim Delahanty	100.00	200.00
82 Gavvy Cravath	100.00	200.00
83 Russ Ford	100.00	200.00
84 Elmer E. Knetzer	100.00	200.00
85 Buck Herzog	100.00	200.00
86 Burt Shotton	100.00	200.00
87 Forrest Cady	100.00	200.00
88 Christy Mathewson	1,750.00	3,500.00
89 Lawrence Cheney	100.00	200.00
90 Frank Smith	100.00	200.00
91 Roger Peckinpaugh	100.00	200.00
92 Al Demaree	100.00	200.00
93 Del Pratt	125.00	250.00
94 Eddie Cicotte	450.00	900.00
95 Ray Keating	100.00	200.00
96 Beals Becker	125.00	250.00
97 John (Rube) Benton	100.00	200.00
98 Frank LaPorte	100.00	200.00
99 Hal Chase	250.00	500.00
100 Thomas Seaton	100.00	200.00
101 Frank Schulte	100.00	200.00
102 Ray Fisher	100.00	200.00
103 Joe Jackson	7,500.00	15,000.00
104 Vic Saier	100.00	200.00
105 James Lavender	100.00	200.00
106 Joe Birmingham	100.00	200.00
107 Thomas Downey	100.00	200.00
108 Sherry Magee	100.00	200.00
109 Fred Blanding	100.00	200.00
110 Bob Bescher	100.00	200.00
111 Herbie Moran	100.00	200.00
112 Ed Sweeney	100.00	200.00
113 George Suggs	100.00	200.00
114 George Moriarity	100.00	200.00
115 Addison Brennan	100.00	200.00
116 Rollie Zeider	100.00	200.00
117 Ted Easterly	100.00	200.00
118 Ed Konetchy	100.00	200.00
119 George Perring	100.00	200.00
120 Mike Doolan	100.00	200.00
121 Hub Perdue	100.00	200.00
122 Owen Bush	100.00	200.00
123 Slim Sallee	100.00	200.00
124 Earl Moore	100.00	200.00
125 Bert Niehoff	100.00	200.00
126 Walter Blair	100.00	200.00
127 Butch Schmidt	100.00	200.00
128 Steve Evans	100.00	200.00
129 Ray Caldwell	100.00	200.00
130 Ivy Wingo	100.00	200.00
131 Geo. Baumgardner	100.00	200.00
132 Les Nunamaker	100.00	200.00
133 Branch Rickey MG	600.00	1,200.00
134 Armando Marsans	125.00	250.00
135 William Killefer	100.00	200.00
136 Rabbit Maranville	300.00	600.00
137 William Rariden	100.00	200.00
138 Hank Gowdy	100.00	200.00
139 Rebel Oakes	100.00	200.00
140 Danny Murphy	100.00	200.00
141 Cy Barger	100.00	200.00
142 Eugene Packard	100.00	200.00
143 Jake Daubert	100.00	200.00
144 James C. Walsh	100.00	200.00
145 Ted Cather	125.00	250.00
146 George Tyler	125.00	250.00
147 Lee Magee	125.00	250.00
148 Owen Wilson	125.00	250.00
149 Hal Janvrin	125.00	250.00
150 Doc Johnston	125.00	250.00
151 George Whitted	125.00	250.00
152 George McQuillen	125.00	250.00
153 Bill James	125.00	250.00
154 Dick Rudolph	125.00	250.00
155 Joe Connolly	125.00	250.00
156 Jean Dubuc	125.00	250.00
157 George Kaiserling	125.00	250.00
158 Fritz Maisel	125.00	250.00
159 Heinie Groh	125.00	250.00
160 Benny Kauff	125.00	250.00
161 Edd Roush	500.00	1,000.00
162 George Stallings MG	125.00	250.00
163 Bert Whaling	125.00	250.00
164 Bob Shawkey	125.00	250.00
165 Eddie Murphy	125.00	250.00
166 Joe Bush	125.00	250.00
167 Clark Griffith	300.00	600.00
168 Vin Campbell	125.00	250.00
169 Raymond Collins	125.00	250.00
170 Hans Lobert	125.00	250.00
171 Earl Hamilton	125.00	250.00
172 Erskine Mayer	125.00	250.00
173 Tilly Walker	125.00	250.00
174 Robert Veach	125.00	250.00
175 Joseph Benz	125.00	250.00
176 Hippo Vaughn	300.00	600.00

1976 Crane Discs

Produced by MSA, these discs were distributed by a wide variety of advertisers and can be found in various regions of the country. There are many different versions of this set, however, we are only pricing the Crane version. Several players changed teams during the printing of this set, however only the more commonly found version is included in the complete set price. These sets are unnumbered and sequenced in alphabetical order. Some of the other sponsors include Buchmans, Carousel (of which many different locations are known), Dairy Isle, Isaly, Orbakers, Red Barn, Safelon and Towne Club. All multiplier values are notated before.

COMPLETE SET (70) 15.00 40.00
*BLANKBACK DISCS: SAME VALUE AS BASIC DISCS
BUCHMANS DISCS: 1.25X BASIC DISCS
*CAROUSEL: 3X BASIC DISCS
*DAIRY ISLE: 2X BASIC DISCS
*ISALYS: SAME VALUE AS BASIC DISCS
*ORBAKERS: 1.25X BASIC DISCS
*RED BARN: 15X BASIC DISCS
*SAFELON: 2X BASIC DISCS
*TOWNE CLUB: 1.25X BASIC DISCS

1 Hank Aaron	1.25	3.00
2 Johnny Bench	.75	2.00
3 Vida Blue	.12	.30
4 Larry Bowa	.10	.25
5 Lou Brock	.75	2.00
6 Jeff Burroughs	.10	.25
7 John Candelaria	.10	.25
8 Jose Cardenal	.10	.25
9 Rod Carew	.75	2.00
10 Steve Carlton	.75	2.00
11 Dave Cash	.10	.25
12 Cesar Cedeno	.12	.30
13 Ron Cey	.12	.30
14 Carlton Fisk	1.00	2.50
15 Tito Fuentes	.10	.25
16 Steve Garvey	.40	1.00
17 Ken Griffey	.12	.30
18 Don Gullett	.10	.25
19 Willie Horton	.10	.25
20 Al Hrabosky	.10	.25
21 Catfish Hunter	.75	2.00
22A Reggie Jackson Oakland Athletics	2.50	6.00
22B Reggie Jackson Baltimore Orioles	.75	2.00
23 Randy Jones	.10	.25
24 Jim Kaat	.25	.60
25 Don Kessinger	.10	.25
26 Dave Kingman	.25	.60
27 Jerry Koosman	.12	.30
28 Mickey Lolich	.12	.30
29 Greg Luzinski	.25	.60
30 Fred Lynn	.25	.60
31 Bill Madlock	.12	.30
32A Carlos May Chicago White Sox	.40	1.00
32B Carlos May New York Yankees	.10	.25
33 John Mayberry	.10	.25
34 Bake McBride	.10	.25
35 Doc Medich	.10	.25
36A Andy Messersmith Los Angeles Dodgers	.40	1.00
36B Andy Messersmith Atlanta Braves	.10	.25
37 Rick Monday	.10	.25
38 John Montefusco	.10	.25
39 Jerry Morales	.10	.25
40 Joe Morgan	.75	2.00
41 Thurman Munson	.75	2.00
42 Bobby Murcer	.25	.60
43 Al Oliver	.25	.60
44 Jim Palmer	.75	2.00
45 Dave Parker	.40	1.00
46 Tony Perez	.40	1.00
47 Jerry Reuss	.10	.25
48 Brooks Robinson	.75	2.00
49 Frank Robinson	.75	2.00
50 Steve Rogers	.10	.25
51 Pete Rose	1.00	2.50
52 Nolan Ryan	2.00	5.00
53 Manny Sanguillen	.10	.25
54 Mike Schmidt	1.25	3.00
55 Tom Seaver	1.00	2.50
56 Ted Simmons	.25	.60
57 Reggie Smith	.12	.30
58 Willie Stargell	.75	2.00
59 Rusty Staub	.25	.60
60 Rennie Stennett	.10	.25
61 Don Sutton	.75	2.00
62A Andre Thornton Chicago Cubs	.40	1.00
62B Andre Thornton Montreal Expos	.10	.25
63 Luis Tiant	.25	.60
64 Joe Torre	.40	1.00
65 Mike Tyson	.10	.25
66 Bob Watson	.12	.30
67 Wilbur Wood	.10	.25
68 Jimmy Wynn	.10	.25
69 Carl Yastrzemski	.75	2.00
70 Richie Zisk	.10	.25

1907 Cubs A.C. Dietsche Postcards PC765

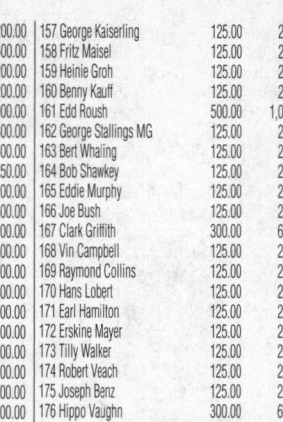

This set of black and white Dietsche postcards was issued in 1907 and feature Chicago Cubs only. Cards have been seen with and without the player's name on the front. There is no current price differential for either variation.

COMPLETE SET	2,000.00	4,000.00
1 Mordecai Brown	200.00	400.00
2 Frank Chance	250.00	500.00
3 Johnny Evers	250.00	500.00
4 Arthur F. Hoffman	100.00	200.00
5 John Kling	125.00	250.00
6 Carl Lundgren	100.00	200.00
7 Patrick J. Moran	100.00	200.00
8 Orvall Overall	125.00	250.00
9 John A. Pfeister	100.00	200.00
10 Ed Reulbach	125.00	250.00
11 Frank Schulte	125.00	250.00
12 James T. Sheckard	100.00	200.00
13 Harry Steinfeldt	125.00	250.00
14 James Slagle	100.00	200.00
15 Joseph B. Tinker	250.00	500.00

1907 Cubs G.F. Grignon Co. PC775

This rather interesting postcard set measures 3 1/2" by 5 1/2", was issued in 1907 and features a Chicago Cub player in a circle in the upper right corner of the front of the card. These cards have green backgrounds featuring a teddy bear in different poses. There is also a head shot in the upper right corner blending comic and photo art. Cards are known to come with an ad for the Boston Oyster House, a popular Chicago restaurant at the time.

COMPLETE SET (16)	1,000.00	2,000.00
1 Mordecai Brown	300.00	600.00
2 Frank Chance	400.00	800.00
3 Johnny Evers	400.00	800.00

4 Arthur Hoffman 150.00 300.00
5 John Kling 200.00 400.00
6 Carl Lundgren 150.00 300.00
7 Pat Moran 200.00 400.00
8 Orvall Overall 200.00 400.00
9 Jack Pfiester 150.00 300.00
10 Ed Reulbach 200.00 400.00
11 Frank Schulte 200.00 400.00
12 Jimmy Sheckard 150.00 300.00
13 James Slagle 150.00 300.00
14 Harry Steinfeldt 200.00 400.00
15 Jack Taylor 150.00 300.00
16 Joe Tinker 400.00 800.00

1908 Cubs Postcards

An unknown Chicago Publisher using a logo of a dollar sign inside a shield produced an attractive set of Cubs players on a gray background in 1908. The known cards in this set are listed below any additions to this checklist are appreciated.

COMPLETE SET (4) 400.00 800.00
1 Frank Chance 200.00 400.00
2 Artie Hoffman 75.00 150.00
3 John Kling 100.00 200.00
4 Harry Steinfeldt 100.00 200.00

1930 Cubs Blue Ribbon Malt

These photographs, which measure 6 1/4" by 8 3/4" and feature fascimile autographs are surrounded by plain white borders. Both Chicago teams were produced; howeverm we have seperated the two teams included in this set. The cards have black backs and are therefore sequenced in alphabetical order. It is possible that other cards may be in the set so all additional information is appreciated. These cards were sent out in special envelopes which included an advertising drawing of Charlie Grimm.

COMPLETE SET 900.00 1,800.00
1 Clyde Beck 40.00 80.00
2 Les Bell 40.00 80.00
3 Clarence Blair 40.00 80.00
4 Fred Blake 40.00 80.00
5 Jimmy Burke CO 40.00 80.00
6 Guy Bush 40.00 80.00
7 Hal Carlson 40.00 80.00
8 Kiki Cuyler 75.00 150.00
9 Woody English 50.00 100.00
10 Charlie Grimm 60.00 120.00
11 Gabby Hartnett 100.00 200.00
12 Cliff Heathcote 40.00 80.00
13 Rogers Hornsby 125.00 250.00
14 Pat Malone 40.00 80.00
15 Joe McCarthy MG 75.00 150.00
16 Malcolm Moss 40.00 80.00
17 Lynn Nelson 40.00 80.00
18 Bob Osborn 40.00 80.00
19 Bobby Smith 40.00 80.00
19 Charlie Root 50.00 100.00
20 Ray Schalk CO 75.00 150.00
21 John Schulte 40.00 80.00
22 Al Shealy 40.00 80.00
23 Riggs Stephenson 60.00 120.00
24 Dan Taylor 40.00 80.00
25 Zach Taylor 40.00 80.00
26 Charles Tolson 40.00 80.00
27 Hal Totten ANN 40.00 80.00
28 Hack Wilson 75.00 150.00

1930 Cubs Team Issue

This 21-card set of the Chicago Cubs features black-and-white player photos with facsimile autographs. The backs are blank. The cards are all 3 1/2" high but have various widths ranging from 1 3/8" to 3". The cards are unnumbered and checklisted below in alphabetical order. A few uncut sheets of this set have survivied.

COMPLETE SET (21) 250.00 500.00
1 Clyde Beck 10.00 25.00
2 Les Bell 10.00 25.00
3 Clarence Blair 10.00 25.00
4 John Blake 10.00 25.00
5 Woody English 15.00 40.00
6 Doc Farrell 10.00 25.00
7 Gabby Hartnett 40.00 80.00
8 Clifton Heathcote 10.00 25.00
9 Rogers Hornsby 60.00 120.00
10 George Kelly 20.00 50.00
11 Pat Malone 10.00 25.00
12 Joe McCarthy MG 20.00 50.00
13 Bob Osborn 10.00 25.00
14 Jesse Petty 10.00 25.00
15 Charlie Root 15.00 40.00
16 Ray Schalk CO 20.00 50.00
17 John Schulte 10.00 25.00
18 Al Shealy 10.00 25.00
19 Zack Taylor 10.00 25.00
20 Bud Teachout 10.00 25.00
21 Hack Wilson 30.00 60.00

1931 Cubs Team Issue

These 31 photos feature players and club personnel involved with the 1931 Chicago Cubs. They measure approximately 6" by 9 1/2" and all the photos have a facsimile autograph as well. All of this is surrounded by white borders. The backs are black and we have sequenced the photos in alphabetical order.

COMPLETE SET (31) 350.00 700.00
1 Ed Baecht 10.00 25.00
2 Clyde Beck 10.00 25.00
3 Les Bell 10.00 25.00
4 Clarence Blair 10.00 25.00
5 Sheriff Blake 15.00 40.00
6 Guy Bush 15.00 40.00
7 KiKi Cuyler 10.00 25.00
8 Margaret Donahue 15.00 40.00
9 Woody English 20.00 50.00
10 Earl Grace 30.00 60.00
11 Charlie Grimm 10.00 25.00
12 Gabby Hartnett 60.00 120.00
13 Rollie Hemsley 15.00 40.00
14 Rogers Hornsby 10.00 25.00
15 Billy Jurges 10.00 25.00
16 Bob Lewis TS 10.00 25.00
17 Andy Lotshaw TR 10.00 25.00
18 Pat Malone 10.00 25.00
19 Jakie May 15.00 40.00
20 John Moore 20.00 50.00
21 Charley O'Leary 10.00 25.00
22 Charlie Root 10.00 25.00
23 Ray Schalk 20.00 50.00
24 John Seys FO 10.00 25.00
25 Bob Smith 10.00 25.00
26 Riggs Stephenson 10.00 25.00
27 Les Sweetland 10.00 25.00
28 Dan Taylor 15.00 40.00
29 Zack Taylor 10.00 25.00
30 Bud Teachout
31 William Veeck PRES 30.00 60.00
32 W.M. Walker FO 15.00 40.00
33 Lon Warneke 15.00 40.00
34 Hack Wilson
35 Phil Wrigley FO
36 William Wrigley OWN

1932 Cubs Denby Postcards

* USE $250 FOR COMMONS* This eight-card postcard set features members of the 1932 Chicago Cubs. The borderless fronts feature a player's photo with a facsimile autograph while the backs promote the use of Denby Cigars. Since these postcards are unnumbered, we have sequenced them in alphabetical order.

1932 Cubs Team Issue

These 35 photos feature members of the 1932 Chicago Cubs. The photos are shot against a black background and feature a player photo and a facsimile signature. The cards measure approximately 6" by 9" are unnumbered and we have sequenced them in alphabetical order. This set was issued late in the season as Mark Koenig who only spent the last part of the season with the Cubs was included.

COMPLETE SET (35) 200.00 450.00
1 Guy Bush 10.00 25.00
2 Gilly Campbell
3 Red Corriden CO 6.00 -15.00
4 Kiki Cuyler 30.00 60.00
5 Frank Demaree 6.00 15.00
6 Margaret Donahue 6.00 15.00
7 Woody English 10.00 25.00
8 Burleigh Grimes 30.00 60.00
9 Charlie Grimm 12.50 30.00
10 Marv Gudat 6.00 15.00
11 Stanley Hack 10.00 25.00
12 Gabby Hartnett 40.00 80.00
13 Rollie Helmsley 6.00 15.00
14 Billy Herman 30.00 60.00
15 Leroy Herrmann 6.00 15.00
16 Billy Jurges 10.00 25.00
17 Mark Koenig 10.00 25.00
18 Bob Lewis 6.00 15.00
19 Pat Malone 6.00 15.00
20 Jake May 6.00 15.00
21 Johnny Moore 6.00 15.00
22 Charley O'Leary CO 6.00 15.00
23 Lance Richbourg 6.00 15.00
24 Charlie Root 10.00 25.00
25 John Seys 6.00 15.00
26 Bob Smith 6.00 15.00
27 Riggs Stephenson 12.50 30.00
28 Harry Taylor
29 Zack Taylor 6.00 15.00
30 Bud Tinning 6.00 15.00
31 William Veeck GM 10.00 25.00
32 W.M. Walker 6.00 15.00
33 Lon Warneke 10.00 25.00
34 Phil Wrigley 10.00 25.00
35 William Wrigley OWN 10.00 25.00

1933 Cubs Team Issue

1 Guy Bush
2 Gilly Campbell
3 Red Corriden
4 Kiki Cuyler
5 Frank Demaree
6 Margaret Donahue
7 Woody English
8 Burleigh Grimes
9 Charlie Grimm
10 Gabby Hartnett
11 Harvey Hendrick
12 Roy Henshaw
13 Babe Herman
14 Billy Herman
15 Billy Jurges
16 Mark Koenig
17 Bob Lewis
18 Pat Malone
19 Charlie Root
20 John Seys
21 Riggs Stephenson
22 John Schulte
23 Zack Taylor
24 Bud Tinning
25 William Veeck
26 W.M. Walker
27 Lon Warneke
28 Phil Wrigley
29 William Wrigley

1936 Cubs Team Issue

This 32-card set of the Chicago Cubs measures approximately 6" by 9" and is printed on black paper with a facimile autograph in white. The backs are blank. The cards are unnumbered and checklisted below in alphabetical order.

COMPLETE SET (32) 225.00 450.00
1 Clay Bryant 6.00 15.00
2 Tex Carleton 6.00 15.00
3 Phil Cavarretta 12.50 30.00
4 John Corriden CO 6.00 15.00
5 Frank Demaree 6.00 15.00
6 Margaret Donahue 6.00 15.00
7 Woody English 6.00 15.00
8 Larry French 8.00 20.00
9 Augie Galan 8.00 20.00
10 Johnny Gill 6.00 15.00
11 Charlie Grimm MG 10.00 25.00
12 Stanley Hack 12.50 30.00
13 Leo Gabby Hartnett 20.00 50.00
14 Roy Henshaw 6.00 15.00
15 Billy Herman 20.00 50.00
16 Roy Johnson 6.00 15.00
17 Bill Jurges 10.00 25.00
18 Chuck Klein 20.00 50.00
19 Fabian Kowalick 6.00 15.00
20 Bill Lee 6.00 15.00
21 Robert Lewis TS 6.00 15.00
22 Gene Lillard 6.00 15.00
23 Andy Lotshaw TR 6.00 15.00
24 Jim O'Dea 6.00 15.00
25 Charlie Root 10.00 25.00
26 John Seys 6.00 15.00
27 Clyde Shoun 6.00 15.00
28 Tuck Stainback 6.00 15.00
29 Riggs Stephenson 12.50 30.00
30 Lon Warneke 10.00 25.00
31 Charles Weber 6.00 15.00
32 Wrigley Field 30.00 60.00

1939 Cubs Team Issue

This set of the Chicago Cubs measures approximately 6 1/2" by 9". The black and white photos display fascimile autographs. The backs are blank. The cards are unnumbered and are checklisted below in alphabetical order.

COMPLETE SET (25) 200.00 400.00
1 Dick Bartell 10.00 25.00
2 Clay Bryant 6.00 15.00
3 Phil Cavarretta 10.00 25.00
4 John Corriden 6.00 15.00
5 Dizzy Dean 40.00 80.00
6 Larry French 8.00 20.00
7 Augie Galan 10.00 25.00
8 Bob Garbark 6.00 15.00
9 Jim Gleeson 6.00 15.00
10 Stanley Hack 10.00 25.00
11 Leo Hartnett 30.00 60.00
12 Billy Herman 30.00 60.00
13 Roy Johnson 6.00 15.00
14 Bill Lee 8.00 20.00
15 Hank Lieber 6.00 15.00
16 Gene Lillard 6.00 15.00
17 Gus Mancuso 6.00 15.00
18 Bobby Mattick 8.00 20.00
19 Vance Page 6.00 15.00
20 Claude Passeau 10.00 25.00
21 Carl Reynolds 6.00 15.00
22 Charlie Root 10.00 25.00
23 Glen Rip Russell 6.00 15.00
24 Jack Russell 6.00 15.00
25 E. Whitehill 6.00 15.00

1941 Cubs Team Issue

These photos measure approximately 6 1/2" by 9". They feature members of the 1941 Chicago Cubs. The set is dated by the appearence of Greek George. The backs are blank and we have sequenced them in alphabetical order. This set was issued twice so there are more than the normal amount of players in this set due to roster manipluations during the season.

COMPLETE SET (25) 125.00 250.00
1 Phil Cavarretta 10.00 25.00
2 Dom Dallessandro 5.00 12.00
3 Paul Erickson 5.00 12.00
4 Larry French 8.00 20.00
5 Augie Galan 8.00 20.00
6 Greek George 5.00 12.00
7 Charlie Gilbert 5.00 12.00
8 Stan Hack 8.00 20.00
9 Johnny Hudson 5.00 12.00
10 Bill Lee 8.00 20.00
11 Hank Leiber 5.00 12.00
12 Clyde McCullough 5.00 12.00
13 Jake Mooty 5.00 12.00
14 Bill Myers 5.00 12.00
15 Bill Nicholson 10.00 25.00
16 Lou Novikoff 6.00 15.00
17 Vern Olsen 5.00 12.00
18 Vance Page 5.00 12.00
19 Claude Passeau 8.00 20.00
20 Tot Pressnell 5.00 12.00
21 Charlie Root 8.00 20.00
22 Bob Scheffing 5.00 12.00
23 Lou Stringer 5.00 12.00
24 Bob Sturgeon 5.00 12.00
25 Cubs Staff 15.00 40.00
Dick Spalding CO
Jimmie Wilson CO

1942 Cubs Team Issue

These 25 photos were issued by the Chicago Cubs. The black and white blank back photos measure 6 1/2" by 9". Since they are unnumbered we have sequenced them in alphabetical order.

COMPLETE SET (25) 125.00 250.00
1 Hiram Bithorn 5.00 12.00
2 Phil Cavarretta 8.00 20.00
3 Dom Dallessandro 5.00 12.00
4 Paul Erickson 5.00 12.00
5 Bill Fleming 5.00 12.00
6 Charlie Gilbert 5.00 12.00
7 Stanley Hack 8.00 20.00
8 Edward Hanyzewski 5.00 12.00
9 Chico Hernandez 5.00 12.00
10 Bill Lee 6.00 15.00
11 Peanuts Lowrey 5.00 12.00
12 Clyde McCullough 5.00 12.00
13 Jake Mooty 5.00 12.00
14 Lennie Merullo 5.00 12.00
15 Bill Nicholson 10.00 25.00
16 Louie Novikoff 5.00 12.00
17 Vern Olsen 5.00 12.00
18 Claude Passeau 8.00 20.00
19 Tot Pressnell 5.00 12.00
20 Glen Russell 5.00 12.00
21 Bob Scheffing 5.00 12.00
22 John Schmitz 5.00 12.00
23 Lou Stringer 5.00 12.00
24 Bob Sturgeon 5.00 12.00
25 Coaches Card 15.00 40.00
Ki Ki Cuyler
Jimmie Wilson
Dick Sp

1943 Cubs Team Issue

This set of photographs measure approximately 6 1/2" by 9". They feature members of the 1943 Chicago Cubs. The black and white photos also feature fascimile autographs. The backs are blank and we have sequenced this set in alphabetical order.

COMPLETE SET (24) 125.00 250.00
1 Dick Barrett 5.00 12.00
2 Heinz Becker 5.00 12.00
3 Hi Bithorn 5.00 12.00
4 Phil Cavarretta 10.00 25.00
5 Dom Dallessandro 5.00 12.00
6 Paul Derringer 8.00 20.00
7 Paul Erickson 5.00 12.00
8 Bill Fleming 5.00 12.00
9 Stan Hack 8.00 20.00
10 Ed Hanyzewski 5.00 12.00
11 Chico Hernandez 5.00 12.00
12 Bill Lee 5.00 12.00
13 Peanuts Lowery 6.00 15.00
14 Stu Martin 5.00 12.00
15 Clyde McCullough 5.00 12.00
16 Lennie Merullo 5.00 12.00
17 Bill Nicholson 10.00 25.00
18 Lou Novikoff 5.00 12.00
19 Claude Passeau 8.00 20.00
20 Ray Prim 5.00 12.00
21 Eddie Stanky 10.00 25.00
22 Al Todd 5.00 12.00
23 Lon Warneke 8.00 20.00
24 Hank Wyse 5.00 12.00
25 Kiki Cuyler CO 15.00 40.00
Jimmie Wilson CO
Dick Spalding CO

1944 Cubs Team Issue

These 1944 Chicago Cub team photos are printed on thin paper stock and measure approximately 6" by 8 1/2". The photos feature a black and white head and shoulders shot, with white borders and the player's autograph inscribed across the picture. The backs are blank. The photos are unnumbered and checklisted below in alphabetical order.

COMPLETE SET (25)	150.00	300.00
1 Heinz Becker	6.00	15.00
2 John Burrows	6.00	15.00
3 Phil Cavarretta	10.00	25.00
4 Dom Dallessandro	6.00	15.00
6 Paul Derringer	10.00	25.00
7 Roy Easterwood	6.00	15.00
8 Paul Erickson	6.00	15.00
9 Bill Fleming	6.00	15.00
10 Jimmie Foxx	30.00	60.00
11 Ival Goodman	6.00	15.00
12 Edward Hanyzewski	6.00	15.00
13 William Holm	6.00	15.00
14 Don Johnson	6.00	15.00
15 Garth Mann	6.00	15.00
16 Lennie Merullo	6.00	15.00
17 John Miklos	6.00	15.00
18 Bill Nicholson	10.00	25.00
19 Lou Novikoff	8.00	20.00
20 Andy Pafko	10.00	25.00
21 Eddie Sauer	6.00	15.00
22 William Schuster	6.00	15.00
23 Eddie Stanky	12.50	30.00
24 Hy Vandenberg	6.00	15.00
25 Hank Wyse	6.00	15.00
26 Tony York	6.00	15.00

1950 Cubs Greats Brace

These 18 photos were issued by noted Chicago photographer George Brace and honored some of the leading players in Cub history. The fronts have a photo of the player along with how long they were in the majors and what years they spent with the Cubs. The backs are blank so we have sequenced this set in alphabetical order.

COMPLETE SET (18)	75.00	150.00
1 Grover C. Alexander	6.00	12.00
2 Cap Anson	6.00	12.00
3 Mordecai Browne	6.00	12.00
4 Frank Chance	6.00	12.00
5 John Evers	6.00	12.00
6 Charlie Grimm	5.00	10.00
7 Stan Hack	4.00	8.00
8 Gabby Hartnett	6.00	12.00
9 Billy Herman	6.00	12.00
10 Charlie Hollocher	3.00	6.00
11 Billy Jurges	4.00	8.00
12 Johnny Kling	3.00	6.00
13 Joe McCarthy MG	5.00	10.00
14 Ed Reulbach	4.00	8.00
15 Albert Spalding	6.00	12.00
16 Joe Tinker	6.00	12.00
17 Hippo Vaughn	3.00	6.00
18 Hack Wilson	6.00	12.00

1952 Cubs Ben Bey

These 8" by 11" photos were issued by Ben Bey and featured members of the Chicago Cubs. The front has a player photo as well as a fascimile signature. The back has the notation; "courtesy of Ben Bey, Lucky Fan WBKB Chicago." Since the photos are unnumbered we have sequenced them in alphabetical order. It is possible that there are more photos in this set so please send any additions you might have.

COMPLETE SET (26)	60.00	120.00
1 Frank Baumholtz	2.50	5.00
2 Bob Borkowski	2.50	5.00
3 Smoky Burgess	3.00	6.00
4 Phil Cavaretta	4.00	8.00
5 Chuck Connors	5.00	10.00
6 Jack Cusick	2.50	5.00
7 Bruce Edwards	2.50	5.00
8 Dee Fondy	2.50	5.00
9 Joe Hatten	2.50	5.00
10 Gene Hermanski	2.50	5.00
11 Frank Hiller	2.50	5.00
12 Ransom Jackson	2.50	5.00
13 Hal Jeffcoat	2.50	5.00
14 Bob Kelly	2.50	5.00
15 John Klippstein	2.50	5.00
16 Dutch Leonard	2.50	5.00
17 Turk Lown	2.50	5.00
18 Cal McLish	2.50	5.00
19 Eddie Miksis	2.50	5.00
20 Paul Minner	2.50	5.00
21 Bob Ramazzotti	2.50	5.00
22 Bob Rush	2.50	5.00
23 Hank Sauer	5.00	10.00
24 Bob Schultz	2.50	5.00
25 Bill Serena	2.50	5.00
26 Roy Smalley	2.50	5.00

1960 Cubs Jay Publishing

This 12-card set of the Chicago Cubs measures approximately 5" by 7" and features black-and-white player photos in a white border. These cards were packaged 12 to a packet. The backs are blank. The cards are unnumbered and checklisted below in alphabetical order.

COMPLETE SET (12)	15.00	40.00
1 George Altman	.75	2.00
2 Bob Anderson	.75	2.00
3 Richie Ashburn	2.50	6.00
4 Ernie Banks	5.00	12.00
5 Moe Drabowsky	.75	2.00
6 Don Elston	.75	2.00
7 Glen Hobbie	.75	2.00
8 Dale Long	.75	2.00
9 Walt Moryn	.75	2.00
10 Sam Taylor	.75	2.00
11 Tony Taylor	.75	2.00
12 Frank Thomas	1.25	3.00

1961 Cubs Jay Publishing

This 12-card set of the Chicago Cubs measures approximately 5" by 7". The fronts feature black-and-white posed player photos with the player's and team name printed below in the white border. These cards were packaged 12 in a packet. The backs are blank. The cards are unnumbered and checklisted below in alphabetical order. Ron Santo appears in his Rookie Card year.

COMPLETE SET	8.00	20.00
1 George Altman	.75	2.00
2 Bob Anderson	.75	2.00
3 Richie Ashburn	2.50	6.00
4 Ernie Banks	5.00	12.00
5 Ed Bouchee	.75	2.00
6 Dick Ellsworth	.75	2.00
7 Don Elston	.75	2.00
8 Glen Hobbie	.75	2.00
9 Jerry Kindall	.75	2.00
10 Ron Santo	2.50	6.00
11 Moe Thacker	.75	2.00
12 Don Zimmer	1.50	4.00

1962 Cubs Jay Publishing

This 12-card set of the Chicago Cubs measures approximately 5" by 7". The fronts feature black-and-white posed player photos with the player's and team name printed below in the white border. These cards were packaged 12 in a packet. The backs are blank. The cards are unnumbered and checklisted below in alphabetical order.

COMPLETE SET (12)	15.00	40.00
1 George Altman	.75	2.00
2 Bob Anderson	.75	2.00
3 Ernie Banks	5.00	12.00
4 Don Cardwell	.75	2.00
5 Jack Curtis	.75	2.00
6 Don Elston	.75	2.00
7 Glen Hobbie	.75	2.00
8 Ken Hubbs	2.00	5.00
9 Ron Santo	2.00	5.00
10 Barney Schultz	.75	2.00
11 Sam Taylor	.75	2.00
12 Billy Williams	3.00	8.00

1963 Cubs Jay Publishing

This 12-card set of the Chicago Cubs measures approximately 5" by 7". The fronts feature black-and-white posed player photos with the player's and team name printed below in the white border. These cards were packaged 12 in a packet. The backs are blank. The cards are unnumbered and checklisted below in alphabetical order.

COMPLETE SET (12)	15.00	40.00
1 Ernie Banks	5.00	12.00
2 Dick Bertell	.75	2.00
3 Lou Brock	5.00	12.00
4 Bob Buhl	.75	2.00
5 Dick Ellsworth	.75	2.00
6 Glen Hobbie	.75	2.00
7 Larry Jackson	.75	2.00
8 Bob Kennedy CO	.75	2.00
9 Lindy McDaniel	.75	2.00
10 Andre Rodgers	.75	2.00
11 Ron Santo	2.00	5.00
12 Billy Williams	3.00	8.00

1964 Cubs Jay Publishing

This 12-card set of the Chicago Cubs measures approximately 5" by 7". The fronts feature black-and-white posed player photos with the player's and team name printed below in the white border. These cards were packaged 12 in a packet. The backs are blank. The cards are unnumbered and checklisted below in alphabetical order.

COMPLETE SET (12)	15.00	40.00
1 Ernie Banks	5.00	12.00
2 Dick Bertell	.75	2.00
3 Lou Brock	4.00	10.00
4 Bob Buhl	.75	2.00
5 Don Elston	.75	2.00
6 Ken Hubbs	2.00	5.00
7 Larry Jackson	.75	2.00
8 Don Landrum	.75	2.00
9 Lindy McDaniel	.75	2.00
10 Andre Rodgers	.75	2.00
11 Ron Santo	2.00	5.00
12 Billy Williams	3.00	8.00

1965 Cubs Announcers

Issued to promote the announcers of the 1965 Chicago Cubs. These two postcards feature both announcers.

COMPLETE SET	6.00	15.00
1 Lou Boudreau Vince Lloyd Color photo in the dugout	2.00	5.00
2 Lou Bourdreau Vince Lloyd Black and White Photo, on the field	4.00	10.00

1965 Cubs Jay Publishing

This 12-card set of the Chicago Cubs measures approximately 5" by 7". The fronts feature black-and-white posed player photos with the player's and team name printed below in the white border. These cards were packaged 12 in a packet. The backs are blank. The cards are unnumbered and checklisted below in alphabetical order.

COMPLETE SET (12)	15.00	40.00
1 George Altman	.75	2.00
2 Ernie Banks	5.00	12.00
3 Dick Bertell	.75	2.00
4 Ernie Broglio	.75	2.00
5 Bob Buhl	.75	2.00
6 Lou Burdette	1.25	3.00
7 Dick Ellsworth	.75	2.00
8 Larry Jackson	.75	2.00
9 Bob Kennedy CO	.75	2.00
10 Ron Santo	2.00	5.00
11 Jim Stewart	.75	2.00
12 Billy Williams	3.00	8.00

1966 Cubs Team Issue

These 12 cards feature members of the 1966 Chicago Cubs, who by finishing last, enabled the New York Mets to finally not finish in the cellar. The cards are unnumbered and we have sequenced them in alphabetical order.

COMPLETE SET (12)	15.00	40.00
1 Ted Abernathy	.75	2.00
2 George Altman	1.25	3.00
3 Ernie Banks	4.00	10.00
4 Glenn Beckert	1.25	3.00
5 Ernie Broglio	.75	2.00
6 Leo Durocher	2.00	5.00
7 Dick Ellsworth	.75	2.00
8 Larry Jackson	.75	2.00
9 Chris Krug	.75	2.00
10 Harvey Kuenn	1.25	3.00
11 Ron Santo	2.00	5.00
12 Billy Williams	2.00	5.00

1968 Cubs Pro's Pizza

This 12-card set measures 4 3/4: in diameter and featured members of the Chicago Cubs. Only the Cubs players are included in this listing.

COMPLETE SET (12)	1,250.00	2,500.00
1 Joe Amalfitano	100.00	200.00
2 Ernie Banks	350.00	700.00
3 Glenn Beckert	125.00	250.00
4 John Boccabella	100.00	200.00
5 Bill Hands	100.00	200.00
6 Ken Holtzman	100.00	200.00
7 Randy Hundley	100.00	200.00
8 Fergie Jenkins	200.00	400.00
9 Don Kessinger	150.00	300.00
10 Adolfo Phillips	100.00	200.00
11 Ron Santo	300.00	600.00
12 Billy Williams	200.00	400.00

1969 Cubs Bumper Stickers

This six-sticker set of the Chicago Cubs measures approximately 7 7/8" by 4" and features color player head photos printed at the end of a baseball bat drawing. Two versions of this set were issued with either "Cub Power" or "Dunkin Donuts" printed inside a ball that looked as if it was being hit by the bat. The stickers are unnumbered and checklisted below in alphabetical order.

COMPLETE SET (6)	50.00	100.00
1 Ernie Banks	15.00	40.00
2 Glenn Beckert	5.00	12.00
3 Randy Hundley	5.00	12.00
4 Don Kessinger	5.00	12.00
5 Ron Santo	10.00	25.00
6 Billy Williams	10.00	25.00

1969 Cubs Jewel Tea

This 20-card set of the Chicago Cubs measures approximately 6" by 9" and were given away over a five week period in 1969. The white-bordered fronts feature color player action and posed photos with a facsimile autograph across the picture. The backs are blank. The cards are unnumbered and checklisted below in alphabetical order.

COMPLETE SET (20)	20.00	50.00
1 Ted Abernathy	.60	1.50
2 Hank Aguirre	.60	1.50
3 Ernie Banks	4.00	10.00
4 Glenn Beckert	.75	2.00
5 Bill Hands	.60	1.50
6 Jim Hickman	.60	1.50
7 Kenny Holtzman	.75	2.00
8 Randy Hundley	.75	2.00
9 Fergie Jenkins	3.00	8.00
10 Don Kessinger	1.00	2.50
11 Rich Nye	.60	1.50
12 Paul Popovich	.60	1.50
13 Jim Qualls	.60	1.50
14 Phil Regan	.60	1.50
15 Ron Santo	1.25	3.00
16 Dick Selma	.60	1.50
17 Willie Smith	.60	1.50
18 Al Spangler	.60	1.50
19 Billy Williams	2.50	6.00
20 Don Young	.60	1.50

1969 Cubs Photos

These photos feature members of the 1969 Chicago Cubs, best known as the team which lost a huge lead so the Miracle Mets could win the pennant. These photos are unnumbered and we have sequenced them in alphabetical order.

COMPLETE SET (12)	12.50	30.00
1 Ted Abernathy	.60	1.50
2 Ernie Banks	3.00	8.00
3 Glenn Beckert	.60	1.50
4 Leo Durocher MG	1.25	3.00
5 Ken Holtzman	.75	2.00
6 Randy Hundley	.75	2.00
7 Ferguson Jenkins	2.00	5.00
8 Don Kessinger	1.00	2.50
9 Phil Regan	.60	1.50
10 Ron Santo	1.25	3.00
11 Al Spangler	.60	1.50
12 Billy Williams	2.00	5.00

1969 Cubs Team Issue Color

This 10-card set of the Chicago Cubs measures approximately 7" by 8 3/4" with the fronts featuring white-bordered color player photos. The player's name and team is printed in black in the white margin below the picture. The backs are blank. The cards are unnumbered and checklisted below in alphabetical order.

COMPLETE SET	12.50	30.00
1 Ernie Banks	3.00	8.00
2 Glenn Beckert	.60	1.50
3 Ken Holtzman	.75	2.00
4 Randy Hundley	1.00	2.50
5 Ferguson Jenkins	2.00	5.00
6 Don Kessinger	1.00	2.50
7 Phil Regan	.60	1.50
8 Ron Santo	1.25	3.00
9 Willie Smith	.60	1.50
10 Billy Williams	2.00	5.00

1970 Cubs Dunkin Donuts

This set of six bumper stickers (apparently commemorating the Cubs near-miss in 1969) was produced and distributed by Dunkin Donuts. The stickers are approximately 4 1/16" by 8 1/16" and are in color. Each sticker features a facsimile autograph in the upper left hand corner. The stickers are unnumbered and are listed below in alphabetical order according to the player's name.

COMPLETE SET (6)	40.00	80.00
1 Ernie Banks	15.00	40.00
2 Glenn Beckert	1.25	3.00
3 Randy Hundley	1.25	3.00
4 Don Kessinger	8.00	20.00

5 Ron Santo 10.00 25.00
6 Billy Williams 6.00 15.00

1972 Cubs Chi-Foursome

These 11" by 14" drawings feature Chicago Cubs players. The attractive color drawings also have a facimilie signature. The backs are blank and we have sequenced this set in alphabetical order.

COMPLETE SET (8) 6.00 15.00
1 Ernie Banks 2.00 5.00
2 Glenn Beckert .40 1.00
3 Fergie Jenkins 1.00 2.50
4 Don Kessinger .40 1.00
5 Milt Pappas .40 1.00
6 Joe Pepitone .75 2.00
7 Ron Santo 1.00 2.50
8 Billy Williams 1.00 2.50

1972 Cubs Team Issue

These 12 photos feature members of the 1972 Chicago Cubs. The photos measure approximately 4 1/4" by 7". The black and white photos are surrounded by white borders and feature a facsimile autograph. The backs are blank and we have sequenced this set in alphabetical order.

COMPLETE SET (12) 12.50 30.00
1 Ernie Banks CO 2.50 6.00
2 Glenn Beckert .75 2.00
3 Bill Hands .60 1.50
4 Jim Hickman .60 1.50
5 Randy Hundley .75 2.00
6 Fergie Jenkins 2.00 5.00
7 Don Kessinger .75 2.00
8 Rick Monday 1.00 2.50
9 Milt Pappas .60 1.50
10 Joe Pepitone .75 2.00
11 Ron Santo 1.25 3.00
12 Billy Williams 2.00 5.00

1973 Cubs Jewel

These blank-backed photos, which measure approximately 6" by 9", feature members of the 1973 Chicago Cubs. These fronts have white borders which surround a full-color player portrait as well as a facsimile autograph. These cards are unnumbered, so we have sequenced them in alphabetical order.

COMPLETE SET 6.00 15.00
1 Jack Aker .20 .50
2 Glenn Beckert .40 1.00
3 Jose Cardenal .40 1.00
4 Carmen Fanzone .20 .50
5 Jim Hickman .20 .50
6 Burt Hooton .20 .50
7 Randy Hundley .40 1.00
8 Fergie Jenkins 1.25 3.00
9 Don Kessinger .40 1.00
10 Bob Locker .20 .50
11 Rick Monday .40 1.00
12 Milt Pappas .40 1.00
13 Rick Reuschel .75 2.00
14 Ken Rudolph .20 .50
15 Ron Santo 1.00 2.50
16 Billy Williams 1.25 3.00

1974 Cubs 1938 Bra-Mac

These 29 photos, which measure 3 1/2" by 5" feature members of the 1938 Chicago Cubs and were issued by Bra-Mac using negatives they had in their massive photo file.

COMPLETE SET 10.00 25.00
1 Phil Cavaretta .60 1.50
2 Bob Garbark .20 .50
3 Jack Russell .20 .50
4 Tony Lazzeri .75 2.00
5 Dizzy Dean 1.25 3.00
6 Coaker Triplett .20 .50
7 Ken O'Dea .20 .50
8 Larry French .40 1.00
9 Stan Hack .40 1.00
10 Gabby Hartnett .75 2.00
11 Bill Lee .60 1.50
12 Kirby Higbe .40 1.00
13 Bobby Mattick .40 1.00
14 Tex Carleton .20 .50
15 Charlie Root .40 1.00
16 Bob Logan .20 .50
17 Steve Mesner .20 .50
18 Newt Kimball .20 .50
19 Clay Bryant .20 .50
20 Rip Collins .40 1.00
21 Augie Galan .40 1.00
22 Frank Demaree .20 .50
23 Al Epperly .20 .50
24 Billy Herman .75 2.00
25 Jim Asbell .20 .50
26 Carl Reynolds .20 .50
27 Vance Page .20 .50
28 Billy Jurges .40 1.00
29 Joe Marty .20 .50

1974 Cubs Team Issue

These blank-backed photos, which measure approximately 7" by 9", feature members of the 1974 Chicago Cubs. The fronts have full color photos surrounded by white borders with the players name and team on the bottom. Since these photos are unnumbered, we have sequenced them in alphabetical order.

COMPLETE SET 3.00 8.00
1 Ray Burris .20 .50
2 Jose Cardenal .30 .75
3 Carmen Fanzone .20 .50
4 Vic Harris .20 .50
5 Burt Hooton UER Spelled Houton .30 .75
6 Don Kessinger .20 .50
7 Bill Madlock .60 1.50
8 George Mitterwald .20 .50
9 Rick Monday .30 .75
10 Jerry Morales .20 .50
11 Steve Stone .30 .75
12 Billy Williams .75 2.00

1976 Cubs TCMA 1938

These cards were issued by TCMA and feature members of the pennant winning 1938 Chicago Cubs. These cards are unnumbered and we have sequenced them in alphabetical order.

COMPLETE SET (33) 8.00 20.00
1 Jim Asbell .20 .50
2 Clay Bryant .20 .50
3 Tex Carleton .20 .50
4 Phil Cavaretta .40 1.00
5 Ripper Collins .20 .50
6 Red Corriden .20 .50
7 Dizzy Dean 1.25 3.00
8 Frank Demaree .20 .50
9 Al Epperly .20 .50
10 Larry French .30 .75
11 Augie Galan .30 .75
12 Bob Garbark .20 .50
13 Charlie Grimm MG .60 1.50
14 Stan Hack .40 1.00
15 Gabby Hartnett P MG .75 2.00
16 Billy Herman .75 2.00
17 Kirby Higbe .30 .75
18 Roy Johnson CO .20 .50
19 Billy Jurges .30 .75
20 Newt Kimball .20 .50
21 Tony Lazzeri .75 2.00
22 Bill Lee .20 .50
23 Bob Logan .20 .50
24 Joe Marty .20 .50
25 Bobby Mattick .30 .75
26 Steve Mesner .20 .50
27 Ken O'Dea .20 .50
28 Vance Page .20 .50
29 Carl Reynolds .20 .50
30 Charlie Root .30 .75
31 Jack Russell .20 .50
32 Coaker Triplett .20 .50
33 Chicago Cub Unidentified Player .20 .50

1976 Cubs Tribune

These 26 cards were issued by the Chicago Tribune and features the members of the 1976 Cubs. They are unnumbered and we have sequenced them in alphabetical order. This set features a "pre-rookie card" of Hall of Famer Bruce Sutter.

COMPLETE SET 10.00 25.00
1 Larry Biittner .40 1.00
2 Bill Bonham .40 1.00
3 Pete Broberg .40 1.00
4 Ray Burris .40 1.00
5 Jose Cardenal .60 1.50
6 Gene Clines .40 1.00
7 Bobby Darwin .40 1.00
8 Ivan DeJesus .40 1.00
9 Herman Franks MG .40 1.00
10 Greg Gross .40 1.00
11 Willie Hernandez 1.00 2.50
12 Mick Kelleher .40 1.00
13 Mike Krukow .40 1.00
14 George Mitterwald .40 1.00
15 Donnie Moore .40 1.00
16 Jerry Morales .40 1.00
17 Bobby Murcer .75 2.00
18 Steve Ontiveros .40 1.00
19 Steve Renko .40 1.00
20 Rick Reuschel .75 2.00
21 Dave Rosello .40 1.00
22 Bruce Sutter 4.00 10.00
23 Steve Swisher .40 1.00
24 Jim Todd .40 1.00
25 Manny Trillo .60 1.50
26 Joe Wallis .40 1.00

1977 Cubs All-Time TCMA

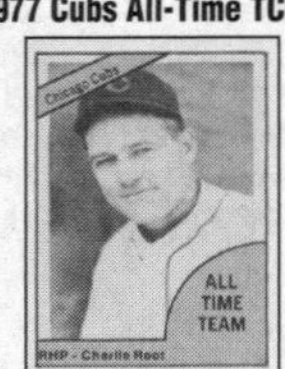

This 13-card set features black-and-white photos with wide white and thin black borders of Chicago Cubs players considered to be the best at their respective positions.The backs carry the checklist for the set. The cards are unnumbered and checklisted below in alphabetical order.

COMPLETE SET (13) 3.00 8.00
1 Ernie Banks .60 1.50
2 Kiki Cuyler .30 .75
3 Larry French .20 .50
4 Charlie Grimm .20 .50
5 Charlie Grimm MG .20 .50
6 Gabby Hartnett .30 .75
7 Billy Herman .30 .75
8 Rogers Hornsby .60 1.50
9 Emil Kush .20 .50
10 Charlie Root .20 .50
11 Ron Santo .40 1.00
12 Billy Williams .40 1.00
13 Hack Wilson .30 .75

1977 Cubs Jewel Tea

This 16-card set of the Chicago Cubs measures approximately 5 7/8" by 9". The white-bordered fronts feature color player head photos with a facsimile autograph. The backs are blank. The cards are unnumbered and checklisted below in alphabetical order.

COMPLETE SET (16) 6.00 15.00
1 Larry Biittner .30 .75
2 Bill Bonham .30 .75
3 Bill Buckner .60 1.50
4 Ray Burris .30 .75
5 Jose Cardenal .30 .75
6 Gene Clines .30 .75
7 Ivan DeJesus .30 .75
8 Willie Hernandez .60 1.50
9 Mike Krukow .30 .75
10 George Mitterwald .30 .75
11 Jerry Morales .30 .75
12 Bobby Murcer .40 1.00
13 Steve Ontiveros .30 .75
14 Rick Reuschel .40 1.00
15 Bruce Sutter 2.00 5.00
16 Manny Trillo .40 1.00

1980 Cubs Greats TCMA

This 12-card standard-size set honors some all-time Chicago Cubs greats. The fronts have a player photo, his name and position. The backs have vital statistics, career totals and a brief biography.

COMPLETE SET (12) 2.00 5.00
1 Billy Williams .40 1.00
2 Charlie Root .20 .50
3 Ron Santo .30 .75
4 Larry French .08 .25
5 Gabby Hartnett .40 1.00
6 Emil Kush .08 .25
7 Charlie Grimm .20 .50
8 Kiki Cuyler .30 .75
9 Billy Herman .30 .75
10 Hack Wilson .30 .75
11 Rogers Hornsby .40 1.00
12 Ernie Banks .60 1.50

1980 Cubs Sun Times

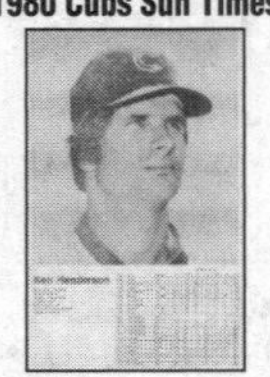

Measuring approximately 7" by 11" when neatly cut, these newspaper "inserts" feature a black and white photo of the player on top along with biographical information on the left and year by year statistics on the right. Since these are unnumbered, we have sequenced them in alphabetical order. The Lee Smith cut predates his Rookie Card by two years.

COMPLETE SET 10.00 25.00
1 Larry Biittner .40 1.00
2 Tim Blackwell .40 1.00
3 Bill Buckner .75 2.00
4 Doug Capilla .40 1.00
5 Bill Caudill .40 1.00
6 Ivan DeJesus .40 1.00
7 Steve Dillard .40 1.00
8 Jesus Figueroa .40 1.00
9 Barry Foote .40 1.00
10 Ken Henderson .40 1.00
11 Dave Kingman 1.25 3.00
12 Mike Krukow .40 1.00
13 Dennis Lamp .40 1.00
14 Jerry Martin .40 1.00
15 Lynn McGlothen .40 1.00
16 Lenny Randle .40 1.00
17 Rick Reuschel .60 1.50
18 Lee Smith 2.00 5.00
19 Scot Thompson .40 1.00
20 Dick Tidrow .40 1.00
21 Mike Tyson .40 1.00
22 Mike Vail .40 1.00

1976 Dallas Convention

This nine-card slightly oversized set features local Dallas players and was issued in conjunction with the annual Dallas Sports Card Convention hosted by noted hobbyist Gervise Ford. Mr. Ford also produced the set with "Life of the Southwest Insurance Co.".

COMPLETE SET (9) .75 2.00
1 Paul Aube .10 .25
2 Jodie Beeler .10 .25
3 Edward Borom/(Red) .10 .25
4 Sal Gliatto .10 .25
5 Richard Herrscher .10 .25
6 Joe Kotrany .10 .25
7 Joe Macko .10 .25
8 Frank Murray .10 .25
9 Ron Samford .10 .25

1954 Dan-Dee

The cards in this 29-card set measure approximately 2 1/2" by 3 5/8". Most of the cards marketed by Dan Dee in bags of potato chips in 1954 depict players from the Cleveland Indians or Pittsburgh Pirates. The Pittsburgh Pirates players in the set are much tougher to find than the Cleveland Indians players. The pictures used for New York Yankees players were also employed in the Briggs and Stahl-Meyer sets. Dan Dee cards have a waxed surface, but are commonly found with product stains. Paul Smith and Walker Cooper are considered the known scarcities. The catalog designation for this set is F342. These unnumbered cards are listed below in alphabetical order.

COMPLETE SET (29) 5,000.00 10,000.00
COMMON CARD (1-29) 50.00 100.00
COMMON PIRATE CARD 50.00 100.00
COMMON PIRATE SP'S 250.00 500.00
1 Bobby Avila 60.00 120.00
2 Hank Bauer 60.00 120.00
3 Walker Cooper SP/Pittsburgh Pirates 300.00 600.00
4 Larry Doby 100.00 200.00
5 Luke Easter 60.00 120.00
6 Bob Feller 150.00 300.00
7 Bob Friend/Pittsburgh Pirates 100.00 200.00
8 Mike Garcia 60.00 120.00
9 Sid Gordon/Pittsburgh Pirates 75.00 150.00
10 Jim Hegan 50.00 100.00
11 Gil Hodges 125.00 250.00
12 Art Houtteman 50.00 100.00
13 Monte Irvin 100.00 200.00
14 Paul LaPalme/Pittsburgh Pirates 60.00 120.00
15 Bob Lemon 100.00 200.00
16 Al Lopez MG 75.00 150.00
17 Mickey Mantle 1,500.00 2,500.00
18 Dale Mitchell 50.00 100.00
19 Phil Rizzuto 200.00 400.00
20 Curt Roberts/Pittsburgh Pirates 60.00 120.00
21 Al Rosen 75.00 150.00
22 Red Schoendienst 100.00 200.00
23 Paul Smith SP/Pittsburgh Pirates 500.00 1,000.00
24 Duke Snider 250.00 500.00
25 George Strickland 50.00 100.00
26 Max Surkont/Pittsburgh Pirates 60.00 120.00
27 Frank Thomas/Pittsburgh Pirates 150.00 300.00
28 Wally Westlake 50.00 100.00
29 Early Wynn 100.00 200.00

1910 Darby Chocolates E271

These 34 cards listed below are what are known of this very scarce set. A major help in cataloguing this set was a find of 22 cards in 1982. Some new cards are always being discovered. We understand that this checklist may be incomplete therefore verified copies of unlisted cards are appreciated. Uncut complete boxes are more desirable when found and are worth a little more than twice the value of the combined cards.

COMPLETE SET (34) 15,000.00 35,000.00
1 Jimmy Archer 1,000.00 2,000.00
2 Chief Bender 2,000.00 4,000.00
3 Bob Bescher 1,000.00 2,000.00
4 Roger Bresnahan 2,000.00 4,000.00
5 Al Bridwell 1,000.00 2,000.00
6 Mordecai Brown 2,000.00 4,000.00
7 Eddie Cicotte 2,000.00 4,000.00
8 Fred Clarke 2,000.00 4,000.00
9 Ty Cobb Batting 6,000.00 15,000.00
10 Ty Cobb Fielding 6,000.00 15,000.00
11 King Cole 1,000.00 2,000.00

12 Eddie Collins	2,500.00	5,000.00
13 Wid Conroy	1,000.00	2,000.00
14 Sam Crawford	2,000.00	4,000.00
15 Bill Dahlen	1,000.00	2,000.00
16 Bill Donovan	1,000.00	2,000.00
17 Patsy Dougherty	1,000.00	2,000.00
18 Kid Elberfeld	1,000.00	2,000.00
19 Johnny Evers	2,000.00	4,000.00
20 Buck Herzog	1,000.00	2,000.00
21 Hugh Jennings MG	2,000.00	4,000.00
22 Walter Johnson	5,000.00	10,000.00
23 Ed Konetchy	1,000.00	2,000.00
24 Tommy Leach	1,000.00	2,000.00
25 Fred Luderus Sic, Luderous	1,000.00	2,000.00
26 John McGraw MG	2,500.00	5,000.00
27 Mike Mowrey	1,000.00	2,000.00
28 Jack Powell	1,000.00	2,000.00
29 Slim Sallee	1,000.00	2,000.00
30 Jimmy Sheckard Sic, Scheckard	1,000.00	2,000.00
31 Fred Snodgrass	1,250.00	2,500.00
32 Tris Speaker	2,500.00	5,000.00
33 Charlie Suggs	1,000.00	2,000.00
34 Fred Tenney	1,000.00	2,000.00
35 Jim Vaughn	1,000.00	2,000.00
36 Honus Wagner	1,250.00	3,000.00

1970 Dayton Daily News M137

These 3 3/4" by 3 1/2" cards were issued inside issues of the Dayton Daily News. The newsprint-stock cards were issued on successive days and were numbered in that order. Tony Perez, card number 11, has been seen with a light or dark cap. There is no pricing difference for either card. The Dave Concepcion card predates his Topps Rookie Card by one year.

COMPLETE SET	300.00	600.00
COMMON CARD (61-160)	1.25	3.00
1 Pete Rose	8.00	20.00
2 Johnny Bench	4.00	10.00
3 Maury Wills	2.00	5.00
4 Harmon Killebrew	2.50	6.00
5 Frank Robinson	3.00	8.00
6 Willie Mays	6.00	15.00
7 Hank Aaron	6.00	15.00
8 Tom Seaver	4.00	10.00
9 Sam McDowell	1.50	4.00
10 Rico Petrocelli	1.50	4.00
11 Tony Perez Dark Cap	2.50	6.00
11A Tony Perez White Cap	2.50	6.00
12 Hoyt Wilhelm	2.50	6.00
13 Alex Johnson	1.00	2.50
14 Gary Nolan	1.00	2.50
15 Al Kaline	3.00	8.00
16 Bob Gibson	3.00	8.00
17 Larry Dierker	1.00	2.50
18 Ernie Banks	3.00	8.00
19 Lee May	1.50	4.00
20 Claude Osteen	1.00	2.50
21 Tony Horton	1.00	2.50
22 Mack Jones	1.00	2.50
23 Wally Bunker	1.00	2.50
24 Bill Hands	1.00	2.50
25 Bobby Tolan	1.00	2.50
26 Jim Wynn	1.50	4.00
27 Tom Haller	1.00	2.50
28 Carl Yastrzemski	3.00	8.00
29 Jim Merritt	1.00	2.50
30 Tony Oliva	2.00	5.00
31 Reggie Jackson	8.00	20.00
32 Bob Clemente	12.50	30.00
33 Tommy Helms	1.00	2.50
34 Boog Powell	2.00	5.00
35 Mickey Lolich	1.50	4.00
36 Frank Howard	1.50	4.00
37 Jim McGlothlin	1.00	2.50
38 Rusty Staub	1.50	4.00
39 Mel Stottlemyre	1.50	4.00
40 Rico Carty	1.00	2.50
41 Nate Colbert	1.00	2.50
42 Wayne Granger	1.00	2.50
43 Mike Hegan	1.00	2.50
44 Jerry Koosman	1.50	4.00
45 Jim Perry	1.00	2.50
46 Pat Corrales	1.00	2.50
47 Dick Bosman	1.00	2.50
48 Bert Campaneris	1.50	4.00
49 Larry Hisle	1.00	2.50
50 Bernie Carbo	1.00	2.50
51 Wilbur Wood	1.00	2.50
52 Dave McNally	1.50	4.00
53 Andy Messersmith	1.50	4.00
54 Jimmy Stewart	1.00	2.50
55 Luis Aparicio	2.50	6.00
56 Mike Cuellar	1.00	2.50
57 Bill Grabarkewitz	1.00	2.50
58 Dick Dietz	1.00	2.50
59 Dave Concepcion	2.50	6.00
60 Gary Gentry	1.00	2.50
61 Don Money	1.25	3.00
62 Rod Carew	4.00	10.00
63 Denis Menke	1.25	3.00
64 Hal McRae	1.50	4.00
65 Felipe Alou	1.50	4.00
66 Richie Hebner	1.25	3.00
67 Don Sutton	2.50	6.00
68 Wayne Simpson	1.25	3.00
69 Art Shamsky	1.25	3.00
70 Luis Tiant	2.00	5.00
71 Clay Carroll	1.25	3.00
72 Jim Hickman	1.25	3.00
73 Clarence Gaston	1.25	3.00
74 Angel Bravo	1.25	3.00
75 Jim Hunter	2.50	6.00
76 Lou Piniella	2.00	5.00
77 Jim Bunning	2.50	6.00
78 Don Gullett	1.25	3.00
80 Richie Allen	2.00	5.00
81 Jim Bouton	1.50	4.00
82 Jim Palmer	4.00	10.00
83 Woody Woodward	1.25	3.00
84 Tom Agee	1.25	3.00
85 Carlos May	1.25	3.00
86 Ray Washburn	1.25	3.00
87 Denny McLain	1.50	4.00
88 Lou Brock	4.00	10.00
89 Ken Henderson	1.25	3.00
90 Roy White	1.50	4.00
91 Chris Cannizzaro	1.25	3.00
92 Willie Horton	1.50	4.00
93 Jose Cardenal	1.25	3.00
94 Jim Fregosi	1.50	4.00
95 Richie Hebner	1.25	3.00
96 Tony Conigliaro	2.00	5.00
97 Tony Cloninger	1.25	3.00
98 Mike Epstein	1.25	3.00
99 Ty Cline	1.25	3.00
100 Tommy Harper	1.25	3.00
101 Jose Azcue	1.25	3.00
102a Ray Fosse	1.25	3.00
102b Glenn Beckert	1.25	3.00
103 not issued		
104 Gerry Moses	1.25	3.00
105 Bud Harrelson	1.25	3.00
106 Joe Torre	2.50	6.00
107 Dave Johnson	1.50	4.00
108 Don Kessinger	1.50	4.00
109 Bill Freehan	1.50	4.00
110 Sandy Alomar	1.25	3.00
111 Matty Alou	1.25	3.00
112 Joe Morgan	2.50	6.00
113 John Odom	1.25	3.00
114 Amos Otis	1.50	4.00
115 Jay Johnstone	1.25	3.00
116 Ron Perranoski	1.25	3.00
117 Manny Mota	1.25	3.00
118 Billy Conigliaro	1.25	3.00
119 Leo Cardenas	1.25	3.00
120 Rich Reese	1.25	3.00
121 Ron Santo	2.00	5.00
122 Gene Michael	1.25	3.00
123 Milt Pappas	1.25	3.00
124 Joe Pepitone	1.50	4.00
125 Jose Cardenal	1.25	3.00
126 Jim Northrup	1.50	4.00
127 Wes Parker	1.25	3.00
128 Fritz Peterson	1.25	3.00
129 Phil Regan	1.25	3.00
130 John Callison	1.25	3.00
131 Cookie Rojas	1.25	3.00
132 Claude Raymond	1.25	3.00
133 Darrell Chaney	1.25	3.00
134 Gary Peters	1.25	3.00
135 Del Unser	1.25	3.00
136 Joey Foy	1.25	3.00
137 Luke Walker	1.25	3.00
138 Bill Mazeroski	2.50	6.00
139 Tony Taylor	1.25	3.00
140 Leron Lee	1.25	3.00
141 Jesus Alou	1.50	4.00
142 Donn Clendenon	1.25	3.00
143 Merv Rettenmund	1.25	3.00
144 Bob Moose	1.25	3.00
145 Jim Kaat	2.00	5.00
146 Randy Hundley	1.25	3.00
147 Jim McAndrew	1.25	3.00
148 Manny Sanguillen	1.25	3.00
149 Bob Allison	1.25	3.00
150 Jim Maloney	1.25	3.00
151 Don Buford	1.25	3.00
152 Gene Alley	1.25	3.00
153 Cesar Tovar	1.25	3.00
154 Brooks Robinson	4.00	10.00
155 Milt Wilcox	1.25	3.00
156 Willie Stargell	2.50	6.00
157 Paul Blair	1.25	3.00
158 Andy Etchebarren	1.25	3.00
159 Mark Belanger	1.25	3.00
160 Elrod Hendricks	1.25	3.00

1971 Dell Today's Team Stamps

This set of stamps consists of 600 stamps contained in 25 stamp books (each containing 24 stamps) labeled Today's 1971 Team. The stamps are usually found still in the team albums. The value of each album intact with all its stamps would be the sum of the prices of all the individual player stamps inside the album. Stamps are unnumbered but are presented here in alphabetical order by team, Atlanta Braves (1-24), Chicago Cubs (25-48), Cincinnati Reds (49-72), Houston Astros (73-96), Los Angeles Dodgers (97-120), Montreal Expos (121-144), New York Mets (145-168), Philadelphia Phillies (169-192), Pittsburgh Pirates (193-216), San Diego Padres (217-240), San Francisco Giants (241-264), St. Louis Cardinals (265-288), Baltimore Orioles AL (289-312), Boston Red Sox (313-336), California Angels (337-360), Chicago White Sox (361-384), Cleveland Indians (385-408), Detroit Tigers (409-432), Kansas City Royals (433-456), Milwaukee Brewers (457-480), Minnesota Twins (481-504), New York Yankees (505-528), Oakland A's (529-552), Washington Senators (553-576) and All-Stars (577-600).

COMPLETE SET (576)	100.00	200.00
1 Hank Aaron	1.50	4.00
2 Tommy Aaron	.08	.20
3 Hank Allen	.08	.20
4 Clete Boyer	.12	.30
5 Oscar Brown	.08	.20
6 Rico Carty	.08	.20
7 Orlando Cepeda	.40	1.00
8 Bob Didier	.08	.20
9 Ralph Garr	.08	.20
10 Gil Garrido	.08	.20
11 Ron Herbel	.08	.20
12 Sonny Jackson	.08	.20
13 Pat Jarvis	.08	.20
14 Larry Jaster	.08	.20
15 Hal King	.08	.20
16 Mike Lum	.08	.20
17 Felix Millan	.08	.20
18 Jim Nash	.08	.20
19 Phil Niekro	.50	1.25
20 Bob Priddy	.08	.20
21 Ron Reed	.08	.20
22 George Stone	.08	.20
23 Cecil Upshaw	.08	.20
24 Hoyt Wilhelm	.40	1.00
25 Ernie Banks	.75	2.00
26 Glenn Beckert	.08	.20
27 Danny Breeden	.08	.20
28 Johnny Callison	.08	.20
29 Jim Colborn	.08	.20
30 Joe Decker	.08	.20
31 Bill Hands	.08	.20
32 Jim Hickman	.08	.20
33 Ken Holtzman	.08	.20
34 Randy Hundley	.08	.20
35 Fergie Jenkins	.40	1.00
36 Don Kessinger	.08	.20
37 J.C. Martin	.08	.20
38 Bob Miller	.08	.20
39 Milt Pappas	.08	.20
40 Joe Pepitone	.08	.20
41 Juan Pizarro	.08	.20
42 Paul Popovich	.08	.20
43 Phil Regan	.08	.20
44 Roberto Rodriguez	.08	.20
45 Ken Rudolph	.08	.20
46 Ron Santo	.15	.40
47 Hector Torres	.08	.20
48 Billy Williams	.50	1.25
49 Johnny Bench	.75	2.00
50 Angel Bravo	.08	.20
51 Bernie Carbo	.08	.20
52 Clay Carroll	.08	.20
53 Darrel Chaney	.08	.20
54 Ty Cline	.08	.20
55 Tony Cloninger	.08	.20
56 Dave Concepcion	.15	.40
57 Pat Corrales	.08	.20
58 Greg Garrett	.08	.20
59 Wayne Granger	.08	.20
60 Don Gullett	.08	.20
61 Tommy Helms	.08	.20
62 Lee May	.08	.20
63 Jim McGlothlin	.08	.20
64 Hal McRae	.08	.20
65 Jim Merritt	.08	.20
66 Gary Nolan	.08	.20
67 Tony Perez	.40	1.00
68 Pete Rose	1.25	3.00
69 Wayne Simpson	.08	.20
70 Jimmy Stewart	.08	.20
71 Bobby Tolan	.08	.20
72 Woody Woodward	.08	.20
73 Jesus Alou	.08	.20
74 Jack Billingham	.08	.20
75 Ron Cook	.08	.20
76 George Culver	.08	.20
77 Larry Dierker	.08	.20
78 Jack DiLauro	.08	.20
79 Johnny Edwards	.08	.20
80 Fred Gladding	.08	.20
81 Tom Griffin	.08	.20
82 Skip Guinn	.08	.20
83 Jack Hiatt	.08	.20
84 Denver Lemaster	.08	.20
85 Marty Martinez	.08	.20
86 John Mayberry	.08	.20
87 Denis Menke	.08	.20
88 Norm Miller	.08	.20
89 Joe Morgan	.40	1.00
90 Doug Rader	.08	.20
91 Jim Ray	.08	.20
92 Scipio Spinks	.08	.20
93 Bob Watkins	.08	.20
94 Bob Watson	.12	.30
95 Don Wilson	.08	.20
96 Jim Wynn	.12	.30
97 Rich Allen	.15	.40
98 Jim Brewer	.08	.20
99 Bill Buckner	.15	.40
100 Willie Crawford	.08	.20
101 Willie Davis	.12	.30
102 Al Downing	.08	.20
103 Steve Garvey	.50	1.25
104 Billy Grabarkewitz	.08	.20
105 Tom Haller	.08	.20
106 Jim LeFebvre	.08	.20
107 Pete Mikkelsen	.08	.20
108 Joe Moeller	.08	.20
109 Manny Mota	.08	.20
110 Claude Osteen	.08	.20
111 Wes Parker	.08	.20
112 Jose Pena	.08	.20
113 Bill Russell	.08	.20
114 Duke Sims	.08	.20
115 Bill Singer	.08	.20
116 Mike Strahler	.08	.20
117 Bill Sudakis	.08	.20
118 Don Sutton	.50	1.25
119 Jeff Torborg	.08	.20
120 Maury Wills	.40	1.00
121 Bob Bailey	.08	.20
122 John Bateman	.08	.20
123 John Boccabella	.08	.20
124 Ron Brand	.08	.20
125 Boots Day	.08	.20
126 Jim Fairey	.08	.20
127 Ron Fairly	.08	.20
128 Jim Gosger	.08	.20
129 Don Hahn	.08	.20
130 Ron Hunt	.08	.20
131 Mack Jones	.08	.20
132 Jose Laboy	.08	.20
133 Mike Marshall	.08	.20
134 Dan McGinn	.08	.20
135 Carl Morton	.08	.20
136 John O'Donoghue	.08	.20
137 Adolpho Phillips	.08	.20
138 Claude Raymond	.08	.20
139 Steve Renko	.08	.20
140 Marv Staehle	.08	.20
141 Rusty Staub	.15	.40
142 Bill Stoneman	.08	.20
143 Gary Sutherland	.08	.20
144 Bobby Wine	.08	.20
145 Tommy Agee	.08	.20
146 Bob Aspromonte	.08	.20
147 Ken Boswell	.08	.20
148 Dean Chance	.08	.20
149 Donn Clendenon	.08	.20
150 Duffy Dyer	.08	.20
151 Dan Frisella	.08	.20
152 Wayne Garrett	.08	.20
153 Gary Gentry	.08	.20
154 Jerry Grote	.08	.20
155 Bud Harrelson	.12	.30
156 Cleon Jones	.08	.20
157 Jerry Koosman	.15	.40
158 Ed Kranepool	.08	.20
159 Dave Marshall	.08	.20
160 Jim McAndrew	.08	.20
161 Tug McGraw	.15	.40
162 Nolan Ryan	4.00	10.00
163 Ray Sadecki	.08	.20
164 Tom Seaver	.75	2.00
165 Art Shamsky	.08	.20
166 Ron Swoboda	.08	.20
167 Ron Taylor	.08	.20
168 Al Weis	.08	.20
169 Larry Bowa	.15	.40
170 Johnny Briggs	.08	.20
171 Byron Browne	.08	.20
172 Jim Bunning	.40	1.00
173 Billy Champion	.08	.20
174 Mike Compton	.08	.20
175 Denny Doyle	.08	.20
176 Roger Freed	.08	.20
177 Woody Fryman	.08	.20
178 Oscar Gamble	.08	.20
179 Terry Harmon	.08	.20
180 Larry Hisle	.08	.20
181 Joe Hoerner	.08	.20
182 Deron Johnson	.08	.20
183 Barry Lersch	.08	.20
184 Tim McCarver	.15	.40
185 Don Money	.08	.20
186 Mike Ryan	.08	.20
187 Dick Selma	.08	.20
188 Chris Short	.08	.20
189 Ron Stone	.08	.20
190 Tony Taylor	.08	.20
191 Rick Wise	.08	.20
192 Billy Wilson	.08	.20
193 Gene Alley	.08	.20
194 Steve Blass	.08	.20
195 Nelson Briles	.08	.20
196 Jim Campanis	.08	.20
197 Dave Cash	.08	.20
198 Roberto Clemente	2.50	6.00
199 Vic Davalillo	.08	.20
200 Dock Ellis	.08	.20
201 Jim Grant	.08	.20
202 Dave Giusti	.08	.20
203 Richie Hebner	.08	.20
204 Jackie Hernandez	.08	.20
205 Johnny Jeter	.08	.20
206 Lou Marone	.08	.20
207 Jose Martinez	.08	.20
208 Bill Mazeroski	.30	.75
209 Bob Moose	.08	.20
210 Al Oliver	.15	.40
211 Jose Pagan	.08	.20
212 Bob Robertson	.08	.20
213 Manny Sanguillen	.08	.20
214 Willie Stargell	.40	1.00
215 Bob Veale	.08	.20
216 Luke Walker	.08	.20
217 Jose Arcia	.08	.20
218 Bob Barton	.08	.20
219 Fred Beene	.08	.20
220 Ollie Brown	.08	.20
221 Dave Campbell	.12	.30
222 Chris Cannizzaro	.08	.20
223 Nate Colbert	.08	.20
224 Mike Corkins	.08	.20
225 Tommy Dean	.08	.20
226 Al Ferrara	.08	.20

Card	Low	High
227 Rod Gaspar	.08	.20
228 Clarence Gaston	.08	.20
229 Enzo Hernandez	.08	.20
230 Clay Kirby	.08	.20
231 Don Mason	.08	.20
232 Ivan Murrell	.08	.20
233 Gerry Nyman	.08	.20
234 Tom Phoebus	.08	.20
235 Dave Roberts	.08	.20
236 Gary Ross	.08	.20
237 Al Santorini	.08	.20
238 Al Severinsen	.08	.20
239 Ron Slocum	.08	.20
240 Ed Spiezio	.08	.20
241 Bobby Bonds	.15	.40
242 Ron Bryant	.08	.20
243 Don Carrithers	.08	.20
244 John Cumberland	.08	.20
245 Mike Davison	.08	.20
246 Dick Dietz	.08	.20
247 Tito Fuentes	.08	.20
248 Russ Gibson	.08	.20
249 Jim Ray Hart	.08	.20
250 Bob Heise	.08	.20
251 Ken Henderson	.08	.20
252 Steve Huntz	.08	.20
253 Frank Johnson	.08	.20
254 Jerry Johnson	.08	.20
255 Hal Lanier	.08	.20
256 Juan Marichal	.40	1.00
257 Willie Mays	1.50	4.00
258 Willie McCovey	.60	1.50
259 Don McMahon	.08	.20
260 Jackie Moyer	.08	.20
261 Gaylord Perry	.50	1.25
262 Frank Reberger	.08	.20
263 Rich Robertson	.08	.20
264 Bernie Williams	.08	.20
265 Matty Alou	.12	.30
266 Jim Beauchamp	.08	.20
267 Frank Bertaina	.08	.20
268 Lou Brock	.60	1.50
269 George Brunet	.08	.20
270 Jose Cardenal	.08	.20
271 Steve Carlton	.60	1.50
272 Moe Drabowsky	.08	.20
273 Bob Gibson	.60	1.50
274 Joe Hague	.08	.20
275 Julian Javier	.08	.20
276 Leron Lee	.08	.20
277 Frank Linzy	.08	.20
278 Dal Maxvill	.08	.20
279 Gerry McNertney	.08	.20
280 Fred Norman	.08	.20
281 Milt Ramirez	.08	.20
282 Dick Schofield	.08	.20
283 Mike Shannon	.08	.20
284 Ted Sizemore	.08	.20
285 Bob Stinson	.08	.20
286 Carl Taylor	.08	.20
287 Joe Torre	.30	.75
288 Mike Torrez	.08	.20
289 Mark Belanger	.08	.20
290 Paul Blair	.08	.20
291 Don Buford	.08	.20
292 Terry Crowley	.08	.20
293 Mike Cuellar	.08	.20
294 Clay Dalrymple	.08	.20
295 Pat Dobson	.08	.20
296 Andy Etchebarren	.08	.20
297 Dick Hall	.08	.20
298 Jim Hardin	.08	.20
299 Elrod Hendricks	.08	.20
300 Grant Jackson	.08	.20
301 Dave Johnson	.15	.40
302 Dave Leonhard	.08	.20
303 Marcelino Lopez	.08	.20
304 Dave McNally	.08	.20
305 Curt Motton	.08	.20
306 Jim Palmer	.60	1.50
307 Boog Powell	.12	.30
308 Merv Rettenmund	.08	.20
309 Brooks Robinson	.60	1.50
310 Frank Robinson	.60	1.50
311 Pete Richert	.08	.20
312 Chico Salmon	.08	.20
313 Luis Aparicio	.40	1.00
314 Bobby Bolin	.08	.20
315 Ken Brett	.08	.20
316 Billy Conigliaro	.08	.20
317 Ray Culp	.08	.20
318 Mike Fiore	.08	.20
319 John Kennedy	.08	.20
320 Cal Koonce	.08	.20
321 Joe Lahoud	.08	.20
322 Bill Lee	.08	.20
323 Jim Lonborg	.08	.20
324 Sparky Lyle	.15	.40
325 Mike Nagy	.08	.20
326 Don Pavletich	.08	.20
327 Gary Peters	.08	.20
328 Rico Petrocelli	.12	.30
329 Vicente Romo	.08	.20
330 Tom Satriano	.08	.20
331 George Scott	.12	.30
332 Sonny Siebert	.08	.20
333 Reggie Smith	.15	.40
334 Jarvis Tatum	.08	.20
335 Ken Tatum	.08	.20
336 Carl Yastrzemski	.75	2.00
337 Sandy Alomar	.08	.20
338 Jose Azcue	.08	.20
339 Ken Berry	.08	.20
340 Gene Brabender	.08	.20
341 Billy Cowan	.08	.20
342 Tony Conigliaro	.15	.40
343 Eddie Fisher	.08	.20
344 Jim Fregosi	.12	.30
345 Tony Gonzales	.08	.20
346 Alex Johnson	.08	.20
347 Fred Lasher	.08	.20
348 Jim Maloney	.08	.20
349 Rudy May	.08	.20
350 Ken McMullen	.08	.20
351 Andy Messersmith	.08	.20
352 Gerry Moses	.08	.20
353 Syd O'Brien	.08	.20
354 Mel Queen	.08	.20
355 Roger Repoz	.08	.20
356 Archie Reynolds	.08	.20
357 Chico Ruiz	.08	.20
358 Jim Spencer	.08	.20
359 Clyde Wright	.08	.20
360 Billy Wynne	.08	.20
361 Mike Andrews	.08	.20
362 Luis Alvarado	.08	.20
363 Tom Egan	.08	.20
364 Steve Hamilton	.08	.20
365 Ed Herrmann	.08	.20
366 Joel Horlen	.08	.20
367 Tommy John	.15	.40
368 Bart Johnson	.08	.20
369 Jay Johnstone	.08	.20
370 Duane Josephson	.08	.20
371 Pat Kelly	.08	.20
372 Bobby Knoop	.08	.20
373 Carlos May	.08	.20
374 Lee Maye	.08	.20
375 Tom McCraw	.08	.20
376 Bill Melton	.08	.20
377 Rich Morales	.08	.20
378 Tom Murphy	.08	.20
379 Don O'Riley	.08	.20
380 Rick Reichardt	.08	.20
381 Bill Robinson	.08	.20
382 Bob Spence	.08	.20
383 Walt Williams	.08	.20
384 Wilbur Wood	.08	.20
385 Rick Austin	.08	.20
386 Buddy Bradford	.08	.20
387 Larry Brown	.08	.20
388 Lou Camilli	.08	.20
389 Vince Colbert	.08	.20
390 Ray Fosse	.08	.20
391 Alan Foster	.08	.20
392 Roy Foster	.08	.20
393 Rich Hand	.08	.20
394 Steve Hargan	.08	.20
395 Ken Harrelson	.15	.40
396 Jack Heidemann	.08	.20
397 Phil Hennigan	.08	.20
398 Dennis Higgins	.08	.20
399 Chuck Hinton	.08	.20
400 Tony Horton	.08	.20
401 Ray Lamb	.08	.20
402 Eddie Leon	.08	.20
403 Sam McDowell	.12	.30
404 Graig Nettles	.15	.40
405 Mike Paul	.08	.20
406 Vada Pinson	.15	.40
407 Ken Suarez	.08	.20
408 Ted Uhlaender	.08	.20
409 Eddie Brinkman	.08	.20
410 Gates Brown	.08	.20
411 Ike Brown	.08	.20
412 Les Cain	.08	.20
413 Norm Cash	.15	.40
414 Joe Coleman	.08	.20
415 Bill Freehan	.12	.30
416 Cesar Gutierrez	.08	.20
417 John Hiller	.08	.20
418 Willie Horton	.12	.30
419 Dalton Jones	.08	.20
420 Al Kaline	.60	1.50
421 Mike Kilkenny	.08	.20
422 Mickey Lolich	.15	.40
423 Dick McAuliffe	.08	.20
424 Joe Niekro	.15	.40
425 Jim Northrup	.08	.20
426 Daryl Patterson	.08	.20
427 Jimmie Price	.08	.20
428 Bob Reed	.08	.20
429 Aurelio Rodriguez	.08	.20
430 Fred Scherman	.08	.20
431 Mickey Stanley	.08	.20
432 Tom Timmerman	.08	.20
433 Ted Abernathy	.08	.20
434 Wally Bunker	.08	.20
435 Tom Burgmeier	.08	.20
436 Bill Butler	.08	.20
437 Bruce Dal Canton	.08	.20
438 Dick Drago	.08	.20
439 Bobby Floyd	.08	.20
440 Gail Hopkins	.08	.20
441 Joe Keough	.08	.20
442 Ed Kirkpatrick	.08	.20
443 Tom Matchick	.08	.20
444 Jerry May	.08	.20
445 Aurelio Monteagudo	.08	.20
446 Dave Morehead	.08	.20
447 Bob Oliver	.08	.20
448 Amos Otis	.08	.20
449 Fred Patek	.08	.20
450 Lou Piniella	.15	.40
451 Cookie Rojas	.08	.20
452 Jim Rooker	.08	.20
453 Paul Schaal	.08	.20
454 Rich Severson	.08	.20
455 George Spriggs	.08	.20
456 Carl Taylor	.08	.20
457 Dave Baldwin	.08	.20
458 Ted Savage	.08	.20
459 Dick Ellsworth	.08	.20
460 John Gelnar	.08	.20
461 Tommy Harper	.08	.20
462 Mike Hegan	.08	.20
463 Bob Humphreys	.08	.20
464 Andy Kosco	.08	.20
465 Lew Krausse	.08	.20
466 Ted Kubiak	.08	.20
467 Skip Lockwood	.08	.20
468 Dave May	.08	.20
469 Bob Meyer	.08	.20
470 John Morris	.08	.20
471 Marty Pattin	.08	.20
472 Roberto Pena	.08	.20
473 Ellie Rodriguez	.08	.20
474 Phil Roof	.08	.20
475 Ken Sanders	.08	.20
476 Russ Snyder	.08	.20
477 Bill Tillman	.08	.20
478 Bill Voss	.08	.20
479 Danny Walton	.08	.20
480 Floyd Wicker	.08	.20
481 Brant Alyea	.08	.20
482 Bert Blyleven	.15	.40
483 Dave Boswell	.08	.20
484 Leo Cardenas	.08	.20
485 Rod Carew	.75	2.00
486 Tom Hall	.08	.20
487 Jim Holt	.08	.20
488 Jim Kaat	.15	.40
489 Harmon Killebrew	.40	1.00
490 Charlie Manuel	.08	.20
491 George Mitterwald	.08	.20
492 Tony Oliva	.15	.40
493 Ron Perranoski	.08	.20
494 Jim Perry	.08	.20
495 Frank Quilici	.08	.20
496 Rich Reese	.08	.20
497 Rick Renick	.08	.20
498 Danny Thompson	.08	.20
499 Luis Tiant	.12	.30
500 Tom Tischinski	.08	.20
501 Cesar Tovar	.08	.20
502 Stan Williams	.08	.20
503 Dick Woodson	.08	.20
504 Bill Zepp	.08	.20
505 Jack Aker	.08	.20
506 Stan Bahnsen	.08	.20
507 Curt Blefary	.08	.20
508 Bill Burbach	.08	.20
509 Danny Cater	.08	.20
510 Horace Clarke	.08	.20
511 John Ellis	.08	.20
512 Jake Gibbs	.08	.20
513 Ron Hansen	.08	.20
514 Mike Kekich	.08	.20
515 Jerry Kenney	.08	.20
516 Ron Klimkowski	.08	.20
517 Steve Kline	.08	.20
518 Mike McCormick	.08	.20
519 Lindy McDaniel	.08	.20
520 Gene Michael	.08	.20
521 Thurman Munson	.75	2.00
522 Bobby Murcer	.15	.40
523 Fritz Peterson	.08	.20
524 Mel Stottlemyre	.15	.40
525 Pete Ward	.08	.20
526 Gary Waslewski	.08	.20
527 Roy White	.12	.30
528 Ron Woods	.08	.20
529 Felipe Alou	.15	.40
530 Sal Bando	.12	.30
531 Vida Blue	.15	.40
532 Bert Campaneris	.12	.30
533 Ron Clark	.08	.20
534 Chuck Dobson	.08	.20
535 Dave Duncan	.08	.20
536 Frank Fernandez	.08	.20
537 Rollie Fingers	.40	1.00
538 Dick Green	.08	.20
539 Steve Hovley	.08	.20
540 Jim Hunter	.60	1.50
541 Reggie Jackson	1.25	3.00
542 Marcel Lachemann	.08	.20
543 Paul Lindblad	.08	.20
544 Bob Locker	.08	.20
545 Don Mincher	.08	.20
546 Rick Monday	.12	.30
547 John Odom	.08	.20
548 Jim Roland	.08	.20
549 Joe Rudi	.12	.30
550 Diego Segui	.08	.20
551 Bob Stickels	.08	.20
552 Gene Tenace	.08	.20
553 Bernie Allen	.08	.20
554 Dick Bosman	.08	.20
555 Jackie Brown	.08	.20
556 Paul Casanova	.08	.20
557 Casey Cox	.08	.20
558 Tim Cullen	.08	.20
559 Mike Epstein	.08	.20
560 Curt Flood	.15	.40
561 Joe Foy	.08	.20
562 Jim French	.08	.20
563 Bill Gogolewski	.08	.20
564 Tom Grieve	.12	.30
565 Joe Grzenda	.08	.20
566 Frank Howard	.15	.40
567 Joe Janeski	.08	.20
568 Darold Knowles	.08	.20
569 Elliott Maddox	.08	.20
570 Denny McLain	.15	.40
571 Dave Nelson	.08	.20
572 Horacio Pina	.08	.20
573 Jim Shellenback	.08	.20
574 Ed Stroud	.08	.20
575 Del Unser	.08	.20
576 Don Wert	.08	.20
577 Hank Aaron	1.50	4.00
578 Luis Aparicio	.40	1.00
579 Ernie Banks	.75	2.00
580 Johnny Bench	.75	2.00
581 Rico Carty	.08	.20
582 Roberto Clemente	2.50	6.00
583 Bob Gibson	.50	1.25
584 Willie Horton	.12	.30
585 Frank Howard	.15	.40
586 Reggie Jackson	1.25	3.00
587 Fergie Jenkins	.40	1.00
588 Alex Johnson	.08	.20
589 Al Kaline	.60	1.50
590 Harmon Killebrew	.40	1.00
591 Willie Mays	1.50	4.00
592 Sam McDowell	.08	.20
593 Denny McLain	.15	.40
594 Boog Powell	.15	.40
595 Brooks Robinson	.60	1.50
596 Frank Robinson	.60	1.50
597 Pete Rose	1.25	3.00
598 Tom Seaver	.75	2.00
599 Rusty Staub	.15	.40
600 Carl Yastrzemski	.75	2.00

1933 DeLong

The cards in this 24-card set measure approximately 2" by 3". The 1933 Delong Gum set of 24 multi-colored cards was, along with the 1933 Goudey Big League series, one of the first baseball card sets issued with chewing gum. It was the only card set issued by this company. The reverse text was written by Austen Lake, who also wrote the sports tips found on the Diamond Stars series which began in 1934, leading to speculation that Delong was bought out by National Chicle.

Card	Low	High
COMPLETE SET (24)	5,000.00	10,000.00
1 Marty McManus	200.00	400.00
2 Al Simmons	250.00	500.00
3 Oscar Melillo	150.00	300.00
4 Bill Terry	300.00	600.00
5 Charlie Gehringer	300.00	600.00
6 Mickey Cochrane	500.00	1,000.00
7 Lou Gehrig	4,000.00	8,000.00
8 Kiki Cuyler	400.00	800.00
9 Bill Urbanski	150.00	300.00
10 Lefty O'Doul	250.00	500.00
11 Fred Lindstrom	300.00	600.00
12 Pie Traynor	400.00	800.00
13 Rabbit Maranville	300.00	600.00
14 Lefty Gomez	400.00	800.00
15 Riggs Stephenson	200.00	400.00
16 Lon Warneke	150.00	300.00
17 Pepper Martin	200.00	400.00
18 Jimmy Dykes	200.00	400.00
19 Chick Hafey	300.00	600.00
20 Joe Vosmik	150.00	300.00
21 Jimmie Foxx	600.00	1,200.00
22 Chuck Klein	300.00	600.00
23 Lefty Grove	500.00	1,000.00
24 Goose Goslin	400.00	800.00

1935 Al Demaree Die Cuts R304

These cards are drawings which were produced approximately in 1935; other cards may exist in this scarce set. The cards measure 1" x 4 1/2". This listing may be incomplete. All additions are welcome and appreciated. A few cards have not yet been discovered with the tab that would enable us to ID the card numbers. They are listed at the end as NNO's

Card	Low	High
COMPLETE SET	2,500.00	50,000.00
3 Earle Combs	400.00	800.00
4 Babe Ruth	2,000.00	4,000.00
5 Sam Byrd	200.00	400.00
6 Tony Lazzeri	300.00	600.00
7 Frank Crosetti	250.00	500.00
9 Lou Gehrig	1,500.00	3,000.00
11 Mule Haas	200.00	400.00
12 Evar Swanson	200.00	400.00
13 Merv Shea	200.00	400.00
14 Al Simmons throwing	300.00	600.00
15 Minter Hayes	200.00	400.00
16 Al Simmons batting	300.00	600.00
17 Jimmy Dykes	250.00	500.00
18 Luke Appling	300.00	600.00
19 Ted Lyons	300.00	600.00
20 Red Kress	200.00	400.00
21 Gee Walker	200.00	400.00
23 Gordon Stanley/(Mickey) Cochrane/(catcher unifor	400.00	800.00
24 Gordon Stanley/(Mickey) Cochrane/(batting - poss	400.00	800.00
25 Pete Fox	200.00	400.00
26 Firpo Marberry	200.00	400.00
28 Mickey Owen	200.00	400.00
35 Joe Vosmik	200.00	400.00
40 Oral Hildebrand	200.00	400.00
41 Jack Burns	200.00	400.00

Card	Low	High
45 Ray Pepper	200.00	400.00
46 Bruce Campbell	200.00	400.00
48 Art Scharein	200.00	400.00
49 George Blaeholder	200.00	400.00
50 Rogers Hornsby	1,000.00	2,000.00
54 Jimmie Foxx	600.00	1,200.00
56 Dib Williams	200.00	400.00
57 Lou Finney	200.00	400.00
59 Bob Johnson	250.00	500.00
60 Roy Mahaffey	200.00	400.00
61 Ossie Bluege	200.00	400.00
64 Joe Cronin	300.00	600.00
66 Buddy Myer	200.00	400.00
67 Earl Whitehill	200.00	400.00
71 Ed Morgan	200.00	400.00
73 Rick Ferrell	400.00	800.00
74 Carl Reynolds	200.00	400.00
76 Bill Cissell	200.00	400.00
77 Johnny Hodapp	200.00	400.00
78 Dusty Cooke	200.00	400.00
79 Lefty Grove	400.00	800.00
82 Gus Mancuso	200.00	400.00
83 Kiddo Davis	200.00	400.00
84 Blondy Ryan	200.00	400.00
86 Travis Jackson	300.00	600.00
87 Mel Ott	600.00	1,200.00
89 Bill Terry	400.00	800.00
90 Carl Hubbell	600.00	1,200.00
91 Tony Cuccinello	200.00	400.00
92 Al Lopez	400.00	800.00
94 John Frederick	200.00	400.00
96 Hack Wilson	400.00	800.00
97 Danny Taylor	200.00	400.00
99 Johnny Frederick	200.00	400.00
100 Sam Leslie	200.00	400.00
101 Sparky Adams	200.00	400.00
107 Syl Johnson	200.00	400.00
108 Jim Bottomley	300.00	600.00
110 Adam Comorosky	200.00	400.00
112 Harvey Hendrick	200.00	400.00
115 Don Hurst	200.00	400.00
117 Prince Oana	200.00	400.00
118 Ed Holley	200.00	400.00
121 Spud Davis	200.00	400.00
122 George Watkins	200.00	400.00
123 Frankie Frisch	300.00	600.00
125 Rip Collins	200.00	400.00
126 Dizzy Dean	600.00	1,200.00
127 Pepper Martin	250.00	500.00
128 Joe Medwick	300.00	600.00
129 Leo Durocher	300.00	600.00
130 Ernie Orsatti	200.00	400.00
132 Shanty Hogan	200.00	400.00
137 Wally Berger	250.00	500.00
138 Hal Lee	200.00	400.00
139 Rabbit Maranville	400.00	800.00
141 Gus Suhr	200.00	400.00
142 Earl Grace	200.00	400.00
144 Arky Vaughan	400.00	800.00
147 Lloyd Waner	400.00	800.00
148 Paul Waner	600.00	1,200.00
149 Pie Traynor	600.00	1,200.00
151 Kiki Cuyler	400.00	800.00
152 Gabby Hartnett	300.00	600.00
154 Chuck Klein	300.00	600.00
156 Woody English	250.00	500.00
158 Billy Herman	300.00	600.00
160 Charlie Grimm	250.00	500.00
162 Bill Klem UMP	300.00	600.00
167 George Hildebrand UMP	200.00	400.00
NNO Willie Kamm	200.00	400.00
NNO Roy Mahaffey	200.00	400.00
NNO Bob Johnson	200.00	400.00
NNO Pinky Higgins	200.00	400.00
NNO Roy Johnson	200.00	400.00
102A Mark Koenig	200.00	400.00
102B Ernie Lombardi	400.00	800.00
133A Wes Schulmerich	200.00	400.00
133B Randy Moore	200.00	400.00

1979 Detroit Convention

This 20 card 3 1/2" by 5" set was issued to commemorate the 10th annual Detroit show. The cards are reproductions of photos provided by various fans and the Detroit Tigers. An interesting mix of players and media members are commemorated in this set. The cards are unnumbered so we have sequenced them in alphabetical order. The set was originally available for $3.

Card	Low	High
COMPLETE SET	4.00	10.00
1 Gates Brown	.20	.50
2 Norm Cash	.60	1.50
3 Al Cicotte	.20	.50
4 Roy Cullenbine	.30	.75
5 Gene Desautels	.20	.50
6 Hoot Evers	.20	.50
7 Joe Falls Columnist	.20	.50
8 Joe Ginsberg	.20	.50
9 Ernie Harwell ANN	.40	1.00
10 Ray Herbert	.20	.50
11 John Hiller	.20	.50
12 Billy Hoeft	.20	.50
13 Ralph Houk MG	.30	.75
14 Cliff Kachline Writer	.20	.50
15 George Kell	.60	1.50
16 Ron LeFlore	.20	.50
17 Barney McCosky	.20	.50
18 Jim Northrup	.20	.50
19 Dick Radatz	.20	.50
20 Tom Timmerman	.20	.50

1935 Detroit Free Press

This newsprint set of the 1935 Detroit Tigers and one boxer measures approximately 9" by 11" and was within the "The Detroit Free Press." The cards are unnumbered and checklisted below in alphabetical order. One boxer -- Joe Lewis is known to be issued as part of this set.

Card	Low	High
COMPLETE SET	162.50	325.00
1 Eldon Auker	5.00	10.00
2 Del Baker	5.00	10.00
3 Tommy Bridges	7.50	15.00
4 Flea Clifton	5.00	10.00
5 Mickey Cochrane	12.50	25.00
6 General Crowder	5.00	10.00
7 Frank Deljack	5.00	10.00
8 Carl Fischer	5.00	10.00
9 Pete Fox	5.00	10.00
10 Charlie Gehringer	10.00	20.00
11 Goose Goslin	10.00	20.00
12 Hank Greenberg	12.50	25.00
13 Luke Hamlin	5.00	10.00
14 Ray Hayworth	5.00	10.00
15 Chief Hogsett	5.00	10.00
17 Firpo Marberry	5.00	10.00
18 Marvin Owen	5.00	10.00
19 Cy Perkins	5.00	10.00
20 Billie Rogell	5.00	10.00
21 Schoolboy Rowe	7.50	15.00
22 Geinie Schuble	5.00	10.00
23 Victor Sorrell	5.00	10.00
24 Joe Sullivan	5.00	10.00
25 Gee Walker	5.00	10.00
26 Jo-Jo White	5.00	10.00

1967 Dexter Press

This 228-card set was produced by Dexter Press and issued in team sets as a premium by the Coca-Cola Bottling Co. Eighteen Major League teams participated in the promotion. The set measures approximately 5 1/2" by 7" and features glossy color waist-to-cap player photos in a white border with a black facsimile autograph at the top. The white backs display player biographical details and career highlights printed in blue. An all-star set was also produced with these players' cards differentiated from their regular cards in the team sets by the lengthier biographies on the back. The cards are unnumbered and checklisted below in alphabetical order. Paul Schaal was also issued as a sample print. This card is considered a SP and is not included in the checklist.

Card	Low	High
COMPLETE SET (228)	400.00	800.00
1 Hank Aaron	8.00	20.00
2 Tommie Agee	1.50	4.00
3 Jack Aker	1.25	3.00
4 Bernie Allen	1.25	3.00
5 Richie Allen	2.00	5.00
6 Gene Alley	1.25	3.00
7 Bob Allison	1.50	4.00
8 Felipe Alou	2.00	5.00
9 Jesus Alou	1.50	4.00
10 Matty Alou	1.50	4.00
11 George Altman	1.25	3.00
12 Max Alvis	1.25	3.00
13 Luis Aparicio	4.00	10.00
14 Bob Aspromonte	1.25	3.00
15 Joe Azcue	1.25	3.00
16 Bob Bailey	1.25	3.00
17 Ernie Banks	6.00	15.00
18 John Bateman	1.25	3.00
19 Earl Battey	1.25	3.00
20 Glenn Beckert	1.25	3.00
21 Gary Bell	1.25	3.00
22 Ken Berry	1.25	3.00
23 Wade Blasingame	1.25	3.00
24 Curt Blefary	1.25	3.00
25 John Boccabella	1.25	3.00
26 Dave Boswell	1.25	3.00
27 Jim Bouton	1.50	4.00
28 Clete Boyer	1.50	4.00
29 Ken Boyer	2.00	5.00
30 Ed Bressoud	1.25	3.00
31 John Briggs	1.25	3.00
32 Ed Brinkman	1.25	3.00
33 Larry Brown	1.25	3.00
34 Ollie Brown	1.25	3.00
35 Bob Bruce	1.25	3.00
36 Don Buford	1.25	3.00
37 Wally Bunker	1.25	3.00
38 Jim Bunning	4.00	10.00
39 Jim Bunning AS	2.00	5.00
40 Johnny Callison	1.50	4.00
41 Bert Campaneris	1.25	3.00
42 Leo Cardenas	1.25	3.00
43 Paul Casanova	1.25	3.00
44 Norm Cash	2.00	5.00
45 Danny Cater	1.25	3.00
46 Dean Chance	1.25	3.00
47 Ed Charles	1.25	3.00
48 Ossie Chavarria	1.25	3.00
49 Horace Clarke	1.25	3.00
50 Roberto Clemente	10.00	25.00
51 Roberto Clemente AS	5.00	12.00
52 Donn Clendenon	1.25	3.00
53 Ty Cline	1.25	3.00
54 Tony Cloninger	1.25	3.00
55 Rocky Colavito	3.00	8.00
56 Gordy Coleman	1.25	3.00
57 Ray Culp	1.25	3.00
58 Clay Dalrymple	1.25	3.00
59 Vic Davalillo	1.25	3.00
60 Jim Davenport	1.25	3.00
61 Ron Davis	1.25	3.00
62 Tommy Davis	1.50	4.00
63 Willie Davis	1.50	4.00
64 Willie Davis AS	1.50	4.00
65 Don Demeter	1.25	3.00
66 Larry Dierker	1.25	3.00
67 Al Downing	1.25	3.00
68 Johnny Edwards	1.25	3.00
69 Andy Etchebarren	1.25	3.00
70 Ron Fairly	1.50	4.00
71 Dick Farrell	1.25	3.00
72 Bill Fischer	1.25	3.00
73 Eddie Fisher	1.25	3.00
74 Jack Fisher	1.25	3.00
75 Joe Foy	1.25	3.00
76 Bill Freehan	1.50	4.00
77 Woodie Fryman	1.25	3.00
78 Tito Fuentes	1.25	3.00
79 Dave Giusti	1.25	3.00
80 Pedro Gonzalez	1.25	3.00
81 Mudcat Grant	1.25	3.00
82 Dick Green	1.25	3.00
83 Dick Groat	1.50	4.00
84 Jerry Grote	1.25	3.00
85 Tom Haller	1.25	3.00
86 Jack Hamilton	1.25	3.00
87 Steve Hamilton	1.25	3.00
88 Ron Hansen	1.25	3.00
89 Tommy Harper	1.25	3.00
90 Ken Harrelson	1.50	4.00
91 Chuck Harrison	1.25	3.00
92 Jim Hart	1.25	3.00
93 Tommy Helms	1.25	3.00
94 Mike Hershberger	1.25	3.00
95 Chuck Hinton	1.25	3.00
96 Ken Holtzman	1.25	3.00
97 Joe Horlen	1.25	3.00
98 Willie Horton	1.50	4.00
99 Elston Howard	2.00	5.00
100 Frank Howard	2.00	5.00
101 Randy Hundley	1.25	3.00
102 Ron Hunt	1.25	3.00
103 Larry Jackson	1.25	3.00
104 Sonny Jackson	1.25	3.00
105 Tommy John	2.00	5.00
106 Davey Johnson	1.50	4.00
107 Deron Johnson	1.25	3.00
108 Ken Johnson	1.25	3.00
109 Lou Johnson	1.25	3.00
110 Cleon Jones	1.25	3.00
111 Dalton Jones	1.25	3.00
112 Al Kaline	6.00	15.00
113 Al Kaline AS	3.00	8.00
114 John Kennedy	1.25	3.00
115 Harmon Killebrew	6.00	15.00
116 Harmon Killebrew AS	3.00	8.00
117 Jim King	1.25	3.00
118 Cal Koonce	1.25	3.00
119 Ed Kranepool	1.25	3.00
120 Lew Krausse	1.25	3.00
121 Jim Landis	1.25	3.00
122 Hal Lanier	1.25	3.00
123 Vern Law	1.25	3.00
124 Jim Lefebvre	1.25	3.00
125 Johnny Lewis	1.25	3.00
126 Don Lock	1.25	3.00
127 Bob Locker	1.25	3.00
128 Mickey Lolich	3.00	8.00
129 Jim Lonborg	1.50	4.00
130 Jerry Lumpe	1.25	3.00
131 Jim Maloney	1.25	3.00
132 Mickey Mantle	50.00	100.00
133 Eddie Mathews	6.00	15.00
134 Willie Mays	12.50	30.00
135 Willie Mays AS	6.00	15.00
136 Bill Mazeroski	3.00	8.00
137 Dick McAuliffe	1.25	3.00
138 Bill McCool	1.25	3.00
139 Mike McCormick	1.25	3.00
140 Willie McCovey	4.00	10.00
141 Tommy McCraw	1.25	3.00
142 Sam McDowell	1.25	3.00
143 Ken McMullen	1.25	3.00
144 Dave McNally	1.25	3.00
145 Jerry McNertney	1.25	3.00
146 Dennis Menke	1.25	3.00
147 Jim Merritt	1.25	3.00
148 Joe Morgan	4.00	10.00
149 Manny Mota	1.50	4.00
150 Jim Nash	1.25	3.00
151 Dick Nen	1.25	3.00
152 Joe Nossek	1.25	3.00
153 Tony Oliva	2.00	5.00
154 Gene Oliver	1.25	3.00
155 Phil Ortega	1.25	3.00
156 Claude Osteen	1.25	3.00
157 Jim O'Toole	1.25	3.00
158 Jim Pagliaroni	1.25	3.00
159 Jim Palmer	6.00	15.00
160 Milt Pappas	1.25	3.00
161 Wes Parker	1.25	3.00
162 Joe Pepitone	1.50	4.00
163 Joe Pepitone AS	1.25	3.00
164 Ron Perranoski	1.25	3.00
165 Gaylord Perry	4.00	10.00
166 Fritz Peterson	1.25	3.00
167 Rico Petrocelli	1.25	3.00
168 Adolfo Phillips	1.25	3.00
169 Vada Pinson	2.00	5.00
170 Johnny Podres	1.50	4.00
171 Boog Powell	2.00	5.00
172 Phil Regan	1.25	3.00
173 Roger Repoz	1.25	3.00
174 Pete Richert	1.25	3.00
175 Brooks Robinson	6.00	15.00
176 Brooks Robinson AS	3.00	8.00
177 Frank Robinson	6.00	15.00
178 Frank Robinson AS	3.00	8.00
179 Cookie Rojas	1.25	3.00
180 Rich Rollins	1.25	3.00
181 Phil Roof	1.25	3.00
182 Pete Rose	8.00	20.00
183 Jose Santiago	1.25	3.00
184 Ron Santo	4.00	10.00
185 Ron Santo AS	2.00	5.00
186 Bob Saverine	1.25	3.00
187 George Scott	1.25	3.00
188 Art Shamsky	1.25	3.00
189 Bob Shaw	1.25	3.00
190 Chris Short	1.25	3.00
191 Norman Siebern	1.25	3.00
192 Moose Skowron	1.50	4.00
193 Charley Smith	1.25	3.00
194 George Smith	1.25	3.00
195 Russ Snyder	1.25	3.00
196 Joe Sparma	1.25	3.00
197 Willie Stargell	4.00	10.00
198 Rusty Staub	2.00	5.00
199 John Stephenson	1.25	3.00
200 Mel Stottlemyre	1.50	4.00
201 Don Sutton	4.00	10.00
202 Ron Swoboda	1.25	3.00
203 Jose Tartabull	1.25	3.00
204 Tony Taylor	1.25	3.00
205 Lee Thomas	1.25	3.00
206 Luis Tiant	2.00	5.00
207 Bob Tillman	1.25	3.00
208 Joe Torre	2.50	6.00
209 Joe Torre AS	2.00	5.00
210 Tom Tresh	1.50	4.00
211 Ted Uhlaender	1.25	3.00
212 Sandy Valdespino	1.25	3.00
213 Fred Valentine	1.25	3.00
214 Bob Veale	1.25	3.00
215 Zoilo Versalles	1.25	3.00
216 Leon Wagner	1.25	3.00
217 Pete Ward	1.25	3.00
218 Don Wert	1.25	3.00
219 Bill White	2.00	5.00
220 Roy White	1.25	3.00
221 Fred Whitfield	1.25	3.00
222 Dave Wickersham	1.25	3.00
223 Billy Williams	4.00	10.00
224 Maury Wills	2.00	5.00
225 Earl Wilson	1.25	3.00
226 Woody Woodward	1.25	3.00
227 Carl Yastrzemski	6.00	15.00
228 Carl Yastrzemski AS	3.00	8.00

1968 Dexter Press

This 77-card set, which measures approximately 3 1/2" by 5 1/2", has beautiful full-color photos on the front of the card with biographical and career information on the back of the card. There are no year by year statistical lines on the back of the card. Dexter Press is another name for cards which the Coca-Cola Company helped to distribute during the mid sixties. The backs of the cards have a facsimile autograph. Dexter Press was located in West Nyack, New York. These unnumbered cards are listed below in alphabetical order.

Card	Low	High
COMPLETE SET (77)	400.00	800.00
1 Hank Aaron	20.00	50.00
2 Jerry Adair	2.50	6.00
3 Richie Allen	4.00	10.00
4 Bob Allison	3.00	8.00
5 Felipe Alou	4.00	10.00
6 Jesus Alou	2.50	6.00
7 Mike Andrews	2.50	6.00
8 Bob Aspromonte	2.50	6.00
9 Johnny Bateman	2.50	6.00
10 Mark Belanger	2.50	6.00
11 Gary Bell	2.50	6.00
12 Paul Blair	2.50	6.00
13 Curt Blefary	2.50	6.00
14 Bobby Bolin	2.50	6.00
15 Ken Boswell	2.50	6.00
16 Clete Boyer	3.00	8.00
17 Ron Brand	2.50	6.00
18 Darrell Brandon	2.50	6.00
19 Don Buford	2.50	6.00
20 Rod Carew	20.00	50.00
21 Clay Carroll	2.50	6.00
22 Rico Carty	3.00	8.00
23 Dean Chance	2.50	6.00
24 Roberto Clemente	75.00	150.00
25 Tony Cloninger	2.50	6.00
26 Mike Cuellar	2.50	6.00
27 Jim Davenport	2.50	6.00
28 Ron Davis	2.50	6.00
29 Moe Drabowsky	2.50	6.00
30 Dick Ellsworth	2.50	6.00
31 Andy Etchebarren	2.50	6.00
32 Joe Foy	2.50	6.00
33 Bill Freehan	3.00	8.00
34 Jim Fregosi	3.00	8.00
35 Julio Gotay	2.50	6.00
36 Dave Giusti	2.50	6.00
37 Jim Ray Hart	2.50	6.00
38 Jack Hiatt	2.50	6.00
39 Ron Hunt	2.50	6.00
40 Sonny Jackson	2.50	6.00
41 Pat Jarvis	2.50	6.00
42 Davey Johnson	3.00	8.00
43 Ken Johnson	2.50	6.00
44 Dalton Jones	2.50	6.00
45 Jim Kaat	4.00	10.00
46 Harmon Killebrew	10.00	25.00
47 Denny Lemaster	2.50	6.00
48 Frank Linzy	2.50	6.00
49 Jim Lonborg	3.00	8.00
50 Juan Marichal	10.00	25.00
51 Willie Mays	40.00	80.00
52 Bill Mazeroski	5.00	12.00
53 Mike McCormick	2.50	6.00
54 Dave McNally	3.00	8.00
55 Denis Menke	2.50	6.00
56 Joe Morgan	8.00	20.00
57 Dave Morehead	2.50	6.00
58 Phil Niekro	8.00	20.00
59 Russ Nixon	2.50	6.00

60 Tony Oliva	4.00	10.00
61 Gaylord Perry	8.00	20.00
62 Rico Petrocelli	3.00	8.00
63 Tom Phoebus	2.50	6.00
64 Boog Powell	3.00	8.00
65 Brooks Robinson	10.00	25.00
66 Frank Robinson	10.00	25.00
67 Rich Rollins	2.50	6.00
68 John Roseboro	2.50	6.00
69 Ray Sadecki	2.50	6.00
70 George Scott	3.00	8.00
71 Rusty Staub	4.00	10.00
72 Cesar Tovar	2.50	6.00
73 Joe Torre	5.00	12.00
74 Ted Uhlaender	2.50	6.00
75 Woody Woodward	2.50	6.00
76 John Wyatt	2.50	6.00
77 Jimmy Wynn	3.00	8.00

1958 Diamond Gallery

These photos which were inserted into copies of the NY Daily News feature leading players in baseball at that time. It is believed that these photos were actually issued over a course of a few seasons and any additions to this checklist is appreciated. There are probably many additions to this checklist so any further information is very appreciated.

COMPLETE SET	15.00	30.00
COMMON CARD		
1 Gus Bell	5.00	10.00
2 Nellie Fox	10.00	20.00
Brooks Lawrence		

1979 Diamond Greats

This 400-card set features black-and-white player portraits with the player's name, life-time statistics, team name, and playing position printed in black in the white margins. The backs are blank.

COMPLETE SET (400)	60.00	120.00
1 Joe DiMaggio	2.50	6.00
2 Ben Chapman	.10	.25
3 Joe Dugan	.10	.25
4 Bob Shawkey	.20	.50
5 Joe Sewell	.30	.75
6 George Pipgras	.10	.25
7 George Selkirk	.10	.25
8 Babe Dahlgren	.10	.25
9 Spud Chandler	.20	.50
10 Duffy Lewis	.10	.25
11 Lefty Gomez	.40	1.00
12 Atley Donald	.10	.25
13 Whitey Witt	.10	.25
14 Marius Russo	.10	.25
15 Buddy Rosar	.10	.25
16 Russ Van Atta	.10	.25
17 Johnny Lindell	.10	.25
18 Bobby Brown	.20	.50
19 Tony Kubek	.20	.50
20 Joe Beggs	.10	.25
21 Don Larsen	.20	.50
22 Andy Carey	.10	.25
23 Johnny Kucks	.10	.25
24 Elston Howard	.20	.50
25 Roger Maris	.75	2.00
26 Rube Marquard	.40	1.00
27 Sam Leslie	.10	.25
28 Freddy Leach	.10	.25
29 Fred Fitzsimmons	.20	.50
30 Bill Terry	.40	1.00
31 Joe Moore	.10	.25
32 Waite Hoyt	.30	.75
33 Travis Jackson	.30	.75
34 Gus Mancuso	.10	.25
35 Carl Hubbell	.60	1.50
36 Bill Voiselle	.10	.25
37 Hank Leiber	.10	.25
38 Burgess Whitehead	.10	.25
39 Johnny Mize	.40	1.00
40 Bill Lohrman	.10	.25
41 Bill Rigney	.10	.25
42 Cliff Melton	.10	.25
43 Willard Marshall	.10	.25
44 Wes Westrum	.10	.25
45 Monte Irvin	.40	1.00
46 Marv Grissom	.10	.25
47 Clyde Castleman	.10	.25
48 Harry Gumbert	.10	.25
49 Daryl Spencer	.10	.25
50 Willie Mays	2.00	5.00
51 Sam West	.10	.25
52 Fred Schulte	.10	.25
53 Cecil Travis	.10	.25
54 Tommy Thomas	.10	.25
55 Dutch Leonard	.10	.25
56 Jimmy Wasdell	.10	.25
57 Doc Cramer	.20	.50
58 Harland Clift	.20	.50
59 Ken Chase	.10	.25
60 Buddy Lewis	.10	.25
61 Ossie Bluege	.10	.25
62 Chuck Stobbs	.10	.25
63 Jimmy DeShong	.10	.25
64 Roger Wolff	.10	.25
65 Luke Sewell	.10	.25
66 Sid Hudson	.10	.25
67 Jack Russell	.10	.25
68 Walt Masterson	.10	.25
69 George Myatt	.10	.25
70 Monte Weaver	.10	.25
71 Cliff Bolton	.10	.25
72 Ray Scarborough	.10	.25
73 Albie Pearson	.10	.25
74 Gil Coan	.10	.25
75 Roy Sievers	.20	.50
76 Burleigh Grimes	.30	.75
77 Charlie Hargreaves	.10	.25
78 Babe Herman	.20	.50
79 Fred Frankhouse	.10	.25
80 Al Lopez	.30	.75
81 Lonny Frey	.10	.25
82 Dixie Walker	.10	.25
83 Kirby Higbe	.10	.25
84 Bobby Bragan	.10	.25
85 Leo Durocher	.30	.75
86 Woody English	.10	.25
87 Preacher Roe	.10	.25
88 Vic Lombardi	.10	.25
89 Clyde Sukeforth	.10	.25
90 Pee Wee Reese	1.00	2.50
91 Joe Hatten	.10	.25
92 Gene Hermanski	.10	.25
93 Ray Benge	.10	.25
94 Duke Snider	1.00	2.50
95 Walter Alston MG	.30	.75
96 Don Drysdale	.75	2.00
97 Andy Pafko	.20	.50
98 Don Zimmer	.20	.50
99 Carl Erskine	.20	.50
100 Dick Williams	.20	.50
101 Charlie Grimm	.20	.50
102 Clarence Blair	.10	.25
103 Johnny Moore	.10	.25
104 Clay Bryant	.10	.25
105 Billy Herman	.30	.75
106 Hy Vandenberg	.10	.25
107 Lennie Merullo	.10	.25
108 Hank Wyse	.10	.25
109 Dom Dallessandro	.10	.25
110 Al Epperly	.10	.25
111 Bill Nicholson	.10	.25
112 Vern Olsen	.10	.25
113 Johnny Schmitz	.10	.25
114 Bob Scheffing	.10	.25
115 Bob Rush	.10	.25
116 Roy Smalley	.10	.25
117 Ransom Jackson	.10	.25
118 Cliff Chambers	.10	.25
119 Harry Chiti	.10	.25
120 Johnny Klippstein	.10	.25
121 Gene Baker	.10	.25
122 Walt Moryn	.10	.25
123 Dick Littlefield	.10	.25
124 Bob Speake	.10	.25
125 Hank Sauer	.10	.25
126 Monty Stratton	.20	.50
127 Johnny Kerr	.10	.25
128 Milt Gaston	.10	.25
129 Eddie Smith	.10	.25
130 Larry Rosenthal	.10	.25
131 Orval Grove	.10	.25
132 Johnny Hodapp	.10	.25
133 Johnny Rigney	.10	.25
134 Willie Kamm	.10	.25
135 Ed Lopat	.20	.50
136 Smead Jolley	.10	.25
137 Ralph Hodgin	.10	.25
138 Ollie Bejma	.10	.25
139 Zeke Bonura	.10	.25
140 Al Hollingsworth	.10	.25
141 Thurman Tucker	.10	.25
142 Cass Michaels	.10	.25
143 Bill Wight	.10	.25
144 Don Lenhardt	.10	.25
145 Sammy Esposito	.10	.25
146 Jack Harshman	.10	.25
147 Turk Lown	.10	.25
148 Jim Landis	.10	.25
149 Bob Shaw	.10	.25
150 Minnie Monoso	.30	.75
151 Les Bell	.10	.25
152 Taylor Douthit	.10	.25
153 Jack Rothrock	.10	.25
154 Terry Moore	.20	.50
155 Max Lanier	.10	.25
156 Don Gutteridge	.10	.25
157 Stu Martin	.10	.25
158 Stan Musial	.75	2.00
159 Frank Crespi	.10	.25
160 Johnny Hopp	.10	.25
161 Ernie Koy	.10	.25
162 Joe Garagiola	.40	1.00
163 Joe Orengo	.10	.25
164 Ed Kazak	.10	.25
165 Howie Krist	.10	.25
166 Enos Slaughter	.30	.75
167 Ray Sanders	.10	.25
168 Walker Cooper	.10	.25
169 Nippy Jones	.10	.25
170 Dick Sisler	.10	.25
171 Harvey Haddix	.10	.25
172 Solly Hemus	.10	.25
173 Ray Jablonski	.10	.25
174 Alex Grammas	.10	.25
175 Joe Cunningham	.20	.50
176 Debs Garms	.10	.25
177 Chief Hogsett	.10	.25
178 Alan Strange	.10	.25
179 Rick Ferrell	.30	.75
180 Jack Kramer	.10	.25
181 Jack Knott	.10	.25
182 Bob Harris	.10	.25
183 Billy Hitchcock	.10	.25
184 Jim Walkup	.10	.25
185 Roy Cullenbine	.10	.25
186 Bob Muncrief	.10	.25
187 Chet Laabs	.10	.25
188 Vern Kennedy	.10	.25
189 Bill Trotter	.10	.25
190 Denny Galehouse	.10	.25
191 Al Zarilla	.10	.25
192 Hank Arft	.10	.25
193 Nelson Potter	.10	.25
194 Ray Coleman	.10	.25
195 Bob Dillinger	.20	.50
196 Dick Kokos	.10	.25
197 Bob Cain	.10	.25
198 Virgil Trucks	.10	.25
199 Duane Pillette	.10	.25
200 Bob Turley	.20	.50
201 Wally Berger	.20	.50
202 John Lanning	.10	.25
203 Buck Jordan	.10	.25
204 Jim Turner	.10	.25
205 Johnny Cooney	.10	.25
206 Hank Majeski	.10	.25
207 Phil Masi	.10	.25
208 Tony Cuccinello	.10	.25
209 Whitey Wietelman	.10	.25
210 Lou Fette	.10	.25
211 Vince Di Maggio	.10	.25
212 Huck Betts	.10	.25
213 Red Barrett	.10	.25
214 Pinkey Whitney	.10	.25
215 Tommy Holmes	.20	.50
216 Ray Berres	.10	.25
217 Mike Sandlock	.10	.25
218 Max Macon	.10	.25
219 Sibby Sisti	.10	.25
220 Johnny Beazley	.10	.25
221 Bill Posedel	.10	.25
222 Connie Ryan	.10	.25
223 Del Crandall	.10	.25
224 Bob Addis	.10	.25
225 Warren Spahn	.60	1.50
227 Dom DiMaggio	.20	.50
228 Emerson Dickman	.10	.25
229 Bobby Doerr	.30	.75
230 Tony Lupien	.10	.25
231 Roy Partee	.10	.25
232 Stan Spence	.10	.25
233 Jim Bagby	.10	.25
234 Buster Mills	.10	.25
235 Fabian Gaffke	.10	.25
236 George Metkovich	.10	.25
237 Tom McBride	.10	.25
238 Charlie Wagner	.10	.25
239 Eddie Pellegrini	.10	.25
240 Harry Dorish	.10	.25
241 Ike Delock	.10	.25
242 Mel Parnell	.10	.25
243 Matt Batts	.10	.25
244 Gene Stephens	.10	.25
245 Milt Bolling	.10	.25
246 Charlie Maxwell	.10	.25
247 Willard Nixon	.10	.25
248 Sammy White	.10	.25
249 Dick Gernert	.10	.25
250 Rico Petrocelli	.10	.25
251 Edd Roush	.30	.75
252 Mark Koenig	.20	.50
253 Jimmy Outlaw	.10	.25
254 Ethan Allen	.10	.25
255 Tony Freitas	.10	.25
256 Frank McCormick	.10	.25
257 Bucky Walters	.20	.50
258 Harry Craft	.10	.25
259 Nate Andrews	.10	.25
260 Ed Lukon	.10	.25
261 Elmer Riddle	.10	.25
262 Lee Grissom	.10	.25
263 Johnny Vander Meer	.20	.50
264 Eddie Joost	.10	.25
265 Kermit Wahl	.10	.25
266 Ival Goodman	.10	.25
267 Clyde Vollmer	.10	.25
268 Graddy Hatten	.10	.25
269 Ted Kluszewski	.40	1.00
270 Johnny Pramesa	.10	.25
271 Joe Black	.20	.50
272 Roy McMillan	.10	.25
273 Wally Post	.10	.25
274 Joe Nuxhall	.10	.25
275 Jerry Lynch	.10	.25
276 Stan Coveleski	.30	.75
277 Bill Wambsganss	.20	.50
278 Bruce Campbell	.10	.25
279 George Uhle	.10	.25
280 Earl Averill	.30	.75
281 Whit Wyatt	.10	.25
282 Oscar Grimes	.10	.25
283 Roy Weatherly	.10	.25
284 Joe Dobson	.10	.25
285 Bob Feller	.75	2.00
286 Jim Hegan	.10	.25
287 Mel Harder	.20	.50
288 Ken Keltner	.10	.25
289 Red Embree	.10	.25
290 Al Milnar	.10	.25
291 Lou Boudreau	.40	1.00
292 Ed Klieman	.10	.25
293 Steve Gromek	.10	.25
294 George Strickland	.10	.25
295 Gene Woodling	.10	.25
296 Hank Edwards	.10	.25
297 Don Mossi	.20	.50
298 Eddie Robinson	.10	.25
299 Sam Dente	.10	.25
300 Herb Score	.20	.50
301 Dolf Camilli	.20	.50
302 Jack Warner	.10	.25
303 Ike Pearson	.10	.25
304 Johnny Peacock	.10	.25
305 Gene Corbett	.10	.25
306 Walt Millies	.10	.25
307 Vance Dinges	.10	.25
308 Joe Marty	.10	.25
309 Hugh Mulcahey	.10	.25
310 Boom Boom Beck	.10	.25
311 Charley Schanz	.10	.25
312 John Bolling	.10	.25
313 Danny Litwhiler	.10	.25
314 Emil Verban	.10	.25
315 Andy Seminick	.10	.25
316 John Antonelli	.10	.25
317 Robin Roberts	.75	2.00
318 Richie Ashburn	.40	1.00
319 Curt Simmons	.10	.25
320 Murry Dickson	.10	.25
321 Jim Greengrass	.10	.25
322 Gene Freese	.10	.25
323 Bobby Morgan	.10	.25
324 Don Demeter	.10	.25
325 Eddie Sawyer	.10	.25
326 Bob Johnson	.10	.25
327 Ace Parker	.30	.75
328 Joe Hauser	.10	.25
329 Walt French	.10	.25
330 Tom Ferrick	.10	.25
331 Bill Werber	.10	.25
332 Walt Masters	.10	.25
333 Les McCrabb	.10	.25
334 Ben McCoy	.10	.25
335 Eric Tipton	.10	.25
336 Al Rubeling	.10	.25
337 Nick Etten	.10	.25
338 Carl Scheib	.10	.25
339 Dario Lodigiani	.10	.25
340 Earle Brucker	.10	.25
341 Al Brancato	.10	.25
342 Lou Limmer	.10	.25
343 Elmer Valo	.10	.25
344 Bob Hooper	.10	.25
345 Joe Astroth	.10	.25
346 Pete Suder	.10	.25
347 Dave Philley	.10	.25
348 Gus Zernial	.10	.25
349 Bobby Shantz	.10	.25
350 Joe DeMaestri	.10	.25
351 Fred Lindstrom	.30	.75
352 Red Lucas	.10	.25
353 Clyde Barnhart	.10	.25
354 Nick Strincevich	.10	.25
355 Lloyd Waner	.30	.75
356 Guy Bush	.10	.25
357 Joe Bowman	.10	.25
358 Al Todd	.10	.25
359 Mace Brown	.10	.25
360 Larry French	.10	.25
361 Elbie Fletcher	.10	.25
362 Woody Jensen	.10	.25
363 Rip Sewell	.10	.25
364 Johnny Dickshot	.10	.25
365 Pete Coscarart	.10	.25
366 Bud Hafey	.10	.25
367 Ken Heintzelman	.10	.25
368 Wally Westlake	.10	.25
369 Frank Gustine	.10	.25
370 Smokey Burgess	.20	.50
371 Vernon Law	.20	.50
372 Dick Groat	.20	.50
373 Bob Skinner	.10	.25
374 Don Cardwell	.10	.25
375 Bob Friend	.10	.25
376 Frank O'Rourke	.10	.25
377 Birdie Tebbetts	.10	.25
378 Charlie Gehringer	.40	1.00
379 Eldon Auker	.10	.25
380 Tuck Stainback	.10	.25
381 Chet Morgan	.10	.25
382 Johnny Lipon	.10	.25
383 Paul Richards	.10	.25
384 Johnny Gorsica	.10	.25
385 Ray Hayworth	.10	.25
386 Jimmy Bloodworth	.10	.25
387 Gene Desautels	.10	.25
388 Jo Jo White	.10	.25
389 Boots Poffenberger	.10	.25
390 Barney McCoskey	.10	.25
391 Dick Wakefield	.10	.25
392 Johnny Groth	.10	.25
393 Steve Souchock	.10	.25
394 George Vico	.10	.25
395 Hal Newhouser	.30	.75
396 Ray Herbert	.10	.25
397 Jim Bunning	.40	1.00
398 Frank Lary	.10	.25
399 Harvey Kuenn	.20	.50
400 Eddie Mathews	.75	2.00

1911 Diamond Gum Pins

This set of 29 (the number of pins known at this time) pins is described on each pin as "Free with Diamond Gum." The border of each pin is blue. Since the pins are unnumbered they are ordered below in alphabetical order. The player's name and team are given on the front of the pin on either side of the black and white player photo. Each pin measures approximately 7/8" in diameter.

COMPLETE SET	4,000.00	8,000.00
1 Babe Adams	75.00	150.00
2 Frank Baker	125.00	250.00
3 Chief Bender	125.00	250.00
4 Mordecai Brown	125.00	250.00
5 Donie Bush	75.00	150.00
6 Bill Carrigan	75.00	150.00
7 Frank Chance	150.00	300.00
8 Hal Chase	125.00	250.00
9 Ty Cobb	750.00	1,500.00
10 Eddie Collins	150.00	300.00
11 Harry Davis	75.00	150.00
12 Red Dooin	75.00	150.00
13 Larry Doyle	87.50	175.00
14 Johnny Evers	125.00	250.00
15 Miller Huggins	125.00	250.00
16 Hugh Jennings	125.00	250.00
17 Napolean Lajoie	200.00	400.00
18 Harry Lord	75.00	150.00
19 C.Mathewson	300.00	600.00
20 Dots Miller	75.00	150.00
21 G.Mullen (Mullin)	75.00	150.00
22 Danny Murphy	75.00	150.00
23 Orval Overall	75.00	150.00
24 Eddie Plank	150.00	300.00
25 H.Simmons Roch.	75.00	150.00
26 Ira Thomas	75.00	150.00
27 Joe Tinker	150.00	300.00
28 Honus Wagner	250.00	500.00
29 Cy Young	200.00	400.00

1934 Diamond Match Co. Silver Border

Issued in 1934, the 200-cover Silver-Bordered set includes many of the day's premier ballplayers. Each cover features four different background colors, red, green, blue and orange. Charlie Grimm is shown in two different poses. Players are listed in alphabetical order. All color variations are equally valued. The complete set price includes both Grimm covers. Complete matchbooks can sell for 60 to 100 percent higher.

COMPLETE SET (200)	1,500.00	3,000.00
1 Earl Adams	6.00	15.00
2 Ethan Allen	6.00	15.00
3 Eldon Auker	6.00	15.00
4 Del Baker	6.00	15.00
5 Dick Bartell	6.00	15.00
6 Walter Beck	6.00	15.00
7 Herman Bell	6.00	15.00
8 Ray Benge	6.00	15.00
9 Larry Benton	6.00	15.00
10 Louis Berger	6.00	15.00
11 Wally Berger	8.00	20.00
12 Ray Berres	6.00	15.00
13 Charlie Berry	6.00	15.00
14 Walter Betts	20.00	50.00
15 Ralph Birkofer	6.00	15.00
16 George Blaeholder	6.00	15.00
17 Jim Bottomley	6.00	15.00
18 Ralph Boyle	6.00	15.00
19 Ed Brandt	6.00	15.00
20 Don Brennan	6.00	15.00
21 Jack Burns	6.00	15.00
22 Guy Bush	6.00	15.00
23 Dolph Camilli	8.00	20.00
24 Ben Cantwell	6.00	15.00
25 Tex Carleton	6.00	15.00
26 Owen Carroll	6.00	15.00
27 Louis Chiozza	6.00	15.00
28 Watson Clark	6.00	15.00
29 James A. Collins	8.00	20.00
30 Phil Collins	6.00	15.00
31 Edward Connolly	6.00	15.00
32 Raymond Coombs	6.00	15.00
33 Roger Doc Cramer	8.00	20.00
34 Cliff Crawford	6.00	15.00
35 Hugh Critz	6.00	15.00
36 General Crowder	6.00	15.00
37 Tony Cuccinello	6.00	15.00
38 Kiki Cuyler	20.00	50.00
39 Virgil Davis	6.00	15.00
40 Dizzy Dean	12.50	30.00
41 Paul Dean	12.50	30.00
42 Edward Delker	6.00	15.00
43 Paul Derringer	12.50	30.00
44 Gene DeSautel	6.00	15.00
45 Bill Dietrich	6.00	15.00
46 Frank F. Doljack	6.00	15.00
47 Edward Durham	6.00	15.00
48 Leo Durocher	10.00	25.00
49 Jim Elliott	6.00	15.00
50 Woody English	6.00	15.00
51 Woody English	6.00	15.00
52 Rick Ferrell	12.50	30.00
53 Wes Ferrell	10.00	25.00
54 Charles Fischer	6.00	15.00
55 Freddy Fitzsimmons	8.00	20.00
56 Lew Fonseca	8.00	20.00
57 Fred Frankhouse	6.00	15.00
58 John Frederick	6.00	15.00
59 Benny Frey	6.00	15.00
60 Linus Frey	6.00	15.00
61 Frankie Frisch	15.00	40.00
62 Chick Fullis	6.00	15.00
63 Augie Galan	6.00	15.00
64 Milton Galatzer	6.00	15.00
65 Dennis Galehouse	6.00	15.00
66 Milton Gaston	6.00	15.00
67 Charlie Gehringer	20.00	50.00
68 Edward Gharrity	6.00	15.00
69 George Gibson	6.00	15.00
70 Isidore Goldstein	75.00	150.00
71 Hank Gowdy	6.00	15.00
72 Earl Grace	6.00	15.00
73 Charlie Grimm	12.50	30.00
74 Charlie Grimm	12.50	30.00
75 Frank Grube	6.00	15.00
76 Richard Gyselman	6.00	15.00
77 Stan Hack	6.00	15.00
78 Bump Hadley	6.00	15.00
79 Chick Hafey	6.00	15.00
80 Harold Haid	6.00	15.00
81 Jesse Haines	6.00	15.00
82 Odell Hale	6.00	15.00
83 Bill Hallahan	6.00	15.00
84 Luke Hamlin	6.00	15.00
85 Roy Hansen	6.00	15.00
86 Mel Harder	8.00	20.00
87 William Harris	6.00	15.00
88 Gabby Hartnett	12.50	30.00
89 Harvey Hendrick	6.00	15.00
90 Babe Herman	8.00	20.00
91 Billy Herman	10.00	25.00
92 Shanty Hogan	6.00	15.00
93 Chief Hogsett	6.00	15.00
94 Waite Hoyt	20.00	50.00
95 Carl Hubbell	30.00	60.00
96 Si Johnson	6.00	15.00
97 Syl Johnson	6.00	15.00
98 Roy Joiner	6.00	15.00
99 Baxter Jordan	6.00	15.00
100 Arndt Jorgens	6.00	15.00
101 Billy Jurges	8.00	20.00
102 Vern Kennedy	6.00	15.00
103 John Kerr	6.00	15.00
104 Chuck Klein	10.00	25.00
105 Ted Kleinhans	6.00	15.00
106 Bill Klem UMP	12.50	30.00
107 Robert Kline	6.00	15.00
108 William Knickerbocker	6.00	15.00
109 Jack Knott	6.00	15.00
110 Mark Koenig	8.00	20.00
111 William Lawrence	6.00	15.00
112 Thornton Lee	6.00	15.00
113 Bill Lee	6.00	15.00
114 Dutch Leonard	6.00	15.00
115 Ernie Lombardi	30.00	60.00
116 Al Lopez	20.00	50.00
117 Red Lucas	6.00	15.00
118 Ted Lyons	8.00	20.00
119 Daniel MacFayden	6.00	15.00
120 Ed. Majeski	6.00	15.00
121 Leroy Mahaffey	6.00	15.00
122 Pat Malone	6.00	15.00
123 Leo Mangum	6.00	15.00
124 Rabbit Maranville	12.50	30.00
125 Charles Marrow	6.00	15.00
126 Bill McKechnie MG	12.50	30.00
127 Justin McLaughlin	6.00	15.00
128 Marty McManus	6.00	15.00
129 Eric McNair	6.00	15.00
130 Joe Medwick	12.50	30.00
131 Jim Mooney	6.00	15.00
132 Joe Moore	6.00	15.00
133 John Moore	6.00	15.00
134 Randy Moore	6.00	15.00
135 Joe Morrisey	6.00	15.00
136 Joseph Mowrey	6.00	15.00
137 Fred Muller	6.00	15.00
138 Van Lingle Mungo	10.00	25.00
139 Glenn Myatt	6.00	15.00
140 Lynn Nelson	6.00	15.00
141 Prince Oana	30.00	60.00
142 Lefty O'Doul	12.50	30.00
143 Robert O'Farrell	6.00	15.00
144 Ernest Orsatti	6.00	15.00
145 Fritz Ostermueller	6.00	15.00
146 Mel Ott	12.50	30.00
147 Roy Parmelee	6.00	15.00
148 Ralph Perkins	6.00	15.00
149 Frank Pytlak	6.00	15.00
150 Ernest Quigley	6.00	15.00
151 George Rensa	6.00	15.00
152 Harry Rice	6.00	15.00
153 Walter Roettger	8.00	20.00
154 William Rogell	6.00	15.00
155 Edwin Rommel	6.00	15.00
156 Charlie Root	4.00	10.00
157 John Rothrock	6.00	15.00
158 Jack Russell	6.00	15.00
159 Blondy Ryan	6.00	15.00
160 Al Schacht CO	8.00	20.00
161 Wes Schultmerick	6.00	15.00
162 Rip Sewell	6.00	15.00
163 Gordon Slade	6.00	15.00
164 Bob Smith	6.00	15.00
165 Moose Solters	6.00	15.00
166 Glenn Spencer	6.00	15.00
167 Al Spohrer	6.00	15.00
168 George Stainback	8.00	20.00
169 Dolly Stark	12.50	30.00
170 Casey Stengel MG	30.00	60.00
171 Riggs Stephenson	12.50	30.00
172 Walter Stewart	6.00	15.00
173 Lin Storti	6.00	15.00
174 Allyn Stout	6.00	15.00
175 Joe Stripp	6.00	15.00
176 Gus Suhr	8.00	20.00
177 Billy Sullivan Jr.	6.00	15.00
178 Benny Tate	6.00	15.00
179 Danny Taylor	6.00	15.00
180 Tommy Thevenow	6.00	15.00
181 Bud Tinning	6.00	15.00
182 Cecil Travis	6.00	15.00
183 Forest Twogood	6.00	15.00
184 Bill Urbanski	6.00	15.00
185 Dazzy Vance	12.50	30.00
186 Arthur Veltman	6.00	15.00
187 John Vergez	6.00	15.00
188 Gee Walker	6.00	15.00
189 Bill Walker	8.00	20.00
190 Lloyd Waner	10.00	25.00
191 Paul Waner	10.00	25.00
192 Lon Warneke	8.00	20.00
193 Rabbit Warstler	6.00	15.00
194 Bill Werber	8.00	20.00
195 Jo Jo White	6.00	15.00
196 Pinky Whitney	6.00	15.00
197 Jimmy Wilson	6.00	15.00
198 Hack Wilson	75.00	150.00
199 Ralph Winegarner	6.00	15.00
200 Thomas Zachary	8.00	20.00

1935 Diamond Match Co. Series 2

The Second baseball set was issued circa 1935 by the Diamond Match Company. Each cover in the 24-cover set features a black border on the front and a brief player biography on the reverse. Covers are either green, red or blue in color. A crossed-bat design appears on the front-side of each cover. Players are listed in alphabetical order. Complete matchbooks are valued at fifty percent higher.

COMPLETE SET (24)	750.00	1,500.00
1 Ethan Allen (red)	30.00	60.00
2 Wally Berger (red)	30.00	60.00
3 Tommy Carey (blue)	20.00	40.00
4 Louis Chiozza (blue)	20.00	40.00
5 Dizzy Dean (green)	75.00	150.00
6 Frankie Frisch (red)	50.00	100.00
7 Charlie Grimm (blue)	40.00	80.00
8 Chick Hafey (red)	40.00	80.00
9 Francis Hogan (red)	20.00	40.00
10 Carl Hubbell (green)	50.00	100.00
11 Chuck Klein (green)	50.00	100.00
12 Ernie Lombardi (blue)	40.00	80.00
13 Al Lopez (blue)	50.00	100.00
14 Rabbit Maranville (green)	50.00	100.00
15 Joe Moore (red)	20.00	40.00
16 Van Lingle Mungo (green)	30.00	60.00
17 Mel Ott (blue)	60.00	120.00
18 Gordon Slade (green)	20.00	40.00
19 Casey Stengel MG (green)	60.00	120.00
20 Tommy Thevenow (red)	20.00	40.00
21 Lloyd Waner (red)	50.00	100.00
22 Paul Waner (green)	50.00	100.00
23 Lon Warneke (blue)	30.00	60.00
24 James Wilson (blue)	20.00	40.00

1935-36 Diamond Match Co. Series 3 Type 1

This set was released over two years (1935-36) by the Diamond Match Company. This set varies from the First and Second set in that the saddle has the "ball" with the players name and team only. Covers come in red, green and blue. Players are listed in alphabetical order. Complete matchbooks are valued fifty percent higher.

COMPLETE SET (151)	900.00	1,800.00
1 Ethan Allen	6.00	15.00
2 Melo Almada	6.00	15.00
3 Eldon Auker	6.00	15.00
4 Dick Bartell	6.00	15.00
5 Aloysius Bejma	6.00	15.00
6 Ollie Bejma	6.00	15.00
7 Roy Bell	6.00	15.00
8 Louis Berger	6.00	15.00
9 Wally Berger	8.00	20.00
10 Ralph Birkofer	6.00	15.00
11 Max Bishop	6.00	15.00
12 George Blaeholder	6.00	15.00
13 Zeke Bonura	8.00	20.00
14 Jim Bottomley	15.00	40.00
15 Ed Brandt	6.00	15.00
16 Don Brennan	6.00	15.00
17 Lloyd Brown	6.00	15.00
18 Walter Brown	6.00	15.00
19 Claiborne Bryant	6.00	15.00
20 Jim Bucher	6.00	15.00
21 John Burnett	6.00	15.00
22 Irving Burns	6.00	15.00
23 Merritt Cain	6.00	15.00
24 Ben Cantwell	6.00	15.00
25 Tommy Carey	6.00	15.00
26 Tex Carleton	6.00	15.00
27 Joseph Cascarella	6.00	15.00
28 Thomas Casey	6.00	15.00
29 George Caster	6.00	15.00
30 Phil Cavaretta	12.50	30.00
31 Louis Chiozza	6.00	15.00
32 Edward Cihocki	6.00	15.00
33 Herman E. Clifton	6.00	15.00
34 Richard Coffman	6.00	15.00
35 Edward Coleman	6.00	15.00
36 James A. Collins	8.00	20.00
37 Jocko Conlon	12.50	30.00
38 Roger Cramer	8.00	20.00
39 Hugh Critz	6.00	15.00
40 Alvin Crowder	6.00	15.00
41 Tony Cuccinello	6.00	15.00
42 Kiki Cuyler	15.00	40.00
43 Virgil Davis	6.00	15.00
44 Dizzy Dean	30.00	60.00
45 Paul Derringer	8.00	20.00
46 James DeShong	6.00	15.00
47 Billy Dietrich	6.00	15.00
48 Leo Durocher	20.00	50.00
49 George Earnshaw	10.00	25.00
50 Woody English	6.00	15.00
51 Louis Finney	6.00	15.00
52 Charles Fischer	6.00	15.00
53 Freddy Fitzsimmons	10.00	25.00
54 Linus Frey	6.00	15.00
55 Frankie Frisch	20.00	50.00
56 Augie Galan	8.00	20.00
57 Milton Galatzer	15.00	40.00
58 Dennis Galehouse	6.00	15.00
59 Debs Garms	6.00	15.00
60 Angelo Giuliani	6.00	15.00
61 Earl Grace	6.00	15.00
62 Charlie Grimm	12.50	30.00
63 Frank Grube	6.00	15.00
64 Stan Hack	12.50	30.00
65 Bump Hadley	6.00	15.00
66 Odell Hale	6.00	15.00
67 Bill Hallahan	6.00	15.00
68 Roy Hanson	6.00	15.00
69 Mel Harder	8.00	20.00
70 Gabby Hartnett	15.00	40.00
71 Clyde Hatter	6.00	15.00
72 Raymond Hayworth	6.00	15.00
73 Babe Herman	12.50	30.00
74 Gordon Hinkle	6.00	15.00
75 George Hockette	6.00	15.00
76 James Holbrook	6.00	15.00
77 Alex Hooks	6.00	15.00
78 Waite Hoyt	12.50	30.00
79 Carl Hubbell	15.00	40.00
80 Roy Joiner	6.00	15.00
81 Sam Jones	8.00	20.00
82 Baxter Jordan	6.00	15.00
83 Arndt Jorgens	6.00	15.00
84 Billy Jurges	8.00	20.00
85 Willie Kamm	8.00	20.00
86 Vern Kennedy	6.00	15.00
87 John Kerr	6.00	15.00
88 Chuck Klein	15.00	40.00
89 Ted Kleinhans	6.00	15.00
90 William Knickerbocker	6.00	15.00
91 Jack Knott	6.00	15.00
92 Mark Koenig	8.00	20.00
93 Fabian Kowalik	6.00	15.00
94 Red Kress	6.00	15.00
95 Bill Lee	6.00	15.00
96 Louis Legett	6.00	15.00
97 Dutch Leonard	6.00	15.00
98 Fred Lindstrom	12.50	30.00
99 Edward Linke	6.00	15.00
100 Ernie Lombardi	12.50	30.00
101 Al Lopez	15.00	40.00
102 John Marcum	6.00	15.00
103 Bill McKechnie MG	12.50	30.00
104 Eric McNair	6.00	15.00
105 Joe Medwick	15.00	40.00
106 Oscar Melillo	6.00	15.00
107 John Michaels	6.00	15.00
108 Joe Moore	6.00	15.00
109 John Moore	6.00	15.00
110 Wally Moses	8.00	20.00
111 Joseph Milligan	6.00	15.00
112 Van Lingle Mungo	10.00	25.00
113 Glenn Myatt	6.00	15.00
114 James O'Dea	6.00	15.00
115 Ernest Orsatti	6.00	15.00
116 Fred Ostermueller	6.00	15.00
117 Mel Ott	20.00	50.00
118 LeRoy Parmelee	6.00	15.00
119 Monte Pearson	6.00	15.00
120 Raymond Pepper	6.00	15.00
121 Raymond Phelps	6.00	15.00
122 George Pipgras	6.00	15.00
123 Frank Pytlak	6.00	15.00
124 Gordon Rhodes	6.00	15.00
125 Charlie Root	8.00	20.00
126 John Rothrock	6.00	15.00
127 Muddy Ruel	6.00	15.00
128 Jack Saltzgaver	6.00	15.00
129 Fred Schulte	6.00	15.00
130 George Selkirk	8.00	20.00
131 Mervyn Shea	6.00	15.00
132 Al Spoher	6.00	15.00
133 George Stainback	6.00	15.00
134 Casey Stengel MG	20.00	50.00
135 Walter Stephenson	6.00	15.00
136 Lee Stine	6.00	15.00
137 John Stone	6.00	15.00
138 Gus Suhr	6.00	15.00
139 Tommy Thevenow	6.00	15.00
140 Fay Thomas	6.00	15.00
141 Leslie Tietje	6.00	15.00
142 Bill Urbanski	6.00	15.00
143 William Walker	6.00	15.00
144 Lloyd Waner	15.00	40.00
145 Paul Waner	15.00	40.00
146 Lon Warneke	8.00	20.00
147 Harold Warstler	6.00	15.00
148 Bill Werber	8.00	20.00
149 Vernon Wiltshere	6.00	15.00
150 James Wilson	6.00	15.00
151 Ralph Winegarner	6.00	15.00

1936 Diamond Match Co. Series 3 Type 2

This 23-player set was issued by the Diamond Match Company around 1936. Each player's cover is featured in three different colors, red, green and blue, All player photos, except "Dizzy" Dean, feature head and shoulders shot. The set was released with two different colors of ink, brown and black. All players are listed in alphabetical order. Complete matchbooks are valued fifty percent higher.

COMPLETE SET (23)	100.00	200.00
1 Claiborne Bryant	4.00	8.00
2 Tex Carleton	4.00	8.00

3 Phil Cavaretta	6.00	12.00
4 James A. Collins	5.00	10.00
5 Curt Davis	4.00	8.00
6 Dizzy Dean	12.50	25.00
7 Frank Demaree	4.00	8.00
8 Larry French	4.00	8.00
9 Linus Frey	4.00	8.00
10 Augie Galan	5.00	10.00
11 Bob Garbark	4.00	8.00
12 Stan Hack	6.00	12.00
13 Gabby Hartnett	10.00	20.00
14 Billy Herman	10.00	20.00
15 Billy Jurges	5.00	10.00
16 Bill Lee	4.00	8.00
17 Joe Marty	4.00	8.00
18 James O'Dea	4.00	8.00
19 LeRoy Parmelee	4.00	8.00
20 Charlie Root	5.00	10.00
21 Clyde Shoun	4.00	8.00
22 George Stainback	5.00	10.00
23 Paul Waner	10.00	20.00

1936 Diamond Match Co. Series 4

This is by far the smallest matchcover set released by the Diamond Match Company during the 1930's. The set is similar to the Third Baseball set other than the players team name shows under his name on the back. All of the covers minus Charlie Grimm were printed using brown ink. The three different Grimm cover feature black ink. The players are listed in alphabetical order. Complete matchbooks are valued fifty percent higher.

COMPLETE SET (12)	75.00	150.00
1 Tommy Carey	4.00	10.00
2 Tony Cuccinello	4.00	10.00
3 Freddy Fitzsimmons	5.00	12.00
4 Frankie Frisch	12.50	30.00
5 Charlie Grimm (3)	8.00	20.00
6 Carl Hubbell	10.00	25.00
7 Baxter Jordan	4.00	10.00
8 Chuck Klein	10.00	25.00
9 Al Lopez	8.00	20.00
10 Joe Medwick	8.00	20.00
11 Van Lingle Mungo	6.00	15.00
12 Mel Ott	12.50	30.00

1934-36 Diamond Stars

The cards in this 108-card set measure approximately 2 3/8" by 2 7/8". The Diamond Stars set, produced by National Chicle from 1934-36, is also commonly known by its catalog designation, R327. The year of production can be determined by the statistics contained on the back of the card. There are 170 possible front/back combinations counting blue (B) and green (G) backs over all three years. The last twelve cards are repeat players and are quite scarce. The checklist below lists the year(s) and back color(s) for the cards. Cards 32 through 72 were issued only in 1935 with green ink on back. Cards 73 through 84 were issued three ways: 35B, 35G, and 36B. Card numbers 85 through 108 were issued only in 1936 with blue ink on back. The complete set price below refers to the set of all variations listed explicitly below. A blank-backed proof sheet of 12 additional (never-issued) cards was discovered in 1980.

COMPLETE SET (119)	9,000.00	15,000.00
COMMON CARD (1-31)	30.00	50.00
COMMON CARD (32-84)	35.00	60.00
COMMON CARD (85-96)	60.00	100.00
COMMON CARD (97-108)	125.00	200.00
WRAPPER (1-CENT, BLUE)	200.00	250.00
WRAPPER (1-CENT, YEL.)	150.00	200.00
WRAPPER (1-CENT, CLR.)	150.00	200.00
1 Lefty Grove (34G, 35G)	800.00	1,500.00
2A Simmons w/Sox (34G,35G)	90.00	150.00
2B Al Simmons w/o Sox (36B)	125.00	200.00
3 Rabbit Maranville (34G,35G)	90.00	150.00
4 Buddy Myer (34G,35G,36B)	35.00	60.00
5 T.Bridges (34G,35G,36B)	35.00	60.00
6 Max Bishop (34G,35G)	35.00	60.00
7 Lew Fonseca (34G,35G)	35.00	60.00
8 Joe Vosmik XRC (34G,35G,36B)	30.00	50.00
9 M.Cochrane (34G,35G,36B)	200.00	400.00
10A L.Mahaffey w/A's(34G,35G)	30.00	50.00
10B L.Mahaffey w/o A's (36B)	50.00	80.00
11 Bill Dickey (34G, 35G)	200.00	400.00
12A Fred Walker XRC (34G)	50.00	80.00
12B Fred Walker (35G)	50.00	80.00
12C Fred Walker (36B)	60.00	100.00
13 G.Blaeholder (34G,35G)	30.00	50.00
14 Bill Terry (34G,35G)	100.00	175.00
15A Dick Bartell (34G)	60.00	100.00
15B Dick Bartell (35G)	50.00	80.00
16 L.Waner (34G,35G,36B)	125.00	250.00
17 Frankie Frisch (34G,35G)	150.00	300.00
18 Chick Hafey XRC (34G,35G)	100.00	200.00
19 Van Mungo XRC (34G,35G)	50.00	80.00
20 Frank Hogan (34G,35G)	35.00	60.00
21A Johnny Vergez (34G)	50.00	80.00
21B Johnny Vergez (35G)	35.00	60.00
22 J.Wilson (34G,35G,36B)	35.00	60.00
23 Bill Hallahan (34G,35G)	30.00	50.00
24 Earl Adams (34G,35G)	30.00	50.00
25 Wally Berger (35G)	35.00	60.00
26 P.Martin (35G,36B)	50.00	80.00
27 Pie Traynor (35G)	90.00	150.00
28 Al Lopez (35G)	90.00	150.00
29 Red Rolfe (35G)	50.00	80.00
30A Manush W/sleeve (35G)	90.00	150.00
30B H.Manush no W (36B)	125.00	200.00
31A Kiki Cuyler (35G)	75.00	125.00
31B Kiki Cuyler (36B)	100.00	175.00
32 Sam Rice (35G)	75.00	125.00
33 Schoolboy Rowe (35G)	50.00	80.00
34 Stan Hack (35G)	50.00	80.00
35 Earl Averill (35G)	75.00	125.00
36A Earnie Lombardi (35G)	175.00	300.00
36B Ernie Lombardi (35G)	125.00	200.00
37 Billy Urbanski (35G)	35.00	60.00
38 Ben Chapman (35G)	50.00	80.00
39 Carl Hubbell (35G)	125.00	200.00
40 Blondy Ryan (35G)	35.00	60.00
41 Harvey Hendrick XRC (35G)	35.00	60.00
42 Jimmy Dykes (35G)	50.00	80.00
43 Ted Lyons (35G)	75.00	125.00
44 Rogers Hornsby (35G)	150.00	300.00
45 Jo Jo White XRC (35G)	35.00	60.00
46 Red Lucas (35G)	35.00	60.00
47 Bob Bolton XRC (35G)	35.00	60.00
48 Rick Ferrell (35G)	75.00	125.00
49 Buck Jordan (35G)	35.00	60.00
50 Mel Ott (35G)	150.00	300.00
51 John Whitehead XRC (35G)	35.00	60.00
52 Tuck Stainback XRC (35G)	35.00	60.00
53 Oscar Melillo (35G)	35.00	60.00
54A Hank Greenburg (35G)	600.00	1,200.00
54B Hank Greenberg (35G)	300.00	600.00
55 Tony Cuccinello (35G)	50.00	80.00
56 Gus Suhr (35G)	35.00	60.00
57 Cy Blanton (35G)	35.00	60.00
58 Glenn Myatt (35G)	35.00	60.00
59 Jim Bottomley (35G)	75.00	125.00
60 Red Ruffing (35G)	90.00	150.00
61 Bill Werber (35G)	50.00	80.00
62 Fred Frankhouse (35G)	35.00	60.00
63 Travis Jackson (35G)	75.00	125.00
64 Jimmie Foxx (35G)	250.00	500.00
65 Zeke Bonura (35G)	35.00	60.00
66 Ducky Medwick (35G)	125.00	200.00
67 Marvin Owen (35G)	50.00	80.00
68 Sam Leslie (35G)	35.00	60.00
69 Earl Grace (35G)	35.00	60.00
70 Hal Trosky (35G)	50.00	80.00
71 Ossie Bluege (35G)	50.00	80.00
72 Tony Piet (35G)	35.00	60.00
73 F.Ostermueller (35G,35B,36B)	50.00	80.00
74 Tony Lazzeri (35G,35B,36B)	125.00	200.00
75 Jack Burns (35G,35B,36B)	50.00	80.00
76 Billy Rogell (35G,35B,36B)	50.00	80.00
77 C.Gehringer (35G,35B,36B)	150.00	300.00
78 Joe Kuhel (35G,35B,36B)	50.00	80.00
79 W.Hudlin (35G,35B,36B)	50.00	80.00
80 Lou Chiozza XRC (35G,35B,36B)	50.00	80.00
81 Bill Delancey XRC (35G,35B,36B)	35.00	60.00
82A Babich w/Dodgers(35G,35B)	50.00	80.00
82B John Babich wo/Dod. (36B)	75.00	125.00
83 P.Waner (35G,35B,36B)	90.00	150.00
84 Sam Byrd (35G,35B,36B)	50.00	80.00
85 Moose Solters (36B)	60.00	100.00
86 Frank Crosetti (36B)	90.00	150.00
87 Steve O'Neill MG (36B)	75.00	125.00
88 George Selkirk XRC (36B)	75.00	125.00
89 Joe Stripp (36B)	75.00	125.00
90 Ray Hayworth (36B)	75.00	125.00
91 Bucky Harris MG XRC (36B)	125.00	200.00
92 Ethan Allen (36B)	60.00	100.00
93 General Crowder (36B)	60.00	100.00
94 Wes Ferrell (36B)	90.00	150.00
95 Luke Appling (36B)	150.00	250.00
96 Lew Riggs XRC (36B)	60.00	100.00
97 Al Lopez (36B)	250.00	400.00
98 Schoolboy Rowe (36B)	125.00	200.00
99 Pie Traynor (36B)	300.00	500.00
100 Earl Averill (36B)	250.00	400.00
101 Dick Bartell (36B)	125.00	200.00
102 Van Lingle Mungo (36B)	150.00	250.00
103 Bill Dickey (36B)	400.00	700.00
104 Red Rolfe (36B)	125.00	200.00
105 Ernie Lombardi (36B)	250.00	400.00
106 Red Lucas (36B)	125.00	200.00
107 Stan Hack (36B)	125.00	200.00
108 Wally Berger (36B)	175.00	300.00

1924 Diaz Cigarettes

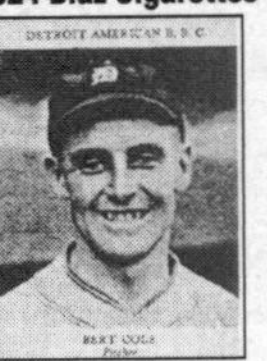

These 136 cards measure 1 3/4" by 2 1/4" with a white band on the top and the bottom. The team name is on the top while the players name is on the bottom. The middle has a player portrait. The back of the card has some information in Spanish Interestingly enough, all the players in this set are pitchers.

COMPLETE SET (136)	25,000.00	50,000.00
1 Walter Johnson	1,250.00	2,500.00
2 Waite Hoyt	500.00	1,000.00
3 Grover Alexander	750.00	1,500.00
4 Tom Sheehan	300.00	600.00
5 Pete Donohue	300.00	600.00
6 Herb Pennock	500.00	1,000.00
7 Adolfo Luque	400.00	800.00
8 Carl Mays	400.00	800.00
9 Fred Marberry	350.00	700.00
10 Red Faber	500.00	1,000.00
11 William Piercy	300.00	600.00
12 Curt Fullerton	300.00	600.00
13 Sloppy Thurston	300.00	600.00
14 Rube Walberg	300.00	600.00
15 Fred Heimach	300.00	600.00
16 Sherry Smith	300.00	600.00
17 Warren Ogden	300.00	600.00
18 Ernest Osborne	300.00	600.00
19 Dutch Ruether	300.00	600.00
20 Burleigh Grimes	500.00	1,000.00
21 Joe Genewich	300.00	600.00
22 Vic Aldridge	300.00	600.00
23 Arnold Stone	300.00	600.00
24 Les Howe	300.00	600.00
25 George Murry	300.00	600.00
26 Herman Pillette	300.00	600.00
27 John Couch	300.00	600.00
28 Tony Kaufmann	300.00	600.00
29 Frank May	300.00	600.00
30 Howard Ehmke	350.00	700.00
31 Bob Hasty	300.00	600.00
32 Dazzy Vance	600.00	1,200.00
33 Gorham Leverette	300.00	600.00
34 Bryan Harris	300.00	600.00
35 Paul Schreiber	300.00	600.00
36 Dewey Hinkle	300.00	600.00
37 Byron Yarrison	300.00	600.00
38 Jesse Haines	400.00	800.00
39 Earl Hamilton	300.00	600.00
40 Wilbur Cooper	350.00	700.00
41 Tom Long	300.00	600.00
42 Alex Ferguson	300.00	600.00
43 Chet Ross	300.00	600.00
44 Jack Quinn	350.00	700.00
45 Ray Kolp	300.00	600.00
46 Art Nehf	350.00	700.00
47 Hugh McQuillan	300.00	600.00
48 George Uhle	350.00	700.00
49 Ed Rommel	350.00	700.00
50 Ted Lyons	500.00	1,000.00
51 Roy Meeker	300.00	600.00
52 John Stuart	300.00	600.00
53 Joe Oeschger	300.00	600.00
54 Wayland Dean	300.00	600.00
55 Guy Morton	300.00	600.00
56 Bill Doak	300.00	600.00
57 Ed Pfeffer	300.00	600.00
58 Sam Gray	300.00	600.00
59 Lou North	300.00	600.00
60 Godfrey Brogan	300.00	600.00
61 Jimmy Ring	300.00	600.00
62 Rube Marquard	500.00	1,000.00
63 Bert Lewis	300.00	600.00
64 Frank Henry	300.00	600.00
65 Dennis Burns	300.00	600.00
66 Roline Naylor	300.00	600.00
67 Walt Huntzinger	300.00	600.00
68 Stan Baumgartner	300.00	600.00
69 Virgil Barnes	300.00	600.00
70 Clarence Mitchell	300.00	600.00
71 Lee Meadows	300.00	600.00
72 Charles Clazner	300.00	600.00
73 Jesse Barnes	300.00	600.00
74 Sam Jones	350.00	700.00
75 Dennis Gearin	300.00	600.00
76 Tom Zachary	350.00	700.00
77 Larry Benton	300.00	600.00
78 Jess Winter	300.00	600.00
79 Red Ruffing	600.00	1,200.00
80 John Cooney	300.00	600.00
81 Joe Bush	350.00	700.00
82 William Harris	300.00	600.00
83 Joe Shaute	300.00	600.00
84 George Pipgras	350.00	700.00
85 Eppa Rixey	500.00	1,000.00
86 Bill Sherdel	300.00	600.00
87 John Benton	300.00	600.00
88 Art Decatur	300.00	600.00
89 Harry Shriver	300.00	600.00
90 John Morrison	300.00	600.00
91 Walter Betts	300.00	600.00
92 Oscar Roettger	300.00	600.00
93 Bob Shawkey	500.00	1,000.00
94 Mike Cvengros	300.00	600.00
95 Leo Dickerman	300.00	600.00
96 Phillip Weinert	300.00	600.00
97 Nicholas Dumovich	300.00	600.00
98 Herb McQuaid	300.00	600.00
99 Tim McNamara	300.00	600.00
100 Alan Russell	300.00	600.00
101 Ted Blankenship	300.00	600.00
102 Howard Baldwin	300.00	600.00
103 Frank Davis	300.00	600.00
104 James Edwards	300.00	600.00
105 Hub Pruett	350.00	700.00
106 Dick Rudolph	300.00	600.00
107 Allan Sothoron	300.00	600.00
108 Claude Jonnard	300.00	600.00
109 Joubert Davenport	300.00	600.00
110 Paul Zahnser	300.00	600.00
111 John Bentley	300.00	600.00
112 Wilfred Ryan	300.00	600.00
113 George Metevier	300.00	600.00
114 John Watson	300.00	600.00
115 Syl Johnson	300.00	600.00
116 Oscar Fuhr	300.00	600.00
117 Warren Collins	300.00	600.00
118 Stan Covelskie	500.00	1,000.00
119 Dave Danforth	300.00	600.00
120 Elam Van Gilder	300.00	600.00
121 Bert Cole	300.00	600.00
122 Ken Holoway	300.00	600.00
123 Charles Robertson	300.00	600.00
124 Ed Wells	300.00	600.00
125 George Davis	300.00	600.00
126 William Bayne	300.00	600.00
127 Urban Shocker	400.00	800.00
128 Slim McGrew	300.00	600.00
129 Philip Bedgood	300.00	600.00
130 Fred Wingfield	300.00	600.00
131 George Modridge	300.00	600.00
132 Joe Martina	300.00	600.00
133 Byron Speece	300.00	600.00
134 Hal Carlson	300.00	600.00
135 Wilbur Hubbell	300.00	600.00
136 Milt Gaston	300.00	600.00

1951 DiMaggio Yankee Clipper Shoes

This one card set, which measures approximately 2 1/2" by 3 1/2" was issued as part of the shoe purchase. These cards were supposed to be tied to the shoe strings. The front has a batting portrait shot of DiMaggio set against a green background while the back a bullet point assortment of career highlights

1 Joe DiMaggio	25.00	50.00

1972-87 DiMaggio Bowery Bank

This one-card standard-size set was actually released three times. The first time was is 1972, the second was in 1979 and third was in 1987. We have priced the 1987 version here. The 1979 version is valued at $25 and the 1972 version is at $50. The front features a full-color photo of Dimaggio framed by the words Yankees on top and his name and position on the bottom. The horizontal backs has his career numbers, a brief biography and his vital statistics.

1 Joe DiMaggio	5.00	12.00

1972-83 Dimanche/Derniere Heure

The blank-backed photo sheets in this multi-sport set measure approximately 8 1/2" by 11" and feature white-bordered color sports star photos from Dimanche Derniere Heure, a Montreal newspaper. The player's name, position and biographical information appear within the lower white margin. All text is in French. A white vinyl album was available for storing the photo sheets. Printed on the album's spine are the words, "Mes Vedettes du Sport" (My Stars of Sport).The photos are unnumbered and are checklisted below in alphabetical order according to sport or team as follows: Montreal Expos baseball players (1-117; National League baseball players (118-130); Montreal Canadiens hockey players (131-177); wrestlers (178-202); prize fighters (203-204); auto racing drivers (205-208); women's golf (209); Patof the circus clown (210); and CFL (211-278).

1 Santo Alcala	1.00	2.00
2 Bill Almon	1.00	2.00
3 Bill Atkinson	1.00	2.00
4 Stan Bahnsen	1.00	2.00
5 Bob Bailey	1.00	2.00
6 Greg Bargar	1.00	2.00
7 Tony Bernazard	1.00	2.00
8 Tim Blackwell	1.00	2.00
9 Dennis Blair	1.00	2.00
10 John Boccabella	1.25	2.50
11 Jim Brewer CO	1.00	2.00
12 Hal Breeden	1.00	2.00
13 Dave Bristol CO	1.00	2.00
14 Jackie Brown	1.25	2.50
15 Ray Burris	1.00	2.00
16 Don Carrithers	1.00	2.00
17 Gary Carter	7.50	15.00
18 Dave Cash	1.00	2.00
19 Jim Cox	1.00	2.00
20 Warren Cromartie	1.00	2.00
21 Terry Crowley	1.00	2.00
22 Willie Davis	1.50	3.00
23 Andre Dawson	5.00	10.00
24 Boots Day	1.00	2.00
25 Don Demola	1.00	2.00
26 Larry Doby CO	2.00	4.00
27 Hal Dues	1.00	2.00
28 Duffy Dyer	1.00	2.00
29 Jim Fairey	1.00	2.00
30 Ron Fairly	1.50	3.00
31 Jim Fanning MG	1.00	2.00
32 Doug Flynn	1.00	2.00
33 Tim Foli	1.25	2.50
34 Barry Foote	1.00	2.00
35 Barry Foote/(Wearing chest protector and shin	1.00	2.00
36 Terry Francona	1.25	2.50
37 Pepe Frias	1.00	2.00
38 Woodie Fryman	1.00	2.00
39 Woodie Fryman Jeff Reardon	1.25	2.50
40 Mike Garman	1.00	2.00
41 Wayne Garrett	1.00	2.00
42 Ross Grimsley	1.00	2.00
43 Bill Gullickson	1.00	2.00
44 Ed Herrmann	1.00	2.00
45 Terry Humphrey	1.00	2.00
46 Ron Hunt	1.25	2.50
47 Tommy Hutton	1.00	2.00
48 Bob James	1.00	2.00
49 Wallace Johnson	1.00	2.00
50 Mike Jorgensen	1.00	2.00
51 Joe Kerrigan	1.00	2.00

52 Darold Knowles 1.00 2.00
53 Coco Laboy 1.25 2.50
54 Charles Lea 1.00 2.00
55 Bill Lee 1.25 2.50
56 Ron LeFlore 1.25 2.50
57 Larry Lintz 1.00 2.00
58 Bryan Little 1.00 2.00
59 Ken Macha 1.00 2.00
60 Jerry Manuel 1.25 2.50
61 Mike Marshall 1.50 3.00
62 Clyde Mashore 1.00 2.00
63 Jim Mason 1.00 2.00
64 Gene Mauch MG 1.50 3.00
65 Rudy May 1.00 2.00
66 Ernie McAnally 1.00 2.00
67 Tim McCarver 2.00 4.00
68 Cal McLish CO 1.00 2.00
69 Sam Mejias 1.00 2.00
70 John Milner 1.00 2.00
71 John Montague 1.00 2.00
72 Willie Montanez 1.00 2.00
73 Balor Moore 1.00 2.00
74 Jose Morales 1.00 2.00
75 Dan Norman 1.00 2.00
76 Fred Norman 1.00 2.00
77 Al Oliver 2.00 4.00
78 David Palmer 1.00 2.00
79 Stan Papi 1.00 2.00
80 Larry Parrish 1.25 2.50
81 Tony Perez 2.00 4.00
82 Tim Raines 2.00 4.00
83 Tim Raines 2.00 4.00
Andre Dawson
Warren Cromartie
84 Bobby Ramos 1.00 2.00
85 Bob Reece 1.00 2.00
86 Steve Renko 1.00 2.00
87 Steve Rogers 1.50 3.00
88 Angel Salazar 1.00 2.00
89 Scott Sanderson 1.00 2.00
90 Dan Schatzeder 1.00 2.00
91 Rodney Scott 1.00 2.00
92 Norm Sherry CO 1.00 2.00
93 Ken Singleton 1.25 2.50
94 Tony Solaita 1.00 2.00
95 Elias Sosa 1.00 2.00
96 Chris Speier 1.00 2.00
97 Don Stanhouse 1.00 2.00
98 Mike Stenhouse 1.00 2.00
99 Bill Stoneman 1.25 2.50
100 John Strohmayer 1.00 2.00
101 John Tamargo 1.00 2.00
102 Frank Taveres 1.00 2.00
103 Chuck Taylor 1.00 2.00
104 Jeff Terpko 1.00 2.00
105 Hector Torres 1.00 2.00
106 Mike Torrez 1.25 2.50
107 Wayne Twitchell 1.00 2.00
108 Del Unser 1.00 2.00
109 Ellis Valentine 1.00 2.00
110 Mickey Vernon CO 1.25 2.50
111 Bill Virdon MG 1.25 2.50
112 Tom Walker 1.00 2.00
113 Tim Wallach 1.00 2.00
114 Dan Warthen 1.00 2.00
115 Jerry White 1.00 2.00
116 Dick Williams MG 1.50 3.00
117 Bobby Wine 1.00 2.00
118 Jim Wohlford 1.00 2.00
119 Ron Woods 1.00 2.00
120 Joel Youngblood 1.00 2.00
121 Hank Aaron 5.00 10.00
122 Johnny Bench 3.00 6.00
123 Larry Bowa 1.25 2.50
124 Steve Carlton 2.00 4.00
125 Roberto Clemente 5.00 10.00
126 Willie Davis 1.00 2.00
127 Bob Gibson 2.00 4.00
128 Ferguson Jenkins 2.00 4.00
129 Willie McCovey 2.00 4.00
130 Willie Montanez 1.00 2.00
131 Pete Rose 4.00 8.00
132 Willie Stargell 2.00 4.00
133 Rusty Staub 1.50 3.00
Mike Jorgensen

1937 Dixie Lids Small

This unnumbered set of lids is actually a combined sport and non-sport set with 24 different lids. The lids are found in more than one size, approximately 2 11/16" in diameter as well as 2 5/16" in diameter. The 1937 lids are distinguished from the 1938 Dixie Lids by the fact that the 1937 lids are printed in black or wine-colored ink where the 1938 lids are printed in blue ink. In the checklist below only the sports subjects are checklisted; non-sport subjects (celebrities) included in this 24-card set are Gene Autry, Freddie Bartholomew, Bill Boyd, Johnny Mack Brown, Madeleine Carroll, Nelson Eddy, Clark Gable, Jean Harlow, Carole Lombard, Myrna Loy, Fred MacMurray, Ken Maynard, Merle Oberon, Eleanor Powell, William Powell, Luisa Rainer, Charles Starrett and Robert Taylor. The catalog designation is F7-1.

COMPLETE SPORT (6) 175.00 350.00
*LARGE: .6X TO 1.5X SMALL
2 Charles Gehringer 50.00 100.00
3 Charles Hartnett 40.00 80.00
4 Carl Hubbell 60.00 120.00
5 Joe Medwick 40.00 80.00

1937 Dixie Premiums

This is a parallel issue to the lids -- an attractive "premium" large picture of each of the subjects in the Dixie Lid set. The premiums are printed on thick stock and feature a large color drawing on the front; each unnumbered premium measures approximately 8" X 10". The 1937 premiums are distinguished from the 1938 Dixie Lid premiums by the fact that the 1937 premiums contain a dark green border whereas the 1938 premiums have a lighter green border completely around the photo. Also, on the reverse, the 1937 premiums have a large gray star and three light gray lines at the top. Only the sports personalities are checklisted below.

COMPLETE SPORT SET (6) 175.00 350.00
2 Charles Gehringer 50.00 100.00
3 Charles Hartnett 40.00 80.00
4 Carl Hubbell 50.00 100.00
5 Joe Medwick 40.00 80.00

1938 Dixie Lids Small

This unnumbered set of lids is actually a combined sport and non-sport set with 24 different lids. The lids are found in more than one size, approximately 2 11/16" in diameter as well as 2 5/16" in diameter. The catalog designation is F7-1. The 1938 lids are distinguished from the 1937 Dixie Lids by the fact that the 1938 lids are printed in blue ink whereas the 1938 lids are printed in black or wine-colored ink. In the checklist below only the sports subjects are checklisted; non-sport subjects (celebrities) included in this 24 card set are Don Ameche, Annabella, Gene Autry, Warner Baxter, William Boyd, Bobby Breen, Gary Cooper, Alice Fay, Sonja Henie, Tommy Kelly, June Lang, Colonel Tim McCoy, Tyrone Power, Tex Ritter, Simone Simon, Bob Steele, The Three Musquiteers and Jane Withers.

COMPLETE SPORT SET (6) 250.00 500.00
*LARGE: .6X TO 1.5X SMALL
2 Bob Feller 40.00 80.00
3 Jimmie Foxx 40.00 80.00
4 Carl Hubbell 40.00 80.00
mouth open
5 Wally Moses 20.00 40.00

1938 Dixie Premiums

This is a parallel issue to the lids -- an attractive "premium" large picture of each of the subjects in the Dixie Lids set. The premiums are printed on thick stock and feature a large color drawing on the front; each unnumbered premium measures approximately 8" X 10". The 1938 premiums are distinguished from the 1937 Dixie Lid premiums by the fact that the 1938 premiums contain a light green border whereas the 1937 premiums have a darker green border completely around the photo. Also, on the reverse, the 1938 premiums have a single gray sline line at the top leading to the player's name in script. Again, we have only checklisted the sports personalities.

COMPLETE SET (6) 375.00 750.00
2 Bob Feller 50.00 100.00
3 Jimmie Foxx 50.00 100.00
4 Carl Hubbell 50.00 100.00
5 Wally Moses 25.00 50.00

1952 Dixie Lids

This scarce 24-lid set features all baseball subjects each measuring 2 11/16". The 1952 set was released very late in the year and in only one size; it is undoubtedly the toughest Dixie baseball set. The lids are found with a blue tint. The catalog designation for this set is F7-2A. Lids found with the tab removed would suffer an approximate 25 percent in value. The asterisked lids below are those that were only available in 1952. The 50s Dixie Lids are distinguished from the 30's lids also by the fact that the 50s lids have the circular picture portion abruptly squared off near the bottom end of the lid where the player's name appears.

COMPLETE SET (24) 3,000.00 6,000.00
1 Richie Ashburn 300.00 600.00
2 Tommy Byrne 150.00 300.00
3 Chico Carrasquel 125.00 250.00
4 Pete Castiglione 125.00 250.00
5 Walker Cooper 150.00 300.00
6 Billy Cox 125.00 250.00
7 Ferris Fain 125.00 250.00
8 Bobby Feller 350.00 700.00
9 Nellie Fox 250.00 500.00
10 Monte Irvin 250.00 500.00
11 Ralph Kiner 250.00 500.00
12 Cass Michaels 125.00 250.00
13 Don Mueller 125.00 250.00
14 Mel Parnell 125.00 250.00
15 Allie Reynolds 175.00 350.00
16 Preacher Roe 175.00 350.00
17 Connie Ryan 125.00 250.00
18 Hank Sauer 150.00 300.00
19 Al Schoendienst 250.00 500.00
20 Andy Seminick 150.00 300.00
21 Bobby Shantz 150.00 300.00
22 Enos Slaughter 250.00 500.00
23 Virgil Trucks 125.00 250.00
24 Gene Woodling 150.00 300.00

1952 Dixie Premiums

The catalog designation is F7-2A. The 1952 Dixie Cup Baseball Premiums contain 1951 statistics. There are 24 (sepia-tinted) black and white photos each measuring approximately 8" by 10". Each photo has a facsimile autograph at the bottom. These large premium photos are blank backed and were printed on thick paper stock.

COMPLETE SET (24) 1,000.00 2,000.00
1 Richie Ashburn 125.00 250.00
2 Tommy Byrne 40.00 80.00
3 Chico Carrasquel 40.00 80.00
4 Pete Castiglione 40.00 80.00
5 Walker Cooper 40.00 80.00
6 Billy Cox 40.00 80.00
7 Ferris Fain 40.00 80.00
8 Bob Feller 150.00 300.00
9 Nellie Fox 200.00 400.00
10 Monte Irvin 100.00 200.00
11 Ralph Kiner 100.00 200.00
12 Cass Michaels 40.00 80.00
13 Don Mueller 40.00 80.00
14 Mel Parnell 40.00 80.00
15 Allie Reynolds 60.00 120.00
16 Preacher Roe 60.00 120.00
17 Connie Ryan 40.00 80.00
18 Hank Sauer 50.00 100.00
19 Al Schoendienst 100.00 200.00
20 Andy Seminick 40.00 80.00
21 Bobby Shantz 50.00 100.00
22 Enos Slaughter 100.00 200.00
23 Virgil Trucks 40.00 80.00
24 Gene Woodling 50.00 100.00

1953 Dixie Lids

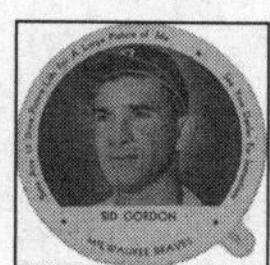

This 24-lid set features all baseball subjects each measuring 2 11/16". There are many different back types in existence. The lids are found with a wine tint. The catalog designation for this set is F7-2. Lids found without the tab attached are considered good condition at best. There is also a smaller size variation, 2 5/16" in diameter. These smaller lids are worth an additional 50 percent more than the prices listed below.

COMPLETE SET (24) 1,200.00 2,400.00
1 Richie Ashburn 100.00 200.00
2 Chico Carrasquel 40.00 80.00
3 Billy Cox 40.00 80.00
4 Ferris Fain 40.00 80.00
5 Nellie Fox 100.00 200.00
6A Sid Gordon 100.00 200.00
Boston Braves
6B Sid Gordon 40.00 80.00
Milwaukee Braves
7 Warren Hacker 40.00 80.00
8 Monte Irvin 100.00 200.00
9 Jackie Jensen 75.00 150.00
10 Ralph Kiner 100.00 200.00
11 Ted Kluszewski 100.00 200.00
12 Bob Lemon 100.00 200.00
13 Don Mueller 40.00 80.00
14 Mel Parnell 40.00 80.00
15 Jerry Priddy 40.00 80.00
16 Allie Reynolds 75.00 150.00
17 Preacher Roe 75.00 150.00
18 Hank Sauer 40.00 80.00
19 Al Schoendienst 100.00 200.00
20 Bobby Shantz 40.00 80.00
21 Enos Slaughter 100.00 200.00
22A Warren Spahn 175.00 350.00
Boston Braves
22B Warren Spahn 175.00 350.00
Milwaukee Braves
23A Virgil Trucks 40.00 80.00
Chicago White Sox
23B Virgil Trucks 40.00 80.00
St. Louis Browns
24 Gene Woodling 40.00 80.00

1953 Dixie Premiums

The catalog designation is F7-2A. The 1953 Dixie Cup Baseball Premiums contain 1952 statistics. There are 24 (sepia-tinted) black and white photos each measuring approximately 8" by 10". Each photo has a facsimile autograph at the bottom. These large premium photos are blank backed and were printed on thick paper stock.

COMPLETE SET (24) 800.00 1,600.00
1 Richie Ashburn 100.00 200.00
2 Chico Carrasquel 30.00 60.00
3 Billy Cox 40.00 80.00
4 Ferris Fain 30.00 60.00
5 Nellie Fox 175.00 350.00
6 Sid Gordon 30.00 60.00
7 Warren Hacker 30.00 60.00
8 Monte Irvin 75.00 150.00
9 Jack Jensen 50.00 100.00
10 Ralph Kiner 75.00 150.00
11 Ted Kluszewski 60.00 120.00
12 Bob Lemon 75.00 150.00
13 Don Mueller 30.00 60.00
14 Mel Parnell 30.00 60.00
15 Jerry Priddy 30.00 60.00
16 Allie Reynolds 50.00 100.00
17 Preacher Roe 75.00 150.00
18 Hank Sauer 40.00 80.00
19 Al Schoendienst 60.00 120.00
20 Bobby Shantz 40.00 80.00
21 Enos Slaughter 60.00 120.00
22 Warren Spahn 100.00 200.00
23 Virgil Trucks 30.00 60.00
24 Gene Woodling 40.00 80.00

1954 Dixie Lids

This 18 lid set features all baseball subjects each measuring 2 11/16". There are many different back types in existence. The lids are typically found with a brown sepia tint. The catalog designation for this set is F7-4. Lids found without the tab attached are considered good condition at best. This year is distinguishable by the fact that the lids say "Get Dixie Lid 3-D Starviewer. Send 25 cents, this lid, name, address, to DIXIE, Box 630, New York 17, N.Y." around the border on the front. The lids have an "L" or "R" on the tab, which distinguished which side of the 3-D viewer was to be used for that particular card. The lids are also seen in a small (2 5/16") and large (3 3/16") size; these variations carry approximately double the prices below.

COMPLETE SET (18) 500.00 1,000.00
1 Richie Ashburn 60.00 120.00
2 Clint Courtney 30.00 60.00
3 Sid Gordon 30.00 60.00
4 Billy Hoeft 30.00 60.00
5 Monte Irvin 60.00 120.00
6 Jackie Jensen 50.00 100.00
7 Ralph Kiner 60.00 120.00
8 Ted Kluszewski 60.00 120.00
9 Gil McDougald 50.00 100.00
10 Minnie Minoso 50.00 100.00
11 Danny O'Connell 30.00 60.00
12 Mel Parnell 30.00 60.00
13 Preacher Roe 50.00 100.00
14 Al Rosen 40.00 80.00
15 Al Schoendienst 40.00 80.00
16 Enos Slaughter 60.00 120.00
17 Gene Woodling 30.00 60.00
18 Gus Zernial 30.00 60.00

1969-72 Dodge Promo Postcards

These postcards were issued by the car maker, Dodge to promote some of their lines of cars. These cards feature players involved in the 1968 World Series and feature a player photo as well as a photo of the card being promoted. The back is blank except for a brief description of the player as well as how it relates to the "Dodge car" pictured on the front. The cards are unnumbered so we have sequenced them in alphabetical order.

COMPLETE SET (4) 15.00 40.00
1 Lou Brock 4.00 10.00
2 Bill Freehan 3.00 8.00
3 Joe Garagiola 4.00 10.00
4 Mickey Lolich 3.00 8.00

1909 Dodgers Daily Eagle Supplement

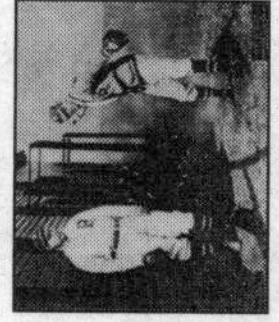

These supplments to the Brooklyn Daily Eagle are sepia toned photos and measure approximately 7" by 9 1/2" and feature members of the Brooklyn Dodgers. Since the photos are unnumbered, we have sequenced them in alphabetical order. Also, it is possible that there are more cards in this set so any additions to this checklist is appreciated.

COMPLETE SET 250.00 500.00
1 George Bell 50.00 100.00
2 George Hunter 50.00 100.00
3 Doc Scanlon 50.00 100.00
4 Kaiser Wilhelm 50.00 100.00
5 Harry McIntire 50.00 100.00
Jimmy Pastorious

1940 Dodgers Team Issue

These photos measure approximately 6 1/2" by 9". They feature members of the 1940 Brooklyn Dodgers. The photos take up nearly all of the card except for a small white border. There is also a facsimile signature of each player. The backs are blank and we have sequenced them in alphabetical order. Pee Wee Reese appears in his rookie season in this set.

COMPLETE SET (25) 150.00 300.00
1 Dolph Camilli 7.50 15.00
2 Tex Carleton 5.00 10.00
3 Hugh Casey 6.00 12.00
4 Pete Coscarart 5.00 10.00
5 Curt Davis 5.00 10.00
6 Leo Durocher 10.00 20.00
7 Fred Fitzsimmons 6.00 12.00
8 Herman Franks 5.00 10.00
9 Joe Gallagher 5.00 10.00
10 Charlie Gilbert 5.00 10.00
11 Luke Hamlin 5.00 10.00
12 Johnny Hudson 5.00 10.00
13 Newt Kimball 5.00 10.00
14 Cookie Lavagetto 6.00 12.00
15 Gus Mancuso 5.00 10.00
16 Joe Medwick 10.00 20.00
17 Van Lingle Mungo 6.00 12.00
18 Babe Phelps 5.00 10.00
19 Tot Pressnell 5.00 10.00
20 Pee Wee Reese 25.00 50.00
21 Vito Tamulis 5.00 10.00
22 Joe Vosmik 5.00 10.00
23 Dixie Walker 7.50 15.00
24 Jimmy Wasdell 5.00 10.00
25 Whit Wyatt 6.00 12.00

1941 Dodgers Team Issue

These are blank-backed, white-bordered, 6 1/2" X 9" black-and-white photos. The photos have facsimile autographs, are unnumbered and checklisted below in alphabetical order.

COMPLETE SET (28)	125.00	250.00
1 Mace Brown	5.00	10.00
2 Dolph Camilli	7.50	15.00
3 Tex Carleton	5.00	10.00
4 Hugh Casey	5.00	10.00
5 Pete Coscarart	5.00	10.00
6 Curt Davis	5.00	10.00
7 Leo Durocher MG	15.00	30.00
8 Fred Fitzsimmons	6.00	12.00
9 Herman Franks	5.00	10.00
10 Joe Gallagher	5.00	10.00
10 Jimmy Wasdell	5.00	10.00
11 Charlie Gilbert	5.00	10.00
11 Kemp Wicker	5.00	10.00
12 Luke Hamlin	5.00	10.00
13 Johnny Hudson	5.00	10.00
14 Newill Kimball	5.00	10.00
15 Cookie Lavagetto	6.00	12.00
16 Gus Mancuso	6.00	12.00
17 Joe Medwick	15.00	30.00
18 Van Mungo	7.50	15.00
19 Babe Phelps	5.00	10.00
20 Tot Pressnell	5.00	10.00
21 Pee Wee Reese	20.00	40.00
22 Lew Riggs	5.00	10.00
23 Bill Swift	5.00	10.00
24 Vito Tamulis	5.00	10.00
25 Joe Vosmik	5.00	10.00
26 Dixie Walker	7.50	15.00
27 Jimmy Wasdell	5.00	10.00
28 Whit Wyatt	5.00	10.00

1942 Dodgers Team Issue

This 25-card set of the Brooklyn Dodgers measures approximately 6 1/2" by 9" and features black-and-white player portraits with a facsimile autograph. The cards are unnumbered and checklisted below in alphabetical order.

COMPLETE SET (25)	125.00	250.00
1 Johnny Allen	5.00	10.00
2 Frenchy Bordagaray	5.00	10.00
3 Dolph Camilli	6.00	12.00
4 Hugh Casey	5.00	10.00
5 Curt Davis	5.00	10.00
6 Leo Durocher	10.00	20.00
7 Larry French	6.00	12.00
8 Augie Galan	5.00	10.00
9 Ed Head	5.00	10.00
10 Billy Herman	10.00	20.00
11 Kirby Higbe	6.00	12.00
12 Alex Kampouris	5.00	10.00
13 Newell Kimball	5.00	10.00
14 Joe Medwick	10.00	20.00
15 Mickey Owen	6.00	12.00
16 Pee Wee Reese	10.00	20.00
17 Pete Reiser	7.50	15.00
18 Lew Riggs	5.00	10.00
19 Johnny Rizzo	5.00	10.00
20 Schoolboy Rowe	6.00	12.00
21 Bill Sullivan	5.00	10.00
22 Arky Vaughn	10.00	20.00
23 Dixie Walker	7.50	15.00
24 Les Webber	5.00	10.00
25 Whitlow Wyatt	6.00	12.00

1943 Dodgers Team Issue

This set of the Brooklyn Dodgers measures approximately 6 1/2" by 9". The black-and-white player photos display fascimile autographs. The backs are blank. The cards are unnumbered and checklisted below in alphabetical order.

COMPLETE SET (25)	100.00	200.00
1 Johnny Allen	6.00	12.00
2 Frenchy Bordagaray	5.00	10.00
3 Bob Bragan	6.00	12.00
4 Dolph Camilli	7.50	15.00
5 John Cooney	5.00	10.00
6 John Corriden	5.00	10.00
7 Curt Davis	5.00	10.00
8 Leo Durocher	10.00	20.00
9 Fred Fitzimmons	6.00	12.00
10 Augie Galan	6.00	12.00
11 Al Glossop	5.00	10.00
12 Ed Head	5.00	10.00
13 Billy Herman	10.00	20.00
14 Kirby Higbe	6.00	12.00
15 Max Macon	5.00	10.00
16 Joe Medwick	10.00	20.00
17 Rube Melton	5.00	10.00
18 Dee Moore	5.00	10.00
19 B. Newsom	7.50	15.00
20 Mickey Owen	6.00	12.00
21 Arky Vaughan	10.00	20.00
22 Dixie Walker	7.50	15.00
23 Paul Waner	10.00	20.00
24 Les Webber	5.00	10.00
25 Whitlow Wyatt	5.00	10.00

1943 Dodgers War Bonds

Issued in conjunction with a war bonds drive in 1943, this card, which measure 2 1/2" by 4 3/8" features a team photo of the 1943 Brooklyn Dodgers. Because of the nature of how it was issued, not many of these cards have survived.

1 Brooklyn Dodgers	250.00	500.00

1946 Dodgers Team Issue

This 25-card set of the Brooklyn Dodgers measures approximately 6 1/2" by 9" and features black-and-white player portraits with white borders. The backs are blank. The cards are unnumbered and checklisted below in alphabetical order.

COMPLETE SET (25)	125.00	250.00
1 Ferrell(Andy) Anderson	4.00	8.00
2 Henry Behrman	4.00	8.00
3 Ralph Branca	7.50	15.00
4 Hugh Casey	4.00	8.00
5 Leo Durocher	7.50	15.00
6 Carl Furillo	7.50	15.00
7 Augie Galan	5.00	10.00
8 Hal Gregg	4.00	8.00
9 Joe Hatten	4.00	8.00
10 Ed Head	4.00	8.00
11 Billy Herman	7.50	15.00
12 Gene Hermanski	4.00	8.00
13 Art Herring	4.00	8.00
14 Kirby Higbe	5.00	10.00
15 Cookie Lavagetto	6.00	12.00
16 Vic Lombardi	4.00	8.00
17 Pee Wee Reese	15.00	30.00
18 Pete Reiser	6.00	12.00
19 Stan Rojek	4.00	8.00
20 Mike Sandlock	4.00	8.00
21 Eddie Stanky	7.50	15.00
22 Ed Stevens	4.00	8.00
23 Dixie Walker	6.00	12.00
24 Les Webber	4.00	8.00
25 Dick Whitman	4.00	8.00

1947 Dodgers Team Issue

This 25-card set of the Brooklyn Dodgers measures approximately 6 1/2" by 9" and features black-and-white player portraits with white borders and facsimile autographs. The backs are blank. The cards are unnumbered and checklisted below in alphabetical order. Carl Furillo, Gil Hodges and Duke Snider are featured in this set, two years before their Rookie Cards. Jackie Robinson is featured in this set as well during his rookie season.

COMPLETE SET (25)	150.00	300.00
1 Ray Blades	4.00	8.00
2 Bob Bragan	5.00	10.00
3 Ralph Branca	6.00	12.00
4 Tommy Brown	4.00	8.00
5 Hugh Casey	4.00	8.00
6 Eddie Chandler	4.00	8.00
7 Carl Furillo	12.50	25.00
8 Hal Gregg	4.00	8.00
9 Joe Hatten	4.00	8.00
10 Gene Hermanski	4.00	8.00
11 Gil Hodges	15.00	30.00
12 John Jorgensen	4.00	8.00
13 Clyde King	4.00	8.00
14 Vic Lombardi	4.00	8.00
15 Rube Melton	4.00	8.00
16 Eddie Miksis	4.00	8.00
17 Pee Wee Reese	7.50	15.00
18 Pete Reiser	6.00	12.00
19 Jackie Robinson	50.00	100.00
20 Stan Fojek	4.00	8.00
21 B.E. Shotton	4.00	8.00
22 Duke Snider	20.00	40.00
23 Eddie Stanky	6.00	12.00
24 Harry Taylor	4.00	8.00
25 Dixie Walker	5.00	10.00

1948 Dodgers Team Issue

This 26-card set of the Brooklyn Dodgers measures approximately 6 1/2" by 9" and features black-and-white player portraits with white borders. The backs are blank. The cards are unnumbered and checklisted below in alphabetical order. This set can be dated to 1948 with the inclusion of Preston Ward in his only season in Brooklyn.

COMPLETE SET (26)	150.00	300.00
1 Rex Barney	5.00	10.00
2 Ray Blades	4.00	8.00
3 Bob Bragan	5.00	10.00
4 Ralph Branca	6.00	12.00
5 Tommy Brown	4.00	8.00
6 Hugh Casey	4.00	8.00
7 Billy Cox	6.00	12.00
8 Leo Durocher	7.50	15.00
9 Bruce Edwards	4.00	8.00
10 Carl Furillo	6.00	12.00
11 Joe Hatten	4.00	8.00
12 Gene Hermanski	4.00	8.00
13 Gil Hodges	12.50	25.00
14 John Jorgensen	4.00	8.00
15 Don Lund	4.00	8.00
16 Eddie Miksis	4.00	8.00
17 Jake Pitler	4.00	8.00
18 Pee Wee Reese	20.00	40.00
19 Pete Reiser	6.00	12.00
20 Jackie Robinson	30.00	60.00
21 Preacher Roe	6.00	12.00
22 B.E. Shotton	4.00	8.00
23 Clyde Sukeforth	4.00	8.00
24 Harry Taylor	4.00	8.00
25 Arky Vaughan	7.50	15.00
26 Preston Ward	4.00	8.00

1949 Dodgers Team Issue

This 25-card set of the Brooklyn Dodgers measures approximately 6 1/2" by 9" and features black-and-white player portraits with white borders. The backs are blank. The cards are unnumbered and checklisted below in alphabetical order. Roy Campanella is featured in his Rookie Card year. Don Newcombe is featured in this set a year prior to his Rookie Card. The Dodgers, Giants, Red Sox and Yankees Team Issue sets were all available at time of issue from Harry M Stevens for 68 cents per set.

COMPLETE SET (25)	200.00	400.00
1 Jack Banta	5.00	10.00
2 Rex Barney	6.00	12.00
3 Ralph Branca	7.50	15.00
4 Tommy Brown	5.00	10.00
5 Roy Campanella	25.00	50.00
6 Billy Cox	7.50	15.00
7 Bruce Edwards	5.00	10.00
8 Carl Furillo	10.00	20.00
9 Joe Hatten	5.00	10.00
10 Gene Hermanski	5.00	10.00
11 Gil Hodges	10.00	20.00
12 Johnny Hopp	5.00	10.00
13 Spider Jorgensen	5.00	10.00
14 Mike McCormick	5.00	10.00
15 Eddie Miksis	5.00	10.00
16 Don Newcombe	10.00	20.00
17 Erv Palica	5.00	10.00
18 Jake Pitler CO	5.00	10.00
19 Pee Wee Reese	25.00	50.00
20 Jackie Robinson	40.00	80.00
21 Preacher Roe	5.00	10.00
22 Burt Shotton MG	5.00	10.00
23 Duke Snider	25.00	50.00
24 Milt Stock CO	5.00	10.00
25 Clyde Sukeforth CO	5.00	10.00

1955 Dodgers Golden Stamps

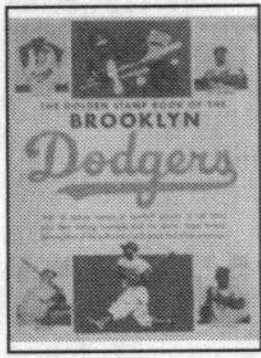

This 32-stamp set features color photos of the Brooklyn Dodgers and measures approximately 2" by 2 5/8". The stamps are designed to be placed in a 32-page album which measures approximately 8 3/8" by 10 15/16". The album contains black-and-white drawings of players with statistics and life stories. The stamps are unnumbered and listed below according to where they fall in the album. Sandy Koufax appears in what was both his rookie and Rookie Card season.

COMPLETE SET (32)	100.00	200.00
1 Walt Alston MG	6.00	12.00
2 Don Newcombe	2.00	4.00
3 Carl Erskine	2.00	4.00
4 Johnny Podres	2.00	4.00
5 Billy Loes	1.25	2.50
6 Russ Meyer	1.25	2.50
7 Jim Hughes	1.25	2.50
8 Sandy Koufax	40.00	80.00
9 Joe Black	1.50	3.00
10 Karl Spooner	1.25	2.50
11 Clem Labine	1.50	3.00
12 Roy Campanella	10.00	20.00
13 Gil Hodges	6.00	12.00
14 Jim Gilliam	2.50	5.00
15 Jackie Robinson	20.00	40.00
16 Pee Wee Reese	10.00	20.00
17 Duke Snider	10.00	20.00
18 Carl Furillo	2.50	5.00
19 Sandy Amoros	2.00	4.00
20 Frank Kellert	1.25	2.50
21 Don Zimmer	2.00	4.00
22 Al Walker	1.25	2.50
23 Tom Lasorda	10.00	20.00
24 Ed Roebuck	1.25	2.50
25 Don Hoak	1.25	2.50
26 George Shuba	1.50	3.00
27 Billy Herman CO	2.00	4.00
28 Jake Pitler CO	1.25	2.50
29 Joe Becker CO	1.25	2.50
30 Doc Wendler Carl Furillo	1.50	3.00
31 Charlie Di Giovanna	1.25	2.50
32 Ebbets Field	10.00	20.00
XX Album	2.50	5.00

1956 Dodgers Team Issue

Issued the year after the Brooklyn Dodgers won their only World Series, these 12 black and white blank-backed photos, which measure 5" by 7" feature some of the key members of the 1956 Brooklyn Dodgers. The pack was issued in an envelope which cost 25 cents upon release in 1956. Since these photos are unnumbered, we have sequenced them in alphabetical order.

COMPLETE SET (12)	75.00	150.00
1 Walt Alston MG	5.00	10.00
2 Roy Campanella	10.00	20.00
3 Carl Erskine	4.00	8.00
4 Carl Furillo	4.00	8.00
5 Gil Hodges	7.50	15.00
6 Randy Jackson	2.50	5.00
7 Clem Labine	3.00	6.00
8 Don Newcombe	4.00	8.00
9 Johnny Podres	4.00	8.00
10 Pee Wee Reese	10.00	20.00
11 Jackie Robinson	12.50	25.00
12 Duke Snider	10.00	20.00

1958 Dodgers Bell Brand

The 1958 Bell Brand Potato Chips set of ten unnumbered cards features members of the Los Angeles Dodgers exclusively. Each card has a 1/4" green border, and the Gino Cimoli, Johnny Podres, Pee Wee Reese and Duke Snider cards are more difficult to find; they are marked with an SP (short printed) in the checklist below. The cards measure approximately 3" by 4". This set marks the first year for the Dodgers in Los Angeles and includes a Campanella card despite the fact that he never played for the team in California. The catalog designation for this set is F339-1. Cards found still inside the original cellophane wrapper are valued at double the prices below. According to printed reports, the promotion went badly for Bell Brand and much of the product was destroyed. The cards were found in both 29 cent and 49 cent packages.

COMPLETE SET (10)	3,000.00	6,000.00
COMMON CARD (1-10)	100.00	200.00
COMMON SP	200.00	400.00
1 Roy Campanella	400.00	800.00
2 Gino Cimoli SP	200.00	400.00
3 Don Drysdale	250.00	500.00
4 Jim Gilliam	100.00	200.00
5 Gil Hodges	200.00	400.00
6 Sandy Koufax	500.00	1,000.00
7 Johnny Podres SP	300.00	600.00
8 Pee Wee Reese SP	400.00	800.00
9 Duke Snider SP	600.00	1,200.00
10 Don Zimmer	100.00	200.00

1958 Dodgers Jay Publishing

This 12-card set of the Los Angeles Dodgers measures approximately 5" by 7" and features black-and-white player photos in a white border. These cards were packaged 12 to a packet. The backs are blank. The cards are unnumbered and checklisted below in alphabetical order.

COMPLETE SET (12)	37.50	75.00
1 Walt Alston MG	2.50	5.00
2 Roy Campanella	7.50	15.00
3 Gino Cimoli	1.50	3.00
4 Don Drysdale	5.00	10.00
5 Carl Furillo	2.50	5.00
6 Gil Hodges	5.00	10.00
7 Clem Labine	1.50	3.00
8 Charley Neal	1.50	3.00
9 Don Newcombe	2.50	5.00
10 Johnny Podres	2.50	5.00
11 Pee Wee Reese	7.50	15.00
12 Duke Snider	5.00	10.00

1958 Dodgers Team Issue

This 25-card set features black-and-white photos of the Los Angeles Dodgers in white borders. The backs are blank. The set could originally be obtained through the mail for $1. Later on this set was also sold at the park for $1 and due to lack of early sales was later reduced to $.50. The cards are unnumbered and checklisted below in alphabetical order.

COMPLETE SET (25)	62.50	125.00
1 Walt Alston MG	3.00	6.00
2 Joe Becker CO	1.50	3.00
3 Don Bessent	1.50	3.00
4 Roger Craig	2.50	5.00
5 Charlie Dressen CO	2.50	5.00
6 Don Drysdale	5.00	10.00
7 Carl Erskine	2.50	5.00
8 Carl Furillo	2.50	5.00
9 Junior Gilliam	2.50	5.00
10 Gil Hodges	5.00	10.00
11 Randy Jackson	1.50	3.00
12 Sandy Koufax	10.00	20.00
13 Clem Labine	2.50	5.00
14 Danny McDevitt	1.50	3.00
15 Greg Mulleavy CO	1.50	3.00
16 Charlie Neal	1.50	3.00
17 Don Newcombe	2.50	5.00
18 Joe Pignatano	1.50	3.00
19 Johnny Podres	2.50	5.00
20 Pee Wee Reese	5.00	10.00
21 Ed Roebuck	1.50	3.00
22 Duke Snider	5.00	10.00
23 Elmer Valo	2.00	4.00
24 Rube Walker	1.50	3.00
25 Don Zimmer	2.50	5.00

1958 Dodgers Volpe

Printed on heavy paper stock, these blank-backed reproductions of artist Nicholas Volpe's charcoal portraits of the 1958 Los Angeles Dodgers were issued in two sizes, 2 5/8" by 3 3/4" and 8" by 10". The player's name appears near the bottom. The smaller size was sold by mail at a cost of 50 cents a protrait. The larger size was also sold by mail by the club for $1.00 a card. The portraits are unnumbered and checklisted below in alphabetical order.

COMPLETE SET (12)	200.00	400.00
1 Walter Alston	15.00	30.00
2 Gino Cimoli	12.50	25.00
3 Don Drysdale	30.00	60.00
4 Carl Erskine	12.50	25.00
5 Carl Furillo	15.00	30.00
6 Jim Gilliam	15.00	30.00
7 Gil Hodges	30.00	60.00
8 Clem Labine	12.50	25.00
9 Don Newcombe	15.00	30.00
10 Johnny Podres	15.00	30.00
11 Pee Wee Reese	40.00	80.00
12 Duke Snider	40.00	80.00

1959 Dodgers Morrell

The cards in this 12-card set measure 2 1/2" by 3 1/2". The 1959 Morrell Meats set of full color, unnumbered cards features Los Angeles Dodger players only. The photos used are the same as those selected for the Dodger team issue postcards in 1959. The Morrell Meats logo is on the backs of the cards. The Clem Labine card actually features a picture of Stan Williams and the Norm Larker card actually features a picture of Joe Pignatano as indicated in the checklist below.

The catalog designation is F172-1.

COMPLETE SET (12)	750.00	1,250.00
1 Don Drysdale	75.00	150.00
2 Carl Furillo	60.00	120.00
3 Jim Gilliam	60.00	120.00
4 Gil Hodges	75.00	150.00
5 Sandy Koufax	150.00	300.00
6 Clem Labine UER/(Photo actually Stan Williams)	40.00	80.00
7 Norm Larker UER/(Photo actually Joe Pignatano)	40.00	80.00
8 Charlie Neal	40.00	80.00
9 Johnny Podres	60.00	120.00
10 John Roseboro	50.00	100.00
11 Duke Snider	150.00	300.00
12 Don Zimmer	50.00	100.00

1959 Dodgers Postcards

These 12 postcards were issued by the Dodgers during the 1959 season and feature some of the leading players from the team. The cards have color photos on the front and brown printing on the back and were produced by the H.S. Crocker Co. in LA. A couple of the players are misidentified and we have notated them as such.

COMPLETE SET (12)	100.00	200.00
901 Duke Snider	12.50	25.00
902 Gil Hodges	10.00	20.00
903 Johnny Podres	6.00	12.00
904 Carl Furillo	6.00	12.00
905 Don Drysdale	12.50	25.00
906 Sandy Koufax	25.00	50.00
907 Jim Gilliam	6.00	12.00
908 Don Zimmer	6.00	12.00
909 Charlie Neal	5.00	10.00
910 Norm Larker UER	5.00	10.00
911 Clem Labine	6.00	12.00
912 John Roseboro	5.00	10.00

1959 Dodgers Team Issue

This 26-card set of the Los Angeles Dodgers measures approximately 5" by 7" and features black-and-white player photos in a white border. The backs are blank. The cards are unnumbered and checklisted below in alphabetical order.

COMPLETE SET (26)	37.50	75.00
1 Walter Alston MG	3.00	6.00
2 Don Bessent	1.50	3.00
3 Roger Craig	1.50	3.00
4 Charlie Dressen CO	1.50	3.00
5 Don Drysdale	5.00	10.00
6 Carl Erskine	2.50	5.00
7 Ron Fairly	2.50	5.00
8 Carl Furillo	2.50	5.00
9 Junior Gilliam	2.50	5.00
10 Gil Hodges	3.00	6.00
11 Fred Kipp	1.50	3.00
12 Sandy Koufax	7.50	15.00
13 Clem Labine	2.00	4.00
14 Norm Larker	1.50	3.00
15 Bob Lillis	1.50	3.00
16 Danny McDevitt	1.50	3.00
17 Wally Moon	1.50	3.00
18 Greg Mulleavy CO	1.50	3.00
19 Charlie Neal	1.50	3.00
20 Joe Pignatano	1.50	3.00
21 Johnny Podres	2.50	5.00
22 Pee Wee Reese	3.00	6.00
23 Rip Repulski	1.50	3.00
24 John Roseboro	1.50	3.00
25 Duke Snider	3.00	6.00
26 Don Zimmer	2.00	4.00

1959 Dodgers Volpe

Issued on thin paper stock, these blank-backed reproductions of artist Nicholas Volpe's charcoal portraits of the 1959 Dodgers measure approximately 8" by 10". The player's name appears near the bottom. The portraits are unnumbered and checklisted below in alphabetical order. The Campanella portrait has his career stats on the back.

COMPLETE SET (15)	125.00	250.00
1 Walter Alston MG	10.00	25.00
2 Roy Campnella TRIB	12.50	30.00
3 Don Drysdale	12.50	30.00
4 Carl Erskine	10.00	25.00
5 Carl Furillo	10.00	25.00
6 Jim Gilliam	10.00	25.00
7 Gil Hodges	12.50	30.00
8 Clem Labine	8.00	20.00
9 Wally Moon	8.00	20.00
10 Don Newcombe	10.00	25.00
11 Johnny Podres	8.00	20.00
12 Pee Wee Reese CO	15.00	40.00
13 Rip Repulski	8.00	20.00
14 Vin Scully ANN Jerry Doggett ANN	8.00	20.00
15 Duke Snider	15.00	40.00

1960 Dodgers Bell Brand

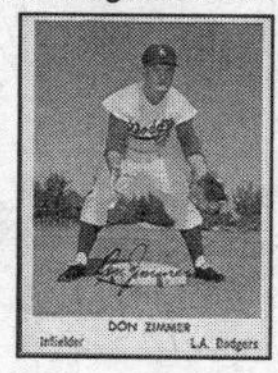

The 1960 Bell Brand Potato Chips set of 20 full color, numbered cards features Los Angeles Dodgers only. Because these cards, measuring approximately 2 1/2" by 3 1/2", were issued in packages of potato chips, many cards suffered from stains. Clem Labine, Johnny Klippstein, and Walt Alston are somewhat more difficult to obtain than other cards in the set; they are marked with SP (short printed) in the checklist below. The catalog designation for this set is F339-2.

COMPLETE SET (20)	500.00	1,000.00
COMMON CARD (1-20)	8.00	20.00
COMMON SP	50.00	100.00
1 Norm Larker	8.00	20.00
2 Duke Snider	50.00	100.00
3 Danny McDevitt	8.00	20.00
4 Jim Gilliam	12.50	30.00
5 Rip Repulski	8.00	20.00
6 Clem Labine SP	60.00	120.00
7 John Roseboro	8.00	20.00
8 Carl Furillo	10.00	25.00
9 Sandy Koufax	100.00	200.00
10 Joe Pignatano	8.00	20.00
11 Chuck Essegian	8.00	20.00
12 John Klippstein SP	50.00	100.00
13 Ed Roebuck	8.00	20.00
14 Don Demeter	8.00	20.00
15 Roger Craig	10.00	25.00
16 Stan Williams	8.00	20.00
17 Don Zimmer	10.00	25.00
18 Walt Alston SP MG	75.00	150.00
19 Johnny Podres	12.50	30.00
20 Maury Wills	15.00	40.00

1960 Dodgers Jay Publishing

This set of the Los Angeles Dodgers measures approximately 5" by 7" and features black-and-white player photos in a white border. The backs are blank. These cards were originally packaged 12 to a packet. The set is more than 12 cards as changes during the season necessitated a second printing. The cards are unnumbered and checklisted below in alphabetical order.

COMPLETE SET (16)	20.00	50.00
1 Roger Craig	1.25	3.00
2 Don Demeter	1.25	3.00
3 Don Drysdale	2.50	6.00
4 Ron Fairly	1.50	4.00
5 Junior Gilliam	2.00	5.00
6 Gil Hodges	2.50	6.00
7 Frank Howard	2.00	5.00
8 Norm Larker	1.25	3.00
9 Wally Moon	1.50	4.00
10 Charlie Neal	1.25	3.00
11 Johnny Podres	2.00	5.00
12 John Roseboro	1.50	4.00
13 Larry Sherry	1.25	3.00
14 Duke Snider	2.50	6.00
15 Stan Williams	1.25	3.00
16 Maury Wills	2.00	5.00

1960 Dodgers Morrell

The cards in this 12-card set measure 2 1/2" by 3 1/2". The 1960 Morrell Meats set of full color, unnumbered cards is similar in format to the 1959 Morrell set but can be distinguished from the 1959 set by a red heart which appears in the Morrell logo on the back. The photos used are the same as those selected for the Dodger team issue postcards in 1960. The Furillo, Hodges, and Snider cards received limited distribution and are hence more scarce. The catalog designation is F172-2. The cards were printed in Japan.

COMPLETE SET (12)	600.00	1,200.00
COMMON CARD (1-12)	12.50	30.00
COMMON SP	60.00	120.00
1 Walt Alston MG	40.00	80.00
2 Roger Craig	15.00	40.00
3 Don Drysdale	60.00	120.00
4 Carl Furillo SP	60.00	120.00
5 Gil Hodges SP	125.00	250.00
6 Sandy Koufax	150.00	300.00
7 Wally Moon	12.50	30.00
8 Charlie Neal	12.50	30.00
9 Johnny Podres	20.00	50.00
10 John Roseboro	12.50	30.00
11 Larry Sherry	12.50	30.00
12 Duke Snider SP	200.00	400.00

1960 Dodgers Postcards

These 12 postcards feature members of the 1960 Los Angeles Dodgers. These cards are unnumbered and we have sequenced them in alphabetical order. The Furillo card is very scarce as he was released midway through the season and this card is thereford presumed no longer circulated after that point. We are considering the Furillo card a SP

COMPLETE SET (12)	30.00	60.00
COMMON PLAYER (1-10)	1.00	2.50
COMMON SP	4.00	10.00
1 Walt Alston MG	2.00	5.00
2 Roger Craig	1.25	3.00
3 Don Drysdale	3.00	8.00
4 Carl Furillo SP	4.00	10.00
5 Gil Hodges	2.00	5.00
6 Sandy Koufax	4.00	10.00
7 Wally Moon	1.25	3.00
8 Charlie Neal	1.00	2.50
9 Johnny Podres	1.50	4.00
10 Johnny Roseboro	1.25	3.00
11 Larry Sherry	1.00	2.50
12 Duke Snider	3.00	8.00

1960 Dodgers Team Issue

These 20 blank-backed, black-and-white photos of the 1960 Dodgers have white borders around posed player shots and measure approximately 5" by 7". The pictures came in a manila envelope that carried the year of issue. The player's facsimile autograph appears in the margin below each photo. The photos are unnumbered and checklisted below in alphabetical order.

COMPLETE SET (20)	40.00	80.00
1 Walter Alston MG	2.00	5.00
2 Bob Bragan CO	1.00	2.50
3 Roger Craig	1.25	3.00
4 Don Demeter	1.00	2.50
5 Don Drysdale	3.00	8.00
6 Chuck Essegian	1.00	2.50
7 Jim Gilliam	1.50	4.00
8 Gil Hodges	3.00	8.00
9 Frank Howard	1.50	4.00
10 Sandy Koufax	6.00	15.00
11 Norm Larker	1.00	2.50
12 Wally Moon	1.00	2.50
13 Charlie Neal	1.00	2.50
14 Johnny Podres	1.50	4.00
15 Pete Reiser CO	1.00	2.50
16 John Roseboro	1.25	3.00
17 Larry Sherry	1.25	3.00
18 Duke Snider	3.00	8.00
19 Stan Williams	1.00	2.50
20 Maury Wills	2.00	5.00

1960 Dodgers Union Oil

The set contains 23, 16-page unnumbered booklets which describe and give more detailed biographies of the player on the front covers. These booklets were given away at Union Oil gas stations and covered members of the 1960 Los Angeles Dodgers. The back page of the booklets had the Dodger schedule on it along with an ad for Union Oil. They are sometimes referenced as "Meet the Dodger Family" booklets. Each booklet measures approximately 5 3/8" by 7 1/2".

COMPLETE SET (23)	40.00	80.00
1 Walt Alston MG	2.00	5.00
2 Roger Craig	1.25	3.00
3 Tom Davis	1.50	4.00
4 Don Demeter	.75	2.00
5 Don Drysdale	4.00	10.00
6 Chuck Essegian	.75	2.00
7 Jim Gilliam	1.50	4.00
8 Gil Hodges	4.00	10.00
9 Frank Howard	1.50	4.00
10 Sandy Koufax	8.00	20.00
11 Norm Larker	.75	2.00
12 Wally Moon	1.25	3.00
13 Charlie Neal	.75	2.00
14 Johnny Podres	1.50	4.00
15 Ed Roebuck	.75	2.00
16 John Roseboro	1.25	3.00
17 Larry Sherry	.75	2.00
18 Norm Sherry	.75	2.00
19 Duke Snider	4.00	10.00
20 Stan Williams	.75	2.00
21 Maury Wills	2.00	5.00
22 Dodger Broadcasters/(Vin Scully and Jerry Dogget	1.25	3.00
23 Dodger Coaches Greg Mulleavy CO Joe Becker CO B	.75	2.00

1961 Dodgers Bell Brand

The 1961 Bell Brand Potato Chips set of 20 full color cards features Los Angeles Dodger players only and is numbered by the uniform numbers of the players. The cards are slightly smaller (approximately 2 7/16" by 3 1/2") than the 1960 Bell Brand cards and are on thinner paper stock. The catalog designation is F339-3.

COMPLETE SET (20)	250.00	500.00
3 Willie Davis	12.50	30.00
4 Duke Snider	50.00	100.00
5 Norm Larker	8.00	20.00
8 John Roseboro	10.00	25.00
9 Wally Moon	10.00	25.00
11 Bob Lillis	8.00	20.00
12 Tommy Davis	12.50	30.00
14 Gil Hodges	15.00	40.00
16 Don Demeter	8.00	20.00
19 Jim Gilliam	12.50	30.00
22 John Podres	12.50	30.00
24 Walt Alston MG	15.00	40.00
30 Maury Wills	15.00	40.00
32 Sandy Koufax	75.00	150.00
34 Norm Sherry	8.00	20.00
37 Ed Roebuck	8.00	20.00
38 Roger Craig	10.00	25.00
40 Stan Williams	8.00	20.00
43 Charlie Neal	8.00	20.00
51 Larry Sherry	8.00	20.00

1961 Dodgers Jay Publishing

This 12-card set of the Los Angeles Dodgers measures approximately 5" by 7". The fronts feature black-and-white posed player portraits with the player's and team name printed below in the white border. The backs are blank. The cards are unnumbered and checklisted below in alphabetical order.

COMPLETE SET (11)	15.00	40.00
1 Walt Alston MG	2.00	5.00
2 Don Drysdale	3.00	8.00
3 Junior Gilliam	1.50	4.00
4 Frank Howard	1.50	4.00
5 Norm Larker	.75	2.00
6 Wally Moon	.75	2.00
7 Charlie Neal	.75	2.00
8 Johnny Podres	1.50	4.00
9 John Roseboro	.75	2.00
10 Larry Sherry	.75	2.00
11 Stan Williams	.75	2.00
12 Maury Wills	2.00	5.00

1961 Dodgers Morrell

The cards in this six-card set measure 2 1/2" by 3 1/2". The 1961 Morrell Meats set of full color, unnumbered cards features Los Angeles Dodger players only and contains statistical information on the backs of the cards in brown print. The catalog designation is F172-3.

COMPLETE SET (6)	600.00	1,200.00
1 Tommy Davis	50.00	100.00
2 Don Drysdale	150.00	300.00
3 Frank Howard	60.00	120.00
4 Sandy Koufax	300.00	600.00
5 Norm Larker	40.00	80.00
6 Maury Wills	75.00	150.00

1961 Dodgers Union Oil

The set contains 24, 16-page unnumbered booklets which describe and give more detailed biographies of the player on the front covers. These booklets were given away by Union Oil at gas stations and covered members of the 1961 Los Angeles Dodgers. The back page of the booklets had the Dodger schedule on it along with an ad for Union Oil. They are sometimes referenced as "Meet the Dodger Family" booklets. Each booklet measures approximately 5 3/8" by 7 1/2".

COMPLETE SET (24)	50.00	100.00
1 Walt Alston MG	2.00	5.00
2 Roger Craig	1.50	4.00
3 Tommy Davis	1.50	4.00
4 Willie Davis	1.50	4.00
5 Don Drysdale	4.00	10.00
6 Dick Farrell	.75	2.00
7 Ron Fairly	1.25	3.00
8 Jim Gilliam	1.50	4.00
9 Gil Hodges	4.00	10.00
10 Frank Howard	2.00	5.00
11 Sandy Koufax	8.00	20.00
12 Norm Larker	.75	2.00
13 Wally Moon	1.25	3.00
14 Charlie Neal	.75	2.00
15 Ron Perranoski	1.25	3.00
16 Johnny Podres	1.50	4.00
17 John Roseboro	1.25	3.00
18 Larry Sherry	.75	2.00
19 Norm Sherry	.75	2.00
20 Duke Snider	4.00	10.00
21 Daryl Spencer	.75	2.00
22 Stan Williams	.75	2.00
23 Maury Wills	2.00	5.00
24 Dodger Broadcasters/(Vin Scully and Jerry Dogget	1.25	3.00

1962 Dodgers Bell Brand

The 1962 Bell Brand Potato Chips set of 20 full color cards features Los Angeles Dodger players only and is numbered by the uniform numbers of the players. These cards were printed on a high quality glossy paper, much better than the previous two years, virtually eliminating the grease stains. This set is distinguished by a 1962 Home schedule on the backs of the cards. The cards measure 2 7/16" by 3 1/2", the same size as the year before. The catalog designation is F339-4.

COMPLETE SET (20)	500.00	1,000.00
3 Willie Davis	20.00	50.00
4 Duke Snider	75.00	150.00
6 Ron Fairly	15.00	40.00
8 John Roseboro	15.00	40.00
9 Wally Moon	15.00	40.00
12 Tommy Davis	20.00	50.00
16 Ron Perranoski	15.00	40.00
19 Jim Gilliam	20.00	50.00
20 Daryl Spencer	12.50	30.00
22 John Podres	20.00	50.00
24 Walt Alston MG	30.00	60.00
25 Frank Howard	20.00	50.00
30 Maury Wills	30.00	60.00
32 Sandy Koufax	125.00	250.00
34 Norm Sherry	12.50	30.00
37 Ed Roebuck	12.50	30.00
40 Stan Williams	12.50	30.00
51 Larry Sherry	12.50	30.00
53 Don Drysdale	50.00	100.00
56 Lee Walls	12.50	30.00

1962 Dodgers Jay Publishing

This 12-card set of the Los Angeles Dodgers measures approximately 5" by 7". The fronts feature black-and-white posed player photos with the player's and team name printed below in the white border. These cards were packaged 12 in a packet. The backs are blank. The cards are unnumbered and checklisted below in alphabetical order.

COMPLETE SET (12)	30.00	60.00
1 Walt Alston MG	2.00	5.00
2 Don Drysdale	3.00	8.00
3 Ron Fairly	1.25	3.00
4 Jim Gilliam	1.50	4.00
5 Frank Howard	1.25	3.00
6 Sandy Koufax	6.00	15.00
7 Wally Moon	1.00	2.50
8 John Podres	1.25	3.00
9 John Roseboro	1.25	3.00
10 Duke Snider	3.00	8.00
11 Stan Williams	1.00	2.50
12 Maury Wills	2.00	5.00

1962-65 Dodgers Postcards

These ten cards were printed by "Plastic Chrome" and distributed by Mitock and Sons Postcards. All the photos were taken at Dodger Stadium. The backs are red and black with a sketch of Dodgers Stadium on the back in the early cards. These same cards were issued through 1965 so it is really difficult to tell the years apart. We are using the last three numbers printed on the postcard to identify the card number.

COMPLETE SET (10)	40.00	80.00
315 Willie Davis	3.00	8.00
316 Larry Sherry	2.00	5.00
317 Ron Perranoski	2.00	5.00
318 Sandy Koufax	8.00	20.00
319 Frank Howard	4.00	10.00
320 Tommy Davis	2.50	6.00
321 Don Drysdale	6.00	15.00
322 John Roseboro	2.50	6.00
323 Ron Fairly	2.00	5.00
324 Maury Wills	4.00	10.00

1962 Dodgers Volpe

These cards measure 8 3/4" by 11". This set, like many others of the period, were drawn by noted sports artist Nicholas Volpe. They were issued by Union Oil Co/Phillips 76. The backs have a brief biography of Volpe. This set was released one per week during the 1962 season.

COMPLETE SET (24)	125.00	250.00
1 Sandy Koufax	15.00	40.00
2 Wally Moon	3.00	8.00
3 Don Drysdale	8.00	20.00
4 Jim Gilliam	5.00	12.00
5 Larry Sherry	3.00	8.00
6 John Roseboro	4.00	10.00
7 Willie Davis	4.00	10.00
8 Norm Sherry	3.00	8.00
9 Lee Walls	3.00	8.00
10 Stan Williams	3.00	8.00
11 Tommy Davis	4.00	10.00
12 Ron Fairly	4.00	10.00
13 Larry Burright	3.00	8.00
14 Duke Snider	8.00	20.00
15 Ron Perranoski	3.00	8.00
16 Maury Wills	6.00	15.00
17 Frank Howard	5.00	12.00
18 Joe Moeller	3.00	8.00
19 Ed Roebuck	3.00	8.00
20 Andy Carey	3.00	8.00
21 Johnny Podres	5.00	12.00
22 Daryl Spencer	3.00	8.00
23 Doug Camilli	3.00	8.00
24 Tim Harkness	3.00	8.00

1963 Dodgers Jay Publishing

The 1963 Dodgers Jay set consists of 13 cards produced by Jay Publishing. The Skowron card establishes the year of the set, since 1963 was Skowron's only year with the Dodgers. The cards measure approximately 4 3/4" by 7 1/4" and are printed on thin photographic paper stock. The white fronts feature a black-and-white player portrait with the player's name and the team name below. The backs are blank. The cards are packaged 12 to a packet. The cards are unnumbered and checklisted below in alphabetical order. As far as we can tell, the Bill Skowron card was added and the Wally Moon card not issued in the second printing.

COMPLETE SET (13)	20.00	50.00
1 Walt Alston MG	2.00	5.00
2 Tom Davis	1.25	3.00
3 Willie Davis	1.25	3.00
4 Don Drysdale	3.00	8.00
5 Ron Fairly	1.25	3.00
6 Jim Gilliam	1.25	3.00
7 Frank Howard	1.50	4.00
8 Sandy Koufax	6.00	15.00
9 Wally Moon	1.25	3.00
10 Johnny Podres	1.25	3.00
11 John Roseboro	1.00	2.50
12 Bill Skowron	1.25	3.00
13 Maury Wills	2.00	5.00

1964 Dodgers Heads Up

This ten-card blank-backed set was issued in 1964 as a way to further merchandise some of the Los Angeles stars. This set features a large full-color head shot of a player which came with instructiions on how to push out the players face and the rest of the torso. The whole cardboard sheet measures approximately 7 1/4" by 8 1/2". There was a quantity of these items found in the late 1980's. Since these are unnumbered, they are checklisted below alphabetically.

COMPLETE SET (10)	15.00	40.00
1 Tom Davis	1.25	3.00
2 Willie Davis	1.25	3.00
3 Don Drysdale	3.00	8.00
4 Ron Fairly	1.25	3.00
5 Frank Howard	1.50	4.00
6 Sandy Koufax	6.00	15.00
7 Joe Moeller	1.00	2.50
8 Ron Perranoski	1.00	2.50
9 John Roseboro	1.25	3.00
10 Maury Wills	2.00	5.00

1964 Dodgers Jay Publishing

This 12-card set of the Los Angeles Dodgers measures approximately 5" by 7". The fronts feature black-and-white posed player photos with the player's and team name printed below in the white border. These cards were packaged 12 to a packet. The backs are blank. The cards are unnumbered and checklisted below in alphabetical order.

COMPLETE SET (12)	20.00	50.00
1 Walt Alston MG	2.00	5.00
2 Tom Davis	1.25	3.00
3 Willie Davis	1.25	3.00
4 Don Drysdale	3.00	8.00
5 Ron Fairly	1.25	3.00
6 Jim Gilliam	1.50	4.00
7 Frank Howard	1.50	4.00
8 Sandy Koufax	6.00	15.00
9 Wally Moon	1.00	2.50
10 John Podres	1.50	4.00
11 John Roseboro	1.00	2.50
12 Maury Wills	2.00	5.00

1964 Dodgers Volpe

This set which measure approximately 8 1/2" by 11" features members of the L.A. Dodgers and were drawn by noted sports artist Nicholas Volpe. These posters were distributed at local Union 76 gas stations. The drawings featured a large full-size facial shot while the background had the player dressed in street clothes.

COMPLETE SET	100.00	200.00
1 Willie Davis	4.00	10.00
2 Tommy Davis	6.00	15.00
3 Don Drysdale	8.00	20.00
4 Ron Fairly	4.00	10.00
5 Jim Gilliam	4.00	10.00
6 Frank Howard	6.00	15.00
7 Sandy Koufax	12.50	30.00
8 Bob Miller	3.00	8.00
9 Joe Moeller	3.00	8.00
10 Wally Moon	4.00	10.00
11 Phil Ortega	3.00	8.00
12 Wes Parker	5.00	12.00
13 Ron Perranoski	3.00	8.00
14 Johnny Podres	4.00	10.00
15 John Roseboro	4.00	10.00
16 Dick Tracewski	3.00	8.00
17 Lee Walls	3.00	8.00
18 Maury Wills	6.00	15.00

1965 Dodgers Jay Publishing

These 12 cards feature members of the World Champion Los Angeles Dodgers. They were issued in a pack as a 12 card set and the cards are unnumbered and checklisted below in alphabetical order. This set was issued twice to correct the Tommy and Willie Davis misidentifications.

COMPLETE SET (14)	30.00	60.00
1 Walter Alston MG	2.00	5.00
2A Tommy Davis ERR Photo is Willie Davis	2.00	5.00
2B Tommy Davis COR	2.00	5.00
3A Willie Davis ERR Photo is Tommy Davis	2.00	5.00
3B Willie Davis COR	2.00	5.00
4 Don Drysdale	3.00	8.00
5 Ron Fairly	1.25	3.00
6 Lou Johnson	1.00	2.50
7 Sandy Koufax	6.00	15.00
8 Jim Lefebvre	1.25	3.00
9 Claude Osteen	1.00	2.50
10 Wes Parker	1.25	3.00
11 John Roseboro	1.25	3.00
12 Maury Wills	2.00	5.00

1965 Dodgers Team Issue

These 21 blank-backed, black-and-white photos of the 1965 Los Angeles Dodgers have white borders around posed player shots and measure approximately 5" by 7". The player's facsimile autograph appears in the bottom margin on each photo. The pictures came in an undated manila envelope. The year of issue was determined to be 1965 because that was Dick Tracewski's last year with the Dodgers and Lou Johnson's first. The photos are unnumbered and checklisted below in alphabetical order.

COMPLETE SET (21)	30.00	60.00
1 Walter Alston MG	1.50	4.00
2 Willie Crawford	.60	1.50
3 Tommy Davis	1.25	3.00
4 Willie Davis	1.25	3.00
5 Don Drysdale	2.50	6.00
6 Ron Fairly	.75	2.00
7 Derrell Griffith	.60	1.50
8 Lou Johnson	.60	1.50
9 John Kennedy	.60	1.50
10 Sandy Koufax	6.00	15.00
11 Bob Miller	.60	1.50
12 Nate Oliver	.60	1.50
13 Claude Osteen	.75	2.00
14 Wes Parker	.75	2.00
15 Ron Perranoski	.75	2.00
16 Johnny Podres	1.25	3.00
17 John Purdin	.60	1.50
18 Howie Reed	.60	1.50
19 John Roseboro	.75	2.00
20 Dick Tracewski	.60	1.50
21 Maury Wills	1.50	4.00

1970 Dodgers Team Issue

These blank-backed cards featured members of the 1970 Los Angeles Dodgers. The fronts have a player photo with the fascimile autograph on the bottom. These photos were sold in a special envelope which said 20 individual pictures 50 cents and photo of the stadium and a drawing on the envelope. Since these cards are unnumbered, we have sequenced them in alphabetical order.

COMPLETE SET	15.00	40.00
1 Walter Alston MG	1.25	3.00
2 Jim Brewer	.75	2.00
3 Willie Crawford	.75	2.00
4 Willie Davis	1.00	2.50
5 Alan Foster	.75	2.00
6 Len Gabrielson	.75	2.00
7 Bill Grabarkewitz	.75	2.00
8 Tom Haller	.75	2.00
9 Andy Kosco	.75	2.00
10 Ray Lamb	.75	2.00
11 Jim Lefebvre	.75	2.00
12 Joe Moeller	.75	2.00
13 Manny Mota	1.00	2.50
14 Fred Norman	.75	2.00
15 Claude Osteen	.75	2.00
16 Wes Parker	.75	2.00
17 Bill Singer	.75	2.00
18 Ted Sizemore	.75	2.00
19 Bill Sudakis	.75	2.00
20 Maury Wills	1.50	4.00

1971 Dodgers Photos

These photos featured the members of the 1971 Los Angeles Dodgers. They are unnumbered and are therefore sequenced alphabetically. It is possible there are more photos so any additions to this list is appreciated.

COMPLETE SET	15.00	40.00
1 Walt Alston MG	2.00	5.00
2 Bill Buckner	1.50	4.00
3 Jim Brewer	.75	2.00
4 Willie Crawford	.75	2.00
5 Bill Grabarkewitz	.75	2.00
6 Jim Lefebvre	1.25	3.00
7 Pete Mikkelsen	.75	2.00
8 Joe Moeller	.75	2.00
9 Manny Mota	1.25	3.00
10 Danny Ozark CO	.75	2.00
11 Jose Pena	.75	2.00
12 Bill Russell	1.50	4.00
13 Duke Sims	.75	2.00
14 Bill Singer	1.25	3.00
15 Mike Strahler	.75	2.00
16 Billy Sudakis	.75	2.00
17 Don Sutton	2.50	6.00
18 Bobby Valentine	1.50	4.00

1971 Dodgers Ticketron

The 1971 Ticketron Los Angeles Dodgers set is a 20-card set with cards measuring approximately 4" by 6". This set has a 1971 Garvey rookie year card as well as 18 other players including Richie Allen in his only year as a Dodger. The fronts are beautiful full-color photos which also have a facsimile autograph on the front and are borderless while the backs contain an advertisement for Ticketron, the 1971 Dodger home schedule and a list of promotional events scheduled for 1971. These unnumbered cards are listed in alphabetical order for convenience.

COMPLETE SET (20)	30.00	60.00
1 Richie Allen	2.00	5.00
2 Walt Alston MG	2.00	5.00
3 Jim Brewer	.75	2.00
4 Willie Crawford	.75	2.00
5 Willie Davis	1.25	3.00
6 Steve Garvey	6.00	15.00
7 Bill Grabarkewitz	.75	2.00
8 Jim Lefebvre	1.25	3.00
9 Pete Mikkelsen	.75	2.00
10 Joe Moeller	.75	2.00
11 Manny Mota	1.25	3.00
12 Claude Osteen	1.25	3.00
13 Wes Parker	1.25	3.00
14 Bill Russell	1.50	4.00
15 Duke Sims	.75	2.00
16 Bill Singer	.75	2.00
17 Bill Sudakis	.75	2.00
18 Don Sutton	3.00	8.00
19 Maury Wills	2.00	5.00
20 Vic Scully ANN and Jerry Doggett ANN	1.50	4.00

1972 Dodgers McDonald's

These borderless discs have color player photos on the front. The backs have the player's name, some biographical information and the 1971 statistics. Since these discs are unnumbered, we have sequenced them in alphabetical order. These items are also known as photoballs.

COMPLETE SET	100.00	200.00
1 Walter Alston MG	6.00	15.00
2 Red Adams CO	4.00	10.00
3 Willie Crawford	4.00	10.00
4 Willie Davis	5.00	12.00
5 Al Downing	4.00	10.00
6 Jim Gilliam CO	5.00	12.00
7 Jim LeFebvre	4.00	10.00
8 Pete Mikkelsen	4.00	10.00
9 Manny Mota	5.00	12.00
10 Wes Parker	5.00	12.00
11 Claude Osteen	4.00	10.00
12 Bill Russell	4.00	10.00
13 Duke Sims	4.00	10.00
14 Bill Sudakis	4.00	10.00
15 Don Sutton	8.00	20.00
16 Bobby Valentine	6.00	15.00
17 Maury Wills	8.00	20.00

1973 Dodgers 1941 TCMA

This 32-card set features blue tinted photos of the 1941 National League Champion Brooklyn Dodgers. The backs carry player information. The cards are unnumbered and checklisted below alphabetically.

COMPLETE SET (32)	12.50	30.00
1 John Allen	.40	1.00
2 Mace Brown	.40	1.00
3 Adolf Camilli	.75	2.00
4 Hugh Casey	.60	1.50
5 Curtis Davis	.40	1.00
6 Thomas Drake	.40	1.00
7 Leo Durocher	1.50	4.00
8 Fred Fitzsimmons	1.00	2.50
9 Herman Franks	.40	1.00
10 August Galan	.60	1.50
11 Angelo Giuliani	.40	1.00
12 Luke Hamlin	.40	1.00
13 William Herman	1.00	2.50
14 Walter Higby	.40	1.00
15 Alex Kampouris	.40	1.00
16 Newell Kimball	.40	1.00
17 Cookie Lavagetto	.60	1.50
18 Joseph Medwick	1.00	2.50
19 Van Lingle Mungo	.60	1.50
20 N.L. Champion Card	.40	1.00
21 Mickey Owen	.40	1.00
22 Babe Phelps	.40	1.00
23 Pee Wee Reese	2.00	5.00
24 Harold Reiser	.60	1.50
25 Lewis Riggs	.40	1.00
26 William Swift	.40	1.00
27 Vitautis Tamulis	.40	1.00
28 Joseph Vosmik	.40	1.00
29 Dixie Walker	.75	2.00
30 Paul Waner	1.25	3.00
31 James Wasdell	.40	1.00
32 John Wyatt	.60	1.50

1973 Dodgers Postcards

These fifteen cards were created by Kolor View Press and were distributed by Mitock and Sonds. The fronts show clear photographs and the backs are in black print and all these cards are labeled KV5251. Since these cards are unnumbered, we have sequenced them in alphabetical order.

COMPLETE SET	12.50	30.00

1 Bill Buckner 1.00 2.50
2 Ron Cey 1.50 4.00
3 Willie Davis 1.00 2.50
4 Joe Ferguson .75 2.00
5 Tommy John 1.25 3.00
6 Lee Lacy .75 2.00
7 Tom Lasorda CO 1.50 4.00
8 Dave Lopes 1.25 3.00
9 Andy Messersmith .75 2.00
10 Manny Mota 1.00 2.50
11 Claude Osteen .75 2.00
12 Tom Paciorek .75 2.00
13 Bill Russell .75 2.00
14 Don Sutton 1.50 4.00
15 Steve Yeager 1.00 2.50

1973 Dodgers Team Issue

These 20 5" by 7" blank-backed black and white photos with fascimile autographs on the bottom feature members of the 1973 Los Angeles Dodgers. They were sold at the ballpark for 50 cents for the 20 photos. Since the photos are unnumbered, we have sequenced them in alphabetical order.

COMPLETE SET (20) 6.00 15.00
1 Walt Alston MG .60 1.50
2 Red Adams CO .20 .50
3 Jim Brewer .20 .50
4 Bill Buckner .40 1.00
5 Ron Cey .60 1.50
6 Willie Davis .30 .75
7 Joe Ferguson .20 .50
8 Steve Garvey 1.25 3.00
9 Jim Gilliam CO .30 .75
10 Charlie Hough .30 .75
11 Tommy John .60 1.50
12 Lee Lacy .20 .50
13 Tom Lasorda CO .60 1.50
14 Davey Lopes .40 1.00
15 Manny Mota .20 .50
16 Tom Paciorek .20 .50
17 Doug Rau .20 .50
18 Pete Richert .20 .50
19 Bill Russell .20 .50
20 Don Sutton .75 2.00

1974 Dodgers 1952 TCMA Black/White Red Names

This 40-card set features players from the 1952 Brooklyn Dodgers team. The player photos can be found in three different color variations: blue and white photos with red names, black and white photos with red names, and blue and white photos with black names.The backs carry player information.

COMPLETE SET (40) 20.00 50.00
1 1952 Cover Card .60 1.50
2 Cal Abrams .40 1.00
3 Sandy Amoros .60 1.50
4 Joe Black 1.00 2.50
5 Rocky Bridges .40 1.00
6 Ralph Branca .60 1.50
7 Roy Campanella 2.00 5.00
8 Billy Cox .75 2.00
9 Chuck Dressen MG .60 1.50
10 Carl Furillo 1.00 2.50
11 Jim Hughes .40 1.00
12 Billy Herman CO .60 1.50
13 Carl Erskine 1.00 2.50
14 Gil Hodges 1.25 3.00
15 Thomas Holmes .40 1.00
16 Richard Williams .60 1.50
17 Clyde King .40 1.00
18 Stephen Lembo .40 1.00
19 Ken Lehman .40 1.00
20 Joe Landrum .40 1.00
21 Clem Labine .75 2.00
22 Ray Moore .40 1.00
23 Bob Morgan .40 1.00
24 Ron Negray .40 1.00
25 Rocky Nelson .40 1.00
26 Jake Pitler CO .40 1.00
27 Billy Loes .40 1.00
28 Cookie Lavagetto .40 1.00
29 Andy Pafko .60 1.50
30 Bud Podbielan .40 1.00
31 Preacher Roe 1.00 2.50
32 John Rutherford .40 1.00
33 Harold Reese 1.25 3.00
34 Jackie Robinson 2.00 5.00
35 George Shuba .40 1.00
36 Johnny Schmitz .40 1.00
37 Duke Snider 1.25 3.00
38 Chris Van Cuyk .40 1.00
39 Ben Wade .40 1.00
40 Rube Walker .40 1.00

1974 Dodgers 1890 Program TCMA

This 16-card set contains copies of information included in the 1890 Brooklyn Dodgers programs. The cards measure approximately 4" by 4 1/4" and feature black-and-white player photos with artistically designed borders. The backs carry a paragraph about the player. The cards are unnumbered and checklisted below in alphabetical order.

COMPLETE SET (16) 3.00 8.00
1 Oyster Burns .30 .75
2 Doc Bushong .30 .75
3 Robert Lee Caruthers .60 1.50
4 Robert H. Clark .20 .50
5 Hubbert Collins .20 .50
6 John S. Corkhill .20 .50
7 Thomas P. Daly .20 .50
8 Dave Foutz .20 .50
9 Michael F. Hughes .20 .50
10 Thomas J. Lovett .20 .50
11 Bill McGunnigle MG .20 .50
12 Wm. D. O'Brien .20 .50
13 George Burton Pinkney .20 .50
14 George J. Smith .20 .50
15 George T. Stallings .30 .75
16 Wm. H. Terry .20 .50

1975 Dodgers All-Time TCMA

This 12-card set features black-and-white photos with white borders of all-time Dodgers great players. The cards are unnumbered and checklisted below in alphabetical order.

COMPLETE SET (12) 8.00 20.00
1 Walter Alston .20 .50
2 Roy Campanella .75 2.00
3 Hugh Casey .20 .50
4 Don Drysdale .75 2.00
5 Junior Gilliam .40 1.00
6 Gil Hodges .75 2.00
7 Sandy Koufax 1.25 3.00
8 Pee Wee Reese 1.00 2.50
9 Jackie Robinson 2.00 5.00
10 Duke Snider 1.25 3.00
11 Dixie Walker .40 1.00
12 Zack Wheat .60 1.50

1975 Dodgers Postcards

These 15 postcards were issued by Kolor View Press and featured members of the 1975 Dodgers. The fronts feature full-color photos while the backs were issued in black print. The Garvey card has the line "1974 National League MVP" added to the back. These cards are numbered with the prefix "KV7813" and we have used the final number in that sequence as our numbering of this set.

COMPLETE SET (15) 8.00 20.00
1 Bill Buckner .60 1.50
2 Jim Wynn .60 1.50
3 Henry Cruz .40 1.00
4 Rick Auerbach .40 1.00
5 Bill Russell .40 1.00
6 Tom Paciorek .40 1.00
7 Steve Yeager .60 1.50
8 Don Sutton 1.00 2.50
9 Mike Marshall .60 1.50
10 Ron Cey .75 2.00
11 Rick Rhoden .40 1.00
13 Joe Ferguson .40 1.00
15 Davey Lopes .75 2.00
31 Doug Rau .40 1.00
57 Willie Crawford .40 1.00

1976 Dodgers Photo Album

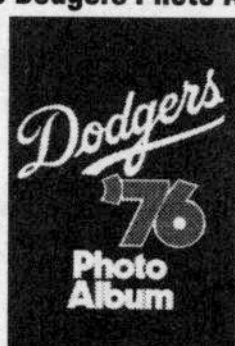

Issued as a photo album, but with easily perforated photos, which measure approximately 5 1/4" by 8 1/2" when seperated, these pictures feature members of the 1976 Los Angeles Dodgers. Since the photos were issued in alphabetical order, we have notated these photos in that order as well.

COMPLETE SET 12.50 30.00
1 Rick Auerbach .40 1.00
2 Dusty Baker .75 2.00
3 Bill Buckner .60 1.50
4 Ron Cey .40 1.00
5 Henry Cruz .40 1.00
6 Al Downing .40 1.00
7 Steve Garvey 1.00 2.50
8 Ed Goodson .40 1.00
9 Burt Hooton .40 1.00
10 Charlie Hough .60 1.50
11 Tommy John 1.00 2.50
12 Lee Lacy .40 1.00
13 Davey Lopes .60 1.50
14 Manny Mota .40 1.00
15 Doug Rau .40 1.00
16 Rick Rhoden .40 1.00
17 Ellie Rodriguez .40 1.00
18 Bill Russell .40 1.00
19 Ted Sizemore .40 1.00
20 Reggie Smith .60 1.50
21 Elias Sosa .40 1.00
22 Don Sutton 1.25 3.00
23 Stan Wall .40 1.00
24 Danny Walton .40 1.00
25 Steve Yeager .40 1.00
26 Walt Alston MG .75 2.00
27 Red Adams CO .40 1.00
Monty Basgall CO
28 Jim Gilliam CO .75 2.00
Tom Lasorda CO

1976 Dodgers Postcards

This 10-card set of the Los Angeles Dodgers measures approximately 3 1/2" by 5 1/2" and features borderless color player photos with a facsimile player autograph printed in white. The backs carry a postcard format.

COMPLETE SET (10) 5.00 12.00
1 Walt Alston .75 2.00
2 Ron Cey .75 2.00
3 Tommy John .75 2.00
4 Davey Lopes .60 1.50
5 Charlie Hough .50 1.25
6 Steve Garvey 1.25 3.00
7 Mike Marshall .40 1.00
8 Joe Ferguson .40 1.00
9 Dusty Baker .60 1.50
10 Burt Hooton .40 1.00

1977-78 Dodgers Photos

This 15-card set of the Los Angeles Dodgers features color player photos in white borders measuring approximately 8" by 10" and with a facsimile autograph. The backs are blank. There is no way to tell if the set was produced in 1977 or 1978. It could be either year. The cards are unnumbered and checklisted below in alphabetical order.

COMPLETE SET (15) 15.00 40.00
1 Ron Cey .75 2.00
2 Steve Garvey 2.00 5.00
3 Burt Hooton .75 2.00
4 Charlie Hough 1.25 3.00
5 Tommy John 1.50 4.00
6 Tom Lasorda MG 2.00 5.00
7 Davey Lopes 1.25 3.00
8 Rick Monday .75 2.00
9 Manny Mota 1.25 3.00
10 Johnny Oates .75 2.00
11 Doug Rau .75 2.00
12 Rick Rhoden .75 2.00
13 Bill Russell .75 2.00
14 Reggie Smith 1.25 3.00
15 Steve Yeager .75 2.00

1978 Dodgers 1941 TCMA

This 43-card set features blue-and-white action photos of the 1941 National League Champion Brooklyn Dodgers in white borders. The backs carry player information. Cards numbers 39 and 40 are oversized and measure 5" by 3".

COMPLETE SET (43) 6.00 15.00
1 Mickey Owen .10 .25
2 Pee Wee Reese .75 2.00
3 Hugh Casey .10 .25
4 Larry French .10 .25
5 Tom Drake .10 .25
6 Ed Albasta .10 .25
7 Tommy Tatum .10 .25
8 Paul Waner .60 1.50
9 Van Lingle Mungo .20 .50
10 Bill Swift .10 .25
11 Dolph Camilli .30 .75
12 Pete Coscarart .10 .25
13 Vito Tamulis .10 .25
14 Johnny Allen .10 .25
15 Lee Grissom .10 .25
16 Billy Herman .40 1.00
17 Joe Vosmik .10 .25
18 Babe Phelps .10 .25
19 Mace Brown .10 .25
20 Freddie Fitzsimmons .20 .50
21 Tony Giuliani .10 .25
22 Lew Riggs .10 .25
23 Jimmy Wasdell .10 .25
24 Herman Franks .10 .25
25 Alex Kampouris .10 .25
26 Kirby Higby .10 .25
27 Ducky Medwick .40 1.00
28 Newt Kimball .10 .25
29 Curt Davis .10 .25
30 Augie Galan .10 .25
31 Luke Hamlin .10 .25
32 Cookie Lavagetto .10 .25
33 Joe Gallagher .10 .25
34 Whit Wyatt .20 .50
35 Dixie Walker .30 .75
36 Pete Reiser .40 1.00
37 Leo Durocher MG .40 1.00
38 Pee Wee Reese .60 1.50
Ducky Medwick
39 Dixie Walker
Joe Medwick
Dolph Camilli
Pete Reiser
40 Joe Medwick
Billy Herman
Pee Wee Reese
Pete Reiser
Mickey Owen
Whit Wyatt
41 Kemp Wicker .10 .25
42 George Pfister CO .10 .25
43 Chuck Dressen CO .10 .25

1979 Dodgers Blue

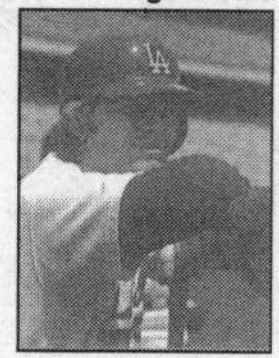

This 15-card standard-size set features full-bleed posed color player photos. The backs are white and carry the slogan "Go Dodger Blue," the player's name, uniform number, batting and throwing preference and a player profile. The cards are unnumbered and checklisted below in alphabetical order.

COMPLETE SET (15) 4.00 10.00
1 Dusty Baker .40 1.00
2 Ron Cey .40 1.00
3 Terry Forster .20 .50
4 Steve Garvey .60 1.50
5 Burt Hooton .20 .50
6 Charlie Hough .30 .75
7 Tom Lasorda MG .60 1.50
8 Davey Lopes .40 1.00
9 Rick Monday .30 .75
10 Manny Mota .30 .75
11 Doug Rau .20 .50
12 Bill Russell .20 .50
13 Reggie Smith .40 1.00
14 Don Sutton .60 1.50
15 Steve Yeager .30 .75

1979 Dodgers Postcards

These were the only new postcards issued of Dodger players in 1979. Other than Bob Welch who was playing his first full season, most of the other players were acquired from other teams.

COMPLETE SET 1.25 3.00
1 Joe Ferguson .20 .50
2 Charlie Hough .30 .75
3 Andy Messersmith .20 .50
4 Derrel Thomas .20 .50
5 Gary Thomasson .20 .50
6 Bob Welch .40 1.00

1980 Dodgers Greats TCMA

This 12-card standard-size set features some leading all-time Brooklyn Dodgers. The fronts have a player photo in the middle with the words "All-Time Dodgers" on top and his name on the bottom. The backs have vital statistics, a biography as well as career totals.

COMPLETE SET (12) 3.00 8.00
1 Gil Hodges .40 1.00
2 Jim Gilliam .20 .50
3 Pee Wee Reese .60 1.50
4 Jackie Robinson 1.00 2.50
5 Sandy Koufax .75 2.00
6 Zach Wheat .20 .50
7 Dixie Walker .20 .50
8 Hugh Casey .08 .25
9 Dazzy Vance .20 .50
10 Duke Snider .60 1.50
11 Roy Campanella .60 1.50
12 Walter Alston MG .20 .50

1980 Dodgers Police

The cards in this 30-card set measure approximately 2 13/16" by 4 1/8". The full color 1980 Police Los Angeles Dodgers set features the player's name, uniform number, position, and biographical data on the fronts in addition to the photo. The backs feature Tips from the Dodgers, the LAPD logo, and the Dodgers' logo. The cards are listed below according to uniform number.

COMPLETE SET (30) 5.00 12.00
5 Johnny Oates .08 .25
6 Steve Garvey .40 1.00

7 Steve Yeager	.20	.50
8 Reggie Smith	.30	.75
9 Gary Thomasson	.08	.25
10 Ron Cey	.30	.75
12 Dusty Baker	.30	.75
13 Joe Ferguson	.08	.25
15 Davey Lopes	.30	.75
16 Rick Monday	.20	.50
18 Bill Russell	.08	.25
20 Don Sutton	.60	1.50
21 Jay Johnstone	.20	.50
23 Teddy Martinez	.08	.25
27 Joe Beckwith	.08	.25
28 Pedro Guerrero	.50	1.25
29 Don Stanhouse	.08	.25
30 Derrel Thomas	.08	.25
31 Doug Rau	.08	.25
34 Ken Brett	.08	.25
35 Bob Welch	.20	.50
37 Robert Castillo	.08	.25
38 Dave Goltz	.08	.25
41 Jerry Reuss	.20	.50
43 Rick Sutcliffe	.60	1.50
44 Mickey Hatcher	.08	.25
46 Burt Hooton	.20	.50
49 Charlie Hough	.30	.75
51 Terry Forster	.20	.50
NNO Team Card	.20	.50

1980 Dodgers TCMA 1959

This 40-card standard-size set features members of the 1959 Los Angeles Dodgers, who became the first team to win a World Series while playing on the West Coast. The cards have white blue with Dodger Blue borders inside them. There is a player photo and his name and position are on the bottom. The horizontal backs have vital stats as well as a blurb about the player and his 1959 and career stats

COMPLETE SET (40)	10.00	25.00
1 Joe Pignatano	.08	.25
2 Carl Furillo	.30	.75
3 Bob Lillis	.08	.25
4 Chuck Essegian	.08	.25
5 Dick Gray	.08	.25
6 Rip Repulski	.08	.25
7 Jim Baxes	.08	.25
8 Frank Howard	.40	1.00
9 Solly Drake	.08	.25
10 Sandy Amoros	.08	.25
11 Norm Sherry	.08	.25
12 Tommy Davis	.20	.50
13 Jim Gilliam	.20	.50
14 Duke Snider	.60	1.50
15 Maury Wills	.40	1.00
16 Don Demeter	.08	.25
17 Wally Moon	.20	.50
18 John Roseboro	.20	.50
19 Ron Fairly	.20	.50
20 Norm Larker	.08	.25
21 Charlie Neal	.08	.25
22 Don Zimmer	.30	.75
23 Chuck Dressen CO	.20	.50
24 Gil Hodges	.40	1.00
25 Joe Becker CO	.08	.25
26 Walter Alston MG	.40	1.00
27 Greg Mulleavy	.08	.25
28 Don Drysdale	.60	1.50
29 Johnny Podres	.08	.25
30 Sandy Koufax	1.00	2.50
31 Roger Craig	.08	.25
32 Danny McDevitt	.08	.25
33 Bill Harris	.08	.25
34 Larry Sherry	.08	.25
35 Stan Williams	.08	.25
36 Clem Labine	.20	.50
37 Chuck Churn	.08	.25
38 Johnny Klippstein	.08	.25
39 Carl Erskine	.20	.50
40 Fred Kipp	.08	.25

1955-62 Don Wingfield

This set of black and white and color postcards was first issued in 1955 and consists of three diffferent types. Type 1 postcards consist of Washington Senatos only and feature the player's name - Washington Nationals, copyright 1955 - Don Wingfield, Griffith Stadium, Washington, D.C., at the base of the front. The type 2 postcards feature players from many teams and present the player's name on the back down the center of the card. The type 3 postcard is in color and consists of but one card (Killebrew). Multiple player poses of several of the Type 2 postcards exist. Cards 1-9 are Type 1 card, Cards 10-43 are Type 2 and Card 44 is Type 3.

COMPLETE SET (43)	250.00	500.00
1 Jim Busby	10.00	20.00
2 Charley Dressen MG	25.00	50.00
3 Ed Fitzgerald	25.00	50.00
4 Bob Porterfield	10.00	20.00
5 Roy Sievers	25.00	50.00
6 Chuck Stobbs	25.00	50.00
7 Dean Stone	25.00	50.00
8 Mickey Vernon	25.00	50.00
9 Eddie Yost	25.00	50.00
10 Ted Abernathy	10.00	20.00
11 Bob Allison (2)	10.00	20.00
12 Ernie Banks	30.00	60.00
13 Earl Battey	10.00	20.00
14 Norm Cash	15.00	30.00
15 Jim Coates	10.00	20.00
16 Rocky Colavito	20.00	40.00
17 Chuck Cottier	10.00	20.00
18 Bennie Daniels	10.00	20.00
19 Dan Dobbek	10.00	20.00
20 Nellie Fox	20.00	40.00
21 Jim Gentile	10.00	20.00
22 Gene Green	10.00	20.00
23 Steve Hamilton	10.00	20.00
24 Ken Hamlin	10.00	20.00
25 Rudy Hernandez	10.00	20.00
26 Ed Hobaugh	10.00	20.00
27 Elston Howard	20.00	40.00
28 Bob Johnson	10.00	20.00
29 Russ Kemmerer	10.00	20.00
30 Harmon Killebrew (3)	25.00	50.00
31 Dale Long	10.00	20.00
32 Mickey Mantle	60.00	120.00
33 Roger Maris	30.00	60.00
34 Willie Mays	40.00	80.00
35 Stan Musial	40.00	80.00
36 Claude Osteen	10.00	20.00
37 Ken Retzer	10.00	20.00
38 Brooks Robinson	25.00	50.00
39 Dick Rudolph	10.00	20.00
40 Dave Stenhouse	10.00	20.00
41 Jose Valdivielso	10.00	20.00
42 Gene Woodling	15.00	30.00
43 Bud Zipfel	10.00	20.00
44 Harmon Killebrew	25.00	50.00

1953-55 Dormand

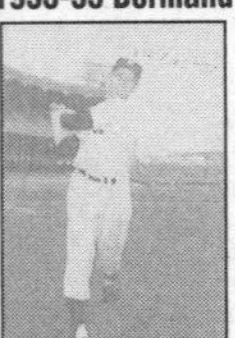

One of the most attractive and popular postcards ever issued are the full color postcards of Louis Dormand, which were issued as premiums by the Mason Candy Company. The cards are numbered on the reverse in the line which seperates the address portion from the message portion of the postcards. Two variations of the McDougald, Collins and Sain exist. Rizzuto and Mantle also exist in a 6" by 9" postcard, and a 9" by 12" postcard also exists. The Hodges card used to be considered quite scarce; however, recent major auction house "warehouse" finds of these cards have significantly increased the supply of these cards to the secondary market..

COMPLETE SET	1,500.00	3,000.00
COMMON POSTCARD	10.00	20.00
COMMON SP	200.00	400.00
101 Phil Rizzuto	25.00	50.00
101A Phil Rizzuto Straight Sig at top	25.00	50.00
101B Phil Rizzuto Straight Sig at top; smaller	25.00	50.00
101C Phil Rizzuto Signature at an angle	25.00	50.00
101D Phil Rizzuto Jumbo 6 by 9	60.00	120.00
102 Yogi Berra	40.00	80.00
103 Ed Lopat	12.50	25.00
104A Hank Bauer Large Sig	20.00	40.00
104B Hank Bauer Smaller Signature	20.00	40.00
105A Joe Collins Patch on Sleeve Signature on Top	10.00	20.00
105B Joe Collins Patch on Sleeve Signature at Bottom	20.00	40.00
105C Joe Collins No Patch on Sleeve Signature at top	20.00	40.00
105D Joe Collins No Patch on Sleeve Signature on Bott	20.00	40.00
106 Ralph Houk	12.50	25.00
107 Bill Miller	10.00	20.00
108 Ray Scarborough	10.00	20.00
109 Allie Reynolds	12.50	25.00
110 Gil McDougald Large Signature	12.50	25.00
110A Gil McDougald Small Signature Variation	20.00	40.00
111 Mickey Mantle Batting Left	60.00	120.00
111A Mickey Mantle Bat on Shoulder	100.00	200.00
111B Mickey Mantle Jumbo 6 by 9	150.00	300.00
111C Mickey Mantle Jumbo 9 by 12	150.00	300.00
112 Johnny Mize	40.00	80.00
113A Casey Stengel MG Signature on Top	40.00	80.00
113B Casey Stengel Signature on Bottom	40.00	80.00
114A Bobby Shantz Signature on Top	10.00	20.00
114B Bobby Shantz Signature at an angle	10.00	20.00
115 Whitey Ford	40.00	80.00
116 Johnny Sain Pitching	12.50	25.00
116A Johnny Sain Winding Up	50.00	100.00
117 Jim McDonald	10.00	20.00
118 Gene Woodling	12.50	25.00
119 Charlie Silvera	10.00	20.00
120 Don Bollweg	10.00	20.00
121 Billy Pierce	12.50	25.00
122 Chico Carrasquel	12.50	25.00
123 Willie Miranda	12.50	25.00
124 Carl Erskine	25.00	50.00
125 Roy Campanella	75.00	150.00
126 Jerry Coleman	12.50	25.00
127 Pee Wee Reese	40.00	80.00
128 Carl Furillo	20.00	40.00
129 Gil Hodges	200.00	400.00
130 Billy Martin	25.00	50.00
132 Irv Noren	10.00	20.00
133 Enos Slaughter	40.00	80.00
134 Tom Gorman	10.00	20.00
135 Eddie Robinson	10.00	20.00
136 Frank Crosetti CO	25.00	50.00
138 Jim Konstanty	50.00	100.00
139 Elston Howard	60.00	120.00
140 Bill Skowron	20.00	40.00

1941 Double Play

The cards in this 75-card set measure approximately 2 1/2" by 3 1/8" was a blank-backed issue distributed by Gum Products. It consists of 75 numbered cards (two consecutive numbers per card), each depicting two players in sepia tone photographs. Cards 81-100 contain action poses, and the last 50 numbers of the set are slightly harder to find. Cards that have been cut in half to form "singles" have a greatly reduced value. These cards have a value from five to ten percent of the uncut strips and are very difficult to sell. The player on the left has an odd number and the other player has an even number. We are using only the odd numbers to identify these panels. Each penny pack contained two cards and they were issued 100 packs to a box.

COMPLETE SET (150)	3,000.00	5,000.00
COMMON PAIRS (1-100)	15.00	40.00
COMMON PAIRS (101-150)	20.00	50.00
WRAPPER (1-CENT)	400.00	500.00
1 L.French/V.Page XRC	50.00	100.00
3 B.Herman/S.Hack	40.00	80.00
5 L.Frey/J.VanderMeer XRC	30.00	60.00
7 P.Derringer/B.Walters	30.00	60.00
9 F.McCormick/B.Werber	15.00	40.00
11 J.Ripple/E.Lombardi	40.00	80.00
13 A.Kampouris/W.Wyatt	15.00	40.00
15 M.Owen/P.Waner	40.00	80.00
17 C.Lavagetto/P.Reiser XRC	20.00	50.00
19 J.Wasdell XRC/D.Camilli	20.00	50.00
21 D.Walker/J.Medwick	40.00	80.00
23 P.Reese XRC/K.Higbe XRC	150.00	300.00
25 H.Danning/C.Melton	15.00	40.00
27 H.Gumbert/B.Whitehead	15.00	40.00
29 J.Orengo XRC/J.Moore	15.00	40.00
31 M.Ott/N.Young	75.00	150.00
33 L.Handley/A.Vaughan	40.00	80.00
35 B.Klinger/S.Brown XRC	15.00	40.00
37 T.Moore XRC/G.Mancuso	20.00	50.00
39 J.Mize XRC/E.Slaughter XRC	125.00	250.00
41 J.Cooney/S.Sisti XRC	15.00	40.00
43 M.West/C.Rowell XRC	15.00	40.00
45 D.Litwhiler XRC/M.May	15.00	40.00
47 F.Hayes/A.Brancato XRC	15.00	40.00
49 B.Johnson/B.Nagel XRC	20.00	50.00
51 B.Newsom/H.Greenberg	75.00	150.00
53 B.McCosky/C.Gehringer	60.00	120.00
55 P.Higgins/D.Bartell	20.00	50.00
57 T.Williams/J.Tabor	400.00	800.00
59 J.Cronin/J.Foxx	150.00	300.00
61 L.Gomez/P.Rizzuto XRC	200.00	400.00
63 J.DiMaggio/C.Keller	300.00	600.00
65 R.Rolfe/B.Dickey	75.00	150.00
67 J.Gordon XRC/R.Ruffing	75.00	150.00
69 M.Tresh XRC/L.Appling	50.00	100.00
71 M.Solters/J.Rigney XRC	15.00	40.00
73 B.Meyer/B.Chapman	20.00	50.00
75 C.Travis/G.Case	20.00	50.00
77 J.Krakauskas/B.Feller	100.00	200.00
79 K.Keltner XRC/H.Trosky	20.00	50.00
81 T.Williams/J.Cronin	250.00	500.00
83 J.Gordon XRC/C.Keller	30.00	60.00
85 H.Greenberg/R.Ruffing	150.00	300.00
87 H.Trosky/G.Case	20.00	50.00
89 M.Ott/B.Whitehead	75.00	150.00
91 H.Danning/H.Gumbert	15.00	40.00
93 N.Young/C.Melton	15.00	40.00
95 J.Ripple/B.Walters	20.00	50.00
97 S.Hack/B.Klinger	20.00	50.00
99 J.Mize XRC/D.Litwhiler XRC	60.00	120.00
101 D.Dallesandro XRC/A.Galan	20.00	50.00
103 B.Lee/P.Cavarretta	30.00	60.00
105 L.Grove/B.Doerr	125.00	250.00
107 F.Pytlak/D.DiMaggio XRC	50.00	100.00
109 J.Priddy XRC/J.Murphy	30.00	60.00
111 T.Henrich/M.Russo XRC	40.00	80.00
113 F.Crosetti/J.Sturm XRC	40.00	80.00
115 I.Goodman/M.McCormick XRC	20.00	50.00
117 E.Joost/E.Koy XRC	20.00	50.00
119 L.Waner/H.Majeski XRC	50.00	100.00
121 B.Hassett/E.Moore	20.00	50.00
123 N.Etten XRC/J.Rizzo	20.00	50.00
125 S.Chapman/W.Moses	20.00	50.00
127 J.Babich/D.Siebert	20.00	50.00
129 N.Potter XRC/B.McCoy XRC	20.00	50.00
131 C.Camp.XRC/L.Boud.XRC	60.00	120.00
133 R.Hemsley/M.Harder	30.00	60.00
135 G.Walker/J.Heving	20.00	50.00
137 J.Rucker/A.Adams XRC	20.00	50.00
139 M.Arnovich/C.Hubbell	75.00	150.00
141 L.Riggs/L.Durocher	60.00	120.00
143 F.Fitzsimmons/J.Vosmik	20.00	50.00
145 F.Crespi XRC/J.Brown	20.00	50.00
147 D.Heffner/H.Clift XRC	20.00	50.00
149 D.Garms/E.Fletcher	30.00	60.00

1978 Dover Publications Baseball Greats

COMPLETE SET (32)	25.00	60.00
1 Grover Cleveland Alexander	1.00	2.50
2 Chief Bender	1.00	2.50
3 Roger Bresnahan	1.00	2.50
4 Joe Bush	.75	2.00
5 Frank Chance	1.00	2.50
6 Ty Cobb	2.00	5.00
7 Eddie Collins	1.00	2.50
8 Stan Coveleski	1.00	2.50
9 Sam Crawford	1.00	2.50
10 Frankie Frisch	1.00	2.50
11 Goose Goslin	1.00	2.50
12 Harry Heilman	1.00	2.50
13 Rogers Hornsby	1.00	2.50
14 Joe Jackson	1.50	4.00
15 Hugh Jennings	1.00	2.50
16 Walter Johnson	1.25	3.00
17 Sam Jones	.75	2.00
18 Rabbit Maranville	1.00	2.50
19 Rube Marquard	1.00	2.50
20 Christy Mathewson	1.25	3.00
21 John McGraw	1.00	2.50
22 Herb Pennock	1.00	2.50
23 Eddie Plank	1.00	2.50
24 Edd Roush	1.00	2.50
25 Babe Ruth	3.00	8.00
26 George Sisler	1.00	2.50
27 Tris Speaker	1.00	2.50
28 Casey Stengel	1.00	2.50
29 Joe Tinker	1.00	2.50
30 Pie Traynor	1.00	2.50
31 Dazzy Vance	1.00	2.50
32 Cy Young	1.25	3.00

1950 Drake's Cookies

The cards in this 36-card set measure approximately 2 1/2" by 2 1/2". The 1950 Drake's Cookies set contains numbered black and white cards. The players are pictured inside a simulated television screen and the caption "TV Baseball Series" appears on the cards. The players selected for this set show a heavy representation of players from New York teams. The catalog designation for this set is D358.

COMPLETE SET (36)	2,500.00	5,000.00
1 Preacher Roe	60.00	120.00
2 Clint Hartung	50.00	100.00
3 Earl Torgeson	50.00	100.00
4 Lou Brissie	50.00	100.00
5 Duke Snider	300.00	600.00
6 Roy Campanella	300.00	600.00
7 Sheldon Jones	50.00	100.00
8 Whitey Lockman	50.00	100.00
9 Bobby Thomson	60.00	120.00
10 Dick Sisler	50.00	100.00
11 Gil Hodges	125.00	250.00
12 Eddie Waitkus	50.00	100.00
13 Bobby Doerr	100.00	200.00
14 Warren Spahn	250.00	500.00
15 Buddy Kerr	50.00	100.00
16 Sid Gordon	50.00	100.00
17 Willard Marshall	50.00	100.00
18 Carl Furillo	60.00	120.00
19 Pee Wee Reese	250.00	500.00
20 Alvin Dark	60.00	120.00
21 Del Ennis	60.00	120.00
22 Ed Stanky	60.00	120.00
23 Tom Henrich	75.00	150.00
24 Yogi Berra	250.00	500.00
25 Phil Rizzuto	125.00	250.00
26 Jerry Coleman	60.00	120.00
27 Joe Page	60.00	120.00
28 Allie Reynolds	60.00	120.00
29 Ray Scarborough	50.00	100.00
30 Birdie Tebbetts	50.00	100.00
31 Maurice McDermott	50.00	100.00
32 Johnny Pesky	60.00	120.00
33 Dom DiMaggio	75.00	150.00
34 Vern Stephens	60.00	120.00
35 Bob Elliott	60.00	120.00
36 Enos Slaughter	125.00	250.00

1894 Duke Cabinets N142

These four cabinets were produced by W.H. Duke. These color cabinets measure approximately 6" X 9 1/2" and a portrait takes up almost the entire card. The player is identified on the bottom.

COMPLETE SET (4)	20,000.00	40,000.00
1 George Davis	5,000.00	10,000.00
2 Ed Delahanty	6,000.00	12,000.00
3 Billy Nash	2,500.00	5,000.00
4 Wilbert Robinson	7,500.00	15,000.00

1893 Duke Talk of the Diamond N135

The 25 cards in Duke's Talk of the Diamond set feature a humorous situation placed alongside a baseball design. Since the reverse lists the manufacturer as a branch of the American Tobacco Company, it is thought that this set was issued about 1893. A list of the 25 titles appears on the back of each card. Most of the baseball designs are similar to those appearing in the Buchner Gold Coin set (N284).

COMPLETE SET (25)	1,250.00	2,500.00
COMMON CARD (1-25)	30.00	80.00

1914 E and S Publishing

These ornate styled postcards produced by the E and S Pub. Co. of Chicago in 1914 are extremely rare. This bluetone cards have a closeup head and shoulders caraciture of the player surrounded by cartoon vignettes of his career done by an obviously gifted cartoonist, possibly from one of the Chicago newspapers. The art is signed T.S. Several additions were made in the past couple years; there are probably others as well; any further additions to this checklist are greatly appreciated.

COMPLETE SET	6,000.00	12,000.00
1 Joe Benz	500.00	1,000.00
2 Ty Cobb	1,500.00	3,000.00
3 Miller Huggins	1,000.00	2,000.00
4 Joe Jackson	1,250.00	2,500.00
5 James Lavender	500.00	1,000.00
6 Christy Mathewson	1,000.00	2,000.00
7 Frank Schulte	500.00	1,000.00
8 Jim Scott	500.00	1,000.00
9 Art Wilson	500.00	1,000.00

1911 Close Candy E94

The cards in this 30-card set measure 1 1/2" by 2 3/4". The E94 format, like that of E93, consists of tinted, black and white photos on solid color backgrounds (seven colors seen; each player seen in more than one color). Issued in 1911, cards from this set may be found with advertising overstamps covering the gray print checklist on the back (begins with Moore). Some blank backs have been found, and the set is identical to M131. Listed pricing for these cards in raw condition references "VG" condition.

COMPLETE SET (30)	50,000.00	100,000.00
1 Jimmy Austin	200.00	350.00
2 Johnny Bates	200.00	350.00
3 Bob Bescher	200.00	350.00
4 Bobby Byrne	200.00	350.00
5 Frank Chance	500.00	800.00
6 Eddie Cicotte	500.00	800.00
7 Ty Cobb	2,500.00	4,000.00
8 Sam Crawford	500.00	800.00
9 Harry Davis	200.00	350.00
10 Art Devlin	200.00	350.00
11 Josh Devore	200.00	350.00
12 Mickey Doolan	200.00	350.00
13 Patsy Dougherty	200.00	350.00
14 Johnny Evers	500.00	800.00
15 Eddie Grant	200.00	350.00
16 Hugh Jennings	350.00	600.00
17 Red Kleinow	200.00	350.00
18 Napoleon Lajoie	500.00	800.00
19 Joe Lake	200.00	350.00
20 Tommy Leach	200.00	350.00
21 Hans Lobert	200.00	350.00
22 Harry Lord	200.00	350.00
23 Sherry Magee	300.00	500.00
24 John McGraw	350.00	600.00
25 Earl Moore	200.00	350.00
26 Red Murray	200.00	350.00
27 Tris Speaker	900.00	1,500.00
28 Terry Turner	200.00	350.00
29 Honus Wagner	1,800.00	3,000.00
30 Cy Young	1,200.00	2,000.00

1909 E92-2 Croft's Candy

The cards in this 50-card set measure 1 1/2" by 2 3/4". Additional advertising backs can also be found for Croft's Candy, Dockman and Son's and Nadja - but pricing for these cards can be found in their own listings. The set contains poses identical to those in E101, E102, and E105. Of note, these cards were printed with the advertising on back done in black, blue and red ink variations. The black ink are most common and our pricing refernces these cards. Blue ink backs are considerably tougher and generally trade for two to three times the listed values. Red ink backs are extremely rare - so much so that establishing consistent values for them remains to this day a nearly impossible task. Finally, our listed prices for raw cards reference VgEx condition given the majority of cards found in this set are typically off-grade. Cards are unnumbered and checklisted alphabetically by each player's last name.

1 Jack Barry	125.00	200.00
2 Harry Bemis	125.00	200.00
3 Chief Bender Striped Cap	350.00	600.00
4 Chief Bender White Cap	350.00	600.00
5 Bill Bergen	125.00	200.00
6 Bob Bescher	125.00	200.00
7 Al Bridwell	125.00	200.00
8 Doc Casey	125.00	200.00
9 Frank Chance	350.00	600.00
10 Hal Chase	175.00	300.00
11 Ty Cobb	3,500.00	6,000.00
12 Eddie Collins	350.00	600.00
13 Sam Crawford	350.00	600.00
14 Harry Davis	125.00	200.00
15 Art Devlin	125.00	200.00
16 Bill Donovan	125.00	200.00
17 Red Dooin	125.00	200.00
18 Mickey Doolan	125.00	200.00
19 Patsy Dougherty	125.00	200.00
20 Larry Doyle Batting	125.00	200.00
21 Larry Doyle Throwing	125.00	200.00
22 Johnny Evers	350.00	600.00
23 George Gibson	125.00	200.00
24 Topsy Hartsel	125.00	200.00
25 Fred Jacklitsch	125.00	200.00
26 Hugh Jennings	125.00	200.00
27 Red Kleinow	125.00	200.00
28 Otto Knabe	125.00	200.00
29 John Knight	125.00	200.00
30 Nap Lajoie	500.00	800.00
31 Hans Lobert	125.00	200.00
32 Sherry Magee	125.00	200.00
33 Christy Mathewson UER	1,200.00	2,000.00
34 John McGraw	350.00	600.00
35 Larry McLean	125.00	200.00
36 Dots Miller Batting	125.00	200.00
37 Dots Miller Fielding	125.00	200.00
38 Danny Murphy	125.00	200.00
39 Bill O'Hara	125.00	200.00
40 Germany Schaefer	125.00	200.00
41 Admiral Schlei	125.00	200.00
42 Boss Smith (Schmidt)	125.00	200.00
43 Dave Shean	125.00	200.00
44 Johnny Seigle (Siegle)	125.00	200.00
45 Frank Smith	125.00	200.00
46 Joe Tinker	350.00	600.00
47 Honus Wagner Batting	2,500.00	4,000.00
48 Honus Wagner Throwing	1,800.00	3,000.00
49 Cy Young	900.00	1,500.00
50 Heinie Zimmerman	125.00	200.00

1909 E92-3 Croft's Cocoa

The cards in this 50-card set measure 1 1/2" by 2 3/4". Additional advertising backs can also be found for Croft's Candy, Dockman and Son's and Nadja - but pricing for these cards can be found in their own listings. The set contains poses identical to those in E101, E102, and E105. Book prices reference VgEx condition given the majority of cards found in this set are typically off-grade. Cards are unnumbered and checklisted alphabetically by each player's last name.

1 Jack Barry	125.00	200.00
2 Harry Bemis	125.00	200.00
3 Chief Bender Striped Cap	350.00	600.00
4 Chief Bender White Cap	350.00	600.00
5 Bill Bergen	125.00	200.00
6 Bob Bescher	125.00	200.00
7 Al Bridwell	125.00	200.00
8 Doc Casey	125.00	200.00
9 Frank Chance	350.00	600.00
10 Hal Chase	175.00	300.00
11 Ty Cobb	3,500.00	6,000.00
12 Eddie Collins	350.00	600.00
13 Sam Crawford	350.00	600.00
14 Harry Davis	125.00	200.00
15 Art Devlin	125.00	200.00
16 Bill Donovan	125.00	200.00
17 Red Dooin	125.00	200.00
18 Mickey Doolan	125.00	200.00
19 Patsy Dougherty	125.00	200.00
20 Larry Doyle Batting	125.00	200.00
21 Larry Doyle Throwing	125.00	200.00
22 Johnny Evers	350.00	600.00
23 George Gibson	125.00	200.00
24 Topsy Hartsel	125.00	200.00
25 Fred Jacklitsch	125.00	200.00
26 Hugh Jennings	350.00	600.00
27 Red Kleinow	125.00	200.00
28 Otto Knabe	125.00	200.00
29 Jack Knight	125.00	200.00
30 Nap Lajoie	500.00	800.00
31 Hans Lobert	125.00	200.00
32 Sherry Magee	125.00	200.00
33 Christy Mathewson UER Matthewson	1,200.00	2,000.00
34 John McGraw	350.00	600.00
35 Larry McLean	125.00	200.00
36 Dots Miller Batting	125.00	200.00
37 Dots Miller Fielding	125.00	200.00
38 Danny Murphy	125.00	200.00
39 Bill O'Hara	125.00	200.00
40 Germany Schaefer	125.00	200.00
41 Admiral Schlei	125.00	200.00
42 Boss Smith (Schmidt)	125.00	200.00
43 Dave Shean	125.00	200.00
44 Johnny Seigle (Siegle)	125.00	200.00
45 Frank Smith	125.00	200.00
46 Joe Tinker	350.00	600.00
47 Honus Wagner Batting	2,500.00	4,000.00
48 Honus Wagner Throwing	1,800.00	3,000.00
49 Cy Young Cleveland	900.00	1,500.00
50 Heinie Zimmerman	125.00	200.00

1909 E92-4 Nadja Caramel

The cards in this 62-card set measure 1 1/2" by 2 3/4". Additional advertising backs can also be found for Croft's Candy, Croft's Cocoa and Dockman and Son's - but pricing for these cards can be found in their own listings. Of note, the Nadja backed set contains a group of St. Louis players unavailable in the other E92 variations. The set contains poses identical to those in E101, E102, and E105. Book prices reference VgEx condition given the majority of cards found in this set are typically off-grade. Cards are unnumbered and checklisted alphabetically by each player's last name.

1 Bill Bailey	125.00	200.00
2 Jack Barry	125.00	200.00
3 Harry Bemis	125.00	200.00
4 Chief Bender Striped Cap	350.00	600.00
5 Chief Bender White Cap	350.00	600.00
6 Bill Bergen	125.00	200.00
7 Bob Bescher	125.00	200.00
8 Roger Bresnahan	350.00	600.00
9 Al Bridwell	125.00	200.00
10 Doc Casey	125.00	200.00
11 Frank Chance	350.00	600.00
12 Hal Chase	175.00	300.00
13 Ty Cobb	3,500.00	6,000.00
14 Eddie Collins	350.00	600.00
15 Sam Crawford	350.00	600.00
16 Harry Davis	125.00	200.00
17 Art Devlin	125.00	200.00
18 Bill Donovan	125.00	200.00
19 Red Dooin	125.00	200.00
20 Mickey Doolan	125.00	200.00
21 Patsy Dougherty	125.00	200.00
22 Larry Doyle Batting	125.00	200.00
23 Larry Doyle Throwing	125.00	200.00
24 Rube Ellis	125.00	200.00
25 Johnny Evers	350.00	600.00
26 George Gibson	125.00	200.00
27 Topsy Hartsel	125.00	200.00
28 Roy Hartzell Batting	125.00	200.00
29 Roy Hartzell Fielding	125.00	200.00
30 Harry Howell Follow Through	125.00	200.00
31 Harry Howell Ready to Pitch	125.00	200.00
32 Fred Jacklitsch	125.00	200.00
33 Hugh Jennings	350.00	600.00
34 Red Kleinow	125.00	200.00
35 Otto Knabe	125.00	200.00
36 Jack Knight	125.00	200.00
37 Nap Lajoie	500.00	800.00
38 Hans Lobert	125.00	200.00
39 Sherry Magee	125.00	200.00
40 Christy Mathewson UER	1,200.00	2,000.00
41 John McGraw	350.00	600.00
42 Larry McLean	125.00	200.00
43 Dots Miller Batting	125.00	200.00
44 Dots Miller Fielding	125.00	200.00
45 Danny Murphy	125.00	200.00
46 Rebel Oakes	125.00	200.00
47 Bill O'Hara	125.00	200.00
48 Ed Phelps	125.00	200.00
49 Germany Schaefer	125.00	200.00
50 Admiral Schlei	125.00	200.00
51 Boss Smith (Schmidt)	125.00	200.00
52 Dave Shean	125.00	200.00
53 Johnny Seigle (Siegle)	125.00	200.00
54 Frank Smith	125.00	200.00
55 George Stone Blue Background	125.00	200.00
56 George Stone Green Background	125.00	200.00
57 Joe Tinker	350.00	600.00
58 Honus Wagner Batting	2,500.00	4,000.00
59 Honus Wagner Throwing	1,800.00	3,000.00
60 Bobby Wallace	250.00	400.00
61 Cy Young	900.00	1,500.00
62 Heinie Zimmerman	125.00	200.00

1910 E98 Set of 30

The cards in this 30-card set measure 1 1/2" by 2 3/4". E98 is an anonymous set with more similarities to Standard Caramel issues than to Briggs. Most players are found with four different background colors and the brown print checklist (starts with "1. Christy Mathewson") has been alphabetized below. The set was issued in 1910. Listed prices for raw cards references "VgEx" condition.

COMPLETE SET (30)	60,000.00	120,000.00
1 Chief Bender	500.00	800.00
2 Roger Bresnahan	500.00	800.00
3 Al Bridwell	300.00	500.00
4 Miner Brown	500.00	800.00
5 Frank Chance	500.00	800.00
6 Hal Chase	300.00	500.00
7 Fred Clarke	500.00	800.00
8 Ty Cobb	3,000.00	5,000.00
9 Eddie Collins	500.00	800.00
10 Jack Coombs	300.00	500.00
11 Bill Dahlen	300.00	500.00
12 Harry Davis	300.00	500.00
13 Red Dooin	300.00	500.00
14 Johnny Evers	500.00	800.00
15 Russ Ford	300.00	500.00
16 Hugh Jennings	500.00	800.00
17 Johnny Kling	300.00	500.00
18 Nap Lajoie	700.00	1,200.00
19 Connie Mack	900.00	1,500.00
20 Christy Mathewson	1,800.00	3,000.00
21 John McGraw	500.00	800.00
22 Larry McLean	300.00	500.00
23 Chief Meyers	300.00	500.00
24 George Mullin	300.00	500.00
25 Fred Tenney	300.00	500.00
26 Joe Tinker	500.00	800.00
27 Hippo Vaughn	300.00	500.00
28 Honus Wagner	2,500.00	4,000.00
29 Ed Walsh	500.00	800.00
30 Cy Young UER	1,800.00	3,000.00

1910 E101 Set of 50

The cards in this 50-card set measure 1 1/2" by 2 3/4". The "Prominent Members of National and American Leagues" portrayed in E101 are identical to the line drawings of E92 and E105. The set was distributed about 1910. The set issuer is not mentioned anywhere on the cards. The complete set price includes all variation cards listed in the checklist below.

COMPLETE SET (50)	6,000.00	12,000.00
1 Jack Barry	300.00	600.00
2 Harry Bemis	300.00	600.00
3A Chief Bender/(white cap)	600.00	1,200.00
3B Chief Bender/(striped cap)	600.00	1,200.00
4 Bill Bergen	300.00	600.00
5 Bob Bescher	300.00	600.00
6 Al Bridwell	300.00	600.00
7 Doc Casey	300.00	600.00
8 Frank Chance	600.00	1,200.00
9 Hal Chase	500.00	1,000.00
10 Ty Cobb	6,000.00	12,000.00
11 Eddie Collins	1,000.00	2,000.00
12 Sam Crawford	600.00	1,200.00
13 Harry Davis	300.00	600.00
14 Art Devlin	300.00	600.00
15 Bill Donovan	300.00	600.00
16 Red Dooin	300.00	600.00
17 Mickey Doolan	300.00	600.00
18 Patsy Dougherty	300.00	600.00
19A Larry Doyle/(batting)	400.00	800.00
19B Larry Doyle/(throwing)	400.00	800.00
20 Johnny Evers	600.00	1,200.00
21 George Gibson	300.00	600.00
22 Topsy Hartsel	300.00	600.00
23 Fred Jacklitsch	300.00	600.00
24 Hugh Jennings	600.00	1,200.00
25 Red Kleinow	300.00	600.00
26 Otto Knabe	300.00	600.00
27 John Knight	300.00	600.00
28 Nap Lajoie	1,000.00	2,000.00
29 Hans Lobert	300.00	600.00
30 Sherry Magee	400.00	800.00
31 Christy Mathewson	2,000.00	4,000.00
32 John McGraw	1,000.00	2,000.00
33 Larry McLean	300.00	600.00
34A J.B. Miller/(batting)	300.00	600.00
34B J.B. Miller/(fielding)	300.00	600.00
35 Danny Murphy	300.00	600.00
36 Bill O'Hara	300.00	600.00
37 Germany Schaefer	400.00	800.00
38 Admiral Schlei	300.00	600.00
39 Boss Schmidt	300.00	600.00
40 Johnny Seigle/(sic& Siegle)	300.00	600.00
41 Dave Shean	300.00	600.00
42 Frank Smith	300.00	600.00
43 Joe Tinker	600.00	1,200.00
44A Honus Wagner/(batting)	2,000.00	4,000.00
44B Honus Wagner/(throwing)	2,000.00	4,000.00
45 Cy Young	1,000.00	2,000.00
46 Heine Zimmerman	300.00	600.00

1910 E102 Set of 25

The cards in this 29-card set measure 1 1/2" by 2 3/4". The player poses in E102 are identical to those in E92. The reverse of each card carries an angled checklist (Begins with "COBB, Detroit") printed in black. Smith is not listed, and two poses exist for Doyle, Miller and Wagner. The set was issued circa 1910. The complete set price includes all variation cards listed in the checklist below.

COMPLETE SET (29)	25,000.00	50,000.00
1 Chief Bender	750.00	1,500.00
2 Bob Bescher	400.00	800.00
3 Hal Chase	600.00	1,200.00
4 Ty Cobb	7,500.00	15,000.00
5 Eddie Collins	750.00	1,500.00
6 Sam Crawford	750.00	1,500.00
7 Bill Donovan	400.00	800.00
8 Red Dooin	400.00	800.00
9 Patsy Dougherty	400.00	800.00
10A Larry Doyle Batting	500.00	1,000.00
10B Larry Doyle Throwing	500.00	1,000.00
11 Johnny Evers	750.00	1,500.00
12 Red Kleinow	400.00	800.00
13 Otto Knabe	400.00	800.00
14 Nap Lajoie	1,500.00	3,000.00
15 Hans Lobert	400.00	800.00
16 Sherry Magee	500.00	1,000.00
17 Christy Mathewson	2,500.00	5,000.00
18A Dots Miller Batting	400.00	800.00
18B Dots Miller Fielding	2,000.00	4,000.00
19 Danny Murphy	400.00	800.00
20 Germany Schaefer	500.00	1,000.00
21 Boss Schmidt	400.00	800.00
22 Boss Smith (Schmidt)	400.00	800.00

23 Dave Shean	400.00	800.00
24 Joe Tinker	750.00	1,500.00
25A Honus Wagner Batting	2,500.00	5,000.00
25B Honus Wagner Throwing	2,500.00	5,000.00
26 Heinie Zimmerman	400.00	800.00

1922 E120 American Caramel Series of 240

The cards in this 240-card set measure 2" by 3 1/2". The 1922 E120 set was issued by American Caramels and contains unnumbered cards which are numbered here alphabetically within team for convenience. The order of teams is alphabeticallly within league: Boston AL (1-15), Chicago AL (16-30), Cleveland (31-45), Detroit (46-60), New York AL (61-75), Philadelphia AL (76-90), St. Louis AL (91-105), Washington (106-120), Boston NL (121-135), Brooklyn (136-150), Chicago NL (151-165), Cincinnati (166-180), New York NL (181-195), Philadelphia NL (196-210), Pittsburgh (211-225) and St. Louis NL (226-240). This set is one of the most popular of the E card sets.

COMPLETE SET (240)	6,000.00	12,000.00
1 George H. Burns	100.00	200.00
2 Shano Collins	100.00	200.00
3 Joe Dugan	125.00	250.00
4 Joe Harris	100.00	200.00
5 Bennie Karr	100.00	200.00
6 Nemo Leibold	100.00	200.00
7 Michael Menosky	100.00	200.00
8 Elmer Myers	100.00	200.00
9 Herb Pennock	200.00	400.00
10 Clarke Pittenger	100.00	200.00
11 Derrill Pratt	100.00	200.00
12 John Quinn	125.00	250.00
13 Muddy Ruel	100.00	200.00
14 Elmer Smith	100.00	200.00
15 Al Walters	100.00	200.00
16 Eddie Collins	300.00	600.00
17 Elmer Cox	100.00	200.00
18 Urban Faber	200.00	400.00
19 Bib Falk	100.00	200.00
20 Clarence Hodge	100.00	200.00
21 Harry Hooper	200.00	400.00
22 Ernie Johnson	100.00	200.00
23 Horace Leverette	100.00	200.00
24 Harvey McClellan	100.00	200.00
25 Johnny Mostil	100.00	200.00
26 Charles Robertson	100.00	200.00
27 Ray Schalk	200.00	400.00
28 Earl Sheely	100.00	200.00
29 Amos Strunk	100.00	200.00
30 Clarence Yaryan	100.00	200.00
31 Jim Bagby	100.00	200.00
32 Stan Coveleskie	200.00	400.00
33 Harry Gardner	100.00	200.00
34 Jack Graney	100.00	200.00
35 Charles Jamieson	100.00	200.00
36 John Mails	100.00	200.00
37 Stuffy McInnis	125.00	250.00
38 Leslie Nunamaker	100.00	200.00
39 Steve O'Neill	125.00	250.00
40 Joe Sewell	200.00	400.00
41 Allen Sothoron	100.00	200.00
42 Tris Speaker	500.00	1,000.00
43 George Uhle	100.00	200.00
44 Bill Wambsganss	125.00	250.00
45 Joe Wood	150.00	300.00
46 John Bassler	100.00	200.00
47 Lu Blue	100.00	200.00
48 Ty Cobb	1,500.00	3,000.00
49 Bert Cole	100.00	200.00
50 George Cutshaw	100.00	200.00
51 George Dauss	100.00	200.00
52 Howard Ehmke	125.00	250.00
53 Ira Flagstead	100.00	200.00
54 Harry Heilman	200.00	400.00
55 Sylvester Johnson	100.00	200.00
56 Bob Jones	100.00	200.00
57 Herman Pillette	100.00	200.00
58 Emory Rigney	100.00	200.00
59 Bob Veach	100.00	200.00
60 Charles Woodall	100.00	200.00
61 Frank Baker	200.00	400.00
62 Joe Bush	125.00	250.00
63 Al DeVormer	100.00	200.00
64 Waite Hoyt	200.00	400.00
65 Sam Jones	125.00	250.00
66 Carl Mays	125.00	250.00
67 Michael McNally	100.00	200.00
68 Bob Meusel	150.00	300.00
69 Elmer Miller	100.00	200.00
70 Wally Pipp	125.00	250.00
71 Babe Ruth	2,000.00	4,000.00
72 Wallie Schang	100.00	200.00
73 Everett Scott	125.00	250.00
74 Bob Shawkey	125.00	250.00
75 Aaron Ward	100.00	200.00
76 Frank Calloway	100.00	200.00
77 Jimmy Dykes	150.00	300.00
78 Alfred Fuhrman	100.00	200.00
79 Chick Galloway	100.00	200.00
80 Bryan Harris	100.00	200.00
81 Robert Hasty	100.00	200.00
82 Joe Hauser	100.00	200.00
83 W.F. (Doc) Johnston	100.00	200.00
84 Bing Miller	100.00	200.00
85 Roy Moore	100.00	200.00
86 Roleine Naylor	100.00	200.00
87 Cy Perkins	100.00	200.00
88 Ed Rommel	125.00	250.00
89 Clarence Walker (Tillie)	100.00	200.00
90 Frank Welch	100.00	200.00
91 William Bayne	100.00	200.00
92 Pat Collins	100.00	200.00
93 David Danforth	100.00	200.00
94 Frank Davis	100.00	200.00
95 Francis Ellerbe	100.00	200.00
96 Walter Gerber	100.00	200.00
97 Will Jacobson	100.00	200.00
98 Marty McManus	100.00	200.00
99 Hank Severeid	100.00	200.00
100 Urban Shocker	125.00	250.00
101 Charles Shorten	100.00	200.00
102 George Sisler	300.00	600.00
103 John Tobin	100.00	200.00
104 Elam Van Gilder	100.00	200.00
105 Ken Williams	125.00	250.00
106 Henry Courtney	100.00	200.00
107 Edward Gharrity	100.00	200.00
108 Goose Goslin	200.00	400.00
109 Bucky Harris	200.00	400.00
110 Walter Johnson	600.00	1,200.00
111 Joe Judge	100.00	200.00
112 Clyde Milan	125.00	250.00
113 George Mogridge	100.00	200.00
114 Roger Peckinpaugh	125.00	250.00
115 Tom Phillips	100.00	200.00
116 Val Picinich	100.00	200.00
117 Sam Rice	200.00	400.00
118 Howard Shanks	100.00	200.00
119 Earl Smith Wash	100.00	200.00
120 Tom Zachary	100.00	200.00
121 Walter Barbare	100.00	200.00
122 Norman Boeckel	100.00	200.00
123 Walton Cruise	100.00	200.00
124 Dana Fillingim	100.00	200.00
125 Horace Ford	100.00	200.00
126 Hank Gowdy	125.00	250.00
127 Walter Holke	100.00	200.00
128 Larry Kopf	100.00	200.00
129 Rube Marquard	200.00	400.00
130 Hugh McQuillan	100.00	200.00
131 Joe Oeschger	100.00	200.00
132 George O'Neil	100.00	200.00
133 Roy Powell	100.00	200.00
134 Billy Southworth	125.00	250.00
135 John Watson	100.00	200.00
136 Leon Cadore	100.00	200.00
137 Samuel Crane	100.00	200.00
138 Hank DeBerry	100.00	200.00
139 Tom Griffith	100.00	200.00
140 Burleigh Grimes	200.00	400.00
141 Bernard Hungling	100.00	200.00
142 Jimmy Johnston	100.00	200.00
143 Al Mamaux	100.00	200.00
144 Clarence Mitchell	100.00	200.00
145 Hy Myers	100.00	200.00
146 Ivan Olson	100.00	200.00
147 Dutch Reuther	125.00	250.00
148 Ray Schmandt	100.00	200.00
149 Sherrod Smith	100.00	200.00
150 Zach Wheat	200.00	400.00
151 Victor Aldridge	100.00	200.00
152 Grover C. Alexander	300.00	600.00
153 Tyrus Barber	100.00	200.00
154 Marty Callaghan	100.00	200.00
155 Virgil Cheeves	100.00	200.00
156 Max Flack	100.00	200.00
157 Oscar Grimes	100.00	200.00
158 Gabby Hartnett	200.00	400.00
159 Charles Hollocher	100.00	200.00
160 Percy Jones	100.00	200.00
161 Johnny Kelleher	100.00	200.00
162 Martin Krug	100.00	200.00
163 Hack Miller	100.00	200.00
164 Bob O'Farrell	125.00	250.00
165 Arnold Statz	100.00	200.00
166 Sammy Bohne	100.00	200.00
167 George J. Burns	100.00	200.00
168 James Caveney	100.00	200.00
169 Jake Daubert	125.00	250.00
170 Pete Donohue	100.00	200.00
171 Pat Duncan	100.00	200.00
172 John Gillespie	100.00	200.00
173 Gene Hargrave (Bubbles)	100.00	200.00
174 Dolph Luque	125.00	250.00
175 Cliff Markle	100.00	200.00
176 Greasy Neale	125.00	250.00
177 Ralph Pinelli	125.00	250.00
178 Eppa Rixey	200.00	400.00
179 Ed Roush	200.00	400.00
180 Ivy Wingo	100.00	200.00
181 Dave Bancroft	200.00	400.00
182 Jesse Barnes	100.00	200.00
183 Bill Cunningham	100.00	200.00
184 Phil Douglas	100.00	200.00
185 Frankie Frisch	300.00	600.00
186 Heine Groh	125.00	250.00
187 George Kelly	200.00	400.00
188 Emil Meusel	125.00	250.00
189 Art Nehf	100.00	200.00
190 John Rawlings	100.00	200.00
191 Ralph Shinners	100.00	200.00
192 Earl Smith New York	100.00	200.00
193 Frank Snyder	100.00	200.00
194 Fred Toney	100.00	200.00
195 Ross Youngs (Pep)	200.00	400.00
196 Walter Betts	100.00	200.00
197 Art Fletcher	100.00	200.00
198 Walter Henline	100.00	200.00
199 Wilbur Hubbell	125.00	250.00
200 Lee King	100.00	200.00
201 Roy Leslie	100.00	200.00
202 Henry Meadows	100.00	200.00
203 Frank Parkinson	100.00	200.00
204 Jack Peters	100.00	200.00
205 Joseph Rapp	100.00	200.00
206 James Ring	100.00	200.00
207 Colonel Snover	100.00	200.00
208 Curtis Walker	100.00	200.00
209 Cy Williams	125.00	250.00
210 Russel Wrightstone	100.00	200.00
211 Babe Adams	150.00	300.00
212 Clyde Barnhart	100.00	200.00
213 Carlson Bigbee	100.00	200.00
214 Max Carey	200.00	400.00
215 Wilbur Cooper	100.00	200.00
216 Charles Glazner	100.00	200.00
217 Johnny Gooch	100.00	200.00
218 Charlie Grimm	125.00	250.00
219 Earl Hamilton	100.00	200.00
220 Rabbit Maranville	200.00	400.00
221 John L. Mokan	100.00	200.00
222 John Morrison	100.00	200.00
223 Walter Schmidt	100.00	200.00
224 James Tierney	100.00	200.00
225 Pie Traynor	250.00	500.00
226 Edward Ainsmith	100.00	200.00
227 Vern Clemons	100.00	200.00
228 William Doak	100.00	200.00
229 John Fournier	100.00	200.00
230 Jesse Haines	200.00	400.00
231 Cliff Heathcoate	100.00	200.00
232 Rogers Hornsby	500.00	1,000.00
233 John Lavan	100.00	200.00
234 Austin McHenry	100.00	200.00
235 Will Pertice	100.00	200.00
236 Joe Schultz	100.00	200.00
237 William Sherdel	100.00	200.00
238 Jack Smith	100.00	200.00
239 Milton Stock	100.00	200.00
240 George Torporcer	100.00	200.00

1922 E121 American Caramel Series of 120

The cards in this set measure 2" by 3 1/2". Many of the photos which appear in the "Series of 80" are duplicated in the so-called "Series of 120". As noted above, the variations in titling and photos have run the known number of cards past the original statement of length and collectors should expect to encounter additions to both E121 lists in the future. The cards have been alphabetized and numbered in the checklist below. The complete set price includes all variation cards listed in the checklist below.

COMPLETE SET (136)	25,000.00	50,000.00
1 Babe Adams	100.00	200.00
2 Grover C. Alexander	300.00	600.00
3 Jim Bagby	75.00	150.00
4 Dave Bancroft	150.00	300.00
5 Turner Barber	75.00	150.00
6A Carlson Bigbee	75.00	150.00
6B Carlson L. Bigbee	75.00	150.00
6C Corson L. Bigbee	75.00	150.00
6D L. Bigbee	75.00	150.00
7 Joe Bush	100.00	200.00
8 Max Carey	150.00	300.00
9 Cecil Causey	75.00	150.00
10A Ty Cobb Batting	1,500.00	3,000.00
10B Ty Cobb Throwing	1,500.00	3,000.00
11 Eddie Collins	200.00	400.00
12 Wilbur Cooper	75.00	150.00
13 Stan Coveleskie	150.00	300.00
14 Dave Danforth	75.00	150.00
15 Jake Daubert	100.00	200.00
16 George Dauss	75.00	150.00
17 Dixie Davis	75.00	150.00
18 Al DeVormer	75.00	150.00
19 William Doak	75.00	150.00
20 Phil Douglas	75.00	150.00
21 Urban Faber	150.00	300.00
22 Bib Falk	75.00	150.00
23 Chick Fewster	75.00	150.00
24 Max Flack	75.00	150.00
25 Ira Flagstead	75.00	150.00
26 Frankie Frisch	250.00	500.00
27 Larry Gardner	75.00	150.00
28 Alexander Gaston	75.00	150.00
29 Edward Gharrity	75.00	150.00
30 George Gibson	75.00	150.00
31 Whitey Glazner	75.00	150.00
32 Kid Gleason MG	100.00	200.00
33 Hank Gowdy	100.00	200.00
34 John Graney	75.00	150.00
35 Tom Griffith	75.00	150.00
36 Charlie Grimm	100.00	200.00
37 Heinie Groh	100.00	200.00
38 Jesse Haines	150.00	300.00
39 Harry Harper	75.00	150.00
40A Harry Heilman	150.00	300.00
40B Harry Heilmann	150.00	300.00
41 Clarence Hodge	75.00	150.00
42A Walter Holke Portrait	75.00	150.00
42B Walter Holke Throwing	75.00	150.00
43 Charles Hollocher	75.00	150.00
44 Harry Hooper	150.00	300.00
45 Rogers Hornsby	300.00	600.00
46 Waite Hoyt	150.00	300.00
47 Miller Huggins MG	150.00	300.00
48 Walter Johnson	250.00	500.00
49 Joe Judge	75.00	150.00
50 George Kelly	150.00	300.00
51 Dick Kerr	100.00	200.00
52 Pete Kilduff	75.00	150.00
53A Bill Killifer w/Bat	75.00	150.00
53B Bill Killifer Throwing	75.00	150.00
54 John Lavan	75.00	150.00
55 Walter Mails	75.00	150.00
56 Rabbit Maranville	150.00	300.00
57 Elwood Martin	75.00	150.00
58 Carl Mays	100.00	200.00
59 John McGraw MG	250.00	500.00
60 Jack McInnis	100.00	200.00
61 M.J. McNally	75.00	150.00
62 Emil Meusel	75.00	150.00
63 Bob Meusel	125.00	250.00
64 Clyde Milan	100.00	200.00
65 Elmer Miller	75.00	150.00
66 Otto Miller	75.00	150.00
67 Johnny Mostil	75.00	150.00
68 Eddie Mulligan	75.00	150.00
69A Hy Myers	75.00	150.00
69B Hy Myers	75.00	150.00
70 Greasy Neale	125.00	250.00
71 Art Nehf	75.00	150.00
72 Leslie Nunamaker	75.00	150.00
73 Joe Oeschger	75.00	150.00
74 Charley O'Leary	75.00	150.00
75 Steve O'Neill	100.00	200.00
76 Del Pratt	75.00	150.00
77 John Rawlings	75.00	150.00
78 Sam Rice	150.00	300.00
79A Eppa J. Rixey	150.00	300.00
79B Eppa Rixey	150.00	300.00
80 Wilbert Robinson MG	150.00	300.00
81 Tom Rogers	75.00	150.00
82A Ed Rommel	100.00	200.00
82B Ed Rounnel	100.00	200.00
83 Ed Roush	150.00	300.00
84 Muddy Ruel	75.00	150.00
85 Walter Ruether	100.00	200.00
86A Babe Ruth Montage	2,500.00	5,000.00
86B 'Babe' Ruth Montage	3,000.00	6,000.00
86C Babe Ruth Holding Bird	2,500.00	5,000.00
86D 'Babe' Ruth Holding Bird	3,000.00	6,000.00
86E Babe Ruth Holding Ball	2,500.00	5,000.00
87 Bill Ryan	75.00	150.00
88A Ray Schalk Catching	150.00	300.00
88B Ray Schalk Bunting	150.00	300.00
89 Wally Schang	75.00	150.00
90 Ferd Schupp	75.00	150.00
91 Everett Scott	100.00	200.00
92 Joe Sewell	150.00	300.00
93 Bob Shawkey	100.00	200.00
94 Pat Shea	75.00	150.00
95 Earl Sheely	75.00	150.00
96 Urban Shocker	100.00	200.00
97A George Sisler Batting	250.00	500.00
97B George Sisler Throwing	250.00	500.00
98 Earl Smith	75.00	150.00
99 Elmer Smith	75.00	150.00
100 Frank Snyder	75.00	150.00
101 Billy Southworth	100.00	200.00
102A Tris Speaker Large Proj	300.00	600.00
102B Tris Speaker Small Proj	300.00	600.00
103A Milton Stock	75.00	150.00
103B Milton J. Stock	75.00	150.00
104 Amos Strunk	75.00	150.00
105 Zeb Terry	75.00	150.00
106 Fred Toney	75.00	150.00
107 George Torporcer	75.00	150.00
108 Bob Veach	75.00	150.00
109 Oscar Vitt	75.00	150.00
110 Curtis Walker	75.00	150.00
111 Bill Wambsganss	100.00	200.00
112 Aaron Ward	75.00	150.00
113 Zach Wheat	150.00	300.00
114A George Whitted Brooklyn	75.00	150.00
114B George Whitted Pittsburgh	75.00	150.00
115 Fred Williams	100.00	200.00
116 Ivy Wingo	75.00	150.00
117 Ross Youngs (Young)	150.00	300.00

1921 E121 American Caramel Series of 80

The cards in this set measure 2" by 3 1/2". The E121 sets contain many errors, misspellings and minor variations in titles and photos, which accounts for the difficulty in collecting the entire set. Many photos were taken from E135 and a fine screen is apparent on the cards. The American Caramel Co. marketed this black and white issue about 1922. Many localized advertising reverses have been found, and these cards more properly belong to the W classification than to E121. The cards have been alphabetized and numbered in the checklist below. The complete set price includes all variation cards listed in the checklist below.

COMPLETE SET (134)	75,000.00	15,000.00
1A G.C. Alexander Arms Above	300.00	600.00
1B Grover Alexander Right Arm	250.00	500.00
2 Jim Bagby	75.00	150.00
3A J. Franklin Baker	150.00	300.00
3B Frank Baker	150.00	300.00
4A Dave Bancroft Batting	150.00	300.00

4B Dave Bancroft Fielding 150.00 300.00
5 Ping Bodie 75.00 150.00
6 George H. Burns 75.00 150.00
7 George J. Burns 75.00 150.00
8 Owen Bush 75.00 150.00
9A Max Carey Batting 150.00 300.00
9B Max Carey Hands at Hips 150.00 300.00
10 Cecil Causey 75.00 150.00
11A Ty Cobb Look Ahead 1,500.00 3,000.00
11B Ty Cobb Look Right Manager 1,500.00 3,000.00
11C Ty Cobb Look Right Mgr. 1,500.00 3,000.00
12 Eddie Collins 200.00 400.00
13 Rip Collins 75.00 150.00
14 Jake Daubert 100.00 200.00
15 George Dauss 75.00 150.00
16A Charles Deal Dark Uni 75.00 150.00
16B Charles Deal Light Uni 75.00 150.00
17 William Doak 75.00 150.00
18 Bill Donovan 75.00 150.00
19 Phil Douglas 75.00 150.00
20A Johnny Evers Manager 150.00 300.00
20B Johnny Evers Mgr. 150.00 300.00
21A Urban Faber Dark Uni 150.00 300.00
21B Urban Faber White Uni 150.00 300.00
22 Wilson Fewster 75.00 150.00
23 Eddie Foster 75.00 150.00
24 Frankie Frisch 200.00 400.00
25 Larry Gardner 75.00 150.00
26 Alexander Gaston 75.00 150.00
27 Kid Gleason MG 100.00 200.00
28 Mike Gonzalez 75.00 150.00
29 Hank Gowdy 100.00 200.00
30 John Graney 75.00 150.00
31 Tom Griffith 75.00 150.00
32 Heinie Groh 100.00 200.00
33 Harry Harper 75.00 150.00
34 Harry Heilmann 150.00 300.00
35A Walter Holke Portrait 75.00 150.00
35B Walter Holke Throwing 75.00 150.00
36 Charles Hollacher 75.00 150.00
37 Harry Hooper 150.00 300.00
38 Rogers Hornsby 300.00 600.00
39 Waite Hoyt 150.00 300.00
40 Miller Huggins MG 150.00 300.00
41 Baby Doll Jacobson 75.00 150.00
42 Hugh Jennings MG 150.00 300.00
43A Walter Johnson Throwing 750.00 1,500.00
43B Walter Johnson Hands at Chest 750.00 1,500.00
44 James Johnston 75.00 150.00
45 Joe Judge 75.00 150.00
46 George Kelly 150.00 300.00
47 Dick Kerr 100.00 200.00
48 Pete Kilduff 75.00 150.00
49A Bill Killefer 75.00 150.00
49B Bill Killifer 75.00 150.00
50 John Lavan 75.00 150.00
51 Nemo Leibold 75.00 150.00
52 Duffy Lewis 75.00 150.00
53 Al Mamaux 75.00 150.00
54 Rabbit Maranville 150.00 300.00
55A Carl Mays UER May 100.00 200.00
55B Carl Mays COR Mays 100.00 200.00
56 John McGraw MG 250.00 500.00
57 Snuffy McInnis 100.00 200.00
58 M.J. McNally 75.00 150.00
59 Emil Muesel 75.00 150.00
60 Bob Meusel 125.00 250.00
61 Clyde Milan 100.00 200.00
62 Elmer Miller 75.00 150.00
63 Otto Miller 75.00 150.00
64 Guy Morton 75.00 150.00
65 Eddie Murphy 75.00 150.00
66 Hy Myers 75.00 150.00
67 Art Nehf 75.00 150.00
68 Steve O'Neill 75.00 150.00
69A Roger Peckinbaugh UER 100.00 200.00
69B Roger Peckinpaugh COR 100.00 200.00
70 Jeff Pfeffer Brooklyn 75.00 150.00
71 Jeff Pfeffer Stl 75.00 150.00
72 Wally Pipp 100.00 200.00
73 Jack Quinn 75.00 150.00
74 John Rawlings 75.00 150.00
75 Sam Rice 150.00 300.00
76 Eppa Rixey 150.00 300.00
77 Wilburt Robinson MG 150.00 300.00
78 Tom Rogers 75.00 150.00
79 Robert Roth 75.00 150.00
80 Bill Ryan 75.00 150.00
81 Ed Roush 150.00 300.00
82A Babe Ruth 2,000.00 4,000.00
82B 'Babe' Ruth 2,500.00 5,000.00
82C George Ruth 2,000.00 4,000.00
83A Slim Sallee Glove 75.00 150.00
83B Slim Sallee No Glove 75.00 150.00
84 Ray Schalk 150.00 300.00
85 Walter Schang 75.00 150.00
86A Ferd Schupp UER 75.00 150.00
86B Fred Schupp COR 75.00 150.00
87 Everett Scott 75.00 150.00
88 Hank Severeid 75.00 150.00
89 Bob Shawkey 100.00 200.00
90A Pat Shea 75.00 150.00
90B Pat Shea 75.00 150.00
91A George Sisler Batting 250.00 500.00
91B George Sisler Throwing 250.00 500.00
92 Earl Smith 75.00 150.00
93 Frank Snyder 75.00 150.00
94A Tris Speaker Manager Large 300.00 600.00
94B Tris Speaker Manager Small 300.00 600.00
94C Tris Speaker Mgr. 300.00 600.00
95 Milton Stock 75.00 150.00
96 Amos Strunk 75.00 150.00
97 Zeb Terry 75.00 150.00
98 Chester Thomas 75.00 150.00
99A Fred Toney Trees 75.00 150.00
99B Fred Toney No Trees 75.00 150.00
100 George Tyler 75.00 150.00
101A Jim Vaughn Dark Hat 75.00 150.00
101B Jim Vaughn White Hat 75.00 150.00
102A Bob Veach Glove in Air 75.00 150.00
102B Bob Veach Arms Crossed 75.00 150.00
103 Oscar Vitt 75.00 150.00
104 Bill Wambsganss 100.00 200.00
105 Aaron Ward 75.00 150.00
106 Zach Wheat 150.00 300.00
107 George Whitted 75.00 150.00
108 Fred Williams 100.00 200.00
109 Ivy Wingo 75.00 150.00
110 Joe Wood 125.00 250.00
111 Pep Young 75.00 150.00

1910 Orange Borders

This unusual card set features black-and-white pictures surrounded by a thin orange border and measures approximately 1 5/8" by 2 5/8". These orange bordered cards apparently were part of a box of candy. Only 24 cards are checklisted below, but the box indicates that there are 144 in the whole set. Any known additions to the checklist would be welcomed.

COMPLETE SET 2,000.00 4,000.00
1 National League Champions, 1909/Pirates 150.00 300.00
2 American League Champions, 1909/Tigers 150.00 300.00
3 Bill Bergen 150.00 300.00
4 Bill Carrigan 150.00 300.00
5 Hal Chase 250.00 500.00
6 Fred Clark UER/(misspelled Clarke) 300.00 600.00
7 Ty Cobb 3,000.00 6,000.00
8 Sam Crawford 300.00 600.00
9 Lou Criger 150.00 300.00
10 Mickey Doolan 150.00 300.00
11 George Gibson 150.00 300.00
12 Frank LaPorte 150.00 300.00
13 Nap Lajoie 750.00 1,500.00
14 Harry Lord 150.00 300.00
15 Christy Mathewson 750.00 1,500.00
16 John McGraw 300.00 600.00
17 Dots Miller 150.00 300.00
18 George Mullin 200.00 400.00
19 Eddie Plank 300.00 600.00
20 Tris Speaker 600.00 1,200.00
21 Jake Stahl 150.00 300.00
22 Heinie Wagner 150.00 300.00
23 Honus Wagner 1,000.00 2,000.00
24 Jack Warhop 150.00 300.00

1889 Edgerton R. Williams Game

The cards measure 2 7/16" by 3 1/2" and have green tinted backs and was issued as part of a parlor game. Each card features two players on the front -- therefore 38 players in total are featured in the set. Only the cards with Baseball players are included in this checklist.

COMPLETE SET (19) 4,000.00 8,000.00
1 Cap Anson 600.00 1,200.00
Buck Ewing
2 Dan Brouthers 500.00 1,000.00
Arlie Latham
3 Charlie Buffington 300.00 600.00
Bob Carruthers
4 Fred Carroll 300.00 600.00
Hick Carpenter
5 Roger Connor 600.00 1,200.00
Charles Comiskey
6 Pop Corkhill 300.00 600.00
Jim Fogarty
7 John Clarkson 600.00 1,200.00
Tim Keefe
8 Jerry Denny 300.00 600.00
Mike Tiernan
9 Dave Foutz 500.00 1,000.00
King Kelly
10 Pud Galvin 500.00 1,000.00
Dave Orr
11 Jack Glasscock 400.00 800.00
Tommy Tucker
12 Mike Griffin 300.00 600.00
Ed McKean
13 Dummy Hoy 400.00 800.00
John Reilly
14 Arthur Irwin 300.00 600.00
Ned Williamson
15 Silver King 300.00 600.00
John Tener
16 Al Myers 300.00 600.00
Cub Stricker
17 Fred Pfeffer 300.00 600.00
Jimmy Wolf
18 Toad Ramsey 300.00 600.00
Gus Weyhing
19 Mickey Ward 300.00 600.00
Curt Welch
20 Game Card 100.00 200.00

1967-73 Equitable Sports Hall of Fame

This set consists of copies of art work found over a number of years in many national magazines, especially "Sports Illustrated," honoring sports heroes that Equitable Life Assurance Society selected to be in its very own Sports Hall of Fame. The cards consists of charcoal-type drawings on white backgrounds by artists, George Loh and Robert Riger, and measure approximately 11" by 7 3/4". The unnumbered cards have been assigned numbers below using a sport prefix (BB- baseball, BK- basketball, FB- football, HK- hockey, OT-other).

COMPLETE SET (95) 250.00 500.00
BB1 Ernie Banks 4.00 8.00
BB2 Roy Campanella 4.00 8.00
BB3 Johnny Evers 3.00 6.00
BB4 Bob Feller 3.00 6.00
BB5 Lou Gehrig 7.50 15.00
BB6 Lefty Grove 3.00 6.00
BB7 Tom Henrich 1.25 2.50
BB8 Carl Hubbell 3.00 6.00
BB9 Al Kaline 3.00 6.00
BB10 Jerry Koosman 2.00 4.00
BB11 Mickey Mantle 7.50 15.00
BB12 Ed Mathews 3.00 6.00
BB13 Willie Mays 6.00 12.00
BB14 Stan Musial 5.00 10.00
BB15 PeeWee Reese 4.00 8.00
BB16 Allie Reynolds 1.25 2.50
BB17 Robin Roberts 3.00 6.00
BB18 Brooks Robinson 4.00 8.00
BB19 Red Ruffing 2.00 4.00
BB20 Babe Ruth 7.50 15.00
BB21 Warren Spahn 3.00 6.00

1949 Eureka Stamps

This set features National League players only. Apparently the promotion was not successful enough to warrant continuing on to do the American League, even though it was pre-announced in the back of the stamp album. Album is available to house the stamps. The album measures 7 1/2" by 9 1/4" whereas the individual stamps measure approximately 1 1/2" by 2". The stamps are numbered and are in full color. The album and stamp numbering is organized by teams (and alphabetically within teams), e.g., Boston Braves (3-27), Brooklyn Dodgers (28-51), Chicago Cubs (52-75), Cincinnati Reds (76-100), New York Giants (101-126), Philadelphia Phillies (127-151), Pittsburgh Pirates (152-176) and St. Louis Cardinals (177-200). At the bottom of the stamp the player's name is given in a narrow yellow strip.

COMPLETE SET (200) 250.00 500.00
1 Happy Chandler COMM 2.50 5.00
2 Ford Frick PRES 2.50 5.00
3 Johnny Antonelli 1.00 2.00
4 Red Barrett .75 1.50
5 Clint Conaster .75 1.50
6 Alvin Dark 1.50 3.00
7 Bob Elliott 1.00 2.00
8 Glenn Elliott .75 1.50
9 Elbie Fletcher .75 1.50
10 Bob Hall .75 1.50
11 Jeff Heath .75 1.50
12 Bobby Hogue .75 1.50
13 Tommy Holmes 1.00 2.00
14 Al Lakeman .75 1.50
15 Phil Masi .75 1.50
16 Nelson Potter .75 1.50
17 Pete Reiser 1.50 3.00
18 Rick Rickert .75 1.50
19 Connie Ryan .75 1.50
20 Jim Russell .75 1.50
21 Johnny Sain 1.50 3.00
22 Bill Salkeld .75 1.50
23 Sibby Sisti .75 1.50
24 Billy Southworth MG .75 1.50
25 Warren Spahn 7.50 15.00
26 Eddie Stanky 1.25 2.50
27 Bill Voiselle .75 1.50
28 Jack Banta .75 1.50
29 Rex Barney 1.00 2.00
30 Ralph Branca 1.50 3.00
31 Tommy Brown .75 1.50
32 Roy Campanella 10.00 20.00
33 Billy Cox 1.00 2.00
34 Bruce Edwards .75 1.50
35 Carl Furillo 2.50 5.00
36 Joe Hatten .75 1.50
37 Gene Hermanski .75 1.50
38 Gil Hodges 5.00 10.00
39 Johnny Jorgensen .75 1.50
40 Lefty Martin .75 1.50
41 Mike McCormick .75 1.50
42 Eddie Miksis .75 1.50
43 Paul Minner .75 1.50
44 Sam Narron .75 1.50
45 Don Newcombe 2.50 5.00
46 Jake Pitler CO .75 1.50
47 Pee Wee Reese 7.50 15.00
48 Jackie Robinson 15.00 30.00
49 Burt Shotton MG .75 1.50
50 Duke Snider 10.00 20.00
51 Dick Whitman .75 1.50
52 Smoky Burgess 1.00 2.00
53 Phil Cavarretta 1.00 2.00
54 Bob Chipman .75 1.50
55 Walt Dubiel .75 1.50
56 Hank Edwards .75 1.50
57 Frankie Gustine .75 1.50
58 Hal Jeffcoat .75 1.50
59 Emil Kush .75 1.50
60 Doyle Lade .75 1.50
61 Dutch Leonard .75 1.50
62 Peanuts Lowrey .75 1.50
63 Gene Mauch 1.25 2.50
64 Cal McLish .75 1.50
65 Rube Novotney .75 1.50
66 Andy Pafko 1.00 2.00
67 Bob Ramazzotti .75 1.50
68 Herman Reich .75 1.50
69 Bob Rush .75 1.50
70 Johnny Schmitz .75 1.50
71 Bob Scheffing .75 1.50
72 Roy Smalley 1.00 2.00
73 Emil Verban .75 1.50
74 Al Walker .75 1.50
75 Harry Walker 1.00 2.00
76 Bobby Adams .75 1.50
77 Ewell Blackwell 1.25 2.50
78 Jimmy Bloodworth .75 1.50
79 Walker Cooper .75 1.50
80 Tony Cuccinello .75 1.50
81 Jess Dobernick .75 1.50
82 Eddie Erautt .75 1.50
83 Frank Fanovich .75 1.50
84 Howie Fox .75 1.50
85 Grady Hatton .75 1.50
86 Homer Howell .75 1.50
87 Ted Kluszewski 2.50 5.00
88 Danny Litwhiler .75 1.50
89 Everett Lively .75 1.50
90 Lloyd Merriman .75 1.50
91 Phil Page .75 1.50
92 Kent Peterson .75 1.50
93 Ken Raffensberger .75 1.50
94 Luke Sewell CO 1.00 2.00
95 Virgil Stallcup .75 1.50
96 John Vander Meer 1.50 3.00
97 Bucky Walters MG 1.25 2.50
98 Herman Wehmeier .75 1.50
99 Johnny Wyrostek .75 1.50
100 Benny Zientara .75 1.50
101 Hank Behrman .75 1.50
102 Leo Durocher MG 2.50 5.00
103 Augie Galan .75 1.50
104 Sid Gordon .75 1.50
105 Bert Haas .75 1.50
106 Andy Hansen .75 1.50
107 Clint Hartung 1.00 2.00
108 Kirby Higbe .75 1.50
109 George Hausman .75 1.50
110 Larry Jansen 1.00 2.00
111 Sheldon Jones .75 1.50
112 Monte Kennedy .75 1.50
113 Buddy Kerr .75 1.50
114 Dave Koslo .75 1.50
115 Joe Lafata .75 1.50
116 Whitey Lockman 1.00 2.00
117 Jack Lohrke .75 1.50
118 Willard Marshall .75 1.50
119 Bill Milne .75 1.50
120 Johnny Mize 5.00 10.00
121 Don Mueller 1.25 2.50
122 Ray Mueller .75 1.50
123 Bill Rigney 1.00 2.00
124 Bobby Thomson 1.50 3.00
125 Sam Webb .75 1.50
126 Wes Westrum 1.00 2.00
127 Richie Ashburn 5.00 10.00
128 Bennie Bengough CO .75 1.50
129 Charlie Bicknell .75 1.50
130 Buddy Blattner .75 1.50
131 Hank Borowy .75 1.50
132 Ralph Caballero .75 1.50
133 Blix Donnelly .75 1.50
134 Del Ennis 1.00 2.00
135 Granville Hamner 1.00 2.00
136 Ken Heintzelman .75 1.50
137 Stan Hollmig .75 1.50
138 Willie Jones .75 1.50
139 Jim Konstanty 1.25 2.50
140 Stan Lopata .75 1.50
141 Jackie Mayo .75 1.50
142 Bill Nicholson 1.00 2.00
143 Robin Roberts 5.00 10.00
144 Schoolboy Rowe 1.25 2.50
145 Eddie Sawyer MG 1.00 2.00
146 Andy Seminick .75 1.50
147 Ken Silvestri .75 1.50
148 Curt Simmons 1.25 2.50
149 Dick Sisler 1.00 2.00
150 Ken Trinkle .75 1.50
151 Eddie Waitkus 1.00 2.00
152 Romanus Basgall .75 1.50
153 Eddie Bockman .75 1.50
154 Ernie Bonham .75 1.50
155 Hugh Casey 1.00 2.00
156 Pete Castiglione .75 1.50
157 Cliff Chambers .75 1.50
158 Murry Dickson .75 1.50
159 Ed Fitzgerald .75 1.50
160 Les Fleming .75 1.50
161 Hal Gregg .75 1.50
162 Goldie Holt .75 1.50
163 Johnny Hopp 1.00 2.00
164 Ralph Kiner 5.00 10.00
165 Vic Lombardi .75 1.50
166 Clyde McCullough .75 1.50
167 Bill Meyer MG 1.00 2.00
168 Danny Murtaugh 1.00 2.00
169 Barnacle Bill Posedel .75 1.50
170 Elmer Riddle .75 1.50
171 Stan Rojek .75 1.50
172 Rip Sewell 1.00 2.00
173 Eddie Stevens .75 1.50
174 Dixie Walker 1.00 2.00
175 Bill Werle .75 1.50
176 Wally Westlake .75 1.50
177 Bill Baker .75 1.50
178 Al Brazle .75 1.50
179 Harry Brecheen 1.00 2.00
180 Chuck Diering .75 1.50
181 Eddie Dyer MG 1.00 2.00
182 Joe Garagiola 5.00 10.00
183 Tom Glaviano .75 1.50
184 Jim Hearn .75 1.50
185 Ken Johnson .75 1.50
186 Nippy Jones .75 1.50

187 Ed Kazak	.75	1.50
188 Lou Klein	.75	1.50
189 Marty Marion	1.50	3.00
190 George Munger	.75	1.50
191 Stan Musial	12.50	25.00
192 Spike Nelson	.75	1.50
193 Howie Pollet	.75	1.50
194 Bill Reeder	.75	1.50
195 Del Rice	.75	1.50
196 Ed Sauer	.75	1.50
197 Red Schoendienst	4.00	8.00
198 Enos Slaughter	5.00	10.00
199 Ted Wilks	.75	1.50
200 Ray Yochim	.75	1.50
XX Album		

1921-24 Exhibits

Although the Exhibit Supply Company issued 64 cards in 1921 and 128 cards in each of the following three years, the category of 1921-24 was created because of the large number of pictures found repeated in all four years. Each exhibit card measures 3 3/8" by 5 3/8". The cards of 1921 are characterized by ornate hand-lettered names while the cards of 1922-24 have players' names hand-written in a plainer style. Also for 1921 cards, the abbreviation used for the junior circuit is "Am.L." In contrast, cards of the 1922-24 period have the American League abbreviated "A.L." All the cards in the 1921-24 category are black and white and have blank backs; some have white borders measuring approximately 3/16" in width. There is some mislabeling of pictures, incorrect assignment of proper names and many misspellings. Some of the cards have a horizontal (HOR) orientation.

COMPLETE SET (193)	4,000.00	8,000.00
1 Chas. B. Adams	20.00	50.00
2 Grover C. Alexander	40.00	80.00
3 James Bagby	15.00	40.00
4 J. Frank Baker	40.00	80.00
5 David Bancroft	40.00	80.00
6 Walter Barbare	15.00	40.00
7 Turner Barber	15.00	40.00
8 Clyde Barnhart	15.00	40.00
9 John Bassler	15.00	40.00
10 Carlson L. Bigbee	15.00	40.00
11 Ray Blades	15.00	40.00
12 Sam Bohne	15.00	40.00
13 James Bottomley	40.00	80.00
14 Geo. Burns (Cinn) portrait	15.00	40.00
15 Geo. J. Burns/(New York NL)	15.00	40.00
16 George Burns/(Boston AL)	15.00	40.00
17 George Burns/(Cleveland)	15.00	40.00
18 Joe Bush	20.00	50.00
19 Owen Bush	15.00	40.00
20 Leon Cadore	15.00	40.00
21 Max G. Carey	40.00	80.00
22 Jim Caveney	15.00	40.00
23 Dan Clark	15.00	40.00
24 Ty R. Cobb	400.00	800.00
25 Eddie T. Collins	40.00	80.00
26 John Collins	15.00	40.00
27 Wilbur Cooper	15.00	40.00
28 Stanley Coveleskie sic, Coveleski	40.00	80.00
29 Walton E. Cruse sic, Cruise	15.00	40.00
30 George Cutshaw	15.00	40.00
31 Dave Danforth	15.00	40.00
32 Jacob E. Daubert	20.00	50.00
33 George Dauss	15.00	40.00
34 Charles A. Deal	15.00	40.00
35 Bill Doak/(Brooklyn)	15.00	40.00
36 Bill Doak/(St. Louis NL)	15.00	40.00
37 Joe Dugan/(Boston AL)	20.00	50.00
38 Joe A. Dugan/(New York AL)	20.00	50.00
39 Joe A. Dugan/(Philadelphia AL)	20.00	50.00
40 Pat Duncan	15.00	40.00
41 James Dykes	20.00	50.00
42 Howard J. Ehmke/(Boston AL)	20.00	50.00
43 Howard Ehmke/(Detroit)/(with border)	20.00	50.00
44 Wm. Evans/(Umpire)	75.00	150.00
45 U.C. Red Faber	40.00	80.00
46 Bib Falk	15.00	40.00
47 Dana Fillingim	15.00	40.00
48 Ira Flagstead/(Boston AL)	15.00	40.00
49 A. Fletcher	15.00	40.00
50 J.F. Fournier/(Brooklyn)	15.00	40.00
51 J.F. Fournier/(St. Louis NL)	15.00	40.00
52 Howard Freigau	15.00	40.00
53 Frank F. Frisch	40.00	80.00
54 C.E. Galloway	15.00	40.00
55 W.L. Gardner/(Cleveland)	15.00	40.00
56 Joe Genewich	15.00	40.00
57 Wally Gerber	15.00	40.00
58 Mike Gonzales	15.00	40.00
59 H.M. Hank Gowdy/(Boston NL)	20.00	50.00
60 H.M. Hank Gowdy/(New York NL)	20.00	50.00
61 Burleigh A. Grimes	40.00	80.00
62 Ray Grimes	15.00	40.00
63 Charles Grimm	20.00	50.00
64 Heinie Groh Cincinnati	20.00	50.00
65 Heinie Groh New York NL	20.00	50.00
66 Jesse Haines	40.00	80.00
67 Chas. L. Hartnett	40.00	80.00
68 George Harper	15.00	40.00
69 Sam Harris	15.00	40.00
70 Slim Harris	15.00	40.00
71 Clifton Heathcote	15.00	40.00
72 Harry Heilmann	40.00	80.00
73 Andy High	15.00	40.00
74 George Hildebrand UMP	20.00	50.00
75 Walter L. Holke Boston NL	15.00	40.00
76 Walter L. Holke Philadelphia NL	15.00	40.00
77 Chas.J. Hollicher sic, Hollocher	15.00	40.00
78 Rogers Hornsby	75.00	150.00
79 Wilbert Hubbell	15.00	40.00
80 Bill Jacobson	15.00	40.00
81 Charles D. Jamieson	15.00	40.00
82 E.R. Johnson	15.00	40.00
83 James H. Johnston	15.00	40.00
84 Walter P. Johnson	150.00	300.00
85 Sam P. Jones	15.00	40.00
86 Joe Judge	15.00	40.00
87 Willie Kamm	15.00	40.00
88 Tony Kaufman	15.00	40.00
89 George L. Kelly	40.00	80.00
90 Dick Kerr	20.00	50.00
91 William L. Killefer	15.00	40.00
92 Bill Klem UMP	75.00	150.00
93 Ed Konetchy	15.00	40.00
94 John Doc Lavan	15.00	40.00
95 Dudley Lee	15.00	40.00
96 Nemo Leibold Boston AL	15.00	40.00
97 Nemo Leibold Washington with border	15.00	40.00
98 Adolph Luque	20.00	50.00
99 Walter Mails	15.00	40.00
100 Geo. Maisel	15.00	40.00
101 Walt. J. Maranville	40.00	80.00
102 W.C. (Wid) Matthews	15.00	40.00
103 Carl W. Mays	20.00	50.00
104 John McGraw	40.00	80.00
105 J. Stuffy McInnis Boston AL	20.00	50.00
106 J. Stuffy McInnis Boston NL	20.00	50.00
107 Lee Meadows	15.00	40.00
108 Clyde Milan	20.00	50.00
109 Ed (Bing) Miller	15.00	40.00
110 Hack Miller	15.00	40.00
111 George Moriarty UMP	20.00	50.00
112 Johnny Morrison	15.00	40.00
113 John A. Mostil	15.00	40.00
114 Robert Meusel	30.00	60.00
115 Harry Myers	15.00	40.00
116 Rollie C. Naylor	15.00	40.00
117 A. Earl Neale	20.00	50.00
118 Arthur Nehf	20.00	50.00
119 Joe Oeschger	15.00	40.00
120 Ivan M. Olson	15.00	40.00
121 Geo. O'Neil	15.00	40.00
122 S.F.Steve O'Neil sic, O'Neill	20.00	50.00
123 J.F. O'Neill	15.00	40.00
124 Ernest Padgett	15.00	40.00
125 Roger Peckinpaugh New York AL with border	20.00	50.00
126 Peckinpaugh Washington	20.00	50.00
127 Ralph Cy Perkins	15.00	40.00
128 Val Picinich Boston AL	15.00	40.00
129 Val Picinich Washington	15.00	40.00
130 Bill Piercy light background	15.00	40.00
131 Bill Piercy dark background	15.00	40.00
132 Herman Pillett	15.00	40.00
133 Wally Pipp	20.00	50.00
134 Raymond R. Powell light background	15.00	40.00
135 Raymond R. Powell dark background	15.00	40.00
136 Del Pratt Detroit	15.00	40.00
137 Derrill Pratt Boston AL	15.00	40.00
138 Joe Goldie Rapp	15.00	40.00
139 Walter Reuther	15.00	40.00
140 Edgar S. Rice	40.00	80.00
141 Cy Rigler UMP	20.00	50.00
142 E. E. Rigney	15.00	40.00
143 Jimmy Ring	15.00	40.00
144 Eppa Rixey	40.00	80.00
145 Chas. Robertson	15.00	40.00
146 Eddie Rommel	20.00	50.00
147 Muddy Ruel	15.00	40.00
148 Babe Ruth	400.00	800.00
149 Babe Ruth with border	800.00	1,600.00
150 J. H. Sand	15.00	40.00
151 Ray W. Schalk	40.00	80.00
152 Wallie Schang	20.00	50.00
153 Everett Scott Boston AL	20.00	50.00
154 Everett Scott New York AL	20.00	50.00
155 Harry Severeid	15.00	40.00
156 Joseph Sewell	40.00	80.00
157 H.S. Shanks photo actually Wally Schang	15.00	40.00
158 Earl Sheely	15.00	40.00
159 Urban Shocker	20.00	50.00
160 Al Simmons	40.00	80.00
161 George H. Sisler	40.00	80.00
162 Earl Smith New York NL with border	15.00	40.00
163 Earl Smith New York NL/2/3 shot	15.00	40.00
164 Elmer Smith Boston AL	15.00	40.00
165 Jack Smith	15.00	40.00
166 R.E. Smith	15.00	40.00
167 Sherrod Smith Brooklyn	15.00	40.00
168 Sherrod Smith Cleveland	15.00	40.00
169 Frank Snyder	15.00	40.00
170 Allan Sothoron	15.00	40.00
171 Tris Speaker	100.00	200.00
172 Arnold Statz	15.00	40.00
173 Casey Stengel	100.00	200.00
174 J.R. Stevenson	15.00	40.00
175 Milton Stock	15.00	40.00
176 James Tierney Boston NL	15.00	40.00
177 James Tierney Pittsburgh	15.00	40.00
178 John Tobin	15.00	40.00
179 George Toporcer	15.00	40.00
180 Robert Veach	15.00	40.00
181 Clar.(Tillie)Walker	15.00	40.00
182 Curtis Walker	15.00	40.00
183 Aaron Ward	15.00	40.00
184 Zack D. Wheat	40.00	80.00
185 Geo. B. Whitted	15.00	40.00
186 Cy Williams	15.00	40.00
187 Kenneth R. Williams	20.00	50.00
188 Ivy B. Wingo	15.00	40.00
189 Joe Wood	30.00	6.00
190 L. Woodall	15.00	40.00
191 Russell G.Wrightstone	15.00	40.00
192 Moses Yellowhorse	15.00	40.00
193 Ross Youngs	40.00	80.00

1925 Exhibits

The most dramatic change in the 1925 series from that of the preceding group was the printed legend which appeared for the first time in this printing. The subject's name, position, team and the line "(Made in U.S.A.)" appear on four separate lines in a bottom corner, enclosed in a small white box. The name of the player is printed in large capitals while the other lines are of a smaller type size. The cards are black and white, have plain backs and are unnumbered. Each exhibit card measures 3 3/8" by 5 3/8". There are 128 cards in the set and numerous misspellings exist. Note: the card marked "Robert Veach" does not picture that player, but is thought to contain a photo of Ernest Vache. A few of the cards are presented in a horizontal (HOR) format. Players are arranged below in alphabetical order by team: Boston NL 1-8, Brooklyn 9-16, Chicago 17-24, Cincinnati 25-32, New York 33-40, Philadelphia 41-48, Pittsburgh 49-56, St. Louis 57-64, Boston AL 65-72, Chicago 73-80, Cleveland 81-88, Detroit 89-96, New York 97-104, Philadelphia 105-112, St. Louis 113-120 and Washington 121-128. There is a very early card of Lou Gehrig in this set.

COMPLETE SET (128)	6,000.00	12,000.00
1 David Bancroft	60.00	120.00
2 Jesse Barnes	40.00	80.00
3 Lawrence Benton	40.00	80.00
4 Maurice Burrus	40.00	80.00
5 Joseph Genewich	40.00	80.00
6 Frank Gibson	40.00	80.00
7 David Harris	40.00	80.00
8 George O'Neil	40.00	80.00
9 John H. Deberry	40.00	80.00
10 Art Decatur	40.00	80.00
11 Jacques F. Fournier	40.00	80.00
12 Burleigh A. Grimes	60.00	120.00
13 James H. Johnson/sic& Johnston	40.00	80.00
14 Milton J. Stock	40.00	80.00
15 A.C. Dazzy Vance	60.00	120.00
16 Zack Wheat	75.00	150.00
17 Sparky Adams	40.00	80.00
18 Grover C. Alexander	100.00	200.00
19 John Brooks	40.00	80.00
20 Howard Freigau	40.00	80.00
21 Charles Grimm	50.00	100.00
22 Leo Hartnett	60.00	120.00
23 Walter Maranville	60.00	120.00
24 A.J. Weis	40.00	80.00
25 Raymond Bressler	40.00	80.00
26 Hugh M. Critz	40.00	80.00
27 Peter Donohue	40.00	80.00
28 Charles Dressen	50.00	100.00
29 John (Stuffy)/McInnes (McInnis)	50.00	100.00
30 Eppa Rixey	60.00	120.00
31 Ed. Roush	75.00	150.00
32 Ivy Wingo	40.00	80.00
33 Frank Frisch	100.00	200.00
34 Heine Groh	50.00	100.00
35 Travis C. Jackson	60.00	120.00
36 Emil Meusel	40.00	80.00
37 Arthur Nehf	50.00	100.00
38 Frank Snyder	40.00	80.00
39 Wm. H. Southworth	50.00	100.00
40 William Terry	100.00	200.00
41 George Harper	40.00	80.00
42 Nelson Hawks	40.00	80.00
43 Walter Henline	40.00	80.00
44 Walter Holke	40.00	80.00
45 Wilbur Hubbell	40.00	80.00
46 John Mokan	40.00	80.00
47 John Sand	40.00	80.00
48 Fred Williams	40.00	80.00
49 Carson Bigbee	40.00	80.00
50 Max Carey	60.00	120.00
51 Hazen Cuyler	60.00	120.00
52 George Grantham	40.00	80.00
53 Ray Kremer	40.00	80.00
54 Earl Smith	40.00	80.00
55 Harold Traynor	75.00	150.00
56 Glenn Wright	40.00	80.00
57 Lester Bell HOR	40.00	80.00
58 Raymond Blates sic, Blades	40.00	80.00
59 James Bottomly sic, Bottomley	60.00	120.00
60 Max Flack	40.00	80.00
61 Rogers Hornsby	125.00	250.00
62 Clarence Mueller	40.00	80.00
63 William Sherdell	40.00	80.00
64 George Toporcer	40.00	80.00
65 Howard Ehmke	50.00	100.00
66 Ira Flagstead	40.00	80.00
67 I.Valentine Picinich	40.00	80.00
68 John Quinn	50.00	100.00
69 Red Ruffing	75.00	150.00
70 Philip Todt	40.00	80.00
71 Robert Veach	40.00	80.00
72 William Wambsganss	40.00	80.00
73 Eddie Collins	75.00	150.00
74 Bib Falk	40.00	80.00
75 Harry Hooper	75.00	150.00
76 Willie Kamm	40.00	80.00
77 I.M. Davis	60.00	120.00
78 Ray Shalk (Schalk)	60.00	120.00
79 Earl Sheely	40.00	80.00
80 Hollis Thurston	40.00	80.00
81 Wilson Fewster	40.00	80.00
82 Charles Jamieson	40.00	80.00
83 Walter Lutzke	40.00	80.00
84 Glenn Myatt	40.00	80.00
85 Joseph Sewell	60.00	120.00
86 Sherrod Smith	40.00	80.00
87 Tristram Speaker	125.00	250.00
88 Homer Summa	40.00	80.00
89 John Bassler	40.00	80.00
90 Tyrus Cobb	350.00	700.00
91 George Dauss	40.00	80.00
92 Harry Heilmann	75.00	150.00
93 Frank O'Rourke	40.00	80.00
94 Emory Rigney	40.00	80.00
95 Al Wings(Wingo) HOR	40.00	80.00
96 Larry Woodall	40.00	80.00
97 Lou Gehrig	5,000.00	7,500.00
98 Robert W. Muesel sic, Meusel	50.00	100.00
99 Walter C. Pipp	60.00	120.00
100 Babe Ruth	700.00	1,400.00
101 Walter H. Shang sic, Schang	50.00	100.00
102 J.R. Shawkey	50.00	100.00
103 Urban J. Shocker	50.00	100.00
104 Aaron Ward	40.00	80.00
105 Max Bishop	40.00	80.00
106 James J. Dykes	50.00	100.00
107 Samuel Gray	40.00	80.00
108 Samuel Hale	40.00	80.00
109 Edmund(Bind) Miller sic& Bing	40.00	80.00
110 Ralph Perkins	40.00	80.00
111 Edwin Rommel	50.00	100.00
112 Frank Welch	40.00	80.00
113 Walter Gerber	40.00	80.00
114 William Jacobson	40.00	80.00
115 Martin McManus	40.00	80.00
116 Henry Severid sic, Severeid	40.00	80.00
117 George Sissler sic, Sisler	100.00	200.00
118 John Tobin	40.00	80.00
119 Kenneth Williams	40.00	80.00
120 Ernest Wingard	40.00	80.00
121 Oswald Bluege	40.00	80.00
122 Stanley Coveleski	60.00	120.00
123 Leon Goslin	75.00	150.00
124 Bucky Harris	60.00	120.00
125 Walter Johnson	200.00	400.00
126 Joseph Judge	50.00	100.00
127 Earl McNeely	40.00	80.00
128 Harold Ruel	40.00	80.00

1926 Exhibits

The year 1926 marked the last of the 128-card sets produced by Exhibit Supply. Of this number, 70 cards are identical to those issued in 1925 but are easily identified because of the new blue-gray color introduced in 1926. Another 21 cards use 1925 pictures but contain the line "Ex. Sup. Co., U.S.A."; these are marked with an asterisk in the checklist below. The 37 photos new to this set have an unboxed legend and carry the new company line. Bischoff is incorrectly placed with Boston, N.L. (should be A.L.); the picture of Galloway is reversed; the photos of Hunnefield and Thomas are wrongly exchanged. Each exhibit card measures 3 3/8" by 5 3/8". Players are in alphabetical order by team: Boston NL 1-8, Brooklyn 9-16, Chicago 17-24, Cincinnati 25-32, New York 33-40, Philadelphia 41-48, Pittsburgh 49-56, St. Louis 57-

64, Boston AL 65-72, Chicago 73-80, Cleveland 81-88, Detroit 89-96, New York 97-104, Philadelphia 105-112, St. Louis 113-120 and Washington 121-128.

COMPLETE SET (128) 4,500.00 9,000.00
1 Lawrence Benton 30.00 60.00
2 Andrew High 30.00 60.00
3 Maurice Burrus 30.00 60.00
4 David Bancroft 50.00 100.00
5 Joseph Genewich 30.00 60.00
6 Bernie F. Neis 30.00 60.00
7 Edward Taylor 30.00 60.00
8 John Taylor 30.00 60.00
9 John Butler 30.00 60.00
10 Jacques F. Furnier/(sic, Fournier) * 30.00 60.00
11 Burleigh A.Grimes 50.00 100.00
12 Wilson Fewster 30.00 60.00
13 Douglas McWeeny 30.00 60.00
14 George O'Neil 30.00 60.00
15 Walter Maranville 50.00 100.00
16 Zach Wheat 60.00 120.00
17 Sparky Adams 30.00 60.00
18 J. Fred Blake 30.00 60.00
19 James E. Cooney 30.00 60.00
20 Howard Freigau 30.00 60.00
21 Charles Grimm 40.00 80.00
22 Leo Hartnett 50.00 100.00
23 C.E. Heathcote 30.00 60.00
24 Joseph M. Munson 30.00 60.00
25 Raymond Bressler 30.00 60.00
26 Hugh M. Critz 30.00 60.00
27 Peter Donohue 30.00 60.00
28 Charles Dressen 40.00 80.00
29 Walter C. Pipp 40.00 80.00
30 Eppa Rixey 50.00 100.00
31 Ed. Roush 60.00 120.00
32 Ivy Wingo 30.00 60.00
33 Edward S. Farrell 30.00 60.00
34 Frank Frisch 100.00 200.00
35 Frank Snyder 30.00 60.00
36 Fredrick Lindstrom/(sic, Frederick) * 60.00 120.00
37 Hugh A.McQuillan 30.00 60.00
38 Emil Musel/(sic, Meusel) 30.00 60.00
39 James J. Ring 30.00 60.00
40 William Terry 100.00 200.00
41 John M. Bentley 30.00 60.00
42 Bernard Friberg 30.00 60.00
43 George Harper 30.00 60.00
44 Walter Henline 30.00 60.00
45 Clarence Huber 30.00 60.00
46 John Makan/(sic, Mokan) 30.00 60.00
47 John Sand 30.00 60.00
48 Russell Wrigtstone/(sic, Wrightstone) * 30.00 60.00
49 Carson Bigbee 30.00 60.00
50 Max Carey 50.00 100.00
51 Hazen Cuyler 50.00 100.00
52 George Grantham 30.00 60.00
53 Ray Kremer 30.00 60.00
54 Earl Smith 30.00 60.00
55 Harold Traynor 75.00 150.00
56 Glen Wright 30.00 60.00
57 Lester Bell 30.00 60.00
58 Raymond Blates/(sic, Blades) 30.00 60.00
59 James Bottomly/(sic, Bottomley) 60.00 120.00
60 Rogers Hornsby 100.00 200.00
61 Clarence Mueller 30.00 60.00
62 Robert O'Farrell 30.00 60.00
63 William Sherdell 30.00 60.00
64 George Torporcer 30.00 60.00
65 Ira Flagstead 30.00 60.00
66 Fred Haney 40.00 80.00
67 Ramon Herrera 30.00 60.00
68 John Quinn 40.00 80.00
69 Emory Rigney 30.00 60.00
70 Red Ruffing 60.00 120.00
71 Philip Todt 30.00 60.00
72 Fred Wingfield 30.00 60.00
73 Ted Blankenship 30.00 60.00
74 Eddie Collins 60.00 120.00
75 Bib Falk 30.00 60.00
76 Wm. Hunnefield/(sic, Tommy Thomas) 30.00 60.00
77 Willie Kamm 30.00 60.00
78 Ray Shalk (Schalk) 50.00 100.00
79 Earl Sheely 30.00 60.00
80 Hollis Thurston 30.00 60.00
81 Geo.H. Burns HOR 30.00 60.00
82 Walter Lutzke 30.00 60.00
83 Glenn Myatt 30.00 60.00
84 Joseph Sewell 50.00 100.00
85 Sherrod Smith 30.00 60.00
86 Tristram Speaker 125.00 250.00
87 Fred Spurgeon 30.00 60.00
88 Homer Summa 30.00 60.00
89 John Bassler 30.00 60.00
90 Lucerne Blue/(sic, Luzerne) 30.00 60.00
91 Tyrus Cobb 450.00 900.00
92 George Dauss 30.00 60.00
93 Harry Heilmann 60.00 120.00
94 Frank O'Rourke 30.00 60.00
95 Charles Gehringer/(batting) 100.00 200.00
96 John Warner 30.00 60.00
97 Patrick T.Collins 30.00 60.00
98 Earle Combs 60.00 120.00
99 Henry L. Gehrig 450.00 900.00
100 Tony Lazzeri 50.00 100.00
101 Robert W. Muesel/(sic, Meusel) 40.00 80.00
102 Babe Ruth 600.00 1,200.00
103 J. R. Shawkey 40.00 80.00
104 Urban J. Shocker 40.00 80.00
105 Max Bishop 30.00 60.00
106 Joseph Galloway 30.00 60.00
107 James J. Dykes 40.00 80.00
108 Joseph Hauser 30.00 60.00
109 Edmund(Bind) Miller 30.00 60.00
sic, Bing
110 Ralph Perkins 30.00 60.00
111 Edwin Rommel 40.00 80.00
112 Wm. Wambsganss 30.00 60.00
113 Wm. Hargrave 30.00 60.00
114 William Jacobson 30.00 60.00
115 Martin McManus 30.00 60.00
116 Oscar Melillo 30.00 60.00
117 Walter Gerber 30.00 60.00
118 George Sissler 100.00 200.00
sic, Sisler
119 Kenneth Williams 40.00 80.00
120 Ernest Wingard 30.00 60.00
121 Oswald Bluege 30.00 60.00
122 Stanley Coveleski 50.00 100.00
123 Leon Goslin 50.00 100.00
124 Bucky Harris 50.00 100.00
125 Walter Johnson 175.00 350.00
126 Joseph Judge 30.00 60.00
127 Earl McNeely 30.00 60.00
128 Harold Ruel 30.00 60.00

1927 Exhibits

Two innovations characterize the 64-card set produced by Exhibit Supply Company for 1927. The first was a radical departure from the color scheme of previous sets marked by this year's light green hue. The second was the installation of the divided legend, whereby the player's name (all caps) and team were set in one corner, and the lines "Ex. Sup. Co., Chgo." and "Made in U.S.A." were set in the other. All the photos employed in this set were taken from the previous issues in 1925 and 1926, although 13 players appear with new teams. The usual misspellings and incorrect labeling of names and initials occurs throughout the set. Note: Genewich and Hunnefield have a different style of print, and Myatt is missing the right side of the legend. Each card measures 3 3/8" by 5 3/8". Players are listed in alphabetical order by team: Boston NL 1-4, Brooklyn 5-8, Chicago 9-12, Cincinnati 13-16, New York 17-20, Philadelphia 21-24, Pittsburgh 25-28, St. Louis 29-32, Boston AL 33-36, Chicago 37-40, Cleveland 41-44, Detroit 45-48, New York 49-52, Philadelphia 53-56, St. Louis 57-60, Washington 61-64.

COMPLETE SET (64) 3,000.00 6,000.00
1 David Bancroft 75.00 150.00
2 Joseph Genewich 40.00 80.00
3 Andrew High 40.00 80.00
4 J. Taylor 40.00 80.00
5 John Buttler (Butler) 40.00 80.00
6 Wilson Fewster 40.00 80.00
7 Burleigh A. Grimes 75.00 150.00
8 Walter Henline 40.00 80.00
9 Sparky Adams 40.00 80.00
10 Charles Grimm 50.00 100.00
11 Leo Hartnett 75.00 150.00
12 Clifton Heathcote 40.00 80.00
13 Raymond Bressler 40.00 80.00
14 Walter C. Pipp 60.00 120.00
15 Eppa Rixey 75.00 150.00
16 Ivy Wingo 40.00 80.00
17 John M. Bentley 40.00 80.00
18 George Harper 40.00 80.00
19 Rogers Hornsby 125.00 250.00
20 Fredrick Lindstrom 75.00 150.00
21 A.R. Decatur 40.00 80.00
22 John Stuffy McInnes/(sic, McInnis) 50.00 100.00
23 John Mokan 40.00 80.00
24 Russell Wrightstone 40.00 80.00
25 Hazen Cuyler 75.00 150.00
26 Ray Kremer 40.00 80.00
27 Earl Smith 40.00 80.00
28 Harold Traynor 75.00 150.00
29 Grover C. Alexander 100.00 200.00
30 James Bottomly/(sic, Bottomley) 100.00 200.00
31 Robert O'Farrell 40.00 80.00
32 Wm. H. Southworth 50.00 100.00
33 Ira Flagstead 40.00 80.00
34 Fred Haney 40.00 80.00
35 Philip Todt 40.00 80.00
36 Fred Wingfield 40.00 80.00
37 Fred Blankenship/(sic, Ted) 40.00 80.00
38 Wm. Hunnefield/(sic, Tommy Thomas) 40.00 80.00
39 Willie Kamm 40.00 80.00
40 Ray Schalk 75.00 150.00
41 Geo. H. Burns HOR 40.00 80.00
42 Walter Lutzke 40.00 80.00
43 Glenn Myatt 40.00 80.00
44 Bernie Neis 40.00 80.00
45 John Bassler 40.00 80.00
46 George Daus/(sic, Dauss) 40.00 80.00
47 Charles Gehringer 100.00 200.00
48 Harry Heilman/(sic, Heilmann) 75.00 150.00
49 Henry L. Gehrig 450.00 900.00
50 Tony Lazzeri 75.00 150.00
51 Robert W. Muesel/(sic, Meusel) 40.00 80.00
52 Babe Ruth 700.00 1,400.00
53 Tyrus Cobb 450.00 900.00
54 Eddie Collins 75.00 150.00
55 William Wambsganns 50.00 100.00
sic, Wambsganss
56 Zach Wheat 75.00 150.00
57 Wm. Hargrave 40.00 80.00
58 Kenneth Williams 50.00 100.00
59 George Sissler 100.00 200.00
sic, Sisler
60 Ernest Wingard 40.00 80.00
61 Leon Goslin 75.00 150.00
62 Walter Johnson 250.00 500.00
63 Harold Ruel 40.00 80.00
64 Tristam Speaker 125.00 250.00
sic, Tristram

1928 Exhibits

In contrast to the green color of the preceding year, the 64 Exhibit cards of 1928 are blue in color. Each card measures 3 3/8" by 5 3/8". They may be found with blank backs, or postcard backs containing a small premium offer clip-off in one corner. The use of the divided legend was continued, with the Roush card being unique in the set as it also cites his position. Of the 64 players in the set, 24 appear for the first time, while 12 of the holdovers show new poses. In addition, four players are shown with new team affiliations. The remaining 24 cards are identical to those issued in 1927 except for color. Once again, there is at least one mistaken identity and many misspellings and wrong names. A few of the cards are presented horizontally (HOR). Players are listed below in alphabetical order by team: Boston NL 1-4, Brooklyn 5-8, Chicago 9-12, Cincinnati 13-16, New York 17-20, Philadelphia 21-24, Pittsburgh 25-28, St. Louis 29-32, Boston AL 33-36, Chicago 37-40, Cleveland 41-44, Detroit 45-48, New York 49-52, Philadelphia 53-56, St. Louis 57-60 and Washington 61-64.

COMPLETE SET (64) 2,500.00 5,000.00
1 Edward Brown 40.00 80.00
2 Rogers Hornsby HOR 150.00 300.00
3 Robert Smith 40.00 80.00
4 John Taylor 40.00 80.00
5 David Bancroft 75.00 150.00
6 Max G. Carey 75.00 150.00
7 Charles R. Hargraves 40.00 80.00
8 Arthur Dazzy Vance 75.00 150.00
9 Woody English 40.00 80.00
10 Leo Hartnett 75.00 150.00
11 Charlie Root 40.00 80.00
12 L.R. (Hack) Wilson 75.00 150.00
13 Hugh M. Critz 40.00 80.00
14 Eugene Hargrave 40.00 80.00
15 Adolph Luque 50.00 100.00
16 William A. Zitzmann 40.00 80.00
17 Virgil Barnes 40.00 80.00
18 J. Francis Hogan 40.00 80.00
19 Fredrick Lindstrom 75.00 150.00
sic, Frederick
20 Edd. Roush, Outfield 75.00 150.00
21 Fred Leach 40.00 80.00
22 James Ring 40.00 80.00
23 Henry Sand HOR 40.00 80.00
24 Fred Williams 50.00 100.00
25 Ray Kremer 40.00 80.00
26 Earl Smith 40.00 80.00
27 Paul Waner 75.00 150.00
28 Glenn Wright 40.00 80.00
29 Grover C. Alexander 75.00 150.00
no emblem
30 Francis R. Blades 40.00 80.00
31 Frank Frisch 100.00 200.00
32 James Wilson 50.00 100.00
33 Ira Flagstead 40.00 80.00
34 Bryan Slim Harriss 40.00 80.00
35 Fred Hoffman 40.00 80.00
36 Philip Todt 40.00 80.00
37 Chalmer W. Cissell HOR 40.00 80.00
38 Bib Falk 40.00 80.00
39 Theodore Lyons 75.00 150.00
40 Harry McCurdy 40.00 80.00
41 Chas. Jamieson 40.00 80.00
42 Glenn Myatt 40.00 80.00
43 Joseph Sewell 75.00 150.00
44 Geo. Uhle 40.00 80.00
45 Robert Fothergill 40.00 80.00
46 Jack Tavener HOR 40.00 80.00
47 Earl G. Whitehill 40.00 80.00
48 Lawrence Woodall 40.00 80.00
49 Pat Collins 40.00 80.00
50 Lou Gehrig 450.00 900.00
51 Babe Ruth 700.00 1,400.00
52 Urban J. Shocker 40.00 80.00
53 Gordon S. Cochrane 100.00 200.00
54 Howard Ehmke 50.00 100.00
55 Joseph Hauser 40.00 80.00
56 Al. Simmons 75.00 150.00
57 L.A. Blue 40.00 80.00
58 John Ogden 40.00 80.00
sic, Warren Ogden
59 Walter Shang 50.00 100.00
sic, Schang
60 Fred Schulte 40.00 80.00
61 Leon Goslin 75.00 150.00
62 Bucky Harris 75.00 150.00
63 Sam Jones 50.00 100.00
64 Harold Ruel 40.00 80.00

1929-30 Exhibits Four-in-One

The years 1929-30 marked the initial appearance of the Exhibit Company's famous "Four-In-One" design. Each of the 32 cards depict four players from one team, with a total of 128 players shown (eight from each of 16 major league teams). Each of these exhibit cards measures 3 3/8" by 5 3/8". The player's names and teams are located under each picture in dark blue or white print. All the reverses are post card style with the premium clip-off across one corner. There are 11 color combinations known for the fronts. The backs may be uncolored, red (black/red front) or yellow (blue/yellow front). The card labeled "Babe Herman" actually depicts Jesse Petty. The catalog designation is W463-1.

COMPLETE SET (32) 1,200.00 2,400.00
1 Pat Collins/Joe Dugan/Edward Farrel/(sic& Farre 40.00 80.00
2 Lance Richbourg/Fred Maguire
Robert Smith/Georg 25.00 50.00
3 Brooklyn Dodgers 30.00 60.00
D'Arcy Flowers
Arthur Dazzy Vance
Nick Cullop
Harvey Hendrick
4 Floyd C. Herman/David Bancroft
John H. Deberry/ 30.00 60.00
5A Leo Hartnett/C.E. Beck/L.R.
(Hack) Wilson/Roger 75.00 150.00
5B Clyde Beck/Gabby Hartnett/Hack Wilson/Rogers Ho
6 Charlie Root/Kiki Cuyler
Woody English/Charlie 30.00 60.00
7 H.M. Critz/W.C. Walker
George L. Kelly/V.J. Pic 30.00 60.00
8 Pid Purdy/Pinky Pittenger
Red Lucas/Hod Ford 25.00 50.00
9 Larry Benton/Melvin Ott
William Terry/Andrew Re 40.00 80.00
10 J.F. Hogan/Travis C. Jackson
J.D. Welsh/Fred Li 40.00 80.00
11 Frank O'Doul/Bernard Friberg
Fresco Thompson/Do 25.00 50.00
12 Cy Williams/A. C. Whitney
Ray Benge/Lester L. S 25.00 50.00
13 Earl J. Adams/R. Bartell
Harold Traynor/Earl Sh 30.00 60.00
14 Lloyd Waner/Charles R.Hargreaves
Ray Kremer/Pau 40.00 80.00
15 Grover C. Alexander/James Wilson
Frank Frisch/J 50.00 100.00
16 Fred G. Haney/Chas. J. Hafey
Taylor Douthit/Cha 30.00 60.00
17 J.A. Heving/J. Rothrock
Red Ruffing/B.Reeves 30.00 60.00
18 Phil Todt/Hal Rhyne
Bill Regan/Doug Taitt 25.00 50.00
19 Chalmer W. Cissell/John W. Clancy
John L. Kerr/ 25.00 50.00
20 Alex Metzler/Alphonse Thomas
Carl Reynolds/Mart 25.00 50.00
21 Lew Fonseca/Joe Sewell
Carl Lind/Jackie Tavener 30.00 60.00
22 K. Holloway/Bibb A. Falk
Luke Sewell/Earl Averi 30.00 60.00
23 Dale Alexander/G.F. McManus
H.F. Rice/C. Gehrin 40.00 80.00
24 M.J. Shea/G.E. Uhle
Harry E. Heilman/(sic& Heil 30.00 60.00
25 Waite Hoyt/Anthony Lazzeri
Benny Bengough/Earle 50.00 100.00
26 New York Yankees 400.00 800.00
Mark Koenig
Babe Ruth
Leo Durocher
Henry L. Gehrig
27 Jimmy Foxx/Gordon S.
Cochrane/Robert M. Grove/G 75.00 150.00
28 Homer Summa/James Dykes
Samuel Hale/Max Bishop 25.00 50.00
29 Heine Manush/W.H. Shang
(sic& Schang)/S. Gray/ 30.00 60.00
30 Oscar Melillo/F.O. Rourke
(sic& O'Rourke)/L.A. 25.00 50.00
31 Leon Goslin/Oswald Bluege
Harold Ruel/Joseph Ju 30.00 60.00
32 Sam Rice/Jack Hayes
Sam P. Jones/Buddy M. Myer 30.00 60.00

1931-32 Exhibits Four-in-One

The collector should refer to the checklists when trying to determine the year of issue of any "Four-In-One" set because the checklist (showing the players as they are, appear in groups of four) and the card color will ultimately provide the right clues. Some of the colors of the previous issue -- black on green, orange, red or yellow, and blue on white -- are repeated in this series, but the 1931-32 cards are distinguishable by the combinations of players which appear. Each card measures 3 3/8" by 5 3/8". The backs contain a description of attainable "Free Prizes" for coupons. The backs also contain the clip-off premium coupon. There are numerous misspellings, as usual, in the set. The catalog designation for this set is W463-2.

COMPLETE SET (32) 2,000.00 4,000.00
1 Walter Maranville/J.T. Zachary
Alfred Sphorer/R 60.00 120.00
2 Lance Richbourg/Fred Maguire
Earl Sheely/Walter 50.00 100.00
3 Brooklyn Dodgers 60.00 120.00
D'Arcy Flowers
Arthur Dazzy Vance
Frank O'Doul
Fresco Thompson
4 Floyd C. Herman/Glenn Wright
Jack Quinn/Del L. 50.00 100.00
5 Leo Hartnett/J.R. Stevenson
(sic& Stephenson)/L 125.00 250.00
6 Charlie Root/Hazen Cuyler
Woody English/Charlie 60.00 120.00
7 Les Durocher/(sic& Leo)
W.C. Walker/Harry Heilm 75.00 150.00

8 W. Roettger/Gooch/C.F. Lucas/H.E. Ford 50.00 100.00
9 J.F. Hogan/Travis C. Jackson
H.M. Critz/Fred Li 60.00 120.00
10 Robert O'Farrell/Melvin Ott
William Terry/Fred 100.00 200.00
11 Chuck Klein/Pinky Whitney
Ray Benge/Buzz Arlett 60.00 120.00
12 Harry McCurdy/Bernard Friberg
Richard Bartell/D 50.00 100.00
13 Adam Comorosky/Gus Suhr
Harold Traynor/T.J. The 60.00 120.00
14 Lloyd Waner/George Grantham
Ray Kremer/Paul Wan 60.00 120.00
15 Earl J. Adams/James Wilson
Frank Frisch/James B 75.00 150.00
16 Bill Hallahan/Chas. J. Hafey
Taylor Douthit/Cha 60.00 120.00
17 Chas. Berry/J. Rothrock
Robt. Reeves/R.R. (R.E. 50.00 100.00
18 Earl Webb/Hal Rhyne/Bill Sweeney
Danny MacFayde 50.00 100.00
19 Luke L. Appling/Ted Lyons
Chalmer W. Cissell/Wi 60.00 120.00
20 Smead Jolley/Lu Blue
Carl Reynolds/Henry Tate 50.00 100.00
21 Hunnefield/J. Goldman
Ed Morgan/Wes Ferrell 50.00 100.00
22 Lew Fonseca/Bibb Falk
Luke Sewell/Earl Averill 60.00 120.00
23 Dale Alexander/G.F. McManus
G.E. Uhle/C. Gehrin 60.00 120.00
24 Wallie Schang/Liz Funk
Mark Koenig/Waite Hoyt 60.00 120.00
25 W. Dickey/Anthony Lazzeri
Herb Pennock/Earl B. 150.00 300.00
26 Lyn Lary/Geo. H. Babe Ruth
James Reese/Henry L. 600.00 1,200.00
27 John Boley/James Dykes
Bing. Miller/Al Simmons 60.00 120.00
28 Jimmy Foxx/Gordon S. Cochrane
Robert M. Grove/G 100.00 200.00
29 O. Melillo/F.O. Rourke
(sic& O'Rourke)/Leon Gos 60.00 120.00
30 W. Stewart/Richard Farrell
(sic& Ferrell)/S. Gr 60.00 120.00
31 Roy Spencer/Heine Manush
Joe Cronin/Fred Marber 60.00 120.00
32 Ossie Bluege/Joe Judge
Sam Rice/Buddy Myer 60.00 120.00

1933 Exhibits Four-in-One

The physical dimensions of the cardboard sheet used by the Exhibit Supply Company in printing their card sets over the years allows the following correlation to be made when one establishes that 32 of the standard-sized cards (3 3/8" by 5 3/8") are printed per sheet. Sets of 128 cards are equal to four sheets, 64 cards to two sheets, 32 cards to one sheet and 16 cards to one-half sheet. Whether it was economics, the Depression, or simplicity of operation, something caused the company to change their set totals in a descending order since 1922 in 1933. The first of a series of 16-card sets was released. The fronts of these cards are black green, orange, red or yellow; the backs are blank. The catalog designation for this set is W463-3.

COMPLETE SET (16) 1,200.00 2,400.00
1 Lance Richbourg 40.00 80.00
Fred Maguire
Earl Sheely
Walter
2 Vincent Lopez (Al) 60.00 120.00
Glenn Wright
Arthur Dazzy Van
3 Riggs Stephenson 40.00 80.00
Charlie Grimm
Woody English
Ch
4 Taylor Douthit 50.00 100.00
George Grantham
G. F. Lucas
Chas
5 Fred Fitzsimmons 50.00 100.00
H. M. Critz
Fred Lindstrom
Rob
6 Chuck Klein 50.00 100.00
Ray Benge
Richard Bartell
Donald Hu
7 Tom J. Thevenow 60.00 120.00
Paul Waner
Gus Suhr
Lloyd Waner
8 Earl J. Adams 60.00 120.00
Frank Frisch
Bill Halloran
Chas.
9 Danny MacFayden 40.00 80.00
Earl Webb
Hal Rhyne
Charlie Ber
10 Charles Berry 50.00 100.00
Bob Seeds
Lu Blue
Ted Lyons
11 Wes Ferrell 50.00 100.00
Luke Sewell
Ed Morgan
Earl Averill
12 Muddy' Ruel/G.E. Uhle
Jonathon Stone/C. Gehri 60.00 120.00
13 Babe Ruth 600.00 1,200.00
Herb Pennock
Anthony Lazzer
14 Mickey Cochrane 125.00 250.00
Jimmy Foxx (Jimmie)
Al Simmons
Robert M.
15 Richard Farrell/(sic& Ferrell) 60.00 120.00
O. Melillo
Leon
16 Heinie Manush 50.00 100.00
Firpo Marberry
Joe Judge
Roy Spen

1934 Exhibits Four-in-One

The emergence of the bubble gum card producers in 1933-34 may have motivated Exhibit Supply to make a special effort to provide a "quality" set for 1934. The new 16-card series was printed in colors of blue, brown, olive green and violet -- all in softer tones than used in previous years. No less than 25 players appeared on cards for the first time, and another 16 were given entirely new poses. For the first time in the history of the Exhibit baseball series, there were no spelling errors. However, perfection is rarely attained in any endeavor, and the "bugaboo" of 1934 was the labeling of Al Lopez as Vincent Lopez (famous band leader and prognosticator). The cards have plain backs. Each card measures 3 3/8" by 5 3/8". ACC catalog designation for this set is W463-4.

COMPLETE SET (16) 900.00 1,800.00
1 Bill Urbansky/Ed Brandt
Walter Berger/Frank Hog 25.00 50.00
2 Vincent Lopez (Al)/Glenn Wright
Sam Leslie/Leon 30.00 60.00
3 Chas. Klein/C.J. Grimm
Woody English/Lon Warnek 30.00 60.00
4 Botchi Lombardi/Tony Piet
Jimmy Bottomley/Chas. 50.00 100.00
5 Blondy Ryan/Bill Terry
Carl Hubbell/Mel Ott 75.00 150.00
6 Jimmy Wilson/Wesley Schulmerich
Richard Bartell# 25.00 50.00
7 T.J. Thevenow/Paul Waner
Pie Traynor/Lloyd Wane 50.00 100.00
8 Pepper Martin/Frank Frisch
Bill Hallahan/John R 40.00 80.00
9 Lefty Grove/Roy Johnson
Bill Cissell/Rick Ferre 50.00 100.00
10 Luke Appling/Al Simmons
Evar Swanson/George Ear 40.00 80.00
11 Wes Ferrell/Frank Pytlak
Willie Kamm/Earl Averi 30.00 60.00
12 Mickey Cochrane/Goose Goslin
Fred Marberry/C. G 75.00 150.00
13 Babe Ruth/Lefty Gomez
Lou Gehrig/B.Dickey 400.00 800.00
14 Mickey Cochrane/Jimmy Foxx
Al Simmons/Robert M. 50.00 100.00
15 Irving Burns/O. Melillo
Irving Hadley/Rollie He 25.00 50.00
16 Heine Manush/Alvin Crowder
Joe Cronin/Joe Kuhel 40.00 80.00

1935 Exhibits Four-in-One W463-5

The year 1935 marked the return of the 16-card Exhibit series to a simple slate blue color. Babe Ruth appears with Boston, N.L., the last time his card would be made while he was playing, after being included in every Exhibit series since 1921. Of the 64 players pictured, 17 are shown for the first time, while 11 of the returnees are graced with new poses. The infamous "Vincent Lopez" card returns with this set, and the photo purportedly showing Tony Cuccinello is really that of George Puccinello. The cards have plain backs. The cards measure 3 3/8" by 5 3/8".

COMPLETE SET (16) 1,200.00 2,400.00
1 Babe Ruth/Frank Hogan
Walter Berger/Ed Brand 400.00 800.00
2 Van Mungo/Vincent Lopez
(Al)/Dan Taylor/Tony Cu 30.00 60.00
3 Chas. Klein/C.J. Grimm
Lon Warneke/Gabby Hartne 40.00 80.00
4 Botchi Lombardi/Paul Derringer
Jimmy Bottomley/ 50.00 100.00
5 Hughie Critz/Bill Terry
Carl Hubbell/Mel Ott 75.00 150.00
6 Philadelphia Phillies 25.00 50.00
Jimmy Wilson
Phil Collins
John Blondy Ryan
George Watkins
7 Paul Waner/Pie Traynor
Guy Bush/Floyd Vaughan 50.00 100.00
8 St. Louis Cardinals 125.00 250.00
Pepper Martin
Frank Frisch
Jerome Dizzy Dean
Paul Dean
9 Lefty Grove/Billy Werber
Joe Cronin/Rick Ferrel 75.00 150.00
10 Al Simmons/Jimmy Dykes
Ted Lyons/Henry Bonura 40.00 80.00
11 Mel Harder/Hal Trosky/Willie
Kamm/Earl Averill 30.00 60.00
12 Mickey Cochrane/Goose Goslin
Linwood Rowe/(sic& 50.00 100.00
13 Tony Lazzeri/Lefty Gomez
Lou Gehrig/Bill Dicke 300.00 600.00
14 Slug Mahaffey/Jimmy Foxx
George Cramer/Bob John 40.00 80.00
15 Irving Burns/Oscar Melillo
L.N. Newson/Rollie H 25.00 50.00
16 Buddy Meyer (Myer)/Earl Whitehill
H. Manush/Fre 30.00 60.00

1936 Exhibits Four-in-One W463-6

In 1936, the 16-card Exhibit set retained the "slate" or blue-gray color of the preceding year, but also added an olive green hue to the set. The cards are blank-backed, but for the first time since the "Four-In-One" design was introduced in 1929, a line reading "Ptd. in U.S.A." was placed in the bottom border on the obverse. The set contains 16 players making their debut in Exhibit cards, while nine holdovers have new poses. The photos of George Puccinelli was correctly identified and placed with Philadelphia, A.L. The cards measure 3 3/8" by 5 3/8".

COMPLETE SET (16) 750.00 1,500.00
1 Bill Urbanski/Pinky Whitney
Walter Berger/Danny 25.00 50.00
2 Van Mungo/Stan Bordagaray
Fred Lindstrom/Dutch 30.00 60.00
3 Billy Herman/Augie Galan
Lon Warneke/Gabby Hart 40.00 80.00
4 Botchie Lombardi/Paul Derringer
Babe Herman/Ale 30.00 60.00
5 Gus. Mancuso/Bill Terry
Carl Hubbell/Mel Ott 75.00 150.00
6 Jimmy Wilson/Curt Davis
Dolph Camilli/Johnny Mo 25.00 50.00
7 Paul Waner/Pie Traynor
Guy Bush/Floyd Vaughan 40.00 80.00
8 St. Louis Cardinals 75.00 150.00
Joe Ducky Medwick
Frank Frisch
Jerome Dizzy Dean
Paul Dean
9 Lefty Grove/Jimmy Foxx
Joe Cronin/Rick Ferrell 75.00 150.00
10 Luke Appling/Jimmy Dykes
Ted Lyons/Henry Bonura 40.00 80.00
11 Mel Harder/Hal Trosky
Joe Vosmik/Earl Averill 30.00 60.00
12 Mickey Cochrane/Goose Goslin
Linwood Rowe/(sic& 75.00 150.00
13 Tony Lazzeri/Vernon Gomez
Lou Gehrig/Red Ruffin 300.00 600.00
14 Charles Berry/Puccinelli
Frank Higgins/Bob John 25.00 50.00
15 Harland Clift/Sammy West
Paul Andrews/Rollie He 25.00 50.00
16 Buddy Meyer (Myer)/Earl Whitehill
Ossie Bluege/ 25.00 50.00

1937 Exhibits Four-in-One

It would appear that Exhibit Supply was merely "flip-flopping" color schemes during the three year period 1935-37. In 1935, the cards were blue-gray; in 1936, the cards were either blue-gray or green; in 1937, the cards appear in green only. As with the previous set, the name and team of each player is printed in two or three lines under his picture, the "Ptd. in U.S.A." line appears in the bottom border (missing on some cards) and the backs are blank. The ACC catalog designation for this set is W463-7

COMPLETE SET (16) 1,000.00 2,000.00
1 Bill Urbanski/Alfonso Lopez
Walter Berger/Danny 40.00 80.00
2 Van Mungo/E. English/Johnny
Moore/(Philadelphia 30.00 60.00
3 Billy Herman/Augie Galan
Bill Lee/Gabby Hartnet 40.00 80.00
4 Botchi Lombardi/Paul Derringer
Lew Riggs/Phil W 30.00 60.00
5 Gus Mancuso/Sam Leslie
Carl Hubbell/Mel Ott 60.00 120.00
6 Pinky Whitney/Wm. Walters
Dolph Camilli/Johnny 30.00 60.00
7 Paul Waner/Gus Suhr/Cy Blanton
Floyd Vaughan 40.00 80.00
8 St. Louis Cardinals 100.00 200.00
Joe Duck Medwick
Lon Warneke
Jerome Dizzy Dean
Stuart Martin
9 Lefty Grove/Jimmy Foxx
Joe Cronin/Dick Ferrell 150.00 300.00
10 Luke Appling/Jimmy Dykes
Vernon Kennedy/Henry B 30.00 60.00
11 Bob Feller/Hal Trosky
Frank Pytlak/Earl Averill 100.00 200.00
12 Mickey Cochrane/Goose Goslin
Linwood Rowe/C. Ge 60.00 120.00
13 Tony Lazzeri/Vernon Gomez
Lou Gehrig/Joe DiMagg 400.00 800.00
14 Billy Weber/(sic& Werber)
Harry Kelly/(sic& Kel 30.00 60.00
15 Harland Clift/Sammy West
Orval Hildebrand/Rolli 30.00 60.00
16 Buddy Meyer (Myer)
Jonathan Stone/Joe Kuhel/L.N 30.00 60.00

1938 Exhibits Four-in-One

The 1938 set of 16 cards demonstrated the fact that one consistent "quality" of Exhibit Supply sets is their inconsistency. For example, the card of Tony Cuccinello once again contains the photo of George Puccinelli, a mistake first made in 1935, corrected in 1936 and now made again in 1938. The set is also rife with name and spelling errors. Of the 64 players depicted, 12 are new arrivals and three are returnees with new poses. Another ten retained their 1937 photos but were designated new team affiliations. The cards have blank backs. The set was the last to employ the "Four-In-One" format. The catalog designation is W463-8. The cards measure 3 3/8" by 5 3/8".

COMPLETE SET (16) 1,200.00 2,400.00
1 Tony Cuccinello/(sic, Geo.Puccinelli) 40.00 80.00
Roy Johnson
Vince DiMaggio
Danny MacFayden
2 Van Mungo 40.00 80.00
Leo Durocher
Dolph Camilli
Gordon Phelps
3 Billy Herman 125.00 250.00
Augie Galan
Jerome Dizzy Dean
Gabby Hartnett
4 Dutch Lombardi 40.00 80.00
Paul Derringer
Lew Riggs
Ival Goodman
5 Hank Leiber 75.00 150.00
Jim Ripple
Carl Hubbell
Mel Ott
6 Pinky Whitney 40.00 80.00
Bucky Walters
Chuck Klein
Morris Arnovich
7 Paul Waner 50.00 100.00
Gus Suhr
Cy Blanton
Floyd Vaughan
8 Joe Ducky Medwick 50.00 100.00
Lon Warneke
John Mize
Stuart Martin
9 Lefty Grove 75.00 150.00
Jimmy Foxx (Jimmie)
Joe Cronin
Joe Vosmik
10 Luke Appling 50.00 100.00
Luke Sewell
Mike Kreevich
Ted Lyons
11 Bob Feller 75.00 150.00
Hal Trosky
Odell Hale
Earl Averill
12 Hank Greenberg 75.00 150.00
Rudy York
Tom Bridges
Charlie Gehringer
13 Bill Dickey 500.00 1,000.00
Lefty Gomez
Lou Gehrig
Joe DiMaggio
14 Billy Weber 40.00 80.00
sic, Werber
Harry Kelly
sic, Kelley
Wallace Moses
Bob Johnson
15 Harland Clift 40.00 80.00
Sammy West
Beau Bell
Bobo Newsom
16 Buddy Meyer (Myer) 40.00 80.00
Jonathan Stone
Wes Ferrell
Rick Ferrell

1939-46 Exhibits Salutation

This collection of exhibit cards shares a common style: the "Personal Greeting" or "Salutation". The specific greeting varies from card to card -- "Yours truly, Best wishes, etc." -- as does the location of the exhibit identification (lower left, LL, or lower right, LR). Some players appear with different teams and there are occasional misspellings. Each card measures 3 3/8" by 5 3/8". The Bob Feller (Yours Truly), Andy Pafko (Yours Truly) and Ted Williams (Sincerely Yours) cards are relatively quite common as they were still being printed into the middle to late 1950s, i.e., basically until the end of their respective careers. The Jeff Heath small picture variation (26B) is differentiated by measuring the distance between the top of his cap and the top edge of the card; for the small picture variation that distance is approximately 5/8" whereas it is only 3/8" for 26A. There is some doubt about whether Camilli #6B exists. An Andy Pafko sincerely yours card is rumored to exist but has never been verified, while the 50B Pafko is a very tough card since it was printed only in 1960.

Card	Low	High
COMPLETE SET (84)	4,000.00	8,000.00
1A Luke Appling LL Sincerely Yours	15.00	25.00
1B Luke Appling LR Sincerely Yours	9.00	15.00
2 Earl Averill Very Best Wishes	500.00	800.00
3 Charles Red Barrett Yours Truly	3.00	5.00
4 Henry Hank Borowy Sincerely Yours	3.00	5.00
5 Lou Boudreau Sincerely	5.00	8.00
6A Adolf Camilli LL Very Truly Yours	15.00	25.00
6B Adolf Camilli LR Very Truly Yours	120.00	200.00
7 Phil Cavarretta Cordially Yours	3.00	5.00
8 Harland Clift Very Truly Yours	12.00	20.00
9 Tony Cuccinello Very Best Wishes	25.00	40.00
10 Dizzy Dean Sincerely	60.00	100.00
11 Paul Derringer Yours Truly	3.00	5.00
12A Bill Dickey LL Cordially Yours	30.00	50.00
12B Bill Dickey LR Cordially Yours	30.00	50.00
13 Joe DiMaggio Cordially	70.00	120.00
14 Bob Elliott Truly Yours	3.00	5.00
15A Bob Feller Best Wishes portrait	70.00	120.00
15B Bob Feller Yours Truly pitching pose	9.00	15.00
16 Dave Ferriss Best of Luck	3.00	5.00
17 Jimmy Foxx Sincerely (Jimmie)	120.00	200.00
18 Lou Gehrig Sincerely	1,200.00	2,000.00
19 Charlie Gehringer Yours Truly	75.00	125.00
20 Lefty Gomez	120.00	200.00
21A Joe Gordon Cleveland Sincerely	15.00	25.00
21B Joe Gordon New York Sincerely	3.00	5.00
22A Hank Greenberg Truly Yours	20.00	35.00
22B Henry Greenberg Very Truly Yours	90.00	150.00
23 Robert Grove Cordially Yours	75.00	125.00
24 Gabby Hartnett Cordially	200.00	350.00
25 Buddy Hassett Yours Truly	15.00	25.00
26A Jeff Heath Best Wishes	15.00	25.00
26B Jeff Heath Small Picture Best Wishes	3.00	5.00
27 Kirby Higbe Sincerely	15.00	25.00
28A Tommy Holmes Sincerely Yours	120.00	200.00
28B Tommy Holmes Yours Truly	3.00	5.00
29 Carl Hubbell Best Wishes	60.00	100.00
30 Bob Johnson Yours Truly	15.00	25.00
31A Charles Keller LL Best Wishes	15.00	25.00
31B Charles Keller LR Best Wishes	6.00	10.00
32 Ken Keltner Sincerly sic	30.00	50.00
33 Chuck Klein Yours Truly	180.00	300.00
34 Mike Kreevich Sincerely	150.00	250.00
35 Joe Kuhel Truly Yours	3.00	5.00
36 Bill Lee Cordially Yours	12.00	20.00
37A Ernie Lombardi 1/2 B Cordially	250.00	400.00
38B Ernie Lombardi Cordially Yours	6.00	10.00
39 Marty Marion Best Wishes	6.00	10.00
40 Merrill May Best Wishes	15.00	25.00
41A Frank McCormick LL Sincerely	15.00	25.00
41B Frank McCormick LR Sincerely	3.00	5.00
42A George McQuinn LL Yours Truly	15.00	25.00
42B George McQuinn LR Yours Truly	3.00	5.00
43 Joe Medwick Very Best Wishes	20.00	35.00
44A Johnny Mize LL Yours Truly	25.00	40.00
44B Johnny Mize LR Yours Truly	9.00	15.00
45 Hugh Mulcahy Cordially	15.00	25.00
46 Hal Newhouser Best Wishes	9.00	15.00
47 Louis Buck Newsom Sincerely	15.00	25.00
48 Buck Newson sic Very Best Wishes	180.00	300.00
49A Mel Ott LL Sincerely Yours	30.00	50.00
49B Mel Ott LR Sincerely Yours	25.00	40.00
50A Andy Pafko Yours Truly	3.00	5.00
50B Andy Pafko Yours Truly plain cap	20.00	40.00
51 Claude Passeau Sincerely	3.00	5.00
52A Howard Pollet LL Best Wishes	15.00	25.00
52B Howard Pollet LR Best Wishes	3.00	5.00
53A Pete Reiser LL Truly Yours	60.00	100.00
53B Pete Reiser LR Truly Yours	5.00	8.00
54 Johnny Rizzo Sincerely Yours	300.00	500.00
55 Glenn Russell Sincerely	180.00	300.00
56 George Stirnweiss Yours Truly	3.00	5.00
57 Cecil Travis Best Wishes	9.00	15.00
58 Paul Trout Truly Yours	3.00	5.00
59 Johnny Vander Meer Cordially Yours	30.00	50.00
60 Arky Vaughan Best Wishes	15.00	25.00
61A Fred Dixie Walker D on Hat Yours Truly	3.00	5.00
61B Fred Dixie Walker Cap blanked out Yours Truly	40.00	75.00
62 Bucky Walters Sincerely Yours	3.00	5.00
63 Lon Warneke Very Truly Yours	12.00	20.00
64A Ted Williams Sincerely #9 Showing	200.00	400.00
64B Ted Williams Sincerely Yours #9 Not Showing	45.00	80.00
65 Rudy York Cordially	3.00	5.00

1947-66 Exhibits

This grouping encompasses a wide time span but displays a common design. The following players have been illegally reprinted in mass quantities on a thinner-than-original cardboard which is also characterized by a dark gray back: Aaron, Ford, Fox, Hodges, Elston Howard, Mantle, Mays, Musial, Newcombe, Reese, Spahn, and Ted Williams. Each card measures 3 3/8" by 5 3/8". In the checklist below SIG refers to signature and SCR refers to script name on card. The abbreviations POR (portrait), BAT (batting), and FIE (fielding) are also used below. There are many levels of scarcity within this "set," essentially based on which year(s) the player's card was printed. The Mickey Mantle portrait card, for example, was only printed in 1966, the last year of production. Those scarce cards which were only produced one or two years are noted parenthetically below by the last two digits of the year(s) of issue. Cards which seem to be especially difficult to obtain are the ones produced only in 1966 which are the aforementioned Mantle Portrait, Ford, Kranepool, Richardson, Skowron (White Sox), Ward and Yastrzemski. Some leading exhibit experts believe that the salutation and these cards should be checklisted together because of the long printing history of some of the salutations. Please note that the following cards have been reprinted: Hank Aaron, Whitey Ford (no glove, throwing), Nelson Fox, Gil Hodges (Brooklyn cap), Elston Howard, Willie May (Batting, New York), Stan Musial (three bats, kneeling), Don Newcombe (Brooklyn cap), Pee Wee Reese (ball not visable), Warren Spahn (Boston).

Card	Low	High
COMPLETE SET (321)	4,000.00	8,000.00
1 Hank Aaron	30.00	60.00
2A Joe Adcock SCR	3.00	8.00
2B Joe Adcock SIG	3.00	8.00
3 Max Alvis 66	30.00	60.00
4A Johnny Antonelli Braves	3.00	8.00
4B Johnny Antonelli Giants	3.00	8.00
5A Luis Aparicio POR	4.00	10.00
5B Luis Aparicio BAT 64	40.00	80.00
6 Luke Appling	4.00	10.00
7A Richie Ashburn Phillies	30.00	60.00
7B Ritchie Ashburn sic, Richie	6.00	15.00
7C Richie Ashburn Cubs 61	40.00	80.00
8 Bob Aspromonte 64/66	3.00	8.00
9 Toby Atwell	3.00	8.00
10A Ed Bailey 61 Cincinnati cap	6.00	15.00
10B Ed Bailey no cap	3.00	8.00
11 Gene Baker	3.00	8.00
12A Ernie Banks SCR	20.00	50.00
12B Ernie Banks SIG	10.00	25.00
12C Ernie Banks POR 64/66	20.00	50.00
13 Steve Barber 64/66	3.00	8.00
14 Earl Battey 64/66	3.00	8.00
15 Matt Batts	4.00	10.00
16A Hank Bauer New York cap	3.00	8.00
16B Hank Bauer 61 plain cap	20.00	50.00
17 Frank Baumholtz	3.00	8.00
18 Gene Bearden	3.00	8.00
19 Joe Beggs 47	12.50	30.00
20A Yogi Berra	6.00	15.00
20B Larry Yogi Berra 64/66	30.00	60.00
21 Steve Bilko	3.00	8.00
22A Ewell Blackwell foot up	4.00	10.00
22B Ewell Blackwell POR	3.00	8.00
23A Don Blasingame St. Louis cap	3.00	8.00
23B Don Blasingame plain cap	4.00	10.00
24 Ken Boyer 64/66	12.50	30.00
25 Ralph Branca	3.00	8.00
26 Jackie Brandt 61	40.00	80.00
27 Harry Brecheen	3.00	8.00
28 Tom Brewer 61	30.00	60.00
29 Lou Brissie	3.00	8.00
30 Bill Bruton	3.00	8.00
31A Lew Burdette side view	3.00	8.00
31B Lew Burdette facing 64	15.00	40.00
32 Johnny Callison 64/66	4.00	10.00
33 Roy Campanella	30.00	60.00
34A Chico Carrasquel White Sox	3.00	8.00
34B Chico Carrasquel plain cap	10.00	25.00
35 George Case 47	12.50	30.00
36 Hugh Casey	6.00	15.00
37 Norm Cash 64/66	10.00	25.00
38A Orlando Cepeda POR 60/61	10.00	25.00
38B Orlando Cepeda BAT 64/66	10.00	25.00
39A Bob Cerv 60 A's uniform	3.00	8.00
39B Bob Cerv 61 plain uniform	30.00	60.00
40 Dean Chance 64/66	3.00	8.00
41 Spud Chandler 47	12.50	30.00
42 Tom Cheney 64/66	3.00	8.00
43 Bubba Church	3.00	8.00
44 Roberto Clemente	75.00	150.00
45A Rocky Colavito POR 61	75.00	150.00
45B Rocky Colavito BAT 64/66	15.00	40.00
46 Choo Choo Coleman 64	15.00	40.00
47 Gordy Coleman 66	30.00	60.00
48 Jerry Coleman	3.00	8.00
49 Mort Cooper 47	15.00	40.00
50 Walker Cooper	3.00	8.00
51 Roger Craig 64/66	6.00	15.00
52 Delmar Crandall	3.00	8.00
53A Joe Cunningham POR 64/66	4.00	10.00
53B Joe Cunningham BAT 61	40.00	80.00
54 Guy Curtwright 47 sic, Curtright	12.50	30.00
55 Bud Daley 61	30.00	60.00
56A Alvin Dark Boston cap	6.00	15.00
56B Alvin Dark New York cap	3.00	8.00
56C Alvin Dark Cubs 60	20.00	50.00
57 Murray Dickson	3.00	8.00
58 Bob Dillinger	6.00	15.00
59 Dom DiMaggio	6.00	15.00
60 Joe Dobson	3.00	8.00
61 Larry Doby	3.00	8.00
62 Bobby Doerr	6.00	15.00
63A Dick Donovan Braves, plain cap	3.00	8.00
63B Dick Donovan White Sox	3.00	8.00
64 Walter Dropo	3.00	8.00
65A Don Drysdale POR/60/61	30.00	60.00
65B Don Drysdale 64/66/POR 1/2	30.00	60.00
66 Luke Easter	3.00	8.00
67 Bruce Edwards	6.00	15.00
68 Del Ennis	3.00	8.00
69 Al Evans	3.00	8.00
70 Walter Evers	3.00	8.00
71A Ferris Fain FIE	6.00	15.00
71B Ferris Fain POR	3.00	8.00
72 Dick Farrell 64/66	3.00	8.00
73A Whitey Ford no glove, throwing	6.00	15.00
73B Whitey Ford POR 66	175.00	350.00
73C Ed 'Whitey' Ford (glove on shoulder)/64/66	30.00	60.00
74 Dick Fowler	3.00	8.00
75 Nelson Fox	10.00	25.00
76 Tito Francona 64/66	3.00	8.00
77 Bob Friend	3.00	8.00
78 Carl Furillo	12.50	30.00
79 Augie Galan	12.50	30.00
80 Jim Gentile 64/66	3.00	8.00
81 Tony Gonzalez 64/66	3.00	8.00
82A Billy Goodman FIE fielding	3.00	8.00
82B Billy Goodman BAT 60/61	12.50	30.00
83 Ted Greengrass sic, Jim	6.00	15.00
84 Dick Groat	3.00	8.00
85 Steve Gromek	6.00	15.00
86 Johnny Groth	3.00	8.00
87 Orval Grove 47	12.50	30.00
88A Frank Gustine Pirates	3.00	8.00
88B Frank GustineCubs	3.00	8.00
89 Berthold Haas	12.50	30.00
90 Grady Hatton	3.00	8.00
91 Jim Hegan	3.00	8.00
92 Tommy Henrich	3.00	8.00
93 Ray Herbert 66	30.00	60.00
94 Gene Hermanski	6.00	15.00
95 Whitey Herzog 60/61	6.00	15.00
96 Kirby Higbe 47	12.50	30.00
97 Chuck Hinton 64/66	3.00	8.00
98 Don Hoak 64	15.00	40.00
99A Gil Hodges Brooklyn cap	6.00	15.00
99B Gil Hodges Los Angeles cap	12.50	30.00
100 Johnny Hopp 47	12.50	30.00
101 Elston Howard	3.00	8.00
102 Frank Howard 64/66	10.00	25.00
103 Ken Hubbs 64	75.00	150.00
104 Tex Hughson 47	12.50	30.00
105 Fred Hutchinson 50	6.00	15.00
106 Monte Irvin	6.00	15.00
107 Joey Jay 64/66	3.00	8.00
108 Jackie Jensen 60	40.00	80.00
109 Sam Jethroe	4.00	10.00
110 Bill Johnson 50	4.00	10.00
111 Walter Judnich 47	12.50	30.00
112A Al Kaline SCR kneeling	12.50	30.00
112B Al Kaline SIG POR	10.00	25.00
113 George Kell	6.00	15.00
114 Charley Keller	6.00	15.00
115 Alex Kellner	3.00	8.00
116 Kenn Keltner sic, Ken	12.50	30.00
117A Harmon Killebrew pinstripes, batting 60/61	30.00	60.00
117B Harmon Killibrew sic, Killebrew POR 66	40.00	80.00
117C Harmon Killebrew throwing 64/66	15.00	40.00
118 Ellis Kinder	3.00	8.00
119 Ralph Kiner	6.00	15.00
120 Billy Klaus 60	30.00	60.00
121A Ted KluszewskiReds	12.50	30.00
121B Ted Kluszewski Pirates	12.50	30.00
121C Ted Kluszewski plain uniform 60/61	40.00	80.00
122 Don Kolloway 50	6.00	15.00
123 Jim Konstanty	4.00	10.00
124 Sandy Koufax 64/66	75.00	150.00
125 Ed Kranepool 66	150.00	300.00
126A Tony Kubek dark background	3.00	8.00
126B Tony Kubek light background	3.00	8.00
127A Harvey Kuenn 60 Detroit	6.00	15.00
127B Harvey Kuenn 61 plain uniform	30.00	60.00
127C Harvey Kuenn San Francisco 64/66	6.00	15.00
128 Whitey Kurowski 50	12.50	30.00
129 Eddie Lake 47	12.50	30.00
130 Jim Landis 64/66	3.00	8.00
131 Don Larsen	3.00	8.00
132A Bob Lemon left arm not shown	4.00	10.00
132B Bob Lemon left arm extended	40.00	80.00
133 Buddy Lewis 47	12.50	30.00
134 Johnny Lindell 50	12.50	30.00
135 Phil Linz 66	30.00	60.00
136 Don Lock 66	30.00	60.00
137 Whitey Lockman	3.00	8.00
138 Johnny Logan	3.00	8.00
139A Dale Long Pirates	3.00	8.00
139B Dale Long Cubs 61	30.00	60.00
140 Ed Lopat	3.00	8.00
141A Harry Lowery sic, Lowrey	6.00	15.00
141B Harry Lowrey	3.00	8.00
142 Sal Maglie	3.00	8.00
143 Art Mahaffey 64/66	3.00	8.00
144 Hank Majeski	3.00	8.00

145 Frank Malzone 3.00 8.00
146A Mickey Mantle/(batting to waist)
(white outline 100.00 200.00
146B Mickey Mantle/(batting to waist)
(no white outli 150.00 300.00
146C Mickey Mantle/(batting full) 64/66 100.00 200.00
146D Mickey Mantle POR/66 400.00 800.00
147 Marty Marion 3.00 8.00
148 Roger Maris 64/66 40.00 80.00
149 Willard Marshall 3.00 8.00
150A Ed Matthews SCR 10.00 25.00
sic, Mathews
150B Eddie Mathews SIG 15.00 40.00
151 Ed Mayo 3.00 8.00
152A Willie Mays Batting 30.00 60.00
New York
152B Willie Mays 30.00 60.00
San Francisco
153A Bill Mazeroski POR 8.00 20.00
60/61
153B Bill Mazeroski BAT 8.00 20.00
64/66
154 Ken McBride 64/66 3.00 8.00
155A Barney McCaskey 15.00 40.00
sic, McCosky
155B Barney McCoskey/(sic, McCosky) 50.00 100.00
156 Lindy McDaniel 60/61 3.00 8.00
157 Gil McDougald 3.00 8.00
158 Albert Mele 30.00 60.00
159 Sam Mele 6.00 15.00
160A Minnie Minoso 3.00 8.00
White Sox
160B Minnie Minoso 6.00 15.00
Cleveland
161 Dale Mitchell 3.00 8.00
162 Wally Moon 3.00 8.00
163 Don Mueller 15.00 40.00
164A Stan Musial 30.00 60.00
three bats, kneeling
164B Stan Musial BAT 64 100.00 200.00
165 Charles Neal 64 15.00 40.00
166A Don Newcombe 6.00 15.00
shaking hands
166B Don Newcombe 3.00 8.00
Brooklyn cap
166C Don Newcombe 10.00 25.00
plain cap
167 Hal Newhouser 6.00 15.00
168 Ron Northey 47 15.00 40.00
169 Bill O'Dell 64/66 3.00 8.00
170 Joe Page 50 12.50 30.00
171 Satchel Paige 75.00 150.00
172 Milt Pappas 64/66 3.00 8.00
173 Camilo Pascual 64/66 3.00 8.00
174 Albie Pearson 66 30.00 60.00
175 Johnny Pesky 3.00 8.00
176 Gary Peters 66 30.00 60.00
177 Dave Philley 3.00 8.00
178 Billy Pierce 60/61 3.00 8.00
179 Jimmy Piersall 66 50.00 100.00
180 Vada Pinson 64/66 10.00 25.00
181 Bob Porterfield 3.00 8.00
182 Boog Powell 66 75.00 150.00
183 Vic Raschi 3.00 8.00
184A Harold Peewee Reese
(ball visible along/bottom 10.00 25.00
184B Harold Peewee Reese 10.00 25.00
ball not visible
185 Del Rice 3.00 8.00
186 Bobby Richardson 66 175.00 350.00
187A Phil Rizzuto 10.00 25.00
small photo
187B Phil Rizzuto 6.00 15.00
larger photo
188A Robin Roberts SIG 6.00 15.00
188B Robin Roberts SCR 8.00 20.00
189 Brooks Robinson 30.00 60.00
190 Eddie Robinson POR 3.00 8.00
191 Floyd Robinson 66 30.00 60.00
192 Frankie Robinson 30.00 60.00
64/66
193 Jackie Robinson 40.00 80.00
194 Preacher Roe 3.00 8.00
195 Bob Rogers 66 30.00 60.00
sic, Rodgers
196 Richard Rollins 66 30.00 60.00
197 Pete Runnels 64 15.00 40.00
198 John Sain 3.00 8.00
199 Ron Santo 64/66 12.50 30.00
200 Henry Sauer 3.00 8.00
201A Carl Sawatski 3.00 8.00
Milwaukee cap
201B Carl Sawatski 3.00 8.00
Philadelphia cap
201C Carl Sawatski 61 15.00 40.00
plain cap
202 Johnny Schmitz 4.00 10.00
203A Red Schoendeinst
(one foot shown&/catching)/(si 15.00 40.00
203B Red Schoendeinst
(both feet shown&/catching)/(s 30.00 60.00
203C Red Schoendinst BAT 6.00 15.00
sic, Schoendienst
204A Herb Score 6.00 15.00
Cleveland cap
204B Herb Score 61 30.00 60.00
plain cap
205 Andy Seminick 3.00 8.00
206 Rip Sewell 47 15.00 40.00
207 Norm Siebern 3.00 8.00
208A Roy Sievers 51 40.00 80.00
Browns
208B Roy Sievers 3.00 8.00
Senators
dark background
208C Roy Sievers 3.00 8.00
Senators
light background
208D Roy Sievers 61 30.00 60.00
plain uniform
209 Curt Simmons 3.00 8.00
210 Dick Sisler 3.00 8.00
211A Bill Skowron 3.00 8.00
New York
211B Bill Moose Skowron 150.00 300.00
White Sox 66
212 Enos Slaughter 6.00 15.00
213A Duke Snider 10.00 25.00
Brooklyn
213B Duke Snider 15.00 40.00
Los Angeles
214A Warren Spahn 6.00 15.00
Boston
214B Warren Spahn 12.50 30.00
Milwaukee
215 Stanley Spence 12.50 30.00
216A Ed Stanky 3.00 8.00
plain uniform
216B Ed Stanky Giants 3.00 8.00
217A Vern Stephens 3.00 8.00
Browns
217B Vern Stephens 4.00 10.00
Red Sox
218 Ed Stewart 3.00 8.00
219 Snuffy Stirnweiss 15.00 40.00
220 George Birdie Tebbets 10.00 25.00
221A Frankie Thomas BAT 30.00 60.00
Bob Skinner picture
59
221B Frank Thomas Cubs 30.00 60.00
60/61
222 Lee Thomas 64/66 3.00 8.00
223 Bobby Thomson 6.00 15.00
224A Earl Torgeson 3.00 8.00
Braves
224B Earl Torgeson 60/61 3.00 8.00
plain uniform
225 Gus Triandos 60/61 6.00 15.00
226 Virgil Trucks 3.00 8.00
227 Johnny Vandermeer 47 40.00 80.00
228 Emil Verban 15.00 40.00
229A Mickey Vernon 3.00 8.00
throwing
229B Mickey Vernon BAT 3.00 8.00
230 Bill Voiselle 47 15.00 40.00
231 Leon Wagner 64/66 3.00 8.00
232A Eddie Waitkus BAT 3.00 8.00
Cub uniform
232B Eddie Waitkus BAT 3.00 8.00
plain uniform
232C Eddie Waitkus POR 30.00 60.00
Phillies uniform
233 Dick Wakefield 3.00 8.00
234 Harry Walker 40.00 80.00
235 Bucky Walters 6.00 15.00
236 Pete Ward 66 125.00 250.00
237 Herman Wehmeier 3.00 8.00
238A Vic Wertz Tigers 3.00 8.00
238B Vic WertzRed Sox 3.00 8.00
239 Wally Westlake 3.00 8.00
240 Wes Westrum 30.00 60.00
241 Billy Williams 64/66 30.00 60.00
242 Maurice Wills 64/66 12.50 30.00
243A Gene Woodling SCR 3.00 8.00
243B Gene Woodling SIG 3.00 8.00
244 Taffy Wright 47 12.50 30.00
245 Carl Yastrzemski 66 250.00 500.00
246 Al Zarilla 51 6.00 15.00
247A Gus Zernial SCR 3.00 8.00
247B Gus Zernial SIG 3.00 8.00
248 Braves Team 1948
249 Dodgers Team 1949
250 Dodgers Team 1952
251 Dodgers Team 1955
252 Dodgers Team 1956
253 Giants Team 1951
254 Giants Team 1954
255 Indians Team 1948
256 Indians Team 1954
257 Phillies Team 1950
258 Yankees Team 1949
259 Yankees Team 1950
260 Yankees Team 1951
261 Yankees Team 1952
262 Yankees Team 1955
263 Yankees Team 1956

1948 Exhibit Hall of Fame

This exhibit set, entitled "Baseball's Great Hall of Fame," consists of black and white photos on gray background. The pictures are framed on the sides by Greek columns and a short biography is printed at the bottom. The cards are blank backed. Twenty four of the cards were reissued in 1974 on extremely white stock. Each card measures 3 3/8" by 5 3/8".

COMPLETE SET (33) 300.00 600.00
1 G.C. Alexander 4.00 8.00
2 Roger Bresnahan 2.50 5.00
3 Frank Chance 3.00 6.00
4 Jack Chesbro 2.50 5.00
5 Fred Clarke 2.50 5.00
6 Ty Cobb 40.00 80.00
7 Mickey Cochrane 4.00 8.00
8 Eddie Collins 2.50 5.00
9 Hugh Duffy 2.50 5.00
10 Johnny Evers 3.00 6.00
11 Frankie Frisch 3.00 6.00
12 Lou Gehrig 40.00 80.00
13 Clark Griffith 2.50 5.00
14 Lefty Grove 4.00 8.00
15 Rogers Hornsby 5.00 10.00
16 Carl Hubbell 3.00 6.00
17 Hughie Jennings 2.50 5.00
18 Walter Johnson 7.50 15.00
19 Willie Keeler 2.50 5.00
20 Nap Lajoie 5.00 10.00
21 Connie Mack 4.00 8.00
22 Christy Mathewson 7.50 15.00
23 John McGraw 5.00 10.00
24 Eddie Plank 3.00 6.00
25A Babe Ruth/(swinging) 25.00 50.00
25B Babe Ruth/(bats in front)/ten bats pose 150.00 300.00
26 George Sisler 3.00 6.00
27 Tris Speaker 5.00 10.00
28 Joe Tinker 3.00 6.00
29 Rube Waddell 2.50 5.00
30 Honus Wagner 7.50 15.00
31 Ed Walsh 2.50 5.00
32 Cy Young 5.00 10.00

1948-56 Exhibits Team

The cards found listed in this classification were not a separate issue from the individual player cards of the same period but have been assembled together in the Price Guide for emphasis. Each of these 1948-1956 Exhibit team cards was issued to honor the champions of the National and American Leagues, except for 1953, when none were printed. Reprints of these popular cards are known to exist. Each card measures 3 3/8" by 5 3/8".

COMPLETE SET (16) 600.00 1,200.00
1 1948 Boston Braves 30.00 60.00
2 1948 Cleveland Indians 30.00 60.00
3 1949 Brooklyn Dodgers 40.00 80.00
4 1949 New York Yankees 40.00 80.00
5 1950 Philadelphia 40.00 80.00
Phillies
6 1950 New York Yankees 40.00 80.00
7 1951 New York Giants 40.00 80.00
8 1951 New York Yankees 30.00 60.00
9 1952 Brooklyn Dodgers 40.00 80.00
10 1952 New York Yankees 40.00 80.00
11 1954 New York Giants 40.00 80.00
12 1954 Cleveland Indians 40.00 80.00
13 1955 Brooklyn Dodgers 150.00 300.00
14 1955 New York Yankees 100.00 200.00
15 1956 Brooklyn Dodgers 200.00 400.00
16 1956 New York Yankees 100.00 200.00

1953 Exhibits Canadian

This numbered, blank-backed set depicts both major league players (reprinted from American Exhibit sets) and International League Montreal Royals. The cards (3 1/4" by 5 1/4") are slightly smaller than regular Exhibit issues and are printed on gray stock. Numbers 1-32 are found in green or wine-red color, while 33-64 are blue or reddish-brown. Cards 1-32 are numbered in a small& diamond-shaped white box at lower right; cards 33-64 have a large, hand-lettered number at upper right.

COMPLETE SET (64) 600.00 1,200.00
COMMON PLAYER (1-32) 4.00 10.00
COMMON PLAYER (33-64) 2.00 5.00
1 Preacher Roe 5.00 12.00
2 Luke Easter 4.00 10.00
3 Gene Bearden 4.00 10.00
4 Chico Carrasquel 4.00 10.00
5 Vic Raschi 5.00 12.00
6 Monte Irvin 8.00 20.00
7 Hank Sauer 4.00 10.00
8 Ralph Branca 5.00 12.00
9 Eddie Stanky 4.00 10.00
10 Sam Jethroe 4.00 10.00
11 Larry Doby 8.00 20.00
12 Hal Newhouser 8.00 20.00
13 Gil Hodges 12.50 30.00
14 Harry Brecheen 4.00 10.00
15 Ed Lopat 6.00 15.00
16 Don Newcombe 6.00 15.00
17 Bob Feller 30.00 60.00
18 Tommy Holmes 4.00 10.00
19 Jackie Robinson 100.00 200.00
20 Roy Campanella 50.00 100.00
21 Pee Wee Reese 20.00 50.00
22 Ralph Kiner 8.00 20.00
23 Dom DiMaggio 6.00 15.00
24 Bobby Doerr 8.00 20.00
25 Phil Rizzuto 15.00 40.00
26 Bob Elliott 4.00 10.00
27 Tom Henrich 5.00 12.00
28 Joe DiMaggio 150.00 300.00
29 Harry Lowery 4.00 10.00
30 Ted Williams 100.00 200.00
31 Bob Lemon 10.00 25.00
32 Warren Spahn 12.50 30.00
33 Don Hoak 4.00 10.00
34 Bob Alexander 2.00 5.00
35 John Simmons 2.00 5.00
36 Steve Lembo 2.00 5.00
37 Norman Larker 5.00 12.00
38 Bob Ludwick 2.00 5.00
39 Walter Moryn 4.00 10.00
40 Charlie Thompson 4.00 10.00
41 Ed Roebuck 4.00 10.00
42 Rose 2.00 5.00
43 Edmundo Amoros 5.00 12.00
44 Bob Milliken 4.00 10.00
45 Art Fabbro 2.00 5.00
46 Forrest Jacobs 4.00 10.00
47 Carmen Mauro 2.00 5.00
48 Walter Fiala 2.00 5.00
49 Rocky Nelson 2.00 5.00
50 Tom Lasorda 40.00 80.00
51 Ronnie Lee 2.00 5.00
52 Hampton Coleman 2.00 5.00
53 Frank Marchio 2.00 5.00
54 William Samson 2.00 5.00
55 Gil Mills 2.00 5.00
56 Al Ronning 2.00 5.00
57 Stan Musial 50.00 100.00
58 Walker Cooper 4.00 10.00
59 Mickey Vernon 5.00 12.00
60 Del Ennis 5.00 12.00
61 Walter Alston MG 20.00 50.00
62 Dick Sisler 4.00 10.00
63 Billy Goodman 4.00 10.00
64 Alex Kellner 4.00 10.00

1960-61 Exhibits Wrigley HOF

ALOYSIUS HARRY SIMMONS

This Exhibit issue was distributed at Wrigley Field in Chicago in the early sixties. The set consists entirely of Hall of Famers, many of whom are depicted in their younger days. The set is complete at 24 cards and is interesting in that the full name of each respective Hall of famer is given on the front of the card. Card backs feature a postcard back on gray card stock. Each card measures 3 3/8" by 5 3/8".

COMPLETE SET (24) 300.00 600.00
1 Grover Cleveland 8.00 20.00
Alexander
2 Cap Anson 8.00 20.00
3 Frank Baker 5.00 12.00
4 Roger Bresnahan 5.00 12.00
5 Mordecai Brown 5.00 12.00
6 Frank Chance 6.00 15.00
7 Tyrus Cobb 40.00 80.00
8 Eddie Collins 6.00 15.00
9 Jimmy Collins 5.00 12.00
10 Johnnie Evers 5.00 12.00
11 Lou Gehrig 40.00 80.00
12 Clark Griffith 5.00 12.00
13 Walter Johnson 15.00 40.00
14 Tony Lazzeri 5.00 12.00
15 Rabbit Maranville 5.00 12.00
16 Christy Mathewson 15.00 40.00
17 John McGraw 8.00 20.00
18 Melvin Ott 10.00 25.00
19 Herb Pennock 5.00 12.00
20 Babe Ruth 75.00 150.00
21 Al Simmons 5.00 12.00
22 Tris Speaker 10.00 25.00
23 Joe Tinker 5.00 12.00
24 Honus Wagner 15.00 40.00

1962 Exhibit Stat Back

The 32-card sheet was a standard production feature of the Exhibit Supply Company, although, generally more than one sheet comprised a set. The 32-card set issued in 1962 thus amounted to one-half a normal printing, and is differentiated from other concurrent Exhibit issues by the inclusion of records, printed in black or red, on the reverse of each card. Each card measures 3 3/8" by 5 3/8". Backs printed in red ink are slightly more difficult to find but there is no difference in price.

COMPLETE SET (32) 400.00 800.00
1 Hank Aaron 40.00 80.00
2 Luis Aparicio 8.00 20.00
3 Ernie Banks 15.00 40.00
4 Yogi Berra 30.00 60.00
5 Ken Boyer 6.00 15.00
6 Lew Burdette 4.00 10.00
7 Norm Cash 8.00 20.00
8 Orlando Cepeda 8.00 20.00
9 Roberto Clemente 60.00 120.00
10 Rocky Colavito 15.00 40.00
11 Whitey Ford 15.00 40.00
12 Nellie Fox 8.00 20.00
13 Tito Francona 2.50 6.00
14 Jim Gentile 2.50 6.00
15 Dick Groat 4.00 10.00
16 Don Hoak 2.50 6.00
17 Al Kaline 15.00 40.00
18 Harmon Killebrew 12.50 30.00
19 Sandy Koufax 50.00 100.00
20 Jim Landis 2.50 6.00
21 Art Mahaffey 2.50 6.00
22 Frank Malzone 2.50 6.00

23 Mickey Mantle 150.00 300.00
24 Roger Maris 30.00 60.00
25 Eddie Mathews 15.00 40.00
26 Willie Mays 40.00 80.00
27 Wally Moon 2.50 6.00
28 Stan Musial 40.00 80.00
29 Milt Pappas 2.50 6.00
30 Vada Pinson 4.00 10.00
31 Norm Siebern 2.50 6.00
32 Warren Spahn 12.50 30.00

1963 Exhibit Stat Back

The 1963 Exhibit issue features 64 thick-stock cards with statistics printed in red on the backs. Each card measures 3 3/8" by 5 3/8". The set is quite similar to the set of the previous year -- but this set can be distinguished by the red print on the backs and the additional year of statistics.

COMPLETE SET (64) 400.00 800.00
1 Hank Aaron 15.00 40.00
2 Luis Aparicio 4.00 10.00
3 Bob Aspromonte 1.25 3.00
4 Ernie Banks 8.00 20.00
5 Steve Barber 1.25 3.00
6 Earl Battey 1.25 3.00
7 Yogi Berra 12.50 30.00
8 Ken Boyer 4.00 10.00
9 Lew Burdette 2.00 5.00
10 Johnny Callison 1.50 4.00
11 Norm Cash 4.00 10.00
12 Orlando Cepeda 4.00 10.00
13 Dean Chance 1.25 3.00
14 Tom Cheney 1.25 3.00
15 Roberto Clemente 30.00 60.00
16 Rocky Colavito 4.00 10.00
17 Choo Choo Coleman 2.00 5.00
18 Roger Craig 2.00 5.00
19 Joe Cunningham 1.50 4.00
20 Don Drysdale 6.00 15.00
21 Dick Farrell 1.25 3.00
22 Whitey Ford 8.00 20.00
23 Nellie Fox 4.00 10.00
24 Tito Francona 1.25 3.00
25 Jim Gentile 1.50 4.00
26 Tony Gonzales 1.25 3.00
27 Dick Groat 2.00 5.00
28 Ray Herbert 1.25 3.00
29 Chuck Hinton 1.25 3.00
30 Don Hoak 1.25 3.00
31 Frank Howard 2.50 6.00
32 Ken Hubbs 8.00 20.00
33 Joey Jay 1.25 3.00
34 Al Kaline 8.00 20.00
35 Harmon Killebrew 6.00 15.00
36 Sandy Koufax 20.00 50.00
37 Harvey Kuenn 2.00 5.00
38 Jim Landis 1.25 3.00
39 Art Mahaffey 1.25 3.00
40 Frank Malzone 1.50 4.00
41 Mickey Mantle 75.00 150.00
42 Roger Maris 15.00 40.00
43 Eddie Mathews 6.00 15.00
44 Willie Mays 15.00 40.00
45 Bill Mazeroski 4.00 10.00
46 Ken McBride 1.25 3.00
47 Wally Moon 1.50 4.00
48 Stan Musial 15.00 40.00
49 Charlie Neal 2.00 5.00
50 Billy O'Dell 1.25 3.00
51 Milt Pappas 1.25 3.00
52 Camilo Pascual 1.25 3.00
53 Jim Piersall 3.00 8.00
54 Vada Pinson 3.00 8.00
55 Brooks Robinson 10.00 25.00
56 Frank Robinson 8.00 20.00
57 Pete Runnels 1.25 3.00
58 Ron Santo 3.00 8.00
59 Norm Siebern 1.25 3.00
60 Warren Spahn 6.00 15.00
61 Lee Thomas 1.25 3.00
62 Leon Wagner 1.25 3.00
63 Billy Williams 6.00 15.00
64 Maury Wills 4.00 10.00

1969 Expos Fud's Photography

This blank-backed set was apparently issued by Bob Solon in the Chicago area. The black-and-white cards measure approximately 3 1/2" by 3" and feature Montreal Expos players of the 1969 season. The fronts carry action player photos with a white border. The player's name appears in a white bar in the lower right corner of the photo. The words "Compliments of" are printed in the upper border, while the words "Fud's Photography" appear in the lower border. The cards are unnumbered and checklisted below in alphabetical order.

COMPLETE SET (14) 8.00 20.00
1 Bob Bailey .50 1.25
2 John Bateman .50 1.25
3 Don Bosch .40 1.00
4 Jim Grant .60 1.50
5 Mack Jones .50 1.25
6 Coco Laboy .50 1.25
7 Dan McGinn .40 1.00
8 Cal McLish CO .40 1.00
9 Carl Morton .50 1.25
10 Manny Mota .75 2.00
11 Rusty Staub 2.00 5.00
12 Gary Sutherland .40 1.00
13 Mike Wegener .40 1.00
14 Floyd Wicker .40 1.00

1969 Expos Postcards

These postcards were issued during the Expos debut season. More cards should exist so all additions to this list is appreciated. These postcards are sequenced by uniform number.

COMPLETE SET 4.00 10.00
17 Howie Reed .40 1.00
18 Steve Renko .40 1.00
19 Jerry Robertson .40 1.00
20 Gary Waslewski .40 1.00
21 Kevin Collins .40 1.00
22 Ron Fairly .75 2.00
23 Jose Herrera .40 1.00
24 Ty Cline .40 1.00
25 Adolfo Phillips .40 1.00
26 Floyd Wicker .40 1.00
27 Gene Mauch MG .60 1.50
28 Peanuts Lowrey CO .40 1.00
29 Cal McLish CO .40 1.00
30 Bob Oldis CO .40 1.00
31 Jerry Zimmerman CO .40 1.00

1970 Expos Postcards

These 16 Montreal Expos postcards measure approximately 3 1/2" by 5 1/2" and feature borderless posed color player photos on their fronts. The player's facsimile autograph appears near the bottom. The backs carry the player's name and bilingual position in black ink at the upper left. The cards are numbered on the back.

COMPLETE SET (16) 8.00 20.00
1 Roy Face .75 2.00
2 Don Shaw .40 1.00
3 Dan McGinn .40 1.00
4 Bill Stoneman .60 1.50
5 Mike Wegener .40 1.00
6 Bob Bailey .60 1.50
7 Gary Sutherland .40 1.00
8 Coco Laboy .50 1.25
9 Bobby Wine UER/(Misspelled Boby on back) .50 1.25
10 Mack Jones .50 1.25
11 Rusty Staub 2.00 5.00
12 Don Bosch .40 1.00
13 Larry Jaster .60 1.50
14 John Bateman .50 1.25
15 John Boccabella .50 1.25
16 Ron Brand .40 1.00

1971 Expos La Pizza Royale

Featuring members of the Montreal Expos, this set, like the Fud's set, is thought to have been issued by Bob Solon in the Chicago area. Printed on thick cardboard paper, the cards measure approximately 2 1/2" by 5". The fronts typically feature blue-tinted player photos on a dark blue background; however the set was also issued in at least three other colors: green, gold, and red. The words "La Pizza Royale" are printed in white letters above the photo, while the player's name and position in French appear under the photo. The backs are blank. The cards are unnumbered and checklisted below in alphabetical order.

COMPLETE SET (14) 10.00 25.00
1 Bob Bailey 1.25 3.00
2 John Boccabella 1.00 2.50
3 Ron Fairly 1.25 3.00
4 Jim Gosger .75 2.00
5 Coco Laboy 1.00 2.50
6 Gene Mauch MG 1.25 3.00
7 Rich Nye .75 2.00
8 John O'Donoghue .75 2.00
9 Adolfo Phillips .75 2.00
10 Howie Reed .75 2.00
11 Marv Staehle .75 2.00
12 Rusty Staub 3.00 8.00
13 Gary Sutherland .75 2.00
14 Bobby Wine 1.00 2.50

1971 Expos Pro Stars

Printed in Canada by Pro Stars Publications, these 28 blank-backed postcards measure approximately 3 1/2" by 5 1/2" and feature white-bordered color player photos. The player's name appears as a facsimile autograph across the bottom of the photo. The postcards are unnumbered and checklisted below in alphabetical order.

COMPLETE SET (28) 20.00 50.00
1 Bob Bailey 1.25 3.00
2 John Bateman 1.00 2.50
3 John Boccabella 1.00 2.50
4 Ron Brand .75 2.00
5 Boots Day .75 2.00
6 Jim Fairey .75 2.00
7 Ron Fairly 1.25 3.00
8 Jim Gosger .75 2.00
9 Don Hahn .75 2.00
10 Ron Hunt 1.25 3.00
11 Mack Jones 1.00 2.50
12 Coco Laboy 1.00 2.50
13 Mike Marshall 1.50 4.00
14 Clyde Mashore .75 2.00
15 Gene Mauch MG 1.25 3.00
16 Dan McGinn .75 2.00
17 Carl Morton 1.00 2.50
18 John O'Donoghue .75 2.00
19 Adolfo Phillips .75 2.00
20 Claude Raymond 1.00 2.50
21 Howie Reed .75 2.00
22 Steve Renko .75 2.00
23 Rusty Staub 3.00 8.00
24 Bill Stoneman 1.25 3.00
25 John Strohmayer .75 2.00
26 Gary Sutherland .75 2.00
27 Mike Wegener .75 2.00
28 Bobby Wine 1.00 2.50

1972 Expos Matchbooks

These seven matchbooks, which measure 2 1/8" by 4 3/8" were issued by the Eddy Match Co. The fronts have a player photo while the backs have the home team schedule. Since these are unnumbered, we have sequenced them in alphabetical order.

COMPLETE SET 6.00 15.00
1 Boots Day .75 2.00
2 Ron Fairly 1.00 2.50
3 Ron Hunt .75 2.00
4 Steve Renko .75 2.00
5 Rusty Staub 1.50 4.00
6 Bobby Wine .75 2.00
7 Scoreboard .75 2.00
Honoring Ron Hunt's 50th Hit by Pitche

1973 Expos Matchbooks

These seven matchbooks, which measure 2 1/8" by 4 3/8" were issued by the Eddy Match Co. The fronts have a player photo while the backs have the home team schedule. Since these are unnumbered, we have sequenced them in alphabetical order.

COMPLETE SET 5.00 12.00
1 Tim Foli .75 2.00
2 Ron Hunt .75 2.00
3 Mike Jorgensen .75 2.00
4 Gene Mauch MG .75 2.00
5 Balor Moore .75 2.00
6 Ken Singleton .75 2.00
7 Bill Stoneman 1.00 2.50
No-hitter congratulations

1973 Expos Postcards

This set features borderless black-and-white player portraits measuring approximately 3 1/2" by 5 1/2". The backs carry the sentence, "Souvenir of the Montreal Expos Baseball Club," in both English and French.The cards are unnumbered and checklisted below in alphabetical order. There are probably many additions to this set so all help is appreciated.

COMPLETE SET 12.50 30.00
COMMON CARD (1-7) 1.50 4.00
1 Jimmy Bragan 1.50 4.00
2 Hal Breeden 1.50 4.00
3 Larry Doby CO 4.00 10.00
4 Ron Fairly 2.00 5.00
5 Mike Jorgensen 1.50 4.00
6 Steve Rogers 2.00 5.00
7 Mike Torrez 2.00 5.00

1974 Expos Weston

This ten-card set, featuring members of the Montreal Expos, measures approximately 3 1/2" by 5 1/2". The fronts have color player photos inside a thin white border with a facsimile autograph in black ink, and the player's name under the photo. The player's uniforms and caps have been airbrushed to remove the Expos insignia. The backs carry biography and statistics in English and French. The cards are unnumbered and checklisted below in alphabetical order. These cards were originally issued one to a package of Weston 39 cent baseball bats.

COMPLETE SET (10) 8.00 20.00
1 Bob Bailey 1.25 3.00
2 John Boccabella 1.00 2.50
3 Boots Day .75 2.00
4 Tim Foli 1.00 2.50
5 Ron Hunt 1.25 3.00
6 Mike Jorgensen 1.00 2.50
7 Ernie McAnally .75 2.00
8 Steve Renko .75 2.00
9 Ken Singleton 2.00 5.00
10 Bill Stoneman 1.50 4.00

1975 Expos Postcards

This 39-card set of the Montreal Expos features player photos on postcard-size cards. The cards are unnumbered and checklisted below in alphabetical order.

COMPLETE SET (39) 8.00 20.00
1 Bob Bailey .20 .50
2 Larry Biittner .20 .50
3 Dennis Blair .20 .50
4 Hal Breeden .20 .50
5 Dave Bristol CO .20 .50
6 Don Carrithers .20 .50
7 Gary Carter 2.00 5.00
8 Rich Coggins .20 .50
9 Nate Colbert .20 .50
10 Don DeMola .20 .50
11 Jim Dwyer .20 .50
12 Tim Foli .20 .50
13 Barry Foote .20 .50
14 Pepe Frias .20 .50
15 Woodie Fryman .20 .50
16 Walt Hriniak .20 .50
17 Mike Jorgensen .20 .50
18 Jim Lyttle .20 .50
19 Pete Mackanin .20 .50
20 Pepe Mangual .20 .50
21 Gene Mauch MG .20 .50
22 Cal McLish .20 .50
23 Dave McNally .30 .75
24 John Montague .20 .50
25 Jose Morales .20 .50
26 Dale Murray .20 .50
27 Larry Parrish .20 .50
28 Steve Renko .20 .50
29 Bombo Rivera .20 .50
30 Steve Rogers .20 .50
31 Pat Scanlon .20 .50
32 Fred Schermann .20 .50
33 Tony Scott .20 .50
34 Duke Snider CO .60 1.50
35 Don Stanhouse .20 .50
36 Chuck Taylor .20 .50
37 Dan Warthen .20 .50
38 Jerry White .20 .50
39 Jerry Zimmerman CO .20 .50

1976 Expos Matchbooks

These seven matchbooks, which measure 2 1/8" by 4 3/8" were issued by the Eddy Match Co. The fronts have a player photo while the backs have the home team schedule. Since these are unnumbered, we have sequenced them in alphabetical order.

COMPLETE SET 5.00 12.00
1 Barry Foote .75 2.00
2 Mike Jorgensen .75 2.00
3 Pete Mackanin .75 2.00
4 Dale Murray .75 2.00
5 Larry Parrish 1.00 2.50
6 Steve Rogers .75 2.00
7 Dan Warthen .75 2.00

1976 Expos Postcards

This 31-card set of the Montreal Expos features player photos on postcard-size cards. The cards are unnumbered and checklisted below in alphabetical order.

COMPLETE SET (31) 6.00 15.00
1 Billy Adair CO .20 .50
2 Larry Bearnarth CO .20 .50
3 Don Carrithers .20 .50
4 Gary Carter 1.50 4.00
5 Nate Colbert .20 .50
6 Jim Cox .20 .50
7 Larry Doby CO .60 1.50
8 Jim Dwyer .20 .50
9 Tim Foli .20 .50
10 Barry Foote .20 .50
11 Pepe Frias .20 .50
12 Woodie Fryman .20 .50
13 Wayne Granger .20 .50
14 Mike Jorgensen .20 .50
15 Clay Kirby .20 .50
16 Karl Kuehl MG .20 .50
17 Chip Lang .20 .50
18 Jim Lyttle .20 .50
19 Pepe Manguel .20 .50
20 Pete MacKanin .20 .50
21 Jose Morales .20 .50
22 Dale Murray .20 .50
23 Larry Parrish .60 1.50
24 Ron Piche CO .20 .50
25 Bombo Rivera .20 .50
26 Steve Rogers .40 1.00
27 Fred Scherman .20 .50
28 Don Stanhouse .20 .50
29 Ozzie Virgil CO .20 .50
30 Dan Warthen .20 .50
31 Jerry White .20 .50

1976 Expos Redpath

This set of 1976 Montreal Expos was issued by the Redpath Sugar company. The sheets measure approximately 3 1/4" by 10" and each sheet features four team members. The white fronts have a color head shot of the player on the right with the player's name and position printed above the photo in French and below the photo in English. To the left of the photo is brief biography and how they were acquired by Montreal Expos written in both French and English. The players are listed below in alphabetical order.

COMPLETE SET 10.00 25.00
1 Bill Adair CO .30 .75
2 Larry Bearnarth CO .30 .75
3 Don Carrithers .30 .75
4 Gary Carter 1.50 4.00
5 Larry Doby CO .75 2.00
6 Steve Dunning .30 .75
7 Jim Dwyer .30 .75
8 Tim Foli .30 .75
9 Barry Foote .30 .75
10 Pepe Frias .30 .75
11 Woodie Fryman .30 .75
12 Wayne Garrett .30 .75
13 Wayne Granger .30 .75
14 Mike Jorgensen .30 .75
15 Joe Kerrigan .30 .75
16 Clay Kirby .30 .75
17 Karl Kuehl MG .30 .75
18 Chip Lang .30 .75
19 Jim Lyttle .30 .75
20 Pete MacKanin .30 .75
21 Jose Mangual .30 .75
22 Jose Morales .30 .75
23 Dale Murray .30 .75
24 Larry Parrish .30 .75
25 Ron Piche CO .30 .75
26 Bombo Rivera .30 .75
27 Steve Rogers .60 1.50
28 Fred Scherman .30 .75
29 Don Stanhouse .30 .75
30 Chuck Taylor .30 .75
31 Andre Thornton .40 1.00
32 Del Unser .30 .75
33 Ellis Valentine .40 1.00
34 Ossie Virgil CO .60 1.50
35 Dan Warthen .30 .75
36 Jerry White .30 .75

1977 Expos Postcards

These 39 postcards feature all sorts of people in the Expos orginization. This was not just issued as one set, but these postcards were continually printed during the season to account for new additions.

COMPLETE SET 15.00 40.00
1 Santo Alcala .30 .75
2 Bill Atkinson .30 .75
3 Bill Atkinson .30 .75
Tree in background
4 Stan Bahnsen .30 .75
5 Tim Blackwell .30 .75
6 Jim Brewer CO .30 .75
7 Jackie Brown CO .30 .75
8 Gary Carter 1.50 4.00
9 Dave Cash .30 .75
10 Warren Cromartie .60 1.50
11 Andre Dawson 2.00 5.00
12 Andre Dawson 2.00 5.00
Wearing batting helmet
13 Barry Foote .30 .75
14 Pepe Frias .30 .75
15 Bill Gardner .30 .75
16 Wayne Garrett .30 .75
17 Gerald Hannahs .30 .75
18 Mike Jorgenson .30 .75
19 Joe Kerrigan .30 .75
20 Pete Mackanin .30 .75
21 Will McEnaney .30 .75
22 Sam Mejias .30 .75
23 Jose Morales .30 .75
24 Larry Parrish .40 1.00
25 Tony Perez .75 2.00
26 Steve Rogers .40 1.00
27 Dan Schatzeder .30 .75
28 Chris Speier .30 .75
29 Don Stanhouse .30 .75
30 Jeff Terpko .30 .75
31 Wayne Twitchell .30 .75
32 Del Unser .30 .75
33 Ellis Valentine .30 .75
34 Mickey Vernon .40 1.00
35 Ozzie Virgil CO .30 .75
36 Tom Walker .30 .75
37 Dan Warthen .30 .75
38 Jerry White .30 .75
39 Dick Williams MG .40 1.00

1978 Expos Postcards

This 15-card set features a borerless front with the player's name and team in a box near the bottom. The player's position is also printed on the front in both French and English. Backs are blank. cards are aphabetically checklisted below.

COMPLETE SET (15) 6.00 15.00
1 Stan Bahnsen .30 .75
2 Gary Carter 1.50 4.00
3 Andre Dawson 1.25 3.00
4 Hal Dues .30 .75
5 Ross Grimsley .30 .75
6 Fred Holdsworth .30 .75
7 Darold Knowles .30 .75
8 Rudy May .30 .75
9 Stan Papi .30 .75
10 Larry Parrish .40 1.00
11 Bob Reece .30 .75
12 Norm Sherry CO .30 .75
13 Dan Schatzeder .30 .75
14 Chris Speier .40 1.00
15 Wayne Twitchell .30 .75

1979 Expos Postcards

These postcards feature members from the Montreal Expos organization. These postcards are blankbacked and are borderless. The only identification is the player's name and billungual player information on the bottom.

COMPLETE SET (32) 10.00 25.00
1 Felipe Alou CO .60 1.50
2 Stan Bahnsen .30 .75
3 Tony Bernazard .30 .75
4 Jim Brewer CO .30 .75
5 Dave Cash .30 .75
6 Warren Cromartie .40 1.00
7 Andre Dawson 1.25 3.00
8 Duffy Dyer .30 .75
9 Woodie Fryman .30 .75
10 Mike Garman .30 .75
11 Ed Herrmann .30 .75
12 Tommy Hutton .30 .75
13 Bill Lee .40 1.00
With facial hair
14 Bill Lee .40 1.00
Clean-shaven
15 Ken Macha .60 1.50
16 Jim Mason .30 .75
17 Pat Mullin .30 .75
18 Dave Palmer .30 .75
19 Tony Perez .75 2.00
20 Vern Rapp CO .30 .75
21 Steve Rogers .40 1.00
22 Scott Sanderson .60 1.50
23 Rodney Scott .30 .75
number 3 on uniform
24 Rodney Scott .30 .75
number 19 on uniform
25 Norm Sherry CO .30 .75
26 Tony Solaita .30 .75
27 Elias Sosa .30 .75
28 Rusty Staub .75 2.00
29 Ellis Valentine .40 1.00
30 Ozzie Virgil CO .40 1.00
31 Jerry White .30 .75
32 Dick Williams MG .40 1.00

1980 Expos Postcards

These postcards feature members of the 1980 Montreal Expos. These postcards are similar to those issued in the three previous seasons but they have no positions on them. These are all new photos that have red and blue shoulder striping. These cards are unnumbered so we have sequenced them in alphabetical order.

COMPLETE SET (35) 6.00 15.00
1 Bill Almon .20 .50
2 Felipe Alou CO .40 1.00
3 Stan Bahnsen .20 .50
4 Tony Bernazard .20 .50
5 Gary Carter 1.00 2.50
6 Galen Cisco CO .20 .50
7 Warren Cromartie .30 .75
8 Andre Dawson .75 2.00
9 Woodie Fryman .20 .50
10 Ross Grimsley .20 .50
11 Bill Gullickson .30 .75
12 Tommy Hutton .20 .50
13 Charlie Lea .20 .50
14 Bill Lee .30 .75
15 Ron LeFlore .20 .50
16 Ken Macha .30 .75
17 Pat Mullin CO .20 .50
18 Dale Murray .20 .50
19 Fred Norman .20 .50
20 Rowland Office .20 .50
21 David Palmer .20 .50
22 Larry Parrish .20 .50
23 Bobby Ramos .20 .50
24 Vern Rapp CO .20 .50
25 Steve Rogers .20 .50
26 Scott Sanderson .20 .50
27 Rodney Scott .20 .50
28 Norm Sherry CO .20 .50
29 Elias Sosa .20 .50
30 Chris Speier .20 .50
31 John Tamargo .20 .50
32 Ellis Valentine .20 .50
33 Ozzie Virgil CO .20 .50
34 Jerry White .20 .50
35 Dick Williams MG .40 1.00

1960 El Roy Face Motel

This one-card set was actually a business card advertising the motel in Penn Run, Pennsylvania, which was owned by El Roy Face of the Pittsburgh Pirates. The front features a black-and-white autographed photo of the player. The back displays the motel information. The card measures approximately 2 1/8" by 3 1/2".

1 Roy Face 6.00 15.00

1922 Fan T231

Little is known about this set. Only two cards, Carson Bigbie (in a photocopy) and Frank Baker have ever been discovered. The card has a sepia toned photo on the front and the back has batting information from the previous few seasons. Also on the back was a entry form for a contest, meaning these cards were probably sent back to the factory.

1 Carson Bigbee
61 Frank Baker 2000

1906 Fan Craze AL WG2

These cards were distributed as part of a baseball game produced in 1906. The cards each measure approximately 2 1/2" by 3 1/2" and have rounded corners. The card fronts show a black and white cameo photo of the player, his name, his team and the game outcome associated with that particular card. The card backs are all the same, each showing "Art Series" and "Fan Craze" in dark blue and white. This set features only players from the American League. Since the cards are unnumbered, they are listed below in alphabetical order. These sets were available, on a league basis, in retail catalogs of the period for 48 cents postpaid.

COMPLETE SET (51) 3,000.00 6,000.00
1 Nick Altrock 50.00 100.00
2 Jim Barrett 50.00 100.00
3 Harry Bay 50.00 100.00
4 Chief Bender 200.00 400.00
5 Bill Bernhardt 50.00 100.00
6 Bill Bradley 50.00 100.00
7 Jack Chesbro 200.00 400.00
8 Jimmy Collins 200.00 400.00
9 Sam Crawford 225.00 450.00
10 Lou Criger 50.00 100.00
11 Lave Cross 50.00 100.00
12 Monty Cross 50.00 100.00
13 Harry Davis 50.00 100.00
14 Bill Dineen 50.00 100.00
15 Pat Donovan 50.00 100.00
16 Pat Dougherty 50.00 100.00
17 Norman Elberfeld 50.00 100.00
18 Hobe Ferris 50.00 100.00
19 Elmer Flick 150.00 300.00
20 Buck Freeman 50.00 100.00
21 Fred Glade 50.00 100.00
22 Clark Griffith 150.00 300.00
23 Charles Hickman 50.00 100.00
24 William Holmes 50.00 100.00
25 Harry Howell 50.00 100.00
26 Frank Isbell 50.00 100.00
27 Albert Jacobson 50.00 100.00
28 Ban Johnson PRES 225.00 450.00
29 Fielder Jones 50.00 100.00
30 Adrian Joss 225.00 450.00
31 Willie Keeler 200.00 400.00
32 Nap Lajoie 225.00 450.00
33 Connie Mack MG 225.00 450.00
34 Jimmy McAleer 50.00 100.00
35 Jim McGuire 50.00 100.00
36 Earl Moore 50.00 100.00
37 George Mullen 75.00 150.00
38 Billy Owen 50.00 100.00
39 Fred Parent 50.00 100.00
40 Case Patten 50.00 100.00
41 Eddie Plank 225.00 450.00
42 Ossie Schreckengost 50.00 100.00
43 Jake Stahl 50.00 100.00
44 Fred Stone 50.00 100.00
45 William Sudhoff 50.00 100.00
46 Roy Turner 50.00 100.00
47 Rube Waddell 150.00 300.00
48 Bob Wallace 100.00 200.00
49 G. Harris White 50.00 100.00
50 George Winter 50.00 100.00
51 Cy Young 600.00 1,200.00

1906 Fan Craze NL WG3

These cards were distributed as part of a baseball game produced in 1906. The game cost 50 cents upon issuance in 1906. The cards each measure approximately 2 1/2" by 3 1/2" and have rounded corners. The card fronts show a black and white cameo photo of the player, his name, his team, and the game outcome associated with that particular card. The card backs are all the same, each showing "Art Series" and "Fan Craze" in dark blue and white. This set features only players from the National League. Since the cards are unnumbered, they are arranged in alphabetical order in our checklist.

COMPLETE SET (54) 3,000.00 6,000.00
1 Red Ames 50.00 100.00
2 Ginger Beaumont 50.00 100.00
3 Jake Beckley 200.00 400.00
4 Billy Bergen 50.00 100.00
5 Roger Bresnahan 200.00 400.00
6 George Brown 50.00 100.00
7 Mordacai Brown 200.00 400.00
8 Doc Casey 50.00 100.00
9 Frank Chance 200.00 400.00
10 Fred Clarke 150.00 300.00
11 Tommy Corcoran 50.00 100.00
12 Bill Dahlen 60.00 120.00
13 Mike Donlin 50.00 100.00
14 Charley Dooin 50.00 100.00
15 Mickey Doolin 50.00 100.00
16 Hugh Duffy 150.00 300.00
17 John E. Dunleavy 50.00 100.00
18 Bob Ewing 50.00 100.00
19 Chick Fraser 50.00 100.00
20 Ned Hanlon MG 150.00 300.00
21 Del Howard 50.00 100.00
22 Miller Huggins 150.00 300.00
23 Joe Kelley 150.00 300.00
24 John Kling 50.00 100.00
25 Tommy Leach 50.00 100.00
26 Harry Lumley 50.00 100.00
27 Carl Lundgren 50.00 100.00
28 Bill Maloney 50.00 100.00
29 Dan McGann 50.00 100.00
30 Joe McGinnity 150.00 300.00
31 John McGraw MG 150.00 300.00
32 Harry McIntire 50.00 100.00
33 Kid Nichols 100.00 200.00
34 Mike O'Neil 50.00 100.00
35 Orval Overall 50.00 100.00
36 Frank Pfeffer 50.00 100.00
37 Deacon Philippe 50.00 100.00
38 Charley Pittinger 50.00 100.00
39 Harry C. Pulliam PRES 50.00 100.00
40 Ed Reulbach 50.00 100.00
41 Claude Ritchey 50.00 100.00
42 Cy Seymour 50.00 100.00
43 Jim Sheckard 50.00 100.00
44 Jack Taylor 50.00 100.00
45 Luther (Dummy) Taylor 50.00 100.00
46 Fred Tenney 50.00 100.00
47 Harry Theilman 50.00 100.00
48 Roy Thomas 50.00 100.00
49 Honus Wagner 1,000.00 2,000.00
50 Jake Weimer 50.00 100.00
51 Bob Wicker 50.00 100.00
52 Vic Willis 150.00 300.00
53 Lew Wiltsie 50.00 100.00
54 Irving Young 50.00 100.00

1939 Father and Son Shoes

These black and white blank-backed cards, which measure approximately 3" by 4" feature members of both Philadelphia area baseball teams. The fronts have a posed action shot with the player's name, position and team on the the bottom. Since these cards are unnumbered, we have sequenced them in alphabetical order.

COMPLETE SET 750.00 1,500.00
1 Moe Arnovich 50.00 100.00
2 Earl Brucker 50.00 100.00
3 George Caster 50.00 100.00
4 Sam Chapman 60.00 120.00
5 Spud Davis 50.00 100.00
6 Joe Gantenbein 50.00 100.00
7 Bob Johnson 60.00 120.00
8 Chuck Klein 100.00 200.00
9 Herschel Martin 50.00 100.00
10 Pinky May 50.00 100.00
11 Wally Moses 60.00 120.00
12 Emmitt Mueller 50.00 100.00
13 Hugh Mulcahy 50.00 100.00
14 Skeeter Newsome 50.00 100.00
15 Claude Passeau 60.00 120.00
16 George Scharein 50.00 100.00
17 Dick Siebert 50.00 100.00

1910-13 Fatima Cigarettes Premiums

These 12 1/2" by 19" black and white blank-backed photos were issued by Fatima as a premium promotion. The player's photo takes up most of the card with a brief biography and advertisment for Fatima on the bottom. There may be additions to this checklist so any additional information is appreciated.

COMPLETE SET 3,000.00 6,000.00
15 Christy Mathewson 750.00 1,500.00
22 Ty Cobb 1,500.00 3,000.00
31 Pittsburgh Pirates/1913 250.00 500.00
51 Walter Johnson 1,000.00 2,000.00

1913 Fatima Teams T200

The cards in this 16-card set measure approximately 2 5/8" by 5 13/16". The 1913 Fatima Cigarettes issue contains unnumbered glossy surface team cards. Both St. Louis team cards are considered difficult to obtain. A large 13" by 21" unnumbered, heavy cardboard parallel premium issue is also known to exist and is quite scarce. These unnumbered team cards are ordered below by team alphabetical order within league. Listed pricing references raw "VgEx" condition.

COMPLETE SET (16)	7,500.00	15,000.00
1 Boston Americans	300.00	500.00
2 Chicago Americans	300.00	500.00
3 Cleveland Americans	600.00	1,000.00
4 Detroit Americans	700.00	1,200.00
5 New York Americans	700.00	1,200.00
6 Philadelphia Americans	175.00	300.00
7 St. Louis Americans	600.00	1,000.00
8 Washington Americans	300.00	500.00
9 Boston Nationals	1,500.00	2,500.00
10 Brooklyn Nationals	300.00	500.00
11 Chicago Nationals	250.00	400.00
12 Cincinnati Nationals	175.00	300.00
13 New York Nationals	350.00	600.00
14 Philadelphia Nationals	175.00	300.00
15 Pittsburgh Nationals	300.00	500.00
16 St. Louis Nationals	300.00	500.00

1913 Fatima Teams Premiums T200

These premiums, which measure approximately 13" by 21" parallel the regular Fatima set. There is no pricing due to scarcity.

1914 Fatima Players T222

The cards in this 52-card set measure approximately 2 1/2" by 4 1/2" and are unnumbered. The cards are quite fragile on thin, brittle paper stock. The set was produced in 1914 by Liggett and Myers Tobacco Co. The players in the set have been alphabetized and numbered for reference in the checklist below.

COMPLETE SET (52)	25,000.00	50,000.00
1 Grover C. Alexander	750.00	1,500.00
2 Jimmy Archer	400.00	800.00
3 James Austin	500.00	1,000.00
4 Jack Barry	400.00	800.00
5 George Baumgardner	400.00	800.00
6 Rube Benton	400.00	800.00
7 Roger Bresnahan	750.00	1,500.00
8 Mordecai Brown	750.00	1,500.00
9 George J. Burns	400.00	800.00
10 Joe Bush	400.00	800.00
11 George Chalmers	400.00	800.00
12 Frank Chance	1,250.00	2,500.00
13 Albert Demaree	400.00	800.00
14 Arthur Fletcher	400.00	800.00
15 Earl Hamilton	400.00	800.00
16 John Henry	500.00	1,000.00
17 Byron Houck	400.00	800.00
18 Miller Huggins	750.00	1,500.00
19 Hugh Jennings MG	750.00	1,500.00
20 Walter Johnson	5,000.00	10,000.00
21 Ray Keating	400.00	800.00
22 John Lapp	400.00	800.00
23 Thomas Leach	400.00	800.00
24 Nemo Leibold	400.00	800.00
25 John Frank Lelivelt	400.00	800.00
26 Hans Lobert	500.00	1,000.00
27 Lee Magee	400.00	800.00
28 Sherry Magee	600.00	1,200.00
29 Fritz Maisel	400.00	800.00
30 Rube Marquard	750.00	1,500.00
31 George McBride	400.00	800.00
32 Stuffy McInnis	400.00	800.00
33 Larry McLean	400.00	800.00
34 Raymond Morgan	400.00	800.00
35 Eddie Murphy	400.00	800.00
36 Red Murray	400.00	800.00
37 Rube Oldring	500.00	1,000.00
38 William J. Orr	400.00	800.00
39 Hub Perdue	500.00	1,000.00
40 Arthur Phelan	400.00	800.00
41 Ed Reulbach	600.00	1,200.00
42 Vic Saier	400.00	800.00
43 Slim Sallee	400.00	800.00
44 Wally Schang	500.00	1,000.00
45 Frank Schulte	500.00	1,000.00
46 Jimmy Smith	400.00	800.00
47 Amos Strunk	400.00	800.00
48 Bill Sweeney	400.00	800.00
49 Lefty Tyler	500.00	1,000.00
50 Oscar Vitt	400.00	800.00
51 Ivy Wingo	400.00	800.00
52 Heinie Zimmerman	400.00	800.00

1951-52 Fischer Baking Labels

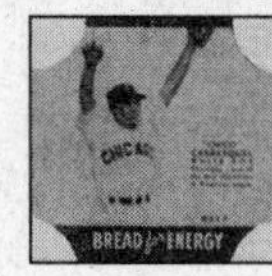

One of the popular "Bread for Energy" end-labels sets, these labels are found with blue, red and yellow backgrounds. Each bread label measures 2 3/4" by 2 3/4". They were distributed mainly in the northeast section of the country and there may be an album associated with the set. These labels are unnumbered and we have sequenced them in alphabetical order. The catalog designation is D290-3.

COMPLETE SET (32)	3,000.00	6,000.00
1 Vern Bickford	125.00	250.00
2 Ralph Branca	150.00	300.00
3 Harry Brecheen	125.00	250.00
4 Chico Carrasquel	125.00	250.00
5 Cliff Chambers	125.00	250.00
6 Hoot Evers	125.00	250.00
7 Ned Garver	125.00	250.00
8 Billy Goodman	125.00	250.00
9 Gil Hodges	250.00	500.00
10 Larry Jansen	125.00	250.00
11 Willie Jones	125.00	250.00
12 Eddie Joost	125.00	250.00
13 George Kell	250.00	300.00
14 Alex Kellner	125.00	500.00
15 Ted Kluszewski	175.00	350.00
16 Jim Konstanty	150.00	300.00
17 Bob Lemon	250.00	500.00
18 Cass Michaels	125.00	250.00
19 Johnny Mize	250.00	500.00
20 Irv Noren	125.00	250.00
21 Andy Pafko	125.00	250.00
22 Joe Page	150.00	300.00
23 Mel Parnell	150.00	300.00
24 Johnny Sain	150.00	300.00
25 Red Schoendienst	150.00	300.00
26 Roy Sievers	150.00	300.00
27 Roy Smalley	125.00	250.00
28 Herm Wehmeier	125.00	250.00
29 Bill Werle	125.00	250.00
30 Wes Westrum	125.00	250.00
31 Early Wynn	250.00	500.00
32 Gus Zernial	150.00	300.00

1959 Fleer Ted Williams

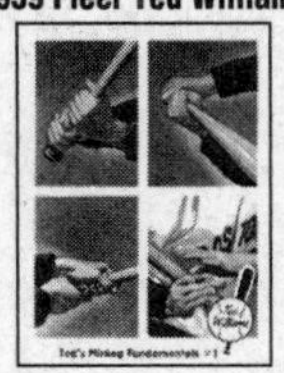

The cards in this 80-card set measure 2 1/2" by 3 1/2". The 1959 Fleer set, with a catalog designation of R418-1, portrays the life of Ted Williams. The wording of the wrapper, "Baseball's Greatest Series," has led to speculation that Fleer contemplated similar sets honoring other baseball immortals, but chose to develop instead the format of the 1960 and 1961 issues. These packs contained either six or eight cards. The packs cost a nickel and were packed 24 to a box which were packed 24 to a case. Card number 68, which was withdrawn early in production, is considered scarce and has even been counterfeited; the fake has a rosy coloration and a cross-hatch pattern visible over the picture area. The card numbering is arranged essentially in chronological order.

COMPLETE SET (80)	900.00	1,500.00
WRAPPER (6-CARD)	100.00	125.00
WRAPPER (8-CARD)	100.00	150.00
1 The Early Years	60.00	100.00
2 Ted's Idol Babe Ruth	60.00	100.00
3 Practice Makes Perfect	7.50	15.00
4 Learns Fine Points	7.50	15.00
5 Ted's Fame Spreads	7.50	15.00
6 Ted Turns Pro	12.50	25.00
7 From Mound to Plate	7.50	15.00
8 1937 First Full Season	7.50	15.00
9 Williams E.Collins	10.00	20.00
10 Gunning as Pastime	7.50	15.00
11 T.Williams J.Foxx	20.00	40.00
12 Burning Up Minors	10.00	20.00
13 1939 Shows Will Stay	7.50	15.00
14 Outstanding Rookie '39	7.50	15.00
15 Licks Sophomore Jinx	10.00	20.00
16 1941 Greatest Year	7.50	15.00
17 How Ted Hit .400	20.00	40.00
18 1941 All Star Hero	10.00	20.00
19 Ted Wins Triple Crown	7.50	15.00
20 On to Naval Training	7.50	15.00
21 Honors for Williams	7.50	15.00
22 1944 Ted Solos	7.50	15.00
23 Williams Wins Wings	7.50	15.00
24 1945 Sharpshooter#	7.50	15.00
25 1945 Ted Discharged	7.50	15.00
26 Off to Flying Start	7.50	15.00
27 7/9/46 One Man Show	7.50	15.00
28 The Williams Shift	7.50	15.00
29 Ted Hits for Cycle	10.00	20.00
30 Beating Williams Shift	7.50	15.00
31 Sox Lose Series	10.00	20.00
32 Most Valuable Player	7.50	15.00
33 Another Triple Crown	7.50	15.00
34 Runs Scored Record	7.50	15.00
35 Sox Miss Pennant	7.50	15.00
36 Banner Year for Ted	7.50	15.00
37 1949 Sox Miss Again	7.50	15.00
38 1949 Power Rampage	7.50	15.00
39 1950 Great Start	12.50	25.00
40 Ted Crashes into Wall	7.50	15.00
41 1950 Ted Recovers	7.50	15.00
42 Williams Tom Yawkey	7.50	15.00
43 Double Play Lead	7.50	15.00
44 Back to Marines	7.50	15.00
45 Farewell to Baseball	7.50	15.00
46 Ready for Combat	7.50	15.00
47 Ted Crash Lands Jet	7.50	15.00
48 1953 Ted Returns	10.00	20.00
49 Smash Return	7.50	15.00
50 1954 Spring Injury	12.50	25.00
51 Ted is Patched Up	7.50	15.00
52 1954 Ted's Comeback	10.00	20.00
53 Comeback is Success	7.50	15.00
54 Ted Hooks Big One	7.50	15.00
55 Retirement No Go	10.00	20.00
56 2,000th Hit 8/11/55	7.50	15.00
57 400th Homer	10.00	20.00
58 Williams Hits .388	7.50	15.00
59 Hot September for Ted	7.50	15.00
60 More Records for Ted	7.50	15.00
61 1957 Outfielder Ted	10.00	20.00
62 1958 Sixth Batting Title	7.50	15.00
63 AS Record w Auto	50.00	80.00
64 Daughter and Daddy	7.50	15.00
65 1958 August 30	10.00	20.00
66 1958 Powerhouse	7.50	15.00
67 Fam.Fishermen w Snead	20.00	40.00
68 Signs for 1959 SP	400.00	700.00
69 A Future Ted Williams	7.50	15.00
70 T.Williams J.Thorpe	20.00	40.00
71 Hitting Fundamental 1	7.50	15.00
72 Hitting Fundamental 2	7.50	15.00
73 Hitting Fundamental 3	7.50	15.00
74 Here's How	7.50	15.00
75 Williams' Value to Sox	30.00	50.00
76 On Base Record	7.50	15.00
77 Ted Relaxes	7.50	15.00
78 Honors for Williams	7.50	15.00
79 Where Ted Stands	12.50	25.00
80 Ted's Goals for 1959	20.00	40.00

1960 Fleer

The cards in this 79-card set measure 2 1/2" by 3 1/2". The cards from the 1960 Fleer series of Baseball Greats are sometimes mistaken for 1930s cards by collectors not familiar with this set. The cards each contain a tinted photo of a baseball immortal, and were issued in one series. There are no known scarcities, although a number 80 card (Pepper Martin reverse with Eddie Collins, Joe Tinker or Lefty Grove obverse) exists (this is not considered part of the set). The catalog designation for 1960 Fleer is R418-2. The cards were printed on a 96-card sheet with 17 double prints. These are noted in the checklist below by DP. On the sheet the second Eddie Collins card is typically found in the number 80 position. According to correspondence sent from Fleers at the time -- no card 80 was issued because of contract problems. Some cards have been discovered with wrong backs. The cards were issued in nickel packs which were packed 24 to a box.

COMPLETE SET (79)	300.00	600.00
WRAPPER (5-CENT)	50.00	100.00
1 Napoleon Lajoie DP	12.50	30.00
2 Christy Mathewson	6.00	15.00
3 Babe Ruth	50.00	100.00
4 Carl Hubbell	3.00	8.00
5 Grover C. Alexander	3.00	8.00
6 Walter Johnson DP	4.00	10.00
7 Chief Bender	1.50	4.00
8 Roger Bresnahan	1.50	4.00
9 Mordecai Brown	1.50	4.00
10 Tris Speaker	3.00	8.00
11 Arky Vaughan DP	1.50	4.00
12 Zach Wheat	1.50	4.00
13 George Sisler	1.50	4.00
14 Connie Mack	3.00	8.00
15 Clark Griffith	1.50	4.00
16 Lou Boudreau DP	3.00	8.00
17 Ernie Lombardi	1.50	4.00
18 Heinie Manush	1.50	4.00
19 Marty Marion	2.50	6.00
20 Eddie Collins DP	1.50	4.00
21 Rabbit Maranville DP	1.50	4.00
22 Joe Medwick	1.50	4.00
23 Ed Barrow	1.50	4.00
24 Mickey Cochrane	2.50	6.00
25 Jimmy Collins	1.50	4.00
26 Bob Feller DP	6.00	15.00
27 Luke Appling	2.50	6.00
28 Lou Gehrig	25.00	60.00
29 Gabby Hartnett	1.50	4.00
30 Chuck Klein	1.50	4.00
31 Tony Lazzeri DP	2.50	6.00
32 Al Simmons	1.50	4.00
33 Wilbert Robinson	1.50	4.00
34 Sam Rice	1.50	4.00
35 Herb Pennock	1.50	4.00
36 Mel Ott DP	3.00	8.00
37 Lefty O'Doul	1.50	4.00
38 Johnny Mize	3.00	8.00
39 Edmund (Bing) Miller	1.50	4.00
40 Joe Tinker	1.50	4.00
41 Frank Baker DP	1.50	4.00
42 Ty Cobb	20.00	50.00
43 Paul Derringer	1.50	4.00
44 Cap Anson	1.50	4.00
45 Jim Bottomley	1.50	4.00
46 Eddie Plank DP	1.50	4.00
47 Denton (Cy) Young	4.00	10.00
48 Hack Wilson	2.50	6.00
49 Ed Walsh UER	1.50	4.00
50 Frank Chance	1.50	4.00
51 Dazzy Vance DP	1.50	4.00
52 Bill Terry	2.50	6.00
53 Jimmie Foxx	4.00	10.00
54 Lefty Gomez	3.00	8.00
55 Branch Rickey	1.50	4.00
56 Ray Schalk DP	1.50	4.00
57 Johnny Evers	1.50	4.00
58 Charley Gehringer	2.50	6.00
59 Burleigh Grimes	1.50	4.00
60 Lefty Grove	3.00	8.00
61 Rube Waddell DP	1.50	4.00
62 Honus Wagner	12.00	30.00
63 Red Ruffing	1.50	4.00
64 Kenesaw M. Landis	1.50	4.00
65 Harry Heilmann	1.50	4.00
66 John McGraw DP	1.50	4.00
67 Hughie Jennings	1.50	4.00
68 Hal Newhouser	2.50	6.00
69 Waite Hoyt	1.50	4.00
70 Bobo Newsom	1.50	4.00
71 Earl Averill DP	1.50	4.00
72 Ted Williams	40.00	80.00
73 Warren Giles	2.50	6.00
74 Ford Frick	2.50	6.00
75 Kiki Cuyler	1.50	4.00
76 Paul Waner DP	2.50	6.00
77 Pie Traynor	1.50	4.00
78 Lloyd Waner	1.50	4.00
79 Ralph Kiner	4.00	10.00
80A P.Martin SP/Eddie Collins	1,250.00	2,500.00
80B P.Martin SP/Lefty Grove	1,000.00	2,000.00
80C P.Martin SP/Joe Tinker	1,000.00	2,000.00

1960 Fleer Stickers

This 20-sticker set measures the standard size. The fronts feature a cartoon depicting the title of the card. The pictures are framed with red and black stars and the words "All Star" printed in blue. First names are printed below and are used to place in the blank box of each sticker to represent the person the sticker depicts. The stickers are unnumbered and checklisted below in alphabetical order.

COMPLETE SET (20)	20.00	50.00
COMMON CARD (1-20)	1.25	3.00

1961 Fleer

The cards in this 154-card set measure 2 1/2" by 3 1/2". In 1961, Fleer continued its Baseball Greats format by issuing this series of cards. The set was released in two distinct series, 1-88 and 89-154 (of which the latter is more difficult to obtain). The players within each series are conveniently numbered in alphabetical order. The catalog number for this set is F418-3. In each first series pack Fleer inserted a Major League team decal and a pennant sticker honoring past World Series winners. The cards were issued in nickel packs which were issued 24 to a box.

COMPLETE SET (154)	600.00	1,200.00
COMMON CARD (1-88)	1.25	3.00
COMMON CARD (89-154)	3.00	8.00
WRAPPER (5-CENT)	50.00	100.00
1 Baker/Cobb/Wheat	20.00	50.00
2 Grover C. Alexander	2.50	6.00
3 Nick Altrock	1.25	3.00
4 Cap Anson	1.50	4.00
5 Earl Averill	1.50	4.00
6 Frank Baker	1.50	4.00
7 Dave Bancroft	1.50	4.00
8 Chief Bender	1.50	4.00
9 Jim Bottomley	1.50	4.00
10 Roger Bresnahan	1.50	4.00
11 Mordecai Brown	1.50	4.00
12 Max Carey	1.50	4.00
13 Jack Chesbro	1.50	4.00
14 Ty Cobb	20.00	50.00
15 Mickey Cochrane	1.50	4.00
16 Eddie Collins	2.50	6.00
17 Earle Combs	1.50	4.00
18 Charles Comiskey	1.50	4.00
19 Kiki Cuyler	1.50	4.00
20 Paul Derringer	1.25	3.00
21 Howard Ehmke	1.25	3.00
22 Billy Evans UMP	1.50	4.00
23 Johnny Evers	1.50	4.00
24 Urban Faber	1.50	4.00
25 Bob Feller	5.00	12.00
26 Wes Ferrell	1.25	3.00
27 Lew Fonseca	1.25	3.00
28 Jimmie Foxx	2.50	6.00
29 Ford Frick	1.25	3.00
30 Frankie Frisch	1.50	4.00
31 Lou Gehrig	25.00	60.00
32 Charley Gehringer	1.50	4.00
33 Warren Giles	1.25	3.00
34 Lefty Gomez	1.50	4.00
35 Goose Goslin	1.50	4.00
36 Clark Griffith	1.50	4.00
37 Burleigh Grimes	1.50	4.00
38 Lefty Grove	2.50	6.00
39 Chick Hafey	1.50	4.00
40 Jesse Haines	1.50	4.00
41 Gabby Hartnett	1.50	4.00
42 Harry Heilmann	1.50	4.00
43 Rogers Hornsby	2.50	6.00
44 Waite Hoyt	1.50	4.00
45 Carl Hubbell	2.50	6.00
46 Miller Huggins	1.50	4.00
47 Hughie Jennings	1.50	4.00

48 Ban Johnson	1.50	4.00
49 Walter Johnson	5.00	12.00
50 Ralph Kiner	2.50	6.00
51 Chuck Klein	1.50	4.00
52 Johnny Kling	1.25	3.00
53 Kenesaw M. Landis	1.50	4.00
54 Tony Lazzeri	1.50	4.00
55 Ernie Lombardi	1.50	4.00
56 Dolf Luque	1.25	3.00
57 Heinie Manush	1.50	4.00
58 Marty Marion	1.25	3.00
59 Christy Mathewson	5.00	12.00
60 John McGraw	1.50	4.00
61 Joe Medwick	1.50	4.00
62 Edmund (Bing) Miller	1.25	3.00
63 Johnny Mize	1.50	4.00
64 John Mostil	1.25	3.00
65 Art Nehf	1.25	3.00
66 Hal Newhouser	1.50	4.00
67 Bobo Newsom	1.25	3.00
68 Mel Ott	2.50	6.00
69 Allie Reynolds	1.25	3.00
70 Sam Rice	1.50	4.00
71 Eppa Rixey	1.50	4.00
72 Edd Roush	1.50	4.00
73 Schoolboy Rowe	1.25	3.00
74 Red Ruffing	1.50	4.00
75 Babe Ruth	60.00	120.00
76 Joe Sewell	1.50	4.00
77 Al Simmons	1.50	4.00
78 George Sisler	1.50	4.00
79 Tris Speaker	1.50	4.00
80 Fred Toney	1.25	3.00
81 Dazzy Vance	1.50	4.00
82 Hippo Vaughn	1.25	3.00
83 Ed Walsh	1.50	4.00
84 Lloyd Waner	1.50	4.00
85 Paul Waner	1.50	4.00
86 Zack Wheat	1.50	4.00
87 Hack Wilson	1.50	4.00
88 Jimmy Wilson	1.25	3.00
89 G.Sisler/P.Traynor	30.00	60.00
90 Babe Adams	3.00	8.00
91 Dale Alexander	3.00	8.00
92 Jim Bagby	3.00	8.00
93 Ossie Bluege	3.00	8.00
94 Lou Boudreau	4.00	10.00
95 Tommy Bridges	3.00	8.00
96 Donie Bush	3.00	8.00
97 Dolph Camilli	3.00	8.00
98 Frank Chance	4.00	10.00
99 Jimmy Collins	4.00	10.00
100 Stan Coveleskie	4.00	10.00
101 Hugh Critz	3.00	8.00
102 Alvin Crowder	3.00	8.00
103 Joe Dugan	3.00	8.00
104 Bibb Falk	3.00	8.00
105 Rick Ferrell	4.00	10.00
106 Art Fletcher	3.00	8.00
107 Dennis Galehouse	3.00	8.00
108 Chick Galloway	3.00	8.00
109 Mule Haas	3.00	8.00
110 Stan Hack	3.00	8.00
111 Bump Hadley	3.00	8.00
112 Billy Hamilton	4.00	10.00
113 Joe Hauser	3.00	8.00
114 Babe Herman	3.00	8.00
115 Travis Jackson	4.00	10.00
116 Eddie Joost	3.00	8.00
117 Addie Joss	4.00	10.00
118 Joe Judge	3.00	8.00
119 Joe Kuhel	3.00	8.00
120 Napoleon Lajoie	5.00	12.00
121 Dutch Leonard	3.00	8.00
122 Ted Lyons	4.00	10.00
123 Connie Mack	5.00	12.00
124 Rabbit Maranville	4.00	10.00
125 Fred Marberry	3.00	8.00
126 Joe McGinnity	4.00	10.00
127 Oscar Melillo	3.00	8.00
128 Ray Mueller	3.00	8.00
129 Kid Nichols	4.00	10.00
130 Lefty O'Doul	4.00	10.00
131 Bob O'Farrell	3.00	8.00
132 Roger Peckinpaugh	3.00	8.00
133 Herb Pennock	4.00	10.00
134 George Pipgras	3.00	8.00
135 Eddie Plank	4.00	10.00
136 Ray Schalk	4.00	10.00
137 Hal Schumacher	3.00	8.00
138 Luke Sewell	3.00	8.00
139 Bob Shawkey	3.00	8.00
140 Riggs Stephenson	3.00	8.00
141 Billy Sullivan	3.00	8.00
142 Bill Terry	5.00	12.00
143 Joe Tinker	4.00	10.00
144 Pie Traynor	4.00	10.00
145 Hal Trosky	3.00	8.00
146 George Uhle	3.00	8.00
147 Johnny VanderMeer	4.00	10.00
148 Arky Vaughan	4.00	10.00
149 Rube Waddell	4.00	10.00
150 Honus Wagner	20.00	50.00
151 Dixie Walker	3.00	8.00
152 Ted Williams	40.00	100.00
153 Cy Young	15.00	40.00
154 Ross Youngs	15.00	40.00

1963 Fleer

The Fleer set of current baseball players was marketed in 1963 in a gum card-style waxed wrapper package which contained a cherry cookie instead of gum. The five cent packs were packaged 24 to a box. The cards were printed in sheets of 66 with the scarce card of Joe Adcock (number 46) replaced by the unnumbered checklist card for the final press run. The complete set price includes the checklist card. The catalog designation for this set is R418-4. The key Rookie Card in this set is Maury Wills. The set is basically arranged numerically in alphabetical order by teams which are also in alphabetical order.

COMPLETE SET (67)	1,000.00	2,000.00
WRAPPER (5-CENT)	50.00	100.00
1 Steve Barber	10.00	25.00
2 Ron Hansen	6.00	15.00
3 Milt Pappas	8.00	20.00
4 Brooks Robinson	20.00	50.00
5 Willie Mays	40.00	100.00
6 Lou Clinton	6.00	15.00
7 Bill Monbouquette	6.00	15.00
8 Carl Yastrzemski	20.00	50.00
9 Ray Herbert	6.00	15.00
10 Jim Landis	6.00	15.00
11 Dick Donovan	6.00	15.00
12 Tito Francona	6.00	15.00
13 Jerry Kindall	6.00	15.00
14 Frank Lary	8.00	20.00
15 Dick Howser	8.00	20.00
16 Jerry Lumpe	6.00	15.00
17 Norm Siebern	6.00	15.00
18 Don Lee	6.00	15.00
19 Albie Pearson	8.00	20.00
20 Bob Rodgers	8.00	20.00
21 Leon Wagner	6.00	15.00
22 Jim Kaat	10.00	25.00
23 Vic Power	8.00	20.00
24 Rich Rollins	8.00	20.00
25 Bobby Richardson	10.00	25.00
26 Ralph Terry	8.00	20.00
27 Tom Cheney	6.00	15.00
28 Chuck Cottier	6.00	15.00
29 Jimmy Piersall	8.00	20.00
30 Dave Stenhouse	6.00	15.00
31 Glen Hobbie	6.00	15.00
32 Ron Santo	10.00	25.00
33 Gene Freese	6.00	15.00
34 Vada Pinson	10.00	25.00
35 Bob Purkey	6.00	15.00
36 Joe Amalfitano	6.00	15.00
37 Bob Aspromonte	6.00	15.00
38 Dick Farrell	6.00	15.00
39 Al Spangler	6.00	15.00
40 Tommy Davis	8.00	20.00
41 Don Drysdale	20.00	50.00
42 Sandy Koufax	50.00	120.00
43 Maury Wills RC	30.00	80.00
44 Frank Bolling	6.00	15.00
45 Warren Spahn	15.00	40.00
46 Joe Adcock SP	25.00	60.00
47 Roger Craig	8.00	20.00
48 Al Jackson	8.00	20.00
49 Rod Kanehl	8.00	20.00
50 Ruben Amaro	6.00	15.00
51 Johnny Callison	8.00	20.00
52 Clay Dalrymple	6.00	15.00
53 Don Demeter	6.00	15.00
54 Art Mahaffey	6.00	15.00
55 Smoky Burgess	8.00	20.00
56 Roberto Clemente	50.00	120.00
57 Roy Face	8.00	20.00
58 Vern Law	8.00	20.00
59 Bill Mazeroski	8.00	20.00
60 Ken Boyer	10.00	25.00
61 Bob Gibson	25.00	60.00
62 Gene Oliver	6.00	15.00
63 Bill White	8.00	20.00
64 Orlando Cepeda	12.50	30.00
65 Jim Davenport	6.00	15.00
66 Billy O'Dell	10.00	25.00
NNO Checklist SP	250.00	500.00

1966 Fleer AS Match Game

The 1966 Fleer All-Star Match Baseball Game set consists of 66 standard-size cards. The front of each card has nine rectangular boxes, one for each inning of a baseball game. These boxes are either blue (for American All Stars) or yellow (for National All Stars). In the lower right corner, a tie breaker rule is listed. When properly placed, the backs of all the cards form a composite black and white photo of Don Drysdale. The cards are numbered on the front. This is a rare instance where the set is worth much more than any individual part.

COMPLETE SET (66)	150.00	300.00
COMMON PLAYER (1-66)	3.00	8.00

1968-72 Fleer Cloth Stickers

This set was issued over a period of four years. This can be determined by the inclusion of the Seattle Pilots, who only played in 1969, as well as the Texas Rangers who did not move to Texas until 1972. This sticker set measures 2 1/2" by 3 1/4" and is comprised of two different types of stickers. The first group (1-24) are all the same design with the team city printed in a banner across the top and the official team logo in a circular design below. Both are designed to peel off. The second group (25-48) are of a different design with the team logo letter being the top portion and the city left off. The team name makes up the bottom section. Again, both are designed to be peeled off. The stickers are unnumbered and checklisted below in alphabetical order within each sticker type.

COMPLETE SET (48)	40.00	80.00
1 Atlanta Braves	.75	2.00
2 Baltimore Orioles	.75	2.00
3 Boston Red Sox	.75	2.00
4 California Angels	.75	2.00
5 Chicago Cubs	.75	2.00
6 Chicago White Sox	.75	2.00
7 Cincinnati Reds	.75	2.00
8 Cleveland Indians	.75	2.00
9 Detroit Tigers	.75	2.00
10 Houston Astros	.75	2.00
11 Kansas City Royals	.75	2.00
12 Los Angeles Dodgers	.75	2.00
13 Minnesota Twins	.75	2.00
14 Montreal Expos	.75	2.00
15 New York Mets	.75	2.00
16 New York Yankees	.75	2.00
17 Oakland A's	.75	2.00
18 Philadelphia Phillies	.75	2.00
19 Pittsburgh Pirates	.75	2.00
20 St. Louis Cardinals	.75	2.00
21 San Francisco Giants	.75	2.00
22 Seattle Pilots	2.00	5.00
23 Texas Rangers	.75	2.00
24 Washington Senators	.75	2.00
25 California Angels	.75	2.00
26 Houston Astros	.75	2.00
27 Atlanta Braves	.75	2.00
28 St. Louis Cardinals	.75	2.00
29 Chicago Cubs	.75	2.00
30 Los Angeles Dodgers	.75	2.00
31 Montreal Expos	.75	2.00
32 San Francisco Giants	.75	2.00
33 Cleveland Indians	.75	2.00
34 New York Mets	.75	2.00
35 Oakland A's	.75	2.00
36 Baltimore Orioles	.75	2.00
37 Philadelphia Phillies	.75	2.00
38 Seattle Pilots	.75	2.00
39 Pittsburgh Pirates	.75	2.00
40 Texas Rangers	.75	2.00
41 Reds	.75	2.00
42 Red Sox	.75	2.00
43 Royals	.75	2.00
44 Senators	.75	2.00
45 Sox	.75	2.00
46 Tigers	.75	2.00
47 Twins	.75	2.00
48 Yankees	.75	2.00

1970 Fleer Laughlin World Series Blue Backs

This set of 66 standard-size cards was distributed by Fleer in 1970 although the cards carry a copyright date of 1968 on the back. The cards are in crude color on the front with light blue printing on white card stock on the back. All the years are represented except for 1904 when no World Series was played. In the list below, the winning series team is listed first. The year of the Series on the obverse is inside a white baseball. The original art for the cards in this set was drawn by sports artist R.G. Laughlin.

COMPLETE SET (66)	75.00	150.00
1 1903 Red Sox Pirates	.60	1.50
2 1905 Giants A's/(Christy Mathewson)	1.50	4.00
3 1906 White Sox Cubs	.60	1.50
4 1907 Cubs Tigers	.60	1.50
5 1908 Cubs Tigers/(Joe Tinker& Johnny Evers& and	1.50	4.00
6 1909 Pirates/Tigers	2.50	6.00
7 1910 A's Cubs/(Chief Bender and Jack Coombs)	1.00	2.50
8 1911 A's Giants/(John McGraw)	1.00	2.50
9 1912 Red Sox Giants	.60	1.50
10 1913 A's Giants	.60	1.50
11 1914 Braves A's	.60	1.50
12 1915 Red Sox Phillies/(Babe Ruth)	3.00	8.00
13 1916 Red Sox Dodgers/(Babe Ruth)	3.00	8.00
14 1917 White Sox Giants	.60	1.50
15 1918 Red Sox Cubs	.60	1.50
16 1919 Reds White Sox	3.00	8.00
17 1920 Indians Dodgers/(Stan Coveleski)	1.00	2.50
18 1921 Giants Yankees/(Commissioner Landis)	.60	1.50
19 1922 Giants Yankees	.60	1.50
20 1923 Yankees Giants/(Babe Ruth)	3.00	8.00
21 1924 Senators Giants/(John McGraw)	1.00	2.50
22 1925 Pirates Senators/(Walter Johnson)	1.50	4.00
23 1926 Cardinals Yankees/(Grover C. Alexander and	1.00	2.50
24 1927 Yankees Pirates	.60	1.50
25 1928 Yankees Cardinals/(Babe Ruth and Lou Gehrig	3.00	8.00
26 1929 A's Cubs	.60	1.50
27 1930 A's Cardinals	.60	1.50
28 1931 Cardinals A's/(Pepper Martin)	.60	1.50
29 1932 Yankees Cubs/(Babe Ruth and Lou Gehrig)	3.00	8.00
30 1933 Giants Senators/(Mel Ott)	1.00	2.50
31 1934 Cardinals Tigers	.60	1.50
32 1935 Tigers Cubs/(Charlie Gehringer and Tommy Br	1.00	2.50
33 1936 Yankees Giants	.60	1.50
34 1937 Yankees Giants/(Carl Hubbell)	1.00	2.50
35 1938 Yankees Cubs/(Lou Gehrig)	2.50	6.00
36 1939 Yankees Reds	.60	1.50
37 1940 Reds Tigers	.60	1.50
38 1941 Yankees Dodgers	.60	1.50
39 1942 Cardinals Yankees	.60	1.50
40 1943 Yankees Cardinals	.60	1.50
41 1944 Cardinals Browns	.60	1.50
42 1945 Tigers Cubs/(Hank Greenberg)	1.50	4.00
43 1946 Cardinals Red Sox/(Enos Slaughter)	1.00	2.50
44 1947 Yankees Dodgers/(Al Gionfriddo)	.60	1.50
45 1948 Indians Braves	.60	1.50
46 1949 Yankees Dodgers/(Allie Reynolds and Preache	.60	1.50
47 1950 Yankees Phillies	.60	1.50
48 1951 Yankees Giants	.60	1.50
49 1952 Yankees Dodgers/(Johnny Mize and Duke Snide	2.50	6.00
50 1953 Yankees Dodgers/(Carl Erskine)	.60	1.50
51 1954 Giants Indians/(Johnny Antonelli)	.60	1.50
52 1955 Dodgers Yankees/(Johnny Podres)	.60	1.50
53 1956 Yankees Dodgers	.60	1.50
54 1957 Braves Yankees/(Lew Burdette)	.60	1.50
55 1958 Yankees Braves/(Bob Turley)	.60	1.50
56 1959 Dodgers White Sox/(Chuck Essegian)	.60	1.50
57 1960 Pirates Yankees	.60	1.50
58 1961 Yankees Reds/(Whitey Ford)	1.00	2.50
59 1962 Yankees Giants	.60	1.50
60 1963 Dodgers Yankees/(Moose Skowron)	.60	1.50
61 1964 Cardinals Yankees/(Bobby Richardson)	1.00	2.50
62 1965 Dodgers Twins	.60	1.50
63 1966 Orioles Dodgers	.60	1.50
64 1967 Cardinals Red Sox	.60	1.50
65 1968 Tigers Cardinals	.60	1.50
66 1969 Mets Orioles	1.00	2.50

1971 Fleer Laughlin World Series Black Backs

This set of standard-size cards was distributed by Fleer in 1971 as a 68-card set. The cards were printed in crude color on the front with black printing on white card stock on the back. All the years since 1903 are represented in this set including 1904, when no World Series was played. While the copyright line on the card back references the year of issue as 1968, these black backed card first appeared in 1971. In 1978, Fleer reissued the entire 68-card set along with 7-update cards for the World Series' 1971-1977.

COMPLETE SET (68) 250.00 500.00
1 1903 Red Sox 1.50 4.00
Pirates/(Cy Young)
2 1904 NO Series/(John McGraw) 1.00 2.50
3 1905 Giants 1.50 4.00
A's/(Christy Mathewson&
Chief Bender
4 1906 White Sox .60 1.50
Cubs/(Fielder Jones)
5 1907 Cubs .60 1.50
Tigers
6 1908 Cubs/Tigers 2.00 5.00
7 1909 Pirates .60 1.50
Tigers
8 1910 A's 1.00 2.50
Cubs/(Eddie Collins)
9 1911 A's 1.00 2.50
Giants/(Home Run Baker)
10 1912 Red Sox .60 1.50
Giants
11 1913 A's 1.50 4.00
Giants/(Christy Mathewson)
12 1914 Braves .60 1.50
A's
13 1915 Red Sox 1.00 2.50
Phillies/(Grover Alexander)
14 1916 Red Sox .60 1.50
Dodgers
15 1917 White Sox 1.00 2.50
Giants/(Red Faber)
16 1918 Red Sox 3.00 8.00
Cubs/(Babe Ruth)
17 1919 Reds 3.00 8.00
White Sox
18 1920 Indians .60 1.50
Dodgers
19 1921 Giants 1.00 2.50
Yankees/(Waite Hoyt)
20 1922 Giants .60 1.50
Yankees
21 1923 Yankees 1.00 2.50
Giants/(Herb Pennock)
22 1924 Senators 1.50 4.00
Giants/(Walter Johnson)
23 1925 Pirates 1.00 2.50
Senators/(Kiki Cuyler and
Walter Jo
24 1926 Cardinals 1.50 4.00
Yankees/(Rogers Hornsby)
25 1927 Yankees .60 1.50
Pirates
26 1928 Yankees 2.00 5.00
Cardinals/(Lou Gehrig)
27 1929 A's .60 1.50
Cubs/(Howard Ehmke)
28 1930 A's 1.50 4.00
Cardinals/(Jimmie Foxx)
29 1931 Cardinals .60 1.50
A's/(Pepper Martin)
30 1932 Yankees 3.00 8.00
Cubs/(Babe Ruth)
31 1933 Giants 1.00 2.50
Senators/(Carl Hubbell)
32 1934 Cardinals .60 1.50
Tigers
33 1935 Tigers 1.00 2.50
Cubs/(Mickey Cochrane)
34 1936 Yankees .60 1.50
Giants/(Red Rolfe)
35 1937 Yankees 1.00 2.50
Giants/(Tony Lazzeri)
36 1938 Yankees .60 1.50
Cubs
37 1939 Yankees .60 1.50
Reds
38 1940 Reds .60 1.50
Tigers
39 1941 Yankees .60 1.50
Dodgers
40 1942 Cardinals .60 1.50
Yankees
41 1943 Yankees .60 1.50
Cardinals
42 1944 Cardinals .60 1.50
Browns
43 1945 Tigers 1.50 4.00
Cubs/(Hank Greenberg)
44 1946 Cardinals 1.00 2.50
Red Sox/(Enos Slaughter)
45 1947 Yankees .60 1.50
Dodgers
46 1948 Indians .60 1.50
Braves
47 1949 Yankees .60 1.50
Dodgers/(Preacher Roe)
48 1950 Yankees .60 1.50
Phillies/(Allie Reynolds)
49 1951 Yankees .60 1.50
Giants/(Ed Lopat)
50 1952 Yankees 1.00 2.50
Dodgers/(Johnny Mize)
51 1953 Yankees .60 1.50
Dodgers
52 1954 Giants .60 1.50
Indians
53 1955 Dodgers 1.00 2.50
Yankees/(Duke Snider)
54 1956 Yankees .60 1.50
Dodgers
55 1957 Braves .60 1.50
Yankees
56 1958 Yankees .60 1.50
Braves/(Hank Bauer)
57 1959 Dodgers 1.00 2.50
Wh.Sox/(Duke Snider)
58 1960 Pirates .60 1.50
Yankees
59 1961 Yankees 1.00 2.50
Reds/(Whitey Ford)
60 1962 Yankees .60 1.50
Giants
61 1963 Dodgers .60 1.50
Yankees
62 1964 Cardinals .60 1.50
Yankees
63 1965 Dodgers .60 1.50
Twins
64 1966 Orioles .60 1.50
Dodgers
65 1967 Cardinals .60 1.50
Red Sox
66 1968 Tigers .60 1.50
Cardinals
67 1969 Mets .60 1.50
Orioles
68 1970 Orioles 1.00 2.50
Reds
69 1971 Pirates 100.00 200.00
Orioles
Roberto Clemente
70 1972 A's 40.00 80.00
Reds
71 1973 A's 40.00 80.00
Mets
72 1974 A's 40.00 80.00
Dodgers
73 1975 Reds 40.00 80.00
Red Sox
74 1976 Reds 40.00 80.00
Yankees
75 1977 Yankees 40.00 80.00
Dodgers

1972 Fleer Famous Feats

This Fleer set of 40 cards features the artwork of sports artist R.G. Laughlin. The set is titled "Baseball's Famous Feats." The cards are numbered both on the front and back. The backs are printed in light blue on white card stock. The cards measure approximately 2 1/2" by 4". This set was licensed by Major League Baseball.

COMPLETE SET (40) 60.00 120.00
1 Joe McGinnity .75 2.00
2 Rogers Hornsby 1.25 3.00
3 Christy Mathewson 2.50 6.00
4 Dazzy Vance .75 2.00
5 Lou Gehrig 5.00 12.00
6 Jim Bottomley .75 2.00
7 Johnny Evers .75 2.00
8 Walter Johnson 2.50 6.00
9 Hack Wilson .75 2.00
10 Wilbert Robinson .75 2.00
11 Cy Young 1.25 3.00
12 Rudy York .50 1.25
13 Grover C. Alexander .75 2.00
14 Fred Toney and .50 1.25
Hippo Vaughan
15 Ty Cobb 5.00 12.00
16 Jimmie Foxx 2.50 6.00
17 Hub Leonard .50 1.25
18 Eddie Collins .75 2.00
19 Joe Oeschger and .50 1.25
Leon Cadore
20 Babe Ruth 10.00 25.00
21 Honus Wagner 1.25 3.00
22 Red Rolfe .50 1.25
23 Ed Walsh .75 2.00
24 Paul Waner .75 2.00
25 Mel Ott 1.00 2.50
26 Eddie Plank .75 2.00
27 Sam Crawford .75 2.00
28 Napoleon Lajoie 1.00 2.50
29 Ed Reulbach .50 1.25
30 Pinky Higgins .50 1.25
31 Bill Klem .75 2.00
32 Tris Speaker 1.00 2.50
33 Hank Gowdy .50 1.25
34 Lefty O'Doul .50 1.25
35 Lloyd Waner .75 2.00
36 Chuck Klein .75 2.00
37 Deacon Phillippe .50 1.25
38 Ed Delahanty .75 2.00
39 Jack Chesbro .75 2.00
40 Willie Keeler .75 2.00

1973 Fleer Wildest Days

This Fleer set of 42 cards is titled "Baseball's Wildest Days and Plays" and features the artwork of sports artist R.G. Laughlin. The sets were available from Bob Laughlin for $3. The backs are printed in dark red on white card stock. The cards measure approximately 2 1/2" by 4". This set was not licensed by Major League Baseball.

COMPLETE SET (42) 60.00 120.00
1 Cubs and Phillies 1.25 3.00
Score 49 Runs in Game
2 Frank Chance .60 1.50
Five HBP's in One Day
3 Jim Thorpe 4.00 10.00
Homered into 3 States
4 Eddie Gaedel 1.50 4.00
Midget in Majors
5 Most Tied Game Ever .60 1.50
6 Seven Errors in .60 1.50
One Inning
7 Four 20-Game Winners .60 1.50
But No Pennant
8 Dummy Hoy 1.25 3.00
Umpires Signal Strikes
9 Fourteen Hits in .60 1.50
One Inning
10 Yankees Not Shut Out .60 1.50
For Two Years
11 Buck Weaver 1.50 4.00
17 Straight Fouls
12 George Sisler .60 1.50
Greatest Thrill
Was as a Pitcher
13 Wrong-Way Baserunner .60 1.50
14 Kiki Cuyler .60 1.50
Sits Out Series
15 Grounder Climbed Wall .60 1.50
16 Gabby Street .60 1.50
Washington Monument
17 Mel Ott 3.00 8.00
Ejected Twice
18 Shortest Pitching .60 1.50
Career
19 Three Homers in .60 1.50
One Inning
20 Bill Byron .60 1.50
Singing Umpire
21 Fred Clarke .60 1.50
Walking Steal of Home
22 Christy Mathewson 3.00 8.00
373rd Win Discovered
23 Hitting Through the .60 1.50
Unglaub Arc
24 Jim O'Rourke .60 1.50
Catching at 52
25 Fired for Striking .60 1.50
Out in Series
26 Eleven Run Inning .60 1.50
on One Hit
27 58 Innings in 3 Days .60 1.50
28 Homer on Warm-Up .60 1.50
Pitch
29 Giants Win 26 Straight .60 1.50
But Finish Fourth
30 Player Who Stole .60 1.50
First Base
31 Ernie Shore .60 1.50
Perfect Game
in Relief
32 Greatest Comeback .60 1.50
33 All-Time Flash- .60 1.50
In-The-Pan
34 Hub Pruett 1.50 4.00
Fanned Ruth
19 out of 31
35 Fixed Batting Race Cobb/Lajoie 3.00 8.00
36 Wild-Pitch Rebound .60 1.50
Play
37 17 Straight Scoring .60 1.50
Innings
38 Wildest Opening Day .60 1.50
39 Baseball's Strike One .60 1.50
40 Opening Day No Hitter .60 1.50
That Didn't Count
41 Jimmie Foxx 3.00 8.00
Six Straight Walks
in One Game
42 Entire Team Hit and 1.25 3.00
Scored in Inning

1974 Fleer Baseball Firsts

This Fleer set of 42 cards is titled "Baseball Firsts" and features the artwork of sports artist R.G. Laughlin. The cards are numbered on the back. The backs are printed in black on gray card stock. The cards measure approximately 2 1/2" by 4". This set was not licensed by Major League Baseball.

COMPLETE SET (42) 50.00 100.00
COMMON PLAYER (1-42) .60 1.50
1 Slide 1.00 2.50
2 Spring Training .60 1.50
3 Bunt .60 1.50
4 Catcher's Mask .60 1.50
5 Lou Gehrig 8.00 20.00
Four straight Homers
6 Radio Broadcast .60 1.50
7 Numbered Uniforms .60 1.50
8 Shin Guards .60 1.50
9 Players Association .60 1.50
10 Knuckleball .60 1.50
11 Player With Glasses .60 1.50
12 Baseball Cards 6.00 15.00
13 Standardized Rules .60 1.50
14 Grand Slam .60 1.50
15 Player Fined .60 1.50
16 Presidential Opener .60 1.50
17 Player Transaction .60 1.50
18 All-Star Game .60 1.50
19 Scoreboard .60 1.50
20 Cork Center Ball .60 1.50
21 Scorekeeping .60 1.50
22 Domed Stadium .60 1.50
23 Batting Helmet .60 1.50
24 Fatality .60 1.50
25 Unassisted Triple Play .60 1.50
26 Home Run At Night .60 1.50
27 Black Major Leaguer 1.00 2.50
28 Pinch Hitter .60 1.50
29 Million-Dollar .60 1.50
World Series
30 Tarpaulin .60 1.50
31 Team Initials .60 1.50
32 Pennant Playoff .60 1.50
33 Glove .60 1.50
34 Curve Ball .60 1.50
35 Night Game .60 1.50
36 Admission Charge .60 1.50
37 Farm System .60 1.50
38 Telecast .60 1.50
39 Commissioner .60 1.50
40 .400 Hitter .60 1.50
41 World Series .60 1.50
42 Player Into Service 1.00 2.50

1975 Fleer Pioneers

This 28-card set of brown and white sepia-toned photos of old timers is subtitled "Pioneers of Baseball. The graphics artwork was done by R.G. Laughlin. The cards measure approximately 2 1/2" X 4". The card backs are a narrative about the particular player.

COMPLETE SET (28) 15.00 40.00
1 Cap Anson 1.25 3.00
2 Harry Wright .75 2.00
3 Buck Ewing .75 2.00
4 Al G. Spalding .75 2.00
5 Old Hoss Radbourn .75 2.00
6 Dan Brouthers .75 2.00
7 Roger Bresnahan .75 2.00
8 Mike Kelly .75 2.00
9 Ned Hanlon .75 2.00
10 Ed Delahanty .75 2.00
11 Pud Galvin .75 2.00
12 Amos Rusie .75 2.00
13 Tommy McCarthy .75 2.00
14 Ty Cobb 4.00 10.00
15 John McGraw .75 2.00
16 Home Run Baker .75 2.00
17 Johnny Evers .75 2.00
18 Nap Lajoie 1.00 2.50
19 Cy Young 1.25 3.00
20 Eddie Collins 1.00 2.50
21 John Glasscock .60 1.50
22 Hal Chase .60 1.50
23 Mordecai Brown .75 2.00
24 Jake Daubert .60 1.50
25 Mike Donlin .60 1.50
26 John Clarkson .75 2.00
27 Buck Herzog .60 1.50
28 Art Nehf .60 1.50

1916 Fleischmann Bread D381

This 103-card set was produced by Fleischmann Breads in 1916. These unnumbered cards are arranged here for convenience in alphabetical order; cards with tabs intact are worth 50 percent more than the prices listed below. The cards measure approximately 2 3/4" by 5 1/2" (with tab) or 2 3/4" by 4 13/16" (without tab). There is also a similar set issued by Ferguson Bread which is harder to find and is distinguished by having the photo caption written on only one line rather than two as with the Fleischmann cards.

COMPLETE SET 5,000.00 10,000.00
1 Babe Adams 300.00 600.00
2 Grover Alexander 1,250.00 2,500.00
3 Walt E. Alexander 250.00 500.00
4 Frank Allen 250.00 500.00
5 Fred Anderson 250.00 500.00
6 Dave Bancroft 500.00 1,000.00
7 Jack Barry 250.00 500.00
8 Beals Becker 250.00 500.00
9 Beals Becker 250.00 500.00
Copyright logo more prevalent
10 Eddie Burns 250.00 500.00
11 George J. Burns 250.00 500.00
12 Bobby Byrne 250.00 500.00
13 Ray B. Caldwell 250.00 500.00
14 James Callahan P/MG 250.00 500.00
15 William Carrigan MG 250.00 500.00
16 Larry Cheney 250.00 500.00
17 Tom Clarke 250.00 500.00
Photo goes to waist
18 Tom Clark 250.00 500.00
Photo shows his pants
19 Ty Cobb 10,000.00 20,000.00
20 Ray W. Collins 250.00 500.00
21 Ray Collins 250.00 500.00
Copyright logo more prominent
22 Jack Coombs 400.00 800.00

1916 Fleischmann Bread D381

23 A. Wilbur Cooper	250.00	500.00
24 George Cutshaw	250.00	500.00
25 Jake Daubert	300.00	600.00
26 Wheezer Dell	250.00	500.00
27 Bill Donovan	250.00	500.00
28 Larry Doyle	300.00	600.00
29 R.J. Egan	250.00	500.00
30 Johnny Evers	750.00	1,500.00
31 Ray Fisher	250.00	500.00
32 Harry Gardner (Sic)	250.00	500.00
33 Joe Gedeon	250.00	500.00
34 Larry Gilbert	250.00	500.00
35 Frank Gilhooley	250.00	500.00
36 Hank Gowdy	300.00	600.00
37 Sylvanus Gregg	250.00	500.00
38 Tom Griffith	250.00	500.00
39 Heinie Groh	300.00	600.00
40 Robert Harmon	250.00	500.00
41 Roy A. Hartzell	250.00	500.00
42 Claude Hendricks	250.00	500.00
43 Olaf Hendriksen	250.00	500.00
44 Buck Herzog P MG	250.00	500.00
45 Hugh High	250.00	500.00
46 Dick Hoblitzell	250.00	500.00
47 Herb H. Hunter	250.00	500.00
48 Harold Janvrin	250.00	500.00
49 Hugh Jennings MG	500.00	1,000.00
50 John Johnston	250.00	500.00
51 Erving Kantlehner	250.00	500.00
52 Bennie Kauff	300.00	600.00
53 Ray H. Keating	250.00	500.00
54 Wade Killefer	250.00	500.00
55 Elmer Knetzer	250.00	500.00
56 Brad W. Kocher	250.00	500.00
57 Ed Konetchy	250.00	500.00
58 Fred Lauderus (Sic)	250.00	500.00
59 Dutch Leonard	300.00	600.00
60 Duffy Lewis	300.00	600.00
61 E.H.(Slim) Love	250.00	500.00
62 Albert L. Mamaux	250.00	500.00
63 Rabbit Maranville	500.00	1,000.00
64 Rube Marquard	500.00	1,000.00
65 Christy Mathewson	2,500.00	5,000.00
66 Bill McKechnie	500.00	1,000.00
67 Chief Meyer (Sic)	300.00	600.00
68 Otto Miller	250.00	500.00
69 Fred Mollwitz	250.00	500.00
70 Herbie Moran	250.00	500.00
71 Mike Mowrey	250.00	500.00
72 Dan Murphy	250.00	500.00
73 Art Nehf	300.00	600.00
74 Rube Oldring	250.00	500.00
75 Oliver O'Mara	250.00	500.00
76 Dode Paskert	250.00	500.00
77 D.C.Pat Ragan	250.00	500.00
78 Wm.A. Rariden	250.00	500.00
79 Davis Robertson	250.00	500.00
80 Wm. Rodgers	250.00	500.00
81 Edw.F.Rousch (Sic)	750.00	1,500.00
82 Nap Rucker	300.00	600.00
83 Dick Rudolph	250.00	500.00
84 Walter Schang	300.00	600.00
85 A.J.(Rube) Schauer	250.00	500.00
86 Pete Schneider	250.00	500.00
87 Ferd M. Schupp	250.00	500.00
88 Ernie Shore	300.00	600.00
89 Red Smith	250.00	500.00
90 Fred Snodgrass	300.00	600.00
91 Tris Speaker	1,250.00	2,500.00
92 George Stallings MG	250.00	500.00
93 Casey Stengel/Sic, Stengle	2,500.00	5,000.00
94 Sailor Stroud	250.00	500.00
95 Amos Strunk	250.00	500.00
96 Chas.(Jeff) Tesreau	250.00	500.00
97 Chester D. Thomas	250.00	500.00
98 Chester D. Thomas Copyright logo more prominent	250.00	500.00
99 Fred Toney	250.00	500.00
100 Walter Tragresser	250.00	500.00
101 Honus Wagner	2,500.00	5,000.00
102 Carl Weilman	250.00	500.00
103 Zack Wheat	500.00	1,000.00
104 George Whitted	250.00	500.00
105 Arthur Wilson	250.00	500.00
106 Ivy Wingo	250.00	500.00
107 Joe Wood	400.00	800.00

1887 Four Base Hits N-Unc.

The fourteen known baseball cards inscribed "Four Base Hits" were catalogued in the N690 classification for two reasons: they are identical in size and format to N690-1, and two players, Mays and Roseman, have the same pictures in both sets. Although it is known that the Charles Gross Company "farmed out" some of its insert designs to other companies, "Four Base Hits" will retain this catalog number until new evidence places them elsewhere. As far as is known, the Mickey Welch card is currently unique.

COMPLETE SET	100,000.00	200,000.00
1 Tom Dailey (sic, Daly)	12,500.00	25,000.00
2 John Clarkson	50,000.00	100,000.00
3 Pat Deasley	12,500.00	25,000.00
4 Buck Ewing	50,000.00	100,000.00
5 Pete Gillespie	12,500.00	25,000.00
6 Frank Hankinson	12,500.00	25,000.00
7 Mike King Kelly	60,000.00	120,000.00
8 Al Mays	12,500.00	25,000.00
9 James Mutrie	12,500.00	25,000.00
10 James (Chief) Roseman	12,500.00	25,000.00
11 Marty Sullivan	12,500.00	25,000.00
12 George Van Haltren	12,500.00	25,000.00
13 John Mont. Ward	50,000.00	100,000.00
14 Mickey Welch	50,000.00	100,000.00

1980 Franchise Babe Ruth

This 80-card set measures the standard size and was manufactured by the Franchise of Bel Air, Maryland. The cards present the life of Babe Ruth and include his activities both on and off the field. The fronts have black and white photos framed by white borders. The set, which had an original print run of 1,000 sets was originally issued in complete set form and available for $8 directly from the manufacturer at the time of the issue

COMPLETE SET (80)	10.00	25.00
COMMON PLAYER (1-80)	.75	1.50

1960 Free Press Hot Stove League Manager

Issued as inserts in the Detroit Free Press, these clippings measure approximately 5 1/2" by 6". These were issued and featured various highlights of what a manager decision was at a key part of a game. Please note that this checklist is basically complete (we still need to id card number 17) and that last addition would be greatly appreciated.

COMPLETE SET	50.00	100.00
1 Duke Snider	6.00	15.00
2 Eddie Sawyer MG	1.00	2.50
3 Elmer Valo	1.25	3.00
4 Joe Gordon MG	1.25	3.00
5 Don Blasingame	1.00	2.50
6 Paul Richards MG	1.00	2.50
7 Billy Consolo	1.00	2.50
8 Leo Kiely	1.00	2.50
9 Dave Philley	1.00	2.50
10 George Strickland MG	1.00	2.50
11 Felipe Alou	3.00	8.00
12 Al Lopez MG	2.00	5.00
13 Yogi Berra	6.00	15.00
14 Don McMahon	1.00	2.50
15 Johnny Temple	1.00	2.50
16 Solly Hemus MG	1.00	2.50
18 Bill Rigney MG	1.00	2.50
19 Bob Cerv	1.00	2.50
20 Walt Alston MG	2.00	5.00
21 Nellie Fox	3.00	8.00
22 Danny Murtaugh MG	1.00	2.50
23 Orlando Cepeda	3.00	8.00
24 George Altman	1.00	2.50

1977-83 Fritsch One Year Winners

This 118-card standard-size set honors players who played roughly a season or less and were thus forgotten in baseball lore. The set was issued as three parts of one series. Cards 1-18 were issued in 1977 and feature black and white player photos, bordered in white and green. Cards 19-54 were issued in 1979 and have color player photos with white borders. Cards 55-118 were issued in 1983 and have colored photois with blue and white borders. The extended caption and Major League statistical record on the horizontally oriented backs are banded above and below by red stripes. The cards are numbered on the back in a baseball diamond in the upper left corner.

COMPLETE SET (118)	12.50	30.00
1 Eddie Gaedel	.60	1.50
2 Chuck Connors	.30	.75
3 Joe Brovia	.10	.25
4 Ross Grimsley Sr.	.10	.25
5 Bob Thorpe	.10	.25
6 Pete Gray	.30	.75
7 Cy Buker	.10	.25
8 Ted Fritsch Sr.	.15	.40
9 Ron Necciai	.15	.40
10 Nino Escalera	.10	.25
11 Bobo Holloman	.15	.40
12 Tony Roig	.10	.25
13 Paul Pettit	.15	.40
14 Paul Schramka	.10	.25
15 Hal Trosky Jr.	.15	.40
16 Floyd Wooldridge	.10	.25
17 Jim Westlake	.10	.25
18 Leon Brinkopf	.10	.25
19 Daryl Robertson	.10	.25
20 Gerry Shoen	.10	.25
21 Jim Brenneman	.10	.25
22 Pat House	.10	.25
23 Ken Poulsen	.10	.25
24 Arlo Brunsberg	.10	.25
25 Jay Hankins	.10	.25
26 Chuck Nieson	.10	.25
27 Dick Joyce	.10	.25
28 Jim Ellis	.10	.25
29 John Duffie	.10	.25
30 Vern Holtgrave	.10	.25
31 Bill Bethea	.10	.25
32 Joe Moock	.10	.25
33 John Hoffman	.10	.25
34 Jorge Rubio	.10	.25
35 Fred Rath	.10	.25
36 Jess Hickman	.10	.25
37 Tom Fisher	.10	.25
38 Dick Scott	.10	.25
39 Jim Hibbs	.10	.25
40 Paul Gilliford	.10	.25
41 Bob Botz	.10	.25
42 Jack Kubiszyn	.10	.25
43 Rich Rusteck	.10	.25
44 Roy Gleason	.10	.25
45 Glenn Vaughan	.10	.25
46 Bill Graham	.40	1.00
47 Dennis Musgraves	.10	.25
48 Ron Henry	.10	.25
49 Mike Jurewicz	.10	.25
50 Pidge Browne	.15	.40
51 Ron Keller	.10	.25
52 Doug Gallagher	.10	.25
53 Dave Thies	.10	.25
54 Don Eaddy	.10	.25
55 Don Prince	.10	.25
56 Tom Granly	.10	.25
57 Roy Heiser	.10	.25
58 Hank Izquierdo	.10	.25
59 Rex Johnston	.10	.25
60 Jack Damaska	.10	.25
61 John Flavin	.10	.25
62 John Glenn	.10	.25
63 Stan Johnson	.10	.25
64 Don Choate	.10	.25
65 Bill Kern	.10	.25
66 Dick Luebke	.10	.25
67 Glen Clark	.10	.25
68 Lamar Jacobs	.10	.25
69 Rick Herrscher	.15	.40
70 Jim McManus	.10	.25
71 Len Church	.10	.25
72 Moose Stubing	.10	.25
73 Cal Emery	.10	.25
74 Lee Gregory	.10	.25
75 Mike Page	.10	.25
76 Benny Valenzuela	.10	.25
77 John Papa	.10	.25
78 Jim Stump	.10	.25
79 Brian McCall	.10	.25
80 Al Kenders	.10	.25
81 Corky Withrow	.10	.25
82 Verle Tiefenthaler	.10	.25
83 Dave Wissman	.10	.25
84 Tom Fletcher	.10	.25
85 Dale Willis	.10	.25
86 Larry Foster	.10	.25
87 Johnnie Seale	.10	.25
88 Jim Lehew	.10	.25
89 Charlie Shoemaker	.10	.25
90 Don Arlich	.10	.25
91 George Gerberman	.10	.25
92 John Pregenger	.10	.25
93 Merlin Nippert	.10	.25
94 Steve Demeter	.10	.25
95 John Paciorek	.15	.40
96 Larry Loughlin	.10	.25
97 Alan Brice	.10	.25
98 Chet Boak	.10	.25
99 Alan Koch	.10	.25
100 Danny Thomas	.10	.25
101 Elder White	.10	.25
102 Jim Snyder	.10	.25
103 Ted Schreiber	.10	.25
104 Evans Killeen	.10	.25
105 Ray Daviault	.10	.25
106 Larry Foss	.10	.25
107 Wayne Graham	.10	.25
108 Santiago Rosario	.10	.25
109 Bob Sprout	.10	.25
110 Tom Hughes	.10	.25
111 Em Lindbeck	.10	.25
112 Ray Blemker	.10	.25
113 Shaun Fitzmaurice	.10	.25
114 Ron Stillwell	.10	.25
115 Carl Thomas	.10	.25
116 Mike DeGerick	.10	.25
117 Jay Dahl	.10	.25
118 Al Lary	.10	.25

1976 Funky Facts

This 40-card standard-size set is subtitled "The Wierd [sic] World of Baseball". A paper insert included with the set carries a checklist on its back. Inside a white outer border and a color inner border, the fronts feature colorful cartoon drawings. A trivia question appears above each picture in a pale yellow bar. Each back shows five trivia questions and their answers. The first question repeats the question found on card fronts.

COMPLETE SET	4.00	10.00
COMMON CARD	.10	.25

1963 Gad Fun Cards

This set of 1963 Fun Cards were issued by a sports illustrator by the name of Gad from Minneapolis, Minnesota. The cards are printed on cardboard stock paper. The borderless fronts have black and white line drawings. A fun sport's fact or player career statistic is depicted in the drawing. The backs of the first six cards display numbers used to play the game explained on card number 6. The other backs carry a cartoon with a joke or riddle. Copyright information is listed on the lower portion of the card.

COMPLETE SET (84)	37.50	75.00
1 Babe Ruth	4.00	8.00
2 Lost Baseballs Fact	.25	.50
3 Baseball Slang Fireman	.25	.50
4 Baseball Hurling Fact	.25	.50
5 Lou Gehrig	2.50	5.00
6 Number Game Directions	.25	.50
7 Baseball Fact Consecutive Home Runs	.25	.50
8 Old Hoss Radbourne	.50	1.00
10 Joe Nuxhall	.38	.75
11 Ty Cobb	2.50	5.00
12 Baseball Slang Jake	.25	.50
13 Pop Schriver	.25	.50
14 Boston Red Sox	.25	.50
15 John Taylor	.25	.50
16 Cincinnati Red Stockings	.25	.50
17 Runs Scored in a Game	.25	.50
18 Baseball Slang Duster	.25	.50
19 1908 Baseball Fact	.25	.50
20 Evar Swanson	.25	.50
21 1929 World Series Pinch Hitters	.25	.50
22 Rogers Hornsby	.75	1.50
23 Highlanders	.25	.50
24 Baseball Slang Strawberry	.25	.50
25 Lew Flick	.25	.50
26 Cy Young	1.50	3.00
27 Jim Konstanty	.25	.50
28 Carl Weilman	.25	.50
29 Warren Rosar	.25	.50
30 Baseball Slang Rabbit Ears	.25	.50
31 Graham McNamee	.25	.50
32 Ty Cobb Batting Record	2.50	5.00
33 Joe DiMaggio	2.50	5.00
34 Babe Ruth Earnings	4.00	8.00
35 Baseball Slang Chinese Homer	.25	.50
36 Ed Delahanty	.38	.75
37 1912 Detroit Tiger Team Strike	.25	.50
38 Bobo Holloman	.25	.50
39 Walter Johnson	1.50	3.00
40 Sam Crawford	.50	1.00
41 Lifetime Record Stolen Bases	.25	.50
42 Baseball Slang Showboat	.25	.50
43 Lou Gehrig/23 Bases-loaded Homers	2.50	5.00
44 Yankee Stadium	.25	.50
45 Nick Altrock	.50	1.00
46 Moses Walker Welday Walker	.50	1.00
47 Joseph Borden	.25	.50
48 Baseball Slang Around the Horn	.25	.50
49 Hugh Duffy	.50	1.00
50 Longest Game Baseball History	.25	.50
51 Jim Scott	.25	.50
52 Longest Homer in 1919	.25	.50
53 Record Runs Scored in One Inning	.25	.50
54 Baseball Slang Jockey	.25	.50
55 Umpires in 1871	.25	.50
57 Eddie Collins	.50	1.00
58 Milwaukee Braves	.25	.50
59 Bill Wambsganss	.25	.50
60 Baseball Slang Annie Oakley	.25	.50
61 Bob Feller	.50	1.00
62 Wally Pipp	.25	.50
63 Shortest World Series Game	.25	.50
64 Chicago White Sox	.25	.50
65 Cleveland Indians	.25	.50
66 Baseball Slang Baltimore Chop	.25	.50
67 14 Pitchers Used in One Game	.25	.50

1888 G and B Chewing Gum Co E223

These cards measure approximately 1" by 2 1/8" and primarily feature players from the National League. This is one of the few nineteenth century issues which are not tobacco related. The set was issued by the G and B Chewing Gum Co and is the first set baseball issue released by a gum or candy company. The cards are unnumbered and we have sequenced them in alphabetical order. If more than one pose is known, we have put the number of said poses next to the player's name. The complete set price only includes one of each variation. Portraits are worth approximately 1.5X times the value of the drawings. Some cards were recently discovered and added to this checklist so any further additions are appreciated.

COMPLETE SET 250,000.00 500,000.00
1 Cap Anson 15,000.00 30,000.00
2 Lady Baldwin (3) 5,000.00 10,000.00
3 Sam Barkley 5,000.00 10,000.00
4 Steve Brady 5,000.00 10,000.00
5 Bill Brown (2) 5,000.00 10,000.00
6 Dan Brouthers 5,000.00 10,000.00
7 Charlie Buffington 5,000.00 10,000.00
8 Oyster Burns 6,000.00 12,000.00
9 Bob Caruthers 5,000.00 10,000.00
10 John Clarkson 10,000.00 20,000.00
11 Pop Smith 5,000.00 10,000.00
12 John Coleman 5,000.00 10,000.00
13 Charles Comiskey 15,000.00 30,000.00
14 Roger Connor (2) 10,000.00 20,000.00
15 Ed Daily 5,000.00 10,000.00
16 Pat Deasley 5,000.00 10,000.00
17 Jim Donahue 5,000.00 10,000.00
18 Pat Dorgan 5,000.00 10,000.00
19 Dude Esterbrook 5,000.00 10,000.00
20 Buck Ewing 10,000.00 20,000.00
21 Charlie Ferguson 6,000.00 12,000.00
22 Frank Flint 6,000.00 12,000.00
23 Charles Getzein 5,000.00 10,000.00
24 Jack Glasscock 5,000.00 10,000.00
25 Kid Gleason 7,500.00 15,000.00
26 Frank Hankinson 5,000.00 10,000.00
27 Ned Hanlon 10,000.00 20,000.00
28 Pete Hotaling 5,000.00 10,000.00
29 Richard Johnston 5,000.00 10,000.00
30 Tim Keefe (3) 10,000.00 20,000.00
31 Mike Kelly (2) 20,000.00 40,000.00
32 August Krock 5,000.00 10,000.00
33 Connie Mack 20,000.00 40,000.00
34 Kid Madden 5,000.00 10,000.00
35 George Miller 5,000.00 10,000.00
36 John Morrill 5,000.00 10,000.00
37 Henry Porter 6,000.00 12,000.00
38 James Mutrie MG 5,000.00 10,000.00
39 Sam Nicoll 5,000.00 10,000.00
40 Tip O'Neill 6,000.00 12,000.00
41 Jim O'Rourke 15,000.00 30,000.00
42 Fred Pfeffer 5,000.00 10,000.00
43 Al Reach 25,000.00 50,000.00
44 Danny Richardson (2) 5,000.00 10,000.00
45 Yank Robinson 5,000.00 10,000.00
46 Chief Roseman 5,000.00 10,000.00
47 Jimmy Ryan (2) 7,500.00 15,000.00
48 William J. Sowders 5,000.00 10,000.00
49 Albert G. Spalding 60,000.00 120,000.00
50 Martin J. Sullivan 5,000.00 10,000.00
51 Billy Sunday (2) 15,000.00 30,000.00
52 Ezra Sutton 5,000.00 10,000.00
53 Mike Tiernan (2) 5,000.00 10,000.00
54 Sam Thompson 15,000.00 30,000.00
55 Lawrence Twitchell 5,000.00 10,000.00
56 George Van Haltren 5,000.00 10,000.00
57 John Montgomery Ward 15,000.00 30,000.00
58 Curt Welch 6,000.00 12,000.00
59 Mickey Welch (2) 15,000.00 30,000.00
60 Grasshopper Whitney 5,000.00 10,000.00
61 Pete Wood 5,000.00 10,000.00

1976 Galasso Baseball's Great Hall of Fame

These 32 cards feature players considered among the all time greats. This was the first of many collector issue sets released by Renato Galasso Inc. Many of these sets were released as premiums with orders to RGI. This set is sequenced in alphabetical order.

COMPLETE SET 10.00 25.00
1 Luke Appling .20 .50
2 Ernie Banks .40 1.00
3 Yogi Berra .40 1.00
4 Roy Campanella .40 1.00
5 Roberto Clemente 1.25 3.00
6 Alvin Dark .10 .25
7 Joe DiMaggio 1.25 3.00
8 Bob Feller .30 .75
9 Whitey Ford .30 .75
10 Jimmy Foxx (Jimmie) .40 1.00
11 Lou Gehrig 1.25 3.00
12 Charlie Gehringer .20 .50
13 Henry Greenberg .20 .50
14 Gabby Hartnett .20 .50
15 Carl Hubbell .30 .75
16 Al Kaline .30 .75
17 Mickey Mantle 1.50 4.00
18 Willie Mays .75 2.00
19 Johnny Mize .20 .50
20 Stan Musial .60 1.50
21 Mel Ott .20 .50
22 Satchell Paige .60 1.50
23 Robin Roberts .30 .75
25 Babe Ruth 1.50 4.00
26 Duke Snider .40 1.00
27 Warren Spahn .30 .75
28 Tris Speaker .30 .75
29 Honus Wagner .40 1.00
30 Ted Williams 1.25 3.00
31 Rudy York .10 .25
32 Cy Young .40 1.00

1977-84 Galasso Glossy Greats

This 270-card standard-size set was issued by Renata Galasso Inc. (a hobby card dealer) and originally offered as a free bonus when ordering hand-collated Topps sets. The set may be subdivided into six series with 45 cards per series, with one series being issued per year as follows: TCMA printed the first four series and Renata Galasso Inc. the last two. The fronts display black and white player photos bordered in white. The player's name, position and team for which he played appear in the bottom white border. The backs are white, printed in red and blue ink and carry a career summary and an advertisement for Renata Galasso Inc. The backs have a red baseball in each of the upper corners with the card number in the left one.

COMPLETE SET (270) 60.00 120.00
1 Joe DiMaggio 1.25 3.00
2 Ralph Kiner .15 .40
3 Don Larsen .12 .30
4 Robin Roberts .15 .40
5 Roy Campanella .30 .75
6 Smoky Burgess .08 .20
7 Mickey Mantle 1.25 3.00
8 Willie Mays .75 2.00
9 George Kell .15 .40
10 Ted Williams 1.00 2.50
11 Carl Furillo .12 .30
12 Bob Feller .15 .40
13 Casey Stengel .30 .75
14 Richie Ashburn .15 .40
15 Gil Hodges .15 .40
16 Stan Musial .75 2.00
17 Don Newcombe .12 .30
18 Jackie Jensen .12 .30
19 Lou Boudreau .15 .40
20 Jackie Robinson .75 2.00
21 Billy Goodman .08 .20
22 Satchel Paige .40 1.00
23 Hoyt Wilhelm .15 .40
24 Duke Snider .30 .75
25 Whitey Ford .40 1.00
26 Monte Irvin .15 .40
27 Hank Sauer .08 .20
28 Sal Maglie .08 .20
29 Ernie Banks .30 .75
30 Billy Pierce .08 .20
31 Pee Wee Reese .30 .75
32 Al Lopez .15 .40
33 Allie Reynolds .08 .20
34 Eddie Mathews .15 .40
35 Al Rosen .08 .20
36 Early Wynn .15 .40
37 Phil Rizzuto .15 .40
38 Warren Spahn .15 .40
39 Bobby Thomson .12 .30
40 Enos Slaughter .15 .40
41 Roberto Clemente 1.00 2.50
42 Luis Aparicio .15 .40
43 Roy Sievers .08 .20
44 Hank Aaron .75 2.00
45 Mickey Vernon .08 .20
46 Lou Gehrig 1.25 3.00
47 Lefty O'Doul .08 .20
48 Chuck Klein .15 .40
49 Paul Waner .15 .40
50 Mel Ott .15 .40
51 Riggs Stephenson .08 .20
52 Dizzy Dean .15 .40
53 Frank Frisch .15 .40
54 Red Ruffing .15 .40
55 Lefty Grove .15 .40
56 Heinie Manush .15 .40
57 Jimmie Foxx .30 .75
58 Al Simmons .15 .40
59 Charlie Root .08 .20
60 Goose Goslin .15 .40
61 Mickey Cochrane .15 .40
62 Gabby Hartnett .15 .40
63 Joe Medwick .15 .40
64 Ernie Lombardi .15 .40
65 Joe Cronin .15 .40
66 Pepper Martin .08 .20
67 Jim Bottomley .15 .40
68 Bill Dickey .30 .75
69 Babe Ruth 1.50 4.00
70 Joe McCarthy MG .12 .30
71 Doc Cramer .08 .20
72 KiKi Cuyler .15 .40
73 Johnny Vander Meer .12 .30
74 Paul Derringer .08 .20
75 Fred Fitzsimmons .08 .20
76 Lefty Gomez .15 .40
77 Arky Vaughan .15 .40
78 Stan Hack .08 .20
79 Earl Averill .15 .40
80 Luke Appling .15 .40
81 Mel Harder .08 .20
82 Hank Greenberg .15 .40
83 Schoolboy Rowe .08 .20
84 Billy Herman .15 .40
85 Gabby Street .08 .20
86 Lloyd Waner .15 .40
87 Jocko Conlon .12 .30
88 Carl Hubbell .30 .75
89 Checklist 1 .08 .20
90 Checklist 2 .08 .20
91 Babe Ruth 1.50 4.00
92 Rogers Hornsby .15 .40
93 Edd Roush .15 .40
94 George Sisler .15 .40
95 Harry Heilmann .15 .40
96 Tris Speaker .30 .75
97 Burleigh Grimes .15 .40
98 John McGraw .30 .75
99 Eppa Rixey .15 .40
100 Ty Cobb 1.25 3.00
101 Zack Wheat .15 .40
102 Pie Traynor .30 .75
103 Max Carey .15 .40
104 Dazzy Vance .15 .40
105 Walter Johnson .40 1.00
106 Herb Pennock .15 .40
107 Joe Sewell .15 .40
108 Sam Rice .15 .40
109 Earle Combs .15 .40
110 Ted Lyons .15 .40
111 Eddie Collins .30 .75
112 Bill Terry .15 .40
113 Hack Wilson .15 .40
114 Rabbit Maranville .15 .40
115 Charlie Grimm .08 .20
116 Tony Lazzeri .15 .40
117 Waite Hoyt .15 .40
118 Stan Coveleski .15 .40
119 George Kelly .15 .40
120 Jimmie Dykes .08 .20
121 Red Faber .15 .40
122 Dave Bancroft .15 .40
123 Judge Landis COMM .12 .30
124 Branch Rickey .12 .30
125 Jesse Haines .15 .40
126 Carl Mays .08 .20
127 Fred Lindstrom .15 .40
128 Miller Huggins .15 .40
129 Sad Sam Jones .08 .20
130 Joe Judge .08 .20
131 Ross Youngs .15 .40
132 Bucky Harris .15 .40
133 Bob Meusel .12 .30
134 Billy Evans .12 .30
135 Checklist 3 .08 .20
136 Ty Cobb 1.25 3.00
137 Nap Lajoie .15 .40
138 Tris Speaker .15 .40
139 Heinie Groh .08 .20
140 Sam Crawford .15 .40
141 Clyde Milan .08 .20
142 Chief Bender .15 .40
143 Big Ed Walsh .15 .40
144 Walter Johnson .30 .75
145 Connie Mack MG .15 .40
146 Hal Chase .12 .30
147 Hugh Duffy .15 .40
148 Honus Wagner .30 .75
149 Tom Connolly UMP .12 .30
150 Clark Griffith .12 .30
151 Zack Wheat .15 .40
152 Christy Mathewson .30 .75
153 Grover Cleveland Alexander .30 .75
154 Joe Jackson .60 1.50
155 Home Run Baker .15 .40
156 Ed Plank .15 .40
157 Larry Doyle .08 .20
158 Rube Marquard .15 .40
159 John Evers .15 .40
160 Joe Tinker .15 .40
161 Frank Chance .15 .40
162 Wilbert Robinson MG .12 .30
163 Roger Peckinpaugh .08 .20
164 Fred Clarke .15 .40
165 Babe Ruth 1.50 4.00
166 Wilbur Cooper .08 .20
167 Germany Schaefer .08 .20
168 Addie Joss .15 .40
169 Cy Young .15 .40
170 Ban Johnson PRES .12 .30
171 Joe Judge .08 .20
172 Harry Hooper .15 .40
173 Bill Klem UMP .12 .30
174 Ed Barrow MG .12 .30
175 Ed Cicotte .12 .30
176 Hughie Jennings MG .12 .30
177 Ray Schalk .15 .40
178 Nick Altrock .12 .30
179 Roger Bresnahan MG .15 .40
180 Checklist 4 .08 .20
The 100&000 Infield
Stuffy McInnis/
181 Lou Gehrig 1.25 3.00
182 Eddie Collins .15 .40
183 Art Fletcher CO .08 .20
184 Jimmie Foxx .15 .40
185 Lefty Gomez .15 .40
186 Oral Hildebrand .08 .20
187 General Crowder .08 .20
188 Bill Dickey .15 .40
189 Wes Ferrell .08 .20
190 Al Simmons .15 .40
191 Tony Lazzeri .15 .40
192 Sam West .08 .20
193 Babe Ruth 1.50 4.00
194 Connie Mack MG .15 .40
195 Lefty Grove .15 .40
196 Eddie Rommel .08 .20
197 Ben Chapman .08 .20
198 Joe Cronin .15 .40
199 Rick Ferrell .15 .40
200 Charlie Gehringer .15 .40
201 Jimmy Dykes .08 .20
202 Earl Averill .15 .40
203 Pepper Martin .08 .20
204 Bill Terry .15 .40
205 Pie Traynor .15 .40
206 Gabby Hartnett .15 .40
207 Frank Frisch .15 .40
208 Carl Hubbell .15 .40
209 Paul Waner .15 .40
210 Woody English .08 .20
211 Bill Hallahan .08 .20
212 Dick Bartell .08 .20
213 Bill McKechnie CO .12 .30
214 Max Carey CO .15 .40
215 John McGraw MG .15 .40
216 Jimmie Wilson .08 .20
217 Chick Hafey .15 .40
218 Chuck Klein .15 .40
219 Lefty O'Doul .08 .20
220 Wally Berger .08 .20
221 Hal Schumacher .08 .20
222 Lon Warneke .08 .20
223 Tony Cuccinello .08 .20
224 Americal League Team Photo .08 .20
225 National League Team Photo .08 .20
226 Roger Maris .30 .75
227 Babe Ruth 1.50 4.00
228 Jackie Robinson .75 2.00
229 Pete Gray .15 .40
230 Ted Williams 1.00 2.50
231 Hank Aaron .75 2.00
232 Mickey Mantle 1.25 3.00
233 Gil Hodges .30 .75
234 Walter Johnson .15 .40
235 Joe DiMaggio 1.25 3.00
236 Lou Gehrig 1.25 3.00
237 Stan Musial .75 2.00
238 Mickey Cochrane .15 .40
239 Denny McLain .08 .20
240 Carl Hubbell .15 .40
241 Harvey Haddix .08 .20
242 Christy Mathewson .15 .40
243 Johnny Vander Meer .08 .20
244 Sandy Koufax .30 .75
245 Willie Mays .75 2.00
246 Don Drysdale .15 .40
247 Bobby Richardson .08 .20
248 Hoyt Wilhelm .15 .40
249 Yankee Stadium .08 .20
250 Bill Terry .15 .40
251 Roy Campanella .30 .75
252 Roberto Clemente 1.00 2.50
253 Casey Stengel .15 .40
254 Ernie Banks .30 .75
255 Bobby Thomson .12 .30
256 Mel Ott .15 .40
257 Tony Oliva .08 .20
258 Satchel Paige .40 1.00
259 Joe Jackson .60 1.50
260 Nap Lajoie .15 .40
261 Bill Mazeroski .12 .30
262 Bill Wambsganss .08 .20
263 Willie McCovey .15 .40
264 Warren Spahn .15 .40
265 Lefty Gomez .15 .40
266 Dazzy Vance .15 .40
267 Sam Crawford .15 .40
268 Tris Speaker .15 .40
269 Lou Brock .30 .75
270 Cy Young .15 .40

1920 Gassler's American Maid Bread D381-1

These cards measure approximately 2" by 3". The cards have a photo on most of the card with the player's name and position on the bottom. The back has an advertisment for Gassler's Bread. The cards are unnumbered and we have sequenced them alphabetically by team which are also sequenced alphabetically.

COMPLETE SET 750.00 1,500.00
1 Kid Gleason MG 150.00 300.00
2 Harry Hooper 200.00 400.00
3 Dick Kerr 150.00 300.00
4 Amos Strunk 100.00 200.00
5 George Burns 100.00 200.00
6 W. L. Gardner 100.00 200.00
7 Rip Collins 100.00 200.00
8 Wm. Fewster 100.00 200.00
9 Harry Harper 100.00 200.00
10 Waite Hoyt 200.00 400.00
11 Miller Huggins MG 200.00 400.00
12 M.J. McNally 100.00 200.00
13 Bob Meusel 150.00 300.00
14 Walter Pipp 125.00 250.00
15 Jack Quinn 100.00 200.00
16 Robert Roth 100.00 200.00
17 Wally Schang 125.00 250.00
18 Aaron Ward 100.00 200.00
19 Wm. Jacobson 100.00 200.00
20 Clyde Milan 125.00 250.00
21 Walter Holke 100.00 200.00
22 P. J. Kilduff 100.00 200.00
23 Zach Wheat 200.00 400.00
24 Charles Deal 100.00 200.00
25 Charles Hollacher 100.00 200.00
26 Zeb Terry 100.00 200.00
27 Geo. J. Burns 100.00 200.00
28 Cecil Causey 100.00 200.00
29 Hugh Jennings MG 200.00 400.00
30 Arthur Nehf 125.00 250.00
31 John Rawlings 100.00 200.00
32 Bill Ryan 100.00 200.00
33 Pat Shea 100.00 200.00
34 Earl Smith 100.00 200.00
35 Frank Snyder 100.00 200.00
36 Jeff Pfeffer 100.00 200.00
37 Ty Cobb 1,250.00 2,500.00

1911-14 General Baking D304

These cards, which measure 1 3/4" by 2 1/2" feature drawings of leading players. Many of the players in this set were members of the 1911 pennant winners, leading one to believe that this set was issued sometime the next summer. Various other bread manufacturers also produced this set, most noticeably Brunner's Bread and Butter Krust. Other companies that issued these cards include Weber Bakery and Martens Bakery.

COMPLETE SET (25)	3,000.00	6,000.00
1 J. Frank Baker	750.00	1,500.00
2 Jack Barry	500.00	1,000.00
3 George Bell	500.00	1,000.00
4 Charles Bender	750.00	1,500.00
5 Frank Chance	1,000.00	2,000.00
6 Hal Chase	1,000.00	2,000.00
7 Ty Cobb	3,000.00	6,000.00
8 Eddie Collins	2,000.00	4,000.00
9 Otis Crandall	500.00	1,000.00
10 Sam Crawford	1,000.00	2,000.00
11 John Evers	1,000.00	2,000.00
12 Arthur Fletcher	500.00	1,000.00
13 Charles Herzog	500.00	1,000.00
14 Billy Kelly	500.00	1,000.00
15 Napoleon Lajoie	1,500.00	3,000.00
16 Rube Marquard	1,000.00	2,000.00
17 Christy Mathewson	2,500.00	5,000.00
18 Fred Merkle	500.00	1,000.00
19 Chief Meyers	500.00	1,000.00
20 Marty O'Toole	500.00	1,000.00
21 Nap Rucker	500.00	1,000.00
22 Arthur Shafer	500.00	1,000.00
23 Fred Tenney	500.00	1,000.00
24 Honus Wagner	3,000.00	6,000.00
25 Cy Young	2,500.00	5,000.00

1956 Gentry Magazine Ty Cobb

NNO Ty Cobb	40.00	100.00

1933 George C. Miller R300

The cards in this 32-card set measure 2 1/2" by 3". This set of soft tone color baseball cards issued in 1933 by the George C. Miller Company consists of 16 players from each league. The bottom portion of the reverse contained a premium offer and many cards are found with this section cut off. Cards without the coupon are considered fair to good condition at best. The Andrews card (with coupon intact) is considered extremely scarce in relation to all other common players. Very few copies are known of the Andrews with the coupon attached.

COMPLETE SET (32)	60,000.00	120,000.00
1 Dale Alexander	1,500.00	3,000.00
2 Ivy Andrews	10,000.00	20,000.00
3 Earl Averill	2,500.00	5,000.00
4 Dick Bartell	1,500.00	3,000.00
5 Wally Berger	1,500.00	3,000.00
6 Jim Bottomley	2,500.00	5,000.00
7 Joe Cronin	2,500.00	5,000.00
8 Dizzy Dean	3,000.00	6,000.00
9 Bill Dickey	3,000.00	6,000.00
10 Jimmy Dykes	1,500.00	3,000.00
11 Wes Ferrell	2,000.00	4,000.00
12 Jimmy Foxx (Jimmie)	3,000.00	6,000.00
13 Frank Frisch	2,500.00	5,000.00
14 Charlie Gehringer	2,500.00	5,000.00
15 Goose Goslin	2,500.00	5,000.00
16 Charlie Grimm	1,500.00	3,000.00
17 Lefty Grove	3,000.00	6,000.00
18 Chick Hafey	2,000.00	4,000.00
19 Ray Hayworth	1,500.00	3,000.00
20 Chuck Klein	2,500.00	5,000.00
21 Rabbit Maranville	2,500.00	5,000.00
22 Oscar Melillo	1,500.00	3,000.00
23 Lefty O'Doul	2,000.00	4,000.00
24 Mel Ott	3,000.00	6,000.00
25 Carl Reynolds	1,500.00	3,000.00
26 Red Ruffing	2,500.00	5,000.00
27 Al Simmons	2,500.00	5,000.00
28 Joe Stripp	1,500.00	3,000.00
29 Bill Terry	2,500.00	5,000.00
30 Lloyd Waner	2,500.00	5,000.00
31 Paul Waner	2,500.00	5,000.00
32 Lon Warneke	1,500.00	3,000.00

1972 Gera Postcard

This postcard was given away at what was supposed to be lady umpire Bernice Gera's first game. As the only game she actually umpired in was one day later, this card features several factual errors. The postcard features a photo of Gera on top and then the basic information about the game she umpired in. Gera only umpired in one game before concluding her professional career.

1 Bernice Gera	4.00	10.00

1886 Giants Old Judge N167

These cards measure approximately 1 1/2" by 2 1/2". All the players portrayed are members of the New York National team which became the Giants. Though their existance has not been confirmed, it was rumored that the Deasley and Mutrie cards may exist. We have sequenced this set in alphabetical order.

COMPLETE SET	150,000.00	300,000.00
1 Roger Connor	25,000.00	50,000.00
2 Larry Corcoran	7,500.00	15,000.00
3 Tom Deasley		
4 Mike Dorgan	7,500.00	15,000.00
5 Dude Esterbrook	7,500.00	15,000.00
6 Buck Ewing	25,000.00	50,000.00
7 Joe Gerhardt	7,500.00	15,000.00
8 Pete Gillespie	7,500.00	15,000.00
9 Tim Keefe	25,000.00	50,000.00
10 Jim Mutrie MG		
11 James O'Rourke	25,000.00	50,000.00
12 Danny Richardson	7,500.00	15,000.00
13 John M. Ward	25,000.00	50,000.00
14 Mickey Welsh (sic)	25,000.00	50,000.00

1886 Giants J.Wood Studio Cabinets

These blank-backed cabinets, which measure 4 1/8" by 6 1/2" were issued by the J.Wood Photo Studios. These images are the same images later used in the Old Judge N167 Giants set. Since these cabinets are unnumbered, we have sequenced them in alphabetical order. Listed prices reference raw VG condition.

1 Roger Connor	2,500.00	4,000.00
2 Larry Corcoran	1,500.00	2,500.00
3 Pat Deasley	1,500.00	2,500.00
4 Mike Dorgan	1,500.00	2,500.00
5 Dude Esterbrook	1,500.00	2,500.00
6 Buck Ewing	2,500.00	4,000.00
7 Joe Gerhardt	1,500.00	2,500.00
8 Pete Gillespie	1,500.00	2,500.00
9 Tim Keefe	2,500.00	4,000.00
10 Jim Mutrie MG	1,500.00	2,500.00
11 Jim O'Rourke	2,500.00	4,000.00
12 Danny Richardson	1,500.00	2,500.00
13 John Ward	2,500.00	4,000.00
14 Mickey Welch	1,500.00	2,500.00
15 New York Giants Team (No Caps)	1,500.00	2,500.00
16 New York Giants Team (with Caps)	3,000.00	5,000.00

1906 Giants Ullman's Art Frame Series

These cards, issued the year after the Giants won their first World Series, show an action view of the player or players inside a brown or green border made to resemble a picture frame. At the bottom is a gold area made to look like an identification tag for a picture containing a description of the scene and players identified. There are probably more cards in this set so additions to the checklist are appreciated. Other postcards, on non-sports related subjects were directly available from the company in 1906 and thus it is therefore possible for these to have been readily available from the company in direct sale format.

COMPLETE SET (3)	1,500.00	3,000.00
1 Red Ames	400.00	800.00
2 Mike Donlin	500.00	1,000.00
3 George Ferguson	300.00	600.00
4 Matty Fitzgerald	300.00	600.00
5 Bill Gilbert	300.00	600.00
6 Christy Mathewson	1,250.00	2,500.00
7 Harry Mathewson	300.00	600.00
8 Dan McGann	300.00	600.00
9 Joe McGinnity	600.00	1,200.00
10 John McGraw MG	600.00	1,200.00
11 Sammy Strang Frank Bowerman	300.00	600.00
12 Hooks Wiltse	300.00	600.00

1909 Giants Derby Cigar

These 12 blank-backed cards measure 1 3/4" by 2 3/4" and were assumed to be issued by the Derby Cigar Co. They feature members of the New York Giants and the players photo is in an oval design in the middle with the name and position at the bottom

COMPLETE SET (12)	6,000.00	12,000.00
1 Josh Devore	1,250.00	2,500.00
2 Larry Doyle	1,500.00	3,000.00
3 Art Fletcher	1,250.00	2,500.00
4 Buck Herzog	1,250.00	2,500.00
5 Rube Marquard	2,500.00	5,000.00
6 Christy Mathewson	4,000.00	8,000.00
7 John McGraw MG	3,000.00	6,000.00
8 Fred Merkle	1,500.00	3,000.00
9 Chief Meyers	1,500.00	3,000.00
10 Red Murray	1,250.00	2,500.00
11 Fred Snodgrass	1,500.00	3,000.00
12 Hooks Wiltse	1,250.00	2,500.00

1913 Giants Evening Sun

This group of 21 newspaper supplements, which measured 12" by 9" were produced to honor the pennant winning 1913 New York Giants. The artist who drew these sketches was Lawrence Semon, who also produced postcards featuring many of these players. Since these are unnumbered, we have sequenced this set in alphabetical order.

COMPLETE SET		
1 George Burns	250.00	500.00
2 Doc Crandall	125.00	250.00
3 Al Demaree	125.00	250.00
4 Art Fletcher	125.00	250.00
5 Art Fromme	125.00	250.00
6 Grover Hartley	125.00	250.00
7 Buck Herzog	150.00	300.00
8 Rube Marquard	250.00	500.00
9 Christy Mathewson	500.00	1,000.00
10 Moose McCormick	125.00	250.00
11 John McGraw MG	250.00	500.00
12 Fred Merkle	125.00	250.00
13 Chief Meyers	150.00	300.00
14 Red Murray	125.00	250.00
15 Wilbert Robinson CO	200.00	400.00
16 Art Shafer	125.00	250.00
17 Fred Snodgrass	150.00	300.00
18 Jeff Tesreau	125.00	250.00
19 Jim Thorpe	1,500.00	3,000.00
20 Hooks Wiltse	125.00	250.00
21 Art Wilson	125.00	250.00

1932 Giants Schedule

This set of the 1932 New York Giants was issued in a postcard format with a black and white action photo on the front. Player information is printed in the wide bottom margin. The back displays the team's schedule. It has been alleged that the Hubbell was counterfeited. However, many dealers believe an inordinate amount of the Hubbell's were printed and a warehouse find made them appear to be too clean to be more than 60 years old. It seems like the Hubbell commonly seen in the marketplace is just a double print and has been noted as such. Some other dealers believe the common Hubbell variety is a proof issue. In addition, cards of Clarence Mitchell and Hall of Famer Fred Lindstrom were recently discovered.

COMPLETE SET	2,500.00	5,000.00
COMMON DP		
1 Ethan Allen	75.00	150.00
2 Herman Bell	75.00	150.00
3 Hugh Critz	75.00	150.00
4 Fred Fitzsimmons	150.00	300.00
5 Chick Fullis	75.00	150.00
6 Sam Gibson	75.00	150.00
7 Fran Healy Sic, Healey	75.00	150.00
8 Frank Hogan	75.00	150.00
9 Carl Hubbell DP	75.00	150.00
10 Carl Hubbell	400.00	800.00
11 Travis Jackson	200.00	400.00
12 Len Koenecke	75.00	150.00
13 Sam Leslie	75.00	150.00
14 Fred Lindstrom	200.00	400.00
15 Dolph Luque	125.00	250.00
16 Clarence Mitchell	75.00	150.00
17 Jim Mooney	75.00	150.00
18 Bob O'Farrell	125.00	250.00
19 Mel Ott	400.00	800.00
20 Roy Parmelee	75.00	150.00
21 Bill Terry	300.00	600.00
22 Johnny Vergez	75.00	150.00
23 Bill Walker	75.00	150.00

1948 Giants Team Issue

This 26-card set, which measures 6 1/2" by 9" features black-and-white photos of the New York Giants with white borders and was issued by Harry M. Stevens, Inc. A facsimile autograph is printed across the front. The backs are blank. The cards are unnumbered and checklisted below in alphabetical order. Mel Ott was originally issued with this set but was pulled after being let go in midseason. He was replaced by Leo Durocher as manager. As far as can be determined there is an even number of Ott and Durocher cards issued. The set is considered complete with either the Ott or the Durocher card.

COMPLETE SET (26)	75.00	150.00
1 Jack Conway	2.50	5.00
2 Walker Cooper	3.00	6.00
3 Leo Durocher MG	12.50	25.00
4 Sid Gordon	2.50	5.00
5 Andy Hansen	2.50	5.00
6 Clint Hartung	2.50	5.00
7 Larry Jansen	4.00	8.00
8 Sheldon Jones	2.50	5.00
9 Monte Kennedy	2.50	5.00
10 Buddy Kerr	2.50	5.00
11 Dave Koslo	2.50	5.00
12 Thornton Lee	2.50	5.00
13 Mickey Livingston	2.50	5.00
14 Whitey Lockman	4.00	8.00
15 Jack Lohrke	2.50	5.00
16 Willard Marshall	2.50	5.00
17 Johnnie McCarthy	2.50	5.00
18 Earl McGowan	2.50	5.00
19 Johnny Mize	7.50	15.00
20 Bobo Newsom	4.00	8.00
21 Mel Ott MG	12.50	25.00
22 Ray Poat	2.50	5.00
23 Bobbie Rhawn	2.50	5.00
24 Bill Rigney	4.00	8.00
25 Bob Thomson	5.00	10.00
26 Ken Trinkle	2.50	5.00
27 Wes Westrum	3.00	6.00

1949 Giants Team Issue

This 25-card set features black-and-white photos of the New York Giants with white borders and was issued by Harry M. Stevens, Inc. A facsimile autograph is printed across the front. The backs are blank. The cards are unnumbered and checklisted below in alphabetical order.

COMPLETE SET (25)	75.00	150.00
1 Hank Behrman	2.50	5.00
2 Walker Cooper	2.50	5.00
3 Leo Durocher MG	10.00	20.00
4 Fred Fitzsimmons CO	2.50	5.00
5 Frank Frisch CO	7.50	15.00
6 Augie Galan	2.50	5.00
7 Sid Gordon	2.50	5.00
8 Bert Haas	2.50	5.00
9 Andy Hansen	2.50	5.00
10 Clint Hartung	2.50	5.00
11 Bob Hofman	2.50	5.00
12 Larry Jansen	4.00	8.00
13 Sheldon Jones	2.50	5.00
14 Monte Kennedy	2.50	5.00
15 Buddy Kerr	2.50	5.00
16 Dave Koslo	2.50	5.00
17 Mickey Livingston	2.50	5.00
18 Whitey Lockman	4.00	8.00
19 Willard Marshall	2.50	5.00
20 Johnny Mize	7.50	15.00
21 Don Mueller	2.50	5.00
22 Ray Poat	2.50	5.00
23 Bobbie Rhawn	2.50	5.00
24 Bill Rigney	4.00	8.00
25 Bob Thomson	5.00	10.00

1954 Giants Jacobellis

These black and white photos, which were issued as Grandstand Magazine premiums, measure approximately 8 1/4" by 10" feature members of the 1954 New York Giants. The fronts feature the players photo, his name and on the bottom a small note that the photo was taken by Bill Jacobellis. Since these photos are unnumbered, we have sequenced them in alphabetical order.

COMPLETE SET	60.00	120.00
1 John Antonelli	6.00	12.00
2 Al Dark	6.00	12.00
3 Ruben Gomez	5.00	10.00
4 Whitey Lockman	6.00	12.00
5 Willie Mays	25.00	50.00
6 Don Mueller	5.00	10.00
7 Dusty Rhodes	5.00	10.00
8 New York Giants	10.00	20.00

1955 Giants Golden Stamps

This 32-stamp set features color photos of the New York Giants and measures approximately 2" by 2 5/8". The stamps are designed to be placed in a 32-page album which measures approximately 8 3/8" by 10 15/16". The album contains black-and-white drawings of players with statistics and life stories. The stamps are unnumbered and listed below according to where they fall in the album.

COMPLETE SET (32)	100.00	200.00
1 1954 Giants Team	6.00	12.00
2 Leo Durocher MG	10.00	20.00
3 Johnny Antonelli	1.25	2.50
4 Sal Maglie	2.00	4.00
5 Ruben Gomez	1.25	2.50
6 Hoyt Wilhelm	6.00	12.00
7 Marv Grissom	1.25	2.50
8 Jim Hearn	1.25	2.50
9 Paul Giel	1.25	2.50
10 Al Corwin	1.25	2.50
11 George Spencer	1.25	2.50
12 Don Liddle	1.25	2.50
13 Windy McCall	1.25	2.50
14 Al Worthington	1.25	2.50
15 Wes Westrum	1.25	2.50
16 Whitey Lockman	1.50	3.00
17 Dave Williams	1.25	2.50
18 Hank Thompson	2.00	4.00
19 Alvin Dark	2.00	4.00
20 Monte Irvin	6.00	12.00
21 Willie Mays	30.00	60.00
22 Don Mueller	1.25	2.50
23 Dusty Rhodes	1.25	2.50
24 Ray Katt	1.25	2.50
25 Joe Amalfitano	1.25	2.50
26 Billy Gardner	1.25	2.50
27 Foster Castleman	1.25	2.50
28 Bobby Hoffman	1.25	2.50
29 Bill Taylor	1.25	2.50
30 Manager and Coaches	2.00	4.00
31 Bobby Weinstein BB	1.25	2.50
32 Polo Grounds	10.00	20.00
XX Album	2.50	5.00

1956 Giants Jay Publishing

This 12-card set of the New York Giants measures approximately 5 1/8" by 7". The fronts feature black-and-white posed player photos with the player's and team name printed below in the white border. These cards were packaged 12 to a packet and originally sold for 25 cents by mail. The backs are blank. The cards are unnumbered and checklisted below in alphabetical order.

COMPLETE SET (12)	30.00	60.00
1 Johnny Antonelli	2.00	4.00
2 Al Dark	2.50	5.00
3 Ruben Gomez	1.50	3.00
4 Monte Irvin	3.00	6.00
5 Whitey Lockman	2.50	5.00
6 Sal Maglie	2.50	5.00

7 Willie Mays	10.00	20.00
8 Don Mueller	1.50	3.00
9 Bill Rigney	2.00	4.00
10 Hank Thompson	2.00	4.00
11 Wes Westrum	1.50	3.00
12 Dave Williams	1.50	3.00

1957 Giants Jay Publishing

This 12-card set of the New York Giants measures approximately 5" by 7". The fronts feature black-and-white posed player photos with the player's and team name printed below in the white border. These cards were packaged 12 to a packet and originally sold for 25 cents by mail. The backs are blank. The cards are unnumbered and checklisted below in alphabetical order. A pre-Rookie Card of Bill White (precedes his Rookie Card by 2 years) is featured in this set.

COMPLETE SET (12)	30.00	60.00
1 Johnny Antonelli	2.50	5.00
2 Jackie Brandt	1.50	3.00
3 Eddie Bressoud	1.50	3.00
4 Ruben Gomez	1.50	3.00
5 Willie Mays	10.00	20.00
6 Don Mueller	1.50	3.00
7 Bill Rigney	2.00	4.00
8 Bill Sarni	1.50	3.00
9 Red Schoendienst	3.00	6.00
10 Daryl Spencer	1.50	3.00
11 Bill White	3.00	6.00
12 Allan Worthington	1.50	3.00

1958 Giants Jay Publishing

This 12-card set of the San Francisco Giants measures approximately 5" by 7" and features black-and-white player photos in a white border. These cards were packaged 12 to a packet. The backs are blank. The cards are unnumbered and checklisted below in alphabetical order.

COMPLETE SET (12)	25.00	50.00
1 John Antonelli	2.00	4.00
2 Curt Barclay	1.50	3.00
3 Paul Giel	1.50	3.00
4 Ruben Gomez	1.50	3.00
5 Willie Kirkland	1.50	3.00
6 Whitey Lockman	2.00	4.00
7 Willie Mays	10.00	20.00
8 Danny O'Connell	1.50	3.00
9 Hank Sauer	2.00	4.00
10 Bob Schmidt	1.50	3.00
11 Daryl Spencer	1.50	3.00
12 Al Worthington	1.50	3.00

1958 Giants S.F. Call-Bulletin

The cards in this 25-card set measure approximately 2" by 4". The 1958 San Francisco Call-Bulletin set of unnumbered cards features black print on orange paper. These cards were given away as inserts in the San Francisco Call-Bulletin newspaper. The backs of the cards list the Giants home schedule and a radio station ad. The cards are entitled "Giant Payoff" and feature San Francisco Giant players only. The bottom part of the card (tab) could be detached as a ticket stub; hence, cards with the tab intact are worth approximately double the prices listed below. The catalog designation for this set is M126. The Tom Bowers card was issued in very short supply; also Bressoud, Jablonski, and Kirkland are tougher to find than the others; all of these tougher cards are indicated as SP's in our checklist.

COMPLETE SET (25)	700.00	1,400.00
COMMON CARD (1-25)	5.00	10.00
COMMON SP	60.00	120.00
1 John Antonelli	6.00	12.00
2 Curt Barclay	5.00	10.00
3 Tom Bowers SP	325.00	600.00
4 Ed Bressoud SP	60.00	120.00
5 Orlando Cepeda	25.00	50.00
6 Ray Crone	5.00	10.00
7 Jim Davenport	6.00	12.00
8 Paul Giel	10.00	20.00
9 Ruben Gomez	5.00	10.00
10 Marv Grissom	5.00	10.00
11 Ray Jablonski SP	60.00	120.00
12 Willie Kirkland SP	75.00	150.00
13 Whitey Lockman	6.00	12.00
14 Willie Mays	125.00	250.00
15 Mike McCormick	6.00	12.00
16 Stu Miller	6.00	12.00
17 Ray Monzant	5.00	10.00
18 Danny O'Connell	5.00	10.00
19 Bill Rigney MG	5.00	10.00
20 Hank Sauer	6.00	12.00
21 Bob Schmidt	5.00	10.00
22 Daryl Spencer	5.00	10.00
23 Valmy Thomas	5.00	10.00
24 Bobby Thomson	10.00	20.00
25 Al Worthington	5.00	10.00

1958-61 Giants Falstaff Beer Team Photos

This four-card set features color photos of the 1958, 1959, 1960, and 1961 San Francisco Giants teams. Each card measures approximately 6 1/4" by 9" and displays the Falstaff logo on the front. The backs carry a team promotional message.

COMPLETE SET (4)	60.00	120.00
COMMON CARD (1-4)	12.50	25.00
1 1958 Giants Team Photo	25.00	50.00
2 1959 Giants Team Photo	20.00	40.00

1959 Giants Jay Publishing

This 12-card set of the San Francisco Giants measures approximately 5" by 7" and features black-and-white player photos in a white border. These cards were packaged 12 to a packet and originally sold for 25 cents. The backs are blank. The cards are unnumbered and checklisted below in alphabetical order.

COMPLETE SET	20.00	50.00
1 Jackie Brandt	1.25	3.00
2 Orlando Cepeda	3.00	8.00
3 Jim Davenport	1.25	3.00
4 Sam Jones	1.25	3.00
5 Willie Kirkland	1.25	3.00
6 Hobie Landrith	1.25	3.00
7 Willie Mays	8.00	20.00
8 Stu Miller	1.25	3.00
9 Jack Sanford	1.25	3.00
10 Hank Sauer	1.50	4.00
11 Bob Schmidt	1.25	3.00
12 Daryl Spencer	1.25	3.00

1960 Giants Jay Publishing

ORLANDO CEPEDA, San Francisco Giants

This 12-card set of the San Francisco Giants measures approximately 5" by 7" and features black-and-white player photos in a white border. These cards were packaged 12 to a packet. The backs are blank. The cards are unnumbered and checklisted below in alphabetical order. Willie McCovey is featured in his Rookie Card year.

COMPLETE SET (12)	30.00	60.00
1 John Antonelli	1.00	2.50
2 Don Blasingame	1.00	2.50
3 Eddie Bressoud	1.00	2.50
4 Orlando Cepeda	2.50	6.00
5 Jim Davenport	1.00	2.50
6 Sam Jones	1.00	2.50
7 Willie Kirkland	1.00	2.50
8 Willie Mays	8.00	20.00
9 Willie McCovey	5.00	12.00
10 Mike McCormick	1.00	2.50
11 Jack Sanford	1.00	2.50
12 Bob Schmidt	1.00	2.50

1961 Giants Jay Publishing

WILLIE MAYS, San Francisco Giants

This 12-card set of the San Francisco Giants measures approximately 5" by 7". The fronts feature black-and-white posed player photos with the player's and team name printed below in the white border. These cards were packaged 12 in a packet. The backs are blank. The cards are unnumbered and checklisted below in alphabetical order. Juan Marichal is featured in his Rookie Card year.

COMPLETE SET (12)	12.50	25.00
1 Felipe Alou	1.00	2.50
2 Don Blasingame	.60	1.50
3 Orlando Cepeda	1.50	4.00
4 Alvin Dark MG	.75	2.00
5 Jim Davenport	.75	2.00
6 Sam Jones	.60	1.50
7 Harvey Kuenn	.75	2.00
8 Juan Marichal	4.00	10.00
9 Willie Mays	5.00	12.00
10 Mike McCormick	.60	1.50
11 Stu Miller	.60	1.50
12 Bob Schmidt	.60	1.50

1962 Giants Jay Publishing

JUAN MARICHAL, San Francisco Giants

This 12-card set of the San Francisco Giants measures approximately 5" by 7". The fronts feature black-and-white posed player photos with the player's and team name printed below in the white border. These cards were packaged 12 in a packet. The backs are blank. The cards are unnumbered and checklisted below in alphabetical order.

COMPLETE SET (12)	30.00	60.00
1 Felipe Alou	1.50	4.00
2 Ed Bailey	1.00	2.50
3 Orlando Cepeda	3.00	8.00
4 Jim Davenport	1.25	3.00
5 Tom Haller	1.00	2.50
6 Chuck Hiller	1.00	2.50
7 Harvey Kuenn	1.25	3.00
8 Juan Marichal	4.00	10.00
9 Willie Mays	8.00	20.00
10 Mike McCormick	1.25	3.00
11 Stu Miller	1.00	2.50
12 Billy Pierce	1.50	4.00

1962 Giants Photo Album

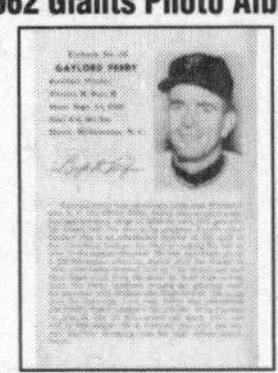

Issued by the San Fransisco News Cal-Bulletin, these photos feature biographical information, a player portrait and a biography of the featured player. Each of these pages were part of a special photo album commemorating the opening of what would be pennant winning season for the 1962 Giants. Since these photos are unnumbered, we have sequenced them in the order they appeared in the photo album. Gaylord Perry appears in this set in his Rookie Card year.

COMPLETE SET	100.00	200.00
1 Al Dark MG	2.50	6.00
2 Mike McCormick	2.50	6.00
3 Stu Miller	2.00	5.00
4 Jack Sanford	2.00	5.00
5 Juan Marichal	8.00	20.00
6 Bob Bolin	2.00	5.00
7 Jim Duffalo	2.00	5.00
8 Don Larsen	3.00	8.00
9 Billy O'Dell	2.00	5.00
10 Billy Pierce	3.00	8.00
11 Dick LeMay	2.00	5.00
12 Gaylord Perry	10.00	25.00
13 Ed Bailey	2.00	5.00
14 Tom Haller	2.00	5.00
15 Joe Pignatano	2.00	5.00
16 Orlando Cepeda	6.00	15.00
17 Chuck Hiller	2.00	5.00
18 Jose Pagan	2.00	5.00
19 Jim Davenport	2.00	5.00
20 Felipe Alou	4.00	10.00
21 Willie Mays	15.00	40.00
22 Harvey Kuenn	2.50	6.00
23 Willie McCovey	8.00	20.00
24 Ernie Bowman	2.00	5.00
25 Dick Phillips	2.00	5.00
26 Manny Mota	4.00	10.00

1963 Giants Jay Publishing

WILLIE McCOVEY, San Francisco Giants

This 12 card set of the San Francisco Giants measures approximately 5" by 7". The fronts feature black-and-white posed player photos with the player's and team name printed below in the white border. These cards were packaged 12 in a packet. The backs are blank. The cards are unnumbered and checklisted below in alphabetical order.

COMPLETE SET (12)	30.00	60.00
1 Felipe Alou	1.50	4.00
2 Orlando Cepeda	3.00	8.00
3 Alvin Dark MG	1.25	3.00
4 Jim Davenport	1.25	3.00
5 Tom Haller	1.00	2.50
6 Chuck Hiller	1.00	2.50
7 Willie Mays	8.00	20.00
8 Willie McCovey	4.00	10.00
9 Billy O'Dell	1.00	2.50
10 Jose Pagan	1.00	2.50
11 Billy Pierce	1.50	4.00
12 Jack Sanford	1.00	2.50

1964 Giants Jay Publishing

WILLIE McCOVEY, San Francisco Giants

This 12-card set of the San Francisco Giants measures approximately 5" X 7". The fronts feature black-and-white posed player photos with the player's and team name printed below in the white border. These cards were packaged 12 to a packet and originally sold for 25 cents. The backs are blank. The cards are unnumbered and checklisted below in alphabetical order.

COMPLETE SET (12)	20.00	50.00
1 Orlando Cepeda	3.00	8.00
2 Del Crandall	1.00	2.50
3 Alvin Dark MG	1.00	2.50
4 Jim Davenport	.75	2.00
5 Tom Haller	.75	2.00
6 Juan Marichal	4.00	10.00
7 Willie Mays	8.00	20.00
8 Willie McCovey	4.00	10.00
9 Billy O'Dell	.75	2.00
10 Jose Pagan	.75	2.00
11 Jack Sanford	.75	2.00
12 Bob Shaw	.75	2.00

1965 Giants Jay Publishing

This 12-card set of the San Francisco Giants measures approximately 5" by 7". The fronts feature black-and-white posed player photos with the player's and team name printed below in the white border. These cards were packaged 12 to a packet. The backs are blank. The cards are unnumbered and checklisted below in alphabetical order.

COMPLETE SET (12)	30.00	60.00
1 Jesus Alou	1.00	2.50
2 Matty Alou	1.25	3.00
3 Orlando Cepeda	2.50	6.00
4 Jim Davenport	.75	2.00
5 Herman Franks MG	.75	2.00
6 Tom Haller	.75	2.00
7 Bob Hendley	.75	2.00
8 Juan Marichal	4.00	10.00
9 Willie Mays	8.00	20.00
10 Willie McCovey	4.00	10.00
11 Jose Pagan	.75	2.00
12 Gaylord Perry	2.00	5.00

1965 Giants Team Issue

WILLIE MAYS

These photos, which measure approximately 5" by 7" feature members of the 1965 San Francisco Giants. The color photos take up most of the cards with the player being identified on the bottom. The backs are blank and we have sequenced them in alphabetical order.

COMPLETE SET (10)	15.00	40.00
1 Jim Davenport	.75	2.00
2 Herman Franks MG	.75	2.00
3 Tom Haller	.75	2.00
4 Jim Ray Hart	.75	2.00
5 Juan Marichal	2.50	6.00
6 Willie Mays	15.00	40.00
7 Willie McCovey	2.50	6.00
8 Lindy McDaniel	.75	2.00
9 Gaylord Perry	2.00	5.00
10 Team Photo	1.50	4.00

1970 Giants

This 12-card set is approximately 4 1/2" X 7", with the player's name and "Giants" printed on front. Cards were printed in black and white on pebbled white stock with a blank back.

COMPLETE SET (12)	12.50	30.00
1 Bobby Bonds	2.00	5.00
2 Dick Dietz	.60	1.50
3 Charles Fox MG	.60	1.50
4 Ken Henderson	.60	1.50
5 Ron Hunt	1.25	3.00
6 Hal Lanier	.75	2.00
7 Frank Linzy	.60	1.50
8 Juan Marichal	2.00	5.00
9 Willie Mays	4.00	10.00
10 Willie McCovey	2.00	5.00
11 Gaylord Perry	2.00	5.00
12 Frank Reberger	.60	1.50

1970 Giants Chevrolet Bonds

This one-card set measures approximately 3" by 5 3/4" with the top half of the card containing a black-and-white photo of Giants outfielder, Bobby Bonds. The bottom white margin was where the collector could have the player sign his Giants autograph card which was issued by Chevrolet and Nor-Cal Leasing Co. The back is blank.

1 Bobby Bonds	4.00	10.00

1971 Giants Ticketron

The 1971 Ticketron San Francisco Giants set is a ten-card set featuring members of the division-winning 1971 San Francisco Giants. The set measures approximately 3 7/8" by 6" and features an attractive full-color photo framed by white borders on the front along with a facsimile autograph. The back contains an ad for Ticketron as well as the 1971 Giants home schedule. These unnumbered cards are listed in alphabetical order for convenience.

COMPLETE SET (10)	50.00	100.00
1 Bobby Bonds	4.00	10.00
2 Dick Dietz	1.25	3.00
3 Charles Fox MG	1.25	3.00
4 Tito Fuentes	1.25	3.00
5 Ken Henderson	2.00	5.00
6 Juan Marichal	6.00	15.00
7 Willie Mays	20.00	50.00
8 Willie McCovey	6.00	15.00
9 Don McMahon	1.25	3.00
10 Gaylord Perry	6.00	15.00

1972-76 Giants Team Issue

This 18-card set features black-and-white photos of the San Francisco Giants. The cards are unnumbered and checklisted below in alphabetical order.

COMPLETE SET (18)	20.00	50.00
1 Bobby Bonds	2.50	6.00
2 Ron Bryant	1.00	2.50
3 Don Carrithers	1.00	2.50
4 Pete Falcone	1.00	2.50
5 Charlie Fox CO	1.00	2.50
6 Alan Gallagher	1.00	2.50
7 Russ Gibson	1.00	2.50
8 Ed Goodson	1.00	2.50
9 Ed Halicki	1.00	2.50
10 Jim Howarth	1.00	2.50
11 Dave Kingman	2.00	5.00
12 Garry Maddox	2.00	5.00
13 Juan Marichal	2.50	6.00
14 Willie McCovey	2.50	6.00
15 Mike Phillips	1.00	2.50
16 Bill Rigney MG	1.00	2.50
17 Chris Speier	1.00	2.50
18 Jim Willoughby	1.00	2.50

1973 Giants TCMA 1886

This set features the New York National League Team of 1886. Since these cards are not numbered, we have sequenced them in alphabetical order.

COMPLETE SET	6.00	15.00
1 Roger Connor	.75	2.00
2 Larry Corcoran	.20	.50
3 Tom Deasley	.20	.50
4 Mike Dorgan	.20	.50
5 Dude Esterbrook	.20	.50

6 Buck Ewing .75 2.00
7 Joe Gerhardt .20 .50
8 Peter Gillespie .20 .50
9 Tim Keefe .75 2.00
10 Jim Mutrie .30 .75
11 Jim O'Rourke .75 2.00
12 Daniel Richardson .20 .50
13 John M. Ward .75 2.00
14 Mickey Welch .75 2.00
15 Bat Boy .20 .50

1974 Giants 1937 TCMA

This 36-card set measures 2 5/8" by 3 3/8".The cards feature orange and black photos on orange card stock. The cards are unnumbered and have been checklisted alphabetically. Reportedly, Dick Bartell objected to being in the set and more than half of the sets originally produced were destroyed.

COMPLETE SET (36) 15.00 40.00
1 Tom Baker .60 1.50
2 Dick Bartell .60 1.50
3 Wally Berger .60 1.50
4 Don Brennan .60 1.50
5 Walter Brown .60 1.50
6 Clydell Castleman .60 1.50
7 Lou Chiozza .60 1.50
8 Dick Coffman .60 1.50
9 Harry Danning .60 1.50
10 George Davis .60 1.50
11 Charlie English .60 1.50
12 Fred Fitzsimmons .60 1.50
13 Frank Gabler .60 1.50
14 Harry Gumbert .60 1.50
15 Mickey Haslin .60 1.50
16 Carl Hubbell 1.00 2.50
17 Travis Jackson .60 1.50
18 Mark Koenig .60 1.50
19 Hank Leiber .60 1.50
20 Sam Leslie .60 1.50
21 Bill Lohrman .60 1.50
22 Eddie Mayo .60 1.50
23 Johnny McCarthy .60 1.50
24 Cliff Melton .60 1.50
25 Jo Jo Moore .60 1.50
26 Mel Ott 1.50 4.00
27 Jimmy Ripple .60 1.50
28 Hal Schumacher .60 1.50
29 Al Smith .60 1.50
30 Roy Spencer .60 1.50
31 Bill Terry .60 1.50
32 Hy Vandenberg .60 1.50
33 Phil Weintraub .60 1.50
34 Burgess Whitehead .60 1.50
35 Babe Young .60 1.50
36 Title Card .60 1.50

1975 Giants

Most of the cards in this 12-card set measure approximately 3" by 5 1/2"; a few measure slightly smaller at 3" by 5". The fronts feature black-and-white portraits of members of the 1975 Giants team. The pictures are 2 1/2" by 3" and rest on a white card face accented only by the player's name printed in black below the photo and a facsimile autograph in the lower white margin. The backs are blank. The cards are unnumbered and checklisted below in alphabetical order.

COMPLETE SET (12) 4.00 10.00
1 Mike Caldwell .50 1.25
2 Pete Falcone .40 1.00
3 Marc Hill .40 1.00
4 Gary Matthews .60 1.50
5 Randy Moffitt .40 1.00
6 Willie Montanez .40 1.00
7 Steve Ontiveros .40 1.00
8 Dave Rader .40 1.00
9 Derrel Thomas .40 1.00
10 Gary Thomasson .40 1.00
11 Wes Westrum MG .40 1.00
12 Charles Williams .40 1.00

1975 Giants All-Time TCMA

This 13-card set features black-and-white photos with white borders of all-time New York Giants great players. The cards are unnumbered and checklisted below in alphabetical order.

COMPLETE SET (13) 5.00 12.00
1 Alvin Dark .20 .50
2 Frankie Frisch .40 1.00
3 Carl Hubbell .60 1.50
4 Fred Lindstrom .30 .75
5 Christy Mathewson .60 1.50
6 Willie Mays 1.25 3.00
7 John McGraw MG .30 .75
8 Mel Ott .60 1.50
Name in black ink
9 Mel Ott .60 1.50
Name in red ink
10 Bill Terry .40 1.00
11 Bobby Thomson .30 .75
12 Wes Westrum .20 .50
13 Hoyt Wilhelm .40 1.00

1975 Giants 1951 TCMA

This 34-card set features the 1951 New York Giants Team. The fronts display black-and-white player photos while the backs carry player statistics. The set includes two jumbo cards which measure approximately 3 1/2" by 5". The cards are unnumbered and checklisted below in alphabetical order with the jumbo cards listed last.

COMPLETE SET (34) 12.50 30.00
1 George Bamberger .20 .50
2 Roger Bowman .20 .50
3 Al Corwin .20 .50
4 Al Dark .60 1.50
5 Allen Gettel .20 .50
6 Clint Hartung .20 .50
7 Jim Hearn .20 .50
8 Monte Irvin .75 2.00
9 Larry Jansen .40 1.00
10 Sheldon Jones .20 .50
11 John Spider Jorgensen .20 .50
12 Monte Kennedy .20 .50
13 Alex Konikowski .20 .50
14 Dave Koslo .20 .50
15 Jack Kramer .20 .50
16 Carroll Whitey Lockman .40 1.00
17 Jack Lucky Lohrke .20 .50
18 Sal Maglie .60 1.50
19 Jack Maguire .20 .50
20 Willie Mays 4.00 10.00
21 Don Mueller .40 1.00
22 Ray Noble .20 .50
23 Earl Rapp .20 .50
24 Bill Rigney .20 .50
25 George Spencer .20 .50
26 Eddie Stanky .40 1.00
27 Bobby Thomson .75 2.00
28 Hank Thompson .20 .50
29 Wes Westrum .40 1.00
30 Davey Williams .20 .50
31 Artie Wilson .20 .50
32 Sal Yvars .20 .50
33 Herman Franks CO/ .60 1.50
34 Leo Durocher MG 2.00 5.00
Willie Mays

1975 Giants Team Issue

This 18-card set of the 1975 San Francisco Giants features player portraits in white borders. The cards are unnumbered and checklisted below in alphabetical order.

COMPLETE SET (18) 3.00 8.00
1 Jim Barr .20 .50
2 Tom Bradley .20 .50
3 Mike Caldwell .20 .50
4 John D'Acquisto .20 .50
5 Pete Falcone .20 .50
6 Marc Hill .20 .50
7 Von Joshua .20 .50
8 Gary Matthews .40 1.00
9 Randy Moffitt .20 .50
10 John Motefusco .20 .50
11 Willie Montanez .20 .50
12 Bobby Murcer .30 .75
13 Steve Ontiveros .20 .50
14 Dave Radar .20 .50
15 Chris Speier .20 .50
16 Derrel Thomas .20 .50
17 Wes Westrum MG .20 .50
18 Charles Williams .20 .50

1976 Giants Postcards

This 24-card set of the San Francisco Giants features player photos on postcard-size cards. The cards are unnumbered and checklisted below in alphabetical order.

COMPLETE SET (24) 4.00 10.00
1 Glenn Adams .20 .50
2 Chris Arnold .20 .50
3 Jim Barr .20 .50
4 Mike Caldwell .20 .50
5 John D'Acquisto .20 .50
6 Rob Dressler .20 .50
7 Ed Halicki .20 .50
8 Dave Heaverlo .20 .50
9 Larry Herndon .20 .50
10 Marc Hill .20 .50
11 Gary Lavelle .20 .50
12 Gary Matthews .40 1.00
13 Randy Moffitt .20 .50
14 John Montefusco .20 .50
15 Bobby Murcer .30 .75
16 Steve Ontiveros .20 .50
17 Dave Rader .20 .50
18 Ken Reitz .20 .50
19 Bill Rigney MG .20 .50
20 Mike Sadek .20 .50
21 Chris Speier .20 .50
22 Derrel Thomas .20 .50
23 Gary Thomasson .20 .50
24 Charles Williams .20 .50

1977 Giants

This 25-card set measures 3 1/2" by 5" and features black-and-white close-up player photos. The pictures are framed by an orange border and set on a black card face. The player's name, position and team name appear below the picture. The backs are blank. The cards are unnumbered and checklisted below in alphabetical order.

COMPLETE SET (25) 8.00 20.00
1 Joe Altobelli MG .30 .75
2 Jim Barr .30 .75
3 Jack Clark .75 2.00
4 Terry Cornutt .30 .75
5 Rob Dressler .30 .75
6 Darrell Evans .60 1.50
7 Frank Funk INS .30 .75
8 Ed Halicki .30 .75
9 Tom Haller CO .40 1.00
10 Marc Hill .30 .75
11 Skip James .30 .75
12 Bob Knepper .30 .75
13 Gary Lavelle .30 .75
14 Bill Madlock .60 1.50
15 Willie McCovey 1.25 3.00
16 Randy Moffitt .30 .75
17 John Montefusco .40 1.00
18 Marty Perez .30 .75
19 Frank Riccelli .30 .75
20 Mike Sadek .30 .75
21 Hank Sauer INS .40 1.00
22 Chris Speier .40 1.00
23 Gary Thomasson .30 .75
24 Tommy Toms .30 .75
25 Bobby Winkles CO .30 .75

1977 Giants Team Issue

This 25-card set of the 1977 San Francisco Giants features player portraits in white borders. The cards are unnumbered and checklisted below in alphabetical order.

COMPLETE SET (25) 5.00 12.00
1 Gary Alexander .20 .50
2 Joe Altobelli MG .20 .50
3 Rob Andrews .20 .50
4 Jim Barr .20 .50
5 Jack Clark 1.25 3.00
6 Terry Cornutt .20 .50
7 Randy Elliott .20 .50
8 Darrell Evans .40 1.00
9 Tim Foli .20 .50
10 Ed Halicki .20 .50
11 Vic Harris .20 .50
12 Dave Heaverlo .20 .50
13 Marc Hill .20 .50
14 Bob Knepper .20 .50
15 Gary Lavelle .20 .50
16 Johnnie LeMaster .20 .50
17 Bill Madlock .30 .75
18 Lynn McGlothen .20 .50
19 Randy Moffitt .20 .50
20 John Montefusco .20 .50
21 Mike Sadek .20 .50
22 Darrel Thomas .20 .50
23 Gary Thomasson .20 .50
24 Terry Whitfield .20 .50
25 Charlie Williams .20 .50

1978 Giants Team Issue

This 25-card set of the 1978 San Francisco Giants features player portraits in white borders. The cards are unnumbered and checklisted below in alphabetical order.

COMPLETE SET (25) 5.00 12.00
1 Joe Altobelli MG .20 .50
2 Rob Andrews .20 .50
3 Jim Barr .20 .50
4 Vida Blue .40 1.00
5 Jack Clark .60 1.50
6 John Curtis .20 .50
7 Darrell Evans .30 .75
8 Ed Halicki .20 .50
9 Vic Harris .20 .50
10 Tom Heintzelman .20 .50
11 Larry Herndon .20 .50
12 Marc Hill .20 .50
13 Mike Ivie .20 .50
14 Skip James .20 .50
15 Bob Knepper .20 .50
16 Gary Lavelle .20 .50
17 Johnnie LeMaster .20 .50
18 Bill Madlock .40 1.00
19 Randy Moffitt .20 .50
20 John Montefusco .20 .50
21 Willie McCovey 1.00 2.50
22 Lynn McGlothen .20 .50
23 Mike Sadek .20 .50
24 Terry Whitfield .20 .50
25 Charlie Williams .20 .50

1979 Giants Police

The cards in this 30-card set measure approximately 2 5/8" by 4 1/8". The 1979 Police Giants set features cards numbered by the player's uniform number. This full color set features the player's photo, the Giants' logo, and the player's name, number and position on the front of the cards. A facsimile autograph in an attractive blue ink is also contained on the front. The backs, printed in orange and black, feature Tips from the Giants, the Giants' and sponsoring radio station, KNBR, logos and a line listing the Giants, KNBR, and the San Francisco Police Department as sponsors of the set. The 15 cards which are shown with an asterisk below were available only from the Police. The other 15 cards were given away at the ballpark on June 17, 1979. These cards look very similar to the Giants police set issued in 1980, the following year. Both sets credit Dennis Desprois photographically on each card but this (1979) set seems to have a fuzzier focus on the pictures. The sets can be distinguished on the front since this set's cards have a number sign before the player's uniform number on the front. Also on the card backs the KNBR logo is usually left justified for the cards in the 1979 set whereas the 1980 set has the KNBR logo centered on the card back.

COMPLETE SET (30) 8.00 20.00
1 Dave Bristol MG .20 .50
2 Marc Hill .20 .50
3 Mike Sadek * .20 .50
5 Tom Haller .20 .50
6 Joe Altobelli CO * .30 .75
8 Larry Shepard CO * .30 .75
9 Heity Cruz .20 .50
10 Johnnie LeMaster .20 .50
12 Jim Davenport CO .30 .75
14 Vida Blue .40 1.00
15 Mike Ivie .20 .50
16 Roger Metzger .20 .50
17 Randy Moffitt .20 .50
18 Bill Madlock .40 1.00
21 Rob Andrews * .20 .50
22 Jack Clark * .60 1.50
25 Dave Roberts .20 .50
26 John Montefusco .30 .75
28 Ed Halicki * .20 .50
30 John Tamargo .20 .50
31 Larry Herndon .20 .50
36 Bill North * .20 .50
39 Bob Knepper * .30 .75
40 John Curtis * .20 .50
41 Darrell Evans * .60 1.50
43 Tom Griffin * .20 .50
44 Willie McCovey * 1.50 4.00
45 Terry Whitfield * .20 .50
46 Gary Lavelle * .20 .50
49 Max Venable * .20 .50

1979 Giants Team Issue

Originally sold by the Giants for 20 cents each, these cards featured members of the 1979 San Francisco Giants. More cards may be known so any additions are appreciated, these cards are not numbered so we have sequenced them in alphabetical order.

COMPLETE SET 4.00 10.00
1 Rob Andrews .20 .50
2 Vida Blue .30 .75
3 Jack Clark .40 1.00
4 Tom Griffin .20 .50
5 Ed Halicki .20 .50
6 Marc Hill .20 .50
7 Mike Ivie .20 .50
8 Willie McCovey 1.00 2.50
9 Roger Metzger .20 .50
10 Greg Minton .20 .50
11 John Montefusco .20 .50
12 Phil Nastu .20 .50
13 Bill North .20 .50
14 Mike Sadek .20 .50
15 Max Venable .20 .50

1980 Giants Eureka Federal Savings

This eight-card set of the San Francisco Giants measures approximately 9 1/2" by 12" and features art work by Todd Alan Gold. Each card displays three color drawings of the same player, two action and one portrait. The backs are blank. These complimentary cards were available at all Eureka Federal Savings branches. The cards are unnumbered and checklisted below in alphabetical order.

COMPLETE SET (8) 4.00 10.00
1 Al Holland .40 1.00
2 Gary Lavelle .40 1.00
3 Johnnie LeMaster .40 1.00
4 Milt May .40 1.00
5 Willie McCovey 2.00 5.00
6 John Montefusco .40 1.00
7 Bill North .40 1.00
8 Rennie Stennett .40 1.00

1980 Giants Greats TCMA

This 12-card standard-size set features some great Giants from both New York and San Francisco. The fronts have red borders with the player's photo inside. The player's name is printed on the bottom. The back carries a biography.

COMPLETE SET (12) 3.00 8.00
1 Willie Mays 1.00 2.50
2 Wes Westrum .08 .25
3 Carl Hubbell .40 1.00
4 Hoyt Wilhelm .20 .50
5 Bobby Thomson .20 .50
6 Frankie Frisch .30 .75
7 Bill Terry .30 .75

8 Alvin Dark	.20	.50
9 Mel Ott	.50	1.25
10 Christy Mathewson	.50	1.25
11 Fred Lindstrom	.20	.50
12 John McGraw MG	.30	.75

1980 Giants Police

The cards in this 31-card set measure approximately 2 5/8" by 4 1/8". The 1980 Police San Francisco Giants set features cards numbered by the player's uniform number. This full color set features the player's photo, the Giants' logo, and the player's name, number and position on the front of the cards. A facsimile autograph in an attractive blue ink is also contained on the front. The backs, printed in orange and black, feature Tips from the Giants, the Giants' and sponsoring radio station, KNBR, logos and a line listing the Giants, KNBR, and the San Francisco Police Department as sponsors of the set. The sets were given away at the ballpark on May 31, 1980.

COMPLETE SET (31)	6.00	15.00
1 Dave Bristol MG	.20	.50
2 Marc Hill	.20	.50
3 Mike Sadek	.20	.50
5 Jim Lefebvre CO	.20	.50
6 Rennie Stennett	.20	.50
7 Milt May	.20	.50
8 Vern Benson CO	.20	.50
9 Jim Wohlford	.20	.50
10 Johnnie LeMaster	.20	.50
12 Jim Davenport CO	.20	.50
14 Vida Blue	.30	.75
15 Mike Ivie	.20	.50
16 Roger Metzger	.20	.50
17 Randy Moffitt	.20	.50
19 Al Holland	.20	.50
20 Joe Strain	.20	.50
22 Jack Clark	.40	1.00
26 John Montefusco	.20	.50
28 Ed Halicki	.20	.50
31 Larry Herndon	.20	.50
32 Ed Whitson	.20	.50
36 Bill North	.20	.50
38 Greg Minton	.20	.50
39 Bob Knepper	.20	.50
41 Darrell Evans	.40	1.00
42 John Van Ornum	.20	.50
43 Tom Griffin	.20	.50
44 Willie McCovey	1.25	3.00
45 Terry Whitfield	.20	.50
46 Gary Lavelle	.20	.50
47 Don McMahon CO	.20	.50

1980 Giants Team Issue

This 30-card set of the 1980 San Francisco Giants features player portraits in white borders. The cards are unnumbered and checklisted below in alphabetical order.

COMPLETE SET (30)	8.00	20.00
1 Dave Bristol	.20	.50
2 Vida Blue	.40	1.00
3 Bill Bordley	.20	.50
4 Jack Clark	.40	1.00
5 Darrell Evans	.40	1.00
6 Tom Griffin	.20	.50
7 Ed Halicki	.20	.50
8 Larry Herndon	.20	.50
9 Marc Hill	.20	.50
10 Al Holland	.20	.50
11 Mike Ivie	.20	.50
12 Bob Knepper	.20	.50
13 Gary Lavelle	.20	.50
14 Johnnie LeMaster	.20	.50
15 Dennis Littlejohn	.20	.50
16 Milt May	.20	.50
17 Roger Metzger	.20	.50
18 Willie McCovey	1.50	4.00
19 Greg Minton	.20	.50
20 Randy Moffitt	.20	.50
21 John Montefusco	.20	.50
22 Rich Murray	.20	.50
23 Bill North	.20	.50
24 Allen Ripley	.20	.50
25 Mike Sadek	.20	.50
26 Rennie Stennett	.20	.50
27 Joe Strain	.20	.50
28 Terry Whitfield	.20	.50
29 Ed Whitson	.20	.50
30 Jim Wohlford	.20	.50

1942 Gillette Razor Label

This label was produced by the Gillette Razor company and honors the 1941 American League and National League Champions. The narrow cardboard label measures 4 3/8" by 1 3/8". The left side has two player photos printed in blue ink, the upper head shot is of "Lefty Gomez of the New York Yankees, and below is Johnny Mize of St. Louis Cardinals. The right side also carries two player head shots in blue ink of Bucky Walters of the Cincinnati Reds, and Red Rolfe of the New York Yankees. The middle portion is printed in red, blue, and yellow and has a navy blue pennant for the American League and a red pennant for the National League. The Gillette logo is printed where the two pennants intersect.

1934 Gold Medal Flour R313A

The 1934 Gold Medal Flour series was believed to have been issued to commemorate the World Series of 1934 which featured the Detroit Tigers and the St. Louis Cardinals as well as some other stars of the early 1930's. Each card measures approximately 3 1/4" by 5 3/8". The cards are blank backed and unnumbered. Some cards have recently been discovered, which were not cards of either Tigers or Cardinals. Therefore, even more additions are possible so any additions to this checklist are appreciated

COMPLETE SET	500.00	1,000.00
1 Earl Averill	150.00	300.00
2 George Blaeholder	75.00	150.00
3 Tommy Bridges	15.00	30.00
4 Irving Burns	75.00	150.00
5 Bruce Campbell	75.00	150.00
6 Tex Carleton	15.00	30.00
7 Mickey Cochrane	30.00	60.00
8 Dizzy Dean	100.00	200.00
9 Paul Dean	25.00	50.00
10 George Earnshaw		
11 Frank Frisch	30.00	60.00
12 Goose Goslin	30.00	60.00
13 Odell Hale	75.00	150.00
14 William Hallahan	15.00	30.00
15 Mel Harder	100.00	200.00
16 Chuck Klein		
17 Jack Knott	75.00	150.00
18 Fred Marberry	15.00	30.00
19 Pepper Martin	25.00	50.00
20 Joe Medwick	30.00	60.00
21 William Rogell	15.00	30.00
22 Al Simmons		
23 Joe Vosmik	75.00	150.00
24 Bill Walker	15.00	30.00
25 Jo-Jo White	15.00	30.00

1969 Globe Imports

These very thin paper-stock blank-backed cards, which measure approximately 1 5/8" by 2 1/4" and feature the playing card ID in both the upper left and lower right corner with a player photo in the middle. Since these were designed as playing card type elements we have sequenced our checklist with A meaning 1, through King at 13.

COMPLETE SET	12.50	30.00
C1 Richie Allen	.40	1.00
C2 Reggie Smith	.30	.75
C3 Jerry Koosman	.30	.75
C4 Tony Oliva	.40	1.00
C5 Bud Harrelson	.20	.50
C6 Rick Reichardt	.10	.25
C7 Billy Williams	.60	1.50
C8 Pete Rose	4.00	10.00
C9 Jim Maloney	.10	.25
C10 Tim McCarver	.40	1.00
C11 Max Alvis	.10	.25
C12 Ron Swoboda	.20	.50
C13 Johnny Callison	.10	.25
D1 Bob Gibson	1.00	2.50
D2 Paul Casanova	.10	.25
D3 Juan Marichal	1.00	2.50
D4 Jim Fregosi	.20	.50
D5 Earl Wilson	.10	.25
D6 Tony Horton	.10	.25
D7 Harmon Killebrew	1.00	2.50
D8 Tom Seaver	2.50	6.00
D9 Curt Flood	.40	1.00
D10 Frank Robinson	1.50	4.00
D11 Bob Aspromonte	.10	.25
D12 Lou Brock	1.00	2.50
D13 Jim Lonborg	.20	.50
H1 Willie Mays	2.50	6.00
H2 Chris Short	.10	.25
H3 Tony Conigliaro	.30	.75
H4 Bill Freehan	.20	.50
H5 Willie McCovey	1.25	3.00
H6 Joel Horlen	.10	.25
H7 Ernie Banks	1.50	4.00
H8 Jim Wynn	.20	.50
H9 Brooks Robinson	1.00	2.50
H10 Orlando Cepeda	1.00	2.50
H11 Al Kaline	1.00	2.50
H12 Gene Alley	.10	.25
H13 Rusty Staub	.30	.75
S1a Ken Harrelson	.20	.50
S1b Mickey Mantle	15.00	40.00
S2 Denny McLain	.20	.50
S3 Rick Monday	.10	.25
S4 Richie Allen	.40	1.00
S5 Mel Stottlemyre	.20	.50
S6 Tommy John	.30	.75
S7 Don Mincher	.10	.25
S8 Chico Cardenas	.10	.25
S9 Willie Davis	.20	.50
S10 Bert Campaneris	.20	.50
S11 Ron Santo	.40	1.00
S12 Al Ferrara	.10	.25
S13 Clete Boyer	.10	.25

1961 Golden Press

The cards in this 33-card set measure 2 1/2" by 3 1/2". The 1961 Golden Press set of full color cards features members of Baseball's Hall of Fame. The cards came in a booklet with perforations for punching the cards out of the book. The catalog designation for this set is W524. The price for the full book intact is double the complete set price listed. Some collectors believe that the three cards which appear on the cover are more difficult to obtain in high-graded third party professional graded condition than the other cards in this set.

COMPLETE SET (33)	150.00	300.00
1 Mel Ott	2.50	6.00
2 Grover C. Alexander	2.00	5.00
3 Babe Ruth	30.00	60.00
4 Hank Greenberg	2.00	5.00
5 Bill Terry	1.25	3.00
6 Carl Hubbell	1.25	3.00
7 Rogers Hornsby	2.50	6.00
8 Dizzy Dean	4.00	10.00
9 Joe DiMaggio	20.00	50.00
10 Charlie Gehringer	.60	1.50
11 Gabby Hartnett	.60	1.50
12 Mickey Cochrane	1.25	3.00
13 George Sisler	.60	1.50
14 Joe Cronin	.60	1.50
15 Pie Traynor	.60	1.50
16 Lou Gehrig	20.00	50.00
17 Lefty Grove	2.00	5.00
18 Chief Bender	.60	1.50
19 Frankie Frisch	.60	1.50
20 Al Simmons	.60	1.50
21 Home Run Baker	.60	1.50
22 Jimmy Foxx (Jimmie)	2.50	6.00
23 John McGraw	.60	1.50
24 Christy Mathewson	4.00	10.00
25 Ty Cobb	20.00	50.00
26 Dazzy Vance	.60	1.50
27 Bill Dickey	1.25	3.00
28 Eddie Collins	1.25	3.00
29 Walter Johnson	5.00	12.00
30 Tris Speaker	2.00	5.00
31 Nap Lajoie	2.00	5.00
32 Honus Wagner	4.00	10.00
33 Cy Young	2.50	6.00
XX Album	3.00	8.00

1888 Goodwin Champions N162

This 50-card set issued by Goodwin was one of the major competitors to the N28 and N29 sets marketed by Allen and Ginter. It contains individuals representing 18 sports, with eight baseball players pictured. Each color card is backlisted and bears advertising for "Old Judge" and "Gypsy Queen" cigarettes on the front. The set was released to the public in 1888 and an album (catalog: A36) is associated with it as a premium issue.

1 Ed Andrews (Baseball)	350.00	700.00
2 Cap Anson (Baseball)	1,750.00	3,500.00
3 Dan Brouthers (Baseball)	700.00	1,400.00
4 Bob Caruthers (Baseball)	400.00	750.00
5 Fred Dunlap (Baseball)	350.00	700.00
6 Jack Glasscock (Baseball)	400.00	750.00
7 Tim Keefe (Baseball)	700.00	1,400.00
8 King Kelly (Baseball)	1,250.00	2,500.00

1933 Goudey

The cards in this 240-card set measure approximately 2 3/8" by 2 7/8". The 1933 Goudey set, was that company's first baseball issue. The four Babe Ruth and two Lou Gehrig cards in the set are extremely popular with collectors. Card number 106, Napoleon Lajoie, was not printed in 1933, and was circulated to a limited number of collectors in 1934 upon request (it was printed along with the 1934 Goudey cards). An album was offered to house the 1933 set. Several minor leaguers are depicted. Card number 1 (Bengough) is very rarely found in mint condition; in fact, as a general rule all the first series cards are more difficult to find in Mint condition. Players with more than one card are also sometimes differentiated below by their pose: BAT (Batting), FIELD (Fielding), PIT (Pitching), THROW (Throwing). One of the Babe Ruth cards was double printed (DP) apparently in place of the Lajoie and hence is easier to obtain than the others. Due to the scarcity of the Lajoie card, the set is considered complete at 239 cards and is priced as such below. One copy of card number 106 as Leo Durocher is known to exist. The card was apparently cut from a proof sheet and is the only known copy to exist. A large window display poster which measured 5 3/8" by 11 1/4" was sent to stores and used the same Babe Ruth photo as in the Goudey Premium set. The gum used was approximately the same dimension as the actual card. At the factory each piece was scored twice so it could be snapped into three pieces. The gum had a spearmint flavor and according to collectors who remember chewing said gum, the flavor did not last very long.

COMPLETE SET (239)	25,000.00	40,000.00
COMMON CARD (1-52)	45.00	75.00
COMMON (41/43/53-240)	35.00	60.00
WRAPPER (1-CENT, BAT.)	75.00	100.00
WRAPPER (1-CENT, AD)	150.00	175.00
1 Benny Bengough RC	1,500.00	2,500.00
2 Dazzy Vance RC	125.00	200.00
3 Hugh Critz BAT RC	40.00	75.00
4 Heinie Schuble RC	45.00	75.00
5 Babe Herman RC	150.00	300.00
6 Jimmy Dykes RC	40.00	75.00
7 Ted Lyons RC	150.00	300.00
8 Roy Johnson RC	45.00	75.00
9 Dave Harris RC	60.00	150.00
10 Glenn Myatt RC	45.00	75.00
11 Billy Rogell RC	50.00	120.00
12 George Pipgras RC	45.00	75.00
13 Fresco Thompson RC	45.00	75.00
14 Henry Johnson RC	60.00	150.00
15 Victor Sorrell RC	60.00	150.00
16 George Blaeholder RC	60.00	150.00
17 Watson Clark RC	60.00	150.00
18 Muddy Ruel RC	60.00	150.00
19 Bill Dickey RC	300.00	600.00
20 Bill Terry THROW RC	250.00	500.00
21 Phil Collins RC	50.00	120.00
22 Pie Traynor RC	300.00	600.00
23 Kiki Cuyler RC	125.00	200.00
24 Horace Ford RC	60.00	150.00
25 Paul Waner RC	250.00	500.00
26 Bill Cissell RC	45.00	75.00
27 George Connally RC	50.00	120.00
28 Dick Bartell RC	40.00	75.00
29 Jimmie Foxx RC	800.00	1,500.00
30 Frank Hogan RC	45.00	75.00
31 Tony Lazzeri RC	400.00	800.00
32 Bud Clancy RC	40.00	75.00
33 Ralph Kress RC	45.00	75.00
34 Bob O'Farrell RC	45.00	75.00
35 Al Simmons RC	300.00	600.00
36 Tommy Thevenow RC	45.00	75.00
37 Jimmy Wilson RC	60.00	150.00
38 Fred Brickell RC	60.00	150.00
39 Mark Koenig RC	40.00	75.00
40 Taylor Douthit RC	45.00	75.00
41 Gus Mancuso CATCH	35.00	60.00
42 Eddie Collins RC	150.00	300.00
43 Lew Fonseca RC	35.00	60.00
44 Jim Bottomley RC	150.00	300.00
45 Larry Benton RC	45.00	75.00
46 Ethan Allen RC	40.00	75.00
47 Heinie Manush BAT RC	100.00	175.00
48 Marty McManus RC	45.00	75.00
49 Frankie Frisch RC	150.00	300.00
50 Ed Brandt RC	45.00	75.00
51 Charlie Grimm RC	150.00	300.00
52 Andy Cohen RC	45.00	75.00
53 Babe Ruth RC	10,000.00	20,000.00
54 Ray Kremer RC	35.00	60.00
55 Pat Malone RC	35.00	60.00
56 Red Ruffing RC	150.00	300.00
57 Earl Clark RC	35.00	60.00
58 Lefty O'Doul RC	75.00	125.00
59 Bing Miller RC	35.00	60.00
60 Waite Hoyt RC	150.00	300.00
61 Max Bishop RC	35.00	60.00
62 Pepper Martin RC	100.00	200.00
63 Joe Cronin BAT RC	150.00	300.00
64 Burleigh Grimes RC	125.00	250.00
65 Milt Gaston RC	35.00	60.00
66 George Grantham RC	35.00	60.00
67 Guy Bush RC	35.00	60.00
68 Horace Lisenbee RC	35.00	60.00
69 Randy Moore RC	35.00	60.00
70 Floyd (Pete) Scott RC	35.00	60.00
71 Robert J. Burke RC	35.00	60.00
72 Owen Carroll RC	35.00	60.00
73 Jesse Haines RC	125.00	250.00
74 Eppa Rixey RC	125.00	250.00
75 Willie Kamm RC	35.00	60.00
76 Mickey Cochrane RC	250.00	500.00
77 Adam Comorosky RC	35.00	60.00
78 Jack Quinn RC	35.00	60.00
79 Red Faber RC	125.00	250.00
80 Clyde Manion RC	35.00	60.00
81 Sam Jones RC	35.00	60.00
82 Dib Williams RC	40.00	100.00
83 Pete Jablonowski RC	35.00	60.00
84 Glenn Spencer RC	35.00	60.00
85 Heinie Sand RC	35.00	60.00
86 Phil Todt RC	35.00	60.00
87 Frank O'Rourke RC	35.00	60.00
88 Russell Rollings RC	35.00	60.00
89 Tris Speaker RET	300.00	600.00
90 Jess Petty RC	35.00	60.00
91 Tom Zachary RC	35.00	60.00
92 Lou Gehrig RC	3,000.00	6,000.00
93 John Welch RC	35.00	60.00
94 Bill Walker RC	35.00	60.00
95 Alvin Crowder RC	35.00	60.00
96 Willis Hudlin RC	35.00	60.00
97 Joe Morrissey RC	35.00	60.00
98 Wally Berger RC	45.00	75.00
99 Tony Cuccinello RC	45.00	75.00
100 George Uhle RC	35.00	60.00
101 Richard Coffman RC	35.00	60.00
102 Travis Jackson RC	150.00	300.00
103 Earle Combs RC	200.00	400.00
104 Fred Marberry RC	35.00	60.00
105 Bernie Friberg RC	35.00	60.00
106 Napoleon Lajoie SP	15,000.00	25,000.00
107 Heinie Manush RC	150.00	300.00
108 Joe Kuhel RC	35.00	60.00
109 Joe Cronin RC	175.00	300.00
110 Goose Goslin RC	125.00	250.00
111 Monte Weaver RC	35.00	60.00
112 Fred Schulte RC	35.00	60.00
113 Oswald Bluege POR RC	35.00	60.00
114 Luke Sewell FIELD RC	45.00	75.00
115 Cliff Heathcote RC	35.00	60.00
116 Eddie Morgan RC	35.00	60.00
117 Rabbit Maranville RC	150.00	300.00
118 Val Picinich RC	40.00	100.00
119 Rogers Hornsby Field RC	500.00	1,000.00
120 Carl Reynolds RC	35.00	60.00
121 Walter Stewart RC	35.00	60.00
122 Alvin Crowder RC	35.00	60.00
123 Jack Russell RC	35.00	60.00
124 Earl Whitehill RC	35.00	60.00
125 Bill Terry RC	150.00	300.00
126 Joe Moore BAT RC	35.00	60.00
127 Mel Ott RC	300.00	600.00
128 Chuck Klein RC	200.00	400.00
129 Hal Schumacher PIT RC	35.00	60.00
130 Fred Fitzsimmons POR RC	35.00	60.00
131 Fred Frankhouse RC	35.00	60.00
132 Jim Elliott RC	35.00	60.00
133 Fred Lindstrom RC	100.00	250.00
134 Sam Rice RC	150.00	300.00
135 Woody English RC	35.00	60.00
136 Flint Rhem RC	35.00	60.00
137 Red Lucas RC	35.00	60.00
138 Herb Pennock RC	150.00	300.00
139 Ben Cantwell RC	35.00	60.00
140 Bump Hadley RC	35.00	60.00
141 Ray Benge RC	35.00	60.00
142 Paul Richards RC	50.00	120.00
143 Glenn Wright RC	35.00	60.00

144 Babe Ruth Bat DP RC 5,000.00 10,000.00
145 Rube Walberg RC 35.00 60.00
146 Walter Stewart PIT RC 35.00 60.00
147 Leo Durocher RC 125.00 200.00
148 Eddie Farrell RC 35.00 60.00
149 Babe Ruth RC 5,000.00 10,000.00
150 Ray Kolp RC 35.00 60.00
151 Jake Flowers RC 35.00 60.00
152 Zack Taylor RC 35.00 60.00
153 Buddy Myer RC 35.00 60.00
154 Jimmie Foxx RC 600.00 1,200.00
155 Joe Judge RC 35.00 60.00
156 Danny MacFayden RC 35.00 60.00
157 Sam Byrd RC 35.00 60.00
158 Moe Berg RC 250.00 500.00
159 Oswald Bluege FIELD RC 35.00 60.00
160 Lou Gehrig RC 2,500.00 5,000.00
161 Al Spohrer RC 35.00 60.00
162 Leo Mangum RC 35.00 60.00
163 Luke Sewell POR RC 45.00 75.00
164 Lloyd Waner RC 150.00 300.00
165 Joe Sewell RC 125.00 250.00
166 Sam West RC 35.00 60.00
167 Jack Russell RC 35.00 60.00
168 Goose Goslin RC 150.00 300.00
169 Al Thomas RC 35.00 60.00
170 Harry McCurdy RC 35.00 60.00
171 Charlie Jamieson RC 35.00 60.00
172 Billy Hargrave RC 35.00 60.00
173 Roscoe Holm RC 35.00 60.00
174 Warren (Curly) Ogden RC 35.00 60.00
175 Dan Howley MG RC 35.00 60.00
176 John Ogden RC 35.00 60.00
177 Walter French RC 35.00 60.00
178 Jackie Warner RC 35.00 60.00
179 Fred Leach RC 35.00 60.00
180 Eddie Moore RC 35.00 60.00
181 Babe Ruth RC 5,000.00 10,000.00
182 Andy High RC 35.00 60.00
183 Rube Walberg RC 35.00 60.00
184 Charley Berry RC 35.00 60.00
185 Bob Smith RC 35.00 60.00
186 John Schulte RC 35.00 60.00
187 Heinie Manush RC 125.00 250.00
188 Rogers Hornsby RC 400.00 800.00
189 Joe Cronin RC 150.00 300.00
190 Fred Schulte RC 35.00 60.00
191 Ben Chapman RC 45.00 75.00
192 Walter Brown RC 35.00 60.00
193 Lynford Lary RC 35.00 60.00
194 Earl Averill RC 125.00 250.00
195 Evar Swanson RC 35.00 60.00
196 Leroy Mahaffey RC 35.00 60.00
197 Rick Ferrell RC 125.00 250.00
198 Jack Burns RC 35.00 60.00
199 Tom Bridges RC 35.00 60.00
200 Bill Hallahan RC 35.00 60.00
201 Ernie Orsatti RC 35.00 60.00
202 Gabby Hartnett RC 150.00 300.00
203 Lon Warneke RC 35.00 60.00
204 Riggs Stephenson RC 35.00 60.00
205 Heinie Meine RC 35.00 60.00
206 Gus Suhr RC 35.00 60.00
207 Mel Ott Bat RC 400.00 800.00
208 Bernie James RC 35.00 60.00
209 Adolfo Luque RC 45.00 75.00
210 Spud Davis RC 35.00 60.00
211 Hack Wilson RC 300.00 600.00
212 Billy Urbanski RC 35.00 60.00
213 Earl Adams RC 35.00 60.00
214 John Kerr RC 35.00 60.00
215 Russ Van Atta RC 35.00 60.00
216 Lefty Gomez RC 200.00 400.00
217 Frank Crosetti RC 125.00 250.00
218 Wes Ferrell RC 45.00 75.00
219 Mule Haas UER RC 35.00 60.00
220 Lefty Grove RC 400.00 800.00
221 Dale Alexander RC 35.00 60.00
222 Charley Gehringer RC 300.00 600.00
223 Dizzy Dean RC 500.00 1,000.00
224 Frank Demaree RC 35.00 60.00
225 Bill Jurges RC 35.00 60.00
226 Charley Root RC 60.00 150.00
227 Billy Herman RC 90.00 150.00
228 Tony Piet RC 35.00 60.00
229 Arky Vaughan RC 90.00 150.00
230 Carl Hubbell PIT RC 300.00 600.00
231 Joe Moore FIELD RC 35.00 60.00
232 Lefty O'Doul RC 75.00 125.00
233 Johnny Vergez RC 35.00 60.00
234 Carl Hubbell RC 250.00 500.00
235 Fred Fitzsimmons PIT RC 35.00 60.00
236 George Davis RC 35.00 60.00
237 Gus Mancuso FIELD RC 35.00 60.00
238 Hugh Critz FIELD RC 35.00 60.00
239 Leroy Parmelee RC 35.00 60.00
240 Hal Schumacher RC 100.00 200.00

1933 World Wide Gum V353

The cards in this 94-card set measure approximately 2 3/8" by 2 7/8". World Wide Gum, the Canadian subsidiary of Goudey issued this set of numbered color cards in 1933. Cards 1 to 52 contain obverses identical to the American issue, but cards 53 to 94 have a slightly different order. The fronts feature white-bordered color player drawings. The words "Big League Chewing Gum" are printed in white lettering within a red stripe near the bottom. The green ink backs are found printed in English only, or in French and English (the latter are slightly harder to find and are valued at a 25 percent premium over the prices listed below). The catalog designation for this set is V353.

COMPLETE SET (94) 12,000.00 20,000.00
1 Benny Bengough 350.00 600.00
2 Dazzy Vance 75.00 120.00
3 Hugh Critz 35.00 60.00
4 Heinie Schulbe 35.00 60.00
5 Babe Herman 60.00 100.00
6 Jimmy Dykes 50.00 80.00
7 Ted Lyons 75.00 120.00
8 Roy Johnson 35.00 60.00
9 Dave Harris 35.00 60.00
10 Glenn Myatt 35.00 60.00
11 Billy Rogell 35.00 60.00
12 George Pipgras 50.00 80.00
13 Lafayette Thompson 35.00 60.00
14 Henry Johnson 35.00 60.00
15 Victor Sorrell 35.00 60.00
16 George Blaeholder 35.00 60.00
17 Watson Clark 35.00 60.00
18 Muddy Ruel 35.00 60.00
19 Bill Dickey 250.00 400.00
20 Bill Terry 125.00 200.00
21 Phil Collins 35.00 60.00
22 Pie Traynor 75.00 120.00
23 Kiki Cuyler 75.00 120.00
24 Horace Ford 35.00 60.00
25 Paul Waner 75.00 120.00
26 Chalmer Cissell 35.00 60.00
27 George Connally 35.00 60.00
28 Dick Bartell 50.00 80.00
29 Jimmy Foxx (Jimmie) 300.00 500.00
30 Frank Hogan 35.00 60.00
31 Tony Lazzeri 125.00 200.00
32 Bud Clancy 35.00 60.00
33 Ralph Kress 35.00 60.00
34 Bob O'Farrell 50.00 80.00
35 Al Simmons 125.00 200.00
36 Tommy Thevenow 35.00 60.00
37 Jimmy Wilson 50.00 80.00
38 Fred Bickell 35.00 60.00
39 Mark Koenig 50.00 80.00
40 Taylor Douthit 35.00 60.00
41 Gus Mancuso 35.00 60.00
42 Eddie Collins 75.00 120.00
43 Lew Fonseca 50.00 80.00
44 Jim Bottomley 75.00 120.00
45 Larry Benton 35.00 60.00
46 Ethan Allen 50.00 80.00
47 Heinie Manush 75.00 120.00
48 Marty McManus 35.00 60.00
49 Frank Frisch 75.00 120.00
50 Ed Brandt 35.00 60.00
51 Charlie Grimm 50.00 80.00
52 Andy Cohen 35.00 60.00
53 Jack Quinn 50.00 80.00
54 Urban Faber 75.00 120.00
55 Lou Gehrig 2,500.00 5,000.00
56 John Welch 35.00 60.00
57 Bill Walker 35.00 60.00
58 Lefty O'Doul 60.00 100.00
59 Bing Miller 50.00 80.00
60 Waite Hoyt 75.00 120.00
61 Max Bishop 50.00 80.00
62 Pepper Martin 60.00 100.00
63 Joe Cronin 75.00 120.00
64 Burleigh Grimes 75.00 120.00
65 Milt Gaston 35.00 60.00
66 George Grantham 35.00 60.00
67 Guy Bush 35.00 60.00
68 Willie Kamm 35.00 60.00
69 Mickey Cochrane 125.00 200.00
70 Adam Comorosky 35.00 60.00
71 Alvin Crowder 35.00 60.00
72 Willis Hudlin 35.00 60.00
73 Eddie Farrell 35.00 60.00
74 Leo Durocher 125.00 200.00
75 Walter Stewart 35.00 60.00
76 George Walberg 35.00 60.00
77 Glenn Wright 50.00 80.00
78 Buddy Myer 50.00 80.00
79 James(Zack) Taylor 35.00 60.00
80 George H.(Babe)Ruth 4,000.00 8,000.00
81 D'Arcy(Jake) Flowers 35.00 60.00
82 Ray Kolp 35.00 60.00
83 Oswald Bluege 35.00 60.00
84 Moe Berg 175.00 300.00
85 Jimmy Foxx (Jimmie) 300.00 500.00
86 Sam Byrd 35.00 60.00
87 Danny MacFayden 35.00 60.00
88 Joe Judge 50.00 80.00
89 Joe Sewell 75.00 120.00
90 Lloyd Waner 75.00 120.00
91 Luke Sewell 50.00 80.00
92 Leo Mangum 35.00 60.00
93 George H.(Babe)Ruth 3,000.00 5,000.00
94 Al Spohrer 50.00 80.00

1934 Goudey

The cards in this 96-card color set measure approximately 2 3/8" by 2 7/8". Cards 1-48 are considered to be the easiest to find (although card number 1, Foxx, is very scarce in mint condition) while 73-96 are much more difficult to find. Cards of this 1934 Goudey series are slightly less abundant than cards of the 1933 Goudey set. Of the 96 cards, 84 contain a "Lou Gehrig Says" line on the front in a blue design, while 12 of the high series (80-91) contain a "Chuck Klein Says" line in a red design. These Chuck Klein cards are indicated in the checklist below by CK and are in fact the 12 National Leaguers in the high series.

COMPLETE SET (96) 9,000.00 16,000.00
COMMON CARD (1-48) 30.00 50.00
COMMON CARD (49-72) 40.00 75.00
COMMON CARD (73-96) 100.00 175.00
WRAPPER (1-CENT, WHT.) 75.00 100.00
WRAPPER (1-CENT, CLR.) 75.00 100.00
1 Jimmie Foxx 450.00 750.00
2 Mickey Cochrane 100.00 175.00
3 Charlie Grimm 35.00 60.00
4 Woody English 30.00 50.00
5 Ed Brandt 30.00 50.00
6 Dizzy Dean 500.00 1,000.00
7 Leo Durocher 125.00 250.00
8 Tony Piet 30.00 50.00
9 Ben Chapman 35.00 60.00
10 Chuck Klein 125.00 250.00
11 Paul Waner 125.00 250.00
12 Carl Hubbell 100.00 175.00
13 Frankie Frisch 125.00 250.00
14 Willie Kamm 30.00 50.00
15 Alvin Crowder 30.00 50.00
16 Joe Kuhel 30.00 50.00
17 Hugh Critz 30.00 50.00
18 Heinie Manush 75.00 125.00
19 Lefty Grove 250.00 500.00
20 Frank Hogan 30.00 50.00
21 Bill Terry 150.00 300.00
22 Arky Vaughan 125.00 250.00
23 Charley Gehringer 200.00 400.00
24 Ray Benge 30.00 50.00
25 Roger Cramer RC 35.00 60.00
26 Gerald Walker RC 30.00 50.00
27 Luke Appling RC 150.00 300.00
28 Ed Coleman RC 30.00 50.00
29 Larry French RC 30.00 50.00
30 Julius Solters RC 30.00 50.00
31 Buck Jordan RC 30.00 50.00
32 Blondy Ryan RC 30.00 50.00
33 Don Hurst RC 30.00 50.00
34 Chick Hafey RC 75.00 125.00
35 Ernie Lombardi RC 90.00 150.00
36 Walter Betts RC 30.00 50.00
37 Lou Gehrig 4,000.00 8,000.00
38 Oral Hildebrand RC 30.00 50.00
39 Fred Walker RC 30.00 50.00
40 John Stone 30.00 50.00
41 George Earnshaw RC 30.00 50.00
42 John Allen RC 30.00 50.00
43 Dick Porter RC 30.00 50.00
44 Tom Bridges 35.00 60.00
45 Oscar Melillo RC 30.00 50.00
46 Joe Stripp RC 30.00 50.00
47 John Frederick RC 30.00 50.00
48 Tex Carleton RC 30.00 50.00
49 Sam Leslie RC 40.00 75.00
50 Walter Beck RC 40.00 75.00
51 Rip Collins RC 40.00 75.00
52 Herman Bell RC 40.00 75.00
53 George Watkins RC 40.00 75.00
54 Wesley Schulmerich RC 40.00 75.00
55 Ed Holley RC 40.00 75.00
56 Mark Koenig 60.00 100.00
57 Bill Swift RC 40.00 75.00
58 Earl Grace RC 40.00 75.00
59 Joe Mowry RC 40.00 75.00
60 Lynn Nelson RC 40.00 75.00
61 Lou Gehrig 3,000.00 6,000.00
62 Hank Greenberg RC 600.00 1,200.00
63 Minter Hayes RC 40.00 75.00
64 Frank Grube RC 40.00 75.00
65 Cliff Bolton RC 40.00 75.00
66 Mel Harder RC 60.00 100.00
67 Bob Weiland RC 40.00 75.00
68 Bob Johnson RC 60.00 100.00
69 John Marcum RC 40.00 75.00
70 Pete Fox RC 40.00 75.00
71 Lyle Tinning RC 40.00 75.00
72 Arndt Jorgens RC 40.00 75.00
73 Ed Wells RC 100.00 175.00
74 Bob Boken RC 100.00 175.00
75 Bill Werber RC 100.00 175.00
76 Hal Trosky RC 125.00 200.00
77 Joe Vosmik RC 100.00 175.00
78 Pinky Higgins RC 125.00 200.00
79 Eddie Durham RC 100.00 175.00
80 Marty McManus CK 100.00 175.00
81 Bob Brown CK RC 100.00 175.00
82 Bill Hallahan CK 100.00 175.00
83 Jim Mooney CK RC 100.00 175.00
84 Paul Derringer CK RC 125.00 225.00
85 Adam Comorosky CK 100.00 175.00
86 Lloyd Johnson CK RC 100.00 175.00
87 George Darrow CK RC 100.00 175.00
88 Homer Peel CK RC 100.00 175.00
89 Linus Frey CK RC 100.00 175.00
90 KiKi Cuyler CK 200.00 400.00
91 Dolph Camilli CK RC 125.00 200.00
92 Steve Larkin RC 100.00 175.00
93 Fred Ostermueller RC 100.00 175.00
94 Red Rolfe RC 150.00 300.00
95 Myril Hoag RC 100.00 175.00
96 James DeShong RC 300.00 500.00

1934 World Wide Gum V354

The cards in this 96-card set measure approximately 2 3/8" by 2 7/8". The 1934 Canadian Goudey set was issued by World Wide Gum Company. Cards 1 to 48 have the same format as the 1933 American Goudey issue while cards 49 to 96 have the same format as the 1934 American Goudey issue. Cards numbers 49 to 96 all have the "Lou Gehrig Says" endorsement on the front of the cards. No Chuck Klein endorsement exists as it does in the 1934 American issue. The fronts feature white-bordered color player drawings. The words "Big League Chewing Gum" are printed in white lettering within a red stripe near the bottom. The green ink backs are found printed in English only, or in French and English (the latter are slightly harder to find and are valued at a 25 percent premium over the prices listed below). It has been recently speculated that the final 24 cards are printed in far greater quantity than the first 72 cards in the set. The catalog designation for this set is V354.

COMPLETE SET (96) 7,800.00 13,000.00
1 Rogers Hornsby 350.00 600.00
2 Eddie Morgan 35.00 60.00
3 Val Picinich 35.00 60.00
4 Rabbit Maranville 75.00 120.00
5 Flint Rhem 35.00 60.00
6 Jim Elliott 35.00 60.00
7 Fred(Red) Lucas 35.00 60.00
8 Fred Marberry 35.00 60.00
9 Clifton Heathcote 35.00 60.00
10 Bernie Friberg 35.00 60.00
11 Woody English 35.00 60.00
12 Carl Reynolds 35.00 60.00
13 Ray Benge 35.00 60.00
14 Ben Cantwell 35.00 60.00
15 Bump Hadley 35.00 60.00
16 Herb Pennock 75.00 120.00
17 Fred Lindstrom 75.00 120.00
18 Sam Rice 75.00 120.00
19 Fred Frankhouse 35.00 60.00
20 Fred Fitzsimmons 50.00 80.00
21 Earle Combs 75.00 120.00
22 George Uhle 35.00 60.00
23 Richard Coffman 35.00 60.00
24 Travis Jackson 75.00 120.00
25 Robert J. Burke 35.00 60.00
26 Randy Moore 35.00 60.00
27 Heinie Sand 35.00 60.00
28 George (Babe) Ruth 3,000.00 5,000.00
29 Tris Speaker 175.00 300.00
30 Perce(Pat) Malone 35.00 60.00
31 Sam Jones 50.00 80.00
32 Eppa Rixey 75.00 120.00
33 Floyd (Pete) Scott 35.00 60.00
34 Pete Jablonowski 35.00 60.00
35 Clyde Manion 35.00 60.00
36 Dib Williams 35.00 60.00
37 Glenn Spencer 35.00 60.00
38 Ray Kremer 35.00 60.00
39 Phil Todt 35.00 60.00
40 Russell Rollings 35.00 60.00
41 Earl Clark 35.00 60.00
42 Jess Petty 35.00 60.00
43 Frank O'Rourke 35.00 60.00
44 Jesse Haines 75.00 120.00
45 Horace Lisenbee 35.00 60.00
46 Owen Carroll 35.00 60.00
47 Tom Zachary 50.00 80.00
48 Red Ruffing 75.00 120.00
49 Ray Benge 35.00 60.00
50 Woody English 35.00 60.00
51 Ben Chapman 50.00 80.00
52 Joe Kuhel 35.00 60.00
53 Bill Terry 125.00 200.00
54 Robert(Lefty) Grove 175.00 300.00
55 Dizzy Dean 500.00 800.00
56 Chuck Klein 75.00 120.00
57 Charley Gehringer 125.00 200.00
58 Jimmie Foxx 250.00 400.00
59 Mickey Cochrane 125.00 200.00
60 Willie Kamm 35.00 60.00
61 Charlie Grimm 60.00 100.00
62 Ed Brandt 35.00 60.00
63 Tony Piet 35.00 60.00
64 Frank Frisch 75.00 120.00
65 Alvin Crowder 35.00 60.00
66 Frank Hogan 35.00 60.00
67 Paul Waner 75.00 120.00
68 Heinie Manush 75.00 120.00
69 Leo Durocher 75.00 120.00
70 Arky Vaughan 75.00 120.00
71 Carl Hubbell 125.00 200.00
72 Hugh Critz 35.00 60.00
73 John(Blondy) Ryan 35.00 60.00
74 Doc Cramer 50.00 80.00
75 Baxter Jordan 35.00 60.00
76 Ed Coleman 35.00 60.00
77 Julius(Moose) Solters 35.00 60.00
78 Chick Hafey 75.00 120.00
79 Larry French 35.00 60.00
80 Frank(Don) Hurst 35.00 60.00
81 Gerald Walker 35.00 60.00
82 Ernie Lombardi 75.00 120.00
83 Walter(Huck) Betts 35.00 60.00
84 Luke Appling 75.00 120.00
85 John Frederick 35.00 60.00
86 Fred(Dixie) Walker 60.00 100.00
87 Tom Bridges 50.00 80.00
88 Dick Porter 35.00 60.00
89 John Stone 35.00 60.00
90 James(Tex) Carleton 35.00 60.00
91 Joe Stripp 35.00 60.00
92 Lou Gehrig 2,500.00 4,000.00
93 George Earnshaw 50.00 80.00
94 Oscar Melillo 35.00 60.00
95 Oral Hildebrand 35.00 60.00
96 John Allen 50.00 80.00

1934 Goudey Card Album

These rare 1934 Goudey American and National League Card

albums were issued one per box of Big League Gum or could be had by redeeming 50 Big League wrappers to the Goudey Gum Company. The American League album is red and the National League album is blue. Each has 10 spaces allocated for each of the teams in their respective leagues and for their All-Star teams. Each team has its own biography printed in the album.

COMPLETE SET (2)	500.00	1,000.00
1 American League/(red)	250.00	500.00
2 National League/(blue)	250.00	500.00

1934 Goudey Premiums R309-1

The most ambitious premium issue of the Goudey Gum Company was the R309-1 set of 1934. Printed on heavy cardboard, the black and white picture was embellished with a gold and frame-like border and a back stand. Each of these thick cards measures approximately 5 1/2" by 8 15/16". The Babe Ruth card seems to be more common than the other cards in this short set. The Ruth card was available as a redemption for 50 wrappers sent to Goudey.

COMPLETE SET (4)	750.00	1,200.00
1 A.L. All-Stars of 1933	200.00	400.00
2 N.L. All-Stars of 1933	200.00	400.00
3 World Champ 1933 Giants	250.00	500.00
4 Babe Ruth	500.00	1,000.00

1935 Goudey Premiums R309-2

The 16 cards in the R309-2 Goudey Premium set are unnumbered, glossy black and white photos on thin paper stock. Teams (1-3) and individual players (4-16) are featured in this relatively scarce premium set from 1935. The ballplayer is identified by his name rendered in longhand in the "wide pen" style of later Goudey issues. This written name is not a facsimile autograph. Each card measures approximately 5 1/2" by 9".

COMPLETE SET (16)	900.00	1,500.00
COMMON TEAM (1-3)	50.00	80.00
COMMON PLAYER (4-16)	50.00	80.00
1 Boston Red Sox	75.00	150.00
2 Cleveland Indians	75.00	150.00
3 Washington Senators	75.00	150.00
4 Elden Auker	75.00	150.00
5 Johnny Babich	75.00	150.00
6 Dick Bartell	75.00	150.00
7 Lester R. Bell	75.00	150.00
8 Wally Berger	100.00	200.00
9 Mickey Cochrane	200.00	400.00
10 Fox Goslin Walker	125.00	250.00
11 Lefty Gomez	150.00	300.00
12 Hank Greenberg	200.00	400.00
13 Oscar Melillo	75.00	150.00
14 Mel Ott	200.00	400.00
15 Schoolboy Rowe	75.00	150.00
16 Vito Tamulis	75.00	150.00

1935 Goudey 4-in-1

The cards in this confusing 36-card set (the number of different front pictures) measure approximately 2 3/8" by 2 7/8". The 1935 Goudey set is sometimes called the Goudey Puzzle set, or the Goudey 4-in-1n set. There are 36 different card fronts but 114 different front/back combinations. Our checklist details all 114 cards, grouped together by the 36 different card front combinations. The player combinations are listed alphabetically by reading the player names in clockwise order starting from the top left corner. The card backs can be arranged to form one of nine different puzzles picturing either a player or a team and each back specifically details both the puzzle (or "picture" as it states on the actual card backs) it belongs too using numbers 1-9 and the specific piece it is within the puzzle (using letters A-M). The following is the list of the puzzle back pictures: 1) Detroit Tigers; 2) Chuck Klein; 3) Frankie Frisch; 4) Mickey Cochrane; 5) Joe Cronin; 6) Jimmy Foxx; 7) Al Simmons; 8) Cleveland Indians; and 9) Washington Senators. The first seven puzzles were actually created in two separate combinations of card fronts; thus the Chuck Klein puzzle (catalogued as "Picture 2" on the card backs) is actually available in two different groups of six card fronts - one group of which has been verified as a short print. The SP cards have all been tagged in our checklist. Finally, a limited number of cards feature blue borders (rather than the standard red borders). Though they're not short-printed, we've tagged the cards for referential purposes.

COMPLETE SET (114)	8,000.00	13,500.00
COMMON CARDS (1-9)	30.00	50.00
COMMON CARDS (11-17)	45.00	80.00
WRAPPER (1-CENT, WHITE)	150.00	200.00
2-Jan Berry/Burk/Kres/Vance 2C SP	60.00	100.00
4-Jan Berry/Burk/Kres/Vance 4C	35.00	60.00
7-Jan Berry/Burk/Kres/Vance 7C	35.00	60.00
8-Feb Burns/Hems/Grub/Weil 8C	30.00	50.00
9-Feb Burns/Hems/Grub/Weil 9C	30.00	50.00
8-Mar Campbell/Mey/Good/Kamp 8D	30.00	50.00
9-Mar Campbell/Mey/Good/Kamp 9D	30.00	50.00
1-Apr Cochrane/Gehringer/Brid/Rog 1D	60.00	120.00
2-Apr Cochrane/Gehringer/Brid/Rog 2D	70.00	120.00
6-Apr Cochrane/Gehringer/Brid/Rog 6D SP	90.00	150.00
7-Apr Cochrane/Gehringer/Brid/Rog 7D SP	90.00	150.00
2-May Critz/Bartell/Ott/Manc 2A SP	90.00	150.00
4-May Critz/Bartell/Ott/Manc 4A	60.00	100.00
7-May Critz/Bartell/Ott/Manc 7A	60.00	100.00
1-Jun Cronin/Reyn/Bish/Ciss 1G SP	60.00	100.00
3-Jun Cronin/Reyn/Bish/Ciss 3E SP	60.00	100.00
5-Jun Cronin/Reyn/Bish/Ciss 5E SP	60.00	100.00
6-Jun Cronin/Reyn/Bish/Ciss 6E	35.00	60.00
8-Jul DeShong/Allen/Rolfe/Walk 8E	30.00	50.00
9-Jul DeShong/Allen/Rolfe/Walk 9E	30.00	50.00
1-Aug Earn/Dyk/Sew/Appling 1I	35.00	60.00
2-Aug Earn/Dyk/Sew/Appling 2F	35.00	60.00
6-Aug Earn/Dyk/Sew/Appling 6F SP	60.00	100.00
7-Aug Earn/Dyk/Sew/Appling 7F SP	60.00	100.00
8-Sep Fox/Greenberg/Walk/Rowe 8F	60.00	100.00
9-Sep Fox/Greenberg/Walk/Rowe 9F	60.00	100.00
1-Oct Frisch/Dean/Ors/Carl 1A	90.00	150.00
2-Oct Frisch/Dean/Ors/Carl 2A	90.00	150.00
6-Oct Frisch/Dean/Ors/Carl 6A SP	150.00	250.00
7-Oct Frisch/Dean/Ors/Carl 7A SP	150.00	250.00
1-Nov Grimes/Klein/Cuyler/Eng 1F	60.00	100.00
3-Nov Grimes/Klein/Cuyler/Eng 3D	60.00	100.00
4-Nov Grimes/Klein/Cuyler/Eng 4D SP	90.00	150.00
5-Nov Grimes/Klein/Cuyler/Eng 5D SP	90.00	150.00
8-Dec Hayes/Lyons/Haas/Bon 8B	35.00	60.00
9-Dec Hayes/Lyons/Haas/Bon 9B	35.00	60.00
13-8 Herman/Suhr/Padd/Blant 8K	35.00	60.00
13-9 Herman/Suhr/Padd/Blant 9K	35.00	60.00
14-1 Hudlin/Myatt/Com/Bottomley 1K SP	60.00	100.00
14-3 Hudlin/Myatt/Com/Bottomley 3B SP	60.00	100.00
14-5 Hudlin/Myatt/Com/Bottomley 5B	35.00	60.00
14-6 Hudlin/Myatt/Com/Bottomley 6B	35.00	60.00
15-8 Johnson/Cole/Marc/Cramer 8J	30.00	50.00
15-9 Johnson/Cole/Marc/Cramer 9J	30.00	50.00
16-1 Kamm/Hild/Averill/Tro 1L	35.00	60.00
16-2 Kamm/Hild/Averill/Tro 2E	35.00	60.00
16-6 Kamm/Hild/Averill/Tro 6E SP	60.00	100.00
16-7 Kamm/Hild/Averill/Tro 7E SP	60.00	100.00
17-8 Koenig/Fitz/Benge/Zach 8A	30.00	50.00
17-8 Koenig/Fitz/Benge/Zach 8M	30.00	50.00
18-8 Kuhel/White/Myer/Stone 8H	30.00	50.00
18-9 Kuhel/White/Myer/Stone 9H	30.00	50.00
19-1 Leslie/Frey/Stripp/Clark 1G	30.00	50.00
19-3 Leslie/Frey/Stripp/Clark 3E	30.00	50.00
19-4 Leslie/Frey/Stripp/Clark 4E SP	45.00	80.00
19-5 Leslie/Frey/Stripp/Clark 5E	30.00	50.00
20-1 Mahaffey/Foxx/Will/Hig 1B	70.00	120.00
20-2 Mahaffey/Foxx/Will/Hig 2B	70.00	120.00
20-6 Mahaffey/Foxx/Will/Hig 6B SP	90.00	150.00
20-7 Mahaffey/Foxx/Will/Hig 7B SP	125.00	200.00
21-1 Manush/Lary/Weav/Had 1C	35.00	60.00
21-2 Manush/Lary/Weav/Had 2C	35.00	60.00
21-6 Manush/Lary/Weav/Had 6C SP	60.00	100.00
21-7 Manush/Lary/Weav/Had 7C SP	60.00	100.00
22-2 Martin/O'Far/Byrd/Mac 2F SP	45.00	80.00
22-4 Martin/O'Far/Byrd/Mac 4F	30.00	50.00
22-7 Martin/O'Far/Byrd/Mac 7F	30.00	50.00
23-2 Moore/Hogan/Frank/Bran 2E SP	45.00	80.00
23-4 Moore/Hogan/Frank/Bran 4E	30.00	50.00
23-7 Moore/Hogan/Frank/Bran 7E	30.00	50.00
24-1 Piet/Com/Bottomley/Adam 1H	35.00	60.00
24-3 Piet/Com/Bottomley/Adam 3F	35.00	60.00
24-4 Piet/Com/Bottomley/Adam 4F SP	60.00	100.00
24-5 Piet/Com/Bottomley/Adam 5F SP	60.00	100.00
25-1 Ruel/Simmons/Kam/Cochrane 1J SP	90.00	150.00
25-3 Ruel/Simmons/Kam/Cochrane 3A SP	90.00	150.00
25-5 Ruel/Simmons/Kam/Cochrane 5A	60.00	100.00
25-6 Ruel/Simmons/Kam/Cochrane 6A	60.00	100.00
26-2 Ruff/Mal/Lazzeri/Dickey 2D SP	150.00	250.00
26-4 Ruff/Mal/Lazzeri/Dickey 4D	90.00	150.00
26-7 Ruff/Mal/Lazzeri/Dickey 7D	90.00	150.00
27-1 Ruth/McM/Bran/Maranville 1J	1,500.00	2,500.00
27-3 Ruth/McM/Bran/Maranville 3A	1,000.00	2,000.00
27-4 Ruth/McM/Bran/Maranville 4A SP	1,500.00	2,500.00
27-5 Ruth/McM/Bran/Maranville 5A SP	1,000.00	1,500.00
28-1 Schuble/Marb/Goslin/Crow 1H SP	60.00	100.00
28-3 Schuble/Marb/Goslin/Crow 3F SP	60.00	100.00
28-5 Schuble/Marb/Goslin/Crow 5F	35.00	60.00
28-6 Schuble/Marb/Goslin/Crow 6F	35.00	60.00
29-8 Spohrer/Rhem/Cant/Bent 8L	30.00	50.00
29-9 Spohrer/Rhem/Cant/Bent 9L	30.00	50.00
30-1 Terry/Schu/Man/Jackson 1K	60.00	100.00
30-3 Terry/Schu/Man/Jackson 3B	60.00	100.00
30-4 Terry/Schu/Man/Jackson 4B SP	90.00	150.00
30-5 Terry/Schu/Man/Jackson 5B SP	90.00	150.00
31-2 Traynor/Luc/Thev/Wright 2B SP	60.00	100.00
31-4 Traynor/Luc/Thev/Wright 4B	35.00	60.00
31-7 Traynor/Luc/Thev/Wright 7B	35.00	60.00
32-8 Vosmik/Knick/Hard/Stew 8I	30.00	50.00
32-9 Vosmik/Knick/Hard/Stew 9I	30.00	50.00
33-1 Waner/Bush/Hoyt/Waner 1E	60.00	100.00
33-3 Waner/Bush/Hoyt/Waner 3C	60.00	100.00
33-4 Waner/Bush/Hoyt/Waner 4C SP	90.00	150.00
33-5 Waner/Bush/Hoyt/Waner 5C	60.00	100.00
34-8 Werber/Ferrell/Ferrell/Ost 8G	35.00	60.00
34-9 Werber/Ferrell/Ferrell/Ost 9G	35.00	60.00
35-1 West/Melillo/Blae/Coff 1F SP	45.00	80.00
35-3 West/Melillo/Blae/Coff 3D SP	45.00	80.00
35-5 West/Melillo/Blae/Coff 5D	30.00	50.00
35-6 West/Melillo/Blae/Coff 6D	30.00	50.00
36-1 Wilson/Allen/Jonnard/Brick 1E SP	45.00	80.00
36-3 Wilson/Allen/Jonnard/Brick 3C SP	45.00	80.00
36-5 Wilson/Allen/Jonnard/Brick 5C SP	45.00	80.00
36-6 Wilson/Allen/Jonnard/Brick 6C	30.00	50.00

1936 Goudey Black and White

The cards in this 25-card black and white set measure approximately 2 3/8" by 2 7/8". In contrast to the color artwork of its previous sets, the 1936 Goudey set contained a simple black and white player photograph. A facsimile autograph appeared within the picture area. Each card was issued with a number of different "game situation" backs, and there may be as many as 200 different front/back combinations. This unnumbered set is checklisted and numbered below in alphabetical order for convenience. The cards were issued in penny packs which came 100 to a box.

COMPLETE SET (25)	1,250.00	2,500.00
WRAPPER (1-CENT)	150.00	200.00
1 Wally Berger	30.00	60.00
2 Zeke Bonura	40.00	80.00
3 Frenchy Bordagaray XRC	40.00	80.00
4 Bill Brubaker XRC	25.00	50.00
5 Dolph Camilli	30.00	60.00
6 Clyde Castleman XRC	25.00	50.00
7 Mickey Cochrane	125.00	250.00
8 Joe Coscarart XRC	25.00	50.00
9 Frank Crosetti	40.00	80.00
10 Kiki Cuyler	50.00	100.00
11 Paul Derringer	30.00	60.00
12 Jimmy Dykes	60.00	120.00
13 Rick Ferrell	50.00	100.00
14 Lefty Gomez	125.00	250.00
15 Hank Greenberg	150.00	300.00
16 Bucky Harris XRC	50.00	100.00
17 Rollie Hemsley	25.00	60.00
18 Pinky Higgins	30.00	60.00
19 Oral Hildebrand	25.00	50.00
20 Chuck Klein	75.00	150.00
21 Pepper Martin	40.00	80.00
22 Bobo Newsom XRC	30.00	60.00
23 Joe Vosmik	25.00	50.00
24 Paul Waner	75.00	150.00
25 Bill Werber	25.00	50.00

1936 Goudey Wide Pen Premiums R314

Each card measures approximately 3 1/4" by 5 1/2". These black and white unnumbered cards could be obtained directly from a retail outlet rather than through the mail only. Four types of this card exist. Type A contains cards, mainly individual players, with "Litho USA" in the bottom border. Type B does not have the "Litho USA" marking and comes both with and without a border. Type C cards are American players on creamy paper stock with medium thickness signatures and no "Litho USA" markings. Type D consists of Canadian players from Montreal (M) or Toronto (T) on creamy stock paper with non-glossy photos.

COMPLETE SET (208)	5,000.00	10,000.00
COMMON CARD (A1-A119)	10.00	20.00
COMMON CARD (B1-B25)	25.00	50.00
COMMON CARD (C1-C25)	25.00	50.00
COMMON CARD (D1-D39)	40.00	80.00
A1 Ethan Allen	15.00	30.00
A2 Earl Averill	25.00	50.00
A3 Dick Bartell	12.50	25.00
A4 Dick Bartell	15.00	30.00
A5 Wally Berger	15.00	30.00
A6 Geo. Blaeholder	12.50	25.00
A7 Cy Blanton	12.50	25.00
A8 Cliff Bolton	12.50	25.00
A9 Stan Bordagaray	12.50	25.00
A10 Tommy Bridges	15.00	30.00
A11 Bill Brubaker	12.50	25.00
A12 Sam Byrd	12.50	25.00
A13 Dolph Camilli	15.00	30.00
A14 Clydell Castleman/(throwing)	12.50	25.00
A15 Clydell Castleman	12.50	25.00
A16 Phil Cavarretta	20.00	40.00
A17 Mickey Cochrane	40.00	80.00
A18 Earle Combs	25.00	50.00
A19 Joe Coscarart	12.50	25.00
A20 Joe Cronin	25.00	50.00
A21 Frank Crosetti	25.00	50.00
A22 Tony Cuccinello	12.50	25.00
A23 KiKi Cuyler	25.00	50.00
A24 Curt Davis	12.50	25.00
A25 Virgil Davis	12.50	25.00
A26 Paul Derringer	15.00	30.00
A27 Bill Dickey	25.00	50.00
A28 Jimmy Dykes kneeling	15.00	30.00
A29 Rick Ferrell	25.00	50.00
A30 Wes Ferrell	20.00	40.00
A31 Lou Finney	12.50	25.00
A32 Ervin Pete Fox	12.50	25.00
A33 Tony Freitas	12.50	25.00
A34 Lonnie Frey	12.50	25.00
A35 Frankie Frisch	40.00	80.00
A36 Augie Galan	12.50	25.00
A37 Charley Gehringer	40.00	80.00
A38 Charlie Gelbert	12.50	25.00
A39 Lefty Gomez	40.00	80.00
A40 Goose Goslin	25.00	50.00
A41 Earl Grace	12.50	25.00
A42 Hank Greenberg	50.00	100.00
A43 Mule Haas	12.50	25.00
A44 Odell Hale	12.50	25.00
A45 Bill Hallahan	12.50	25.00
A46 Mel Harder	15.00	30.00
A47 Bucky Harris	25.00	50.00
A48 Gabby Hartnett	25.00	50.00
A49 Ray Hayworth	12.50	25.00
A50 Rollie Hemsley	12.50	25.00
A51 Babe Herman	20.00	40.00
A52 Frank Higgins	12.50	25.00
A53 Oral Hildebrand	12.50	25.00
A54 Myril Hoag	12.50	25.00
A55 Waite Hoyt	25.00	50.00
A56 Woody Jensen	12.50	25.00
A57 Bob Johnson	15.00	30.00
A58 Buck Jordan	12.50	25.00
A59 Alex Kampouris	12.50	25.00
A60 Chuck Klein	25.00	50.00
A61 Joe Kuhel	12.50	25.00
A62 Lyn Lary	12.50	25.00
A63 Cookie Lavagetto	15.00	30.00
A64 Sam Leslie	12.50	25.00
A64 Fred Lindstrom	25.00	50.00
A66 Ernie Lombardi	25.00	50.00
A67 Al Lopez	25.00	50.00
A68 Dan MacFayden	12.50	25.00
A69 John Marcum	12.50	25.00
A70 Pepper Martin	20.00	40.00
A71 Eric McNair	12.50	25.00
A72 Joe Medwick	25.00	50.00
A73 Gene Moore	12.50	25.00
A74 Randy Moore	12.50	25.00
A75 Terry Moore	15.00	30.00
A76 Edward Moriarty	12.50	25.00
A77 Wally Moses	12.50	25.00
A78 Buddy Myer	12.50	25.00
A79 Buck Newsom	15.00	30.00
A80 Fred Ostermueller	12.50	25.00
A81 Marvin Owen	12.50	25.00
A82 Tommy Padden	12.50	25.00
A83 Ray Pepper	12.50	25.00
A84 Tony Piet	12.50	25.00
A85 Rabbit Pytlak	12.50	25.00
A86 Rip Radcliff	12.50	25.00
A87 Bobby Reis	12.50	25.00
A88 Lew Riggs	12.50	25.00
A89 Bill Rogell	12.50	25.00
A90 Red Rolfe	15.00	30.00
A91 Schoolboy Rowe	15.00	30.00
A92 Al Schacht	20.00	40.00
A93 Luke Sewell	15.00	30.00
A94 Al Simmons	40.00	80.00
A95 John Stone	12.50	25.00
A96 Gus Suhr	12.50	25.00
A97 Joe Sullivan	12.50	25.00
A98 Bill Swift	12.50	25.00
A99 Vito Tamulis	12.50	25.00
A100 Dan Taylor	12.50	25.00
A101 Cecil Travis	12.50	25.00
A102 Hal Trosky	15.00	30.00
A103 Bill Urbanski	12.50	25.00
A104 Russ Van Atta	12.50	25.00
A105 Arky Vaughan	25.00	50.00
A106 Gerald Walker	12.50	25.00
A107 Bucky Walters	20.00	40.00
A108 Lloyd Waner	25.00	50.00
A109 Paul Waner	25.00	50.00
A110 Lon Warneke	12.50	25.00
A111 Rabbit Warstler	12.50	25.00
A112 Bill Werber	12.50	25.00
A113 Jo-Jo White	12.50	25.00
A114 Burgess Whitehead	12.50	25.00
A115 John Whitehead	12.50	25.00
A116 Whitlow Wyatt	12.50	25.00
A117 J.DiMaggio McCarthy	200.00	400.00
A118 W.Ferrell R.Ferrell	25.00	50.00
A119 F.Pytlak S.O'Neill	12.50	25.00
B1 Mel Almada	25.00	50.00
B2 Luke Appling	50.00	100.00
B3 Henry Bonura	25.00	50.00
B4 B. Chapman B. Werber	25.00	50.00
B5 Herman Clifton	25.00	50.00
B6 Roger Doc Cramer	30.00	60.00
B7 Joe Cronin	50.00	100.00
B8 Jimmy Dykes	30.00	60.00
B9 Ervin Pete Fox	25.00	50.00
B10 Jimmie Foxx	125.00	250.00
B11 Hank Greenberg	50.00	100.00
B12 Oral Hildebrand	25.00	50.00
B13 Alex Hooks	25.00	50.00
B14 Willis Hudlin	25.00	50.00
B15 Bill Knickerbocker	25.00	50.00
B16 Heinie Manush	40.00	80.00
B17 Steve O'Neill	25.00	50.00
B18 Marvin Owen	25.00	50.00
B19 Al Simmons	50.00	100.00
B20 Lem Moose Solters	25.00	50.00
B21 Hal Trosky (batting)	30.00	60.00
B22 Joe Vosmik	25.00	50.00
B23 Joe Vosmik(batting)	25.00	50.00
B24 Joe Vosmik(fielding)	25.00	50.00
B25 Earl Whitehill	25.00	50.00
C1 Luke Appling batting	50.00	100.00
C2 Earl Averill	50.00	100.00
C3 Cy Blanton	25.00	50.00
C4 Zeke Bonura batting	25.00	50.00
C5 Tom Bridges	25.00	50.00
C6 Joe DiMaggio	800.00	1,500.00
C7 Bobby Doerr	50.00	100.00
C8 Jimmy Dykes	25.00	50.00
C9 Bob Feller	150.00	300.00

C10 Elbie Fletcher	25.00	50.00
C11 Pete Fox (batting)	25.00	50.00
C12 Gus Galan batting	25.00	50.00
C13 Charley Gehringer	50.00	100.00
C14 Hank Greenberg	100.00	200.00
C15 Mel Harder	40.00	80.00
C16 Gabby Hartnett	50.00	100.00
C17 Pinky Higgins	25.00	50.00
C18 Carl Hubbell	100.00	200.00
C19 Wally Moses batting	25.00	50.00
C20 Lou Newsom	30.00	60.00
C21 Schoolboy Rowe throwing	30.00	60.00
C22 Julius Solters	25.00	50.00
C23 Hal Trosky	30.00	60.00
C24 Joe Vosmik kneeling	25.00	50.00
C25 Johnnie Whitehead throwing	25.00	50.00
D1 Buddy Bates M	40.00	80.00
D2 Del Bissonette M	40.00	80.00
D3 Lincoln Blakely T	40.00	80.00
D4 Isaac J. Boone T	40.00	80.00
D5 John H. Burnett T	40.00	80.00
D6 Leon Chagnon M	40.00	80.00
D7 Gus Dugas M	40.00	80.00
D8 Henry N. Erickson	40.00	80.00
D9 Art Funk T	40.00	80.00
D10 George Granger M	40.00	80.00
D11 Thomas G. Heath	40.00	80.00
D12 Phil Hensich M	40.00	80.00
D13 LeRoy Hermann T	40.00	80.00
D14 Henry Johnson M	40.00	80.00
D15 Hal King M	40.00	80.00
D16 Charles S. Lucas T	40.00	80.00
D17 Edward S. Miller T	40.00	80.00
D18 Jake F. Mooty T	40.00	80.00
D19 Guy Moreau	40.00	80.00
D20 George Murray T	40.00	80.00
D21 Glenn Myatt M	40.00	80.00
D22 Lauri Myllykangas M	40.00	80.00
D23 Franci J. Nicholas T	40.00	80.00
D24 Bill O'Brien	40.00	80.00
D25 Thomas Oliver T	40.00	80.00
D26 James Pattison T	40.00	80.00
D27 Crip Polli M	40.00	80.00
D28 Harlin Pool T	40.00	80.00
D29 Walter Purcey T	40.00	80.00
D30 Bill Rhiel M	40.00	80.00
D31 Ben Sankey M	40.00	80.00
D32 Leslie Scarsella T	40.00	80.00
D33 Bob Seeds M	40.00	80.00
D34 Frank Shaughnessy M	40.00	80.00
D35 Harry Smythe M	40.00	80.00
D36 Ben Tate M	40.00	80.00
D37 Fresco Thompson M	50.00	100.00
D38 Charles Wilson M	40.00	80.00
D39 Francis Wistert T	40.00	80.00

1937 Goudey Knot Hole R325

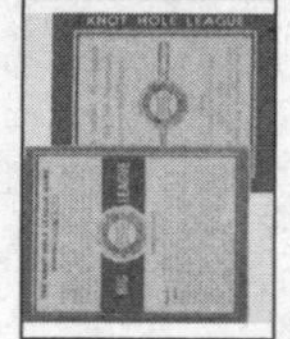

The cards in this 24-card set measure approximately 2 3/8" by 2 7/8". The 1937 "Knot Hole League Game" was another of the many innovative marketing ideas of the Goudey Gum Company. Advertised as a series of 100 game cards promising "exciting" baseball action, the set actually was limited to the 24 cards listed below.

COMPLETE SET (24)	90.00	150.00
COMMON PLAYER (1-24)	5.00	8.00

1937 Goudey Thum Movies R342

These numbered booklets are the same dimensions (2" by 3") as the R326 Flip Movies except that these are twice the thickness as they comprise both parts within a single cover. They were produced by Goudey Gum. The desirability of the set is decreased by the fact that the outside of the Thum Movie booklet does not show any picture of the player; this is in contrast to the R326 Flip Movie style which shows an inset photo of the player on the cover.

COMPLETE SET (13)	850.00	1,400.00
1 John Irving Burns	50.00	80.00
2 Joe Vosmik	50.00	80.00
3 Mel Ott	90.00	150.00
4 Joe DiMaggio	250.00	400.00
5 Wally Moses	50.00	80.00
6 Van Lingle Mungo	50.00	80.00
7 Luke Appling	90.00	150.00
8 Bob Feller	90.00	150.00
9 Paul Derringer	50.00	80.00
10 Paul Waner	90.00	150.00
11 Joe Medwick	90.00	150.00
12 James Emory Foxx	90.00	150.00
13 Wally Berger	60.00	100.00

1937 Goudey Flip Movies R326

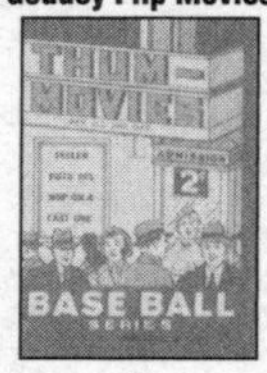

The 26 "Flip Movies" which comprise this set are a miniature version (2" by 3") of the popular penny arcade features of the period. Each movie comes in two parts, clearly labeled, and there are several cover colors as well as incorrect photos known to exist.

COMPLETE SET (13)	750.00	1,250.00
1A John Irving Burns Poles Two Bagger	25.00	50.00
1B John Irving Burns Poles Two Bagger	25.00	50.00
2A Joe Vosmik Triples	25.00	50.00
2B Joe Vosmik Triples	25.00	50.00
3A Mel Ott Puts It Over The Fence	50.00	100.00
3B Mel Ott Puts It Over The Fence	50.00	100.00
4A Joe DiMaggio Socks A Sizzling Long Drive	150.00	300.00
4B Joe DiMaggio Socks A Sizzling Long Drive	150.00	300.00
5A Wally Moses Leans Against A Fast Ball	25.00	50.00
5B Wally Moses Leans Against A Fast Ball	25.00	50.00
6A Van Lingle Mungo Tosses Fire-Ball	25.00	50.00
6B Van Lingle Mungo Tosses Fire-Ball	25.00	50.00
7A Luke Appling Gets Set For Double Play	50.00	100.00
7B Luke Appling Gets Set For Double Play	50.00	100.00
8A Bob Feller Puts His Hop On A Fast One	50.00	100.00
8B Bob Feller/(Puts His Hop On A Fast One)	50.00	100.00
9A Paul Derringer Demonstrates Sharp Curve	25.00	50.00
9B Paul Derringer Demonstrates Sharp Curve	25.00	50.00
10A Paul Waner Big Poison Smacks A Triple	50.00	100.00
10B Paul Waner Big Poison Smacks A Triple	50.00	100.00
11A Joe Medwick Bats Hard Grounder	50.00	100.00
11B Joe Medwick Bats Hard Grounder	50.00	100.00
12A James Emory Foxx Smacks A Homer	50.00	100.00
12B James Emory Foxx Smacks A Homer	50.00	100.00
13A Wally Berger Puts One In The Bleachers	30.00	60.00
13B Wally Berger Puts One In The Bleachers	30.00	60.00

1938 Goudey Heads-Up

The cards in this 48-card set measure approximately 2 3/8" by 2 7/8". The 1938 Goudey set is commonly referred to as the Heads-Up set. These very popular but difficult to obtain cards came in two series of the same 24 players. The first series, numbers 241-264, is distinguished from the second series, numbers 265-288, in that the second contains etched cartoons and comments surrounding the player picture. Although the set starts with number 241, it is not a continuation of the 1933 Goudey set, but a separate set in its own right.

COMPLETE SET (48)	9,000.00	15,000.00
COMMON CARD (241-264)	60.00	100.00
COMMON CARD (265-288)	60.00	100.00
WRAPPER (1-CENT, 6-FIG.)	700.00	800.00
241 Charley Gehringer	175.00	300.00
242 Pete Fox	60.00	100.00
243 Joe Kuhel	60.00	100.00
244 Frank Demaree	60.00	100.00
245 Frank Pytlak XRC	60.00	100.00
246 Ernie Lombardi	100.00	175.00
247 Joe Vosmik	60.00	100.00
248 Dick Bartell	60.00	100.00
249 Jimmie Foxx	300.00	600.00
250 Joe DiMaggio XRC	2,500.00	5,000.00
251 Bump Hadley	60.00	100.00
252 Zeke Bonura	60.00	100.00
253 Hank Greenberg	250.00	400.00
254 Van Lingle Mungo	75.00	125.00
255 Moose Solters	60.00	100.00
256 Vernon Kennedy XRC	60.00	100.00
257 Al Lopez	125.00	200.00
258 Bobby Doerr XRC	150.00	250.00
259 Billy Werber	60.00	100.00
260 Rudy York XRC	75.00	125.00
261 Rip Radcliff XRC	60.00	100.00
262 Joe Medwick	150.00	250.00
263 Marvin Owen	60.00	100.00
264 Bob Feller XRC	800.00	1,500.00
265 Charley Gehringer	175.00	300.00
266 Pete Fox	60.00	100.00
267 Joe Kuhel	60.00	100.00
268 Frank Demaree	60.00	100.00
269 Frank Pytlak XRC	60.00	100.00
270 Ernie Lombardi	250.00	500.00
271 Joe Vosmik	60.00	100.00
272 Dick Bartell	60.00	100.00
273 Jimmie Foxx	400.00	800.00
274 Joe DiMaggio XRC	2,500.00	5,000.00
275 Bump Hadley	60.00	100.00
276 Zeke Bonura	60.00	100.00
277 Hank Greenberg	250.00	400.00
278 Van Lingle Mungo	75.00	125.00
279 Moose Solters	60.00	100.00
280 Vernon Kennedy XRC	60.00	100.00
281 Al Lopez	150.00	250.00
282 Bobby Doerr XRC	150.00	250.00
283 Billy Werber	60.00	100.00
284 Rudy York XRC	75.00	125.00
285 Rip Radcliff XRC	60.00	100.00
286 Joe Medwick	150.00	250.00
287 Marvin Owen	60.00	100.00
288 Bob Feller XRC	800.00	1,500.00

1939 Goudey Premiums R303A

This series of 48 paper premiums were issued in 1939 by the Goudey Company. Each premium photo measures approximately 4" by 6 3/16". This set carries the name Diamond Stars Gum on the reverse, although the National Chicle Company who produced the Diamond Stars baseball cards is in no way connected with this set. The backs contain instructions on various baseball disciplines. The color of the set is brown, not the more reddish color of sepia normally listed for this set.

COMPLETE SET (48)	2,000.00	4,000.00
1 Luke Appling	40.00	80.00
2 Earl Averill	40.00	80.00
3 Wally Berger	30.00	60.00
4 Darrell Blanton	25.00	50.00
5 Zeke Bonura	25.00	50.00
6 Mace Brown	25.00	50.00
7 George Case	25.00	50.00
8 Ben Chapman	25.00	50.00
9 Joe Cronin	40.00	80.00
10 Frank Crosetti	30.00	60.00
11 Paul Derringer	30.00	60.00
12 Bill Dickey	50.00	100.00
13 Joe DiMaggio	300.00	600.00
14 Bob Feller	100.00	200.00
15 Jimmie Foxx	75.00	150.00
16 Charley Gehringer	50.00	100.00
17 Lefty Gomez	50.00	100.00
18 Ival Goodman	30.00	60.00
19 Joe Gordon	30.00	60.00
20 Hank Greenberg	60.00	120.00
21 Buddy Hassett	25.00	50.00
22 Jeff Heath	25.00	50.00
23 Tommy Henrich	40.00	80.00
24 Billy Herman	40.00	80.00
25 Frank Higgins	25.00	50.00
26 Fred Hutchinson	30.00	60.00
27 Bob Johnson	25.00	50.00
28 Ken Keltner	25.00	50.00
29 Mike Kreevich	25.00	50.00
30 Ernie Lombardi	40.00	80.00
31 Gus Mancuso	25.00	50.00
32 Eric McNair	25.00	50.00
33 Van Mungo	30.00	60.00
34 Buck Newsom	30.00	60.00
35 Mel Ott	50.00	100.00
36 Marvin Owen	25.00	50.00
37 Frankie Pytlak	25.00	50.00
38 Woody Rich	25.00	50.00
39 Charlie Root	25.00	50.00
40 Al Simmons	40.00	80.00
41 Jim Tabor	25.00	50.00
42 Cecil Travis	25.00	50.00
43 Hal Trosky	30.00	60.00
44 Arky Vaughan	40.00	80.00
45 Joe Vosmik	25.00	50.00
46 Lon Warneke	25.00	50.00
47 Ted Williams	300.00	600.00
48 Rudy York	30.00	60.00

1939 Goudey Premiums R303B

This set of 24 paper photos is slightly larger than its counterpart R303A and was also issued in 1939. Each premium photo measures approximately 4 3/4" by 7 5/16". The photos of R303A series are the same ones depicted on these cards, and the reverses contain "How to" instructions and the Diamond Stars Gum name. The photos are the same as R303A. This set comes in two distinct colors, black and sepia.

COMPLETE SET (24)	1,000.00	2,000.00
1 Luke Appling	40.00	80.00
2 George Case	25.00	50.00
3 Ben Chapman	25.00	50.00
4 Joe Cronin	40.00	80.00
5 Bill Dickey	50.00	100.00
6 Joe DiMaggio	350.00	700.00
7 Bob Feller	125.00	250.00
8 Jimmie Foxx	100.00	200.00
9 Lefty Gomez	50.00	100.00
10 Ival Goodman	25.00	50.00
11 Joe Gordon	30.00	60.00
12 Hank Greenberg	75.00	150.00
13 Jeff Heath	25.00	50.00
14 Billy Herman	40.00	80.00
15 Frank Higgins	25.00	50.00
16 Ken Keltner	25.00	50.00
17 Mike Kreevich	25.00	50.00
18 Ernie Lombardi	40.00	80.00
19 Gus Mancuso	25.00	50.00
20 Mel Ott	75.00	150.00
21 Al Simmons	40.00	80.00
22 Arky Vaughan	40.00	80.00
23 Joe Vosmik	25.00	50.00
24 Rudy York	30.00	60.00

1941 Goudey

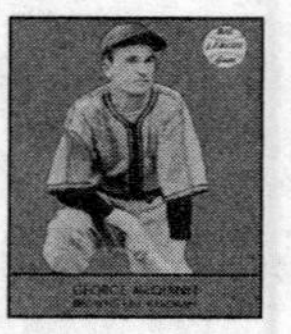

The cards in this 33-card set measure 2 3/8" by 2 7/8". The 1941 Series of blank backed baseball cards was the last baseball issue marketed by Goudey before the war closed the door on that company for good. Each black and white player photo comes with four color backgrounds (blue, green, red, or yellow). Cards without numbers are probably miscut. Cards 21-25 are especially scarce in relation to the rest of the set. In fact the eight hardest to find cards in the set are, in order, 22, 24, 23, 25, 21, 27, 29 and 32.

COMPLETE SET (33)	1,200.00	2,000.00
COMMON PLAYER (1-33)	15.00	30.00
COMMON SP		
WRAPPER (1-CENT)	150.00	200.00
1 Hugh Mulcahy	15.00	30.00
2 Harland Clift XRC	15.00	30.00
3 Louis Chiozza	15.00	30.00
4 Buddy Rosar XRC	15.00	30.00
5 George McQuinn	15.00	30.00
6 George Dickman	15.00	30.00
7 Wayne Ambler	15.00	30.00
8 Bob Muncrief XRC	15.00	30.00
9 Bill Dietrich XRC	15.00	30.00
10 Taft Wright	15.00	30.00
11 Don Heffner	15.00	30.00
12 Fritz Ostermueller	15.00	30.00
13 Frank Hayes	15.00	30.00
14 John Kramer XRC	15.00	30.00
15 Dario Lodigiani XRC	15.00	30.00
16 George Case	15.00	30.00
17 Vito Tamulis	15.00	30.00
18 Whitlow Wyatt	20.00	40.00
19 Bill Posedel	15.00	30.00
20 Carl Hubbell	50.00	80.00
21 Harold Warstler SP	60.00	120.00
22 Joe Sullivan SP XRC	175.00	300.00
23 Norman Young SP	100.00	200.00
24 Stanley Andrews SP XRC	125.00	250.00
25 Morris Arnovich SP	60.00	120.00
26 Elbert Fletcher	15.00	30.00
27 Bill Crouch XRC	40.00	60.00
28 Al Todd XRC	15.00	30.00
29 Debs Garms	30.00	50.00
30 Jim Tobin	15.00	30.00
31 Chester Ross XRC	15.00	30.00
32 George Coffman	20.00	40.00
33 Mel Ott	75.00	125.00

1978 Grand Slam

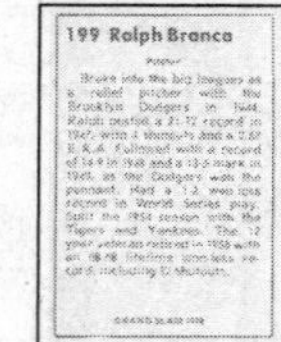

Issued by Renata Galasso, Inc., these 200 cards, which measure 2 1/4" by 3 1/4" features some of the leading figures in baseball history. All the players in this set were alive at time of issue and many collectors wrote to these players to get autographs.

COMPLETE SET (200)	60.00	120.00
1 Leo Durocher	.60	1.50
2 Bob Lemon	.60	1.50
3 Earl Averill	.60	1.50
4 Dale Alexander	.10	.25
5 Hank Greenberg	.75	2.00
6 Waite Hoyt	.60	1.50
7 Al Lopez	.60	1.50
8 Lloyd Waner	.40	1.00
9 Bob Feller	1.25	3.00
10 Guy Bush	.10	.25
11 Stan Hack	.20	.50
12 Zeke Bonura	.10	.25
13 Wally Moses	.10	.25
14 Fred Fitzsimmons	.10	.25
15 Johnny Vander Meer	.20	.50
16 Riggs Stephenson	.20	.50
17 Bucky Walters	.40	1.00
18 Charlie Grimm	.40	1.00

19 Phil Cavaretta .30 .75
20 Wally Berger .20 .50
21 Joe Sewell .40 1.00
22 Edd Roush .40 1.00
23 Johnny Mize .60 1.50
24 Bill Dickey .75 2.00
25 Lou Boudreau .60 1.50
26 Bill Terry 1.25 3.00
27 Willie Kamm .10 .25
28 Charlie Gehringer .75 2.00
29 Stanley Coveleskie .60 1.50
30 Larry French .10 .25
31 George Kelly .30 .75
32 Terry Moore .20 .50
33 Billy Herman .40 1.00
34 Babe Herman .30 .75
35 Carl Hubbell 1.25 3.00
36 Buck Leonard 1.25 3.00
37 Gus Suhr .10 .25
38 Burleigh Grimes .40 1.00
39 Lew Fonseca .10 .25
40 Travis Jackson .30 .75
41 Enos Slaughter .60 1.50
42 Fred Lindstrom .30 .75
43 Rick Ferrell .30 .75
44 Cookie Lavagetto .10 .25
45 Stan Musial 2.50 6.00
46 Hal Trosky .10 .25
47 Hal Newhouser .40 1.00
48 Paul Dean .10 .25
49 George Halas 1.25 3.00
50 Jocko Conlan .40 1.00
51 Joe DiMaggio 5.00 12.00
52 Bobby Doerr .60 1.50
53 Carl Reynolds .10 .25
54 Pete Reiser .30 .75
55 Frank McCormick .10 .25
56 Mel Harder .20 .50
57 George Uhle .10 .25
58 Doc Cramer .10 .25
59 Taylor Douthit .10 .25
60 Cecil Travis .10 .25
61 James Cool Papa Bell 1.25 3.00
62 Charlie Keller .30 .75
63 Bill Hallahan .10 .25
64 Debs Garms .10 .25
65 Rube Marquard .40 1.00
66 Rube Walberg .10 .25
67 Augie Galan .20 .50
68 George Pipgras .10 .25
69 Hal Schumacher .10 .25
70 Dolf Camilli .20 .50
71 Paul Richards .10 .25
72 Judy Johnson 1.25 3.00
73 Frank Crosetti .30 .75
74 Peanuts Lowery .10 .25
75 Walter Alston .30 .75
76 Dutch Leonard .10 .25
77 Barney McCosky .10 .25
78 Joe Dobson .10 .25
79 George Kell .60 1.50
80 Ted Lyons .40 1.00
81 Johnny Pesky .20 .50
82 Hank Borowy .10 .25
83 Ewell Blackwell .10 .25
84 Pee Wee Reese 1.25 3.00
85 Monte Irvin .75 2.00
86 Joe Moore .10 .25
87 Joe Wood .40 1.00
88 Babe Dahlgren .10 .25
89 Bibb Falk .10 .25
90 Ed Lopat .30 .75
91 Rip Sewell .10 .25
92 Marty Marion .20 .50
93 Taft Wright .10 .25
94 Allie Reynolds .30 .75
95 Harry Walker .20 .50
96 Tex Hughson .10 .25
97 George Selkirk .10 .25
98 Dom DiMaggio .40 1.00
99 Walker Cooper .10 .25
100 Phil Rizzuto 1.25 3.00
101 Robin Roberts 1.25 3.00
102 Joe Adcock .30 .75
103 Hank Bauer .30 .75
104 Frank Baumholtz .10 .25
105 Ray Boone .10 .25
106 Smoky Burgess .10 .25
107 Walt Dropo .10 .25
108 Alvin Dark .20 .50
109 Carl Erskine .20 .50
110 Dick Donovan .10 .25
111 Dee Fondy .10 .25
112 Mike Garcia .10 .25
113 Bob Friend .10 .25
114 Ned Garver .10 .25
115 Billy Goodman .10 .25
116 Larry Jansen .10 .25
117 Jackie Jensen .20 .50
118 John Antonelli .10 .25
119 Ted Kluszewski .40 1.00
120 Harvey Kuenn .20 .50
121 Clem Labine .10 .25
122 Red Schoendienst .40 1.00
123 Don Larsen .30 .75
124 Vern Law .20 .50
125 Charlie Maxwell .10 .25
126 Wally Moon .10 .25
127 Bob Nieman .10 .25
128 Don Newcombe .20 .50
129 Wally Post .10 .25
130 Johnny Podres .20 .50
131 Vic Raschi .20 .50
132 Dusty Rhodes .10 .25
133 Jim Rivera .10 .25
134 Pete Runnels .10 .25
135 Hank Sauer .20 .50
136 Roy Sievers .20 .50
137 Bobby Shantz .20 .50
138 Curt Simmons .10 .25
139 Bob Skinner .10 .25
140 Bill Skowron .30 .75
141 Warren Spahn .75 2.00
142 Gerry Staley .10 .25
143 Frank Thomas .20 .50
144 Bobby Thomson .30 .75
145 Bob Turley .10 .25
146 Vic Wertz .10 .25
147 Bill Virdon .10 .25
148 Gene Woodling .10 .25
149 Eddie Yost .10 .25
150 Sandy Koufax 2.50 6.00
151 Lefty Gomez .75 2.00
152 Al Rosen .40 1.00
153 Vince DiMaggio .20 .50
154 Bill Nicholson .10 .25
155 Mark Koenig .10 .25
156 Max Lanier .10 .25
157 Ken Keltner .10 .25
158 Whit Wyatt .10 .25
159 Marv Owen .10 .25
160 Red Lucas .10 .25
161 Babe Phelps .10 .25
162 Pete Donohue .10 .25
163 Johnny Cooney .10 .25
164 Glenn Wright .10 .25
165 Willis Hudlin .10 .25
166 Tony Cuccinello .10 .25
167 Bill Bevens .10 .25
168 Dave Ferriss .10 .25
169 Whitey Kurowski .10 .25
170 Buddy Hassett .10 .25
171 Ossie Bluege .10 .25
172 Hoot Evers .10 .25
173 Thornton Lee .10 .25
174 Spud Davis .10 .25
175 Bob Shawkey .30 .75
176 Smead Jolley .10 .25
177 Andy High .10 .25
178 George McQuinn .10 .25
179 Mickey Vernon .20 .50
180 Birdie Tebbetts .10 .25
181 Jack Kramer .10 .25
182 Don Kolloway .10 .25
183 Claude Passeau .10 .25
184 Frank Shea .10 .25
185 Bob O'Farrell .10 .25
186 Bob Johnson .10 .25
187 Ival Goodman .10 .25
188 Mike Kreevich .10 .25
189 Joe Stripp .10 .25
190 Mickey Owen .10 .25
191 Hughie Critz .10 .25
192 Ethan Allen .10 .25
193 Billy Rogell .10 .25
194 Joe Kuhel .10 .25
195 Dale Mitchell .20 .50
196 Eldon Auker .10 .25
197 Johnny Beazley .10 .25
198 Spud Chandler .20 .50
199 Ralph Branca .20 .50
200 Joe Cronin .75 2.00

1975-76 Great Plains Greats

This 42-card set measures approximately 2 1/2" by 3 3/4". The set was issued by the Great Plains Sports Collectors Association in conjunction with their annual show. The first series cards have the photos surrounded by a green border while the second series cards have an orange border. The Lloyd Waner card with a green border is an extra addition to the first series. The card is only available as a single when cut from an uncut sheet. Since it was not issued with the regular set, we are calling it a Short Print. Waner was never distributed since he did not sign a release form. The 1st series was available directly from the producer at time of issue for $4.25. The 2nd series was available from the producer at time of issue for $2.25. 2,000 1st series sets were printed.

COMPLETE SET (42) 10.00 25.00
MINOR STARS .20 .50
COMMON SP
1 Bob Feller .40 1.00
2 Carl Hubbell .40 1.00
3 Jocko Conlan .20 .50
4 Hal Trosky .10 .25
5 Allie Reynolds .10 .25
6 Burleigh Grimes .30 .75
7 Jake Beckley .20 .50
8 Al Simmons .40 1.00
9 Paul Waner .40 1.00
10 Chief Bender .30 .75
11 Fred Clarke .20 .50
12 Jim Bottomley .10 .25
13 Dave Bancroft .20 .50
14 Bing Miller .10 .25
15 Walter Johnson .75 2.00
16 Grover Alexander .75 2.00
17 Bob Johnson .10 .25
18 Roger Maris .40 1.00
19 Ken Keltner .10 .25
20 Red Faber .20 .50
21 Cool Papa Bell .40 1.00
22 Yogi Berra .40 1.00
23 Fred Lindstrom .20 .50
24 Ray Schalk .20 .50
25A Lloyd Waner SP
26 John Hopp .10 .25
27 Mel Harder .10 .25
28 Dutch Leonard .10 .25
29 Bob O'Farrell .10 .25
30 Cap Anson .30 .75
31 Dazzy Vance .20 .50
32 Red Schoendienst .20 .50
33 George Pipgras .10 .25
34 Harvey Kuenn .10 .25
35 Red Ruffing .20 .50
36 Roy Sievers .10 .25
37 Ken Boyer .20 .50
38 Al Smith .10 .25
39 Casey Stengel .40 1.00
40 Bob Gibson .30 .75
41 Mickey Mantle 1.50 4.00
42 Denny McLain .20 .50

1974 Greyhound Heroes of Base Paths

Beginning in 1965, the Greyhound Award for Stolen Bases was given to the champions in each league and the second-place finishers. The 1974 Heroes of the Base Paths pamphlet unfolds to reveal five 4" by 9" panels. The first panel is the title page and features on the back a picture of Joe Black holding the trophy. The second and third panels have on the fronts the history of the award and major league statistics pertaining to stolen bases, while the backs have an essay on the art of base stealing. Finally, the fourth and fifth panels display six player cards; after perforation, the cards measure 4" by 3". Cards 1-4 feature the AL and NL winners and the runner-ups for each league, in that order. The player cards display a black and white head shot of the player on the left half, with player information and number of stolen bases on the right half. The backs have statistics. Both sides of the cards are framed by thin brown border stripes. Cards 5-6 display black and white player photos of past winners in the AL and NL, respectively. The cards are unnumbered.

COMPLETE SET (6) 5.00 12.00
1 Bill North .50 1.25
2 Lou Brock 1.50 4.00
3 Rod Carew 1.50 4.00
4 Davey Lopes .60 1.50
5 American League .50 1.25
Dagoberto Campaneris
Tommy Harpe
6 National League .60 1.50
Lou Brock
Maury Wills
Bobby Tol

1975 Greyhound Heroes of Base Paths

The Greyhound Award for Stolen Bases was given to the champions in each league and the second-place finishers. The 1975 Heroes of the Base Paths pamphlet unfolds to reveal five 4" by 9" panels. The first panel is the title page and features on the back a picture of Maury Wills holding the trophy. The second and third panels have on the fronts the history of the award and major league statistics pertaining to stolen bases, while backs have an essay on the art of bases stealing. The fourth and fifth panels display six player cards; after perforation, cards measure approximately 4" by 3". Cards 1-4 feature the AL and NL winners and the runner-ups for each league, in that order. The player cards display a black and white head shot of the player on the left half, with player information and number of stolen bases on the right half. The backs have statistics. Both sides of the cards are framed by thin powder blue border stripes. Cards 5-6 display black and white player photos of Billy North and Davey Lopes. The cards are unnumbered.

COMPLETE SET (6) 4.00 10.00
1 Mickey Rivers .20 .50
2 Davey Lopes .30 .75
3 Claudell Washington .20 .50
4 Joe Morgan 1.00 2.50
5 Billy North .20 .50
6 Davey Lopes .30 .75

1976 Greyhound Heroes of Base Paths

The Greyhound Award for Stolen Bases was given to the champions in each league and the second-place finishers. The 1976 Heroes of the Base Paths pamphlet unfolds to reveal five 4" by 9" panels. The first panel is the title page and features on the back a picture of Maury Wills holding the trophy. The second and third panels have on the fronts the history of the award and major league statistics pertaining to stolen bases& while the backs have an essay on the art of base stealing. The fourth and fifth panels display six player cards; after perforation, cards measure approximately 4" by 3". Cards 1-4 feature the AL and NL winners and the runner-ups for each league, in that order. The player cards display a black and white head shot of the player on the left half, with player information and number of stolen bases on the right half. The backs have statistics. Both sides of the cards are framed by thin powder reddish-brown stripes. Cards 5-6 display black and white player photos of Billy North and Davey Lopes. The cards are unnumbered.

COMPLETE SET (6) 1.50 4.00
1 Bill North .20 .50
2 Davey Lopes .30 .75
3 Ron LeFlore .20 .50
4 Joe Morgan .75 2.00
5 Billy North .20 .50
6 Davey Lopes .30 .75

1977 Burleigh Grimes Daniels

This 16-card set features black-and-white photos with blue borders of different aspects in the life of Hall of Famer and last legal spitball pitcher Burleigh Grimes. Card number 12 comes with or without an autograph. Sets were available from the producer upon release for $3.49 or in uncut sheet form for $6.49.

COMPLETE SET (16) 15.00 40.00
1 Burleigh Grimes .75 2.00
Dodger Manager 1937-38
2 Burleigh Grimes .75 2.00
Lord Burleigh
3 Burleigh Grimes .75 2.00
Clarence Mitchell
Last Spitballe
4 Burleigh Grimes .75 2.00
Rogers Hornsby
John McGraw
Edd
5 Burleigh Grimes .75 2.00
Zack Wheat
Winning Combination
6 Burleigh Grimes .75 2.00
World Champion
7 Burleigh Grimes .75 2.00
Old Stubblebeard
8 Burleigh Grimes .75 2.00
Joe McCarthy MG
9 Burleigh Grimes .75 2.00
Dazzy Vance
Van Mungo
Watson Cl
10 Burleigh Grimes .75 2.00
Babe Ruth
11 Burleigh Grimes .75 2.00
Babe Ruth
Leo Durocher
Dodger S
12 Burleigh Grimes .75 2.00
Chief Bender
12A Burleigh Grimes AU 8.00 20.00
Chief Bender
13 Burleigh Grimes .75 2.00
Robin Roberts
Number 270
14 Burleigh Grimes .75 2.00
The Origin
15 Burleigh Grimes .75 2.00
Red Faber
Luke Appling
Heinie M
16 Burleigh Grimes .75 2.00
Lord Burleigh 1977

1973 Hall of Fame Picture Pack

This 20-card set issued in a special envelope measures approximately 5" by 6 3/4" and features black-and-white photos of players who are in the Baseball Hall of Fame in Cooperstown, New York. Player information and statistics are printed on the front in the bottom margin. The backs are blank. The cards are unnumbered and checklisted below in alphabetical order. These sets were also issued in a 4 7/8" by 7 1/2" format and an easy way to tell the difference is that the "shorter" photos have career statistical information while the "longer" photos have just career batting average (for players) and length of major league service.

COMPLETE SET (20) 15.00 40.00
1 Yogi Berra 1.00 2.50
2 Roy Campanella 1.00 2.50
3 Ty Cobb 1.25 3.00
4 Joe Cronin .40 1.00
5 Dizzy Dean .75 2.00
6 Joe DiMaggio 1.50 4.00
7 Bob Feller .40 1.00
8 Lou Gehrig 1.50 4.00

9 Rogers Hornsby	.60	1.50
10 Sandy Koufax	1.00	2.50
11 Christy Mathewson	.60	1.50
12 Stan Musial	1.00	2.50
13 Satchel Paige	.60	1.50
14 Jackie Robinson	1.25	3.00
15 Babe Ruth	2.00	5.00
16 Warren Spahn	.40	1.00
17 Casey Stengel	.40	1.00
18 Honus Wagner	.75	2.00
19 Ted Williams	1.25	3.00
20 Cy Young	.60	1.50

1978 Hall of Fame Plaque Postcards Dexter

This 54-card set was produced by Dexter Press and measures approximately 3 1/2" by 5 1/2". The fronts feature a facsimile Cooperstown National Baseball Hall of Fame player's plaque. The backs display a postcard format. The cards are unnumbered and checklisted below in alphabetical order.

COMPLETE SET (53)	40.00	80.00
1 Grover Alexander	.60	1.50
2 Lou Boudreau	.20	.50
3 Roy Campanella	.40	1.00
5 Roberto Clemente	2.00	5.00
6 Ty Cobb	3.00	8.00
7 Stan Coveleskie	.20	.50
8 Sam Crawford	.20	.50
9 Martin Dihigo	.20	.50
10 Joe DiMaggio	3.00	8.00
11 Billy Evans	.20	.50
12 Johnny Evers	.20	.50
13 Red Faber	.20	.50
14 Elmer Flick	.20	.50
15 Ford Frick	.20	.50
16 Frankie Frisch	.20	.50
17 Pud Galvin	.20	.50
18 Lou Gehrig	3.00	8.00
19 Warren Giles	.20	.50
20 Will Harridge	.20	.50
21 Harry Heilmann	.20	.50
22 Harry Hooper	.20	.50
23 Waite Hoyt	.20	.50
24 Miller Huggins	.20	.50
25 Judy Johnson	.20	.50
26 Addie Joss	.20	.50
27 Tim Keefe	.20	.50
28 Willie Keeler	.20	.50
29 George Kelly	.20	.50
30 Sandy Koufax	1.25	3.00
31 Nap Lajoie	.20	.50
32 Pop Lloyd	.20	.50
33 Connie Mack	.75	2.00
34 Larry MacPhail	.20	.50
35 Mickey Mantle	3.00	8.00
36 Heinie Manush	.20	.50
37 Eddie Mathews	.75	2.00
38 Willie Mays	2.00	5.00
39 Ducky Medwick	.20	.50
40 Stan Musial	1.25	3.00
41 Herb Pennock	.20	.50
42 Edd Roush	.20	.50
43 Amos Rusie	.20	.50
44 Babe Ruth	4.00	10.00
45 Ray Schalk	.20	.50
46 Al Simmons	.20	.50
47 Albert Spalding	.20	.50
48 Joe Tinker	.40	1.00
49 Harold Traynor	.20	.50
50A Dazzy Vance 67557-D code on back	.20	.50
51 Lloyd Waner	.20	.50
52 Ted Williams	3.00	8.00
53 Hack Wilson	.20	.50
54 Ross Youngs	.20	.50

1978 Halsey Hall Recalls

This 21-card set measures 2 1/2" by 3 3/4". The players featured were all local Minneapolis-St. Paul heroes whose exploits were remembered by local legend Halsey Hall. These sets were available upon issue from the producer for $3.50. The set was produced by Olde Cards Inc.

COMPLETE SET (21)	15.00	40.00
1 Halsey Hall	.60	1.50
2 Ray Dandridge	1.25	3.00
3 Bruno Haas	.30	.75
4 Fabian Gaffke	.30	.75
5 George Stumpf	.30	.75
6 Roy Campanella	3.00	8.00
7 Babe Barna	.30	.75
8 Tom Sheehan	.30	.75
9 Ray Moore	.30	.75
10 Ted Williams	8.00	20.00
11 Harley Davidson	.30	.75
12 Jack Cassini	.30	.75
13 Pea Ridge Day	.30	.75
14 Oscar Roettger	.30	.75
15 Buzz Arlett	.30	.75
16 Joe Hauser	.30	.75
17 Rube Benton	.30	.75
18 Dave Barnhill	.30	.75
19 Hoyt Wilhelm	1.25	3.00
20 Willie Mays	4.00	10.00
21 Nicollet Park CL	.30	.75
26 Ray Moore	.30	.75

1912 Hassan Triple Folders T202

The cards in this 132-card set measure approximately 2 1/4" by 5 1/4". The 1912 T202 Hassan Triple Folder issue is perhaps the most ingenious baseball card ever issued. The two end cards of each panel are full color, T205-like individual cards whereas the black and white center panel pictures an action photo or portrait. The end cards can be folded across the center panel and stored in this manner. Seventy-six different center panels are known to exist; however, many of the center panels contain more than one combination of end cards. The center panel titles are listed below in alphabetical order while the different combinations of end cards are listed below each center panel as they appear left to right on the front of the card. A total of 132 different card fronts exist. The set price below includes all panel and player combinations listed in the checklist. Back color variations (red or black) also exist. The Birmingham's Home Run card is difficult to obtain as are other cards whose center panel exists with but one combination of end cards. The Devlin with Mathewson end panels on numbers 29A and 74C picture Devlin as a Giant. Devlin is pictured as a Rustler on 29B and 74D. Listed pricing references cards in raw "EX" condition.

COMPLETE SET (132)	20,000.00	35,000.00
1 A Close (Wallace/LaPorte)	150.00	250.00
2 A Close (Wallace/Pelty)	150.00	250.00
3 A Desperate (O'Leary/Cobb)	900.00	1,500.00
4 A Great (Barger/Bergen)	125.00	200.00
5 A Great (Rucker/Bergen)	125.00	200.00
6 A Wide (Mullin/Stanage)	125.00	200.00
7 Ambrose (Blair/Quinn)	125.00	200.00
8 Baker Gets (Collins/Baker)	250.00	400.00
9 Birmingham Gets (Johnson/Street)	350.00	600.00
10 Birmingham's HR (Birmingham/Turner)	150.00	250.00
11 Bush Just (Moran/Magee)	125.00	200.00
12 Carrigan (Gaspar/McLean)	125.00	200.00
13 Carrigan (Wagner/Carrigan)	125.00	200.00
14 Catching (Oakes/Bresnahan)	150.00	250.00
15 Caught (Bresnahan/Harmon)	150.00	250.00
16 Chance (Chance/Foxen)	150.00	250.00
17 Chance (McIntire/Archer)	125.00	200.00
18 Chance (Overall/Archer)	125.00	200.00
19 Chance (Rowan/Archer)	125.00	200.00
20 Chance (Shean/Chance)	150.00	250.00
21 Chase Dives (Chase/Wolter)	125.00	200.00
22 Chase Dives (Gibson/Clarke)	150.00	250.00
23 Chase Dives (Phillippe/Gibson)	125.00	200.00
24 Chase Gets (Egan/Mitchell)	125.00	200.00
25 Chase Gets (Wolter/Chase)	125.00	200.00
26 Chase Guard (Chase/Wolter)	125.00	200.00
27 Chase Guard (Gibson/Clarke)	125.00	200.00
28 Chase Guard (Leifield/Gibson)	125.00	200.00
29 Chase Ready (Paskert/Magee)	125.00	200.00
30 Chase Safe (Barry/Baker)	300.00	500.00
31 Chief (Bender/Thomas)	150.00	250.00
32 Clarke Hikes (Bridwell/Kling)	125.00	200.00
33 Close First (Ball/Stovall)	125.00	200.00
34 Close Plate (Payne/White)	125.00	200.00
35 Close Plate (Walsh/Payne)	150.00	250.00
36 Close Third (Carrigan/Wagner)	125.00	200.00
37 Close Third (Wood/Speaker)	300.00	500.00
38 Collins (Byrne/Clarke)	150.00	250.00
39 Collins (Collins/Baker)	250.00	400.00
40 Collins (Collins/Murphy)	150.00	250.00
41 Crawford (Stanage/Summers)	125.00	200.00
42 Cree Rolls (Daubert/Hummel)	125.00	200.00
43 Davy Jones (Delahanty/Jones)	125.00	200.00
44 Devlin (Devlin G/Mathewson)	500.00	800.00
45 Devlin (Devlin R/Mathewson)	500.00	800.00
46 Devlin (Fletcher/Mathewson)	350.00	600.00
47 Devlin (Meyers/Mathewson)	300.00	500.00
48 Donlin (Camnitz/Gibson)	125.00	200.00
49 Donlin (Dooin/Magee)	125.00	200.00
50 Donlin (Doyle/Merkle)	125.00	200.00
51 Donlin (Gibson/Phillippe)	125.00	200.00
52 Donlin (Leach/Wilson)	125.00	200.00
53 Dooin (Dooin/Doolan)	125.00	200.00
54 Dooin (Dooin/Lobert)	125.00	200.00
55 Dooin (Dooin/Titus)	125.00	200.00
56 Easy (Doyle/Merkle)	125.00	200.00
57 Elberfeld Beats (Elberfeld/Milan)	125.00	200.00
58 Elberfeld Gets (Elberfeld/Milan)	125.00	200.00
59 Engle (Speaker/Engle)	175.00	300.00
60 Evers (Archer/Evers)	150.00	250.00
61 Evers (Archer/Overall)	125.00	200.00
62 Evers (Archer/Reulbach)	125.00	200.00
63 Evers (Chance/Evers)	250.00	400.00
64 Evers (Tinker/Chance)	500.00	800.00
65 Fast Work (O'Leary/Cobb)	900.00	1,500.00
66 Ford (Ford/Sweeney)	125.00	200.00
67 Ford (Ford/Vaughn)	125.00	200.00
68 Good Play (Moriarty/Cobb)	900.00	1,500.00
69 Grant (Grant/Hoblitzell)	125.00	200.00
70 Hal Chase (McConnell/McIntyre)	125.00	200.00
71 Hal Chase (McLean/Suggs)	125.00	200.00
72 Harry Lord (Lennox/Tinker)	150.00	250.00
73 Hartsel Strikes (Gray/Groom)	125.00	200.00
74 Hartzell (Dahlen/Scanlan)	125.00	200.00
75 Held (Lord/Tannehill)	125.00	200.00
76 Jake Stahl (Cicotte/Stahl)	125.00	200.00
77 Jim Delahanty (Delahanty/Jones)	125.00	200.00
78 Just Before (Ames/Meyers)	125.00	200.00
79 Just Before (Becker/Devore)	125.00	200.00
80 Just Before (Bresnahan/McGraw)	250.00	400.00
81 Just Before (Crandall/Meyers)	125.00	200.00
82 Just Before (Fletcher/Mathewson)	350.00	600.00
83 Just Before (Marquard/Meyers)	150.00	250.00
84 Just Before (McGraw/Jennings)	250.00	400.00
85 Just Before (Meyers/Mathewson)	300.00	500.00
86 Just Before (Meyers/Wiltse)	125.00	200.00
87 Just Before (Murray/Snodgrass)	125.00	200.00
88 Knight (Knight/Johnson)	350.00	600.00
89 Lobert Almost (Bridwell/Kling)	125.00	200.00
90 Lobert Almost (Kling/Steinfeldt)	125.00	200.00
91 Lobert Almost (Kling/Young)	350.00	600.00
92 Lobert Almost (Mattern/Kling)	125.00	200.00
93 Lobert Gets (Dooin/Tenney)	125.00	200.00
94 Lobert Catches (Lord/L.Tannehill)	125.00	200.00
95 McConnell (Needham/Richie)	125.00	200.00
96 McIntyre (McConnell/McIntyre)	125.00	200.00
97 Moriarty (Stanage/Willett)	125.00	200.00
98 Nearly (Bates/Bescher)	125.00	200.00
99 Oldring (Lord/Oldring)	125.00	200.00
100 Schaefer On (McBride/Milan)	125.00	200.00
101 Schaefer Steals (McBride/Griffith)	125.00	200.00
102 Scoring (Lord/Oldring)	125.00	200.00
103 Scrambling (Barger/B.Bergen)	125.00	200.00
104 Scrambling (Chase/Wolter)	125.00	200.00
105 Speaker Almost (Miller/Clarke)	150.00	250.00
106 Speaker Round (Wood/Speaker)	350.00	600.00
107 Speaker Scores (Speaker/Engle)	300.00	500.00
108 Stahl Safe (Austin/Stovall)	125.00	200.00
109 Stone (Schulte/Sheckard)	125.00	200.00
110 Sullivan (Evans/Huggins)	150.00	250.00
111 Sullivan (Gray/Groom)	125.00	200.00
112 Sweeney (Ford/Sweeney)	125.00	200.00
113 Sweeney (Ford/Vaughn)	125.00	200.00
114 Tenney (Latham/Raymond)	125.00	200.00
115 The Athletic (Barry/Baker)	175.00	300.00
116 The Athletic (Brown/Graham)	150.00	250.00
117 The Athletic (Hauser/Konetchy)	125.00	200.00
118 The Athletic (Krause/Thomas)	125.00	200.00
119 The Pinch (Egan/Hoblitzell)	125.00	200.00
120 The Scissors (Birmingham/Turner)	125.00	200.00
121 Tom Jones (Fromme/McLean)	125.00	200.00
122 Tom Jones (Gaspar/McLean)	125.00	200.00
123 Too Late (Ames/Meyers)	125.00	200.00
124 Too Late (Crandall/Meyers)	125.00	200.00
125 Too Late (Devlin G/Mathewson)	700.00	1,200.00
126 Too Late (Devlin R/Mathewson)	900.00	1,500.00
127 Too Late (Marquard/Meyers)	250.00	400.00
128 Too Late (Meyers/Wiltse)	125.00	200.00
129 Ty Cobb Steals (Jennings/Cobb)	1,200.00	2,000.00
130 Ty Cobb Steals (Moriarty/Cobb)	1,200.00	2,000.00
131 Ty Cobb Steals (Stovall/Austin)	600.00	1,000.00
132 Wheat Strikes (Dahlen/Wheat)	150.00	250.00

1911 Helmar Stamps

Each stamp measures 1 1/8" by 1 3/8". The stamps are very thin and have an ornate, bright colorful border surrounding the black-and-white photo of the player. There are many differnet border color combinations. There is no identification of issuer to be found anywhere on the stamp. Since the stamps are unnumbered, they are listed below alphabetically within team: Boston Red Sox (1-5), Chicago White Sox (6-20), Cleveland Indians (21-26), Detroit Tigers (27-38), New York Yankees (39-51), Philadelphia A's (52-59), St. Louis Browns (60-66), Washington Senators (67-76), Boston Bees NL (77-81), Brooklyn Dodgers (82-89), Chicago Cubs (90-108), Cincinnati Reds (109-119), New York Giants (120-139), Philadelphia Phillies (140-152), Pittsburgh Pirates (153-166), and St. Louis Cardinals (166-177).

COMPLETE SET (178)	5,000.00	10,000.00
1 Bill Carrigan	25.00	50.00
2 Ed Cicotte	75.00	150.00
3 Hack Engle	25.00	50.00
4 Tris Speaker	50.00	100.00
5 Heine Wagner	25.00	50.00
6 Bruno Block	25.00	50.00
7 Ping Bodie	25.00	50.00
8 Nixey Callahan	25.00	50.00
9 Shano Collins	25.00	50.00
10 Patsy Dougherty	25.00	50.00
11 Bristol Lord	25.00	50.00
12 Ambrose McConnell	25.00	50.00
13 Matthew McIntyre	25.00	50.00
14 Freddy Parent	25.00	50.00
15 Jim Scott	25.00	50.00
16 William Sullivan	25.00	50.00
17 Lee Ford Tannehill	25.00	50.00
18 Ed Walsh	50.00	100.00
19 Guy White	25.00	50.00
20 Irving Young	100.00	200.00
21 Neal Ball	25.00	50.00
22 Dode Birmingham	25.00	50.00
23 George Davis	50.00	100.00
24 Napoleon Lajoie	100.00	200.00
25 Paddy Livingston	25.00	50.00
26 Terry Turner	25.00	50.00
27 Donie Bush	25.00	50.00
28 Ty Cobb	250.00	500.00
29 Sam Crawford	50.00	100.00
30 Jim Delahanty	25.00	50.00
31 Patsy Donovan	25.00	50.00
32 Hughie Jennings	50.00	100.00
33 Davy Jones	25.00	50.00
34 George Moriarity	25.00	50.00
35 George Mullin	30.00	60.00
36 Boss Schmidt	25.00	50.00
37 Oscar Strange	25.00	50.00
38 Robert Willett	25.00	50.00
39 Lew Brockett	25.00	50.00
40 Hal Chase	50.00	100.00
41 Birdie Cree	25.00	50.00
42 Ray Fisher	25.00	50.00
43 Russ Ford	25.00	50.00
44 Earl Gardner	25.00	50.00
45 Jack Quinn	30.00	60.00
46 Gabby Street	25.00	50.00
47 Ed Sweeney	25.00	50.00
48 James(Hippo) Vaughn	30.00	60.00
49 John Warhop	25.00	50.00
50 Harry Wolter	25.00	50.00
51 Harry Wolverton	25.00	50.00
52 Frank Baker	50.00	100.00
53 Jack Barry	25.00	50.00
54 Chief Bender	50.00	100.00
55 Eddie Collins	50.00	100.00
56 Harry Krause	25.00	50.00
57 Danny Murphy	25.00	50.00
58 Rube Oldring	25.00	50.00
59 Ira Thomas	25.00	50.00
60 Jimmy Austin	25.00	50.00
61 Joe Lake	25.00	50.00
62 Frank LaPorte	25.00	50.00
63 Barney Pelty	25.00	50.00
64 John Powell	25.00	50.00
65 George Stovall	25.00	50.00
66 Bobby Wallace	50.00	100.00
67 Wid Conroy	25.00	50.00
68 Dolly Gray	25.00	50.00
69 Clark Griffith	50.00	100.00
70 Bob Groom	25.00	50.00
71 Tom Hughes	25.00	50.00
72 Walter Johnson	100.00	200.00
73 John Knight	25.00	50.00
74 George McBride	25.00	50.00
75 Clyde Milan	30.00	60.00
76 Germany Schaefer	25.00	50.00
77 Al Bridwell	25.00	50.00
78 Hank Gowdy	25.00	50.00
79 Johnny Kling	25.00	50.00
80 Al Mattern	25.00	50.00
81 Ed Sweeney	25.00	50.00
82 Cy Barger	25.00	50.00
83 George Bell	25.00	50.00
84 Bill Dahlen	25.00	50.00
85 Jake Daubert	40.00	80.00
86 Tex Erwin	25.00	50.00
87 John Hummel	25.00	50.00
88 Nap Rucker	40.00	80.00
89 Zach Wheat	50.00	100.00
90 Jimmy Archer	25.00	50.00
91 Mordecai Brown	50.00	100.00
92 Frank Chance	50.00	100.00
93 Leonard(King) Cole	25.00	50.00
94 Johnny Evers	50.00	100.00
95 George(Peaches) Graham	25.00	50.00
96 Solly Hoffman	25.00	50.00
97 Ed Lennox	25.00	50.00
98 Harry McIntire	25.00	50.00
99 Tom Needham	25.00	50.00
100 Ed Reulbach	25.00	50.00
101 Lewis Richie	25.00	50.00
102 Richter	25.00	50.00
103 John Rowan	25.00	50.00
104 Frank Schulte	25.00	50.00
105 Dave Shean	25.00	50.00
106 Jimmy Sheckard	25.00	50.00
107 Joe Tinker	50.00	100.00
108 Fred Toney	25.00	50.00
109 Johnny Bates	25.00	50.00
110 Bob Bescher	25.00	50.00
111 Ed Burns	25.00	50.00
112 Fred Clarke	50.00	100.00
113 Art Fromme	25.00	50.00
114 Harry Gaspar	25.00	50.00
115 Ed Grant	25.00	50.00
116 Doc Hoblitzell	25.00	50.00
117 Larry McLean	25.00	50.00
118 Clarence Mitchell	25.00	50.00
119 George Suggs	25.00	50.00
120 Red Ames	25.00	50.00
121 Beals Becker	25.00	50.00
122 Doc Crandall	25.00	50.00
123 Art Devlin	25.00	50.00
124 Josh Devore	25.00	50.00
125 Larry Doyle	30.00	60.00
126 Louis Drucke	25.00	50.00
127 Arthur Fletcher	25.00	50.00
128 Grover Hartley	25.00	50.00
129 Buck Herzog	30.00	60.00
130 Rube Marquard	50.00	100.00
131 Christy Mathewson	100.00	200.00
132 John McGraw	50.00	100.00
133 Fred Merkle	30.00	60.00
134 John(Chief) Meyers	30.00	60.00
135 Red Murray	25.00	50.00
136 Shafer	25.00	50.00
137 Fred Snodgrass	30.00	60.00
138 John(Chief) Wilson	30.00	60.00
139 Hooks Wiltse	25.00	50.00
140 Zinn Beck	25.00	50.00
141 Red Dooin	25.00	50.00
142 Mickey Doolan	25.00	50.00
143 Tom Downey	25.00	50.00
144 Otto Knabe	25.00	50.00
145 Hans Lobert	25.00	50.00
146 Fred Luderus	25.00	50.00
147 Sherry Magee	40.00	80.00
148 Earl Moore	25.00	50.00
149 Pat Moran	25.00	50.00
150 Dode Paskert	25.00	50.00
151 William(Doc) Scanlan	25.00	50.00
152 John Titus	25.00	50.00
153 Bert Adams	25.00	50.00
154 Bobby Byrne	25.00	50.00
155 Howard Camnitz	25.00	50.00
156 Max Carey	50.00	100.00
157 Fred Clarke	50.00	100.00
158 Mike Donlin	30.00	60.00
159 John Ferry	25.00	50.00
160 George Gibson	25.00	50.00
161 Thomas Leach	25.00	50.00

162 Albert(Lefty) Leifield	25.00	50.00
163 Roy(Doc) Miller	25.00	50.00
164 Martin O'Toole	25.00	50.00
165 Michael Simon	25.00	50.00
166 John(Chief) Wilson	30.00	60.00
167 John Bliss	25.00	50.00
168 Roger Bresnahan	50.00	100.00
169 Louis Evans	25.00	50.00
170 Robert Harmon	25.00	50.00
171 Arnold Hauser	25.00	50.00
172 Miller Huggins	50.00	100.00
173 Ed Konetchy	25.00	50.00
174 Mike Mowrey	25.00	50.00
175 Ennis(Rebel) Oakes	25.00	50.00
176 Edward Phelps	25.00	50.00
177 Slim Sallee	25.00	50.00
178 Bill Steele	25.00	50.00

1962 H.F. Gardner Sports Stars PC768

This colorful 1960's set feature people of color stars only. The reverses can be identified by the line "Color by H.F. Gardner" at the lower left. A short biography of the subject player(s) is present on the reverse.

COMPLETE SET (5)	50.00	100.00
1 Hank Aaron Tommy Aaron	25.00	50.00
2 Billy Bruton	2.50	5.00
3 Lee Maye	2.50	5.00
4 Billy Williams	10.00	20.00

1958 Hires Root Beer

The cards in this 66-card set measure approximately 2 5/16" by 3 1/2" or 2 5/16" by 7" with tabs. The 1958 Hires Root Beer set of numbered, colored cards was issued with detachable coupons as inserts with Hires Root Beer cartons. Cards with the coupon still intact are worth 2.5 times the prices listed below. The card front picture is surrounded by a wood grain effect which makes it look like the player is seen through a knot hole. The numbering of this set is rather strange in that it begins with 10 and skips 69.

COMPLETE SET (66)	1,000.00	2,000.00
10 Richie Ashburn	60.00	120.00
11 Chico Carrasquel	12.50	25.00
12 Dave Philley	12.50	25.00
13 Don Newcombe	15.00	30.00
14 Wally Post	12.50	25.00
15 Rip Repulski	12.50	25.00
16 Chico Fernandez	12.50	25.00
17 Larry Doby	30.00	60.00
18 Hector Brown	12.50	25.00
19 Danny O'Connell	12.50	25.00
20 Granny Hamner	12.50	25.00
21 Dick Groat	15.00	30.00
22 Ray Narleski	12.50	25.00
23 Pee Wee Reese	60.00	120.00
24 Bob Friend	12.50	25.00
25 Willie Mays	200.00	400.00
26 Bob Nieman	12.50	25.00
27 Frank Thomas	15.00	30.00
28 Curt Simmons	15.00	30.00
29 Stan Lopata	12.50	25.00
30 Bob Skinner	12.50	25.00
31 Ron Kline	12.50	25.00
32 Willie Miranda	12.50	25.00
33 Bobby Avila	12.50	25.00
34 Clem Labine	15.00	30.00
35 Ray Jablonski	12.50	25.00
36 Bill Mazeroski	40.00	80.00
37 Billy Gardner	12.50	25.00
38 Pete Runnels	12.50	25.00
39 Jack Sanford	12.50	25.00
40 Dave Sisler	12.50	25.00
41 Don Zimmer	15.00	30.00
42 Johnny Podres	15.00	30.00
43 Dick Farrell	12.50	25.00
44 Hank Aaron	200.00	400.00
45 Bill Virdon	12.50	25.00
46 Bobby Thomson	15.00	30.00
47 Willard Nixon	12.50	25.00
48 Billy Loes	12.50	25.00
49 Hank Sauer	15.00	30.00
50 Johnny Antonelli	15.00	30.00
51 Daryl Spencer	12.50	25.00
52 Ken Lehman	12.50	25.00
53 Sammy White	12.50	25.00
54 Charley Neal	12.50	25.00
55 Don Drysdale	60.00	120.00
56 Jackie Jensen	25.00	50.00
57 Ray Katt	12.50	25.00
58 Frank Sullivan	12.50	25.00
59 Roy Face	15.00	30.00
60 Willie Jones	12.50	25.00
61 Duke Snider	60.00	120.00
62 Whitey Lockman	12.50	25.00
63 Gino Cimoli	12.50	25.00
64 Marv Grissom	12.50	25.00
65 Gene Baker	12.50	25.00
66 George Zuverink	12.50	25.00
67 Ted Kluszewski	25.00	50.00
68 Jim Busby	12.50	25.00
69 Not Issued		
70 Curt Barclay	12.50	25.00
71 Hank Foiles	12.50	25.00
72 Gene Stephens	12.50	25.00
73 Al Worthington	12.50	25.00
74 Al Walker	12.50	25.00
75 Bob Boyd	12.50	25.00
76 Al Pilarcik	12.50	25.00

1958 Hires Root Beer Test

The cards in this eight-card test set measure approximately 2 5/16" by 3 1/2" or 2 5/16" by 7" with tabs. The 1958 Hires Root Beer test set features unnumbered, color cards. The card front photos are shown on a yellow or orange back ground instead of the wood grain background used in the Hires regular set. The cards contain a detachable coupon just as the regular Hires issue does. Cards were test marketed on a very limited basis in a few cities. Cards with the coupon still intact are especially tough to find and are worth triple the prices in the checklist below. The checklist below is ordered alphabetically.

COMPLETE SET (8)	750.00	1,500.00
1 Johnny Antonelli	100.00	200.00
2 Jim Busby	75.00	150.00
3 Chico Fernandez	75.00	150.00
4 Bob Friend	100.00	200.00
5 Vern Law	100.00	200.00
6 Stan Lopata	75.00	150.00
7 Willie Mays	500.00	1,000.00
8 Al Pilarcik	75.00	150.00

1959 Home Run Derby

Though commonly referenced as a 1959 release, this 20-card set was most likely produced in 1960 by American Motors to publicize a 1959 television program. Though the show was filmed in the 1959 off-season, it appears that the set was released in early 1960 based on the fact that Rocky Colavito was traded to the Tigers in April, 1960 and his card in the set lists him with the Tigers while showing him in an Indians uniform. The cards are black and white and blank backed. The cards measure approximately 3 1/8" by 5 1/4". The cards are unnumbered and are ordered alphabetically below for convenience. During 1988, the 19 player cards in this set were publicly reprinted.

COMPLETE SET (20)	3,000.00	6,000.00
1 Hank Aaron	300.00	600.00
2 Bob Allison	60.00	150.00
3 Ernie Banks	150.00	300.00
4 Ken Boyer	60.00	150.00
5 Bob Cerv	50.00	120.00
6 Rocky Colavito	150.00	300.00
7 Gil Hodges	150.00	300.00
8 Jackie Jensen	60.00	150.00
9 Al Kaline	200.00	400.00
10 Harmon Killabrew	250.00	500.00
11 Jim Lemon	50.00	120.00
12 Mickey Mantle	1,000.00	2,000.00
13 Eddie Mathews	200.00	400.00
14 Willie Mays	400.00	800.00
15 Wally Post	50.00	120.00
16 Frank Robinson	250.00	500.00
17 Mark Scott ANN	50.00	120.00
18 Duke Snider	200.00	400.00
19 Dick Stuart	60.00	150.00
20 Gus Triandos	50.00	120.00

1947 Homogenized Bond

The cards in this 48-card set measure approximately 2 1/4" by 3 1/2". The 1947 W571/D305 Homogenized Bread are sets of unnumbered cards containing 44 baseball players and four boxers. The W571 set exists in two styles. Style one is identical to the D305 set except for the back printing while style two has perforated edges and movie stars depicted on the backs. The second style of W571 cards contains only 13 cards. The four boxers in the checklist below are indicated by BOX. The checklist below is ordered alphabetically. There are 24 cards in the set which were definitely produced in greater supply. These 24 (marked by DP below) are quite a bit more common than the other 24 cards in the set.

COMPLETE SET	500.00	1,000.00
1 Rex Barney	6.00	12.00
2 Yogi Berra	100.00	200.00
3 Ewell Blackwell DP	1.00	2.00
4 Lou Boudreau DP	2.50	5.00
5 Ralph Branca	6.00	12.00
6 Harry Brecheen DP	1.00	2.00
9 Dom DiMaggio	7.50	15.00
10 Joe DiMaggio	125.00	250.00
11 Bobby Doerr DP	2.50	5.00
12 Bruce Edwards	6.00	12.00
13 Bob Elliott DP	1.00	2.00
14 Del Ennis DP	1.00	2.00
15 Bob Feller DP	6.00	12.00
16 Carl Furillo	10.00	20.00
17 Joe Gordon DP	1.00	2.00
18 Sid Gordon	6.00	12.00
19 Joe Hatten	6.00	12.00
20 Gil Hodges	40.00	80.00
21 Tommy Holmes DP	1.00	2.00
22 Larry Jansen	6.00	12.00
23 Sheldon Jones	6.00	12.00
24 Edwin Joost	6.00	12.00
25 Charlie Keller	7.50	15.00
26 Ken Keltner DP	1.00	2.00
27 Buddy Kerr	6.00	12.00
28 Ralph Kiner DP	4.00	8.00
30 John Lindell	6.00	12.00
31 Whitey Lockman	6.00	12.00
33 Willard Marshall	6.00	12.00
34 Johnny Mize DP	4.00	8.00
35 Stan Musial DP	25.00	50.00
36 Andy Pafko DP	1.00	2.00
37 Johnny Pesky DP	1.00	2.00
38 Pee Wee Reese	30.00	60.00
39 Phil Rizzuto DP	6.00	12.00
40 Aaron Robinson DP	1.00	2.00
41 Jackie Robinson DP	40.00	80.00
42 John Sain DP	2.50	5.00
43 Enos Slaughter DP	4.00	8.00
44 Vern Stephens DP	1.00	2.00
45 Birdie Tebbetts	6.00	12.00
46 Bobby Thomson	7.50	15.00
47 Johnny VanderMeer	7.50	15.00
48 Ted Williams DP	25.00	50.00

1927 Honey Boy Ice Cream

These 21 cards, which measure approximately 1 5/8" by 2 /38" feature a mix of major and minor league players.Honey Boy was a Canadian product. Some collectors refer to this set as the "Purity" set since that was the specific brand that these cards were inserted in. The first half of this set is dedicated to Canadian players while the second half is devoted to major leaguers. The cards were redeemable for a "brick" of Honey Boy Ice Cream. When all 21 cards were accumulated and sent in, the cards were then given a punch hole and returned to the lucky collector along with the brick.

COMPLETE SET (21)	7,000.00	14,000.00
COMMON MINORS (1-9)	150.00	300.00
COMMON MAJORS (10-21)	400.00	800.00
1 Steamer Maxwell Arenas	150.00	300.00
2 Cecil Brown Dominion Express	150.00	300.00
3 Carson McVey Transcona	150.00	300.00
4 Sam Perlman Tigers	150.00	300.00
5 Snake Siddle Arenas	150.00	300.00
6 Eddie Cass Columbus	150.00	300.00
7 Jimmy Bradley Columbus	150.00	300.00
8 Gordon Caslake Dominion Express	150.00	300.00
9 Ward McVey Tigers	150.00	300.00
10 Tris Speaker	750.00	1,500.00
11 George Sisler	750.00	1,500.00
12 Emil Meusel	400.00	800.00
13 Edd Roush	600.00	1,200.00
14 Babe Ruth	1,500.00	3,000.00
15 Harry Heilmann	600.00	1,200.00
16 Heinie Groh	400.00	800.00
17 Eddie Collins	750.00	1,500.00
18 Grover Alexander	750.00	1,500.00
19 Dave Bancroft	600.00	1,200.00
20 Frank Frisch	750.00	1,500.00
21 George Burns	400.00	800.00

1905-10 Carl Horner Cabinets

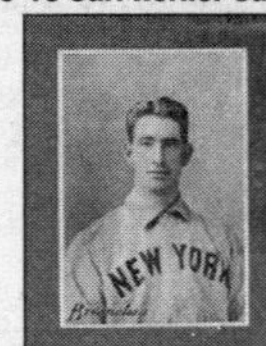

These portraits, which measure an approximate 5 1/2" by 7" feature photographs which were also used in the W600 set or later in the T206 set. These are rarely seen in the secondary market and since several cards were discovered recently, it is believed that there should be many additions to this checklists. Since these are unnumbered, we have sequenced them in alphabetical order.

COMPLETE SET	30,000.00	60,000.00
1 Doug Altizer		
2 Nick Altrock	1,000.00	2,000.00
3 Frank Arrelanes	1,000.00	2,000.00
4 Harry Barton	1,000.00	2,000.00
5 Jake Beckley	2,000.00	4,000.00
6 Heinie Berger		
7 Frank Bowerman		
8 Dave Brain		
9 Bill Bradley		
10 Kitty Bransfield		
11 Roger Bresnahan	2,000.00	4,000.00
12 Ray Collins		
13 Jack Cronin		
14 Bill Dahlen	1,000.00	2,000.00
15 Don Daub	1,000.00	2,000.00
16 Frank Delahanty		
17 Red Dooin		
18 Pat Donahue		
19 Mickey Doolan		
20 Fred Dunlap		
21 Kid Elberfeld	1,000.00	2,000.00
22 Rube Ellis	1,000.00	2,000.00
23 Dave Foutz MG	1,000.00	2,000.00
24 Billy Gilbert	1,000.00	2,000.00
25 Danny Green	1,000.00	2,000.00
26 John Grim	1,000.00	2,000.00
27 Mike Griffin	1,000.00	2,000.00
28 Otto Hess	1,000.00	2,000.00
29 Tom Jones		
30 Addie Joss	2,500.00	5,000.00
31 Brickyard Kennedy	1,000.00	2,000.00
32 Red Kleinow		
33 Harry Krause		
34 Rube Kroh	1,000.00	2,000.00
35 Nap Lajoie		
36 Tommy Leach		
37 Lefty Leifeld		
38 Bris Lord		
39 Sherry Magee		
40 George McBride		
41 Dan McGann		
42 Joe McGinnity	2,000.00	4,000.00
43 Deacon McGuire		
44 Sam Mertes		
45 Joe Mulvey	1,000.00	2,000.00
46 Danny Murphy		
47 Harry Niles	1,000.00	2,000.00
48 Fred Odwell		
49 Boss Schmidt		
50 Tris Speaker		
51 George Stovall	1,000.00	2,000.00
52 Sammy Strang		
53 Bill Sweeney		
54 John Taylor OWN		
55 Fred Tenney		
56 Joe Tinker	2,500.00	5,000.00
57 Kirby White		
58 Vic Willis	2,000.00	4,000.00
59 Hooks Wiltse	1,000.00	2,000.00
60 Art Wilson		
61 Joe Wood		
62 Cy Young	5,000.00	10,000.00

1975 Hostess

The cards in this 150-card set measure approximately 2 1/4" by 3 1/4" individually or 3 1/4" by 7 1/4" as panels of three. The 1975 Hostess set was issued in panels of three cards each on the backs of family-size packages of Hostess cakes. Card number 125, Bill Madlock, was listed correctly as an infielder and incorrectly as a pitcher. Number 11, Burt Hooton, and number 89, Doug Rader, are spelled two different ways. Some panels are more difficult to find than others as they were issued only on the backs of less popular Hostess products. These scarcer cards are shown with SP in the checklist. Although complete panel prices are not explicitly listed, they would generally have a value of 20-30 percent greater than the sum of the values of the individual players on that panel. One of the more interesting cards in the set is that of Robin Yount; Hostess issued one of the few Yount cards available in 1975, his rookie year for cards. An album to hold these cards was issued. The albums were originally intended to be given out in grocery stores. However, most seemingly were distributed through Hostess stores.

COMPLETE INDIV.SET (150)	100.00	200.00
COMMON CARD (1-150)	.15	.40
COMMON SP	.25	.60
1 Bob Tolan	.15	.40
2 Cookie Rojas	.15	.40
3 Darrell Evans	.25	.60
4 Sal Bando	.25	.60
5 Joe Morgan	1.25	3.00
6 Mickey Lolich	.25	.60
7 Don Sutton	1.25	3.00
8 Bill Melton	.15	.40
9 Tim Foli	.15	.40
10 Joe Lahoud	.15	.40
11A Burt Hooton ERR Misspelled Bert Hooten on card	.30	.75
11B Burt Hooton COR	.30	.75
12 Paul Blair	.15	.40
13 Jim Barr	.15	.40
14 Toby Harrah	.15	.40
15 John Milner	.15	.40
16 Ken Holtzman	.15	.40
17 Cesar Cedeno	.15	.40
18 Dwight Evans	.50	1.25
19 Willie McCovey	1.00	2.50
20 Tony Oliva	.50	1.25
21 Manny Sanguillen	.15	.40
22 Mickey Rivers	.15	.40
23 Lou Brock	1.25	3.00
24 Graig Nettles UER Craig on front	.50	1.25
25 Jim Wynn	.15	.40
26 George Scott	.15	.40
27 Greg Luzinski	.30	.75
28 Bert Campaneris	.25	.60
29 Pete Rose	3.00	8.00
30 Buddy Bell	.30	.75
31 Gary Matthews	.25	.60
32 Freddie Patek	.15	.40
33 Mike Lum	.15	.40
34 Ellie Rodriguez	.15	.40
35 Milt May UER Photo actually Lee May	.15	.40
36 Willie Horton	.25	.60
37 Dave Winfield	6.00	15.00
38 Tom Grieve	.15	.40
39 Barry Foote	.15	.40
40 Joe Rudi	.15	.40
41 Bake McBride	.15	.40
42 Mike Cuellar	.15	.40
43 Garry Maddox	.15	.40
44 Carlos May	.15	.40
45 Bud Harrelson	.15	.40
46 Dave Chalk	.15	.40
47 Dave Concepcion	.50	1.25
48 Carl Yastrzemski	1.50	4.00
49 Steve Garvey	.75	2.00
50 Amos Otis	.15	.40
51 Rick Reuschel	.15	.40
52 Rollie Fingers	1.00	2.50
53 Bob Watson	.25	.60
54 John Ellis	.15	.40
55 Bob Bailey	.15	.40
56 Rod Carew	1.50	4.00
57 Rich Hebner	.15	.40
58 Nolan Ryan	12.50	30.00
59 Reggie Smith	.25	.60
60 Joe Coleman	.15	.40
61 Ron Cey	.25	.60
62 Darrell Porter	.25	.60
63 Steve Carlton	1.50	4.00
64 Gene Tenace	.15	.40
65 Jose Cardenal	.15	.40
66 Bill Lee	.15	.40

67 Dave Lopes	.25	.60
68 Wilbur Wood	.15	.40
69 Steve Renko	.15	.40
70 Joe Torre	.50	1.25
71 Ted Sizemore	.15	.40
72 Bobby Grich	.25	.60
73 Chris Speier	.15	.40
74 Bert Blyleven	.30	.75
75 Tom Seaver	3.00	8.00
76 Nate Colbert	.15	.40
77 Don Kessinger	.15	.40
78 George Medich	.15	.40
79 Andy Messersmith SP	.25	.60
80 Robin Yount SP	12.50	30.00
81 Al Oliver SP	.30	.75
82 Bill Singer SP	.25	.60
83 Johnny Bench SP	4.00	10.00
84 Gaylord Perry SP	1.25	3.00
85 Dave Kingman SP	.60	1.50
86 Ed Herrmann SP	.25	.60
87 Ralph Garr SP	.25	.60
88 Reggie Jackson SP	4.00	10.00
89A Doug Rader ERR SP Misspelled Radar	.50	1.25
89B Doug Rader COR SP	2.00	5.00
90 Elliott Maddox SP	.25	.60
91 Bill Russell SP	.50	1.25
92 John Mayberry SP	.25	.60
93 Dave Cash SP	.25	.60
94 Jeff Burroughs SP	.25	.60
95 Ted Simmons SP	.60	1.50
96 Joe Decker SP	.25	.60
97 Bill Buckner SP	.50	1.25
98 Bobby Darwin SP	.25	.60
99 Phil Niekro SP	1.25	3.00
100 Jim Sundberg	.15	.40
101 Greg Gross	.15	.40
102 Luis Tiant	.30	.75
103 Glenn Beckert	.15	.40
104 Hal McRae	.25	.60
105 Mike Jorgensen	.15	.40
106 Mike Hargrove	.50	1.25
107 Don Gullett	.25	.60
108 Tito Fuentes	.15	.40
109 John Grubb	.15	.40
110 Jim Kaat	.30	.75
111 Felix Millan	.15	.40
112 Don Money	.15	.40
113 Rick Monday	.15	.40
114 Dick Bosman	.15	.40
115 Roger Metzger	.15	.40
116 Fergie Jenkins	1.00	2.50
117 Dusty Baker	.30	.75
118 Billy Champion SP	.25	.60
119 Bob Gibson SP	1.50	4.00
120 Bill Freehan SP	.30	.75
121 Cesar Geronimo	.15	.40
122 Jorge Orta	.15	.40
123 Cleon Jones	.15	.40
124 Steve Busby	.15	.40
125A Bill Madlock ERR Pitcher	.50	1.25
125B Bill Madlock COR Infielder	.50	1.25
126 Jim Palmer	1.25	3.00
127 Tony Perez	.75	2.00
128 Larry Hisle	.15	.40
129 Rusty Staub	.30	.75
130 Hank Aaron SP	6.00	15.00
131 Rennie Stennett SP	.25	.60
132 Rico Petrocelli SP	.30	.75
133 Mike Schmidt	6.00	15.00
134 Sparky Lyle	.30	.75
135 Willie Stargell	1.00	2.50
136 Ken Henderson	.15	.40
137 Willie Montanez	.15	.40
138 Thurman Munson	1.00	2.50
139 Richie Zisk	.15	.40
140 George Hendrick UER named spelled Hendricks	.15	.40
141 Bobby Murcer	.25	.60
142 Lee May UER name in all CAPS on back	.15	.40
143 Carlton Fisk	3.00	8.00
144 Brooks Robinson	1.50	4.00
145 Bobby Bonds	.50	1.25
146 Gary Sutherland	.15	.40
147 Oscar Gamble	.15	.40
148 Jim Hunter	1.25	3.00
149 Tug McGraw	.30	.75
150 Dave McNally	.25	.60
NNO Album	2.50	6.00

1975 Hostess Twinkie

The cards in this 60-card set measure approximately 2 1/4" by 3 1/4". The 1975 Hostess Twinkie set was issued on a limited basis in the far western part of the country. The set contains the same numbers as the regular set to number 36; however, the set is skip numbered after number 36. The cards were issued as the backs for 25-cent Twinkies packs. The fronts are indistinguishable from the regular Hostess cards; however the card backs are different in that the Twinkie cards have a thick black bar in the middle of the reverse. The cards are frequently found with product stains. One of the more interesting cards in the set is that of Robin Yount; Hostess issued one of the few Yount cards available in 1975, his rookie year for cards.

COMPLETE SET (60)	75.00	150.00
1 Bob Tolan	.40	1.00
2 Cookie Rojas	.40	1.00
3 Darrell Evans	.60	1.50
4 Sal Bando	.60	1.50
5 Joe Morgan	2.50	6.00
6 Mickey Lolich	.75	2.00
7 Don Sutton	2.00	5.00
8 Bill Melton	.40	1.00
9 Tim Foli	.40	1.00
10 Joe Lahoud	.40	1.00
11 Burt Hooton UER/(Misspelled Bert Hooten on card)	.40	1.00
12 Paul Blair	.40	1.00
13 Jim Barr	.40	1.00
14 Toby Harrah	.40	1.00
15 John Milner	.40	1.00
16 Ken Holtzman	.40	1.00
17 Cesar Cedeno	.60	1.50
18 Dwight Evans	1.00	2.50
19 Willie McCovey	2.00	5.00
20 Tony Oliva	.75	2.00
21 Manny Sanguillen	.40	1.00
22 Mickey Rivers	.40	1.00
23 Lou Brock	2.50	6.00
24 Graig Nettles UER/(Craig on front)	1.00	2.50
25 Jim Wynn	.60	1.50
26 George Scott	.40	1.00
27 Greg Luzinski	.60	1.50
28 Bert Campaneris	.60	1.50
29 Pete Rose	6.00	15.00
30 Buddy Bell	.75	2.00
31 Gary Matthews	.60	1.50
32 Freddie Patek	.40	1.00
33 Mike Lum	.40	1.00
34 Ellie Rodriguez	.40	1.00
35 Milt May UER/(Lee May picture)	.40	1.00
36 Willie Horton	.60	1.50
40 Joe Rudi	.60	1.50
43 Garry Maddox	.40	1.00
46 Dave Chalk	.40	1.00
49 Steve Garvey	1.50	4.00
52 Rollie Fingers	2.00	5.00
58 Nolan Ryan	20.00	50.00
61 Ron Cey	.75	2.00
64 Gene Tenace	.40	1.00
65 Jose Cardenal	.40	1.00
67 Dave Lopes	.75	2.00
68 Wilbur Wood	.40	1.00
73 Chris Speier	.40	1.00
77 Don Kessinger	.40	1.00
79 Andy Messersmith	.40	1.00
80 Robin Yount	12.50	40.00
82 Bill Singer	.40	1.00
103 Glenn Beckert	.40	1.00
110 Jim Kaat	.75	2.00
112 Don Money	.60	1.50
113 Rick Monday	.60	1.50
122 Jorge Orta	.40	1.00
125 Bill Madlock	.75	2.00
130 Hank Aaron	8.00	20.00
136 Ken Henderson	.40	1.00
XX Checklist	10.00	25.00

1976 Hostess

The cards in this 150-card set measure approximately 2 1/4" by 3 1/4" individually or 3 1/4" by 7 1/4" as panels of three. The 1976 Hostess set contains full-color, numbered cards issued in panels of three cards each on family-size packages of Hostess cakes. Scarcer panels (those only found on less popular Hostess products) are listed in the checklist below with SP. Complete panels of three have a value 20-30 percent more than the sum of the individual cards on the panel. Nine additional numbers (151-159) were apparently planned but never actually issued. These exist as proof cards and are quite scarce, e.g., 151 Ferguson Jenkins (even though he already appears in the set as card number 138), 152 Mike Cuellar, 153 Tom Murphy, 154 Al Cowens, 155 Barry Foote, 156 Steve Carlton, 157 Richie Zisk, 158 Ken Holtzman, and 159 Cliff Johnson. One of the more interesting cards in the set is that of Dennis Eckersley; Hostess issued one of the few Eckersley cards available in 1976, his rookie year for cards. An album to hold these cards were issued. Many of these cards were issued with brown printing on the back, those cards are valued the same as the black printed cards.

COMPLETE INDIV.SET (150)	150.00	300.00
COMMON CARD (1-150)	.20	.50
COMMON SP	.30	.75
1 Fred Lynn	.60	1.50
2 Joe Morgan	1.50	4.00
3 Phil Niekro	1.50	4.00
4 Gaylord Perry	1.25	3.00
5 Bob Watson	.30	.75
6 Bill Freehan	.30	.75
7 Lou Brock	1.50	4.00
8 Al Fitzmorris	.20	.50
9 Rennie Stennett	.20	.50
10 Tony Oliva	.60	1.50
11 Robin Yount	8.00	20.00
12 Rick Manning	.20	.50
13 Bobby Grich	.30	.75
14 Terry Forster	.20	.50
15 Dave Kingman	.40	1.00
16 Thurman Munson	1.25	3.00
17 Rick Reuschel	.20	.50
18 Bobby Bonds	.60	1.50
19 Steve Garvey	1.00	2.50
20 Vida Blue	.30	.75
21 Dave Rader	.20	.50
22 Johnny Bench	3.00	8.00
23 Luis Tiant	.30	.75
24 Darrell Evans	.30	.75
25 Larry Dierker	.20	.50
26 Willie Horton	.30	.75
27 John Ellis	.20	.50
28 Al Cowens	.20	.50
29 Jerry Reuss	.20	.50
30 Reggie Smith	.30	.75
31 Bobby Darwin SP	.30	.75
32 Fritz Peterson SP	.30	.75
33 Rod Carew SP	4.00	10.00
34 Carlos May SP	.30	.75
35 Tom Seaver SP	6.00	15.00
36 Brooks Robinson SP	4.00	10.00
37 Jose Cardenal	.20	.50
38 Ron Blomberg	.20	.50
39 Leroy Stanton	.20	.50
40 Dave Cash	.20	.50
41 John Montefusco	.20	.50
42 Bob Tolan	.20	.50
43 Carl Morton	.20	.50
44 Rick Burleson	.20	.50
45 Don Gullett	.20	.50
46 Vern Ruhle	.20	.50
47 Cesar Cedeno	.30	.75
48 Toby Harrah	.20	.50
49 Willie Stargell	1.25	3.00
50 Al Hrabosky	.20	.50
51 Amos Otis	.20	.50
52 Bud Harrelson	.20	.50
53 Jim Hughes	.20	.50
54 George Scott	.20	.50
55 Mike Vail SP	.30	.75
56 Jim Palmer SP	2.50	6.00
57 Jorge Orta SP	.30	.75
58 Chris Chambliss SP	.40	1.00
59 Dave Chalk SP	.30	.75
60 Ray Burris SP	.30	.75
61 Bert Campaneris SP	.40	1.00
62 Gary Carter SP	6.00	15.00
63 Ron Cey SP	.60	1.50
64 Carlton Fisk SP	6.00	15.00
65 Marty Perez SP	.30	.75
66 Pete Rose SP	8.00	20.00
67 Roger Metzger SP	.30	.75
68 Jim Sundberg SP	.30	.75
69 Ron LeFlore SP	.30	.75
70 Ted Sizemore SP	.30	.75
71 Steve Busby SP	.30	.75
72 Manny Sanguillen SP	.30	.75
73 Larry Hisle SP	.30	.75
74 Pete Broberg SP	.30	.75
75 Boog Powell SP	.75	2.00
76 Ken Singleton SP	.40	1.00
77 Goose Gossage SP	.75	2.00
78 Jerry Grote SP	.30	.75
79 Nolan Ryan SP	20.00	50.00
80 Rick Monday SP	.40	1.00
81 Graig Nettles SP	.75	2.00
82 Chris Speier	.20	.50
83 Dave Winfield	5.00	12.00
84 Mike Schmidt	6.00	15.00
85 Buzz Capra	.20	.50
86 Tony Perez	1.00	2.50
87 Dwight Evans	.60	1.50
88 Mike Hargrove	.30	.75
89 Joe Coleman	.20	.50
90 Greg Gross	.20	.50
91 John Mayberry	.20	.50
92 John Candelaria	.30	.75
93 Bake McBride	.20	.50
94 Hank Aaron	6.00	15.00
95 Buddy Bell	.30	.75
96 Steve Braun	.20	.50
97 Jon Matlack	.20	.50
98 Lee May	.20	.50
99 Wilbur Wood	.20	.50
100 Bill Madlock	.30	.75
101 Frank Tanana	.30	.75
102 Mickey Rivers	.20	.50
103 Mike Ivie	.20	.50
104 Rollie Fingers	1.25	3.00
105 Dave Lopes	.30	.75
106 George Foster	.40	1.00
107 Denny Doyle	.20	.50
108 Earl Williams	.20	.50
109 Tom Veryzer	.20	.50
110 J.R. Richard	.20	.50
111 Jeff Burroughs	.20	.50
112 Al Oliver	.30	.75
113 Ted Simmons	.40	1.00
114 George Brett	12.50	40.00
115 Frank Duffy	.20	.50
116 Bert Blyleven	.40	1.00
117 Darrell Porter	.20	.50
118 Don Baylor	.40	1.00
119 Bucky Dent	.30	.75
120 Felix Millan	.20	.50
121 Mike Cuellar	.20	.50
122 Gene Tenace	.20	.50
123 Bobby Murcer	.30	.75
124 Willie McCovey	1.25	3.00
125 Greg Luzinski	.30	.75
126 Larry Parrish	.20	.50
127 Jim Rice	.75	2.00
128 Dave Concepcion	.40	1.00
129 Jim Wynn	.20	.50
130 Tom Grieve	.20	.50
131 Mike Cosgrove	.20	.50
132 Dan Meyer	.20	.50
133 Dave Parker	.75	2.00
134 Don Kessinger	.20	.50
135 Hal McRae	.30	.75
136 Don Money	.20	.50
137 Dennis Eckersley	8.00	20.00
138 Fergie Jenkins	1.25	3.00
139 Mike Torrez	.20	.50
140 Jerry Morales	.20	.50
141 Jim Hunter	1.25	3.00
142 Gary Matthews	.20	.50
143 Randy Jones	.20	.50
144 Mike Jorgensen	.20	.50
145 Larry Bowa	.30	.75
146 Reggie Jackson	4.00	10.00
147 Steve Yeager	.20	.50
148 Dave May	.20	.50
149 Carl Yastrzemski	2.50	6.00
150 Cesar Geronimo	.20	.50
XX Album	3.00	8.00

1976 Hostess Twinkie

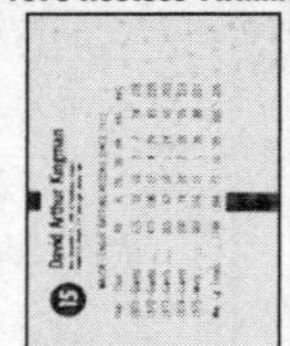

The cards in this 60-card set measure approximately 2 1/4" by 3 1/4". The 1976 Hostess Twinkies set contains the first 60 cards of the 1976 Hostess set. These cards were issued as backs on 25-cent Twinkie packages as in the 1975 Twinkies set. The fronts are indistinguishable from the regular Hostess cards; however the card backs are different in that the Twinkie cards have a thick black bar in the middle of the reverse. The cards are frequently found with product stains.

COMPLETE SET (60)	60.00	120.00
1 Fred Lynn	1.00	2.50
2 Joe Morgan	2.50	6.00
3 Phil Niekro	2.00	5.00
4 Gaylord Perry	2.00	5.00
5 Bob Watson	.60	1.50
6 Bill Freehan	.60	1.50
7 Lou Brock	2.00	5.00
8 Al Fitzmorris	.40	1.00
9 Rennie Stennett	.40	1.00
10 Tony Oliva	1.00	2.50
11 Robin Yount	6.00	15.00
12 Rick Manning	.40	1.00
13 Bobby Grich	.60	1.50
14 Terry Forster	.40	1.00
15 Dave Kingman	1.00	2.50
16 Thurman Munson	2.50	6.00
17 Rick Reuschel	.60	1.50
18 Bobby Bonds	1.00	2.50
19 Steve Garvey	2.50	6.00
20 Vida Blue	.75	2.00
21 Dave Rader	.40	1.00
22 Johnny Bench	4.00	10.00
23 Luis Tiant	.60	1.50
24 Darrell Evans	.60	1.50
25 Larry Dierker	.40	1.00
26 Willie Horton	.60	1.50
27 John Ellis	.40	1.00
28 Al Cowens	.40	1.00
29 Jerry Reuss	.60	1.50
30 Reggie Smith	.60	1.50
31 Bobby Darwin	.40	1.00
32 Fritz Peterson	.40	1.00
33 Rod Carew	2.50	6.00
34 Carlos May	.40	1.00
35 Tom Seaver	4.00	10.00
36 Brooks Robinson	2.50	6.00
37 Jose Cardenal	.40	1.00
38 Ron Blomberg	.40	1.00
39 Leroy Stanton	.40	1.00
40 Dave Cash	.40	1.00
41 John Montefusco	.40	1.00
42 Bob Tolan	.40	1.00
43 Carl Morton	.40	1.00
44 Rick Burleson	.60	1.50
45 Don Gullett	.60	1.50
46 Vern Ruhle	.40	1.00
47 Cesar Cedeno	.60	1.50
48 Toby Harrah	.60	1.50
49 Willie Stargell	2.00	5.00
50 Al Hrabosky	.60	1.50
51 Amos Otis	.60	1.50
52 Bud Harrelson	.60	1.50
53 Jim Hughes	.60	1.50
54 George Scott	.60	1.50
55 Mike Vail	.60	1.50
56 Jim Palmer	2.00	5.00
57 Jorge Orta	.40	1.00
58 Chris Chambliss	.75	2.00
59 Dave Chalk	.40	1.00
60 Ray Burris	.40	1.00

1977 Hostess

The cards in this 150-card set measure approximately 2 1/4" by 3 1/4" individually or 3 1/4" by 7 1/4" as panels of three.

The 1977 Hostess set contains full-color, numbered cards issued in panels of three cards each with Hostess family-size cake products. Scarcer cards are listed in the checklist below with SP. Although complete panel prices are not explicitly listed below, they would generally have a value 20-30 percent greater than the sum of the individual players on the panel. There were ten additional cards proofed, but not produced or distributed; they are 151 Ed Kranepool, 152 Ross Grimsley, 153 Ken Brett, 154 Rowland Office, 155 Rick Wise, 156 Paul Splittorff, 157 Gerald Augustine, 158 Ken Forsch, 159 Jerry Reuss (Reuss is also number 119 in the set), and 160 Nelson Briles. An album to hold these cards were issued.

COMPLETE INDIV.SET (150) 125.00 250.00
COMMON CARD (1-150) .20 .50
COMMON SP .30 .75
1 Jim Palmer 1.50 4.00
2 Joe Morgan 1.50 4.00
3 Reggie Jackson 4.00 10.00
4 Carl Yastrzemski 2.50 6.00
5 Thurman Munson 1.25 3.00
6 Johnny Bench 3.00 8.00
7 Tom Seaver 3.00 8.00
8 Pete Rose 4.00 10.00
9 Rod Carew 1.50 4.00
10 Luis Tiant .30 .75
11 Phil Garner .30 .75
12 Sixto Lezcano .20 .50
13 Mike Torrez .20 .50
14 Dave Lopes .30 .75
15 Doug DeCinces .20 .50
16 Jim Spencer .20 .50
17 Hal McRae .30 .75
18 Mike Hargrove .30 .75
19 Willie Montanez SP .30 .75
20 Roger Metzger SP .30 .75
21 Dwight Evans SP .75 2.00
22 Steve Rogers SP .30 .75
23 Jim Rice SP 1.00 2.50
24 Pete Falcone SP .30 .75
25 Greg Luzinski SP .60 1.50
26 Randy Jones SP .30 .75
27 Willie Stargell SP 2.00 5.00
28 John Hiller SP .30 .75
29 Bobby Murcer SP .75 2.00
30 Rick Monday SP .40 1.00
31 John Montefusco SP .30 .75
32 Lou Brock SP 2.00 5.00
33 Bill North SP .30 .75
34 Robin Yount SP 10.00 25.00
35 Steve Garvey SP 2.00 5.00
36 George Brett SP 12.50 35.00
37 Toby Harrah SP .30 .75
38 Jerry Royster SP .30 .75
39 Bob Watson SP .40 1.00
40 George Foster .30 .75
41 Gary Carter 1.50 4.00
42 John Denny .20 .50
43 Mike Schmidt 5.00 12.00
44 Dave Winfield 4.00 10.00
45 Al Oliver .30 .75
46 Mark Fidrych 1.25 3.00
47 Larry Herndon .20 .50
48 Dave Goltz .20 .50
49 Jerry Morales .20 .50
50 Ron LeFlore .20 .50
51 Fred Lynn .30 .75
52 Vida Blue .30 .75
53 Rick Manning .20 .50
54 Bill Buckner .30 .75
55 Lee May .30 .75
56 John Mayberry .20 .50
57 Darrel Chaney .20 .50
58 Cesar Cedeno .30 .75
59 Ken Griffey .40 1.00
60 Dave Kingman .40 1.00
61 Ted Simmons .40 1.00
62 Larry Bowa .30 .75
63 Frank Tanana .30 .75
64 Jason Thompson .20 .50
65 Ken Brett .20 .50
66 Roy Smalley .20 .50
67 Ray Burris .20 .50
68 Rick Burleson .20 .50
69 Buddy Bell .30 .75
70 Don Sutton 1.50 4.00
71 Mark Belanger .20 .50
72 Dennis Leonard .20 .50
73 Gaylord Perry 1.25 3.00
74 Dick Ruthven .20 .50
75 Jose Cruz .30 .75
76 Cesar Geronimo .20 .50
77 Jerry Koosman .30 .75
78 Garry Templeton .20 .50
79 Jim Hunter 1.25 3.00
80 John Candelaria .20 .50
81 Nolan Ryan 12.50 40.00
82 Rusty Staub .30 .75
83 Jim Barr .20 .50
84 Butch Wynegar .30 .75
85 Jose Cardenal .20 .50
86 Claudell Washington .20 .50
87 Bill Travers .20 .50
88 Rick Waits .20 .50
89 Ron Cey .30 .75
90 Al Bumbry .20 .50
91 Bucky Dent .30 .75
92 Amos Otis .20 .50
93 Tom Grieve .20 .50
94 Enos Cabell .20 .50
95 Dave Concepcion .40 1.00
96 Felix Millan .20 .50
97 Bake McBride .20 .50
98 Chris Chambliss .30 .75
99 Butch Metzger .20 .50
100 Rennie Stennett .20 .50
101 Dave Roberts .20 .50
102 Lyman Bostock .30 .75
103 Rick Reuschel .20 .50
104 Carlton Fisk 4.00 10.00
105 Jim Slaton .20 .50
106 Dennis Eckersley 3.00 8.00
107 Ken Singleton .20 .50
108 Ralph Garr .20 .50
109 Freddie Patek SP .30 .75
110 Jim Sundberg SP .30 .75
111 Phil Niekro SP 2.00 5.00
112 J.R. Richard SP .30 .75
113 Gary Nolan SP .30 .75
114 Jon Matlack SP .30 .75
115 Keith Hernandez SP .75 2.00
116 Graig Nettles SP .60 1.50
117 Steve Carlton SP 3.00 8.00
118 Bill Madlock SP .60 1.50
119 Jerry Reuss SP .40 1.00
120 Aurelio Rodriguez SP .30 .75
121 Dan Ford SP .30 .75
122 Ray Fosse SP .30 .75
123 George Hendrick SP .30 .75
124 Alan Ashby .20 .50
125 Joe Lis .20 .50
126 Sal Bando .20 .50
127 Richie Zisk .20 .50
128 Rich Gossage .60 1.50
129 Don Baylor .30 .75
130 Dave McKay .20 .50
131 Bob Grich .30 .75
132 Dave Pagan .20 .50
133 Dave Cash .20 .50
134 Steve Braun .20 .50
135 Dan Meyer .20 .50
136 Bill Stein .20 .50
137 Rollie Fingers 1.25 3.00
138 Brian Downing .20 .50
139 Bill Singer .20 .50
140 Doyle Alexander .20 .50
141 Gene Tenace .20 .50
142 Gary Matthews .20 .50
143 Don Gullett .20 .50
144 Wayne Garland .20 .50
145 Pete Broberg .20 .50
146 Joe Rudi .20 .50
147 Glenn Abbott .20 .50
148 George Scott .20 .50
149 Bert Campaneris .20 .50
150 Andy Messersmith .20 .50
XX Album 3.00 8.00

1977 Hostess Twinkie

COMPLETE SET (150) 175.00 350.00
1 Jim Palmer 2.50 6.00
2 Joe Morgan 2.50 6.00
3 Reggie Jackson 6.00 15.00
4 Carl Yastrzemski 4.00 10.00
5 Thurman Munson 2.00 5.00
6 Johnny Bench 5.00 12.00
7 Tom Seaver 5.00 12.00
8 Pete Rose 6.00 15.00
9 Rod Carew 2.50 6.00
10 Luis Tiant .50 1.25
11 Phil Garner .50 1.25
12 Sixto Lezcano .30 .75
13 Mike Torrez .30 .75
14 Dave Lopes .50 1.25
15 Doug DeCinces .30 .75
16 Jim Spencer .30 .75
17 Hal McRae .50 1.25
18 Mike Hargrove .50 1.25
19 Willie Montanez .50 1.25
20 Roger Metzger .50 1.25
21 Dwight Evans 1.25 3.00
22 Steve Rogers .50 1.25
23 Jim Rice 1.50 4.00
24 Pete Falcone .50 1.25
25 Greg Luzinski 1.00 2.50
26 Randy Jones .50 1.25
27 Willie Stargell 3.00 8.00
28 John Hiller .50 1.25
29 Bobby Murcer 1.25 3.00
30 Rick Monday .60 1.50
31 John Montefusco .50 1.25
32 Lou Brock 3.00 8.00
33 Bill North .50 1.25
34 Robin Yount 15.00 40.00
35 Steve Garvey 3.00 8.00
36 George Brett 20.00 50.00
37 Toby Harrah .50 1.25
38 Jerry Royster .50 1.25
39 Bob Watson .60 1.50
40 George Foster .50 1.25
41 Gary Carter 2.50 6.00
42 John Denny .30 .75
43 Mike Schmidt 8.00 20.00
44 Dave Winfield 6.00 15.00
45 Al Oliver .50 1.25
46 Mark Fidrych 2.00 5.00
47 Larry Herndon .30 .75
48 Dave Goltz .30 .75
49 Jerry Morales .30 .75
50 Ron LeFlore .30 .75
51 Fred Lynn .50 1.25
52 Vida Blue .50 1.25
53 Rick Manning .30 .75
54 Bill Buckner .50 1.25
55 Lee May .50 1.25
56 John Mayberry .30 .75
57 Darrel Chaney .30 .75
58 Cesar Cedeno .50 1.25
59 Ken Griffey .60 1.50
60 Dave Kingman .60 1.50
61 Ted Simmons .60 1.50
62 Larry Bowa .50 1.25
63 Frank Tanana .50 1.25
64 Jason Thompson .30 .75
65 Ken Brett .30 .75
66 Roy Smalley .30 .75
67 Ray Burris .30 .75
68 Rick Burleson .30 .75
69 Buddy Bell .50 1.25
70 Don Sutton 2.50 6.00
71 Mark Belanger .30 .75
72 Dennis Leonard .30 .75
73 Gaylord Perry 2.00 5.00
74 Dick Ruthven .30 .75
75 Jose Cruz .50 1.25
76 Cesar Geronimo .30 .75
77 Jerry Koosman .50 1.25
78 Garry Templeton .30 .75
79 Jim Hunter 2.00 5.00
80 John Candelaria .30 .75
81 Nolan Ryan 20.00 50.00
82 Rusty Staub .50 1.25
83 Jim Barr .30 .75
84 Butch Wynegar .50 1.25
85 Jose Cardenal .30 .75
86 Claudell Washington .30 .75
87 Bill Travers .30 .75
88 Rick Waits .30 .75
89 Ron Cey .50 1.25
90 Al Bumbry .30 .75
91 Bucky Dent .50 1.25
92 Amos Otis .30 .75
93 Tom Grieve .30 .75
94 Enos Cabell .30 .75
95 Dave Concepcion .60 1.50
96 Felix Millan .30 .75
97 Bake McBride .30 .75
98 Chris Chambliss .50 1.25
99 Butch Metzger .30 .75
100 Rennie Stennett .30 .75
101 Dave Roberts .30 .75
102 Lyman Bostock .50 1.25
103 Rick Reuschel .30 .75
104 Carlton Fisk 6.00 15.00
105 Jim Slaton .30 .75
106 Dennis Eckersley 5.00 12.00
107 Ken Singleton .30 .75
108 Ralph Garr .30 .75
109 Freddie Patek .50 1.25
110 Jim Sundberg .50 1.25
111 Phil Niekro 3.00 8.00
112 J.R. Richard .50 1.25
113 Gary Nolan .50 1.25
114 Jon Matlack .50 1.25
115 Keith Hernandez 1.25 3.00
116 Graig Nettles 1.00 2.50
117 Steve Carlton 5.00 12.00
118 Bill Madlock 1.00 2.50
119 Jerry Reuss .60 1.50
120 Aurelio Rodriguez .50 1.25
121 Dan Ford .50 1.25
122 Ray Fosse .50 1.25
123 George Hendrick .50 1.25
124 Alan Ashby .30 .75
125 Joe Lis .30 .75
126 Sal Bando .30 .75
127 Richie Zisk .30 .75
128 Rich Gossage 1.00 2.50
129 Don Baylor .50 1.25
130 Dave McKay .30 .75
131 Bob Grich .50 1.25
132 Dave Pagan .30 .75
133 Dave Cash .30 .75
134 Steve Braun .30 .75
135 Dan Meyer .30 .75
136 Bill Stein .30 .75
137 Rollie Fingers 2.00 5.00
138 Brian Downing .30 .75
139 Bill Singer .30 .75
140 Doyle Alexander .30 .75
141 Gene Tenace .30 .75
142 Gary Matthews .30 .75
143 Don Gullett .30 .75
144 Wayne Garland .30 .75
145 Pete Broberg .30 .75
146 Joe Rudi .30 .75
147 Glenn Abbott .30 .75
148 George Scott .30 .75
149 Bert Campaneris .30 .75
150 Andy Messersmith .30 .75

1978 Hostess

The cards in this 150-card set measure approximately 2 1/4" by 3 1/4" individually or 3 1/4" by 7 1/4" as panels of three. The 1978 Hostess set contains full-color, numbered cards issued in panels of three cards each on family packages of Hostess cake products. Scarcer cards are listed in the checklist with SP. The 1978 Hostess panels are considered by some collectors to be somewhat more difficult to obtain than Hostess panels of other years. Although complete panel prices are not explicitly listed below, they would generally have a value 20-25 percent greater than the sum of the individual players on the panel. There is additional interest in Eddie Murray number 31, since this card corresponds to his rookie year in cards. An album to hold all these cards were issued. There was an album issued for these cards. It is priced below.

COMPLETE INDIV.SET (150) 125.00 250.00
COMMON CARD (1-150) .20 .50
COMMON SP .30 .75
1 Butch Hobson .20 .50
2 George Foster .30 .75
3 Bob Forsch .20 .50
4 Tony Perez .60 1.50
5 Bruce Sutter .60 1.50
6 Hal McRae .30 .75
7 Tommy John .60 1.50
8 Greg Luzinski .30 .75
9 Enos Cabell .20 .50
10 Doug DeCinces .20 .50
11 Willie Stargell 1.25 3.00
12 Ed Halicki .20 .50
13 Larry Hisle .20 .50
14 Jim Slaton .20 .50
15 Buddy Bell .30 .75
16 Earl Williams .20 .50
17 Glenn Abbott .20 .50
18 Dan Ford .20 .50
19 Gary Matthews .20 .50
20 Eric Soderholm .20 .50
21 Bump Wills .20 .50
22 Keith Hernandez .60 1.50
23 Dave Cash .20 .50
24 George Scott .20 .50
25 Ron Guidry .60 1.50
26 Dave Kingman .40 1.00
27 George Brett 10.00 25.00
28 Bob Watson SP .40 1.00
29 Bob Boone SP .60 1.50
30 Reggie Smith SP .40 1.00
31 Eddie Murray SP 12.50 40.00
32 Gary Lavelle SP .30 .75
33 Rennie Stennett SP .30 .75
34 Duane Kuiper SP .30 .75
35 Sixto Lezcano SP .30 .75
36 Dave Rozema SP .30 .75
37 Butch Wynegar SP .30 .75
38 Mitchell Page SP .30 .75
39 Bill Stein SP .30 .75
40 Elliott Maddox .20 .50
41 Mike Hargrove .30 .75
42 Bobby Bonds .60 1.50
43 Garry Templeton .20 .50
44 Johnny Bench 3.00 8.00
45 Jim Rice .75 2.00
46 Bill Buckner .30 .75
47 Reggie Jackson 3.00 8.00
48 Freddie Patek .20 .50
49 Steve Carlton 1.50 4.00
50 Cesar Cedeno .30 .75
51 Steve Yeager .20 .50
52 Phil Garner .30 .75
53 Lee May .30 .75
54 Darrell Evans .30 .75
55 Steve Kemp .20 .50
56 Dusty Baker .30 .75
57 Ray Fosse .20 .50
58 Manny Sanguillen .20 .50
59 Tom Johnson .20 .50
60 Lee Stanton .20 .50
61 Jeff Burroughs .20 .50
62 Bobby Grich .30 .75
63 Dave Winfield 3.00 8.00
64 Dan Driessen .20 .50
65 Ted Simmons .40 1.00
66 Jerry Remy .20 .50
67 Al Cowens .20 .50
68 Sparky Lyle .30 .75
69 Manny Trillo .20 .50
70 Don Sutton 1.25 3.00
71 Larry Bowa .30 .75
72 Jose Cruz .30 .75
73 Willie McCovey 1.25 3.00
74 Bert Blyleven .40 1.00
75 Ken Singleton .20 .50
76 Bill North .20 .50
77 Jason Thompson .20 .50
78 Dennis Eckersley 2.00 5.00
79 Jim Sundberg .20 .50
80 Jerry Koosman .30 .75
81 Bruce Bochte .20 .50
82 George Hendrick .20 .50
83 Nolan Ryan 12.50 40.00
84 Roy Howell .20 .50
85 Butch Metzger .20 .50
86 Doc Medich .20 .50
87 Joe Morgan 1.50 4.00
88 Dennis Leonard .20 .50
89 Willie Randolph .40 1.00
90 Bobby Murcer .30 .75
91 Rick Manning .20 .50
92 J.R. Richard .20 .50
93 Ron Cey .30 .75
94 Sal Bando .20 .50
95 Ron LeFlore .20 .50
96 Dave Goltz .20 .50
97 Dan Meyer .20 .50
98 Chris Chambliss .30 .75
99 Biff Pocoroba .20 .50
100 Oscar Gamble .20 .50
101 Frank Tanana .30 .75
102 Len Randle .20 .50
103 Tommy Hutton .20 .50
104 John Candelaria .20 .50
105 Jorge Orta .20 .50
106 Ken Reitz .20 .50
107 Bill Campbell .20 .50
108 Dave Concepcion .40 1.00
109 Joe Ferguson .20 .50
110 Mickey Rivers .30 .75
111 Paul Splittorff .20 .50
112 Dave Lopes .20 .50
113 Mike Schmidt 4.00 10.00
114 Joe Rudi .20 .50
115 Milt May .20 .50
116 Jim Palmer 1.50 4.00
117 Bill Madlock .30 .75
118 Roy Smalley .20 .50

119 Cecil Cooper .30 .75
120 Rick Langford .20 .50
121 Ruppert Jones .20 .50
122 Phil Niekro 1.25 3.00
123 Toby Harrah .20 .50
124 Chet Lemon .20 .50
125 Gene Tenace .20 .50
126 Steve Henderson .20 .50
127 Mike Torrez .20 .50
128 Pete Rose 4.00 10.00
129 John Denny .20 .50
130 Darrell Porter .20 .50
131 Rick Reuschel .20 .50
132 Graig Nettles .40 1.00
133 Garry Maddox .20 .50
134 Mike Flanagan .20 .50
135 Dave Parker .60 1.50
136 Terry Whitfield .20 .50
137 Wayne Garland .20 .50
138 Robin Yount 6.00 15.00
139 Gaylord Perry 1.25 3.00
140 Rod Carew 1.50 4.00
141 Wayne Gross .20 .50
142 Barry Bonnell .20 .50
143 Willie Montanez .20 .50
144 Rollie Fingers 1.25 3.00
145 Lyman Bostock .30 .75
146 Gary Carter 1.25 3.00
147 Ron Blomberg .20 .50
148 Bob Bailor .20 .50
149 Tom Seaver 2.50 6.00
150 Thurman Munson 1.25 3.00
XX Album 3.00 8.00

1979 Hostess

The cards in this 150-card set measure approximately 2 1/4" by 3 1/4" individually or 3 1/4" by 7 1/4" as panels of three. The 1979 Hostess set contains full color, numbered cards issued in panels of three cards each on the backs of family sized Hostess cake products. Scarcer cards are listed in the checklist below with SP. Although complete panel prices are not explicitly listed below they would generally have a value 20-25 percent greater than the sum of the individual players on the panel. The collectors who don't consider 1978 to be the most difficult Hostess to acquire, believe that 1979's are the toughest to get. The shelf life on the 1979's seemed to be slightly shorter than other years.There is additional interest in Ozzie Smith (102) since this card corresponds to his rookie year in cards. An album to hold these cards were issued.

COMPLETE INDIV.SET (150) 200.00 400.00
COMMON CARD (1-150) .20 .50
COMMON SP .30 .75
1 John Denny .30 .75
2 Jim Rice 1.00 2.50
3 Doug Bair .30 .75
4 Darrell Porter .30 .75
5 Ross Grimsley .30 .75
6 Bobby Murcer .50 1.25
7 Lee Mazzilli .50 1.25
8 Steve Garvey .75 2.00
9 Mike Schmidt 6.00 15.00
10 Terry Whitfield .30 .75
11 Jim Palmer 2.50 6.00
12 Omar Moreno .30 .75
13 Duane Kuiper .30 .75
14 Mike Caldwell .30 .75
15 Steve Kemp .30 .75
16 Dave Goltz .30 .75
17 Mitchell Page .30 .75
18 Bill Stein .30 .75
19 Gene Tenace .30 .75
20 Jeff Burroughs .30 .75
21 Francisco Barrios .30 .75
22 Mike Torrez .30 .75
23 Ken Reitz .30 .75
24 Gary Carter 2.00 5.00
25 Al Hrabosky .30 .75
26 Thurman Munson 2.00 5.00
27 Bill Buckner .50 1.25
28 Ron Cey SP .60 1.50
29 J.R. Richard SP .60 1.50
30 Greg Luzinski SP .60 1.50
31 Ed Ott SP .50 1.25
32 Dennis Martinez SP 2.00 5.00
33 Darrell Evans SP .60 1.50
34 Ron LeFlore .30 .75
35 Rick Waits .30 .75
36 Cecil Cooper .50 1.25
37 Leon Roberts .30 .75
38 Rod Carew 2.50 6.00
39 John Henry Johnson .30 .75
40 Chet Lemon .30 .75
41 Craig Swan .30 .75
42 Gary Matthews .30 .75
43 Lamar Johnson .30 .75
44 Ted Simmons .50 1.25
45 Ken Griffey .50 1.25
46 Fred Patek .30 .75
47 Frank Tanana .50 1.25
48 Goose Gossage .60 1.50
49 Burt Hooton .30 .75
50 Ellis Valentine .30 .75
51 Ken Forsch .30 .75
52 Bob Knepper .30 .75
53 Dave Parker 1.00 2.50
54 Doug DeCinces .30 .75
55 Robin Yount 6.00 15.00
56 Rusty Staub .50 1.25
57 Gary Alexander .30 .75
58 Julio Cruz .30 .75
59 Matt Keough .30 .75
60 Roy Smalley .30 .75
61 Joe Morgan 2.50 6.00
62 Phil Niekro 2.00 5.00
63 Don Baylor .50 1.25
64 Dwight Evans .60 1.50
65 Tom Seaver 4.00 10.00
66 George Hendrick .30 .75
67 Rick Reuschel .30 .75
68 George Brett 10.00 25.00
69 Lou Piniella .50 1.25
70 Enos Cabell .30 .75
71 Steve Carlton 2.50 6.00
72 Reggie Smith .50 1.25
73 Rick Dempsey SP .60 1.50
74 Vida Blue SP 1.00 2.50
75 Phil Garner SP .60 1.50
76 Rick Manning SP .50 1.25
77 Mark Fidrych SP 1.50 4.00
78 Mario Guerrero SP .50 1.25
79 Bob Stinson SP .50 1.25
80 Al Oliver SP 1.00 2.50
81 Doug Flynn SP .50 1.25
82 John Mayberry .30 .75
83 Gaylord Perry 2.00 5.00
84 Joe Rudi .30 .75
85 Dave Concepcion .60 1.50
86 John Candelaria .30 .75
87 Pete Vuckovich .30 .75
88 Ivan DeJesus .30 .75
89 Ron Guidry .60 1.50
90 Hal McRae .50 1.25
91 Cesar Cedeno .30 .75
92 Don Sutton 2.00 5.00
93 Andre Thornton .30 .75
94 Roger Erickson .30 .75
95 Larry Hisle .30 .75
96 Jason Thompson .30 .75
97 Jim Sundberg .30 .75
98 Bob Horner .50 1.25
99 Ruppert Jones .30 .75
100 Willie Montanez .30 .75
101 Nolan Ryan 20.00 50.00
102 Ozzie Smith 20.00 50.00
103 Eric Soderholm .30 .75
104 Willie Stargell 2.00 5.00
105A Bob Bailor ERR/(Reverse negative) .50 1.25
105B Bob Bailor COR 1.00 2.50
106 Carlton Fisk 5.00 12.00
107 George Foster .50 1.25
108 Keith Hernandez 1.00 2.50
109 Dennis Leonard .30 .75
110 Graig Nettles .60 1.50
111 Jose Cruz .50 1.25
112 Bobby Grich .50 1.25
113 Bob Boone .50 1.25
114 Dave Lopes .30 .75
115 Eddie Murray 10.00 25.00
116 Jack Clark .60 1.50
117 Lou Whitaker 2.50 6.00
118 Miguel Dilone .30 .75
119 Sal Bando .30 .75
120 Reggie Jackson 6.00 15.00
121 Dale Murphy 5.00 12.00
122 Jon Matlack .30 .75
123 Bruce Bochte .30 .75
124 John Stearns .30 .75
125 Dave Winfield 5.00 12.00
126 Jorge Orta .30 .75
127 Garry Templeton .30 .75
128 Johnny Bench 4.00 10.00
129 Butch Hobson .30 .75
130 Bruce Sutter .50 1.25
131 Bucky Dent .50 1.25
132 Amos Otis .30 .75
133 Bert Blyleven .60 1.50
134 Larry Bowa .50 1.25
135 Ken Singleton .30 .75
136 Sixto Lezcano .30 .75
137 Roy Howell .30 .75
138 Bill Madlock .50 1.25
139 Dave Revering .30 .75
140 Richie Zisk .30 .75
141 Butch Wynegar .30 .75
142 Alan Ashby .30 .75
143 Sparky Lyle .50 1.25
144 Pete Rose 6.00 15.00
145 Dennis Eckersley 1.50 4.00
146 Dave Kingman .60 1.50
147 Buddy Bell .50 1.25
148 Mike Hargrove .50 1.25
149 Jerry Koosman .50 1.25
150 Toby Harrah .30 .75
XX Album 5.00 12.00

1976 Houston Post Dierker

This one-card set was distributed by the Houston Post and honors Larry Dierker's no hitter.

COMPLETE SET (1) 2.00 5.00
1 Larry Dierker 2.00 5.00

1979 Elston Howard Sausage

This one-card set features a small black-and-white head photo of Elston Howard of the New York Yankees on a black card with white printing. The white back displays information about the player. Some of the cards were personally autographed. The card was used as a business card advertising Elston Howard's Sausage, a division of Piedmont Provision Co.

1 Elston Howard 4.00 10.00

1953-59 Howard Photo Service PC751

The Howard Photo Service late 1950's postcard set was, until recently, thought to contain only the Bob Turley card. However, the recently discovered cards indicates that additional cards may be found in the future. These black and white postcards were issued in New York.

COMPLETE SET (5) 40.00 80.00
1 Ned Garver 5.00 10.00
2 Billy Hitchcock 5.00 10.00
3 Dave Madison 5.00 10.00
4 Willie Mays 20.00 40.00
5 Bob Turley 7.50 15.00

1905 Indians Souvenir Postcard Shop of Cleveland PC785

These distinguished looking black and white cards measures 3 1/4" by 5 1/2" and is similar to PC 782 in appearance and it was also issued in 1905. The Souvenir Postcard Shop of Cleveland identification appears on the front of the card. The backs are devoid of company identification.

COMPLETE SET 1,750.00 3,500.00
1 Harry Bay 400.00 800.00
2 Harry Bemis 400.00 800.00
3 Bill Bernhard 400.00 800.00
4 Bill Bradley 400.00 800.00
5 Fred Buelow 400.00 800.00
6 Chuck Carr 400.00 800.00
7 Frank Donahue 400.00 800.00
8 Elmer Flick 750.00 1,500.00
9 Otto Hess 400.00 800.00
10 Jay Jackson 400.00 800.00
11 Addie Joss 750.00 1,500.00
12 Nick Kahl 400.00 800.00
13 Nap Lajoie 1,500.00 3,000.00
14 Earl Moore 400.00 800.00
15 Robert Rhoads 400.00 800.00
16 George Stovall 600.00 1,200.00
17 Terry Turner 600.00 1,200.00
18 Ernest Vinson 400.00 800.00

1913-14 Indians Postcards

These seven postcards were issued over the 1913-14 time period. We are gathering them together since they seem to be team issued to promote appearences by both opposing players and to honor the Indians star players of that time.

COMPLETE SET (7) 1,000.00 2,000.00
1 Joe Birmingham 50.00 100.00
2 Ray Chapman 150.00 300.00
3 Joe Jackson 750.00 1,500.00
4 Doc Johnston 50.00 100.00
5 Willie Mitchell 50.00 100.00
6 I.Olson G.Stovall 50.00 100.00
7 Heinie Zimmerman 50.00 100.00

1947 Indians Team Issue

These 26 photos measure 6" by 8 1/2". They have player photos and a facsimile autograph. All of this is framed by white borders. The backs are blank and we have sequenced these photos in alphabetical order.

COMPLETE SET (26) 60.00 120.00
1 Don Black 2.00 4.00
2 Eddie Bockman 2.00 4.00
3 Lou Boudreau P MG 5.00 10.00
4 Jack Conway 2.00 4.00
5 Larry Doby 5.00 10.00
6 Hank Edwards 2.00 4.00
7 Red Embree 2.00 4.00
8 Bob Feller 7.50 15.00
9 Les Fleming 2.00 4.00
10 Allen Gettel 2.00 4.00
11 Joe Gordon 4.00 8.00
12 Steve Gromek 2.00 4.00
13 Mel Harder 3.00 6.00
14 Jim Hegan 2.50 5.00
15 Ken Keltner 2.50 5.00
16 Ed Klieman 2.00 4.00
17 Bob Lemon 5.00 10.00
18 Al Lopez 5.00 10.00
19 George Catfish Metkovich 2.00 4.00
20 Dale Mitchell 2.50 5.00
21 Hal Peck 2.00 4.00
22 Eddie Robinson 2.00 4.00
23 Hank Ruszkowksi 2.00 4.00
24 Pat Seerey 2.00 4.00
25 Bryan Stephens 2.00 4.00
26 Les Willis 2.00 4.00

1947 Indians Van Patrick PC-761

This set of 26 black and white postcards was issued in 1947 and features only Cleveland Indians. The cards were obtained by writing to Van Patrick, then the Cleveland announcer. The backs of the postcards features the name of the player on the front in a short note from Van Patrick. Two cards of Bob Feller exist; they are noted in the listings below. According to advanced postcard collectors, it is possible that other members of the 47 Indians have cards as well but they have yet to be discovered.

COMPLETE SET 500.00 1,000.00
1 Don Black 15.00 30.00
2 Eddie Bockman 15.00 30.00
3 Lou Boudreau P MG 30.00 60.00
4 Jack Conway 15.00 30.00
5 Hank Edwards 15.00 30.00
6 Red Embree 15.00 30.00
7A Bob Feller Pitching, abode wall 40.00 80.00
7B Bob Feller Pitching, Leg up, fuzzy card back 40.00 80.00
8 Les Fleming 15.00 30.00
9 Al Gettel 15.00 30.00
10 Joe Gordon 25.00 50.00
11 Steve Gromek 15.00 30.00
12 Mel Harder 25.00 50.00
13 Jim Hegan 20.00 40.00
14 Ken Keltner 20.00 40.00
15 Eddie Klieman 15.00 30.00
16 Bob Lemon 30.00 60.00
17 Al Lopez 30.00 60.00
18 George Metkovich 15.00 30.00
19 Dale Mitchell 15.00 30.00
20 Hal Peck 15.00 30.00
21 Eddie Robinson 15.00 30.00
22 Hank Ruszowski 15.00 30.00
23 Pat Seerey 15.00 30.00
24 Bryan Stephens 15.00 30.00
25 Les Willis 15.00 30.00

1948 Indians Team Issue

This set commemorates the members of the World Champion 1948 Cleveland Indians. The black and white photos measure approximately 6 1/2" by 9" and are blank backed. We have arranged this checklist in alphabetical order.

COMPLETE SET (31) 100.00 200.00
1 Gene Bearden 2.50 5.00
2 Johnny Berardino 6.00 12.00
3 Don Black 2.00 4.00
4 Lou Boudreau 6.00 12.00
5 Russ Christopher 2.00 4.00
6 Allie Clark 2.00 4.00
7 Larry Doby 7.50 15.00
8 Hank Edwards 2.00 4.00
9 Bob Feller 7.50 15.00
10 Joe Gordon 3.00 6.00
11 Hank Greenberg GM In Uniform 10.00 20.00
12 Hank Greenberg GM In Street Clothes 7.50 15.00
13 Steve Gromek 2.00 4.00
14 Mel Harder 3.00 6.00
15 Jim Hegan 2.50 5.00
16 Walt Judnich 2.00 4.00
17 Ken Keltner 2.50 5.00
18 Bob Kennedy 2.50 5.00
19 Ed Klieman 2.00 4.00
20 Bob Lemon 4.00 8.00
21 Bill McKechnie CO 4.00 8.00
22 Dale Mitchell 2.50 5.00
23 Bob Muncrief 2.00 4.00
24 Satchel Paige 10.00 20.00
25 Hal Peck 2.00 4.00
26 Eddie Robinson 2.00 4.00
27 Muddy Ruel CO 2.00 4.00
28 Joe Tipton 2.00 4.00
29 Thurman Tucker 2.00 4.00
30 Bill Veeck OWN 4.00 8.00
31 Sam Zoldak 2.00 4.00

1949 Indians Sun

These "self-developing" photos feature members of the 1949 Cleveland Indians. These photos were issued in groups of four negatives and five pieces of photo paper for 25 cents per envelope. Since these photos are unnumbered, we have sequenced them in alphabetical order.

COMPLETE SET (20) 400.00 800.00
1 Gene Bearden 12.50 25.00
2 Al Benton 12.50 25.00
3 Ray Boone 12.50 25.00
4 Lou Boudreau 30.00 60.00
5 Allie Clark 12.50 25.00
6 Larry Doby 30.00 60.00
7 Bob Feller 50.00 100.00
8 Mike Garcia 15.00 30.00
9 Joe Gordon 25.00 50.00
10 Steve Gromek 12.50 25.00
11 Jim Hegan 12.50 25.00
12 Ken Keltner 15.00 30.00
13 Bob Kennedy 12.50 25.00
14 Bob Lemon 30.00 60.00
15 Dale Mitchell 15.00 30.00
16 Hal Peck 12.50 25.00
17 Satchel Paige 75.00 150.00
18 Thurman Tucker 12.50 25.00
19 Mickey Vernon 20.00 40.00
20 Early Wynn 30.00 60.00

1949 Indians Team Issue Action Photos

These 30 photos measure approximatley 6 1/2" by 9". They feature members of the 1949 Cleveland Indians in action poses. The black and white photos are framed by white borders. The backs are blank and we have sequenced this set in alphabetical order. This set was available from the Cleveland Indians for 50 cents at time of issue.

COMPLETE SET (30)	100.00	200.00
1 Bob Avila	2.50	5.00
2 Al Benton	2.00	4.00
3 Gene Bearden	2.00	4.00
4 John Berardino	3.00	6.00
5 Ray Boone	2.50	5.00
6 Lou Boudreau	7.50	15.00
7 Allie Clark	2.00	4.00
8 Larry Doby	7.50	15.00
9 Bob Feller	7.50	15.00
10 Mike Garcia	2.50	5.00
11 Joe Gordon	3.00	6.00
12 Hank Greenberg GM	7.50	15.00
13 Steve Gromek	2.00	4.00
14 Jim Hegan	2.50	5.00
15 Ken Keltner	2.50	5.00
16 Bob Kennedy	2.00	4.00
17 Bob Lemon	6.00	12.00
18 Dale Mitchell	2.50	5.00
19 Satchel Paige	10.00	20.00
20 Frank Papish	2.00	4.00
21 Hal Peck	2.00	4.00
22 Al Rosen	4.00	8.00
23 Mike Tresh	2.00	4.00
24 Thurman Tucker	2.00	4.00
25 Bill Veeck OWN	4.00	8.00
26 Mickey Vernon	3.00	6.00
27 Early Wynn	6.00	12.00
28 Sam Zoldak	2.00	4.00
29 Indians Coaches George Susce Muddy Ruel Bill Mc	2.50	5.00
30 Cleveland Stadium	5.00	10.00

1950 Indians Num Num

This issue features members of the 1950 Cleveland Indians. The black and white photos measure 6 1/2" by 9". Complete sets were sent out by Num Num in special envelopes. Some backs feature a redemption offer for other photos. We have checklisted the set alphabetically.

COMPLETE SET (23)	800.00	1,600.00
1 Bob Avila	40.00	80.00
2 Gene Bearden	30.00	60.00
3 Al Benton	30.00	60.00
4 Ray Boone	40.00	80.00
5 Lou Boudreau	60.00	120.00
6 Allie Clark	30.00	60.00
7 Larry Doby	60.00	120.00
8 Luke Easter	50.00	100.00
9 Bob Feller	125.00	250.00
10 Mike Garcia	40.00	80.00
11 Joe Gordon	100.00	200.00
12 Steve Gromek	30.00	60.00
13 Jim Hegan	40.00	80.00
14 Bob Kennedy	40.00	80.00
15 Bob Lemon	60.00	120.00
16 Dale Mitchell	40.00	80.00
17 Ray Murray	30.00	60.00
18 Chick Pieretti	30.00	60.00
19 Al Rosen	50.00	100.00
20 Mike Tresh	30.00	60.00
21 Thurman Tucker	30.00	60.00
22 Early Wynn	60.00	210.00
23 Sam Zoldak	30.00	60.00

1950 Indians Team Issue

These 26 black and white photos measure approximately 6 1/2" by 9". They feature members of the Cleveland Indians. The photos are surrounded by a white border and have facsimile autographs. The photos are unnumbered and we have sequenced them in alphabetical order.

COMPLETE SET (27)	75.00	150.00
1 Bob Avila	2.50	5.00
2 Gene Bearden	2.00	4.00
3 Al Benton	2.00	4.00
4 Ray Boone	2.50	5.00
5 Lou Boudreau P MG	6.00	12.00
6 Allie Clark	2.00	4.00
7 Larry Doby	10.00	20.00
8 Luke Easter	3.00	6.00
9 Bob Feller	10.00	20.00
10 Jess Flores	2.00	4.00
11 Mike Garcia	2.50	5.00
12 Joe Gordon	3.00	6.00
13 Hank Greenberg GM	12.50	25.00
14 Steve Gromek	2.00	4.00
15 Jim Hegan	2.50	5.00
16 Bob Kennedy	2.50	5.00
17 Bob Lemon	6.00	12.00
18 Dale Mitchell	2.50	5.00
19 Ray Murray	2.00	4.00
20 Chick Pieretti	2.00	4.00
21 Al Rosen	3.00	6.00
22 Dick Rozek	2.00	4.00
23 Ellis Ryan OWN	2.00	4.00
24 Thurman Tucker	2.00	4.00
25 Early Wynn	7.50	15.00
26 Sam Zoldak	2.00	4.00
27 Cleveland Stadium	12.50	25.00

1951 Indians Hage's

This seven-card set of the Cleveland Indians was issued by Hage's Ice Cream and features green-and-brown tinted player photos printed on black-backed cards. The cards are unnumbered and checklisted below in alphabetical order.

COMPLETE SET (7)	750.00	1,500.00
1 Ray Boone	125.00	250.00
2 Allie Clark	100.00	200.00
3 Luke Easter	125.00	250.00
4 Jesse Flores	100.00	200.00
5 Al Olsen	100.00	200.00
6 Al Rosen	200.00	400.00
7 George Zuverink	100.00	200.00

1951 Indians Team Issue

These 6 1/2" by 9" photos were issued by the Cleveland Indians and featured members of the 1951 Indians. The black and white photos are surrounded by a white border and have fascimile autographs. The photos are unnumbered and we have sequenced them in alphabetical order. This list may be incomplete and any additions are welcome.

COMPLETE SET	100.00	200.00
1 Bobby Avila	3.00	6.00
2 Johnny Beardino	4.00	8.00
3 Lou Boudreau Batting	5.00	10.00
4 Lou Boudreau Throwing	5.00	10.00
5 Ray Boone	2.50	5.00
6 Lou Brissie	2.50	5.00
7 Allie Clark	2.50	5.00
8 Merrill Combs	2.50	5.00
9 Bob Chakales	2.50	5.00
10 Sam Chapman	2.50	5.00
11 Larry Doby	5.00	10.00
12 Luke Easter	2.50	5.00
13 Red Fahr	2.50	5.00
14 Bob Feller	6.00	12.00
15 Jess Flores	2.50	5.00
16 Mike Garcia	3.00	6.00
17 Joe Gordon	4.00	8.00
18 Steve Gromek	2.50	5.00
19 Jim Hegan	3.00	6.00
20 Bob Kennedy	3.00	6.00
21 Bob Lemon Facing Straight Ahead	5.00	10.00
22 Bob Lemon Facing Left	5.00	10.00
23 Dale Mitchell	3.00	6.00
24 Ray Murray	2.50	5.00
25 Al Rosen	4.00	8.00
26 Dick Rozek	2.50	5.00
27 Harry Simpson	2.50	5.00
28 Snuffy Stirnweiss	2.50	5.00
29 Thurman Tucker	2.50	5.00
30 Mickey Vernon	3.00	6.00
31 Early Wynn	5.00	10.00
32 Sam Zoldak	2.50	5.00

1952 Indians Num Num

The cards in this 20-card set measure approximately 3 1/2" by 4 1/2". The 1952 Num Num Potato Chips issue features black and white, numbered cards of the Cleveland Indians. Cards came with and without coupons (tabs). The cards were issued without coupons directly by the Cleveland baseball club. When the complete set was obtained the tabs were cut off and exchanged for an autographed baseball. Card Number 16, Kennedy, is rather scarce. Cards with the tabs still intact are worth approximately double the values listed below. The catalog designation for this set is F337-2.

COMPLETE SET (20)	1,750.00	3,500.00
COMMON CARD (1-20)	50.00	100.00
COMMON SP	750.00	1,500.00
1 Lou Brissie	150.00	300.00
2 Jim Hegan	60.00	120.00
3 Birdie Tebbetts	60.00	120.00
4 Bob Lemon	100.00	200.00
5 Bob Feller	250.00	500.00
6 Early Wynn	100.00	200.00
7 Mike Garcia	60.00	120.00
8 Steve Gromek	50.00	100.00
9 Bob Chakales	50.00	100.00
10 Al Rosen	75.00	150.00
11 Dick Rozek	50.00	100.00
12 Luke Easter	60.00	120.00
13 Ray Boone	60.00	120.00
14 Bobby Avila	60.00	120.00
15 Dale Mitchell	60.00	120.00
16 Bob Kennedy SP	750.00	1,500.00
17 Harry Simpson	50.00	100.00
18 Larry Doby	100.00	200.00
19 Sam Jones	60.00	120.00
20 Al Lopez MG	100.00	200.00

1953 Indians Team Issue

These photos which measure approximately 6" by 9" feature members of the 1953 Indians. The black and white photos are produced with a glossy paper and have fascimile autographs. Since these cards are unnumbered, we have sequenced them in alphabetical order.

COMPLETE SET	50.00	100.00
1 Al Aber	2.50	5.00
2 Bob Avila	3.00	6.00
3 Ray Boone	2.50	5.00
4 Larry Doby	5.00	10.00
5 Luke Easter	2.50	5.00
6 Bob Feller	6.00	12.00
7 Mike Garcia	3.00	6.00
8 Bill Glynn	2.50	5.00
9 Jim Hegan	2.50	5.00
10 Bob Hooper	2.50	5.00
11 Dave Hoskins	2.50	5.00
12 Bob Kennedy	2.50	5.00
13 Bob Lemon	5.00	10.00
14 Jim Lemon	2.50	5.00
15 Al Lopez MG	5.00	10.00
16 Dale Mitchell	2.50	5.00
17 Al Rosen	4.00	8.00
18 Harry Simpson	2.50	5.00
19 George Strickland	2.50	5.00
20 Early Wynn	5.00	10.00

1954 Indians Team Issue

These photos, which measure approximately 6" by 8 3/4" feature members of the American League champions Cleveland Indians. These photos are similar to the 1953 Indians in style but are slightly smaller and are printed on heavier paper. Since these are unnumbered, we have sequenced them in alphabetical order.

COMPLETE SET	75.00	150.00
1 Bob Avila	2.50	5.00
2 Sam Dente	2.50	5.00
3 Larry Doby	5.00	10.00
4 Bob Feller	6.00	12.00
5 Mike Garcia	3.00	6.00
6 Bill Glynn	2.50	5.00
7 Jim Hegan	2.50	5.00
8 Bob Hooper	2.50	5.00
9 Dave Hoskins	2.50	5.00
10 Art Houtteman	2.50	5.00
11 Bob Lemon	5.00	10.00
12 Al Lopez MG	5.00	10.00
13 Hank Majeski	2.50	5.00
14 Dale Mitchell	2.50	5.00
15 Don Mossi	4.00	8.00
16 Hal Naragon	2.50	5.00
17 Ray Narleski	3.00	6.00
18 Hal Newhouser	5.00	10.00
19 Dave Philley	2.50	5.00
20 Dave Pope	2.50	5.00
21 Rudy Regalado	2.50	5.00
22 Al Rosen	4.00	8.00
23 Al Smith	2.50	5.00
24 George Strickland	2.50	5.00
25 Vic Wertz	2.50	5.00
26 Wally Westlake	2.50	5.00
27 Early Wynn	5.00	10.00

1955 Indians Team Issue

These cards which measure approximately 6" by 8 3/4" feature members of the 1955 Indians. Most of these cards have fascimile autographs printed on them except for Foiles, Kiner, Score and Wertz. This checklist comes from a set purchased directly from the Indians in July, 1955 so there might have been additions both before and after these were issued. Since these cards are unnumbered, we have sequenced them in alphabetical order.

COMPLETE SET	60.00	120.00
1 Bob Avila	3.00	6.00
2 Sam Dente	2.50	5.00
3 Larry Doby	5.00	10.00
4 Bob Feller	6.00	12.00
5 Hank Foiles	2.50	5.00
6 Mike Garcia	3.00	6.00
7 Jim Hegan	2.50	5.00
8 Art Houtteman	2.50	5.00
9 Ralph Kiner	5.00	10.00
10 Bob Lemon	5.00	10.00
11 Dale Mitchell	2.50	5.00
12 Don Mossi	3.00	6.00
13 Hal Naragon	2.50	5.00
14 Ray Narleski	2.50	5.00
15 Dave Philley	2.50	5.00
16 Al Rosen	4.00	8.00
17 Herb Score	5.00	10.00
18 Al Smith	2.50	5.00
19 George Strickland	2.50	5.00
20 Vic Wertz	2.50	5.00
21 Wally Westlake	2.50	5.00
22 Early Wynn	5.00	10.00

1955 Indians Golden Stamps

This 32-stamp set features color photos of the Cleveland Indians and measures approximately 2" by 2 5/8". The stamps are designed to be placed in a 32-page album which measures approximately 8 3/8" by 10 15/16". The album contains black-and-white drawings of players with statistics and life stories. The stamps are unnumbered and listed below according to where they fall in the album.

COMPLETE SET (32)	75.00	150.00
1 Al Lopez MG	2.50	5.00
2 Bob Lemon	6.00	12.00
3 Early Wynn	6.00	12.00
4 Mike Garcia	1.50	3.00
5 Bob Feller	10.00	20.00
6 Art Houtteman	1.25	2.50
7 Herb Score	2.50	5.00
8 Don Mossi	2.00	4.00
9 Ray Narleski	1.25	2.50
10 Jim Hegan	1.50	3.00
11 Vic Wertz	1.25	2.50
12 Bobby Avila	1.25	2.50
13 George Strickland	1.25	2.50
14 Al Rosen	2.00	4.00
15 Larry Doby	6.00	12.00
16 Ralph Kiner	2.50	5.00
17 Al Smith	1.25	2.50
18 Wally Westlake	1.25	2.50
19 Hal Naragon	1.25	2.50
20 Hank Foiles	1.25	2.50
21 Hank Majeski	1.25	2.50
22 Bill Wight	1.25	2.50
23 Sam Dente	1.25	2.50
24 Dave Pope	1.25	2.50
25 Dave Philley	1.25	2.50
26 Dale Mitchell	1.50	3.00
27 Hank Greenberg GM	10.00	20.00
28 Mel Harder CO	1.50	3.00
29 Ralph Kress CO	1.25	2.50
30 Tony Cuccinello CO	1.25	2.50
31 Bill Lobe CO	1.25	2.50
32 Cleveland Stadium	5.00	10.00
XX Album	2.50	5.00

1955-56 Indians Carling Black Label

This ten-card, approximately 8 1/2" by 12", set was issued by Carling Beer and celebrated members of the (then) perennial contending Cleveland Indians. These cards feature a black and white photo with the printed name of the player inserted in the photo. Underneath the photo is a joint advertisement for Carling Black Label Beer and The Cleveland Indians. The set looks like it could be easily replicated and may indeed have been reprinted. The checklist for this unnumbered set is ordered alphabetically.

COMPLETE SET (10)	60.00	120.00
1 Bob Feller	15.00	30.00
2 Mike Garcia	5.00	10.00
3 Jim Hegan	5.00	10.00
4 Art Houtteman	4.00	8.00
5 Ralph Kiner	7.50	15.00
6 Bob Lemon	7.50	15.00
7 Al Rosen	6.00	12.00
8 Herb Score	7.50	15.00
9 Al Smith	4.00	8.00
10 George Strickland	4.00	8.00
11 Early Wynn	7.50	15.00

1956 Indians Team Issue

These cards, which measure approximately 6" by 9" feature members of the 1956 Cleveland Indians. Similar to the 1955 set and many of the photos were also repeats from the 1955 set. This set was produced early in the season so additions to this checklist is appreciated. These cards are not numbered, so we have sequenced them in alphabetical order. Rocky Colavito appears in this set before his Rookie Card year.

COMPLETE SET	60.00	120.00
1 Earl Averill	2.50	5.00
2 Bob Avila	3.00	6.00
3 Rocky Colavito	7.50	20.00
4 Bob Feller	6.00	12.00
5 Mike Garcia	3.00	6.00
6 Jim Hegan	2.50	5.00
7 Art Houtteman	2.50	5.00
8 Bob Lemon	5.00	10.00
9 Al Lopez MG	5.00	10.00
10 Sam Mele	2.50	5.00
11 Dale Mitchell	2.50	5.00
12 Don Mossi	3.00	6.00
13 Ray Narleski	2.50	5.00
14 Rudy Regalado	2.50	5.00
15 Al Rosen	4.00	8.00
16 Al Smith	2.50	5.00
17 George Strickland	2.50	5.00
18 Gene Woodling	2.50	5.00
19 Early Wynn	5.00	10.00

1956 Indians Team Issue Mail

Unlike the other 1956 Indians Team Issue, this set was available to mail order customers. Thes cards, which measure approximately 6 1/2" by 9" are slightly thinner in card stock than the other Indian team issue. Rocky Colavito appears in this photo set a year before his Topps Rookie Card was issued.

COMPLETE SET	75.00	150.00
1 Earl Averill	2.50	5.00
2 Bob Avila	3.00	6.00
3 Jim Busby	2.50	5.00
4 Chico Carrasquel	2.50	5.00
5 Rocky Colavito	15.00	30.00

6 Bud Daley	2.50	5.00
7 Bob Feller	6.00	12.00
8 Mike Garcia	3.00	6.00
9 Mel Harder CO Bill Lobe CO Tony Cuccinello CO R	2.50	5.00
10 Jim Hegan	2.50	5.00
11 Kenny Kuhn	2.50	5.00
12 Bob Lemon	5.00	10.00
13 Al Lopez MG	5.00	10.00
14 Sam Mele	2.50	5.00
15 Dale Mitchell	2.50	5.00
16 Don Mossi	3.00	6.00
17 Hal Naragon	2.50	5.00
18 Ray Narleski	2.50	5.00
19 Al Rosen	4.00	8.00
20 Herb Score	4.00	8.00
21 Al Smith	2.50	5.00
22 George Strickland	2.50	5.00
23 Vic Wertz	2.50	5.00
24 Gene Woodling	2.50	5.00
25 Early Wynn	5.00	10.00

1957 Indians Sohio

The 1957 Sohio Cleveland Indians set consists of 18 perforated photos; originally issued in strips of three cards, which after perforation measure approximately 5" by 7". These black and white cards were issued with facsimile autographs on the front which were designed to be pasted into a special photo album issued by SOHIO (Standard Oil of Ohio). The set features one of the earliest Roger Maris cards which even predates his 1958 Topps rookie card. In addition, the Rocky Colavito card is popular as well as 1957 was Rocky's rookie year for cards. These unnumbered cards are listed below in alphabetical order for convenience. It has been alleged that counterfeits of this set have been recently produced.

COMPLETE SET (18)	125.00	250.00
1 Bob Avila	3.00	6.00
2 Jim Busby	2.00	4.00
3 Chico Carrasquel	2.00	4.00
4 Rocky Colavito	40.00	80.00
5 Mike Garcia	3.00	6.00
6 Jim Hegan	2.00	4.00
7 Bob Lemon	15.00	30.00
8 Roger Maris	60.00	120.00
9 Don Mossi	3.00	6.00
10 Ray Narleski	2.00	4.00
11 Russ Nixon	2.00	4.00
12 Herb Score	4.00	8.00
13 Al Smith	2.00	4.00
14 George Strickland	2.00	4.00
15 Bob Usher	2.00	4.00
16 Vic Wertz	3.00	6.00
17 Gene Woodling	3.00	6.00
18 Early Wynn	15.00	30.00

1957 Indians Team Issue

This 29-card set of the Cleveland Indians features black-and-white player photos measuring approximately 6 1/2" by 9". The backs are blank. The cards are unnumbered and checklisted below in alphabetical order. An very eary card of Roger Maris is in this set.

COMPLETE SET (29)	50.00	100.00
1 Joe Altobelli	1.50	3.00
2 Bob Avila	2.00	4.00
3 Alfonso Carrasquel	1.50	3.00
4 Rocky Colavito	10.00	20.00
5 Bud Daley	1.50	3.00
6 Kerby Ferrell MG	1.50	3.00
7 Mike Garcia	1.50	3.00
8 Mel Harder CO Red Kress CO Kerby Farrell CO Eddie Stanky CO	2.00	4.00
9 Jim Hegan	1.50	3.00
10 Art Houtteman	1.50	3.00
11 Kenny Kuhn	1.50	3.00
12 Bob Lemon	5.00	10.00
13 Roger Maris	12.50	25.00
14 Don Mossi	2.00	4.00
15 Hal Naragon	1.50	3.00
16 Ray Narleski	1.50	3.00
17 Russ Nixon	1.50	3.00
18 Stan Pitula	1.50	3.00
19 Lawrence Raines	1.50	3.00
20 Herb Score	2.50	5.00
21 Al Smith	1.50	3.00
22 George Strickland	1.50	3.00
23 Dick Tomanek	1.50	3.00
24 Bob Usher	1.50	3.00
25 Preston Ward	1.50	3.00
26 Vic Wertz	2.00	4.00
27 Dick Williams	2.50	5.00
28 Gene Woodling	2.00	4.00
29 Early Wynn	5.00	10.00

1958 Indians Team Issue

This 30-card set of the Cleveland Indians features black-and-white player photos measuring approximately 6 1/2" by 9" with white borders and facsimile autographs. The backs are blank. The first 24 cards were issued in the set in May. The last five cards were found in the August set with several of the other players dropped. The set could be obtained by mail for 50 cents from the club.

COMPLETE SET (30)	75.00	150.00
1 Bob Avila	2.00	4.00
2 Bobby Bragan MG	1.50	3.00
3 Dick Brown	1.50	3.00
4 Alfonso(Chico) Carrasquel	1.50	3.00
5 Rocky Colavito	10.00	20.00
6 Larry Doby	5.00	10.00
7 Mike Garcia	2.00	4.00
8 Gary Geiger	1.50	3.00
9 Jim Grant	1.50	3.00
10 Bill Harrell	1.50	3.00
11 Red Kress CO Bobby Bragan MG Eddie Stanky CO Me	2.00	4.00
12 Roger Maris	10.00	20.00
13 Cal McLish	1.50	3.00
14 Minnie Minoso	3.00	6.00
15 Bill Moran	1.50	3.00
16 Don Mossi	2.00	4.00
17 Ray Narleski	1.50	3.00
18 Russ Nixon	1.50	3.00
19 J.W. Porter	1.50	3.00
20 Herb Score	2.50	5.00
21 Dick Tomanek	1.50	3.00
22 Mickey Vernon	2.00	4.00
23 Preston Ward	1.50	3.00
24 Hoyt Wilhelm	5.00	10.00
25 Gary Bell	1.50	3.00
26 Rocky Colavito	7.50	15.00
27 Woodie Held	2.00	4.00
28 Bill Hunter	1.50	3.00
29 Don Mossi	2.00	4.00
30 Vic Power	3.00	6.00

1959 Indians

This set features black-and-white photos of the 1959 Cleveland Indians and measures approximately 6 1/2" by 9". Some of the photos have a facsimile autograph identifying the player while others have the player's name printed in a small bar in a bottom corner. The backs are blank. The cards are unnumbered and checklisted below in alphabetical order.

COMPLETE SET (26)	40.00	80.00
1 Gary Bell	1.50	3.00
2 Jim Bolger	1.50	3.00
3 Dick Brodowski	1.50	3.00
4 Al Cicotte	1.50	3.00
5 Rocky Colavito	5.00	10.00
6 Don Ferrarese	1.50	3.00
7 Tito Francona	2.00	4.00
8 Mike Garcia	2.00	4.00
9 Joe Gordon MG	2.50	5.00
10 Jim Grant	1.50	3.00
11 Mel Harder CO	2.00	4.00
12 Carroll Hardy	1.50	3.00
13 Woodie Held	1.50	3.00
14 Frank Lane GM	1.50	3.00
15 Billy Martin	5.00	10.00
16 Cal McLish	1.50	3.00
17 Minnie Minoso	3.00	6.00
18 Hal Naragon	1.50	3.00
19 Russ Nixon	1.50	3.00
20 Jim Perry	2.00	4.00
21 Jim Piersall	2.50	5.00
22 Vic Power	2.00	4.00
23 Herb Score	2.50	5.00
24 George Strickland	1.50	3.00
25 Mickey Vernon	2.00	4.00
26 Ray Webster	1.50	3.00

1960 Indians Jay Publishing

This 12-card set of the Cleveland Indians measures approximately 5" by 7". The fronts feature black-and-white posed player photos with the player's and team name printed below in the white border. These cards were packaged 12 to a packet and originally sold for 25 cents. The backs are blank. The cards are unnumbered and checklisted below in alphabetical order.

COMPLETE SET (12)	20.00	40.00
1 Tito Francona	2.50	6.00
2 Jim Grant	2.00	5.00
3 Woody Held	2.00	5.00
4 Harvey Kuenn	2.50	6.00
5 Barry Latman	2.00	5.00
6 Russ Nixon	2.00	5.00
7 Bubba Phillips	2.00	5.00
8 Jimmy Piersall	3.00	8.00
9 Vic Power	2.50	6.00
10 John Romano	2.00	5.00
11 George Strickland	2.00	5.00
12 John Temple	2.00	5.00

1961 Indians Team Issue

These black-backed photos, which measure approximately 6" by 9" feature members of the 1961 Cleveland Indians. These photos are unnumbered and are sequenced in alphabetical order.

COMPLETE SET	15.00	40.00
1 John Antonelli	1.00	2.50
2 Gary Bell	.75	2.00
3 Mike de la Hoz	.75	2.00
4 Jimmie Dykes MG	1.00	2.50
5 Tito Francona	.75	2.00
6 Jim Grant	1.00	2.50
7 Wynn Hawkins	.75	2.00
8 Woodie Held	.75	2.00
9 Willie Kirkland	.75	2.00
10 Barry Latman	.75	2.00
11 Bobby Locke	.75	2.00
12 Jim Perry	1.25	3.00
13 Bubba Phillips	.75	2.00
14 Jim Piersall	1.50	4.00
15 Vic Power	.75	2.00
16 John Romano	.75	2.00
17 Dick Stigman	.75	2.00
18 John Temple	.75	2.00
19 Indians Coaches	1.25	3.00
20 Municipal Stadium	.75	2.00

1962 Indians Jay Publishing

This 12-card set of the Cleveland Indians measures approximately 5" by 7". The fronts feature black-and-white posed player photos with the player's and team name printed below in the white border. These cards were packaged 12 to a packet. The backs are blank. The cards are unnumbered and checklisted below in alphabetical order.

COMPLETE SET (12)	20.00	40.00
1 Gary Bell	2.00	5.00
2 Dick Donovan	2.00	5.00
3 Tito Francona	2.50	6.00
4 Jim Grant	2.50	6.00
5 Woody Held	2.50	6.00
6 Willie Kirkland	2.00	5.00
7 Barry Latman	2.00	5.00
8 Mel McGaha MG	2.00	5.00
9 Bob Nieman	2.00	5.00
10 Bubba Phillips	2.00	5.00
11 Pedro Ramos	2.00	5.00
12 John Romano	2.00	5.00

1963 Indians Jay Publishing

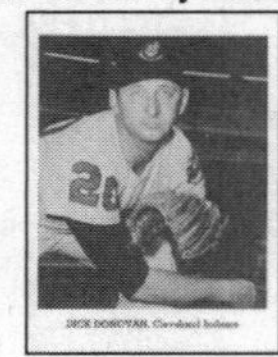

This 12-card set of the Cleveland Indians measures approximately 5" by 7". The fronts feature black-and-white posed player photos with the player's and team name printed below in the white border. These cards were packaged 12 to a packet. The backs are blank. The cards are unnumbered and checklisted below in alphabetical order.

COMPLETE SET (12)	25.00	50.00
1 Joe Adcock	3.00	8.00
2 Gary Bell	2.00	5.00
3 Vic Davalillo	2.00	5.00
4 Mike De La Hoz	2.00	5.00
5 Dick Donovan	2.00	5.00
6 Tito Francona	2.50	6.00
7 Jim Grant	2.50	6.00
8 Woody Held	2.00	5.00
9 Willie Kirkland	2.00	5.00
10 Barry Latman	2.00	5.00
11 John Romano	2.00	5.00
12 Birdie Tebbetts MG	2.50	6.00

1964 Indians Jay Publishing

This 12-card set of the Cleveland Indians measures approximately 5" by 7". The fronts feature black-and-white posed player photos with the player's and team name printed below in the white border. These cards were packaged 12 to a packet. The backs are blank. The cards are unnumbered and checklisted below in alphabetical order.

COMPLETE SET (12)	10.00	25.00
1 Max Alvis	1.00	2.50
2 Joe Azcue	.75	2.00
3 Vic Davalillo	.75	2.00
4 Dick Donovan	.75	2.00
5 Tito Francona	1.00	2.50
6 Jim Grant	1.00	2.50
7 Woody Held	.75	2.00
8 Jack Kralick	.75	2.00
9 Pedro Ramos	.75	2.00
10 John Romano	.75	2.00
11 Al Smith	.75	2.00
12 Birdie Tebbetts MG	1.00	2.50

1965 Indians Jay Publishing

This 12-card set of the Cleveland Indians measures approximately 5" by 7". The fronts feature black-and-white posed player photos with the player's and team name printed below in the white border. These cards were packaged 12 to a packet. The backs are blank. The cards are unnumbered and checklisted below in alphabetical order. Luis Tiant appears in his Rookie Card season.

COMPLETE SET (12)	25.00	50.00
1 Max Alvis	2.00	5.00
2 Gary Bell	2.00	5.00
3 Larry Brown	2.00	5.00
4 Rocky Colavito	4.00	10.00
5 Dick Donovan	2.00	5.00
6 Chuck Hinton	2.00	5.00
7 Jack Kralick	2.00	5.00
8 Sam McDowell	3.00	8.00
9 Birdie Tebbetts MG	2.00	5.00
10 Ralph Terry	2.50	6.00
11 Luis Tiant	4.00	10.00
12 Leon Wagner	2.00	5.00

1966 Indians Photos

These photos, which measure 8" by 10" feature members of the 1966 Cleveland Indians. Since these photos are unnumbered, we have sequenced them in alphabetical order.

COMPLETE SET	10.00	25.00
1 Max Alvis	1.25	3.00
2 Joe Azcue	1.25	3.00
3 Gary Bell	1.25	3.00
4 Larry Brown	1.25	3.00
5 Rocky Colavito	2.00	5.00
6 Del Crandall	1.25	3.00
7 Vic Davalillo	1.25	3.00
8 Steve Hargan	1.25	3.00
9 Chuck Hinton	1.25	3.00
10 Dick Howser	1.25	3.00
11 Pedro Gonzalez	1.25	3.00
12 Tom Kelly	1.25	3.00
13 Jack Kralick	1.25	3.00
14 Jim Landis	1.25	3.00
15 Sam McDowell	2.00	5.00
16 Chico Salmon	1.25	3.00
17 Sonny Siebert	1.25	3.00
18 Duke Sims	1.25	3.00
19 Birdie Tebbetts MG Early Wynn CO George Strickla	1.50	4.00
20 Luis Tiant	2.50	6.00
21 Leon Wagner	1.25	3.00
22 Fred Whitfield	1.25	3.00

1966 Indians Team Issue

This 12-card set of the Cleveland Indians measures approximately 4 7/8" by 7 1/8" and features black-and-white player photos in a white border. These cards were packaged 12 to a packet and originally sold for 25 cents. The backs are blank. The cards are unnumbered and checklisted below in alphabetical order.

COMPLETE SET (12)	12.50	30.00
1 Max Alvis	.75	2.00
2 Joe Azcue	.75	2.00
3 Rocky Colavito	1.50	4.00
4 Vic Davalillo	1.00	2.50
5 Chuck Hinton	.75	2.00
6 Dick Howser	1.00	2.50
7 Jack Kralick	.75	2.00
8 Sam McDowell	1.25	3.00
9 Don McMahon	.75	2.00
10 Birdie Tebbetts MG	.75	2.00
11 Luis Tiant	1.50	4.00
12 Leon Wagner	.75	2.00

1970 Indians

This 12-card set of the Cleveland Indians measures approximately 4 1/4" by 7" and features white-bordered black-and-white player photos. The player's name and team are printed in the wide top margin. The backs are blank. The cards are unnumbered and checklisted below in alphabetical order.

COMPLETE SET (12)	8.00	20.00
1 Buddy Bradford	.60	1.50
2 Larry Brown	.60	1.50
3 Alvin Dark	.75	2.00
4 Ray Fosse	.75	2.00
5 Steve Hargan	.60	1.50
6 Ken Harrelson	1.00	2.50
7 Dennis Higgins	.60	1.50
8 Sam McDowell	1.00	2.50
9 Graig Nettles	1.25	3.00
10 Vada Pinson	1.25	3.00
11 Ken Suarez	.60	1.50
12 Ted Uhlaender	.60	1.50

1971 Indians

These 12 cards featuring members of the Cleveland Indians measure approximately 7" by 8 3/4" with the fronts having white-bordered color player photos. The player's name and team is printed in black in the white margin below the picture. The backs are blank. The cards are unnumbered and checklisted below in alphabetical order.

COMPLETE SET (12)	8.00	20.00
1 Buddy Bradford	.60	1.50
2 Alvin Dark MG	1.00	2.50
3 Steve Dunning	.60	1.50
4 Ray Fosse	.75	2.00
5 Steve Hargan	.60	1.50
6 Ken Harrelson	1.00	2.50

7 Chuck Hinton .60 1.50
8 Ray Lamb .60 1.50
9 Sam McDowell 1.25 3.00
10 Vada Pinson 1.25 3.00
11 Ken Suarez .60 1.50
12 Ted Uhlaender .60 1.50

1972 Indians Brown Derby Poster

Issued through the Brown Derby restaurant chain, these posters measured 22" by 27" and featured members of the 1972 Cleveland Indians. They were apparently issued each Sunday, but incomplete information is known as to which players were actually produced for this set or whether all 16 players which were supposed to be issued were issued. Since these cards are not numbered, we have sequenced them in alphabetical information. Obviously, more information on this set would be greatly appreciated.

COMPLETE SET 15.00 40.00
1 Chris Chambliss 3.00 8.00
2 Ray Fosse 2.00 5.00
3 Roy Foster 2.00 5.00
4 Graig Nettles 3.00 8.00
5 Gaylord Perry 5.00 12.00
6 Dick Tidrow 2.00 5.00
7 Del Unser 2.00 5.00

1973 Indians Team Issue

This set features color photos of the 1973 Cleveland Indians printed on postcard-size cards with postcard backs. The cards are unnumbered and checklisted below in alphabetical order. Four of the cards had numbers on them, and these numbers are listed after the player's names. These cards were published by Cleveland Sports Pro Enterprises and the photos were taken by Axel Studios. A collector could order these postcards, as they were issued in 25-card sets and evolved during the year from the producer for $3 per set.

COMPLETE SET 12.50 30.00
1 Dwain Anderson 332 .40 1.00
2 Ken Aspromonte MG .40 1.00
3 Fred Beene 322 .40 1.00
4 Buddy Bell 1.00 2.50
5 Dick Bosman .40 1.00
6 Jack Brohamer .40 1.00
7 Leo Cardenas .40 1.00
8 Chris Chambliss .75 2.00
9 Frank Duffy .40 1.00
10 Dave Duncan .40 1.00
11 John Ellis .40 1.00
12 Ed Farmer .40 1.00
13 Oscar Gamble .60 1.50
14 George Hendrick .60 1.50
15 Tom Hilgendorf .40 1.00
16 Jerry Johnson .40 1.00
17 Ray Lamb .40 1.00
18 Ron Lolich .40 1.00
19 John Lowenstein .40 1.00
20 Joe Lutz CO 1
21 Steve Mingori .40 1.00
22 Tony Pacheco CO 327 .40 1.00
23 Gaylord Perry 1.50 4.00
24 Tom Ragland .40 1.00
25 Warren Spahn CO 1.50 4.00
26 Charlie Spikes .40 1.00
27 Brent Strom .40 1.00
28 Dick Tidrow .40 1.00
29 Rosendo Rusty Torres 342 .40 1.00
30 Rusty Torres .40 1.00
Back says Leo Cardenas
31 Milt Wilcox .40 1.00
32 Walt Williams .40 1.00

1974 Indians Team Issue

These postcards feature players who made their debut with the Indians in 1974. Many of the 1973 players also appeared in 1974 but they are not listed here. Since these cards are not numbered, we have sequenced them in alphabetical order.

COMPLETE SET 8.00 20.00
1 Luis Alvarado .40 1.00
2 Dwain Anderson .40 1.00
3 Steve Arlin .40 1.00
4 Alan Ashby .40 1.00
5 Fred Beene .40 1.00
6 Ossie Blanco .40 1.00
7 Clay Bryant .40 1.00
8 Tom Buskey .40 1.00
9 Ed Crosby .40 1.00
10 Larry Doby CO 1.00 2.50
11 Bruce Ellingsen .40 1.00
12 Bob Johnson .40 1.00
13 Steve Kline .40 1.00
14 Leron Lee .40 1.00
15 Joe Lis .40 1.00
16 Tony Pacheco CO .40 1.00
17 Jim Perry .60 1.50
18 Fritz Peterson .40 1.00
19 Ken Sanders .40 1.00

1975 Indians 1954 TCMA

The 39-card set of the 1954 Cleveland Indians features black-and-white player photos in white borders. The backs carry player statistics for 1954. The cards are unnumbered and checklisted below in alphabetical order with cards 37, 38, and 39 being jumbo cards.

COMPLETE SET (39) 12.50 30.00
1 Bobby Avila .40 1.00
2 Bob Chakales .20 .50
3 Tony Cuccinello .20 .50
4 Sam Dente .20 .50
5 Larry Doby 1.25 3.00
6 Luke Easter .20 .50
7 Bob Feller 2.00 5.00
8 Mike Garcia .20 .50
9 Joe Ginsberg .20 .50
10 Billy Glynn .20 .50
11 Mickey Grasso .20 .50
12 Mel Harder .40 1.00
13 Jim Hegan .40 1.00
14 Bob Hooper .20 .50
15 Dave Hoskins .20 .50
16 Art Houtteman .20 .50
17 Bob Kennedy .20 .50
18 Bob Lemon .75 2.00
19 Al Lopez .60 1.50
20 Hank Majeski .20 .50
21 Dale Mitchell .40 1.00
22 Don Mossi .60 1.50
23 Hal Naragon .20 .50
24 Ray Narleski .20 .50
25 Rocky Nelson .20 .50
26 Hal Newhouser .75 2.00
27 Dave Philley .20 .50
28 Dave Pope .20 .50
29 Rudy Regalado .20 .50
30 Al Rosen .75 2.00
31 Jose Santiago .20 .50
32 Al Smith .20 .50
33 George Strickland .20 .50
34 Vic Wertz .20 .50
35 Wally Westlake .20 .50
36 Early Wynn 1.25 3.00
37 Dave Pope .40 1.00
Dave Philley
Larry Doby
Al Smith
38 Bill Lobe .40 1.00
Tony Cuccinello
Red Kress
Mel Harder#
39 Wynn .75 2.00
Lem
Hoop
Hout
Sant
Narl
Garc
Newh
Lopez

1975 Indians JB Robinson

This seven-card set was issued by JB Robinson Jewelers and features 8 1/2" by 8 1/2" color photos of the Cleveland Indians. The cards are unnumbered and checklisted below in alphabetical order.

COMPLETE SET (7) 5.00 12.00
1 Buddy Bell 1.00 2.50
2 Jack Brohamer .40 1.00
3 Rico Carty .75 2.00
4 Frank Duffy .40 1.00
5 Oscar Gamble .60 1.50
6 Boog Powell 1.00 2.50
7 Frank Robinson MG 1.00 2.50

1975 Indians Postcards

This 25-card set of the Cleveland Indians features player photos on postcard-size cards. The cards are unnumbered and checklisted below in alphabetical order.

COMPLETE SET (25) 5.00 12.00
1 Alan Ashby .30 .75
2 Fred Beene .20 .50
3 Buddy Bell .60 1.50
4 Ken Berry .20 .50
5 Dick Bosman .20 .50
6 Jack Brohamer .20 .50
7 Tom Buskey .20 .50
8 Rico Carty .30 .75
9 Ed Crosby .20 .50
10 Frank Duffy .20 .50
11 John Ellis .20 .50
12 Oscar Gamble .30 .75
13 George Hendrick .30 .75
14 Don Hood .20 .50
15 Jim Kern .20 .50
16 Dave LaRoche .20 .50
17 Leron Lee .20 .50
18 John Lowenstein .20 .50
19 Gaylord Perry .75 2.00
20 Jim Perry .30 .75
21 Fritz Peterson .20 .50
22 John Boog Powell .60 1.50
23 Frank Robinson P MG .75 2.00
24 Charlie Spikes .20 .50
25 Coaching Staff .20 .50

1976 Indians Team Issue

This nine-card set of the Cleveland Indians features color player photos printed on postcard-size cards. The cards are unnumbered and checklisted below in alphabetical order.

COMPLETE SET (9) 3.00 8.00
1 Larvell Banks .20 .50
2 Tom Buskey .20 .50
3 Dennis Eckersley 2.00 5.00
4 Ray Fosse .20 .50
5 Don Hood .20 .50
6 Dave LaRoche .20 .50
7 Boog Powell .60 1.50
8 Ron Pruitt .20 .50
9 Stan Thomas .20 .50

1977 Indians 1920 TCMA

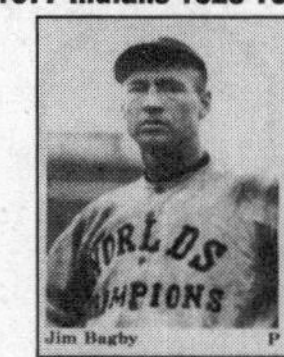

This 22-card set commemorates the 1920 World Champion Cleveland Indians. The fronts feature black-and-white player photos, while the backs display player statistics. One jumbo card measuring approximately 3 3/4" by 5" carries a story about the 1920 Cleveland Indians Team. The cards are unnumbered and checklisted below in alphabetical order with the jumbo card listed as number 22.

COMPLETE SET (22) 8.00 20.00
1 Jim Bagby .40 1.00
2 George Burns .20 .50
3 Ray Caldwell .20 .50
4 Ray Chapman .60 1.50
5 Stan Coleleski .75 2.00
6 Joe Evans .20 .50
7 Larry Gardner .20 .50
8 Jack Graney .20 .50
9 Charlie Jamieson .20 .50
10 Wheeler Doc Johnston .20 .50
11 Harry Lunte .20 .50
12 John Duster Mails .20 .50
13 Guy Morton .20 .50
14 Les Nunamaker .20 .50
15 Steve O'Neill .40 1.00
16 Joe Sewell .75 2.00
17 Elmer Smith .20 .50
18 Tris Speaker P MG 2.00 5.00
19 Goerge Uhle .20 .50
20 Bill Wambsganss .60 1.50
21 Joe Wood .60 1.50
22 World Series Foes .75 2.00
Wilbert Robinson
Tris Speaker

1977 Indians Team Issue

This 25-card set features black-and-white, glossy photos of the Cleveland Indians printed on postcard-size cards. Jim Bibby's card (number 1) is the only color photo. The cards are unnumbered and checklisted below in alphabetical order.

COMPLETE SET (25) 6.00 15.00
1 Jim Bibby .40 1.00
2 Larvell Blanks .20 .50
3 Bruce Bochte .20 .50
4 Tom Buskey .20 .50
5 Rico Carty .30 .75
6 Rocky Colavito CO .60 1.50
7 Pat Dobson .20 .50
8 Frank Duffy .20 .50
9 Dennis Eckersley 1.25 3.00
10 Al Fitzmorris .20 .50
11 Ray Fosse .20 .50
12 Fred Kendall .20 .50
13 Jim Kern .20 .50
14 Dave LaRoche .20 .50
15 John Lowenstein .20 .50
16 Rick Manning .20 .50
17 Bill Melton .20 .50
18 Sid Monge .20 .50
19 Jim Norris .20 .50
20 Joe Nossek CO .20 .50
21 Ron Pruitt .20 .50
22 Frank Robinson MG .60 1.50
23 Andre Thornton .40 1.00
24 Jeff Torborg CO .20 .50
25 Rick Waits .20 .50

1978 Indians Team Issue

This 31-card set of the Cleveland Indians features black-and-white photos on postcard-size cards. The cards are unnumbered and checklisted below in alphabetical order.

COMPLETE SET (31) 5.00 12.00
1 Buddy Bell .40 1.00
2 Larvell Blanks .20 .50
3 Wayne Cage .20 .50
4 David Clyde .20 .50
5 Rocky Colavito CO .60 1.50
6 Ted Cox .20 .50
7 Paul Dade .20 .50
8 Bo Diaz .20 .50
9 Dave Duncan CO .20 .50
10 Al Fitzmorris .20 .50
11 Wayne Garland .20 .50
12 Johnny Grubb .20 .50
13 Harvey Haddix CO .20 .50
14 Ron Hassey .20 .50
15 Don Hood .20 .50
16 Willie Horton .30 .75
17 Jim Kern .20 .50
18 Dennis Kinney .20 .50
19 Duane Kuiper .20 .50
20 Rick Manning .20 .50
21 Sid Monge .20 .50
22 Jim Norris .20 .50
23 Joe Nossek CO .20 .50
24 Mike Paxton .20 .50
25 Ron Pruitt .20 .50
26 Horace Speed .20 .50
27 Andre Thornton .40 1.00
28 Jeff Torborg MG .20 .50
29 Tom Veryzer .20 .50
30 Rick Waits .20 .50
31 Rick Wise .20 .50

1979 Indians Team Issue

These cards are similar to the other Indians team issues around this period. These cards are black and white with a light paper stock. These cards are unnumbered so we have sequenced them in alphabetical order.

COMPLETE SET 6.00 15.00
1 Gary Alexander .20 .50
2 Del Alston .20 .50
3 Larry Anderson .20 .50
4 Len Barker .20 .50
5 Bobby Bonds .40 1.00
6 Wayne Cage .20 .50
7 David Clyde .20 .50
8 Ted Cox .20 .50
9 Victor Cruz .20 .50
10 Paul Dade .20 .50
11 Bo Diaz .20 .50
12 Dave Duncan .20 .50
13 Dave Garcia MG .20 .50
14 Wayne Garland .20 .50
15 Mike Hargrove .30 .75
16 Toby Harrah .30 .75
17 Chuck Hartenstein .20 .50
18 Don Hood .20 .50
19 Cliff Johnson .20 .50
20 Duane Kuiper .20 .50
21 Rick Manning .20 .50
22 Sid Monge .20 .50
23 Joe Nossek .20 .50
24 Mike Paxton .20 .50
25 Paul Reuschel .20 .50
26 Ron Pruitt .20 .50
27 Dave Rosello .20 .50
28 Horace Speed .20 .50
29 Dan Spillner .20 .50
30 Andre Thornton .30 .75
31 Jeff Torborg MG .20 .50
32 Tom Veryzer .20 .50
33 Rick Waits .20 .50
34 Eric Wilkins .20 .50
35 Rick Wise .20 .50

1980 Indians Team Issue

This 31-card set of the Cleveland Indians features black-and-white player photos printed on postcard-size cards. The cards are unnumbered and checklisted below in alphabetical order. The postcards numbered from 32 through 38 were late additions as the Indians made player moves during the season

COMPLETE SET (31) 6.00 15.00
1 Gary Alexander .20 .50
2 Del Alston .20 .50
3 Len Barker .20 .50
5 Victor Cruz .20 .50
6 John Denny .20 .50
6 Joe Charboneau .60 1.50
7 Bo Diaz .20 .50
8 Dave Duncan CO .20 .50
9 Jerry Dybzinski .20 .50
10 Dave Garcia MG .20 .50
11 Wayne Garland .20 .50
12 Mike Hargrove .40 1.00
13 Toby Harrah .30 .75
14 Ron Hassey .20 .50
15 Cliff Johnson .20 .50
16 Duane Kuiper .20 .50
17 Rick Manning .20 .50
18 Tom McCraw CO .20 .50
19 Sid Monge .20 .50
20 Andres Mora .20 .50
21 Joe Nossek CO .20 .50
22 Jorge Orta .20 .50
23 Bob Owchinko .20 .50
24 Ron Pruitt .20 .50
25 Dave Rosello .20 .50
26 Dennis Sommers CO .20 .50
27 Dan Spillner .20 .50
28 Mike Stanton .20 .50
29 Andre Thornton .30 .75
30 Tom Veryzer .20 .50
31 Rick Waits .20 .50
32 Baseball Bug .20 .50
33 Alan Bannister .20 .50
34 Jack Brohamer .20 .50
35 Miguel Dilone .20 .50
36 Gary Gray .20 .50
37 Ross Grimsley .20 .50
38 Sandy Withol .20 .50

1980 Italian American Sports Hall of Fame

These exhibit-sized cards were issued to commemorate the first inductees into the Italian American Sports Hall of Fame. The fronts have sepia toned photos of the athlete as well as their name and identification in the lower left column. The bottom right of the card is dedicated to the "Unity" logo. The back is a standard postcard back. Since these cards are unnumbered we have sequenced them in alphabetical order.

COMPLETE SET 5.00 10.00
2 Phil Cavarretta .40 1.00
3 Joe DiMaggio 2.00 5.00
5 Vince Lombardi .75 2.00

1910 J.H. Dockman All-Star Baseball E-Unc.

Produced by J.H. Dockman and Son, this unattractive issue is actually the sides of a candy package. The package measures approximately 1 7/8" by 3 3/8" and is 3/4" thick. Each package features two players, crudely drawn, one on each side. The words "All Star Baseball Package" appear on the side of the package and at the top of each player panel. The other side panel displays the words, "Candy and Gift." The end panel indicates a serial number, Dockman's name and reference to the Food and Drugs Act of 1906. A complete box is worth four times the individual value.

COMPLETE SET (16) 2,500.00 5,000.00

1 Henry Beckendorf 175.00 350.00
2 Roger Bresnahan 300.00 600.00
3 Al Burch 175.00 350.00
4 Frank Chance 350.00 700.00
5 Wid Conroy 175.00 350.00
6 Jack Coombs 250.00 500.00
7 George Gibson 175.00 350.00
8 Doc Hoblitzel 175.00 350.00
9 Johnny Kling 175.00 350.00
10 Frank LaPorte 175.00 350.00
11 Connie Mack 600.00 1,200.00
12 Christy Mathewson 900.00 1,800.00
13 Matthew McIntyre 175.00 350.00
14 Jimmy Sheckard 175.00 350.00
15 Al Schweitzer 175.00 350.00
16 Harry Wolter 175.00 350.00

1950-54 J.J.K. Copyart Photographers

This set measures 3 1/2" by 5 1/2" and features New York Giants, Boston Braves, Philadelphia Phillies and one Brooklyn Dodger. The postcards are black and white glossy photos with no company identification on the back.

COMPLETE SET (24) 150.00 300.00
1 Johnny Antonelli (2) 5.00 10.00
2 Sam Calderone 4.00 8.00
3 Del Crandall 5.00 10.00
4 Del Ennis 4.00 8.00
5 Jim Hearn (2) 4.00 8.00
6 Tommy Holmes 5.00 10.00
7 Larry Jansen 5.00 10.00
8 Whitey Lockman (2) 4.00 8.00
9 Williard Marhsall 4.00 8.00
10 Eddie Mathews 15.00 30.00
11 Don Mueller 4.00 8.00
12 Danny O'Connell 4.00 8.00
13 Bill Rigney 5.00 10.00
14 Robin Roberts 12.50 25.00
15 Jackie Robinson 40.00 80.00
16 Hank Sauer 5.00 10.00
17 Red Schoendienst 12.50 25.00
18 Curt Simmons 5.00 10.00
19 Sibby Sisti 4.00 8.00
20 Eddie Stanky 7.50 15.00
Boston Braves
21 Eddie Stanly 7.50 15.00
New York Giants
22 Wes Westrum 4.00 8.00
23 Hoyt Wilhelm 12.50 25.00
24 Al Worthington 4.00 8.00

1969 Reggie Jackson Regiment

This one card set was issued during the early days of Reggie Jackson's career. It was issued as a ballpark promotion during his sensational first half of the 1969 season in which he hit 37 homers.

1 Reggie Jackson 40.00 80.00

1956 Jay Publishing World Series Pack

This 50-card set of the 1956 World Series Participants measure approximately 5 1/8" by 7". The fronts feature black-and-white posed player photos with the player's and team name printed below in the white border. The backs are blank. The cards are unnumbered and checklisted below in alphabetical order.

COMPLETE SET (50) 150.00 300.00
1 Walt Alston MG 3.00 6.00
2 Sandy Amoros 2.00 4.00
3 Hank Bauer 2.50 5.00
4 Joe Becker CO 1.50 3.00
5 Yogi Berra 5.00 10.00
6 Don Bessent 1.50 3.00
7 Tommy Byrne 1.50 3.00
8 Roy Campanella 5.00 10.00
9 Andy Carey 2.00 4.00
10 Bob Cerv 2.00 4.00
11 Jerry Coleman 2.50 5.00
12 Joe Collins 2.00 4.00
13 Roger Craig 2.00 4.00
14 Frank Crosetti CO 2.00 4.00
15 Bill Dickey CO 3.00 6.00
16 Don Drysdale 10.00 20.00
17 Carl Erskine 3.00 6.00
18 Chico Fernandez 1.50 3.00
19 Whitey Ford 7.50 15.00
20 Carl Furillo 3.00 6.00
21 Jim Gilliam 2.50 5.00
22 Bob Grim 1.50 3.00
23 Billy Herman CO 3.00 6.00
24 Gil Hodges 5.00 10.00
25 Elston Howard 4.00 8.00
26 Billy Hunter 1.50 3.00
27 Randy Jackson 1.50 3.00
28 Sandy Koufax 10.00 20.00
29 Johnny Kucks 1.50 3.00
30 Clem Labine 1.50 3.00
31 Don Larsen 3.00 6.00
32 Sal Maglie 3.00 6.00
33 Mickey Mantle 12.50 25.00
34 Billy Martin 4.00 8.00
35 Gil McDougald 3.00 6.00
36 Tom Morgan 1.50 3.00
37 Don Newcombe 2.50 5.00
38 Jake Pitler CO 1.50 3.00
39 Johnny Podres 2.50 5.00
40 Pee Wee Reese 5.00 10.00
41 Ed Roebuck 1.50 3.00
42 Jackie Robinson 10.00 20.00
43 Charlie Silvera 1.50 3.00
44 Bill Skowron 3.00 6.00
45 Duke Snider 7.50 15.00
46 Casey Stengel MG 4.00 8.00
47 Tom Sturdivant 1.50 3.00
48 Jim Turner CO 1.50 3.00
49 Bob Turley 1.50 3.00
50 Rube Walker 1.50 3.00

1959 Jay Publishing All-Stars

The 23 blank-backed photos comprising the 1958 Jay Publishing All-Stars set measure 5" by 7" and feature white-bordered black-and-white posed player shots. The player's name appears in black lettering within the bottom white margin. The pictures are unnumbered and checklisted below in alphabetical order.

COMPLETE SET (23) 50.00 150.00
1 Henry Aaron 10.00 20.00
2 Luis Aparicio 4.00 8.00
3 Bob Cerv .75 2.00
4 Delmar Crandall .75 2.00
5 Whitey Ford 4.00 8.00
6 Nelson Fox 4.00 8.00
7 Bob Friend .75 2.00
8 Fred Haney MG .75 2.00
9 Jack Jensen 1.50 3.00
10 Frank Malzone .75 2.00
11 Mickey Mantle 20.00 40.00
12 Willie Mays 20
Bill White in Background
12 Bill Mazeroski 2.50 6.00
13 Roy McMillan .75 2.00
14 Stan Musial 7.50 15.00
15 Bill Pierce .75 2.00
16 Robin Roberts 4.00 8.00
17 Bob Skinner .75 2.00
18 Bill Skowron 1.50 3.00
19 Warren Spahn 4.00 8.00
20 Casey Stengel MG 4.00 8.00
21 Frank Thomas .75 2.00
22 Gus Triandos .75 2.00
23 Bob Turley .75 2.00

1958 Jay Publishing All-Time Greats

This 10-card set features glossy black-and-white photos of Baseball's all-time great players. The backs are blank. The cards are unnumbered and checklisted below in alphabetical order.

COMPLETE SET (10) 35.00 70.00
1 Ty Cobb 7.50 15.00
2 Joe DiMaggio 7.50 15.00
3 Lou Gehrig 7.50 15.00
4 Rogers Hornsby 2.50 5.00
Spelled Roger
5 Carl Hubbell 1.00 2.00
6 Connie Mack 1.00 2.00
7 Christy Mathewson 2.00 4.00
8 Johnny Mize 1.00 2.00
9 Babe Ruth 10.00 20.00
10 Casey Stengel 2.00 4.00

1958 Jay Publishing Sluggers

This 10-card set features glossy black-and-white photos of some of Baseball's great hitters. The backs are blank. The cards are unnumbered and checklisted below in alphabetical order.

COMPLETE SET (10) 50.00 100.00
1 Hank Aaron 7.50 15.00
2 Larry Berra 4.00 8.00
3 Nelson Fox 2.50 5.00
4 Al Kaline 3.00 6.00
5 Mickey Mantle 12.50 25.00
6 Ed Mathews 3.00 6.00
7 Willie Mays 7.50 15.00
8 Stan Musial 5.00 10.00
9 Duke Snider 4.00 8.00
10 Ted Williams 10.00 20.00

1962 Jello

The cards in this 200-card (only 197 were ever issued) set measure 2 1/2" by 3 3/8". The 1962 Jello set has the same checklist as the Post Cereal set of the same year, but is considered by some to be a test issue. The cards are grouped numerically by team. For example: New York Yankees (1-13), Detroit (14-26), Baltimore (27-36), Cleveland (37-45), Chicago White Sox (46-55), Boston (56-64), Washington (65-73), Los Angeles Angels (74-82), Minnesota (83-91), Kansas City (92-100), Los Angeles Dodgers (101-115), Cincinnati (116-130), San Francisco (131-144), Milwaukee (145-157), St. Louis (158-168), Pittsburgh (169-181), Chicago Cubs (182-191), and Philadelphia (192-200). Although the players and numbers are identical in both sets, the Jello series has its own list of scarce and difficult cards. Numbers 29, 82 and 176 were never issued. A Jello card is easily distinguished from its counterpart in Post by the absence of the Post logo. The catalog designation for this set is F229-1.

COMPLETE SET (197) 2,500.00 5,000.00
1 Bill Skowron 10.00 25.00
2 Bobby Richardson 225.00 450.00
3 Cletis Boyer 5.00 12.00
4 Tony Kubek 8.00 20.00
5 Mickey Mantle 500.00 1,000.00
6 Roger Maris 100.00 200.00
7 Yogi Berra 60.00 120.00
8 Elston Howard 5.00 12.00
9 Whitey Ford 40.00 80.00
10 Ralph Terry 4.00 10.00
11 John Blanchard 4.00 10.00
12 Luis Arroyo 4.00 10.00
13 Bill Stafford 6.00 15.00
14 Norm Cash 5.00 12.00
15 Jake Wood 2.50 6.00
16 Steve Boros 2.50 6.00
17 Chico Fernandez 2.50 6.00
18 Bill Bruton 2.50 6.00
19 Ken Aspromonte 2.50 6.00
20 Al Kaline 30.00 60.00
21 Dick Brown 2.50 6.00
22 Frank Lary 2.50 6.00
23 Don Mossi 4.00 10.00
24 Phil Regan 2.50 6.00
25 Charley Maxwell 2.50 6.00
26 Jim Bunning 12.50 30.00
27 Jim Gentile 4.00 10.00
28 Marv Breeding 2.50 6.00
29 Not issued
30 Ron Hansen 2.50 6.00
31 Jackie Brandt 10.00 25.00
32 Dick Williams 5.00 12.00
33 Gus Triandos 2.50 6.00
34 Milt Pappas 2.50 6.00
35 Hoyt Wilhelm 20.00 50.00
36 Chuck Estrada 2.50 6.00
37 Vic Power 2.50 6.00
38 Johnny Temple 2.50 6.00
39 Bubba Phillips 10.00 25.00
40 Tito Francona 2.50 6.00
41 Willie Kirkland 2.50 6.00
42 John Romano 2.50 6.00
43 Jim Perry 4.00 10.00
44 Woodie Held 2.50 6.00
45 Chuck Essegian 2.50 6.00
46 Roy Sievers 2.50 6.00
47 Nellie Fox 15.00 40.00
48 Al Smith 2.50 6.00
49 Luis Aparicio 15.00 40.00
50 Jim Landis 2.50 6.00
51 Minnie Minoso 10.00 25.00
52 Andy Carey 10.00 25.00
53 Sherman Lollar 2.50 6.00
54 Billy Pierce 4.00 10.00
55 Early Wynn 12.50 30.00
56 Chuck Schilling 10.00 25.00
57 Pete Runnels 4.00 10.00
58 Frank Malzone 4.00 10.00
59 Don Buddin 4.00 10.00
60 Gary Geiger 10.00 25.00
61 Carl Yastrzemski 150.00 300.00
62 Jackie Jensen 12.50 30.00
63 Jim Pagliaroni 10.00 25.00
64 Don Schwall 4.00 10.00
65 Dale Long 4.00 10.00
66 Chuck Cottier 4.00 10.00
67 Billy Klaus 10.00 25.00
68 Coot Veal 4.00 10.00
69 Marty Keough 15.00 40.00
70 Willie Tasby 15.00 40.00
71 Gene Woodling 4.00 10.00
72 Gene Green 15.00 40.00
73 Dick Donovan 4.00 10.00
74 Steve Bilko 4.00 10.00
75 Rocky Bridges 10.00 25.00
76 Eddie Yost 6.00 15.00
77 Leon Wagner 5.00 12.00
78 Albie Pearson 4.00 10.00
79 Ken Hunt 6.00 15.00
80 Earl Averill 15.00 40.00
81 Ryne Duren 5.00 12.00
82 Not issued
83 Bob Allison 4.00 10.00
84 Billy Martin 12.50 30.00
85 Harmon Killebrew 20.00 50.00
86 Zoilo Versalles 4.00 10.00
87 Lenny Green 12.50 30.00
88 Bill Tuttle 2.50 6.00
89 Jim Lemon 2.50 6.00
90 Earl Battey 10.00 25.00
91 Camilo Pascual 2.50 6.00
92 Norm Siebern 4.00 10.00
93 Jerry Lumpe 4.00 10.00
94 Dick Howser 5.00 12.00
95 Gene Stephens 15.00 40.00
96 Leo Posada 5.00 12.00
97 Joe Pignatano 4.00 10.00
98 Jim Archer 4.00 10.00
99 Haywood Sullivan 10.00 25.00
100 Art Ditmar 4.00 10.00
101 Gil Hodges 20.00 50.00
102 Charlie Neal 4.00 10.00
103 Daryl Spencer 4.00 10.00
104 Maury Wills 12.50 30.00
105 Tommy Davis 6.00 15.00
106 Willie Davis 6.00 15.00
107 Johnny Roseboro 15.00 40.00
108 John Podres 6.00 15.00
109 Sandy Koufax 60.00 120.00
110 Don Drysdale 30.00 60.00
111 Larry Sherry 10.00 25.00
112 Jim Gilliam 12.50 30.00
113 Norm Larker 15.00 40.00
114 Duke Snider 40.00 80.00
115 Stan Williams 10.00 25.00
116 Gordy Coleman 40.00 80.00
117 Don Blasingame 10.00 25.00
118 Gene Freese 15.00 40.00
119 Ed Kasko 15.00 40.00
120 Gus Bell 12.50 30.00
121 Vada Pinson 6.00 15.00
122 Frank Robinson 15.00 40.00
123 Bob Purkey 4.00 10.00
124 Joey Jay 4.00 10.00
125 Jim Brosnan 4.00 10.00
126 Jim O'Toole 4.00 10.00
127 Jerry Lynch 4.00 10.00
128 Wally Post 4.00 10.00
129 Ken Hunt 4.00 10.00
130 Jerry Zimmerman 4.00 10.00
131 Willie McCovey 30.00 60.00
132 Jose Pagan 12.50 30.00
133 Felipe Alou 6.00 15.00
134 Jim Davenport 5.00 12.00
135 Harvey Kuenn 6.00 15.00
136 Orlando Cepeda 12.50 30.00
137 Ed Bailey 4.00 10.00
138 Sam Jones 4.00 10.00
139 Mike McCormick 4.00 10.00
140 Juan Marichal 40.00 80.00
141 Jack Sanford 4.00 10.00
142 Willie Mays 125.00 250.00
143 Stu Miller 30.00 60.00
144 Joe Amalfitano 4.00 10.00
145 Joe Adcock 4.00 10.00
146 Frank Bolling 2.50 6.00
147 Eddie Mathews 20.00 50.00
148 Roy McMillan 2.50 6.00
149 Hank Aaron 100.00 200.00
150 Gino Cimoli 10.00 25.00
151 Frank Thomas 4.00 10.00
152 Joe Torre 8.00 20.00
153 Lew Burdette 5.00 12.00
154 Bob Buhl 2.50 6.00
155 Carlton Willey 2.50 6.00
156 Lee Maye 10.00 25.00
157 Al Spangler 15.00 40.00
158 Bill White 30.00 60.00
159 Ken Boyer 10.00 25.00
160 Joe Cunningham 4.00 10.00
161 Carl Warwick 4.00 10.00
162 Carl Sawatski 2.50 6.00
163 Lindy McDaniel 2.50 6.00
164 Ernie Broglio 4.00 10.00
165 Larry Jackson 2.50 6.00
166 Curt Flood 12.50 30.00
167 Curt Simmons 12.50 30.00
168 Alex Grammas 10.00 25.00
169 Dick Stuart 2.50 6.00
170 Bill Mazeroski 12.50 30.00
171 Don Hoak 4.00 10.00
172 Dick Groat 5.00 12.00
173 Roberto Clemente 150.00 300.00
174 Bob Skinner 10.00 25.00
175 Bill Virdon 12.50 30.00
176 Not issued
177 Roy Face 5.00 12.00
178 Bob Friend 2.50 6.00
179 Vern Law 12.50 30.00
180 Harvey Haddix 15.00 40.00
181 Hal Smith 10.00 25.00
182 Ed Bouchee 10.00 25.00
183 Don Zimmer 5.00 12.00
184 Ron Santo 8.00 20.00
185 Andre Rodgers 2.50 6.00
186 Richie Ashburn 15.00 40.00
187 George Altman 2.50 6.00
188 Ernie Banks 15.00 40.00
189 Sam Taylor 2.50 6.00
190 Don Elston 2.50 6.00
191 Jerry Kindall 8.00 20.00
192 Pancho Herrera 2.50 6.00
193 Tony Taylor 4.00 10.00
194 Ruben Amaro 8.00 20.00
195 Don Demeter 2.50 6.00
196 Bobby Gene Smith 2.50 6.00
197 Clay Dalrymple 2.50 6.00
198 Robin Roberts 12.50 30.00
199 Art Mahaffey 2.50 6.00
200 John Buzhardt 2.50 6.00

1963 Jello

The cards in this 200-card set measure 2 1/2" by 3 3/8". The 1963 Jello set contains the same players and numbers as the Post Cereal set of the same year. The players are grouped by team with American Leaguers comprising 1-100 and National Leaguers 101-200. The ordering of teams is as follows: Minnesota (1-11), New York Yankees (12-23), Los Angeles Angels (24-34), Chicago White Sox (35-45), Detroit (46-56), Baltimore (57-66), Cleveland (67-76), Boston (77-84), Kansas City (85-92), Washington (93-100), San Francisco (101-112), Los Angeles Dodgers (113-124), Cincinnati (125-136), Pittsburgh (137-147), Milwaukee (148-157), St. Louis (158-168), Chicago Cubs (169-176), Philadelphia (177-184), Houston (185-192) and New York Mets (193-200). As in 1962, the Jello series has its own list of scarcities (many resulting from an unpopular package size). Since the Post Cereal logo was removed from the 1963 cereal set, Jello cards are primarily distinguishable by (1) smaller card size and (2) smaller print. The catalog esignation is F229-2.

COMPLETE SET (200)	1,500.00	3,000.00
1 Vic Power	1.50	4.00
2 Bernie Allen	8.00	20.00
3 Zoilo Versalles	10.00	25.00
4 Rich Rollins	1.50	4.00
5 Harmon Killebrew	6.00	15.00
6 Lenny Green	10.00	25.00
7 Bob Allison	2.50	6.00
8 Earl Battey	6.00	15.00
9 Camilo Pascual	2.50	6.00
10 Jim Kaat	20.00	50.00
11 Jack Kralick	1.50	4.00
12 Bill Skowron	10.00	25.00
13 Bobby Richardson	3.00	8.00
14 Cletis Boyer	2.50	6.00
15 Mickey Mantle	125.00	250.00
16 Roger Maris	50.00	100.00
17 Yogi Berra	12.50	30.00
18 Elston Howard	20.00	50.00
19 Whitey Ford	8.00	20.00
20 Ralph Terry	1.50	4.00
21 John Blanchard	6.00	15.00
22 Bill Stafford	8.00	20.00
23 Tom Tresh	4.00	10.00
24 Steve Bilko	1.50	4.00
25 Bill Moran	1.50	4.00
26 Joe Koppe	1.50	4.00
27 Felix Torres	1.50	4.00
28 Leon Wagner	1.50	4.00
29 Albie Pearson	1.50	4.00
30 Lee Thomas	1.50	4.00
31 Bob Rodgers	8.00	20.00
32 Dean Chance	3.00	8.00
33 Ken McBride	8.00	20.00
34 George Thomas	8.00	20.00
35 Joe Cunningham	8.00	20.00
36 Nellie Fox	4.00	10.00
37 Luis Aparicio	4.00	10.00
38 Al Smith	2.50	6.00
39 Floyd Robinson	1.50	4.00
40 Jim Landis	1.50	4.00
41 Charlie Maxwell	1.50	4.00
42 Sherman Lollar	2.50	6.00
43 Early Wynn	4.00	10.00
44 Juan Pizarro	8.00	20.00
45 Ray Herbert	10.00	25.00
46 Norm Cash	3.00	8.00
47 Steve Boros	12.50	30.00
48 Dick McAuliffe	3.00	8.00
49 Bill Bruton	8.00	20.00
50 Rocky Colavito	4.00	10.00
51 Al Kaline	6.00	15.00
52 Dick Brown	8.00	20.00
53 Jim Bunning	4.00	10.00
54 Hank Aguirre	1.50	4.00
55 Frank Lary	8.00	20.00
56 Don Mossi	10.00	25.00
57 Jim Gentile	3.00	8.00
58 Jackie Brandt	2.50	6.00
59 Brooks Robinson	6.00	15.00
60 Ron Hansen	1.50	4.00
61 Jerry Adair	15.00	40.00
62 Boog Powell	3.00	8.00
63 Russ Snyder	10.00	25.00
64 Steve Barber	2.50	6.00
65 Milt Pappas	8.00	20.00
66 Robin Roberts	5.00	12.00
67 Tito Francona	1.50	4.00
68 Jerry Kindall	8.00	20.00
69 Woody Held	1.50	4.00
70 Bubba Phillips	1.50	4.00
71 Chuck Essegian	1.50	4.00
72 Willie Kirkland	8.00	20.00
73 Al Luplow	1.50	4.00
74 Ty Cline	15.00	40.00
75 Dick Donovan	1.50	4.00
76 John Romano	1.50	4.00
77 Pete Runnels	3.00	8.00
78 Ed Bressoud	8.00	20.00
79 Frank Malzone	2.50	6.00
80 Carl Yastrzemski	40.00	80.00
81 Gary Geiger	2.50	6.00
82 Lou Clinton	8.00	20.00
83 Earl Wilson	2.50	6.00
84 Bill Monbouquette	1.50	4.00
85 Norm Siebern	1.50	4.00
86 Jerry Lumpe	1.50	4.00
87 Manny Jimenez	1.50	4.00
88 Gino Cimoli	2.50	6.00
89 Ed Charles	15.00	40.00
90 Ed Rakow	2.50	6.00
91 Bobby Del Greco	15.00	40.00
92 Haywood Sullivan	8.00	20.00
93 Chuck Hinton	1.50	4.00
94 Ken Retzer	8.00	20.00
95 Harry Bright	8.00	20.00
96 Bob Johnson	2.50	6.00
97 Dave Stenhouse	6.00	15.00
98 Chuck Cottier	2.50	6.00
99 Tom Cheney	2.50	6.00
100 Claude Osteen	10.00	25.00
101 Orlando Cepeda	4.00	10.00
102 Chuck Hiller	6.00	15.00
103 Jose Pagan	8.00	20.00
104 Jim Davenport	1.50	4.00
105 Harvey Kuenn	2.50	6.00
106 Willie Mays	50.00	100.00
107 Felipe Alou	3.00	8.00
108 Tom Haller	2.50	6.00
109 Juan Marichal	4.00	10.00
110 Jack Sanford	1.50	4.00
111 Bill O'Dell	1.50	4.00
112 Willie McCovey	60.00	120.00
113 Lee Walls	8.00	20.00
114 Jim Gilliam	12.50	30.00
115 Maury Wills	3.00	8.00
116 Ron Fairly	2.50	6.00
117 Tommy Davis	2.50	6.00
118 Duke Snider	5.00	12.00
119 Willie Davis	2.50	6.00
120 John Roseboro	1.50	4.00
121 Sandy Koufax	15.00	40.00
122 Stan Williams	1.50	4.00
123 Don Drysdale	4.00	10.00
124 Daryl Spencer	1.50	4.00
125 Gordy Coleman	2.50	6.00
126 Don Blasingame	8.00	20.00
127 Leo Cardenas	1.50	4.00
128 Eddie Kasko	8.00	20.00
129 Jerry Lynch	1.50	4.00
130 Vada Pinson	4.00	10.00
131 Frank Robinson	5.00	12.00
132 Johnny Edwards	8.00	20.00
133 Joey Jay	1.50	4.00
134 Bob Purkey	1.50	4.00
135 Marty Keough	15.00	40.00
136 Jim O'Toole	8.00	20.00
137 Dick Stuart	1.50	4.00
138 Bill Mazeroski	4.00	10.00
139 Dick Groat	2.50	6.00
140 Don Hoak	1.50	4.00
141 Bob Skinner	1.50	4.00
142 Bill Virdon	2.50	6.00
143 Roberto Clemente	60.00	120.00
144 Smoky Burgess	3.00	8.00
145 Bob Friend	1.50	4.00
146 Al McBean	10.00	25.00
147 Roy Face	2.50	6.00
148 Joe Adcock	2.50	6.00
149 Frank Bolling	1.50	4.00
150 Roy McMillan	2.50	6.00
151 Eddie Mathews	6.00	15.00
152 Hank Aaron	50.00	100.00
153 Del Crandall	10.00	25.00
154 Bob Shaw	2.50	6.00
155 Lew Burdette	2.50	6.00
156 Joe Torre	20.00	50.00
157 Tony Cloninger	15.00	40.00
158 Bill White	4.00	10.00
159 Julian Javier	8.00	20.00
160 Ken Boyer	4.00	10.00
161 Julio Gotay	10.00	25.00
162 Curt Flood	2.50	6.00
163 Charlie James	20.00	50.00
164 Gene Oliver	10.00	25.00
165 Ernie Broglio	1.50	4.00
166 Bob Gibson	50.00	100.00
167 Lindy McDaniel	8.00	20.00
168 Ray Washburn	2.50	6.00
169 Ernie Banks	6.00	15.00
170 Ron Santo	3.00	8.00
171 George Altman	1.50	4.00
172 Billy Williams	40.00	80.00
173 Andre Rodgers	10.00	25.00
174 Ken Hubbs	3.00	8.00
175 Don Landrum	8.00	20.00
176 Dick Bertell	8.00	20.00
177 Roy Sievers	2.50	6.00
178 Tony Taylor	10.00	25.00
179 Johnny Callison	2.50	6.00
180 Don Demeter	1.50	4.00
181 Tony Gonzalez	8.00	20.00
182 Wes Covington	8.00	20.00
183 Art Mahaffey	1.50	4.00
184 Clay Dalrymple	2.50	6.00
185 Al Spangler	1.50	4.00
186 Roman Mejias	1.50	4.00
187 Bob Aspromonte	12.50	30.00
188 Norm Larker	1.50	4.00
189 Johnny Temple	1.50	4.00
190 Carl Warwick	8.00	20.00
191 Bob Lillis	8.00	20.00
192 Dick Farrell	15.00	40.00
193 Gil Hodges	5.00	12.00
194 Marv Throneberry	2.50	6.00
195 Charlie Neal	10.00	25.00
196 Frank Thomas	2.50	6.00
197 Richie Ashburn	4.00	10.00
198 Felix Mantilla	8.00	20.00
199 Rod Kanehl	8.00	20.00
200 Roger Craig	12.50	30.00

1963 Jewish Sports Champions

The 16 cards in this set, measuring roughly 2 2/3" x 3", are cut out of an "Activity Funbook" entitled Jewish Sports Champions. The set pays tribute to famous Jewish athletes from baseball, football, bull fighting to chess. The cards have a green border with a yellow background and a player close-up illustration. Cards that are still attached carry a premium over those that have been cut-out. The cards are unnumbered and listed below in alphabetical order with an assigned sport prefix (BB-baseball, BK- basketball, BX- boxing, FB-football, OT- other).

COMPLETE SET (16)	100.00	200.00
BB1 Hank Greenberg BB	10.00	20.00
BB2 Johnny Kling BB	5.00	10.00
BB3 Sandy Koufax BB	20.00	40.00

1973 Jewish Sports Champions

The 16 cards in this set, measuring roughly 2 2/3" x 3", are cut out of a sequel to the 1968 Activity Funbook. This time, the cards come from a funbook entitled "More Jewish Sports Champions". There are two variations to each card that are valued equally. One has a pink border with a yellow background and blue ink on the player close-up illustration. The other has a blue background and black ink on the player illustration. Cards that are still attached carry a premium over those that have been cut-out. The cards are unnumbered and listed below in alphabetical order.

COMPLETE SET (16)	65.00	125.00
12 Al (Flip) Rosen BB	6.00	12.00

1959 Jimmy Fund Membership Card

This one card "set" is presumed to be issued in 1959 and features a photo of the Jimmy Fund building on the front. The back contains a "photo" of Ted Williams along with a statement thanking the member for their support of the Jimmy Fund.

1 Jimmy Fund Building	4.00	8.00

1976 Jimmy Fund

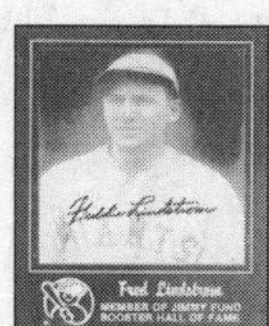

These oversize cards were issued in 1976 and featured members of the Baseball Hall of Fame. These cards are rarely seen and have black and white photos on the front with the players names and their Jimmy Fund affiliation on the bottom. As far as is known, the only players issued are in the Hall of Fame. As the cards are blank backed and unnumbered we have sequenced them in alphabetical order. There may be additions to this checklist so any additional information is appreciated.

COMPLETE SET	300.00	600.00
1 Cool Papa Bell	20.00	50.00
2 Jocko Conlan UER Spelled Conlin	20.00	50.00
3 Stan Coveleskie	20.00	50.00
4 Charlie Gehringer	30.00	60.00
5 Hank Greenberg	40.00	80.00
6 Burleigh Grimes	20.00	50.00
7 Waite Hoyt	20.00	50.00
8 Monte Irvin	30.00	60.00
9 George Kelly	20.00	50.00
10 Sandy Koufax	75.00	150.00
11 Fred Lindstrom	20.00	50.00

1976 Jerry Jonas Promotion Cards

These eight cards were issued by Jerry Jonas Promotions as part of an attempt to secure a major league lisense. These cards were presented at the World Series meetings in 1975. These cards, featuring all time greats, were in the format of the regular 1975 Topps issue. The set is also sometimes found as an uncut sheet of all eight players. According to published reports no more than 100 sets of these were printed.

COMPLETE SET	300.00	600.00
1 Sandy Koufax	50.00	100.00
2 Mel Ott	30.00	60.00
3 Willie Mays	75.00	150.00
4 Stan Musial	50.00	100.00
5 Rogers Hornsby	20.00	50.00
6 Honus Wagner	40.00	80.00
7 Grover Alexander	40.00	80.00
8 Robin Roberts	30.00	60.00

1911 Jones, Keyser and Arras Cabinets

These 4 3/4" by 7 1/4" cabinets were issued in 1911 from this New York City based company. The fronts feature a player photo with the image number on the bottom of the photo and the players name on the bottom of the card. There may be more cabinets in this set so any additional information is appreciated.

COMPLETE SET	5,000.00	12,000.00
301 Russ Ford	400.00	800.00
303 Jack Warhop	400.00	800.00
304 Bill Dahlen MG	400.00	800.00
306 Zack Wheat	750.00	1,500.00
307 Al Bridwell	400.00	800.00
308 Red Murray	400.00	800.00
310 Fred Snodgrass	500.00	1,000.00
311 Red Ames	400.00	800.00
312 Fred Merkle	600.00	1,200.00
313 Art Devlin	400.00	800.00
314 Hooks Wiltse	400.00	800.00
315 Josh Devore	400.00	800.00
316 Eddie Collins	1,250.00	2,500.00
317 Ed Reulbach	400.00	800.00
318 Jimmy Sheckard	400.00	800.00
320 Wildfire Schulte	500.00	1,000.00
321 Solly Hofman	400.00	800.00
322 Bill Bergen	400.00	800.00
323 George Bell	400.00	800.00
325 Fred Clarke MG	750.00	1,500.00
326 Clark Griffith MG	750.00	1,500.00
327 Roger Bresnahan	750.00	1,500.00
328 Fred Tenney	400.00	800.00
329 Harry Lord	400.00	800.00
331 Walter Johnson	2,000.00	4,000.00
332 Nap Lajoie	1,500.00	3,000.00
333 Joe Tinker	1,250.00	2,500.00
334 Mordecai Brown	750.00	1,500.00
336 Jimmy Archer	400.00	800.00
340 Hal Chase	600.00	1,200.00
341 Larry Doyle	500.00	1,000.00
342 Chief Meyers	500.00	1,000.00
343 Christy Mathewson	2,000.00	4,000.00
344 Bugs Raymond	400.00	800.00
345 John McGraw MG	1,500.00	3,000.00
346 Honus Wagner	2,000.00	4,000.00
347 Ty Cobb	3,000.00	6,000.00
348 Johnnie Evers	1,250.00	2,500.00
349 Frank Chance	1,250.00	2,500.00

1886-88 Joseph Hall Cabinets

In 1888, Joseph Hall produced a 14-card set of cabinets. The cabinet cards feature major league team photos. The horizontal cabinets measure 6 1/2" by 4 1/4". The cards have says Joseph Hall directly under the team photo.

COMPLETE SET	40,000.00	80,000.00
1 Baltimore, 1888	4,000.00	8,000.00
2 Boston, 1888	6,000.00	12,000.00
3 Brooklyn, 1888	4,000.00	8,000.00
4 Chicago, 1888	6,000.00	12,000.00
5 Cincinnati, 1888	4,000.00	8,000.00
6 Cleveland, 1888	4,000.00	8,000.00
7 Detroit, 1888	5,000.00	10,000.00
8 Indianapolis, 1888	4,000.00	8,000.00
9 Kansas City, 1888	4,000.00	8,000.00
10 Louisville, 1888	4,000.00	8,000.00
11 New York, 1888	4,000.00	8,000.00
12 Athletic, 1888	5,000.00	10,000.00
13 St. Louis, 1888	4,000.00	8,000.00
14 Washington, 1888	4,000.00	8,000.00

1910 Ju Ju Drums E286

These round "cards" have a diameter measure of 1 7/16". They were issued by Ju Ju Drums gum. The set can be dated to 1910 by the inclusion of Elmer Zacher who had his only major league season that year. These cards are unnumbered and we have sequenced them in alphabetical order.

COMPLETE SET (43)	7,500.00	15,000.00
1 Eddie Ainsmith	250.00	500.00
2 Jimmy Austin	250.00	500.00
3 Chief Bender	500.00	1,000.00
4 Bruno Block	250.00	500.00
5 Jimmy Burke	250.00	500.00
6 Donie Bush	250.00	500.00
7 Frank Chance	600.00	1,200.00
8 Harry Cheek	250.00	500.00
9 Eddie Cicotte	500.00	1,000.00
10 Ty Cobb	3,000.00	6,000.00
11 King Cole	250.00	500.00
12 Jack Coombs	500.00	1,000.00
13 Bill Dahlen	250.00	500.00
14 Bert Daniels	250.00	500.00
15 George Davis	500.00	1,000.00
16 Larry Doyle	300.00	600.00
17 Rube Ellis	250.00	500.00
18 George Ferguson	250.00	500.00
19 Russ Ford	250.00	500.00
20 Robert Harmon	250.00	500.00
21 Robert Hyatt	250.00	500.00
22 William Killefer	250.00	500.00
23 Arthur Krueger	250.00	500.00
24 Thomas Leach	300.00	600.00
25 Christy Mathewson	1,500.00	3,000.00
26 John McGraw	750.00	1,500.00
27 Deacon McGuire	250.00	500.00
28 Chief Meyers	300.00	600.00
29 Roy Miller	250.00	500.00
30 George Mullin	300.00	600.00
31 Tom Needham	250.00	500.00
32 Rube Oldring	250.00	500.00
33 Barney Pelty	250.00	500.00
34 Ed Reulbach	300.00	600.00
35 John Rowan	250.00	500.00
36 David Shean	250.00	500.00
37 Tris Speaker	1,000.00	2,000.00
38 Ed Sweeney	250.00	500.00
39 Jimmy Walsh	250.00	500.00
40 Honus Wagner	1,500.00	3,000.00
41 Doc White	250.00	500.00
42 Ralph Works	250.00	500.00
43 Elmer Zacher	250.00	500.00

1893 Just So

These 14 cards measure 2 1/2" by 3 7/8" and feature members of the Cleveland Spiders. So far, these cards have been checklisted but others may exist. We have sequenced these cards in alphabetical order. The earliest known Cy Young card is in this set.

COMPLETE SET (13)	200,000.00	400,000.00
1 Frank Boyd	15,000.00	30,000.00
2 Jesse Burkett	30,000.00	60,000.00
3 Cupid Childs	15,000.00	30,000.00
4 John Clarkson	30,000.00	60,000.00
5 George Cuppy	15,000.00	30,000.00
6 George Davies	30,000.00	60,000.00
7 Charlie Hastings	15,000.00	30,000.00
8 Ed McKean	15,000.00	30,000.00
9 Jack O'Connor	15,000.00	30,000.00
10 Patsy Tebeau	20,000.00	40,000.00
11 Jake Virtue	15,000.00	30,000.00
12 Tom Williams	15,000.00	30,000.00
13 Cy Young	50,000.00	100,000.00
14 Chief Zimmer	15,000.00	30,000.00

1955 Kahn's

The cards in this six-card set measure 3 1/4" X 4". The 1955 Kahn's Wieners set received very limited distribution. The cards were supposedly given away at an amusement park. The set portrays the players in street clothes rather than in uniform and hence are sometimes referred to as "street clothes" Kahn's. All Kahn's sets from 1955 through 1963 are black and white and contain a 1/2" tab. Cards with the tab still intact are worth approximately 50 percent more than cards without the tab. Cards feature a facsimile autograph of the player on the front. Cards are blank-backed. Only Cincinnati Redlegs players are featured.

COMPLETE SET (6)	3,400.00	6,800.00
1 Gus Bell	750.00	1,500.00
2 Ted Kluszewski	1,250.00	2,500.00
3 Roy McMillan	600.00	1,200.00
4 Joe Nuxhall	750.00	1,500.00
5 Wally Post	600.00	1,200.00
6 Johnny Temple	600.00	1,200.00

1956 Kahn's

The cards in this 15-card set measure 3 1/4" X 4". The 1956 Kahn's set was the first set to be issued with Kahn's meat products. The cards are blank backed. The set is distinguished by the old style, short sleeve shirts on the players and the existence of backgounds (Kahn's cards of later years utilize a blank backgound). Cards which have the tab still intact are worth approximately 50 percent more than cards without the tab. Only Cincinnati Redlegs players are featured. The cards are listed and numbered below in alphabetical order by the subject's name. This set contains a very early Frank Robinson card.

COMPLETE SET (15)	1,000.00	1,600.00
1 Ed Bailey	50.00	80.00
2 Gus Bell	55.00	100.00
3 Joe Black	60.00	120.00
4 Smoky Burgess	55.00	100.00
5 Art Fowler	50.00	80.00
6 Herschel Freeman	50.00	80.00
7 Ray Jablonski	50.00	80.00
8 John Klippstein	50.00	80.00
9 Ted Kluszewski	120.00	200.00
10 Brooks Lawrence	55.00	100.00
11 Roy McMillan	55.00	100.00
12 Joe Nuxhall	55.00	100.00
13 Wally Post	55.00	100.00
14 Frank Robinson	300.00	500.00
15 Johnny Temple	55.00	100.00

1957 Kahn's

The cards in this 29-card set measure 3 1/4" by 4". The 1957 Kahn's Wieners set contains black and white, blank backed, unnumbered cards. The set features only the Cincinnati Redlegs and Pittsburgh Pirates. The cards feature a light background. Each card features a facsimile autograph of the player on the front. The Groat card exists with a "Richard Groat" autograph and also exists with the printed name "Dick Groat" on the card. The set price includes both Groats. The catalog designation is F155-3. The cards are listed and numbered below in alphabetical order by the subject's name. A Bill Mazeroski card was printed during this, his Rookie Card season.

COMPLETE SET (29)	1,800.00	3,000.00
1 Tom Acker	35.00	60.00
2 Ed Bailey	35.00	60.00
3 Gus Bell	50.00	80.00
4 Smoky Burgess	50.00	80.00
5 Roberto Clemente	600.00	1,000.00
6 George Crowe	35.00	60.00
7 Roy Face	60.00	100.00
8 Herschel Freeman	35.00	60.00
9 Bob Friend	50.00	80.00
10 Dick Groat	60.00	100.00
11 Richard Groat	100.00	200.00
12 Don Gross	35.00	60.00
13 Warren Hacker	35.00	60.00
14 Don Hoak	50.00	80.00
15 Hal Jeffcoat	35.00	60.00
16 Ron Kline	35.00	60.00
17 John Klippstein	35.00	60.00
18 Ted Kluszewski	100.00	200.00
19 Brooks Lawrence	50.00	80.00
20 Dale Long	35.00	60.00
21 Bill Mazeroski	150.00	250.00
22 Roy McMillan	50.00	80.00
23 Joe Nuxhall	35.00	60.00
24 Wally Post	50.00	80.00
25 Frank Robinson	250.00	400.00
26 John Temple	50.00	80.00
27 Frank Thomas	35.00	60.00
28 Bob Thurman	35.00	60.00
29 Lee Walls	35.00	60.00

1958 Kahn's

The cards in this 29-card set measure approximately 3 1/4" X 4". The 1958 Kahn's Wieners set of unnumbered, black and white cards features Cincinnati Redlegs, Philadelphia Phillies and Pittsburgh Pirates. The backs present a story for each player entitled "My Greatest Thrill in Baseball". A method of distinguishing 1958 Kahn's from 1959 Kahn's is that the word Wieners is found on the front of the 1958 but not on the front of the 1959 cards. Cards of Wally Post, Charlie Rabe and Frank Thomas are somewhat more difficult to find and are designated SP in the our checklist. The cards are listed and numbered below in alphabetical order by the subject's name.

COMPLETE SET (29)	2,000.00	3,200.00
COMMON PLAYER (1-29)	30.00	50.00
COMMON SP	150.00	300.00
1 Ed Bailey	30.00	50.00
2 Gene Baker	30.00	50.00
3 Gus Bell	35.00	60.00
4 Smoky Burgess	35.00	60.00
5 Roberto Clemente	300.00	600.00
6 George Crowe	35.00	60.00
7 Roy Face	50.00	80.00
8 Hank Foiles	30.00	50.00
9 Dee Fondy	30.00	50.00
10 Bob Friend	35.00	60.00
11 Dick Groat	50.00	80.00
12 Harvey Haddix	35.00	60.00
13 Don Hoak	30.00	50.00
14 Hal Jeffcoat	30.00	50.00
15 Ron Kline	30.00	50.00
16 Ted Kluszewski	75.00	125.00
17 Vernon Law	35.00	60.00
18 Brooks Lawrence	35.00	60.00
19 Bill Mazeroski	75.00	125.00
20 Roy McMillan	35.00	60.00
21 Joe Nuxhall	35.00	60.00
22 Wally Post SP	175.00	350.00
23 John Powers	30.00	50.00
24 Bob Purkey	30.00	50.00
25 Charlie Rabe SP	150.00	300.00
26 Frank Robinson	150.00	250.00
27 Bob Skinner	30.00	50.00
28 Johnny Temple	35.00	60.00
29 Frank Thomas SP	175.00	350.00

1959 Kahn's

The cards in this 38-card set measure approximately 3 1/4" X 4". The 1959 Kahn's set features members of the Cincinnati Reds, Cleveland Indians and Pittsburgh Pirates. Backs feature stories entitled "The Toughest Play I have to Make," or "The Toughest Batter I Have To Face." The Brodowski card is very scarce while Haddix, Held and McLish are considered quite difficult to obtain; these scarcities are designated SP in the checklist below. The cards are listed and numbered below in alphabetical order by the subject's name.

COMPLETE SET (38)	2,500.00	4,500.00
COMMON PLAYER (1-38)	30.00	50.00
COMMON SP	200.00	400.00
1 Ed Bailey	30.00	50.00
2 Gary Bell	30.00	50.00
3 Gus Bell	35.00	60.00
4 Dick Brodowski SP	300.00	600.00
5 Smoky Burgess	35.00	60.00
6 Roberto Clemente	300.00	600.00
7 Rocky Colavito	75.00	125.00
8 Roy Face	50.00	80.00
9 Bob Friend	35.00	60.00
10 Joe Gordon MG	35.00	60.00
11 Jim Grant	35.00	60.00
12 Dick Groat	50.00	80.00
13 Harvey Haddix SP/(Blank back)	200.00	400.00
14 Woodie Held SP	200.00	400.00
15 Don Hoak	30.00	50.00
16 Ron Kline	30.00	50.00
17 Ted Kluszewski	75.00	125.00
18 Vernon Law	35.00	60.00
19 Jerry Lynch	30.00	50.00
20 Billy Martin	75.00	125.00
21 Bill Mazeroski	75.00	125.00
22 Cal McLish SP	200.00	400.00
23 Roy McMillan	30.00	50.00
24 Minnie Minoso	60.00	100.00
25 Russ Nixon	30.00	50.00
26 Joe Nuxhall	35.00	60.00
27 Jim Perry	50.00	80.00
28 Vada Pinson	60.00	100.00
29 Vic Power	30.00	50.00
30 Bob Purkey	30.00	50.00
31 Frank Robinson	120.00	200.00
32 Herb Score	50.00	80.00
33 Bob Skinner	30.00	50.00
34 George Strickland	30.00	50.00
35 Dick Stuart	35.00	60.00
36 Johnny Temple	30.00	50.00
37 Frank Thomas	35.00	60.00
38 George Witt	30.00	50.00

1960 Kahn's

The cards in this 42-card set measure 3 1/4" X 4". The 1960 Kahn's set features players of the Chicago Cubs, Chicago White Sox, Cincinnati Redlegs, Cleveland Indians, Pittsburgh Pirates and St. Louis Cardinals. The backs give vital player information and records through the 1959 season. Kline appears with either St. Louis or Pittsburgh. The set price includes both Kline's. The Harvey Kuenn card in this set appears with a blank back and is scarce. The cards are listed and numbered below in alphabetical order by the subject's name.

COMPLETE SET (43)	1,000.00	2,000.00
1 Ed Bailey	10.00	25.00
2 Gary Bell	10.00	25.00
3 Gus Bell	12.50	30.00
4 Smoky Burgess	12.50	30.00
5 Gino Cimoli	10.00	25.00
6 Roberto Clemente	250.00	500.00
7 Roy Face	12.50	30.00
8 Tito Francona	10.00	25.00
9 Bob Friend	12.50	30.00
10 Jim Grant	12.50	30.00
11 Dick Groat	15.00	40.00
12 Harvey Haddix	12.50	30.00
13 Woodie Held	10.00	25.00
14 Bill Henry	10.00	25.00
15 Don Hoak	10.00	25.00
16 Jay Hook	10.00	25.00
17 Eddie Kasko	10.00	25.00
18A Ron Kline/(Pittsburgh)	20.00	50.00
18B Ron Kline/(St. Louis)	20.00	50.00
19 Ted Kluszewski	30.00	60.00
20 Harvey Kuenn SP/(Blank back)	200.00	400.00
21 Vernon Law	12.50	30.00
22 Brooks Lawrence	12.50	30.00
23 Jerry Lynch	10.00	25.00
24 Billy Martin	30.00	60.00
25 Bill Mazeroski	30.00	60.00
26 Cal McLish	10.00	25.00
27 Roy McMillan	10.00	25.00
28 Don Newcombe	15.00	40.00
29 Russ Nixon	10.00	25.00
30 Joe Nuxhall	12.50	30.00
31 Jim O'Toole	10.00	25.00
32 Jim Perry	12.50	30.00
33 Vada Pinson	20.00	50.00
34 Vic Power	10.00	25.00
35 Bob Purkey	10.00	25.00
36 Frank Robinson	75.00	150.00
37 Herb Score	12.50	30.00
38 Bob Skinner	10.00	25.00
39 Dick Stuart	12.50	30.00
40 Johnny Temple	12.50	30.00
41 Frank Thomas	12.50	30.00
42 Lee Walls	10.00	25.00

1961 Kahn's

The cards in this 43-card set measure approximately 3 1/4" X 4". The 1961 Kahn's Wieners set of black and white, unnumbered cards features members of the Cincinnati Reds, Cleveland Indians and Pittsburgh Pirates. This year was the first year Kahn's made complete sets available to the public; hence they are more available, especially in the better condition grades than the Kahn's of the previous years. The backs give vital player information and year by year career statistics through 1960. The catalog designation is F155-7. The cards are listed and numbered below in alphabetical order by the subject's name.

COMPLETE SET (43)	500.00	1,000.00
1 John Antonelli	5.00	12.00
2 Ed Bailey	5.00	12.00
3 Gary Bell	5.00	12.00
4 Gus Bell	6.00	15.00
5 Jim Brosnan	6.00	15.00
6 Smoky Burgess	6.00	15.00
7 Gino Cimoli	5.00	12.00
8 Roberto Clemente	200.00	400.00
9 Gordie Coleman	5.00	12.00
10 Jimmy Dykes MG	6.00	15.00
11 Roy Face	6.00	15.00
12 Tito Francona	5.00	12.00
13 Gene Freese	5.00	12.00
14 Bob Friend	6.00	15.00
15 Jim Grant	6.00	15.00
16 Dick Groat	6.00	15.00
17 Harvey Haddix	6.00	15.00
18 Woodie Held	5.00	12.00
19 Don Hoak	5.00	12.00
20 Jay Hook	5.00	12.00
21 Joey Jay	5.00	12.00
22 Eddie Kasko	5.00	12.00
23 Willie Kirkland	5.00	12.00
24 Vernon Law	6.00	15.00
25 Jerry Lynch	5.00	12.00
26 Jim Maloney	8.00	20.00
27 Bill Mazeroski	15.00	40.00
28 Wilmer Mizell	6.00	15.00
29 Rocky Nelson	5.00	12.00
30 Jim O'Toole	5.00	12.00
31 Jim Perry	6.00	15.00
32 Bubba Phillips	5.00	12.00
33 Vada Pinson	12.50	30.00
34 Wally Post	5.00	12.00
35 Vic Power	5.00	12.00
36 Bob Purkey	5.00	12.00
37 Frank Robinson	50.00	100.00
38 John Romano	5.00	12.00
39 Dick Schofield	5.00	12.00
40 Bob Skinner	5.00	12.00
41 Hal Smith	5.00	12.00
42 Dick Stuart	6.00	15.00
43 Johnny Temple	5.00	12.00

1962 Kahn's

The cards in this 38-card set measure approximately 3 1/4" X 4". The 1962 Kahn's Wieners set of black and white, unnumbered cards features Cincinnati, Cleveland, Minnesota and Pittsburgh players. Card numbers 1 Bell, 33 Power and 34 Purkey exist in two different forms; these variations are listed in the checklist below. The backs of the cards contain career information. The catalog designation is F155-8. The set price below includes the set with all variation cards. The cards are listed and numbered below in alphabetical order by the subject's name.

COMPLETE SET (41)	1,000.00	2,000.00
1A Gary Bell/(With fat man)	100.00	200.00
1B Gary Bell/(No fat man)	40.00	80.00
2 Jim Brosnan	10.00	25.00
3 Smoky Burgess	10.00	25.00
4 Chico Cardenas	10.00	25.00
5 Roberto Clemente	300.00	600.00
6 Ty Cline	8.00	20.00
7 Gordon Coleman	10.00	25.00
8 Dick Donovan	8.00	20.00
9 John Edwards	8.00	20.00
10 Tito Francona	8.00	20.00
11 Gene Freese	8.00	20.00
12 Bob Friend	10.00	25.00
13 Joe Gibbon	60.00	120.00
14 Jim Grant	12.50	25.00
15 Dick Groat	12.50	30.00
16 Harvey Haddix	10.00	25.00
17 Woodie Held	8.00	20.00
18 Bill Henry	8.00	20.00
19 Don Hoak	8.00	20.00
20 Ken Hunt	8.00	20.00
21 Joey Jay	8.00	20.00
22 Eddie Kasko	8.00	20.00
23 Willie Kirkland	8.00	20.00
24 Barry Latman	8.00	20.00
25 Jerry Lynch	8.00	20.00
26 Jim Maloney	12.50	30.00
27 Bill Mazeroski	15.00	40.00
28 Jim O'Toole	8.00	20.00
29 Jim Perry	10.00	25.00
30 Bubba Phillips	8.00	20.00
31 Vada Pinson	12.50	30.00
32 Wally Post	8.00	20.00
33A Vic Power (Indians)	40.00	80.00
33B Vic Power (Twins)	100.00	200.00
34A Bob Purkey/(With autograph)	40.00	80.00
34B Bob Purkey/(No autograph)	100.00	200.00
35 Frank Robinson	100.00	200.00
36 John Romano	8.00	20.00
37 Dick Stuart	10.00	25.00
38 Bill Virdon	12.50	30.00

1963 Kahn's

The cards in this 30-card set measure approximately 3 1/4" X 4". The 1963 Kahn's Wieners set of black and white, unnumbered cards features players from Cincinnati, Cleveland, St. Louis, Pittsburgh and the New York Yankees. The cards feature a white border around the picture of the players. The backs contain career information. The catalog designation for this set is F155-10. The cards are listed and numbered below in alphabetical order by the subject's name.

COMPLETE SET (30)	1,000.00	2,000.00
1 Bob Bailey	12.50	30.00
2 Don Blasingame	12.50	30.00
3 Clete Boyer	20.00	50.00
4 Smoky Burgess	15.00	40.00
5 Chico Cardenas	15.00	40.00
6 Roberto Clemente	400.00	800.00
7 Donn Clendenon	15.00	40.00

8 Gordon Coleman	15.00	40.00
9 John Edwards	12.50	30.00
10 Gene Freese	12.50	30.00
11 Bob Friend	15.00	40.00
12 Joe Gibbon	12.50	30.00
13 Dick Groat	20.00	50.00
14 Harvey Haddix	15.00	40.00
15 Elston Howard	40.00	80.00
16 Joey Jay	12.50	30.00
17 Eddie Kasko	12.50	30.00
18 Tony Kubek	50.00	100.00
19 Jerry Lynch	12.50	30.00
20 Jim Maloney	20.00	50.00
21 Bill Mazeroski	50.00	100.00
22 Joe Nuxhall	15.00	40.00
23 Jim O'Toole	12.50	30.00
24 Vada Pinson	30.00	60.00
25 Bob Purkey	12.50	30.00
26 Bobby Richardson	50.00	100.00
27 Frank Robinson	150.00	300.00
28 Bill Stafford	12.50	30.00
29 Ralph Terry	15.00	40.00
30 Bill Virdon	15.00	40.00

1964 Kahn's

The cards in this 31-card set measure 3" X 3 1/2". The 1964 Kahn's set marks the beginning of the full color cards and the elimination of the tabs which existed on previous Kahn's cards. The set of unnumbered cards contains player information through the 1963 season on the backs. The set features Cincinnati, Cleveland and Pittsburgh players. The cards are listed and numbered below in alphabetical order by the subject's name. An early card of Pete Rose highlights this set.

COMPLETE SET (31)	600.00	1,200.00
1 Max Alvis	5.00	12.00
2 Bob Bailey	5.00	12.00
3 Chico Cardenas	6.00	15.00
4 Roberto Clemente	200.00	400.00
5 Donn Clendenon	6.00	15.00
6 Vic Davalillo	5.00	12.00
7 Dick Donovan	5.00	12.00
8 John Edwards	5.00	12.00
9 Bob Friend	6.00	15.00
10 Jim Grant	6.00	15.00
11 Tommy Harper	6.00	15.00
12 Woodie Held	6.00	15.00
13 Joey Jay	5.00	12.00
14 Jack Kralick	5.00	12.00
15 Jerry Lynch	5.00	12.00
16 Jim Maloney	6.00	15.00
17 Bill Mazeroski	12.50	30.00
18 Alvin McBean	5.00	12.00
19 Joe Nuxhall	6.00	15.00
20 Jim Pagliaroni	5.00	12.00
21 Vada Pinson	10.00	25.00
22 Bob Purkey	5.00	12.00
23 Pedro Ramos	5.00	12.00
24 Frank Robinson	60.00	120.00
25 John Romano	5.00	12.00
26 Pete Rose	250.00	500.00
27 John Tsitouris	5.00	12.00
28 Bob Veale	6.00	15.00
29 Bill Virdon	6.00	15.00
30 Leon Wagner	5.00	12.00
31 Fred Whitfield	5.00	12.00

1965 Kahn's

The cards in this 45-card set measure 3" X 3 1/2". The 1965 Kahn's set contains full-color, unnumbered cards. The set features Cincinnati, Cleveland, Pittsburgh and Milwaukee players. Backs contain statistical information through the 1964 season. The cards are listed and numbered below in alphabetical order by the subject's name.

COMPLETE SET (45)	1,250.00	2,500.00
1 Henry Aaron	200.00	400.00
2 Max Alvis	12.50	30.00
3 Joe Azcue	10.00	25.00
4 Bob Bailey	10.00	25.00
5 Frank Bolling	10.00	25.00
6 Chico Cardenas	12.50	30.00
7 Rico Carty	15.00	40.00
8 Donn Clendenon	12.50	30.00
9 Tony Cloninger	12.50	30.00
10 Gordon Coleman	10.00	25.00
11 Vic Davalillo	10.00	25.00
12 John Edwards	10.00	25.00
13 Sammy Ellis	10.00	25.00
14 Bob Friend	12.50	30.00
15 Tommy Harper	10.00	25.00
16 Chuck Hinton	12.50	30.00
17 Dick Howser	12.50	30.00
18 Joey Jay	10.00	25.00
19 Deron Johnson	12.50	30.00
20 Jack Kralick	10.00	25.00
21 Denver LeMaster	10.00	25.00
22 Jerry Lynch	10.00	25.00
23 Jim Maloney	15.00	40.00
24 Lee Maye	10.00	25.00
25 Bill Mazeroski	30.00	60.00
26 Alvin McBean	10.00	25.00
27 Bill McCool	10.00	25.00
28 Sam McDowell	15.00	40.00
29 Don McMahon	10.00	25.00
30 Denis Menke	10.00	25.00
31 Joe Nuxhall	12.50	30.00
32 Gene Oliver	10.00	25.00
33 Jim O'Toole	10.00	25.00
34 Jim Pagliaroni	10.00	25.00
35 Vada Pinson	20.00	50.00
36 Frank Robinson	125.00	250.00
37 Pete Rose	250.00	500.00
38 Willie Stargell	125.00	250.00
39 Ralph Terry	12.50	30.00
40 Luis Tiant	20.00	50.00
41 Joe Torre	30.00	60.00
42 John Tsitouris	10.00	25.00
43 Bob Veale	12.50	30.00
44 Bill Virdon	12.50	30.00
45 Leon Wagner	10.00	25.00

1966 Kahn's

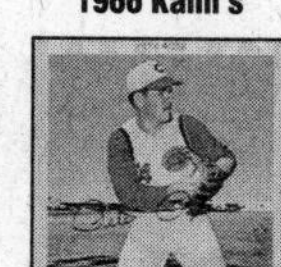

The cards in this 32-card set measure 2 13/16" X 4". 1966 Kahn's full-color, unnumbered set features players from Atlanta, Cincinnati, Cleveland and Pittsburgh. The set is identified by yellow and white vertical stripes and the name Kahn's written in red across a red rose at the top. The cards contain a 1 5/16" ad in the form of a tab. Cards with the ad (tab) are worth twice as much as cards without the ad. (double the prices below) The cards are listed and numbered below in alphabetical order by the subject's name.

COMPLETE SET (32)	400.00	800.00
1 Henry Aaron/(Portrait& no wind- breaker under je	75.00	150.00
2 Felipe Alou: Braves/(Full pose& batting screen i	10.00	25.00
3 Max Alvis: Indians/(Kneeling& full pose& with ba	5.00	12.00
4 Bob Bailey	5.00	12.00
5 Wade Blasingame	5.00	12.00
6 Frank Bolling	5.00	12.00
7 Chico Cardenas: Reds Fielding feet at base	6.00	15.00
8 Roberto Clemente	100.00	200.00
9 Tony Cloninger: Braves (Pitching& foulpole in b	6.00	15.00
10 Vic Davalillo	5.00	12.00
11 John Edwards: Reds Catching	5.00	12.00
12 Sam Ellis: Reds White hat	5.00	12.00
13 Pedro Gonzalez	5.00	12.00
14 Tommy Harper: Reds Arm cocked	6.00	15.00
15 Deron Johnson: Reds (Batting with batting cage i	6.00	15.00
16 Mack Jones	5.00	12.00
17 Denver Lemaster	5.00	12.00
18 Jim Maloney: Reds Pitching white hat	6.00	15.00
19 Bill Mazeroski: Pirates Throwing	12.50	30.00
20 Bill McCool: Reds White hat	5.00	12.00
21 Sam McDowell: Indians Kneeling	6.00	15.00
22 Denis Menke: Braves/(White windbreaker under jer	5.00	12.00
23 Joe Nuxhall	6.00	15.00
24 Jim Pagliaroni: Pirates Catching	5.00	12.00
25 Milt Pappas	6.00	15.00
26 Vada Pinson: Reds/(Fielding ball on ground	10.00	25.00
27 Pete Rose: Reds With glove	75.00	150.00
28 Sonny Siebert: Indians (Pitching& signature at f	6.00	15.00
29 Willie Stargell: Pirates (Batting& clouds in sky	30.00	60.00
30 Joe Torre: Braves Catching with hand on mask	12.50	30.00
31 Bob Veale: Pirates Hands at knee with glasses	6.00	15.00
32 Fred Whitfield	5.00	12.00

1967 Kahn's

The cards in this 41-player set measure 2 13/16" X 4". The 1967 Kahn's set of full-color, unnumbered cards is almost identical in style to the 1966 issue. Different meat products had different background colors (yellow and white stripes, red and white stripes, etc.). The set features players from Atlanta, Cincinnati, Cleveland, New York Mets and Pittsburgh. Cards with the ads (see 1966 set) are worth twice as much as cards without the ad, i.e., double the prices below. The complete set price below includes all variations. The cards are listed and numbered below in alphabetical order by the subject's name. Examples have been seen in which the top borders have a very small indentation.

COMPLETE SET (51)	800.00	1,600.00
1A Henry Aaron: Braves/(Swinging pose& batting glov	125.00	250.00
1B Henry Aaron: Braves Swinging pose, batting glove, ball, and hat on ground; Cut Along Dotted Lines printed on lower tab	150.00	300.00
2 Gene Alley: Pirates Portrait	10.00	25.00
3 Felipe Alou: Braves Full pose, bat on shoulder	15.00	40.00
4A Matty Alou: Pirates (Portrait with bat/Matio	10.00	25.00
4B Matty Alou: Pirates (Portrait with bat/Matio	12.50	30.00
5 Max Alvis: Indians Fielding, hands on knees	8.00	20.00
6A Ken Boyer Batting righthanded; autograph at waist	12.50	30.00
6B Ken Boyer Batting righthanded; autograph at shoulders; Cut Along Dotted Lines printed on lower tab	15.00	40.00
7 Chico Cardenas: Reds Fielding hand on knee	10.00	25.00
8 Rico Carty	10.00	25.00
9 Tony Cloninger: Braves Pitching, no foul- pole in background	10.00	25.00
10 Tommy Davis	10.00	25.00
11 John Edwards: Reds Kneeling with bat	8.00	20.00
12A Sam Ellis: Reds All red hat	8.00	20.00
12B Sam Ellis: Reds All red hat; Cut Along Dotted Lines printed on lower tab	10.00	25.00
13 Jack Fisher	8.00	20.00
14 Steve Hargan: Indians Pitching, no clouds blue sky	8.00	20.00
15 Tommy Harper: Reds Fielding, glove on ground	10.00	25.00
16A Tommy Helms Batting righthanded; top of bat visible	10.00	25.00
16B Tommy Helms Batting righthanded; bat chopped above hat; Cut Along Dotted Lines printed on lower tab	12.50	30.00
17 Deron Johnson: Reds Batting, blue sky	10.00	25.00
18 Ken Johnson	8.00	20.00
19 Cleon Jones	10.00	25.00
20A Ed Kranepool Ready for throw; yellow stripes	10.00	25.00
20B Ed Kranepool Ready for throw; red stripes	10.00	25.00
21A Jim Maloney: Reds Pitching, red hat, follow thru delivery; yellow stripes	10.00	25.00
21B Jim Maloney: Reds Pitching, red hat, follow thru delivery; red stripes	12.50	30.00
22 Lee May: Reds Hands on knee	10.00	25.00
23A Bill Mazeroski: Pirates Portrait; autograph below waist	20.00	50.00
23B Bill Mazeroski: Pirates Portrait; autograph above waist; Cut Along Dotted Lines printed on lower tab	30.00	60.00
24 Bill McCool: Reds Red hat, left hand out	8.00	20.00
25 Sam McDowell: Indians Pitching, left hand under glove	12.50	30.00
26 Denis Menke: Braves Blue sleeves	8.00	20.00
27 Jim Pagliaroni: Pirates Catching no chest protector	8.00	20.00
28 Don Pavletich	8.00	20.00
29 Tony Perez: Reds Throwing	50.00	100.00
30 Vada Pinson: Reds Ready to throw	15.00	40.00
31 Dennis Ribant	8.00	20.00
32 Pete Rose: Reds Batting	125.00	250.00
33 Art Shamsky: Reds	8.00	20.00
34 Bob Shaw	8.00	20.00
35 Sonny Siebert: Indians Pitching signature at knees	8.00	20.00
36 Willie Stargell: Pirates Batting no clouds	50.00	100.00
37A Joe Torre: Braves Catching, mask on ground	15.00	40.00
37B Joe Torre: Braves Catching, mask on ground; Cut Along Dotted Lines printed on lower tab	30.00	60.00
38 Bob Veale: Pirates Portrait, hands not shown	8.00	20.00
39 Leon Wagner: Indians Fielding	8.00	20.00
40A Fred Whitfield Batting lefthanded	8.00	20.00
40B Fred Whitfield Batting lefthanded; Cut Along Dotted Lines printed on lower tab	8.00	20.00
41 Woody Woodward	8.00	20.00

1968 Kahn's

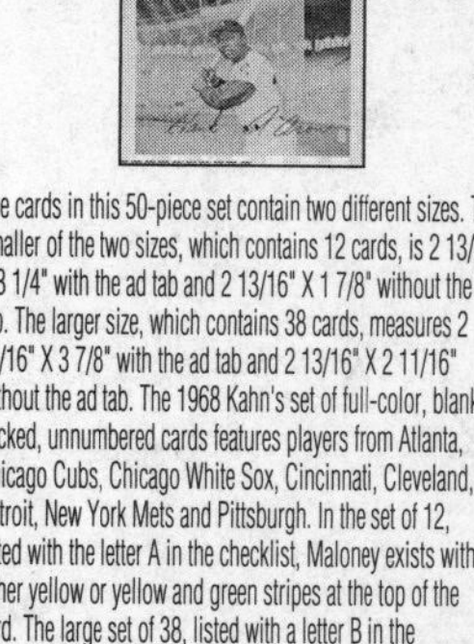

The cards in this 50-piece set contain two different sizes. The smaller of the two sizes, which contains 12 cards, is 2 13/16" X 3 1/4" with the ad tab and 2 13/16" X 1 7/8" without the ad tab. The larger size, which contains 38 cards, measures 2 13/16" X 3 7/8" with the ad tab and 2 13/16" X 2 11/16" without the ad tab. The 1968 Kahn's set of full-color, blank backed, unnumbered cards features players from Atlanta, Chicago Cubs, Chicago White Sox, Cincinnati, Cleveland, Detroit, New York Mets and Pittsburgh. In the set of 12, listed with the letter A in the checklist, Maloney exists with either yellow or yellow and green stripes at the top of the card. The large set of 38, listed with a letter B in the checklist, contains five cards which exist in two variations. The variations in this large set have either yellow or red stripes at the top of the cards, with Maloney being an exception. Maloney has either a yellow stripe or a Blue Mountain ad at the top. Cards with the ad tabs (see other Kahn's sets) are worth twice as much as cards without the ad, i.e., double the prices below. The cards are listed and numbered below in alphabetical order (within each subset) by the subject's name. The set features a card of Johnny Bench in his Rookie Card year.

COMPLETE SET (50)	1,100.00	2,200.00
A1 Hank Aaron	75.00	150.00
A2 Gene Alley	15.00	40.00
A3 Max Alvis	12.50	30.00
A4 Clete Boyer	20.00	50.00
A5 Chico Cardenas	15.00	40.00
A6 Bill Freehan	20.00	50.00
A7 Jim Maloney 2	20.00	50.00
A8 Lee May	20.00	50.00
A9 Bill Mazeroski	50.00	100.00
A10 Vada Pinson	30.00	60.00
A11 Joe Torre	40.00	80.00
A12 Bob Veale	15.00	40.00
B1 Hank Aaron: Braves Full pose batting bat cocked	75.00	150.00
B2 Tommy Agee	15.00	40.00
B3 Gene Alley: Pirates Fielding, full pose	12.50	30.00
B4 Felipe Alou Full pose batting, swinging player in background	30.00	60.00
B5 Matty Alou: Pirates Portrait with bat Matio Alou 2	15.00	40.00
B6 Max Alvis Fielding glove on ground	12.50	30.00
B7 Gerry Arrigo: Reds Pitching followthru delivery	12.50	30.00
B8 John Bench	200.00	400.00
B9 Clete Boyer	20.00	50.00
B10 Larry Brown	12.50	30.00
B11 Leo Cardenas: Reds Leaping in the air	15.00	40.00
B12 Bill Freehan	20.00	50.00
B13 Steve Hargan: Indians Pitching clouds in background	12.50	30.00
B14 Joel Horlen White Sox Portrait	12.50	30.00
B15 Tony Horton: Indians Portrait signed Anthony	20.00	50.00
B16 Willie Horton	20.00	50.00
B17 Fergie Jenkins	60.00	120.00
B18 Deron Johnson: Braves	15.00	40.00
B19 Mack Jones: Reds	12.50	30.00
B20 Bob Lee	12.50	30.00
B21 Jim Maloney: Reds Red hat	20.00	50.00

Card	Low	High
pitching hands up 2		
B22 Lee May: Reds	15.00	40.00
Batting		
B23 Bill Mazeroski:	50.00	100.00
Pirates		
Fielding		
hands in front		
of body		
B24 Dick McAuliffe	12.50	30.00
B25 Bill McCool	12.50	30.00
Red hat		
left hand down		
B26 Sam McDowell:	20.00	50.00
Indians		
Pitching		
left hand over glove 2		
B27 Tony Perez	50.00	100.00
Fielding ball in glove 2		
B28 Gary Peters	12.50	30.00
White Sox		
Portrait		
B29 Vada Pinson: Reds	20.00	50.00
Batting		
B30 Chico Ruiz	12.50	30.00
B31 Ron Santo: Cubs	50.00	100.00
Batting		
follow thru 2		
B32 Art Shamsky: Mets	12.50	30.00
B33 Luis Tiant: Indians	30.00	60.00
Hands over head		
B34 Joe Torre: Braves	40.00	80.00
Batting		
B35 Bob Veale: Pirates	12.50	30.00
Hands chest high		
B36 Leon Wagner: Indians	12.50	30.00
Batting		
B37 Billy Williams: Cubs	60.00	120.00
Bat behind back		
B38 Earl Wilson	12.50	30.00

1969 Kahn's

The cards in this 25-piece set contain two different sizes. The three small cards (see 1968 description) measure 2 13/16" X 3 1/4" and the 22 large cards (see 1968 description) measure 2 13/16" X 3 15/16". The 1969 Kahn's Wieners set of full-color, unnumbered cards features players from Atlanta, Chicago Cubs, Chicago White Sox, Cincinnati, Cleveland, Pittsburgh and St. Louis. The small cards have the letter A in the checklist while the large cards have the letter B in the checklist. Four of the larger cards exist in two variations (red or yellow color stripes at the top of the card). These variations are identified in the checklist below. Cards with the ad tabs (see other Kahn's sets) are worth twice as much as cards without the ad, i.e., double the prices below. The cards are listed and numbered below in alphabetical order (within each subset) by the subject's name.

Card	Low	High
COMPLETE SET (25)	650.00	1,300.00
A1 Hank Aaron	150.00	300.00
Portrait		
A2 Jim Maloney	15.00	40.00
Pitching		
hands at side		
A3 Tony Perez	50.00	100.00
Glove on		
B1 Hank Aaron	150.00	300.00
B2 Matty Alou	15.00	40.00
Batting		
B3 Max Alvis/69 patch	12.50	30.00
B4 Gerry Arrigo	12.50	30.00
Leg up		
B5 Steve Blass	15.00	40.00
B6 Clay Carroll	12.50	30.00
B7 Tony Cloninger: Reds	12.50	30.00
B8 George Culver	12.50	30.00
B9 Joel Horlen	15.00	40.00
Pitching		
B10 Tony Horton	20.00	50.00
Batting		
B11 Alex Johnson	15.00	40.00
B12 Jim Maloney	15.00	40.00
B13 Lee May	15.00	40.00
Foot on bag (2)		
B14 Bill Mazeroski	50.00	100.00
Hands on knees (2)		
B15 Sam McDowell	15.00	40.00
Leg up (2)		
B16 Tony Perez	60.00	120.00
B17 Gary Peters	12.50	30.00
Pitching		
B18 Ron Santo	40.00	80.00
Emblem (2)		
B19 Luis Tiant	30.00	60.00
Glove at knee		
B20 Joe Torre: Cardinals	40.00	80.00
B21 Bob Veale	15.00	40.00
Hands at knees		
no glasses		
B22 Billy Williams	60.00	120.00
Bat behind head		

1887 Kalamazoo Bats N690-1

The Charles Gross Company of Philadelphia marketed this series of baseball players in 1887 in packages of tobacco with the intriguing name Kalamazoo Bats. This name involved a two-fold meaning since the word "bat" also referred to a wad of tobacco. There are 61 sepia photographs of baseball players known; most cards are blank backed although some are found with a list of premiums printed on the reverse. A Tom McLaughlin card was found recently, so this checklist may not be complete and all additions are appreciated. There is only one card known of both the Tom Poorman and the Wilbert Robinson/Fred Mann combo so we are not pricing those cards due to market scarcity. Cards with advertising backs are valued at 1.5X the prices listed in our data base.

Card	Low	High
COMMON PHILADELPHIA	750.00	1,500.00
COMMON N.Y. GIANTS	4,000.00	8,000.00
COMMON METS	4,000.00	8,000.00
1 George Andrews: Phila.	4,000.00	8,000.00
2 Charlie Bastian	4,000.00	8,000.00
Denny Lyons:		
Philadelphia		
3 Louis Bierbauer:	4,000.00	8,000.00
Athletics		
4 Louis Bierbauer	4,000.00	8,000.00
Gallagher:		
Athletics		
5 Charlie Buffington:	4,000.00	8,000.00
Philadelphia		
6 Dan Casey: Phila.	4,000.00	8,000.00
7 Jack Clements: Phila.	4,000.00	8,000.00
8 Roger Connor: New York	40,000.00	80,000.00
9 Larry Corcoran:	7,500.00	15,000.00
New York		
10 Ed Cushman	12,500.00	25,000.00
11 Pat Deasley	7,500.00	15,000.00
12 Jim Devlin: Phila.	4,000.00	8,000.00
13 Jim Donahue: Mets	12,500.00	25,000.00
14 Mike Dorgan: New York	7,500.00	15,000.00
15 Dude Esterbrooke (sic):	12,500.00	25,000.00
Mets		
16 Buck Ewing	40,000.00	80,000.00
New York		
17 Sid Farrar: Phila.	5,000.00	10,000.00
18 Charlie Ferguson	4,000.00	8,000.00
Philadelphia		
19 Jim Fogarty: Phila.	4,000.00	8,000.00
20 Jim Fogarty	4,000.00	8,000.00
James McGuire:		
Philadelphia		
21 Elmer E. Foster: Mets	12,500.00	25,000.00
22 Gibson: Philadelphia	4,000.00	8,000.00
23 Pete Gillespie:	7,500.00	15,000.00
New York		
24 Tom Gunning: Phila.	4,000.00	8,000.00
25 Art Irwin: Phila.	4,000.00	8,000.00
26 Irwin (Capt.) and Maul:	4,000.00	8,000.00
Philadelphia		
27 Tim Keefe	12,500.00	25,000.00
28 Ted Larkin: Athletics	4,000.00	8,000.00
29 Jack Lynch: Mets	12,500.00	25,000.00
30 Denny Lyons: Phila.	4,000.00	8,000.00
31 Denny Lyons	4,000.00	8,000.00
Billy Taylor:		
Philadelphia		
32 Fred Mann: Athletics	4,000.00	8,000.00
33 Charlie Mason MG	4,000.00	8,000.00
34 Bobby Mathews:	4,000.00	8,000.00
Athletics		
35 Al Maul: Philadelphia	4,000.00	8,000.00
36 Al Mays: Mets	12,500.00	25,000.00
37 Jim McGarr	4,000.00	8,000.00
38 James McGuire (one hand	4,000.00	8,000.00
at chin throwing):		
Phila		
39 James McGuire (both	4,000.00	8,000.00
hands at chin catch-		
ing): P		
40 Tom McLaughlin	10,000.00	20,000.00
Mets		
41 Jocko Milligan	4,000.00	8,000.00
Henry Larkin:		
Athletics		
42 Joe Mulvey: Phila.	4,000.00	8,000.00
43 Jack Nelson: Mets	12,500.00	25,000.00
44 Jim O'Rourke: New York	40,000.00	80,000.00
45 Dave Orr: Mets	12,500.00	25,000.00
46 Tom Poorman	4,000.00	8,000.00
47 Danny Richardson	7,500.00	15,000.00
New York		
48 Wilbert Robinson:	7,500.00	15,000.00
Athletics		
49 Wilbert Robinson	4,000.00	8,000.00
Fred Mann: Athletics		
50 James(Chief)Roseman:	12,500.00	25,000.00
Mets		
51 Harry Stowe (sic&	6,000.00	12,000.00
Stovey) (hands at		
hips standin		
52 Harry Stowe (sic&	6,000.00	12,000.00
Stovey)(hands raised		
catching)		
53 Harry Stowe (sic)	7,500.00	15,000.00
Jocko Milligan		
Athletics		
54 George Townsend:	4,000.00	8,000.00
Athletics		
55 George Townsend	4,000.00	8,000.00
Jocko Milligan		
Athletics		
56 John M. Ward	40,000.00	80,000.00
57 Mickey Welch	40,000.00	80,000.00
58 Gus Weyhing	4,000.00	8,000.00
59 George Wood: Phila.	4,000.00	8,000.00
60 Harry Wright:	10,000.00	20,000.00
Phila.-Mgr.		
61 New York	4,000.00	8,000.00
Players Composite		

1887 Kalamazoo Teams N690-2

Like the cards of set N690-1, the team cards of this set are sepia photographs and are blank-backed. There are only six teams known at the present time, and the cards themselves are slightly larger than those of the individual ballplayers in N690-1. They also appear to have been issued in 1887. There are only two copies known of the Pittsburg card and one copy of the Althletic and Philadelphia cards and we are not pricing those card due to market scarcity.

Card	Low	High
COMPLETE SET (6)	10,000.00	40,000.00
1 Athletics Club	7,500.00	15,000.00
2 Baltimore B.B.C.	20,000.00	40,000.00
3 Boston B.B.C.	10,000.00	20,000.00
4 Detroit B.B.C.	15,000.00	30,000.00
5 Philadelphia B.B.C.	10,000.00	20,000.00
6 Pittsburg B.B.C.	20,000.00	40,000.00

1974 Kaline Sun-Glo Pop

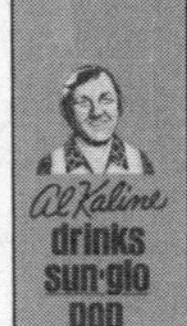

Sun-Glo Pop issued this card attached to a bottle of pop. The bright green card has a black and white portrait of Al Kaline (not in uniform) with his name printed in black script lettering below followed by the words "drinks Sun-Glo pop". The back is blank.

Card	Low	High
1 Al Kaline	4.00	10.00

1910 Kallis and Dane

These two 6 1/2" by 5 1/2" blank backed cards were produced by Kallis and Dane printers and featured pictures and highlights from the 1910 World Series. Any additions to the checklist as well as comments are greatly appreciated.

Card	Low	High
COMPLETE SET	200.00	400.00
1 Johnny Evers	150.00	300.00
Stealing Home		
Harry Steinfeldt at b		
2 Paddy Livingston	50.00	100.00
Cutting off a Run		
Connie Mack M		

1928 Kashin Publications R315

This listing is actually an amalgamation of different issued sets. The cards all measure 3 1/4" by 5 1/4" and are all blank-backed. Cissell, Clancy, Hendrick, Jolley and Traynor were all issued in a sepia toned version which are both made of thicker stock than the regular photos and are considerably more difficult to acquire than the other cards in the set.

Card	Low	High
COMPLETE SET (88)	2,500.00	5,000.00
COMMON PLAYER A/B	10.00	20.00
COMMON PLAYER C/D	12.50	25.00
A1 Earl Averill	50.00	100.00
A2 Benny Bengough	20.00	40.00
A3 Laurence Benton	20.00	40.00
A4 Max Bishop	20.00	40.00
A5 Jim Bottomley	50.00	100.00
A6 Freddy Fitzsimmons	20.00	40.00
A7 Jimmie Foxx	200.00	400.00
A8 Johnny Fredericks	20.00	40.00
A9 Frank Frisch	75.00	150.00
A10 Lou Gehrig	400.00	800.00
A11 Goose Goslin	50.00	100.00
A12 Burleigh Grimes	50.00	100.00
A13 Lefty Grove	125.00	250.00
A14 Mule Haas	20.00	40.00
A15 Babe Herman	25.00	50.00
A16 Rogers Hornsby	200.00	400.00
A17 Carl Hubbell	75.00	150.00
A18 Travis Jackson	40.00	80.00
A19 Chuck Klein	75.00	150.00
A20 Mark Koenig	20.00	40.00
A21 Tony Lazzeri	40.00	80.00
A22 Fred Leach	20.00	40.00
A23 Fred Lindstrom	40.00	80.00
A24 Fred Marberry	20.00	40.00
A25 Bing Miller	20.00	40.00
A26 Lefty O'Doul	30.00	60.00
A27 Bob O'Farrell	20.00	40.00
A28 Herb Pennock	50.00	100.00
A29 George Pipgras	20.00	40.00
A30 Andrew Reese	20.00	40.00
A31 Babe Ruth	500.00	1,000.00
A32 Bob Shawkey	25.00	50.00
A33 Al Simmons	50.00	100.00
A34 Riggs Stephenson	30.00	60.00
A35 Bill Terry	75.00	150.00
A36 Pie Traynor	100.00	200.00
A37 Dazzy Vance	50.00	100.00
A38 Paul Waner	50.00	100.00
A39 Hack Wilson	75.00	150.00
A40 Tom Zachary	20.00	40.00
B1 Earl Averill	50.00	100.00
B2 Benny Bengough	20.00	40.00
B3 Laurence Benton	20.00	40.00
B4 Max Bishop	20.00	40.00
B5 Jim Bottomley	50.00	100.00
B6 Freddy Fitzsimmons	20.00	40.00
B7 Jimmie Foxx	150.00	300.00
B8 Johnny Fredericks	20.00	40.00
B9 Frank Frisch	125.00	250.00
B10 Lou Gehrig	400.00	800.00
B11 Goose Goslin	50.00	100.00
B12 Burleigh Grimes	50.00	100.00
B13 Lefty Grove	125.00	250.00
B14 Mule Haas	20.00	40.00
B15 Babe Herman	25.00	50.00
B16 Rogers Hornsby	200.00	400.00
B17 Carl Hubbell	100.00	200.00
B18 Travis Jackson	50.00	100.00
B19 Chuck Klein	75.00	150.00
B20 Mark Koenig	20.00	40.00
B21 Tony Lazzeri	40.00	80.00
B22 Fred Leach	20.00	40.00
B23 Fred Lindstrom	50.00	100.00
B24 Fred Marberry	20.00	40.00
B25 Bing Miller	20.00	40.00
B26 Lefty O'Doul	30.00	60.00
B27 Bob O'Farrell	20.00	40.00
B28 Herb Pennock	50.00	100.00
B29 George Pipgras	20.00	40.00
B30 Andrew Reese	20.00	40.00
B31 Babe Ruth	500.00	1,000.00
B32 Bob Shawkey	20.00	40.00
B33 Al Simmons	50.00	100.00
B34 Riggs Stephenson	30.00	60.00
B35 Bill Terry	100.00	200.00
B36 Pie Traynor	75.00	150.00
B37 Dazzy Vance	50.00	100.00
B38 Paul Waner	50.00	100.00
B39 Hack Wilson	75.00	150.00
B40 Tom Zachary	20.00	40.00
C1 Bill Cissell	25.00	50.00
C2 Harvey Hendricks	25.00	50.00
C3 Smead Jolley	25.00	50.00
C4 Carl Reynolds	25.00	50.00
C5 Art Shires	25.00	50.00
D1 Bill Cissell	25.00	50.00
D2 Bud Clancy	25.00	50.00
D3 Smead Jolley	25.00	50.00

1929 Kashin Publications R316

The 1929 R316 Portraits and Action Baseball set features 101 unnumbered, blank backed, black and white cards each measuring 3 1/2" by 4 1/2". The name of the player is written in script at the bottom of the card. The Hadley, Haines, Siebold and Todt cards are considered scarce. The Babe Ruth card seems to be one of the more plentiful cards in the set. These cards were issued in 25 count boxes which had the checklist printed on the reverse. There were four different boxes issued: Orange, Blue, Coral and Canary and Babe Ruth is the only player included in all four of these boxes. This set was issued by Kashin Publications.

Card	Low	High
COMPLETE SET (101)	2,250.00	4,500.00
1 Ethan N. Allen	15.00	30.00
2 Dale Alexander	15.00	30.00
3 Larry Benton	15.00	30.00
4 Moe Berg	30.00	60.00
5 Max Bishop	15.00	30.00
6 Del Bissonette	15.00	30.00
7 Lucerne A. Blue	15.00	30.00
8 Jim Bottomley	25.00	50.00
9 Guy T. Bush	15.00	30.00
10 Harold G. Carlson	15.00	30.00
11 Owen Carroll	15.00	30.00
12 Chalmers W. Cissell	15.00	30.00
13 Earle Combs	25.00	50.00
14 Hugh M. Critz	15.00	30.00
15 H.J. DeBerry	15.00	30.00
16 Pete Donohue	15.00	30.00
17 Taylor Douthit	15.00	30.00
18 Chuck Dressen	20.00	40.00
19 Jimmy Dykes	20.00	40.00
20 Howard Ehmke	15.00	30.00
21 Woody English	15.00	30.00
22 Urban Faber	25.00	50.00
23 Fred Fitzsimmons	20.00	40.00
24 Lewis A. Fonseca	15.00	30.00
25 Horace H. Ford	15.00	30.00
26 Jimmie Foxx	40.00	80.00
27 Frankie Frisch	30.00	60.00
28 Lou Gehrig	200.00	400.00
29 Charley Gehringer	30.00	60.00
30 Goose Goslin	25.00	50.00
31 George Grantham	15.00	30.00
32 Burleigh Grimes	25.00	50.00
33 Lefty Grove	30.00	60.00
34 Bump Hadley	100.00	200.00
35 Chick Hafey	25.00	50.00
36 Jesse Haines	125.00	250.00
37 Harvey Hendrick	15.00	30.00
38 Babe Herman	20.00	40.00
39 Andy High	15.00	30.00
40 Urban J. Hodapp	15.00	30.00
41 Frank Hogan	15.00	30.00
42 Rogers Hornsby	40.00	80.00
43 Waite Hoyt	25.00	50.00
44 Willis Hudlin	15.00	30.00
45 Frank O. Hurst	15.00	30.00
46 Charlie Jamieson	15.00	30.00
47 Roy C. Johnson	15.00	30.00
48 Percy Jones	15.00	30.00
49 Sam Jones	20.00	40.00
50 Joseph Judge	15.00	30.00
51 Willie Kamm	15.00	30.00
52 Chuck Klein	25.00	50.00
53 Mark Koenig	15.00	30.00
54 Ralph Kress	15.00	30.00
55 Fred M. Leach	15.00	30.00
56 Fred Lindstrom	25.00	50.00
57 Ad Liska	15.00	30.00

58 Fred Lucas	15.00	30.00
59 Fred Maguire	15.00	30.00
60 Perce L. Malone	15.00	30.00
61 Heinie Manush	25.00	50.00
62 Rabbit Maranville	25.00	50.00
63 Douglas McWeeney	15.00	30.00
64 Oscar Melillo	15.00	30.00
65 Bing Miller	15.00	30.00
66 Lefty O'Doul	20.00	40.00
67 Mel Ott	40.00	80.00
68 Herb Pennock	25.00	50.00
69 William W. Regan	15.00	30.00
70 Harry F. Rice	15.00	30.00
71 Sam Rice	25.00	50.00
72 Lance Richbourg	15.00	30.00
73 Eddie Rommel	15.00	30.00
74 Chas. H. Root	15.00	30.00
75 Ed Roush	25.00	50.00
76 Harold Ruel	15.00	30.00
77 Red Ruffing	25.00	50.00
78 Jack Russell	15.00	30.00
79 Babe Ruth QP	200.00	400.00
80 Fred Schulte	15.00	30.00
81 Joe Sewell	25.00	50.00
82 Luke Sewell	20.00	40.00
83 Art Shires	15.00	30.00
84 Henry Seibold	100.00	200.00
85 Al Simmons	25.00	50.00
86 Bob Smith	15.00	30.00
87 Riggs Stephenson	20.00	40.00
88 Bill Terry	30.00	60.00
89 Alphonse Thomas	15.00	30.00
90 Lafayette Thompson	15.00	30.00
91 Phil Todt	100.00	200.00
92 Pie Traynor	25.00	50.00
93 Dazzy Vance	25.00	50.00
94 Lloyd Waner	25.00	50.00
95 Paul Waner	25.00	50.00
96 Jimmy Welsh	15.00	30.00
97 Earl Whitehill	15.00	30.00
98 A.C. Whitney	15.00	30.00
99 Claude Willoughby	15.00	30.00
100 Hack Wilson	30.00	60.00
101 Tom Zachary	15.00	30.00

1937 Kellogg's Pep Stamps

Kellogg's distributed these multi-sport stamps inside specially marked Pep brand cereal boxes in 1937. They were originally issued in four-stamp blocks along with an instructional type tab at the top. The tab contained the sheet number. We've noted the sheet number after each athlete's name below. Note that six athletes appear on two sheets, thereby making those six double prints. There were 24-different sheets produced. We've catalogued the unnumbered stamps below in single loose form according to sport (AR- auto racing, AV- aviation, BB- baseball, BX- boxing, FB- football, GO- golf, HO- horses, SW- swimming, TN- tennis). Stamps can often be found intact in blocks of four along with the tab. Complete blocks of stamps are valued at roughly 50 percent more than the total value of the four individual stamps as priced below. An album was also produced to house the set.

COMPLETE SET (90)	1,000.00	2,000.00
BB1 Luke Appling 7	12.50	25.00
BB2 Mordecai Brown 22	12.50	25.00
BB3 Leo Durocher 3	12.50	25.00
BB4 Johnny Evers 17	12.50	25.00
BB5 Rick Ferrell 16	10.00	20.00
BB6 Lew Fonseca 15	5.00	10.00
BB7 Gabby Hartnett 5	12.50	25.00
BB8 Billy Herman 6	12.50	25.00
BB9 Walter Johnson 13	25.00	50.00
BB10 Ducky Medwick 1	12.50	25.00
BB11 Buddy Myer 19	5.00	10.00
BB12 George Selkirk 12	5.00	10.00
BB13 Tris Speaker 20/23	12.50	25.00
BB14 Bill Terry 11	12.50	25.00
BB15 Joe Tinker 21	12.50	25.00
BB16 Arky Vaughan 8	12.50	25.00
BB17 Paul Waner 9	12.50	25.00
BB18 Sam West 18	5.00	10.00

1948 Kellogg's All Wheat Sport Tips Series 1

13 Baseball: Placing Hits	3.00	8.00
14 Baseball: Hook Slide	3.00	8.00

1948 Kellogg's All Wheat Sport Tips Series 2

7 Baseball: Batting Trick	3.00	8.00
15 Baseball: Fly Ball	3.00	8.00
18 Baseball: Head Position	3.00	8.00
20 Baseball: Infield Stance	3.00	8.00
21 Baseball: Base Running	3.00	8.00

1948 Kellogg's Pep

These small cards measure approximately 1 7/16" by 1 5/8". The card front presents a black and white head-and-shoulders shot of the player, with a white border. The back has the player's name and a brief description of his accomplishments. The cards are unnumbered, but have been assigned numbers below using a sport (BB- baseball, FB- football, BK- basketball, OT- other) prefix. Other Movie Star Kellogg's Pep cards exist, but they are not listed below. The catalog designation for this set is F273-19. An album was also produced to house the set.

COMPLETE SET (20)	700.00	1,400.00
BB1 Phil Cavarretta	15.00	30.00
BB2 Orval Grove	10.00	20.00
BB3 Mike Tresh	10.00	20.00
BB4 Paul(Dizzy) Trout	15.00	30.00
BB5 Dick Wakefield	10.00	20.00

1970 Kellogg's

The cards in this 75-card set measure approximately 2 1/4" by 3 1/2". The 1970 Kellogg's set was Kellogg's first venture into the baseball card producing field. The design incorporates a brilliant color photo of the player set against an indistinct background, which is then covered with a layer of plastic to simulate a 3-D look. Some veteran card dealers consider cards 16-30 to be in shorter supply than the other cards in the set. The cards were individually inserted one per specially marked boxes of Kellogg's cereal. Cards still found with the wrapper intact are valued 50 percent greater than the values listed below. Kellogg's also distributed six-card packs which were available when collectors bought two card team patches. These packs, are still occassionally seen in the hobby and have a current value of $35.

COMPLETE SET (75)	150.00	300.00
1 Ed Kranepool	.60	1.50
2 Pete Rose	8.00	20.00
3 Cleon Jones	.60	1.50
4 Willie McCovey	3.00	8.00
5 Mel Stottlemyre	.60	1.50
6 Frank Howard	.60	1.50
7 Tom Seaver	8.00	20.00
8 Don Sutton	2.50	6.00
9 Jim Wynn	.60	1.50
10 Jim Maloney	.40	1.00
11 Tommie Agee	.60	1.50
12 Willie Mays	10.00	25.00
13 Juan Marichal	2.50	6.00
14 Dave McNally	.60	1.50
15 Frank Robinson	4.00	10.00
16 Carlos May	.40	1.00
17 Bill Singer	.40	1.00
18 Rick Reichardt	.40	1.00
19 Boog Powell	.75	2.00
20 Gaylord Perry	3.00	8.00
21 Brooks Robinson	6.00	15.00
22 Luis Aparicio	2.50	6.00
23 Joel Horlen	.40	1.00
24 Mike Epstein	.40	1.00
25 Tom Haller	.40	1.00
26 Willie Crawford	.40	1.00
27 Roberto Clemente	12.50	40.00
28 Matty Alou	.40	1.00
29 Willie Stargell	4.00	10.00
30 Tim Cullen	.40	1.00
31 Randy Hundley	.40	1.00
32 Reggie Jackson	10.00	25.00
33 Rich Allen	1.00	2.50
34 Tim McCarver	.75	2.00
35 Ray Culp	.40	1.00
36 Jim Fregosi	.40	1.00
37 Billy Williams	2.50	6.00
38 Johnny Odom	.40	1.00
39 Bert Campaneris	.60	1.50
40 Ernie Banks	5.00	12.00
41 Chris Short	.40	1.00
42 Ron Santo	.75	2.00
43 Glenn Beckert	.60	1.50
44 Lou Brock	3.00	8.00
45 Larry Hisle	.40	1.00
46 Reggie Smith	.60	1.50
47 Rod Carew	4.00	10.00
48 Curt Flood	.60	1.50
49 Jim Lonborg	.40	1.00
50 Sam McDowell	.60	1.50
51 Sal Bando	.60	1.50
52 Al Kaline	5.00	12.00
53 Gary Nolan	.40	1.00
54 Rico Petrocelli	.60	1.50
55 Ollie Brown	.40	1.00
56 Luis Tiant	.60	1.50
57 Bill Freehan	.60	1.50
58 Johnny Bench	10.00	25.00
59 Joe Pepitone	.60	1.50
60 Bobby Murcer	.60	1.50
61 Harmon Killebrew	4.00	10.00
62 Don Wilson	.40	1.00
63 Tony Oliva	1.00	2.50
64 Jim Perry	.40	1.00
65 Mickey Lolich	.60	1.50
66 Jose Laboy	.40	1.00
67 Dean Chance	.40	1.00
68 Ken Harrelson	.60	1.50
69 Willie Horton	.60	1.50
70 Wally Bunker	.40	1.00
71A Bob Gibson ERR (1959 innings/pitched is blank)	3.00	8.00
71B Bob Gibson COR (1959 innings is 76)	3.00	8.00
72 Joe Morgan	2.50	6.00
73 Denny McLain	.60	1.50
74 Tommy Harper	.40	1.00
75 Don Mincher	.40	1.00

1971 Kellogg's

The cards in this 75-card set measure approximately 2 1/4" by 3 1/2". The 1971 set of 3-D cards marketed by the Kellogg Company is the scarcest of all that company's issues. It was distributed as single cards, one in each package of cereal, without the usual complete set mail-in offer. In addition, card dealers were unable to obtain this set in quantity, as they have in other years. All the cards are available with and without the year 1970 before XOGRAPH on the back in the lower left corner; the version without carries a slight premium for most numbers. Prices listed below are for the more common variety with the year 1970. Cards still found with the wrapper intact are valued 50 percent greater than the values listed below.

COMP.MASTER SET (92)	750.00	1,500.00
COMPLETE SET (75)	600.00	1,200.00
1A Wayne Simpson 119 SO	5.00	12.00
1B Wayne Simpson 120 SO	5.00	12.00
2 Tom Seaver	20.00	50.00
3A Jim Perry 2238 IP	5.00	12.00
3B Jim Perry 2239 IP	5.00	12.00
4A Bob Robertson 94 RBI	5.00	12.00
4B Bob Robertson 95 RBI	5.00	12.00
5 Roberto Clemente	40.00	80.00
6A Gaylord Perry 2014 IP	10.00	25.00
6B Gaylord Perry 2015 IP	10.00	25.00
7A Felipe Alou Oakland NL	5.00	12.00
7B Felipe Alou Oakland AL	5.00	12.00
8 Denis Menke	5.00	12.00
9A Don Kessinger No 1970 Date	5.00	12.00
9B Don Kessinger Dated 1970, 849 Hits	5.00	12.00
9C Don Kessinger Dated 1970, 850 Hits	5.00	12.00
10 Willie Mays	30.00	60.00
11 Jim Hickman	5.00	12.00
12 Tony Oliva	8.00	20.00
13 Manny Sanguillen	5.00	12.00
14A Frank Howard Washington NL	5.00	12.00
14B Frank Howard Washington AL	5.00	12.00
15 Frank Robinson	12.50	30.00
16 Willie Davis	5.00	12.00
17 Lou Brock	12.50	30.00
18 Cesar Tovar	5.00	12.00
19 Luis Aparicio	10.00	25.00
20 Boog Powell	6.00	15.00
21A Dick Selma 584 SO	5.00	12.00
21B Dick Selma 587 SO	5.00	12.00
22 Danny Walton	5.00	12.00
23 Carl Morton	5.00	12.00
24A Sonny Siebert 1054 SO	5.00	12.00
24B Sonny Siebert 1055 SO	5.00	12.00
25 Jim Merritt	5.00	12.00
26A Jose Cardenal 828 Hits	5.00	12.00
26B Jose Cardenal 829 Hits	5.00	12.00
27 Don Mincher	5.00	12.00
28A Clyde Wright No 1970 Date, Angels Logo	6.00	15.00
28B Clyde Wright No 1970 Date, California Logo	6.00	15.00
28C Clyde Wright Dated 1970, California Logo	5.00	12.00
29 Les Cain	5.00	12.00
30 Danny Cater	5.00	12.00
31 Don Sutton	10.00	25.00
32 Chuck Dobson	5.00	12.00
33 Willie McCovey	12.50	30.00
34 Mike Epstein	5.00	12.00
35A Paul Blair 386 Runs	5.00	12.00
35B Paul Blair 385 Runs	5.00	12.00
36A Gary Nolan No 1970 Date	5.00	12.00
36B Gary Nolan Dated 1970, 577 SO	5.00	12.00
36C Gary Nolan Dated 1970, 581 SO	5.00	12.00
37 Sam McDowell	5.00	12.00
38 Amos Otis	5.00	12.00
39A Ray Fosse 69 RBI	5.00	12.00
39B Ray Fosse 70 RBI	5.00	12.00
40 Mel Stottlemyre	5.00	12.00
41 Clarence Gaston	5.00	12.00
42 Dick Dietz	5.00	12.00
43 Roy White	5.00	12.00
44 Al Kaline	12.50	40.00
45 Carlos May	5.00	12.00
46A Tommie Agee 313 RBI	5.00	12.00
46B Tommie Agee 314 RBI	5.00	12.00
47 Tommy Harper	5.00	12.00
48 Larry Dierker	5.00	12.00
49 Mike Cuellar	5.00	12.00
50 Ernie Banks	12.50	40.00
51 Bob Gibson	12.50	30.00
52 Reggie Smith	5.00	12.00
53A Matty Alou 273 RBI	5.00	12.00
53B Matty Alou 274 RBI	5.00	12.00
54A Alex Johnson No 1970 Date, Angels Logo	6.00	15.00
54B Alex Johnson No 1970 Date, California Logo	6.00	15.00
54C Alex Johnson Dated 1970, California Logo	5.00	12.00
55 Harmon Killebrew	12.50	30.00
56 Bill Grabarkewitz	5.00	12.00
57 Richie Allen	6.00	15.00
58 Tony Perez	10.00	25.00
59A Dave McNally 1065 SO	5.00	12.00
59B Dave McNally 1067 SO	5.00	12.00
60A Jim Palmer 564 SO	12.50	30.00
60B Jim Palmer 567 SO	12.50	30.00
61 Billy Williams	10.00	25.00
62 Joe Torre	8.00	20.00
63A Jim Northrup 2773 AB	5.00	12.00
63B Jim Northrup 2772 AB	5.00	12.00
64A Jim Fregosi No 1970 Date, Angels Logo	6.00	15.00
64B Jim Fregosi No 1970 Date, California Logo	6.00	15.00
64C Jim Fregosi Dated 1970, California Logo, 1326 Hits	5.00	12.00
64D Jim Fregosi Dated 1970, California Logo, 1327 Hits	5.00	12.00
65 Pete Rose	20.00	50.00
66A Bud Harrelson No 1970 Date	5.00	12.00
66B Bud Harrelson Dated 1970, 112 RBI	5.00	12.00
66C Bud Harrelson Dated 1970, 113 RBI	5.00	12.00
67 Tony Taylor	5.00	12.00
68 Willie Stargell	10.00	25.00
69 Tony Horton	6.00	15.00
70A Claude Osteen No 1970 Date, Card Number Missing	6.00	15.00
70B Claude Osteen No 1970 Date, Number 70 on Back	6.00	15.00
70C Claude Osteen Dated 1970, Number 70 on Back	5.00	12.00
71 Glenn Beckert	5.00	12.00
72 Nate Colbert	5.00	12.00
73A Rick Monday No 1970 Date	5.00	12.00
73B Rick Monday Dated 1970 1705 AB	5.00	12.00
73C Rick Monday Dated 1970 1704 AB	5.00	12.00
74A Tommy John 444 BB	6.00	15.00
74B Tommy John 443 BB	6.00	15.00
75 Chris Short	5.00	12.00

1972 Kellogg's

The cards in this 54-card set measure approximately 2 1/8" by 3 1/4". The dimensions of the cards in the 1972 Kellogg's set were reduced in comparison to those of the 1971 series. In addition, the length of the set was set at 54 cards rather than the 75 of the previous year. The cards of this Kellogg's set are characterized by the diagonal bands found on the obverse. Cards still found with the wrapper intact are valued 50 percent greater than the values listed below.

COMP.MASTER SET (75)	100.00	200.00
COMPLETE SET (54)	60.00	120.00
1A Tom Seaver ERA 2.85	8.00	20.00
1B Tom Seaver ERA 2.81	4.00	10.00
2 Amos Otis	.40	1.00
3A Willie Davis Runs 842	.75	2.00
3B Willie Davis Runs 841	.40	1.00
4 Wilbur Wood	.40	1.00
5 Bill Parsons	.40	1.00
6 Pete Rose	6.00	15.00
7A Willie McCovey HR 360	3.00	8.00
7B Willie McCovey HR 370	1.50	4.00
8 Ferguson Jenkins	1.50	4.00
9A Vida Blue ERA 2.35	.75	2.00
9B Vida Blue ERA 2.31	.40	1.00
10 Joe Torre	.75	2.00
11 Merv Rettenmund	.40	1.00
12 Bill Melton	.40	1.00
13A Jim Palmer Games 170	4.00	10.00
13B Jim Palmer Games 168	2.00	5.00
14 Doug Rader	.40	1.00
15A Dave Roberts League Leader	.75	2.00
15B Dave Roberts NL Leader	.40	1.00
16 Bobby Murcer	.60	1.50
17 Wes Parker	.40	1.00
18A Joe Coleman BB 294	.75	2.00
18B Joe Coleman BB 393	.40	1.00
19 Manny Sanguillen	.40	1.00
20 Reggie Jackson	4.00	10.00
21 Ralph Garr	.40	1.00
22 Jim Hunter	1.50	4.00
23 Rick Wise	.40	1.00
24 Glenn Beckert	.40	1.00
25 Tony Oliva	1.00	2.50
26A Bob Gibson SO 2577	3.00	8.00
26B Bob Gibson SO 2578	1.50	4.00
27A Mike Cuellar ERA 3.80	.75	2.00
27B Mike Cuellar ERA 3.08	.40	1.00
28 Chris Speier	.40	1.00
29A Dave McNally ERA 3.18	.75	2.00
29B Dave McNally ERA 3.15	.40	1.00
30 Leo Cardenas	.40	1.00
31A Bill Freehan Runs 497	.75	2.00
31B Bill Freehan Runs 500	.40	1.00
32A Bud Harrelson Hits 634	.75	2.00
32B Bud Harrelson Hits 624	.40	1.00
33A Sam McDowell Less than 200	.75	2.00
33B Sam McDowell Less than 225	.40	1.00
34A Claude Osteen ERA 3.25	.75	2.00
34B Claude Osteen ERA 3.51	.40	1.00
35 Reggie Smith	.60	1.50
36 Sonny Siebert	.40	1.00
37 Lee May	.60	1.50
38 Mickey Lolich	.60	1.50
39A Cookie Rojas 2B 149	.75	2.00
39B Cookie Rojas 2B 150	.40	1.00
40A Dick Drago Poyals	.75	2.00
40B Dick Drago Royals	.40	1.00
41 Nate Colbert	.40	1.00
42 Andy Messersmith	.40	1.00
43A Dave Johnson Avg .262	.75	2.00
43B Dave Johnson Avg .264	.60	1.50
44 Steve Blass	.40	1.00
45 Bob Robertson	.40	1.00
46A Billy Williams Missed Only 1	2.50	6.00
46B Billy Williams Phrase Omitted	1.50	4.00
47 Juan Marichal	1.50	4.00
48 Lou Brock	1.50	4.00
49 Roberto Clemente	8.00	20.00
50 Mel Stottlemyre	.40	1.00
51 Don Wilson	.40	1.00
52A Sal Bando RBI 355	.75	2.00
52B Sal Bando RBI 356	.40	1.00
53A Willie Stargell 2B 197	3.00	8.00
53B Willie Stargell 2B 196	1.50	4.00
54A Willie Mays RBI 1855	10.00	25.00
54B Willie Mays RBI 1856	5.00	12.00

1972 Kellogg's ATG

The cards in this 15-card set measure 2 1/4" by 3 1/2". The 1972 All-Time Greats 3-D set was issued with Kellogg's Danish Go Rounds. The set contains two different cards of Babe Ruth. The set is a reissue of a 1970 set issued by Rold Gold Pretzels to commemorate baseball's first 100 years. The Rold Gold cards are copyrighted 1970 on the reverse and are valued at approximately double the prices listed below.

COMPLETE SET (15)	30.00	60.00
1 Walter Johnson	1.00	2.50
2 Rogers Hornsby	.60	1.50
3 John McGraw	.60	1.50
4 Mickey Cochrane	.60	1.50
5 George Sisler	.60	1.50
6 Babe Ruth	4.00	10.00
7 Lefty Grove	.60	1.50
8 Pie Traynor	.40	1.00
9 Honus Wagner	1.00	2.50
10 Eddie Collins	.40	1.00
11 Tris Speaker	.60	1.50
12 Cy Young	1.00	2.50
13 Lou Gehrig	3.00	8.00
14 Babe Ruth	4.00	10.00
15 Ty Cobb	3.00	8.00

1973 Kellogg's

The cards in this 54-card set measure approximately 2 1/4" by 3 1/2". The 1973 Kellogg's set is the only non-3D set produced by the Kellogg Company. Apparently Kellogg's decided to have the cards produced through Visual Panographics rather than by Xograph, as in the other years. The complete set could be obtained from the company through a box-top redemption procedure. The card size is slightly larger than the previous year. According to published reports at the time, the redemption for this set cost either $1.50 and one Raisin Bran box top or $1.25 and two Raisin Bran box tops.

COMPLETE SET (54)	40.00	80.00
1 Amos Otis	.30	.75
2 Ellie Rodriguez	.20	.50
3 Mickey Lolich	.30	.75
4 Tony Oliva	.60	1.50
5 Don Sutton	1.25	3.00
6 Pete Rose	5.00	12.00
7 Steve Carlton	2.00	5.00
8 Bobby Bonds	.60	1.50
9 Wilbur Wood	.20	.50
10 Billy Williams	1.50	4.00
11 Steve Blass	.20	.50
12 Jon Matlack	.20	.50
13 Cesar Cedeno	.30	.75
14 Bob Gibson	1.50	4.00
15 Sparky Lyle	.40	1.00
16 Nolan Ryan	10.00	25.00
17 Jim Palmer	2.00	5.00
18 Ray Fosse	.20	.50
19 Bobby Murcer	.30	.75
20 Jim Hunter	1.25	3.00
21 Tug McGraw	.20	.50
22 Reggie Jackson	4.00	10.00
23 Bill Stoneman	.20	.50
24 Lou Piniella	.40	1.00
25 Willie Stargell	2.00	5.00
26 Dick Allen	.60	1.50
27 Carlton Fisk	5.00	12.00
28 Ferguson Jenkins	1.50	4.00
29 Phil Niekro	1.50	4.00
30 Gary Nolan	.20	.50
31 Joe Torre	.60	1.50
32 Bobby Tolan	.20	.50
33 Nate Colbert	.20	.50
34 Joe Morgan	1.50	4.00
35 Bert Blyleven	.40	1.00
36 Joe Rudi	.30	.75
37 Ralph Garr	.20	.50
38 Gaylord Perry	1.50	4.00
39 Bobby Grich	.30	.75
40 Lou Brock	1.50	4.00
41 Pete Broberg	.20	.50
42 Manny Sanguillen	.20	.50
43 Willie Davis	.30	.75
44 Dave Kingman	.60	1.50
45 Carlos May	.20	.50
46 Tom Seaver	4.00	10.00
47 Mike Cuellar	.20	.50
48 Joe Coleman	.20	.50
49 Claude Osteen	.20	.50
50 Steve Kline	.20	.50
51 Rod Carew	2.00	5.00
52 Al Kaline	2.50	6.00
53 Larry Dierker	.20	.50
54 Ron Santo	.40	1.00

1974 Kellogg's

The cards in this 54-card set measure 2 1/8" by 3 1/4". In 1974 the Kellogg's set returned to its 3-D format; it also returned to the smaller-size card. Complete sets could be obtained from the company through a box-top offer. The cards are numbered on the back. Cards still found with the wrapper intact are valued 25 percent greater than the values listed below.

COMPLETE SET (54)	50.00	100.00
1 Bob Gibson	1.25	3.00
2 Rick Monday	.20	.50
3 Joe Coleman	.20	.50
4 Bert Campaneris	.30	.75
5 Carlton Fisk	2.50	6.00
6 Jim Palmer	1.25	3.00
7A Ron Santo Cubs	2.50	6.00
7B Ron Santo White Sox	.30	.75
8 Nolan Ryan	8.00	20.00
9 Greg Luzinski	.30	.75
10A Buddy Bell 134 Runs	.30	.75
10B Buddy Bell 135 Runs		
11 Bob Watson	.30	.75
12 Bill Singer	.20	.50
13 Dave May	.20	.50
14 Jim Brewer	.20	.50
15 Manny Sanguillen	.20	.50
16 Jeff Burroughs	.30	.75
17 Amos Otis	.20	.50
18 Ed Goodson	.20	.50
19 Nate Colbert	.20	.50
20 Reggie Jackson	4.00	10.00
21 Ted Simmons	.40	1.00
22 Bobby Murcer	.30	.75
23 Willie Horton	.30	.75
24 Orlando Cepeda	1.25	3.00
25 Ron Hunt	.20	.50
26 Wayne Twitchell	.20	.50
27 Ron Fairly	.20	.50
28 Johnny Bench	2.50	6.00
29 John Mayberry	.20	.50
30 Rod Carew	1.50	4.00
31 Ken Holtzman	.20	.50
32 Billy Williams	1.25	3.00
33 Dick Allen	.60	1.50
34A Wilbur Wood K 198	1.25	3.00
34B Wilbur Wood K 199	.20	.50
35 Danny Thompson	.20	.50
36 Joe Morgan	1.25	3.00
37 Willie Stargell	1.25	3.00
38 Pete Rose	4.00	10.00
39 Bobby Bonds	.60	1.50
40 Chris Speier	.20	.50
41 Sparky Lyle	.30	.75
42 Cookie Rojas	.20	.50
43 Tommy Davis	.20	.50
44 Jim Hunter	1.25	3.00
45 Willie Davis	.20	.50
46 Bert Blyleven	.30	.75
47 Pat Kelly	.20	.50
48 Ken Singleton	.20	.50
49 Manny Mota	.30	.75
50 Dave Johnson	.40	1.00
51 Sal Bando	.30	.75
52 Tom Seaver	4.00	10.00
53 Felix Millan	.20	.50
54 Ron Blomberg	.20	.50

1975 Kellogg's

The cards in this 57-card set measure approximately 2 1/8" by 3 1/4". The 1975 Kellogg's 3-D set could be obtained card by card in cereal boxes or as a set from a box-top offer from the company. Card number 44, Jim Hunter, exists with the A's emblem or the Yankees emblem on the back of the card. Cards still found with the wrapper intact are valued 25 percent greater than the values listed below. This set was available from Kellogg's for 2 box tops and a $2 charge.

COMPLETE SET (57)	200.00	400.00
1 Roy White	6.00	15.00
2 Ross Grimsley	2.50	6.00
3 Reggie Smith	2.50	6.00
4A Bob Grich 1973 Work	2.50	6.00
4B Bob Grich Because	2.50	6.00
5 Greg Gross	2.50	6.00
6 Bob Watson	2.50	6.00
7 Johnny Bench	12.50	30.00
8 Jeff Burroughs	2.50	6.00
9 Elliott Maddox	2.50	6.00
10 Jon Matlack	2.50	6.00
11 Pete Rose	15.00	40.00
12 Lee Stanton	2.50	6.00
13 Bake McBride	2.50	6.00
14 Jorge Orta	2.50	6.00
15 Al Oliver	2.50	6.00
16 John Briggs	2.50	6.00
17 Steve Garvey	3.00	8.00
18 Brooks Robinson	8.00	20.00
19 John Hiller	2.50	6.00
20 Lynn McGlothen	2.50	6.00
21 Cleon Jones	2.50	6.00
22 Fergie Jenkins	3.00	8.00
23 Bill North	2.50	6.00
24 Steve Busby	2.50	6.00
25 Richie Zisk	2.50	6.00
26 Nolan Ryan	30.00	60.00
27 Joe Morgan	4.00	10.00
28 Joe Rudi	2.50	6.00
29 Jose Cardenal	2.50	6.00
30 Andy Messersmith	2.50	6.00
31 Willie Montanez	2.50	6.00
32 Bill Buckner	2.50	6.00
33 Rod Carew	4.00	10.00
34 Lou Piniella	2.50	6.00
35 Ralph Garr	2.50	6.00
36 Mike Marshall	2.50	6.00
37 Garry Maddox	2.50	6.00
38 Dwight Evans	3.00	8.00
39 Lou Brock	4.00	10.00
40 Ken Singleton	2.50	6.00
41 Steve Braun	2.50	6.00
42 Rich Allen	5.00	12.00
43 John Grubb	2.50	6.00
44A Jim Hunter A's Logo	5.00	12.00
44B Jim Hunter Yankees Logo	3.00	8.00
45 Gaylord Perry	3.00	8.00
46 George Hendrick	2.50	6.00
47 Sparky Lyle	2.50	6.00
48 Dave Cash	2.50	6.00
49 Luis Tiant	2.50	6.00
50 Cesar Geronimo	2.50	6.00
51 Carl Yastrzemski	8.00	20.00
52 Ken Brett	2.50	6.00
53 Hal McRae	2.50	6.00
54 Reggie Jackson	8.00	20.00
55 Rollie Fingers	4.00	10.00
56 Mike Schmidt	8.00	20.00
57 Richie Hebner	5.00	12.00

1976 Kellogg's

The cards in this 57-card set measure approximately 2 1/8" by 3 1/4". The 1976 Kellogg's 3-D set could be obtained card by card in cereal boxes or as a set from the company for box-tops. Card numbers 1-3 (marked in the checklist below with SP) were apparently printed apart from the other 54 and are in shorter supply. Cards still found with the wrapper intact are valued 25 percent greater than the values listed below.

COMP.MASTER SET (68)	75.00	150.00
COMPLETE SET (57)	40.00	80.00
COMMON CARD (4-57)	.20	.50
SHORT PRINT COMMONS	4.00	10.00
1 Steve Hargan SP	4.00	10.00
2 Claudell Washington SP	4.00	10.00
3 Don Gullett SP	4.00	10.00
4 Randy Jones	.20	.50
5 Jim Hunter	1.25	3.00
6A Clay Carroll/(Team logo Cincinnati Reds on bac	1.25	3.00
6B Clay Carroll/(Team logo Chicago White Sox on bac	.40	1.00
7 Joe Rudi	.20	.50
8 Reggie Jackson	2.50	6.00
9 Felix Millan	.20	.50
10 Jim Rice	1.25	3.00
11 Bert Blyleven	.30	.75
12 Ken Singleton	.20	.50
13 Don Sutton	1.00	2.50
14 Joe Morgan	1.25	3.00
15 Dave Parker	.75	2.00
16 Dave Cash	.20	.50
17 Ron LeFlore	.20	.50
18 Greg Luzinski	.30	.75
19 Dennis Eckersley	6.00	15.00
20 Bill Madlock	.20	.50
21 George Scott	.20	.50
22 Willie Stargell	1.25	3.00
23 Al Hrabosky	.20	.50
24 Carl Yastrzemski	2.50	6.00
25A Jim Kaat Team logo Chicago White Sox on back	1.25	3.00
25B Jim Kaat/(Team logo Philadelphia Phillies on	.60	1.50
26 Marty Perez	.20	.50
27 Bob Watson	.30	.75
28 Eric Soderholm	.20	.50
29 Bill Lee	.20	.50
30A Frank Tanana ERR/1975 ERA 2.63	.40	1.00
30B Frank Tanana COR/1975 ERA 2.62	.30	.75
31 Fred Lynn	.40	1.00
32A Tom Seaver ERR/(1967 Pct. 552 with no decimal po	3.00	8.00
32B Tom Seaver COR/1967 Pct. .552	3.00	8.00
33 Steve Busby	.20	.50
34 Gary Carter	1.50	4.00
35 Rick Wise	.20	.50
36 Johnny Bench	2.50	6.00
37 Jim Palmer	1.25	3.00
38 Bobby Murcer	.30	.75
39 Von Joshua	.20	.50
40 Lou Brock	1.50	4.00
41A Mickey Rivers/(Missing line in bio about Yankees	.75	2.00
41B Mickey Rivers Bio has Yankees obtained ...	.30	.75
42 Manny Sanguillen	.20	.50
43 Jerry Reuss	.20	.50
44 Ken Griffey	.40	1.00
45A Jorge Orta ERR Lifetime AB 1615	.30	.75
45B Jorge Orta COR Lifetime AB 1616	.30	.75
46 John Mayberry	.20	.50
47A Vida Blue Bio struck out more batters	.30	.75
47B Vida Blue Bio pitched more innings	.30	.75
48 Rod Carew	1.50	4.00
49A Jon Matlack ERR/1975 ER 87	.30	.75
49B Jon Matlack COR/1975 ER 86	.30	.75
50 Boog Powell	.40	1.00
51A Mike Hargrove ERR Lifetime AB 935	.40	1.00
51B Mike Hargrove COR Lifetime AB 934	.40	1.00
52A Paul Lindblad ERR/1975 ERA 2.43	.30	.75
52B Paul Lindblad COR/1975 ERA 2.72	.30	.75
53 Thurman Munson	1.50	4.00
54 Steve Garvey	1.00	2.50
55 Pete Rose	5.00	12.00
56A Greg Gross ERR Lifetime games 334	.30	.75
56B Greg Gross COR Lifetime games 302	.30	.75
57 Ted Simmons	.40	1.00

1977 Kellogg's

The cards in this 57-card set measure approximately 2 1/8" by 3 1/4". The 1977 Kellogg's series of 3-D baseball player cards could be obtained card by card from cereal boxes or by sending in box-tops and money. Each player's picture appears in miniature form on the reverse, an idea begun in 1971 and replaced in subsequent years by the use of a picture of the Kellogg's mascot. Cards still found with the wrapper intact are valued 25 percent greater than the values listed below.

COMPLETE SET (57)	40.00	80.00
1 George Foster	.30	.75
2 Bert Campaneris	.20	.50
3 Fergie Jenkins	1.25	3.00
4 Dock Ellis	.20	.50
5 John Montefusco	.20	.50
6 George Brett	8.00	20.00
7 John Candelaria	.20	.50
8 Fred Norman	.20	.50
9 Bill Travers	.20	.50
10 Hal McRae	.30	.75
11 Doug Rau	.20	.50
12 Greg Luzinski	.30	.75
13 Ralph Garr	.20	.50
14 Steve Garvey	.75	2.00
15 Rick Manning	.20	.50
16A Lyman Bostock ERR Ellis Photo	1.25	3.00
16B Lyman Bostock COR	.30	.75
17 Randy Jones	.20	.50
18A Ron Cey 48 HR	.30	.75
18B Ron Cey 58 HR	.30	.75
19 Dave Parker	.60	1.50
20 Pete Rose	3.00	8.00
21A Wayne Garland No Trade	.20	.50
21B Wayne Garland Trade	.60	1.50
22 Bill North	.20	.50
23 Thurman Munson	1.25	3.00
24 Tom Poquette	.20	.50
25 Ron LeFlore	.20	.50
26 Mark Fidrych	2.00	5.00
27 Sixto Lezcano	.20	.50
28 Dave Winfield	3.00	8.00
29 Jerry Koosman	.30	.75
30 Mike Hargrove	.30	.75
31 Willie Montanez	.20	.50
32 Don Stanhouse	.20	.50
33 Jay Johnstone	.20	.50
34 Bake McBride	.20	.50
35 Dave Kingman	.60	1.50
36 Fred Patek	.20	.50
37 Garry Maddox	.20	.50
38A Ken Reitz No Trade	.20	.50
38B Ken Reitz Trade	.60	1.50
39 Bobby Grich	.30	.75
40 Cesar Geronimo	.20	.50
41 Jim Lonborg	.20	.50
42 Ed Figueroa	.20	.50
43 Bill Madlock	.30	.75
44 Jerry Remy	.20	.50
45 Frank Tanana	.30	.75
46 Al Oliver	.30	.75
47 Charlie Hough	.30	.75
48 Lou Piniella	.30	.75
49 Ken Griffey	.60	1.50
50 Jose Cruz	.30	.75
51 Rollie Fingers	1.25	3.00
52 Chris Chambliss	.30	.75
53 Rod Carew	2.00	5.00
54 Andy Messersmith	.20	.50
55 Mickey Rivers	.30	.75
56 Butch Wynegar	.20	.50
57 Steve Carlton	2.00	5.00

1978 Kellogg's

The cards in this 57-card set measure 2 1/8" by 3 1/4". This 1978 3-D Kellogg's series marks the first year in which Tony the Tiger appears on the reverse of each card next to the team and MLB logos. Once again the set could be obtained as individually wrapped cards in cereal boxes or as a set via a mail-in offer. The key card in the set is Eddie Murray, as it was one of Murray's few card issues in 1978, the year of his Topps Rookie Card. Cards still found with the wrapper intact are valued 25 percent greater than the values listed below.

COMPLETE SET (57)	30.00	60.00
1 Steve Carlton	1.25	3.00
2 Bucky Dent	.30	.75
3 Mike Schmidt	2.50	6.00
4 Ken Griffey	.40	1.00
5 Al Cowens	.20	.50
6 George Brett	6.00	15.00
7 Lou Brock	1.25	3.00
8 Goose Gossage	.40	1.00
9 Tom Johnson	.20	.50
10 George Foster	.30	.75
11 Dave Winfield	1.50	4.00
12 Dan Meyer	.20	.50
13 Chris Chambliss	.30	.75
14 Paul Dade	.20	.50
15 Jeff Burroughs	.20	.50
16 Jose Cruz	.30	.75
17 Mickey Rivers	.30	.75
18 John Candelaria	.20	.50
19 Ellis Valentine	.20	.50
20 Hal McRae	.20	.50
21 Dave Rozema	.20	.50
22 Lenny Randle	.20	.50
23 Willie McCovey	1.25	3.00
24 Ron Cey	.30	.75
25 Eddie Murray	8.00	20.00
26 Larry Bowa	.30	.75
27 Tom Seaver	2.00	5.00
28 Garry Maddox	.20	.50
29 Rod Carew	1.50	4.00
30 Thurman Munson	1.00	2.50
31 Garry Templeton	.30	.75
32 Eric Soderholm	.20	.50
33 Greg Luzinski	.30	.75
34 Reggie Smith	.30	.75
35 Dave Goltz	.20	.50
36 Tommy John	.40	1.00
37 Ralph Garr	.20	.50
38 Alan Bannister	.20	.50
39 Bob Bailor	.20	.50
40 Reggie Jackson	1.50	4.00
41 Cecil Cooper	.30	.75
42 Burt Hooton	.20	.50
43 Sparky Lyle	.30	.75
44 Steve Ontiveros	.20	.50
45 Rick Reuschel	.20	.50
46 Lyman Bostock	.30	.75
47 Mitchell Page	.20	.50
48 Bruce Sutter	.40	1.00
49 Jim Rice	.60	1.50
50 Ken Forsch	.20	.50
51 Nolan Ryan	6.00	15.00
52 Dave Parker	.40	1.00
53 Bert Blyleven	.30	.75
54 Frank Tanana	.30	.75
55 Ken Singleton	.20	.50
56 Mike Hargrove	.30	.75
57 Don Sutton	1.00	2.50

1979 Kellogg's

The cards in this 60-card set measure approximately 1 15/16" by 3 1/4". The 1979 edition of Kellogg's 3-D baseball cards have a 3/16" reduced width from the previous year; a nicely designed curved panel above the picture gives this set a distinctive appearance. The set contains the largest number of cards issued in a Kellogg's set since the 1971 series. Three different press runs produced numerous variations in this set. The first two printings were included in cereal boxes, while the third printing was for the complete set mail-in offer. Forty-seven cards have three variations, while thirteen cards (4, 6, 9, 15, 19, 20, 30, 33, 41, 43, 45, 51, and 54) are unchanged from the second and third printings. The three printings may be distinguished by the placement of the registered symbol by Tony the Tiger and by team logos. In the third printing, four cards (16, 18, 22, 44) show the "P" team logo (no registered symbol), and card numbers 56 and 57 omit the registered symbol by Tony. Cards still found with the wrapper intact are valued 25 percent greater than the values listed below. The set was available from Kellogg's for two boxtops and $2 and the offer was available until April 30, 1980.

COMPLETE SET (60)	15.00	40.00
1 Bruce Sutter	.75	2.00
2 Ted Simmons	.20	.50
3 Ross Grimsley	.10	.25
4 Wayne Nordhagen	.10	.25
5A Jim Palmer Pct. .649	1.25	3.00
5B Jim Palmer Pct. .650		
6 John Henry Johnson	.10	.25
7 Jason Thompson	.10	.25
8 Pat Zachry	.10	.25
9 Dennis Eckersley	1.25	3.00
10A Paul Splittorff IP 1665	.10	.25
10B Paul Splittorff IP 1666		
11A Ron Guidry Hits 397	.30	.75
11B Ron Guidry Hits 396		
12 Jeff Burroughs	.10	.25
13 Rod Carew	1.25	3.00
14A Buddy Bell No Trade	.60	1.50
14B Buddy Bell Trade	.20	.50
15 Jim Rice	.40	1.00
16 Garry Maddox	.10	.25
17 Willie McCovey	.75	2.00
18 Steve Carlton	1.25	3.00
19A J.R. Richard Stats 1972	.10	.25
19B J.R. Richard Stats 1971		
20 Paul Molitor	2.50	6.00
21A Dave Parker Avg. 281	.30	.75
21B Dave Parker Avg. 318		
22A Pete Rose 1978 3B 3	2.00	5.00
22B Pete Rose 1978 3B 33		
23A Vida Blue Runs 819	.20	.50
23B Vida Blue Runs 818		
24 Richie Zisk	.10	.25
25A Darrell Porter 2B 101	.10	.25
25B Darrell Porter 2B 111		
26A Dan Driessen Games 742	.10	.25
26B Dan Driessen Games 642		
27A Geoff Zahn Minnesota	.10	.25
27B Geoff Zahn Minnesota		
28 Phil Niekro	.75	2.00
29 Tom Seaver	1.50	4.00
30 Fred Lynn	.20	.50
31 Bill Bonham	.10	.25
32 George Foster	.20	.50
33A Terry Puhl His Lively	.10	.25
33B Terry Puhl Terry Stole		
34A John Candelaria Age 24	.10	.25
34B John Candelaria Age 25		
35 Bob Knepper	.10	.25
36 Fred Patek	.10	.25
37 Chris Chambliss	.20	.50
38A Bob Forsch 1977 Games 86	.10	.25
38B Bob Forsch 1977 Games 35		
39A Ken Griffey 1978 AB 674	.20	.50
39B Ken Griffey 1978 AB 614		
40 Jack Clark	.20	.50
41A Dwight Evans 1978 Hits 13	.20	.50
41B Dwight Evans 1978 Hits 123		
42 Lee Mazzilli	.10	.25
43 Mario Guerrero	.10	.25
44 Larry Bowa	.20	.50
45A Carl Yastrzemski AB 9930	1.50	4.00
45B Carl Yastrzemski AB 9929		
46A Reggie Jackson 1978 Games 162	1.50	4.00
46B Reggie Jackson 1978 Games 139		
47 Rick Reuschel	.10	.25
48A Mike Flanagan 1976 SO 57	.20	.50
48B Mike Flanagan 1976 SO 56		
49A Gaylord Perry 1973 Hits 315	.75	2.00
49B Gaylord Perry 1973 Hits 325		
50 George Brett	4.00	10.00
51A Craig Reynolds He Spent	.10	.25
51B Craig Reynolds In Those		
52 Dave Lopes	.20	.50
53A Bill Almon 2B 31	.10	.25
53B Bill Almon 2B 41		
54 Roy Howell	.10	.25
55 Frank Tanana	.10	.25
56A Doug Rau 1978 Pct. .577	.10	.25
56B Doug Rau 1978 Pct. .625		
57A Rick Monday 1976 Runs 107	.10	.25
57B Rick Monday 1976 Runs 197		
58 Jon Matlack	.10	.25
59A Ron Jackson His Best	.10	.25
59B Ron Jackson The Twins		
60 Jim Sundberg	.10	.25

1980 Kellogg's

The cards in this 60-card set measure approximately 1 7/8" by 3 1/4". The 1980 Kellogg's 3-D set is quite similar to, but smaller (narrower) than, the other recent Kellogg's issues. Sets could be obtained card by card from cereal boxes or as a set from a box-top offer from the company. Cards still found with the wrapper intact are valued 25 percent greater than the values listed below.

COMPLETE SET (60)	15.00	40.00
1 Ross Grimsley	.08	.25
2 Mike Schmidt	1.50	4.00
3 Mike Flanagan	.08	.25
4 Ron Guidry	.20	.50
5 Bert Blyleven	.20	.50
6 Dave Kingman	.30	.75
7 Jeff Newman	.08	.25
8 Steve Rogers	.08	.25
9 George Brett	3.00	8.00
10 Bruce Sutter	.60	1.50
11 Gorman Thomas	.08	.25
12 Darrell Porter	.08	.25
13 Roy Smalley	.08	.25
14 Steve Carlton	.75	2.00
15 Jim Palmer	.75	2.00
16 Bob Bailor	.08	.25
17 Jason Thompson	.08	.25
18 Graig Nettles	.20	.50
19 Ron Cey	.20	.50
20 Nolan Ryan	3.00	8.00
21 Ellis Valentine	.08	.25
22 Larry Hisle	.08	.25
23 Dave Parker	.30	.75
24 Eddie Murray	1.50	4.00
25 Willie Stargell	.75	2.00
26 Reggie Jackson	1.50	4.00
27 Carl Yastrzemski	1.25	3.00
28 Andre Thornton	.08	.25
29 Dave Lopes	.20	.50
30 Ken Singleton	.08	.25
31 Steve Garvey	.40	1.00
32 Dave Winfield	.75	2.00
33 Steve Kemp	.08	.25
34 Claudell Washington	.08	.25
35 Pete Rose	1.50	4.00
36 Cesar Cedeno	.08	.25
37 John Stearns	.08	.25
38 Lee Mazzilli	.08	.25
39 Larry Bowa	.20	.50
40 Fred Lynn	.20	.50
41 Carlton Fisk	1.50	4.00
42 Vida Blue	.20	.50
43 Keith Hernandez	.20	.50
44 Jim Rice	.40	1.00
45 Ted Simmons	.20	.50
46 Chet Lemon	.08	.25
47 Ferguson Jenkins	.75	2.00
48 Gary Matthews	.20	.50
49 Tom Seaver	1.50	4.00
50 George Foster	.20	.50
51 Phil Niekro	.75	2.00
52 Johnny Bench	1.25	3.00
53 Buddy Bell	.20	.50
54 Lance Parrish	.20	.50
55 Joaquin Andujar	.08	.25
56 Don Baylor	.30	.75
57 Jack Clark	.20	.50
58 J.R. Richard	.08	.25
59 Bruce Bochte	.08	.25
60 Rod Carew	1.25	3.00

1977 Jim Rowe 4-in-1 Exhibits

COMPLETE SET (16)	20.00	50.00
1 Luke Appling Ted Lyons Red Ruffing Red Faber	2.00	5.00
2 Jim Bottomley Earle Combs George Sisler Rogers Hornsby	2.00	5.00
3 Dizzy Dean Stan Musial Jesse Haines Frank Frisch	3.00	8.00
4 Joe DiMaggio Lefty Gomez Lou Gehrig Bill Dickey	3.00	8.00
5 Bob Feller Lou Boudreau Earl Averill Bob Lemon	2.00	5.00
6 Jimmie Foxx Grover Alexander Robin Roberts Eppa Rixey	2.00	5.00
7 Hank Greenberg Charlie Gehringer Ty Cobb Goose Goslin	3.00	8.00
8 Chick Hafey Edd Roush Bill McKechnie George Kelly	2.00	5.00
9 Freddy Lindstrom Billy Herman Kiki Kyler Gabby Hartnett	2.00	5.00
10 Heinie Manush Walter Johnson Bucky Harris Sam Rice	2.00	5.00
11 Joe Medwick Max Carey Dazzy Vance Burleigh Grimes	2.00	5.00
12 Mel Ott Carl Hubbell Dave Bancroft Bill Terry	2.00	5.00
13 Al Simmons Lefty Grove Mickey Cochrane Eddie Collins	2.00	5.00
14 Warren Spahn Al Lopez Casey Stengel Rabbit Marrinville	2.00	5.00
15 Pie Traynor Lloyd Waner Honus Wagner Paul Waner	3.00	8.00
16 Ted Williams Herb Pennock Babe Ruth Joe Cronin	4.00	10.00

1888 Kimball's N184

This set of 50 color pictures of contemporary athletes was Kimball's answer to the sets produced by Allen and Ginter (N28 and N29) and Goodwin (N162). Issued in 1888, the cards are backlisted but are not numbered. The cards are listed below in alphabetical order without regard to sport. There are four baseball players in the set. An album (catalog: A42) was offered as a premium in exchange for coupons found in the tobacco packages. The baseball players are noted in the checklist below by BB after their name; boxers are noted by BOX.

COMPLETE SET (50)		7000
6 E.A.(Ernie) Burch BB	350.00	700.00
10 Dell Darling BB	350.00	700.00
19 Hardie Henderson BB	350.00	700.00
33 James O'Neil BB UER#	400.00	800.00

1962 Kluszewski Charcoal Steak House

This one card postcard set features former Cincinnati Reds slugger Ted Kluszewski. The front features a photo of Klu wearing an Los Angeles Angels cap while the back features information about the Charcoal Steak House. Please note that the date of this card is noted by the cap that big Klu is wearing.

1 Ted Kluszewski	12.50	30.00

1921 Koester Bread D383

Issued in conjunction with the first all New York World Series, these cards feature members of the Giants and Yankees. The cards measure approximately 2" by 3 1/2" and are unnumbered. Therefore, we have sequenced them in alphabetical order by team. The following players are not known in the E121 issue: Ferguson, Mitchell, O'Leary, Barnes, Berry, Brown, Burkett, Cunningham and Stengel. These players sell at a premium over the other regular cards in this set.

COMPLETE SET	1,500.00	3,000.00
1 Dave Bancroft	100.00	200.00
2 Jesse Barnes	50.00	100.00
3 Joe Berry	50.00	100.00
4 Eddie Brown	50.00	100.00
5 Jesse Burkett	100.00	200.00
6 George Burns	50.00	100.00
7 Red Causey	50.00	100.00
8 Bill Cunningham	50.00	100.00
9 Phil Douglas	50.00	100.00
10 Frank Frisch	100.00	200.00
11 Alex Gaston	50.00	100.00
12 Mike Gonzalez	50.00	100.00
13 Hugh Jennings CO	100.00	200.00
14 George Kelly	100.00	200.00
15 John McGraw MG	100.00	200.00
16 Irish Meusel	50.00	100.00
17 Art Nehf	75.00	150.00
18 Johnny Rawlings	50.00	100.00
19 Rosy Ryan	50.00	100.00
20 Slim Sallee	50.00	100.00
21 Pat Shea	50.00	100.00
22 Earl Smith	50.00	100.00
23 Frank Snyder	50.00	100.00
24 Casey Stengel	150.00	300.00
25 Fred Toney	50.00	100.00
26 Ross Youngs	100.00	200.00
27 Frank Baker	100.00	200.00
28 Ping Bodie	60.00	120.00
29 Rip Collins	50.00	100.00
30 Al DeVormer	50.00	100.00
31 Alex Ferguson	50.00	100.00
32 Chick Fewster	50.00	100.00
33 Harry Harper	50.00	100.00
34 Chicken Hawks	50.00	100.00
35 Fred Hofmann	50.00	100.00
36 Waite Hoyt	100.00	200.00
37 Miller Huggins MG	100.00	200.00
38 Carl Mays	75.00	150.00
39 Mike McNally	50.00	100.00
40 Bob Meusel	75.00	150.00
41 Elmer Miller	50.00	100.00
42 Johnny Mitchell	50.00	100.00
43 Charlie O'Leary CO	50.00	100.00
44 Roger Peckinpaugh	75.00	150.00
45 Bill Piercy	50.00	100.00
46 Jack Quinn	75.00	150.00
47 Tom Rogers	50.00	100.00
48 Braggo Roth	50.00	100.00
49 Babe Ruth	500.00	1,000.00
50 Wally Schang	75.00	150.00
51 Bob Shawkey	75.00	150.00
52 Aaron Ward	50.00	100.00

1911 L1 Leathers

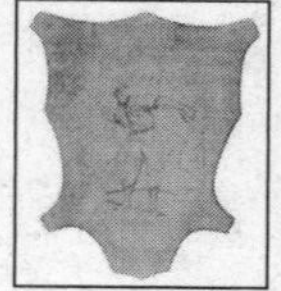

This highly prized set of baseball player pictures on a piece of leather shaped to resemble the hide of a small animal was issued during the 1911 time period. Each "leather" measures 10" by 12". While the pictures are those of the T3 Turkey Red card premium set, only the most popular players of the time are depicted. The cards are numbered at the bottom part of the leather away from the central image.

111 Rube Marquard	1,750.00	3,500.00
112 Marty O'Toole	1,250.00	2,500.00
113 Rube Benton	1,250.00	2,500.00
114 Grover C. Alexander	2,500.00	5,000.00
115 Russ Ford	1,250.00	2,500.00
116 John McGraw MG	2,250.00	4,500.00
117 Nap Rucker	1,500.00	3,000.00
118 Mike Mitchell	1,250.00	2,500.00
119 Chief Bender	2,250.00	4,500.00
120 Frank Baker	2,250.00	4,500.00
121 Napoleon Lajoie	2,250.00	4,500.00
122 Joe Tinker	2,250.00	4,500.00
123 Sherry Magee	1,500.00	3,000.00
124 Howie Camnitz	1,250.00	2,500.00
125 Eddie Collins	2,250.00	4,500.00
126 Red Dooin	1,250.00	2,500.00
127 Ty Cobb	10,000.00	20,000.00
128 Hugh Jennings MG	1,750.00	3,500.00
129 Roger Bresnahan	1,750.00	3,500.00
130 Jake Stahl	1,250.00	2,500.00
131 Tris Speaker	2,250.00	4,500.00
132 Ed Walsh	1,750.00	3,500.00
133 Christy Mathewson	5,000.00	10,000.00
134 Johnny Evers	2,250.00	4,500.00
135 Walter Johnson	6,000.00	12,000.00

1913 Lajoie Game

These cards were issued as part of a game of a baseball game. Each card in that game featured a photo of Napoleon Lajoie. Due to their distribution, these cards are farily common for vintage cards and show up in the secondary market with some frequency.

1 Nap Lajoie	10.00	25.00

1967 Laughlin World Series

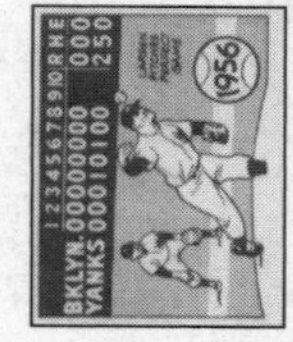

This set of 64 cards was apparently a limited test issue by sports artist R.G. Laughlin for the World Series set concept that was mass marketed by Fleer two and three years later. The cards are slightly oversized, (2 3/4" by 3 1/2") and are black and white on the front and red and white on the back. All the years are represented except for 1904 when no World Series was played. In the list below, the winning series team is listed first. According to an ad placed by Mr. Laughlin, only 300 of these sets were produced. Although these cards have a 1967 copyright; it is believed they were not released until 1968.

COMPLETE SET (64)	150.00	300.00
1 1903 Red Sox Pirates Deacon Phillippe	1.00	2.50
2 1905 Giants A's/(Christy Mathewson)	1.50	4.00
3 1906 White Sox Cubs	1.00	2.50
4 1907 Cubs Tigers	1.00	2.50
5 1908 Cubs Tigers Joe Tinker Johnny Evers Frank Chance	2.00	5.00
6 1909 Pirates Tigers/(Honus Wagner Ty Cobb)	2.00	5.00
7 1910 A's Cubs	1.00	2.50
8 1911 A's Giants John McGraw MG	1.50	4.00

9 1912 Red Sox 1.00 2.50
Giants
10 1913 A's 1.00 2.50
Giants
11 1914 Braves 1.00 2.50
A's
12 1915 Red Sox 4.00 10.00
Phillies/(Babe Ruth)
13 1916 Red Sox 4.00 10.00
Dodgers/(Babe Ruth)
14 1917 White Sox 1.00 2.50
Giants
15 1918 Red Sox 1.00 2.50
Cubs
16 1919 Reds 2.00 5.00
White Sox
17 1920 Indians 1.00 2.50
Dodgers
Bill Wambsganss
18 1921 Giants 1.25 3.00
Yankees/(Waite Hoyt)
19 1922 Giants 1.25 3.00
Yankees
Frank Frisch
Heinie Groh
20 1923 Yankees 4.00 10.00
Giants/(Babe Ruth)
21 1924 Senators 1.00 2.50
Giants
22 1925 Pirates 2.00 5.00
Senators/(Walter Johnson)
23 1926 Cardinals 1.50 4.00
Yankees
Grover C. Alexander
Tony Lazzeri
24 1927 Yankees 1.25 3.00
Pirates
25 1928 Yankees 4.00 10.00
Cardinals
Babe Ruth
Lou Gehrig
26 1929 A's 1.00 2.50
Cubs
27 1930 A's 1.00 2.50
Cardinals
28 1931 Cardinals 1.25 3.00
A's/(Pepper Martin)
29 1932 Yankees 4.00 10.00
Cubs/(Babe Ruth)
30 1933 Giants 1.50 4.00
Senators/(Mel Ott)
31 1934 Cardinals 2.00 5.00
Tigers
Dizzy Dean
Paul Dean
32 1935 Tigers 1.00 2.50
Cubs
33 1936 Yankees 1.00 2.50
Giants
34 1937 Yankees 1.25 3.00
Giants/(Carl Hubbell)
35 1938 Yankees 1.00 2.50
Cubs
36 1939 Yankees 2.00 5.00
Reds/(Joe DiMaggio)
37 1940 Reds 1.00 2.50
Tigers
38 1941 Yankees 1.25 3.00
Dodgers/(Mickey Owen)
39 1942 Cardinals 1.00 2.50
Yankees
40 1943 Yankees 1.25 3.00
Cardinals
Joe McCarthy MG
41 1944 Cardinals 1.00 2.50
Browns
42 1945 Tigers 1.50 4.00
Cubs/(Hank Greenberg)
43 1946 Cardinals 1.50 4.00
Red Sox/(Enos Slaughter)
44 1947 Yankees 1.25 3.00
Dodgers/(Al Gionfriddo)
45 1948 Indians 1.50 4.00
Braves/(Bob Feller)
46 1949 Yankees 1.25 3.00
Dodgers
Allie Reynolds
Preacher Roe
47 1950 Yankees 1.00 2.50
Phillies
48 1951 Yankees 1.00 2.50
Giants
49 1952 Yankees 1.50 4.00
Dodgers
Johnny Mize
Duke Snider
50 1953 Yankees 1.50 4.00
Dodgers
Casey Stengel MG
51 1954 Giants 1.00 2.50
Indians/(Dusty Rhodes)
52 1955 Dodgers 1.25 3.00
Yankees/(Johnny Podres)
53 1956 Yankees 1.25 3.00
Dodgers/(Don Larsen)
54 1957 Braves 1.00 2.50
Yankees/(Lew Burdette)
55 1958 Yankees 1.00 2.50
Braves/(Hank Bauer)
56 1959 Dodgers 1.00 2.50
Wh.Sox/(Larry Sherry)
57 1960 Pirates 1.25 3.00
Yankees
58 1961 Yankees 1.50 4.00
Reds/(Whitey Ford)
59 1962 Yankees 1.00 2.50
Giants
60 1963 Dodgers 12.50 30.00
Yankees/(Sandy Koufax)
61 1964 Cardinals 40.00 80.00
Yankees/(Mickey Mantle)
62 1965 Dodgers 1.50 4.00
Twins
Sandy Koufax
63 1966 Orioles 1.00 2.50
Dodgers
64 1967 Cardinals 1.50 4.00
Red Sox/(Bob Gibson)

1972 Laughlin Great Feats

This 51 card-set is printed on white card stock. Sports artist R.G. Laughlin is copyrighted only on the unnumbered title card but not on each card. The obverses are line drawings in black and white inside a red border. The cards measure 2 9/16" by 3 9/16". The set features "Great Feats" from baseball's past. The cards are blank backed and hence are numbered and captioned on the front. There is a variation set with a blue border and colored in flesh tones in the players pictured; this variation is a little more attractive and hence is valued a little higher. The blue-bordered variation set has larger type in the captions; in fact, the type has been reset and there are some minor wording differences. The blue-bordered set is also 1/16" wider. These sets were originally available from the artist for $3.25.

COMPLETE SET (51) 20.00 50.00
1 Joe DiMaggio 2.00 5.00
2 Walter Johnson .60 1.50
3 Rudy York .20 .50
4 Sandy Koufax .60 1.50
5 George Sisler .30 .75
6 Iron Man McGinnity .30 .75
7 Johnny VanderMeer .20 .50
8 Lou Gehrig 2.00 5.00
9 Max Carey .30 .75
10 Ed Delahanty .30 .75
11 Pinky Higgins .20 .50
12 Jack Chesbro .30 .75
13 Jim Bottomley .30 .75
14 Rube Marquard .30 .75
15 Rogers Hornsby .40 1.00
16 Lefty Grove .40 1.00
17 Johnny Mize .30 .75
18 Lefty Gomez .30 .75
19 Jimmie Foxx .40 1.00
20 Casey Stengel .40 1.00
21 Dazzy Vance .30 .75
22 Jerry Lynch .20 .50
23 Hughie Jennings .30 .75
24 Stan Musial .75 2.00
25 Christy Mathewson .60 1.50
26 Roy Face .20 .50
27 Hack Wilson .30 .75
28 Smoky Burgess .20 .50
29 Cy Young .60 1.50
30 Wilbert Robinson .30 .75
31 Wee Willie Keeler .30 .75
32 Babe Ruth 2.00 5.00
33 Mickey Mantle 2.50 6.00
34 Hub Leonard .20 .50
35 Ty Cobb 1.50 4.00
36 Carl Hubbell .30 .75
37 Joe Oeschger and .20 .50
Leon Cadore
38 Don Drysdale .30 .75
39 Fred Toney and .20 .50
Hippo Vaughn
40 Joe Sewell .30 .75
41 Grover C. Alexander .40 1.00
42 Joe Adcock .20 .50
43 Eddie Collins .40 1.00
44 Bob Feller .60 1.50
45 Don Larsen .20 .50
46 Dave Philley .20 .50
47 Bill Fischer .20 .50
48 Dale Long .20 .50
49 Bill Wambsganss .20 .50
50 Roger Maris .60 1.50
NNO Title Card .40 1.00

1973 Laughlin Stand-Ups

These "stand-ups" which measure approximately 7" by 11" were created by noted sports artist Robert Laughlin. The fronts feature drawings of a mix of then current superstars and retired greats while the back is signed Bob Laughlin. Since these are unnumbered, we have sequenced them in alphabetical order. It is believed this checklist is incomplete so any additions are appreciated.

COMPLETE SET 1,000.00 2,000.00
1 Hank Aaron 100.00 200.00
2 Johnny Bench 60.00 120.00
3 Roberto Clemente 100.00 200.00
4 Joe DiMaggio 125.00 250.00
5 Lou Gehrig 125.00 250.00
6 Gil Hodges 50.00 100.00
7 Sandy Koufax 125.00 250.00
8 Mickey Mantle 125.00 250.00
9 Babe Ruth 150.00 300.00
10 Ted Williams 125.00 250.00

1974 Laughlin All-Star Games

This 40-card set is printed on white card stock. Sports artist R.G. Laughlin is copyrighted at the bottom of the reverse of each card. The obverses are line drawings primarily in red, light blue, black and white inside a white border. The cards measure approximately 2 11/16" by 3 3/8". The set features memorable moments from each year's All-Star Game. The cards are numbered on the back according to the last two digits of the year and captioned on the front. The backs are printed in blue on white stock. There is no card No. 45 in the set as there was no All-Star Game played in 1945 because of World War II. This set was available from Bob Laughlin for $3.50.

COMPLETE SET (40) 60.00 120.00
33 Babe Ruth 4.00 10.00
Homer
34 Carl Hubbell .75 2.00
Fans Five
35 Jimmie Foxx .75 2.00
Smashes Homer
36 Dizzy Dean .75 2.00
Fogs 'Em
37 Ducky Medwick .60 1.50
Four Hits
38 John VanderMeer .60 1.50
No-Hit
39 Joe DiMaggio 2.50 6.00
Homers
40 Max West's/3-Run Shot .40 1.00
41 Arky Vaughan .60 1.50
Busts Two
42 Rudy York/2-Run Smash .40 1.00
43 Bobby Doerr/3-Run Blast .60 1.50
44 Phil Cavarretta .40 1.00
Reaches
46 Ted Williams 2.50 6.00
Field Day
47 Johnny Mize .60 1.50
Plants One
48 Vic Raschi .40 1.00
Pitches
49 Jackie Robinson 2.00 5.00
Scores
50 Red Schoendienst .60 1.50
Breaks
51 Ralph Kiner .60 1.50
Homers
52 Hank Sauer .40 1.00
Shot
53 Enos Slaughter .60 1.50
Hustles
54 Al Rosen .40 1.00
Hits
55 Stan Musial 1.25 3.00
Homer
56 Ken Boyer .40 1.00
Super
57 Al Kaline .75 2.00
Hits
58 Nellie Fox .60 1.50
Gets Two
59 Frank Robinson .75 2.00
Perfect
60 Willie Mays/3-for-4 2.00 5.00
61 Jim Bunning .60 1.50
Hitless
62 Roberto Clemente 2.50 6.00
Perfect
63 Dick Radatz .40 1.00
Monster Strikeouts
64 John Callison .40 1.00
Homer
65 Willie Stargell .60 1.50
Big Day
66 Brooks Robinson .75 2.00
Hits
67 Fergie Jenkins .60 1.50
Fans Six
68 Tom Seaver 1.25 3.00
Terrific
69 Willie McCovey .60 1.50
Belts Two
70 Carl Yatrzemski .75 2.00
Four Hits
71 Reggie Jackson 1.25 3.00
Unloads
72 Henry Aaron 2.00 5.00
Hammers
73 Bobby Bonds .60 1.50
Perfect

1974 Laughlin Old Time Black Stars

This 36-card set is printed on flat (non-glossy) white card stock. Sports artist R.G. Laughlin's work is evident but there are no copyright notices or any mention of him anywhere on any of the cards in this set. The obverses are line drawings in tan and brown. The cards measure approximately 2 5/8" by 3 1/2". The set features outstanding black players form the past. The backs are printed in brown on white stock. These sets were available from Bob Laughlin for $3.

COMPLETE SET (36) 60.00 120.00
1 Smokey Joe Williams 1.50 4.00
2 Rap Dixon .75 2.00
3 Oliver Marcelle .75 2.00
4 Bingo DeMoss 1.00 2.50
5 Willie Foster 1.00 2.50
6 John Beckwith .75 2.00
7 Floyd(Jelly) Gardner .75 2.00
8 Josh Gibson 4.00 10.00
9 Jose Mendez .75 2.00
10 Pete Hill 3.00 8.00
11 Buck Leonard 2.50 6.00
12 Jud Wilson .75 2.00
13 Willie Wells 1.25 3.00
14 Jimmie Lyons .75 2.00
15 Satchel Paige 4.00 10.00
16 Louis Santop .75 2.00
17 Frank Grant .75 2.00
18 Christobel Torrienti 1.00 2.50
19 Bullet Rogan 1.00 2.50
20 Dave Malarcher 1.00 2.50
21 Spot Poles .75 2.00
22 Home Run Johnson .75 2.00
23 Charlie Grant .75 2.00
24 Cool Papa Bell 2.50 6.00
25 Cannonball Dick Redding .75 2.00
26 Ray Dandridge 1.50 4.00
27 Biz Mackey 1.25 3.00
28 Fats Jenkins .75 2.00
29 Martin Dihigo 2.50 6.00
30 Mule Suttles .75 2.00
31 Bill Monroe .75 2.00
32 Dan McClellan .75 2.00
33 John Henry Lloyd 2.50 6.00
34 Oscar Charleston 2.50 6.00
35 Andrew(Rube) Foster 2.50 6.00
36 William(Judy) Johnson 2.50 6.00

1974 Laughlin Sportslang

This 41-card set is printed on white card stock. Sports artist R.G. Laughlin 1974 is copyrighted at the bottom of every reverse. The obverses are drawings in red and blue on a white enamel card stock. The cards measure approximately 2 3/4" by 3 3/8". The set actually features the slang of several sports, not just baseball. The cards are numbered on the back and captioned on the front. The card back also provides an explanation of the slang term pictured on the card front.

COMPLETE SET (41) 50.00 100.00
COMMON PLAYER (1-41) .60 1.50

1975 Laughlin Batty Baseball

This 25-card set is printed on white card stock. Sports artist R.G. Laughlin 1975 is copyrighted on the title card. The obverses are line drawings primarily in orange, black and white. The cards measure 2 9/16" X 3 7/16". The set features a card for each team with a depiction of a fractured nickname for the team. The cards are numbered on the front. The backs are blank on white stock.

COMPLETE SET (25) 60.00 120.00
COMMON PLAYER (1-24) 2.00 5.00

1976 Laughlin Diamond Jubilee

This 32-card set is printed on non-glossy white card stock. Sports artist R.Laughlin 1976 is copyrighted at the bottom of the reverse of each card. The obverses are line drawings primarily in red, blue, black and white inside a red border. The cards measure approximately 2 13/16" by 3 15/16". The set features memorable moments voted by the media and fans in each major league city. The cards are numbered on the back and captioned on the front and the back. The backs are printed in dark blue on white stock. The set was available from the artist for $3.50.

COMPLETE SET (32) 75.00 150.00
1 Nolan Ryan 30.00 60.00
2 Ernie Banks 1.25 3.00
3 Mickey Lolich .40 1.00
4 Sandy Koufax 2.50 6.00
5 Frank Robinson 1.25 3.00
6 Bill Mazeroski .50 1.50
7 Jim Hunter .50 1.50
8 Hank Aaron 4.00 10.00
9 Carl Yastrzemski 1.25 3.00
10 Jim Bunning .50 1.50
11 Brooks Robinson 1.25 3.00
12 John VanderMeer .50 1.50
13 Harmon Killebrew 1.25 3.00
14 Lou Brock 1.25 3.00
15 Steve Busby .40 1.00
16 Nate Colbert .40 1.00
17 Don Larsen .50 1.50
18 Willie Mays 2.50 6.00
19 David Clyde .40 1.00
20 Mack Jones .40 1.00
21 Mike Hegan .40 1.00
22 Jerry Koosman .40 1.00
23 Early Wynn .50 1.50
24 Nellie Fox .50 1.50

25 Joe DiMaggio	5.00	12.00
26 Jackie Robinson	3.00	8.00
27 Ted Williams	5.00	12.00
28 Lou Gehrig	5.00	12.00
29 Bobby Thomson	.50	1.50
30 Roger Maris	1.25	3.00
31 Harvey Haddix	.40	1.00
32 Babe Ruth	6.00	15.00

1976 Laughlin Indianapolis Clowns

This 42-card set was issued to commemorate the Indianapolis Clowns, a black team that began touring in 1929 and played many games for charity. The cards measure 2 5/8" by 4 1/4". The front design has blackand-white player photos inside a white frame against a light blue card face. The team name is printed in red and white above the picture. In red courier-style print on white, the backs present extended captions. The cards are numbered on the front.

COMPLETE SET (42)	40.00	80.00
1 Ed Hamman	1.25	3.00
Ed the Clown		
2 Dero Austin	.75	2.00
3 James Williams	.75	2.00
Nickname Natureboy		
4 Sam Brison	.75	2.00
Nickname Birmingham		
5 Richard King	.75	2.00
Nickname King Tut		
6 Syd Pollock	.75	2.00
Founder		
7 Nataniel(Lefty) Small	.75	2.00
8 Grant Greene	.75	2.00
Nickname Double Duty		
9 Nancy Miller	.75	2.00
Lady umpire		
10 Billy Vaughn	.75	2.00
11 Sam Brison	.75	2.00
Putout for Sam		
12 Ed Hamman	1.25	3.00
13 Dero Austin	.75	2.00
Home delivery		
14 Steve(Nub) Anderson	.75	2.00
15 Joe Cherry	.75	2.00
16 Reece(Goose) Tatum	3.00	8.00
17 James Williams	.75	2.00
Natureboy		
18 Byron Purnell	.75	2.00
19 Bat boy	.75	2.00
20 Spec BeBop	.75	2.00
21 Satchel Paige	4.00	10.00
22 Prince Jo Henry	.75	2.00
23 Ed Hamman	.75	2.00
Syd Pollock		
24 Paul Casanova	1.25	3.00
25 Steve(Nub) Anderson	.75	2.00
Nub singles		
26 Comiskey Park	1.25	3.00
27 Toni Stone	2.00	5.00
Second basewoman		
28 Dero Austin	.75	2.00
Small target		
29 Sam Brison and	.75	2.00
Natureboy Williams		
Calling Dr. Ki		
30 Oscar Charleston	2.00	5.00
31 Richard King	.75	2.00
King Tut		
32 Ed Hamman	.75	2.00
Joe Cherry		
Hal King		
Ed and prospects		
33 In style	.75	2.00
Team bus		
34 Hank Aaron	4.00	10.00
35 The Great Yogi	2.00	5.00
36 W.H.(Chauff) Wilson	.75	2.00
37 Sam Brison	1.25	3.00
Sonny Jackson		
Doin' their thing		
38 Billy Vaughn	.75	2.00
The hard way		
39 James Williams/1B the easy way	.75	2.00
40 Ed Hamman	2.00	5.00
Casey Stengel		
Casey and Ed		

xx Title Card	.75	2.00
xx Baseball Laff Book	.75	2.00

1977 Laughlin Erorrs

This set of 39 blank-backed cards is printed on white card stock and measures 2 5/8" by 3 3/4". Sports artist R.G. Laughlin has created illustrations for actual errors made on baseball cards over the years, a sampling of the hundreds of mistakes that found their way into print. The illustrations are bordered in green with "Erorrs" (incorrect spelling intentional) in wide white script at the top of the cards. Each card lists the year, card make and number depicted in the line drawing. The cards are unnumbered and checklisted below in chronological order. This set was available from the artist for $3 at the time of issue.

COMPLETE SET (39)	75.00	150.00
COMMON PLAYER (1-39)	2.00	5.00

1978 Laughlin Long Ago Black Stars

This set of 36 cards is printed on non-glossy white card stock. Sports artist R.G. Laughlin's work is evident and the reverse of each card indicates copyright by R.G. Laughlin 1978. The obverses are line drawings in light and dark green. The cards measure 2 5/8" by 3 1/2". The set features outstanding black players form the past. The cards are numbered on the back. The backs are printed in black on white stock. This is not a reissue of the similar Laughlin set from 1974 Old Time Black Stars but is actually in effect a second series with all new players and was available from Mr. Laughlin at time of issue for $3.75.

COMPLETE SET (36)	60.00	120.00
1 Ted Trent	1.50	4.00
2 Larry Brown	1.25	3.00
3 Newt Allen	2.50	6.00
4 Norman Stearns	1.25	3.00
5 Leon Day	4.00	10.00
6 Dick Lundy	1.25	3.00
7 Bruce Petway	1.50	4.00
8 Bill Drake	1.25	3.00
9 Chaney White	1.25	3.00
10 Webster McDonald	1.25	3.00
11 Tommy Butts	1.25	3.00
12 Ben Taylor	1.25	3.00
13 James(Joe) Greene	1.25	3.00
14 Dick Seay	1.25	3.00
15 Sammy Hughes	1.25	3.00
16 Ted Page	3.00	8.00
17 Willie Cornelius	1.25	3.00
18 Pat Patterson	1.25	3.00
19 Frank Wickware	1.25	3.00
20 Albert Haywood	1.25	3.00
21 Bill Holland	1.25	3.00
22 Sol White	1.25	3.00
23 Chet Brewer	2.50	6.00
24 Crush Holloway	1.25	3.00
25 George Johnson	1.25	3.00
26 George Scales	1.25	3.00
27 Dave Brown	1.25	3.00
28 John Donaldson	1.25	3.00
29 William Johnson	3.00	8.00
30 Bill Yancey	2.50	6.00
31 Sam Bankhead	1.50	4.00
32 Leroy Matlock	1.25	3.00
33 Quincy Troupe	1.50	4.00
34 Hilton Smith	4.00	10.00
35 Jim Crutchfield	1.50	4.00
36 Ted Radcliffe	2.50	6.00

1980 Laughlin 300/400/500

This square (approximately 3 1/4" square) set of 30 players features members of the 300/400/500 club, namely 300 pitching wins, batting .400 or better, or hitting 500 homers since 1900. Cards are blank backed but are numbered on the front. The cards feature the artwork of R.G. Laughlin for the player's body connected to an out of proportion head shot stock photo. This creates an effect faintly reminiscent of the Goudey Heads Up cards.

COMPLETE SET (30)	10.00	25.00
1 Title Card	.30	.75
2 Babe Ruth	2.00	5.00
3 Walter Johnson	.60	1.50
4 Ty Cobb	.75	2.00
5 Christy Mathewson	.75	2.00
6 Ted Williams	1.50	4.00
7 Bill Terry	.30	.75
8 Grover C. Alexander	.40	1.00
9 Napoleon Lajoie	.40	1.00
10 Willie Mays	.75	2.00
11 Cy Young	.60	1.50
12 Mel Ott	.40	1.00
13 Joe Jackson	.75	2.00
14 Harmon Killebrew	.40	1.00
15 Warren Spahn	.40	1.00
16 Hank Aaron	1.25	3.00
17 Rogers Hornsby	.75	2.00
18 Mickey Mantle	2.00	5.00
19 Lefty Grove	.50	1.00
20 Ted Williams	.75	2.00
21 Jimmie Foxx	.60	1.50
22 Eddie Plank	.30	.75
23 Frank Robinson	.40	1.00
24 George Sisler	.30	.75
25 Eddie Mathews	.40	1.00
26 Early Wynn	.30	.75
27 Ernie Banks	.60	1.50
28 Harry Heilmann	.30	.75
29 Lou Gehrig	1.25	3.00
30 Willie McCovey	.40	1.00

1980 Laughlin Famous Feats

This set of 40 standard-size cards is printed on white card stock. Sports artist R.G. Laughlin 1980 is copyrighted at the bottom of every obverse. The obverses are line drawings primarily in many colors. The set is subtitled "Second Series" of Famous Feats. The cards are numbered on the front. The backs are blank on white stock.

COMPLETE SET (40)	8.00	20.00
1 Honus Wagner	.40	1.00
2 Herb Pennock	.20	.50
3 Al Simmons	.20	.50
4 Hack Wilson	.20	.50
5 Dizzy Dean	.30	.75
6 Chuck Klein	.20	.50
7 Nellie Fox	.20	.50
8 Lefty Grove	.30	.75
9 George Sisler	.20	.50
10 Lou Gehrig	.75	2.00
11 Rube Waddell	.20	.50
12 Max Carey	.20	.50
13 Thurman Munson	.30	.75
14 Mel Ott	.30	.75
15 Doc White	.08	.25
16 Babe Ruth	1.00	2.50
17 Schoolboy Rowe	.08	.25
18 Jackie Robinson	.60	1.50
19 Joe Medwick	.20	.50
20 Casey Stengel	.40	1.00
21 Roberto Clemente	.75	2.00
22 Christy Mathewson	.40	1.00
23 Jimmie Foxx	.30	.75
24 Joe Jackson	.60	1.50
25 Walter Johnson	.40	1.00
26 Tony Lazzeri	.20	.50
27 Hugh Casey	.08	.25
28 Ty Cobb	.75	2.00
29 Stuffy McInnis	.08	.25
30 Cy Young	.30	.75
31 Lefty O'Doul	.08	.25
32 Eddie Collins	.20	.50
33 Joe McCarthy	.20	.50
34 Ed Walsh	.20	.50
35 George Burns	.08	.25
36 Walt Dropo	.08	.25
37 Connie Mack	.30	.75
38 Babe Adams	.08	.25
39 Rogers Hornsby	.30	.75
40 Grover C. Alexander	.30	.75

1914 Lawrence Semon Postcards

These seven postcards were produced by photographer Lawrence Semon. These postcards feature a large photo of the player using most of the space of the card with the players name and some information on the bottom. Six additions to this checklist were discovered in recent years -- so there might be more and additions to this checklist are welcome.

COMPLETE SET	2,000.00	4,000.00
1 George Burns	100.00	200.00
2 Frank Chance	200.00	400.00
3 Ty Cobb	600.00	1,200.00
4 Walter Johnson	400.00	800.00
5 Connie Mack MG	300.00	600.00
6 Rube Marquard	200.00	400.00
7 John McGraw MG	300.00	600.00

1949 Leaf

The cards in this 98-card set measure 2 3/8" by 2 7/8". The 1949 Leaf set was the first post-war baseball series issued in color. This effort was not entirely successful due to a lack of refinement which resulted in many color variations and cards out of register. In addition, the set was skip numbered from 1-168, with 49 of the 98 cards printed in limited quantities (marked with SP in the checklist). Cards 102 and 136 have variations, and cards are sometimes found with overprinted, incorrect or blank backs. Some cards were produced with a 1948 copyright date but overwhelming evidence seemed to indicate that this set was not actually released until early in 1949. An album to hold these cards was available as a premium. The album could only be obtained by sending in five wrappers and 25 cents. Since so few albums appear on the secondary market, no value is attached to them. Notable Rookie Cards in this set include Stan Musial, Satchel Paige, and Jackie Robinson. A proof card of Hal Newhouser; with a different photo and back biography recently surfaced. So far; there is only one known copy of this card.

COMPLETE SET (98)	25,000.00	40,000.00
COMMON CARD (1-168)	15.00	25.00
COMMON SP's	200.00	300.00
WRAPPER (1-CENT)	120.00	160.00
1 Joe DiMaggio	1,000.00	2,000.00
3 Babe Ruth	2,000.00	4,000.00
4 Stan Musial	1,500.00	3,000.00
5 Virgil Trucks SP RC	250.00	400.00
8 S.Paige SP RC	9,000.00	15,000.00
10 Dizzy Trout	25.00	40.00
11 Phil Rizzuto	150.00	300.00
13 Cass Michaels SP RC	200.00	300.00
14 Billy Johnson	25.00	40.00
17 Frank Overmire RC	15.00	25.00
19 Johnny Wyrostek SP	200.00	300.00
20 Hank Sauer SP	250.00	400.00
22 Al Evans RC	15.00	25.00
26 Sam Chapman	25.00	40.00
27 Mickey Harris RC	15.00	25.00
28 Jim Hegan RC	25.00	40.00
29 Elmer Valo RC	25.00	40.00
30 Billy Goodman SP RC	250.00	400.00
31 Lou Brissie RC	15.00	25.00
32 Warren Spahn	400.00	800.00
33 Peanuts Lowrey SP RC	200.00	300.00
36 Al Zarilla SP	200.00	300.00
38 Ted Kluszewski RC	125.00	200.00
39 Ewell Blackwell	35.00	60.00
42A Kent Peterson RC	15.00	25.00
42B Kent Peterson Red Cap		
43 Ed Stevens SP RC	200.00	300.00
45 Ken Keltner SP RC	200.00	300.00
46 Johnny Mize	60.00	100.00
47 George Vico RC	15.00	25.00
48 Johnny Schmitz SP RC	200.00	300.00
49 Del Ennis RC	35.00	60.00
50 Dick Wakefield RC	15.00	25.00
51 Alvin Dark SP RC	300.00	500.00
53 Johnny VanderMeer	60.00	100.00
54 Bobby Adams SP RC	200.00	300.00
55 Tommy Henrich SP	300.00	500.00
56 Larry Jansen	25.00	40.00
57 Bob McCall RC	15.00	25.00
59 Luke Appling	60.00	100.00
61 Jake Early RC	15.00	25.00
62 Eddie Joost SP	200.00	300.00
63 Barney McCosky SP	200.00	300.00
65 Bob Elliott UER	60.00	100.00
66 Orval Grove SP RC	200.00	300.00
68 Eddie Miller SP	200.00	300.00
70 Honus Wagner	250.00	500.00
72 Hank Edwards RC	15.00	25.00
73 Pat Seerey RC	15.00	25.00
75 Dom DiMaggio SP	350.00	600.00
76 Ted Williams	800.00	1,500.00
77 Roy Smalley RC	15.00	25.00
78 Hoot Evers SP RC	200.00	300.00
79 Jackie Robinson RC	6,000.00	12,000.00
81 Whitey Kurowski SP RC	200.00	300.00
82 Johnny Lindell	25.00	40.00
83 Bobby Doerr	60.00	100.00
84 Sid Hudson	15.00	25.00
85 Dave Philley SP RC	250.00	400.00
86 Ralph Weigel RC	15.00	25.00
88 Frank Gustine SP RC	200.00	300.00
91 Ralph Kiner	125.00	250.00
93 Bob Feller SP	1,400.00	2,000.00
95 Snuffy Stirnweiss	25.00	40.00
97 Marty Marion	35.00	60.00
98 Hal Newhouser SP RC	350.00	600.00
98A Hal Newhouser Proof		
102A G.Hermansk ERR	150.00	250.00
102B Gene Hermanski COR RC	25.00	40.00
104 Eddie Stewart SP RC	200.00	300.00
106 Lou Boudreau MG RC	60.00	100.00
108 Matt Batts SP RC	200.00	300.00
111 Jerry Priddy RC	15.00	25.00
113 Dutch Leonard SP	200.00	300.00
117 Joe Gordon RC	25.00	40.00
120 George Kell SP RC	350.00	600.00
121 Johnny Pesky SP RC	250.00	400.00
123 Cliff Fannin SP RC	200.00	300.00
125 Andy Pafko RC	15.00	25.00
127 Enos Slaughter SP	500.00	800.00
128 Buddy Rosar	15.00	25.00
129 Kirby Higbe SP	200.00	300.00
131 Sid Gordon SP	200.00	300.00
133 Tommy Holmes SP RC	300.00	500.00
136A C.Aberson Full Slv RC	15.00	25.00
136B C.Aberson Short Slv	150.00	250.00
137 Harry Walker SP RC	250.00	400.00
138 Larry Doby SP RC	400.00	700.00
139 Johnny Hopp RC	15.00	25.00
142 D.Murtaugh SP RC	250.00	400.00
143 Dick Sisler SP RC	200.00	300.00
144 Bob Dillinger SP RC	200.00	300.00
146 Pete Reiser SP	300.00	500.00
149 Hank Majeski SP RC	200.00	300.00
153 Floyd Baker SP RC	200.00	300.00
158 H.Brecheen SP RC	250.00	400.00
159 Mizell Platt RC	15.00	25.00
160 Bob Scheffing SP RC	200.00	300.00
161 V.Stephens SP RC	250.00	400.00
163 F.Hutchinson SP RC	250.00	400.00
165 Dale Mitchell SP RC	250.00	400.00
168 Phil Cavarretta SP RC	300.00	500.00
NNO Album		

1949 Leaf Premiums

This set of eight large, blank-backed premiums is rather scarce. They were issued as premiums with the 1949 Leaf Gum set. The catalog designation is R401-4. The set is subtitled "Baseball's Immortals" and there is no reference anywhere on the premium to Leaf, the issuing company. These large photos measure approximately 5 1/2" x 7 3/16" and are printed on thin paper.

COMPLETE SET (8)	2,500.00	5,000.00
1 Grover C. Alexander	200.00	400.00
2 Mickey Cochrane	200.00	400.00
3 Lou Gehrig	500.00	1,000.00

4 Walter Johnson	300.00	600.00
5 Christy Mathewson	300.00	600.00
6 John McGraw	200.00	400.00
7 Babe Ruth	750.00	1,500.00
8 Ed Walsh	150.00	300.00

1960 Leaf

The cards in this 144-card set measure the standard size. The 1960 Leaf set was issued in a regular gum package style but with a marble instead of gum. This set was issued in five card nickel packs which came 24 to a box. The series was a joint production by Sports Novelties, Inc., and Leaf, two Chicago-based companies. Cards 73-144 are more difficult to find than the lower numbers. Photo variations exist (probably proof cards) for the eight cards listed with an asterisk and there is a well-known error card, number 25 showing Brooks Lawrence (in a Reds uniform) with Jim Grant's name on front, and Grant's biography and record on back. The corrected version with Grant's photo is the more difficult variety. The only notable Rookie Card in this set is Dallas Green. The complete set price below includes both versions of Jim Grant.

COMPLETE SET (144)	1,000.00	2,000.00
COMMON CARD (1-72)	1.25	3.00
COMMON CARD (73-144)	12.50	30.00
WRAPPER (5-CENT)	20.00	50.00
1 Luis Aparicio *	10.00	25.00
2 Woody Held	1.25	3.00
3 Frank Lary	1.50	4.00
4 Camilo Pascual	2.00	5.00
5 Pancho Herrera	1.25	3.00
6 Felipe Alou	3.00	8.00
7 Benjamin Daniels	1.25	3.00
8 Roger Craig	2.00	5.00
9 Eddie Kasko	1.25	3.00
10 Bob Grim	1.50	4.00
11 Jim Busby	1.50	4.00
12 Ken Boyer*	3.00	8.00
13 Bob Boyd	1.25	3.00
14 Sam Jones	1.50	4.00
15 Larry Jackson	1.50	4.00
16 Roy Face	1.50	4.00
17 Walt Moryn *	1.25	3.00
18 Jim Gilliam	2.00	5.00
19 Don Newcombe	2.00	5.00
20 Glen Hobbie	1.25	3.00
21 Pedro Ramos	1.50	4.00
22 Ryne Duren	1.25	3.00
23 Joey Jay *	1.50	4.00
24 Lou Berberet	1.25	3.00
25A Jim Grant ERR	6.00	15.00
25B Jim Grant COR	10.00	25.00
26 Tom Borland RC	1.25	3.00
27 Brooks Robinson	20.00	50.00
28 Jerry Adair RC	1.25	3.00
29 Ron Jackson	1.25	3.00
30 George Strickland	1.25	3.00
31 Rocky Bridges	1.25	3.00
32 Bill Tuttle	1.50	4.00
33 Ken Hunt RC	1.25	3.00
34 Hal Griggs	1.25	3.00
35 Jim Coates *	1.25	3.00
36 Brooks Lawrence	1.25	3.00
37 Duke Snider	15.00	40.00
38 Al Spangler RC	1.25	3.00
39 Jim Owens	1.25	3.00
40 Bill Virdon	2.00	5.00
41 Ernie Broglio	1.25	3.00
42 Andre Rodgers	1.25	3.00
43 Julio Becquer	1.50	4.00
44 Tony Taylor	1.50	4.00
45 Jerry Lynch	1.50	4.00
46 Clete Boyer	3.00	8.00
47 Jerry Lumpe	1.25	3.00
48 Charlie Maxwell	1.50	4.00
49 Jim Perry	1.50	4.00
50 Danny McDevitt	1.25	3.00
51 Juan Pizarro	1.25	3.00
52 Dallas Green RC	3.00	8.00
53 Bob Friend	1.50	4.00
54 Jack Sanford	1.50	4.00
55 Jim Rivera	1.25	3.00
56 Ted Wills RC	1.25	3.00
57 Milt Pappas	1.50	4.00
58A Hal Smith *	1.25	3.00
58B Hal Smith Blacked out team		
58C Hal Smith No team on back	75.00	200.00
59 Bobby Avila	1.25	3.00
60 Clem Labine	2.00	5.00
61 Norman Rehm RC *	1.25	3.00
62 John Gabler RC	1.50	4.00
63 John Tsitouris RC	1.25	3.00
64 Dave Sisler	1.25	3.00
65 Vic Power	1.50	4.00
66 Earl Battey	1.25	3.00
67 Bob Purkey	1.25	3.00
68 Moe Drabowsky	1.50	4.00
69 Hoyt Wilhelm	6.00	15.00
70 Humberto Robinson	1.25	3.00
71 Whitey Herzog	3.00	8.00
72 Dick Donovan *	1.25	3.00
73 Gordon Jones	12.50	30.00
74 Joe Hicks RC	12.50	30.00
75 Ray Culp RC	15.00	40.00
76 Dick Drott	12.50	30.00
77 Bob Duliba RC	12.50	30.00
78 Art Ditmar	12.50	30.00
79 Steve Korcheck	12.50	30.00
80 Henry Mason RC	12.50	30.00
81 Harry Simpson	12.50	30.00
82 Gene Green	12.50	30.00
83 Bob Shaw	12.50	30.00
84 Howard Reed	12.50	30.00
85 Dick Stigman	12.50	30.00
86 Rip Repulski	12.50	30.00
87 Seth Morehead	12.50	30.00
88 Camilo Carreon RC	12.50	30.00
89 Johnny Blanchard	15.00	40.00
90 Billy Hoeft	12.50	30.00
91 Fred Hopke RC	12.50	30.00
92 Joe Martin RC	12.50	30.00
93 Wally Shannon RC	12.50	30.00
94 Hal R. Hal W. Smith	15.00	40.00
95 Al Schroll	12.50	30.00
96 John Kucks	12.50	30.00
97 Tom Morgan	12.50	30.00
98 Willie Jones	12.50	30.00
99 Marshall Renfroe RC	12.50	30.00
100 Willie Tasby	12.50	30.00
101 Irv Noren	12.50	30.00
102 Russ Snyder RC	12.50	30.00
103 Bob Turley	15.00	40.00
104 Jim Woods RC	12.50	30.00
105 Ronnie Kline	12.50	30.00
106 Steve Bilko	12.50	30.00
107 Elmer Valo	12.50	30.00
108 Tom McAvoy RC	12.50	30.00
109 Stan Williams	12.50	30.00
110 Earl Averill Jr.	12.50	30.00
111 Lee Walls	12.50	30.00
112 Paul Richards MG	12.50	30.00
113 Ed Sadowski	12.50	30.00
114 Stover McIlwain RC	12.50	30.00
115 Chuck Tanner UER	15.00	40.00
116 Lou Klimchock RC	12.50	30.00
117 Neil Chrisley	12.50	30.00
118 Johnny Callison	20.00	50.00
119 Hal Smith	12.50	30.00
120 Carl Sawatski	12.50	30.00
121 Frank Leja	12.50	30.00
122 Earl Torgeson	12.50	30.00
123 Art Schult	12.50	30.00
124 Jim Brosnan	12.50	30.00
125 Sparky Anderson	30.00	60.00
126 Joe Pignatano	12.50	30.00
127 Rocky Nelson	12.50	30.00
128 Orlando Cepeda	40.00	80.00
129 Daryl Spencer	12.50	30.00
130 Ralph Lumenti	12.50	30.00
131 Sam Taylor	12.50	30.00
132 Harry Brecheen CO	15.00	40.00
133 Johnny Groth	12.50	30.00
134 Wayne Terwilliger	12.50	30.00
135 Kent Hadley	12.50	30.00
136 Faye Throneberry	12.50	30.00
137 Jack Meyer	12.50	30.00
138 Chuck Cottier RC	12.50	30.00
139 Joe DeMaestri	12.50	30.00
140 Gene Freese	12.50	30.00
141 Curt Flood	20.00	50.00
142 Gino Cimoli	12.50	30.00
143 Clay Dalrymple RC	12.50	30.00
144 Jim Bunning	40.00	80.00

1960 Leaf Full Face

This eight-card set, which measures the standard size, was probably issued as promos to display the general design of the 1960 Leaf Set. These cards feature full facial shots of the featured players. There has been discussion that these cards were samples used to promote the Leaf product as most of the known examples surfaced in the Chicago area where Leaf Gum had their headquarters.

COMPLETE SET (8)	1,500.00	3,000.00
1 Luis Aparicio	400.00	800.00
12 Ken Boyer	300.00	600.00
17 Walt Moryn	150.00	300.00
23 Joey Jay	150.00	300.00
35 Jim Coates	200.00	400.00
58 Hal Smith	150.00	300.00
61 Vic Rehm	150.00	300.00
72 Dick Donovan	150.00	300.00

1923 Lections

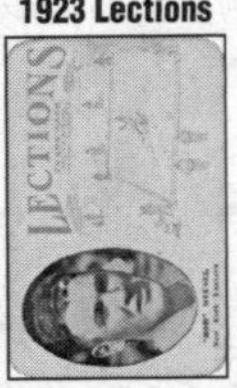

These 2 1/2" by 4" blank-backed horizontal cards are on heavy cardboard stock. The player's picture is on the left side and a game diagram is one the right. It is believed that these cards were issued in the Albany, New York area.Any additional findings to this checklist are appreciated.

COMPLETE SET	7,500.00	15,000.00
1 Frank Chance	1,250.00	2,500.00
2 Howard Ehmke	500.00	1,000.00
3 Frank Frisch	1,250.00	2,500.00
4 Rogers Horsnby	2,500.00	5,000.00
5 Charlie Jamieson	500.00	1,000.00
6 Bob Meusel	1,000.00	2,000.00
7 Irish Meusel	500.00	1,000.00
8 Babe Ruth	4,250.00	8,500.00
9 Charles Schmidt	500.00	1,000.00
10 Bob Shawkey	750.00	1,500.00

1973-74 Linnett Portraits

Measuring 8 1/2" by 11", these 179 charcoal drawings are facial portraits by noted sports artist Charles Linnett. The player's facsimile autograph is inscribed across the lower right corner. The backs are blank. Three portraits of players from the same team or major stars issued in those groups of three were included in each clear plastic packet. A checklist was also included in each packet, with an offer to order individual player portraits for 50 cents each. Originally, the suggested retail price was 99 cents. In later issues, the price was raised to $1.19. The portraits are unnumbered and listed alphabetically by teams as follows: Atlanta Braves (1-6), Baltimore Orioles (7-13), Boston Red Sox (14-32), California Angels (33-38), Chicago Cubs (39-46), Chicago White Sox (47-53), Cincinnati Reds (54-59), Cleveland Indians (60-67), Detroit Tigers (68-79), Houston Astros (80-86), Kansas City Royals (87-91), Los Angeles Dodgers (92-97), Milwaukee Brewers (98-103), Minnesota Twins (104-109), New York Mets (110-125), New York Yankees (126-136), Oakland A's (137-141), Philadelphia Phillies (142-147), Pittsburgh Pirates (148-153), San Diego Padres (154-156), San Francisco Giants (157-164), St. Louis Cardinals (165-171), and Texas Rangers (172-179). The Mets packages were as follows: Jon Matlack, Felix Millan and Duffy Dyer; Rusty Staub, Jerry Koosman and John Milner; and Wayne Garrett, Cleon Jones and Bud Harrelson.

COMPLETE SET	350.00	700.00
1 Hank Aaron	6.00	15.00
2 Darrell Evans	3.00	8.00
3 Ralph Garr	2.50	6.00
4 Dave Johnson	3.00	8.00
5 Mike Lum	2.00	5.00
6 Carl Morton	2.00	5.00
7 Mark Belanger	2.50	6.00
8 Paul Blair	2.00	5.00
9 Al Bumbry	2.00	5.00
10 Bobby Grich	3.00	8.00
11 Lee May	2.50	6.00
12 Jim Palmer	5.00	12.00
13 Brooks Robinson	6.00	15.00
14 Luis Aparicio	5.00	12.00
15 Bob Bolin	2.00	5.00
16 Danny Cater	2.00	5.00
17 Orlando Cepeda	5.00	12.00
18 John Curtis	2.00	5.00
19 Dwight Evans	4.00	10.00
20 Carlton Fisk	5.00	12.00
21 Doug Griffin	2.00	5.00
22 Mario Guerrero	2.00	5.00
23 Tommy Harper	2.00	5.00
24 John Kennedy	2.00	5.00
25 Bill Lee	3.00	8.00
26 Rick Miller	2.00	5.00
27 Bob Montgomery	2.00	5.00
28 Marty Pattin	2.00	5.00
29 Rico Petrocelli	2.50	6.00
30 Luis Tiant	4.00	10.00
31 Bob Veale	2.00	5.00
32 Carl Yastrzemski	10.00	25.00
33 Bob Oliver	2.00	5.00
34 Frank Robinson	5.00	12.00
35 Nolan Ryan	8.00	20.00
36 Bill Singer	2.00	5.00
37 Lee Stanton	2.00	5.00
38 Bobby Valentine	3.00	8.00
39 Bill Bonham	2.00	5.00
40 Jose Cardenal	2.00	5.00
41 Don Kessinger	2.50	6.00
42 Bob Locker	2.00	5.00
43 Rick Monday	2.50	6.00
44 Ron Santo	4.00	10.00
45 Steve Stone	2.50	6.00
46 Billy Williams	5.00	12.00
47 Dick Allen	4.00	10.00
48 Ed Herrmann	2.00	5.00
49 Eddie Leon	2.00	5.00
50 Bill Melton	2.00	5.00
51 Jorge Orta	2.00	5.00
52 Rick Reichardt	2.00	5.00
53 Wilbur Wood	2.00	5.00
54 Johnny Bench	5.00	12.00
55 Cesar Geronimo	2.00	5.00
56 Don Gullett	2.00	5.00
57 Joe Morgan	5.00	12.00
58 Tony Perez	5.00	12.00
59 Pete Rose	6.00	15.00
60 Buddy Bell	3.00	8.00
61 Chris Chambliss	2.50	6.00
62 John Ellis	2.00	5.00
63 George Hendrick	2.00	5.00
64 Steve Kline	2.00	5.00
65 Gaylord Perry	5.00	12.00
66 Jim Perry	2.50	6.00
67 Charlie Spikes	2.00	5.00
68 Norm Cash	4.00	10.00
69 Bill Freehan	3.00	8.00
70 John Hiller	2.00	5.00
71 Willie Horton	2.50	6.00
72 Al Kaline	5.00	12.00
73 Mickey Lolich	4.00	10.00
74 Dick McAuliffe	2.50	6.00
75 Jim Northrup	2.50	6.00
76 Ben Oglivie	2.00	5.00
77 Aurelio Rodriguez	2.00	5.00
78 Fred Scherman	2.00	5.00
79 Mickey Stanley	2.00	5.00
80 Cesar Cedeno	2.50	6.00
81 Greg Gross	2.00	5.00
82 Roger Metzger	2.00	5.00
83 Jerry Reuss	2.50	6.00
84 Dave Roberts (P)	2.00	5.00
85 Bob Watson	2.50	6.00
86 Don Wilson	2.00	5.00
87 John Mayberry	2.00	5.00
88 Amos Otis	2.00	5.00
89 Fred Patek	2.00	5.00
90 Cookie Rojas	2.00	5.00
91 Paul Splittorff	2.00	5.00
92 Bill Buckner	2.50	6.00
93 Willie Crawford	2.00	5.00
94 Joe Ferguson	2.00	5.00
95 Dave Lopes	2.50	6.00
96 Bill Russell	2.50	6.00
97 Don Sutton	5.00	12.00
98 John Briggs	2.00	5.00
99 Jim Colborn	2.00	5.00
100 Pedro Garcia	2.00	5.00
101 Dave May	2.00	5.00
102 Don Money	2.00	5.00
103 George Scott	2.50	6.00
104 Bert Blyleven	4.00	10.00
105 Steve Braun	2.00	5.00
106 Steve Brye	2.00	5.00
107 Rod Carew	5.00	12.00
108 Bobby Darwin	2.00	5.00
109 Danny Thompson	2.00	5.00
110 Duffy Dyer	2.00	5.00
111 Wayne Garrett	2.00	5.00
112 Bud Harrelson	2.00	5.00
113 Cleon Jones	2.00	5.00
114 Jerry Koosman	2.50	6.00
115 Teddy Martinez	2.00	5.00
116 Jon Matlack	2.00	5.00
117 Jim McAndrew	2.00	5.00
118 Tug McGraw	3.00	8.00
119 Felix Millan	2.00	5.00
120 John Milner	2.00	5.00
121 Harry Parker	2.00	5.00
122 Tom Seaver	6.00	15.00
123 Rusty Staub	4.00	10.00
124 George Stone	2.00	5.00
125 George Theodore	2.00	5.00
126 Bernie Allen	2.00	5.00
127 Felipe Alou	4.00	10.00
128 Matty Alou	3.00	8.00
129 Ron Blomberg	2.00	5.00
130 Sparky Lyle	3.00	8.00
131 Gene Michael	2.00	5.00
132 Thurman Munson	5.00	12.00
133 Bobby Murcer	3.00	8.00
134 Graig Nettles	4.00	10.00
135 Lou Piniella	3.00	8.00
136 Mel Stottlemyre	2.50	6.00
137 Sal Bando	2.50	6.00
138 Bert Campaneris	3.00	8.00
139 Rollie Fingers	5.00	12.00
140 Jim Hunter	5.00	12.00
141 Reggie Jackson	6.00	15.00
142 Bob Boone	3.00	8.00
143 Larry Bowa	2.50	6.00
144 Steve Carlton	5.00	12.00
145 Dave Cash	2.00	5.00
146 Greg Luzinski	3.00	8.00
147 Willie Montanez	2.00	5.00
148 Ken Brett	2.00	5.00
149 Dave Giusti	2.00	5.00
150 Ed Kirkpatrick	2.00	5.00
151 Al Oliver	4.00	10.00
152 Manny Sanguillen	2.50	6.00
153 Willie Stargell	5.00	12.00
154 Nate Colbert	2.00	5.00
155 John Grubb	2.00	5.00
156 Dave Roberts (3B)	2.00	5.00
157 Bobby Bonds	4.00	10.00
158 Ron Bryant	2.00	5.00
159 Dave Kingman	4.00	10.00
160 Garry Maddox	2.00	5.00
161 Gary Matthews	2.50	6.00
162 Willie McCovey	5.00	12.00
163 Sam McDowell	2.50	6.00
164 Chris Speier	2.00	5.00
165 Lou Brock	5.00	12.00
166 Bernie Carbo	2.00	5.00
167 Bob Gibson	5.00	12.00
168 Lynn McGlothen	2.00	5.00
169 Ted Simmons	4.00	10.00
170 Reggie Smith	3.00	8.00
171 Joe Torre	4.00	10.00
172 Jim Bibby	2.00	5.00
173 Jeff Burroughs	2.50	6.00
174 David Clyde	2.00	5.00
175 Jim Fregosi	2.50	6.00
176 Toby Harrah	2.00	5.00
177 Vic Harris	2.00	5.00
178 Ferguson Jenkins	5.00	12.00
179 Dave Nelson	2.00	5.00

1976 Linnett Superstars

The Linnett Superstars set contains 36 oversized cards measuring approximately 4" by 5 5/8". The cards feature black and white facial portraits of the players, with various color borders. In the corners of the portrait appear four different logos: MLB, MLBPA, team and PeeWee's. The backs have a picture and discussion of either great cars of the world or sailing ships. The cards are checklisted below according to teams as follows: Cincinnati Reds, (90-101) Boston Red Sox, (102-113) and Los Angeles Dodgers (114-125).

COMPLETE SET	40.00	80.00
90 Don Gullett	.40	1.00
91 Johnny Bench	3.00	8.00
92 Tony Perez	2.00	5.00
93 Mike Lum	.40	1.00
94 Ken Griffey	.75	2.00
95 George Foster	.60	1.50
96 Joe Morgan	2.00	5.00
97 Pete Rose	4.00	10.00

98 Dave Concepcion	.75	2.00
99 Cesar Geronimo	.40	1.00
100 Dan Driessen	.40	1.00
101 Pedro Borbon	.40	1.00
102 Carl Yastrzemski	3.00	8.00
103 Fred Lynn	.75	2.00
104 Dwight Evans	.75	2.00
105 Ferguson Jenkins	2.00	5.00
106 Rico Petrocelli	.60	1.50
107 Denny Doyle	.40	1.00
108 Luis Tiant	.75	2.00
109 Carlton Fisk	2.00	5.00
110 Rick Burleson	.60	1.50
111 Bill Lee	.60	1.50
112 Rick Wise	.40	1.00
113 Jim Rice	1.00	2.50
114 Davey Lopes	.60	1.50
115 Steve Garvey	.75	2.00
116 Bill Russell	.40	1.00
117 Ron Cey	.75	2.00
118 Steve Yeager	.40	1.00
119 Doug Rau	.40	1.00
120 Don Sutton	1.25	3.00
121 Joe Ferguson	.40	1.00
122 Mike Marshall	.40	1.00
123 Bill Buckner	.40	1.00
124 Rick Rhoden	.40	1.00
125 Ted Sizemore	.40	1.00

1968 Lolich Macomb Mall

This one card set, which is a photograph which measures 8 1/2" by 11" features Mickey Lolich and was given away to commemorate his appearance at the Macomb Mall in 1968.

1 Mickey Lolich	4.00	10.00

1887 Lone Jack N370

There are rulers and celebrities as well as baseball players in this set of sepia photographs issued by the Lone Jack Cigarette Company of Lynchburg, Va. The ballplayers are all members of the 1886 St. Louis Club which won the World Championship, and the pictures are identical to those found in set N172.

COMPLETE SET	30,000.00	60,000.00
1 Al Bushong	4,000.00	8,000.00
2 Arlie Latham	600.00	12,000.00
4 Bill (Yank) Robinson	4,000.00	8,000.00
6 Bob Caruthers	5,000.00	10,000.00
7 Charles Commiskey(sic)	7,500.00	15,000.00
8 Chris Von Der Ahe OWN	600.00	12,000.00
9 Curt Welsh (sic)	5,000.00	10,000.00
10 Dave Foutz	4,000.00	8,000.00
15 Hugh Nicol	4,000.00	8,000.00
16 James O'Neil (sic)	5,000.00	10,000.00
23 Nat Hudson	4,000.00	8,000.00
32 Rudy Kimler (sic)	4,000.00	8,000.00
36 William Gleason	5,000.00	10,000.00

1886 Lorillard Team Cards

These four cards, which measure approximately 4" by 5" feature composite "head" shots of members of four National League teams. The backs feature schedules for these teams, as well as an advertisement for Lorillard Tobacco. All of these cards are extremely condition sensitive and finding ex-mt examples of these cards is a real challenge.

COMPLETE SET (4)	9,000.00	18,000.00
1 Chicago NL	4,000.00	8,000.00
2 Detroit NL	5,000.00	10,000.00
3 New York NL	6,000.00	12,000.00
4 Philadelphia NL	3,000.00	6,000.00

1953 MacGregor Staff

This set features black-and-white photos of players on the MacGregor Sporting Goods Advisory Staff. The cards measure approximately 8" by 9 1/8" with facsimile autographs on the fronts and blank backs. The cards are unnumbered and checklisted below in alphabetical order. The checklist may be incomplete.

COMPLETE SET	125.00	250.00
1 Ralph Kiner	40.00	80.00
2 Ted Kluszewski	30.00	60.00
3 Robin Roberts	40.00	80.00
4 Al Schoendienst	30.00	60.00
5 Warren Spahn	40.00	80.00

1960 MacGregor Staff

This 25-card set represents members of the MacGregor Sporting Goods Advisory Staff. Since the cards are unnumbered they ordered below in alphabetical order. The cards are blank backed and measure approximately 3 3/4" by 5". The photos are in black and white. The catalog designation for the set is H801-10. Cards have a facsimile autograph in white lettering on the front. These cards were sent out as complete sets as mailing envelopes have been seen.

COMPLETE SET (25)	300.00	600.00
1 Hank Aaron	60.00	120.00
2 Richie Ashburn	8.00	20.00
3 Gus Bell	5.00	12.00
4 Lou Berberet	4.00	10.00
5 Jerry Casale	4.00	10.00
6 Del Crandall	5.00	12.00
7 Art Ditmar	4.00	10.00
8 Gene Freese	4.00	10.00
9 James Gilliam	6.00	15.00
10 Ted Kluszewski	8.00	20.00
11 Jim Landis	4.00	10.00
12 Al Lopez MG	6.00	15.00
13 Willie Mays	75.00	150.00
14 Bill Mazeroski	8.00	20.00
15 Mike McCormick	5.00	12.00
16 Gil McDougald	6.00	15.00
17 Russ Nixon	4.00	10.00
18 Bill Rigney MG	4.00	10.00
19 Robin Roberts	8.00	20.00
20 Frank Robinson	15.00	40.00
21 John Roseboro	5.00	12.00
22 Red Schoendienst	8.00	20.00
23 Bill Skowron	6.00	15.00
24 Daryl Spencer	4.00	10.00
25 Johnny Temple	4.00	10.00

1965 MacGregor Staff

This ten-card set represents members of the MacGregor Sporting Goods Advisory Staff. Since the cards are unnumbered they are ordered below in alphabetical order. The cards are blank backed and measure approximately 3 9/16" by 5 1/8". The photos are in black and white. The catalog designation for the set is H825-2.

COMPLETE SET (10)	500.00	1,000.00
1 Roberto Clemente	250.00	500.00
2 Al Downing	12.50	30.00
3 Johnny Edwards	12.50	30.00
4 Ron Hansen	12.50	30.00
5 Deron Johnson	12.50	30.00
6 Willie Mays	200.00	400.00
7 Tony Oliva	30.00	60.00
8 Claude Osteen	12.50	30.00
9 Bobby Richardson	30.00	60.00
10 Zoilo Versalles	12.50	30.00

1950 Mack 66 Years in the Big Leagues

These four black and white (with a seeming sepia tone) cards were issued in conjuction with the release of Connie Mack's Book "My 66 Years in the Big Leagues". The players featured are Mack's most memorable three personalities. The cards were also shipped in a special promotional envelope to inspire more sales of the book. The cards measure 2 1/4" by 3 1/2" and were printed on thin white stock.

COMPLETE SET (4)	750.00	1,500.00
1 Connie Mack	125.00	250.00
2 Christy Mathewson	200.00	400.00
3 Babe Ruth	400.00	800.00
4 Rube Waddell	100.00	200.00

1926 Major League Die-Cuts

Measuring approximately 2 5/8" by 1 1/8" these die-cut cards feature a drawing on the top as well as the player's name, position and team on the bottom. Since these are unnumbered, we have sequenced them in alphabetical order by team. This checklist is incomplete, so all additions are appreciated.

COMPLETE SET	1,500.00	3,000.00
1 John Bischoff	15.00	30.00
2 Ira Flagstead	15.00	30.00
3 Alex Gaston	15.00	30.00
4 Fred Haney	15.00	30.00
5 Slim Harriss	15.00	30.00
6 Fred Heimach	15.00	30.00
7 Baby Doll Jacobson	15.00	30.00
8 Bill Regan	15.00	30.00
9 Topper Rigney	15.00	30.00
10 Red Ruffing	30.00	60.00
11 Wally Shaner	15.00	30.00
12 Phil Todt	15.00	30.00
13 Hal Wiltse	15.00	30.00
14 Ted Wingfield	15.00	30.00
15 Bill Barrett	15.00	30.00
16 Ted Blankenship	15.00	30.00
17 Wilbur Cooper	15.00	30.00
18 Buck Crouse	15.00	30.00
19 Jim Joe Edwards	15.00	30.00
20 Bibb Falk	15.00	30.00
21 Bill Hunnefield	15.00	30.00
22 Willie Kamm	15.00	30.00
23 Ted Lyons	30.00	60.00
24 John Mostil	15.00	30.00
25 Ray Schalk	30.00	60.00
26 Earl Sheely	15.00	30.00
27 Tommy Thomas	15.00	30.00
28 George Burns	15.00	30.00
29 Charlie Jamieson	15.00	30.00
30 Benn Karr	15.00	30.00
31 Dutch Levsen	15.00	30.00
32 Glenn Myatt	15.00	30.00
33 Joe Sewell	30.00	60.00
34 Joe Shaute	15.00	30.00
35 Sherry Smith	15.00	30.00
36 Tris Speaker	50.00	100.00
37 Freddy Spurgeon	15.00	30.00
38 Homer Summa	15.00	30.00
39 George Uhle	15.00	30.00
40 Max Bishop	15.00	30.00
41 Mickey Cochrane	40.00	80.00
42 Eddie Collins	60.00	120.00
43 Jimmy Dykes	20.00	40.00
44 Howard Ehmke	15.00	30.00
45 Walter French	15.00	30.00
46 Sam Gray	15.00	30.00
47 Lefty Grove	75.00	150.00
48 Joe Hauser	20.00	40.00
49 Bill Lamar	15.00	30.00
50 Cy Perkins	15.00	30.00
51 Ed Rommel	20.00	40.00
52 Al Simmons	50.00	100.00
53 Rube Walberg	15.00	30.00
54 Benny Bengough	15.00	30.00
55 Pat Collins	15.00	30.00
56 Earl Combs	30.00	60.00
57 Joe Dugan	20.00	40.00
58 Lou Gehrig	100.00	200.00
59 Waite Hoyt	30.00	60.00
60 Sam Jones	20.00	40.00
61 Mark Koenig	20.00	40.00
62 Tony Lazzeri	30.00	60.00
63 Bob Meusel	25.00	50.00
64 Herb Pennock	30.00	60.00
65 Babe Ruth	150.00	300.00
66 Urban Shocker	20.00	40.00
67 Myles Thomas	15.00	30.00
68 Dixie Davis	15.00	30.00
69 Cedric Durst	15.00	30.00
70 Milt Gaston	15.00	30.00
71 Wally Gerber	15.00	30.00
72 Joe Giard	15.00	30.00
73 Pinky Hargrave	15.00	30.00
74 Marty McManus	15.00	30.00
75 Oscar Melillo	15.00	30.00
76 Bing Miller	15.00	30.00
77 Harry Rice	15.00	30.00
78 Wally Schang	20.00	40.00
79 George Sisler	40.00	80.00
80 Tom Zachary	15.00	30.00

1956 Mantle Holiday Inn Postcard

This one-card set features a borderless color photo of Mickey Mantle in the Dugout Lounge at the Holiday Inn in Joplin, Missouri, which was operated by him. The back displays a postcard format. It is believed that there may be at least four different poses of this postcard. Any further information is greatly appreciated.

1980 Mantle Reserve Life

This one-card set features a painting of Mickey Mantle in various baseball playing action with a facsimile autograph printed in the top right. The set commemorates him as the Director of Public Relations for Reserve Life Insurance Company. The back displays player information and career statistics.

1 Mickey Mantle	5.00	10.00

1923 Maple Crispette V117

This 30-card set was produced by Maple Crispette Co. of Montreal around 1923. The cards are black and white and measure approximately 1 3/8" by 2 1/4". The card backs explain a send-in offer for a ball, bat or glove in return for 30 baseball (or hockey) cards collected. The cards are numbered on the front. The Stengel card was undoubtedly the short-printed card in the set that made the send-in offer a very difficult task to fulfill.

COMPLETE SET (30)	6,000.00	12,000.00
1 J. Barnes	100.00	200.00
2 Pie Traynor	200.00	400.00
3 Ray Schalk	200.00	400.00
4 Eddie Collins	200.00	400.00
5 Lee Fohl MG	100.00	200.00
6 Howard Summa	100.00	200.00
7 Waite Hoyt	200.00	400.00
8 Babe Ruth	5,000.00	10,000.00
9 Cozy Dolan CO	100.00	200.00
10 Johnny Bassler	100.00	200.00
11 George Dauss	100.00	200.00
12 Joe Sewell	200.00	400.00
13 Syl Johnson	100.00	200.00
14 Ivy Wingo	100.00	200.00
15 Casey Stengel SP	6,000.00	12,000.00
16 Arnold Statz	100.00	200.00
17 Emil Meusel	100.00	200.00
18 Bill Jacobson	100.00	200.00
19 Jim Bottomley	200.00	400.00
20 Sam Bohne	100.00	200.00
21 Bucky Harris	200.00	400.00
22 Ty Cobb	3,000.00	6,000.00
23 Roger Peckinpaugh	125.00	250.00
24 Muddy Ruel	100.00	200.00
25 Bill McKechnie	200.00	400.00
26 Riggs Stephenson	125.00	250.00
27 Herb Pennock	200.00	400.00
28 Ed Roush	200.00	400.00
29 Bill Wambsganss	125.00	250.00
30 Walter Johnson	750.00	1,500.00

1980 Marchant Exhibits

These 32 exhibit cards, which measure the same as the original issue, was relased in 1980 and made by card dealer Paul Marchant who issued this set to honor various popular players. This set, clearly marked as reprints, are unnumbered and are sequenced in alphabetical order. According to the manufacturer only 5,000 of these sets were produced.

COMPLETE SET	6.00	15.00
1 Johnny Antonelli	.02	.10
2 Richie Ashburn	.10	.30
3 Earl Averill	.07	.20
4 Ernie Banks	.10	.30
5 Ewell Blackwell	.02	.10
6 Lou Brock	.10	.30
7 Dean Chance	.02	.10
8 Roger Craig	.02	.10
9 Lou Gehrig	.40	1.00
10 Gil Hodges	.10	.30
11 Jackie Jensen	.02	.10
12 Charlie Keller	.02	.10
13 George Kell	.07	.20
14 Alex Kellner	.02	.10
15 Harmon Killebrew	.07	.20
16 Dale Long	.02	.10
17 Sal Maglie	.02	.10
18 Roger Maris	.20	.50
19 Willie Mays	.30	.75
20 Minnie Minoso	.07	.20
21 Stan Musial	.20	.50
22 Billy Pierce	.02	.10
23 Jim Piersall	.02	.10
24 Eddie Plank	.07	.20
25 Pete Reiser	.02	.10
26 Brooks Robinson	.10	.30
27 Pete Runnels	.02	.10
28 Herb Score	.02	.10
29 Warren Spahn	.10	.30
30 Billy Williams	.10	.30
31 1948 Indians Team	.02	.10
32 1948 Braves Team	.02	.10

1980 Marchant Exhibits HOF Blue

Noted long-time dealer Paul Marchant bought out the rights to use the exhibit name in 1980. He then issued this set, which measured the same size as the original exhibits to honor various Hall of Famers. This set was very noticeably marked as a "reprint" so there would be no confusion with the original cards. According to the manufacturer, 10,000 of these sets were produced.

COMPLETE SET	5.00	12.00
1 Grover C. Alexander	.07	.20
2 Lou Boudreau	.07	.20
3 Roger Bresnahan	.02	.10
4 Roy Campanella	.10	.30
5 Frank Chance	.02	.10
6 Ty Cobb	.30	.75
7 Mickey Cochrane	.07	.20
8 Dizzy Dean	.20	.50
9 Bill Dickey	.07	.20
10 Joe DiMaggio	.40	1.00
11 Johnny Evers	.07	.20
12 Jimmy Foxx (Jimmie)	.10	.30
13 Lefty Gomez	.07	.20
14 Hank Greenberg	.07	.20
15 Lefty Grove	.07	.20
16 Rogers Hornsby	.10	.30
17 Carl Hubbell	.07	.20
18 Hughie Jennings	.02	.10
19 Walter Johnson	.20	.50
20 Nap Lajoie	.10	.30
21 Bob Lemon	.07	.20
22 Mickey Mantle	.40	1.00
23 Christy Mathewson	.10	.30
24 Mel Ott	.07	.20
25 Satchel Paige	.20	.50
26 Jackie Robinson	.40	1.00
27 Babe Ruth	.60	1.50
28 Tris Speaker	.10	.30
29 Joe Tinker	.07	.20
30 Honus Wagner	.10	.30
31 Ted Williams	.30	.75
32 Cy Young	.10	.30

1977-78 Mariners Postcards

This 23-card set features photos of the 1978 Seattle Mariners printed on 3 1/2" by 3 5/8" black and white postcard-size cards. They either have standard postcard backs or blank backs. The cards are unnumbered and checklisted below in alphabetical order.

COMPLETE SET (23)	4.00	10.00
1 Glenn Abbott Long Hair	.20	.50
2 Glenn Abbott Short Hair	.20	.50
3 Jose Baez	.20	.50
4 Bruce Bochte	.20	.50
5 Don Bryant CO	.20	.50
6 Steve Burke	.20	.50
7 Jim Busby CO	.20	.50
8 Julio Cruz	.20	.50
9 John Hale	.20	.50
10 Rick Honeycutt	.20	.50
11 Tom House	.20	.50
12 Darrell Johnson MG	.20	.50
13 Rick Jones	.20	.50
14 Ruppert Jones	.20	.50
15 Bill Laxton	.20	.50
16 Byron McLaughlin	.20	.50
17 Dan Meyer	.20	.50
18 Larry Milbourne	.20	.50
19 Paul Mitchell	.20	.50
20 John Montague	.20	.50
21 Dave Pagan	.20	.50
22 Mike Parrott	.20	.50
23 Vada Pinson CO	.30	.75
24 Dick Pole	.20	.50
25 Shane Rawley	.20	.50
26 Craig Reynolds	.20	.50
27 Leon Roberts	.20	.50
28 Bob Robertson	.20	.50
29 Enrique Romo	.20	.50
30 Tommy Smith	.20	.50
31 Lee Stanton(Smiling	.20	.50
32 Lee Stanton Letters on Uniform	.20	.50
33 Bill Stein Mountain Background	.20	.50
34 Bill Stein Fence Background	.20	.50
35 Bob Stinson Fence Background	.20	.50
36 Bob Stinson Hill Background	.20	.50
37 Wes Stock CO	.20	.50
38 Fred Thomas	.20	.50
39 Jim Todd	.20	.50
40 Gary Wheelock	.20	.50

1978 Mariners Fred Meyer

These thirteen portraits were issued by Fred Meyer and featured members of the Seattle Mariners. The fronts feature player portraits against a blue background and the backs are blank. We have sequenced this set in alphabetical order. Interestingly a cover sheet was issued for this set and included photos of Darrell Johnson (who was the Mariners first manager) and Dick Pole. Neither Johnson nor Pole was included in the set.

COMPLETE SET (12)	20.00	50.00
1 Glenn Abbott	2.00	5.00
2 Jose Baez	2.00	5.00
3 Bruce Bochte	2.00	5.00
4 Julio Cruz	2.00	5.00
5 John Hale	2.00	5.00
6 Ruppert Jones	2.00	5.00
7 Danny Meyer	2.00	5.00
8 Craig Reynolds	2.00	5.00
9 Enrique Romo	2.00	5.00
10 Lee Stanton	2.00	5.00
11 Bill Stein	2.00	5.00
12 Bob Stinson	2.00	5.00
13 Cover Sheet Bill Stein Julio Cruz Danny Meyer/	4.00	10.00

1979 Mariners Postcards

These 29 postcards, which measure 3 3/4" by 5 1/2" feature members of the 1979 Seattle Mariners. The fronts have a player photo, a facsimile signature as well as the "Seattle Mariners" team logo on the bottom. The backs are standard postcard backs. Since these cards are unnumbered, we have sequenced this set in alphabetical order.

COMPLETE SET (29)	6.00	15.00
1 Glenn Abbott	.20	.50
2 Floyd Bannister	.20	.50
3 Bruce Bochte	.20	.50
4 Don Bryant CO	.20	.50
5 Larry Cox	.20	.50
6 Julio Cruz	.20	.50
7 Joe Decker	.20	.50
8 Rob Dressler	.20	.50
9 John Hale	.20	.50
10 Rick Honeycutt	.20	.50
11 Willie Horton	.30	.75
12 Darrell Johnson MG	.20	.50
13 Odell Jones	.20	.50
14 Ruppert Jones	.20	.50
15 Byron McLaughlin	.20	.50
16 Mario Mendoza	.20	.50
17 Dan Meyer	.20	.50
18 Larry Milbourne	.20	.50
19 John Montague	.20	.50
20 Tom Paciorek	.20	.50
21 Mike Parrott	.20	.50
22 Vada Pinson CO	.30	.75
23 Shane Rawley	.20	.50
24 Leon Roberts	.20	.50
25 Joe Simpson	.20	.50
26 Bill Stein	.20	.50
27 Bob Stinson	.20	.50
28 Wes Stock CO	.20	.50
29 Bobby Valentine	.30	.75

1980 Mariners Postcards

These postcards which measure 3 3/4" by 5 1/2" feature members of the 1980 Seattle Mariners. These are unnumbered so we have sequenced them in alphabetical order. One way to differentiate these postcards from earlier Mariner postcards is that the the words "Baseball Club" were absent from under Mariners on the front. The two late season cards; Wills and Walton, come without a postcard back

COMPLETE SET	5.00	12.00
1 Glenn Abbott	.20	.50
2 Jim Anderson	.20	.50
3 Floyd Bannister	.20	.50
4 Jim Beattie	.20	.50
5 Juan Beniquez	.20	.50
6 Bruce Bochte	.20	.50
7 Don Bryant CO	.20	.50
8 Ted Cox	.20	.50
9 Rodney Craig	.20	.50
10 Julo Cruz	.20	.50
11 Rob Dressler	.20	.50
12 Dave Heaverlo	.20	.50
13 Marc Hill	.20	.50
14 Rick Honeycutt	.20	.50
15 Willie Horton	.30	.75
16 Darrell Johnson MG	.20	.50
17 Bill Mazeroski CO	.60	1.50
18 Byron McLaughlin	.20	.50
19 Mario Mendoza	.20	.50
20 Larry Milbourne	.20	.50
21 Dan Meyer	.20	.50
22 Tom Paciorek	.20	.50
23 Mike Parrott	.20	.50
24 Vada Pinson CO	.30	.75
25 Shane Rawley	.20	.50
26 Dave Roberts	.20	.50
27 Leon Roberts	.20	.50
28 Joe Simpson	.20	.50
29 Bill Stein	.20	.50
30 Wes Stock CO	.20	.50
31 Reggie Walton	.20	.50
32 Maury Wills MG	.40	1.00

1962 Maris Game

These cards, were issued as part of the Roger Maris board game issued in 1962. Since each of the 88 cards in the set feature the same photo, we are only listing one card from the set. Each card is the same value. These cards came from the "Roger Maris Baseball Game" which was produced by Play-Rite.

1 Roger Maris	4.00	10.00

1962 Maris Gehl's

These black and white photos 4" by 5" photos were issued in packages of Gehl's ice-cream and feature cards of then single-season home run king, Roger Maris.

COMPLETE SET (6)	6,000.00	9,000.00

1909-17 Max Stein/United States Publishing House PC758

These sepia-colored postcards were issued from the 1909-16 time period. The Marquard and Zimmerman cards have "United States Pub." marked on the back, leading to the theory that perhaps these two cards belong to another postcard set. The backs are quite attractive.

COMPLETE SET (25)	4,000.00	8,000.00
1 Ping Bodie	75.00	150.00
2 Frank Chance	150.00	300.00
3 Ty Cobb	600.00	1,200.00
4 Johnny Evers	125.00	250.00
5 Rube Marquard	125.00	250.00
6 Christy Mathewson	300.00	600.00
7 John McGraw MG	150.00	300.00
8 Chief Meyers	100.00	200.00
9 Marty O'Toole	75.00	150.00
10 Frank Schulte	75.00	150.00
11 Tris Speaker	150.00	300.00
12 Jake Stahl	75.00	150.00
13 Jim Thorpe	400.00	800.00
14 Joe Tinker	150.00	300.00
15 Honus Wagner	300.00	600.00
16 Ed Walsh	150.00	300.00
17 Buck Weaver	200.00	400.00
18 Joe Wood	100.00	200.00
19 Heinie Zimmerman	75.00	150.00
20 Johnny	125.00	250.00
21 Doc Miller	75.00	150.00
22 Boston American Team	150.00	300.00
23 Chicago Cubs 1916	150.00	300.00
24 Cincinnati Reds 1916	150.00	300.00
25 N.Y. National Team	150.00	300.00

1895 Mayo's Cut Plug N300

The Mayo Tobacco Works of Richmond, Va., issued this set of 48 ballplayers about 1895. Some recent speculation has been made that this set was issued beginning in 1894. The cards contain sepia portraits although some pictures appear to be black and white. There are 40 different individuals known in the set; cards 1 to 28 appear in uniform, while the last twelve (29-40) appear in street clothes. Eight of the former also appear with variations in uniform. The player's name appears within the picture area and a "Mayo's Cut Plug" ad is printed in a panel at the base of the card. Similar to the football set issued around the same time, the cards have black blank backs. Due to the fact that N300's are found in off-grade, our pricing references the technical grade of "EX".

COMPLETE SET (48)	75,000.00	150,000.00
1 Charlie S. Abbey CF:/Washington	600.00	1,000.00
2 Cap Anson: Chicago	5,000.00	8,000.00
3 Jimmy Bannon RF:/Boston	600.00	1,000.00
4A Dan Brouthers 1B:/Baltimore	3,000.00	5,000.00
4B Dan Brouthers 1B:/Louisville	3,000.00	5,000.00
5 Ed W. Cartwright FB:/Washington	600.00	1,000.00
6 Dad Clarkson P:/St. Louis	1,500.00	2,500.00
7 Tommy W. Corcoran SS/Brooklyn	600.00	1,000.00
8 Lave Cross 2B:/Philadelphia	600.00	1,000.00
9 William F. Dahlen SS:/Chicago	600.00	1,000.00
10 Tom P. Daly 2B:/Brooklyn	600.00	1,000.00
11 Ed J. Delehanty LF:/Phila.	3,500.00	6,000.00
12 Hugh Duffy CF:/Boston	1,800.00	3,000.00
13A Buck Ewing RF:/Cincinnati	3,000.00	5,000.00
13B Buck Ewing RF:/Cleveland	3,000.00	5,000.00
14 Dave Foutz 1B:/Brooklyn	600.00	1,000.00
15 Bill Joyce CF:/Brooklyn	600.00	1,000.00
16 Charlie Ganzel C:/Boston	600.00	1,000.00
17A Jack Glasscock SS:/Louisville	600.00	1,000.00
17B Jack Glasscock SS:/Pittsburgh	600.00	1,000.00
18 Mike Griffin CF:/Brooklyn	600.00	1,000.00
19A George Haddock P:/no team	600.00	1,000.00
19B George Haddock P:/Philadelphia	600.00	1,000.00
20 Bill W. Hallman 2B:/Phila.	600.00	1,000.00
21 Billy Hamilton CF:/Phila.	2,500.00	4,000.00
22 Wm.(Brickyard) Kennedy/P: Brooklyn	600.00	1,000.00
23A Tom F. Kinslow C:/no team	900.00	1,200.00
23B Tom F. Kinslow C:/Pitts.	900.00	1,200.00
24 Arlie Latham 3B:/Cincinnati	600.00	1,000.00
25 Herman Long SS: Boston	600.00	1,000.00
26 Tom Lovett P: Boston	600.00	1,000.00
27 Link Lowe 2B: Boston	600.00	1,000.00
28 Tommy McCarthy LF:/Boston	1,800.00	3,000.00
29 Yale Murphy SS:/New York	600.00	1,000.00
30 Billy Nash 3B: Boston	600.00	1,000.00
31 Kid Nicols P: Boston	3,500.00	6,000.00
32A Fred Pfeffer 2B:/Louisville	600.00	1,000.00
32B Fred Pfeffer/(Retired)	600.00	1,000.00
33 Wilbert Robinson C:/Baltimore	2,500.00	4,000.00
34A Amos Rusie P:/New York	2,500.00	4,000.00
34B Amos Russie (Sic) P:/New York	2,500.00	4,000.00
35 James Ryan RF:/Chicago	600.00	1,000.00
36 Billy Shindle 3B:/Brooklyn	600.00	1,000.00
37 George J. Smith SS:/Cinc.	600.00	1,000.00
38 Otis H. Stockdale P:/Washington	600.00	1,000.00
39 Tommy Tucker 1B:/Boston	600.00	1,000.00
40A John Ward 2B:/New York	2,500.00	4,000.00
40B John Ward (Retired)	2,500.00	4,000.00

1950-69 J.D. McCarthy PC753

One of the most prolific producers of postward postcards was J.D McCarthy on Michigan. During the 1950's and 1960's, thousands of these black and white postcards were issued. Most of the popular players of that era have been featured on the McCarthy postcards and a checklist is not provided. Some McCarthy postcards are much more difficult to obtain. Among the scarcities known are Jehoise Heard (less than 10 have been proven to exist) and Gus Triandos Orioles portrait card. We are interested in any additions to this currently short list of scarcities.

COMMON PLAYER (1950'S)	5.00	10.00
COMMON PLAYER (1960'S)	2.50	5.00

1964 Meadow Gold Dairy

Issued as a four-card panel on Meadow Gold milk cartons, these cards feature some of the leading players at the time. Another part of the unopened milk carton features an advertisement for the 1964 Auravision records. When cut from the milk carton and the panels, these cards measure approximately 1 3/4" by 2 1/16". Since these are unnumbered, we have sequenced these in alphabetical order.

COMPLETE SET (4)	250.00	500.00
1 Sandy Koufax	60.00	120.00
2 Mickey Mantle	125.00	250.00
3 Willie Mays	60.00	120.00
4 Bill Mazeroski	30.00	60.00
5 Full Sheet		

1911 Mecca Double Folders T201

The cards in this 50-card set measure approximately 2 1/4" by 4 11/16". The 1911 Mecca Double Folder issue contains unnumbered cards. This issue was one of the first to list statistics of players portrayed on the cards. Each card portrays two players, one when the card is folded, another when the card is unfolded. The card of Dougherty and Lord is considered scarce.

COMPLETE SET (50)	4,000.00	6,000.00
1 Abstein/Butler	90.00	150.00
2 Baker/Downey	90.00	150.00
3 Barrett/McGlyn	90.00	150.00
4 Bender/Oldring	125.00	200.00
5 Brown/Hofman	125.00	200.00
6 Chase/Sweeney	125.00	200.00
7 Cicotte/Thoney	125.00	200.00
8 Clarke/Byrne	125.00	200.00
9 F.Baker/E.Collins	175.00	300.00
10 Crawford/Cobb	1,200.00	2,000.00
11 Donovan/Stroud	90.00	150.00
12 Downs/Odell	90.00	150.00
13 Doyle/Meyers	90.00	150.00
14 Evers/Chance	250.00	400.00
15 Ford/Johnson	90.00	150.00
16 Foster/Ward	90.00	150.00
17 Gasper/Clarke	90.00	150.00
18 Grant/McLean	90.00	150.00
19 W.Blair/R.Hartzell	90.00	150.00
20 Hickman/Hinchman	90.00	150.00
21 R.Bresnahan/M.Huggins	175.00	300.00
22 Johnson/Street	400.00	700.00
23 Killian/Fitzpatrick	90.00	150.00
24 Kling/Cole	90.00	150.00
25 Lajoie/Falkenberg	250.00	400.00
26 Lake/Wallace	125.00	200.00
27 LaPorte/Stephens	90.00	150.00
28 J.Barry/J.Lapp	90.00	150.00
29 Leach/Gibson	90.00	150.00
30 Leifield/Simon	90.00	150.00
31 Lobert/Moore	90.00	150.00
32 Lord/Dougherty	150.00	250.00
33 Lush/Hauser	90.00	150.00
34 Mattern/Graham	90.00	150.00
35 Mathewson/Bridwell UER	400.00	700.00
36 McBride/Elberfeld	90.00	150.00
37 McCabe/Starr	90.00	150.00
38 McGinnity/McCarty	125.00	200.00
39 Miller/Herzog	90.00	150.00
40 Rucker/Daubert	90.00	150.00
41 Seymour/Dygert	90.00	150.00
42 Speaker/Gardner	250.00	400.00
43 Summers/Jennings	125.00	200.00
44 Thomas/Coombs	90.00	150.00
45 Titus/Dooin	90.00	150.00
46 Turner/Stovall	90.00	150.00
47 Walsh/Payne	125.00	200.00
48 B.Bergen/Z.Wheat	125.00	200.00
49 Wiltse/Merkle	90.00	150.00
50 Woodruff/Williams	90.00	150.00

1910 Mello Mint E105

The cards in this 50-card set measure 1 1/2" by 2 3/4". The cards were manufactured by the Texas Gum Company. The cards themselves are unnumbered and the fronts are identical to these found in E92. Printed on paper, the backs are horizontally aligned and carry advertising for "Smith's Mello-Mint". The set was issued about 1910. The cards have been alphabetized and numbered in the checklist below. The complete set price includes all variation cards listed in the checklist below.

COMPLETE SET (50)	50,000.00	100,000.00
1 Jack Barry	600.00	1,200.00
2 Harry Bemis	600.00	1,200.00
3A Chief Bender/(blue background)	800.00	1,600.00
3B Chief Bender/(green background)	800.00	1,600.00
4 Bill Bergen	600.00	1,200.00
5 Bob Bescher	600.00	1,200.00
6 Al Bridwell	600.00	1,200.00
7 Doc Casey	600.00	1,200.00
8 Frank Chance	600.00	1,200.00
9 Hal Chase	750.00	1,500.00
10 Ty Cobb	12,500.00	25,000.00
11 Eddie Collins	1,500.00	3,000.00
12 Sam Crawford	900.00	1,800.00
13 Harry Davis	600.00	1,200.00
14 Art Devlin	700.00	1,400.00
15 Bill Donovan	600.00	1,200.00

16 Red Dooin	600.00	1,200.00
17 Mickey Doolan	600.00	1,200.00
18 Patsy Dougherty	600.00	1,200.00
19A Larry Doyle/batting	700.00	1,400.00
19B Larry Doyle/throwing	700.00	1,400.00
20 Johnny Evers	1,250.00	2,500.00
21 George Gibson	600.00	1,200.00
22 Topsy Hartsel	600.00	1,200.00
23 Fred Jacklitsch	600.00	1,200.00
24 Hugh Jennings	900.00	1,800.00
25 Red Kleinow	600.00	1,200.00
26 Otto Knabe	600.00	1,200.00
27 John Knight	600.00	1,200.00
28 Nap Lajoie	2,250.00	4,500.00
29 Hans Lobert	600.00	1,200.00
30 Sherry Magee	700.00	1,400.00
31 Christy Mathewson	5,000.00	10,000.00
32 John McGraw MG	1,500.00	3,000.00
33 Larry McLean	600.00	1,200.00
34A Dots Miller/batting	600.00	1,200.00
34B Dots Miller/fielding	600.00	1,200.00
35 Danny Murphy	600.00	1,200.00
36 William O'Hara	600.00	1,200.00
37 Germany Schaefer	700.00	1,400.00
38 George Schlei	600.00	1,200.00
39 Charles Schmidt	600.00	1,200.00
40 Johnny Seigle	600.00	1,200.00
41 David Shean	600.00	1,200.00
42 Frank Smith	600.00	1,200.00
43 Joe Tinker	1,250.00	2,500.00
44A Honus Wagner/batting	10,000.00	20,000.00
44B Honus Wagner/throwing	10,000.00	20,000.00
45 Cy Young	2,000.00	4,000.00
46 Heinie Zimmerman	600.00	1,200.00

1979 Metallic Creations

These 3" by 5" portrait cards were issued with a 3 1/2" statuette. The cards were drawn by P. Herek and feature a full drawing of the player as well as two action shots In the background. Each player also has a fascimile autograph on the front. The back has career statistics on them. The cards are unnumbered and we have sequenced them in alphabetical order. While the Cedeno, Koufax and Ryan cards are known, there have been extremely few statues spotted of, these players, therefore we are calling these cards SP's. The statues and the cards were available for $7.95 upon release. The players listed as SP's were produced late in the run and are available in lesser quantities than the other players listed in our checklist.

COMPLETE SET	200.00	400.00
COMMON CARD	4.00	10.00
COMMON SP	8.00	20.00
1 Hank Aaron	8.00	20.00
2 Rod Carew	5.00	12.00
3 Cesar Cedeno SP	8.00	20.00
4 Ty Cobb	8.00	20.00
5 Steve Garvey	4.00	10.00
6 Lou Gehrig	8.00	20.00
7 Ron Guidry	4.00	10.00
8 Rogers Hornsby	6.00	15.00
9 Walter Johnson	6.00	15.00
10 Ralph Kiner	5.00	12.00
11 Sandy Koufax SP	30.00	60.00
12 Dave Lopes	4.00	10.00
13 Christy Mathewson	5.00	12.00
14 Willie Mays	8.00	20.00
15 Willie McCovey	5.00	12.00
16 Mel Ott	6.00	15.00
17 Babe Ruth	12.50	30.00
18 Nolan Ryan SP	40.00	80.00
19 Tris Speaker	5.00	12.00
20 Honus Wagner	6.00	15.00

1970 Metropolitan Museum of Art Burdick

This eight-card set consists of West German-made cards from Jefferson Burdick's collection at the Metropolitan Museum of Art. The cards feature black-and-white player photos measuring approximately 2 3/4" by 3 3/4". The cards are unnumbered and checklisted below in alphabetical order.

COMPLETE SET (8)	20.00	50.00
1 Max Bishop R315	2.00	5.00
2 Lou Gehrig R315	10.00	25.00
3 Carl Hubbell R315	6.00	15.00
4 Kores Portland	2.00	5.00
5 Leard Venice	2.00	5.00
6 Babe Ruth R315	12.50	30.00
7 Dazzy Vance R315	4.00	10.00
8 Zacher Oaks	2.00	5.00

1962 Mets Jay Publishing

This 12-card set of the original New York Mets measures approximately 5" X 7". The fronts feature black-and-white posed player photos with the player's and team name printed below in the white border. These cards were packaged 12 to a packet. The backs are blank. The cards are unnumbered and checklisted below in alphabetical order. A complete set in the original envelope is valued at fifty percent higher.

COMPLETE SET (12)	30.00	60.00
1 Gus Bell	1.50	4.00
2 Elio Chacon	1.25	3.00
3 Roger Craig	2.00	5.00
4 Gil Hodges	6.00	15.00
5 Jay Hook	1.25	3.00
6 Al Jackson	1.50	4.00
7 Hobie Landrith	1.25	3.00
8 Bob Miller	1.25	3.00
9 Charlie Neal	1.50	4.00
10 Casey Stengel MG	6.00	15.00
11 Frank Thomas	2.00	5.00
12 Don Zimmer	2.50	6.00

1962-65 Mets Requena Photo

These 8" by 10" color photographs feature members of the New York Mets and were taken by known sports photographer Louis Requenna. These photos were taken throughout the early seasons of the Mets. Since these photos are unnumbered, we have sequenced them in alphabetical order.

COMPLETE SET	250.00	500.00
1 George Altman	6.00	15.00
2 Ed Bauta	6.00	15.00
3 Larry Bearnarth	6.00	15.00
4 Yogi Berra CO	15.00	40.00
5 Chris Cannizzaro Portrait	6.00	15.00
6 Chris Cannizzaro Batting	6.00	15.00
7 Chris Cannizzaro Kneeling	6.00	15.00
8 Chris Cannizzaro Squatting	6.00	15.00
9 Duke Carmel	6.00	15.00
10 Joe Christopher Kneeling	6.00	15.00
11 Joe Christopher Standing	6.00	15.00
12 Roger Craig	8.00	20.00
13 Ray Daviault	6.00	15.00
14 John DeMerit	6.00	15.00
15 Don Heffner CO	6.00	15.00
16 Jay Hook	6.00	15.00
17 Ron Hunt Ralph Kiner ANN	10.00	25.00
18 Ed Kranepool	8.00	20.00
19 Felix Mantilla	6.00	15.00
20 Jim Marshall	6.00	15.00
21 Danny Napoleon	6.00	15.00
22 Charlie Neal	6.00	15.00
23 Jimmy Piersall	8.00	20.00
24 Joe Pignatano	6.00	15.00
25 Duke Snider Full Length Photo	12.50	30.00
26 Duke Snider Portrait	12.50	30.00
27 Casey Stengel MG	15.00	40.00
28 Ron Swoboda	8.00	20.00

1963 Mets Jay Publishing

This 12-card set of the New York Mets measures approximately 5" by 7". The fronts feature black-and-white posed player photos with the player's and team name printed below in the white border. These cards were packaged 12 to a packet.The backs are blank. The cards are unnumbered and checklisted below in alphabetical order.

COMPLETE SET (12)	20.00	50.00
1 Larry Burright	1.00	2.50
2 Roger Craig	1.50	4.00
3 Jim Hickman	1.25	3.00
4 Gil Hodges	5.00	12.00
5 Jay Hook	1.25	3.00
6 Al Jackson	1.25	3.00
7 Rod Kanehl	1.25	3.00
8 Charlie Neal	1.25	3.00
9 Duke Snider	5.00	12.00
10 Casey Stengel MG	5.00	12.00
11 Frank Thomas	1.25	3.00
12 Marv Throneberry	1.50	4.00

1964 Mets Jay Publishing

This 12-card set of the New York Mets measures approximately 5" by 7". The fronts feature black and white posed player photos with the player's and team name printed below in the white border. These cards were packaged 12 to an oversized envelope. The backs are blank. The cards are unnumbered and sequenced below in alphabetical order.

COMPLETE SET (12)	15.00	40.00
1 Larry Bearnarth	1.00	2.50
2 Duke Carmel	1.00	2.50
3 Choo Choo Coleman	1.25	3.00
4 Jesse Gonder	1.00	2.50
5 Tim Harkness	1.00	2.50
6 Jim Hickman	1.25	3.00
7 Ron Hunt	1.50	4.00
8 Al Jackson	1.25	3.00
9 Rod Kanehl	1.25	3.00
10 Duke Snider	4.00	10.00
11 Casey Stengel MG	4.00	10.00
12 Carlton Willey	1.00	2.50

1964 Mets Team Issue

This 12-card set of the New York Mets measures approximately 5" by 7". The fronts feature black and white posed player photos. The set was sold at the ballpark or could be obtained through mail order. The backs are blank. The cards are unnumbered and sequenced below in alphabetical order.

COMPLETE SET (12)	12.50	30.00
1 George Altman	.75	2.00
2 Larry Bearnarth	.75	2.00
3 Jesse Gonder	.75	2.00
4 Tim Harkness	.75	2.00
5 Jim Hickman	.75	2.00
6 Jay Hook	.75	2.00
7 Ron Hunt	1.25	3.00
8 Al Jackson	.75	2.00
9 Tracy Stallard	.75	2.00
10 Casey Stengel MG	3.00	8.00
11 Frank Thomas	1.25	3.00
12 Carl Willey	.75	2.00

1965 Mets Jay Publishing

This 12-card set of the New York Mets measures approximately 5" by 7". The fronts feature black and white posed player photos with the player's and team name printed below in the white border. These cards were packaged 12 to an envelope. The backs are blank and are sequenced in alphabetical order.

COMPLETE SET (12)	15.00	40.00
1 Larry Bearnarth	.75	2.00
2 Yogi Berra	4.00	10.00
3 Chris Cannizzaro	.75	2.00
4 Galen Cisco	.75	2.00
5 Jack Fisher	.75	2.00
6 Jim Hickman	.75	2.00
7 Ron Hunt	.75	2.00
8 Al Jackson	.75	2.00
9 Ed Kranepool	1.00	2.50
10 Roy McMillan	.75	2.00
11 Warren Spahn	3.00	8.00
12 Casey Stengel MG	3.00	8.00

1965 Mets Postcards

This 10-card set were issued by B and E, feature color player photos and measures approximately 3" by 5". The backs display the player's statistical record and the Mets insignia in green. The cards are unnumbered and checklisted below in alphabetical order.

COMPLETE SET (10)	60.00	120.00
1 Yogi Berra	10.00	25.00
2 Joe Christopher	6.00	15.00
3 Jack Fisher	6.00	15.00
4 Ron Hunt	6.00	15.00
5 Al Jackson	6.00	15.00
6 Ed Kranepool	8.00	20.00
7 Roy McMillan	6.00	15.00
8 Warren Spahn	10.00	25.00
9 Casey Stengel MG	10.00	25.00
10 Carl Willey	6.00	15.00

1966 Mets Postcards

This six-card set features color player photos in the same style as the 1965 Mets Postcards set and measures approximately 3" by 5". The backs carry the player's name, Mets insignia, and B and E Advertising in Haledon, NJ as the publisher. There is no reference to the player's statistical record.

COMPLETE SET (6)	40.00	80.00
1 Al Jackson	6.00	15.00
2 Ron Hunt	8.00	20.00
3 Ed Kranepool	6.00	15.00
4 Wes Westrum MG	6.00	15.00
5 Cleon Jones	8.00	20.00
6 Tug McGraw	10.00	25.00

1966 Mets Team Issue

This 12-card set of the New York Mets measures approximately 5" by 7". The fronts feature black and white posed player photos. The set was sold at the ballpark or could be obtained through mail order. The backs are blank. The cards are unnumbered and sequenced below in alphabetical order.

COMPLETE SET (12)	12.50	30.00
1 Yogi Berra CO	3.00	8.00
2 Ken Boyer	2.00	5.00
3 Don Cardwell	.75	2.00
4 Tommy Davis	1.25	3.00
5 Jack Fisher	.75	2.00
6 Jerry Grote	1.25	3.00
7 Chuck Hiller	.75	2.00
8 Cleon Jones	1.25	3.00
9 Ed Kranepool	1.25	3.00
10 Don Shaw	.75	2.00
11 Ron Swoboda	1.25	3.00
12 Wes Westrum MG	.75	2.00

1967 Mets Postcards

This five-card set features color player photos and measure approximately 3" by 5". The backs carry the player's name printed in black. The cards are unnumbered and checklisted below in alphabetical order. Tom Seaver has a card in his Rookie Card year.

COMPLETE SET (5)	40.00	80.00
1 Tommy Davis	3.00	8.00
2 Jack Fisher	2.00	5.00
3 Jerry Grote	3.00	8.00
4 Ed Kranepool	3.00	8.00
5 Tom Seaver	40.00	80.00

1967 Mets Team Issue

This 12-card set of the New York Mets measures approximately 4 13/16" by 7" and features black-and-white player photos in a white border with blank backs. These cards were originally packaged 12 to a packet. The cards are unnumbered and checklisted below in alphabetical order.

COMPLETE SET (12)	20.00	50.00
1 Yogi Berra CO	6.00	15.00
2 Ken Boyer	3.00	8.00
3 Don Cardwell	1.50	4.00
4 Tommy Davis	2.50	6.00
5 Jack Fisher	1.50	4.00
6 Jerry Grote	2.50	6.00
7 Chuck Hiller	1.50	4.00
8 Cleon Jones	1.50	4.00
9 Ed Kranepool	2.50	6.00
10 Bob Shaw	1.50	4.00
11 Ron Swoboda	2.50	6.00
12 Wes Westrum MG	1.50	4.00

1969 Mets Citgo

These eight 8" by 10" prints were drawn by John Wheeldon. These prints were available at Citgo for a nominal fee after a gasoline fill-up. The fronts feature a large portait pose and a smaller action pose on a colorful background. The backs have the CITGO, MLB and Mets skyline logos, the player's biography and lifetime records. There is also a picture and bio of the artist on the back. The prints are unnumbered and listed in alphabetical order.

COMPLETE SET (8)	30.00	60.00
1 Tommie Agee	2.50	6.00
2 Ken Boswell	2.00	5.00
3 Gary Gentry	2.00	5.00
4 Jerry Grote	2.50	6.00
5 Ed Kranepool	2.50	6.00
6 Jerry Koosman	3.00	8.00
7 Cleon Jones	2.00	5.00
8 Tom Seaver	8.00	20.00

1969 Mets New York Daily News

These 9" by 12" blank-backed charcoal drawings were issued by the Daily News to celebrate the Miracle Mets. An artist named Bruce Stark drew the pictures which were put on white textured paper. Each drawing has a fascimile autograph on the lower left. The blank-backed items are unnumbered and are sequenced in alphabetical order and came in a special folder which featured additional artwork.

COMPLETE SET (20)	60.00	120.00
1 Tommie Agee	2.00	5.00
2 Ken Boswell	1.50	4.00
3 Don Cardwell	1.50	4.00
4 Donn Clendenon	2.00	5.00
5 Wayne Garrett	1.50	4.00
6 Gary Gentry	1.50	4.00
7 Jerry Grote	2.00	5.00
8 Derrel(Bud) Harrelson	3.00	8.00
9 Gil Hodges MG	8.00	20.00
10 Cleon Jones	3.00	8.00
11 Jerry Koosman	3.00	8.00
12 Ed Kranepool	2.00	5.00
13 Jim McAndrew	1.50	4.00
14 Frank(Tug) McGraw	3.00	8.00
15 Nolan Ryan	20.00	50.00
16 Tom Seaver	15.00	40.00
17 Art Shamsky	1.50	4.00
18 Ron Swoboda	2.00	5.00

19 Ron Taylor 1.50 4.00
20 Al Weis 1.50 4.00

1969 Mets Team Issue

This 16-card set of the New York Mets features black and white posed player photos with a facsimile player autograph. The set was sold at the ballpark or could be obtained through mail order. The backs are blank. The cards are unnumbered and sequenced below in alphabetical order.

COMPLETE SET (16) 40.00 80.00
1 Tommie Agee 1.50 4.00
2 Yogi Berra CO 3.00 8.00
3 Ken Boswell 1.50 4.00
4 Ed Charles 1.25 3.00
5 Kevin Collins 1.25 3.00
6 Bud Harrelson 1.50 4.00
7 Gil Hodges MG 2.50 6.00
8 Al Jackson 1.25 3.00
9 Cleon Jones 1.50 4.00
10 Jerry Koosman 2.50 6.00
11 Ed Kranepool 1.50 4.00
12 Nolan Ryan 8.00 20.00
13 Tom Seaver 6.00 15.00
14 Art Shamsky 1.25 3.00
15 Ron Swoboda 1.50 4.00
16 Ron Taylor 1.25 3.00

1969 Mets Team Issue Color

This five-card set of the New York Mets features color player photos measuring approximately 7" by 8 3/4". The backs are blank. The cards are unnumbered and checklisted below in alphabetical order.

COMPLETE SET (5) 15.00 40.00
1 Bud Harrelson 2.00 5.00
2 Jerry Koosman 3.00 8.00
3 Ed Kranepool 2.00 5.00
4 Tom Seaver 8.00 20.00
5 Ron Swoboda 2.00 5.00

1970 Mets Nestle's Quik

These cards, which measure approximately 3" by 5" when cut from the back of Nestle Quik containers feature members of the 1969 Mets in highlights from different games of the 1969 World Series. This list is incomplete and all additions are appreciated to this checklist.

COMPLETE SET 12.50 30.00
2 Jerry Koosman 5.00 12.00
3 Tommie Agee 4.00 10.00
4 Ron Swoboda 4.00 10.00

1970 Mets Team Issue

This 12-card set of the New York Mets features black-and-white player photos measuring approximately 4 3/4" by 7 1/2". The player's name and team name is printed above the photo. The backs are blank. The set was originally sold at the ballpark or through mail order. The cards are unnumbered and checklisted below in alphabetical order.

COMPLETE SET (12) 12.50 30.00
1 Tommie Agee 1.00 2.50
2 Ken Boswell .75 2.00
3 Donn Clendenon .75 2.00
4 Joe Foy .75 2.00
5 Jerry Grote 1.00 2.50
6 Bud Harrelson .75 2.00
7 Gil Hodges MG 1.50 4.00
8 Cleon Jones 1.00 2.50
9 Jerry Koosman 1.25 3.00
10 Tom Seaver 2.50 6.00
11 Art Shamsky .75 2.00
12 Ron Swoboda 1.00 2.50

1970 Mets Team Issue Color

This five-card set of the New York Mets features color player photos measuring approximately 7" by 8 3/4". The backs are blank. The cards are unnumbered and checklisted below in alphabetical order.

COMPLETE SET (5) 6.00 15.00
1 Bud Harrelson .75 2.00
2 Jerry Koosman 1.25 3.00
3 Ed Kranepool .75 2.00
4 Tom Seaver 2.50 6.00
5 Ron Swoboda .75 2.00

1971 Mets Team Issue

This 20-card set of the New York Mets features black and white posed player photos with a facsimile player autograph and measures approximately 4 7/8" by 6 3/4". The set was originally sold at the ballpark or could be obtained through mail order. The backs are blank. The cards are unnumbered and checklisted below in alphabetical order.

COMPLETE SET (20) 20.00 50.00
1 Tommie Agee .40 1.00
2 Yogi Berra CO 1.25 3.00
3 Donn Clendenon .40 1.00
4 Duffy Dyer .40 1.00
5 Danny Frisella .40 1.00
6 Gary Gentry .40 1.00
7 Jerry Grote .60 1.50
8 Bud Harrelson .60 1.50
9 Gil Hodges MG 1.00 2.50
10 Cleon Jones .60 1.50
11 Jerry Koosman .75 2.00
12 Ed Kranepool .60 1.50
13 Dave Marshall .40 1.00
14 Jim McAndrew .40 1.00
15 Tug McGraw .75 2.00
16 Nolan Ryan 6.00 15.00
17 Tom Seaver 4.00 10.00
18 Art Shamsky .40 1.00
19 Ken Singleton 1.00 2.50
20 Ron Taylor .40 1.00

1971 Mets Team Issue Autographs

This seven-card set of the New York Mets features black-and-white player photos measuring approximately 5 1/4" by 6 1/2" with a blue facsimile autograph printed across the front of the player's jersey. The cards are unnumbered and checklisted below in alphabetical order.

COMPLETE SET (7) 6.00 15.00
1 Tommie Agee 1.25 3.00
2 Danny Frisella .75 2.00
3 Gary Gentry .75 2.00
4 Jim McAndrew .75 2.00
5 Art Shamsky .75 2.00
6 Ken Singleton 1.25 3.00
7 Ron Taylor .75 2.00

1971 Mets Team Issue Color

This set of the New York Mets features color player photos measuring approximately 7" by 8 3/4". Only six players are listed below, all these players are from the "A" set. Since most teams from this period also had a "B" set, it is presumed that there are six other players in this set as well. Cards have blank backs.The cards are unnumbered and checklisted below in alphabetical order.

COMPLETE SET 5.00 12.00
1 Tommie Agee 1.25 3.00
2 Bob Aspromonte .75 2.00
3 Ken Boswell .75 2.00
4 Donn Clendenon .75 2.00
5 Jerry Grote 1.25 3.00
6 Jerry Koosman 1.50 4.00

1972 Mets Team Issue

The 1972 New York Mets Team Issue set was distributed in two different six-photo packs as Set A and Set B. The sets feature player photos measuring approximately 7" by 8 3/4". The cards are unnumbered and checklisted below alphabetically within each set. Set A consists of cards 1-6, and Set B contains cards 7-12.

COMPLETE SET (12) 12.50 30.00
1 Tommie Agee 1.25 3.00
2 Ken Boswell .75 2.00
3 Jerry Grote .75 2.00
4 Cleon Jones .75 2.00
5 Tom Seaver 4.00 10.00
6 Rusty Staub 2.00 5.00
7 Jim Fregosi .75 2.00
8 Wayne Garrett .75 2.00
9 Gary Gentry .75 2.00
10 Bud Harrelson 1.25 3.00
11 Jerry Koosman 1.50 4.00
12 Ed Kranepool 1.25 3.00

1973 Mets Team Issue

This 1973 New York Mets Team set was distributed in two different six-photo packs. The set features color player photos measuring approximately 7" by 8 3/4". The cards are unnumbered and checklisted below alphabetically. No distinction is made in the checklist as to which pack contains each player's photo as there is in the 1972 set.

COMPLETE SET (12) 12.50 30.00
1 Ken Boswell .75 2.00
2 Jim Fregosi 1.00 2.50
3 Jerry Grote 1.00 2.50
4 Bud Harrelson 1.00 2.50
5 Cleon Jones 1.00 2.50
6 Jerry Koosman 1.25 3.00
7 Ed Kranepool 1.00 2.50
8 Willie Mays 3.00 8.00
9 Tug McGraw 1.00 2.50
10 Felix Millan .75 2.00
11 Tom Seaver 2.00 5.00
12 Rusty Staub 1.50 4.00

1974 Mets Dairylea Photo Album

This set was issued in two fold-out strip booklets, each of which measures 8" by 8" in size. The inside front cover contains several small photos; the rest of the bookley contains white bordered portraits. The complete set comes in a white folder. Both the folder and booklets have the Mets logo on the front and the Dairylea trademark on the back. The books and photos are unnumbered and are sequenced the way they came in the booklet. Card numbers 1-13 are from the first book while numbers 14-20 are from the second book. The complete set in booklet form is valued at $45. Individual photos are valued below. Players from George Theodore to Bob Apodaca are all on the inside front cover in the first album. All people listed from Yogi Berra to the end of the set were in the inside front cover of the second booklet.

COMPLETE SET (20) 15.00 40.00
1 George Theodore .60 1.50
2 Ron Hodges .60 1.50
3 George Stone .60 1.50
4 Duffy Dyer .60 1.50
5 Jack Aker .60 1.50
6 Jim Gosger .60 1.50
7 Bob Apodaca .60 1.50
8 Tom Seaver 5.00 12.00
9 Bud Harrelson .75 2.00
10 Ed Kranepool .75 2.00
11 Rusty Staub 1.25 3.00
12 Ray Sadecki .60 1.50
13 Yogi Berra MG 4.00 10.00
Willie Mays CO
14 Ken Boswell .60 1.50
15 Cleon Jones .75 2.00
16 Jerry Grote 1.25 3.00
17 Jerry Koosman 1.25 3.00
18 Wayne Garrett .60 1.50

1974 Mets Japan Ed Broder

This 11-card set of the New York Mets features black-and-white player photos measuring approximately 1 7/8" by 3" and commemorates the 1974 New York Mets Tour of Japan. The backs carry the player's name, team name, tour, and the Mets logo. The cards are unnumbered and checklisted below alphabetically. This set was originally available from Broder for $1.50.

COMPLETE SET (11) 8.00 20.00
1 Yogi Berra MG 1.00 2.50
2 Wayne Garrett .40 1.00
3 Gil Hodges 1.00 2.50
4 Jerry Koosman .75 2.00
5 Ed Kranepool .40 1.00
John Milner
Joe Torre
6 Jon Matlack .40 1.00
7 Felix Millan .40 1.00
8 John Milner .40 1.00
9 Tom Seaver 2.00 5.00
10 George Theodore .40 1.00
11 Joe Torre 1.00 2.50

1975 Mets 1963 Morey

These 3 1/2" by 5 1/2" photos feature members of the 1963 Mets and were issued in color. This set was produced by long time hobbyist Jeffrey Morey.

COMPLETE SET 6.00 15.00
1 Craig Anderson .20 .50
2 Ed Bauta .20 .50
3 Larry Bearnarth .20 .50
4 Chris Cannizzaro .20 .50
5 Duke Carmel .20 .50
6 Chico Fernandez .20 .50
7 Jesse Gonder .20 .50
8 Pumpsie Green .20 .50
9 Tim Harkness .20 .50
10 Solly Hemus CO .20 .50
11 Jim Hickman .20 .50
12 Joe Hicks .20 .50
13 Will Huckle .20 .50
14 Rod Kanehl .20 .50
15 Ed Kranepool .30 .75
16 Joe Christopher .20 .50
17 Marty Kutyna .20 .50
18 Cookie Lavagetto CO .20 .50
19 Al Moran .20 .50
20 Choo Choo Coleman .20 .50
21 Roger Craig .30 .75
22 Steve Dillon .20 .50
23 Grover Powell .20 .50
24 Ted Schreiber .20 .50
25 Norm Sherry .20 .50
26 Dick Smith .20 .50
27 Tracy Stallard .20 .50
28 Casey Stengel MG 1.25 3.00
29 Ernie White CO .20 .50
30 Polo Grounds .40 1.00

1975 Mets SSPC

This 22-card standard-size set of New York Mets features white-bordered posed color player photos on their fronts, which are free of any other markings. The white back carries the player's name in red lettering above his blue-lettered biography and career highlights. The cards are numbered on the back within a circle formed by the player's team name. A similar set of New York Yankees was produced at the same time. The set is dated to 1975 because that year was Dave Kingman's first year as a Met and George Stone's last year.

COMPLETE SET (22) 6.00 15.00
1 John Milner .20 .50
2 Henry Webb .20 .50
3 Tom Hall .20 .50
4 Del Unser .20 .50
5 Wayne Garrett .20 .50
6 Jesus Alou .30 .75
7 Rusty Staub .60 1.50
8 John Stearns .30 .75
9 Dave Kingman .40 1.00
10 Ed Kranepool .30 .75
11 Cleon Jones .30 .75
12 Tom Seaver 3.00 8.00
13 George Stone .20 .50
14 Jerry Koosman .40 1.00
15 Bob Apodaca .20 .50
16 Felix Millan .30 .75
17 Gene Clines .20 .50
18 Mike Phillips .20 .50
19 Yogi Berra MG 1.50 4.00
20 Joe Torre .60 1.50
21 Jon Matlack .40 1.00
22 Ricky Baldwin .20 .50

1976 Mets '63 SSPC

These 18 standard-size cards honored members of the 1963 New York Mets. These cards have color photos covering almost all of the front except for a small white border. The horizontal backs have vital statistics; a biography written as it would have been after the '63 season and career information up to that point. The cards are unnumbered and we have sequenced them in alphabetical order. These cards were inserted in the 1976 Summer edition of Collectors Quarterly.

COMPLETE SET (18) 10.00 25.00
1 Ed Bauta .40 1.00
2 Duke Carmel .40 1.00
3 Joe Christopher .40 1.00
4 Choo Choo Coleman .75 2.00
5 Steve Dillon .40 1.00
6 Jesse Gonder .40 1.00
7 Pumpsie Green .40 1.00
8 Jim Hickman .60 1.50
9 Rod Kanehl .40 1.00
10 Al Moran .40 1.00
11 Grover Powell .40 1.00
12 Ted Schreiber .40 1.00
13 Norm Sherry .40 1.00
14 Dick Smith .40 1.00
15 Duke Snider 2.00 5.00
16 Tracy Stallard .40 1.00
17 Casey Stengel MG 2.00 5.00
18 Ernie White CO .40 1.00

1976 Mets MSA Placemats

This set of four placemats was produced by Creative Dimensions, liscensed by Major League Baseball, and issued by MSA. Each placemat measures 14 1/4" by 11 1/4", has a clear matte finish, and pictures three players, each appearing in a 3" diameter circle. Player statistics and additional artwork complete the placemat. Logos have been airbrushed from the caps as is typical of all MSA products. Placemats are unnumbered and listed below in first player uniform number.

COMPLETE SET (4) 8.00 20.00
1 Bud Harrelson 6.00 15.00
Tom Seaver
Jerry Grote
2 Ed Kranepool 2.50 6.00
Dave Kingman
Joe Torre
3 Bob Apodaca 1.25 3.00
Felix Millan
Del Unser
4 Jerry Koosman 2.00 5.00
Mickey Lolich
Jon Matlack

1977 Mets Dairylea Photo Album

This 27-card set features 8" by 8" player photos and was issued in an album that was given away at the Mets game of April 17th in Shea Stadium. The cards are unnumbered and checklisted below in alphabetical order.

COMPLETE SET (27) 10.00 25.00
1 Luis Alvarado .30 .75
Leo Foster
2 Bob Apodaca .30 .75
3 Rick Baldwin .30 .75
4 Bruce Boisclair .30 .75
5 Nino Espinosa .30 .75
6 Jerry Grote .40 1.00
7 Bud Harrelson .40 1.00
8 Ron Hodges .30 .75
9 Dave Kingman .75 2.00
10 Jerry Koosman .60 1.50
11 Ed Kranepool .30 .75
12 Skip Lockwood .30 .75
13 Joe Frazier MG .30 .75
Joe Pignatano CO
Tom Burgess CO/
14 Jon Matlack .30 .75
15 Lee Mazzilli .75 2.00
16 Felix Millan .30 .75
17 John Milner .30 .75
18 Bob Myrick .30 .75
19 Mike Phillips .30 .75
20 Ray Sadecki .30 .75
21 Tom Seaver 1.50 4.00
22 Roy Staiger .30 .75
23 John Stearns .30 .75
24 Craig Swan .30 .75
25 Jackson Todd .30 .75
26 Joe Torre .75 2.00
27 Mike Vail .30 .75

1978 Mets Dairylea Photo Album

This photo album was distributed at the Mets home game of May 30, 1978. This edition consists of a single booklet, 8" by 8" in size, bound on the left side. Each page contains a white-bordered, unnumbered portrait. They are listed below in the order they appear in the album.

COMPLETE SET (27)	10.00	25.00
1 Joe Torre MG With Coaches	1.00	2.50
2 Bruce Boisclair	.40	1.00
3 Mike Bruhert	.40	1.00
4 Mardie Cornejo	.40	1.00
5 Nino Espinosa	.40	1.00
6 Doug Flynn	.40	1.00
7 Tim Foli	.40	1.00
8 Tom Grieve	.75	2.00
9 Ken Henderson	.40	1.00
10 Steve Henderson	.40	1.00
11 Ron Hodges	.40	1.00
12 Jerry Koosman	1.00	2.50
13 Ed Kranepool	.75	2.00
14 Skip Lockwood	.40	1.00
15 Elliott Maddox	.40	1.00
16 Lee Mazzilli	.75	2.00
17 Butch Metzger	.40	1.00
18 Willie Montanez	.40	1.00
19 Bob Myrick	.40	1.00
20 Len Randle	.40	1.00
21 Paul Siebert	.40	1.00
22 John Stearns	.40	1.00
23 Craig Swan	.40	1.00
24 Bobby Valentine	.75	2.00
25 Joel Youngblood	.40	1.00
26 Pat Zachry	.40	1.00
27 Bob Apodaca Sergio Ferrer	.40	1.00

1980 Mets Subway Promotional Posters

These six very oversized posters were plastered in the New York Subway trains in early 1980 as a way to hype up the New York Mets, who were then suffering from both bad performance on the field and at Shea Stadium. These posters were in black and white and the backs were back since they were used as advertisments for people riding the trains. Since these are unnumbered, we have sequenced them in alphabetical order.

COMPLETE SET (6)	25.00	60.00
1 Doug Flynn	5.00	10.00
2 Steve Henderson	5.00	10.00
3 Lee Mazzilli	10.00	20.00
4 Craig Swan	5.00	10.00
5 Frank Taveras	5.00	10.00
6 Joel Youngblood	5.00	10.00

1927 Middy Bread

These 44 cards blank-backed, which measure approximately 2 1/4" by 4" were issued in the St Louis area and feature members of the Browns and Cardinals. It seems as if 22 cards for each of the teams were issued. Since the cards are unnumbered, we have sequenced them alphabetically by team with the Cardinals from card 1 through 22 and the Browns from 23 through 44. A Ross Youngs card was recently discovered and looks as if it fits in this set. More information about that card is certainly appreciated.

COMPLETE SET (44)	40,000.00	80,000.00
1 Grover Alexander	4,000.00	8,000.00
2 Herman Bell	1,000.00	2,000.00
3 Lester Bell	1,000.00	2,000.00
4 Ray Blades	1,000.00	2,000.00
5 Jim Bottomley	2,000.00	4,000.00
6 Danny Clark	1,000.00	2,000.00
7 Taylor Douthit	1,000.00	2,000.00
8 Frank Frisch	2,500.00	5,000.00
9 Chick Hafey	2,000.00	4,000.00
10 Jesse Haines	2,000.00	4,000.00
11 Vic Keen	1,000.00	2,000.00
12 Bob McGraw	1,000.00	2,000.00
13 Bob O'Farrell	1,000.00	2,000.00
14 Art Reinhardt	1,000.00	2,000.00
15 Jimmy Ring	1,000.00	2,000.00
16 Walter Roettger	1,000.00	2,000.00
17 Robert Schang	1,000.00	2,000.00
18 Willie Sherdel	1,000.00	2,000.00
19 Billy Southworth	1,250.00	2,500.00
20 Tommy Thevenow	1,000.00	2,000.00
21 George Toporcer	1,000.00	2,000.00
22 Spencer Adams	1,000.00	2,000.00
23 Win Ballou	1,000.00	2,000.00
24 Walter Beck	1,000.00	2,000.00
25 Herschel Bennett	1,000.00	2,000.00
26 Stewart Bolen	1,000.00	2,000.00
27 Leo Dixon	1,000.00	2,000.00
28 Chester Falk	1,000.00	2,000.00
29 Milt Gaston	1,000.00	2,000.00
30 Walter Gerber	1,000.00	2,000.00
31 Sam Jones	1,250.00	2,500.00
32 Carlisle Littlejohn	1,000.00	2,000.00
33 Oscar Melillo	1,000.00	2,000.00
34 Bing Miller	1,250.00	2,500.00
35 Otis Miller	1,000.00	2,000.00
36 Billie Mullen	1,000.00	2,000.00
37 Ernie Nevers	2,000.00	4,000.00
38 Steve O'Neil	1,250.00	2,500.00
39 Harry Rice	1,000.00	2,000.00
40 George Sisler	2,500.00	5,000.00
41 Walter Stewart	1,000.00	2,000.00
42 Elom Van Gilder	1,000.00	2,000.00
43 Ken Williams	1,500.00	3,000.00
44 Ernie Wingard	1,000.00	2,000.00
45 Ross Youngs	2,000.00	4,000.00

1971 Milk Duds

The cards in this 69-card set measure 1 13/16" by 2 5/8". The 1971 Milk Duds set contains 32 American League cards and 37 National League cards. The cards are actually numbered, but the very small number appears only on the flap of the box; nevertheless the numbers below are ordered alphabetically by player's name within league. American Leaguers are numbered 1-32 and National Leaguers 33-69. The cards are sepia toned on a tan background and were issued on the backs of five-cent boxes of Milk Duds candy. The prices listed in the checklist are for complete boxes. Cards cut from boxes are approximately one-half of the listed price. The names of three of the players in the set were misspelled and are noted in the checklist below as errors. Three of the boxes were double printed, i.e., twice as many were produced or printed compared to the other players. These double-printed players are indicated below by DP in the checklist after the player's name. According to published reports around the time of issue, Dick Bosman was supposedly going to be in this set but a bad photo negated his card being printed.

COMPLETE SET (69)	400.00	800.00
COMMON DP	4.00	10.00
1 Luis Aparicio	8.00	20.00
2 Stan Bahnsen	4.00	10.00
3 Danny Cater	4.00	10.00
4 Ray Culp	4.00	10.00
5 Ray Fosse	4.00	10.00
6 Bill Freehan	5.00	12.00
7 Jim Fregosi	5.00	12.00
8 Tommy Harper	4.00	10.00
9 Frank Howard	5.00	12.00
10 Jim Hunter	10.00	25.00
11 Tommy John	5.00	12.00
12 Alex Johnson	4.00	10.00
13 Dave Johnson	5.00	12.00
14 Harmon Killebrew DP	6.00	15.00
15 Sam McDowell	5.00	12.00
16 Dave McNally	4.00	10.00
17 Bill Melton	4.00	10.00
18 Andy Messersmith	4.00	10.00
19 Thurman Munson	20.00	50.00
20 Tony Oliva	6.00	15.00
21 Jim Palmer	8.00	20.00
22 Jim Perry	5.00	12.00
23 Fritz Peterson	4.00	10.00
24 Rico Petrocelli	4.00	10.00
25 Boog Powell	5.00	12.00
26 Brooks Robinson DP	6.00	15.00
27 Frank Robinson	12.50	30.00
28 George Scott	4.00	10.00
29 Reggie Smith	5.00	12.00
30 Mel Stottlemyer ERR/(sic, Stottlemyre)	5.00	12.00
31 Cesar Tovar	4.00	10.00
32 Roy White	4.00	10.00
33 Hank Aaron	30.00	60.00
34 Ernie Banks	12.50	40.00
35 Glen Beckert ERR/(sic, Glenn)	4.00	10.00
36 Johnny Bench	20.00	50.00
37 Lou Brock	12.50	30.00
38 Rico Carty	5.00	12.00
39 Orlando Cepeda	8.00	20.00
40 Roberto Clemente	50.00	100.00
41 Willie Davis	4.00	10.00
42 Dick Dietz	4.00	10.00
43 Bob Gibson	8.00	20.00
44 Bill Grabarkewitz	4.00	10.00
45 Bud Harrelson	4.00	10.00
46 Jim Hickman	4.00	10.00
47 Ken Holtzman	4.00	10.00
48 Randy Hundley	4.00	10.00
49 Fergie Jenkins	8.00	20.00
50 Don Kessinger	5.00	12.00
51 Willie Mays	50.00	100.00
52 Willie McCovey	8.00	20.00
53 Dennis Menke	4.00	10.00
54 Jim Merritt	4.00	10.00
55 Felix Millan	4.00	10.00
56 Claud Osteen ERR/(sic& Claude)	4.00	10.00
57 Milt Pappas/(pictured in Oriole uniform)	5.00	12.00
58 Tony Perez	8.00	20.00
59 Gaylord Perry	8.00	20.00
60 Pete Rose DP	40.00	80.00
61 Manny Sanguillen	5.00	12.00
62 Ron Santo	6.00	15.00
63 Tom Seaver	20.00	50.00
64 Wayne Simpson	4.00	10.00
65 Rusty Staub	5.00	12.00
66 Bobby Tolan	4.00	10.00
67 Joe Torre	6.00	15.00
68 Luke Walker	4.00	10.00
69 Billy Williams	8.00	20.00

1969 Milton Bradley

These cards were distributed as part of a baseball game produced by Milton Bradley in 1969. The cards each measure approximately 2" by 3" and have square corners. The card fronts show a black and white photo of the player with his name above the photo in a white border. The game outcomes are printed on the card backs. The game was played by rolling two dice. The outcomes (two through twelve) on the back of the player's card related to the sum of the two dice. The card backs are printed in red and black on white card stock; the player's name on back and successful outcomes for the batter such as hits are printed in red. Team logos have been airbrushed from the photos in this set. The cards are typically found with perforation notches visible. Since the cards are unnumbered, they are listed below in alphabetical order. One way to tell the 1969 and 1972 Milton Bradley sets apart is that the 1969 cards all the red digits 1 do not have a base while the 1972 red digit cards all have a base.

COMPLETE SET (296)	250.00	500.00
1 Hank Aaron	8.00	20.00
2 Ted Abernathy	.40	1.00
3 Jerry Adair	.40	1.00
4 Tommy Agee	.40	1.00
5 Bernie Allen	.40	1.00
6 Hank Allen	.40	1.00
7 Richie Allen	1.25	3.00
8 Gene Alley	.40	1.00
9 Bob Allison	.60	1.50
10 Felipe Alou	1.25	3.00
11 Jesus Alou	.40	1.00
12 Matty Alou	.60	1.50
13 Max Alvis	.40	1.00
14 Mike Andrews	.40	1.00
15 Luis Aparicio	3.00	8.00
16 Jose Arcia	.40	1.00
17 Bob Aspromonte	.40	1.00
18 Joe Azcue	.40	1.00
19 Ernie Banks	5.00	12.00
20 Steve Barber	.40	1.00
21 John Bateman	.40	1.00
22 Glenn Beckert	.40	1.00
23 Gary Bell	.40	1.00
24 Johnny Bench	8.00	20.00
25 Ken Berry	.40	1.00
26 Frank Bertaina	.40	1.00
27 Paul Blair	.40	1.00
28 Wade Blasingame	.40	1.00
29 Curt Blefary	.40	1.00
30 John Boccabella	.40	1.00
31 Bobby Bonds	3.00	8.00
32 Sam Bowens	.40	1.00
33 Ken Boyer	1.25	3.00
34 Charles Bradford	.40	1.00
35 Darrell Brandon	.40	1.00
36 Jim Brewer	.40	1.00
37 John Briggs	.40	1.00
38 Nelson Briles	.40	1.00
39 Ed Brinkman	.40	1.00
40 Lou Brock	5.00	12.00
41 Gates Brown	.40	1.00
42 Larry Brown	.40	1.00
43 George Brunet	.40	1.00
44 Jerry Buchek	.40	1.00
45 Don Buford	.40	1.00
46 Jim Bunning	3.00	8.00
47 Johnny Callison	1.00	2.50
48 Bert Campaneris	1.00	2.50
49 Jose Cardenal	.40	1.00
50 Leo Cardenas	.40	1.00
51 Don Cardwell	.40	1.00
52 Rod Carew	5.00	12.00
53 Paul Casanova	.40	1.00
54 Norm Cash	1.25	3.00
55 Danny Cater	.40	1.00
56 Orlando Cepeda	2.50	6.00
57 Dean Chance	.60	1.50
58 Ed Charles	.40	1.00
59 Horace Clarke	.40	1.00
60 Roberto Clemente	12.50	30.00
61 Donn Clendenon	.40	1.00
62 Ty Cline	.40	1.00
63 Nate Colbert	.40	1.00
64 Joe Coleman	.40	1.00
65 Bob Cox	2.50	6.00
66 Mike Cuellar	1.25	3.00
67 Ray Culp	.40	1.00
68 Clay Dalrymple	.40	1.00
69 Jim Davenport	.40	1.00
70 Vic Davalillo	.40	1.00
71 Ron Davis	.40	1.00
72 Tommy Davis	1.00	2.50
73 Willie Davis	.60	1.50
74 Chuck Dobson	.40	1.00
75 John Donaldson	.40	1.00
76 Al Downing	.40	1.00
77 Moe Drabowsky	.40	1.00
78 Dick Ellsworth	.40	1.00
79 Mike Epstein	.40	1.00
80 Andy Etchebarren	.40	1.00
81 Ron Fairly	.60	1.50
82 Dick Farrell	.40	1.00
83 Curt Flood	1.25	3.00
84 Joe Foy	.40	1.00
85 Tito Francona	.40	1.00
86 Bill Freehan	1.25	3.00
87 Jim Fregosi	1.00	2.50
88 Woodie Fryman	.40	1.00
89 Len Gabrielson	.40	1.00
90 Clarence Gaston	1.00	2.50
91 Jake Gibbs	.40	1.00
92 Russ Gibson	.40	1.00
93 Dave Giusti	.40	1.00
94 Tony Gonzalez	.40	1.00
95 Jim Gosger	.40	1.00
96 Julio Gotay	.40	1.00
97 Dick Green	.40	1.00
98 Jerry Grote	.60	1.50
99 Jimmie Hall	.40	1.00
100 Tom Haller	.40	1.00
101 Steve Hamilton	.40	1.00
102 Ron Hansen	.40	1.00
103 Jim Hardin	.40	1.00
104 Tommy Harper	.60	1.50
105 Bud Harrelson	.60	1.50
106 Ken Harrelson	1.25	3.00
107 Jim Ray Hart	.40	1.00
108 Woodie Held	.40	1.00
109 Tommy Helms	.40	1.00
110 Elrod Hendricks	.40	1.00
111 Mike Hershberger	.40	1.00
112 Jack Hiatt	.40	1.00
113 Jim Hickman	.40	1.00
114 John Hiller	.40	1.00
115 Chuck Hinton	.40	1.00
116 Ken Holtzman	.60	1.50
117 Joel Horlen	.40	1.00
118 Tony Horton	.60	1.50
119 Willie Horton	1.00	2.50
120 Frank Howard	1.25	3.00
121 Dick Howser	.40	1.00
122 Randy Hundley	.40	1.00
123 Ron Hunt	.40	1.00
124 Jim Hunter	3.00	8.00
125 Al Jackson	.40	1.00
126 Larry Jackson	.40	1.00
127 Reggie Jackson	10.00	25.00
128 Sonny Jackson	.40	1.00
129 Pat Jarvis	.40	1.00
130 Julian Javier	.40	1.00
131 Ferguson Jenkins	3.00	8.00
132 Manny Jimenez	.40	1.00
133 Tommy John	1.50	4.00
134 Bob Johnson	.40	1.00
135 Dave Johnson	1.25	3.00
136 Deron Johnson	.40	1.00
137 Lou Johnson	.40	1.00
138 Jay Johnstone	1.25	3.00
139 Cleon Jones	.60	1.50
140 Dalton Jones	.40	1.00
141 Duane Josephson	.40	1.00
142 Jim Kaat	1.50	4.00
143 Al Kaline	5.00	12.00
144 Don Kessinger	.60	1.50
145 Harmon Killebrew	4.00	10.00
146 Hal King	.40	1.00
147 Ed Kirkpatrick	.40	1.00
148 Fred Klages	.40	1.00
149 Ron Kline	.40	1.00
150 Bobby Knoop	.40	1.00
151 Gary Kolb	.40	1.00
152 Andy Kosco	.40	1.00
153 Ed Kranepool	.60	1.50
154 Lew Krausse	.40	1.00
155 Hal Lanier	.40	1.00
156 Jim LeFebvre	.40	1.00
157 Denny Lemaster	.40	1.00
158 Dave Leonhard	.40	1.00
159 Don Lock	.40	1.00
160 Mickey Lolich	1.25	3.00
161 Jim Lonborg	1.00	2.50
162 Mike Lum	.40	1.00
163 Sparky Lyle	2.00	5.00
164 Jim Maloney	.60	1.50
165 Juan Marichal	3.00	8.00
166 J.C. Martin	.40	1.00
167 Marty Martinez	.40	1.00
168 Tom Matchick	.40	1.00
169 Ed Mathews	4.00	10.00
170 Jerry May	.40	1.00
171 Lee May	.60	1.50
172 Lee Maye	.40	1.00
173 Willie Mays	8.00	20.00
174 Dal Maxvill	.40	1.00
175 Bill Mazeroski	1.50	4.00
176 Dick McAuliffe	.40	1.00
177 Al McBean	.40	1.00
178 Tim McCarver	1.25	3.00
179 Bill McCool	.40	1.00
180 Mike McCormick	.60	1.50
181 Willie McCovey	4.00	10.00
182 Tom McCraw	.40	1.00
183 Lindy McDaniel	.40	1.00
184 Sam McDowell	1.00	2.50
185 Orlando McFarlane	.40	1.00
186 Jim McGlothlin	.40	1.00
187 Denny McLain	1.25	3.00
188 Ken McMullen	.40	1.00
189 Dave McNally	1.00	2.50
190 Gerry McNertney	.40	1.00
191 Denis Menke	.40	1.00
192 Felix Millan	.40	1.00
193 Don Mincher	.40	1.00
194 Rick Monday	.60	1.50
195 Joe Morgan	4.00	10.00
196 Bubba Morton	.40	1.00
197 Manny Mota	.60	1.50
198 Jim Nash	.40	1.00
199 Dave Nelson	.40	1.00
200 Dick Nen	.40	1.00
201 Phil Niekro	3.00	8.00
202 Jim Northrup	.60	1.50
203 Rich Nye	.40	1.00
204 Johnny Odom	.40	1.00
205 Tony Oliva	1.50	4.00
206 Gene Oliver	.40	1.00
207 Phil Ortega	.40	1.00
208 Claude Osteen	.60	1.50
209 Ray Oyler	.40	1.00
210 Jose Pagan	.40	1.00
211 Jim Pagliaroni	.40	1.00
212 Milt Pappas	.60	1.50
213 Wes Parker	.40	1.00
214 Camilo Pascual	.40	1.00
215 Don Pavletich	.40	1.00
216 Joe Pepitone	1.00	2.50

217 Tony Perez 2.50 6.00
218 Gaylord Perry 3.00 8.00
219 Jim Perry 1.25 3.00
220 Gary Peters .40 1.00
221 Rico Petrocelli .60 1.50
222 Adolpho Phillips .40 1.00
223 Tom Phoebus .40 1.00
224 Vada Pinson 1.25 3.00
225 Boog Powell 1.50 4.00
226 Frank Quilici .40 1.00
227 Doug Rader .40 1.00
228 Rich Reese .40 1.00
229 Phil Regan .40 1.00
230 Rick Reichardt .40 1.00
231 Rick Renick .40 1.00
232 Roger Repoz .40 1.00
233 Dave Ricketts .40 1.00
234 Bill Robinson .40 1.00
235 Brooks Robinson 5.00 12.00
236 Frank Robinson 5.00 12.00
237 Bob Rodgers .40 1.00
238 Cookie Rojas .40 1.00
239 Rich Rollins .40 1.00
240 Phil Roof .40 1.00
241 Pete Rose 6.00 15.00
242 John Roseboro .60 1.50
243 Chico Ruiz .40 1.00
244 Ray Sadecki .40 1.00
245 Chico Salmon .40 1.00
246 Jose Santiago .40 1.00
247 Ron Santo 1.25 3.00
248 Tom Satriano .40 1.00
249 Paul Schaal .40 1.00
250 Tom Seaver 6.00 15.00
251 Art Shamsky .40 1.00
252 Mike Shannon 1.00 2.50
253 Chris Short .40 1.00
254 Dick Simpson .40 1.00
255 Duke Sims .40 1.00
256 Reggie Smith 1.25 3.00
257 Willie Smith .40 1.00
258 Russ Snyder .40 1.00
259 Al Spangler .40 1.00
260 Larry Stahl .40 1.00
261 Lee Stange .40 1.00
262 Mickey Stanley .40 1.00
263 Willie Stargell 4.00 10.00
264 Rusty Staub 1.25 3.00
265 Mel Stottlemyre 1.25 3.00
266 Ed Stroud .40 1.00
267 Don Sutton 3.00 8.00
268 Ron Swoboda .60 1.50
269 Jose Tartabull .40 1.00
270 Tony Taylor .60 1.50
271 Luis Tiant 1.25 3.00
272 Bill Tillman .40 1.00
273 Bobby Tolan .40 1.00
274 Jeff Torborg .40 1.00
275 Joe Torre 2.00 5.00
276 Cesar Tovar .40 1.00
277 Dick Tracewski .40 1.00
278 Tom Tresh 1.25 3.00
279 Ted Uhlaender .40 1.00
280 Del Unser .40 1.00
281 Sandy Valdespino .40 1.00
282 Fred Valentine .40 1.00
283 Bob Veale .40 1.00
284 Zoilo Versalles .60 1.50
285 Pete Ward .40 1.00
286 Al Weis .40 1.00
287 Don Wert .40 1.00
288 Bill White 1.25 3.00
289 Roy White .60 1.50
290 Fred Whitfield .40 1.00
291 Hoyt Wilhelm 3.00 8.00
292 Billy Williams 3.00 8.00
293 Maury Wills 1.50 4.00
294 Earl Wilson .40 1.00
295 Wilbur Wood .40 1.00
296 Jerry Zimmerman .40 1.00

1970 Milton Bradley

TOM SEAVER
P 11/17/44 6-1 TR RR

These cards were distributed as part of a baseball game produced by Milton Bradley in 1970. The cards each measure approximately 2 3/16" by 3 1/2" and have rounded corners. The card fronts show a black and white photo of the player with his name and vital statistics below the photo in a white border. The game outcomes are printed on the card backs. The card backs are printed in red and black on white card stock; the player's name is printed in red at the top of the card. Team logos have been airbrushed from the photos in this set. Since the cards are unnumbered, they are listed below in alphabetical order. Thirty two game cards were also included in the original box, those cards are not priced here. This set is sometimes found in the original box and unwrapped. If the cards are in that condition, there is a 25 percent premium for the set.

COMPLETE SET (28) 50.00 100.00
1 Hank Aaron 4.00 10.00
2 Lou Brock 2.50 6.00
3 Ernie Banks 2.50 6.00
4 Rod Carew 3.00 8.00
5 Roberto Clemente 8.00 20.00
6 Tommy Davis .50 1.25
7 Bill Freehan .50 1.25
8 Jim Fregosi .50 1.25
9 Tom Haller .40 1.00
10 Frank Howard .60 1.50
11 Reggie Jackson 5.00 12.00
12 Harmon Killebrew 1.50 4.00
13 Mickey Lolich .60 1.50
14 Juan Marichal 1.50 4.00
15 Willie Mays 6.00 15.00
16 Willie McCovey 2.00 5.00
17 Sam McDowell .50 1.25
18 Denis Menke .40 1.00
19 Don Mincher .40 1.00
20 Phil Niekro 1.50 4.00
21 Rico Petrocelli .50 1.25
22 Boog Powell .75 2.00
23 Frank Robinson 2.50 6.00
24 Pete Rose 4.00 10.00
25 Ron Santo .75 2.00
26 Tom Seaver 4.00 10.00
27 Mel Stottlemyre .50 1.25
28 Tony Taylor .40 1.00

1972 Milton Bradley

These cards were distributed as part of a baseball game produced by Milton Bradley in 1972. The cards each measure approximately 2" by 3" and have square corners. The card fronts show a black and white photo of the player with his name above the photo in a white border. The game outcomes are printed on the card backs. The game was played by rolling two dice. The outcomes (two through twelve) on the back of the player's card related to the sum of the two dice. The card backs are printed in red and black on white card stock; successful outcomes for the batter such as hits are printed in red. Team logos have been airbrushed from the photos in this set. The cards are typically found with perforation notches visible. Since the cards are unnumbered, they are listed below in alphabetical order.

COMPLETE SET (372) 350.00 700.00
1 Hank Aaron 12.50 30.00
2 Tommie Aaron .20 .50
3 Ted Abernathy .20 .50
4 Jerry Adair .20 .50
5 Tommy Agee .40 1.00
6 Bernie Allen .20 .50
7 Hank Allen .20 .50
8 Richie Allen 1.25 3.00
9 Gene Alley .20 .50
10 Bob Allison .20 .50
11 Sandy Alomar .20 .50
12 Felipe Alou .75 2.00
13 Jesus Alou .40 1.00
14 Matty Alou .60 1.50
15 Max Alvis .20 .50
16 Brant Alyea .20 .50
17 Mike Andrews .20 .50
18 Luis Aparicio 2.50 6.00
19 Jose Arcia .20 .50
20 Jerry Arrigo .20 .50
21 Bob Aspromonte .20 .50
22 Joe Azcue .20 .50
23 Bob Bailey .20 .50
24 Sal Bando .75 2.00
25 Ernie Banks 6.00 15.00
26 Steve Barber .20 .50
27 Bob Barton .20 .50
28 John Bateman .20 .50
29 Glenn Beckert .40 1.00
30 Johnny Bench 15.00 40.00
31 Ken Berry .20 .50
32 Frank Bertaina .20 .50
33 Paul Blair .40 1.00
34 Steve Blass .20 .50
35 Curt Blefary .20 .50
36 Bobby Bolin .20 .50
37 Bobby Bonds 1.25 3.00
38 Don Bosch .20 .50
39 Dick Bosman .20 .50
40 Dave Boswell .20 .50
41 Ken Boswell .20 .50
42 Cletis Boyer .60 1.50
43 Charles Bradford .20 .50
44 Ron Brand .20 .50
45 Ken Brett .20 .50
46 Jim Brewer .20 .50
47 John Briggs .20 .50
48 Nelson Briles .20 .50
49 Ed Brinkman .20 .50
50 Jim Britton .20 .50
51 Lou Brock 5.00 12.00
52 Gates Brown .20 .50
53 Larry Brown .20 .50
54 Ollie Brown .20 .50
55 George Brunet .20 .50
56 Don Buford .20 .50
57 Wally Bunker .20 .50
58 Jim Bunning 2.50 6.00
59 Bill Butler .20 .50
60 Johnny Callison .60 1.50
61 Bert Campaneris .60 1.50
62 Jose Cardenal .20 .50
63 Leo Cardenas .20 .50
64 Don Cardwell .20 .50
65 Rod Carew 5.00 12.00
66 Cisco Carlos .20 .50
67 Steve Carlton 6.00 15.00
68 Clay Carroll .20 .50
69 Paul Casanova .20 .50
70 Norm Cash 1.25 3.00
71 Danny Cater .20 .50
72 Orlando Cepeda 2.00 5.00
73 Dean Chance .40 1.00
74 Horace Clarke .20 .50
75 Roberto Clemente 40.00 80.00
76 Donn Clendenon .20 .50
77 Ty Cline .20 .50
78 Nate Colbert .20 .50
79 Joe Coleman .20 .50
80 Billy Conigliaro .20 .50
81 Casey Cox .20 .50
82 Mike Cuellar .60 1.50
83 Ray Culp .20 .50
84 George Culver .20 .50
85 Jim Davenport .20 .50
86 Vic Davalillo .20 .50
87 Tommy Davis .60 1.50
88 Willie Davis .40 1.00
89 Larry Dierker .20 .50
90 Dick Dietz .20 .50
91 Chuck Dobson .20 .50
92 Pat Dobson .20 .50
93 John Donaldson .20 .50
94 Al Downing .20 .50
95 Moe Drabowsky .20 .50
96 John Edwards .20 .50
97 Thomas Egan .20 .50
98 Dick Ellsworth .20 .50
99 Mike Epstein .20 .50
100 Andy Etchebarren .20 .50
101 Ron Fairly .60 1.50
102 Frank Fernandez .20 .50
103 Al Ferrara .20 .50
104 Mike Fiore .20 .50
105 Curt Flood .75 2.00
106 Joe Foy .20 .50
107 Tito Francona .20 .50
108 Bill Freehan .75 2.00
109 Jim Fregosi .60 1.50
110 Woodie Fryman .20 .50
111 Vern Fuller .20 .50
112 Phil Gagliano .20 .50
113 Clarence Gaston .20 .50
114 Jake Gibbs .20 .50
115 Russ Gibson .20 .50
116 Dave Giusti .20 .50
117 Fred Gladding .20 .50
118 Tony Gonzalez .20 .50
119 Jim Gosger .20 .50
120 Jim Grant .20 .50
121 Dick Green .20 .50
122 Tom Griffin .20 .50
123 Jerry Grote .20 .50
124 Tom Hall .20 .50
125 Tom Haller .20 .50
126 Steve Hamilton .20 .50
127 Bill Hands .20 .50
128 Jim Hannan .20 .50
129 Ron Hansen .20 .50
130 Jim Hardin .20 .50
131 Steve Hargan .20 .50
132 Tommy Harper .40 1.00
133 Bud Harrelson .40 1.00
134 Ken Harrelson .75 2.00
135 Jim Ray Hart .20 .50
136 Richie Hebner .40 1.00
137 Mike Hedlund .20 .50
138 Tommy Helms .20 .50
139 Elrod Hendricks .20 .50
140 Ron Herbel .20 .50
141 Jackie Hernandez .20 .50
142 Mike Hershberger .20 .50
143 Jack Hiatt .20 .50
144 Dennis Higgins .20 .50
146 John Hiller .20 .50
147 Chuck Hinton .20 .50
148 Larry Hisle .20 .50
149 Ken Holtzman .40 1.00
150 Joel Horlen .20 .50
151 Tony Horton .20 .50
152 Willie Horton .60 1.50
153 Frank Howard .75 2.00
154 Bob Humphreys .20 .50
155 Randy Hundley .20 .50
156 Ron Hunt .20 .50
157 Jim Hunter 2.50 6.00
158 Grant Jackson .20 .50
159 Reggie Jackson 15.00 40.00
160 Sonny Jackson .20 .50
161 Pat Jarvis .20 .50
162 Larry Jaster .20 .50
163 Julian Javier .20 .50
164 Ferguson Jenkins 2.50 6.00
165 Tommy John 1.25 3.00
166 Alex Johnson .40 1.00
167 Bob Johnson .20 .50
168 Dave Johnson .75 2.00
169 Deron Johnson .20 .50
170 Jay Johnstone .40 1.00
171 Cleon Jones .40 1.00
172 Dalton Jones .20 .50
173 Mack Jones .20 .50
174 Rick Joseph .20 .50
175 Duane Josephson .20 .50
176 Jim Kaat 1.25 3.00
177 Al Kaline 5.00 12.00
178 Dick Kelley .20 .50
179 Pat Kelly .20 .50
180 Jerry Kenney .20 .50
181 Don Kessinger .40 1.00
182 Harmon Killebrew 4.00 10.00
183 Ed Kirkpatrick .20 .50
184 Bobby Knoop .20 .50
185 Cal Koonce .20 .50
186 Jerry Koosman .75 2.00
187 Andy Kosco .20 .50
188 Ed Kranepool .40 1.00
189 Ted Kubiak .20 .50
190 Jose Laboy .20 .50
191 Joe Lahoud .20 .50
192 Bill Landis .20 .50
193 Hal Lanier .20 .50
194 Fred Lasher .20 .50
195 John Lazar .20 .50
196 Jim LeFebvre .20 .50
197 Denny Lemaster .20 .50
198 Dave Leonhard .20 .50
199 Frank Linzy .20 .50
200 Mickey Lolich .75 2.00
201 Jim Lonborg .40 1.00
202 Sparky Lyle .75 2.00
203 Jim Maloney .40 1.00
204 Juan Marichal 3.00 8.00
205 David Marshall .20 .50
206 J.C. Martin .20 .50
207 Marty Martinez .20 .50
208 Tom Matchick .20 .50
209 Carlos May .20 .50
210 Jerry May .20 .50
211 Lee May .40 1.00
212 Lee Maye .20 .50
213 Willie Mays 10.00 25.00
214 Dal Maxvill .20 .50
215 Bill Mazeroski .75 2.00
216 Dick McAuliffe .40 1.00
217 Al McBean .20 .50
218 Tim McCarver .75 2.00
219 Bill McCool .20 .50
220 Mike McCormick .40 1.00
221 Willie McCovey 4.00 10.00
222 Tom McCraw .20 .50
223 Lindy McDaniel .20 .50
224 Sam McDowell .60 1.50
225 Leon McFadden .20 .50
226 Dan McGinn .20 .50
227 Jim McGlothlin .20 .50
228 Tug McGraw .75 2.00
229 Denny McLain .75 2.00
230 Ken McMullen .20 .50
231 Dave McNally .60 1.50
232 Gerry McNertney .20 .50
233 Bill Melton .20 .50
234 Denis Menke .20 .50
235 Andy Messersmith .40 1.00
236 Felix Millan .20 .50
237 Norm Miller .20 .50
238 Don Mincher .20 .50
239 Rick Monday .40 1.00
240 Don Money .20 .50
241 Barry Moore .20 .50
242 Bob Moose .20 .50
243 Dave Morehead .20 .50
244 Joe Morgan 4.00 10.00
245 Manny Mota .40 1.00
246 Curt Motton .20 .50
247 Bob Murcer .75 2.00
248 Tom Murphy .20 .50
249 Ivan Murrell .20 .50
250 Jim Nash .20 .50
251 Joe Niekro .75 2.00
252 Phil Niekro 3.00 8.00
253 Gary Nolan .20 .50
254 Jim Northrup .40 1.00
255 Rich Nye .20 .50
256 Johnny Odom .20 .50
257 John O'Donoghue .20 .50
258 Tony Oliva .75 2.00
259 Bob Oliver .20 .50
260 Claude Osteen .40 1.00
261 Ray Oyler .20 .50
262 Jose Pagan .20 .50
263 Jim Palmer 3.00 8.00
264 Milt Pappas .40 1.00
265 Wes Parker .40 1.00
266 Freddie Patek .20 .50
267 Mike Paul .20 .50
268 Joe Pepitone .60 1.50
269 Tony Perez 2.00 5.00
270 Gaylord Perry 3.00 8.00
271 Jim Perry .60 1.50
272 Gary Peters .20 .50
273 Rico Petrocelli .60 1.50
274 Tom Phoebus .20 .50
275 Lou Piniella .75 2.00
276 Vada Pinson .75 2.00
277 Boog Powell .75 2.00
278 Jimmie Price .20 .50
279 Frank Quilici .20 .50
280 Doug Rader .20 .50
281 Ron Reed .20 .50
282 Rich Reese .20 .50
283 Phil Regan .20 .50
284 Rick Reichardt .20 .50
285 Rick Renick .20 .50
286 Roger Repoz .20 .50
287 Merv Rettenmund .20 .50
288 Dave Ricketts .20 .50
289 Juan Rios .20 .50
290 Bill Robinson .20 .50
291 Brooks Robinson 5.00 12.00
292 Frank Robinson 5.00 12.00
293 Aurelio Rodriguez .20 .50
294 Ellie Rodriguez .20 .50
295 Cookie Rojas .20 .50
296 Rich Rollins .20 .50
297 Vincente Romo .20 .50
298 Phil Roof .20 .50
299 Pete Rose 40.00 80.00
300 John Roseboro .40 1.00
301 Chico Ruiz .20 .50
302 Mike Ryan .20 .50
303 Ray Sadecki .20 .50
304 Chico Salmon .20 .50
305 Manny Sanguillen .40 1.00
306 Ron Santo .75 2.00
307 Tom Satriano .20 .50
308 Ted Savage .20 .50
309 Paul Schaal .20 .50
310 Dick Schofield .20 .50
311 George Scott .40 1.00
312 Tom Seaver 8.00 20.00
313 Art Shamsky .20 .50
314 Mike Shannon .60 1.50
315 Chris Short .20 .50
316 Duke Sims .20 .50

317 Bill Singer .20 .50
318 Reggie Smith .75 2.00
319 Willie Smith .20 .50
320 Russ Snyder .20 .50
321 Al Spangler .20 .50
322 Jim Spencer .20 .50
323 Ed Spiezio .20 .50
324 Larry Stahl .20 .50
325 Lee Stange .20 .50
326 Mickey Stanley .40 1.00
327 Willie Stargell 5.00 12.00
328 Rusty Staub .75 2.00
329 Jim Stewart .20 .50
330 George Stone .20 .50
331 Bill Stoneman .40 1.00
332 Mel Stottlemyre .75 2.00
333 Ed Stroud .20 .50
334 Ken Suarez .20 .50
335 Gary Sutherland .20 .50
336 Don Sutton 2.50 6.00
337 Ron Swoboda .40 1.00
338 Fred Talbot .20 .50
339 Jose Tartabull .20 .50
340 Ken Tatum .20 .50
341 Tony Taylor .40 1.00
342 Luis Tiant .75 2.00
343 Bob Tillman .20 .50
344 Bobby Tolan .20 .50
345 Jeff Torborg .20 .50
346 Joe Torre .75 2.00
347 Cesar Tovar .20 .50
348 Tom Tresh .75 2.00
349 Ted Uhlaender .20 .50
350 Del Unser .20 .50
351 Bob Veale .20 .50
352 Zoilo Versalles .40 1.00
353 Luke Walker .20 .50
354 Pete Ward .20 .50
355 Eddie Watt .20 .50
356 Ramon Webster .20 .50
357 Al Weis .20 .50
358 Don Wert .20 .50
359 Bill White .75 2.00
360 Roy White .60 1.50
361 Hoyt Wilhelm 2.00 5.00
362 Billy Williams 4.00 10.00
363 Walt Williams .20 .50
364 Maury Wills .75 2.00
365 Don Wilson .20 .50
366 Earl Wilson .20 .50
367 Bobby Wine .20 .50
368 Rick Wise .40 1.00
369 Wilbur Wood .20 .50
370 Woody Woodward .20 .50
371 Clyde Wright .20 .50
372 Jim Wynn .75 2.00

1977 Johnny Mize

This 20-card set measures 3 1/8" by 3 3/4" and features both vertical and horizontal black-and-white photos of Johnny Mize at various stages of his life. The photos are bordered in gold and gray by a design similar to picture frame. The card title is printed below the photo in script. The backs are white and carry a variety of information. Some contain statistics, while others have quotes from other ball players or career information. The cards are unnumbered and checklisted below in alphabetical order according to either the card's title or the last name of an individual pictured with Johnny Mize. Two postage paid postcards were also included for buyers of the set to send to HOF Veteran Committee voters to support Mize's case for the HOF.

COMPLETE SET 6.00 15.00
COMMON CARD .30 .75
1 Buddy Blattner .60 1.50
Sid Gordon
Ernie Lombardi
Willar
5 Johnny Mize .60 1.50
Happy Chandler COMM
Bucky Harris MG
11 Johnny Mize .40 1.00
Terry Moore
13 Johnny Mize .40 1.00
Allie Reynolds
Billy Johnson
14 Johnny Mize .75 2.00
Roy Rogers
16 Johnny Mize .75 2.00
Enos Slaughter/1939
20 Johnny Mize .40 1.00
Gene Woodling
Vic Raschi/1952

1969 MLB PhotoStamps

Each team is represented by nine players; hence the set consists of 216 player stamps each measuring approximately 1 3/4" by 2 7/8". There are two large albums available, one for each league. Also there are four smaller divisional albums each measuring approximately 4" by 7" and holding all the player stamps for a particular division. Stamps are unnumbered but are presented here in alphabetical order by team, Baltimore Orioles (1-9), Boston Red Sox (10-18), California Angels (19-27), Chicago White Sox (28-36), Cleveland Indians (37-45), Detroit Tigers (46-54), Kansas City Royals (55-63), Minnesota Twins (64-72), New York Yankees (73-81), Oakland A's (82-90), Seattle Pilots (91-99), Washington Senators (100-108), Atlanta Braves (109-117), Chicago Cubs (118-126), Cincinnati Reds (127-135), Houston Astros (136-144), Los Angeles Dodgers (145-153), Montreal Expos (154-162), New York Mets (163-171), Philadelphia Phillies (172-180), Pittsburgh Pirates (181-189), San Diego Padres (190-198), San Francisco Giants (199-207), and St. Louis Cardinals (208-216).

COMPLETE SET (216) 40.00 80.00
1 Paul Blair .12 .30
2 Don Buford .08 .20
3 Andy Etchebarren .08 .20
4 Dave Johnson .15 .40
5 Dave McNally .12 .30
6 Tom Phoebus .08 .20
7 Boog Powell .20 .50
8 Brooks Robinson .60 1.50
9 Frank Robinson .60 1.50
10 Mike Andrews .08 .20
11 Ray Culp .08 .20
12 Dick Ellsworth .08 .20
13 Ken Harrelson .15 .40
14 Jim Lonborg .12 .30
15 Rico Petrocelli .12 .30
16 Jose Santiago .08 .20
17 George Scott .12 .30
18 Reggie Smith .15 .40
19 George Brunet .08 .20
20 Vic Davalillo .08 .20
21 Jim Fregosi .15 .40
22 Chuck Hinton .08 .20
23 Bobby Knoop .08 .20
24 Jim McGlothlin .08 .20
25 Rick Reichardt .08 .20
26 Roger Repoz .08 .20
27 Bob Rodgers .15 .40
28 Luis Aparicio .40 1.00
29 Ken Berry .08 .20
30 Joe Horlen .08 .20
31 Tommy John .20 .50
32 Duane Josephson .08 .20
33 Tom McCraw .08 .20
34 Gary Peters .08 .20
35 Pete Ward .08 .20
36 Wilbur Wood .12 .30
37 Max Alvis .08 .20
38 Joe Azcue .08 .20
39 Larry Brown .08 .20
40 Jose Cardenal .08 .20
41 Tony Horton .12 .30
42 Sam McDowell .12 .30
43 Sonny Siebert .08 .20
44 Luis Tiant .15 .40
45 Zoilo Versalles .08 .20
46 Norm Cash .15 .40
47 Bill Freehan .15 .40
48 Willie Horton .15 .40
49 Al Kaline .60 1.50
50 Mickey Lolich .15 .40
51 Dick McAuliffe .08 .20
52 Denny McLain .20 .50
53 Jim Northrup .08 .20
54 Mickey Stanley .08 .20
55 Jerry Adair .08 .20
56 Wally Bunker .08 .20
57 Moe Drabowsky .08 .20
58 Joe Foy .08 .20
59 Ed Kirkpatrick .08 .20
60 Dave Morehead .08 .20
61 Roger Nelson .08 .20
62 Paul Schaal .08 .20
63 Steve Whitaker .08 .20
64 Bob Allison .12 .30
65 Rod Carew .60 1.50
66 Dean Chance .12 .30
67 Jim Kaat .20 .50
68 Harmon Killebrew .40 1.00
69 Tony Oliva .20 .50
70 John Roseboro .08 .20
71 Cesar Tovar .08 .20
72 Ted Uhlaender .08 .20
73 Horace Clarke .08 .20
74 Jake Gibbs .08 .20
75 Steve Hamilton .08 .20
76 Joe Pepitone .12 .30
77 Fritz Peterson .08 .20
78 Bill Robinson .12 .30
79 Mel Stottlemyre .12 .30
80 Tom Tresh .15 .40
81 Roy White .12 .30
82 Sal Bando .12 .30
83 Bert Campaneris .15 .40
84 Danny Cater .08 .20
85 John Donaldson .08 .20
86 Mike Hershberger .08 .20
87 Jim Hunter .40 1.00
88 Rick Monday .12 .30
89 Jim Nash .08 .20
90 John Odom .08 .20
91 Jack Aker .08 .20
92 Steve Barber .08 .20
93 Gary Bell .08 .20
94 Tommy Davis .12 .30
95 Tommy Harper .08 .20
96 Don Mincher .08 .20
97 Ray Oyler .08 .20
98 Rich Rollins .08 .20
99 Chico Salmon .08 .20
100 Bernie Allen .08 .20
101 Ed Brinkman .08 .20
102 Paul Casanova .08 .20
103 Joe Coleman Jr. .08 .20
104 Mike Epstein .08 .20
105 Frank Howard .20 .50
106 Ken McMullen .08 .20
107 Camilo Pascual .08 .20
108 Ed Stroud .08 .20
109 Hank Aaron 1.00 2.50
110 Felipe Alou .15 .40
111 Bob Aspromonte .08 .20
112 Rico Carty .12 .30
113 Orlando Cepeda .30 .75
114 Pat Jarvis .08 .20
115 Felix Millan .08 .20
116 Phil Niekro .30 .75
117 Milt Pappas .08 .20
118 Ernie Banks .60 1.50
119 Glenn Beckert .08 .20
120 Bill Hands .08 .20
121 Randy Hundley .08 .20
122 Fergie Jenkins .30 .75
123 Don Kessinger .12 .30
124 Phil Regan .08 .20
125 Ron Santo .20 .50
126 Billy Williams .40 1.00
127 Johnny Bench .60 1.50
128 Tony Cloninger .08 .20
129 Tommy Helms .08 .20
130 Jim Maloney .12 .30
131 Lee May .12 .30
132 Jim Merritt .08 .20
133 Gary Nolan .08 .20
134 Tony Perez .30 .75
135 Pete Rose .75 2.00
136 Jesus Alou .08 .20
137 Curt Blefary .08 .20
138 Larry Dierker .08 .20
139 Johnny Edwards .08 .20
140 Denis Menke .08 .20
141 Joe Morgan .40 1.00
142 Doug Rader .12 .30
143 Don Wilson .08 .20
144 Jim Wynn .12 .30
145 Willie Davis .12 .30
146 Ron Fairly .12 .30
147 Len Gabrielson .08 .20
148 Tom Haller .08 .20
149 Jim LeFebvre .08 .20
150 Claude Osteen .08 .20
151 Wes Parker .12 .30
152 Bill Singer .08 .20
153 Don Sutton .30 .75
154 Bob Bailey .08 .20
155 John Bateman .08 .20
156 Ty Cline .08 .20
157 Jim Fairey .08 .20
158 Jim Grant .08 .20
159 Mack Jones .08 .20
160 Manny Mota .12 .30
161 Rusty Staub .20 .50
162 Maury Wills .20 .50
163 Tommy Agee .08 .20
164 Ed Charles .08 .20
165 Jerry Grote .12 .30
166 Bud Harrelson .15 .40
167 Cleon Jones .12 .30
168 Jerry Koosman .15 .40
169 Ed Kranepool .08 .20
170 Tom Seaver .75 2.00
171 Ron Swoboda .08 .20
172 Richie Allen .20 .50
173 Johnny Briggs .08 .20
174 Johnny Callison .12 .30
175 Woody Fryman .08 .20
176 Cookie Rojas .08 .20
177 Mike Ryan .08 .20
178 Chris Short .08 .20
179 Tony Taylor .08 .20
180 Rick Wise .12 .30
181 Gene Alley .08 .20
182 Matty Alou .12 .30
183 Jim Bunning .30 .75
184 Roberto Clemente 1.50 4.00
185 Ron Davis .08 .20
186 Jerry May .08 .20
187 Bill Mazeroski .20 .50
188 Willie Stargell .40 1.00
189 Bob Veale .08 .20
190 Ollie Brown .08 .20
191 Al Ferrara .08 .20
192 Tony Gonzales .08 .20
193 Dick Kelley .08 .20
194 Bill McCool .08 .20
195 Dick Selma .08 .20
196 Tommy Sisk .08 .20
197 Ed Spiezio .08 .20
198 Larry Stahl .08 .20
199 Jim Ray Hart .12 .30
200 Ron Hunt .08 .20
201 Hal Lanier .15 .40
202 Frank Linzy .08 .20
203 Juan Marichal .40 1.00
204 Willie Mays 1.00 2.50
205 Mike McCormick .12 .30
206 Willie McCovey .40 1.00
207 Gaylord Perry .30 .75
208 Nelson Briles .08 .20
209 Lou Brock .50 1.25
210 Curt Flood .20 .50
211 Bob Gibson .50 1.25
212 Julian Javier .08 .20
213 Dal Maxvill .08 .20
214 Tim McCarver .20 .50
215 Mike Shannon .12 .30
216 Joe Torre .20 .50

1970 MLB PhotoStamps

These unnumbered stamps are organized below alphabetically within teams; there are 24 teams each featuring 12 player stamps. This set is much tougher to find than the set produced the year before. They are essentially the same size at 1 7/8" by 2 15/16" and as with the prior set they are not gummed on the back. Stamps are unnumbered but are presented here in alphabetical order by team, Atlanta Braves (1-12), Chicago Cubs (13-24), Cincinnati Reds (25-36), Houston Astros (37-48), Los Angeles Dodgers (49-60), Montreal Expos (61-72), New York Mets (73-84), Philadelphia Phillies (85-96), Pittsburgh Pirates (97-108), San Diego Padres (109-120), San Francisco Giants (121-132), St. Louis Cardinals (133-144), Baltimore Orioles (145-156), Boston Red Sox (157-168), California Angels (169-180), Chicago White Sox (181-192), Cleveland Indians (193-204), Detroit Tigers (205-216), Kansas City Royals (217-228), Minnesota Twins (229-240), New York Yankees (241-252), Oakland A's (253-264), Seattle Pilots (265-276) and Washington Senators (277-288).

COMPLETE SET (288) 75.00 150.00
1 Hank Aaron 2.00 5.00
2 Bob Aspromonte .08 .20
3 Rico Carty .12 .30
4 Orlando Cepeda .20 .50
5 Bob Didier .08 .20
6 Tony Gonzales .08 .20
7 Pat Jarvis .08 .20
8 Felix Millan .08 .20
9 Jim Nash .08 .20
10 Phil Niekro .60 1.50
11 Milt Pappas .12 .30
12 Ron Reed .08 .20
13 Ernie Banks 1.00 2.50
14 Glenn Beckert .12 .30
15 Johnny Callison .12 .30
16 Bill Hands .08 .20
17 Randy Hundley .08 .20
18 Ken Holtzman .12 .30
19 Fergie Jenkins .60 1.50
20 Don Kessinger .12 .30
21 Phil Regan .08 .20
22 Ron Santo .20 .50
23 Dick Selma .08 .20
24 Billy Williams .60 1.50
25 Johnny Bench 1.00 2.50
26 Tony Cloninger .08 .20
27 Wayne Granger .08 .20
28 Tommy Helms .08 .20
29 Jim Maloney .12 .30
30 Lee May .12 .30
31 Jim McGlothlin .08 .20
32 Jim Merritt .08 .20
33 Gary Nolan .08 .20
34 Tony Perez .60 1.50
35 Pete Rose 1.50 4.00
36 Bobby Tolan .08 .20
37 Jesus Alou .08 .20
38 Tommy Davis .12 .30
39 Larry Dierker .08 .20
40 Johnny Edwards .08 .20
41 Fred Gladding .08 .20
42 Denver Lemaster .08 .20
43 Denis Menke .08 .20
44 Joe Morgan .60 1.50
45 Joe Pepitone .12 .30
46 Doug Rader .08 .20
47 Don Wilson .08 .20
48 Jim Wynn .12 .30
49 Willie Davis .12 .30
50 Len Gabrielson .08 .20
51 Tom Haller .08 .20
52 Jim LeFebvre .08 .20
53 Manny Mota .12 .30
54 Claude Osteen .12 .30
55 Wes Parker .12 .30
56 Bill Russell .20 .50
57 Bill Singer .08 .20
58 Ted Sizemore .08 .20
59 Don Sutton .60 1.50
60 Maury Wills .20 .50
61 Johnny Bateman .08 .20
62 Bob Bailey .08 .20
63 Ron Brand .08 .20
64 Ty Cline .08 .20
65 Ron Fairly .12 .30
66 Mack Jones .08 .20
67 Jose Laboy .08 .20
68 Claude Raymond .08 .20
69 Joe Sparma .08 .20
70 Rusty Staub .20 .50
71 Bill Stoneman .08 .20
72 Bobby Wine .08 .20
73 Tommy Agee .12 .30
74 Donn Clendenon .08 .20
75 Joe Foy .08 .20
76 Jerry Grote .12 .30
77 Bud Harrelson .12 .30
78 Cleon Jones .12 .30
79 Jerry Koosman .15 .40
80 Ed Kranepool .12 .30
81 Nolan Ryan 6.00 15.00
82 Tom Seaver 1.25 3.00
83 Ron Swoboda .12 .30
84 Al Weis .08 .20
85 Johnny Briggs .08 .20
86 Jim Bunning .60 1.50
87 Curt Flood .20 .50
88 Woody Fryman .08 .20
89 Larry Hisle .12 .30

90 Joe Hoerner	.08	.20
91 Grant Jackson	.08	.20
92 Tim McCarver	.20	.50
93 Mike Ryan	.08	.20
94 Chris Short	.08	.20
95 Tony Taylor	.08	.20
96 Rick Wise	.12	.30
97 Gene Alley	.08	.20
98 Matty Alou	.12	.30
99 Roberto Clemente	4.00	10.00
100 Ron Davis	.08	.20
101 Richie Hebner	.08	.20
102 Jerry May	.08	.20
103 Bill Mazeroski	.30	.75
104 Bob Moose	.08	.20
105 Al Oliver	.20	.50
106 Manny Sanguillen	.12	.30
107 Willie Stargell	.75	2.00
108 Bob Veale	.08	.20
109 Ollie Brown	.08	.20
110 Dave Campbell	.15	.40
111 Nate Colbert	.08	.20
112 Pat Dobson	.12	.30
113 Al Ferrara	.08	.20
114 Dick Kelley	.08	.20
115 Clay Kirby	.08	.20
116 Bill McCool	.08	.20
117 Frank Reberger	.08	.20
118 Tommie Sisk	.08	.20
119 Ed Spiezio	.08	.20
120 Larry Stahl	.08	.20
121 Bobby Bonds	.20	.50
122 Jim Davenport	.12	.30
123 Dick Dietz	.08	.20
124 Jim Ray Hart	.12	.30
125 Ron Hunt	.08	.20
126 Hal Lanier	.15	.40
127 Frank Linzy	.08	.20
128 Juan Marichal	.60	1.50
129 Willie Mays	3.00	8.00
130 Mike McCormick	.12	.30
131 Willie McCovey	.60	1.50
132 Gaylord Perry	.60	1.50
133 Richie Allen	.20	.50
134 Nelson Briles	.08	.20
135 Lou Brock	.75	2.00
136 Jose Cardenal	.08	.20
137 Steve Carlton	1.00	2.50
138 Vic Davalillo	.08	.20
139 Bob Gibson	.75	2.00
140 Julian Javier	.08	.20
141 Dal Maxvill	.08	.20
142 Cookie Rojas	.12	.30
143 Mike Shannon	.15	.40
144 Joe Torre	.20	.50
145 Mark Belanger	.12	.30
146 Paul Blair	.12	.30
147 Don Buford	.08	.20
148 Mike Cuellar	.12	.30
149 Andy Etchebarren	.08	.20
150 Dave Johnson	.15	.40
151 Dave McNally	.12	.30
152 Tom Phoebus	.08	.20
153 Boog Powell	.20	.50
154 Brooks Robinson	1.00	2.50
155 Frank Robinson	1.00	2.50
156 Chico Salmon	.08	.20
157 Mike Andrews	.08	.20
158 Ray Culp	.08	.20
159 Jim Lonborg	.12	.30
160 Sparky Lyle	.20	.50
161 Gary Peters	.08	.20
162 Rico Petrocelli	.15	.40
163 Vicente Romo	.08	.20
164 Tom Satriano	.08	.20
165 George Scott	.12	.30
166 Sonny Siebert	.08	.20
167 Reggie Smith	.15	.40
168 Carl Yastrzemski	1.00	2.50
169 Sandy Alomar	.12	.30
170 Jose Azcue	.08	.20
171 Tom Egan	.08	.20
172 Jim Fregosi	.15	.40
173 Alex Johnson	.12	.30
174 Jay Johnstone	.12	.30
175 Rudy May	.08	.20
176 Andy Messersmith	.12	.30
177 Rick Reichardt	.08	.20
178 Roger Repoz	.08	.20
179 Aurelio Rodriguez	.08	.20
180 Ken Tatum	.08	.20
181 Luis Aparicio	.60	1.50
182 Ken Berry	.08	.20
183 Buddy Bradford	.08	.20
184 Ron Hansen	.08	.20
185 Joe Horlen	.08	.20
186 Tommy John	.40	1.00
187 Duane Josephson	.08	.20
188 Bobby Knoop	.08	.20
189 Tom McCraw	.08	.20
190 Bill Melton	.08	.20
191 Walt Williams	.08	.20
192 Wilbur Wood	.12	.30
193 Max Alvis	.08	.20
194 Larry Brown	.08	.20
195 Dean Chance	.08	.20
196 Dick Ellsworth	.12	.30
197 Vern Fuller	.08	.20
198 Ken Harrelson	.20	.50
199 Chuck Hinton	.08	.20
200 Tony Horton	.12	.30
201 Sam McDowell	.15	.40
202 Vada Pinson	.20	.50
203 Duke Sims	.08	.20
204 Ted Uhlaender	.08	.20
205 Norm Cash	.15	.40
206 Bill Freehan	.15	.40
207 Willie Horton	.15	.40
208 Al Kaline	.75	2.00
209 Mike Kilkenny	.08	.20
210 Mickey Lolich	.20	.50
211 Dick McAuliffe	.12	.30
212 Denny McLain	.20	.50
213 Jim Northrup	.12	.30
214 Mickey Stanley	.12	.30
215 Tom Tresh	.12	.30
216 Earl Wilson	.08	.20
217 Jerry Adair	.08	.20
218 Wally Bunker	.08	.20
219 Bill Butler	.08	.20
220 Moe Drabowsky	.08	.20
221 Jackie Hernandez	.08	.20
222 Pat Kelly	.08	.20
223 Ed Kirkpatrick	.08	.20
224 Dave Morehead	.08	.20
225 Roger Nelson	.08	.20
226 Bob Oliver	.08	.20
227 Lou Piniella	.20	.50
228 Paul Schaal	.08	.20
229 Bob Allison	.12	.30
230 Dave Boswell	.08	.20
231 Leo Cardenas	.08	.20
232 Rod Carew	1.00	2.50
233 Jim Kaat	.40	1.00
234 Harmon Killebrew	.75	2.00
235 Tony Oliva	.20	.50
236 Jim Perry	.12	.30
237 Ron Perranoski	.12	.30
238 Rich Reese	.08	.20
239 Luis Tiant	.20	.50
240 Cesar Tovar	.12	.30
241 Jack Aker	.08	.20
242 Curt Blefary	.08	.20
243 Danny Cater	.08	.20
244 Horace Clarke	.08	.20
245 Jake Gibbs	.08	.20
246 Steve Hamilton	.08	.20
247 Bobby Murcer	.20	.50
248 Fritz Peterson	.08	.20
249 Bill Robinson	.08	.20
250 Mel Stottlemyre	.15	.40
251 Pete Ward	.08	.20
252 Roy White	.12	.30
253 Felipe Alou	.15	.40
254 Sal Bando	.15	.40
255 Bert Campaneris	.12	.30
256 Chuck Dobson	.08	.20
257 Tito Francona	.08	.20
258 Dick Green	.08	.20
259 Jim Hunter	.60	1.50
260 Reggie Jackson	2.00	5.00
261 Don Mincher	.08	.20
262 Rick Monday	.12	.30
263 John Odom	.08	.20
264 Ray Oyler	.08	.20
265 Steve Barber	.08	.20
266 Bobby Bolin	.08	.20
267 George Brunet	.08	.20
268 Wayne Comer	.08	.20
269 John Donaldson	.08	.20
270 Tommy Harper	.12	.30
271 Mike Hegan	.08	.20
272 Mike Hershberger	.08	.20
273 Steve Hovley	.08	.20
274 Bob Locker	.08	.20
275 Gerry McNertney	.08	.20
276 Rich Rollins	.08	.20
277 Bernie Allen	.08	.20
278 Dick Bosman	.08	.20
279 Ed Brinkman	.08	.20
280 Paul Casanova	.08	.20
281 Joe Coleman	.08	.20
282 Mike Epstein	.08	.20
283 Frank Howard	.20	.50
284 Ken McMullen	.08	.20
285 John Roseboro	.12	.30
286 Ed Stroud	.08	.20
287 Del Unser	.08	.20
288 Zoilo Versalles	.12	.30

1977 Montefusco/D'Acquisto Restaurant

This postcard which features action shots of 1970's pitchers John "The Count" Montefusco as well as John D'Acquisto. In addition, there is a photo of the two Giant pitchers sitting at a table in their eatery. The back has information about this place.

1 John Montefusco John D'Acuqisto	1.25	3.00

1976 Motorola Old Timers

This 11-card standard-size set, issued by Motorola for their stockholders meeting in 1976, honored some of Baseball's all-time greats. The front of the cards were about the player while the backs of the cards talked in technical terms about Motorola products. The cards are also made on a thin (paper-like) card stock and are very flimsy. Certain dealers have reported that there was also an edible version made of organic substances of these cards issued. There are reports that this set was privately produced for Motorola by long time hobbyist Mike Cramer.

COMPLETE SET (11)	12.50	30.00
1 Honus Wagner	2.00	5.00
2 Nap Lajoie	1.00	2.50
3 Ty Cobb	3.00	8.00
4 William Wambsganss	.40	1.00
5 Mordecai Brown	.60	1.50
6 Ray Schalk	.60	1.50
7 Frank Frisch	.75	2.00
8 Pud Galvin	.60	1.50
9 Babe Ruth	4.00	10.00
10 Grover C. Alexander	1.00	2.50
11 Frank L. Chance	.75	2.00

1943 MP and Co. R302-1

The 1943 MP and Co. baseball card set consists of 24 player drawings each measuring 2 11/16" by 2 1/4". This company specialized in producing strips of cards to be sold in candy stores and provided a low quality but persistent challenge to other current sets. These unnumbered cards have been alphabetized and numbered in the checklist below. There is a variation on Foxx due to his acquisition by the Cubs from the Red Sox on June 1, 1942.

COMPLETE SET (24)	400.00	800.00
1 Ernie Bonham	7.50	15.00
2 Lou Boudreau	15.00	30.00
3 Dolph Camilli	10.00	20.00
4 Mort Cooper	7.50	15.00
5 Walker Cooper	7.00	12.00
6 Joe Cronin	15.00	30.00
7 Hank Danning	7.50	15.00
8 Bill Dickey	20.00	40.00
9 Joe DiMaggio	60.00	120.00
10 Bob Feller	20.00	40.00
11 Jimmy Foxx/(Chicago Cubs) (Jimmie)	30.00	60.00
12 Hank Greenberg	30.00	60.00
13 Stan Hack	7.50	15.00
14 Tommy Henrich	12.50	25.00
15 Carl Hubbell	15.00	30.00
16 Joe Medwick	15.00	30.00
17 John Mize	15.00	30.00
18 Lou Novikoff	7.50	15.00
19 Mel Ott	20.00	40.00
20 Pee Wee Reese	20.00	40.00
21 Pete Reiser	12.50	25.00
22 Red Ruffing	15.00	30.00
23 Johnny Vander Meer	12.50	25.00
24 Ted Williams	60.00	120.00

1949 MP and Co. R302-2

The 1949 rendition of MP and Co. was basically a re-issue of the 1943 set with different players and numbers on the back. Cards again measure approximately 2 11/16" by 2 1/4". The card fronts are even more washed out than the previous set. Card numbers 104, 118, and 120 are unknown and may be related to the two unnumbered cards found in the set. The catalog also lists this set as W523.

COMPLETE SET	200.00	400.00
100 Lou Boudreau	10.00	20.00
101 Ted Williams	50.00	80.00
102 Buddy Kerr	5.00	10.00
103 Bob Feller	12.50	25.00
104 Unknown		
105 Joe DiMaggio	50.00	80.00
106 Pee Wee Reese	12.50	25.00
107 Ferris Fain	5.00	10.00
108 Andy Pafko	5.00	10.00
109 Del Ennis	7.50	15.00
110 Ralph Kiner	12.50	25.00
111 Nippy Jones	5.00	10.00
112 Del Rice	5.00	10.00
113 Hank Sauer	6.00	12.00
114 Gil Coan	5.00	10.00
115 Eddie Joost	5.00	10.00
116 Alvin Dark	7.50	15.00
117 Larry Berra	15.00	30.00
118 Unknown		
119 Bob Lemon	10.00	20.00
120 Unknown		
121 Johnny Pesky	7.50	15.00
122 Johnny Sain	7.50	15.00
123 Hoot Evers	5.00	10.00
124 Larry Doby	12.50	25.00
xx Tom Henrich/(unnumbered)	7.50	15.00
xx Al Kozar/(unnumbered)	5.00	10.00

1977 MSA Discs

Produced under the auspices of Michael Scheter Associates (MSA) in 1977, the ballplayer on disc format was distributed by a number of different advertisers. There are many different back variations based on the particular area of distribution and sponsor. The discs are approximately 3 3/8" in diameter. Since these discs are unnumbered we have sequenced them in alphabetical order. Some of the other sponsors include Chilly Willie, Customized Sports, Dairy Isle, Detroit Ceasars, Dairy Isle, Holiday Inn, Saga, Wendy's and Zip'z. Unlike 1976, where these discs can be based off Crane Discs; these are priced only in each sponsor's area. Please check all the various sponsors for listings.

1910 Murad College Silks S21

Each of these silks was issued by Murad Cigarettes around 1910 with a college emblem and an artist's rendering of a generic athlete on the front. The backs are blank. Each of the S21 silks measures roughly 5" by 7" and there was a smaller version created (roughly 3 1/2" by 5 1/2") of each and cataloged as S22.

*SMALLER S22: .3X TO .8X LARGER S21

1BB Army (West Point) baseball batter	30.00	60.00
2BB Brown baseball batter	30.00	60.00
3BB California baseball batter	30.00	60.00
4BB Chicago baseball batter	30.00	60.00
5BB Colorado baseball batter	30.00	60.00
6BB Columbia baseball batter	30.00	60.00
7BB Cornell baseball batter	30.00	60.00
8BB Dartmouth baseball batter	30.00	60.00
9BB Georgetown baseball batter	30.00	60.00
10BB Harvard baseball batter	30.00	60.00
11BB Illinois baseball batter	30.00	60.00
12BB Michigan baseball batter	30.00	60.00
13BB Minnesota baseball batter	30.00	60.00
14BB Missouri baseball batter	30.00	60.00
15BB Navy (Annapolis) baseball batter	30.00	60.00
16BB Ohio State baseball batter	30.00	60.00
17BB Pennsylvania baseball batter	30.00	60.00
18BB Purdue baseball batter	30.00	60.00
19BB Stanford baseball batter	30.00	60.00
1BBP Army (West Point) baseball pitcher	30.00	60.00
20BB Stanford baseball batter	30.00	60.00
21BB Syracuse baseball batter	30.00	60.00
22BB Texas baseball batter	30.00	60.00
23BB Wisconsin baseball batter	30.00	60.00
24BB Yale baseball batter	30.00	60.00
2BBP Brown baseball pitcher	30.00	60.00
3BBP California baseball pitcher	30.00	60.00
4BBP Chicago baseball pitcher	30.00	60.00
5BBP Colorado baseball pitcher	30.00	60.00
6BBP Columbia baseball pitcher	30.00	60.00
7BBP Cornell baseball pitcher	30.00	60.00
8BBP Dartmouth baseball pitcher	30.00	60.00
9BBP Georgetown baseball pitcher	30.00	60.00
10BBP Harvard baseball pitcher	30.00	60.00
11BBP Illinois baseball pitcher	30.00	60.00
12BBP Michigan baseball pitcher	30.00	60.00
13BBP Minnesota baseball pitcher	30.00	60.00
14BBP Missouri baseball pitcher	30.00	60.00
15BBP Navy (Annapolis) baseball pitcher	30.00	60.00
16BBP Ohio State baseball pitcher	30.00	60.00
17BBP Pennsylvania baseball pitcher	30.00	60.00
18BBP Purdue baseball pitcher	30.00	60.00
19BBP Stanford baseball pitcher	30.00	60.00
20BBP Stanford baseball pitcher	30.00	60.00
21BBP Syracuse baseball pitcher	30.00	60.00
22BBP Texas baseball pitcher	30.00	60.00
23BBP Wisconsin baseball pitcher	30.00	60.00
24BBP Yale baseball pitcher	30.00	60.00

1911 Murad College Series Premiums T6

9 Fordham Baseball fielder	250.00	400.00
19 State(Penn State) Baseball batter	250.00	400.00

1911 Murad College Series T51

These colorful cigarette cards featured several colleges and a variety of sports and recreations of the day and were issued in packs of Murad Cigarettes. The cards measure approximately 2" by 3". Two variations of each of the first 50 cards were produced; one variation says "College Series" on back, the other, "2nd Series". The drawings on cards of the 2nd Series are slightly different from those of the College Series. There are 6 different series of 25 in the College Series and they are listed here in the order that they appear on the checklist on the cardbacks. There is also a larger version (5" x 8") that was available for the first 25 cards as a premium (catalog designation T6) offer that could be obtained in exchange for 15 Murad cigarette coupons; the offers expired June 30, 1911.

*2ND SERIES: .4X TO 1X COLLEGE SERIES

9 Fordham Baseball fielder	25.00	50.00
19 State(Penn State) Baseball batter	25.00	50.00
38 S.U.K.(State Univ. of Kentucky) Baseball	25.00	50.00
92 O.S.U.(Ohio State) Baseball	25.00	50.00
109 H (Haverford) Baseball	25.00	50.00
128 Antioch#(Baseball	25.00	50.00
131 Bethany Baseball	25.00	50.00
146 K.W.C./(Kentucky Wesleyan College) Baseball	25.00	50.00

1963 Musial Colt 45 Tribute

This 5" by 7" one-card blank-backed set was issued to commemorate Stan Musial's last series in Houston during the 1963 season. The front has a posed photo of Stan along with the words "Farewell Houston Appearance August 23-24-25, 1963.

1 Stan Musial	6.00	15.00

1889 N526 No. 7 Cigars

This set is comprised exclusively of members of the Boston Baseball Club, who are portrayed in black and white line drawings. The tobacco brand No. 7 Cigars has not yet been linked to a specific manufacturer. These cards were issued in 1889 and are similar to another series bearing Diamond S brand advertising.

COMPLETE SET (15)	3,000.00	6,000.00
1 Charles W. Bennett	400.00	800.00
2 Dennis (Dan) Brouthers	600.00	1,200.00
3 Tom T. Brown	400.00	800.00
4 John G. Clarkson	600.00	1,200.00
5 Charles W. Ganzell	400.00	800.00
6 James A. Hart	400.00	800.00
7 Richard F. Johnston	400.00	800.00
8 Mike King Kelly Captain	1,000.00	2,000.00
9 M.J. (Kid) Madden	400.00	800.00
10 William Nash	400.00	800.00
11 Jos. Quinn	400.00	800.00
12 Charles Radbourne	600.00	1,200.00
13 J.B. Ray (sic)	400.00	800.00
14 Hardie Richardson	400.00	800.00
15 William Sowders	400.00	800.00

1976 Nabisco Sugar Daddy 1

This set of 25 tiny (approximately 1 1/16" by 2 3/4") cards features action scenes from a variety of popular sports from around the world. One card was included in specially marked Sugar Daddy and Sugar Mama candy bars. The set is referred to as "Sugar Daddy Sports World - Series 1" on the backs of the cards. The cards are in color with a relatively wide white border around the front of the cards.

COMPLETE SET (25)	40.00	80.00
12 Baseball Pete Rose	10.00	20.00

1976 Nabisco Sugar Daddy 2

This set of 25 tiny (approximately 1 1/16" by 2 3/4") cards features action scenes from a variety of popular sports from around the world. One card was included in specially marked Sugar Daddy and Sugar Mama candy bars. The set is referred to as "Sugar Daddy Sports World - Series 2" on the backs of the cards. The cards are in color with a relatively wide white border around the front of the cards.

COMPLETE SET (25)	40.00	80.00
25 Baseball	6.00	12.00

1969 Nabisco Team Flakes

The cards in this 24-card set measure either 1 15/16" by 3" or 1 3/4" by 2 15/16" depending on the amount of yellow border area provided between the "cut lines." The 1969 Nabisco Team Flakes set of full color, blank-backed and unnumbered cards was issued on the backs of Team Flakes cereal boxes. The cards are numbered in the checklist below in alphabetical order. There were three different panels or box backs containing eight cards each. The cards have yellow borders and are devoid of team insignias. The wider cards are tougher and should be valued at approximately 1.5X to 2X the narrower cards. The catalog designation is F275-34. Based on the alphabetical order of the player on the top left corner, we have identified the sheet that each player was on. The Aaron sheet is labelled S1, Pete Rose is labelled S2 and Ron Santo is labelled S3. These cards are actually called Mini Posters by Nabisco and all of these photos were also available in 2 feet by 3 feet posters that a kid could mail away for.

COMPLETE SET (24)	300.00	600.00
1 Hank Aaron S1	40.00	80.00
2 Richie Allen S1	6.00	15.00
3 Lou Brock S2	15.00	40.00
4 Paul Casanova S1	2.50	6.00
5 Roberto Clemente S3	50.00	100.00
6 Al Ferrara S3	2.50	6.00
7 Bill Freehan S2	4.00	10.00
8 Jim Fregosi S1	4.00	10.00
9 Bob Gibson S3	15.00	40.00
10 Tony Horton S2	4.00	10.00
11 Tommy John S3	6.00	15.00
12 Al Kaline S3	15.00	40.00
13 Jim Lonborg S2	2.50	6.00
14 Juan Marichal S1	15.00	40.00
15 Willie Mays S2	40.00	80.00
16 Rick Monday S2	2.50	6.00
17 Tony Oliva S1	6.00	15.00
18 Brooks Robinson S1	15.00	40.00
19 Frank Robinson S3	15.00	40.00
20 Pete Rose S2	30.00	60.00
21 Ron Santo S3	8.00	20.00
22 Tom Seaver S2	30.00	60.00
23 Rusty Staub S1	4.00	10.00
24 Mel Stottlemyre S3	2.50	6.00

1909 E92-1 Dockman and Sons

The cards in this 40-card set measure 1 1/2" by 2 3/4". Additional advertising backs can also be found for Croft's Candy, Croft's Cocoa and Nadja - but pricing for these cards can be found in their own listings. The set contains poses identical to those in E101, E102, and E105. Book prices reference VgEx condition given the majority of cards found in this set are typically off-grade. Cards are unnumbered and checklisted alphabetically by each player's last name.

COMPLETE SET (62)	12,500.00	25,000.00
1 Harry Bemis	125.00	200.00
2 Chief Bender	350.00	600.00
3 Bill Bergen	125.00	200.00
4 Bob Bescher	125.00	200.00
5 Al Bridwell	125.00	200.00
6 Joe Casey	125.00	200.00
7 Frank Chance	350.00	600.00
8 Hal Chase	175.00	300.00
9 Sam Crawford	350.00	600.00
10 Harry Davis	125.00	200.00
11 Art Devlin	125.00	200.00
12 Bill Donovan	125.00	200.00
13 Mickey Doolan	125.00	200.00
14 Patsy Dougherty	125.00	200.00
15 Larry Doyle Batting	125.00	200.00
16 Larry Doyle Throwing	125.00	200.00
17 George Gibson	125.00	200.00
18 Topsy Hartsel	125.00	200.00
19 Hugh Jennings	350.00	600.00
20 Red Kleinow	125.00	200.00
21 Nap Lajoie	500.00	800.00
22 Hans Lobert	125.00	200.00
23 Sherry Magee	125.00	200.00
24 Christy Mathewson UER (Matthewson)	1,200.00	2,000.00
25 John McGraw	350.00	600.00
26 Larry McLean	125.00	200.00
27 Dots Miller Batting	125.00	200.00
28 Danny Murphy	125.00	200.00
29 Bill O'Hara	125.00	200.00
30 Germany Schaefer	125.00	200.00
31 Admiral Schlei	125.00	200.00
32 Boss Smith (Schmidt)	125.00	200.00
33 Johnny Seigle (Siegle)	125.00	200.00
34 Dave Shean	125.00	200.00
35 Frank Smith	125.00	200.00
36 Joe Tinker	350.00	600.00
37 Honus Wagner Batting	2,500.00	4,000.00
38 Honus Wagner Throwing	1,800.00	3,000.00
39 Cy Young Cleveland	900.00	1,500.00
40 Heinie Zimmerman	125.00	200.00

1910 Nadja E104

The cards in this 59-card set measure 1 1/2" by 2 3/4". The title of this set comes from the distinctive "Play Ball and eat Nadja Caramels" advertisement found on the reverse of some of the cards. The great majority of the known cards, however, are blank backed. They are grouped together because they have similar obverses and captions in blue print ("Nadja" cards with brown print captions belong to set E92). The cards are unnumbered and were issued in 1910. They have been alphabetized and numbered in our checklist Nadja reverses are valued at three times the prices below.

COMPLETE SET (59)	40,000.00	80,000.00
1 Bill Abstein	600.00	1,200.00
2 Babe Adams	750.00	1,500.00
3 Red Ames	600.00	1,200.00
4 Home Run Baker	1,000.00	2,000.00
5 Jack Barry	500.00	1,000.00
6 Johnny Bates	600.00	1,200.00
7 Chief Bender	1,000.00	2,000.00
8 Kitty Bransfield	600.00	1,200.00
9 Al Bridwell	600.00	1,200.00
10 Hal Chase	750.00	1,500.00
11 Fred Clarke	1,000.00	2,000.00
12 Eddie Collins	1,000.00	2,000.00
13 Doc Crandall	600.00	1,200.00
14 Sam Crawford	2,000.00	4,000.00
15 Harry Davis	500.00	1,000.00
16 Jim Delehanty (Delahanty)	600.00	1,200.00
17 Art Devlin	500.00	1,000.00
18 Red Dooin	500.00	1,000.00
19 Mickey Doolan	500.00	1,000.00
20 Larry Doyle	600.00	1,200.00
21 Jimmy Dygert	500.00	1,000.00
22 George Gibson	500.00	1,000.00
23 Eddie Grant	600.00	1,200.00
24 Topsy Hartsel	500.00	1,000.00
25 Ham Hyatt	500.00	1,000.00
26 Fred Jacklitsch	600.00	1,200.00
27 Hugh Jennings	2,000.00	4,000.00
28 Davy Jones	600.00	1,200.00
29 Tom Jones	600.00	1,200.00
30 Otto Knabe	600.00	1,200.00
31 Harry Krause	500.00	1,000.00
32 John Lapp	500.00	1,000.00
33 Tommy Leach	500.00	1,000.00
34 Sam Leever	500.00	1,000.00
35 Paddy Livingstone (Livingston)	500.00	1,000.00
36 Bris Lord	500.00	1,000.00
37 Connie Mack	2,000.00	4,000.00
38 Nick Maddox	500.00	1,000.00
39 Sherry Magee	500.00	1,000.00
40 John McGraw	2,000.00	4,000.00
41 Matthew McIntyre	600.00	1,200.00
42 Dots Miller	500.00	1,000.00
43 Earl Moore	600.00	1,200.00
44 Pat Moren (Moran)	600.00	1,200.00
45 Cy Morgan	500.00	1,000.00
46 George Moriarty	600.00	1,200.00
47 George Mullin	600.00	1,200.00
48 Danny Murphy	500.00	1,000.00
49 Red Murray	600.00	1,200.00
50 Simon Nicholls	600.00	1,200.00
51 Rube Oldring	500.00	1,000.00
52 Charlie O'Leary	600.00	1,200.00
53 Deacon Phillippe	600.00	1,200.00
54 Eddie Plank	1,500.00	3,000.00
55 Admiral Schlei	600.00	1,200.00
56 Boss Schmidt	500.00	1,000.00
57 Cy Seymore (Seymour)	600.00	1,200.00
58 Tully Sparks	600.00	1,200.00
59 Amos Strunk	500.00	1,000.00
60 Ed Summers	600.00	1,200.00
62 Ira Thomas	500.00	1,000.00
63 Honus Wagner	6,000.00	10,000.00
64 Ed Willett	600.00	1,200.00
65 Vic Willis	1,000.00	2,000.00
66 Owen Wilson	500.00	1,000.00
67 Hooks Wiltse	500.00	1,000.00
61 Fred Tenney 3		

1967 Nassau Health Ford

This one-card set was issued by Nassau Tuberculosis and Respiratory Disease Association and features a black-and-white photo of Whitey Ford. The back carries player information and a message about the dangers of cigarette smoking.

1 Whitey Ford	20.00	50.00

1921-23 National Caramel E220

The cards in this 120-card set measure 2" by 3 1/4". There are 114 different players and six variations known for the "Baseball Stars" set marketed by the National Caramel Company. The cards are unnumbered and contain black and white photos; they are similar to set E122 but the coarse screening effect of the latter is missing. Some players appear in two poses, Burns is found with two teams, and three names are misspelled on the cards. The set was probably issued in 1922, the same year as was E122. The cards have been alphabetized and numbered in the checklist below. The complete set price includes all variation cards listed in the checklist below.

COMPLETE SET (120)	8,000.00	16,000.00
1 Babe Adams	75.00	150.00
2 Grover C. Alexander	150.00	300.00
3 James Austin	60.00	120.00
4 Jim Bagbyk/(sic& Bagby)	60.00	120.00
5 Frank Baker	100.00	200.00
6 Dave Bancroft	100.00	200.00
7 Turner Barber	60.00	120.00
8 Geo.H. Burns/Cleveland	60.00	120.00
9 Geo.J. Burns/Cincinnati	60.00	120.00
10 Joe Bush	75.00	150.00
11 Leon Cadore	60.00	120.00
12 Max Carey	100.00	200.00
13 Ty Cobb	900.00	1,800.00
14 Eddie Collins	150.00	300.00
15 John Collins	60.00	120.00
16 Wilbur Cooper	60.00	120.00
17 Stan Coveleskie	100.00	200.00
18 Walton Cruise	60.00	120.00
19 William Cunningham	60.00	120.00
20 George Cutshaw	60.00	120.00
21 Jake Daubert	75.00	150.00
22 Chas.A. Deal	60.00	120.00
23 Bill Doak	60.00	120.00
24 Joe Dugan	75.00	150.00
25A Jimmy Dykes/batting	75.00	150.00
25B Jimmy Dykes/fielding	75.00	150.00
26 Red Faber	100.00	200.00
27A Chick Fewster	75.00	150.00
27B Wilson Fewster	75.00	150.00
28 Ira Flagstead	60.00	120.00
29 Art Fletcher	60.00	120.00
30 Frankie Frisch	100.00	200.00
31 Larry Gardner	60.00	120.00
32 Walter Gerber	60.00	120.00
33 Charles Glazner	60.00	120.00
34 Hank Gowdy	75.00	150.00
35 J.C. Graney	60.00	120.00
36 Tommy Griffith	60.00	120.00
37 Charlie Grimm	75.00	150.00
38 Heine Groh	75.00	150.00
39 Byron Harris	60.00	120.00
40 Sam Harris	60.00	120.00
41 Harry Heilmann	100.00	200.00
42 Claude Hendrix	60.00	120.00
43 Walter Henline	60.00	120.00
44 Chas. Hollocher	60.00	120.00
45 Harry Hooper	100.00	200.00
46 Rogers Hornsby	300.00	600.00
47 Waite Hoyt	100.00	200.00
48 Wilbert Hubbell	75.00	150.00
49 Bill Jacobson	60.00	120.00
50 Walter Johnson	400.00	800.00
51 Jimmy Johnston	60.00	120.00
52 Joe Judge	60.00	120.00
53 George Kelly/N.Y. Giants	100.00	200.00
54 Dick Kerr	75.00	150.00
55A Pete Kilduff/bending	60.00	120.00
55B Pete Kilduff/leaping	60.00	120.00
56 Larry Kopf	60.00	120.00
57 Dutch Leonard	75.00	150.00
58 Nemo Leibold	60.00	120.00
59 Walter Mails	75.00	150.00
60 Walter Maranville	100.00	200.00
61 Carl Mays	75.00	150.00
62 Lee Meadows	60.00	120.00
63 Bob Meusel	75.00	150.00
64 Emil Meusel	60.00	120.00
65 Clyde Milan	75.00	150.00
66 Earl Neale	75.00	150.00
67 Robert Nehf/(picture actually/Arthur Nehf)	75.00	150.00
68 Bernie Neis	60.00	120.00
69 Joe Oeschger	60.00	120.00
70 Robert O'Farrell	75.00	150.00
71 Ivan Olson	60.00	120.00
72 Steve O'Neill	75.00	150.00
73 Geo. Paskert	60.00	120.00
74 Roger Peckinpaugh	75.00	150.00
75 Herb Pennock	100.00	200.00
76 Cy Perkins	60.00	120.00
77 Scott Perry	60.00	120.00
78 Jeff Pfeffer	60.00	120.00
79 Val Picinich	60.00	120.00
80 Wally Pipp	75.00	150.00
81 Derrill Pratt	60.00	120.00
82 Goldie Rapp	60.00	120.00
83 Edgar Rice	100.00	200.00
84 Jimmy Ring	60.00	120.00
85 Ed Roush	100.00	200.00
86 Babe Ruth	1,100.00	2,200.00
87 Wally Schang	60.00	120.00
88 Raymond Schmandt	60.00	120.00
89 Everett Scott	75.00	150.00
90 Joe Sewell	100.00	200.00
91 Maurice Shannon	60.00	120.00
92 Bob Shawkey	75.00	150.00
93 Urban Shocker	75.00	150.00
94 George Sisler	100.00	200.00
95 Earl Smith	60.00	120.00
96 John Smith	60.00	120.00
97 Sherrod Smith	60.00	120.00
98A Frank Snyder/crouching	60.00	120.00
98B Frank Snyder/standing	60.00	120.00
99 Tris Speaker	150.00	300.00
100 Vernon Spencer	60.00	120.00
101 Casey Stengel	250.00	500.00
102A Milton Stock/fielding	60.00	120.00
102B Milton Stock/batting	60.00	120.00
103 James Vaughn	60.00	120.00
104 Robert Veach	60.00	120.00
105 Bill Wambsganss	60.00	120.00
106 Aaron Ward	60.00	120.00
107 Zach Wheat	100.00	200.00
108A George Whitted/batting	60.00	120.00
108B George Whitted/fielding	60.00	120.00
109 Fred C. Williams	75.00	150.00
110 Art Wilson	60.00	120.00
111 Ivy Wingo	60.00	120.00
112 Lawton Witt	60.00	120.00
113 Pep Young	60.00	120.00
114 Ross Young	100.00	200.00

1936 National Chicle Fine Pen Premiums R313

The 1936 Fine Pen Premiums were issued anonymously by the National Chicle Company. The set is complete at 120 cards. Each card measures approximately 3 1/4" by 5 3/8". The cards are blank backed, unnumbered and could be obtained directly from a retail outlet rather than through the mail only. Three types of cards exist. The catalog designation for this set is R313.

COMPLETE SET (120)	1,250.00	2,500.00
1 Melo Almada	15.00	30.00
2 Paul Andrews	15.00	30.00
3 Elden Auker	15.00	30.00
4 Earl Averill	30.00	60.00
5 Jim Bucher	15.00	30.00
6 Moe Berg	75.00	150.00
7 Wally Berger	25.00	50.00
8 Charles Berry	15.00	30.00
9 Ralph Birkhofer	15.00	30.00
10 Cy Blanton	15.00	30.00
11 Ossie Bluege	20.00	40.00
12 Cliff Bolton	15.00	30.00
13 Zeke Bonura	15.00	30.00
14 Thos. Bridges	20.00	40.00
15 Sam Byrd	15.00	30.00
16 Dolph Camilli	25.00	50.00
17 Bruce Campbell	15.00	30.00
18 Walter Kit Carson	15.00	30.00
19 Ben Chapman	20.00	40.00
20 Rip Collins	20.00	40.00
21 Joe Cronin	30.00	60.00
22 Frank Crosetti	25.00	50.00
23 Paul Derringer	20.00	40.00
24 Bill Dietrich	15.00	30.00
25 Carl Doyle	15.00	30.00
26 Pete Fox	15.00	30.00
27 Frankie Frisch	30.00	60.00
28 Milton Galatzer	15.00	30.00
29 Charley Gehringer	30.00	60.00
30 Charley Gelbert	15.00	30.00
31 Jose Gomez	15.00	30.00
32 Lefty Gomez	30.00	60.00
33 Goose Goslin	30.00	60.00
34 Hank Gowdy	20.00	40.00
35 Hank Greenberg	30.00	60.00
36 Lefty Grove	30.00	60.00
37 Stan Hack	20.00	40.00
38 Odell Hale	15.00	30.00
39 Wild Bill Hallahan	15.00	30.00
40 Mel Harder	20.00	40.00
41 Bucky Harris	30.00	60.00
42 Frank Higgins	15.00	30.00
43 Oral C. Hildebrand	15.00	30.00
44 Myril Hoag	15.00	30.00
45 Rogers Hornsby	50.00	100.00
46 Waite Hoyt	30.00	60.00
47 Willis G. Hudlin(2)	15.00	30.00
48 Woody Jensen (2)	15.00	30.00
49 Wm. Knickerbocker	15.00	30.00
50 Joseph Kuhel	15.00	30.00
51 Cookie Lavagetto	20.00	40.00
52 Thornton Lee	15.00	30.00
53 Red Lucas	15.00	30.00
54 Pepper Martin	25.00	50.00
55 Joe Medwick	30.00	60.00
56 Oscar Melillo	15.00	30.00
57 Buddy Myer	15.00	30.00
58 Wally Moses	15.00	30.00

59 Van L. Mungo	15.00	30.00
60 Lamar Newsom	15.00	30.00
61 Buck Newsom	25.00	50.00
62 Steve O'Neill	20.00	40.00
63 Tommie Padden	15.00	30.00
64 Babe Phillips/(sic, Phelps)	15.00	30.00
65 Bill Rogel/(sic, Rogell)	15.00	30.00
66 Schoolboy Rowe	20.00	40.00
67 Al Simmons	30.00	60.00
68 Casey Stengel MG	60.00	120.00
69 Bill Swift	15.00	30.00
70 Cecil Travis	15.00	30.00
71 Pie Traynor	30.00	60.00
72 Wm. Urbansky/(sic, Urbanski)	15.00	30.00
73 Arky Vaughan	30.00	60.00
74 Joe Vosmik	15.00	30.00
75 Honus Wagner	60.00	120.00
76 Rube Walberg	20.00	40.00
77 Bill Walker	15.00	30.00
78 Gerald Walker	15.00	30.00
79 Bill Werber	15.00	30.00
80 Sam West	15.00	30.00
81 Pinkey Whitney	15.00	30.00
82 Vernon Wiltshere/(sic, Wilshere)	15.00	30.00
83 Pep Young	15.00	30.00
84 Babe and his babes	15.00	30.00
85 Bordagaray Earnshaw	15.00	30.00
86 James Bucher and John Babich	15.00	30.00
87 B. Chapman B. Werber	15.00	30.00
88 Chicago White Sox/1936	15.00	30.00
89 Fence Busters	15.00	30.00
90 Fox Simmons Cochrane	30.00	60.00
91 G. Hartnett K. Cuyler	30.00	60.00
92 L. Gomez R. Ruffing	50.00	100.00
93 G. Hartnett L. Warneke	30.00	60.00
94 C. Mack J. McGraw	60.00	120.00
95 B. Myer C. Dressen MG	15.00	30.00
96 P. Waner L. Waner Weaver	30.00	60.00
97 Wes Ferrell Rick Ferrell	30.00	60.00
98 Nick Altrock Al Schacht	20.00	40.00
99 Big Bosses Clash Dykes safe	15.00	30.00
100 Bottomley tagging Gelbert	20.00	40.00
101 Camilli catches Jurges off first	20.00	40.00
102 CCS: Radcliffe safe Harnett catching	20.00	40.00
103 CCS: L.Sewell blocks runner at plate	15.00	30.00
104 CCS: Washington safe	15.00	30.00
105 Joe DiMaggio	250.00	500.00
106 Double Play-McQuinn to Stine	15.00	30.00
107 J. Dykes F. Crosetti	20.00	40.00
108 Glenn uses football play at plate	15.00	30.00
109 H. Greenberg B. Dickey	30.00	60.00
110 Hasset makes the out/(sic, Hassett)	15.00	30.00
111 Ernie Lombardi	30.00	60.00
112 McQuinn gets his man	15.00	30.00
113 Randy Moore hurt stealing second	15.00	30.00
114 T. Moore out at plate, Wilson catching	20.00	40.00
115 Sewell waits for ball while Clift scores	15.00	30.00
116 Talking it over	15.00	30.00
117 There she goes, CCS	15.00	30.00
118 Ump says No Cleveland vs. Detroit	15.00	30.00
119 L. Waner G. Hartnett	30.00	60.00
120 World Series 1935	30.00	60.00

1936 National Chicle Maranville Secrets R344

This paper set of 20 was issued in 1936 by the National Chicle Company. Each "card" measures 3 5/8" by 6". It carries the printing "Given only With Batter-Up Gum" on the back page. While the illustration shows the issue to be elongated. the papers were meant to be folded to create a four-page booklet. As the title implies. the set features instructional tips by Rabbit Maranville.

COMPLETE SET (20)	225.00	450.00
COMMON CARD (1-20)	12.50	25.00

1898 National Copper Plate

Measuring 9" by 12", these photos feature star players from the turn of the century. These photos were issued by National Copper Plate Co of Michigan. Since these are unnumbered, we have sequenced them in alphabetical order. There might be more photos known so any additions to this checklist is appreciated.

COMPLETE SET	3,000.00	6,000.00
1 Cap Anson	600.00	1,200.00
2 Bob Becker	200.00	400.00
3 Tom Dowd	200.00	400.00
4 George Gillpatrick	200.00	400.00
5 Jot Goar	200.00	400.00
6 Mike Griffin	200.00	400.00
7 Clark Griffith	400.00	800.00
8 Bill Joyce	200.00	400.00
9 John McGraw	600.00	1,200.00
10 Kid Nichols	400.00	800.00
11 Chief Zimmer	200.00	400.00

1913 National Game WG5

These cards were distributed as part of a baseball game produced in 1913 as indicated by the patent date on the backs of the cards. The cards each measure approximately 2 7/16" by 3 7/16" and have rounded corners. The card fronts show a sepia photo of the player, his name, his team, and the game outcome associated with that particular card. The card backs are all the same, each showing an ornate red and white design with "The National Game" and "Baseball" right in the middle all surrounded by a thick white outer border. Since the cards are unnumbered, they are listed below in alphabetical order. Some of the card photos are oriented horizontally (HOR).

COMPLETE SET (45)	2,000.00	4,000.00
COMMON ACTION CARD	10.00	25.00
1 Grover Alexander	300.00	600.00
2 Frank Baker	50.00	100.00
3 Chief Bender	40.00	80.00
4 Bob Bescher	15.00	40.00
5 Joe Birmingham	15.00	40.00
6 Roger Bresnahan	50.00	100.00
7 Nixey Callahan	15.00	40.00
8 Frank Chance	50.00	100.00
9 Hal Chase	20.00	50.00
10 Fred Clarke	40.00	80.00
11 Ty Cobb	300.00	600.00
12 Sam Crawford	50.00	100.00
13 Bill Dahlen	15.00	40.00
14 Jake Daubert	15.00	40.00
15 Red Dooin	15.00	40.00
16 Johnny Evers	50.00	100.00
17 Vean Gregg	15.00	40.00
18 Clark Griffith MG	40.00	80.00
19 Dick Hoblitzel	15.00	40.00
20 Miller Huggins	40.00	80.00
21 Joe Jackson	750.00	1,500.00
22 Hugh Jennings MG	40.00	80.00
23 Walter Johnson	100.00	200.00
24 Ed Konetchy	15.00	40.00
25 Nap Lajoie	60.00	120.00
26 Connie Mack MG	50.00	100.00
27 Rube Marquard	40.00	80.00
28 Christy Mathewson	100.00	200.00
29 John McGraw MG	50.00	100.00
30 Larry McLean	15.00	40.00
31 Clyde Milan	15.00	40.00
32 Marty O'Toole	15.00	40.00
33 Nap Rucker	15.00	40.00
34 Tris Speaker	60.00	120.00
35 Jake Stahl	15.00	40.00
36 George Stallings MG	15.00	40.00
37 George Stovall	15.00	40.00
38 Bill Sweeney	15.00	40.00
39 Joe Tinker	50.00	100.00
40 Honus Wagner	300.00	600.00
41 Ed Walsh	50.00	100.00
42 Joe Wood	40.00	80.00
43 Cy Young	125.00	250.00
44 Batter Swinging Looking forward		
45 Batter Swinging Looking back		
46 Play at the plate		
47 Runner looking back		
48 Sliding Fielder at base		
49 Ty Cobb Sliding		
50 Slider Hand on base		
51 Sliding at the plate Ump left		
52 Sliding at the plate Ump right		
53 Rules Card		
54 Score Card		

1952 National Tea Labels

The bread labels in this set are often called "Red Borders" because of their distinctive trim. Each label measures 2 3/4" by 2 11/16". Issued with the bakery products of the National Tea Company, there are thought to be 48 different labels in the set. The six missing labels are thought to consist of two Yankees, two Indians and two Red Sox -- so that there would be exactly three representatives from each of the 16 teams. The labels are also known as the "Bread For Health" set and may have included an album. This set is the toughest of the bread label sets listed. These labels are unnumbered so we have sequenced them in alphabetical order. The catalog designation is D290-2.

COMPLETE SET (42)	5,500.00	11,000.00
1 Gene Bearden	175.00	350.00
2 Yogi Berra	300.00	600.00
3 Lou Brissie	175.00	350.00
4 Sam Chapman	175.00	350.00
5 Chuck Diering	175.00	350.00
6 Dom DiMaggio	300.00	600.00
7 Hank Edwards	175.00	350.00
8 Del Ennis	200.00	400.00
9 Ferris Fain	175.00	350.00
10 Howie Fox	175.00	350.00
11 Sid Gordon	200.00	400.00
12 Johhny Groth	175.00	350.00
13 Granny Hamner	175.00	350.00
14 Sam Jones	175.00	350.00
15 Howie Judson	175.00	350.00
16 Sherm Lollar	175.00	350.00
17 Clarence Marshall	175.00	350.00
18 Don Mueller	175.00	350.00
19 Danny Murtaugh	200.00	400.00
20 Dave Philley	175.00	350.00
21 Jerry Priddy	175.00	350.00
22 Bill Rigney	200.00	400.00
23 Robin Roberts	300.00	600.00
24 Eddie Robinson	175.00	350.00
25 Preacher Roe	250.00	500.00
26 Stan Rojek	175.00	350.00
27 Al Rosen	250.00	500.00
28 Bob Rush	175.00	350.00
29 Hank Sauer	200.00	400.00
30 Johnny Schmitz	175.00	350.00
31 Enos Slaughter	300.00	600.00
32 Duke Snider	600.00	1,200.00
33 Warren Spahn	350.00	700.00
34 Gerry Staley	175.00	350.00
35 Virgil Stallcup	175.00	350.00
36 George Stirnweiss	175.00	350.00
37 Earl Torgeson	175.00	350.00
38 Dizzy Trout	200.00	400.00
39 Mickey Vernon	250.00	500.00
40 Wally Westlake	175.00	350.00
41 Johnny Wyrostek	175.00	350.00
42 Eddie Yost	200.00	400.00

1922 Neilson's Chocolates V61

The 1922 Neilson's Chocolate set, titled "Big League Baseball Stars", contains 120 cards and is essentially a reproduction of the E120 set. The cards measure approximately 2" by 3 1/4". The fronts feature oval-shaped black-and-white player photos with ornamented borders. The player's name, position and team also appear on the front. The backs give information about this set and carry an ad for Neilson's chocolate. There are two versions of this set: a numbered paper issue and an unnumbered cardboard issue. Cards of the unnumbered cardboard issue are worth approximately 50 percent more than the values listed in the checklist below.

COMPLETE SET (120)	4,250.00	8,500.00
1 George Burns	60.00	120.00
2 John Tobin	50.00	100.00
3 Tom Zachary	60.00	120.00
4 Joe Bush	60.00	120.00
5 Lu Blue	50.00	100.00
6 Tillie Walker	50.00	100.00
7 Carl Mays	60.00	120.00
8 Goose Goslin	100.00	200.00
9 Ed Rommel	60.00	120.00
10 Charles Robertson	50.00	100.00
11 Ralph Perkins	50.00	100.00
12 Joe Sewell	100.00	200.00
13 Harry Hooper	100.00	200.00
14 Red Faber	100.00	200.00
15 Bibb Falk	50.00	100.00
16 George Uhle	60.00	120.00
17 Emory Rigney	50.00	100.00
18 George Dauss	50.00	100.00
19 Herman Pillette	50.00	100.00
20 Wally Schang	60.00	120.00
21 Lawrence Woodall	50.00	100.00
22 Steve O'Neill	60.00	120.00
23 Bing Miller	50.00	100.00
24 Sylvester Johnson	50.00	100.00
25 Henry Severeid	50.00	100.00
26 Dave Danforth	50.00	100.00
27 Harry Heilmann	100.00	200.00
28 Bert Cole	50.00	100.00
29 Eddie Collins	100.00	200.00
30 Ty Cobb	1,500.00	3,000.00
31 Bill Wambsganss	60.00	120.00
32 George Sisler	100.00	200.00
33 Bob Veach	50.00	100.00
34 Earl Sheely	50.00	100.00
35 Pat Collins	50.00	100.00
36 Frank Davis	50.00	100.00
37 Babe Ruth	2,500.00	5,000.00
38 Bryan Harris	50.00	100.00
39 Bob Shawkey	75.00	150.00
40 Urban Shocker	60.00	120.00
41 Martin McManus	50.00	100.00
42 Clark Pittenger	50.00	100.00
43 Sam Jones	60.00	120.00
44 Waite Hoyt	100.00	200.00
45 Johnny Mostil	50.00	100.00
46 Mike Menosky	50.00	100.00
47 Walter Johnson	500.00	1,000.00
48 Wally Pipp	60.00	120.00
49 Walter Gerber	50.00	100.00
50 Ed Gharrity	50.00	100.00
51 Frank Ellerbe	50.00	100.00
52 Kenneth Williams	75.00	150.00
53 Joe Hauser	60.00	120.00
54 Carson Bigbee	50.00	100.00
55 Irish Meusel	50.00	100.00
56 Milton Stock	50.00	100.00
57 Wilbur Cooper	60.00	120.00
58 Tom Griffith	50.00	100.00
59 Butch Henline	50.00	100.00
60 Bubbles Hargrave	50.00	100.00
61 Russel Wrightstone	50.00	100.00
62 Frankie Frisch	100.00	200.00
63 Frank Parkinson	50.00	100.00
64 Walter Ruether	60.00	120.00
65 Bill Doak	50.00	100.00
66 Marty Callaghan	50.00	100.00
67 Sammy Bohne	50.00	100.00
68 Earl Hamilton	50.00	100.00
69 Grover Alexander	200.00	400.00
70 George Burns	50.00	100.00
71 Max Carey	100.00	200.00
72 Adolph Luque	75.00	150.00
73 Dave Bancroft	100.00	200.00
74 Vic Aldridge	50.00	100.00
75 Jack Smith	50.00	100.00
76 Bob O'Farrell	60.00	120.00
77 Pete Donohue	50.00	100.00
78 Babe Pinelli	60.00	120.00
79 Ed Roush	100.00	200.00
80 Norman Boeckel	50.00	100.00
81 Rogers Hornsby	300.00	600.00
82 George Toporcer	50.00	100.00
83 Ivy Wingo	50.00	100.00
84 Virgil Cheeves	50.00	100.00
85 Vern Clemons	50.00	100.00
86 Lawrence Miller	50.00	100.00
87 Johnny Kelleher	50.00	100.00
88 Heinie Groh	60.00	120.00
89 Burleigh Grimes	100.00	200.00
90 Rabbit Maranville	100.00	200.00
91 Babe Adams	60.00	120.00
92 Lee King	50.00	100.00
93 Art Nehf	60.00	120.00
94 Frank Snyder	50.00	100.00
95 Raymond Powell	50.00	100.00
96 Wilbur Hubbell	50.00	100.00
97 Leon Cadore	50.00	100.00
98 Joe Oeschger	50.00	100.00
99 Jake Daubert	50.00	100.00
100 Will Sherdel	50.00	100.00
101 Hank DeBerry	50.00	100.00
102 Johnny Lavan	50.00	100.00
103 Jesse Haines	100.00	200.00
104 Joe Rapp	50.00	100.00
105 Oscar Ray Grimes	50.00	100.00
106 Ross Youngs	100.00	200.00
107 Art Fletcher	50.00	100.00
108 Clyde Barnhart	50.00	100.00
109 Pat Duncan	50.00	100.00
110 Charlie Hollocher	50.00	100.00
111 Horace Ford	50.00	100.00
112 Bill Cunningham	50.00	100.00
113 Walter Schmidt	50.00	100.00
114 Joe Schultz	50.00	100.00
115 John Morrison	50.00	100.00
116 Jimmy Caveney	50.00	100.00
117 Zach Wheat	100.00	200.00
118 Cy Williams	60.00	120.00
119 George Kelly	100.00	200.00
120 Jimmy Ring	50.00	100.00

1895 Newsboy N566

Newsboy Cut Plug was a tobacco brand by the National Tobacco Works of New York. The cabinet cards associated with this brand were offered as premiums in exchange for coupons or tags found in or on the packages. They were believed to have been issued around 1895. Although a number 841 has been seen, this series-which also contains actresses-has never been completely checklisted, and its exact length is not known. At this time, only 12 baseball players have been discovered. We have checklisted only the baseball players and priced them.

COMPLETE SET (13)	6,000.00	15,000.00
174 W.H. Murphy	1,000.00	2,000.00
175 Amos Rusie	4,000.00	8,000.00
176 Michael Tiernan	1,000.00	2,000.00
177 Eddie Burke	1,000.00	2,000.00
178 Jack Doyle	1,000.00	2,000.00
179 Shorty Fuller	1,000.00	2,000.00
180 George van Haltren	1,000.00	2,000.00
181 Dave Foutz	1,000.00	2,000.00
182 Jouett Meekin	1,000.00	2,000.00
201 W.H. (Dad) Clark/(street clothes)	1,000.00	2,000.00
202 Parke Wilson/(street clothes)	1,000.00	2,000.00
586 John M. Ward portrait arms folded	2,000.00	4,000.00
587 John M. Ward standing full length	2,000.00	4,000.00

1969 New York Boy Scouts

This set of the New York Mets and Yankees, which measures 2 1/2" by 3 1/2" is believed to be a regional Long Island Boy Scout release and features black-and-white player photos with facsimile autographs. The backs carry the words, "Boy power-Manpower" and "Go Team for 1969." The following checklist may be incomplete and known additions are welcomed. Since these cards are unnumbered, we have sequenced them in alphabetical order.

COMPLETE SET	200.00	400.00
1 Tommie Agee	40.00	80.00
2 Bud Harrelson	40.00	80.00
3 Cleon Jones	40.00	80.00
4 Joe Pepitone	40.00	80.00
5 Tom Seaver	100.00	200.00
6 Art Shamsky	30.00	60.00
7 Mel Stottlemyre	40.00	80.00
8 Ron Swoboda	40.00	80.00

1954 New York Journal American

The cards in this 59-card set measure approximately 2" by 4". The 1954 New York Journal American set contains black and white, unnumbered cards issued in conjunction with the newspaper. News stands were given boxes of cards to be distributed with purchases and each card had a serial number for redemption in the contest. The set spotlights New York teams only and carries game schedules on the reverse. The cards have been assigned numbers in the listing below alphabetically within team so that Brooklyn Dodgers are 1-19, New York Giants are 20-39, and New York Yankees are 40-59. There is speculation that a 20th Dodger card may exist. The catalog designation for this set is M127.

COMPLETE SET (59)	1,250.00	2,500.00
1 Joe Black	7.50	15.00
2 Roy Campanella	60.00	120.00
3 Billy Cox	7.50	15.00
4 Carl Erskine	12.50	25.00
5 Carl Furillo	12.50	25.00
6 Jim Gilliam	12.50	25.00
7 Gil Hodges	40.00	80.00
8 Jim Hughes	7.50	15.00
9 Clem Labine	10.00	20.00
10 Billy Loes	7.50	15.00
11 Russ Meyer	7.50	15.00
12 Don Newcombe	12.50	25.00
13 Ervin Palica	7.50	15.00
14 Pee Wee Reese	60.00	120.00
15 Jackie Robinson	125.00	250.00
16 Preacher Roe	12.50	25.00
17 George Shuba	7.50	15.00
18 Duke Snider	75.00	150.00
19 Dick Williams	10.00	20.00
20 John Antonelli	7.50	15.00
21 Alvin Dark	10.00	20.00
22 Marv Grissom	7.50	15.00
23 Ruben Gomez	7.50	15.00
24 Jim Hearn	7.50	15.00
25 Bobby Hofman	7.50	15.00
26 Monte Irvin	25.00	50.00
27 Larry Jansen	7.50	15.00
28 Ray Katt	7.50	15.00
29 Don Liddle	7.50	15.00
30 Whitey Lockman	10.00	20.00
31 Sal Maglie	12.50	25.00
32 Willie Mays	150.00	300.00
33 Don Mueller	7.50	15.00
34 Dusty Rhodes	7.50	15.00
35 Hank Thompson	7.50	15.00
36 Wes Westrum	7.50	15.00
37 Hoyt Wilhelm	25.00	50.00
38 Davey Williams	7.50	15.00
39 Al Worthington	7.50	15.00
40 Hank Bauer	12.50	25.00
41 Yogi Berra	75.00	150.00
42 Harry Byrd	7.50	15.00
43 Andy Carey	7.50	15.00
44 Jerry Coleman	10.00	20.00
45 Joe Collins	7.50	15.00
46 Whitey Ford	50.00	100.00
47 Steve Kraly	7.50	15.00
48 Bob Kuzava	7.50	15.00
49 Frank Leja	7.50	15.00
50 Ed Lopat	12.50	25.00
51 Mickey Mantle	400.00	800.00
52 Gil McDougald	12.50	25.00
53 Bill Miller	7.50	15.00
54 Tom Morgan	7.50	15.00
55 Irv Noren	7.50	15.00
56 Allie Reynolds	12.50	25.00
57 Phil Rizzuto	40.00	80.00
58 Eddie Robinson	7.50	15.00
59 Gene Woodling	10.00	20.00

1973 New York Sunday News M138

These 22 newspaper cutouts feature color caricatures that measure 11 1/4" X 14 3/4". The complete page featuring both players measures 22.5" by 29.5". These are printed on newsprint and are unnumbered. Cards feature Mets and Yankees players. Two cards (One Yankee and one Met) were issued every Sunday from 6/17/73 through 8/26/73 in Cartoon section centerfold. Each pair of players played the same position.

COMPLETE SET (22)	75.00	150.00
1 Yogi Berra MG	5.00	12.00
2 Ralph Houk MG	2.50	6.00
3 Tom Seaver	6.00	15.00
4 Mel Stottlemyre	2.50	6.00
5 Ron Blomberg	2.00	5.00
6 John Milner	2.00	5.00
7 Horace Clarke	2.00	5.00
8 Felix Millan	2.00	5.00
9 Bud Harrelson	2.00	5.00
10 Gene Michael	2.00	5.00
11 Jim Fregosi	2.00	5.00
12 Graig Nettles	3.00	8.00
13 Jerry Grote	2.50	6.00
14 Thurman Munson	5.00	12.00
15 Cleon Jones	2.00	5.00
16 Roy White	2.50	6.00
17 Willie Mays	8.00	20.00
18 Bobby Murcer	3.00	8.00
19 Matty Alou	2.50	6.00
20 Rusty Staub	3.00	8.00
21 Sparky Lyle	2.50	6.00
22 Tug McGraw	4.00	10.00

1974 New York News This Day in Sports

These cards are newspaper clippings of drawings by Hollreiser and are accompanied by textual description highlighting a player's unique sports feat. Cards are approximately 2" X 4 1/4". These are multisport cards and aranged in chronological order.

COMPLETE SET	50.00	120.00
1 Johnny Bench Yogi Berra June 2, 1972; 1951	2.00	4.00
3 Ted Williams 13-Jun-57	2.00	4.00
5 Ezzard Charles Sandy Koufax June 22, 1949; 1959	2.00	4.00
6 Bobby Murcer 24-Jun-70	1.00	2.00
7 Gil Hodges Ralph Kiner June 25, 1949; 1950	2.00	4.00
9 Dizzy Dean 1-Jul-34	1.25	2.50
10 Billie Jean King Carl Hubbell July 2, 1966; 1933	1.25	2.50
11 Yogi Berra 3-Jul-57	1.25	2.50
12 Arky Vaughan Ted Williams July 8, 1941	2.00	4.00
13 Tom Seaver July 9, 1969; 1970	2.00	4.00
14 Willie Stargell 11-Jul-73	1.25	2.50
15 Nolan Ryan 15-Jul-73	5.00	10.00
17 Casey Stengel July 26, 1916; 1955	2.00	4.00
18 Mickey Mantle Whitey Ford July 29, 1966; 1955	5.00	10.00
19 Robin Roberts Aug. 19, 1955	1.25	2.50
20 Lou Gehrig Aug. 21, 1935; 1937	2.00	4.00
21 Warren Spahn Roy Face Aug. 30. 1960; 1959	1.25	2.50
22 George Sisler Pete Rose Sept. 4, 1920; 1973	1.50	3.00
23 Sal Maglie Tommy Henrich Sept. 9, 1950; 1941	1.00	2.00
24 Hank Aaron Sept. 21, 1958	2.00	4.00
26 Dick Sisler Oct. 1, 1950	1.00	2.00
28 Pepper Martin Yogi Berra Oct. 7, 1931; 1961	2.00	4.00
29 Dizzy Dean Daffy Dean Oct. 9, 1934	1.25	2.50
30 Walter Johnson Oct. 11, 1925	1.25	2.50

1916 New York World Advertisements

These 9" by 4" card features four New York Area players. The cards have a player portrait and the rest of the card is devoted to advertising information about the New York World newspaper. Since the cards are unnumbered we have sequenced them in alphabetical order.

COMPLETE SET	250.00	800.00
1 Frank Baker	500.00	1,000.00
2 Dave Bancroft	500.00	1,000.00
3 Jake Daubert	500.00	1,000.00
4 Buck Herzog	300.00	600.00
5 Dave Robertson	250.00	500.00

1953 Northland Bread Labels

This 32-label set features two players from each major league team and is one of the popular "Bread For Energy" sets. Each bread label measures 2 11/16" by 2 11/16". Although the labels are printed in black and white, the 1953 Northland Bread set includes a "Baseball Stars" album which provides additional information concerning "Baseball Immortals" and "Baseball Tips." These labels are unnumbered so we have checklisted them in alphabetical order. The amended catalog designation is D290-3A.

COMPLETE SET (32)	3,500.00	7,000.00
1 Cal Abrams	150.00	300.00
2 Richie Ashburn	250.00	500.00
3 Gus Bell	175.00	350.00
4 Jim Busby	150.00	300.00
5 Clint Courtney	150.00	300.00
6 Billy Cox	150.00	300.00
7 Jim Dyck	150.00	300.00
8 Nellie Fox	350.00	700.00
9 Sid Gordon	150.00	300.00
10 Warren Hacker	150.00	300.00
11 Jim Hearn	150.00	300.00
12 Fred Hutchinson	150.00	300.00
13 Monte Irvin	225.00	450.00
14 Jackie Jensen	175.00	350.00
15 Ted Kluszewski	225.00	450.00
16 Bob Lemon	225.00	450.00
17 Mickey McDermott	150.00	300.00
18 Minnie Minoso	175.00	350.00
19 Johnny Mize	225.00	450.00
20 Mel Parnell	150.00	300.00
21 Howie Pollet	150.00	300.00
22 Jerry Priddy	150.00	300.00
23 Allie Reynolds	175.00	350.00
24 Preacher Roe	175.00	350.00
25 Al Rosen	175.00	350.00
26 Connie Ryan	150.00	300.00
27 Hank Sauer	175.00	350.00
28 Red Schoendienst	225.00	450.00
29 Bobby Shantz	175.00	350.00
30 Enos Slaughter	225.00	450.00
31 Warren Spahn	350.00	700.00
32 Gus Zernial	175.00	350.00

1910 Notebook Covers

These eight cards are similar in size and appearance to the T-3 set. These cards measure 5" by 7 1/2". The cards are in full colors with red borders. We have checklisted the set in alphabetical order.

COMPLETE SET	2,000.00	4,000.00
1 Roger Breshnahan	200.00	400.00
2 Ty Cobb	750.00	1,500.00
3 Eddie Collins	300.00	600.00
4 Johnny Evers	250.00	500.00
5 Clark Griffith	200.00	400.00
6 Nap Lajoie	300.00	600.00
7 Christy Mathewson	400.00	800.00
8 Honus Wagner	400.00	800.00

1960 Nu-Card Hi-Lites

The cards in this 72-card set measure approximately 3 1/4" by 5 3/8". In 1960, the Nu-Card Company introduced its Baseball Hi-Lites set of newspaper style cards. Each card singled out an individual baseball achievement with a picture and story. The reverses contain a baseball quiz. Cards 1-18 are more valuable if found printed totally in black on the front; these are copy-righted CVC as opposed to the NCI designation found on the red and black printed fronts.

COMPLETE SET (72)	400.00	800.00
1 Babe Ruth Hits 3 Homers In A Series Game	20.00	50.00
2 Johnny Podres Pitching Wins Series	1.50	4.00
3 Bill Bevans Pitches No-Hitter, Almost	1.50	4.00
4 Box Score Devised By Reporter	1.50	4.00
5 Johnny VanderMeer Pitches Two No Hitters	1.50	4.00
6 Indians Take Bums	1.50	4.00
7 Joe DiMaggio Comes Thru	15.00	40.00
8 Christy Mathewson Pitches Three WS Shutouts	2.50	6.00
9 Harvey Haddix Pitches 12 Perfect Innings	1.50	4.00
10 Bobby Thomson Homer Sinks Dodgers	5.00	12.00
11 Carl Hubbell Strikes Out 5 A.L. Stars	2.50	6.00
12 Pickoff Ends Series	1.50	4.00
13 Cards Take Series From Yanks	1.50	4.00
14 Dizzy And Daffy Dean Win Series	2.50	6.00
15 Mickey Owen Drops Third Strike	1.50	4.00
16 Babe Ruth Calls Shot	20.00	50.00
17 Fred Merkle Pulls Boner	2.00	5.00
18 Don Larsen Hurls Perfect W.S. Game	2.50	6.00
19 Mickey Cochrane Bean Ball Ends Career	2.00	5.00
20 Ernie Banks Belts 47 Homers Earns MVP	8.00	20.00
21 Stan Musial Hits 5 Homers in One Day	8.00	20.00
22 Mickey Mantle Hits Longest Homer	30.00	60.00
23 Roy Sievers Captures Home Run Title	1.50	4.00
24 Lou Gehrig/2130 Consecutive Game Record Ends	15.00	40.00
25 Red Schoendienst Key Player Braves Pennant	2.00	5.00
26 Midget Pinch-Hits For St. Louis	2.00	5.00
27 Willie Mays Makes Greatest Catch	12.50	30.00
28 Yogi Berra Homer Puts Yanks In 1st	6.00	15.00
29 Roy Campanella NL MVP	6.00	15.00
30 Bob Turley Hurls Yankees To WS Champions	1.50	4.00
31 Dodgers Take Series From Sox in Six	1.50	4.00
32 Carl Furillo Hero as Dodgers Beat Chicago in 3rd	1.50	4.00
33 Joe Adcock Gets 4 Homers And A Double	1.50	4.00
34 Bill Dickey Chosen All-Star Catcher	2.00	5.00
35 Lew Burdette Beats Yanks In Three World Series G	1.50	4.00
36 Umpires Clear White Sox Bench	1.50	4.00
37 Pee Wee Reese	5.00	12.00
38 Joe DiMaggio Hits In 56 Straight	15.00	40.00
39 Ted Williams Hits .406 For Season	20.00	50.00
40 Walter Johnson Pitches 56 Straight	3.00	8.00
41 Gil Hodges Hits 4 Home Runs In Nite Game	2.00	5.00
42 Hank Greenberg Returns to Tigers From Army	2.50	6.00
43 Ty Cobb	8.00	20.00
44 Robin Roberts Wins 28 Games	2.00	5.00
45 Phil Rizzuto Two Runs Save 1st Place	3.00	8.00
46 Tigers Beat Out Senators For Pennant	1.50	4.00
47 Babe Ruth Hits 60th Home Run	20.00	50.00
48 Cy Young Honored	2.00	5.00
49 Harmon Killebrew Starts Spring Training	5.00	12.00
50 Mickey Mantle Hits Longest Homer at Stadium	20.00	50.00
51 Braves Take Pennant	1.50	4.00
52 Ted Williams Hero Of All-Star Game	15.00	40.00
53 Jackie Robinson Saves Dodgers For Play-off Serie	15.00	40.00
54 Fred Snodgrass Muffs Fly	1.50	4.00
55 Duke Snider Belts 2 Homers, Ties Record	8.00	20.00
56 Giants Win 26 Straight	1.50	4.00
57 Ted Kluszewski Stars In 1st Series Win	3.00	8.00
58 Mel Ott Walks 5 Times In Single Game	2.00	5.00
59 Harvey Kuenn Takes A.L. Batting Title	1.50	4.00
60 Bob Feller Hurls 3rd No-Hitter of Career	3.00	8.00
61 Yankees Champs Again	1.50	4.00
62 Hank Aaron Bat Beats Yankees In Series	8.00	20.00
63 Warren Spahn Beats Yanks in W.S.	3.00	8.00
64 Ump's Wrong Call Helps Dodgers Beat Yanks	1.50	4.00
65 Al Kaline Hits 3 Homers Two In Same Inning	5.00	12.00
66 Bob Allison Named AL ROY	1.50	4.00
67 Willie McCovey Blasts Way Into Giant Lineup	3.00	8.00
68 Rocky Colavito Hits 4 Homers in One Game	8.00	20.00
69 Carl Erskine Sets Strike Out Record in World Ser	1.50	4.00
70 Sal Maglie Pitches No-Hit Game	1.50	4.00
71 Early Wynn Victory Crushes Yanks	2.00	5.00
72 Nellie Fox AL MVP	8.00	20.00

1961 Nu-Card Scoops

The cards in this 80-card set measure 2 1/2" by 3 1/2". This series depicts great moments in the history of individual ballplayers. Each card is designed as a miniature newspaper front-page, complete with data and picture. Both the number (401-480) and title are printed in red on the obverse, and the story is found on the back. An album was issued to hold the set. The set has been illegally reprinted, which has served to suppress the demand for the originals as well as the reprints.

COMPLETE SET (80)	200.00	400.00
401 Jim Gentile	.60	1.50
402 Warren Spahn/(No-hitter)	1.25	3.00
403 Bill Mazeroski	.75	2.00
404 Willie Mays:/(Three triples)	6.00	15.00
405 Woodie Held	.60	1.50
406 Vern Law	.60	1.50
407 Pete Runnels	.60	1.50
408 Lew Burdette/(No-hitter)	.60	1.50
409 Dick Stuart	.60	1.50
410 Don Cardwell	.60	1.50
411 Camilo Pascual	.60	1.50
412 Eddie Mathews	1.25	3.00
413 Dick Groat	.60	1.50
414 Gene Autry OWN	2.00	5.00
415 Bobby Richardson	.75	2.00
416 Roger Maris	4.00	10.00
417 Fred Merkle	.60	1.50
418 Don Larsen	.60	1.50
419 Mickey Cochrane	.75	2.00
420 Ernie Banks	1.50	4.00
421 Stan Musial	4.00	10.00
422 Mickey Mantle/(Longest homer)	12.50	30.00
423 Roy Sievers	.60	1.50
424 Lou Gehrig	8.00	20.00
425 Red Schoendienst	.75	2.00
426 Eddie Gaedel	1.25	3.00
427 Willie Mays/(Greatest catch)	8.00	20.00
428 Jackie Robinson	8.00	20.00
429 Roy Campanella	4.00	10.00
430 Bob Turley	.60	1.50
431 Larry Sherry	.60	1.50
432 Carl Furillo	.75	2.00
433 Joe Adcock	.60	1.50
434 Bill Dickey	.75	2.00
435 Lew Burdette 3 wins	.60	1.50

436 Umpire Clears Bench .60 1.50
437 Pee Wee Reese 1.25 3.00
438 Joe DiMaggio/(56 Game Hit Streak) 8.00 20.00
439 Ted Williams/(Hits .406) 8.00 20.00
440 Walter Johnson 1.25 3.00
441 Gil Hodges .75 2.00
442 Hank Greenberg 1.25 3.00
443 Ty Cobb 6.00 15.00
444 Robin Roberts 1.25 3.00
445 Phil Rizzuto 1.25 3.00
446 Hal Newhouser 1.25 3.00
447 Babe Ruth 60th Homer 15.00 40.00
448 Cy Young 1.25 3.00
449 Harmon Killebrew 1.25 3.00
450 Mickey Mantle/(Longest homer) 15.00 40.00
451 Braves Take Pennant .60 1.50
452 Ted Williams/(All-Star Hero) 8.00 20.00
453 Yogi Berra 4.00 10.00
454 Fred Snodgrass .60 1.50
455 Babe Ruth 3 Homers 12.50 30.00
456 Giants 26 Game Streak .60 1.50
457 Ted Kluszewski .60 1.50
458 Mel Ott .75 2.00
459 Harvey Kuenn .60 1.50
460 Bob Feller 1.50 4.00
461 Casey Stengel 1.25 3.00
462 Hank Aaron 8.00 20.00
463 Spahn Beats Yanks .75 2.00
464 Ump's Wrong Call .60 1.50
465 Al Kaline 1.50 4.00
466 Bob Allison .60 1.50
467 Joe DiMaggio/(Four Homers) 8.00 20.00
468 Rocky Colavito 1.25 3.00
469 Carl Erskine .60 1.50
470 Sal Maglie .60 1.50
471 Early Wynn .75 2.00
472 Nellie Fox 1.00 2.50
473 Marty Marion .60 1.50
474 Johnny Podres .60 1.50
475 Mickey Owen .60 1.50
476 Dean Brothers/(Dizzy and Daffy) 1.00 2.50
477 Christy Mathewson 1.25 3.00
478 Harvey Haddix .60 1.50
479 Carl Hubbell .75 2.00
480 Bobby Thomson .75 2.00

1937 O-Pee-Chee Batter Ups V300

The cards in this 40-card set measure approximately 2 3/8" by 2 7/8". The fronts feature black-and-white die-cut player photos against a ballpark background with small players. The backs carry a short biography and career summary in English and French. The set is peculiar in that card numbering begins with 101. Cards without tops have greatly reduced value. The small ballplayer designs on the obverses are similar to those used on the 1934 American Goudey cards.

COMPLETE SET (40) 10,000.00 20,000.00
101 John Lewis 125.00 250.00
102 Jack Hayes 125.00 250.00
103 Earl Averill 250.00 500.00
104 Harland Clift 125.00 250.00
105 Beau Bell 125.00 250.00
106 Jimmie Foxx 750.00 1,500.00
107 Hank Greenberg 750.00 1,500.00
108 George Selkirk 150.00 300.00
109 Wally Moses 150.00 300.00
110 Gerry Walker 125.00 250.00
111 Goose Goslin 250.00 500.00
112 Charlie Gehringer 500.00 1,000.00
113 Hal Trosky 125.00 250.00
114 Buddy Myer 125.00 250.00
115 Luke Appling 250.00 500.00
116 Zeke Bonura 125.00 250.00
117 Tony Lazzeri 250.00 500.00
118 Joe DiMaggio 5,000.00 10,000.00
119 Bill Dickey 600.00 1,200.00
120 Bob Feller 1,500.00 3,000.00
121 Harry Kelley 125.00 250.00
122 Johnny Allen 150.00 300.00
123 Bob Johnson 150.00 300.00
124 Joe Cronin 250.00 500.00
125 Rip Radcliff 125.00 250.00
126 Cecil Travis 150.00 300.00
127 Joe Kuhel 125.00 250.00
128 Odell Hale 125.00 250.00
129 Sam West 125.00 250.00
130 Ben Chapman 150.00 300.00
131 Monte Pearson 125.00 250.00
132 Rick Ferrell 250.00 500.00
133 Tommy Bridges 150.00 300.00
134 Schoolboy Rowe 150.00 300.00
135 Vernon Kennedy 125.00 250.00
136 Red Ruffing 250.00 500.00
137 Lefty Grove 600.00 1,200.00
138 Wes Ferrell 200.00 400.00
139 Buck Newsom 200.00 400.00
140 Rogers Hornsby 1,000.00 2,000.00

1965 O-Pee-Chee

The cards in this 283-card set measure the standard size. This set is essentially the same as the regular 1965 Topps set, except that the words "Printed in Canada" appear on the bottom of the back. On a white border, the fronts feature color player photos with rounded corners. The team name appears within a pennant design below the photo. The player's name and position are also printed on the front. On a blue background, the horizontal backs carry player biography and statistics on a gray card stock. Remember the prices below apply only to the O-Pee- Chee cards -- NOT to the 1965 Topps cards which are much more plentiful. Notable Rookie Cards include Bert Campaneris, Denny McLain, Joe Morgan and Luis Tiant.

COMPLETE SET (283) 1,250.00 2,500.00
COMMON PLAYER (1-198) 1.50 4.00
COMMON PLAYER (199-283) 2.50 6.00
1 Oliva 12.50 30.00
Howard
Brooks LL !
2 Clemente 15.00 40.00
Aaron
Carty LL
3 Kill 40.00 80.00
Mantle
Powell LL
4 Mays 10.00 25.00
Will
Cepeda
LL
5 Brooks 30.00 60.00
Kill
Mantle
LL
6 Boyer 8.00 20.00
Mays
Santo LL
7 Dean Chance 4.00 10.00
Joel Horlen LL
8 Koufax 12.50 30.00
Drysdale LL
9 AL Pitching Leaders 4.00 10.00
Dean Chance
Gary Peters
Dav
10 NL Pitching Leaders 4.00 10.00
Larry Jackson
Ray Sadecki
J
11 AL Strikeout Leaders 4.00 10.00
Al Downing
Dean Chance
Cam
12 Veale 4.00 10.00
Drysdale
Gibson LL
13 Pedro Ramos 2.50 6.00
14 Len Gabrielson 1.50 4.00
15 Robin Roberts 6.00 15.00
16 Joe Morgan RC DP ! 50.00 100.00
17 John Romano 1.50 4.00
18 Bill McCool 1.50 4.00
19 Gates Brown 2.50 6.00
20 Jim Bunning 6.00 15.00
21 Don Blasingame 1.50 4.00
22 Charlie Smith 1.50 4.00
23 Bob Tiefenauer 1.50 4.00
24 Twins Team 4.00 10.00
25 Al McBean 1.50 4.00
26 Bob Knoop 1.50 4.00
27 Dick Bertell 1.50 4.00
28 Barney Schultz 1.50 4.00
29 Felix Mantilla 1.50 4.00
30 Jim Bouton 4.00 10.00
31 Mike White 1.50 4.00
32 Herman Franks MG 1.50 4.00
33 Jackie Brandt 1.50 4.00
34 Cal Koonce 1.50 4.00
35 Ed Charles 1.50 4.00
36 Bob Wine 1.50 4.00
37 Fred Gladding 1.50 4.00
38 Jim King 1.50 4.00
39 Gerry Arrigo 1.50 4.00
40 Frank Howard 3.00 8.00
41 Bruce Howard 1.50 4.00
Marv Staehle
42 Earl Wilson 2.50 6.00
43 Mike Shannon 2.50 6.00
44 Wade Blasingame 1.50 4.00
45 Roy McMillan 2.50 6.00
46 Bob Lee 1.50 4.00
47 Tommy Harper 2.50 6.00
48 Claude Raymond 2.50 6.00
49 Curt Blefary RC 2.50 6.00
50 Juan Marichal 6.00 15.00
51 Bill Bryan 1.50 4.00
52 Ed Roebuck 1.50 4.00
53 Dick McAuliffe 2.50 6.00
54 Joe Gibbon 1.50 4.00
55 Tony Conigliaro 8.00 20.00
56 Ron Kline 1.50 4.00
57 Cardinals Team 4.00 10.00
58 Fred Talbot 1.50 4.00
59 Nate Oliver 1.50 4.00
60 Jim O'Toole 2.50 6.00
61 Chris Cannizzaro 1.50 4.00
62 Jim Kaat UER/(Misspelled Katt) 3.00 8.00
63 Ty Cline 1.50 4.00
64 Lou Burdette 2.50 6.00
65 Tony Kubek 6.00 15.00
66 Bill Rigney MG 1.50 4.00
67 Harvey Haddix 2.50 6.00
68 Del Crandall 2.50 6.00
69 Bill Virdon 2.50 6.00
70 Bill Skowron 3.00 8.00
71 John O'Donoghue 1.50 4.00
72 Tony Gonzalez 1.50 4.00
73 Dennis Ribant 1.50 4.00
74 Rico Petrocelli RC 6.00 15.00
75 Deron Johnson 2.50 6.00
76 Sam McDowell 3.00 8.00
77 Doug Camilli 1.50 4.00
78 Dal Maxvill 2.50 6.00
79 Checklist 1-88 4.00 10.00
80 Turk Farrell 1.50 4.00
81 Don Buford 2.50 6.00
82 Sandy Alomar RC 3.00 8.00
83 George Thomas 1.50 4.00
84 Ron Herbel 1.50 4.00
85 Willie Smith 1.50 4.00
86 Buster Narum 1.50 4.00
87 Nelson Mathews 1.50 4.00
88 Jack Lamabe 1.50 4.00
89 Mike Hershberger 1.50 4.00
90 Rich Rollins 2.50 6.00
91 Cubs Team 4.00 10.00
92 Dick Howser 2.50 6.00
93 Jack Fisher 1.50 4.00
94 Charlie Lau 2.50 6.00
95 Bill Mazeroski 6.00 15.00
96 Sonny Siebert 2.50 6.00
97 Pedro Gonzalez 1.50 4.00
98 Bob Miller 1.50 4.00
99 Gil Hodges MG 4.00 10.00
100 Ken Boyer 6.00 15.00
101 Fred Newman 1.50 4.00
102 Steve Boros 1.50 4.00
103 Harvey Kuenn 2.50 6.00
104 Checklist 89-176 4.00 10.00
105 Chico Salmon 1.50 4.00
106 Gene Oliver 1.50 4.00
107 Pat Corrales RC 2.50 6.00
108 Don Mincher 1.50 4.00
109 Walt Bond 1.50 4.00
110 Ron Santo 3.00 8.00
111 Lee Thomas 2.50 6.00
112 Derrell Griffith 1.50 4.00
113 Steve Barber 1.50 4.00
114 Jim Hickman 2.50 6.00
115 Bobby Richardson 6.00 15.00
116 Bob Tolan RC 2.50 6.00
117 Wes Stock 1.50 4.00
118 Hal Lanier 2.50 6.00
119 John Kennedy 1.50 4.00
120 Frank Robinson 30.00 60.00
121 Gene Alley 2.50 6.00
122 Bill Pleis 1.50 4.00
123 Frank Thomas 2.50 6.00
124 Tom Satriano 1.50 4.00
125 Juan Pizarro 1.50 4.00
126 Dodgers Team 4.00 10.00
127 Frank Lary 1.50 4.00
128 Vic Davalillo 1.50 4.00
129 Bennie Daniels 1.50 4.00
130 Al Kaline 30.00 60.00
131 Johnny Keane MG 1.50 4.00
132 World Series Game 1 4.00 10.00
Cards take opener/(Mike Shan
133 Mel Stottlemyre WS 4.00 10.00
134 Mickey Mantle WS3 60.00 120.00
135 Ken Boyer WS 6.00 15.00
136 Tim McCarver WS 4.00 10.00
137 Jim Bouton WS 4.00 10.00
138 Bob Gibson WS7 8.00 20.00
139 World Series Summary 4.00 10.00
Cards celebrate
140 Dean Chance 2.50 6.00
141 Charlie James 1.50 4.00
142 Bill Monbouquette 1.50 4.00
143 John Gelnar 1.50 4.00
Jerry May
144 Ed Kranepool 2.50 6.00
145 Luis Tiant RC 8.00 20.00
146 Ron Hansen 1.50 4.00
147 Dennis Bennett 1.50 4.00
148 Willie Kirkland 1.50 4.00
149 Wayne Schurr 1.50 4.00
150 Brooks Robinson 30.00 60.00
151 Athletics Team 4.00 10.00
152 Phil Ortega 1.50 4.00
153 Norm Cash 4.00 10.00
154 Bob Humphreys 1.50 4.00
155 Roger Maris 50.00 100.00
156 Bob Sadowski 1.50 4.00
157 Zoilo Versalles 2.50 6.00
158 Dick Sisler MG 1.50 4.00
159 Jim Duffalo 1.50 4.00
160 Roberto Clemente ! 125.00 250.00
161 Frank Baumann 1.50 4.00
162 Russ Nixon 1.50 4.00
163 John Briggs 1.50 4.00
164 Al Spangler 1.50 4.00
165 Dick Ellsworth 1.50 4.00
166 Tommie Agee RC 3.00 8.00
167 Bill Wakefield 1.50 4.00
168 Dick Green 2.50 6.00
169 Dave Vineyard 1.50 4.00
170 Hank Aaron 100.00 200.00
171 Jim Roland 1.50 4.00
172 Jim Piersall 3.00 8.00
173 Tigers Team 4.00 10.00
174 Joe Jay 1.50 4.00
175 Bob Aspromonte 1.50 4.00
176 Willie McCovey 12.50 30.00
177 Pete Mikkelsen 1.50 4.00
178 Dalton Jones 1.50 4.00
179 Hal Woodeschick 1.50 4.00
180 Bob Allison 2.50 6.00
181 Don Loun 1.50 4.00
Joe McCabe
182 Mike de la Hoz 1.50 4.00
183 Dave Nicholson 1.50 4.00
184 John Boozer 1.50 4.00
185 Max Alvis 1.50 4.00
186 Bill Cowan 1.50 4.00
187 Casey Stengel MG 10.00 25.00
188 Sam Bowens 1.50 4.00
189 Checklist 177-264 4.00 10.00
190 Bill White 3.00 8.00
191 Phil Regan 2.50 6.00
192 Jim Coker 1.50 4.00
193 Gaylord Perry 10.00 25.00
194 Bill Kelso 2.50 6.00
Rick Reichardt
195 Bob Veale 2.50 6.00
196 Ron Fairly 2.50 6.00
197 Diego Segui 1.50 4.00
198 Smoky Burgess 2.50 6.00
199 Bob Heffner 2.50 6.00
200 Joe Torre 4.00 10.00
201 Cesar Tovar RC 2.50 6.00
202 Leo Burke 2.50 6.00
203 Dallas Green 2.50 6.00
204 Russ Snyder 2.50 6.00
205 Warren Spahn 20.00 50.00
206 Willie Horton 4.00 10.00
207 Pete Rose 125.00 250.00
208 Tommy John 4.00 10.00
209 Pirates Team 4.00 10.00
210 Jim Fregosi 3.00 8.00
211 Steve Ridzik 2.50 6.00
212 Ron Brand 2.50 6.00
213 Jim Davenport 2.50 6.00
214 Bob Purkey 2.50 6.00
215 Pete Ward 2.50 6.00
216 Al Worthington 2.50 6.00
217 Walt Alston MG 4.00 10.00
218 Dick Schofield 2.50 6.00
219 Bob Meyer 2.50 6.00
220 Billy Williams 6.00 15.00
221 John Tsitouris 2.50 6.00
222 Bob Tillman 2.50 6.00
223 Dan Osinski 2.50 6.00
224 Bob Chance 2.50 6.00
225 Bo Belinsky 3.00 8.00
226 Elvio Jimenez 3.00 8.00
Jake Gibbs
227 Bobby Klaus 2.50 6.00
228 Jack Sanford 2.50 6.00
229 Lou Clinton 2.50 6.00
230 Ray Sadecki 2.50 6.00
231 Jerry Adair 2.50 6.00
232 Steve Blass 2.50 6.00
233 Don Zimmer 3.00 8.00
234 White Sox Team 4.00 10.00
235 Chuck Hinton 2.50 6.00
236 Denny McLain RC 15.00 40.00
237 Bernie Allen 2.50 6.00
238 Joe Moeller 2.50 6.00
239 Doc Edwards 2.50 6.00
240 Bob Bruce 2.50 6.00
241 Mack Jones 2.50 6.00
242 George Brunet 2.50 6.00
243 Tommy Helms RC 3.00 8.00
244 Lindy McDaniel 3.00 8.00
245 Joe Pepitone 3.00 8.00
246 Tom Butters 3.00 8.00
247 Wally Moon 3.00 8.00
248 Gus Triandos 2.50 6.00
249 Dave McNally 3.00 8.00
250 Willie Mays 100.00 200.00
251 Billy Herman MG 3.00 8.00
252 Pete Richert 2.50 6.00
253 Danny Cater 2.50 6.00
254 Roland Sheldon 2.50 6.00
255 Camilo Pascual 3.00 8.00
256 Tito Francona 2.50 6.00
257 Jim Wynn 3.00 8.00
258 Larry Bearnarth 2.50 6.00
259 Jim Northrup RC 4.00 10.00
260 Don Drysdale 12.50 30.00
261 Duke Carmel 2.50 6.00
262 Bud Daley 2.50 6.00
263 Marty Keough 2.50 6.00
264 Bob Buhl 2.50 6.00
265 Jim Pagliaroni 2.50 6.00
266 Bert Campaneris RC 5.00 12.00
267 Senators Team 4.00 10.00
268 Ken McBride 2.50 6.00
269 Frank Bolling 2.50 6.00
270 Milt Pappas 2.50 6.00
271 Don Wert 2.50 6.00
272 Chuck Schilling 2.50 6.00
273 4th Series Checklist 5.00 12.00
274 Lum Harris MG 2.50 6.00
275 Dick Groat 4.00 10.00
276 Hoyt Wilhelm 6.00 15.00
277 Johnny Lewis 2.50 6.00
278 Ken Retzer 2.50 6.00
279 Dick Tracewski 2.50 6.00
280 Dick Stuart 3.00 8.00
281 Bill Stafford 2.50 6.00
282 Masanori Murakami RC 30.00 60.00
283 Fred Whitfield 3.00 8.00

1966 O-Pee-Chee

The cards in this 196-card set measure 2 1/2" by 3 1/2". This set is essentially the same as the regular 1966 Topps set, except that the words "Printed in Canada" appear on the bottom of the back, and the background colors are slightly different. On a white border, the fronts feature color player photos. The team name appears within a tilted bar in the top right corner, while the player's name and position are printed inside a bar under the photo. The horizontal backs carry player biography and statistics. The set was issued in five-card nickel packs which came 36 to a box. Remember the prices below apply only to the O-Pee- Chee cards -- NOT to the 1966 Topps cards which are much more plentiful. Notable Rookie Cards include Jim Palmer.

COMPLETE SET (196) 750.00 1,500.00
1 Willie Mays 200.00 400.00
2 Ted Abernathy 1.25 3.00
3 Sam Mele MG 1.25 3.00

4 Ray Culp 1.25 3.00
5 Jim Fregosi 1.50 4.00
6 Chuck Schilling 1.25 3.00
7 Tracy Stallard 1.25 3.00
8 Floyd Robinson 1.25 3.00
9 Clete Boyer 1.50 4.00
10 Tony Cloninger 1.25 3.00
11 Brant Alyea 1.50 4.00
Pete Craig
12 John Tsitouris 1.25 3.00
13 Lou Johnson 1.50 4.00
14 Norm Siebern 1.25 3.00
15 Vern Law 1.50 4.00
16 Larry Brown 1.25 3.00
17 John Stephenson 1.25 3.00
18 Roland Sheldon 1.25 3.00
19 Giants Team 2.50 6.00
20 Willie Horton 1.50 4.00
21 Don Nottebart 1.25 3.00
22 Joe Nossek 1.25 3.00
23 Jack Sanford 1.25 3.00
24 Don Kessinger RC 2.50 6.00
25 Pete Ward 1.50 4.00
26 Ray Sadecki 1.25 3.00
27 Darold Knowles 1.25 3.00
Andy Etchebarren
28 Phil Niekro 12.50 30.00
29 Mike Brumley 1.25 3.00
30 Pete Rose 75.00 150.00
31 Jack Cullen 1.50 4.00
32 Adolfo Phillips 1.25 3.00
33 Jim Pagliaroni 1.25 3.00
34 Checklist 1-88 5.00 12.00
35 Ron Swoboda 2.50 6.00
36 Jim Hunter 12.50 30.00
37 Billy Herman MG 1.50 4.00
38 Ron Nischwitz 1.25 3.00
39 Ken Henderson 1.25 3.00
40 Jim Grant 1.25 3.00
41 Don LeJohn 1.25 3.00
42 Aubrey Gatewood 1.25 3.00
43 Don Landrum 1.25 3.00
44 Bill Davis 1.25 3.00
Tom Kelley
45 Jim Gentile 1.50 4.00
46 Howie Koplitz 1.25 3.00
47 J.C. Martin 1.25 3.00
48 Paul Blair 1.50 4.00
49 Woody Woodward 1.25 3.00
50 Mickey Mantle 250.00 500.00
51 Gordon Richardson 1.25 3.00
52 Wes Covington 2.50 6.00
Johnny Callison
53 Bob Duliba 1.25 3.00
54 Jose Pagan 1.25 3.00
55 Ken Harrelson 1.50 4.00
56 Sandy Valdespino 1.25 3.00
57 Jim Lefebvre 1.50 4.00
58 Dave Wickersham 1.25 3.00
59 Reds Team 2.50 6.00
60 Curt Flood 3.00 8.00
61 Bob Bolin 1.25 3.00
62 Merritt Ranew/(with sold line) 1.25 3.00
63 Jim Stewart 1.25 3.00
64 Bob Bruce 1.25 3.00
65 Leon Wagner 1.25 3.00
66 Al Weis 1.25 3.00
67 Cleon Jones 2.50 6.00
Dick Selma
68 Hal Reniff 1.25 3.00
69 Ken Hamlin 1.25 3.00
70 Carl Yastrzemski 20.00 50.00
71 Frank Carpin 1.25 3.00
72 Tony Perez 15.00 40.00
73 Jerry Zimmerman 1.25 3.00
74 Don Mossi 1.50 4.00
75 Tommy Davis 1.50 4.00
76 Red Schoendienst MG 2.50 6.00
77 Johnny Orsino 1.25 3.00
78 Frank Linzy 1.25 3.00
79 Joe Pepitone 2.50 6.00
80 Richie Allen 3.00 8.00
81 Ray Oyler 1.25 3.00
82 Bob Hendley 1.25 3.00
83 Albie Pearson 1.50 4.00
84 Jim Beauchamp 1.25 3.00
Dick Kelley
85 Eddie Fisher 1.25 3.00
86 John Bateman 1.25 3.00
87 Dan Napoleon 1.25 3.00
88 Fred Whitfield 1.25 3.00
89 Ted Davidson 1.25 3.00
90 Luis Aparicio 5.00 12.00
91 Bob Uecker/(with traded line) 6.00 15.00
92 Yankees Team 10.00 25.00
93 Jim Lonborg 1.50 4.00
94 Matty Alou 1.50 4.00
95 Pete Richert 1.25 3.00
96 Felipe Alou 2.50 6.00
97 Jim Merritt 1.25 3.00
98 Don Demeter 1.25 3.00
99 W.Stargell 3.00 8.00
Clendenon
100 Sandy Koufax 75.00 150.00
101 Checklist 89-176 5.00 12.00
102 Ed Kirkpatrick 1.25 3.00
103 Dick Groat/(with traded line) 1.50 4.00
104 Alex Johnson/(with traded line) 1.50 4.00
105 Milt Pappas 1.50 4.00
106 Rusty Staub 2.50 6.00
107 Larry Stahl 1.25 3.00
Ron Tompkins
108 Bobby Klaus 1.25 3.00
109 Ralph Terry 1.50 4.00
110 Ernie Banks 20.00 50.00
111 Gary Peters 1.25 3.00
112 Manny Mota 1.50 4.00
113 Hank Aguirre 1.25 3.00
114 Jim Gosger 1.25 3.00
115 Bill Henry 1.25 3.00
116 Walt Alston MG 2.50 6.00
117 Jake Gibbs 1.25 3.00
118 Mike McCormick 1.25 3.00
119 Art Shamsky 1.25 3.00
120 Harmon Killebrew 10.00 25.00
121 Ray Herbert 1.25 3.00
122 Joe Gaines 1.25 3.00
123 Frank Bork 1.25 3.00
Jerry May
124 Tug McGraw 2.50 6.00
125 Lou Brock 12.50 30.00
126 Jim Palmer RC 75.00 150.00
127 Ken Berry 1.25 3.00
128 Jim Landis 1.25 3.00
129 Jack Kralick 1.25 3.00
130 Joe Torre 3.00 8.00
131 Angels Team 3.00 8.00
132 Orlando Cepeda 5.00 12.00
133 Don McMahon 1.25 3.00
134 Wes Parker 1.50 4.00
135 Dave Morehead 1.25 3.00
136 Woody Held 1.25 3.00
137 Pat Corrales 1.25 3.00
138 Roger Repoz 1.25 3.00
139 Byron Browne 1.25 3.00
Don Young
140 Jim Maloney 1.50 4.00
141 Tom McCraw 1.25 3.00
142 Don Dennis 1.25 3.00
143 Jose Tartabull 1.50 4.00
144 Don Schwall 1.25 3.00
145 Bill Freehan 1.50 4.00
146 George Altman 1.25 3.00
147 Lum Harris MG 1.25 3.00
148 Bob Johnson 1.25 3.00
149 Dick Nen 1.25 3.00
150 Rocky Colavito 5.00 12.00
151 Gary Wagner 1.25 3.00
152 Frank Malzone 1.50 4.00
153 Rico Carty 1.50 4.00
154 Chuck Hiller 1.25 3.00
155 Marcelino Lopez 1.25 3.00
156 Dick Schofield 1.25 3.00
Hal Lanier
157 Rene Lachemann 1.50 4.00
158 Jim Brewer 1.25 3.00
159 Chico Ruiz 1.25 3.00
160 Whitey Ford 20.00 50.00
161 Jerry Lumpe 1.25 3.00
162 Lee Maye 1.25 3.00
163 Tito Francona 1.25 3.00
164 Tommie Agee 1.50 4.00
Marv Staehle
165 Don Lock 1.25 3.00
166 Chris Krug 1.25 3.00
167 Boog Powell 3.00 8.00
168 Dan Osinski 1.25 3.00
169 Duke Sims 1.25 3.00
170 Cookie Rojas 1.50 4.00
171 Nick Willhite 1.25 3.00
172 Mets Team 3.00 8.00
173 Al Spangler 1.25 3.00
174 Ron Taylor 1.50 4.00
175 Bert Campaneris 2.50 6.00
176 Jim Davenport 1.25 3.00
177 Hector Lopez 1.25 3.00
178 Bob Tillman 1.25 3.00
179 Dennis Aust 1.50 4.00
Bob Tolan
180 Vada Pinson 2.50 6.00
181 Al Worthington 1.25 3.00
182 Jerry Lynch 1.25 3.00
183 Checklist 177-264 5.00 12.00
184 Denis Menke 1.25 3.00
185 Bob Buhl 1.50 4.00
186 Ruben Amaro 1.25 3.00
187 Chuck Dressen MG 1.50 4.00
188 Al Luplow 1.25 3.00
189 John Roseboro 1.50 4.00
190 Jimmie Hall 1.25 3.00
191 Darrell Sutherland 1.25 3.00
192 Vic Power 1.50 4.00
193 Dave McNally 1.50 4.00
194 Senators Team 3.00 8.00
195 Joe Morgan 10.00 25.00
196 Don Pavletich 1.50 4.00

1967 O-Pee-Chee

The cards in this 196-card set measure 2 1/2" by 3 1/2". This set is essentially the same as the regular 1967 Topps set, except that the words "Printed in Canada" appear on the bottom right corner of the back. On a white border, fronts feature color player photos with a thin black border. The player's name and position appear in the top part, while the team name is printed in big letters in the bottom part of the photo. On a green background, the backs carry player biography and statistics and two cartoon-like facts. Each checklist card features a small circular picture of a popular player included in that series. The set was issued in five card nickel packs which came 36 packs to a box. Remember the prices below apply only to the O-Pee-Chee cards -- NOT to the 1967 Topps cards which are much more plentiful.

COMPLETE SET (196) 600.00 1,200.00
1 The Champs 12.50 30.00
Frank Robinson
Hank Bauer
Brooks Rob
2 Jack Hamilton 1.25 3.00
3 Duke Sims 1.25 3.00
4 Hal Lanier 1.25 3.00
5 Whitey Ford 10.00 25.00
6 Dick Simpson 1.25 3.00
7 Don McMahon 1.25 3.00
8 Chuck Harrison 1.25 3.00
9 Ron Hansen 1.25 3.00
10 Matty Alou 1.50 4.00
11 Barry Moore 1.25 3.00
12 Jim Campanis 1.50 4.00
Bill Singer
13 Joe Sparma 1.25 3.00
14 Phil Linz 1.50 4.00
15 Earl Battey 1.25 3.00
16 Bill Hands 1.25 3.00
17 Jim Gosger 1.25 3.00
18 Gene Oliver 1.25 3.00
19 Jim McGlothlin 1.25 3.00
20 Orlando Cepeda 4.00 10.00
21 Dave Bristol MG 1.25 3.00
22 Gene Brabender 1.25 3.00
23 Larry Elliot 1.25 3.00
24 Bob Allen 1.25 3.00
25 Elston Howard 2.50 6.00
26 Bob Priddy/(with traded line) 1.25 3.00
27 Bob Saverine 1.25 3.00
28 Barry Latman 1.25 3.00
29 Tommy McCraw 1.25 3.00
30 Al Kaline 10.00 25.00
31 Jim Brewer 1.25 3.00
32 Bob Bailey 1.50 4.00
33 Sal Bando RC 3.00 8.00
34 Pete Cimino 1.25 3.00
35 Rico Carty 1.50 4.00
36 Bob Tillman 1.25 3.00
37 Rick Wise 1.50 4.00
38 Bob Johnson 1.25 3.00
39 Curt Simmons 1.50 4.00
40 Rick Reichardt 1.25 3.00
41 Joe Hoerner 1.25 3.00
42 Mets Team 5.00 12.00
43 Chico Salmon 1.25 3.00
44 Joe Nuxhall 1.50 4.00
45 Roger Maris 30.00 60.00
46 Lindy McDaniel 1.50 4.00
47 Ken McMullen 1.25 3.00
48 Bill Freehan 1.50 4.00
49 Roy Face 1.50 4.00
50 Tony Oliva 3.00 8.00
51 Dave Adlesh 1.25 3.00
Wes Bales
52 Dennis Higgins 1.25 3.00
53 Clay Dalrymple 1.25 3.00
54 Dick Green 1.25 3.00
55 Don Drysdale 8.00 20.00
56 Jose Tartabull 1.50 4.00
57 Pat Jarvis 1.50 4.00
58 Paul Schaal 1.25 3.00
59 Ralph Terry 1.50 4.00
60 Luis Aparicio 4.00 10.00
61 Gordy Coleman 1.25 3.00
62 Checklist 1-109 5.00 12.00
Frank Robinson
63 Lou Brock 3.00 8.00
Curt Flood
64 Fred Valentine 1.25 3.00
65 Tom Haller 1.50 4.00
66 Manny Mota 1.50 4.00
67 Ken Berry 1.25 3.00
68 Bob Buhl 1.50 4.00
69 Vic Davalillo 1.25 3.00
70 Ron Santo 3.00 8.00
71 Camilo Pascual 1.50 4.00
72 Tigers Rookies 1.50 4.00
George Korince/(photo actually
J
73 Rusty Staub 3.00 8.00
74 Wes Stock 1.25 3.00
75 George Scott 1.50 4.00
76 Jim Barbieri 1.25 3.00
77 Dooley Womack 1.25 3.00
78 Pat Corrales 1.25 3.00
79 Bubba Morton 1.25 3.00
80 Jim Maloney 1.50 4.00
81 Eddie Stanky MG 1.50 4.00
82 Steve Barber 1.25 3.00
83 Ollie Brown 1.25 3.00
84 Tommie Sisk 1.25 3.00
85 Johnny Callison 1.50 4.00
86 Mike McCormick/(with traded line) 1.50 4.00
87 George Altman 1.25 3.00
88 Mickey Lolich 2.50 6.00
89 Felix Millan 1.50 4.00
90 Jim Nash 1.25 3.00
91 Johnny Lewis 1.25 3.00
92 Ray Washburn 1.25 3.00
93 S.Bahnsen RC 2.50 6.00
B.Murcer
94 Ron Fairly 1.50 4.00
95 Sonny Siebert 1.25 3.00
96 Art Shamsky 1.25 3.00
97 Mike Cuellar 2.50 6.00
98 Rich Rollins 1.25 3.00
99 Lee Stange 1.25 3.00
100 Frank Robinson 8.00 20.00
101 Ken Johnson 1.25 3.00
102 Phillies Team 2.50 6.00
103 Mickey Mantle CL2 DP 10.00 25.00
104 Minnie Rojas 1.25 3.00
105 Ken Boyer 3.00 8.00
106 Randy Hundley 1.50 4.00
107 Joel Horlen 1.25 3.00
108 Alex Johnson 1.50 4.00
109 R.Colavito 3.00 8.00
L.Wagner
110 Jack Aker 1.25 3.00
111 John Kennedy 1.25 3.00
112 Dave Wickersham 1.25 3.00
113 Dave Nicholson 1.25 3.00
114 Jack Baldschun 1.25 3.00
115 Paul Casanova 1.25 3.00
116 Herman Franks MG 1.25 3.00
117 Darrell Brandon 1.25 3.00
118 Bernie Allen 1.25 3.00
119 Wade Blasingame 1.25 3.00
120 Floyd Robinson 1.25 3.00
121 Ed Bressoud 1.25 3.00
122 George Brunet 1.25 3.00
123 Jim Price 1.50 4.00
Luke Walker
124 Jim Stewart 1.25 3.00
125 Moe Drabowsky 1.50 4.00
126 Tony Taylor 1.25 3.00
127 John O'Donoghue 1.25 3.00
128 Ed Spiezio 1.25 3.00
129 Phil Roof 1.25 3.00
130 Phil Regan 1.50 4.00
131 Yankees Team 5.00 12.00
132 Ozzie Virgil 1.25 3.00
133 Ron Kline 1.25 3.00
134 Gates Brown 1.25 3.00
135 Deron Johnson 1.50 4.00
136 Carroll Sembera 1.25 3.00
137 Ron Clark RC 1.25 3.00
Jim Ollom RC
138 Dick Kelley 1.25 3.00
139 Dalton Jones 1.25 3.00
140 Willie Stargell 10.00 25.00
141 John Miller 1.25 3.00
142 Jackie Brandt 1.25 3.00
143 Pete Ward 2.50 6.00
Don Buford
144 Bill Hepler 1.25 3.00
145 Larry Brown 1.25 3.00
146 Steve Carlton 30.00 60.00
147 Tom Egan 1.25 3.00
148 Adolfo Phillips 1.25 3.00
149 Joe Moeller 1.25 3.00
150 Mickey Mantle 200.00 400.00
151 World Series Game 1 2.50 6.00
Moe mows down 11/(Moe Drabow
152 Jim Palmer WS2 4.00 10.00
153 World Series Game 3 2.50 6.00
Paul Blair's homer
defeats L
154 World Series Game 4 2.50 6.00
Orioles four straight/(Brook
155 World Series Summary 2.50 6.00
Winners celebrate
156 Ron Herbel 1.25 3.00
157 Danny Cater 1.25 3.00
158 Jimmie Coker 1.25 3.00
159 Bruce Howard 1.25 3.00
160 Willie Davis 1.50 4.00
161 Dick Williams MG 1.50 4.00
162 Billy O'Dell 1.25 3.00
163 Vic Roznovsky 1.25 3.00
164 Dwight Siebler 1.25 3.00
165 Cleon Jones 1.50 4.00
166 Eddie Mathews 8.00 20.00
167 Joe Coleman 1.25 3.00
Tim Cullen
168 Ray Culp 1.25 3.00
169 Horace Clarke 1.25 3.00
170 Dick McAuliffe 1.50 4.00
171 Calvin Koonce 1.25 3.00
172 Bill Heath 1.25 3.00
173 Cardinals Team 2.50 6.00
174 Dick Radatz 1.50 4.00
175 Bobby Knoop 1.25 3.00
176 Sammy Ellis 1.25 3.00
177 Tito Fuentes 1.25 3.00
178 John Buzhardt 1.25 3.00
179 Charles Vaughan 1.50 4.00
Cecil Upshaw
180 Curt Blefary 1.25 3.00
181 Terry Fox 1.25 3.00
182 Ed Charles 1.25 3.00
183 Jim Pagliaroni 1.25 3.00
184 George Thomas 1.25 3.00
185 Ken Holtzman RC 2.50 6.00
186 Ed Kranepool 2.50 6.00
Ron Swoboda
187 Pedro Ramos 1.25 3.00
188 Ken Harrelson 1.50 4.00
189 Chuck Hinton 1.25 3.00
190 Turk Farrell 1.25 3.00
191 Checklist 197-283/(Willie Mays) 6.00 15.00
192 Fred Gladding 1.25 3.00
193 Jose Cardenal 1.50 4.00
194 Bob Allison 1.50 4.00
195 Al Jackson 1.25 3.00
196 Johnny Romano 1.50 4.00

1967 O-Pee-Chee Paper Inserts

These posters measure approximately 5" by 7" and are very similar to the American Topps poster (paper insert) issue, except that they say "Ptd. in Canada" on the bottom. The fronts feature color player photos with thin borders. The player's name and position, team name, and the card number appear inside a circle in the lower right. A facsimile player autograph rounds out the front. The backs are blank. This Canadian version is much more difficult to find than the American version. These numbered "All-Star" inserts have fold lines which are generally not very noticeable when stored carefully. There is some confusion as to whether these posters were issued in 1967 or 1968.

COMPLETE SET (32) 175.00 350.00
1 Boog Powell 2.00 5.00
2 Bert Campaneris 1.25 3.00

3 Brooks Robinson 8.00 20.00
4 Tommie Agee 1.00 2.50
5 Carl Yastrzemski 10.00 25.00
6 Mickey Mantle 50.00 100.00
7 Frank Howard 1.50 4.00
8 Sam McDowell 1.25 3.00
9 Orlando Cepeda 3.00 8.00
10 Chico Cardenas 1.00 2.50
11 Bob Clemente 75.00 150.00
12 Willie Mays 15.00 40.00
13 Cleon Jones 1.00 2.50
14 John Callison 1.00 2.50
15 Hank Aaron 12.50 30.00
16 Don Drysdale 6.00 15.00
17 Bobby Knoop 1.00 2.50
18 Tony Oliva 2.00 5.00
19 Frank Robinson 6.00 15.00
20 Denny McLain 2.00 5.00
21 Al Kaline 10.00 25.00
22 Joe Pepitone 1.25 3.00
23 Harmon Killebrew 8.00 20.00
24 Leon Wagner 1.00 2.50
25 Joe Morgan 6.00 15.00
26 Ron Santo 2.00 5.00
27 Joe Torre 2.00 5.00
28 Juan Marichal 5.00 12.00
29 Matty Alou 1.25 3.00
30 Felipe Alou 1.50 4.00
31 Ron Hunt 1.00 2.50
32 Willie McCovey 6.00 15.00

1968 O-Pee-Chee

The cards in this 196-card set measure 2 1/2" by 3 1/2". This set is essentially the same as the regular 1968 Topps set, except that the words "Printed in Canada" appear on the bottom of the back and the backgrounds have a different color. The fronts feature color player photos with rounded corners. The player's name is printed under the photo, while his position and team name appear in a circle in the lower right. On a light brown background, the backs carry player biography and statistics and a cartoon-like trivia question. Each checklist card features a small circular picture of a popular player included in that series. Remember the prices below apply only to the O-Pee-Chee cards -- NOT to the 1968 Topps cards which are much more plentiful. The key card in the set is Nolan Ryan in his Rookie Card year. The first OPC cards of Hall of Famers Rod Carew and Tom Seaver also appear in this set.

COMPLETE SET (196) 1,000.00 2,000.00
1 Clemente 15.00 40.00
Gon
M.Alou LL !
2 Yaz 8.00 20.00
F.Rob
Kaline LL
3 Cepeda 10.00 25.00
Clemente
Aar LL
4 Yaz 8.00 20.00
Killebrew
F.Rob LL
5 Aaron 4.00 10.00
Santo
McCovey LL
6 Yaz 4.00 10.00
Killebrew
Howard LL
7 NL ERA Leaders 2.50 6.00
Phil Niekro
Jim Bunning
Chris Sh
8 AL ERA Leaders 2.50 6.00
Joel Horlen
Gary Peters
Sonny Si
9 McCorm 2.50 6.00
Jenk
Bunn
Ost LL
10 AL Pitching Leaders 2.50 6.00
Jim Lonborg
Earl Wilson
Dea
11 Bunning 3.00 8.00
Jenkins
Perry LL
12 AL Strikeout Leaders 2.50 6.00
Jim Lonborg
Sam McDowell
D
13 Chuck Hartenstein 1.25 3.00
14 Jerry McNertney 1.25 3.00
15 Ron Hunt 1.25 3.00
16 Lou Piniella 3.00 8.00
17 Dick Hall 1.25 3.00
18 Mike Hershberger 1.25 3.00
19 Juan Pizarro 1.25 3.00
20 Brooks Robinson 12.50 30.00
21 Ron Davis 1.25 3.00
22 Pat Dobson 1.50 4.00
23 Chico Cardenas 1.50 4.00
24 Bobby Locke 1.25 3.00
25 Julian Javier 1.50 4.00
26 Darrell Brandon 1.25 3.00
27 Gil Hodges MG 4.00 10.00
28 Ted Uhlaender 1.25 3.00
29 Joe Verbanic 1.25 3.00
30 Joe Torre 3.00 8.00
31 Ed Stroud 1.25 3.00
32 Joe Gibbon 1.25 3.00
33 Pete Ward 1.50 4.00
34 Al Ferrara 1.25 3.00
35 Steve Hargan 1.25 3.00
36 Bob Moose 1.50 4.00
Bob Robertson
37 Billy Williams 4.00 10.00
38 Tony Pierce 1.25 3.00
39 Cookie Rojas 1.25 3.00
40 Denny McLain 4.00 10.00
41 Julio Gotay 1.25 3.00
42 Larry Haney 1.25 3.00
43 Gary Bell 1.25 3.00
44 Frank Kostro 1.25 3.00
45 Tom Seaver 30.00 60.00
46 Dave Ricketts 1.25 3.00
47 Ralph Houk MG 1.50 4.00
48 Ted Davidson 1.25 3.00
49 Ed Brinkman 1.25 3.00
50 Willie Mays 40.00 80.00
51 Bob Locker 1.25 3.00
52 Hawk Taylor 1.25 3.00
53 Gene Alley 1.50 4.00
54 Stan Williams 1.25 3.00
55 Felipe Alou 2.50 6.00
56 Dave May RC 1.25 3.00
57 Dan Schneider 1.25 3.00
58 Eddie Mathews 8.00 20.00
59 Don Lock 1.25 3.00
60 Ken Holtzman 1.50 4.00
61 Reggie Smith 2.50 6.00
62 Chuck Dobson 1.25 3.00
63 Dick Kenworthy 1.25 3.00
64 Jim Merritt 1.25 3.00
65 John Roseboro 1.50 4.00
66 Casey Cox 1.25 3.00
67 Checklist 1-109 3.00 8.00
Jim Kaat
68 Ron Willis 1.25 3.00
69 Tom Tresh 1.50 4.00
70 Bob Veale 1.50 4.00
71 Vern Fuller 1.25 3.00
72 Tommy John 3.00 8.00
73 Jim Ray Hart 1.50 4.00
74 Milt Pappas 1.50 4.00
75 Don Mincher 1.25 3.00
76 Jim Britton 1.50 4.00
Ron Reed
77 Don Wilson 1.50 4.00
78 Jim Northrup 3.00 8.00
79 Ted Kubiak 1.25 3.00
80 Rod Carew 30.00 60.00
81 Larry Jackson 1.25 3.00
82 Sam Bowens 1.25 3.00
83 John Stephenson 1.25 3.00
84 Bob Tolan 1.25 3.00
85 Gaylord Perry 4.00 10.00
86 Willie Stargell 4.00 10.00
87 Dick Williams MG 1.50 4.00
88 Phil Regan 1.50 4.00
89 Jake Gibbs 1.50 4.00
90 Vada Pinson 2.50 6.00
91 Jim Ollom 1.25 3.00
92 Ed Kranepool 1.50 4.00
93 Tony Cloninger 1.25 3.00
94 Lee Maye 1.25 3.00
95 Bob Aspromonte 1.25 3.00
96 Frank Coggins 1.25 3.00
Dick Nold
97 Tom Phoebus 1.25 3.00
98 Gary Sutherland 1.25 3.00
99 Rocky Colavito 4.00 10.00
100 Bob Gibson 12.50 30.00
101 Glenn Beckert 1.50 4.00
102 Jose Cardenal 1.50 4.00
103 Don Sutton 4.00 10.00
104 Dick Dietz 1.25 3.00
105 Al Downing 1.50 4.00
106 Dalton Jones 1.25 3.00
107 Checklist 110-196 3.00 8.00
Juan Marichal
108 Don Pavletich 1.25 3.00
109 Bert Campaneris 1.50 4.00
110 Hank Aaron 40.00 80.00
111 Rich Reese 1.25 3.00
112 Woody Fryman 1.25 3.00
113 Tom Matchick 1.50 4.00
Daryl Patterson
114 Ron Swoboda 1.50 4.00
115 Sam McDowell 1.50 4.00
116 Ken McMullen 1.25 3.00
117 Larry Jaster 1.25 3.00
118 Mark Belanger 1.50 4.00
119 Ted Savage 1.25 3.00
120 Mel Stottlemyre 2.50 6.00
121 Jimmie Hall 1.25 3.00
122 Gene Mauch MG 1.50 4.00
123 Jose Santiago 1.50 4.00
124 Nate Oliver 1.25 3.00
125 Joel Horlen 1.25 3.00
126 Bobby Etheridge 1.25 3.00
127 Paul Lindblad 1.25 3.00
128 Tom Dukes 1.25 3.00
Alonzo Harris
129 Mickey Stanley 3.00 8.00
130 Tony Perez 4.00 10.00
131 Frank Bertaina 1.25 3.00
132 Bud Harrelson 1.50 4.00
133 Fred Whitfield 1.25 3.00
134 Pat Jarvis 1.25 3.00
135 Paul Blair 1.50 4.00
136 Randy Hundley 1.50 4.00
137 Twins Team 2.50 6.00
138 Ruben Amaro 1.25 3.00
139 Chris Short 1.25 3.00
140 Tony Conigliaro 4.00 10.00
141 Dal Maxvill 1.25 3.00
142 Buddy Bradford 1.25 3.00
Bill Voss
143 Pete Cimino 1.25 3.00
144 Joe Morgan 6.00 15.00
145 Don Drysdale 6.00 15.00
146 Sal Bando 1.50 4.00
147 Frank Linzy 1.25 3.00
148 Dave Bristol MG 1.25 3.00
149 Bob Saverine 1.25 3.00
150 Roberto Clemente 50.00 100.00
151 Lou Brock WS1 5.00 12.00
152 Carl Yastrzemski WS2 5.00 12.00
153 Nellie Briles WS3 2.50 6.00
154 Bob Gibson WS4 5.00 12.00
155 Jim Lonborg WS 2.50 6.00
156 Rico Petrocelli WS 2.50 6.00
157 World Series Game 7 2.50 6.00
St. Louis wins it
158 World Series Summary 2.50 6.00
Cardinals celebrate
159 Don Kessinger 1.50 4.00
160 Earl Wilson 1.50 4.00
161 Norm Miller 1.25 3.00
162 Hal Gilson 1.50 4.00
Mike Torrez
163 Gene Brabender 1.25 3.00
164 Ramon Webster 1.25 3.00
165 Tony Oliva 3.00 8.00
166 Claude Raymond 1.50 4.00
167 Elston Howard 3.00 8.00
168 Dodgers Team 2.50 6.00
169 Bob Bolin 1.25 3.00
170 Jim Fregosi 1.50 4.00
171 Don Nottebart 1.25 3.00
172 Walt Williams 1.25 3.00
173 John Boozer 1.25 3.00
174 Bob Tillman 1.25 3.00
175 Maury Wills 3.00 8.00
176 Bob Allen 1.25 3.00
177 N.Ryan 300.00 600.00
J.Koosman RC !
178 Don Wert 1.50 4.00
179 Bill Stoneman 1.25 3.00
180 Curt Flood 2.50 6.00
181 Jerry Zimmerman 1.25 3.00
182 Dave Giusti 1.25 3.00
183 Bob Kennedy MG 1.50 4.00
184 Lou Johnson 1.25 3.00
185 Tom Haller 1.25 3.00
186 Eddie Watt 1.25 3.00
187 Sonny Jackson 1.25 3.00
188 Cap Peterson 1.25 3.00
189 Bill Landis 1.25 3.00
190 Bill White 1.50 4.00
191 Dan Frisella 1.25 3.00
192 Checklist 3 4.00 10.00
Carl Yastrzemski
193 Jack Hamilton 1.25 3.00
194 Don Buford 1.25 3.00
195 Joe Pepitone 1.50 4.00
196 Gary Nolan 1.50 4.00

1969 O-Pee-Chee

The cards in this 218-card set measure 2 1/2" by 3 1/2". This set is essentially the same as the regular 1969 Topps set, except that the words "Printed in Canada" appear on the bottom of the back and the backgrounds have a purple color. The fronts feature color player photos with rounded corners and thin black borders. The player's name and position are printed inside a circle in the top right corner, while the team name appears in the lower part of the photo. On a magenta background, the backs carry player biography and statistics. Each checklist card features a small circular picture of a popular player included in that series. Remember the prices below apply only to the O-Pee-Chee cards -- NOT to the 1969 Topps cards which are much more plentiful. Notable Rookie Cards include Graig Nettles.

COMPLETE SET (218) 500.00 1,000.00
1 Yaz 8.00 20.00
Cater
Oliva LL DP!
2 Rose 4.00 10.00
M.Alou
F.Alou LL
3 AL RBI Leaders 2.50 6.00
Ken Harrelson
Frank Howard
Jim N
4 McCov 3.00 8.00
Santo
B.Will LL
5 AL Home Run Leaders 2.50 6.00
Frank Howard
Willie Horton/
6 McCov 3.00 8.00
R.Allen
Banks LL
7 AL ERA Leaders 2.50 6.00
Luis Tiant
Sam McDowell
Dave McN
8 Gibson 3.00 8.00
Bolin
Veale LL
9 AL Pitching Leaders 2.50 6.00
Denny McLain
Dave McNally
L
10 Marich 4.00 10.00
Gibson
Jenk LL
11 AL Strikeout Leaders 3.00 8.00
Sam McDowell
Denny McLain/
12 Gibson 2.50 6.00
Jenkins
LL DP
13 Mickey Stanley 1.50 4.00
14 Al McBean .75 2.00
15 Boog Powell 2.50 6.00
16 Cesar Gutierrez .75 2.00
Rich Robertson
17 Mike Marshall 1.50 4.00
18 Dick Schofield .75 2.00
19 Ken Suarez .75 2.00
20 Ernie Banks 10.00 25.00
21 Jose Santiago .75 2.00
22 Jesus Alou 1.50 4.00
23 Lew Krausse .75 2.00
24 Walt Alston MG 2.50 6.00
25 Roy White 1.50 4.00
26 Clay Carroll 1.50 4.00
27 Bernie Allen .75 2.00
28 Mike Ryan .75 2.00
29 Dave Morehead .75 2.00
30 Bob Allison 1.50 4.00
31 Amos Otis 2.50 6.00
G.Gentry RC
32 Sammy Ellis .75 2.00
33 Wayne Causey .75 2.00
34 Gary Peters .75 2.00
35 Joe Morgan 5.00 12.00
36 Luke Walker .75 2.00
37 Curt Motton .75 2.00
38 Zoilo Versalles 1.50 4.00
39 Dick Hughes .75 2.00
40 Mayo Smith MG .75 2.00
41 Bob Barton .75 2.00
42 Tommy Harper 1.50 4.00
43 Joe Niekro 1.50 4.00
44 Danny Cater .75 2.00
45 Maury Wills 2.50 6.00
46 Fritz Peterson 1.50 4.00
47 Paul Popovich .75 2.00
48 Brant Alyea .75 2.00
49 Steve Jones .75 2.00
Ellie Rodriguez
50 Roberto Clemente/(Bob on card) 40.00 80.00
51 Woody Fryman 1.50 4.00
52 Mike Andrews .75 2.00
53 Sonny Jackson .75 2.00
54 Cisco Carlos .75 2.00
55 Jerry Grote 1.50 4.00
56 Rich Reese .75 2.00
57 Denny McLain CL 3.00 8.00
58 Fred Gladding .75 2.00
59 Jay Johnstone 1.50 4.00
60 Nelson Briles 1.50 4.00
61 Jimmie Hall .75 2.00
62 Chico Salmon .75 2.00
63 Jim Hickman .75 2.00
64 Bill Monbouquette .75 2.00
65 Willie Davis 1.50 4.00
66 Mike Adamson .75 2.00
Merv Rettenmund
67 Bill Stoneman 1.50 4.00
68 Dave Duncan 1.50 4.00
69 Steve Hamilton 1.50 4.00
70 Tommy Helms 1.50 4.00
71 Steve Whitaker 1.50 4.00
72 Ron Taylor 1.50 4.00
73 Johnny Briggs .75 2.00
74 Preston Gomez MG .75 2.00
75 Luis Aparicio 3.00 8.00
76 Norm Miller .75 2.00
77 Ron Perranoski 1.50 4.00
78 Tom Satriano .75 2.00
79 Milt Pappas 1.50 4.00
80 Norm Cash 1.50 4.00
81 Mel Queen .75 2.00
82 Al Oliver RC 4.00 10.00
83 Mike Ferraro 1.50 4.00
84 Bob Humphreys .75 2.00
85 Lou Brock 10.00 25.00
86 Pete Richert .75 2.00
87 Horace Clarke 1.50 4.00
88 Rich Nye .75 2.00
89 Russ Gibson .75 2.00
90 Jerry Koosman 2.50 6.00
91 Al Dark MG 1.50 4.00
92 Jack Billingham 1.50 4.00
93 Joe Foy .75 2.00
94 Hank Aguirre .75 2.00
95 Johnny Bench 30.00 60.00
96 Denver LeMaster .75 2.00
97 Buddy Bradford .75 2.00
98 Dave Giusti .75 2.00
99 Twins Rookies 8.00 20.00
Danny Morris
Graig Nettles
100 Hank Aaron 30.00 60.00
101 Daryl Patterson .75 2.00
102 Jim Davenport .75 2.00
103 Roger Repoz .75 2.00
104 Steve Blass .75 2.00
105 Rick Monday 1.50 4.00
106 Jim Hannan .75 2.00
107 Checklist 110-218 3.00 8.00
Bob Gibson
108 Tony Taylor 1.50 4.00
109 Jim Lonborg 1.50 4.00
110 Mike Shannon 1.50 4.00
111 John Morris .75 2.00

112 J.C. Martin 1.50 4.00
113 Dave May .75 2.00
114 Alan Closter 1.50 4.00
John Cumberland
115 Bill Hands .75 2.00
116 Chuck Harrison .75 2.00
117 Jim Fairey 1.50 4.00
118 Stan Williams .75 2.00
119 Doug Rader 1.50 4.00
120 Pete Rose 30.00 60.00
121 Joe Grzenda .75 2.00
122 Ron Fairly 1.50 4.00
123 Wilbur Wood 1.50 4.00
124 Hank Bauer MG 1.50 4.00
125 Ray Sadecki .75 2.00
126 Dick Tracewski .75 2.00
127 Kevin Collins 1.50 4.00
128 Tommie Aaron 1.50 4.00
129 Bill McCool .75 2.00
130 Carl Yastrzemski 10.00 25.00
131 Chris Cannizzaro .75 2.00
132 Dave Baldwin .75 2.00
133 Johnny Callison 1.50 4.00
134 Jim Weaver .75 2.00
135 Tommy Davis 1.50 4.00
136 Steve Huntz .75 2.00
Mike Torrez
137 Wally Bunker .75 2.00
138 John Bateman .75 2.00
139 Andy Kosco .75 2.00
140 Jim Lefebvre 1.50 4.00
141 Bill Dillman .75 2.00
142 Woody Woodward .75 2.00
143 Joe Nossek .75 2.00
144 Bob Hendley .75 2.00
145 Max Alvis .75 2.00
146 Jim Perry 1.50 4.00
147 Leo Durocher MG 2.50 6.00
148 Lee Stange .75 2.00
149 Ollie Brown .75 2.00
150 Denny McLain 2.50 6.00
151 Clay Dalrymple/(Catching, Phillies) 1.50 4.00
152 Tommie Sisk .75 2.00
153 Ed Brinkman .75 2.00
154 Jim Britton .75 2.00
155 Pete Ward 1.50 4.00
156 Hal Gilson .75 2.00
Leon McFadden
157 Bob Rodgers 1.50 4.00
158 Joe Gibbon .75 2.00
159 Jerry Adair .75 2.00
160 Vada Pinson 2.50 6.00
161 John Purdin .75 2.00
162 Bob Gibson WS1 4.00 10.00
163 World Series Game 2 3.00 8.00
Tiger homers
deck the Cards#
164 T.McCarver 6.00 15.00
Maris WS3 DP
165 Lou Brock WS4 4.00 10.00
166 Al Kaline WS5 4.00 10.00
167 Jim Northrup WS 3.00 8.00
168 M.Lolich 4.00 10.00
B.Gibson WS7
169 World Series Summary 3.00 8.00
Tigers celebrate/(Dick McAu
170 Frank Howard 1.50 4.00
171 Glenn Beckert 1.50 4.00
172 Jerry Stephenson .75 2.00
173 Bob Christian .75 2.00
Gerry Nyman
174 Grant Jackson .75 2.00
175 Jim Bunning 3.00 8.00
176 Joe Azcue .75 2.00
177 Ron Reed .75 2.00
178 Ray Oyler 1.50 4.00
179 Don Pavletich .75 2.00
180 Willie Horton 1.50 4.00
181 Mel Nelson .75 2.00
182 Bill Rigney MG .75 2.00
183 Don Shaw 1.50 4.00
184 Roberto Pena .75 2.00
185 Tom Phoebus .75 2.00
186 John Edwards .75 2.00
187 Leon Wagner .75 2.00
188 Rick Wise 1.50 4.00
189 Joe Lahoud .75 2.00
John Thibodeau
190 Willie Mays 50.00 100.00
191 Lindy McDaniel 1.50 4.00
192 Jose Pagan .75 2.00
193 Don Cardwell 1.50 4.00
194 Ted Uhlaender .75 2.00
195 John Odom .75 2.00
196 Lum Harris MG .75 2.00
197 Dick Selma .75 2.00
198 Willie Smith .75 2.00
199 Jim French .75 2.00
200 Bob Gibson 6.00 15.00
201 Russ Snyder .75 2.00
202 Don Wilson 1.50 4.00
203 Dave Johnson 1.50 4.00
204 Jack Hiatt .75 2.00
205 Rick Reichardt .75 2.00
206 Larry Hisle 1.50 4.00
Barry Lersch
207 Roy Face 1.50 4.00
208 Donn Clendenon/(Montreal Expos) 1.50 4.00
209 Larry Haney UER/(Reversed negative) .75 2.00
210 Felix Millan .75 2.00
211 Galen Cisco .75 2.00
212 Tom Tresh 1.50 4.00
213 Gerry Arrigo .75 2.00
214 Checklist 3 3.00 8.00
With 69T deckle CL
on back (no playe
215 Rico Petrocelli 1.50 4.00
216 Don Sutton 3.00 8.00
217 John Donaldson .75 2.00
218 John Roseboro 1.50 4.00

1969 O-Pee-Chee Deckle

This set is very similar to the U.S. deckle version produced by Topps. The cards measure approximately 2 1/8" by 3 1/8" (slightly smaller than the American issue) and are cut with deckle edges. The fronts feature black-and-white player photos with white borders and facsimile autographs in black ink (instead of blue ink like the Topps issue). The backs are blank. The cards are unnumbered and checklisted below in alphabetical order. Remember the prices below apply only to the O-Pee-Chee Deckle cards -- NOT to the 1969 Topps Deckle cards which are much more plentiful.

COMPLETE SET (24) 125.00 250.00
1 Richie Allen 2.00 5.00
2 Luis Aparicio 3.00 8.00
3 Rod Carew 4.00 10.00
4 Roberto Clemente 75.00 150.00
5 Curt Flood 1.50 4.00
6 Bill Freehan 1.50 4.00
7 Bob Gibson 4.00 10.00
8 Ken Harrelson 1.50 4.00
9 Tommy Helms 1.25 3.00
10 Tom Haller 1.25 3.00
11 Willie Horton 1.50 4.00
12 Frank Howard 2.00 5.00
13 Willie McCovey 4.00 10.00
14 Denny McLain 2.00 5.00
15 Juan Marichal 4.00 10.00
16 Willie Mays 40.00 80.00
17 Boog Powell 2.00 5.00
18 Brooks Robinson 6.00 15.00
19 Ron Santo 2.50 6.00
20 Rusty Staub 1.50 4.00
21 Mel Stottlemyre 1.25 3.00
22 Luis Tiant 1.25 3.00
23 Maury Wills 1.50 4.00
24 Carl Yastrzemski 8.00 20.00

1970 O-Pee-Chee

The cards in this 546-card set measure 2 1/2" by 3 1/2". This set is essentially the same as the regular 1970 Topps set, except that the words "Printed in Canada" appear on the backs and the backs are bilingual. On a gray border, the fronts feature color player photos with thin white borders. The player's name and position are printed under the photo, while the team name appears in the upper part of the picture. The horizontal backs carry player biography and statistics in French and English. The card stock is a deeper shade of yellow on the reverse for the O-Pee-Chee cards. The set was issued in eight-card dime packs which came 36 packs to a box. Remember the prices below apply only to the O-Pee-Chee cards -- NOT to the 1970 Topps cards which are much more plentiful. Notable Rookie Cards include Thurman Munson.

COMPLETE SET (546) 750.00 1,500.00
COMMON PLAYER (1-459) .60 1.50
COMMON PLAYER (460-546) 1.00 2.50
1 Mets Team ! 12.50 40.00
2 Diego Segui .75 2.00
3 Darrel Chaney .60 1.50
4 Tom Egan .60 1.50
5 Wes Parker .75 2.00
6 Grant Jackson .60 1.50
7 Gary Boyd .60 1.50
Russ Nagelson
8 Jose Martinez .60 1.50
9 Checklist 1-132 6.00 15.00
10 Carl Yastrzemski 10.00 25.00
11 Nate Colbert .60 1.50
12 John Hiller .75 2.00
13 Jack Hiatt .60 1.50
14 Hank Allen .60 1.50
15 Larry Dierker .60 1.50
16 Charlie Metro MG .60 1.50
17 Hoyt Wilhelm 2.50 6.00
18 Carlos May .75 2.00
19 John Boccabella .60 1.50
20 Dave McNally .75 2.00
21 Vida Blue 2.50 6.00
G.Tenace RC
22 Ray Washburn .60 1.50
23 Bill Robinson .75 2.00
24 Dick Selma .60 1.50
25 Cesar Tovar .60 1.50
26 Tug McGraw 1.50 4.00
27 Chuck Hinton .60 1.50
28 Billy Wilson .60 1.50
29 Sandy Alomar .75 2.00
30 Matty Alou .75 2.00
31 Marty Pattin .75 2.00
32 Harry Walker MG .60 1.50
33 Don Wert .60 1.50
34 Willie Crawford .60 1.50
35 Joel Horlen .60 1.50
36 Danny Breeden .75 2.00
Bernie Carbo
37 Dick Drago .60 1.50
38 Mack Jones .60 1.50
39 Mike Nagy .60 1.50
40 Richie Allen 1.50 4.00
41 George Lauzerique .60 1.50
42 Tito Fuentes .60 1.50
43 Jack Aker .60 1.50
44 Roberto Pena .60 1.50
45 Dave Johnson .75 2.00
46 Ken Rudolph .60 1.50
47 Bob Miller .60 1.50
48 Gil Garrido .60 1.50
49 Tim Cullen .60 1.50
50 Tommie Agee .75 2.00
51 Bob Christian .60 1.50
52 Bruce Dal Canton .60 1.50
53 John Kennedy .60 1.50
54 Jeff Torborg .75 2.00
55 John Odom .60 1.50
56 Joe Lis .60 1.50
Scott Reid
57 Pat Kelly .60 1.50
58 Dave Marshall .60 1.50
59 Dick Ellsworth .60 1.50
60 Jim Wynn .75 2.00
61 Rose 6.00 15.00
Clemente
Jones LL
62 R.Carew 1.25 3.00
T.Oliva
LL
63 McCovey 1.25 3.00
Santo
Perez LL
64 Kill 2.50 6.00
Powell
Reggie LL
65 McCovey 2.50 6.00
Aaron
May LL
66 Kill 2.50 6.00
Howard
Reggie LL
67 Marich 3.00 8.00
Carlton
Gibs LL
68 Bosm .75 2.00
Palmer
Cuellar LL
69 Seav 3.00 8.00
Niek
Jenk
Mar LL
70 AL Pitching Leaders .75 2.00
Dennis McLain
Mike Cuellar/
71 F.Jenkins 1.25 3.00
B.Gibson
LL
72 AL Strikeout Leaders .75 2.00
Sam McDowell
Mickey Lolich#
73 Wayne Granger .60 1.50
74 Greg Washburn .60 1.50
Wally Wolf
75 Jim Kaat .75 2.00
76 Carl Taylor .60 1.50
77 Frank Linzy .60 1.50
78 Joe Lahoud .60 1.50
79 Clay Kirby .60 1.50
80 Don Kessinger .75 2.00
81 Dave May .60 1.50
82 Frank Fernandez .60 1.50
83 Don Cardwell .60 1.50
84 Paul Casanova .60 1.50
85 Max Alvis .60 1.50
86 Lum Harris MG .60 1.50
87 Steve Renko .75 2.00
88 Miguel Fuentes .75 2.00
Dick Baney
89 Juan Rios .60 1.50
90 Tim McCarver 1.25 3.00
91 Rich Morales .60 1.50
92 George Culver .60 1.50
93 Rick Renick .60 1.50
94 Fred Patek .75 2.00
95 Earl Wilson .75 2.00
96 Jerry Reuss RC 1.25 3.00
97 Joe Moeller .60 1.50
98 Gates Brown .75 2.00
99 Bobby Pfeil .60 1.50
100 Mel Stottlemyre .75 2.00
101 Bobby Floyd .60 1.50
102 Joe Rudi .75 2.00
103 Frank Reberger .60 1.50
104 Gerry Moses .60 1.50
105 Tony Gonzalez .60 1.50
106 Darold Knowles .60 1.50
107 Bobby Etheridge .60 1.50
108 Tom Burgmeier .60 1.50
109 Garry Jestadt .75 2.00
Carl Morton
110 Bob Moose .60 1.50
111 Mike Hegan .75 2.00
112 Dave Nelson .60 1.50
113 Jim Ray .60 1.50
114 Gene Michael .75 2.00
115 Alex Johnson .75 2.00
116 Sparky Lyle 1.25 3.00
117 Don Young .60 1.50
118 George Mitterwald .60 1.50
119 Chuck Taylor .60 1.50
120 Sal Bando .75 2.00
121 Fred Beene .60 1.50
Terry Crowley
122 George Stone .60 1.50
123 Don Gutteridge MG .60 1.50
124 Larry Jaster .60 1.50
125 Deron Johnson .60 1.50
126 Marty Martinez .60 1.50
127 Joe Coleman .60 1.50
128 Checklist 133-263 3.00 8.00
129 Jimmie Price .60 1.50
130 Ollie Brown .60 1.50
131 Ray Lamb .60 1.50
Bob Stinson
132 Jim McGlothlin .60 1.50
133 Clay Carroll .60 1.50
134 Danny Walton .60 1.50
135 Dick Dietz .60 1.50
136 Steve Hargan .60 1.50
137 Art Shamsky .60 1.50
138 Joe Foy .60 1.50
139 Rich Nye .60 1.50
140 Reggie Jackson 30.00 60.00
141 Dave Cash .75 2.00
Johnny Jeter
142 Fritz Peterson .60 1.50
143 Phil Gagliano .60 1.50
144 Ray Culp .60 1.50
145 Rico Carty .75 2.00
146 Danny Murphy .60 1.50
147 Angel Hermoso .60 1.50
148 Earl Weaver MG 2.00 5.00
149 Billy Champion .60 1.50
150 Harmon Killebrew 4.00 10.00
151 Dave Roberts .60 1.50
152 Ike Brown .60 1.50
153 Gary Gentry .60 1.50
154 Jim Miles .60 1.50
Jan Dukes
155 Denis Menke .60 1.50
156 Eddie Fisher .60 1.50
157 Manny Mota 1.25 3.00
158 Jerry McNertney .75 2.00
159 Tommy Helms .75 2.00
160 Phil Niekro 2.50 6.00
161 Richie Scheinblum .60 1.50
162 Jerry Johnson .60 1.50
163 Syd O'Brien .60 1.50
164 Ty Cline .60 1.50
165 Ed Kirkpatrick .60 1.50
166 Al Oliver 1.50 4.00
167 Bill Burbach .60 1.50
168 Dave Watkins .60 1.50
169 Tom Hall .60 1.50
170 Billy Williams 3.00 8.00
171 Jim Nash .60 1.50
172 Ralph Garr RC 1.25 3.00
173 Jim Hicks .60 1.50
174 Ted Sizemore .75 2.00
175 Dick Bosman .60 1.50
176 Jim Ray Hart .75 2.00
177 Jim Northrup .75 2.00
178 Denny LeMaster .60 1.50
179 Ivan Murrell .60 1.50
180 Tommy John 1.25 3.00
181 Sparky Anderson MG 3.00 8.00
182 Dick Hall .60 1.50
183 Jerry Grote .75 2.00
184 Ray Fosse .60 1.50
185 Don Mincher .75 2.00
186 Rick Joseph .60 1.50
187 Mike Hedlund .60 1.50
188 Manny Sanguillen .75 2.00
189 Thurman Munson RC 50.00 100.00
190 Joe Torre 1.50 4.00
191 Vicente Romo .60 1.50
192 Jim Qualls .60 1.50
193 Mike Wegener .60 1.50
194 Chuck Manuel RC 1.50 4.00
195 Tom Seaver NLCS1 8.00 20.00
196 Ken Boswell NLCS 1.50 4.00
197 Nolan Ryan NLCS3 12.50 40.00
198 Mets Celebrate 8.00 20.00
N.Ryan
199 AL Playoff Game 1 1.50 4.00
Orioles win squeaker/(Mike Cue
200 Boog Powell ALCS 1.50 4.00
201 AL Playoff Game 3 1.50 4.00
Birds wrap it up/(Boog Powell
202 AL Playoff Summary 1.50 4.00
Orioles celebrate
203 Rudy May .60 1.50
204 Len Gabrielson .60 1.50
205 Bert Campaneris .75 2.00
206 Clete Boyer .75 2.00
207 Norman McRae .60 1.50
Bob Reed
208 Fred Gladding .60 1.50
209 Ken Suarez .60 1.50
210 Juan Marichal 3.00 8.00
211 Ted Williams MG 8.00 20.00
212 Al Santorini .60 1.50
213 Andy Etchebarren .60 1.50
214 Ken Boswell .60 1.50
215 Reggie Smith 1.25 3.00
216 Chuck Hartenstein .60 1.50
217 Ron Hansen .60 1.50
218 Ron Stone .60 1.50
219 Jerry Kenney .60 1.50
220 Steve Carlton 8.00 20.00
221 Ron Brand .60 1.50
222 Jim Rooker .60 1.50
223 Nate Oliver .60 1.50
224 Steve Barber .75 2.00
225 Lee May .75 2.00
226 Ron Perranoski .60 1.50
227 John Mayberry RC .75 2.00
228 Aurelio Rodriguez .60 1.50
229 Rich Robertson .60 1.50
230 Brooks Robinson 8.00 20.00
231 Luis Tiant 1.25 3.00
232 Bob Didier .60 1.50
233 Lew Krausse .60 1.50
234 Tommy Dean .60 1.50
235 Mike Epstein .60 1.50
236 Bob Veale .60 1.50
237 Russ Gibson .60 1.50
238 Jose Laboy .75 2.00
239 Ken Berry .60 1.50

240 Fergie Jenkins 3.00 8.00
241 Al Fitzmorris .60 1.50
Scott Northey
242 Walt Alston MG 1.50 4.00
243 Joe Sparma .75 2.00
244 Checklist 264-372 3.00 8.00
245 Leo Cardenas .60 1.50
246 Jim McAndrew .60 1.50
247 Lou Klimchock .60 1.50
248 Jesus Alou .60 1.50
249 Bob Locker .60 1.50
250 Willie McCovey 5.00 12.00
251 Dick Schofield .60 1.50
252 Lowell Palmer .60 1.50
253 Ron Woods .60 1.50
254 Camilo Pascual .60 1.50
255 Jim Spencer .60 1.50
256 Vic Davalillo .60 1.50
257 Dennis Higgins .60 1.50
258 Paul Popovich .60 1.50
259 Tommie Reynolds .60 1.50
260 Claude Osteen .75 2.00
261 Curt Motton .60 1.50
262 Jerry Morales .60 1.50
Jim Williams
263 Duane Josephson .60 1.50
264 Rich Hebner .60 1.50
265 Randy Hundley .60 1.50
266 Wally Bunker .60 1.50
267 Herman Hill .60 1.50
Paul Ratliff
268 Claude Raymond .75 2.00
269 Cesar Gutierrez .60 1.50
270 Chris Short .60 1.50
271 Greg Goossen .75 2.00
272 Hector Torres .60 1.50
273 Ralph Houk MG .75 2.00
274 Gerry Arrigo .60 1.50
275 Duke Sims .60 1.50
276 Ron Hunt .60 1.50
277 Paul Doyle .60 1.50
278 Tommie Aaron .60 1.50
279 Bill Lee 1.25 3.00
280 Donn Clendenon .75 2.00
281 Casey Cox .60 1.50
282 Steve Huntz .60 1.50
283 Angel Bravo .60 1.50
284 Jack Baldschun .60 1.50
285 Paul Blair .75 2.00
286 Bill Buckner RC 3.00 8.00
287 Fred Talbot .60 1.50
288 Larry Hisle .75 2.00
289 Gene Brabender .60 1.50
290 Rod Carew 10.00 25.00
291 Leo Durocher MG 1.50 4.00
292 Eddie Leon .60 1.50
293 Bob Bailey .75 2.00
294 Jose Azcue .60 1.50
295 Cecil Upshaw .60 1.50
296 Woody Woodward .60 1.50
297 Curt Blefary .60 1.50
298 Ken Henderson .60 1.50
299 Buddy Bradford .60 1.50
300 Tom Seaver 12.50 40.00
301 Chico Salmon .60 1.50
302 Jeff James .60 1.50
303 Brant Alyea .60 1.50
304 Bill Russell RC 3.00 8.00
305 Don Buford WS 1.50 4.00
306 World Series Game 2 1.50 4.00
Donn Clendenon's homer
break
307 World Series Game 3 1.50 4.00
Tommie Agee's catch
saves th
308 World Series Game 4 1.50 4.00
J.C. Martin's bunt
ends dead
309 Jerry Koosman WS 1.50 4.00
310 WS Celebration Mets 3.00 8.00
311 Dick Green .60 1.50
312 Mike Torrez .60 1.50
313 Mayo Smith MG .60 1.50
314 Bill McCool .60 1.50
315 Luis Aparicio 3.00 8.00
316 Skip Guinn .60 1.50
317 Billy Conigliaro .75 2.00
Luis Alvarado
318 Willie Smith .60 1.50
319 Clay Dalrymple .60 1.50
320 Jim Maloney .75 2.00
321 Lou Piniella 1.25 3.00
322 Luke Walker .60 1.50
323 Wayne Comer .60 1.50
324 Tony Taylor .75 2.00
325 Dave Boswell .60 1.50
326 Bill Voss .60 1.50
327 Hal King RC .60 1.50
328 George Brunet .60 1.50
329 Chris Cannizzaro .60 1.50
330 Lou Brock 5.00 12.00
331 Chuck Dobson .60 1.50
332 Bobby Wine .75 2.00
333 Bobby Murcer 1.25 3.00
334 Phil Regan .60 1.50
335 Bill Freehan .75 2.00
336 Del Unser .60 1.50
337 Mike McCormick .75 2.00
338 Paul Schaal .60 1.50
339 Johnny Edwards .60 1.50
340 Tony Conigliaro 1.50 4.00
341 Bill Sudakis .60 1.50
342 Wilbur Wood .75 2.00
343 Checklist 373-459 3.00 8.00
344 Marcelino Lopez .60 1.50
345 Al Ferrara .60 1.50
346 Red Schoendienst MG .75 2.00
347 Russ Snyder .60 1.50
348 Mike Jorgensen .75 2.00
Jesse Hudson
349 Steve Hamilton .60 1.50
350 Roberto Clemente 40.00 80.00
351 Tom Murphy .60 1.50
352 Bob Barton .60 1.50
353 Stan Williams .60 1.50
354 Amos Otis .75 2.00
355 Doug Rader .60 1.50
356 Fred Lasher .60 1.50
357 Bob Burda .60 1.50
358 Pedro Borbon RC .75 2.00
359 Phil Roof .60 1.50
360 Curt Flood 1.25 3.00
361 Ray Jarvis .60 1.50
362 Joe Hague .60 1.50
363 Tom Shopay .60 1.50
364 Dan McGinn .75 2.00
365 Zoilo Versalles .60 1.50
366 Barry Moore .60 1.50
367 Mike Lum .60 1.50
368 Ed Herrmann .60 1.50
369 Alan Foster .60 1.50
370 Tommy Harper .75 2.00
371 Rod Gaspar .60 1.50
372 Dave Giusti .60 1.50
373 Roy White .75 2.00
374 Tommie Sisk .60 1.50
375 Johnny Callison 1.25 3.00
376 Lefty Phillips MG .60 1.50
377 Bill Butler .60 1.50
378 Jim Davenport .60 1.50
379 Tom Tischinski .60 1.50
380 Tony Perez 3.00 8.00
381 Bobby Brooks .60 1.50
Mike Olivo
382 Jack DiLauro .60 1.50
383 Mickey Stanley .75 2.00
384 Gary Neibauer .60 1.50
385 George Scott .75 2.00
386 Bill Dillman .60 1.50
387 Orioles Team 1.50 4.00
388 Byron Browne .60 1.50
389 Jim Shellenback .60 1.50
390 Willie Davis 1.25 3.00
391 Larry Brown .60 1.50
392 Walt Hriniak .75 2.00
393 John Gelnar .60 1.50
394 Gil Hodges MG 1.50 4.00
395 Walt Williams .60 1.50
396 Steve Blass .75 2.00
397 Roger Repoz .60 1.50
398 Bill Stoneman .60 1.50
399 Yankees Team 1.50 4.00
400 Denny McLain 1.50 4.00
401 John Harrell .60 1.50
Bernie Williams
402 Ellie Rodriguez .60 1.50
403 Jim Bunning 3.00 8.00
404 Rich Reese .60 1.50
405 Bill Hands .60 1.50
406 Mike Andrews .60 1.50
407 Bob Watson .75 2.00
408 Paul Lindblad .60 1.50
409 Bob Tolan .60 1.50
410 Boog Powell 1.50 4.00
411 Dodgers Team 1.50 4.00
412 Larry Burchart .60 1.50
413 Sonny Jackson .60 1.50
414 Paul Edmondson .60 1.50
415 Julian Javier .75 2.00
416 Joe Verbanic .60 1.50
417 John Bateman .60 1.50
418 John Donaldson .60 1.50
419 Ron Taylor .75 2.00
420 Ken McMullen .75 2.00
421 Pat Dobson .75 2.00
422 Royals Team 1.50 4.00
423 Jerry May .60 1.50
424 Mike Kilkenny .75 2.00
425 Bobby Bonds 3.00 8.00
426 Bill Rigney MG .60 1.50
427 Fred Norman .60 1.50
428 Don Buford .60 1.50
429 Randy Bobb .60 1.50
Jim Cosman
430 Andy Messersmith .75 2.00
431 Ron Swoboda .75 2.00
432 Checklist 460-546 3.00 8.00
433 Ron Bryant .60 1.50
434 Felipe Alou 1.25 3.00
435 Nelson Briles .75 2.00
436 Phillies Team 1.50 4.00
437 Danny Cater .60 1.50
438 Pat Jarvis .60 1.50
439 Lee Maye .60 1.50
440 Bill Mazeroski 3.00 8.00
441 John O'Donoghue .60 1.50
442 Gene Mauch MG .75 2.00
443 Al Jackson .60 1.50
444 Billy Farmer .60 1.50
John Matias
445 Vada Pinson 1.25 3.00
446 Billy Grabarkewitz .60 1.50
447 Lee Stange .60 1.50
448 Astros Team 1.50 4.00
449 Jim Palmer 6.00 15.00
450 Willie McCovey AS 3.00 8.00
451 Boog Powell AS 1.50 4.00
452 Felix Millan AS 1.25 3.00
453 Rod Carew AS 3.00 8.00
454 Ron Santo AS 1.50 4.00
455 Brooks Robinson AS 3.00 8.00
456 Don Kessinger AS 1.25 3.00
457 Rico Petrocelli AS 1.50 4.00
458 Pete Rose AS 8.00 20.00
459 Reggie Jackson AS 6.00 15.00
460 Matty Alou AS 1.50 4.00
461 Carl Yastrzemski AS 5.00 12.00
462 Hank Aaron AS 8.00 20.00
463 Frank Robinson AS 4.00 10.00
464 Johnny Bench AS 8.00 20.00
465 Bill Freehan AS 1.50 4.00
466 Juan Marichal AS 2.50 6.00
467 Denny McLain AS 2.50 6.00
468 Jerry Koosman AS 1.50 4.00
469 Sam McDowell AS 1.50 4.00
470 Willie Stargell 5.00 12.00
471 Chris Zachary 1.00 2.50
472 Braves Team 1.50 4.00
473 Don Bryant 1.00 2.50
474 Dick Kelley 1.00 2.50
475 Dick McAuliffe 1.50 4.00
476 Don Shaw 1.00 2.50
477 Al Severinsen 1.00 2.50
Roger Freed
478 Bob Heise 1.00 2.50
479 Dick Woodson 1.00 2.50
480 Glenn Beckert 1.50 4.00
481 Jose Tartabull 1.00 2.50
482 Tom Hilgendorf 1.00 2.50
483 Gail Hopkins 1.00 2.50
484 Gary Nolan 1.50 4.00
485 Jay Johnstone 1.50 4.00
486 Terry Harmon 1.00 2.50
487 Cisco Carlos 1.00 2.50
488 J.C. Martin 1.00 2.50
489 Eddie Kasko MG 1.00 2.50
490 Bill Singer 1.50 4.00
491 Graig Nettles 2.50 6.00
492 Keith Lampard 1.00 2.50
Scipio Spinks
493 Lindy McDaniel 1.50 4.00
494 Larry Stahl 1.00 2.50
495 Dave Morehead 1.00 2.50
496 Steve Whitaker 1.00 2.50
497 Eddie Watt 1.00 2.50
498 Al Weis 1.00 2.50
499 Skip Lockwood 1.00 2.50
500 Hank Aaron 30.00 60.00
501 White Sox Team 1.50 4.00
502 Rollie Fingers 5.00 12.00
503 Dal Maxvill 1.00 2.50
504 Don Pavletich 1.00 2.50
505 Ken Holtzman 1.50 4.00
506 Ed Stroud 1.00 2.50
507 Pat Corrales 1.00 2.50
508 Joe Niekro 1.50 4.00
509 Expos Team 2.50 6.00
510 Tony Oliva 2.50 6.00
511 Joe Hoerner 1.00 2.50
512 Billy Harris 1.00 2.50
513 Preston Gomez MG 1.00 2.50
514 Steve Hovley 1.00 2.50
515 Don Wilson 1.50 4.00
516 John Ellis 1.00 2.50
Jim Lyttle
517 Joe Gibbon 1.00 2.50
518 Bill Melton 1.00 2.50
519 Don McMahon 1.00 2.50
520 Willie Horton 1.50 4.00
521 Cal Koonce 1.00 2.50
522 Angels Team 1.50 4.00
523 Jose Pena 1.00 2.50
524 Alvin Dark MG 1.50 4.00
525 Jerry Adair 1.00 2.50
526 Ron Herbel 1.00 2.50
527 Don Bosch 1.50 4.00
528 Elrod Hendricks 1.00 2.50
529 Bob Aspromonte 1.00 2.50
530 Bob Gibson 8.00 20.00
531 Ron Clark 1.00 2.50
532 Danny Murtaugh MG 1.50 4.00
533 Buzz Stephen 1.00 2.50
534 Twins Team 1.50 4.00
535 Andy Kosco 1.00 2.50
536 Mike Kekich 1.00 2.50
537 Joe Morgan 5.00 12.00
538 Bob Humphreys 1.00 2.50
539 Larry Bowa RC 4.00 10.00
540 Gary Peters 1.00 2.50
541 Bill Heath 1.00 2.50
542 Checklist 547-633 3.00 8.00
543 Clyde Wright 1.00 2.50
544 Reds Team 2.50 6.00
545 Ken Harrelson 1.50 4.00
546 Ron Reed 1.50 4.00

1971 O-Pee-Chee

The cards in this 752-card set measure 2 1/2" by 3 1/2". The 1971 O-Pee-Chee set is a challenge to complete in "Mint" condition because the black borders are easily scratched and damaged. The O-Pee-Chee cards seem to have been cut (into individual cards) not as sharply as the Topps cards; the borders frequently appear slightly frayed. The players are also pictured in black and white on the back of the card. The next-to-last series (524-643) and the last series (644-752) are somewhat scarce. The O-Pee-Chee cards can be distinguished from Topps cards by the "Printed in Canada" on the bottom of the reverse. The reverse color is yellow instead of the green found on the backs of the 1971 Topps cards. The card backs are written in both French and English, except for cards 524-752 which were printed in English only. There are several cards which are different from the corresponding Topps card with a different pose or different team noted in bold type, i.e. "Recently Traded to ..." These changed cards are numbers 31, 32, 73, 144, 151, 161, 172, 182, 191, 202, 207, 248, 289 and 578. These cards were issued in eight-card dime packs which came 36 packs to a box. Remember, the prices below apply only to the 1971 O-Pee-Chee cards -- NOT Topps cards which are much more plentiful. Notable Rookie Cards include Dusty Baker and Don Baylor (Sharing the same card), Bert Blyleven, Dave Concepcion and Steve Garvey.

COMPLETE SET (752) 1,250.00 2,500.00
COMMON PLAYER (1-393) .60 1.50
COMMON PLAYER (394-523) 1.25 3.00
COMMON PLAYER (524-643) 1.50 4.00
COMMON PLAYER (644-752) 4.00 10.00
1 Orioles Team 10.00 25.00
2 Dock Ellis .60 1.50
3 Dick McAuliffe .75 2.00
4 Vic Davalillo .60 1.50
5 Thurman Munson 75.00 150.00
6 Ed Spiezio .60 1.50
7 Jim Holt .60 1.50
8 Mike McQueen .60 1.50
9 George Scott .75 2.00
10 Claude Osteen .75 2.00
11 Elliott Maddox .60 1.50
12 Johnny Callison .75 2.00
13 Charlie Brinkman .60 1.50
Dick Moloney
14 Dave Concepcion RC 10.00 25.00
15 Andy Messersmith .75 2.00
16 Ken Singleton RC 1.25 3.00
17 Billy Sorrell .60 1.50
18 Norm Miller .60 1.50
19 Skip Pitlock .60 1.50
20 Reggie Jackson 30.00 60.00
21 Dan McGinn .75 2.00
22 Phil Roof .60 1.50
23 Oscar Gamble .60 1.50
24 Rich Hand .60 1.50
25 Cito Gaston .75 2.00
26 Bert Blyleven RC 10.00 25.00
27 Fred Cambria .60 1.50
Gene Clines
28 Ron Klimkowski .60 1.50
29 Don Buford .60 1.50
30 Phil Niekro 3.00 8.00
31 John Bateman/(different pose) 1.25 3.00
32 Jerry DeVanon .75 2.00
Recently Traded To Orioles
33 Del Unser .60 1.50
34 Sandy Vance .60 1.50
35 Lou Piniella 1.25 3.00
36 Dean Chance .75 2.00
37 Rich McKinney .60 1.50
38 Jim Colborn .60 1.50
39 Gene Lamont RC .75 2.00
40 Lee May .75 2.00
41 Rick Austin .60 1.50
42 Boots Day .75 2.00
43 Steve Kealey .60 1.50
44 Johnny Edwards .60 1.50
45 Jim Hunter 3.00 8.00
46 Dave Campbell .75 2.00
47 Johnny Jeter .60 1.50
48 Dave Baldwin .60 1.50
49 Don Money .60 1.50
50 Willie McCovey 5.00 12.00
51 Steve Kline .60 1.50
52 Earl Williams RC .60 1.50
53 Paul Blair .75 2.00
54 Checklist 1-132 4.00 10.00
55 Steve Carlton 10.00 25.00
56 Duane Josephson .60 1.50
57 Von Joshua .60 1.50
58 Bill Lee .75 2.00
59 Gene Mauch MG .75 2.00
60 Dick Bosman .60 1.50
61 A.Johnson 1.25 3.00
Yaz
Oliva LL
62 NL Batting Leaders .75 2.00
Rico Carty
Joe Torre
Manny S
63 AL RBI Leaders 1.25 3.00
Frank Howard
Tony Conigliaro
B
64 Bench 3.00 8.00
Perez
B.Will LL
65 F.Howard 1.25 3.00
Kill
Yaz LL
66 Bench 3.00 8.00
B.Will
Perez LL
67 Segui 1.25 3.00
Palmer
Wright LL
68 Seaver 1.25 3.00
Simpson
Walker LL
69 AL Pitching Leaders .75 2.00
Mike Cuellar
Dave McNally
J
70 Gibson 3.00 8.00
Perry
Jenk LL
71 AL Strikeout Leaders .75 2.00
Sam McDowell
Mickey Lolich#
72 Seaver 3.00 8.00

Gibson
Jenk LL
73 George Brunet/(St. Louis Cardinals) .60 1.50
74 Pete Hamm .60 1.50
Jim Nettles
75 Gary Nolan .75 2.00
76 Ted Savage .60 1.50
77 Mike Compton .60 1.50
78 Jim Spencer .60 1.50
79 Wade Blasingame .60 1.50
80 Bill Melton .60 1.50
81 Felix Millan .60 1.50
82 Casey Cox .60 1.50
83 Tim Foli RC .75 2.00
84 Marcel Lachemann RC .60 1.50
85 Bill Grabarkewitz .60 1.50
86 Mike Kilkenny .75 2.00
87 Jack Heidemann .60 1.50
88 Hal King .60 1.50
89 Ken Brett .60 1.50
90 Joe Pepitone .75 2.00
91 Bob Lemon MG .75 2.00
92 Fred Wenz .60 1.50
93 Norm McRae .60 1.50
Denny Riddleberger
94 Don Hahn .75 2.00
95 Luis Tiant .75 2.00
96 Joe Hague .60 1.50
97 Floyd Wicker .60 1.50
98 Joe Decker .60 1.50
99 Mark Belanger .75 2.00
100 Pete Rose 50.00 100.00
101 Les Cain .60 1.50
102 Ken Forsch .75 2.00
Larry Howard
103 Rich Severson .60 1.50
104 Dan Frisella .60 1.50
105 Tony Conigliaro .75 2.00
106 Tom Dukes .60 1.50
107 Roy Foster .60 1.50
108 John Cumberland .60 1.50
109 Steve Hovley .60 1.50
110 Bill Mazeroski 3.00 8.00
111 Loyd Colson .60 1.50
Bobby Mitchell
112 Manny Mota .75 2.00
113 Jerry Crider .60 1.50
114 Billy Conigliaro .75 2.00
115 Donn Clendenon .75 2.00
116 Ken Sanders .60 1.50
117 Ted Simmons RC 4.00 10.00
118 Cookie Rojas .75 2.00
119 Frank Lucchesi MG .60 1.50
120 Willie Horton .75 2.00
121 Jim Dunegan .60 1.50
Roe Skidmore
122 Eddie Watt .60 1.50
123 Checklist 133-263 4.00 10.00
124 Don Gullett RC .75 2.00
125 Ray Fosse .60 1.50
126 Danny Coombs .60 1.50
127 Danny Thompson .75 2.00
128 Frank Johnson .60 1.50
129 Aurelio Monteagudo .60 1.50
130 Denis Menke .60 1.50
131 Curt Blefary .60 1.50
132 Jose Laboy .75 2.00
133 Mickey Lolich .75 2.00
134 Jose Arcia .60 1.50
135 Rick Monday .75 2.00
136 Duffy Dyer .60 1.50
137 Marcelino Lopez .60 1.50
138 Joe Lis .75 2.00
Willie Montanez
139 Paul Casanova .60 1.50
140 Gaylord Perry 3.00 8.00
141 Frank Quilici MG .60 1.50
142 Mack Jones .75 2.00
143 Steve Blass .75 2.00
144 Jackie Hernandez .75 2.00
145 Bill Singer .75 2.00
146 Ralph Houk MG .75 2.00
147 Bob Priddy .60 1.50
148 John Mayberry .75 2.00
149 Mike Hershberger .60 1.50
150 Sam McDowell .75 2.00
151 Tommy Davis/(Oakland A's) 1.25 3.00
152 Lloyd Allen .60 1.50
Winston Llenas
153 Gary Ross .60 1.50
154 Cesar Gutierrez .60 1.50
155 Ken Henderson .60 1.50
156 Bart Johnson .60 1.50
157 Bob Bailey 1.25 3.00
158 Jerry Reuss .75 2.00
159 Jarvis Tatum .60 1.50
160 Tom Seaver 12.50 40.00
161 Ron Hunt/(different pose) 2.50 6.00
162 Jack Billingham .60 1.50
163 Buck Martinez .75 2.00
164 Frank Duffy .75 2.00
Milt Wilcox
165 Cesar Tovar .60 1.50
166 Joe Hoerner .60 1.50
167 Tom Grieve RC .75 2.00
168 Bruce Dal Canton .60 1.50
169 Ed Herrmann .60 1.50
170 Mike Cuellar .75 2.00
171 Bobby Wine .75 2.00
172 Duke Sims/(Los Angeles Dodgers) .75 2.00
173 Gil Garrido .60 1.50
174 Dave LaRoche .60 1.50
175 Jim Hickman .60 1.50
176 Bob Montgomery RC .75 2.00
177 Hal McRae .75 2.00
178 Dave Duncan .75 2.00
179 Mike Corkins .60 1.50
180 Al Kaline 10.00 25.00
181 Hal Lanier .60 1.50
182 Al Downing/(Los Angeles Dodgers) .75 2.00
183 Gil Hodges MG 1.25 3.00
184 Stan Bahnsen .60 1.50
185 Julian Javier .60 1.50
186 Bob Spence .60 1.50
187 Ted Abernathy .60 1.50
188 Bobby Valentine RC 3.00 8.00
189 George Mitterwald .60 1.50
190 Bob Tolan .60 1.50
191 Mike Andrews/(Chicago White Sox) .75 2.00
192 Billy Wilson .60 1.50
193 Bob Grich RC 1.25 3.00
194 Mike Lum .60 1.50
195 Boog Powell ALCS .75 2.00
196 AL Playoff Game 2 .75 2.00
Dave McNally makes it
two stra
197 Jim Palmer ALCS2 1.25 3.00
198 AL Playoff Summary .75 2.00
Orioles Celebrate
199 NL Playoff Game 1 .75 2.00
Ty Cline pinch-triple
decides
200 NL Playoff Game 2 .75 2.00
Bobby Tolan scores for
third t
201 Ty Cline NLCS .75 2.00
202 Claude Raymond/(different pose) 2.50 6.00
203 Larry Gura .75 2.00
204 Bernie Smith .60 1.50
George Kopacz
205 Gerry Moses .60 1.50
206 Checklist 264-393 5.00 12.00
207 Alan Foster/(Cleveland Indians) .75 2.00
208 Billy Martin MG 1.25 3.00
209 Steve Renko .75 2.00
210 Rod Carew 8.00 20.00
211 Phil Hennigan .60 1.50
212 Rich Hebner .75 2.00
213 Frank Baker .60 1.50
214 Al Ferrara .60 1.50
215 Diego Segui .60 1.50
216 Reggie Cleveland .75 2.00
Luis Melendez
217 Ed Stroud .60 1.50
218 Tony Cloninger .60 1.50
219 Elrod Hendricks .60 1.50
220 Ron Santo 1.25 3.00
221 Dave Morehead .60 1.50
222 Bob Watson .75 2.00
223 Cecil Upshaw .60 1.50
224 Alan Gallagher .60 1.50
225 Gary Peters .60 1.50
226 Bill Russell .75 2.00
227 Floyd Weaver .60 1.50
228 Wayne Garrett .60 1.50
229 Jim Hannan .60 1.50
230 Willie Stargell 8.00 20.00
231 John Lowenstein RC .75 2.00
232 John Strohmayer .75 2.00
233 Larry Bowa .75 2.00
234 Jim Lyttle .60 1.50
235 Nate Colbert .60 1.50
236 Bob Humphreys .60 1.50
237 Cesar Cedeno RC .75 2.00
238 Chuck Dobson .60 1.50
239 Red Schoendienst MG .75 2.00
240 Clyde Wright .60 1.50
241 Dave Nelson .60 1.50
242 Jim Ray .60 1.50
243 Carlos May .60 1.50
244 Bob Tillman .60 1.50
245 Jim Kaat .75 2.00
246 Tony Taylor .60 1.50
247 Jerry Cram .75 2.00
Paul Splittorff
248 Hoyt Wilhelm/(Atlanta Braves) 4.00 10.00
249 Chico Salmon .60 1.50
250 Johnny Bench 30.00 60.00
251 Frank Reberger .60 1.50
252 Eddie Leon .60 1.50
253 Bill Sudakis .60 1.50
254 Cal Koonce .60 1.50
255 Bob Robertson .75 2.00
256 Tony Gonzalez .60 1.50
257 Nelson Briles .75 2.00
258 Dick Green .60 1.50
259 Dave Marshall .60 1.50
260 Tommy Harper .75 2.00
261 Darold Knowles .60 1.50
262 Jim Williams .60 1.50
Dave Robinson
263 John Ellis .60 1.50
264 Joe Morgan 4.00 10.00
265 Jim Northrup .75 2.00
266 Bill Stoneman .75 2.00
267 Rich Morales .60 1.50
268 Phillies Team 1.25 3.00
269 Gail Hopkins .60 1.50
270 Rico Carty .75 2.00
271 Bill Zepp .60 1.50
272 Tommy Helms .75 2.00
273 Pete Richert .60 1.50
274 Ron Slocum .60 1.50
275 Vada Pinson .75 2.00
276 George Foster RC 4.00 10.00
277 Gary Waslewski .60 1.50
278 Jerry Grote .75 2.00
279 Lefty Phillips MG .60 1.50
280 Fergie Jenkins 3.00 8.00
281 Danny Walton .60 1.50
282 Jose Pagan .60 1.50
283 Dick Such .60 1.50
284 Jim Gosger .75 2.00
285 Sal Bando .75 2.00
286 Jerry McNertney .60 1.50
287 Mike Fiore .60 1.50
288 Joe Moeller .60 1.50
289 Rusty Staub/(Different pose) 4.00 10.00
290 Tony Oliva 1.25 3.00
291 George Culver .60 1.50
292 Jay Johnstone .75 2.00
293 Pat Corrales .75 2.00
294 Steve Dunning .60 1.50
295 Bobby Bonds 2.50 6.00
296 Tom Timmermann .60 1.50
297 Johnny Briggs .60 1.50
298 Jim Nelson .60 1.50
299 Ed Kirkpatrick .75 2.00
300 Brooks Robinson 10.00 25.00
301 Earl Wilson .60 1.50
302 Phil Gagliano .60 1.50
303 Lindy McDaniel .75 2.00
304 Ron Brand .75 2.00
305 Reggie Smith .75 2.00
306 Jim Nash .60 1.50
307 Don Wert .60 1.50
308 Cardinals Team 1.25 3.00
309 Dick Ellsworth .60 1.50
310 Tommie Agee .75 2.00
311 Lee Stange .60 1.50
312 Harry Walker MG .60 1.50
313 Tom Hall .60 1.50
314 Jeff Torborg .75 2.00
315 Ron Fairly 1.25 3.00
316 Fred Scherman .60 1.50
317 Jim Driscoll .60 1.50
Angel Mangual
318 Rudy May .60 1.50
319 Ty Cline .60 1.50
320 Dave McNally .75 2.00
321 Tom Matchick .60 1.50
322 Jim Beauchamp .60 1.50
323 Billy Champion .60 1.50
324 Graig Nettles 1.25 3.00
325 Juan Marichal 4.00 10.00
326 Richie Scheinblum .60 1.50
327 World Series Game 1 .75 2.00
Boog Powell homers to
opposi
328 Don Buford WS .75 2.00
329 Frank Robinson WS3 1.25 3.00
330 World Series Game 4 .75 2.00
Reds stay alive
331 Brooks Robinson WS5 3.00 8.00
332 World Series Summary .75 2.00
Orioles Celebrate
333 Clay Kirby .60 1.50
334 Roberto Pena .60 1.50
335 Jerry Koosman .75 2.00
336 Tigers Team 1.25 3.00
337 Jesus Alou .60 1.50
338 Gene Tenace .75 2.00
339 Wayne Simpson .60 1.50
340 Rico Petrocelli .75 2.00
341 Steve Garvey RC 20.00 50.00
342 Frank Tepedino .75 2.00
343 Milt May RC .75 2.00
344 Ellie Rodriguez .60 1.50
345 Joel Horlen .60 1.50
346 Lum Harris MG .60 1.50
347 Ted Uhlaender .60 1.50
348 Fred Norman .60 1.50
349 Rich Reese .60 1.50
350 Billy Williams 3.00 8.00
351 Jim Shellenback .60 1.50
352 Denny Doyle .60 1.50
353 Carl Taylor .60 1.50
354 Don McMahon .60 1.50
355 Bud Harrelson 1.25 3.00
356 Bob Locker .60 1.50
357 Reds Team 1.25 3.00
358 Danny Cater .60 1.50
359 Ron Reed .60 1.50
360 Jim Fregosi .75 2.00
361 Don Sutton 3.00 8.00
362 Mike Adamson .60 1.50
Roger Freed
363 Mike Nagy .60 1.50
364 Tommy Dean .60 1.50
365 Bob Johnson .60 1.50
366 Ron Stone .60 1.50
367 Dalton Jones .60 1.50
368 Bob Veale .75 2.00
369 Checklist 394-523 4.00 10.00
370 Joe Torre 2.50 6.00
371 Jack Hiatt .60 1.50
372 Lew Krausse .60 1.50
373 Tom McCraw .60 1.50
374 Clete Boyer .75 2.00
375 Steve Hargan .60 1.50
376 Clyde Mashore .75 2.00
Ernie McAnally
377 Greg Garrett .60 1.50
378 Tito Fuentes .60 1.50
379 Wayne Granger .60 1.50
380 Ted Williams MG 6.00 15.00
381 Fred Gladding .60 1.50
382 Jake Gibbs .60 1.50
383 Rod Gaspar .60 1.50
384 Rollie Fingers 3.00 8.00
385 Maury Wills 2.50 6.00
386 Red Sox Team 1.25 3.00
387 Ron Herbel .60 1.50
388 Al Oliver 1.25 3.00
389 Ed Brinkman .60 1.50
390 Glenn Beckert .75 2.00
391 Steve Brye .75 2.00
Cotton Nash
392 Grant Jackson .60 1.50
393 Merv Rettenmund .75 2.00
394 Clay Carroll 1.25 3.00
395 Roy White 1.50 4.00
396 Dick Schofield 1.25 3.00
397 Alvin Dark MG 1.50 4.00
398 Howie Reed 1.50 4.00
399 Jim French 1.25 3.00
400 Hank Aaron 40.00 80.00
401 Tom Murphy 1.25 3.00
402 Dodgers Team 2.50 6.00
403 Joe Coleman 1.25 3.00
404 Buddy Harris 1.25 3.00
Roger Metzger
405 Leo Cardenas 1.25 3.00
406 Ray Sadecki 1.25 3.00
407 Joe Rudi 1.50 4.00
408 Rafael Robles 1.25 3.00
409 Don Pavletich 1.25 3.00
410 Ken Holtzman 1.50 4.00
411 George Spriggs 1.25 3.00
412 Jerry Johnson 1.25 3.00
413 Pat Kelly 1.25 3.00
414 Woodie Fryman 1.25 3.00
415 Mike Hegan 1.25 3.00
416 Gene Alley 1.25 3.00
417 Dick Hall 1.25 3.00
418 Adolfo Phillips 1.50 4.00
419 Ron Hansen 1.25 3.00
420 Jim Merritt 1.25 3.00
421 John Stephenson 1.25 3.00
422 Frank Bertaina 1.25 3.00
423 Dennis Saunders 1.25 3.00
Tim Marting
424 Roberto Rodriquez 1.25 3.00
425 Doug Rader 1.50 4.00
426 Chris Cannizzaro 1.25 3.00
427 Bernie Allen 1.25 3.00
428 Jim McAndrew 1.25 3.00
429 Chuck Hinton 1.25 3.00
430 Wes Parker 1.50 4.00
431 Tom Burgmeier 1.25 3.00
432 Bob Didier 1.25 3.00
433 Skip Lockwood 1.25 3.00
434 Gary Sutherland 1.50 4.00
435 Jose Cardenal 1.50 4.00
436 Wilbur Wood 1.50 4.00
437 Danny Murtaugh MG 1.50 4.00
438 Mike McCormick 1.50 4.00
439 Greg Luzinski RC 2.50 6.00
440 Bert Campaneris 1.50 4.00
441 Milt Pappas 1.50 4.00
442 Angels Team 2.50 6.00
443 Rich Robertson 1.25 3.00
444 Jimmie Price 1.25 3.00
445 Art Shamsky 1.25 3.00
446 Bobby Bolin 1.25 3.00
447 Cesar Geronimo 1.50 4.00
448 Dave Roberts 1.25 3.00
449 Brant Alyea 1.25 3.00
450 Bob Gibson 8.00 20.00
451 Joe Keough 1.25 3.00
452 John Boccabella 1.50 4.00
453 Terry Crowley 1.25 3.00
454 Mike Paul 1.25 3.00
455 Don Kessinger 1.50 4.00
456 Bob Meyer 1.25 3.00
457 Willie Smith 1.25 3.00
458 Ron Lolich 1.25 3.00
Dave Lemonds
459 Jim Lefebvre 1.25 3.00
460 Fritz Peterson 1.25 3.00
461 Jim Ray Hart 1.25 3.00
462 Senators Team 2.50 6.00
463 Tom Kelley 1.25 3.00
464 Aurelio Rodriguez 1.25 3.00
465 Tim McCarver 2.50 6.00
466 Ken Berry 1.25 3.00
467 Al Santorini 1.25 3.00
468 Frank Fernandez 1.25 3.00
469 Bob Aspromonte 1.25 3.00
470 Bob Oliver 1.25 3.00
471 Tom Griffin 1.25 3.00
472 Ken Rudolph 1.25 3.00
473 Gary Wagner 1.25 3.00
474 Jim Fairey 1.50 4.00
475 Ron Perranoski 1.25 3.00
476 Dal Maxvill 1.25 3.00
477 Earl Weaver MG 3.00 8.00
478 Bernie Carbo 1.25 3.00
479 Dennis Higgins 1.25 3.00
480 Manny Sanguillen 1.50 4.00
481 Daryl Patterson 1.25 3.00
482 Padres Team 2.50 6.00
483 Gene Michael 1.25 3.00
484 Don Wilson 1.25 3.00
485 Ken McMullen 1.25 3.00
486 Steve Huntz 1.25 3.00
487 Paul Schaal 1.25 3.00
488 Jerry Stephenson 1.25 3.00
489 Luis Alvarado 1.25 3.00
490 Deron Johnson 1.25 3.00
491 Jim Hardin 1.25 3.00
492 Ken Boswell 1.25 3.00
493 Dave May 1.25 3.00
494 Ralph Garr 1.50 4.00
Rick Kester
495 Felipe Alou 1.50 4.00
496 Woody Woodward 1.25 3.00
497 Horacio Pina 1.25 3.00
498 John Kennedy 1.25 3.00
499 Checklist 524-643 3.00 8.00
500 Jim Perry 1.50 4.00
501 Andy Etchebarren 1.25 3.00
502 Cubs Team 2.50 6.00
503 Gates Brown 1.50 4.00
504 Ken Wright 1.25 3.00

Card	Low	High
505 Ollie Brown	1.25	3.00
506 Bobby Knoop	1.25	3.00
507 George Stone	1.25	3.00
508 Roger Repoz	1.25	3.00
509 Jim Grant	1.25	3.00
510 Ken Harrelson	1.50	4.00
511 Chris Short	1.50	4.00
512 Dick Mills	1.25	3.00
Mike Garman		
513 Nolan Ryan	100.00	200.00
514 Ron Woods	1.25	3.00
515 Carl Morton	1.50	4.00
516 Ted Kubiak	1.25	3.00
517 Charlie Fox MG	1.25	3.00
518 Joe Grzenda	1.25	3.00
519 Willie Crawford	1.25	3.00
520 Tommy John	2.50	6.00
521 Leron Lee	1.25	3.00
522 Twins Team	2.50	6.00
523 John Odom	1.25	3.00
524 Mickey Stanley	2.50	6.00
525 Ernie Banks	40.00	80.00
526 Ray Jarvis	1.50	4.00
527 Cleon Jones	2.50	6.00
528 Wally Bunker	1.50	4.00
529 Bill Buckner	2.50	6.00
530 Carl Yastrzemski	20.00	50.00
531 Mike Torrez	1.50	4.00
532 Bill Rigney MG	1.50	4.00
533 Mike Ryan	1.50	4.00
534 Luke Walker	1.50	4.00
535 Curt Flood	2.50	6.00
536 Claude Raymond	2.50	6.00
537 Tom Egan	1.50	4.00
538 Angel Bravo	1.50	4.00
539 Larry Brown	1.50	4.00
540 Larry Dierker	2.50	6.00
541 Bob Burda	1.50	4.00
542 Bob Miller	1.50	4.00
543 Yankees Team	6.00	15.00
544 Vida Blue	2.50	6.00
545 Dick Dietz	1.50	4.00
546 John Matias	1.50	4.00
547 Pat Dobson	1.50	4.00
548 Don Mason	1.50	4.00
549 Jim Brewer	1.50	4.00
550 Harmon Killebrew	12.50	40.00
551 Frank Linzy	1.50	4.00
552 Buddy Bradford	1.50	4.00
553 Kevin Collins	1.50	4.00
554 Lowell Palmer	1.50	4.00
555 Walt Williams	1.50	4.00
556 Jim McGlothlin	1.50	4.00
557 Tom Satriano	1.50	4.00
558 Hector Torres	1.50	4.00
559 AL Rookie Pitchers	1.50	4.00
Terry Cox		
Bill Gogolewski		
Ga		
560 Rusty Staub	3.00	8.00
561 Syd O'Brien	1.50	4.00
562 Dave Giusti	1.50	4.00
563 Giants Team	3.00	8.00
564 Al Fitzmorris	1.50	4.00
565 Jim Wynn	2.50	6.00
566 Tim Cullen	1.50	4.00
567 Walt Alston MG	4.00	10.00
568 Sal Campisi	1.50	4.00
569 Ivan Murrell	1.50	4.00
570 Jim Palmer	20.00	50.00
571 Ted Sizemore	1.50	4.00
572 Jerry Kenney	1.50	4.00
573 Ed Kranepool	2.50	6.00
574 Jim Bunning	4.00	10.00
575 Bill Freehan	2.50	6.00
576 Cubs Rookies	1.50	4.00
Adrian Garrett		
Brock Davis		
Garry J		
577 Jim Lonborg	2.50	6.00
578 Eddie Kasko/(Topps 578 is Ron Hunt)	2.50	6.00
579 Marty Pattin	1.50	4.00
580 Tony Perez	12.50	30.00
581 Roger Nelson	1.50	4.00
582 Dave Cash	2.50	6.00
583 Ron Cook	1.50	4.00
584 Indians Team	3.00	8.00
585 Willie Davis	2.50	6.00
586 Dick Woodson	1.50	4.00
587 Sonny Jackson	1.50	4.00
588 Tom Bradley	1.50	4.00
589 Bob Barton	1.50	4.00

Card	Low	High
590 Alex Johnson	2.50	6.00
591 Jackie Brown	1.50	4.00
592 Randy Hundley	2.50	6.00
593 Jack Aker	1.50	4.00
594 Al Hrabosky RC	2.50	6.00
595 Dave Johnson	2.50	6.00
596 Mike Jorgensen	1.50	4.00
597 Ken Suarez	1.50	4.00
598 Rick Wise	2.50	6.00
599 Norm Cash	2.50	6.00
600 Willie Mays	75.00	150.00
601 Ken Tatum	1.50	4.00
602 Marty Martinez	1.50	4.00
603 Pirates Team	3.00	8.00
604 John Gelnar	1.50	4.00
605 Orlando Cepeda	4.00	10.00
606 Chuck Taylor	1.50	4.00
607 Paul Ratliff	1.50	4.00
608 Mike Wegener	2.50	6.00
609 Leo Durocher MG	3.00	8.00
610 Amos Otis	2.50	6.00
611 Tom Phoebus	1.50	4.00
612 Indians Rookies	1.50	4.00
Lou Camilli		
Ted Ford		
Steve Ming		
613 Pedro Borbon	1.50	4.00
614 Billy Cowan	1.50	4.00
615 Mel Stottlemyre	2.50	6.00
616 Larry Hisle	2.50	6.00
617 Clay Dalrymple	1.50	4.00
618 Tug McGraw	2.50	6.00
619 Checklist 644-752	4.00	10.00
620 Frank Howard	2.50	6.00
621 Ron Bryant	1.50	4.00
622 Joe Lahoud	1.50	4.00
623 Pat Jarvis	1.50	4.00
624 Athletics Team	3.00	8.00
625 Lou Brock	20.00	50.00
626 Freddie Patek	2.50	6.00
627 Steve Hamilton	1.50	4.00
628 John Bateman	2.50	6.00
629 John Hiller	3.00	8.00
630 Roberto Clemente	100.00	200.00
631 Eddie Fisher	1.50	4.00
632 Darrel Chaney	1.50	4.00
633 AL Rookie Outfielders	1.50	4.00
Bobby Brooks		
Pete Koegel/		
634 Phil Regan	1.50	4.00
635 Bobby Murcer	2.50	6.00
636 Denny LeMaster	1.50	4.00
637 Dave Bristol MG	1.50	4.00
638 Stan Williams	1.50	4.00
639 Tom Haller	1.50	4.00
640 Frank Robinson	30.00	60.00
641 Mets Team	10.00	25.00
642 Jim Roland	1.50	4.00
643 Rick Reichardt	1.50	4.00
644 Jim Stewart	4.00	10.00
645 Jim Maloney	5.00	12.00
646 Bobby Floyd	4.00	10.00
647 Juan Pizarro	4.00	10.00
648 Jon Matlack RC SP	8.00	20.00
649 Sparky Lyle	6.00	15.00
650 Richie Allen SP !	20.00	50.00
651 Jerry Robertson	4.00	10.00
652 Braves Team	6.00	15.00
653 Russ Snyder	4.00	10.00
654 Don Shaw	4.00	10.00
655 Mike Epstein	4.00	10.00
656 Gerry Nyman	4.00	10.00
657 Jose Azcue	4.00	10.00
658 Paul Lindblad	4.00	10.00
659 Byron Browne	4.00	10.00
660 Ray Culp	4.00	10.00
661 Chuck Tanner MG	6.00	15.00
662 Mike Hedlund	4.00	10.00
663 Marv Staehle	4.00	10.00
664 Rookie Pitchers	6.00	15.00
Archie Reynolds		
Bob Reynolds		
Ke		
665 Ron Swoboda	6.00	15.00
666 Gene Brabender	4.00	10.00
667 Pete Ward	5.00	12.00
668 Gary Neibauer	4.00	10.00
669 Ike Brown	4.00	10.00
670 Bill Hands	4.00	10.00
671 Bill Voss	4.00	10.00
672 Ed Crosby	4.00	10.00
673 Gerry Janeski	4.00	10.00
674 Expos Team	6.00	15.00

Card	Low	High
675 Dave Boswell	4.00	10.00
676 Tommie Reynolds	4.00	10.00
677 Jack DiLauro	4.00	10.00
678 George Thomas	4.00	10.00
679 Don O'Riley	4.00	10.00
680 Don Mincher	4.00	10.00
681 Bill Butler	4.00	10.00
682 Terry Harmon	4.00	10.00
683 Bill Burbach	4.00	10.00
684 Curt Motton	4.00	10.00
685 Moe Drabowsky	4.00	10.00
686 Chico Ruiz	4.00	10.00
687 Ron Taylor	5.00	12.00
688 Sparky Anderson MG	20.00	50.00
689 Frank Baker	4.00	10.00
690 Bob Moose	4.00	10.00
691 Bob Heise	4.00	10.00
692 AL Rookie Pitchers	4.00	10.00
Hal Haydel		
Rogelio Moret		
Way		
693 Jose Pena	4.00	10.00
694 Rick Renick	4.00	10.00
695 Joe Niekro	5.00	12.00
696 Jerry Morales	4.00	10.00
697 Rickey Clark	4.00	10.00
698 Brewers Team	8.00	20.00
699 Jim Britton	5.00	12.00
700 Boog Powell	12.50	40.00
701 Bob Garibaldi	4.00	10.00
702 Milt Ramirez	4.00	10.00
703 Mike Kekich	4.00	10.00
704 J.C. Martin	4.00	10.00
705 Dick Selma	4.00	10.00
706 Joe Foy	4.00	10.00
707 Fred Lasher	4.00	10.00
708 Russ Nagelson	4.00	10.00
709 D.Baylor	60.00	120.00
D.Baker RC SP !		
710 Sonny Siebert	4.00	10.00
711 Larry Stahl	4.00	10.00
712 Jose Martinez	4.00	10.00
713 Mike Marshall	8.00	20.00
714 Dick Williams MG	6.00	15.00
715 Horace Clarke	4.00	10.00
716 Dave Leonhard	4.00	10.00
717 Tommie Aaron	5.00	12.00
718 Billy Wynne	4.00	10.00
719 Jerry May	4.00	10.00
720 Matty Alou	5.00	12.00
721 John Morris	4.00	10.00
722 Astros Team	8.00	20.00
723 Vicente Romo	4.00	10.00
724 Tom Tischinski	4.00	10.00
725 Gary Gentry	4.00	10.00
726 Paul Popovich	4.00	10.00
727 Ray Lamb	4.00	10.00
728 NL Rookie Outfielders	4.00	10.00
Wayne Redmond		
Keith Lampar		
729 Dick Billings	4.00	10.00
730 Jim Rooker	4.00	10.00
731 Jim Qualls	4.00	10.00
732 Bob Reed	4.00	10.00
733 Lee Maye	4.00	10.00
734 Rob Gardner	4.00	10.00
735 Mike Shannon	6.00	15.00
736 Mel Queen	4.00	10.00
737 Preston Gomez MG	4.00	10.00
738 Russ Gibson	4.00	10.00
739 Barry Lersch	4.00	10.00
740 Luis Aparicio	20.00	50.00
741 Skip Guinn	4.00	10.00
742 Royals Team	6.00	15.00
743 John O'Donoghue	5.00	12.00
744 Chuck Manuel	4.00	10.00
745 Sandy Alomar	5.00	12.00
746 Andy Kosco	4.00	10.00
747 NL Rookie Pitchers	4.00	10.00
Al Severinsen		
Scipio Spinks/		
748 John Purdin	4.00	10.00
749 Ken Szotkiewicz	4.00	10.00
750 Denny McLain	12.50	40.00
751 Al Weis	6.00	15.00
752 Dick Drago	5.00	12.00

1972 O-Pee-Chee

The cards in this 525-card set measure 2 1/2" by 3 1/2". The 1972 O-Pee-Chee set is very similar to the 1972 Topps set. On a white background, the fronts feature color player photos with multicolored frames, rounded bottom corners and the top part of the photo also rounded. The player's name and team name appear on the front. The horizontal backs carry player biography and statistics in French and English and have a different color than the 1972 Topps cards. Features appearing for the first time were "Boyhood Photos" (KP: 341-348 and 491-498) and "In Action" cards. The O-Pee-Chee cards can be distinguished from Topps cards by the "Printed in Canada" on the bottom of the back. This was the first year the cards denoted O.P.C. in the copyright line rather than T.C.G. There is one card in the set which is notably different from the corresponding Topps number on the back, No. 465 Gil Hodges, which notes his death in April of 1972. Remember, the prices below apply only to the O-Pee-Chee cards -- NOT Topps cards which are much more plentiful. The cards were packaged in 36 count boxes with eight cards per pack which cost ten cents each. Notable Rookie Cards include Carlton Fisk.

Card	Low	High
COMPLETE SET (525)	1,000.00	2,000.00
COMMON PLAYER (1-132)	.40	1.00
COMMON PLAYER (133-263)	.60	1.50
COMMON PLAYER (264-394)	.75	2.00
COMMON PLAYER (395-525)	1.00	2.50
1 Pirates Team	5.00	12.00
2 Ray Culp	.40	1.00
3 Bob Tolan	.40	1.00
4 Checklist 1-132	2.50	6.00
5 John Bateman	.75	2.00
6 Fred Scherman	.40	1.00
7 Enzo Hernandez	.40	1.00
8 Ron Swoboda	.75	2.00
9 Stan Williams	.40	1.00
10 Amos Otis	.75	2.00
11 Bobby Valentine	.75	2.00
12 Jose Cardenal	.40	1.00
13 Joe Grzenda	.40	1.00
14 Phillies Rookies	.40	1.00
Pete Koegel		
Mike Anderson		
Wayn		
15 Walt Williams	.40	1.00
16 Mike Jorgensen	.40	1.00
17 Dave Duncan	.75	2.00
18 Juan Pizarro	.40	1.00
19 Billy Cowan	.40	1.00
20 Don Wilson	.40	1.00
21 Braves Team	.75	2.00
22 Rob Gardner	.40	1.00
23 Ted Kubiak	.40	1.00
24 Ted Ford	.40	1.00
25 Bill Singer	.40	1.00
26 Andy Etchebarren	.40	1.00
27 Bob Johnson	.40	1.00
28 Bob Gebhard	.40	1.00
Steve Brye		
Hal Haydel		
29 Bill Bonham	.40	1.00
30 Rico Petrocelli	.75	2.00
31 Cleon Jones	.75	2.00
32 Cleon Jones IA	.40	1.00
33 Billy Martin MG	2.50	6.00
34 Billy Martin IA	1.50	4.00
35 Jerry Johnson	.40	1.00
36 Jerry Johnson IA	.40	1.00
37 Carl Yastrzemski	8.00	20.00
38 Carl Yastrzemski IA	3.00	8.00
39 Bob Barton	.40	1.00
40 Bob Barton IA	.40	1.00
41 Tommy Davis	.75	2.00
42 Tommy Davis IA	.40	1.00
43 Rick Wise	.75	2.00
44 Rick Wise IA	.40	1.00
45 Glenn Beckert	.75	2.00
46 Glenn Beckert IA	.40	1.00
47 John Ellis	.40	1.00
48 John Ellis IA	.40	1.00
49 Willie Mays	30.00	60.00
50 Willie Mays IA !	12.50	30.00
51 Harmon Killebrew	5.00	12.00
52 Harmon Killebrew IA	2.50	6.00

Card	Low	High
53 Bud Harrelson	.75	2.00
54 Bud Harrelson IA	.40	1.00
55 Clyde Wright	.40	1.00
56 Rich Chiles	.40	1.00
57 Bob Oliver	.40	1.00
58 Ernie McAnally	.75	2.00
59 Fred Stanley	.40	1.00
60 Manny Sanguillen	.75	2.00
61 Burt Hooton RC	.75	2.00
62 Angel Mangual	.40	1.00
63 Duke Sims	.40	1.00
64 Pete Broberg	.40	1.00
65 Cesar Cedeno	.75	2.00
66 Ray Corbin	.40	1.00
67 Red Schoendienst MG	1.50	4.00
68 Jim York	.40	1.00
69 Roger Freed	.40	1.00
70 Mike Cuellar	.75	2.00
71 Angels Team	.75	2.00
72 Bruce Kison	.40	1.00
73 Steve Huntz	.40	1.00
74 Cecil Upshaw	.40	1.00
75 Bert Campaneris	.75	2.00
76 Don Carrithers	.40	1.00
77 Ron Theobald	.40	1.00
78 Steve Arlin	.40	1.00
79 Carlton Fisk	40.00	80.00
Cooper RC !		
80 Tony Perez	3.00	8.00
81 Mike Hedlund	.40	1.00
82 Ron Woods	.75	2.00
83 Dalton Jones	.40	1.00
84 Vince Colbert	.40	1.00
85 NL Batting Leaders	1.50	4.00
Joe Torre		
Ralph Garr		
Glenn B		
86 AL Batting Leaders	1.50	4.00
Tony Oliva		
Bobby Murcer		
Merv		
87 Torre	2.50	6.00
Starg		
Aaron LL		
88 Kill	2.50	6.00
F.Rob		
R.Smith LL		
89 Stargell	1.50	4.00
Aaron		
May LL		
90 Melton	1.50	4.00
Cash		
Reggie LL		
91 Seaver	1.50	4.00
Roberts		
Wilson LL		
92 Blue	1.50	4.00
Wood		
Palmer LL		
93 Jenk	2.50	6.00
Carlton		
Seaver LL		
94 AL Pitching Leaders	1.50	4.00
Mickey Lolich		
Vida Blue		
Wil		
95 Seaver	2.50	6.00
Jenkins		
Stone LL		
96 AL Strikeout Leaders	1.50	4.00
Mickey Lolich		
Vida Blue		
Jo		
97 Tom Kelley	.40	1.00
98 Chuck Tanner MG	.75	2.00
99 Ross Grimsley	.40	1.00
100 Frank Robinson	4.00	10.00
101 J.R.Richard RC	1.50	4.00
102 Lloyd Allen	.40	1.00
103 Checklist 133-263	2.50	6.00
104 Toby Harrah RC	.75	2.00
105 Gary Gentry	.40	1.00
106 Brewers Team	.75	2.00
107 Jose Cruz RC	.75	2.00
108 Gary Waslewski	.40	1.00
109 Jerry May	.40	1.00
110 Ron Hunt	.75	2.00
111 Jim Grant	.40	1.00
112 Greg Luzinski	.75	2.00
113 Rogelio Moret	.40	1.00
114 Bill Buckner	.75	2.00
115 Jim Fregosi	.75	2.00
116 Ed Farmer	.40	1.00

Card	Low	High
117 Cleo James	.40	1.00
118 Skip Lockwood	.40	1.00
119 Marty Perez	.40	1.00
120 Bill Freehan	.75	2.00
121 Ed Sprague	.40	1.00
122 Larry Biittner	.40	1.00
123 Ed Acosta	.40	1.00
124 Yankees Rookies	.40	1.00
Alan Closter		
Rusty Torres		
Roger		
125 Dave Cash	.75	2.00
126 Bart Johnson	.40	1.00
127 Duffy Dyer	.40	1.00
128 Eddie Watt	.40	1.00
129 Charlie Fox MG	.40	1.00
130 Bob Gibson	4.00	10.00
131 Jim Nettles	.40	1.00
132 Joe Morgan	3.00	8.00
133 Joe Keough	.60	1.50
134 Carl Morton	1.00	2.50
135 Vada Pinson	1.00	2.50
136 Darrel Chaney	.60	1.50
137 Dick Williams MG	1.00	2.50
138 Mike Kekich	.60	1.50
139 Tim McCarver	1.00	2.50
140 Pat Dobson	1.00	2.50
141 Mets Rookies	1.00	2.50
Buzz Capra		
Leroy Stanton		
Jon Matla		
142 Chris Chambliss RC	2.00	5.00
143 Garry Jestadt	.60	1.50
144 Marty Pattin	.60	1.50
145 Don Kessinger	1.00	2.50
146 Steve Kealey	.60	1.50
147 Dave Kingman RC	3.00	8.00
148 Dick Billings	.60	1.50
149 Gary Neibauer	.60	1.50
150 Norm Cash	1.00	2.50
151 Jim Brewer	.60	1.50
152 Gene Clines	.60	1.50
153 Rick Auerbach	.60	1.50
154 Ted Simmons	2.00	5.00
155 Larry Dierker	1.00	2.50
156 Twins Team	1.00	2.50
157 Don Gullett	.60	1.50
158 Jerry Kenney	.60	1.50
159 John Boccabella	1.00	2.50
160 Andy Messersmith	1.00	2.50
161 Brock Davis	.60	1.50
162 Darrell Porter RC UER	1.00	2.50
163 Tug McGraw	2.00	5.00
164 Tug McGraw IA	1.00	2.50
165 Chris Speier RC	1.00	2.50
166 Chris Speier IA	.60	1.50
167 Deron Johnson	.60	1.50
168 Deron Johnson IA	.60	1.50
169 Vida Blue	2.00	5.00
170 Vida Blue IA	1.00	2.50
171 Darrell Evans	2.00	5.00
172 Darrell Evans IA	1.00	2.50
173 Clay Kirby	.60	1.50
174 Clay Kirby IA	.60	1.50
175 Tom Haller	.60	1.50
176 Tom Haller IA	.60	1.50
177 Paul Schaal	.60	1.50
178 Paul Schaal IA	.60	1.50
179 Dock Ellis	.60	1.50
180 Dock Ellis IA	.60	1.50
181 Ed Kranepool	1.00	2.50
182 Ed Kranepool IA	.60	1.50
183 Bill Melton	.60	1.50
184 Bill Melton IA	.60	1.50
185 Ron Bryant	.60	1.50
186 Ron Bryant IA	.60	1.50
187 Gates Brown	.60	1.50
188 Frank Lucchesi MG	.60	1.50
189 Gene Tenace	1.00	2.50
190 Dave Giusti	.60	1.50
191 Jeff Burroughs RC	2.00	5.00
192 Cubs Team	1.00	2.50
193 Kurt Bevacqua	.60	1.50
194 Fred Norman	.60	1.50
195 Orlando Cepeda	3.00	8.00
196 Mel Queen	.60	1.50
197 Johnny Briggs	.60	1.50
198 Charlie Hough RC	3.00	8.00
199 Mike Fiore	.60	1.50
200 Lou Brock	4.00	10.00
201 Phil Roof	.60	1.50
202 Scipio Spinks	.60	1.50
203 Ron Blomberg	.60	1.50
204 Tommy Helms	.60	1.50
205 Dick Drago	.60	1.50
206 Dal Maxvill	.60	1.50
207 Tom Egan	.60	1.50
208 Milt Pappas	1.00	2.50
209 Joe Rudi	1.00	2.50
210 Denny McLain	1.00	2.50
211 Gary Sutherland	1.00	2.50
212 Grant Jackson	.60	1.50
213 Angels Rookies	.60	1.50
Billy Parker		
Art Kusnyer		
Tom Sil		
214 Mike McQueen	.60	1.50
215 Alex Johnson	1.00	2.50
216 Joe Niekro	1.00	2.50
217 Roger Metzger	.60	1.50
218 Eddie Kasko MG	.60	1.50
219 Rennie Stennett	1.00	2.50
220 Jim Perry	1.00	2.50
221 NL Playoffs	1.00	2.50
Bucs champs		
222 Brooks Robinson ALCS	2.00	5.00
223 Dave McNally WS	1.00	2.50
224 World Series Game 2/(Dave Johnson	1.00	2.50
and Mark Belan		
225 Manny Sanguillen WS	1.00	2.50
226 Roberto Clemente WS4	4.00	10.00
227 Nellie Briles WS	1.00	2.50
228 World Series Game 6		
(Frank Robinson and	2.00	5.00
Manny Sa		
229 Steve Blass WS	1.00	2.50
230 World Series Summary	1.00	2.50
Pirates celebrate		
231 Casey Cox	.60	1.50
232 Chris Arnold	.60	1.50
Jim Barr		
Dave Rader		
233 Jay Johnstone	1.00	2.50
234 Ron Taylor	2.00	5.00
235 Merv Rettenmund	.60	1.50
236 Jim McGlothlin	.60	1.50
237 Yankees Team	1.00	2.50
238 Leron Lee	.60	1.50
239 Tom Timmermann	.60	1.50
240 Richie Allen	1.00	2.50
241 Rollie Fingers	3.00	8.00
242 Don Mincher	.60	1.50
243 Frank Linzy	.60	1.50
244 Steve Braun	.60	1.50
245 Tommie Agee	1.00	2.50
246 Tom Burgmeier	.60	1.50
247 Milt May	.60	1.50
248 Tom Bradley	.60	1.50
249 Harry Walker MG	.60	1.50
250 Boog Powell	1.00	2.50
251 Checklist 264-394	2.50	6.00
252 Ken Reynolds	.60	1.50
253 Sandy Alomar	1.00	2.50
254 Boots Day	1.00	2.50
255 Jim Lonborg	1.00	2.50
256 George Foster	1.00	2.50
257 Jim Foor	.60	1.50
Tim Hosley		
Paul Jata		
258 Randy Hundley	.60	1.50
259 Sparky Lyle	1.00	2.50
260 Ralph Garr	1.00	2.50
261 Steve Mingori	.60	1.50
262 Padres Team	1.00	2.50
263 Felipe Alou	1.00	2.50
264 Tommy John	1.25	3.00
265 Wes Parker	1.25	3.00
266 Bobby Bolin	.75	2.00
267 Dave Concepcion	2.50	6.00
268 Dwain Anderson	.75	2.00
Chris Floethe		
269 Don Hahn	.75	2.00
270 Jim Palmer	4.00	10.00
271 Ken Rudolph	.75	2.00
272 Mickey Rivers RC	1.25	3.00
273 Bobby Floyd	.75	2.00
274 Al Severinsen	.75	2.00
275 Cesar Tovar	.75	2.00
276 Gene Mauch MG	1.25	3.00
277 Elliott Maddox	.75	2.00
278 Dennis Higgins	.75	2.00
279 Larry Brown	.75	2.00
280 Willie McCovey	3.00	8.00
281 Bill Parsons	.75	2.00
282 Astros Team	1.25	3.00
283 Darrell Brandon	.75	2.00
284 Ike Brown	.75	2.00
285 Gaylord Perry	4.00	10.00
286 Gene Alley	.75	2.00
287 Jim Hardin	.75	2.00
288 Johnny Jeter	.75	2.00
289 Syd O'Brien	.75	2.00
290 Sonny Siebert	.75	2.00
291 Hal McRae	1.25	3.00
292 Hal McRae IA	.75	2.00
293 Danny Frisella	.75	2.00
294 Danny Frisella IA	.75	2.00
295 Dick Dietz	.75	2.00
296 Dick Dietz IA	.75	2.00
297 Claude Osteen	1.25	3.00
298 Claude Osteen IA	.75	2.00
299 Hank Aaron	30.00	60.00
300 Hank Aaron IA	12.50	30.00
301 George Mitterwald	.75	2.00
302 George Mitterwald IA	.75	2.00
303 Joe Pepitone	1.25	3.00
304 Joe Pepitone IA	.75	2.00
305 Ken Boswell	.75	2.00
306 Ken Boswell IA	.75	2.00
307 Steve Renko	1.25	3.00
308 Steve Renko IA	.75	2.00
309 Roberto Clemente	40.00	80.00
310 Roberto Clemente IA	12.50	40.00
311 Clay Carroll	.75	2.00
312 Clay Carroll IA	.75	2.00
313 Luis Aparicio	4.00	10.00
314 Luis Aparicio IA	2.50	6.00
315 Paul Splittorff	.75	2.00
316 Cardinals Rookies	1.25	3.00
Jim Bibby		
Jorge Roque		
Santiag		
317 Rich Hand	.75	2.00
318 Sonny Jackson	.75	2.00
319 Aurelio Rodriguez	.75	2.00
320 Steve Blass	1.25	3.00
321 Joe Lahoud	.75	2.00
322 Jose Pena	.75	2.00
323 Earl Weaver MG	3.00	8.00
324 Mike Ryan	.75	2.00
325 Mel Stottlemyre	1.25	3.00
326 Pat Kelly	.75	2.00
327 Steve Stone RC	1.25	3.00
328 Red Sox Team	1.25	3.00
329 Roy Foster	.75	2.00
330 Jim Hunter	4.00	10.00
331 Stan Swanson	1.25	3.00
332 Buck Martinez	.75	2.00
333 Steve Barber	.75	2.00
334 Rangers Rookies	.75	2.00
Bill Fahey		
Jim Mason		
Tom Raglan		
335 Bill Hands	.75	2.00
336 Marty Martinez	.75	2.00
337 Mike Kilkenny	1.25	3.00
338 Bob Grich	1.25	3.00
339 Ron Cook	.75	2.00
340 Roy White	1.25	3.00
341 Joe Torre KP	1.25	3.00
342 Wilbur Wood KP	.75	2.00
343 Willie Stargell KP	1.25	3.00
344 Dave McNally KP	.75	2.00
345 Rick Wise KP	.75	2.00
346 Jim Fregosi KP	.75	2.00
347 Tom Seaver KP	3.00	8.00
348 Sal Bando KP	.75	2.00
349 Al Fitzmorris	.75	2.00
350 Frank Howard	1.25	3.00
351 Braves Rookies	1.25	3.00
Tom House		
Rick Kester		
Jimmy Brit		
352 Dave LaRoche	.75	2.00
353 Art Shamsky	.75	2.00
354 Tom Murphy	.75	2.00
355 Bob Watson	1.25	3.00
356 Gerry Moses	.75	2.00
357 Woodie Fryman	.75	2.00
358 Sparky Anderson MG	3.00	8.00
359 Don Pavletich	.75	2.00
360 Dave Roberts	.75	2.00
361 Mike Andrews	.75	2.00
362 Mets Team	2.50	6.00
363 Ron Klimkowski	.75	2.00
364 Johnny Callison	1.25	3.00
365 Dick Bosman	1.25	3.00
366 Jimmy Rosario	.75	2.00
367 Ron Perranoski	.75	2.00
368 Danny Thompson	.75	2.00
369 Jim LeFebvre	1.25	3.00
370 Don Buford	.75	2.00
371 Denny LeMaster	.75	2.00
372 Lance Clemons	.75	2.00
Monty Montgomery		
373 John Mayberry	1.25	3.00
374 Jack Heidemann	.75	2.00
375 Reggie Cleveland	1.25	3.00
376 Andy Kosco	.75	2.00
377 Terry Harmon	.75	2.00
378 Checklist 395-525	3.00	8.00
379 Ken Berry	.75	2.00
380 Earl Williams	.75	2.00
381 White Sox Team	1.25	3.00
382 Joe Gibbon	.75	2.00
383 Brant Alyea	.75	2.00
384 Dave Campbell	1.25	3.00
385 Mickey Stanley	1.25	3.00
386 Jim Colborn	.75	2.00
387 Horace Clarke	1.25	3.00
388 Charlie Williams	.75	2.00
389 Bill Rigney MG	.75	2.00
390 Willie Davis	1.25	3.00
391 Ken Sanders	.75	2.00
392 Fred Cambria	1.25	3.00
Richie Zisk RC		
393 Curt Motton	.75	2.00
394 Ken Forsch	1.25	3.00
395 Matty Alou	1.25	3.00
396 Paul Lindblad	1.00	2.50
397 Phillies Team	2.50	6.00
398 Larry Hisle	1.25	3.00
399 Milt Wilcox	1.25	3.00
400 Tony Oliva	2.50	6.00
401 Jim Nash	1.00	2.50
402 Bobby Heise	1.00	2.50
403 John Cumberland	1.00	2.50
404 Jeff Torborg	1.25	3.00
405 Ron Fairly	1.25	3.00
406 George Hendrick RC	1.25	3.00
407 Chuck Taylor	1.00	2.50
408 Jim Northrup	1.25	3.00
409 Frank Baker	1.00	2.50
410 Fergie Jenkins	4.00	10.00
411 Bob Montgomery	1.00	2.50
412 Dick Kelley	1.00	2.50
413 Don Eddy	1.00	2.50
Dave Lemonds		
414 Bob Miller	1.00	2.50
415 Cookie Rojas	1.00	2.50
416 Johnny Edwards	1.00	2.50
417 Tom Hall	1.00	2.50
418 Tom Shopay	1.00	2.50
419 Jim Spencer	1.00	2.50
420 Steve Carlton	12.50	30.00
421 Ellie Rodriguez	1.00	2.50
422 Ray Lamb	1.00	2.50
423 Oscar Gamble	1.25	3.00
424 Bill Gogolewski	1.00	2.50
425 Ken Singleton	1.25	3.00
426 Ken Singleton IA	1.00	2.50
427 Tito Fuentes	1.00	2.50
428 Tito Fuentes IA	1.00	2.50
429 Bob Robertson	1.00	2.50
430 Bob Robertson IA	1.00	2.50
431 Cito Gaston	1.25	3.00
432 Cito Gaston IA	1.00	2.50
433 Johnny Bench	12.50	40.00
434 Johnny Bench IA	8.00	20.00
435 Reggie Jackson	20.00	50.00
436 Reggie Jackson IA !	10.00	25.00
437 Maury Wills	2.50	6.00
438 Maury Wills IA	1.25	3.00
439 Billy Williams	3.00	8.00
440 Billy Williams IA	2.50	6.00
441 Thurman Munson	10.00	25.00
442 Thurman Munson IA	5.00	12.00
443 Ken Henderson	1.00	2.50
444 Ken Henderson IA	1.00	2.50
445 Tom Seaver	20.00	50.00
446 Tom Seaver IA	10.00	25.00
447 Willie Stargell	4.00	10.00
448 Willie Stargell IA	2.50	6.00
449 Bob Lemon MG	1.25	3.00
450 Mickey Lolich	1.25	3.00
451 Tony LaRussa	3.00	8.00
452 Ed Herrmann	1.00	2.50
453 Barry Lersch	1.00	2.50
454 A's Team	2.50	6.00
455 Tommy Harper	1.25	3.00
456 Mark Belanger	1.25	3.00
457 Padres Rookies	1.00	2.50
Darcy Fast		
Derrel Thomas		
Mike Iv		
458 Aurelio Monteagudo	1.00	2.50
459 Rick Renick	1.00	2.50
460 Al Downing	1.00	2.50
461 Tim Cullen	1.00	2.50
462 Rickey Clark	1.00	2.50
463 Bernie Carbo	1.00	2.50
464 Jim Roland	1.00	2.50
465 Gil Hodges MG/(Mentions his	12.50	40.00
death on 4/2/72)		
466 Norm Miller	1.00	2.50
467 Steve Kline	1.00	2.50
468 Richie Scheinblum	1.00	2.50
469 Ron Herbel	1.00	2.50
470 Ray Fosse	1.00	2.50
471 Luke Walker	1.00	2.50
472 Phil Gagliano	1.00	2.50
473 Dan McGinn	1.00	2.50
474 J.Oates RC	10.00	25.00
Don Baylor		
475 Gary Nolan	1.00	2.50
476 Lee Richard	1.00	2.50
477 Tom Phoebus	1.00	2.50
478 Checklist 5th Series	3.00	8.00
479 Don Shaw	1.00	2.50
480 Lee May	1.25	3.00
481 Billy Conigliaro	1.00	2.50
482 Joe Hoerner	1.00	2.50
483 Ken Suarez	1.00	2.50
484 Lum Harris MG	1.00	2.50
485 Phil Regan	1.00	2.50
486 John Lowenstein	1.00	2.50
487 Tigers Team	2.50	6.00
488 Mike Nagy	1.00	2.50
489 Terry Humphrey	1.00	2.50
Keith Lampard		
490 Dave McNally	1.25	3.00
491 Lou Piniella KP	1.25	3.00
492 Mel Stottlemyre KP	1.25	3.00
493 Bob Bailey KP	1.25	3.00
494 Willie Horton KP	1.25	3.00
495 Bill Melton KP	1.00	2.50
496 Bud Harrelson KP	1.25	3.00
497 Jim Perry KP	1.25	3.00
498 Brooks Robinson KP	2.50	6.00
499 Vicente Romo	1.00	2.50
500 Joe Torre	3.00	8.00
501 Pete Hamm	1.00	2.50
502 Jackie Hernandez	1.00	2.50
503 Gary Peters	1.00	2.50
504 Ed Spiezio	1.00	2.50
505 Mike Marshall	1.25	3.00
506 Terry Ley	1.25	3.00
Jim Moyer		
Dick Tidrow		
507 Fred Gladding	1.00	2.50
508 Ellie Hendricks	1.00	2.50
509 Don McMahon	1.00	2.50
510 Ted Williams MG	8.00	20.00
511 Tony Taylor	1.00	2.50
512 Paul Popovich	1.00	2.50
513 Lindy McDaniel	1.25	3.00
514 Ted Sizemore	1.00	2.50
515 Bert Blyleven	2.50	6.00
516 Oscar Brown	1.00	2.50
517 Ken Brett	1.00	2.50
518 Wayne Garrett	1.00	2.50
519 Ted Abernathy	1.00	2.50
520 Larry Bowa	1.25	3.00
521 Alan Foster	1.00	2.50
522 Dodgers Team	2.50	6.00
523 Chuck Dobson	1.00	2.50
524 Ed Armbrister	1.00	2.50
Mel Behney		
525 Carlos May	1.25	3.00

1973 O-Pee-Chee

The cards in this 660-card set measure 2 1/2" by 3 1/2". This set is essentially the same as the regular 1973 Topps set, except that the words "Printed in Canada" appear on the backs and the backs are bilingual. On a white border, the fronts feature color player photos with rounded corners and thin black borders. The player's name and position and the team name are also printed on the front. An "All-Time Leaders" series (471-478) appears in this set. Kid pictures appeared again for the second year in a row (341-346). The backs carry player biography and statistics in French and English. The cards are numbered on the back. The backs appear to be more "yellow" than the Topps backs. Remember, the prices below apply only to the O-Pee-Chee cards -- NOT Topps cards which are more plentiful. Unlike the 1973 Topps set, all cards in this set were issued equally and at the same time, i.e., there were no scarce series with the O-Pee-Chee cards. Although there are no scarce series, cards 529-660 attract a slight premium. Because of the premium that high series Topps cards attract, there is a perception that O-Pee-Chee cards of the same number sequence are less available. The key card in this set is the Mike Schmidt Rookie Card. The cards were packaged in 10 count packs with 36 cards in a box which cost 10 cents. Other Rookie Cards of note in this set include Bob Boone and Dwight Evans.

COMPLETE SET (660)	500.00	1,000.00
COMMON PLAYER (1-528)	.30	.75
COMMON PLAYER (529-660)	1.25	3.00
1 Aaron	20.00	50.00
Ruth		
Mays !		
2 Rich Hebner	.60	1.50
3 Jim Lonborg	.60	1.50
4 John Milner	.30	.75
5 Ed Brinkman	.30	.75
6 Mac Scarce	.30	.75
7 Texas Rangers Team	.60	1.50
8 Tom Hall	.30	.75
9 Johnny Oates	.30	.75
10 Don Sutton	2.50	6.00
11 Chris Chambliss	.60	1.50
12 Padres Leaders	.60	1.50
Don Zimmer MG		
Dave Garcia CO		
Joh		
13 George Hendrick	.60	1.50
14 Sonny Siebert	.30	.75
15 Ralph Garr	.60	1.50
16 Steve Braun	.30	.75
17 Fred Gladding	.30	.75
18 Leroy Stanton	.30	.75
19 Tim Foli	.30	.75
20 Stan Bahnsen	.30	.75
21 Randy Hundley	.60	1.50
22 Ted Abernathy	.30	.75
23 Dave Kingman	.60	1.50
24 Al Santorini	.30	.75
25 Roy White	.60	1.50
26 Pirates Team	.60	1.50
27 Bill Gogolewski	.30	.75
28 Hal McRae	.60	1.50
29 Tony Taylor	.60	1.50
30 Tug McGraw	.60	1.50
31 Buddy Bell RC	1.00	2.50
32 Fred Norman	.30	.75
33 Jim Breazeale	.30	.75
34 Pat Dobson	.30	.75
35 Willie Davis	.60	1.50
36 Steve Barber	.30	.75
37 Bill Robinson	.60	1.50
38 Mike Epstein	.30	.75
39 Dave Roberts	.30	.75
40 Reggie Smith	.60	1.50
41 Tom Walker	.30	.75
42 Mike Andrews	.30	.75
43 Randy Moffitt	.30	.75
44 Rick Monday	.60	1.50
45 Ellie Rodriguez/(photo actually	.30	.75
John Felske)		
46 Lindy McDaniel	.60	1.50
47 Luis Melendez	.30	.75
48 Paul Splittorff	.30	.75
49 Twins Leaders	.60	1.50
Frank Quilici MG		
Vern Morgan CO		
B		
50 Roberto Clemente	20.00	50.00
51 Chuck Seelbach	.30	.75
52 Denis Menke	.30	.75
53 Steve Dunning	.30	.75
54 Checklist 1-132	1.25	3.00
55 Jon Matlack	.60	1.50
56 Merv Rettenmund	.30	.75
57 Derrel Thomas	.30	.75
58 Mike Paul	.30	.75
59 Steve Yeager RC	.60	1.50
60 Ken Holtzman	.60	1.50
61 B.Williams	1.50	4.00
R.Carew LL		
62 J.Bench	1.00	2.50
D.Allen LL		
63 J.Bench	1.00	2.50
D.Allen LL		
64 L.Brock	.60	1.50
Campaneris LL		
65 S.Carlton	.60	1.50
L.Tiant LL		
66 Carlton	.60	1.50
Perry		
Wood LL		
67 S.Carlton	12.50	40.00
N.Ryan LL		
68 C.Carroll	.60	1.50
S.Lyle LL		
69 Phil Gagliano	.30	.75
70 Milt Pappas	.60	1.50
71 Johnny Briggs	.30	.75
72 Ron Reed	.30	.75
73 Ed Herrmann	.30	.75
74 Billy Champion	.30	.75
75 Vada Pinson	.60	1.50
76 Doug Rader	.30	.75
77 Mike Torrez	.60	1.50
78 Richie Scheinblum	.30	.75
79 Jim Willoughby	.30	.75
80 Tony Oliva	1.50	4.00
81 Chicago Cubs Leaders	.60	1.50
Whitey Lockman MG		
Hank Agui		
82 Fritz Peterson	.30	.75
83 Leron Lee	.30	.75
84 Rollie Fingers	2.50	6.00
85 Ted Simmons	.60	1.50
86 Tom McCraw	.30	.75
87 Ken Boswell	.30	.75
88 Mickey Stanley	.60	1.50
89 Jack Billingham	.30	.75
90 Brooks Robinson	4.00	10.00
91 Dodgers Team	.60	1.50
92 Jerry Bell	.30	.75
93 Jesus Alou	.30	.75
94 Dick Billings	.30	.75
95 Steve Blass	.60	1.50
96 Doug Griffin	.30	.75
97 Willie Montanez	.60	1.50
98 Dick Woodson	.30	.75
99 Carl Taylor	.30	.75
100 Hank Aaron	20.00	50.00
101 Ken Henderson	.30	.75
102 Rudy May	.30	.75
103 Celerino Sanchez	.30	.75
104 Reggie Cleveland	.60	1.50
105 Carlos May	.30	.75
106 Terry Humphrey	.30	.75
107 Phil Hennigan	.30	.75
108 Bill Russell	.60	1.50
109 Doyle Alexander	.60	1.50
110 Bob Watson	.60	1.50
111 Dave Nelson	.30	.75
112 Gary Ross	.30	.75
113 Jerry Grote	.60	1.50
114 Lynn McGlothen	.30	.75
115 Ron Santo	1.50	4.00
116 Yankees Leaders	.60	1.50
Ralph Houk MG		
Jim Hegan CO		
Elst		
117 Ramon Hernandez	.30	.75
118 John Mayberry	.60	1.50
119 Larry Bowa	.60	1.50
120 Joe Coleman	.30	.75
121 Dave Rader	.30	.75
122 Jim Strickland	.30	.75
123 Sandy Alomar	.60	1.50
124 Jim Hardin	.30	.75
125 Ron Fairly	.60	1.50
126 Jim Brewer	.30	.75
127 Brewers Team	.60	1.50
128 Ted Sizemore	.30	.75
129 Terry Forster	.60	1.50
130 Pete Rose	12.50	40.00
131 Red Sox Leaders	.60	1.50
Eddie Kasko MG		
Doug Camilli CO/		
132 Matty Alou	.60	1.50
133 Dave Roberts	.30	.75
134 Milt Wilcox	.30	.75
135 Lee May	.60	1.50
136 Orioles Leaders	1.50	4.00
Earl Weaver MG		
George Bamberger		
137 Jim Beauchamp	.30	.75
138 Horacio Pina	.30	.75
139 Carmen Fanzone	.30	.75
140 Lou Piniella	1.00	2.50
141 Bruce Kison	.30	.75
142 Thurman Munson	4.00	10.00
143 John Curtis	.30	.75
144 Marty Perez	.30	.75
145 Bobby Bonds	1.50	4.00
146 Woodie Fryman	.30	.75
147 Mike Anderson	.30	.75
148 Dave Goltz	.30	.75
149 Ron Hunt	.30	.75
150 Wilbur Wood	.60	1.50
151 Wes Parker	.60	1.50
152 Dave May	.30	.75
153 Al Hrabosky	.60	1.50
154 Jeff Torborg	.60	1.50
155 Sal Bando	.60	1.50
156 Cesar Geronimo	.30	.75
157 Denny Riddleberger	.30	.75
158 Astros Team	.60	1.50
159 Cito Gaston	.60	1.50
160 Jim Palmer	3.00	8.00
161 Ted Martinez	.30	.75
162 Pete Broberg	.30	.75
163 Vic Davalillo	.30	.75
164 Monty Montgomery	.30	.75
165 Luis Aparicio	2.50	6.00
166 Terry Harmon	.30	.75
167 Steve Stone	.60	1.50
168 Jim Northrup	.60	1.50
169 Ron Schueler RC	.60	1.50
170 Harmon Killebrew	2.50	6.00
171 Bernie Carbo	.30	.75
172 Steve Kline	.30	.75
173 Hal Breeden	.60	1.50
174 Goose Gossage RC	3.00	8.00
175 Frank Robinson	3.00	8.00
176 Chuck Taylor	.30	.75
177 Bill Plummer	.30	.75
178 Don Rose	.30	.75
179 Oakland A's Leaders	.60	1.50
Dick Williams MG		
Jerry Adair		
180 Fergie Jenkins	2.00	5.00
181 Jack Brohamer	.30	.75
182 Mike Caldwell RC	.60	1.50
183 Don Buford	.30	.75
184 Jerry Koosman	.60	1.50
185 Jim Wynn	.60	1.50
186 Bill Fahey	.30	.75
187 Luke Walker	.30	.75
188 Cookie Rojas	.60	1.50
189 Greg Luzinski	1.00	2.50
190 Bob Gibson	4.00	10.00
191 Tigers Team	.60	1.50
192 Pat Jarvis	.30	.75
193 Carlton Fisk	5.00	12.00
194 Jorge Orta	.30	.75
195 Clay Carroll	.30	.75
196 Ken McMullen	.30	.75
197 Ed Goodson	.30	.75
198 Horace Clarke	.30	.75
199 Bert Blyleven	1.50	4.00
200 Billy Williams	2.50	6.00
201 A.L. Playoffs	.60	1.50
A's over Tigers;		
George Hendrick s		
202 N.L. Playoffs	.60	1.50
Reds over Pirates		
George Foster's#		
203 Gene Tenace WS	.60	1.50
204 World Series Game 2	.60	1.50
A's two straight		
205 World Series Game 3	1.00	2.50
Reds win squeeker/(Tony Pere		
206 Gene Tenace WS	.60	1.50
207 Blue Moon Odom WS	.60	1.50
208 World Series Game 6	2.50	6.00
Reds' slugging		
ties series/		
209 World Series Game 7	.60	1.50
Bert Campaneris stars		
winnin		
210 World Series Summary	.60	1.50
World champions:		
A's Win		
211 Balor Moore	.30	.75
212 Joe Lahoud	.30	.75
213 Steve Garvey	2.50	6.00
214 Dave Hamilton	.30	.75
215 Dusty Baker	1.50	4.00
216 Toby Harrah	.60	1.50
217 Don Wilson	.30	.75
218 Aurelio Rodriguez	.30	.75
219 Cardinals Team	.60	1.50
220 Nolan Ryan	50.00	100.00
221 Fred Kendall	.30	.75
222 Rob Gardner	.30	.75
223 Bud Harrelson	.60	1.50
224 Bill Lee	.60	1.50
225 Al Oliver	.60	1.50
226 Ray Fosse	.30	.75
227 Wayne Twitchell	.30	.75
228 Bobby Darwin	.30	.75
229 Roric Harrison	.30	.75
230 Joe Morgan	3.00	8.00
231 Bill Parsons	.30	.75
232 Ken Singleton	.60	1.50
233 Ed Kirkpatrick	.30	.75
234 Bill North	.30	.75
235 Jim Hunter	2.50	6.00
236 Tito Fuentes	.30	.75
237 Braves Leaders	1.50	4.00
Eddie Mathews MG		
Lew Burdette CO#		
238 Tony Muser	.30	.75
239 Pete Richert	.30	.75
240 Bobby Murcer	1.00	2.50
241 Dwain Anderson	.30	.75
242 George Culver	.30	.75
243 Angels Team	.60	1.50
244 Ed Acosta	.30	.75
245 Carl Yastrzemski	5.00	12.00
246 Ken Sanders	.30	.75
247 Del Unser	.30	.75
248 Jerry Johnson	.30	.75
249 Larry Biittner	.30	.75
250 Manny Sanguillen	.60	1.50
251 Roger Nelson	.30	.75
252 Giants Leaders	.60	1.50
Charlie Fox MG		
Joe Amalfitano CO#		
253 Mark Belanger	.60	1.50
254 Bill Stoneman	.60	1.50
255 Reggie Jackson	8.00	20.00
256 Chris Zachary	.30	.75
257 N.Y. Mets Leaders	1.50	4.00
Yogi Berra MG		
Roy McMillan CO#		
258 Tommy John	1.00	2.50
259 Jim Holt	.30	.75
260 Gary Nolan	.60	1.50
261 Pat Kelly	.30	.75
262 Jack Aker	.30	.75
263 George Scott	.60	1.50
264 Checklist 133-264	1.00	2.50
265 Gene Michael	.60	1.50
266 Mike Lum	.30	.75
267 Lloyd Allen	.30	.75
268 Jerry Morales	.30	.75
269 Tim McCarver	1.00	2.50
270 Luis Tiant	1.00	2.50
271 Tom Hutton	.30	.75
272 Ed Farmer	.30	.75
273 Chris Speier	.30	.75
274 Darold Knowles	.30	.75
275 Tony Perez	2.50	6.00
276 Joe Lovitto	.30	.75
277 Bob Miller	.30	.75
278 Orioles Team	.60	1.50
279 Mike Strahler	.30	.75
280 Al Kaline	4.00	10.00
281 Mike Jorgensen	.30	.75
282 Steve Hovley	.30	.75
283 Ray Sadecki	.30	.75
284 Glenn Borgmann	.30	.75
285 Don Kessinger	.60	1.50
286 Frank Linzy	.30	.75
287 Eddie Leon	.30	.75
288 Gary Gentry	.30	.75
289 Bob Oliver	.30	.75
290 Cesar Cedeno	.60	1.50
291 Rogelio Moret	.30	.75
292 Jose Cruz	.60	1.50
293 Bernie Allen	.30	.75
294 Steve Arlin	.30	.75
295 Bert Campaneris	.60	1.50
296 Sparky Anderson MG	1.50	4.00
297 Walt Williams	.30	.75
298 Ron Bryant	.30	.75
299 Ted Ford	.30	.75
300 Steve Carlton	5.00	12.00
301 Billy Grabarkewitz	.30	.75
302 Terry Crowley	.30	.75
303 Nelson Briles	.30	.75
304 Duke Sims	.30	.75
305 Willie Mays	20.00	50.00
306 Tom Burgmeier	.30	.75
307 Boots Day	.30	.75
308 Skip Lockwood	.30	.75
309 Paul Popovich	.30	.75
310 Dick Allen	1.00	2.50
311 Joe Decker	.30	.75
312 Oscar Brown	.30	.75
313 Jim Ray	.30	.75
314 Ron Swoboda	.60	1.50
315 John Odom	.30	.75
316 Padres Team	.60	1.50
317 Danny Cater	.30	.75
318 Jim McGlothlin	.30	.75
319 Jim Spencer	.30	.75
320 Lou Brock	4.00	10.00
321 Rich Hinton	.30	.75
322 Garry Maddox RC	.60	1.50
323 Billy Martin MG	1.00	2.50
324 Al Downing	.30	.75
325 Boog Powell	.60	1.50
326 Darrell Brandon	.30	.75
327 John Lowenstein	.30	.75
328 Bill Bonham	.30	.75
329 Ed Kranepool	.60	1.50
330 Rod Carew	4.00	10.00
331 Carl Morton	.30	.75
332 John Felske	.30	.75
333 Gene Clines	.30	.75
334 Freddie Patek	.30	.75
335 Bob Tolan	.30	.75
336 Tom Bradley	.30	.75
337 Dave Duncan	.60	1.50
338 Checklist 265-396	1.00	2.50
339 Dick Tidrow	.30	.75
340 Nate Colbert	.30	.75
341 Jim Palmer KP	1.00	2.50
342 Sam McDowell KP	.60	1.50
343 Bobby Murcer KP	.60	1.50
344 Jim Hunter KP	1.00	2.50
345 Chris Speier KP	.30	.75
346 Gaylord Perry KP	.60	1.50
347 Royals Team	.60	1.50
348 Rennie Stennett	.30	.75
349 Dick McAuliffe	.30	.75
350 Tom Seaver	6.00	15.00
351 Jimmy Stewart	.30	.75
352 Don Stanhouse	.30	.75
353 Steve Brye	.30	.75
354 Billy Parker	.30	.75
355 Mike Marshall	.60	1.50
356 White Sox Leaders	.60	1.50
Chuck Tanner MG		
Joe Lonnett CO		
357 Ross Grimsley	.30	.75
358 Jim Nettles	.30	.75
359 Cecil Upshaw	.30	.75
360 Joe Rudi/(photo actually	.60	1.50
Gene Tenace)		
361 Fran Healy	.30	.75
362 Eddie Watt	.30	.75
363 Jackie Hernandez	.30	.75
364 Rick Wise	.30	.75
365 Rico Petrocelli	.60	1.50
366 Brock Davis	.30	.75
367 Burt Hooton	.60	1.50
368 Bill Buckner	.60	1.50
369 Lerrin LaGrow	.30	.75
370 Willie Stargell	2.50	6.00
371 Mike Kekich	.30	.75
372 Oscar Gamble	.30	.75
373 Clyde Wright	.30	.75
374 Darrell Evans	1.00	2.50
375 Larry Dierker	.60	1.50
376 Frank Duffy	.30	.75
377 Expos Leaders	1.00	2.50
Gene Mauch MG		
Dave Bristol CO		
Lar		
378 Lenny Randle	.30	.75
379 Cy Acosta	.30	.75
380 Johnny Bench	6.00	15.00
381 Vicente Romo	.30	.75
382 Mike Hegan	.30	.75
383 Diego Segui	.30	.75
384 Don Baylor	1.50	4.00
385 Jim Perry	.60	1.50
386 Don Money	.30	.75
387 Jim Barr	.30	.75
388 Ben Oglivie	.60	1.50
389 Mets Team	2.00	5.00
390 Mickey Lolich	.60	1.50

391 Lee Lacy RC .60 1.50
392 Dick Drago .30 .75
393 Jose Cardenal .30 .75
394 Sparky Lyle .60 1.50
395 Roger Metzger .30 .75
396 Grant Jackson .30 .75
397 Dave Cash .60 1.50
398 Rich Hand .30 .75
399 George Foster .60 1.50
400 Gaylord Perry 2.50 6.00
401 Clyde Mashore .30 .75
402 Jack Hiatt .30 .75
403 Sonny Jackson .30 .75
404 Chuck Brinkman .30 .75
405 Cesar Tovar .30 .75
406 Paul Lindblad .30 .75
407 Felix Millan .30 .75
408 Jim Colborn .30 .75
409 Ivan Murrell .30 .75
410 Willie McCovey 3.00 8.00
411 Ray Corbin .30 .75
412 Manny Mota .60 1.50
413 Tom Timmerman .30 .75
414 Ken Rudolph .30 .75
415 Marty Pattin .30 .75
416 Paul Schaal .30 .75
417 Scipio Spinks .30 .75
418 Bobby Grich .60 1.50
419 Casey Cox .30 .75
420 Tommie Agee .30 .75
421 Angels Leaders .60 1.50
Bobby Winkles MG
Tom Morgan CO
S
422 Bob Robertson .30 .75
423 Johnny Jeter .30 .75
424 Denny Doyle .30 .75
425 Alex Johnson .30 .75
426 Dave LaRoche .30 .75
427 Rick Auerbach .30 .75
428 Wayne Simpson .30 .75
429 Jim Fairey .30 .75
430 Vida Blue .60 1.50
431 Gerry Moses .30 .75
432 Dan Frisella .30 .75
433 Willie Horton .60 1.50
434 Giants Team 1.00 2.50
435 Rico Carty .60 1.50
436 Jim McAndrew .30 .75
437 John Kennedy .30 .75
438 Enzo Hernandez .30 .75
439 Eddie Fisher .30 .75
440 Glenn Beckert .30 .75
441 Gail Hopkins .30 .75
442 Dick Dietz .30 .75
443 Danny Thompson .30 .75
444 Ken Brett .30 .75
445 Ken Berry .30 .75
446 Jerry Reuss .60 1.50
447 Joe Hague .30 .75
448 John Hiller .60 1.50
449 Indians Leaders 2.00 5.00
Ken Aspromonte MG
Rocky Colavito
450 Joe Torre 1.00 2.50
451 John Vuckovich .30 .75
452 Paul Casanova .30 .75
453 Checklist 397-528 1.00 2.50
454 Tom Haller .30 .75
455 Bill Melton .30 .75
456 Dick Green .30 .75
457 John Strohmayer .30 .75
458 Jim Mason .30 .75
459 Jimmy Howarth .30 .75
460 Bill Freehan .60 1.50
461 Mike Corkins .30 .75
462 Ron Blomberg .30 .75
463 Ken Tatum .30 .75
464 Chicago Cubs Team 1.00 2.50
465 Dave Giusti .30 .75
466 Jose Arcia .30 .75
467 Mike Ryan .30 .75
468 Tom Griffin .30 .75
469 Dan Monzon .30 .75
470 Mike Cuellar .60 1.50
471 Ty Cobb LDR 5.00 12.00
472 Lou Gehrig LDR 8.00 20.00
473 Hank Aaron LDR 5.00 12.00
474 Babe Ruth LDR 10.00 25.00
475 Ty Cobb LDR 4.00 10.00
476 Walter Johnson ATL/113 Shutouts 1.00 2.50
477 Cy Young ATL/511 Wins 1.00 2.50
478 Walter Johnson ATL/3508 Strikeouts 1.00 2.50
479 Hal Lanier .30 .75
480 Juan Marichal 2.50 6.00
481 White Sox Team Card 1.00 2.50
482 Rick Reuschel RC 1.00 2.50
483 Dal Maxvill .30 .75
484 Ernie McAnally .30 .75
485 Norm Cash .60 1.50
486 Phillies Leaders .60 1.50
Danny Ozark MG
Carroll Beringer
487 Bruce Dal Canton .30 .75
488 Dave Campbell .60 1.50
489 Jeff Burroughs .60 1.50
490 Claude Osteen .60 1.50
491 Bob Montgomery .30 .75
492 Pedro Borbon .30 .75
493 Duffy Dyer .30 .75
494 Rich Morales .30 .75
495 Tommy Helms .30 .75
496 Ray Lamb .30 .75
497 Cardinals Leaders 1.00 2.50
Red Schoendienst MG
Vern Benso
498 Graig Nettles 1.50 4.00
499 Bob Moose .30 .75
500 Oakland A's Team 1.00 2.50
501 Larry Gura .30 .75
502 Bobby Valentine 1.00 2.50
503 Phil Niekro 2.50 6.00
504 Earl Williams .30 .75
505 Bob Bailey .30 .75
506 Bart Johnson .30 .75
507 Darrel Chaney .30 .75
508 Gates Brown .30 .75
509 Jim Nash .30 .75
510 Amos Otis .60 1.50
511 Sam McDowell .60 1.50
512 Dalton Jones .30 .75
513 Dave Marshall .30 .75
514 Jerry Kenney .30 .75
515 Andy Messersmith .60 1.50
516 Danny Walton .30 .75
517 Pirates Leaders 1.00 2.50
Bill Virdon MG
Don Leppert CO
B
518 Bob Veale .30 .75
519 John Edwards .30 .75
520 Mel Stottlemyre .60 1.50
521 Atlanta Braves Team 1.00 2.50
522 Leo Cardenas .30 .75
523 Wayne Granger .30 .75
524 Gene Tenace .60 1.50
525 Jim Fregosi .60 1.50
526 Ollie Brown .30 .75
527 Dan McGinn .30 .75
528 Paul Blair .60 1.50
529 Milt May 1.25 3.00
530 Jim Kaat 1.50 4.00
531 Ron Woods 1.25 3.00
532 Steve Mingori 1.25 3.00
533 Larry Stahl 1.25 3.00
534 Dave Lemonds 1.25 3.00
535 John Callison 1.50 4.00
536 Phillies Team 2.50 6.00
537 Bill Slayback 1.25 3.00
538 Jim Ray Hart 1.50 4.00
539 Tom Murphy 1.25 3.00
540 Cleon Jones 1.50 4.00
541 Bob Bolin 1.25 3.00
542 Pat Corrales 1.50 4.00
543 Alan Foster 1.25 3.00
544 Von Joshua 1.25 3.00
545 Orlando Cepeda 4.00 10.00
546 Jim York 1.25 3.00
547 Bobby Heise 1.25 3.00
548 Don Durham 1.25 3.00
549 Whitey Herzog MG 1.50 4.00
550 Dave Johnson 1.50 4.00
551 Mike Kilkenny 1.50 4.00
552 J.C. Martin 1.25 3.00
553 Mickey Scott 1.25 3.00
554 Dave Concepcion 2.50 6.00
555 Bill Hands 1.25 3.00
556 Yankees Team 2.50 6.00
557 Bernie Williams 1.25 3.00
558 Jerry May 1.25 3.00
559 Barry Lersch 1.25 3.00
560 Frank Howard 1.50 4.00
561 Jim Geddes 1.25 3.00
562 Wayne Garrett 1.25 3.00
563 Larry Haney 1.25 3.00
564 Mike Thompson 1.25 3.00
565 Jim Hickman 1.25 3.00
566 Lew Krausse 1.25 3.00
567 Bob Fenwick 1.25 3.00
568 Ray Newman 1.25 3.00
569 Walt Alston MG 3.00 8.00
570 Bill Singer 1.50 4.00
571 Rusty Torres 1.25 3.00
572 Gary Sutherland 1.25 3.00
573 Fred Beene 1.25 3.00
574 Bob Didier 1.25 3.00
575 Dock Ellis 1.25 3.00
576 Expos Team 3.00 8.00
577 Eric Soderholm 1.25 3.00
578 Ken Wright 1.25 3.00
579 Tom Grieve 1.50 4.00
580 Joe Pepitone 1.50 4.00
581 Steve Kealey 1.25 3.00
582 Darrell Porter 1.50 4.00
583 Bill Greif 1.25 3.00
584 Chris Arnold 1.25 3.00
585 Joe Niekro 1.50 4.00
586 Bill Sudakis 1.25 3.00
587 Rich McKinney 1.25 3.00
588 Checklist 529-660 8.00 20.00
589 Ken Forsch 1.25 3.00
590 Deron Johnson 1.25 3.00
591 Mike Hedlund 1.25 3.00
592 John Boccabella 1.25 3.00
593 Royals Leaders 1.25 3.00
Jack McKeon MG
Galen Cisco CO
Ha
594 Vic Harris 1.25 3.00
595 Don Gullett 1.50 4.00
596 Red Sox Team 2.50 6.00
597 Mickey Rivers 1.50 4.00
598 Phil Roof 1.25 3.00
599 Ed Crosby 1.25 3.00
600 Dave McNally 1.50 4.00
601 Rookie Catchers 1.50 4.00
Sergio Robles
George Pena
Rick
602 Rookie Pitchers 1.50 4.00
Mel Behney
Ralph Garcia
Doug Ra
603 Rookie 3rd Basemen 1.50 4.00
Terry Hughes
Bill McNulty
Ke
604 Rookie Pitchers 1.50 4.00
Jesse Jefferson
Dennis O'Toole/
605 Enos Cabell RC 1.50 4.00
606 Gary Matthews RC 2.50 6.00
607 Rookie Shortstops 1.50 4.00
Pepe Frias
Ray Busse
Mario Gu
608 Steve Busby RC 2.50 6.00
609 Davey Lopes RC 2.50 6.00
610 Charlie Hough 1.50 4.00
611 Rookie Outfielders 1.50 4.00
Rich Coggins
Jim Wohlford
Ri
612 Rookie Pitchers 1.50 4.00
Steve Lawson
Bob Reynolds
Brent
613 Bob Boone RC 6.00 15.00
614 Dwight Evans RC 8.00 20.00
615 Mike Schmidt RC 100.00 250.00
Cey !
616 Rookie Pitchers 1.50 4.00
Norm Angelini
Steve Blateric
Mi
617 Rich Chiles 1.25 3.00
618 Andy Etchebarren 1.25 3.00
619 Billy Wilson 1.25 3.00
620 Tommy Harper 1.50 4.00
621 Joe Ferguson 1.50 4.00
622 Larry Hisle 1.50 4.00
623 Steve Renko 1.25 3.00
624 Leo Durocher MG 3.00 8.00
625 Angel Mangual 1.25 3.00
626 Bob Barton 1.25 3.00
627 Luis Alvarado 1.25 3.00
628 Jim Slaton 1.25 3.00
629 Indians Team 2.50 6.00
630 Denny McLain 2.50 6.00
631 Tom Matchick 1.25 3.00
632 Dick Selma 1.25 3.00
633 Ike Brown 1.25 3.00
634 Alan Closter 1.25 3.00
635 Gene Alley 1.50 4.00
636 Rickey Clark 1.25 3.00
637 Norm Miller 1.25 3.00
638 Ken Reynolds 1.25 3.00
639 Willie Crawford 1.25 3.00
640 Dick Bosman 1.25 3.00
641 Reds Team 2.50 6.00
642 Jose Laboy 1.25 3.00
643 Al Fitzmorris 1.25 3.00
644 Jack Heidemann 1.25 3.00
645 Bob Locker 1.25 3.00
646 Brewers Leaders 1.50 4.00
Del Crandall MG
Harvey Kuenn CO#
647 George Stone 1.25 3.00
648 Tom Egan 1.25 3.00
649 Rich Folkers 1.25 3.00
650 Felipe Alou 2.50 6.00
651 Don Carrithers 1.25 3.00
652 Ted Kubiak 1.25 3.00
653 Joe Hoerner 1.25 3.00
654 Twins Team 2.50 6.00
655 Clay Kirby 1.25 3.00
656 John Ellis 1.25 3.00
657 Bob Johnson 1.25 3.00
658 Elliott Maddox 1.25 3.00
659 Jose Pagan 1.25 3.00
660 Fred Scherman 2.50 6.00

1973 O-Pee-Chee Blue Team Checklists

This 24-card standard-size set is somewhat difficult to find. These blue-bordered team checklist cards are very similar in design to the mass produced red trim team checklist cards issued by O-Pee-Chee the next year and obviously very similar to the Topps issue. The primary difference compared to the Topps issue is the existence of a little French language on the reverse of the O-Pee-Chee. The fronts feature facsimile autographs on a white background. On an orange background, the backs carry the team checklists. The words "Team Checklist" are printed in French and English. The cards are unnumbered and checklisted below in alphabetical order.

COMPLETE SET (24) 60.00 120.00
COMMON TEAM (1-24) 2.50 6.00

1974 O-Pee-Chee

The cards in this 660-card set measure 2 1/2" by 3 1/2". The 1974 O-Pee-Chee cards are very similar to the 1974 Topps cards. Since the O-Pee-Chee cards were printed substantially later than the Topps cards, there was no "San Diego rumored moving to Washington" problem in the O-Pee-Chee set. On a white background, the fronts feature color player photos with rounded corners and blue borders. The player's name and position and the team name also appear on the front. The horizontal backs are golden yellow instead of green like the 1974 Topps and carry player biography and statistics in French and English. There are a number of obverse differences between the two sets as well; they are numbers 3, 4, 5, 6, 7, 8, 9, 99, 166 and 196. The Aaron Specials generally feature two past cards per card instead of four as in the Topps. Remember, the prices below apply only to O-Pee-Chee cards -- they are NOT prices for Topps cards as the Topps cards are generally much more available. The cards were issued in eight card packs with 36 packs to a box. Notable Rookie Cards include Dave Parker and Dave Winfield.

COMPLETE SET (660) 600.00 1,000.00
1 Hank Aaron 30.00 60.00
Complete ML record
2 Aaron Special 54-57 5.00 12.00
Special 54-57
Records on back
3 Aaron Special 58-59 5.00 12.00
Special 58-59
4 Aaron Special 60-61 5.00 12.00
Special 60-61
5 Aaron Special 62-63 5.00 12.00
Special 62-63
6 Aaron Special 64-65 5.00 12.00
Special 64-65
7 Aaron Special 66-67 5.00 12.00
Special 66-67
8 Aaron Special 68-69 5.00 12.00
Special 68-69
9 Aaron Special 70-73 5.00 12.00
Special 70-73
Milestone homers
10 Johnny Bench 10.00 25.00
11 Jim Bibby .40 1.00
12 Dave May .40 1.00
13 Tom Hilgendorf .40 1.00
14 Paul Popovich .40 1.00
15 Joe Torre 1.50 4.00
16 Orioles Team .75 2.00
17 Doug Bird .40 1.00
18 Gary Thomasson .40 1.00
19 Gerry Moses .40 1.00
20 Nolan Ryan 40.00 80.00
21 Bob Gallagher .40 1.00
22 Cy Acosta .40 1.00
23 Craig Robinson .40 1.00
24 John Hiller .75 2.00
25 Ken Singleton .75 2.00
26 Bill Campbell .40 1.00
27 George Scott .75 2.00
28 Manny Sanguillen .75 2.00
29 Phil Niekro 2.50 6.00
30 Bobby Bonds 1.50 4.00
31 Astros Leaders .75 2.00
Preston Gomez MG
Roger Craig CO/
32 Johnny Grubb .40 1.00
33 Don Newhauser .40 1.00
34 Andy Kosco .40 1.00
35 Gaylord Perry 2.50 6.00
36 Cardinals Team .75 2.00
37 Dave Sells .40 1.00
38 Don Kessinger .75 2.00
39 Ken Suarez .40 1.00
40 Jim Palmer 5.00 12.00
41 Bobby Floyd .40 1.00
42 Claude Osteen .75 2.00
43 Jim Wynn .75 2.00
44 Mel Stottlemyre .75 2.00
45 Dave Johnson .75 2.00
46 Pat Kelly .40 1.00
47 Dick Ruthven .40 1.00
48 Dick Sharon .40 1.00
49 Steve Renko .75 2.00
50 Rod Carew 5.00 12.00
51 Bob Heise .40 1.00
52 Al Oliver .75 2.00
53 Fred Kendall .40 1.00
54 Elias Sosa .40 1.00
55 Frank Robinson 5.00 12.00
56 New York Mets Team .75 2.00
57 Darold Knowles .40 1.00
58 Charlie Spikes .40 1.00
59 Ross Grimsley .40 1.00
60 Lou Brock 4.00 10.00
61 Luis Aparicio 2.50 6.00
62 Bob Locker .40 1.00
63 Bill Sudakis .40 1.00
64 Doug Rau .40 1.00
65 Amos Otis .75 2.00
66 Sparky Lyle .75 2.00
67 Tommy Helms .40 1.00
68 Grant Jackson .40 1.00
69 Del Unser .40 1.00
70 Dick Allen 1.25 3.00
71 Dan Frisella .40 1.00
72 Aurelio Rodriguez .40 1.00
73 Mike Marshall 1.25 3.00
74 Twins Team .75 2.00
75 Jim Colborn .40 1.00
76 Mickey Rivers .75 2.00
77 Rich Troedson .40 1.00
78 Giants Leaders .75 2.00
Charlie Fox MG
John McNamara CO/
79 Gene Tenace .75 2.00
80 Tom Seaver 8.00 20.00
81 Frank Duffy .40 1.00
82 Dave Giusti .40 1.00
83 Orlando Cepeda 2.50 6.00

Card	Low	High
84 Rick Wise	.40	1.00
85 Joe Morgan	5.00	12.00
86 Joe Ferguson	.75	2.00
87 Fergie Jenkins	2.50	6.00
88 Fred Patek	.75	2.00
89 Jackie Brown	.40	1.00
90 Bobby Murcer	.75	2.00
91 Ken Forsch	.40	1.00
92 Paul Blair	.75	2.00
93 Rod Gilbreath	.40	1.00
94 Tigers Team	.75	2.00
95 Steve Carlton	5.00	12.00
96 Jerry Hairston	.40	1.00
97 Bob Bailey	.75	2.00
98 Bert Blyleven	1.50	4.00
99 George Theodore/(Topps 99 is	1.25	3.00
Brewers Leaders)		
100 Willie Stargell	5.00	12.00
101 Bobby Valentine	.75	2.00
102 Bill Greif	.40	1.00
103 Sal Bando	.75	2.00
104 Ron Bryant	.40	1.00
105 Carlton Fisk	8.00	20.00
106 Harry Parker	.40	1.00
107 Alex Johnson	.40	1.00
108 Al Hrabosky	.75	2.00
109 Bobby Grich	.75	2.00
110 Billy Williams	2.50	6.00
111 Clay Carroll	.40	1.00
112 Davey Lopes	1.25	3.00
113 Dick Drago	.40	1.00
114 Angels Team	.75	2.00
115 Willie Horton	.75	2.00
116 Jerry Reuss	.75	2.00
117 Ron Blomberg	.40	1.00
118 Bill Lee	.75	2.00
119 Phillies Leaders	.75	2.00
Danny Ozark MG		
Ray Rippelmeyer		
120 Wilbur Wood	.40	1.00
121 Larry Lintz	.40	1.00
122 Jim Holt	.40	1.00
123 Nellie Briles	.75	2.00
124 Bobby Coluccio	.40	1.00
125 Nate Colbert	.40	1.00
126 Checklist 1-132	2.00	5.00
127 Tom Paciorek	.75	2.00
128 John Ellis	.40	1.00
129 Chris Speier	.40	1.00
130 Reggie Jackson	10.00	25.00
131 Bob Boone	1.25	3.00
132 Felix Millan	.40	1.00
133 David Clyde	.40	1.00
134 Denis Menke	.40	1.00
135 Roy White	.75	2.00
136 Rick Reuschel	.75	2.00
137 Al Bumbry	.75	2.00
138 Eddie Brinkman	.40	1.00
139 Aurelio Monteagudo	.40	1.00
140 Darrell Evans	1.25	3.00
141 Pat Bourque	.40	1.00
142 Pedro Garcia	.40	1.00
143 Dick Woodson	.40	1.00
144 Walt Alston MG	1.50	4.00
145 Dock Ellis	.40	1.00
146 Ron Fairly	.75	2.00
147 Bart Johnson	.40	1.00
148 Dave Hilton	.40	1.00
149 Mac Scarce	.40	1.00
150 John Mayberry	.75	2.00
151 Diego Segui	.40	1.00
152 Oscar Gamble	.75	2.00
153 Jon Matlack	.75	2.00
154 Astros Team	.75	2.00
155 Bert Campaneris	.75	2.00
156 Randy Moffitt	.40	1.00
157 Vic Harris	.40	1.00
158 Jack Billingham	.40	1.00
159 Jim Ray Hart	.40	1.00
160 Brooks Robinson	5.00	12.00
161 Ray Burris	.75	2.00
162 Bill Freehan	.75	2.00
163 Ken Berry	.40	1.00
164 Tom House	.40	1.00
165 Willie Davis	.75	2.00
166 Mickey Lolich/(Topps 166 is	1.50	4.00
Royals Leaders)		
167 Luis Tiant	1.25	3.00
168 Danny Thompson	.40	1.00
169 Steve Rogers RC	1.25	3.00
170 Bill Melton	.40	1.00
171 Eduardo Rodriguez	.40	1.00
172 Gene Clines	.40	1.00
173 Randy Jones RC	1.25	3.00
174 Bill Robinson	.75	2.00
175 Reggie Cleveland	.75	2.00
176 John Lowenstein	.40	1.00
177 Dave Roberts	.40	1.00
178 Garry Maddox	.75	2.00
179 Yogi Berra MG	3.00	8.00
180 Ken Holtzman	.75	2.00
181 Cesar Geronimo	.40	1.00
182 Lindy McDaniel	.75	2.00
183 Johnny Oates	.40	1.00
184 Rangers Team	.75	2.00
185 Jose Cardenal	.40	1.00
186 Fred Scherman	.40	1.00
187 Don Baylor	1.25	3.00
188 Rudy Meoli	.40	1.00
189 Jim Brewer	.40	1.00
190 Tony Oliva	1.25	3.00
191 Al Fitzmorris	.40	1.00
192 Mario Guerrero	.40	1.00
193 Tom Walker	.40	1.00
194 Darrell Porter	.75	2.00
195 Carlos May	.40	1.00
196 Jim Hunter/(Topps 196 is	2.50	6.00
Jim Fregosi)		
197 Vicente Romo	.40	1.00
198 Dave Cash	.40	1.00
199 Mike Kekich	.40	1.00
200 Cesar Cedeno	.75	2.00
201 Rod Carew	3.00	8.00
Pete Rose LL		
202 Reggie	3.00	8.00
W.Stargell LL		
203 Reggie	3.00	8.00
W.Stargell LL		
204 T.Harper	1.25	3.00
Lou Brock LL		
205 Wilbur Wood	.75	2.00
Ron Bryant LL		
206 Jim Palmer	2.50	6.00
T.Seaver LL		
207 Nolan Ryan	8.00	20.00
T.Seaver LL		
208 John Hiller	.75	2.00
Mike Marshall LL		
209 Ted Sizemore	.40	1.00
210 Bill Singer	.40	1.00
211 Chicago Cubs Team	.75	2.00
212 Rollie Fingers	2.50	6.00
213 Dave Rader	.40	1.00
214 Bill Grabarkewitz	.40	1.00
215 Al Kaline	6.00	15.00
216 Ray Sadecki	.40	1.00
217 Tim Foli	.40	1.00
218 John Briggs	.40	1.00
219 Doug Griffin	.40	1.00
220 Don Sutton	2.50	6.00
221 White Sox Leaders	.75	2.00
Chuck Tanner MG		
Jim Mahoney CO		
222 Ramon Hernandez	.40	1.00
223 Jeff Burroughs	1.25	3.00
224 Roger Metzger	.40	1.00
225 Paul Splittorff	.40	1.00
226 Padres Team Card	1.25	3.00
227 Mike Lum	.40	1.00
228 Ted Kubiak	.40	1.00
229 Fritz Peterson	.40	1.00
230 Tony Perez	2.50	6.00
231 Dick Tidrow	.40	1.00
232 Steve Brye	.40	1.00
233 Jim Barr	.40	1.00
234 John Milner	.40	1.00
235 Dave McNally	.75	2.00
236 Red Schoendienst MG	1.50	4.00
237 Ken Brett	.40	1.00
238 Fran Healy	.40	1.00
239 Bill Russell	.75	2.00
240 Joe Coleman	.40	1.00
241 Glenn Beckert	.40	1.00
242 Bill Gogolewski	.40	1.00
243 Bob Oliver	.40	1.00
244 Carl Morton	.40	1.00
245 Cleon Jones	.40	1.00
246 A's Team	1.25	3.00
247 Rick Miller	.40	1.00
248 Tom Hall	.40	1.00
249 George Mitterwald	.40	1.00
250 Willie McCovey	4.00	10.00
251 Graig Nettles	1.25	3.00
252 Dave Parker RC	6.00	15.00
253 John Boccabella	.40	1.00
254 Stan Bahnsen	.40	1.00
255 Larry Bowa	.75	2.00
256 Tom Griffin	.40	1.00
257 Buddy Bell	1.25	3.00
258 Jerry Morales	.40	1.00
259 Bob Reynolds	.40	1.00
260 Ted Simmons	1.50	4.00
261 Jerry Bell	.40	1.00
262 Ed Kirkpatrick	.40	1.00
263 Checklist 133-264	1.50	4.00
264 Joe Rudi	.75	2.00
265 Tug McGraw	1.50	4.00
266 Jim Northrup	.75	2.00
267 Andy Messersmith	.75	2.00
268 Tom Grieve	.75	2.00
269 Bob Johnson	.40	1.00
270 Ron Santo	1.50	4.00
271 Bill Hands	.40	1.00
272 Paul Casanova	.40	1.00
273 Checklist 265-396	1.50	4.00
274 Fred Beene	.40	1.00
275 Ron Hunt	.40	1.00
276 Angels Leaders	.75	2.00
Bobby Winkles MG		
John Roseboro CO		
277 Gary Nolan	.75	2.00
278 Cookie Rojas	.75	2.00
279 Jim Crawford	.40	1.00
280 Carl Yastrzemski	8.00	20.00
281 Giants Team	.75	2.00
282 Doyle Alexander	.75	2.00
283 Mike Schmidt	12.50	40.00
284 Dave Duncan	.75	2.00
285 Reggie Smith	.75	2.00
286 Tony Muser	.40	1.00
287 Clay Kirby	.40	1.00
288 Gorman Thomas	1.25	3.00
289 Rick Auerbach	.40	1.00
290 Vida Blue	.75	2.00
291 Don Hahn	.40	1.00
292 Chuck Seelbach	.40	1.00
293 Milt May	.40	1.00
294 Steve Foucault	.40	1.00
295 Rick Monday	.75	2.00
296 Ray Corbin	.40	1.00
297 Hal Breeden	.40	1.00
298 Roric Harrison	.40	1.00
299 Gene Michael	.40	1.00
300 Pete Rose	12.50	30.00
301 Bob Montgomery	.40	1.00
302 Rudy May	.40	1.00
303 George Hendrick	.75	2.00
304 Don Wilson	.40	1.00
305 Tito Fuentes	.40	1.00
306 Earl Weaver MG	1.50	4.00
307 Luis Melendez	.40	1.00
308 Bruce Dal Canton	.40	1.00
309 Dave Roberts	.40	1.00
310 Terry Forster	.75	2.00
311 Jerry Grote	.75	2.00
312 Deron Johnson	.40	1.00
313 Barry Lersch	.40	1.00
314 Brewers Team	.40	1.00
315 Ron Cey	1.25	3.00
316 Jim Perry	.75	2.00
317 Richie Zisk	.75	2.00
318 Jim Merritt	.40	1.00
319 Randy Hundley	.40	1.00
320 Dusty Baker	1.25	3.00
321 Steve Braun	.40	1.00
322 Ernie McAnally	.40	1.00
323 Richie Scheinblum	.40	1.00
324 Steve Kline	.40	1.00
325 Tommy Harper	.75	2.00
326 Sparky Anderson MG	1.50	4.00
327 Tom Timmermann	.40	1.00
328 Skip Jutze	.40	1.00
329 Mark Belanger	.75	2.00
330 Juan Marichal	2.50	6.00
331 Carlton Fisk	3.00	8.00
J.Bench AS		
332 Dick Allen	4.00	10.00
H.Aaron AS		
333 Rod Carew	2.00	5.00
J.Morgan AS		
334 B.Robinson	1.50	4.00
R.Santo AS		
335 Bert Campaneris	.75	2.00
Chris Speier AS		
336 Bobby Murcer	2.50	6.00
P.Rose AS		
337 Amos Otis	.75	2.00
Cesar Cedeno AS		
338 R.Jackson	3.00	8.00
B.Williams AS		
339 Jim Hunter	1.50	4.00
R.Wise AS		
340 Thurman Munson	5.00	12.00
341 Dan Driessen RC	.75	2.00
342 Jim Lonborg	.75	2.00
343 Royals Team	.75	2.00
344 Mike Caldwell	.40	1.00
345 Bill North	.40	1.00
346 Ron Reed	.40	1.00
347 Sandy Alomar	.75	2.00
348 Pete Richert	.40	1.00
349 John Vukovich	.40	1.00
350 Bob Gibson	4.00	10.00
351 Dwight Evans	1.50	4.00
352 Bill Stoneman	.40	1.00
353 Rich Coggins	.40	1.00
354 Chicago Cubs Leaders	.75	2.00
Whitey Lockman MG		
J.C. Mart		
355 Dave Nelson	.40	1.00
356 Jerry Koosman	.75	2.00
357 Buddy Bradford	.40	1.00
358 Dal Maxvill	.40	1.00
359 Brent Strom	.40	1.00
360 Greg Luzinski	1.25	3.00
361 Don Carrithers	.40	1.00
362 Hal King	.40	1.00
363 Yankees Team	1.25	3.00
364 Cito Gaston	.75	2.00
365 Steve Busby	.75	2.00
366 Larry Hisle	.75	2.00
367 Norm Cash	1.25	3.00
368 Manny Mota	.75	2.00
369 Paul Lindblad	.40	1.00
370 Bob Watson	.75	2.00
371 Jim Slaton	.40	1.00
372 Ken Reitz	.40	1.00
373 John Curtis	.40	1.00
374 Marty Perez	.40	1.00
375 Earl Williams	.40	1.00
376 Jorge Orta	.40	1.00
377 Ron Woods	.40	1.00
378 Burt Hooton	.75	2.00
379 Billy Martin MG	1.25	3.00
380 Bud Harrelson	.75	2.00
381 Charlie Sands	.40	1.00
382 Bob Moose	.40	1.00
383 Phillies Team	.75	2.00
384 Chris Chambliss	.75	2.00
385 Don Gullett	.75	2.00
386 Gary Matthews	1.25	3.00
387 Rich Morales	.40	1.00
388 Phil Roof	.40	1.00
389 Gates Brown	.40	1.00
390 Lou Piniella	1.25	3.00
391 Billy Champion	.40	1.00
392 Dick Green	.40	1.00
393 Orlando Pena	.40	1.00
394 Ken Henderson	.40	1.00
395 Doug Rader	.40	1.00
396 Tommy Davis	.75	2.00
397 George Stone	.40	1.00
398 Duke Sims	.40	1.00
399 Mike Paul	.40	1.00
400 Harmon Killebrew	4.00	10.00
401 Elliott Maddox	.40	1.00
402 Jim Rooker	.40	1.00
403 Red Sox Leaders	.75	2.00
Darrell Johnson MG		
Eddie Popowsk		
404 Jim Howarth	.40	1.00
405 Ellie Rodriguez	.40	1.00
406 Steve Arlin	.40	1.00
407 Jim Wohlford	.40	1.00
408 Charlie Hough	.75	2.00
409 Ike Brown	.40	1.00
410 Pedro Borbon	.40	1.00
411 Frank Baker	.40	1.00
412 Chuck Taylor	.40	1.00
413 Don Money	.75	2.00
414 Checklist 397-528	1.50	4.00
415 Gary Gentry	.40	1.00
416 White Sox Team	.75	2.00
417 Rich Folkers	.40	1.00
418 Walt Williams	.40	1.00
419 Wayne Twitchell	.40	1.00
420 Ray Fosse	.40	1.00
421 Dan Fife	.40	1.00
422 Gonzalo Marquez	.40	1.00
423 Fred Stanley	.40	1.00
424 Jim Beauchamp	.40	1.00
425 Pete Broberg	.40	1.00
426 Rennie Stennett	.40	1.00
427 Bobby Bolin	.40	1.00
428 Gary Sutherland	.40	1.00
429 Dick Lange	.40	1.00
430 Matty Alou	.75	2.00
431 Gene Garber RC	.75	2.00
432 Chris Arnold	.40	1.00
433 Lerrin LaGrow	.40	1.00
434 Ken McMullen	.40	1.00
435 Dave Concepcion	1.25	3.00
436 Don Hood	.40	1.00
437 Jim Lyttle	.40	1.00
438 Ed Herrmann	.40	1.00
439 Norm Miller	.40	1.00
440 Jim Kaat	1.50	4.00
441 Tom Ragland	.40	1.00
442 Alan Foster	.40	1.00
443 Tom Hutton	.40	1.00
444 Vic Davalillo	.40	1.00
445 George Medich	.40	1.00
446 Len Randle	.40	1.00
447 Twins Leaders	.75	2.00
Frank Quilici MG		
Ralph Rowe CO		
Bo		
448 Ron Hodges	.40	1.00
449 Tom McCraw	.40	1.00
450 Rich Hebner	.75	2.00
451 Tommy John	1.50	4.00
452 Gene Hiser	.40	1.00
453 Balor Moore	.40	1.00
454 Kurt Bevacqua	.40	1.00
455 Tom Bradley	.40	1.00
456 Dave Winfield RC	30.00	60.00
457 Chuck Goggin	.40	1.00
458 Jim Ray	.40	1.00
459 Reds Team	1.25	3.00
460 Boog Powell	1.25	3.00
461 John Odom	.40	1.00
462 Luis Alvarado	.40	1.00
463 Pat Dobson	.40	1.00
464 Jose Cruz	1.25	3.00
465 Dick Bosman	.40	1.00
466 Dick Billings	.40	1.00
467 Winston Llenas	.40	1.00
468 Pepe Frias	.40	1.00
469 Joe Decker	.40	1.00
470 Reggie Jackson ALCS	3.00	8.00
471 N.L. Playoffs	.75	2.00
Mets over Reds/(Jon Matlack pitchi		
472 Darold Knowles WS	.75	2.00
473 Willie Mays WS2	5.00	12.00
474 Bert Campaneris WS	.75	2.00
475 Rusty Staub WS	.75	2.00
476 Cleon Jones WS	.75	2.00
477 Reggie Jackson WS6	3.00	8.00
478 Bert Campaneris WS	.75	2.00
479 World Series Summary	.75	2.00
A's Celebrate; Win/2nd cons		
480 Willie Crawford	.40	1.00
481 Jerry Terrell	.40	1.00
482 Bob Didier	.40	1.00
483 Braves Team	.75	2.00
484 Carmen Fanzone	.40	1.00
485 Felipe Alou	1.25	3.00
486 Steve Stone	.75	2.00
487 Ted Martinez	.40	1.00
488 Andy Etchebarren	.40	1.00
489 Pirates Leaders	.75	2.00
Danny Murtaugh MG		
Don Osborn CO#		
490 Vada Pinson	1.25	3.00
491 Roger Nelson	.40	1.00
492 Mike Rogodzinski	.40	1.00
493 Joe Hoerner	.40	1.00
494 Ed Goodson	.40	1.00
495 Dick McAuliffe	.75	2.00
496 Tom Murphy	.40	1.00
497 Bobby Mitchell	.40	1.00
498 Pat Corrales	.40	1.00
499 Rusty Torres	.40	1.00
500 Lee May	.75	2.00
501 Eddie Leon	.40	1.00
502 Dave LaRoche	.40	1.00
503 Eric Soderholm	.40	1.00
504 Joe Niekro	.75	2.00
505 Bill Buckner	.75	2.00
506 Ed Farmer	.40	1.00
507 Larry Stahl	.40	1.00
508 Expos Team	1.25	3.00
509 Jesse Jefferson	.40	1.00
510 Wayne Garrett	.40	1.00
511 Toby Harrah	.75	2.00

512 Joe Lahoud .40 1.00
513 Jim Campanis .40 1.00
514 Paul Schaal .40 1.00
515 Willie Montanez .40 1.00
516 Horacio Pina .40 1.00
517 Mike Hegan .40 1.00
518 Derrel Thomas .40 1.00
519 Bill Sharp .40 1.00
520 Tim McCarver 1.25 3.00
521 Indians Leaders .75 2.00
Ken Aspromonte MG
Clay Bryant CO
522 J.R. Richard 1.25 3.00
523 Cecil Cooper 1.25 3.00
524 Bill Plummer .40 1.00
525 Clyde Wright .40 1.00
526 Frank Tepedino .75 2.00
527 Bobby Darwin .40 1.00
528 Bill Bonham .40 1.00
529 Horace Clarke .75 2.00
530 Mickey Stanley .75 2.00
531 Expos Leaders 1.25 3.00
Gene Mauch MG
Dave Bristol CO
Cal
532 Skip Lockwood .40 1.00
533 Mike Phillips .40 1.00
534 Eddie Watt .40 1.00
535 Bob Tolan .40 1.00
536 Duffy Dyer .40 1.00
537 Steve Mingori .40 1.00
538 Cesar Tovar .40 1.00
539 Lloyd Allen .40 1.00
540 Bob Robertson .40 1.00
541 Indians Team .75 2.00
542 Goose Gossage 1.25 3.00
543 Danny Cater .40 1.00
544 Ron Schueler .40 1.00
545 Billy Conigliaro .75 2.00
546 Mike Corkins .40 1.00
547 Glenn Borgmann .40 1.00
548 Sonny Siebert .40 1.00
549 Mike Jorgensen .40 1.00
550 Sam McDowell .75 2.00
551 Von Joshua .40 1.00
552 Denny Doyle .40 1.00
553 Jim Willoughby .40 1.00
554 Tim Johnson .40 1.00
555 Woody Fryman .40 1.00
556 Dave Campbell .75 2.00
557 Jim McGlothlin .40 1.00
558 Bill Fahey .40 1.00
559 Darrell Chaney .40 1.00
560 Mike Cuellar .75 2.00
561 Ed Kranepool .75 2.00
562 Jack Aker .40 1.00
563 Hal McRae .75 2.00
564 Mike Ryan .40 1.00
565 Milt Wilcox .40 1.00
566 Jackie Hernandez .40 1.00
567 Red Sox Team .75 2.00
568 Mike Torrez .75 2.00
569 Rick Dempsey .75 2.00
570 Ralph Garr .75 2.00
571 Rich Hand .40 1.00
572 Enzo Hernandez .40 1.00
573 Mike Adams .40 1.00
574 Bill Parsons .40 1.00
575 Steve Garvey 1.50 4.00
576 Scipio Spinks .40 1.00
577 Mike Sadek .40 1.00
578 Ralph Houk MG .75 2.00
579 Cecil Upshaw .40 1.00
580 Jim Spencer .40 1.00
581 Fred Norman .40 1.00
582 Bucky Dent RC 2.50 6.00
583 Marty Pattin .40 1.00
584 Ken Rudolph .40 1.00
585 Merv Rettenmund .40 1.00
586 Jack Brohamer .40 1.00
587 Larry Christenson .40 1.00
588 Hal Lanier .40 1.00
589 Boots Day .75 2.00
590 Rogelio Moret .40 1.00
591 Sonny Jackson .40 1.00
592 Ed Bane .40 1.00
593 Steve Yeager .75 2.00
594 Leroy Stanton .40 1.00
595 Steve Blass .75 2.00
596 Rookie Pitchers .40 1.00
Wayne Garland
Fred Holdsworth
M
597 Rookie Shortstops .75 2.00
Dave Chalk
John Gamble
Pete M
598 Ken Griffey Sr. RC 6.00 15.00
599 Rookie Pitchers 1.25 3.00
Ron Diorio
Dave Freisleben
Fran
600 Bill Madlock RC 3.00 8.00
601 Brian Downing RC 1.50 4.00
602 Rookie Pitchers .75 2.00
Glenn Abbott
Rick Henninger
Cra
603 Rookie Catchers .75 2.00
Barry Foote
Tom Lundstedt
Charl
604 A.Thornton 3.00 8.00
F.White RC
605 Frank Tanana RC 2.00 5.00
606 Rookie Outfielders .75 2.00
Jim Fuller
Wilbur Howard
Tom
607 Rookie Shortstops .75 2.00
Leo Foster
Tom Heintzelman
Da
608 Rookie Pitchers 1.25 3.00
Bob Apodaca
Dick Baney
John D'A
609 Rico Petrocelli .75 2.00
610 Dave Kingman 1.50 4.00
611 Rich Stelmaszek .40 1.00
612 Luke Walker .40 1.00
613 Dan Monzon .40 1.00
614 Adrian Devine .40 1.00
615 John Jeter .40 1.00
616 Larry Gura .40 1.00
617 Ted Ford .40 1.00
618 Jim Mason .40 1.00
619 Mike Anderson .40 1.00
620 Al Downing .40 1.00
621 Bernie Carbo .40 1.00
622 Phil Gagliano .40 1.00
623 Celerino Sanchez .40 1.00
624 Bob Miller .40 1.00
625 Ollie Brown .40 1.00
626 Pirates Team .75 2.00
627 Carl Taylor .40 1.00
628 Ivan Murrell .40 1.00
629 Rusty Staub 1.25 3.00
630 Tommy Agee .75 2.00
631 Steve Barber .40 1.00
632 George Culver .40 1.00
633 Dave Hamilton .40 1.00
634 Eddie Mathews MG 1.50 4.00
635 John Edwards .40 1.00
636 Dave Goltz .40 1.00
637 Checklist 529-660 1.50 4.00
638 Ken Sanders .40 1.00
639 Joe Lovitto .40 1.00
640 Milt Pappas .75 2.00
641 Chuck Brinkman .40 1.00
642 Terry Harmon .40 1.00
643 Dodgers Team .75 2.00
644 Wayne Granger .40 1.00
645 Ken Boswell .40 1.00
646 George Foster 1.25 3.00
647 Juan Beniquez .40 1.00
648 Terry Crowley .40 1.00
649 Fernando Gonzalez .40 1.00
650 Mike Epstein .40 1.00
651 Leron Lee .40 1.00
652 Gail Hopkins .40 1.00
653 Bob Stinson .75 2.00
654 Jesus Alou .75 2.00
655 Mike Tyson .40 1.00
656 Adrian Garrett .40 1.00
657 Jim Shellenback .40 1.00
658 Lee Lacy .40 1.00
659 Joe Lis .40 1.00
660 Larry Dierker 1.25 3.00

1974 O-Pee-Chee Team Checklists

The cards in this 24-card set measure 2 1/2" by 3 1/2". The fronts have red borders and feature the year and team name in a green panel decorated by a crossed bats design, below which is a white area containing facsimile autographs of various players. On a light yellow background, the backs list team members alphabetically, along with their card number, uniform number and position. The words "Team Checklist" appear in French and English. The cards are unnumbered and checklisted below in alphabetical order.

COMPLETE SET (24) 20.00 50.00
COMMON TEAM (1-24) 1.00 2.50

1975 O-Pee-Chee

The cards in this 660-card set measure 2 1/2" by 3 1/2". The 1975 O-Pee-Chee cards are very similar to the 1975 Topps cards, yet rather different from previous years' issues. The most prominent change for the fronts is the use of a two-color fram colors surrounding the picture area rather than a single, subdued color. The fronts feature color player photos with rounded corners. The player's name and position, the team name and a facsimile autograph round out the front. The backs are printed in red and green on a yellow-vanilla card stock and carry player biography and statistics in French and English. Cards 189-212 depict the MVPs of both leagues from 1951 through 1974. The first six cards (1-6) feature players breaking records or achieving milestones during the previous season. Cards 306-313 picture league leaders in various statistical categories. Cards 459-466 depict the results of post-season action. Team cards feature a checklist back for players on that team. Remember, the prices below apply only to O-Pee-Chee cards -- they are NOT prices for Topps cards as the Topps cards are generally much more available. The cards were issued in eight card packs which cost 10 cents and came 48 packs to a box. Notable Rookie Cards include George Brett, Fred Lynn, Keith Hernandez, Jim Rice and Robin Yount.

COMPLETE SET (660) 500.00 1,000.00
1 Hank Aaron HL 12.50 40.00
2 Lou Brock HL 1.50 4.00
3 Bob Gibson HL 1.50 4.00
4 Al Kaline HL 3.00 8.00
5 Nolan Ryan HL 12.50 30.00
6 Mike Marshall RB .60 1.50
Hurls 106 Games
7 S.Busby 5.00 12.00
Bosman
N.Ryan HL
8 Rogelio Moret .30 .75
9 Frank Tepedino .60 1.50
10 Willie Davis .60 1.50
11 Bill Melton .30 .75
12 David Clyde .30 .75
13 Gene Locklear .60 1.50
14 Milt Wilcox .30 .75
15 Jose Cardenal .60 1.50
16 Frank Tanana 1.00 2.50
17 Dave Concepcion 1.00 2.50
18 Tigers Team CL 1.00 2.50
Ralph Houk MG
19 Jerry Koosman .60 1.50
20 Thurman Munson 4.00 10.00
21 Rollie Fingers 2.00 5.00
22 Dave Cash .30 .75
23 Bill Russell .60 1.50
24 Al Fitzmorris .30 .75
25 Lee May .60 1.50
26 Dave McNally .60 1.50
27 Ken Reitz .30 .75
28 Tom Murphy .30 .75
29 Dave Parker 1.50 4.00
30 Bert Blyleven 1.00 2.50
31 Dave Rader .30 .75
32 Reggie Cleveland .60 1.50
33 Dusty Baker 1.00 2.50
34 Steve Renko .30 .75
35 Ron Santo .60 1.50
36 Joe Lovitto .30 .75
37 Dave Freisleben .30 .75
38 Buddy Bell 1.00 2.50
39 Andre Thornton .60 1.50
40 Bill Singer .30 .75
41 Cesar Geronimo .60 1.50
42 Joe Coleman .30 .75
43 Cleon Jones .60 1.50
44 Pat Dobson .30 .75
45 Joe Rudi .60 1.50
46 Phillies Team CL(Danny Ozark MG 1.00 2.50
47 Tommy John 1.00 2.50
48 Freddie Patek .60 1.50
49 Larry Dierker .60 1.50
50 Brooks Robinson 4.00 10.00
51 Bob Forsch .60 1.50
52 Darrell Porter .60 1.50
53 Dave Giusti .30 .75
54 Eric Soderholm .30 .75
55 Bobby Bonds 1.50 4.00
56 Rick Wise .60 1.50
57 Dave Johnson .60 1.50
58 Chuck Taylor .30 .75
59 Ken Henderson .30 .75
60 Fergie Jenkins 2.00 5.00
61 Dave Winfield 10.00 25.00
62 Fritz Peterson .30 .75
63 Steve Swisher .30 .75
64 Dave Chalk .30 .75
65 Don Gullett .60 1.50
66 Willie Horton .60 1.50
67 Tug McGraw 1.00 2.50
68 Ron Blomberg .30 .75
69 John Odom .30 .75
70 Mike Schmidt 12.50 30.00
71 Charlie Hough .60 1.50
72 Royals Team CL(Jack McKeon MG 1.00 2.50
73 J.R. Richard .60 1.50
74 Mark Belanger .60 1.50
75 Ted Simmons 1.00 2.50
76 Ed Sprague .30 .75
77 Richie Zisk .60 1.50
78 Ray Corbin .30 .75
79 Gary Matthews .60 1.50
80 Carlton Fisk 4.00 10.00
81 Ron Reed .30 .75
82 Pat Kelly .30 .75
83 Jim Merritt .30 .75
84 Enzo Hernandez .30 .75
85 Bill Bonham .30 .75
86 Joe Lis .30 .75
87 George Foster 1.00 2.50
88 Tom Egan .30 .75
89 Jim Ray .30 .75
90 Rusty Staub 1.00 2.50
91 Dick Green .30 .75
92 Cecil Upshaw .30 .75
93 Davey Lopes 1.00 2.50
94 Jim Lonborg .60 1.50
95 John Mayberry .60 1.50
96 Mike Cosgrove .30 .75
97 Earl Williams .30 .75
98 Rich Folkers .30 .75
99 Mike Hegan .30 .75
100 Willie Stargell 2.50 6.00
101 Expos Team CL(Gene Mauch MG 1.00 2.50
102 Joe Decker .30 .75
103 Rick Miller .30 .75
104 Bill Madlock 1.00 2.50
105 Buzz Capra .30 .75
106 Mike Hargrove RC 1.50 4.00
107 Jim Barr .30 .75
108 Tom Hall .30 .75
109 George Hendrick .60 1.50
110 Wilbur Wood .30 .75
111 Wayne Garrett .30 .75
112 Larry Hardy .30 .75
113 Elliott Maddox .30 .75
114 Dick Lange .30 .75
115 Joe Ferguson .30 .75
116 Lerrin LaGrow .30 .75
117 Orioles Team CL 1.50 4.00
Earl Weaver MG
118 Mike Anderson .30 .75
119 Tommy Helms .30 .75
120 Steve Busby/(photo actually .60 1.50
Fran Healy)
121 Bill North .30 .75
122 Al Hrabosky .60 1.50
123 Johnny Briggs .30 .75
124 Jerry Reuss .60 1.50
125 Ken Singleton .60 1.50
126 Checklist 1-132 1.50 4.00
127 Glenn Borgmann .30 .75
128 Bill Lee .60 1.50
129 Rick Monday .60 1.50
130 Phil Niekro 1.50 4.00
131 Toby Harrah .60 1.50
132 Randy Moffitt .30 .75
133 Dan Driessen .60 1.50
134 Ron Hodges .30 .75
135 Charlie Spikes .30 .75
136 Jim Mason .30 .75
137 Terry Forster .60 1.50
138 Del Unser .30 .75
139 Horacio Pina .30 .75
140 Steve Garvey 1.50 4.00
141 Mickey Stanley .60 1.50
142 Bob Reynolds .30 .75
143 Cliff Johnson RC .60 1.50
144 Jim Wohlford .30 .75
145 Ken Holtzman .60 1.50
146 Padres Team CL 1.00 2.50
John McNamara MG
147 Pedro Garcia .30 .75
148 Jim Rooker .30 .75
149 Tim Foli .30 .75
150 Bob Gibson 3.00 8.00
151 Steve Brye .30 .75
152 Mario Guerrero .30 .75
153 Rick Reuschel .60 1.50
154 Mike Lum .30 .75
155 Jim Bibby .30 .75
156 Dave Kingman 1.00 2.50
157 Pedro Borbon .60 1.50
158 Jerry Grote .30 .75
159 Steve Arlin .30 .75
160 Graig Nettles 1.00 2.50
161 Stan Bahnsen .30 .75
162 Willie Montanez .30 .75
163 Jim Brewer .30 .75
164 Mickey Rivers .60 1.50
165 Doug Rader .60 1.50
166 Woodie Fryman .30 .75
167 Rich Coggins .30 .75
168 Bill Greif .30 .75
169 Cookie Rojas .30 .75
170 Bert Campaneris .60 1.50
171 Ed Kirkpatrick .30 .75
172 Red Sox Team CL(Darrell Johnson MG 1.50 4.00
173 Steve Rogers .60 1.50
174 Bake McBride .60 1.50
175 Don Money .60 1.50
176 Burt Hooton .60 1.50
177 Vic Correll .30 .75
178 Cesar Tovar .30 .75
179 Tom Bradley .30 .75
180 Joe Morgan 3.00 8.00
181 Fred Beene .30 .75
182 Don Hahn .30 .75
183 Mel Stottlemyre .60 1.50
184 Jorge Orta .30 .75
185 Steve Carlton 4.00 10.00
186 Willie Crawford .30 .75
187 Denny Doyle .30 .75
188 Tom Griffin .30 .75
189 Y.Berra 2.50 6.00
R.Campanella MVP
190 Bobby Shantz 1.00 2.50
Hank Sauer MVP
191 Al Rosen 1.00 2.50
R.Campanella MV
192 Yogi Berra 2.50 6.00
W.Mays MVP
193 Y.Berra 1.50 4.00
R.Campanella MVP
194 M.Mantle 6.00 15.00
D.Newcombe MVP
195 Mickey Mantle 8.00 20.00
H.Aaron MV
196 Jackie Jensen 1.00 2.50
Ernie Banks MVP
197 Nellie Fox 1.50 4.00
E.Banks MVP
198 Roger Maris 1.00 2.50
Dick Groat MVP
199 Rog.Maris 1.50 4.00
F.Robinson MVP
200 Mickey Mantle 6.00 15.00
M.Wills MV
201 Els.Howard 1.00 2.50
S.Koufax MVP
202 B.Robinson 1.00 2.50
K.Boyer MVP

203 Zoilo Versalles 1.00 2.50
W.Mays M
204 R.Clemente 3.00 8.00
F.Robinson MV
205 C.Yastrzemski 1.00 2.50
Cepeda MVP
206 Denny McLain 1.00 2.50
B.Gibson MV
207 H.Killebrew 1.00 2.50
W.McCovey MV
208 Boog Powell 1.00 2.50
J.Bench MVP
209 Vida Blue 1.00 2.50
Joe Torre MVP
210 Dick Allen 1.00 2.50
J.Bench MVP
211 Reggie Jackson 3.00 8.00
P.Rose MV
212 Jeff Burroughs 1.00 2.50
Steve Garvey MVP
213 Oscar Gamble .60 1.50
214 Harry Parker .30 .75
215 Bobby Valentine .60 1.50
216 Giants Team CL 1.00 2.50
Wes Westrum MG
217 Lou Piniella 1.00 2.50
218 Jerry Johnson .30 .75
219 Ed Herrmann .30 .75
220 Don Sutton 1.50 4.00
221 Aurelio Rodriguez .30 .75
222 Dan Spillner .30 .75
223 Robin Yount RC 30.00 60.00
224 Ramon Hernandez .30 .75
225 Bob Grich .60 1.50
226 Bill Campbell .30 .75
227 Bob Watson .60 1.50
228 George Brett RC 50.00 100.00
229 Barry Foote .60 1.50
230 Jim Hunter 2.00 5.00
231 Mike Tyson .30 .75
232 Diego Segui .30 .75
233 Billy Grabarkewitz .30 .75
234 Tom Grieve .60 1.50
235 Jack Billingham .60 1.50
236 Angels Team CL 1.00 2.50
Dick Williams MG
237 Carl Morton .30 .75
238 Dave Duncan .60 1.50
239 George Stone .30 .75
240 Garry Maddox .60 1.50
241 Dick Tidrow .30 .75
242 Jay Johnstone .60 1.50
243 Jim Kaat 1.00 2.50
244 Bill Buckner .60 1.50
245 Mickey Lolich 1.00 2.50
246 Cardinals Team CL 1.00 2.50
Red Schoendienst MG
247 Enos Cabell .30 .75
248 Randy Jones 1.00 2.50
249 Danny Thompson .30 .75
250 Ken Brett .30 .75
251 Fran Healy .30 .75
252 Fred Scherman .30 .75
253 Jesus Alou .30 .75
254 Mike Torrez .60 1.50
255 Dwight Evans 1.00 2.50
256 Billy Champion .30 .75
257 Checklist 133-264 1.50 4.00
258 Dave LaRoche .30 .75
259 Len Randle .30 .75
260 Johnny Bench 8.00 20.00
261 Andy Hassler .30 .75
262 Rowland Office .30 .75
263 Jim Perry .60 1.50
264 John Milner .30 .75
265 Ron Bryant .30 .75
266 Sandy Alomar .60 1.50
267 Dick Ruthven .30 .75
268 Hal McRae .60 1.50
269 Doug Rau .30 .75
270 Ron Fairly .60 1.50
271 Jerry Moses .30 .75
272 Lynn McGlothen .30 .75
273 Steve Braun .30 .75
274 Vicente Romo .30 .75
275 Paul Blair .60 1.50
276 White Sox Team CL 1.00 2.50
Chuck Tanner MG
277 Frank Taveras .30 .75
278 Paul Lindblad .30 .75
279 Milt May .30 .75
280 Carl Yastrzemski 6.00 15.00
281 Jim Slaton .30 .75
282 Jerry Morales .30 .75
283 Steve Foucault .30 .75
284 Ken Griffey Sr. 2.00 5.00
285 Ellie Rodriguez .30 .75
286 Mike Jorgensen .30 .75
287 Roric Harrison .30 .75
288 Bruce Ellingsen .30 .75
289 Ken Rudolph .30 .75
290 Jon Matlack .30 .75
291 Bill Sudakis .30 .75
292 Ron Schueler .30 .75
293 Dick Sharon .30 .75
294 Geoff Zahn .30 .75
295 Vada Pinson 1.00 2.50
296 Alan Foster .30 .75
297 Craig Kusick .30 .75
298 Johnny Grubb .30 .75
299 Bucky Dent 1.00 2.50
300 Reggie Jackson 8.00 20.00
301 Dave Roberts .30 .75
302 Rick Burleson .60 1.50
303 Grant Jackson .30 .75
304 Pirates Team CL 1.00 2.50
Danny Murtaugh MG
305 Jim Colborn .30 .75
306 Rod Carew 1.00 2.50
R.Garr LL
307 Dick Allen 2.00 5.00
M.Schmidt LL
308 Jeff Burroughs 1.00 2.50
Bench LL
309 Billy North 1.00 2.50
Brock LL
310 Hunter 1.00 2.50
Jenk
Niekro LL
311 Jim Hunter 1.00 2.50
B.Capra LL
312 Nolan Ryan 8.00 20.00
S.Carlton LL
313 Terry Forster .60 1.50
Mike Marshall LL
314 Buck Martinez .30 .75
315 Don Kessinger .60 1.50
316 Jackie Brown .30 .75
317 Joe Lahoud .30 .75
318 Ernie McAnally .30 .75
319 Johnny Oates .30 .75
320 Pete Rose 12.50 40.00
321 Rudy May .30 .75
322 Ed Goodson .30 .75
323 Fred Holdsworth .30 .75
324 Ed Kranepool .60 1.50
325 Tony Oliva 1.00 2.50
326 Wayne Twitchell .30 .75
327 Jerry Hairston .30 .75
328 Sonny Siebert .30 .75
329 Ted Kubiak .30 .75
330 Mike Marshall .60 1.50
331 Indians Team CL(Frank Robinson MG 1.00 2.50
332 Fred Kendall .30 .75
333 Dick Drago .30 .75
334 Greg Gross .30 .75
335 Jim Palmer 3.00 8.00
336 Rennie Stennett .30 .75
337 Kevin Kobel .30 .75
338 Rick Stelmaszek .30 .75
339 Jim Fregosi .60 1.50
340 Paul Splittorff .30 .75
341 Hal Breeden .30 .75
342 Leroy Stanton .30 .75
343 Danny Frisella .30 .75
344 Ben Oglivie .60 1.50
345 Clay Carroll .60 1.50
346 Bobby Darwin .30 .75
347 Mike Caldwell .30 .75
348 Tony Muser .30 .75
349 Ray Sadecki .30 .75
350 Bobby Murcer .60 1.50
351 Bob Boone 1.00 2.50
352 Darold Knowles .30 .75
353 Luis Melendez .30 .75
354 Dick Bosman .30 .75
355 Chris Cannizzaro .30 .75
356 Rico Petrocelli .60 1.50
357 Ken Forsch .30 .75
358 Al Bumbry .60 1.50
359 Paul Popovich .30 .75
360 George Scott .60 1.50
361 Dodgers Team CL 1.00 2.50
Walter Alston MG
362 Steve Hargan .30 .75
363 Carmen Fanzone .30 .75
364 Doug Bird .30 .75
365 Bob Bailey .30 .75
366 Ken Sanders .30 .75
367 Craig Robinson .30 .75
368 Vic Albury .30 .75
369 Merv Rettenmund .30 .75
370 Tom Seaver 6.00 15.00
371 Gates Brown .30 .75
372 John D'Acquisto .30 .75
373 Bill Sharp .30 .75
374 Eddie Watt .30 .75
375 Roy White .60 1.50
376 Steve Yeager .60 1.50
377 Tom Hilgendorf .30 .75
378 Derrel Thomas .30 .75
379 Bernie Carbo .30 .75
380 Sal Bando .60 1.50
381 John Curtis .30 .75
382 Don Baylor 1.00 2.50
383 Jim York .30 .75
384 Brewers Team CL 1.00 2.50
Del Crandall MG
385 Dock Ellis .30 .75
386 Checklist 265-396 1.50 4.00
387 Jim Spencer .30 .75
388 Steve Stone .60 1.50
389 Tony Solaita .30 .75
390 Ron Cey 1.00 2.50
391 Don DeMola .30 .75
392 Bruce Bochte RC .60 1.50
393 Gary Gentry .30 .75
394 Larvell Blanks .30 .75
395 Bud Harrelson .60 1.50
396 Fred Norman .60 1.50
397 Bill Freehan .60 1.50
398 Elias Sosa .30 .75
399 Terry Harmon .30 .75
400 Dick Allen 1.00 2.50
401 Mike Wallace .30 .75
402 Bob Tolan .30 .75
403 Tom Buskey .30 .75
404 Ted Sizemore .30 .75
405 John Montague .30 .75
406 Bob Gallagher .30 .75
407 Herb Washington RC 1.00 2.50
408 Clyde Wright .30 .75
409 Bob Robertson .30 .75
410 Mike Cueller .60 1.50
sic, Cuellar
411 George Mitterwald .30 .75
412 Bill Hands .30 .75
413 Marty Pattin .30 .75
414 Manny Mota .60 1.50
415 John Hiller .60 1.50
416 Larry Lintz .30 .75
417 Skip Lockwood .30 .75
418 Leo Foster .30 .75
419 Dave Goltz .30 .75
420 Larry Bowa 1.00 2.50
421 Mets Team CL 1.50 4.00
Yogi Berra MG
422 Brian Downing .60 1.50
423 Clay Kirby .30 .75
424 John Lowenstein .30 .75
425 Tito Fuentes .30 .75
426 George Medich .30 .75
427 Clarence Gaston .60 1.50
428 Dave Hamilton .30 .75
429 Jim Dwyer .30 .75
430 Luis Tiant 1.00 2.50
431 Rod Gilbreath .30 .75
432 Ken Berry .30 .75
433 Larry Demery .30 .75
434 Bob Locker .30 .75
435 Dave Nelson .30 .75
436 Ken Frailing .30 .75
437 Al Cowens .60 1.50
438 Don Carrithers .30 .75
439 Ed Brinkman .30 .75
440 Andy Messersmith .60 1.50
441 Bobby Heise .30 .75
442 Maximino Leon .30 .75
443 Twins Team 1.00 2.50
Frank Quilici MG
444 Gene Garber .60 1.50
445 Felix Millan .30 .75
446 Bart Johnson .30 .75
447 Terry Crowley .30 .75
448 Frank Duffy .30 .75
449 Charlie Williams .30 .75
450 Willie McCovey 3.00 8.00
451 Rick Dempsey .60 1.50
452 Angel Mangual .30 .75
453 Claude Osteen .60 1.50
454 Doug Griffin .30 .75
455 Don Wilson .30 .75
456 Bob Coluccio .30 .75
457 Mario Mendoza .30 .75
458 Ross Grimsley .30 .75
459 1974 AL Champs .60 1.50
A's over Orioles/(Second base
ac
460 Steve Garvey NLCS 1.00 2.50
461 Reggie Jackson WS1 2.50 6.00
462 World Series Game 2/(Dodger dugout).60 1.50
463 Rollie Fingers WS3 1.00 2.50
464 World Series Game 4/(A's batter) .60 1.50
465 Joe Rudi WS .60 1.50
466 WS Summary 1.00 2.50
A's
467 Ed Halicki .30 .75
468 Bobby Mitchell .30 .75
469 Tom Dettore .30 .75
470 Jeff Burroughs .60 1.50
471 Bob Stinson .30 .75
472 Bruce Dal Canton .30 .75
473 Ken McMullen .30 .75
474 Luke Walker .30 .75
475 Darrell Evans .60 1.50
476 Ed Figueroa .30 .75
477 Tom Hutton .30 .75
478 Tom Burgmeier .30 .75
479 Ken Boswell .30 .75
480 Carlos May .30 .75
481 Will McEnaney .60 1.50
482 Tom McCraw .30 .75
483 Steve Ontiveros .30 .75
484 Glenn Beckert .60 1.50
485 Sparky Lyle .60 1.50
486 Ray Fosse .30 .75
487 Astros Team CL 1.00 2.50
Preston Gomez MG
488 Bill Travers .30 .75
489 Cecil Cooper 1.00 2.50
490 Reggie Smith .60 1.50
491 Doyle Alexander .60 1.50
492 Rich Hebner .60 1.50
493 Don Stanhouse .30 .75
494 Pete LaCock .30 .75
495 Nelson Briles .60 1.50
496 Pepe Frias .30 .75
497 Jim Nettles .30 .75
498 Al Downing .30 .75
499 Marty Perez .30 .75
500 Nolan Ryan 40.00 80.00
501 Bill Robinson .60 1.50
502 Pat Bourque .30 .75
503 Fred Stanley .30 .75
504 Buddy Bradford .30 .75
505 Chris Speier .30 .75
506 Leron Lee .30 .75
507 Tom Carroll .30 .75
508 Bob Hansen .30 .75
509 Dave Hilton .30 .75
510 Vida Blue .60 1.50
511 Rangers Team CL 1.00 2.50
Billy Martin MG
512 Larry Milbourne .30 .75
513 Dick Pole .30 .75
514 Jose Cruz 1.00 2.50
515 Manny Sanguillen .60 1.50
516 Don Hood .30 .75
517 Checklist 397-528 1.50 4.00
518 Leo Cardenas .30 .75
519 Jim Todd .30 .75
520 Amos Otis .60 1.50
521 Dennis Blair .30 .75
522 Gary Sutherland .30 .75
523 Tom Paciorek .60 1.50
524 John Doherty .30 .75
525 Tom House .30 .75
526 Larry Hisle .60 1.50
527 Mac Scarce .30 .75
528 Eddie Leon .30 .75
529 Gary Thomasson .30 .75
530 Gaylord Perry 1.50 4.00
531 Reds Team 2.50 6.00
532 Gorman Thomas .60 1.50
533 Rudy Meoli .30 .75
534 Alex Johnson .30 .75
535 Gene Tenace .60 1.50
536 Bob Moose .30 .75
537 Tommy Harper .60 1.50
538 Duffy Dyer .30 .75
539 Jesse Jefferson .30 .75
540 Lou Brock 3.00 8.00
541 Roger Metzger .30 .75
542 Pete Broberg .30 .75
543 Larry Biittner .30 .75
544 Steve Mingori .30 .75
545 Billy Williams 1.50 4.00
546 John Knox .30 .75
547 Von Joshua .30 .75
548 Charlie Sands .30 .75
549 Bill Butler .30 .75
550 Ralph Garr .60 1.50
551 Larry Christenson .30 .75
552 Jack Brohamer .30 .75
553 John Boccabella .30 .75
554 Goose Gossage 1.00 2.50
555 Al Oliver 1.00 2.50
556 Tim Johnson .30 .75
557 Larry Gura .30 .75
558 Dave Roberts .30 .75
559 Bob Montgomery .30 .75
560 Tony Perez 2.00 5.00
561 A's Team CL 1.00 2.50
Alvin Dark MG
562 Gary Nolan .60 1.50
563 Wilbur Howard .30 .75
564 Tommy Davis .60 1.50
565 Joe Torre 1.00 2.50
566 Ray Burris .30 .75
567 Jim Sundberg RC 1.00 2.50
568 Dale Murray .30 .75
569 Frank White .60 1.50
570 Jim Wynn .60 1.50
571 Dave Lemanczyk .30 .75
572 Roger Nelson .30 .75
573 Orlando Pena .30 .75
574 Tony Taylor .30 .75
575 Gene Clines .30 .75
576 Phil Roof .30 .75
577 John Morris .30 .75
578 Dave Tomlin .30 .75
579 Skip Pitlock .30 .75
580 Frank Robinson 3.00 8.00
581 Darrel Chaney .30 .75
582 Eduardo Rodriguez .30 .75
583 Andy Etchebarren .30 .75
584 Mike Garman .30 .75
585 Chris Chambliss .60 1.50
586 Tim McCarver 1.00 2.50
587 Chris Ward .30 .75
588 Rick Auerbach .30 .75
589 Braves Team CL 1.00 2.50
Clyde King MG
590 Cesar Cedeno .60 1.50
591 Glenn Abbott .30 .75
592 Balor Moore .30 .75
593 Gene Lamont .30 .75
594 Jim Fuller .30 .75
595 Joe Niekro .60 1.50
596 Ollie Brown .30 .75
597 Winston Llenas .30 .75
598 Bruce Kison .30 .75
599 Nate Colbert .30 .75
600 Rod Carew 4.00 10.00
601 Juan Beniquez .30 .75
602 John Vukovich .30 .75
603 Lew Krausse .30 .75
604 Oscar Zamora .30 .75
605 John Ellis .30 .75
606 Bruce Miller .30 .75
607 Jim Holt .30 .75
608 Gene Michael .30 .75
609 Elrod Hendricks .30 .75
610 Ron Hunt .30 .75
611 Yankees: Team 1.00 2.50
MG
Bill Virdon
612 Terry Hughes .30 .75
613 Bill Parsons .30 .75
614 Rookie Pitchers .60 1.50
Jack Kucek
Dyar Miller
Vern Ruh
615 Dennis Leonard RC 1.00 2.50
616 Jim Rice RC 8.00 20.00
617 Doug DeCinces RC 1.00 2.50
618 Rick Rhoden .60 1.50
McGregor RC
619 Rookie Outfielders .60 1.50
Benny Ayala
Nyls Nyman
Tommy
620 Gary Carter RC 10.00 25.00
621 John Denny RC 1.00 2.50
622 Fred Lynn RC 4.00 10.00

623 K.Hernandez 5.00 12.00
P.Garner RC
624 Rookie Pitchers .60 1.50
Doug Konieczny
Gary Lavelle
Jim
625 Boog Powell 1.00 2.50
626 Larry Haney/(photo actually .30 .75
Dave Duncan)
627 Tom Walker .30 .75
628 Ron LeFlore RC .60 1.50
629 Joe Hoerner .30 .75
630 Greg Luzinski 1.00 2.50
631 Lee Lacy .30 .75
632 Morris Nettles .30 .75
633 Paul Casanova .30 .75
634 Cy Acosta .30 .75
635 Chuck Dobson .30 .75
636 Charlie Moore .30 .75
637 Ted Martinez .30 .75
638 Cubs Team CL 1.00 2.50
Jim Marshall MG
639 Steve Kline .30 .75
640 Harmon Killebrew 3.00 8.00
641 Jim Northrup .60 1.50
642 Mike Phillips .30 .75
643 Brent Strom .30 .75
644 Bill Fahey .30 .75
645 Danny Cater .30 .75
646 Checklist 529-660 1.50 4.00
647 Claudell Washington RC 1.00 2.50
648 Dave Pagan .60 1.50
649 Jack Heidemann .30 .75
650 Dave May .30 .75
651 John Morlan .30 .75
652 Lindy McDaniel .60 1.50
653 Lee Richard .30 .75
654 Jerry Terrell .30 .75
655 Rico Carty .60 1.50
656 Bill Plummer .30 .75
657 Bob Oliver .30 .75
658 Vic Harris .30 .75
659 Bob Apodaca .30 .75
660 Hank Aaron 12.50 40.00

1976 O-Pee-Chee

This is a 660-card standard-size set. The 1976 O-Pee-Chee cards are very similar to the 1976 Topps cards, yet rather different from previous years' issues. The most prominent change is that the backs are much brighter than their American counterparts. The cards parallel the American issue and it is a challenge to find well centered examples of these cards. Notable Rookie Cards include Dennis Eckersley and Ron Guidry.

COMPLETE SET (660) 400.00 800.00
1 Hank Aaron RB 10.00 25.00
Most RBI's, 2262
2 Bobby Bonds RB 1.25 3.00
Most leadoff
homers& 32;
Plus 3
3 Mickey Lolich RB .60 1.50
Lefthander& Most
Strikeouts 267
4 Dave Lopes RB .60 1.50
Most consecutive
SB attempts& 38
5 Tom Seaver RB 3.00 8.00
Most cons. seasons
with 200 SO's&
6 Rennie Stennett RB .60 1.50
Most hits in a 9
inning game&
7 Jim Umbarger .30 .75
8 Tito Fuentes .30 .75
9 Paul Lindblad .30 .75
10 Lou Brock 3.00 8.00
11 Jim Hughes .30 .75
12 Richie Zisk .60 1.50
13 John Wockenfuss .30 .75
14 Gene Garber .60 1.50
15 George Scott .60 1.50
16 Bob Apodaca .30 .75
17 New York Yankees 1.25 3.00
Team Card
18 Dale Murray .30 .75
19 George Brett 30.00 60.00
20 Bob Watson .60 1.50
21 Dave LaRoche .30 .75
22 Bill Russell .60 1.50
23 Brian Downing .30 .75
24 Cesar Geronimo .60 1.50
25 Mike Torrez .60 1.50
26 Andre Thornton .60 1.50
27 Ed Figueroa .30 .75
28 Dusty Baker 1.25 3.00
29 Rick Burleson .60 1.50
30 John Montefusco RC .60 1.50
31 Len Randle .30 .75
32 Danny Frisella .30 .75
33 Bill North .30 .75
34 Mike Garman .30 .75
35 Tony Oliva 1.25 3.00
36 Frank Taveras .30 .75
37 John Hiller .60 1.50
38 Garry Maddox .60 1.50
39 Pete Broberg .30 .75
40 Dave Kingman 1.25 3.00
41 Tippy Martinez .60 1.50
42 Barry Foote .60 1.50
43 Paul Splittorff .30 .75
44 Doug Rader .60 1.50
45 Boog Powell 1.25 3.00
46 Los Angeles Dodgers 1.25 3.00
Team Card
Walt Alston MG/(C
47 Jesse Jefferson .30 .75
48 Dave Concepcion 1.25 3.00
49 Dave Duncan .60 1.50
50 Fred Lynn 1.25 3.00
51 Ray Burris .30 .75
52 Dave Chalk .30 .75
53 Mike Beard RC .30 .75
54 Dave Rader .30 .75
55 Gaylord Perry 2.00 5.00
56 Bob Tolan .30 .75
57 Phil Garner .60 1.50
58 Ron Reed .30 .75
59 Larry Hisle .60 1.50
60 Jerry Reuss .60 1.50
61 Ron LeFlore .60 1.50
62 Johnny Oates .60 1.50
63 Bobby Darwin .30 .75
64 Jerry Koosman .60 1.50
65 Chris Chambliss .60 1.50
66 Father and Son .60 1.50
Gus
Buddy Bell
67 Bob .60 1.50
Ray Boone FS
68 Father and Son .30 .75
Joe Coleman
Joe Coleman Jr.
69 Father and Son .30 .75
Jim
Mike Hegan
70 Father and Son .60 1.50
Roy Smalley
Roy Smalley Jr.
71 Steve Rogers 1.25 3.00
72 Hal McRae .60 1.50
73 Baltimore Orioles 1.25 3.00
Team Card
Earl Weaver MG/(Che
74 Oscar Gamble .60 1.50
75 Larry Dierker .60 1.50
76 Willie Crawford .30 .75
77 Pedro Borbon .60 1.50
78 Cecil Cooper .60 1.50
79 Jerry Morales .30 .75
80 Jim Kaat 1.50 4.00
81 Darrell Evans .60 1.50
82 Von Joshua .30 .75
83 Jim Spencer .30 .75
84 Brent Strom .30 .75
85 Mickey Rivers .60 1.50
86 Mike Tyson .30 .75
87 Tom Burgmeier .30 .75
88 Duffy Dyer .30 .75
89 Vern Ruhle .30 .75
90 Sal Bando .60 1.50
91 Tom Hutton .30 .75
92 Eduardo Rodriguez .30 .75
93 Mike Phillips .30 .75
94 Jim Dwyer .30 .75
95 Brooks Robinson 4.00 10.00
96 Doug Bird .30 .75
97 Wilbur Howard .30 .75
98 Dennis Eckersley RC 20.00 50.00
99 Lee Lacy .30 .75
100 Jim Hunter 2.00 5.00
101 Pete LaCock .30 .75
102 Jim Willoughby .30 .75
103 Biff Pocoroba RC .30 .75
104 Reds Team 1.50 4.00
105 Gary Lavelle .30 .75
106 Tom Grieve .60 1.50
107 Dave Roberts .30 .75
108 Don Kirkwood .30 .75
109 Larry Lintz .30 .75
110 Carlos May .30 .75
111 Danny Thompson .30 .75
112 Kent Tekulve RC 1.25 3.00
113 Gary Sutherland .30 .75
114 Jay Johnstone .60 1.50
115 Ken Holtzman .60 1.50
116 Charlie Moore .30 .75
117 Mike Jorgensen .30 .75
118 Boston Red Sox 1.25 3.00
Team Card
Darrell Johnson/(Check
119 Checklist 1-132 1.25 3.00
120 Rusty Staub .60 1.50
121 Tony Solaita .30 .75
122 Mike Cosgrove .30 .75
123 Walt Williams .30 .75
124 Doug Rau .30 .75
125 Don Baylor 1.50 4.00
126 Tom Dettore .30 .75
127 Larvell Blanks .30 .75
128 Ken Griffey Sr. 1.50 4.00
129 Andy Etchebarren .30 .75
130 Luis Tiant 1.25 3.00
131 Bill Stein .30 .75
132 Don Hood .30 .75
133 Gary Matthews .60 1.50
134 Mike Ivie .30 .75
135 Bake McBride .60 1.50
136 Dave Goltz .30 .75
137 Bill Robinson .60 1.50
138 Lerrin LaGrow .30 .75
139 Gorman Thomas .60 1.50
140 Vida Blue .60 1.50
141 Larry Parrish RC 1.25 3.00
142 Dick Drago .30 .75
143 Jerry Grote .30 .75
144 Al Fitzmorris .30 .75
145 Larry Bowa .60 1.50
146 George Medich .30 .75
147 Houston Astros 1.25 3.00
Team Card
Bill Virdon MG/(Checkl
148 Stan Thomas .30 .75
149 Tommy Davis .60 1.50
150 Steve Garvey 1.50 4.00
151 Bill Bonham .30 .75
152 Leroy Stanton .30 .75
153 Buzz Capra .30 .75
154 Bucky Dent .60 1.50
155 Jack Billingham .60 1.50
156 Rico Carty .60 1.50
157 Mike Caldwell .30 .75
158 Ken Reitz .30 .75
159 Jerry Terrell .30 .75
160 Dave Winfield 8.00 20.00
161 Bruce Kison .30 .75
162 Jack Pierce .30 .75
163 Jim Slaton .30 .75
164 Pepe Mangual .30 .75
165 Gene Tenace .60 1.50
166 Skip Lockwood .30 .75
167 Freddie Patek .60 1.50
168 Tom Hilgendorf .30 .75
169 Graig Nettles 1.25 3.00
170 Rick Wise .30 .75
171 Greg Gross .30 .75
172 Texas Rangers 1.25 3.00
Team Card
Frank Lucchesi MG/(Chec
173 Steve Swisher .30 .75
174 Charlie Hough .60 1.50
175 Ken Singleton .60 1.50
176 Dick Lange .30 .75
177 Marty Perez .30 .75
178 Tom Buskey .30 .75
179 George Foster 1.25 3.00
180 Goose Gossage 1.50 4.00
181 Willie Montanez .30 .75
182 Harry Rasmussen .30 .75
183 Steve Braun .30 .75
184 Bill Greif .30 .75
185 Dave Parker 1.50 4.00
186 Tom Walker .30 .75
187 Pedro Garcia .30 .75
188 Fred Scherman .30 .75
189 Claudell Washington .60 1.50
190 Jon Matlack .30 .75
191 NL Batting Leaders .60 1.50
Bill Madlock
Ted Simmons
Man
192 R.Carew 1.50 4.00
Lynn
T.Munson LL
193 Schmidt 2.00 5.00
Kingman
Luz LL
194 Reggie 2.00 5.00
Scott
Mayb LL
195 Luzin 1.25 3.00
Bench
Perez LL
196 AL RBI Leaders .60 1.50
George Scott
John Mayberry
Fred
197 Lopes 1.25 3.00
Morgan
Brock LL
198 AL Steals Leaders .60 1.50
Mickey Rivers
Claudell Washing
199 Seaver 1.50 4.00
Jones
Messers LL
200 Hunter 1.25 3.00
Palmer
Blue LL
201 R.Jones 1.25 3.00
Messer
Seaver LL
202 Palmer 2.00 5.00
Hunter
Eck LL
203 Seaver 1.50 4.00
Montef
Messer LL
204 Tanana .60 1.50
Blylev
Perry LL
205 Leading Firemen .60 1.50
Al Hrabosky
Rich Gossage
206 Manny Trillo .30 .75
207 Andy Hassler .30 .75
208 Mike Lum .30 .75
209 Alan Ashby .60 1.50
210 Lee May .60 1.50
211 Clay Carroll .60 1.50
212 Pat Kelly .30 .75
213 Dave Heaverlo .30 .75
214 Eric Soderholm .30 .75
215 Reggie Smith .60 1.50
216 Montreal Expos 1.25 3.00
Team Card
Karl Kuehl MG/(Checkli
217 Dave Freisleben .30 .75
218 John Knox .30 .75
219 Tom Murphy .30 .75
220 Manny Sanguillen .60 1.50
221 Jim Todd .30 .75
222 Wayne Garrett .30 .75
223 Ollie Brown .30 .75
224 Jim York .30 .75
225 Roy White .60 1.50
226 Jim Sundberg .60 1.50
227 Oscar Zamora .30 .75
228 John Hale .30 .75
229 Jerry Remy .30 .75
230 Carl Yastrzemski 6.00 15.00
231 Tom House .30 .75
232 Frank Duffy .30 .75
233 Grant Jackson .30 .75
234 Mike Sadek .30 .75
235 Bert Blyleven 1.50 4.00
236 Kansas City Royals 1.25 3.00
Team Card
Whitey Herzog MG/(
237 Dave Hamilton .30 .75
238 Larry Biittner .30 .75
239 John Curtis .30 .75
240 Pete Rose 12.50 40.00
241 Hector Torres .30 .75
242 Dan Meyer .30 .75
243 Jim Rooker .30 .75
244 Bill Sharp .30 .75
245 Felix Millan .30 .75
246 Cesar Tovar .30 .75
247 Terry Harmon .30 .75
248 Dick Tidrow .30 .75
249 Cliff Johnson .60 1.50
250 Fergie Jenkins 2.00 5.00
251 Rick Monday .60 1.50
252 Tim Nordbrook .30 .75
253 Bill Buckner .60 1.50
254 Rudy Meoli .30 .75
255 Fritz Peterson .30 .75
256 Rowland Office .30 .75
257 Ross Grimsley .30 .75
258 Nyls Nyman .30 .75
259 Darrel Chaney .30 .75
260 Steve Busby .30 .75
261 Gary Thomasson .30 .75
262 Checklist 133-264 1.25 3.00
263 Lyman Bostock RC 1.25 3.00
264 Steve Renko .30 .75
265 Willie Davis .60 1.50
266 Alan Foster .30 .75
267 Aurelio Rodriguez .30 .75
268 Del Unser .30 .75
269 Rick Austin .30 .75
270 Willie Stargell 2.00 5.00
271 Jim Lonborg .60 1.50
272 Rick Dempsey .60 1.50
273 Joe Niekro .60 1.50
274 Tommy Harper .60 1.50
275 Rick Manning .30 .75
276 Mickey Scott .30 .75
277 Chicago Cubs 1.25 3.00
Team Card
Jim Marshall MG/(Checkli
278 Bernie Carbo .30 .75
279 Roy Howell .30 .75
280 Burt Hooton .60 1.50
281 Dave May .30 .75
282 Dan Osborn .30 .75
283 Merv Rettenmund .30 .75
284 Steve Ontiveros .30 .75
285 Mike Cuellar .60 1.50
286 Jim Wohlford .30 .75
287 Pete Mackanin .30 .75
288 Bill Campbell .30 .75
289 Enzo Hernandez .30 .75
290 Ted Simmons .60 1.50
291 Ken Sanders .30 .75
292 Leon Roberts .30 .75
293 Bill Castro .30 .75
294 Ed Kirkpatrick .30 .75
295 Dave Cash .30 .75
296 Pat Dobson .30 .75
297 Roger Metzger .30 .75
298 Dick Bosman .30 .75
299 Champ Summers .30 .75
300 Johnny Bench 8.00 20.00
301 Jackie Brown .30 .75
302 Rick Miller .30 .75
303 Steve Foucault .30 .75
304 California Angels 1.25 3.00
Team Card
Dick Williams MG/(C
305 Andy Messersmith .60 1.50
306 Rod Gilbreath .30 .75
307 Al Bumbry .60 1.50
308 Jim Barr .30 .75
309 Bill Melton .30 .75
310 Randy Jones .60 1.50
311 Cookie Rojas .30 .75
312 Don Carrithers .30 .75
313 Dan Ford .30 .75
314 Ed Kranepool .30 .75
315 Al Hrabosky .60 1.50
316 Robin Yount 10.00 25.00
317 John Candelaria RC 1.25 3.00
318 Bob Boone 1.25 3.00
319 Larry Gura .30 .75
320 Willie Horton .60 1.50
321 Jose Cruz 1.25 3.00
322 Glenn Abbott .30 .75
323 Rob Sperring .30 .75
324 Jim Bibby .30 .75
325 Tony Perez 2.00 5.00
326 Dick Pole .30 .75
327 Dave Moates .30 .75
328 Carl Morton .30 .75
329 Joe Ferguson .30 .75
330 Nolan Ryan 20.00 50.00

331 San Diego Padres 1.25 3.00
Team Card
John McNamara MG/(Ch
332 Charlie Williams .30 .75
333 Bob Coluccio .30 .75
334 Dennis Leonard .60 1.50
335 Bob Grich .60 1.50
336 Vic Albury .30 .75
337 Bud Harrelson .60 1.50
338 Bob Bailey .30 .75
339 John Denny .60 1.50
340 Jim Rice 2.50 6.00
341 Lou Gehrig ATG 8.00 20.00
342 Rogers Hornsby ATG 1.50 4.00
343 Pie Traynor ATG 1.25 3.00
344 Honus Wagner ATG 3.00 8.00
345 Babe Ruth ATG 10.00 25.00
346 Ty Cobb ATG 8.00 20.00
347 Ted Williams ATG 8.00 20.00
348 Mickey Cochrane ATG 1.25 3.00
349 Walter Johnson ATG 3.00 8.00
350 Lefty Grove ATG 1.25 3.00
351 Randy Hundley .60 1.50
352 Dave Giusti .30 .75
353 Sixto Lezcano .60 1.50
354 Ron Blomberg .30 .75
355 Steve Carlton 4.00 10.00
356 Ted Martinez .30 .75
357 Ken Forsch .30 .75
358 Buddy Bell .60 1.50
359 Rick Reuschel .60 1.50
360 Jeff Burroughs .60 1.50
361 Detroit Tigers 1.25 3.00
Team Card
Ralph Houk MG/(Checkli
362 Will McEnaney .60 1.50
363 Dave Collins RC .60 1.50
364 Elias Sosa .30 .75
365 Carlton Fisk 3.00 8.00
366 Bobby Valentine .60 1.50
367 Bruce Miller .30 .75
368 Wilbur Wood .30 .75
369 Frank White .60 1.50
370 Ron Cey .60 1.50
371 Ellie Hendricks .30 .75
372 Rick Baldwin .30 .75
373 Johnny Briggs .30 .75
374 Dan Warthen .30 .75
375 Ron Fairly .60 1.50
376 Rich Hebner .60 1.50
377 Mike Hegan .30 .75
378 Steve Stone .60 1.50
379 Ken Boswell .30 .75
380 Bobby Bonds 1.50 4.00
381 Denny Doyle .30 .75
382 Matt Alexander .30 .75
383 John Ellis .30 .75
384 Philadelphia Phillies 1.25 3.00
Team Card
Danny Ozark MG/
385 Mickey Lolich .60 1.50
386 Ed Goodson .30 .75
387 Mike Miley .30 .75
388 Stan Perzanowski .30 .75
389 Glenn Adams .30 .75
390 Don Gullett .60 1.50
391 Jerry Hairston .30 .75
392 Checklist 265-396 1.25 3.00
393 Paul Mitchell .30 .75
394 Fran Healy .30 .75
395 Jim Wynn .60 1.50
396 Bill Lee .30 .75
397 Tim Foli .30 .75
398 Dave Tomlin .30 .75
399 Luis Melendez .30 .75
400 Rod Carew 3.00 8.00
401 Ken Brett .30 .75
402 Don Money .60 1.50
403 Geoff Zahn .30 .75
404 Enos Cabell .30 .75
405 Rollie Fingers 2.00 5.00
406 Ed Herrmann .30 .75
407 Tom Underwood .30 .75
408 Charlie Spikes .30 .75
409 Dave Lemanczyk .30 .75
410 Ralph Garr .60 1.50
411 Bill Singer .30 .75
412 Toby Harrah .60 1.50
413 Pete Varney .30 .75
414 Wayne Garland .30 .75
415 Vada Pinson 1.50 4.00
416 Tommy John 1.50 4.00
417 Gene Clines .30 .75
418 Jose Morales RC .60 1.50
419 Reggie Cleveland .30 .75
420 Joe Morgan 3.00 8.00
421 Oakland A's 1.25 3.00
Team Card/(No MG on front;
checklis
422 Johnny Grubb .30 .75
423 Ed Halicki .30 .75
424 Phil Roof .30 .75
425 Rennie Stennett .30 .75
426 Bob Forsch .30 .75
427 Kurt Bevacqua .30 .75
428 Jim Crawford .30 .75
429 Fred Stanley .30 .75
430 Jose Cardenal .60 1.50
431 Dick Ruthven .30 .75
432 Tom Veryzer .30 .75
433 Rick Waits .30 .75
434 Morris Nettles .30 .75
435 Phil Niekro 2.00 5.00
436 Bill Fahey .30 .75
437 Terry Forster .30 .75
438 Doug DeCinces .60 1.50
439 Rick Rhoden .60 1.50
440 John Mayberry .60 1.50
441 Gary Carter 3.00 8.00
442 Hank Webb .30 .75
443 San Francisco Giants 1.25 3.00
Team Card/(No MG on front;#
444 Gary Nolan .60 1.50
445 Rico Petrocelli .60 1.50
446 Larry Haney .30 .75
447 Gene Locklear .60 1.50
448 Tom Johnson .30 .75
449 Bob Robertson .30 .75
450 Jim Palmer 3.00 8.00
451 Buddy Bradford .30 .75
452 Tom Hausman .30 .75
453 Lou Piniella 1.25 3.00
454 Tom Griffin .30 .75
455 Dick Allen 1.25 3.00
456 Joe Coleman .30 .75
457 Ed Crosby .30 .75
458 Earl Williams .30 .75
459 Jim Brewer .30 .75
460 Cesar Cedeno .60 1.50
461 NL and AL Champs .60 1.50
Reds sweep Bucs;
Bosox surprise
462 World Series .60 1.50
Reds Champs
463 Steve Hargan .30 .75
464 Ken Henderson .30 .75
465 Mike Marshall .60 1.50
466 Bob Stinson .30 .75
467 Woodie Fryman .30 .75
468 Jesus Alou .30 .75
469 Rawly Eastwick .60 1.50
470 Bobby Murcer .60 1.50
471 Jim Burton .30 .75
472 Bob Davis .30 .75
473 Paul Blair .60 1.50
474 Ray Corbin .30 .75
475 Joe Rudi .60 1.50
476 Bob Moose .30 .75
477 Cleveland Indians 1.25 3.00
Team Card
Frank Robinson MG/(
478 Lynn McGlothen .30 .75
479 Bobby Mitchell .30 .75
480 Mike Schmidt 10.00 25.00
481 Rudy May .30 .75
482 Tim Hosley .30 .75
483 Mickey Stanley .30 .75
484 Eric Raich .30 .75
485 Mike Hargrove .60 1.50
486 Bruce Dal Canton .30 .75
487 Leron Lee .30 .75
488 Claude Osteen .60 1.50
489 Skip Jutze .30 .75
490 Frank Tanana .60 1.50
491 Terry Crowley .30 .75
492 Martin Pattin .30 .75
493 Derrel Thomas .30 .75
494 Craig Swan .60 1.50
495 Nate Colbert .30 .75
496 Juan Beniquez .30 .75
497 Joe McIntosh .30 .75
498 Glenn Borgmann .30 .75
499 Mario Guerrero .30 .75
500 Reggie Jackson 8.00 20.00
501 Billy Champion .30 .75
502 Tim McCarver 1.25 3.00
503 Elliott Maddox .30 .75
504 Pittsburgh Pirates 1.25 3.00
Team Card
Danny Murtaugh MG/
505 Mark Belanger .60 1.50
506 George Mitterwald .30 .75
507 Ray Bare .30 .75
508 Duane Kuiper .30 .75
509 Bill Hands .30 .75
510 Amos Otis .60 1.50
511 Jamie Easterley .30 .75
512 Ellie Rodriguez .30 .75
513 Bart Johnson .30 .75
514 Dan Driessen .60 1.50
515 Steve Yeager .60 1.50
516 Wayne Granger .30 .75
517 John Milner .30 .75
518 Doug Flynn .30 .75
519 Steve Brye .30 .75
520 Willie McCovey 3.00 8.00
521 Jim Colborn .30 .75
522 Ted Sizemore .30 .75
523 Bob Montgomery .30 .75
524 Pete Falcone .30 .75
525 Billy Williams 2.00 5.00
526 Checklist 397-528 1.25 3.00
527 Mike Anderson .30 .75
528 Dock Ellis .30 .75
529 Deron Johnson .30 .75
530 Don Sutton 2.00 5.00
531 New York Mets 1.25 3.00
Team Card
Joe Frazier MG/(Checkli
532 Milt May .30 .75
533 Lee Richard .30 .75
534 Stan Bahnsen .30 .75
535 Dave Nelson .30 .75
536 Mike Thompson .30 .75
537 Tony Muser .30 .75
538 Pat Darcy .30 .75
539 John Balaz .30 .75
540 Bill Freehan .60 1.50
541 Steve Mingori .30 .75
542 Keith Hernandez 1.25 3.00
543 Wayne Twitchell .30 .75
544 Pepe Frias .30 .75
545 Sparky Lyle .60 1.50
546 Dave Rosello .30 .75
547 Roric Harrison .30 .75
548 Manny Mota .60 1.50
549 Randy Tate .30 .75
550 Hank Aaron 12.50 40.00
551 Jerry DaVanon .30 .75
552 Terry Humphrey .30 .75
553 Randy Moffitt .30 .75
554 Ray Fosse .30 .75
555 Dyar Miller .30 .75
556 Minnesota Twins 1.25 3.00
Team Card
Gene Mauch MG/(Checkl
557 Dan Spillner .30 .75
558 Clarence Gaston .60 1.50
559 Clyde Wright .30 .75
560 Jorge Orta .30 .75
561 Tom Carroll .30 .75
562 Adrian Garrett .30 .75
563 Larry Demery .30 .75
564 Kurt Bevacqua Gum 1.25 3.00
565 Tug McGraw 1.25 3.00
566 Ken McMullen .30 .75
567 George Stone .30 .75
568 Rob Andrews .30 .75
569 Nelson Briles .60 1.50
570 George Hendrick .60 1.50
571 Don DeMola .30 .75
572 Rich Coggins .30 .75
573 Bill Travers .30 .75
574 Don Kessinger .60 1.50
575 Dwight Evans 1.25 3.00
576 Maximino Leon .30 .75
577 Marc Hill .30 .75
578 Ted Kubiak .30 .75
579 Clay Kirby .30 .75
580 Bert Campaneris .60 1.50
581 St. Louis Cardinals 1.25 3.00
Team Card
Red Schoendienst M
582 Mike Kekich .30 .75
583 Tommy Helms .30 .75
584 Stan Wall .30 .75
585 Joe Torre 1.50 4.00
586 Ron Schueler .30 .75
587 Leo Cardenas .30 .75
588 Kevin Kobel .30 .75
589 Mike Flanagan RC 1.25 3.00
590 Chet Lemon RC .60 1.50
591 Rookie Pitchers .60 1.50
Steve Grilli
Craig Mitchell
Jos
592 Willie Randolph RC 4.00 10.00
593 Rookie Pitchers .60 1.50
Larry Anderson
Ken Crosby
Mark
594 Rookie Catchers .60 1.50
OF
Andy Merchant
Ed Ott
Royle S
595 Rookie Pitchers .60 1.50
Art DeFillipis
Randy Lerch
Sid
596 Rookie Infielders .60 1.50
Craig Reynolds
Lamar Johnson/
597 Rookie Pitchers .60 1.50
Don Aase
Jack Kucek
Frank LaCor
598 Rookie Outfielders .60 1.50
Hector Cruz
Jamie Quirk
Jerr
599 Ron Guidry RC ! 5.00 12.00
600 Tom Seaver 6.00 15.00
601 Ken Rudolph .30 .75
602 Doug Konieczny .30 .75
603 Jim Holt .30 .75
604 Joe Lovitto .30 .75
605 Al Downing .30 .75
606 Milwaukee Brewers 1.25 3.00
Team Card
Alex Grammas MG/(Ch
607 Rich Hinton .30 .75
608 Vic Correll .30 .75
609 Fred Norman .30 .75
610 Greg Luzinski 1.25 3.00
611 Rich Folkers .30 .75
612 Joe Lahoud .30 .75
613 Tim Johnson .30 .75
614 Fernando Arroyo .30 .75
615 Mike Cubbage .30 .75
616 Buck Martinez .60 1.50
617 Darold Knowles .30 .75
618 Jack Brohamer .30 .75
619 Bill Butler .30 .75
620 Al Oliver .60 1.50
621 Tom Hall .30 .75
622 Rick Auerbach .30 .75
623 Bob Allietta .30 .75
624 Tony Taylor .30 .75
625 J.R. Richard .60 1.50
626 Bob Sheldon .30 .75
627 Bill Plummer .30 .75
628 John D'Acquisto .30 .75
629 Sandy Alomar .60 1.50
630 Chris Speier .30 .75
631 Atlanta Braves 1.25 3.00
Team Card
Dave Bristol MG/(Check
632 Rogelio Moret .30 .75
633 John Stearns RC .60 1.50
634 Larry Christenson .30 .75
635 Jim Fregosi .60 1.50
636 Joe Decker .30 .75
637 Bruce Bochte .30 .75
638 Doyle Alexander .60 1.50
639 Fred Kendall .30 .75
640 Bill Madlock 1.25 3.00
641 Tom Paciorek .60 1.50
642 Dennis Blair .30 .75
643 Checklist 529-660 1.25 3.00
644 Tom Bradley .30 .75
645 Darrell Porter .60 1.50
646 John Lowenstein .30 .75
647 Ramon Hernandez .30 .75
648 Al Cowens .30 .75
649 Dave Roberts .30 .75
650 Thurman Munson 4.00 10.00
651 John Odom .30 .75
652 Ed Armbrister .30 .75
653 Mike Norris RC .60 1.50
654 Doug Griffin .30 .75
655 Mike Vail .30 .75
656 Chicago White Sox 1.25 3.00
Team Card
Chuck Tanner MG/(Ch
657 Roy Smalley RC .60 1.50
658 Jerry Johnson .30 .75
659 Ben Oglivie .60 1.50
660 Davey Lopes ! 1.25 3.00

1977 O-Pee-Chee

The 1977 O-Pee-Chee set of 264 standard-size cards is not only much smaller numerically than its American counterpart, but also contains many different poses and is loaded with players from the two Canadian teams, including many players from the inaugural year of the Blue Jays and many single cards of players who were on multiplayer rookie cards. On a white background, the fronts feature color player photos with thin black borders. The player's name and position, a facsimile autograph, and the team name also appear on the front. The horizontal backs carry player biography and statistics in French and English. The numbering of this set is different than the U.S. issue, the backs have different colors and the words "O-Pee-Chee Printed in Canada" are printed on the back.

COMPLETE SET (264) 150.00 300.00
1 George Brett 4.00 10.00
Bill Madlock LL
2 Graig Nettles .75 2.00
Mike Schmidt LL
3 Lee May .60 1.50
George Foster LL
4 Bill North .30 .75
Dave Lopes LL
5 Jim Palmer .60 1.50
Randy Jones LL
6 Nolan Ryan 8.00 20.00
Tom Seaver LL
7 Mark Fidrych .30 .75
John Denny LL
8 Bill Campbell .30 .75
Rawly Eastwick LL
9 Mike Jorgensen .30 .75
10 Jim Hunter 1.00 2.50
11 Ken Griffey Sr. .60 1.50
12 Bill Campbell .12 .30
13 Otto Velez .30 .75
14 Milt May .12 .30
15 Dennis Eckersley 2.00 5.00
16 John Mayberry .30 .75
17 Larry Bowa .30 .75
18 Don Carrithers .30 .75
19 Ken Singleton .30 .75
20 Bill Stein .12 .30
21 Ken Brett .12 .30
22 Gary Woods .30 .75
23 Steve Swisher .12 .30
24 Don Sutton 1.00 2.50
25 Willie Stargell 1.00 2.50
26 Jerry Koosman .30 .75
27 Del Unser .30 .75
28 Bob Grich .30 .75
29 Jim Slaton .12 .30
30 Thurman Munson 2.00 5.00
31 Dan Driessen .12 .30
32 Tom Bruno .30 .75
33 Larry Hisle .30 .75
34 Phil Garner .12 .30
35 Mike Hargrove .30 .75
36 Jackie Brown .30 .75
37 Carl Yastrzemski 3.00 8.00
38 Dave Roberts .12 .30
39 Ray Fosse .12 .30
40 Dave McKay .30 .75
41 Paul Splittorff .12 .30
42 Garry Maddox .12 .30
43 Phil Niekro 1.00 2.50
44 Roger Metzger .12 .30
45 Gary Carter 1.00 2.50
46 Jim Spencer .12 .30
47 Ross Grimsley .12 .30
48 Bob Bailor .30 .75
49 Chris Chambliss .30 .75
50 Will McEnaney .30 .75
51 Lou Brock 1.50 4.00
52 Rollie Fingers 1.00 2.50
53 Chris Speier .12 .30

Card	Low	High
54 Bombo Rivera	.30	.75
55 Pete Broberg	.12	.30
56 Bill Madlock	.75	2.00
57 Rick Rhoden	.30	.75
58 Blue Jays Coaches	.30	.75
Don Leppert		
Bob Miller		
Jackie		
59 John Candelaria	.12	.30
60 Ed Kranepool	.12	.30
61 Dave LaRoche	.12	.30
62 Jim Rice	.75	2.00
63 Don Stanhouse	.30	.75
64 Jason Thompson RC	.30	.75
65 Nolan Ryan	12.50	40.00
66 Tom Poquette	.12	.30
67 Leon Hooten	.30	.75
68 Bob Boone	.30	.75
69 Mickey Rivers	.30	.75
70 Gary Nolan	.12	.30
71 Sixto Lezcano	.12	.30
72 Larry Parrish	.30	.75
73 Dave Goltz	.12	.30
74 Bert Campaneris	.30	.75
75 Vida Blue	.30	.75
76 Rick Cerone	.30	.75
77 Ralph Garr	.30	.75
78 Ken Forsch	.12	.30
79 Willie Montanez	.12	.30
80 Jim Palmer	1.50	4.00
81 Jerry White	.30	.75
82 Gene Tenace	.30	.75
83 Bobby Murcer	.30	.75
84 Garry Templeton	.60	1.50
85 Bill Singer	.30	.75
86 Buddy Bell	.30	.75
87 Luis Tiant	.30	.75
88 Rusty Staub	.60	1.50
89 Sparky Lyle	.30	.75
90 Jose Morales	.30	.75
91 Dennis Leonard	.30	.75
92 Tommy Smith	.12	.30
93 Steve Carlton	2.00	5.00
94 John Scott	.30	.75
95 Bill Bonham	.12	.30
96 Dave Lopes	.30	.75
97 Jerry Reuss	.30	.75
98 Dave Kingman	.60	1.50
99 Dan Warthen	.30	.75
100 Johnny Bench	4.00	10.00
101 Bert Blyleven	.60	1.50
102 Cecil Cooper	.30	.75
103 Mike Willis	.30	.75
104 Dan Ford	.12	.30
105 Frank Tanana	.30	.75
106 Bill North	.12	.30
107 Joe Ferguson	.12	.30
108 Dick Williams MG	.30	.75
109 John Denny	.30	.75
110 Willie Randolph	.60	1.50
111 Reggie Cleveland	.30	.75
112 Doug Howard	.30	.75
113 Randy Jones	.12	.30
114 Rico Carty	.30	.75
115 Mark Fidrych RC	2.00	5.00
116 Darrell Porter	.30	.75
117 Wayne Garrett	.30	.75
118 Greg Luzinski	.60	1.50
119 Jim Barr	.12	.30
120 George Foster	.60	1.50
121 Phil Roof	.30	.75
122 Bucky Dent	.30	.75
123 Steve Braun	.12	.30
124 Checklist 1-132	.60	1.50
125 Lee May	.30	.75
126 Woodie Fryman	.30	.75
127 Jose Cardenal	.30	.75
128 Doug Rau	.12	.30
129 Rennie Stennett	.12	.30
130 Pete Vuckovich RC	.30	.75
131 Cesar Cedeno	.30	.75
132 Jon Matlack	.12	.30
133 Don Baylor	.60	1.50
134 Darrel Chaney	.12	.30
135 Tony Perez	1.00	2.50
136 Aurelio Rodriguez	.12	.30
137 Carlton Fisk	2.50	6.00
138 Wayne Garland	.12	.30
139 Dave Hilton	.30	.75
140 Rawly Eastwick	.12	.30
141 Amos Otis	.30	.75
142 Tug McGraw	.30	.75
143 Rod Carew	2.50	6.00

Card	Low	High
144 Mike Torrez	.30	.75
145 Sal Bando	.30	.75
146 Dock Ellis	.12	.30
147 Jose Cruz	.30	.75
148 Alan Ashby	.30	.75
149 Gaylord Perry	1.00	2.50
150 Keith Hernandez	.30	.75
151 Dave Pagan	.12	.30
152 Richie Zisk	.12	.30
153 Steve Rogers	.30	.75
154 Mark Belanger	.30	.75
155 Andy Messersmith	.30	.75
156 Dave Winfield	6.00	15.00
157 Chuck Hartenstein	.30	.75
158 Manny Trillo	.12	.30
159 Steve Yeager	.30	.75
160 Cesar Geronimo	.12	.30
161 Jim Rooker	.12	.30
162 Tim Foli	.30	.75
163 Fred Lynn	.30	.75
164 Ed Figueroa	.12	.30
165 Johnny Grubb	.12	.30
166 Pedro Garcia	.12	.30
167 Ron LeFlore	.30	.75
168 Rich Hebner	.30	.75
169 Larry Herndon RC	.30	.75
170 George Brett	12.50	30.00
171 Joe Kerrigan	.30	.75
172 Bud Harrelson	.30	.75
173 Bobby Bonds	.75	2.00
174 Bill Travers	.12	.30
175 John Lowenstein	.30	.75
176 Butch Wynegar RC	.30	.75
177 Pete Falcone	.12	.30
178 Claudell Washington	.30	.75
179 Checklist 133-264	.60	1.50
180 Dave Cash	.30	.75
181 Fred Norman	.12	.30
182 Roy White	.30	.75
183 Marty Perez	.12	.30
184 Jesse Jefferson	.30	.75
185 Jim Sundberg	.30	.75
186 Dan Meyer	.30	.75
187 Fergie Jenkins	1.00	2.50
188 Tom Veryzer	.12	.30
189 Dennis Blair	.30	.75
190 Rick Manning	.12	.30
191 Doug Bird	.12	.30
192 Al Bumbry	.30	.75
193 Dave Roberts	.12	.30
194 Larry Christenson	.12	.30
195 Chet Lemon	.30	.75
196 Ted Simmons	.30	.75
197 Ray Burris	.12	.30
198 Expos Coaches	.30	.75
Jim Brewer		
Billy Gardner		
Mickey V		
199 Ron Cey	.30	.75
200 Reggie Jackson	4.00	10.00
201 Pat Zachry	.12	.30
202 Doug Ault	.30	.75
203 Al Oliver	.30	.75
204 Robin Yount	4.00	10.00
205 Tom Seaver	3.00	8.00
206 Joe Rudi	.30	.75
207 Barry Foote	.30	.75
208 Toby Harrah	.30	.75
209 Jeff Burroughs	.30	.75
210 George Scott	.30	.75
211 Jim Mason	.30	.75
212 Vern Ruhle	.12	.30
213 Fred Kendall	.12	.30
214 Rick Reuschel	.30	.75
215 Hal McRae	.30	.75
216 Chip Lang	.30	.75
217 Graig Nettles	.60	1.50
218 George Hendrick	.30	.75
219 Glenn Abbott	.12	.30
220 Joe Morgan	2.00	5.00
221 Sam Ewing	.30	.75
222 George Medich	.12	.30
223 Reggie Smith	.30	.75
224 Dave Hamilton	.12	.30
225 Pepe Frias	.30	.75
226 Jay Johnstone	.30	.75
227 J.R. Richard	.30	.75
228 Doug DeCinces	.30	.75
229 Dave Lemanczyk	.30	.75
230 Rick Monday	.30	.75
231 Manny Sanguillen	.30	.75
232 John Montefusco	.12	.30
233 Duane Kuiper	.12	.30

Card	Low	High
234 Ellis Valentine	.30	.75
235 Dick Tidrow	.12	.30
236 Ben Oglivie	.30	.75
237 Rick Burleson	.30	.75
238 Roy Hartsfield MG	.30	.75
239 Lyman Bostock	.30	.75
240 Pete Rose	8.00	20.00
241 Mike Ivie	.12	.30
242 Dave Parker	.60	1.50
243 Bill Greif	.30	.75
244 Freddie Patek	.30	.75
245 Mike Schmidt	6.00	15.00
246 Brian Downing	.30	.75
247 Steve Hargan	.12	.30
248 Dave Collins	.30	.75
249 Felix Millan	.12	.30
250 Don Gullett	.30	.75
251 Jerry Royster	.12	.30
252 Earl Williams	.30	.75
253 Frank Duffy	.12	.30
254 Tippy Martinez	.12	.30
255 Steve Garvey	.75	2.00
256 Alvis Woods	.30	.75
257 John Hiller	.30	.75
258 Dave Concepcion	.60	1.50
259 Dwight Evans	.60	1.50
260 Pete MacKanin	.30	.75
261 George Brett RB	5.00	12.00
Most Consec. Games		
Three Or More		
262 Minnie Minoso RB	.30	.75
Oldest Player To		
Hit Safely		
263 Jose Morales RB	.30	.75
Most Pinch-hits, Season		
264 Nolan Ryan RB	6.00	15.00
Most Seasons 300		
Or More Strikeout		

1978 O-Pee-Chee

The 242 standard-size cards comprising the 1978 O-Pee-Chee set differ from the cards of the 1978 Topps set by having a higher ratio of cards of players from the two Canadian teams, a practice begun by O-Pee-Chee in 1977 and continued to 1988. The fronts feature white-bordered color player photos, each framed by a colored line. The player's name appears in black lettering at the right of lower white margin. His team name appears in colored cursive lettering, interrupting the framing line at the bottom left of the photo; his position appears within a white baseball icon in an upper corner. The tan and brown horizontal backs carry the player's name, team and position in the brown border at the bottom. Biography, major league statistics, career highlights in both French and English and a bilingual result of an "at bat" in the "Play Ball" game also appear. The asterisked cards have an extra line on the front indicating team change. Double-printed (DP) cards are also noted below. The key card in this set is the Eddie Murray Rookie Card.

Card	Low	High
COMPLETE SET (242)	100.00	200.00
COMMON PLAYER (1-242)	.10	.25
COMMON PLAYER DP (1-242)	.08	.20
1 Dave Parker	.60	1.50
Rod Carew LL		
2 George Foster	.25	.60
Jim Rice LL DP		
3 George Foster	.25	.60
Larry Hisle LL		
4 Stolen Base Leaders DP	.10	.25
Frank Taveras		
Freddie Pat		
5 Victory Leaders	1.00	2.50
Steve Carlton		
Dave Goltz		
Dennis		
6 Phil Niekro	2.50	6.00
Nolan Ryan LL DP		
7 John Candelaria	.25	.60
Frank Tanana LL DP		
8 Rollie Fingers	.50	1.25
Bill Campbell LL		
9 Steve Rogers DP	.12	.30
10 Graig Nettles DP	.30	.75
11 Doug Capilla	.10	.25
12 George Scott	.25	.60
13 Gary Woods	.25	.60
14 Tom Veryzer	.25	.60
Now with Cleveland as of 12-9-77		
15 Wayne Garland	.10	.25
16 Amos Otis	.25	.60
17 Larry Christenson	.10	.25
18 Dave Cash	.25	.60
19 Jim Barr	.10	.25
20 Ruppert Jones	.10	.25
21 Eric Soderholm	.10	.25
22 Jesse Jefferson	.25	.60
23 Jerry Morales	.10	.25
24 Doug Rau	.10	.25
25 Rennie Stennett	.10	.25
26 Lee Mazzilli	.10	.25
27 Dick Williams MG	.25	.60
28 Joe Rudi	.25	.60
29 Robin Yount	4.00	10.00
30 Don Gullett DP	.10	.25
31 Roy Howell DP	.08	.20
32 Cesar Geronimo	.10	.25
33 Rick Langford DP	.08	.20
34 Dan Ford	.10	.25
35 Gene Tenace	.25	.60
36 Santo Alcala	.25	.60
37 Rick Burleson	.25	.60
38 Dave Rozema	.10	.25
39 Duane Kuiper	.10	.25
40 Ron Fairly	.25	.60
Now with California as of 12-8-77		
41 Dennis Leonard	.25	.60
42 Greg Luzinski	.50	1.25
43 Willie Montanez	.25	.60
Now with N.Y. Mets as of 12-8-77		
44 Enos Cabell	.10	.25
45 Ellis Valentine	.25	.60
46 Steve Stone	.25	.60
47 Lee May DP	.12	.30
48 Roy White	.25	.60
49 Jerry Garvin	.10	.25
50 Johnny Bench	3.00	8.00
51 Garry Templeton	.25	.60
52 Doyle Alexander	.25	.60
53 Steve Henderson	.10	.25
54 Stan Bahnsen	.10	.25
55 Dan Meyer	.10	.25
56 Rick Reuschel	.25	.60
57 Reggie Smith	.25	.60
58 Blue Jays Team DP CL	.30	.75
59 John Montefusco	.10	.25
60 Dave Parker	.50	1.25
61 Jim Bibby	.10	.25
62 Fred Lynn	.25	.60
63 Jose Morales	.25	.60
64 Aurelio Rodriguez	.10	.25
65 Frank Tanana	.25	.60
66 Darrell Porter	.25	.60
67 Otto Velez	.10	.25
68 Larry Bowa	.50	1.25
69 Jim Hunter	1.00	2.50
70 George Foster	.50	1.25
71 Cecil Cooper DP	.12	.30
72 Gary Alexander DP	.08	.20
73 Paul Thormodsgard	.10	.25
74 Toby Harrah	.25	.60
75 Mitchell Page	.10	.25
76 Alan Ashby	.10	.25
77 Jorge Orta	.10	.25
78 Dave Winfield	4.00	10.00
79 Andy Messersmith	.25	.60
Now with N.Y. Yankees as of 12-8-		
80 Ken Singleton	.25	.60
81 Will McEnaney	.25	.60
82 Lou Piniella	.25	.60
83 Bob Forsch	.10	.25
84 Dan Driessen	.10	.25
85 Dave Lemanczyk	.10	.25
86 Paul Dade	.10	.25
87 Bill Campbell	.10	.25
88 Ron LeFlore	.25	.60
89 Bill Madlock	.25	.60
90 Tony Perez DP	.50	1.25
91 Freddie Patek	.25	.60
92 Glenn Abbott	.10	.25
93 Garry Maddox	.25	.60
94 Steve Staggs	.10	.25
95 Bobby Murcer	.25	.60
96 Don Sutton	1.00	2.50
97 Al Oliver	1.00	2.50
Now with Texas Rangers as of 12-8-77		
98 Jon Matlack	.25	.60
Now with Texas Rangers as of 12-8-77		
99 Sam Mejias	.25	.60
100 Pete Rose DP	5.00	12.00
101 Randy Jones	.10	.25
102 Sixto Lezcano	.10	.25
103 Jim Clancy DP	.12	.30
104 Butch Wynegar	.10	.25
105 Nolan Ryan	12.50	40.00
106 Wayne Gross	.10	.25
107 Bob Watson	.25	.60
108 Joe Kerrigan	.25	.60
Now with Baltimore as of 12-8-77		
109 Keith Hernandez	.25	.60
110 Reggie Jackson	3.00	8.00
111 Denny Doyle	.10	.25
112 Sam Ewing	.25	.60
113 Bert Blyleven	1.00	2.50
Now with Pittsburgh as of 12-8-77		
114 Andre Thornton	.25	.60
115 Milt May	.10	.25
116 Jim Colborn	.10	.25
117 Warren Cromartie RC	.50	1.25
118 Ted Sizemore	.10	.25
119 Checklist 1-121	.50	1.25
120 Tom Seaver	2.50	6.00
121 Luis Gomez	.25	.60
122 Jim Spencer	.25	.60
Now with N.Y. Yankees as of 12-12-77		
123 Leroy Stanton	.10	.25
124 Luis Tiant	.25	.60
125 Mark Belanger	.25	.60
126 Jackie Brown	.10	.25
127 Bill Buckner	.25	.60
128 Bill Robinson	.25	.60
129 Rick Cerone	.25	.60
130 Ron Cey	.50	1.25
131 Jose Cruz	.25	.60
132 Len Randle DP	.08	.20
133 Bob Grich	.25	.60
134 Jeff Burroughs	.25	.60
135 Gary Carter	1.00	2.50
136 Milt Wilcox	.10	.25
137 Carl Yastrzemski	2.50	6.00
138 Dennis Eckersley	1.25	3.00
139 Tim Nordbrook	.10	.25
140 Ken Griffey Sr.	.50	1.25
141 Bob Boone	.50	1.25
142 Dave Goltz DP	.08	.20
143 Al Cowens	.10	.25
144 Bill Atkinson	.10	.25
145 Chris Chambliss	.25	.60
146 Jim Slaton	.25	.60
Now with Detroit Tigers as of 12-9-77		
147 Bill Stein	.10	.25
148 Bob Bailor	.25	.60
149 J.R. Richard	.25	.60
150 Ted Simmons	.25	.60
151 Rick Manning	.10	.25
152 Lerrin LaGrow	.10	.25
153 Larry Parrish	.50	1.25
154 Eddie Murray RC!	30.00	60.00
155 Phil Niekro	1.00	2.50
156 Bake McBride	.25	.60
157 Pete Vuckovich	.25	.60
158 Ivan DeJesus	.10	.25
159 Rick Rhoden	.25	.60
160 Joe Morgan	1.25	3.00
161 Ed Ott	.10	.25
162 Don Stanhouse	.25	.60
163 Jim Rice	.50	1.25
164 Bucky Dent	.25	.60
165 Jim Kern	.10	.25
166 Doug Rader	.10	.25
167 Steve Kemp	.10	.25
168 John Mayberry	.25	.60
169 Tim Foli	.25	.60
Now with N.Y. Mets as of 12-7-77		
170 Steve Carlton	1.50	4.00
171 Pepe Frias	.25	.60
172 Pat Zachry	.10	.25
173 Don Baylor	.50	1.25
174 Sal Bando DP	.12	.30
175 Alvis Woods	.25	.60
176 Mike Hargrove	.25	.60
177 Vida Blue	.25	.60
178 George Hendrick	.25	.60
179 Jim Palmer	1.25	3.00
180 Andre Dawson	5.00	12.00
181 Paul Moskau	.10	.25
182 Mickey Rivers	.25	.60
183 Checklist 122-242	.50	1.25
184 Jerry Johnson	.25	.60
185 Willie McCovey	1.25	3.00
186 Enrique Romo	.10	.25
187 Butch Hobson	.10	.25
188 Rusty Staub	.50	1.25

189 Wayne Twitchell .25 .60
190 Steve Garvey 1.00 2.50
191 Rick Waits .10 .25
192 Doug DeCinces .25 .60
193 Tom Murphy .10 .25
194 Rich Hebner .25 .60
195 Ralph Garr .25 .60
196 Bruce Sutter .50 1.25
197 Tom Poquette .10 .25
198 Wayne Garrett .10 .25
199 Pedro Borbon .10 .25
200 Thurman Munson 1.50 4.00
201 Rollie Fingers 1.00 2.50
202 Doug Ault .25 .60
203 Phil Garner DP .08 .20
204 Lou Brock 1.25 3.00
205 Ed Kranepool .25 .60
206 Bobby Bonds .50 1.25
Now with White Sox as of 12-15-77
207 Expos Team DP .50 1.25
208 Bump Wills .10 .25
209 Gary Matthews .25 .60
210 Carlton Fisk 1.50 4.00
211 Jeff Byrd .25 .60
212 Jason Thompson .25 .60
213 Larvell Blanks .10 .25
214 Sparky Lyle .25 .60
215 George Brett 8.00 20.00
216 Del Unser .10 .25
217 Manny Trillo .10 .25
218 Roy Hartsfield MG .25 .60
219 Carlos Lopez .25 .60
Now with Baltimore as of 12-7-77
220 Dave Concepcion .50 1.25
221 John Candelaria .25 .60
222 Dave Lopes .25 .60
223 Tim Blackwell DP .12 .30
Now with Chicago Cubs as of 2-1-7
224 Chet Lemon .25 .60
225 Mike Schmidt 5.00 12.00
226 Cesar Cedeno .25 .60
227 Mike Willis .25 .60
228 Willie Randolph .50 1.25
229 Doug Bair .10 .25
230 Rod Carew 1.50 4.00
231 Mike Flanagan .25 .60
232 Chris Speier .10 .25
233 Don Aase .25 .60
Now with California as of 12-8-77
234 Buddy Bell .25 .60
235 Mark Fidrych 1.00 2.50
236 Lou Brock RB 1.25 3.00
Most Steals& Lifetime
237 Sparky Lyle RB .25 .60
Most Games Pure
Relief& Lifetime
238 Willie McCovey RB 1.00 2.50
Most Times 2 HR's
in Inning& L
239 Brooks Robinson RB 1.00 2.50
Most Consecutive
Seasons with
240 Pete Rose RB 3.00 8.00
Most Hits& Switch-
hitter& Lifetime
241 Nolan Ryan RB 6.00 15.00
Most games 10 or More
Strikeouts&
242 Reggie Jackson RB 1.50 4.00
Most Homers& One
World Series

1979 O-Pee-Chee

This set is an abridgement of the 1979 Topps set. The 374 standard-size cards comprising the 1979 O-Pee-Chee set differ from the cards of the 1979 Topps set by having a higher ratio of cards of players from the two Canadian teams, a practice begun by O-Pee-Chee in 1977 and continued to 1988. The 1979 O-Pee-Chee set was the largest (374) original baseball card set issued (up to that time) by O-Pee-Chee. The fronts feature white-bordered color player photos. The player's name, position, and team appear in colored lettering within the lower white margin. The green and white horizontal backs carry the player's name, team and position at the top. Biography, major league statistics, career highlights in both French and English and a bilingual trivia question and answer also appear. The asterisked cards have an extra line on the front indicating team change. Double-printed (DP) cards are also noted below. The fronts have an O-Pee-Chee logo in the lower left corner comparable to the Topps logo on the 1979 American Set. The cards are sequenced in the same order as the Topps cards; the O-Pee-Chee cards are in effect a compressed version of the Topps set. The key card in this set is the Ozzie Smith Rookie Card. This set was issued in 15 cent wax packs which came 24 boxes to a case.

COMPLETE SET (374) 100.00 200.00
COMMON PLAYER (1-374) .10 .25
COMMON PLAYER DP (1-374) .08 .20
1 Lee May .40 1.00
2 Dick Drago .10 .25
3 Paul Dade .10 .25
4 Ross Grimsley .10 .25
5 Joe Morgan DP 1.00 2.50
6 Kevin Kobel .10 .25
7 Terry Forster .10 .25
8 Paul Molitor 6.00 15.00
9 Steve Carlton 1.50 4.00
10 Dave Goltz .10 .25
11 Dave Winfield 2.50 6.00
12 Dave Rozema .10 .25
13 Ed Figueroa .10 .25
14 Alan Ashby .20 .50
Trade with Blue Jays 11-28-78
15 Dale Murphy 1.50 4.00
16 Dennis Eckersley .75 2.00
17 Ron Blomberg .10 .25
18 Wayne Twitchell .20 .50
Free Agent as of 3-1-79
19 Al Hrabosky .10 .25
20 Fred Norman .10 .25
21 Steve Garvey DP .40 1.00
22 Willie Stargell .75 2.00
23 John Hale .10 .25
24 Mickey Rivers .20 .50
25 Jack Brohamer .10 .25
26 Tom Underwood .10 .25
27 Mark Belanger .20 .50
28 Elliott Maddox .10 .25
29 John Candelaria .20 .50
30 Shane Rawley .10 .25
31 Steve Yeager .20 .50
32 Warren Cromartie .40 1.00
33 Jason Thompson .20 .50
34 Roger Erickson .10 .25
35 Gary Matthews .20 .50
36 Pete Falcone .20 .50
Traded 12-5-78
37 Dick Tidrow .10 .25
38 Bob Boone .40 1.00
39 Jim Bibby .10 .25
40 Len Barker .20 .50
Trade with Rangers 10-3-78
41 Robin Yount 2.50 6.00
42 Sam Mejias .20 .50
Traded 12-14-78
43 Ray Burris .10 .25
44 Tom Seaver DP 2.00 5.00
45 Roy Howell .10 .25
46 Jim Todd .20 .50
Free Agent 3-1-79
47 Frank Duffy .10 .25
48 Joel Youngblood .10 .25
49 Vida Blue .20 .50
50 Cliff Johnson .10 .25
51 Nolan Ryan 12.50 30.00
52 Ozzie Smith RC 40.00 80.00
53 Jim Sundberg .20 .50
54 Mike Paxton .10 .25
55 Lou Whitaker 2.50 6.00
56 Dan Schatzeder .10 .25
57 Rick Burleson .10 .25
58 Doug Bair .10 .25
59 Ted Martinez .10 .25
60 Bob Watson .20 .50
61 Jim Clancy .20 .50
62 Rowland Office .10 .25
63 Bobby Murcer .20 .50
64 Don Gullett .20 .50
65 Tom Paciorek .10 .25
66 Rick Rhoden .10 .25
67 Duane Kuiper .10 .25
68 Bruce Boisclair .10 .25
69 Manny Sarmiento .10 .25
70 Wayne Cage .10 .25
71 John Hiller .20 .50
72 Rick Cerone .10 .25
73 Dwight Evans .40 1.00
74 Buddy Solomon .10 .25
75 Roy White .20 .50
76 Mike Flanagan .40 1.00
77 Tom Johnson .10 .25
78 Glenn Burke .10 .25
79 Frank Taveras .10 .25
80 Don Sutton .75 2.00
81 Leon Roberts .10 .25
82 George Hendrick .40 1.00
83 Aurelio Rodriguez .10 .25
84 Ron Reed .10 .25
85 Alvis Woods .10 .25
86 Jim Beattie DP .08 .20
87 Larry Hisle .10 .25
88 Mike Garman .10 .25
89 Tim Johnson .10 .25
90 Paul Splittorff .10 .25
91 Darrel Chaney .10 .25
92 Mike Torrez .20 .50
93 Eric Soderholm .10 .25
94 Ron Cey .20 .50
95 Randy Jones .10 .25
96 Bill Madlock .20 .50
97 Steve Kemp DP .08 .20
98 Bob Apodaca .10 .25
99 Johnny Grubb .10 .25
100 Larry Milbourne .10 .25
101 Johnny Bench DP 2.50 6.00
102 Dave Lemanczyk .10 .25
103 Reggie Cleveland .10 .25
104 Larry Bowa .20 .50
105 Denny Martinez .60 1.50
106 Bill Travers .10 .25
107 Willie McCovey 1.00 2.50
108 Wilbur Wood .10 .25
109 Dennis Leonard .20 .50
110 Roy Smalley .20 .50
111 Cesar Geronimo .10 .25
112 Jesse Jefferson .20 .50
113 Dave Revering .10 .25
114 Goose Gossage .40 1.00
115 Steve Stone .20 .50
Free Agent 11-25-78
116 Doug Flynn .10 .25
117 Bob Forsch .10 .25
118 Paul Mitchell .10 .25
119 Toby Harrah .20 .50
Traded 12-8-78
120 Steve Rogers .20 .50
121 Checklist 1-125 DP .08 .20
122 Balor Moore .10 .25
123 Rick Reuschel .20 .50
124 Jeff Burroughs .20 .50
125 Willie Randolph .20 .50
126 Bob Stinson .10 .25
127 Rick Wise .10 .25
128 Luis Gomez .20 .50
129 Tommy John .60 1.50
Signed as Free Agent 11-22-78
130 Richie Zisk .10 .25
131 Mario Guerrero .10 .25
132 Oscar Gamble .20 .50
Trade with Padres 10-25-78
133 Don Money .10 .25
134 Joe Rudi .20 .50
135 Woodie Fryman .10 .25
136 Butch Hobson .20 .50
137 Jim Colborn .10 .25
138 Tom Grieve .20 .50
Traded 12-5-78
139 Andy Messersmith .20 .50
Free Agent 2-7-79
140 Andre Thornton .20 .50
141 Ken Kravec .10 .25
142 Bobby Bonds .60 1.50
Trade with Rangers 10-3-78
143 Jose Cruz .40 1.00
144 Dave Lopes .20 .50
145 Jerry Garvin .10 .25
146 Pepe Frias .10 .25
147 Mitchell Page .20 .50
148 Ted Sizemore .20 .50
Traded 2-23-79
149 Rich Gale .10 .25
150 Steve Ontiveros .10 .25
151 Rod Carew 1.50 4.00
Traded 2-5-79
152 Lary Sorensen DP .08 .20
153 Willie Montanez .10 .25
154 Floyd Bannister .20 .50
Traded 12-8-78
155 Bert Blyleven .40 1.00
156 Ralph Garr .20 .50
157 Thurman Munson 1.50 4.00
158 Bob Robertson .20 .50
Free Agent 3-1-79
159 Jon Matlack .10 .25
160 Carl Yastrzemski 2.50 6.00
161 Gaylord Perry .75 2.00
162 Mike Tyson .10 .25
163 Cecil Cooper .20 .50
164 Pedro Borbon .10 .25
165 Art Howe DP .08 .20
166 Joe Coleman .20 .50
Free Agent 3-1-79
167 George Brett 8.00 20.00
168 Gary Alexander .10 .25
169 Chet Lemon .20 .50
170 Craig Swan .10 .25
171 Chris Chambliss .20 .50
172 John Montague .10 .25
173 Ron Jackson .20 .50
Traded 12-4-78
174 Jim Palmer 1.25 3.00
175 Willie Upshaw .40 1.00
176 Tug McGraw .20 .50
177 Bill Buckner .20 .50
178 Doug Rau .10 .25
179 Andre Dawson 2.50 6.00
180 Jim Wright .10 .25
181 Garry Templeton .20 .50
182 Bill Bonham .10 .25
183 Lee Mazzilli .10 .25
184 Alan Trammell 3.00 8.00
185 Amos Otis .20 .50
186 Tom Dixon .10 .25
187 Mike Cubbage .10 .25
188 Sparky Lyle .40 1.00
Traded 11-10-78
189 Juan Bernhardt .10 .25
190 Bump Wills/(Texas Rangers) .40 1.00
191 Dave Kingman .40 1.00
192 Lamar Johnson .10 .25
193 Lance Rautzhan .10 .25
194 Ed Herrmann .10 .25
195 Bill Campbell .10 .25
196 Gorman Thomas .20 .50
197 Paul Moskau .10 .25
198 Dale Murray .10 .25
199 John Mayberry .20 .50
200 Phil Garner .10 .25
201 Dan Ford .20 .50
Traded 12-4-78
202 Gary Thomasson .20 .50
Traded 2-15-79
203 Rollie Fingers .75 2.00
204 Al Oliver .20 .50
205 Doug Ault .20 .50
206 Scott McGregor .20 .50
207 Dave Cash .10 .25
208 Bill Plummer .10 .25
209 Ivan DeJesus .10 .25
210 Jim Rice .40 1.00
211 Ray Knight .20 .50
212 Paul Hartzell .20 .50
Traded 2-5-79
213 Tim Foli .10 .25
214 Butch Wynegar DP .08 .20
215 Darrell Evans .40 1.00
216 Ken Griffey Sr. .20 .50
217 Doug DeCinces .20 .50
218 Ruppert Jones .10 .25
219 Bob Montgomery .10 .25
220 Rick Manning .10 .25
221 Chris Speier .10 .25
222 Bobby Valentine .20 .50
223 Dave Parker .20 .50
224 Larry Biittner .10 .25
225 Ken Clay .10 .25
226 Gene Tenace .20 .50
227 Frank White .20 .50
228 Rusty Staub .40 1.00
229 Lee Lacy .10 .25
230 Doyle Alexander .10 .25
231 Bruce Bochte .10 .25
232 Steve Henderson .10 .25
233 Jim Lonborg .20 .50
234 Dave Concepcion .40 1.00
235 Jerry Morales .20 .50
Traded 12-4-78
236 Len Randle .10 .25
237 Bill Lee DP .12 .30
Traded 12-7-78
238 Bruce Sutter .75 2.00
239 Jim Essian .10 .25
240 Graig Nettles .40 1.00
241 Otto Velez .10 .25
242 Checklist 126-250 DP .08 .20
243 Reggie Smith .20 .50
244 Stan Bahnsen DP .08 .20
245 Garry Maddox DP .08 .20
246 Joaquin Andujar .20 .50
247 Dan Driessen .10 .25
248 Bob Grich .20 .50
249 Fred Lynn .20 .50
250 Skip Lockwood .10 .25
251 Craig Reynolds .20 .50
Traded 12-5-78
252 Willie Horton .20 .50
253 Rick Waits .10 .25
254 Bucky Dent .20 .50
255 Bob Knepper .10 .25
256 Miguel Dilone .10 .25
257 Bob Owchinko .10 .25
258 Al Cowens .10 .25
259 Bob Bailor .10 .25
260 Larry Christenson .10 .25
261 Tony Perez .75 2.00
262 Blue Jays Team .60 1.50
Roy Hartsfield MG/(Team checklist
263 Glenn Abbott .10 .25
264 Ron Guidry .20 .50
265 Ed Kranepool .10 .25
266 Charlie Hough .20 .50
267 Ted Simmons .40 1.00
268 Jack Clark .20 .50
269 Enos Cabell .10 .25
270 Gary Carter .75 2.00
271 Sam Ewing .10 .25
272 Tom Burgmeier .10 .25
273 Freddie Patek .10 .25
274 Frank Tanana .20 .50
275 Leroy Stanton .10 .25
276 Ken Forsch .10 .25
277 Ellis Valentine .10 .25
278 Greg Luzinski .20 .50
279 Rick Bosetti .10 .25
280 John Stearns .10 .25
281 Enrique Romo .20 .50
Traded 12-5-78
282 Bob Bailey .10 .25
283 Sal Bando .20 .50
284 Matt Keough .10 .25
285 Biff Pocoroba .10 .25
286 Mike Lum .20 .50
Free Agent 3-1-79
287 Jay Johnstone .20 .50
288 John Montefusco .10 .25
289 Ed Ott .10 .25
290 Dusty Baker .40 1.00
291 Rico Carty .40 1.00
Waivers from A's 10-2-78
292 Nino Espinosa .10 .25
293 Rich Hebner .20 .50
294 Cesar Cedeno .20 .50
295 Darrell Porter .20 .50
296 Rod Gilbreath .10 .25
297 Jim Kern .20 .50
Trade with Indians 10-3-78
298 Claudell Washington .20 .50
299 Luis Tiant .40 1.00
Signed as Free Agent 11-14-78
300 Mike Parrott .10 .25
301 Pete Broberg .20 .50
Free Agent 3-1-79
302 Greg Gross .20 .50
Traded 2-23-79
303 Darold Knowles .20 .50
Free Agent 2-12-79
304 Paul Blair .20 .50
305 Julio Cruz .10 .25
306 Hal McRae .40 1.00
307 Ken Reitz .10 .25
308 Tom Murphy .10 .25
309 Terry Whitfield .10 .25
310 J.R. Richard .20 .50
311 Mike Hargrove .40 1.00
Trade with Rangers 10-25-78
312 Rick Dempsey .20 .50
313 Phil Niekro .75 2.00
314 Bob Stanley .10 .25
315 Jim Spencer .10 .25
316 George Foster .20 .50
317 Dave LaRoche .10 .25
318 Rudy May .10 .25
319 Jeff Newman .10 .25
320 Rick Monday DP .08 .20
321 Omar Moreno .10 .25
322 Dave McKay .20 .50

Card	Low	High
323 Mike Schmidt	4.00	10.00
324 Ken Singleton	.20	.50
325 Jerry Remy	.10	.25
326 Bert Campaneris	.20	.50
327 Pat Zachry	.10	.25
328 Larry Herndon	.10	.25
329 Mark Fidrych	.60	1.50
330 Del Unser	.10	.25
331 Gene Garber	.20	.50
332 Bake McBride	.20	.50
333 Jorge Orta	.10	.25
334 Don Kirkwood	.10	.25
335 Don Baylor	.40	1.00
336 Bill Robinson	.20	.50
337 Manny Trillo	.20	.50
Traded 2-23-79		
338 Eddie Murray	10.00	25.00
339 Tom Hausman	.10	.25
340 George Scott DP	.08	.20
341 Rick Sweet	.10	.25
342 Lou Piniella	.20	.50
343 Pete Rose	6.00	15.00
Free Agent 12-5-79		
344 Stan Papi	.20	.50
Traded 12-7-78		
345 Jerry Koosman	.40	1.00
Traded 12-8-78		
346 Hosken Powell	.10	.25
347 George Medich	.10	.25
348 Ron LeFlore DP	.08	.20
349 Montreal Expos Team	.60	1.50
Dick Williams MG/(Team check		
350 Lou Brock	1.25	3.00
351 Bill North	.10	.25
352 Jim Hunter DP	.60	1.50
353 Checklist 251-374 DP	.12	.30
354 Ed Halicki	.10	.25
355 Tom Hutton	.10	.25
356 Mike Caldwell	.10	.25
357 Larry Parrish	.40	1.00
358 Geoff Zahn	.10	.25
359 Derrel Thomas	.20	.50
Signed as Free Agent 11-14-78		
360 Carlton Fisk	1.25	3.00
361 John Henry Johnson	.10	.25
362 Dave Chalk	.10	.25
363 Dan Meyer DP	.08	.20
364 Sixto Lezcano	.10	.25
365 Rennie Stennett	.10	.25
366 Mike Willis	.20	.50
367 Buddy Bell DP	.08	.20
Traded 12-8-78		
368 Mickey Stanley	.10	.25
369 Dave Rader	.20	.50
Traded 2-23-79		
370 Burt Hooton	.20	.50
371 Keith Hernandez	.40	1.00
372 Bill Stein	.10	.25
373 Hal Dues	.10	.25
374 Reggie Jackson DP	2.50	6.00

1980 O-Pee-Chee

This set is an abridgement of the 1980 Topps set. The cards are printed on white stock rather than the gray stock used by Topps. The 374 standard-size cards also differ from their Topps counterparts by having a higher ratio of cards of players from the two Canadian teams, a practice begun by O-Pee-Chee in 1977 and continued to 1988. The fronts feature white-bordered color player photos framed by a colored line. The player's name appears in the white border at the top and also as a simulated autograph across the photo. The player's position appears within a colored banner at the upper left; his team name appears within a colored banner at the lower right. The blue and white horizontal backs carry the player's name, team and position at the top. Biography, major league statistics and career highlights in both French and English also appear. The cards are numbered on the back. The asterisked cards have an extra line, "Now with (new team name)" on the front indicating team change. Color changes, to correspond to the new team, are apparent on the pennant name and frame on the front. Double-printed (DP) cards are also noted below. The cards in this set were produced in lower quantities than other O-Pee-Chee sets of this era reportedly due to the company being on strike. The cards are sequenced in the same order as the Topps cards.

Card	Low	High
COMPLETE SET (374)	75.00	150.00
COMMON PLAYER (1-374)	.08	.25
COMMON CARD DP (1-374)	.02	.10
1 Craig Swan	.08	.25
2 Dennis Martinez	.40	1.00
3 Dave Cash (Now With Padres)	.15	.40
4 Bruce Sutter	.60	1.50
5 Ron Jackson	.08	.25
6 Balor Moore	.15	.40
7 Dan Ford	.08	.25
8 Pat Putnam	.08	.25
9 Derrel Thomas	.08	.25
10 Jim Slaton	.08	.25
11 Lee Mazzilli	.15	.40
12 Del Unser	.08	.25
13 Mark Wagner	.08	.25
14 Vida Blue	.30	.75
15 Jay Johnstone	.15	.40
16 Julio Cruz DP	.02	.10
17 Tony Scott	.08	.25
18 Jeff Newman DP	.02	.10
19 Luis Tiant	.15	.40
20 Carlton Fisk	1.25	3.00
21 Dave Palmer	.08	.25
22 Bombo Rivera	.08	.25
23 Bill Fahey	.08	.25
24 Frank White	.30	.75
25 Rico Carty	.15	.40
26 Bill Bonham DP	.02	.10
27 Rick Miller	.08	.25
28 J.R. Richard	.15	.40
29 Joe Ferguson DP	.02	.10
30 Bill Madlock	.15	.40
31 Pete Vuckovich	.08	.25
32 Doug Flynn	.08	.25
33 Bucky Dent	.15	.40
34 Mike Ivie	.08	.25
35 Bob Stanley	.08	.25
36 Al Bumbry	.15	.40
37 Gary Carter	.75	2.00
38 John Milner DP	.02	.10
39 Sid Monge	.08	.25
40 Bill Russell	.15	.40
41 John Stearns	.08	.25
42 Dave Stieb	.40	1.00
43	.15	.40
44 Bob Owchinko	.08	.25
45 Ron LeFlore	.30	.75
Now with Expos		
46 Ted Sizemore	.08	.25
47 Ted Simmons	.15	.40
48 Pepe Frias	.15	.40
Now with Rangers		
49 Ken Landreaux	.08	.25
50 Manny Trillo	.15	.40
51 Rick Dempsey	.15	.40
52 Cecil Cooper	.15	.40
53 Bill Lee	.15	.40
54 Victor Cruz	.08	.25
55 Johnny Bench	2.00	5.00
56 Rich Dauer	.08	.25
57 Frank Tanana	.15	.40
58 Francisco Barrios	.08	.25
59 Bob Horner	.15	.40
60 Fred Lynn DP	.07	.20
61 Bob Knepper	.08	.25
62 Sparky Lyle	.15	.40
63 Larry Cox	.08	.25
64 Dock Ellis	.15	.40
Now with Pirates		
65 Phil Garner	.15	.40
66 Greg Luzinski	.15	.40
67 Checklist 1-125	.30	.75
68 Dave Lemanczyk	.08	.25
69 Tony Perez	.60	1.50
Now with Red Sox		
70 Gary Thomasson	.08	.25
71 Craig Reynolds	.08	.25
72 Amos Otis	.15	.40
73 Biff Pocoroba	.08	.25
74 Matt Keough	.08	.25
75 Bill Buckner	.15	.40
76 John Castino	.08	.25
77 Goose Gossage	.40	1.00
78 Gary Alexander	.08	.25
79 Phil Huffman	.08	.25
80 Bruce Bochte	.08	.25
81 Darrell Evans	.15	.40
82 Terry Puhl	.15	.40
83 Jason Thompson	.08	.25
84 Lary Sorensen	.08	.25
85 Jerry Remy	.08	.25
86 Tony Brizzolara	.08	.25
87 Willie Wilson DP	.07	.20
88 Eddie Murray	6.00	12.00
89 Larry Christenson	.08	.25
90 Bob Randall	.08	.25
91 Greg Pryor	.08	.25
92 Glenn Abbott	.08	.25
93 Jack Clark	.15	.40
94 Rick Waits	.08	.25
95 Luis Gomez	.15	.40
Now with Braves		
96 Burt Hooton	.15	.40
97 John Henry Johnson	.08	.25
98 Ray Knight	.15	.40
99 Rick Reuschel	.15	.40
100 Champ Summers	.08	.25
101 Ron Davis	.08	.25
102 Warren Cromartie	.15	.40
103 Ken Reitz	.08	.25
104 Hal McRae	.15	.40
105 Alan Ashby	.08	.25
106 Kevin Kobel	.08	.25
107 Buddy Bell	.15	.40
108 Dave Goltz	.15	.40
Now with Dodgers		
109 John Montefusco	.08	.25
110 Lance Parrish	.15	.40
111 Mike LaCoss	.08	.25
112 Jim Rice	.15	.40
113 Steve Carlton	1.25	3.00
114 Sixto Lezcano	.08	.25
115 Ed Halicki	.08	.25
116 Jose Morales	.08	.25
117 Dave Concepcion	.30	.75
118 Joe Cannon	.08	.25
119 Willie Montanez	.15	.40
Now with Padres		
120 Lou Piniella	.30	.75
121 Bill Stein	.08	.25
122 Dave Winfield	2.00	5.00
123 Alan Trammell	.75	2.00
124 Andre Dawson	1.25	3.00
125 Marc Hill	.08	.25
126 Don Aase	.08	.25
127 Dave Kingman	.30	.75
128 Checklist 126-250	.30	.75
129 Dennis Lamp	.08	.25
130 Phil Niekro	.75	2.00
131 Tim Foli DP	.02	.10
132 Jim Clancy	.15	.40
133 Bill Atkinson	.15	.40
Now with White Sox		
134 Paul Dade DP	.02	.10
135 Dusty Baker	.15	.40
136 Al Oliver	.30	.75
137 Dave Chalk	.08	.25
138 Bill Robinson	.08	.25
139 Robin Yount	2.50	6.00
140 Dan Schatzeder	.15	.40
Now with Tigers		
141 Mike Schmidt DP	2.00	5.00
142 Ralph Garr	.15	.40
Now with Angels		
143 Dale Murphy	.75	2.00
144 Jerry Koosman	.15	.40
145 Tom Veryzer	.08	.25
146 Rick Bosetti	.08	.25
147 Jim Spencer	.08	.25
148 Gaylord Perry	.75	2.00
Now with Rangers		
149 Paul Blair	.15	.40
150 Don Baylor	.30	.75
151 Dave Rozema	.08	.25
152 Steve Garvey	.40	1.00
153 Elias Sosa	.08	.25
154 Larry Gura	.08	.25
155 Tim Johnson	.08	.25
156 Steve Henderson	.08	.25
157 Ron Guidry	.15	.40
158 Mike Edwards	.08	.25
159 Butch Wynegar	.08	.25
160 Randy Jones	.08	.25
161 Denny Walling	.08	.25
162 Mike Hargrove	.15	.40
163 Dave Parker	.40	1.00
164 Roger Metzger	.08	.25
165 Johnny Grubb	.08	.25
166 Steve Kemp	.08	.25
167 Bob Lacey	.08	.25
168 Chris Speier	.08	.25
169 Dennis Eckersley	.60	1.50
170 Keith Hernandez	.15	.40
171 Claudell Washington	.15	.40
172 Tom Underwood	.15	.40
Now with Yankees		
173 Dan Driessen	.08	.25
174 Al Cowens	.15	.40
Now with Angels		
175 Rich Hebner	.15	.40
Now with Tigers		
176 Willie McCovey	.75	2.00
177 Carney Lansford	.15	.40
178 Ken Singleton	.15	.40
179 Jim Essian	.08	.25
180 Mike Vail	.08	.25
181 Randy Lerch	.08	.25
182 Larry Parrish	.30	.75
183 Checklist 251-374	.30	.75
184 George Hendrick	.15	.40
185 Bob Davis	.08	.25
186 Gary Matthews	.15	.40
187 Lou Whitaker	.75	2.00
188 Darrell Porter DP	.07	.20
189 Wayne Gross	.08	.25
190 Bobby Murcer	.15	.40
191 Willie Aikens	.15	.40
Now with Royals		
192 Jim Kern	.08	.25
193 Cesar Cedeno	.15	.40
194 Joel Youngblood	.08	.25
195 Ross Grimsley	.08	.25
196 Jerry Mumphrey	.15	.40
Now with Padres		
197 Kevin Bell	.08	.25
198 Garry Maddox	.15	.40
199 Dave Freisleben	.08	.25
200 Ed Ott	.08	.25
201 Enos Cabell	.08	.25
202 Pete LaCock	.08	.25
203 Fergie Jenkins	.75	2.00
204 Milt Wilcox	.08	.25
205 Ozzie Smith	7.50	15.00
206 Ellis Valentine	.15	.40
207 Dan Meyer	.08	.25
208 Barry Foote	.08	.25
209 George Foster	.15	.40
210 Dwight Evans	.15	.40
211 Paul Molitor	5.00	10.00
212 Tony Solaita	.08	.25
213 Bill North	.08	.25
214 Paul Splittorff	.08	.25
215 Bobby Bonds	.40	1.00
Now with Cardinals		
216 Butch Hobson	.08	.25
217 Mark Belanger	.15	.40
218 Grant Jackson	.08	.25
219 Tom Hutton DP	.02	.10
220 Pat Zachry	.08	.25
221 Duane Kuiper	.08	.25
222 Larry Hisle DP	.02	.10
223 Mike Krukow	.08	.25
224 Johnnie LeMaster	.08	.25
225 Billy Almon	.15	.40
Now with Expos		
226 Joe Niekro	.15	.40
227 Dave Revering	.08	.25
228 Don Sutton	.60	1.50
229 John Hiller	.15	.40
230 Alvis Woods	.08	.25
231 Mark Fidrych	.40	1.00
232 Duffy Dyer	.08	.25
233 Nino Espinosa	.08	.25
234 Doug Bair	.08	.25
235 George Brett	7.50	16.00
236 Mike Torrez	.08	.25
237 Frank Taveras	.08	.25
238 Bert Blyleven	.40	1.00
239 Willie Randolph	.15	.40
240 Mike Sadek DP	.02	.10
241 Jerry Royster	.08	.25
242 John Denny	.15	.40
Now with Indians		
243 Rick Monday	.08	.25
244 Jesse Jefferson	.15	.40
245 Aurelio Rodriguez	.15	.40
Now with Padres		
246 Bob Boone	.30	.75
247 Cesar Geronimo	.08	.25
248 Bob Shirley	.08	.25
249 Expos Checklist	.40	1.00
250 Bob Watson	.30	.75
Now with Yankees		
251 Mickey Rivers	.15	.40
252 Mike Tyson DP	.07	.20
Now with Cubs		
253 Wayne Nordhagen	.08	.25
254 Roy Howell	.08	.25
255 Lee May	.15	.40
256 Jerry Martin	.08	.25
257 Bake McBride	.08	.25
258 Silvio Martinez	.08	.25
259 Jim Mason	.08	.25
260 Tom Seaver	2.00	5.00
261 Rich Wortham DP	.02	.10
262 Mike Cubbage	.08	.25
263 Gene Garber	.15	.40
264 Bert Campaneris	.15	.40
265 Tom Buskey	.08	.25
266 Leon Roberts	.08	.25
267 Ron Cey	.30	.75
268 Steve Ontiveros	.08	.25
269 Mike Caldwell	.08	.25
270 Nelson Norman	.08	.25
271 Steve Rogers	.15	.40
272 Jim Morrison	.08	.25
273 Clint Hurdle	.15	.40
274 Dale Murray	.08	.25
275 Jim Barr	.08	.25
276 Jim Sundberg DP	.07	.20
277 Willie Horton	.15	.40
278 Andre Thornton	.15	.40
279 Bob Forsch	.08	.25
280 Joe Strain	.08	.25
281 Rudy May	.15	.40
Now with Yankees		
282 Pete Rose	6.00	12.00
283 Jeff Burroughs	.15	.40
284 Rick Langford	.08	.25
285 Ken Griffey Sr.	.30	.75
286 Bill Nahorodny	.15	.40
Now with Braves		
287 Art Howe	.15	.40
288 Ed Figueroa	.08	.25
289 Joe Rudi	.15	.40
290 Alfredo Griffin	.15	.40
291 Dave Lopes	.15	.40
292 Rick Manning	.08	.25
293 Dennis Leonard	.15	.40
294 Bud Harrelson	.15	.40
295 Skip Lockwood	.15	.40
Now with Red Sox		
296 Roy Smalley	.08	.25
297 Kent Tekulve	.15	.40
298 Scot Thompson	.08	.25
299 Ken Kravec	.08	.25
300 Blue Jays Checklist	.40	1.00
301 Scott Sanderson	.15	.40
302 Charlie Moore	.08	.25
303 Nolan Ryan	12.50	25.00
Now with Astros		
304 Bob Bailor	.15	.40
305 Bob Stinson	.08	.25
306 Al Hrabosky	.15	.40
Now with Braves		
307 Mitchell Page	.08	.25
308 Garry Templeton	.08	.25
309 Chet Lemon	.15	.40
310 Jim Palmer	.75	2.00
311 Rick Cerone	.15	.40
Now with Yankees		
312 Jon Matlack	.08	.25
313 Don Money	.08	.25
314 Reggie Jackson	2.50	6.00
315 Brian Downing	.08	.25
316 Woodie Fryman	.08	.25
317 Alan Bannister	.08	.25
318 Ron Reed	.08	.25
319 Willie Stargell	.75	2.00
320 Jerry Garvin DP	.02	.10
321 Cliff Johnson	.08	.25
322 Doug DeCinces	.15	.40
323 Gene Richards	.08	.25
324 Joaquin Andujar	.15	.40
325 Richie Zisk	.08	.25
326 Bob Grich	.15	.40
327 Gorman Thomas	.15	.40
328 Chris Chambliss	.30	.75
Now with Braves		
329 Blue Jays Prospects	.30	.75
Butch Edge		
Pat Kelly		
Ted Wi		
330 Larry Bowa	.15	.40
331 Barry Bonnell	.15	.40
Now with Blue Jays		
332 John Candelaria	.15	.40
333 Toby Harrah	.15	.40
334 Larry Biittner	.08	.25
335 Mike Flanagan	.15	.40
336 Ed Kranepool	.08	.25

337 Ken Forsch DP	.02	.10
338 John Mayberry	.15	.40
339 Rick Burleson	.08	.25
340 Milt May	.15	.40
Now with Giants		
341 Roy White	.15	.40
342 Joe Morgan	.75	2.00
343 Rollie Fingers	.75	2.00
344 Mario Mendoza	.08	.25
345 Stan Bahnsen	.08	.25
346 Tug McGraw	.15	.40
347 Rusty Staub	.15	.40
348 Tommy John	.30	.75
349 Ivan DeJesus	.08	.25
350 Reggie Smith	.15	.40
351 Expos Prospects	.40	1.00
Tony Bernazard		
Randy Miller		
Joh		
352 Floyd Bannister	.08	.25
353 Rod Carew DP	.60	1.50
354 Otto Velez	.08	.25
355 Gene Tenace	.15	.40
356 Freddie Patek	.15	.40
Now with Angels		
357 Elliott Maddox	.08	.25
358 Pat Underwood	.08	.25
359 Graig Nettles	.30	.75
360 Rodney Scott	.08	.25
361 Terry Whitfield	.08	.25
362 Fred Norman	.15	.40
Now with Expos		
363 Sal Bando	.15	.40
364 Greg Gross	.08	.25
365 Carl Yastrzemski DP	.75	2.00
366 Paul Hartzell	.08	.25
367 Jose Cruz	.15	.40
368 Shane Rawley	.08	.25
369 Jerry White	.08	.25
370 Rick Wise	.15	.40
Now with Padres		
371 Steve Yeager	.30	.75
372 Omar Moreno	.08	.25
373 Bump Wills	.08	.25
374 Craig Kusick	.15	.40
Now with Padres		

1959 Oklahoma Today Major Leaguers

These 20 cards which measure 1 11/16" by 2 3/4" were featured on the back cover of the Summer 1959 Issue of Oklahoma Today. The card fronts feature Black and White photos on color backgrounds (8 green, 8 gold and 4 light blue). The bottom 1/4" of the front has a white panel with the players name in red. The backs are grey with the player's name, position team and league. The checklist below is as the players appear on the uncut covers in 4 rows of 5 cards starting on the top left. In the complete book form -- this set is valued at two to three times the values listed below.

COMPLETE SET (20)	125.00	250.00
1 Paul Waner	7.50	15.00
2 Lloyd Waner	7.50	15.00
3 Jerry Walker	3.00	6.00
4 Tom Sturdivant	3.00	6.00
5 Warren Spahn	12.50	25.00
6 Allie Reynolds	5.00	10.00
7 Dale Mitchell	3.00	6.00
8 Cal McLish	3.00	6.00
9 Von McDaniel	3.00	6.00
10 Lindy McDaniel	3.00	6.00
11 Pepper Martin	6.00	12.00
12 Mickey Mantle	150.00	300.00
13 Carl Hubbell	7.50	15.00
14 Paul Dean	3.00	6.00
15 Dizzy Dean	7.50	15.00
16 Don Demeter	3.00	6.00
17 Alvin Dark	5.00	10.00
18 Johnny Callison	5.00	10.00
19 Harry Brecheen	3.00	6.00
20 Jerry Adair	3.00	6.00

1887-90 Old Judge N172

The Goodwin Company's baseball series depicts hundreds of ballplayers from more than 40 major and minor league teams as well as boxers and wrestlers. The cards (approximately 1 1/2" by 2 1/2") are actually photographs from the Hall studio in New York which were pasted onto thick cardboard. The pictures are sepia in color with either a white or pink cast, and the cards are blank backed. They are found either numbered or unnumbered, with or without a copyright date, and with hand printed or machine printed names. All known cards have the name "Goodwin Co., New York" at the base. The cards were marketed during the period 1887-1890 in packs of "Old Judge" and "Gypsy Queen" cigarettes (cards marked with the latter brand are worth double the values listed below). They have been listed alphabetically and assigned numbers in the checklist below for simplicity's sake; the various poses known for some players also have not been listed for the same reason. Some of the players are pictured in horizontal (HOR) poses. In all, more than 2300 different Goodwin cards are known to collectors, with more being discovered every year. Cards from the "Spotted Tie" sub-series are denoted in the checklist below by SPOT. The Lee Gibson and Egyptian Healey cards are currently considered unique and are not priced due to market scarcity. The Stephen Behel card is drawing extra interest as there is debate as to whether or not he is the first Jewish player depicted on a card.

COMPLETE SET	500,000.00	1,000,000.00
COMMON PLAYER	150.00	300.00
COMMON PLAYER (DOUBLE)	200.00	400.00
COMMON BROWNS CHAMP	250.00	500.00
COMMON PLAYER (PCL)	20,000.00	50,000.00
COMMON SPOTTED TIE	500.00	1,000.00
1 Gus Albert	300.00	500.00
2 Charles Alcott	300.00	500.00
3 Alexander	300.00	500.00
4 Myron Allen	300.00	500.00
5 Bob Allen	300.00	500.00
6 Uncle Bill Alvord	300.00	500.00
7 Varney Anderson	300.00	500.00
8 Ed Andrews	300.00	500.00
9 Ed Andrews w B.Hoover	350.00	600.00
10 Wally Andrews	300.00	500.00
11 Bill Annis	300.00	500.00
12A Cap Anson in Uniform		
12B Cap Anson Street Clothes	5,000.00	8,000.00
13 Old Hoss Ardner	300.00	500.00
14 Tug Arundel	300.00	500.00
15 Jersey Bakley	300.00	500.00
16 Clarence Baldwin	300.00	500.00
17 Mark (Fido) Baldwin	300.00	500.00
18 Lady Baldwin	350.00	600.00
19 James Banning	300.00	500.00
20 Samuel Barkley	300.00	500.00
21 Bald Billy Barnie MG	350.00	600.00
22 Charles Bassett	300.00	500.00
23 Charles Bastian	300.00	500.00
24 Charles Bastian w P.Schriver	350.00	600.00
25 Ebenezer Beatin	300.00	500.00
26 Jake Beckley	2,500.00	4,000.00
27 Stephen Behel SPOT	6,000.00	10,000.00
28 Charles Bennett	300.00	500.00
29 Louis Bierbauer	300.00	500.00
30 Louis Bierbauer w R.Gamble	350.00	600.00
31 Bill Bishop	300.00	500.00
32 William Blair	300.00	500.00
33 Ned Bligh	300.00	500.00
34 Bogart	300.00	500.00
35 Boyce	300.00	500.00
36 Jake Boyd	350.00	600.00
37 Honest John Boyle	300.00	500.00
38 Handsome Henry Boyle	300.00	500.00
39 Nick Bradley	300.00	500.00
40 George (Grin) Bradley	300.00	500.00
41 Stephen Brady SPOT	900.00	1,500.00
42 E.L. Breckinridge PCL		
43 Timothy Brosnan Minn	300.00	500.00
44 Timothy Brosnan Sioux	300.00	500.00
45 Cal Broughton	300.00	500.00
46 Big Dan Brouthers	1,500.00	2,500.00
47 Thomas Brown	300.00	500.00
48 California Brown	300.00	500.00
49 Pete Browning	3,000.00	5,000.00
50 Charles Brynan	300.00	500.00
51 Al Buckenberger MG	300.00	500.00
52 Dick Buckley	300.00	500.00
53 Charles Buffington	300.00	500.00
54 Ernest Burch	300.00	500.00
55 Bill Burdick	300.00	500.00
56 Black Jack Burdock	300.00	500.00
57 Robert Burks	300.00	500.00
58 George (Watch) Burnham MG	350.00	600.00
59 James Burns Omaha	300.00	500.00
60 Jimmy Burns KC	300.00	500.00
61 Tommy (Oyster) Burns	350.00	600.00
62 Thomas E. Burns	300.00	500.00
63 Doc Bushong Brooklyn	300.00	500.00
64 Doc Bushong Browns Champs	500.00	800.00
65 Patsy Cahill	300.00	500.00
66 Count Campau	300.00	500.00
67 Jimmy Canavan	300.00	500.00
68 Bart Cantz	300.00	500.00
69 Handsome Jack Carney	300.00	500.00
70 Hick Carpenter	300.00	500.00
71 Cliff Carroll	300.00	500.00
72 Scrappy Carroll	300.00	500.00
73 Frederick Carroll	300.00	500.00
74 Jumbo Cartwright	300.00	500.00
75 Bob Caruthers Brooklyn	500.00	800.00
76 Bob Caruthers Browns Champs	500.00	800.00
77 Daniel Casey	300.00	500.00
78 Icebox Chamberlain	300.00	500.00
79 Cupid Childs	300.00	500.00
80 Bob Clark	300.00	500.00
81 Owen Clark	300.00	500.00
82 William H. Clarke w/M.Hughes	350.00	600.00
83 William (Dad) Clarke	300.00	500.00
84 Pete Connell	300.00	500.00
85 John Clarkson	1,200.00	2,000.00
86 Jack Clements	300.00	500.00
87 Elmer Cleveland	300.00	500.00
88 Monk Cline	300.00	500.00
89 Mike Cody	300.00	500.00
90 John Coleman	300.00	500.00
91 Bill Collins	300.00	500.00
92 Hub Collins	300.00	500.00
93 Charles Comiskey	2,500.00	4,000.00
94 Commy Comiskey	1,800.00	3,000.00
95 Roger Connor Script	2,500.00	4,000.00
96 Roger Connor New York	2,500.00	4,000.00
97 Richard Conway	300.00	500.00
98 Peter Conway	300.00	500.00
99 James Conway	300.00	500.00
100 Paul Cook	300.00	500.00
101 Jimmy Cooney	300.00	500.00
102 Larry Corcoran	500.00	800.00
103 Pop Corkhill	300.00	500.00
104 Cannon Ball Crane	300.00	500.00
105 Samuel Crane	300.00	500.00
106 Jack Crogan	350.00	600.00
107 John Crooks	300.00	500.00
108 Lave Cross	300.00	500.00
109 Bill Crossley	300.00	500.00
110 Joe Crotty SPOT	900.00	1,500.00
111 Joe Crotty	300.00	500.00
112 Billy Crowell	300.00	500.00
113 Jim Cudworth	300.00	500.00
114 Bert Cunningham	300.00	500.00
115 Tacks Curtis	300.00	500.00
116 Ed Cushman SPOT	900.00	1,500.00
117 Ed Cushman	300.00	500.00
118 Tony Cusick	300.00	500.00
119 Vincent Dailey PCL		
120 Edward Dailey Phi-Wash	300.00	500.00
121 Edward Dailey Columbus	500.00	800.00
122 Bill Daley	300.00	500.00
123 Con Daley	300.00	500.00
124 Abner Dalrymple	300.00	500.00
125 Tom Daly	350.00	600.00
126 James Daly	300.00	500.00
127 Law Daniels	300.00	500.00
128 Dell Darling	300.00	500.00
129 William Darnbrough	300.00	500.00
130 D. Davin	300.00	1,500.00
131 Jumbo Davis	300.00	500.00
132 Pat Dealey	300.00	500.00
133 Thomas Deasley Throwing	300.00	500.00
134 Thomas Deasley Fielding	300.00	500.00
135 Edward Decker	300.00	500.00
136 Big Ed Delahanty	5,000.00	8,000.00
137 Jeremiah Denny	300.00	500.00
138 James Devlin	300.00	500.00
139 Thomas Dolan	300.00	500.00
140 Jack Donahue PCL		
141 James Donahue SPOT	900.00	1,500.00
142 James Donahue	300.00	500.00
143 James Donnelly	300.00	500.00
144 Charles Dooley PCL		
145 J. Doran		
146 Michael Dorgan	300.00	500.00
147 Cornelius Doyle PCL		
148 Home Run Duffe	300.00	500.00
149 Hugh Duffy	1,500.00	2,500.00
150 Dan Dugdale	350.00	600.00
151 Duck Duke	300.00	500.00
152 Sure Shot Dunlap	300.00	500.00
153 J. Dunn	350.00	600.00
154 Jesse (Cyclone) Duryea	300.00	500.00
155 John Dwyer	350.00	600.00
156 Billy Earle	300.00	500.00
157 Buck Ebright	300.00	500.00
158 Red Ehret	300.00	500.00
159 R. Emmerke	300.00	500.00
160 Dude Esterbrook	300.00	500.00
161 Henry Esterday	300.00	500.00
162 Long John Ewing	300.00	500.00
163 Buck Ewing	1,500.00	2,500.00
164 Buck Ewing w Mascot	1,500.00	2,500.00
165 Jay Faatz	300.00	500.00
166 Clinkgers Fagan	300.00	500.00
167 William Farmer	300.00	500.00
168 Sidney Farrar	350.00	600.00
169 John (Moose) Farrell	300.00	500.00
170 Charles(Duke) Farrell	300.00	500.00
171 Frank Fennelly	300.00	500.00
172 Charlie Ferguson	300.00	500.00
173 Colonel Ferson	300.00	500.00
174 Wallace Fessenden UMP	350.00	600.00
175 Jocko Fields	300.00	500.00
176 Fischer	350.00	600.00
177 Thomas Flanigan	300.00	500.00
178 Silver Flint	300.00	500.00
179 Thomas Flood	300.00	500.00
180 Flynn		1500
181 James Fogarty	300.00	500.00
182 Frank (Monkey) Foreman	300.00	500.00
183 Thomas Forster	300.00	500.00
184 Elmer E. Foster SPOT	900.00	1,500.00
185 Elmer Foster NY-Chi	300.00	500.00
186 F.W. Foster SPOT	900.00	1,500.00
187 Scissors Foutz Browns Champ	500.00	800.00
188 Scissors Foutz Brooklyn	300.00	500.00
189 Julie Freeman	300.00	500.00
190 Will Fry	300.00	500.00
191 Fred Fudger PCL		
192 William Fuller	300.00	500.00
193 Shorty Fuller	300.00	500.00
194 Christopher Fullmer	300.00	500.00
195 Christopher Fullmer w T.Tucker	350.00	600.00
196 Honest John Gaffney MGR	500.00	800.00
197 Pud Galvin	1,800.00	3,000.00
198 Robert Gamble	300.00	500.00
199 Charles Ganzel	300.00	500.00
200 Gid Gardner	300.00	500.00
201 Gid Gardner w M.Murray	350.00	600.00
202 Hank Gastreich	300.00	500.00
203 Emil Geiss	300.00	500.00
204 Frenchy Genins	300.00	500.00
205 William George	300.00	500.00
206 Joe Gerhardt	300.00	500.00
207 Pretzels Getzein	300.00	500.00
208 Lee Gibson	300.00	500.00
209 Robert Gilks	300.00	500.00
210 Pete Gillespie	300.00	500.00
211 Barney Gilligan	300.00	500.00
212 Frank Gilmore	300.00	500.00
213 Pebbly Jack Glasscock	500.00	800.00
214 Kid Gleason	500.00	800.00
215 Brother Bill Gleason	300.00	500.00
216 William Bill Gleason	500.00	800.00
217 Mouse Glenn	300.00	500.00
218 Michael Goodfellow	300.00	500.00
219 George (Piano Legs) Gore	300.00	500.00
220 Frank Graves: Minn.	300.00	500.00
221 William Greenwood	300.00	500.00
222 Michael Greer	300.00	500.00
223 Mike Griffin	300.00	500.00
224 Clark Griffith	1,800.00	3,000.00
225 Henry Gruber	300.00	500.00
226 Addison Gumbert	300.00	500.00
227 Thomas Gunning	300.00	500.00
228 Joseph Gunson	300.00	500.00
229 George Haddock	300.00	500.00
230 William Hafner	300.00	500.00
231 Willie Hahm Mascot	300.00	500.00
232 William Hallman	300.00	500.00
233 Billy Hamilton	1,200.00	2,000.00
234 Willie Hamm w N.Williamson	500.00	800.00
235 Frank Hankinson SPOT	900.00	1,500.00
236 Frank Hankinson	300.00	500.00
237 Ned Hanlon	1,200.00	2,000.00
238 William Hanrahan	350.00	600.00
239 A.G. Hapeman PCL		
240 Pa Harkins	300.00	500.00
241 William Hart	300.00	500.00
242 William (Bill) Hasamdear	300.00	500.00
243 Colonel Hatfield	300.00	500.00
244 Egyptian Healey Wash-Ind	300.00	500.00
245 Egyptian Healey Washington	300.00	500.00
246 J.C. Healy	300.00	500.00
247 Guy Hecker	300.00	500.00
248 Tony Hellman	300.00	500.00
249 Hardie Henderson	300.00	500.00
250 Hardie Henderson w M.Greer	350.00	600.00
251 Moxie Hengle	350.00	600.00
252 John Henry	300.00	500.00
253 Edward Herr	300.00	500.00
254 Hunkey Hines	300.00	500.00
255 Paul Hines	300.00	500.00
256 Texas Wonder Hoffman	300.00	500.00
257 Eddie Hogan	300.00	500.00
258 William Holbert SPOT	900.00	1,500.00
259 William Holbert	300.00	500.00
260 James (Bugs) Holliday	300.00	500.00
261 Charles Hoover	350.00	600.00
262 Buster Hoover	300.00	500.00
263 Jack Horner	300.00	500.00
264 Jack Horner w E.Warner	350.00	600.00
265 Michael Horning	300.00	500.00
266 Pete Hotaling	300.00	500.00
267 William Howes	300.00	500.00
268 Dummy Hoy	1,800.00	3,000.00
269 Nat Hudson Browns Champs	500.00	800.00
270 Nat Hudson St. Louis	300.00	500.00
271 Mickey Hughes	300.00	500.00
272 Hungler	300.00	500.00
273 Wild Bill Hutchinson	300.00	500.00
274 John Irwin	300.00	500.00
275 Arthur (Cut Rate) Irwin	300.00	500.00
276 A.C. Jantzen	300.00	500.00
277 Frederick Jevne	300.00	500.00
278 John Johnson	300.00	500.00
279 Richard Johnston	300.00	500.00
280 Jordan	300.00	500.00
281 Heinie Kappell	300.00	500.00
282 Timothy Keefe	1,200.00	2,000.00
283 Tim Keefe w D.Richardson	700.00	1,200.00
284 George Keefe	300.00	500.00
285 James Keenan	300.00	500.00
286 King Kelly 10,000-Bos-Chic	3,000.00	5,000.00
287 Honest John Kelly MGR	500.00	800.00
288 Kelly UMP	350.00	600.00
289 Charles Kelly	600.00	1,000.00
290 Kelly and Powell UMP-MGR	350.00	600.00
291 Rudolph Kemmler Browns Champs	500.00	800.00
292 Rudolph Kemmler St. Paul	300.00	500.00
293 Theodore Kennedy	350.00	600.00
294 J.J. Kenyon	300.00	500.00
295 John Kerins	300.00	500.00
296 Matthew Kilroy	300.00	500.00
297 Charles King	300.00	500.00
298 August Kloff	300.00	500.00
299 William Klusman	300.00	500.00
300 Phillip Knell	300.00	500.00
301 Fred Knouf	300.00	500.00
302 Charles Kremmeyer PCL		
303 William Krieg	300.00	500.00
304 William Krieg w/A.Kloff	350.00	600.00
305 Gus Krock	300.00	500.00
306 Willie Kuehne	300.00	500.00
307 Frederick Lange	350.00	600.00
308 Ted Larkin	300.00	500.00
309 Arlie Latham Browns Champs	600.00	1,000.00
310 Arlie Latham Stl-Chi	500.00	800.00
311 John Lauer	300.00	500.00
312 John Leighton	300.00	500.00
313 Rube Levy PCL		
314 Tom Loftus MGR	300.00	500.00
315 Herman (Germany) Long	500.00	800.00
316 Danny Long PCL		
317 Tom Lovett	300.00	500.00
318 Bobby (Link) Lowe	500.00	800.00
319 Jack Lynch SPOT	900.00	1,500.00

320 John Lynch	300.00	500.00
321 Dennis Lyons	300.00	500.00
322 Harry Lyons	300.00	500.00
323 Connie Mack	3,500.00	6,000.00
324 Joe (Reddie) Mack	300.00	500.00
325 James (Little Mack) Macullar	300.00	500.00
326 Kid Madden	300.00	500.00
327 Daniel Mahoney	300.00	500.00
328 Willard (Grasshopper) Maines	300.00	500.00
329 Fred Mann	300.00	500.00
330 Jimmy Manning	300.00	500.00
331 Charles (Lefty) Marr	300.00	500.00
332 Mascot (Willie) Breslin	350.00	600.00
333 Samuel Maskery	300.00	500.00
334 Bobby Mathews	300.00	500.00
335 Michael Mattimore	300.00	500.00
336 Albert Maul	300.00	500.00
337 Albert Mays SPOT	900.00	1,500.00
338 Albert Mays	300.00	500.00
339 James McAleer	300.00	500.00
340 Thomas McCarthy	1,500.00	2,500.00
341 John McCarthy	300.00	500.00
342 James McCauley	350.00	600.00
343 William McClellan	300.00	500.00
344 John McCormack	300.00	500.00
345 Big Jim McCormick	300.00	500.00
346 McCreachery MGR		
347 James (Chippy) McGarr	300.00	500.00
348 Jack McGeachy	300.00	500.00
349 John McGlone	300.00	500.00
350 James (Deacon) McGuire	300.00	500.00
351 Bill McGunnigle MGR	500.00	800.00
352 Ed McKean	300.00	500.00
353 Alex McKinnon	300.00	500.00
354 Thomas McLaughlin SPOT	900.00	1,500.00
355 John (Bid) McPhee	3,000.00	5,000.00
356 James McQuaid	300.00	500.00
357 John McQuaid UMP	350.00	600.00
358 Jame McTamany	300.00	500.00
359 George McVey	300.00	500.00
360 Peter Meegan PCL		
361 John Messitt	300.00	500.00
362 George (Doggie) Miller	300.00	500.00
363 Joseph Miller	300.00	500.00
364 Jocko Milligan	300.00	500.00
365 E.L. Mills	300.00	500.00
366 Daniel Minnehan	300.00	500.00
367 Samuel Moffet	300.00	500.00
368 Honest Morrell	300.00	500.00
369 Ed Morris	300.00	500.00
370 Morrisey	300.00	500.00
371 Tony (Count) Mullane	500.00	800.00
372 Joseph Mulvey	300.00	500.00
373 P.L. Murphy	300.00	500.00
374 Pat J. Murphy	300.00	500.00
375 Miah Murray	300.00	500.00
376 Truthful Mutrie MGR	350.00	600.00
377 George Myers	300.00	500.00
378 Al (Cod) Myers	300.00	500.00
379 Thomas Nagle	300.00	500.00
380 Billy Nash	300.00	500.00
381 Candy Nelson SPOT	900.00	1,500.00
382 Kid Nichols	2,500.00	4,000.00
383 Samuel Nichols	300.00	500.00
384 J.W. Nicholson	350.00	600.00
385 Tom Nicholson (Parson)	300.00	500.00
386 Nicholls Nicol	500.00	800.00
387 Hugh Nicol	300.00	500.00
388 Hugh Nicol w J.Reilly	350.00	600.00
389 Frederick Nyce	300.00	500.00
390 Doc Oberlander	300.00	500.00
391 Jack O'Brien	300.00	500.00
392 William O'Brien	300.00	500.00
393 William O'Brien w/J.Irwin	350.00	600.00
394 Darby O'Brien	300.00	500.00
395 John O'Brien	300.00	500.00
396 P.J. O'Connell	300.00	500.00
397 John O'Connor	300.00	500.00
398 Hank O'Day	500.00	800.00
399 O'Day	300.00	500.00
400 James O'Neil Stl-Chi	300.00	500.00
401 James O'Neil Browns Champs	500.00	800.00
402 Norris (Tip) O'Neill PCL		
403 Jim O'Rourke	1,800.00	3,000.00
404 Thomas O'Rourke	300.00	500.00
405 David Orr SPOT	900.00	1,500.00
406 David Orr	300.00	500.00
407 Parsons	300.00	500.00
408 Owen Patton	300.00	500.00
409 James Peeples	300.00	500.00
410 James Peeples w H.Henderson	350.00	600.00
411 Hip Perrier PCL		
412 Patrick Pettee	300.00	500.00
413 Patrick Pettee w B.Lowe	350.00	600.00
414 Dandelion Pfeffer	300.00	500.00
415 Dick Phelan	300.00	500.00
416 William Phillips	300.00	500.00
417 John Pickett	300.00	500.00
418 George Pinkney	300.00	500.00
419 Thomas Poorman	300.00	500.00
420 Henry Porter	300.00	500.00
421 James Powell	300.00	500.00
422 Tom Powers PCL		
423 Bill (Blondie) Purcell	300.00	500.00
424 Thomas Quinn	300.00	500.00
425 Joseph Quinn	300.00	500.00
426 Old Hoss Radbourne Portrait	2,500.00	4,000.00
427 Old Hoss Radbourne Non-Portrait	2,500.00	4,000.00
428 Shorty Radford	300.00	500.00
429 Tom Ramsey	300.00	500.00
430 Rehse	300.00	500.00
431 Long John Reilly	300.00	500.00
432 Charles (Princeton) Reilly	300.00	500.00
433 Charles Reynolds	300.00	500.00
434 Hardie Richardson	300.00	500.00
435 Danny Richardson	300.00	500.00
436 Charles Ripslager SPOT	900.00	1,500.00
437 John Roach	300.00	500.00
438 Wilbert (Uncle Robbie) Robinson	1,500.00	2,500.00
439 M.C. Robinson	300.00	500.00
440 Yank Robinson Stl	300.00	500.00
441 Yank Robinson Browns Champs	500.00	800.00
442 George Rooks	350.00	600.00
443 James (Chief) Roseman SPOT	900.00	1,500.00
444 Davis Rowe MGR	300.00	500.00
445 Jack Rowe	300.00	500.00
446 Amos Rusie Indianapolis	3,500.00	6,000.00
447 Amos Rusie New York	3,500.00	6,000.00
448 James Ryan	500.00	800.00
449 Henry Sage	300.00	500.00
450 Henry Sage w W.Van Dyke	350.00	600.00
451 Sanders	300.00	500.00
452 Al (Ben) Sanders	300.00	500.00
453 Frank Scheibeck	300.00	500.00
454 Albert Schellhase	300.00	500.00
455 William Schenkle	300.00	500.00
456 Bill Schildknecht	300.00	500.00
457 Gus (Pink Whiskers) Schmelz MGR	300.00	500.00
458 Lewis (Jumbo) Schoeneck	350.00	600.00
459 Pop Schriver	300.00	500.00
460 John Seery	300.00	500.00
461 William Serad	300.00	500.00
462 Edward Seward	300.00	500.00
463 George (Orator) Shafer	300.00	500.00
464 Frank Shafer	300.00	500.00
465 Daniel Shannon	300.00	500.00
466 William Sharsig	350.00	600.00
467 Samuel Shaw	300.00	500.00
468 John Shaw	300.00	500.00
469 William Shindle	300.00	500.00
470 George Shock	300.00	500.00
471 Otto Shomberg	300.00	500.00
472 Lev Shrev	300.00	500.00
473 Ed (Baldy) Silch	300.00	500.00
474 Michael Slattery	300.00	500.00
475 Sam (Sky Rocket) Smith	300.00	500.00
476 John (Phenomenal) Smith Portrait	1,500.00	2,500.00
477 John (Phenomenal) Smith Non-Portrait	300.00	500.00
478 Elmer Smith	300.00	500.00
479 Fred (Sam) Smith	300.00	500.00
480 George (Germany) Smith	300.00	500.00
481 Pop Smith	300.00	500.00
482 Nick Smith	300.00	500.00
483 P.T. Somers	300.00	500.00
484 Joe Sommer	300.00	500.00
485 Pete Sommers	300.00	500.00
486 William Sowders	300.00	500.00
487 John Sowders	300.00	500.00
488 Charles Sprague	350.00	600.00
489 Edward Sproat	300.00	500.00
490 Harry Staley	300.00	500.00
491 Daniel Stearns	300.00	500.00
492 Billy (Cannonball) Stemmyer	300.00	500.00
493 B.F. Stephens	300.00	500.00
494 John C. Sterling	300.00	500.00
495 Leonard Stockwell PCL		
496 Harry Stovey	600.00	1,000.00
497 C. Scott Stratton	300.00	500.00
498 Joseph Straus	300.00	500.00
499 John (Cub) Stricker	300.00	500.00
500 Marty Sullivan	300.00	500.00
501 Michael Sullivan	300.00	500.00
502 Billy Sunday	900.00	1,500.00
503 Sy Sutcliffe	300.00	500.00
504 Ezra Sutton	300.00	500.00
505 Ed Cyrus Swartwood	300.00	500.00
506 Parke Swartzel	300.00	500.00
507 Peter Sweeney	300.00	500.00
508 Louis Sylvester PCL		
509 Ed (Dimples) Tate	300.00	500.00
510 Patsy Tebeau	500.00	800.00
511 John Tener	350.00	600.00
512 Bill (Adonis) Terry	300.00	500.00
513 Big Sam Thompson	1,500.00	2,500.00
514 Silent Mike Tiernan	350.00	600.00
515 Ledell Titcomb	300.00	500.00
516 Phillip Tomney	300.00	500.00
517 Stephen Toole	300.00	500.00
518 George Townsend	300.00	500.00
519 William Traffley	300.00	500.00
520 George Treadway	300.00	500.00
521 Samuel Trott	300.00	500.00
522 Samuel Trott w T.Burns	350.00	600.00
523 Tom (Foghorn) Tucker	300.00	500.00
524 William Tuckerman	300.00	500.00
525 George Turner	300.00	500.00
526 Lawrence Twitchell	300.00	500.00
527 James Tyng	300.00	500.00
528 William Van Dyke	300.00	500.00
529 George (Rip) Van Haltren	300.00	500.00
530 Farmer Harry Vaughn	300.00	500.00
531 Peek-a-Boo Veach	500.00	800.00
532 Veach PCL		
533 Leon Viau	300.00	500.00
534 William Vinton	300.00	500.00
535 Joseph Visner	300.00	500.00
536 Christian Von Der Ahe OWNER	500.00	800.00
537 Joseph Walsh	300.00	500.00
538 John M. Ward	1,800.00	3,000.00
539 E.H. Warner	500.00	800.00
540 William Watkins MGR	350.00	600.00
541 Farmer Bill Weaver	300.00	500.00
542 Charles Weber	300.00	500.00
543 George (Stump) Weidman	300.00	500.00
544 William Weidner	300.00	500.00
545 Curtis Welch Browns Champ	500.00	800.00
546 Curtis Welch A's	350.00	600.00
547 Curtis Welch w B.Gleason	500.00	800.00
548 Smilin' Mickey Welch	1,800.00	3,000.00
549 Jake Wells	300.00	500.00
550 Frank Wells	350.00	600.00
551 Joseph Werrick	300.00	500.00
552 Milton (Buck) West	300.00	500.00
553 Gus (Cannonball) Weyhing	300.00	500.00
554 John Weyhing	300.00	500.00
555 Bobby Wheelock	300.00	500.00
556 Whitacre	300.00	500.00
557 Pat Whitaker	300.00	500.00
558 Deacon White	500.00	800.00
559 William White	300.00	500.00
560 Jim (Grasshopper) Whitney	300.00	500.00
561 Arthur Whitney	300.00	500.00
562 G. Whitney	300.00	500.00
563 James Williams MGR	350.00	600.00
564 Ned Williamson	500.00	800.00
565 Williamson and Mascot	350.00	600.00
566 C.H. Willis	300.00	500.00
567 Walt Wilmot	300.00	500.00
568 George Winkleman Hartford	600.00	1,000.00
569 Samuel Wise	300.00	500.00
570 William (Chicken) Wolf	300.00	500.00
571 George (Dandy) Wood	300.00	500.00
572 Peter Wood	300.00	500.00
573 Harry Wright MGR	5,000.00	8,000.00
574 Charles (Chief) Zimmer	300.00	500.00
575 Frank Zinn	300.00	500.00
576 John Barnes (Barns) MG	500.00	800.00

1887-89 Old Judge Cabinets N173

These cabinets measuure approximately 4 1/2" by 6". These feature the same poses as on the N172 Old Judge Set. As a note we are listing these cabinets by player's name and not by poses. This list is in alphabetical order and all additions to the checklist are appreciated.

COMPLETE SET

1949 Olmes Studios

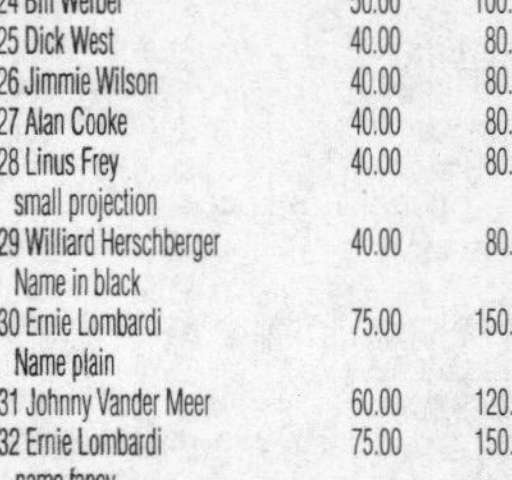

This set measures 3 1/2" by 5 1/2" and features Philadelphia players only. Seven poses of Ferris Fain exist. The Olmes Studio identification is printed on the back of the postcard. There have been several additions to this set in recent years so any further additions are appreciated.

COMPLETE SET	400.00	800.00
1 Lou Brissie	25.00	50.00
2 Sam Chapman	25.00	50.00
3 Joe Coleman	25.00	50.00
4 Ferris Fain	40.00	80.00
5 Frank Fanovich	25.00	50.00
6 Dick Fowler	25.00	50.00
7 Bob Hooper	25.00	50.00
8 Skeeter Kell	25.00	50.00
9 Paul Lehner	25.00	50.00
10 Lou Limmer	25.00	50.00
11 Barney McCoskey	25.00	50.00
12 Robin Roberts	50.00	100.00
13 Carl Scheib	25.00	50.00
14 Joe Tipton	25.00	50.00
15 Gus Zernial	25.00	50.00

1979 Open Pantry

This set is an unnumbered, 12-card issue featuring players from Milwaukee area professional sports teams with five Brewers baseball (1-5), five Bucks basketball (6-10), and two Packers football (11-12). Cards are black and white with red trim and measure approximately 5" by 6". Cards were sponsored by Open Pantry, Lake to Lake, and MACC (Milwaukee Athletes against Childhood Cancer). The cards are unnumbered and hence are listed and numbered below alphabetically within sport.

COMPLETE SET (12)	12.50	25.00
1 Jerry Augustine	1.00	2.00
2 Sal Bando	1.50	3.00
3 Cecil Cooper	1.50	3.00
4 Larry Hisle	1.25	2.50
5 Lary Sorensen	1.00	2.00

1939 Orcajo Photo Art PC786

The postcards in this set measures 3 1/2" by 5 1/2" and comes in three styles. The first contains an Orcajo Photo Art back. Type 2 is marked "Courtesy of Val Decker Packing Co., Piquality Brand Meats" on the front. Type 3 is marked "Metropolitan Clothing Co" on the front. The cards are listed in the checklist below by type. The set is broken down this way: Type 1 are cards 1-26; Type 2 are 27-31 and Type 3 are cards 32-33. The set was issued in 1939 and features a card of Joe DiMaggio, the only apparent non-Cincinnati player. The cards are sepia in color and feature white borders.

COMPLETE SET (33)	1,750.00	3,500.00
1 Wally Berger	50.00	100.00
2 Nino Bongiovanni	40.00	80.00
3 Frenchy Bordagray	40.00	80.00
4 Harry Craft	50.00	100.00
5 Ray Davis	40.00	80.00
6 Paul Derringer	50.00	100.00
7 Joe DiMaggio	400.00	800.00
8 Linus Frey	40.00	80.00
9 Lee Gamble	40.00	80.00
10 Ival Goodman	40.00	80.00
11 Hank Gowdy CO	40.00	80.00
12 Lee Grissom	40.00	80.00
13 Williard Herschberger Name in White	50.00	100.00
14 Eddie Joost	50.00	100.00
15 Frank McCormick	50.00	100.00
16 Bill McKecknie MG	75.00	150.00
17 Billy Meyers	40.00	80.00
18 Whitey Moore	40.00	80.00
19 Lew Riggs	40.00	80.00
20 Les Scarsella	40.00	80.00
21 Milburn Shoffner	40.00	80.00
22 Junior Thompson	40.00	80.00
23 Bucky Walters	60.00	120.00
24 Bill Werber	50.00	100.00
25 Dick West	40.00	80.00
26 Jimmie Wilson	40.00	80.00
27 Alan Cooke	40.00	80.00
28 Linus Frey small projection	40.00	80.00
29 Williard Herschberger Name in black	40.00	80.00
30 Ernie Lombardi Name plain	75.00	150.00
31 Johnny Vander Meer	60.00	120.00
32 Ernie Lombardi name fancy	75.00	150.00
33 Johnny Vander Meer	60.00	120.00

1894 Orioles Alpha

These cards which measure 3 7/8" by 2 3/8" featured players from the great Baltimore Oriole teams of the 1890's. This set has the players photographed in black tie regalia. The back of each card credits the Alpha Photo Engraving Company of Baltimore, Maryland.

COMPLETE SET (14)	6,000.00	12,000.00
1 Frank Bonner	10,000.00	20,000.00
2 Walter Brodie	10,000.00	20,000.00
3 Dan Brouthers	20,000.00	40,000.00
4 Charles Esper	10,000.00	20,000.00
5 Kid Gleason	12,500.00	25,000.00
6 Ned Hanlon MG	15,000.00	30,000.00
7 William Hawke	10,000.00	20,000.00
8 George Hemmings	10,000.00	20,000.00
9 Hugh Jennings	20,000.00	40,000.00
10 Joe Kelley	20,000.00	40,000.00
11 John McGraw	25,000.00	50,000.00
12 John McMahon	10,000.00	20,000.00
13 Henry Reitz	10,000.00	20,000.00
14 Wilbert Robinson	20,000.00	40,000.00

1954 Orioles Esskay

The cards in this 36-card set measure 2 1/4" by 3 1/2". The 1954 Esskay Meats set contains color, unnumbered cards featuring Baltimore Orioles only. The cards were issued in panels of two on boxes of Esskay hot dogs; consequently, many have grease stains on the cards and are quite difficult to obtain in mint condition. The 1954 Esskay set can be distinguished from the 1955 Esskay set supposedly by the white or off-white (the 1955 set) backs of the cards. The backs of the 1954 cards are also supposedly "waxed" to a greater degree than the 1955 cards. The catalog designation is F181-1. Since the cards are unnumbered, they are ordered below in alphabetical order for convenience. These cards were issued in conjunction with the "Bobo Newsome" TV Show. In addition, 8 by 10 photos of Bobo Newsome pitching Esskay photos are known to exist. It is considered a photo premium for this product

COMPLETE SET (36)	10,000.00	20,000.00
1 Cal Abrams	300.00	600.00
2 Neil Berry	300.00	600.00
3 Michael Blyzka	300.00	600.00
4 Harry Brecheen	400.00	800.00
5 Gil Coan	300.00	600.00
6 Joe Coleman	300.00	600.00
7 Clint Courtney	400.00	800.00
8 Charles E. Diering	300.00	600.00
9 Jimmie Dykes	400.00	800.00
10 Frank Fanovich	300.00	600.00
11 Howard Fox	300.00	600.00
12 Jim Fridley	300.00	600.00
13 Chico Garcia	300.00	600.00
14 Jehosie Heard	300.00	600.00
15 Darrell Johnson	400.00	800.00
16 Robert D. Kennedy	400.00	800.00
17 Dick Kokos	300.00	600.00
18 Dave Koslo	300.00	600.00
19 Lou Kretlow	300.00	600.00
20 Dick Kryhoski	300.00	600.00
21 Bob Kuzava	300.00	600.00

22 Don Larsen	600.00	1,200.00
23 Don Lenhardt	300.00	600.00
24 Dick Littlefield	300.00	600.00
25 Sam Mele	300.00	600.00
26 Les Moss	300.00	600.00
27 Ray L. Murray	300.00	600.00
28 Bobo Newsom	400.00	800.00
29 Tom Oliver	300.00	600.00
30 Duane Pillette	300.00	600.00
31 Francis M. Skaff	300.00	600.00
32 Marlin Stuart	300.00	600.00
33 Bob Turley	600.00	1,200.00
34 Eddie Waitkus	300.00	600.00
35 Vic Wertz	400.00	800.00
36 Robert G. Young	300.00	600.00
NNO Bobo Newsom Photo	500.00	1,000.00

1954 Orioles Photos

These blank-backed black and white photos featured members of the 1954 Baltimore Orioles, in their first year in Baltimore. This listing we are running was found as a set, however it is possible that these photos were issued throughout the 1954 season. Since these are unnumbered, we have sequenced them in alphabetical order.

COMPLETE SET	250.00	500.00
1 Cal Abrams	10.00	20.00
2 Neil Berry	10.00	20.00
3 Vern Bickford	10.00	20.00
4 Gil Coan	10.00	20.00
5 Joe Coleman	10.00	20.00
6 Chuck Diering	10.00	20.00
7 Jim Dyck	10.00	20.00
8 Howie Fox	10.00	20.00
9 Jim Fridley	10.00	20.00
10 Jehosie Heard	10.00	20.00
11 Billy Hunter	10.00	20.00
12 Darrell Johnson	10.00	20.00
13 Dick Kokos	10.00	20.00
14 Lou Kretlow	10.00	20.00
15 Dick Kryhoski	10.00	20.00
16 Don Larsen	20.00	40.00
17 Don Lenhardt	10.00	20.00
18 Dick Littlefield	10.00	20.00
19 Sam Mele	10.00	20.00
20 Les Moss	10.00	20.00
21 Duane Pillette	10.00	20.00
22 Vern Stephens	12.50	25.00
23 Marlin Stuart	10.00	20.00
24 Bob Turley	20.00	40.00
25 Vic Wertz	12.50	25.00
26 Bob Young	10.00	20.00

1954-55 Orioles Postcards

This set features glossy black-and-white portraits of the Baltimore Orioles with white borders. The backs carry a postcard format. The cards are unnumbered and checklisted below in alphabetical order.

COMPLETE SET	1,500.00	3,000.00
1 Cal Abrams	40.00	80.00
2 Bob Alexander	40.00	80.00
3 Mike Blyzka	40.00	80.00
4 Jim Brideweser	40.00	80.00
5 Hal Brown	40.00	80.00
6 Harry Byrd	40.00	80.00
7 Bob Chakales	40.00	80.00
8 Wayne Causey	40.00	80.00
9 Gil Coan	40.00	80.00
10 Joe Coleman	40.00	80.00
11 Clint Courtney	40.00	80.00
12 Billy Cox	50.00	100.00
13 Chuck Diering	40.00	80.00
14 Harry Dorish	40.00	80.00
15 Jim Dyck	40.00	80.00
16 Jimmy Dykes	50.00	100.00
17 Howie Fox	40.00	80.00
18 Jim Fridley	40.00	80.00
19 Chico Garcia	40.00	80.00
20 Ted Gray	40.00	80.00
21 Bob Hale	40.00	80.00
22 Bill Hunter	50.00	100.00
23 Don Johnson	40.00	80.00
24 Bob Kennedy	40.00	80.00
25 Lou Kretlow	40.00	80.00
26 Dick Kryhoski	40.00	80.00
27 Bob Kuzava	40.00	80.00
28 Don Larsen	60.00	120.00
29 Don Leppert	40.00	80.00
30 Ed Lopat	50.00	100.00
31 Fred Marsh	40.00	80.00
32 Jim McDonald	40.00	80.00
33 Sam Mele	40.00	80.00
34 Willie Miranda	40.00	80.00
35 Les Moss	40.00	80.00
36 Ray Murray	40.00	80.00
37 Bob Nelson	40.00	80.00
38 Billy O'Dell	40.00	80.00
39 Dave Philley	40.00	80.00
40 Erv Palica	40.00	80.00
41 Duane Pillette	40.00	80.00
42 Dave Pope	40.00	80.00
43 Paul Richards	50.00	100.00
44 Saul Rogovin	40.00	80.00
45 Art Schallock	40.00	80.00
46 Frank Skaff	40.00	80.00
47 Hal Smith	40.00	80.00
48 Vern Stephens	50.00	100.00
49 Marlin Stuart	40.00	80.00
50 Gus Triandos	50.00	100.00
51 Bob Turley/(Portrait)	50.00	100.00
52 Bob Turley/(Throwing)	50.00	100.00
53 Eddie Waitkus	50.00	100.00
54 Wally Westlake	40.00	80.00
55 Bill Wright	40.00	80.00
56 Gene Woodling	50.00	100.00
57 Bobby Young	40.00	80.00
58 George Zuverink	40.00	80.00

1954 Orioles Zip Large

Little is known about these cards, which were issued over a two-year period. Believed to be called Zip Cards. These cards measure 2 3/4" by 3 5/8" and a total of twenty-five total cards are known to be issued between 1954 and 1955. The biggest difference between the large and small zip cards is in the larger photos, the photos are basically full bordered and take up a great deal of the card while in the small cards, the player's photo are in a circle. All the cards have a year and card number along with the zip cards name on the bottom.

COMPLETE SET (4)	400.00	800.00
1 Billy O'Dell	100.00	200.00
2 Joe Durham	100.00	200.00
3 Eddie Waitkus	100.00	200.00
4 Chuck Diering	100.00	200.00

1954 Orioles Zip Small

These cards, measure 2" and 2 5/8" and are significantly smaller than their larger counterparts

1 Marlin Stuart	100.00	200.00
2 Chico Garcia	100.00	200.00
3 Jim Fridley	100.00	200.00
4 Jimmy Dykes MG	100.00	200.00
5 Bob Chakales	100.00	200.00
6 Jim Bridewesser	100.00	200.00
7 Tom Oliver CO	100.00	200.00
8 Frank Skaff CO	100.00	200.00

1955 Orioles Esskay

The cards in this 27-card set measure 2 1/4" by 3 1/2". The 1955 Esskay Meats set was issued in panels of two on boxes of Esskay hot dogs. This set of full color, blank back, unnumbered cards features Baltimore Orioles only. Many of the players in the 1954 Esskay set were also issued in this set. The catalog designation is F181-2. Since the cards are unnumbered, they are ordered below in alphabetical order for convenience. The 1955 set is supposedly somewhat more difficult to find than the 1954 set.

COMPLETE SET (27)	7,500.00	15,000.00
1 Cal Abrams	300.00	600.00
2 Robert Alexander	300.00	600.00
3 Harry Brecheen	400.00	800.00
4 Harry Byrd	300.00	600.00
5 Gil Coan	300.00	600.00
6 Joe Coleman	300.00	600.00
7 William Cox	400.00	800.00
8 Charles E. Diering	300.00	600.00
9 Walter Evers	400.00	800.00
10 Don Johnson	300.00	600.00
11 Robert D. Kennedy	400.00	800.00
12 Lou Kretlow	300.00	600.00
13 Bob Kuzava	300.00	600.00
14 Fred Marsh	300.00	600.00
15 Charles Maxwell	400.00	800.00
16 Jim McDonald	300.00	600.00
17 Bill Miller	300.00	600.00
18 Willie Miranda	400.00	800.00
19 Raymond L. Moore	300.00	600.00
20 Les Moss	300.00	600.00
21 Bobo Newsom	400.00	800.00
22 Duane Pillette	300.00	600.00
23 Harold W. Smith	300.00	600.00
24 Gus Triandos	400.00	800.00
25 Eddie Waitkus	300.00	600.00
26 Gene Woodling	500.00	1,000.00
27 Robert G. Young	300.00	600.00

1955 Orioles Zip Large

For the second year, the company "zip cards" issued a few cards of the fledgling Baltimore Orioles. These cards, just as the 1954 cards measure 2 3/4" by 3 5/8". Any further information about these cards as well as additions to our checklists is very appreciated.

COMPLETE SET (5)	500.00	1,000.00
1 Les Moss	100.00	200.00
2 Don Leppert	100.00	200.00
3 Bobby Young	100.00	200.00
4 Hoot Evers	100.00	200.00
5 Bob Kennedy	100.00	200.00

1955 Orioles Zip Small

COMPLETE SET (8)	750.00	1,500.00
1 Wayne Causey	100.00	200.00
2 Bob Hale	100.00	200.00
3 Dave Philley	100.00	200.00
4 Tom Gastall	100.00	200.00
5 Jim Dyck	100.00	200.00
6 Lum Harris	100.00	200.00
7 Art Schallock	100.00	200.00
8 Bob Nelson	100.00	200.00

1956 Orioles Postcards

This 38-card set features glossy black-and-white portraits of the Baltimore Orioles in white borders and printed on a postcard format. Cards 1-28 were blank in the bottom margins for autographs. Card 29-37 had the player's name and nickname printed on the front. There were two cards of different players numbered 20. Please note that there is some duplications in the Orioles Postcards lists and years. We will continue to work on further clarifying each set and year.

COMPLETE SET (38)	750.00	1,500.00
1 George Zuverink	30.00	60.00
2 Wayne Causey	30.00	60.00
3 Bob Nelson	30.00	60.00
4 Jim Pyburn	30.00	60.00
5 Willie Miranda	30.00	60.00
6 Jim Dyck	30.00	60.00
7 Dave Philley	30.00	60.00
8 Erv Palica	30.00	60.00
9 Gus Triandos	40.00	80.00
10 Hal Smith	30.00	60.00
11 Dave Pope	30.00	60.00
12 Tom Gastall	30.00	60.00
13 Jim Wilson	30.00	60.00
14 Hal Brown	30.00	60.00
15 Harry Dorish	30.00	60.00
16 Ray Moore	30.00	60.00
17 Bob Hale	30.00	60.00
18 Tito Francona	30.00	60.00
19 Don Ferrarese	30.00	60.00
20 Bob Boyd	30.00	60.00
20 George Kell	60.00	120.00
21 Babe Birrer	30.00	60.00
22 Bill Wright	30.00	60.00
23 Billy Gardner	40.00	80.00
24 Paul Richards MG	40.00	80.00
25 Mel Held	30.00	60.00
26 Chuck Diering	30.00	60.00
27 Fred Marsh	30.00	60.00
28 Bobby Adams	30.00	60.00
29 Walter Evers	30.00	60.00
30 Robert Nieman	30.00	60.00
31 George Kell	60.00	120.00
32 Jose Fornieles	30.00	60.00
33 William Loes	40.00	80.00
34 John Schmitz	30.00	60.00
35 Clifford Johnson	30.00	60.00
36 Joseph Frazier	30.00	60.00
37 Richard Williams	40.00	80.00

1958 Orioles Jay Publishing

This 12-card set of the Baltimore Orioles measures approximately 5" by 7" and features black-and-white player photos in a white border. These cards were packaged 12 to a packet. The backs are blank. The cards are unnumbered and checklisted below in alphabetical order.

COMPLETE SET (12)	20.00	40.00
1 Bob Boyd	1.50	3.00
2 Jim Busby	1.50	3.00
3 Billy Gardner	1.50	3.00
4 Connie Johnson	1.50	3.00
5 Billy Loes	2.00	4.00
6 Willy Miranda	1.50	3.00
7 Bob Nieman	1.50	3.00
8 Bill O'Dell	1.50	3.00
9 Al Pilarcik	1.50	3.00
10 Paul Richards MG	2.50	5.00
11 Gus Triandos	2.50	5.00
12 George Zuverink	1.50	3.00

1959 Orioles Jay Publishing

This 12-card set of the Baltimore Orioles measures approximately 5" by 7" and features black-and-white player photos in a white border. These cards were packaged 12 to a packet. The backs are blank. The cards are unnumbered and checklisted below in alphabetical order.

COMPLETE SET (12)	25.00	50.00
1 Bob Boyd	1.50	3.00
2 Chico Carrasquel	1.50	3.00
3 Billy Gardner	1.50	3.00
4 Bob Nieman	1.50	3.00
5 Billy O'Dell	1.50	3.00
6 Milt Pappas	2.50	5.00
7 Brooks Robinson	7.50	15.00
8 Willie Tasby	1.50	3.00
9 Gus Triandos	1.50	3.00
10 Jerry Walker	1.50	3.00
11 James(Hoyt) Wilhelm	5.00	10.00
12 Gene Woodling	1.50	3.00

1960 Orioles Jay Publishing

This 12-card set of the Baltimore Orioles measures approximately 5" by 7" and features black-and-white player photos in a white border. These cards were packaged 12 to a packet and originally sold for 25 cents. The backs are blank. The cards are unnumbered and checklisted below in alphabetical order.

COMPLETE SET (12)	15.00	40.00
1 Jackie Brandt	1.00	2.50
2 Marv Breeding	1.00	2.50
3 Jack Fisher	1.00	2.50
4 Ron Hansen	1.00	2.50
5 Milt Pappas	1.25	3.00
6 Paul Richards MG	1.25	3.00
7 Brooks Robinson	5.00	12.00
8 Willie Tasby	1.00	2.50
9 Gus Triandos	1.00	2.50
10 Jerry Walker	1.00	2.50
11 Hoyt Wilhelm	3.00	8.00
12 Gene Woodling	1.25	3.00

1960 Orioles Postcards

This 12-card set of the Baltimore Orioles features black-and-white player portraits in white borders. The backs are blank. The cards are unnumbered and checklisted below in alphabetical order.

COMPLETE SET (12)	75.00	150.00
1 Jackie Brandt	8.00	20.00
2 Harry Brecheen	8.00	20.00
3 Marv Breeding	8.00	20.00
4 Chuck Estrada	8.00	20.00
5 Jack Fisher	8.00	20.00
6 Jim Gentil/(After Swing)	10.00	25.00
7 Gordon Jones/(Pitching)	8.00	20.00
8 Dave Philley	8.00	20.00
9 Willie Tasby	8.00	20.00
10 Gus Triandos	8.00	20.00
11 Jerry Walker	8.00	20.00
12 Gene Woodling	10.00	25.00

1961 Orioles Jay Publishing

This 12-card set of the Baltimore Orioles measures approximately 5" by 7". The fronts feature black-and-white posed player photos with the player's and team name printed below in the white border. These cards were packaged 12 in a packet. The backs are blank. The cards are unnumbered and checklisted below in alphabetical order.

COMPLETE SET (12)	8.00	20.00
1 Jackie Brandt	1.25	3.00
2 Chuck Estrada	1.25	3.00
3 Jack Fisher	1.25	3.00
4 Jim Gentile	1.50	4.00
5 Ron Hansen	1.25	3.00
6 Whitey Herzog		
7 Milt Pappas	1.50	4.00
8 Paul Richards MG	1.25	3.00
9 Brooks Robinson	4.00	10.00
10 Russ Snyder	1.25	3.00
11 Gus Triandos	1.25	3.00
12 Jerry Walker	1.25	3.00

1961 Orioles Postcards

This 22-card set features black-and-white portraits of the Baltimore Orioles with white borders and printed on a cream colored paper. The backs are blank. The cards are unnumbered and checklisted below in alphabetical order.

COMPLETE SET (22)	150.00	300.00
1 Jerry Adair	8.00	20.00
2 Jackie Brandt	8.00	20.00
3 Marv Breeding	8.00	20.00
4 Hal Brown	8.00	20.00
5 Jim Busby	8.00	20.00
6 Walt Dropo	8.00	20.00
7 Chuck Estrada	8.00	20.00
8 Jack Fisher	8.00	20.00
9 Hank Foiles	8.00	20.00
10 Jim Gentile	8.00	20.00
11 Ron Hansen	8.00	20.00
12 Whitey Herzog	8.00	20.00
13 Billy Hoeft	8.00	20.00
14 Milt Pappas	8.00	20.00
15 Dave Philley	8.00	20.00
16 Brooks Robinson	10.00	25.00
17 Russ Snyder	8.00	20.00
18 Gene Stephens	8.00	20.00
19 Wes Stock	8.00	20.00
20 Gus Triandos	8.00	20.00
21 Jerry Walker	8.00	20.00
22 Hoyt Wilhelm	8.00	20.00

1962 Orioles Jay Publishing

This 12-card set of the Baltimore Orioles measures approximately 5" by 7". The fronts feature black-and-white posed player photos with the player's and team name printed below in the white border. These cards were packaged 12 to a packet. The backs are blank. The cards are unnumbered and checklisted below in alphabetical order.

COMPLETE SET (12)	12.50	30.00
1 Jerry Adair	.75	2.00
2 Steve Barber	.75	2.00
3 Jackie Brandt	.75	2.00
4 Marv Breeding	.75	2.00
5 Hector Brown	.75	2.00
6 Chuck Estrada	.75	2.00
7 Jim Gentile	1.25	3.00
8 Ron Hansen	.75	2.00
9 Milt Pappas	1.00	2.50
10 Brooks Robinson	4.00	10.00
11 Earl Robinson	.75	2.00
12 Gus Triandos	.75	2.00

1962 Orioles Postcards

This 33-card set features black-and-white player portraits with white borders. The backs are blank. The cards are unnumbered and checklisted below in alphabetical order. Boog Powell appears in his Rookie Card season.

COMPLETE SET (33)	200.00	400.00
1 Jerry Adair	4.00	10.00
2 Steve Barber/(Portrait)	4.00	10.00
3 Steve Barber/(Ready to throw)	4.00	10.00
4 Jackie Brandt	4.00	10.00
5 Marv Breeding	4.00	10.00
6 Hal Brown	4.00	10.00
7 Chuck Estrada	4.00	10.00
8 Jack Fisher	4.00	10.00
9 Jim Gentile	6.00	15.00
10 Dick Hall	4.00	10.00
11 Ron Hansen	4.00	10.00
12 Whitey Herzog	6.00	15.00
13 Billy Hitchcock	6.00	15.00
14 Billy Hoeft	4.00	10.00
15 Hobie Landrith	4.00	10.00
16 Charlie Lau	4.00	10.00
17 Jim Lehew	4.00	10.00
18 Dave Nicholson	4.00	10.00
19 Milt Pappas	6.00	15.00
20 Boog Powell	10.00	25.00
21 Art Quirk	4.00	10.00
22 Robin Roberts	8.00	20.00
23 Brooks Robinson	10.00	25.00
24 Earl Robinson	4.00	10.00
25 Billy Short	4.00	10.00
26 Russ Snyder	4.00	10.00

27 Wes Stock	4.00	10.00
28 Johnny Temple	4.00	10.00
29 Marv Throneberry	5.00	12.00
30 Gus Triandos	4.00	10.00
31 Ozzie Virgil	4.00	10.00
32 Hoyt Wilhelm	8.00	20.00
33 Dick Williams	5.00	12.00

1963 Orioles Jay Publishing

This 12-card set of the Baltimore Orioles measures approximately 5" by 7". The fronts feature black-and-white posed player photos with the player's and team name printed below in the white border. These cards were packaged 12 to a packet. The backs are blank. The cards are unnumbered and checklisted below in alphabetical order.

COMPLETE SET (12)	15.00	40.00
1 Jerry Adair	.75	2.00
2 Luis Aparicio	2.50	6.00
3 Steve Barber	.75	2.00
4 Jackie Brandt	.75	2.00
5 Chuck Estrada	.75	2.00
6 Jim Gentile	1.25	3.00
7 Billy Hitchcock MG	.75	2.00
8 John Orsino	.75	2.00
9 Milt Pappas	1.25	3.00
10 Robin Roberts	2.50	6.00
11 Brooks Robinson	3.00	8.00
12 Wes Stock	.75	2.00

1963 Orioles Postcards

This 34-card set features black-and-white portraits of the Baltimore Orioles with white borders. The backs are blank. The cards are unnumbered and checklisted below in alphabetical order.

COMPLETE SET (34)	200.00	400.00
1 Jerry Adair	4.00	10.00
2 Luis Aparicio	8.00	20.00
3 Luke Appling	8.00	20.00
4 Steve Barber	6.00	15.00
5 Hank Bauer CO	6.00	15.00
6 Jack Brandt	4.00	10.00
7 Harry Brecheen CO	6.00	15.00
8 Dick Brown	4.00	10.00
9 Pete Burnside	4.00	10.00
10 Chuck Estrada	4.00	10.00
11 Joe Gaines	4.00	10.00
12 Jim Gentile	6.00	15.00
13 Dick Hall	4.00	10.00
14 Billy Hitchcock MG	6.00	15.00
15 Bob Johnson	4.00	10.00
16 Hobie Landrith	4.00	10.00
17 Charlie Lau	5.00	12.00
18 Mike McCormick	4.00	10.00
19 Dave McNally	8.00	20.00
20 John Miller	4.00	10.00
21 Stu Miller	4.00	10.00
22 Buster Narum	4.00	10.00
23 John Orsino/(Catching)	4.00	10.00
24 John Orsino	4.00	10.00
25 Milt Pappas	6.00	15.00
26 Boog Powell	8.00	20.00
27 Robin Roberts	8.00	20.00
28 Brooks Robinson	10.00	25.00
29 Bob Saverine	4.00	10.00
30 Al Smith	4.00	10.00
31 Russ Snyder	4.00	10.00
32 Wes Stock	4.00	10.00
33 Dean Stone	4.00	10.00
34 Fred Valentine	4.00	10.00

1964 Orioles Jay Publishing

This 12-card set of the Baltimore Orioles measures approximately 5" by 7". The fronts feature black-and-white posed player photos with the player's and team name printed below in the white border. These cards were packaged 12 to a packet. The backs are blank. The cards are unnumbered and checklisted below in alphabetical order.

COMPLETE SET (12)	15.00	40.00
1 Luis Aparicio	2.00	5.00
2 Steve Barber	1.25	3.00
3 Hank Bauer MG	1.50	4.00
4 Jackie Brandt	1.00	2.50
5 Chuck Estrada	1.00	2.50
6 Willie Kirkland	1.00	2.50
7 John Orsino	1.00	2.50
8 Milt Pappas	1.25	3.00
9 Boog Powell	2.00	5.00
10 Robin Roberts	2.00	5.00
11 Brooks Robinson	4.00	10.00
12 Norm Siebern	1.00	2.50

1964 Orioles Postcards

This 36-card set features black-and-white portraits of the Baltimore Orioles with white borders. The backs are blank. The cards are unnumbered and checklisted below in alphabetical order.

COMPLETE SET (36)	150.00	300.00
1 Jerry Adair	3.00	8.00
2 Luis Aparicio	6.00	15.00
3 Steve Barber/(Light ink autograph)	5.00	12.00
4 Steve Barber/(Dark ink autograph)	5.00	12.00
5 Hank Bauer MG	5.00	12.00
6 Frank Bertaina	3.00	8.00
7 Sam Bowens/(Closer head shot)	3.00	8.00
8 Sam Bowens	3.00	8.00
9 Jack Brandt	3.00	8.00
10 Harry Brecheen CO	5.00	12.00
11 Dick Brown	3.00	8.00
12 Wally Bunker	3.00	8.00
13 Chuck Estrada	3.00	8.00
14 Joe Gaines	3.00	8.00
15 Harvey Haddix	3.00	8.00
16 Dick Hall	3.00	8.00
17 Larry Haney	3.00	8.00
18 Billy Hunter CO	3.00	8.00
19 Lou Jackson	3.00	8.00
20 Bob Johnson	3.00	8.00
21 Willie Kirkland	3.00	8.00
22 Charley Lau	3.00	8.00
23 Mike McCormick	3.00	8.00
24 Dave McNally	5.00	12.00
25 Stu Miller	3.00	8.00
26 John Orsino	3.00	8.00
27 Milt Pappas	5.00	12.00
28 Boog Powell	6.00	15.00
29 Robin Roberts	6.00	15.00
30 Brooks Robinson	8.00	20.00
31 Earl Robinson	3.00	8.00
32 Bob Saverine	3.00	8.00
33 Norm Siebern	3.00	8.00
34 Russ Snyder	3.00	8.00
35 Wes Stock	3.00	8.00
36 Dave Vinyard	3.00	8.00

1965 Orioles Jay Publishing

This 12-card set of the Pittsburgh Pirates measures approximately 5" by 7". The fronts feature black-and-white posed player photos with the player's and team name printed below in the white border. These cards were packaged 12 to a packet. The backs are blank. The cards are unnumbered and checklisted below in alphabetical order.

COMPLETE SET (12)	12.50	30.00
1 Jerry Adair	.75	2.00
2 Luis Aparicio	1.50	4.00
3 Steve Barber	1.00	2.50
4 Hank Bauer MG	1.25	3.00
5 Sam Bowens	.75	2.00
6 Wally Bunker	.75	2.00
7 John Orsino	.75	2.00
8 Milt Pappas	1.00	2.50
9 Boog Powell	1.50	4.00
10 Brooks Robinson	2.50	6.00
11 Norm Siebern	.75	2.00
12 Dave Vineyard	.75	2.00

1965 Orioles Postcards

This 34-card set features black-and-white portraits of the Baltimore Orioles with white borders. The backs are blank. The cards are unnumbered and checklisted below in alphabetical order. Jim Palmer's postcard predates his Rookie Card.

COMPLETE SET (34)	150.00	300.00
1 Jerry Adair	3.00	8.00
2 Luis Aparicio	6.00	15.00
3 Steve Barber	5.00	12.00
4 Hank Bauer MG	5.00	12.00
5 Paul Blair	5.00	12.00
6 Curt Blefary	3.00	8.00
7 Sam Bowens	3.00	8.00
8 Jack Brandt	3.00	8.00
9 Harry Brecheen CO	4.00	10.00
10 Dick Brown	3.00	8.00
11 Wally Bunker	3.00	8.00
12 Sam Bowens	3.00	8.00
13 Dick Hall	3.00	8.00
14 Billy Hunter CO	4.00	10.00
15 Bob Johnson	3.00	8.00
16 Davey Johnson	6.00	15.00
17 Darold Knowles	3.00	8.00
18 Don Larsen	6.00	15.00
19 Charley Lau	3.00	8.00
20 Sherm Lollar CO	3.00	8.00
21 Dave McNally	6.00	15.00
22 John Miller	3.00	8.00
23 Stu Miller	3.00	8.00
24 John Orsino	3.00	8.00
25 Jim Palmer	12.50	30.00
26 Milt Pappas	5.00	12.00
27 Boog Powell	6.00	15.00
28 Robin Roberts	6.00	15.00
29 Brooks Robinson	10.00	25.00
30 Norm Siebern	3.00	8.00
31 Russ Snyder	3.00	8.00
32 Dave Vineyard	3.00	8.00
33 Carl Warwick	3.00	8.00
34 Gene Woodling CO	4.00	10.00

1966 Orioles Postcards

This 34-card set features black-and-white portraits of the Baltimore Orioles with white borders. The backs are blank. The cards are unnumbered and checklisted below in alphabetical order. Jim Palmer has a postcard in his Rookie Card year.

COMPLETE SET (34)	150.00	300.00
1 Luis Aparicio	6.00	15.00
2 Steve Barber	4.00	10.00
3 Frank Bertaina	3.00	8.00
4 Paul Blair	4.00	10.00
5 Curt Blefary	3.00	8.00
6 Sam Bowens	3.00	8.00
7 Gene Brabender	3.00	8.00
8 Harry Brecheen	3.00	8.00
9 Wally Bunker/(Looking forward)	3.00	8.00
10 Wally Bunker/(Looking to the side)	3.00	8.00
11 Camilo Carreon	3.00	8.00
12 Moe Drabowsky	3.00	8.00
13 Andy Etchebarren	3.00	8.00
14 Eddie Fisher	3.00	8.00
15 Dick Hall	3.00	8.00
16 Woodie Held	3.00	8.00
17 Billy Hunter	3.00	8.00
18 Bob Johnson	3.00	8.00
19 Davey Johnson	5.00	12.00
20 Charley Lau	3.00	8.00
21 Sherm Lollar/(Closer head photo)	3.00	8.00
22 Sherm Lollar	3.00	8.00
23 Dave McNally	4.00	10.00
24 John Miller	3.00	8.00
25 Stu Miller	3.00	8.00
26 Jim Palmer	6.00	15.00
27 Boog Powell	6.00	15.00
28 Brooks Robinson	8.00	20.00
29 Frank Robinson	8.00	20.00
30 Vic Roznovsky	3.00	8.00
31 Billy Short	3.00	8.00
32 Russ Snyder	3.00	8.00
33 Eddie Watt	3.00	8.00
34 Gene Woodling	3.00	8.00

1967-69 Orioles Postcards

This 107-card set features black-and-white portraits of the Baltimore Orioles with white borders. The backs are blank. Some of the cards carry facsimile autographs. The cards are unnumbered and checklisted below in alphabetical order.

COMPLETE SET (107)	300.00	600.00
1 Mike Adamson	2.00	5.00
2 Luis Aparicio	4.00	10.00
3 George Bamberger CO Larger head shot	2.00	5.00
4 George Bamberger CO	2.00	5.00
5 Steve Barber	2.00	5.00
6 Hank Bauer MG	3.00	8.00
7 Fred Beene	2.00	5.00
8 Mark Belanger	2.50	6.00
9 Mark Belanger Closer head shot	2.50	6.00
10 Mark Belanger Artist's rendition	2.50	6.00
11 Frank Bertaina	2.00	5.00
12 Frank Bertaina Lighter portrait	2.00	5.00
13 Paul Blair Lighter looking to left	2.50	6.00
14 Paul Blair Darker looking to left	2.50	6.00
15 Paul Blair Looking straight ahead	2.50	6.00
16 Curt Blefary	2.00	5.00
17 Sam Bowens	2.00	5.00
18 Gene Brabender	2.00	5.00
19 Harry Brecheen CO	2.00	5.00
20 Don Buford Looking straight ahead	2.00	5.00
21 Don Buford Dark closer head shot	2.00	5.00
22 Don Buford Lighter closer head shot	2.00	5.00
23 Don Buford Name in bold print	2.00	5.00
24 Wally Bunker Dark portrait	2.00	5.00
25 Wally Bunker Lighter prctrait	2.00	5.00
26 Terry Crowley	2.00	5.00
27 Mike Cuellar Light portrait	3.00	8.00
28 Mike Cuellar Dark portrait	3.00	8.00
29 Clay Dalrymple	2.00	5.00
30 Bill Dillman	2.00	5.00
31 Moe Drabowsky Looking to the left	2.00	5.00
32 Moe Drabowsky Looking straight ahead	2.00	5.00
33 Mike Epstein	2.00	5.00
34 Andy Etchebarren Looking to the left	2.00	5.00
35 Andy Etchebarren Cream colored paper	2.00	5.00
36 Andy Etchebarren Clearer looking to left	2.00	5.00
37 Andy Etchebarren Looking straight ahead	2.00	5.00
38 Chico Fernandez	2.00	5.00
39 Eddie Fisher	2.00	5.00
40 Bobby Floyd	2.00	5.00
41 Jim Frey CO	2.00	5.00
42 Dick Hall	2.00	5.00
43 Larry Haney	2.00	5.00
44 Larry Haney Larger portrait	2.00	5.00
45 Jim Hardin	2.00	5.00
46 Elrod Hendricks Looking straight ahead	2.00	5.00
47 Elrod Hendricks Looking slightly to the left	2.00	5.00
48 Elrod Hendricks Closer looking to the left photo	2.00	5.00
49 Vern Hoscheit CO	2.00	5.00
50 Bruce Howard	2.00	5.00
51 Billy Hunter CO Looking to the left	2.00	5.00
52 Bill Hunter CO Darker looking to left	2.00	5.00
53 Billy Hunter/(Autographed and looking straight ah	2.00	5.00
54 Bob Johnson	2.00	5.00
55 Dave Johnson Autographed artist's version	3.00	8.00
56 Davey Johnson	3.00	8.00
57 Dave Johnson Darker portrait	3.00	8.00
58 Charlie Lau	2.00	5.00
59 Dave Leonhard Autographed	2.00	5.00
60 Dave Leonhard Name is spelled as Leonard	2.00	5.00
61 Dave Leonhard Closer head view	2.00	5.00
62 Dave Leonhard Different cap	2.00	5.00
63 Sherm Lollar CO	2.00	5.00
64 Marcelino Lopez	2.00	5.00
65 Dave May	2.00	5.00
66 Dave May Closer head shot	2.00	5.00
67 Dave McNally Looking to left	3.00	8.00
68 Dave McNally Looking straight ahead	3.00	8.00
69 Stu Miller	2.00	5.00
70 John Morris	2.00	5.00
71 Curt Motton Light portrait	2.00	5.00
72 Curt Motton Darker portrait	2.00	5.00
73 Roger Nelson	2.00	5.00
74 John O'Donoghue	2.00	5.00
75 Jim Palmer Looking to the right	6.00	15.00
76 Jim Palmer Head turned straight	6.00	15.00
77 Jim Palmer Looking to the left	6.00	15.00
78 Tom Phoebus	2.00	5.00
79 Tom Phoebus Darker portrait	2.00	5.00
80 Tom Phoebus Lighter portrait	2.00	5.00
81 Boog Powell Light portrait	4.00	10.00
82 Boog Powell Larger head shot	4.00	10.00
83 Boog Powell Lighter portrait	4.00	10.00
84 Merv Rettenmund	2.00	5.00
85 Merv Rettenmund Darker portrait	2.00	5.00
86 Merv Rettenmund Lighter portrait	2.00	5.00
87 Pete Richert Not smiling	2.00	5.00
88 Pete Richert Smiling	2.00	5.00
89 Brooks Robinson	6.00	15.00
90 Brooks Robinson Darker autographed version	6.00	15.00
91 Brooks Robinson Lighter portrait	6.00	15.00
92 Brooks Robinson Shows mail cancellation	6.00	15.00
93 Brooks Robinson Farther away head shot	6.00	15.00
94 Frank Robinson	6.00	15.00
95 Vic Roznovsky	2.00	5.00
96 Chico Salmon	2.00	5.00
97 Ray Scarborough CO	2.00	5.00
98 Al Severinsen	2.00	5.00
99 Russ Snyder	2.00	5.00
100 George Staller CO	2.00	5.00
101 Fred Valentine	2.00	5.00
102 Eddie Watt	2.00	5.00
103 Ed Watt Autographed	2.00	5.00
104 Earl Weaver MG	4.00	10.00
105 Gene Woodling CO Looking straight ahead	2.00	5.00
106 Gene Woodling CO Autographed and darker	2.00	5.00
107 Gene Woodling CO Autographed and lighter	2.00	5.00

1968 Orioles Dexter Press/Coca Cola Postcards

This 12-card set features posed borderless color photos of the Baltimore Orioles printed on postcard-size cards. The backs carry the player's biography and a facsimile autograph with a Dexter press serial number.

COMPLETE SET (12)	40.00	80.00
1 Mark Belanger	2.50	6.00
2 Paul Blair	2.50	6.00
3 Curt Blefary	2.00	5.00
4 Don Buford	2.00	5.00
5 Moe Drabowsky	2.00	5.00
6 Andy Etchebarren	2.00	5.00
7 Dave Johnson	4.00	10.00

8 Dave McNally 3.00 8.00
9 Tom Phoebus 2.00 5.00
10 Boog Powell 4.00 10.00
11 Brooks Robinson 6.00 15.00
12 Frank Robinson 6.00 15.00

1969 Orioles Postcards Color

This three-card set features borderless color portraits of the Baltimore Orioles printed on postcard size cards. The backs are blank. The cards are unnumbered and checklisted below in alphabetical order.

COMPLETE SET (3) 10.00 25.00
1 Bob Grich 3.00 8.00
2 Dave Johnson 3.00 8.00
3 Brooks Robinson 6.00 15.00

1970 Orioles Black and White

This 15-piece set features blank-backed, white-bordered, 8" X 10" black-and-white photos. The player's name appears in black within the bottom border. A facsimile autograph is printed across the photo. The word "Tadder" is pasted into photos at lower right. Photos are unnumbered and checklisted below in alphabetical order.

COMPLETE SET (15) 20.00 50.00
1 Mark Belanger 2.00 5.00
2 Don Buford 1.25 3.00
3 Mike Cuellar 2.00 5.00
4 Clay Dalrymple 1.25 3.00
5 Andy Etchebarren 1.25 3.00
6 Dave Johnson 2.50 6.00
7 Dave McNally 2.00 5.00
8 Curt Motton 1.25 3.00
9 Jim Palmer 4.00 10.00
10 Boog Powell 2.50 6.00
11 Merv Rettenmund 1.25 3.00
12 Frank Robinson 4.00 10.00
13 Chico Salmon 1.25 3.00
14 Eddie Watt 1.25 3.00
15 Earl Weaver MG 2.50 6.00

1970 Orioles Matchbooks

These matchbooks are known to be issued by Universal Match and are known to be an 24 matchbook set. The front shows a portrait of the featured player in an team logo while the reverse has the Baltimore Oriole mascot. Since these are unnumbered, we have sequenced them in alphabetical order and any help in finishing this checklist is appreciated.

COMPLETE SET (24) 100.00 175.00
1 Mike Cuellar 3.00 8.00
2 Clay Dalrymple 3.00 8.00
3 Andy Etchebarren 3.00 8.00
4 Bobby Floyd 3.00 8.00
5 Dick Hall 3.00 8.00
6 Jim Hardin 3.00 8.00
7 Elrod Hendricks 3.00 8.00
8 Dave Leonhard 3.00 8.00
9 Dave McNally 3.00 8.00
10 Jim Palmer 6.00 15.00
11 Tom Phoebus 3.00 8.00
12 Boog Powell 10.00 25.00
13 Merv Rettenmund 3.00 8.00
14 Pete Richert 3.00 8.00
15 Brooks Robinson 20.00 50.00
16 Frank Robinson 15.00 40.00
17 Chico Salmon 3.00 8.00
18 Eddie Watt 3.00 8.00
19 Earl Weaver MG 3.00 8.00

1970 Orioles Postcards

This 32-card set features color portraits of the Baltimore Orioles with white borders and printed on postcard size cards. The backs are blank. The cards are unnumbered and checklisted below in alphabetical order. According to information published at the time, these cards could be ordered from the Orioles at 10 cents each, 12 cards for a dollar or $2.50 for the whole set.

COMPLETE SET (32) 75.00 150.00
1 George Bamberger CO 1.50 4.00
2 Mark Belanger 2.00 5.00
3 Paul Blair 2.50 6.00
4 Don Buford 1.50 4.00
5 Terry Crowley 1.50 4.00
6 Mike Cuellar 2.50 6.00
7 Clay Dalrymple 1.50 4.00
8 Moe Drabowsky 1.50 4.00
9 Andy Etchebarren 1.50 4.00
10 Jim Frey CO 1.50 4.00
11 Dick Hall 1.50 4.00
12 Jim Hardin 1.50 4.00
13 Elrod Hendricks/(No buttons showing) 1.50 4.00
14 Elrod Hendricks/(One button showing) 1.50 4.00
15 Billy Hunter CO 1.50 4.00
16 Dave Johnson 2.50 6.00
17 Dave Leonhard 1.50 4.00
18 Marcelino Lopez 1.50 4.00
19 Dave McNally 2.50 6.00
20 Dave McNally/(Darker portrait) 2.50 6.00
21 Curt Motton 1.50 4.00
22 Jim Palmer 5.00 12.00
23 Tom Phoebus 1.50 4.00
24 Boog Powell 3.00 8.00
25 Merv Rettenmund 1.50 4.00
26 Pete Richert 1.50 4.00
27 Brooks Robinson 5.00 12.00
28 Frank Robinson 5.00 12.00
29 Chico Salmon 1.50 4.00
30 George Staller CO 1.50 4.00
31 Eddie Watt 1.50 4.00
32 Earl Weaver MG 3.00 8.00

1971 Orioles Aldana

This crude 12 card blank backed cards are credited to artist Carl Aldana. A drawing of the player along with his last name is on the front. There are two different Brooks Robinson cards in this set.

COMPLETE SET (12) 75.00 150.00
1 Mark Belanger 1.00 2.50
2 Paul Blair .75 2.00
3 Mike Cuellar 1.25 3.00
4 Ellie Hendricks .75 2.00
5 Dave Johnson 2.00 5.00
6 Dave McNally 1.25 3.00
7 Jim Palmer 6.00 15.00
8 Boog Powell 2.00 5.00
9 Brooks Robinson 15.00 40.00
Uniform number visible on back
10 Brooks Robinson 15.00 40.00
Facing front
11 Frank Robinson 12.50 30.00
12 Earl Weaver MG 3.00 8.00

1971 Orioles Champions

Subtitled "Pictures of Champions," this 16-card set measures 2 1/8" by 2 3/4". Since the card stock is orange, the close-up photos on the fronts are orange-tinted and have orange borders. The orange backs have the jersey number, player's name and the set subtitle. The cards are unnumbered and checklisted below in alphabetical order.

COMPLETE SET (16) 75.00 150.00
1 Mark Belanger 4.00 10.00
2 Don Buford 2.50 6.00
3 Mike Cuellar 4.00 10.00
4 Andy Etchebarren 2.50 6.00
5 Dick Hall 2.50 6.00
6 Ellie Hendricks 2.50 6.00
7 Dave Johnson 5.00 12.00
8 Dave Leonhard 2.50 6.00
9 Dave May 2.50 6.00
10 Dave McNally 4.00 10.00
11 Jim Palmer 8.00 20.00
12 Pete Richert 2.50 6.00
13 Brooks Robinson 15.00 40.00
14 Frank Robinson 12.50 30.00
15 Eddie Watt 2.50 6.00
16 Earl Weaver MG 5.00 12.00

1971 Orioles Postcards

This 30-card set features color portraits of the Baltimore Orioles with white borders and printed on postcard size cards. The backs are blank. The cards are unnumbered and checklisted below in alphabetical order.

COMPLETE SET (30) 75.00 150.00
1 George Bamberger CO 1.50 4.00
2 Mark Belanger 2.00 5.00
3 Paul Blair 2.50 6.00
4 Don Buford 1.50 4.00
5 Mike Cuellar 2.50 6.00
6 Clay Dalrymple 1.50 4.00
7 Jerry DaVanon 1.50 4.00
8 Pat Dobson 2.00 5.00
9 Tom Dukes 1.50 4.00
10 Andy Etchebarren 1.50 4.00
11 Jim Frey CO 1.50 4.00
12 Dick Hall 1.50 4.00
13 Jim Hardin 1.50 4.00
14 Elrod Hendricks 1.50 4.00
15 Billy Hunter CO 1.50 4.00
16 Grant Jackson 1.50 4.00
17 Dave Johnson 2.50 6.00
18 Dave McNally 2.50 6.00
19 Curt Motton 1.50 4.00
20 Jim Palmer 4.00 10.00
21 Boog Powell 3.00 8.00
22 Merv Rettenmund 1.50 4.00
23 Pete Richert 1.50 4.00
24 Brooks Robinson 4.00 10.00
25 Frank Robinson 4.00 10.00
26 Chico Salmon 1.50 4.00
27 Tom Shopay 1.50 4.00
28 George Staller CO 1.50 4.00
29 Ed Watt 1.50 4.00
30 Earl Weaver MG 3.00 8.00

1972 Orioles DMV

The 1972 Baltimore Orioles Police/Safety set was issued on a thin unperforated cardboard sheet measuring 12 1/2" by 8". When the players are cut into individual cards, they measure approximately 2 1/2" by 4". The color of the sheet is pale yellow, and consequently the black and white borderless player photos have a similar cast. The player's name, position, and team name appear below the pictures. The backs have different safety messages sponsored by the Office of Traffic Safety, D.C. Department of Motor Vehicles. The cards are unnumbered and checklisted below in alphabetical order.

COMPLETE SET (10) 15.00 40.00
1 Mark Belanger 1.50 4.00
2 Paul Blair 1.25 3.00
3 Don Buford 1.25 3.00
4 Mike Cuellar 1.25 3.00
5 Dave Johnson 1.50 4.00
6 Dave McNally 1.50 4.00
7 Boog Powell 2.00 5.00
8 Brooks Robinson 4.00 10.00
9 Merv Rettenmund .75 2.00
10 Earl Weaver MG 2.00 5.00

1972 Orioles Postcards

This 33-card set features color portraits of the Baltimore Orioles with white borders and printed on postcard size cards. The backs are blank. The cards are unnumbered and checklisted below in alphabetical order.

COMPLETE SET (33) 75.00 150.00
1 Doyle Alexander 1.50 4.00
2 George Bamberger CO 1.50 4.00
3 Don Baylor 2.50 6.00
4 Mark Belanger 2.00 5.00
5 Paul Blair 2.50 6.00
6 Dave Boswell 1.50 4.00
7 Don Buford 1.50 4.00
8 Richie Coggins 1.50 4.00
9 Terry Crowley 1.50 4.00
10 Mike Cuellar 2.50 6.00
11 Pat Dobson 1.50 4.00
12 Andy Etchebarren 1.50 4.00
13 Jim Frey CO 1.50 4.00
14 Bobby Grich 2.50 6.00
15 Roric Harrison 1.50 4.00
16 Elrod Hendricks 1.50 4.00
17 Billy Hunter CO 1.50 4.00
18 Grant Jackson 1.50 4.00
19 Dave Johnson 2.50 6.00
20 Dave Leonhard 1.50 4.00
21 Dave McNally 2.50 6.00
22 Johnny Oates 2.00 5.00
23 Jim Palmer 5.00 12.00
24 Boog Powell 3.00 8.00
25 John Boog Powell 3.00 8.00
26 Merv Rettenmund 1.50 4.00
27 Brooks Robinson 5.00 12.00
28 Chico Salmon 1.50 4.00
29 Mickey Scott 1.50 4.00
30 Tom Shopay 1.50 4.00
31 George Staller CO 1.50 4.00
32 Eddie Watt 1.50 4.00
33 Earl Weaver MG 3.00 8.00

1973 Orioles Johnny Pro

This 25-card set measures approximately 4 1/4" by 7 1/4" and features members of the 1973 Baltimore Orioles. The cards were designed to be pushed-out in a style similar to the 1964 Topps Stand Ups. The sides of the cards have a small advertisement for Johnny Pro Enterprises and even gives a phone number where they could have been reached. Oddly, the Orlando Pena card was not available in a die-cut version. The cards have the player's photo against a distinctive solid green background. The cards are blank backed. There are several variations within the set; the complete set price below includes all of the variation cards. The set is checklisted in order by uniform number. According to informed sources, there were 15,000 sets produced.

COMPLETE SET (25) 100.00 200.00
1 Al Bumbry 1.50 4.00
2 Rich Coggins 1.50 4.00
3A Bobby Grich/(Fielding) 3.00 8.00
3B Bobby Grich/(Batting) 12.50 30.00
4 Earl Weaver 4.00 10.00
5A Brooks Robinson/(Fielding) 8.00 20.00
5B Brooks Robinson/(Batting) 12.50 40.00
6 Paul Blair 2.50 6.00
7 Mark Belanger 2.50 6.00
8 Andy Etchebarren 1.50 4.00
10 Elrod Hendricks 1.50 4.00
11 Terry Crowley 1.50 4.00
12 Tommy Davis 2.50 6.00
13 Doyle Alexander 2.50 6.00
14 Merv Rettenmund 1.50 4.00
15 Frank Baker 1.50 4.00
19 Dave McNally 2.50 6.00
21 Larry Brown 1.50 4.00
22A Jim Palmer 8.00 20.00
22B Jim Palmer/(Pitching) 12.50 30.00
23 Grant Jackson 1.50 4.00
25 Don Baylor 3.00 8.00
26 John(Boog) Powell 5.00 12.00
27 Orlando Pena/(NOT die-cut) 1.50 4.00
32 Earl Williams 1.50 4.00
34 Bob Reynolds 1.50 4.00
35 Mike Cuellar 2.50 6.00
39 Eddie Watt 1.50 4.00

1973-74 Orioles Postcards

These 43 cards feature color portraits of the Baltimore Orioles with white borders and printed on postcard size cards. The backs are blank. The cards are unnumbered and checklisted below in alphabetical order.

COMPLETE SET (43) 30.00 60.00
1 Doyle Alexander/(Dark) .40 1.00
2 Doyle Alexander/(Light) .40 1.00
3 Frank Baker .40 1.00
4 George Bamberger CO .40 1.00
5 Don Baylor 1.00 2.50
6 Mark Belanger .75 2.00
7 Paul Blair .60 1.50
8 Larry Brown .40 1.00
9 Al Bumbry .40 1.00
10 Al Bumbry .40 1.00
11 Enos Cabell .40 1.00
12 Rich Coggins .40 1.00
13 Terry Crowley .40 1.00
14 Jim Fuller .40 1.00
15 Wayne Garland .40 1.00
16 Mike Cuellar .60 1.50
17 Tommy Davis .60 1.50
18 Andy Etchebarren .40 1.00
19 Jim Frey CO .40 1.00
20 Bob Grich 1.00 2.50
21 Ross Grimsley .40 1.00
22 Roric Harrison .40 1.00
23 Ellie Hendricks .40 1.00
24 Don Hood .40 1.00
25 Billy Hunter CO .40 1.00
26 Grant Jackson .40 1.00
27 Jesse Jefferson .40 1.00
28 Dave McNally/(Looking right) .75 2.00
29 Dave McNally/(Looking left) .75 2.00
30 Johnny Oates .40 1.00
31 Jim Palmer/(Autographed) 2.00 5.00
32 Jim Palmer/(Eyes looking left) 2.00 5.00
33 Orlando Pena .40 1.00
34 Boog Powell 1.25 3.00
35 Merv Rettenmund .40 1.00
36 Bob Reynolds .40 1.00
37 Brooks Robinson 2.00 5.00
38 Mickey Scott .40 1.00
39 George Staller .40 1.00
40 Eddie Watt .40 1.00
41 Earl Weaver MG 1.00 2.50
42 Earl Williams/(Smiling) .40 1.00
43 Earl Williams/(Non-smiling) .40 1.00

1975 Orioles Postcards

This 30-card set of the Baltimore Orioles features player photos on postcard-size cards. The cards are unnumbered and checklisted below in alphabetical order.

COMPLETE SET (30) 12.50 30.00
1 Doyle Alexander .30 .75
2 George Bamberger CO .30 .75
3 Don Baylor .75 2.00
4 Mark Belanger .30 .75
5 Paul Blair .40 1.00
6 Al Bumbry .30 .75
7 Mike Cuellar .40 1.00
8 Tommy Davis .40 1.00
9 Doug DeCinces .60 1.50
10 Dave Duncan .30 .75
11 Jim Frey CO .30 .75
12 Wayne Garland .30 .75
13 Bob Grich .30 .75
14 Ross Grimsley .30 .75
15 Elrod Hendricks .30 .75
16 Billy Hunter CO .30 .75
17 Grant Jackson .30 .75
18 Jesse Jefferson .30 .75
19 Dave Johnson .30 .75
20 Lee May .40 1.00
21 Tim Nordbrook .30 .75
22 Jim Northrup .30 .75
23 Jim Palmer 1.50 4.00
24 Bob Reynolds .30 .75
25 Brooks Robinson 2.00 5.00
26 Tom Shopay .30 .75
27 Ken Singleton .60 1.50
28 George Staller CO .30 .75
29 Mike Torrez .30 .75
30 Earl Weaver MG .75 2.00

1976 Orioles English's Chicken Lids

This set features round black-and-white player photos and measures approximately 8 1/4" in diameter. The backs are blank. The cards are unnumbered and checklisted below in alphabetical order; however, the checklist is incomplete. Cuellar, Holtzman and Palmer are all the large size cards. Ten other cards were issued and those lids measure 7" in diameter.

COMPLETE SET 40.00 80.00
1 Mark Belanger 2.50 6.00
2 Paul Blair 2.00 5.00
3 Al Bumbry 2.00 5.00
4 Mike Cuellar 2.00 5.00
5 Dave Duncan 2.50 6.00
6 Bobby Grich 2.00 5.00
7 Ross Grimsley 2.00 5.00
8 Ellie Hendricks 2.00 5.00
9 Ken Holtzman 2.00 5.00
10 Lee May 2.50 6.00
11 Jim Palmer 5.00 12.00
12 Brooks Robinson 5.00 12.00
13 Ken Singleton 2.50 6.00

1976 Orioles Postcards

This 38-card set of the Baltimore Orioles features glossy

player photos with white borders on postcard-size cards. The cards are unnumbered and checklisted below in alphabetical order. An important card in this set is of Reggie Jackson, during his only season as an Oriole and one of the few Jackson Oriole cards available.

COMPLETE SET (38)	15.00	40.00
1 Doyle Alexander	.30	.75
2 Bob Bailor	.30	.75
3 George Bamberger CO	.30	.75
4 Mark Belanger	.60	1.50
5 Paul Blair	.30	.75
6 Al Bumbry	.30	.75
7 Terry Crowley	.30	.75
8 Mike Cuellar	.40	1.00
9 Doug DeCinces	.40	1.00
10 Rick Dempsey	.40	1.00
11 Dave Duncan	.30	.75
12 Mike Flanagan	.30	.75
13 Jim Frey CO	.30	.75
14 Wayne Garland	.30	.75
15 Bobby Grich	.40	1.00
16 Ross Grimsley	.30	.75
17 Tommy Harper	.30	.75
18 Elrod Hendricks	.30	.75
19 Fred Holdsworth	.30	.75
20 Bill Hunter CO	.30	.75
21 Grant Jackson	.30	.75
22 Reggie Jackson	4.00	10.00
23 Tippy Martinez	.30	.75
24 Lee May	.40	1.00
25 Rudy May	.30	.75
26 Dyar Miller	.30	.75
27 Andres Mora	.30	.75
28 Tony Muser	.30	.75
29 Tim Nordbrook	.30	.75
30 Dave Pagan	.30	.75
31 Jim Palmer	1.50	4.00
32 Cal Ripken Sr. CO	.30	.75
33 Brooks Robinson	1.50	4.00
34 Brooks Robinson Triangle in lower right corner	1.50	4.00
35 Tom Shopay	.30	.75
36 Ken Singleton	.40	1.00
37 Royle Stillman	.30	.75
38 Earl Weaver MG	.75	2.00

1977 Orioles Photo Album

Issued as a photo album, but with easily perforated photos, which measure approximately 5 1/4" by 8 1/2" when seperated, these pictures feature members of the Baltimore Orioles. Since the photos were issued in alphabetical order, we have notated these photos in that order as well. This set is noticable for one of the very first appearences of Eddie Murray.

COMPLETE SET	10.00	25.00
1 Earl Weaver MG	.60	1.50
2 George Bamberger CO	.30	.75
3 Jim Frey CO	.30	.75
4 Cal Ripken Sr CO	.30	.75
5 Mark Belanger	.40	1.00
6 Al Bumbry	.30	.75
7 Rich Dauer	.30	.75
8 Doug DeCinces	.40	1.00
9 Rick Dempsey	.40	1.00
10 Dick Drago	.30	.75
11 Mike Flanagan	.30	.75
12 Kiko Garcia	.30	.75
13 Ross Grimsley	.30	.75
14 Pat Kelly	.30	.75
15 Elliott Maddox	.30	.75
16 Dennis Martinez	.40	1.00
17 Tippy Martinez	.30	.75
18 Lee May	.40	1.00
19 Rudy May	.30	.75
20 Scott McGregor	.30	.75
21 Andres Mora	.30	.75
22 Eddie Murray	3.00	8.00
23 Tony Muser	.30	.75
24 Jim Palmer	1.25	3.00
25 Brooks Robinson	1.25	3.00
26 Tom Shopay	.30	.75
27 Ken Singleton	.40	1.00
28 Dave Skaggs	.30	.75
29 Billy Smith	.30	.75
30 Dave Criscione	.30	.75
31 Ken Rudolph	.30	.75

1977 Orioles Postcards

This 22-card set features glossy color portraits of the Baltimore Orioles with white borders and measures approximately 3 3/8" by 5 1/4". The backs are blank. The cards are unnumbered and checklisted below in alphabetical order. The Eddie Murray postcard predates his Rookie Card.

COMPLETE SET (22)	10.00	25.00
1 Mark Belanger	.40	1.00
2 Al Bumbry	.30	.75
3 Rich Dauer	.30	.75
4 Doug DeCinces	.40	1.00
5 Rick Dempsey	.40	1.00
6 Kiko Garcia	.30	.75
7 Ross Grimsley	.30	.75
8 Larry Harlow	.30	.75
9 Fred Holdsworth	.30	.75
10 Bill Hunter CO	.30	.75
11 Pat Kelly	.30	.75
12 Dennis Martinez	.75	2.00
13 Tippy Martinez	.30	.75
14 Scott McGregor	.30	.75
15 Eddie Murray	3.00	8.00
16 Brooks Robinson/(Light background)	1.50	4.00
17 Brooks Robinson/(Dark background)	1.50	4.00
18 Tom Shopay	.30	.75
19 Ken Singleton	.40	1.00
20 Dave Skaggs	.30	.75
21 Billy Smith	.30	.75
22 Earl Weaver MG	.75	2.00

1978 Orioles Postcards

This 34-card set features glossy color portraits of the Baltimore Orioles with white borders and measures approximately 3 3/8" by 5 1/4". The backs are blank. The cards are unnumbered and checklisted below in alphabetical order.

COMPLETE SET (34)	12.50	30.00
1 Mark Belanger	.40	1.00
2 Nelson Briles	.30	.75
3 Al Bumbry	.40	1.00
4 Terry Crowley	.30	.75
5 Rich Dauer	.30	.75
6 Doug DeCinces	.40	1.00
7 Rick Dempsey	.40	1.00
8 Mike Flanagan	.60	1.50
9 Jim Frey CO	.30	.75
10 Kiko Garcia	.30	.75
11 Larry Harlow	.30	.75
12 Ellie Hendricks	.30	.75
13 Pat Kelly	.30	.75
14 Joe Kerrigan	.30	.75
15 Carlos Lopez	.30	.75
16 Dennis Martinez	.75	2.00
17 Tippy Martinez	.30	.75
18 Lee May	.40	1.00
19 Scott McGregor	.30	.75
20 Ray Miller CO	.30	.75
21 Andres Mora	.30	.75
22 Eddie Murray	1.25	3.00
23 Tony Muser	.30	.75
24 Jim Palmer	1.25	3.00
25 Cal Ripken Sr. CO	.30	.75
26 Frank Robinson CO	.75	2.00
27 Gary Roenicke	.30	.75
28 Ken Singleton	.40	1.00
29 Dave Skaggs	.30	.75
30 Billy Smith	.30	.75
31 Don Stanhouse	.30	.75
32 Earl Stephenson	.30	.75
33 Tim Stoddard	.40	1.00
34 Earl Weaver MG	.75	2.00

1979 Orioles Postcards

This 18-card set features glossy color portraits of the Baltimore Orioles with white borders and measures approximately 3 3/8" by 5 1/4". The backs are blank. The cards are unnumbered and checklisted below in alphabetical order.

COMPLETE SET (18)	6.00	15.00
1 Benny Ayala	.30	.75
2 Al Bumbry	.30	.75
3 Rich Dauer	.30	.75
4 Doug DeCinces	.40	1.00
5 Rick Dempsey	.40	1.00
6 Mike Flanagan	.40	1.00
7 Jim Frey CO	.30	.75
8 Joe Kerrigan	.30	.75
9 John Lowenstein	.30	.75
10 Scott McGregor	.30	.75
11 Ray Miller CO	.30	.75
12 Eddie Murray	1.25	3.00
13 Jim Palmer	1.25	3.00
14 Sammy Stewart/(Red trim)	.30	.75
15 Sammy Stewart/(Orange trim)	.30	.75
16 Steve Stone	.60	1.50
17 Earl Weaver MG	.75	2.00
18 The Bird(Mascot)	.30	.75

1980 Orioles Postcards

This 24-card blank-backed set features glossy color portraits of the Baltimore Orioles with white borders and measures approximately 3 3/8" by 5 1/4". The cards are unnumbered and checklisted below in alphabetical order. Any of these cards were available from the team for 10 cents each.

COMPLETE SET (24)	8.00	20.00
1 Benny Ayala	.20	.50
2 Mark Belanger	.20	.50
3 Al Bumbry		
4 Terry Crowley	.20	.50
5 Rich Dauer		
6 Doug DeCinces	.30	.75
7 Rick Dempsey		
8 Mike Flanagan	.30	.75
9 Dave Ford	.20	.50
10 Kiko Garcia	.20	.50
11 Dan Graham	.20	.50
12 Ellie Hendricks	.20	.50
13 Pat Kelly	.20	.50
14 Joe Kerrigan	.20	.50
15 John Lowenstein	.20	.50
16 Dennis Martinez		
17 Tippy Martinez		
18 Lee May		
19 Scott McGregor	.20	.50
20 Ray Miller	.20	.50
21 Eddie Murray	1.50	4.00
22 Jim Palmer	1.25	3.00
23 Cal Ripken Sr. CO		
24 Frank Robinson CO		
25 Gary Roenicke	.20	.50
26 Lenn Sakata	.20	.50
27 Ken Singleton	.30	.75
27 Tim Stoddard	.30	.75
28 Steve Stone	.30	.75
29 Earl Weaver	.60	1.50
30 The Bird(Mascot)	.20	.50
31 Memorial Stadium	.20	.50

1936-41 Overland Candy R301

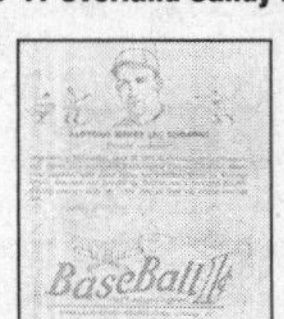

These unnumbered cards (which are actually wrappers) measure 5" by 5 1/4" and were issued over a period of time in the 1930's. A drawing of the player is on the top of the wrapper with his name and biography underneath him. The Overland Candy Co logo is noted on the bottom. Wrappers are known with or without the ingredient list. No extra value is given for either variation.

COMPLETE SET	7,500.00	15,000.00
1 Mel Almada	200.00	400.00
2 Luke Appling	400.00	800.00
3 Earl Averill	400.00	800.00
4 Wally Berger	250.00	500.00
5 Zeke Bonura	250.00	500.00
6 Dolph Camilli	250.00	500.00
7 Phil Cavaretta	250.00	500.00
8 Ben Chapman	200.00	400.00
9 Harland Clift	200.00	400.00
10A Johnny Cooney Boston	200.00	400.00
10B Johnny Cooney Brooklyn	200.00	400.00
11A Bill Dietrich Chicago	200.00	400.00
11B Bill Dietrich Philadelphia	200.00	400.00
12 Joe DiMaggio	2,000.00	4,000.00
13 Jimmie Foxx	400.00	800.00
14 Lou Gehrig	1,500.00	3,000.00
15 Charley Gehringer	400.00	800.00
16 Jose Luis Gomez	200.00	400.00
17 Lefty Gomez	400.00	800.00
18 Joe Gordon	300.00	600.00
19 Hank Greenberg	400.00	800.00
20 Lefty Grove	400.00	800.00
21 Mule Haas	200.00	400.00
22 Rollie Hemsley	200.00	400.00
23 Pinky Higgins	200.00	400.00
24 Oral Hildebrand	200.00	400.00
25 Bob Johnson	250.00	500.00
26 Buck Jordan	200.00	400.00
27 Fabian Kowalik	200.00	400.00
28 Ken Keltner	250.00	500.00
29 Cookie Lavagetto	200.00	400.00
30 Tony Lazzeri	400.00	800.00
31 Samuel A. Leslie	200.00	400.00
32 Danny Litwhiler	200.00	400.00
33 Ted Lyons	400.00	800.00
34 George McQuinn	200.00	400.00
35 Johnny Mize	400.00	800.00
36 Terry Moore	200.00	400.00
37 Bill Nicholson	200.00	400.00
38 Frankie Pytlak	200.00	400.00
39 Rip Radcliff	200.00	400.00
40 Pete Reiser	300.00	600.00
41 Red Rolfe	250.00	500.00
42 Schoolboy Rowe	250.00	500.00
43 Al Simmons	400.00	800.00
44 Cecil Travis	250.00	500.00
45 Hal Trosky	250.00	500.00
46 Joe Vosmik	200.00	400.00
47 Bill Werber	200.00	400.00
48 Max West	200.00	400.00
49 Sam West	200.00	400.00
50 Whit Wyatt	200.00	400.00

1921 Oxford Confectionery E253

This 20 card set measures 1 5/8" by 2 3/4" and almost the whole front is a player photo. The player's name and team is on the bottom. The backs note that these cards are produced solely for the Oxford Confectionery Company and lists a player checklist.

COMPLETE SET (20)	3,000.00	6,000.00
1 Grover C. Alexander	750.00	1,500.00
2 Dave Bancroft	400.00	800.00
3 Max Carey	400.00	800.00
4 Ty Cobb	3,000.00	6,000.00
5 Eddie Collins	750.00	1,500.00
6 Frankie Frisch	600.00	1,200.00
7 Burleigh Grimes	400.00	800.00
8 Bill Holke	200.00	400.00
9 Rogers Hornsby	1,000.00	2,000.00
10 Walter Johnson	1,500.00	3,000.00
11 Lee Meadows	200.00	400.00
12 Cy Perkins	200.00	400.00
13 Del Pratt	200.00	400.00
14 Ed Roush	400.00	800.00
15 Babe Ruth	5,000.00	10,000.00
16 Ray Schalk	400.00	800.00
17 George Sisler	600.00	1,200.00
18 Tris Speaker	750.00	1,500.00
19 Cy Williams	200.00	400.00
20 Whitey Witt	200.00	400.00

1980-83 Pacific Legends

This 120-card standard-size set is actually four 30-card subsets plus a four-card wax box bottom panel (cards 121-124). The golden-toned set was distributed by series over several years beginning in 1980 with the first 30 cards. The set was produced by Pacific Trading Cards and is frequently referred to as Cramer Legends, for the founder of Pacific Trading cards, Mike Cramer. Even though the wax box cards are numbered from 121-124 and called "Series 5," the set is considered complete without them. Each series was originally available from Pacific Trading card for $2.95 each.

COMPLETE SET (120)	12.50	30.00
COMMON PLAYER (1-120)		.1
COMMON PLAYER (121-124)		.5
1 Babe Ruth	1.25	3.00
2 Heinie Manush	.07	.20
3 Rabbit Maranville	.07	.20
4 Earl Averill	.07	.20
5 Joe DiMaggio	1.00	2.50
6 Mickey Mantle	1.25	3.00
7 Hank Aaron	.60	1.50
8 Stan Musial	.30	.75
9 Bill Terry	.07	.20
10 Sandy Koufax	.20	.50
11 Ernie Lombardi	.07	.20
12 Dizzy Dean	.20	.50
13 Lou Gehrig	1.00	2.50
14 Walter Alston	.07	.20
15 Jackie Robinson	.60	1.50
16 Jimmie Foxx	.10	.30
17 Billy Southworth	.02	.10
18 Honus Wagner	.30	.75
19 Duke Snider	.20	.50
20 Rogers Hornsby UER (At bat total of/1873 is inco	.20	.50
21 Paul Waner	.07	.20
22 Luke Appling	.07	.20
23 Billy Herman	.07	.20
24 Lloyd Waner	.07	.20
25 Fred Hutchinson	.02	.10
26 Eddie Collins	.07	.20
27 Lefty Grove	.10	.30
28 Chuck Connors	.10	.30
29 Lefty O'Doul	.02	.10
30 Hank Greenberg	.20	.50
31 Ty Cobb	.75	2.00
32 Enos Slaughter	.07	.20
33 Ernie Banks	.20	.50
34 Christy Mathewson	.20	.50
35 Mel Ott	.10	.30
36 Pie Traynor	.07	.20
37 Clark Griffith	.07	.20
38 Mickey Cochrane	.07	.20
39 Joe Cronin	.07	.20
40 Leo Durocher	.07	.20
41 Home Run Baker	.07	.20
42 Joe Tinker	.07	.20
43 John McGraw	.07	.20
44 Bill Dickey	.07	.20
45 Walter Johnson	.20	.50
46 Frankie Frisch	.07	.20
47 Casey Stengel	.10	.30
48 Willie Mays	.60	1.50
49 Johnny Mize	.07	.20
50 Roberto Clemente	.75	2.00
51 Burleigh Grimes	.07	.20
52 Pee Wee Reese	.20	.50
53 Bob Feller	.20	.50
54 Brooks Robinson	.20	.50
55 Sam Crawford	.07	.20
56 Robin Roberts	.10	.30
57 Warren Spahn	.10	.30
58 Joe McCarthy	.07	.20
59 Jocko Conlan	.07	.20
60 Satchel Paige		1
61 Ted Williams	.75	2.00
62 George Kelly	.07	.20
63 Gil Hodges	.10	.30
64 Jim Bottomley	.07	.20
65 Al Kaline	.20	.50
66 Harvey Kuenn	.02	.10
67 Yogi Berra	.20	.50
68 Nellie Fox	.02	.10
69 Harmon Killebrew	.10	.30
70 Edd Roush	.07	.20
71 Mordecai Brown	.07	.20
72 Gabby Hartnett	.07	.20
73 Early Wynn	.07	.20
74 Nap Lajoie	.07	.20
75 Charlie Grimm	.02	.10
76 Joe Garagiola	.07	.20
77 Ted Lyons	.07	.20
78 Mickey Vernon	.02	.10
79 Lou Boudreau	.07	.20
80 Al Dark	.02	.10
81 Ralph Kiner	.10	.30
82 Phil Rizzuto	.10	.30
83 Stan Hack	.02	.10
84 Frank Chance	.07	.20
85 Ray Schalk	.07	.20
86 Bill McKechnie	.07	.20
87 Travis Jackson	.07	.20
88 Pete Reiser	.02	.10
89 Carl Hubbell	.10	.30
90 Roy Campanella	.20	.50
91 Cy Young	.10	.30
92 Kiki Cuyler	.07	.20
93 Chief Bender	.07	.20
94 Richie Ashburn	.10	.30
95 Riggs Stephenson	.02	.10
96 Minnie Minoso	.02	.10
97 Hack Wilson	.07	.20
98 Al Lopez	.07	.20
99 Willie Keeler	.07	.20
100 Fred Lindstrom	.07	.20
101 Roger Maris	.10	.30
102 Roger Bresnahan	.07	.20
103 Monty Stratton	.07	.20
104 Goose Goslin	.07	.20
105 Earle Combs	.07	.20
106 Pepper Martin	.02	.10
107 Joe Jackson	.60	1.50
108 George Sisler	.07	.20
109 Red Ruffing	.07	.20
110 Johnny Vander Meer	.02	.10

111 Herb Pennock .07 .20
112 Chuck Klein .07 .20
113 Paul Derringer .02 .10
114 Addie Joss .07 .20
115 Bobby Thomson .02 .10
116 Chick Hafey .07 .20
117 Lefty Gomez .07 .20
118 George Kell .07 .20
119 Al Simmons .07 .20
120 Bob Lemon .07 .20
121 Hoyt Wilhelm/(Wax box card) .20 .50
122 Arky Vaughan/(Wax box card) .20 .50
123 Frank Robinson/(Wax box card) .60 1.50
124 Grover Alexander/(Wax box card) 1

1958 Packard Bell

This seven-card set includes members of the Los Angeles Dodgers and San Francisco Giants and was issued in both teams' first year on the West Coast. This black and white, unnumbered set features cards measuring approximately 3 3/8" by 5 3/8". The backs are advertisements for Packard Bell (a television and radio manufacturer) along with a schedule for either the Giants or Dodgers. There were four Giants printed and three Dodgers. The catalog designation for this set is H805-5. Since the cards are unnumbered, they are listed below alphabetically.

COMPLETE SET (7) 600.00 1,200.00
1 Walt Alston MG 125.00 250.00
2 Johnny Antonelli 60.00 120.00
3 Jim Gilliam 75.00 150.00
4 Gil Hodges 150.00 300.00
5 Willie Mays 400.00 800.00
6 Bill Rigney MG 60.00 120.00
7 Hank Sauer 60.00 120.00

1969 Padres Team Issue

Measuring approximately 5" by 7", these cards feature members of the 1969 San Diego Padres during their debut season. Since these cards are unnumbered, we have sequenced them in alphabetical order. This list may be incomplete so any additions are appreciated.

COMPLETE SET 30.00 60.00
1 Nate Colbert 3.00 8.00
2 Bill Davis 2.00 5.00
3 Tom Dukes 2.00 5.00
4 Tony Gonzalez 2.00 5.00
5 Walt Hriniak 3.00 8.00
6 Chris Krug 2.00 5.00
7 Billy McCool 2.00 5.00
8 Ivan Murrell 2.00 5.00
9 John Podres 2.50 6.00
10 Frank Reberger 2.00 5.00
11 Rafael Robles 2.00 5.00
12 John Ruberto
13 John Sipin 2.00 5.00
14 Tommie Sisk 2.00 5.00
15 Larry Stahl 2.00 5.00

1969 Padres Volpe

These eight 8 1/2" by 11 cards feature members of the San Diego Padres in their inagural season. These cards feature two drawings (a large portrait shot as well as an smaller action pose) by noted sport artist Nicholas Volpe on the front. The backs have the Padres logo as well as a biography of Volpe. These cards are unnumbered and we have sequenced them in alphabetical order.

COMPLETE SET (8) 10.00 25.00
1 Ollie Brown 1.25 3.00
2 Tommy Dean 1.00 2.50
3 Al Ferrera 1.00 2.50
4 Clarence Gaston 2.00 5.00
5 Preston Gomez MG 1.25 3.00
6 Johnny Podres 1.50 4.00
7 Al Santorini 1.00 2.50
8 Ed Spiezio 1.00 2.50

1971 Padres Team Issue

Measuring approximately 5" by 7", these cards feature members of the 1971 San Diego Padres. Since these cards are unnumbered, we have sequenced them in alphabetical order.

COMPLETE SET 5.00 12.00
1 Dave Campbell .75 2.00
2 Chris Cannizzaro .40 1.00
3 Tommy Dean .40 1.00
4 Al Ferrara .40 1.00
5 Enzo Hernandez .40 1.00
6 Steve Huntz .40 1.00
7 Van Kelly .40 1.00
8 Bill Laxton .40 1.00
9 Gerry Nyman .40 1.00
10 Tom Phoebus .40 1.00
11 Al Santorini .40 1.00
12 Ron Slocum .40 1.00
13 Ramon Webster .40 1.00

1972 Padres Colbert Commemorative

This 8 1/2" by 11" photo features Nate Colbert and honors his spectacular doubleheader feat of August 1, 1972 in which he hit five homers and drove in 13 runs. Colbert is posed with a bat and balls which show what occured that day.

1 Nate Colbert 4.00 10.00

1972 Padres Postcards

This 28-card set of the San Diego Padres features borderless black-and-white player photos measuring approximately 3 3/8" by 5 3/8". The backs are blank. The cards are unnumbered and checklisted below in alphabetical order.

COMPLETE SET (28) 50.00 100.00
1 Ed Acosta 1.50 4.00
2 Steve Arlin 1.50 4.00
3 Bob Barton 1.50 4.00
4 Ollie Brown 2.00 5.00
5 Mike Caldwell 1.50 4.00
6 Dave Campbell 2.50 6.00
7 Nate Colbert 2.50 6.00
8 Mike Corkins 1.50 4.00
9 Roger Craig 2.50 6.00
10 Clarence Gaston 3.00 8.00
11 Bill Greif 1.50 4.00
12 Enzo Hernandez 1.50 4.00
13 Gary Jestadt 1.50 4.00
14 John Jeter 1.50 4.00
15 Fred Kendall 1.50 4.00
16 Clay Kirby 1.50 4.00
17 Leron Lee 1.50 4.00
18 Jerry Morales 1.50 4.00
19 Ivan Murrell 1.50 4.00
20 Fred Norman 1.50 4.00
21 Raefle Robles 1.50 4.00
22 Gary Ross 1.50 4.00
23 Mark Schaeffer 1.50 4.00
24 Ed Spiezio 1.50 4.00
25 Ron Taylor 1.50 4.00
26 Darrel Thomas 1.50 4.00
27 W. Whiettlemann CO 1.50 4.00
28 Don Zimmer MG 2.50 6.00

1973 Padres Dean's

This 30-card set of the San Diego Padres was issued in five series. The cards measure 5 1/2" by 8 1/2" and are printed on very thin paper. The fronts feature white-bordered black-and-white player portraits with the player's name and position, sponsor and team logos below the photo. The backs are blank. The cards are unnumbered and checklisted below in alphabetical order. Dave Winfield is featured in his rookie season in an item which predates his Rookie Card.

COMPLETE SET (30) 40.00 80.00
1 Steve Arlin .75 2.00
2 Mike Caldwell .75 2.00
3 Dave Campbell 1.50 4.00
4 Nate Colbert 1.25 3.00
5 Mike Corkins .75 2.00
6 Pat Corrales .75 2.00
7 Dave Garcia .75 2.00
8 Clarence Gaston 1.25 3.00
9 Bill Greif .75 2.00
10 John Grubb .75 2.00
11 Enzo Hernandez .75 2.00
12 Randy Jones 2.00 5.00
13 Fred Kendall .75 2.00
14 Clay Kirby .75 2.00
15 Leron Lee .75 2.00
16 Dave Marshall .75 2.00
17 Don Mason .75 2.00
18 Jerry Morales .75 2.00
19 Ivan Murrell .75 2.00
20 Fred Norman .75 2.00
21 Johnny Podres 1.25 3.00
22 Dave Roberts .75 2.00
23 Vicente Romo .75 2.00
24 Gary Ross .75 2.00
25 Bob Skinner .75 2.00
26 Derrel Thomas .75 2.00
27 Rich Troedson .75 2.00
28 Whitey Wietelmann CO .75 2.00
29 Dave Winfield 20.00 50.00
30 Don Zimmer 1.25 3.00

1974 Padres Dean's

These cards measure 5 1/2" by 8 1/2" and are printed on very thin paper. The fronts feature white-bordered black-and-white player photos with the player's name and position, and sponsor and team logos below the photo. The backs carry the player's career summary, biography and statistics. The cards are unnumbered and checklisted below in alphabetical order. Some of these cards are also known to come with blank backs. Dave Winfield appears in his Rookie Card season.

COMPLETE SET (30) 40.00 80.00
1 Matty Alou 1.25 3.00
2 Bob Barton .75 2.00
3 Glenn Beckert .75 2.00
4 Jack Bloomfield CO .75 2.00
5 Nate Colbert .75 2.00
6 Mike Corkins .75 2.00
7 Jim Davenport CO .75 2.00
8 Dave Freisleben .75 2.00
9 Cito Gaston 1.50 4.00
10 Bill Greif .75 2.00
11 John Grubb .75 2.00
12 Larry Hardy .75 2.00
13 Enzo Hernandez .75 2.00
14 Dave Hilton .75 2.00
15 Randy Jones 1.50 4.00
16 Fred Kendall .75 2.00
17 Gene Locklear .75 2.00
18 Willie McCovey 4.00 10.00
19 John McNamara MG .75 2.00
20 Rich Morales .75 2.00
21 Bill Poesdel CO .75 2.00
22 Dave Roberts .75 2.00
23 Vicente Romo .75 2.00
24 Dan Spillner .75 2.00
25 Derrel Thomas .75 2.00
26 Bob Tolan .75 2.00
27 Rich Troedson .75 2.00
28 Whitey Wietelmann CO 1.25 3.00
29 Bernie Williams .75 2.00
30 Dave Winfield 8.00 20.00

1974 Padres McDonald Discs

Measuring approximately 2 3/8" in diameter, members of the 1974 Padres are featured in this set. Among the players featured in this set is Dave Winfield during his Rookie Card season. These items were given out at the July 30th Padres game. According to informed sources, 60,000 photo balls were produced for the event. A baseball holder was also produced. These have a value of approximately $25. The set was originally available for $3 from the manufacturer.

COMPLETE SET (15) 20.00 50.00
1 Matty Alou 2.00 5.00
2 Glen Beckert 1.25 3.00
3 Nate Colbert 1.50 4.00
4 Bill Greif 1.25 3.00
5 John Grubb 1.25 3.00
6 Enzo Hernandez 1.25 3.00
7 Randy Jones 1.50 4.00
8 Fred Kendall 1.25 3.00
9 Willie McCovey 4.00 10.00
10 John McNamara MG 1.25 3.00
11 Dave Roberts 1.25 3.00
12 Bobby Tolan 1.50 4.00
13 Dave Winfield 8.00 20.00
14 Ronald McDonald 1.25 3.00
Has giveaway dates
15 Padres Sked 1.25 3.00

1974 Padres Team Issue

This 18-card set features black-and-white photos of the San Diego Padres measuring approximately 3 5/16" by 5 5/16". The cards are unnumbered and checklisted below in alphabetical order.

COMPLETE SET (18) 8.00 20.00
1 Bob Barton .20 .50
2 Glenn Beckert .20 .50
3 Mike Corkins .20 .50
4 Dave Freisleben .20 .50
5 Bill Greif .20 .50
6 Larry Hardy .20 .50
7 Randy Jones .30 .75
8 Willie McCovey/(Batting) 2.00 5.00
9 Willie McCovey/(Leaning on bat) 2.00 5.00
10 Dave Roberts/(Catching) .20 .50
11 Dave Roberts/(Leaning on bat) .20 .50
12 Vicente Romo .20 .50
13 Dan Spillner .20 .50
14 Derrel Thomas .20 .50
15 Bobby Tolan .20 .50
16 Dave Tomlin .20 .50
17 Rich Troedson .20 .50
18 Dave Winfield 4.00 10.00

1975 Padres Dean's

These cards measure 5 1/2" by 8 1/2" and are printed on very thin paper. The fronts feature black-and-white player photos with the player's name and position, and sponsor and team logos below the photo. The backs carry the player's career summary, biography and statistics. The cards are unnumbered and checklisted below in alphabetical order. Randy Hundley and Hector Torres were late season trade and their cards have blank backs.

COMPLETE SET (30) 40.00 80.00
1 Jim Davenport CO .75 2.00
2 Bob Davis .75 2.00
3 Rich Folkers .75 2.00
4 Alan Foster .75 2.00
5 Dave Freisleben .75 2.00
6 Tito Fuentes .75 2.00
7 Danny Frisella .75 2.00
8 Bill Greif .75 2.00
9 Johnny Grubb .75 2.00
10 Enzo Hernandez .75 2.00
11 Randy Hundley 1.25 3.00
12 Mike Ivie .75 2.00
13 Jerry Johnson .75 2.00
14 Randy Jones 1.50 4.00
15 Fred Kendall .75 2.00
16 Ted Kubiak .75 2.00
17 Gene Locklear .75 2.00
18 Willie McCovey 4.00 10.00
19 Joe McIntosh .75 2.00
20 John McNamara MG .75 2.00
21 Tom Morgan CO .75 2.00
22 Dick Sharon .75 2.00
23 Dick Sisler CO .75 2.00
24 Dan Spillner .75 2.00
25 Brent Strom .75 2.00
26 Bobby Tolan .75 2.00
27 Dave Tomlin .75 2.00
28 Hector Torres .75 2.00
29 Whitey Wietelmann CO .75 2.00
30 Dave Winfield 6.00 15.00

1977 Padres Family Fun

This set of the San Diego Padres was produced by Huish Family Fun Centers and measures approximately 5 1/2" by 8 1/2". The fronts feature black-and-white player photos with white borders. The backs carry biographical information and career statistics. The set was distributed in eight-card packs with sponsor coupons printed on the pack wrappers. The cards are unnumbered and checklisted below in alphabetical order.

COMPLETE SET (8) 6.00 15.00
1 Joey Amalfitano CO .75 2.00
2 Alvin Dark MG 1.25 3.00
3 Randy Jones 1.00 2.50
4 Bob Owchinko .75 2.00
5 Dave Roberts .75 2.00
6 Rick Sawyer .75 2.00
7 Pat Scanlon .75 2.00
8 Jerry Turner .75 2.00

1977 Padres Schedule Cards

This 89-card set was issued in 1977 and features members of the 1977 San Diego Padres as well as former Padres and others connected with the Padres in some capacity. The cards measure approximately 2 1/4" by 3 3/8" and have brown and white photos on the front of the cards with a schedule of the 1977 Padres special events on the back. A thin line borders the front photo with the team name and player name appearing below in the same sepia tone. The set is checklisted alphabetically in the list below. The complete set price below refers to the set with all variations listed. The blank-backed cards may have been issued in a different year than the other schedule-back cards.

COMPLETE SET (89) 20.00 50.00
1A Bill Almon .20 .50
Kneeling
1B Bill Almon .30 .75
Shown chest up
bat on shoulder
2 Matty Alou .30 .75
3 Joe Amalfitano CO .10 .25
4A Steve Arlin .20 .50
Follow through
4B Steve Arlin .20 .50
Glove to chest
5 Bob Barton .30 .75
6 Buzzie Bavasi GM .20 .50
7 Glenn Beckert .30 .75
8 Vic Bernal .10 .25
9 Ollie Brown .30 .75
10A Dave Campbell .30 .75
Bat on shoulder
10B Dave Campbell .30 .75
Kneeling, capless
11 Mike Champion .10 .25
12 Mike Champion and .10 .25
Bill Almon
13A Nate Colbert .30 .75
Shown waist up
13B Nate Colbert .40 1.00
Shown full figure;
blank back
14 Nate Colbert and .30 .75
friend Kneeling next
to child with bat
15 Jerry Coleman ANN .30 .75
16 Roger Craig CO .20 .50
17 John D'Acquisto .10 .25
18 Bob Davis .10 .25
19 Willie Davis .40 1.00
20 Jim Eakle .10 .25
Tuba Man
21A Rollie Fingers .75 2.00
Shown waist up
both hands in glove
in front of body
21B Rollie Fingers .75 2.00
Head shot
22A Dave Freisleben 1.00 2.50
Washington jersey and
cap blank back
22B Dave Freisleben .20 .50
Kneeling
23A Clarence Gaston .40 1.00
Bat on shoulder Padres on jersey
23B Clarence Gaston .40 1.00
Bat on shoulder Padre on jersey
24 Tom Griffin .10 .25
25 Johnny Grubb .20 .50
26A George Hendrick .30 .75
Shown chest up

wearing warm-up jacket
26B George Hendrick .30 .75
Shown waist up
wearing white jersey
27 Enzo Hernandez .10 .25
28 Enzo Hernandez and .30 .75
Nate Colbert
29A Mike Ivie .30 .75
Batting pose, shown
from thighs up
29B Mike Ivie .30 .75
Batting pose
shown from shoulders up
blank back
29C Mike Ivie/(Bat on shoulder) .30 .75
30A Randy Jones .30 .75
Following Through
30B Randy Jones .40 1.00
Holding Cy Young Award
31 Randy Jones and .40 1.00
Bowie Kuhn COMM
Randy holding trophy
32A Fred Kendall .30 .75
Batting pose
32B Fred Kendall .30 .75
Ball in right hand
33 Mike Kilkenny .30 .75
Blank back
34A Clay Kirby .30 .75
Follow through
34B Clay Kirby .30 .75
Glove near to chest
35 Ray Kroc OWN .40 1.00
Blank back
36 Dave Marshall .30 .75
37A Willie McCovey 1.25 3.00
With mustache
bat on shoulder
37B Willie McCovey 1.25 3.00
Without mustache
blank back
38A John McNamara MG .30 .75
Looking to his left
blank back
38B John McNamara MG .30 .75
Looking to his right
38C John McNamara MG .30 .75
Looking straight
ahead, smiling
39 Luis Melendez .10 .25
40 Butch Metzger .10 .25
41 Bob Miller CO .10 .25
42A Fred Norman .30 .75
Short hair, kneeling
42B Fred Norman .30 .75
Long hair, arms
over head
43 Bob Owchinko .10 .25
44 Doug Rader .30 .75
45 Merv Rettenmund .10 .25
46A Gene Richards .30 .75
Shown chest up
stands in background
46B Gene Richards .20 .50
Shown from thighs up
47 Dave Roberts .10 .25
48 Rick Sawyer .10 .25
49 Bob Shirley .10 .25
50 Bob Skinner CO .20 .50
51 Ballard Smith GM .30 .75
52 Ed Spiezio .30 .75
53 Dan Spillner .10 .25
54 Brent Strom .10 .25
55 Gary Sutherland .10 .25
56 Gene Tenace .30 .75
57A Derrell Thomas .30 .75
Head shot
wearing glasses
57B Derrell Thomas .30 .75
Kneeling, not
wearing glasses
58A Bobby Tolan .30 .75
Batting pose
58B Bobby Tolan .30 .75
Kneeling, holding
cleats in hand
59 Dave Tomlin .10 .25
60A Jerry Turner .30 .75
Batting pose, gloveless
wall in background
60B Jerry Turner .30 .75
Batting pose
both hands gloved
61 Bobby Valentine .40 1.00
62 Dave Wehrmeister .10 .25
63 Whitey Wietelmann CO .10 .25
64 Don Williams CO .10 .25
65A Dave Winfield 4.00 10.00
Batting pose, waist up#field in background
65B Dave Winfield 4.00 10.00
Batting, stands in
background, black bat
telescoped
65C Dave Winfield 4.00 10.00
Two bats on shoulder
65D Dave Winfield 4.00 10.00
Full figure, leaning
on bat, blank back

1978 Padres Family Fun

This 39-card set features members of the 1978 San Diego Padres. These large cards measure approximately 3 1/2" by 5 1/2" and are framed in a style similar to the 1962 Topps set with wood-grain borders. The cards have full color photos on the front of the card along with the Padres logo and Family Fun Centers underneath the photo in circles and the name of the player on the bottom of the card. The backs of the card asked each person what their greatest thrill in baseball was. This set is especially noteworthy for having one of the earliest Ozzie Smith cards printed. The set is checklisted alphabetically in the list below. This set was also available in uncut sheet form.

COMPLETE SET (39) 20.00 50.00
1 Bill Almon .20 .50
2 Tucker Ashford .20 .50
3 Chuck Baker .20 .50
4 Dave Campbell ANN .30 .75
5 Mike Champion .20 .50
6 Jerry Coleman ANN .30 .75
7 Roger Craig MG .40 1.00
8 John D'Acquisto .20 .50
9 Bob Davis .20 .50
10 Chuck Estrada CO .20 .50
11 Rollie Fingers 1.50 4.00
12 Dave Freisleben .20 .50
13 Oscar Gamble .30 .75
14 Fernando Gonzalez .20 .50
15 Billy Herman CO .60 1.50
16 Randy Jones .30 .75
17 Ray Kroc OWN .60 1.50
18 Mark Lee .20 .50
19 Mickey Lolich .40 1.00
20 Bob Owchinko .20 .50
21 Broderick Perkins .20 .50
22 Gaylord Perry 1.50 4.00
23 Eric Rasmussen .20 .50
24 Don Reynolds .20 .50
25 Gene Richards .20 .50
26 Dave Roberts .20 .50
27 Phil Roof CO .20 .50
28 Bob Shirley .20 .50
29 Ozzie Smith 10.00 25.00
30 Dan Spillner .20 .50
31 Rick Sweet .20 .50
32 Gene Tenace .30 .75
33 Derrel Thomas .20 .50
34 Jerry Turner .20 .50
35 Dave Wehrmeister .20 .50
36 Whitey Wietelmann CO .20 .50
37 Don Williams CO .20 .50
38 Dave Winfield 4.00 10.00
39 1978 All-Star Game .30 .75

1979 Padres Family Fun

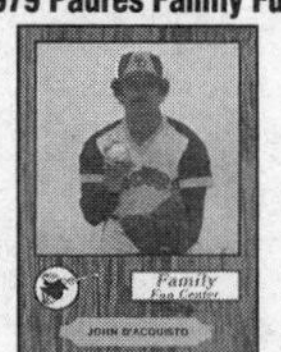

This set features photos of the San Diego Padres and has Family Fun Center printed in a bar on the front. These cards were also produced by Dean's photo processors.

COMPLETE SET 12.50 30.00
1 Roger Craig MG .20 .50
2 John D'Acquisto .20 .50
3 Ozzie Smith 4.00 10.00
4 KGB Chicken .60 1.50
5 Gene Richards .20 .50
6 Jerry Turner .20 .50
7 Bob Owchinko .20 .50
8 Gene Tenace .40 1.00
9 Whitey Wietelmann CO .20 .50
10 Bill Almon .20 .50
11 Dave Winfield 2.00 5.00
12 Mike Hargrove .30 .75
13 Fernando Gonzalez .20 .50
14 Barry Evans .20 .50
15 Steve Mura .20 .50
16 Chuck Estrada CO .20 .50
17 Bill Fahey .20 .50
18 Gaylord Perry 1.25 3.00
19 Dan Briggs .20 .50
20 Billy Herman CO .60 1.50
21 Mickey Lolich .40 1.00
22 Broderick Perkins .20 .50
23 Fred Kendall .20 .50
24 Rollie Fingers 1.25 3.00
25 Kurt Bevacqua .20 .50
26 Jerry Coleman ANN .40 1.00
27 Don Williams .20 .50
28 Paul Dade .20 .50
29 Randy Jones .30 .75
30 Eric Rasmussen .20 .50
31 Bobby Tolan .20 .50
32 Doug Rader .20 .50
33 Dave Campbell .30 .75
34 Jay Johnstone .40 1.00
35 Mark Lee .20 .50
36 Bob Shirley .20 .50

1980 Padres Family Fun

This 36 card set was issued in six card increments six times during the 1980 season. We have sequenced these cards in the order they were given out during the season.

COMPLETE SET 10.00 25.00
1 Randy Jones .30 .75
2 John D'Acquisto .20 .50
3 Jerry Coleman CO .60 1.50
4 Ozzie Smith 2.00 5.00
5 Gene Richards .20 .50
6 Bill Fahey .20 .50
7 John Curtis .20 .50
8 Al Heist CO .20 .50
9 Gary Lucas .20 .50
10 Gene Tenace .20 .50
11 Willie Montanez .20 .50
12 Aurelio Rodriguez .20 .50
13 Eric Rasmussen .20 .50
14 Tim Flannery .20 .50
15 Chuck Estrada CO .20 .50
16 Eddie Doucette ANN .20 .50
17 Bob Shirley .20 .50
18 The Chicken .60 1.50
19 Dave Winfield 1.25 3.00
20 Kurt Bevacqua .20 .50
21 Paul Dade .20 .50
22 Dave Cash .20 .50
23 Don Williams CO .20 .50
24 Rollie Fingers .75 2.00
25 Jerry Mumphrey .20 .50
26 Fred Kendall .20 .50
27 Steve Mura .20 .50
28 Dennis Kinney .20 .50
29 Von Joshua .20 .50
30 Dick Phillips CO .20 .50
31 Dave Campbell .30 .75
32 Juan Eichelberger .20 .50
33 Rick Wise .20 .50
34 Bobby Tolan .20 .50
35 Jerry Turner .20 .50
36 Barry Evans .20 .50

1978 Papa Gino's Discs

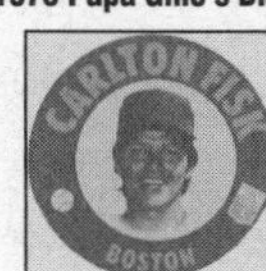

This 40-disc set consists of all American League players with more than half the set being Boston Red Sox players. Papa Gino's was a chain of restaurants located throughout central New England.The discs are 3 3/8" in diameter and have a distinctive thick dark blue border on the front with orange printing. The set was approved by the Major League Baseball Players Association under the auspices of Mike Schechter Associates (MSA) and as such has team logos airbrushed away. The discs are numbered on the back at the bottom; the uniform number is also given at the top of the reverse. The first 25 players in the set are members of the Boston Red Sox. Supposedly eight discs were printed in smaller quantities; these short printed discs are marked SP in the checklist below.

COMPLETE SET (40) 20.00 50.00
COMMON PLAYER (1-40) .20 .50
COMMON SP .40 1.00
1 Allen Ripley .20 .50
2 Jerry Remy .20 .50
3 Jack Brohamer .20 .50
4 Butch Hobson .20 .50
5 Dennis Eckersley 1.25 3.00
6 Sam Bowen SP .40 1.00
7 Rick Burleson .20 .50
8 Carl Yastrzemski 1.50 4.00
9 Bill Lee .40 1.00
10 Bob Montgomery .20 .50
11 Dick Drago SP .40 1.00
12 Bob Stanley SP .40 1.00
13 Fred Kendall SP .40 1.00
14 Jim Rice SP .75 2.00
15 George Scott .40 1.00
16 Tom Burgmeier .20 .50
17 Frank Duffy SP .40 1.00
18 Jim Wright .20 .50
19 Fred Lynn .60 1.50
20 Bob Bailey SP .40 1.00
21 Mike Torrez .20 .50
22 Bill Campbell SP .40 1.00
23 Luis Tiant .60 1.50
24 Dwight Evans .75 2.00
25 Carlton Fisk 1.50 4.00
26 Reggie Jackson 2.00 5.00
27 Thurman Munson 1.25 3.00
28 Ron Guidry .75 2.00
29 Bruce Bochte .20 .50
30 Richie Zisk .20 .50
31 Jim Palmer 1.25 3.00
32 Mark Fidrych 1.25 3.00
33 Frank Tanana .40 1.00
34 Buddy Bell .60 1.50
35 Rod Carew 1.25 3.00
36 George Brett 3.00 8.00
37 Ralph Garr .20 .50
38 Larry Hisle .20 .50
39 Mitchell Page .20 .50
40 John Mayberry .20 .50

1943-48 Parade Sportive

These blank-backed photo sheets of sports figures from the Montreal area around 1945 measure approximately 5" by 8 1/4". They were issued to promote a couple of Montreal radio stations that used to broadcast interviews with some of the pictured athletes. The sheets feature white-bordered black-and-white player photos, some of them crudely retouched. The player's name appears in the bottom white margin and also as a facsimile autograph across the photo. The sheets are unnumbered and are checklisted below in alphabetical order within sport as follows: hockey (1-75), baseball (76-95) and various other sports (96-101). Additions to this checklist are appreciated. Many players are known to appear with two different poses. Since the values are the same for both poses, we have put a (2) next to the players name but have placed a value on only one of the photos.

COMPLETE SET 1,250.00 2,500.00
77 Jack Banta 15.00 30.00
78 Stan Breard 12.50 25.00
79 Les Burge 12.50 25.00
80 Al Campanis 15.00 30.00
81 Red Durrett 12.50 25.00
82 Herman Franks 15.00 30.00
83 John Gabbard 12.50 25.00
84 Roland Gladu 12.50 25.00
85 Ray Hathaway 12.50 25.00
86 John Jorgensen 12.50 25.00
87 Paul Pepper Martin 12.50 25.00
88 Steve Nagy 12.50 25.00
89 Jackie Robinson 100.00 200.00
90 Marvin Rackley 12.50 25.00
91 Jean-Pierre Roy 12.50 25.00
92 Roland Gaddy 12.50 25.00
Jean-Pierre Roy
Stan Breard
93 Montreal Royals 1944 25.00 50.00
94 Montreal Royals 1945 12.50 25.00
95 Montreal Royals 1946 25.00 50.00

1977-81 Bob Parker Hall of Fame

These 103 cards measure 3 1/2" by 5 1/2". The cards are checklisted in alphabetical order. Noted sports artist Bob Parker drew these pictures of Hall of Famers. Between 1977 and 1981 two different continuation series of 23 postcards were issued. They are each entered in order of issue. A couple of other notes. All three series have unnumbered header cards. The first series header does list the cards in numerical order while the other header cards do not. Also the first and third series card are made of similar stock while the middle series consists of a darker tan paper stock.

COMPLETE SET (103) 100.00 200.00
1 Grover C. Alexander .60 1.50
2 Cap Anson .60 1.50
3 Luke Appling .30 .75
4 Ernie Banks 10.00 25.00
5 Chief Bender .30 .75
6 Jim Bottomley .20 .50
7 Dan Brouthers .20 .50
8 Morgan Bulkeley .10 .25
9 Roy Campanella .40 1.00
10 Alex Cartwright .10 .25
11 Henry Chadwick .10 .25
12 John Clarkson .20 .50
13 Ty Cobb 2.00 5.00
14 Eddie Collins .40 1.00
15 Jimmy Collins .20 .50
16 Charles Comiskey .40 1.00
17 Sam Crawford .30 .75
18 Dizzy Dean .40 1.00
19 Joe DiMaggio 2.00 5.00
20 Buck Ewing .30 .75
21 Bob Feller .60 1.50
22 Lou Gehrig 2.00 5.00
23 Goose Goslin .30 .75
24 Burleigh Grimes .30 .75
25 Chick Hafey .20 .50
26 Rogers Hornsby .60 1.50
27 Carl Hubbell .40 1.00
28 Miller Huggins .20 .50
29 Tim Keefe .20 .50
30 Mike Kelly .30 .75
31 Nap Lajoie .40 1.00
32 Fred Lindstrom .20 .50
33 Connie Mack .40 1.00
34 Mickey Mantle 30.00 60.00
35 Heine Manush .30 .75
36 Joe McGinnity .20 .50
37 John McGraw .40 1.00
38 Eddie Plank .30 .75
39 Eppa Rixey .20 .50
40 Jackie Robinson 1.50 4.00
41 Eddie Roush .30 .75
42 Babe Ruth 3.00 8.00
43 Al Simmons .30 .75
44 Albert Spalding .20 .50
45 Tris Speaker .60 1.50
46 Casey Stengel .40 1.00
47 Bill Terry .30 .75
48 Rube Waddell .20 .50
49 Hans Wagner .75 2.00
50 Paul Waner .30 .75
51 John M. Ward .20 .50
52 Ted Williams 8.00 20.00
53 George Wright .20 .50
54 Harry Wright .20 .50
55 Mordecai Brown .20 .50
56 Frank Chance .30 .75
57 Candy Cummings .20 .50
58 Frank Frisch .20 .50
59 Gabby Hartnett .20 .50
60 Billy Herman .20 .50
61 Waite Hoyt .20 .50
62 Walter Johnson .60 1.50
63 Kenesaw Landis .10 .25
64 Rube Marquard .20 .50
65 Christy Mathewson .60 1.50
66 Eddie Mathews .30 .75
67 Willie Mays 1.50 4.00
68 Bill McKechnie .10 .25
69 Stan Musial 6.00 15.00
70 Mel Ott .40 1.00
71 Satchel Paige .40 1.00
72 Robin Roberts .30 .75

Card	Low	High
73 George Sisler	.20	.50
74 Warren Spahn	.30	.75
75 Joe Tinker	.10	.25
76 Dazzy Vance	.10	.25
77 Cy Young	.40	1.00
78 Home Run Baker	.30	.75
79 Yogi Berra	.40	1.00
80 Max Carey	.10	.25
81 Roberto Clemente	15.00	40.00
82 Mickey Cochrane	.20	.50
83 Roger Connor	.10	.25
84 Joe Cronin	.30	.75
85 Kiki Cuyler	.20	.50
86 Johnny Evers	.30	.75
87 Jimmy Foxx	.40	1.00
(Jimmie)		
88 Charlie Gehringer	.30	.75
89 Lefty Gomez	.30	.75
90 Jesse Haines	.10	.25
91 Will Harridge	.10	.25
92 Monte Irvin	.20	.50
93 Addie Joss	.20	.50
94 Al Kaline	6.00	15.00
95 Sandy Koufax	8.00	20.00
96 Rabbit Maranville	.10	.25
97 Jim O'Rourke	.10	.25
98 Wilbert Robinson	.20	.50
99 Pie Traynor	.20	.50
100 Zach Wheat	.10	.25
NNO 3rd series Header	.10	.25
NNO 1st series Header	.10	.25
NNO 2nd series Header	.10	.25

1977 Bob Parker More Baseball Cartoons

These 24 cartoons feature imporant players in Baseball History as drawn by noted sports artist Bob Parker. These cards feature drawings on the front and are blank-backed

Card	Low	High
COMPLETE SET (24)	15.00	40.00
1 Hank Aaron	2.00	5.00
Babe Ruth		
2 Ernie Banks	.60	1.50
3 Rod Carew	.40	1.00
4 Joe DiMaggio	2.00	5.00
5 Doug Flynn	.10	.25
6 Mike Garcia	.10	.25
7 Steve Garvey	.20	.50
Greg Luzinski		
8 Lou Gehrig	2.00	5.00
9 Chuck Klein	.20	.50
Hack Wilson		
10 Don Larsen	.20	.50
11 Fred Lynn	.20	.50
12 Roy Majtyka	.10	.25
13 Pepper Martin	.20	.50
14 Christy Mathewson	.40	1.00
15 Cal McVey	.30	.75
16 Tony Perez	.30	.75
17 Babe Ruth	2.00	5.00
Lou Gehrig		
18 Everett Scott	.10	.25
19 Bobby Thomson	.20	.50
20 Ted Williams/1939 Version of Williams	2.00	5.00
Drawn in 7		
21 Ted Williams	2.00	5.00
Last .400 Hitter		
Drawn in 76		
22 Bill Madlock	.20	.50
23 Honus Wagner	.30	.75
Al Spalding		
Buck Ewing		
Henry Chadw		
24 Checklist	.10	.25

1968-70 Partridge Meats

These black and white (with some red trim and text) photo-like cards feature players from all three Cincinnati major league sports teams of that time: Cincinnati Reds baseball (BB1-BB20), Cincinnati Bengals football (FB1-FB5), and Cincinnati Royals basketball (BK1-BK2). The cards measure approximately 4" by 5" or 3-3/4" by 5-1/2" and were issued over a period of years. The cards are blank backed and a "Mr. Whopper" card was also issued in honor of the 7'-3" company spokesperson. The Tom Rhoads football card was only recently discovered, in 2012, adding to the prevailing thought that these cards were issued over a period of years since its format matches some of the baseball cards and not the other four more well-known football cards in the set. Joe Morgan was also recently added to the checklist indicating that more cards could turn up in the future. This card follows the same format as Gullett, May, Perez, and Tolan (all measuring 3-3/4" by 5-1/2") missing the team's logo on the cap, missing the team's nickname in the text, and missing the company's slogan below the image. Some collectors believe this style to be consistent with a 1972 release.

Card	Low	High
COMPLETE SET (14)	400.00	800.00
BB1 Ted Abernathy SP	25.00	50.00
BB2 Johnny Bench	60.00	120.00
(measures 4" x 5")		
BB3 Jimmy Bragan CO	12.50	25.00
(measures 4" x 5")		
BB4 Dave Bristol MG SP	25.00	50.00
BB5 Don Gullett	15.00	30.00
(measures 3 3/4" x 5 1/2")		
BB6 Tommy Harper SP	25.00	50.00
BB7 Tommy Helms	12.50	25.00
(measures 4" x 5")		
BB8 Lee May	20.00	40.00
(measures 3 3/4" x 5 1/2")		
BB9 Denis Menke SP	25.00	50.00
BB10 Jim Merritt SP	25.00	50.00
BB11 Joe Morgan SP	75.00	150.00
(measures 3 3/4" x 5 1/2")		
BB12 Gary Nolan	12.50	25.00
(measures 4" x 5")		
BB13 Gary Nolan		
(measures 3 3/4" x 5 1/2")		
BB14 Milt Pappas SP	25.00	50.00
BB15 Don Pavletich SP	25.00	50.00
BB16 Tony Perez	40.00	80.00
(measures 3 3/4" x 5 1/2")		
BB17 Mel Queen	12.50	25.00
(measures 4" x 5")		
BB18 Pete Rose	75.00	150.00
(measures 4" x 5")		
BB19 Jim Stewart SP	25.00	50.00
BB20 Bob Tolan	12.50	25.00
(measures 3 3/4" x 5 1/2")		

1914 Pastime Novelty Postcard

This postcard, issued by the Pastime Novelty company featured Christy Mathewson in a photo taken during the 1913 World Series. Little else is known about ths postcard so all additional information is appreciated.

Card	Low	High
1 Christy Mathewson	400.00	800.00

1868-71 Peck and Snyder Trade Cards

Issued over a period of years, these cards feature rare photos of some of the earliest professional teams. The Lowells card is currently known as only a photocopy.

Card	Low	High
COMPLETE SET	50,000.00	100,000.00
1 Lowells/1868	20,000.00	40,000.00
2 Atlantics/1868	12,500.00	25,000.00
3 Chicago White Sox 1870	12,500.00	25,000.00
4 Mutuals/1870	12,500.00	25,000.00
5 Philadelphia Athletics 1870	12,500.00	25,000.00

1914 People's Tobacco Kotton T216

The cards in this 59-player set measure 1 1/2" by 2 5/8" and contains unnumbered cards. The players have been alphabetized and numbered for reference in the checklist below. Back variations, listed in order of scarcity from hardest to easiest, within this set include Kotton, Mino and Virginia Brights Cigarettes.

Card	Low	High
COMPLETE SET	30,000.00	60,000.00
1A Jack Barry	400.00	800.00
Batting		
1B Jack Barry	400.00	800.00
Fielding		
2 Harry Bemis	400.00	800.00
3A Chief Bender	750.00	1,500.00
Striped Cap		
Phila Am.		
3B Chief Bender	750.00	1,500.00
Striped Cap		
Baltimore Fed		
3C Chief Bender	750.00	1,500.00
White Cap		
Phila Am.		
3D Chief Bender	750.00	1,500.00
White Cap		
Baltimore Fed		
4 Bill Bergen	400.00	800.00
5A Bob Bescher	400.00	800.00
Cincinnati		
5B Bob Bescher	400.00	800.00
St. Louis Fed		
6 Roger Bresnahan	750.00	1,500.00
7A Al Bridwell	400.00	800.00
batting		
7B Al Bridwell	400.00	800.00
Sliding		
New York Nat'l		
7C Al Bridwell	400.00	800.00
Sliding		
St. Louis Feds		
8 Donie Bush	450.00	900.00
9 Doc Casey	400.00	800.00
10 Frank Chance	900.00	1,800.00
11A Hal Chase	750.00	1,500.00
Portrait		
11B Hal Chase	750.00	1,500.00
Fielding		
New York Am.		
11C Hal Chase	750.00	1,500.00
Fielding		
Buffalo		
12A Ty Cobb Standing Detroit Am.	7,500.00	15,000.00
12B Ty Cobb Standing Detroit Americans	7,500.00	15,000.00
12C Ty Cobb Batting	7,500.00	15,000.00
13 Sam Crawford	750.00	1,500.00
13A Eddie Collins	750.00	1,500.00
Philadelphia Amer.		
13B Eddie Collins	750.00	1,500.00
Phila Am.		
13C Eddie Collins	750.00	1,500.00
Chicago Americans		
14 Harry Davis	400.00	800.00
15 Ray Demmitt	400.00	800.00
17A Bill Donovan	400.00	800.00
Detroit Amer.		
17B Bill Donovan	400.00	800.00
N.Y. Americans		
18A Red Dooin	400.00	800.00
Phila Nat.		
18B Red Dooin	400.00	800.00
Cincinnati		
19A Mickey Doolan	400.00	800.00
Phila Nat.		
19B Mickey Doolan	400.00	800.00
Baltimore Fed.		
20 Patsy Dougherty	400.00	800.00
21A Larry Doyle	450.00	900.00
N.Y. Nat'l		
21B Larry Doyle	450.00	900.00
New York Nat'l		
21C Larry Doyle	450.00	900.00
Throwing		
22 Clyde Engle	400.00	800.00
23A Johnny Evers	750.00	1,500.00
Chicago Nat'l		
23B Johnny Evers	750.00	1,500.00
Boston National		
24 Art Fromme	400.00	800.00
25A George Gibson	400.00	800.00
Back		
Pittsburg Nat'l		
25B George Gibson	400.00	800.00
Back		
Pittsburgh Nat'l.		
25C George Gibson	400.00	800.00
Front		
Pittsburg Nat'l		
25D George Gibson	400.00	800.00
Front		
Pittsburgh Nat'l		
26A Topsy Hartsel	400.00	800.00
Phila Am.		
26B Topsy Hartsel	400.00	800.00
Philadelphia Amer.		
27A Roy Hartzell	400.00	800.00
Catching		
27B Roy Hartzell	400.00	800.00
Batting		
28A Fred Jacklitsch	400.00	800.00
Phila Nat.		
28B Fred Jacklitsch	400.00	800.00
Baltimore Feds		
29A Hugh Jennings	750.00	1,500.00
Dance: Red		
29B Hugh Jennings	750.00	1,500.00
Dance; Orange		
30 Red Kleinow	400.00	800.00
31A Otto Knabe	400.00	800.00
Phila Nat.		
31B Otto Knabe	400.00	800.00
Baltimore Fed.		
32 John Knight	400.00	800.00
33A Nap Lajoie	1,750.00	3,500.00
Portrait		
33B Nap Lajoie	1,750.00	3,500.00
Fielding		
Cleveland		
33C Nap Lajoie	1,750.00	3,500.00
Fielding		
Phila Amer.		
34A Hans Lobert	400.00	800.00
Cincinnati		
34B Hans Lobert	400.00	800.00
New York Nat'l		
35 Sherry Magee	450.00	900.00
36 Rube Marquard	750.00	1,500.00
37A Christy Mathewson	1,500.00	3,000.00
Small Print		
37B Christy Mathewson	1,500.00	3,000.00
Large Print		
38A John McGraw MG	750.00	1,500.00
Small Print		
38B John McGraw MG	750.00	1,500.00
Large Print		
39 Larry McLean	400.00	800.00
40 George McQuillan	400.00	800.00
41A Dots Miller	400.00	800.00
Batting		
41B Dots Miller	400.00	800.00
Fielding		
Pittsburg		
41C Dots Miller	400.00	800.00
Fielding		
St. Louis Nat'l		
42A Danny Murphy	400.00	800.00
Phila Amer.		
42B Danny Murphy	400.00	800.00
Brooklyn Feds.		
43 Rebel Oakes	400.00	800.00
44 Bill O'Hara	400.00	800.00
45 Eddie Plank	750.00	1,500.00
46A Germany Schaefer	450.00	900.00
Washington		
46B Germany Schaefer	450.00	900.00
Newark Fed.		
47 Admiral Schlei	400.00	800.00
48 Boss Schmidt	400.00	800.00
49 Dave Shean	400.00	800.00
50 Johnny Siegle	400.00	800.00
51 Tris Speaker	1,750.00	3,500.00
52 Oscar Stanage	400.00	800.00
53 George Stovall	400.00	800.00
54 Ed Sweeney	400.00	800.00
55A Joe Tinker	750.00	1,500.00
Portrait		
55B Joe Tinker	750.00	1,500.00
Batting		
Chicago Nat'l		
55C Joe Tinker	750.00	1,500.00
Batting		
Chicago Feds		
56A Honus Wagner	4,000.00	8,000.00
Batting		
Pittsburg Nat'l		
56B Honus Wagner	4,000.00	8,000.00
Batting		
Pittsburgh Nat'l		
56C Honus Wagner	4,000.00	8,000.00
Throwing		
S.S		
56D Honus Wagner	4,000.00	8,000.00
Throwing/#2b		
57 Hooks Wiltse	400.00	800.00
58 Cy Young	1,750.00	3,500.00
59A Heinie Zimmerman/2B	400.00	800.00
59B Heinie Zimmerman/3B	400.00	800.00

1977 Pepsi Glove Discs

These discs actually form the middle of a glove-shaped tab which was inserted in cartons of Pepsi-Cola during a baseball related promotion. The disc itself measures 3 3/8" in diameter whereas the glove tab is approximately 9" tall. The backs of the discs and the tab tell how you can get a personalized superstar shirt of Pete Rose, Rico Carty, Joe Morgan, or Rick Manning by sending in Pepsi cap liners. The players are shown in "generic" hats, i.e., the team logos have been airbrushed. This set was sanctioned by the Major League Baseball Players Association. The set is quite heavy in Cleveland Indians and Cincinnati Reds.

Card	Low	High
COMPLETE SET (72)	40.00	80.00
1 Robin Yount	2.00	5.00
2 Rod Carew	2.00	5.00
3 Butch Wynegar	.20	.50
4 Manny Sanguillen	.10	.25
5 Mike Hargrove	.20	.50
6 Larvell Blanks	.10	.25
7 Jim Kern	.10	.25
8 Pat Dobson	.10	.25
9 Rico Carty	.10	.25
10 John Grubb	.10	.25
11 Buddy Bell	.20	.50
12 Rick Manning	.10	.25
13 Dennis Eckersley	2.00	5.00
14 Wayne Garland	.10	.25
15 Dave Laroche	.10	.25
16 Rick Waits	.10	.25
17 Ray Fosse	.10	.25
18 Frank Duffy	.10	.25
19 Duane Kuiper	.10	.25
20 Jim Palmer	2.00	5.00
21 Fred Lynn	.20	.50
22 Carlton Fisk	2.00	5.00
23 Carl Yastrzemski	2.00	5.00
24 Nolan Ryan	4.00	10.00
25 Bobby Grich	.20	.50
26 Ralph Garr	.10	.25
27 Richie Zisk	.10	.25
28 Ron LeFlore	.10	.25
29 Rusty Staub	.40	1.00
30 Mark Fidrych	1.50	4.00
31 Willie Horton	.20	.50
32 George Brett	4.00	10.00
33 Amos Otis	.10	.25
34 Reggie Jackson	2.00	5.00
35 Don Gullett	.10	.25
36 Thurman Munson	.60	1.50
37 Al Hrabosky	.10	.25
38 Mike Tyson	.10	.25
39 Gene Tenace	.20	.50
40 George Hendrick	.10	.25
41 Chris Speier	.10	.25
42 John Montefusco	.10	.25
43 Pete Rose	2.00	5.00
44 Johnny Bench	2.00	5.00
45 Dan Driessen	.10	.25
46 Joe Morgan	1.25	3.00
47 Dave Concepcion	.40	1.00
48 George Foster	.40	1.00
49 Cesar Geronimo	.10	.25
50 Ken Griffey	.40	1.00
51 Gary Nolan	.10	.25
52 Santo Alcala	.10	.25
53 Jack Billingham	.10	.25
54 Pedro Borbon	.10	.25
55 Rawly Eastwick	.10	.25
56 Fred Norman	.10	.25
57 Pat Zachry	.10	.25
58 Jeff Burroughs	.10	.25
59 Manny Trillo	.10	.25
60 Bob Watson	.20	.50
61 Steve Garvey	.60	1.50
62 Don Sutton	1.25	3.00
63 John Candelaria	.10	.25
64 Willie Stargell	1.25	3.00
65 Jerry Reuss	.10	.25
66 Dave Cash	.10	.25
67 Tom Seaver	2.00	5.00
68 Jon Matlack	.10	.25
69 Dave Kingman	.60	1.50
70 Mike Schmidt	2.00	5.00
71 Jay Johnstone	.20	.50
72 Greg Luzinski	.40	1.00

1978 Pepsi

Sponsored by Pepsi-Cola and produced by MSA, this set of 40 collector cards measures approximately 2 1/8" by 9 1/2" and features members of the Cincinnati Reds and 15 national players. A checklist for the Cincinnati Reds (1-25) and for the 15 National players (26-40) is printed. The bottom part of the front has information on how to get a deck of Superstar playing cards free for 250 Pepsi capliners. The backs carry an order form and more detailed information. The cards are unnumbered and checklisted below in alphabetical order by grouping.

Card	Low	High
COMPLETE SET (40)	50.00	100.00
1 Sparky Anderson MG	1.00	2.50
2 Rick Auerbach	.40	1.00
3 Doug Bair UER	.40	1.00

Name is spelled Blair
4 Johnny Bench 3.00 8.00
5 Bill Bonham .40 1.00
6 Pedro Borbon .40 1.00
7 Dave Collins .40 1.00
8 Dave Concepcion 1.00 2.50
9 Dan Driessen .60 1.50
10 George Foster .75 2.00
11 Cesar Geronimo .40 1.00
12 Ken Griffey 1.00 2.50
13 Ken Henderson .40 1.00
14 Tom Hume .40 1.00
15 Junior Kennedy .40 1.00
16 Ray Knight .75 2.00
17 Mike Lum .40 1.00
18 Joe Morgan 2.00 5.00
19 Paul Moskau UER .40 1.00
Name is spelled Moscau
20 Fred Norman .40 1.00
21 Pete Rose 3.00 8.00
22 Manny Sarmiento .40 1.00
23 Tom Seaver 3.00 8.00
24 Dave Tomlin .40 1.00
25 Don Werner .40 1.00
26 Buddy Bell .75 2.00
27 Larry Bowa .60 1.50
28 George Brett 6.00 15.00
29 Jeff Burroughs .40 1.00
30 Rod Carew 2.00 5.00
31 Steve Garvey 1.00 2.50
32 Reggie Jackson 3.00 8.00
33 Dave Kingman .75 2.00
34 Jerry Koosman .60 1.50
35 Bill Madlock .60 1.50
36 Jim Palmer 2.00 5.00
37 Nolan Ryan 8.00 20.00
38 Ted Simmons .75 2.00
39 Carl Yastrzemski 2.00 5.00
40 Richie Zisk .40 1.00

1980-02 Perez-Steele Hall of Fame Postcards

President Ronald Reagan was given the first numbered set issued on May 27th, 1981 at the White House.The sets were also issued with continuation rights. These rights have been transferable over the years. These 3 1/2" by 5 1/2" cards feature noted sports artist Dick Perez drawings. The cards were distributed through Perez-Steele galleries. According to the producer, many of these cards are sold to art or postcard collectors. Just 10,000 of these sets were produced.

COMPLETE SET (260) 1,000.00 1,500.00
1 Ty Cobb 15.00 40.00
2 Walter Johnson 4.00 10.00
3 Christy Mathewson 4.00 10.00
4 Babe Ruth 25.00 60.00
5 Honus Wagner 4.00 10.00
6 Morgan Bulkeley .40 1.00
7 Ban Johnson .40 1.00
8 Nap Lajoie 2.00 5.00
9 Connie Mack 2.00 5.00
10 John McGraw 2.00 5.00
11 Tris Speaker 2.00 5.00
12 George Wright .40 1.00
13 Cy Young 2.00 5.00
14 Grover Alexander 2.00 5.00
15 Alex. Cartwright .40 1.00
16 Henry Chadwick .40 1.00
17 Cap Anson 1.00 2.50
18 Eddie Collins 2.00 5.00
19 Candy Cummings .60 1.50
20 Charles Comiskey .40 1.00
21 Buck Ewing .60 1.50
22 Lou Gehrig 15.00 40.00
23 Willie Keeler .60 1.50
24 Hoss Radbourne .60 1.50
25 George Sisler 6.00 15.00
26 A.G. Spalding .60 1.50
27 Rogers Hornsby 2.00 5.00
28 Kenesaw Landis .40 1.00
29 Roger Bresnahan .60 1.50
30 Dan Brouthers .60 1.50
31 Fred Clarke .60 1.50
32 Jimmy Collins .60 1.50
33 Ed Delahanty .60 1.50
34 Hugh Duffy .60 1.50
35 Hughie Jennings .60 1.50
36 King Kelly 1.00 2.50
37 Jim O'Rourke .60 1.50
38 Wilbert Robinson .60 1.50
39 Jesse Burkett .60 1.50
40 Frank Chance 2.00 5.00
41 Jack Chesbro .60 1.50
42 Johnny Evers 2.00 5.00
43 Clark Griffith .60 1.50
44 Thomas McCarthy .60 1.50
45 Joe McGinnity .60 1.50
46 Eddie Plank .60 1.50
47 Joe Tinker 2.00 5.00
48 Rube Waddell .60 1.50
49 Ed Walsh .60 1.50
50 Mickey Cochrane 2.00 5.00
51 Frankie Frisch 2.00 5.00
52 Lefty Grove 2.00 5.00
53 Carl Hubbell 4.00 10.00
54 Herb Pennock .60 1.50
55 Pie Traynor 1.00 2.50
56 Mordecai Brown .60 1.50
57 Charlie Gehringer 1.00 2.50
58 Kid Nichols .60 1.50
59 Jimmy Foxx 6.00 15.00
(Jimmie)
60 Mel Ott 4.00 10.00
61 Harry Heilmann .60 1.50
62 Paul Waner 2.00 5.00
63 Edward Barrow .40 1.00
64 Chief Bender 2.00 5.00
65 Tom Connolly .40 1.00
66 Dizzy Dean 6.00 15.00
67 Bill Klem .40 1.00
68 Al Simmons 2.00 5.00
69 Bobby Wallace .60 1.50
70 Harry Wright .60 1.50
71 Bill Dickey 2.00 5.00
72 Rabbit Maranville .60 1.50
73 Bill Terry 2.00 5.00
74 Frank Baker .60 1.50
75 Joe DiMaggio 25.00 60.00
76 Gabby Hartnett .60 1.50
77 Ted Lyons .60 1.50
78 Ray Schalk .60 1.50
79 Dazzy Vance .60 1.50
80 Joe Cronin 1.00 2.50
81 Hank Greenberg 8.00 20.00
82 Sam Crawford 2.00 5.00
83 Joe McCarthy .40 1.00
84 Zack Wheat .60 1.50
85 Max Carey .60 1.50
86 Billy Hamilton .60 1.50
87 Bob Feller 6.00 15.00
88 Bill McKechnie .40 1.00
89 Jackie Robinson 10.00 25.00
90 Edd Roush 1.00 2.50
91 John Clarkson .60 1.50
92 Elmer Flick .60 1.50
93 Sam Rice 2.00 5.00
94 Eppa Rixey .60 1.50
95 Luke Appling 1.00 2.50
96 Red Faber .60 1.50
97 Burleigh Grimes .60 1.50
98 Miller Huggins .60 1.50
99 Tim Keefe .60 1.50
100 Heinie Manush .60 1.50
101 John Ward .60 1.50
102 Pud Galvin .60 1.50
103 Casey Stengel 4.00 10.00
104 Ted Williams 25.00 60.00
105 Branch Rickey .60 1.50
106 Red Ruffing .60 1.50
107 Lloyd Waner .60 1.50
108 Kiki Cuyler .60 1.50
109 Goose Goslin 2.00 5.00
110 Joe Medwick .60 1.50
111 Roy Campanella 4.00 10.00
112 Stan Coveleski .60 1.50
113 Waite Hoyt .60 1.50
114 Stan Musial 15.00 40.00
115 Lou Boudreau 5.00 12.00
116 Earle Combs .60 1.50
117 Ford Frick .40 1.00
118 Jesse Haines .60 1.50
119 David Bancroft .60 1.50
120 Jake Beckley .60 1.50
121 Chick Hafey .40 1.00
122 Harry Hooper .60 1.50
123 Joe Kelley .60 1.50
124 Rube Marquard 2.00 5.00
125 Satchel Paige 10.00 25.00
126 George Weiss .40 1.00
127 Yogi Berra 6.00 15.00
128 Josh Gibson 2.00 5.00
129 Lefty Gomez 1.00 2.50
130 William Harridge .40 1.00
131 Sandy Koufax 8.00 20.00
132 Buck Leonard 6.00 15.00
133 Early Wynn 2.00 5.00
134 Ross Youngs .60 1.50
135 Roberto Clemente 20.00 50.00
136 Billy Evans .40 1.00
137 Monte Irvin 3.00 8.00
138 George Kelly .60 1.50
139 Warren Spahn 4.00 10.00
140 Mickey Welch .60 1.50
141 Cool Papa Bell 3.00 8.00
142 Jim Bottomley .60 1.50
143 Jocko Conlan .40 1.00
144 Whitey Ford 8.00 20.00
145 Mickey Mantle 25.00 60.00
146 Sam Thompson .60 1.50
147 Earl Averill 1.00 2.50
148 Bucky Harris .60 1.50
149 Billy Herman 1.00 2.50
150 Judy Johnson 4.00 10.00
151 Ralph Kiner 4.00 10.00
152 Oscar Charleston 1.00 2.50
153 Roger Connor .60 1.50
154 Cal Hubbard .40 1.00
155 Bob Lemon 2.00 5.00
156 Fred Lindstrom .60 1.50
157 Robin Roberts 4.00 10.00
158 Ernie Banks 6.00 15.00
159 Martin Dihigo 2.00 5.00
160 John Lloyd 2.00 5.00
161 Al Lopez 5.00 12.00
162 Amos Rusie .60 1.50
163 Joe Sewell .60 1.50
164 Addie Joss .60 1.50
165 Larry MacPhail .40 1.00
166 Eddie Mathews 4.00 10.00
167 Warren Giles .40 1.00
168 Willie Mays 15.00 40.00
169 Hack Wilson .60 1.50
170 Al Kaline 6.00 15.00
171 Chuck Klein .60 1.50
172 Duke Snider 8.00 20.00
173 Tom Yawkey .40 1.00
174 Rube Foster .40 1.00
175 Bob Gibson 4.00 10.00
176 Johnny Mize 1.00 2.50
177 Hank Aaron 8.00 20.00
178 Happy Chandler .40 1.00
179 Travis Jackson .60 1.50
180 Frank Robinson 8.00 20.00
181 Walter Alston 3.00 8.00
182 George Kell 3.00 8.00
183 Juan Marichal 2.00 5.00
184 Brooks Robinson 6.00 15.00
185 Luis Aparicio 4.00 10.00
186 Don Drysdale 2.00 5.00
187 Rick Ferrell .60 1.50
188 Harmon Killebrew 4.00 10.00
189 Pee Wee Reese 6.00 15.00
190 Lou Brock 6.00 15.00
191 Enos Slaughter 3.00 8.00
192 Arky Vaughan .60 1.50
193 Hoyt Wilhelm 3.00 8.00
194 Bobby Doerr 3.00 8.00
195 Ernie Lombardi .60 1.50
196 Willie McCovey 2.00 5.00
197 Ray Dandridge 2.00 5.00
198 Catfish Hunter 2.00 5.00
199 Billy Williams 3.00 8.00
200 Willie Stargell 2.50 6.00
201 Al Barlick 1.00 2.50
202 Johnny Bench 2.00 5.00
203 Red Schoendienst 3.00 8.00
204 Carl Yastrzemski 8.00 20.00
205 Joe Morgan 6.00 15.00
206 Jim Palmer 2.00 5.00
207 Rod Carew 6.00 15.00
208 Ferguson Jenkins 4.00 10.00
209 Tony Lazzeri .60 1.50
210 Gaylord Perry 3.00 8.00
211 Bill Veeck .40 1.00
212 Rollie Fingers 3.00 8.00
213 Bill McGowan .40 1.00
214 Hal Newhouser 4.00 10.00
215 Tom Seaver 8.00 20.00
216 Reggie Jackson 8.00 20.00
217 Steve Carlton 6.00 15.00
218 Leo Durocher 2.00 5.00
219 Phil Rizzuto 8.00 20.00
220 Richie Ashburn 4.00 10.00
221 Leon Day 1.00 2.50
222 William Hulbert .40 1.00
223 Mike Schmidt 8.00 20.00
224 Vic Willis 2.00 5.00
225 Jim Bunning 4.00 10.00
226 Bill Foster 2.00 5.00
227 Ned Hanlon 2.00 5.00
228 Earl Weaver 4.00 10.00
229 Nellie Fox .60 1.50
230 Tom Lasorda 4.00 10.00
231 Phil Niekro 3.00 8.00
232 Willie Wells .60 1.50
233 George Davis .60 1.50
234 Larry Doby 3.00 8.00
235 Lee MacPhail .40 1.00
236 Joe Rogan .60 1.50
237 Don Sutton 3.00 8.00
238 George Brett 8.00 20.00
239 Orlando Cepeda 10
240 Nestor Chylak .40 1.00
241 Nolan Ryan 10.00 25.00
242 Frank Selee .40 1.00
243 Joe Williams .40 1.00
244 Robin Yount 4.00 10.00
245 Sparky Anderson 1.00 2.50
246 Carlton Fisk 4.00 10.00
247 Bid McPhee .60 1.50
248 Tony Perez 3.00 8.00
249 Turkey Stearnes 2.00 5.00
250 Bill Mazeroski 2.00 5.00
251 Kirby Puckett 6.00 15.00
252 Hilton Smith .60 1.50
253 Dave Winfield 4.00 10.00
F George H.W. Bush 1.00 2.50
Edward W. Stack
G Franklin A. Steele MEM .40 1.00
A Abner Doubleday 2.00 5.00
B Stephen C. Clark .40 1.00
C Paul S. Kerr .40 1.00
D Edward W. Stack .40 1.00
E Perez-Steele Galleries .40 1.00

1974 Pete Ward Clinic

These six 5" by 7" blank-back photos feature guest instructors at the Pete Ward Baseball Clinic. These photos, which were issued by the Fred Meyer Company all came in one mailing envelope. Since these photos are unnumbered, we have sequenced them in alphabetical order.

1 Mickey Mantle
2 Billy Martin
3 Pete Rose
4 Harry Walker
5 Pete Ward
6 Maury Wills

1889 Philadelphia Stage

This 14 card set of prints ran in the Stage, a paper issued in Philadelphia late in the 19th century. These prints measure approximately 9" by 12" and filled up an entire newspaper page. Since these were unnumbered, we have sequenced these prints in alphabetical order.

1909 Philadelphia Caramel E95

The cards in this 25-card set measure 1 1/2" by 2 3/4". This set of color drawings was issued by the Philadelphia Caramel Company about 1909. The back is checklisted with its own numbering system (begins with "1. Wagner"), but has been alphabetized for convenience in this listing. Blank backs found in this set are probably cut from advertising panels and should not be considered as proof cards. Of note, our pricing for raw cards is provided in VgEx condition due to the fact that most cards from this set are found in off-grade shape.

COMPLETE SET (25) 15,000.00 30,000.00
1 Chief Bender 350.00 600.00
2 Bill Carrigan 125.00 200.00
3 Frank Chance 300.00 500.00
4 Ed Cicotte 350.00 600.00
5 Ty Cobb 2,500.00 4,000.00
6 Eddie Collins 300.00 500.00
7 Sam Crawford 300.00 500.00
8 Art Devlin 125.00 200.00
9 Larry Doyle 125.00 200.00
10 Johnny Evers 300.00 500.00
11 Solly Hoffman 125.00 200.00
12 Harry Krause 125.00 200.00
13 Tommy Leach 125.00 200.00
14 Harry Lord 125.00 200.00
15 Nick Maddox 125.00 200.00
16 Christy Mathewson 900.00 1,500.00
17 Matty McIntyre 125.00 200.00
18 Fred Merkle 150.00 250.00
19 Harry (Cy) Morgan 125.00 200.00
20 Eddie Plank 900.00 1,500.00
21 Ed Reulbach 125.00 200.00
22 Honus Wagner 1,500.00 2,500.00
23 Ed Willett 125.00 200.00
24 Vic Willis 300.00 500.00
25 Hooks Wiltse 125.00 200.00

1910 Philadelphia Caramel E96

The cards in this 30-card set measure 1 1/2" by 2 3/4". The red printed backs in this set carry the statement "previous Series 25, making total issue 55 cards", and for this reason it is often referred to as the second series of E95. Issued about 1912, the numbering of the original checklist (starts with "1. Davis") has been rearranged alphabetically below. Some blank backs are known. Listed pricing for raw cards references "VgEx" condition.

COMPLETE SET (30) 2,500.00 5,000.00
1 Babe Adams 200.00 350.00
2 Red Ames 200.00 350.00
3 Frank Arrelanes 200.00 350.00
4 Frank Baker 350.00 600.00
5 Mordecai Brown 350.00 600.00
6 Fred Clark 300.00 500.00
7 Harry Davis 200.00 350.00
8 Jim Delehanty 200.00 350.00
9 Bill Donovan 200.00 350.00
10 Red Dooin 200.00 350.00
11 George Gibson 200.00 350.00
12 Buck Herzog 200.00 350.00
13 Hugh Jennings MG 300.00 500.00
14 Ed Karger 200.00 350.00
15 Johnny Kling 200.00 350.00
16 Ed Konetchy 200.00 350.00
17 Napoleon Lajoie 600.00 1,000.00
18 Connie Mack MG 600.00 1,000.00
19 Rube Marquard 300.00 500.00
20 George McQuillan 200.00 350.00
21 Chief Meyers 200.00 350.00
22 Mike Mowrey 200.00 350.00
23 George Mullin 200.00 350.00
24 Red Murray 200.00 350.00
25 Jack Pfeister 200.00 350.00
26 Claude Rossman 200.00 350.00
27 Nap Rucker 200.00 350.00
28 Tubby Spencer 200.00 350.00
29 Ira Thomas 200.00 350.00
30 Joe Tinker 300.00 500.00

1930 Philadelphia Badge Pins

These pins, which measure 1 1/2" in diameter were issued by the Philadelphia Badge company. The fronts have a player photo against a black background with the player's name and team on the bottom

COMPLETE SET (2) 1,250.00 2,500.00
1 Rogers Hornsby 750.00 1,500.00
2 Paul Waner 500.00 1,000.00

1949 Philadelphia Bulletin

This 59-card set features black-and-white portraits of the Philadelphia A's and Phillies. Six of the portraits were inserted each week in the "Fun Book" section of the "Philadelphia Sunday Bulletin" from May 22 through July 24, 1949. Only five portraits were inserted in the paper the last Sunday. The cards are unnumbered and checklisted below in alphabetical order.

COMPLETE SET (59) 150.00 300.00
1 Richie Ashburn 12.50 25.00
2 Joe Astroth 2.00 4.00
3 Bennie Bengough CO 2.50 5.00

4 Hank Biasetti	2.00	4.00
5 Charles Bicknell	2.00	4.00
6 Buddy Blattner	2.00	4.00
7 Hank Borowy	2.00	4.00
8 Lou Brissie	2.00	4.00
9 Earle Brucker CO	2.00	4.00
10 Ralph Caballero	2.00	4.00
11 Sam Chapman	2.50	5.00
12 Joe Coleman	2.50	5.00
13 Dusty Cooke CO	2.00	4.00
14 Thomas Davis	2.00	4.00
15 Blix Donnelly	2.00	4.00
16 Jimmy Dykes CO	3.00	6.00
17 Del Ennis	3.00	6.00
18 Ferris Fain	3.00	6.00
19 Dick Fowler	2.00	4.00
20 Nellie Fox	12.50	25.00
21 Mike Guerra	2.00	4.00
22 Granny Hamner	3.00	6.00
23 Charley Harris	2.00	4.00
24 Ken Heintzleman	2.00	4.00
25 Stan Hollmig	2.00	4.00
26 Willie Jones	2.00	4.00
27 Eddie Joost	2.50	5.00
28 Alex Kellner	2.00	4.00
29 Jim Konstanty	3.00	6.00
30 Stan Lopata	2.50	5.00
31 Connie Mack MG	12.50	25.00
32 Earle Mack CO	2.50	5.00
33 Hank Majeskie	2.00	4.00
34 Phil Marchildon	2.00	4.00
35 Jackie Mayo	2.00	4.00
36 Bill McCahan	2.00	4.00
37 Barney McCoskey	2.00	4.00
38 Russ Meyer	2.50	5.00
39 Eddie Miller	2.00	4.00
40 Wally Moses	2.00	4.00
41 Bill Nicholson	2.00	4.00
42 Cy Perkins CO	2.00	4.00
43 Robin Roberts	10.00	20.00
44 Buddy Rosar	2.00	4.00
45 Schoolboy Rowe	3.00	6.00
46 Eddie Sawyer	2.00	4.00
47 Carl Scheib	2.00	4.00
48 Andy Seminick	3.00	6.00
49 Bobby Shantz	4.00	8.00
50 Ken Silvestri	2.00	4.00
51 Al Simmons CO	6.00	12.00
52 Curt Simmons	6.00	12.00
53 Dick Sisler	2.00	4.00
54 Pete Suder	2.00	4.00
55 Ken Trinkle	2.00	4.00
56 Elmer Valo	2.00	4.00
57 Eddie Waitkus	3.00	6.00
58 Don White	2.00	4.00
59 Taft Wright	2.00	4.00

1979 Philadelphia Doubleheaders

These 27 cards were issued to promote the EPSCC shows that have been put on in the Philadelphia area since the 1970's The set features two 1950 Philadelphia players on each card along with a back that either promoted the March 1979 EPSCC show or the Philadelphia Phillies checklist book. The two managers are the only people who have cards to themselves.

COMPLETE SET (30)	12.50	30.00
1 Connie Mack MG	1.25	3.00
2 Joe Astroth Dick Fowler	.40	1.00
3 Sam Chapman Lou Brissie	.40	1.00
4 Bob Dillinger Billy Hitchcock	.60	1.50
5 Ben Guintini Joe Tipton	.40	1.00
6 Bob Hooper Barney McCosky	.40	1.00
7 Eddie Joost Kermit Wahl	.40	1.00
8 Ed Klieman Mike Guerra	.40	1.00
9 Paul Lehner Ferris Fain	.60	1.50
10 Earl Mack AMG Mickey Cochrane CO	1.00	2.50
11 Wally Moses Carl Scheib	.40	1.00
12 Pete Suder Alex Kellner	.40	1.00
13 Elmer Valo Bobby Shantz	.60	1.50
14 Hank Wyse Gene Markland	.40	1.00
15 Robert Wellman Joe Coleman	.40	1.00
16 Eddie Sawyer MG	.60	1.50
17 Johnny Blatnik Taffy Wright	.40	1.00
18 Ralph Caballero Bubba Church	.40	1.00
19 Milo Candini Hank Bowory	.40	1.00
20 Blix Donnelly Bill Nicholson	.60	1.50
21 Mike Goliat Dick Whitman	.40	1.00
22 Granny Hamner Richie Ashburn	1.00	2.50
23 Ken Heintzelman Del Ennis	.40	1.00
24 Willie Jones Russ Meyer	.40	1.00
25 Jim Konstanty Ken Silvestri	.40	1.00
26 Stan Lopata Eddie Waitkus	.40	1.00
27 Ed Sanicki Robin Roberts	1.00	2.50
28 Andy Seminick/Ken Trickle	.40	1.00
29 Dick Sisler Stan Hollmig	.40	1.00
30 Jocko Thompson Curt Simmons	.60	1.50

1911 Philadelphia Evening Times Supplements

Issued as a supplement within the Philadelphia Evening Times, these 15 known supplements feature mainly members of the Philadelphia A's and the New York Giants, who squared off against each other in the 1911 World Series.

COMPLETE SET (15)	2,000.00	4,000.00

1977 Philadelphia Favorites

This 25-card set was used as promotional give-aways for the EPSCC in the Delaware Valley area during the summer of 1977 and measures approximately 3 3/4" by 2 1/4". Some complete sets were also available by mail at the time of issue for $2.75 from the set's producer. The fronts feature a sepia photo of a former Phillies or Athletics player with white borders. The player's name, position, team, and years played are printed in the bottom margin.

COMPLETE SET (25)	20.00	50.00
1 Connie Mack	2.00	5.00
2 Nap Lajoie	2.00	5.00
3 Eddie Collins	2.00	5.00
4 Lefty Grove	2.00	5.00
5 Al Simmons	1.00	2.50
6 Jimmy Foxx (Jimmie)	2.00	5.00
7 Frank Baker	1.00	2.50
8 Ferris Fain	.40	1.00
9 Jimmy Dykes	.40	1.00
10 Willie Jones	.40	1.00
11 Del Ennis	.40	1.00
12 Granny Hamner	.40	1.00
13 Andy Seminick	.40	1.00
14 Robin Roberts	2.00	5.00
15 Ed Delahanty	1.00	2.50
16 Gavvy Cravath	.75	2.00
17 Cy Williams	.40	1.00
18 Chuck Klein	1.00	2.50
19 Richie Ashburn	2.00	5.00
20 Bobby Shantz	.40	1.00
21 Gus Zernial	.40	1.00
22 Eddie Sawyer	.40	1.00
23 G.C. Alexander	1.00	2.50
24 Wally Moses	.40	1.00
25 Connie Mack Stadium/(nee Shibe Park)	.40	1.00

1940 Phillies Team Issue

These 31 5 7/8" by 8 1/2" blank backed photos were issued by the Philadelphia Phillies. They are unnumbered and we have sequenced them in alphabetical order.

COMPLETE SET	90.00	180.00
1 Morrie Arnovich	5.00	10.00
2 Bill Atwood	5.00	10.00
3 Walter Beck	5.00	10.00
4 Stan Benjamin	5.00	10.00
5 Wally Berger	7.50	15.00
6 Cy Blanton	5.00	10.00
7 Bob Bragan	10.00	20.00
8 Lloyd Brown	5.00	10.00
9 Roy Bruner	5.00	10.00
10 Kirby Higbe	6.00	12.00
11 Frank Hoerst	5.00	10.00
12 Si Johnson	5.00	10.00
13 Syl Johnson	5.00	10.00
14 Chuck Klein	15.00	30.00
15 Ed Levy	5.00	10.00
16 Dan Litwhiler	6.00	12.00
17 Hans Lobert CO	6.00	12.00
18 Art Mahan	5.00	10.00
19 Hershel Martin	5.00	10.00
20 Joe Marty	5.00	10.00
21 Merrill May	5.00	10.00
22 Mel Mazzera	5.00	10.00
23 Walt Millies	5.00	10.00
24 Alex Monchak	5.00	10.00
25 Heinie Mueller	5.00	10.00
26 Hugh Mulcahy	5.00	10.00
27 Ike Pearson	5.00	10.00
28 Doc Prothro MG	5.00	10.00
29 John Rizzo	5.00	10.00
30 George Scharein	5.00	10.00
31 Ham Schulte	5.00	10.00
32 Clyde Smoll	5.00	10.00
33 Gus Suhr	6.00	12.00
34 Ben Warren	5.00	10.00
35 Del Young	5.00	10.00
36 Philadelphia Phillies	10.00	20.00

1941 Phillies Team Issue

This 26-card set of the Philadelphia Phillies measuring approximately 6" by 8 1/2" features black-and-white player photos with fascimile autographs. The backs are blank. The cards are unnumbered and checklisted below in alphabetical order.

COMPLETE SET (26)	125.00	250.00
1 Morrie Arnovich	5.00	10.00
2 Bill Atwood	5.00	10.00
3 Walter Beck	5.00	10.00
4 Stan Benjamin	5.00	10.00
5 Bob Bragan	7.50	15.00
6 Roy Bruner	5.00	10.00
7 Kirby Higbe	6.00	12.00
8 Frank Hoerst	5.00	10.00
9 Si Johnson	5.00	10.00
10 Syl Johnson	5.00	10.00
11 Chuck Klein	15.00	30.00
12 Ed Levy	5.00	10.00
13 Dan Litwhiler	6.00	12.00
14 Hans Lobert	6.00	12.00
15 Hershel Martin	5.00	10.00
16 Joe Marty	5.00	10.00
17 Merrill May	5.00	10.00
18 Walt Millies	5.00	10.00
19 Hugh Mulcahy	5.00	10.00
20 Ike Pearson	5.00	10.00
21 Doc Prothro	5.00	10.00
22 George Scharein	5.00	10.00
23 Clyde Smoll	5.00	10.00
24 Gus Suhr	6.00	12.00
25 Ben Warren	5.00	10.00
26 Del Young	5.00	10.00

1943 Phillies Team Issue

This 23-card set of the Philadelphia Phillies measures approximately 6" by 8 1/2" and features black-and-white player photos with white borders. The backs are blank. The cards are unnumbered and checklisted below in alphabetical order. This set is so large as it presumed that the Phillies kept issuing photos during the year as players were shuttling in and out of the majors during World War II.

COMPLETE SET (23)	200.00	400.00
1 Buster Adams	5.00	10.00
2 Walter Beck	5.00	10.00
3 Stan Benjamin	5.00	10.00
4 Cy Blanton	5.00	10.00
5 Bobby Bragan	6.00	12.00
6 Charlie Brewster	5.00	10.00
7 Paul Busby	5.00	10.00
8 Bennie Culp	5.00	10.00
9 Babe Dahlgren	6.00	12.00
10 Lloyd Dietz	5.00	10.00
11 Nick Etten	6.00	12.00
12 George Eyrich	5.00	10.00
13 Charlie Fuchs	5.00	10.00
14 Al Glossop	5.00	10.00
14 Al Gerheauser	5.00	10.00
15 Frank Hoerst	5.00	10.00
16 Si Johnson	5.00	10.00
17 Bill Killefer	5.00	10.00
18 Newell Kimball	5.00	10.00
19 Chuck Klein	20.00	40.00
20 Ernie Koy	6.00	12.00
22 Danny Litwhiler	6.00	12.00
23 Jack Kraus	5.00	10.00
24 Mickey Livingston	5.00	10.00
25 Hans Lobert	5.00	10.00
26 Harry Marnie	5.00	10.00
27 Merrill May	5.00	10.00
28 Rube Melton	5.00	10.00
29 Danny Murtaugh	8.00	20.00
30 Sam Nahem	5.00	10.00
31 Earl Naylor	5.00	10.00
32 Ron Northey	5.00	10.00
33 Tom Padden	5.00	10.00
34 Ike Pearson	5.00	10.00
35 Johnny Podgajny	5.00	10.00
36 Schoolboy Rowe	6.00	12.00
37 Neb Stewart	5.00	10.00
38 Coaker Triplett	5.00	10.00
39 Lloyd Waner	12.50	25.00
40 Ben Warren	5.00	10.00
41 Jimmie Wasdell	5.00	10.00

1949 Phillies Lummis Peanut Butter

The cards in this 12-card set measure 3 1/4" by 4 1/4". The 1949 Lummis set of black and white, unnumbered action poses depicts Philadelphia Phillies only. These "cards" are actually stickers and were distributed locally by Lummis Peanut Butter and Sealtest Dairy Products. The prices listed below are for the Sealtest cards. The harder-to-find Lummis variety are worth double the listed values below. The catalog designation is F343.

COMPLETE SET (12)	5,000.00	10,000.00
1 Rich Ashburn	2,000.00	4,000.00
2 Hank Borowy	500.00	1,000.00
3 Del Ennis	800.00	1,600.00
4 Granny Hamner	500.00	1,000.00
5 Puddinhead Jones	500.00	1,000.00
6 Russ Meyer	500.00	1,000.00
7 Bill Nicholson	500.00	1,000.00
8 Robin Roberts	1,500.00	3,000.00
9 Schoolboy Rowe	600.00	1,200.00
10 Andy Seminick	750.00	1,500.00
11 Curt Simmons	750.00	1,500.00
12 Ed Waitkus	600.00	1,200.00

1950 Phillies Philadelphia Inquirer

This set of cards have posed color photos and measure 4 1/4" X 5 3/4". Cards are printed on newsprint and have facsimile autographs. A brief biography of the player is printed underneath his name. The set is titled on the bottom "Inquirer Fightin' Phillies Album".

COMPLETE SET (24)	125.00	250.00
1 Richie Ashburn	12.50	25.00
2 Jimmy Bloodworth	5.00	10.00
3 Putsy Caballero	5.00	10.00
4 Milo Candini	5.00	10.00
5 Bubba Church	5.00	10.00
6 Blix Donnelly	5.00	10.00
7 Del Ennis	7.50	15.00
8 Mike Goliat	5.00	10.00
9 Granny Hamner	6.00	12.00
10 Ken Heintzelman	5.00	10.00
11 Stan Hollmig	5.00	10.00
12 Ken Johnson	5.00	10.00
13 Willie Puddin-Head Jones	6.00	12.00
14 Stan Lopata	5.00	10.00
15 Russ Meyer	5.00	10.00
16 Bob Miller	5.00	10.00
17 Bill Nicholson	6.00	12.00
18 Robin Roberts	12.50	25.00
19 Andy Seminick	5.00	10.00
20 Ken Silvestri	5.00	10.00
21 Curt Simmons	7.50	15.00
22 Dick Sisler	6.00	12.00
23 Eddie Waitkus	6.00	12.00
24 Dick Whitman	5.00	10.00

1955 Phillies Felin's Franks

These horizontal 4" by 3 5/8" cards, with rounded corners, features members of the 1955 Philadelphia Phillies.The red bordered cards have the player photo on the left with biographical information underneath. The right side of the card lists a different players information from the 1954 season and asks the collector to identify who the player is. The back has information about the contest these cards are involved with. While 30 cards were printed for this set, this set is scarce enough that not all cards are known so any additional information on missing cards are appreciated.

COMPLETE SET	30,000.00	60,000.00
1 Mayo Smith MG	1,500.00	3,000.00
3 Wally Moses CO	1,500.00	3,000.00
4 Whit Wyatt CO	1,500.00	3,000.00
5 Maje McDonell CO	1,500.00	3,000.00
6 Frank Wiechec TR	1,500.00	3,000.00
7 Murry Dickson	1,500.00	3,000.00
8 Earl Torgeson	1,500.00	3,000.00
9 Bobby Morgan	1,500.00	3,000.00
10 Jack Meyer	1,500.00	3,000.00
11 Bob Miller	1,500.00	3,000.00
12 Jim Owens	1,500.00	3,000.00
13 Steve Ridzik	1,500.00	3,000.00
14 Robin Roberts	3,000.00	6,000.00
16 Herm Wehmeier	1,500.00	3,000.00
17 Smoky Burgess	2,000.00	4,000.00
18 Stan Lopata	1,500.00	3,000.00
19 Gus Niarhos	1,500.00	3,000.00
20 Floyd Baker	1,500.00	3,000.00
21 Merv Blaylock	1,500.00	3,000.00
22 Granny Hamner	2,000.00	4,000.00
23 Willie Jones	2,000.00	4,000.00
26 Richie Ashburn	2,500.00	5,000.00
27 Joe Lonnett	1,500.00	3,000.00
28 Mel Clark	1,500.00	3,000.00
29 Bob Greenwood	1,500.00	3,000.00

1956 Phillies Postcards

These six 3 1/4" by 5 1/2" cards feature white borders, autographs on the picture and were sent by the club in relation to fan requests. These cards are unnumbered and we have sequenced them in alphabetical order.

COMPLETE SET (6)	20.00	40.00
1 Richie Ashburn	5.00	10.00
2 Granny Hammer	2.50	5.00
3 Willie Jones	3.00	6.00
4 Stan Lopata	2.50	5.00
5 Robin Roberts	5.00	10.00
6 Curt Simmons	3.00	6.00

1958 Phillies Jay Publishing

This 12-card set of the Philadelphia Phillies measures approximately 5" by 7" and features black-and-white player photos in a white border. These cards were packaged 12 to a packet. The backs are blank. The cards are unnumbered and checklisted below in alphabetical order.

COMPLETE SET (12)	25.00	50.00
1 Harry Anderson	1.50	3.00
2 Richie Ashburn	6.00	12.00
3 Bob Bowman	1.50	3.00
4 Dick Farrell	1.50	3.00
5 Chico Fernandez	1.50	3.00
6 Granny Hamner	1.50	3.00
7 Stan Lopata	1.50	3.00

8 Rip Repulski	1.50	3.00
9 Robin Roberts	6.00	12.00
10 Jack Sanford UER Sandford	1.50	3.00
11 Curt Simmons	2.50	5.00
12 Mayo Smith MG	1.50	3.00

1958-60 Phillies Team Issue

This 19-card blank-backed set features black-and-white photos of the Philadelphia Phillies measuring approximately 3 1/4" by 5 1/2". The cards are unnumbered and checklisted below in alphabetical order.

COMPLETE SET (19)	37.50	75.00
1 Harry Anderson	1.50	3.00
2 Richie Ashburn	5.00	10.00
3 Ed Bouchee	1.50	3.00
4 John Buzhardt	1.50	3.00
5 Johnny Callison	3.00	6.00
6 Jim Coker	1.50	3.00
7 Clay Dalrymple	1.50	3.00
8 Tony Gonzalez	1.50	3.00
9 Granny Hamner	1.50	3.00
10 Willie Jones	2.00	4.00
11 Stan Lopata	1.50	3.00
12 Art Mahaffey	2.00	4.00
13 Gene Mauch MG	2.50	5.00
14 Wally Post	1.50	3.00
15 Robin Roberts	4.00	8.00
16 Eddie Sawyer MG	1.50	3.00
17 Ray Semproch	1.50	3.00
18 Chris Short	2.50	5.00
19 Curt Simmons	2.50	5.00

1959 Phillies Jay Publishing

This 12-card set of the Philadelphia Phillies measures approximately 5" by 7" and features black-and-white player photos in a white border. These cards were packaged 12 to a packet. The backs are blank. The cards are unnumbered and checklisted below in alphabetical order.

COMPLETE SET	20.00	50.00
1 Harry Anderson	1.50	4.00
2 Richie Ashburn	5.00	12.00
3 Ed Bouchee	1.50	4.00
4 Dick Farrell	1.50	4.00
5 Chico Fernandez	1.50	4.00
6 Ruben Gomez	1.50	4.00
7 Harry Hanebrink	1.50	4.00
8 Wally Post	1.50	4.00
9 Robin Roberts	5.00	12.00
10 Eddie Sawyer MG	1.50	4.00
11 Roman Semproch	1.50	4.00
12 Curt Simmons	2.00	5.00

1960 Phillies Jay Publishing

This 12-card set of the Philadelphia Phillies measures approximately 5" X 7". The fronts feature black-and-white posed player photos with the player's and team name printed below in the white border. These cards were packaged 12 to a packet and originally sold for 25 cents. The backs are blank. The cards are unnumbered and checklisted below in alphabetical order.

COMPLETE SET (12)	20.00	50.00
1 Ruben Amaro	1.50	4.00
2 Harry Anderson	1.50	4.00
3 Ed Bouchee	1.50	4.00
4 John Callison	2.50	6.00
5 Jim Coker	1.50	4.00
6 Al Dark	2.50	6.00
7 Dick Farrell	1.50	4.00
8 Pancho Herrera	1.50	4.00
9 Jim Owens	1.50	4.00
10 Wally Post	2.50	6.00
11 Robin Roberts	6.00	15.00
12 Eddie Sawyer MG	1.50	4.00

1961 Phillies Jay Publishing

This 12-card set of the Philadelphia Phillies measures approximately 5" X 7". The fronts feature black-and-white posed player photos with the player's and team name printed below in the white border. These cards were packaged 12 to a packet and originally sold for 25 cents. The backs are blank. The cards are unnumbered and checklisted below in alphabetical order.

COMPLETE SET (12)	10.00	25.00
1 Ruben Amaro	1.00	2.50
2 Johnny Callison	1.00	2.50
3 Bobby Del Greco	1.00	2.50
4 Dick Farrell	1.00	2.50
5 Dallas Green	1.25	3.00
6 Pancho Herrera	1.00	2.50
7 Gene Mauch MG	1.00	2.50
8 Bob Malkmus	1.00	2.50
9 Robin Roberts	3.00	8.00
10 Tony Taylor	1.25	3.00
11 Lee Walls	1.00	2.50
12 Ken Walters	1.00	2.50

1962 Phillies Jay Publishing

This 12-card set of the Philadelphia Phillies measures approximately 5" by 7". The fronts feature black-and-white posed player photos with the player's and team name printed below in the white border. These cards were packaged 12 to a packet. The backs are blank. The cards are unnumbered and checklisted below in alphabetical order.

COMPLETE SET (12)	15.00	40.00
1 Jack Baldschun	1.50	4.00
2 John Callison	2.50	6.00
3 Clay Dalrymple	1.50	4.00
4 Don Demeter	1.50	4.00
5 Dallas Green	2.00	5.00
6 Art Mahaffey	1.50	4.00
7 Gene Mauch MG	1.50	4.00
8 Cal McLish	1.50	4.00
9 Roy Sievers	2.00	5.00
10 Frank Sullivan	1.50	4.00
11 Tony Taylor	2.00	5.00
12 Ken Walters	1.50	4.00

1963 Phillies Jay Publishing

This 12-card set of the Philadelphia Phillies measures approximately 5" by 7". The fronts feature black-and-white posed player photos with the player's and team name printed below in the white border. These cards were packaged 12 to a packet. The backs are blank. The cards are unnumbered and checklisted below in alphabetical order.

COMPLETE SET (12)	20.00	50.00
1 Ruben Amaro	1.50	4.00
2 Jack Baldschun	1.50	4.00
3 John Callison	3.00	8.00
4 Clay Dalrymple	1.50	4.00
5 Don Demeter	1.50	4.00
6 Art Mahaffey	1.50	4.00
7 Gene Mauch MG	1.50	4.00
8 Cal McLish	1.50	4.00
9 Chris Short	2.00	5.00
10 Roy Sievers	2.00	5.00
11 Tony Taylor	2.00	5.00
12 Bobby Wine	1.50	4.00

1964 Phillies Jay Publishing

This 12-card set of the Philadelphia Phillies measures approximately 5" by 7". The fronts feature black-and-white posed player photos with the player's and team name printed below in the white border. These cards were packaged 12 to a packet. The backs are blank. The cards are unnumbered and checklisted below in alphabetical order.

COMPLETE SET (12)	8.00	20.00
1 Jack Baldschun	.75	2.00
2 John Callison	1.25	3.00
3 Wes Covington	.75	2.00
4 Clay Dalrymple	.75	2.00
5 Tony Gonzalez	.75	2.00
6 Dallas Green	1.00	2.50
7 Don Hoak	.75	2.00
8 Art Mahaffey	.75	2.00
9 Gene Mauch MG	.75	2.00
10 Roy Sievers	1.00	2.50
11 Tony Taylor	1.00	2.50
12 Bob Wine	.75	2.00

1964 Phillies Philadelphia Bulletin

This 27-subject set was produced by the Philadelphia Bulletin newspaper. The catalog designation for this set is M130-5. These large, approximately 8" by 10", photo cards are unnumbered and blank backed. The complete set price below includes both Bunning variation cards.

COMPLETE SET (27)	100.00	200.00
1 Richie Allen	10.00	25.00
2 Ruben Amaro	2.50	6.00
3 Jack Baldschun	2.50	6.00
4 Dennis Bennett	2.50	6.00
5 John Boozer	2.50	6.00
6 Johnny Briggs	2.50	6.00
7 Jim Bunning (2)	10.00	25.00
8 Johnny Callison	3.00	8.00
9 Danny Cater	2.50	6.00
10 Wes Covington	2.50	6.00
11 Ray Culp	2.50	6.00
12 Clay Dalrymple	2.50	6.00
13 Tony Gonzalez	2.50	6.00
14 John Herrnstein	2.50	6.00
15 Alex Johnson	2.50	6.00
16 Art Mahaffey	2.50	6.00
17 Gene Mauch MG	3.00	8.00
18 Vic Power	2.50	6.00
19 Ed Roebuck	2.50	6.00
20 Cookie Rojas	3.00	8.00
21 Bobby Shantz	3.00	8.00
22 Chris Short	3.00	8.00
23 Tony Taylor	3.00	8.00
24 Frank Thomas	3.00	8.00
25 Gus Triandos	2.50	6.00
26 Bobby Wine	2.50	6.00
27 Rick Wise	3.00	8.00

1964 Phillies Team Set

This six-card set of the Philadelphia Phillies measures approximately 3 1/4" by 5 1/2" and feature black-and-white player portraits with a facsimile autograph. The backs are blank. The cards are unnumbered and checklisted below in alphabetical order.

COMPLETE SET (7)	8.00	20.00
1 Jim Bunning	3.00	8.00
2 Johnny Callison	1.50	4.00
3 Clay Dalrymple	1.25	3.00
4 Tony Gonzalez	1.25	3.00
5 Cookie Rojas	1.50	4.00
6 Chris Short	1.50	4.00
7 Roy Sievers	1.50	4.00

1965 Phillies Ceramic Tiles

These tiles, which measure 6" square, feature members of the Philadelphia Phillies. The players photo and a fascimile autograph are set against a white background. Since these are unnumbered, we have sequenced them in alphabetical order.

COMPLETE SET	300.00	600.00
1 Richie Allen	100.00	200.00
2 Bo Belinsky	60.00	120.00
3 Jim Bunning	75.00	150.00
4 John Callison	60.00	120.00
5 Clay Dalrymple	50.00	100.00
6 Gene Mauch MG	50.00	100.00
7 Tony Taylor	50.00	100.00

1965 Phillies Jay Publishing

This 12-card set of the Philadelphia Phillies measures approximately 5" X 7". The fronts feature black-and-white posed player photos with the player's and team's names printed below in the white border. These cards were packaged 12 to a packet and originally sold for 25 cents. The backs are blank. The cards are unnumbered and checklisted below in alphabetical order.

COMPLETE SET (12)	20.00	50.00
1 Ruben Amaro	1.50	4.00
2 Jack Baldschun	1.50	4.00
3 Jim Bunning	5.00	12.00
4 John Callison	2.50	6.00
5 Clay Dalrymple	1.50	4.00
6 Dallas Green	2.00	5.00
7 Art Mahaffey	1.50	4.00
8 Gene Mauch MG	2.00	5.00
9 Chris Short	2.00	5.00
10 Tony Taylor	2.00	5.00
11 Gus Triandos	1.50	4.00
12 Bob Wine	1.50	4.00

1966 Phillies Team Issue

This 12-card set features black-and-white photos of the 1966 Philadelphia Phillies. The cards are unnumbered and checklisted below in alphabetical order.

COMMON CARD (1-12)	12.50	30.00
1 Richie Allen	1.50	4.00
2 Jackie Brandt	.75	2.00
3 Jim Bunning	2.50	6.00
4 John Callison	1.25	3.00
5 Ray Culp	.75	2.00
6 Clay Dalrymple	.75	2.00
7 Tony Gonzalez	.75	2.00
8 Dick Groat	1.25	3.00
9 Phil Linz	.75	2.00
10 Cookie Rojas	1.00	2.50
11 Chris Short	.75	2.00
12 Bill White	1.25	3.00

1967 Phillies Police

The 1967 Philadelphia Phillies Police/Safety set contains 13 cards measuring approximately 2 13/16" by 4 7/16". The black and white posed player photos on the fronts are bordered in white and have the player's signature inscribed across the picture. In blue print on white, the backs have biography, player profile, and a "Safe Driving" emblem at the bottom. Cards can be found where the players' pictured on the fronts do not match the card backs. For example, the Jim Bunning card has a Dick Ellsworth back, the John Briggs card has a Dick Groat back, the Johnny Callison card has a Bill White back, the Clay Dalrymple card has a Chris Short back, and the Gene Mauch card has a Tony Gonzalez back. The cards are unnumbered and checklisted below in alphabetical order.

COMPLETE SET (13)	50.00	100.00
1 Richie Allen	4.00	10.00
2 Jim Bunning	12.50	30.00
3 John Briggs	2.00	5.00
4 Johnny Callison	3.00	8.00
5 Clay Dalrymple	2.00	5.00
6 Dick Ellsworth	2.00	5.00
7 Tony Gonzalez	2.00	5.00
8 Dick Groat	3.00	8.00
9 Larry Jackson	2.50	6.00
10 Gene Mauch MG	2.50	6.00
11 Cookie Rojas	2.50	6.00
12 Chris Short	2.50	6.00
13 Bill White	3.00	8.00

1969 Phillies Team Issue

This 12-card set of the Philadelphia Phillies measures approximately 4 1/4" by 7". The fronts freature black-and-white player portraits in a white border. The player's name and team name are printed above. The backs are blank. The cards are unnumbered and checklisted below in alphabetical order.

COMPLETE SET (12)	10.00	25.00
1 Richie Allen	1.50	4.00
2 John Callison	1.25	3.00
3 Woody Fryman	.75	2.00
4 Larry Hisle	1.00	2.50
5 Deron Johnson	1.00	2.50
6 Don Money	1.00	2.50
7 Cookie Rojas	1.00	2.50
8 Mike Ryan	.75	2.00
9 Chris Short	1.00	2.50
10 Bob Skinner	.75	2.00
11 Tony Taylor	1.00	2.50
12 Rick Wise	1.00	2.50

1970 Phillies Team Issue

This 12-card set of the Philadelphia Phillies measures approximately 4 1/4" by 7" and features black-and-white player photos in a white border. Packaged 12 to a packet with blank backs, the cards are unnumbered and checklisted below in alphabetical order.

COMPLETE SET (12)	10.00	25.00
1 Larry Bowa	1.50	4.00
2 John Briggs	.75	2.00
3 Denny Doyle	.75	2.00
4 Larry Hisle	1.00	2.50
5 Grant Jackson	.75	2.00
6 Deron Johnson	1.00	2.50
7 Rick Joseph	.75	2.00
8 Tim McCarver	1.50	4.00
9 Don Money	1.00	2.50
10 Chris Short	1.00	2.50
11 Tony Taylor	1.00	2.50
12 Rick Wise	1.00	2.50

1971 Phillies Arco Oil

Sponsored by Arco Oil, these 13 pictures of the 1971 Philadelphia Phillies measure approximately 8" by 10" and feature on their fronts white-bordered posed color player photos. The player's name is shown in black lettering within the white margin below the photo. His facsimile autograph appears across the picture. The white back carries the team's and player's names at the top, followed below by position, biography, career highlights, and statistics. An ad at the bottom for picture frames rounds out the back. The cards are unnumbered and checklisted below in alphabetical order.

COMPLETE SET (13)	15.00	40.00
1 Larry Bowa	2.00	5.00
2 Jim Bunning	3.00	8.00
3 Roger Freed	1.00	2.50
4 Terry Harmon	1.00	2.50
5 Larry Hisle	1.25	3.00
6 Joe Hoerner	1.00	2.50
7 Deron Johnson	1.25	3.00
8 Tim McCarver	2.00	5.00
9 Don Money	1.25	3.00
10 Dick Selma	1.00	2.50
11 Chris Short	1.25	3.00
12 Tony Taylor	1.25	3.00
13 Rick Wise	1.25	3.00

1972 Phillies Ticketron

These cards, featuring members of the 1972 Phillies, were issued in conjunction with Ticketron. Since these cards are unnumbered, we have sequenced them in alphabetical order.

COMPLETE SET	30.00	60.00
1 Mike Anderson	2.00	5.00
2 Larry Bowa	2.50	6.00
3 Steve Carlton	6.00	15.00
4 Deron Johnson	2.00	5.00
5 Frank Lucchesi MG	2.00	5.00
6 Greg Luzinski	4.00	10.00
7 Tim McCarver	4.00	10.00
8 Don Money	2.00	5.00

9 Willie Montanez	2.00	5.00
10 Dick Selma	2.00	5.00

1973 Phillies Team Issue

This 29-card set of the Philadelphia Phillies measures approximately 3 1/4" by 5 1/2" and features black-and-white player photos with white borders. The backs are blank. The cards are unnumbered and checklisted below in alphabetical order. An early card of Mike Schmidt is in this set.

COMPLETE SET (29)	15.00	40.00
1 Mike Anderson	.40	1.00
2 Bob Boone	1.25	3.00
3 Larry Bowa	1.25	3.00
4 Darrell Brandon	.40	1.00
5 Ken Brett	.40	1.00
6 Steve Carlton	2.50	6.00
7 Denny Doyle	.40	1.00
8 Terry Harmon	.40	1.00
9 Tommy Hutton	.40	1.00
10 Barry Lersch	.40	1.00
11 Jim Lonborg	.75	2.00
12 Greg Luzinski	1.25	3.00
13 Willie Montanez	.40	1.00
14 Jose Pagan	.40	1.00
15 Bill Robinson	.40	1.00
16 Dick Ruthven	.40	1.00
17 Mike Ryan	.40	1.00
18 Mac Scarce	.40	1.00
19 Mike Schmidt	6.00	15.00
20 Cesar Tovar	.40	1.00
21 Mike Rogodzinski	.40	1.00
22 Wayne Twitchell	.40	1.00
23 Del Unser	.40	1.00
24 Billy Wilson	.40	1.00
25 Danny Ozark MG	.40	1.00
26 Ray Rippelmeyer CO	.40	1.00
27 Carroll Beringer CO	.40	1.00
28 Billy Demars CO	.40	1.00
29 Bobby Wine CO	.40	1.00

1974 Phillies Johnny Pro

This 12-card set measures approximately 3 3/4" by 7 1/8" and features members of the 1974 Philadelphia Phillies. The most significant player in this series is an early card of Mike Schmidt. The cards are designed to be pushed out and have the players photo against a solid white background. The backs are blank and marked the second straight year that Johnny Pro issued cards of a major league team. The set is checklisted by uniform number. According to informed sources, there were less than 15,000 sets produced.

COMPLETE SET (12)	100.00	200.00
8 Bob Boone	4.00	10.00
10 Larry Bowa	3.00	8.00
16 Dave Cash	2.00	5.00
19 Greg Luzinski	4.00	10.00
20 Mike Schmidt	75.00	150.00
22 Mike Anderson	2.00	5.00
24 Bill Robinson	2.50	6.00
25 Del Unser	2.00	5.00
27 Willie Montanez	2.00	5.00
32 Steve Carlton	12.50	30.00
37 Ron Schueler	2.50	6.00
41 Jim Lonborg	3.00	8.00

1975 Phillies 1950 TCMA

This 31-card set features black-and-white photos of the 1950 Philadelphia Phillies Baseball team with red lettering. The cards are unnumbered and checklisted below alphabetically.

COMPLETE SET (31)	8.00	20.00
1 Richie Ashburn	1.50	4.00
2 Benny Bengough CO	.20	.50
3 Jimmy Bloodworth	.20	.50
4 Hank Borowy	.20	.50
5 Putsy Caballero	.20	.50
6 Emory Church	.20	.50
7 Dusty Cooke CO	.20	.50
8 Blix Donnelly	.20	.50
9 Del Ennis	.60	1.50
10 Mike Goliat	.20	.50
11 Granny Hamner	.30	.75
12 Ken Heintzleman	.20	.50
13 Stan Hollmig	.20	.50
14 Ken Johnson	.20	.50
15 Willie Jones	.30	.75
16 Jim Konstantly	.40	1.00
17 Stan Lopata	.20	.50
18 Eddie Mayo	.20	.50
19 Russ Meyer	.20	.50
20 Bob Miller	.20	.50
21 Bill Nicholson	.20	.50
22 Cy Perkins CO	.20	.50
23 Robin Roberts	1.25	3.00
24 Eddie Sawyer MG	.20	.50
25 Andy Seminick	.20	.50
26 Ken Silvestri	.20	.50
27 Curt Simmons	.30	.75
28 Dick Sisler	.30	.75
29 Jocko Thompson	.20	.50
30 Eddie Waitkus	.30	.75
31 Dick Whitman	.20	.50

1975 Phillies Photo Album

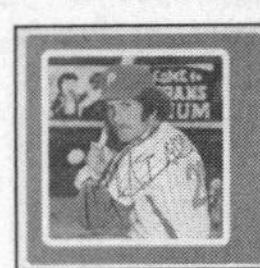

These seven 6" by 9" photos were issued by the Philadelphia Phillies and feature some of their leading players in 1975. The player photos are surrounded by red borders and have a fascimile signature. The backs look as they are taken from the Phillies Media Guide. The backs have a small photo, biographical information, a brief blurb and career statistics. Since the photos are unnumbered we have sequenced them in alphabetical order.

COMPLETE SET (7)	8.00	20.00
1 Dick Allen	1.25	3.00
2 Larry Bowa	1.00	2.50
3 Dave Cash	.40	1.00
4 Jay Johnstone	.60	1.50
5 Greg Luzinski	.75	2.00
6 Garry Maddox	.40	1.00
7 Mike Schmidt	4.00	10.00

1975 Phillies Postcards

This 31-card set of the Philadelphia Phillies features player photos on postcard-size cards. The cards are unnumbered and checklisted below in alphabetical order.

COMPLETE SET (31)	8.00	20.00
1 Dick Allen	.60	1.50
2 Mike Anderson	.20	.50
3 Alan Bannister	.20	.50
4 Carroll Beringer CO	.20	.50
5 Bob Boone	.60	1.50
6 Larry Bowa	.20	.50
7 Ollie Brown	.20	.50
8 Steve Carlton	1.25	3.00
9 Dave Cash	.20	.50
10 Larry Christenson	.20	.50
11 Larry Cox	.20	.50
12 Billy DeMars CO	.20	.50
13 Gene Garber	.30	.75
14 Terry Harmon	.20	.50
15 Tom Hilgendorf	.20	.50
16 Joe Hoerner	.20	.50
17 Tommy Hutton	.20	.50
18 Jay Johnstone	.40	1.00
19 Jim Lonborg	.30	.75
20 Greg Luzinski	.60	1.50
21 Garry Maddox	.30	.75
22 Tim McCarver	.40	1.00
23 Tug McGraw	.40	1.00
24 Danny Ozark MG	.20	.50
25 Ray Ripplemeyer CO	.20	.50
26 Mike Schmidt	2.50	6.00
27 Ron Schueler	.20	.50
28 Tony Taylor	.30	.75
29 Wayne Twitchell	.20	.50
30 Tom Underwood	.20	.50
31 Bobby Wine	.20	.50

1976 Phillies Photo Album

Issued as a photo album, but with easily perforated photos, which measure approximately 5 1/4" by 8 1/2" when seperated, these pictures feature members of the Eastern Division Champion Philadelphia Phillies. Since the photos were issued in alphabetical order, we have notated these photos in that order as well.

COMPLETE SET	10.00	25.00
1 Dick Allen	.75	2.00
2 Bob Boone	.60	1.50
3 Larry Bowa	.60	1.50
4 Ollie Brown	.30	.75
5 Steve Carlton	1.50	4.00
6 Dave Cash	.30	.75
7 Larry Christenson	.30	.75
8 Gene Garber	.30	.75
9 Terry Harmon	.30	.75
10 Tommy Hutton	.30	.75
11 Jay Johnstone	.30	.75
12 Jim Kaat	.75	2.00
13 Jim Lonborg	.40	1.00
14 Greg Luzinski	.60	1.50
15 Garry Maddox	.40	1.00
16 Jerry Martin	.30	.75
17 Tim McCarver	.75	2.00
18 Tug McGraw	.75	2.00
19 Johnny Oates	.30	.75
20 Ron Reed	.30	.75
21 Mike Schmidt	2.50	6.00
22 Ron Schueler	.30	.75
23 Tony Taylor	.30	.75
24 Bobby Tolan	.30	.75
25 Wayne Twitchell	.30	.75
26 Tom Underwood	.30	.75
27 Danny Ozark MG	.30	.75
28 Billy DeMars CO Ray Ripplemeyer CO Bobby Wine CO Carroll Beringer CO	.30	.75

1976 Phillies Postcards

This 31-card set of the Philadelphia Phillies features player photos on postcard-size cards. The cards are unnumbered and checklisted below in alphabetical order.

COMPLETE SET (31)	10.00	25.00
1 Dick Allen	.60	1.50
2 Carroll Beringer CO	.20	.50
3 Bob Boone	.60	1.50
4 Larry Bowa	.20	.50
5 Ollie Brown	.20	.50
6 Steve Carlton	1.25	3.00
7 Dave Cash	.20	.50
8 Larry Christenson	.20	.50
9 Billy DeMars CO	.20	.50
10 Gene Garber	.30	.75
11 Terry Harmon	.20	.50
12 Tommy Hutton	.20	.50
13 Jay Johnstone	.40	1.00
14 Jim Kaat	.40	1.00
15 Jim Lonborg	.30	.75
16 Greg Luzinski	.40	1.00
17 Garry Maddox	.20	.50
18 Jerry Martin	.20	.50
19 Tim McCarver	.60	1.50
20 Tug McGraw	.40	1.00
21 Johnny Oates	.20	.50
22 Danny Ozark CO	.20	.50
23 Ron Reed	.20	.50
24 Ray Ripplemeyer CO	.20	.50
25 Mike Schmidt	2.00	5.00
26 Ron Schueler	.20	.50
27 Tony Taylor	.30	.75
28 Bobby Tolan	.20	.50
29 Wayne Twitchell	.20	.50
30 Tom Underwood	.20	.50
31 Bobby Wine	.20	.50

1979 Phillies Burger King

The cards in this 23-card set measure 2 1/2" by 3 1/2". The 1979 Burger King Phillies set follows the regular format of 22 player cards and one unnumbered checklist card. The asterisk indicates where the pose differs from the Topps card of that year. The set features the first card of Pete Rose as a member of the Philadelphia Phillies.

COMPLETE SET (23)	4.00	10.00
1 Danny Ozark MG *	.08	.20
2 Bob Boone	.20	.50
3 Tim McCarver	.20	.50
4 Steve Carlton	1.00	2.50
5 Larry Christenson	.08	.20
6 Dick Ruthven	.08	.20
7 Ron Reed	.08	.20
8 Randy Lerch	.08	.20
9 Warren Brusstar	.08	.20
10 Tug McGraw	.12	.30
11 Nino Espinosa *	.08	.20
12 Doug Bird *	.08	.20
13 Pete Rose */(Shown as Reds in 1979 Topps)	1.50	4.00
14 Manny Trillo *	.08	.20
15 Larry Bowa	.12	.30
16 Mike Schmidt	1.50	4.00
17 Pete Mackanin *	.08	.20
18 Jose Cardenal	.08	.20
19 Greg Luzinski	.12	.30
20 Garry Maddox	.08	.20
21 Bake McBride	.08	.20
22 Greg Gross *	.08	.20
NNO Checklist Card TP	.08	.20

1979 Phillies Postcards

These attractive postcards were issued in black and white and many of them featured facsmile autographs. Since the cards are unnumbered, we have sequenced them in alphabetical order.

COMPLETE SET	12.50	30.00
1 Ramon Aviles	.20	.50
2 Doug Bird	.20	.50
3 Bob Boone	.40	1.00
4 Larry Bowa	.60	1.50
5 Warren Brusstar	.20	.50
6 Jose Cardenal	.20	.50
7 Steve Carlton	1.25	3.00
8 Larry Christenson	.20	.50
9 Rawly Eastwick	.20	.50
10 Nino Espinosa	.20	.50
11 Greg Gross	.20	.50
12 Bud Harrelson	.20	.50
13 Jim Kaat	.60	1.50
14 Randy Lerch	.20	.50
15 Jim Lonborg	.30	.75
16 Greg Luzinski	.40	1.00
17 Pete Mackanin	.20	.50
18 Garry Maddox	.20	.50
19 Rudy Meoli	.20	.50
20 Bake McBride	.20	.50
21 Tim McCarver	.30	.75
22 Tug McGraw	.30	.75
23 Dickie Noles	.20	.50
24 Danny Ozark MG	.20	.50
25 Dave Rader	.20	.50
26 Ron Reed	.20	.50
27 Pete Rose	2.00	5.00
28 Dick Ruthven	.20	.50
29 Kevin Saucier	.20	.50
30 Mike Schmidt	2.00	5.00
31 Lonnie Smith	.20	.50
32 Tony Taylor CO	.20	.50
33 Bob Tiefenauer CO	.20	.50
34 Manny Trillo Batting	.30	.75
35 Manny Trillo Portrait	.30	.75
36 Del Unser	.20	.50
37 Bobby Wine CO	.20	.50

1979 Phillies Team Issue Drawings

This 10-card set of the Philadelphia Phillies was issued in a clear front envelope and was likely sold at the stadium. The set measures approximately 8 3/4" by 11 5/8" and features art work by Todd Alan Gold. Each card displays two action drawings and a portrait of the same player. The backs are blank. The cards are unnumbered and checklisted below in alphabetical order.

COMPLETE SET (10)	8.00	20.00
1 Rich Ashburn	1.50	4.00
2 Bob Boone	1.25	3.00
3 Larry Bowa	.75	2.00
4 Greg Luzinski	.75	2.00
5 Garry Maddox	.60	1.50
6 Bake McBride	.60	1.50
7 Robin Roberts	1.25	3.00
8 Pete Rose	1.50	4.00
9 Mike Schmidt	1.50	4.00
10 Manny Trillo	.60	1.50

1980 Phillies Burger King

The cards in this 23-card set measure 2 1/2" by 3 1/2". The 1980 edition of Burger King Phillies follows the established pattern of 22 numbered player cards and one unnumbered checklist. Cards marked with asterisks contain poses different from those found in the regular 1980 Topps cards. This was the first Burger King set to carry the Burger King logo and hence does not generate the same confusion that the three previous years do for collectors trying to distinguish Burger King cards from the very similar Topps cards of the same years.

COMPLETE SET (23)	3.00	8.00
1 Dallas Green MG *	.07	.20
2 Bob Boone	.10	.30
3 Keith Moreland *	.10	.30
4 Pete Rose	1.50	4.00
5 Manny Trillo	.07	.20
6 Mike Schmidt	1.50	4.00
7 Larry Bowa	.07	.20
8 John Vukovich *	.02	.10
9 Bake McBride	.02	.10
10 Garry Maddox	.07	.20
11 Greg Luzinski	.07	.20
12 Greg Gross	.02	.10
13 Del Unser	.02	.10
14 Lonnie Smith *	.07	.20
15 Steve Carlton	1.00	2.50
16 Larry Christenson	.02	.10
17 Nino Espinosa	.02	.10
18 Randy Lerch	.02	.10
19 Dick Ruthven	.02	.10
20 Tug McGraw	.10	.30
21 Ron Reed	.02	.10
22 Kevin Saucier *	.02	.10
NNO Checklist Card TP	.01	.05

1980 Phillies 1950 TCMA

This 31-card set features black-and-white photos of the 1950 Philadelphia Phillies Baseball team in red borders. The words, "Whiz Kids" are printed in white at the top. The backs carry player information and career statistics. The cards are unnumbered and checklisted below alphabetically.

COMPLETE SET (31)	10.00	25.00
1 Richie Ashburn	.40	1.00
2 Benny Bengough CO	.20	.50
3 Jimmy Bloodworth	.08	.25
4 Hank Borowy	.08	.25
5 Putsy Caballero	.08	.25
6 Emory Church	.08	.25
7 Dusty Cooke	.08	.25
8 Blix Donnelly	.08	.25
9 Del Ennis	.30	.75
10 Mike Goliat	.08	.25
11 Granny Hamner	.20	.50
12 Ken Heintzleman	.08	.25
13 Stan Hollmig	.08	.25
14 Ken Johnson	.08	.25
15 Willie Jones	.20	.50
16 Jim Konstantly	.20	.50
17 Stan Lopata	.08	.25
18 Jackie Mayo	.08	.25
19 Russ Meyer	.08	.25

20 Bob Miller	.08	.25
21 Bill Nicholson	.20	.50
22 Cy Perkins	.08	.25
23 Robin Roberts	.40	1.00
24 Eddie Sawyer MG	.08	.25
25 Andy Seminick	.20	.50
26 Ken Silvestri	.08	.25
27 Curt Simmons	.20	.50
28 Dick Sisler	.08	.25
29 Jocko Thompson	.08	.25
30 Eddie Waitkus	.20	.50
31 Dick Whitman	.08	.25

1980 Phillies Postcards

These black and white postcards were issued by the Phillies during their World Championship season. Since the cards are unnumbered we have sequenced them in alphabetical order.

COMPLETE SET	10.00	25.00
1 Ruben Amaro CO	.20	.50
2 Luis Aguayo	.20	.50
3 Ramon Aviles	.20	.50
4 Bob Boone	.40	1.00
5 Larry Bowa	.60	1.50
6 Warren Brusstar	.20	.50
7 Steve Carlton	1.25	3.00
8 Larry Christenson	.20	.50
9 Billy DeMars CO	.20	.50
10 Lee Elia CO	.20	.50
11 Nino Espinosa	.20	.50
12 Dallas Green MG	.20	.50
13 Greg Gross	.20	.50
14 Lerrin LaGrow	.20	.50
15 Dan Larson	.20	.50
16 Randy Lerch	.20	.50
17 Greg Luzinski	.40	1.00
18 Bake McBride	.30	.75
19 Tug McGraw	.40	1.00
20 Keith Moreland	.20	.50
21 Scott Munninghoff	.20	.50
22 Ron Reed	.20	.50
23 Pete Rose	2.00	5.00
24 Dick Ruthven	.20	.50
25 Mike Ryan CO	.20	.50
26 Kevin Saucier	.20	.50
27 Mike Schmidt	2.00	5.00
28 Lonnie Smith	.30	.75
29 Herm Starrette CO	.20	.50
30 Manny Trillo	.30	.75
31 Del Unser	.20	.50
32 George Vukovich	.20	.50
33 Bob Walk	.20	.50
34 Bobby Wine CO	.20	.50

1914 Piedmont Stamps T330-2

These attractive stamps are approximately 1 7/16" by 2 5/8" and are unnumbered. Unlike most stamps, these have blue printing on the back. On the back there is an offer for an album to house these stamps. This offer expired on June 30, 1915." The front designs are similar to T205.

COMPLETE SET	7,500.00	15,000.00
1 Leon Ames	60.00	120.00
2 Jimmy Archer	60.00	120.00
3 Jimmy Austin	60.00	120.00
4 Frank Baker	125.00	250.00
5 Cy Barger	60.00	120.00
6 Jack Barry	60.00	120.00
7 Johnny Bates	60.00	120.00
8 Beals Becker	60.00	120.00
9 Chief Bender	125.00	250.00
10 Bob Bescher	60.00	120.00
11 Joe Birmingham	60.00	120.00
12 Walter Blair	60.00	120.00
13 Roger Breshnahan	125.00	250.00
14 Al Bridwell	60.00	120.00
15 Mordecai Brown	125.00	250.00
16 Robert Byrne	60.00	120.00
17 Howie Camnitz	60.00	120.00
18 Bill Carrigan	60.00	120.00
19 Frank Chance	200.00	400.00
20 Hal Chase Identified as Hal Chase	125.00	250.00
21 Hal Chase Indentified only as Chase	100.00	200.00
22 Eddie Cicotte	125.00	250.00
23 Fred Clarke	125.00	250.00
24 Ty Cobb	750.00	1,500.00
25 Eddie Collins Mouth Open	150.00	300.00
26 Eddie Collins Mouth Closed	250.00	500.00
27 Doc Crandall	60.00	120.00
28 Bill Dahlen	75.00	150.00
29 Jake Daubert	100.00	200.00
30 Jim Delahanty	60.00	120.00
31 Josh Devore	60.00	120.00
32 Red Dooin	60.00	120.00
33 Mike Doolan	60.00	120.00
34 Tom Downey	60.00	120.00
35 Larry Doyle	75.00	150.00
36 Joe Egan	60.00	120.00
37 Kid Elberfeld	60.00	120.00
38 Clyde Engle	60.00	120.00
39 Steve Evans	60.00	120.00
40 Johnny Evers	200.00	400.00
41 Ray Fisher	60.00	120.00
42 Art Fletcher	60.00	120.00
43 Russ Ford White Cap	60.00	120.00
44 Russ Ford Dark Cap	60.00	120.00
45 Arthur Fromme	60.00	120.00
46 George Gibson	60.00	120.00
47 William Goode	60.00	120.00
48 Eddie Grant	75.00	150.00
49 Clark Griffith	125.00	250.00
50 Bob Groom	60.00	120.00
51 Bob Harmon	60.00	120.00
52 Arnold Hauser	60.00	120.00
53 Buck Herzog	60.00	120.00
54 Doc Hoblitzell	60.00	120.00
55 Miller Huggins	125.00	250.00
56 John Hummel	60.00	120.00
57 Hugh Jennings MG	200.00	400.00
58 Walter Johnson	300.00	600.00
59 Davy Jones	60.00	120.00
60 William Killifer	100.00	200.00
61 Ed Konetchy	60.00	120.00
62 John Knight	60.00	120.00
63 Frank LaPorte	60.00	120.00
64 Tommy Leach	75.00	150.00
65 Ed Lennox	60.00	120.00
66 Hans Lobert	75.00	150.00
67 Bris Lord	60.00	120.00
68 Sherry Magee	75.00	150.00
69 Rube Marquard	125.00	250.00
70 Christy Mathewson	300.00	600.00
71 George McBride	60.00	120.00
72 John McGraw MG	200.00	400.00
73 Larry McLean	60.00	120.00
74 Chief Meyers	75.00	150.00
75 Fred Merkle	75.00	150.00
76 Clyde Milan	75.00	150.00
77 Dots Miller	60.00	120.00
78 Michael Mitchell	60.00	120.00
79 Pat Moran	60.00	120.00
80 George Moriarty	60.00	120.00
81 George Mullin	75.00	150.00
82 Danny Murphy	60.00	120.00
83 Jack Murray	60.00	120.00
84 Tom Needham	60.00	120.00
85 Rebel Oakes	60.00	120.00
86 Rube Oldring	60.00	120.00
87 Freddy Parent	60.00	120.00
88 Dode Paskert	60.00	120.00
89 Jack Quinn	75.00	150.00
90 Ed Reulbach	100.00	200.00
91 Lewis Ritchie	60.00	120.00
92 John A. Rowan	60.00	120.00
93 Nap Rucker	75.00	150.00
94 Germany Schaefer	75.00	150.00
95 Fred Schulte	75.00	150.00
96 Jim Scott	60.00	120.00
97 Fred Snodgrass	60.00	120.00
98 Tris Speaker	200.00	400.00
99 Oscar Stanage	60.00	120.00
100 George Stovall	60.00	120.00
101 George Suggs	60.00	120.00
102 Jeff Sweeney	60.00	120.00
103 Ira Thomas	60.00	120.00
104 Joe Tinker	125.00	250.00
105 Terry Turner	75.00	150.00
106 Hippo Vaughn	60.00	120.00
107 Heinie Wagner	60.00	120.00
108 Bobby Wallace With Cap	125.00	250.00
109 Bobby Wallace No Cap	125.00	250.00
110 Ed Walsh	125.00	250.00
111 Zach Wheat	125.00	250.00
112 Kaiser Wilhelm	60.00	120.00
113 Ed Willett	60.00	120.00
114 J. Owen Wilson	60.00	120.00
115 Hooks Wiltse	60.00	120.00
116 Joe Wood	100.00	200.00

1954 Piersall Colonial Meat Products

These black and white postcards measure 3 1/2" by 5 3/8" and were issued by Colonial Meat Products. Both of these cards feature Jimmy Piersall; however, the cropping and the color of the facsimile autograph on the front of the card are different. The backs of the cards contain a Colonial Meat advertisement and endorsement by Piersall.

COMPLETE SET (2)	15.00	30.00
1 Jimmy Piersall	15.00	30.00
2 Jimmy Piersall	15.00	30.00

1957 Piersall Neptune Sardines

This black and white postcard features a batting photo of Jimmy Piersall on the front and a back message with an ad for Neptune Sardines.

COMPLETE SET		
1 Jimmy Piersall	7.50	15.00

1969 Pilots Post-Intelligencer

This set was originally inserted into copies of the Seattle Post-Intelligencer in 1969. They were drawn by Stu Moldrem, the Post-Intellingencer staff artist. The reprint cards measure approximately 2 3/8" by 4 7/8". The fronts feature drawings; and year by year stats. This set is dated 1969 as that was the only year of the Pilots existence. According to reports, the reprint set was issued with the Post-Intelligencer permission. The original cards measure approximately 7" by 3" but there is considerable variation with these numbers. Card number five was printed in the fashion section, rather than the sports section, making this a much harder item to find in 1969 and years later. Therefore, Card number five was never issued in the reprint set. The set was reprinted as a collectors issue in 1977 and is priced seperately. Card number 34 is larger than the other cards in this set.

COMPLETE SET (38)	200.00	400.00
COMMON CARD (1-39)	4.00	10.00
COMMON SP	15.00	40.00
1 Don Mincher	4.00	10.00
2 Tommy Harper	5.00	12.00
3 Ray Oyler	4.00	10.00
4 Jerry McNertney	4.00	10.00
5 Joe Schultz MG SP	15.00	40.00
6 Tommy Davis	6.00	15.00
7 Gary Bell	4.00	10.00
8 Chico Salmon	5.00	12.00
9 Jack Aker	4.00	10.00
10 Rich Rollins	4.00	10.00
11 Diego Segui	5.00	12.00
12 Steve Barber	5.00	12.00
13 Wayne Comer	4.00	10.00
14 John Kennedy	4.00	10.00
15 Buzz Stephen	4.00	10.00
16 Jim Gosger	4.00	10.00
17 Mike Ferraro	4.00	10.00
18 Marty Pattin	4.00	10.00
19 Gerry Schoen	4.00	10.00
20 Steve Hovely	4.00	10.00
21 Frank Crosetti CO	8.00	20.00
22 Dick Bates	4.00	10.00
23 Jose Vidal	4.00	10.00
24 Bob Richmond	4.00	10.00
25 Lou Piniella	15.00	40.00
26 John Miklos	4.00	10.00
27 John Morris	4.00	10.00
28 Larry Haney	4.00	10.00
29 Mike Marshall	6.00	15.00
30 Marv Staehle	4.00	10.00
31 Gus Gil	4.00	10.00
32 Sal Maglie CO	6.00	15.00
33 Ron Plaza CO	4.00	10.00
34 Ed O'Brien CO	4.00	10.00
35 Jim Bouton	12.50	30.00
36 Bill Stafford	4.00	10.00
37 Darrell Brandon	4.00	10.00
38 Mike Hegan	4.00	10.00
39 Dick Baney	4.00	10.00

1969 Pilots Wheeldon

This eight-card set features color player portraits by artist, John Wheeldon, printed on cards measuring approximately 8 1/2" by 11" in white borders. The fronts carry a facsimile autograph with the player's name printed in the wide bottom margin. The backs display player information, career statistics, and a paragraph about the artist. The cards are unnumbered and checklisted below in alphabetical order.

COMPLETE SET (8)	12.50	30.00
1 Wayne Comer	1.50	4.00
2 Tommy Harper	1.50	4.00
3 Mike Hegan	1.50	4.00
4 Jerry McNertney	1.50	4.00
5 Don Mincher	1.50	4.00
6 Ray Oyler	1.50	4.00
7 Marty Pattin	1.50	4.00
8 Diego Segui	1.50	4.00

1977 Pilots Post-Intelligencer Reprints

These are the reprint cards referenced to in the 1969 write-up. Please note that the 1969 and 1977 sets are different sizes and were issued almost 10 years apart. They were produced by Frank Caruso, who also produced minor league sets during this period. Please note that card number 5 does not exist in this set.The reprint cards measure approximately 2 3/8" by 4 7/8."

COMPLETE SET (38)	50.00	100.00
1 Don Mincher	1.50	4.00
2 Tommy Harper	2.00	5.00
3 Ray Oyler	1.50	4.00
4 Jerry McNertney	1.50	4.00
6 Tommy Davis	2.50	6.00
7 Gary Bell	1.50	4.00
8 Chico Salmon	1.50	4.00
9 Jack Aker	1.50	4.00
10 Rich Rollins	1.50	4.00
11 Diego Segui	2.00	5.00
12 Steve Barber	2.00	5.00
13 Wayne Comer	1.50	4.00
14 John Kennedy	1.50	4.00
15 Buzz Stephen	1.50	4.00
16 Jim Gosger	1.50	4.00
17 Mike Ferraro	1.50	4.00
18 Marty Pattin	1.50	4.00
19 Gerry Schoen	1.50	4.00
20 Steve Hovely	1.50	4.00
21 Frank Crosetti CO	3.00	8.00
22 Dick Bates	1.50	4.00
23 Jose Vidal	1.50	4.00
24 Bob Richmond	1.50	4.00
25 Lou Piniella	8.00	20.00
26 John Miklos	1.50	4.00
27 John Morris	1.50	4.00
28 Larry Haney	1.50	4.00
29 Mike Marshall	2.50	6.00
30 Marv Staehle	1.50	4.00
31 Gus Gil	1.50	4.00
32 Sal Maglie CO	3.00	8.00
33 Ron Plaza CO	1.50	4.00
34 Ed O'Brien CO	1.50	4.00
35 Jim Bouton	3.00	8.00
36 Bill Stafford	1.50	4.00
37 Darrell Brandon	1.50	4.00
38 Mike Hegan	1.50	4.00
39 Dick Baney	1.50	4.00

1911 Pinkerton T5

This 376-card set is called a true Cabinet card set meaning a player photograph is affixed to a cardboard backing. The set was produced by the Pinkerton Tobacco Company and could be obtained by sending in a certain number of coupons from Pinkerton tobacco products. Cards numbered 101-875 are Major League player cards while cards numbered 901-1115 are Minor League players. This is the original checklist as Pinkerton provided in 1911. No individual cards are priced due to scarcity and it is possible that not all exist. A Joe Jackson in ex/mt condition sold for more than $180,000 in an Mile High Auction while a Jackson in vg/ex sold for more than $40,000 in an Mastro Auction in 2006. A recently discovered card number 1510, indicates that the checklist may be incomplete. Any pricing information or checklist verification is appreciated.

1910 American Caramel Pirates E90-2

The cards in this 11-card set measure 1 1/2" by 2 3/4". The 1910 E90-2 American Caramels Baseball Star set contains unnumbered cards featuring players from the 1909 Pittsburgh Pirates. The backs of these cards are exactly like the E90-1 cards; however, blue print is used for the names of the players and the teams on the fronts of the cards. Listed pricing for raw cards references "VgEx" conditon.

COMPLETE SET (11)	7,500.00	15,000.00
1 Babe Adams	300.00	500.00
2 Fred Clarke	600.00	1,000.00
3 George Gibson	300.00	500.00
4 Ham Hyatt	300.00	500.00
5 Tommy Leach	300.00	500.00
6 Sam Leever	300.00	500.00
7 Nick Maddox	300.00	500.00
8 Dots Miller	300.00	500.00
9 Deacon Phillippe	300.00	500.00
10 Honus Wagner	7,000.00	10,000.00
11 Chief Wilson	300.00	500.00

1910 Pirates Tip-Top D322

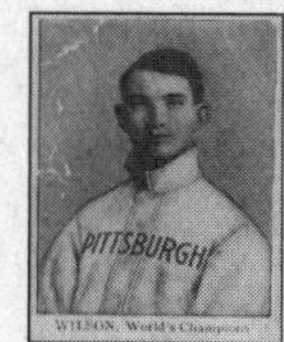

This 25-card set of the Pittsburgh Pirates was distributed by Tip-Top Bread at a rate of one per bread loaf and measures approximately 1 13/15" by 2 3/8". The fronts feature pastel paintings of the World Champion Team. The backs carry a checklist, ad for the bakery, and offer to send the complete set for 50 bread labels.

COMPLETE SET (25)	60,000.00	120,000.00
1 Barney Dreyfuss	2,500.00	5,000.00
2 William Locke	2,000.00	4,000.00
3 Fred Clarke	4,000.00	8,000.00
4 Honus Wagner	12,500.00	25,000.00
5 Tom Leach	2,000.00	4,000.00
6 George Gibson	2,000.00	4,000.00
7 Dots Miller	2,000.00	4,000.00
8 Howie Camnitz	2,000.00	4,000.00
9 Babe Adams	2,500.00	5,000.00
10 Lefty Leifield	2,000.00	4,000.00
11 Nick Maddox	2,000.00	4,000.00
12 Deacon Phillippe	2,500.00	5,000.00
13 Bobby Byrne	2,000.00	4,000.00
14 Ed Abbaticchio	2,000.00	4,000.00
15 Lefty Webb	2,000.00	4,000.00
16 Vin Campbell	2,000.00	4,000.00
17 Owen Wilson	2,500.00	5,000.00
18 Sam Leever	2,000.00	4,000.00
19 Mike Simon	2,000.00	4,000.00
20 Ham Hyatt	2,000.00	4,000.00
21 Paddy O'Connor	2,000.00	4,000.00

22 John Flynn 2,000.00 4,000.00
23 Kirby White 2,000.00 4,000.00
24 Boy Mascot 2,000.00 4,000.00
25 Forbes Field 2,000.00 4,000.00

1913 Pirates Voskamps

These cards, which measure approximately 3 5/8" by 2 1/4" feature members of the 1913 Pittsburgh Pirates. Both Hoffman and O'Toole are known to exist in two different versions. Since these cards were unnumbered, we have sequenced them in alphabetical order.

COMPLETE SET 6,000.00 12,000.00
1 Babe Adams 600.00 1,200.00
2 Everitt Booe 500.00 1,000.00
3 Bobby Byrne 500.00 1,000.00
4 Howie Camnitz 500.00 1,000.00
5 Max Carey 1,500.00 3,000.00
6 Joe Conzelman 500.00 1,000.00
7 Jack Ferry 500.00 1,000.00
8 George Gibson 500.00 1,000.00
9 Claude Hendrix 500.00 1,000.00
10 Solly Hofman 500.00 1,000.00
11 Ham Hyatt 500.00 1,000.00
12 Bill Kelly 500.00 1,000.00
13 Ed Mensor 500.00 1,000.00
14 Dots Miller 500.00 1,000.00
15 Marty O'Toole 500.00 1,000.00
16 Hank Robinson 500.00 1,000.00
17 Mike Simon 500.00 1,000.00
18 Jim Viox 500.00 1,000.00
19 Honus Wagner 5,000.00 10,000.00
20 Chief Wilson 600.00 1,200.00

1950 Pirates Team Issue

This set of the Pittsburgh Pirates measures approximately 6 1/2" by 9" and features black-and-white player photos. The backs are blank. The cards are unnumbered and checklisted below in alphabetical order.

COMPLETE SET (25) 75.00 150.00
1 Ted Beard 2.50 5.00
2 Gus Bell 4.00 8.00
3 Pete Castiglione 2.50 5.00
4 Cliff Chambers 2.50 5.00
5 Dale Coogan 2.50 5.00
6 Murry Dickson 3.00 6.00
7 Froilan Fernandez 2.50 5.00
8 Johnny Hopp 3.00 6.00
9 Ralph Kiner 10.00 20.00
10 Vernon Law 5.00 10.00
11 Vic Lombardi 2.50 5.00
12 William MacDonald 2.50 5.00
13 Clyde McCullough 2.50 5.00
14 Bill Meyer MG 2.50 5.00
15 Ray Mueller 2.50 5.00
16 Danny Murtaugh 4.00 8.00
17 Jack Phillips 2.50 5.00
18 Mel Queen 2.50 5.00
19 Stan Rojek 2.50 5.00
20 Henry Schenz 2.50 5.00
21 George Strickland 2.50 5.00
22 Earl Turner 2.50 5.00
23 Jim Walsh 2.50 5.00
24 Bill Werle 2.50 5.00
25 Wally Westlake 2.50 5.00

1956 Pirates Team Issue

This 24-card set of the Pittsburgh Pirates features black-and-white player photos with white borders and was sold by the club for 15 cents each. The backs are blank. The cards are unnumbered and checklisted below in alphabetical order. The Bill Mazeroski card in this set predates his Rookie Card.

COMPLETE SET (24) 100.00 200.00
1 Luis Arroyo 2.00 4.00
2 Bobby Bragan MG 3.00 6.00
3 Roberto Clemente 50.00 100.00
4 Dick Cole 2.00 4.00
5 Roy Face 3.00 6.00
6 Hank Foiles 2.00 4.00
7 Gene Freese 2.00 4.00
8 Bob Friend 3.00 6.00
9 Dick Groat 3.00 6.00
10 Dick Hall 2.00 4.00
11 Nelson King 2.00 4.00
12 Ronnie Kline 2.00 4.00
13 Danny Kravitz 2.00 4.00
14 Vernon Law 3.00 6.00
15 Dale Long 2.00 4.00
16 Jerry Lynch 2.00 4.00
17 Bill Mazeroski 20.00 40.00
18 Johnny O'Brien 2.00 4.00
19 Curt Roberts 2.00 4.00
20 Jack Shepard 2.00 4.00
21 Bob Skinner 2.00 4.00
22 Frank Thomas 3.00 6.00
23 Bill Virdon 3.00 6.00
24 Lee Walls 2.00 4.00

1957 Pirates Team Issue

This 10-card set of the Pittsburgh Pirates features black-and-white player photos with white borders. The backs are blank. The cards are unnumbered and checklisted below in alphabetical order. The checklist might be incomplete and any confirmed addtions are welcomed. Bill Mazerosi appears in his Rookie Card year.

COMPLETE SET (10) 30.00 60.00
1 Roberto Clemente 12.50 25.00
2 Dick Groat 2.50 5.00
3 Danny Kravitz 1.50 3.00
4 Vernon Law 2.00 4.00
5 Dale Long 1.50 3.00
6 Bill Mazeroski 6.00 12.00
7 Johnny O'Brien 1.50 3.00
8 Bob Skinner 1.50 3.00
9 Frank Thomas 2.00 4.00
10 Bill Virdon 2.50 5.00

1958 Pirates Team Issue

This set of the Pittsburgh Pirates measures approximately 5" by 7" and features black-and-white player portraits with white borders. The set was sold by the club through the mail for 50 cents. The cards are unnumbered and checklisted below in alphabetical order. An 8 1/2" by 11" team photo was added to the set along with an 8 1/4" by 10 1/4" glossy photo of Dick Groat (card number 13) with a printed autograph and name in the white border.

COMPLETE SET (12) 40.00 80.00
1 Roberto Clemente 12.50 25.00
2 Hank Foiles 1.50 3.00
3 Bob Friend 1.50 3.00
4 Dick Groat 2.50 5.00
5 Ronald Kline 1.50 3.00
6 Bill Mazeroski 6.00 12.00
7 Roman Mejias 1.50 3.00
8 Danny Murtaugh 2.50 5.00
9 Bob Skinner 1.50 3.00
10 Dick Stuart 1.50 3.00
11 Frank Thomas 1.50 3.00
12 Bill Virdon 2.50 5.00
13 Dick Groat 3.00 6.00
14 Team Picture 7.50 15.00

1959 Pirates Jay Publishing

This 12-card set of the Pittsburgh Pirates measures approximately 5" by 7" and features black-and-white player photos in a white border. These cards were packaged 12 to a packet. The backs are blank. The cards are unnumbered and checklisted below in alphabetical order.

COMPLETE SET 40.00 80.00
1 Roberto Clemente 12.50 25.00
2 Hank Foiles 2.50 6.00
3 Bob Friend 2.50 6.00
4 Dick Groat 4.00 10.00
5 Don Hoak 2.50 6.00
6 Ron Kline 2.50 6.00
7 Ted Kluszewski 5.00 12.00
8 Bill Mazeroski 6.00 15.00
9 Danny Murtaugh MG 2.50 6.00
10 Bob Skinner 2.50 6.00
11 Dick Stuart 2.50 6.00
12 Bill Virdon 3.00 8.00

1960 Pirates Jay Publishing

This 12-card set of the Pittsburgh Pirates measures approximately 5" by 7". The fronts feature black-and-white posed player photos with the player's and team name printed below in the white border. These cards were packaged 12 to a packet and originally sold for 50 cents. The backs are blank. The cards are unnumbered and checklisted below in alphabetical order.

COMPLETE SET (12) 30.00 60.00
1 Smoky Burgess 1.50 4.00
2 Gino Cimoli 1.00 2.50
3 Roberto Clemente 10.00 25.00
4 Roy Face 1.50 4.00
5 Bob Friend 1.25 3.00
6 Dick Groat 2.00 5.00
7 Harvey Haddix 1.25 3.00
8 Don Hoak 1.25 3.00
9 Bill Mazeroski 3.00 8.00
10 Danny Murtaugh MG 1.50 4.00
11 Bob Skinner 1.00 2.50
12 Dick Stuart 1.25 3.00

1960 Pirates Tag-Ons

This 10-card set originally sold for $1.98 and features individually die-cut self-sticking figures in full color on one large sheet measuring approximately 10" by 15 1/2". These flexible color-fast Tag-ons are weatherproof and can be applied to any surface. The figures are checklisted below according to the small black numbers printed on their shoulders.

COMPLETE SET (10) 40.00 80.00
4 Robert Skinner 2.00 5.00
6 Forrest Burgess 2.00 5.00
7 Dick Stuart 2.50 6.00
9 Bill Mazeroski 4.00 10.00
12 Don Hoak 2.00 5.00
18 Bill Virdon 2.50 6.00
19 Bob Friend 2.00 5.00
21 Roberto Clemente 10.00 25.00
24 Dick Groat 3.00 8.00
26 Roy Face 2.50 6.00
XX Complete Sheet 40.00 80.00

1961 Pirates Riger Ford

This six-card set was distributed by Ford Motor Company and measures approximately 11" by 14". The fronts feature pencil drawings by Robert Riger of six of the 1960 World Champion Pittsburgh Pirates. The cards are unnumbered and checklisted below in alphabetical order.

COMPLETE SET (6) 40.00 80.00
1 Roberto Clemente 20.00 50.00
2 Bob Friend 4.00 10.00
3 Dick Groat 8.00 20.00
4 Don Hoak 4.00 10.00
5 Vernon Law 6.00 15.00
6 Bill Mazeroski 10.00 25.00

1962 Pirates Jay Publishing

This 12-card set of the Pittsburgh Pirates measures approximately 5" by 7". The fronts feature black-and-white posed player photos with the player's and team name printed below in the white border. These cards were packaged 12 to a packet. The backs are blank. The cards are unnumbered and checklisted below in alphabetical order.

COMPLETE SET (12) 30.00 60.00
1 Smoky Burgess 1.25 3.00
2 Roberto Clemente 10.00 25.00
3 Roy Face 1.50 4.00
4 Bob Friend 1.25 3.00
5 Dick Groat 1.50 4.00
6 Don Hoak 1.00 2.50
7 Vern Law 1.25 3.00
8 Bill Mazeroski 3.00 8.00
9 Danny Murtaugh MG 1.25 3.00
10 Bob Skinner 1.00 2.50
11 Dick Stuart 1.25 3.00
12 Bill Virdon 1.25 3.00

1963 Pirates IDL

This 26-card set measures approximately 4" by 5" and is blank-backed. The fronts have black and white photos on the top of the card along with the IDL Drug Store logo in the lower left corner of the card and the players name printed in block letters underneath the picture. The only card which has any designation as to position is the manager card of Danny Murtaugh. These cards are unnumbered and feature members of the Pittsburgh Pirates. The catalog designation for the set is H801-13 although it is infrequently referenced. The Stargell card is one of his few cards from 1963, his rookie year for cards.

COMPLETE SET (26) .150.00 300.00
1 Bob Bailey 3.00 8.00
2 Smoky Burgess 4.00 10.00
3 Don Cardwell 3.00 8.00
4 Roberto Clemente 75.00 150.00
5 Donn Clendenon 4.00 10.00
6 Roy Face 5.00 12.00
7 Earl Francis 3.00 8.00
8 Bob Friend 4.00 10.00
9 Joe Gibbon 3.00 8.00
10 Julio Gotay 3.00 8.00
11 Harvey Haddix 4.00 10.00
12 Johnny Logan 3.00 8.00
13 Bill Mazeroski 10.00 25.00
14 Al McBean 3.00 8.00
15 Danny Murtaugh MG 4.00 10.00
16 Sam Narron CO 3.00 8.00
17 Ron Northey CO 3.00 8.00
18 Frank Oceak CO 3.00 8.00
19 Jim Pagliaroni 3.00 8.00
20 Ted Savage 3.00 8.00
21 Dick Schofield 3.00 8.00
22 Willie Stargell 15.00 40.00
23 Tom Sturdivant 3.00 8.00
24 Virgil Trucks CO 3.00 8.00
25 Bob Veale 3.00 8.00
26 Bill Virdon 4.00 10.00

1963 Pirates Jay Publishing

This 12-card set of the Pittsburgh Pirates measures approximately 5" by 7". The fronts feature black-and-white posed player photos with the player's and team name printed below in the white border. These cards were packaged 12 to a packet. The backs are blank. The cards are unnumbered and checklisted below in alphabetical order.

COMPLETE SET (12) 20.00 50.00
1 Bob Bailey 1.00 2.50
2 Smoky Burgess 1.25 3.00
3 Roberto Clemente 10.00 25.00
4 Donn Clendenon 1.00 2.50
5 Roy Face 1.50 4.00
6 Bob Friend 1.25 3.00
7 Harvey Haddix 1.25 3.00
8 Vern Law 1.25 3.00
9 Bill Mazeroski 3.00 8.00
10 Danny Murtaugh MG 1.25 3.00
11 Bob Skinner 1.00 2.50
12 Bill Virdon 1.25 3.00

1964 Pirates Jay Publishing

This 12-card set of the Pittsburgh Pirates measures approximately 5" by 7". The fronts feature black-and-white posed player photos with the player's and team name printed below in the white border. These cards were packaged 12 to a packet. The backs are blank. The cards are unnumbered and checklisted below in alphabetical order.

COMPLETE SET (12) 20.00 50.00
1 Bob Bailey .75 2.00
2 Smoky Burgess 1.00 2.50
3 Roberto Clemente 10.00 25.00
4 Donn Clendenon 1.00 2.50
5 Roy Face 1.25 3.00
6 Bob Friend 1.00 2.50
7 Bill Mazeroski 3.00 8.00
8 Danny Murtaugh MG 1.00 2.50
9 Dick Schofield .75 2.00
10 Willie Stargell 5.00 12.00
11 Bob Veale .75 2.00
12 Bill Virdon 1.00 2.50

1964 Pirates KDKA

This set featured members of the 1964 Pittsburgh Pirates. It was issued by radio station KDKA. The set can be dated to 1964 by the card of Rex Johnston, who only played for the Pirates in that season.

COMPLETE SET (28) 1,500.00 3,000.00
1 Gene Alley 40.00 80.00
2 Bob Bailey 40.00 80.00
3 Frank Bork 40.00 80.00
4 Smoky Burgess 50.00 100.00
5 Tom Butters 40.00 80.00
6 Don Cardwell 40.00 80.00
7 Roberto Clemente 500.00 1,000.00
8 Donn Clendenon 50.00 100.00
9 Roy Face 60.00 120.00
10 Gene Freese 40.00 80.00
11 Bob Friend 50.00 100.00
12 Joe Gibbon 40.00 80.00
13 Julio Gotay 40.00 80.00
14 Rex Johnston 40.00 80.00
15 Vernon Law 60.00 120.00
16 Jerry Lynch 40.00 80.00
17 Bill Mazeroski 200.00 400.00
18 Al McBean 40.00 80.00
19 Orlando McFarlane 40.00 80.00
20 Manny Mota 60.00 120.00
21 Danny Murtaugh MG 50.00 100.00
22 Jim Pagliaroni 60.00 120.00
23 Dick Schofield 40.00 80.00
24 Don Schwall 40.00 80.00
25 Tommie Sisk 40.00 80.00
26 Willie Stargell 200.00 400.00
27 Bob Veale 40.00 80.00
28 Bill Virdon 50.00 100.00

1965 Pirates Jay Publishing

This 12-card set of the Pittsburgh Pirates measures approximately 5" by 7". The fronts feature black-and-white posed player photos with the player's and team name printed below in the white border. These cards were packaged 12 to a packet. The backs are blank. The cards are unnumbered and checklisted below in alphabetical order.

COMPLETE SET (12) 40.00 80.00
1 Bob Bailey 1.50 4.00
2 Roberto Clemente 15.00 40.00
3 Donn Clendenon 2.00 5.00
4 Del Crandall 2.00 5.00
5 Vern Law 2.50 6.00
6 Bill Mazeroski 6.00 15.00
7 Manny Mota 2.00 5.00
8 Jim Pagliaroni 1.50 4.00
9 Dick Schofield 1.50 4.00
10 Willie Stargell 8.00 20.00
11 Bill Virdon 2.00 5.00
12 Harry Walker MG 1.50 4.00

1965 Pirates KDKA Posters

These posters, which measure approximately 8" by 12" feature members of the 1965 Pirates and give the collector a chance to win an Emenee Electric Guitar. The top of the poster has the player's photo as well as his hame while the bottom half is dedicated to information about the contest. We have sequenced the known players in alphabetical order but it would be suspected that there would be additions to this checklist.

COMPLETE SET 75.00 150.00
1 Tom Butters 20.00 50.00
2 Joe Gibbon 75.00 150.00

1966 Pirates East Hills

The 1966 East Hills Pirates set consists of 25 large (approximately 3 1/4" by 4 1/4"), full color photos of Pittsburgh Pirate ballplayers. These blank-backed cards are numbered in the lower right corner according to the uniform number of the individual depicted. The set was distributed by various stores located in the East Hills Shopping Center. The catalog number for this set is F405.

COMPLETE SET (25)	40.00	80.00
3 Harry Walker MG	.30	.75
7 Bob Bailey	.20	.50
8 Willie Stargell	10.00	25.00
9 Bill Mazeroski	2.00	5.00
10 Jim Pagliaroni	.20	.50
11 Jose Pagan	.20	.50
12 Jerry May	.20	.50
14 Gene Alley	.40	1.00
15 Manny Mota	.40	1.00
16 Andre Rodgers UER/(Andy on card)	.20	.50
17 Donn Clendenon	.40	1.00
18 Matty Alou	1.25	3.00
19 Pete Mikkelsen	.20	.50
20 Jesse Gonder	.20	.50
21 Roberto Clemente	20.00	50.00
22 Woody Fryman	.30	.75
24 Jerry Lynch	.20	.50
25 Tommie Sisk	.20	.50
26 Roy Face	.40	1.00
28 Steve Blass	.40	1.00
32 Vernon Law	.40	1.00
34 Al McBean	.20	.50
39 Bob Veale	.30	.75
43 Don Cardwell	.20	.50
45 Gene Michael	.30	.75

1967 Pirates Stickers Topps

This was a limited production "test" issue for Topps. It is very similar to the Red Sox "test" issue following. The stickers are blank backed and measure 2 1/2" by 3 1/2". The stickers look like cards from the front and are somewhat attractive in spite of the "no neck" presentation of many of the players' photos. The cards are numbered on the front.

COMPLETE SET (33)	500.00	1,000.00
WRAPPERS	20.00	50.00
1 Gene Alley	10.00	25.00
2 Matty Alou	10.00	25.00
3 Dennis Ribant	8.00	20.00
4 Steve Blass	10.00	25.00
5 Juan Pizarro	8.00	20.00
6 Roberto Clemente	250.00	500.00
7 Donn Clendenon	10.00	25.00
8 Roy Face	12.50	30.00
9 Woodie Fryman	8.00	20.00
10 Jesse Gonder	8.00	20.00
11 Vern Law	10.00	25.00
12 Al McBean	8.00	20.00
13 Jerry May	8.00	20.00
14 Bill Mazeroski	30.00	60.00
15 Pete Mikkelsen	8.00	20.00
16 Manny Mota	10.00	25.00
17 Bill O'Dell	8.00	20.00
18 Jose Pagan	8.00	20.00
19 Jim Pagliaroni	8.00	20.00
20 Johnny Pesky CO	10.00	25.00
21 Tommie Sisk	8.00	20.00
22 Willie Stargell	75.00	150.00
23 Bob Veale	10.00	25.00
24 Harry Walker MG	8.00	20.00
25 I Love the Pirates	8.00	20.00
26 Let's Go Pirates	8.00	20.00
27 Roberto Clemente for Mayor	125.00	250.00
28 Matty Alou NL Batting Champ	10.00	25.00
29 Happiness is a Pirate Win	8.00	20.00
30 Donn Clendenon is my Hero	10.00	25.00
31 Willie Stargell Pirates HR Champ	50.00	100.00
32 Pirates Logo	8.00	20.00
33 Pirates Pennant	8.00	20.00

1967 Pirates Team Issue

This 24-card set of the Pittsburgh Pirates features color player photos with white borders and measures approximately 3 1/4" by 4 1/4". A facsimile autograph is printed in the wide bottom border. The backs are blank. The cards are unnumbered and checklisted below in alphabetical order. The complete set of 24 was available for $1 from Pitt Sportservice at time of issue.

COMPLETE SET (24)	50.00	100.00
1 Gene Alley	1.25	3.00
2 Matty Alou	1.50	4.00
3 Steve Blass	1.25	3.00
4 Roberto Clemente	8.00	20.00
5 Donn Clendenon	1.50	4.00
6 Roy Face	2.00	5.00
7 Woody Fryman	1.25	3.00
8 Jesse Gonder	1.25	3.00
9 Vernon Law	2.00	5.00
10 Jerry May	1.25	3.00
11 Bill Mazeroski	3.00	8.00
12 Al McBean	1.25	3.00
13 Pete Mikkelsen	1.25	3.00
14 Manny Mota	1.50	4.00
15 Jose Pagan	1.25	3.00
16 Jim Pagliaroni	1.25	3.00
17 Juan Pizarro	1.25	3.00
18 Dennis Ribant	1.25	3.00
19 Andy Rodgers	1.25	3.00
20 Tommie Sisk	1.25	3.00
21 Willie Stargell	4.00	10.00
22 Bob Veale	1.25	3.00
23 Harry Walker	1.50	4.00
24 Maury Wills	2.50	6.00

1967 Pirates Team Issue 8 by 10

These 24 blank-backed photos, which measure approximately 8" by 10", feature members of the 1967 Pittsburgh Pirates. From the description given, these were promotional shots mailed out to members of the press at the start of the 1967 season. Since these photos are unnumbered, we have sequenced them in alphabetical order.

COMPLETE SET (24)	75.00	150.00
1 Gene Alley	2.00	5.00
2 Matty Alou	2.50	6.00
3 Steve Blass	2.00	5.00
4 Roberto Clemente	15.00	40.00
5 Donn Clendenon	2.00	5.00
6 Roy Face	2.50	6.00
7 Woodie Fryman	2.00	5.00
8 Jesse Gonder	2.00	5.00
9 Vern Law	2.50	6.00
10 Jerry May	2.00	5.00
11 Bill Mazeroski	6.00	15.00
12 Al McBean	2.00	5.00
13 Pete Mikkelsen	2.00	5.00
14 Manny Mota	2.50	6.00
15 Billy O'Dell	2.00	5.00
16 Jose Pagan	2.00	5.00
17 Jim Pagliaroni	2.00	5.00
18 Juan Pizarro	2.00	5.00
19 Dennis Ribant	2.00	5.00
20 Tommie Sisk	2.00	5.00
21 Willie Stargell	6.00	15.00
22 Bob Veale	2.00	5.00
23 Harry Walker MG	2.00	5.00
24 Maury Wills	4.00	10.00

1968 Pirates KDKA

This 23-card set measures approximately 2 3/8" by 4" and was issued by radio and television station KDKA to promote the Pittsburgh Pirates, whom they were covering at the time. The fronts have the players' photo on the top 2/3 of the card and a facsimile autograph, the players name and position and uniform number on the lower left hand corner and an ad for KDKA on the lower right corner of the card. The back has an advertisment for both KDKA radio and television. The set is checklisted below by uniform number.

COMPLETE SET (23)	40.00	80.00
7 Larry Shepard MG	.60	1.50
8 Willie Stargell	6.00	15.00
9 Bill Mazeroski	3.00	8.00
10 Gary Kolb	.60	1.50
11 Jose Pagan	.60	1.50
12 Jerry May	.60	1.50
14 Jim Bunning	2.50	6.00
15 Manny Mota	.75	2.00
17 Donn Clendenon	.75	2.00
18 Matty Alou	.75	2.00
21 Roberto Clemente	12.50	30.00
22 Gene Alley	.75	2.00
25 Tommy Sisk	.60	1.50
26 Roy Face	1.25	3.00
27 Ron Kline	.60	1.50
28 Steve Blass	.75	2.00
29 Juan Pizzaro	.60	1.50
30 Maury Wills	1.50	4.00
34 Al McBean	.60	1.50
35 Manny Sanguillen	1.25	3.00
38 Bob Moose	.75	2.00
39 Bob Veale	.60	1.50
40 Dave Wickersham	.60	1.50

1968 Pirates Team Issue

This 24-card set of the Pittsburgh Pirates features color player photos with white borders and measures approximately 3 1/4" by 4 1/4". A facsimile autograph is printed in the wide bottom border. The backs are blank. The cards are unnumbered and checklisted below in alphabetical order.

COMPLETE SET (24)	50.00	100.00
1 Gene Alley	1.25	3.00
2 Matty Alou	2.00	5.00
3 Steve Blass	1.25	3.00
4 Jim Bunning	3.00	8.00
5 Roberto Clemente	8.00	20.00
6 Donn Clendenon	1.50	4.00
7 Roy Face	2.00	5.00
8 Ronnie Kline	1.25	3.00
9 Gary Kolb	1.25	3.00
10 Jerry May	1.25	3.00
11 Bill Mazeroski	3.00	8.00
12 Al McBean	1.25	3.00
13 Bob Moose	1.25	3.00
14 Manny Mota	1.50	4.00
15 Jose Pagan	1.25	3.00
16 Juan Pizarro	1.25	3.00
17 Manny Sanguillen	1.50	4.00
18 Jim Shellenback	1.25	3.00
19 Larry Shepard	1.25	3.00
20 Tommie Sisk	1.25	3.00
21 Willie Stargell	4.00	10.00
22 Bob Veale	1.25	3.00
23 Dave Wickersham	1.25	3.00
24 Maury Wills	2.50	6.00

1969 Pirates Jack in the Box

This 12-card set measures approximately 2 1/16" by 3 5/8" and features black-and-white player photos on a white card face. The player's name, team name, position, and batting or pitching record appear below the photo. The backs are blank. The cards are unnumbered and checklisted below in alphabetical order. Pittsburgh is misspelled Pittsburg on the front of the cards.

COMPLETE SET (12)	20.00	50.00
1 Gene Alley	1.25	3.00
2 Dave Cash	1.50	4.00
3 Dock Ellis	1.25	3.00
4 Dave Giusti	.75	2.00
5 Jerry May	.75	2.00
6 Bill Mazeroski	3.00	8.00
7 Al Oliver	2.50	6.00
8 Jose Pagan	.75	2.00
9 Fred Patek	1.25	3.00
10 Bob Robertson	.75	2.00
11 Manny Sanguillen	1.25	3.00
12 Willie Stargell	8.00	20.00

1969 Pirates Greiner

This eight-card set of the Pittsburgh Pirates, sponsored by Greiner Tire Service, measures approximately 5 1/2" by 8 1/2" and features black-and-white player portraits inside a white border. The player's name and team is printed with a "good luck" message in the wide bottom margin along with the sponsor name, address and phone number. The backs are blank. The cards are unnumbered and checklisted below in alphabetical order.

COMPLETE SET (8)	20.00	50.00
1 Gene Alley	2.00	5.00
2 Matty Alou	2.50	6.00
3 Steve Blass	1.50	4.00
4 Roberto Clemente	15.00	40.00
5 Jerry May	1.50	4.00
6 Bill Mazeroski	4.00	10.00
7 Larry Shepard MG	1.50	4.00
8 Willie Stargell	5.00	12.00

1969 Pirates Team Issue

This 26-card set of the Pittsburgh Pirates was issued in two series and measures approximately 3 1/4" by 4 1/4". The fronts feature color player photos in white borders with a facsimile autograph printed in the wide bottom margin. The backs are blank. The cards are unnumbered and checklisted below in alphabetical order.

COMPLETE SET (24)	40.00	80.00
1 Gene Alley	.75	2.00
2 Matty Alou	1.25	3.00
3 Steve Blass	.75	2.00
4 Jim Bunning	2.00	5.00
5 Roberto Clemente	8.00	20.00
6 Bruce Dal Canton	.75	2.00
7 Doc Ellis	1.00	2.50
8 Chuck Hartenstein	.75	2.00
9 Richie Hebner	1.00	2.50
10 Ronnie Kline	.75	2.00
11 Gary Kolb	.75	2.00
12 Vernon Law CO	1.00	2.50
13 Jose Martinez	.75	2.00
14 Jerry May	.75	2.00
15 Bill Mazeroski	2.50	6.00
16 Bob Moose	.75	2.00
17 Al Oliver	1.50	4.00
18 Jose Pagan	.75	2.00
19 Fred Patek	1.00	2.50
20 Manny Sanguillen	1.00	2.50
21 Larry Shepard MG	.75	2.00
22 Willie Stargell	4.00	10.00
23 Carl Taylor	.75	2.00
24 Bob Veale	.75	2.00
25 Bill Virdon CO	1.00	2.50
26 Luke Walker	.75	2.00

1970 Pirates Team Issue

This 20-card set of the Pittsburgh Pirates was issued in two series of 10 cards each measuring approximately 3 1/4" by 4 1/4". The fronts feature color player portraits in white borders. A facsimile autograph is printed in the wide bottom margin. The backs are blank. The cards are unnumbered and checklisted below in alphabetical order.

COMPLETE SET (20)	100.00	175.00
1 Gene Alley	2.00	5.00
2 Matty Alou	3.00	8.00
3 Steve Blass	2.00	5.00
4 Bob Clemente	15.00	40.00
5 Bruce Dal Canton	2.00	5.00
6 Dock Ellis	2.00	5.00
7 Chuck Hartenstein	2.00	5.00
8 Richie Hebner	2.50	6.00
9 Gary Kolb	2.00	5.00
10 Jerry May	2.00	5.00
11 Bill Mazeroski	6.00	15.00
12 Bob Moose	2.00	5.00
13 Al Oliver	4.00	10.00
14 Jose Pagan	2.00	5.00
15 Fred Patek	2.50	6.00
16 Manny Sanguillen	2.50	6.00
17 Willie Stargell	8.00	20.00
18 Bob Veale	2.00	5.00
19 Bill Virdon CO	2.50	6.00
20 Luke Walker	2.00	5.00

1971 Pirates

The six blank-backed photos comprising this Set "A" of the '71 Pirates measure approximately 7" by 8 3/4" and feature white-bordered posed color player shots. The player's name appears in black lettering within the bottom white margin. The pictures are unnumbered and checklisted below in alphabetical order.

COMPLETE SET (6)	12.50	30.00
1 Nelson Briles	2.00	5.00
2 Dave Cash	1.50	4.00
3 Roberto Clemente	50.00	100.00
4 Richie Hebner	2.00	5.00
5 Bob Robertson	1.50	4.00
6 Luke Walker	1.50	4.00

1971 Pirates Action Photos

These unnumbered cards feature members of the World Champion Pittsburgh Pirates. These cards were issued in two series (1-12, 13-24) and each group is sequenced into alphabetical order.

COMPLETE SET (24)	100.00	200.00
1 Gene Alley	1.50	4.00
2 Nelson Briles	1.00	2.50
3 Dave Cash	1.00	2.50
4 Roberto Clemente	50.00	100.00
5 Dock Ellis	2.00	5.00
6 Mudcat Grant	1.00	2.50
7 Bob Johnson	1.00	2.50
8 Milt May	1.00	2.50
9 Jose Pagan	1.00	2.50
10 Manny Sanguillen	2.00	5.00
11 Bob Veale	1.00	2.50
12 Luke Walker	1.00	2.50
13 Steve Blass	1.50	4.00
14 Gene Clines	1.00	2.50
15 Vic Davalillo	1.00	2.50
16 Dave Giusti	1.00	2.50
17 Richie Hebner	1.50	4.00
18 Jackie Hernandez	1.00	2.50
19 Bill Mazeroski	10.00	25.00
20 Bob Moose	1.00	2.50
21 Al Oliver	2.50	6.00
22 Bob Robertson	1.00	2.50
23 Charlie Sands	1.00	2.50
24 Willie Stargell	6.00	15.00

1971 Pirates Arco Oil

Sponsored by Arco Oil, this 12-card set features photos of

the 1971 Pittsburgh Pirates. The cards are unnumbered and checklisted below in alphabetical order.

COMPLETE SET (12) 40.00 80.00
1 Gene Alley 2.00 5.00
2 Steve Blass 2.50 6.00
3 Roberto Clemente 10.00 25.00
4 Dave Giusti 2.00 5.00
5 Richie Hebner 2.00 5.00
6 Bill Mazeroski 5.00 12.00
7 Bob Moose 2.00 5.00
8 Al Oliver 3.00 8.00
9 Bob Robertson 2.00 5.00
10 Manny Sanguillen 3.00 8.00
11 Willie Stargell 6.00 15.00
12 Luke Walker 2.00 5.00

1971 Pirates Post-Gazette Inserts

These inserts, which feature members of the 1971 Pittsburgh Pirates, were inserted daily into the Post-Gazette newspaper. These inserts are numbered and this list may be incomplete so any further information is appreciated.

COMPLETE SET 50.00 100.00
5 Dave Cash 5.00 12.00
7 Bob Johnson 4.00 10.00
8 Nelson Briles 4.00 10.00
11 Dave Giusti 4.00 10.00
12 Luke Walker 4.00 10.00
13 Gene Clines 4.00 10.00
14 Milt May 4.00 10.00
15 Bob Robertson 4.00 10.00
17 Gene Alley 4.00 10.00
18 Bruce Kison 4.00 10.00
19 Jose Pagan 4.00 10.00
20 Dock Ellis 4.00 10.00
22 Bob Miller 4.00 10.00
23 Jackie Hernandez 4.00 10.00

1972 Pirates Team Issue

This eight-card set of the Pittsburgh Pirates measures approximately 3 1/4" by 4 1/4" and features color player portraits with a facsimile autograph in the wide bottom margin. The cards are unnumbered and checklisted below in alphabetical order.

COMPLETE SET 30.00 60.00
1 Steve Blass 1.25 3.00
2 Roberto Clemente 8.00 20.00
3 Dock Ellis 1.50 4.00
4 Richie Hebner 1.25 3.00
5 Dave Giusti 1.25 3.00
6 Bob Johnson 1.25 3.00
7 Bob Moose 1.25 3.00
8 Al Oliver 2.50 6.00
9 Jose Pagan 1.25 3.00
10 Bob Robertson 1.25 3.00
11 Manny Sanguillen 1.50 4.00
12 Willie Stargell 3.00 8.00

1973 Pirates Post/Gazette Inserts

These photos were inserted each day into the Pittsburgh Post Gazette. This listing is incomplete and any further information is appreciated. There may be other photos so all additional information is appreciated.

COMPLETE SET 20.00 50.00
6 Vic Davalillo 2.00 5.00
10 Ramon Hernandez 2.00 5.00
12 Bob Johnson 2.00 5.00
14 Milt May 2.00 5.00
15 Bob Miller 2.00 5.00
19 Charlie Sands 2.00 5.00
23 Luke Walker 2.00 5.00
24 Bill Virdon MG 2.00 5.00
NNO Gene Alley 2.00 5.00
NNO Steve Blass 2.00 5.00
NNO Nelson Briles 2.00 5.00
NNO Dave Cash 2.00 5.00

1974 Pirates 1938 Bra-Mac

These 26 photos, which measure 3 1/2" by 5" feature members of the 1938 Pittsburgh Pirates who lost the battle for the NL pennant very late in that season.

COMPLETE SET 6.00 15.00
1 Paul Waner .75 2.00
2 Lloyd Waner .60 1.50
3 Bill Swift .20 .50
4 Woody Jensen .20 .50
5 Jim Tobin .20 .50
6 Ray Berres .20 .50
7 Tommy Thevenow .20 .50
8 Bob Klinger .20 .50
9 Arky Vaughan .60 1.50
10 Pep Young .20 .50
11 Heinie Manush .60 1.50
12 Bill Brubaker .20 .50
13 Pie Traynor .75 2.00
14 Lee Handley .20 .50
15 Rip Sewell .20 .50
16 Johnny Dickshot .20 .50
17 Cy Blanton .20 .50
18 Gus Suhr .30 .75
19 Mace Brown .20 .50
20 Johnny Rizzo .20 .50
21 Al Todd .20 .50
22 Russ Bauers .20 .50
23 Ed Brandt .20 .50
24 Red Lucas .20 .50
25 Joe Bowman .20 .50
26 Ken Heintzleman .20 .50

1975 Pirates Postcards

This 29-card set of the Pittsburgh Pirates features player photos on postcard-size cards. The average size is 3 3/4" by 5 1/4". The fronts feature white-bordered black and white portraits. The player's name is printed in the wider bottom margin. Also a fascimile autograph in blue ink is inscribed across each picture. The backs are blank. The cards are unnumbered and checklisted below in alphabetical order.

COMPLETE SET (29) 8.00 20.00
1 Ken Brett .20 .50
2 John Candelaria .60 1.50
3 Larry Demery .20 .50
4 Duffy Dyer .20 .50
5 Dock Ellis .20 .50
6 Dave Giusti .20 .50
7 Richie Hebner .30 .75
8 Ramon Hernandez .20 .50
9 Art Howe .60 1.50
10 Ed Kirkpatrick .20 .50
11 Bruce Kison .20 .50
12 Don Leppert CO .20 .50
13 Mario Mendoza .20 .50
14 Bob Moose .20 .50
15 Danny Murtaugh MG .20 .50
16 Al Oliver .60 1.50
17 Don Osborne CO .20 .50
18 Jose Pagan CO .20 .50
19 Dave Parker 1.00 2.50
20 Paul Popovich .20 .50
21 Jerry Reuss .40 1.00
22 Bill Robinson .20 .50
23 Bob Robertson .20 .50
24 Jim Rooker .30 .75
25 Manny Sanguillen .30 .75
26 Willie Stargell 1.50 4.00
27 Rennie Stennett .20 .50
28 Frank Taveras .20 .50
29 Richie Zisk .20 .50

1976 Pirates Postcards

This 27-card set of the Pittsburgh Pirates features player photos on postcard-size cards. The cards are unnumbered and checklisted below in alphabetical order.

COMPLETE SET (27) 10.00 25.00
1 John Candelaria 1.25 3.00
2 Larry Demery .40 1.00
3 Dave Giusti .40 1.00
4 Richie Hebner .60 1.50
5 Tommy Helms .40 1.00
6 Ramon Hernandez .40 1.00
7 Ed Kirkpatrick .40 1.00
8 Bruce Kison .40 1.00
9 Don Leppert CO .40 1.00
10 George Medich .40 1.00
11 Mario Mendoza .40 1.00
12 Bob Moose .40 1.00
13 Danny Murtaugh MG .40 1.00
14 Al Oliver 1.25 3.00
15 Ed Ott .40 1.00
16 Dave Parker 1.25 3.00
17 Jerry Reuss .60 1.50
18 Bob Robertson .40 1.00
19 Bill Robinson .40 1.00
20 Jim Rooker .40 1.00
21 Manny Sanguillen .40 1.00
22 Bob Skinner CO .40 1.00
23 Willie Stargell 2.50 6.00
24 Rennie Stennett .40 1.00
25 Frank Taveras .40 1.00
26 Kent Tekulve .75 2.00
27 Richie Zisk .40 1.00

1977 Pirates Post-Gazette Portraits

This 30-card set was distributed in an 8 1/2" by 11" book from the Pittsburgh Post-Gazette. The black-and-white player portraits were detachable and measured approximately 8" by 11". The backs are blank. The cards are unnumbered and checklisted below in alphabetical order.

COMPLETE SET (30) 40.00 80.00
1 John Candelaria 1.50 4.00
2 Larry Demery 1.00 2.50
3 Miguel Dilone 1.00 2.50
4 Duffy Dyer 1.00 2.50
5 Terry Forster 1.00 2.50
6 Jim Fregosi 1.00 2.50
7 Phil Garner 1.50 4.00
8 Fernando Gonzalez 1.00 2.50
9 Goose Gossage 3.00 8.00
10 Grant Jackson 1.00 2.50
11 Odell Jones 1.00 2.50
12 Bruce Kison 1.00 2.50
13 Joe Lonnett CO 1.00 2.50
14 Mario Mendoza 1.00 2.50
15 Al Monchak CO 1.00 2.50
16 Omar Moreno 1.50 4.00
17 Al Oliver 3.00 8.00
18 Ed Ott 1.00 2.50
19 Jose Pagan CO 1.00 2.50
20 Dave Parker 3.00 8.00
21 Jerry Reuss 1.50 4.00
22 Bill Robinson 1.00 2.50
23 Jim Rooker 1.00 2.50
24 Larry Sherry CO 1.00 2.50
25 Willie Stargell 6.00 15.00
26 Rennie Stennett 1.00 2.50
27 Chuck Tanner MG 1.00 2.50
28 Frank Taveras 1.00 2.50
29 Kent Tekulve 1.50 4.00
30 Bobby Tolan 1.00 2.50

1977 Pirates 1960 World Champions TCMA

This 41-card set features black-and-white photos of the 1960 World Champion Pittsburgh Pirates in orange borders. The backs carry player information and statistics. (There is no card number 35 in the checklist.)

COMPLETE SET (41) 30.00 60.00
1 Danny Murtaugh MG .60 1.50
2 Dick Stuart .60 1.50
3 Bill Mazeroski 2.50 6.00
4 Dick Groat 1.00 2.50
5 Don Hoak .60 1.50
6 Roberto Clemente 6.00 15.00
7 Bill Virdon 1.00 2.50
8 Bob Skinner .60 1.50
9 Smoky Burgess 1.00 2.50
10 Gino Cimoli .60 1.50
11 Rocky Nelson .60 1.50
12 Hal Smith .60 1.50
13 Dick Schofield .60 1.50
14 Joe Christopher .60 1.50
15 Gene Baker .60 1.50
16 Bob Oldis .60 1.50
17 Vern Law 1.00 2.50
18 Bob Friend .60 1.50
19 Vinegar Bend Mizell .60 1.50
20 Havey Haddix .60 1.50
21 Roy Face 1.00 2.50
22 Freddie Green .60 1.50
23 Joe Gibbon .60 1.50
24 Clem Labine .60 1.50
25 Paul Giel .60 1.50
26 Tom Chaney .60 1.50
27 Earl Francis .60 1.50
28 Jim Umbricht .60 1.50
29 George Witt .60 1.50
30 Bennie Daniels .60 1.50
31 Don Gross .60 1.50
32 Diomedes Olivo .60 1.50
33 Ramon Mejias .60 1.50
34 Mickey Vernon 1.00 2.50
36 Danny Kravitz .60 1.50
37 Harry Bright .60 1.50
38 Dick Barone .60 1.50
39 Bill Burwell CO .60 1.50
40 Lenny Levy .60 1.50
41 Sam Narron CO .60 1.50
42 Bob Friend 1.00 2.50

1980 Pirates 1960 TCMA

This 41 card set was issued in 1980 and can be differentiated from the earlier TCMA 1960 Pirates set as the photos are clearer and the 1960 Pirates and player's name are on the front.

COMPLETE SET 8.00 20.00
1 Clem Labine .20 .50
2 Bob Friend .20 .50
3 Roy Face .30 .75
4 Vern Law .30 .75
5 Harvey Haddix .20 .50
6 Wilmer Mizell .08 .25
7 Bill Burwell .08 .25
8 Diomedes Olivo .08 .25
9 Don Gross .08 .25
10 Fred Green .08 .25
11 Jim Umbricht .08 .25
12 George Witt .08 .25
13 Tom Cheney .08 .25
14 Bennie Daniels .08 .25
15 Earl Francis .08 .25
16 Joe Gibbon .08 .25
17 Paul Giel .08 .25
18 Danny Kravitz .08 .25
19 R.C. Stevens .08 .25
20 Roman Mejias .08 .25
21 Dick Barone .08 .25
22 Sam Narron .08 .25
23 Harry Bright .08 .25
24 Mickey Vernon .20 .50
25 Bob Skinner .08 .25
26 Smoky Burgess .08 .25
27 Bill Virdon .08 .25
28 Roberto Clemente 2.00 5.00
No Number on back
29 Don Hoak .20 .50
30 Bill Mazeroski 1.00 2.50
31 Dick Stuart .30 .75
32 Dick Groat .40 1.00
33 Bob Oldis .08 .25
34 Gene Baker .08 .25
35 Joe Christopher .08 .25
36 Dick Schofield .08 .25
37 Hal W. Smith .08 .25
38 Rocky Nelson .08 .25
39 Gino Cimoli .08 .25
40 Danny Murtaugh MG .08 .25
41 Leo Levy .08 .25

1939 Play Ball

The cards in this 161-card set measure approximately 2 1/2" by 3 1/8". Gum Incorporated introduced a brief (war-shortened) but innovative era of baseball card production with its set of 1939. The combination of actual player photos (black and white), large card size, and extensive biography proved extremely popular. Player names are found either entirely capitalized or with initial caps only, and a "sample card" overprint is not uncommon. The "sample card" overprint variations are valued at double the prices below. Card number 126 was never issued, and cards 116-162 were produced in lesser quantities than cards 1-115. A card of Ted Williams in his rookie season as well as an early card of Joe DiMaggio are the key cards in the set.

COMPLETE SET (161) 6,000.00 10,000.00
COMMON CARD (1-115) 12.00 20.00
COMMON CARD (116-162) 40.00 75.00
WRAPPER (1-CENT) 150.00 200.00
1 Jake Powell RC 30.00 60.00
2 Lee Grissom RC 12.00 20.00
3 Red Ruffing 40.00 75.00
4 Eldon Auker RC 12.00 20.00
5 Luke Sewell 15.00 25.00
6 Leo Durocher 60.00 100.00
7 Bobby Doerr RC 40.00 75.00
8 Henry Pippen RC 12.00 20.00
9 James Tobin RC 12.00 20.00
10 James DeShong 12.00 20.00
11 Johnny Rizzo RC 12.00 20.00
12 Hershel Martin RC 12.00 20.00
13 Luke Hamlin RC 12.00 20.00
14 Jim Tabor RC 12.00 20.00
15 Paul Derringer 18.00 30.00
16 John Peacock RC 12.00 20.00
17 Emerson Dickman RC 12.00 20.00
18 Harry Danning RC 12.00 20.00
19 Paul Dean RC 25.00 40.00
20 Joe Heving RC 12.00 20.00
21 Dutch Leonard RC 18.00 30.00
22 Bucky Walters RC 18.00 30.00
23 Burgess Whitehead RC 12.00 20.00
24 Richard Coffman 12.00 20.00
25 George Selkirk RC 25.00 40.00
26 Joe DiMaggio RC 1,000.00 2,000.00
27 Fred Ostermueller 12.00 20.00
28 Sylvester Johnson RC 12.00 20.00
29 John(Jack) Wilson RC 12.00 20.00
30 Bill Dickey 75.00 125.00
31 Sam West 12.00 20.00
32 Bob Seeds RC 12.00 20.00
33 Del Young RC 12.00 20.00
34 Frank Demaree 12.00 20.00
35 Bill Jurges 12.00 20.00
36 Frank McCormick RC 12.00 20.00
37 Virgil Davis 12.00 20.00
38 Billy Myers RC 12.00 20.00
39 Rick Ferrell 40.00 75.00
40 James Bagby Jr. RC 12.00 20.00
41 Lon Warneke 15.00 25.00
42 Arndt Jorgens 12.00 20.00
43 Melo Almada RC 15.00 25.00
44 Don Heffner RC 12.00 20.00
45 Merrill May RC 12.00 20.00
46 Morris Arnovich RC 12.00 20.00
47 Buddy Lewis RC 12.00 20.00
48 Lefty Gomez 75.00 125.00
49 Eddie Miller RC 12.00 20.00
50 Charley Gehringer 75.00 125.00
51 Mel Ott 75.00 125.00
52 Tommy Henrich RC 25.00 40.00
53 Carl Hubbell 75.00 125.00
54 Harry Gumpert RC 12.00 20.00
55 Arky Vaughan 40.00 75.00
56 Hank Greenberg 125.00 200.00
57 Buddy Hassett RC 12.00 20.00
58 Lou Chiozza RC 12.00 20.00
59 Ken Chase RC 12.00 20.00
60 Schoolboy Rowe RC 25.00 40.00
61 Tony Cuccinello 15.00 25.00
62 Tom Carey RC 12.00 20.00
63 Emmett Mueller RC 12.00 20.00
64 Wally Moses RC 15.00 25.00
65 Harry Craft RC 15.00 25.00
66 Jimmy Ripple RC 12.00 20.00
67 Ed Joost RC 15.00 25.00
68 Fred Sington RC 12.00 20.00
69 Elbie Fletcher RC 12.00 20.00
70 Fred Frankhouse 12.00 20.00
71 Monte Pearson RC 18.00 30.00
72 Debs Garms RC 12.00 20.00
73 Hal Schumacher 15.00 25.00
74 Cookie Lavagetto RC 15.00 25.00
75 Stan Bordagaray RC 12.00 20.00
76 Goody Rosen RC 12.00 20.00
77 Lew Riggs RC 12.00 20.00
78 Julius Solters 12.00 20.00
79 Jo Jo Moore 12.00 20.00
80 Pete Fox 12.00 20.00
81 Babe Dahlgren RC 18.00 30.00
82 Chuck Klein 60.00 100.00
83 Gus Suhr 12.00 20.00
84 Skeeter Newsom RC 12.00 20.00
85 Johnny Cooney RC 12.00 20.00
86 Dolph Camilli 15.00 25.00
87 Milburn Shoffner RC 12.00 20.00
88 Charlie Keller RC 25.00 40.00
89 Lloyd Waner 40.00 75.00
90 Robert Klinger RC 12.00 20.00
91 John Knott RC 12.00 20.00
92 Ted Williams RC 3,000.00 6,000.00

93 Charles Gelbert RC 12.00 20.00
94 Heinie Manush 40.00 75.00
95 Whit Wyatt RC 15.00 25.00
96 Babe Phelps RC 12.00 20.00
97 Bob Johnson 18.00 30.00
98 Pinky Whitney RC 12.00 20.00
99 Wally Berger 18.00 30.00
100 Buddy Myer 15.00 25.00
101 Roger Cramer 15.00 25.00
102 Lem (Pep) Young RC 12.00 20.00
103 Moe Berg 75.00 125.00
104 Tom Bridges 15.00 25.00
105 Rabbit McNair RC 12.00 20.00
106 Dolly Stark UMP 18.00 30.00
107 Joe Vosmik 12.00 20.00
108 Frank Hayes 12.00 20.00
109 Myril Hoag 12.00 20.00
110 Fred Fitzsimmons 15.00 25.00
111 Van Lingle Mungo RC 18.00 30.00
112 Paul Waner 60.00 100.00
113 Al Schacht 18.00 30.00
114 Cecil Travis RC 15.00 25.00
115 Ralph Kress 12.00 20.00
116 Gene Desautels RC 40.00 75.00
117 Wayne Ambler RC 40.00 75.00
118 Lynn Nelson 40.00 75.00
119 Will Hershberger RC 50.00 100.00
120 Rabbit Warstler RC 40.00 75.00
121 Bill Posedel RC 40.00 75.00
122 George McQuinn RC 40.00 75.00
123 Ray T. Davis RC 40.00 75.00
124 Walter Brown 40.00 75.00
125 Cliff Melton RC 40.00 75.00
127 Gil Brack RC 40.00 75.00
128 Joe Bowman RC 40.00 75.00
129 Bill Swift 40.00 75.00
130 Bill Brubaker RC 40.00 75.00
131 Mort Cooper RC 50.00 100.00
132 Jim Brown RC 40.00 75.00
133 Lynn Myers RC 40.00 75.00
134 Tot Presnell RC 40.00 75.00
135 Mickey Owen RC 50.00 100.00
136 Roy Bell RC 40.00 75.00
137 Pete Appleton 40.00 75.00
138 George Case RC 50.00 100.00
139 Vito Tamulis RC 40.00 75.00
140 Ray Hayworth RC 40.00 75.00
141 Pete Coscarart RC 40.00 75.00
142 Ira Hutchinson RC 40.00 75.00
143 Earl Averill 100.00 175.00
144 Zeke Bonura RC 50.00 100.00
145 Hugh Mulcahy RC 40.00 75.00
146 Tom Sunkel RC 40.00 75.00
147 George Coffman RC 40.00 75.00
148 Bill Trotter RC 40.00 75.00
149 Max West RC 40.00 75.00
150 James Walkup RC 40.00 75.00
151 Hugh Casey RC 50.00 100.00
152 Roy Weatherly RC 40.00 75.00
153 Dizzy Trout RC 50.00 100.00
154 Johnny Hudson RC 40.00 75.00
155 Jimmy Outlaw RC 40.00 75.00
156 Ray Berres RC 40.00 75.00
157 Don Padgett RC 40.00 75.00
158 Bud Thomas RC 40.00 75.00
159 Red Evans RC 40.00 75.00
160 Gene Moore RC 40.00 75.00
161 Lonnie Frey 40.00 75.00
162 Whitey Moore RC 50.00 100.00

1940 Play Ball

The cards in this 240-card series measure approximately 2 1/2" by 3 1/8". Gum Inc. improved upon its 1939 design by enclosing the 1940 black and white player photo with a frame line and printing the player's name in a panel below the picture (often using a nickname). The set included many Hall of Famers and Old Timers. Cards 1-114 are numbered in team groupings. Cards 181-240 are scarcer than cards 1-180. The backs contain an extensive biography and a dated copyright line. The key cards in the set are the cards of Joe DiMaggio, Shoeless Joe Jackson, and Ted Williams.

COMPLETE SET (240) 10,000.00 15,000.00
COMMON CARD (1-120) 12.00 20.00
COMMON CARD (121-180) 12.00 20.00
COMMON CARD (181-240) 35.00 70.00
WRAP.(1-CENT, DIFF. COL.) 700.00 800.00
1 Joe DiMaggio 1,500.00 3,000.00
2 Art Jorgens 15.00 25.00
3 Babe Dahlgren 15.00 25.00
4 Tommy Henrich 25.00 50.00
5 Monte Pearson 15.00 25.00
6 Lefty Gomez 90.00 150.00
7 Bill Dickey 100.00 175.00
8 George Selkirk 15.00 25.00
9 Charlie Keller 25.00 50.00
10 Red Ruffing 50.00 90.00
11 Jake Powell 15.00 25.00
12 Johnny Schulte 12.00 20.00
13 Jack Knott 12.00 20.00
14 Rabbit McNair 12.00 20.00
15 George Case 15.00 25.00
16 Cecil Travis 15.00 25.00
17 Buddy Myer 15.00 25.00
18 Charlie Gelbert 12.00 20.00
19 Ken Chase 12.00 20.00
20 Buddy Lewis 12.00 20.00
21 Rick Ferrell 45.00 80.00
22 Sammy West 12.00 20.00
23 Dutch Leonard 15.00 25.00
24 Frank Hayes 12.00 20.00
25 Bob Johnson 15.00 25.00
26 Wally Moses 15.00 25.00
27 Ted Williams 800.00 1,500.00
28 Gene Desautels 12.00 20.00
29 Doc Cramer 15.00 25.00
30 Moe Berg 90.00 150.00
31 Jack Wilson 12.00 20.00
32 Jim Bagby 12.00 20.00
33 Fritz Ostermueller 12.00 20.00
34 John Peacock 12.00 20.00
35 Joe Heving 12.00 20.00
36 Jim Tabor 12.00 20.00
37 Emerson Dickman 12.00 20.00
38 Bobby Doerr 50.00 90.00
39 Tom Carey 12.00 20.00
40 Hank Greenberg 100.00 200.00
41 Charley Gehringer 90.00 150.00
42 Bud Thomas 12.00 20.00
43 Pete Fox 12.00 20.00
44 Dizzy Trout 15.00 25.00
45 Red Kress 12.00 20.00
46 Earl Averill 50.00 90.00
47 Oscar Vitt RC 12.00 20.00
48 Luke Sewell 15.00 25.00
49 Stormy Weatherly 12.00 20.00
50 Hal Trosky 15.00 25.00
51 Don Heffner 12.00 20.00
52 Myril Hoag 12.00 20.00
53 George McQuinn 15.00 25.00
54 Bill Trotter 12.00 20.00
55 Slick Coffman 12.00 20.00
56 Eddie Miller RC 15.00 25.00
57 Max West 12.00 20.00
58 Bill Posedel 12.00 20.00
59 Rabbit Warstler 12.00 20.00
60 John Cooney 12.00 20.00
61 Tony Cuccinello 15.00 25.00
62 Buddy Hassett 12.00 20.00
63 Pete Coscarart 12.00 20.00
64 Van Lingle Mungo 15.00 25.00
65 Fred Fitzsimmons 15.00 25.00
66 Babe Phelps 12.00 20.00
67 Whit Wyatt 15.00 25.00
68 Dolph Camilli 15.00 25.00
69 Cookie Lavagetto 15.00 25.00
70 Luke Hamlin/(Hot Potato) 12.00 20.00
71 Mel Almada 12.00 20.00
72 Chuck Dressen RC 15.00 25.00
73 Bucky Walters 15.00 25.00
74 Paul(Duke) Derringer 15.00 25.00
75 Frank (Buck) McCormick 15.00 25.00
76 Lonny Frey 12.00 20.00
77 Willard Hershberger 15.00 25.00
78 Lew Riggs 12.00 20.00
79 Harry Craft 15.00 25.00
80 Billy Myers 12.00 20.00
81 Wally Berger 15.00 25.00
82 Hank Gowdy CO 15.00 25.00
83 Cliff Melton 12.00 20.00
84 Jo Jo Moore 12.00 20.00
85 Hal Schumacher 15.00 25.00
86 Harry Gumbert 12.00 20.00
87 Carl Hubbell 75.00 125.00
88 Mel Ott 100.00 175.00
89 Bill Jurges 12.00 20.00
90 Frank Demaree 12.00 20.00
91 Bob Seeds 12.00 20.00
92 Whitey Whitehead 12.00 20.00
93 Harry Danning 12.00 20.00
94 Gus Suhr 12.00 20.00
95 Hugh Mulcahy 12.00 20.00
96 Heinie Mueller 12.00 20.00
97 Morry Arnovich 12.00 20.00
98 Pinky May 12.00 20.00
99 Syl Johnson 12.00 20.00
100 Hersh Martin 12.00 20.00
101 Del Young 12.00 20.00
102 Chuck Klein 60.00 100.00
103 Elbie Fletcher 12.00 20.00
104 Paul Waner 50.00 90.00
105 Lloyd Waner 45.00 80.00
106 Pep Young 12.00 20.00
107 Arky Vaughan 45.00 80.00
108 Johnny Rizzo 12.00 20.00
109 Don Padgett 12.00 20.00
110 Tom Sunkel 12.00 20.00
111 Mickey Owen 15.00 25.00
112 Jimmy Brown 12.00 20.00
113 Mort Cooper 15.00 25.00
114 Lon Warneke 15.00 25.00
115 Mike Gonzalez CO 15.00 25.00
116 Al Schacht 15.00 25.00
117 Dolly Stark UMP 15.00 25.00
118 Waite Hoyt 50.00 90.00
119 Grover C. Alexander 100.00 175.00
120 Walter Johnson 100.00 200.00
121 Atley Donald RC 15.00 25.00
122 Sandy Sundra RC 15.00 25.00
123 Hildy Hildebrand 15.00 25.00
124 Earle Combs 60.00 100.00
125 Art Fletcher RC 15.00 25.00
126 Jake Solters 12.00 20.00
127 Muddy Ruel 12.00 20.00
128 Pete Appleton 12.00 20.00
129 Bucky Harris MG RC 45.00 80.00
130 Clyde Milan RC 15.00 25.00
131 Zeke Bonura 15.00 25.00
132 Connie Mack MG RC 75.00 150.00
133 Jimmie Foxx 100.00 200.00
134 Joe Cronin 60.00 100.00
135 Line Drive Nelson 12.00 20.00
136 Cotton Pippen 12.00 20.00
137 Bing Miller 12.00 20.00
138 Beau Bell 12.00 20.00
139 Elden Auker 12.00 20.00
140 Dick Coffman 12.00 20.00
141 Casey Stengel MG RC 100.00 175.00
142 George Kelly RC 50.00 90.00
143 Gene Moore 12.00 20.00
144 Joe Vosmik 12.00 20.00
145 Vito Tamulis 12.00 20.00
146 Tot Pressnell 12.00 20.00
147 Johnny Hudson 12.00 20.00
148 Hugh Casey 15.00 25.00
149 Pinky Shoffner 12.00 20.00
150 Whitey Moore 12.00 20.00
151 Edwin Joost 15.00 25.00
152 Jimmy Wilson 12.00 20.00
153 Bill McKechnie MG RC 45.00 80.00
154 Jumbo Brown 12.00 20.00
155 Ray Hayworth 12.00 20.00
156 Daffy Dean 25.00 50.00
157 Lou Chiozza 12.00 20.00
158 Travis Jackson 50.00 90.00
159 Pancho Snyder RC 12.00 20.00
160 Hans Lobert CO 12.00 20.00
161 Debs Garms 12.00 20.00
162 Joe Bowman 12.00 20.00
163 Spud Davis 12.00 20.00
164 Ray Berres 12.00 20.00
165 Bob Klinger 12.00 20.00
166 Bill Brubaker 12.00 20.00
167 Frankie Frisch MG 50.00 90.00
168 Honus Wagner CO 100.00 200.00
169 Gabby Street 12.00 20.00
170 Tris Speaker 100.00 175.00
171 Harry Heilmann 45.00 80.00
172 Chief Bender 45.00 80.00
173 Napoleon Lajoie 100.00 175.00
174 Johnny Evers 50.00 90.00
175 Christy Mathewson 150.00 250.00
176 Heinie Manush 50.00 90.00
177 Frank Baker 60.00 100.00
178 Max Carey 50.00 90.00
179 George Sisler 75.00 125.00
180 Mickey Cochrane 90.00 150.00
181 Spud Chandler RC 45.00 80.00
182 Knick Knickerbocker RC 35.00 70.00
183 Marvin Breuer RC 35.00 70.00
184 Mule Haas 35.00 70.00
185 Joe Kuhel 35.00 70.00
186 Taft Wright RC 35.00 70.00
187 Jimmy Dykes MG 45.00 80.00
188 Joe Krakauskas RC 35.00 70.00
189 Jim Bloodworth RC 35.00 70.00
190 Charley Berry 35.00 70.00
191 John Babich RC 35.00 70.00
192 Dick Siebert RC 35.00 70.00
193 Chubby Dean RC 35.00 70.00
194 Sam Chapman RC 35.00 70.00
195 Dee Miles RC 35.00 70.00
196 Red (Nonny) Nonnenkamp RC 35.00 70.00
197 Lou Finney RC 35.00 70.00
198 Denny Galehouse RC 35.00 70.00
199 Pinky Higgins 35.00 70.00
200 Soup Campbell RC 35.00 70.00
201 Barney McCosky RC 35.00 70.00
202 Al Milnar RC 35.00 70.00
203 Bad News Hale RC 35.00 70.00
204 Harry Eisenstat RC 35.00 70.00
205 Rollie Hemsley RC 35.00 70.00
206 Chet Laabs RC 35.00 70.00
207 Gus Mancuso 35.00 70.00
208 Lee Gamble RC 35.00 70.00
209 Hy Vandenberg RC 35.00 70.00
210 Bill Lohrman RC 35.00 70.00
211 Pop Joiner RC 35.00 70.00
212 Babe Young RC 35.00 70.00
213 John Rucker RC 35.00 70.00
214 Ken O'Dea RC 35.00 70.00
215 Johnnie McCarthy RC 35.00 70.00
216 Joe Marty RC 35.00 70.00
217 Walter Beck 35.00 70.00
218 Wally Millies RC 35.00 70.00
219 Russ Bauers RC 35.00 70.00
220 Mace Brown RC 35.00 70.00
221 Lee Handley RC 35.00 70.00
222 Max Butcher RC 35.00 70.00
223 Hughie Jennings 90.00 150.00
224 Pie Traynor 100.00 175.00
225 Joe Jackson 1,500.00 2,500.00
226 Harry Hooper 90.00 150.00
227 Jesse Haines 90.00 150.00
228 Charlie Grimm 45.00 80.00
229 Buck Herzog 35.00 70.00
230 Red Faber 100.00 175.00
231 Dolf Luque 60.00 100.00
232 Goose Goslin 90.00 150.00
233 George Earnshaw 45.00 80.00
234 Frank Chance 90.00 150.00
235 John McGraw 100.00 175.00
236 Jim Bottomley 90.00 150.00
237 Willie Keeler 100.00 175.00
238 Tony Lazzeri 100.00 175.00
239 George Uhle 35.00 70.00
240 Bill Atwood RC 60.00 100.00

1941 Play Ball

HARRY "GUNBOAT" GUMBERT

The cards in this 72-card set measure approximately 2 1/2" by 3 1/8". Many of the cards in the 1941 Play Ball series are simply color versions of pictures appearing in the 1940 set. This was the only color baseball card set produced by Gum, Inc.. Card numbers 49-72 are slightly more difficult to obtain as they were not issued until 1942. In 1942, numbers 1-48 were also reissued but without the copyright date. The cards were also printed on paper without a cardboard backing; these are generally encountered in sheets or strips. The set features a card of Pee Wee Reese in his rookie year.

COMPLETE SET (72) 6,000.00 10,000.00
COMMON CARD (1-48) 20.00 40.00
COMMON CARD (49-72) 30.00 60.00
WRAPPER (1-CENT) 700.00 800.00
1 Eddie Miller 75.00 125.00
2 Max West 20.00 40.00
3 Bucky Walters 25.00 45.00
4 Paul Derringer 30.00 50.00
5 Frank (Buck) McCormick 25.00 45.00
6 Carl Hubbell 100.00 175.00
7 Harry Danning 20.00 40.00
8 Mel Ott 150.00 300.00
9 Pinky May 20.00 40.00
10 Arky Vaughan 60.00 100.00
11 Debs Garms 20.00 40.00
12 Jimmy Brown 20.00 40.00
13 Jimmie Foxx 200.00 400.00
14 Ted Williams 1,000.00 2,000.00
15 Joe Cronin 75.00 125.00
16 Hal Trosky 25.00 45.00
17 Roy Weatherly 20.00 40.00
18 Hank Greenberg 150.00 300.00
19 Charley Gehringer 100.00 200.00
20 Red Ruffing 75.00 125.00
21 Charlie Keller 35.00 60.00
22 Bob Johnson 30.00 50.00
23 George McQuinn 20.00 40.00
24 Dutch Leonard 25.00 45.00
25 Gene Moore 20.00 40.00
26 Harry Gumpert 20.00 40.00
27 Babe Young 20.00 40.00
28 Joe Marty 20.00 40.00
29 Jack Wilson 20.00 40.00
30 Lou Finney 20.00 40.00
31 Joe Kuhel 20.00 40.00
32 Taft Wright 20.00 40.00
33 Al Milnar 20.00 40.00
34 Rollie Hemsley 20.00 40.00
35 Pinky Higgins 25.00 45.00
36 Barney McCosky 20.00 40.00
37 Bruce Campbell RC 20.00 40.00
38 Atley Donald 30.00 50.00
39 Tommy Henrich 35.00 60.00
40 John Babich 20.00 40.00
41 Frank (Blimp) Hayes 20.00 40.00
42 Wally Moses 25.00 45.00
43 Al Brancato RC 20.00 40.00
44 Sam Chapman 20.00 40.00
45 Eldon Auker 20.00 40.00
46 Sid Hudson RC 20.00 40.00
47 Buddy Lewis 20.00 40.00
48 Cecil Travis 25.00 45.00
49 Babe Dahlgren 35.00 65.00
50 Johnny Cooney 30.00 60.00
51 Dolph Camilli 35.00 65.00
52 Kirby Higbe RC 30.00 60.00
53 Luke Hamlin 30.00 60.00
54 Pee Wee Reese RC 400.00 800.00
55 Whit Wyatt 35.00 65.00
56 Johnny VanderMeer RC 60.00 100.00
57 Moe Arnovich 30.00 60.00
58 Frank Demaree 30.00 60.00
59 Bill Jurges 30.00 60.00
60 Chuck Klein 90.00 150.00
61 Vince DiMaggio RC 125.00 225.00
62 Elbie Fletcher 30.00 60.00
63 Dom DiMaggio RC 150.00 250.00
64 Bobby Doerr 100.00 175.00
65 Tommy Bridges 35.00 65.00
66 Harland Clift RC 30.00 60.00
67 Walt Judnich RC 30.00 60.00
68 John Knott 30.00 60.00
69 George Case 35.00 65.00
70 Bill Dickey 250.00 400.00
71 Joe DiMaggio 1,500.00 3,000.00
72 Lefty Gomez 200.00 400.00

1912 Plow's Candy E300

The cards in this set measure 3" X 4" with a sepia photograph measuring 2 1/4" X 3 5/16". This set was issued by Plow's Candy Company in 1912 on thin cardboard with wide borders. The subject's name is printed in block letters outside the bottom frame, and his team is listed directly beneath. The title "Plow's Candy Collection" is printed at the top; the cards are unnumbered and blank-backed. A few cards have been discovered with "premium or offer" backs. Those cards do trade at a premium. The cards have been alphabetized and numbered in the checklist below. The Doyle card was just discovered recently, leading many to believe that there might be other additions to this checklist. Any additions are therefore appreciated.

1 Babe Adams 1,250.00 2,500.00
2 Frank Baker 2,000.00 4,000.00
3 Cy Barger 1,000.00 2,000.00
4 Jack Barry 1,000.00 2,000.00
5 Johnny Bates 1,000.00 2,000.00
6 Chief Bender 2,000.00 4,000.00
7 Joe Benz 1,000.00 2,000.00
8 Bill Bergen 1,000.00 2,000.00
UER Berger
9 Roger Breshnahan 2,000.00 4,000.00
10 Mordecai Brown 2,000.00 4,000.00
11 Donie Bush 1,000.00 2,000.00

12 Bobby Byrne 1,000.00 2,000.00
13 Nixey Callahan 1,000.00 2,000.00
14 Hal Chase 1,500.00 3,000.00
15 Fred Clarke 2,000.00 4,000.00
16 Ty Cobb 7,500.00 15,000.00
17 King Cole 1,000.00 2,000.00
18 Eddie Collins 2,000.00 4,000.00
19 Jack Coombs 1,000.00 2,000.00
20 Bill Dahlen 1,000.00 2,000.00
21 Bert Daniels 1,000.00 2,000.00
22 Harry Davis 2,000.00 4,000.00
23 Jim Delahanty 1,000.00 2,000.00
24 Josh Devore 1,000.00 2,000.00
25 Bill Donovan 1,250.00 2,500.00
26 Red Dooin 1,000.00 2,000.00
27 Larry Doyle 1,250.00 2,500.00
28 Johnny Evers 2,000.00 4,000.00
29 Russ Ford 1,000.00 2,000.00
30 Del Gainor 1,000.00 2,000.00
31 Vean Gregg 1,000.00 2,000.00
32 Robert Harmon 1,000.00 2,000.00
33 Arnold Hauser 1,000.00 2,000.00
34 Dick Hoblitzell 1,000.00 2,000.00
UER Hoblitzelle
35 Solly Hofman 1,000.00 2,000.00
36 Miller Huggins 2,000.00 4,000.00
37 John Hummel 1,000.00 2,000.00
38 Walter Johnson 4,000.00 8,000.00
39 Johnny Kling 1,000.00 2,000.00
40 Nap Lajoie 2,000.00 4,000.00
41 John Lapp 1,000.00 2,000.00
42 Fred Luderus 1,000.00 2,000.00
43 Sherry Magee 1,250.00 2,500.00
44 Rube Marquard 2,000.00 4,000.00
45 Christy Mathewson 4,000.00 8,000.00
46 Stuffy McInnis 1,250.00 2,500.00
UER McInnes
47 Larry McLean 1,000.00 2,000.00
48 Fred Merkle 1,500.00 3,000.00
49 Cy Morgan 1,000.00 2,000.00
50 George Moriarity 1,000.00 2,000.00
51 Harry Mowrey 1,000.00 2,000.00
52 Chief Meyers 1,250.00 2,500.00
UER Myers
53 Rube Oldring 1,000.00 2,000.00
54 Martin O'Toole 1,000.00 2,000.00
55 Eddie Plank 2,000.00 4,000.00
56 Nap Rucker 1,250.00 2,500.00
57 Slim Sallee 1,000.00 2,000.00
58 Boss Schmidt 1,000.00 2,000.00
59 Jimmy Sheckard 1,000.00 2,000.00
60 Tris Speaker 2,000.00 4,000.00
61 Billy Sullivan 1,000.00 2,000.00
62 Ira Thomas 1,000.00 2,000.00
63 Joe Tinker 2,000.00 4,000.00
64 John Titus 1,000.00 2,000.00
65 Hippo Vaughn 1,000.00 2,000.00
UER Vaughan
66 Honus Wagner 4,000.00 8,000.00
67 Ed Walsh 2,000.00 4,000.00
68 Bob Williams 1,000.00 2,000.00

1910-12 Plow Boy Tobacco

Measuring approximately 5 3/4" by 8", these cards were issued with Large tins of Plow Boy tobacco. These cards feature only members of the Chicago Cubs and Chicago White Sox. Since these cards are unnumbered, we have sequenced them in alphabetical order. In addition, there is a good chance that additions to this checklist may still be found; if so, we appreciate the help to our checklist in advance.

COMPLETE SET 40,000.00 80,000.00
1 Jimmy Archer 750.00 1,500.00
2 Ginger Beaumont 750.00 1,500.00
3 Lena Blackburne 750.00 1,500.00
4 Bruno Block 750.00 1,500.00
5 Ping Bodie 750.00 1,500.00
6 Mordecai Brown 2,000.00 4,000.00
7 Al Carson 750.00 1,500.00
8 Frank Chance 2,000.00 4,000.00
9 Eddie Cicotte 2,500.00 5,000.00
10 King Cole 750.00 1,500.00
11 Shano Collins 750.00 1,500.00
12 George Davis 750.00 1,500.00
13 Patsy Dougherty 750.00 1,500.00
14 Chick Gandil 1,500.00 3,000.00
15 Ed Hahn 750.00 1,500.00
16 George Howard 750.00 1,500.00
17 Bill Jones 750.00 1,500.00
18 Johnny Kling 1,000.00 2,000.00
19 Rube Kroh 750.00 1,500.00
20 Frank Lange 750.00 1,500.00
21 Fred Luderus 750.00 1,500.00
22 Harry McIntyre 750.00 1,500.00
23 Ward Miller 750.00 1,500.00
24 Charlie Mullen 750.00 1,500.00
25 Fred Olmstead 750.00 1,500.00
26 Orvie Overall 1,000.00 2,000.00
27 Fred Parent 750.00 1,500.00
28 Fred Payne 750.00 1,500.00
29 Jeff Pfeffer 750.00 1,500.00
30 Jeff Pfeister 750.00 1,500.00
31 Billy Purtell 750.00 1,500.00
32 Ed Reulbach 1,250.00 2,500.00
33 Lew Richie 750.00 1,500.00
34 Frank Schulte 1,250.00 2,500.00
35 Jim Scott 750.00 1,500.00
Sic, Scotts
36 Jim Scott 750.00 1,500.00
37 Frank Smith 750.00 1,500.00
38 Jimmy Sheckard 1,000.00 2,000.00
39 Harry Steinfeldt 1,000.00 2,000.00
40 Billy Sullivan 750.00 1,500.00
41 Lee Tannehill 750.00 1,500.00
42 Joe Tinker 2,000.00 4,000.00
43 Ed Walsh 2,000.00 4,000.00
44 Doc White 1,000.00 2,000.00
45 Irv Young 750.00 1,500.00
46 Rollie Zeider 750.00 1,500.00
47 Heinie Zimmerman 1,000.00 2,000.00

1901-17 Police Gazette Supplements

These 11" by 16" premiums were issued with copies of the "Police Gazette" magazine. The high quality photos have the police gazette ID on the top and an ID of the athlete as well as some information about him on the bottom. We have just listed the Baseball players here but it is believed many more should exist. Although this list is alphabetical, when 2 or more supplements are confirmed for the same player we have put the supplement number next to the player's name.

COMPLETE SET 15,000.00 30,000.00
1 Grover C. Alexander 500.00 1,000.00
2 Leon Ames 150.00 300.00
3 Jimmy Archer 125.00 250.00
4 Harry Bay 125.00 250.00
5 Frank Baker 300.00 600.00
6 Ping Bodie 125.00 250.00
7 Frank Bowerman 125.00 250.00
8 Roger Bresnahan 250.00 500.00
9 Al Bridwell 125.00 250.00
10 Mordecai Brown 300.00 600.00
11 Al Burch 125.00 250.00
12 Owen Bush 125.00 250.00
13 Ray Caldwell 125.00 250.00
14 Jimmy Casey 125.00 250.00
15 Frank Chance 400.00 800.00
16 Hal Chase 300.00 600.00
17 Hal Chase 250.00 500.00
Charlie Armbruster
18 Jack Chesbro 300.00 600.00
19 Ty Cobb 1,250.00 2,500.00
20 Eddie Collins 400.00 800.00
21 Jack Coombs 150.00 300.00
22 Harry Coveleski 125.00 250.00
23 Stan Coveleskie 250.00 500.00
24 Sam Crawford 250.00 500.00
25 Birdie Cree 125.00 250.00
26 Jack Cronin 125.00 250.00
27 Nick Cullop 125.00 250.00
28 Bill Dahlen 150.00 300.00
29 Tom Dalton 125.00 250.00
30 Bert Daniels 125.00 250.00
31 Jake Daubert 150.00 300.00
32 George Davis 250.00 500.00
33 Harry Davis 125.00 250.00
34 Josh Devore 125.00 250.00
35 Mike Donlin 150.00 300.00
36 Red Dooin 125.00 250.00
37 Larry Doyle 150.00 300.00
38 Louis Drucke 125.00 250.00
39 Cecil Ferguson 125.00 250.00
40 Dave Fultz 125.00 250.00
41 Russ Ford 125.00 250.00
42 Clark Griffith 250.00 500.00
43 Charley Hemphill 125.00 250.00
44 Dick Hoblitzel 125.00 250.00
45 Danny Hoffman 125.00 250.00
46 Buck Herzog 150.00 300.00
47 Bill Hogg 125.00 250.00
48 Del Howard 125.00 250.00
49 Joe Jackson 1,000.00 2,000.00
50 Walter Johnson 750.00 1,500.00
51 Benny Kauff 125.00 250.00
52 Willie Keeler 300.00 600.00
53 Willie Keeler 250.00 500.00
Jack Kleinow
54 Malachi Kittredge 125.00 250.00
55 Jack Kleinow 125.00 250.00
56 Napoleon Lajoie 400.00 800.00
57 Tommy Leach 125.00 250.00
58 Hans Lobert/1660 125.00 250.00
59 Hans Lobert/1975 125.00 250.00
60 Hans Lobert/2074 125.00 250.00
61 Fred Luderus 125.00 250.00
62 Harry Lumley 125.00 250.00
63 Sherry Magee/1722 150.00 300.00
64 Sherry Magee/1970 150.00 300.00
65 Fritz Maisel 125.00 250.00
66 Rabbit Maranville 250.00 500.00
67 Rube Marquard 250.00 500.00
68 Christy Mathewson/1251 750.00 1,500.00
69 Christy Mathewson/1771 750.00 1,500.00
70 Dan McGann 125.00 250.00
71 Joe McGinnity 250.00 500.00
72 John McGraw 400.00 800.00
73 Sandow Mertes 125.00 250.00
74 Clarence Mitchell 125.00 250.00
75 George Moriarty 125.00 250.00
76 Dick Morris 125.00 250.00
77 Jack Myers 125.00 250.00
78 Orval Overall 125.00 250.00
79 Pol Perritt 125.00 250.00
80 Philadelphia A's/1914 150.00 300.00
81 Pittsburgh Pirates/1905 150.00 300.00
82 Eddie Plank 300.00 600.00
83 Maurice Powers 125.00 250.00
84 Bugs Raymond 125.00 250.00
85 Dave Robertson 125.00 250.00
86 Nap Rucker 150.00 300.00
87 Dick Rudolph 125.00 250.00
88 Cy Seymour 125.00 250.00
89 Nap Shea 125.00 250.00
90 George Sisler 300.00 600.00
91 Alec Smith 125.00 250.00
92 Jake Stahl 125.00 250.00
93 Sammy Strang 125.00 250.00
94 Roy Thomas 125.00 250.00
95 Jim Thorpe 1,000.00 2,000.00
96 Honus Wagner 1,000.00 2,000.00
97 Honus Wagner 1,000.00 2,000.00
Roger Bresnahan
98 Jack Warhop 125.00 250.00
99 Jack Warner 125.00 250.00
100 Zach Wheat 250.00 500.00
101 Arthur Wilson 125.00 250.00
102 Joe Wood 200.00 400.00
103 Heinie Zimmerman 150.00 300.00

1914 Polo Grounds Game WG4

These cards were distributed as part of a baseball game produced around 1914. The cards each measure approximately 2 1/2" by 3 1/2" and have rounded corners. The card fronts show a photo of the player, his name, his team, and the game outcome associated with that particular card. The card backs are printed in green and white and are all the same each showing a panoramic picture of the Polo Grounds inside an ornate frame with a white outer border. Since the cards are unnumbered, they are listed below in alphabetical order.

COMPLETE SET (30) 1,500.00 3,000.00
1 Jimmy Archer 15.00 25.00
2 Frank Baker 35.00 60.00
3 Frank Chance 30.00 50.00
4 Larry Cheney 15.00 25.00
5 Ty Cobb 175.00 300.00
6 Eddie Collins 35.00 60.00
7 Larry Doyle 15.00 25.00
8 Art Fletcher 15.00 25.00
9 Claude Hendrix 15.00 25.00
10 Joe Jackson 300.00 500.00
11 Hugh Jennings MG 35.00 60.00
12 Nap Lajoie 50.00 80.00
13 Jimmy Lavender 15.00 25.00
14 Fritz Maisel 15.00 25.00
15 Rabbit Maranville 35.00 60.00
16 Rube Marquard 35.00 60.00
17 Christy Mathewson 90.00 150.00
18 John McGraw MG 35.00 60.00
19 Stuffy McInnis 15.00 25.00
20 Chief Meyers 15.00 25.00
21 Red Murray 15.00 25.00
22 Eddie Plank 35.00 60.00
23 Nap Rucker 15.00 25.00
24 Reb Russell 15.00 25.00
25 Frank Schulte 15.00 25.00
26 Jim Scott 15.00 25.00
27 Tris Speaker 50.00 80.00
28 Honus Wagner 150.00 250.00
29 Ed Walsh 35.00 60.00
30 Joe Wood 35.00 60.00

1930 Post Famous North Americans

This blank-backed card, which measures approximately 2 3/8" by 3 3/8" was cut from a strip of 4 cards and features a photo of Christy Mathewson on the front. Mathewson is the only sports personage featured in this set of 32 cards.

8 Christy Mathewson 75.00 150.00

1960 Post Cereal

These large cards measure approximately 7" by 8 3/4". The 1960 Post Cereal Sports Stars set contains nine cards depicting current baseball, football and basketball players. Each card comprised the entire back of a Grape Nuts Flakes Box and is blank backed. The color player photos are set on a colored background surrounded by a wooden frame design, and they are unnumbered (assigned numbers below for reference according to sport). The catalog designation is F278-26.

COMPLETE SET (9) 3,000.00 5,000.00
BB1 Don Drysdale 150.00 300.00
BB2 Al Kaline 200.00 400.00
BB3 Harmon Killebrew 250.00 500.00
BB4 Ed Mathews 200.00 400.00
BB5 Mickey Mantle 1,000.00 2,000.00

1961 Post

The cards in this 200-card set measure 2 1/2" by 3 1/2". The 1961 Post set was this company's first major set. The cards were available on thick cardbox stock, singly or in various panel sizes from cereal boxes (BOX), or in team sheets, printed on thinner cardboard stock, directly from the Post Cereal Company (COM). It is difficult to differentiate the COM cards from the BOX cards; the thickness of the card stock is the best indicator. Many variations exist and are noted in the checklist below. There are many cards which were produced in lesser quantities; the prices below reflect the relative scarcity of the cards. Cards 10, 23, 70, 73, 94, 113, 135, 163, and 183 are examples of cards printed in limited quantities and hence commanding premium prices. The cards are numbered essentially in team groups, i.e., New York Yankees (1-18), Chicago White Sox (19-34), Detroit (35-46), Boston (47-56), Cleveland (57-67), Baltimore (68-80), Kansas City (81-90), Minnesota (91-100), Milwaukee (101-114), Philadelphia (115-124), Pittsburgh (125-140), San Francisco (141-155), Los Angeles Dodgers (156-170), St. Louis (171-180), Cincinnati (181-190), and Chicago Cubs (191-200). The catalog number is F278-33. The complete set price refers to the set with all variations (357). There was also an album produced by Post to hold the cards.

COMPLETE MASTER SET (357) 1,700.00 3,400.00
1A Yogi Berra COM 15.00 40.00
1B Yogi Berra BOX 15.00 40.00
2A Elston Howard COM 2.50 6.00
2B Elston Howard BOX 2.50 6.00
3A Bill Skowron COM 2.50 6.00
3B Bill Skowron BOX 2.50 6.00
4A Mickey Mantle COM 100.00 200.00
4B Mickey Mantle BOX 100.00 200.00
5 Bob Turley COM only 10.00 25.00
6A Whitey Ford COM 6.00 15.00
6B Whitey Ford BOX 6.00 15.00
7A Roger Maris COM 15.00 40.00
7B Roger Maris BOX 15.00 40.00
8A Bobby Richardson COM 2.50 6.00
8B Bobby Richardson BOX 2.50 6.00
9A Tony Kubek COM 2.50 6.00
9B Tony Kubek BOX 2.50 6.00
10 G.McDougald BOX only 30.00 60.00
11 Cletis Boyer BOX only 2.50 6.00
12A Hector Lopez COM 1.50 4.00
12B Hector Lopez BOX 1.50 4.00
13 Bob Cerv BOX only 1.50 4.00
14 Ryne Duren BOX only 1.50 4.00
15 Bobby Shantz BOX only 1.50 4.00
16 Art Ditmar BOX only 1.50 4.00
17 Jim Coates BOX only 1.50 4.00
18 Johnny Blanchard BOX only 1.50 4.00
19A Luis Aparicio COM 4.00 10.00
19B Luis Aparicio BOX 4.00 10.00
20A Nellie Fox COM 4.00 10.00
20B Nellie Fox BOX 4.00 10.00
21A Billy Pierce COM 2.50 6.00
21B Billy Pierce BOX 2.50 6.00
22A Early Wynn COM 8.00 20.00
22B Early Wynn BOX 8.00 20.00
23 Bob Shaw BOX only 60.00 120.00
24A Al Smith COM 2.50 6.00
24B Al Smith BOX 2.50 6.00
25A Minnie Minoso COM 3.00 8.00
25B Minnie Minoso BOX 3.00 8.00
26A Roy Sievers COM 1.50 4.00
26B Roy Sievers BOX 1.50 4.00
27A Jim Landis COM 1.50 4.00
27B Jim Landis BOX 1.50 4.00
28A Sherm Lollar COM 1.50 4.00
28B Sherm Lollar BOX 1.50 4.00
29 Gerry Staley BOX only 1.50 4.00
30A G.Freese COM(Reds) 6.00 15.00
30B G.Freese BOX (WS) 1.50 4.00
31 T.Kluszewski BOX only 3.00 8.00
32 Turk Lown BOX only 1.50 4.00
33A Jim Rivera COM 1.50 4.00
33B Jim Rivera BOX 1.50 4.00
34 Frank Baumann BOX only 1.50 4.00
35A Al Kaline COM 10.00 25.00
35B Al Kaline BOX 10.00 25.00
36A Rocky Colavito COM 5.00 12.00
36B Rocky Colavito BOX 5.00 12.00
37A Charlie Maxwell COM 2.50 6.00
37B Charlie Maxwell BOX 2.50 6.00
38A Frank Lary COM 2.50 6.00
38B Frank Lary BOX 2.50 6.00
39A Jim Bunning COM 4.00 10.00
39B Jim Bunning BOX 4.00 10.00
40A Norm Cash COM 2.50 6.00
40B Norm Cash BOX 2.50 6.00
41A F.Bolling COM Braves 2.50 6.00
41B F.Bolling BOX Tigers 4.00 10.00
42A Don Mossi COM 1.50 4.00
42B Don Mossi BOX 1.50 4.00
43A Lou Berberet COM 1.50 4.00
43B Lou Berberet BOX 1.50 4.00
44 Dave Sisler BOX only 1.50 4.00
45 Eddie Yost BOX only 1.50 4.00
46 Pete Burnside BOX only 1.50 4.00
47A Pete Runnels COM 2.50 6.00
47B Pete Runnels BOX 2.50 6.00
48A Frank Malzone COM 1.50 4.00
48B Frank Malzone BOX 1.50 4.00
49A Vic Wertz COM 2.50 6.00
49B Vic Wertz BOX 2.50 6.00
50A Tom Brewer COM 1.50 4.00
50B Tom Brewer BOX 1.50 4.00
51A W.Tasby COM(S 4.00 10.00
Wash.)
51B W.Tasby BOX (No sale) 2.50 6.00
52A Russ Nixon COM 1.50 4.00
52B Russ Nixon BOX 1.50 4.00
53A Don Buddin COM 1.50 4.00
53B Don Buddin BOX 1.50 4.00
54A Bill Monbouquette COM 1.50 4.00
54B Bill Monbouquette BOX 1.50 4.00
55A F.Sullivan COM Phillies 5.00 12.00
55B F.Sullivan BOX Red Sox 1.50 4.00
56A Haywood Sullivan COM 1.50 4.00
56B Haywood Sullivan BOX 1.50 4.00
57A H.Kuenn COM Giants 4.00 10.00
57B H.Kuenn BOX Indians 3.00 8.00
58A Gary Bell COM 2.50 6.00
58B Gary Bell BOX 2.50 6.00
59A Jim Perry COM 1.50 4.00
59B Jim Perry BOX 1.50 4.00
60A Jim Grant COM 2.50 6.00
60B Jim Grant BOX 2.50 6.00
61A Johnny Temple COM 2.50 6.00
61B Johnny Temple BOX 2.50 6.00
62A Paul Foytack COM 1.50 4.00
62B Paul Foytack BOX 1.50 4.00
63A Vic Power COM 1.50 4.00
63B Vic Power BOX 1.50 4.00
64A Tito Francona COM 1.50 4.00
64B Tito Francona BOX 1.50 4.00
65A K.Aspromonte COM Sold LA 4.00 10.00

65B K.Aspromonte BOX No sale	4.00	10.00
66 Bob Wilson BOX only	1.50	4.00
67A John Romano COM	1.50	4.00
67B John Romano BOX	1.50	4.00
68A Jim Gentile COM	2.50	6.00
68B Jim Gentile BOX	2.50	6.00
69A Gus Triandos COM	2.50	6.00
69B Gus Triandos BOX	2.50	6.00
70 G.Woodling BOX only	15.00	40.00
71A Milt Pappas COM	2.50	6.00
71B Milt Pappas BOX	2.50	6.00
72A Ron Hansen COM	1.50	4.00
72B Ron Hansen BOX	1.50	4.00
73 C.Estrada COM only	75.00	150.00
74A Steve Barber COM	1.50	4.00
74B Steve Barber BOX	1.50	4.00
75A Brooks Robinson COM	12.50	30.00
75B Brooks Robinson BOX	12.50	30.00
76A Jackie Brandt COM	1.50	4.00
76B Jackie Brandt BOX	1.50	4.00
77A Marv Breeding COM	1.50	4.00
77B Marv Breeding BOX	1.50	4.00
78 Hal Brown BOX only	1.50	4.00
79 Billy Klaus BOX only	1.50	4.00
80A Hoyt Wilhelm COM	4.00	10.00
80B Hoyt Wilhelm BOX	4.00	10.00
81A Jerry Lumpe COM	2.50	6.00
81B Jerry Lumpe BOX	2.50	6.00
82A Norm Siebern COM	1.50	4.00
82B Norm Siebern BOX	1.50	4.00
83A Bud Daley COM	2.50	6.00
83B Bud Daley BOX	2.50	6.00
84A Bill Tuttle COM	1.50	4.00
84B Bill Tuttle BOX	1.50	4.00
85A Marv Throneberry COM	2.50	6.00
85B Marv Throneberry BOX	2.50	6.00
86A Dick Williams COM	2.50	6.00
86B Dick Williams BOX	2.50	6.00
87A Ray Herbert COM	1.50	4.00
87B Ray Herbert BOX	1.50	4.00
88A Whitey Herzog COM	3.00	8.00
88B Whitey Herzog BOX	3.00	8.00
89A K.Hamlin COM Sold LA	10.00	25.00
89B K.Hamlin BOX No sold	1.50	4.00
90A Hank Bauer COM	2.50	6.00
90B Hank Bauer BOX	2.50	6.00
91A B.Allison COM Minnesota	3.00	8.00
91B B.Allison BOX Minneapolis	3.00	8.00
92A H.Killebrew COM Minnesota	30.00	60.00
92B H.Killebrew BOX Minneapolis	20.00	50.00
93A J.Lemon COM Minnesota	12.50	30.00
93B J.Lemon BOX Minneapolis	50.00	100.00
94A C.Stobbs COM only Minnesota	125.00	250.00
95A R.Bertoia COM Minnesota	2.50	6.00
95B R.Bertoia BOX Minneapolis	1.50	4.00
96A B.Gardner COM Minnesota	2.50	6.00
96B B.Gardner BOX Minneapolis	1.50	4.00
97A E.Battey COM Minnesota	2.50	6.00
97B E.Battey BOX Minneapolis	1.50	4.00
98A P.Ramos COM Minnesota	2.50	6.00
98B P.Ramos BOX Minneapolis	1.50	4.00
99A C.Pascual COM Minnesota	2.50	6.00
99B C.Pascual BOX Minneapolis	1.50	4.00
100A B.Consolo COM Minnesota	2.50	6.00
100B B.Consolo BOX Minneapolis	1.50	4.00
101A Warren Spahn COM	12.50	30.00
101B Warren Spahn BOX	12.50	30.00
102A Lew Burdette COM	2.50	6.00
102B Lew Burdette BOX	2.50	6.00
103A Bob Buhl COM	1.50	4.00
103B Bob Buhl BOX	1.50	4.00
104A Joe Adcock COM	2.50	6.00
104B Joe Adcock BOX	2.50	6.00
105A Johnny Logan COM	2.50	6.00
105B Johnny Logan BOX	2.50	6.00
106 E.Mathews COM only	20.00	50.00
107A Hank Aaron COM	15.00	40.00
107B Hank Aaron BOX	15.00	40.00
108A Wes Covington COM	1.50	4.00
108B Wes Covington BOX	1.50	4.00
109A B.Bruton COM Tigers	3.00	8.00
109B B.Bruton BOX Braves	3.00	8.00
110A Del Crandall COM	2.50	6.00
110B Del Crandall BOX	2.50	6.00
111 E.Schoendienst BOX only	3.00	8.00
112 J.Pizarro BOX only	1.50	4.00
113 C.Cottier BOX only	8.00	20.00
114 Al Spangler BOX only	1.50	4.00
115A Dick Farrell COM	2.50	6.00
115B Dick Farrell BOX	2.50	6.00
116A Jim Owens COM	2.50	6.00
116B Jim Owens BOX	2.50	6.00
117A Robin Roberts COM	5.00	12.00
117B Robin Roberts BOX	4.00	10.00
118A Tony Taylor COM	1.50	4.00
118B Tony Taylor BOX	1.50	4.00
119A Lee Walls COM	1.50	4.00
119B Lee Walls BOX	1.50	4.00
120A Tony Curry COM	1.50	4.00
120B Tony Curry BOX	1.50	4.00
121A Pancho Herrera COM	2.50	6.00
121B Pancho Herrera BOX	2.50	6.00
122A Ken Walters COM	2.50	6.00
122B Ken Walters BOX	2.50	6.00
123A John Callison COM	2.50	6.00
123B John Callison BOX	2.50	6.00
124A G.Conley COM Red Sox	6.00	15.00
124B G.Conley BOX Phillies	1.50	4.00
125A Bob Friend COM	2.50	6.00
125B Bob Friend BOX	2.50	6.00
126A Vern Law COM	2.50	6.00
126B Vern Law BOX	2.50	6.00
127A Dick Stuart COM	2.50	6.00
127B Dick Stuart BOX	2.50	6.00
128A Bill Mazeroski COM	3.00	8.00
128B Bill Mazeroski BOX	3.00	8.00
129A Dick Groat COM	2.50	6.00
129B Dick Groat BOX	2.50	6.00
130A Don Hoak COM	1.50	4.00
130B Don Hoak BOX	1.50	4.00
131A Bob Skinner COM	1.50	4.00
131B Bob Skinner BOX	1.50	4.00
132A R.Clemente COM	40.00	80.00
132B R.Clemente BOX	40.00	80.00
133 Roy Face BOX only	2.50	6.00
134 H.Haddix BOX only	1.50	4.00
135 Bill Virdon BOX only	20.00	50.00
136A Gino Cimoli COM	1.50	4.00
136B Gino Cimoli BOX	1.50	4.00
137 R.Nelson BOX only	1.50	4.00
138A Smoky Burgess COM	2.50	6.00
138B Smoky Burgess BOX	2.50	6.00
139 Hal W. Smith BOX only	1.50	4.00
140 Wilmer Mizell BOX only	1.50	4.00
141A Mike McCormick COM	1.50	4.00
141B Mike McCormick BOX	1.50	4.00
142A J. Antonelli COM Cleve	3.00	8.00
142B J.Antonelli BOX S.F.	2.50	6.00
143A Sam Jones COM	2.50	6.00
143B Sam Jones BOX	2.50	6.00
144A Orlando Cepeda COM	5.00	12.00
144B Orlando Cepeda BOX	5.00	12.00
145A Willie Mays COM	20.00	50.00
145B Willie Mays BOX	20.00	50.00
146A W.Kirkland COM Cleve	4.00	10.00
146B W.Kirkland BOX S.F.	3.00	8.00
147A Willie McCovey COM	5.00	12.00
147B Willie McCovey BOX	5.00	12.00
148A Don Blasingame COM	1.50	4.00
148B Don Blasingame BOX	1.50	4.00
149A Jim Davenport COM	2.50	6.00
149B Jim Davenport BOX	2.50	6.00
150A Hobie Landrith COM	1.50	4.00
150B Hobie Landrith BOX	1.50	4.00
151 Bob Schmidt BOX only	1.50	4.00
152A Ed Bressoud COM	1.50	4.00
152B Ed Bressoud BOX	1.50	4.00
153A A.Rodgers BOX no trade	10.00	25.00
153B A.Rodgers BOX Traded	2.50	6.00
154 Jack Sanford BOX only	1.50	4.00
155 Billy O'Dell BOX only	1.50	4.00
156A Norm Larker COM	1.50	4.00
156B Norm Larker BOX	1.50	4.00
157A Charlie Neal COM	2.50	6.00
157B Charlie Neal BOX	2.50	6.00
158A Jim Gilliam COM	4.00	10.00
158B Jim Gilliam BOX	4.00	10.00
159A Wally Moon COM	3.00	8.00
159B Wally Moon BOX	3.00	8.00
160A Don Drysdale COM	8.00	20.00
160B Don Drysdale BOX	8.00	20.00
161A Larry Sherry COM	2.50	6.00
161B Larry Sherry BOX	2.50	6.00
162 S.Williams BOX only	4.00	10.00
163 Mel Roach BOX only	60.00	120.00
164A Maury Wills COM	5.00	12.00
164B Maury Wills BOX	5.00	12.00
165 Tommy Davis BOX only	2.50	6.00
166A John Roseboro COM	1.50	4.00
166B John Roseboro BOX	1.50	4.00
167A Duke Snider COM	4.00	10.00
167B Duke Snider BOX	4.00	10.00
168A Gil Hodges COM	4.00	10.00
168B Gil Hodges BOX	4.00	10.00
169 John Podres BOX only	2.50	6.00
170 Ed Roebuck BOX only	2.50	6.00
171A Ken Boyer COM	5.00	12.00
171B Ken Boyer BOX	5.00	12.00
172A Joe Cunningham COM	1.50	4.00
172B Joe Cunningham BOX	1.50	4.00
173A Daryl Spencer COM	1.50	4.00
173B Daryl Spencer BOX	1.50	4.00
174A Larry Jackson COM	2.50	6.00
174B Larry Jackson BOX	2.50	6.00
175A Lindy McDaniel COM	1.50	4.00
175B Lindy McDaniel BOX	1.50	4.00
176A Bill White COM	2.50	6.00
176B Bill White BOX	2.50	6.00
177A Alex Grammas COM	1.50	4.00
177B Alex Grammas BOX	1.50	4.00
178A Curt Flood COM	3.00	8.00
178B Curt Flood BOX	3.00	8.00
179A Ernie Broglio COM	1.50	4.00
179B Ernie Broglio BOX	1.50	4.00
180A Hal Smith COM	1.50	4.00
180B Hal Smith BOX	1.50	4.00
181A Vada Pinson COM	2.50	6.00
181B Vada Pinson BOX	2.50	6.00
182A Frank Robinson COM	20.00	50.00
182B Frank Robinson BOX	20.00	50.00
183 R.McMillan BOX only	60.00	120.00
184A Bob Purkey COM	1.50	4.00
184B Bob Purkey BOX	1.50	4.00
185A Ed Kasko COM	1.50	4.00
185B Ed Kasko BOX	1.50	4.00
186A Gus Bell COM	1.50	4.00
186B Gus Bell BOX	1.50	4.00
187A Jerry Lynch COM	1.50	4.00
187B Jerry Lynch BOX	1.50	4.00
188A Ed Bailey COM	1.50	4.00
188B Ed Bailey BOX	1.50	4.00
189A Jim O'Toole COM	1.50	4.00
189B Jim O'Toole BOX	1.50	4.00
190A B.Martin COM Sold Milw	5.00	12.00
190B B.Martin BOX No sold	3.00	8.00
191A Ernie Banks COM	15.00	40.00
191B Ernie Banks BOX	15.00	40.00
192A Richie Ashburn COM	5.00	12.00
192B Richie Ashburn BOX	5.00	12.00
193A Frank Thomas COM	30.00	60.00
193B Frank Thomas BOX	30.00	60.00
194A Don Cardwell COM	2.50	6.00
194B Don Cardwell BOX	2.50	6.00
195A George Altman COM	1.50	4.00
195B George Altman BOX	1.50	4.00
196A Ron Santo COM	3.00	8.00
196B Ron Santo BOX	3.00	8.00
197A Glen Hobbie COM	1.50	4.00
197B Glen Hobbie BOX	1.50	4.00
198A Sam Taylor COM	1.50	4.00
198B Sam Taylor BOX	1.50	4.00
199A Jerry Kindall COM	1.50	4.00
199B Jerry Kindall BOX	1.50	4.00
200A Don Elston COM	2.50	6.00
200B Don Elston BOX	2.50	6.00
XX Album		

1962 Post

The cards in this 200-player series measure 2 1/2" by 3 1/2" and are oriented horizontally. The 1962 Post set is the easiest of the Post sets to complete. The cards are grouped numerically by team, for example, New York Yankees (1-13), Detroit (14-26), Baltimore (27-36), Cleveland (37-45), Chicago White Sox (46-55), Boston (56-64), Washington (65-73), Los Angeles Angels (74-82), Minnesota (83-91), Kansas City (92-100), Los Angeles Dodgers (101-115), Cincinnati (116-130), San Francisco (131-144), Milwaukee (145-157), St. Louis (158-168), Pittsburgh (169-181), Chicago Cubs (182-191), and Philadelphia (192-200). Cards 5B and 6B were printed on thin stock in a two-card panel and distributed in a Life magazine promotion. The scarce cards are 55, 69, 83, 92, 101, 103, 113, 116, 122, 125, 127, 131, 140, 144, and 158. The checklist for this set is the same as that of 1962 Jello and 1962 Post Canadian, but those sets are considered separate issues. The catalog number for this set is F278-37.

COMPLETE MASTER SET (210)	1,300.00	2,600.00
1 Bill Skowron	3.00	8.00
2 Bobby Richardson	3.00	8.00
3 Cletis Boyer	2.50	6.00
4 Tony Kubek	3.00	8.00
5A Mickey Mantle	100.00	200.00
5B Mickey Mantle AD	100.00	200.00
6A Roger Maris	12.50	30.00
6B Roger Maris AD	12.50	30.00
7 Yogi Berra	12.50	30.00
8 Elston Howard	2.50	6.00
9 Whitey Ford	5.00	12.00
10 Ralph Terry	2.50	5.00
11 John Blanchard	1.50	4.00
12 Luis Arroyo	2.50	5.00
13 Bill Stafford	1.50	4.00
14A N.Cash ERR(T:right)	10.00	25.00
14B N.Cash COR(T:left)	3.00	8.00
15 Jake Wood	1.50	4.00
16 Steve Boros	1.50	4.00
17 Chico Fernandez	1.50	4.00
18 Bill Bruton	1.50	4.00
19 Rocky Colavito	4.00	10.00
20 Al Kaline	8.00	20.00
21 Dick Brown	1.50	4.00
22 Frank Lary	1.50	4.00
23 Don Mossi	1.50	4.00
24 Phil Regan	1.50	4.00
25 Charley Maxwell	1.50	4.00
26 Jim Bunning	4.00	10.00
27A J.Gentile H-Baltimore	2.50	5.00
27B J.Gentile H-San Lorenzo	10.00	25.00
28 Marv Breeding	1.50	4.00
29 Brooks Robinson	8.00	20.00
30A Ron Hansen (At-Bats)	2.50	6.00
30B Ron Hansen (At Bats)	2.50	6.00
31 Jackie Brandt	1.50	4.00
32 Dick Williams	2.50	5.00
33 Gus Triandos	1.50	4.00
34 Milt Pappas	2.50	5.00
35 Hoyt Wilhelm	4.00	10.00
36 Chuck Estrada	5.00	12.00
37 Vic Power	1.50	4.00
38 Johnny Temple	1.50	4.00
39 Bubba Phillips	1.50	4.00
40 Tito Francona	1.50	4.00
41 Willie Kirkland	1.50	4.00
42 John Romano	1.50	4.00
43 Jim Perry	1.50	4.00
44 Woodie Held	1.50	4.00
45 Chuck Essegian	1.50	4.00
46 Roy Sievers	1.50	4.00
47 Nellie Fox	4.00	10.00
48 Al Smith	1.50	4.00
49 Luis Aparicio	4.00	10.00
50 Jim Landis	1.50	4.00
51 Minnie Minoso	2.50	6.00
52 Andy Carey	1.50	4.00
53 Sherman Lollar	1.50	4.00
54 Billy Pierce	2.50	5.00
55 Early Wynn	15.00	40.00
56 Chuck Schilling	2.50	5.00
57 Pete Runnels	1.50	4.00
58 Frank Malzone	1.50	4.00
59 Don Buddin	1.50	4.00
60 Gary Geiger	1.50	4.00
61 Carl Yastrzemski	20.00	50.00
62 Jackie Jensen	2.50	5.00
63 Jim Pagliaroni	1.50	4.00
64 Don Schwall	1.50	4.00
65 Dale Long	1.50	4.00
66 Chuck Cottier	1.50	4.00
67 Billy Klaus	1.50	4.00
68 Coot Veal	2.50	5.00
69 Marty Keough	20.00	50.00
70 Willie Tasby	1.50	4.00
71 Gene Woodling	1.50	4.00
72 Gene Green	2.50	5.00
73 Dick Donovan	1.50	4.00
74 Steve Bilko	1.50	4.00
75 Rocky Bridges	1.50	4.00
76 Eddie Yost	1.50	4.00
77 Leon Wagner	1.50	4.00
78 Albie Pearson	2.50	5.00
79 Ken Hunt	1.50	4.00
80 Earl Averill	1.50	4.00
81 Ryne Duren	1.50	4.00
82 Ted Kluszewski	5.00	12.00
83 Bob Allison	15.00	40.00
84 Billy Martin	4.00	10.00
85 Harmon Killebrew	5.00	12.00
86 Zoilo Versalles	1.50	4.00
87 Lenny Green	1.50	4.00
88 Bill Tuttle	1.50	4.00
89 Jim Lemon	1.50	4.00
90 Earl Battey	1.50	4.00
91 Camilo Pascual	1.50	4.00
92 Norm Siebern	50.00	100.00
93 Jerry Lumpe	1.50	4.00
94 Dick Howser	2.50	5.00
95A G.Stephens (BD:Jan. 5)	2.50	6.00
95B G.Stephens(BD:Jan.20)	10.00	25.00
96 Leo Posada	1.50	4.00
97 Joe Pignatano	1.50	4.00
98 Jim Archer	1.50	4.00
99 Haywood Sullivan	1.50	4.00
100 Art Ditmar	1.50	4.00
101 Gil Hodges	60.00	120.00
102 Charlie Neal	1.50	4.00
103 Daryl Spencer	15.00	40.00
104 Maury Wills	5.00	12.00
105 Tommy Davis	2.50	5.00
106 Willie Davis	2.50	5.00
107 John Roseboro	1.50	4.00
108 Johnny Podres	2.50	5.00
109A Sandy Koufax	20.00	50.00
109B S.Koufax(w/blue lines)	100.00	200.00
110 Don Drysdale	6.00	15.00
111 Larry Sherry	2.50	5.00
112 Jim Gilliam	2.50	6.00
113 Norm Larker	20.00	50.00
114 Duke Snider	4.00	10.00
115 Stan Williams	1.50	4.00
116 Gordy Coleman	60.00	120.00
117 Don Blasingame	1.50	4.00
118 Gene Freese	1.50	4.00
119 Ed Kasko	1.50	4.00
120 Gus Bell	1.50	4.00
121 Vada Pinson	2.50	5.00
122 Frank Robinson	15.00	40.00
123 Bob Purkey	1.50	4.00
124A Joey Jay	2.50	5.00
124B Joey Jay(w/blue lines)	10.00	25.00
125 Jim Brosnan	15.00	40.00
126 Jim O'Toole	1.50	4.00
127 Jerry Lynch	50.00	100.00
128 Wally Post	1.50	4.00
129 Ken Hunt	1.50	4.00
130 Jerry Zimmerman	1.50	4.00
131 Willie McCovey	60.00	120.00
132 Jose Pagan	1.50	4.00
133 Felipe Alou UER	2.50	5.00
134 Jim Davenport	1.50	4.00
135 Harvey Kuenn	2.50	5.00
136 Orlando Cepeda	3.00	8.00
137 Ed Bailey	1.50	4.00
138 Sam Jones	1.50	4.00
139 Mike McCormick	2.50	5.00
140 Juan Marichal	75.00	150.00
141 Jack Sanford	1.50	4.00
142 Willie Mays	30.00	60.00
143 Stu Miller	3.00	8.00
144 Joe Amalfitano	12.50	30.00
145A Joe Adock (sic) ERR	50.00	100.00
145B Joe Adcock COR	2.50	6.00
146 Frank Bolling	1.50	4.00
147 Eddie Mathews	6.00	15.00
148 Roy McMillan	1.50	4.00
149 Hank Aaron	30.00	60.00
150 Gino Cimoli	1.50	4.00
151 Frank Thomas	1.50	4.00
152 Joe Torre	3.00	8.00
153 Lew Burdette	2.50	5.00
154 Bob Buhl	1.50	4.00
155 Carlton Willey	1.50	4.00
156 Lee Maye	1.50	4.00
157 Al Spangler	1.50	4.00
158 Bill White	20.00	50.00
159 Ken Boyer	3.00	8.00
160 Joe Cunningham	1.50	4.00
161 Carl Warwick	1.50	4.00
162 Carl Sawatski	1.50	4.00
163 Lindy McDaniel	1.50	4.00
164 Ernie Broglio	1.50	4.00
165 Larry Jackson	1.50	4.00
166 Curt Flood	2.50	5.00
167 Curt Simmons	2.50	5.00
168 Alex Grammas	1.50	4.00
169 Dick Stuart	2.50	6.00
170 Bill Mazeroski UER	3.00	8.00
171 Don Hoak	1.50	4.00
172 Dick Groat	2.50	5.00
173A Roberto Clemente	50.00	100.00
173B Clemente(w/blue lines)	150.00	300.00
174 Bob Skinner	1.50	4.00
175 Bill Virdon	2.50	5.00
176 Smoky Burgess	1.50	4.00
177 Roy Face	2.50	5.00
178 Bob Friend	1.50	4.00
179 Vernon Law	1.50	4.00
180 Harvey Haddix	1.50	4.00
181 Hal Smith	1.50	4.00
182 Ed Bouchee	1.50	4.00
183 Don Zimmer	1.50	4.00
184 Ron Santo	2.50	6.00
185 Andre Rodgers	1.50	4.00
186 Richie Ashburn	4.00	10.00
187 George Altman	1.50	4.00

188 Ernie Banks 8.00 20.00
189 Sam Taylor 2.50 5.00
190 Don Elston 1.50 4.00
191 Jerry Kindall 1.50 4.00
192 Pancho Herrera 2.50 5.00
193 Tony Taylor 1.50 4.00
194 Ruben Amaro 1.50 4.00
195 Don Demeter 1.50 4.00
196 Bobby Gene Smith 1.50 4.00
197 Clay Dalrymple 1.50 4.00
198 Robin Roberts 4.00 10.00
199 Art Mahaffey 2.50 5.00
200 John Buzhardt 5.00 12.00

1962 Post Canadian

The 200 blank-backed cards comprising the 1962 Post Canadian set measure approximately 2 1/2" by 3 1/2". The set is similar in appearance to the Jell-O set released in the U.S. that same year. The fronts feature a posed color player photo at the upper right. To the left of the photo, the player's name appears in blue cursive lettering, followed below by bilingual biography and career highlights. The cards are numbered on the front. The cards are grouped by team as follows: New York Yankees (1-13), Detroit (14-26), Baltimore (27-36), Cleveland (37-45), Chicago White Sox (46-55), Boston (56-64), Washington (65-73), Los Angeles Angels (74-82), Minnesota (83-91), Kansas City (92-100), Los Angeles Dodgers (101-115), Cincinnati (116-130), San Francisco (131-144), Milwaukee (145-157), St. Louis (158-168), Pittsburgh (169-181), Chicago Cubs (182-191) and Philadelphia (192-200). Maris (6) and Mays (142) are somewhat scarce. Whitey Ford is listed incorrectly with the Dodgers and correctly with the Yankees. The complete set price includes both Whitey Ford variations.

COMPLETE SET (201) 1,500.00 3,000.00
1 Bill Skowron 5.00 12.00
2 Bobby Richardson 5.00 12.00
3 Cletis Boyer 4.00 10.00
4 Tony Kubek 5.00 12.00
5 Mickey Mantle 200.00 400.00
6 Roger Maris 60.00 120.00
7 Yogi Berra 30.00 60.00
8 Elston Howard 5.00 12.00
9A Whitey Ford ERR/(Los Angeles Dodgers) 40.00 80.00
9B Whitey Ford COR/(New York Yankees) 40.00 80.00
10 Ralph Terry 3.00 8.00
11 John Blanchard 3.00 8.00
12 Luis Arroyo 2.50 6.00
13 Bill Stafford 2.50 6.00
14 Norm Cash 5.00 12.00
15 Jake Wood 2.50 6.00
16 Steve Boros 2.50 6.00
17 Chico Fernandez 2.50 6.00
18 Bill Bruton 2.50 6.00
19A Rocky Colavito 8.00 20.00
Colavito spelled in Large Letter
19B Rocky Colavito 8.00 20.00
Name is in small letter
20 Al Kaline 15.00 40.00
21 Dick Brown 2.50 6.00
22A Frank Lary 8.00 20.00
The word residence is in his vital sta
22B Frank Lary 8.00 20.00
No word residence in french vital stat
23 Don Mossi 3.00 8.00
24 Phil Regan 2.50 6.00
25 Charlie Maxwell 2.50 6.00
26 Jim Bunning 6.00 15.00
27A Jim Gentile 6.00 15.00
Partie is in third line
27B Jim Gentile 6.00 15.00
Partie in on final line of French tex
28 Marv Breeding 2.50 6.00
29 Brooks Robinson 15.00 40.00
30 Ron Hansen 2.50 6.00
31 Jackie Brandt 2.50 6.00
32 Dick Williams 5.00 12.00
33 Gus Triandos 2.50 6.00
34 Milt Pappas 4.00 10.00
35 Hoyt Wilhelm 20.00 50.00
36 Chuck Estrada 2.50 6.00
37 Vic Power 2.50 6.00
38 Johnny Temple 2.50 6.00
39 Bubba Phillips 2.50 6.00
40 Tito Francona 8.00 20.00
41 Willie Kirkland 2.50 6.00
42 John Romano 2.50 6.00
43 Jim Perry 4.00 10.00
44 Woodie Held 2.50 6.00
45 Chuck Essegian 2.50 6.00
46 Roy Sievers 4.00 10.00
47 Nellie Fox 6.00 15.00
48 Al Smith 2.50 6.00
49 Luis Aparicio 20.00 50.00
50 Jim Landis 2.50 6.00
51 Minnie Minoso 5.00 12.00
52 Andy Carey 2.50 6.00
53 Sherman Lollar 2.50 6.00
54 Bill Pierce 4.00 10.00
55 Early Wynn 6.00 15.00
56 Chuck Schilling 2.50 6.00
57 Pete Runnels 3.00 8.00
58 Frank Malzone 3.00 8.00
59 Don Buddin 2.50 6.00
60 Gary Geiger 2.50 6.00
61 Carl Yastrzemski 30.00 60.00
62 Jackie Jensen 4.00 10.00
63 Jim Pagliaroni 2.50 6.00
64 Don Schwall 8.00 20.00
65 Dale Long 2.50 6.00
66 Chuck Cottier 2.50 6.00
67 Billy Klaus 2.50 6.00
68 Coot Veal 2.50 6.00
69 Marty Keough 2.50 6.00
70 Willie Tasby 2.50 6.00
71 Gene Woodling 3.00 8.00
72 Gene Green 2.50 6.00
73 Dick Donovan 2.50 6.00
74 Steve Bilko 2.50 6.00
75 Rocky Bridges 2.50 6.00
76 Eddie Yost 2.50 6.00
77 Leon Wagner 8.00 20.00
78 Albie Pearson 2.50 6.00
79 Ken L. Hunt 2.50 6.00
80 Earl Averill 2.50 6.00
81 Ryne Duren 3.00 8.00
82 Ted Kluszewski 5.00 12.00
83 Bob Allison 2.50 6.00
84 Billy Martin 5.00 12.00
85 Harmon Killebrew 12.50 30.00
86 Zoilo Versalles 4.00 10.00
87 Lenny Green 8.00 20.00
88 Bill Tuttle 2.50 6.00
89 Jim Lemon 2.50 6.00
90 Earl Battey 2.50 6.00
91 Camilo Pascual 3.00 8.00
92 Norm Siebern 2.50 6.00
93 Jerry Lumpe 2.50 6.00
94 Dick Howser 3.00 8.00
95 Gene Stephens 2.50 6.00
96 Leo Posada 2.50 6.00
97 Joe Pignatano 2.50 6.00
98 Jim Archer 2.50 6.00
99 Haywood Sullivan 2.50 6.00
100 Art Ditmar 2.50 6.00
101 Gil Hodges 12.50 30.00
102 Charlie Neal 2.50 6.00
103 Daryl Spencer 2.50 6.00
104 Maury Wills 6.00 15.00
105 Tommy Davis 10.00 25.00
106 Willie Davis 3.00 8.00
107 John Roseboro 3.00 8.00
108 John Podres 4.00 10.00
109 Sandy Koufax 30.00 60.00
110 Don Drysdale 12.50 30.00
111 Larry Sherry 3.00 8.00
112 Jim Gilliam 10.00 25.00
113 Norm Larker 2.50 6.00
114 Duke Snider 15.00 40.00
115 Stan Williams 2.50 6.00
116 Gordy Coleman 2.50 6.00
117 Don Blasingame 8.00 20.00
118 Gene Freese 2.50 6.00
119 Ed Kasko 2.50 6.00
120 Gus Bell 2.50 6.00
121 Vada Pinson 4.00 10.00
122 Frank Robinson 12.50 30.00
123 Bob Purkey 8.00 20.00
124 Joey Jay 2.50 6.00
125 Jim Brosnan 3.00 8.00
126 Jim O'Toole 2.50 6.00
127 Jerry Lynch 2.50 6.00
128 Wally Post 3.00 8.00
129 Ken R. Hunt 2.50 6.00
130 Jerry Zimmerman 3.00 8.00
131 Willie McCovey 12.50 30.00
132 Jose Pagan 2.50 6.00
133 Felipe Alou 5.00 12.00
134 Jim Davenport 2.50 6.00
135 Harvey Kuenn 3.00 8.00
136 Orlando Cepeda 8.00 20.00
137 Ed Bailey 8.00 20.00
138 Sam Jones 2.50 6.00
139 Mike McCormick 2.50 6.00
140 Juan Marichal 12.50 30.00
141 Jack Sanford 2.50 6.00
142 Willie Mays 50.00 100.00
143 Stu Miller 2.50 6.00
144 Joe Amalfitano 15.00 40.00
145 Joe Adcock 3.00 8.00
146 Frank Bolling 2.50 6.00
147 Eddie Mathews 10.00 25.00
148 Roy McMillan 2.50 6.00
149 Hank Aaron 50.00 100.00
150 Gino Cimoli 2.50 6.00
151 Frank Thomas 3.00 8.00
152 Joe Torre 8.00 20.00
153 Lew Burdette 4.00 10.00
154 Bob Buhl 2.50 6.00
155 Carlton Willey 2.50 6.00
156 Lee Maye 2.50 6.00
157 Al Spangler 2.50 6.00
158 Bill White 4.00 10.00
159 Ken Boyer 5.00 12.00
160 Joe Cunningham 3.00 8.00
161 Carl Warwick 8.00 20.00
162 Carl Sawatski 2.50 6.00
163 Lindy McDaniel 2.50 6.00
164 Ernie Broglio 2.50 6.00
165 Larry Jackson 2.50 6.00
166 Curt Flood 4.00 10.00
167 Curt Simmons 2.50 6.00
168 Alex Grammas 2.50 6.00
169 Dick Stuart 2.50 6.00
170 Bill Mazeroski 6.00 15.00
171 Don Hoak 2.50 6.00
172 Dick Groat 4.00 10.00
173 Roberto Clemente 75.00 150.00
174 Bob Skinner 2.50 6.00
175 Bill Virdon 2.50 6.00
176 Smoky Burgess 8.00 20.00
177 Roy Face 4.00 10.00
178 Bob Friend 2.50 6.00
179 Vernon Law 3.00 8.00
180 Harvey Haddix 2.50 6.00
181 Hal Smith 2.50 6.00
182 Ed Bouchee 8.00 20.00
183 Don Zimmer 3.00 8.00
184 Ron Santo 6.00 15.00
185 Andre Rodgers 2.50 6.00
186 Richie Ashburn 6.00 15.00
187 George Altman 2.50 6.00
188 Ernie Banks 15.00 40.00
189 Sam Taylor 2.50 6.00
190 Don Elston 2.50 6.00
191 Jerry Kindall 2.50 6.00
192 Pancho Herrera 2.50 6.00
193 Tony Taylor 3.00 8.00
194 Ruben Amaro 2.50 6.00
195 Don Demeter 2.50 6.00
196 Bobby Gene Smith 2.50 6.00
197 Clay Dalrymple 2.50 6.00
198 Robin Roberts 10.00 25.00
199 Art Mahaffey 2.50 6.00
200 John Buzhardt 2.50 6.00

1963 Post

The cards in this 200-card set measure 2 1/2" by 3 1/2". The players are grouped by team with American Leaguers comprising 1-100 and National Leaguers 101-200. The ordering of teams is as follows: Minnesota (1-11), New York Yankees (12-23), Los Angeles Angels (24-34), Chicago White Sox (35-45), Detroit (46-56), Baltimore (57-66), Cleveland (67-76), Boston (77-84), Kansas City (85-92), Washington (93-100), San Francisco (101-112), Los Angeles Dodgers (113-124), Cincinnati (125-136), Pittsburgh (137-147), Milwaukee (148-157), St. Louis (158-168), Chicago Cubs (169-176), Philadelphia (177-184), Houston (185-192), and New York Mets (193-200). In contrast to the 1962 issue, the 1963 Post baseball card series is very difficult to complete. There are many card scarcities reflected in the price list below. Cards of the Post set are easily confused with those of the 1963 Jello set, which are 1/4" narrower (a difference which is often eliminated by bad cutting). The catalog designation is F278-38. There was also an album produced by Post to hold the cards. The album could only hold 120 cards.

COMPLETE SET (206) 2,400.00 4,800.00
1 Vic Power 3.00 8.00
2 Bernie Allen 2.50 5.00
3 Zoilo Versalles 2.50 5.00
4 Rich Rollins 2.50 5.00
5 Harmon Killebrew 10.00 25.00
6 Lenny Green 30.00 60.00
7 Bob Allison 2.50 6.00
8 Earl Battey 2.50 6.00
9 Camilo Pascual 2.50 5.00
10 Jim Kaat 3.00 8.00
11 Jack Kralick 2.50 5.00
12 Bill Skowron 3.00 8.00
13 Bobby Richardson 5.00 12.00
14 Cletis Boyer 2.50 5.00
15 Mickey Mantle 200.00 400.00
16 Roger Maris 125.00 250.00
17 Yogi Berra 12.50 30.00
18 Elston Howard 3.00 8.00
19 Whitey Ford 8.00 20.00
20 Ralph Terry 2.50 5.00
21 John Blanchard 2.50 6.00
22 Bill Stafford 2.50 5.00
23 Tom Tresh 2.50 5.00
24 Steve Bilko 2.50 6.00
25 Bill Moran 2.50 5.00
26A Joe Koppe (BA: .277) 2.50 6.00
26B Joe Koppe (BA: .227) 10.00 25.00
27 Felix Torres 2.50 5.00
28A L.Wagner (BA: .278) 2.50 5.00
28B L.Wagner (BA: .272) 10.00 25.00
29 Albie Pearson 2.50 5.00
30 Lee Thomas UER 75.00 150.00
31 Bob Rodgers 2.50 5.00
32 Dean Chance 2.50 5.00
33 Ken McBride 2.50 5.00
34 George Thomas UER 2.50 5.00
35 Joe Cunningham 2.50 5.00
36 Nellie Fox 5.00 12.00
37 Luis Aparicio 4.00 10.00
38 Al Smith 30.00 60.00
39 Floyd Robinson 75.00 150.00
40 Jim Landis 2.50 5.00
41 Charlie Maxwell 2.50 5.00
42 Sherman Lollar 2.50 5.00
43 Early Wynn 4.00 10.00
44 Juan Pizarro 2.50 5.00
45 Ray Herbert 2.50 6.00
46 Norm Cash 2.50 6.00
47 Steve Boros 2.50 5.00
48 Dick McAuliffe 12.50 30.00
49 Bill Bruton 2.50 6.00
50 Rocky Colavito 3.00 8.00
51 Al Kaline 12.50 30.00
52 Dick Brown 2.50 5.00
53 Jim Bunning 125.00 250.00
54 Hank Aguirre 2.50 5.00
55 Frank Lary 2.50 5.00
56 Don Mossi 2.50 5.00
57 Jim Gentile 2.50 5.00
58 Jackie Brandt 2.50 5.00
59 Brooks Robinson 12.50 30.00
60 Ron Hansen 2.50 6.00
61 Jerry Adair 125.00 250.00
62 Boog Powell 3.00 8.00
63 Russ Snyder 2.50 5.00
64 Steve Barber 2.50 5.00
65 Milt Pappas 2.50 5.00
66 Robin Roberts 4.00 10.00
67 Tito Francona 2.50 5.00
68 Jerry Kindall 2.50 5.00
69 Woody Held 2.50 5.00
70 Bubba Phillips 8.00 20.00
71 Chuck Essegian 2.50 5.00
72 Willie Kirkland 2.50 5.00
73 Al Luplow 2.50 5.00
74 Ty Cline 2.50 5.00
75 Dick Donovan 2.50 5.00
76 John Romano 2.50 5.00
77 Pete Runnels 2.50 5.00
78 Ed Bressoud 2.50 5.00
79 Frank Malzone 2.50 5.00
80 Carl Yastrzemski 175.00 350.00
81 Gary Geiger 2.50 5.00
82 Lou Clinton 2.50 5.00
83 Earl Wilson 2.50 5.00
84 Bill Monbouquette 2.50 5.00
85 Norm Siebern 2.50 5.00
86 Jerry Lumpe 75.00 150.00
87 Manny Jimenez 75.00 150.00
88 Gino Cimoli 2.50 5.00
89 Ed Charles 2.50 5.00
90 Ed Rakow 2.50 5.00
91 Bob Del Greco 2.50 5.00
92 Haywood Sullivan 2.50 5.00
93 Chuck Hinton 2.50 5.00
94 Ken Retzer 2.50 5.00
95 Harry Bright 2.50 5.00
96 Bob Johnson 2.50 5.00
97 Dave Stenhouse 8.00 20.00
98 Chuck Cottier 12.50 30.00
99 Tom Cheney 2.50 5.00
100 Claude Osteen 8.00 20.00
101 Orlando Cepeda 4.00 10.00
102 Chuck Hiller 2.50 5.00
103 Jose Pagan 2.50 5.00
104 Jim Davenport 2.50 5.00
105 Harvey Kuenn 2.50 6.00
106 Willie Mays 30.00 60.00
107 Felipe Alou 2.50 6.00
108 Tom Haller 75.00 150.00
109 Juan Marichal 5.00 12.00
110 Jack Sanford 2.50 5.00
111 Bill O'Dell 2.50 5.00
112 Willie McCovey 5.00 12.00
113 Lee Walls 2.50 5.00
114 Jim Gilliam 3.00 8.00
115 Maury Wills 3.00 8.00
116 Ron Fairly 2.50 6.00
117 Tommy Davis 2.50 6.00
118 Duke Snider 5.00 12.00
119 Willie Davis 125.00 250.00
120 John Roseboro 2.50 5.00
121 Sandy Koufax 30.00 60.00
122 Stan Williams 2.50 5.00
123 Don Drysdale 5.00 12.00
124 Daryl Spencer 2.50 5.00
125 Gordy Coleman 2.50 5.00
126 Don Blasingame 2.50 5.00
127 Leo Cardenas 2.50 5.00
128 Eddie Kasko 125.00 250.00
129 Jerry Lynch 8.00 20.00
130 Vada Pinson 3.00 8.00
131A F.Robinson(No stripes) 12.50 30.00
131B F.Robinson(Stripes/hat) 30.00 60.00
132 John Edwards 2.50 6.00
133 Joey Jay 2.50 5.00
134 Bob Purkey 2.50 5.00
135 Marty Keough 15.00 40.00
136 Jim O'Toole 2.50 5.00
137 Dick Stuart 2.50 5.00
138 Bill Mazeroski 5.00 12.00
139 Dick Groat 2.50 6.00
140 Don Hoak 20.00 50.00
141 Bob Skinner 10.00 25.00
142 Bill Virdon 2.50 6.00
143 Roberto Clemente 60.00 120.00
144 Smoky Burgess 2.50 6.00
145 Bob Friend 2.50 5.00
146 Al McBean 2.50 5.00
147 Roy Face 2.50 6.00
148 Joe Adcock 2.50 6.00
149 Frank Bolling 2.50 5.00
150 Roy McMillan 2.50 5.00
151 Eddie Mathews 10.00 25.00
152 Hank Aaron 100.00 200.00
153 Del Crandall 20.00 50.00
154A Bob Shaw COR 2.50 5.00
154B Bob Shaw ERR (Two in 1959) 8.00 20.00
155 Lew Burdette 3.00 8.00
156 Joe Torre 3.00 8.00
157 Tony Cloninger 2.50 5.00
158A Bill White (Ht. 6'0) 2.50 6.00
158B Bill White (Ht. 6';) 2.50 6.00
159 Julian Javier 2.50 5.00
160 Ken Boyer 4.00 10.00
161 Julio Gotay 2.50 5.00
162 Curt Flood 75.00 150.00
163 Charlie James 2.50 5.00
164 Gene Oliver 2.50 5.00
165 Ernie Broglio 2.50 5.00
166 Bob Gibson 5.00 12.00
167A Lindy McDaniel (No *) 4.00 10.00
167B L.McDaniel (w/*trade) 4.00 10.00
168 Ray Washburn 2.50 5.00
169 Ernie Banks 10.00 25.00
170 Ron Santo 3.00 8.00
171 George Altman 2.50 5.00
172 Billy Williams 125.00 250.00
173 Andre Rodgers 8.00 20.00
174 Ken Hubbs 15.00 40.00
175 Don Landrum 2.50 5.00
176 Dick Bertell 10.00 25.00
177 Roy Sievers 2.50 5.00
178 Tony Taylor 2.50 6.00
179 John Callison 2.50 5.00
180 Don Demeter 2.50 6.00
181 Tony Gonzalez 8.00 20.00
182 Wes Covington 12.50 30.00
183 Art Mahaffey 2.50 5.00
184 Clay Dalrymple 2.50 5.00
185 Al Spangler 2.50 5.00
186 Roman Mejias 2.50 5.00
187 Bob Aspromonte 250.00 500.00
188 Norm Larker 20.00 50.00
189 Johnny Temple 2.50 5.00
190 Carl Warwick 2.50 5.00
191 Bob Lillis 2.50 5.00
192 Dick Farrell 2.50 5.00
193 Gil Hodges 5.00 12.00

194 Marv Throneberry 2.50 6.00
195 Charlie Neal 5.00 12.00
196 Frank Thomas 150.00 300.00
197 Richie Ashburn 15.00 40.00
198 Felix Mantilla 2.50 5.00
199 Rod Kanehl 10.00 25.00
200 Roger Craig 2.50 6.00
XX Album

1979 Post Garvey Tips

These "Baseball Tips" were printed on boxes of Post Raisin Bran cereal in 1979. Cards 1-6 were on 15 oz. boxes and cards 7-12 were on the larger 20 oz. boxes. The cards are blank backed and feature a lime green background color with a red stitching border around the card. The cards measure approximately 7" by 2 1/16" although as with most cereal cards they are frequently found badly cut. The set essentially consists of Steve Garvey's advice or tips on various segments and aspects of the game of baseball. Each card shows a crude line drawing demonstrating the skill discussed in the narrative on the card. Each card contains a color drawing of Steve Garvey in the upper left corner of the card along with his facsimile autograph. Cards on full boxes are worth 3x the listed price.

COMPLETE SET (12) 30.00 60.00
COMMON CARD (1-6) 2.00 5.00
COMMON CARD (7-12) 3.00 8.00

1950 Prest-o-Lite Postcards

These postcards were issued to promote the "Prest-O-Lite" batteries. The front contains an action photo of the star while the back has a promotion for those batteries. There might be more photos so any additions are appreiciated.

2 Tommy Henrich 10.00 20.00
3 Ted Williams 30.00 60.00

1967 Pro's Pizza

This set, which features members of both Chicago teams features a square design with the words "The Pro's Pizza" in a black box in the upper right. These photos are in black and white. Since these cards are unnumbered, we have sequenced them in alphabetical order. Ron Santo was involved in management of Pro's Pizza at the time this set was issued.

COMPLETE SET 1,500.00 3,000.00
1 Ted Abernathy 50.00 100.00
2 George Altman 50.00 100.00
3 Joe Amalfitano 50.00 100.00
4 Ernie Banks 400.00 800.00
5 Glenn Beckert 50.00 100.00
6 Ernie Broglio 50.00 100.00
7 Byron Browne 50.00 100.00
8 Don Buford 50.00 100.00
9 Billy Connors 50.00 100.00
10 Dick Ellsworth 50.00 100.00
11 Billy Hoeft 50.00 100.00
12 Ken Holtzman 100.00 200.00
13 Joel Horlen 50.00 100.00
14 Randy Hundley 50.00 100.00
15 Fergie Jenkins 250.00 500.00
16 Don Kessinger 50.00 100.00
17 Chris Krug 50.00 100.00
18 Gary Peters 50.00 100.00
19 Ron Santo 125.00 250.00
20 Carl Warwick 50.00 100.00
21 Billy Williams 250.00 500.00

1972 Pro Stars Postcards

Printed in Canada by Pro Star Promotions, these 37 blank-backed postcards measure approximately 3 1/2" by 5 1/2" and feature white-bordered color player photos. The player's name appears within the lower white border and also as a facsimile autograph across the bottom of the photo. The postcards are unnumbered and checklisted below in alphabetical order within the Expos team (1-12), National League (13-24) and American League (25-36). In addition to the 36 players listed below, the checklist also carries a listing for 12 posters of major league players.

COMPLETE SET (37) 150.00 300.00
COMMON EXPOS (1-12) .60 1.50
COMMON ALL-STAR (13-36) .75 2.00
1 Bob Bailey .75 2.00
2 John Boccabella .75 2.00
3 Boots Day .60 1.50
4 Jim Fairey .60 1.50
5 Tim Foli .60 1.50
6 Ron Hunt .60 1.50
7 Mike Jorgensen .60 1.50
8 Ernie McAnally .60 1.50
9 Carl Morton .60 1.50
10 Steve Renko .60 1.50
11 Ken Singleton 1.25 3.00
12 Bill Stoneman .75 2.00
13 Hank Aaron 4.00 10.00
14 Johnny Bench 20.00 50.00
15 Roberto Clemente 50.00 100.00
16 Ferguson Jenkins 1.50 4.00
17 Juan Marichal 1.50 4.00
18 Willie Mays 50.00 100.00
19 Willie McCovey 2.50 6.00
20 Frank Robinson 2.50 6.00
21 Pete Rose 40.00 80.00
22 Tom Seaver 2.50 6.00
23 Willie Stargell 1.50 4.00
24 Joe Torre 1.25 3.00
25 Vida Blue 1.25 3.00
26 Reggie Jackson 2.50 6.00
27 Al Kaline 2.50 6.00
28 Harmon Killebrew 15.00 40.00
29 Mickey Lolich 1.25 3.00
30 Dave McNally 1.25 3.00
31 Bill Melton .75 2.00
32 Bobby Murcer 1.25 3.00
33 Fritz Peterson .75 2.00
34 Boog Powell 8.00 20.00
35 Merv Rettenmund .75 2.00
36 Brooks Robinson 12.50 30.00
37 Checklist Card .75 2.00

1954 Quaker Sports Oddities

This 27-card set features strange moments in sports and was issued as an insert inside Quaker Puffed Rice cereal boxes. Fronts of the cards are drawings depicting the person or the event. In a stripe at the top of the card face appear the words "Sports Oddities." Two colorful drawings fill the remaining space: the left half is a portrait, while the right half is action-oriented. A variety of sports are included. The cards measure approximately 2 1/4" by 3 1/2" and have rounded corners. The last line on the back of each card declares, "It's Odd but True." A person could also buy the complete set for fifteen cents and two box tops from Quaker Puffed Wheat or Quaker Rice. If a collector did send in their material to Quaker Oats the set came back in a specially marked box with the cards in cellophane wrapping. Sets in original wrapping are valued at 1.25x to 1.5X the high column listings in our checklist.

COMPLETE SET (27) 125.00 250.00
27 Yankee Stadium 7.50 15.00

1936 R311 Premiums

The 1936 R311 set of Portraits and Team Baseball Photos exist in two different forms, each measuring 6" by 8". Fifteen leather-like or uneven surface cards comprise the first type; these are indicated by the prefix L in the checklist below and are listed first. Twenty eight glossy surface, sepia or black and white cards comprise the second type. These glossy cards are indicated by the prefix G in the checklist below. The Boston Red Sox team exists with or without a sky above the building at the right of the card. Scarcities within the glossy subset include Pepper Martin, Mel Harder, Schoolboy Rowe, and the Dodgers, Pirates, Braves and Columbus team cards; these are asterisked in the checklist below.

COMPLETE SET (44) 1,200.00 2,400.00
COMMON GLOSSY (G1-G28) 10.00 20.00
COMMON LEATHER (L1-L15) 15.00 30.00
G1 Earl Averill 25.00 50.00
G2 Jim Bottomley 25.00 50.00
G3 Mickey Cochrane 30.00 60.00
G4 Joe Cronin 25.00 50.00
G5 Dizzy Dean 50.00 100.00
G6 Jimmy Dykes 12.50 25.00
G7 Jimmie Foxx 50.00 100.00
G8 Frankie Frisch 30.00 60.00
G9 Hank Greenberg 30.00 60.00
G10 Mel Harder 20.00 40.00
G11 Ken Keltner 15.00 30.00
G12 Pepper Martin 100.00 200.00
G13 Schoolboy Rowe 15.00 30.00
G14 Bill Terry 25.00 50.00
G15 Pie Traynor 25.00 50.00
G16 American League All Stars 1935 12.50 25.00
G17 Detroit Tigers 1934 25.00 50.00
G18 Boston Braves 1935 125.00 250.00
G19A Boston Red Sox with sky above building at right of the card 12.50 25.00
G19B Boston Red Sox without sky 50.00 100.00
G20 Brooklyn Dodgers1935 125.00 250.00
G21 Chicago White Sox/1935 12.50 25.00
G22 Columbus Red Birds 1934 Pennant Winners of Amer. Assoc. 12.50 25.00
G23 National League All Stars 1934 12.50 25.00
G24 National League Champions 1935 Chicago Cubs 12.50 25.00
G25 New York Yankees/1935 25.00 50.00
G26 Pittsburgh Pirates/1935 * 25.00 50.00
G27 St. Louis Browns/1935 12.50 25.00
G28 World Champions 1934 St. Louis Cardinals 12.50 25.00
L1 Paul Derringer 20.00 40.00
L2 Wes Ferrell 20.00 40.00
L3 Jimmie Foxx 60.00 120.00
L4 Charley Gehringer 40.00 80.00
L5 Mel Harder 20.00 40.00
L6 Gabby Hartnett 40.00 80.00
L7 Rogers Hornsby 60.00 120.00
L8 Connie Mack MG 50.00 100.00
L9 Van Mungo 20.00 40.00
L10 Steve O'Neill 20.00 40.00
L11 Red Ruffing 40.00 80.00
L12 Joe DiMaggio Frank Crosetti Tony Lazzeri 250.00 500.00
L13 Arky Vaughan Honus Wagner CO 60.00 120.00
L14 American League Pennant Winners 1935 Detroit Tigers 20.00 40.00
L15 National League Pennant Winners 1935 Chicago Cubs 20.00 40.00

1936 R312 Pastel Photos

The 1936 R312 Baseball Photos set contains 25 color tinted, single player cards, listed with the letter A in the checklist; 14 multiple player cards, listed with the letter B in the checklist; 6 action cards with handwritten signatures, listed with the letter C in the checklist; and 5 action cards with printed titles, listed with the letter D in the checklist. The pictures are reminiscent of a water-color type painting in soft pastels. The Allen card is reportedly more difficult to obtain than other cards in the set.

COMPLETE SET (50) 2,500.00 5,000.00
1 Johnny Allen 125.00 250.00
2 Cy Blanton 30.00 60.00
3 Mace Brown 30.00 60.00
4 Dolph Camilli 30.00 60.00
5 Mickey Cochrane 75.00 150.00
6 Rip Collins 30.00 60.00
7 KiKi Cuyler 60.00 120.00
8 Bill Dickey 75.00 150.00
9 Joe DiMaggio UER 600.00 1,200.00
10 Chuck Dressen 40.00 80.00
11 Benny Frey 30.00 60.00
12 Hank Greenberg 75.00 150.00
13 Mel Harder 40.00 80.00
14 Rogers Hornsby 125.00 250.00
15 Ernie Lombardi 60.00 120.00
16 Pepper Martin 40.00 80.00
17 Johnny Mize 75.00 150.00
18 Van Lingle Mungo 30.00 60.00
19 Bud Parmalee 30.00 60.00
20 Red Ruffing 60.00 120.00
21 Eugene Schott 30.00 60.00
22 Casey Stengel 125.00 250.00
23 Billy Sullivan 30.00 60.00
24 Bill Swift 30.00 60.00
25 Ralph Winegarner 30.00 60.00
26 Ollie Bejma and Rollie Hemsley 30.00 60.00
27 Cliff Bolton and Earl Whitehill 30.00 60.00
28 Stan Bordagaray and George Earnshaw 30.00 60.00
29 Herman Cavarretta Hack 40.00 80.00
30 Fox White Goslin 40.00 80.00
31 Galan Herman Lindstrom Hartnett 40.00 80.00
32 Bucky Harris Joe Cronin 60.00 120.00
33 G. Hartnett L. Warneke 40.00 80.00
34 Myril Hoag Lefty Gomez 60.00 120.00
35 A. Sothoron R. Hornsby 60.00 120.00
36 Connie Mack Lefty Grove 100.00 200.00
37 Taylor Speaker Cuyler 60.00 120.00
38 Dixie Walker Mule Haas Mike Kreevich 30.00 60.00
39 P. Waner L.Waner Weaver 60.00 120.00
40 Nick Altrock Al Schacht 40.00 80.00
41 Bell (St. Louis) Out At First Zeke Bonura 30.00 60.00
42 Jim Collins (Safe) and Stan Hack 30.00 60.00
43 Jimmie Foxx Luke Sewell 60.00 120.00
44 Al Lopez Traps Two Cubs on Third Base 60.00 120.00
45 Pie Traynor Augie Galan 60.00 120.00
46 Alvin Crowder after victory in the World Series 30.00 60.00
48 Gabby Hartnett Crossing home plate after hitting homer 60.00 120.00
49 Schoolboy Rowe 30.00 60.00
50 Russ Van Atta/St. Louis pitcher out at plate/Rick Ferrell 30.00 60.00

1933 R337 Eclipse Import Series Of 24

The cards in this 24-card set measure 2 5/16" by 2 13/16". The "Series of 24" is similar to the MP and Co. issues in terms of style and quality. Produced in 1933, this set is numbered 401-424. The three missing numbers, 403, 413, and 414, probably correspond to the three known unnumbered players. Some dealers believe this is known as the "Eclipse Import" set.

COMPLETE SET (24) 1,200.00 2,400.00
401 Johnny Vergez 50.00 100.00
402 Babe Ruth 1,000.00 2,000.00
404 George Pipgras 50.00 100.00
405 Bill Terry 100.00 200.00
406 George Connally 50.00 100.00
407 Wilson Clark 50.00 100.00
408 Lefty Grove 150.00 300.00
409 Henry Johnson 50.00 100.00
410 Jimmy Dykes 50.00 100.00
411 Henry Hine Schuble 50.00 100.00
412 Washington Harris Makes Home Run 75.00 150.00
415 Al Simmons 100.00 200.00
416 Heinie Manush 75.00 150.00
417 Glen Myatt 50.00 100.00
418 Babe Herman 75.00 150.00
419 Frank Frisch# 100.00 200.00
420 A Safe Slide to the Home Plate 50.00 100.00
421 Paul Waner 75.00 150.00
422 Jimmy Wilson 50.00 100.00
423 Charles Grimm 75.00 150.00
424 Dick Bartell 50.00 100.00
NNO Jimmy Fox/(sic& Jimmie Foxx) Athletics/(unnumbe 150.00 300.00
NNO Roy Johnson unnumbered 50.00 100.00
NNO Traynor Pitts/(sic& Pittsburgh) is out/(unnumbe 100.00 200.00

1950 R423

Many numbers of these small and unattractive cards may be yet unknown for this issue of the early 1950s. The cards are printed on thin stock and measure 5/8" by 3/4"; sometimes they are found as a long horizontal strip of 13 cards connected by a perforation. Complete strips intact are worth 50 percent more than the sum of the individual players on the strip. The cards were available with a variety of back colors, red, green, blue, or purple, with the red and blue being the rarest of the varieties. The cards on the strip are in no apparent order, numerically or alphabetically. The producer's numbering of the cards in the set is very close to alphabetical order. Cards are so small they are sometimes lost. These strips were premiums or prizes in one-cent bubblegum machines; they were folded accordion style and held together by a small metal clip.

COMPLETE SET 600.00 1,200.00
1 Grover C. Alexander 7.50 15.00
2 Richie Ashburn 7.50 15.00
3 Frank Baumholtz 2.50 5.00
4 Ralph Branca 3.00 6.00
5 Yogi Berra 20.00 40.00
6 Ewell Blackwell 3.00 6.00
7 Lou Boudreau 5.00 10.00
8 Harry Brecheen 2.50 5.00
9 Chico Carrasquel 2.50 5.00
10 Jerry Coleman 3.00 6.00
11 Walker Cooper 2.50 5.00
12 Roy Campanella 20.00 40.00
13 Phil Cavarretta 3.00 6.00
14A Ty Cobb Facsimile Auto 40.00 80.00
14B Ty Cobb No Auto 40.00 80.00
15 Mickey Cochrane 5.00 10.00
16 Eddie Collins 5.00 10.00
17 Frank Crosetti 3.00 6.00
18 Larry Doby 5.00 10.00
19 Walter Dropo 2.50 5.00
20 Alvin Dark 3.00 6.00
21 Dizzy Dean 15.00 30.00
22 Bill Dickey 5.00 10.00
23 Murray Dickson 2.50 5.00
24 Dom DiMaggio 5.00 10.00
25 Joe DiMaggio 40.00 80.00
26 Leo Durocher MG 5.00 10.00
27 Mel Parnell 3.00 6.00
28 Bob Elliott 3.00 6.00
29 Del Ennis 2.50 5.00
31 Bob Feller 15.00 30.00
32 Frank Frisch 5.00 10.00
33 Billy Goodman 2.50 5.00
34 Lefty Gomez
35 Lou Gehrig 40.00 80.00
36 Joe Gordon 3.00 6.00
38 Hank Greenberg 5.00 10.00
39 Lefty Grove 5.00 10.00
42 Ken Heintzelman 2.50 5.00
44 Jim Hearn 2.50 5.00
45 Gil Hodges 7.50 15.00
46 Harry Heilmann 5.00 10.00
47 Tommy Henrich 4.00 8.00
48 Roger Hornsby 12.50 25.00
49 Carl Hubbell 5.00 10.00
50 Eddie Joost 2.50 5.00
51 Nippy Jones 2.50 5.00
53 Nippy Jones 2.50 5.00
54 Walter Johnson 12.50 25.00
55 Ellis Kinder 2.50 5.00
56 Jim Konstanty 3.00 6.00
57 George Kell 5.00 10.00
58 Ralph Kiner 5.00 10.00
59 Bob Lemon 5.00 10.00
60 Whitey Lockman 3.00 6.00
61 Ed Lopat 3.00 6.00
62 Tony Lazzeri 5.00 10.00
63 Cass Michaels 2.50 5.00
64 Cliff Mapes 2.50 5.00
65 Willard Marshall 2.50 5.00
66 Clyde McCullough 2.50 5.00
67 Connie Mack 5.00 10.00
68 Christy Mathewson 12.50 25.00
69 Joe Medwick 5.00 10.00
70 Johnny Mize 5.00 10.00
71 Terry Moore 2.50 5.00
72 Stan Musial 25.00 50.00
73 Hal Newhouser 5.00 10.00

74 Don Newcombe 4.00 8.00
75 Lefty O'Doul 3.00 6.00
76 Mel Ott 5.00 10.00
77 Mel Parnell 2.50 5.00
79 Gerald Priddy 2.50 5.00
80 Dave Philley 2.50 5.00
81 Bob Porterfield 2.50 5.00
82 Andy Pafko 2.50 5.00
83 Howie Pollet 2.50 5.00
84 Herb Pennock 5.00 10.00
85 Al Rosen 3.00 6.00
86 Pee Wee Reese 5.00 10.00
87 Del Rice 2.50 5.00
88 Vic Raschi 3.00 6.00
89 Allie Reynolds 3.00 6.00
90 Phil Rizzuto 5.00 10.00
91 Jackie Robinson 40.00 80.00
92 Babe Ruth 50.00 100.00
93 Casey Stengel 5.00 10.00
94 Vern Stephens 3.00 6.00
95 Duke Snider 7.50 15.00
96 Enos Slaughter 5.00 10.00
97 Al Schoendienst 5.00 10.00
98 Gerald Staley 2.50 5.00
99 Clyde Shoun 2.50 5.00
102 Al Simmons 5.00 10.00
103 George Sisler 5.00 10.00
104 Tris Speaker 5.00 10.00
105 Ed Stanky 3.00 6.00
106 Virgil Trucks 2.50 5.00
107 Henry Thompson 2.50 5.00
109 Dazzy Vance 5.00 10.00
110 Lloyd Waner 5.00 10.00
111 Paul Waner 5.00 10.00
112 Gene Woodling 2.50 5.00
113 Ted Williams 40.00 80.00
114 Vic Wertz 2.50 5.00
115 Wes Westrum 2.50 5.00
116 Johnny Wyrostek 2.50 5.00
117 Eddie Yost 2.50 5.00
118 Al Zarilla 2.50 5.00
119 Gus Zernial 2.50 5.00
120 Sam Zoldak 2.50 5.00
XX Strip of 13 cards 10.00 20.00

1909 Ramly T204

The cards in this 121-card set measure approximately 2" by 2 1/2". The Ramly baseball series, designated T204 in the catalog, contains unnumbered cards. This set is one of the most distinguished ever produced, containing ornate gold borders around a black and white portrait of each player. There are spelling errors, and two distinct backs, "Ramly" and "TTT", are known. There is a premium of up to 25 percent for the "TTT" back. Much of the obverse card detail is actually embossed. The players have been alphabetized and numbered for reference in the checklist below. A few players (so far only six are confirmed, and a seventh is rumored) are known with square frames with blank backs. It is possible that these are proofs. The confirmed square players are John Anderson, Frank Bancroft, Kitty Bransfield, Jesse Burkett, Bill Dineen and Pat Moran. Of note, pricing for raw cards is provided in VgEx condition due to the fact that most cards from this set are found in off-grade shape.

COMPLETE SET (121) 25,000.00 50,000.00
1 Whitey Alperman 250.00 500.00
2 John J. Anderson 150.00 300.00
3 Jimmy Archer 150.00 300.00
4 Frank Arrelanes 250.00 500.00
5 Jim Ball 150.00 300.00
6 Neal Ball 150.00 300.00
7 Frank Bancroft 150.00 300.00
8 Johnny Bates 150.00 300.00
9 Fred Beebe 150.00 300.00
10 George Bell 150.00 300.00
11 Chief Bender 600.00 1,200.00
12 Walter Blair 150.00 300.00
13 Cliff Blankenship 150.00 300.00
14 Frank Bowerman 150.00 300.00
15 Kitty Bransfield 150.00 300.00
16 Roger Bresnahan 500.00 1,000.00
17 Al Bridwell 150.00 300.00
18 Mordecai Brown 600.00 1,200.00
19 Fred Burchell 150.00 300.00
20 Jesse Burkett 3,000.00 6,000.00
21 Bobby Byrne (Byrnes) 150.00 300.00
22 Bill Carrigan 150.00 300.00
23 Frank Chance 500.00 1,000.00
24 Charles Chech 150.00 300.00
25 Eddie Cicolte 500.00 1,000.00
26 Otis Clymer 150.00 300.00
27 Andrew Coakley 150.00 300.00
28 Eddie Collins 600.00 1,200.00
29 Jimmy Collins 500.00 1,000.00
30 Wid Conroy 150.00 300.00
31 Jack Coombs 250.00 500.00
32 Doc Crandall 150.00 300.00
33 Lou Criger 150.00 300.00
34 Harry Davis 150.00 300.00
35 Art Devlin 150.00 300.00
36 Bill Dineen 150.00 300.00
37 Pat Donahue 150.00 300.00
38 Mike Donlin 150.00 300.00
39 Bill Donovan 150.00 300.00
40 Gus Dorner 150.00 300.00
41 Joe Dunn 150.00 300.00
42 Kid Elberfield 150.00 300.00
43 Johnny Evers 600.00 1,200.00
44 Bob Ewing 150.00 300.00
45 George Ferguson 150.00 300.00
46 Hobe Ferris 150.00 300.00
47 Jerry Freeman 150.00 300.00
48 Art Fromme 150.00 300.00
49 Bob Ganley 150.00 300.00
50 Doc Gessler 150.00 300.00
51 Peaches Graham 150.00 300.00
52 Clark Griffith 500.00 1,000.00
53 Roy Hartzell 150.00 300.00
54 Charlie Hemphill 150.00 300.00
55 Dick Hoblitzell 150.00 300.00
56 George Howard 150.00 300.00
57 Harry Howell 150.00 300.00
58 Miller Huggins 500.00 1,000.00
59 John Hummel 150.00 300.00
60 Walter Johnson 10,000.00 20,000.00
61 Tom Jones 150.00 300.00
62 Mike Kahoe 150.00 300.00
63 Ed Kargar 150.00 300.00
64 Willie Keeler 600.00 1,200.00
65 Red Kleinon 150.00 300.00
66 John Knight 150.00 300.00
67 Ed Konetchey 150.00 300.00
68 Vive Lindaman 150.00 300.00
69 Hans Loebert 150.00 300.00
70 Harry Lord 150.00 300.00
71 Harry Lumley 150.00 300.00
72 Ernie Lush 150.00 300.00
73 Rube Manning 150.00 300.00
74 Jimmy McAleer 150.00 300.00
75 Amby McConnell 150.00 300.00
76 Moose McCormick 150.00 300.00
77 Matty McIntyre 150.00 300.00
78 Larry McLean 150.00 300.00
79 Fred Merkle 250.00 500.00
80 Clyde Milan 150.00 300.00
81 Mike Mitchell 150.00 300.00
82 Pat Moran 150.00 300.00
83 Harry Cy Morgan 150.00 300.00
84 Tim Murname 150.00 300.00
85 Danny Murphy 150.00 300.00
86 Red Murray 150.00 300.00
87 Doc Newton 150.00 300.00
88 Simon Nichols 150.00 300.00
89 Harry Niles 150.00 300.00
90 Bill O'Hare 150.00 300.00
91 Charley O'Leary 150.00 300.00
92 Dode Paskert 150.00 300.00
93 Barney Pelty 150.00 300.00
94 Jack Pfeister 150.00 300.00
95 Eddie Plank 1,500.00 3,000.00
96 Jack Powell 150.00 300.00
97 Bugs Raymond 150.00 300.00
98 Tom Reilly 150.00 300.00
99 Claude Ritchey 150.00 300.00
100 Nap Rucker 150.00 300.00
101 Ed Ruelbach 150.00 300.00
102 Slim Sallee 150.00 300.00
103 Germany Schaefer 150.00 300.00
104 Jimmy Schekard 150.00 300.00
105 Admiral Schlei 150.00 300.00
106 Wildfire Schulte 150.00 300.00
107 Jimmy Sebring 150.00 300.00
108 Bill Shipke 150.00 300.00
109 Charlie Smith 150.00 300.00
110 Tubby Spencer 150.00 300.00
111 Jake Stahl 250.00 500.00
112 Jim Stephens 150.00 300.00
113 Harry Stienfeldt (Steinfeldt) 250.00 500.00
114 Gabby Street 150.00 300.00
115 Bill Sweeney 150.00 300.00
116 Fred Tenney 150.00 300.00
117 Ira Thomas 150.00 300.00
118 Joe Tinker 700.00 1,400.00
119 Bob Unglane 150.00 300.00
120 Heinie Wagner 150.00 300.00
121 Bobby Wallace 500.00 1,000.00

1909 Ramly Square Frame T204

These few cards are known to exist with square picture frames. They can also be identfied as the players full name is printed on the card. It is possible, although unlikely, that a few other players in this set may exist but no confirmation is known at this time.

COMPLETE SET 12,500.00 25,000.00
1 John Anderson 3,000.00 6,000.00
2 Frank Bancroft 3,000.00 6,000.00
3 Kitty Bransfield 3,000.00 6,000.00
4 Jesse Burkett 7,500.00 15,000.00
5 Bill Dineen 3,000.00 6,000.00
6 Pat Moran 5,000.00 10,000.00

1972 Rangers Team Issue

This 32-card set of the 1972 Texas Rangers measures approximately 3 1/2" by 5 3/4" and features black-and-white player portraits with white borders. A facsimile autograph is printed on the photo. Name, position, and Texas Rangers are printed across the bottom of the photo. The backs are blank. The cards are unnumbered and checklisted below in alphabetical order.

COMPLETE SET (32) 40.00 80.00
1 Larry Biittner .75 2.00
2 Dick Billings .75 2.00
3 Dick Bosman 1.25 3.00
4 Pete Broberg .75 2.00
5 Jeff Burroughs 2.00 5.00
6 Casey Cox .75 2.00
7 Jim Driscoll .75 2.00
8 Ted Ford .75 2.00
9 Bill Gogolewski .75 2.00
10 Tom Grieve 1.50 4.00
11 Rich Hand .75 2.00
12 Toby Harrah 2.00 5.00
13 Frank Howard 2.00 5.00
14 Sid Hudson CO .75 2.00
15 Dalton Jones .75 2.00
16 Hal King .75 2.00
17 Ted Kubiak .75 2.00
18 Paul Lindblad .75 2.00
19 Joe Lovitto .75 2.00
20 Elliott Maddox .75 2.00
21 Don Mincher .75 2.00
22 Dave Nelson .75 2.00
23 Jim Panther .75 2.00
24 Mike Paul .75 2.00
25 Horacio Pina .75 2.00
26 Lenny Randle .75 2.00
27 Jim Shellenback .75 2.00
28 Don Stanhouse 1.25 3.00
29 Ken Suarez .75 2.00
30 George Susce CO .75 2.00
31 Wayne Terwilliger CO .75 2.00
32 Ted Williams MG 6.00 15.00

1973 Rangers Team Issue

This set of the Texas Rangers measures approximately 3 1/2" by 5 3/4" and features black-and-white player portraits in a white border. The backs are blank. The cards are unnumbered and checklisted below in alphabetical order. Since the Rangers changed managers during the 1973 season, both Whitey Herzog and Billy Martin are listed as managers in our checklist.

COMPLETE SET 15.00 40.00
1 Lloyd Allen .40 1.00
2 Jim Bibby .75 2.00
3 Larry Biittner .40 1.00
4 Rich Billings .40 1.00
5 Pete Broberg .40 1.00
6 Jeff Burroughs 1.50 4.00
7 Rico Carty .75 2.00
8 David Clyde .75 2.00
9 Steve Dunning .40 1.00
10 Chuck Estrada CO .40 1.00
11 Steve Foucalt .40 1.00
12 Bill Gogolewski .40 1.00
13 Rich Hand .40 1.00
14 Toby Harrah 1.25 3.00
15 Vic Harris .40 1.00
16 Whitey Herzog .75 2.00
17 Chuck Hiller CO .40 1.00
18 Charlie Hudson .40 1.00
19 Alex Johnson .75 2.00
20 Elliot Maddox .40 1.00
21 Billy Martin MG 2.00 5.00
22 Jim Mason .40 1.00
23 Jim Merritt .40 1.00
24 Dave Nelson .40 1.00
25 Mike Paul .40 1.00
26 Lenny Randle .40 1.00
27 Sonny Siebert .40 1.00
28 Don Stanhouse .40 1.00
29 Ken Suarez .40 1.00

1974 Rangers Team Issue

This set, which measured 3 1/2" by 5 3/4" featured members of the 1974 Texas Rangers. These black and white blank-backed cards feature the player's photo along with their name, position and Texas Rangers name on the bottom. Since these cards are unnumbered, we have sequenced them in alphabetical order. It is believed but not confirmed that cards were issued for Dick Billings and Don Stanhouse.

COMPLETE SET 12.50 30.00
1 Jim Bibby .40 1.00
2 Pete Broberg .40 1.00
3 Jackie Brown .40 1.00
4 Larry Brown .40 1.00
5 Jeff Burroughs .60 1.50
6 Leo Cardenas .40 1.00
7 David Clyde .40 1.00
8 Merrill Combs CO .40 1.00
9 Mike Cubbage .40 1.00
10 Don Durham .40 1.00
11 Steve Dunning .40 1.00
12 Chuck Estrada CO .40 1.00
13 Steve Foucault .40 1.00
14 Art Fowler CO .40 1.00
15 Jim Fregosi .40 1.00
16 Tom Grieve .60 1.50
17 Toby Harrah .40 1.00
18 Steve Hargan .40 1.00
19 Mike Hargrove 1.00 2.50
20 Fergie Jenkins 1.25 3.00
21 Alex Johnson .40 1.00
22 Joe Lovitto .40 1.00
23 Frank Lucchesi CO .40 1.00
24 Billy Martin MG 1.25 3.00
25 Jim Merritt .40 1.00
26 Jackie Moore .40 1.00
27 Dave Nelson .40 1.00
28 Lenny Randle .40 1.00
29 Jim Shellenback .40 1.00
30 Charlie Silvera CO .40 1.00
31 Jim Spencer .40 1.00
32 Jim Sundberg 1.00 2.50
33 Cesar Tovar .40 1.00

1975 Rangers Postcards

This 37-card set of the Texas Rangers features player photos on postcard-size cards. The cards are unnumbered and checklisted below in alphabetical order.

COMPLETE SET (37) 8.00 20.00
1 Mike Bacsik .20 .50
2 Jim Bibby .20 .50
3 Jackie Brown .20 .50
4 Jeff Burroughs .30 .75
5 Leo Cardenas .20 .50
6 Merrill Combs CO .20 .50
7 Mike Cubbage .20 .50
8 Bill Fahey .20 .50
9 Steve Foucault .20 .50
10 Art Fowler CO .20 .50
11 Jim Fregosi .30 .75
12 Tom Grieve .30 .75
13 Bill Hands .20 .50
14 Steve Hargan .20 .50
15 Mike Hargrove .60 1.50
16 Toby Harrah .30 .75
17 Roy Howell .20 .50
18 Fergie Jenkins .75 2.00
19 Joe Lovitto .20 .50
20 Frank Lucchesi CO .20 .50
21 Billy Martin MG .60 1.50
22 Jim Merritt .20 .50
23 Dave Moates .20 .50
24 Jackie Moore .20 .50
25 Tommy Joe Moore .20 .50
26 Dave Nelson .20 .50
27 Dave Nelson/(Autographed) .20 .50
28 Gaylord Perry .75 2.00
29 Lenny Randle .20 .50
30 Lenny Randle/(Autographed) .20 .50
31 Charlie Silvera CO .20 .50
32 Roy Smalley .30 .75
33 Jim Spencer .20 .50
34 Jim Sundberg .30 .75
35 Jim Sundberg/(Last year's picture) .30 .75
36 Stan Thomas .20 .50
37 Cesar Tovar .20 .50
38 Jim Umbarger .20 .50
39 Clyde Wright .20 .50

1976 Rangers Team Issue

This photo card set featured members of the 1976 Texas Rangers. The 3 1/2" by 5 3/4" blank-backed cards black and white cards feature player photos surrounded by a white border. The player's name is identified at the bottom of the card. Since the cards are unnumbered, we have sequenced them in alphabetical order.

COMPLETE SET 12.50 30.00
1 Steve Barr .40 1.00
2 Juan Beniquez .40 1.00
3 Bert Blyleven 1.00 2.50
4 Nelson Briles .40 1.00
5 Jeff Burroughs .40 1.00
6 Gene Clines .40 1.00
7 Pat Corrales CO .40 1.00
8 John Ellis .40 1.00
9 Bill Fahey .40 1.00
10 Steve Foucault .40 1.00
11 Jim Fregosi .40 1.00
12 Dick Gernert CO .40 1.00
13 Tom Grieve .60 1.50
14 Steve Hargan .40 1.00
15 Mike Hargrove .60 1.50
16 Toby Harrah .40 1.00
17 Joe Hoerner .40 1.00
18 Roy Lee Howell .40 1.00
19 Sid Hudson CO .40 1.00
20 Joe Lahoud .40 1.00
21 Dave Moates .40 1.00
22 Jackie Moore .40 1.00
23 Gaylord Perry 1.25 3.00
24 Lenny Randle .40 1.00
25 Jim Sundberg .60 1.50
26 Danny Thompson .40 1.00
27 Jim Umbarger .40 1.00
28 Bill Zeigler .40 1.00

1977 Rangers Team Issue

This set was issued to promote the members of the 1977 Texas Rangers. The black and white blank-backed cards measures approximately 3 1/2" by 5 3/4". The player's photo are surrounded by white borders. This checklist may be incomplete and any additions are appreciated. Since these cards are unnumbered, we have sequenced them in alphabetical order.

COMPLETE SET 10.00 25.00
1 Doyle Alexander .40 1.00
2 Bert Blyleven .75 2.00
3 Nelson Briles .40 1.00
4 Bert Campaneris .75 2.00
5 Adrian Devine .40 1.00
6 Dock Ellis .40 1.00
7 Bill Fahey .40 1.00
8 Tom Grieve .60 1.50
9 Mike Hargrove .60 1.50
10 Toby Harrah .40 1.00
11 Ken Henderson .40 1.00
12 Willie Horton .60 1.50
13 Billy Hunter MG .40 1.00
14 Darold Knowles .40 1.00
15 Paul Lindblad .40 1.00
16 Mike Marshall .40 1.00
17 Jim Mason .40 1.00
18 Dave May .40 1.00
19 Gaylord Perry 1.25 3.00
20 Jim Sundberg .60 1.50
21 Claudell Washington .40 1.00
22 Bump Wills .60 1.50

1978 Rangers Burger King

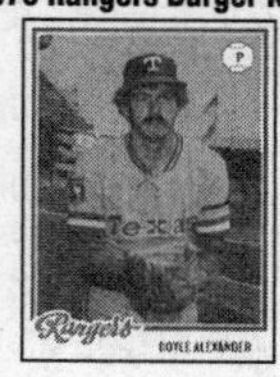

The cards in this 23-card set measure 2 1/2" by 3 1/2". This set of 22 numbered player cards (featuring the Texas Rangers) and one unnumbered checklist was issued regionally by Burger King in 1978. Asterisks denote poses different from those found in the regular Topps cards of this year.

COMPLETE SET (23)	6.00	15.00
1 Billy Hunter MG	.20	.50
2 Jim Sundberg	.40	1.00
3 John Ellis	.20	.50
4 Doyle Alexander	.30	.75
5 Jon Matlack *	.30	.75
6 Dock Ellis	.20	.50
7 Doc Medich	.20	.50
8 Fergie Jenkins *	1.50	4.00
9 Len Barker	.20	.50
10 Reggie Cleveland *	.20	.50
11 Mike Hargrove	.60	1.50
12 Bump Wills	.20	.50
13 Toby Harrah	.40	1.00
14 Bert Campaneris	.40	1.00
15 Sandy Alomar	.30	.75
16 Kurt Bevacqua	.20	.50
17 Al Oliver *	.60	1.50
18 Juan Beniquez	.20	.50
19 Claudell Washington	.40	1.00
20 Richie Zisk	.30	.75
21 John Lowenstein *	.20	.50
22 Bobby Thompson *	.20	.50
NNO Checklist Card TP	.10	.25

1978-79 Rangers Team Issue

Issued over a period of years, these cards feature members of the late 1970's Texas Rangers. These black and white blank-backed cards measure 3 1/2" by 5 1/2". The player's photo is surrounded by white borders while his name is located at the bottom. Since the cards are unnumbered, we have sequenced this set in alphabetical order.

COMPLETE SET	12.50	30.00
1 Doyle Alexander	.40	1.00
2 Sandy Alomar	.40	1.00
3 Len Barker	.60	1.50
4 Buddy Bell	.60	1.50
5 Juan Beniquez	.40	1.00
6 Kurt Bevacqua	.40	1.00
7 Bobby Bonds	1.00	2.50
8 Bert Campaneris	.60	1.50
9 Reggie Cleveland	.40	1.00
10 Steve Comer	.40	1.00
11 Pat Corrales CO	.40	1.00
12 John Ellis	.40	1.00
13 Bill Fahey	.40	1.00
14 Mike Hargrove	.60	1.50
15 Toby Harrah	.40	1.00
16 Sid Hudson CO	.40	1.00
17 Billy Hunter MG	.40	1.00
18 Mike Jorgensen	.40	1.00
19 Jim Kern	.40	1.00
20 Fred Koenig CO	.40	1.00
21 Paul Lindblad	.40	1.00
22 John Lowenstein	.40	1.00
23 Sparky Lyle	.60	1.50
24 Jim Mason	.40	1.00
25 Jon Matlack	.40	1.00
26 George Doc Medich	.40	1.00
27 Roger Moret	.40	1.00
28 Al Oliver	.75	2.00
29 Jim Sundberg	.60	1.50
30 Jim Umbarger	.40	1.00
31 Bump Wills	.40	1.00
32 Richie Zisk	.40	1.00

1980 Rangers Postcards

These postcards came in black and white with the player's name in a white border on the bottom. For some unexplained reason, both Billy Sample and Bump Wills have two poses. These cards are not numbered so we have sequenced them in alphabetical order.

COMPLETE SET	8.00	20.00
1 Buddy Bell	.40	1.00
2 Steve Comer	.20	.50
3 Pat Corrales MG	.20	.50
4 Danny Darwin	.20	.50
5 Adrian Devine	.20	.50
6 Rich Donnelly CO	.20	.50
7 John Ellis	.20	.50
8 Pepe Frias	.20	.50
9 John Grubb	.20	.50
10 Bud Harrelson	.20	.50
11 Fergie Jenkins	.75	2.00
12 Jim Kern	.20	.50
13 Fred Koenig CO	.20	.50
14 Sparky Lyle	.30	.75
15 Jon Matlack	.20	.50
16 Doc Medich	.20	.50
17 Jackie Moore CO	.20	.50
18 Nelson Norman	.20	.50
19 Jim Norris	.20	.50
20 Al Oliver	.40	1.00
21 Gaylord Perry	.75	2.00
22 Pat Putnam	.20	.50
23 Dave Rajsich	.20	.50
24 Mickey Rivers	.30	.75
25 Dave Roberts	.20	.50
26 Billy Sample Patch on Uniform	.20	.50
27 Billy Sample No Patch	.20	.50
28 Rusty Staub	.60	1.50
29 Jim Sundberg	.20	.50
30 Jim Umbarger	.20	.50
31 Bump Wills With facial hair	.20	.50
32 Bump Wills Clean shaven	.20	.50
33 Richie Zisk	.30	.75

1964-66 Rawlings Photos

These 8" by 9 1/2" photos parallel the glove box cut cards. These photos were given away with a purchase of a Rawlings Glove

COMPLETE SET
COMMON CARD

1955 Rawlings Musial

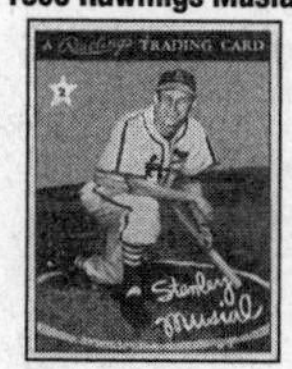

This six-card set was actually the side panels of the box containing a Rawlings baseball glove. Rawlings Sporting Goods was headquartered in St. Louis. The cards are numbered and come in two sizes. Cards 1-4 are larger, 2 5/8" by 3 3/4" whereas numbers 1A and 2A are smaller, 2 1/8" by 3 1/8". The cards are blank backed and have a black and white picture on a light blue background.

COMPLETE SET (6)	750.00	1,500.00
1 Stan Musial/(portrait)	150.00	300.00
1A Stan Musial/(portrait with hand and bat visible)	100.00	200.00
2 Stan Musial/(kneeling)	150.00	300.00
2A Stan Musial/(portrait& same picture as number 1	100.00	200.00
3 Stan Musial/(swinging HOR)	150.00	300.00
4 Stan Musial/(batting stance)	150.00	300.00

1961 Rawlings

This set measures approximately 8 1/8" by 10 1/8" and features white-bordered, black-and-white player photos. A facsimile autograph and sponsor name is printed in a white box on one side of the picture. The backs are blank. The cards are unnumbered and checklisted below in alphabetical order. More photos, from more years, are believed to exist so any additions to this checklist are appreciated.

COMPLETE SET	300.00	600.00
1 Joe Adcock	8.00	20.00
2 Hank Aguirre	5.00	12.00
3 Bob Bailey	5.00	12.00
4 Ed Bailey	5.00	12.00
5 Dick Bertell	5.00	12.00
6 John Blanchard	5.00	12.00
7 Clete Boyer	8.00	20.00
8 Ken Boyer/2 different photos known	10.00	25.00
9 Lew Burdette	6.00	15.00
10 Bob Cerv	5.00	12.00
11 Gordon Coleman	5.00	12.00
12 Tony Conigliaro	5.00	12.00
13 Wes Covington	5.00	12.00
14 Joe Cunningham	5.00	12.00
15 Tommy Davis	6.00	15.00
16 Don Demeter	5.00	12.00
17 Jim Grant	5.00	12.00
18 Dick Groat	5.00	12.00
19 Harvey Haddix	5.00	12.00
20 Elston Howard	10.00	25.00
21 Larry Jackson	5.00	12.00
22 Tony Kubek	10.00	25.00
23 Vern Law	5.00	12.00
24 Sherm Lollar	5.00	12.00
25 Mickey Mantle	40.00	80.00
26 Eddie Mathews	12.50	30.00
27 Dal Maxvill	5.00	12.00
28 Wilmer Mizell	5.00	12.00
29 Wally Moon	6.00	15.00
30 Stan Musial	12.50	30.00
31 Charlie Neal	5.00	12.00
32 Rocky Nelson	5.00	12.00
33 Brooks Robinson	30.00	60.00
34 Herb Score	6.00	15.00
35 Roy Sievers	6.00	15.00
36 Bob Skinner	5.00	12.00
37 Duke Snider	40.00	80.00
38 Warren Spahn	40.00	80.00
39 Bob Turley	6.00	15.00
40 Billy Williams	6.00	15.00

1964-66 Rawlings

This set features borderless color player photos that measure 2 3/8" by 4" when properly cut off the glove boxes on which they were printed. The photos are of stars of the day posing with their Rawlings glove prominently displayed, and a facsimile autograph is printed across the bottom of the picture. The cards are unnumbered and checklisted below in alphabetical order. There was also a picture issue of 8" by 9 1/2" Advisory Staff photos given away upon purchase. The same players featured on the boxes were featured on these photos.

COMPLETE SET	100.00	200.00
1 Ken Boyer Cards	6.00	15.00
2 Ken Boyer Mets	6.00	15.00
3 Gordy Coleman	4.00	10.00
4 Tommy Davis	4.00	10.00
5 Willie Davis	5.00	12.00
6 Dick Groat	6.00	15.00
7 Mickey Mantle	20.00	50.00
8 Dal Maxvill	4.00	10.00
9 Brooks Robinson	10.00	25.00
10 Warren Spahn	8.00	20.00
11 Tom Tresh	5.00	12.00
12 Bill White Phillies	6.00	15.00
13 Billy Williams	8.00	20.00

1976 Rawlings

This card was distributed by Rawlings Sporting Goods Company honoring Cesar Cedeno on the winning of his 4th consecutive Golden Glove Award. It measures approximately 5" by 7" and features a color photo in a white border with a white facsimile autograph. The back displays player information and career statistics. This set may be incomplete.

1 Cesar Cedeno	1.25	3.00

1978 Reading Remembers

This 23-card set measures 3" by 4". The fronts feature brown and white tinted player action and posted photos. The backs carry the player's name, jersey number, position, biography, statistics, and other player facts. The cards are unnumbered and checklisted below in alphabetical order. This set was issued in three-card strips. This set was available upon release for $4 postpaid from the producers.

COMPLETE SET (23)	8.00	20.00
1 Tommy Brown	.20	.50
2 Doug Clemens	.20	.50
3 Dom Dallessandro	.20	.50
4 George Eyrich	.20	.50
5 Carl Furillo	.60	1.50
6 Dick Gernert	.20	.50
7 Randy Gumpert	.20	.50
8 Bob Katz	.20	.50
9 Betz Klopp	.20	.50
10 Whitey Kurowski	.30	.75
11 Lauer's Park	.20	.50
12 Jesse Levan	.20	.50
13 Carl Mathias	.20	.50
14 Roger Maris	2.00	5.00
15 Lenny Moore	1.25	3.00
16 Robin Roberts	2.00	5.00
17 Harry Schaeffer	.20	.50
18 Herb Score	.60	1.50
19 Ty Stofflet	.20	.50
20 John Updike	.30	.75
21 Charlie Wagner	.20	.50
22 Stan Wentzel	.20	.50
23 Vic Wertz	.20	.50

1910-13 Red Cross T215

The cards in this set measure 1 1/2" by 2 5/8." There are actually three distinct groupings or types. Type 1 cards have brown captions. Type 2 cards have blue captions. Type 3 cards are distinguished by their "Pirate Cigarettes" backs printed in green ink. According to leading dealers and collectors, these cards were produced for Americans serving their country in the South Seas. The players have been alphabetized within Type and numbered for reference in the checklist below.

COMMON TYPE 1 (1-88)	75.00	150.00
COMMON TYPE 2 (89-167)	50.00	100.00
COMMON TYPE 3 (168-259)		
1 Red Ames	200.00	400.00
2 Frank Baker	400.00	800.00
3 Neal Ball	200.00	400.00
4 Chief Bender (2)	400.00	800.00
5 Chief Bender (2)	400.00	800.00
6 Al Bridwell	200.00	400.00
7 Bobby Byrne	200.00	400.00
8 Howie Camnitz	200.00	400.00
9 Frank Chance	600.00	1,200.00
10 Hal Chase	400.00	800.00
11 Ty Cobb	3,000.00	6,000.00
12 Eddie Collins	400.00	800.00
13 Wid Conroy	200.00	400.00
14 Doc Crandall	200.00	400.00
15 Sam Crawford	400.00	800.00
16 Birdie Cree	200.00	400.00
17 Harry Davis	200.00	400.00
18 Josh Devore	200.00	400.00
19 Mike Donlin	250.00	500.00
20 Mickey Doolan	200.00	400.00
21 Patsy Dougherty	200.00	400.00
22 Larry Doyle	250.00	500.00
23 Larry Doyle	250.00	500.00
24 Kid Elberfeld	200.00	400.00
25 Russ Ford	200.00	400.00
26 Art Fromme	200.00	400.00
27 Clark Griffith	400.00	800.00
28 Topsy Hartsel	200.00	400.00
29 Doc Hoblitzell	200.00	400.00
30 Danny Hofman	200.00	400.00
31 Del Howard	200.00	400.00
32 Miller Huggins	400.00	800.00
33 John Hummell	200.00	400.00
34 Hugh Jennings (2)	400.00	800.00
35 Hugh Jennings (2)	400.00	800.00
36 Walter Johnson	1,000.00	2,000.00
37 Ed Konetchy	200.00	400.00
38 Harry Krause	200.00	400.00
39 Nap Lajoie	750.00	1,500.00
40 Bill Lange		
41 Arlie Latham	200.00	400.00
42 Tommy Leach	200.00	400.00
43 Lefty Leifield	200.00	400.00
44 Harry Lord	200.00	400.00
45 Sherry Magee	300.00	600.00
46 Rube Marquard (2)	400.00	800.00
47 Rube Marquard (2)	400.00	800.00
48 Christy Mathewson	1,000.00	2,000.00
49 Christy Mathewson	1,000.00	2,000.00
50 Joe McGinnity	400.00	800.00
51 John McGraw (2)	600.00	1,200.00
52 John McGraw (2)	600.00	1,200.00
53 Matty McIntyre	200.00	400.00
54 Fred Merkle	300.00	600.00
55 Chief Meyers	250.00	500.00
56 Dots Miller	200.00	400.00
57 George Mullin	250.00	500.00
58 Danny Murphy	200.00	400.00
59 Red Murray	200.00	400.00
60 Rebel Oakes	200.00	400.00
61 Charley O'Leary	200.00	400.00
62 Dode Paskert	200.00	400.00
63 Barney Pelty	200.00	400.00
64 Jack Quinn	200.00	400.00
65 Ed Reulbach	250.00	500.00
66 Nap Rucker	250.00	500.00
67 Germany Schaefer	300.00	600.00
68 Frank Schulte	250.00	500.00
69 Jimmy Sheckard	200.00	400.00
70 Frank Smith	200.00	400.00
71 Smither	200.00	400.00
72 Tris Speaker	750.00	1,500.00
73 Jake Stahl	250.00	500.00
74 Harry Steinfeldt	250.00	500.00
75 Gabby Street (2)	200.00	400.00
76 Gabby Street (2)	200.00	400.00
77 William Sweeney	200.00	400.00
78 Lee Tannehill	200.00	400.00
79 Joe Tinker (2)	400.00	800.00
80 Joe Tinker (2)	400.00	800.00
81 Honus Wagner	1,000.00	2,000.00
82 Jack Warhop	200.00	400.00
83 Zach Wheat	400.00	800.00
84 Doc White	200.00	400.00
85 Ed Willett	200.00	400.00
86 Owen Wilson	200.00	400.00
87 Hooks Wiltse (2)	200.00	400.00
88 Hooks Wiltse (2)	200.00	400.00
89 Cy Young	1,250.00	2,500.00
90 Red Ames	200.00	400.00
91 Chief Bender (2)	400.00	800.00
92 Chief Bender (2)	400.00	800.00
93 Roger Bresnahan	400.00	800.00
94 Mordecai Brown	400.00	800.00
95 Bobby Byrne	200.00	400.00
96 Howie Camnitz	200.00	400.00
97 Frank Chance	750.00	1,500.00
98 Ty Cobb	4,000.00	8,000.00
99 Eddie Collins	400.00	800.00
100 Doc Crandall	200.00	400.00
101 Birdie Cree	200.00	400.00
102 Harry Davis	200.00	400.00
103 Josh Devore	200.00	400.00
104 Mike Donlin	250.00	500.00
105 Mickey Doolan (2)	200.00	400.00
106 Mickey Doolan (2)	200.00	400.00
107 Patsy Dougherty	200.00	400.00
108 Larry Doyle (2)	250.00	500.00
109 Larry Doyle (2)	250.00	500.00
110 Jean Dubuc	200.00	400.00
111 Kid Elberfeld	200.00	400.00
112 Johnny Evers	400.00	800.00
113 Russ Ford	200.00	400.00
114 Art Fromme	200.00	400.00
115 Clark Griffith	400.00	800.00
116 Bob Groom	200.00	400.00
117 Topsy Hartsel	200.00	400.00
118 Buck Herzog	200.00	400.00
119 Doc Hoblitzell	200.00	400.00
120 Solly Hofman	200.00	400.00
121 Miller Huggins (2)	750.00	1,500.00
122 Miller Huggins (2)	750.00	1,500.00
123 John Hummel	200.00	400.00
124 Hugh Jennings	400.00	800.00
125 Walter Johnson	1,250.00	2,500.00
126 Joe Kelley	400.00	800.00
127 Ed Konetchy	200.00	400.00
128 Harry Krause	200.00	400.00
129 Napolean Lajoie	1,000.00	2,000.00
130 Lake	200.00	400.00
131 Tommy Leach	200.00	400.00
132 Lefty Leifield	200.00	400.00
133 Harry Lord	200.00	400.00
134 Rube Marquard	400.00	800.00
135 Christy Mathewson	1,250.00	2,500.00
136 John McGraw (2)	600.00	1,200.00
137 John McGraw (2)	600.00	1,200.00
138 Larry McLean	200.00	400.00
139 Dots Miller	200.00	400.00
140 Michael Mitchell	200.00	400.00

141 Mike Mowrey	200.00	400.00
142 George Mullin	250.00	500.00
143 Danny Murphy	200.00	400.00
144 Red Murray	200.00	400.00
145 Rebel Oakes	200.00	400.00
146 Rube Oldring	200.00	400.00
147 Charley O'Leary	200.00	400.00
148 Dode Paskert	200.00	400.00
149 Barney Pelty	200.00	400.00
150 William Purtell	200.00	400.00
151 Ed Reulbach	250.00	500.00
152 Nap Rucker	250.00	500.00
153 Germany Schaefer (2)	250.00	500.00
154 Germany Schaefer (2)	250.00	500.00
155 Frank Schulte	250.00	500.00
156 Frank Smith (2)	200.00	400.00
157 Frank Smith (2)	200.00	400.00
158 Tris Speaker	1,000.00	2,000.00
159 Jake Stahl	200.00	400.00
160 Harry Steinfeldt	250.00	500.00
161 Ed Summers	200.00	400.00
162 William Sweeney	200.00	400.00
163 Joe Tinker	400.00	800.00
164 Honus Wagner	1,250.00	2,500.00
165 Jack Warhop	200.00	400.00
166 Doc White	200.00	400.00
167 Hooks Wiltse (2)	200.00	400.00
168 Hooks Wiltse (2)	200.00	400.00
169 Red Ames	500.00	1,000.00
170 Frank Baker	1,250.00	2,500.00
171 Neal Ball	500.00	1,000.00
172 Chief Bender	1,250.00	2,500.00
173 Al Bridwell	500.00	1,000.00
174 Bobby Byrne	500.00	1,000.00
175 Howie Camnitz	500.00	1,000.00
176 Frank Chance	1,500.00	3,000.00
177 Hal Chase	1,000.00	2,000.00
178 Eddie Collins	2,000.00	4,000.00
179 Doc Crandall	500.00	1,000.00
180 Sam Crawford	1,500.00	3,000.00
181 Birdie Cree	500.00	1,000.00
182 Harry Davis	500.00	1,000.00
183 Josh Devore	500.00	1,000.00
184 Mike Donlin	600.00	1,200.00
185 Mickey Doolan	500.00	1,000.00
186 Mickey Doolan	500.00	1,000.00
187 Patsy Dougherty	500.00	1,000.00
188 Larry Doyle	600.00	1,200.00
189 Larry Doyle	600.00	1,200.00
190 Jean Dubuc	500.00	1,000.00
191 Kid Eberfeld	500.00	1,000.00
192 Steve Evans	500.00	1,000.00
193 Johnny Evers	1,500.00	3,000.00
194 Russ Ford	500.00	1,000.00
195 Art Fromme	500.00	1,000.00
196 Clark Griffith	1,500.00	3,000.00
197 Bob Groom	500.00	1,000.00
198 Topsy Hartsell	500.00	1,000.00
199 Buck Herzog	1,000.00	2,000.00
200 Dick Hoblitzell	500.00	1,000.00
201 Solly Hofman	500.00	1,000.00
202 Del Howard	500.00	1,000.00
203 Miller Huggins	1,000.00	2,000.00
204 Miller Huggins	1,000.00	2,000.00
205 John Hummel	500.00	1,000.00
206 Hugh Jennings	1,000.00	2,000.00
207 Hugh Jennings	1,000.00	2,000.00
208 Walter Johnson	2,500.00	5,000.00
209 Joe Kelley	2,500.00	5,000.00
210 Ed Konetchy	500.00	1,000.00
211 Harry Krause	500.00	1,000.00
212 Nap Lajoie	1,500.00	3,000.00
213 Joe Lake	500.00	1,000.00
214 Lefty Leifield	500.00	1,000.00
215 Harry Lord	500.00	1,000.00
216 Sherry Magee	600.00	1,200.00
217 Rube Marquard	1,000.00	2,000.00
218 Rube Marquard	1,000.00	2,000.00
219 Joe McGinnity	1,000.00	2,000.00
220 John McGraw	1,250.00	2,500.00
221 John McGraw	1,250.00	2,500.00
222 Matty McIntyre Chicago Nat'l	500.00	1,000.00
223 Matty McIntyre Bkln. and Chicago Nat'l	500.00	1,000.00
224 Larry McLean	500.00	1,000.00
225 Fred Merkle	600.00	1,200.00
226 Chief Meyers	600.00	1,200.00
227 Michael Mitchell	500.00	1,000.00
228 Mike Mowrey	500.00	1,000.00
229 George Mullin	600.00	1,200.00
230 Danny Murphy	500.00	1,000.00
231 Red Murray.	500.00	1,000.00
232 Rebel Oakes	500.00	1,000.00
233 Rube Oldring	500.00	1,000.00
234 Charley O'Leary	500.00	1,000.00
235 Dode Paskert	500.00	1,000.00
236 Barney Pelty	500.00	1,000.00
237 William Purtell	500.00	1,000.00
238 Jack Quinn	600.00	1,200.00
239 Ed Reulbach	750.00	1,500.00
240 Nap Rucker	600.00	1,200.00
241 Germany Schaefer	600.00	1,200.00
242 Frank Schulte	600.00	1,200.00
243 Jimmy Sheckard	600.00	1,200.00
244 Frank Smith	500.00	1,000.00
245 Tris Speaker	2,000.00	4,000.00
246 Jake Stahl	500.00	1,000.00
247 Harry Steinfeldt	600.00	1,200.00
248 Gabby Street	500.00	1,000.00
249 Ed Summers	500.00	1,000.00
250 William Sweeney	500.00	1,000.00
251 Lee Tannehill	500.00	1,000.00
252 Ira Thomas	500.00	1,000.00
253 Joe Tinker	1,500.00	3,000.00
254 Heinie Wagner	500.00	1,000.00
255 Jack Warhop	500.00	1,000.00
256 Zack Wheat	1,000.00	2,000.00
257 Ed Willett	500.00	1,000.00
258 Owen Wilson	600.00	1,200.00
259 Hooks Wiltse	500.00	1,000.00
260 Hooks Wiltse	500.00	1,000.00

1954 Red Heart

The cards in this 33-card set measure approximately 2 5/8" by 3 3/4". The 1954 Red Heart baseball series was marketed by Red Heart dog food, which, incidentally, was a subsidiary of Morrell Meats. The set consists of three series of eleven unnumbered cards each of which could be ordered from the company via an offer (two can labels plus ten cents for each series) on the can label. Each series has a specific color background (red, green or blue) behind the color player photo. Cards with red backgrounds are considered scarcer and are marked with SP in the checklist (which has been alphabetized and numbered for reference). The catalog designation is F156. It is believed that some of the cards were available directly from Red Heart well into the 1970's.

COMPLETE SET (33)	2,000.00	4,000.00
COMMON CARD	25.00	50.00
COMMON CARD SP	30.00	60.00
1 Richie Ashburn SP	60.00	120.00
2 Frank Baumholtz SP	30.00	60.00
3 Gus Bell	25.00	50.00
4 Billy Cox	40.00	80.00
5 Alvin Dark	30.00	60.00
6 Carl Erskine SP	50.00	100.00
7 Ferris Fain	30.00	60.00
8 Dee Fondy	25.00	50.00
9 Nellie Fox	60.00	120.00
10 Jim Gilliam	40.00	80.00
11 Jim Hegan SP	50.00	100.00
12 George Kell	50.00	100.00
13 Ralph Kiner SP	60.00	120.00
14 Ted Kluszewski SP	60.00	120.00
15 Harvey Kuenn	40.00	80.00
16 Bob Lemon SP	50.00	100.00
17 Sherman Lollar	30.00	60.00
18 Mickey Mantle	500.00	1,000.00
19 Billy Martin	50.00	100.00
20 Gil McDougald SP	40.00	80.00
21 Roy McMillan	30.00	60.00
22 Minnie Minoso	50.00	100.00
23 Stan Musial SP	200.00	400.00
24 Billy Pierce	30.00	60.00
25 Al Rosen SP	50.00	100.00
26 Hank Sauer	30.00	60.00
27 Red Schoendienst SP	60.00	120.00
28 Enos Slaughter	50.00	100.00
29 Duke Snider	50.00	100.00
30 Warren Spahn	60.00	120.00
31 Sammy White	25.00	50.00
32 Eddie Yost	25.00	50.00
33 Gus Zernial	30.00	60.00

1952 Red Man

The cards in this 52-card set measure approximately 3 1/2" by 4" (or 3 1/2" by 3 5/8" without the tab). This Red Man issue was the first nationally available tobacco issue since the T cards of the teens early in this century. This 52-card set contains 26 top players from each league. Cards that have the tab (coupon) attached are generally worth a multiplier of cards without tabs. Please refer to multiplier line below. The 1952 Red Man cards are considered to be the most difficult (of the Red Man sets) to find with tabs. Card numbers are located on the tabs. The prices listed below refer to cards without tabs. The numbering of the set is alphabetical by player within league with the exception of the managers who are listed first.

COMPLETE SET (52)	500.00	1,000.00
*CARDS WITH TABS: 3X VALUES		
AL1 Casey Stengel MG	15.00	30.00
AL2 Bobby Avila	5.00	10.00
AL3 Yogi Berra	25.00	50.00
AL4 Gil Coan	5.00	10.00
AL5 Dom DiMaggio	10.00	20.00
AL6 Larry Doby	12.50	25.00
AL7 Ferris Fain	5.00	10.00
AL8 Bob Feller	15.00	30.00
AL9 Nellie Fox	12.50	25.00
AL10 Johnny Groth	5.00	10.00
AL11 Jim Hegan	5.00	10.00
AL12 Eddie Joost	5.00	10.00
AL13 George Kell	12.50	25.00
AL14 Gil McDougald	7.50	15.00
AL15 Minnie Minoso	7.50	15.00
AL16 Billy Pierce	6.00	12.00
AL17 Bob Porterfield	5.00	10.00
AL18 Eddie Robinson	5.00	10.00
AL19 Saul Rogovin	5.00	10.00
AL20 Bobby Shantz	6.00	12.00
AL21 Vern Stephens	5.00	10.00
AL22 Vic Wertz	5.00	10.00
AL23 Ted Williams	500.00	1,000.00
AL24 Early Wynn	12.50	25.00
AL25 Eddie Yost	5.00	10.00
AL26 Gus Zernial	6.00	12.00
NL1 Leo Durocher MG	10.00	20.00
NL2 Richie Ashburn	12.50	25.00
NL3 Ewell Blackwell	5.00	10.00
NL4 Cliff Chambers	5.00	10.00
NL5 Murry Dickson	5.00	10.00
NL6 Sid Gordon	5.00	10.00
NL7 Granny Hamner	5.00	10.00
NL8 Jim Hearn	5.00	10.00
NL9 Monte Irvin	12.50	25.00
NL10 Larry Jansen	5.00	10.00
NL11 Willie Jones	5.00	10.00
NL12 Ralph Kiner	12.50	25.00
NL13 Whitey Lockman	5.00	10.00
NL14 Sal Maglie	6.00	12.00
NL15 Willie Mays	250.00	500.00
NL16 Stan Musial	50.00	100.00
NL17 Pee Wee Reese	15.00	30.00
NL18 Robin Roberts	12.50	25.00
NL19 Red Schoendienst	12.50	25.00
NL20 Enos Slaughter	12.50	25.00
NL21 Duke Snider	30.00	60.00
NL22 Warren Spahn	15.00	30.00
NL23 Eddie Stanky	6.00	12.00
NL24 Bobby Thomson	7.50	15.00
NL25 Earl Torgeson	5.00	10.00
NL26 Wes Westrum	5.00	10.00

1953 Red Man

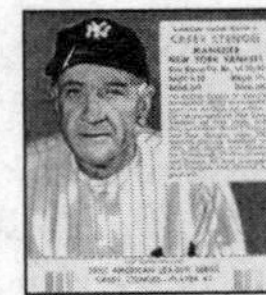

The cards in this 52-card set measure approximately 3 1/2" by 4" (or 3 1/2" by 3 5/8" without the tab). The 1953 Red Man set contains 26 National League stars and 26 American League stars. Card numbers are located both on the write-up of the player and on the tab. Cards that have the tab (coupon) attached are worth a multiplier of cards without tabs. Please refer to the multiplier line below. The prices listed below refer to cards without tabs.

COMPLETE SET (52)	400.00	800.00
*CARDS WITH TABS: 2.5X VALUES		
AL1 Casey Stengel MG	15.00	30.00
AL2 Hank Bauer	5.00	10.00
AL3 Yogi Berra	25.00	50.00
AL4 Walt Dropo	4.00	8.00
AL5 Nellie Fox	12.50	25.00
AL6 Jackie Jensen	5.00	10.00
AL7 Eddie Joost	4.00	8.00
AL8 George Kell	10.00	20.00
AL9 Dale Mitchell	4.00	8.00
AL10 Phil Rizzuto	15.00	30.00
AL11 Eddie Robinson	4.00	8.00
AL12 Gene Woodling	6.00	12.00
AL13 Gus Zernial	6.00	12.00
AL14 Early Wynn	10.00	20.00
AL15 Joe Dobson	4.00	8.00
AL16 Billy Pierce	6.00	12.00
AL17 Bob Lemon	10.00	20.00
AL18 Johnny Mize	10.00	20.00
AL19 Bob Porterfield	4.00	8.00
AL20 Bobby Shantz	6.00	12.00
AL21 Mickey Vernon	6.00	12.00
AL22 Dom DiMaggio	7.50	15.00
AL23 Gil McDougald	5.00	10.00
AL24 Al Rosen	5.00	10.00
AL25 Mel Parnell	4.00	8.00
AL26 Bobby Avila	4.00	8.00
NL1 Charlie Dressen MG	4.00	8.00
NL2 Bobby Adams	4.00	8.00
NL3 Richie Ashburn	12.50	25.00
NL4 Joe Black	5.00	10.00
NL5 Roy Campanella	30.00	60.00
NL6 Ted Kluszewski	7.50	15.00
NL7 Whitey Lockman	4.00	8.00
NL8 Sal Maglie	5.00	10.00
NL9 Andy Pafko	4.00	8.00
NL10 Pee Wee Reese	15.00	30.00
NL11 Robin Roberts	10.00	20.00
NL12 Red Schoendienst	10.00	20.00
NL13 Enos Slaughter	10.00	20.00
NL14 Duke Snider	30.00	60.00
NL15 Ralph Kiner	10.00	20.00
NL16 Hank Sauer	5.00	10.00
NL17 Del Ennis	5.00	10.00
NL18 Granny Hamner	5.00	10.00
NL19 Warren Spahn	15.00	30.00
NL20 Wes Westrum	4.00	8.00
NL21 Hoyt Wilhelm	10.00	20.00
NL22 Murry Dickson	4.00	8.00
NL23 Warren Hacker	4.00	8.00
NL24 Gerry Staley	4.00	8.00
NL25 Bobby Thomson	7.50	15.00
NL26 Stan Musial	50.00	100.00

1954 Red Man

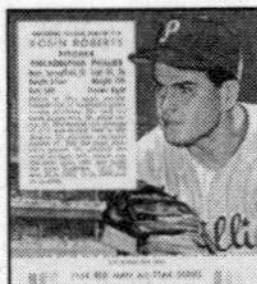

The cards in this 50-card set measure approximately 3 1/2" by 4" (or 3 1/2" by 3 5/8" without the tab). The 1954 Red Man set witnessed a reduction to 25 players from each league. George Kell, Sam Mele, and Dave Philley are known to exist with two different teams. Card number 19 of the National League exists as Enos Slaughter and as Gus Bell. Card numbers are on the write-ups of the players. Cards that have the tab (coupon) attached are worth a multiple of cards without tabs. Please refer to the values below for cards with tabs. The prices listed below refer to cards without tabs. The complete set price below refers to all 54 cards including the four variations.

COMPLETE SET (54)	500.00	800.00
*CARDS WITH TABS:2.5X VALUES		
AL1 Bobby Avila	4.00	8.00
AL2 Jim Busby	4.00	8.00
AL3 Nellie Fox	12.00	20.00
AL4 George Kell/(Boston)	15.00	25.00
AL4 George Kell/(Chicago)	35.00	60.00
AL5 Sherman Lollar	4.00	8.00
AL6 Sam Mele/(Baltimore)	7.00	12.00
AL6 Sam Mele/(Chicago)	25.00	40.00
AL7 Minnie Minoso	6.00	10.00
AL8 Mel Parnell	4.00	8.00
AL9 Dave Philley/(Cleveland)	7.00	12.00
AL9 Dave Philley/(Philadelphia)	25.00	40.00
AL10 Billy Pierce	6.00	10.00
AL11 Jimmy Piersall	6.00	10.00
AL12 Al Rosen	6.00	10.00
AL13 Mickey Vernon	6.00	10.00
AL14 Sammy White	4.00	8.00
AL15 Gene Woodling	6.00	10.00
AL16 Whitey Ford	15.00	25.00
AL17 Phil Rizzuto	12.00	20.00
AL18 Bob Porterfield	4.00	8.00
AL19 Chico Carrasquel	4.00	8.00
AL20 Yogi Berra	25.00	40.00
AL21 Bob Lemon	9.00	15.00
AL22 Ferris Fain	4.00	8.00
AL23 Hank Bauer	6.00	10.00
AL24 Jim Delsing	4.00	8.00
AL25 Gil McDougald	6.00	10.00
NL1 Richie Ashburn	12.00	20.00
NL2 Billy Cox	6.00	10.00
NL3 Del Crandall	6.00	10.00
NL4 Carl Erskine	6.00	10.00
NL5 Monte Irvin	7.00	12.00
NL6 Ted Kluszewski	7.00	12.00
NL7 Don Mueller	4.00	8.00
NL8 Andy Pafko	4.00	8.00
NL9 Del Rice	4.00	8.00
NL10 Red Schoendienst	9.00	15.00
NL11 Warren Spahn	12.00	20.00
NL12 Curt Simmons	6.00	10.00
NL13 Roy Campanella	30.00	50.00
NL14 Jim Gilliam	6.00	10.00
NL15 Pee Wee Reese	15.00	25.00
NL16 Duke Snider	30.00	50.00
NL17 Rip Repulski	4.00	8.00
NL18 Robin Roberts	9.00	15.00
NL19 Enos Slaughter	35.00	60.00
NL19 Gus Bell	15.00	25.00
NL20 Johnny Logan	4.00	8.00
NL21 John Antonelli	4.00	8.00
NL22 Gil Hodges	12.00	20.00
NL23 Eddie Mathews	12.00	20.00
NL24 Lew Burdette	6.00	10.00
NL25 Willie Mays	50.00	80.00

1955 Red Man

The cards in this 50-card set measure approximately 3 1/2" by 4" (or 3 1/2" by 3 5/8" without the tab). The 1955 Red Man set contains 25 players from each league. Card numbers are on the write-ups of the players. Cards that have the tab (coupon) attached are generally worth a multiple of cards which have had their tabs removed. Please see mulitplier values below. The prices listed below refer to cards without tabs.

COMPLETE SET (50)	300.00	600.00
*CARDS WITH TABS:2.5X VALUES		
AL1 Ray Boone	4.00	8.00
AL2 Jim Busby	4.00	8.00
AL3 Whitey Ford	15.00	30.00
AL4 Nellie Fox	12.50	25.00
AL5 Bob Grim	4.00	8.00
AL6 Jack Harshman	4.00	8.00
AL7 Jim Hegan	4.00	8.00
AL8 Bob Lemon	10.00	20.00
AL9 Irv Noren	4.00	8.00
AL10 Bob Porterfield	4.00	8.00
AL11 Al Rosen	5.00	10.00
AL12 Mickey Vernon	6.00	12.00
AL13 Vic Wertz	4.00	8.00
AL14 Early Wynn	10.00	20.00
AL15 Bobby Avila	4.00	8.00
AL16 Yogi Berra	25.00	50.00
AL17 Joe Coleman	4.00	8.00
AL18 Larry Doby	10.00	20.00
AL19 Jackie Jensen	6.00	12.00
AL20 Pete Runnels	4.00	8.00
AL21 Jimmy Piersall	5.00	10.00
AL22 Hank Bauer	5.00	10.00
AL23 Chico Carrasquel	4.00	8.00
AL24 Minnie Minoso	6.00	12.00
AL25 Sandy Consuegra	4.00	8.00
NL1 Richie Ashburn	12.50	25.00
NL2 Del Crandall	4.00	8.00
NL3 Gil Hodges	12.50	25.00
NL4 Brooks Lawrence	4.00	8.00
NL5 Johnny Logan	4.00	8.00
NL6 Sal Maglie	5.00	10.00
NL7 Willie Mays	60.00	120.00
NL8 Don Mueller	4.00	8.00
NL9 Bill Sarni	4.00	8.00

NL10 Warren Spahn	12.50	25.00
NL11 Hank Thompson	4.00	8.00
NL12 Hoyt Wilhelm	10.00	20.00
NL13 John Antonelli	4.00	8.00
NL14 Carl Erskine	6.00	12.00
NL15 Granny Hamner	4.00	8.00
NL16 Ted Kluszewski	7.50	15.00
NL17 Pee Wee Reese	15.00	30.00
NL18 Red Schoendienst	10.00	20.00
NL19 Duke Snider	30.00	60.00
NL20 Frank Thomas	5.00	10.00
NL21 Ray Jablonski	4.00	8.00
NL22 Dusty Rhodes	5.00	10.00
NL23 Gus Bell	5.00	10.00
NL24 Curt Simmons	5.00	10.00
NL25 Marv Grissom	4.00	8.00

1912 Red Sox Boston American Series PC742-1

These cream-colored cards with sepia photo and printing were issued in 1912 by the Boston American newspaper. The set features players from the 1912 Red Sox, who won the World Series. It is reasonable to assume that additional cards will be found. All additions to this checklist are appreciated. Unlike the PC 742-2 Boston Daily American Souvenir set, this set features excellent quality photos. The two most commonly found postcards from this set are Tris Speaker and Joe Wood, the others are found only on rare occassions.

COMPLETE SET (6)	500.00	1,000.00
1 Forest Cady	150.00	300.00
2 Hub Perdue	150.00	300.00
3 Tris Speaker	300.00	600.00
4 Jake Stahl	150.00	300.00
5 Heinie Wagner	150.00	300.00
6 Joe Wood	250.00	500.00

1912 Red Sox Boston Daily American Souvenir PC742-2

This black and white postcard set was issued in 1912 and features players from the World Champion Boston Red Sox of that year. The printing quality of the cards are rather poor. It is thought that this checklist may be incomplete, so any additions are appreciated.

COMPLETE SET (4)	300.00	600.00
1 Forest Cady	150.00	300.00
2 Ray Collins	150.00	300.00
3 Hub Perdue	150.00	300.00
4 Heinie Wagner	150.00	300.00

1940 Red Sox Team Issue

These 25 blank-backed cards, which measure 6 1/2" by 9" feature the players photo along with a facsimile autograph. The cards are unnumbered, so we have sequenced them in alphabetical order.

COMPLETE SET	150.00	300.00
1 Jim Bagby Jr	5.00	10.00
2 Bull Butland	5.00	10.00
3 Tom Carey	5.00	10.00
4 Doc Cramer	6.00	12.00
5 Joe Cronin	10.00	20.00
6 Gene Desautels	5.00	10.00
7 Emerson Dickman	5.00	10.00
8 Dom DiMaggio	12.50	25.00
9 Bobby Doerr	10.00	20.00
10 Lou Finney	5.00	10.00
11 Jimmie Foxx	20.00	40.00
12 Denny Galehouse	5.00	10.00
13 Joe Glenn	5.00	10.00
14 Lefty Grove	15.00	30.00
15 Mickey Harris	5.00	10.00
16 Herb Hash	5.00	10.00
17 Joe Hevering	5.00	10.00
18 Leo Nonnenkamp	5.00	10.00
19 Fritz Ostermueller	5.00	10.00
20 Marv Owen	5.00	10.00
21 John Peacock	5.00	10.00
22 Jim Tabor	5.00	10.00
23 Charlie Wagner	5.00	10.00
24 Ted Williams	30.00	60.00
25 Jack Wilson	5.00	10.00

1941 Red Sox Team Issue

These 25 blank-backed cards, which measure 6 1/2" by 9" feature the players photo along with a facsimile autograph. Since these cards are unnumbered, we have sequenced them in alphabetical order.

1 Tom Carey	5.00	10.00
2 Joe Cronin	10.00	20.00
3 Emerson Dickman	5.00	10.00
4 Dom DiMaggio	10.00	20.00
5 Joe Dobson	5.00	10.00
6 Bobby Doerr	10.00	20.00
7 Lou Finney	5.00	10.00
8 Bill Fleming	5.00	10.00
9 Pete Fox	5.00	10.00
10 Jimmie Foxx	15.00	30.00
11 Lefty Grove	12.50	25.00
12 Odell Hale	5.00	10.00
13 Mickey Harris	5.00	10.00
14 Earl Johnson	5.00	10.00
15 Lefty Judd	5.00	10.00
16 Skeeter Newsome	5.00	10.00
17 Dick Newsome	5.00	10.00
18 John Peacock	5.00	10.00
19 Frank Pytlak	5.00	10.00
20 Mike Ryba	5.00	10.00
21 Stan Spence	5.00	10.00
22 Jim Tabor	5.00	10.00
23 Charlie Wagner	5.00	10.00
24 Ted Williams	40.00	80.00
25 Jack Wilson	5.00	10.00

1942 Red Sox Team Issue

This set of the Boston Red Sox measures approximately 6 1/2" by 9". The black and white photos display fascimile autographs. The backs are blank. The cards are unnumbered and are checklisted below in alphabetical order.

COMPLETE SET (25)	150.00	300.00
1 Mace Brown	5.00	10.00
2 Bill Butland	5.00	10.00
3 Paul Campbell	5.00	10.00
4 Tom Carey	5.00	10.00
5 Ken Chase	5.00	10.00
6 Bill Conroy	5.00	10.00
7 Joe Cronin	10.00	20.00
8 Dominic DiMaggio	10.00	20.00
9 Joe Dobson	5.00	10.00
10 Bob Doerr	10.00	20.00
11 Lou Finney	5.00	10.00
12 Pete Fox	5.00	10.00
13 Jimmie Foxx	20.00	40.00
14 Tex Hughson	5.00	10.00
15 Oscar Judd	5.00	10.00
16 Tony Lupien	5.00	10.00
17 Dick Newsome	5.00	10.00
18 Skeeter Newsome	5.00	10.00
19 John Peacock	5.00	10.00
20 Johnny Pesky	7.50	15.00
21 Mike Ryba	5.00	10.00
22 Jim Tabor	5.00	10.00
23 Yank Terry	5.00	10.00
24 Charles Wagner	5.00	10.00
25 Ted Williams	40.00	80.00

1943 Red Sox Team Issue

This 24-card set of the Boston Red Sox measures approximately 6 1/2" by 9" and features black-and-white player portraits with a facsimile autograph. The cards are unnumbered and checklisted below in alphabetical order.

COMPLETE SET (24)	125.00	250.00
1 Mace Brown	5.00	10.00
2 Ken Chase	5.00	10.00
3 Bill Conroy	5.00	10.00
4 Joe Cronin	10.00	20.00
5 Joe Dobson	5.00	10.00
6 Bob Doerr	10.00	20.00
7 Pete Fox	5.00	10.00
8 Ford Garrison	5.00	10.00
9 Tex Hughson	5.00	10.00
10 Oscar Judd	5.00	10.00
11 Andy Karl	5.00	10.00
12 Eddie Lake	5.00	10.00
13 John Lazor	5.00	10.00
14 Lou Luceer	5.00	10.00
15 Tony Lupien	5.00	10.00
16 Dee Miles	5.00	10.00
17 Dick Newsome	5.00	10.00
18 Skeeter Newsome	5.00	10.00
19 Roy Partee	5.00	10.00
20 John Peacock	5.00	10.00
21 Mike Ryba	5.00	10.00
22 Al Simmons	25.00	50.00
23 Jim Tabor	5.00	10.00
24 Yank Terry	5.00	10.00

1946 Red Sox Team Issue

These 25 cards measure approximately 6 1/2" by 9". They feature members of the 1946 American League pennant winners Red Sox. The set can be dated by Ernie Andres whose only year in the majors was 1946.

COMPLETE SET (25)	150.00	300.00
1 Ernie Andres	4.00	8.00
2 Jim Bagby Jr	4.00	8.00
3 Mace Brown	4.00	8.00
4 Joe Cronin	12.50	25.00
5 Leon Culberson	4.00	8.00
6 Mel Deutsch	4.00	8.00
7 Dom DiMaggio	12.50	25.00
8 Joe Dobson	4.00	8.00
9 Bob Doerr	12.50	25.00
10 Dave Ferriss	4.00	8.00
11 Mickey Harris	4.00	8.00
12 Randy Heflin	4.00	8.00
13 Tex Hughson	4.00	8.00
14 Earl Johnson	4.00	8.00
15 Ed McGah	4.00	8.00
16 George Metkovich	4.00	8.00
17 Roy Partee	4.00	8.00
18 Eddie Pellagrini	4.00	8.00
19 Johnny Pesky	6.00	12.00
20 Rip Russell	4.00	8.00
21 Mike Ryba	4.00	8.00
22 Charlie Wagner	4.00	8.00
23 Hal Wagner	4.00	8.00
24 Ted Williams	40.00	80.00
25 Rudy York	6.00	12.00

1947 Red Sox Team Issue

This 25-card set of the Boston Red Sox team measures approximately 6 1/2" by 9" and features black-and-white player portraits. A fascimile autograph is printed on each photo. The backs are blank. The cards are unnumbered and checklisted below in alphabetical order.

COMPLETE SET (25)	150.00	300.00
1 Joe Cronin MG	7.50	15.00
2 Leon Culberson	4.00	8.00
3 Dom DiMaggio	7.50	15.00
4 Joseph Dobson	4.00	8.00
5 Bob Doerr	7.50	15.00
6 Harry Dorish	4.00	8.00
7 David Boo Ferriss	4.00	8.00
8 Tommy Fine	4.00	8.00
9 Don Gutteridge	4.00	8.00
10 Mickey Harris	4.00	8.00
11 Tex Hughson	4.00	8.00
12 Earl Johnson	4.00	8.00
13 Bob Klinger	4.00	8.00
14 Sam Mele	4.00	8.00
15 Wally Moses	5.00	10.00
16 Johnny Murphy	4.00	8.00
17 Mel Parnell	5.00	10.00
18 Roy Partee	4.00	8.00
19 Eddie Pellagrini	4.00	8.00
20 Johnny Pesky	6.00	12.00
21 Rip Russell	4.00	8.00
22 Birdie Tebbetts	5.00	10.00
23 Ted Williams	40.00	80.00
24 Rudy York	6.00	12.00
25 Bill Zuber	4.00	8.00

1948 Red Sox Team Issue

These 25 photos measure approximately 6 1/2" by 9". They feature members of the 1948 Boston Red Sox. The photos take up almost the entire surface and are surrounded by white borders. A fascimile autograph is also on each photo. The backs are blank and we have sequenced this set in alphabetical order.

COMPLETE SET (25)	150.00	300.00
1 Matt Batts	4.00	8.00
2 Dom DiMaggio	10.00	20.00
3 Joe Dobson	4.00	8.00
4 Bobby Doerr	10.00	20.00
5 Harry Dorish	4.00	8.00
6 Dave Boo Ferriss	4.00	8.00
7 Denny Galehouse	4.00	8.00
8 Bill Goodman	6.00	12.00
9 Mickey Harris	4.00	8.00
10 Billy Hitchcock	4.00	8.00
11 Earl Johnson	4.00	8.00
12 Jake Jones	4.00	8.00
13 Ellis Kinder	4.00	8.00
14 Jack Kramer	4.00	8.00
15 Joe McCarthy MG	10.00	20.00
16 Maurice McDermott	4.00	8.00
17 Sam Mele	4.00	8.00
18 Wally Moses	4.00	8.00
19 Mel Parnell	6.00	12.00
20 Johnny Pesky	6.00	12.00
21 Stan Spence	4.00	8.00
22 Vern Stephens	6.00	12.00
23 Chuck Stobbs	4.00	8.00
24 Birdie Tebbetts	4.00	8.00
25 Ted Williams	40.00	80.00

1949 Red Sox Team Issue

This 25-card set of the Boston Red Sox team measures approximately 6 1/2" by 9" and features black-and-white player portraits with white borders. A fascimile autograph is printed on each photo. The backs are blank. The cards are unnumbered and checklisted below in alphabetical order.

COMPLETE SET (25)	150.00	300.00
1 Matt Batts	4.00	8.00
2 Merrill Combs	4.00	8.00
3 Dom DiMaggio	7.50	15.00
4 Joe Dobson	4.00	8.00
5 Bob Doerr	7.50	15.00
6 David Boo Ferriss	4.00	8.00
7 Bill Goodman	6.00	12.00
8 Mickey Harris	4.00	8.00
9 Billy Hitchcock	4.00	8.00
10 Tex Hughson	4.00	8.00
11 Earl Johnson	4.00	8.00
12 Ellis Kinder	4.00	8.00
13 Jack Kramer	4.00	8.00
14 Joe McCarthy MG	7.50	15.00
15 Sam Mele	4.00	8.00
16 Tommy O'Brien	4.00	8.00
17 Mel Parnell	6.00	12.00
18 Johnny Pesky	6.00	12.00
19 Frank Quinn	4.00	8.00
20 Vern Stephens	6.00	12.00
21 Chuck Stobbs	4.00	8.00
22 Lou Stringer	4.00	8.00
23 Birdie Tebbetts	4.00	8.00
24 Ted Williams	40.00	80.00
25 Al Zarilla	4.00	8.00

1950 Red Sox Clark Locksmith

This four-card set features black-and-white photos of Boston Red Sox players and measures approximately 2 3/4" bvy 3 3/4".

COMPLETE SET (4)	25.00	50.00
1 Bobby Doerr	5.00	10.00
2 Ted Williams	12.50	25.00
3 Dom DiMaggio	7.50	15.00
4 Johnny Pesky	2.50	5.00

1950 Red Sox Team Issue

This 30-card set of the Boston Red Sox team measures approximately 6 1/2" by 9" and features black-and-white player portraits with white borders. A fascimile autograph is printed on each photo. The backs are blank. The cards are unnumbered and checklisted below in alphabetical order. Earl Johnson, Ken Keltner, Joe McCarthy, Al Papai and Charley Schanz were issued originally and were replaced in the second series with Dick Littlefield, Williard Nixon, Steve O'Neill, George Susce, and Clyde Vollmer. All of these 10 people are notated with SP's below.

COMPLETE SET (30)	125.00	250.00
COMMON CARD (1-30)	2.00	4.00
COMMON SP	5.00	10.00
1 Matt Batts	2.00	4.00
2 Earle Combs CO	4.00	8.00
3 Dom DiMaggio	4.00	8.00
4 Joe Dobson	2.00	4.00
5 Bob Doerr	4.00	8.00
6 Walter Dropo	2.50	5.00
7 Bill Goodman	2.00	4.00
8 Earl Johnson SP	5.00	10.00
9 Ken Keltner SP	6.00	12.00
10 Ellis Kinder	2.00	4.00
11 Dick Littlefield SP	5.00	10.00
12 Walter Masterson	2.00	4.00
13 Joe McCarthy MG SP	10.00	20.00
14 Maurice McDermott	2.00	4.00
15 Willard Nixon SP	5.00	10.00
16 Steve O'Neill MG SP	6.00	12.00
17 Al Papai SP	5.00	10.00
18 Mel Parnell	3.00	6.00
19 Johnny Pesky	3.00	6.00
20 Buddy Rosar	2.00	4.00
21 Charley Schanz SP	5.00	10.00
22 Vern Stephens	3.00	6.00
23 Chuck Stobbs	2.00	4.00
24 Lou Stringer	2.00	4.00
25 George Susce SP	5.00	10.00
26 Birdie Tebbetts	2.50	5.00
27 Clyde Vollmer SP	10.00	20.00
28 Ted Williams	20.00	40.00
29 Tom Wright	2.00	4.00
30 Al Zarilla	2.00	4.00

1953 Red Sox First National Super Market Stores

This four-card set features black-and-white player photos and measures approximately 3 3/4" by 5". The backs carry advertising for the stores. The cards are unnumbered and checklisted below in alphabetical order. A reprint of this set was made in the early 80's.

COMPLETE SET (4)	150.00	300.00
1 Bill Goodman	40.00	80.00
2 Ellis Kinder	40.00	80.00
3 Mel Parnell	50.00	100.00
4 Sammy White	40.00	80.00

1953 Red Sox Team Issue

This set of the Boston Red Sox measures approximately 6 1/2" by 9". The black-and-white player photos display fascimile autographs. The backs are blank. The cards are unnumbered and checklisted below in alphabetical order.

COMPLETE SET (30)	125.00	250.00
1 Milt Bolling	4.00	8.00
2 Lou Boudreau	7.50	15.00
3 Harold Brown	4.00	8.00
4 Bill Consolo	4.00	8.00
5 Dom DiMaggio	7.50	15.00
6 Hoot Evers	4.00	8.00
7 Ben Flowers	4.00	8.00
8 Hershell Freeman	4.00	8.00
9 Dick Gernert	4.00	8.00
10 Bill Goodman	6.00	12.00
11 Marv Grissom	4.00	8.00
12 Ken Holcombe	4.00	8.00
13 Sid Hudson	4.00	8.00
14 George Kell	7.50	15.00
15 Bill Kennedy	4.00	8.00
16 Ellis Kinder	6.00	12.00
17 Ted Lepcio	4.00	8.00
18 Johnny Lipon	4.00	8.00
19 Maurice McDermott	4.00	8.00
20 John Merson	4.00	8.00
21 Gus Niarhos	4.00	8.00
22 Willard Nixon	4.00	8.00
23 Mel Parnell	6.00	12.00
24 Jimmy Piersall	7.50	15.00
25 Gene Stephens	4.00	8.00
26 Tommy Umphlett	4.00	8.00
27 Bill Werle	4.00	8.00
28 Sam White	4.00	8.00
29 Del Wilber	4.00	8.00
30 Al Zarilla	4.00	8.00

1954 Red Sox Team Issue

These 30 blank-backed cards, which measure 6 1/2" by 9" feature members of the 1954 Boston Red Sox. The fronts feature the players photo along with a fascimile autograph. Since these cards are unnumbered, we have sequenced them in alphabetical order. One of the very few Harry Agganis cards printed during his short career is in this set.

COMPLETE SET	150.00	300.00
1 Harry Agganis	15.00	30.00
2 Milt Bolling	4.00	8.00
3 Lou Boudreau MG	7.50	15.00

4 Tom Brewer	4.00	8.00
5 Hal Brown	4.00	8.00
6 Tex Clevenger	4.00	8.00
7 Billy Consolo	4.00	8.00
8 Joe Dobson	4.00	8.00
9 Hoot Evers	4.00	8.00
10 Dick Gernert	4.00	8.00
11 Billy Goodman	5.00	10.00
12 Bill Henry	4.00	8.00
13 Tom Herrin	4.00	8.00
14 Sid Hudson	4.00	8.00
15 Jackie Jensen	6.00	12.00
16 George Kell	7.50	15.00
17 Leo Kiely	4.00	8.00
18 Ellis Kinder	4.00	8.00
19 Ted Lepcio	4.00	8.00
20 Charlie Maxwell	4.00	8.00
21 Willard Nixon	4.00	8.00
22 Karl Olson	4.00	8.00
23 Mickey Owen CO	4.00	8.00
24 Mel Parnell	5.00	10.00
25 Jimmy Piersall	6.00	12.00
26 Frank Sullivan	4.00	8.00
27 Bill Werle	4.00	8.00
28 Sammy White	4.00	8.00
29 Del Wilber	4.00	8.00
30 Ted Williams	40.00	80.00

1958 Red Sox Jay Publishing

This 12-card set of the Boston Red Sox measures approximately 5" by 7" and features black-and-white player photos in a white border. These cards were packaged 12 to a packet. The backs are blank. The cards are unnumbered and checklisted below in alphabetical order.

COMPLETE SET (12)	30.00	60.00
1 Tom Brewer	1.50	3.00
2 Don Buddin	1.50	3.00
3 Dick Gernert	1.50	3.00
4 Mike Higgins MG	1.50	3.00
5 Jack Jensen	2.50	5.00
6 Frank Malzone	2.50	5.00
7 Jim Piersall	2.50	5.00
8 Pete Runnels	2.00	4.00
9 Gene Stephens	1.50	3.00
10 Frank Sullivan	1.50	3.00
11 Sam White	1.50	3.00
12 Ted Williams	12.50	25.00

1959 Red Sox Jay Publishing

This 12-card set of the Boston Red Sox measures approximately 5" by 7" and features black-and-white player photos in a white border. These cards were packaged 12 to a packet and originally sold for 25 cents. The backs are blank. The cards are unnumbered and checklisted below in alphabetical order.

COMPLETE SET (12)	30.00	60.00
1 Tom Brewer	1.50	3.00
2 Dick Gernert	1.50	3.00
3 Mike Higgins	1.50	3.00
4 Jackie Jensen	2.50	5.00
5 Frank Malzone	2.50	5.00
6 Gene Mauch	1.50	3.00
7 Jimmy Piersall	2.50	5.00
8 Dave Sisler	1.50	3.00
9 Gene Stephens	1.50	3.00
10 Frank Sullivan	1.50	3.00
11 Sammy White	1.50	3.00
12 Ted Williams	12.50	25.00

1960 Red Sox Jay Publishing

This 12-card set of the Boston Red Sox measures approximately 5" by 7" and features black-and-white player photos in a white border. These cards were packaged 12 to a packet. The backs are blank. The cards are unnumbered and checklisted below in alphabetical order.

COMPLETE SET (12)	15.00	40.00
1 Tom Brewer	.75	2.00
2 Don Buddin	.75	2.00
3 Jerry Casale	.75	2.00
4 Ike Delock	.75	2.00
5 Jerry(Pumpsie) Green	.75	2.00
6 Bill Jurges MG	.75	2.00
7 Frank Malzone	1.25	3.00
8 Pete Runnels	1.00	2.50
9 Gene Stephens	.75	2.00
10 Bobby Thomson	1.50	4.00
11 Vic Wertz	.75	2.00
12 Ted Williams	10.00	25.00

1962 Red Sox Jay Publishing

Like other Jay Publishing issues these black-and-white, blank-backed, white-bordered, 5" X 7" photos. The player's name and team are printed in black within the lower margin. The photos are unnumbered and checklisted below in alphabetical order. This set has more than 12 cards since two different versions were issued during 1962.

COMPLETE SET	15.00	40.00
1 Ed Bressoud	.75	2.00
2 Lou Clinton	.75	2.00
3 Gene Conley	1.00	2.50
4 Gary Geiger	.75	2.00
5 Carroll Hardy	.75	2.00
6 Mike Higgins MG	.75	2.00
7 Frank Malzone	1.25	3.00
8 Bill Monbouquette	.75	2.00
9 Russ Nixon	.75	2.00
10 Pete Runnels	.75	2.00
11 Chuck Schilling	.75	2.00
12 Don Schwall	.75	2.00
13 Carl Yastrzemski UER Misspelled Yastremski	8.00	20.00

1963 Red Sox Jay Publishing

This 12-card set of the Boston Red Sox measures approximately 5" by 7". The fronts feature black-and-white posed player photos with the player's and team name printed below in the white border. These cards were packaged 12 to a packet. The backs are blank. The cards are unnumbered and checklisted below in alphabetical order.

COMPLETE SET (12)	20.00	50.00
1 Ed Bressoud	.75	2.00
2 Lou Clinton	.75	2.00
3 Gary Geiger	.75	2.00
4 Frank Malzone	1.25	3.00
5 Roman Mejias	.75	2.00
6 Bill Monbouquette	.75	2.00
7 Johnny Pesky MG	1.00	2.50
8 Dick Radatz	1.00	2.50
9 Chuck Schilling	.75	2.00
10 Dick Stuart	.75	2.00
11 Bob Tillman	.75	2.00
12 Carl Yastrzemski	8.00	20.00

1964 Red Sox Jay Publishing

This 12-card set of the Boston Red Sox measures approximately 5" by 7". The fronts feature black-and-white posed player photos with the player's and team name printed below in the white border. These cards were packaged 12 to a packet. The backs are blank. The cards are unnumbered and checklisted below in alphabetical order.

COMPLETE SET (12)	20.00	50.00
1 Ed Bressoud	.75	2.00
2 Lou Clinton	.75	2.00
3 Gary Geiger	.75	2.00
4 Frank Malzone	1.25	3.00
5 Felix Mantilla	.75	2.00
6 Bill Monbouquette	.75	2.00
7 Russ Nixon	.75	2.00
8 Johnny Pesky MG	1.00	2.50
9 Dick Radatz	1.00	2.50
10 Chuck Schilling	.75	2.00
11 Dick Stuart	1.00	2.50
12 Carl Yastrzemski	8.00	20.00

1964 Red Sox Team Issue

This eight-card set of the Boston Red Sox measures approximately 8" by 10" and features color portraits with a white border and a facsimile autograph. The backs are blank. The photos were packaged eight to a clear plastic packet and originally sold for 50 cents at the park or through the mail. They were also inserted one to each Red Sox year book. The cards are unnumbered and checklisted below in alphabetical order.

COMPLETE SET (8)	15.00	40.00
1 Ed Bressoud	1.50	4.00
2 Jack Lamabe	1.50	4.00
3 Frank Malzone	2.50	6.00
4 Bill Monbouquette	2.00	5.00
5 Johnny Pesky	2.00	5.00
6 Dick Radatz	2.00	5.00
7 Dick Stuart	2.00	5.00
8 Carl Yastrzemski	8.00	20.00

1965 Red Sox Jay Publishing

This 12-card set of the Boston Red Sox measures approximately 5" by 7". The fronts feature black-and-white posed player photos with the player's and team name printed below in the white border. These cards were packaged 12 to a packet. The backs are blank. The cards are unnumbered and checklisted below in alphabetical order.

COMPLETE SET (12)	15.00	40.00
1 Dennis Bennett	.75	2.00
2 Ed Bressoud	.75	2.00
3 Tony Conigliaro	2.00	5.00
4 Billy Herman MG	1.50	4.00
5 Frank Malzone	1.25	3.00
6 Felix Mantilla	.75	2.00
7 Bill Monbouquette	.75	2.00
8 Dick Radatz	1.00	2.50
9 Lee Thomas	.75	2.00
10 John Tillman	.75	2.00
11 Earl Wilson	.75	2.00
12 Carl Yastrzemski	8.00	20.00

1965 Red Sox Team Issue

This 18-card set of the 1965 Boston Red Sox features color player photos measuring approximately 7 7/8" by 9 7/8" with a white border. A facsimile autograph is printed across the bottom of the photo. The cards were packaged in a clear plastic packet and was originally sold for $1 at the park or through the mail. They were also inserted one to each Red Sox year book. The backs are blank. The cards are unnumbered and checklisted below in alphabetical order. Although the photos were sold 16 at a time, turnover within the team's roster made for an expanded set

COMPLETE SET	40.00	80.00
1 Dennis Bennett	1.50	4.00
2 Ed Bressoud	1.50	4.00
3 Tony Conigliaro	5.00	12.00
4 Bob Heffner	1.50	4.00
5 Billy Herman MG	3.00	8.00
6 Tony Horton		
7 Jack Lamabe	1.50	4.00
8 Frank Malzone	2.50	6.00
9 Felix Mantilla	1.50	4.00
10 Bill Monbouquette	1.50	4.00
11 Dave Morehead	1.50	4.00
12 Dick Radatz	2.00	5.00
13 Jerry Stephenson	1.50	4.00
14 Dick Stuart		
15 Lee Thomas	1.50	4.00
16 Bob Tillman	1.50	4.00
17 Earl Wilson	1.50	4.00
18 Carl Yastrzemski	12.50	30.00

1966 Red Sox Team Issue

This 16-card set of the 1966 Boston Red Sox features color player photos measuring approximately 7 3/4" by 9 7/8" with a white border. A facsimile autograph is printed at the bottom of the photo. The photos were packaged in a clear plastic packet and was originally sold for $1 at the park or through the mail. They were also inserted one to each Red Sox year book. The backs are blank. The cards are unnumbered and checklisted below in alphabetical order.

COMPLETE SET (16)	40.00	80.00
1 Dennis Bennett	1.50	4.00
2 Tony Conigliaro	3.00	8.00
3 Joe Foy	1.50	4.00
4 Jim Gosger	1.50	4.00
5 Tony Horton	2.00	5.00
6 Jim Lonborg	2.50	6.00
7 Dave Morehead	1.50	4.00
8 Dan Osinski	1.50	4.00
9 Rico Petrocelli	2.50	6.00
10 Dick Radatz	2.00	5.00
11 Mike Ryan	1.50	4.00
12 Bob Sadowski	1.50	4.00
13 George Smith	1.50	4.00
14 George Thomas	1.50	4.00
15 Earl Wilson	1.50	4.00
16 Carl Yastrzemski	10.00	25.00

1967 Red Sox Stickers Topps

This was a limited production "test" issue for Topps. It is very similar to the Pirates "test" issue preceding. The stickers are blank backed and measure 2 1/2" by 3 1/2". The stickers look like cards from the front and are somewhat attractive in spite of the "no neck" presentation of many of the players' photos. The cards are numbered on the front.

COMPLETE SET (33)	350.00	700.00
WRAPPER (5-CENT)	20.00	50.00
1 Dennis Bennett	10.00	25.00
2 Darrell Brandon	10.00	25.00
3 Tony Conigliaro	15.00	40.00
4 Don Demeter	10.00	25.00
5 Hank Fischer	10.00	25.00
6 Joe Foy	10.00	25.00
7 Mike Andrews	10.00	25.00
8 Dalton Jones	10.00	25.00
9 Jim Lonborg	12.50	30.00
10 Don McMahon	10.00	25.00
11 Dave Morehead	10.00	25.00
12 Reggie Smith	15.00	40.00
13 Rico Petrocelli	12.50	30.00
14 Mike Ryan	10.00	25.00
15 Jose Santiago	10.00	25.00
16 George Scott	12.50	30.00
17 Sal Maglie CO	12.50	30.00
18 George Smith	10.00	25.00
19 Lee Stange	10.00	25.00
20 Jerry Stephenson	10.00	25.00
21 Jose Tartabull	10.00	25.00
22 George Thomas	10.00	25.00
23 Bob Tillman	10.00	25.00
24 John Wyatt	10.00	25.00
25 Carl Yastrzemski	100.00	200.00
26 Dick Williams MG	15.00	40.00
27 I Love the Red Sox	10.00	25.00
28 Let's Go Red Sox	10.00	25.00
29 Carl Yastrzemski for Mayor	50.00	100.00
30 Tony Conigliaro is my Hero	20.00	50.00
31 Happiness is a Boston Win	10.00	25.00
32 Red Sox Logo	10.00	25.00
33 Red Sox Pennant	10.00	25.00

1967 Red Sox Team Issue

These 16 blank backed cards measure approximately 4" by 5 5/8" and have white borders. They were issued in two series and were available at the ball park or via the mail for 50 cents per pack. They were issued in two series and we have sequenced them alphabetically by series.

COMPLETE SET (16)	15.00	40.00
1 Tony Conigliaro A	1.50	4.00
2 Joe Foy A	.75	2.00
3 Jim Lonborg A	1.25	3.00
4 Don McMahon A	.75	2.00
5 Rico Petrocelli A	1.25	3.00
6 George Scott A	1.00	2.50
7 Lee Stange A	.75	2.00
8 Carl Yastrzemski A	4.00	10.00
9 Darrell Brandon B	.75	2.00
10 Russ Gibson B	.75	2.00
11 Bill Rohr B	.75	2.00
12 Mike Ryan B	.75	2.00
13 Reggie Smith B	2.50	6.00
14 Jose Tartabull B	.75	2.00
15 George Thomas B	.75	2.00
16 John Wyatt B	.75	2.00

1968 Red Sox Team Issue

This eight-card set of the 1968 Boston Red Sox measures approximately 5 1/2" by 7 1/2". The fronts feature black-and-white player portraits with facsimile autographs and white borders. The backs are blank. The cards are unnumbered and checklisted below in alphabetical order. The set may be incomplete and any confirmed additions would be appreciated.

COMPLETE SET (8)	10.00	25.00
1 Mike Andrews	.75	2.00
2 Darrell Brandon	.75	2.00
3 Bobby Doerr	2.00	5.00
4 Ken Harrelson	2.00	5.00
5 Jim Lonborg	1.50	4.00
6 Rico Petrocelli	2.00	5.00
7 Reggie Smith	2.00	5.00
8 Dick Williams MG	2.00	5.00

1969 Red Sox Arco Oil

Sponsored by Arco Oil, this 12-card set features photos of the 1969 Boston Red Sox. The cards are unnumbered and checklisted below in alphabetical order.

COMPLETE SET (12)	40.00	80.00
1 Mike Andrews	2.00	5.00
2 Tony Conigliaro	4.00	10.00
3 Ray Culp	2.00	5.00
4 Russ Gibson	2.00	5.00
5 Dalton Jones	2.00	5.00
6 Jim Lonborg	3.00	8.00
7 Sparky Lyle	4.00	10.00
8 Syd O'Brien	2.00	5.00
9 Rico Petrocelli	3.00	8.00
10 Geo. Scott	2.50	6.00
11 Reggie Smith	3.00	8.00
12 Carl Yastrzemski	8.00	20.00

1969 Red Sox Team Issue

This 12-card set of the Boston Red Sox measures approximately 4 1/4" by 7". The fronts display black-and-white player portraits bordered in white. The player's name and team are printed in the top margin. The backs are blank. The cards are unnumbered and checklisted below in alphabetical order.

COMPLETE SET (12)	12.50	30.00
1 Mike Andrews	.75	2.00
2 Tony Conigliaro	1.50	4.00
3 Russ Gibson	.75	2.00
4 Dalton Jones	.75	2.00
5 Bill Landis	.75	2.00
6 Jim Lonborg	1.25	3.00
7 Sparky Lyle	1.50	4.00
8 Rico Petrocelli	1.25	3.00
9 George Scott	1.00	2.50
10 Reggie Smith	1.00	2.50
11 Dick Williams MG	1.00	2.50
12 Carl Yastrzemski	3.00	8.00

1969 Red Sox Team Issue Color

This 10-card set features color portraits of the Boston Red Sox with white borders and measures approximately 7" by 8 3/4". The backs are blank. The cards are unnumbered and checklisted below in alphabetical order.

COMPLETE SET (10)	15.00	40.00
1 Mike Andrews	1.25	3.00
2 Tony Conigliaro	2.50	6.00
3 Ray Culp	1.25	3.00
4 Russ Gibson	1.25	3.00
5 James Lonborg	2.00	5.00
6 Rico Petrocelli	2.00	5.00
7 George Scott	1.50	4.00
8 Reggie Smith	2.00	5.00
9 Dick Williams	1.50	4.00
10 Carl Yastrzemski	4.00	10.00

1970 Red Sox Color Photo Post Cards

This set features members of the 1970 Boston Red Sox. These color post cards are unnumbered and we have sequenced them in alphabetical order.

COMPLETE SET	12.50	30.00
1 Luis Alvarado	.40	1.00
2 Mike Andrews	.40	1.00
3 Ken Brett	.60	1.50
4 Bill Conigliaro	.60	1.50
5 Tony Conigliaro	1.00	2.50
6 Ray Culp	.40	1.00
7 Sparky Lyle	1.00	2.50
8 Gerry Moses	.40	1.00
9 Mike Nagy	.40	1.00
10 Gary Peters	.60	1.50
11 Rico Petrocelli	.75	2.00
12 George Scott	.60	1.50
13 Sonny Siebert	.40	1.00
14 Reggie Smith	.75	2.00
15 Lee Stange	.40	1.00
16 Carl Yastrzemski	3.00	8.00
17 Jim Lonborg (oversize)	.75	2.00

1971 Red Sox Arco Oil

Sponsored by Arco Oil, these 12 pictures of the 1971 Boston Red Sox measure approximately 8" by 10" and feature on their fronts white-bordered posed color player photos. The player's name is shown in black lettering within the white margin below the photo. His facsimile autograph appears across the picture. The white back carries the team's and player's names at the top, followed below by position, biography, career highlights, and statistics. An ad at the bottom for picture frames rounds out the back. The cards are unnumbered and checklisted below in alphabetical order.

COMPLETE SET (12)	30.00	60.00
1 Luis Aparicio	4.00	10.00
2 Ken Brett	2.00	5.00
3 Billy Conigliaro	2.50	6.00
4 Ray Culp	2.00	5.00
5 Doug Griffin	2.00	5.00
6 Bob Montgomery	2.00	5.00
7 Gary Peters	2.00	5.00
8 George Scott	2.50	6.00
9 Sonny Siebert	2.00	5.00
10 Reggie Smith	2.50	6.00
11 Ken Tatum	2.00	5.00
12 Carl Yastrzemski	5.00	12.00

1971 Red Sox Team Issue

These 12 photos measure approximately 4 1/4" by 7". The player's name and team are noted on the top with the rest of the front dedicated to a photo. The backs are blank. We have sequenced this set in alphabetical order. The set is dated 1971 as that was Luis Aparicio's first year with the Red Sox and Sparky Lyle's last season with the club.

COMPLETE SET (12)	10.00	25.00
1 Luis Aparicio	1.25	3.00
2 Billy Conigliaro	.75	2.00
3 Ray Culp	.60	1.50
4 Duane Josephson	.60	1.50
5 Jim Lonborg	1.00	2.50
6 Sparky Lyle	1.00	2.50
7 Gary Peters	.60	1.50
8 Rico Petrocelli	1.00	2.50
9 George Scott	.75	2.00
10 Sonny Siebert	.60	1.50
11 Reggie Smith	.75	2.00
12 Carl Yastrzemski	2.00	5.00

1972 Red Sox Team Issue

This 23-card set of the Boston Red Sox features borderless black-and-white player portraits with a facsimile autograph. The backs are blank. The cards are unnumbered and checklisted below in alphabetical order. Carlton Fisk has a card in his Rookie Card year.

COMPLETE SET (23)	8.00	20.00
1 Juan Beniquez	.20	.50
2 Bob Bolin	.20	.50
3 Danny Cater	.20	.50
4 John Curtis	.20	.50
5 Mike Fiore	.20	.50
6 Carlton Fisk	3.00	8.00
7 Phil Gagliano	.20	.50
8 Doug Griffin	.20	.50
9 Tommy Harper	.30	.75
10 John Kennedy	.20	.50
11 Lew Krausse	.20	.50
12 Joe Lahoud	.20	.50
13 Bill Lee	.40	1.00
14 Lynn McGlothlin	.20	.50
15 Rick Miller	.30	.75
16 Bob Montgomery	.20	.50
17 Roger Moret	.20	.50
18 Ben Oglivie	.30	.75
19 Marty Pattin	.20	.50
20 Don Pavletich	.20	.50
21 Ken Tatum	.20	.50
22 Luis Tiant	.40	1.00
23 Carl Yastrzemski	3.00	8.00

1975 Red Sox Herald

This 26 card set was issued as an insert in the two Boston Herald papers over a period of time and featured drawings by sports artist Phil Bissell.

COMPLETE SET	12.50	30.00
1 Carl Yastrzemski	2.00	5.00
2 Fred Lynn	2.00	5.00
3 Jim Rice	2.00	5.00
4 Carlton Fisk	2.00	5.00
5 Bill Lee	.40	1.00
6 Rick Wise	.20	.50
7 Rico Petrocelli	.40	1.00
8 Luis Tiant	.75	2.00
9 Bernie Carbo	.20	.50
10 Bob Heise	.20	.50
11 Juan Beniquez	.20	.50
12 Jim Willoughby	.20	.50
13 Jim Burton	.20	.50
14 Dick Pole	.20	.50
15 Reggie Cleveland	.20	.50
16 Tim Blackwell	.20	.50
17 Cecil Cooper	.40	1.00
18 Dick Drago	.20	.50
19 Dwight Evans	.75	2.00
20 Rick Burleson	.60	1.50
21 Doug Griffin	.20	.50
22 Rick Miller	.20	.50
23 Roger Moret	.20	.50
24 Diego Segui	.20	.50
25 Bob Montgomery	.20	.50
26 Denny Doyle	.20	.50

1975 Red Sox 1946 TCMA

This 43-card set of the 1946 Boston Red Sox team was printed in 1975 by TCMA and features white-and-blue tinted player photos with red lettering. The backs carry player information. The cards are unnumbered and checklisted below in alphabetical order. Card number 43 pictures five players and measures 3 1/2" by 5" instead of the standard size.

COMPLETE SET (43)	10.00	25.00
1 Jim Bagby	.20	.50
2 Floyd Baker	.20	.50
3 Mace Brown	.20	.50
4 Bill Butland	.20	.50
5 Paul Campbell	.20	.50
6 Tom Carey	.20	.50
7 Joe Cronin P MG	.75	2.00
8 Leon Culbertson	.20	.50
9 Tom Daly CO	.20	.50
10 Dom DiMaggio	.60	1.50
11 Joe Dobson	.20	.50
12 Bob Doerr	.75	2.00
13 Clem Dreisewerd	.20	.50
14 Boo Ferriss	.20	.50
15 Andy Gilbert	.20	.50
16 Don Gutteridge	.20	.50
17 Mickey Harris	.20	.50
18 Randy Heflin	.20	.50
19 Pinky Higgins	.20	.50
20 Tex Hughson	.20	.50
21 Earl Johnson	.20	.50
22 Bob Klinger	.20	.50
23 John Lazor	.20	.50
24 Thomas McBride	.20	.50
25 Ed McGah	.20	.50
26 Catfish Metkovich	.20	.50
27 Wally Moses	.40	1.00
28 Roy Partee	.20	.50
29 Eddie Pellargini	.20	.50
30 Johnny Pesky	.60	1.50
31 Frank Pytlak	.20	.50
32 Rip Russell	.20	.50
33 Mike Ryba	.20	.50
34 Ben Steiner	.20	.50
35 Charlie Wagner	.20	.50
36 Hal Wagner	.20	.50
37 Ted Williams	2.00	5.00
38 Larry Woodall CO	.20	.50
39 Larry Woodall CO Charlie Wagner Floyd Baker	.20	.50
40 Rudy York	.40	1.00
41 B. Zuber	.20	.50
42 Six player card	.40	1.00
43 Five player card	.40	1.00

1976 Red Sox Star Market

This 16-card set of the Boston Red Sox measures approximately 5 7/8" by 9". The white-bordered fronts feature color player head photos with a facsimile autograph. The backs are blank. The cards are unnumbered and checklisted below in alphabetical order.

COMPLETE SET (16)	15.00	40.00
1 Rick Burleson	.75	2.00
2 Reggie Cleveland	.40	1.00
3 Cecil Cooper	1.00	2.50
4 Denny Doyle	.40	1.00
5 Dwight Evans	1.50	4.00
6 Carlton Fisk	3.00	8.00
7 Tom House	.40	1.00
8 Fergie Jenkins	1.50	4.00
9 Bill Lee	.75	2.00
10 Fred Lynn	1.00	2.50
11 Rick Miller	.40	1.00
12 Rico Petrocelli	.75	2.00
13 Jim Rice	1.50	4.00
14 Luis Tiant	1.00	2.50
15 Rick Wise	.40	1.00
16 Carl Yastrzemski	3.00	8.00

1976-77 Red Sox

This nine-card set of the Boston Red Sox measures approximately 7" by 8 1/2". The fronts feature white-bordered color player action photos with the player's name printed in black in the bottom margin. The backs are blank. The cards are unnumbered and checklisted below in alphabetical order. These cards were issued over a two year period as eight card sets. They are listed together since there is no difference other than Rico Petrocelli retired after the 1976 season and was replaced by George Scott.

COMPLETE SET (9)	8.00	20.00
1 Rick Burleson	.75	2.00
2 Denny Doyle	.60	1.50
3 Dwight Evans	1.25	3.00
4 Carlton Fisk	2.00	5.00
5 Fred Lynn	1.25	3.00
6 Rico Petrocelli '76	1.00	2.50
7 Jim Rice	1.25	3.00
8 George Scott '77	1.00	2.50
9 Carl Yastrzemski	1.25	3.00

1979 Red Sox Early Favorites

This 25-card set measures 2 1/2" by 3 3/4". The set covers the early years of Tom Yawkey's ownership. The photos are all black and white.

COMPLETE SET (25)	8.00	20.00
1 New Fenway Park	.40	1.00
2 Mrs. Tom Yawkey Mrs. Eddie Collins	.30	.75
3 1932 Outfielders Tom Oliver Earl Webb Jack Roth	.30	.75
4 Ace Pitchers John Marcum Wes Ferrell Lefty Grov	.30	.75
5 John Gooch	.30	.75
6 Pitching recruits with (Joe Cronin Lee Rogers B	.40	1.00
7 Danny MacFayden	.30	.75
8 Dale Alexander	.30	.75
9 Robert Fothergill/(Fatsy)	.30	.75
10 Sunday Morning Workout	.30	.75
11 Jimmy Foxx (Jimmie) signs ball for Mrs. Tom Yawkey	.40	1.00
12 Lefty Grove receiving key for new car	.40	1.00
13 Lefty Grove Fireball	.40	1.00
14 Jack Rothrock Urbane Pickering	.30	.75
15 Tom Daly CO Al Schact CO Herb Pennock CO	.30	.75
16 Heinie Manush Eddie Collins	.40	1.00
17 Tris Speaker	.60	1.50
18 Jimmy Foxx (Jimmie)	.75	2.00
19 Smead Jolley	.30	.75
20 Hal Trosky James Foxx	.30	.75
21 Harold (Muddy) Ruel Wilcy (Fireman) Moore	.30	.75
22 Bob Quinn PR Shano Collins MG	.30	.75
23 Tom Oliver	.30	.75
24 Joe Cronin CO Herb Pennock CO Bud Buetter	.40	1.00
25 Jimmie Foxx	2.00	5.00

1979 Red Sox Vendor Cards

This standard-size set of the Boston Red Sox features black-and-white player portraits with biographical and statistical information on the backs except for one card which displays a picture of Garry Hancodk on one side and Stan Papi on the other. There are three other double player cards who need identifying. For now they are listed as two player cards. Any help on these three other cards is appreciated. According to the back, The Phantom Co. issued these cards. The cards came in a white packet with a picture of a Red Sox (apparently Yaz) rounding the bases.

COMPLETE SET	10.00	25.00
1 Gary Allenson	.20	.50
2 Jack Brohamer	.20	.50
3 Tom Burgmeier	.20	.50
4 Rick Burleson	.30	.75
5 Bill Campbell	.20	.50
6 Dick Drago	.20	.50
7 Dennis Eckersley	1.25	3.00
8 Dwight Evans	.60	1.50
9 Carlton Fisk	2.00	5.00
10 Andy Hassler	.20	.50
11 Butch Hobson	.20	.50
12 Fred Lynn	.60	1.50
13 Bob Montgomery	.20	.50
14 Mike O'Berry	.20	.50
15 Jerry Remy	.20	.50
16 Steve Renko	.20	.50
17 Jim Rice	.75	2.00
18 George Scott	.30	.75
19 Bob Stanley	.20	.50
20 Mike Torrez	.20	.50
21 Larry Wolfe	.20	.50
22 Jim Wright	.20	.50
23 Carl Yastrzemski	2.00	5.00
24 Garry Hancock Stan Papi	.20	.50
25 Two Player Card	.20	.50
26 Two Player Card	.20	.50
27 Two Player Card	.20	.50

1980 Red Sox Postcards

Issued by the team, these 19 cards are black and white and are postcard sized. Some of these cards were known to come with facsimile autographs. Since these cards are unnumbered we have sequenced them in alphabetical order.

COMPLETE SET	8.00	20.00
1 Gary Allenson	.20	.50
2 Jack Billingham	.20	.50
3 Jack Brohamer	.20	.50
4 Rick Burleson	.20	.50
5 Dick Drago	.20	.50
6 Dennis Eckersley	.75	2.00
7 Dwight Evans	.60	1.50
8 Carlton Fisk	1.25	3.00
9 Butch Hobson	.20	.50
10 Glenn Hoffman	.20	.50
11 Fred Lynn	.60	1.50
12 Tony Perez	.75	2.00
13 Chuck Rainey	.20	.50
14 Jerry Remy	.20	.50
15 Steve Renko	.20	.50
16 Jim Rice	.60	1.50
17 Bob Stanley	.20	.50
18 Mike Torrez	.20	.50
19 Carl Yastrzemski	2.00	5.00

1869 Red Stockings Peck and Snyder

This card was issued by Peck and Snyder as an advertising trade piece. It comes in two versions (either with red or black borders). The black version is usually larger than the red version. Most of these cards are found trimmed to fit into CdV albums. The front features a photo of the 1869 Red Stockings while the back is an advertisment for Peck and Snyder.

1 Red Stockings Team	35,000.00	70,000.00

1891 Reds Cabinets Conly

These Cabinets feature members of the 1891 Cincinnati Reds. The players are all pictured in suit and tie. The back features an ad for Conly studios. This set is not numbered so we have sequenced them in alphabetical order.

COMPLETE SET	7,500.00	15,000.00
1 Tom Brown	1,000.00	2,000.00
2 Charlie Buffington	1,000.00	2,000.00
3 Bill Daley	1,000.00	2,000.00
4 Duke Farrell	1,000.00	2,000.00
5 Arthur Irwin	1,000.00	2,000.00
6 John Irwin	1,000.00	2,000.00
7 Morgan Murphy	1,000.00	2,000.00
8 Darby O'Brien	1,000.00	2,000.00
9 Paul Radford	1,000.00	2,000.00
10 Hardy Richardson	1,000.00	2,000.00
11 John Striker	1,000.00	2,000.00

1919-20 Reds World's Champions Postcards

This black and white set of Cincinnati players was issued in 1920 and appears with either of two captions in the border on the front of the card -- World Champions 1919 or National League Champions 1919. A glossy version of this set also exists.

COMPLETE SET	900.00	1,800.00
1 Nick Allen	50.00	100.00
2 Rube Bressler	50.00	100.00
3 Jake Daubert	50.00	100.00
4 Pat Duncan	50.00	100.00
5 Hod Eller	50.00	100.00

Card	Low	High
6 Ray Fisher	50.00	100.00
7 Eddie Gerner	50.00	100.00
8 Heine Groh	75.00	150.00
9 Larry Kopf	50.00	100.00
10 Adolfo Luque	75.00	150.00
11 Sherwood Magee	60.00	120.00
12 Roy Mitchell	50.00	100.00
13 Pat Moran MG	50.00	100.00
14 Greasy Neale	75.00	150.00
15 Bill Rariden	50.00	100.00
16 Morris Rath	50.00	100.00
17 Jimmy Ring	50.00	100.00
18 Edd Roush	100.00	200.00
19 Walter Reuther	50.00	100.00
20 Harry Sallee	50.00	100.00
21 Hank Schreiber	50.00	100.00
22 Charles See	50.00	100.00
23 Jimmy Smith	50.00	100.00
24 Ivy Wingo	50.00	100.00
25 Team Card	300.00	600.00

1938-39 Reds Orange/Gray W711-1

The cards in this 32-card set measure approximately 2" by 3". The 1938-39 Cincinnati Reds Baseball player set was printed in orange and gray tones. Many back variations exist and there are two poses of Johnny VanderMeer, portrait (PORT) and an action (ACT) poses. The set was sold at the ballpark and was printed on thin cardboard stock. The cards are unnumbered but have been alphabetized and numbered in the checklist below.

Card	Low	High
COMPLETE SET (32)	600.00	1,200.00
1 Wally Berger (2)	25.00	50.00
2 Nino Bongiovanni (39)	50.00	100.00
3 Stanley Bordagaray Frenchy (39)	50.00	100.00
4 Joe Cascarella (38)	15.00	30.00
5 Allen Dusty Cooke (38)	15.00	30.00
6 Harry Craft	20.00	40.00
7 Ray(Peaches) Davis	15.00	30.00
8 Paul Derringer (2)	30.00	60.00
9 Linus Frey (2)	15.00	30.00
10 Lee Gamble (2)	15.00	30.00
11 Ival Goodman (2)	15.00	30.00
12 Hank Gowdy CO	20.00	40.00
13 Lee Grissom (2)	15.00	30.00
14 Willard Hershberger (2)	20.00	40.00
15 Eddie Joost (39)	20.00	40.00
16 Wes Livengood (39)	100.00	200.00
17 Ernie Lombardi (2)	60.00	120.00
18 Frank McCormick	25.00	50.00
19 Bill McKechnie (2) MG	30.00	60.00
20 Lloyd Whitey Moore (2)	15.00	30.00
21 Billy Myers (2)	15.00	30.00
22 Lew Riggs (2)	15.00	30.00
23 Eddie Roush CO (38)	50.00	100.00
24 Les Scarsella (39)	15.00	30.00
25 Gene Schott (38)	15.00	30.00
26 Eugene Thompson	15.00	30.00
27 Johnny VanderMeer PORT	30.00	60.00
28 Johnny VanderMeer ACT	30.00	60.00
29 Wm.(Bucky) Walters (2)	25.00	50.00
30 Jim Weaver	15.00	30.00
31 Bill Werber (39)	15.00	30.00
32 Jimmy Wilson (39)	15.00	30.00

1939 Reds Team Issue

This 25-card set of the Cincinnati Reds features player photos printed on cards with blank backs. The cards are unnumbered and checklisted below in alphabetical order. The cards measure approximaley 2" by 3", were printed in grey sepia and the players' name is printed in orange. It is believed that this set was issued by Kroger's. Although this set is similar to the W711-1 set, the difference in these cards is believed to be the distribution method

Card	Low	High
1 Wally Berger	15.00	30.00
2 Nino Bongiovanni	12.50	25.00
3 Frenchy Bordagaray	12.50	25.00
4 Joe Cascarella	12.50	25.00
5 Harry Craft	12.50	25.00
6 Paul Derringer	15.00	30.00
7 Linus Frey	12.50	25.00
8 Lee Gamble	12.50	25.00
9 Ival Goodman	12.50	25.00
10 Hank Gowdy CO	12.50	25.00
11 Willard Hershberger	20.00	40.00
12 Eddie Joost	15.00	30.00
13 Ernie Lombardi	25.00	50.00
14 Frank McCormick	15.00	30.00
15 Bill McKechnie MG	25.00	50.00
16 Whitey Moore	12.50	25.00
17 Billy Myers	12.50	25.00
18 Lew Riggs	12.50	25.00
19 Eddie Roush CO	25.00	50.00
20 Les Scarsella	12.50	25.00
21 Junior Thompson	12.50	25.00
22 Johnny VanderMeer	20.00	40.00
23 Jimmy Wilson CO	15.00	30.00
24 Bill Werber	15.00	30.00
25 Bucky Walters	20.00	40.00

1941 Reds Harry Hartman W711-2

The cards in this 34-card set measure approximately 2 1/8" by 2 5/8". The W711-2 Cincinnati Reds set contains unnumbered, black and white cards and was issued in boxes which had a reverse side resembling a mailing label. This issue is sometimes called the "Harry Hartman" set. The cards are numbered below in alphabetical order by player's name with non-player cards listed at the end. The set is worth about $100 more when it is in the original mailing box. The set originally cost 20 cents when ordered in 1940.

Card	Low	High
COMPLETE SET (34)	300.00	600.00
COMMON CARD (1-28)	7.50	15.00
COMMON CARD (29-34)	7.50	15.00
1 Morris Arnovich	12.50	25.00
2 William(Bill) Baker	12.50	25.00
3 Joseph Beggs	12.50	25.00
4 Harry Craft	15.00	30.00
5 Paul Derringer	25.00	50.00
6 Linus Frey	12.50	25.00
7 Ival Goodman	12.50	25.00
8 Hank Gowdy CO	15.00	30.00
9 Witt Guise	12.50	25.00
10 Willard Hershberger	15.00	30.00
11 John Hutchings	12.50	25.00
12 Edwin Joost	15.00	30.00
13 Ernie Lombardi	30.00	60.00
14 Frank McCormick	20.00	40.00
15 Myron McCormick	12.50	25.00
16 Bill McKechnie MG	25.00	50.00
17 Whitey Moore	12.50	25.00
18 William(Bill) Myers	12.50	25.00
19 Elmer Riddle	12.50	25.00
20 Lewis Riggs	12.50	25.00
21 James A. Ripple	12.50	25.00
22 Milburn Shoffner	12.50	25.00
23 Eugene Thompson	12.50	25.00
24 James Turner	15.00	30.00
25 John VanderMeer	25.00	50.00
26 Bucky Walters	20.00	40.00
27 Bill Werber	15.00	30.00
28 James Wilson	12.50	25.00
29 Results 1940 World Series	12.50	25.00
30 The Cincinnati Reds/(Title Card)	12.50	25.00
31 The Cincinnati Reds World's Champions/(Title Car	12.50	25.00
32 Debt of Gratitude to Wm. Koehl Co.	12.50	25.00
33 Tell the World About Our Reds	12.50	25.00
34 Harry Hartman ANN	12.50	25.00

1954-55 Reds Postcards

These cards, which were issued over a two year period, have four distinct styles to them. They are: no name in the white 3/4" inch space at the bottom; no name in the box but a blue fascimile autograph; printed name and fascimile autograph in the bottom white box and printed name, Cincinnatie Redleg in white space plus the blue fascimile autograph. This set carries a catalog naming of PC746. These cards are unnumbered, so we have sequenced them in alphabetical order. At least 20 more players are considered to be possible additions to this set so any help is appreciated.

Card	Low	High
COMPLETE SET	250.00	500.00
1 Bobby Adams Portrait	3.00	6.00
2 Bobby Adams Fielding	3.00	6.00
3 Fred Baczewski	3.00	6.00
4 Ed Bailey	3.00	6.00
5 Dick Bartell CO Neck Shows	3.00	6.00
6 Dick Bartell CO No-Neck	3.00	6.00
7 Matt Batts	3.00	6.00
8 Gus Bell Hitting	4.00	8.00
9 Gus Bell Portrait	4.00	8.00
10 Joe Black	4.00	8.00
11 Bob Borkowski	3.00	6.00
12 Rocky Bridges	3.00	6.00
13 Smoky Burgess	3.00	6.00
14 Jackie Collum Portrait	3.00	6.00
15 Jackie Collum Pitching	3.00	6.00
16 Powell Crosley Jr. PRES	3.00	6.00
17 Jimmy Dykes MG	4.00	8.00
18 Nico Escalera	3.00	6.00
19 Tom Ferrick	3.00	6.00
20 Art Fowler Portrait	3.00	6.00
21 Art Fowler Pitching	3.00	6.00
22 Herschel Freeman	3.00	6.00
23 Jim Greengrass	3.00	6.00
24 Don Gross	3.00	6.00
25 Charley Harmon	3.00	6.00
26 Ray Jablonski	3.00	6.00
27 Howie Judson	3.00	6.00
28 Johnny Klippstein	3.00	6.00
29 Ted Kluszewski Neck Shows, looking right	10.00	20.00
30 Ted Kluszewski No-Beck, leaning right	10.00	20.00
31 Ted Kluszewski Standing, holding 4 bats	10.00	20.00
32 Ted Kluszewski Ready to hit; cut-out sleeves	10.00	20.00
33 Ted Kluszewski Uniform number visible	10.00	20.00
34 Ted Kluszewski Stretching at 1st	10.00	20.00
35 Ted Kluszewski Ready to hit; hands at belt	10.00	20.00
36 Ted Kluszewski Batting follow-through, lookin up	10.00	20.00
37 Ted Kluszewski Batting follow-through; stands vis	10.00	20.00
38 Hobie Landrith	3.00	6.00
39 Bill McKechnie Jr.	3.00	6.00
40 Roy McMillan Portrait	4.00	8.00
41 Roy McMillan Batting	4.00	8.00
42 Lloyd Merriman	3.00	6.00
43 Rudy Minarcin Neck shows	3.00	6.00
44 Rudy Minarcin No-Neck	3.00	6.00
45 Joe Nuxhall Portrait	4.00	8.00
46 Joe Nuxhall Pitching	4.00	8.00
47 Stan Palys	3.00	6.00
48 Bud Podbielan No Belt	3.00	6.00
49 Bud Podbielan Belt	3.00	6.00
50 Wally Post Ready to hit; only to hips	4.00	8.00
51 Wally Post Ready to hit; belt shows	4.00	8.00
52 Wally Post Follow-through; one pole	4.00	8.00
53 Wally Post Follow-through; two posts	4.00	8.00
54 Wally Post Portrait	4.00	8.00
56 Ken Raffensberger	3.00	6.00
57 Steve Ridzik	3.00	6.00
58 Connie Ryan	3.00	6.00
59 Andy Seminick	3.00	6.00
60 Al Silvera	3.00	6.00
61 Frank Smith	3.00	6.00
62 Milt Smith	3.00	6.00
63 Gerry Staley	3.00	6.00
64 Birdie Tebbetts Neck	3.00	6.00
65 Birdie Tebbetts No-Neck	3.00	6.00
66 Johnny Temple Mouth closed	3.00	6.00
67 Johnny Temple Mouth open	3.00	6.00
68 Corky Valentine	3.00	6.00
69 George Zuverink	3.00	6.00
70 Crosley Field	3.00	6.00

1956-65 Reds Burger Beer

This 23-card set features 8 1/2" by 11" black-and-white photos of various Cincinnati Reds from 1956 through 1965. Most of the backs are blank, but the 1959 photos have a Burger Beer ad on them. The cards are unnumbered and checklisted below in alphabetical order.

Card	Low	High
COMPLETE SET	250.00	500.00
COMMON BURGER BEER AD	15.00	40.00
1 Ed Bailey 60-61	6.00	12.00
2 Mel Bailey 57-58	7.50	15.00
3 Gus Bell 59-61	7.50	15.00
4 Smoky Burgess 56	12.50	25.00
5 Gordon Coleman 60-65	6.00	12.00
6 John Edwards 61-65	6.00	12.00
7 Gene Freese 61-63	6.00	12.00
8 Waite Hoyt ANN 60-65 Black Suit	7.50	15.00
9 Waite Hoyt ANN 60-65 Checkered Suit	7.50	15.00
10 Fred Hutchinson 1960-65	6.00	12.00
11 Joey Jay 60-65	6.00	12.00
12 Hal Jeffcoat 57-58	7.50	15.00
13 Eddie Kasko 60-63	6.00	12.00
14 Gene Kelly ANN 60-65	6.00	12.00
15 Jerry Lynch 59	7.50	15.00
16 Jim Maloney 60-65	6.00	12.00
17 Ray McMillan 56-58	10.00	20.00
18 Joe Nuxhall 60, 62-65	6.00	12.00
19 Jim O'Toole 60-65 Winding Up	6.00	12.00
20 Jim O'Toole 60-65 Follow Through	6.00	12.00
21 Vada Pinson 60-65 Hands on Knee	12.50	25.00
22 Vada Pinson 60-65 Catching Fly Ball	12.50	25.00
23 Vada Pinson 60-65 Batting	12.50	25.00
24 Wally Post 56	10.00	20.00
25 Bob Purkey 59-64 Portrait	7.50	15.00
26 Bob Purkey 59-64 Pitching	7.50	15.00
27 Frank Robinson 59-65 Portrait	25.00	50.00
28 Frank Robinson 59-65 Fielding	25.00	50.00
29 Pete Rose 63-65	30.00	60.00
30 Johnny Temple 58-59	6.00	12.00
31 Frank Thomas 58-59	7.50	15.00

1957 Reds Sohio

The 1957 Sohio Cincinnati Reds set consists of 18 perforated photos, approximately 5" by 7", in black and white with facsimile autographs on the front which were designed to be pasted into a special photo album issued by SOHIO (Standard Oil of Ohio). The set features an early Frank Robinson card. These unnumbered cards are listed below in alphabetical order for convenience.

Card	Low	High
COMPLETE SET (18)	125.00	250.00
1 Ed Bailey	4.00	10.00
2 Gus Bell	5.00	12.00
3 Rocky Bridges	4.00	10.00
4 Smoky Burgess	5.00	12.00
5 Hersh Freeman	4.00	10.00
6 Alex Grammas	4.00	10.00
7 Don Gross	4.00	10.00
8 Warren Hacker	4.00	10.00
9 Don Hoak	5.00	12.00
10 Hal Jeffcoat	4.00	10.00
11 Johnny Klippstein	4.00	10.00
12 Ted Kluszewski	20.00	40.00
13 Brooks Lawrence	4.00	10.00
14 Roy McMillan	4.00	10.00
15 Joe Nuxhall	5.00	12.00
16 Wally Post	5.00	12.00
17 Frank Robinson	40.00	80.00
18 John Temple	5.00	12.00

1957 Reds Team Issue

These 8" by 10" photos feature members of the 1957 Cincinnati Reds. The fronts have the players photo along with their name on the bottom. The backs are blank so we have sequenced these photos in alphabetical order. Some of these photos are also know with the Cincinnati Baseball Club stamp on the back.

Card	Low	High
COMPLETE SET	40.00	80.00
1 Tom Acker	2.00	4.00
2 Gus Bell	2.00	4.00
3 George Crowe	2.00	4.00
4 Jimmy Dykes CO	2.50	5.00
5 Tom Ferrick	2.00	4.00
6 Art Fowler	2.00	4.00
7 Hersh Freeman	2.00	4.00
8 Alex Grammas	2.00	4.00
9 Don Gross	2.00	4.00
10 Bobby Henrich	2.00	4.00
11 Don Hoak	2.00	4.00
12 Johnny Klippstein	2.00	4.00
13 Brooks Lawrence	2.00	4.00
14 Frank McCormick CO	2.00	4.00
15 Roy McMillan	2.00	4.00
16 Joe Nuxhall	2.50	5.00
17 Gabe Paul GM	2.00	4.00
18 Frank Robinson	7.50	15.00
19 Raul Sanchez	2.00	4.00
20 Birdie Tebbetts MG	2.00	4.00
21 Pete Whisenant	2.00	4.00

1958 Reds Enquirer

This set consists of Lou Smith's Redleg Scrapbook newspaper clippings from the Cincinnati Enquirer and features black-and-white photos of the members of the 1958 Cincinnati Reds team with information about the players. The clippings were designed to be placed in an album. They are unnumbered and checklisted below in alphabetical order.

Card	Low	High
COMPLETE SET (44)	40.00	80.00
1 Tom Acker	.75	1.50
2 Chico Alvarez	.75	1.50
3 Ed Bailey	.75	1.50
4 Gus Bell	.75	1.50
5 Steve Bilko	.75	1.50
6 Smoky Burgess	1.00	2.00
7 Jerry Cade	.75	1.50
8 George Crowe	1.00	2.00
9 Dutch Dotterer	.75	1.50
10 Jimmy Dykes CO	1.25	2.50
11 Tom Ferrick CO	.75	1.50
12 Dee Fondy	.75	1.50
13 Hersh Freeman	.75	1.50
14 Buddy Gilbert	.75	1.50
15 Harvey Haddix	1.25	2.50
16 Bob Henrich	.75	1.50
17 Don Hoak	1.00	2.00
18 Ken Hommel	.75	1.50
19 Jay Hook	.75	1.50
20 Hal Jeffcoat	.75	1.50
21 Bob Kelly	.75	1.50
22 John Klippstein	.75	1.50
23 Marty Kutyna	.75	1.50
24 Brooks Lawrence	1.00	2.00
25 Jerry Lynch	.75	1.50
26 Roy McMillan	.75	1.50
27 Joe Nuxhall	1.50	3.00
28 Jim O'Toole	.75	1.50
29 Stan Palys	.75	1.50
30 Bob Purkey	.75	1.50
31 Charley Rabe	.75	1.50
32 Johnny Riddle CO	.75	1.50
33 Frank Robinson	5.00	10.00
34 Haven Schmidt	.75	1.50
35 Willard Schmidt	.75	1.50
36 Dave Skaugstad	.75	1.50
37 John Smith	.75	1.50
38 Birdie Tebbetts MG	.75	1.50
39 John Temple	.75	1.50
40 Bob Thurman	.75	1.50
41 Pete Whisenant	.75	1.50
42 Ted Wieand	.75	1.50
43 Bill Wight	.75	1.50
44 Album	7.50	15.00

1958 Reds Jay Publishing

This 12-card set of the Cincinnati Reds measures approximately 5" by 7" and features black-and-white player photos in a white border. These cards were packaged 12 to a packet. The backs are blank. The cards are unnumbered and checklisted below in alphabetical order.

Card	Low	High
COMPLETE SET (12)	20.00	40.00
1 Ed Bailey	1.50	3.00
2 Gus Bell	1.50	3.00
3 Steve Bilko	1.50	3.00
4 Smoky Burgess	2.00	4.00
5 George Crowe	2.00	4.00

6 Harvey Haddix	2.00	4.00
7 Don Hoak	1.50	3.00
8 Hal Jeffcoat	1.50	3.00
9 Roy McMillan	2.50	5.00
10 Bob Purkey	1.50	3.00
11 Frank Robinson	5.00	10.00
12 Birdie Tebbetts MG	2.00	4.00

1959 Reds Enquirer

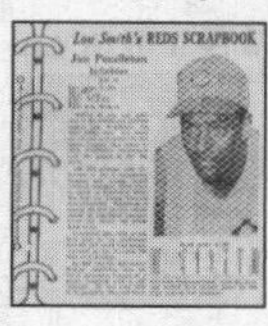

This set consists of Lou Smith's Reds Scrapbook newspaper clippings from the Cincinnati Enquirer and features black-and-white photos of the members of the 1959 Cincinnati Reds team with information about the players. The clippings are unnumbered and checklisted below in alphabetical order.

COMPLETE SET (28)	40.00	80.00
1 Tom Acker	2.00	5.00
2 Ed Bailey	2.00	5.00
3 Chuck Coles	2.00	5.00
4 Dutch Dotterer	2.00	5.00
5 Walt Dropo	2.00	5.00
6 Del Ennis	2.50	6.00
7 Jim Fridley	2.00	5.00
8 Buddy Gilbert	2.00	5.00
9 Jesse Gonder	2.00	5.00
10 Bob Henrich	2.00	5.00
11 Hal Jeffcoat	2.00	5.00
12 Brooks Lawrence	2.00	5.00
13 Bobbie Mabe	2.00	5.00
14 Roy McMillan	2.00	5.00
15 Don Newcombe	4.00	10.00
16 Joe Nuxhall	3.00	8.00
17 Claude Osteen	3.00	8.00
18 Don Pavletich	2.00	5.00
19 Orlando Pena	2.00	5.00
20 Jim Pendleton	2.00	5.00
21 John Powers	2.00	5.00
22 Charley Rabe	2.00	5.00
23 Willard Schmidt	2.00	5.00
24 Mayo Smith MG	2.50	6.00
25 Johnny Temple	2.00	5.00
26 Frank Thomas	3.00	8.00
27 Bob Thurman	2.00	5.00
28 Ted Wieand	2.00	5.00

1959 Reds Jay Publishing

This 12-card set of the Cincinnati Reds measures approximately 5" by 7" and features black-and-white player photos in a white border. These cards were packaged 12 to a packet. The backs are blank. The cards are unnumbered and checklisted below in alphabetical order.

COMPLETE SET	15.00	40.00
1 Ed Bailey	1.50	3.00
2 Gus Bell	1.50	3.00
3 Brooks Lawrence	1.50	3.00
4 Jerry Lynch	1.50	3.00
5 Roy McMillan	2.00	4.00
6 Don Newcombe	2.00	4.00
7 Joe Nuxhall	2.00	4.00
8 Vada Pinson	3.00	6.00
9 Bob Purkey	1.50	3.00
10 Johnny Temple	1.50	3.00
11 Frank Robinson	6.00	12.00
12 Frank Thomas	1.50	3.00

1960 Reds Jay Publishing

This 12-card set of the Cincinnati Reds measures approximately 5" by 7". The fronts feature black-and-white posed player photos with the player's and team name printed below in the white border. These cards were packaged 12 in a packet and originally sold for 25 cents. The backs are blank. The cards are unnumbered and checklisted below in alphabetical order.

COMPLETE SET (12)	15.00	40.00
1 Gus Bell	1.25	3.00
2 Dutch Dotterer	.75	2.00
3 Jay Hook	.75	2.00
4 Fred Hutchinson MG	1.25	3.00
5 Roy McMillan	1.25	3.00
6 Don Newcombe	1.50	4.00
7 Joe Nuxhall	1.25	3.00
8 Jim O'Toole	.75	2.00
9 Orlanda Pena	.75	2.00
10 Vada Pinson	1.50	4.00
11 Bob Purkey	.75	2.00
12 Frank Robinson	5.00	12.00

1961 Reds Jay Publishing

This 12-card set of the Cincinnati Reds measures approximately 5" by 7". The fronts feature black-and-white posed player photos with the player's and team name printed below in the white border. These cards were packaged 12 in a packet. The backs are blank. The cards are unnumbered and checklisted below in alphabetical order.

COMPLETE SET (12)	6.00	15.00
1 Ed Bailey	.75	2.00
2 Jim Baumer	.75	2.00
3 Gus Bell	1.25	3.00
4 Gordon Coleman	.75	2.00
5 Fred Hutchinson MG	1.25	3.00
6 Joey Jay	1.00	2.50
7 Willie Jones	.75	2.00
8 Eddie Kasko	.75	2.00
9 Jerry Lynch	.75	2.00
10 Claude Osteen	1.00	2.50
11 Vada Pinson	1.50	4.00
12 Frank Robinson	5.00	12.00

1961 Reds Postcards

These postcards feature members of the NL Champion Cincinnati Reds. Many of these cards have stamped blue signatures which appear to be the only year this approach was used. Since these cards are unnumbered, we have sequenced them in alphabetical order.

COMPLETE SET	75.00	150.00
1 Gus Bell	2.00	5.00
2 Don Blasingame	2.00	5.00
3 Marshall Bridges	2.00	5.00
4 Jim Brosnan	2.00	5.00
5 Leo Cardenas	2.00	5.00
6 Elio Chacon	2.00	5.00
7 Gordy Coleman	2.00	5.00
8 Otis Douglas	2.00	5.00
9 John Edwards	2.00	5.00
10 Gene Freese	2.00	5.00
11 Dick Gernert	2.00	5.00
12 Bill Henry	2.00	5.00
13 Ken Hunt	2.00	5.00
14 Fred Hutchinson MG Black Background	2.00	5.00
15 Fred Hutchinson MG Smiling	2.00	5.00
16 Joey Jay	2.00	5.00
17 Ken Johnson	2.00	5.00
18 Sherman Jones	2.00	5.00
19 Eddie Kasko	2.00	5.00
20 Jerry Lynch Dark Background	2.00	5.00
21 Jerry Lynch number 4 on back	2.00	5.00
22 Jim Maloney	3.00	8.00
23 Howie Nunn	2.00	5.00
24 Reggie Otero	2.00	5.00
25 Jim O'Toole	2.00	5.00
26 Vada Pinson	4.00	10.00
27 Wally Post	2.00	5.00
28 Bob Purkey	2.00	5.00
29 Frank Robinson	6.00	15.00
30 Dick Sisler	2.00	5.00
31 Bob Schmidt	2.00	5.00
32 Jim Turner CO	2.00	5.00
33 Pete Whisenant	2.00	5.00
34 Jerry Zimmerman	2.00	5.00

1962 Reds Enquirer

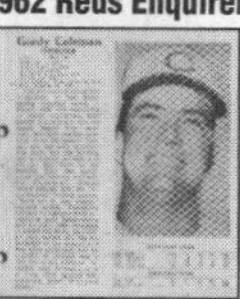

This set consists of newspaper clippings from the Cincinnati Enquirer and features black-and-white photos of the members of the 1962 Cincinnati Reds team with information about the players. They are unnumbered and checklisted below in alphabetical order.

COMPLETE SET (32)	50.00	100.00
1 Don Blasingame	1.25	3.00
2 Jim Brosnan	1.25	3.00
3 Leo Cardenas	1.50	4.00
4 Gordy Coleman	1.25	3.00
5 Cliff Cook	1.25	3.00
6 Myron Drabowsky	1.25	3.00
7 John Edwards	1.25	3.00
8 Gene Freese	1.25	3.00
9 Joe Gaines	1.25	3.00
10 Jesse Gonder	1.25	3.00
11 Tom Harper	1.50	4.00
12 Bill Henry	1.25	3.00
13 Dave Hillman	1.25	3.00
14 Ken Hunt	1.25	3.00
15 Fred Hutchinson MG	1.50	4.00
16 Joey Jay	1.25	3.00
17 Darrell Johnson	1.25	3.00
18 Eddie Kasko	1.25	3.00
19 Marty Keough	1.25	3.00
20 John Klippstein	1.25	3.00
21 Jerry Lynch	1.25	3.00
22 Jim Maloney	1.50	4.00
23 Bob Miller	1.25	3.00
24 Jim O'Toole	1.25	3.00
25 Don Pavletich	1.25	3.00
26 Vada Pinson	2.00	5.00
27 Wally Post	1.50	4.00
28 Bob Purkey	1.25	3.00
29 Frank Robinson	6.00	15.00
30 Octavio Rojas	2.00	5.00
31 Hiraldo Ruiz	1.25	3.00
32 Dave Sisler	1.25	3.00

1962 Reds Jay Publishing

This 12-card set features members of the Cincinnati Reds. Originally, this set came in a brown envelope that included a "picture pak order form". Printed on thin stock paper, the cards measure approximately 5" by 7". On a white background the fronts have a black-and-white posed player photo. The player's name and team appear in black letters under the photo. The backs are blank. The cards are unnumbered and checklisted below in alphabetical order.

COMPLETE SET (12)	15.00	40.00
1 Jim Brosnan	.75	2.00
2 Leo Cardenas	1.00	2.50
3 Gordon Coleman	.75	2.00
4 Jess Gonder	.75	2.00
5 Fred Hutchinson MG	1.25	3.00
6 Joey Jay	1.25	3.00
7 Eddie Kasko	.75	2.00
8 Jerry Lynch	.75	2.00
9 Jim O'Toole	1.00	2.50
10 Vada Pinson	1.50	4.00
11 Wally Post	1.25	3.00
12 Frank Robinson	5.00	12.00

1962 Reds Postcards

These cards feature members of the 1962 Cincinnati Reds. For the first time, the stamped autographs are no longer on the card. Since these cards are unnumbered, we have sequenced them in alphabetical order.

COMPLETE SET	75.00	150.00
1 Don Blasingame	2.00	5.00
2 Jim Brosnan	2.00	5.00
3 Leo Cardenas	2.00	5.00
4 Gordy Coleman	2.00	5.00
5 Otis Douglas	2.00	5.00
6 Moe Drabowsky	2.00	5.00
7 John Edwards	2.00	5.00
8 Sammy Ellis	2.00	5.00
9 Hank Foiles	2.00	5.00
10 Gene Freese	2.00	5.00
11 Joe Gaines	2.00	5.00
12 Bill Henry	2.00	5.00
13 Fred Hutchinson MG	2.00	5.00
14 Joey Jay	2.00	5.00
15 Eddie Kasko	2.00	5.00
16 Marty Keough	2.00	5.00
17 Johnny Klippstein	2.00	5.00
18 Jerry Lynch	2.00	5.00
19 Howie Nunn	2.00	5.00
20 Reggie Otero CO	2.00	5.00
21 Jim O'Toole	2.00	5.00
22 Don Pavletich	2.00	5.00
23 Vada Pinson	4.00	10.00
24 Bob Purkey	2.00	5.00
25 Dr. Richard Rohde	2.00	5.00
26 Cookie Rojas	2.50	6.00
27 Ray Shore	2.00	5.00
28 Dave Sisler	2.00	5.00
29 Dick Sisler	2.00	5.00
30 Jim Turner CO	2.00	5.00
31 Pete Whisenant	2.00	5.00
32 Ted Wills	2.00	5.00
33 Don Zimmer	3.00	8.00

1963 Reds Enquirer

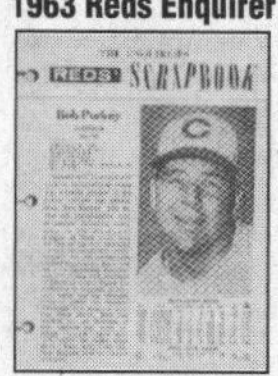

This set consists of newspaper clippings from the Reds' Scrapbook found in the Cincinnati Enquirer and features black-and-white photos of the members of the 1963 Cincinnati Reds team with information about the players. They are unnumbered and checklisted below in alphabetical order. Pete Rose appears in his rookie year.

COMPLETE SET (33)	100.00	200.00
1 Don Blasingame	1.25	3.00
2 Harry Bright	1.25	3.00
3 Jim Brosnan	1.25	3.00
4 Leo Cardenas	1.50	4.00
5 Gordy Coleman	1.25	3.00
6 John Edwards	1.25	3.00
7 Sam Ellis	1.25	3.00
8 Hank Foiles	1.25	3.00
9 Gene Freese	1.25	3.00
10 Jesse Gonder	1.25	3.00
11 Tom Harper	1.50	4.00
12 Bill Henry	1.25	3.00
13 Ken Hunt	1.25	3.00
14 Fred Hutchinson MG	2.00	5.00
15 Joey Jay	1.25	3.00
16 Eddie Kasko	1.25	3.00
17 Marty Keough	1.25	3.00
18 John Klippstein	1.25	3.00
19 Jerry Lynch	1.25	3.00
20 Jim Maloney	2.00	5.00
21 Joe Nuxall	2.00	5.00
22 Jim O'Toole	1.25	3.00
23 Jim Owens	1.25	3.00
24 Don Pavletich	1.25	3.00
25 Vada Pinson	2.50	6.00
26 Wally Post	1.50	4.00
27 Bob Purkey	1.25	3.00
28 Frank Robinson	8.00	20.00
29 Dave Sisler	1.25	3.00
30 John Tsitouris	1.25	3.00
31 Ken Walters	1.25	3.00
32 Pete Rose	20.00	50.00
33 Al Worthington	1.25	3.00

1963 Reds French Bauer Caps

These are a 32 "card" set of (cardboard) milk bottle caps featuring personnel of the Cincinnati Reds. These unattractive cardboard caps are blank-backed and unnumbered; they are numbered below for convenience in alphabetical order. The caps are approximately 1 1/4" in diameter. Blasingame was traded to the Senators early in the '63 season and Spencer was picked up from the Dodgers early in the '63 season; hence their caps are tougher to find than the others. Ken Walters and Don Pavletich also seem to be harder to find. We are listing those caps as SP's. Pete Rose has a cap in his rookie year.

COMPLETE SET (32)	250.00	500.00
COMMON PLAYER CAP	2.50	6.00
COMMON SP	6.00	15.00
1 Don Blasingame SP	6.00	15.00
2 Leo Cardenas	3.00	8.00
3 Gordon Coleman	2.50	6.00
4 Wm. O. DeWitt OWN	2.50	6.00
5 John Edwards	2.50	6.00
6 Jesse Gonder	2.50	6.00
7 Tommy Harper	3.00	8.00
8 Bill Henry	2.50	6.00
9 Fred Hutchinson MG	4.00	10.00
10 Joey Jay	3.00	8.00
11 Eddie Kasko	2.50	6.00
12 Marty Keough	2.50	6.00
13 Jim Maloney	4.00	10.00
14 Joe Nuxhall	4.00	10.00
15 Reggie Otero CO	2.50	6.00
16 Jim O'Toole	3.00	8.00
17 Jim Owens	2.50	6.00
18 Don Pavletich SP	6.00	15.00
19 Vada Pinson	5.00	12.00
20 Bob Purkey	2.50	6.00
21 Dr. Richard Rohde	2.50	6.00
22 Frank Robinson	30.00	60.00
23 Pete Rose	100.00	200.00
24 Ray Shore CO	2.50	6.00
25 Dick Sisler CO	2.50	6.00
26 Bob Skinner	2.50	6.00
27 Daryl Spencer SP	12.50	30.00
28 John Tsitouris	2.50	6.00
29 Jim Turner CO	3.00	8.00
30 Ken Walters SP	6.00	15.00
31 Al Worthington	2.50	6.00
32 Dom Zanni	2.50	6.00

1963 Reds Jay Publishing

This 12-card set features members of the Cincinnati Reds. Printed on thin stock paper, the cards measure approximately 5" by 7". On a white background the fronts have a black-and-white posed player photo. The player's name and team appear in black letters under the photo. The backs are blank. The cards are unnumbered and checklisted below in alphabetical order.

COMPLETE SET (12)	12.50	30.00
1 Jim Brosnan	.75	2.00
2 Gordy Coleman	.75	2.00
3 Fred Hutchinson MG	1.25	3.00
4 Joey Jay	1.00	2.50
5 Eddie Kasko	.75	2.00
6 Marty Keough	.75	2.00
7 Jerry Lynch	.75	2.00
8 Jim O'Toole	1.00	2.50
9 Don Pavletich	.75	2.00
10 Vada Pinson	1.50	4.00
11 Bob Purkey	.75	2.00
12 Frank Robinson	5.00	12.00

1963 Reds Postcards

These cards feature members of the 1963 Cincinnati Reds. Since these cards are unnumbered, we have sequenced them in alphabetical order. A card of Pete Rose, issued during his rookie season, is included in this set.

COMPLETE SET	125.00	250.00
1 Jim Brosnan	2.00	5.00
2 Leo Cardenas Hitting	2.00	5.00
3 Leo Cardenas Fielding	2.00	5.00
4 Jim Coates	2.00	5.00
5 Gordy Coleman	2.00	5.00
6 John Edwards	2.00	5.00
7 Gene Freese Fielding	2.00	5.00
8 Gene Freese Hitting	2.00	5.00
9 Jesse Gonder	2.00	5.00
10 Gene Green	2.50	6.00
11 Tommy Harper	2.00	5.00
12 Bill Henry	2.00	5.00
13 Joey Jay	2.00	5.00
14 Eddie Kasko	2.00	5.00
15 Marty Keough	2.00	5.00
16 Jim Maloney	3.00	8.00
17 Charlie Neal	2.00	5.00
18 Jim O'Toole	2.00	5.00
19 Reggie Otero	2.00	5.00
20 Jim Owens	2.00	5.00
21 Don Pavletich	2.00	5.00
22 Vada Pinson	4.00	10.00
23 Bob Purkey	2.00	5.00
24 Frank Robinson Batting	6.00	15.00
25 Frank Robinson Portrait	6.00	15.00

26 Dr. Richard Rohde	2.00	5.00
27 Pete Rose	100.00	200.00
28 Ray Shore	2.00	5.00
29 Dick Sisler	2.00	5.00
30 Bob Skinner	2.00	5.00
31 Hal Smith	2.00	5.00
32 Daryl Spencer	2.00	5.00
33 Sammy Taylor	2.00	5.00
34 John Tsitouris	2.00	5.00
35 Ken Walters	2.00	5.00
36 Al Worthington	2.00	5.00
37 Don Zanni	2.00	5.00

1964 Reds Enquirer Scrapbook

These newspaper "clippings" measure about 5" by 7" when cut from the Cincinnati Enquirer Newspaper. Each time, a different member of the 1964 Reds was featured with some biographical information, his statistics as well as a brief biography. Since these are unnumbered, we have sequenced them in alphabetical order.

COMPLETE SET	40.00	80.00
1 Steve Boros	.75	2.00
2 Leo Cardenas	.75	2.00
3 Gordy Coleman	.75	2.00
4 Lincoln Curtis	.75	2.00
5 Jim Dickson	.75	2.00
6 John Edwards	.75	2.00
7 Sam Ellis	.75	2.00
8 Tommy Harper	.75	2.00
9 Bill Henry	.75	2.00
10 Fred Hutchinson MG	.75	2.00
11 Joey Jay	.75	2.00
12 Deron Johnson	.75	2.00
13 Marty Keough	.75	2.00
14 Jim Maloney	1.00	2.50
15 Billy McCool	.75	2.00
16 Charley Neal	.75	2.00
17 Chet Nichols	.75	2.00
18 Joe Nuxhall	1.25	3.00
19 Vada Pinson	1.50	4.00
20 Bob Purkey	.75	2.00
21 Mel Queen	.75	2.00
22 Frank Robinson	3.00	8.00
23 Pete Rose	10.00	25.00
24 Chico Ruiz	.75	2.00
25 Bob Skinner	.75	2.00
26 Hal Smith	.75	2.00
27 John Tsitouris	.75	2.00
28 Al Worthington	.75	2.00

1964 Reds Jay Publishing

This 12-card set of the Cincinnati Reds measures approximately 5" by 7". The fronts feature black-and-white posed player photos with the player's and team name printed below in the white border. These cards were packaged 12 in a packet. The backs are blank. The cards are unnumbered and checklisted below in alphabetical order.

COMPLETE SET (12)	30.00	60.00
1 Leo Cardenas	.75	2.00
2 Gordy Coleman	.75	2.00
3 Tommy Harper	1.00	2.50
4 Fred Hutchinson MG	.75	2.00
5 Joey Jay	1.00	2.50
6 Jim Maloney	1.25	3.00
7 Joe Nuxhall	1.25	3.00
8 Jim O'Toole	1.00	2.50
9 Vada Pinson	1.50	4.00
10 Bob Purkey	.75	2.00
11 Frank Robinson	5.00	12.00
12 Pete Rose	10.00	25.00

1964 Reds Postcards

This set features members of the 1964 Cincinnati Reds. These cards had no PC markings on the back. Since these cards were unnumbered, we have sequenced them in alphabetical order. A Pre-Rookie Card Tony Perez is in this set.

COMPLETE SET	125.00	250.00
1 Steve Boros	2.00	5.00
2 Leo Cardenas	2.00	5.00
3 Jim Coker Arms Crossed	2.00	5.00
4 Jim Coker Near the dugout	2.00	5.00
5 Gordy Coleman	2.00	5.00
6 Ryne Duren	2.00	5.00
7 John Edwards	2.00	5.00
8 Sam Ellis	2.00	5.00
9 Tommy Harper	2.00	5.00
10 Bill Henry	2.00	5.00
11 Fred Hutchinson MG	2.00	5.00
12 Joey Jay	2.00	5.00
13 Deron Johnson	2.00	5.00
14 Marty Keough	2.00	5.00
15 Bobby Klaus	2.00	5.00
16 Jim Maloney	2.50	6.00
17 Billy McCool	2.00	5.00
18 Tom Murphy TR	2.00	5.00
19 Joe Nuxhall	3.00	8.00
20 Reggie Otero CO	2.00	5.00
21 Jim O'Toole	2.00	5.00
22 Don Pavletich	2.00	5.00
23 Tony Perez	8.00	20.00
24 Vada Pinson	4.00	10.00
25 Bob Purkey	2.00	5.00
26 Mel Queen	2.00	5.00
27 Frank Robinson	6.00	15.00
28 Pete Rose	30.00	60.00
29 Chico Ruiz	2.00	5.00
30 Ray Shore	2.00	5.00
31 Dick Sisler CO	2.00	5.00
32 Johnny Temple	2.00	5.00
33 John Tsitouris	2.00	5.00
34 Jim Turner CO	2.00	5.00

1965 Reds Enquirer

This set consists of newspaper clippings from the Cincinnati Enquirer and features black-and-white photos of the members of the 1965 Cincinnati Reds team with information about the players. They are unnumbered and checklisted below in alphabetical order.

COMPLETE SET (29)	30.00	60.00
1 Gerry Arrigo	.60	1.50
2 Steve Boros	.60	1.50
3 Leo Cardenas	.60	1.50
4 Jim Coker	.60	1.50
5 Gordy Coleman	.60	1.50
6 Roger Craig	.75	2.00
7 Ryne Duren	.75	2.00
8 John Edwards	.60	1.50
9 Sammy Ellis	.60	1.50
10 Tommy Harper	.75	2.00
11 Tommy Helms	.75	2.00
12 Bill Henry	.60	1.50
13 Charley James	.60	1.50
14 Joey Jay	.60	1.50
15 Deron Johnson	.60	1.50
16 Marty Keough	.60	1.50
17 Jim Maloney	1.00	2.50
18 Bill McCool	.60	1.50
19 Joe Nuxhall	1.00	2.50
20 Jim O'Toole	.60	1.50
21 Don Pavletich	.60	1.50
22 Tony Perez	3.00	8.00
23 Vada Pinson	1.25	3.00
24 Frank Robinson	4.00	10.00
25 Pete Rose	8.00	20.00
26 Hiraldo S.(Chico) Ruiz	.60	1.50
27 Art Shamsky	.60	1.50
28 Dick Sisler MG	.60	1.50
29 John Tsitouris	.60	1.50

1965 Reds Jay Publishing

This 12-card set of the Cincinnati Reds measures approximately 5" by 7". The fronts feature black-and-white posed player photos with the player's and team name printed below in the white border. These cards were packaged 12 to a packet. The backs are blank. The cards are unnumbered and checklisted below in alphabetical order.

COMPLETE SET (12)	20.00	50.00
1 Gerry Arrigo	.75	2.00
2 Gordy Coleman	.75	2.00
3 Sammy Ellis	.75	2.00
4 Joey Jay	1.00	2.50
5 Marty Keough	.75	2.00
6 Jim Maloney	1.25	3.00
7 Jim O'Toole	1.00	2.50
8 Vada Pinson	1.50	4.00
9 Mel Queen	.75	2.00
10 Frank Robinson	5.00	12.00
11 Pete Rose	10.00	25.00
12 Dick Sisler MG	.75	2.00

1965 Reds Postcards

Issued by the team, these postcards feature members of the 1965 Cincinnati Reds. Since these are unnumbered, we have sequenced them in alphabetical order. A Tony Perez card is in this series, which is also his Rookie Card year.

COMPLETE SET	100.00	200.00
1 Gerry Arrigo	2.00	5.00
2 Leo Cardenas	2.00	5.00
3 Jimmy Coker	2.00	5.00
4 Gordy Coleman	2.00	5.00
5 Roger Craig	2.00	5.00
6 Jim Duffalo	2.00	5.00
7 Johnny Edwards	2.00	5.00
8 Sammy Ellis	2.00	5.00
9 Tommy Harper	2.50	6.00
10 Charlie James	2.00	5.00
11 Joey Jay	2.00	5.00
12 Deron Johnson	2.00	5.00
13 Marty Keough	2.00	5.00
14 Jim Maloney	2.50	6.00
15 Billy McCool	2.00	5.00
16 Joe Nuxhall	3.00	8.00
17 Frank Oceak	2.00	5.00
18 Reggie Otero CO	2.00	5.00
19 Jim O'Toole	2.00	5.00
20 Don Pavletich	2.00	5.00
21 Tony Perez	40.00	80.00
22 Vada Pinson	4.00	10.00
23 Frank Robinson	8.00	20.00
24 Pete Rose	50.00	100.00
25 Chico Ruiz	2.00	5.00
26 Art Shamsky	2.00	5.00
27 Ray Shore	2.00	5.00
28 Dick Sisler MG	2.00	5.00
29 John Tsitouris	2.00	5.00
30 Jim Turner CO Portrait to Belt	2.00	5.00
31 Jim Turner CO Portrait shows entire right shoulde	2.00	5.00

1966 Reds Postcards

These 33 postcards were issued by the Cincinnati Reds and featured members of the 1966 Reds. Since they are unnumbered, we have sequenced them in alphabetical order. These cards can be identified as they were the last year the Reds printed cards on glossy stock.

COMPLETE SET	100.00	200.00
1 Jack Baldschun	2.00	5.00
2 Dave Bristol CO	2.00	5.00
3 Leo Cardenas	2.00	5.00
4 Jimmie Coker	2.00	5.00
5 Gordy Coleman	2.00	5.00
6 Ted Davidson	2.00	5.00
7 Johnny Edwards	2.00	5.00
8 Sammy Ellis	2.00	5.00
9 Bill Fischer	2.00	5.00
10 Mel Harder CO	2.00	5.00
11 Tommy Harper	2.50	6.00
12 Don Heffner MG	2.00	5.00
13 Tommy Helms	2.00	5.00
14 Joey Jay	2.00	5.00
15 Alex Johnson	2.00	5.00
16 Jim Maloney	2.50	6.00
17 Bill McCool	2.00	5.00
18 Don Nottebart	2.00	5.00
19 Joe Nuxhall	3.00	8.00
20 Darrell Osteen	2.00	5.00
21 Jim O'Toole	2.00	5.00
22 Milt Pappas	2.50	6.00
23 Don Pavletich	2.00	5.00
24 Tony Perez	6.00	15.00
25 Vada Pinson	4.00	10.00
26 Mel Queen	2.00	5.00
27 Pete Rose	15.00	40.00
28 Chico Ruiz	2.00	5.00
29 Art Shamsky	2.00	5.00
30 Ray Shore CO	2.00	5.00
31 Roy Sievers	2.50	6.00
32 Dick Simpson	2.00	5.00
33 Whitey Wietelmann	2.00	5.00

1966 Reds Team Issue

These 5" by 7" black and white glossy photos featured members of the 1966 Cincinnati Reds. Since they are unnumbered, we have sequenced them in alphabetical order. It is possible that there are more photos so any additions are greatly appreciated.

COMPLETE SET	40.00	80.00
1 Gerry Arrigo	1.50	4.00
2 Jack Baldschun	1.50	4.00
3 Leo Cardenas	1.50	4.00
4 Jim Coker	1.50	4.00
5 Gordy Coleman	1.50	4.00
6 Ted Davidson	1.50	4.00
7 Johnny Edwards	1.50	4.00
8 Sammy Ellis	1.50	4.00
9 Tommy Helms	1.50	4.00
10 Deron Johnson	1.50	4.00
11 Jim Maloney	2.00	5.00
12 Billy McCool	1.50	4.00
13 Don Nottebart	1.50	4.00
14 Milt Pappas	2.00	5.00
15 Vada Pinson	3.00	8.00
16 Pete Rose	8.00	20.00

1967 Reds Postcards

These 38 blank-backed black and white postcards measure 3 1/2" by 5 1/2" and feature members of the 1967 Reds. The fronts have a player photo, a blue fascimile autograph as well as the Cincinnati Reds in red lettering. Since the photos are unnumbered, we have sequenced them in alphabetical order. Darrell Osteen, who was pictured in the special folder made available to put these photos in, was not published as a postcard. A Johnny Bench postcard is known in this series which predates his Rookie Card.

COMPLETE SET (38)	75.00	150.00
1 Ted Abernathy	1.50	4.00
2 Gerry Arrigo	1.50	4.00
3 Jack Baldschun	1.50	4.00
4 Johnny Bench	12.50	30.00
5 Vern Benson CO	1.50	4.00
6 Jimmy Bragan CO	1.50	4.00
7 Dave Bristol MG	1.50	4.00
8 Leo Cardenas	1.50	4.00
9 Jim Coker	1.50	4.00
10 Ted Davidson	1.50	4.00
11 John Edwards	1.50	4.00
12 Sammy Ellis	1.50	4.00
13 Ray Evans CP	1.50	4.00
14 Mel Harder CO	2.00	5.00
15 Tommy Harper	1.50	4.00
16 Tommy Helms	1.50	4.00
17 Deron Johnson	1.50	4.00
18 Bob Lee	1.50	4.00
19 Jim Maloney	2.00	5.00
20 Lee May	2.00	5.00
21 Bill McCool	1.50	4.00
22 Tom Murphy CP	1.50	4.00
23 Gary Nolan	1.50	4.00
24 Don Nottebart	1.50	4.00
25 Don Pavletich	1.50	4.00
26 Milt Pappas	2.00	5.00
27 Tony Perez	4.00	10.00
28 Vada Pinson	3.00	8.00
29 Mel Queen	1.50	4.00
30 Floyd Robinson	1.50	4.00
31 Pete Rose	50.00	100.00
32 Chico Ruiz	1.50	4.00
33 Art Shamsky	1.50	4.00
34 Ray Shore CO	1.50	4.00
35 Dick Simpson	1.50	4.00
36 Jake Wood	1.50	4.00
37 Whitey Wietelmann CO	1.50	4.00
38 Al Wylder CP	1.50	4.00

1968 Reds Postcards

These 30 blank-backed black and white postcards features members of the 1968 Reds. The fronts have a player photo, a blue fascimile signature and "Cincinnati Reds" in red lettering. Since the cards are unnumbered, we have sequenced them in alphabetical order. John Bench is featured during his rookie season.

COMPLETE SET (30)	75.00	150.00
1 Ted Abernathy	1.50	4.00
2 Gerry Arrigo	1.50	4.00
3 Johnny Bench	40.00	80.00
4 Vern Benson CO	1.50	4.00
5 Jimmy Bragan CO	1.50	4.00
6 Dave Bristol MG	1.50	4.00
7 Leo Cardenas	1.50	4.00
8 Clay Carroll	1.50	4.00
9 Tony Cloninger	1.50	4.00
10 George Culver	1.50	4.00
11 Tommy Helms	1.50	4.00
12 Alex Johnson	1.50	4.00
13 Mack Jones	1.50	4.00
14 Bill Kelso	1.50	4.00
15 Bob Lee	1.50	4.00
16 Jim Maloney	2.00	5.00
17 Lee May	2.00	5.00
18 Bill McCool	1.50	4.00
19 Gary Nolan	1.50	4.00
20 Don Pavletich	1.50	4.00
21 Tony Perez	4.00	10.00
22 Vada Pinson	3.00	8.00
23 Mel Queen	1.50	4.00
24 Jay Ritchie	1.50	4.00
25 Pete Rose	8.00	20.00
26 Chico Ruiz	1.50	4.00
27 Jim Schaffer	1.50	4.00
28 Hal Smith CO	1.50	4.00
29 Fred Whitfield	1.50	4.00
30 Woody Woodward	1.50	4.00

1969 Reds Postcards

These 28 blank-backed black and white postcards feature members of the 1969 Cincinnati Reds. These postcards have a player photo, a black fascimile autograph and "Cincinnati Reds" in red lettering. Since these are unnumbered, we have sequenced them in alphabetical order.

COMPLETE SET (28)	50.00	100.00
1 Gerry Arrigo	1.25	3.00
2 Johnny Bench	6.00	15.00
3 Jim Beauchamp	1.25	3.00
4 Vern Benson CO	1.25	3.00
5 Jimmy Bragan CO	1.25	3.00
6 Dave Bristol MG	1.25	3.00
7 Clay Carroll	1.25	3.00
8 Darrel Chaney	1.25	3.00
9 Tony Cloninger	1.25	3.00
10 Pat Corrales	1.25	3.00
11 George Culver	1.25	3.00
12 Jack Fisher	1.25	3.00
13 Wayne Granger	1.25	3.00
14 Harvey Haddix CO	1.25	3.00
15 Tommy Helms	1.25	3.00
16 Alex Johnson	1.25	3.00
17 Jim Maloney	1.25	3.00
18 Lee May	1.50	4.00
19 Jim Merritt	1.25	3.00
20 Tony Perez	3.00	8.00
21 Pete Rose	6.00	15.00
22 Chico Ruiz	1.25	3.00
23 Ted Savage	1.25	3.00
24 Hal Smith CO	1.25	3.00
25 Jim Stewart	1.25	3.00
26 Bob Tolan	1.25	3.00
27 Fred Whitfield	1.25	3.00
28 Woody Woodward	1.25	3.00

1970 Reds Team Issue

These two 5" by 7" blank-backed cards feature members of the Cincinnati Reds circa 1970. It is probable that there are many more cards in this set and grouping so all additional information is appreciated. These cards are unnumbered so we have put them in alphabetical order. Interestingly enough,

these are the same photos used in Partridge meats set around the same era.
COMPLETE SET 15.00 40.00
1 Johnny Bench 8.00 20.00
2 Pete Rose 8.00 20.00

1971 Reds Postcards

These 33 black and white blank-backed postcards feature members of the 1971 Cincinnati Reds. The fronts have a player photo, a black fascimile autograph and "Cincinnati Reds" in black lettering. Since these cards are unnumbered, we have sequenced them in alphabetical order.

COMPLETE SET 40.00 80.00
1 Sparky Anderson MG 2.00 5.00
2 Johnny Bench 4.00 10.00
3 Buddy Bradford .75 2.00
4 Bernie Carbo .75 2.00
5 Clay Carroll .75 2.00
6 Ty Cline .75 2.00
7 Tony Cloninger .75 2.00
8 Dave Concepcion 2.00 5.00
9 Pat Corrales .75 2.00
10 Al Ferrara .75 2.00
11 George Foster 2.50 6.00
12 Joe Gibbon .75 2.00
13 Alex Grammas CO .75 2.00
14 Wayne Granger .75 2.00
15 Ross Grimsley .75 2.00
16 Don Gullett 1.25 3.00
17 Tommy Helms .75 2.00
18 Ted Kluszewski 2.00 5.00
19 Lee May 1.25 3.00
20 Jim McGlothlin .75 2.00
21 Hal McRae .75 2.00
22 Jim Merritt .75 2.00
23 Gary Nolan .75 2.00
24 Tony Perez 2.50 6.00
25 Pete Rose 6.00 15.00
26 George Scherger CO .75 2.00
27 Larry Shepard .75 2.00
28 Willie Smith .75 2.00
29 Wayne Simpson .75 2.00
30 Jim Stewart .75 2.00
31 Bobby Tolan .75 2.00
32 Milt Wilcox .75 2.00
33 Woody Woodward .75 2.00

1973 Reds Postcards

These blank-backed cards feature members of the 1973 Cincinnati Reds. Each of the cards have the player's fascimile autograph in a white box with a Cincinnati Reds logo below the signature. It is believed that many of these cards were also issued during the 1974 season. Since these cards are unnumbered, we have sequenced them in alphabetical order.

COMPLETE SET 30.00 60.00
1 Sparky Anderson MG 1.00 2.50
2 Dick Baney .40 1.00
3 Bob Barton .40 1.00
4 Johnny Bench 2.00 5.00
5 Jack Billingham .40 1.00
6 Jack Billingham .40 1.00
Photo credit given
7 Pedro Borbon .40 1.00
8 Clay Carroll .40 1.00
9 Darrel Chaney .40 1.00
10 Dave Concepcion 1.00 2.50
11 Ed Crosby .40 1.00
12 Dan Driessen .40 1.00
13 Phil Gagliano .40 1.00
14 Cesar Geronimo .40 1.00
15 Alex Grammas CO .40 1.00
16 Ken Griffey 1.00 2.50
17 Ross Grimsley .40 1.00
18 Don Gullett .60 1.50
19 Joe Hague .40 1.00
20 Tom Hall .40 1.00
21 Hal King .40 1.00
22 Ted Kluszewski CO 1.00 2.50
23 Andy Kosco .40 1.00
24 Gene Locklear .40 1.00
25 Jim McGlothlin .40 1.00
26 Denis Menke .40 1.00
27 Joe Morgan 1.50 4.00
28 Roger Nelson .40 1.00
29 Gary Nolan .40 1.00
30 Fred Norman .40 1.00
31 Tony Perez 1.25 3.00
32 Bill Plummer .40 1.00
33 Pete Rose 3.00 8.00
34 Richie Scheinblum .40 1.00
35 George Scherger CO .40 1.00
36 Larry Shepard CO .40 1.00
37 Ed Sprague .40 1.00
38 Larry Stahl .40 1.00
39 Bobby Tolan .40 1.00
40 Dave Tomlin .40 1.00

1974 Reds 1939-40 Bra-Mac

This 48 card set, which measured 3 1/2" by 5" featured members of the NL Champions Cincinnati Reds and were issued by Bra-Mac using their extensive photo library. The 1939-40 Reds won consecutive NL pennants during that period.

COMPLETE SET 10.00 25.00
1 John Vander Meer .60 1.50
2 Jimmie Wilson .30 .75
3 Wally Berger .30 .75
4 Bucky Walters .60 1.50
5 Vince DiMaggio .30 .75
6 Johnny Rizzo .20 .50
7 Ival Goodman .20 .50
8 Junior Thompson .20 .50
9 Jim Turner .20 .50
10 Milt Shoffner .20 .50
11 Whitey Moore .20 .50
12 Moe Arnovich .20 .50
13 Ernie Lombardi .75 2.00
14 Mike Dejan .20 .50
15 Dick West .20 .50
16 Johnny Ripple .20 .50
17 Joe Beggs .20 .50
18 Harry Craft .20 .50
19 Lew Riggs .20 .50
20 Mike McCormick .30 .75
21 Red Barrett .20 .50
22 Paul Derringer .40 1.00
23 Johnny Riddle .20 .50
24 Witt Guise .20 .50
25 Billy Werber .30 .75
26 Johnny Hutchings .20 .50
27 Billy Myers .20 .50
28 Williard Hershberger .30 .75
29 Lonnie Frey .20 .50
30 Frank McCormick .30 .75
31 Bill Baker .20 .50
32 Lee Gamble .20 .50
33 Eddie Joost .30 .75
34 Nino Bongiovani .20 .50
35 French Bordagaray .20 .50
36 Peaches Davis .20 .50
37 Johnny Niggeling .20 .50
38 Les Scarsella .20 .50
39 Lee Grissom .20 .50
40 Wes Livengood .20 .50
41 Milt Galatzer .20 .50
42 Pete Noktenis .20 .50
43 Jim Weaver .20 .50
44 Art Jacobs .20 .50
45 Nolen Richardson .20 .50
46 Al Simmons .75 2.00
47 Hank Johnson .20 .50
48 Bill McKechnie MG .60 1.50

1976 Reds Icee Lids

This unnumbered and blank-backed set of "lids" is complete at 12. Cards are listed below in alphabetical order. They are circular cards with the bottom squared off. The circle is approximately 2" in diameter. The fronts contain the MLB logo as well as the player's name, position and team. The player photo is in black and white with the cap logo removed. If a collector acquired all 12 of these discs, they were then eligible to win free tickets to a Cincinnati Reds game. These discs were on the bottom of 12 ounce Icee drinks.

COMPLETE SET 40.00 80.00
1 Johnny Bench 8.00 20.00
2 Dave Concepcion 2.00 5.00
3 Rawley Eastwick .50 1.25
4 George Foster 1.50 4.00
5 Cesar Geronimo .50 1.25
6 Ken Griffey 1.50 4.00
7 Don Gullett .50 1.25
8 Will McEnaney .50 1.25
9 Joe Morgan 5.00 12.00
10 Gary Nolan .50 1.25
11 Tony Perez 4.00 10.00
12 Pete Rose 15.00 40.00

1976 Reds Kroger

This 16-card set of the Cincinnati Reds measures approximately 5 7/8" by 9". The white-bordered fronts feature color player head photos with a facsimile autograph below. The backs are blank. The cards are unnumbered and checklisted below in alphabetical order. They were printed on thin glossy paper.

COMPLETE SET (19) 10.00 25.00
1 Ed Armbrister .40 1.00
2 Bob Bailey .40 1.00
3 Johnny Bench 2.00 5.00
4 Jack Billingham .40 1.00
5 Dave Concepcion .75 2.00
6 Dan Driessen .40 1.00
7 Rawly Eastwick .40 1.00
8 George Foster .75 2.00
9 Cesar Geronimo .40 1.00
10 Ken Griffey 1.00 2.50
11 Don Gullett .40 1.00
12 Joe Morgan 1.50 4.00
13 Gary Nolan .40 1.00
14 Fred Norman .40 1.00
15 Tony Perez 1.00 2.50
16 Pete Rose 3.00 8.00

1976 Reds Parker Classic

These 24 cartoons honor various people who have been involved with the Reds as either a player or manager. These cartoons were drawn by noted sports artist Bob Parker.

COMPLETE SET (24) 50.00 100.00
1 Sparky Anderson MG 5.00 12.00
2 Wally Berger 1.50 4.00
3 Pedro Borbon 1.50 4.00
4 Rube Bressler 1.50 4.00
5 Gordy Coleman 1.50 4.00
6 Dave Concepcion 3.00 8.00
7 Harry Craft 1.50 4.00
8 Hugh Critz 1.50 4.00
9 Dan Driessen 1.50 4.00
10 Pat Duncan 1.50 4.00
11 Lonnie Frey 1.50 4.00
12 Ival Goodman 1.50 4.00
13 Heinie Groh 1.50 4.00
14 Noodles Hahn 2.50 6.00
15 Mike Lum 1.50 4.00
16 Bill McKechnie 5.00 12.00
17 Pat Moran 1.50 4.00
18 Billy Myers 1.50 4.00
19 Gary Nolan 1.50 4.00
20 Fred Norman 1.50 4.00
21 Jim O'Toole 1.50 4.00
22 Vada Pinson 3.00 8.00
23 Bucky Walters 3.00 8.00
24 Checklist 1.50 4.00

1977 Reds Cartoons Parker

This 24-card set features drawings of famous Cincinnati Reds players by cartoonist and photographer, Bob Parker. The set displays player head drawings along with cartoon illustrated player facts and could be obtained by mail for $3.50.

COMPLETE SET (24) 60.00 120.00
1 Ted Kluszewski 6.00 15.00
2 Johnny Bench 15.00 40.00
3 Jim Maloney .75 2.00
4 Bub Hargrave .75 2.00
5 Don Gullett .75 2.00
6 Joe Nuxhall .75 2.00
7 Eddie Roush 1.50 4.00
8 Wally Post 4.00 10.00
9 George Wright 2.50 6.00
10 George Foster 1.25 3.00
11 Pete Rose 20.00 50.00
12 Red Lucas .75 2.00
13 Joe Morgan 6.00 15.00
14 Eppa Rixey 1.50 4.00
15 Bill Werber .75 2.00
16 Frank Robinson 6.00 15.00
17 Dolf Luque .75 2.00
18 Frank McCormick .75 2.00
18 Paul Derringer .75 2.00
20 Ken Griffey 1.25 3.00
21 Jack Billingham .75 2.00
22 Larry Kopf .75 2.00
23 Ernie Lombardi 1.50 4.00
24 John Vandermeer 1.25 3.00

1977 Reds 1939-40 TCMA

This 45-card set features black-and-white player photos of the 1939-40 Cincinnati Reds in red borders. The backs carry 1939 and 1940 player statistics.

COMPLETE SET (45) 8.00 20.00
1 Vince DiMaggio .40 1.00
2 Wally Berger .40 1.00
3 Nolen Richardson .20 .50
4 Ernie Lombardi .75 2.00
5 Ival Goodman .20 .50
6 Jim Turner .40 1.00
7 Bucky Walters .60 1.50
8 Jimmy Ripple .20 .50
9 Hank Johnson .20 .50
10 Bill Baker .20 .50
11 Al Simmons .75 2.00
12 Johnny Hutchings .20 .50
13 Peaches Davis .20 .50
14 Willard Hershberger .40 1.00
15 Bill Werber .40 1.00
16 Harry Craft .20 .50
17 Milt Galatzer .20 .50
18 Dick West .20 .50
19 Art Jacobs .20 .50
20 Joe Beggs .20 .50
21 Frenchy Bordagary .20 .50
22 Lee Gamble .20 .50
23 Lee Grissom .20 .50
24 Eddie Joost .40 1.00
25 Milt Shofner .20 .50
26 Morrie Arnovich .20 .50
27 Pete Naktenis .20 .50
28 Jim Weaver .20 .50
29 Mike McCormick .20 .50
30 Johnny Niggeling .20 .50
31 Les Scarsella .20 .50
32 Lonny Frey .20 .50
33 Billy Myers .20 .50
34 Frank McCormick .40 1.00
35 Lew Riggs .20 .50
36 Nino Bongiovanni .20 .50
37 Johnny Rizzo .20 .50
38 Wes Livengood .20 .50
39 Junior Thompson .20 .50
40 Mike Dejan .20 .50
41 Jimmy Wilson .20 .50
42 Paul Derringer .40 1.00
43 Johnny VanderMeer .40 1.00
44 Whitey Moore .20 .50
45 Bill McKechnie MG .40 1.00

1980 Reds Enquirer

This set features members of the 1980 Cincinnati Reds. The cards are sequenced by uniform numbers of the organization. When cut out, these cards measure 3" by 4 7/16".

COMPLETE SET 5.00 12.00
2 Russ Nixon CO .08 .25
3 John McNamara MG .08 .25
4 Harry Dunlop CO .08 .25
5 Johnny Bench 1.50 4.00
6 Bill Fischer CO .08 .25
7 Hector Cruz .08 .25
9 Vic Correll .08 .25
11 Ron Plaza CO .08 .25
12 Harry Spilman .08 .25
13 Dave Concepcion .40 1.00
15 George Foster .40 1.00
16 Ron Oester .08 .25
19 Don Werner .08 .25
20 Cesar Geronimo .08 .25
22 Dan Driessen .08 .25
23 Rick Auerbach .08 .25
25 Ray Knight .20 .50
26 Junior Kennedy .08 .25
28 Sam Mejias .08 .25
29 Dave Collins .08 .25
30 Ken Griffey .40 1.00
31 Paul Moskau .08 .25
34 Sheldon Burnside .08 .25
35 Frank Pastore .08 .25
36 Mario Soto .20 .50
37 Dave Tomlin .08 .25
40 Doug Bair .08 .25
41 Tom Seaver 1.00 2.50
42 Bill Bonham .08 .25
44 Charlie Leibrandt .08 .25
47 Tom Hume .08 .25
51 Mike LaCoss .08 .25

1980 Reds 1961 TCMA

This 41-card set features photos of the 1961 Cincinnati Reds team with red lettering. The backs carry player information and statistics.

COMPLETE SET (41) 10.00 25.00
1 Eddie Kasko .08 .25
2 Wally Post .08 .25
3 Vada Pinson .30 .75
4 Frank Robinson .40 1.00
5 Pete Whisenant .08 .25
6 Reggie Otero CO .08 .25
7 Dick Sisler CO .08 .25
8 Jim Turner CO .20 .50
9 Fred Hutchinson MG .08 .25
10 Gene Freese .08 .25
11 Gordy Coleman .08 .25
12 Don Blasingame .08 .25
13 Gus Bell .08 .25
14 Leo Cardenas .08 .25
15 Elio Chacon .08 .25
16 Dick Gernert .08 .25
17 Jim Baumer .08 .25
18 Willie Jones .08 .25
19 Joe Gaines .08 .25
20 Cliff Cook .08 .25
21 Harry Anderson .08 .25
22 Jerry Zimmerman .08 .25
23 Johnny Edwards .08 .25
24 Bob Schmidt .08 .25
25 Darrell Johnson .08 .25
26 Ed Bailey .08 .25
27 Joey Jay .08 .25
28 Jim O'Toole .08 .25
29 Bob Purkey .08 .25
30 Jim Brosnan .08 .25
31 Ken Hunt .08 .25
32 Ken Johnson .08 .25
33 Jim Maloney .20 .50
34 Bill Henry .08 .25
35 Jerry Lynch .08 .25
36 Hal Bevan .08 .25
37 Howie Nunn .08 .25
38 Sherman Jones .08 .25
39 Jay Hook .08 .25
40 Claude Osteen .08 .25
41 Marshall Bridges .08 .25

1933 Rittenhouse Candy E285

These cards measure 2 1/4" by 1 7/16" and are found in four

colors: red, green, orange or blue. The fronts feature a player photo in the middle surrounded by the suits symbol. The backs either feature one alphabetical character from the words "Rittnehouse Candy Co" or a description of the premium offers. We have sequenced the set in playing order by suit and numbers are assigned to Aces (1), Jacks (11A), Queens (12) and Kings (13). All colors are priced equally.

COMPLETE SET (52)	1,875.00	3,750.00
1C Doc Cramer	30.00	60.00
1D Babe Herman	50.00	100.00
1H Mule Haas	30.00	60.00
1S Babe Ruth	300.00	600.00
2C Bing Miller	30.00	60.00
2D Chick Hafey	60.00	120.00
2H Gus Mancuso	30.00	60.00
2S Billy Herman	60.00	120.00
3C Lefty O'Doul	60.00	120.00
3D Chuck Klein	60.00	120.00
3H George Earnshaw	40.00	80.00
3S Frankie Frisch	100.00	200.00
4C Mel Ott	100.00	200.00
4D Fred Brickell	30.00	60.00
4H Leroy Mahaffey	30.00	60.00
4S Dick Bartell	30.00	60.00
5C Kiki Cuyler	60.00	120.00
5D George Davis	30.00	60.00
5H Jimmy Dykes	40.00	80.00
5S Paul Waner	60.00	120.00
6C Hugh Critz	30.00	60.00
6D Paul Waner	60.00	120.00
6H Rogers Hornsby	125.00	250.00
6S Don Hurst	30.00	60.00
7C Walter Berger	40.00	80.00
7D Sugar Cain	30.00	60.00
7H Joe Cronin	60.00	120.00
7S Frankie Frisch	60.00	120.00
8C Dib Williams	30.00	60.00
8D Lefty Grove	100.00	200.00
8H Lou Finney	30.00	60.00
8S Ed. Cihocki	30.00	60.00
9C Hack Wilson	60.00	120.00
9D Al Simmons	60.00	120.00
9H Spud Davis	30.00	60.00
9S Hack Wilson	60.00	120.00
10C Pie Traynor	60.00	120.00
10D Bill Terry	60.00	120.00
10H Lloyd Waner	60.00	120.00
10S Jimmy Foxx	100.00	200.00
(Jimmie)		
11C Jumbo Elliott	30.00	60.00
11D Don Hurst	30.00	60.00
11H Pinky Higgins	30.00	60.00
11S Jim Bottomley	60.00	120.00
12C Pinky Whitney	30.00	60.00
12D Lloyd Waner	60.00	120.00
12H Eric McNair	30.00	60.00
12S Rube Walberg	30.00	60.00
13C Babe Ruth	300.00	600.00
13D Phil Collins	30.00	60.00
13H Gabby Hartnett	60.00	120.00
13S Max Bishop	30.00	60.00

1955 Robert Gould W605

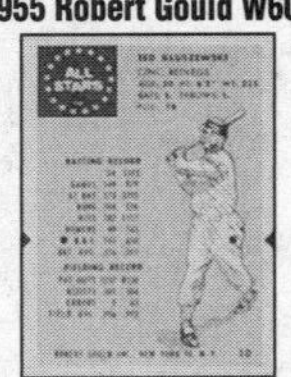

The cards in this 28-card set measure 2 1/2" by 3 1/2". The 1955 Robert F. Gould set of black and white on green cards were toy store cardboard holders for small plastic statues. The statues were attached to the card by a rubber band through two holes on the side of the card. The catalog designation is W605. The cards are numbered in the bottom right corner of the obverse and are blank-backed.

COMPLETE SET (28)	5,000.00	10,000.00
1 Willie Mays	1,250.00	2,500.00
2 Gus Zernial	100.00	200.00
3 Red Schoendienst	200.00	400.00
4 Chico Carrasquel	100.00	200.00
5 Jim Hegan	100.00	200.00
6 Curt Simmons	125.00	250.00
7 Bob Porterfield	100.00	200.00
8 Jim Busby	100.00	200.00
9 Don Mueller	100.00	200.00
10 Ted Kluszewski	200.00	400.00
11 Ray Boone	100.00	200.00
12 Smoky Burgess	125.00	250.00
13 Bob Rush	100.00	200.00
14 Early Wynn	200.00	400.00
15 Bill Bruton	100.00	200.00
16 Gus Bell	100.00	200.00
17 Jim Finigan	100.00	200.00
18 Granny Hamner	100.00	200.00
19 Hank Thompson	100.00	200.00
20 Joe Coleman	100.00	200.00
21 Don Newcombe	150.00	300.00
22 Richie Ashburn	300.00	600.00
23 Bobby Thomson	150.00	300.00
24 Sid Gordon	100.00	200.00
25 Gerry Coleman	125.00	250.00
26 Ernie Banks	600.00	1,200.00
27 Billy Pierce	125.00	250.00
28 Mel Parnell	125.00	250.00

1947 Jackie Robinson Bond Bread

The 1947 Bond Bread Jackie Robinson set features 13 unnumbered cards of Jackie in different action or portrait poses; each card measures approximately 2 1/4" by 3 1/2". Card number 7, which is the only card in the set to contain a facsimile autograph, was apparently issued in greater quantity than other cards in the set and has been noted as a double print (DP) in the checklist below. Several of the cards have a horizontal format; these are marked in the checklist below by HOR. The catalog designation for this set is D302.

COMPLETE SET (13)	4,000.00	8,000.00
COMMON DP		
1 Jackie Robinson	400.00	800.00
Sliding into base		
cap, ump in photo, HOR		
2 Jackie Robinson	400.00	800.00
Running down 3rd base line		
3 Jackie Robinson	400.00	800.00
Batting		
bat behind head		
facing camera		
4 Jackie Robinson	400.00	800.00
Moving towards second		
throw almost to glove		
HOR		
5 Jackie Robinson	400.00	800.00
Taking throw at first, HOR		
6 Jackie Robinson	400.00	800.00
Jumping high in the air for ball		
7 Jackie Robinson	250.00	500.00
Profile with glove in		
front of head		
facsimile autograph DP		
8 Jackie Robinson	400.00	800.00
Leaping over second base		
ready to throw		
9 Jackie Robinson	400.00	800.00
Portrait		
holding glove over head		
10 Jackie Robinson	400.00	800.00
Portrait		
holding bat perpendicular		
to body		
11 Jackie Robinson	400.00	800.00
Reaching for throw		
glove near ankle		
12 Jackie Robinson	400.00	800.00
Leaping for throw		
no scoreboard		
in background		
13 Portrait, holding/bat parallel/to body	400.00	800.00
XX Jackie Robinson/6 1/2 by 9 Premium Photo		750.00
1,500.00		

1930 Rogers Peet

The Rogers Peet Department Store in New York released this set in early 1930. The cards were given out four at time to employees at the store for enrolling boys in Ropeco (the store's magazine club). Employees who completed the set, and pasted them in the album designed to house the cards, were eligible to win prizes. The blankbacked cards measure roughly 1 3/4" by 2 1/2" and feature a black and white photo of the famous athlete with his name and card number below the picture. Additions to this list are appreciated.

5 Dazzy Vance BB	60.00	100.00
13 Walter Johnson BB	200.00	400.00
16 Rogers Hornsby BB	100.00	200.00
18 Herb Pennock BB	60.00	100.00
28 Lou Gehrig BB	375.00	750.00
34 Ty Cobb BB	500.00	800.00
38 Tris Speaker BB	62.50	125.00
48 Babe Ruth BB	2,500.00	4,000.00

1964 Rollins Sheels Hardware

This blank-backed photograph, which measures approximately 7 1/2" by 9 1/2" features Twins star third baseman Rich Rollins. The front has a photo of Rollins along with a note at the bottom for Sheels Hardware which then had 3 locations in the Fargo-Moorehead, North Dakota area.

1 Rich Rollins	4.00	10.00

1908-09 Rose Company PC760

One of the most attractive postcards ever issued, The Rose Company postcards were issued during the end of the 20th century's first decade. The set features a black and white photo in a circle surrounded by a yellow and green baseball field, crossed bats and small figures. Imprints on the reverse contain the letters TRC, with the loop around the bottom of the C possibly accounting for a lower case "o," giving Co. The Rose Co. baseball series is listed in alphabetical order by teams in the checklist below-research indicates that each of the 16 major league teams is represented by 12 Rose postcards (to date not all have been found). And several minor league franchises are now believed to have 10 or more cards for them as well. The cards we currently list as 192 through 204 all feature members of the Springfield Mass baseball team. Although it is not confirmed that these are Rose postcards, the similarities are obvious enough that to add these to these listings makes sense.

COMPLETE SET	25,000.00	50,000.00
1 Ralph Glaze	300.00	600.00
2 Dad Hale	300.00	600.00
3 Frank LaPorte	300.00	600.00
4 Bris Lord	300.00	600.00
5 Tex Pruiett	300.00	600.00
6 Jack Thoney	300.00	600.00
7 Bob Unglaub	300.00	600.00
8 Heinie Wagner	300.00	600.00
9 George Winter	300.00	600.00
10 Cy Young	1,500.00	3,000.00
11 Nick Altrock	400.00	800.00
12 John Anderson	300.00	600.00
13 Jiggs Donohue	300.00	600.00
14 Fielder Jones	300.00	600.00
15 Freddy Parent	300.00	600.00
16 Frank Smith	300.00	600.00
17 Billy Sullivan	300.00	600.00
18 Lee Tannehill	300.00	600.00
19 Doc White	300.00	600.00
20 Harry Bemis	300.00	600.00
21 Joe Birmingham	300.00	600.00
22 Bill Bradley	300.00	600.00
23 Josh Clarke	300.00	600.00
24 Bill Hinchman	300.00	600.00
25 Addie Joss	1,000.00	2,000.00
26 Nap Lajoie	600.00	1,200.00
27 Glen Liebhardt	300.00	600.00
28 Bob Rhoads	300.00	600.00
Spelled Rhoades on card		
29 George Stovall	300.00	600.00
30 Terry Turner	300.00	600.00
31 Ty Cobb	3,000.00	6,000.00
32 Bill Coughlin	300.00	600.00
33 Sam Crawford	600.00	1,200.00
34 Bill Donovan	400.00	800.00
35 Ed Killian	300.00	600.00
36 Matty McIntyre	300.00	600.00
37 George Mullin	400.00	800.00
38 Charley O'Leary	300.00	600.00
39 Claude Rossman	300.00	600.00
40 Germany Schaefer	400.00	800.00
41 Boss Schmidt	300.00	600.00
42 Ed Summers	300.00	600.00
43 Hal Chase	600.00	1,200.00
44 Jack Chesbro	600.00	1,200.00
45 Wid Conroy	300.00	600.00
46 Kid Elberfeld	300.00	600.00
47 Fred Glade	300.00	600.00
48 Charlie Hemphill	300.00	600.00
49 Willie Keeler	600.00	1,200.00
50 Red Kleinow	300.00	600.00
51 Doc Newton	300.00	600.00
52 Harry Niles	300.00	600.00
53 Al Orth	300.00	600.00
54 Jake Stahl	300.00	600.00
55 Chief Bender	600.00	1,200.00
56 Jimmy Collins	600.00	1,200.00
57 Jack Coombs	300.00	600.00
58 Harry Davis	300.00	600.00
59 Jimmy Dygert	300.00	600.00
60 Topsy Hartsel	300.00	600.00
61 Danny Murphy	300.00	600.00
62 Simon Nicholls	300.00	600.00
63 Rube Oldring	300.00	600.00
64 Eddie Plank	600.00	1,200.00
65 Ossee Schreck	300.00	600.00
66 Socks Seybold	300.00	600.00
67 Hobe Ferris	300.00	600.00
68 Danny Hoffman	300.00	600.00
69 Harry Howell	300.00	600.00
70 Tom Jones	300.00	600.00
71 Jack Powell	300.00	600.00
72 Tubby Spencer	300.00	600.00
73 George Stone	300.00	600.00
74 Rube Waddell	600.00	1,200.00
75 Jimmy Williams	300.00	600.00
76 Otis Clymer	300.00	600.00
77 Frank Delahanty	300.00	600.00
78 Bob Ganley	300.00	600.00
79 Jerry Freeman	300.00	600.00
80 Tom Hughes	300.00	600.00
81 Walter Johnson	2,000.00	4,000.00
82 George McBride	300.00	600.00
83 Casey Patten	300.00	600.00
84 Clyde Milan	400.00	800.00
85 Bill Shipke	300.00	600.00
86 Charlie Smith	300.00	600.00
87 Jack Warner	300.00	600.00
88 Ginger Beaumont	300.00	600.00
89 Sam Brown	300.00	600.00
90 Bill Dahlen	300.00	600.00
91 George Ferguson	300.00	600.00
92 Vive Lindaman	300.00	600.00
93 Claude Ritchey	300.00	600.00
94 Whitey Alperman	300.00	600.00
95 John Hummel	300.00	600.00
96 Phil Lewis	300.00	600.00
97 Harry Lumley	300.00	600.00
98 Billy Maloney	300.00	600.00
99 Harry MacIntyre	300.00	600.00
100 Nap Rucker	300.00	600.00
101 Tommy Sheehan	300.00	600.00
102 Mordecai Brown	600.00	1,200.00
103 Frank Chance	1,000.00	2,000.00
104 Johnny Evers	1,000.00	2,000.00
105 Solly Hofman	300.00	600.00
106 John Kling	300.00	600.00
107 Orvall Overall	300.00	600.00
108 Ed Reulbach	300.00	600.00
109 Frank Schulte	400.00	800.00
110 Jimmy Sheckard	300.00	600.00
111 Jimmy Slagle	300.00	600.00
112 Harry Steinfeldt	400.00	800.00
113 Joe Tinker	1,000.00	2,000.00
114 Billy Campbell	300.00	600.00
115 Andy Coakley	300.00	600.00
116 Bob Ewing	300.00	600.00
117 John Ganzel	300.00	600.00
118 Miller Huggins	600.00	1,200.00
119 Rudy Hulswitt	300.00	600.00
120 Hans Lobert	300.00	600.00
121 Larry McLean	300.00	600.00
122 Mike Mitchell	300.00	600.00
123 Mike Mowery	300.00	600.00
124 Dode Paskert	300.00	600.00
125 Jake Weimer	300.00	600.00
126 Roger Bresnahan	600.00	1,200.00
127 Al Bridwell	300.00	600.00
128 Art Devlin	300.00	600.00
129 Mike Donlin	400.00	800.00
130 Joe Doyle	300.00	600.00
131 Christy Mathewson	2,000.00	4,000.00
132 Joe McGinnity	600.00	1,200.00
133 Cy Seymour	300.00	600.00
134 Spike Shannon	300.00	600.00
135 Dummy Taylor	400.00	800.00
136 Fred Tenney	300.00	600.00
137 Hooks Wiltse	300.00	600.00
138 Kitty Bransfield	300.00	600.00
139 Buster Brown	300.00	600.00
140 Frank Corridon	300.00	600.00
141 Red Dooin	300.00	600.00
142 Mickey Doolan	300.00	600.00
143 Eddie Grant	400.00	800.00
144 Otto Knabe	300.00	600.00
145 Sherry Magee	500.00	1,000.00
146 George McQuillan	300.00	600.00
Spelled McQuillen on card		
147 Fred Osborn	300.00	600.00
148 Tully Sparks	300.00	600.00
149 John Titus	300.00	600.00
150 Ed Abbaticchio	300.00	600.00
151 Bill Abstein	300.00	600.00
152 Howie Camnitz	300.00	600.00
153 Fred Clarke	600.00	1,200.00
154 George Gibson	300.00	600.00
155 Jim Kane	300.00	600.00
156 Tommy Leach	300.00	600.00
157 Nick Maddox	300.00	600.00
158 Deacon Philippe	400.00	800.00
159 Roy Thomas	300.00	600.00
160 Honus Wagner	2,000.00	4,000.00
161 Owen Wilson	400.00	800.00
162 Irv Young	300.00	600.00
163 Shad Barry	300.00	600.00
164 Fred Beebe	300.00	600.00
165 Bobby Byrne	300.00	600.00
166 Joe Delahanty	300.00	600.00
167 Billy Gilbert	300.00	600.00
168 Art Hoelskoetter	300.00	600.00
169 Ed Karger	300.00	600.00
170 Ed Konetchy	300.00	600.00
171 Johnny Lush	300.00	600.00
172 Stoney McGlynn	300.00	600.00
173 Red Murray	300.00	600.00
174 Patsy O'Rourke	300.00	600.00
175 Beckendorf	300.00	600.00
Scranton		
176 Bills	300.00	600.00
177 Graham	300.00	600.00
178 Groh	300.00	600.00
Scranton		
179 Halligan	300.00	600.00
180 Houser	300.00	600.00
181 Isbel	300.00	600.00
182 Kellogg	300.00	600.00
Scranton		
183 Kittredge	300.00	600.00
Scranton		
184 Moran	300.00	600.00
185 Schultz	300.00	600.00
186 Steele	300.00	600.00
187 Andy Coakley	300.00	600.00
188 Knight	300.00	600.00
189 Schlei	300.00	600.00
190 Spade	300.00	600.00
191 Tris Speaker	600.00	1,200.00
192 Thomas	300.00	600.00
193 Harl Maggert	300.00	600.00
194 Parker	300.00	600.00
195 James Burns	300.00	600.00
196 Edwin Warner	300.00	600.00
197 Rising	300.00	600.00
198 Connor	300.00	600.00
199 Wachob	300.00	600.00
200 McLean	300.00	600.00
201 Chet Waite	300.00	600.00
202 Luby	300.00	600.00
203 George Tacy	300.00	600.00
204 Collins	300.00	600.00
205 Louis Barbour	300.00	600.00
206 Big Jeff Pfeffer		

1968 Rose Jamesway Trucking

This one card set, which measures 4" by 5 1/4" featured a batting pose of Pete Rose and the "Jamesway Trucking Logo" on the bottom.

1 Pete Rose	200.00	400.00

1905 Rotograph Co. PC782

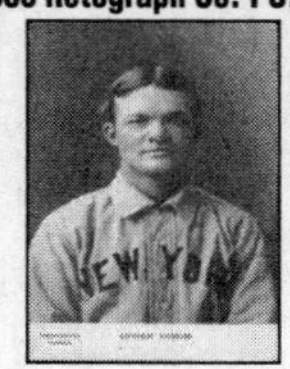

This rather distinguished looking set mesaures 3 1/4" by 5 3/8" and was printed by the Rotograph Company of New York in 1905. Some of the cards are numbered while others are not. The Clark Griffith card was initially issued with the name misspelled and was later corrected. The Rotograph identification is printed on the back of the card. Only New York teams are portrayed.

COMPLETE SET (9)	875.00	1,750.00
1 Ambrose Puttman	100.00	200.00
2 Jack Chesbro (2)	200.00	400.00
3 George Brown	100.00	200.00
4 Bill Dahlen	100.00	200.00
5 John McGraw	300.00	600.00
6 Clark Griffill	200.00	400.00
Sic, Griffith		
7 Clark Griffith	200.00	400.00
8 Joe McGinnity	200.00	400.00
Spelled Josep		
9 Joe McGinnity	200.00	400.00
Spelled Joseph		
10 Luther Taylor	100.00	200.00

1976 Rowe Exhibits

These collector issued exhibits feature the best major leaguers of the pre- World War 2 era. The cards are unnumbered and we have sequenced in alphabetical order by who appears in the upper left corner.

COMPLETE SET (16)	4.00	10.00
1 Luke Appling	.15	.40
Ted Lyons		
Red Ruffing		
Red Faber		
2 Jim Bottomley	.20	.50
Earle Combs		
George Sisler		
Roger H		
3 Dizzy Dean	.30	.75
Stan Musial		
Jesse Haines		
Frank Frisc		
4 Joe DiMaggio	.40	1.00
Lou Gehrig		
Lefty Gomez		
Bill Dickey		
5 Bob Feller	.20	.50
Lou Boudreau		
Earl Averill		
Bob Lemon		
6 Jimmie Foxx	.15	.40
Grover C. Alexander		
Robin Roberts		
E		
7 Hank Greenberg	.40	1.00
Charlie Gehringer		
Ty Cobb		
Goose		
8 Chick Hafey	.15	.40
Edd Roush		
Bill McKechnie		
George Kel		
9 Fred Lindstrom	.15	.40
Billy Herman		
Kiki Cuyler		
Gabby H		
10 Heinie Manush	.20	.50
Walter Johnson		
Bucky Harris		
Sam R		
11 Joe Medwick	.15	.40
Max Carey		
Dazzy Vance		
Burleigh Grim		
12 Mel Ott	.20	.50
Carl Hubbell		
Dave Bancroft		
Bill Terry		
13 Al Simmons	.20	.50
Lefty Grove		
Mickey Cochrane		
Eddie Co		
14 Warren Spahn	.20	.50
Al Lopez		
Casey Stengel		
Rabbit Mara		
15 Pie Traynor	.20	.50
Lloyd Waner		
Honus Wagner		
Paul Waner		
16 Ted Williams	.40	1.00
Herb Pennock		
Babe Ruth		
Joe Cronin		

1950-53 Royal Desserts

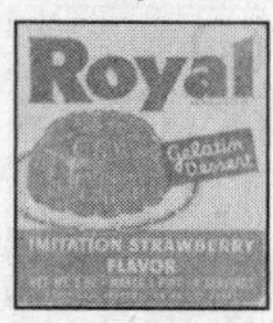

These cards were issued by Royal desserts over a period of years. These cards measure 2 1/2" by 3 1/2" and even though the same players are featured, variations exist when biographies were changed to keep the cards current. The backs are blank but the cards are numbered on the front. A set is considered complete with only one of each variation. These items were also made in blue. They have a value of 1X to2X the values listed below.

COMPLETE SET	1,250.00	2,500.00
COMMON PLAYER (1-24)	15.00	30.00
COMMON DP		
1 Stan Musial DP	200.00	400.00
2 Pee Wee Reese DP	75.00	150.00
3 George Kell	60.00	120.00
4 Dom DiMaggio	40.00	80.00
5 Warren Spahn	75.00	150.00
6A Andy Pafko	20.00	40.00
Chicago Cubs		
6B Andy Pafko	75.00	150.00
Brooklyn Dodgers		
7A Andy Seminick	20.00	40.00
Philadelphia Phillies		
7B Andy Seminick	20.00	40.00
Cincinnati Reds		
8A Lou Brissie	20.00	40.00
Philadelphia A's		
8B Lou Brissie	75.00	150.00
Cleveland Indians		
9 Ewell Blackwell	20.00	40.00
10 Bobby Thomson	40.00	80.00
11 Phil Rizzuto DP	75.00	150.00
12 Tommy Henrich	40.00	80.00
13 Joe Gordon	40.00	80.00
14A Ray Scarborough	20.00	40.00
Washington Senators		
14B Ray Scarborough	75.00	150.00
Chicago White Sox		
14C Ray Scarborough	20.00	40.00
Boston Red Sox		
15A Stan Rojek	20.00	40.00
Pittsburgh Pirates		
15B Stan Rojek	75.00	150.00
St. Louis Browns		
16 Luke Appling	60.00	120.00
17 Willard Marshall	20.00	40.00
18 Alvin Dark	40.00	80.00
19A Dick Sisler	20.00	40.00
Philadelphia Phillies		
19B Dick Sisler	20.00	40.00
Cincinnati Reds		
20 Johnny Ostrowski	20.00	40.00
21A Virgil Trucks	20.00	40.00
Detroit Tigers		
21B Virgil Trucks	75.00	150.00
St. Louis Browns		
22 Eddie Robinson	20.00	40.00
23 Nanny Fernandez	75.00	150.00
24 Ferris Fain	20.00	40.00

1952 Royal Premiums

These 16 photos measure approximately 5" by 7". These black and white photos are all facsimile signed with the expression "To a Royal Fan". The backs are blank and sequenced in alphabetical order.

COMPLETE SET (16)	400.00	800.00
1 Ewell Blackwell	15.00	30.00
2 Leland Brissie Jr.	15.00	30.00
3 Alvin Dark	20.00	40.00
4 Dom DiMaggio	30.00	60.00
5 Ferris Fain	15.00	30.00
6 George Kell	30.00	60.00
7 Stan Musial	100.00	200.00
8 Andy Pafko	15.00	30.00
9 Pee Wee Reese	50.00	100.00
10 Phil Rizzuto	50.00	100.00
11 Eddie Robinson	15.00	30.00
12 Ray Scarborough	15.00	30.00
13 Andy Seminick	15.00	30.00
14 Dick Sisler	15.00	30.00
15 Warren Spahn	50.00	100.00
16 Bobby Thomson	20.00	40.00

1969 Royals Solon

These 15 blank-backed cards measure approximately 2 1/8" by 3 3/8" and feature blue-screened posed player photos on their white-bordered fronts. The player's name and position, along with the Royals logo, appear in blue lettering in the lower white margin. The cards are unnumbered and checklisted below in alphabetical order. The set is given the appelation Solon because long-time hobbyist Bob Solon produced these cards.

COMPLETE SET (15)	6.00	15.00
1 Jerry Adair	.40	1.00
2 Wally Bunker	.40	1.00
3 Moe Drabowsky	.40	1.00
4 Dick Drago	.40	1.00
5 Joe Foy	.40	1.00
6 Joe Gordon MG	.60	1.50
7 Chuck Harrison	.40	1.00
8 Mike Hedlund	.40	1.00
9 Jack Hernandez	.40	1.00
10 Pat Kelly	.40	1.00
11 Roger Nelson	.40	1.00
12 Bob Oliver	.40	1.00
13 Lou Piniella	1.50	4.00
14 Ellie Rodriguez	.40	1.00
15 Dave Wickersham	.40	1.00

1969 Royals Team Issue

This 12-card set of the Kansas City Royals measures approximately 4 1/4" by 7". The fronts display black-and-white player portraits bordered in white. The player's name and team are printed in the top margin. The backs are blank. The cards are unnumbered and checklisted below in alphabetical order.

COMPLETE SET	6.00	15.00
1 Jerry Adair	.60	1.50
2 Jimmy Campanis	.60	1.50
3 Moe Drabowsky	.60	1.50
4 Mike Fiore	.60	1.50
5 Joe Foy	.60	1.50
6 Joe Gordon MG	1.00	2.50
7 Pat Kelly	.60	1.50
8 Joe Keough	.60	1.50
9 Roger Nelson	.60	1.50
10 Bob Oliver	.60	1.50
11 Juan Rios	.60	1.50
12 Dave Wickersham	.60	1.50

1970 Royals Team Issue

This 38-card set measures approximately 3 3/8" by 5" and features black-and-white player portraits in a white border. A facsimile autograph across the bottom of the picture. The backs are blank. The cards are unnumbered and checklisted below in alphabetical order.

COMPLETE SET (38)	15.00	40.00
1 Ted Abernathy	.40	1.00
2 Jerry Adair	.40	1.00
3 Luis Alcaraz	.40	1.00
4 Wally Bunker	.40	1.00
5 Tom Burgmeier	.40	1.00
6 Bill Butler	.40	1.00
7 Jim Campanis	.40	1.00
8 Dan Carnevale CO	.40	1.00
9 Moe Drabowsky	.40	1.00
10 Dick Drago	.40	1.00
11 Harry Dunlop CO	.40	1.00
12 Mike Fiore	.40	1.00
13 Al Fitzmorris	.40	1.00
14 Jack Hernandez	.40	1.00
15 Bob Johnson	.40	1.00
16 Pat Kelly	.40	1.00
17 Joe Keough	.40	1.00
18 Ed Kirkpatrick	.40	1.00
19 Bob Lemon MG	1.00	2.50
20 Pat Locanto	.40	1.00
21 Tommy Matchick	.40	1.00
22 Charlie Metro CO	.40	1.00
23 Aurelio Monteagudo	.40	1.00
24 Dave Morehead	.40	1.00
25 Bob Oliver	.40	1.00
26 Amos Otis	.60	1.50
27 Lou Piniella	1.00	2.50
28 Ellie Rodriguez	.40	1.00
29 Cookie Rojas	.60	1.50
30 Jim Rooker	.40	1.00
31 Paul Schaal	.40	1.00
32 Joe Schultz CO	.60	1.50
33 Bill Sorrell	.40	1.00
34 Rich Stevenson	.40	1.00
35 George Strickland CO	.40	1.00
36 Cedric Tallis GM	.40	1.00
37 Bob Hawk Taylor	.40	1.00
38 Ken Wright	.40	1.00

1971 Royals Signature Series Team

These photos feature members of the 1971 Kansas City Royals. The photos are unnumbered and feature fascimile signatures on them and we have sequenced them in alphabetical order.

COMPLETE SET	12.50	30.00
1 Ted Abernathy	.40	1.00
2 Wally Bunker	.40	1.00
3 Galen Cisco	.40	1.00
4 Bruce Dal Canton	.40	1.00
5 Dick Drago	.40	1.00
6 Harry Dunlop CO	.40	1.00
7 Al Fitzmorris	.60	1.50
8 Mike Hedlund	.40	1.00
9 Chuck Harrison	.40	1.00
10 Gail Hopkins	.40	1.00
11 Pat Kelly	.40	1.00
12 Ed Kirkpatrick	.40	1.00
13 Bobby Knoop	.40	1.00
14 Charley Lau CO	.60	1.50
15 Bob Lemon MG	1.00	2.50
16 Jerry May	.40	1.00
17 Dave Morehead	.40	1.00
18 Roger Nelson	.40	1.00
19 Bob Oliver	.75	2.00
20 Amos Otis	1.00	2.50
21 Dennis Paepke	.40	1.00
22 Fred Patek	.75	2.00
23 Lou Piniella	1.00	2.50
24 Lou Piniella	1.00	2.50
25 Cookie Rojas	.60	1.50
26 Ted Savage	.40	1.00
27 Paul Splittorff	.60	1.50
28 George Strickland CO	.40	1.00
29 Cedric Talles GM	.40	1.00
30 Carl Taylor	.40	1.00
31 Ken Wright	.40	1.00
32 Jim York	.40	1.00

1972 Royals Team Issue

These photos feature members of the 1972 Kansas City Royals. They are unnumbered so we have sequenced them in alphabetical order.

COMPLETE SET	6.00	15.00
1 Ted Abernathy	.20	.50
2 Tom Burgmeier	.20	.50
3 Harry Dunlop GM	.20	.50
4 Al Fitzmorris	.20	.50
5 Bob Floyd	.20	.50
6 Mike Hedlund	.20	.50
7 Gail Hopkins	.20	.50
8 Steve Hovley	.20	.50
9 Joe Keough	.20	.50
10 Ed Kirkpatrick	.20	.50
11 Bobby Knoop	.20	.50
12 Charley Lau CO	.40	1.00
13 Bob Lemon MG	.60	1.50
14 Jerry May	.20	.50
15 John Mayberry	.40	1.00
16 Roger Nelson	.20	.50
17 Amos Otis	.60	1.50
18 Fred Patek	.40	1.00
19 Lou Pinella	.60	1.50
20 Cookie Rojas	.30	.75
21 Jim Rooker	.20	.50
22 Paul Schaal	.20	.50
23 Richie Scheinblum	.20	.50
24 Paul Splittorff	.30	.75
25 George Strickland CO	.20	.50
26 Carl Taylor	.20	.50
27 Ken Wright	.20	.50

1974 Royals Postcards

This 29-card set of the Kansas City Royals features black-and-white player protraits measuring approximately 3 1/4" by 5" with a facsimile autograph. The set could originally be bought from the team for $2 or 10 cards for $1. The cards are unnumbered and checklisted below in alphabetical order. George Brett has a postcard in this set, a year before his Rookie Card.

COMPLETE SET (29)	15.00	40.00
1 Kurt Bevacqua	.30	.75
2 Doug Bird	.20	.50
3 George Brett	10.00	25.00
4 Nelson Briles	.20	.50
5 Steve Busby	.20	.50
6 Orlando Cepeda	2.00	5.00
7 Galen Cisco CO	.20	.50
8 Al Cowens	.30	.75
9 Bruce Dal Canton	.20	.50
10 Harry Dunlop CO	.20	.50
11 Al Fitzmorris	.20	.50
12 Fran Healy	.40	1.00
13 Joe Hoerner	.20	.50
14 Charley Lau CO	.30	.75
Card does not have a fascimile aut		
15 Buck Martinez	.30	.75
16 John Mayberry	.40	1.00
17 Lindy McDaniel	.20	.50
18 Jack McKeon MG	.20	.50
19 Hal McRae	.40	1.00
20 Steve Mingori	.20	.50
21 Amos Otis	.40	1.00
22 Fred Patek	.30	.75
23 Marty Pattin	.20	.50
24 Vada Pinson	.60	1.50
25 Cookie Rojas	.30	.75
26 Tony Solaita	.20	.50
27 Paul Spittorff	.20	.50
28 Frank White	1.25	3.00
29 Jim Wohlford	.20	.50

1975 Royals Postcards

This 32-card set of the Kansas City Royals features player photos on postcard-size cards. The cards are unnumbered and checklisted below in alphabetical order.

COMPLETE SET (32)	10.00	25.00
1 Doug Bird	.20	.50
2 George Brett	4.00	10.00
3 Steve Boros CO	.20	.50
4 Nelson Briles	.20	.50
5 Joe Burke GM	.20	.50
6 Steve Busby	.20	.50
7 Bruce Dal Canton	.20	.50
8 Galen Cisco CO	.20	.50
9 Al Cowens	.20	.50
10 Harry Dunlop CO	.20	.50
11 Al Fitzmorris	.20	.50
12 Fran Healy	.20	.50
13 Whitey Herzog MG	.20	.50
14 Harmon Killebrew	1.25	3.00
15 Charlie Lau CO	.20	.50
16 Dennis Leonard	.20	.50
17 Burck Martinez	.30	.75
18 John Mayberry	.20	.50
19 Lindy McDaniel	.30	.75
20 Jack McKeon FO	.20	.50
21 Hal McRae	.40	1.00
22 Steve Mingori	.20	.50
23 Amos Otis	.40	1.00

24 Fred Patek	.30	.75
25 Marty Pattin	.20	.50
26 Vada Pinson	.60	1.50
27 Cookie Rojas	.30	.75
28 Tony Solaita	.20	.50
29 Paul Splittorff	.20	.50
30 Bob Stinson	.20	.50
31 Frank White	.60	1.50
32 Jim Wohlford	.20	.50

1976 Royals A and P

This 16-card set features color photos of the Kansas City Royals and is believed to measure approximately 5 7/8" by 9". The set was produced by the Atlantic and Pacific Tea Company and distributed in Missouri and surrounding areas. The cards are unnumbered and checklisted below in alphabetical order. These cards were issued over a four week period at a rate of four each week. The cards were available when a customer bought two specially priced items at the A and P.

COMPLETE SET (16)	8.00	20.00
1 Doug Bird	.40	1.00
2 George Brett	3.00	8.00
3 Steve Busby	.40	1.00
4 Al Cowens	.40	1.00
5 Al Fitzmorris	.40	1.00
6 Dennis Leonard	.40	1.00
7 Buck Martinez	.60	1.50
8 John Mayberry	.40	1.00
9 Hal McRae	.75	2.00
10 Amos Otis	.75	2.00
11 Fred Patek	.60	1.50
12 Tom Poquette	.40	1.00
13 Cookie Rojas	.60	1.50
14 Tony Solaita	.40	1.00
15 Paul Splittorff	.40	1.00
16 Jim Wohlford	.40	1.00

1976 Royals Postcards

This 33-card set of the Kansas City Royals features player photos on postcard-size cards. The cards are unnumbered and checklisted below in alphabetical order.

COMPLETE SET (33)	8.00	20.00
1 Doug Bird	.20	.50
2 Steve Boros CO	.20	.50
3 George Brett	2.50	6.00
4 Joe Burke GM	.20	.50
5 Steve Busby	.20	.50
6 Galen Cisco CO	.20	.50
7 Al Cowens	.20	.50
8 Al Fitzsimmons	.20	.50
9 Larry Gura	.20	.50
10 Tom Hall	.20	.50
11 Fran Healy	.20	.50
12 Whitey Herzog MG	.60	1.50
13 Chuck Hiller CO	.20	.50
14 Charley Lau CO	.20	.50
15 Dennis Leonard	.20	.50
16 Mark Littell	.20	.50
17 Buck Martinez	.30	.75
18 John Mayberry	.30	.75
19 Hal McRae	.40	1.00
20 Steve Mingori	.20	.50
21 Dave Nelson	.20	.50
22 Amos Otis	.40	1.00
23 Fred Patek	.30	.75
24 Marty Pattin	.20	.50
25 Tom Poquette	.20	.50
26 Jamie Quirk	.20	.50
27 Cookie Rojas	.30	.75
28 Tony Solaita	.20	.50
29 Paul Splittorff	.20	.50
30 Bob Stinson	.20	.50
31 John Wathan	.30	.75
32 Frank White	.40	1.00
33 Jim Wohlford	.20	.50

1978 Royals

This 27-card set features the Kansas City Royals. The cards measure approximately 3 1/4" by 5". The fronts have black-and-white player portraits with a thin white border. The player's name, position, and team name are printed in a wider border beneath the picture. The backs are blank. The cards are unnumbered and checklisted below in alphabetical order.

COMPLETE SET (27)	10.00	25.00
1 Doug Bird	.30	.75
2 Steve Braun	.30	.75
3 George Brett	2.00	5.00
4 Al Cowens	.30	.75
5 Rich Gale	.30	.75
6 Larry Gura	.30	.75
7 Whitey Herzog MG	.60	1.50
8 Al Hrabosky	.40	1.00
9 Clint Hurdle	.60	1.50
10 Pete LaCock	.30	.75
11 Dennis Leonard	.30	.75
12 John Mayberry	.40	1.00
13 Hal McRae	.60	1.50
14 Steve Mingori	.30	.75
15 Dave Nelson	.30	.75
16 Amos Otis	.60	1.50
17 Fred Patek	.40	1.00
18 Marty Pattin	.30	.75
19 Tom Poquette	.30	.75
20 Darrell Porter	.60	1.50
21 Paul Splittorff	.30	.75
22 Jerry Terrell	.30	.75
23 U.L. Washington	.30	.75
24 John Wathan	.30	.75
25 Frank White	.60	1.50
26 Willie Wilson	.75	2.00
27 Joe Zdeb	.30	.75

1979-80 Royals Team Issue

These color photos feature members of the Kansas City Royals. The photos measure approximately 4" by 5 1/4" and have blank backs. A fascimile signature is on each photo and we have sequenced these photos in alphabetical order.

COMPLETE SET (13)	8.00	20.00
1 Willie Mays Aikens	.30	.75
2 Steve Braun	.20	.50
3 George Brett	2.00	5.00
4 Steve Busby	.20	.50
5 Al Cowens	.20	.50
6 Rich Gale	.20	.50
7 Larry Gura	.20	.50
8 Whitey Herzog MG	.40	1.00
9 Al Hrabosky	.20	.50
10 Clint Hurdle	.40	1.00
11 Pete LaCock	.20	.50
12 Dennis Leonard	.30	.75
13 Renie Martin	.20	.50
14 Hal McRae	.40	1.00
15 Steve Mingori	.20	.50
16 Amos Otis	.40	1.00
17 Fred Patek	.20	.50
18 Marty Pattin	.20	.50
19 Tom Poquette	.20	.50
20 Darrell Porter	.30	.75
21 Jamie Quirk	.20	.50
22 Dan Quisenberry	.60	1.50
23 Ed Rodriguez	.20	.50
24 Paul Splitorff	.20	.50
25 Jerry Terrell	.20	.50
26 U.L Washington	.20	.50
27 John Wathan	.20	.50
28 Frank White	.40	1.00
29 Willie Wilson	.40	1.00
30 Joe Zdeb	.20	.50
31 Steve Boros CO Galen Cisco CO	.20	.50
32 John Sullivan CO Chuck Hiller CO	.20	.50

1933 Blue Bird Soda

This card, which measures approximately 3 7/8" by 5 7/" features all-time slugger Babe Ruth. The photo shows the Babe in a batting pose, while the back has an advertisment for Blue Bird drink.

1 Babe Ruth Front View	500.00	1,000.00
2 Babe Ruth Side View	500.00	1,000.00

1928 Ruth Fro Joy

The cards in this six-card set measure approximately 2 1/16" by 4". The Fro Joy set of 1928 was designed to exploit the advertising potential of the mighty Babe Ruth. Six black and white cards explained specific baseball techniques while the reverse advertising extolled the virtues of Fro Joy ice cream and ice cream cones. Unfortunately this small set has been illegally reprinted (several times) and many of these virtually worthless fakes have been introduced into the hobby. The easiest fakes to spot are those cards (or uncut sheets) that are slightly over-sized and blue tinted; however some of the other fakes are more cleverly faithful to the original. Be very careful before purchasing Fro-Joys; obtain a qualified opinion on authenticity from an experienced dealer (preferably one who is unrelated to the dealer trying to sell you his cards). You might also show the cards (before you commit to purchase them) to an experienced printer who can advise you on the true age of the paper stock. More than one dealer has been quoted as saying that 99 percent of the Fro Joys seen are fakes. In addition, a 8 1/2" by 12" premium photo was also issued as part of the release of this promotion.

COMPLETE SET (6)	300.00	600.00
1 Babe Ruth George Herman Babe Ruth	150.00	300.00
2 Babe Ruth Look Out Mr. Pitcher	100.00	200.00
3 Babe Ruth Bang The Babe Lines one out	100.00	200.00
4 Babe Ruth/When the Babe Comes Out	100.00	200.00
5 Babe Ruth Babe Ruth's Grip	100.00	200.00
6 Babe Ruth Ruth is a Crack Fielder	100.00	200.00
P1 Babe Ruth Premium	150.00	300.00
NNO Uncut Sheet		

1920 Ruth Heading Home

This six card blank-back set, which measure approximately 1 1/2" by 2 3/8", was issued to promote Babe Ruth in his first starring movie vehichle. That film was titled "Heading Home" and each card shows the Babe with a bat in his hand

COMPLETE SET (6)	4000
COMMON CARD	750

1928 Ruth Home Run Candy Membership

This one card set was issued to people who purchased a ruth's home run candy which cost a nickel and featured a photo of the Babe on the front and ten general rules for members on the back. Very few copies are known to exist of this card and any additional information is greatly appreciated. A few wrappers are also known to exist of this product.

1 Babe Ruth	1,000.00	2,000.00

1921 Ruth Pathe

This 7" by 9" card was issued as a premium card by the Pathe Freres Phonograph Company. This card is printed in green and gray tones and shows the Babe with his hands at the waist. The back describes his 1920 season when he set a then record with 54 homers in a season. This item was actually the sleeve of a 78 RPM record commemorating the great Babe.

1 Babe Ruth	1,500.00	3,000.00

1938 Ruth Quaker Oats

This 8" by 10" blank backed poster of Babe Ruth was produced in the 1930's by the Quaker Oats company.The poster features Ruth swinging and has a facsimile autograph with the words "To My Pal from "Babe" Ruth. The bottom of the poster has the words "Presented to Members of the the Babe Ruth Base Ball Clun by the Quaker Oats Company, Makers of the Quaker Puffed Wheat and Puffed Rice." Like most promotional photos, it was sent in a mailing envelope to insure delivery in good condition

1 Babe Ruth	250.00	500.00

1936 S and S (Green Backs) WG8

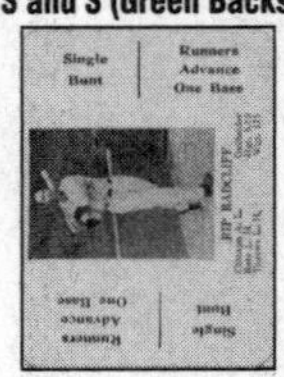

These cards were distributed as part of a baseball game produced in 1936. The cards each measure approximately 2 1/4" by 3 1/2" and have rounded corners. The card fronts are all oriented horizontally and show a small black and white photo of the player, his name, position, his team, vital statistics and the game outcome associated with that particular card. The card backs are evenly split between a plain green back with a thin white border or a plain back on a tannish paper stock. Since the cards are unnumbered, they are listed below in alphabetical order. Interestingly there are actually two box sizes. The box, which contained these fifty-two cards, and some other accoutrements to play the game, retailed for fifty cents when issued in 1936.

COMPLETE SET (52)	400.00	800.00
1 Luke Appling	15.00	30.00
2 Earl Averill	15.00	30.00
3 Zeke Bonura	7.50	15.00
4 Dolph Camilli	10.00	20.00
5 Ben Cantwell	7.50	15.00
6 Phil Cavarretta	12.50	25.00
7 Rip Collins	10.00	20.00
8 Joe Cronin	25.00	50.00
9 Frank Crosetti	12.50	25.00
10 Kiki Cuyler	15.00	30.00
11 Virgil Davis	7.50	15.00
12 Frank Demaree	10.00	20.00
13 Paul Derringer	15.00	30.00
14 Bill Dickey	30.00	60.00
15 Woody English	7.50	15.00
16 Fred Fitzsimmons	10.00	20.00
17 Rick Ferrell	15.00	30.00
18 Pete Fox	7.50	15.00
19 Jimmy Foxx (Jimmie)	40.00	80.00
20 Larry French	7.50	15.00
21 Frank Frisch	25.00	50.00
22 August Galan	10.00	20.00
23 Charlie Gehringer	25.00	50.00
24 John Gill	7.50	15.00
25 Charles Grimm	12.50	25.00
26 Mule Haas	10.00	20.00
27 Stan Hack	12.50	25.00
28 Bill Hallahan	10.00	20.00
29 Mel Harder	12.50	25.00
30 Gabby Hartnett	15.00	30.00
31 Ray Hayworth	7.50	15.00
32 Ralston Hemsley	7.50	15.00
33 Bill Herman	15.00	30.00
34 Frank Higgins	7.50	15.00
35 Carl Hubbell	30.00	60.00
36 Bill Jurges	7.50	15.00
37 Vernon Kennedy	7.50	15.00
38 Chuck Klein	15.00	30.00
39 Mike Kreevich	7.50	15.00
40 Bill Lee	7.50	15.00
41 Joe Medwick	15.00	30.00
42 Van Mungo	10.00	20.00
43 James O'Dea	7.50	15.00
44 Mel Ott	30.00	60.00
45 Rip Radcliff	7.50	15.00
46 Pie Traynor	15.00	30.00
47 Arky Vaughan	15.00	30.00
48 Joe Vosmik	7.50	15.00
49 Lloyd Waner	15.00	30.00
50 Paul Waner	15.00	30.00
51 Lon Warneke	10.00	20.00
52 Floyd Young	7.50	15.00

1911 S74 Silks

Issued around 1911, these silk fabric collectibles have designs similar to the designs in the T205 Cigarette card set. The silk itself is 2" by 3" and the image is 1 1/4" by 2 3/8". The line work on the silks is in one color only, with colors of blue, red, brown and several variations between red and brown known to exist. The field or stock color is known in white and several pastel tints. The cards are unnumbered but have been numbered and listed by team alphabetical order and then player alphabetical order within the teams in the checklist below. Turkey Red and Old Mill Cigarettes are among the issuers of these silks. These silks were produced in more than one year and in fact may possibly be broken into two distinct sets. Silks with Helmar and Reu Sun backs can also be found; although the Red Sun variations seem to be very scarce. White backgroung silks ave valued 25% higher. Silks which still have the paper ad backing attached are worth double the prices listed below.

COMPLETE SET (122)	4,000.00	8,000.00
1 Bill Carrigan	50.00	100.00
2 Ed Cicotte	200.00	400.00
3 Tris Speaker	250.00	500.00
4 Jake Stahl	50.00	100.00
5 Hugh Duffy	150.00	300.00
6 Amby McConnell	50.00	100.00
7 Freddie Parent	50.00	100.00
8 Fred Payne	50.00	100.00
9 Lee Tannehill	50.00	100.00
10 Doc White	50.00	100.00
11 Terry Turner	50.00	100.00
12 Cy Young	250.00	500.00
13 Ty Cobb	1,000.00	2,000.00
14 Jim Delahanty	50.00	100.00
15 Davy Jones	50.00	100.00
16 George Moriarity	50.00	100.00
17 George Mullin	60.00	120.00
18 Ed Summers	50.00	100.00
19 Ed Willett	50.00	100.00
20 Hal Chase	100.00	200.00
21 Russ Ford	50.00	100.00
22 Charlie Hemphill	50.00	100.00
23 John Knight	50.00	100.00
24 John Quinn	60.00	120.00
25 Harry Wolter	50.00	100.00
26 Frank Baker	150.00	300.00
27 Jack Barry	50.00	100.00
28 Chief Bender	150.00	300.00
29 Eddie Collins	150.00	300.00
30 Jimmy Dygert	50.00	100.00
31 Topsy Hartsel	50.00	100.00
32 Harry Krause	50.00	100.00
33 Danny Murphy	50.00	100.00
34 Rube Oldring	50.00	100.00
35 Barney Pelty	50.00	100.00
36 George Stone	50.00	100.00
37 Bobby Wallace	150.00	300.00
38 Kid Elberfeld	50.00	100.00
39 Walter Johnson	500.00	1,000.00
40 Germany Schaefer	60.00	120.00
41 Gabby Street	50.00	100.00
42 Fred Beck	50.00	100.00
43 Peaches Graham	50.00	100.00

44 Buck Herzog	50.00	100.00
45 Al Mattern	50.00	100.00
46 Dave Shean	50.00	100.00
47 Harry Steinfeldt	60.00	120.00
48 Cy Barger (2)	50.00	100.00
49 George Bell	50.00	100.00
50 Bill Bergen	50.00	100.00
51 Bill Dahlen	60.00	120.00
52 Jake Daubert	60.00	120.00
53 John Hummel	50.00	100.00
54 Nap Rucker	60.00	120.00
55 Doc Scanlan	50.00	100.00
56 Red Smith	50.00	100.00
57 Tony Smith	50.00	100.00
58 Zach Wheat	150.00	300.00
59 Mordecai Brown	150.00	300.00
60 Frank Chance	200.00	400.00
61 Johnny Evers	200.00	400.00
62 Bill Foxen	50.00	100.00
63 Peaches Graham	50.00	100.00
64 Johnny Kling	60.00	120.00
65 Harry McIntire	50.00	100.00
66 Tom Needham	50.00	100.00
67 Orval Overall	60.00	120.00
68 Ed Reulbach	60.00	120.00
69 Frank Schulte	60.00	120.00
70 Jimmy Sheckard	50.00	100.00
71 Harry Steinfeldt	60.00	120.00
72 Joe Tinker	200.00	400.00
73 Bob Bescher	50.00	100.00
74 Tom Downey	50.00	100.00
75 Art Fromme	50.00	100.00
76 Eddie Grant	50.00	100.00
77 Clark Griffith	150.00	300.00
78 Dick Hoblitzell	50.00	100.00
79 Mike Mitchell	50.00	100.00
80 Red Ames	50.00	100.00
81 Beals Becker	50.00	100.00
82 Al Bridwell	50.00	100.00
83 Doc Crandall	50.00	100.00
84 Art Devlin	50.00	100.00
85 Josh Devore	50.00	100.00
86 Larry Doyle	60.00	120.00
87 Art Fletcher	50.00	100.00
88 Rube Marquard	150.00	300.00
89 Christy Mathewson	500.00	1,000.00
90 John McGraw MG	200.00	400.00
91 Fred Merkle	60.00	120.00
92 Chief Meyers	60.00	120.00
93 Red Murray	50.00	100.00
94 Bugs Raymond	50.00	100.00
95 Admiral Schlei	50.00	100.00
96 Fred Snodgrass	50.00	100.00
97 Hooks Wiltse (2)	50.00	100.00
98 Johnny Bates	50.00	100.00
99 Red Dooin	50.00	100.00
100 Mickey Doolan	50.00	100.00
101 Bob Ewing	50.00	100.00
102 Hans Lobert	50.00	100.00
103 Pat Moran	50.00	100.00
104 Dode Paskert	50.00	100.00
105 Jack Rowan	50.00	100.00
106 John Titus	50.00	100.00
107 Bobby Byrne	50.00	100.00
108 Howie Camnitz	50.00	100.00
109 Fred Clarke	150.00	300.00
110 John Flynn	50.00	100.00
111 George Gibson	50.00	100.00
112 Tommy Leach	50.00	100.00
113 Lefty Leifield	50.00	100.00
114 Dots Miller	50.00	100.00
115 Deacon Phillippe	60.00	120.00
116 Kirby White	50.00	100.00
117 Owen Wilson	50.00	100.00
118 Roger Bresnahan (2)	150.00	300.00
119 Steve Evans	50.00	100.00
120 Arnold Hauser	50.00	100.00
121 Miller Huggins	150.00	300.00
122 Ed Konetchy	50.00	100.00
123 Rebel Oakes	50.00	100.00

1911 S81 Large Silks

These large and attractive silks are found in two sizes, approximately 5" by 7" or 7" by 9". Unlike the smaller S74 Baseball Silks, these silks are numbered, beginning with number 86 and ending at number 110. The pose of the picture is the same as that of the T3 Turkey Red baseball cards. The silks were issued in 1911 and are frequently found grouped on pillow covers. For some reason the silk of Mathewson appears to be the most plentiful member of this admittedly scarce issue. Therefore no premium typically associated with a Hall of Famer exists for this card.

COMPLETE SET (25)	25,000.00	35,000.00
86 Rube Marquard	900.00	1,500.00
87 Marty O'Toole	500.00	800.00
88 Rube Benton	500.00	800.00
89 Grover C. Alexander	900.00	1,500.00
90 Russ Ford	500.00	800.00
91 John McGraw MG	900.00	1,500.00
92 Nap Rucker	500.00	800.00
93 Mike Mitchell	500.00	800.00
94 Chief Bender	900.00	1,500.00
95 Frank Baker	900.00	1,500.00
96 Napoleon Lajoie	900.00	1,500.00
97 Joe Tinker	900.00	1,500.00
98 Sherry Magee	600.00	1,000.00
99 Howie Camnitz	500.00	800.00
100 Eddie Collins	900.00	1,500.00
101 Red Dooin	500.00	800.00
102 Ty Cobb	12,500.00	25,000.00
103 Hugh Jennings MG	900.00	1,500.00
104 Roger Bresnahan	900.00	1,500.00
105 Jake Stahl	500.00	800.00
106 Tris Speaker	900.00	1,500.00
107 Ed Walsh	900.00	1,500.00
108 Christy Mathewson	800.00	1,200.00
109 Johnny Evers	900.00	1,500.00
110 Walter Johnson	6,000.00	12,000.00

1889 S.F.Hess and Co. N338-2

In contrast to the color drawings in Hess' California League set N321, the players in this series of big league ballplayers are shown in sepia photographs. The cards are blank-backed and unnumbered; they have no printed detail except for the player's name and the advertisement for S.F. Hess and Co.'s Cigarettes found below the picture. Cards denoted by SPOT are "Spotted Ties".

COMPLETE SET	30,000.00	60,000.00
1 Bill Brown: New York	2,500.00	5,000.00
2 Roger Conner (sic) New York	10,000.00	20,000.00
3 Ed Crane: New York	2,500.00	5,000.00
4 Buck Ewing: New York SPOT	10,000.00	20,000.00
5 Elmer Foster: New York	2,500.00	5,000.00
6 William George: New York	2,500.00	5,000.00
7 Joe Gerhardt: New York SPOT	2,500.00	5,000.00
8 Charles Getzein: Detroit	2,500.00	5,000.00
9 George Gore: New York	2,500.00	5,000.00
10 Gil Hatfield: New York	2,500.00	5,000.00
11 Arlie Latham: St.Louis	4,000.00	8,000.00
12 Pat Murphy: New York	2,500.00	5,000.00
13 Jim Mutrie: New York	4,000.00	8,000.00
14 Dave Orr: New York SPOT	2,500.00	5,000.00
15 Danny Richardson: New York	2,500.00	5,000.00
16 Mike Slattery: New York	2,500.00	5,000.00
17 Lidell Titcomb: New York	2,500.00	5,000.00
18 John M. Ward: New York	10,000.00	20,000.00
19 Curt Welch: St. Louis	3,000.00	6,000.00
20 Mickey Welch: New York SPOT	10,000.00	20,000.00
21 Arthur Whitney: New York	2,500.00	5,000.00

1948-1950 Safe-T-Card

Cards from this set were issued in the Washington D.C. area in the late 1940s and early 1950s. Each card was printed in either black or red and features an artist's rendering of a famous area athlete or personality from a variety of sports. The card backs feature an ad for Jim Gibbons Cartoon-A-Quiz television show along with an ad from a local business. The player's facsimile autograph and team or sport affiliation is included on the fronts.

11 Ossie Bluege Mgr BB	15.00	30.00
13 Gilbert Coan BB	15.00	30.00
19 Sam Dente BB	15.00	30.00
21 Jacob Early BB	20.00	40.00
23 Al Evans BB	15.00	30.00
29 Calvin Griffith BB	15.00	30.00
30 Clark Griffith BB	20.00	40.00
34 Bucky Harris BB	25.00	50.00
37 Sid Hudson BB	15.00	30.00
40 Joe Kuhel BB	15.00	30.00
41 Bob Lemon BB	25.00	50.00
45 Bill McGowan Ump BB	15.00	30.00
46 George McQuinn BB	15.00	30.00
48 Don Newcombe BB	25.00	50.00
50 Joe Ostrowski BB	15.00	30.00
52 Sam Rice BB	25.00	50.00
56 Ray Scarborough BB	15.00	30.00
57 Bert Shepard BB	15.00	30.00
62 Mickey Vernon BB	20.00	40.00
66 Early Wynn BB	25.00	50.00
67 Eddie Yost BB	20.00	40.00

1978 Saga Discs

This set is a parallel to the 1978 Tastee-Freez discs. They were issued through Saga and are significantly more difficult than the regular Tastee-Freez discs.

COMPLETE SET (26)	100.00	200.00
1 Buddy Bell	2.00	5.00
2 Jim Palmer	8.00	20.00
3 Steve Garvey	3.00	8.00
4 Jeff Burroughs	1.00	2.50
5 Greg Luzinski	2.00	5.00
6 Lou Brock	6.00	15.00
7 Thurman Munson	4.00	10.00
8 Rod Carew	6.00	15.00
9 George Brett	20.00	50.00
10 Tom Seaver	8.00	20.00
11 Willie Stargell	6.00	15.00
12 Jerry Koosman	1.00	2.50
13 Bill North	1.00	2.50
14 Richie Zisk	1.00	2.50
15 Bill Madlock	2.00	5.00
16 Carl Yastrzemski	6.00	15.00
17 Dave Cash	1.00	2.50
18 Bob Watson	2.00	5.00
19 Dave Kingman	4.00	10.00
20 Gene Tenace	1.00	2.50
21 Ralph Garr	1.00	2.50
22 Mark Fidrych	6.00	15.00
23 Frank Tanana	2.00	5.00
24 Larry Hisle	1.00	2.50
25 Bruce Bochte	1.00	2.50
26 Bob Bailor	1.00	2.50

1962 Sain Spinner Postcard

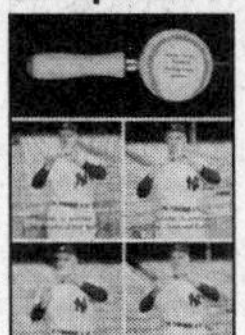

This one-card set features four small color photos of the New York Yankee's pitching coach, John Sain, demonstrating how to use the Spinner, a device to teach the mechanics of a Curveball, Fast Ball, Sinker, and Screwball. The back displays a postcard format with an ad for the Spinner and instructions on how to obtain it.

1 John Sain CO	8.00	20.00

1932 Sanella Margarine

The cards in this set measure approximately 2 3/4" by 4 1/8" and feature color images of famous athletes printed on thin stock. The cards were created in Germany and originally designed to be pasted into an album called "Handbook of Sports." The Ruth, and possibly the other cards in the set, was created in four versions with slight differences being found on the cardbacks.

1 Japanese catcher	5.00	10.00
83A Babe Ruth Type 1 (Sanella Centered)	50.00	100.00
83B Babe Ruth Type 2 (Sanella at Bottom)	50.00	100.00
83C Babe Ruth Type 3 (Sanella at Bottom with 83)	75.00	150.00
83D Babe Ruth Type 4 (Sanella Centered with 83)	100.00	200.00

1968 SCFS Old Timers

This 72-card set measures 3 1/2" X 4 1/4" and features black-and-white artistic renderings of old time baseball players. The player's name, position and years played are printed at the bottom. The first series backs are blank except for a small stamp at the bottom with the 1968 copyright date. The second series has more complete player information and have a 1969 copyright date. The cards are numbered on the front. The cards were produced by long time hobbyist Mike Aronstein. This set was available from the producer at time of issue for $6.50.

COMPLETE SET	125.00	250.00
1 Babe Ruth	20.00	50.00
2 Rube Marquard	3.00	8.00
3 Zack Wheat	3.00	8.00
4 John Clarkson	3.00	8.00
5 Honus Wagner	4.00	10.00
6 Crab Evers	3.00	8.00
7 Bill Dickey	3.00	8.00
8 Elmer Smith	1.00	2.50
9 Ty Cobb	10.00	25.00
10 Happy Jack Chesbro	3.00	8.00
11 Moon Gibson	1.00	2.50
12 Bullet Joe Bush	1.00	2.50
13 George Mullin	1.00	2.50
14 Buddy Myer	1.00	2.50
15 James Collins	3.00	8.00
16 William Wambsganss	1.00	2.50
17 Jack Barry	1.00	2.50
18 Dickie Kerr	1.00	2.50
19 Connie Mack	3.00	8.00
20 Rabbit Maranville	3.00	8.00
21 Roger Peckinpaugh	1.00	2.50
22 Mickey Cochrane	3.00	8.00
23 George Kelly	3.00	8.00
24 John Baker	1.00	2.50
25 Wally Schang	1.00	2.50
26 Eddie Plank	3.00	8.00
27 Bill Donovan	1.00	2.50
28 Red Faber	3.00	8.00
29 Hack Wilson	3.00	8.00
30 Three Fingered Brown	3.00	8.00
31 Frederick Merkle	1.00	2.50
32 Heinie Groh	1.00	2.50
33 Stuffy McInnis	1.00	2.50
34 Prince Hal Chase	3.00	8.00
35 Kenesaw Mountain Landis COMM	2.00	5.00
36 Chief Bender	3.00	8.00
38 Tony Lazzeri		
39 John McGraw		
40 Mel Ott		
41 Grover Cleveland Alexander		
42 Rube Waddell		
43 Wilbert Robinson		
44 Cap Anson		
45 Eddie Cicotte		
46 Hank Gowdy		
47 Frankie Frisch		
48 Charles Comiskey		
49 Clyde Milan		
50 Jimmy Wilson	1.00	2.50
51 Christy Mathewson		
52 Tim Keefe		
53 Abner Doubleday		
54 Ed Walsh		
55 Jim Thorpe	10.00	25.00
56 Roger Bresnahan		
57 Frank Chance		
58 Heinie Manush		
59 Max Carey		
72 Bill Dineen		
73 Kid Gleason		

1921 Schapira Bros.

This seven card set, which measures approximately 1 3/4" by 2 1/2, were used as part of a contest by Schapira brothers for people to collect and turn in 250 of the portrait photos plus any one of the action photos for a signed Babe Ruth baseball. Since more portraits were needed for the contest than action shots, we are presuming that those cards were printed in greater supply and are more available then the action shots in this set.

COMPLETE SET (6)	2,000.00	4,000.00
1 Babe Ruth Portrait (without Arrows)	400.00	800.00
2 Babe Ruth Portrait (with Arrows)	400.00	800.00
3 Babe Ruth Clear the Bags	500.00	1,000.00
4 Babe Ruth Home Run	500.00	1,000.00
5 Babe Ruth Over the Fence	500.00	1,000.00
6 Babe Ruth They Passed Him	500.00	1,000.00
7 Babe Ruth Waiting for a High One	500.00	1,000.00

1950 Schumacher Gas

Little is known about these two cards which measure approximately 2 1/2" by 3 1/2" and were cut fairly unevenly. The fronts feature a black and white picture of the player while the horizontal backs feature the then "Gulf" logo and just some basic details about Schumacher service station. Since these cards are unnumbered, we have sequenced them in alphabetical order. There may be more players in this set so any further checklisting help is appreciated.

COMPLETE SET	100.00	200.00
COMMON CARD	50.00	100.00
1 George Munger	50.00	100.00
2 Vern Stephens	60.00	120.00

1935 Schutter-Johnson R332

This set of 50 cards was issued by the Schutter-Johnson Candy Corporation around 1935. Each card measures 2 1/4" by 2 7/8". While each card in the series is numbered, the ones in the checklist below are the only ones known at the present time. These black line-drawing cards on a red field are entitled "Major League Secrets" and feature tips from major league players on the reverse.

COMPLETE SET (50)	2,000.00	4,000.00
1 Al Simmons Swings 2 or 3 bats	150.00	300.00
2 Lloyd Waner's Batting Stance	150.00	300.00
3 Kiki Cuyler's Baserunning Tips	150.00	300.00
4 Frank Frisch Chop Bunt	200.00	400.00
5 Chick Hafey Get Jump On Fly Balls	150.00	300.00
6 Bill Klem UMP Balk	200.00	400.00
7 How to Practice Control (Rogers Hornsby Pitch-/	300.00	600.00
8 Carl Mays Underhand Ball	100.00	200.00
9 Umpire Charles Wrig- ley (Pitcher's feet with no	100.00	200.00
10 Christy Mathewson Fade-Away Pitch	400.00	800.00
11 Bill Dickey Waste Ball	200.00	400.00
12 Walter Berger don't step in the bucket	100.00	200.00
13 George Earnshaw Curve	100.00	200.00
14 Hack Wilson grip bat at extreme end	200.00	400.00
15 Charley Grimm testing pitcher at first	100.00	200.00
16 Waner Brothers word signs in outfield	150.00	300.00
17 Chuck Klein keep eye on ball	150.00	300.00
18 Woody English bunt flat-footed	100.00	200.00
19 Grover Alexander side arm fastball	200.00	400.00
20 Lou Gehrig hit ball where pitched)	1,000.00	2,000.00
21 Wes Ferrell Wind-up	100.00	200.00
22 Carl Hubbell Wind-up Pitching Tips	200.00	400.00

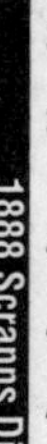

23 Pie Traynor Bunting Tips	150.00	300.00
24 Gus Mancuso getting under foul ball	100.00	200.00
25 Ben Cantwell curve ball grip	100.00	200.00
26 Babe Ruth Advice	2,000.00	4,000.00
27 Goose Goslin throw from outfield	150.00	300.00
28 Earle Combs Hands Apart Grip	150.00	300.00
29 Kiki Cuyler halfslide	150.00	300.00
30 Jimmy Wilson delayed steal	100.00	200.00
31 Dizzy Dean curveball	300.00	600.00
32 Mickey Cochrane signs	200.00	400.00
33 Ted Lyons Knuckle Ball	200.00	400.00
34 Si Johnson Slow Ball	100.00	200.00
35 Dizzy Dean Fork Ball	300.00	600.00
36 Pepper Martin bunting	100.00	200.00
37 Joe Cronin Battery Tips	150.00	300.00
38 Gabby Hartnett Simple Batting Signs	150.00	300.00
39 Oscar Melillo (play ball& don't let ball play yo	100.00	200.00
40 Ben Chapman hook slide)	100.00	200.00
41 John McGraw MG Coaching Signs	200.00	400.00
42 Babe Ruth choke grip	2,000.00	4,000.00
43 Red Lucas illegal action	100.00	200.00
44 Charley Root Holding Runners on First	100.00	200.00
45 Dazzy Vance drop pitch	150.00	300.00
46 Hugh Critz second baseman's throw	100.00	200.00
47 Firpo Marberry Raise Ball	100.00	200.00
48 Grover Alexander Full Windup	200.00	400.00
49 Lefty Grove fast ball grip	200.00	400.00
50 Heine Meine three types of curves	100.00	200.00

1888 Scrapps Die Cuts

These cards are unnumbered; they are ordered below alphabetially within team. The first nine players (1-9) are St. Louis and the second nine (10-18) are Detroit players.

COMPLETE SET (18)	7,500.00	15,000.00
1 Doc Bushong	500.00	1,000.00
2 Bob Caruthers	500.00	1,000.00
3 Charles Comiskey	1,500.00	3,000.00
4 Dave. Foutz	500.00	1,000.00
5 Bill Gleason	750.00	1,500.00
6 Arlie Latham	600.00	1,200.00
7 Tip O'Neill	500.00	1,000.00
8 Yank Robinson	500.00	1,000.00
9 Curt Welch	600.00	1,200.00
10 C.W. Bennett	500.00	1,000.00
11 Dan Brouthers	2,000.00	4,000.00
12 Fred Dunlap	500.00	1,000.00
13 Charlie Getzen (sic)	500.00	1,000.00
14 Ned Hanlon	1,000.00	2,000.00
15 Hardie Richardson	500.00	1,000.00
16 Jack Rowe	500.00	1,000.00
17 Sam Thompson	1,500.00	3,000.00
18 Deacon White	500.00	1,000.00

1946 Sears-East St. Louis PC783

This black and white blank-backed set measures 3 1/2" by 5 3/8" and was issued in 1946 and given away by Sears at their East St. Louis location. The set features players from St. Louis teams. Two poses of John Miller exist. The cards are unnumbered so we have listed them alphabetically. Famed broadcaster Joe Garagiola has an early card in this set.

COMPLETE SET	3,000.00	6,000.00
1 Buster Adams	40.00	80.00
2 Red Barrett	40.00	80.00
3 Johnny Beazley	40.00	80.00
4 John Berardino	60.00	120.00
5 Frank Biscan	40.00	80.00
6 Al Brazle	40.00	80.00
7 Harry Breechen	50.00	100.00
8 Ken Burkhardt	40.00	80.00
9 Jerry Burmeister	40.00	80.00
10 Mark Christman	40.00	80.00
11 Joffre Cross	40.00	80.00
12 Babe Dahlgren	50.00	100.00
13 Murray Dickson	40.00	80.00
14 Bob Dillinger	50.00	100.00
15 George Duckins	40.00	80.00
16 Blix Donnelly	40.00	80.00
17 Erv Dusak	40.00	80.00
18 Eddie Dyer MG	40.00	80.00
19 Bill Endicott	40.00	80.00
20 Stanley Ferens	40.00	80.00
21 Denny Galehouse	40.00	80.00
22 Joe Garagiola	100.00	200.00
23 Mike Gonzales CO	40.00	80.00
24 Joe Grace	40.00	80.00
25 Jeff Heath	40.00	80.00
26 Henry Helf	40.00	80.00
27 Fred Hoffman	40.00	80.00
28 Walt Judnich	40.00	80.00
29 Ellis Kinder	40.00	80.00
30 Lou Klein	40.00	80.00
31 Clyde Kluttz	40.00	80.00
32 Jack Kramer	40.00	80.00
33 Howard Krist	40.00	80.00
34 Whitey Kurowski	50.00	100.00
35 Chet Laabs	40.00	80.00
36 Al LaMacchia	40.00	80.00
37 John Lucadello	40.00	80.00
38 Frank Mancuso	40.00	80.00
39 Marty Marion	60.00	120.00
40 Fred Martin	40.00	80.00
41 George McQuillen	40.00	80.00
42 John Miller (2)	40.00	80.00
43 Al Milnar	40.00	80.00
44 Terry Moore	60.00	120.00
45 Bob Muncrief	40.00	80.00
46 Stan Musial	1,000.00	2,000.00
47 Ken O'Dea	40.00	80.00
48 Howie Pollet	40.00	80.00
49 Nelson Potter	40.00	80.00
50 Del Rice	40.00	80.00
51 Len Schulte	40.00	80.00
51 Red Schoendienst	75.00	150.00
53 Ken Sears	40.00	80.00
54 Walt Sessi	40.00	80.00
55 Luke Sewell MG	50.00	100.00
56 Joe Schultz	40.00	80.00
57 Tex Shirley	40.00	80.00
58 Dick Sisler	40.00	80.00
59 Enos Slaughter	75.00	150.00
60 Vern Stephens	60.00	120.00
61 Chuck Stevens	40.00	80.00
62 Max Surkont	40.00	80.00
63 Zack Taylor MG	40.00	80.00
64 Harry Walker	50.00	100.00
65 Buzzy Wares	40.00	80.00
66 Ernie White	40.00	80.00
67 Ted Wilks	40.00	80.00
68 Al Zarilla	40.00	80.00
69 Sam Zoldak	40.00	80.00

1894 Senators Cabinets Bell

These cabinets feature members of the 19th century Washington Senators and were produced at the Bell Studio on Pennsylvania Avenue. These cabinets feature mainly players in uniform but a couple of players are posed in suit and tie. Since these cabinets are unnumbered, we have sequenced them in alphabetical order.

COMPLETE SET	6,000.00	12,000.00
1 Charles Abbey	750.00	1,500.00
2 Ed Cartwright	750.00	1,500.00
3 Dan Dugdale	750.00	1,500.00
4 Jim McGuire	750.00	1,500.00
5 Tim O'Rourke	750.00	1,500.00
6 Al Selbach	750.00	1,500.00
7 Otis Stocksdale	750.00	1,500.00
8 Mike Sullivan	750.00	1,500.00
9 George Tebeau	750.00	1,500.00
10 Frank Ward	750.00	1,500.00

1909 Senators Barr-Farnham Postcards

This extremely rare set of real photo postcards was produced by Barr-Farnham Picture Postcards Co. located in Washington, DC in 1909. Ten cards have been positively identified but there are undoubtedly others, probably every member of the team. There is a strong possibility there is a team postcard as well. All additions to this checklist are greatly appreciated. All views show a full body close up of the player taken on the outfield grass with the ball park in the background.

COMPLETE SET (10)	1,250.00	2,500.00
11 Bob Unglaub	100.00	200.00
1 Otis Clymer	100.00	200.00
2 Wid Conroy	100.00	200.00
3 Bob Ganley	100.00	200.00
4 Dolly Gray	100.00	200.00
5 Bob Groom	100.00	200.00
6 Tom Hughes	100.00	200.00
7 Walter Johnson	400.00	800.00
8 George McBride	100.00	200.00
9 Charlie Smith	100.00	200.00
10 Jesse Tannehill	100.00	200.00

1912 Senators National Photo Company

The National Photo Company located in Washington, DC published a rare set of real photo postcards. The Postcards were also titled "The Climbers" and was probably produced in 1912 when the Senators climbed to second place from a seventh place finish the season before. The two known players are all time great pitcher Walter Johnson and fleet outfielder Clyde Milan. Both players had superb seasons in 1912. There might be other players in this set so additions to the checklist are appreciated.

COMPLETE SET (2)	350.00	700.00
1 Walter Johnson	300.00	600.00
2 Clyde Milan	100.00	200.00

1925 Senators Holland Creameries

These 18 cards, which feature members of the Washington Senators, were issued in Canada by an ice cream company. These cards, which measure approximately 1 1/2" by 3", feature the players photo and his position on the front and the back describes the prize is all 18 cards are returned. Roger Peckinpaugh, number 16, is believed to have been deliberately short printed to make winning the prize extremely hard.

COMPLETE SET (18)	1,500.00	3,000.00
COMMON CARD (1-18)	60.00	120.00
COMMON SP		
1 Ralph Miller	300.00	600.00
2 Earl McNeely	300.00	600.00
3 Allan Russell	300.00	600.00
4 Ernest Shirley	300.00	600.00
5 Sam Rice	600.00	1,200.00
6 Muddy Ruel	300.00	600.00
7 Ossie Bluege	400.00	800.00
8 Nemo Leibold	300.00	600.00
9 Paul Zahniser	300.00	600.00
10 Firpo Marberry	400.00	800.00
11 Warren Ogden	300.00	600.00
12 George Mogridge	300.00	600.00
13 Tom Zachary	300.00	600.00
14 Goose Goslin	600.00	1,200.00
15 Joe Judge	400.00	800.00
16 Roger Peckinpaugh SP	1,000.00	2,000.00
17 Bucky Harris	600.00	1,200.00
18 Walter Johnson	2,500.00	5,000.00

1925 Senators Oakland Tribune

This one-card set measures approximately 3" by 4 3/4" and was issued to commemorate the Washington Senators 1924 Series victory. The card features a blue tinted photo of Walter Johnson who was close to purchasing the Oakland minor league team at the time.

1 Walter Johnson	2,500.00	5,000.00

1931 Senators Team Issue Photos W-UNC

This 30-card team set of the Washington Senators measures approximately 6 1/8" by 9 3/8" and features sepia-toned player photos printed on thin paper stock. The backs are blank. The cards are unnumbered and checklisted below in alphabetical order.

COMPLETE SET (30)	125.00	250.00
1 Nick Altrock CO	6.00	12.00
2 Oswald Bluege	7.50	15.00
3 Cliff Bolton	5.00	10.00
4 Lloyd Brown	5.00	10.00
5 Robert Burke	5.00	10.00
6 Joe Cronin	20.00	40.00
7 Alvin Crowder	5.00	10.00
8 E.B. Eynon Jr.	5.00	10.00
9 Charles Fischer	5.00	10.00
10 Edward Gharrity	5.00	10.00
11 Clark Griffith OWN	20.00	40.00
12 Irving Hadley	5.00	10.00
13 William Hargrave	5.00	10.00
14 David Harris	5.00	10.00
15 Jack Hayes	5.00	10.00
16 Walter Johnson MG	75.00	150.00
17 Sam Jones	6.00	12.00
18 Baxter Jordan	5.00	10.00
19 Joe Judge	5.00	10.00
20 Joe Kuhel	5.00	10.00
21 Henry Manush	10.00	20.00
22 Fred Marberry	6.00	12.00
23 Mike Martin	5.00	10.00
24 Walter Masters	5.00	10.00
25 Charles Myer	6.00	12.00
26 Harry Rice	5.00	10.00
27 Sam Rice	20.00	40.00
28 Al Schacht CO	10.00	20.00
29 Ray Spencer	5.00	10.00
30 Sam West	5.00	10.00

1947 Senators Gunther Beer PC

These postcards usually featuring two players on the front were issued around 1947-48 based on the players in the set. The cards feature the players photos on the front along with their names in big bold black letters on the bottom. The backs have room for messages to be sent, usually from the Senators announcer at the time, Arch MacDonald. This listing may be incomplete so additions are welcome.

COMMON PLAYER	500.00	1,000.00
1 Joe Kuhel	50.00	100.00
2 Al Evans Scott Cary	50.00	100.00
3 Tom Ferrick Harold Keller	50.00	100.00
4 Mickey Haefner Forrest Thompson	50.00	100.00
5 Sid Hudson Al Kozar	50.00	100.00
6 Walter Masterson Rick Ferrell	60.00	120.00
7 Tom McBride Milo Candini	50.00	100.00
8 Marino Pieretti Leon Culberson	50.00	100.00
9 Sherrard Robertson Eddie Lyons	50.00	100.00
10 Ray Scarborough Kenneth McCreight	50.00	100.00
11 Mickey Vernon Gil Coan	60.00	120.00

1958 Senators Jay Publishing

This 12-card set of the Washington Senators measures approximately 5" by 7" and features black-and-white player photos in a white border. These cards were packaged 12 to a packet. The backs are blank. The cards are unnumbered and checklisted below in alphabetical order.

COMPLETE SET (12)	20.00	40.00
1 Rocky Bridges	2.00	4.00
2 Truman Clevenger	1.50	3.00
3 Clint Courtney	1.50	3.00
4 Dick Hyde	1.50	3.00
5 Cookie Lavagetto MG	2.00	4.00
6 Jim Lemon	1.50	3.00
7 Camilo Pascual	2.50	5.00
8 Albie Pearson	2.00	4.00
9 Herb Plews	1.50	3.00
10 Pedro Ramos	1.50	3.00
11 Roy Sievers	2.00	4.00
12 Eddie Yost	2.00	4.00

1958 Senators Team Issue

This 29-card set of the Washington Senators measures approximately 4" by 5" and features black-and-white player photos in a white border with a facsimile autograph printed on the front. These cards were originally sold through the mail by the club for 10 cents each. The cards are unnumbered and checklisted below in alphabetical order.

COMPLETE SET (29)	75.00	150.00
1 Ozzie Alvarez	2.50	5.00
2 Ken Aspromonte	2.50	5.00
3 Boom-Boom Beck CO	2.50	5.00
4 Julio Becquer	2.50	5.00
5 Rocky Bridges	3.00	6.00
6 Neil Chrisley	2.50	5.00
7 Ellis Clary CO	2.50	5.00
8 Truman Clevenger	2.50	5.00
9 Clint Courtney	2.50	5.00
10 Ed Fitzgerald	2.50	5.00
11 Hal Griggs	2.50	5.00
12 Dick Hyde	2.50	5.00
13 Walter Johnson	5.00	10.00
14 Bill Jurges CO	2.50	5.00
15 Russ Kemmerer	2.50	5.00
16 Steve Korcheck	2.50	5.00
17 Cookie Lavagetto MG	3.00	6.00
18 Jim Lemon	2.50	5.00
19 Bob Malkmus	2.50	5.00
20 Camilio Pascual	4.00	8.00
21 Albie Pearson	3.00	6.00
22 Herb Plews	2.50	5.00
23 Pedro Ramos	2.50	5.00
24 Roy Sievers	4.00	8.00
25 Faye Throneberry	2.50	5.00
26 Vito Valentinetti	2.50	5.00
27 Eddie Yost	3.00	6.00
28 Norm Zauchin	2.50	5.00
29 Team Picture	10.00	20.00

1959 Senators Team Issue

This Washington Senators team set features black-and-white player photos in a white border and measures approximately 4" by 5". The cards are unnumbered and checklisted below in alphabetical order. This checklist may be incomplete and any known additions are welcomed.

COMPLETE SET	40.00	80.00
1 Ken Aspromonte	2.50	5.00
2 Julio Becquer	2.50	5.00
3 Reno Bertoia	2.50	5.00
4 Tex Clevenger	2.50	5.00
5 Billy Consolo	2.50	5.00
6 Clint Courtney	2.50	5.00
7 Bill Fischer	2.50	5.00
8 Hal Griggs	2.50	5.00
9 Russ Kemmerer	2.50	5.00
10 Ralph Lumenti	2.50	5.00
11 Hal Naragon	2.50	5.00
12 Camilo Pascual	4.00	8.00
13 J.W. Porter	2.50	5.00
14 Pedro Ramos	2.50	5.00
15 John Romonosky	2.50	5.00
16 Ron Samford	2.50	5.00
17 Jose Valdivielso	2.50	5.00
18 Hal Woodeshick	2.50	5.00

1959 Senators Team Issue 5 by 7

Measuring 5" by 7", these photos were issued by the Senators in 1959. Since these photos are unnumbered, we have sequenced them in alphabetical order.

COMPLETE SET	10.00	25.00
1 Reno Bertoia	1.50	3.00
2 Clint Courtney	1.50	3.00
3 Ed Fitzgerald	1.50	3.00

4 Dick Hyde	1.50	3.00
5 Cookie Lavagetto MG	1.50	3.00
6 Jim Lemon	1.50	3.00
7 Camilio Pascual	2.00	4.00
8 Albie Pearson	1.50	3.00
9 Herb Plews	1.50	3.00
10 Pedro Ramos	1.50	3.00
11 Roy Sievers	2.00	4.00
12 Norm Zauchin	1.50	3.00

1960 Senators Universal Match Corp.

This 20-cover set produced by the Universal Match Corp. of Washington, D.C. titled "Famous Senators" features a facial cut-out of a player on a cream. The "Mr. Senator" logo is printed in red, blue and black. The set was sponsored by 1st Federal Savings and Loan Associatiion. Complete matchbooks carry a fifty percent premium.

COMPLETE SET (20)	60.00	120.00
1 Nick Altrock	2.50	6.00
2 Ossie Bluege	2.50	6.00
3 Joe Cronin	5.00	12.00
4 Alvin Crowder	2.50	6.00
5 Goose Goslin	5.00	12.00
6 Clark Griffith	5.00	12.00
7 Bucky Harris	5.00	12.00
8 Walter Johnson	6.00	15.00
9 Joe Judge	2.50	6.00
10 Harmon Killebrew	6.00	15.00
11 Joe Kuhel	2.50	6.00
12 Buddy Lewis	2.50	6.00
13 Clyde Milan	2.50	6.00
14 Buddy Myer	2.50	6.00
15 Roger Peckinpaugh	2.50	6.00
16 Sam Rice	5.00	12.00
17 Roy Sievers	3.00	8.00
18 Stan Spence	2.50	6.00
19 Mickey Vernon	3.00	8.00
20 Sam West	2.50	6.00

1960 Senators Jay Publishing

This 12-card set of the Washington Senators measures approximately 5" by 7" and features black-and-white player photos in a white border. These cards were packaged 12 to a packet. The backs are blank. The cards are unnumbered and checklisted below in alphabetical order.

COMPLETE SET (12)	12.50	30.00
1 Bob Allison	1.25	3.00
2 Julio Becquer	.75	2.00
3 Truman Clevenger	.75	2.00
4 Billy Consolo	.75	2.00
5 Dan Dobbek	.75	2.00
6 William(Billy) Gardner	.75	2.00
7 Harmon Killebrew	4.00	10.00
8 Steve Korchek	.75	2.00
9 Cookie Lavagetto MG	1.00	2.50
10 Jim Lemon	.75	2.00
11 Camilo Pascual	1.25	3.00
12 Pedro Ramos	.75	2.00

1961 Senators Jay Publishing

This 12-card set of the first year expansion Washington Senators measures approximately 5" by 7". The fronts feature black-and-white posed player photos with the player's and team name printed below in the white border. These cards were packaged 12 in a packet. The backs are blank. The cards are unnumbered and checklisted below in alphabetical order.

COMPLETE SET (12)	8.00	20.00
1 Harry Bright	.75	2.00
2 Pete Daley	.75	2.00
3 Bennie Daniels	.75	2.00
4 Dick Donovan	.75	2.00
5 Bob Johnson	.75	2.00
6 Marty Keough	.75	2.00
7 R.C. Stevens	.75	2.00
8 Willie Tasby	.75	2.00
9 Coot Veal	.75	2.00
10 Mickey Vernon MG	1.00	2.50
11 Gene Woodling	1.00	2.50
12 Bud Zipfel	.75	2.00

1962 Senators Jay Publishing

Produced by Jay Publishing, this 12-card set features members of the Washington Senators. Originally, this set came in a plastic sack that included a "picture pak order form" and sold for 25 cents. Printed on thin stock paper, the cards measure approximately 5" by 7". On a white background the fronts have a black-and-white posed player photo. The player's name and team appear in black letters under the photo. The backs are blank. The cards are unnumbered and checklisted below in alphabetical order.

COMPLETE SET (12)	15.00	40.00
1 Pete Burnside	1.50	4.00
2 Chuck Cottier	1.50	4.00
3 Bernie Daniels	1.50	4.00
4 Bob Johnson	1.50	4.00
5 Marty Kutyna	1.50	4.00
6 Joe McClain	1.50	4.00
7 Danny O'Connell	1.50	4.00
8 Ken Retzer	1.50	4.00
9 Willie Tasby	1.50	4.00
10 Mickey Vernon MG	2.50	6.00
11 Gene Wooding	2.00	5.00
12 Bud Zipfel	1.50	4.00

1962 Senators Newberrys Little Pro

This one-card set was a promotional card for a batting practice device. The card measures approximately 4" by 5" and features a photo of Jimmy Piersall. The back displays a statement by Roger Maris as to the effectiveness of the device as a batting aid and a list of six reasons as to why it is a good batting tool.

1 Jimmy Piersall	6.00	15.00

1963 Senators Jay Publishing

This 12-card set of the Washington Senators measures approximately 5" by 7". The fronts feature black-and-white posed player photos with the player's and team name printed below in the white border. These cards were packaged 12 to a packet. The backs are blank. The cards are unnumbered and checklisted below in alphabetical order.

COMPLETE SET (12)	15.00	40.00
1 Tom Cheney	1.50	4.00
2 Bennie Daniels	1.50	4.00
3 Ken Hamlin	1.50	4.00
4 Chuck Hinton	1.50	4.00
5 Don Lock	1.50	4.00
6 Claude Osteen	2.50	6.00
7 Jim Piersall	3.00	8.00
8 Ken Retzer	1.50	4.00
9 Don Rudolph	1.50	4.00
10 Bob Schmidt	1.50	4.00
11 Dave Stenhouse	1.50	4.00
12 Mickey Vernon MG	2.00	5.00

1964 Senators Jay Publishing

This 12-card set of the Washington Senators measures approximately 5" by 7". The fronts feature black-and-white posed player photos with the player's and team name printed below in the white border. These cards were packaged 12 to a packet. The backs are blank. The cards are unnumbered and checklisted below in alphabetical order.

COMPLETE SET (12)	20.00	50.00
1 Don Blasingame	1.50	4.00
2 Tom Cheney	1.50	4.00
3 Chuck Cottier	1.50	4.00
4 Chuck Hinton	1.50	4.00
5 Gil Hodges MG	4.00	10.00
6 Jim King	1.50	4.00
7 Ron Kline	1.50	4.00
8 Don Leppert	1.50	4.00
9 Don Lock	1.50	4.00
10 Claude Osteen	2.50	6.00
11 Ed Roebuck	1.50	4.00
12 Don Rudolph	1.50	4.00

1965 Senators Jay Publishing

This 12-card set of the Washington Senators measures approximately 5" by 7". The fronts feature black-and-white posed player photos with the player's and team name printed below in the white border. These cards were packaged 12 to a packet. The backs are blank. The cards are unnumbered and checklisted below in alphabetical order.

COMPLETE SET (12)	8.00	20.00
1 Don Blasingame	.75	2.00
2 Ed Brinkman	.75	2.00
3 Mike Brumley	.75	2.00
4 Woodie Held	.75	2.00
5 Gil Hodges MG	2.00	5.00
6 Frank Howard	1.50	4.00
7 Jim King	.75	2.00
8 Don Lock	.75	2.00
9 Ken McMullen	.75	2.00
10 Buster Narum	.75	2.00
11 Phil Ortega	.75	2.00
12 Pete Richert	.75	2.00

1966 Senators Team Issue

This 12-card set of the Washington Senators measures approximately 5" by 7" and is printed on textured paper stock. The fronts feature black-and-white posed player photos with the player's and team name printed below in the white border. These cards were packaged 12 to a packet and could be obtained from the team through a mail-in offer. The twelfth player in the pack is unknown. The backs are blank. The cards are unnumbered and checklisted below in alphabetical order.

COMPLETE SET (12)	12.50	30.00
1 Don Blasingame	1.00	2.50
2 Ed Brinkman/(Without hat)	1.00	2.50
3 Mike Brumley	1.00	2.50
4 Bob Chance	1.00	2.50
5 Bennie Daniels	1.00	2.50
6 Woodie Held	1.00	2.50
7 Gil Hodges	2.50	6.00
8 Frank Howard	2.00	5.00
9 Don Lock	1.00	2.50
10 Phil Ortega	1.00	2.50
11 Pete Richert/(With plain cap)	1.00	2.50
12 Unknown player		

1967 Senators Postcards

This 22-card set of the Washington Senators features borderless black-and-white player photos with a facsimile autograph in a white bar at the bottom. The cards measure approximately 3 1/2" by 5 13/16". The backs are blank. The cards are unnumbered and checklisted below in alphabetical order.

COMPLETE SET (22)	8.00	20.00
1 Bernie Allen	.40	1.00
2 Hank Allen	.40	1.00
3 Dave Baldwin	.40	1.00
4 Frank Bertaina	.40	1.00
5 Ed Brinkman	.40	1.00
6 Doug Camilli	.40	1.00
7 Paul Casanova	.40	1.00
8 Joe Coleman	.40	1.00
9 Tim Cullen	.40	1.00
10 Mike Esptein	.40	1.00
11 Frank Howard	2.00	5.00
12 Bob Humphreys	.40	1.00
13 Darold Knowles	.40	1.00
14 Dick Lines	.40	1.00
15 Ken McMullen	.40	1.00
16 Dick Nen	.40	1.00
17 Phil Ortega	.40	1.00
18 Camilo Pascual	.60	1.50
19 Cap Peterson	.40	1.00
20 Bob Priddy	.40	1.00
21 Bob Saverine	.40	1.00
22 Fred Valentine	.40	1.00

1967 Senators Team Issue

This 12-card set of the Washington Senators measures approximately 5" by 7" and is printed on textured paper stock. The fronts feature black-and-white posed player photos with the player's and team name printed below in the white border. These cards were packaged 12 to a packet and could be obtained from the team through a mail-in offer. The backs are blank. The cards are unnumbered and checklisted below in alphabetical order.

COMPLETE SET (12)	10.00	25.00
1 Bernie Allen	.75	2.00
2 Ed Brinkman/(With hat)	.75	2.00
3 Paul Casanova	.75	2.00
4 Ken Harrelson	1.50	4.00
5 Gil Hodges	2.50	6.00
6 Frank Howard	2.00	5.00
7 Jim Lemon	.75	2.00
8 Ken McMullen	.75	2.00
9 Phil Ortega	.75	2.00
10 Camilo Pascual	1.25	3.00
11 Pete Richert/(With Senators cap)	.75	2.00
12 Fred Valentine	.75	2.00

1968 Senators Team Issue

This 12-card set of the Washington Senators measures approximately 5" by 7" and is printed on textured paper stock. The fronts feature black-and-white posed player photos with the player's and team name printed below in the white border. These cards were packaged 12 to a packet and could be obtained from the team through a mail-in offer. The backs are blank. The cards are unnumbered and checklisted below in alphabetical order.

COMPLETE SET (12)	10.00	25.00
1 Frank Bertaina	1.00	2.50
2 Paul Casanova	1.00	2.50
3 Frank Coggins	1.00	2.50
4 Mike Epstein	1.00	2.50
5 Ron Hansen	1.00	2.50
6 Frank Howard	2.00	5.00
7 Jim Lemon	1.00	2.50
8 Ken McMullen	1.00	2.50
9 Phil Ortega	1.00	2.50
10 Camilo Pascual	1.25	3.00
11 Cap Peterson	1.00	2.50
12 Fred Valentine	1.00	2.50

1968 Senators Team Issue 8 1/2x 11

This set features black-and-white player photos in white borders and measures 8 1/2" by 11". The backs are blank. The cards are unnumbered and checklisted below in alphabetical order. The checklist is incomplete and any known additions are welcomed.

COMPLETE SET	8.00	20.00
1 Ed Brinkman	4.00	10.00
2 Sid Hudson CO	4.00	10.00

1969-70 Senators Team Issue

This 16-card set of the Washington Senators measures approximately 4 1/4" by 7". The fronts display black-and-white player portraits bordered in white and printed on a grainy, textured card stock. The player's name and team are printed in the top margin. The backs are blank. The cards are unnumbered and checklisted below in alphabetical order.

COMPLETE SET (16)	15.00	40.00
1 Hank Allen	.75	2.00
2 Dick Bosman	.75	2.00
3 Ed Brinkman	.75	2.00
4 George Brunet	.75	2.00
5 Paul Casanova	.75	2.00
6 Joe Coleman	1.00	2.50
7 Mike Epstein	.75	2.00
8 Jim Hannan	.75	2.00
9 Frank Howard	1.50	4.00
10 Lee Maye	.75	2.00
11 Ken McMullen	.75	2.00
12 Camilo Pascual	1.25	3.00
13 Aurelio Rodriguez	.75	2.00
14 Ed Stroud	.75	2.00
15 Del Unser	.75	2.00
16 Ted Williams	6.00	15.00

1969 Senators Team Issue 8x10

This 20-card set features black-and-white player photos in white borders and measuring 8" by 10". The backs are blank. The cards are unnumbered and checklisted below in alphabetical order.

COMPLETE SET (20)	40.00	80.00
1 Bernie Allen	1.25	3.00
2 Hank Allen	1.25	3.00
3 Dave Baldwin	1.25	3.00
4 Dick Bosman	1.25	3.00
5 Ed Brinkman/(Batting)	1.25	3.00
6 Ed Brinkman/(Throwing)	1.25	3.00
7 Doug Camilli	1.25	3.00
8 Joe Coleman	1.50	4.00
9 Casey Cox	1.25	3.00
10 Mike Epstein	1.25	3.00
11 Nellie Fox CO	4.00	10.00
12 Frank Howard	2.50	6.00
13 Darold Knowles	1.25	3.00
14 Ken McMullen	1.25	3.00
15 Phil Ortega	1.25	3.00
16 Camilo Pascual	2.00	5.00
17 Cap Peterson	1.25	3.00
18 Del Unser	1.25	3.00
19 Fred Valentine	1.25	3.00
20 Ted Williams MG	8.00	20.00

1970 Senators Police Yellow

The 1970 Washington Senators Police set was issued on a thin unperforated cardboard sheet measuring approximately 12 1/2" by 8". The sheet is divided into ten cards by thin black lines. When the players are cut into individual cards, they measure approximately 2 1/2" by 4". The color of the sheet is yellow, and consequently the black and white borderless player photos have a similar cast. The player's name, position, and team name appear below the pictures. The backs have different safety messages sponsored by the Office of Traffic Safety, D.C. Department of Motor Vehicles. The cards are unnumbered and checklisted below in alphabetical order.

COMPLETE SET (10)	12.50	30.00
1 Dick Bosman	1.25	3.00
2 Eddie Brinkman	1.00	2.50
3 Paul Casanova	1.00	2.50
4 Mike Epstein	1.25	3.00
5 Frank Howard	3.00	8.00
6 Darold Knowles	1.00	2.50
7 Lee Maye	1.00	2.50
8 Aurelio Rodriguez	1.25	3.00
9 John Roseboro	1.25	3.00
10 Ed Stroud	1.00	2.50

1971 Senators Police Pink

The 1971 Washington Senators Police set was issued on a thin unperforated cardboard sheet measuring approximately 12 1/2" by 8". In contrast to the previous year's issue, the sheet is not divided up into separate cards by thin black lines. If the sheet were cut into individual player cards, each player's card would measure approximately 2 1/2" by 4". The color of the sheet ranges from pink to peach, and consequently the black and white borderless player photos have a similar cast. The player's name, position, and team name appear below the pictures. The backs have different safety messages sponsored by the Office of Traffic Safety, D.C. Department of Motor Vehicles. The cards are unnumbered and checklisted below in alphabetical order. The set is dated by the fact that it is Denny McLain's only year on the Senators.

COMPLETE SET (10)	12.50	30.00
1 Dick Bosman	1.25	3.00
2 Paul Casanova	1.00	2.50
3 Tim Cullen	1.00	2.50
4 Joe Foy	1.00	2.50
5 Toby Harrah	2.00	5.00
6 Frank Howard	3.00	8.00
7 Elliott Maddox	1.25	3.00
8 Tom McCraw	1.00	2.50
9 Denny McLain	2.00	5.00
10 Don Wert	1.00	2.50

1971 Senators Team Issue W-UNC

This 24-card set of the Washington Senators features black-and-white player photos with a facsimile autograph in the bottom margin. The cards measure approximately 3 1/2" by 5 3/4" and have blank backs. The cards are unnumbered and checklisted below in alphabetical order.

COMPLETE SET (24)	40.00	80.00
1 Bernie Allen	1.25	3.00
2 Larry Biittner	1.25	3.00
3 Dick Billings	1.25	3.00
4 Dick Bosman	1.50	4.00
5 Pete Broberg	1.25	3.00
6 Jackie Brown	1.25	3.00
7 Paul Casanova	1.25	3.00

8 Casey Cox 1.25 3.00
9 Tim Cullen 1.25 3.00
10 Bill Gogolewski 1.25 3.00
11 Joe Grzenda 1.25 3.00
12 Toby Harrah 2.50 6.00
13 Frank Howard 2.50 6.00
14 Paul Lindblad 1.25 3.00
15 Elliott Maddox 1.25 3.00
16 Denny McLain 2.50 6.00
17 Don Mincher 1.25 3.00
18 Dave Nelson 1.25 3.00
19 Horacio Pina 1.25 3.00
20 Lenny Randle 1.25 3.00
21 Denny Riddleberger 1.25 3.00
22 Jim Shellenback 1.25 3.00
23 Mike Thompson 1.25 3.00
24 Del Unser 1.25 3.00

1975 Senators 1924-25 TCMA

This 40-card set features black-and-white photos of the 1924-25 Washington Senators in white borders. The cards measure approximately 2 3/8" by 3 3/8". The backs carry player information and statistics. The cards are unnumbered and checklisted below in alphabetical order except for cards 38-40 which are jumbo cards.

COMPLETE SET (41) 10.00 25.00
1 Spencer Adams .20 .50
2 Nick Altrock .75 2.00
3 Ossie Bluege .40 1.00
4 Stan Coveleski .75 2.00
5 Alex Ferguson .20 .50
6 Showboat Fischer .20 .50
7 Goose Goslin .75 2.00
8 Bert Griffith .20 .50
9 Pinky Hargrave .20 .50
10 Bucky Harris P MG .75 2.00
11 Joe Harris .20 .50
12 Tex Jeans .20 .50
13 Walter Johnson 1.50 4.00
14 Joe Judge .60 1.50
15 Wade Lefler .20 .50
16 Nemo Leibold .20 .50
17 Fripo Marberry .20 .50
18 Joe Martina .20 .50
19 Wid Matthews .20 .50
20 Mike McNally .20 .50
21 Ralph Miller .20 .50
22 George Mogridge .20 .50
23 Buddy Myer .20 .50
24 Curly Ogden .20 .50
25 Roger Peckinpaugh .40 1.00
26 Sam Rice .20 .50
27 Muddy Ruel .20 .50
28 Dutch Ruether .20 .50
29 Allen Russell .20 .50
30 Hank Severeid .20 .50
31 Everett Scott .20 .50
32 Mule Shirley .20 .50
33 By Speece .20 .50
34 Bennie Tate .20 .50
35 Bobby Veach .20 .50
36 Tom Zachary .20 .50
37 Paul Zahniser .20 .50
38 Bucky Harris Bill McKechnie .40 1.00
39 Ossie Bluege Roger Peckinpaugh Harris Joe Judge .40 1.00
40 Tom Zachary Firpo Marberry Alex Ferguson Walter .75 2.00
41 Earl McNeely .40 1.00

1910 Sepia Anon PC796

This sepia with white border set measures 3 1/2" by 5 1/2", was issued circa 1910 and features 25 cards of popular players of the era. No markings are found either on the front or on the backs to indicate a manufacturer or issuer. The Cobb and Wagner card spells Honus' name as Honas. The same checklist is also used for the PC Novelty Cultery Co set. The pictures in that set have been reduced and enclosed in an ornate frame border. Postcards by either issuer are valued the same.

COMPLETE SET (25) 3,750.00 7,500.00
1 Roger Bresnahan Full catching pose 500.00 1,000.00
2 Al Bridwell Stooped fielding 250.00 500.00
3 Mordecai Brown Pitching - left leg up 400.00 800.00
4 Ty Cobb Batting to Hips 2,000.00 4,000.00
5 T.Cobb/H.Wagner Shaking Hands 1,250.00 2,500.00
6 Frank Chance MG Throwing 500.00 1,000.00
7 Hal Chase Fielding at first 400.00 800.00
8 Eddie Collins Batting 400.00 800.00
9 Sam Crawford Batting 400.00 800.00
10 Johnny Evers Germany Schaefer Standing 500.00 1,000.00
11 Art Devlin Glove outstretched 250.00 500.00
12 Red Dooin Arms High Ball in one hand; Glove the 250.00 500.00
13 Sam Frock Portrait 250.00 500.00
14 George Gibson Full catching position 250.00 500.00
15 Artie Hoffman Fielding for high one 250.00 500.00
16 Walter Johnson Pitching 1,000.00 2,000.00
17 Nap Lajoie Full batting pose 500.00 1,000.00
18 Harry Lord Throwing 250.00 500.00
19 Christy Mathewson Pitching -- right leg up 1,000.00 2,000.00
20 Orvall Overall Pitching -- left leg up 250.00 500.00
21 Eddie Plank Portrait -- hand over head 400.00 800.00
22 Tris Speaker Batting pose 500.00 1,000.00
23 Charley Street Full catching about to throw 250.00 500.00
24 Honus Wagner Full batting pose 1,000.00 2,000.00
25 Ed Walsh Full bunting pose 400.00 800.00

1977 Sertoma Stars

1 Hank Aaron 6.00 15.00
2 Bob Allison 2.50 6.00
3 Clete Boyer 2.50 6.00
4 Don Buford 2.50 6.00
5 Rod Carew 3.00 8.00
6 Rico Carty 2.50 6.00
7 Roberto Clemente 10.00 25.00
8 Jim Ray Hart 2.50 6.00
9 Dave Johnson 2.50 6.00
10 Harmon Killebrew 4.00 10.00
11 Mickey Mantle 12.50 30.00
12 Juan Marichal 3.00 8.00
13 Bill Mazeroski 3.00 8.00
14 Joe Morgan 3.00 8.00
15 Phil Niekro 3.00 8.00
16 Tony Oliva 3.00 8.00
17 Gaylord Perry 3.00 8.00
18 Boog Powell 2.50 6.00
19 Brooks Robinson 3.00 8.00
20 Frank Robinson 3.00 8.00
21 John Roseboro 2.50 6.00
22 Rusty Staub 2.50 6.00
23 Joe Torre 3.00 8.00
24 Jim Wynn 2.50 6.00

1977 Sertoma Stars Puzzle Backs

This 25-card set, measures approximately 2 3/4" by 4 1/4". The fronts feature a black-and-white player portrait in a black-framed circle on a yellow background. The player's name, position, sponsor logo, and card name are printed in black and red between a top and bottom row of black stars which border the card. The backs carry a puzzle piece which, when placed in the right position, form a picture of the 1913 Pittsburgh Nationals. The cards are unnumbered and checklisted below in alphabetical order. Although a 1978 set was planned and a checklist was distributed into the hobby; those cards were never produced.

COMPLETE SET (25) 30.00 60.00
1 Bernie Allen .20 .50
2 Frank(Home Run) Baker .75 2.00
3 Ted Beard .20 .50
4 Don Buford .20 .50
5 Eddie Cicotte .75 2.00
6 Roberto Clemente 2.50 6.00
7 Dom Dallessandro .20 .50
8 Carl Erskine .40 1.00
9 Nellie Fox .75 2.00
10 Lou Gehrig 2.50 6.00
11 Joe Jackson 2.50 6.00
12 Len Johnston .20 .50
13 Benny Kauff .20 .50
14 Dick Kenworthy .20 .50
15 Harmon Killebrew .75 2.00
16 Bob(Lefty) Logan .20 .50
17 Willie Mays 2.50 6.00
18 Satchell Paige 2.50 6.00
19 Edd Roush .75 2.00
20 Chico Ruiz .20 .50
21 Babe Ruth 4.00 10.00
22 Herb Score .40 1.00
23 George Sisler .75 2.00
24 George(Buck) Weaver .75 2.00
25 Early Wynn .75 2.00

1961 Seven-Eleven

The 1961 7-Eleven set consists of 30 cards, each measuring approximately 2 7/16" by 3 3/8". The checklist card states that this is the first series, and that a new series was to be released every two weeks (though apparently no other series were issued). The cards are printed on pink cardboard stock and the backs are blank and were available as seven cards for five cents. The fronts have a black and white headshot in the upper left portion and brief biographical information to the right of the picture. The player's name appears across the top of each front. The remainder of the front carries "1960 Hi Lites," which consist of a list of dates and the player's achievements on those dates. The team name across the bottom of the card rounds out the front. The cards are numbered on the front in the lower right corner.

COMPLETE SET (30) 1,100.00 2,200.00
1 Dave Sisler 100.00 200.00
2 Don Mossi 30.00 60.00
3 Joey Jay 20.00 50.00
4 Bob Purkey 20.00 50.00
5 Jack Fisher 20.00 50.00
6 John Romano 20.00 50.00
7 Russ Snyder 20.00 50.00
8 Johnny Temple 20.00 50.00
9 Roy Sievers 30.00 60.00
10 Ron Hansen 20.00 50.00
11 Pete Runnels 30.00 60.00
12 Gene Woodling 30.00 60.00
13 Clint Courtney 20.00 50.00
14 Whitey Herzog 40.00 80.00
15 Warren Spahn 75.00 150.00
16 Stan Musial 150.00 300.00
17 Willie Mays 150.00 300.00
18 Ken Boyer 40.00 80.00
19 Joe Cunningham 30.00 60.00
20 Orlando Cepeda 50.00 100.00
21 Gil Hodges 50.00 100.00
22 Yogi Berra 100.00 200.00
23 Ernie Banks 200.00 400.00
24 Lou Burdette 40.00 80.00
25 Roger Maris 200.00 400.00
26 Charlie Smith 20.00 50.00
27 Jimmie Foxx 50.00 100.00
28 Mel Ott 50.00 100.00
29 Don Nottebart 20.00 50.00
NNO Checklist Card 150.00 300.00

1975 Shakey's Pizza

This 18-card set measures 2 3/4" by 3 1/2" and features black-and-white players photos on a white card face. The red Shakey's Pizza logo overlaps the lower left corner of the picture. The phrase "West Coast Greats" cuts diagonally across the upper left corner of the picture. The player's name is printed below the photo in red. Red and brown stars accent the margins. The backs carry a Shakey's Pizza advertisement encouraging consumers to visit Shakey's Pizza parlors in Bellevue, Lake City, Aurora and West Seattle. The DiMaggio back has an offer for $1.00 off on a family-size pizza and were given away to the 1st 1,000 attendees at a Seattle card convention. The cards are numbered on the front below the picture.

COMPLETE SET (18) 40.00 80.00
1 Joe DiMaggio 6.00 15.00
2 Paul Waner 1.50 4.00
3 Lefty Gomez 1.50 4.00
4 Earl Averill 1.50 4.00
5 Ernie Lombardi 1.50 4.00
6 Joe Cronin 1.50 4.00
7 George Burns 1.25 3.00
8 Casey Stengel 2.50 6.00
9 Sam Crawford 1.50 4.00
10 Ted Williams 6.00 15.00
11 Fred Hutchinson 1.25 3.00
12 Duke Snider 2.50 6.00
13 Hal Chase 1.25 3.00
14 Bobby Doerr 1.50 4.00
15 Arky Vaughan 1.50 4.00
16 Tony Lazzeri 1.50 4.00
17 Lefty O'Doul 1.25 3.00
18 Stan Hack 1.25 3.00

1976 Shakey's Pizza

The 1976 Shakey's Pizza set contains 159 standard-size cards. The cards were part of a promotion at five Seattle-area Shakey's restaurants, and the "A" card could be exchanged for $1.00 off on any family-size pizza. The set is arranged according to year of induction into the Baseball Hall of Fame. The fronts feature vintage black and white player photos framed by red and white border stripes against a blue card face. The player's name appears in a baseball icon at the bottom of the picture. The backs have biography, career summary and player statistics.

COMPLETE SET (159) 50.00 100.00
1 Ty Cobb 2.50 6.00
2 Babe Ruth 4.00 10.00
3 Walter Johnson .75 2.00
4 Christy Mathewson .75 2.00
5 Honus Wagner 1.00 2.50
6 Nap Lajoie .75 2.00
7 Tris Speaker .60 1.50
8 Cy Young .75 2.00
9 Morgan G. Bulkeley .10 .25
10 Ban Johnson PRES .10 .25
11 John McGraw .60 1.50
12 Connie Mack .60 1.50
13 George Wright .20 .50
14 Grover Cleveland Alexander .40 1.00
15 Alexander Cartwright .10 .25
16 Henry Chadwick .10 .25
17 Eddie Collins .60 1.50
18 Lou Gehrig 2.50 6.00
19 Willie Keeler .20 .50
20 George Sisler .60 1.50
21 Cap Anson .60 1.50
22 Charles Comiskey .20 .50
23 Candy Cummings .20 .50
24 Buck Ewing .20 .50
25 Old Hoss Radbourne .20 .50
26 Al Spalding .20 .50
27 Rogers Hornsby .60 1.50
28 Kenesaw Landis COMM .10 .25
29 Roger Bresnahan .20 .50
30 Dan Brouthers .20 .50
31 Fred Clarke .20 .50
32 Jimmy Collins .20 .50
33 Ed Delahanty .20 .50
34 Hugh Duffy .20 .50
35 Hugh Jennings .20 .50
36 Mike King Kelly .20 .50
37 Jim O'Rourke .20 .50
38 Wilbert Robinson .20 .50
39 Jesse Burkett .20 .50
40 Frank Chance .60 1.50
41 Jack Chesbro .20 .50
42 Johnny Evers .60 1.50
43 Clark Griffith .20 .50
44 Tommy McCarthy .20 .50
45 Joe McGinnity .20 .50
46 Eddie Plank .20 .50
47 Joe Tinker .60 1.50
48 Rube Waddell .20 .50
49 Ed Walsh .20 .50
50 Mickey Cochrane .60 1.50
51 Frankie Frisch .20 .50
52 Lefty Grove .60 1.50
53 Carl Hubbell .20 .50
54 Herb Pennock .20 .50
55 Pie Traynor .60 1.50
56 Charley Gehringer .20 .50
57 Mordecai Brown .20 .50
58 Kid Nichols .20 .50
59 Jimmie Foxx .75 2.00
60 Mel Ott .60 1.50
61 Harry Heilmann .20 .50
62 Paul Waner .20 .50
63 Dizzy Dean .75 2.00
64 Al Simmons .20 .50
65 Ed Barrow .10 .25
66 Chief Bender .20 .50
67 Tommy Connolly .10 .25
68 Bill Klem .10 .25
69 Bobby Wallace .20 .50
70 Harry Wright .20 .50
71 Bill Dickey .60 1.50
72 Rabbit Maranville .20 .50
73 Bill Terry .20 .50
74 Joe DiMaggio 2.50 6.00
75 Gabby Hartnett .20 .50
76 Ted Lyons .20 .50
77 Dazzy Vance .20 .50
78 Home Run Baker .20 .50
79 Ray Schalk .20 .50
80 Joe Cronin .20 .50
81 Hank Greenberg .60 1.50
82 Sam Crawford .20 .50
83 Joe McCarthy MG .10 .25
84 Zack Wheat .20 .50
85 Max Carey .20 .50
86 Billy Hamilton .20 .50
87 Bob Feller .75 2.00
88 Jackie Robinson 2.50 6.00
89 Bill McKechnie .10 .25
90 Edd Roush .20 .50
91 John Clarkson .20 .50
92 Elmer Flick .20 .50
93 Sam Rice .20 .50
94 Eppa Rixey .20 .50
95 Luke Appling .20 .50
96 Red Faber .20 .50
97 Burleigh Grimes .20 .50
98 Miller Huggins .20 .50
99 Tim Keefe .20 .50
100 Heinie Manush .20 .50
101 Monte Ward .20 .50
102 Pud Galvin .20 .50
103 Ted Williams 2.50 6.00
104 Casey Stengel .60 1.50
105 Red Ruffing .20 .50
106 Branch Rickey .10 .25
107 Lloyd Waner .20 .50
108 Joe Medwick .20 .50
109 Kiki Cuyler .20 .50
110 Goose Goslin .20 .50
111 Roy Campanella .75 2.00
112 Stan Musial 1.00 2.50
113 Stan Coveleski .20 .50
114 Waite Hoyt .20 .50
115 Lou Boudreau .20 .50
116 Earle Combs .20 .50
117 Ford Frick COMM .10 .25
118 Jesse Haines .20 .50

119 Dave Bancroft	.20	.50
120 Jake Beckley	.20	.50
121 Chick Hafey	.20	.50
122 Harry Hooper	.20	.50
123 Joe Kelley	.20	.50
124 Rube Marquard	.20	.50
125 Satchel Paige	1.00	2.50
126 George Weiss GM	.10	.25
127 Yogi Berra	.60	1.50
128 Josh Gibson	1.00	2.50
129 Lefty Gomez	.20	.50
130 Will Harridge PRES	.10	.25
131 Sandy Koufax	.60	1.50
132 Buck Leonard	.20	.50
133 Early Wynn	.20	.50
134 Ross Youngs	.20	.50
135 Roberto Clemente	2.50	6.00
136 Billy Evans	.10	.25
137 Monte Irvin	.20	.50
138 George Kelly	.20	.50
139 Warren Spahn	.20	.50
140 Mickey Welch	.10	.25
141 Cool Papa Bell	.10	.25
142 Jim Bottomley	.10	.25
143 Jocko Conlan	.10	.25
144 Whitey Ford	.10	.25
145 Mickey Mantle	4.00	10.00
146 Sam Thompson	.20	.50
147 Earl Averill	.20	.50
148 Bucky Harris	.20	.50
149 Billy Herman	.20	.50
150 Judy Johnson	.20	.50
151 Ralph Kiner	.40	1.00
152 Oscar Charleston	.20	.50
153 Roger Connor	.20	.50
154 Cal Hubbard	.20	.50
155 Bob Lemon	.20	.50
156 Fred Lindstrom	.20	.50
157 Robin Roberts	.40	1.00
158 Robin Roberts Same picture and text as previous	.40	1.00
A Earl Averill	.10	.25

1977 Shakey's Pizza

In this 28-card commemorative set, cards A-C were issued in honor of baseball's "1977 WASSCA Convention Superstars." Cards 1-25 honor "All-Time Superstars." They were available at five Seattle area Shakey's: Bellevue, Lake City, Aurora, West Seattle and at Elliott and Broad. The cards measure 2 1/4" by 3" and feature posed and action black-and-white player photos with faded maroon borders. A blue facsimile autograph runs across the bottom of each picture. The backs carry the player's name, career highlights and statistics in the form of "Seasonal Bests."

COMPLETE SET (28)	20.00	50.00
1 Connie Mack	.60	1.50
2 John McGraw	.40	1.00
3 Cy Young	.60	1.50
4 Walter Johnson	.60	1.50
5 Grover C. Alexander	.60	1.50
6 Christy Mathewson	.60	1.50
7 Lefty Grove	.60	1.50
8 Mickey Cochrane	.40	1.00
9 Bill Dickey	.40	1.00
10 Lou Gehrig	2.50	6.00
11 George Sisler	.40	1.00
12 Cap Anson	.40	1.00
13 Jimmie Foxx	.60	1.50
14 Rogers Hornsby	1.00	2.50
15 Nap Lajoie	.60	1.50
16 Eddie Collins	.40	1.00
17 Pie Traynor	.40	1.00
18 Honus Wagner	.60	1.50
19 Ty Cobb	2.50	6.00
20 Babe Ruth	3.00	8.00
21 Joe Jackson	2.00	5.00
22 Tris Speaker	.60	1.50
23 Ted Williams	2.00	5.00
24 Joe DiMaggio	2.00	5.00
25 Stan Musial	1.00	2.50
A Earl Averill	.30	.75
B Johnny Mize	.30	.75
C Bob Johnson	.20	.50

1949 R447 Smack-A-Roo

1 Pop Fly	10.00	25.00
2 Ball Hits Home Plate	10.00	25.00
3 Ball Hits Batter	10.00	25.00
4 Hit by Pitcher	10.00	25.00
5 Scoring Descision	10.00	25.00
6 Pitcher Drops Ball	10.00	25.00
7 Fan Reaches Over Fence	10.00	25.00
8 Municipal Stadium	10.00	25.00
9 Longest Distances	10.00	25.00
10 Longest Game in History	10.00	25.00
11 Double Play	10.00	25.00
12 Babe Ruth	12.50	30.00
13 New York Giants	10.00	25.00
14 Base Measurements	10.00	25.00
15 Fielder Throws Glove	10.00	25.00
16 Bunted Ball	10.00	25.00

1926 Sport Company of America

This 151-card set encompasses athletes from a multitude of different sports. There are 49-cards representing baseball and 14-cards for football. Each includes a black-and-white player photo within a fancy frame border. The player's name and sport are printed at the bottom. The backs carry a short player biography and statistics. The cards originally came in a small glassine envelope along with a coupon that could be redeemed for sporting equipment and are often still found in this form. The cards are unnumbered and have been checklisted below in alphabetical order within sport. We've assigned prefixes to the card numbers which serves to group the cards by sport (BB- baseball, FB- football).

BB1 Babe Adams	40.00	80.00
BB2 Grover Alexander	75.00	150.00
BB3 Nick Altrock	25.00	50.00
BB4 Dave Bancroft	75.00	150.00
BB5 Jesse Barnes	25.00	50.00
BB6 Ossie Bluege	25.00	50.00
BB7 Jim Bottomley	50.00	100.00
BB8 Max Carey	50.00	100.00
BB9 Ty Cobb	500.00	800.00
BB10 Mickey Cochrane	75.00	150.00
BB11 Eddie Collins	75.00	150.00
BB12 Stan Coveleski	50.00	100.00
BB13 Kiki Cuyler	50.00	100.00
BB14 Hank DeBerry	25.00	50.00
BB15 Jack Fournier	25.00	50.00
BB16 Goose Goslin	50.00	100.00
BB17 Charley Grimm	40.00	80.00
BB18 Bucky Harris	50.00	100.00
BB19 Gabby Hartnett	50.00	100.00
BB20 Fred Hofmann	25.00	50.00
BB21 Rogers Hornsby	100.00	200.00
BB22 Waite Hoyt	50.00	100.00
BB23 Walter Johnson	200.00	400.00
BB24 Joe Judge	25.00	50.00
BB25 Willie Kamm	25.00	50.00
BB26 Tony Lazzeri	50.00	100.00
BB27 Rabbit Maranville	50.00	100.00
BB28 Firpo Marberry	25.00	50.00
BB29 Rube Marquard	50.00	100.00
BB30 Stuffy McInnis	25.00	50.00
BB31 Babe Pinelli	25.00	50.00
BB32 Wally Pipp	25.00	50.00
BB33 Sam Rice	50.00	100.00
BB34 Emory Rigney	25.00	50.00
BB35 Dutch Ruether	25.00	50.00
BB36 Babe Ruth	600.00	1,000.00
BB37 Ray Schalk	50.00	100.00
BB38 Joe Sewell	50.00	100.00
BB39 Urban Shocker	40.00	80.00
BB40 Al Simmons	50.00	100.00
BB41 George Sisler	75.00	150.00
BB42 Tris Speaker	100.00	200.00
BB43 Pie Traynor	75.00	150.00
BB44 George Uhle	25.00	50.00
BB45 Paul Waner	75.00	150.00
BB46 Aaron Ward	25.00	50.00
BB47 Ken Williams	40.00	80.00
BB48 Glenn Wright	25.00	50.00
BB49 Emil Yde	25.00	50.00

1967-71 Sport Hobbyist Famous Cards

This 48-card set was issued in two series. The first two series (1-30), measuring approximately 2 1/4" by 3 3/4", features black-and-white player photos. The card numbered 2 is unknown. The second series (31-51), measuring approximately 2" by 3", features black-and-white player photos with red borders. There are no cards numbered 42, 44, nor 46. Each of the first two series cost $1 from the producer of these cards.

COMPLETE SET (48)	30.00	60.00
1 Honus Wagner T206	4.00	10.00
2 Unknown		
3 Simmons C46	.40	1.00
4 Christy Mathewson M116	1.00	2.50
5 Jack Barry M101-5	.40	1.00
6 Mordecai Brown T204	1.00	2.50
7 Webb D322 Tip Top Bread	.40	1.00
8 Lou Criger S74	.40	1.00
9 Kiki Cuyler R333	.75	2.00
10 Nap Lajoie R319	1.00	2.50
11 John McGraw T205	1.00	2.50
12 Addie Joss E107	.75	2.00
13 George Sisler W502	.75	2.00
14 Buck Ewing Allen & Ginter #29	.60	1.50
15 Chief Bender E90	.60	1.50
16 George Mullin E104	.40	1.00
17 Fred Merkle E95	.40	1.00
18 Walter Schang E121	.40	1.00
19 Tim Keefe Allen & Ginter #28	.40	1.00
20 Harold Muddy Ruel E120	.40	1.00
21 Irving Jack Burns D382	.40	1.00
22 George Connally D382	.40	1.00
23 Myril Hoag D382	.40	1.00
24 Willie Kamm D382	.40	1.00
25 Dutch Leonard D382	.40	1.00
26 Clyde Manion D382	.40	1.00
27 Johnny Vergez D382	.40	1.00
28 Tom Zachary D382	.40	1.00
29 Ty Cobb E145	.40	1.00
30 Richardson Playing Card	.40	1.00
31 Ed Abbaticchio T206	.40	1.00
32 Barbeau T206	.40	1.00
33 Burch T206	.40	1.00
34 Mordecai Brown T206	1.00	2.50
35 Hal Chase T206	.75	2.00
36 Ball T206	.40	1.00
37 Abstein T206	.40	1.00
38 Bowerman T206	.40	1.00
39 Hal Chase T206	.75	2.00
40 Criss T206	.40	1.00
41 Beck T206	.40	1.00
43 Bradley T206	.40	1.00
45 Kitty Bransfield T206	.40	1.00
47 Bell T206	.40	1.00
48 Bergen T206	.40	1.00
49 Chief Bender T206	.75	2.00
50 Bush T206	.40	1.00
51 Jack Chesbro T206	.60	1.50

1910-11 Sporting Life M116

The cards in this 288-card set (326 with all variations) measure approximately 1 1/2" by 2 5/8". The Sporting Life set was offered as a premium to the publication's subscribers in 1910 and 1911. Each of the 24 series of 12 cards, which cost four cents for each series, came in an envelope printed with a list of the players within. Cards marked with S1 or S2 followed by an asterisk can be found with both a blue background and a more common pastel background. Cards marked with S3 followed with an asterisk are found with either a blue or black printed Sporting Life advertisement on the reverse. McConnell appears with both Boston AL (common) and Chicago White Sox (scarce). Pricing is unavailable on the McConnell White Sox card, but a copy was sold at auction in 2007 graded EX+ by SGC for $31,024. McQuillan appears with Phillies (common) and Cincinnati (scarce). A card featuring Johnny Bates as a member of the Cincinnati Reds was recently discovered, and the first known copy sold for slightly more than $20,000 early in 2006.

COMPLETE SET (290)	20,000.00	40,000.00
COMMON MAJOR (1-280)	40.00	80.00
COMMON MINOR (280-288)	40.00	80.00
COMMON S19-S24	50.00	120.00
1 Ed Abbaticchio	70.00	120.00
2A Babe Adams Black Back	70.00	120.00
2B Babe Adams Blue Back	70.00	120.00
3 Red Ames	70.00	120.00
4 Jimmy Archer	70.00	120.00
5 Frank Arellanes	70.00	120.00
6 Tommy Atkins	70.00	120.00
7 Jimmy Austin	70.00	120.00
8 Les Bachman	70.00	120.00
9 Bill Bailey	70.00	120.00
10A Frank Baker Black Back	250.00	400.00
10B Frank Baker Blue Back	250.00	400.00
11 Cy Barger	70.00	120.00
12 Jack Barry	70.00	120.00
13A Johnny Bates Phil	70.00	120.00
13B Johnny Bates Cinc		
14 Ginger Beaumont	70.00	120.00
15 Fred Beck	70.00	120.00
16 Heine Beckendorf	70.00	120.00
17 Fred Beebe	70.00	120.00
18 George Bell	70.00	120.00
19 Harry Bemis	70.00	120.00
20A Chief Bender Blue	300.00	500.00
20B Chief Bender Pastel	250.00	400.00
21 Bill Bergen	70.00	120.00
22 Charles Berger	70.00	120.00
23 Bob Bescher	70.00	120.00
24 Joseph Birmingham	70.00	120.00
25 Lena Blackburn	70.00	120.00
26 Jack Bliss	70.00	120.00
27 James J. Block	70.00	120.00
28 Hugh Bradley	70.00	120.00
29 Kitty Bransfield	70.00	120.00
30A Roger Bresnahan Blue	300.00	500.00
30B Roger Bresnahan Pastel	250.00	400.00
31 Al Bridwell	70.00	120.00
32 Buster Brown	70.00	120.00
33A Mordecai Brown Blue	300.00	500.00
33B Mordecai Brown Pastel	250.00	400.00
34 Al Burch	70.00	120.00
35 Donie Bush	70.00	120.00
36 Bobby Byrne	70.00	120.00
37 Howie Camnitz	70.00	120.00
38 Vin Campbell	70.00	120.00
39 Bill Carrigan	70.00	120.00
40A Frank Chance Blue	300.00	500.00
40B Frank Chance Pastel	250.00	400.00
41 Chappy Charles	70.00	120.00
42A Hal Chase Blue	250.00	400.00
42B Hal Chase Pastel	175.00	300.00
43 Ed Cicotte	250.00	400.00
44A Fred Clarke Black Back	250.00	400.00
44B Fred Clarke Blue Back	250.00	400.00
45 Nig Clarke	70.00	120.00
46 Tommy Clarke	70.00	120.00
47A Ty Cobb Blue	2,500.00	4,000.00
47B Ty Cobb Pastel	1,800.00	3,000.00
48A Eddie Collins Blue	350.00	600.00
48B Eddie Collins Pastel	300.00	500.00
49 Ray Collins	70.00	120.00
50 Wid Conroy	70.00	120.00
51 Jack Coombs	70.00	120.00
52 Frank Corridon	70.00	120.00
53 Harry Coveleski	90.00	150.00
54 Doc Crandall	70.00	120.00
55A Sam Crawford Blue	300.00	500.00
55B Sam Crawford Pastel	250.00	400.00
56 Birdie Cree	70.00	120.00
57 Lou Criger	70.00	120.00
58 Dode Criss	70.00	120.00
59 Cliff Curtis	70.00	120.00
60 Bill Dahlen MG	70.00	120.00
61 William Davidson	70.00	120.00
62A Harry Davis Blue	90.00	150.00
62B Harry Davis Pastel	70.00	120.00
63 Jim Delehanty	70.00	120.00
64 Ray Demmitt	70.00	120.00
65 Frank Dessau	70.00	120.00
66A Art Devlin Black Back	70.00	120.00
66B Art Devlin Blue Back	70.00	120.00
67 Josh Devore	70.00	120.00
68 Pat Donahue	70.00	120.00
69 Patsy Donovan MG	70.00	120.00
70A Bill Donovan Blue	70.00	120.00
70B Bill Donovan Pastel	70.00	120.00
71A Red Dooin Blue	90.00	150.00
71B Red Dooin Pastel	70.00	120.00
72 Mickey Doolan	70.00	120.00
73 Patsy Dougherty	70.00	120.00
74 Tom Downey	70.00	120.00
75 Jim Doyle	70.00	120.00
76A Larry Doyle Blue	90.00	150.00
76B Larry Doyle Pastel	70.00	120.00
77 Hugh Duffy MG	250.00	400.00
78 Jimmy Dygert	70.00	120.00
79 Dick Eagan	70.00	120.00
80 Kid Elberfeld	70.00	120.00
81 Rube Ellis	70.00	120.00
82 Arthur Engle	70.00	120.00
83 Tex Erwin	70.00	120.00
84 Steve Evans	70.00	120.00
85A Johnny Evers Black Back	300.00	500.00
85B Johnny Evers Blue Back	300.00	500.00
86 Bob Ewing	70.00	120.00
87 Cy Falkenberg	70.00	120.00
88 George Ferguson	70.00	120.00
89 Art Fletcher	70.00	120.00
90 Elmer Flick	250.00	400.00
91 John Flynn	70.00	120.00
92 Russ Ford	70.00	120.00
93 Ed Foster	70.00	120.00
94 Bill Foxen	70.00	120.00
95 John Frill	70.00	120.00
96 Samuel Frock	70.00	120.00
97 Art Fromme	70.00	120.00
98 Earle Gardner New York	70.00	120.00
99 Larry Gardner Boston	70.00	120.00
100 Harry Gaspar	70.00	120.00
101 Doc Gessler	70.00	120.00
102A George Gibson Blue	90.00	150.00
102B George Gibson Pastel	70.00	120.00
103 Bert Graham	70.00	120.00
104 Peaches Graham	70.00	120.00
105 Eddie Grant	70.00	120.00
106 Clark Griffith MG	250.00	400.00
107 Ed Hahn	70.00	120.00
108 Charles Hall	70.00	120.00
109 Bob Harmon	70.00	120.00
110 Topsy Hartsel	70.00	120.00
111 Roy Hartzell	70.00	120.00
112 Heinie Heitmuller	70.00	120.00
113 Buck Herzog	70.00	120.00
114 Doc Hoblitzel	70.00	120.00
115 Danny Hoffman	70.00	120.00
116 Solly Hofman	70.00	120.00
117 Harry Hooper	250.00	400.00
118 Harry Howell	70.00	120.00
119 Miller Huggins	250.00	400.00
120 Tom Hughes ML	70.00	120.00
121 Rudy Hulswitt	70.00	120.00
122 John Hummel	70.00	120.00
123 George Hunter	70.00	120.00
124 Ham Hyatt	70.00	120.00
125 Fred Jacklitsch	70.00	120.00
126A Hugh Jennings MG Blue	300.00	500.00
126B Hugh Jennings MG Pastel	250.00	400.00
127 Walter Johnson	900.00	1,500.00
128A Davy Jones Blue	70.00	120.00
128B Davy Jones Pastel	70.00	120.00
129 Tom Jones	70.00	120.00
130A Tim Jordan Blue	90.00	150.00
130B Tim Jordan Pastel	70.00	120.00
131 Addie Joss	250.00	400.00
132 John Kane	70.00	120.00

1910-11 Sporting Life M116

133 Edwin Karge	70.00	120.00
134 Red Killifer	70.00	120.00
135 Johnny Kling	70.00	120.00
136 Otto Knabe	70.00	120.00
137 John Knight	70.00	120.00
138 Ed Konetchy	70.00	120.00
139 Harry Krause	70.00	120.00
140 Rube Kroh	70.00	120.00
141 Otto Krueger ML	70.00	120.00
142A Napoleon Lajoie Blue	600.00	1,000.00
142B Napoleon Lajoie Pastel	500.00	800.00
143 Joe Lake	70.00	120.00
144 Fred Lake MG	70.00	120.00
145 Frank LaPorte	70.00	120.00
146 Jack Lapp	70.00	120.00
147 Chick Lathers	70.00	120.00
148A Tommy Leach Blue	90.00	150.00
148B Tommy Leach Pastel	70.00	120.00
149 Sam Leever	70.00	120.00
150 Lefty Leifield	70.00	120.00
151 Ed Lennox	70.00	120.00
152 Frederick Link	70.00	120.00
153 Paddy Livingstone	70.00	120.00
154 Hans Lobert	70.00	120.00
155 Bris Lord	70.00	120.00
156A Harry Lord Blue	90.00	150.00
156B Harry Lord Pastel	70.00	120.00
157 Johnny Lush	70.00	120.00
158 Connie Mack MG	350.00	600.00
159 Thomas Madden	70.00	120.00
160 Nick Maddox	70.00	120.00
161 Sherry Magee	70.00	120.00
162A Christy Mathewson Blue	900.00	1,500.00
162B Christy Mathewson Pastel	900.00	1,500.00
163 Al Mattern	70.00	120.00
164 Jimmy McAleer MG	70.00	120.00
165 George McBride	70.00	120.00
166A Amby McConnell Bos	70.00	120.00
166B Amby McConnell Chi		
167 Pryor McElveen	70.00	120.00
168 John McGraw MG	300.00	500.00
169 Deacon McGuire MG	70.00	120.00
170 Stuffy McInnis	70.00	120.00
171 Harry McIntire	70.00	120.00
172 Matty McIntyre	70.00	120.00
173 Larry McLean	70.00	120.00
174 Tommy McMillan	70.00	120.00
175A G.McQuillan Cinc	3,500.00	6,000.00
175B G.McQuillan Phil Blue	90.00	150.00
175C G.McQuillan Phil Pastel	70.00	120.00
176 Paul Meloan	70.00	120.00
177 Fred Merkle	70.00	120.00
178 Chief Meyers	70.00	120.00
179 Clyde Milan	70.00	120.00
180 Dots Miller	70.00	120.00
181 Warren Miller	70.00	120.00
182 Fred Mitchell ML	70.00	120.00
183 Mike Mitchell	70.00	120.00
184 Earl Moore	70.00	120.00
185 Pat Moran	70.00	120.00
186A Lew Moren Black Back	70.00	120.00
186B Lew Moren Blue Back	90.00	150.00
187 Cy Morgan	70.00	120.00
188 George Moriarty	70.00	120.00
189 Mike Mowery	70.00	120.00
190A George Mullin Black Back	70.00	120.00
190B George Mullin Blue Back	90.00	150.00
191 Danny Murphy	70.00	120.00
192 Red Murray	70.00	120.00
193 Tom Needham	70.00	120.00
194 Harry Niles	70.00	120.00
195 Rebel Oakes	70.00	120.00
196 Jack O'Conner	70.00	120.00
197 Paddy O'Connor	70.00	120.00
198 Bill O'Hara ML	70.00	120.00
199 Rube Oldring	70.00	120.00
200 Charley O'Leary	70.00	120.00
201 Orvie Overall	70.00	120.00
202 Fred Parent	70.00	120.00
203 Dode Paskert	70.00	120.00
204 Frederick Payne	70.00	120.00
205 Barney Pelty	70.00	120.00
206 Hub Pernoll	70.00	120.00
207 George Perring ML	70.00	120.00
208 Big Jeff Pfeffer	70.00	120.00
209 Jack Pfiester	70.00	120.00
210 Art Phelan	70.00	120.00
211 Ed Phelps	70.00	120.00
212 Deacon Phillipe	70.00	120.00
213 Eddie Plank	700.00	1,200.00
214 Jack Powell	70.00	120.00
215 Billy (William) Purtell	70.00	120.00
216 Farmer Ray ML	70.00	120.00
217 Bugs Raymond	70.00	120.00
218 Doc Reisling	70.00	120.00
219 Ed Reulbach	70.00	120.00
220 Lew Richie	70.00	120.00
221 Jack Rowan	70.00	120.00
222A Nap Rucker Black Back	70.00	120.00
222B Nap Rucker Blue Back	70.00	120.00
223 Slim Sallee	70.00	120.00
224 Doc Scanlon	70.00	120.00
225 Germany Schaefer	70.00	120.00
226 Lou Schettler	70.00	120.00
227 Admiral Schlei	70.00	120.00
228 Boss Schmidt	70.00	120.00
229 Frank Schulte	70.00	120.00
230 Al Schweitzer	70.00	120.00
231 James Scott	70.00	120.00
232 James Seymour	70.00	120.00
233 Tillie Shafer	70.00	120.00
234 David Shean	70.00	120.00
235 Bayard Sharpe	70.00	120.00
236 Jimmy Sheckard	70.00	120.00
237 Mike Simon	70.00	120.00
238 Charlie Smith	70.00	120.00
239 Frank Smith	70.00	120.00
240 Harry Smith	70.00	120.00
241 Fred Snodgrass	70.00	120.00
242 Bob Spade UER	70.00	120.00
243 Tully Sparks	70.00	120.00
244 Tris Speaker	1,200.00	2,000.00
245 Jake Stahl	70.00	120.00
246 George Stallings MG	70.00	120.00
247 Oscar Stanage	70.00	120.00
248 Harry Steinfeldt	70.00	120.00
249 Jim Stephens	70.00	120.00
250 George Stone	70.00	120.00
251 George Stovall	70.00	120.00
252 Gabby Street	70.00	120.00
253 Sailor Stroud	70.00	120.00
254 Amos Strunk	70.00	120.00
255 George Suggs	70.00	120.00
256 Billy Sullivan	70.00	120.00
257A Ed Summers Black Back	70.00	120.00
257B Ed Summers Blue Back	70.00	120.00
258 Bill Sweeney	70.00	120.00
259 Jeff Sweeney	70.00	120.00
260 Lee Tannehill	70.00	120.00
261A Fred Tenney Blue	90.00	150.00
262B Fred Tenney Pastel	70.00	120.00
262A Ira Thomas Blue	90.00	150.00
262B Ira Thomas Pastel	70.00	120.00
263 John Thoney	70.00	120.00
264A Joe Tinker Black Back	250.00	400.00
264B Joe Tinker Blue Back	250.00	400.00
265 John Titus	70.00	120.00
266 Terry Turner	70.00	120.00
267 Bob Unglaub	70.00	120.00
268A Rube Waddell Black Back	250.00	400.00
268B Rube Waddell Blue Back	250.00	400.00
269A Hans Wagner Blue	5,000.00	8,000.00
269B Hans Wagner Pastel	3,000.00	5,000.00
270 Heinie Wagner	70.00	120.00
271 Bobby Wallace	175.00	300.00
272 Ed Walsh	250.00	400.00
273 Jimmy Walsh Gray	175.00	300.00
274 Jimmy Walsh White	175.00	300.00
275 Doc White	70.00	120.00
276 Kaiser Wilhelm	70.00	120.00
277 Ed Willett	70.00	120.00
278 Vic Willis	250.00	400.00
279 Art Wilson	70.00	120.00
280 Chief Wilson	70.00	120.00
281 Hooks Wiltse	70.00	120.00
282 Harry Wolter	70.00	120.00
283 Joe Wood	1,200.00	2,000.00
284 Ralph Works	70.00	120.00
285A Cy Young Black Back	900.00	1,500.00
285B Cy Young Blue Back	900.00	1,500.00
286 Irv Young	70.00	120.00
287 Heinie Zimmerman	70.00	120.00
288 Dutch Zwilling	70.00	120.00

1910-11 Sporting Life M116 Blank Backs

20A Chief Bender Blue
40A Frank Chance Blue
42A Hal Chase Blue
47A Ty Cobb Blue
48A Eddie Collins Blue
62A Harry Davis Blue
71A Red Dooin Blue
76A Larry Doyle Blue
126A Hugh Jennings Blue MG
162A Christy Mathewson Blue
175B George McQuillan Philadelphia Blue
269A Hans Wagner Blue

1911 Sporting Life Cabinets M110

This six-card set which measures approximately 5 5/8" by 7 1/2" was issued as a premium offer to the Sporting Life card set. These cards have a player photo surrounded by green borders with the players name on the bottom. The backs contain an advertisement for the Sporting Life newspaper. Since the cards are unnumbered, we have put them in alphabetical order.

COMPLETE SET (6)	20,000.00	40,000.00
1 Frank Chance	3,000.00	6,000.00
2 Hal Chase	2,500.00	5,000.00
3 Ty Cobb	6,000.00	12,000.00
4 Larry Lajoie	4,000.00	8,000.00
5 Christy Mathewson	5,000.00	10,000.00
6 Honus Wagner	5,000.00	10,000.00

1902-11 Sporting Life Cabinets W600

These large and attractive cabinet-type cards were issued by the Sporting Life Publishing Company over a period of years between 1902 and 1911. The exact number of cards in the set is not known but is estimated to be about 450. The cards are not numbered and might appear to have a slight reddish or sepia tinit. Many are found still in the glassine envelope in which they were issued. The backs are blank.

COMPLETE SET	75,000.00	150,000.00
1 Bill Abstein	600.00	1,200.00
2 Babe Adams	600.00	1,200.00
3 Whitey Alperman	600.00	1,200.00
4 Nick Altrock	750.00	1,500.00
5 Red Ames	600.00	1,200.00
6 Frank Arelanes	600.00	1,200.00
7 Charlie Armbruster	600.00	1,200.00
8 Bill Armour MG	600.00	1,200.00
9 Harry Arndt	600.00	1,200.00
10 Harry Aubrey	600.00	1,200.00
11 Jimmy Austin	750.00	1,500.00
12 Charlie Babb	600.00	1,200.00
13 Frank Baker	2,000.00	4,000.00
14 Jap Barbeau	600.00	1,200.00
15 George Barclay	600.00	1,200.00
16 Cy Barger	600.00	1,200.00
17 Jimmy Barrett	600.00	1,200.00
18 Shad Barry	600.00	1,200.00
19 Jack Barry	600.00	1,200.00
20 Harry Barton	600.00	1,200.00
21 Emil Batch	600.00	1,200.00
22 Johnny Bates	600.00	1,200.00
23 Harry Bay	600.00	1,200.00
24 Ginger Beaumont	600.00	1,200.00
25 Fred Beck	600.00	1,200.00
26 Henie Beckendorf	600.00	1,200.00
26a Jake Beckley		
27 Fred Beebe	600.00	1,200.00
28 George Bell	600.00	1,200.00
29 Harry Bemis	600.00	1,200.00
30 Chief Bender	1,250.00	2,500.00
31 Pug Bennett	600.00	1,200.00
32 Bill Bergen	600.00	1,200.00
33 C. Berger	600.00	1,200.00
34 Bill Bernhard	600.00	1,200.00
35 Bob Bescher	600.00	1,200.00
36 W. Beville	600.00	1,200.00
37 Lena Blackburne	600.00	1,200.00
38 Elmer Bliss	600.00	1,200.00
39 Frank Bowerman	600.00	1,200.00
40 Bill Bradley	600.00	1,200.00
41 W. Bradley	600.00	1,200.00
42 Dave Brain	600.00	1,200.00
43 Kitty Bransfield	600.00	1,200.00
44 Roger Bresnahan	1,250.00	2,500.00
45 Al Bridwell	600.00	1,200.00
46 Buster Brown	600.00	1,200.00
47 Mordecai Brown	1,250.00	2,500.00
48 Sam Brown	600.00	1,200.00
49 George Browne	600.00	1,200.00
50 Jimmy Burke	600.00	1,200.00
51 Jesse Burkett	1,250.00	2,500.00
52 Nixey Callahan	600.00	1,200.00
53 Howie Camnitz	600.00	1,200.00
54 Rip Cannell	600.00	1,200.00
55 Joe Cantillon MG	600.00	1,200.00
56 Pat Carney	600.00	1,200.00
57 Charlie Carr	600.00	1,200.00
58 Bill Carrigan	600.00	1,200.00
59 Doc Casey	600.00	1,200.00
60 Louis Castro		
61 Frank Chance	3,000.00	6,000.00
62 Hal Chase	1,000.00	2,000.00
63 Jack Chesbro	1,250.00	2,500.00
64 Eddie Cicotte	1,250.00	2,500.00
65 Fred Clarke	1,250.00	2,500.00
66 Nig Clarke	600.00	1,200.00
67 T. Clarke	600.00	1,200.00
68 Walter Clarkson	600.00	1,200.00
69 Otis Clymer	600.00	1,200.00
70 Andy Coakley	600.00	1,200.00
71 Ty Cobb	10,000.00	20,000.00
72 Eddie Collins	1,250.00	2,500.00
73 Jimmy Collins	2,000.00	4,000.00
74 Bunk Congalton	600.00	1,200.00
75 Wid Conroy	600.00	1,200.00
76 Duff Cooley	600.00	1,200.00
77 Jack Coombs	750.00	1,500.00
78 Frank Corridon	600.00	1,200.00
79 Bill Coughlin	600.00	1,200.00
80 Ernie Courtney	600.00	1,200.00
81 Doc Crandall	600.00	1,200.00
82 Sam Crawford	1,250.00	2,500.00
83 Lou Criger	600.00	1,200.00
84 Dode Criss	600.00	1,200.00
85 John Cronin	750.00	1,500.00
86 Lave Cross	600.00	1,200.00
87 Monte Cross	600.00	1,200.00
88 Clarence Currie	600.00	1,200.00
89 Bill Dahlen	750.00	1,500.00
90 George Davis	2,000.00	4,000.00
91 Harry Davis	600.00	1,200.00
92 Jim Delehanty	750.00	1,500.00
93 Art Devlin	750.00	1,500.00
94 Pop Dillon	600.00	1,200.00
95 Bill Dineen	600.00	1,200.00
96 John Dobbs	600.00	1,200.00
97 Ed Doheny	600.00	1,200.00
98 Cozy Dolan	600.00	1,200.00
99 Jiggs Donahue	600.00	1,200.00
100 Mike Donlin	1,000.00	2,000.00
101 Patsy Donovan	600.00	1,200.00
102 Bill Donovan	600.00	1,200.00
103 Red Dooin	600.00	1,200.00
104 Mickey Doolan	600.00	1,200.00
105 Tom Doran	600.00	1,200.00
106 Gus Dorner	600.00	1,200.00
107 Patsy Dougherty	600.00	1,200.00
108 Tom Downey	600.00	1,200.00
109 Red Downs	600.00	1,200.00
110 Jim Doyle	600.00	1,200.00
111 Joe Doyle	600.00	1,200.00
112 Larry Doyle	750.00	1,500.00
113 Hugh Duffy	1,250.00	2,500.00
114 Bill Duggleby	600.00	1,200.00
115 Gus Dundon	600.00	1,200.00
116 Jack Dunleavy	600.00	1,200.00
117 Jack Dunn	750.00	1,500.00
118 Jimmy Dygert	600.00	1,200.00
119 Dick Egan	600.00	1,200.00
120 Kid Elberfeld	750.00	1,500.00
121 Claude Elliott	600.00	1,200.00
122 Rube Ellis	600.00	1,200.00
123 Johnny Evers	2,000.00	4,000.00
124 Bob Ewing	600.00	1,200.00
125 Cy Falkenberg	600.00	1,200.00
126 John Farrell	600.00	1,200.00
127 George Ferguson	600.00	1,200.00
128 Hobe Ferris	600.00	1,200.00
129 Tom Fisher	600.00	1,200.00
130 Patsy Flaherty	600.00	1,200.00
131 Elmer Flick	1,250.00	2,500.00
132 John Flynn	600.00	1,200.00
133 Bill Foxen	600.00	1,200.00
134 Chick Fraser	600.00	1,200.00
135 Bill Friel	600.00	1,200.00
136 Art Fromme	600.00	1,200.00
137 Dave Fultz	600.00	1,200.00
138 Bob Ganley	600.00	1,200.00
139 John Ganzel	600.00	1,200.00
140 Ned Garvin	600.00	1,200.00
141 Harry Gasper	600.00	1,200.00
142 Phil Geier	600.00	1,200.00
143 Doc Gessler	600.00	1,200.00
144 George Gibson	600.00	1,200.00
145 Norwood Gibson	600.00	1,200.00
146 Billy Gilbert	600.00	1,200.00
147 Fred Glade	600.00	1,200.00
148 Harry Gleason	750.00	1,500.00
149 Eddie Grant	750.00	1,500.00
150 Danny Green	600.00	1,200.00
151 Ed Gremminger	600.00	1,200.00
152 Clark Griffith	1,250.00	2,500.00
153 Moose Grimshaw	600.00	1,200.00
154 H. Hackett	600.00	1,200.00
155 Ed Hahn	600.00	1,200.00
156 Noodles Hahn	750.00	1,500.00
157 Charley Hall	600.00	1,200.00
158 Bill Hallman	600.00	1,200.00
159 Ned Hanlon MG	1,250.00	2,500.00
160 Bob Harmon	600.00	1,200.00
161 Jack Harper	600.00	1,200.00
162 Hub Hart	600.00	1,200.00
163 Topsy Hartsel	600.00	1,200.00
164 Roy Hartzell	600.00	1,200.00
165 Charlie Hemphill	600.00	1,200.00
166 Weldon Henley	600.00	1,200.00
167 Otto Hess	600.00	1,200.00
168 Mike Heydon	600.00	1,200.00
169 Piano Legs Hickman	600.00	1,200.00
170 Hunter Hill	600.00	1,200.00
171 Homer Hillebrand	600.00	1,200.00
172 Harry Hinchman	600.00	1,200.00
173 Bill Hinchman	600.00	1,200.00
174 Dick Hoblitzel	600.00	1,200.00
175 Danny Hoffman	600.00	1,200.00
176 Solly Hofman	600.00	1,200.00
177 Bill Hogg	600.00	1,200.00
178 A. Holesketter	600.00	1,200.00
179 Ducky Holmes	600.00	1,200.00
180 Del Howard	600.00	1,200.00
181 Harry Howell	600.00	1,200.00
182 J. Huelsman	600.00	1,200.00
183 Miller Huggins	1,250.00	2,500.00
184 Jim Hughes	600.00	1,200.00
185 Tom Hughes	600.00	1,200.00
186 Rudy Hulswitt	600.00	1,200.00
187 John Hummell	600.00	1,200.00
189 Ham Hyatt	600.00	1,200.00
188 Berthold Hustings		
190 Frank Isbell	600.00	1,200.00
191 Fred Jacklitsch	600.00	1,200.00
192 Joe Jackson	6,000.00	12,000.00
193 H. Jacobson	600.00	1,200.00
194 Hugh Jennings MG	1,250.00	2,500.00
195 Charlie Jones	600.00	1,200.00
196 Davy Jones	600.00	1,200.00
197 Oscar Jones	600.00	1,200.00
198 Tom Jones	600.00	1,200.00
199 Dutch Jordan	600.00	1,200.00
200 Addie Joss	1,250.00	2,500.00
201 Mike Kahoe	600.00	1,200.00
202 Ed Karger	600.00	1,200.00
203 Bob Keefe	600.00	1,200.00
204 Willie Keeler	2,500.00	5,000.00
205 Bill Keister	600.00	1,200.00
206 Joe Kelley	1,250.00	2,500.00
207 Brickyard Kennedy	600.00	1,200.00
208 Ed Killian	600.00	1,200.00
209 J. Kissinger	600.00	1,200.00
210 Frank Kitson	600.00	1,200.00
211 Mal Kittridge	600.00	1,200.00
212 Red Kleinrow	600.00	1,200.00
213 Johnny Kling	750.00	1,500.00
214 Ben Koehler	600.00	1,200.00
215 Ed Konetchy	600.00	1,200.00
216 Harry Krause	600.00	1,200.00
217 Otto Krueger	600.00	1,200.00
218 Candy LaChance	600.00	1,200.00
219 Nap Lajoie	3,000.00	6,000.00
220 Joe Lake	600.00	1,200.00
221 Frank Laporte	600.00	1,200.00
222 L. Laroy	600.00	1,200.00
223 Tommy Leach	750.00	1,500.00
224 Watty Lee	600.00	1,200.00
225 Sam Leever	600.00	1,200.00
226 Phil Lewis	600.00	1,200.00
227 Vive Lindaman	600.00	1,200.00
228 Paddy Livingstone	600.00	1,200.00
229 Hans Lobert	750.00	1,500.00
230 Herman Long	600.00	1,200.00
231 Bris Lord	600.00	1,200.00
232 Harry Lord	750.00	1,500.00
233 Harry Lumley	600.00	1,200.00

234 Carl Lundgren	600.00	1,200.00
235 Johnny Lush	600.00	1,200.00
236 Connie Mack MG	2,500.00	5,000.00
237 Nick Maddox	600.00	1,200.00
238 Sherry Magee	1,000.00	2,000.00
239 George Magoon	600.00	1,200.00
240 John Malarkey	600.00	1,200.00
241 Billy Maloney	600.00	1,200.00
242 Doc Marshall	600.00	1,200.00
243 Christy Mathewson	5,000.00	10,000.00
244 Jimmy McAleer	600.00	1,200.00
245 Sport McAlister	600.00	1,200.00
246 Jack McCarthy	600.00	1,200.00
247 John McCloskey	600.00	1,200.00
248 Amby McConnell	600.00	1,200.00
249 Moose McCormick	600.00	1,200.00
250 Chappie McFarland	600.00	1,200.00
251 Herm McFarland	600.00	1,200.00
252 Dan McGann	600.00	1,200.00
253 Joe McGinnity	1,250.00	2,500.00
254 John McGraw MG	2,500.00	5,000.00
255 Deacon McGuire	750.00	1,500.00
256 Harry McIntyre	600.00	1,200.00
257 Matty McIntyre	600.00	1,200.00
258 Larry McLean	600.00	1,200.00
259 Fred Merkle	1,000.00	2,000.00
260 Sam Mertes	600.00	1,200.00
261 Clyde Milan	750.00	1,500.00
262 Dots Miller	600.00	1,200.00
263 Billy Milligan	600.00	1,200.00
264 Fred Mitchell	600.00	1,200.00
265 Mike Mitchell	600.00	1,200.00
266 Earl Moore	600.00	1,200.00
267 Pat Moran	750.00	1,500.00
268 Lew Moren	600.00	1,200.00
269 Cy Morgan	600.00	1,200.00
270 E. Moriarty	600.00	1,200.00
271 Jack Morrissey	600.00	1,200.00
272 Mike Mowery	600.00	1,200.00
273 George Mullin	750.00	1,500.00
274 Danny Murphy	600.00	1,200.00
275 Red Murray	600.00	1,200.00
276 W. Murray	600.00	1,200.00
277 Jim Nealon	600.00	1,200.00
278 D. Needham	600.00	1,200.00
279 Doc Newton	600.00	1,200.00
280 Harry Niles	600.00	1,200.00
281 Rabbit Nill	600.00	1,200.00
282 Pete Noonan	600.00	1,200.00
283 Jack O'Brien	600.00	1,200.00
284 Pete O'Brien	600.00	1,200.00
285 Rube Oldring	600.00	1,200.00
286 Charley O'Leary	600.00	1,200.00
287 Jack O'Neil	600.00	1,200.00
288 Mike O'Neil	600.00	1,200.00
289 Al Orth	600.00	1,200.00
290 Orvie Overall	600.00	1,200.00
291 Frank Owens	600.00	1,200.00
292 Freddie Parent	600.00	1,200.00
293 Dode Paskert	600.00	1,200.00
294 Jim Pastorious	600.00	1,200.00
295 Roy Paterson	600.00	1,200.00
296 Fred Payne	600.00	1,200.00
297 Barney Pelty	600.00	1,200.00
298 Big Jeff Pfeiffer	600.00	1,200.00
299 Jack Pfiester	600.00	1,200.00
300 Ed Phelps	600.00	1,200.00
301 Deacon Phillippe	750.00	1,500.00
302 Bill Phillips	600.00	1,200.00
303 Ollie Pickering	600.00	1,200.00
304 Eddie Plank	2,500.00	5,000.00
305 Ed Poole	600.00	1,200.00
306 Jack Powell	600.00	1,200.00
307 Maurice Powers		
308 Billy Purtell	600.00	1,200.00
309 Ambrose Puttman	600.00	1,200.00
310 Tommy Raub	600.00	1,200.00
311 Fred Raymer	600.00	1,200.00
312 Bill Reidy	600.00	1,200.00
313 Ed Reulbach	1,000.00	2,000.00
314 Bob Rhoads	600.00	1,200.00
315 D. Richie	600.00	1,200.00
316 Claude Ritchey	600.00	1,200.00
317 Lew Ritter	600.00	1,200.00
318 C. Robinson	600.00	1,200.00
319 George Rohe	600.00	1,200.00
320 Claude Rossman	600.00	1,200.00
321 Frank Roth	600.00	1,200.00
322 Jack Rowan	600.00	1,200.00
323 Slim Sallee	600.00	1,200.00
324 Germany Schaefer	750.00	1,500.00
325 Admiral Schiel	600.00	1,200.00
326 Boss Schmidt	600.00	1,200.00
327 Harry Schmidt		
328 Ossie Schreckengost		
329 Frank Schulte	600.00	1,200.00
330 T. Sebring	600.00	1,200.00
331 Al Schweitzer	600.00	1,200.00
332 Kip Selbach	600.00	1,200.00
333 Cy Seymour	600.00	1,200.00
334 Spike Shannon	600.00	1,200.00
335 Danny Shay	600.00	1,200.00
336 Ralph Seybold		
337 Dave Shean	600.00	1,200.00
338 Jimmy Sheckard	600.00	1,200.00
339 Ed Siever	600.00	1,200.00
340 Jimmy Slagle	600.00	1,200.00
341 Jack Slattery	600.00	1,200.00
342 Charlie Smith	600.00	1,200.00
343 E. Smith	600.00	1,200.00
344 Frank Smith	600.00	1,200.00
345 Harry Smith	600.00	1,200.00
346 Homer Smoot	600.00	1,200.00
347 Tully Sparks	600.00	1,200.00
348 Chick Stahl	750.00	1,500.00
349 Jake Stahl	750.00	1,500.00
350 Joe Stanley	600.00	1,200.00
351 Harry Steinfeldt	750.00	1,500.00
352 George Stone	600.00	1,200.00
353 George Stovall	600.00	1,200.00
354 Jesss Stovall	600.00	1,200.00
355 Sammy Strang	600.00	1,200.00
356 Elmer Stricklett	600.00	1,200.00
357 Willie Sudhoff	600.00	1,200.00
358 Joe Sugden	600.00	1,200.00
359 Billy Sullivan	600.00	1,200.00
360 Ed Summers	600.00	1,200.00
361 Bill Sweeney	600.00	1,200.00
362 Lee Tannehill	600.00	1,200.00
363 Jack Taylor	600.00	1,200.00
364 Dummy Taylor	600.00	1,200.00
365 Fred Tenney	600.00	1,200.00
366 Ira Thomas	600.00	1,200.00
367 Jack Thoney	600.00	1,200.00
368 Joe Tinker	1,250.00	2,500.00
369 Terry Turner	600.00	1,200.00
370 Bob Unglaub	600.00	1,200.00
371 George Van Haltren	600.00	1,200.00
372 Bucky Veil	600.00	1,200.00
373 Rube Waddell	2,000.00	4,000.00
374 Heinie Wagner	600.00	1,200.00
375 Honus Wagner	4,000.00	8,000.00
376 Bobby Wallace	1,250.00	2,500.00
377 Ed Walsh	2,000.00	4,000.00
378 Jack Warner	600.00	1,200.00
379 Art Weaver	600.00	1,200.00
380 Jake Weimer	600.00	1,200.00
381 Kirby White	600.00	1,200.00
382 Bob Wicker	600.00	1,200.00
383 F. Wilhelm	600.00	1,200.00
384 Ed Willett	600.00	1,200.00
385 Jimmy Williams	600.00	1,200.00
386 Otto Williams	600.00	1,200.00
387 Hooks Wiltse	750.00	1,500.00
388 George Winter	600.00	1,200.00
389 Bill Wolfe	600.00	1,200.00
390 Harry Wolverton	600.00	1,200.00
391 Howard Wilson		
392 Joe Yeager	600.00	1,200.00
393 Cy Young	4,000.00	8,000.00
394 Irv Young	600.00	1,200.00
395 Chief Zimmer	600.00	1,200.00
396 Henie Zimmerman	600.00	1,200.00

1899-00 Sporting News Supplements M101-1

Measuring approximately 9" by 11", these photos were issued as supplements in the Sporting News. This list is far from complete, so any additions are appreciated.

COMPLETE SET	7,500.00	15,000.00
1 Ted Breitenstein	250.00	500.00
2 Frank Chance	400.00	800.00
3 Jack Chesbro	300.00	600.00
4 Tom Corcoran	200.00	400.00
5 Bill Dahlen	250.00	500.00
6 Lou Criger	150.00	300.00
7 Lave Cross	150.00	300.00
8 George Davis	400.00	800.00
9 Ed Delahanty	300.00	600.00
10 Hugh Duffy	400.00	800.00
11 Frank Donahue	150.00	300.00
12 Patsy Donovan	200.00	400.00
13 Bill Dineen	200.00	400.00
14 Buck Freeman	200.00	400.00
15 Noodles Hahn	200.00	400.00
16 Ned Hanlon MG	300.00	600.00
18 Cowboy Jones	150.00	300.00
17 Hugh Jennings	400.00	800.00
19 Sam Leever	150.00	300.00
20 Herman Long	200.00	400.00
21 John McGraw	500.00	1,000.00
22 Heinie Peitz	150.00	300.00
23 Deacon Phillippe	250.00	500.00
24 Wilbert Robinson	400.00	800.00
25 Ed Scott	150.00	300.00
26 Chick Stahl	200.00	400.00
27 Jesse Tannehill	200.00	400.00
28 Roy Thomas	200.00	400.00
29 Honus Wagner	1,000.00	2,000.00
30 James Williams	150.00	300.00
31 Vic Willis	400.00	800.00
32 Cy Young	750.00	1,500.00
33 George Yeager	200.00	400.00

1909-13 Sporting News Supplements M101-2

These 100 8" x 10" sepia supplements were inserted in various issues of the Sporting News. We have identified the player and then given the date of the issue in which this supplement appears. The set is sequenced in order of appearence. No photos were issued between 4/14 and 8/25 in 1910. No photos were issued between 3/30 and 10/19 in 1911. No photos were issued between 1/18 and 10/03 in 1912.

COMPLETE SET (101)	6,000.00	12,000.00
1 Roger Bresnahan St. Louis NL/7/22/09	75.00	150.00
2 Denton T. Young Cleveland AL and Louis Criger#	100.00	200.00
3 Christopher Mathewson New York-N/8/5/09	200.00	400.00
4 Nap Lajoie Cleve/8/10/09	125.00	250.00
5 Tyrus R. Cobb 8/12/09	300.00	600.00
6 Nap Lajoie Cleveland/8/19/09	125.00	250.00
7 Sherwood N. Magee Philadelphia-N/8/26/09	30.00	60.00
8 Frank L. Chance Chicago-N/9/02/09	125.00	250.00
9 Edward Walsh Chicago-A/9/9/09	50.00	100.00
10 Nap Rucker Brooklyn/9/16/09	25.00	50.00
11 Honus Wagner Pittsburgh/9/23/09	200.00	400.00
12 Hugh Jennings MG Detroit/9/30/09	50.00	100.00
13 Fred C. Clarke Pittsburgh/10/07/09	100.00	200.00
14 Ban Johnson AL PRES/10/14/09	100.00	200.00
15 Charles Comiskey OWN Chicago White Sox/10/21/09	75.00	150.00
16 Eddie Collins Philadelphia-A/10/28/09	75.00	150.00
17 James A. McAleer Washington/11/04/09	25.00	50.00
18 Pittsburgh Pirates/11/11/09	50.00	100.00
19 Detroit Team/11/18/09	50.00	100.00
20 George Bell Brooklyn/11/25/09	25.00	50.00
21 Tris Speaker Boston-A/12/02/09	150.00	300.00
22 Mordecai Brown Chicago-N/12/09/09	100.00	200.00
23 Hal Chase New York-A/12/16/09	50.00	100.00
24 Thomas W. Leach Pittsburgh/12/23/09	30.00	60.00
25 Owen Bush Detroit/12/30/09	25.00	50.00
26 John J. Evers Chicago-N/1/6/10	75.00	150.00
27 Harry Krause Philadelphia-A/1/13/10	25.00	50.00
28 Babe Adams Pittsburgh/1/20/10	30.00	60.00
29 Addie Joss Cleveland/1/27/10	125.00	250.00
30 Orval Overall Chicago-N/2/3/10	25.00	50.00
31 Samuel E. Crawford Detroit/2/10/10	100.00	200.00
32 Fred Merkle New York-N/2/17/10	30.00	60.00
33 George Mullin Detroit/2/24/10	30.00	60.00
34 Edward Konetchy St. Louis-N/3/3/10	25.00	50.00
35 George Gibson Pitt. Bugs Raymond NY NL/3/10/10	25.00	50.00
36 T.Cobb/H.Wagner 3/17/10	250.00	500.00
37 Connie Mack MG Phila.-AL/3/24/10	150.00	300.00
38 Bill Evans UMP Silk O'Loughlin UMP Bill Klem UMP	25.00	50.00
39 Edward Plank Philadelphia-AL/4/7/10	75.00	150.00
40 Walter Johnson Gabby Street Wash./9/1/10	150.00	300.00
41 John C. Kling Chicago-N/9/8/10	25.00	50.00
42 Frank Baker Philadelphia-A/9/15/10	75.00	150.00
43 Charles S. Dooin Philadelphia-A/9/22/10	25.00	50.00
44 Wm. F. Carrigan Boston-A/9/29/10	25.00	50.00
45 John B. McLean Cincinnati/10/06/10	25.00	50.00
46 John W. Coombs Philadelphia-A/10/13/10	30.00	60.00
47 Jos. B. Tinker Chicago-N/10/20/10	100.00	200.00
48 John I. Taylor OWN Boston-A/10/27/10	25.00	50.00
49 Russell Ford New York-A/11/03/10	25.00	50.00
50 Leonard L. Cole Chicago-N/11/10/10	25.00	50.00
51 Harry Lord Chicago-A/11/17/10	25.00	50.00
52 Philadelphia-A Team/11/24/10	50.00	100.00
53 Chicago-N Team/12/1/10	50.00	100.00
54 Charles A. Bender Philadelphia-A/12/08/10	50.00	100.00
55 Arthur Hofman Chicago-N/12/15/10	25.00	50.00
56 Bobby Wallace St. Louis-A/12/21/10	50.00	100.00
57 John J. McGraw MG New York-N/12/28/10	150.00	300.00
58 Harry H. Davis/1/5/11 Philadelphia-A	25.00	50.00
59 James P. Archer Chicago-N/1/12/11	25.00	50.00
60 Ira Thomas Philadelphia-A/1/19/11	25.00	50.00
61 Robert Byrnes Pittsbutrgh/1/26/11	25.00	50.00
62 Clyde Milan Washington/2/2/11	30.00	60.00
63 John T. Meyer New York-N/2/9/11	30.00	60.00
64 Robert Bescher Cincinnati/2/16/11	25.00	50.00
65 John J. Barry Philadelphia-A/2/23/11	25.00	50.00
66 Frank Schulte Chicago-N/3/2/11	30.00	60.00
67 C. Harris White Chicago-A/3/9/11	25.00	50.00
68 Lawrence Doyle New York-N/3/16/11	30.00	60.00
69 Joe Jackson Cleveland/3/23/11	400.00	800.00
70 Martin O'Toole William Kelly Pittsburgh/10/26/1	25.00	50.00
71 Vean Gregg Cleveland/11/2/11	25.00	50.00
72 Richard W. Marquard New York-N/11/9/11	75.00	150.00
73 John E. McInnis Philadelphia-N/11/16/11	30.00	60.00
74 Grover C. Alexander Philadelphia-N/11/23/11	125.00	250.00
75 Del Gainor Detroit/11/30/11	25.00	50.00
76 Fred Snodgrass New York-N/12/7/11	30.00	60.00
77 James J. Callahan Chicago-A/12/14/11	30.00	60.00
78 Robert Harmon St. Louis-N/12/21/11	25.00	50.00
79 George Stovall Cleveland/12/28/11	25.00	50.00
80 Zack D. Wheat Brooklyn/1/4/12	75.00	150.00
81 Frank 'Ping' Bodie Chicago-A/1/11/12	25.00	50.00
82 Boston-A Team/10/10/1912	50.00	100.00
83 New York-NTeam/10/17/1912	50.00	100.00
84 Jake Stahl MG Boston-A/10/24/12	30.00	60.00
85 Joe Wood Boston-A/10/31/12	40.00	80.00
86 Charles Wagner Boston-A/11/07/12	25.00	50.00
87 Lew Ritchie Chicago-N/11/14/12	25.00	50.00
88 Clark Griffith MG Washington/11/21/12	50.00	100.00
89 Arnold Houser St. Louis-N/11/28/12	25.00	50.00
90 Charles Herzog New York-N/12/05/12	25.00	50.00
91 James Lavender Chicago-N/12/12/12	25.00	50.00
92 Jeff Tesreau New York-N/12/19/12	25.00	50.00
93 August Herrrman OWN Cincinnati	30.00	60.00
94 Jake Daubert Brooklyn/10/23/13	30.00	60.00
95 Heinie Zimmerman Chicago-N/10/30/13	25.00	50.00
96 Ray Schalk Chicago-A/11/07/13	75.00	150.00
97 Hans Lobert Philadelphia-N/11/13/13	25.00	50.00
98 Albert W. Demaree New York-N/11/20/13	25.00	50.00
99 Arthur Fletcher New York-N/11/27/13	25.00	50.00
100 Charles A. Somers OWN Cleveland/12/04/13	25.00	50.00
101 Joe Birmingham MG Cleveland/12/11/13	25.00	50.00

1911 Sporting News

Little is know about this set. The front featured an posed action photo of the featured player along with his name, position and year and team on the bottom. The back is stamped "a picture given with every 5 cents in trade at". Any more information on this set is very appreciated.

COMPLETE SET
1 Solly Hofman

1916 M101-5 Blank Back

The cards in this set measure approximately 1 5/8" by 3". Issued in 1916 as a premium offer, the M101-5 set features black and white photos of current ballplayers. Each card is numbered on the front and the backs carry either a blank back or a sponsoring company's information. The fronts are the same as D329, H801-9 and the unclassified Famous and Barr set. Most of the players in this set also appear in the M101-4 set but the majority feature a different card number in both sets. Those cards which are asterisked in the checklist below are those cards which appeared in both the M101-5 and M101-4 sets identically and those have only been cataloged once in their respective M101-5 versions. The M101-5 cards are known to exist in these back variations but not every card has been confirmed to exist in every version: blank back, Block and Kuhl, Famous and Barr, Gimbels (large block letters), Gimbels (small block letters),

Herpolsheimer, Holmes to Holmes, Morehouse Baking, Standard Biscuit, and Successful Farming. It is thought that the blank backs, Famous and Barr and Standard Biscuit versions are the most common with Holmes to Homes being the most difficult to find.

COMPLETE SET (200) 12,500.00 25,000.00
1 Babe Adams * 60.00 120.00
2 Sam Agnew Browns 50.00 100.00
3 Eddie Ainsmith * 50.00 100.00
4 Grover Alexander * 250.00 500.00
5 Leon Ames * 50.00 100.00
6 Jimmy Archer * 50.00 100.00
7 Jimmy Austin * 50.00 100.00
8 Frank Baker 100.00 200.00
9 Dave Bancroft 100.00 200.00
10 Jack Barry 60.00 120.00
11 Zinn Beck 50.00 100.00
12A Beals Becker SP
12B Lute Boone * 60.00 120.00
13 Joe Benz 50.00 100.00
14 Bob Bescher 50.00 100.00
15 Al Betzel 3rd B. 50.00 100.00
16 Roger Bresnahan 100.00 200.00
17 Eddie Burns 50.00 100.00
18 Geo. J. Burns 50.00 100.00
19 Joe Bush 60.00 120.00
20 Owen J. Bush 60.00 120.00
21 Art Butler 50.00 100.00
22 Bobby Byrne 50.00 100.00
23A Mordecai Brown 100.00 200.00
23B Forrest Cady SP
24 Jimmy Callahan 50.00 100.00
25 Ray Caldwell 50.00 100.00
26 Max Carey 100.00 200.00
27 George Chalmers 50.00 100.00
28 Frank Chance 150.00 300.00
29 Ray Chapman 60.00 120.00
30 Larry Cheney 50.00 100.00
31 Eddie Cicotte 150.00 300.00
32 Tom Clarke 50.00 100.00
33 Eddie Collins 100.00 200.00
34 Shauno Collins 50.00 100.00
35 Charles Comiskey UER 100.00 200.00
(Misspelled Comisky)
36 Joe Connolly 50.00 100.00
37 Luther Cook 60.00 120.00
38 Jack Coombs 100.00 200.00
39 Dan Costello 60.00 120.00
40 Harry Coveleski UER 60.00 120.00
(misspelled Coveleskie)
41 Gavvy Cravath 60.00 120.00
42 Sam Crawford 100.00 200.00
43 Jean Dale 50.00 100.00
44 Jake Daubert 60.00 120.00
45 George Davis Jr. 60.00 120.00
46 Charles Deal 50.00 100.00
47 Al Demaree 50.00 100.00
48 William Doak 50.00 100.00
49 Bill Donovan 50.00 100.00
50 Charles Dooin 50.00 100.00
51 Mike Doolan 50.00 100.00
52 Larry Doyle 60.00 120.00
53 Jean Dubuc 50.00 100.00
54 Oscar Dugey 50.00 100.00
55 Johnny Evers 150.00 300.00
56 Urban Faber 100.00 200.00
57 Hap Felsch R.F. 150.00 300.00
58 Bill Fischer 50.00 100.00
59 Ray Fisher Hands Over Head 50.00 100.00
60 Max Flack 50.00 100.00
61 Art Fletcher 50.00 100.00
62 Eddie Foster 50.00 100.00
63 Jacques Fournier 50.00 100.00
64 Del Gainer UER 50.00 100.00
(misspelled Gainor)
65 Larry Gardner * 50.00 100.00
66 Joe Gedeon * 50.00 100.00
67 Gus Getz * 50.00 100.00
68 Geo. Gibson (eo Not Missing) 50.00 100.00
69 Wilbur Good * 50.00 100.00
70 Hank Gowdy * 60.00 120.00
71 Jack Graney * 60.00 120.00
72 Tom Griffith 50.00 100.00
73 Heinie Groh 60.00 120.00
74 Earl Hamilton 50.00 100.00
75 Bob Harmon 50.00 100.00
76 Roy Hartzell Am. 50.00 100.00
77 Claude Hendrix 50.00 100.00
78 Olaf Henriksen 50.00 100.00
79 John Henry 50.00 100.00
80 Buck Herzog 50.00 100.00
81 Hugh High 50.00 100.00
82 Dick Hoblitzell 50.00 100.00
83 Harry Hooper 100.00 200.00
84 Ivan Howard 1st B. 50.00 100.00
85 Miller Huggins 100.00 200.00
86 Joe Jackson 4,000.00 8,000.00
87 William James 50.00 100.00
88 Harold Janvrin 50.00 100.00
89 Hughie Jennings 100.00 200.00
90 Walter Johnson 600.00 1,200.00
91 Fielder Jones 50.00 100.00
92 Benny Kauff 50.00 100.00
93 Bill Killefer Jr. 50.00 100.00
94 Ed Konetchy 50.00 100.00
95 Napoleon Lajoie 300.00 600.00
96 Jack Lapp 50.00 100.00
97 John Lavan 50.00 100.00
98 Jimmy Lavender 50.00 100.00
99 Nemo Leibold 50.00 100.00
100 Hubert Leonard 60.00 120.00
101 Duffy Lewis 60.00 120.00
102 Hans Lobert 50.00 100.00
103 Tom Long 50.00 100.00
104 Fred Luderus 50.00 100.00
105 Connie Mack 200.00 400.00
106 Lee Magee 2nd B. 50.00 100.00
107 Albert Mamaux 50.00 100.00
108 Leslie Mann C.F. 50.00 100.00
109 Rabbit Maranville 100.00 200.00
110 Rube Marquard 100.00 200.00
111 Armando Marsans 60.00 120.00
112 J. Erskine Mayer 50.00 100.00
113 George McBride 50.00 100.00
114 John J. McGraw 150.00 300.00
115 Jack McInnis 60.00 120.00
116 Fred Merkle 60.00 120.00
117 Chief Meyers 50.00 100.00
118 Clyde Milan 60.00 120.00
119 Otto Miller 50.00 100.00
120 Willie Mitchell UER 50.00 100.00
(misspelled Mitchel)
121 Fred Mollwitz 50.00 100.00
122 J. Herbert Moran 60.00 120.00
123 Pat Moran 50.00 100.00
124 Ray Morgan 60.00 120.00
125 George Moriarty 50.00 100.00
126 Guy Morton 50.00 100.00
127 Ed. Murphy UER Photo 50.00 100.00
128 John Murray 60.00 120.00
129 Hy Myers 50.00 100.00
130 J. A. Niehoff 50.00 100.00
131 Leslie Nunamaker 60.00 120.00
132 Rube Oldring 50.00 100.00
133 Oliver O'Mara 50.00 100.00
134 Steve O'Neill 60.00 120.00
135 Dode Paskert C. 50.00 100.00
136 Roger Peckinpaugh UER Photo 60.00 120.00
137 E. J. Pfeffer 60.00 120.00
138 George Pierce UER 60.00 120.00
(misspelled Pearce)
139 Wally Pipp 60.00 120.00
140 Derrill Pratt UER 50.00 100.00
(misspelled Derril)
141 Bill Rariden * 50.00 100.00
142 Eppa Rixey * 100.00 200.00
143 Davey Robertson * 50.00 100.00
144 Wilbert Robinson * 150.00 300.00
145 Bob Roth C.F. 50.00 100.00
146 Edd Roush C.F. 100.00 200.00
147 Clarence Rowland * 50.00 100.00
148 Nap Rucker * 60.00 120.00
149 Dick Rudolph * 50.00 100.00
150 Reb Russell * 50.00 100.00
151 Babe Ruth * 50,000.00 80,000.00
152 Vic Saier * 50.00 100.00
153 Slim Sallee * 50.00 100.00
154 Germany Schaefer 60.00 120.00
155 Ray Schalk 100.00 200.00
156 Walter Schang 60.00 120.00
157 Charles Schmidt 60.00 120.00
158 Frank Schulte 50.00 100.00
159 Jim Scott 50.00 100.00
160 Everett Scott 60.00 120.00
161 Tom Seaton 50.00 100.00
162 Howard Shanks 50.00 100.00
163 Bob Shawkey UER Photo 60.00 120.00
164 Ernie Shore 60.00 120.00
165 Burt Shotton 50.00 100.00
166 George Sisler P 150.00 300.00
167 J. Carlisle Smith 50.00 100.00
168 Fred Snodgrass 60.00 120.00
169 George Stallings 50.00 100.00
170 Oscar Stanage UER Photo 50.00 100.00
171 Casey Stengel 600.00 1,200.00
172 Milton Stock 50.00 100.00
173 Amos Strunk UER Photo 50.00 100.00
174 Billy Sullivan 60.00 120.00
175 Jeff Tesreau 50.00 100.00
176 Jim Thorpe 4,000.00 8,000.00
177 Joe Tinker 150.00 300.00
178 Fred Toney 50.00 100.00
179 Terry Turner 3rd B. 50.00 100.00
180 Jim Vaughn 50.00 100.00
181 Bob Veach 50.00 100.00
182 James Viox 2nd B. 50.00 100.00
183 Oscar Vitt 50.00 100.00
184 Honus Wagner 1,000.00 2,000.00
185 Clarence Walker Browns UER Photo 50.00 100.00
186A Zach Wheat 100.00 200.00
186B Bobby Wallace SP
187 Ed Walsh 100.00 200.00
188 Buck Weaver S.S. 200.00 400.00
189 Carl Weilman 50.00 100.00
190 George Whitted Nat'ls 50.00 100.00
191 Fred Williams 50.00 100.00
192 Art Wilson 50.00 100.00
193 J. Owen Wilson 50.00 100.00
194 Ivy Wingo 50.00 100.00
195 Mel Wolfgang 50.00 100.00
196 Joe Wood 100.00 200.00
197 Steve Yerkes 50.00 100.00
198 Rollie Zeider * 50.00 100.00
199 Heiny Zimmerman * 50.00 100.00
200 Edward Zwilling * 50.00 100.00

1916 M101-5 Block and Kuhl

BLOCK AND KUHL TOO SCARCE TO PRICE

1916 M101-5 Famous and Barr

*FAMOUS AND BARR: .4X TO 1X BLANK BACK

1916 M101-5 Gimbels (Large Block)

GIMBELS (LARGE) TOO SCARCE TO PRICE

1916 M101-5 Gimbels (Small Block)

GIMBELS (SMALL) TOO SCARCE TO PRICE

1916 M101-5 Herpolsheimer

HERPOLSHEIMER TOO SCARCE TO PRICE

1916 M101-5 Holmes to Homes

HOLMES TO HOMES TOO SCARCE TO PRICE

1916 M101-5 Morehouse Baking

MOREHOUSE BAKING TOO SCARCE TO PRICE

1916 M101-5 Standard Biscuit

*STANDARD BISCUIT: .4X TO 1X BLANK BACK

1916 M101-5 Successful Farming

SUCCESSFUL FARMING TOO SCARCE TO PRICE

1915 Sporting News Postcards M101-3

These 3 1/2" by 5 1/2" borderless postcards feature color, a rare commodity in early baseball postcards. The inscription "published by the Sporting News" appears on the front of the card along with the player's name and team. The postcards are believed to have been issued as premiums and mailed in an envelope, and the set is believed to be complete at six cards.

COMPLETE SET (6) 750.00 1,500.00
1 Roger Bresnahan 100.00 200.00
2 Ty Cobb 400.00 800.00
3 Eddie Collins 100.00 200.00
4 Vean Gregg 50.00 100.00
5 Walter Johnson 150.00 300.00
Gabby Street
6 Rube Marquard 100.00 200.00

1916 M101-4 Blank Back

The cards in this set measure approximately 1 5/8" by 3". Issued in 1916 as a premium offer, the M101-4 set features black and white photos of current ballplayers with each card numbered on the front and the backs carry either a blank back, a Sporting News advertisement, or another company's sponsoring information. The fronts are the same as D329, H801-9 and the Famous and Barr set. Most of the players in this also appear in the M101-5 set, issued earlier that same year, but the majority feature a different card number in both sets. Block and Kuhl, Famous and Barr, Herpolsheimer, Morehouse Baking and Standard Baking sets identically are checklisted only in the M101-5 set and not listed below since there is no distinction between the two (cards: 1/3/4/5/6/7/65/66/67/69/70/71/141/142/143/144/147/148/149/150/151/152/153/198/199/200). At present, 17 different backs are known for M101-4: Altoona Tribune, blank back, Block and Kuhl, Burgess-Nash, Everybody's, Famous and Barr, Gimbels (Italic lettering), Globe, Green-Joyce, Herposheimer, Indianapolis Brewing Co, Mall Theatre, Morehouse Baking, Sporting News, Standard Biscuit, Ware's Basement, and Weil Baking. It is thought that the blank backs, Sporting News, Famous and Barr and Standard Biscuit versions are the most common with Everybody's, Green-Joyce, and Mall Theatre being the most difficult to find.

COMPLETE SET (200) 10,000.00 20,000.00
2 Sam Agnew Red Sox 50.00 100.00
4 Grover Alexander 250.00 500.00
8 H. D. Baird C.F. 50.00 100.00
9 Frank Baker 75.00 150.00
10 Dave Bancroft 60.00 120.00
11 Jack Barry 50.00 100.00
12 Zinn Beck 40.00 80.00
13 Chief Bender 75.00 150.00
14 Joe Benz 40.00 80.00
15 Bob Bescher 40.00 80.00
16 Al Betzel 2nd B. 40.00 80.00
17 Mordecai Brown 60.00 120.00
18 Eddie Burns 40.00 80.00
19 George Burns 50.00 100.00
20 Geo. J. Burns 40.00 80.00
21 Joe Bush 50.00 100.00
22 Donie Bush 50.00 100.00
23 Art Butler 40.00 80.00
24 Bobbie Byrne 40.00 80.00
25 Forrest Cady 50.00 100.00
26 Jimmy Callahan 40.00 80.00
27 Ray Caldwell 40.00 80.00
28 Max Carey 60.00 120.00
29 George Chalmers 40.00 80.00
30 Ray Chapman 50.00 100.00
31 Larry Cheney 40.00 80.00
32 Eddie Cicotte 150.00 300.00
33 Tom Clarke 40.00 80.00
34 Eddie Collins 75.00 150.00
35 Shauno Collins 40.00 80.00
36 Charles Comiskey 75.00 150.00
37 Joe Connolly 40.00 80.00
38 Ty Cobb 2,000.00 4,000.00
39 Harry Coveleski UER 40.00 80.00
(misspelled Coveleskie)
40 Gavvy Cravath 50.00 100.00
41 Sam Crawford 60.00 120.00
42 Jean Dale 40.00 80.00
43 Jake Daubert 50.00 100.00
44 Charles Deal 40.00 80.00
45 Al Demaree 40.00 80.00
46 Josh Devore 50.00 100.00
47 William Doak 40.00 80.00
48 Bill Donovan 40.00 80.00
49 Charles Dooin 40.00 80.00
50 Mike Doolan 50.00 100.00
51 Larry Doyle 50.00 100.00
52 Jean Dubuc 40.00 80.00
53 Oscar Dugey 40.00 80.00
54 Johnny Evers 75.00 150.00
55 Urban Faber 60.00 120.00
56 Hap Felsch C.F. 150.00 300.00
57 Bill Fischer 40.00 80.00
58 Ray Fisher Pitching 40.00 80.00
59 Max Flack 40.00 80.00
60 Art Fletcher 40.00 80.00
61 Eddie Foster 40.00 80.00
62 Jacques Fournier 40.00 80.00
63 Del Gainer UER 40.00 80.00
(misspelled Gainor)
64 Chic Gandil 100.00 200.00
68 Geo. Gibson (eo Missing) 50.00 100.00
72 Clark Griffith 75.00 150.00
73 Tom Griffith 40.00 80.00
74 Heinie Groh 50.00 100.00
75 Earl Hamilton 40.00 80.00
76 Bob Harmon 40.00 80.00
77 Roy Hartzell Americans 40.00 80.00
78 Claude Hendrix 40.00 80.00
79 Olaf Henriksen 40.00 80.00
80 John Henry 40.00 80.00
81 Buck Herzog 40.00 80.00
82 Hugh High 40.00 80.00
83 Dick Hoblitzell 40.00 80.00
84 Harry Hooper 60.00 120.00
85 Ivan Howard 3rd B. 40.00 80.00
86 Miller Huggins 60.00 120.00
87 Joe Jackson 5,000.00 10,000.00
88 William James 40.00 80.00
89 Harold Janvrin 40.00 80.00
90 Hughie Jennings 60.00 120.00
91 Walter Johnson 300.00 600.00
92 Fielder Jones 40.00 80.00
93 Joe Judge 50.00 100.00
94 Benny Kauff 40.00 80.00
95 Bill Killefer Jr. 40.00 80.00
96 Ed Konetchy 40.00 80.00
97 Napoleon Lajoie 250.00 500.00
98 Jack Lapp 40.00 80.00
99 John Lavan 40.00 80.00
100 Jimmy Lavender 40.00 80.00
101 Nemo Leibold 40.00 80.00
102 Hubert Leonard 50.00 100.00
103 Duffy Lewis 50.00 100.00
104 Hans Lobert 40.00 80.00
105 Tom Long 40.00 80.00
106 Fred Luderus 40.00 80.00
107 Connie Mack 200.00 400.00
108 Lee Magee L.F. 40.00 80.00
109 Sherwood Magee 50.00 100.00
110 Al Mamaux 40.00 80.00
111 Leslie Mann L.F. 40.00 80.00
112 Rabbit Maranville 60.00 120.00
113 Rube Marquard 60.00 120.00
114 J. Erskine Mayer 40.00 80.00
115 George McBride 40.00 80.00
116 John J. McGraw 150.00 300.00
117 Jack McInnis 50.00 100.00
118 Fred Merkle 50.00 100.00
119 Chief Meyers 50.00 100.00
120 Clyde Milan 40.00 80.00
121 John Miller 50.00 100.00
122 Otto Miller 40.00 80.00
123 Willie Mitchell 40.00 80.00
124 Fred Mollwitz 40.00 80.00
125 Pat Moran 40.00 80.00
126 Ray Morgan 40.00 80.00
127 George Moriarty 40.00 80.00
128 Guy Morton 40.00 80.00
129 Mike Mowrey 50.00 100.00
130 Edward Murphy 40.00 80.00
131 Hy Myers 40.00 80.00
132 J. A. Niehoff 40.00 80.00
133 Rube Oldring 40.00 80.00
134 Oliver O'Mara 40.00 80.00
135 Steve O'Neill 50.00 100.00
136 Dode Paskert C.F. 40.00 80.00
137 Roger Peckinpaugh 50.00 100.00
138 Wally Pipp 50.00 100.00
139 Derrill Pratt UER 40.00 80.00
(misspelled Derril)
140 Pat Ragan 50.00 100.00
142 Eppa Rixey 100.00 200.00
144 Wilbert Robinson 150.00 300.00
145 Bob Roth R.F. 40.00 80.00
146 Edd Roush R.F. UER 75.00 150.00
(misspelled Rousch)
151 Babe Ruth 50,000.00 80,000.00
154 Ray Schalk 60.00 120.00
155 Walter Schang 50.00 100.00
156 Frank Schulte 40.00 80.00
157 Everett Scott 50.00 100.00
158 Jim Scott 40.00 80.00
159 Tom Seaton 40.00 80.00
160 Howard Shanks 40.00 80.00
161 Bob Shawkey 50.00 100.00
162 Ernie Shore 50.00 100.00
163 Burt Shotton 40.00 80.00
164 George Sisler 1st B. 150.00 300.00
165 J. Carlisle Smith 40.00 80.00
166 Fred Snodgrass 50.00 100.00
167 George Stallings 40.00 80.00
168A Oscar Stanage Portrait SP
168B Oscar Stanage Catching 40.00 80.00
169 Casey Stengel 600.00 1,200.00
170 Milton Stock 40.00 80.00
171 Amos Strunk 40.00 80.00
172 Billy Sullivan 50.00 100.00
173 Jeff Tesreau 40.00 80.00
174 Joe Tinker 75.00 150.00
175 Fred Toney 40.00 80.00
176 Terry Turner 2nd B. 40.00 80.00
177 George Tyler 50.00 100.00
178 Jim Vaughn 40.00 80.00
179 Bob Veach 40.00 80.00
180 James Viox 3rd B. 40.00 80.00
181 Oscar Vitt 40.00 80.00
182 Honus Wagner 600.00 1,200.00
183 Clarence Walker Red Sox 40.00 80.00
184 Ed Walsh 60.00 120.00
185 W. Wambsganss UER Photo 50.00 100.00
186 Buck Weaver 3rd B. 200.00 400.00
187 Carl Weilman 40.00 80.00
188 Zach Wheat 60.00 120.00
189 George Whitted Nationals 40.00 80.00
190 Fred Williams 40.00 80.00
191 Art Wilson 40.00 80.00

192 J. Owen Wilson	40.00	80.00
193 Ivy Wingo	40.00	80.00
194 Mel Wolfgang	40.00	80.00
195 Joe Wood	60.00	120.00
196 Steve Yerkes	40.00	80.00
197 Pep Young	50.00	100.00

1916 M101-4 Altoona Tribune

ALTOONA TRIBUNE TOO SCARCE TO PRICE

1916 M101-4 Block and Kuhl

BLOCK AND KUHL TOO SCARCE TO PRICE

1916 M101-4 Burgess-Nash

BURGESS-NASH TOO SCARCE TO PRICE

1916 M101-4 Everybody's

EVERYBODY'S TOO SCARCE TO PRICE

1916 M101-4 Famous and Barr

*FAMOUS AND BARR: .4X TO 1X BLANK BACK

1916 M101-4 Gimbels Italic

GIMBLES ITALIC TOO SCARCE TO PRICE

1916 M101-4 Globe

GLOBE TOO SCARCE TO PRICE

1916 M101-4 Green-Joyce

GREEN-JOYCE TOO SCARCE TO PRICE

1916 M101-4 Herpolsheimer

HERPOLSHEIMER TOO SCARCE TO PRICE

1916 M101-4 Indianapolis Brewing

INDY BREWING TOO SCARCE TO PRICE

1916 M101-4 Mall Theatre

MALL THEATRE TOO SCARCE TO PRICE

1916 M101-4 Morehouse Baking

MOREHOUSE BAKING TOO SCARCE TO PRICE

1916 M101-4 Sporting News

*SPORTING NEWS: .4X TO 1X BLANK BACK

1 Babe Adams	50.00	100.00
3 Eddie Ainsmith	40.00	80.00
4 Grover Alexander	250.00	500.00
5 Leon Ames	50.00	100.00
6 Jimmy Archer	50.00	100.00
7 Jimmy Austin	50.00	100.00
65 Larry Gardner	50.00	100.00
66 Joe Gedeon	50.00	100.00
67 Gus Getz	50.00	100.00
69 Wilbur Good	40.00	80.00
70 Hank Gowdy	50.00	100.00
71 John Graney	50.00	100.00
141 Bill Rariden	40.00	80.00
142 Eppa Rixey	60.00	120.00
143 Davey Robertson	40.00	80.00
147 Clarence Rowland	40.00	80.00
148 Nap Rucker	50.00	100.00
149 Dick Rudolph	50.00	100.00
150 Reb Russell	40.00	80.00
151 Babe Ruth	50,000.00	80,000.00
152 Vic Saier	40.00	80.00
153 Slim Sallee	50.00	100.00
168A Stanage Port SP		
198 Rollie Zeider	50.00	100.00
199 Heiny Zimmerman	50.00	100.00
200 Edward Zwilling	50.00	100.00

1916 M101-4 Ware's Basement

WARE'S BASEMENT TOO SCARCE TO PRICE

1916 M101-4 Weil Baking

WEIL BAKING TOO SCARCE TO PRICE

1926-27 Sporting News Supplements M101-7

These 11 cards were included as inserts of the "Sporting News" publication. They are known to come in two sizes, 7" by 10" and 10" by 14 1/2". We have basically sequenced this set in alphabetical order.

COMPLETE SET (11)	600.00	1,200.00
1 Kiki Cuyler	60.00	120.00
16-Dec		
2 Babe Ruth	250.00	500.00
30-Dec		
3 Rogers Hornsby	125.00	250.00
2-Dec		
4 Tony Lazzeri	60.00	120.00
5 Heinie Manush	60.00	120.00
11-Nov		
6 John Mostil	40.00	80.00
7 Harry Rice	60.00	120.00
January 13,1927		
8 Al Simmons	75.00	150.00
23-Dec		
9 Pie Traynor	75.00	150.00
26-Nov		
10 George Uhle	40.00	80.00
11 Glenn Wright	40.00	80.00
4-Nov		
12 New York Yankees		
13 St. Louis Cardinals		

1932 Sporting News Supplement M101-8

These four supplements were issued in 1932 as an supplement to the popular Baseball weekly, the Sporting News. Unlike most of the other supplements, these photos have biographical information and stats on the back. Since these are unnumbered, we have sequenced them in alphabetical order.

COMPLETE SET (4)	250.00	500.00
1 Kiki Cuyler	150.00	300.00
2 Dizzy Dean	200.00	400.00
3 Charlie Grimm	100.00	200.00
4 Lon Warneke	75.00	150.00

1939 Sporting News Premiums

All of these premiums are blank-backed. The players premiums measure approximately 8" by 10" while the team premiums measure approximately 11" by 16". The catalog number on this set is M101-9.

1 New York Yankees	100.00	200.00
Double Size		
Octoer 19		
2 Joe DiMaggio	150.00	300.00
26-Oct-39		
3 Bob Feller	125.00	250.00
9-Nov-39		
4 Cincinnati Reds	50.00	100.00
November 2, 1939		
Double Size		
5 St. Louis Cardinals	50.00	100.00
November 16,1939		

1888-89 Sporting Times M117

These 27 cards which measure 7 1/2" by 4 1/2" were included as premiums in the Sporting Times weekly newspaper. The cards are sequenced in alphabetical order and some of the other photos (most noticably) the Anson were used in other sets.

COMPLETE SET (27)	100,000.00	200,000.00
1 Cap Anson	12,500.00	25,000.00
2 Jersey Bakely	3,000.00	6,000.00
3 Dan Brouthers	6,000.00	12,000.00
4 Doc Bushong	3,000.00	6,000.00
5 Jack Clements	3,000.00	6,000.00
6 Charles Comiskey	6,000.00	12,000.00
7 Hank O'Day	3,000.00	6,000.00
8 Jerry Denny	3,000.00	6,000.00
9 Buck Ewing	5,000.00	12,000.00
10 Dude Esterbrook	3,000.00	6,000.00
11 Jay Faatz	3,000.00	6,000.00
12 Pud Galvin	6,000.00	12,000.00
13 Jack Glasscock	4,000.00	8,000.00
14 Tim Keefe	6,000.00	12,000.00
15 King Kelly	6,000.00	12,000.00
16 Matt Kilroy	3,000.00	6,000.00
17 Arlie Latham	4,000.00	8,000.00
18 Doggie Miller	3,000.00	6,000.00
19 Fred Pfeffer	3,000.00	6,000.00
20 Henry Porter	3,000.00	6,000.00
21 Toad Ramsey	3,000.00	6,000.00
22 John Reilly	3,000.00	6,000.00
23 Elmer Smith	3,000.00	6,000.00
24 Harry Stovey	4,000.00	8,000.00
25 Sam Thompson	6,000.00	12,000.00
26 John Montgomery Ward	6,000.00	12,000.00
27 Curt Welch	4,000.00	8,000.00

1933 Sport Kings

The cards in this 48-card set measure 2 3/8" by 2 7/8". The 1933 Sport Kings set, issued by the Goudey Gum Company, contains cards for the most famous athletic heroes of the times. No less than 18 different sports are represented in the set. The baseball cards of Cobb, Hubbell, and Ruth, and the football cards of Rockne, Grange and Thorpe command premium prices. The cards were issued in one-card penny packs which came 100 packs to a box along with a piece of gum. The catalog designation for this set is R338.

COMPLETE SET	10,000.00	16,000.00
1 Ty Cobb BB	2,000.00	4,000.00
2 Babe Ruth BB	5,000.00	10,000.00
42 Carl Hubbell BB	300.00	600.00

1953 Sport Magazine Premiums

This 10-card set features 5 1/2" by 7" color portraits and was issued as a subscription premium by Sport Magazine. These photos were taken by noted sports photographer Ozzie Sweet. Each features a top player from a number of different sports. The photo backs are blank and unnumbered. We've checklisted the set below in alphabetical order.

COMPLETE SET (10)	30.00	60.00
1 Joe Black BB	5.00	10.00
6 Stan Musial BB	7.50	15.00
8 Allie Reynolds BB	5.00	10.00
9 Robin Roberts BB	6.00	12.00
10 Bobby Shantz BB	4.00	8.00

1968-73 Sport Pix

These 8" by 10" blank-backed photos feature black and white photos with the players name and the words "Sport Pix" on the bottom. The address for Sport Pix is also on the bottom. Since the cards are not numbered, we have sequenced them in alphabetical order.

COMPLETE SET (22)	150.00	300.00
12 Willie Mays	12.50	25.00
15 Casey Stengel	7.50	15.00
22 Ted Williams	12.50	25.00

1970 Sports Cards for Collectors Old-Timer Postcards

This 32-card set was issued by Sports Cards for Collectors of New York and features black-and-white portraits and action photos of some of baseball's old-timer great players in white borders. Some of the cards display facsimile player autographs. The backs carry a postcard format.

COMPLETE SET (32)	20.00	50.00
1 Title Card	1.50	4.00
Babe Ruth		
Lou Gehrig		
2 Larry Doby	.40	1.00
3 Mike Garcia	.20	.50
4 Bob Feller	.60	1.50
5 Early Wynn	.40	1.00
6 Burleigh Grimes	.40	1.00
7 Rabbit Maranville	.40	1.00
8 Babe Ruth	2.00	5.00
Batting		
9 Lou Gehrig	1.50	4.00
10 Joe Dimaggio	1.50	4.00
11 Ty Cobb	1.50	4.00
12 Lou Boudreau	.40	1.00
13 Jimmy Foxx	1.25	3.00
(Jimmie)		
14 Casey Stengle	.60	1.50
15 Kenesaw Landis	.40	1.00
16 Max Carey	.40	1.00
17 Wilbert Robinson	.40	1.00
18 Paul Richards	.20	.50
19 Zack Wheat	.40	1.00
20 Rube Marquard	.40	1.00
21 Dave Bancroft	.20	.50
22 Bobby Thomson	.20	.50
23 Melvin Ott	.60	1.50
24 Bobo Newsom	.20	.50
25 John Mize	.40	1.00
26 Walker Cooper	.20	.50
27 Dixie Walker	.20	.50
28 Augie Galan	.20	.50
29 George Stirnweiss	.20	.50
30 Floyd Herman	.20	.50
31 Babe Ruth	2.00	5.00
Glove on knee		
32 Babe Ruth	2.00	5.00
Waist up		

1977-79 Sportscaster Series 1

COMPLETE SET (24)	17.50	35.00
121 Tom Seaver	2.00	4.00

1977-79 Sportscaster Series 2

COMPLETE SET (24)	30.00	60.00
208 Joe DiMaggio	5.00	10.00
216 1969 Mets	5.00	10.00

1977-79 Sportscaster Series 3

COMPLETE SET (24)	15.00	30.00
316 Henry Aaron	2.50	5.00

1977-79 Sportscaster Series 4

COMPLETE SET (24)	15.00	30.00
422 Johnny Bench	2.00	4.00

1977-79 Sportscaster Series 5

COMPLETE SET (24)	12.50	25.00
511 Babe Ruth	4.00	8.00
514 Bobby Thomson	.75	1.50
522 The 1927 Yankees	1.00	2.00

1977-79 Sportscaster Series 6

COMPLETE SET (24)	12.50	25.00
624 Johnny Vander Meer	.75	1.50

1977-79 Sportscaster Series 7

COMPLETE SET (24)	15.00	30.00
716 Roger Maris	5.00	10.00

1977-79 Sportscaster Series 8

COMPLETE SET (24)	12.50	25.00
804 Pete Rose	2.50	5.00

1977-79 Sportscaster Series 9

COMPLETE SET (24)	15.00	30.00
923 Jackie Robinson	7.50	15.00

1977-79 Sportscaster Series 10

COMPLETE SET (24)	17.50	35.00
1006 The Hall of Fame	.75	1.50
1007 Rod Carew	1.25	2.50

1977-79 Sportscaster Series 11

COMPLETE SET (25)	20.00	40.00
1106 Willie Mays	2.50	5.00
1109 The Rules	1.50	3.00
Hank Aaron		

1977-79 Sportscaster Series 12

COMPLETE SET (24)	12.50	25.00
1207 Ernie Banks	1.50	3.00

1977-79 Sportscaster Series 13

COMPLETE SET (24)	12.50	25.00
1303 Ted Williams	4.00	8.00
1305 Glenn Davis	.75	1.50

1977-79 Sportscaster Series 14

COMPLETE SET (24)	17.50	35.00
1410 Jim Hunter	1.25	2.50
1411 Maury Wills	.75	1.50

1977-79 Sportscaster Series 15

COMPLETE SET (24)	12.50	25.00
1509 A Century and a Half of History	1.00	2.00
Johnny Bench		

1977-79 Sportscaster Series 16

COMPLETE SET (24)	15.00	30.00
1607 Brooks Robinson	1.25	2.50

1977-79 Sportscaster Series 17

COMPLETE SET (24)	10.00	20.00
1704 Randy Jones	.50	1.00

1977-79 Sportscaster Series 18

COMPLETE SET (24)	12.50	25.00
1805 Joe Morgan	1.25	2.50
1811 Mark Fidrych	1.50	3.00
1816 Lingo II	.75	1.50

1977-79 Sportscaster Series 19

COMPLETE SET (24)	25.00	50.00
1920 Gaylord Perry	.75	1.50

1977-79 Sportscaster Series 20

COMPLETE SET (24)	7.50	15.00
2002 The Astrodome	.25	.50
2005 Thurman Munson	1.50	3.00

1977-79 Sportscaster Series 21

COMPLETE SET (24)	15.00	30.00
2104 Lingo I	.50	1.00
2105 Joe Rudi	.50	1.00
2109 Vada Pinson	.50	1.00
2116 Stan Musial	2.00	4.00

1977-79 Sportscaster Series 23

COMPLETE SET (24)	20.00	40.00
2304 Nolan Ryan	15.00	30.00
2323 Warren Spahn	1.50	3.00

1977-79 Sportscaster Series 24

COMPLETE SET (24)	10.00	20.00
2416 Lou Brock	1.25	2.50

1977-79 Sportscaster Series 25

COMPLETE SET (24)	10.00	20.00
2518 Frank Tanana	.75	1.50

1977-79 Sportscaster Series 26

COMPLETE SET (24)	15.00	30.00
2615 Jim Palmer	1.50	3.00

1977-79 Sportscaster Series 27

COMPLETE SET (24)	12.50	25.00
2702 Steve Carlton	1.50	3.00
2721 Dave Kingman	.75	1.50

1977-79 Sportscaster Series 29

COMPLETE SET (24)	17.50	35.00
2902 The Perfect Game	2.00	4.00
2922 At-A-Glance	1.00	2.00

1977-79 Sportscaster Series 30

COMPLETE SET (24)	12.50	25.00
3003 Triple Crown	1.25	2.50
3016 Ron Cey	.75	1.50

1977-79 Sportscaster Series 31

COMPLETE SET (24)	12.50	25.00
3101 Instruction	1.25	2.50

1977-79 Sportscaster Series 32

COMPLETE SET (24)	17.50	35.00
3201 The 3000 Hit Club	10.00	20.00
3204 Tommy John	.75	1.50
3217 Cy Young Award	1.25	2.50

1977-79 Sportscaster Series 33

COMPLETE SET (24)	10.00	20.00
3305 Keeping Score	.25	.50

1977-79 Sportscaster Series 34

COMPLETE SET (24)	15.00	30.00
3402 Four Home Runs In	4.00	8.00
3419 All-Star Game	1.25	2.50
3424 Greg Luzinski	.50	1.00

1977-79 Sportscaster Series 35

COMPLETE SET (24)	15.00	30.00
3502 Infield Fly Rule	.75	1.50
3504 John Candelaria	.75	1.50
3515 Interference	1.50	3.00

1977-79 Sportscaster Series 36

COMPLETE SET (24)	15.00	30.00
3601 Ron LeFlore	.50	1.00

1977-79 Sportscaster Series 37

Please note that cards number 4 and 17 are not listed. Any information on the two missing cards is very appreciated.

COMPLETE SET (24)	12.50	25.00
3709 Pickoff	.75	1.50
3722 NCAA Tournament	.50	1.00

1977-79 Sportscaster Series 38

COMPLETE SET (24)	20.00	40.00
3809 George Brett	7.50	15.00
3810 Jim Rice	1.00	2.00

1977-79 Sportscaster Series 39

COMPLETE SET (24)	7.50	15.00
3902 Rundown	.75	1.50
3904 Measurements	.25	.50

1977-79 Sportscaster Series 40

COMPLETE SET (24)	10.00	20.00
4001 Garry Templeton	.50	1.00
4002 Jeff Burroughs	.50	1.00

1977-79 Sportscaster Series 41

COMPLETE SET (24)	20.00	40.00
4103 Relief Pitching	.50	1.00
4107 Triple Play	.50	1.00

1977-79 Sportscaster Series 42

COMPLETE SET (24)	15.00	30.00
4208 Dave Parker	.75	1.50
4209 Bert Blyleven	.75	1.50

1977-79 Sportscaster Series 43

COMPLETE SET (24)	12.50	25.00
4307 Rick Reuschel	.50	1.00

1977-79 Sportscaster Series 44

COMPLETE SET (24)	12.50	25.00
4417 Hidden Ball Trick	.75	1.50

1977-79 Sportscaster Series 45

Card number 11 is not in our checklist. Any information on this missing card is greatly appreciated.

COMPLETE SET (24)	20.00	40.00
4517 Hit and Run	.75	1.50
4522 Hitting the Cutoff	.75	1.50

1977-79 Sportscaster Series 46

COMPLETE SET (24)	12.50	25.00
4622 Amateur Draft	.50	1.00

1977-79 Sportscaster Series 47

COMPLETE SET (24)	17.50	35.00
4702 Great Moments	1.00	2.00
4705 Great Moments	1.25	2.50

1977-79 Sportscaster Series 50

COMPLETE SET (24)	15.00	30.00
5007 Dennis Eckersley	2.00	4.00

1977-79 Sportscaster Series 51

COMPLETE SET (24)	20.00	40.00
5102 The Double Steal	.75	1.50
5103 Cy Young	1.50	3.00

1977-79 Sportscaster Series 52

COMPLETE SET (24)	10.00	20.00
5202 Gene Tenace	.50	1.00
5209 Great Moments	.75	1.50

1977-79 Sportscaster Series 53

COMPLETE SET (24)	15.00	30.00
5307 Andre Thornton	.50	1.00

1977-79 Sportscaster Series 54

COMPLETE SET (24)	15.00	30.00
5408 Great Moments	1.25	2.50
5409 Freddie Patek	.50	1.00

1977-79 Sportscaster Series 55

COMPLETE SET (24)	12.50	25.00
5503 Lyman Bostock	.75	1.50

1977-79 Sportscaster Series 56

COMPLETE SET (24)	37.50	75.00
5613 Carlton Fisk	5.00	10.00

1977-79 Sportscaster Series 57

COMPLETE SET (24)	40.00	80.00
5702 Dave Winfield	6.00	12.00

1977-79 Sportscaster Series 58

COMPLETE SET (24)	25.00	50.00
5801 Shea Stadium	1.00	2.00
5802 Busch Memorial	1.00	2.00
5805 Fenway Park	2.50	5.00
5812 Baltimore Memorial	1.00	2.00
5814 Yankee Stadium	2.50	5.00
5818 Candlestick Park	2.00	4.00
5821 Veterans Stadium	1.00	2.00
5823 Dodger Stadium	1.00	2.00

1977-79 Sportscaster Series 59

COMPLETE SET (24)	50.00	100.00
5920 Frank Robinson	4.00	8.00

1977-79 Sportscaster Series 60

COMPLETE SET (24)	37.50	75.00
6023 Sandy Koufax	5.00	10.00

1977-79 Sportscaster Series 61

COMPLETE SET (24)	50.00	100.00
6102 Ron Guidry	2.00	4.00
6116 Roberto Clemente	12.50	25.00

1977-79 Sportscaster Series 62

COMPLETE SET (24)	40.00	80.00
6204 Don Larsen's	2.50	5.00

1977-79 Sportscaster Series 63

COMPLETE SET (24)	30.00	60.00
6318 Gil Hodges	4.00	8.00

1977-79 Sportscaster Series 65

COMPLETE SET (24)	40.00	80.00
6518 Vida Blue	1.50	3.00

1977-79 Sportscaster Series 66

COMPLETE SET (24)	37.50	75.00
6615 Designated Hitter	2.50	5.00

1977-79 Sportscaster Series 67

COMPLETE SET (24)	40.00	80.00
6701 Steve Garvey	2.50	5.00
6715 The Presidential	2.50	5.00

1977-79 Sportscaster Series 68

COMPLETE SET (24)	40.00	80.00
6810 7th Game of the	2.00	4.00
6818 Babe Ruth Baseball	2.00	4.00

1977-79 Sportscaster Series 69

COMPLETE SET (24)	40.00	80.00
6906 Roy Campanella	5.00	10.00
6917 Little League To	2.00	4.00

1977-79 Sportscaster Series 70

COMPLETE SET (24)	30.00	60.00
7013 The Dean Brothers	2.50	5.00

1977-79 Sportscaster Series 71

COMPLETE SET (24)	40.00	80.00
7103 J.R. Richard	2.00	4.00

1977-79 Sportscaster Series 72

COMPLETE SET (24)	50.00	100.00
7209 High School Record	2.00	4.00
7213 Hitting Pitchers	4.00	8.00

1977-79 Sportscaster Series 73

COMPLETE SET (24)	40.00	80.00
7315 Emmett Ashford	2.00	4.00

1977-79 Sportscaster Series 74

COMPLETE SET (24)	200.00	400.00
7401 Forever Blowing	2.50	5.00
7410 Phil Niekro	4.00	8.00
7423 The Forsch Brothers	2.00	4.00

1977-79 Sportscaster Series 75

COMPLETE SET (24)	30.00	60.00
7509 Tommy Lasorda	4.00	8.00
7513 Fellowship of	2.00	4.00
7515 Hack Wilson	2.50	5.00
7524 The Firemen	4.00	8.00

1977-79 Sportscaster Series 76

COMPLETE SET (24)	30.00	60.00
7611 Iron Mike	1.00	2.00
7619 Training Camps	1.00	2.00

1977-79 Sportscaster Series 77

COMPLETE SET (24)	150.00	300.00
7708 Monty Stratton	2.50	5.00
7713 Ron Taylor	2.00	4.00

1977-79 Sportscaster Series 78

COMPLETE SET (24)	150.00	300.00
7816 Willie McCovey	4.00	8.00

1977-79 Sportscaster Series 79

COMPLETE SET (24)	60.00	120.00
7911 Craig Swan	1.50	3.00

1977-79 Sportscaster Series 80

COMPLETE SET (24)	62.50	125.00
8021 Umpires Strike	2.50	5.00

1977-79 Sportscaster Series 81

COMPLETE SET (24)	62.50	125.00
8124 Wrigley Marathon	7.50	15.00

1977-79 Sportscaster Series 82

COMPLETE SET (24)	50.00	100.00
8219 Bobby Bonds	3.00	6.00

1977-79 Sportscaster Series 83

COMPLETE SET (24)	62.50	125.00
8309 Billy Martin	4.00	8.00
8321 Brother vs. Brother	3.00	6.00

1977-79 Sportscaster Series 84

COMPLETE SET (24)	60.00	120.00
8408 Triple Play	3.00	6.00
8415 The Money Game	4.00	8.00
8418 Clemente Award	3.00	6.00

1977-79 Sportscaster Series 85

COMPLETE SET (24)	62.50	125.00
8504 Like Father	2.50	5.00
8513 Walkie-Talkie	6.00	12.00

1977-79 Sportscaster Series 86

COMPLETE SET (24)	50.00	100.00
8608 Danny Ainge	15.00	40.00

1977-79 Sportscaster Series 87

This series contains two cards numbered 4.

COMPLETE SET (24)	60.00	120.00
8712 Lee Mazzilli	3.00	6.00
8718 Steve Dembowski	2.00	4.00
8720 Hutch Award	7.50	15.00

1977-79 Sportscaster Series 88

COMPLETE SET (24)	50.00	100.00
8803 Dave Winfield	7.50	15.00
8824 Cape Cod League	2.50	5.00

1977-79 Sportscaster Series 101

COMPLETE SET (24)	62.50	125.00
10122 400-Homer Club	4.00	8.00

1977-79 Sportscaster Series 102

COMPLETE SET (24)	75.00	150.00
10201 Mike Flanagan	3.00	6.00
10210 Boston's Fenway	3.00	6.00
10224 Jim Piersall	3.00	6.00

1946-49 Sports Exchange W603

These cards measuring approximately 7" by 10" were issued by Sports Exchange between 1946 and 1949. The cards are numbered but we have sequenced them alphabetically within series. This set is considered one of the first "collector-issued" sets as many copies were sold through what was then considered a small group of dedicated collectors.

COMPLETE SET (117)	1,250.00	2,500.00
1-1A Phil Cavaretta	7.50	15.00
1-1B Bill Dickey	25.00	50.00
2-Jan John 'Al' Benton	6.00	12.00
3-Jan Harry Brecheen	7.50	15.00
4-Jan Jimmy Foxx (Jimmie)	30.00	60.00
5-Jan Edwin Dyer	6.00	12.00
6-Jan Ewell Blackwell	7.50	15.00
7-Jan Floyd Bevens	6.00	12.00
8-Jan Nick Altrock	6.00	12.00
9-Jan George Case	6.00	12.00
10-Jan Lu Blue	6.00	12.00
11-Jan Ralph Branca-Ken Keltner	7.50	15.00
12-Jan Gene Bearden	6.00	12.00
2-1A Walker Cooper	6.00	12.00
2-1B Bob Doerr	10.00	20.00
2-Feb Lou Boudreau	20.00	40.00
3-Feb Dom DiMaggio	10.00	20.00
4-Feb Frank Frisch	20.00	40.00
5-Feb Charlie Grimm	7.50	15.00
6-Feb Jimmy Outlaw	6.00	12.00
7-Feb Hugh Casey	6.00	12.00
8-Feb Mark Christman	6.00	12.00
9-Feb Jake Early	6.00	12.00
10-Feb Bruce Edwards	6.00	12.00
11-Feb Mickey Cochrane-Bob Dillinger	10.00	20.00
12-Feb Ben Chapman	6.00	12.00
3-1A Dave Ferriss	6.00	12.00
3-1B Bob Feller	20.00	40.00
2-Mar Spud Chandler	7.50	15.00
3-Mar Del Ennis	7.50	15.00
4-Mar Lou Gehrig	125.00	250.00
5-Mar William Herman	12.50	25.00
6-Mar Andy Pafko	7.50	15.00
7-Mar Sam Chapman	6.00	12.00
8-Mar Earle Combs	12.50	25.00
9-Mar Carl Furillo	10.00	20.00
10-Mar Elbie Fletcher	6.00	12.00
11-Mar Dizzy Dean-Edwin Joost	12.50	25.00
12-Mar Steve Gromek	6.00	12.00
4-1A George Kurowski	6.00	12.00
4-1B Hank Greenberg	12.50	25.00
2-Apr Jeff Heath	6.00	12.00
3-Apr Al Evans	6.00	12.00
4-Apr Lefty Grove	30.00	60.00
5-Apr Ted Lyons	12.50	25.00
6-Apr Pee Wee Reese	12.50	25.00
7-Apr Joe DiMaggio	100.00	200.00
8-Apr Travis Jackson	10.00	20.00
9-Apr Augie Galan	6.00	12.00
10-Apr Joe Gordon	7.50	15.00
11-Apr Joe Jackson-Wally Westlake	75.00	150.00
12-Apr Jim Hegan	6.00	12.00
5-1A Marty Marion	7.50	15.00
5-1B George McQuinn	6.00	12.00
2-May Kirby Higbe	6.00	12.00
3-May John Lindell	6.00	12.00
4-May Bill Hallahan	6.00	12.00
5-May Lefty O'Doul	7.50	15.00
6-May Phil Rizzuto	25.00	50.00
7-May Tommy Henrich	7.50	15.00
8-May Bob Muncrief	6.00	12.00
9-May Berthold Haas	6.00	12.00
10-May Tommy Holmes	7.50	15.00
11-May Larry Jansen-Yogi Berra	12.50	25.00
12-May Bob Lemon	12.50	25.00
6-1A Truett'Rip' Sewell	6.00	12.00
6-1B Ray Mueller	6.00	12.00
2-Jun Tex Hughson	6.00	12.00
3-Jun John Mize	12.50	25.00
4-Jun Rogers Hornsby	30.00	60.00
5-Jun Steve O'Neil	6.00	12.00
6-Jun Buddy Rosar	6.00	12.00
7-Jun Ralph Kiner	12.50	25.00
9-Jun John Hopp	6.00	12.00
10-Jun Bill Johnson	6.00	12.00
11-Jun Harry Lowrey-Heinie Manush	7.50	15.00
12-Jun Billy Meyer	6.00	12.00
7-1A Ed Stanky	7.50	15.00
7-1B Hal Newhouser	10.00	20.00
2-Jul Stan Musial	50.00	100.00
3-Jul Johnny Pesky	7.50	15.00
4-Jul Carl Hubbell	12.50	25.00
5-Jul Herb Pennock	12.50	25.00
6-Jul Johnny Sain	7.50	15.00
7-Jul Harry Lavagetto	7.50	15.00
8-Jul Joe Page	7.50	15.00
9-Jul John 'Buddy' Kelly	6.00	12.00
10-Jul Phil Masi	6.00	12.00
12-Jul Dale Mitchell	6.00	12.00
8-1A Fred'Dixie' Walker	6.00	12.00
8-1B Dick Wakefield	6.00	12.00
2-Aug Howie Pollet	6.00	12.00
3-Aug Harold Reiser	7.50	15.00
4-Aug Babe Ruth	150.00	300.00
5-Aug Luke Sewell	7.50	15.00
6-Aug Dizzy Trout	6.00	12.00
7-Aug Vic Lombardi	6.00	12.00
8-Aug Honus Wagner	50.00	100.00
9-Aug Ray Lamanno	6.00	12.00
10-Aug George Munger	6.00	12.00
12-Aug Red Rolfe	6.00	12.00
9-1B Ted Williams	75.00	150.00
2-Sep Enos Slaughter	12.50	25.00
3-Sep Aaron Robinson	6.00	12.00
4-Sep Hack Wilson	12.50	25.00
5-Sep William Southworth	6.00	12.00
6-Sep Harry Walker	6.00	12.00
7-Sep Cecil Travis	6.00	12.00
8-Sep Mickey Witek	6.00	12.00
9-Sep Warren Spahn	20.00	40.00
10-Sep Vern Stephens	6.00	12.00
12-Sep Sibbi Sisti	6.00	12.00
3-Oct Bos. Red Sox-1946	7.50	15.00
12-Oct Zach Taylor	6.00	12.00
3-Nov St.L.Cardinals-1946	7.50	15.00
12-Nov Earl Torgeson	6.00	12.00
12-Dec Mickey Vernon	7.50	15.00

1977 Sports Illustrated Ad Cards

This set is a multi-sport set and features cards with action player photos from various sports as they appeared on different covers of Sports Illustrated Magazine. The cards measure approximately 3 1/2" by 4 3/4" with the backs displaying the player's name and team name and information on how to subscribe to the magazine at a special rate. It was issued by Mrs. Carter Breads.

COMPLETE SET	12.50	25.00
1 George Brett	4.00	10.00
2 George Foster	1.50	3.00
3 Bump Wills	1.50	3.00

1968 Sports Memorabilia All-Time Greats

This 15-card standard-size set features some of the leading players of all-time. The fronts have crude drawings of the players, while the backs have a player biography. The drawings were done by sports artist Art Ouellette.

COMPLETE SET (15)	50.00	100.00
1 Checklist	2.00	5.00
2 Connie Mack	3.00	8.00
3 Walter Johnson	4.00	10.00
4 Warren Spahn	3.00	8.00
5 Christy Mathewson	4.00	10.00
6 Lefty Grove	3.00	8.00
7 Mickey Cochrane	2.00	5.00
8 Bill Dickey	2.00	5.00
9 Tris Speaker	3.00	8.00
10 Ty Cobb	6.00	15.00
11 Babe Ruth	10.00	25.00
12 Lou Gehrig	6.00	15.00
13 Rogers Hornsby	4.00	10.00
14 Honus Wagner	4.00	10.00
15 Pie Traynor	2.00	5.00

1973 Sports Scoop HOF Candidates

This 14-card set measures approximately 3 1/2" by 5 1/2" and features borderless black-and-white photos of National Baseball Hall of Fame Nominees according to Sports Scoop. The backs display the players name and why he might be considered for the Hall of Fame. The cards are unnumbered and checklisted below in alphabetical order.

COMPLETE SET (14)	5.00	12.00
1 Earl Averill/(Batting)	.40	1.00
2 Earl Averill/(Holding bat)	.40	1.00
3 Earl Averill/(Ready to catch ball)	.40	1.00
4 George Burns	.20	.50
5 Jack Fournier	.20	.50
6 Jeff Heath	.20	.50
7 Joe Jackson	1.50	4.00
8 Fred Lindstrom/(Holding bat)	.40	1.00
9 Fred Lindstrom/(Portrait)	.40	1.00
10 Fred Lindstrom/(Sitting)	.40	1.00
11 Barney McCoskey	.20	.50
12 Johnny Mize/(Holding bat in front)	.60	1.50
13 Johnny Mize/(Kneeling with bat)	.60	1.50
14 Johnny Mize/(Swinging bat)	.60	1.50

1976 Sportstix

This set features color action photos of some of the favorite sport stars printed on various geometric shaped stickers with peel off backing. These are all that are known to date -- however, other groups may surface -- if so -- any additions to this checklist are appreciated.

COMMON PLAYER (1-10)	60.00	120.00
1 Dave Kingman	4.00	10.00
2 Steve Busby	2.00	5.00
3 Bill Madlock	2.50	6.00
4 Jeff Burroughs	2.00	5.00
5 Ted Simmons	3.00	8.00
6 Randy Jones	2.00	5.00
7 Buddy Bell	2.50	6.00
8 Dave Cash	2.00	5.00
9 Jerry Grote	2.00	5.00
10 Dave Lopes	2.00	5.00
A Willie Mays	6.00	15.00
B Roberto Clemente	20.00	50.00
C Mickey Mantle	12.50	35.00

1975 SSPC 18

This 18-card promo standard-size set was released the year before the 1976 SSPC 630-card set. Like the 1976 "Pure Card" set, the cards feature white-bordered color player photos on their otherwise plain fronts. The back carries the player's position, team, and biography in red lettering at the upper right. The player's uniform number appears in red within a black-lettered circle formed by the words "Sample Card 1976" at the upper left. Shown below are the player's full name and his career highlights in black lettering. The card number appears on the back at the bottom, as does the copyright date, 1975. These cards were also included as inserts in the Winter 1975 issue of Collectors Quarterly.

COMPLETE SET (18)	8.00	20.00
1 Harry Parker	.25	.60
2 Jim Bibby	.25	.60
3 Mike Wallace	.25	.60
4 Tony Muser	.25	.60
5 Yogi Berra MG	3.00	8.00
6 Preston Gomez MG	.25	.60
7 Jack McKeon MG	.25	.60
8 Sam McDowell	.50	1.25
9 Gaylord Perry	2.50	6.00
10 Fred Scherman	.25	.60
11 Willie Davis	.25	.60
12 Don Hopkins	.25	.60
13 Whitey Herzog MG	.50	1.25
14 Ray Sadecki	.25	.60
15 Stan Bahnsen	.25	.60
16 Bob Oliver	.25	.60
17 Denny Doyle	.25	.60
18 Deron Johnson	.25	.60

1975 SSPC 42

This 42-card standard-size set features posed color player photos with white borders. The horizontal backs are plain white card stock and carry the player's name, biographical information, career highlights, and statistics.

COMPLETE SET (42)	40.00	80.00
1 Wilbur Wood	.25	.60
2 Johnny Sain CO	.50	1.25
3 Bill Melton	.25	.60
4 Dick Allen	.75	2.00
5 Jim Palmer	2.50	6.00
6 Brooks Robinson	3.00	8.00
7 Tommy Davis	.50	1.25
8 Frank Robinson MG	2.50	6.00
9 Vada Pinson	.50	1.25

10 Nolan Ryan	12.50	30.00
11 Reggie Jackson	4.00	10.00
12 Vida Blue	.50	1.25
13 Sal Bando	.50	1.25
14 Bert Campaneris	.50	1.25
15 Tom Seaver	3.00	8.00
16 Bud Harrelson	.50	1.25
17 Jerry Koosman	.50	1.25
18 David Nelson	.25	.60
19 Ted Williams	5.00	12.00
20 Tony Oliva	.75	2.00
21 Mickey Lolich	.50	1.25
22 Amos Otis	.25	.60
23 Carl Yastrzemski	2.50	6.00
24 Mike Cuellar	.50	1.25
25 Doc Medich	.25	.60
26 Cesar Cedeno	.25	.60
27 Jeff Burroughs	.50	1.25
28 Sparky Lyle and Ted Williams	2.50	6.00
29 Johnny Bench	3.00	8.00
30 Gaylord Perry	2.00	5.00
31 John Mayberry	.25	.60
32 Rod Carew	2.50	6.00
33 Whitey Ford CO	2.50	6.00
34 Al Kaline	2.50	6.00
35 Willie Mays CO	5.00	12.00
36 Warren Spahn	2.50	6.00
37 Mickey Mantle	10.00	25.00
38 Norm Cash	.75	2.00
39 Steve Busby	.25	.60
40 Yogi Berra MG	2.50	6.00
41 Harvey Kuenn CO	.25	.60
42 The Alou Brothers Felipe Alou Matty Alou Jesus	.50	1.25

1975 SSPC Puzzle Back

The 24 cards in this set measure approximately 3 1/2" by 4 1/4" and feature posed color player photos with white borders on the front. The player's name, position, and team are printed at the bottom. The backs are the pieces of a puzzle that shows a 17" by 21" black-and-white photo of Nolan Ryan and Catfish Hunter. When the puzzle is assembled, the player's names appear at the bottom. The name and address of Sports Stars Publishing Company is printed around the left, top, and right edges. The cards are unnumbered and checklisted below in alphabetical order.

COMPLETE SET (24)	12.50	30.00
1 Hank Aaron	2.50	6.00
2 Johnny Bench	1.25	3.00
3 Bobby Bonds	.40	1.00
4 Jeff Burroughs	.10	.25
5 Rod Carew	.75	2.00
6 Dave Cash	.10	.25
7 Cesar Cedeno	.10	.25
8 Bucky Dent	.40	1.00
9 Rollie Fingers	.60	1.50
10 Steve Garvey	.40	1.00
11 John Grubb	.10	.25
12 Reggie Jackson	2.00	5.00
13 Jim Kaat	.40	1.00
14 Greg Luzinski	.20	.50
15 Fred Lynn	.40	1.00
16 Bill Madlock	.20	.50
17 Andy Messersmith	.10	.25
18 Thurman Munson	.75	2.00
19 Jim Palmer	1.00	2.50
20 Dave Parker	.60	1.50
21 Jim Rice	.40	1.00
22 Pete Rose	1.25	3.00
23 Tom Seaver	1.25	3.00
24 Chris Speier	.10	.25

1975 SSPC Samples

This six-card standard-size set features posed color player photos with white borders. The backs are white card stock and have either a horizontal or vertical format. Each card carries the player's name, biographical information, and career highlights. The horizontal backs also carry statistics. The cards are unnumbered, and checklisted below in alphabetical order.

COMPLETE SET (6)	12.50	30.00
1 Hank Aaron	4.00	10.00
2 Catfish Hunter	1.25	3.00
3 Dave Kingman	.50	1.25
4 Mickey Mantle	8.00	20.00
5 Willie Mays	4.00	10.00
6 Tom Seaver	2.50	6.00

1976 SSPC Promos

These standard-size cards were issued by SSPC/TCMA to promote their first (and would prove to be their only) major set. These cards feature the photos used in the 1975 SSPC Samples set on the front. The only difference between this set and the 1975 SSPC Samples set are the card backs. There might be additions to this checklist so any additional information would be appreciated. These cards are not numbered, so we have sequenced them in alphabetical order.

COMPLETE SET	12.50	30.00
1 Hank Aaron	6.00	15.00
2 Jim Hunter	6.00	15.00
3 Dave Kingman	6.00	15.00
4 Mickey Mantle	8.00	20.00
5 Willie Mays	6.00	15.00
6 Tom Seaver	6.00	15.00

1976 SSPC

The cards in this 630-card set measure 2 1/2" by 3 1/2". The 1976 "Pure Card" set issued by TCMA derives its name from the lack of borders, logos, signatures, etc., which often clutter up the picture areas of some baseball sets. It differs from other sets produced by this company in that it cannot be re-issued due to an agreement entered into by the manufacturer. Thus, while not technically a legitimate issue, it is significant because it cannot be reprinted, unlike other collector issues. The cards are numbered in team groups, i.e., Atlanta (1-21), Cincinnati (22-46), Houston (47-65), Los Angeles (66-91), San Francisco (92-113), San Diego (114-133), Chicago White Sox (134-158), Kansas City (159-185), California (186-204), Minnesota (205-225), Milwaukee (226-251), Texas (252-273), St. Louis (274-300), Chicago Cubs (301-321), Montreal (322-351), Detroit (352-373), Baltimore (374-401), Boston (402-424), New York Yankees (425-455), Philadelphia (456-477), Oakland (478-503), Cleveland (504-532), New York Mets (533-560), and Pittsburgh (561-586). The rest of the numbers are filled in with checklists (589-595), miscellaneous players, and a heavy dose of coaches. There are a few instances in the set where the team identified on the back is different from the team shown on the front due to trades made after the completion of the 1975 season. The set features rookie year cards of Dennis Eckersley and Willie Randolph as well as early cards of George Brett, Gary Carter, and Robin Yount. The card backs were edited by Keith Olbermann, prior to his network broadcasting days. Although some of these cards were copyrighted in 1975, they were not released until spring of 1976 and have always been considered cards from 1976 within the hobby. These cards were originally available directly from SSPC for $10.99 per set.

COMPLETE SET (630)	40.00	80.00
1 Buzz Capra	.08	.20
2 Tom House	.08	.20
3 Max Leon	.08	.20
4 Carl Morton	.08	.20
5 Phil Niekro	1.50	4.00
6 Mike Thompson	.08	.20
7 Elias Sosa	.08	.20
8 Larvell Blanks	.08	.20
9 Darrell Evans	.08	.20
10 Rod Gilbreath	.08	.20
11 Mike Lum	.08	.20
12 Craig Robinson	.08	.20
13 Earl Williams	.08	.20
14 Vic Correll	.08	.20
15 Biff Pocoroba	.08	.20
16 Dusty Baker	.12	.30
17 Ralph Garr	.08	.20
18 Cito Gaston	.08	.20
19 Dave May	.08	.20
20 Rowland Office	.08	.20
21 Bob Beall	.08	.20
22 Sparky Anderson MG	.30	.75
23 Jack Billingham	.08	.20
24 Pedro Borbon	.08	.20
25 Clay Carroll	.08	.20
26 Pat Darcy	.08	.20
27 Don Gullett	.08	.20
28 Clay Kirby	.08	.20
29 Gary Nolan	.08	.20
30 Fred Norman	.08	.20
31 Johnny Bench	2.50	6.00
32 Bill Plummer	.08	.20
33 Darrel Chaney	.08	.20
34 Dave Concepcion	.12	.30
35 Terry Crowley	.08	.20
36 Dan Driessen	.08	.20
37 Doug Flynn	.08	.20
38 Joe Morgan	1.25	3.00
39 Tony Perez	1.00	2.50
40 Ken Griffey	.40	1.00
41 Pete Rose	3.00	8.00
42 Ed Armbrister	.08	.20
43 John Vukovich	.08	.20
44 George Foster	.20	.50
45 Cesar Geronimo	.08	.20
46 Merv Rettenmund	.08	.20
47 Jim Crawford	.08	.20
48 Ken Forsch	.08	.20
49 Doug Konieczny	.08	.20
50 Joe Niekro	.08	.20
51 Cliff Johnson	.08	.20
52 Skip Jutze	.08	.20
53 Milt May	.08	.20
54 Rob Andrews	.08	.20
55 Ken Boswell	.08	.20
56 Tommy Helms	.08	.20
57 Roger Metzger	.08	.20
58 Larry Milbourne	.08	.20
59 Doug Rader	.08	.20
60 Bob Watson	.12	.30
61 Enos Cabell	.08	.20
62 Jose Cruz	.08	.20
63 Cesar Cedeno	.08	.20
64 Greg Gross	.08	.20
65 Wilbur Howard	.08	.20
66 Al Downing	.08	.20
67 Burt Hooton	.08	.20
68 Charlie Hough	.12	.30
69 Tommy John	.30	.75
70 Andy Messersmith	.08	.20
71 Doug Rau	.08	.20
72 Rick Rhoden	.08	.20
73 Don Sutton	1.00	2.50
74 Rick Auerbach	.08	.20
75 Ron Cey	.12	.30
76 Ivan DeJesus	.08	.20
77 Steve Garvey	.60	1.50
78 Lee Lacy	.08	.20
79 Dave Lopes	.08	.20
80 Ken McMullen	.08	.20
81 Joe Ferguson	.08	.20
82 Paul Powell	.08	.20
83 Steve Yeager	.08	.20
84 Willie Crawford	.08	.20
85 Henry Cruz	.08	.20
86 Charlie Manuel	.08	.15
87 Manny Mota	.08	.20
88 Tom Paciorek	.08	.20
89 Jim Wynn	.08	.20
90 Walt Alston MG	.30	.75
91 Bill Buckner	.12	.30
92 Jim Barr	.08	.20
93 Mike Caldwell	.08	.20
94 John D'Acquisto	.08	.20
95 Dave Heaverlo	.08	.20
96 Gary Lavelle	.08	.20
97 John Montefusco	.08	.20
98 Charlie Williams	.08	.20
99 Chris Arnold	.08	.20
100 Marc Hill	.08	.20
101 Dave Rader	.08	.20
102 Bruce Miller	.08	.20
103 Willie Montanez	.08	.20
104 Steve Ontiveros	.08	.20
105 Chris Speier	.08	.20
106 Derrel Thomas	.08	.20
107 Gary Thomasson	.08	.20
108 Glenn Adams	.08	.20
109 Von Joshua	.08	.20
110 Gary Matthews	.08	.20
111 Bobby Murcer	.12	.30
112 Horace Speed	.08	.20
113 Wes Westrum MG	.08	.20
114 Rich Folkers	.08	.20
115 Alan Foster	.08	.20
116 Dave Freisleben	.08	.20
117 Dan Frisella	.08	.20
118 Randy Jones	.08	.20
119 Dan Spillner	.08	.20
120 Larry Hardy	.08	.20
121 Randy Hundley	.08	.20
122 Fred Kendall	.08	.20
123 John McNamara MG	.08	.20
124 Tito Fuentes	.08	.20
125 Enzo Hernandez	.08	.20
126 Steve Huntz	.08	.20
127 Mike Ivie	.08	.20
128 Hector Torres	.08	.20
129 Ted Kubiak	.08	.20
130 John Grubb	.08	.20
131 John Scott	.08	.20
132 Bob Tolan	.08	.20
133 Dave Winfield	5.00	12.00
134 Bill Gogolewski	.08	.20
135 Dan Osborn	.08	.20
136 Jim Kaat	.30	.75
137 Claude Osteen	.08	.20
138 Cecil Upshaw	.08	.20
139 Wilbur Wood	.08	.20
140 Lloyd Allen	.08	.20
141 Brian Downing	.08	.20
142 Jim Essian	.08	.20
143 Bucky Dent	.08	.20
144 Jorge Orta	.08	.20
145 Lee Richard	.08	.20
146 Bill Stein	.08	.20
147 Ken Henderson	.08	.20
148 Carlos May	.08	.20
149 Nyls Nyman	.08	.20
150 Bob Coluccio	.08	.20
151 Chuck Tanner MG	.08	.20
152 Pat Kelly	.08	.20
153 Jerry Hairston	.08	.20
154 Pete Varney	.08	.20
155 Bill Melton	.08	.20
156 Goose Gossage	.50	1.25
157 Terry Forster	.08	.20
158 Rich Hinton	.08	.20
159 Nelson Briles	.08	.20
160 Al Fitzmorris	.08	.20
161 Steve Mingori	.08	.20
162 Marty Pattin	.08	.20
163 Paul Splittorff	.08	.20
164 Dennis Leonard	.08	.20
165 Buck Martinez	.08	.20
166 Bob Stinson	.08	.20
167 George Brett	8.00	20.00
168 Harmon Killebrew	1.25	3.00
169 John Mayberry	.08	.20
170 Fred Patek	.08	.20
171 Cookie Rojas	.08	.20
172 Rodney Scott	.08	.20
173 Tony Solaita	.08	.20
174 Frank White	.12	.30
175 Al Cowens	.08	.20
176 Hal McRae	.12	.30
177 Amos Otis	.08	.20
178 Vada Pinson	.12	.30
179 Jim Wohlford	.08	.20
180 Doug Bird	.08	.20
181 Mark Littell	.08	.20
182 Bob McClure	.08	.20
183 Steve Busby	.08	.20
184 Fran Healy	.08	.20
185 Whitey Herzog MG	.08	.20
186 Andy Hassler	.08	.20
187 Nolan Ryan	10.00	25.00
188 Bill Singer	.08	.20
189 Frank Tanana	.12	.30
190 Ed Figueroa	.08	.20
191 Dave Collins	.08	.20
192 Dick Williams MG	.08	.20
193 Ellie Rodriguez	.08	.20
194 Dave Chalk	.08	.20
195 Winston Llenas	.08	.20
196 Rudy Meoli	.08	.20
197 Orlando Ramirez	.08	.20
198 Jerry Remy	.08	.20
199 Billy Smith	.08	.20
200 Bruce Bochte	.08	.20
201 Joe Lahoud	.08	.20
202 Morris Nettles	.08	.20
203 Mickey Rivers	.08	.20
204 Leroy Stanton	.08	.20
205 Vic Albury	.08	.20
206 Tom Burgmeier	.08	.20
207 Bill Butler	.08	.20
208 Bill Campbell	.08	.20
209 Ray Corbin	.08	.20
210 Joe Decker	.08	.20
211 Jim Hughes	.08	.20
212 Ed Bane UER/(Photo actually Mike Pazik)	.08	.20
213 Glenn Borgmann	.08	.20
214 Rod Carew	2.00	5.00
215 Steve Brye	.08	.20
216 Dan Ford	.08	.20
217 Tony Oliva	.30	.75
218 Dave Goltz	.08	.20
219 Bert Blyleven	.20	.50
220 Larry Hisle	.08	.20
221 Steve Braun	.08	.20
222 Jerry Terrell	.08	.20
223 Eric Soderholm	.08	.20
224 Phil Roof	.08	.20
225 Danny Thompson	.08	.20
226 Jim Colborn	.08	.20
227 Tom Murphy	.08	.20
228 Ed Rodriguez	.08	.20
229 Jim Slaton	.08	.20
230 Ed Sprague	.08	.20
231 Charlie Moore	.08	.20
232 Darrell Porter	.08	.20
233 Kurt Bevacqua	.08	.20
234 Pedro Garcia	.08	.20
235 Mike Hegan	.08	.20
236 Don Money	.08	.20
237 George Scott	.08	.20
238 Robin Yount	5.00	12.00
239 Hank Aaron	4.00	10.00
240 Rob Ellis	.08	.20
241 Sixto Lezcano	.08	.20
242 Bob Mitchell	.08	.20
243 Gorman Thomas	.08	.20
244 Bill Travers	.08	.20
245 Pete Broberg	.08	.20
246 Bill Sharp	.08	.20
247 Bobby Darwin	.08	.20
248 Rick Austin UER/(Photo actually Larry Anderson)	.08	.20
249 Larry Anderson UER/(Photo actually Rick Austin)	.08	.20
250 Tom Bianco	.08	.20
251 Lafayette Currence	.08	.20
252 Steve Foucault	.08	.20
253 Bill Hands	.08	.20
254 Steve Hargan	.08	.20
255 Fergie Jenkins	1.25	3.00
256 Bob Sheldon	.08	.20
257 Jim Umbarger	.08	.20
258 Clyde Wright	.08	.20
259 Bill Fahey	.08	.20
260 Jim Sundberg	.08	.20
261 Leo Cardenas	.08	.20
262 Jim Fregosi	.08	.20
263 Mike Hargrove	.08	.20
264 Toby Harrah	.08	.20
265 Roy Howell	.08	.20
266 Lenny Randle	.08	.20
267 Roy Smalley	.08	.20
268 Jim Spencer	.08	.20
269 Jeff Burroughs	.08	.20
270 Tom Grieve	.08	.20
271 Joe Lovitto	.08	.20
272 Frank Lucchesi MG	.08	.20
273 Dave Nelson	.08	.20
274 Ted Simmons	.30	.75
275 Lou Brock	1.50	4.00
276 Ron Fairly	.08	.20
277 Bake McBride	.08	.20
278 Reggie Smith	.08	.20
279 Willie Davis	.08	.20
280 Ken Reitz	.08	.20
281 Buddy Bradford	.08	.20
282 Luis Melendez	.08	.20
283 Mike Tyson	.08	.20
284 Ted Sizemore	.08	.20
285 Mario Guerrero	.08	.20
286 Larry Lintz	.08	.20
287 Ken Rudolph	.08	.20
288 Dick Billings	.08	.20
289 Jerry Mumphrey	.08	.20
290 Mike Wallace	.08	.20
291 Al Hrabosky	.08	.20
292 Ken Reynolds	.08	.20
293 Mike Garman	.08	.20
294 Bob Forsch	.08	.20
295 John Denny	.08	.20

296 Harry Rasmussen .08 .20
297 Lynn McGlothen .08 .20
298 Mike Barlow .08 .20
299 Greg Terlecky .08 .20
300 Red Schoendienst MG .20 .50
301 Rick Reuschel .08 .20
302 Steve Stone .08 .20
303 Bill Bonham .08 .20
304 Oscar Zamora .08 .20
305 Ken Frailing .08 .20
306 Milt Wilcox .08 .20
307 Darold Knowles .08 .20
308 Jim Marshall MG .08 .20
309 Bill Madlock .20 .50
310 Jose Cardenal .08 .20
311 Rick Monday .08 .20
312 Jerry Morales .08 .20
313 Tim Hosley .08 .20
314 Gene Hiser .08 .20
315 Don Kessinger .08 .20
316 Manny Trillo .08 .20
317 Pete LaCock .08 .20
318 George Mitterwald .08 .20
319 Steve Swisher .08 .20
320 Rob Sperring .08 .20
321 Vic Harris .08 .20
322 Ron Dunn .08 .20
323 Jose Morales .08 .20
324 Pete Mackanin .08 .20
325 Jim Cox .08 .20
326 Larry Parrish .08 .20
327 Mike Jorgensen .08 .20
328 Tim Foli .08 .20
329 Hal Breeden .08 .20
330 Nate Colbert .08 .20
331 Pepe Frias .08 .20
332 Pat Scanlon .08 .20
333 Bob Bailey .08 .20
334 Gary Carter 2.00 5.00
335 Pepe Mangual .08 .20
336 Larry Biittner .08 .20
337 Jim Lyttle .08 .20
338 Gary Roenicke .08 .20
339 Tony Scott .08 .20
340 Jerry White .08 .20
341 Jim Dwyer .08 .20
342 Ellis Valentine .08 .20
343 Fred Scherman .08 .20
344 Dennis Blair .08 .20
345 Woodie Fryman .08 .20
346 Chuck Taylor .08 .20
347 Dan Warthen .08 .20
348 Dan Carrithers .08 .20
349 Steve Rogers .08 .20
350 Dale Murray .08 .20
351 Duke Snider CO .75 2.00
352 Ralph Houk MG .08 .20
353 John Hiller .08 .20
354 Mickey Lolich .12 .30
355 Dave Lemancyzk .08 .20
356 Lerrin LaGrow .08 .20
357 Fred Arroyo .08 .20
358 Joe Coleman .08 .20
359 Ben Oglivie .08 .20
360 Willie Horton .08 .20
361 John Knox .08 .20
362 Leon Roberts .08 .20
363 Ron LeFlore .08 .20
364 Gary Sutherland .08 .20
365 Dan Meyer .08 .20
366 Aurelio Rodriguez .08 .20
367 Tom Veryzer .08 .20
368 Jack Pierce .08 .20
369 Gene Michael .08 .20
370 Billy Baldwin .08 .20
371 Gates Brown .08 .20
372 Mickey Stanley .08 .20
373 Terry Humphrey .08 .20
374 Doyle Alexander .08 .20
375 Mike Cuellar .08 .20
376 Wayne Garland .08 .20
377 Ross Grimsley .08 .20
378 Grant Jackson .08 .20
379 Dyar Miller .08 .20
380 Jim Palmer 1.50 4.00
381 Mike Torrez .08 .20
382 Mike Willis .08 .20
383 Dave Duncan .08 .20
384 Ellie Hendricks .08 .20
385 Jim Hutto .08 .20
386 Bob Bailor .08 .20
387 Doug DeCinces .08 .20
388 Bob Grich .08 .20
389 Lee May .08 .20
390 Tony Muser .08 .20
391 Tim Nordbrook .08 .20
392 Brooks Robinson 1.50 4.00
393 Royle Stillman .08 .20
394 Don Baylor .30 .75
395 Paul Blair .08 .20
396 Al Bumbry .08 .20
397 Larry Harlow .08 .20
398 Tommy Davis .08 .20
399 Jim Northrup .08 .20
400 Ken Singleton .08 .20
401 Tom Shopay .08 .20
402 Fred Lynn .30 .75
403 Carlton Fisk 2.00 5.00
404 Cecil Cooper .12 .30
405 Jim Rice .75 2.00
406 Juan Beniquez .08 .20
407 Denny Doyle .08 .20
408 Dwight Evans .40 1.00
409 Carl Yastrzemski 2.00 5.00
410 Rick Burleson .08 .20
411 Bernie Carbo .08 .20
412 Doug Griffin .08 .20
413 Rico Petrocelli .08 .20
414 Bob Montgomery .08 .20
415 Tim Blackwell .08 .20
416 Rick Miller .08 .20
417 Darrell Johnson MG .08 .20
418 Jim Burton .08 .20
419 Jim Willoughby .08 .20
420 Rogelio Moret .08 .20
421 Bill Lee .08 .20
422 Dick Drago .08 .20
423 Diego Segui .08 .20
424 Luis Tiant .12 .30
425 Jim Hunter 1.25 3.00
426 Rick Sawyer .08 .20
427 Rudy May .08 .20
428 Dick Tidrow .08 .20
429 Sparky Lyle .12 .30
430 Doc Medich .08 .20
431 Pat Dobson .08 .20
432 Dave Pagan .08 .20
433 Thurman Munson 1.25 3.00
434 Chris Chambliss .12 .30
435 Roy White .08 .20
436 Walt Williams .08 .20
437 Graig Nettles .20 .50
438 Rick Dempsey .08 .20
439 Bobby Bonds .30 .75
440 Ed Herrmann .08 .20
441 Sandy Alomar .08 .20
442 Fred Stanley .08 .20
443 Terry Whitfield .08 .20
444 Rich Bladt .08 .20
445 Lou Piniella .20 .50
446 Rich Coggins .08 .20
447 Ed Brinkman .08 .20
448 Jim Mason .08 .20
449 Larry Murray .08 .20
450 Ron Blomberg .08 .20
451 Elliott Maddox .08 .20
452 Kerry Dineen .08 .20
453 Billy Martin MG .30 .75
454 Dave Bergman .08 .20
455 Otto Velez .08 .20
456 Joe Hoerner .08 .20
457 Tug McGraw .12 .30
458 Gene Garber .08 .20
459 Steve Carlton 2.00 5.00
460 Larry Christenson .08 .20
461 Tom Underwood .08 .20
462 Jim Lonborg .08 .20
463 Jay Johnstone .08 .20
464 Larry Bowa .08 .20
465 Dave Cash .08 .20
466 Ollie Brown .08 .20
467 Greg Luzinski .12 .30
468 Johnny Oates .08 .20
469 Mike Anderson .08 .20
470 Mike Schmidt 6.00 15.00
471 Bob Boone .20 .50
472 Tom Hutton .08 .20
473 Rich Allen .30 .75
474 Tony Taylor .08 .20
475 Jerry Martin .08 .20
476 Danny Ozark MG .08 .20
477 Dick Ruthven .08 .20
478 Jim Todd .08 .20
479 Paul Lindblad .08 .20
480 Rollie Fingers 1.25 3.00
481 Vida Blue .08 .20
482 Ken Holtzman .08 .20
483 Dick Bosman .08 .20
484 Sonny Siebert .08 .20
485 Glenn Abbott .08 .20
486 Stan Bahnsen .08 .20
487 Mike Norris .08 .20
488 Alvin Dark MG .08 .20
489 Claudell Washington .08 .20
490 Joe Rudi .08 .20
491 Bill North .08 .20
492 Bert Campaneris .08 .20
493 Gene Tenace .08 .20
494 Reggie Jackson 3.00 8.00
495 Phil Garner .20 .50
496 Billy Williams 1.25 3.00
497 Sal Bando .08 .20
498 Jim Holt .08 .20
499 Ted Martinez .08 .20
500 Ray Fosse .08 .20
501 Matt Alexander .08 .20
502 Larry Haney .08 .20
503 Angel Mangual .08 .20
504 Fred Beene .08 .20
505 Tom Buskey .08 .20
506 Dennis Eckersley 5.00 12.00
507 Roric Harrison .08 .20
508 Don Hood .08 .20
509 Jim Kern .08 .20
510 Dave LaRoche .08 .20
511 Fritz Peterson .08 .20
512 Jim Strickland .08 .20
513 Rick Waits .08 .20
514 Alan Ashby .08 .20
515 John Ellis .08 .20
516 Rick Cerone .08 .20
517 Buddy Bell .08 .20
518 Jack Brohamer .08 .20
519 Rico Carty .08 .20
520 Ed Crosby .08 .20
521 Frank Duffy .08 .20
522 Duane Kuiper UER/(Photo actually Rick Manning) .08 .20
523 Joe Lis .08 .20
524 Boog Powell .40 1.00
525 Frank Robinson 1.50 4.00
526 Oscar Gamble .08 .20
527 George Hendrick .08 .20
528 John Lowenstein .08 .20
529 Rick Manning UER/(Photo actually Duane Kuiper) .08 .20
530 Tommy Smith .08 .20
531 Charlie Spikes .08 .20
532 Steve Kline .08 .20
533 Ed Kranepool .08 .20
534 Mike Vail .08 .20
535 Del Unser .08 .20
536 Felix Millan .08 .20
537 Rusty Staub .12 .30
538 Jesus Alou .08 .20
539 Wayne Garrett .08 .20
540 Mike Phillips .08 .20
541 Joe Torre .20 .50
542 Dave Kingman .20 .50
543 Gene Clines .08 .20
544 Jack Heidemann .08 .20
545 Bud Harrelson .08 .20
546 John Stearns .08 .20
547 John Milner .08 .20
548 Bob Apodaca .08 .20
549 Skip Lockwood .08 .20
550 Ken Sanders .08 .20
551 Tom Seaver 2.50 6.00
552 Rick Baldwin .08 .20
553 Jon Matlack .08 .20
554 Hank Webb .08 .20
555 Randy Tate .08 .20
556 Tom Hall .08 .20
557 George Stone .08 .20
558 Craig Swan .08 .20
559 Jerry Cram .08 .20
560 Roy Staiger .08 .20
561 Kent Tekulve .12 .30
562 Jerry Reuss .08 .20
563 John Candelaria .08 .20
564 Larry Demery .08 .20
565 Dave Giusti .08 .20
566 Jim Rooker .08 .20
567 Ramon Hernandez .08 .20
568 Bruce Kison .08 .20
569 Ken Brett .08 .20
570 Bob Moose .08 .20
571 Manny Sanguillen .08 .20
572 Dave Parker 1.00 2.50
573 Willie Stargell 1.25 3.00
574 Richie Zisk .08 .20
575 Rennie Stennett .08 .20
576 Al Oliver .20 .50
577 Bill Robinson .08 .20
578 Bob Robertson .08 .20
579 Rich Hebner .08 .20
580 Ed Kirkpatrick .08 .20
581 Duffy Dyer .08 .20
582 Craig Reynolds .08 .20
583 Frank Taveras .08 .20
584 Willie Randolph 1.25 3.00
585 Art Howe .08 .20
586 Danny Murtaugh MG .08 .20
587 Rick McKinney .08 .20
588 Ed Goodson .08 .20
589 George Brett 1.50 4.00
Al Cowens CL
590 Keith Hernandez .40 1.00
Lou Brock CL
591 Jerry Koosman .40 1.00
Duke Snider CL
592 Maury Wills .08 .20
John Knox CL
593A Checklist 5 ERR 6.00 15.00
Jim Hunter
Nolan Ryan/(Noland o
593B Jim Hunter 2.00 5.00
Nolan Ryan CL COR
594 Checklist 6 .08 .20
Ralph Branca
Carl Erskine
Pee Wee R
595 Willie Mays .60 1.50
Herb Score CL
596 Larry Cox .08 .20
597 Gene Mauch MG .08 .20
598 Whitey Wietelmann CO .08 .20
599 Wayne Simpson .08 .20
600 Erskine Thomason .08 .20
601 Ike Hampton .08 .20
602 Ken Crosby .08 .20
603 Ralph Rowe .08 .20
604 Jim Tyrone .08 .20
605 Mick Kelleher .08 .20
606 Mario Mendoza .08 .20
607 Mike Rogodzinski .08 .20
608 Bob Gallagher .08 .20
609 Jerry Koosman .08 .20
610 Joe Frazier MG .08 .20
611 Karl Kuehl MG .08 .20
612 Frank LaCorte .08 .20
613 Ray Bare .08 .20
614 Billy Muffett CO .08 .20
615 Bill Laxton .08 .20
616 Willie Mays CO 3.00 8.00
617 Phil Cavarretta CO .08 .20
618 Ted Kluszewski CO .12 .30
619 Elston Howard CO .08 .20
620 Alex Grammas CO .08 .20
621 Mickey Vernon CO .08 .20
622 Dick Sisler CO .08 .20
623 Harvey Haddix CO .08 .20
624 Bobby Winkles CO .08 .20
625 John Pesky CO .08 .20
626 Jim Davenport CO .08 .20
627 Dave Tomlin .08 .20
628 Roger Craig CO .08 .20
629 Joe Amalfitano CO .08 .20
630 Jim Reese CO .12 .30

1976 SSPC 1887 World Series

This 18-card standard-size set was inserted into the Fall 1976 Collectors Quarterly issue. Many of the players featured have few cards issued of them during their career. The fronts feature drawings while the backs talk about the 1887 World Series.

COMPLETE SET (18) 5.00 12.00
1 Bob Caruthers .30 .75
2 Dave Foutz .20 .50
3 Arlie Latham .30 .75
4 Charlie Getzein .20 .50
5 Jack Rowe .20 .50
6 Fred Dunlap .20 .50
7 Tip O'Neill .30 .75
8 Curt Welch .30 .75
9 Kid Gleason .40 1.00
10 Sam Thompson .60 1.50
11 Ned Hanlon .60 1.50
12 Dan Brouthers .60 1.50
13 Doc Bushong .20 .50
14 Charles Comiskey 1.25 3.00
15 Yank Robinson .20 .50
16 Charlie Bennett .30 .75
17 Hardy Richardson .20 .50
18 Deacon White .30 .75

1976 SSPC Yankees Old-Timers Day

These nine standard-size cards were inserted in the Collectors Quarterly Spring 1976 edition. The cards feature the player's photo and his name on the bottom. The backs form a puzzle of four Yankee greats: Billy Martin, Joe DiMaggio, Whitey Ford and Mickey Mantle. The cards are unnummbered and thus sequenced in alphabetical order.

COMPLETE SET (9) 3.00 8.00
1 Earl Averill .30 .75
2 Joe DiMaggio 1.25 3.00
3 Tommy Henrich .20 .50
4 Billy Herman .30 .75
5 Monte Irvin .30 .75
6 Jim Konstanty .10 .25
7 Mickey Mantle 1.25 3.00
8 Pee Wee Reese .40 1.00
9 Bobby Thomson .20 .50

1978 SSPC 270

This 270-card set was issued as magazine (All-Star Gallery) inserts in sets of three panels, with each panel measuring approximately 7 1/4" by 10 3/4". Each of the three panels contains nine cards. If cut, the individual cards would measure the standard size (2 1/2" by 3 1/2"). The fronts display color posed and action player photos with thin black inner borders and white outer borders. The backs carry the player's name, biographical information, and career summary. The cards are checklisted below alphabetically according to teams as follows: New York Yankees (1-27)), Philadelphia Phillie (28-54), Los Angeles Dodgers (55-81), Texas Rangers (82-108), Cincinnati Reds (109-135), Chicago White Sox (136-162), Boston Red Sox (163-189), California Angels (190-216), Kansas City Royals (217-243), and Chicago Cubs (244-270). The pricing below is for individual cards.

COMPLETE SET (270) 50.00 100.00
1 Thurman Munson .75 2.00
2 Cliff Johnson .08 .20
3 Lou Piniella .15 .40
4 Dell Alston .08 .20
5 Yankee Stadium .08 .20
6 Ken Holtzman .08 .20
7 Chris Chambliss .12 .30
8 Roy White .08 .20
9 Ed Figueroa .08 .20
10 Dick Tidrow .08 .20
11 Sparky Lyle .12 .30
12 Fred Stanley .08 .20
13 Mickey Rivers .08 .20
14 Billy Martin MG .15 .40
15 George Zeber .08 .20
16 Ken Clay .08 .20
17 Ron Guidry .12 .30
18 Don Gullett .08 .20
19 Fran Healy .08 .20
20 Paul Blair .08 .20
21 Mickey Klutts .08 .20
22 Yankees Team Photo .08 .20
23 Catfish Hunter .75 2.00
24 Bucky Dent .08 .20
25 Graig Nettles .15 .40
26 Reggie Jackson 1.50 4.00
27 Willie Randolph .12 .30
28 Garry Maddox .08 .20
29 Steve Carlton 1.25 3.00
30 Ron Reed .08 .20
31 Greg Luzinski .12 .30
32 Bobby Wine CO .08 .20
33 Bob Boone .12 .30
34 Carroll Beringer CO .08 .20
35 Richie Hebner .08 .20
36 Ray Rippelmeyer CO .08 .20
37 Terry Harmon .08 .20

38 Gene Garber .08 .20
39 Ted Sizemore .08 .20
40 Barry Foote .08 .20
41 Tony Taylor CO .08 .20
42 Tug McGraw .15 .40
43 Jay Johnstone .12 .30
44 Randy Lerch .08 .20
45 Billy DeMars CO .08 .20
46 Mike Schmidt 2.00 5.00
47 Larry Christenson .08 .20
48 Tim McCarver .15 .40
49 Larry Bowa .12 .30
50 Danny Ozark MG .08 .20
51 Jerry Martin .08 .20
52 Jim Lonborg .08 .20
53 Bake McBride .08 .20
54 Warren Brusstar .08 .20
55 Burt Hooton .08 .20
56 Bill Russell .08 .20
57 Dusty Baker .12 .30
58 Reggie Smith .12 .30
59 Rick Rhoden .08 .20
60 Jerry Grote .08 .20
61 Bill Butler .08 .20
62 Ron Cey .12 .30
63 Tom Lasorda MG .30 .75
64 Teddy Martinez .08 .20
65 Ed Goodson .08 .20
66 Vic Davalillo .08 .20
67 Davey Lopes .08 .20
68 Terry Forster .08 .20
69 Lee Lacy .08 .20
70 Mike Garman .08 .20
71 Steve Garvey .30 .75
72 Johnny Oates .08 .20
73 Steve Yeager .08 .20
74 Rafael Landestoy .08 .20
75 Tommy John .15 .40
76 Glenn Burke .08 .20
77 Rick Monday .08 .20
78 Doug Rau .08 .20
79 Manny Mota .08 .20
80 Don Sutton .40 1.00
81 Charlie Hough .12 .30
82 Mike Hargrove .08 .20
83 Jim Sundberg .08 .20
84 Fergie Jenkins .60 1.50
85 Paul Lindblad .08 .20
86 Sandy Alomar .08 .20
87 John Lowenstein .08 .20
88 Claudell Washington .08 .20
89 Toby Harrah .08 .20
90 Jim Umbarger .08 .20
91 Len Barker .08 .20
92 Dave May .08 .20
93 Kurt Bevacqua .08 .20
94 Jim Mason .08 .20
95 Bump Wills .08 .20
96 Dock Ellis .08 .20
97 Bill Fahey .08 .20
98 Richie Zisk .08 .20
99 Jon Matlack .08 .20
100 John Ellis .08 .20
101 Bert Campaneris .08 .20
102 Doc Medich .08 .20
103 Juan Beniquez .08 .20
104 Billy Hunter MG .08 .20
105 Doyle Alexander .08 .20
106 Roger Moret .08 .20
107 Mike Jorgensen .08 .20
108 Al Oliver .12 .30
109 Fred Norman .08 .20
110 Ray Knight .15 .40
111 Pedro Borbon .08 .20
112 Bill Bonham .08 .20
113 George Foster .15 .40
114 Doug Bair .08 .20
115 Cesar Geronimo .08 .20
116 Tom Seaver 1.00 2.50
117 Mario Soto .08 .20
118 Ken Griffey .12 .30
119 Mike Lum .08 .20
120 Tom Hume .08 .20
121 Joe Morgan .75 2.00
122 Manny Sarmiento .08 .20
123 Dan Driessen .08 .20
124 Ed Armbrister .08 .20
125 Champ Summers .08 .20
126 Rick Auerbach .08 .20
127 Doug Capilla .08 .20
128 Johnny Bench 1.00 2.50
129 Sparky Anderson MG .15 .40
130 Raul Ferreyra .08 .20
131 Dale Murray .08 .20
132 Pete Rose 1.25 3.00
133 Dave Concepcion .12 .30
134 Junior Kennedy .08 .20
135 Dave Collins .08 .20
136 Mike Eden .08 .20
137 Lamar Johnson .08 .20
138 Ron Schueler .08 .20
139 Bob Lemon MG .15 .40
140 Bobby Bonds .15 .40
141 Thad Bosley .08 .20
142 Jorge Orta .08 .20
143 Wilbur Wood .08 .20
144 Francisco Barrios .08 .20
145 Greg Prior .08 .20
146 Chet Lemon .08 .20
147 Mike Squires .08 .20
148 Eric Soderholm .08 .20
149 Reggie Sanders .08 .20
150 Kevin Bell .08 .20
151 Alan Bannister .08 .20
152 Henry Cruz .08 .20
153 Larry Doby CO .15 .40
154 Don Kessinger .08 .20
155 Ralph Garr .08 .20
156 Bill Nahorodny .08 .20
157 Ron Blomberg .08 .20
158 Bob Molinaro .08 .20
159 Junior Moore .08 .20
160 Minnie Minoso CO .12 .30
161 Lerrin LaGrow .08 .20
162 Wayne Nordhagen .08 .20
163 Ramon Aviles .08 .20
164 Bob Stanley .12 .30
165 Reggie Cleveland .08 .20
166 Jack Brohamer .08 .20
167 Bill Lee .08 .20
168 Jim Burton .08 .20
169 Bill Campbell .08 .20
170 Mike Torrez .08 .20
171 Dick Drago .08 .20
172 Butch Hobson .08 .20
173 Bob Bailey .08 .20
174 Fred Lynn .08 .20
175 Rick Burleson .08 .20
176 Luis Tiant .12 .30
177 Ted Williams CO 3.00 8.00
178 Dennis Eckersley 1.50 4.00
179 Don Zimmer MG .08 .20
180 Carlton Fisk 1.50 4.00
181 Dwight Evans .15 .40
182 Fred Kendall .08 .20
183 George Scott .08 .20
184 Frank Duffy .08 .20
185 Bernie Carbo .08 .20
186 Jerry Remy .08 .20
187 Carl Yastrzemski 1.50 4.00
188 Allen Ripley .08 .20
189 Jim Rice .40 1.00
190 Ken Landreaux .08 .20
191 Paul Hartzell .08 .20
192 Ken Brett .08 .20
193 Dave Garcia MG .08 .20
194 Bobby Grich .12 .30
195 Lyman Bostock Jr. .12 .30
196 Ike Hampton .08 .20
197 Dave LaRoche .08 .20
198 Dave Chalk .08 .20
199 Rick Miller .08 .20
200 Floyd Rayford .08 .20
201 Willie Aikens .08 .20
202 Balor Moore .08 .20
203 Nolan Ryan 8.00 20.00
204 Danny Goodwin .08 .20
205 Ron Fairly .08 .20
206 Dyar Miller .08 .20
207 Carney Lansford .15 .40
208 Don Baylor .15 .40
209 Gil Flores .08 .20
210 Terry Humphrey .08 .20
211 Frank Tanana .15 .40
212 Chris Knapp .08 .20
213 Ron Jackson .08 .20
214 Joe Rudi .08 .20
215 Tony Solaita .08 .20
216 Rance Mulliniks .08 .20
217 George Brett 6.00 15.00
218 Doug Bird .08 .20
219 Hal McRae .15 .40
220 Dennis Leonard .08 .20
221 Darrell Porter .08 .20
222 Randy McGilberry .08 .20
223 Pete LaCock .08 .20
224 Whitey Herzog MG .12 .30
225 Andy Hassler .08 .20
226 Joe Lahoud .08 .20
227 Amos Otis .08 .20
228 Al Hrabosky .08 .20
229 Clint Hurdle .15 .40
230 Paul Splittorff .08 .20
231 Marty Pattin .08 .20
232 Frank White .12 .30
233 John Wathan .08 .20
234 Freddie Patek .08 .20
235 Rich Gale .08 .20
236 U.L. Washington .08 .20
237 Larry Gura .08 .20
238 Jim Colborn .08 .20
239 Tom Poquette .08 .20
240 Al Cowens .08 .20
241 Willie Wilson .15 .40
242 Steve Mingori .08 .20
243 Jerry Terrell .08 .20
244 Larry Biittner .08 .20
245 Rick Reuschel .08 .20
246 Dave Rader .08 .20
247 Paul Reuschel .08 .20
248 Heity Cruz .08 .20
249 Woodie Fryman .08 .20
250 Steve Ontiveros .08 .20
251 Mike Gordon .08 .20
252 Dave Kingman .15 .40
253 Gene Clines .08 .20
254 Bruce Sutter .30 .75
255 Willie Hernandez .08 .20
256 Ivan DeJesus .08 .20
257 Greg Gross .08 .20
258 Larry Cox .08 .20
259 Joe Wallis .08 .20
260 Dennis Lamp .08 .20
261 Ray Burris .08 .20
262 Bill Caudill .08 .20
263 Donnie Moore .08 .20
264 Bill Buckner .12 .30
265 Bobby Murcer .12 .30
266 Dave Roberts .08 .20
267 Mike Krukow .08 .20
268 Herman Franks MG .08 .20
269 Mick Kelleher .08 .20
270 Rudy Meoli .08 .20

1980-87 SSPC HOF

The 1980 SSPC set was commonly known as the Baseball Immortals set. This standard-size set honored all of the members of the Hall of Fame. When the set was first issued the first 10,000 sets made indicated first printing on the back. This set continued to be issued as new additions were inducted into the Hall of Fame. Baseball writers Bill Madden and Fred McMane wrote the text used on the backs.

COMPLETE SET (199) 40.00 80.00
1 Babe Ruth .75 2.00
2 Ty Cobb .60 1.50
3 Walter Johnson .30 .75
4 Christy Mathewson .30 .75
5 Honus Wagner 1
6 Morgan Bulkeley .05
7 Ban Johnson .05
8 Larry Lajoie .20 .50
9 Connie Mack .08 .25
10 John McGraw .08 .25
11 Tris Speaker .08 .25
12 George Wright .05
13 Cy Young .30 .75
14 Grover Alexander .30 .75
15 Alexander Cartwright .05
16 Henry Chadwick .05
17 Cap Anson .08 .25
18 Eddie Collins .05 .15
19 Charles Comiskey .05
20 Candy Cummings .05
21 Buck Ewing .05
22 Lou Gehrig .60 1.50
23 Willie Keeler .05
24 Hoss Radbourne .05
25 George Sisler .05 .15
26 Albert Spalding .05
27 Rogers Hornsby .30 .75
28 Judge Landis .05
29 Roger Bresnahan .05
30 Dan Brouthers .05
31 Fred Clarke .05
32 James Collins .05
33 Ed Delahanty .05
34 Hugh Duffy .05
35 Hughie Jennings .05
36 Mike King Kelly .05 .15
37 James O'Rourke .05
38 Wilbert Robinson .05
39 Jesse Burkett .05
40 Frank Chance .05 .15
41 Jack Chesbro .05
42 John Evers .05 .15
43 Clark Griffith .05
44 Thomas McCarthy .05
45 Joe McGinnity .05
46 Eddie Plank .05 .15
47 Joe Tinker .05 .15
48 Rube Waddell .05
49 Ed Walsh .05
50 Mickey Cochrane .05 .15
51 Frankie Frisch .05 .15
52 Lefty Grove .05 .15
53 Carl Hubbell .08 .25
54 Herb Pennock .05
55 Pie Traynor .05 .15
56 Three Finger Brown .05
57 Charlie Gehringer .05 .15
58 Kid Nichols .05
59 Jimmie Foxx .30 .75
60 Mel Ott .20 .50
61 Harry Heilmann .05
62 Paul Waner .05 .15
63 Ed Barrow .05
64 Chief Bender .05
65 Tom Connolly .05
66 Dizzy Dean .30 .75
67 Bill Klem .05
68 Al Simmons .05 .15
69 Bobby Wallace .05
70 Harry Wright .05
71 Bill Dickey .08 .25
72 Rabbit Maranville .05
73 Bill Terry .05 .15
74 Home Run Baker .05 .15
75 Joe DiMaggio .60 1.50
76 Gabby Hartnett .05
77 Ted Lyons .05
78 Ray Schalk .05
79 Dazzy Vance .05
80 Joe Cronin .05 .15
81 Hank Greenberg .05 .15
82 Sam Crawford .05
83 Joe McCarthy .05
84 Zack Wheat .05
85 Max Carey .05
86 Billy Hamilton .05
87 Bob Feller .30 .75
88 Bill McKechnie .05
89 Jackie Robinson 1
90 Ed Roush .05
91 John Clarkson .05
92 Elmer Flick .05
93 Sam Rice .05
94 Eppa Rixey .05
95 Luke Appling .05
96 Red Faber .05
97 Burleigh Grimes .05
98 Miller Huggins .05
99 Tim Keefe .05
100 Heinie Manush .05
101 John Ward .05
102 Pud Galvin .05
103 Casey Stengel .08 .25
104 Ted Williams 1
105 Branch Rickey .05 .15
106 Red Ruffing .05
107 Lloyd Waner .05
108 Kiki Cuyler .05
109 Goose Goslin .05
110 Joe Medwick .05
111 Roy Campanella .20 .50
112 Stan Coveleski .05
113 Waite Hoyt .05
114 Stan Musial .30 .75
115 Lou Boudreau .05
116 Earle Combs .05
117 Ford Frick .05
118 Jesse Haines .05
119 Dave Bancroft .05
120 Jake Beckley .05
121 Chick Hafey .05
122 Harry Hooper .05
123 Joe Kelley .05
124 Rube Marquard .05
125 Satchel Paige .20 .50
126 George Weiss .05
127 Yogi Berra .20 .50
128 Josh Gibson .20 .50
129 Lefty Gomez .05 .15
130 Will Harridge .05
131 Sandy Koufax .30 .75
132 Buck Leonard .05 .15
133 Early Wynn .05 .15
134 Ross Youngs .05
135 Roberto Clemente 1
136 Billy Evans .05
137 Monte Irvin .05 .15
138 George Kelly .05
139 Warren Spahn .05 .15
140 Mickey Welch .05
141 Cool Papa Bell .05 .15
142 Jim Bottomley .05
143 Jocko Conlan .05
144 Whitey Ford .08 .25
145 Mickey Mantle .60 1.50
146 Sam Thompson .05
147 Earl Averill .05
148 Bucky Harris .05
149 Billy Herman .05
150 Judy Johnson .05
151 Ralph Kiner .05 .15
152 Oscar Charleston .05
153 Roger Connor .05
154 Cal Hubbard .05
155 Bob Lemon .05
156 Fred Lindstrom .05
157 Robin Roberts .05 .15
158 Ernie Banks .20 .50
159 Martin Dihigo .05
160 John Henry Lloyd .05
161 Al Lopez .05
162 Amos Rusie .05
163 Joe Sewell .05
164 Addie Joss .05
165 Larry McPhail .05
166 Eddie Mathews .20 .50
167 Warren Giles .05
168 Willie Mays 1
169 Hack Wilson .05
170 Duke Snider .40 1.00
171 Al Kaline .40 1.00
172 Chuck Klein .05
173 Tom Yawkey .05
174 Bob Gibson .30 .75
175 Rube Foster .05
176 Johnny Mize .05
177 Hank Aaron .75 2.00
178 Frank Robinson .30 .75
179 Happy Chandler .05
180 Travis Jackson .05
181 Brooks Robinson .08 .25
182 Juan Marichal .08 .25
183 George Kell .05 .15
184 Walter Alston .05
185 Harmon Killebrew .08 .25
186 Luis Aparicio .05 .15
187 Don Drysdale .05 .15
188 Pee Wee Reese .08 .25
189 Rick Ferrell .05
190 Willie McCovey .08 .25
191 Ernie Lombardi .05
192 Bobby Doerr .05
193 Arky Vaughan .05
194 Enos Slaughter .20 .50
195 Lou Brock .20 .50
196 Hoyt Wilhelm .20 .50
197 Billy Williams .20 .50
198 Jim Hunter .20 .50
199 Ray Dandridge .05 .15

1953 Stahl Meyer

The cards in this nine-card set measure approximately 3 1/4" by 4 1/2". The 1953 Stahl Meyer set of full color, unnumbered cards includes three players from each of the three New York teams. The cards have white borders. The Lockman card is the most plentiful of any card in the set.

Some batting and fielding statistics and short biography are included on the back. The cards are ordered in the checklist below by alphabetical order without regard to team affiliation. A promotional kit, titled a "Baseball Kit" was also issued and sent to stores to promote this set. Information about the cards and a checklist was included in that kit.

COMPLETE SET (9)	7,500.00	15,000.00
1 Hank Bauer	250.00	500.00
2 Roy Campanella	1,000.00	2,000.00
3 Gil Hodges	250.00	500.00
4 Monte Irvin	300.00	600.00
5 Whitey Lockman	200.00	400.00
6 Mickey Mantle	4,000.00	8,000.00
7 Phil Rizzuto	500.00	1,000.00
8 Duke Snider	1,000.00	2,000.00
9 Bobby Thomson	250.00	500.00

1954 Stahl Meyer

The cards in this 12-card set measure approximately 3 1/4" by 4 1/2". The 1954 Stahl Meyer set of full color, unnumbered cards includes four players from each of the three New York teams. The cards have yellow borders and the backs, oriented horizontally, include an ad for a baseball kit and the player's statistics. No player biography is included on the back. The cards are ordered in the checklist below by alphabetical order without regard to team affiliation.

COMPLETE SET (12)	7,500.00	15,000.00
1 Hank Bauer	250.00	500.00
2 Carl Erskine	250.00	500.00
3 Gil Hodges	400.00	800.00
4 Monte Irvin	300.00	600.00
5 Whitey Lockman	200.00	400.00
6 Mickey Mantle	4,000.00	8,000.00
7 Willie Mays	2,000.00	4,000.00
8 Gil McDougald	250.00	500.00
9 Don Mueller	200.00	400.00
10 Don Newcombe	250.00	500.00
11 Phil Rizzuto	400.00	800.00
12 Duke Snider	750.00	1,500.00

1955 Stahl Meyer

The cards in this 12-card set measure approximately 3 1/4" by 4 1/2". The 1955 Stahl Meyer set of full color, unnumbered cards contains four players each from the three New York teams. As in the 1954 set, the cards have yellow borders; however, the back of the cards contain a sketch of Mickey Mantle with an ad for a baseball cap or a pennant. The cards are ordered in the checklist below by alphabetical order without regard to team affiliation.

COMPLETE SET (12)	6,000.00	12,000.00
1 Hank Bauer	250.00	500.00
2 Carl Erskine	250.00	500.00
3 Gil Hodges	400.00	800.00
4 Monte Irvin	300.00	600.00
5 Whitey Lockman	200.00	400.00
6 Mickey Mantle	4,000.00	8,000.00
7 Gil McDougald	250.00	500.00
8 Don Mueller	200.00	400.00
9 Don Newcombe	250.00	500.00
10 Dusty Rhodes	200.00	400.00
11 Phil Rizzuto	400.00	800.00
12 Duke Snider	750.00	1,500.00

1910 Standard Caramel E93

The cards in this 30-card set measure 1 1/2" by 2 3/4". The E93 set was distributed by Standard Caramel in 1910. It consists of black and white player photos which were tinted and placed against solid color backgrounds. A checklist, starting with Ames, is printed in brown ink on the reverse. Some blank backs are known and all poses also appear in W555. Listed pricing for raw cards references "VgEx" condition.

COMPLETE SET (30)	60,000.00	120,000.00
1 Red Ames	250.00	400.00
2 Chief Bender	350.00	600.00
3 Mordecai Brown	500.00	800.00
4 Frank Chance	350.00	600.00
5 Hal Chase	250.00	400.00
6 Ty Cobb	2,500.00	4,000.00
7 Eddie Collins	300.00	500.00
8 Harry Coveleskie (Coveleski)	250.00	400.00
9 Fred Clarke	300.00	500.00
10 Jim Delehanty	250.00	400.00
11 Bill Donovan	250.00	400.00
12 Red Dooin	250.00	400.00
13 Johnny Evers	350.00	600.00
14 George Gibson	250.00	400.00
15 Clark Griffith	300.00	500.00
16 Hugh Jennings	300.00	500.00
17 Davy Jones	250.00	400.00
18 Addie Joss	350.00	600.00
19 Napoleon Lajoie	500.00	800.00
20 Tommy Leach	250.00	400.00
21 Christy Mathewson	1,500.00	2,500.00
22 John McGraw	300.00	500.00
23 Jim Pastorius	250.00	400.00
24 Deacon Phillippe	250.00	400.00
25 Eddie Plank	500.00	800.00
26 Joe Tinker	300.00	500.00
27 Rube Waddell	300.00	500.00
28 Honus Wagner	2,500.00	4,000.00
29 Hooks Wiltse	250.00	400.00
30 Cy Young	1,500.00	2,500.00

1952 Star Cal Large

Type One of the Star Cal Decal set, issued in 1952, contains the cards listed in the checklist below. Each decal sheet measures 4 1/8" by 6 1/8". When the decal is taken from the paper wrapper, a checklist of existing decals is revealed on the wrapper. The set was issued by the Meyercord Company of Chicago and carries a catalog designation of W625-1.

COMPLETE SET (70)	4,000.00	8,000.00
70A Allie Reynolds	30.00	60.00
70B Ed Lopat	30.00	60.00
70C Yogi Berra	100.00	200.00
70D Vic Raschi	25.00	50.00
70E Jerry Coleman	25.00	50.00
70F Phil Rizzuto	60.00	120.00
70G Mickey Mantle	1,000.00	2,000.00
71A Mel Parnell	25.00	50.00
71B Ted Williams	250.00	500.00
71C Ted Williams	250.00	500.00
71D Vern Stephens	25.00	50.00
71E Billy Goodman	25.00	50.00
71F Dom DiMaggio	30.00	60.00
71G Dick Gernert	20.00	40.00
71H Hoot Evers	100.00	200.00
72A George Kell	60.00	120.00
72B Hal Newhouser	50.00	100.00
72C Hoot Evers	20.00	40.00
72D Vic Wertz	20.00	40.00
72E Fred Hutchinson	25.00	50.00
72F Johnny Groth	20.00	40.00
73A Al Zarilla	20.00	40.00
73B Billy Pierce	30.00	60.00
73C Eddie Robinson	20.00	40.00
73D Chico Carrasquel	25.00	50.00
73E Minnie Minoso	40.00	80.00
73F Jim Busby	20.00	40.00
73G Nellie Fox	50.00	100.00
73H Sam Mele	100.00	200.00
74A Larry Doby	50.00	100.00
74B Al Rosen	30.00	60.00
74C Bob Lemon	50.00	100.00
74D Jim Hegan	20.00	40.00
74E Bob Feller	100.00	200.00
74F Dale Mitchell	25.00	50.00
75A Ned Garver	20.00	40.00
76A Gus Zernial	25.00	50.00
76B Ferris Fain	20.00	40.00
76C Bobby Shantz	100.00	200.00
77A Richie Ashburn	50.00	100.00
77B Ralph Kiner	60.00	120.00
77C Curt Simmons	100.00	200.00
78A Bobby Thomson	25.00	50.00
78B Alvin Dark	25.00	50.00
78C Sal Maglie	25.00	50.00
78D Larry Jansen	20.00	40.00
78E Willie Mays	400.00	800.00
78F Monte Irvin	60.00	120.00
78G Whitey Lockman	20.00	40.00
79A Gil Hodges	60.00	120.00
79B Pee Wee Reese	75.00	150.00
79C Roy Campanella	200.00	400.00
79D Don Newcombe	40.00	80.00
79E Duke Snider	125.00	250.00
79F Preacher Roe	30.00	60.00
79G Jackie Robinson	250.00	500.00
80A Eddie Miksis	20.00	40.00
80B Dutch Leonard	20.00	40.00
80C Randy Jackson	20.00	40.00
80D Bob Rush	20.00	40.00
80E Hank Sauer	20.00	40.00
80F Phil Cavarretta	25.00	50.00
80G Warren Hacker	20.00	40.00
81A Red Schoendienst	50.00	100.00
81B Wally Westlake	20.00	40.00
81C Cliff Chambers	20.00	40.00
81D Enos Slaughter	50.00	100.00
81E Stan Musial	150.00	300.00
81F Stan Musial	150.00	300.00
81G Gerry Staley	20.00	40.00

1952 Star Cal Small

Type Two of the Star Cal Decal set features a decal package half the size of the W625-1 set, each sheet contains two decals, each of which is approximately half the size of the large decal found in the W625-1 set. Each decal package (sheet) measures 3 1/16" by 4 1/8". The set was issued by the Meyercord Company of Chicago and carries a catalog designation of W625-2. The checklist below features two players per "card".

COMPLETE SET (32)	750.00	1,500.00
84A A. Reynolds	25.00	50.00
V. Raschi		
84B E. Lopat	40.00	80.00
Y. Berra		
84C P. Rizzuto	30.00	60.00
J. Coleman		
85A T. Williams	250.00	500.00
T. Williams		
85B D. DiMaggio	25.00	50.00
M. Parnell		
85C V. Stephens	20.00	40.00
B. Goodman		
86A G. Kell	40.00	80.00
H. Newhouser		
86B H. Evers	20.00	40.00
V. Wertz		
86C J. Groth	20.00	40.00
F. Hutchinson		
87A E. Robinson	20.00	40.00
E. Robinson		
87B C. Carrasquel	25.00	50.00
M. Minoso		
87C B. Pierce	60.00	120.00
N. Fox		
87D A. Zarilla	20.00	40.00
J. Busby		
88A B. Lemon	25.00	50.00
J. Hegan		
88B L. Doby	50.00	100.00
B. Feller		
88C D. Mitchell	25.00	50.00
A. Rosen		
89A N. Garver	20.00	40.00
N. Garver		
89B F. Fain	20.00	40.00
G. Zernial		
89C R. Ashburn	40.00	80.00
R. Ashburn		
89D R. Kiner	50.00	100.00
R. Kiner		
90A W. Mays	150.00	300.00
M. Irvin		
90B L. Jansen	25.00	50.00
S. Maglie		
90C B. Thomson	25.00	50.00
A. Dark		
91A G. Hodges	75.00	150.00
P. Reese		
91B R. Campanella	150.00	300.00
J. Robinson		
91C D. Snider	50.00	100.00
P. Roe		
92A P. Cavarretta	20.00	40.00
D. Leonard		
92B R. Jackson	20.00	40.00
E. Miksis		
92C B. Rush	20.00	40.00
H. Sauer		
93A S. Musial	200.00	400.00
S. Musial		
93B R. Schoendienst	30.00	60.00
E. Slaughter		
93C C. Chambers	20.00	40.00
W. Westlake		

1928 Star Player Candy

This set is presumed to have been inserts to a candy box named "Star Player Candy" produced by Dockman and Sons candy company. The cards are sepia colored and measure approximately 1 7/8" by 2 7/8" with blank backs. The fronts feature full length action shots except for Dave Bancroft which is a portrait. The player's name is printed in brown capital letters in the bottom border. A second version of some cards in this set were recently discovered as part of a multi-sport product (issued by Dockman and Son) entitled "Headliners and Gum." This version features card numbers and bios on the backs and the baseball players were issued with golfers and aviators.

COMPLETE SET	60,000.00	120,000.00
1 Dave Bancroft	1,500.00	3,000.00
2 Emile Barnes	500.00	1,000.00
3 Lu Blue	500.00	1,000.00
4 Garland Buckeye	500.00	1,000.00
5 George Burns	500.00	1,000.00
6 Guy Bush	500.00	1,000.00
7 Owen Carroll	500.00	1,000.00
8 Bud Cissell	500.00	1,000.00
9 Ty Cobb	12,500.00	25,000.00
10 Mickey Cochrane	1,500.00	3,000.00
11 Richard Coffman	500.00	1,000.00
12 Eddie Collins	2,500.00	5,000.00
13 Stan Coveleskie	1,500.00	3,000.00
14 Hugh Critz	500.00	1,000.00
15 Kiki Cuyler	1,500.00	3,000.00
16 Chuck Dressen	600.00	1,200.00
17 Joe Dugan	600.00	1,200.00
18 Woody English	500.00	1,000.00
19 Bibb Falk	500.00	1,000.00
20 Ira Flagstead	500.00	1,000.00
21 Bob Fothergill	500.00	1,000.00
22 Frank Frisch	1,500.00	3,000.00
23 Foster Ganzel	1,500.00	3,000.00
24 Lou Gehrig	6,000.00	12,000.00
25 Charley Gehringer	1,500.00	3,000.00
26 George Gerken	500.00	1,000.00
27 Grant Gillis	500.00	1,000.00
28 Mike Gonzales	500.00	1,000.00
29 Sam Gray	500.00	1,000.00
30 Charlie Grimm	750.00	1,500.00
31 Lefty Grove	2,000.00	4,000.00
32 Chick Hafey	1,500.00	3,000.00
33 Jesse Haines	1,500.00	3,000.00
34 Gabby Hartnett	1,500.00	3,000.00
35 Clifton Heathcote	500.00	1,000.00
36 Harry Heilmann	1,000.00	2,000.00
37 John Heving	500.00	1,000.00
38 Waite Hoyt	1,000.00	2,000.00
39 Charles Jamieson	500.00	1,000.00
40 Joe Judge	500.00	1,000.00
41 Willie Kamm	500.00	1,000.00
42 George Kelly	1,000.00	2,000.00
43 Tony Lazzeri	1,000.00	2,000.00
44 Adolfo Luque	750.00	1,500.00
45 Ted Lyons	1,000.00	2,000.00
46 Hugh McMullen	500.00	1,000.00
47 Bob Meusel	750.00	1,500.00
48 Wilcy Moore	500.00	1,000.00
49 Ed Morgan	500.00	1,000.00
50 Buddy Myer	600.00	1,200.00
51 Herb Pennock	1,000.00	2,000.00
52 Everett Purdy	500.00	1,000.00
53 William Regan	500.00	1,000.00
54 Eppa Rixey	1,000.00	2,000.00
55 Charles Root	500.00	1,000.00
56 Jack Rothrock	500.00	1,000.00
57 Muddy Ruel	500.00	1,000.00
58 Babe Ruth	12,500.00	25,000.00
59 Wally Schang	500.00	1,000.00
60 Joe Sewell	1,000.00	2,000.00
61 Luke Sewell	500.00	1,000.00
62 Joe Shaute	500.00	1,000.00
63 George Sisler	750.00	1,500.00
64 Tris Speaker	2,000.00	4,000.00
65 Riggs Stephenson	750.00	1,500.00
66 Jack Tavener	500.00	1,000.00
67 Al Thomas	500.00	1,000.00
68 Pie Traynor	1,000.00	2,000.00
69 George Uhle	500.00	1,000.00
70 Dazzy Vance	1,000.00	2,000.00
71 Cy Williams	600.00	1,200.00
72 Ken Williams	600.00	1,200.00
73 Hack Wilson	1,000.00	2,000.00

1965 Stengel Dugan Brothers

This one card set was issued to commemorate the retirement of Casey Stengel from baseball. The black and white front features him in a Mets uniform while the back contains biographical information.

1 Casey Stengel	75.00	150.00

1962 Sugardale

The 1962 Sugardale Meats set of 22 black and white, numbered and lettered cards featuring the Cleveland Indians and Pittsburgh Pirates. The Indians are numbered while the Pirates are lettered. The backs, in red print, give player tips. The Bob Nieman card is considered to be scarce. The catalog numbering for this set is F174-1.

COMPLETE SET (22)	1,500.00	3,000.00
COMMON CARD (1-22)	40.00	100.00
COMMON SP	200.00	400.00
1 Barry Latman	40.00	100.00
2 Gary Bell	40.00	100.00
3 Dick Donovan	40.00	100.00
4 Frank Funk	40.00	100.00
5 Jim Perry	60.00	120.00
7 John Romano	40.00	100.00
8 Ty Cline	40.00	100.00
9 Tito Francona	40.00	100.00
10 Bob Nieman SP	200.00	400.00
11 Willie Kirkland	40.00	100.00
12 Woody Held	40.00	100.00
13 Jerry Kindall	40.00	100.00
14 Bubba Phillips	40.00	100.00
15 Mel Harder CO	60.00	120.00
16 Salty Parker CO	40.00	100.00
17 Ray Katt CO	40.00	100.00
18 Mel McGaha MG	40.00	100.00
19 Pedro Ramos	40.00	100.00
A Dick Groat	75.00	150.00
B Roberto Clemente	1,000.00	2,000.00
C Don Hoak	40.00	100.00
D Dick Stuart	40.00	100.00

1963 Sugardale

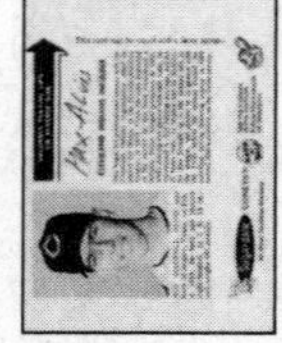

The 1963 Sugardale Meats set of 31 black and white, numbered and lettered cards, features the Cleveland Indians and Pittsburgh Pirates. The Indians cards are numbered while the Pirates cards are lettered. The backs are printed in red and give player tips. The 1963 Sugardale set can be distinguished from the 1962 set by examing the biographies on the card for mentions of the 1962 season. The Perry and Skinner cards were withdrawn after June trades and are quite scarce

COMPLETE SET (31)	3,000.00	6,000.00
COMMON CARD	100.00	200.00
COMMON SP	200.00	400.00
1 Barry Latman	100.00	200.00

Card	Low	High
2 Gary Bell	100.00	200.00
3 Dick Donovan	100.00	200.00
4 Joe Adcock	150.00	300.00
5 Jim Perry SP	200.00	400.00
7 John Romano	100.00	200.00
8 Mike de la Hoz	100.00	200.00
9 Tito Francona	100.00	200.00
10 Gene Green	100.00	200.00
11 Willie Kirkland	100.00	200.00
12 Woody Held	100.00	200.00
13 Jerry Kindall	100.00	200.00
14 Max Alvis	100.00	200.00
15 Mel Harder CO	125.00	250.00
16 George Strickland CO	100.00	200.00
17 Elmer Valo CO	100.00	200.00
18 Birdie Tebbetts MG	100.00	200.00
19 Pedro Ramos	100.00	200.00
20 Al Luplow	100.00	200.00
23 Jim Grant	100.00	200.00
24 Vic Davalillo	100.00	200.00
25 Jerry Walker	100.00	200.00
26 Sam McDowell	200.00	400.00
27 Fred Whitfield	100.00	200.00
28 Jack Kralick	100.00	200.00
33 Bob Allen	100.00	200.00
A Don Cardwell	100.00	200.00
B Bob Skinner SP	200.00	400.00
C Don Schwall	100.00	200.00
D Jim Pagliaroni	100.00	200.00
E Dick Schofield	100.00	200.00

1962 Swan-Virdon Postcard

This one-card postcard set features Bill Virdon in which the front is a portrait shot of Virdon and the back promotes the Swan-Virdon company of Missouri. Like so many other postcards at that time, the photo was taken by noted sports photographer J.D. McCarthy.

Card	Low	High
1 Bill Virdon	6.00	15.00

1948 Swell Sport Thrills

The cards in this 20-card set measure approximately 2 7/16" by 3". The 1948 Swell Gum Sports Thrills set of black and white, numbered cards highlights events from baseball history. The cards have picture framed borders with the title "Sports Thrills Highlights in the World of Sport" on the front. The backs of the cards give the story of the event pictured on the front and most of the cards also promote the then recently printed "How to Pitch" book written by Bob Feller. Cards numbered 9, 11, 16, and 20 are more difficult to obtain than the other cards in this set. The catalog designation is R448. These cards were issued as one card packaged with two pieces of gum.

Card	Low	High
COMPLETE SET (20)	500.00	1,000.00
1 Greatest Single Inning Athletics' 10 Run Rally	17.50	35.00
2 Amazing Record: Pete Reiser's Debut With Dodgers	12.50	25.00
3 Dramatic Debut: Jackie Robinson ROY	75.00	150.00
4 Greatest Pitcher of Them All: Walter Johnson	30.00	60.00
5 Three Strikes Not Out: Lost Third Strike Changes	12.50	25.00
6 Home Run Wins Series: Bill Dickey's Last Home Ru	20.00	40.00
7 Never Say Die Pitcher: Hal Schumacher Pitching	12.50	25.00
8 Five Strikeouts: Nationals Lose All Star Game/(	20.00	40.00
9 Greatest Catch: Al Gionfriddo's Catch	15.00	30.00
10 No Hits No Runs: Johnny VanderMeer Comes Back	15.00	30.00
11 Bases Loaded:/(Grover C.) Alexander The Great	20.00	40.00
12 Most Dramatic Homer: Babe Ruth Points	100.00	200.00
13 Winning Run: Tommy Bridges' Pitching and Goose G	12.50	25.00
14 Great Slugging: Lou Gehrig's Four Homers	60.00	120.00
15 Four Men To Stop Him: Joe DiMaggio's Bat Streak	17.50	35.00
16 Three Run Homer in Ninth: Ted Williams' Homer	100.00	200.00
17 Football Block: Johnny Lindell's Football Block	12.50	25.00
18 Home Run To Fame: PeeWee Reese's Grand Slam	20.00	40.00
19 Strikeout Record: Bob Feller Whiffs Five	20.00	40.00
20 Rifle Arm: Carl Furillo	17.50	35.00

1957 Swift Meats

The cards in this 18-card set measure approximately 3 1/2" by 4". These full color, numbered cards issued in 1957 by the Swift Company are die-cut and have rounded corners. Each card consists of several pieces which can be punched out and assembled to form a stand-up model of the player. The cards and a game board were available directly from the company. The company-direct set consisted of three panels each containing six cards; sets found in this "uncut" state carry a value 25 percent higher than the values listed below. The catalog designation for this set is F162. Rocky Colavito appears in his Rookie Card year.

Card	Low	High
COMPLETE SET (18)	750.00	1,500.00
1 John Podres	30.00	60.00
2 Gus Triandos	25.00	50.00
3 Dale Long	25.00	50.00
4 Billy Pierce	30.00	60.00
5 Ed Bailey	25.00	50.00
6 Vic Wertz	25.00	50.00
7 Nelson Fox	75.00	150.00
8 Ken Boyer	40.00	80.00
9 Gil McDougald	30.00	60.00
10 Junior Gilliam	30.00	60.00
11 Eddie Yost	25.00	50.00
12 Johnny Logan	25.00	50.00
13 Hank Aaron	200.00	400.00
14 Bill Tuttle	25.00	50.00
15 Jackie Jensen	40.00	80.00
16 Frank Robinson		250
17 Richie Ashburn	75.00	150.00
18 Rocky Colavito	60.00	120.00

1911 T205 Gold Border

The cards in this 218-card set measure approximately 1 1/2" by 2 5/8". The T205 set (catalog designation), also known as the "Gold Border" set, was issued in 1911 in packages of the following cigarette brands: American Beauty, Broadleaf, Cycle, Drum, Hassan, Honest Long Cut, Piedmont, Polar Bear, Sovereign and Sweet Caporal. All the above were products of the American Tobacco Company, and the ads for the various brands appear below the biographical section on the back of each card. There are pose variations noted in the checklist (which is alphabetized and numbered for reference) and there are 12 minor league cards of a more ornate design which are somewhat scarce. The numbers below correspond to alphabetical order within category, i.e., major leaguers and minor leaguers are alphabetized separately. The gold borders of T205 cards chip easily and they are hard to find in "Mint" or even "Near Mint" condition, due to this there is a high premium on these high condition cards. Listed pricing for raw cards references "EX" condition.

Card	Low	High
COMPLETE SET (218)	25,000.00	50,000.00
COMMON MAJOR (1-186)	90.00	150.00
COM. MINOR (187-198)	150.00	300.00
1 Ed Abbaticchio	60.00	100.00
2 Merle (Doc) Adkins	125.00	200.00
3 Red Ames	60.00	100.00
4 Jimmy Archer	60.00	100.00
5 Jimmy Austin	60.00	100.00
6 Bill Bailey	60.00	100.00
7 Frank Baker	175.00	300.00
8 Neal Ball	60.00	100.00
9 Cy Barger Full B	60.00	100.00
10 Cy Barger Part B	250.00	400.00
11 Jack Barry	60.00	100.00
12 Emil Batch	125.00	200.00
13 Johnny Bates	60.00	100.00
14 Fred Beck	60.00	100.00
15 Beals Becker	60.00	100.00
16 George Bell	60.00	100.00
17 Chief Bender	175.00	300.00
18 Bill Bergen	60.00	100.00
19 Bob Bescher	60.00	100.00
20 Joe Birmingham	60.00	100.00
21 Russ Blackburne	60.00	100.00
22 Kitty Bransfield	60.00	100.00
23 R.Bresnahan Closed	175.00	300.00
24 R.Bresnahan Open	300.00	500.00
25 Al Bridwell	60.00	100.00
26 Mordecai Brown	175.00	300.00
27 Bobby Byrne	60.00	100.00
28 Hick Cady	150.00	250.00
29 Howie Camnitz	60.00	100.00
30 Bill Carrigan	60.00	100.00
31 Frank Chance	175.00	300.00
32A Hal Chase Both - Ends	125.00	200.00
32B Hal Chase Both - Extends	125.00	200.00
33 Hal Chase Left Ear	300.00	500.00
34 Eddie Cicotte	250.00	400.00
35 Fred Clarke	150.00	250.00
36 Ty Cobb	2,500.00	4,000.00
37 E.Collins Mouth Closed	175.00	300.00
38 E.Collins Mouth Open	350.00	600.00
39 Jimmy Collins	250.00	400.00
40 Frank Corridon	60.00	100.00
41A Otis Crandall (Otis)	150.00	250.00
41B Otis Crandall (Olis)	90.00	150.00
42 Lou Criger	60.00	100.00
43 Bill Dahlen	250.00	400.00
44 Jake Daubert	60.00	100.00
45 Jim Delahanty	60.00	100.00
46 Art Devlin	60.00	100.00
47 Josh Devore	60.00	100.00
48 Walt Dickson	60.00	100.00
49 Jiggs Donohue	250.00	400.00
50 Red Dooin	60.00	100.00
51 Mickey Doolan	60.00	100.00
52A Patsy Dougherty Red	150.00	250.00
52B Patsy Dougherty White	150.00	250.00
53 Tom Downey	60.00	100.00
54 Larry Doyle	60.00	100.00
55 Hugh Duffy	175.00	300.00
56 Jack Dunn	175.00	300.00
57 Jimmy Dygert	60.00	100.00
58 Dick Egan	60.00	100.00
59 Kid Elberfeld	60.00	100.00
60 Clyde Engle	60.00	100.00
61 Steve Evans	60.00	100.00
62 Johnny Evers	300.00	500.00
63 Bob Ewing	60.00	100.00
64 George Ferguson	60.00	100.00
65 Ray Fisher	175.00	300.00
66 Art Fletcher	60.00	100.00
67 John Flynn	60.00	100.00
68 Russ Ford Dark Cap	60.00	100.00
69 Russ Ford Light Cap	250.00	400.00
70 Bill Foxen	60.00	100.00
71 James Frick	150.00	250.00
72 Art Fromme	60.00	100.00
73 Earl Gardner	60.00	100.00
74 Harry Gaspar	60.00	100.00
75 George Gibson	60.00	100.00
76 Wilbur Good	60.00	100.00
77 P.Graham Cubs	250.00	400.00
78 P.Graham Rustlers	60.00	100.00
79 Eddie Grant	250.00	400.00
80A Dolly Gray w/o Stats	150.00	250.00
80B Dolly Gray w/Stats	600.00	1,000.00
81 Clark Griffith	175.00	300.00
82 Bob Groom	60.00	100.00
83 Charles Hanford	150.00	250.00
84 Robert Harmon Both ears	60.00	100.00
85 Robert Harmon Left ear only	250.00	400.00
86 Topsy Hartsel	60.00	100.00
87 Arnold Hauser	60.00	100.00
88 Charlie Hemphill	60.00	100.00
89 Buck Herzog	60.00	100.00
90A D.Hoblitzell No Stats	7,000.00	12,000.00
90B D.Hoblitzell w/CIN	90.00	150.00
90C D.Hoblitzell (Hoblitzel)	350.00	600.00
90D D.Hoblitzell w/o CIN	350.00	600.00
91 Danny Hoffman	60.00	100.00
92 Miller Huggins	175.00	300.00
93 John Hummell	60.00	100.00
94 Fred Jacklitsch	60.00	100.00
95 Hughie Jennings MG	175.00	300.00
96 Walter Johnson	1,000.00	1,800.00
97 Davy Jones	60.00	100.00
98 Tom Jones	60.00	100.00
99 Addie Joss	900.00	1,500.00
100 Ed Karger	250.00	400.00
101 Ed Killian	60.00	100.00
102 Red Kleinow	250.00	400.00
103 John Kling	60.00	100.00
104 John Knight	60.00	100.00
105 Ed Konetchy	60.00	100.00
106 Harry Krause	60.00	100.00
107 Rube Kroh	60.00	100.00
108 Frank Lang	60.00	100.00
109 Frank LaPorte	60.00	100.00
110A Arlie Latham (A.)	125.00	200.00
110B Arlie Latham (W.A.)	250.00	400.00
111 Tommy Leach	60.00	100.00
112 Wyatt Lee	90.00	150.00
113 Sam Leever	60.00	100.00
114A Lefty Leifield (A.)	150.00	250.00
114B Lefty Leifield (A.P.)	250.00	400.00
115 Ed Lennox	60.00	100.00
116 Paddy Livingston	60.00	100.00
117 Hans Lobert	60.00	100.00
118 Bris Lord	60.00	100.00
119 Harry Lord	60.00	100.00
120 John Lush	60.00	100.00
121 Nick Maddox	60.00	100.00
122 Sherry Magee	60.00	100.00
123 Rube Marquard	175.00	300.00
124 Christy Mathewson	1,000.00	1,800.00
125 Al Mattern	60.00	100.00
126 Lewis McAllister	90.00	150.00
127 George McBride	60.00	100.00
128 Amby McConnell	60.00	100.00
129 Pryor McElveen	60.00	100.00
130 John McGraw MG	175.00	300.00
131 Harry McIntire	60.00	100.00
132 Matty McIntyre	60.00	100.00
133 Larry McLean	60.00	100.00
134 Fred Merkle	60.00	100.00
135 George Merritt	150.00	250.00
136 Chief Meyers	60.00	100.00
137 Clyde Milan	60.00	100.00
138 Dots Miller	60.00	100.00
139 Mike Mitchell	60.00	100.00
140A Pat Moran Extra Stat	900.00	1,500.00
140B Pat Moran	60.00	100.00
141 George Moriarity	60.00	100.00
142 George Mullin	60.00	100.00
143 Danny Murphy	60.00	100.00
144 Red Murray	60.00	100.00
145 John Nee	150.00	250.00
146 Tom Needham	60.00	100.00
147 Rebel Oakes	60.00	100.00
148 Rube Oldring	60.00	100.00
149 Charley O'Leary	60.00	100.00
150 Fred Olmstead	60.00	100.00
151 Orval Overall	60.00	100.00
152 Freddy Parent	60.00	100.00
153 Dode Paskert	60.00	100.00
154 Fred Payne	60.00	100.00
155 Barney Pelty	60.00	100.00
156 Jack Pfiester	60.00	100.00
157 James Phelan	150.00	250.00
158 Ed Phelps	60.00	100.00
159 Decon Phillippe	60.00	100.00
160 Jack Quinn	60.00	100.00
161 Bugs Raymond	250.00	400.00
162 Ed Reulbach	60.00	100.00
163 Lewis Richie	60.00	100.00
164 Jack Rowan	175.00	300.00
165 Nap Rucker	60.00	100.00
166 Doc Scanlan	250.00	400.00
167 Germany Schaefer	60.00	100.00
168 Admiral Schlei	60.00	100.00
169 Boss Schmidt	60.00	100.00
170 Wildfire Schulte	60.00	100.00
171 Jim Scott	60.00	100.00
172 Bayard Sharpe	60.00	100.00
173 David Shean Chicago Cubs	175.00	300.00
174 David Shean Boston Rustlers	60.00	100.00
175 Jimmy Sheckard	60.00	100.00
176 Hack Simmons	60.00	100.00
177 Tony Smith	60.00	100.00
178 Fred Snodgrass	60.00	100.00
179 Tris Speaker	500.00	800.00
180 Jake Stahl	60.00	100.00
181 Oscar Stanage	60.00	100.00
182 Harry Steinfeldt	60.00	100.00
183 George Stone	60.00	100.00
184 George Stovall	60.00	100.00
185 Gabby Street	60.00	100.00
186 George Suggs	250.00	400.00
187 Ed Summers	60.00	100.00
188 Jeff Sweeney	250.00	400.00
189 Lee Tannehill	60.00	100.00
190 Ira Thomas	60.00	100.00
191 Joe Tinker	175.00	300.00
192 John Titus	60.00	100.00
193 Terry Turner	250.00	400.00
194 Hippo Vaughn	300.00	500.00
195 Heinie Wagner	175.00	300.00
196 B.Wallace w/cap	150.00	250.00
197A B.Wallace w/o Cap 1 Line	1,200.00	2,000.00
197B B.Wallace w/o Cap 2 Lines	700.00	1,200.00
198 Ed Walsh	500.00	800.00
199 Zach Wheat	175.00	300.00
200 Doc White	60.00	100.00
201 Kirby White	250.00	400.00
202A Irvin K. Wilhelm	350.00	600.00
202B Irvin K. Wilhelm Missing Letter	175.00	300.00
203 Ed Willett	60.00	100.00
204 Owen Wilson	60.00	100.00
205 H.Wiltse Both Ears	60.00	100.00
206 H.Wiltse Right Ear	250.00	400.00
207 Harry Wolter	60.00	100.00
208 Cy Young	1,000.00	1,800.00

1909-11 T206

The T206 set was and is the most popular of all the tobacco issues. The set was issued from 1909 to 1911 with sixteen different brands of cigarettes: American Beauty, Broadleaf, Cycle, Carolina Brights, Drum, El Principe de Gales, Hindu, Lenox, Old Mill, Piedmont, Polar Bear, Sovereign, Sweet Caporal, Tolstoi, and Uzit. There was also an extremely rare Ty Cobb back version for the Ty Cobb Red Portrait that it's believed was issued as a promotional card. Pricing for the Cobb back card is unavailable and it's typically not considered part of the complete 524-card set. The minor league cards are supposedly slightly more difficult to obtain than the cards of the major leaguers, with the Southern League player cards being definitively more difficult. Minor League players were obtained from the American Association and the Eastern league. Southern League players were obtained from a variety of leagues including the following: South Atlantic League, Southern League, Texas League, and Virginia League. Series 150 (notated as such on the card backs) was issued between February 1909 thru the end of May, 1909. Series 350 was issued from the end of May, 1909 thru April, 1910. The last series 350 to 460 was issued in late December 1910 through early 1911. The set price below does not include ultra-expensive Wagner, Plank, Magie error, or Doyle variation. The Wagner card is one of the most sought after cards in the hobby. This card was pulled from circulation almost immediately after being issued. Estimates of how many Wagners are in existence generally settle on around 50 to 60 copies. The backs vary in scarcity as follows: Exceedingly Rare: Ty Cobb; Rare: Drum, Uzit, Lenox, Broadleaf 460 and Hindu; Scarce: Broadleaf 350, Carolina brights, Hindu Red; Less Common: American Beauty, Cycle and Tolstoi; Readily Available: El Principe de Gales, Old Mill, Polar Bear and Sovereign and Common: Piedmont and Sweet Caporal. Listed prices refer to the Piedmont and Sweet caporal backs in raw "EX" condition. Of note, the O'Hara St. Louis and Demmitt St. Louis cards were only issued with Polar Bear backs and are are priced as such. Pricing is unavailable for the unbelieveably rare Joe Doyle Nat'l variation (perhaps a dozen or fewer copies exist) in addition to the Bud Shappe and Fred nodgrass printing variaitons. Finally, unlike the other cards in this set, listed raw pricing for the famed Honus Wagner references "Good" condition insetad of "EX".

Card	Low	High
COMPLETE SET (520)	30,000.00	55,000.00

COMMON MAJOR (1-389)	50.00	100.00
COMMON MINOR (390-475)	50.00	100.00
COM. SO. LEA. (476-523)	125.00	250.00
CARDS PRICED IN EXMT CONDITION		
HONUS WAGNER PRICED IN GOOD CONDITION		
1 Ed Abbaticchio Blue	85.00	135.00
2 Ed Abbaticchio Brown	85.00	135.00
3 Fred Abbott	60.00	100.00
4 Bill Abstein	60.00	100.00
5 Doc Adkins	125.00	200.00
6 Whitey Alperman	60.00	100.00
7 Red Ames Hands at	150.00	250.00
8 Red Ames Hands over	60.00	100.00
9 Red Ames	60.00	100.00
Portrait		
10 John Anderson	60.00	100.00
11 Frank Arellanes	60.00	100.00
12 Herman Armbruster	60.00	100.00
13 Harry Arndt	70.00	120.00
14 Jake Atz	60.00	100.00
15 Home Run Baker	250.00	400.00
16 Neal Ball	60.00	100.00
Cleveland		
17 Neal Ball	60.00	100.00
New York		
18 Jap Barbeau	60.00	100.00
19 Cy Barger	60.00	100.00
20 Jack Barry	60.00	100.00
21 Shad Barry	60.00	100.00
22 Jack Bastian	175.00	300.00
23 Emil Batch	60.00	100.00
24 Johnny Bates	60.00	100.00
25 Harry Bay	175.00	300.00
26 Ginger Beaumont	60.00	100.00
27 Fred Beck	60.00	100.00
28 Beals Becker	60.00	100.00
29 Jake Beckley	175.00	300.00
30 George Bell Follow	60.00	100.00
31 George Bell Hands above	60.00	100.00
32 Chief Bender Pitching	250.00	400.00
33 Chief Bender	250.00	400.00
Pitching Trees in Back		
34 Chief Bender	300.00	500.00
Portrait		
35 Bill Bergen	60.00	100.00
Batting		
36 Bill Bergen	60.00	100.00
Catching		
37 Heinie Berger	60.00	100.00
38 Bill Bernhard	175.00	300.00
39 Bob Bescher Hands	60.00	100.00
40 Bob Bescher	60.00	100.00
Portrait		
41 Joe Birmingham	90.00	150.00
42 Lena Blackburne	60.00	100.00
43 Jack Bliss	60.00	100.00
44 Frank Bowerman	60.00	100.00
45 Bill Bradley with Bat	60.00	100.00
46 Bill Bradley	60.00	100.00
Portrait		
47 David Brain	60.00	100.00
48 Kitty Bransfield	60.00	100.00
49 Roy Brashear	60.00	100.00
50 Ted Breitenstein	175.00	300.00
51 Roger Bresnahan	175.00	300.00
Portrait		
52 Roger Bresnahan	175.00	300.00
with Bat		
53 Al Bridwell	60.00	100.00
No Cap		
54 Al Bridwell	60.00	100.00
with Cap		
55 George Brown Chicago	125.00	200.00
56 George Brown Washington	300.00	500.00
57 Mordecai Brown Chicago	200.00	350.00
58 Mordecai Brown Cubs	350.00	600.00
59 Mordecai Brown	300.00	500.00
Portrait		
60 Al Burch	125.00	200.00
Batting		
61 Al Burch	60.00	100.00
Fielding		
62 Fred Burchell	60.00	100.00
63 Jimmy Burke	60.00	100.00
64 Bill Burns	60.00	100.00
65 Donie Bush	60.00	100.00
66 John Butler	60.00	100.00
67 Bobby Byrne	60.00	100.00
68 Howie Camnitz	60.00	100.00
Arm at Side		
69 Howie Camnitz Folded	60.00	100.00
70 Howie Camnitz Hands	60.00	100.00
71 Billy Campbell	60.00	100.00
72 Scoops Carey	175.00	300.00
73 Charley Carr	60.00	100.00
74 Bill Carrigan	60.00	100.00
75 Doc Casey	60.00	100.00
76 Peter Cassidy	60.00	100.00
77 Frank Chance	250.00	400.00
Batting		
78 F.Chance Portrait Red	300.00	500.00
79 F.Chance Portrait Yel	250.00	400.00
80 Bill Chappelle	60.00	100.00
81 Chappie Charles	60.00	100.00
82 Hal Chase Dark Cap	90.00	150.00
83 Hal Chase	150.00	250.00
Holding Trophy		
84 Hal Chase	90.00	150.00
Portrait Blue		
85 Hal Chase	250.00	400.00
Portrait Pink		
86 Hal Chase White Cap	125.00	200.00
87 Jack Chesbro	250.00	400.00
88 Ed Cicotte	175.00	300.00
89 Bill Clancy (Clancey)	60.00	100.00
90 Fred Clarke	250.00	400.00
Holding Bat		
91 Fred Clarke	250.00	400.00
Portrait		
92 Josh Clark (Clarke) ML	60.00	100.00
93 J.J. (Nig) Clarke	60.00	100.00
94 Bill Clymer	60.00	100.00
95 Ty Cobb	1,500.00	2,500.00
Bat off Shoulder		
96 Ty Cobb	1,500.00	2,500.00
Bat on Shoulder		
97 Ty Cobb	3,500.00	5,000.00
Portrait Green		
98 Ty Cobb	1,200.00	2,000.00
Portrait Red		
99 Cad Coles	175.00	300.00
100 Eddie Collins	200.00	350.00
101 Jimmy Collins	175.00	300.00
102 Bunk Congalton ML	60.00	100.00
103 Wid Conroy	60.00	100.00
Fielding		
104 Wid Conroy	60.00	100.00
with Bat		
105 Harry Covaleski (Coveleski)	60.00	100.00
106 Doc Crandall	60.00	100.00
No Cap		
107 Doc Crandall	60.00	100.00
with Cap		
108 Bill Cranston	175.00	300.00
109 Gavvy Cravath	60.00	100.00
110 Sam Crawford	250.00	400.00
Throwing		
111 Sam Crawford	250.00	400.00
with Bat		
112 Birdie Cree	60.00	100.00
113 Lou Criger	60.00	100.00
114 Dode Criss UER	60.00	100.00
115 Monte Cross	60.00	100.00
116 Bill Dahlen	90.00	150.00
Boston		
117 Bill Dahlen	300.00	500.00
Brooklyn		
118 Paul Davidson	60.00	100.00
119 George Davis	175.00	300.00
120 Harry Davis	60.00	100.00
Davis on Front		
121 Harry Davis	60.00	100.00
H.Davis on Front		
122 Frank Delehanty	60.00	100.00
123 Jim Delehanty	60.00	100.00
124 Ray Demmitt	70.00	120.00
New York		
125 Ray Demmitt	6,000.00	10,000.00
St. Louis		
126 Rube Dessau	85.00	135.00
127 Art Devlin	60.00	100.00
128 Josh Devore	60.00	100.00
129 Bill Dineen	60.00	100.00
130 Mike Donlin	125.00	200.00
Fielding		
131 Mike Donlin Sitting	60.00	100.00
132 Mike Donlin	60.00	100.00
with Bat		
133 Jiggs Donahue (Donohue)	60.00	100.00
134 Wild Bill Donovan	60.00	100.00
Portrait		
135 Wild Bill Donovan	60.00	100.00
Throwing		
136 Red Dooin	60.00	100.00
137 Mickey Doolan	60.00	100.00
Batting		
138 Mickey Doolan	60.00	100.00
Fielding		
139 Mickey Doolin	60.00	100.00
Portrait (Doolan)		
140 Gus Dorner ML	60.00	100.00
141 Gus Dorner		
Card Spelled Dopner on Back		
142 Patsy Dougherty	60.00	100.00
Arm in Air		
143 Patsy Dougherty	60.00	100.00
Portrait		
144 Tom Downey	60.00	100.00
Batting		
145 Tom Downey	60.00	100.00
Fielding		
146 Jerry Downs	60.00	100.00
147 Joe Doyle	350.00	600.00
148 Joe Doyle Nat'l		
149 Larry Doyle Portrait	60.00	100.00
150 Larry Doyle	60.00	100.00
Throwing		
151 Larry Doyle	60.00	100.00
with Bat		
152 Jean Dubuc	60.00	100.00
153 Hugh Duffy	175.00	300.00
154 Jack Dunn Baltimore	60.00	100.00
155 Joe Dunn	60.00	100.00
Brooklyn		
156 Bull Durham	60.00	100.00
157 Jimmy Dygert	60.00	100.00
158 Ted Easterly	60.00	100.00
159 Dick Egan	90.00	150.00
160 Kid Elberfeld	60.00	100.00
Fielding		
161 Kid Elberfeld Port NY	60.00	100.00
162 Kid Elberfeld Port Wash	1,800.00	3,000.00
163 Roy Ellam	175.00	300.00
164 Clyde Engle	60.00	100.00
165 Steve Evans	60.00	100.00
166 J.Evers Portrait	350.00	600.00
167 J.Evers Chi Shirt	250.00	400.00
168 J.Evers Cubs Shirt	500.00	800.00
169 Bob Ewing	60.00	100.00
170 Cecil Ferguson	60.00	100.00
171 Hobe Ferris	60.00	100.00
172 Lou Fiene	60.00	100.00
Portrait		
173 Lou Fiene	60.00	100.00
Throwing		
174 Steamer Flanagan	60.00	100.00
175 Art Fletcher	60.00	100.00
176 Elmer Flick	175.00	300.00
177 Russ Ford	60.00	100.00
178 Ed Foster	175.00	300.00
179 Jerry Freeman	60.00	100.00
180 John Frill	60.00	100.00
181 Charlie Fritz	175.00	300.00
182 Art Fromme	60.00	100.00
183 Chick Gandil	175.00	300.00
184 Bob Ganley	60.00	100.00
185 John Ganzel	60.00	100.00
186 Harry Gasper (Gaspar)	60.00	100.00
187 Rube Geyer	60.00	100.00
188 George Gibson	60.00	100.00
189 Billy Gilbert	60.00	100.00
190 Wilbur Goode (Good)	60.00	100.00
191 Bill Graham	60.00	100.00
St. Louis		
192 Peaches Graham	70.00	120.00
193 Dolly Gray	60.00	100.00
194 Ed Greminger	175.00	300.00
195 Clark Griffith	175.00	300.00
Batting		
196 Clark Griffith	175.00	300.00
Portrait		
197 Moose Grimshaw	60.00	100.00
198 Bob Groom	60.00	100.00
199 Tom Guiheen	175.00	300.00
200 Ed Hahn	60.00	100.00
201 Bob Hall	60.00	100.00
202 Bill Hallman	60.00	100.00
203 Jack Hannifan (Hannifin)	60.00	100.00
204 Bill Hart Little Rock	175.00	300.00
205 Jimmy Hart Montgomery	175.00	300.00
206 Topsy Hartsel	60.00	100.00
207 Jack Hayden	60.00	100.00
208 J.Ross Helm	175.00	300.00
209 Charlie Hemphill	60.00	100.00
210 Buck Herzog	60.00	100.00
Boston		
211 Buck Herzog	60.00	100.00
New York		
212 Gordon Hickman	175.00	300.00
213 Bill Hinchman	60.00	100.00
214 Harry Hinchman	60.00	100.00
215 Doc Hoblitzell	60.00	100.00
216 Danny Hoffman	60.00	100.00
St. Louis		
217 Izzy Hoffman Providence	60.00	100.00
218 Solly Hofman	60.00	100.00
219 Buck Hooker	175.00	300.00
220 Del Howard	60.00	100.00
Chicago		
221 Ernie Howard Savannah	175.00	300.00
222 Harry Howell	60.00	100.00
Hand at Waist		
223 Harry Howell	60.00	100.00
Portrait		
224 M.Huggins Mouth	175.00	300.00
225 M.Huggins Portrait	175.00	300.00
226 Rudy Hulswitt	60.00	100.00
227 John Hummel	60.00	100.00
228 George Hunter	60.00	100.00
229 Frank Isbell	60.00	100.00
230 Fred Jacklitsch	60.00	100.00
231 Jimmy Jackson	60.00	100.00
232 H.Jennings Both	175.00	300.00
233 H.Jennings One	175.00	300.00
234 H.Jennings Portrait	175.00	300.00
235 Walter Johnson Hands	700.00	1,200.00
236 Walter Johnson Port	1,000.00	1,800.00
237 Davy Jones	60.00	100.00
Detroit		
238 Fielder Jones	60.00	100.00
Hands at Hips		
239 Fielder Jones	60.00	100.00
Portrait		
240 Tom Jones	60.00	100.00
St. Louis		
241 Dutch Jordan Atlanta	175.00	300.00
242 Tim Jordan Batting	60.00	100.00
243 Tim Jordan Portrait	60.00	100.00
244 Addie Joss	175.00	300.00
Pitching		
245 Addie Joss	250.00	400.00
Portrait		
246 Ed Karger	60.00	100.00
247 Willie Keeler	350.00	600.00
Portrait		
248 Willie Keeler Batting	350.00	600.00
249 Joe Kelley	150.00	250.00
250 J.F. Kiernan	300.00	500.00
251 Ed Killian	60.00	100.00
Pitching		
252 Ed Killian	60.00	100.00
Portrait		
253 Frank King	175.00	300.00
254 Rube Kisinger (Kissinger)	60.00	100.00
255 Red Kleinow	300.00	500.00
Boston		
256 Red Kleinow NY Catch	60.00	100.00
257 Red Kleinow NY Bat	60.00	100.00
258 Johnny Kling	60.00	100.00
259 Otto Knabe	60.00	100.00
260 Jack Knight	60.00	100.00
Portrait		
261 Jack Knight	60.00	100.00
with Bat		
262 Ed Konetchy Glove Lo	60.00	100.00
263 Ed Konetchy Glove Hi	60.00	100.00
264 Harry Krause	60.00	100.00
Pitching		
265 Harry Krause	60.00	100.00
Portrait		
266 Rube Kroh	60.00	100.00
267 Otto Kruger (Krueger)	60.00	100.00
268 James LaFitte	175.00	300.00
269 Nap Lajoie	500.00	800.00
Portrait		
270 Nap Lajoie	400.00	700.00
Throwing		
271 Nap Lajoie	400.00	700.00
with Bat		
272 Joe Lake NY	60.00	100.00
273 Joe Lake Stl No Ball	60.00	100.00
274 Joe Lake Stl with Ball	60.00	100.00
275 Frank LaPorte	60.00	100.00
276 Arlie Latham	60.00	100.00
277 Bill Lattimore	60.00	100.00
278 Jimmy Lavender	60.00	100.00
279 Tommy Leach	60.00	100.00
Bending Over		
280 Tommy Leach	60.00	100.00
Portrait		
281 Lefty Leifield	60.00	100.00
Batting		
282 Lefty Leifield	60.00	100.00
Pitching		
283 Ed Lennox	60.00	100.00
284 Harry Lentz	250.00	400.00
(Sentz) SL		
285 Glenn Liebhardt	60.00	100.00
286 Vive Lindaman	60.00	100.00
287 Perry Lipe	175.00	300.00
288 Paddy Livingstone	60.00	100.00
(Livingston)		
289 Hans Lobert	60.00	100.00
290 Harry Lord	60.00	100.00
291 Harry Lumley	60.00	100.00
292 Carl Lundgren	500.00	800.00
Chicago		
293 Carl Lundgren Kansas City	125.00	200.00
294 Sherry Magie Portrait ERR	15,000.00	25,000.00
294 Nick Maddox	60.00	100.00
295 Sherry Magee	60.00	100.00
with Bat		
296 Sherry Magee	150.00	250.00
Portrait		
298 Bill Malarkey	60.00	100.00
299 Bill Maloney	60.00	100.00
300 George Manion	175.00	300.00
301 Rube Manning	60.00	100.00
Batting		
302 Rube Manning	60.00	100.00
Pitching		
303 R.Marquard Follow	175.00	300.00
304 R.Marquard Hands	175.00	300.00
305 R.Marquard Portrait	200.00	350.00
306 Doc Marshall	60.00	100.00
307 C.Mathewson Drk Cap	700.00	1,200.00
308 C.Mathewson Portrait	900.00	1,500.00
309 C.Mathewson Wht Cap	900.00	1,500.00
310 Al Mattern	60.00	100.00
311 John McAleese	60.00	100.00
312 George McBride	60.00	100.00
313 Pat McCauley	175.00	300.00
314 Moose McCormick	60.00	100.00
315 Pryor McElveen	60.00	100.00
316 Dennis McGann	60.00	100.00
317 Jim McGinley	60.00	100.00
318 Iron Man McGinnity	175.00	300.00
319 Stoney McGlynn	60.00	100.00
320 J.McGraw Finger	250.00	400.00
321 J.McGraw Glove-Hip	250.00	400.00
322 J.McGraw w/o Cap	250.00	400.00
323 J.McGraw w/Cap	250.00	400.00
324 Harry McIntyre	60.00	100.00
Brooklyn		
325 Harry McIntyre	60.00	100.00
Brooklyn-Chicago		
326 Matty McIntyre	60.00	100.00
Detroit		
327 Larry McLean	60.00	100.00
328 George McQuillan	60.00	100.00
Ball in Hand		
329 George McQuillan	60.00	100.00
with Bat		
330 Fred Merkle Portrait	70.00	120.00
331 Fred Merkle Throwing	90.00	150.00
332 George Merritt	60.00	100.00
333 Chief Meyers	60.00	100.00
334 Chief Myers	70.00	120.00
Batting (Meyers)		
335 Chief Myers	60.00	100.00
Fielding (Meyers)		
336 Clyde Milan	60.00	100.00
337 Molly Miller Dallas	175.00	300.00
338 Dots Miller	60.00	100.00
Pittsburgh		
339 Bill Milligan	60.00	100.00
340 Fred Mitchell Toronto	60.00	100.00
341 Mike Mitchell	60.00	100.00
Cincinnati		
342 Dan Moeller	60.00	100.00
343 Carleton Molesworth	175.00	300.00
344 Herbie Moran Providence	60.00	100.00
345 Pat Moran	60.00	100.00
Chicago		
346 George Moriarty	60.00	100.00
347 Mike Mowrey	60.00	100.00
348 Dom Mullaney	175.00	300.00
349 George Mullen	60.00	100.00
(Mullin)		
350 George Mullin	60.00	100.00
with Bat		
351 George Mullin Throwing	60.00	100.00
352 Danny Murphy	60.00	100.00
Batting		
353 Danny Murphy	60.00	100.00

Throwing		
354 Red Murray	60.00	100.00
Batting		
355 Red Murray	60.00	100.00
Portrait		
356 Billy Nattress	60.00	100.00
357 Tom Needham	60.00	100.00
358 Simon Nicholls	60.00	100.00
Hands on Knees		
359 Simon Nichols	60.00	100.00
Batting (Nicholls)		
360 Harry Niles	60.00	100.00
361 Rebel Oakes	60.00	100.00
362 Frank Oberlin	60.00	100.00
363 Peter O'Brien	60.00	100.00
364 Bill O'Hara NY	60.00	100.00
365 Bill O'Hara Stl	6,000.00	10,000.00
366 Rube Oldring	60.00	100.00
Batting		
367 Rube Oldring	60.00	100.00
Fielding		
368 Charley O'Leary	60.00	100.00
Hands on Knees		
369 Charley O'Leary	60.00	100.00
Portrait		
370 William O'Neil	150.00	250.00
371 Albert Orth	175.00	300.00
372 William Otey	175.00	300.00
373 Orval Overall	60.00	100.00
Hand at Face		
374 Orval Overall	60.00	100.00
Hands at Waist		
375 Orval Overall	60.00	100.00
Portrait		
376 Frank Owen (Owens)	60.00	100.00
377 George Paige	175.00	300.00
378 Freddy Parent	60.00	100.00
379 Dode Paskert	60.00	100.00
380 Jim Pastorius	60.00	100.00
381 Harry Pattee	60.00	100.00
382 Fred Payne	60.00	100.00
383 Barney Pelty	60.00	100.00
Horizontal		
384 Barney Pelty	60.00	100.00
Vertical		
385 Hub Perdue	175.00	300.00
386 George Perring	60.00	100.00
387 Arch Persons	175.00	300.00
388 Jeff Pfeffer	60.00	100.00
389 Jeff Pfeffer ERR		
Chicago		
390 Jake Pfeister	60.00	100.00
Seated (Pfiester)		
391 Jake Pfeister	60.00	100.00
Throwing (Pfiester)		
392 Jimmy Phelan	60.00	100.00
393 Ed Phelps	60.00	100.00
394 Deacon Phillippe.	60.00	100.00
395 Ollie Pickering	60.00	100.00
396 Eddie Plank	45,000.00	60,000.00
397 Phil Poland	60.00	100.00
398 Jack Powell	60.00	100.00
399 Mike Powers	60.00	100.00
400 Billy Purtell	60.00	100.00
401 Ambrose Puttman (Puttmann)	85.00	135.00
402 Lee Quillen (Quillin)	60.00	100.00
403 Jack Quinn	60.00	100.00
404 Newt Randall	60.00	100.00
405 Bugs Raymond	60.00	100.00
406 Ed Reagan	175.00	300.00
407 Ed Reulbach Glove	60.00	100.00
408 Ed Reulbach	70.00	120.00
No Glove		
409 Dutch Revelle	175.00	300.00
410 Bob Rhoades Hands	60.00	100.00
411 Bob Rhoades Right	60.00	100.00
412 Charlie Rhodes	60.00	100.00
413 Claude Ritchey	60.00	100.00
414 Lou Ritter	60.00	100.00
415 Ike Rockenfeld	175.00	300.00
416 Claude Rossman	60.00	100.00
417 Nap Rucker	60.00	100.00
Portrait		
418 Nap Rucker	60.00	100.00
Throwing		
419 Dick Rudolph	60.00	100.00
420 Ray Ryan	175.00	300.00
421 Germany Schaefer Det	60.00	100.00
422 Germany Schaefer Wash	60.00	100.00
423 George Schirm	85.00	135.00
424 Larry Schlafly	60.00	100.00
425 Admiral Schlei	60.00	100.00
Batting		
426 Admiral Schlei	60.00	100.00
Catching		
427 Admiral Schlei	60.00	100.00
Portrait		
428 Boss Schmidt	60.00	100.00
Portrait		
429 Boss Schmidt	60.00	100.00
Throwing		
430 Ossee Schreck (Schreckengost)	70.00	120.00
431 Wildfire Schulte	60.00	100.00
Back View		
432 Wildfire Schulte	175.00	300.00
Front View		
433 Jim Scott	60.00	100.00
434 Charles Seitz	175.00	300.00
435 Cy Seymour	60.00	100.00
Batting		
436 Cy Seymour	60.00	100.00
Portrait		
437 Cy Seymour	60.00	100.00
Throwing		
438 Spike Shannon	60.00	100.00
439 Bud Sharpe	60.00	100.00
440 Bud Shappe ERR		
(Sharpe) ML		
441 Frank Shaughnessy SL	175.00	300.00
442 Al Shaw	60.00	100.00
St. Louis		
443 Hunky Shaw Providence	60.00	100.00
444 Jimmy Sheckard Glove	60.00	100.00
445 Jimmy Sheckard	60.00	100.00
No Glove		
446 Bill Shipke	60.00	100.00
447 Jimmy Slagle	60.00	100.00
448 Carlos Smith Shreveport	175.00	300.00
449 Frank Smith Chi-Bos	350.00	600.00
450 Frank Smith Chi F.Smith	60.00	100.00
451 Frank Smith Chi Whit Cap	60.00	100.00
452 Heinie Smith Buffalo	60.00	100.00
453 Happy Smith	60.00	100.00
Brooklyn		
454 Sid Smith Atlanta	175.00	300.00
455 F.Snodgrass Batting	60.00	100.00
456 F.nodgrass Batting ERR		
457 F.Snodgrass Catching	60.00	100.00
458 Bob Spade	60.00	100.00
459 Tris Speaker	600.00	1,000.00
460 Tubby Spencer	60.00	100.00
461 Jake Stahl Glove	85.00	135.00
462 Jake Stahl No Glove	60.00	100.00
463 Oscar Stanage	60.00	100.00
464 Dolly Stark	175.00	300.00
465 Charlie Starr	60.00	100.00
466 Harry Steinfeldt	60.00	100.00
with Bat		
467 Harry Steinfeldt	60.00	100.00
Portrait		
468 Jim Stephens	60.00	100.00
469 George Stone	60.00	100.00
470 George Stovall	60.00	100.00
Batting		
471 George Stovall	60.00	100.00
Portrait		
472 Sam Strang	60.00	100.00
473 Gabby Street	60.00	100.00
Catching		
474 Gabby Street	60.00	100.00
Portrait		
475 Billy Sullivan	60.00	100.00
476 Ed Summers	60.00	100.00
477 Bill Sweeney	60.00	100.00
Boston		
478 Jeff Sweeney	60.00	100.00
New York		
479 Jesse Tannehill	60.00	100.00
Washington		
480 Lee Tannehill Chi L.Tannehill	60.00	100.00
481 Lee Tannehill Chi Tannehill	60.00	100.00
482 Dummy Taylor	60.00	100.00
483 Fred Tenney	60.00	100.00
484 Tony Thebo	175.00	300.00
485 Jake Thielman	90.00	150.00
486 Ira Thomas	60.00	100.00
487 Woodie Thornton	175.00	300.00
488 J.Tinker Bat off Shldr	250.00	400.00
489 J.Tinker Bat on Shldr	400.00	800.00
490 J.Tinker Hand-Knee	350.00	600.00
491 J.Tinker Portrait	350.00	600.00
492 John Titus	60.00	100.00
493 Terry Turner	60.00	100.00
494 Bob Unglaub	60.00	100.00
495 Juan Violat (Viola)	175.00	300.00
496 R.Waddell Portrait	250.00	400.00
497 R.Waddell Throwing	250.00	400.00
498 Heinie Wagner on Left	60.00	100.00
499 Heinie Wagner on Right	60.00	100.00
500 Honus Wagner	250,000.00	350,000.00
501 Bobby Wallace	175.00	300.00
502 Ed Walsh	250.00	400.00
503 Jack Warhop	60.00	100.00
504 Jake Weimer	60.00	100.00
505 James Westlake	175.00	300.00
506 Zack Wheat	200.00	350.00
507 Doc White Pitching	60.00	100.00
508 Doc White Portrait	60.00	100.00
509 Foley White Houston	175.00	300.00
510 Jack White Buffalo	60.00	100.00
511 Kaiser Wilhelm Hands	60.00	100.00
512 Kaiser Wilhelm	60.00	100.00
with Bat		
513 Ed Willett	60.00	100.00
with Bat		
514 Ed Willetts	60.00	100.00
Throwing (Willett)		
515 Jimmy Williams	60.00	100.00
516 Vic Willis Pitt	200.00	350.00
517 Vic Willis Stl Throw	175.00	300.00
518 Vic Willis Stl Bat	175.00	300.00
519 Owen Wilson	60.00	100.00
520 Hooks Wiltse	60.00	100.00
Pitching		
521 Hooks Wiltse Portrait	60.00	100.00
522 Hooks Wiltse Sweater	60.00	100.00
523 Lucky Wright	60.00	100.00
524 Cy Young Bare Hand	700.00	1,200.00
525 Cy Young w/Glove	700.00	1,200.00
526 Cy Young	1,000.00	1,800.00
Portrait		
527 Irv Young Minneapolis	70.00	120.00
528 Heinie Zimmerman:	60.00	100.00

1909-11 T206 Ty Cobb Back

1 Ty Cobb Portrait

1912 T207 Brown Background

The cards in this 207-card set measure approximately 1 1/2" by 2 5/8". The T207 set, also known as the "Brown Background" set was issued beginning in May with Broadleaf, Cycle, Napoleon, Recruit and anonymous (Factories no. 2, 3 or 25) backs in 1912. Broadleaf, Cycle and anonymous backs are difficult to obtain. Although many scarcities and cards with varying degrees of difficulty to obtain exist (see prices below), the Loudermilk, Lewis (Boston NL) and Miller (Chicago NL) cards are the rarest, followed by Saier and Tyler. The cards are numbered below for reference in alphabetical order by player's name. The complete set price below does include the Lewis variation missing the Braves patch on the sleeve. Listed pricing references raw "VgEx" condition.

COMPLETE SET (208)	15,000.00	30,000.00
1 Bert Adams	175.00	300.00
2 Eddie Ainsmith	30.00	50.00
3 Rafael Almeida	125.00	200.00
4 Jimmy Austin Insignia	30.00	50.00
5 Jimmy Austin No Insignia	60.00	100.00
6 Neal Ball	60.00	100.00
7 Cy Barger	30.00	50.00
8 Jack Barry	30.00	50.00
9 Paddy Bauman	125.00	200.00
10 Beals Becker	30.00	50.00
11 Chief Bender	90.00	150.00
12 Joe Benz	125.00	200.00
13 Bob Bescher	30.00	50.00
14 Joe Birmingham	125.00	200.00
15 Lena Blackburne	60.00	100.00
16 Fred Blanding	90.00	150.00
17 Bruno Block	60.00	100.00
18 Ping Bodie	35.00	60.00
19 Hugh Bradley	30.00	50.00
20 Roger Bresnahan	90.00	150.00
21 Jack Bushelman	125.00	200.00
22 Hank Butcher	90.00	150.00
23 Bobby Byrne	30.00	50.00
24 Nixey Callahan	30.00	50.00
25 Howie Camnitz	30.00	50.00
26 Max Carey	150.00	250.00
27 Bill Carrigan Correct Back	30.00	50.00
28 Bill Carrigan Wagner Back	60.00	100.00
29 George Chalmers	30.00	50.00
30 Frank Chance	90.00	150.00
31 Eddie Cicotte	300.00	500.00
32 Tommy Clarke	30.00	50.00
33 King Cole	30.00	50.00
34 Shano Collins	30.00	50.00
35 Bob Coulson	30.00	50.00
36 Tex Covington	30.00	50.00
37 Doc Crandall	30.00	50.00
38 Bill Cunningham	90.00	150.00
39 Dave Danforth	30.00	50.00
40 Bert Daniels	30.00	50.00
41 Jake Daubert	60.00	100.00
42 Harry Davis	30.00	50.00
43 Jim Delahanty	30.00	50.00
44 Claud Derrick	30.00	50.00
45 Art Devlin	30.00	50.00
46 Josh Devore	30.00	50.00
47 Mike Donlin	90.00	150.00
48 Ed Donnelly	60.00	100.00
49 Red Dooin	30.00	50.00
50 Tom Downey	125.00	200.00
51 Larry Doyle	30.00	50.00
52 Dellos Drake	35.00	60.00
53 Ted Easterly	30.00	50.00
54 Rube Ellis	90.00	150.00
55 Clyde Engle	50.00	80.00
56 Tex Erwin	35.00	60.00
57 Steve Evans	30.00	50.00
58 Jack Ferry	30.00	50.00
59 Ray Fisher Blue Cap	60.00	100.00
60 Ray Fisher White Cap	60.00	100.00
61 Art Fletcher	30.00	50.00
62 Jack Fournier	125.00	200.00
63 Art Fromme	30.00	50.00
64 Del Gainor	30.00	50.00
65 Larry Gardner	30.00	50.00
66 Lefty George	30.00	50.00
67 Roy Golden	30.00	50.00
68 Hank Gowdy	35.00	60.00
69 Peaches Graham	60.00	100.00
70 Jack Graney	35.00	60.00
71 Vean Gregg	60.00	100.00
72 Casey Hageman	30.00	50.00
73 Sea Lion Hall	30.00	50.00
74 Ed Hallinan	35.00	60.00
75 Earl Hamilton	30.00	50.00
76 Bob Harmon	30.00	50.00
77 Grover Hartley	60.00	100.00
78 Olaf Henriksen	30.00	50.00
79 John Henry	60.00	100.00
80 Buck Herzog	90.00	150.00
81 Bob Higgins	35.00	60.00
82 Red Hoff	70.00	120.00
83 Willie Hogan	35.00	60.00
84 Harry Hooper	300.00	500.00
85 Ben Houser	90.00	150.00
86 Ham Hyatt	70.00	120.00
87 Walter Johnson	350.00	600.00
88 George Kaler (Kahler)	30.00	50.00
89 Billy Kelly	60.00	100.00
90 Jay Kirke	70.00	120.00
91 Johnny Kling	90.00	150.00
92 Otto Knabe	30.00	50.00
93 Elmer Knetzer	30.00	50.00
94 Ed Konetchy	30.00	50.00
95 Harry Krause	30.00	50.00
96 Walt Kuhn	90.00	150.00
97 Joe Kutina	90.00	150.00
98 Frank Lange	60.00	100.00
99 Jack Lapp	35.00	60.00
100 Arlie Latham	30.00	50.00
101 Tommy Leach	30.00	50.00
102 Lefty Leifield	35.00	60.00
103 Ed Lennox	30.00	50.00
104 Duffy Lewis Boston	125.00	200.00
105A Irving Lewis Emblem on Sleeve	3,500.00	6,000.00
105B Irving Lewis No Emblem on Sleeve	3,500.00	6,000.00
106 Jack Lively	30.00	50.00
107 Paddy Livingston A on Shirt	125.00	200.00
108 Paddy Livingston Big C on Shirt	70.00	120.00
109 Paddy Livingston c Shirt	50.00	80.00
110 Bris Lord Philadelphia	35.00	60.00
111 Harry Lord Chicago	35.00	60.00
112 Louis Lowdermilk	2,500.00	4,000.00
113 Rube Marquard	90.00	150.00
114 Armando Marsans	60.00	100.00
115 George McBride	30.00	50.00
116 Alex McCarthy	125.00	200.00
117 Ed McDonald	30.00	50.00
118 John McGraw	90.00	150.00
119 Harry McIntire	30.00	50.00
120 Matty McIntyre	35.00	60.00
121 Bill McKechnie	300.00	500.00
122 Larry McLean	30.00	50.00
123 Clyde Milan	30.00	50.00
124 Doc Miller Boston	175.00	300.00
125 Dots Miller Pittsburgh	30.00	50.00
126 Otto Miller Brookyln	60.00	100.00
127 Ward Miller Chicago	1,200.00	2,000.00
128 Mike Mitchell Cincinnati	35.00	60.00
129 Willie Mitchell Cleveland	30.00	50.00
130 George Mogridge	60.00	100.00
131 Earl Moore	60.00	100.00
132 Pat Moran	30.00	50.00
133 Cy Morgan Philadelphia	50.00	80.00
134 Ray Morgan Washington	50.00	80.00
135 George Moriarity	70.00	120.00
136 George Mullin D Cap	60.00	100.00
137 George Mullin d Cap	70.00	120.00
138 Tom Needham	30.00	50.00
139 Red Nelson	90.00	150.00
140 Hub Northen	30.00	50.00
141 Les Nunamaker	30.00	50.00
142 Rebel Oakes	30.00	50.00
143 Buck O'Brien	30.00	50.00
144 Rube Oldring	30.00	50.00
145 Ivy Olson	30.00	50.00
146 Marty O'Toole	30.00	50.00
147 Dode Paskert	30.00	50.00
148 Barney Pelty	90.00	150.00
149 Hub Perdue	30.00	50.00
150 Rube Peters	35.00	60.00
151 Art Phelan	90.00	150.00
152 Jack Quinn	30.00	50.00
153 Pat Ragan	175.00	300.00
154 Rasmussen	175.00	300.00
155 Morrie Rath	125.00	200.00
156 Ed Reulbach	30.00	50.00
157 Nap Rucker	60.00	100.00
158 Bud Ryan	150.00	250.00
159 Vic Saier	600.00	1,000.00
160 Doc Scanlon (Scanlan)	30.00	50.00
161 Germany Schaefer	30.00	50.00
162 Bill Schardt	50.00	80.00
163 Frank Schulte	50.00	80.00
164 Jim Scott	60.00	100.00
165 Hank Severeid	30.00	50.00
166 Mike Simon	30.00	50.00
167 Frank Smith Cincinnati	35.00	60.00
168 Wally Smith St. Louis	35.00	60.00
169 Fred Snodgrass	30.00	50.00
170 Tris Speaker	500.00	800.00
171 Harry Spratt	30.00	50.00
172 Eddie Stack	35.00	60.00
173 Oscar Stanage	30.00	50.00
174 Bill Steele	90.00	150.00
175 Harry Steinfeldt	35.00	60.00
176 George Stovall	30.00	50.00
177 Gabby Street	30.00	50.00
178 Amos Strunk	35.00	60.00
179 Billy Sullivan	35.00	60.00
180 Bill Sweeney	90.00	150.00
181 Lee Tannehill	30.00	50.00
182 Claude Thomas	90.00	150.00
183 Joe Tinker	125.00	200.00
184 Bert Tooley	30.00	50.00
185 Terry Turner	30.00	50.00
186 Lefty Tyler	350.00	600.00
187 Hippo Vaughn	60.00	100.00
188 Heine Wagner Correct Back	60.00	100.00
189 Dixie Walker	30.00	50.00
190 Bobby Wallace	125.00	200.00
191 Jack Warhop	30.00	50.00
192 Buck Weaver	900.00	1,500.00
193 Zack Wheat	125.00	200.00
194 Doc White	35.00	60.00
195 Dewey Wilie	30.00	50.00
196 Bob Williams	50.00	80.00
197 Art Wilson New York	35.00	60.00
198 Chief Wilson Pittsburgh	30.00	50.00
199 Hooks Wiltse	30.00	50.00
200 Ivey Wingo	50.00	80.00
201 Harry Wolverton	30.00	50.00
202 Joe Wood	500.00	800.00
203 Gene Woodburn	125.00	200.00
204 Ralph Works	300.00	500.00
205 Steve Yerkes	50.00	80.00
206 Rollie Zeider	50.00	80.00

1912 T227 Series of Champions

The cards in this four-card set measure approximately 2 5/16" by 3 3/8". Actually these four baseball players are but a small part of a larger set featuring a total of 21 other "Champions." The set was produced in 1912. These cards are unnumbered; the players have been alphabetized and numbered for reference in the checklist below. Card backs can be found with either Miners Extra or Honest Long Cut. The complete set price refers only to the four subjects listed immediately below and does not include any non-baseball subjects that may be in the set.

COMPLETE SET (4)	10,000.00	20,000.00
1 Frank Baker	1,500.00	3,000.00
2 Chief Bender	1,250.00	2,500.00
3 Ty Cobb	7,500.00	15,000.00
4 Rube Marquard	1,250.00	2,500.00

1916 Tango Brand Eggs

This 20-card set of 1916 Tango Brand Eggs Baseball cards was issued by the L. Frank Company in New Orleans as a promotion to increase egg sales. Less than 500 examples are known to exist, with some of the cards having quantities of less than 10 copies found. The cards have a glazed finish, a process used in several other sets of this vintage (E106, D303, T213 and T216). The fronts display a player color photo in a mix of poses (portrait, throwing, fielding, and batting). The player's name, position, and team are printed below the photo. Some of the cards are off center and poorly cut. The backs carry promotional information for the Tango Brand Eggs. The cards do not carry the Federal League designation since the league dissolved in 1915 and players moved back to the National and American League teams. One irregularity is the fact that Demmitt, Dooin, Jacklitsch, and Tinker of the E106 set appear as cards of Meyer, Morgan, Meyer, and Weaver in the Tango Brand Egg set. The set can be dated 1916, as "Germany" Schaefer appears in the set as a Brooklyn player, and prior to that year he played for Neward of the Federal League. During the 1916 season he was sold to the New York Americans, making that the only year he played for Brooklyn. The cards are unnumbered and checklisted below alphabetically.

COMPLETE SET (20)	12,500.00	25,000.00
1 Bob Bescher	250.00	500.00
2 Roger Bresnahan	400.00	800.00
3 Al Bridwell	250.00	500.00
4 Hal Chase	400.00	800.00
5 Ty Cobb	5,000.00	10,000.00
6 Eddie Collins	1,250.00	2,500.00
7 Sam Crawford	1,250.00	2,500.00
8 Red Dooin	25.00	500.00
9 Johnny Evers	500.00	1,000.00
10 Hap Felsch	500.00	1,000.00
Photo of Ray Demmitt		
11 Hugh Jennings	400.00	800.00
12 George McQuillen	250.00	500.00
13 Billy Meyer	300.00	600.00
Photo of Fred Jacklitsch		
14 Ray Morgan	300.00	600.00
Photo of Red Dooin		
15 Eddie Murphy	250.00	500.00
16 Germany Schaefer	300.00	600.00
17 Joe Tinker	500.00	1,000.00
18 Honus Wagner	750.00	1,500.00
19 Buck Weaver	1,500.00	3,000.00
Photo of Joe Tinker		
20 Heinie Zimmerman	250.00	500.00

1934 Tarzan Thoro Bread D382

These cards measuring approximately 2 1/2"" by 3 1/8"and featuring attractive black and white photos were issued with Tarzan Thoro Bread. The players name is in the upper right hand corner. Since the cards are unnumbered, we have sequenced them in alphabetical order. New additions have been found in recent years to our checklist; therefore, more additions if found are appeciated.

COMPLETE SET	3,750.00	7,500.00
1 Sparky Adams	750.00	1,500.00
2 Walter Betts	750.00	1,500.00
3 George Blaeholder	750.00	1,500.00
4 Edward Brandt	750.00	1,500.00
5 Tommy Bridges	1,000.00	2,000.00
6 Irving 'Jack' Burns	750.00	1,500.00
7 Bruce Campbell	750.00	1,500.00
8 Tex Carleton	750.00	1,500.00
9 Dick Coffman	750.00	1,500.00
10 George Connally	750.00	1,500.00
11 Tony Cuccinello	750.00	1,500.00
12 Debs Garms	750.00	1,500.00
13 Alex Gaston	750.00	1,500.00
14 Bill Hallahan	750.00	1,500.00
15 Myril Hoag	750.00	1,500.00
16 Chief Hogsett	750.00	1,500.00
17 Arndt Jorgens	750.00	1,500.00
18 Willie Kamm	1,000.00	2,000.00
19 Dutch Leonard	750.00	1,500.00
20 Clyde Manion	750.00	1,500.00
21 Eric McNair	750.00	1,500.00
22 Oscar Mellilo	750.00	1,500.00
23 Randy Moore	750.00	1,500.00
24 Bob O'Farrell	750.00	1,500.00
25 Gus Suhr	750.00	1,500.00
26 Evar Swanson	750.00	1,500.00
27 Billy Urbanski	750.00	1,500.00
28 Johnny Vergez	750.00	1,500.00
29 Red Worthington	750.00	1,500.00
30 Tom Zachary	750.00	1,500.00

1969 Tasco Associates

These oversized crude caricatures were issued by Tasco Associates and featured some of the leading players in baseball. It is presumed that the set was skewed towards the more popular teams since certain teams have many more players known to exist than other less popular teams. This checklist may be incomplete so any additions are appreciated. We have sequenced this set in alphabetical order.

COMPLETE SET	150.00	300.00
1 Hank Aaron	6.00	15.00
2 Richie Allen	4.00	10.00
3 Mike Andrews	2.00	5.00
4 Luis Aparicio	5.00	12.00
5 Ernie Banks	5.00	12.00
6 Glenn Beckert	2.00	5.00
7 Johnny Bench	8.00	20.00
8 Norm Cash	4.00	10.00
9 Danny Cater	2.00	5.00
10 Tony Conigliaro	4.00	10.00
11 Ray Culp	2.00	5.00
12 Don Drysdale	5.00	12.00
13 Bill Freehan	2.50	6.00
14 Jim Fregosi	2.00	5.00
15 Bob Gibson	5.00	12.00
16 Bill Hands	2.00	5.00
17 Ken Holtzman	2.00	5.00
18 Frank Howard	2.50	6.00
19 Randy Hundley	2.00	5.00
20 Ferguson Jenkins	5.00	12.00
21 Jerry Koosman	3.00	8.00
22 Juan Marichal	5.00	12.00
23 Willie Mays	8.00	20.00
24 Bill Mazeroski	5.00	12.00
25 Dick McAuliffe	2.00	5.00
26 Dave McNally	2.00	5.00
27 Jim Northrup	2.00	5.00
28 Tony Oliva	4.00	10.00
29 Rico Petrocelli	2.00	5.00
30 Adolpho Phillips	2.00	5.00
31 Brooks Robinson	5.00	12.00
32 Pete Rose	8.00	20.00
33 Ron Santo	4.00	10.00
34 George Scott	2.00	5.00
35 Reggie Smith	2.50	6.00
36 Mel Stottlemyre	2.00	5.00
37 Luis Tiant	2.50	6.00
38 Billy Williams	5.00	12.00
39 Carl Yastrzemski	6.00	15.00

1978 Tastee-Freez Discs

This set of 26 discs were given out at participating Big T and Tastee-Freez restaurants. The discs measure 3 3/8" in diameter and were produced by MSA. The front design features a black and white headshot inside a white baseball diamond pattern. Four red stars adorn the top of the discs, and the white diamond is bordered by various colors on different discs. The backs are printed in red and blue on white and provide the disc number, player's name, his batting average or won/loss record, and sponsors' advertisements.

COMPLETE SET (26)	15.00	40.00
1 Buddy Bell	.40	1.00
2 Jim Palmer	1.50	4.00
3 Steve Garvey	.60	1.50
4 Jeff Burroughs	.20	.50
5 Greg Luzinski	.40	1.00
6 Lou Brock	1.25	3.00
7 Thurman Munson	.75	2.00
8 Rod Carew	1.25	3.00
9 George Brett	4.00	10.00
10 Tom Seaver	1.50	4.00
11 Willie Stargell	1.25	3.00
12 Jerry Koosman	.20	.50
13 Bill North	.20	.50
14 Richie Zisk	.20	.50
15 Bill Madlock	.40	1.00
16 Carl Yastrzemski	1.25	3.00
17 Dave Cash	.20	.50
18 Bob Watson	.40	1.00
19 Dave Kingman	.75	2.00
20 Gene Tenace	.20	.50
21 Ralph Garr	.20	.50
22 Mark Fidrych	1.25	3.00
23 Frank Tanana	.40	1.00
24 Larry Hisle	.20	.50
25 Bruce Bochte	.20	.50
26 Bob Bailor	.20	.50

1933 Tattoo Orbit

The cards in this 60-card set measure 2" by 2 1/4". The 1933 Tatoo Orbit set contains unnumbered, color cards. Blaeholder and Hadley, and to a lesser degree Andrews and Hornsby are considered more difficult to obtain than the other cards in this set. The cards are ordered and numbered below alphabetically by the player's name.

COMPLETE SET (60)	7,500.00	15,000.00
1 Dale Alexander	100.00	200.00
2 Ivy Andrews	300.00	600.00
3 Earl Averill	200.00	400.00
4 Dick Bartell	100.00	200.00
5 Wally Berger	100.00	200.00
6 George Blaeholder	500.00	1,000.00
7 Irving Burns	100.00	200.00
8 Guy Bush	100.00	200.00
9 Bruce Campbell	100.00	200.00
10 Chalmers Cissell	100.00	200.00
11 Watson Clark	100.00	200.00
12 Mickey Cochrane	300.00	600.00
13 Phil Collins	100.00	200.00
14 Kiki Cuyler	200.00	400.00
15 Dizzy Dean	500.00	1,000.00
16 Jimmy Dykes	125.00	250.00
17 George Earnshaw	100.00	200.00
18 Woody English	100.00	200.00
19 Lou Fonseca	100.00	200.00
20 Jimmy Foxx	400.00	800.00
(Jimmie)		
21 Burleigh Grimes	200.00	400.00
22 Charlie Grimm	150.00	300.00
23 Lefty Grove	300.00	600.00
24 Frank Grube	100.00	200.00
25 George Haas	100.00	200.00
26 Bump Hadley	500.00	1,000.00
27 Chick Hafey	200.00	400.00
28 Jess Haines	200.00	400.00
29 Bill Hallahan	100.00	200.00
30 Mel Harder	125.00	250.00
31 Gabby Hartnett	200.00	400.00
32 Babe Herman	150.00	300.00
33 Billy Herman	200.00	400.00
34 Rogers Hornsby	600.00	1,200.00
35 Roy Johnson	100.00	200.00
36 Smead Jolley	100.00	200.00
37 Billy Jurges	100.00	200.00
38 Willie Kamm	100.00	200.00
39 Mark Koenig	100.00	200.00
40 Jim Levey	100.00	200.00
41 Ernie Lombardi	200.00	400.00
42 Red Lucas	100.00	200.00
43 Ted Lyons	200.00	400.00
44 Connie Mack MG	250.00	500.00
45 Pat Malone	100.00	200.00
46 Pepper Martin	150.00	300.00
47 Marty McManus	100.00	200.00
48 Lefty O'Doul	150.00	300.00
49 Dick Porter	100.00	200.00
50 Carl N. Reynolds	100.00	200.00
51 Charlie Root	125.00	250.00
52 Bob Seeds	100.00	200.00
53 Al Simmons	200.00	400.00
54 Riggs Stephenson	125.00	250.00
55 Lyle Tinning	100.00	200.00
56 Joe Vosmik	100.00	200.00
57 Rube Walberg	100.00	200.00
58 Paul Waner	200.00	400.00
59 Lon Warneke	100.00	200.00
60 Arthur Whitney	100.00	200.00

1933 Tattoo Orbit Self Develop R308

These very small (1 1/4" by 1 7/8") cards are very scarce. They were produced by Tattoo Orbit around 1933. The set is presumed to include the numbers between 151 and 210; a few of the numbers are still unknown at this time. Badly over exposed cards are very difficult to identify and are considered (graded) fair at best. Two types of these cards are known: A larger card (of which only very few are known) and are very rare, and a smaller type -- which is considered the normal card. We are pricing the smaller cards. The larger cards are valued at approximately 5X the listed prices. An album is known for these cards

COMPLETE SET	2,000.00	4,000.00
151 Vernon Gomez	150.00	300.00
152 Kiki Cuyler	125.00	250.00
153 Jimmy Foxx	400.00	800.00
(Jimmie)		
154 Al Simmons	150.00	300.00
155 Gordon Cochrane	150.00	300.00
156 Woody English	75.00	150.00
157 Chuck Klein	125.00	250.00
158 Dick Bartell	75.00	150.00
159 Pepper Martin	100.00	200.00
160 Earl Averill	125.00	250.00
161 William Dickey	150.00	300.00
162 Wesley Ferrell	100.00	200.00
163 Oral Hildebrand	75.00	150.00
164 Willie Kamm	75.00	150.00
165 Earl Whitehill	75.00	150.00
166 Charles Fullis	75.00	150.00
167 Jimmy Dykes	75.00	150.00
168 Ben Cantwell	75.00	150.00
169 George Earnshaw	75.00	150.00
170 Jackson Stephenson	100.00	200.00
171 Randy Moore	75.00	150.00
172 Ted Lyons	125.00	250.00
173 Goose Goslin	125.00	250.00
174 Evar Swanson	75.00	150.00
175 Leroy Mahaffey	75.00	150.00
176 Joe Cronin	150.00	300.00
177 Tom Bridges	75.00	150.00
178 Henry Manush	125.00	250.00
179 Walter Stewart	75.00	150.00
180 Frank Pytlak	75.00	150.00
181 Dale Alexander	75.00	150.00
182 Robert Grove	200.00	400.00
183 Charles Gehringer	150.00	300.00
184 Lewis Fonseca	75.00	150.00
185 Alvin Crowder	75.00	150.00
186 Mickey Cochrane	150.00	300.00
187 Max Bishop	75.00	150.00
188 Connie Mack MG	150.00	300.00
189 Guy Bush	75.00	150.00
190 Charlie Root	75.00	150.00
191 Burleigh Grimes	125.00	250.00
Gabby Hartnett		
192 Pat Malone	75.00	150.00
193 Woody English	75.00	150.00
194 Lonnie Warneke	75.00	150.00
195 Babe Herman	100.00	200.00
200 Gabby Hartnett	125.00	250.00
201 Paul Waner	150.00	300.00
202 Dizzy Dean	400.00	800.00
205 Jim Bottomley	125.00	250.00
207 Charles Hafey	125.00	250.00
XX Album	25.00	50.00

1976 Taylor/Schmierer Bowman 47

This set which measures 2 1/16" by 2 1/2" was issued by show promoters Bob Schmierer and Ted Taylor to promote what would become their long running EPSCC shows in the Philadelphia area. The set is designed in the style of the 1948 Bowman set and according to printed stories even some of the same paper stock was used for these sets as was used in 1948. The first series (1-49) cards sell for considerably more than the later two series. A reprint card of the T-206 Wagner along with a card of show promoter and long time hobbyist Ted Taylor were also produced. They are not considered part of the complete set. Each series was available from the producers at the time of issue for $4.50 each.

COMPLETE SET (113)	100.00	200.00
COMMON CARD (1-49)	.40	1.00
COMMON CARD (50-113)	.10	.25
1 Bobby Doerr	1.50	4.00
2 Stan Musial	4.00	10.00
3 Babe Ruth	8.00	20.00
4 Joe DiMaggio	6.00	15.00
5 Andy Pafko	.40	1.00
6 Johnny Pesky	.75	2.00
7 Gil Hodges	3.00	8.00
8 Tommy Holmes	.40	1.00
9 Ralph Kiner	3.00	8.00
10 Yogi Berra	4.00	10.00
11 Bob Feller	1.50	4.00
12 Sid Gordon	.40	1.00
13 Eddie Joost	.40	1.00
14 Del Ennis	.40	1.00
15 Johnny Mize	3.00	8.00
16 Pee Wee Reese	4.00	10.00
17 Jackie Robinson	6.00	15.00
18 Enos Slaughter	1.50	4.00
19 Vern Stephens	.40	1.00
20 Bobby Thomson	.75	2.00
21 Ted Williams	6.00	15.00
22 Bob Elliott	.40	1.00
23 Mickey Vernon	.40	1.00
24 Ewell Blackwell	.40	1.00
25 Lou Boudreau	1.50	4.00
26 Ralph Branca	.40	1.00
27 Harry Brechen	.40	1.00
28 Dom DiMaggio	1.25	3.00
29 Bruce Edwards	.40	1.00
30 Sam Chapman	.40	1.00
31 George Kell	1.50	4.00
32 Jack Kramer	.40	1.00
33 Hal Newhouser	1.50	4.00
34 Charlie Keller	.40	1.00
35 Ken Keltner	.40	1.00
36 Hank Greenberg	3.00	8.00
37 Howie Pollet	.40	1.00
38 Luke Appling	1.50	4.00
39 Pete Suder	.40	1.00
40 Johnny Sain	1.25	3.00
41 Phil Cavaretta	.75	2.00
42 Johnny Vander Meer	.75	2.00
43 Mel Ott	3.00	8.00
44 Walker Cooper	.40	1.00
45 Birdie Tebbetts	.40	1.00
46 Snuffy Stirnweiss	.40	1.00
47 Connie Mack MG	1.50	4.00
48 Jimmie Foxx	3.00	8.00
49 Joe DiMaggio	6.00	15.00
Babe Ruth		
Checklist Back		
50 Schoolboy Rowe	.10	.25
51 Andy Seminick	.10	.25
52 Dixie Walker	.10	.25

53 Virgil Trucks .10 .25
54 Dizzy Trout .10 .25
55 Hoot Evers .10 .25
56 Thurman Tucker .10 .25
57 Fritz Ostermuller .10 .25
58 Augie Galan .10 .25
59 Babe Young .10 .25
60 Skeeter Newsome .10 .25
61 Jack Lohrke .10 .25
62 Rudy York .20 .50
63 Tex Hughson .10 .25
64 Sam Mele .10 .25
65 Fred Hutchinson .20 .50
66 Don Black .10 .25
67 Les Fleming .10 .25
68 George McQuinn .10 .25
69 Mike McCormick .10 .25
70 Mickey Witek .10 .25
71 Blix Donnelly .10 .25
72 Elbie Fletcher .10 .25
73 Hal Gregg .10 .25
74 Dick Whitman .10 .25
75 Johnny Neun MG .10 .25
76 Doyle Lade .10 .25
77 Ron Northey .10 .25
78 Mort Cooper .10 .25
79 Warren Spahn 1.25 3.00
80 Happy Chandler COMM .40 1.00
81 Connie Mack .40 1.00
Roy Mack
Connie Mack III
Checklist
82 Earle Mack Asst MG .10 .25
83 Buddy Rosar .10 .25
84 Walt Judnich .10 .25
85 Bob Kennedy .10 .25
86 Tom Tresh .10 .25
87 Sid Hudson .10 .25
88 Gene Thompson .10 .25
89 Bill Nicholson .10 .25
90 Stan Hack .10 .25
91 Terry Moore .20 .50
92 Ted Lyons MG .40 1.00
93 Barney McCoskey .10 .25
94 Stan Spence .10 .25
95 Larry Jensen .10 .25
96 Whitey Kurowski .10 .25
97 Honus Wagner CO 1.50 4.00
98 Billy Herman MG .40 1.00
99 Jim Tabor .10 .25
100 Phil Marchildon .10 .25
101 Dave Ferriss .10 .25
102 Al Zarilla .10 .25
103 Bob Dillinger .20 .50
104 Bob Lemon .75 2.00
105 Jim Hegan .10 .25
106 Johnny Lindell .10 .25
107 Williard Marshall .10 .25
108 Walt Masterson .10 .25
109 Carl Scheib .10 .25
110 Bobby Brown .30 .75
111 Cy Block .10 .25
112 Sid Gordon .20 .50
113 Ty Cobb 3.00 8.00
Babe Ruth
Tris Speaker
Checklist Back
NNO Honus Wagner 2.00 5.00
NNO Ted Taylor .10 .25

1972 TCMA the 1930's Panels

This set consists of two 9" by 12" panels of 12 uncut cards each which feature black-and-white photos of players who played during the 1930's. The photos measure approximately 2 1/16" by 2 7/8" each. One panel contains cards #169-180, while the other panel consists of cards #193-204.

COMPLETE SET 12.50 30.00
169 Alvin Crowder .40 1.00
170 August Suhr .40 1.00
171 Monty Stratton .75 2.00
172 Louis Berger .40 1.00
173 John Whitehead .40 1.00
174 Joe Heving .40 1.00
175 Mervyn Shea .40 1.00
176 Ed Durham .40 1.00
177 Buddy Myer .75 2.00
178 Carl Whitehill .40 1.00
179 Joe Cronin 1.50 4.00
180 Zeke Bonura .75 2.00
193 George Myatt .40 1.00
194 Bill Werber .75 2.00
195 Red Lucas .40 1.00
196 Hal Luby .40 1.00
197 Vic Sorell .40 1.00
198 Mickey Cochrane 1.50 4.00
199 Rudy York 1.00 2.00
200 Ray Mack .40 1.00
201 Vince DiMaggio .75 2.00
202 Mel Ott 1.50 4.00
203 John Lucadello .40 1.00
204 Debs Garms .40 1.00

1972 TCMA's the 30's

This 120-card set features borderless black-and-white photos of players who played during the 1930's and measures approximately 2" by 2 7/8". The backs carry the player's name, team and years during the 1930's in which he played. Cards numbered 1-72 are unnumbered and checklisted below alphabetically. Cards numbered 73-120 are listed according to the number on their backs.

COMPLETE SET (120) 50.00 100.00
1 Beau Bell .20 .50
2 Max Bishop .20 .50
3 Robert Boken .20 .50
4 Cliff Bolton .20 .50
5 John Broaca .20 .50
6 Bill Brubaker .20 .50
7 Slick Castleman .20 .50
8 Dick Coffman .20 .50
9 Philip Collins .20 .50
10 Earle Combs .75 2.00
11 Doc Cramer .40 1.00
12 Joseph Cronin .75 2.00
13 Jack Crouch .20 .50
14 Anthony Cuccinello .20 .50
15 Babe Dahlgren .40 1.00
16 Spud Davis .20 .50
17 Daffy Dean .40 1.00
18 Dizzy Dean 1.25 3.00
19 Bill Dickey .75 2.00
20 Joe DiMaggio 3.00 8.00
21 George Earnshaw .20 .50
22 Woody English/(Portrait) .20 .50
23 Woody English/(Batting) .20 .50
24 Harold Finney .20 .50
25 Freddie Fitzsimmons .40 1.00
Hadley Fitzsimmons
26 Tony Freitas .20 .50
27 Frank Frisch .75 2.00
28 Milt Gaston .20 .50
29 Sidney Gautreaux .20 .50
30 Charles Gehringer .75 2.00
31 Charles Gelbert .20 .50
32 Lefty Gomez .75 2.00
33 Lefty Grove .75 2.00
34 Charles Hafey .60 1.50
35 Jesse Haines .60 1.50
36 William Hallahan .40 1.00
37 Bucky Harris .75 2.00
38 Edward Heusser .20 .50
39 Carl Hubbell/(Portrait) .75 2.00
40 Carl Hubbell/(Throwing) .75 2.00
41 James Jordan .20 .50
42 Joseph Judge .40 1.00
43 Leonard Koenecke .20 .50
44 Mark Koenig .40 1.00
45 Cookie Lavagetto .40 1.00
46 Alfred Lawson .20 .50
47 Tony Lazzeri .75 2.00
48 Gus Mancuso .20 .50
49 John McCarthy .20 .50
50 Joe Medwick .75 2.00
51 Clifford Melton .20 .50
52 Terry Moore .60 1.50
53 John Murphy .40 1.00
54 Ken O'Dea .20 .50
55 Robert O'Farrell .20 .50
56 Manuel Onis .20 .50
57 Marcellus Pearson .20 .50
58 Paul Richards .40 1.00
59 Max Rosenfeld .20 .50
60 Red Ruffing/(Side view throwing) .75 2.00
61 Red Ruffing/(Front view throwing) .75 2.00
62 Harold Schumacher .40 1.00
63 George Selkirk .20 .50
64 Joseph Shaute .20 .50
65 Gordon Slade .20 .50
66 Lindo Storti .20 .50
67 Stephen Sundra .20 .50
68 Bill Terry .75 2.00
69 John Tising .20 .50
70 Joseph Vance .20 .50
71 Rube Walberg .40 1.00
72 Samuel West .40 1.00
73 Vic Tamulis .20 .50
74 Kemp Wicker .20 .50
75 Robert Seeds .20 .50
76 Jack Saltzgaver .20 .50
77 Walter Brown .20 .50
78 Spud Chandler .40 1.00
79 Myril Hoag .20 .50
80 Joseph Glenn .20 .50
81 Lefty Gomez .75 2.00
82 Art Jorgens .20 .50
83 Jesse Hill .20 .50
84 Red Rolfe .60 1.50
85 Wesley Ferrell .60 1.50
86 Joseph Morrissey .20 .50
87 Anthony Piet .20 .50
88 Fred Walker .60 1.50
89 William Dietrich .20 .50
90 Lynford Lary/(Portrait) .20 .50
91 Lynford Lary/(Batting) .20 .50
92 Lynford Lary/(Batting in striped uniform) .20 .50
93 Lynford Lary/(Batting facing forward) .20 .50
94 Ralph Boyle .20 .50
95 Tony Malinosky .20 .50
96 Al Lopez .75 2.00
97 Lonny Frey .20 .50
98 Anthony Malinosky .20 .50
99 Owen Carroll .20 .50
100 John Hassett .20 .50
101 Gib Brack .20 .50
102 Samuel Leslie .20 .50
103 Fred Heimach .20 .50
104 Burleigh Grimes .75 2.00
105 Ray Benge .20 .50
106 Joseph Stripp .20 .50
107 Joseph Becker .20 .50
108 Oscar Melillo .20 .50
109 Charles O'Leary CO .75 2.00
Roger Hornsby MG
110 Luke Appling .75 2.00
111 Stanley Hack .40 1.00
112 Raymond Hayworth .20 .50
113 Charles Wilson .20 .50
114 Hal Trosky .60 1.50
115 Wes Ferrell .60 1.50
116 Lyn Lary/(Throwing) .20 .50
117 Nathaniel Gaston .20 .50
118 Eldon Auker .40 1.00
119 Heinie Manush .75 2.00
120 James Foxx 2.00 5.00

1973-79 TCMA All-Time Greats

This set eatures black-and-white photos of some of the greatest baseball players of all time. These cards measure approximately 3 1/2" by 5 1/2". The cards are unnumbered and checklisted below in alphabetical order in order of the series they were released in. The Cy Young card in 1st series of 1973 did not have the 1973 information on the back.

COMPLETE SET 125.00 250.00
1 Luke Appling .40 1.00
2 Mickey Cochrane .75 2.00
3 Eddie Collins 1.00 2.50
4 Kiki Cuyler .40 1.00
5 Bill Dickey .60 1.50
6 Joe DiMaggio 4.00 10.00
7 Bob Feller 1.50 4.00
8 Frankie Frisch .60 1.50
9 Lou Gehrig 2.50 6.00
10 Goose Goslin .40 1.00
11 Chick Hafey .40 1.00
12 Gabby Hartnett .60 1.50
13 Rogers Hornsby 1.00 2.50
14 Ted Lyons .40 1.00
15 Connie Mack .60 1.50
16 Heinie Manush .40 1.00
17 Rabbit Maranville .40 1.00
18 Joe Medwick .40 1.00
19 Al Simmons .60 1.50
20 Bill Terry .60 1.50
21 Pie Traynor .60 1.50
22 Dazzy Vance .40 1.00
23 Cy Young 1.50 4.00
24 Gabby Hartnett 2.00 5.00
Babe Ruth
25 Roger Bresnahan .40 1.00
26 Dizzy Dean .75 2.00
27 Buck Ewing .40 1.00
Mascot
28 Jimmy Foxx 1.00 2.50
(Jimmie)
29 Hank Greenberg 1.00 2.50
30 Burleigh Grimes .40 1.00
31 Harry Heilman .40 1.00
32 Waite Hoyt .40 1.00
33 Walter Johnson 1.00 2.50
34 George Kelly .40 1.00
35 Stan Musial 2.00 5.00
36 Christy Mathewson 1.00 2.50
37 John McGraw .60 1.50
38 Mel Ott 1.00 2.50
39 Satchel Paige 1.00 2.50
40 Sam Rice .40 1.00
41 Edd Roush .40 1.00
42 Red Ruffing .40 1.00
43 Casey Stengel .75 2.00
44 Harry Wright .40 1.00
45 Paul Waner .60 1.50
46 Honus Wagner 1.00 2.50
47 Lloyd Waner .40 1.00
48 Ross Youngs .40 1.00
49 Frank Baker .60 1.50
50 Chief Bender .60 1.50
51 Jim Bottomley .40 1.00
52 Lou Boudreau .60 1.50
53 Mordecai Brown .75 2.00
54 Roy Campanella 1.00 2.50
55 Max Carey .40 1.00
56 Ty Cobb 2.00 5.00
57 Earle Combs .60 1.50
58 Jocko Conlan .40 1.00
59 Hugh Duffy .40 1.00
60 Red Faber .40 1.00
61 Lefty Grove 1.00 2.50
62 Kennesaw M. Landis .40 1.00
63 Eddie Plank .60 1.50
64 Hoss Radbourne .40 1.00
Sic, spelled without an E
65 Eppa Rixey .40 1.00
66 Jackie Robinson 2.50 6.00
67 Babe Ruth 4.00 10.00
68 George Sisler .60 1.50
69 Zack Wheat .60 1.50
70 Ted Williams 3.00 8.00
71 Mel Ott 2.50 6.00
Babe Ruth
72 Tris Speaker 1.00 2.50
Wilbert Robinson
73 Grover C. Alexander 1.25 3.00
74 Cap Anson 1.25 3.00
75 Earl Averill .60 1.50
76 Ed Barrow .40 1.00
77 Yogi Berra 1.00 2.50
78 Roberto Clemente 2.00 5.00
79 Jimmy Collins .60 1.50
80 Whitey Ford 1.00 2.50
81 Ford Frick .40 1.00
82 Lefty Gomez .75 2.00
83 Bucky Harris .60 1.50
84 Billy Herman .60 1.50
85 Carl Hubbell 1.00 2.50
86 Miller Huggins .60 1.50
87 Monte Irvin .60 1.50
88 Bill Klem .40 1.00
89 Sandy Koufax 1.50 4.00
90 Napoleon Lajoie 1.00 2.50
91 Bob Lemon .60 1.50
92 Ralph Kiner .75 2.00
93 Mickey Mantle 2.50 6.00
94 Rube Marquard .60 1.50
95 Joe McCarthy .40 1.00
96 Bill McKechnie .40 1.00
97 Herb Pennock .60 1.50
98 Warren Spahn 1.00 2.50
99 Joe Tinker 1.00 2.50
100 Early Wynn .75 2.00
101 Joe Cronin 1.00 2.50
Honus Wagner
Bill Terry
102 Jimmie Foxx 1.25 3.00
Lou Gehrig
103 Hank Greenberg 1.00 2.50
Ralph Kiner
104 Walter Johnson 1.00 2.50
Connie Mack
105 Connie Mack 1.00 2.50
Bob Feller
106 Mel Ott 1.25 3.00
Lou Gehrig
107 Al Simmons 1.25 3.00
Tris Speaker
Ty Cobb
108 Ted Williams 1.25 3.00
Lou Boudreau
109 Dave Bancroft .40 1.00
110 Ernie Banks 1.25 3.00
111 Frank Chance 1.00 2.50
112 Stan Covaleskie .40 1.00
113 Billy Evans .40 1.00
114 Clark Griffith .60 1.50
115 Jesse Haines .40 1.00
116 Will Harridge .40 1.00
117 Harry Hooper .40 1.00
118 Cal Hubbard .40 1.00
119 Hugh Jennings .60 1.50
120 Willie Keeler 1.00 2.50
121 Fred Lindstrom .40 1.00
122 John Henry Lloyd .75 2.00
123 Al Lopez .40 1.00
124 Robin Roberts 1.00 2.50
125 Amos Rusie .40 1.00
126 Ray Schalk .40 1.00
127 Joe Sewell .40 1.00
128 Rube Waddell .60 1.50
129 George Weiss .40 1.00
130 Dizzy Dean .60 1.50
Gabby Hartnett
131 Joe DiMaggio 4.00 10.00
Mickey Mantle
132 Ted Williams 4.00 10.00
Joe DiMaggio
133 Jack Chesbro .40 1.00
134 Tom Connolly .40 1.00
135 Sam Crawford .60 1.50
136 Elmer Flick .40 1.00
137 Charlie Gehringer .60 1.50
138 Warren Giles .40 1.00
139 Ban Johnson .40 1.00
140 Addie Joss .40 1.00
141 Al Kaline 1.25 3.00
142 Willie Mays 2.00 5.00
143 Joe McGinnity .40 1.00
144 Larry MacPhail .40 1.00
145 Branch Rickey .40 1.00
146 Wilbert Robinson .40 1.00
147 Duke Snider 1.50 4.00
148 Tris Speaker 1.00 2.50
149 Bobby Wallace .40 1.00
150 Hack Wilson .40 1.00
151 Yogi Berra 2.00 5.00
Casey Stengel
152 Warren Giles 2.00 5.00
Roberto Clemente
153 Mickey Mantle 4.00 10.00
Willie Mays
154 John McGraw 2.50 6.00
Babe Ruth
155 Satchel Paige 2.50 6.00
Bob Feller
156 Paul Waner 2.00 5.00
Lloyd Waner

1973 TCMA Autograph Series

These blank-backs cards measure 3.5 x 5.5 and feature black and white photos. Below the player's photo is a white strip where collectors could have the player sign the card. These were quite popular with collectors, and finding a complete, unsigned set, is quite rare. Prices listed are for unsigned cards.

COMPLETE CARD (36) 50.00 100.00
1 Stachel Paige 2.00 5.00
2 Phil Rizzuto 1.25 3.00
3 Sid Gordon .75 2.00
4 Ernie Lombardi .75 2.00
5 Jesse Haines .75 2.00
6 Joe Gordon .75 2.00
7 Billy Terry .75 2.00
8 Bill Dickey 1.25 3.00
9 Joe DiMaggio 6.00 15.00
10 Carl Hubbell 2.00 5.00
11 Freddie Lindstrom .75 2.00
12 Ted Lyons .75 2.00
13 Red Ruffing .75 2.00
14 Joe Gordon .75 2.00
15 Bob Feller 3.00 8.00
16 Yogi Berra 2.00 5.00
17 Whitey Ford/Ford Frick 2.00 5.00
18 Sandy Koufax 3.00 8.00
19 Ted Williams 5.00 12.00
20 Warren Spahn 2.00 5.00
21 Al Rosen .75 2.00
22 Luke Appling .75 2.00
23 Joe Bush .75 2.00
24 Joe Medwick .75 2.00
25 Lou Boudreau 1.25 3.00
26 Ralph Kiner 2.00 5.00
27 Lloyd Waner .75 2.00
28 Pee Wee Reese 1.25 3.00

29 Duke Snider	3.00	8.00
30 Sal Maglie	.75	2.00
31 Monte Irvin	1.25	3.00
32 Lefty Gomez	2.00	5.00
33 George Kelly	.75	2.00
34 Joe Adcock	.75	2.00
35 Max Carey	.75	2.00
36 Rube Marquard	1.25	3.00

1973 TCMA Drawings

These postcards measure 3.5 by 5.5 and feature black and white player illustrations and a facsimile signature.

1 Mickey Cochrane	.75	2.00
2 Christy Mathewson	1.00	2.50
3 Roberto Clemente	20.00	50.00
4 Rogers Hornsby	1.00	2.50
5 Pie Traynor	.60	1.50
6 Frank Frisch	.60	1.50
7 Ty Cobb	2.00	5.00
8 Connie Mack	.60	1.50
9 Babe Ruth	4.00	10.00
10 Lou Gehrig	2.50	6.00
11 Gil Hodges	1.00	2.50
12 Jackie Robinson	2.50	6.00

1974 TCMA Nicknames

This 27-card set features black-and-white player photos with red printing and measures approximately 2 1/4" by 3 1/2". The backs carry player information.

COMPLETE SET (27)	12.50	30.00
1 Bob Feller	1.00	2.50
2 Babe Dahlgren	.40	1.00
3 Spud Chandler	.60	1.50
4 Ducky Medwick	1.00	2.50
5 Cal Benge	.40	1.00
6 Goose Goslin	1.00	2.50
7 Mule Haas	.40	1.00
8 Dizzy Dean	1.00	2.50
9 Ray Harrell	.40	1.00
10 Ralph Boyle	.40	1.00
11 Curtis Davis	.40	1.00
12 Moose Solters	.40	1.00
13 Sam Jones	.40	1.00
14 Bad News Hale	.40	1.00
15 Bucky Harris	1.00	2.50
16 Jim Jordan	.40	1.00
17 Zeke Bonura	.60	1.50
18 Tom Hafey	.40	1.00
19 Virgil Davis	.40	1.00
20 Bing Miller	.40	1.00
21 Preacher Roe	.60	1.50
22 Bill Hallahan	.40	1.00
23 Bob Johnson	.40	1.00
24 Joe Gordon	.60	1.50
25 Tot Presnell	.40	1.00
26 Luke Hamlin	.40	1.00
27 Tommy Henrich	.75	2.00

1975 TCMA All-Time Greats

This 36-card set measures approximately 2 3/8" by 3 3/4". The first printing of the set features blue and white player photos, while the second printing features black and white. The cards were issued in six-card strips, with six different strips in all. Reportedly, each strip had spot in the upper-right hand corner for retail pricing.The pictures are framed in blue with a bat and ball in each top corner. The card name and player's name are in the top and bottom margins respectively. The backs carry the player's name, position, team name and career stats. The cards are unnumbered and checklisted below in alphabetical order.

COMPLETE SET (36)	20.00	50.00
1 Earl Averill	.40	1.00
2 Jim Bottomley	.40	1.00
3 Lou Boudreau	.40	1.00
4 Fred Clarke	.40	1.00
5 Roberto Clemente	2.00	5.00
6 Ty Cobb	2.00	5.00
7 Jocko Conlon	.40	1.00
8 Hugh Duffy	.40	1.00
9 Red Faber	.40	1.00
10 Whitey Ford	1.00	2.50
11 Jimmy Foxx	1.00	2.50
(Jimmie)		
12 Burleigh Grimes	.40	1.00
13 Lefty Grove	.75	2.00
14 Bucky Harris	.40	1.00
15 Billy Herman	.40	1.00
16 Miller Huggins	.40	1.00
17 Monte Irvin	.40	1.00
18 Ralph Kiner	.75	2.00
19 Sandy Koufax	1.00	2.50
20 Judge Landis	.40	1.00
21 Mickey Mantle	2.00	5.00
22 Joe McCarthy	.40	1.00
23 John McGraw	.40	1.00
24 Bill McKechnie	.40	1.00
25 Ducky Medwick	.40	1.00
26 Hoss Radborn	.40	1.00
27 Sam Rice	.40	1.00
28 Jackie Robinson	2.00	5.00
29 Wilbert Robinson	.40	1.00
30 Babe Ruth	3.00	8.00
31 Babe Ruth/(Closer head photo)	3.00	8.00
32 George Sisler	.40	1.00
33 Tris Speaker	.40	1.00
34 Zack Wheat	.40	1.00
35 Ted Williams	2.00	5.00
36 Ross Youngs	.40	1.00

1975 TCMA Guam

This 18-card set measures approximately 3 1/2" by 5 1/2" and features black and white photos of baseball players who served in the Navy in Guam during World War II. The backs display an on-going story about the team by Harrington Crissey.

COMPLETE SET (18)	8.00	20.00
1 Phil Rizzuto	1.00	2.50
Terry Moore		
2 Gab Gab Guam 1945	.40	1.00
3 Team Photo	.40	1.00
4 Merrill May	.75	2.00
Pee Wee Reese		
Johnny Vander Meer		
5 Team Photo	.40	1.00
6 Team Photo	.40	1.00
7 Del Ennis	.60	1.50
8 Mace Brown	.60	1.50
9 Pee Wee Reese	1.00	2.50
Joe Gordon		
Bill Dickey		
10 Glenn McQuillen	.40	1.00
11 Mike Budnick	.40	1.00
12 Team Photo	.40	1.00
13 Skeets Dickey	.40	1.00
14 Connie Ryan	.40	1.00
15 Hal White	.40	1.00
16 Mickey Cochrane	1.00	2.50
17 Barney McCosky	.40	1.00
18 Ben Huffman	.40	1.00

1975 TCMA House of Jazz

This 35-card set features black-and-white player photos printed on thin card stock and measuring approximately 2 3/8" by 3 1/2". The cards are unnumbered and checklisted below in alphabetical order.

COMPLETE SET (35)	30.00	60.00
1 John Antonelli	.20	.50
2 Richie Ashburn	.75	2.00
3 Ernie Banks	1.25	3.00
4 Hank Bauer	.40	1.00
5 Joe DiMaggio	2.00	5.00
6 Bobby Doerr	.20	.50
7 Herman Franks	.20	.50
8 Lou Gehrig	2.00	5.00
9 Granny Hamner	.20	.50
10 Al Kaline	.75	2.00
11 Harmon Killebrew	.75	2.00
12 Jim Konstanty	.20	.50
13 Bob Lemon	.60	1.50
14 Ed Lopat	.20	.50
15 Stan Lopata	.20	.50
16 Peanuts Lowrey	.20	.50
17 Mickey Mantle	3.00	8.00
18 Phil Marchildon	.20	.50
19 Walt Masterson	.20	.50
20 Ed Mathews	.75	2.00
21 Willie Mays	2.00	5.00
22 Don Newcombe	.40	1.00
23 Joe Nuxhall	.20	.50
24 Satchel Paige	1.50	4.00
25 Roy Partee	.20	.50
26 Jackie Robinson	2.00	5.00
27 Babe Ruth	3.00	8.00
28 Carl Scheib	.20	.50
29 Bobby Shantz	.20	.50
30 Burt Shotten	.20	.50
31 Duke Snider	.75	2.00
32 Warren Spahn	.75	2.00
33 Johnny Temple	.20	.50
34 Ted Williams	2.00	5.00
35 Early Wynn	.75	2.00

1975 TCMA Larry French Postcards

This six-card set features black-and-white pictures of Larry French printed in a postcard format. The backs when put together become a life story of French. It is written by French as told to Harrington Crissey.

COMPLETE SET (6)	8.00	20.00
COMMON CARD (1-6)	1.50	4.00
3 Bill Lee	1.50	4.00
Charlie Root		
Larry French		
Tuck Stainba		
4 Larry French	1.50	4.00
Charlie Grimm		
Fred Lindstrom		
6 Larry French	1.50	4.00
Mickey Owen		

1976 TCMA Umpires

This three-card set was produced by TCMA for the three umpires pictured on the cards and was distributed through the umpires themselves. The cards are unnumbered and checklisted below in alphabetical order.

COMPLETE SET (8)	2.00	5.00
1 Larry Barnett	.75	2.00
2 Al Clark	.75	2.00
3 Nick Colosi	.75	2.00
4 Don Denkinger	.75	2.00
5 Art Frantz	.75	2.00
6 Marty Springstead	.75	2.00
7 Ed Sudol	.75	2.00
8 Bill Williams	.75	2.00

1977-80 TCMA The War Years

This standard-size set features players who stayed at home and played major league baseball during the Second World War. The set was released in two 45-card series. Cards 1-45 were issued as Series 1 in 1977. Series 2, cards 46-90, were released in 1980. Reportedly, Series 1 cards are available in shorter supply.

COMPLETE SET (90)	20.00	50.00
1 Sam Narron	.20	.50
2 Ray Mack	.20	.50
3 Mickey Owen	.20	.50
4 John Gaston Peacock	.20	.50
5 Dizzy Trout	.20	.50
6 Birdie Tebbetts	.20	.50
7 Alfred Todd	.20	.50
8 Harland Clift	.20	.50
9 Don Gilberto Nunez	.20	.50
Gil Torres		
10 Al Lopez	.50	1.25
11 Tony Lupien	.20	.50
12 Luke Appling	.50	1.25
13 Pat Seerey	.20	.50
14 Phil Masi	.20	.50
15 Thomas Turner	.20	.50
16 Nicholas Picciuto	.20	.50
17 Mel Ott	1.00	2.50
18 Red Treadway	.20	.50
19 Samuel Naham	.20	.50
20 Rip Sewell	.20	.50
21 Roy Partee	.20	.50
22 Richard Siebert	.20	.50
23 Red Barrett	.20	.50
24 Lefty O'Dea	.20	.50
25 Louis Parisse	.20	.50
26 Martin Marion	.40	1.00
27 Eugene Moore Jr.	.20	.50
28 Walter Boom Boom Beck	.20	.50
29 Donald Manno	.20	.50
30 Hal Newhouser	.50	1.25
31 Gus Mancuso	.20	.50
32 Pinky May	.20	.50
33 Gerald Priddy	.20	.50
34 Herman Besse	.20	.50
35 Luis Olmo	.20	.50
36 Robert O'Neill	.20	.50
37 John Barrett	.20	.50
38 Gordon Maltzberger	.20	.50
39 William Nicholson	.30	.75
40 Ron Northey	.20	.50
41 Howard Pollet	.20	.50
42 Aloysius Piechota	.20	.50
43 Robert Shepard	.20	.50
44 Alfred Anderson	.20	.50
45 Damon Phillips	.20	.50
46 Herman Franks	.20	.50
47 Aldon Wilkie	.20	.50
48 Max Macon	.20	.50
49 Lester Webber	.20	.50
50 Robert Swift	.20	.50
51 Philip Weintraub	.20	.50
52 Nicholas Strincevich	.20	.50
53 Michael Tresh	.20	.50
54 William Trotter	.20	.50
55 1943 New York Yankees	.40	1.00
Starting World Series		
Line		
56 Johnny Sturm	.20	.50
57 Silas Johnson	.20	.50
58 Don Kolloway	.20	.50
59 Cecil Porter Vaughan	.20	.50
60 St. Louis Browns	.20	.50
Belters		
George McQuinn		
Chet La		
61 Harold Wagner	.20	.50
62 Alva Javery	.20	.50
63 Boston Bees Rookie	.30	.75
Pitchers		
George Barnicle		
Bob		
64 Dolf Camilli	.40	1.00
65 Mike McCormick	.20	.50
66 Dick Wakefield	.20	.50
67 Mickey Vernon	.40	1.00
68 John Vander Meer	.40	1.00
69 Mack McDonnell	.20	.50
70 Thomas Jordan	.20	.50
71 Maurice Van Robays	.20	.50
72 Charles Stanceu	.20	.50
73 Samuel Zoldak	.20	.50
74 Ray Starr	.20	.50
75 Roger Wolff	.20	.50
76 Cecil Travis	.30	.75
77 Arthur Johnson	.20	.50
78 Louis Riggs	.20	.50
79 Peter Suder	.20	.50
80 Thomas Warren	.20	.50
81 John Welaj	.20	.50
82 Gee Walker	.20	.50
83 Dee Williams	.20	.50
84 Leonard Merullo	.20	.50
85 Swede Johnson	.20	.50
86 Junior Thompson	.20	.50
87 William Zuber	.20	.50
88 Earl Johnson	.20	.50
89 Babe Young	.20	.50
90 Jim Wallace	.20	.50

1978 TCMA 60'S I

The TCMA Stars of the 60's consists of 293 standard-size cards. This set was issued through hobby dealers at the time and was TCMA's second set of retired players. The set uses many photos from Mike Aronstein's library of photos. Many of the great and not so great players of the 60's are featured. No card numbers 43 or 98 were printed.

COMPLETE SET (293)	40.00	80.00
1 Smoky Burgess	.20	.50
2 Juan Marichal	1.25	3.00
3 Don Drysdale	1.25	3.00
4 Jim Gentile	.10	.25
5 Roy Face	.20	.50
6 Joe Pepitone	.20	.50
7 Joe Christopher	.10	.25
8 Wayne Causey	.10	.25
9 Frank Bolling	.10	.25
10 Jim Maloney	.20	.50
11 Roger Maris	1.50	4.00
12 Bill White	.30	.75
13 Roberto Clemente	4.00	10.00
14 Bob Saverine	.10	.25
15 Barney Schultz	.10	.25
16 Albie Pearson	.10	.25
17 Denny LeMaster	.10	.25
18 Ernie Broglio	.10	.25
19 Bobby Klaus	.10	.25
20 Tony Cloninger	.10	.25
21 Whitey Ford	1.25	3.00
22 Ron Santo	.30	.75
23 Jim Duckworth	.10	.25
24 Willie Davis	.20	.50
25 Ed Charles	.10	.25
26 Bob Allison	.20	.50
27A Fritz Ackley	.30	.75
27B Gary Kroll	.30	.75
28 Ruben Amaro	.10	.25
29 Johnny Callison	.20	.50
30 Greg Bollo	.10	.25
31 Felix Millan	.10	.25
32 Camilo Pascual	.20	.50
33 Jackie Brandt	.10	.25
34 Don Lock	.10	.25
35 Chico Ruiz	.10	.25
36 Joe Azcue	.10	.25
37 Ed Bailey	.10	.25
38 Pete Ramos	.10	.25
39 Eddie Bressoud	.10	.25
40 Al Kaline	1.50	4.00
41 Ron Brand	.10	.25
42 Bob Lillis	.10	.25
44 Buster Narum	.10	.25
45 Junior Gilliam	.30	.75
46 Claude Raymond	.10	.25
47 Billy Bryan	.10	.25
48 Marshall Bridges	.10	.25
49 Norm Cash	.30	.75
50 Orlando Cepeda	.60	1.50
51 Lee Maye	.10	.25
52 Andy Rodgers	.10	.25
53 Ken Berry	.10	.25
54 Don Mincher	.10	.25
55 Jerry Lumpe	.10	.25
56 Milt Pappas	.10	.25
57 Steve Barber	.10	.25
58 Dennis Menke	.10	.25
59 Larry Maxie	.10	.25
60 Bob Gibson	1.25	3.00
61 Larry Bearnarth	.10	.25
62 Bill Mazeroski	.60	1.50
63 Bob Rodgers	.10	.25
64 Jerry Arrigo	.10	.25
65 Joe Nuxhall	.20	.50
66 Dean Chance	.20	.50
67 Ken Boyer	.30	.75
68 John Odom	.10	.25
69 Chico Cardenas	.10	.25
70 Maury Wills	.30	.75
71 Tony Oliva	.30	.75
72 Don Nottebart	.10	.25
73 Joe Adcock	.20	.50
74 Felipe Alou	.30	.75
75 Matty Alou	.20	.50
76 Dick Radatz	.10	.25
77 Jim Bouton	.30	.75
78 John Blanchard	.10	.25
79 Juan Pizarro	.10	.25
80 Boog Powell	.30	.75
81 Earl Robinson	.10	.25
82 Bob Chance	.10	.25
83 Max Alvis	.10	.25
84 Don Blasingame	.10	.25
85 Tom Cheney	.10	.25
86 Jerry Arrigo	.10	.25
87 Tommy Davis	.20	.50

88 Steve Boros .10 .25
89 Don Cardwell .10 .25
90 Harmon Killebrew .75 2.00
91 Jim Pagliaroni .10 .25
92 Jim O'Toole .10 .25
93 Dennis Bennett .10 .25
94 Dick McAuliffe .20 .50
95 Dick Brown .10 .25
96 Joe Amalfitano .10 .25
97 Phil Linz .10 .25
99 Dave Nicholson .10 .25
100 Hoyt Wilhelm .60 1.50
101 Don Leppert .10 .25
102 Jose Pagan .10 .25
103 Sam McDowell .20 .50
104 Jack Baldschun .10 .25
105 Jim Perry .20 .50
106 Hal Reniff .10 .25
107 Lee Maye .10 .25
108 Joe Adcock .20 .50
109 Bob Bolin .10 .25
110 Don Leppert .10 .25
111 Bill Monbouquette .10 .25
112 Bobby Richardson .30 .75
113 Earl Battey .10 .25
114 Bob Veale .10 .25
115 Lou Jackson .10 .25
116 Frank Kreutzer .10 .25
117 Jerry Zimmerman .10 .25
118 Don Schwall .10 .25
119 Rich Rollins .10 .25
120 Pete Ward .10 .25
121 Moe Drabowsky .10 .25
122 Jesse Gonder .10 .25
123 Hal Woodeschick .10 .25
124 John Herrnstein .10 .25
125A Leon Wagner .30 .75
125B Gary Peters .30 .75
126 Dwight Siebler .10 .25
127 Gary Kroll .10 .25
128 Tony Horton .10 .25
129 John DeMerit .10 .25
130 Sandy Koufax 2.50 6.00
131 Jim Davenport .10 .25
132 Wes Covington .10 .25
133 Tony Taylor .20 .50
134 Jack Kralick .10 .25
135 Bill Pleis .10 .25
136 Russ Snyder .10 .25
137 Joe Torre .30 .75
138 Ted Wills .10 .25
139 Wes Stock .10 .25
140 Frank Robinson 1.25 3.00
141 Dave Stenhouse .10 .25
142 Ron Hansen .10 .25
143 Don Elston .10 .25
144 Del Crandall .10 .25
145 Bennie Daniels .10 .25
146 Vada Pinson .20 .50
147 Bill Spanswick .10 .25
148 Earl Wilson .10 .25
149 Ty Cline .10 .25
150 Dick Groat .20 .50
151 Jim Duckworth .10 .25
152 Jim Schaffer .10 .25
153 George Thomas .10 .25
154 Wes Stock .10 .25
155 Mike White .10 .25
156 John Podres .20 .50
157 Willie Crawford .10 .25
158 Fred Gladding .10 .25
159 John Wyatt .10 .25
160 Bob Friend .10 .25
161 Ted Uhlaender .10 .25
162 Dick Stigman .10 .25
163 Don Wert .10 .25
164 Eddie Bressoud .10 .25
165A Ed Roebuck .30 .75
165B Leon Wagner .30 .75
166 Al Spangler .10 .25
167 Bob Sadowski .10 .25
168 Ralph Terry .10 .25
169 Jim Schaffer .10 .25
170 Jim Fregosi .20 .50
170 Dick Hall .10 .25
171 Al Spangler .10 .25
172 Bob Tillman .10 .25
173 Ed Bailey .10 .25
174 Cesar Tovar .10 .25
175 Morrie Stevens .10 .25
176 Floyd Weaver .10 .25
177 Frank Malzone .10 .25
178 Norm Siebern .10 .25
179 Dick Phillips .10 .25
181 Bobby Wine .10 .25
182 Masanori Murakami 1.50 4.00
183 Chuck Schilling .10 .25
184 Jim Schaffer .10 .25
185 John Roseboro .20 .50
186 Jake Wood .10 .25
187 Dallas Green .20 .50
188 Tom Haller .10 .25
189 Chuck Cottier .10 .25
190 Brooks Robinson 1.25 3.00
191 Ty Cline .10 .25
192 Bubba Phillips .10 .25
193 Al Jackson .10 .25
194 Herm Starrette .10 .25
195 Dave Wickersham .10 .25
196 Vic Power .10 .25
197 Ray Culp .10 .25
198 Don Demeter .10 .25
199 Dick Schofield .10 .25
200 Mudcat Grant .10 .25
201 Roger Craig .20 .50
202 Dick Farrell .10 .25
203 Clay Dalrymple .10 .25
204 Jim Duffalo .10 .25
205 Tito Francona .10 .25
206 Tony Conigliaro .30 .75
207 Jim King .10 .25
208 Joel Gibson .10 .25
209 Arnold Earley .10 .25
210 Denny McLain .30 .75
211 Don Larsen .20 .50
212 Ron Hunt .10 .25
213 Deron Johnson .10 .25
214 Harry Bright .10 .25
215 Ernie Fazio .10 .25
216 Joey Jay .10 .25
217 Jim Coates .10 .25
218 Jerry Kindall .10 .25
219 Joe Gibbon .10 .25
220 Frank Howard .30 .75
221 Howie Koplitz .10 .25
222 Larry Jackson .10 .25
223 Dale Long .10 .25
224 Jimmy Dykes MG .20 .50
225 Hank Aguirre .10 .25
226 Earl Francis .10 .25
227 Vic Wertz .10 .25
228 Larry Haney .10 .25
229 Tony LaRussa .30 .75
230 Moose Skowron .20 .50
231 Lee Thomas .10 .25
231 Tito Francona .10 .25
232 Ken Johnson .10 .25
233 Dick Howser .10 .25
234 Bobby Knoop .10 .25
236 Elston Howard .30 .75
237 Donn Clendenon .10 .25
238 Jesse Gonder .10 .25
239 Vern Law .20 .50
240 Curt Flood .30 .75
241 Dal Maxvill .10 .25
242 Roy Sievers .20 .50
243 Jim Brewer .10 .25
244 Harry Craft MG .10 .25
245 Dave Eilers .10 .25
246 Dave DeBusschere .30 .75
247 Ken Harrelson .20 .50
248 Jim Duffalo UER .10 .25
Card #'d 249
249 Ed Kasko .10 .25
250 Luis Aparicio .60 1.50
251 Ron Kline .10 .25
252 Chuck Hinton .10 .25
253 Frank Lary .10 .25
254 Stu Miller .10 .25
255 Ernie Banks 1.50 4.00
256 Dick Farrell .10 .25
257 Bud Daley .10 .25
258 Luis Arroyo .10 .25
259 Bob Del Greco .10 .25
260 Ted Williams 4.00 10.00
261 Mike Epstein .10 .25
262 Mickey Mantle 6.00 15.00
263 Jim LeFebvre .10 .25
264 Pat Jarvis .10 .25
265 Chuck Hinton .10 .25
266 Don Larsen .30 .75
267 Jim Coates .10 .25
268 Gary Kolb .10 .25
269 Jim Hart .10 .25
270 Dave McNally .20 .50
271 Jerry Kindall .10 .25
272 Hector Lopez .10 .25
273 Claude Osteen .10 .25
274 Jack Aker .10 .25
275 Mike Shannon .20 .50
276 Lew Burdette .20 .50
277 Mack Jones .10 .25
278 Art Shamsky .10 .25
279 Bob Johnson .10 .25
280 Willie Mays 3.00 8.00
281 Rich Nye .10 .25
282 Bill Cowan .10 .25
283 Gary Kolb .10 .25
284 Woody Held .10 .25
285 Bill Freehan .20 .50
286 Larry Jackson .10 .25
287 Mike Hershberger .10 .25
288 Julian Javier .10 .25
289 Charley Smith .10 .25
290 Hank Aaron 3.00 8.00
291 John Boccabella .10 .25
292 Charley James .10 .25
293 Sammy Ellis .10 .25

1979 TCMA 50'S

The TCMA Stars of the 50's set contains 291 standard-size cards featuring the players of the 50's. The set features a good mix of superstars and not so important players of the era. This set was TCMA's attempt at issuing cards after Topps successfully enjoined them from issuing current players. Using the style which was typical of most of the TCMA issues, the fronts are clear with an informative biography on the back. The Hutchinson and Wertz cards were also issued with the word "SAMPLE" stamped on the back.

COMPLETE SET (291) 40.00 80.00
1 Joe DiMaggio 4.00 10.00
2 Yogi Berra 1.50 4.00
3 Warren Spahn 1.25 3.00
4 Robin Roberts .60 1.50
5 Ernie Banks 1.50 4.00
6 Willie Mays 3.00 8.00
7 Mickey Mantle 6.00 15.00
8 Roy Campanella 1.50 4.00
9 Stan Musial 2.00 5.00
10 Ted Williams 4.00 10.00
11 Ed Bailey .10 .25
12 Ted Kluszewski .40 1.00
13 Ralph Kiner .60 1.50
14 Dick Littlefield .10 .25
15 Nellie Fox .60 1.50
16 Billy Pierce .20 .50
17 Richie Ashburn .60 1.50
18 Del Ennis .20 .50
19 Bob Lemon .60 1.50
20 Early Wynn .60 1.50
21 Joe Collins .10 .25
22 Hank Bauer .20 .50
23 Roberto Clemente 4.00 10.00
24 Frank Thomas .20 .50
25 Alvin Dark .20 .50
26 Whitey Lockman .10 .25
27 Larry Doby .60 1.50
28 Bob Feller 1.50 4.00
29 Willie Jones .10 .25
30 Granny Hamner .10 .25
31 Clem Labine .20 .50
32 Ralph Branca .20 .50
33 Jack Harshman .10 .25
34 Dick Donovan .10 .25
35 Tommy Henrich .30 .75
36 Jerry Coleman .20 .50
37 Billy Hoeft .10 .25
38 Johnny Groth .10 .25
39 Harvey Haddix .20 .50
40 Gerry Staley .10 .25
41 Dale Long .10 .25
42 Vernon Law .20 .50
43 Dodger Power .75 2.00
44 Sam Jethroe .20 .50
45 Vic Wertz .20 .50
45A Vic Wertz .20 .50
Sample Back
46 Wes Westrum .10 .25
47 Dee Fondy .10 .25
48 Gene Baker .10 .25
49 Sandy Koufax 2.00 5.00
50 Billy Loes .10 .25
51 Chuck Diering .10 .25
52 Joe Ginsberg .10 .25
53 Jim Konstanty .20 .50
54 Curt Simmons .20 .50
55 Alex Kellner .10 .25
56 Charlie Dressen MG .20 .50
57 Frank Sullivan .20 .50
58 Mel Parnell .10 .25
59 Bobby Hofman .10 .25
60 Bill Connelly .10 .25
61 Corky Valentine .10 .25
62 Johnny Klippstein .10 .25
63 Chuck Tanner .20 .50
64 Dick Drott .10 .25
65 Dean Stone .10 .25
66 Jim Busby .10 .25
67 Sid Gordon .10 .25
68 Del Crandall .20 .50
69 Walker Cooper .10 .25
70 Hank Sauer .20 .50
71 Gil Hodges .40 1.00
72 Duke Snider 1.50 4.00
73 Sherman Lollar .10 .25
74 Chico Carrasquel .10 .25
75 Gus Triandos .20 .50
76 Bob Harrison .10 .25
77 Eddie Waitkus .10 .25
78 Ken Heintzelman .10 .25
79 Harry Simpson .10 .25
80 Luke Easter .20 .50
81 Ed Dick .10 .25
82 Jim DePalo .10 .25
83 Billy Cox .20 .50
84 Pee Wee Reese 1.25 3.00
85 Virgil Trucks .10 .25
86 George Kell .40 1.00
87 Mickey Vernon .20 .50
88 Eddie Yost .10 .25
89 Gus Bell .10 .25
91 Eddie Lopat .20 .50
92 Dick Wakefield .10 .25
93 Solly Hemus .10 .25
94 Al Schoendienst .60 1.50
95 Sammy White .10 .25
96 Billy Goodman .10 .25
97 Jim Hearn .10 .25
98 Ruben Gomez .10 .25
99 Marty Marion .20 .50
100 Bill Virdon .20 .50
101 Chuck Stobbs .10 .25
102 Ron Samford .10 .25
103 Bill Tuttle .10 .25
104 Harvey Kuenn .20 .50
105 Joe Cunningham .20 .50
106 Bill Sarni .10 .25
107 Jack Kramer .10 .25
108 Eddie Stanky .20 .50
109 Carmen Mauro .10 .25
110 Wayne Belardi .10 .25
111 Preston Ward .10 .25
112 Jack Shepard .10 .25
113 Buddy Kerr .10 .25
114 Vern Bickford .10 .25
115 Ellis Kinder .10 .25
116 Walt Dropo .10 .25
117 Duke Maas .10 .25
118 Billy Hunter .10 .25
119 Ewell Blackwell .20 .50
120 Hershell Freeman .10 .25
121 Freddie Martin .10 .25
122 Erv Dusak .10 .25
123 Roy Hartsfield .10 .25
124 Willard Marshall .10 .25
125 Jack Sanford .10 .25
126 Herman Wehmeier .10 .25
127 Hal Smith .10 .25
128 Jim Finigan .10 .25
129 Bob Hale .10 .25
130 Jim Wilson .10 .25
131 Bill Wight .10 .25
132 Mike Fornieles .10 .25
133 Steve Gromek .10 .25
134 Herb Score .20 .50
135 Ryne Duren .20 .50
136 Bob Turley .20 .50
137 Wally Moon .20 .50
138 Fred Hutchinson .20 .50
138A Fred Hutchinson .20 .50
Sample Back
139 Jim Hegan .10 .25
140 Dale Mitchell .10 .25
141 Walt Moryn .10 .25
142 Cal Neeman .10 .25
143 Billy Martin .40 1.00
144 Phil Rizzuto 1.25 3.00
145 Preacher Roe .30 .75
146 Carl Erskine .30 .75
147 Vic Power .10 .25
148 Elmer Valo .10 .25
149 Don Mueller .20 .50
150 Hank Thompson .10 .25
151 Stan Lopata .10 .25
152 Dick Sisler .10 .25
153 Willard Schmidt .10 .25
154 Roy McMillan .10 .25
155 Gil McDougald .20 .50
156 Gene Woodling .20 .50
157 Eddie Mathews .75 2.00
158 Johnny Logan .20 .50
159 Dan Bankhead .10 .25
160 Joe Black .20 .50
161 Roger Maris 2.00 5.00
162 Bob Cerv .10 .25
163 Paul Minner .10 .25
164 Bob Rush .10 .25
165 Gene Hermanski .10 .25
166 Harry Brecheen .10 .25
167 Davey Williams .10 .25
168 Monte Irvin .60 1.50
169 Clint Courtney .10 .25
170 Sandy Consuegra .10 .25
171 Bobby Shantz .20 .50
172 Harry Byrd .10 .25
173 Marv Throneberry .20 .50
174 Woody Held .10 .25
175 Al Rosen .30 .75
176 Rance Pless .10 .25
177 Steve Bilko .10 .25
178 Joe Presko .10 .25
179 Ray Boone .10 .25
180 Jim Lemon .10 .25
181 Andy Pafko .20 .50
182 Don Newcombe .30 .75
183 Frank Lary .10 .25
184 Al Kaline 1.50 4.00
185 Allie Reynolds .30 .75
186 Vic Raschi .20 .50
187 Dodger Braintrust .30 .75
188 Jimmy Piersall .20 .50
189 George Wilson .10 .25
190 Dusty Rhodes .10 .25
191 Duane Pillette .10 .25
192 Dave Philley .10 .25
193 Bobby Morgan .10 .25
194 Russ Meyer .10 .25
195 Hector Lopez .10 .25
196 Arnie Portocarrero .10 .25
197 Joe Page .20 .50
198 Tommy Byrne .10 .25
199 Ray Monzant .30 .75
200 John McCall .10 .25
201 Leo Durocher .40 1.00
202 Bobby Thomson .30 .75
203 Jack Banta .10 .25
204 Joe Pignatano .10 .25
205 Carlos Paula .10 .25
206 Roy Sievers .20 .50
207 Mickey McDermott .10 .25
208 Ray Scarborough .10 .25
209 Bill Miller .10 .25
210 Bill Skowron .30 .75
211 Bob Nieman .10 .25
212 Al Pilarcik .10 .25
213 Jerry Priddy .10 .25
214 Frank House .10 .25
215 Don Mossi .20 .50
216 Rocky Colavito .40 1.00
217 Brooks Lawrence .10 .25
218 Ted Wilks .10 .25
219 Zack Monroe .10 .25
220 Art Ditmar .10 .25
221 Cal McLish .10 .25
222 Gene Bearden .10 .25
223 Norm Siebern .10 .25
224 Bob Wiesler .10 .25
225 Foster Castleman .10 .25
226 Daryl Spencer .10 .25
227 Dick Williams .20 .50
228 Don Zimmer .20 .50
229 Jackie Jensen .20 .50
230 Billy Johnson .10 .25
231 Dave Koslo .10 .25
232 Al Corwin .10 .25
233 Erv Palica .10 .25
234 Bob Milliken .10 .25
235 Ray Kaat .10 .25
236 Sammy Calderone .10 .25
237 Don Demeter .10 .25
238 Karl Spooner .10 .25
239 Preacher Roe .20 .50
Johnny Podres
240 Enos Slaughter .40 1.00
241 Dick Kryhoski .10 .25
242 Art Houtteman .10 .25

Card	Low	High
243 Andy Carey	.10	.25
244 Tony Kubek	.30	.75
245 Mike McCormick	.10	.25
246 Bob Schmidt	.10	.25
247 Nelson King	.10	.25
248 Bob Skinner	.10	.25
249 Dick Bokelmann	.10	.25
250 Eddie Kazak	.10	.25
251 Billy Klaus	.10	.25
252 Norm Zauchin	.10	.25
253 Art Schult	.10	.25
254 Bob Martyn	.10	.25
255 Larry Jansen	.10	.25
256 Sal Maglie	.20	.50
257 Bob Darnell	.10	.25
258 Ken Lehman	.10	.25
259 Jim Blackburn	.10	.25
260 Bob Purkey	.10	.25
261 Harry Walker	.10	.25
262 Joe Garagiola	.40	1.00
263 Gus Zernial	.10	.25
264 Walter Evers	.10	.25
265 Mark Freeman	.10	.25
266 Charlie Silvera	.10	.25
267 Johnny Podres	.30	.75
268 Jim Hughes	.10	.25
269 Al Worthington	.10	.25
270 Hoyt Wilhelm	.40	1.00
271 Elston Howard	.40	1.00
272 Don Larsen	.30	.75
273 Don Hoak	.10	.25
274 Chico Fernandez	.10	.25
275 Gail Harris	.10	.25
276 Valmy Thomas	.10	.25
277 George Shuba	.10	.25
278 Al Walker	.10	.25
279 Willard Ramsdell	.10	.25
280 Lindy McDaniel	.10	.25
281 Bob Wilson	.10	.25
282 Chuck Templeton	.10	.25
283 Eddie Robinson	.10	.25
284 Bob Porterfield	.10	.25
285 Larry Miggins	.10	.25
286 Minnie Minoso	.40	1.00
287 Lou Boudreau	.40	1.00
288 Jim Davenport	.10	.25
289 Bob Miller	.10	.25
290 Jim Gilliam	.30	.75
291 Jackie Robinson	4.00	10.00
BC1 1955 Brooklyn Dodgers Bonus Card	.30	.75
BC2 1957 Milwaukee Braves Bonus Card	.30	.75

1914 Texas Tommy E224

There are two types of these cards:Type I are 1-50 and Type II are 51-64. The type one cards measure 2 3/8" by 3 1/2" while the type two cards measure 1 7/8" by 3". The type one cards have stats on the back while the type 2 cards have blank backs. Harry Hooper and Rube Marquard only exist in type two fashion. Some more cards were recently discovered and as it is currently the only one known there is no pricing on this card at this time

Card	Low	High
COMPLETE SET	50,000.00	100,000.00
COMMON CARD (1-51)	200.00	400.00
COMMON CARD (52-66)	500.00	1,000.00
1 Jimmy Archer	4,000.00	8,000.00
2 Jimmy Austin	4,000.00	8,000.00
3 Frank Baker	7,500.00	15,000.00
4 Chief Bender	7,500.00	15,000.00
5 Bob Bescher	4,000.00	8,000.00
6 Ping Bodie	5,000.00	10,000.00
7 Donie Bush	4,000.00	8,000.00
8 Bobby Byrne	4,000.00	8,000.00
9 Nixey Callahan	4,000.00	8,000.00
10 Howie Camnitz	4,000.00	8,000.00
11 Frank Chance	7,500.00	15,000.00
12 Hal Chase	7,500.00	15,000.00
13 Ty Cobb	50,000.00	100,000.00
14 Jack Coombs	5,000.00	10,000.00
15 Sam Crawford	7,500.00	15,000.00
16 Birdie Cree	4,000.00	8,000.00
17 Al Demaree	4,000.00	8,000.00
18 Red Dooin	5,000.00	10,000.00
19 Larry Doyle	7,500.00	15,000.00
20 Johnny Evers	7,500.00	15,000.00
21 Vean Gregg	4,000.00	8,000.00
22 Bob Harmon	4,000.00	8,000.00
23 Joe Jackson	60,000.00	120,000.00
24 Walter Johnson	12,500.00	25,000.00
25 Otto Knabe	4,000.00	8,000.00
26 Nap Lajoie	7,500.00	15,000.00
27 Harry Lord	4,000.00	8,000.00
28 Connie Mack MG	7,500.00	15,000.00
29 Armando Marsans	4,000.00	8,000.00
30 Christy Mathewson	12,500.00	25,000.00
31 George McBride	4,000.00	8,000.00
32 John McGraw MG	15,000.00	30,000.00
33 Snuffy McInnis	5,000.00	10,000.00
34 Chief Meyers	5,000.00	10,000.00
35 Earl Moore	4,000.00	8,000.00
36 Mike Mowrey	4,000.00	8,000.00
37 Rebel Oakes	4,000.00	8,000.00
38 Marty O'Toole	4,000.00	8,000.00
39 Eddie Plank	7,500.00	15,000.00
40 Buddy Ryan	4,000.00	8,000.00
41 Tris Speaker	12,500.00	25,000.00
42 Jake Stahl	4,000.00	8,000.00
43 Oscar Stanage	4,000.00	8,000.00
44 Bill Sweeney	4,000.00	8,000.00
45 Honus Wagner	30,000.00	60,000.00
46 Ed Walsh	7,500.00	15,000.00
47 Zack Wheat	4,000.00	8,000.00
48 Harry Wolter	4,000.00	8,000.00
49 Joe Wood	7,500.00	15,000.00
50 Steve Yerkes	6,000.00	12,000.00
51 Heinie Zimmerman	5,000.00	10,000.00
52 Ping Bodie	6,000.00	12,000.00
53 Larry Doyle	10,000.00	20,000.00
54 Vean Gregg	6,000.00	12,000.00
55 Harry Hooper	12,500.00	25,000.00
56 Walter Johnson	30,000.00	60,000.00
57 Connie Mack MG	12,500.00	25,000.00
58 Rube Marquard	12,500.00	25,000.00
59 Christy Mathewson	12,500.00	25,000.00
60 John McGraw MG	12,500.00	25,000.00
61 Chief Meyers	7,500.00	15,000.00
62 Fred Snodgrass	7,500.00	15,000.00
63 Jake Stahl	6,000.00	12,000.00
64 Honus Wagner	50,000.00	100,000.00
65 Joe Wood	12,500.00	25,000.00
66 Steve Yerkes	6,000.00	12,000.00

1948 Thom McAn Feller

This one-card set was distributed by Thom McAn Shoe Stores and features a black-and-white picture of Bob Feller of the Cleveland Indians with a facsimile autograph. The back carrys a Baseball Quiz with the answers to the questions at the bottom.

Card	Low	High
1 Bob Feller	40.00	80.00

1937 Thrilling Moments

Doughnut Company of America produced these cards and distributed them on the outside of doughnut boxes twelve per box. The cards were to be cut from the boxes and affixed to an album that housed the set. The set's full name is Thrilling Moments in the Lives of Famous Americans. Only seven athletes were included among 65-other famous non-sport American figures. Each blankbacked card measures roughly 1 7/8" by 2 7/8" when neatly trimmed. The set was produced in four different colored backgrounds: blue, green, orange, and yellow with each subject being printed in only one background color.

Card	Low	High
59 Babe Ruth Y BB	800.00	1,200.00

1907-09 Tigers A.C. Dietsche Postcards PC765

These postcards were issued over a three year period. The cards numbered from 1 through 15 are known as series one and issued in 1907 with a 1907 copyright. Cards numbered from 16 to 29 are known as series two and have 1908 or 1909 copyrights. An oversize team card has been rumored to exist but it has never been verified.

Card	Low	High
COMPLETE SET (29)	750.00	1,500.00
1 Ty Cobb	150.00	300.00
2 William Coughlin	30.00	60.00
3 Sam Crawford	60.00	120.00
4 Bill Donovan	40.00	80.00
5 Jerome W. Downs	30.00	60.00
6 Hugh Jennings MG	60.00	120.00
7 Davy Jones	30.00	60.00
8 Ed Killian	30.00	60.00
9 George Mullin	30.00	60.00
10 Charles O'Leary	30.00	60.00
11 Fred T. Payne	30.00	60.00
12 Claude Rossman	30.00	60.00
13 Germany Schaefer	40.00	80.00
14 Boss Schmidt	30.00	60.00
15 Edward Siever	30.00	60.00
16 Henry Beckendorf 08	30.00	60.00
17 Owen Bush 08	30.00	60.00
18 Ty Cobb 08 Batting	150.00	300.00
19 James Delehanty 09	30.00	60.00
20 Bill Donovan 08	40.00	80.00
21 Hugh Jennings MG 08	60.00	120.00
22 Tom Jones 09	30.00	60.00
23 Matthew McIntrye 08	30.00	60.00
24 George Moriarty 08	30.00	60.00
25 Oscar Stanage 08	30.00	60.00
26 Oren Edgar Summers 08	30.00	60.00
27 Edgar Willett 08	30.00	60.00
28 Ralph Works 09	30.00	60.00
29 Team Picture 09	50.00	100.00

1908 Tigers Fred G.Wright Postcard

Fred G. Wright was the photographer for several cards including the Detroit Tigers set produced by H.M. Taylor, established his own company. The only card positively identified is one of "Wild Bill" Donovan, a star pitcher for the Tigers. All additions to this checklist are appreciated.

Card	Low	High
1 Bill Donovan	125.00	250.00

1909-11 Tigers H.M. Taylor PC773-2

The H.M. Taylor postcard set measures 3 1/2" by 5 1/2" and was issued during the 1909-11 time period and features Detroit Tigers players only. The cards are black and white with a rather large border around the card. The H.M Taylor identification is presented on the back of the card.

Card	Low	High
COMPLETE SET (9)	1,375.00	2,750.00
1 Ty Cobb At Bat	750.00	1,500.00
2 Bill Coughlin Batting	100.00	200.00
3 Sam Crawford Ready for the ball	150.00	300.00
4 Detroit Team Card	400.00	800.00
5 Wild Bill Donovan/	100.00	200.00
6 Wild Bill Donovan Batting	100.00	200.00
7 Hugh Jennings Wee Ah; Yours Truly	200.00	400.00
8 Wild Bill Donovan Hugh Jennings Frank Chance	100.00	200.00
9 Hugh Jennings MG and his Tigers Caraciture	150.00	300.00

1909-10 Tigers Topping and Company PC773-1

This set of Detroit Tiger stars is believed to have been issued in late 1909 and early 1910. This distinctive set features yellow bands at the top and bottom and a face shot of the player in a center of a six-pointed star, which also contains a yellow outline. The words "Tiger Stars" are printed in the upper yellow band whereas the player's name and position appears in the lower band. Topping and Publishers Company, Detroit, is identified on the reverse.

Card	Low	High
COMPLETE SET (20)	2,250.00	4,500.00
1 Henry Beckendorf	100.00	200.00
2 Donie Bush	100.00	200.00
3 Ty Cobb	1,250.00	2,500.00
4 Sam Crawford	200.00	400.00
5 Jim Delahanty	100.00	200.00
6 Bill Donovan	100.00	200.00
7 Hugh Jennings MG	200.00	400.00
8 Davy Jones	100.00	200.00
9 Tom Jones	100.00	200.00
10 Ed Killian	100.00	200.00
11 Matty McIntyre	100.00	200.00
12 George Moriarty	100.00	200.00
13 George Mullin	125.00	250.00
14 Charlie O'Leary	100.00	200.00
15 Charlie Schmidt	100.00	200.00
16 George Speer	100.00	200.00
17 Oscar Stanage	100.00	200.00
18 Eddie Summers	100.00	200.00
19 Edgar Willet	100.00	200.00
20 Ralph Works	100.00	200.00

1909 Tigers Wolverine News Postcards PC773-3

The Wolverine News Company features Detroit Tigers. Two poses each of Ty Cobb and Sam Crawford highlight this black and white set. The Wolverine News Company identification is printed on the back of the card.

Card	Low	High
COMPLETE SET	1,000.00	2,000.00
1 Ty Cobb at bat	400.00	800.00
2 Ty Cobb Portrait	400.00	800.00
3 Bill Coughlin Capt. and Third Baseman	40.00	80.00
4 Sam Crawford Bunting	75.00	150.00
5 Sam Crawford Center Field	75.00	150.00
6 Wild Bill Donovan Pitcher	50.00	100.00
7 Wild Bill Donovan At the Water Wagon	50.00	100.00
8 Jerry Downs Utility	40.00	80.00
9 Hugh Jennings MG On the Coaching Line HOR	75.00	150.00
10 Hugh (ey) Jennings Manager	75.00	150.00
11 Davy Jones Left Fielder	40.00	80.00
12 Ed Killian Pitcher	40.00	80.00
13 George Mullin Pitcher	40.00	80.00
14 Charlie O'Leary Short Stop	40.00	80.00
15 Fred Payne Catcher	40.00	80.00
16 Claude Rossman/1st Baseman	40.00	80.00
17 Herman Schaefer/2d. Baseman	40.00	80.00
18 Schaefer and O'Leary working double play HOR	50.00	100.00
19 Charlie Schmidt Catcher	40.00	80.00
20 Eddie Siever Pitcher	40.00	80.00

1910 Tigers Brush Postcards

These postcards, which measure 3 1/2" by 5 1/2" feature members of the then three-time defending American League champions Detroit Tigers. The fronts have a photo of players posed with Brush automobiles along with a poetic description of the player. The backs have traditional post-card markings. Since these cards are unnumbered; we have sequenced them in alphabetical order. It is possible there are more postcards in this set so any help is greatly appreciated.

Card	Low	High
1 Ty Cobb	2,500.00	5,000.00
3 George Mullin	500.00	1,000.00
2 Hugh Jennings MG	1,000.00	2,000.00

1934 Tigers Annis Furs

These 23 photos, which measure approximately 3 1/2" by 5 1/2" features members of the 1934 Tigers. This set has recently been identified as being produced by Annis Furs as some discovered promotional material matches these cards. The set's year is identifiable by the Frank Doljack photo who only played for the Tigers in 1934. The player's name and position is located in the upper left corner. This set is also known as W-UNC.

Card	Low	High
COMPLETE SET (23)	400.00	800.00
1 Eldon Auker	15.00	40.00
2 Del Baker CO	15.00	40.00
3 Tommy Bridges	30.00	60.00
4 Mickey Cochrane	60.00	120.00
5 Alvin Crowder	15.00	40.00
6 Frank Doljack	15.00	40.00
7 Carl Fischer	15.00	40.00
8 Pete Fox	15.00	40.00
9 Charlie Gehringer	60.00	120.00
10 Goose Goslin	40.00	80.00
11 Hank Greenberg	75.00	150.00
12 Luke Hamlin	15.00	40.00
13 Ray Hayworth	15.00	40.00
14 Chief Hogsett	15.00	40.00
15 Firpo Marberry	15.00	40.00
16 Marv Owen	15.00	40.00
17 Cy Perkins CO	15.00	40.00
18 Bill Rogell	15.00	40.00
19 Schoolboy Rowe	15.00	40.00
20 Heinie Schuble	15.00	40.00
21 Vic Sorrell	15.00	40.00
22 Gee Walker	15.00	40.00
23 Jo Jo White	15.00	40.00

1939 Tigers Sportservice

These cards which measure 6 3/8"" by 4 1/8" are sepia toned and feature members of the 1939 Detroit Tigers. The fronts feature a player photo as well as a short biography. There may be more cards so any additions are appreciated.

Card	Low	High
COMPLETE SET	75.00	150.00
1 Earl Averill	20.00	40.00
2 Beau Bell	10.00	20.00
3 Tommy Bridges	10.00	20.00
4 Pinky Higgins	10.00	20.00
5 Red Kress	10.00	20.00
6 Barney McCoskey	10.00	20.00
7 Bobo Newsom	10.00	20.00
8 Birdie Tebbetts	10.00	20.00

1953 Tigers Glendale

The cards in this 28-card set measure approximately 2 5/8" by 3 3/4". The 1953 Glendale Meats set of full-color, unnumbered cards features Detroit Tiger ballplayers exclusively and was distributed one per package of Glendale Meats in the Detroit area. The back contains the complete major and minor league record through the 1952 season. The scarcer cards of the set command higher prices, with the Houtteman card being the most difficult to find. There is an album associated with the set (which also is quite scarce now). The catalog designation for this scarce regional set is F151. Since the cards are unnumbered, they are ordered below alphabetically.

Card	Low	High
COMPLETE SET (28)	7,500.00	15,000.00
COMMON CARD (1-28)	100.00	200.00
COMMON SP	150.00	300.00
1 Matt Batts	200.00	400.00
2 Johnny Bucha	200.00	400.00
3 Frank Carswell	200.00	400.00

4 Jim Delsing	250.00	500.00
5 Walt Dropo	250.00	500.00
6 Hal Erickson	200.00	400.00
7 Paul Foytack	200.00	400.00
8 Owen Friend	200.00	400.00
9 Ned Garver	250.00	500.00
10 Joe Ginsberg SP	600.00	1,200.00
11 Ted Gray	200.00	400.00
12 Fred Hatfield	200.00	400.00
13 Ray Herbert	200.00	400.00
14 Billy Hitchcock	200.00	400.00
15 Billy Hoeft SP	300.00	600.00
16 Art Houtteman SP	2,500.00	5,000.00
17 Milt Jordan	200.00	400.00
18 Harvey Kuenn	600.00	1,200.00
19 Don Lund	200.00	400.00
20 Dave Madison	200.00	400.00
21 Dick Marlowe	200.00	400.00
22 Pat Mullin	200.00	400.00
23 Bob Nieman	200.00	400.00
24 Johnny Pesky	250.00	500.00
25 Jerry Priddy	200.00	400.00
26 Steve Souchock	200.00	400.00
27 Russ Sullivan	200.00	400.00
28 Bill Wight	200.00	400.00

1959 Tigers Graphic Arts Service PC749

The Graphic Art Service postcards were issued in the late 1950's and early 60's in Cincinnati, Ohio. Despite being issued in Cincinnati, the players featured are all Detroit Tigers. These black and white, unnumbered cards feature facsimile autographs on the front. Two poses of Reno Bertoia exist.

COMPLETE SET (16)	37.50	75.00
1 Al Aber	1.50	3.00
2 Hank Aguirre	2.50	5.00
3 Reno Bertoia (2)	1.50	3.00
4 Frank Bolling	1.50	3.00
5 Jim Bunning	7.50	15.00
6 Paul Foytack	1.50	3.00
7 Jim Hegan	1.50	3.00
8 Tom Heinrich CO	5.00	10.00
9 Bill Hoeft	1.50	3.00
10 Frank House	1.50	3.00
11 Harvey Kuenn	2.50	5.00
12 Billy Martin	5.00	10.00
13 Tom Morgan	2.50	5.00
14 Bob Shaw	1.50	3.00
15 Lou Slater	1.50	3.00
16 Tim Thompson	1.50	3.00

1960 Tigers Jay Publishing

This 12-card set of the Detroit Tigers measures approximately 5" by 7" and features black-and-white player photos in a white border. These cards were packaged 12 to a packet. The backs are blank. The cards are unnumbered and checklisted below in alphabetical order.

COMPLETE SET (12)	20.00	50.00
1 Lou Berberet	1.00	2.50
2 Frank Bolling	1.00	2.50
3 Rocky Bridges	1.00	2.50
4 Jim Bunning	3.00	8.00
5 Rocky Colavito	2.00	5.00
6 Paul Foytack	1.00	2.50
7 Al Kaline	5.00	12.00
8 Frank Lary	1.00	2.50
9 Charlie Maxwell	1.00	2.50
10 Don Mossi	1.25	3.00
11 Ray Narleski	1.00	2.50
12 Eddie Yost	1.00	2.50

1961 Tigers Jay Publishing

This 12-card set of the Detroit Tigers measures approximately 5" by 7". The fronts feature black-and-white posed player photos with the player's and team name printed below in the white border. These cards were packaged 12 in a packet. The backs are blank. The cards are unnumbered and checklisted below in alphabetical order.

COMPLETE SET (12)	15.00	40.00
1 Steve Boros	1.00	2.50
2 Dick Brown	1.00	2.50
3 Bill Bruton	1.00	2.50
4 Jim Bunning	3.00	8.00
5 Norm Cash	1.50	4.00
6 Rocky Colavito	2.00	5.00
7 Chuck Cottier	1.00	2.50
8 Dick Gernert	1.00	2.50
9 Al Kaline	5.00	12.00
10 Frank Lary	1.00	2.50
11 Charlie Maxwell	1.00	2.50
12 Bob Sheffing MG	1.00	2.50

1962 Tigers Jay Publishing

This 12-card set of the Detroit Tigers measures approximately 5" by 7". The fronts feature black-and-white posed player photos with the player's and team name printed below in the white border. These cards were packaged 12 in a packet. The backs are blank. The cards are unnumbered and checklisted below in alphabetical order.

COMPLETE SET (12)	20.00	50.00
1 Steve Boros	1.00	2.50
2 Dick Brown	1.00	2.50
3 Jim Bunning	3.00	8.00
4 Norm Cash	2.00	5.00
5 Rocky Colavito	3.00	8.00
6 Chico Fernandez	1.00	2.50
7 Al Kaline	5.00	12.00
8 Frank Lary	1.00	2.50
9 Charley Maxwell	1.00	2.50
10 Don Mossi	1.25	3.00
11 Bob Scheffing MG	1.00	2.50
12 Jake Wood	1.00	2.50

1962 Tigers Post Cards Ford

These postcards feature members of the 1962 Detroit Tigers. They are unnumbered and we have sequenced them in alphabetical order. These cards are usually seen with real autographs.

COMPLETE SET	500.00	1,000.00
1 Hank Aguirre	40.00	80.00
2 Steve Boros	30.00	60.00
3 Dick Brown	30.00	60.00
4 Jim Bunning	100.00	200.00
5 Phil Cavarretta CO	40.00	80.00
6 Rocky Colavito	75.00	150.00
7 Terry Fox	30.00	60.00
8 Purnal Goldy	30.00	60.00
9 Jack Hommel TR	30.00	60.00
10 Dave Jolley	30.00	60.00
11 Ron Kline	30.00	60.00
12 Don Mossi	40.00	80.00
13 George Myatt CO	40.00	80.00
14 Ron Nischwitz	30.00	60.00
15 Larry Osborne	30.00	60.00
16 Phil Regan	30.00	60.00
17 Mike Roarke	30.00	60.00

1963 Tigers Jay Publishing

This 12-card set of the Detroit Tigers measures approximately 5" by 7". The fronts feature black-and-white posed player photos with the player's and team name printed below in the white border. These cards were packaged 12 in a packet. The backs are blank. The cards are unnumbered and checklisted below in alphabetical order.

COMPLETE SET (12)	15.00	40.00
1 Hank Aguirre	.75	2.00
2 Bill Bruton	.75	2.00
3 Jim Bunning	3.00	8.00
4 Norm Cash	1.50	4.00
5 Rocky Colavito	2.50	6.00
6 Chico Fernandez	.75	2.00
7 Paul Foytack	.75	2.00
8 Al Kaline	5.00	12.00
9 Frank Lary	1.00	2.50
10 Bob Sheffing MG	.75	2.00
11 Gus Triandos	1.00	2.50
12 Jake Wood	.75	2.00

1964 Tigers Jay Publishing

This 12-card set of the Detroit Tigers measures approximately 5" by 7". The fronts feature black-and-white posed player photos with the player's and team name printed below in the white border. These cards were packaged 12 in a packet. The backs are blank. The cards are unnumbered and checklisted below in alphabetical order.

COMPLETE SET (12)	15.00	40.00
1 Hank Aguirre	.75	2.00
2 Bill Bruton	.75	2.00
3 Norm Cash	1.50	4.00
4 Chuck Dressen MG	1.00	2.50
5 Bill Freehan	1.50	4.00
6 Al Kaline	5.00	12.00
7 Frank Lary	1.00	2.50
8 Jerry Lumpe	.75	2.00
9 Ed Rakow	.75	2.00
10 Phil Regan	.75	2.00
11 Mike Roarke	.75	2.00
12 Jake Wood	.75	2.00

1964 Tigers Lids

This set of 14 lids was produced in 1964 and features members of the Detroit Tigers. The catalog designation for this set is F96-5. These lids are actually milk bottle caps. Each lid is blank backed and measures approximately 1 1/4" in diameter. Since the lids are unnumbered, they are ordered below in alphabetical order. The players are drawn on the lids in blue and the player's name is written in orange. The lids say "Visit Tiger Stadium" at the top and "See the Tigers More in '64" at the bottom of every lid.

COMPLETE SET	100.00	200.00
1 Hank Aguirre	5.00	12.00
2 Billy Bruton	5.00	12.00
3 Norm Cash	15.00	40.00
4 Don Demeter	5.00	12.00
5 Chuck Dressen MG	6.00	15.00
6 Bill Freehan	10.00	25.00
7 Al Kaline	50.00	100.00
8 Frank Lary	6.00	15.00
9 Jerry Lumpe	5.00	12.00
10 Dick McAuliffe	6.00	15.00
11 Bubba Phillips	5.00	12.00
12 Ed Rakow	5.00	12.00
13 Phil Regan	5.00	12.00
14 Dave Wickersham	5.00	12.00

1965 Tigers Jay Publishing

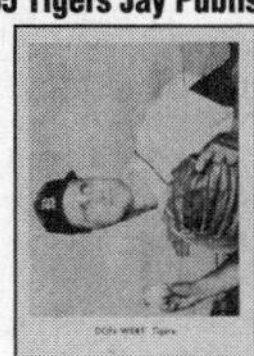

These blank-backed photos measure approximately 5" by 7" and feature white-bordered black-and-white posed player photos. The photos are printed on thin paper stock. The player's name and team appear below the photo within the bottom margin. The cards are unnumbered and checklisted below in alphabetical order. More than 12 photos are listed since the players were changed during the season

COMPLETE SET (19)	15.00	40.00
1 Hank Aguirre	.75	2.00
2 Gates Brown	.75	2.00
3 Norm Cash	1.50	4.00
4 Don Demeter	.75	2.00
5 Charlie Dressen MG	1.00	2.50
6 Bill Faul	.75	2.00
7 Bill Freehan	1.25	3.00
8 Al Kaline	5.00	12.00
9 Mickey Lolich	1.50	4.00
10 Jerry Lumpe	.75	2.00
11 Dick McAuliffe	1.00	2.50
12 Bubba Phillips	.75	2.00
13 Ed Rakow	.75	2.00
14 Phil Regan	.75	2.00
15 Larry Sherry	.75	2.00
16 George Thomas	.75	2.00
17 Don Wert	.75	2.00
18 Dave Wickersham	.75	2.00
19 Jake Wood	.75	2.00

1966 Tigers Team Issue

This 24 card issue measures 9 13/16" by 7 11/16" and features full color photos of members of the 1966 Detroit Tigers. Since the cards are unnumbered, we have sequenced them in alphabetical order.

COMPLETE SET (24)	30.00	60.00
1 Hank Aguirre	.75	2.00
2 Gates Brown	.75	2.00
3 Norm Cash	2.00	5.00
4 Don Demeter	.75	2.00
5 Chuck Dressen MG	.75	2.00
6 Bill Freehan	1.50	4.00
7 Fred Gladding	.75	2.00
8 Willie Horton	1.25	3.00
9 Al Kaline	4.00	10.00
10 Mickey Lolich	2.00	5.00
11 Jerry Lumpe	.75	2.00
12 Dick McAuliffe	1.25	3.00
13 Denny McLain	2.50	6.00
14 Bill Monbouquette	.75	2.00
15 Jim Northrup	1.25	3.00
16 Ray Oyler	.75	2.00
17 Orlando Pena	.75	2.00
18 Larry Sherry	.75	2.00
19 Joe Sparma	.75	2.00
20 Mickey Stanley	1.25	3.00
21 Dick Tracewski	.75	2.00
22 Don Wert	.75	2.00
23 Dave Wickersham	.75	2.00
24 Jake Wood	.75	2.00

1967 Tigers Dexter Press

This set, which features 11 photo cards that measure approximately 5 1/2" by 7", has white-bordered posed color player photos on its fronts. The set was produced by Dexter Press located in West Nyack, New York and features Detroit Tigers' players. A facsimile autograph is printed across the top of the picture. The white backs carry a short biography printed in blue ink, with only one line providing statistics for the 1966 season. The cards are unnumbered and checklisted below in alphabetical order.

COMPLETE SET (11)	12.50	30.00
1 Norm Cash	2.00	5.00
2 Bill Freehan	1.50	4.00
3 Willie Horton	1.25	3.00
4 Al Kaline	3.00	8.00
5 Jerry Lumpe	1.00	2.50
6 Dick McAuliffe	1.25	3.00
7 Johnny Podres	1.25	3.00
8 Joe Sparma	1.00	2.50
9 Don Wert	1.00	2.50
10 Dave Wickersham	1.00	2.50
11 Earl Wilson	1.00	2.50

1968 Tigers Detroit Free Press Bubblegumless

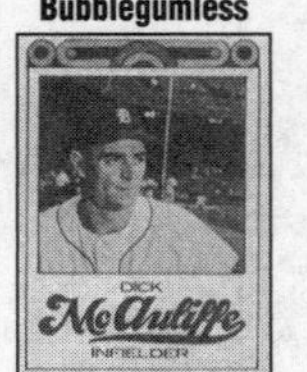

This set features members of the World Champion 1968 Detroit Tigers. The cards are unnumbered so we have sequenced them in alphabetical order.

COMPLETE SET	30.00	60.00
1 Gates Brown	.60	1.50
2 Norm Cash	2.00	5.00
3 Tony Cuccinello CO	.60	1.50
4 Pat Dobson	.60	1.50
5 Bill Freehan	2.00	5.00
6 John Hiller	.60	1.50
7 Willie Horton	1.00	2.50
8 Al Kaline	4.00	10.00
9 Fred Lasher	.60	1.50
10 Mickey Lolich	2.00	5.00
11 Dick McAuliffe	.75	2.00
12 Denny McLain	2.00	5.00
13 Don McMahon	.60	1.50
14 Tom Matchick	.60	1.50
15 Wally Moses CO	.60	1.50
16 Jim Northrup	.75	2.00
17 Ray Oyler	.60	1.50
18 Jim Price	.60	1.50
19 Daryl Patterson	.60	1.50
20 Johnny Sain CO	1.00	2.50
21 Mayo Smith MG	.60	1.50
22 Joe Sparma	.60	1.50
23 Mickey Stanley	.75	2.00
24 Dick Tracewski	.60	1.50
25 Jon Warden	.60	1.50
26 Don Wert	.60	1.50
27 Earl Wilson	.60	1.50
28 John Wyatt	.60	1.50

1968 Tigers News Super Posters

Issued to commemorate the Detroit Tigers would championship in 1968, these posters which measure approximately 13 1/2" by 23" feature all the players who participated in the World Series that year. Since these are unnumbered, we have sequenced them in alphabetical order.

COMPLETE SET (26)	75.00	150.00
1 Gates Brown	2.00	5.00
2 Norm Cash	3.00	8.00
3 Wayne Comer	2.00	5.00
4 Pat Dobson	2.00	5.00
5 Bill Freehan	2.50	6.00
6 John Hiller	2.00	5.00
7 Willie Horton	2.50	6.00
8 Al Kaline	6.00	15.00
9 Fred Lasher	2.00	5.00
10 Mickey Lolich	2.50	6.00
11 Tom Matchick	2.00	5.00
12 Eddie Mathews	5.00	12.00
13 Dick McAuliffe	2.50	6.00
14 Denny McLain	4.00	10.00
15 Don McMahon	2.00	5.00
16 Jim Northrup	2.50	6.00
17 Ray Oyler	2.00	5.00
18 Daryl Patterson	2.00	5.00
19 Jim Price	2.00	5.00
20 Mayo Smith MG	2.00	5.00
21 Joe Sparma	2.00	5.00
22 Mickey Stanley	2.50	6.00
23 Dick Tracewski	2.00	5.00
24 Jon Warden	2.00	5.00
25 Don Wert	2.00	5.00
26 Earl Wilson	2.00	5.00
27 John Wyatt	2.00	5.00
28 Detroit Tigers team	2.50	6.00

1968 Tigers Team Issue

These blank-backed cards, which measure approximately 5" by 7" feature members of the World Champion Detroit Tigers. Since these cards are unnumbered, we have sequenced them in alphabetical order. Since different players were substituted during the season -- there are more than 12 players in this set.

COMPLETE SET (12)	12.50	30.00
1 Norm Cash	1.50	4.00
2 Bill Freehan	1.00	2.50
3 Willie Horton	1.00	2.50
4 Al Kaline	3.00	8.00
5 Mike Kilkenny	.75	2.00
6 Eddie Mathews	2.00	5.00
7 Dick McAuliffe	1.00	2.50
8 Denny McLain	1.50	4.00
9 Jim Northrup	1.00	2.50
10 Mayo Smith MG	.75	2.00
11 Mickey Stanley	.75	2.00
12 Don Wert	.75	2.00
13 Earl Wilson	.75	2.00

1969 Tigers Farmer Jack

This set features six-inch iron-on transfers of player faces of the 1969 Detroit Tigers team and was distributed by Farmer Jack's Supermarket. An iron-on facsimile autograph is printed below the head. The transfers are unnumbered and checklisted below in alphabetical order. The checklist may be incomplete and additions are welcomed.

COMPLETE SET	30.00	60.00
1 Gates Brown	2.00	5.00
2 Norm Cash	4.00	10.00
3 Bill Freehan	3.00	8.00
4 Willie Horton	2.50	6.00
5 Al Kaline	10.00	25.00
6 Mickey Lolich	4.00	10.00
7 Dick McAuliffe	2.00	5.00
8 Denny McLain	4.00	10.00
9 Jim Northrup	2.50	6.00
10 Joe Sparma	2.00	5.00
11 Mickey Stanley	2.50	6.00
12 Earl Wilson	2.00	5.00

1969 Tigers Strip-Posters

Inserted into each Sunday issue of the Detroit Free Press were these "strip-posters" which featured various members of the Detroit Tigers. When properly cut out of the paper, these color drawings (by Dick Mayer) measure 4: by 15". Please note that this checklist is far from complete and any additions are greatly appreciated.

COMPLETE SET	12.50	30.00
1 Bill Freehan	5.00	12.00
2 Denny McLain	6.00	15.00
3 Jim Northrup	4.00	10.00
4 Mickey Stanley	3.00	8.00

1969 Tigers Team Issue

This 12-card set of the Detroit Tigers measures approximately 4 1/4" by 7". The fronts display black-and-white player portraits bordered in white. The player's name and team are printed in the top margin. The backs are blank. The cards are unnumbered and checklisted below in alphabetical order.

COMPLETE SET (12)	10.00	25.00
1 Norm Cash	1.25	3.00
2 Bill Freehan	1.25	3.00
3 Willie Horton	.75	2.00
4 Al Kaline	2.50	6.00
5 Mike Kilkenny	.60	1.50
6 Mickey Lolich	1.25	3.00
7 Dick McAuliffe	.75	2.00
8 Denny McLain	1.25	3.00
9 Jim Northrup	1.00	2.50
10 Mayo Smith MG	.60	1.50
11 Mickey Stanley	.75	2.00
12 Don Wert	.60	1.50

1969 Tigers Team Issue Color

This 20-card set of the Detroit Tigers measures approximately 7" by 8 3/4" with the fronts featuring white-bordered color player photos. The player's name and team is printed in black in the white margin below the picture. The backs are blank. The cards are unnumbered and checklisted below in alphabetical order.

COMPLETE SET (20)	20.00	50.00
1 Gates Brown	.75	2.00
2 Norm Cash	1.50	4.00
3 Pat Dobson	.75	2.00
4 Bill Freehan	1.50	4.00
5 John Hiller	.75	2.00
6 Willie Horton	1.00	2.50
7 Al Kaline	4.00	10.00
8 Fred Lasher	.75	2.00
9 Mickey Lolich	1.50	4.00
10 Tom Matchick	.75	2.00
11 Dick McAuliffe	1.00	2.50
12 Denny McLain	1.50	4.00
13 Jim Northrup	1.25	3.00
14 Jim Price	.75	2.00
15 Mayo Smith	.75	2.00
16 Joe Sparma	.75	2.00
17 Mickey Stanley	1.00	2.50
18 Dick Tracewski	.75	2.00
19 Don Wert	.75	2.00
20 Earl Wilson	.75	2.00

1972 Tigers Team Issue

This 12-card set of the Detroit Tigers measures approximately 4 1/4" by 7". The fronts display black-and-white player portraits bordered in white. The player's name and team are printed in the top margin. The backs are blank. The cards are unnumbered and checklisted below in alphabetical order.

COMPLETE SET (12)	8.00	20.00
1 Ed Brinkman	.40	1.00
2 Norm Cash	1.00	2.50
3 Joe Coleman	.40	1.00
4 Bill Freehan	.75	2.00
5 Willie Horton	.60	1.50
6 Al Kaline	2.00	5.00
7 Mickey Lolich	1.00	2.50
8 Billy Martin MG	1.25	3.00
9 Dick McAuliffe	.60	1.50
10 Jim Northrup	.60	1.50
11 Aurelio Rodriguez	.40	1.00
12 Mickey Stanley	.40	1.00

1973 Tigers Jewel

This 20-card set of the Detroit Tigers was produced by Jewel Food Stores and was issued in two series of ten cards each. Measuring approximately 7" by 8 3/4", the set features color posed player photos with white borders with blank backs. The cards are unnumbered and checklisted below in alphabetical order.

COMPLETE SET (20)	40.00	80.00
1 Ed Brinkman	1.50	4.00
2 Gates Brown	1.50	4.00
3 Ike Brown	1.50	4.00
4 Les Cain	1.50	4.00
5 Norman Cash	3.00	8.00
6 Joe Coleman	1.50	4.00
7 Bill Freehan	3.00	8.00
8 Tom Haller	1.50	4.00
9 Willie Horton	2.50	6.00
10 Al Kaline	6.00	15.00
11 Mickey Lolich	2.50	6.00
12 Billy Martin	3.00	8.00
13 Dick McAuliffe	2.00	5.00
14 Joe Niekro	2.00	5.00
15 Jim Northrup	2.00	5.00
16 Aurelio Rodriguez	1.50	4.00
17 Red Scherman	1.50	4.00
18 Mickey Stanley	2.50	6.00
19 Tony Taylor	1.50	4.00
20 Tom Timmerman	1.50	4.00

1974 Tigers

This 12-piece set of photos are blank-backed, white-bordered and 7" X 8 3/4". The player's name and team in black are within lower margin. The photos are unnumbered and checklisted below in alphabetical order.

COMPLETE SET (12)	8.00	20.00
1 Gates Brown	.75	2.00
2 Ron Cash	.60	1.50
3 Joe Coleman	.60	1.50
4 Bill Freehan	1.25	3.00
5 John Hiller	.60	1.50
6 Al Kaline	2.00	5.00
7 John Knox	.60	1.50
8 Jim Northrup	.75	2.00
9 Ben Oglivie	.75	2.00
10 Jim Ray	.60	1.50
11 Chuck Seelbach	.60	1.50
12 Dick Sharon	.60	1.50

1974 Tigers TCMA 1934-35 AL Champions

This 36-card set of the 1934-35 American League Champion Detroit Tigers features black-and-white player photos measuring approximately 2 1/8" by 3 11/16". The backs carry 1934 and 1935 player statistics. The cards are unnumbered and checklisted below in alphabetical order with cards 35 and 36 being jumbo cards.

COMPLETE SET (36)	10.00	25.00
1 Elden Auker	.20	.50
2 Del Baker CO	.20	.50
3 Tommy Bridges	.20	.50
4 Flea Clifton	.20	.50
5 Mickey Cochrane	.75	2.00
6 Alvin Crowder	.20	.50
7 Frank Doljack	.20	.50
8 Carl Fisher	.20	.50
9 Pete Fox	.20	.50
10 Vic Frasier	.20	.50
11 Charles Gehringer	.75	2.00
12 Goose Goslin	.75	2.00
13 Hank Greenberg	1.25	3.00
14 Luke Hamlin	.20	.50
15 Clyde Hatter	.20	.50
16 Ray Hayworth	.20	.50
17 Chief Hogsett	.20	.50
18 Roxie Lawson	.20	.50
19 Fred Marberry	.20	.50
20 Chet Morgan	.20	.50
21 Marv Owen	.20	.50
22 Cy Perkins CO	.20	.50
23 Red Phillips	.20	.50
24 Frank Reiber	.20	.50
25 Bill Rogell	.20	.50
26 Schoolboy Rowe	.60	1.50
27 Henry Schuble	.20	.50
28 Hugh Shelly	.20	.50
29 Vic Sorrell	.20	.50
30 Joe Sullivan	.20	.50
31 Gee Walker	.20	.50
32 Harvey Walker	.20	.50
33 Jo Jo White	.20	.50
34 Rudy York	.40	1.00
35 Elden Auker Firpo Marberry Tommy Bridges School	.75	2.00
36 Goose Goslin Jo Jo White Pete Fox	.75	2.00

1975 Tigers Postcards

This 36-card set of the Detroit Tigers features player photos on postcard-size cards. The cards are unnumbered and checklisted below in alphabetical order.

COMPLETE SET (36)	8.00	20.00
1 Fred Arroyo	.20	.50
2 Billy Baldwin	.20	.50
3 Ray Bare	.20	.50
4 Gates Brown	.30	.75
5 Nate Colbert	.20	.50
6 Joe Coleman	.20	.50
7 Bill Freeman	.40	1.00
8 Steve Hamilton CO	.20	.50
9 Jim Hegan CO	.20	.50
10 John Hiller	.30	.75
11 Ralph Houk MG	.30	.75
12 Willie Horton	.60	1.50
13 Terry Humphrey	.20	.50
14 Art James	.20	.50
15 John Knox	.20	.50
16 Lerrin LaGrow	.20	.50
17 Gene Lamont	.20	.50
18 Ron LeFlore	.40	1.00
19 Dave Lemanczyk	.20	.50
20 Mickey Lolich	.60	1.50
21 Dan Meyer	.20	.50
22 Gene Michael	.30	.75
23 Ben Oglivie	.30	.75
24 Gene Pentz	.20	.50
25 Jack Pierce	.20	.50
26 Bob Reynolds	.20	.50
27 Leon Roberts	.20	.50
28 Aurelio Rodriguez	.20	.50
29 Vern Ruhle	.20	.50
30 Joe Schultz CO	.20	.50
31 Mickey Stanley	.20	.50
32 Gary Sutherland	.20	.50
33 Dick Tracewski	.20	.50
34 Tom Veryzer	.20	.50
35 Tom Walker	.20	.50
36 John Wockenfuss	.20	.50

1976 Tigers Old-Timers Troy Show

This 23-card set was available at the 7th Annual Midwest Sports Collectors Convention held July 16-18, 1976 in Troy-Hilton, Michigan. The cards measure 2 3/8" by 2 7/8" and feature portrait and action black-and-white illustrations of players. The player's name is near the top as is a small paragraph giving career history. A box at the bottom contains unusual personal facts. The backs carry information about the card show. The cards are unnumbered and checklisted below in alphabetical order.

COMPLETE SET (23)	3.00	8.00
1 Elden Auker	.10	.25
2 Tommy Bridges	.30	.75
3 Flea Clifton	.10	.25
4 Mickey Cochrane	.40	1.00
5 General Crowder	.10	.25
6 Frank Doljack	.10	.25
7 Carl Fischer	.10	.25
8 Pete Fox	.10	.25
9 Charles Gehringer	.40	1.00
10 Goose Goslin	.40	1.00
11 Hank Greenberg	.40	1.00
12 Luke Hamlin	.10	.25
13 Ray Hayworth	.10	.25
14 Chief Hogsett	.10	.25
15 Firpo Marberry	.10	.25
16 Marvin Owen	.30	.75
17 Cy Perkins	.10	.25
18 Bill Rogell	.10	.25
19 Schoolboy Rowe	.40	1.00
20 Heinie Schuble	.10	.25
21 Vic Sorrell	.10	.25
22 Gerald Walker	.10	.25
23 Jo Jo White	.10	.25

1976 Tigers Postcards

This 35-card set of the Detroit Tigers features player photos on postcard-size cards. The cards are unnumbered and checklisted below in alphabetical order.

COMPLETE SET (35)	8.00	20.00
1 Ray Bare	.20	.50
2 Joe Coleman	.20	.50
3 Jim Crawford	.20	.50
4 Mark Fidrych	1.50	4.00
5 Bill Freehan	.40	1.00
6 Pedro Garcia	.20	.50
7 Fred Gladding CO	.20	.50
8 Steve Grilli	.20	.50
9 Jim Hegan CO	.20	.50
10 John Hiller	.30	.75
11 Willie Horton	.40	1.00
12 Ralph Houk MG	.30	.75
13 Alex Johnson	.20	.50
14 Bruce Kimm	.20	.50
15 Bill Laxton	.20	.50
16 Ron LeFlore	.30	.75
17 Dave Lemanczyk	.20	.50
18 Frank MacCormack	.20	.50
19 Jerry Manuel	.20	.50
20 Milt May	.20	.50
21 Dan Meyer	.20	.50
22 Ben Oglivie	.30	.75
23 Dave Roberts	.20	.50
24 Aurelio Rodriguez	.20	.50
25 Vern Ruhle	.20	.50
26 Joe Schultz CO	.20	.50
27 Chuck Scrivener	.20	.50
28 Mickey Stanley	.20	.50
29 Rusty Staub	.40	1.00
30 Gary Sutherland	.20	.50
31 Jason Thompson	.60	1.50
32 Dick Tracewski CO	.20	.50
33 Tom Veryzer	.20	.50
34 John Wockenfuss	.20	.50
35 Tiger Stadium	.20	.50

1977 Tigers Burger King

This four-card set was issued in 1977 by Burger King and features Detroit Tigers. The photo cards measure approximately 8" by 10" and carry posed player color portraits. The backs are blank and the set is checklisted below in alphabetical order.

COMPLETE SET (4)	4.00	10.00
1 Mark Fidyrich	1.50	4.00
2 Ron LeFlore	1.00	2.50
3 Dave Rozema	.75	2.00
4 Mickey Stanley	1.00	2.50

1978 Tigers Burger King

The cards in this 23-card set measure 2 1/2" by 3 1/2". Twenty-three color cards, 22 players and one numbered checklist, comprise the 1978 Burger King Tigers set issued in the Detroit area. The cards marked with an asterisk contain photos different from those appearing on the Topps regular issue cards of that year. For example, Jack Morris, Alan Trammell, and Lou Whitaker (in the 1978 Topps regular issue cards) each appear on rookie prospect cards with three other young players; whereas in this Burger King set, each has his own individual card.

COMPLETE SET (23)	20.00	50.00
1 Ralph Houk MG	.30	.75
2 Milt May	.10	.25
3 John Wockenfuss	.10	.25
4 Mark Fidrych	.30	.75
5 Dave Rozema	.10	.25
6 Jack Billingham *	.10	.25
7 Jim Slaton *	.10	.25
8 Jack Morris *	6.00	15.00
9 John Hiller	.20	.50
10 Steve Foucault	.10	.25
11 Milt Wilcox	.10	.25
12 Jason Thompson	.30	.75
13 Lou Whitaker *	12.00	30.00
14 Aurelio Rodriguez	.10	.25
15 Alan Trammell *	12.00	30.00
16 Steve Dillard *	.10	.25
17 Phil Mankowski	.10	.25
18 Steve Kemp	.20	.50
19 Ron LeFlore	.30	.75
20 Tim Corcoran	.10	.25
21 Mickey Stanley	.30	.75
22 Rusty Staub	.40	1.00
NNO Checklist Card TP	.08	.15

1978-80 Tigers Dearborn Card Show

These 2 5/8" by 3 5/8" cards were issued in conjuction with the annual Detroit area Dearborn card show. They feature Tiger greats from the past. For the 1978 set, 1,200 of each set were printed; 900 for promotional purposes and 300 for collector sales. For the 1980 set (issued in 1979), 1000 sets were produced; 600 for promotional purposes and 400 for collector sales. The first 18 cards were originally available for $2 per set.

COMPLETE SET	12.50	30.00
1 Rocky Colavito	.75	2.00
2 Ervin Fox	.30	.75
3 Schoolboy Rowe	.30	.75
4 Gerald Walker	.30	.75
5 Leon Goslin	.60	1.50

6 Harvey Kuenn	.40	1.00
7 Frank Howard	.40	1.00
8 Woodie Fryman	.30	.75
9 Don Wert	.30	.75
10 Jim Perry	.40	1.00
11 Mayo Smith MG	.30	.75
12 Al Kaline	1.25	3.00
13 Norm Cash	.60	1.50
14 Mickey Cochrane	.40	1.00
15 Fred Marberry	.30	.75
16 Bill Freehan	.40	1.00
17 Charley Gehringer	.60	1.50
18 Jim Northrup	.30	.75
19 Slick Coffman	.30	.75
20 Bruce Campbell	.30	.75
21 Jack Burns	.30	.75
22 Herman Flea Clifton	.30	.75
23 Vic Frasier	.30	.75
24 Pete Fox	.30	.75
25 Al Simmons	.75	2.00
26 Woodrow Davis	.30	.75
27 Dick Conger	.30	.75
28 John Corsica	.30	.75
29 Frank Croucher	.30	.75
30 Hank Greenberg	1.25	3.00
31 Tommy Bridges	.30	.75
32 William Hargrave	.30	.75
33 Chad Kimsey	.30	.75
34 Harry Eisenstat	.30	.75
35 Gene Desaultels	.30	.75
36 Dizzy Trout	.40	1.00

1978 Tigers Team Issue

These 3" by 5" photos feature the members of the 1978 Detroit Tigers. They are unnumbered so we have sequenced them in alphabetical order. Photos of Alan Trammell, Lou Whitaker, Jack Morris and Lance Parrish are included in their rookie season.

COMPLETE SET	15.00	40.00
1 Fernando Arroyo	.20	.50
2 Steve Baker	.20	.50
3 Jack Billingham	.20	.50
4 Gates Brown CO	.20	.50
5 Tim Corcoran	.20	.50
6 Jim Crawford	.20	.50
7 Steve Dillard	.20	.50
8 Mark Fidrych	.60	1.50
9 Steve Foucault	.20	.50
10 Fred Gladding CO	.20	.50
11 Fred Hatfield CO	.20	.50
12 Steve Hackett	.20	.50
13 Jim Hegan CO	.20	.50
14 John Hiller	.20	.50
15 Ralph Houk MG	.20	.50
16 Steve Kemp	.30	.75
17 Ron LeFlore	.30	.75
18 Phil Mankowski	.20	.50
19 Milt May	.20	.50
20 Jack Morris	3.00	8.00
21 Lance Parrish	1.50	4.00
22 Aurelio Rodriguez	.20	.50
23 Dave Rozema	.20	.50
24 Jim Slaton	.20	.50
25 Charlie Spikes	.20	.50
26 Mickey Stanley	.20	.50
27 Rusty Staub	.40	1.00
28 Bob Sykes	.20	.50
29 Bruce Taylor	.20	.50
30 Jason Thompson	.20	.50
31 Dick Tracewski CO	.20	.50
32 Alan Trammell	4.00	10.00
33 Mark Wayne	.20	.50
34 Lou Whitaker	3.00	8.00
35 Milt Wilcox	.20	.50
36 John Wockenfuss	.20	.50
37 Tiger Stadium	.20	.50

1979 Tigers Free Press

These 10" by 15" posters was published in the Detroit Free Press Newspaper and displays a black-and-white player photo with player information and statistics including a printed feature on the player with his career highlights. There may be even more posters and all additions to the checklist are welcomed.

COMPLETE SET	6.00	15.00
1 Jason Thompson	1.25	3.00
4 Ron LeFlore	1.25	3.00
5 Dave Rozema	1.25	3.00
6 Mickey Stanley	1.50	4.00
8 Milt May	1.25	3.00
9 Jim Slaton	1.25	3.00

1979 Tigers Team Issue

These cards, which originally sold from the Tigers directly for 20 cents each, feature members of the 1979 Detroit Tigers. This list consists solely of the new members of the 1979 Tigers that season and since they are unnumbered are sequenced in alphabetical order. Please note that there are 2 different manager cards as Sparky Anderson replaced Les Moss early in the 1979 season.

COMPLETE SET	4.00	10.00
1 Sparky Anderson MG	1.00	2.50
2 Steve Baker	.20	.50
3 Tom Brookens	.20	.50
4 Sheldon Burnside	.20	.50
5 Steve Baker	.20	.50
6 Mike Chris	.20	.50
7 Billy Consolo CO	.20	.50
8 Tim Corcoran	.20	.50
9 Danny Gonzalez	.20	.50
10 Al Greene	.20	.50
11 John Grodzicki CO	.20	.50
12 John Hiller	.30	.75
13 Lynn Jones	.20	.50
14 Aurelio Lopez	.20	.50
15 Dave Machemer	.20	.50
16 Milt May	.20	.50
17 Jerry Morales	.20	.50
18 Les Moss MG	.30	.75
19 Dan Petry	.30	.75
20 Ed Putnam	.20	.50
21 Bruce Robbins	.20	.50
22 Champ Summers	.20	.50
23 Dave Tobik	.20	.50
24 Pat Underwood	.20	.50
25 Kip Young	.20	.50

1980 Tigers Greats TCMA

This 12-card standard-size set features some of the best Detroit Tigers of all time. The fronts have a black-and-white player photo while the horizontal backs have vital statistics, a biography and career statistics.

COMPLETE SET (12)	2.50	6.00
1 George Kell	.20	.50
2 Billy Rogell	.08	.25
3 Ty Cobb	.60	1.50
4 Hank Greenberg	.40	1.00
5 Al Kaline	.40	1.00
6 Charlie Gehringer	.30	.75
7 Harry Heilmann	.20	.50
8 Hal Newhouser	.20	.50
9 Steve O'Neill MG	.08	.25
10 Denny McLain	.20	.50
11 Mickey Cochrane	.30	.75
12 John Hiller	.08	.25

1947 Tip Top

The cards in this 163-card set measure approximately 2 1/4" by 3". The 1947 Tip Top Bread issue contains unnumbered cards with black and white player photos. The set is of interest to baseball historians in that it contains cards of many players not appearing in any other card sets. The cards were issued locally for the eleven following teams: Red Sox (1-15), White Sox (16-30), Tigers (31-45), Yankees (46-60), Browns (61-75), Braves (76-90), Dodgers (91-104), Cubs (105-119), Giants (120-134), Pirates (135-148), and Cardinals (149-163). Players of the Red Sox, Tigers, White Sox, Braves, and the Cubs are scarcer than those of the other teams; players from these tougher teams are marked by SP below to indicate their scarcity. The catalog designation is D323. These unnumbered cards are listed in alphabetical order within teams (with teams also alphabetized within league) for convenience. It was thought that a card for the Giants Eugene Thompson was to be issued but it does not exist.

COMPLETE SET (163)	5,000.00	10,000.00
COMMON CARD (1-163)	12.50	25.00
COMMON SP PLAYER	50.00	80.00
1 Leon Culberson SP	50.00	80.00
2 Dom DiMaggio SP	90.00	150.00
3 Joe Dobson SP	50.00	80.00
4 Bob Doerr SP	175.00	300.00
5 Dave(Boo) Ferris SP	50.00	80.00
6 Mickey Harris SP	50.00	80.00
7 Frank Hayes SP	50.00	80.00
8 Cecil Hughson SP	50.00	80.00
9 Earl Johnson SP	50.00	80.00
10 Roy Partee SP	50.00	80.00
11 Johnny Pesky SP	60.00	100.00
12 Rip Russell SP	50.00	80.00
13 Hal Wagner SP	50.00	80.00
14 Rudy York SP	60.00	100.00
15 Bill Zuber SP	50.00	80.00
16 Floyd Baker SP	50.00	80.00
17 Earl Caldwell SP	50.00	80.00
18 Loyd Christopher SP	50.00	80.00
19 George Dickey SP	50.00	80.00
20 Ralph Hodgin SP	50.00	80.00
21 Bob Kennedy SP	50.00	80.00
22 Joe Kuhel SP	50.00	80.00
23 Thornton Lee SP	50.00	80.00
24 Ed Lopat SP	90.00	150.00
25 Cass Michaels SP	50.00	80.00
26 John Rigney SP	50.00	80.00
27 Mike Tresh SP	50.00	80.00
28 Thurman Tucker SP	50.00	80.00
29 Jack Wallasca SP	50.00	80.00
30 Taft Wright SP	50.00	80.00
31 Walter(Hoot)Evers SP	50.00	80.00
32 John Gorsica SP	50.00	80.00
33 Fred Hutchinson SP	60.00	100.00
34 George Kell SP		500
35 Eddie Lake SP	50.00	80.00
36 Ed Mayo SP	50.00	80.00
37 Arthur Mills SP	50.00	80.00
38 Pat Mullin SP	50.00	80.00
39 James Outlaw SP	50.00	80.00
40 Frank Overmire SP	50.00	80.00
41 Bob Swift SP	50.00	80.00
42 Birdie Tebbetts SP	50.00	80.00
43 Dizzy Trout SP	60.00	100.00
44 Virgil Trucks SP	60.00	100.00
45 Dick Wakefield SP	50.00	80.00
46 Yogi Berra/(Listed as Larry on card)		500
47 Floyd(Bill) Bevans	15.00	30.00
48 Bobby Brown	20.00	40.00
49 Thomas Byrne	15.00	30.00
50 Frank Crosetti	25.00	50.00
51 Tommy Henrich	25.00	50.00
52 Charlie Keller	25.00	50.00
53 Johnny Lindell	15.00	30.00
54 Joe Page	20.00	40.00
55 Mel Queen	15.00	30.00
56 Allie Reynolds	25.00	50.00
57 Phil Rizzuto	100.00	200.00
58 Aaron Robinson	15.00	30.00
59 George Stirnweiss	15.00	30.00
60 Charles Wensloff	15.00	30.00
61 John Berardino	25.00	50.00
62 Clifford Fannin	15.00	30.00
63 Dennis Galehouse	15.00	30.00
64 Jeff Heath	15.00	30.00
65 Walter Judnich	15.00	30.00
66 Jack Kramer	15.00	30.00
67 Paul Lehner	15.00	30.00
68 Les Moss	15.00	30.00
69 Bob Muncrief	15.00	30.00
70 Nelson Potter	15.00	30.00
71 Fred Sanford	15.00	30.00
72 Joe Schultz	15.00	30.00
73 Vern Stephens	20.00	40.00
74 Jerry Witte	15.00	30.00
75 Al Zarilla	15.00	30.00
76 Charles Barrett SP	50.00	80.00
77 Hank Camelli SP	50.00	80.00
78 Dick Culler SP	50.00	80.00
79 Nanny Fernandez SP	50.00	80.00
80 Si Johnson SP	50.00	80.00
81 Danny Litwhiler SP	50.00	80.00
82 Phil Masi SP	50.00	80.00
83 Carvel Rowell SP	50.00	80.00
84 Connie Ryan SP	50.00	80.00
85 John Sain SP	70.00	120.00
86 Ray Sanders SP	50.00	80.00
87 Sibby Sisti SP	50.00	80.00
88 Billy Southworth SP MG	60.00	100.00
89 Warren Spahn SP		600
90 Ed Wright SP	50.00	80.00
91 Bob Bragan	20.00	40.00
92 Ralph Branca	20.00	40.00
93 Hugh Casey	15.00	30.00
94 Bruce Edwards	15.00	30.00
95 Hal Gregg	15.00	30.00
96 Joe Hatten	15.00	30.00
97 Gene Hermanski	15.00	30.00
98 John Jorgensen	15.00	30.00
99 Harry Lavagetto	20.00	40.00
100 Vic Lombardi	15.00	30.00
101 Frank Melton	15.00	30.00
102 Ed Miksis	15.00	30.00
103 Marv Rackley	15.00	30.00
104 Ed Stevens	15.00	30.00
105 Phil Cavarretta SP	70.00	120.00
106 Bob Chipman SP	50.00	80.00
107 Stan Hack SP	60.00	100.00
108 Don Johnson SP	50.00	80.00
109 Emil Kush SP	50.00	80.00
110 Bill Lee SP	60.00	100.00
111 Mickey Livingston SP	50.00	80.00
112 Harry Lowrey SP	50.00	80.00
113 Clyde McCullough SP	50.00	80.00
114 Andy Pafko SP	60.00	100.00
115 Marv Rickert SP	50.00	80.00
116 John Schmitz SP	50.00	80.00
117 Bobby Sturgeon SP	50.00	80.00
118 Ed Waitkus SP	60.00	100.00
119 Henry Wyse SP	50.00	80.00
120 Bill Ayers	15.00	30.00
121 Buddy Blattner	15.00	30.00
122 Mike Budnick	15.00	30.00
123 Sid Gordon	15.00	30.00
124 Clint Hartung	15.00	30.00
125 Monte Kennedy	15.00	30.00
126 Dave Koslo	15.00	30.00
127 Whitey Lockman	20.00	40.00
128 Jack Lohrke	15.00	30.00
129 Ernie Lombardi		100
130 Willard Marshall	15.00	30.00
131 John Mize	75.00	150.00
132 Ken Trinkle	15.00	30.00
133 Bill Voiselle	15.00	30.00
134 Mickey Witek	15.00	30.00
135 Eddie Basinski	15.00	30.00
136 Ernie Bonham	15.00	30.00
137 Billy Cox	20.00	40.00
138 Elbie Fletcher	15.00	30.00
139 Frank Gustine	15.00	30.00
140 Kirby Higbe	15.00	30.00
141 Leroy Jarvis	15.00	30.00
142 Ralph Kiner	75.00	150.00
143 Fred Ostermueller	15.00	30.00
144 Preacher Roe	25.00	50.00
145 Jim Russell	15.00	30.00
146 Rip Sewell	15.00	30.00
147 Nick Strincevich	15.00	30.00
148 Honus Wagner CO	75.00	150.00
149 Alpha Brazle	15.00	30.00
150 Ken Burkhart	15.00	30.00
151 Bernard Creger	15.00	30.00
152 Joffre Cross	15.00	30.00
153 Chuck Diering	15.00	30.00
154 Ervin Dusak	15.00	30.00
155 Joe Garagiola		100
156 Tony Kaufmann	15.00	30.00
157 Whitey Kurowski	15.00	30.00
158 Marty Marion	25.00	50.00
159 George Munger	15.00	30.00
160 Del Rice	15.00	30.00
161 Dick Sisler	20.00	40.00
162 Enos Slaughter	75.00	150.00
163 Ted Wilks	15.00	30.00

1952 Tip Top

This set of 48 bread end-labels was issued by Tip Top in 1952. The labels measure 2 3/4" by 2 1/2". An album distributed with the labels names 47 ball players and has one blank slot with advertising. A second pose of Rizzuto -- which appears "cropped" from the first photo -- suggests either a last minute substitution for another player, or simply his popularity in the market area. These labels are unnumbered so we have sequenced them in alphabetical order. The catalog designation is D290-1.

COMPLETE SET (48)	7,500.00	15,000.00
1 Hank Bauer	250.00	500.00
2 Yogi Berra	600.00	1,200.00
3 Ralph Branca	250.00	500.00
4 Lou Brissie	150.00	300.00
5 Roy Campanella	800.00	1,600.00
6 Phil Cavarretta	250.00	500.00
7 Murray Dickson	150.00	300.00
8 Ferris Fain	150.00	300.00
9 Carl Furillo	300.00	600.00
10 Ned Garver	150.00	300.00
11 Sid Gordon	250.00	500.00
12 Johnny Groth	150.00	300.00
13 Granny Hamner	150.00	300.00
14 Jim Hearn	150.00	300.00
15 Gene Hermanski	150.00	300.00
16 Gil Hodges	500.00	1,000.00
17 Larry Jansen	200.00	400.00
18 Eddie Joost	150.00	300.00
19 George Kell	400.00	800.00
20 Dutch Leonard	150.00	300.00
21 Whitey Lockman	150.00	300.00
22 Eddie Lopat	250.00	500.00
23 Sal Maglie	250.00	500.00
24 Mickey Mantle	2,500.00	5,000.00
25 Gil McDougald	250.00	500.00
26 Dale Mitchell	200.00	400.00
27 Don Mueller	150.00	300.00
28 Andy Pafko	150.00	300.00
29 Bob Porterfield	150.00	300.00
30 Ken Raffensberger	150.00	300.00
31 Allie Reynolds	250.00	500.00
32 Phil Rizzuto (large)	300.00	600.00
33 Phil Rizzuto (small)	300.00	600.00
34 Robin Roberts	500.00	1,000.00
35 Saul Rogovin	150.00	300.00
36 Ray Scarborough	150.00	300.00
37 Red Schoendienst	300.00	600.00
38 Dick Sisler	150.00	300.00
39 Enos Slaughter	400.00	800.00
40 Duke Snider	600.00	1,200.00
41 Warren Spahn	500.00	1,000.00
42 Vern Stephens	150.00	300.00
43 Earl Torgeson	150.00	300.00
44 Mickey Vernon	200.00	400.00
45 Eddie Waitkus	150.00	300.00
46 Wes Westrum	150.00	300.00
47 Eddie Yost	150.00	300.00
48 Al Zarilla	150.00	300.00
XX Album		

1887 Tobin Lithographs

This 11 card set measures 3" by 4 1/2" and were issued in either black and white or color. The color cards have "56" listed in the lower left hand corner with and advertisement in the upper right corner. The card features a player drawing along with an humourus statement. The player's team identification is in the upper left corner. The backs come with or without advertising. We have listed these cards in alphabetical order with the description afterwards.

COMPLETE SET	1,000.00	2,000.00
1 Ed Andrews Go it Old Boy	300.00	600.00
2 Cap Anson Oh, Come Off	600.00	1,200.00
3 Dan Brouthers Watch me soak it	500.00	1,000.00
4 Charlie Ferguson Not onto it	300.00	600.00
5 Jack Glasscock Struck by a cyclone	300.00	600.00
6 Paul Hines An Anxious Moment	300.00	600.00
7 Tim Keefe Where'l you have it	500.00	1,000.00
8 Mike King Kelly The Flower of our Flock Identified as our own Kelly	600.00	1,200.00
9 Mike King Kelly/15,000 in his pocket Black and White Measures approximately 2 1/2 by 4 Does not have 56 in corner	600.00	1,200.00

10 Jim McCormick 300.00 600.00
A slide for Hoome
11 Mickey Welch 500.00 1,000.00
Aint it a daisy

1913 Tom Barker Game WG6

These cards were distributed as part of a baseball game produced in 1913 as indicated by the patent date on the backs of the cards. The cards each measure approximately 2 7/16" by 3 7/16" and have rounded corners. The card fronts show a sepia photo of the player, his name, his team, and the game outcome associated with that particular card. The card backs are all the same, each showing an ornate red and white design with "Tom Barker Baseball Card Game" at the bottom under a drawing of a lefthanded batter all surrounded by a thick white outer border. Since the cards are unnumbered, they are listed below in alphabetical order. The last nine cards in the set feature action photos oriented horizontally.

COMPLETE SET 3,000.00 6,000.00
COMMON ACTION CARD 7.50 15.00
1 Grover Alexander 250.00 400.00
2 Frank Baker 50.00 100.00
3 Chief Bender 30.00 50.00
4 Bob Bescher 15.00 25.00
5 Joe Birmingham 15.00 25.00
6 Roger Bresnahan 35.00 60.00
7 Nixey Callahan 15.00 25.00
8 Bill Carrigan 15.00 25.00
9 Frank Chance 35.00 60.00
10 Hal Chase 18.00 30.00
11 Fred Clarke 30.00 50.00
12 Ty Cobb 250.00 400.00
13 Sam Crawford 35.00 60.00
14 Jake Daubert 15.00 25.00
15 Red Dooin 15.00 25.00
16 Johnny Evers 35.00 60.00
17 Vean Gregg 15.00 25.00
18 Clark Griffith MG 30.00 50.00
19 Dick Hoblitzel 15.00 25.00
20 Miller Huggins 30.00 50.00
21 Joe Jackson 700.00 1,200.00
22 Hugh Jennings MG 30.00 50.00
23 Walter Johnson 90.00 150.00
24 Ed Konetchy 15.00 25.00
25 Nap Lajoie 50.00 80.00
26 Connie Mack MG 35.00 60.00
27 Rube Marquard 30.00 50.00
28 Christy Mathewson 90.00 150.00
29 John McGraw MG 35.00 60.00
30 Chief Meyers 15.00 25.00
31 Clyde Milan 15.00 25.00
32 Marty O'Toole 15.00 25.00
33 Nap Rucker 15.00 25.00
34 Tris Speaker 50.00 80.00
35 George Stallings MG 15.00 25.00
36 Bill Sweeney 15.00 25.00
37 Joe Tinker 35.00 60.00
38 Honus Wagner 250.00 400.00
39 Ed Walsh 35.00 60.00
40 Zack Wheat 30.00 50.00
41 Ivy Wingo 15.00 25.00
42 Joe Wood 30.00 50.00
43 Cy Young 90.00 150.00
A1 Batter Swinging, Looking Forward
A2 Batter Swinging, Looking Back
A3 Runner Sliding, Fielder at Bag
A4 Runner Sliding, Umpire Behind
A5 Runner Sliding, Hugging Base
A6 Sliding Play at Plate, Umpire Left
A7 Sliding Play at Plate, Umpire Right
A8 Play at Plate, Runner Standing
A9 Runner Looking Backwards

1948 Topps Magic Photos

The 1948 Topps Magic Photos set contains 252 small (approximately 7/8" by 1 7/16") individual cards featuring sport and non-sport subjects. They were issued in 19 lettered series with cards numbered within each series. The fronts were developed, much like a photograph, from a "blank" appearance by using moisture and sunlight. Due to varying degrees of photographic sensitivity, the clarity of these cards ranges from fully developed to poorly developed. This set contains Topps' first baseball cards. A premium album holding 126-cards was also issued. The set is sometimes confused with Topps' 1956 Hocus-Focus set, although the cards in this set are slightly smaller than those in the Hocus-Focus set. The checklist below is presented by series. Poorly developed cards are considered in lesser condition and hence have lesser value. The catalog designation for this set is R714-27. Each type of card subject has a letter prefix as follows: Boxing Champions (A), All-American Basketball (B), All-American Football (C), Wrestling Champions (D), Track and Field Champions (E), Stars of Stage and Screen (F), American Dogs (G), General Sports (H), Movie Stars (J), Baseball Hall of Fame (K), Aviation Pioneers (L), Famous Landmarks (M), American Inventors (N), American Military Leaders (O), American Explorers (P), Basketball Thrills (Q), Football Thrills (R), Figures of the Wild West (S), and General Sports (T).

COMPLETE SET (252) 3,000.00 5,000.00
K1 Lou Boudreau 30.00 60.00
K2 Cleveland Indians 20.00 40.00
K3 Bob Elliott 7.50 15.00
K4 Cleveland Indians 4-3 7.50 15.00
K5 Cleveland Indians 4-1 10.00 20.00
K6 Babe Ruth 714 300.00 500.00
K7 Tris Speaker 793 40.00 80.00
K8 Rogers Hornsby 60.00 120.00
K9 Connie Mack 60.00 120.00
K10 Christy Mathewson 90.00 150.00
K11 Hans Wagner 90.00 150.00
K12 Grover Alexander 60.00 120.00
K13 Ty Cobb 175.00 350.00
K14 Lou Gehrig 175.00 350.00
K15 Walter Johnson 100.00 200.00
K16 Cy Young 90.00 150.00
K17 George Sisler 257 40.00 80.00
K18 Tinker and Evers 40.00 80.00
K19 Third Base& 10.00 20.00

1951 Topps Blue Backs

The cards in this 52-card set measure approximately 2" by 2 5/8". The 1951 Topps series of blue-backed baseball cards could be used to play a baseball game by shuffling the cards and drawing them from a pile. These cards (packaged two adjoined in a penny pack) were marketed with a piece of caramel candy, which often melted or was squashed in such a way as to damage the card and wrapper (despite the fact that a paper shield was inserted between candy and card). Blue Backs are more difficult to obtain than the similarly styled Red Backs. The set is denoted on the cards as "Set B" and the Red Back set is correspondingly Set A. The only notable Rookie Card in the set is Billy Pierce.

COMPLETE SET (52) 800.00 1,500.00
WRAPPER (1-CENT) 150.00 200.00
1 Eddie Yost 35.00 60.00
2 Hank Majeski 15.00 30.00
3 Richie Ashburn 125.00 200.00
4 Del Ennis 15.00 30.00
5 Johnny Pesky 15.00 30.00
6 Red Schoendienst 60.00 100.00
7 Gerry Staley RC 15.00 30.00
8 Dick Sisler 15.00 30.00
9 Johnny Sain 30.00 50.00
10 Joe Page 30.00 50.00
11 Johnny Groth 15.00 30.00
12 Sam Jethroe 20.00 40.00
13 Mickey Vernon 15.00 30.00
14 George Munger 15.00 30.00
15 Eddie Joost 15.00 30.00
16 Murry Dickson 15.00 30.00
17 Roy Smalley 15.00 30.00
18 Ned Garver 15.00 30.00
19 Phil Masi 15.00 30.00
20 Ralph Branca 30.00 50.00
21 Billy Johnson 15.00 30.00
22 Bob Kuzava 15.00 30.00
23 Dizzy Trout 20.00 40.00
24 Sherman Lollar 15.00 30.00
25 Sam Mele 15.00 30.00
26 Chico Carrasquel RC 20.00 40.00
27 Andy Pafko 15.00 30.00
28 Harry Brecheen 15.00 30.00
29 Granville Hamner 15.00 30.00
30 Enos Slaughter 60.00 100.00
31 Lou Brissie 15.00 30.00
32 Bob Elliott 20.00 40.00
33 Don Lenhardt RC 15.00 30.00
34 Earl Torgeson 15.00 30.00
35 Tommy Byrne RC 15.00 30.00
36 Cliff Fannin 15.00 30.00
37 Bobby Doerr 60.00 100.00
38 Irv Noren 15.00 30.00
39 Ed Lopat 30.00 50.00
40 Vic Wertz 15.00 30.00
41 Johnny Schmitz 15.00 30.00
42 Bruce Edwards 15.00 30.00
43 Willie Jones 15.00 30.00
44 Johnny Wyrostek 15.00 30.00
45 Billy Pierce RC 30.00 50.00
46 Gerry Priddy 15.00 30.00
47 Herman Wehmeier 15.00 30.00
48 Billy Cox 20.00 40.00
49 Hank Sauer 20.00 40.00
50 Johnny Mize 60.00 100.00
51 Eddie Waitkus 20.00 40.00
52 Sam Chapman 30.00 50.00

1951 Topps Red Backs

The cards in this 52-card set measure approximately 2" by 2 5/8". The 1951 Topps Red Back set is identical in style to the Blue Back set of the same year. The cards have rounded corners and were designed to be used as a baseball game. Zernial, number 36, is listed with either the White Sox or Athletics, and Holmes, number 52, with either the Braves or Hartford. The set is denoted on the cards as "Set A" and the Blue Back set is correspondingly Set B. The cards were packaged as two connected cards along with a piece of caramel in a penny pack. There were 120 penny packs in a box. The most notable Rookie Card in the set is Monte Irvin.

COMPLETE SET (54) 400.00 800.00
WRAPPER (1-CENT) 4.00 5.00
1 Yogi Berra 100.00 250.00
2 Sid Gordon 5.00 10.00
3 Ferris Fain 6.00 12.00
4 Vern Stephens 6.00 12.00
5 Phil Rizzuto 35.00 60.00
6 Allie Reynolds 10.00 20.00
7 Howie Pollet 5.00 10.00
8 Early Wynn 12.50 25.00
9 Roy Sievers 7.50 15.00
10 Mel Parnell 6.00 15.00
11 Gene Hermanski 6.00 15.00
12 Jim Hegan 6.00 15.00
13 Dale Mitchell 6.00 15.00
14 Wayne Terwilliger 5.00 12.00
15 Ralph Kiner 12.50 25.00
16 Preacher Roe 7.50 15.00
17 Gus Bell RC 7.50 15.00
18 Jerry Coleman 7.50 15.00
19 Dick Kokos 5.00 10.00
20 Dom DiMaggio 10.00 20.00
21 Larry Jansen 6.00 12.00
22 Bob Feller 30.00 80.00
23 Ray Boone RC 7.50 15.00
24 Hank Bauer 10.00 20.00
25 Cliff Chambers 5.00 10.00
26 Luke Easter RC 7.50 15.00
27 Wally Westlake 6.00 12.00
28 Elmer Valo 5.00 10.00
29 Bob Kennedy RC 6.00 12.00
30 Warren Spahn 35.00 60.00
31 Gil Hodges 30.00 50.00
32 Henry Thompson 6.00 12.00
33 William Werle 5.00 10.00
34 Grady Hatton 5.00 10.00
35 Al Rosen 7.50 15.00
36A Gus Zernial Chic 20.00 40.00
36B Gus Zernial Phila 10.00 20.00
37 Wes Westrum RC 6.00 12.00
38 Duke Snider 35.00 60.00
39 Ted Kluszewski 12.50 25.00
40 Mike Garcia 7.50 15.00
41 Whitey Lockman 6.00 12.00
42 Ray Scarborough 5.00 10.00
43 Maurice McDermott 5.00 10.00
44 Sid Hudson 5.00 10.00
45 Andy Seminick 6.00 12.00
46 Billy Goodman 6.00 12.00
47 Tommy Glaviano RC 6.00 12.00
48 Eddie Stanky 6.00 12.00
49 Al Zarilla 5.00 10.00
50 Monte Irvin RC 20.00 40.00
51 Eddie Robinson 5.00 10.00
52A T.Holmes Boston 20.00 40.00
52B T.Holmes Hartford 12.50 25.00

1951 Topps Connie Mack's All-Stars

The cards in this 11-card set measure approximately 2 1/16" by 5 1/4". The series of die-cut cards which comprise the set entitled Connie Mack All-Stars was one of Topps' most distinctive and fragile card designs. Printed on thin cardboard, these elegant cards were protected in the wrapper by panels of accompanying Red Backs, but once removed were easily damaged (after all, they were intended to be folded and used as toy figures). Cards without tops have a value less than one-half of that listed below. The cards are unnumbered and are listed below in alphabetical order.

COMPLETE SET (11) 3,000.00 6,000.00
WRAPPER (5-CENT) 300.00 350.00
CARDS PRICED IN EX CONDITION
1 Grover C. Alexander 250.00 500.00
2 Mickey Cochrane 150.00 300.00
3 Eddie Collins 150.00 300.00
4 Jimmy Collins 150.00 300.00
5 Lou Gehrig 1,000.00 1,500.00
6 Walter Johnson 400.00 800.00
7 Connie Mack 250.00 500.00
8 Christy Mathewson 400.00 800.00
9 Babe Ruth 1,500.00 2,000.00
10 Tris Speaker 200.00 400.00
11 Honus Wagner 300.00 600.00

1951 Topps Major League All-Stars

The cards in this 11-card set measure approximately 2 1/16" by 5 1/4". The 1951 Topps Current All-Star series is probably the rarest of all legitimate, nationally issued, post war baseball issues. The set price listed below does not include the prices for the cards of Konstanty, Roberts and Stanky, which likely never were released to the public in gum packs. These three cards (SP in the checklist below) were probably obtained directly from the company and exist in extremely limited numbers. As with the Connie Mack set, cards without the die-cut background are worth half of the value listed below. The cards are unnumbered and are listed below in alphabetical order. These cards were issued in two card packs (one being a Current AS the other being a Topps Team card).

COMP.SET w/o SP's (8) 2,000.00 4,000.00
WRAPPER (5-CENT) 400.00 500.00
1 Yogi Berra 1,000.00 1,500.00
2 Larry Doby 250.00 400.00
3 Walt Dropo 150.00 250.00
4 Hoot Evers 150.00 250.00
5 George Kell 350.00 600.00
6 Ralph Kiner 450.00 750.00
7 Jim Konstanty SP 7,500.00 12,500.00
8 Bob Lemon 350.00 600.00
9 Phil Rizzuto 500.00 800.00
10 Robin Roberts SP 9,000.00 15,000.00
11 Eddie Stanky SP 7,500.00 12,500.00

1951 Topps Teams

The cards in this nine-card set measure approximately 2 1/16" by 5 1/4". These unnumbered team cards issued by Topps in 1951 carry black and white photographs framed by a yellow border. These cards were issued in the same five-cent wrapper as the Connie Mack and Current All Stars. They have been assigned reference numbers in the checklist alphabetically by team city and name. They are found with or without "1950" printed in the name panel before the team name. Although the dated variations are slightly more difficult to find, there is usually no difference in value.

COMPLETE SET (9) 1,500.00 3,000.00
1 Boston Red Sox 250.00 500.00
2 Brooklyn Dodgers 250.00 500.00
3 Chicago White Sox 150.00 300.00
4 Cincinnati Reds 150.00 300.00
5 New York Giants 200.00 400.00
6 Philadelphia Athletics 150.00 300.00
7 Philadelphia Phillies 150.00 300.00
8 St. Louis Cardinals 250.00 500.00
9 Washington Senators 150.00 300.00

1952 Topps

The cards in this 407-card set measure approximately 2 5/8" by 3 3/4". The 1952 Topps set is Topps' first truly major set. Card numbers 1 to 80 were issued with red or black backs, both of which are less plentiful than card numbers 81 to 250. In fact, the first series is considered the most difficult with respect to finding perfect condition cards. Card number 48 (Joe Page) and number 49 (Johnny Sain) can be found with each other's write-up on their back. However, many dealers today believe that all cards numbered 1-250 were produced in the same quantities. Card numbers 251 to 310 are somewhat scarce and numbers 311 to 407 are quite scarce. Cards 281-300 were single printed compared to the other cards in the next to last series. Cards 311-313 were double printed on the last high number printing sheet. The key card in the set is Mickey Mantle, number 311, which was Mickey's first of many Topps cards. A minor variation on cards from 311 through 313 is that they exist with the stitching on the number circle in the back pointing right or left. There seems to be no print run difference between the two versions. Card number 307, Frank Campos, can be found in a scarce version with with one red star and one black star next to the words "Topps Baseball" on the back. In the early 1980's, Topps issued a standard-size reprint set of the 52 Topps set. These cards were issued only as a factory set. Five people portrayed in the regular set: Billy Loes (number 20), Dom DiMaggio (number 22), Saul Rogovin (number 159), Solly Hemus (number 196) and Tommy Holmes (number 289) are not in the reprint set. Although rarely seen, salesman sample panels of three cards containing the fronts of regular cards with ad information on the back do exist.

COMP.MASTER SET (487) 100,000.00 200,000.00
COMPLETE SET (407) 75,000.00 150,000.00
COMMON CARD (1-80) 35.00 60.00
COMMON CARD (81-250) 20.00 40.00
COMMON CARD (251-310) 30.00 50.00
COMMON CARD (311-407) 150.00 250.00
WRAPPER (1-CENT) 200.00 250.00
WRAPPER (5-CENT) 75.00 100.00
1 Andy Pafko 3,000.00 5,000.00
1A Andy Pafko Black 1,800.00 3,000.00
2 Pete Runnels RC 150.00 250.00
2A Pete Runnels Black RC 150.00 250.00
3 Hank Thompson 40.00 70.00
3A Hank Thompson Black 40.00 70.00
4 Don Lenhardt 60.00 150.00
4A Don Lenhardt Black 50.00 120.00
5 c 50.00 120.00
5A Larry Jansen Black 50.00 120.00
6 Grady Hatton 35.00 60.00
6A Grady Hatton Black 35.00 60.00
7 Wayne Terwilliger 35.00 60.00
7A Wayne Terwilliger Black 35.00 60.00
8 Fred Marsh RC 40.00 100.00
8A Fred Marsh Black RC 40.00 100.00
9 Robert Hogue RC 35.00 60.00
9A Robert Hogue Black RC 35.00 60.00
10 Al Rosen 40.00 70.00
10A Al Rosen Black 40.00 70.00
11 Phil Rizzuto 250.00 400.00
11A Phil Rizzuto Black 200.00 350.00
12 Monty Basgall RC 35.00 60.00
12A Monty Basgall Black RC 35.00 60.00
13 Johnny Wyrostek 40.00 100.00
13A Johnny Wyrostek Black 40.00 100.00
14 Bob Elliott 40.00 70.00
14A Bob Elliott Black 40.00 70.00
15 Johnny Pesky 40.00 70.00
15A Johnny Pesky Black 40.00 70.00
16 Gene Hermanski 35.00 60.00
16A Gene Hermanski Black 35.00 60.00
17 Jim Hegan 40.00 70.00
17A Jim Hegan Black 40.00 70.00
18 Merrill Combs RC 35.00 60.00
18A Merrill Combs Black RC 35.00 60.00
19 Johnny Bucha RC 35.00 60.00
19A Johnny Bucha Black RC 35.00 60.00
20 Billy Loes SP RC 90.00 150.00
20A Billy Loes Black RC 90.00 150.00
21 Ferris Fain 40.00 70.00
21A Ferris Fain Black 40.00 70.00

Card	Low	High
22 Dom DiMaggio	75.00	125.00
22A Dom DiMaggio Black	60.00	100.00
23 Billy Goodman	40.00	70.00
23A Billy Goodman Black	40.00	70.00
24 Luke Easter	50.00	80.00
24A Luke Easter Black	50.00	80.00
25 Johnny Groth	35.00	60.00
25A Johnny Groth Black	35.00	60.00
26 Monte Irvin	75.00	200.00
26A Monte Irvin Black	75.00	200.00
27 Sam Jethroe	40.00	70.00
27A Sam Jethroe Black	40.00	70.00
28 Jerry Priddy	40.00	100.00
28A Jerry Priddy Black	40.00	100.00
29 Ted Kluszewski	75.00	125.00
29A Ted Kluszewski Black	75.00	125.00
30 Mel Parnell	40.00	70.00
30A Mel Parnell Black	40.00	70.00
31 Gus Zernial Baseballs	50.00	80.00
31A Gus Zernial Black	50.00	80.00
Posed with six baseballs		
32 Eddie Robinson	35.00	60.00
32A Eddie Robinson Black	35.00	60.00
33 Warren Spahn	175.00	300.00
33A Warren Spahn Black	175.00	300.00
34 Elmer Valo	40.00	100.00
34A Elmer Valo Black	40.00	100.00
35 Hank Sauer	40.00	70.00
35A Hank Sauer Black	40.00	70.00
36 Gil Hodges	200.00	400.00
36A Gil Hodges Black	200.00	400.00
37 Duke Snider	150.00	400.00
37A Duke Snider Black	150.00	400.00
38 Wally Westlake	35.00	60.00
38A Wally Westlake Black	35.00	60.00
39 Dizzy Trout	40.00	70.00
39A Dizzy Trout Black	40.00	70.00
40 Irv Noren	40.00	70.00
40A Irv Noren Black	40.00	70.00
41 Bob Wellman RC	35.00	60.00
41A Bob Wellman Black RC	35.00	60.00
42 Lou Kretlow RC	35.00	60.00
42A Lou Kretlow Black RC	35.00	60.00
43 Ray Scarborough	35.00	60.00
43A Ray Scarborough Black	35.00	60.00
44 Con Dempsey RC	35.00	60.00
44A Con Dempsey Black RC	35.00	60.00
45 Eddie Joost	35.00	60.00
45A Eddie Joost Black	35.00	60.00
46 Gordon Goldsberry RC	35.00	60.00
46A Gordon Goldsberry Black RC	35.00	60.00
47 Willie Jones	40.00	70.00
47A Willie Jones Black	40.00	70.00
48A Joe Page ERR BLA	250.00	400.00
48B Joe Page COR BLA	75.00	125.00
48C Joe Page COR Red	75.00	125.00
49A John Sain ERR BLA	250.00	400.00
49B John Sain COR BLA	75.00	125.00
49C Joe Page COR Red	75.00	125.00
50 Marv Rickert RC	35.00	60.00
50A Marv Rickert Black RC	35.00	60.00
51 Jim Russell	35.00	60.00
51A Jim Russell Black	35.00	60.00
52 Don Mueller	40.00	70.00
52A Don Mueller Black	40.00	70.00
53 Chris Van Cuyk RC	30.00	80.00
53A Chris Van Cuyk Black RC	30.00	80.00
54 Leo Kiely RC	40.00	100.00
54A Leo Kiely Black RC	35.00	60.00
55 Ray Boone	50.00	80.00
55A Ray Boone Black	50.00	80.00
56 Tommy Glaviano	35.00	60.00
56A Tommy Glaviano Black	35.00	60.00
57 Ed Lopat	60.00	100.00
57A Ed Lopat Black	60.00	100.00
58 Bob Mahoney RC	35.00	60.00
58A Bob Mahoney Black RC	35.00	60.00
59 Robin Roberts	75.00	200.00
59A Robin Roberts Black	75.00	200.00
60 Sid Hudson	35.00	60.00
60A Sid Hudson Black	35.00	60.00
61 Tookie Gilbert	35.00	60.00
61A Tookie Gilbert Black	35.00	60.00
62 Chuck Stobbs RC	35.00	60.00
62A Chuck Stobbs Black RC	35.00	60.00
63 Howie Pollet	50.00	120.00
63A Howie Pollet Black	50.00	120.00
64 Roy Sievers	40.00	70.00
64A Roy Sievers Black	40.00	70.00
65 Enos Slaughter	75.00	200.00
65A Enos Slaughter Black	75.00	200.00
66 Preacher Roe	60.00	100.00
66A Preacher Roe Black	60.00	100.00
67 Allie Reynolds	75.00	125.00
67A Allie Reynolds Black	75.00	125.00
68 Cliff Chambers	35.00	60.00
68A Cliff Chambers Black	35.00	60.00
69 Virgil Stallcup	35.00	60.00
69A Virgil Stallcup Black	35.00	60.00
70 Al Zarilla	35.00	60.00
70A Al Zarilla Black	35.00	60.00
71 Tom Upton RC	35.00	60.00
71A Tom Upton Black RC	35.00	60.00
72 Karl Olson RC	35.00	60.00
72A Karl Olson Black RC	35.00	60.00
73 Bill Werle	35.00	60.00
73A Bill Werle Black	35.00	60.00
74 Andy Hansen RC	35.00	60.00
74A Andy Hansen Black RC	35.00	60.00
75 Wes Westrum	40.00	70.00
75A Wes Westrum Black	40.00	70.00
76 Eddie Stanky	50.00	120.00
76A Eddie Stanky Black	40.00	70.00
77 Bob Kennedy	40.00	70.00
77A Bob Kennedy Black	40.00	70.00
78 Ellis Kinder	40.00	100.00
78A Ellis Kinder Black	40.00	100.00
79 Gerry Staley	35.00	60.00
79A Gerry Staley Black	35.00	60.00
80 Herman Wehmeier	50.00	80.00
80A Herman Wehmeier Black	50.00	80.00
81 Vernon Law	50.00	80.00
82 Duane Pillette	20.00	40.00
83 Billy Johnson	20.00	40.00
84 Vern Stephens	30.00	50.00
85 Bob Kuzava	30.00	50.00
86 Ted Gray	20.00	40.00
87 Dale Coogan	20.00	50.00
88 Bob Feller	150.00	300.00
89 Johnny Lipon	20.00	50.00
90 Mickey Grasso	20.00	40.00
91 Red Schoendienst	60.00	150.00
92 Dale Mitchell	30.00	50.00
93 Al Sima RC	20.00	40.00
94 Sam Mele	20.00	40.00
95 Ken Holcombe	25.00	60.00
96 Willard Marshall	20.00	40.00
97 Earl Torgeson	25.00	60.00
98 Billy Pierce	30.00	50.00
99 Gene Woodling	35.00	60.00
100 Del Rice	30.00	80.00
101 Max Lanier	20.00	40.00
102 Bill Kennedy	20.00	40.00
103 Cliff Mapes	20.00	50.00
104 Don Kolloway	20.00	50.00
105 Johnny Pramesa	20.00	40.00
106 Mickey Vernon	20.00	50.00
107 Connie Ryan	20.00	40.00
108 Jim Konstanty	35.00	60.00
109 Ted Wilks	20.00	50.00
110 Dutch Leonard	20.00	40.00
111 Peanuts Lowrey	20.00	40.00
112 Hank Majeski	20.00	40.00
113 Dick Sisler	30.00	50.00
114 Willard Ramsdell	20.00	40.00
115 George Munger	20.00	50.00
116 Carl Scheib	20.00	40.00
117 Sherm Lollar	30.00	50.00
118 Ken Raffensberger	20.00	40.00
119 Mickey McDermott	20.00	40.00
120 Bob Chakales RC	25.00	60.00
121 Gus Niarhos	20.00	40.00
122 Jackie Jensen	50.00	80.00
123 Eddie Yost	30.00	50.00
124 Monte Kennedy	20.00	50.00
125 Bill Rigney	20.00	40.00
126 Fred Hutchinson	30.00	50.00
127 Paul Minner RC	20.00	40.00
128 Don Bollweg RC	20.00	40.00
129 Johnny Mize	60.00	150.00
130 Sheldon Jones	25.00	60.00
131 Morrie Martin RC	20.00	40.00
132 Clyde Kluttz RC	20.00	40.00
133 Al Widmar	20.00	40.00
134 Joe Tipton	20.00	40.00
135 Dixie Howell	20.00	40.00
136 Johnny Schmitz	20.00	40.00
137 Roy McMillan RC	30.00	50.00
138 Bill MacDonald	20.00	40.00
139 Ken Wood	20.00	40.00
140 Johnny Antonelli	35.00	60.00
141 Clint Hartung	20.00	40.00
142 Harry Perkowski RC	20.00	40.00
143 Les Moss	20.00	40.00
144 Ed Blake RC	20.00	40.00
145 Joe Haynes	20.00	40.00
146 Frank House RC	20.00	40.00
147 Bob Young RC	20.00	40.00
148 Johnny Klippstein	20.00	40.00
149 Dick Kryhoski	20.00	40.00
150 Ted Beard	20.00	40.00
151 Wally Post RC	30.00	50.00
152 Al Evans	20.00	40.00
153 Bob Rush	20.00	40.00
154 Joe Muir RC	20.00	40.00
155 Frank Overmire	20.00	40.00
156 Frank Hiller RC	20.00	40.00
157 Bob Usher	20.00	40.00
158 Eddie Waitkus	20.00	40.00
159 Saul Rogovin RC	20.00	40.00
160 Owen Friend	20.00	40.00
161 Bud Byerly RC	20.00	40.00
162 Del Crandall	30.00	50.00
163 Stan Rojek	20.00	40.00
164 Walt Dubiel	20.00	40.00
165 Eddie Kazak	20.00	40.00
166 Paul LaPalme RC	20.00	40.00
167 Bill Howerton	20.00	40.00
168 Charlie Silvera RC	35.00	60.00
169 Howie Judson	20.00	40.00
170 Gus Bell	30.00	50.00
171 Ed Erautt RC	20.00	40.00
172 Eddie Miksis	30.00	80.00
173 Roy Smalley	20.00	40.00
174 Clarence Marshall RC	35.00	60.00
175 Billy Martin RC	300.00	500.00
176 Hank Edwards	20.00	40.00
177 Bill Wight	20.00	40.00
178 Cass Michaels	20.00	40.00
179 Frank Smith RC	20.00	40.00
180 Charlie Maxwell RC	30.00	50.00
181 Bob Swift	20.00	40.00
182 Billy Hitchcock	20.00	40.00
183 Erv Dusak	20.00	40.00
184 Bob Ramazzotti	20.00	40.00
185 Bill Nicholson	30.00	50.00
186 Walt Masterson	20.00	40.00
187 Bob Miller	20.00	40.00
188 Clarence Podbielan RC	20.00	40.00
189 Pete Reiser	35.00	60.00
190 Don Johnson RC	20.00	40.00
191 Yogi Berra	500.00	800.00
192 Myron Ginsberg RC	30.00	80.00
193 Harry Simpson RC	30.00	50.00
194 Joe Hatten	20.00	40.00
195 Minnie Minoso RC	100.00	250.00
196 Solly Hemus RC	35.00	60.00
197 George Strickland RC	20.00	40.00
198 Phil Haugstad RC	20.00	40.00
199 George Zuverink RC	20.00	40.00
200 Ralph Houk RC	50.00	80.00
201 Alex Kellner	20.00	50.00
202 Joe Collins RC	30.00	80.00
203 Curt Simmons	35.00	60.00
204 Ron Northey	20.00	40.00
205 Clyde King	35.00	60.00
206 Joe Ostrowski RC	20.00	40.00
207 Mickey Harris	20.00	40.00
208 Marlin Stuart RC	20.00	40.00
209 Howie Fox	20.00	40.00
210 Dick Fowler	20.00	40.00
211 Ray Coleman	20.00	40.00
212 Ned Garver	20.00	40.00
213 Nippy Jones	20.00	40.00
214 Johnny Hopp	30.00	50.00
215 Hank Bauer	40.00	100.00
216 Richie Ashburn	75.00	200.00
217 Snuffy Stirnweiss	30.00	50.00
218 Clyde McCullough	20.00	40.00
219 Bobby Shantz	35.00	60.00
220 Joe Presko RC	20.00	50.00
221 Granny Hamner	20.00	40.00
222 Hoot Evers	20.00	40.00
223 Del Ennis	30.00	50.00
224 Bruce Edwards	20.00	40.00
225 Frank Baumholtz	20.00	40.00
226 Dave Philley	20.00	40.00
227 Joe Garagiola	40.00	100.00
228 Al Brazle	20.00	40.00
229 Gene Bearden UER	20.00	40.00
230 Matt Batts	20.00	40.00
231 Sam Zoldak	20.00	50.00
232 Billy Cox	30.00	50.00
233 Bob Friend RC	50.00	80.00
234 Steve Souchock RC	20.00	40.00
235 Walt Dropo	25.00	60.00
236 Ed Fitzgerald	20.00	40.00
237 Jerry Coleman	30.00	80.00
238 Art Houtteman	20.00	40.00
239 Rocky Bridges RC	30.00	50.00
240 Jack Phillips RC	20.00	50.00
241 Tommy Byrne	25.00	60.00
242 Tom Poholsky RC	20.00	40.00
243 Larry Doby	50.00	120.00
244 Vic Wertz	20.00	40.00
245 Sherry Robertson	20.00	40.00
246 George Kell	40.00	100.00
247 Randy Gumpert	20.00	40.00
248 Frank Shea	20.00	40.00
249 Bobby Adams	20.00	40.00
250 Carl Erskine	50.00	120.00
251 Chico Carrasquel	30.00	50.00
252 Vern Bickford	30.00	50.00
253 Johnny Berardino	30.00	80.00
254 Joe Dobson	30.00	50.00
255 Clyde Vollmer	30.00	50.00
256 Pete Suder	30.00	50.00
257 Bobby Avila	40.00	100.00
258 Steve Gromek	35.00	60.00
259 Bob Addis RC	30.00	50.00
260 Pete Castiglione	30.00	50.00
261 Willie Mays	3,000.00	6,000.00
262 Virgil Trucks	30.00	80.00
263 Harry Brecheen	35.00	60.00
264 Roy Hartsfield	30.00	50.00
265 Chuck Diering	30.00	50.00
266 Murry Dickson	30.00	50.00
267 Sid Gordon	35.00	60.00
268 Bob Lemon	90.00	150.00
269 Willard Nixon	30.00	50.00
270 Lou Brissie	30.00	50.00
271 Jim Delsing	30.00	80.00
272 Mike Garcia	50.00	80.00
273 Erv Palica	30.00	50.00
274 Ralph Branca	75.00	125.00
275 Pat Mullin	30.00	50.00
276 Jim Wilson RC	30.00	50.00
277 Early Wynn	100.00	250.00
278 Allie Clark	30.00	80.00
279 Eddie Stewart	30.00	50.00
280 Cloyd Boyer	50.00	80.00
281 Tommy Brown SP	50.00	80.00
282 Birdie Tebbetts SP	50.00	80.00
283 Phil Masi SP	35.00	60.00
284 Hank Arft SP	35.00	60.00
285 Cliff Fannin SP	40.00	100.00
286 Joe DeMaestri SP RC	35.00	60.00
287 Steve Bilko SP	30.00	80.00
288 Chet Nichols SP RC	50.00	80.00
289 Tommy Holmes SP	60.00	100.00
290 Joe Astroth SP	35.00	60.00
291 Gil Coan SP	35.00	60.00
292 Floyd Baker SP	35.00	60.00
293 Sibby Sisti SP	35.00	60.00
294 Walker Cooper SP	35.00	60.00
295 Phil Cavarretta SP	50.00	80.00
296 Red Rolfe MG SP	40.00	100.00
297 Andy Seminick SP	35.00	60.00
298 Bob Ross SP RC	35.00	60.00
299 Ray Murray SP RC	50.00	80.00
300 Barney McCosky SP	50.00	80.00
301 Bob Porterfield	30.00	50.00
302 Max Surkont RC	25.00	60.00
303 Harry Dorish	30.00	50.00
304 Sam Dente	30.00	50.00
305 Paul Richards MG	35.00	60.00
306 Lou Sleater RC	25.00	60.00
307 Frank Campos RC	30.00	50.00
Two red stars on back in copyright line		
307A Frank Campos Star		
307B Frank Campos RC		
Partial top left border on front		
308 Luis Aloma	30.00	50.00
309 Jim Busby	35.00	60.00
310 George Metkovich	60.00	100.00
311 Mickey Mantle DP	50,000.00	80,000.00
311B Mickey Mantle DP	50,000.00	80,000.00
312 Jackie Robinson	2,500.00	5,000.00
312B Jackie Robinson Stitch	2,500.00	5,000.00
313 Bobby Thomson DP	200.00	350.00
313B Bobby Thomson Stitch	200.00	350.00
314 Roy Campanella	1,500.00	2,500.00
315 Leo Durocher MG	350.00	600.00
316 Dave Williams RC	175.00	300.00
317 Conrado Marrero	175.00	300.00
318 Harold Gregg RC	175.00	300.00
319 Rube Walker RC	150.00	400.00
320 John Rutherford RC	175.00	300.00
321 Joe Black RC	350.00	500.00
322 Randy Jackson RC	175.00	300.00
323 Bubba Church	150.00	250.00
324 Warren Hacker	125.00	300.00
325 Bill Serena	175.00	300.00
326 George Shuba RC	350.00	500.00
327 Al Wilson RC	125.00	300.00
328 Bob Borkowski RC	175.00	300.00
329 Ike Delock RC	175.00	300.00
330 Turk Lown RC	175.00	300.00
331 Tom Morgan RC	175.00	300.00
332 Tony Bartirome RC	1,500.00	2,500.00
333 Pee Wee Reese	1,000.00	1,500.00
334 Wilmer Mizell RC	175.00	300.00
335 Ted Lepcio RC	150.00	250.00
336 Dave Koslo	150.00	250.00
337 Jim Hearn	175.00	300.00
338 Sal Yvars RC	175.00	300.00
339 Russ Meyer	175.00	300.00
340 Bob Hooper	175.00	300.00
341 Hal Jeffcoat	175.00	300.00
342 Clem Labine RC	350.00	500.00
343 Dick Gernert RC	150.00	250.00
344 Ewell Blackwell	175.00	300.00
345 Sammy White RC	150.00	250.00
346 George Spencer RC	150.00	250.00
347 Joe Adcock	250.00	400.00
348 Robert Kelly RC	150.00	250.00
349 Bob Cain	175.00	300.00
350 Cal Abrams	175.00	300.00
351 Alvin Dark	175.00	300.00
352 Karl Drews	175.00	300.00
353 Bobby Del Greco RC	175.00	300.00
354 Fred Hatfield RC	175.00	300.00
355 Bobby Morgan	175.00	300.00
356 Toby Atwell RC	175.00	300.00
357 Smoky Burgess	175.00	300.00
358 John Kucab RC	175.00	300.00
359 Dee Fondy RC	150.00	400.00
360 George Crowe RC	175.00	300.00
361 Bill Posedel CO	150.00	250.00
362 Ken Heintzelman	175.00	300.00
363 Dick Rozek RC	175.00	300.00
364 Clyde Sukeforth CO RC	175.00	300.00
365 Cookie Lavagetto CO	200.00	500.00
366 Dave Madison RC	150.00	250.00
367 Ben Thorpe RC	175.00	300.00
368 Ed Wright RC	175.00	300.00
369 Dick Groat RC	350.00	500.00
370 Billy Hoeft RC	250.00	600.00
371 Bobby Hofman	150.00	250.00
372 Gil McDougald RC	300.00	500.00
373 Jim Turner CO RC	250.00	400.00
374 Al Benton RC	150.00	250.00
375 John Merson RC	150.00	250.00
376 Faye Throneberry RC	150.00	250.00
377 Chuck Dressen MG	250.00	400.00
378 Leroy Fusselman RC	175.00	300.00
379 Joe Rossi RC	150.00	250.00
380 Clem Koshorek RC	150.00	250.00
381 Milton Stock CO RC	175.00	300.00
382 Sam Jones RC	200.00	350.00
383 Del Wilber RC	150.00	250.00
384 Frank Crosetti CO	300.00	500.00
385 Herman Franks CO RC	150.00	250.00
386 Ed Yuhas RC	175.00	300.00
387 Billy Meyer MG	150.00	250.00
388 Bob Chipman	150.00	250.00
389 Ben Wade RC	175.00	300.00
390 Rocky Nelson RC	175.00	300.00
391 Ben Chapman CO UER	150.00	250.00
392 Hoyt Wilhelm RC	800.00	1,500.00
393 Ebba St.Claire RC	175.00	300.00
394 Billy Herman CO	350.00	600.00
395 Jake Pitler CO	175.00	300.00
396 Dick Williams RC	300.00	500.00
397 Forrest Main RC	150.00	250.00
398 Hal Rice	150.00	250.00
399 Jim Fridley RC	150.00	250.00
400 Bill Dickey CO	500.00	1,200.00
401 Bob Schultz RC	175.00	300.00
402 Earl Harrist RC	175.00	300.00
403 Bill Miller RC	175.00	300.00
404 Dick Brodowski RC	175.00	300.00
405 Eddie Pellagrini	175.00	300.00
406 Joe Nuxhall RC	250.00	400.00
407 Eddie Mathews RC	3,000.00	8,000.00

1953 Topps

WILLIE MAYS

The cards in this 274-card set measure 2 5/8" by 3 3/4". Card number 69, Dick Brodowksi, features the first known drawing of a player during a night game. Although the last card is numbered 280, there are only 274 cards in the set since numbers 253, 261, 267, 268, 271, and 275 were never issued. The 1953 Topps series contains line drawings of players in full color. The name and team panel at the card base is easily damaged, making it very difficult to complete a mint set. The high number series, 221 to 280, was produced in shorter supply late in the year and hence is more difficult to complete than the lower numbers. The key cards in the set are Mickey Mantle (82) and Willie Mays (244). The key Rookie Cards in this set are Roy Face, Jim Gilliam, and Johnny Podres, all from the last series. There are a number of double-printed cards (actually not double but 50 percent more of each of these numbers were printed compared to the other cards in the series) indicated by DP in the checklist below. There were five players (10 Smoky Burgess, 44 Ellis Kinder, 61 Early Wynn, 72 Fred Hutchinson, and 81 Joe Black) held out of the first run of 1-85 (but printed in with numbers 86-165), who are each marked by SP in the checklist below. In addition, there are five numbers which were printed with the more plentiful series 166-220; these cards (94, 107, 131, 145, and 156) are also indicated by DP in the checklist below. All these aforementioned cards from 86 through 165 and the five short prints come with the biographical information on the back in either white or black lettering. These seem to be printed in equal quantities and no price differential is given for either variety. The cards were issued in one-card penny packs or six-card nickel packs. The nickel packs were issued 24 to a box. There were some three-card advertising panels produced by Topps; the players include Johnny Mize/Clem Koshorek/Toby Atwell; Jim Hearn/Johnny Groth/Sherman Lollar and Mickey Mantle/Johnny Wyrostek/

Card	Low	High
COMPLETE SET (274)	10,000.00	20,000.00
COMMON CARD (1-165)	15.00	30.00
COMMON DP (1-165)	7.50	15.00
COMMON CARD (166-220)	12.50	25.00
COMMON CARD (221-280)	50.00	100.00
NOT ISSUED (253/261/267)		
NOT ISSUED (268/271/275)		
WRAP.(1-CENT, DATED)	150.00	200.00
WRAP.(1-CENT,NO DATE)	250.00	300.00
WRAP.(5-CENT, DATED)	300.00	400.00
WRAP.(5-CENT,NO DATE)	275.00	350.00
1 Jackie Robinson DP	600.00	1,200.00
2 Luke Easter DP	10.00	20.00
3 George Crowe	25.00	40.00
4 Ben Wade	15.00	30.00
5 Joe Dobson	15.00	30.00
6 Sam Jones	25.00	40.00
7 Bob Borkowski DP	7.50	15.00
8 Clem Koshorek DP	7.50	15.00
9 Joe Collins	35.00	60.00
10 Smoky Burgess SP	50.00	80.00
11 Sal Yvars	15.00	30.00
12 Howie Judson DP	7.50	15.00
13 Conrado Marrero DP	12.00	30.00
14 Clem Labine DP	10.00	20.00
15 Bobo Newsom DP RC	10.00	20.00
16 Peanuts Lowrey DP	7.50	15.00
17 Billy Hitchcock	15.00	30.00
18 Ted Lepcio DP	7.50	15.00
19 Mel Parnell DP	10.00	20.00
20 Hank Thompson	25.00	40.00
21 Billy Johnson	15.00	30.00
22 Howie Fox	15.00	30.00
23 Toby Atwell DP	7.50	15.00
24 Ferris Fain	25.00	40.00
25 Ray Boone	25.00	40.00
26 Dale Mitchell DP	10.00	20.00
27 Roy Campanella DP	100.00	250.00
28 Eddie Pellagrini	15.00	30.00
29 Hal Jeffcoat	15.00	30.00
30 Willard Nixon	15.00	30.00
31 Ewell Blackwell	35.00	60.00
32 Clyde Vollmer	15.00	30.00
33 Bob Kennedy DP	12.00	30.00
34 George Shuba	25.00	40.00
35 Irv Noren DP	7.50	15.00
36 Johnny Groth DP	7.50	15.00
37 Eddie Mathews DP	75.00	200.00
38 Jim Hearn DP	7.50	15.00
39 Eddie Miksis	15.00	30.00
40 John Lipon	15.00	40.00
41 Enos Slaughter	40.00	100.00
42 Gus Zernial DP	10.00	20.00
43 Gil McDougald	35.00	60.00
44 Ellis Kinder SP	35.00	60.00
45 Grady Hatton DP	7.50	15.00
46 Johnny Klippstein DP	7.50	15.00
47 Bubba Church DP	7.50	15.00
48 Bob Del Greco DP	7.50	15.00
49 Faye Throneberry DP	7.50	15.00
50 Chuck Dressen MG DP	10.00	20.00
51 Frank Campos DP	7.50	15.00
52 Ted Gray DP	7.50	15.00
53 Sherm Lollar DP	10.00	20.00
54 Bob Feller DP	75.00	200.00
55 Maurice McDermott DP	7.50	15.00
56 Gerry Staley DP	7.50	15.00
57 Carl Scheib	15.00	30.00
58 George Metkovich	15.00	30.00
59 Karl Drews DP	7.50	15.00
60 Cloyd Boyer DP	7.50	15.00
61 Early Wynn SP	40.00	100.00
62 Monte Irvin DP	25.00	40.00
63 Gus Niarhos DP	7.50	15.00
64 Dave Philley	15.00	30.00
65 Earl Harrist	15.00	30.00
66 Minnie Minoso	35.00	60.00
67 Roy Sievers DP	10.00	20.00
68 Del Rice	15.00	30.00
69 Dick Brodowski	15.00	30.00
70 Ed Yuhas	15.00	30.00
71 Tony Bartirome	15.00	30.00
72 Fred Hutchinson SP	35.00	60.00
73 Eddie Robinson	15.00	30.00
74 Joe Rossi	15.00	30.00
75 Mike Garcia	25.00	40.00
76 Pee Wee Reese	75.00	200.00
77 Johnny Mize DP	40.00	100.00
78 Red Schoendienst	50.00	80.00
79 Johnny Wyrostek	15.00	30.00
80 Jim Hegan	25.00	40.00
81 Joe Black SP	50.00	80.00
82 Mickey Mantle	5,000.00	10,000.00
83 Howie Pollet	15.00	30.00
84 Bob Hooper DP	7.50	15.00
85 Bobby Morgan DP	7.50	15.00
86 Billy Martin	75.00	200.00
87 Ed Lopat	40.00	100.00
88 Willie Jones DP	7.50	15.00
89 Chuck Stobbs DP	7.50	15.00
90 Hank Edwards DP	7.50	15.00
91 Ebba St.Claire DP	15.00	40.00
92 Paul Minner DP	7.50	15.00
93 Hal Rice DP	7.50	15.00
94 Bill Kennedy DP	7.50	15.00
95 Willard Marshall DP	7.50	15.00
96 Virgil Trucks	25.00	40.00
97 Don Kolloway DP	12.00	30.00
98 Cal Abrams DP	7.50	15.00
99 Dave Madison	15.00	30.00
100 Bill Miller	15.00	30.00
101 Ted Wilks	15.00	30.00
102 Connie Ryan DP	7.50	15.00
103 Joe Astroth DP	7.50	15.00
104 Yogi Berra	250.00	400.00
105 Joe Nuxhall DP	10.00	20.00
106 Johnny Antonelli	25.00	40.00
107 Danny O'Connell DP	7.50	15.00
108 Bob Porterfield DP	12.00	30.00
109 Alvin Dark	35.00	60.00
110 Herman Wehmeier DP	7.50	15.00
111 Hank Sauer DP	15.00	40.00
112 Ned Garver DP	12.00	30.00
113 Jerry Priddy	15.00	30.00
114 Phil Rizzuto	100.00	250.00
115 George Spencer	15.00	30.00
116 Frank Smith DP	7.50	15.00
117 Sid Gordon DP	12.00	30.00
118 Gus Bell DP	10.00	20.00
119 Johnny Sain SP	40.00	100.00
120 Davey Williams	25.00	40.00
121 Walt Dropo	25.00	40.00
122 Elmer Valo	15.00	30.00
123 Tommy Byrne DP	12.00	30.00
124 Sibby Sisti DP	7.50	15.00
125 Dick Williams DP	10.00	20.00
126 Bill Connelly DP RC	7.50	15.00
127 Clint Courtney DP RC	7.50	15.00
128 Wilmer Mizell DP Inconsistent design, logo on front with black birds	10.00	20.00
129 Keith Thomas RC	15.00	30.00
130 Turk Lown DP	15.00	40.00
131 Harry Byrd DP RC	7.50	15.00
132 Tom Morgan	15.00	30.00
133 Gil Coan	15.00	30.00
134 Rube Walker	25.00	40.00
135 Al Rosen DP	10.00	20.00
136 Ken Heintzelman DP	7.50	15.00
137 John Rutherford DP	7.50	15.00
138 George Kell	50.00	80.00
139 Sammy White	15.00	30.00
140 Tommy Glaviano	15.00	30.00
141 Allie Reynolds DP	25.00	60.00
142 Vic Wertz	25.00	40.00
143 Billy Pierce	20.00	50.00
144 Bob Schultz DP	7.50	15.00
145 Harry Dorish DP	7.50	15.00
146 Granny Hamner	15.00	30.00
147 Warren Spahn	100.00	250.00
148 Mickey Grasso	15.00	30.00
149 Dom DiMaggio DP	20.00	50.00
150 Harry Simpson DP	12.00	30.00
151 Hoyt Wilhelm	60.00	100.00
152 Bob Adams DP	7.50	15.00
153 Andy Seminick DP	7.50	15.00
154 Dick Groat	40.00	100.00
155 Dutch Leonard	15.00	30.00
156 Jim Rivera DP RC	10.00	25.00
157 Bob Addis DP	15.00	40.00
158 Johnny Logan RC	20.00	50.00
159 Wayne Terwilliger DP	7.50	15.00
160 Bob Young	15.00	30.00
161 Vern Bickford DP	7.50	15.00
162 Ted Kluszewski	40.00	100.00
163 Fred Hatfield DP	7.50	15.00
164 Frank Shea DP	7.50	15.00
165 Billy Hoeft	15.00	30.00
166 Billy Hunter RC	15.00	40.00
167 Art Schult RC	15.00	40.00
168 Willard Schmidt RC	12.50	25.00
169 Dizzy Trout	15.00	30.00
170 Bill Werle	12.50	25.00
171 Bill Glynn RC	12.00	30.00
172 Rip Repulski RC	12.50	25.00
173 Preston Ward	12.50	25.00
174 Billy Loes	15.00	30.00
175 Ron Kline RC	12.50	25.00
176 Don Hoak RC	25.00	40.00
177 Jim Dyck RC	12.00	30.00
178 Jim Waugh RC	12.50	25.00
179 Gene Hermanski	12.50	25.00
180 Virgil Stallcup	12.50	25.00
181 Al Zarilla	12.50	25.00
182 Bobby Hofman	12.50	25.00
183 Stu Miller RC	25.00	40.00
184 Hal Brown RC	12.50	25.00
185 Jim Pendleton RC	12.50	25.00
186 Charlie Bishop RC	15.00	40.00
187 Jim Fridley	12.50	25.00
188 Andy Carey RC	25.00	60.00
189 Ray Jablonski RC	12.50	25.00
190 Dixie Walker CO	15.00	30.00
191 Ralph Kiner	50.00	120.00
192 Wally Westlake	12.00	30.00
193 Mike Clark RC	12.50	25.00
194 Eddie Kazak	12.50	25.00
195 Ed McGhee RC	12.50	25.00
196 Bob Keegan RC	12.50	25.00
197 Del Crandall	25.00	40.00
198 Forrest Main	12.50	25.00
199 Marion Fricano RC	12.50	25.00
200 Gordon Goldsberry	12.50	25.00
201 Paul LaPalme	12.50	25.00
202 Carl Sawatski RC	12.50	25.00
203 Cliff Fannin	12.50	25.00
204 Dick Bokelman RC	12.50	25.00
205 Vern Benson RC	12.50	25.00
206 Ed Bailey RC	15.00	30.00
207 Whitey Ford	100.00	250.00
208 Jim Wilson	12.00	30.00
209 Jim Greengrass RC	12.50	25.00
210 Bob Cerv RC	25.00	40.00
211 J.W. Porter RC	12.50	25.00
212 Jack Dittmer RC	15.00	40.00
213 Ray Scarborough	20.00	50.00
214 Bill Bruton RC	25.00	40.00
215 Gene Conley RC	15.00	30.00
216 Jim Hughes RC	12.50	25.00
217 Murray Wall RC	12.50	25.00
218 Les Fusselman	12.50	25.00
219 Pete Runnels UER Photo actually Don Johnson	15.00	30.00
220 Satchel Paige UER	500.00	1,000.00
221 Bob Milliken RC	50.00	100.00
222 Vic Janowicz DP RC	25.00	50.00
223 Johnny O'Brien DP RC	25.00	50.00
224 Lou Sleater DP	25.00	50.00
225 Bobby Shantz	75.00	125.00
226 Ed Erautt	50.00	100.00
227 Morrie Martin	50.00	100.00
228 Hal Newhouser	90.00	150.00
229 Rocky Krsnich RC	50.00	100.00
230 Johnny Lindell DP	25.00	50.00
231 Solly Hemus DP	25.00	50.00
232 Dick Kokos	50.00	100.00
233 Al Aber RC	50.00	100.00
234 Ray Murray DP	25.00	50.00
235 John Hetki DP RC	25.00	50.00
236 Harry Perkowski DP	25.00	50.00
237 Bud Podbielan DP	25.00	50.00
238 Cal Hogue DP RC	25.00	50.00
239 Jim Delsing	25.00	60.00
240 Fred Marsh	50.00	100.00
241 Al Sima DP	25.00	50.00
242 Charlie Silvera	75.00	125.00
243 Carlos Bernier DP RC	25.00	50.00
244 Willie Mays	2,000.00	4,000.00
245 Bill Norman CO	50.00	100.00
246 Roy Face RC DP RC	40.00	100.00
247 Mike Sandlock DP RC	25.00	50.00
248 Gene Stephens DP RC	25.00	50.00
249 Eddie O'Brien RC	50.00	100.00
250 Bob Wilson RC	50.00	100.00
251 Sid Hudson	75.00	200.00
252 Hank Foiles RC	50.00	100.00
254 Preacher Roe DP	50.00	80.00
255 Dixie Howell	50.00	100.00
256 Les Peden RC	50.00	100.00
257 Bob Boyd RC	50.00	100.00
258 Jim Gilliam RC	250.00	400.00
259 Roy McMillan DP	25.00	50.00
260 Sam Calderone RC	50.00	100.00
262 Bob Oldis RC	50.00	100.00
263 Johnny Podres RC	150.00	400.00
264 Gene Woodling DP	30.00	60.00
265 Jackie Jensen	75.00	125.00
266 Bob Cain	50.00	100.00
269 Duane Pillette	50.00	100.00
270 Vern Stephens	75.00	125.00
272 Bill Antonello RC	30.00	80.00
273 Harvey Haddix RC	100.00	250.00
274 John Riddle CO	50.00	100.00
276 Ken Raffensberger	50.00	100.00
277 Don Lund RC	50.00	100.00
278 Willie Miranda RC	50.00	100.00
279 Joe Coleman DP	25.00	50.00
280 Milt Bolling RC	200.00	350.00

1954 Topps

The cards in this 250-card set measure approximately 2 5/8" by 3 3/4". Each of the cards in the 1954 Topps set contains a large "head" shot of the player in color plus a smaller full-length photo in black and white set against a color background. The cards were issued in one-card penny packs or five-card nickel packs. Fifteen-card cello packs have also been seen. The penny packs came 120 to a box while the nickel packs came 24 to a box. The nickel boxes had a drawing of Ted Williams along with his name printed on the box to indicate that Williams was part of this product. This set contains the Rookie Cards of Hank Aaron, Ernie Banks, and Al Kaline and two separate cards of Ted Williams (number 1 and number 250). Conspicuous by his absence is Mickey Mantle who apparently was the exclusive property of Bowman during 1954 (and 1955). The first two issues of Sports Illustrated magazine contained "card" inserts on regular paper stock. The first issue showed actual cards in the set in color, while the second issue showed some created cards of New York Yankees players in black and white, including Mickey Mantle. There was also a Canadian printing of the first 50 cards. These cards can be easily discerned as they have "grey" backs rather than the white backs of the American printed cards. To celebrate this set as the first Topps set to feature Ted Williams, his visage is also featured on the five cent box. The Canadian cards came four cards to a pack and 36 packs to a box and cost five cents when issued.

Card	Low	High
COMPLETE SET (250)	6,000.00	12,000.00
COMMON (1-50/76-250)	7.50	15.00
COMMON CARD (51-75)	12.50	25.00
WRAP.(1-CENT, DATED)	150.00	200.00
WRAP.(1-CENT, UNDAT)	100.00	150.00
WRAP.(5-CENT, DATED)	250.00	300.00
WRAP.(5-CENT, UNDAT)	200.00	250.00
1 Ted Williams	400.00	800.00
2 Gus Zernial	12.50	25.00
3 Monte Irvin	30.00	80.00
4 Hank Sauer	12.50	25.00
5 Ed Lopat	12.50	25.00
6 Pete Runnels	12.50	25.00
7 Ted Kluszewski	15.00	40.00
8 Bob Young	7.50	15.00
9 Harvey Haddix	12.50	25.00
10 Jackie Robinson	250.00	600.00
11 Paul Leslie Smith RC	7.50	15.00
12 Del Crandall	12.50	25.00
13 Billy Martin	60.00	100.00
14 Preacher Roe UER	12.00	30.00
15 Al Rosen	12.50	25.00
16 Vic Janowicz	12.50	25.00
17 Phil Rizzuto	40.00	100.00
18 Walt Dropo	12.50	25.00
19 Johnny Lipon	7.50	15.00
20 Warren Spahn	75.00	125.00
21 Bobby Shantz	12.50	25.00
22 Jim Greengrass	7.50	15.00
23 Luke Easter	12.50	25.00
24 Granny Hamner	7.50	15.00
25 Harvey Kuenn RC	20.00	40.00
26 Ray Jablonski	7.50	15.00
27 Ferris Fain	12.50	25.00
28 Paul Minner	7.50	15.00
29 Jim Hegan	12.50	25.00
30 Eddie Mathews	50.00	120.00
31 Johnny Klippstein	7.50	15.00
32 Duke Snider	50.00	120.00
33 Johnny Schmitz	7.50	15.00
34 Jim Rivera	7.50	15.00
35 Junior Gilliam	25.00	50.00
36 Hoyt Wilhelm	25.00	60.00
37 Whitey Ford	60.00	150.00
38 Eddie Stanky MG	12.50	25.00
39 Sherm Lollar	12.50	25.00
40 Mel Parnell	12.50	25.00
41 Willie Jones	7.50	15.00
42 Don Mueller	12.50	25.00
43 Dick Groat	12.50	25.00
44 Ned Garver	7.50	15.00
45 Richie Ashburn	50.00	80.00
46 Ken Raffensberger	7.50	15.00
47 Ellis Kinder	7.50	15.00
48 Billy Hunter	12.50	25.00
49 Ray Murray	7.50	15.00
50 Yogi Berra	100.00	250.00
51 Johnny Lindell	12.50	25.00
52 Vic Power RC	15.00	30.00
53 Jack Dittmer	12.50	25.00
54 Vern Stephens	15.00	30.00
55 Phil Cavarretta MG	15.00	30.00
56 Willie Miranda	12.50	25.00
57 Luis Aloma	12.50	25.00
58 Bob Wilson	12.50	25.00
59 Gene Conley	15.00	30.00
60 Frank Baumholtz	12.50	25.00
61 Bob Cain	12.50	25.00
62 Eddie Robinson	12.50	25.00
63 Johnny Pesky	15.00	30.00
64 Hank Thompson	12.50	25.00
65 Bob Swift CO	12.50	25.00
66 Ted Lepcio	12.50	25.00
67 Jim Willis RC	12.50	25.00
68 Sam Calderone	12.50	25.00
69 Bud Podbielan	12.50	25.00
70 Larry Doby	50.00	120.00
71 Frank Smith	12.50	25.00
72 Preston Ward	12.50	25.00
73 Wayne Terwilliger	12.50	25.00
74 Bill Taylor RC	12.50	25.00
75 Fred Haney MG RC	12.50	25.00
76 Bob Scheffing CO	10.00	25.00
77 Ray Boone	12.50	25.00
78 Ted Kazanski RC	7.50	15.00
79 Andy Pafko	12.50	25.00
80 Jackie Jensen	12.50	25.00
81 Dave Hoskins RC	7.50	15.00
82 Milt Bolling	7.50	15.00
83 Joe Collins	12.00	30.00
84 Dick Cole RC	7.50	15.00
85 Bob Turley RC	20.00	40.00
86 Billy Herman CO	12.50	25.00
87 Roy Face	12.50	25.00
88 Matt Batts	7.50	15.00
89 Howie Pollet	7.50	15.00
90 Willie Mays	400.00	800.00
91 Bob Oldis	7.50	15.00
92 Wally Westlake	7.50	15.00
93 Sid Hudson	7.50	15.00
94 Ernie Banks RC	1,000.00	2,500.00
95 Hal Rice	7.50	15.00
96 Charlie Silvera	12.50	25.00

Card	Low	High
97 Jerald Hal Lane RC	7.50	15.00
98 Joe Black	20.00	40.00
99 Bobby Hofman	7.50	15.00
100 Bob Keegan	7.50	15.00
101 Gene Woodling	12.50	25.00
102 Gil Hodges	40.00	100.00
103 Jim Lemon RC	7.50	15.00
104 Mike Sandlock	7.50	15.00
105 Andy Carey	12.50	25.00
106 Dick Kokos	12.00	30.00
107 Duane Pillette	7.50	15.00
108 Thornton Kipper RC	7.50	15.00
109 Bill Bruton	12.50	25.00
110 Harry Dorish	7.50	15.00
111 Jim Delsing	7.50	15.00
112 Bill Renna RC	7.50	15.00
113 Bob Boyd	7.50	15.00
114 Dean Stone RC	7.50	15.00
115 Rip Repulski	7.50	15.00
116 Steve Bilko	7.50	15.00
117 Solly Hemus	7.50	15.00
118 Carl Scheib	7.50	15.00
119 Johnny Antonelli	12.50	25.00
120 Roy McMillan	12.50	25.00
121 Clem Labine	12.00	30.00
122 Johnny Logan	12.50	25.00
123 Bobby Adams	7.50	15.00
124 Marion Fricano	7.50	15.00
125 Harry Perkowski	7.50	15.00
126 Ben Wade	7.50	15.00
127 Steve O'Neill MG	7.50	15.00
128 Hank Aaron RC	2,500.00	5,000.00
129 Forrest Jacobs RC	7.50	15.00
130 Hank Bauer	12.50	25.00
131 Reno Bertoia RC	12.50	25.00
132 Tommy Lasorda RC	125.00	300.00
133 Del Baker CO	7.50	15.00
134 Cal Hogue	7.50	15.00
135 Joe Presko	7.50	15.00
136 Connie Ryan	7.50	15.00
137 Wally Moon RC	20.00	40.00
138 Bob Borkowski	7.50	15.00
139 J.O'Brien/E.O'Brien	25.00	50.00
140 Tom Wright	7.50	15.00
141 Joey Jay RC	12.50	25.00
142 Tom Poholsky	7.50	15.00
143 Rollie Hemsley CO	7.50	15.00
144 Bill Werle	7.50	15.00
145 Elmer Valo	7.50	15.00
146 Don Johnson	7.50	15.00
147 Johnny Riddle CO	7.50	15.00
148 Bob Trice RC	7.50	15.00
149 Al Robertson	7.50	15.00
150 Dick Kryhoski	7.50	15.00
151 Alex Grammas RC	7.50	15.00
152 Michael Blyzka RC	7.50	15.00
153 Al Walker	12.50	25.00
154 Mike Fornieles RC	7.50	15.00
155 Bob Kennedy	12.50	25.00
156 Joe Coleman	12.50	25.00
157 Don Lenhardt	12.50	25.00
158 Peanuts Lowrey	7.50	15.00
159 Dave Philley	7.50	15.00
160 Ralph Kress CO	7.50	15.00
161 John Hetki	7.50	15.00
162 Herman Wehmeier	7.50	15.00
163 Frank House	7.50	15.00
164 Stu Miller	12.50	25.00
165 Jim Pendleton	7.50	15.00
166 Johnny Podres	20.00	50.00
167 Don Lund	7.50	15.00
168 Morrie Martin	12.50	25.00
169 Jim Hughes	20.00	40.00
170 Dusty Rhodes RC	12.50	25.00
171 Leo Kiely	10.00	25.00
172 Harold Brown RC	7.50	15.00
173 Jack Harshman RC	7.50	15.00
174 Tom Qualters RC	7.50	15.00
175 Frank Leja RC	12.50	25.00
176 Robert Keely CO	12.00	30.00
177 Bob Milliken	7.50	15.00
178 Bill Glynn UER	7.50	15.00
179 Gair Allie RC	7.50	15.00
180 Wes Westrum	12.50	25.00
181 Mel Roach RC	7.50	15.00
182 Chuck Harmon RC	7.50	15.00
183 Earle Combs CO	12.50	25.00
184 Ed Bailey	7.50	15.00
185 Chuck Stobbs	7.50	15.00
186 Karl Olson	7.50	15.00
187 Heinie Manush CO	12.50	25.00
188 Dave Jolly RC	7.50	15.00
189 Bob Ross	7.50	15.00
190 Ray Herbert RC	7.50	15.00
191 Dick Schofield RC	12.50	25.00
192 Ellis Deal CO	7.50	15.00
193 Johnny Hopp CO	12.50	25.00
194 Bill Sarni RC	7.50	15.00
195 Billy Consolo RC	7.50	15.00
196 Stan Jok RC	7.50	15.00
197 Lynwood Rowe CO	12.50	25.00
198 Carl Sawatski	7.50	15.00
199 Glenn Rocky Nelson	7.50	15.00
200 Larry Jansen	12.50	25.00
201 Al Kaline RC	600.00	1,200.00
202 Bob Purkey RC	12.50	25.00
203 Harry Brecheen CO	12.50	25.00
204 Angel Scull RC	7.50	15.00
205 Johnny Sain	20.00	50.00
206 Ray Crone RC	7.50	15.00
207 Tom Oliver CO RC	7.50	15.00
208 Grady Hatton	7.50	15.00
209 Chuck Thompson RC	7.50	15.00
210 Bob Buhl RC	12.50	25.00
211 Don Hoak	12.50	25.00
212 Bob Micelotta RC	7.50	15.00
213 Johnny Fitzpatrick CO RC	7.50	15.00
214 Arnie Portocarrero RC	7.50	15.00
215 Ed McGhee	12.50	25.00
216 Al Sima	7.50	15.00
217 Paul Schreiber CO RC	7.50	15.00
218 Fred Marsh	7.50	15.00
219 Chuck Kress RC	7.50	15.00
220 Ruben Gomez RC	12.50	25.00
221 Dick Brodowski	7.50	15.00
222 Bill Wilson RC	7.50	15.00
223 Joe Haynes CO	12.00	30.00
224 Dick Weik RC	7.50	15.00
225 Don Liddle RC	7.50	15.00
226 Jehosie Heard RC	12.50	25.00
227 Buster Mills CO RC	7.50	15.00
228 Gene Hermanski	7.50	15.00
229 Bob Talbot RC	7.50	15.00
230 Bob Kuzava	12.50	25.00
231 Roy Smalley	7.50	15.00
232 Lou Limmer RC	7.50	15.00
233 Augie Galan CO	10.00	25.00
234 Jerry Lynch RC	7.50	15.00
235 Vern Law	12.50	25.00
236 Paul Penson RC	7.50	15.00
237 Mike Ryba CO RC	7.50	15.00
238 Al Aber	7.50	15.00
239 Bill Skowron RC	30.00	80.00
240 Sam Mele	12.50	25.00
241 Robert Miller RC	7.50	15.00
242 Curt Roberts RC	7.50	15.00
243 Ray Blades CO RC	7.50	15.00
244 Leroy Wheat RC	7.50	15.00
245 Roy Sievers	12.50	25.00
246 Howie Fox	7.50	15.00
247 Ed Mayo CO	7.50	15.00
248 Al Smith RC	12.50	25.00
249 Wilmer Mizell	12.50	25.00
250 Ted Williams	300.00	600.00

1955 Topps

The cards in this 206-card set measure approximately 2 5/8" by 3 3/4". Both the large "head" shot and the smaller full-length photos used on each card of the 1955 Topps set are in color. The card fronts were designed horizontally for the first time in Topps' history. The first card features Dusty Rhodes, hitting star and MVP in the New York Giants' 1954 World Series sweep over the Cleveland Indians. A "high" series, 161 to 210, is more difficult to find than cards 1 to 160. Numbers 175, 186, 203, and 209 were never issued. To fill in for the four cards not issued in the high number series, Topps double printed four players, those appearing on cards 170, 172, 184, and 188. Cards were issued in one-card penny packs or six-card nickel packs (which came 36 packs to a box) and 15-card cello packs (rarely seen). Although rarely seen, there exist salesman sample panels of three cards containing the fronts of regular cards with ad information for the 1955 Topps regular and the 1955 Topps Doubleheaders on the back. One panel depicts (from top to bottom) Danny Schell, Jake Thies, and Howie Pollet. Another Panel consists of Jackie Robinson, Bill Taylor and Curt Roberts. The key Rookie Cards in this set are Ken Boyer, Roberto Clemente, Harmon Killebrew, and Sandy Koufax.

The Frank Sullivan card has a very noticable print dot which appears on some of the cards but not all of the cards. We are not listing that card as a variation at this point, but we will continue to monitor information about that card.

Card	Low	High
COMPLETE SET (206)	6,000.00	12,000.00
COMMON CARD (1-150)	6.00	12.00
COMMON CARD (151-160)	10.00	20.00
COMMON CARD (161-210)	15.00	30.00
NOT ISSUED (175/186/203/209)		
WRAP.(1-CENT, DATED)	100.00	150.00
WRAP.(1-CENT, UNDAT)	40.00	50.00
WRAP.(5-CENT, DATED)	100.00	150.00
WRAP.(5-CENT, UNDAT)	75.00	100.00
1 Dusty Rhodes	25.00	60.00
2 Ted Williams	300.00	600.00
3 Art Fowler RC	7.50	15.00
4 Al Kaline	60.00	150.00
5 Jim Gilliam	20.00	50.00
6 Stan Hack MG RC	12.50	25.00
7 Jim Hegan	20.00	50.00
8 Harold Smith RC	6.00	12.00
9 Robert Miller	6.00	12.00
10 Bob Keegan	6.00	12.00
11 Ferris Fain	7.50	15.00
12 Vernon Jake Thies RC	6.00	12.00
13 Fred Marsh	6.00	12.00
14 Jim Finigan RC	6.00	12.00
15 Jim Pendleton	6.00	12.00
16 Roy Sievers	7.50	15.00
17 Bobby Hofman	6.00	12.00
18 Russ Kemmerer RC	6.00	12.00
19 Billy Herman CO	7.50	15.00
20 Andy Carey	7.50	15.00
21 Alex Grammas	6.00	12.00
22 Bill Skowron	15.00	40.00
23 Jack Parks RC	6.00	12.00
24 Hal Newhouser	20.00	50.00
25 Johnny Podres	20.00	50.00
26 Dick Groat	20.00	50.00
27 Billy Gardner RC	7.50	15.00
28 Ernie Banks	100.00	250.00
29 Herman Wehmeier	6.00	12.00
30 Vic Power	7.50	15.00
31 Warren Spahn	50.00	120.00
32 Warren McGhee	6.00	12.00
33 Tom Qualters	6.00	12.00
34 Wayne Terwilliger	10.00	25.00
35 Dave Jolly	6.00	12.00
36 Leo Kiely	6.00	12.00
37 Joe Cunningham RC	7.50	15.00
38 Bob Turley	12.00	30.00
39 Bill Glynn	6.00	12.00
40 Don Hoak	7.50	15.00
41 Chuck Stobbs	10.00	25.00
42 John Windy McCall RC	6.00	12.00
43 Harvey Haddix	7.50	15.00
44 Harold Valentine RC	6.00	12.00
45 Hank Sauer	7.50	15.00
46 Ted Kazanski	6.00	12.00
47 Hank Aaron	300.00	600.00
48 Bob Kennedy	7.50	15.00
49 J.W. Porter	6.00	12.00
50 Jackie Robinson	300.00	600.00
51 Jim Hughes	7.50	15.00
52 Bill Tremel RC	6.00	12.00
53 Bill Taylor	6.00	12.00
54 Lou Limmer	6.00	12.00
55 Rip Repulski	6.00	12.00
56 Ray Jablonski	6.00	12.00
57 Billy O'Dell RC	6.00	12.00
58 Jim Rivera	10.00	25.00
59 Gair Allie	8.00	20.00
60 Dean Stone	8.00	20.00
61 Forrest Jacobs	6.00	12.00
62 Thornton Kipper	6.00	12.00
63 Joe Collins	12.00	30.00
64 Gus Triandos RC	12.00	30.00
65 Ray Boone	7.50	15.00
66 Ron Jackson RC	6.00	12.00
67 Wally Moon	7.50	15.00
68 Jim Davis RC	6.00	12.00
69 Ed Bailey	7.50	15.00
70 Al Rosen	12.00	30.00
71 Ruben Gomez	6.00	12.00
72 Karl Olson	6.00	15.00
73 Jack Shepard RC	6.00	12.00
74 Bob Borkowski	10.00	25.00
75 Sandy Amoros RC	12.00	30.00
76 Howie Pollet	6.00	12.00
77 Arnie Portocarrero	6.00	12.00
78 Gordon Jones RC	6.00	12.00
79 Clyde Danny Schell RC	6.00	12.00
80 Bob Grim RC	7.50	15.00
81 Gene Conley	7.50	15.00
82 Chuck Harmon	6.00	12.00
83 Tom Brewer RC	6.00	12.00
84 Camilo Pascual RC	7.50	15.00
85 Don Mossi RC	12.50	25.00
86 Bill Wilson	6.00	12.00
87 Frank House	6.00	12.00
88 Bob Skinner RC	7.50	15.00
89 Joe Frazier RC	7.50	15.00
90 Karl Spooner RC	7.50	15.00
91 Milt Bolling	6.00	12.00
92 Don Zimmer RC	25.00	60.00
93 Steve Bilko	6.00	12.00
94 Reno Bertoia	6.00	12.00
95 Preston Ward	6.00	12.00
96 Chuck Bishop	6.00	12.00
97 Carlos Paula RC	6.00	12.00
98 John Riddle CO	6.00	12.00
99 Frank Leja	6.00	12.00
100 Monte Irvin	25.00	60.00
101 Johnny Gray RC	6.00	12.00
102 Wally Westlake	10.00	25.00
103 Chuck White RC	6.00	12.00
104 Jack Harshman	8.00	20.00
105 Chuck Diering	6.00	12.00
106 Frank Sullivan RC	15.00	40.00
107 Curt Roberts	6.00	12.00
108 Rube Walker	7.50	15.00
109 Ed Lopat	12.00	30.00
110 Gus Zernial	8.00	20.00
111 Bob Milliken	7.50	15.00
112 Nelson King RC	6.00	12.00
113 Harry Brecheen CO	7.50	15.00
114 Louis Ortiz RC	6.00	12.00
115 Ellis Kinder	10.00	25.00
116 Tom Hurd RC	6.00	12.00
117 Mel Roach	10.00	25.00
118 Bob Purkey	12.00	30.00
119 Bob Lennon RC	6.00	12.00
120 Ted Kluszewski	20.00	50.00
121 Bill Renna	10.00	25.00
122 Carl Sawatski	6.00	12.00
123 Sandy Koufax RC	800.00	1,500.00
124 Harmon Killebrew RC	150.00	400.00
125 Ken Boyer RC	30.00	80.00
126 Dick Hall RC	6.00	12.00
127 Dale Long RC	7.50	15.00
128 Ted Lepcio	6.00	12.00
129 Elvin Tappe	7.50	15.00
130 Mayo Smith MG RC	10.00	25.00
131 Grady Hatton	6.00	12.00
132 Bob Trice	6.00	12.00
133 Dave Hoskins	6.00	12.00
134 Joey Jay	7.50	15.00
135 Johnny O'Brien	7.50	15.00
136 Veston (Bunky) Stewart RC	6.00	12.00
137 Harry Elliott RC	6.00	12.00
138 Ray Herbert	6.00	12.00
139 Steve Kraly RC	6.00	12.00
140 Mel Parnell	7.50	15.00
141 Tom Wright	6.00	12.00
142 Jerry Lynch	10.00	25.00
143 John Schofield	7.50	15.00
144 Joe Amalfitano RC	6.00	12.00
145 Elmer Valo	6.00	12.00
146 Dick Donovan RC	6.00	12.00
147 Hugh Pepper RC	6.00	12.00
148 Hal Brown	6.00	12.00
149 Ray Crone	6.00	12.00
150 Mike Higgins MG	6.00	12.00
151 Ralph Kress CO	10.00	20.00
152 Harry Agganis RC	60.00	100.00
153 Bud Podbielan	12.50	25.00
154 Willie Miranda	15.00	40.00
155 Eddie Mathews	60.00	150.00
156 Joe Black	30.00	50.00
157 Robert Miller	12.00	30.00
158 Tommy Carroll RC	12.50	25.00
159 Johnny Schmitz	10.00	20.00
160 Ray Narleski RC	10.00	20.00
161 Chuck Tanner RC	20.00	40.00
162 Joe Coleman	15.00	30.00
163 Faye Throneberry	15.00	30.00
164 Roberto Clemente RC	2,500.00	5,000.00
165 Don Johnson	15.00	30.00
166 Hank Bauer	50.00	80.00
167 Tom Casagrande RC	15.00	30.00
168 Duane Pillette	15.00	30.00
169 Bob Oldis	20.00	40.00
170 Jim Pearce DP RC	7.50	15.00
171 Dick Brodowski	15.00	30.00
172 Frank Baumholtz DP	7.50	15.00
173 Bob Kline RC	15.00	30.00
174 Rudy Minarcin RC	15.00	30.00
176 Norm Zauchin RC	15.00	30.00
177 Al Robertson	15.00	40.00
178 Bobby Adams	15.00	30.00
179 Jim Bolger RC	25.00	60.00
180 Clem Labine	30.00	80.00
181 Roy McMillan	20.00	40.00
182 Humberto Robinson RC	15.00	30.00
183 Anthony Jacobs RC	15.00	30.00
184 Harry Perkowski DP	7.50	15.00
185 Don Ferrarese RC	15.00	30.00
187 Gil Hodges	60.00	150.00
188 Charlie Silvera DP	7.50	15.00
189 Phil Rizzuto	60.00	150.00
190 Gene Woodling	25.00	60.00
191 Eddie Stanky MG	20.00	40.00
192 Jim Delsing	20.00	40.00
193 Johnny Sain	30.00	60.00
194 Willie Mays	500.00	1,000.00
195 Ed Roebuck RC	40.00	100.00
196 Gale Wade RC	15.00	30.00
197 Al Smith	30.00	60.00
198 Yogi Berra	150.00	400.00
199 Bert Hamric RC	20.00	40.00
200 Jackie Jensen	30.00	60.00
201 Sherman Lollar	20.00	40.00
202 Jim Owens RC	30.00	80.00
204 Frank Smith	15.00	30.00
205 Gene Freese RC	40.00	100.00
206 Pete Daley RC	15.00	30.00
207 Billy Consolo	30.00	80.00
208 Ray Moore RC	20.00	40.00
210 Duke Snider	250.00	500.00

1955 Topps Double Header

The cards in this 66-card set measure approximately 2 1/16" by 4 7/8". Borrowing a design from the T201 Mecca series, Topps issued a 132-player "Double Header" set in a separate wrapper in 1955. Each player is numbered in the biographical section on the reverse. When open, with perforated flap up, one player is revealed; when the flap is lowered, or closed, the player design on top incorporates a portion of the inside player artwork. When the cards are placed side by side, a continuous ballpark background is formed. Some cards have been found without perforations, and all players pictured appear in the low series of the 1955 regular issue. The cards were issued in one-card penny packs which came 120 packs to a box with a piece of bubble gum.

Card	Low	High
COMPLETE SET (66)	2,500.00	4,000.00
WRAPPER (5-CENT)	150.00	200.00
1 A. Rosen C. Diering	30.00	50.00
3 M.Irvin R.Kemmerer	35.00	60.00
5 Ted Kazanski and 6 Gordon Jones	25.00	40.00
7 Bill Taylor and 8 Billy O'Dell	25.00	40.00
9 J.W. Porter and 10 Thornton Kipper	25.00	40.00
11 Curt Roberts and 12 Arnie Portocarrero	25.00	40.00
13 Wally Westlake and 14 Frank House	30.00	50.00
15 Rube Walker and 16 Lou Limmer	30.00	50.00
17 Dean Stone and 18 Charlie White	25.00	40.00
19 Karl Spooner and 20 Jim Hughes	30.00	50.00
21 B.Skowron F.Sullivan	35.00	60.00
23 Jack Shepard and 24 Stan Hack MG	25.00	40.00
25 J.Robinson D.Hoak	150.00	250.00
27 Dusty Rhodes and 28 Jim Davis	30.00	50.00
29 Vic Power and 30 Ed Bailey	25.00	40.00
31 H.Pollet E.Banks	125.00	200.00
33 Jim Pendleton and 34 Gene Conley	25.00	40.00

35 Karl Olson and 36 Andy Carey	25.00	40.00
37 W. Moon J. Cunningham	30.00	50.00
39 Freddie Marsh and/40 Vernon Thies	25.00	40.00
41 E.Lopat H.Haddix	35.00	60.00
43 Leo Kiely and 44 Chuck Stobbs	25.00	40.00
45 A.Kaline H.Valentine	125.00	200.00
47 Forrest Jacobs and 48 Johnny Gray	25.00	40.00
49 Ron Jackson and 50 Jim Finigan	25.00	40.00
51 Ray Jablonski and 52 Bob Keegan	25.00	40.00
53 B.Herman S.Amoros	50.00	80.00
55 Chuck Harmon and 56 Bob Skinner	25.00	40.00
57 Dick Hall and 58 Bob Grim	25.00	40.00
59 Billy Glynn and 60 Bob Miller	30.00	50.00
61 Billy Gardner and 62 John Hetki	25.00	40.00
63 B. Borkowski B. Turley	25.00	40.00
65 Joe Collins and 66 Jack Harshman	25.00	40.00
67 Jim Hegan and 68 Jack Parks	25.00	40.00
69 T.Williams M.Smith	250.00	500.00
71 Gair Allie and 72 Grady Hatton	25.00	40.00
73 Jerry Lynch and 74 Harry Brecheen CO	25.00	40.00
75 Tom Wright and 76 Vernon Stewart	25.00	40.00
77 Dave Hoskins and 78 Warren McGhee	25.00	40.00
79 Roy Sievers and 80 Art Fowler	30.00	50.00
81 Danny Schell and 82 Gus Triandos	25.00	40.00
83 Joe Frazier and 84 Don Mossi	25.00	40.00
85 Elmer Valo and 86 Hector Brown	25.00	40.00
87 Bob Kennedy and 88 Windy McCall	30.00	50.00
89 Ruben Gomez and 90 Jim Rivera	25.00	40.00
91 Louis Ortiz and 92 Milt Bolling	25.00	40.00
93 Carl Sawatski and 94 El Tappe	25.00	40.00
95 Dave Jolly and 96 Bobby Hofman	25.00	40.00
97 P.Ward D.Zimmer	35.00	60.00
99 B. Renna D. Groat	30.00	50.00
101 Bill Wilson and 102 Bill Tremel	25.00	40.00
103 H. Sauer C. Pascual	30.00	50.00
105 H.Aaron R.Herbert	300.00	500.00
107 Alex Grammas and 108 Tom Qualters	25.00	40.00
109 H.Newhouser C.Bishop	35.00	60.00
111 H.Killebrew J.Podres	125.00	200.00
113 Ray Boone and 114 Bob Purkey	25.00	40.00
115 Dale Long and 116 Ferris Fain	30.00	50.00
117 Steve Bilko and 118 Bob Milliken	25.00	40.00
119 Mel Parnell and 120 Tom Hurd	30.00	50.00
121 T.Kluszewski J.Owens	50.00	80.00
123 Gus Zernial and 124 Bob Trice	25.00	40.00
125 Rip Repulski and 126 Ted Lepcio	25.00	40.00
127 W.Spahn T.Brewer	90.00	150.00
129 J.Gilliam E.Kinder	50.00	80.00
131 Herm Wehmeier and 132 Wayne Terwilliger	25.00	40.00

1955 Topps Test Stamps

These test issues stamps "are full-size versions of regular first series cards, but with blank, gummed backs and perforated edges." These stamps are listed in alphabetical order with their corresponding card number listed immediately after their name. Since these "stamps" show up very infrequently in the hobby -- any additions to this checklist are appreciated.

COMPLETE SET	3,000.00	6,000.00
1 Ray Boone Card number 65	400.00	800.00
2 Joe Cunningham Card number 37	400.00	800.00
3 Jim Davis Card number 68	400.00	800.00
4 Ruben Gomez Card number 71	400.00	800.00
5 Alex Grammas Card number 21	400.00	800.00
6 Stan Hack MG Card number 6	500.00	1,000.00
7 Harvey Haddix Card number 43	400.00	800.00
8 Bobby Hofman Card number 17	400.00	800.00
9 Ray Jablonski Card number 56	400.00	800.00
10 Dave Jolly Card number 35	400.00	800.00
11 Don Mossi Card number 85	600.00	1,200.00
12 Jim Pendleton Card number 15	400.00	800.00
13 Howie Pollet Card number 76	400.00	800.00
14 Jack Shepard Card number 73	400.00	800.00
15 Bob Skinner Card number 88	500.00	1,000.00
16 Bill Skowron Card number 22	750.00	1,500.00
17 Karl Spooner Card number 90	500.00	1,000.00
18 Bill Tremel Card number 52	400.00	800.00
19 Corky Valentine Card number 44	400.00	800.00
20 Rube Walker Card number 108	500.00	1,000.00
21 Charlie White Card number 103	400.00	800.00

1956 Topps

The cards in this 340-card set measure approximately 2 5/8" by 3 3/4". Following up with another horizontally oriented card in 1956, Topps improved the format by layering the color "head" shot onto an actual action sequence involving the player. Cards 1 to 180 come with either white or gray backs: in the 1 to 100 sequence gray backs are less common and in the 101 to 180 sequence white backs are less common. The team cards, used for the first time in a regular set by Topps, are found dated 1955, or undated, with the team name appearing on either side. The dated team cards in the first series were not printed on the gray stock. The two unnumbered checklist cards are highly prized (must be unmarked to qualify as excellent or mint). The complete set price below does not include the unnumbered checklist cards or any of the variations. The set was issued in one-card penny packs or six-card nickel packs. The six card nickel packs came 24 to a box with 24 boxes in a case while the once cent packs came 120 to a box. Both types of packs included a piece of bubble gum. Promotional three card strips were issued for this set. Among those strips were one featuring Johnny O'Brien/Harvey Haddix and Frank House. The key Rookie Cards in this set are Walt Alston, Luis Aparicio, and Roger Craig. There are ten double-printed cards in the first series as evidenced by the discovery of an uncut sheet of 110 cards (10 by 11); these DP's are listed below.

COMPLETE SET (340)	5,000.00	10,000.00
COMMON CARD (1-100)	5.00	10.00
COMMON CARD (101-180)	6.00	12.00
COMMON CARD (261-340)	6.00	12.00
COMMON CARD (181-260)	7.50	15.00
WRAP.(1-CENT)	200.00	250.00
WRAP.(1-CENT, REPEAT)	75.00	100.00
WRAPPER (5-CENT)	150.00	200.00
*1-100 GRAY BACK: .5X TO 1.2X		
*101-180 WHITE BACK: .5X TO 1.2X		
1 Will Harridge PRES	75.00	125.00
2 Warren Giles PRES DP	15.00	40.00
3 Elmer Valo	7.50	15.00
4 Carlos Paula	7.50	15.00
5 Ted Williams	300.00	500.00
6 Ray Boone	15.00	25.00
7 Ron Negray RC	5.00	10.00
8 Walter Alston MG RC	25.00	40.00
9 Ruben Gomez DP	5.00	10.00
10 Warren Spahn	40.00	100.00
11A Chicago Cubs TC Center	15.00	30.00
11B Chicago Cubs TC D'55	50.00	80.00
11C Chicago Cubs TC Left	15.00	30.00
12 Andy Carey	7.50	15.00
13 Roy Face	7.50	15.00
14 Ken Boyer DP	12.00	30.00
15 Ernie Banks DP	75.00	200.00
16 Hector Lopez RC	8.00	20.00
17 Gene Conley	7.50	15.00
18 Dick Donovan	5.00	10.00
19 Chuck Diering DP	5.00	10.00
20 Al Kaline	50.00	120.00
21 Joe Collins DP	7.50	15.00
22 Jim Finigan	5.00	10.00
23 Fred Marsh	5.00	10.00
24 Dick Groat	10.00	25.00
25 Ted Kluszewski	20.00	50.00
26 Grady Hatton	5.00	10.00
27 Nelson Burbrink DP RC	5.00	10.00
28 Bobby Hofman	5.00	10.00
29 Jack Harshman	5.00	10.00
30 Jackie Robinson DP	300.00	600.00
31 Hank Aaron UER DP	150.00	400.00
32 Frank House	5.00	10.00
33 Roberto Clemente	250.00	600.00
34 Tom Brewer DP	5.00	10.00
35 Al Rosen	12.00	30.00
36 Rudy Minarcin	7.50	15.00
37 Alex Grammas	10.00	25.00
38 Bob Kennedy	7.50	15.00
39 Don Mossi	7.50	15.00
40 Bob Turley	7.50	15.00
41 Hank Sauer	7.50	15.00
42 Sandy Amoros	20.00	50.00
43 Ray Moore	5.00	10.00
44 Windy McCall	5.00	10.00
45 Gus Zernial	7.50	15.00
46 Gene Freese DP	5.00	10.00
47 Art Fowler	5.00	10.00
48 Jim Hegan	12.00	30.00
49 Pedro Ramos RC	8.00	20.00
50 Dusty Rhodes DP	7.50	15.00
51 Ernie Oravetz RC	5.00	10.00
52 Bob Grim DP	7.50	15.00
53 Arnie Portocarrero	5.00	10.00
54 Bob Keegan	5.00	10.00
55 Wally Moon	7.50	15.00
56 Dale Long	7.50	15.00
57 Duke Maas RC	5.00	10.00
58 Ed Roebuck	15.00	25.00
59 Jose Santiago RC	5.00	10.00
60 Mayo Smith MG DP	5.00	10.00
61 Bill Skowron	20.00	50.00
62 Hal Smith	7.50	15.00
63 Roger Craig RC	25.00	40.00
64 Luis Arroyo RC	5.00	10.00
65 Johnny O'Brien	7.50	15.00
66 Bob Speake DP RC	5.00	10.00
67 Vic Power	7.50	15.00
68 Chuck Stobbs	5.00	10.00
69 Chuck Tanner	7.50	15.00
70 Jim Rivera	5.00	10.00
71 Frank Sullivan	5.00	10.00
72A Philadelphia Phillies TC Center	15.00	30.00
72B Philadelphia Phillies TC D'55	50.00	80.00
72C Philadelphia Phillies TC Left DP	15.00	30.00
73 Wayne Terwilliger	5.00	10.00
74 Jim King RC	5.00	10.00
75 Roy Sievers DP	7.50	15.00
76 Ray Crone	5.00	10.00
77 Harvey Haddix	10.00	25.00
78 Herman Wehmeier	5.00	10.00
79 Sandy Koufax	200.00	400.00
80 Gus Triandos DP	5.00	10.00
81 Wally Westlake	5.00	10.00
82 Bill Renna DP	5.00	10.00
83 Karl Spooner	7.50	15.00
84 Babe Birrer RC	5.00	10.00
85A Cleveland Indians TC Center	15.00	30.00
85B Cleveland Indians TC D'55	50.00	80.00
85C Cleveland Indians TC Left	15.00	30.00
86 Ray Jablonski DP	5.00	10.00
87 Dean Stone	5.00	10.00
88 Johnny Kucks RC	7.50	15.00
89 Norm Zauchin	5.00	10.00
90A Cincinnati Redlegs TC Center	15.00	30.00
90B Cincinnati Reds TC D'55	50.00	80.00
90C Cincinnati Reds TC Left	15.00	30.00
91 Gail Harris RC	5.00	10.00
92 Bob Red Wilson	5.00	10.00
93 George Susce	5.00	10.00
94 Ron Kline UER	5.00	10.00
Facimile auto is J.Robert Klein		
95A Milwaukee Braves TC Center	20.00	40.00
95B Milwaukee Braves TC D'55	50.00	80.00
95C Milwaukee Braves TC Left	20.00	40.00
96 Bill Tremel	5.00	10.00
97 Jerry Lynch	7.50	15.00
98 Camilo Pascual	7.50	15.00
99 Don Zimmer	15.00	40.00
100A Baltimore Orioles TC Center	20.00	40.00
100B Baltimore Orioles TC D'55	50.00	80.00
100C Baltimore Orioles TC Left	20.00	40.00
101 Roy Campanella	90.00	150.00
102 Jim Davis	6.00	12.00
103 Willie Miranda	6.00	12.00
104 Bob Lennon	6.00	12.00
105 Al Smith	6.00	12.00
106 Joe Astroth	6.00	12.00
107 Eddie Mathews	40.00	100.00
108 Laurin Pepper	6.00	12.00
109 Enos Slaughter	20.00	50.00
110 Yogi Berra	75.00	200.00
111 Boston Red Sox TC	20.00	40.00
112 Dee Fondy	6.00	12.00
113 Phil Rizzuto	50.00	120.00
114 Jim Owens	7.50	15.00
115 Jackie Jensen	7.50	15.00
116 Eddie O'Brien	6.00	12.00
117 Virgil Trucks	7.50	15.00
118 Nellie Fox	20.00	50.00
119 Larry Jackson RC	8.00	20.00
120 Richie Ashburn	35.00	60.00
121 Pittsburgh Pirates TC	20.00	40.00
122 Willard Nixon	6.00	12.00
123 Roy McMillan	7.50	15.00
124 Don Kaiser	6.00	12.00
125 Minnie Minoso	20.00	50.00
126 Jim Brady RC	6.00	12.00
127 Willie Jones	7.50	15.00
128 Eddie Yost	7.50	15.00
129 Jake Martin RC	6.00	12.00
130 Willie Mays	200.00	500.00
131 Bob Roselli RC	6.00	12.00
132 Bobby Avila	6.00	12.00
133 Ray Narleski	6.00	12.00
134 St. Louis Cardinals TC	20.00	40.00
135 Mickey Mantle	1,250.00	2,500.00
136 Johnny Logan	7.50	15.00
137 Al Silvera RC	6.00	12.00
138 Johnny Antonelli	7.50	15.00
139 Tommy Carroll	7.50	15.00
140 Herb Score RC	20.00	50.00
141 Joe Frazier	6.00	12.00
142 Gene Baker	6.00	12.00
143 Jim Piersall	7.50	15.00
144 Leroy Powell RC	6.00	12.00
145 Gil Hodges	30.00	80.00
146 Washington Nationals TC	20.00	40.00
147 Earl Torgeson	6.00	12.00
148 Alvin Dark	12.00	30.00
149 Dixie Howell	6.00	12.00
150 Duke Snider	50.00	120.00
151 Spook Jacobs	7.50	15.00
152 Billy Hoeft	7.50	15.00
153 Frank Thomas	10.00	25.00
154 Dave Pope	6.00	12.00
155 Harvey Kuenn	7.50	15.00
156 Wes Westrum	7.50	15.00
157 Dick Brodowski	6.00	12.00
158 Wally Post	7.50	15.00
159 Clint Courtney	6.00	12.00
160 Billy Pierce	7.50	15.00
161 Joe DeMaestri	6.00	12.00
162 Dave Gus Bell	7.50	15.00
163 Gene Woodling	7.50	15.00
164 Harmon Killebrew	60.00	150.00
165 Red Schoendienst	25.00	60.00
166 Brooklyn Dodgers TC	50.00	120.00
167 Harry Dorish	6.00	12.00
168 Sammy White	6.00	12.00
169 Bob Nelson RC	6.00	12.00
170 Bill Virdon	7.50	15.00
171 Jim Wilson	6.00	12.00
172 Frank Torre RC	7.50	15.00
173 Johnny Podres	20.00	50.00
174 Glen Gorbous RC	6.00	12.00
175 Del Crandall	7.50	15.00
176 Alex Kellner	6.00	12.00
177 Hank Bauer	15.00	40.00
178 Joe Black	7.50	15.00
179 Harry Chiti	6.00	12.00
180 Robin Roberts	30.00	50.00
181 Billy Martin	40.00	100.00
182 Paul Minner	8.00	20.00
183 Stan Lopata	10.00	20.00
184 Don Bessent RC	12.00	30.00
185 Bill Bruton	10.00	20.00
186 Ron Jackson	7.50	15.00
187 Early Wynn	20.00	50.00
188 Chicago White Sox TC	30.00	50.00
189 Ned Garver	7.50	15.00
190 Carl Furillo	15.00	40.00
191 Frank Lary	10.00	20.00
192 Smoky Burgess	10.00	20.00
193 Wilmer Mizell	10.00	20.00
194 Monte Irvin	25.00	60.00
195 George Kell	15.00	40.00
196 Tom Poholsky	7.50	15.00
197 Granny Hamner	7.50	15.00
198 Ed Fitzgerald	7.50	15.00
199 Hank Thompson	10.00	20.00
200 Bob Feller	60.00	150.00
201 Rip Repulski	7.50	15.00
202 Jim Hearn	7.50	15.00
203 Bill Tuttle	7.50	15.00
204 Art Swanson RC	7.50	15.00
205 Whitey Lockman	10.00	20.00
206 Erv Palica	7.50	15.00
207 Jim Small RC	7.50	15.00
208 Elston Howard	25.00	60.00
209 Max Surkont	7.50	15.00
210 Mike Garcia	10.00	20.00
211 Murry Dickson	7.50	15.00
212 Johnny Temple	7.50	15.00
213 Detroit Tigers	35.00	60.00
214 Bob Rush	7.50	15.00
215 Tommy Byrne	10.00	25.00
216 Jerry Schoonmaker RC	7.50	15.00
217 Billy Klaus	7.50	15.00
218 Joe Nuxhall UER	10.00	20.00
219 Lew Burdette	12.00	30.00
220 Del Ennis	10.00	20.00
221 Bob Friend	10.00	25.00
222 Dave Philley	7.50	15.00
223 Randy Jackson	7.50	15.00
224 Bud Podbielan	7.50	15.00
225 Gil McDougald	15.00	40.00
226 New York Giants	25.00	60.00
227 Russ Meyer	7.50	15.00
228 Mickey Vernon	10.00	20.00
229 Harry Brecheen CO	10.00	20.00
230 Chico Carrasquel	10.00	25.00
231 Bob Hale RC	7.50	15.00
232 Toby Atwell	7.50	15.00
233 Carl Erskine	18.00	30.00
234 Pete Runnels	12.00	30.00
235 Don Newcombe	25.00	60.00
236 Kansas City Athletics	20.00	40.00
237 Jose Valdivielso RC	7.50	15.00
238 Walt Dropo	10.00	20.00
239 Harry Simpson	7.50	15.00
240 Whitey Ford	50.00	120.00
241 Don Mueller UER	10.00	20.00
242 Hershell Freeman	7.50	15.00
243 Sherm Lollar	10.00	20.00
244 Bob Buhl	15.00	40.00
245 Billy Goodman	10.00	20.00
246 Tom Gorman	7.50	15.00
247 Bill Sarni	7.50	15.00
248 Bob Porterfield	7.50	15.00

249 Johnny Klippstein 7.50 15.00
250 Larry Doby 25.00 60.00
251 New York Yankees TC UER 75.00 200.00
252 Vern Law 10.00 20.00
253 Irv Noren 18.00 30.00
254 George Crowe 7.50 15.00
255 Bob Lemon 15.00 40.00
256 Tom Hurd 7.50 15.00
257 Bobby Thomson 18.00 30.00
258 Art Ditmar 7.50 15.00
259 Sam Jones 10.00 20.00
260 Pee Wee Reese 50.00 120.00
261 Bobby Shantz 7.50 15.00
262 Howie Pollet 6.00 12.00
263 Bob Miller 6.00 12.00
264 Ray Monzant RC 6.00 12.00
265 Sandy Consuegra 6.00 12.00
266 Don Ferrarese 6.00 12.00
267 Bob Nieman 6.00 12.00
268 Dale Mitchell 7.50 15.00
269 Jack Meyer RC 8.00 20.00
270 Billy Loes 12.00 30.00
271 Foster Castleman RC 6.00 12.00
272 Danny O'Connell 6.00 12.00
273 Walker Cooper 6.00 12.00
274 Frank Baumholtz 6.00 12.00
275 Jim Greengrass 6.00 12.00
276 George Zuverink 6.00 12.00
277 Daryl Spencer 6.00 12.00
278 Chet Nichols 6.00 12.00
279 Johnny Groth 6.00 12.00
280 Jim Gilliam 25.00 40.00
281 Art Houtteman 6.00 12.00
282 Warren Hacker 6.00 12.00
283 Hal Smith RC UER 10.00 25.00
Wrong Facsimile Autograph, belongs to Hal W. Smith
284 Ike Delock 6.00 12.00
285 Eddie Miksis 6.00 12.00
286 Bill Wight 6.00 12.00
287 Bobby Adams 6.00 12.00
288 Bob Cerv 25.00 60.00
289 Hal Jeffcoat 6.00 12.00
290 Curt Simmons 10.00 25.00
291 Frank Kellert RC 6.00 12.00
292 Luis Aparicio RC 50.00 200.00
293 Stu Miller 15.00 25.00
294 Ernie Johnson 7.50 15.00
295 Clem Labine 12.00 30.00
296 Andy Seminick 6.00 12.00
297 Bob Skinner 7.50 15.00
298 Johnny Schmitz 6.00 12.00
299 Charlie Neal 25.00 40.00
300 Vic Wertz 7.50 15.00
301 Marv Grissom 6.00 12.00
302 Eddie Robinson 6.00 12.00
303 Jim Dyck 6.00 12.00
304 Frank Malzone 7.50 15.00
305 Brooks Lawrence 6.00 12.00
306 Curt Roberts 6.00 12.00
307 Hoyt Wilhelm 20.00 50.00
308 Chuck Harmon 6.00 12.00
309 Don Blasingame RC 10.00 25.00
310 Steve Gromek 6.00 12.00
311 Hal Naragon 6.00 12.00
312 Andy Pafko 7.50 15.00
313 Gene Stephens 6.00 12.00
314 Hobie Landrith 6.00 12.00
315 Milt Bolling 6.00 12.00
316 Jerry Coleman 10.00 25.00
317 Al Aber 6.00 12.00
318 Fred Hatfield 6.00 12.00
319 Jack Crimian RC 6.00 12.00
320 Joe Adcock 7.50 15.00
321 Jim Konstanty 7.50 15.00
322 Karl Olson 6.00 12.00
323 Willard Schmidt 6.00 12.00
324 Rocky Bridges 7.50 15.00
325 Don Liddle 6.00 12.00
326 Connie Johnson RC 6.00 12.00
327 Bob Wiesler RC 6.00 12.00
328 Preston Ward 6.00 12.00
329 Lou Berberet RC 6.00 12.00
330 Jim Busby 7.50 15.00
331 Dick Hall 6.00 12.00
332 Don Larsen 30.00 80.00
333 Rube Walker 10.00 25.00
334 Bob Miller 7.50 15.00
335 Don Hoak 8.00 20.00
336 Ellis Kinder 10.00 25.00
337 Bobby Morgan 6.00 12.00
338 Jim Delsing 6.00 12.00
339 Rance Pless RC 6.00 12.00
340 Mickey McDermott 35.00 60.00
CL1 Checklist 1/3 175.00 300.00
CL2 Checklist 2/4 175.00 300.00

1956 Topps Hocus Focus

The 1956 Topps Hocus Focus set is very similar in size and design to the 1948 Topps Magic Photos set. It contains at least 96 small (approximately 7/8" by 1 5/8") individual cards featuring a variety of sports and non-sport subjects. They were printed with both a series card number (by subject matter) on the back as well as a card number reflecting the entire set. The fronts were developed, much like a photograph, from a blank appearance by using moisture and sunlight. Due to varying degrees of photographic sensitivity, the clarity of these cards ranges from fully developed to poorly developed. A premium album holding 126-cards was also issued leading to the theory that there are actually 126 different cards. A few High Series (#97-126) cards have been discovered and cataloged below although a full 126-card checklist is yet unknown. The cards do reference the set name "Hocus Focus" on the backs unlike the 1948 Magic Photos. Finally, a slightly smaller version (roughly 7/8" by 1 7/16") of some of the cards has also been found, but a full checklist is not known.

5 Ted Williams 5 750.00 1,500.00
8 Spook Jacobs 60 100.00 200.00
13 Jackie Robinson 13 600.00 1,200.00
26 Harvey Haddix 26 125.00 250.00
30 Hank Sauer 30 125.00 250.00
31 Ray Boone 31 100.00 200.00
42 Hal Smith 100.00 200.00
43 Dick Groat 125.00 250.00
44 Ed Lopat 150.00 300.00
49 Gus Zernial 100.00 200.00
51 Mayo Smith MG 100.00 200.00
67 Jim Rivera 100.00 200.00
69 Al Rosen 150.00 300.00
79 Ted Kluszewski 200.00 400.00
84 Johnny Schmitz 100.00 200.00
86 Dusty Rhodes 86 125.00 250.00
87 Warren Spahn 87 400.00 800.00
103 Wally Moon 150.00 300.00
109 Ed Mathews 109 500.00 1,000.00
117 Babe Ruth 1,500.00 3,000.00
118 Mel Parnell 125.00 250.00
122 Karl Spooner 100.00 200.00

1956 Topps Pins

This set of 60 full-color pins was Topps first and only baseball player pin set. Each pin measures 1 3/16" in diameter. Although the set was advertised to contain 90 pins, only 60 were issued. The checklist below lists the players in alphabetical order within team, e.g., Baltimore Orioles (1-4), Chicago Cubs (5-7), Cleveland Indians (8-11), Kansas City A's (12-15), Milwaukee Braves (16-19), Philadelphia Phillies (20-22), Boston Red Sox (23-26), New York Yankees (27-31), Chicago White Sox (32-35), Detroit Tigers (36-38), New York Giants (39-41), Pittsburgh Pirates (42-44), St. Louis Cardinals (45-48), Brooklyn Dodgers (49-53), Cincinnati Redlegs (54-57) and Washington Senators (58-60). Chuck Diering, Hector Lopez and Chuck Stobbs (noted below with SP) are more difficult to obtain than other pins in the set. The "packs" were issued as five cent packs with a piece of bubble gum which came 24 to a box. The box featured a photo of Ted Williams on the front.

COMPLETE SET (60) 2,500.00 5,000.00
PIN BOX (5-CENT) 150.00 200.00
1 Chuck Diering SP 250.00 500.00
2 Willie Miranda 15.00 30.00
3 Hal Smith 15.00 30.00
4 Gus Triandos 20.00 40.00
5 Ernie Banks 75.00 150.00
6 Hank Sauer 20.00 40.00
7 Bill Tremel 15.00 30.00
8 Jim Hegan 15.00 30.00
9 Don Mossi 20.00 40.00
10 Al Rosen 30.00 60.00
11 Al Smith 15.00 30.00
12 Jim Finigan 15.00 30.00
13 Hector Lopez SP 200.00 400.00
14 Vic Power 15.00 30.00
15 Gus Zernial 20.00 40.00
16 Hank Aaron 125.00 250.00
17 Gene Conley 15.00 30.00
18 Eddie Mathews 75.00 150.00
19 Warren Spahn 75.00 150.00
20 Ron Negray 15.00 30.00
21 Mayo Smith MG 15.00 30.00
22 Herman Wehmeier 15.00 30.00
23 Grady Hatton 15.00 30.00
24 Jackie Jensen 30.00 60.00
25 Frank Sullivan 15.00 30.00
26 Ted Williams 150.00 300.00
27 Yogi Berra 100.00 200.00
28 Joe Collins 20.00 40.00
29 Phil Rizzuto 50.00 100.00
30 Bill Skowron 50.00 100.00
31 Bob Turley 30.00 60.00
32 Dick Donovan 15.00 30.00
33 Jack Harshman 15.00 30.00
34 Bob Kennedy 15.00 30.00
35 Jim Rivera 15.00 30.00
36 Ray Boone 20.00 40.00
37 Frank House 15.00 30.00
38 Al Kaline 75.00 150.00
39 Ruben Gomez 15.00 30.00
40 Bobby Hofman 15.00 30.00
41 Willie Mays 125.00 250.00
42 Dick Groat 30.00 60.00
43 Dale Long 20.00 40.00
44 Johnny O'Brien 15.00 30.00
45 Luis Arroyo 15.00 30.00
46 Ken Boyer 30.00 60.00
47 Harvey Haddix 20.00 40.00
48 Wally Moon 20.00 40.00
49 Sandy Amoros 20.00 40.00
50 Gil Hodges 50.00 100.00
51 Jackie Robinson 125.00 250.00
52 Duke Snider 100.00 200.00
53 Karl Spooner 20.00 40.00
54 Joe Black 25.00 50.00
55 Art Fowler 15.00 30.00
56 Ted Kluszewski 30.00 60.00
57 Roy McMillan 15.00 30.00
58 Carlos Paula 15.00 30.00
59 Roy Sievers 15.00 30.00
60 Chuck Stobbs SP 200.00 400.00

1957 Topps

The cards in this 407-card set measure 2 1/2" by 3 1/2". In 1957, Topps returned to the vertical obverse, adopted what we now call the standard card size, and used a large, uncluttered color photo for the first time since 1952. Cards in the series 265 to 352 and the unnumbered checklist cards are scarcer than other cards in the set. However within this scarce series (265-352) there are 22 cards which were printed in double the quantity of the other cards in the series; these 22 double prints are indicated by DP in the checklist below. The first star combination cards, cards 400 and 407, are quite popular with collectors. They feature the big stars of the previous season's World Series teams, the Dodgers (Furillo, Hodges, Campanella, and Snider) and Yankees (Berra and Mantle). The complete set price below does not include the unnumbered checklist cards. Confirmed packaging includes one-cent penny packs and six-card nickel packs. Cello packs are definately known to exist and some collectors remember buying rack packs of 57's as well. The key Rookie Cards in this set are Jim Bunning, Rocky Colavito, Don Drysdale, Whitey Herzog, Tony Kubek, Bill Mazeroski, Bobby Richardson, Brooks Robinson, and Frank Robinson.

COMPLETE SET (407) 7,000.00 14,000.00
COMMON CARD (1-88) 5.00 10.00
COMMON CARD (89-176) 4.00 8.00
COMMON CARD (177-264) 4.00 8.00
COMMON CARD (265-352) 10.00 20.00
COMMON CARD (353-407) 4.00 8.00
COMMON DP (265-352) 6.00 12.00
WRAPPER (1-CENT) 250.00 300.00
WRAPPER (5-CENT) 150.00 200.00
1 Ted Williams 150.00 400.00
2 Yogi Berra 60.00 150.00
3 Dale Long 10.00 20.00
4 Johnny Logan 10.00 20.00
5 Sal Maglie 10.00 25.00
6 Hector Lopez 7.50 15.00
7 Luis Aparicio 15.00 40.00
8 Don Mossi 7.50 15.00
9 Johnny Temple 7.50 15.00
10 Willie Mays 125.00 300.00
11 George Zuverink 5.00 10.00
12 Dick Groat 10.00 20.00
13 Wally Burnette RC 5.00 10.00
14 Bob Nieman 10.00 25.00
15 Robin Roberts 20.00 50.00
16 Walt Moryn 5.00 10.00
17 Billy Gardner 5.00 10.00
18 Don Drysdale RC 150.00 250.00
19 Bob Wilson 5.00 10.00
20 Hank Aaron UER 125.00 300.00
21 Frank Sullivan 5.00 10.00
22 Jerry Snyder UER 5.00 10.00
23 Sherm Lollar 7.50 15.00
24 Bill Mazeroski RC 40.00 100.00
25 Whitey Ford 50.00 120.00
26 Bob Boyd 5.00 10.00
27 Ted Kazanski 5.00 10.00
28 Gene Conley 7.50 15.00
29 Whitey Herzog RC 15.00 30.00
30 Pee Wee Reese 40.00 100.00
31 Ron Northey 5.00 10.00
32 Hershell Freeman 5.00 10.00
33 Jim Small 5.00 10.00
34 Tom Sturdivant RC 7.50 15.00
35 Frank Robinson RC 200.00 400.00
36 Bob Grim 5.00 10.00
37 Frank Torre 7.50 15.00
38 Nellie Fox 12.00 30.00
39 Al Worthington RC 5.00 10.00
40 Early Wynn 10.00 25.00
41 Hal W. Smith 5.00 10.00
42 Dee Fondy 5.00 10.00
43 Connie Johnson 5.00 10.00
44 Joe DeMaestri 5.00 10.00
45 Carl Furillo 15.00 40.00
46 Robert J. Miller 5.00 10.00
47 Don Blasingame 5.00 10.00
48 Bill Bruton 7.50 15.00
49 Daryl Spencer 5.00 10.00
50 Herb Score 15.00 30.00
51 Clint Courtney 5.00 10.00
52 Lee Walls 5.00 10.00
53 Clem Labine 10.00 20.00
54 Elmer Valo 5.00 10.00
55 Ernie Banks 50.00 120.00
56 Dave Sisler RC 5.00 10.00
57 Jim Lemon 7.50 15.00
58 Ruben Gomez 5.00 10.00
59 Dick Williams 7.50 15.00
60 Billy Hoeft 7.50 15.00
61 Dusty Rhodes 7.50 15.00
62 Billy Martin 25.00 60.00
63 Ike Delock 5.00 10.00
64 Pete Runnels 7.50 15.00
65 Wally Moon 7.50 15.00
66 Brooks Lawrence 5.00 10.00
67 Chico Carrasquel 5.00 10.00
68 Ray Crone 5.00 10.00
69 Roy McMillan 7.50 15.00
70 Richie Ashburn 20.00 50.00
71 Murry Dickson 5.00 10.00
72 Bill Tuttle 5.00 10.00
73 George Crowe 5.00 10.00
74 Vito Valentinetti RC 5.00 10.00
75 Jimmy Piersall 7.50 15.00
76 Roberto Clemente 100.00 250.00
77 Paul Foytack RC 5.00 10.00
78 Vic Wertz 7.50 15.00
79 Lindy McDaniel RC 7.50 15.00
80 Gil Hodges 30.00 50.00
81 Herman Wehmeier 5.00 10.00
82 Elston Howard 15.00 30.00
83 Lou Skizas RC 5.00 10.00
84 Moe Drabowsky RC 7.50 15.00
85 Larry Doby 20.00 50.00
86 Bill Sarni 5.00 10.00
87 Tom Gorman 5.00 10.00
88 Harvey Kuenn 7.50 15.00
89 Roy Sievers 7.50 15.00
90 Warren Spahn 50.00 80.00
91 Mack Burk RC 4.00 8.00
92 Mickey Vernon 7.50 15.00
93 Hal Jeffcoat 4.00 8.00
94 Bobby Del Greco 4.00 8.00
95 Mickey Mantle 600.00 1,200.00
96 Hank Aguirre RC 4.00 8.00
97 New York Yankees TC 30.00 80.00
98 Alvin Dark 7.50 15.00
99 Bob Keegan 4.00 8.00
100 W.Giles/W.Harridge 7.50 15.00
101 Chuck Stobbs 4.00 8.00
102 Ray Boone 7.50 15.00
103 Joe Nuxhall 7.50 15.00
104 Hank Foiles 4.00 8.00
105 Johnny Antonelli 7.50 15.00
106 Ray Moore 4.00 8.00
107 Jim Rivera 4.00 8.00
108 Tommy Byrne 7.50 15.00
109 Hank Thompson 4.00 8.00
110 Bill Virdon 7.50 15.00
111 Hal R. Smith 4.00 8.00
112 Tom Brewer 4.00 8.00
113 Wilmer Mizell 7.50 15.00
114 Milwaukee Braves TC 10.00 20.00
115 Jim Gilliam 7.50 15.00
116 Mike Fornieles 4.00 8.00
117 Joe Adcock 10.00 20.00
118 Bob Porterfield 4.00 8.00
119 Stan Lopata 4.00 8.00
120 Bob Lemon 15.00 30.00
121 Clete Boyer RC 15.00 30.00
122 Ken Boyer 10.00 25.00
123 Steve Ridzik 4.00 8.00
124 Dave Philley 4.00 8.00
125 Al Kaline 40.00 100.00
126 Bob Wiesler 4.00 8.00
127 Bob Buhl 7.50 15.00
128 Ed Bailey 7.50 15.00
129 Saul Rogovin 4.00 8.00
130 Don Newcombe 12.00 30.00
131 Milt Bolling 4.00 8.00
132 Art Ditmar 7.50 15.00
133 Del Crandall 7.50 15.00
134 Don Kaiser 4.00 8.00
135 Bill Skowron 15.00 40.00
136 Jim Hegan 7.50 15.00
137 Bob Rush 4.00 8.00
138 Minnie Minoso 10.00 25.00
139 Lou Kretlow 4.00 8.00
140 Frank Thomas 7.50 15.00
141 Al Aber 4.00 8.00
142 Charley Thompson 4.00 8.00
143 Andy Pafko 8.00 20.00
144 Ray Narleski 4.00 8.00
145 Al Smith 4.00 8.00
146 Don Ferrarese 4.00 8.00
147 Al Walker 4.00 8.00
148 Don Mueller 7.50 15.00
149 Bob Kennedy 7.50 15.00
150 Bob Friend 7.50 15.00
151 Willie Miranda 4.00 8.00
152 Jack Harshman 4.00 8.00
153 Karl Olson 4.00 8.00
154 Red Schoendienst 15.00 30.00
155 Jim Brosnan 7.50 15.00
156 Gus Triandos 7.50 15.00
157 Wally Post 7.50 15.00
158 Curt Simmons 7.50 15.00
159 Solly Drake RC 4.00 8.00
160 Billy Pierce 7.50 15.00
161 Pittsburgh Pirates TC 7.50 15.00
162 Jack Meyer 4.00 8.00
163 Sammy White 4.00 8.00
164 Tommy Carroll 4.00 8.00
165 Ted Kluszewski 30.00 80.00
166 Roy Face 7.50 15.00
167 Vic Power 7.50 15.00
168 Frank Lary 7.50 15.00
169 Herb Plews RC 4.00 8.00
170 Duke Snider 40.00 100.00
171 Boston Red Sox TC 7.50 15.00
172 Gene Woodling 7.50 15.00
173 Roger Craig 7.50 15.00
174 Willie Jones 4.00 8.00
175 Don Larsen 15.00 40.00
176A Gene Bakep ERR 200.00 350.00
176B Gene Baker COR 7.50 15.00
177 Eddie Yost 7.50 15.00
178 Don Bessent 4.00 8.00
179 Ernie Oravetz 4.00 8.00
180 Gus Bell 7.50 15.00
181 Dick Donovan 4.00 8.00
182 Hobie Landrith 4.00 8.00
183 Chicago Cubs TC 7.50 15.00
184 Tito Francona RC 4.00 8.00
185 Johnny Kucks 7.50 15.00
186 Jim King 7.50 15.00
187 Virgil Trucks 7.50 15.00
188 Felix Mantilla RC 7.50 15.00
189 Willard Nixon 4.00 8.00
190 Randy Jackson 4.00 8.00
191 Joe Margoneri RC 4.00 8.00
192 Jerry Coleman 7.50 15.00
193 Del Rice 4.00 8.00
194 Hal Brown 4.00 8.00
195 Bobby Avila 4.00 8.00
196 Larry Jackson 7.50 15.00
197 Hank Sauer 7.50 15.00
198 Detroit Tigers TC 7.50 15.00
199 Vern Law 7.50 15.00

200 Gil McDougald	10.00	25.00
201 Sandy Amoros	7.50	15.00
202 Dick Gernert	4.00	8.00
203 Hoyt Wilhelm	10.00	25.00
204 Kansas City Athletics TC	7.50	15.00
205 Charlie Maxwell	7.50	15.00
206 Willard Schmidt	4.00	8.00
207 Gordon Billy Hunter	4.00	8.00
208 Lou Burdette	7.50	15.00
209 Bob Skinner	7.50	15.00
210 Roy Campanella	40.00	100.00
211 Camilo Pascual	7.50	15.00
212 Rocky Colavito RC	40.00	100.00
213 Les Moss	4.00	8.00
214 Philadelphia Phillies TC	7.50	15.00
215 Enos Slaughter	15.00	40.00
216 Marv Grissom	4.00	8.00
217 Gene Stephens	4.00	8.00
218 Ray Jablonski	4.00	8.00
219 Tom Acker RC	4.00	8.00
220 Jackie Jensen	10.00	20.00
221 Dixie Howell	4.00	8.00
222 Alex Grammas	4.00	8.00
223 Frank House	4.00	8.00
224 Marv Blaylock	4.00	8.00
225 Harry Simpson	4.00	8.00
226 Preston Ward	4.00	8.00
227 Gerry Staley	4.00	8.00
228 Smoky Burgess UER	7.50	15.00
229 George Susce	4.00	8.00
230 George Kell	10.00	25.00
231 Solly Hemus	4.00	8.00
232 Whitey Lockman	7.50	15.00
233 Art Fowler	4.00	8.00
234 Dick Cole	4.00	8.00
235 Tom Poholsky	4.00	8.00
236 Joe Ginsberg	4.00	8.00
237 Foster Castleman	4.00	8.00
238 Eddie Robinson	4.00	8.00
239 Tom Morgan	4.00	8.00
240 Hank Bauer	20.00	50.00
241 Joe Lonnett RC	4.00	8.00
242 Charlie Neal	7.50	15.00
243 St. Louis Cardinals TC	7.50	15.00
244 Billy Loes	7.50	15.00
245 Rip Repulski	4.00	8.00
246 Jose Valdivielso	4.00	8.00
247 Turk Lown	4.00	8.00
248 Jim Finigan	4.00	8.00
249 Dave Pope	4.00	8.00
250 Eddie Mathews	25.00	60.00
251 Baltimore Orioles TC	7.50	15.00
252 Carl Erskine	7.50	15.00
253 Gus Zernial	7.50	15.00
254 Ron Negray	4.00	8.00
255 Charlie Silvera	7.50	15.00
256 Ron Kline	4.00	8.00
257 Walt Dropo	4.00	8.00
258 Steve Gromek	4.00	8.00
259 Eddie O'Brien	4.00	8.00
260 Del Ennis	7.50	15.00
261 Bob Chakales	4.00	8.00
262 Bobby Thomson	7.50	15.00
263 George Strickland	4.00	8.00
264 Bob Turley	7.50	15.00
265 Harvey Haddix DP	6.00	12.00
266 Ken Kuhn DP RC	6.00	12.00
267 Danny Kravitz RC	10.00	20.00
268 Jack Collum	10.00	20.00
269 Bob Cerv	15.00	30.00
270 Washington Senators TC	35.00	60.00
271 Danny O'Connell DP	6.00	12.00
272 Bobby Shantz	15.00	40.00
273 Jim Davis	10.00	20.00
274 Don Hoak	7.50	15.00
275 Cleveland Indians TC UER	35.00	60.00
276 Jim Pyburn RC	10.00	20.00
277 Johnny Podres DP	25.00	60.00
278 Fred Hatfield DP	6.00	12.00
279 Bob Thurman RC	10.00	20.00
280 Alex Kellner	10.00	20.00
281 Gail Harris	10.00	20.00
282 Jack Dittmer DP	6.00	12.00
283 Wes Covington DP RC	6.00	12.00
284 Don Zimmer	20.00	40.00
285 Ned Garver	10.00	20.00
286 Bobby Richardson RC	50.00	120.00
287 Sam Jones	10.00	20.00
288 Ted Lepcio	10.00	20.00
289 Jim Bolger DP	6.00	12.00
290 Andy Carey DP	20.00	40.00
291 Windy McCall	10.00	20.00
292 Billy Klaus	10.00	20.00
293 Ted Abernathy RC	10.00	20.00
294 Rocky Bridges DP	6.00	12.00
295 Joe Collins DP	20.00	40.00
296 Johnny Klippstein	10.00	20.00
297 Jack Crimian	10.00	20.00
298 Irv Noren DP	6.00	12.00
299 Chuck Harmon	10.00	20.00
300 Mike Garcia	15.00	30.00
301 Sammy Esposito DP RC	10.00	20.00
302 Sandy Koufax DP	150.00	300.00
303 Billy Goodman	15.00	30.00
304 Joe Cunningham	15.00	30.00
305 Chico Fernandez	10.00	20.00
306 Darrell Johnson DP RC	6.00	12.00
307 Jack D. Phillips DP	6.00	12.00
308 Dick Hall	10.00	20.00
309 Jim Busby DP	6.00	12.00
310 Max Surkont DP	6.00	12.00
311 Al Pilarcik DP RC	6.00	12.00
312 Tony Kubek DP RC	40.00	100.00
313 Mel Parnell	7.50	15.00
314 Ed Bouchee DP RC	6.00	12.00
315 Lou Berberet DP	6.00	12.00
316 Billy O'Dell	10.00	20.00
317 New York Giants TC	50.00	80.00
318 Mickey McDermott	10.00	20.00
319 Gino Cimoli RC	10.00	20.00
320 Neil Chrisley RC	10.00	20.00
321 John Red Murff RC	10.00	20.00
322 Cincinnati Reds TC	50.00	80.00
323 Wes Westrum	15.00	30.00
324 Brooklyn Dodgers TC	40.00	100.00
325 Frank Bolling	10.00	20.00
326 Pedro Ramos	10.00	20.00
327 Jim Pendleton	10.00	20.00
328 Brooks Robinson RC	300.00	600.00
329 Chicago White Sox TC	35.00	60.00
330 Jim Wilson	10.00	20.00
331 Ray Katt	10.00	20.00
332 Bob Bowman RC	10.00	20.00
333 Ernie Johnson	10.00	20.00
334 Jerry Schoonmaker	10.00	20.00
335 Granny Hamner	10.00	20.00
336 Haywood Sullivan RC	20.00	40.00
337 Rene Valdes RC	12.50	25.00
338 Jim Bunning RC	90.00	150.00
339 Bob Speake	10.00	20.00
340 Bill Wight	10.00	20.00
341 Don Gross RC	10.00	20.00
342 Gene Mauch	15.00	30.00
343 Taylor Phillips RC	7.50	15.00
344 Paul LaPalme	10.00	20.00
345 Paul Smith	10.00	20.00
346 Dick Littlefield	10.00	20.00
347 Hal Naragon	10.00	20.00
348 Jim Hearn	10.00	20.00
349 Nellie King	10.00	20.00
350 Eddie Miksis	10.00	20.00
351 Dave Hillman RC	10.00	20.00
352 Ellis Kinder	10.00	20.00
353 Cal Neeman RC	4.00	8.00
354 Rip Coleman RC	4.00	8.00
355 Frank Malzone	7.50	15.00
356 Faye Throneberry	4.00	8.00
357 Earl Torgeson	4.00	8.00
358 Jerry Lynch	7.50	15.00
359 Tom Cheney RC	4.00	8.00
360 Johnny Groth	4.00	8.00
361 Curt Barclay RC	4.00	8.00
362 Roman Mejias RC	7.50	15.00
363 Eddie Kasko RC	4.00	8.00
364 Cal McLish RC	7.50	15.00
365 Ozzie Virgil RC	4.00	8.00
366 Ken Lehman	4.00	8.00
367 Ed Fitzgerald	4.00	8.00
368 Bob Purkey	4.00	8.00
369 Milt Graff RC	4.00	8.00
370 Warren Hacker	4.00	8.00
371 Bob Lennon	4.00	8.00
372 Norm Zauchin	4.00	8.00
373 Pete Whisenant RC	4.00	8.00
374 Don Cardwell RC	4.00	8.00
375 Jim Landis RC	7.50	15.00
376 Don Elston RC	4.00	8.00
377 Andre Rodgers RC	4.00	8.00
378 Elmer Singleton	4.00	8.00
379 Don Lee RC	4.00	8.00
380 Walker Cooper	4.00	8.00
381 Dean Stone	4.00	8.00
382 Jim Brideweser	4.00	8.00
383 Juan Pizarro RC	4.00	8.00
384 Bobby G. Smith RC	4.00	8.00
385 Art Houtteman	4.00	8.00
386 Lyle Luttrell RC	4.00	8.00
387 Jack Sanford RC	7.50	15.00
388 Pete Daley	4.00	8.00
389 Dave Jolly	4.00	8.00
390 Reno Bertoia	4.00	8.00
391 Ralph Terry RC	7.50	15.00
392 Chuck Tanner	8.00	20.00
393 Raul Sanchez RC	4.00	8.00
394 Luis Arroyo	7.50	15.00
395 Bubba Phillips	4.00	8.00
396 Casey Wise RC	4.00	8.00
397 Roy Smalley	4.00	8.00
398 Al Cicotte RC	7.50	15.00
399 Billy Consolo	4.00	8.00
400 Fur/Hodges/Campy/Snider	50.00	150.00
401 Earl Battey RC	7.50	15.00
402 Jim Pisoni RC	4.00	8.00
403 Dick Hyde RC	4.00	8.00
404 Harry Anderson RC	4.00	8.00
405 Duke Maas	4.00	8.00
406 Bob Hale	4.00	8.00
407 Y.Berra/M.Mantle	150.00	400.00
CC1 Contest May 4	60.00	100.00
CC2 Contest May 25	60.00	100.00
CC3 Contest June 22	75.00	125.00
CC4 Contest July 19	75.00	125.00
NNO Checklist 1/2 Bazooka	150.00	250.00
NNO Checklist 1/2 Blony	150.00	250.00
NNO Checklist 2/3 Bazooka	250.00	400.00
NNO Checklist 2/3 Blony	250.00	400.00
NNO Checklist 3/4 Bazooka	500.00	800.00
NNO Checklist 3/4 Blony	350.00	600.00
NNO Checklist 4/5 Bazooka	600.00	1,000.00
NNO Checklist 4/5 Blony	500.00	800.00
NNO Lucky Penny Charm	60.00	100.00

1958 Topps

This is a 494-card standard-size set. Card number 145, which was supposedly to be Ed Bouchee, was not issued. The 1958 Topps set contains the first Sport Magazine All-Star Selection series (475-495) and expanded use of combination cards. For the first time team cards carried series checklists on back (Milwaukee, Detroit, Baltimore, and Cincinnati are also found with players listed alphabetically). In the first series some cards were issued with yellow name (YN) or team (YT) lettering, as opposed to the common white lettering. They are explicity noted below. Cards were issued in one-card penny packs or six-card nickel packs. In the last series, All-Star cards of Stan Musial and Mickey Mantle were triple printed; the cards they replaced (443, 446, 450, and 462) on the printing sheet were hence printed in shorter supply than other cards in the last series and are marked with an SP in the list below. The All-Star card of Musial marked his first appearence on a Topps card. Technically the New York Giants team card (19) is an error as the Giants had already moved to San Francisco. The key Rookie Cards in this set are Orlando Cepeda, Curt Flood, Roger Maris, and Vada Pinson. These cards were issued in varying formats, including one cent packs which were issued 120 to a box.

COMP. MASTER SET (534)	6,000.00	12,000.00
COMPLETE SET (494)	4,000.00	8,000.00
COMMON CARD (1-110)	6.00	12.00
COMMON CARD (111-495)	4.00	8.00
WRAPPER (1-CENT)	75.00	100.00
WRAPPER (5-CENT)	100.00	125.00
1 Ted Williams	200.00	400.00
2A Bob Lemon	15.00	30.00
2B Bob Lemon YT	35.00	60.00
3 Alex Kellner	6.00	12.00
4 Hank Foiles	6.00	12.00
5 Willie Mays	125.00	300.00
6 George Zuverink	6.00	12.00
7 Dale Long	7.50	15.00
8A Eddie Kasko	6.00	12.00
8B Eddie Kasko YN	20.00	40.00
9 Hank Bauer	10.00	20.00
10 Lou Burdette	10.00	20.00
11A Jim Rivera	6.00	12.00
11B Jim Rivera YT	20.00	40.00
12 George Crowe	6.00	12.00
13A Billy Hoeft	6.00	12.00
13B Billy Hoeft YN	20.00	40.00
14 Rip Repulski	6.00	12.00
15 Jim Lemon	7.50	15.00
16 Charlie Neal	7.50	15.00
17 Felix Mantilla	6.00	12.00
18 Frank Sullivan	6.00	12.00
19 San Francisco Giants TC	20.00	40.00
20A Gil McDougald	10.00	20.00
20B Gil McDougald YN	35.00	60.00
21 Curt Barclay	6.00	12.00
22 Hal Naragon	6.00	12.00
23A Bill Tuttle	6.00	12.00
23B Bill Tuttle YN	20.00	40.00
24A Hobie Landrith	6.00	12.00
24B Hobie Landrith YN	20.00	50.00
25 Don Drysdale	30.00	80.00
26 Ron Jackson	6.00	12.00
27 Bud Freeman	6.00	12.00
28 Jim Busby	6.00	12.00
29 Ted Lepcio	6.00	12.00
30A Hank Aaron	125.00	300.00
30B Hank Aaron YN	250.00	500.00
31 Tex Clevenger RC	6.00	12.00
32A J.W. Porter	6.00	12.00
32B J.W. Porter YN	20.00	40.00
33A Cal Neeman	6.00	12.00
33B Cal Neeman YT	20.00	40.00
34 Bob Thurman	6.00	12.00
35A Don Mossi	7.50	15.00
35B Don Mossi YT	20.00	40.00
36 Ted Kazanski	6.00	12.00
37 Mike McCormick UER RC	7.50	15.00
38 Dick Gernert	6.00	12.00
39 Bob Martyn RC	6.00	12.00
40 George Kell	10.00	25.00
41 Dave Hillman	6.00	12.00
42 John Roseboro RC	15.00	30.00
43 Sal Maglie	7.50	15.00
44 Washington Senators TC	10.00	20.00
45 Dick Groat	7.50	15.00
46A Lou Sleater	6.00	12.00
46B Lou Sleater YN	20.00	40.00
47 Roger Maris RC	300.00	500.00
48 Chuck Harmon	6.00	12.00
49 Smoky Burgess	7.50	15.00
50A Billy Pierce	7.50	15.00
50B Billy Pierce YT	20.00	40.00
51 Del Rice	6.00	12.00
52A Roberto Clemente	175.00	300.00
52B Roberto Clemente YT	300.00	500.00
53A Morrie Martin	6.00	12.00
53B Morrie Martin YN	20.00	40.00
54 Norm Siebern RC	10.00	20.00
55 Chico Carrasquel	6.00	12.00
56 Bill Fischer RC	6.00	12.00
57A Tim Thompson	6.00	12.00
57B Tim Thompson YN	20.00	40.00
58A Art Schult	6.00	12.00
58B Art Schult YT	20.00	40.00
59 Dave Sisler	6.00	12.00
60A Del Ennis	7.50	15.00
60B Del Ennis YN	20.00	40.00
61A Darrell Johnson	6.00	12.00
61B Darrell Johnson YN	20.00	40.00
62 Joe DeMaestri	6.00	12.00
63 Joe Nuxhall	7.50	15.00
64 Joe Lonnett	6.00	12.00
65A Von McDaniel RC	6.00	12.00
65B Von McDaniel YN	20.00	40.00
66 Lee Walls	6.00	12.00
67 Joe Ginsberg	6.00	12.00
68 Daryl Spencer	6.00	12.00
69 Wally Burnette	6.00	12.00
70A Al Kaline	60.00	100.00
70B Al Kaline YN	150.00	250.00
71 Los Angeles Dodgers TC	35.00	60.00
72 Bud Byerly UER	6.00	12.00
73 Pete Daley	6.00	12.00
74 Roy Face	7.50	15.00
75 Gus Bell	7.50	15.00
76A Dick Farrell RC	6.00	12.00
76B Dick Farrell YT	20.00	40.00
77A Don Zimmer	7.50	15.00
77B Don Zimmer YT	20.00	40.00
78A Ernie Johnson	7.50	15.00
78B Ernie Johnson YN	20.00	40.00
79A Dick Williams	7.50	15.00
79B Dick Williams YT	20.00	40.00
80 Dick Drott RC	6.00	12.00
81A Steve Boros RC	6.00	12.00
81B Steve Boros YT	20.00	40.00
82 Ron Kline	6.00	12.00
83 Bob Hazle RC	6.00	12.00
84 Billy O'Dell	6.00	12.00
85A Luis Aparicio	15.00	30.00
85B Luis Aparicio YT	50.00	80.00
86 Valmy Thomas RC	6.00	12.00
87 Johnny Kucks	6.00	12.00
88 Duke Snider	25.00	60.00
89 Billy Klaus	6.00	12.00
90 Robin Roberts	25.00	60.00
91 Chuck Tanner	7.50	15.00
92A Clint Courtney	6.00	12.00
92B Clint Courtney YN	20.00	40.00
93 Sandy Amoros	7.50	15.00
94 Bob Skinner	7.50	15.00
95 Frank Bolling	6.00	12.00
96 Joe Durham RC	6.00	12.00
97A Larry Jackson	6.00	12.00
97B Larry Jackson YN	20.00	40.00
98A Billy Hunter	6.00	12.00
98B Billy Hunter YN	20.00	40.00
99 Bobby Adams	6.00	12.00
100A Early Wynn	15.00	30.00
100B Early Wynn YT	50.00	80.00
101A Bobby Richardson	15.00	30.00
101B B.Richardson YN	35.00	60.00
102 George Strickland	6.00	12.00
103 Jerry Lynch	7.50	15.00
104 Jim Pendleton	6.00	12.00
105 Billy Gardner	6.00	12.00
106 Dick Schofield	7.50	15.00
107 Ossie Virgil	6.00	12.00
108A Jim Landis	6.00	12.00
108B Jim Landis YT	20.00	40.00
109 Herb Plews	6.00	12.00
110 Johnny Logan	7.50	15.00
111 Stu Miller	5.00	10.00
112 Gus Zernial	5.00	10.00
113 Jerry Walker RC	4.00	8.00
114 Irv Noren	5.00	10.00
115 Jim Bunning	12.00	30.00
116 Dave Philley	4.00	8.00
117 Frank Torre	5.00	10.00
118 Harvey Haddix	5.00	10.00
119 Harry Chiti	4.00	8.00
120 Johnny Podres	10.00	25.00
121 Eddie Miksis	4.00	8.00
122 Walt Moryn	4.00	8.00
123 Dick Tomanek RC	4.00	8.00
124 Bobby Usher	4.00	8.00
125 Alvin Dark	5.00	10.00
126 Stan Palys RC	4.00	8.00
127 Tom Sturdivant	8.00	20.00
128 Willie Kirkland RC	4.00	8.00
129 Jim Derrington RC	4.00	8.00
130 Jackie Jensen	5.00	10.00
131 Bob Henrich RC	4.00	8.00
132 Vern Law	5.00	10.00
133 Russ Nixon RC	4.00	8.00
134 Philadelphia Phillies TC	7.50	15.00
135 Mike MoeDrabowsky	5.00	10.00
136 Jim Finigan	4.00	8.00
137 Russ Kemmerer	4.00	8.00
138 Earl Torgeson	4.00	8.00
139 George Brunet RC	4.00	8.00
140 Wes Covington	5.00	10.00
141 Ken Lehman	4.00	8.00
142 Enos Slaughter	12.00	30.00
143 Billy Muffett RC	4.00	8.00
144 Bobby Morgan	4.00	8.00
146 Dick Gray RC	4.00	8.00
147 Don McMahon RC	4.00	8.00
148 Billy Consolo	4.00	8.00
149 Tom Acker	4.00	8.00
150 Mickey Mantle	500.00	1,000.00
151 Buddy Pritchard RC	4.00	8.00
152 Johnny Antonelli	5.00	10.00
153 Les Moss	4.00	8.00
154 Harry Byrd	4.00	8.00
155 Hector Lopez	5.00	10.00
156 Dick Hyde	4.00	8.00
157 Dee Fondy	4.00	8.00
158 Cleveland Indians TC	7.50	15.00
159 Taylor Phillips	4.00	8.00
160 Don Hoak	5.00	10.00
161 Don Larsen	10.00	25.00
162 Gil Hodges	20.00	50.00
163 Jim Wilson	4.00	8.00
164 Bob Taylor RC	4.00	8.00
165 Bob Nieman	4.00	8.00
166 Danny O'Connell	4.00	8.00
167 Frank Baumann RC	4.00	8.00
168 Joe Cunningham	4.00	8.00
169 Ralph Terry	5.00	10.00
170 Vic Wertz	5.00	10.00
171 Harry Anderson	4.00	8.00
172 Don Gross	4.00	8.00
173 Eddie Yost	4.00	8.00
174 Kansas City Athletics TC	7.50	15.00
175 Marv Throneberry RC	7.50	15.00
176 Bob Buhl	5.00	10.00
177 Al Smith	4.00	8.00
178 Ted Kluszewski	12.50	25.00
179 Willie Miranda	4.00	8.00
180 Lindy McDaniel	5.00	10.00
181 Willie Jones	4.00	8.00
182 Joe Caffie RC	4.00	8.00
183 Dave Jolly	4.00	8.00

184 Elvin Tappe	4.00	8.00
185 Ray Boone	5.00	10.00
186 Jack Meyer	4.00	8.00
187 Sandy Koufax	75.00	200.00
188 Milt Bolling UER	4.00	8.00
189 George Susce	4.00	8.00
190 Red Schoendienst	12.50	25.00
191 Art Ceccarelli RC	4.00	8.00
192 Milt Graff	4.00	8.00
193 Jerry Lumpe RC	4.00	8.00
194 Roger Craig	5.00	10.00
195 Whitey Lockman	5.00	10.00
196 Mike Garcia	5.00	10.00
197 Haywood Sullivan	5.00	10.00
198 Bill Virdon	5.00	10.00
199 Don Blasingame	4.00	8.00
200 Bob Keegan	4.00	8.00
201 Jim Bolger	4.00	8.00
202 Woody Held RC	4.00	8.00
203 Al Walker	4.00	8.00
204 Leo Kiely	4.00	8.00
205 Johnny Temple	5.00	10.00
206 Bob Shaw RC	4.00	8.00
207 Solly Hemus	4.00	8.00
208 Cal McLish	4.00	8.00
209 Bob Anderson RC	4.00	8.00
210 Wally Moon	5.00	10.00
211 Pete Burnside RC	4.00	8.00
212 Bubba Phillips	4.00	8.00
213 Red Wilson	4.00	8.00
214 Willard Schmidt	4.00	8.00
215 Jim Gilliam	7.50	15.00
216 St. Louis Cardinals TC	7.50	15.00
217 Jack Harshman	4.00	8.00
218 Dick Rand RC	4.00	8.00
219 Camilo Pascual	5.00	10.00
220 Tom Brewer	4.00	8.00
221 Jerry Kindall RC	4.00	8.00
222 Bud Daley RC	4.00	8.00
223 Andy Pafko	5.00	10.00
224 Bob Grim	5.00	10.00
225 Billy Goodman	5.00	10.00
226 Bob Smith RC	4.00	8.00
227 Gene Stephens	4.00	8.00
228 Duke Maas	4.00	8.00
229 Frank Zupo RC	4.00	8.00
230 Richie Ashburn	15.00	40.00
231 Lloyd Merritt RC	4.00	8.00
232 Reno Bertoia	4.00	8.00
233 Mickey Vernon	5.00	10.00
234 Carl Sawatski	4.00	8.00
235 Tom Gorman	4.00	8.00
236 Ed Fitzgerald	4.00	8.00
237 Bill Wight	4.00	8.00
238 Bill Mazeroski	15.00	40.00
239 Chuck Stobbs	4.00	8.00
240 Bill Skowron	15.00	40.00
241 Dick Littlefield	4.00	8.00
242 Johnny Klippstein	4.00	8.00
243 Larry Raines RC	4.00	8.00
244 Don Demeter RC	4.00	8.00
245 Frank Lary	5.00	10.00
246 New York Yankees TC	30.00	80.00
247 Casey Wise	4.00	8.00
248 Herman Wehmeier	4.00	8.00
249 Ray Moore	4.00	8.00
250 Roy Sievers	5.00	10.00
251 Warren Hacker	4.00	8.00
252 Bob Trowbridge RC	4.00	8.00
253 Don Mueller	5.00	10.00
254 Alex Grammas	4.00	8.00
255 Bob Turley	5.00	10.00
256 Chicago White Sox TC	7.50	15.00
257 Hal Smith	4.00	8.00
258 Carl Erskine	7.50	15.00
259 Al Pilarcik	4.00	8.00
260 Frank Malzone	5.00	10.00
261 Turk Lown	4.00	8.00
262 Johnny Groth	4.00	8.00
263 Eddie Bressoud RC	5.00	10.00
264 Jack Sanford	5.00	10.00
265 Pete Runnels	5.00	10.00
266 Connie Johnson	4.00	8.00
267 Sherm Lollar	5.00	10.00
268 Granny Hamner	4.00	8.00
269 Paul Smith	4.00	8.00
270 Warren Spahn	30.00	80.00
271 Billy Martin	15.00	40.00
272 Ray Crone	4.00	8.00
273 Hal Smith	4.00	8.00
274 Rocky Bridges	4.00	8.00
275 Elston Howard	15.00	40.00
276 Bobby Avila	4.00	8.00
277 Virgil Trucks	5.00	10.00
278 Mack Burk	4.00	8.00
279 Bob Boyd	4.00	8.00
280 Jim Piersall	5.00	10.00
281 Sammy Taylor RC	4.00	8.00
282 Paul Foytack	4.00	8.00
283 Ray Shearer RC	4.00	8.00
284 Ray Katt	4.00	8.00
285 Frank Robinson	60.00	100.00
286 Gino Cimoli	4.00	8.00
287 Sam Jones	5.00	10.00
288 Harmon Killebrew	40.00	100.00
289 B.Shantz/L.Burdette	5.00	10.00
290 Dick Donovan	4.00	8.00
291 Don Landrum RC	4.00	8.00
292 Ned Garver	4.00	8.00
293 Gene Freese	4.00	8.00
294 Hal Jeffcoat	4.00	8.00
295 Minnie Minoso	12.50	25.00
296 Ryne Duren RC	15.00	40.00
297 Don Buddin RC	4.00	8.00
298 Jim Hearn	4.00	8.00
299 Harry Simpson	4.00	8.00
300 W.Harridge/W.Giles	7.50	15.00
301 Randy Jackson	4.00	8.00
302 Mike Baxes RC	4.00	8.00
303 Neil Chrisley	4.00	8.00
304 H.Kuenn/A.Kaline	12.50	25.00
305 Clem Labine	5.00	10.00
306 Whammy Douglas RC	4.00	8.00
307 Brooks Robinson	50.00	120.00
308 Paul Giel	5.00	10.00
309 Gail Harris	4.00	8.00
310 Ernie Banks	50.00	120.00
311 Bob Purkey	4.00	8.00
312 Boston Red Sox TC	7.50	15.00
313 Bob Rush	4.00	8.00
314 D.Snider/W.Alston	15.00	40.00
315 Bob Friend	5.00	10.00
316 Tito Francona	5.00	10.00
317 Albie Pearson RC	5.00	10.00
318 Frank House	4.00	8.00
319 Lou Skizas	4.00	8.00
320 Whitey Ford	30.00	80.00
321 T.Kluszewski/T.Williams	25.00	60.00
322 Harding Peterson RC	5.00	10.00
323 Elmer Valo	4.00	8.00
324 Hoyt Wilhelm	12.50	25.00
325 Joe Adcock	5.00	10.00
326 Bob Miller	4.00	8.00
327 Chicago Cubs TC	7.50	15.00
328 Ike Delock	4.00	8.00
329 Bob Cerv	5.00	10.00
330 Ed Bailey	5.00	10.00
331 Pedro Ramos	4.00	8.00
332 Jim King	4.00	8.00
333 Andy Carey	5.00	10.00
334 B.Friend/B.Pierce	5.00	10.00
335 Ruben Gomez	4.00	8.00
336 Bert Hamric	4.00	8.00
337 Hank Aguirre	4.00	8.00
338 Walt Dropo	5.00	10.00
339 Fred Hatfield	4.00	8.00
340 Don Newcombe	15.00	40.00
341 Pittsburgh Pirates TC	7.50	15.00
342 Jim Brosnan	5.00	10.00
343 Orlando Cepeda RC	60.00	150.00
344 Bob Porterfield	4.00	8.00
345 Jim Hegan	5.00	10.00
346 Steve Bilko	4.00	8.00
347 Don Rudolph RC	4.00	8.00
348 Chico Fernandez	4.00	8.00
349 Murry Dickson	4.00	8.00
350 Ken Boyer	12.50	25.00
351 Cran/Math/Aaron/Adcock	30.00	80.00
352 Herb Score	7.50	15.00
353 Stan Lopata	4.00	8.00
354 Art Ditmar	5.00	10.00
355 Bill Bruton	5.00	10.00
356 Bob Malkmus RC	4.00	8.00
357 Danny McDevitt RC	4.00	8.00
358 Gene Baker	4.00	8.00
359 Billy Loes	5.00	10.00
360 Roy McMillan	5.00	10.00
361 Mike Fornieles	4.00	8.00
362 Ray Jablonski	4.00	8.00
363 Don Elston	4.00	8.00
364 Earl Battey	4.00	8.00
365 Tom Morgan	4.00	8.00
366 Gene Green RC	4.00	8.00
367 Jack Urban RC	4.00	8.00
368 Rocky Colavito	25.00	60.00
369 Ralph Lumenti RC	4.00	8.00
370 Yogi Berra	50.00	120.00
371 Marty Keough RC	4.00	8.00
372 Don Cardwell	4.00	8.00
373 Joe Pignatano RC	4.00	8.00
374 Brooks Lawrence	4.00	8.00
375 Pee Wee Reese	20.00	50.00
376 Charley Rabe RC	4.00	8.00
377A Milwaukee Braves TC Alpha	7.50	15.00
377B Milwaukee Braves TC Num	60.00	100.00
378 Hank Sauer	5.00	10.00
379 Ray Herbert	4.00	8.00
380 Charlie Maxwell	5.00	10.00
381 Hal Brown	4.00	8.00
382 Al Cicotte	4.00	8.00
383 Lou Berberet	4.00	8.00
384 John Goryl RC	4.00	8.00
385 Wilmer Mizell	5.00	10.00
386 Bailey/Tebbets/F.Rob	7.50	15.00
387 Wally Post	5.00	10.00
388 Billy Moran RC	4.00	8.00
389 Bill Taylor	4.00	8.00
390 Del Crandall	5.00	10.00
391 Dave Melton RC	4.00	8.00
392 Bennie Daniels RC	4.00	8.00
393 Tony Kubek	15.00	30.00
394 Jim Grant RC	4.00	8.00
395 Willard Nixon	4.00	8.00
396 Dutch Dotterer RC	4.00	8.00
397A Detroit Tigers TC Alpha	7.50	15.00
397B Detroit Tigers TC Num	60.00	100.00
398 Gene Woodling	5.00	10.00
399 Marv Grissom	4.00	8.00
400 Nellie Fox	12.00	30.00
401 Don Bessent	4.00	8.00
402 Bobby Gene Smith	4.00	8.00
403 Steve Korcheck RC	4.00	8.00
404 Curt Simmons	5.00	10.00
405 Ken Aspromonte RC	4.00	8.00
406 Vic Power	5.00	10.00
407 Carlton Willey RC	5.00	10.00
408A Baltimore Orioles TC Alpha	7.50	15.00
408B Baltimore Orioles TC Num	60.00	100.00
409 Frank Thomas	5.00	10.00
410 Murray Wall	4.00	8.00
411 Tony Taylor RC	5.00	10.00
412 Gerry Staley	4.00	8.00
413 Jim Davenport RC	4.00	8.00
414 Sammy White	4.00	8.00
415 Bob Bowman	4.00	8.00
416 Foster Castleman	4.00	8.00
417 Carl Furillo	7.50	15.00
418 M.Mantle/H.Aaron	125.00	300.00
419 Bobby Shantz	5.00	10.00
420 Vada Pinson RC	20.00	50.00
421 Dixie Howell	4.00	8.00
422 Norm Zauchin	4.00	8.00
423 Phil Clark RC	4.00	8.00
424 Larry Doby UER	15.00	40.00
425 Sammy Esposito	4.00	8.00
426 Johnny O'Brien	5.00	10.00
427 Al Worthington	4.00	8.00
428A Cincinnati Reds TC Alpha	7.50	15.00
428B Cincinnati Reds TC Num	60.00	100.00
429 Gus Triandos	5.00	10.00
430 Bobby Thomson	5.00	10.00
431 Gene Conley	5.00	10.00
432 John Powers RC	4.00	8.00
433A Pancho Herrera COR RC	5.00	10.00
433B Pancho Herrer ERR	350.00	600.00
433C Pancho Herre ERR		
433D Pancho Herr ERR		
434 Harvey Kuenn	5.00	10.00
435 Ed Roebuck	5.00	10.00
436 W.Mays/D.Snider	25.00	60.00
437 Bob Speake	4.00	8.00
438 Whitey Herzog	5.00	10.00
439 Ray Narleski	4.00	8.00
440 Eddie Mathews	25.00	60.00
441 Jim Marshall RC	5.00	10.00
442 Phil Paine RC	4.00	8.00
443 Billy Harrell SP RC	10.00	20.00
444 Danny Kravitz	4.00	8.00
445 Bob Smith RC	4.00	8.00
446 Carroll Hardy SP RC	10.00	20.00
447 Ray Monzant	4.00	8.00
448 Charlie Lau RC	5.00	10.00
449 Gene Fodge RC	4.00	8.00
450 Preston Ward SP	10.00	20.00
451 Joe Taylor RC	4.00	8.00
452 Roman Mejias	4.00	8.00
453 Tom Qualters	4.00	8.00
454 Harry Hanebrink RC	4.00	8.00
455 Hal Griggs RC	4.00	8.00
456 Dick Brown RC	4.00	8.00
457 Milt Pappas RC	5.00	10.00
458 Julio Becquer RC	4.00	8.00
459 Ron Blackburn RC	4.00	8.00
460 Chuck Essegian RC	4.00	8.00
461 Ed Mayer RC	4.00	8.00
462 Gary Geiger SP RC	10.00	20.00
463 Vito Valentinetti	4.00	8.00
464 Curt Flood RC	20.00	50.00
465 Arnie Portocarrero	4.00	8.00
466 Pete Whisenant	4.00	8.00
467 Glen Hobbie RC	4.00	8.00
468 Bob Schmidt RC	4.00	8.00
469 Don Ferrarese	4.00	8.00
470 R.C. Stevens RC	4.00	8.00
471 Lenny Green RC	4.00	8.00
472 Joey Jay	5.00	10.00
473 Bill Renna	4.00	8.00
474 Roman Semproch RC	4.00	8.00
475 F.Haney/C.Stengel AS	15.00	40.00
476 Stan Musial AS TP	30.00	50.00
477 Bill Skowron AS	5.00	10.00
478 Johnny Temple AS UER	4.00	8.00
479 Nellie Fox AS	7.50	15.00
480 Eddie Mathews AS	15.00	40.00
481 Frank Malzone AS	4.00	8.00
482 Ernie Banks AS	25.00	60.00
483 Luis Aparicio AS	10.00	25.00
484 Frank Robinson AS	25.00	60.00
485 Ted Williams AS	50.00	120.00
486 Willie Mays AS	40.00	100.00
487 Mickey Mantle AS TP	75.00	200.00
488 Hank Aaron AS	30.00	80.00
489 Jackie Jensen AS	5.00	10.00
490 Ed Bailey AS	4.00	8.00
491 Sherm Lollar AS	4.00	8.00
492 Bob Friend AS	10.00	25.00
493 Bob Turley AS	5.00	10.00
494 Warren Spahn AS	12.50	25.00
495 Herb Score AS	7.50	15.00
NNO Contest Cards	20.00	40.00
NNO Felt Emblem Insert		

1959 Topps

The cards in this 572-card set measure 2 1/2" by 3 1/2". The 1959 Topps set contains bust pictures of the players in a colored circle. Card numbers 551 to 572 are Sporting News All-Star Selections. High numbers 507 to 572 have the card number in a black background on the reverse rather than a green background as in the lower numbers. The high numbers are more difficult to obtain. Several cards in the 300s exist with or without an extra traded or option line on the back of the card. Cards 199 to 286 exist with either white or gray backs. There is no price differential for either colored back. Cards 461 to 470 contain "Highlights" while cards 116 to 146 give an alphabetically ordered listing of "Rookie Prospects." These Rookie Prospects (RP) were Topps' first organized inclusion of untested "Rookie" cards. Card 440 features Lew Burdette erroneously posing as a left-handed pitcher. Cards were issued in one-card penny packs or six-card nickel packs. There were some three-card advertising panels produced by Topps; the players included are from the first series. Panels which had Ted Kluszewski's card back on the back included Don McMahon/Red Wilson/Bob Boyd; Joe Pignatano/Sam Jones/Jack Urban also with Kluszewski's card back on back, Strips with Nellie Fox on the back included Billy Hunter/Chuck Stobbs/Carl Sawatski; Vito Valentinetti/Ken Lehman/Ed Bouchee; Mel Roach/Brooks Lawrence/Warren Spahn. Other panels include Harvey Kuenn/Alex Grammas/ Bob Cerv; and Bob Cerv/Jim Bolger/Mickey Mantle. When separated, these advertising cards are distinguished by the non-standard card back, i.e., part of an advertisement for the 1959 Topps set instead of the typical statistics and biographical information about the player pictured. The key Rookie Cards in this set are Felipe Alou, Sparky Anderson (called George on the card), Norm Cash, Bob Gibson, and Bill White.

COMPLETE SET (572)	4,000.00	8,000.00
COMMON CARD (1-110)	3.00	6.00
COMMON CARD (111-506)	2.00	4.00
COMMON CARD (507-572)	7.50	15.00
WRAPPER (1-CENT)	100.00	125.00
WRAPPER (5-CENT)	75.00	100.00
1 Ford Frick COMM	40.00	100.00
2 Eddie Yost	4.00	8.00
3 Don McMahon	4.00	8.00
4 Albie Pearson	4.00	8.00
5 Dick Donovan	4.00	8.00
6 Alex Grammas	3.00	6.00
7 Al Pilarcik	3.00	6.00
8 Philadelphia Phillies CL	50.00	80.00
9 Paul Giel	4.00	8.00
10 Mickey Mantle	400.00	800.00
11 Billy Hunter	4.00	8.00
12 Vern Law	4.00	8.00
13 Dick Gernert	3.00	6.00
14 Pete Whisenant	3.00	6.00
15 Dick Drott	3.00	6.00
16 Joe Pignatano	3.00	6.00
17 Thomas/Murtaugh/Klusz	4.00	8.00
18 Jack Urban	3.00	6.00
19 Eddie Bressoud	3.00	6.00
20 Duke Snider	25.00	60.00
21 Connie Johnson	3.00	6.00
22 Al Smith	4.00	8.00
23 Murry Dickson	4.00	8.00
24 Red Wilson	3.00	6.00
25 Don Hoak	4.00	8.00
26 Chuck Stobbs	3.00	6.00
27 Andy Pafko	4.00	8.00
28 Al Worthington	3.00	6.00
29 Jim Bolger	3.00	6.00
30 Nellie Fox	15.00	30.00
31 Ken Lehman	3.00	6.00
32 Don Buddin	3.00	6.00
33 Ed Fitzgerald	3.00	6.00
34 Al Kaline/C.Maxwell	12.00	30.00
35 Ted Kluszewski	10.00	25.00
36 Hank Aguirre	3.00	6.00
37 Gene Green	3.00	6.00
38 Morrie Martin	3.00	6.00
39 Ed Bouchee	3.00	6.00
40A Warren Spahn ERR	50.00	80.00
40B Warren Spahn ERR	60.00	100.00
40C Warren Spahn COR	35.00	60.00
41 Bob Martyn	3.00	6.00
42 Murray Wall	3.00	6.00
43 Steve Bilko	3.00	6.00
44 Vito Valentinetti	3.00	6.00
45 Andy Carey	4.00	8.00
46 Bill R. Henry	3.00	6.00
47 Jim Finigan	3.00	6.00
48 Baltimore Orioles CL	12.50	25.00
49 Bill Hall RC	3.00	6.00
50 Willie Mays	60.00	150.00
51 Rip Coleman	3.00	6.00
52 Coot Veal RC	3.00	6.00
53 Stan Williams RC	4.00	8.00
54 Mel Roach	3.00	6.00
55 Tom Brewer	3.00	6.00
56 Carl Sawatski	3.00	6.00
57 Al Cicotte	3.00	6.00
58 Eddie Miksis	3.00	6.00
59 Irv Noren	4.00	8.00
60 Bob Turley	4.00	8.00
61 Dick Brown	3.00	6.00
62 Tony Taylor	4.00	8.00
63 Jim Hearn	3.00	6.00
64 Joe DeMaestri	3.00	6.00
65 Frank Torre	4.00	8.00
66 Joe Ginsberg	3.00	6.00
67 Brooks Lawrence	3.00	6.00
68 Dick Schofield	4.00	8.00
69 San Francisco Giants CL	12.50	25.00
70 Harvey Kuenn	4.00	8.00
71 Don Bessent	3.00	6.00
72 Bill Renna	3.00	6.00
73 Ron Jackson	4.00	8.00
74 Lemon/Lavagetto/Sievers	4.00	8.00
75 Sam Jones	4.00	8.00
76 Bobby Richardson	12.00	30.00
77 John Goryl	3.00	6.00
78 Pedro Ramos	3.00	6.00
79 Harry Chiti	3.00	6.00
80 Minnie Minoso	6.00	12.00
81 Hal Jeffcoat	3.00	6.00
82 Bob Boyd	3.00	6.00
83 Bob Smith	3.00	6.00
84 Reno Bertoia	3.00	6.00
85 Harry Anderson	3.00	6.00
86 Bob Keegan	4.00	8.00
87 Danny O'Connell	3.00	6.00
88 Herb Score	6.00	12.00
89 Billy Gardner	3.00	6.00
90 Bill Skowron	6.00	12.00
91 Herb Moford RC	3.00	6.00
92 Dave Philley	3.00	6.00
93 Julio Becquer	3.00	6.00

94 Chicago White Sox CL	20.00	40.00
95 Carl Willey	3.00	6.00
96 Lou Berberet	3.00	6.00
97 Jerry Lynch	4.00	8.00
98 Arnie Portocarrero	3.00	6.00
99 Ted Kazanski	3.00	6.00
100 Bob Cerv	4.00	8.00
101 Alex Kellner	3.00	6.00
102 Felipe Alou RC	15.00	30.00
103 Billy Goodman	4.00	8.00
104 Del Rice	4.00	8.00
105 Lee Walls	3.00	6.00
106 Hal Woodeshick RC	3.00	6.00
107 Norm Larker RC	4.00	8.00
108 Zack Monroe RC	4.00	8.00
109 Bob Schmidt	3.00	6.00
110 George Witt RC	4.00	8.00
111 Cincinnati Redlegs CL	7.50	15.00
112 Billy Consolo	2.00	4.00
113 Taylor Phillips	2.00	4.00
114 Earl Battey	4.00	8.00
115 Mickey Vernon	4.00	8.00
116 Bob Allison RS RC	6.00	12.00
117 John Blanchard RS RC	6.00	12.00
118 John Buzhardt RS RC	2.50	5.00
119 Johnny Callison RS RC	6.00	12.00
120 Chuck Coles RS RC	2.50	5.00
121 Bob Conley RS RC	2.50	5.00
122 Bennie Daniels RS	2.50	5.00
123 Don Dillard RS RC	2.50	5.00
124 Dan Dobbek RS RC	2.50	5.00
125 Ron Fairly RS RC	6.00	12.00
126 Eddie Haas RS RC	2.50	5.00
127 Kent Hadley RS RC	2.50	5.00
128 Bob Hartman RS RC	2.50	5.00
129 Frank Herrera RS	2.50	5.00
130 Lou Jackson RS RC	2.50	5.00
131 Deron Johnson RS RC	6.00	12.00
132 Don Lee RS	2.50	5.00
133 Bob Lillis RS RC	2.50	5.00
134 Jim McDaniel RS RC	2.50	5.00
135 Gene Oliver RS RC	2.50	5.00
136 Jim O'Toole RS RC	2.50	5.00
137 Dick Ricketts RS RC	2.50	5.00
138 John Romano RS RC	2.50	5.00
139 Ed Sadowski RS RC	2.50	5.00
140 Charlie Secrest RS RC	2.50	5.00
141 Joe Shipley RS RC	2.50	5.00
142 Dick Stigman RS RC	2.50	5.00
143 Willie Tasby RS RC	2.50	5.00
144 Jerry Walker RS	2.50	5.00
145 Dom Zanni RS RC	2.50	5.00
146 Jerry Zimmerman RS RC	2.50	5.00
147 Long/Banks/Moryn	15.00	30.00
148 Mike McCormick	4.00	8.00
149 Jim Bunning	10.00	25.00
150 Stan Musial	40.00	100.00
151 Bob Malkmus	2.00	4.00
152 Johnny Klippstein	2.00	4.00
153 Jim Marshall	2.00	4.00
154 Ray Herbert	2.00	4.00
155 Enos Slaughter	10.00	25.00
156 B.Pierce/R.Roberts	6.00	12.00
157 Felix Mantilla	2.00	4.00
158 Walt Dropo	2.00	4.00
159 Bob Shaw	4.00	8.00
160 Dick Groat	4.00	8.00
161 Frank Baumann	2.00	4.00
162 Bobby G. Smith	2.00	4.00
163 Sandy Koufax	90.00	150.00
164 Johnny Groth	2.00	4.00
165 Bill Bruton	2.00	4.00
166 Minoso/Colavito/Doby	15.00	30.00
167 Duke Maas	2.00	4.00
168 Carroll Hardy	2.00	4.00
169 Ted Abernathy	2.00	4.00
170 Gene Woodling	4.00	8.00
171 Willard Schmidt	2.00	4.00
172 Kansas City Athletics CL	7.50	15.00
173 Bill Monbouquette RC	4.00	8.00
174 Jim Pendleton	2.00	4.00
175 Dick Farrell	4.00	8.00
176 Preston Ward	2.00	4.00
177 John Briggs RC	2.00	4.00
178 Ruben Amaro RC	6.00	12.00
179 Don Rudolph	2.00	4.00
180 Yogi Berra	40.00	100.00
181 Bob Porterfield	2.00	4.00
182 Milt Graff	2.00	4.00
183 Stu Miller	4.00	8.00
184 Harvey Haddix	4.00	8.00
185 Jim Busby	2.00	4.00
186 Mudcat Grant	4.00	8.00
187 Bubba Phillips	4.00	8.00
188 Juan Pizarro	2.00	4.00
189 Neil Chrisley	2.00	4.00
190 Bill Virdon	4.00	8.00
191 Russ Kemmerer	2.00	4.00
192 Charlie Beamon RC	2.00	4.00
193 Sammy Taylor	2.00	4.00
194 Jim Brosnan	4.00	8.00
195 Rip Repulski	2.00	4.00
196 Billy Moran	2.00	4.00
197 Ray Semproch	2.00	4.00
198 Jim Davenport	4.00	8.00
199 Leo Kiely	2.00	4.00
200 W.Giles NL PRES	4.00	8.00
201 Tom Acker	2.00	4.00
202 Roger Maris	50.00	120.00
203 Ossie Virgil	2.00	4.00
204 Casey Wise	2.00	4.00
205 Don Larsen	4.00	8.00
206 Carl Furillo	6.00	12.00
207 George Strickland	2.00	4.00
208 Willie Jones	2.00	4.00
209 Lenny Green	2.00	4.00
210 Ed Bailey	2.00	4.00
211 Bob Blaylock RC	2.00	4.00
212 H.Aaron/E.Mathews	25.00	60.00
213 Jim Rivera	4.00	8.00
214 Marcelino Solis RC	2.00	4.00
215 Jim Lemon	4.00	8.00
216 Andre Rodgers	2.00	4.00
217 Carl Erskine	6.00	12.00
218 Roman Mejias	2.00	4.00
219 George Zuverink	2.00	4.00
220 Frank Malzone	4.00	8.00
221 Bob Bowman	2.00	4.00
222 Bobby Shantz	4.00	8.00
223 St. Louis Cardinals CL	7.50	15.00
224 Claude Osteen RC	4.00	8.00
225 Johnny Logan	4.00	8.00
226 Art Ceccarelli	2.00	4.00
227 Hal W. Smith	2.00	4.00
228 Don Gross	2.00	4.00
229 Vic Power	4.00	8.00
230 Bill Fischer	2.00	4.00
231 Ellis Burton RC	2.00	4.00
232 Eddie Kasko	2.00	4.00
233 Paul Foytack	2.00	4.00
234 Chuck Tanner	4.00	8.00
235 Valmy Thomas	2.00	4.00
236 Ted Bowsfield RC	2.00	4.00
237 McDougald/Turley/B.Rich	6.00	12.00
238 Gene Baker	2.00	4.00
239 Bob Trowbridge	2.00	4.00
240 Hank Bauer	6.00	15.00
241 Billy Muffett	2.00	4.00
242 Ron Samford RC	2.00	4.00
243 Marv Grissom	2.00	4.00
244 Dick Gray	2.00	4.00
245 Ned Garver	2.00	4.00
246 J.W. Porter	2.00	4.00
247 Don Ferrarese	2.00	4.00
248 Boston Red Sox CL	7.50	15.00
249 Bobby Adams	2.00	4.00
250 Billy O'Dell	2.00	4.00
251 Clete Boyer	6.00	12.00
252 Ray Boone	4.00	8.00
253 Seth Morehead RC	2.00	4.00
254 Zeke Bella RC	2.00	4.00
255 Del Ennis	4.00	8.00
256 Jerry Davie RC	2.00	4.00
257 Leon Wagner RC	4.00	8.00
258 Fred Kipp RC	2.00	4.00
259 Jim Pisoni	2.00	4.00
260 Early Wynn UER	10.00	25.00
261 Gene Stephens	2.00	4.00
262 Podres/Labine/Drysdale	6.00	12.00
263 Bud Daley	2.00	4.00
264 Chico Carrasquel	2.00	4.00
265 Ron Kline	2.00	4.00
266 Woody Held	2.00	4.00
267 John Romonosky RC	2.00	4.00
268 Tito Francona	4.00	8.00
269 Jack Meyer	2.00	4.00
270 Gil Hodges	15.00	30.00
271 Orlando Pena RC	2.00	4.00
272 Jerry Lumpe	2.00	4.00
273 Joey Jay	4.00	8.00
274 Jerry Kindall	4.00	8.00
275 Jack Sanford	4.00	8.00
276 Pete Daley	2.00	4.00
277 Turk Lown	4.00	8.00
278 Chuck Essegian	2.00	4.00
279 Ernie Johnson	2.00	4.00
280 Frank Bolling	2.00	4.00
281 Walt Craddock RC	2.00	4.00
282 R.C. Stevens	2.00	4.00
283 Russ Heman RC	2.00	4.00
284 Steve Korcheck	2.00	4.00
285 Joe Cunningham	2.00	4.00
286 Dean Stone	2.00	4.00
287 Don Zimmer	6.00	12.00
288 Dutch Dotterer	2.00	4.00
289 Johnny Kucks	4.00	8.00
290 Wes Covington	2.00	4.00
291 P.Ramos/C.Pascual	2.00	4.00
292 Dick Williams	4.00	8.00
293 Ray Moore	2.00	4.00
294 Hank Foiles	2.00	4.00
295 Billy Martin	10.00	25.00
296 Ernie Broglio RC	2.00	4.00
297 Jackie Brandt RC	2.00	4.00
298 Tex Clevenger	2.00	4.00
299 Billy Klaus	2.00	4.00
300 Richie Ashburn	15.00	40.00
301 Earl Averill Jr. RC	2.00	4.00
302 Don Mossi	4.00	8.00
303 Marty Keough	2.00	4.00
304 Chicago Cubs CL	7.50	15.00
305 Curt Raydon RC	2.00	4.00
306 Jim Gilliam	4.00	8.00
307 Curt Barclay	2.00	4.00
308 Norm Siebern	2.00	4.00
309 Sal Maglie	4.00	8.00
310 Luis Aparicio	12.00	30.00
311 Norm Zauchin	2.00	4.00
312 Don Newcombe	4.00	8.00
313 Frank House	2.00	4.00
314 Don Cardwell	2.00	4.00
315 Joe Adcock	4.00	8.00
316A Ralph Lumenti UER	2.00	4.00
316B Ralph Lumenti UER	50.00	80.00
317 R.Ashburn/W.Mays	20.00	50.00
318 Rocky Bridges	2.00	4.00
319 Dave Hillman	2.00	4.00
320 Bob Skinner	4.00	8.00
321A Bob Giallombardo RC	4.00	8.00
321B Bob Giallombardo ERR	50.00	80.00
322A Harry Hanebrink TR	4.00	8.00
322B H.Hanebrink ERR	50.00	80.00
323 Frank Sullivan	2.00	4.00
324 Don Demeter	2.00	4.00
325 Ken Boyer	6.00	12.00
326 Marv Throneberry	4.00	8.00
327 Gary Bell RC	2.00	4.00
328 Lou Skizas	2.00	4.00
329 Detroit Tigers CL	7.50	15.00
330 Gus Triandos	4.00	8.00
331 Steve Boros	2.00	4.00
332 Ray Monzant	2.00	4.00
333 Harry Simpson	2.00	4.00
334 Glen Hobbie	2.00	4.00
335 Johnny Temple	4.00	8.00
336A Billy Loes TR	4.00	8.00
336B Billy Loes ERR	50.00	80.00
337 George Crowe	2.00	4.00
338 Sparky Anderson RC	20.00	50.00
339 Roy Face	4.00	8.00
340 Roy Sievers	4.00	8.00
341 Tom Qualters	2.00	4.00
342 Ray Jablonski	2.00	4.00
343 Billy Hoeft	2.00	4.00
344 Russ Nixon	2.00	4.00
345 Gil McDougald	6.00	15.00
346 D.Sisler/T.Brewer	2.00	4.00
347 Bob Buhl	2.00	4.00
348 Ted Lepcio	2.00	4.00
349 Hoyt Wilhelm	8.00	20.00
350 Ernie Banks	40.00	100.00
351 Earl Torgeson	2.00	4.00
352 Robin Roberts	12.00	30.00
353 Curt Flood	4.00	8.00
354 Pete Burnside	2.00	4.00
355 Jimmy Piersall	4.00	8.00
356 Bob Mabe RC	2.00	4.00
357 Dick Stuart RC	4.00	8.00
358 Ralph Terry	4.00	8.00
359 Bill White RC	10.00	20.00
360 Al Kaline	25.00	60.00
361 Willard Nixon	2.00	4.00
362A Dolan Nichols RC	2.00	4.00
362B Dolan Nichols ERR	50.00	80.00
363 Bobby Avila	2.00	4.00
364 Danny McDevitt	2.00	4.00
365 Gus Bell	4.00	8.00
366 Humberto Robinson	2.00	4.00
367 Cal Neeman	2.00	4.00
368 Don Mueller	4.00	8.00
369 Dick Tomanek	2.00	4.00
370 Pete Runnels	4.00	8.00
371 Dick Brodowski	2.00	4.00
372 Jim Hegan	4.00	8.00
373 Herb Plews	2.00	4.00
374 Art Ditmar	4.00	8.00
375 Bob Nieman	2.00	4.00
376 Hal Naragon	2.00	4.00
377 John Antonelli	4.00	8.00
378 Gail Harris	2.00	4.00
379 Bob Miller	2.00	4.00
380 Hank Aaron	75.00	200.00
381 Mike Baxes	2.00	4.00
382 Curt Simmons	4.00	8.00
383 D.Larsen/C.Stengel	6.00	12.00
384 Dave Sisler	2.00	4.00
385 Sherm Lollar	4.00	8.00
386 Jim Delsing	2.00	4.00
387 Don Drysdale	15.00	40.00
388 Bob Will RC	2.00	4.00
389 Joe Nuxhall	4.00	8.00
390 Orlando Cepeda	12.00	30.00
391 Milt Pappas	4.00	8.00
392 Whitey Herzog	4.00	8.00
393 Frank Lary	4.00	8.00
394 Randy Jackson	2.00	4.00
395 Elston Howard	10.00	25.00
396 Bob Rush	2.00	4.00
397 Washington Senators CL	7.50	15.00
398 Wally Post	4.00	8.00
399 Larry Jackson	2.00	4.00
400 Jackie Jensen	4.00	8.00
401 Ron Blackburn	2.00	4.00
402 Hector Lopez	4.00	8.00
403 Clem Labine	4.00	8.00
404 Hank Sauer	4.00	8.00
405 Roy McMillan	4.00	8.00
406 Solly Drake	2.00	4.00
407 Moe Drabowsky	4.00	8.00
408 N.Fox/L.Aparicio	20.00	40.00
409 Gus Zernial	4.00	8.00
410 Billy Pierce	4.00	8.00
411 Whitey Lockman	4.00	8.00
412 Stan Lopata	2.00	4.00
413 Camilo Pascual UER	4.00	8.00
414 Dale Long	4.00	8.00
415 Bill Mazeroski	10.00	25.00
416 Haywood Sullivan	4.00	8.00
417 Virgil Trucks	4.00	8.00
418 Gino Cimoli	2.00	4.00
419 Milwaukee Braves CL	7.50	15.00
420 Rocky Colavito	15.00	30.00
421 Herman Wehmeier	2.00	4.00
422 Hobie Landrith	2.00	4.00
423 Bob Grim	4.00	8.00
424 Ken Aspromonte	2.00	4.00
425 Del Crandall	4.00	8.00
426 Gerry Staley	4.00	8.00
427 Charlie Neal	4.00	8.00
428 Kline/Friend/Law/Face	2.00	4.00
429 Bobby Thomson	4.00	8.00
430 Whitey Ford	20.00	50.00
431 Whammy Douglas	2.00	4.00
432 Smoky Burgess	4.00	8.00
433 Billy Harrell	2.00	4.00
434 Hal Griggs	2.00	4.00
435 Frank Robinson	25.00	60.00
436 Granny Hamner	2.00	4.00
437 Ike Delock	2.00	4.00
438 Sammy Esposito	2.00	4.00
439 Brooks Robinson	25.00	60.00
440 Lew Burdette UER	4.00	8.00
441 John Roseboro	4.00	8.00
442 Ray Narleski	2.00	4.00
443 Daryl Spencer	2.00	4.00
444 Ron Hansen RC	4.00	8.00
445 Cal McLish	2.00	4.00
446 Rocky Nelson	2.00	4.00
447 Bob Anderson	2.00	4.00
448 Vada Pinson UER	10.00	25.00
449 Tom Gorman	2.00	4.00
450 Eddie Mathews	25.00	60.00
451 Jimmy Constable RC	2.00	4.00
452 Chico Fernandez	2.00	4.00
453 Les Moss	2.00	4.00
454 Phil Clark	2.00	4.00
455 Larry Doby	10.00	25.00
456 Jerry Casale RC	2.00	4.00
457 Los Angeles Dodgers CL	15.00	30.00
458 Gordon Jones	2.00	4.00
459 Bill Tuttle	2.00	4.00
460 Bob Friend	4.00	8.00
461 Mickey Mantle BT	40.00	100.00
462 Rocky Colavito BT	6.00	12.00
463 Al Kaline BT	15.00	30.00
464 Willie Mays BT	25.00	60.00
465 Roy Sievers BT	4.00	8.00
466 Billy Pierce BT	4.00	8.00
467 Hank Aaron BT	20.00	50.00
468 Duke Snider BT	10.00	20.00
469 Ernie Banks BT	12.00	30.00
470 Stan Musial BT	15.00	30.00
471 Tom Sturdivant	2.00	4.00
472 Gene Freese	2.00	4.00
473 Mike Fornieles	2.00	4.00
474 Moe Thacker RC	2.00	4.00
475 Jack Harshman	2.00	4.00
476 Cleveland Indians CL	7.50	15.00
477 Barry Latman RC	2.00	4.00
478 Roberto Clemente UER	60.00	150.00
479 Lindy McDaniel	4.00	8.00
480 Red Schoendienst	10.00	25.00
481 Charlie Maxwell	4.00	8.00
482 Russ Meyer	2.00	4.00
483 Clint Courtney	2.00	4.00
484 Willie Kirkland	2.00	4.00
485 Ryne Duren	4.00	8.00
486 Sammy White	2.00	4.00
487 Hal Brown	2.00	4.00
488 Walt Moryn	2.00	4.00
489 John Powers	2.00	4.00
490 Frank Thomas	4.00	8.00
491 Don Blasingame	2.00	4.00
492 Gene Conley	4.00	8.00
493 Jim Landis	4.00	8.00
494 Don Pavletich RC	2.00	4.00
495 Johnny Podres	8.00	20.00
496 Wayne Terwilliger UER	2.00	4.00
497 Hal R. Smith	2.00	4.00
498 Dick Hyde	2.00	4.00
499 Johnny O'Brien	4.00	8.00
500 Vic Wertz	4.00	8.00
501 Bob Tiefenauer RC	2.00	4.00
502 Alvin Dark	4.00	8.00
503 Jim Owens	2.00	4.00
504 Ossie Alvarez RC	2.00	4.00
505 Tony Kubek	10.00	25.00
506 Bob Purkey	2.00	4.00
507 Bob Hale	7.50	15.00
508 Art Fowler	7.50	15.00
509 Norm Cash RC	30.00	80.00
510 New York Yankees CL	30.00	80.00
511 George Susce	7.50	15.00
512 George Altman RC	7.50	15.00
513 Tommy Carroll	7.50	15.00
514 Bob Gibson RC	400.00	800.00
515 Harmon Killebrew	40.00	100.00
516 Mike Garcia	10.00	20.00
517 Joe Koppe RC	7.50	15.00
518 Mike Cueller UER RC Sic, Cuellar	15.00	40.00
519 Runnels/Gernert/Malzone	10.00	20.00
520 Don Elston	7.50	15.00
521 Gary Geiger	7.50	15.00
522 Gene Snyder RC	7.50	15.00
523 Harry Bright RC	7.50	15.00
524 Larry Osborne RC	7.50	15.00
525 Jim Coates RC	10.00	20.00
526 Bob Speake	7.50	15.00
527 Solly Hemus	7.50	15.00
528 Pittsburgh Pirates CL	50.00	80.00
529 George Bamberger RC	10.00	20.00
530 Wally Moon	10.00	20.00
531 Ray Webster RC	7.50	15.00
532 Mark Freeman RC	7.50	15.00
533 Darrell Johnson	10.00	20.00
534 Faye Throneberry	7.50	15.00
535 Ruben Gomez	7.50	15.00
536 Danny Kravitz	7.50	15.00
537 Rudolph Arias RC	7.50	15.00
538 Chick King	7.50	15.00
539 Gary Blaylock RC	7.50	15.00
540 Willie Miranda	7.50	15.00
541 Bob Thurman	7.50	15.00
542 Jim Perry RC	12.00	30.00
543 Skinner/Virdon/Clemente	25.00	60.00
544 Lee Tate RC	7.50	15.00
545 Tom Morgan	7.50	15.00
546 Al Schroll	7.50	15.00
547 Jim Baxes RC	7.50	15.00
548 Elmer Singleton	7.50	15.00
549 Howie Nunn RC	7.50	15.00
550 R.Campanella Courage	40.00	100.00
551 Fred Haney AS MG	7.50	15.00
552 Casey Stengel AS MG	18.00	30.00

553 Orlando Cepeda AS 18.00 30.00
554 Bill Skowron AS 10.00 20.00
555 Bill Mazeroski AS 15.00 40.00
556 Nellie Fox AS 20.00 40.00
557 Ken Boyer AS 18.00 30.00
558 Frank Malzone AS 7.50 15.00
559 Ernie Banks AS 25.00 60.00
560 Luis Aparicio AS 25.00 40.00
561 Hank Aaron AS 40.00 100.00
562 Al Kaline AS 20.00 50.00
563 Willie Mays AS 40.00 100.00
564 Mickey Mantle AS 125.00 300.00
565 Wes Covington AS 10.00 20.00
566 Roy Sievers AS 7.50 15.00
567 Del Crandall AS 7.50 15.00
568 Gus Triandos AS 7.50 15.00
569 Bob Friend AS 7.50 15.00
570 Bob Turley AS 7.50 15.00
571 Warren Spahn AS 30.00 50.00
572 Billy Pierce AS 25.00 40.00

1959 Topps Venezuelan

This set is a parallel version of the first 196 cards of the regular 1959 Topps set and is similar in design. The difference is found in the words "Impreso en Venezuela por Benco Co." printed on the bottom of the card back. The cards were issued for the Venezuelan market.

COMPLETED SET (196) 6,000.00 12,000.00
1 Ford Frick COMM 150.00 300.00
2 Eddie Yost 15.00 30.00
3 Don McMahon 15.00 30.00
4 Albie Pearson 15.00 30.00
5 Dick Donovan 15.00 30.00
6 Alex Grammas 15.00 30.00
7 Al Pilarcik 15.00 30.00
8 Phillies Team CL 200.00 400.00
9 Paul Giel 15.00 30.00
10 Mickey Mantle 2,000.00 4,000.00
11 Billy Hunter 15.00 30.00
12 Vern Law 15.00 30.00
13 Dick Gernert 15.00 30.00
14 Pete Whisenant 15.00 30.00
15 Dick Drott 15.00 30.00
16 Joe Pignatano 15.00 30.00
17 Danny's Stars 20.00 40.00
Frank Thomas
Danny Murtaugh MG
Te
18 Jack Urban 15.00 30.00
19 Eddie Bressoud 15.00 30.00
20 Duke Snider 200.00 400.00
21 Connie Johnson 15.00 30.00
22 Al Smith 15.00 30.00
23 Murry Dickson 15.00 30.00
24 Red Wilson 15.00 30.00
25 Don Hoak 15.00 30.00
26 Chuck Stobbs 15.00 30.00
27 Andy Pafko 15.00 30.00
28 Al Worthington 15.00 30.00
29 Jim Bolger 15.00 30.00
30 Nellie Fox 30.00 60.00
31 Ken Lehman 15.00 30.00
32 Don Buddin 15.00 30.00
33 Ed Fitzgerald 15.00 30.00
34 Al Kaline 50.00 100.00
Charley Maxwell
35 Ted Kluszewski 60.00 120.00
36 Hank Aguirre 15.00 30.00
37 Gene Green 15.00 30.00
38 Morrie Martin 15.00 30.00
39 Ed Bouchee 15.00 30.00
40 Warren Spahn 150.00 300.00
41 Bob Martyn 15.00 30.00
42 Murray Wall 15.00 30.00
43 Steve Bilko 15.00 30.00
44 Vito Valentinetti 15.00 30.00
45 Andy Carey 15.00 30.00
46 Bill R. Henry 15.00 30.00
47 Jim Finigan 15.00 30.00
48 Orioles Team CL 60.00 120.00
49 Bill Hall 15.00 30.00
50 Willie Mays 500.00 1,000.00
51 Rip Coleman 15.00 30.00
52 Coot Veal 15.00 30.00
53 Stan Williams 15.00 30.00
54 Mel Roach 15.00 30.00
55 Tom Brewer 15.00 30.00
56 Carl Sawatski 15.00 30.00
57 Al Cicotte 15.00 30.00
58 Eddie Miksis 15.00 30.00
59 Irv Noren 15.00 30.00
60 Bob Turley 20.00 40.00
61 Dick Brown 15.00 30.00
62 Tony Taylor 15.00 30.00
63 Jim Hearn 15.00 30.00
64 Joe DeMaestri 15.00 30.00
65 Frank Torre 15.00 30.00
66 Joe Ginsberg 15.00 30.00
67 Brooks Lawrence 15.00 30.00
68 Dick Schofield 15.00 30.00
69 Giants Team CL 60.00 120.00
70 Harvey Kuenn 20.00 40.00
71 Don Bessent 15.00 30.00
72 Bill Renna 15.00 30.00
73 Ron Jackson 15.00 30.00
74 Directing Power 15.00 30.00
Jim Lemon
Cookie Lavagetto MG
R
75 Sam Jones 15.00 30.00
76 Bobby Richardson 75.00 150.00
77 John Goryl 15.00 30.00
78 Pedro Ramos 15.00 30.00
79 Harry Chiti 15.00 30.00
80 Minnie Minoso 30.00 60.00
81 Hal Jeffcoat 15.00 30.00
82 Bob Boyd 15.00 30.00
83 Bob Smith 15.00 30.00
84 Reno Bertoia 15.00 30.00
85 Harry Anderson 15.00 30.00
86 Bob Keegan 15.00 30.00
87 Danny O'Connell 15.00 30.00
88 Herb Score 30.00 60.00
89 Billy Gardner 15.00 30.00
90 Bill Skowron 50.00 100.00
91 Herb Moford 15.00 30.00
92 Dave Philley 15.00 30.00
93 Julio Becquer 15.00 30.00
94 White Sox Team CL 40.00 80.00
95 Carl Willey 15.00 30.00
96 Lou Berberet 15.00 30.00
97 Jerry Lynch 15.00 30.00
98 Arnie Portocarrero 15.00 30.00
99 Ted Kazanski 15.00 30.00
100 Bob Cerv 15.00 30.00
101 Alex Kellner 15.00 30.00
102 Felipe Alou 100.00 200.00
103 Billy Goodman 15.00 30.00
104 Del Rice 15.00 30.00
105 Lee Walls 15.00 30.00
106 Hal Woodeshick 15.00 30.00
107 Norm Larker 15.00 30.00
108 Zack Monroe 15.00 30.00
109 Bob Schmidt 15.00 30.00
110 George Witt 15.00 30.00
111 Redlegs Team CL 30.00 60.00
112 Billy consolo 15.00 30.00
113 Taylor Phillips 15.00 30.00
114 Earl Battey 15.00 30.00
115 Mickey Vernon 20.00 40.00
116 Bob Allison RP 25.00 50.00
117 John Blanchard RP 15.00 30.00
118 John Buzhardt RP 15.00 30.00
119 John Callison RP 30.00 60.00
120 Chuck Coles RP 15.00 30.00
121 Bob Conley RP 15.00 30.00
122 Bennie Daniels RP 15.00 30.00
123 Don Dillard RP 15.00 30.00
124 Dan Dobbek RP 15.00 30.00
125 Ron Fairly RP 25.00 50.00
126 Eddie Haas RP 15.00 30.00
127 Kent Hadley RP 15.00 30.00
128 Bob Hartman RP 15.00 30.00
129 Frank Herrera RP 15.00 30.00
130 Lou Jackson RP 15.00 30.00
131 Deron Johnson RP 15.00 30.00
132 Don Lee RP 15.00 30.00
133 Bob Lillis RP 15.00 30.00
134 Jim McDaniel RP 15.00 30.00
135 Gene Oliver RP 15.00 30.00
136 Jim O'Toole RP 15.00 30.00
137 Dick Ricketts RP 15.00 30.00
138 John Romano RP 15.00 30.00
139 Ed Sadowski RP 15.00 30.00
140 Charlie Secrest RP 15.00 30.00
141 Joe Shipley RP 15.00 30.00
142 Dick Stigman RP 15.00 30.00
143 Willie Tasby RP 15.00 30.00
144 Jerry Walker RP 15.00 30.00
145 Dom Zanni RP 15.00 30.00
146 Jerry Zimmerman RP 15.00 30.00
147 Dale Long 75.00 150.00
Ernie Banks
Walt Moryn
148 Mike McCormick 20.00 40.00
149 Jim Bunning 60.00 120.00
150 Stan Musial 400.00 800.00
151 Bob Malkmus 15.00 30.00
152 Johnny Klippstein 15.00 30.00
153 Jim Marshall 15.00 30.00
154 Ray Herbert 15.00 30.00
155 Enos Slaughter 60.00 120.00
156 Billy Pierce 30.00 60.00
Robin Roberts
157 Felix Mantilla 15.00 30.00
158 Walt Dropo 15.00 30.00
159 Bob Shaw 15.00 30.00
160 Dick Groat 20.00 40.00
161 Frank Baumann 15.00 30.00
162 Bobby G. Smith 15.00 30.00
163 Sandy Koufax 500.00 1,000.00
164 Johnny Groth 15.00 30.00
165 Bill Burton 15.00 30.00
166 Destruction Crew 75.00 150.00
Minnie Minoso
Rocky Colavito(Mi
167 Duke Maas 15.00 30.00
168 Carroll Hardy 15.00 30.00
169 Ted Abernathy 15.00 30.00
170 Gene Woodling 15.00 30.00
171 Willard Schmidt 15.00 30.00
172 Athletics Team CL 30.00 60.00
173 Bill Monbouquette 15.00 30.00
174 Jim Pendleton 15.00 30.00
175 Dick Farrell 15.00 30.00
176 Preston Ward 15.00 30.00
177 John Briggs 15.00 30.00
178 Ruben Amaro 15.00 30.00
179 Don Rudolph 15.00 30.00
180 Yogi Berra 250.00 500.00
181 Bob Porterfield 15.00 30.00
182 Milt Graff 15.00 30.00
183 Stu Miller 15.00 30.00
184 Harvey Haddix 15.00 30.00
185 Jim Busby 15.00 30.00
186 Mudcat Grant 15.00 30.00
187 Bubba Phillips 15.00 30.00
188 Juan Pizarro 15.00 30.00
189 Neil Chrisley 15.00 30.00
190 Bill Virdon 15.00 30.00
191 Russ Kemmerer 15.00 30.00
192 Charlie Beamon 15.00 30.00
193 Sammy Taylor 15.00 30.00
194 Jim Brosnan 15.00 30.00
195 Rip Repulski 15.00 30.00
196 Billy Moran 15.00 30.00

1960 Topps

The cards in this 572-card set measure 2 1/2" by 3 1/2". The 1960 Topps set is the first Topps standard size issue to use a horizontally oriented front. World Series cards appeared for the first time (385 to 391), and there is a Rookie Prospect (RP) series (117-148), the most famous of which is Carl Yastrzemski, and a Sport Magazine All-Star Selection (AS) series (553-572). There are 16 manager cards listed alphabetically from 212 through 227. The 1959 Topps All-Rookie team is featured on cards 316-325. This was the first time the Topps All-Rookie team was ever selected and the only time that all of the cards were placed together in a subset. The coaching staff of each team was also afforded their own card in a 16-card subset (455-470). There is no price differential for either color back. The high series (507-572) were printed on a more limited basis than the rest of the set. The team cards have series checklists on the reverse. Cards were issued in one-card penny packs, six-card nickel packs (which came 24 to a box), 10 cent cello packs (which came 36 packs to a box) and 36-card rack packs which cost 29 cents . Three card ad-sheets have been seen. One such sheet features Wayne Terwilliger, Kent Hadley and Faye Throneberry on the front with Gene Woodling and an Ad on the back. Another sheet featured Hank Foiles/Hobie Landrith and Hal Smith on the front. The key Rookie Cards in this set are Jim Kaat, Willie McCovey and Carl Yastrzemski. Recently, a Kent Hadley was discovered with a Kansas City A's logo on the front, while this card was rumoured to exist for years, this is the first known spotting of the card. According the published reports at the time, seven copies of the Hadley card, along with the Gino Cimoli and the Faye Throneberry cards were produced. Each series of this set had different card backs. Cards numbered 1-110 had cream colored white back, cards numbered 111-198 had grey backs, cards numbered 119-286 had cream colored white backs, cards numbered 287-

COMPLETE SET (572) 2,500.00 5,000.00
COMMON CARD (1-440) 1.50 4.00
COMMON CARD (441-506) 3.00 8.00
COMMON CARD (507-572) 6.00 15.00
WRAPPER (1-CENT) 500.00 1,000.00
WRAP. (1-CENT REPEAT) 250.00 500.00
WRAPPER (5-CENT) 15.00 40.00
1 Early Wynn 20.00 50.00
2 Roman Mejias 1.50 4.00
3 Joe Adcock 2.50 6.00
4 Bob Purkey 1.50 4.00
5 Wally Moon 2.50 6.00
6 Lou Berberet 1.50 4.00
7 W.Mays/B.Rigney 12.00 30.00
8 Bud Daley 1.50 4.00
9 Faye Throneberry 1.50 4.00
9A Faye Throneberry
10 Ernie Banks 40.00 100.00
11 Norm Siebern 1.50 4.00
12 Milt Pappas 2.50 6.00
13 Wally Post 2.50 6.00
14 Jim Grant 2.50 6.00
15 Pete Runnels 2.50 6.00
16 Ernie Broglio 2.50 6.00
17 Johnny Callison 2.50 6.00
18 Los Angeles Dodgers CL 20.00 50.00
19 Felix Mantilla 1.50 4.00
20 Roy Face 2.50 6.00
21 Dutch Dotterer 1.50 4.00
22 Rocky Bridges 1.50 4.00
23 Eddie Fisher RC 1.50 4.00
24 Dick Gray 1.50 4.00
25 Roy Sievers 2.50 6.00
26 Wayne Terwilliger 1.50 4.00
27 Dick Drott 1.50 4.00
28 Brooks Robinson 25.00 60.00
29 Clem Labine 2.50 6.00
30 Tito Francona 1.50 4.00
31 Sammy Esposito 1.50 4.00
32 J.O'Toole/V.Pinson 1.50 4.00
33 Tom Morgan 1.50 4.00
34 Sparky Anderson 6.00 15.00
35 Whitey Ford 20.00 50.00
36 Russ Nixon 1.50 4.00
37 Bill Bruton 1.50 4.00
38 Jerry Casale 1.50 4.00
39 Earl Averill Jr. 1.50 4.00
40 Joe Cunningham 1.50 4.00
41 Barry Latman 1.50 4.00
42 Hobie Landrith 1.50 4.00
43 Washington Senators CL 4.00 10.00
44 Bobby Locke RC 1.50 4.00
45 Roy McMillan 2.50 6.00
46 Jack Fisher RC 1.50 4.00
47 Don Zimmer 2.50 6.00
48 Hal W. Smith 1.50 4.00
49 Curt Raydon 1.50 4.00
50 Al Kaline 25.00 60.00
51 Jim Coates 2.50 6.00
52 Dave Philley 1.50 4.00
53 Jackie Brandt 1.50 4.00
54 Mike Fornieles 1.50 4.00
55 Bill Mazeroski 12.00 30.00
56 Steve Korcheck 1.50 4.00
57 T.Lown/G.Staley 1.50 4.00
58 Gino Cimoli 1.50 4.00
58A Gino Cimoli Cards
59 Juan Pizarro 1.50 4.00
60 Gus Triandos 2.50 6.00
61 Eddie Kasko 1.50 4.00
62 Roger Craig 2.50 6.00
63 George Strickland 1.50 4.00
64 Jack Meyer 1.50 4.00
65 Elston Howard 2.50 6.00
66 Bob Trowbridge 1.50 4.00
67 Jose Pagan RC 1.50 4.00
68 Dave Hillman 1.50 4.00
69 Billy Goodman 2.50 6.00
70 Lew Burdette UER 2.50 6.00
71 Marty Keough 1.50 4.00
72 Detroit Tigers CL 10.00 25.00
73 Bob Gibson 40.00 100.00
74 Walt Moryn 1.50 4.00
75 Vic Power 2.50 6.00
76 Bill Fischer 1.50 4.00
77 Hank Foiles 1.50 4.00
78 Bob Grim 1.50 4.00
79 Walt Dropo 1.50 4.00
80 Johnny Antonelli 2.50 6.00
81 Russ Snyder RC 1.50 4.00
82 Ruben Gomez 1.50 4.00
83 Tony Kubek 8.00 20.00
84 Hal R. Smith 1.50 4.00
85 Frank Lary 2.50 6.00
86 Dick Gernert 1.50 4.00
87 John Romonosky 1.50 4.00
88 John Roseboro 2.50 6.00
89 Hal Brown 1.50 4.00
90 Bobby Avila 1.50 4.00
91 Bennie Daniels 1.50 4.00
92 Whitey Herzog 2.50 6.00
93 Art Schult 1.50 4.00
94 Leo Kiely 1.50 4.00
95 Frank Thomas 2.50 6.00
96 Ralph Terry 2.50 6.00
97 Ted Lepcio 1.50 4.00
98 Gordon Jones 1.50 4.00
99 Lenny Green 1.50 4.00
100 Nellie Fox 15.00 40.00
101 Bob Miller RC 1.50 4.00
102 Kent Hadley 1.50 4.00
102A Kent Hadley A's
103 Dick Farrell 2.50 6.00
104 Dick Schofield 2.50 6.00
105 Larry Sherry RC 2.50 6.00
106 Billy Gardner 1.50 4.00
107 Carlton Willey 1.50 4.00
108 Pete Daley 1.50 4.00
109 Clete Boyer 6.00 15.00
110 Cal McLish 1.50 4.00
111 Vic Wertz 2.50 6.00
112 Jack Harshman 1.50 4.00
113 Bob Skinner 1.50 4.00
114 Ken Aspromonte 1.50 4.00
115 R.Face/H.Wilhelm 2.50 6.00
116 Jim Rivera 1.50 4.00
117 Tom Borland RS 1.50 4.00
118 Bob Bruce RS RC 1.50 4.00
119 Chico Cardenas RS RC 2.50 6.00
120 Duke Carmel RS RC 1.50 4.00
121 Camilo Carreon RS RC 1.50 4.00
122 Don Dillard RS 1.50 4.00
123 Dan Dobbek RS 1.50 4.00
124 Jim Donohue RS RC 1.50 4.00
125 Dick Ellsworth RS RC 2.50 6.00
126 Chuck Estrada RS RC 1.50 4.00
127 Ron Hansen RS 2.50 6.00
128 Bill Harris RS RC 1.50 4.00
129 Bob Hartman RS 1.50 4.00
130 Frank Herrera RS 1.50 4.00
131 Ed Hobaugh RS RC 1.50 4.00
132 Frank Howard RS RC 12.00 30.00
133 Julian Javier RS RC 2.50 6.00
134 Deron Johnson RS 2.50 6.00
135 Ken Johnson RS RC 1.50 4.00
136 Jim Kaat RS RC 20.00 50.00
137 Lou Klimchock RS RC 1.50 4.00
138 Art Mahaffey RS RC 2.50 6.00
139 Carl Mathias RS RC 1.50 4.00
140 Julio Navarro RS RC 1.50 4.00
141 Jim Proctor RS RC 1.50 4.00
142 Bill Short RS RC 1.50 4.00
143 Al Spangler RS RC 1.50 4.00
144 Al Stieglitz RS RC 1.50 4.00
145 Jim Umbricht RS RC 1.50 4.00
146 Ted Wieand RS RC 1.50 4.00
147 Bob Will RS 1.50 4.00
148 C.Yastrzemski RS RC 100.00 250.00
149 Bob Nieman 1.50 4.00
150 Billy Pierce 2.50 6.00
151 San Francisco Giants CL 4.00 10.00
152 Gail Harris 1.50 4.00
153 Bobby Thomson 2.50 6.00
154 Jim Davenport 2.50 6.00
155 Charlie Neal 2.50 6.00
156 Art Ceccarelli 1.50 4.00
157 Rocky Nelson 2.50 6.00
158 Wes Covington 2.50 6.00
159 Jim Piersall 2.50 6.00
160 M.Mantle/K.Boyer 40.00 100.00
161 Ray Narleski 1.50 4.00
162 Sammy Taylor 1.50 4.00
163 Hector Lopez 2.50 6.00
164 Cincinnati Reds CL 4.00 10.00
165 Jack Sanford 2.50 6.00
166 Chuck Essegian 1.50 4.00

167 Valmy Thomas 1.50 4.00
168 Alex Grammas 1.50 4.00
169 Jake Striker RC 1.50 4.00
170 Del Crandall 2.50 6.00
171 Johnny Groth 1.50 4.00
172 Willie Kirkland 1.50 4.00
173 Billy Martin 10.00 25.00
174 Cleveland Indians CL 4.00 10.00
175 Pedro Ramos 1.50 4.00
176 Vada Pinson 2.50 6.00
177 Johnny Kucks 1.50 4.00
178 Woody Held 1.50 4.00
179 Rip Coleman 1.50 4.00
180 Harry Simpson 1.50 4.00
181 Billy Loes 2.50 6.00
182 Glen Hobbie 1.50 4.00
183 Eli Grba RC 1.50 4.00
184 Gary Geiger 1.50 4.00
185 Jim Owens 1.50 4.00
186 Dave Sisler 1.50 4.00
187 Jay Hook RC 1.50 4.00
188 Dick Williams 2.50 6.00
189 Don McMahon 1.50 4.00
190 Gene Woodling 2.50 6.00
191 Johnny Klippstein 1.50 4.00
192 Danny O'Connell 1.50 4.00
193 Dick Hyde 1.50 4.00
194 Bobby Gene Smith 1.50 4.00
195 Lindy McDaniel 2.50 6.00
196 Andy Carey 2.50 6.00
197 Ron Kline 1.50 4.00
198 Jerry Lynch 2.50 6.00
199 Dick Donovan 2.50 6.00
200 Willie Mays 75.00 200.00
201 Larry Osborne 1.50 4.00
202 Fred Kipp 1.50 4.00
203 Sammy White 1.50 4.00
204 Ryne Duren 2.50 6.00
205 Johnny Logan 2.50 6.00
206 Claude Osteen 2.50 6.00
207 Bob Boyd 1.50 4.00
208 Chicago White Sox CL 4.00 10.00
209 Ron Blackburn 1.50 4.00
210 Harmon Killebrew 25.00 60.00
211 Taylor Phillips 1.50 4.00
212 Walter Alston MG 4.00 10.00
213 Chuck Dressen MG 2.50 6.00
214 Jimmy Dykes MG 2.50 6.00
215 Bob Elliott MG 2.50 6.00
216 Joe Gordon MG 2.50 6.00
217 Charlie Grimm MG 2.50 6.00
218 Solly Hemus MG 1.50 4.00
219 Fred Hutchinson MG 2.50 6.00
220 Billy Jurges MG 1.50 4.00
221 Cookie Lavagetto MG 1.50 4.00
222 Al Lopez MG 4.00 10.00
223 Danny Murtaugh MG 2.50 6.00
224 Paul Richards MG 2.50 6.00
225 Bill Rigney MG 1.50 4.00
226 Eddie Sawyer MG 1.50 4.00
227 Casey Stengel MG 12.00 30.00
228 Ernie Johnson 2.50 6.00
229 Joe M. Morgan RC 1.50 4.00
230 Burdette/Spahn/Buhl 4.00 10.00
231 Hal Naragon 1.50 4.00
232 Jim Busby 1.50 4.00
233 Don Elston 1.50 4.00
234 Don Demeter 1.50 4.00
235 Gus Bell 2.50 6.00
236 Dick Ricketts 1.50 4.00
237 Elmer Valo 1.50 4.00
238 Danny Kravitz 1.50 4.00
239 Joe Shipley 1.50 4.00
240 Luis Aparicio 12.00 30.00
241 Albie Pearson 2.50 6.00
242 St. Louis Cardinals CL 4.00 10.00
243 Bubba Phillips 1.50 4.00
244 Hal Griggs 1.50 4.00
245 Eddie Yost 2.50 6.00
246 Lee Maye RC 2.50 6.00
247 Gil McDougald 4.00 10.00
248 Del Rice 1.50 4.00
249 Earl Wilson RC 2.50 6.00
250 Stan Musial 50.00 100.00
251 Bob Malkmus 1.50 4.00
252 Ray Herbert 1.50 4.00
253 Eddie Bressoud 1.50 4.00
254 Arnie Portocarrero 1.50 4.00
255 Jim Gilliam 2.50 6.00
256 Dick Brown 1.50 4.00
257 Gordy Coleman RC 1.50 4.00
258 Dick Groat 2.50 6.00
259 George Altman 1.50 4.00
260 R.Colavito/T.Francona 6.00 15.00
261 Pete Burnside 1.50 4.00
262 Hank Bauer 2.50 6.00
263 Darrell Johnson 1.50 4.00
264 Robin Roberts 10.00 25.00
265 Rip Repulski 1.50 4.00
266 Joey Jay 2.50 6.00
267 Jim Marshall 1.50 4.00
268 Al Worthington 1.50 4.00
269 Gene Green 1.50 4.00
270 Bob Turley 2.50 6.00
271 Julio Becquer 1.50 4.00
272 Fred Green RC 2.50 6.00
273 Neil Chrisley 1.50 4.00
274 Tom Acker 1.50 4.00
275 Curt Flood 2.50 6.00
276 Ken McBride RC 1.50 4.00
277 Harry Bright 1.50 4.00
278 Stan Williams 2.50 6.00
279 Chuck Tanner 2.50 6.00
280 Frank Sullivan 1.50 4.00
281 Ray Boone 2.50 6.00
282 Joe Nuxhall 2.50 6.00
283 Johnny Blanchard 2.50 6.00
284 Don Gross 1.50 4.00
285 Harry Anderson 1.50 4.00
286 Ray Semproch 1.50 4.00
287 Felipe Alou 2.50 6.00
288 Bob Mabe 1.50 4.00
289 Willie Jones 1.50 4.00
290 Jerry Lumpe 1.50 4.00
291 Bob Keegan 1.50 4.00
292 J.Pignatano/J.Roseboro 2.50 6.00
293 Gene Conley 2.50 6.00
294 Tony Taylor 2.50 6.00
295 Gil Hodges 12.00 30.00
296 Nelson Chittum RC 1.50 4.00
297 Reno Bertoia 1.50 4.00
298 George Witt 1.50 4.00
299 Earl Torgeson 1.50 4.00
300 Hank Aaron 100.00 250.00
301 Jerry Davie 1.50 4.00
302 Philadelphia Phillies CL 4.00 10.00
303 Billy O'Dell 1.50 4.00
304 Joe Ginsberg 1.50 4.00
305 Richie Ashburn 10.00 25.00
306 Frank Baumann 1.50 4.00
307 Gene Oliver 1.50 4.00
308 Dick Hall 1.50 4.00
309 Bob Hale 1.50 4.00
310 Frank Malzone 2.50 6.00
311 Raul Sanchez 1.50 4.00
312 Charley Lau 2.50 6.00
313 Turk Lown 1.50 4.00
314 Chico Fernandez 1.50 4.00
315 Bobby Shantz 4.00 10.00
316 W.McCovey ASR RC 100.00 250.00
317 Pumpsie Green ASR RC 2.50 6.00
318 Jim Baxes ASR 2.50 6.00
319 Joe Koppe ASR 2.50 6.00
320 Bob Allison ASR 2.50 6.00
321 Ron Fairly ASR 2.50 6.00
322 Willie Tasby ASR 2.50 6.00
323 John Romano ASR 2.50 6.00
324 Jim Perry ASR 2.50 6.00
325 Jim O'Toole ASR 2.50 6.00
326 Roberto Clemente 100.00 200.00
327 Ray Sadecki RC 1.50 4.00
328 Earl Battey 1.50 4.00
329 Zack Monroe 1.50 4.00
330 Harvey Kuenn 2.50 6.00
331 Henry Mason RC 1.50 4.00
332 New York Yankees CL 20.00 50.00
333 Danny McDevitt 1.50 4.00
334 Ted Abernathy 1.50 4.00
335 Red Schoendienst 10.00 25.00
336 Ike Delock 1.50 4.00
337 Cal Neeman 1.50 4.00
338 Ray Monzant 1.50 4.00
339 Harry Chiti 1.50 4.00
340 Harvey Haddix 2.50 6.00
341 Carroll Hardy 1.50 4.00
342 Casey Wise 1.50 4.00
343 Sandy Koufax 60.00 120.00
344 Clint Courtney 1.50 4.00
345 Don Newcombe 2.50 6.00
346 J.C. Martin UER RC 2.50 6.00
347 Ed Bouchee 1.50 4.00
348 Barry Shetrone RC 1.50 4.00
349 Moe Drabowsky 2.50 6.00
350 Mickey Mantle 400.00 800.00
351 Don Nottebart RC 1.50 4.00
352 Bell/F.Robinson/Lynch 4.00 10.00
353 Don Larsen 10.00 25.00
354 Bob Lillis 1.50 4.00
355 Bill White 2.50 6.00
356 Joe Amalfitano 1.50 4.00
357 Al Schroll 1.50 4.00
358 Joe DeMaestri 1.50 4.00
359 Buddy Gilbert RC 1.50 4.00
360 Herb Score 2.50 6.00
361 Bob Oldis 2.50 6.00
362 Russ Kemmerer 1.50 4.00
363 Gene Stephens 1.50 4.00
364 Paul Foytack 1.50 4.00
365 Minnie Minoso 6.00 15.00
366 Dallas Green RC 4.00 10.00
367 Bill Tuttle 1.50 4.00
368 Daryl Spencer 1.50 4.00
369 Billy Hoeft 1.50 4.00
370 Bill Skowron 4.00 10.00
371 Bud Byerly 1.50 4.00
372 Frank House 1.50 4.00
373 Don Hoak 2.50 6.00
374 Bob Buhl 2.50 6.00
375 Dale Long 4.00 10.00
376 John Briggs 1.50 4.00
377 Roger Maris 50.00 100.00
378 Stu Miller 2.50 6.00
379 Red Wilson 1.50 4.00
380 Bob Shaw 1.50 4.00
381 Milwaukee Braves CL 4.00 10.00
382 Ted Bowsfield 1.50 4.00
383 Leon Wagner 1.50 4.00
384 Don Cardwell 1.50 4.00
385 Charlie Neal WS1 3.00 8.00
386 Charlie Neal WS2 3.00 8.00
387 Carl Furillo WS3 3.00 8.00
388 Gil Hodges WS4 5.00 12.00
389 L.Aparicio WS5 w/M.Wills 4.00 10.00
390 Scrambling After Ball WS6 3.00 8.00
391 Champs Celebrate WS 3.00 8.00
392 Tex Clevenger 1.50 4.00
393 Smoky Burgess 2.50 6.00
394 Norm Larker 2.50 6.00
395 Hoyt Wilhelm 8.00 20.00
396 Steve Bilko 1.50 4.00
397 Don Blasingame 1.50 4.00
398 Mike Cuellar 2.50 6.00
399 Pappas/Fisher/Walker 2.50 6.00
400 Rocky Colavito 8.00 20.00
401 Bob Duliba RC 1.50 4.00
402 Dick Stuart 6.00 15.00
403 Ed Sadowski 1.50 4.00
404 Bob Rush 1.50 4.00
405 Bobby Richardson 10.00 25.00
406 Billy Klaus 1.50 4.00
407 Gary Peters UER RC 2.50 6.00
408 Carl Furillo 4.00 10.00
409 Ron Samford 1.50 4.00
410 Sam Jones 2.50 6.00
411 Ed Bailey 1.50 4.00
412 Bob Anderson 1.50 4.00
413 Kansas City Athletics CL 4.00 10.00
414 Don Williams RC 1.50 4.00
415 Bob Cerv 1.50 4.00
416 Humberto Robinson 1.50 4.00
417 Chuck Cottier RC 1.50 4.00
418 Don Mossi 2.50 6.00
419 George Crowe 1.50 4.00
420 Eddie Mathews 20.00 50.00
421 Duke Maas 1.50 4.00
422 John Powers 1.50 4.00
423 Ed Fitzgerald 1.50 4.00
424 Pete Whisenant 1.50 4.00
425 Johnny Podres 2.50 6.00
426 Ron Jackson 1.50 4.00
427 Al Grunwald RC 1.50 4.00
428 Al Smith 1.50 4.00
429 Nellie Fox/H.Kuenn 4.00 10.00
430 Art Ditmar 1.50 4.00
431 Andre Rodgers 1.50 4.00
432 Chuck Stobbs 1.50 4.00
433 Irv Noren 1.50 4.00
434 Brooks Lawrence 2.50 6.00
435 Gene Freese 1.50 4.00
436 Marv Throneberry 2.50 6.00
437 Bob Friend 2.50 6.00
438 Jim Coker RC 1.50 4.00
439 Tom Brewer 1.50 4.00
440 Jim Lemon 2.50 6.00
441 Gary Bell 4.00 10.00
442 Joe Pignatano 3.00 8.00
443 Charlie Maxwell 3.00 8.00
444 Jerry Kindall 3.00 8.00
445 Warren Spahn 25.00 60.00
446 Ellis Burton 3.00 8.00
447 Ray Moore 3.00 8.00
448 Jim Gentile RC 8.00 20.00
449 Jim Brosnan 3.00 8.00
450 Orlando Cepeda 20.00 50.00
451 Curt Simmons 3.00 8.00
452 Ray Webster 3.00 8.00
453 Vern Law 10.00 25.00
454 Hal Woodeshick 3.00 8.00
455 Baltimore Coaches 3.00 8.00
456 Red Sox Coaches 4.00 10.00
457 Cubs Coaches 3.00 8.00
458 White Sox Coaches 3.00 8.00
459 Reds Coaches 3.00 8.00
460 Indians Coaches 6.00 15.00
461 Tigers Coaches 4.00 10.00
462 Athletics Coaches 3.00 8.00
463 Dodgers Coaches 3.00 8.00
464 Braves Coaches 3.00 8.00
465 Yankees Coaches 10.00 25.00
466 Phillies Coaches 3.00 8.00
467 Pirates Coaches 3.00 8.00
468 Cardinals Coaches 3.00 8.00
469 Giants Coaches 3.00 8.00
470 Senators Coaches 3.00 8.00
471 Ned Garver 3.00 8.00
472 Alvin Dark 3.00 8.00
473 Al Cicotte 3.00 8.00
474 Haywood Sullivan 3.00 8.00
475 Don Drysdale 25.00 60.00
476 Lou Johnson RC 3.00 8.00
477 Don Ferrarese 3.00 8.00
478 Frank Torre 3.00 8.00
479 Georges Maranda RC 3.00 8.00
480 Yogi Berra 40.00 100.00
481 Wes Stock RC 3.00 8.00
482 Frank Bolling 3.00 8.00
483 Camilo Pascual 3.00 8.00
484 Pittsburgh Pirates CL 15.00 40.00
485 Ken Boyer 6.00 15.00
486 Bobby Del Greco 3.00 8.00
487 Tom Sturdivant 3.00 8.00
488 Norm Cash 10.00 25.00
489 Steve Ridzik 3.00 8.00
490 Frank Robinson 25.00 60.00
491 Mel Roach 3.00 8.00
492 Larry Jackson 3.00 8.00
493 Duke Snider 25.00 60.00
494 Baltimore Orioles CL 10.00 25.00
495 Sherm Lollar 3.00 8.00
496 Bill Virdon 4.00 10.00
497 John Tsitouris 3.00 8.00
498 Al Pilarcik 3.00 8.00
499 Johnny James RC 4.00 10.00
500 Johnny Temple 3.00 8.00
501 Bob Schmidt 3.00 8.00
502 Jim Bunning 10.00 25.00
503 Don Lee 3.00 8.00
504 Seth Morehead 3.00 8.00
505 Ted Kluszewski 10.00 25.00
506 Lee Walls 3.00 8.00
507 Dick Stigman 6.00 15.00
508 Billy Consolo 6.00 15.00
509 Tommy Davis RC 20.00 50.00
510 Gerry Staley 6.00 15.00
511 Ken Walters RC 6.00 15.00
512 Joe Gibbon RC 6.00 15.00
513 Chicago Cubs CL 12.50 30.00
514 Steve Barber RC 6.00 15.00
515 Stan Lopata 6.00 15.00
516 Marty Kutyna RC 6.00 15.00
517 Charlie James RC 10.00 25.00
518 Tony Gonzalez RC 6.00 15.00
519 Ed Roebuck 6.00 15.00
520 Don Buddin 6.00 15.00
521 Mike Lee RC 6.00 15.00
522 Ken Hunt RC 12.50 30.00
523 Clay Dalrymple RC 6.00 15.00
524 Bill Henry 6.00 15.00
525 Marv Breeding RC 6.00 15.00
526 Paul Giel 10.00 25.00
527 Jose Valdivielso 10.00 25.00
528 Ben Johnson RC 6.00 15.00
529 Norm Sherry RC 8.00 20.00
530 Mike McCormick 6.00 15.00
531 Sandy Amoros 10.00 25.00
532 Mike Garcia 8.00 20.00
533 Lu Clinton RC 6.00 15.00
534 Ken MacKenzie RC 6.00 15.00
535 Whitey Lockman 6.00 15.00
536 Wynn Hawkins RC 6.00 15.00
537 Boston Red Sox CL 12.50 30.00
538 Frank Barnes RC 6.00 15.00
539 Gene Baker 6.00 15.00
540 Jerry Walker 6.00 15.00
541 Tony Curry RC 6.00 15.00
542 Ken Hamlin RC 6.00 15.00
543 Elio Chacon RC 6.00 15.00
544 Bill Monbouquette 8.00 20.00
545 Carl Sawatski 6.00 15.00
546 Hank Aguirre 6.00 15.00
547 Bob Aspromonte RC 8.00 20.00
548 Don Mincher RC 6.00 15.00
549 John Buzhardt 6.00 15.00
550 Jim Landis 6.00 15.00
551 Ed Rakow RC 6.00 15.00
552 Walt Bond RC 6.00 15.00
553 Bill Skowron AS 8.00 20.00
554 Willie McCovey AS 30.00 80.00
555 Nellie Fox AS 10.00 25.00
556 Charlie Neal AS 6.00 15.00
557 Frank Malzone AS 6.00 15.00
558 Eddie Mathews AS 15.00 40.00
559 Luis Aparicio AS 12.50 30.00
560 Ernie Banks AS 30.00 80.00
561 Al Kaline AS 20.00 50.00
562 Joe Cunningham AS 6.00 15.00
563 Mickey Mantle AS 125.00 300.00
564 Willie Mays AS 50.00 120.00
565 Roger Maris AS 50.00 100.00
566 Hank Aaron AS 40.00 100.00
567 Sherm Lollar AS 6.00 15.00
568 Del Crandall AS 6.00 15.00
569 Camilo Pascual AS 6.00 15.00
570 Don Drysdale AS 25.00 60.00
571 Billy Pierce AS 6.00 15.00
572 Johnny Antonelli AS 12.50 30.00
NNO Iron-On Team Transfer

1960 Topps Tattoos

In 1960 this tattoo set was issued separately by both Topps and O-Pee-Chee. The Topps boxes had 120 one cent packs in it while the O-Pee-Chee boxes had 240 one cent packs in them. They are actually the reverses (inside surfaces) of the wrappers in which the (one cent) product "Tattoo Bubble Gum" was packaged. The dimensions given (1 9/16" by 3 1/2") are for the entire wrapper. The wrapper lists instructions on how to apply the tattoo. The "tattoos" were to be applied by moistening the skin and then pressing the tattoo to the moistened spot. The tattoos are unnumbered and are colored. There are 96 tattoos in the set: 55 players, 16 team logos, 15 action shots and ten autographed balls. In the checklist below the player tattoos are numbered 1-55 in alphabetical order, the team tattoos (56-71) are numbered in alphabetical team order (within league), the action photos (72-86) are numbered in alphabetical order by title and the facsimile autographed ball tattoos (87-96) are numbered in alphabetical order according to the autographing player.

COMPLETE SET (96) 2,000.00 4,000.00
COMMON TATTOO 3.00 8.00
COMMON TEAM (56-71) 2.00 5.00
COMMON ACTION (72-86) 1.00 2.50
COMMON BALL (87-96) 1.00 2.50
WRAPPER 4.00 10.00
1 Hank Aaron 125.00 250.00
2 Bob Allison 8.00 20.00
3 Johnny Antonelli 8.00 20.00
4 Richie Ashburn 30.00 60.00
5 Ernie Banks 50.00 100.00
6 Yogi Berra 100.00 200.00
7 Lew Burdette 8.00 20.00
8 Orlando Cepeda 20.00 50.00
9 Rocky Colavito 20.00 50.00
10 Joe Cunningham 8.00 20.00
11 Bud Daley 6.00 15.00
12 Don Drysdale 40.00 80.00
13 Ryne Duren 10.00 25.00
14 Roy Face 10.00 25.00
15 Whitey Ford 40.00 80.00
16 Nellie Fox 30.00 60.00
17 Tito Francona 6.00 15.00
18 Gene Freese 6.00 15.00
19 Jim Gilliam 12.50 30.00
20 Dick Groat 10.00 25.00
21 Ray Herbert 6.00 15.00
22 Glen Hobbie 6.00 15.00
23 Jackie Jensen 12.50 30.00
24 Sam Jones 6.00 15.00

25 Al Kaline 50.00 100.00
26 Harmon Killebrew 40.00 80.00
27 Harvey Kuenn 12.50 30.00
28 Frank Lary 8.00 20.00
29 Vern Law 10.00 25.00
30 Frank Malzone 8.00 20.00
31 Mickey Mantle 400.00 800.00
32 Roger Maris 50.00 100.00
33 Eddie Mathews 40.00 80.00
34 Willie Mays 150.00 300.00
35 Cal McLish 6.00 15.00
36 Wally Moon 8.00 20.00
37 Walt Moryn 6.00 15.00
38 Don Mossi 8.00 20.00
39 Stan Musial 75.00 150.00
40 Charlie Neal 8.00 20.00
41 Don Newcombe 10.00 25.00
42 Milt Pappas 8.00 20.00
43 Camilo Pascual 8.00 20.00
44 Billy Pierce 8.00 20.00
45 Robin Roberts 30.00 60.00
46 Frank Robinson 40.00 80.00
47 Pete Runnels 8.00 20.00
48 Herb Score 10.00 25.00
49 Warren Spahn 40.00 80.00
50 Johnny Temple 8.00 20.00
51 Gus Triandos 8.00 20.00
52 Jerry Walker 6.00 15.00
53 Bill White 12.50 30.00
54 Gene Woodling 8.00 20.00
55 Early Wynn 30.00 60.00
56 Chicago Cubs 4.00 10.00
57 Cincinnati Reds 4.00 10.00
58 Los Angeles Dodgers 6.00 15.00
59 Milwaukee Braves 4.00 10.00
60 Philadelphia Phillies 4.00 10.00
61 Pittsburgh Pirates 4.00 10.00
62 St. Louis Cardinals 4.00 10.00
63 San Francisco Giants 4.00 10.00
64 Baltimore Orioles 4.00 10.00
65 Boston Red Sox 6.00 15.00
66 Chicago White Sox 4.00 10.00
67 Cleveland Indians 4.00 10.00
68 Detroit Tigers 4.00 10.00
69 Kansas City Athletics 4.00 10.00
70 New York Yankees 8.00 20.00
71 Washington Senators 4.00 10.00
72 Circus Catch 2.00 5.00
73 Double Play 2.00 5.00
74 Grand Slam Homer 2.00 5.00
75 Great Catch 2.00 5.00
76 Left Hand Batter 2.00 5.00
77 Left Hand Pitcher 2.00 5.00
78 Out at First 2.00 5.00
79 Out at Home 2.00 5.00
80 Right Hand Batter 2.00 5.00
81 Right Hand Pitcher 2.00 5.00
82 Right Hand Pitcher/(Different pose) 2.00 5.00
83 Run Down 2.00 5.00
84 Stolen Base 2.00 5.00
85 The Final Word 2.00 5.00
86 Twisting Foul 2.00 5.00
87 Richie Ashburn/(Autographed ball) 6.00 15.00
88 Rocky Colavito/(Autographed ball) 6.00 15.00
89 Roy Face/(Autographed ball) 2.00 5.00
90 Jackie Jensen/(Autographed ball) 3.00 8.00
91 Harmon Killebrew/(Autographed ball) 8.00 20.00
92 Mickey Mantle/(Autographed ball) 200.00 400.00
93 Willie Mays/(Autographed ball) 40.00 80.00
94 Stan Musial/(Autographed ball) 20.00 50.00
95 Billy Pierce/(Autographed ball) 2.50 6.00
96 Jerry Walker/(Autographed ball) 2.00 5.00

1960 Topps Venezuelan

This set is a parallel version of the first 196 cards of the regular 1960 Topps set and are similar in design. The cards were issued for the Venezuelan market. Although the cards were printed in the United States, they are faded compared to the American issued cards.

COMPLETE SET (196) 5,000.00 10,000.00
1 Early Wynn 100.00 200.00
2 Roman Mejias 12.50 30.00
3 Joe Adcock 15.00 40.00
4 Bob Purkey 12.50 30.00
5 Wally Moon 12.50 30.00
6 Lou Berberet 12.50 30.00
7 Willie Mays 75.00 150.00
Bill Rigney MG
8 Bud Daley 12.50 30.00
9 Faye Throneberry 12.50 30.00
10 Ernie Banks 150.00 300.00
11 Norm Siebern 12.50 30.00
12 Milt Pappas 15.00 40.00
13 Wally Post 12.50 30.00
14 Jim Grant 12.50 30.00
15 Pete Runnels 12.50 30.00
16 Ernie Broglio 12.50 30.00
17 Johnny Callison 12.50 30.00
18 Dodgers Team CL 125.00 250.00
19 Felix Mantilla 12.50 30.00
20 Roy Face 15.00 40.00
21 Dutch Dotterer 12.50 30.00
22 Rocky Bridges 12.50 30.00
23 Eddie Fisher 12.50 30.00
24 Dick Gray 12.50 30.00
25 Roy Sievers 15.00 40.00
26 Wayne Terwilliger 12.50 30.00
27 Dick Drott 12.50 30.00
28 Brooks Robinson 150.00 300.00
29 Clem Labine 12.50 30.00
30 Tito Francona 12.50 30.00
31 Sammy Esposito 12.50 30.00
32 Jim O'Toole 12.50 30.00
Vada Pinson
33 Tom Morgan 12.50 30.00
34 Sparky Anderson 50.00 100.00
35 Whitey Ford 150.00 300.00
36 Russ Nixon 12.50 30.00
37 Bill Bruton 12.50 30.00
38 Jerry Casale 12.50 30.00
39 Earl Averill 12.50 30.00
40 Joe Cunningham 15.00 40.00
41 Barry Latman 12.50 30.00
42 Hobie Landrith 12.50 30.00
43 Senators Team CL 20.00 50.00
44 Bobby Locke 12.50 30.00
45 Roy McMillan 12.50 30.00
46 Jerry Fisher 12.50 30.00
47 Don Zimmer 12.50 30.00
48 Hal W. Smith 12.50 30.00
49 Curt Raydon 12.50 30.00
50 Al Kaline 150.00 300.00
51 Jim Coates 12.50 30.00
52 Dave Philley 12.50 30.00
53 Jackie Brandt 12.50 30.00
54 Mike Fornieles 12.50 30.00
55 Bill Mazeroski 50.00 100.00
56 Steve Korcheck 12.50 30.00
57 Win Savers 12.50 30.00
Turk Lown
Gerry Straley
58 Gino Cimoli 12.50 30.00
59 Juan Pizarro 12.50 30.00
60 Gus Triandos 12.50 30.00
61 Eddie Kasko 12.50 30.00
62 Roger Craig 12.50 30.00
63 George Strickland 12.50 30.00
64 Jack Meyer 12.50 30.00
65 Elston Howard 20.00 50.00
66 Bob Trowbridge 12.50 30.00
67 Jose Pagan 12.50 30.00
68 Dave Hillman 12.50 30.00
69 Billy Goodman 12.50 30.00
70 Lew Burdette 15.00 40.00
71 Marty Keough 12.50 30.00
72 Tigers Team CL 60.00 120.00
73 Bob Gibson 150.00 300.00
74 Walt Moryn 12.50 30.00
75 Vic Power 12.50 30.00
76 Bill Fischer 12.50 30.00
77 Hank Foiles 12.50 30.00
78 Bob Grim 12.50 30.00
79 Walt Dropo 12.50 30.00
80 Johnny Antonelli 12.50 30.00
81 Russ Snyder 12.50 30.00
82 Ruben Gomez 12.50 30.00
83 Tony Kubek 15.00 40.00
84 Hal R. Smith 12.50 30.00
85 Frank Lary 12.50 30.00
86 Dick Gernert 12.50 30.00
87 John Romonosky 12.50 30.00
88 John Roseboro 12.50 30.00
89 Hal Brown 12.50 30.00
90 Bobby Avila 12.50 30.00
91 Bennie Daniels 12.50 30.00
92 Whitey Herzog 12.50 30.00
93 Art Schult 12.50 30.00
94 Leo Kiely 12.50 30.00
95 Frank Thomas 12.50 30.00
96 Ralph Terry 12.50 30.00
97 Ted Lepcio 12.50 30.00
98 Gordon Jones 12.50 30.00
99 Lenny Green 12.50 30.00
100 Nellie Fox 50.00 100.00
101 Bob Miller 12.50 30.00
102 Kent Hadley 12.50 30.00
103 Dick Farrell 12.50 30.00
104 Dick Schofield 12.50 30.00
105 Larry Sherry 12.50 30.00
106 Billy Gardner 12.50 30.00
107 Carlton Willey 12.50 30.00
108 Pete Daley 12.50 30.00
109 Clete Boyer 12.50 30.00
110 Cal McLish 12.50 30.00
111 Vic Wertz 12.50 30.00
112 Jack Harshman 12.50 30.00
113 Bob Skinner 12.50 30.00
114 Ken Aspromonte 12.50 30.00
115 Roy Face 15.00 40.00
Hoyt Wilhelm
116 Jim Rivera 12.50 30.00
117 Tom Borland RP 12.50 30.00
118 Bob Bruce RP 12.50 30.00
119 Chico Cardenas RP 12.50 30.00
120 Duke Carmel RP 12.50 30.00
121 Camilo Carreon RP 12.50 30.00
122 Don Dillard Rp 12.50 30.00
123 Dan Dobbek RP 12.50 30.00
124 Jim Donohue RP 12.50 30.00
125 Dick Ellsworth RP 12.50 30.00
126 Chuck Estrada RP 12.50 30.00
127 Ron Hansen RP 12.50 30.00
128 Bill Harris RP 12.50 30.00
129 Bob Hartman RP 12.50 30.00
130 Frank Herrera RP 12.50 30.00
131 Ed Hobaugh RP 12.50 30.00
132 Frank Howard RP 60.00 120.00
133 Julian Javier RP 12.50 30.00
134 Deron Johnson RP 12.50 30.00
135 Ken Johnson RP 12.50 30.00
136 Jim Kaat RP 125.00 250.00
137 Lou Klimchock RP 12.50 30.00
138 Art Mahaffey RP 12.50 30.00
139 Carl Mathias RP 12.50 30.00
140 Julio Navarro RP 12.50 30.00
141 Jim Proctor RP 12.50 30.00
142 Bill Short RP 12.50 30.00
143 Al Spangler RP 12.50 30.00
144 Al Stieglitz RP 12.50 30.00
145 Jim Umbricht RP 12.50 30.00
146 Ted Wieand RP 12.50 30.00
147 Bob Will RP 12.50 30.00
148 Carl Yastrzemski RP 500.00 1,000.00
149 Bob Nieman 12.50 30.00
150 Billy Pierce 15.00 40.00
151 Giants Team CL 20.00 50.00
152 Gail Harris 12.50 30.00
153 Bobby Thomson 15.00 40.00
154 Jim Davenport 12.50 30.00
155 Charlie Neal 12.50 30.00
156 Art Ceccarelli 12.50 30.00
157 Rocky Nelson 12.50 30.00
158 Wes Covington 12.50 30.00
159 Jim Piersall 15.00 40.00
160 Mickey Mantle 500.00 1,000.00
Ken Boyer
161 Ray Narleski 12.50 30.00
162 Sammy Taylor 12.50 30.00
163 Hector Lopez 12.50 30.00
164 Reds Team CL 20.00 50.00
165 Jack Sanford 12.50 30.00
166 Chuck Essegian 12.50 30.00
167 Valmy Thomas 12.50 30.00
168 Alex Grammas 12.50 30.00
169 Jake Striker 12.50 30.00
170 Del Crandall 12.50 30.00
171 Johnny Groth 12.50 30.00
172 Willie Kirkland 12.50 30.00
173 Billy Martin 50.00 100.00
174 Indians Team CL 20.00 50.00
175 Pedro Ramos 12.50 30.00
176 Vada Pinson 15.00 40.00
177 Johnny Kucks 12.50 30.00
178 Woody Held 12.50 30.00
179 Rip Coleman 12.50 30.00
180 Harry Simpson 12.50 30.00
181 Billy Loes 12.50 30.00
182 Glen Hobbie 12.50 30.00
183 Eli Grba 12.50 30.00
184 Gary Geiger 12.50 30.00
185 Jim Owens 12.50 30.00
186 Dave Sisler 12.50 30.00
187 Jay Hook 12.50 30.00
188 Dick Williams 12.50 30.00
189 Don McMahon 12.50 30.00
190 Gene Woodling 12.50 30.00
191 Johnny Klippstein 12.50 30.00
192 Danny O'Connell 12.50 30.00
193 Dick Hyde 12.50 30.00
194 Bobby Gene Smith 12.50 30.00
195 Lindy McDaniel 12.50 30.00
196 Andy Carey 12.50 30.00

1961 Topps

The cards in this 587-card set measure 2 1/2" by 3 1/2". In 1961, Topps returned to the vertical obverse format. Introduced for the first time were "League Leaders" (41-50) and separate, numbered checklist cards. Two number 463s exist: the Braves team card carrying that number was meant to be number 426. There are three versions of the second series checklist card number 98; the variations are distinguished by the color of the "CHECKLIST" headline on the front of the card, the color of the printing of the card number on the bottom of the reverse, and the presence of the copyright notice running vertically on the card back. There are two groups of managers (131-139/219-226) as well as separate subsets of World Series cards (306-313), Baseball Thrills (401-410), MVP's of the 1950's (AL 471-478/NL 479-486) and Sporting News All-Stars (566-589). The usual last series scarcity (523-589) exists. Some collectors believe that 61 high numbers are the toughest of all the Topps hi series numbers. The set actually totals 587 cards since numbers 587 and 588 were never issued. These card advertising promos have been seen: Dan Dobbek/Russ Nixon/60 NL Pitching Leaders on the front along with an ad and Roger Maris on the back.Other strips feature Jack Kralick/Dick Stigman/Joe Christopher; Ed Roebuck/Bob Schmidt/Zoilo Versalles; Lindy (McDaniel) Shows Larry (Jackson)/John Blanchard/Johnny Kucks. Cards were issued in one-card penny packs, five-card nickel packs, 10 cent cello packs (which came 36 to a box) and 36-card rack packs which cost 29 cents. The one card packs came 120 to a box. The key Rookie Cards in this set are Juan Marichal, Ron Santo and Billy Williams.

COMPLETE SET (587) 3,500.00 7,000.00
COMMON CARD (1-370) 1.25 3.00
COMMON CARD (371-446) 1.50 4.00
COMMON CARD (447-522) 3.00 8.00
COMMON CARD (523-589) 12.50 30.00
NOT ISSUED (587/588)
WRAPPER (1-CENT) 100.00 200.00
WRAP.(1-CENT, REPEAT) 50.00 100.00
WRAPPER (5-CENT) 15.00 40.00
1 Dick Groat 12.00 30.00
2 Roger Maris 60.00 150.00
3 John Buzhardt 1.25 3.00
4 Lenny Green 1.25 3.00
5 John Romano 1.25 3.00
6 Ed Roebuck 1.25 3.00
7 Chicago White Sox TC 3.00 8.00
8 Dick Williams UER 2.50 6.00
Blurb states career high in RBI, however his career high in RBI was in 1959
9 Bob Purkey 1.25 3.00
10 Brooks Robinson 15.00 40.00
11 Curt Simmons 2.50 6.00
12 Moe Thacker 1.25 3.00
13 Chuck Cottier 1.25 3.00
14 Don Mossi 2.50 6.00
15 Willie Kirkland 1.25 3.00
16 Billy Muffett 1.25 3.00
17 Checklist 1 4.00 10.00
18 Jim Grant 2.50 6.00
19 Clete Boyer 3.00 8.00
20 Robin Roberts 8.00 20.00
21 Zoilo Versalles UER RC 3.00 8.00
22 Clem Labine 2.50 6.00
23 Don Demeter 1.25 3.00
24 Ken Johnson 2.50 6.00
25 Pinson/Bell/F.Robinson 3.00 8.00
26 Wes Stock 1.25 3.00
27 Jerry Kindall 1.25 3.00
28 Hector Lopez 2.50 6.00
29 Don Nottebart 1.25 3.00
30 Nellie Fox 10.00 25.00
31 Bob Schmidt 1.25 3.00
32 Ray Sadecki 1.25 3.00
33 Gary Geiger 1.25 3.00
34 Wynn Hawkins 1.25 3.00
35 Ron Santo RC 30.00 80.00
36 Jack Kralick RC 1.25 3.00
37 Charley Maxwell 2.50 6.00
38 Bob Lillis 1.25 3.00
39 Leo Posada RC 1.25 3.00
40 Bob Turley 2.50 6.00
41 Groat/Mays/Clemente LL 10.00 25.00
42 Runnels/Minoso/Skow LL 3.00 8.00
43 Banks/Aaron/Mathews LL 10.00 25.00
44 Mante/Maris/Colavito LL 25.00 60.00
45 McCormick/Drysdale LL 3.00 8.00
46 Baumann/Bunning/Dit LL 3.00 8.00
47 Broglio/Spahn/Burdette LL 3.00 8.00
48 Estrada/Perry/Daley LL 3.00 8.00
49 Drysdale/Koufax LL 8.00 20.00
50 Bunning/Ramos/Wynn LL 3.00 8.00
51 Detroit Tigers TC 3.00 8.00
52 George Crowe 1.25 3.00
53 Russ Nixon 1.25 3.00
54 Earl Francis RC 1.25 3.00
55 Jim Davenport 2.50 6.00
56 Russ Kemmerer 1.25 3.00
57 Marv Throneberry 2.50 6.00
58 Joe Schaffernoth RC 1.25 3.00
59 Jim Woods 1.25 3.00
60 Woody Held 1.25 3.00
61 Ron Piche RC 1.25 3.00
62 Al Pilarcik 1.25 3.00
63 Jim Kaat 3.00 8.00
64 Alex Grammas 1.25 3.00
65 Ted Kluszewski 3.00 8.00
66 Bill Henry 1.25 3.00
67 Ossie Virgil 1.25 3.00
68 Deron Johnson 2.50 6.00
69 Earl Wilson 2.50 6.00
70 Bill Virdon 2.50 6.00
71 Jerry Adair 1.25 3.00
72 Stu Miller 2.50 6.00
73 Al Spangler 1.25 3.00
74 Joe Pignatano 1.25 3.00
75 L.McDaniel/L.Jackson 2.50 6.00
76 Harry Anderson 1.25 3.00
77 Dick Stigman 1.25 3.00
78 Lee Walls 2.50 6.00
79 Joe Ginsberg 1.25 3.00
80 Harmon Killebrew 12.00 30.00
81 Tracy Stallard RC 1.25 3.00
82 Joe Christopher RC 1.25 3.00
83 Bob Bruce 1.25 3.00
84 Lee Maye 1.25 3.00
85 Jerry Walker 1.25 3.00
86 Los Angeles Dodgers TC 3.00 8.00
87 Joe Amalfitano 1.25 3.00
88 Richie Ashburn 6.00 15.00
89 Billy Martin 10.00 25.00
90 Gerry Staley 1.25 3.00
91 Walt Moryn 1.25 3.00
92 Hal Naragon 1.25 3.00
93 Tony Gonzalez 1.25 3.00
94 Johnny Kucks 1.25 3.00
95 Norm Cash 3.00 8.00
96 Billy O'Dell 1.25 3.00
97 Jerry Lynch 2.50 6.00
98A Checklist 2 Red 4.00 10.00
98B Checklist 2 Yellow B/W 4.00 10.00
98C Checklist 2 Yellow W/B 4.00 10.00
99 Don Buddin UER 1.25 3.00
100 Harvey Haddix 2.50 6.00
101 Bubba Phillips 1.25 3.00
102 Gene Stephens 1.25 3.00
103 Ruben Amaro 1.25 3.00
104 John Blanchard 3.00 8.00
105 Carl Willey 1.25 3.00
106 Whitey Herzog 1.25 3.00
107 Seth Morehead 1.25 3.00
108 Dan Dobbek 1.25 3.00
109 Johnny Podres 3.00 8.00
110 Vada Pinson 3.00 8.00
111 Jack Meyer 1.25 3.00
112 Chico Fernandez 1.25 3.00
113 Mike Fornieles 1.25 3.00
114 Hobie Landrith 1.25 3.00
115 Johnny Antonelli 2.50 6.00
116 Joe DeMaestri 1.25 3.00
117 Dale Long 2.50 6.00
118 Chris Cannizzaro RC 1.25 3.00
119 Siebern/Bauer/Lumpe 2.50 6.00
120 Eddie Mathews 12.50 30.00
121 Eli Grba 2.50 6.00
122 Chicago Cubs TC 3.00 8.00

Card	Low	High
123 Billy Gardner	1.25	3.00
124 J.C. Martin	1.25	3.00
125 Steve Barber	1.25	3.00
126 Dick Stuart	2.50	6.00
127 Ron Kline	1.25	3.00
128 Rip Repulski	1.25	3.00
129 Ed Hobaugh	1.25	3.00
130 Norm Larker	1.25	3.00
131 Paul Richards MG	2.50	6.00
132 Al Lopez MG	3.00	8.00
133 Ralph Houk MG	2.50	6.00
134 Mickey Vernon MG	2.50	6.00
135 Fred Hutchinson MG	2.50	6.00
136 Walter Alston MG	3.00	8.00
137 Chuck Dressen MG	2.50	6.00
138 Danny Murtaugh MG	2.50	6.00
139 Solly Hemus MG	2.50	6.00
140 Gus Triandos	2.50	6.00
141 Billy Williams RC	30.00	60.00
142 Luis Arroyo	2.50	6.00
143 Russ Snyder	1.25	3.00
144 Jim Coker	1.25	3.00
145 Bob Buhl	2.50	6.00
146 Marty Keough	1.25	3.00
147 Ed Rakow	1.25	3.00
148 Julian Javier	2.50	6.00
149 Bob Oldis	1.25	3.00
150 Willie Mays	40.00	100.00
151 Jim Donohue	1.25	3.00
152 Earl Torgeson	1.25	3.00
153 Don Lee	1.25	3.00
154 Bobby Del Greco	1.25	3.00
155 Johnny Temple	2.50	6.00
156 Ken Hunt	2.50	6.00
157 Cal McLish	1.25	3.00
158 Pete Daley	1.25	3.00
159 Baltimore Orioles TC	3.00	8.00
160 Whitey Ford UER	20.00	50.00
161 Sherman Jones UER RC	1.25	3.00
162 Jay Hook	1.25	3.00
163 Ed Sadowski	1.25	3.00
164 Felix Mantilla	1.25	3.00
165 Gino Cimoli	1.25	3.00
166 Danny Kravitz	1.25	3.00
167 San Francisco Giants TC	3.00	8.00
168 Tommy Davis	3.00	8.00
169 Don Elston	1.25	3.00
170 Al Smith	1.25	3.00
171 Paul Foytack	1.25	3.00
172 Don Dillard	1.25	3.00
173 Malzone/Wertz/Jensen	2.50	6.00
174 Ray Semproch	1.25	3.00
175 Gene Freese	1.25	3.00
176 Ken Aspromonte	1.25	3.00
177 Don Larsen	2.50	6.00
178 Bob Nieman	1.25	3.00
179 Joe Koppe	1.25	3.00
180 Bobby Richardson	8.00	20.00
181 Fred Green	1.25	3.00
182 Dave Nicholson RC	1.25	3.00
183 Andre Rodgers	1.25	3.00
184 Steve Bilko	2.50	6.00
185 Herb Score	2.50	6.00
186 Elmer Valo	2.50	6.00
187 Billy Klaus	1.25	3.00
188 Jim Marshall	1.25	3.00
189A Checklist 3 Copyright 263	4.00	10.00
189B Checklist 3 Copyright 264	4.00	10.00
190 Stan Williams	2.50	6.00
191 Mike de la Hoz RC	1.25	3.00
192 Dick Brown	1.25	3.00
193 Gene Conley	2.50	6.00
194 Gordy Coleman	2.50	6.00
195 Jerry Casale	1.25	3.00
196 Ed Bouchee	1.25	3.00
197 Dick Hall	1.25	3.00
198 Carl Sawatski	1.25	3.00
199 Bob Boyd	1.25	3.00
200 Warren Spahn	15.00	40.00
201 Pete Whisenant	1.25	3.00
202 Al Neiger RC	1.25	3.00
203 Eddie Bressoud	1.25	3.00
204 Bob Skinner	2.50	6.00
205 Billy Pierce	2.50	6.00
206 Gene Green	1.25	3.00
207 S.Koufax/J.Podres	15.00	40.00
208 Larry Osborne	1.25	3.00
209 Ken McBride	1.25	3.00
210 Pete Runnels	2.50	6.00
211 Bob Gibson	20.00	50.00
212 Haywood Sullivan	2.50	6.00
213 Bill Stafford RC	1.25	3.00
214 Danny Murphy RC	2.50	6.00
215 Gus Bell	2.50	6.00
216 Ted Bowsfield	1.25	3.00
217 Mel Roach	1.25	3.00
218 Hal Brown	1.25	3.00
219 Gene Mauch MG	2.50	6.00
220 Alvin Dark MG	2.50	6.00
221 Mike Higgins MG	1.25	3.00
222 Jimmy Dykes MG	2.50	6.00
223 Bob Scheffing MG	1.25	3.00
224 Joe Gordon MG	2.50	6.00
225 Bill Rigney MG	2.50	6.00
226 Cookie Lavagetto MG	2.50	6.00
227 Juan Pizarro	1.25	3.00
228 New York Yankees TC	15.00	40.00
229 Rudy Hernandez RC	1.25	3.00
230 Don Hoak	2.50	6.00
231 Dick Drott	1.25	3.00
232 Bill White	2.50	6.00
233 Joey Jay	2.50	6.00
234 Ted Lepcio	1.25	3.00
235 Camilo Pascual	2.50	6.00
236 Don Gile RC	1.25	3.00
237 Billy Loes	2.50	6.00
238 Jim Gilliam	2.50	6.00
239 Dave Sisler	1.25	3.00
240 Ron Hansen	1.25	3.00
241 Al Cicotte	1.25	3.00
242 Hal Smith	1.25	3.00
243 Frank Lary	2.50	6.00
244 Chico Cardenas	2.50	6.00
245 Joe Adcock	2.50	6.00
246 Bob Davis RC	1.25	3.00
247 Billy Goodman	2.50	6.00
248 Ed Keegan RC	1.25	3.00
249 Cincinnati Reds TC	3.00	8.00
250 V.Law/R.Face	2.50	6.00
251 Bill Bruton	1.25	3.00
252 Bill Short	1.25	3.00
253 Sammy Taylor	1.25	3.00
254 Ted Sadowski RC	2.50	6.00
255 Vic Power	2.50	6.00
256 Billy Hoeft	1.25	3.00
257 Carroll Hardy	1.25	3.00
258 Jack Sanford	2.50	6.00
259 John Schaive RC	1.25	3.00
260 Don Drysdale	15.00	40.00
261 Charlie Lau	2.50	6.00
262 Tony Curry	1.25	3.00
263 Ken Hamlin	1.25	3.00
264 Glen Hobbie	1.25	3.00
265 Tony Kubek	5.00	12.00
266 Lindy McDaniel	2.50	6.00
267 Norm Siebern	1.25	3.00
268 Ike Delock	1.25	3.00
269 Harry Chiti	1.25	3.00
270 Bob Friend	2.50	6.00
271 Jim Landis	1.25	3.00
272 Tom Morgan	1.25	3.00
273A Checklist 4 Copyright 336	6.00	15.00
273B Checklist 4 Copyright 339	4.00	10.00
274 Gary Bell	1.25	3.00
275 Gene Woodling	2.50	6.00
276 Ray Rippelmeyer RC	1.25	3.00
277 Hank Foiles	1.25	3.00
278 Don McMahon	1.25	3.00
279 Jose Pagan	1.25	3.00
280 Frank Howard	3.00	8.00
281 Frank Sullivan	1.25	3.00
282 Faye Throneberry	1.25	3.00
283 Bob Anderson	1.25	3.00
284 Dick Gernert	1.25	3.00
285 Sherm Lollar	2.50	6.00
286 George Witt	1.25	3.00
287 Carl Yastrzemski	40.00	100.00
288 Albie Pearson	2.50	6.00
289 Ray Moore	1.25	3.00
290 Stan Musial	30.00	80.00
291 Tex Clevenger	1.25	3.00
292 Jim Baumer RC	1.25	3.00
293 Tom Sturdivant	1.25	3.00
294 Don Blasingame	1.25	3.00
295 Milt Pappas	2.50	6.00
296 Wes Covington	2.50	6.00
297 Kansas City Athletics TC	3.00	8.00
298 Jim Golden RC	1.25	3.00
299 Clay Dalrymple	1.25	3.00
300 Mickey Mantle	300.00	600.00
301 Chet Nichols	1.25	3.00
302 Al Heist RC	1.25	3.00
303 Gary Peters	2.50	6.00
304 Rocky Nelson	1.25	3.00
305 Mike McCormick	2.50	6.00
306 Bill Virdon WS1	4.00	10.00
307 Mickey Mantle WS2	30.00	80.00
308 Bobby Richardson WS3	5.00	12.00
309 Gino Cimoli WS4	4.00	10.00
310 Roy Face WS5	4.00	10.00
311 Whitey Ford WS6	6.00	15.00
312 Bill Mazeroski WS7	20.00	50.00
313 Pirates Celebrate WS	6.00	15.00
314 Bob Miller	1.25	3.00
315 Earl Battey	2.50	6.00
316 Bobby Gene Smith	1.25	3.00
317 Jim Brewer RC	1.25	3.00
318 Danny O'Connell	1.25	3.00
319 Valmy Thomas	1.25	3.00
320 Lou Burdette	2.50	6.00
321 Marv Breeding	1.25	3.00
322 Bill Kunkel RC	2.50	6.00
323 Sammy Esposito	1.25	3.00
324 Hank Aguirre	1.25	3.00
325 Wally Moon	2.50	6.00
326 Dave Hillman	1.25	3.00
327 Matty Alou RC	8.00	20.00
328 Jim O'Toole	2.50	6.00
329 Julio Becquer	1.25	3.00
330 Rocky Colavito	8.00	20.00
331 Ned Garver	1.25	3.00
332 Dutch Dotterer UER	1.25	3.00
333 Fritz Brickell RC	1.25	3.00
334 Walt Bond	1.25	3.00
335 Frank Bolling	1.25	3.00
336 Don Mincher	2.50	6.00
337 Wynn/Lopez/Score	3.00	8.00
338 Don Landrum	1.25	3.00
339 Gene Baker	1.25	3.00
340 Vic Wertz	2.50	6.00
341 Jim Owens	1.25	3.00
342 Clint Courtney	1.25	3.00
343 Earl Robinson RC	1.25	3.00
344 Sandy Koufax	50.00	100.00
345 Jimmy Piersall	3.00	8.00
346 Howie Nunn	1.25	3.00
347 St. Louis Cardinals TC	3.00	8.00
348 Steve Boros	1.25	3.00
349 Danny McDevitt	1.25	3.00
350 Ernie Banks	20.00	50.00
351 Jim King	1.25	3.00
352 Bob Shaw	1.25	3.00
353 Howie Bedell RC	1.25	3.00
354 Billy Harrell	2.50	6.00
355 Bob Allison	3.00	8.00
356 Ryne Duren	1.25	3.00
357 Daryl Spencer	1.25	3.00
358 Earl Averill Jr.	2.50	6.00
359 Dallas Green	1.25	3.00
360 Frank Robinson	20.00	50.00
361A Checklist 5 No Ad on Back	6.00	15.00
361B Checklist 5 Ad on Back	6.00	15.00
362 Frank Funk RC	1.25	3.00
363 John Roseboro	2.50	6.00
364 Moe Drabowsky	2.50	6.00
365 Jerry Lumpe	1.25	3.00
366 Eddie Fisher	1.25	3.00
367 Jim Rivera	1.25	3.00
368 Bennie Daniels	1.25	3.00
369 Dave Philley	1.25	3.00
370 Roy Face	2.50	6.00
371 Bill Skowron SP	12.00	30.00
372 Bob Hendley RC	1.50	4.00
373 Boston Red Sox TC	3.00	8.00
374 Paul Giel	1.50	4.00
375 Ken Boyer	5.00	12.00
376 Mike Roarke RC	2.50	6.00
377 Ruben Gomez	1.50	4.00
378 Wally Post	2.50	6.00
379 Bobby Shantz	1.50	4.00
380 Minnie Minoso	3.00	8.00
381 Dave Wickersham RC	1.50	4.00
382 Frank Thomas	2.50	6.00
383 McCormick/Sanford/O'Dell	2.50	6.00
384 Chuck Essegian	1.50	4.00
385 Jim Perry	2.50	6.00
386 Joe Hicks	1.50	4.00
387 Duke Maas	1.50	4.00
388 Roberto Clemente	50.00	120.00
389 Ralph Terry	2.50	6.00
390 Del Crandall	3.00	8.00
391 Winston Brown RC	1.50	4.00
392 Reno Bertoia	1.50	4.00
393 D.Cardwell/G.Hobbie	1.50	4.00
394 Ken Walters	1.50	4.00
395 Chuck Estrada	2.50	6.00
396 Bob Aspromonte	1.50	4.00
397 Hal Woodeshick	1.50	4.00
398 Hank Bauer	2.50	6.00
399 Cliff Cook RC	1.50	4.00
400 Vernon Law	40.00	100.00
401 Babe Ruth 60th HR	25.00	60.00
402 Don Larsen Perfect SP	10.00	25.00
403 26 Inning Tie/Oeschger/Cadore	3.00	8.00
404 Rogers Hornsby .424	5.00	12.00
405 Lou Gehrig Streak	20.00	50.00
406 Mickey Mantle 565 HR	25.00	60.00
407 Jack Chesbro Wins 41	3.00	8.00
408 Christy Mathewson K's SP	8.00	20.00
409 Walter Johnson Shutout	8.00	20.00
410 Harvey Haddix 12 Perfect	3.00	8.00
411 Tony Taylor	2.50	6.00
412 Larry Sherry	2.50	6.00
413 Eddie Yost	2.50	6.00
414 Dick Donovan	2.50	6.00
415 Hank Aaron	75.00	200.00
416 Dick Howser RC	3.00	8.00
417 Juan Marichal SP RC	75.00	200.00
418 Ed Bailey	2.50	6.00
419 Tom Borland	1.50	4.00
420 Ernie Broglio	2.50	6.00
421 Ty Cline SP RC	8.00	20.00
422 Bud Daley	1.50	4.00
423 Charlie Neal SP	8.00	20.00
424 Turk Lown	1.50	4.00
425 Yogi Berra	40.00	100.00
426 Milwaukee Braves TC UER	5.00	12.00
427 Dick Ellsworth	2.50	6.00
428 Ray Barker SP RC	8.00	20.00
429 Al Kaline	15.00	40.00
430 Bill Mazeroski SP	10.00	25.00
431 Chuck Stobbs	1.50	4.00
432 Coot Veal	2.50	6.00
433 Art Mahaffey	1.50	4.00
434 Tom Brewer	1.50	4.00
435 Orlando Cepeda UER	10.00	25.00
436 Jim Maloney SP RC	8.00	20.00
437A Checklist 6 440 Louis	6.00	15.00
437B Checklist 6 440 Luis	6.00	15.00
438 Curt Flood	3.00	8.00
439 Phil Regan RC	2.50	6.00
440 Luis Aparicio	8.00	20.00
441 Dick Bertell RC	1.50	4.00
442 Gordon Jones	1.50	4.00
443 Duke Snider	12.00	30.00
444 Joe Nuxhall	2.50	6.00
445 Frank Malzone	2.50	6.00
446 Bob Taylor	1.50	4.00
447 Harry Bright	3.00	8.00
448 Del Rice	6.00	15.00
449 Bob Bolin RC	3.00	8.00
450 Jim Lemon	3.00	8.00
451 Spencer/White/Broglio	3.00	8.00
452 Bob Allen RC	3.00	8.00
453 Dick Schofield	3.00	8.00
454 Pumpsie Green	3.00	8.00
455 Early Wynn	6.00	15.00
456 Hal Bevan	3.00	8.00
457 Johnny James	3.00	8.00
458 Willie Tasby	3.00	8.00
459 Terry Fox RC	4.00	10.00
460 Gil Hodges	10.00	25.00
461 Smoky Burgess	6.00	15.00
462 Lou Klimchock	3.00	8.00
463 Jack Fisher See 426	3.00	8.00
464 Lee Thomas RC	4.00	10.00
465 Roy McMillan	6.00	15.00
466 Ron Moeller RC	3.00	8.00
467 Cleveland Indians TC	5.00	12.00
468 John Callison	4.00	10.00
469 Ralph Lumenti	3.00	8.00
470 Roy Sievers	4.00	10.00
471 Phil Rizzuto MVP	12.00	30.00
472 Yogi Berra MVP	25.00	60.00
473 Bob Shantz MVP	3.00	8.00
474 Al Rosen MVP	4.00	10.00
475 Mickey Mantle MVP	100.00	250.00
476 Jackie Jensen MVP	4.00	10.00
477 Nellie Fox MVP	6.00	15.00
478 Roger Maris MVP	25.00	60.00
479 Jim Konstanty MVP	3.00	8.00
480 Roy Campanella MVP	15.00	40.00
481 Hank Sauer MVP	3.00	8.00
482 Willie Mays MVP	25.00	60.00
483 Don Newcombe MVP	5.00	12.00
484 Hank Aaron MVP	25.00	60.00
485 Ernie Banks MVP	20.00	50.00
486 Dick Groat MVP	4.00	10.00
487 Gene Oliver	3.00	8.00
488 Joe McClain RC	4.00	10.00
489 Walt Dropo	3.00	8.00
490 Jim Bunning	10.00	25.00
491 Philadelphia Phillies TC	5.00	12.00
492A R.Fairly White	4.00	10.00
492B R.Fairly Green	8.00	20.00
493 Don Zimmer UER	5.00	12.00
494 Tom Cheney	4.00	10.00
495 Elston Howard	10.00	25.00
496 Ken MacKenzie	3.00	8.00
497 Willie Jones	3.00	8.00
498 Ray Herbert	3.00	8.00
499 Chuck Schilling RC	3.00	8.00
500 Harvey Kuenn	6.00	15.00
501 John DeMerit RC	3.00	8.00
502 Choo Choo Coleman RC	4.00	10.00
503 Tito Francona	3.00	8.00
504 Billy Consolo	3.00	8.00
505 Red Schoendienst	8.00	20.00
506 Willie Davis RC	8.00	20.00
507 Pete Burnside	3.00	8.00
508 Rocky Bridges	3.00	8.00
509 Camilo Carreon	3.00	8.00
510 Art Ditmar	3.00	8.00
511 Joe M. Morgan	3.00	8.00
512 Bob Will	3.00	8.00
513 Jim Brosnan	3.00	8.00
514 Jake Wood RC	3.00	8.00
515 Jackie Brandt	3.00	8.00
516A Checklist 7 (C on front partially covers Braves cap)	6.00	15.00
516B Checklist 7 (C on front fully above Braves cap)	6.00	15.00
517 Willie McCovey	15.00	40.00
518 Andy Carey	3.00	8.00
519 Jim Pagliaroni RC	3.00	8.00
520 Joe Cunningham	3.00	8.00
521 N.Sherry/L.Sherry	3.00	8.00
522 Dick Farrell UER	6.00	15.00
523 Joe Gibbon	15.00	40.00
524 Johnny Logan	12.00	30.00
525 Ron Perranoski RC	30.00	60.00
526 R.C. Stevens	12.50	30.00
527 Gene Leek RC	12.50	30.00
528 Pedro Ramos	12.50	30.00
529 Bob Roselli	12.50	30.00
530 Bob Malkmus	12.50	30.00
531 Jim Coates	20.00	50.00
532 Bob Hale	12.50	30.00
533 Jack Curtis RC	12.50	30.00
534 Eddie Kasko	15.00	40.00
535 Larry Jackson	12.50	30.00
536 Bill Tuttle	12.50	30.00
537 Bobby Locke	12.50	30.00
538 Chuck Hiller RC	12.50	30.00
539 Johnny Klippstein	12.50	30.00
540 Jackie Jensen	15.00	40.00
541 Roland Sheldon RC	20.00	50.00
542 Minnesota Twins TC	30.00	60.00
543 Roger Craig	15.00	40.00
544 George Thomas RC	20.00	50.00
545 Hoyt Wilhelm	30.00	60.00
546 Marty Kutyna	12.50	30.00
547 Leon Wagner	12.50	30.00
548 Ted Wills	12.50	30.00
549 Hal R. Smith	12.50	30.00
550 Frank Baumann	12.50	30.00
551 George Altman	15.00	40.00
552 Jim Archer RC	12.50	30.00
553 Bill Fischer	12.50	30.00
554 Pittsburgh Pirates TC	40.00	80.00
555 Sam Jones	12.50	30.00
556 Ken R. Hunt RC	12.50	30.00
557 Jose Valdivielso	12.50	30.00
558 Don Ferrarese	12.50	30.00
559 Jim Gentile	30.00	80.00
560 Barry Latman	15.00	40.00
561 Charley James	12.50	30.00
562 Bill Monbouquette	12.50	30.00
563 Bob Cerv	30.00	80.00
564 Don Cardwell	12.50	30.00
565 Felipe Alou	20.00	50.00
566 Paul Richards AS MG	12.50	30.00
567 Danny Murtaugh AS MG	12.50	30.00
568 Bill Skowron AS	12.00	30.00
569 Frank Herrera AS	15.00	40.00
570 Nellie Fox AS	30.00	60.00
571 Bill Mazeroski AS	30.00	60.00
572 Brooks Robinson AS	25.00	60.00
573 Ken Boyer AS	15.00	40.00
574 Luis Aparicio AS	30.00	60.00
575 Ernie Banks AS	40.00	80.00
576 Roger Maris AS	50.00	120.00
577 Hank Aaron AS	50.00	120.00
578 Mickey Mantle AS	150.00	400.00
579 Willie Mays AS	50.00	120.00

580 Al Kaline AS	20.00	50.00
581 Frank Robinson AS	25.00	60.00
582 Earl Battey AS	12.50	30.00
583 Del Crandall AS	12.50	30.00
584 Jim Perry AS	12.50	30.00
585 Bob Friend AS	12.50	30.00
586 Whitey Ford AS	25.00	60.00
589 Warren Spahn AS	30.00	80.00

1961 Topps Magic Rub-Offs

There are 36 "Magic Rub-Offs" in this set of inserts also marketed in packages of 1961 Topps baseball cards. Each rub off measures 2 1/16" by 3 1/16". Of this number, 18 are team designs (numbered 1-18 below), while the remaining 18 depict players (numbered 19-36 below). The latter, one from each team, were apparently selected for their unusual nicknames.

COMPLETE SET (36)	150.00	300.00
COMMON RUB-OFF (1-18)	.75	2.00
COMMON PLAYER (19-36)	2.00	5.00
1 Detroit Tigers	2.00	5.00
2 New York Yankees	2.50	6.00
3 Minnesota Twins	1.25	3.00
4 Washington Senators	1.25	3.00
5 Boston Red Sox	2.00	5.00
6 Los Angeles Angels	1.25	3.00
7 Kansas City A's	1.25	3.00
8 Baltimore Orioles	1.25	3.00
9 Chicago White Sox	1.25	3.00
10 Cleveland Indians	1.25	3.00
11 Pittsburgh Pirates	1.25	3.00
12 San Francisco Giants	1.25	3.00
13 Los Angeles Dodgers	2.50	6.00
14 Philadelphia Phillies	1.25	3.00
15 Cincinnati Redlegs	1.25	3.00
16 St. Louis Cardinals	1.25	3.00
17 Chicago Cubs	1.25	3.00
18 Milwaukee Braves	1.25	3.00
19 John Romano	4.00	10.00
20 Ray Moore	4.00	10.00
21 Ernie Banks	20.00	50.00
22 Charlie Maxwell	4.00	10.00
23 Yogi Berra	20.00	50.00
24 Henry Dutch Dotterer	4.00	10.00
25 Jim Brosnan	4.00	10.00
26 Billy Martin	8.00	20.00
27 Jackie Brandt	4.00	10.00
28 Duke Mass/(sic, Maas)	5.00	12.00
29 Pete Runnels	5.00	12.00
30 Joe Gordon MG	5.00	12.00
31 Sam Jones	4.00	10.00
32 Walt Moryn	4.00	10.00
33 Harvey Haddix	5.00	12.00
34 Frank Howard	6.00	15.00
35 Turk Lown	4.00	10.00
36 Frank Herrera	4.00	10.00

1961 Topps Stamps

There are 207 different baseball players depicted in this stamp series, which was issued as an insert in packages of the regular Topps cards of 1961. The set is actually comprised of 208 stamps: 104 players are pictured on brown stamps and 104 players appear on green stamps, with Kaline found in both colors. The stamps were issued in attached pairs and an album was sold separately (10 cents) at retail outlets. Each stamp measures 1 3/8" by 1 3/16". Stamps are unnumbered but are presented here in alphabetical order by team, Chicago Cubs (1-12), Cincinnati Reds (13-24), Los Angeles Dodgers (25-36), Milwaukee Braves (37-48), Philadelphia Phillies (49-60), Pittsburgh Pirates (61-72), San Francisco Giants (73-84), St. Louis Cardinals (85-96), Baltimore Orioles AL (97-107), Boston Red Sox (108-119), Chicago White Sox (120-131), Cleveland Indians (132-143), Detroit Tigers (144-155), Kansas City A's (156-168), Los Angeles Angels (169-175), Minnesota Twins (176-187), New York Yankees (188-200) and Washington Senators (201-207).

COMPLETE SET (207)	300.00	600.00
1 George Altman	.75	2.00
2 Bob Anderson brown	.75	2.00
3 Richie Ashburn	2.00	5.00
4 Ernie Banks	3.00	8.00
5 Ed Bouchee	.75	2.00
6 Jim Brewer	.75	2.00
7 Dick Ellsworth	.75	2.00
8 Don Elston	.75	2.00
9 Ron Santo	2.00	5.00
10 Sammy Taylor	.75	2.00
11 Bob Will	.75	2.00
12 Billy Williams	2.00	5.00
13 Ed Bailey	.75	2.00
14 Gus Bell	.75	2.00
15 Jim Brosnan brown	.75	2.00
16 Chico Cardenas	.75	2.00
17 Gene Freese	.75	2.00
18 Eddie Kasko	.75	2.00
19 Jerry Lynch	.75	2.00
20 Billy Martin	2.00	5.00
21 Jim O'Toole	.75	2.00
22 Vada Pinson	1.25	3.00
23 Wally Post brown	.75	2.00
24 Frank Robinson	3.00	8.00
25 Tommy Davis	1.25	3.00
26 Don Drysdale	2.00	5.00
27 Frank Howard Brown	1.25	3.00
28 Norm Larker	.75	2.00
29 Wally Moon brown	.75	2.00
30 Charlie Neal	.75	2.00
31 Johnny Podres	1.25	3.00
32 Ed Roebuck	.75	2.00
33 Johnny Roseboro	.75	2.00
34 Larry Sherry	.75	2.00
35 Duke Snider	3.00	8.00
36 Stan Williams	.75	2.00
37 Hank Aaron	10.00	25.00
38 Joe Adcock	.75	2.00
39 Bill Bruton	.75	2.00
40 Bob Buhl	.75	2.00
41 Wes Covington brown	.75	2.00
42 Del Crandall	.75	2.00
43 Joey Jay	.75	2.00
44 Felix Mantilla	.75	2.00
45 Eddie Mathews	3.00	8.00
46 Roy McMillan	.75	2.00
47 Warren Spahn	3.00	8.00
48 Carlton Willey brown	.75	2.00
49 John Buzhardt	.75	2.00
50 Johnny Callison	.75	2.00
51 Tony Curry	.75	2.00
52 Clay Dalrymple brown	.75	2.00
53 Bobby Del Greco brown	.75	2.00
54 Dick Farrell brown	.75	2.00
55 Tony Gonzalez	.75	2.00
56 Pancho Herrera	.75	2.00
57 Art Mahaffey	.75	2.00
58 Robin Roberts	1.25	3.00
59 Tony Taylor	.75	2.00
60 Lee Walls	.75	2.00
61 Smoky Burgess	.75	2.00
62 Roy Face (brown)	.75	2.00
63 Bob Friend	.75	2.00
64 Dick Groat	1.25	3.00
65 Don Hoak	.75	2.00
66 Vern Law	.75	2.00
67 Bill Mazeroski	1.25	3.00
68 Rocky Nelson	.75	2.00
69 Bob Skinner	.75	2.00
70 Hal Smith	.75	2.00
71 Dick Stuart	.75	2.00
72 Bill Virdon	.75	2.00
73 Don Blasingame	.75	2.00
74 Eddie Bressoud brown	.75	2.00
75 Orlando Cepeda	1.25	3.00
76 Jim Davenport	.75	2.00
77 Harvey Kuenn Brown	1.25	3.00
78 Hobie Landrith	.75	2.00
79 Juan Marichal	2.00	5.00
80 Willie Mays	10.00	25.00
81 Mike McCormick	.75	2.00
82 Willie McCovey	3.00	8.00
83 Billy O'Dell	.75	2.00
84 Jack Sanford	.75	2.00
85 Ken Boyer	1.25	3.00
86 Curt Flood	1.25	3.00
87 Alex Grammas brown	.75	2.00
88 Larry Jackson	.75	2.00
89 Julian Javier	.75	2.00
90 Ron Kline brown	.75	2.00
91 Lindy McDaniel	.75	2.00
92 Stan Musial	6.00	15.00
93 Curt Simmons brown	.75	2.00
94 Hal Smith	.75	2.00
95 Daryl Spencer	.75	2.00
96 Bill White brown	.75	2.00
97 Steve Barber	.75	2.00
98 Jackie Brandt brown	.75	2.00
99 Marv Breeding	.75	2.00
100 Chuck Estrada	.75	2.00
101 Jim Gentile	.75	2.00
102 Ron Hansen	.75	2.00
103 Milt Pappas	.75	2.00
104 Brooks Robinson	3.00	8.00
105 Gene Stephens	.75	2.00
106 Gus Triandos	.75	2.00
107 Hoyt Wilhelm	1.25	3.00
108 Tom Brewer	.75	2.00
109 Gene Conley brown	.75	2.00
110 Ike Delock brown	.75	2.00
111 Gary Geiger	.75	2.00
112 Jackie Jensen	1.25	3.00
113 Frank Malzone	.75	2.00
114 Bill Monbouquette	.75	2.00
115 Russ Nixon	.75	2.00
116 Pete Runnels	.75	2.00
117 Willie Tasby	.75	2.00
118 Vic Wertz brown	.75	2.00
119 Carl Yastrzemski	6.00	15.00
120 Luis Aparicio	1.25	3.00
121 Russ Kemmerer brown	.75	2.00
122 Jim Landis	.75	2.00
123 Sherman Lollar	.75	2.00
124 J.C. Martin	.75	2.00
125 Minnie Minoso	1.25	3.00
126 Billy Pierce	.75	2.00
127 Bob Shaw	.75	2.00
128 Roy Sievers	.75	2.00
129 Al Smith	.75	2.00
130 Gerry Staley brown	.75	2.00
131 Early Wynn	1.25	3.00
132 Johnny Antonelli brown	.75	2.00
133 Ken Aspromonte	.75	2.00
134 Tito Francona	.75	2.00
135 Jim Grant	.75	2.00
136 Woody Held	.75	2.00
137 Barry Latman	.75	2.00
138 Jim Perry	.75	2.00
139 Jimmy Piersall	1.25	3.00
140 Bubba Phillips	.75	2.00
141 Vic Power	.75	2.00
142 John Romano	.75	2.00
143 Johnny Temple	.75	2.00
144 Hank Aguirre brown	.75	2.00
145 Frank Bolling	.75	2.00
146 Steve Boros brown	.75	2.00
147 Jim Bunning	1.25	3.00
148 Norm Cash	1.25	3.00
149 Harry Chiti	.75	2.00
150 Chico Fernandez	.75	2.00
151 Dick Gernert	.75	2.00
152A Al Kaline (green)	3.00	8.00
152B Al Kaline (brown)	3.00	8.00
153 Frank Lary	.75	2.00
154 Charlie Maxwell	.75	2.00
155 Dave Sisler	.75	2.00
156 Hank Bauer	.75	2.00
157 Bob Boyd (brown)	.75	2.00
158 Andy Carey	.75	2.00
159 Bud Daley	.75	2.00
160 Dick Hall	.75	2.00
161 J.C. Hartman	.75	2.00
162 Ray Herbert	.75	2.00
163 Whitey Herzog	1.25	3.00
164 Jerry Lumpe brown	.75	2.00
165 Norm Siebern	.75	2.00
166 Marv Throneberry	.75	2.00
167 Bill Tuttle	.75	2.00
168 Dick Williams	.75	2.00
169 Jerry Casale brown	.75	2.00
170 Bob Cerv	.75	2.00
171 Ned Garver	.75	2.00
172 Ken Hunt	.75	2.00
173 Ted Kluszewski	2.00	5.00
174 Ed Sadowski brown	.75	2.00
175 Eddie Yost	.75	2.00
176 Bob Allison	.75	2.00
177 Earl Battey brown	.75	2.00
178 Reno Bertoia	.75	2.00
179 Billy Gardner	.75	2.00
180 Jim Kaat	1.25	3.00
181 Harmon Killebrew	3.00	8.00
182 Jim Lemon	.75	2.00
183 Camilo Pascual	.75	2.00
184 Pedro Ramos	.75	2.00
185 Chuck Stobbs	.75	2.00
186 Zoilo Versalles	.75	2.00
187 Pete Whisenant	.75	2.00
188 Luis Arroyo brown	.75	2.00
189 Yogi Berra	5.00	12.00
190 John Blanchard	.75	2.00
191 Clete Boyer	.75	2.00
192 Art Ditmar	.75	2.00
193 Whitey Ford	5.00	12.00
194 Elston Howard	2.00	5.00
195 Tony Kubek	2.00	5.00
196 Mickey Mantle	50.00	100.00
197 Roger Maris	10.00	25.00
198 Bobby Shantz	.75	2.00
199 Bill Stafford	.75	2.00
200 Bob Turley	.75	2.00
201 Bud Daley brown	.75	2.00
202 Dick Donovan	.75	2.00
203 Bobby Klaus	.75	2.00
204 Johnny Klippstein	.75	2.00
205 Dale Long	.75	2.00
206 Ray Semproch	.75	2.00
207 Gene Woodling	.75	2.00
XX Stamp Album	8.00	20.00

1961 Topps Dice Game

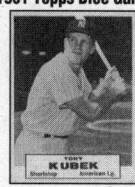

This 18-card standard-size set may never have been issued by Topps; it is considered a very obscure "test" issue and is quite scarce. The cards are printed completely in black and white on white card stock. There is no reference to Topps anywhere on the front or back of the card. The card back lays out the batter's outcome depending on the type of pitch thrown and the sum of two dice rolled. The cards are unnumbered and hence they are ordered below and assigned numbers alphabetically.

1 Earl Battey	500.00	1,000.00
2 Del Crandall	500.00	1,000.00
3 Jim Davenport	500.00	1,000.00
4 Don Drysdale	3,000.00	6,000.00
5 Dick Groat	600.00	1,200.00
6 Al Kaline	3,000.00	6,000.00
7 Tony Kubek	750.00	1,500.00
8 Mickey Mantle	50,000.00	100,000.00
9 Willie Mays	20,000.00	40,000.00
10 Bill Mazeroski	1,000.00	2,000.00
11 Stan Musial	20,000.00	40,000.00
12 Camilo Pascual	500.00	1,000.00
13 Bobby Richardson	750.00	1,500.00
14 Brooks Robinson	3,000.00	6,000.00
15 Frank Robinson	3,000.00	6,000.00
16 Norm Siebern	500.00	1,000.00
17 Leon Wagner	500.00	1,000.00
18 Bill White	600.00	1,200.00

1962 Topps

The cards in this 598-card set measure 2 1/2" by 3 1/2". The 1962 Topps set contains a mini-series spotlighting Babe Ruth (135-144). Other subsets in the set include League Leaders (51-60), World Series cards (232-237), In Action cards (311-319), NL All Stars (390-399), AL All Stars (466-475), and Rookie Prospects (591-598). The All-Star selections were again provided by Sport Magazine, as in 1958 and 1960. The second series had two distinct printings which are distinguishable by numerous color and pose variations. Those cards with a distinctive "green tint" are valued at a slight premuim as they are basically the result of a flawed printing process occurring early in the second series run. Card number 139 exists as A: Babe Ruth Special card, B: Hal Reniff with arms over head, or C: Hal Reniff in the same pose as card number 159. In addition, two poses exist for these cards: 129, 132, 134, 147, 174, 176, and 190. The high number series, 523 to 598, is somewhat more difficult to obtain than other cards in the set. Within the last series (523-598) there are 43 cards which were printed in lesser quantities; these are marked SP in the checklist below. In particular, the Rookie Parade subset (591-598) of this last series is even more difficult. This was the first year Topps produced multi-player Rookie Cards. The set price listed does not include the pose variations (see checklist below for individual values). A three card ad sheet has been seen. The players on the front include AL HR leaders, Barney Schultz and Carl Sawatski, while the back features an ad and a Roger Maris card. Cards were issued in one-card penny packs as well as five-card nickel packs. The five card packs came 24 to a box. The key Rookie Cards in this set are Lou Brock, Tim McCarver, Gaylord Perry, and Bob Uecker.

COMP. MASTER SET (689)	5,000.00	10,000.00
COMPLETE SET (598)	4,000.00	8,000.00
COMMON CARD (1-370)	2.00	5.00
COMMON CARD (371-446)	2.50	6.00
COMMON CARD (447-522)	5.00	12.00
COMMON CARD (523-598)	8.00	20.00
WRAPPER (1-CENT)	50.00	100.00
WRAPPER (5-CENT)	12.50	30.00
1 Roger Maris	100.00	250.00
2 Jim Brosnan	2.00	5.00
3 Pete Runnels	2.00	5.00
4 John DeMerit	3.00	8.00
5 Sandy Koufax UER	50.00	120.00
6 Marv Breeding	2.00	5.00
7 Frank Thomas	4.00	10.00
8 Ray Herbert	2.00	5.00
9 Jim Davenport	3.00	8.00
10 Roberto Clemente	60.00	150.00
11 Tom Morgan	2.00	5.00
12 Harry Craft MG	3.00	8.00
13 Dick Howser	3.00	8.00
14 Bill White	3.00	8.00
15 Dick Donovan	2.00	5.00
16 Darrell Johnson	2.00	5.00
17 Johnny Callison	3.00	8.00
18 M.Mantle/W.Mays	60.00	150.00
19 Ray Washburn RC	2.00	5.00
20 Rocky Colavito	6.00	15.00
21 Jim Kaat	3.00	8.00
22A Checklist 1 ERR	5.00	12.00
22B Checklist 1 COR	5.00	12.00
23 Norm Larker	2.00	5.00
24 Detroit Tigers TC	4.00	10.00
25 Ernie Banks	25.00	60.00
26 Chris Cannizzaro	3.00	8.00
27 Chuck Cottier	2.00	5.00
28 Minnie Minoso	4.00	10.00
29 Casey Stengel MG	10.00	25.00
30 Eddie Mathews	15.00	40.00
31 Tom Tresh RC	8.00	20.00
32 John Roseboro	3.00	8.00
33 Don Larsen	3.00	8.00
34 Johnny Temple	3.00	8.00
35 Don Schwall RC	4.00	10.00
36 Don Leppert RC	2.00	5.00
37 Latman/Stigman/Perry	2.00	5.00
38 Gene Stephens	2.00	5.00
39 Joe Koppe	2.00	5.00
40 Orlando Cepeda	10.00	25.00
41 Cliff Cook	2.00	5.00
42 Jim King	2.00	5.00
43 Los Angeles Dodgers TC	4.00	10.00

Card	Low	High
44 Don Taussig RC	2.00	5.00
45 Brooks Robinson	20.00	50.00
46 Jack Baldschun RC	2.00	5.00
47 Bob Will	2.00	5.00
48 Ralph Terry	3.00	8.00
49 Hal Jones RC	2.00	5.00
50 Stan Musial	30.00	80.00
51 Cash/Kaline/Howard LL	3.00	8.00
52 Clemente/Pins/Boyer LL	10.00	25.00
53 Maris/Mantle/Kill LL	30.00	80.00
54 Cepeda/Mays/F.Rob LL	8.00	20.00
55 Donovan/Staff/Mossi LL	3.00	8.00
56 Spahn/O'Toole/Simm LL	3.00	8.00
57 Ford/Lary/Bunning LL	3.00	8.00
58 Spahn/Jay/O'Toole LL	3.00	8.00
59 Pascual/Ford/Bunning LL	3.00	8.00
60 Koufax/Will/Drysdale LL	8.00	20.00
61 St. Louis Cardinals TC	4.00	10.00
62 Steve Boros	2.00	5.00
63 Tony Cloninger RC	3.00	8.00
64 Russ Snyder	2.00	5.00
65 Bobby Richardson	4.00	10.00
66 Cuno Barragan RC	2.00	5.00
67 Harvey Haddix	3.00	8.00
68 Ken Hunt	2.00	5.00
69 Phil Ortega RC	2.00	5.00
70 Harmon Killebrew	15.00	40.00
71 Dick LeMay RC	2.00	5.00
72 Boros/Scheffing/Wood	2.00	5.00
73 Nellie Fox	8.00	20.00
74 Bob Lillis	3.00	8.00
75 Milt Pappas	3.00	8.00
76 Howie Bedell	2.00	5.00
77 Tony Taylor	3.00	8.00
78 Gene Green	2.00	5.00
79 Ed Hobaugh	2.00	5.00
80 Vada Pinson	3.00	8.00
81 Jim Pagliaroni	2.00	5.00
82 Deron Johnson	3.00	8.00
83 Larry Jackson	2.00	5.00
84 Lenny Green	2.00	5.00
85 Gil Hodges	10.00	25.00
86 Donn Clendenon RC	3.00	8.00
87 Mike Roarke	2.00	5.00
88 Ralph Houk MG	3.00	8.00
89 Barney Schultz RC	2.00	5.00
90 Jimmy Piersall	3.00	8.00
91 J.C. Martin	2.00	5.00
92 Sam Jones	2.00	5.00
93 John Blanchard	3.00	8.00
94 Jay Hook	3.00	8.00
95 Don Hoak	3.00	8.00
96 Eli Grba	2.00	5.00
97 Tito Francona	2.00	5.00
98 Checklist 2	5.00	12.00
99 Boog Powell RC	12.50	30.00
100 Warren Spahn	15.00	40.00
101 Carroll Hardy	2.00	5.00
102 Al Schroll	2.00	5.00
103 Don Blasingame	2.00	5.00
104 Ted Savage RC	2.00	5.00
105 Don Mossi	3.00	8.00
106 Carl Sawatski	2.00	5.00
107 Mike McCormick	3.00	8.00
108 Willie Davis	3.00	8.00
109 Bob Shaw	2.00	5.00
110 Bill Skowron	3.00	8.00
110A Bill Skowron Green Tint	3.00	8.00
111 Dallas Green	3.00	8.00
111A Dallas Green Green Tint	3.00	8.00
112 Hank Foiles	2.00	5.00
112A Hank Foiles Green Tint	2.00	5.00
113 Chicago White Sox TC	4.00	10.00
113A Chicago White Sox TC Green Tint	4.00	10.00
114 Howie Koplitz RC	2.00	5.00
114A Howie Koplitz Green Tint	2.00	5.00
115 Bob Skinner	3.00	8.00
115A Bob Skinner Green Tint	3.00	8.00
116 Herb Score	3.00	8.00
116A Herb Score Green Tint	3.00	8.00
117 Gary Geiger	3.00	8.00
117A Gary Geiger Green Tint	3.00	8.00
118 Julian Javier	3.00	8.00
118A Julian Javier Green Tint	3.00	8.00
119 Danny Murphy	2.00	5.00
119A Danny Murphy Green Tint	2.00	5.00
120 Bob Purkey	2.00	5.00
120A Bob Purkey Green Tint	2.00	5.00
121 Billy Hitchcock	2.00	5.00
121A Billy Hitchcock Green Tint	2.00	5.00
122 Norm Bass RC	2.00	5.00
122A Norm Bass Green Tint	2.00	5.00
123 Mike de la Hoz	2.00	5.00
123A Mike de la Hoz Green Tint	2.00	5.00
124 Bill Pleis RC	2.00	5.00
124A Bill Pleis Green Tint	2.00	5.00
125 Gene Woodling	3.00	8.00
125A Gene Woodling Green Tint	3.00	8.00
126 Al Cicotte	2.00	5.00
126A Al Cicotte Green Tint	2.00	5.00
127 Siebern/Bauer/Lumpe	2.00	5.00
127A Siebern/Bauer/Lumpe Green Tint	2.00	5.00
128 Art Fowler	2.00	5.00
128A Art Fowler Green Tint	2.00	5.00
129A Lee Walls Facing Right	2.00	5.00
129B Lee Walls Face Lft Grn	12.50	30.00
130 Frank Bolling	2.00	5.00
130A Frank Bolling Green Tint	2.00	5.00
131 Pete Richert RC	2.00	5.00
131A Pete Richert Green Tint	2.00	5.00
132A Los Angeles Angels TC w/o inset	4.00	10.00
132B Los Angeles Angels TC w/inset	12.50	30.00
133 Felipe Alou	3.00	8.00
133A Felipe Alou Green Tint	3.00	8.00
134A Billy Hoeft Blue Sky	2.00	5.00
134B Billy Hoeft Green Sky	12.50	30.00
135 Babe as a Boy	8.00	20.00
135A Babe as a Boy Green	8.00	20.00
136 Babe Joins Yanks	8.00	20.00
136A Babe Joins Yanks Green	8.00	20.00
137 Babe with Mgr. Huggins	10.00	25.00
137A Babe with Mgr. Huggins Green	10.00	25.00
138 The Famous Slugger	8.00	20.00
138A The Famous Slugger Green	8.00	20.00
139A1 Babe Hits 60 (Pole)	12.50	30.00
139A2 Babe Hits 60 (No Pole)	12.50	30.00
139B Hal Reniff Portrait	6.00	15.00
139C Hal Reniff Pitching	30.00	60.00
140 Gehrig and Ruth	20.00	50.00
140A Gehrig and Ruth Green	20.00	50.00
141 Twilight Years	12.00	30.00
141A Twilight Years Green	12.00	30.00
142 Coaching the Dodgers	8.00	20.00
142A Coaching the Dodgers Green	8.00	20.00
143 Greatest Sports Hero	8.00	20.00
143A Greatest Sports Hero Green	8.00	20.00
144 Farewell Speech	8.00	20.00
144A Farewell Speech Green	8.00	20.00
145 Barry Latman	2.00	5.00
145A Barry Latman Green Tint	2.00	5.00
146 Don Demeter	2.00	5.00
146A Don Demeter Green Tint	2.00	5.00
147A Bill Kunkel Portrait	2.00	5.00
147B Bill Kunkel Pitching	12.50	30.00
148 Wally Post	2.00	5.00
148A Wally Post Green Tint	2.00	5.00
149 Bob Duliba	2.00	5.00
149A Bob Duliba Green Tint	2.00	5.00
150 Al Kaline	20.00	50.00
150A Al Kaline Green Tint	20.00	50.00
151 Johnny Klippstein	2.00	5.00
151A Johnny Klippstei Green Tint	2.00	5.00
152 Mickey Vernon MG	3.00	8.00
152A Mickey Vernon MG Green Tint	3.00	8.00
153 Pumpsie Green	2.50	6.00
153A Pumpsie Green Green Tint	2.50	6.00
154 Lee Thomas	2.50	6.00
154A Lee Thomas Green Tint	2.50	6.00
155 Stu Miller	2.50	6.00
155A Stu Miller Green Tint	2.50	6.00
156 Merritt Ranew RC	2.00	5.00
156A Merritt Ranew Green Tint	2.00	5.00
157 Wes Covington	3.00	8.00
157A Wes Covington Green Tint	3.00	8.00
158 Milwaukee Braves TC	4.00	10.00
158A Milwaukee Braves TC Green Tint	6.00	15.00
159 Hal Reniff RC	3.00	8.00
160 Dick Stuart	3.00	8.00
160A Dick Stuart Green Tint	3.00	8.00
161 Frank Baumann	2.00	5.00
161A Frank Baumann Green Tint	2.00	5.00
162 Sammy Drake RC	2.00	5.00
162A Sammy Drake Green Tint	2.00	5.00
163 B.Gardner/C.Boyer	3.00	8.00
163A B.Gardner/C.Boyer Green Tint	3.00	8.00
164 Hal Naragon	2.00	5.00
164A Hal Naragon Green Tint	2.00	5.00
165 Jackie Brandt	2.00	5.00
165A Jackie Brandt Green Tint	2.00	5.00
166 Don Lee	2.00	5.00
166A Don Lee Green Tint	2.00	5.00
167 Tim McCarver RC	15.00	40.00
167A Tim McCarver Green Tint	12.50	30.00
168 Leo Posada	2.00	5.00
168A Leo Posada Green Tint	2.00	5.00
169 Bob Cerv	4.00	10.00
169A Bob Cerv Green Tint	4.00	10.00
170 Ron Santo	12.00	30.00
170A Ron Santo Green Tint	12.00	30.00
171 Dave Sisler	2.00	5.00
171A Dave Sisler Green Tint	2.00	5.00
172 Fred Hutchinson MG	3.00	8.00
172A Fred Hutchinson MG Green Tint	3.00	8.00
173 Chico Fernandez	2.00	5.00
173A Chico Fernandez Green Tint	2.00	5.00
174A Carl Willey w/o Cap	2.00	5.00
174B Carl Willey w/Cap	12.50	30.00
175 Frank Howard	4.00	10.00
175A Frank Howard Green Tint	4.00	10.00
176A Eddie Yost Portrait	2.00	5.00
176B Eddie Yost Batting	12.50	30.00
177 Bobby Shantz	3.00	8.00
177A Bobby Shantz Green Tint	3.00	8.00
178 Camilo Carreon	2.00	5.00
178A Camilo Carreon Green Tint	2.00	5.00
179 Tom Sturdivant	2.00	5.00
179A Tom Sturdivant Green Tint	2.00	5.00
180 Bob Allison	4.00	10.00
180A Bob Allison Green Tint	4.00	10.00
181 Paul Brown RC	2.00	5.00
181A Paul Brown Green Tint	2.00	5.00
182 Bob Nieman	2.00	5.00
182A Bob Nieman Green Tint	2.00	5.00
183 Roger Craig	3.00	8.00
183A Roger Craig Green Tint	3.00	8.00
184 Haywood Sullivan	3.00	8.00
184A Haywood Sullivan Green Tint	3.00	8.00
185 Roland Sheldon	4.00	10.00
185A Roland Sheldon Green Tint	4.00	10.00
186 Mack Jones RC	2.00	5.00
186A Mack Jones Green Tint	2.00	5.00
187 Gene Conley	2.00	5.00
187A Gene Conley Green Tint	2.00	5.00
188 Chuck Hiller	2.00	5.00
188A Chuck Hiller Green Tint	2.00	5.00
189 Dick Hall	2.00	5.00
189A Dick Hall Green Tint	2.00	5.00
190A Wally Moon Portrait	3.00	8.00
190B Wally Moon Batting	12.50	30.00
191 Jim Brewer	2.00	5.00
191A Jim Brewer Green Tint	2.00	5.00
192A Checklist 3 w/o Comma	5.00	12.00
192B Checklist 3 w/Comma	6.00	15.00
193 Eddie Kasko	2.00	5.00
193A Eddie Kasko Green Tint	2.00	5.00
194 Dean Chance RC	3.00	8.00
194A Dean Chance Green Tint	3.00	8.00
195 Joe Cunningham	2.00	5.00
195A Joe Cunningham Green Tint	2.00	5.00
196 Terry Fox	2.00	5.00
196A Terry Fox Green Tint	2.00	5.00
197 Daryl Spencer	2.00	5.00
198 Johnny Keane MG	2.00	5.00
199 Gaylord Perry RC	40.00	100.00
200 Mickey Mantle	400.00	800.00
201 Ike Delock	2.00	5.00
202 Carl Warwick RC	2.00	5.00
203 Jack Fisher	2.00	5.00
204 Johnny Weekly RC	2.00	5.00
205 Gene Freese	2.00	5.00
206 Washington Senators TC	4.00	10.00
207 Pete Burnside	2.00	5.00
208 Billy Martin	8.00	20.00
209 Jim Fregosi RC	6.00	15.00
210 Roy Face	3.00	8.00
211 F.Bolling/R.McMillan	2.00	5.00
212 Jim Owens	2.00	5.00
213 Richie Ashburn	8.00	20.00
214 Dom Zanni	2.00	5.00
215 Woody Held	2.00	5.00
216 Ron Kline	2.00	5.00
217 Walter Alston MG	4.00	10.00
218 Joe Torre RC	40.00	100.00
219 Al Downing RC	3.00	8.00
220 Roy Sievers	3.00	8.00
221 Bill Short	2.00	5.00
222 Jerry Zimmerman	2.00	5.00
223 Alex Grammas	2.00	5.00
224 Don Rudolph	2.00	5.00
225 Frank Malzone	3.00	8.00
226 San Francisco Giants TC	4.00	10.00
227 Bob Tiefenauer	2.00	5.00
228 Dale Long	4.00	10.00
229 Jesus McFarlane RC	2.00	5.00
230 Camilo Pascual	3.00	8.00
231 Ernie Bowman RC	2.00	5.00
232 Ellie Howard WS1	4.00	10.00
233 Joey Jay WS2	4.00	10.00
234 Roger Maris WS3	15.00	40.00
235 Whitey Ford WS4	6.00	15.00
236 Yanks Crush Reds WS5	4.00	10.00
237 Yanks Celebrate WS	4.00	10.00
238 Norm Sherry	2.00	5.00
239 Cecil Butler RC	2.00	5.00
240 George Altman	2.00	5.00
241 Johnny Kucks	2.00	5.00
242 Mel McGaha MG RC	2.00	5.00
243 Robin Roberts	6.00	15.00
244 Don Gile	2.00	5.00
245 Ron Hansen	2.00	5.00
246 Art Ditmar	2.00	5.00
247 Joe Pignatano	2.00	5.00
248 Bob Aspromonte	3.00	8.00
249 Ed Keegan	2.00	5.00
250 Norm Cash	4.00	10.00
251 New York Yankees TC	20.00	50.00
252 Earl Francis	2.00	5.00
253 Harry Chiti CO	2.00	5.00
254 Gordon Windhorn RC	2.00	5.00
255 Juan Pizarro	2.00	5.00
256 Elio Chacon	3.00	8.00
257 Jack Spring RC	2.00	5.00
258 Marty Keough	2.00	5.00
259 Lou Klimchock	2.00	5.00
260 Billy Pierce	3.00	8.00
261 George Alusik RC	2.00	5.00
262 Bob Schmidt	2.00	5.00
263 Purkey/Turner/Jay	2.00	5.00
264 Dick Ellsworth	3.00	8.00
265 Joe Adcock	3.00	8.00
266 John Anderson RC	2.00	5.00
267 Dan Dobbek	2.00	5.00
268 Ken McBride	2.00	5.00
269 Bob Oldis	2.00	5.00
270 Dick Groat	3.00	8.00
271 Ray Rippelmeyer	2.00	5.00
272 Earl Robinson	2.00	5.00
273 Gary Bell	2.00	5.00
274 Sammy Taylor	2.00	5.00
275 Norm Siebern	2.00	5.00
276 Hal Kolstad RC	2.00	5.00
277 Checklist 4	6.00	15.00
278 Ken Johnson	3.00	8.00
279 Hobie Landrith UER	3.00	8.00
280 Johnny Podres	3.00	8.00
281 Jake Gibbs RC	4.00	10.00
282 Dave Hillman	2.00	5.00
283 Charlie Smith RC	2.00	5.00
284 Ruben Amaro	2.00	5.00
285 Curt Simmons	3.00	8.00
286 Al Lopez MG	4.00	10.00
287 George Witt	2.00	5.00
288 Billy Williams	20.00	50.00
289 Mike Krsnich RC	2.00	5.00
290 Jim Gentile	3.00	8.00
291 Hal Stowe RC	2.00	5.00
292 Jerry Kindall	2.00	5.00
293 Bob Miller	3.00	8.00
294 Philadelphia Phillies TC	4.00	10.00
295 Vern Law	3.00	8.00
296 Ken Hamlin	2.00	5.00
297 Ron Perranoski	3.00	8.00
298 Bill Tuttle	2.00	5.00
299 Don Wert RC	2.00	5.00
300 Willie Mays	100.00	250.00
301 Galen Cisco RC	2.00	5.00
302 Johnny Edwards RC	2.00	5.00
303 Frank Torre	3.00	8.00
304 Dick Farrell	3.00	8.00
305 Jerry Lumpe	2.00	5.00
306 L.McDaniel/L.Jackson	2.00	5.00
307 Jim Grant	3.00	8.00
308 Neil Chrisley	3.00	8.00
309 Moe Morhardt RC	2.00	5.00
310 Whitey Ford	20.00	50.00
311 Tony Kubek IA	3.00	8.00
312 Warren Spahn IA	6.00	15.00
313 Roger Maris IA	40.00	80.00
314 Rocky Colavito IA	3.00	8.00
315 Whitey Ford IA	6.00	15.00
316 Harmon Killebrew IA	6.00	15.00
317 Stan Musial IA	8.00	20.00
318 Mickey Mantle IA	40.00	100.00
319 Mike McCormick IA	2.00	5.00
320 Hank Aaron	60.00	150.00
321 Lee Stange RC	2.00	5.00
322 Alvin Dark MG	3.00	8.00
323 Don Landrum	2.00	5.00
324 Joe McClain	2.00	5.00
325 Luis Aparicio	10.00	25.00
326 Tom Parsons RC	2.00	5.00
327 Ozzie Virgil	2.00	5.00
328 Ken Walters	2.00	5.00
329 Bob Bolin	2.00	5.00
330 John Romano	2.00	5.00
331 Moe Drabowsky	3.00	8.00
332 Don Buddin	2.00	5.00
333 Frank Cipriani RC	2.00	5.00
334 Boston Red Sox TC	4.00	10.00
335 Bill Bruton	2.00	5.00
336 Billy Muffett	2.00	5.00
337 Jim Marshall	3.00	8.00
338 Billy Gardner	2.00	5.00
339 Jose Valdivielso	2.00	5.00
340 Don Drysdale	15.00	40.00
341 Mike Hershberger RC	2.00	5.00
342 Ed Rakow	2.00	5.00
343 Albie Pearson	3.00	8.00
344 Ed Bauta RC	2.00	5.00
345 Chuck Schilling	2.00	5.00
346 Jack Kralick	2.00	5.00
347 Chuck Hinton RC	2.00	5.00
348 Larry Burright RC	3.00	8.00
349 Paul Foytack	2.00	5.00
350 Frank Robinson	30.00	80.00
351 J.Torre/D.Crandall	3.00	8.00
352 Frank Sullivan	2.00	5.00
353 Bill Mazeroski	6.00	15.00
354 Roman Mejias	3.00	8.00
355 Steve Barber	2.00	5.00
356 Tom Haller RC	2.00	5.00
357 Jerry Walker	2.00	5.00
358 Tommy Davis	3.00	8.00
359 Bobby Locke	2.00	5.00
360 Yogi Berra	40.00	80.00
361 Bob Hendley	2.00	5.00
362 Ty Cline	2.00	5.00
363 Bob Roselli	2.00	5.00
364 Ken Hunt	2.00	5.00
365 Charlie Neal	3.00	8.00
366 Phil Regan	3.00	8.00
367 Checklist 5	6.00	15.00
368 Bob Tillman RC	2.00	5.00
369 Ted Bowsfield	2.00	5.00
370 Ken Boyer	4.00	10.00
371 Earl Battey	2.50	6.00
372 Jack Curtis	2.50	6.00
373 Al Heist	2.50	6.00
374 Gene Mauch MG	4.00	10.00
375 Ron Fairly	4.00	10.00
376 Bud Daley	3.00	8.00
377 John Orsino RC	2.50	6.00
378 Bennie Daniels	2.50	6.00
379 Chuck Essegian	2.50	6.00
380 Lou Burdette	4.00	10.00
381 Chico Cardenas	4.00	10.00
382 Dick Williams	3.00	8.00
383 Ray Sadecki	2.50	6.00
384 Kansas City Athletics TC	4.00	10.00
385 Early Wynn	6.00	15.00
386 Don Mincher	3.00	8.00
387 Lou Brock RC	100.00	250.00
388 Ryne Duren	3.00	8.00
389 Smoky Burgess	4.00	10.00
390 Orlando Cepeda AS	4.00	10.00
391 Bill Mazeroski AS	4.00	10.00
392 Ken Boyer AS UER	3.00	8.00
393 Roy McMillan AS	2.50	6.00
394 Hank Aaron AS	25.00	60.00
395 Willie Mays AS	20.00	50.00
396 Frank Robinson AS	10.00	25.00
397 John Roseboro AS	2.50	6.00
398 Don Drysdale AS	6.00	15.00
399 Warren Spahn AS	8.00	20.00
400 Elston Howard	4.00	10.00
401 O.Cepeda/R.Maris	15.00	40.00
402 Gino Cimoli	2.50	6.00
403 Chet Nichols	2.50	6.00
404 Tim Harkness RC	3.00	8.00
405 Jim Perry	3.00	8.00
406 Bob Taylor	2.50	6.00
407 Hank Aguirre	2.50	6.00
408 Gus Bell	3.00	8.00
409 Pittsburgh Pirates TC	4.00	10.00
410 Al Smith	2.50	6.00
411 Danny O'Connell	2.50	6.00
412 Charlie James	2.50	6.00
413 Matty Alou	4.00	10.00
414 Joe Gaines RC	2.50	6.00
415 Bill Virdon	4.00	10.00
416 Bob Scheffing MG	2.50	6.00
417 Joe Azcue RC	2.50	6.00
418 Andy Carey	2.50	6.00

419 Bob Bruce	3.00	8.00
420 Gus Triandos	3.00	8.00
421 Ken MacKenzie	3.00	8.00
422 Steve Bilko	2.50	6.00
423 R.Face/H.Wilhelm	4.00	10.00
424 Al McBean RC	2.50	6.00
425 Carl Yastrzemski	40.00	100.00
426 Bob Farley RC	2.50	6.00
427 Jake Wood	2.50	6.00
428 Joe Hicks	2.50	6.00
429 Billy O'Dell	2.50	6.00
430 Tony Kubek	6.00	15.00
431 Bob Buck Rodgers RC	3.00	8.00
432 Jim Pendleton	2.50	6.00
433 Jim Archer	2.50	6.00
434 Clay Dalrymple	2.50	6.00
435 Larry Sherry	3.00	8.00
436 Felix Mantilla	3.00	8.00
437 Ray Moore	2.50	6.00
438 Dick Brown	2.50	6.00
439 Jerry Buchek RC	2.50	6.00
440 Joey Jay	2.50	6.00
441 Checklist 6	6.00	15.00
442 Wes Stock	2.50	6.00
443 Del Crandall	3.00	8.00
444 Ted Wills	2.50	6.00
445 Vic Power	3.00	8.00
446 Don Elston	2.50	6.00
447 Willie Kirkland	5.00	12.00
448 Joe Gibbon	5.00	12.00
449 Jerry Adair	5.00	12.00
450 Jim O'Toole	6.00	15.00
451 Jose Tartabull RC	6.00	15.00
452 Earl Averill Jr.	5.00	12.00
453 Cal McLish	5.00	12.00
454 Floyd Robinson RC	5.00	12.00
455 Luis Arroyo	6.00	15.00
456 Joe Amalfitano	6.00	15.00
457 Lou Clinton	5.00	12.00
458A Bob Buhl Emblem	6.00	15.00
458B Bob Buhl No Emblem	20.00	50.00
459 Ed Bailey	5.00	12.00
460 Jim Bunning	8.00	20.00
461 Ken Hubbs RC	10.00	25.00
462A Willie Tasby Emblem	5.00	12.00
462B Willie Tasby No Emblem	20.00	50.00
463 Hank Bauer MG	6.00	15.00
464 Al Jackson RC	6.00	15.00
465 Cincinnati Reds TC	8.00	20.00
466 Norm Cash AS	6.00	15.00
467 Chuck Schilling AS	5.00	12.00
468 Brooks Robinson AS	12.00	30.00
469 Luis Aparicio AS	6.00	15.00
470 Al Kaline AS	20.00	50.00
471 Mickey Mantle AS	100.00	250.00
472 Rocky Colavito AS	6.00	15.00
473 Elston Howard AS	6.00	15.00
474 Frank Lary AS	5.00	12.00
475 Whitey Ford AS	8.00	20.00
476 Baltimore Orioles TC	8.00	20.00
477 Andre Rodgers	5.00	12.00
478 Don Zimmer	8.00	20.00
479 Joel Horlen RC	5.00	12.00
480 Harvey Kuenn	6.00	15.00
481 Vic Wertz	6.00	15.00
482 Sam Mele MG	5.00	12.00
483 Don McMahon	5.00	12.00
484 Dick Schofield	5.00	12.00
485 Pedro Ramos	5.00	12.00
486 Jim Gilliam	6.00	15.00
487 Jerry Lynch	5.00	12.00
488 Hal Brown	5.00	12.00
489 Julio Gotay RC	5.00	12.00
490 Clete Boyer UER	6.00	15.00
491 Leon Wagner	5.00	12.00
492 Hal W. Smith	6.00	15.00
493 Danny McDevitt	5.00	12.00
494 Sammy White	5.00	12.00
495 Don Cardwell	5.00	12.00
496 Wayne Causey RC	5.00	12.00
497 Ed Bouchee	6.00	15.00
498 Jim Donohue	5.00	12.00
499 Zoilo Versalles	6.00	15.00
500 Duke Snider	20.00	50.00
501 Claude Osteen	6.00	15.00
502 Hector Lopez	6.00	15.00
503 Danny Murtaugh MG	6.00	15.00
504 Eddie Bressoud	5.00	12.00
505 Juan Marichal	15.00	40.00
506 Charlie Maxwell	6.00	15.00
507 Ernie Broglio	6.00	15.00
508 Gordy Coleman	6.00	15.00
509 Dave Giusti RC	6.00	15.00
510 Jim Lemon	5.00	12.00
511 Bubba Phillips	5.00	12.00
512 Mike Fornieles	5.00	12.00
513 Whitey Herzog	6.00	15.00
514 Sherm Lollar	6.00	15.00
515 Stan Williams	6.00	15.00
516A Checklist 7 White	6.00	15.00
516B Checklist 7 Yellow	6.00	15.00
517 Dave Wickersham	5.00	12.00
518 Lee Maye	5.00	12.00
519 Bob Johnson RC	5.00	12.00
520 Bob Friend	6.00	15.00
521 Jacke Davis UER RC	5.00	12.00
522 Lindy McDaniel	6.00	15.00
523 Russ Nixon SP	12.50	30.00
524 Howie Nunn SP	12.50	30.00
525 George Thomas	8.00	20.00
526 Hal Woodeshick SP	12.50	30.00
527 Dick McAuliffe RC	12.50	30.00
528 Turk Lown	8.00	20.00
529 John Schaive SP	12.50	30.00
530 Bob Gibson SP	60.00	150.00
531 Bobby G. Smith	8.00	20.00
532 Dick Stigman	8.00	20.00
533 Charley Lau SP	12.50	30.00
534 Tony Gonzalez SP	12.50	30.00
535 Ed Roebuck	8.00	20.00
536 Dick Gernert	8.00	20.00
537 Cleveland Indians TC	20.00	50.00
538 Jack Sanford	8.00	20.00
539 Billy Moran	8.00	20.00
540 Jim Landis	12.50	30.00
541 Don Nottebart SP	12.50	30.00
542 Dave Philley	8.00	20.00
543 Bob Allen SP	12.50	30.00
544 Willie McCovey SP	60.00	150.00
545 Hoyt Wilhelm SP	20.00	50.00
546 Moe Thacker SP	12.50	30.00
547 Don Ferrarese	8.00	20.00
548 Bobby Del Greco	8.00	20.00
549 Bill Rigney MG SP	12.50	30.00
550 Art Mahaffey SP	12.50	30.00
551 Harry Bright	8.00	20.00
552 Chicago Cubs TC	20.00	50.00
553 Jim Coates	12.50	30.00
554 Bubba Morton SP RC	12.50	30.00
555 John Buzhardt SP	12.50	30.00
556 Al Spangler	8.00	20.00
557 Bob Anderson SP	12.50	30.00
558 John Goryl	8.00	20.00
559 Mike Higgins MG	8.00	20.00
560 Chuck Estrada SP	12.50	30.00
561 Gene Oliver SP	12.50	30.00
562 Bill Henry	8.00	20.00
563 Ken Aspromonte	8.00	20.00
564 Bob Grim	8.00	20.00
565 Jose Pagan	8.00	20.00
566 Marty Kutyna SP	12.50	30.00
567 Tracy Stallard SP	12.50	30.00
568 Jim Golden	8.00	20.00
569 Ed Sadowski SP	12.50	30.00
570 Bill Stafford SP	12.50	30.00
571 Billy Klaus SP	12.50	30.00
572 Bob G. Miller SP	12.50	30.00
573 Johnny Logan	8.00	20.00
574 Dean Stone	8.00	20.00
575 Red Schoendienst SP	20.00	50.00
576 Russ Kemmerer SP	12.50	30.00
577 Dave Nicholson SP	12.50	30.00
578 Jim Duffalo RC	8.00	20.00
579 Jim Schaffer SP RC	12.50	30.00
580 Bill Monbouquette	8.00	20.00
581 Mel Roach	8.00	20.00
582 Ron Piche	8.00	20.00
583 Larry Osborne	8.00	20.00
584 Minnesota Twins TC SP	30.00	60.00
585 Glen Hobbie SP	12.50	30.00
586 Sammy Esposito SP	12.50	30.00
587 Frank Funk SP	12.50	30.00
588 Birdie Tebbetts MG	8.00	20.00
589 Bob Turley	12.50	30.00
590 Curt Flood	12.50	30.00
591 Sam McDowell SP RC	40.00	80.00
592 Jim Bouton SP RC	30.00	80.00
593 Rookie Pitchers SP	20.00	50.00
594 Bob Uecker SP RC	100.00	250.00
595 Rookie Infielders SP	20.00	50.00
596 Joe Pepitone SP RC	40.00	100.00
597 Rookie Infield SP	20.00	50.00
598 Rookie Outfielders SP	40.00	80.00

1962 Topps Bucks

There are 96 "Baseball Bucks" in this unusual set released in its own one-cent package in 1962. Each "buck" measures 1 3/4" by 4 1/8". Each depicts a player with accompanying biography and facsimile autograph to the left. To the right is found a drawing of the player's home stadium. His team and position are listed under the ribbon design containing his name. The team affiliation and league are also indicated within circles on the reverse.

COMPLETE SET (96)	600.00	1,200.00
WRAPPER (1-CENT)	20.00	50.00
1 Hank Aaron	30.00	60.00
2 Joe Adcock	2.50	6.00
3 George Altman	2.00	5.00
4 Jim Archer	2.00	5.00
5 Richie Ashburn	10.00	25.00
6 Ernie Banks	15.00	40.00
7 Earl Battey	2.00	5.00
8 Gus Bell	2.00	5.00
9 Yogi Berra	15.00	40.00
10 Ken Boyer	3.00	8.00
11 Jackie Brandt	2.00	5.00
12 Jim Bunning	10.00	25.00
13 Lew Burdette	2.50	6.00
14 Don Cardwell	2.00	5.00
15 Norm Cash	3.00	8.00
16 Orlando Cepeda	8.00	20.00
17 Roberto Clemente	100.00	200.00
18 Rocky Colavito	6.00	15.00
19 Chuck Cottier	2.00	5.00
20 Roger Craig	2.50	6.00
21 Bennie Daniels	2.00	5.00
22 Don Demeter	2.00	5.00
23 Don Drysdale	12.50	30.00
24 Chuck Estrada	2.00	5.00
25 Dick Farrell	2.00	5.00
26 Whitey Ford	15.00	40.00
27 Nellie Fox	10.00	25.00
28 Tito Francona	2.00	5.00
29 Bob Friend	2.00	5.00
30 Jim Gentile	2.50	6.00
31 Dick Gernert	2.00	5.00
32 Lenny Green	2.00	5.00
33 Dick Groat	2.50	6.00
34 Woodie Held	2.00	5.00
35 Don Hoak	2.00	5.00
36 Gil Hodges	10.00	25.00
37 Elston Howard	6.00	15.00
38 Frank Howard	3.00	8.00
39 Dick Howser	2.50	6.00
40 Ken Hunt	2.00	5.00
41 Larry Jackson	2.00	5.00
42 Joey Jay	2.00	5.00
43 Al Kaline	15.00	40.00
44 Harmon Killebrew	10.00	25.00
45 Sandy Koufax	40.00	80.00
46 Harvey Kuenn	2.50	6.00
47 Jim Landis	2.00	5.00
48 Norm Larker	2.00	5.00
49 Frank Lary	2.00	5.00
50 Jerry Lumpe	2.00	5.00
51 Art Mahaffey	2.00	5.00
52 Frank Malzone	2.00	5.00
53 Felix Mantilla	2.00	5.00
54 Mickey Mantle	100.00	200.00
55 Roger Maris	20.00	50.00
56 Eddie Mathews	10.00	25.00
57 Willie Mays	30.00	60.00
58 Ken McBride	2.00	5.00
59 Mike McCormick	2.00	5.00
60 Stu Miller	2.00	5.00
61 Minnie Minoso	3.00	8.00
62 Wally Moon	2.50	6.00
63 Stan Musial	30.00	60.00
64 Danny O'Connell	2.00	5.00
65 Jim O'Toole	2.00	5.00
66 Camilo Pascual	2.00	5.00
67 Jim Perry	2.50	6.00
68 Jimmy Piersall	2.50	6.00
69 Vada Pinson	3.00	8.00
70 Juan Pizarro	2.00	5.00
71 Johnny Podres	2.50	6.00
72 Vic Power	2.00	5.00
73 Bob Purkey	2.00	5.00
74 Pedro Ramos	2.00	5.00
75 Brooks Robinson	15.00	40.00
76 Floyd Robinson	2.00	5.00
77 Frank Robinson	15.00	40.00
78 John Romano	2.00	5.00
79 Pete Runnels	2.00	5.00
80 Don Schwall	2.00	5.00
81 Bobby Shantz	2.00	5.00
82 Norm Siebern	2.00	5.00
83 Roy Sievers	2.00	5.00
84 Hal Smith	2.00	5.00
85 Warren Spahn	10.00	25.00
86 Dick Stuart	2.50	6.00
87 Tony Taylor	2.00	5.00
88 Lee Thomas	2.50	6.00
89 Gus Triandos	2.00	5.00
90 Leon Wagner	2.00	5.00
91 Jerry Walker	2.00	5.00
92 Bill White	3.00	8.00
93 Billy Williams	10.00	25.00
94 Gene Woodling	2.50	6.00
95 Early Wynn	10.00	25.00
96 Carl Yastrzemski	15.00	40.00

1962 Topps Stamps

The 201 baseball player stamps inserted into the Topps regular issue of 1962 are color photos set upon red or yellow backgrounds (100 players for each color). They came in two-stamp panels with a small additional strip which contained advertising for an album. Roy Sievers appears with Kansas City or Philadelphia; the set price includes both versions. Each stamp measures 1 3/8" by 1 7/8". Stamps are unnumbered but are presented here in alphabetical order by team, Baltimore Orioles AL (1-10), Boston Red Sox (11-20), Chicago White Sox (21-30), Cleveland Indians (31-40), Detroit Tigers (41-50), Kansas City A's (51-61), Los Angeles Angels (62-71), Minnesota Twins (72-81), New York Yankees (82-91), Washington Senators (92-101), Chicago Cubs NL (102-111), Cincinnati Reds (112-121), Houston Colt .45's (122-131), Los Angeles Dodgers (132-141), Milwaukee Braves (142-151), New York Mets (152-161), Philadelphia Phillies (162-171), Pittsburgh Pirates (172-181), St. Louis Cardinals (182-191) and San Francisco Giants (192-201). For some time there has been the rumored existence of a Roy Sievers stamp wearing an A's cap but it has yet to be confirmed.

COMPLETE SET (201)	200.00	400.00
1 Baltimore Emblem	.40	1.00
2 Jerry Adair	.40	1.00
3 Jackie Brandt	.40	1.00
4 Chuck Estrada	.40	1.00
5 Jim Gentile	.60	1.50
6 Ron Hansen	.40	1.00
7 Milt Pappas	.60	1.50
8 Brooks Robinson	3.00	8.00
9 Gus Triandos	.60	1.50
10 Hoyt Wilhelm	1.00	2.50
11 Boston Emblem	.40	1.00
12 Mike Fornieles	.40	1.00
13 Gary Geiger	.40	1.00
14 Frank Malzone	.60	1.50
15 Bill Monbouquette	.40	1.00
16 Russ Nixon	.40	1.00
17 Pete Runnels	.60	1.50
18 Chuck Schilling	.40	1.00
19 Don Schwall	.40	1.00
20 Carl Yastrzemski	5.00	12.00
21 Chicago Emblem	.40	1.00
22 Luis Aparicio	1.00	2.50
23 Camilo Carreon	.40	1.00
24 Nellie Fox	1.50	4.00
25 Ray Herbert	.40	1.00
26 Jim Landis	.40	1.00
27 J.C. Martin	.40	1.00
28 Juan Pizzaro	.40	1.00
29 Floyd Robinson	.40	1.00
30 Early Wynn	1.00	2.50
31 Cleveland Emblem	.40	1.00
32 Ty Cline	.40	1.00
33 Dick Donovan	.40	1.00
34 Tito Francona	.40	1.00
35 Woody Held	.40	1.00
36 Barry Latman	.40	1.00
37 Jim Perry	.60	1.50
38 Bubba Phillips	.40	1.00
39 Vic Power	.40	1.00
40 Johnny Romano	.40	1.00
41 Detroit Emblem	.40	1.00
42 Steve Boros	.40	1.00
43 Bill Bruton	.40	1.00
44 Jim Bunning	1.00	2.50
45 Norm Cash	1.00	2.50
46 Rocky Colavito	1.00	2.50
47 Al Kaline	3.00	8.00
48 Frank Lary	.60	1.50
49 Don Mossi	.60	1.50
50 Jake Wood	.40	1.00
51 Kansas City Emblem	.40	1.00
52 Jim Archer	.40	1.00
53 Dick Howser	1.00	2.50
54 Jerry Lumpe	.40	1.00
55 Leo Posada	.40	1.00
56 Bob Shaw	.40	1.00
57 Norm Siebern	.40	1.00
59 Gene Stephens	.40	1.00
60 Haywood Sullivan	.40	1.00
61 Jerry Walker	.40	1.00
62 Los Angeles Emblem	.40	1.00
63 Steve Bilko	.40	1.00
64 Ted Bowsfield	.40	1.00
65 Ken Hunt	.40	1.00
66 Ken McBride	.40	1.00
67 Albie Pearson	.40	1.00
68 Bob Rodgers	.60	1.50
69 George Thomas	.40	1.00
70 Lee Thomas	.60	1.50
71 Leon Wagner	.40	1.00
72 Minnesota Emblem	.40	1.00
73 Bob Allison	.60	1.50
74 Earl Battey	.40	1.00
75 Lenny Green	.40	1.00
76 Harmon Killebrew	2.50	6.00
77 Jack Kralick	.40	1.00
78 Camilo Pascual	.60	1.50
79 Pedro Ramos	.40	1.00
80 Bill Tuttle	.40	1.00
81 Zoilo Versailles	.40	1.00
82 New York Emblem	.60	1.50
83 Yogi Berra	5.00	12.00
84 Clete Boyer	1.00	2.50
85 Whitey Ford	4.00	10.00
86 Elston Howard	1.50	4.00
87 Tony Kubek	1.00	2.50
88 Mickey Mantle	30.00	60.00
89 Roger Maris	8.00	20.00
90 Bobby Richardson	1.00	2.50
91 Bill Skowron	1.00	2.50
92 Washington Emblem	.40	1.00
93 Chuck Cottier	.40	1.00
94 Pete Daley	.40	1.00
95 Bennie Daniels	.40	1.00
96 Chuck Hinton	.40	1.00
97 Bob Johnson	.40	1.00
98 Joe McClain	.40	1.00
99 Danny O'Connell	.40	1.00
100 Jimmy Piersall	1.00	2.50
101 Gene Woodling	.60	1.50
102 Chicago Emblem	.40	1.00
103 George Altman	.40	1.00
104 Ernie Banks	3.00	8.00
105 Dick Bertell	.40	1.00
106 Don Cardwell	.40	1.00
107 Dick Ellsworth	.40	1.00
108 Glen Hobbie	.40	1.00
109 Ron Santo	1.00	2.50
110 Barney Schultz	.40	1.00
111 Billy Williams	1.00	2.50
112 Cincinnati Emblem	.40	1.00
113 Gordon Coleman	.40	1.00
114 Johnny Edwards	.40	1.00
115 Gene Freese	.40	1.00
116 Joey Jay	.40	1.00
117 Eddie Kasko	.40	1.00
118 Jim O'Toole	.40	1.00
119 Vada Pinson	1.00	2.50
120 Bob Purkey	.40	1.00
121 Frank Robinson	3.00	8.00
122 Houston Emblem	.40	1.00
123 Joe Amalfitano	.40	1.00
124 Bob Aspromonte	.40	1.00
125 Dick Farrell	.40	1.00
126 Al Heist	.40	1.00
127 Sam Jones	.40	1.00
128 Bobby Shantz	.60	1.50
129 Hal W. Smith	.40	1.00
130 Al Spangler	.40	1.00
131 Bob Tiefenauer	.40	1.00
132 Los Angeles Emblem	.40	1.00
133 Don Drysdale	2.50	6.00
134 Ron Fairly	.60	1.50
135 Frank Howard	1.00	2.50
136 Sandy Koufax	6.00	15.00
137 Wally Moon	.60	1.50
138 Johnny Podres	1.00	2.50
139 John Roseboro	.40	1.00
140 Duke Snider	4.00	10.00
141 Daryl Spencer	.40	1.00

Card	Low	High
142 Milwaukee Emblem	.40	1.00
143 Hank Aaron	6.00	15.00
144 Joe Adcock	.60	1.50
145 Frank Bolling	.40	1.00
146 Lou Burdette	1.00	2.50
147 Del Crandall	.40	1.00
148 Eddie Mathews	2.50	6.00
149 Roy McMillan	.40	1.00
150 Warren Spahn	3.00	8.00
151 Joe Torre	2.00	5.00
152 New York Emblem	.60	1.50
153 Gus Bell	.60	1.50
154 Roger Craig	1.00	2.50
155 Gil Hodges	2.50	6.00
156 Jay Hook	.60	1.50
157 Hobie Landrith	.60	1.50
158 Felix Mantilla	.60	1.50
159 Bob L. Miller	.60	1.50
160 Lee Walls	.60	1.50
161 Don Zimmer	1.00	2.50
162 Philadelphia Emblem	.40	1.00
163 Ruben Amaro	.40	1.00
164 Jack Baldschun	.40	1.00
165 Johnny Callison UER	.60	1.50
Name spelled Callizon		
166 Clay Dalrymple	.40	1.00
167 Don Demeter	.40	1.00
168 Tony Gonzalez	.40	1.00
169 Roy Sievers	1.00	2.50
Phils, see also 58		
170 Tony Taylor	.60	1.50
171 Art Mahaffey	.40	1.00
172 Pittsburgh Emblem	.40	1.00
173 Smoky Burgess	.60	1.50
174 Roberto Clemente	15.00	40.00
175 Roy Face	1.00	2.50
176 Bob Friend	.60	1.50
177 Dick Groat	1.00	2.50
178 Don Hoak	.40	1.00
179 Bill Mazeroski	1.50	4.00
180 Dick Stuart	.60	1.50
181 Bill Virdon	1.00	2.50
182 St. Louis Emblem	.40	1.00
183 Ken Boyer	1.00	2.50
184 Larry Jackson	.40	1.00
185 Julian Javier	.40	1.00
186 Tim McCarver	1.50	4.00
187 Lindy McDaniel	.40	1.00
188 Minnie Minoso	1.00	2.50
189 Stan Musial	6.00	15.00
190 Ray Sadecki	.40	1.00
191 Bill White	1.00	2.50
192 San Francisco Emblem	.40	1.00
193 Felipe Alou	1.00	2.50
194 Ed Bailey	.40	1.00
195 Orlando Cepeda	1.00	2.50
196 Jim Davenport	.40	1.00
197 Harvey Kuenn	1.00	2.50
198 Juan Marichal	1.50	4.00
199 Willie Mays	8.00	20.00
200 Mike McCormick	.60	1.50
201 Stu Miller	.40	1.00
NNO Stamp Album	8.00	20.00

1962 Topps Venezuelan

These 198 cards are parallel to the first 198 cards of the regular 1962 Topps set. They were issued for the Venezuelan market and are printed in Spanish. Also note this is not quite an exact parallel as cards numbered 197 and 198 were not printed but were replaced by Elio Chacon and Luis Aparicio as cards numbered 199 and 200. Both Chacon and Aparicio were natives of Venezuela.

Card	Low	High
COMPLETE SET (198)	3,000.00	6,000.00
1 Roger Maris	600.00	1,200.00
2 Jim Brosnan	6.00	15.00
3 Pete Runnels	6.00	15.00
4 John DeMerit	6.00	15.00
5 Sandy Koufax	300.00	600.00
6 Marv Breeding	6.00	15.00
7 Frank Thomas	6.00	15.00
8 Ray Herbert	6.00	15.00
9 Jim Davenport	6.00	15.00
10 Roberto Clemente	400.00	800.00
11 Tom Morgan	6.00	15.00
12 Harry Craft MG	6.00	15.00
13 Dick Howser	6.00	15.00
14 Bill White	8.00	20.00
15 Dick Donovan	6.00	15.00
16 Darrell Johnson	6.00	15.00
17 John Callison	6.00	15.00
18 M.Mantle	300.00	600.00
W.Mays		
19 Ray Washburn	6.00	15.00
20 Rocky Colavito	30.00	60.00
21 Jim Kaat	15.00	40.00
22 Checklist 1	12.50	30.00
23 Norm Larker	6.00	15.00
24 Tigers Team	10.00	25.00
25 Ernie Banks	75.00	150.00
26 Chris Cannizzaro	6.00	15.00
27 Chuck Cottier	6.00	15.00
28 Minnie Minoso	10.00	25.00
29 Casey Stengel MG	30.00	60.00
30 Eddie Mathews	40.00	80.00
31 Tom Tresh RC	20.00	50.00
32 John Roseboro	6.00	15.00
33 Don Larsen	8.00	20.00
34 Johnny Temple	6.00	15.00
35 Don Schwall	6.00	15.00
36 Don Leppert	6.00	15.00
37 Tribe Hill Trio	6.00	15.00
Barry Latman		
Dick Stigman		
Jim P		
38 Gene Stephens	6.00	15.00
39 Joe Koppe	6.00	15.00
40 Orlando Cepeda	20.00	50.00
41 Cliff Cook	6.00	15.00
42 Jim King	6.00	15.00
43 Los Angeles Dodgers	10.00	25.00
Team Card		
44 Don Taussig	6.00	15.00
45 Brooks Robinson	75.00	150.00
46 Jack Baldschun	6.00	15.00
47 Bob Will	6.00	15.00
48 Ralph Terry	6.00	15.00
49 Hal Jones	6.00	15.00
50 Stan Musial	150.00	300.00
51 Cash	8.00	20.00
Pier		
Kaline		
How LL		
52 Clemente	15.00	40.00
Boyer		
Moon LL		
53 Maris	150.00	300.00
Mantle		
Kill LL		
54 Cepeda	20.00	50.00
Mays		
F.Rob LL		
55 AL ERA Leaders	8.00	20.00
Dick Donovan		
Bill Stafford		
Don M		
56 Spahn	8.00	20.00
O'Toole		
Simm		
LL		
57 Ford	8.00	20.00
Lary		
Barb		
Bunn LL		
58 Spahn	8.00	20.00
Jay		
O'Toole LL		
59 Pasc	8.00	20.00
Ford		
Bunn		
Pizz LL		
60 Koufax	12.50	30.00
Drys		
O'Toole LL		
61 Cardinals Team	10.00	25.00
62 Steve Boros	6.00	15.00
63 Tony Cloninger RC	6.00	15.00
64 Russ Snyder	6.00	15.00
65 Bobby Richardson	12.50	30.00
66 Cuno Barragan	6.00	15.00
67 Harvey Haddix	6.00	15.00
68 Ken Hunt	6.00	15.00
69 Phil Ortega	6.00	15.00
70 Harmon Killebrew	40.00	80.00
71 Dick LeMay	6.00	15.00
72 Bob's Pupils	6.00	15.00
Steve Boros		
Bob Scheffing MG		
Jake		
73 Nellie Fox	12.50	30.00
74 Bob Lillis	6.00	15.00
75 Milt Pappas	8.00	20.00
76 Howie Bedell	6.00	15.00
77 Tony Taylor	6.00	15.00
78 Gene Green	6.00	15.00
79 Ed Hobaugh	6.00	15.00
80 Vada Pinson	8.00	20.00
81 Jim Pagliaroni	6.00	15.00
82 Deron Johnson	6.00	15.00
83 Larry Jackson	6.00	15.00
84 Lenny Green	6.00	15.00
85 Gil Hodges	20.00	50.00
86 Donn Clendenon RC	8.00	20.00
87 Mike Roarke	6.00	15.00
88 Ralph Houk MG/(Berra in background)	6.00	15.00
89 Barney Schultz	6.00	15.00
90 Jim Piersall	8.00	20.00
91 J.C. Martin	6.00	15.00
92 Sam Jones	6.00	15.00
93 John Blanchard	8.00	20.00
94 Jay Hook	6.00	15.00
95 Don Hoak	6.00	15.00
96 Eli Grba	6.00	15.00
97 Tito Francona	6.00	15.00
98 Checklist 2	12.50	30.00
99 Boog Powell RC	50.00	100.00
100 Warren Spahn	50.00	100.00
101 Carroll Hardy	6.00	15.00
102 Al Schroll	6.00	15.00
103 Don Blasingame	6.00	15.00
104 Ted Savage	6.00	15.00
105 Don Mossi	6.00	15.00
106 Carl Sawatski	6.00	15.00
107 Mike McCormick	6.00	15.00
108 Willie Davis	6.00	15.00
109 Bob Shaw	6.00	15.00
110 Bill Skowron	10.00	25.00
111 Dallas Green	6.00	15.00
112 Hank Foiles	6.00	15.00
113 Chicago White Sox	10.00	25.00
Team Card		
114 Howie Koplitz	6.00	15.00
115 Bob Skinner	6.00	15.00
116 Herb Score	8.00	20.00
117 Gary Geiger	6.00	15.00
118 Julian Javier	6.00	15.00
119 Danny Murphy	6.00	15.00
120 Bob Purkey	6.00	15.00
121 Billy Hitchcock MG	6.00	15.00
122 Norm Bass	6.00	15.00
123 Mike de la Hoz	6.00	15.00
124 Bill Pleis	6.00	15.00
125 Gene Woodling	6.00	15.00
126 Al Cicotte	6.00	15.00
127 Pride of A's	6.00	15.00
Norm Siebern		
Hank Bauer MG		
Jerry L		
128 Art Fowler	6.00	15.00
129 Lee Walls	6.00	15.00
130 Frank Bolling	6.00	15.00
131 Pete Richert	6.00	15.00
132 Angels Team	10.00	25.00
133 Felipe Alou	8.00	20.00
134 Billy Hoeft	6.00	15.00
135 Babe Ruth Special 1	30.00	60.00
Babe as a Boy		
136 Babe Ruth Special 2	30.00	60.00
Babe Joins Yanks		
137 Babe Ruth Special 3	30.00	60.00
With Miller Huggins		
138 Babe Ruth Special 4	30.00	60.00
Famous Slugger		
139 Babe Ruth Story: 5	40.00	80.00
140 Babe Ruth	30.00	60.00
Lou Gehrig		
141 Babe Ruth Special 7	30.00	60.00
Twilight Years		
142 Babe Ruth Special 8	30.00	60.00
Coaching Dodgers		
143 Babe Ruth Special 9	30.00	60.00
Greatest Sports Hero		
144 Babe Ruth Special 10	30.00	60.00
Farewell Speech		
145 Barry Latman	6.00	15.00
146 Don Demeter	6.00	15.00
147 Bill Kunkel	6.00	15.00
148 Wally Post	6.00	15.00
149 Bob Duliba	6.00	15.00
150 Al Kaline	75.00	150.00
151 Johnny Klippstein	6.00	15.00
152 Mickey Vernon MG	6.00	15.00
153 Pumpsie Green	6.00	15.00
154 Lee Thomas	6.00	15.00
155 Stu Miller	6.00	15.00
156 Merritt Ranew	6.00	15.00
157 Wes Covington	8.00	20.00
158 Braves Team	10.00	25.00
159 Hal Reniff RC	6.00	15.00
160 Dick Stuart	6.00	15.00
161 Frank Baumann	6.00	15.00
162 Sammy Drake	6.00	15.00
163 Billy Gardner	6.00	15.00
Cletis Boyer		
164 Hal Naragon	6.00	15.00
165 Jackie Brandt	6.00	15.00
166 Don Lee	6.00	15.00
167 Tim McCarver RC	50.00	100.00
168 Leo Posada	6.00	15.00
169 Bob Cerv	6.00	15.00
170 Ron Santo	20.00	50.00
171 Dave Sisler	6.00	15.00
172 Fred Hutchinson MG	6.00	15.00
173 Chico Fernandez	6.00	15.00
174 Carl Willey	6.00	15.00
175 Frank Howard	8.00	20.00
176 Eddie Yost	6.00	15.00
177 Bobby Shantz	6.00	15.00
178 Camilo Carreon	6.00	15.00
179 Tom Sturdivant	6.00	15.00
180 Bob Allison	6.00	15.00
181 Paul Brown	6.00	15.00
182 Bob Nieman	6.00	15.00
183 Roger Craig	10.00	25.00
184 Haywood Sullivan	6.00	15.00
185 Roland Sheldon	6.00	15.00
186 Mack Jones	6.00	15.00
187 Gene Conley	6.00	15.00
188 Chuck Hiller	6.00	15.00
189 Dick Hall	6.00	15.00
190 Wally Moon	6.00	15.00
191 Jim Brewer	6.00	15.00
192 Checklist 3	12.50	30.00
193 Eddie Kasko	6.00	15.00
194 Dean Chance RC	6.00	15.00
195 Joe Cunningham	8.00	20.00
196 Terry Fox	6.00	15.00
199 Elio Chacon	15.00	40.00
200 Luis Aparicio	40.00	80.00

1963 Topps

The cards in this 576-card set measure 2 1/2" by 3 1/2". The sharp color photographs of the 1963 set are a vivid contrast to the drab pictures of 1962. In addition to the "League Leaders" series (1-10) and World Series cards (142-148), the seventh and last series of cards (523-576) contains seven rookie cards (each depicting four players). Cards were issued, among other ways, in one-card penny packs and five-card nickel packs. There were some three-card advertising panels produced by Topps; the players included are from the first series; one panel shows Hoyt Wilhelm, Don Lock, and Bob Duliba on the front with a Stan Musial ad/endorsement on one of the backs. Key Rookie Cards in this set are Bill Freehan, Tony Oliva, Pete Rose, Willie Stargell and Rusty Staub.

Card	Low	High
COMPLETE SET (576)	3,000.00	6,000.00
COMMON CARD (1-196)	1.50	4.00
COMMON CARD (197-283)	2.00	5.00
COMMON CARD (284-370)	2.00	5.00
COMMON CARD (371-446)	2.00	5.00
COMMON CARD (447-522)	10.00	25.00
COMMON CARD (523-576)	6.00	15.00
WRAPPER (1-CENT)	15.00	40.00
WRAPPER (5-CENT)	12.50	30.00
1 F.Rob/Musial/Aaron LL	10.00	25.00
2 Runnels/Mantle/Rob LL	20.00	50.00
3 Mays/Aaron/Rob/Cep/Banks LL	20.00	50.00
4 Kill/Cash/Colav/Maris LL	10.00	25.00
5 Koufax/Gibson/Drysdale LL	10.00	25.00
6 Aguirre/Roberts/Ford LL	4.00	10.00
7 Drysdale/Sanf/Purk LL	4.00	10.00
8 Terry/Donovan/Bunning LL	3.00	8.00
9 Drysdale/Koufax/Gibson LL	12.50	30.00
10 Pascual/Bunning/Kaat LL	3.00	8.00
11 Lee Walls	1.50	4.00
12 Steve Barber	1.50	4.00
13 Philadelphia Phillies TC	3.00	8.00
14 Pedro Ramos	1.50	4.00
15 Ken Hubbs UER NPO	4.00	10.00
16 Al Smith	1.50	4.00
17 Ryne Duren	3.00	8.00
18 Burg/Stu/Clemente/Skin	20.00	50.00
19 Pete Burnside	1.50	4.00
20 Tony Kubek	6.00	15.00
21 Marty Keough	1.50	4.00
22 Curt Simmons	3.00	8.00
23 Ed Lopat MG	3.00	8.00
24 Bob Bruce	1.50	4.00
25 Al Kaline	20.00	50.00
26 Ray Moore	1.50	4.00
27 Choo Choo Coleman	3.00	8.00
28 Mike Fornieles	1.50	4.00
29A Rookie Stars 1962	4.00	10.00
29B Rookie Stars 1963	1.50	4.00
30 Harvey Kuenn	3.00	8.00
31 Cal Koonce RC	1.50	4.00
32 Tony Gonzalez	1.50	4.00
33 Bo Belinsky	3.00	8.00
34 Dick Schofield	1.50	4.00
35 John Buzhardt	1.50	4.00
36 Jerry Kindall	1.50	4.00
37 Jerry Lynch	1.50	4.00
38 Bud Daley	3.00	8.00
39 Los Angeles Angels TC	3.00	8.00
40 Vic Power	3.00	8.00
41 Charley Lau	3.00	8.00
42 Stan Williams	3.00	8.00
43 C.Stengel/G.Woodling	3.00	8.00
44 Terry Fox	1.50	4.00
45 Bob Aspromonte	1.50	4.00
46 Tommie Aaron RC	3.00	8.00
47 Don Lock RC	1.50	4.00
48 Birdie Tebbetts MG	3.00	8.00
49 Dal Maxvill RC	3.00	8.00
50 Billy Pierce	3.00	8.00
51 George Alusik	1.50	4.00
52 Chuck Schilling	1.50	4.00
53 Joe Moeller RC	3.00	8.00
54A Dave DeBusschere 62	6.00	15.00
54B Dave DeBusschere 63 RC	3.00	8.00
55 Bill Virdon	3.00	8.00
56 Dennis Bennett RC	1.50	4.00
57 Billy Moran	1.50	4.00
58 Bob Will	1.50	4.00
59 Craig Anderson	1.50	4.00
60 Elston Howard	3.00	8.00
61 Ernie Bowman	1.50	4.00
62 Bob Hendley	1.50	4.00
63 Cincinnati Reds TC	3.00	8.00
64 Dick McAuliffe	3.00	8.00
65 Jackie Brandt	1.50	4.00
66 Mike Joyce RC	1.50	4.00
67 Ed Charles	1.50	4.00
68 G.Hodges/D.Snider	10.00	25.00
69 Bud Zipfel RC	1.50	4.00
70 Jim O'Toole	3.00	8.00
71 Bobby Wine RC	3.00	8.00
72 Johnny Romano	1.50	4.00
73 Bobby Bragan MG RC	3.00	8.00
74 Denny Lemaster RC	1.50	4.00
75 Bob Allison	3.00	8.00
76 Earl Wilson	3.00	8.00
77 Al Spangler	1.50	4.00
78 Marv Throneberry	3.00	8.00
79 Checklist 1	5.00	12.00
80 Jim Gilliam	3.00	8.00
81 Jim Schaffer	1.50	4.00
82 Ed Rakow	1.50	4.00
83 Charley James	1.50	4.00
84 Ron Kline	1.50	4.00
85 Tom Haller	3.00	8.00
86 Charley Maxwell	3.00	8.00
87 Bob Veale	3.00	8.00
88 Ron Hansen	1.50	4.00
89 Dick Stigman	1.50	4.00
90 Gordy Coleman	3.00	8.00
91 Dallas Green	3.00	8.00
92 Hector Lopez	3.00	8.00
93 Galen Cisco	1.50	4.00
94 Bob Schmidt	1.50	4.00
95 Larry Jackson	1.50	4.00
96 Lou Clinton	1.50	4.00
97 Bob Duliba	1.50	4.00
98 George Thomas	1.50	4.00
99 Jim Umbricht	1.50	4.00
100 Joe Cunningham	1.50	4.00
101 Joe Gibbon	1.50	4.00
102A Checklist 2 Red	5.00	12.00
Yellow		
102B Checklist 2 White	5.00	12.00
Red		
103 Chuck Essegian	1.50	4.00
104 Lew Krausse RC	1.50	4.00
105 Ron Fairly	3.00	8.00
106 Bobby Bolin	1.50	4.00
107 Jim Hickman	3.00	8.00
108 Hoyt Wilhelm	4.00	10.00
109 Lee Maye	1.50	4.00
110 Rich Rollins	3.00	8.00

111 Al Jackson 1.50 4.00
112 Dick Brown 1.50 4.00
113 Don Landrum UER 1.50 4.00
114 Dan Osinski RC 1.50 4.00
115 Carl Yastrzemski 25.00 60.00
116 Jim Brosnan 3.00 8.00
117 Jacke Davis 1.50 4.00
118 Sherm Lollar 1.50 4.00
119 Bob Lillis 1.50 4.00
120 Roger Maris 40.00 100.00
121 Jim Hannan RC 1.50 4.00
122 Julio Gotay 1.50 4.00
123 Frank Howard 3.00 8.00
124 Dick Howser 3.00 8.00
125 Robin Roberts 8.00 20.00
126 Bob Uecker 25.00 60.00
127 Bill Tuttle 1.50 4.00
128 Matty Alou 3.00 8.00
129 Gary Bell 1.50 4.00
130 Dick Groat 3.00 8.00
131 Washington Senators TC 3.00 8.00
132 Jack Hamilton 1.50 4.00
133 Gene Freese 1.50 4.00
134 Bob Scheffing MG 1.50 4.00
135 Richie Ashburn 10.00 25.00
136 Ike Delock 1.50 4.00
137 Mack Jones 1.50 4.00
138 W.Mays/S.Musial 20.00 50.00
139 Earl Averill Jr. 1.50 4.00
140 Frank Lary 3.00 8.00
141 Manny Mota RC 3.00 8.00
142 Whitey Ford WS1 8.00 20.00
143 Jack Sanford WS2 3.00 8.00
144 Roger Maris WS3 10.00 25.00
145 Chuck Hiller WS4 3.00 8.00
146 Tom Tresh WS5 3.00 8.00
147 Billy Pierce WS6 3.00 8.00
148 Ralph Terry WS7 3.00 8.00
149 Marv Breeding 1.50 4.00
150 Johnny Podres 3.00 8.00
151 Pittsburgh Pirates TC 3.00 8.00
152 Ron Nischwitz 1.50 4.00
153 Hal Smith 1.50 4.00
154 Walter Alston MG 3.00 8.00
155 Bill Stafford 1.50 4.00
156 Roy McMillan 3.00 8.00
157 Diego Segui RC 3.00 8.00
158 Tommy Harper RC 3.00 8.00
159 Jim Pagliaroni 1.50 4.00
160 Juan Pizarro 1.50 4.00
161 Frank Torre 3.00 8.00
162 Minnesota Twins TC 3.00 8.00
163 Don Larsen 3.00 8.00
164 Bubba Morton 1.50 4.00
165 Jim Kaat 3.00 8.00
166 Johnny Keane MG 1.50 4.00
167 Jim Fregosi 3.00 8.00
168 Russ Nixon 1.50 4.00
169 Gaylord Perry 10.00 25.00
170 Joe Adcock 3.00 8.00
171 Steve Hamilton RC 1.50 4.00
172 Gene Oliver 1.50 4.00
173 Tresh/Mantle/Richardson 40.00 100.00
174 Larry Burright 1.50 4.00
175 Bob Buhl 3.00 8.00
176 Jim King 1.50 4.00
177 Bubba Phillips 1.50 4.00
178 Johnny Edwards 1.50 4.00
179 Ron Piche 1.50 4.00
180 Bill Skowron 3.00 8.00
181 Sammy Esposito 1.50 4.00
182 Albie Pearson 3.00 8.00
183 Joe Pepitone 3.00 8.00
184 Vern Law 3.00 8.00
185 Chuck Hiller 1.50 4.00
186 Jerry Zimmerman 1.50 4.00
187 Willie Kirkland 1.50 4.00
188 Eddie Bressoud 1.50 4.00
189 Dave Giusti 3.00 8.00
190 Minnie Minoso 3.00 8.00
191 Checklist 3 5.00 12.00
192 Clay Dalrymple 1.50 4.00
193 Andre Rodgers 1.50 4.00
194 Joe Nuxhall 3.00 8.00
195 Manny Jimenez 1.50 4.00
196 Doug Camilli 1.50 4.00
197 Roger Craig 3.00 8.00
198 Lenny Green 2.00 5.00
199 Joe Amalfitano 2.00 5.00
200 Mickey Mantle 300.00 600.00
201 Cecil Butler 2.00 5.00
202 Boston Red Sox TC 3.00 8.00
203 Chico Cardenas 3.00 8.00
204 Don Nottebart 2.00 5.00
205 Luis Aparicio 6.00 15.00
206 Ray Washburn 2.00 5.00
207 Ken Hunt 2.00 5.00
208 Rookie Stars 2.00 5.00
209 Hobie Landrith 2.00 5.00
210 Sandy Koufax 75.00 200.00
211 Fred Whitfield RC 2.00 5.00
212 Glen Hobbie 2.00 5.00
213 Billy Hitchcock MG 2.00 5.00
214 Orlando Pena 2.00 5.00
215 Bob Skinner 3.00 8.00
216 Gene Conley 3.00 8.00
217 Joe Christopher 2.00 5.00
218 Lary/Mossi/Bunning 3.00 8.00
219 Chuck Cottier 2.00 5.00
220 Camilo Pascual 3.00 8.00
221 Cookie Rojas RC 3.00 8.00
222 Chicago Cubs TC 3.00 8.00
223 Eddie Fisher 2.00 5.00
224 Mike Roarke 2.00 5.00
225 Joey Jay 2.00 5.00
226 Julian Javier 3.00 8.00
227 Jim Grant 3.00 8.00
228 Tony Oliva RC 30.00 80.00
229 Willie Davis 3.00 8.00
230 Pete Runnels 3.00 8.00
231 Eli Grba UER 2.00 5.00
232 Frank Malzone 3.00 8.00
233 Casey Stengel MG 8.00 20.00
234 Dave Nicholson 2.00 5.00
235 Billy O'Dell 2.00 5.00
236 Bill Bryan RC 2.00 5.00
237 Jim Coates 3.00 8.00
238 Lou Johnson 2.00 5.00
239 Harvey Haddix 3.00 8.00
240 Rocky Colavito 6.00 15.00
241 Billy Smith RC 2.00 5.00
242 E.Banks/H.Aaron 30.00 80.00
243 Don Leppert 2.00 5.00
244 John Tsitouris 2.00 5.00
245 Gil Hodges 8.00 20.00
246 Lee Stange 2.00 5.00
247 New York Yankees TC 25.00 60.00
248 Tito Francona 2.00 5.00
249 Leo Burke RC 2.00 5.00
250 Stan Musial 40.00 100.00
251 Jack Lamabe 2.00 5.00
252 Ron Santo 12.00 30.00
253 Rookie Stars 2.00 5.00
254 Mike Hershberger 2.00 5.00
255 Bob Shaw 2.00 5.00
256 Jerry Lumpe 2.00 5.00
257 Hank Aguirre 2.00 5.00
258 Alvin Dark MG 3.00 8.00
259 Johnny Logan 3.00 8.00
260 Jim Gentile 3.00 8.00
261 Bob Miller 2.00 5.00
262 Ellis Burton 2.00 5.00
263 Dave Stenhouse 2.00 5.00
264 Phil Linz 2.00 5.00
265 Vada Pinson 3.00 8.00
266 Bob Allen 2.00 5.00
267 Carl Sawatski 2.00 5.00
268 Don Demeter 2.00 5.00
269 Don Mincher 2.00 5.00
270 Felipe Alou 3.00 8.00
271 Dean Stone 2.00 5.00
272 Danny Murphy 2.00 5.00
273 Sammy Taylor 2.00 5.00
274 Checklist 4 5.00 12.00
275 Eddie Mathews 15.00 40.00
276 Barry Shetrone 2.00 5.00
277 Dick Farrell 2.00 5.00
278 Chico Fernandez 2.00 5.00
279 Wally Moon 3.00 8.00
280 Bob Buck Rodgers 2.00 5.00
281 Tom Sturdivant 2.00 5.00
282 Bobby Del Greco 2.00 5.00
283 Roy Sievers 3.00 8.00
284 Dave Sisler 2.00 5.00
285 Dick Stuart 3.00 8.00
286 Stu Miller 3.00 8.00
287 Dick Bertell 2.00 5.00
288 Chicago White Sox TC 4.00 10.00
289 Hal Brown 2.00 5.00
290 Bill White 3.00 8.00
291 Don Rudolph 2.00 5.00
292 Pumpsie Green 3.00 8.00
293 Bill Pleis 2.00 5.00
294 Bill Rigney MG 2.00 5.00
295 Ed Roebuck 2.00 5.00
296 Doc Edwards 2.00 5.00
297 Jim Golden 2.00 5.00
298 Don Dillard 2.00 5.00
299 Rookie Stars 3.00 8.00
300 Willie Mays 75.00 200.00
301 Bill Fischer 2.00 5.00
302 Whitey Herzog 3.00 8.00
303 Earl Francis 2.00 5.00
304 Harry Bright 2.00 5.00
305 Don Hoak 2.00 5.00
306 E.Battey/E.Howard 4.00 10.00
307 Chet Nichols 2.00 5.00
308 Camilo Carreon 2.00 5.00
309 Jim Brewer 2.00 5.00
310 Tommy Davis 3.00 8.00
311 Joe McClain 2.00 5.00
312 Houston Colts TC 10.00 25.00
313 Ernie Broglio 2.00 5.00
314 John Goryl 2.00 5.00
315 Ralph Terry 3.00 8.00
316 Norm Sherry 3.00 8.00
317 Sam McDowell 3.00 8.00
318 Gene Mauch MG 3.00 8.00
319 Joe Gaines 2.00 5.00
320 Warren Spahn 30.00 60.00
321 Gino Cimoli 2.00 5.00
322 Bob Turley 3.00 8.00
323 Bill Mazeroski 6.00 15.00
324 Vic Davalillo RC 3.00 8.00
325 Jack Sanford 2.00 5.00
326 Hank Foiles 2.00 5.00
327 Paul Foytack 2.00 5.00
328 Dick Williams 3.00 8.00
329 Lindy McDaniel 3.00 8.00
330 Chuck Hinton 2.00 5.00
331 Stafford/Pierce 3.00 8.00
332 Joel Horlen 3.00 8.00
333 Carl Warwick 2.00 5.00
334 Wynn Hawkins 2.00 5.00
335 Leon Wagner 2.00 5.00
336 Ed Bauta 2.00 5.00
337 Los Angeles Dodgers TC 10.00 25.00
338 Russ Kemmerer 2.00 5.00
339 Ted Bowsfield 2.00 5.00
340 Yogi Berra P CO 50.00 100.00
341 Jack Baldschun 2.00 5.00
342 Gene Woodling 3.00 8.00
343 Johnny Pesky MG 3.00 8.00
344 Don Schwall 2.00 5.00
345 Brooks Robinson 20.00 50.00
346 Billy Hoeft 2.00 5.00
347 Joe Torre 8.00 20.00
348 Vic Wertz 3.00 8.00
349 Zoilo Versalles 3.00 8.00
350 Bob Purkey 2.00 5.00
351 Al Luplow 2.00 5.00
352 Ken Johnson 2.00 5.00
353 Billy Williams 20.00 50.00
354 Dom Zanni 2.00 5.00
355 Dean Chance 3.00 8.00
356 John Schaive 2.00 5.00
357 George Altman 2.00 5.00
358 Milt Pappas 3.00 8.00
359 Haywood Sullivan 3.00 8.00
360 Don Drysdale 20.00 50.00
361 Clete Boyer 4.00 10.00
362 Checklist 5 5.00 12.00
363 Dick Radatz 3.00 8.00
364 Howie Goss 2.00 5.00
365 Jim Bunning 8.00 20.00
366 Tony Taylor 3.00 8.00
367 Tony Cloninger 2.00 5.00
368 Ed Bailey 2.00 5.00
369 Jim Lemon 2.00 5.00
370 Dick Donovan 2.00 5.00
371 Rod Kanehl 3.00 8.00
372 Don Lee 2.00 5.00
373 Jim Campbell RC 2.00 5.00
374 Claude Osteen 3.00 8.00
375 Ken Boyer 6.00 15.00
376 John Wyatt RC 2.00 5.00
377 Baltimore Orioles TC 4.00 10.00
378 Bill Henry 2.00 5.00
379 Bob Anderson 2.00 5.00
380 Ernie Banks UER 50.00 100.00
381 Frank Baumann 2.00 5.00
382 Ralph Houk MG 4.00 10.00
383 Pete Richert 2.00 5.00
384 Bob Tillman 2.00 5.00
385 Art Mahaffey 2.00 5.00
386 Rookie Stars 2.00 5.00
387 Al McBean 2.00 5.00
388 Jim Davenport 3.00 8.00
389 Frank Sullivan 2.00 5.00
390 Hank Aaron 75.00 200.00
391 Bill Dailey RC 2.00 5.00
392 Romano/Francona 2.00 5.00
393 Ken MacKenzie 3.00 8.00
394 Tim McCarver 6.00 15.00
395 Don McMahon 2.00 5.00
396 Joe Koppe 2.00 5.00
397 Kansas City Athletics TC 4.00 10.00
398 Boog Powell 15.00 40.00
399 Dick Ellsworth 2.00 5.00
400 Frank Robinson 30.00 80.00
401 Jim Bouton 10.00 25.00
402 Mickey Vernon MG 3.00 8.00
403 Ron Perranoski 3.00 8.00
404 Bob Oldis 2.00 5.00
405 Floyd Robinson 2.00 5.00
406 Howie Koplitz 2.00 5.00
407 Rookie Stars 3.00 8.00
408 Billy Gardner 2.00 5.00
409 Roy Face 3.00 8.00
410 Earl Battey 2.00 5.00
411 Jim Constable 2.00 5.00
412 Podres/Drysdale/Koufax 30.00 80.00
413 Jerry Walker 2.00 5.00
414 Ty Cline 2.00 5.00
415 Bob Gibson 30.00 80.00
416 Alex Grammas 2.00 5.00
417 San Francisco Giants TC 4.00 10.00
418 John Orsino 2.00 5.00
419 Tracy Stallard 2.00 5.00
420 Bobby Richardson 6.00 15.00
421 Tom Morgan 2.00 5.00
422 Fred Hutchinson MG 3.00 8.00
423 Ed Hobaugh 2.00 5.00
424 Charlie Smith 2.00 5.00
425 Smoky Burgess 3.00 8.00
426 Barry Latman 2.00 5.00
427 Bernie Allen 2.00 5.00
428 Carl Boles RC 2.00 5.00
429 Lou Burdette 3.00 8.00
430 Norm Siebern 2.00 5.00
431A Checklist 6 White Red 5.00 12.00
431B Checklist 6 Black Orange 12.50 30.00
432 Roman Mejias 2.00 5.00
433 Denis Menke 2.00 5.00
434 John Callison 3.00 8.00
435 Woody Held 2.00 5.00
436 Tim Harkness 3.00 8.00
437 Bill Bruton 2.00 5.00
438 Wes Stock 2.00 5.00
439 Don Zimmer 3.00 8.00
440 Juan Marichal 15.00 40.00
441 Lee Thomas 3.00 8.00
442 J.C. Hartman RC 2.00 5.00
443 Jimmy Piersall 3.00 8.00
444 Jim Maloney 3.00 8.00
445 Norm Cash 4.00 10.00
446 Whitey Ford 20.00 50.00
447 Felix Mantilla 10.00 25.00
448 Jack Kralick 10.00 25.00
449 Jose Tartabull 10.00 25.00
450 Bob Friend 12.50 30.00
451 Cleveland Indians TC 15.00 40.00
452 Barney Schultz 10.00 25.00
453 Jake Wood 10.00 25.00
454A Art Fowler White 10.00 25.00
454B Art Fowler Orange 12.50 30.00
455 Ruben Amaro 10.00 25.00
456 Jim Coker 10.00 25.00
457 Tex Clevenger 10.00 25.00
458 Al Lopez MG 12.50 30.00
459 Dick LeMay 10.00 25.00
460 Del Crandall 12.50 30.00
461 Norm Bass 10.00 25.00
462 Wally Post 10.00 25.00
463 Joe Schaffernoth 10.00 25.00
464 Ken Aspromonte 10.00 25.00
465 Chuck Estrada 10.00 25.00
466 Bill Freehan SP RC 20.00 50.00
467 Phil Ortega 10.00 25.00
468 Carroll Hardy 12.50 30.00
469 Jay Hook 12.50 30.00
470 Tom Tresh SP 30.00 60.00
471 Ken Retzer 10.00 25.00
472 Lou Brock 40.00 100.00
473 New York Mets TC 50.00 100.00
474 Jack Fisher 10.00 25.00
475 Gus Triandos 12.50 30.00
476 Frank Funk 10.00 25.00
477 Donn Clendenon 12.50 30.00
478 Paul Brown 10.00 25.00
479 Ed Brinkman RC 10.00 25.00
480 Bill Monbouquette 10.00 25.00
481 Bob Taylor 10.00 25.00
482 Felix Torres 10.00 25.00
483 Jim Owens UER 10.00 25.00
484 Dale Long SP 12.50 30.00
485 Jim Landis 10.00 25.00
486 Ray Sadecki 10.00 25.00
487 John Roseboro 12.50 30.00
488 Jerry Adair 10.00 25.00
489 Paul Toth RC 10.00 25.00
490 Willie McCovey 30.00 80.00
491 Harry Craft MG 10.00 25.00
492 Dave Wickersham 10.00 25.00
493 Walt Bond 10.00 25.00
494 Phil Regan 10.00 25.00
495 Frank Thomas SP 12.50 30.00
496 Rookie Stars 12.50 30.00
497 Bennie Daniels 10.00 25.00
498 Eddie Kasko 10.00 25.00
499 J.C. Martin 10.00 25.00
500 Harmon Killebrew SP 40.00 100.00
501 Joe Azcue 10.00 25.00
502 Daryl Spencer 10.00 25.00
503 Milwaukee Braves TC 15.00 40.00
504 Bob Johnson 10.00 25.00
505 Curt Flood 15.00 40.00
506 Gene Green 10.00 25.00
507 Roland Sheldon 12.50 30.00
508 Ted Savage 10.00 25.00
509A Checklist 7 Centered 12.50 30.00
509B Checklist 7 Right 12.50 30.00
510 Ken McBride 10.00 25.00
511 Charlie Neal 12.50 30.00
512 Cal McLish 10.00 25.00
513 Gary Geiger 10.00 25.00
514 Larry Osborne 10.00 25.00
515 Don Elston 10.00 25.00
516 Purnell Goldy RC 10.00 25.00
517 Hal Woodeshick 10.00 25.00
518 Don Blasingame 10.00 25.00
519 Claude Raymond RC 10.00 25.00
520 Orlando Cepeda 15.00 40.00
521 Dan Pfister 10.00 25.00
522 Rookie Stars 12.50 30.00
523 Bill Kunkel 6.00 15.00
524 St. Louis Cardinals TC 12.50 30.00
525 Nellie Fox 15.00 40.00
526 Dick Hall 6.00 15.00
527 Ed Sadowski 6.00 15.00
528 Carl Willey 6.00 15.00
529 Wes Covington 6.00 15.00
530 Don Mossi 8.00 20.00
531 Sam Mele MG 6.00 15.00
532 Steve Boros 6.00 15.00
533 Bobby Shantz 8.00 20.00
534 Ken Walters 6.00 15.00
535 Jim Perry 8.00 20.00
536 Norm Larker 6.00 15.00
537 Pete Rose RC 800.00 1,500.00
538 George Brunet 6.00 15.00
539 Wayne Causey 6.00 15.00
540 Roberto Clemente 100.00 250.00
541 Ron Moeller 6.00 15.00
542 Lou Klimchock 6.00 15.00
543 Russ Snyder 6.00 15.00
544 Rusty Staub RC 20.00 50.00
545 Jose Pagan 6.00 15.00
546 Hal Reniff 8.00 20.00
547 Gus Bell 6.00 15.00
548 Tom Satriano RC 6.00 15.00
549 Rookie Stars 6.00 15.00
550 Duke Snider 20.00 50.00
551 Billy Klaus 6.00 15.00
552 Detroit Tigers TC 10.00 25.00
553 Willie Stargell RC 125.00 300.00
554 Hank Fischer RC 6.00 15.00
555 John Blanchard 8.00 20.00
556 Al Worthington 6.00 15.00
557 Cuno Barragan 6.00 15.00
558 Ron Hunt RC 8.00 20.00
559 Danny Murtaugh MG 6.00 15.00
560 Ray Herbert 6.00 15.00
561 Mike De La Hoz 6.00 15.00
562 Dave McNally RC 12.50 30.00
563 Mike McCormick 6.00 15.00
564 George Banks RC 6.00 15.00
565 Larry Sherry 6.00 15.00
566 Cliff Cook 6.00 15.00
567 Jim Duffalo 6.00 15.00
568 Bob Sadowski 6.00 15.00
569 Luis Arroyo 8.00 20.00

570 Frank Bolling 6.00 15.00
571 Johnny Klippstein 6.00 15.00
572 Jack Spring 6.00 15.00
573 Coot Veal 6.00 15.00
574 Hal Kolstad 6.00 15.00
575 Don Cardwell 6.00 15.00
576 Johnny Temple 12.50 30.00

1963 Topps Peel-Offs

Stick-on inserts were found in several series of the 1963 Topps cards. Each sticker measures 1 1/4" by 2 3/4". They are found either with blank backs or with instructions on the reverse. Stick-ons with the instruction backs are a little tougher to find. The player photo is in color inside an oval with name, team and postion below. Since these inserts were unnumbered, they are ordered below alphabetically.

COMPLETE SET (46) 300.00 600.00
1 Hank Aaron 15.00 40.00
2 Luis Aparicio 5.00 12.00
3 Richie Ashburn 6.00 15.00
4 Bob Aspromonte 1.50 4.00
5 Ernie Banks 8.00 20.00
6 Ken Boyer 2.50 6.00
7 Jim Bunning 60.00 120.00
8 Johnny Callison 1.50 4.00
9 Roberto Clemente 30.00 60.00
10 Orlando Cepeda 5.00 12.00
11 Rocky Colavito 4.00 10.00
12 Tommy Davis 2.00 5.00
13 Dick Donovan 1.50 4.00
14 Don Drysdale 6.00 15.00
15 Dick Farrell 1.50 4.00
16 Jim Gentile 2.00 5.00
17 Ray Herbert 1.50 4.00
18 Chuck Hinton 1.50 4.00
19 Ken Hubbs 2.50 6.00
20 Al Jackson 1.50 4.00
21 Al Kaline 8.00 20.00
22 Harmon Killebrew 5.00 12.00
23 Sandy Koufax 12.50 30.00
24 Jerry Lumpe 1.50 4.00
25 Art Mahaffey 1.50 4.00
26 Mickey Mantle 50.00 100.00
27 Willie Mays 20.00 50.00
28 Bill Mazeroski 4.00 10.00
29 Bill Monbouquette 1.50 4.00
30 Stan Musial 12.50 30.00
31 Camilo Pascual 1.50 4.00
32 Bob Purkey 1.50 4.00
33 Bobby Richardson 2.50 6.00
34 Brooks Robinson 8.00 20.00
35 Floyd Robinson 1.50 4.00
36 Frank Robinson 8.00 20.00
37 Bob Rodgers 1.50 4.00
38 Johnny Romano 1.50 4.00
39 Jack Sanford 1.50 4.00
40 Norm Siebern 1.50 4.00
41 Warren Spahn 5.00 12.00
42 Dave Stenhouse 1.50 4.00
43 Ralph Terry 1.50 4.00
44 Lee Thomas 2.00 5.00
45 Bill White 2.00 5.00
46 Carl Yastrzemski 10.00 25.00

1964 Topps

The cards in this 587-card set measure 2 1/2" by 3 1/2". Players in the 1964 Topps baseball series were easy to sort by team due to the giant block lettering found at the top of each card. The name and position of the player are found underneath the picture, and the card is numbered in a ball design on the orange-colored back. The usual last series scarcity holds for this set (523 to 587). Subsets within this set include League Leaders (1-12) and World Series cards (136-140). Among other vehicles, cards were issued in one-card penny packs as well as five-card nickel packs. There were some three-card advertising panels produced by Topps; the players included are from the first series; Panels with Mickey Mantle card backs include Walt Alston/Bill Henry/Vada Pinson; Carl Willey/White Sox Rookies/Bob Friend; and Jimmie Hall/Ernie Broglio/A.L. ERA Leaders on the front with a Mickey Mantle card back on one of the backs. The key Rookie Cards in this set are Richie Allen, Tony Conigliaro, Tommy John, Tony LaRussa, Phil Niekro and Lou Piniella.

COMPLETE SET (587) 2,750.00 3,500.00
COMMON CARD (1-196) 1.25 3.00
COMMON CARD (197-370) 1.50 4.00
COMMON CARD (371-522) 3.00 8.00
COMMON CARD (523-587) 6.00 15.00
WRAPPER (1-CENT) 50.00 100.00
WRAP.(1-CENT, REPEAT) 60.00 120.00
WRAPPER (5-CENT) 12.50 30.00
WRAPPER (5-CENT, COIN) 15.00 40.00
1 Koufax/Ells/Friend LL 12.50 30.00
2 Peters/Pizarro/Pascual LL 3.00 8.00
3 Koufax/Marichal/Spahn LL 8.00 20.00
4 Ford/Pascual/Bouton LL 3.00 8.00
5 Koufax/Malon/Drysdale LL 6.00 15.00
6 Pascual/Bunning/Stigman LL 3.00 8.00
7 Clemente/Groat/Aaron LL 12.00 30.00
8 Yaz/Kaline/Rollins LL 10.00 25.00
9 Aaron/McCov/Mays/Cep LL 20.00 50.00
10 Killebrew/Stuart/Allison LL 3.00 8.00
11 Aaron/Boyer/White LL 10.00 25.00
12 Stuart/Kaline/Killebrew LL 3.00 8.00
13 Hoyt Wilhelm 8.00 20.00
14 D.Nen RC/N.Willhite RC 1.25 3.00
15 Zoilo Versalles 2.50 6.00
16 John Boozer 1.25 3.00
17 Willie Kirkland 1.25 3.00
18 Billy O'Dell 1.25 3.00
19 Don Wert 1.25 3.00
20 Bob Friend 2.50 6.00
21 Yogi Berra MG 25.00 60.00
22 Jerry Adair 1.25 3.00
23 Chris Zachary RC 1.25 3.00
24 Carl Sawatski 1.25 3.00
25 Bill Monbouquette 1.25 3.00
26 Gino Cimoli 1.25 3.00
27 New York Mets TC 3.00 8.00
28 Claude Osteen 2.50 6.00
29 Lou Brock 25.00 60.00
30 Ron Perranoski 2.50 6.00
31 Dave Nicholson 1.25 3.00
32 Dean Chance 2.50 6.00
33 S.Ellis/M.Queen 2.50 6.00
34 Jim Perry 2.50 6.00
35 Eddie Mathews 20.00 30.00
36 Hal Reniff 1.25 3.00
37 Smoky Burgess 2.50 6.00
38 Jim Wynn RC 3.00 8.00
39 Hank Aguirre 1.25 3.00
40 Dick Groat 2.50 6.00
41 W.McCovey/L.Wagner 3.00 8.00
42 Moe Drabowsky 2.50 6.00
43 Roy Sievers 2.50 6.00
44 Duke Carmel 1.25 3.00
45 Milt Pappas 2.50 6.00
46 Ed Brinkman 1.25 3.00
47 J.Alou RC/R.Herbel 2.50 6.00
48 Bob Perry RC 1.25 3.00
49 Bill Henry 1.25 3.00
50 Mickey Mantle 200.00 500.00
51 Pete Richert 1.25 3.00
52 Chuck Hinton 1.25 3.00
53 Denis Menke 1.25 3.00
54 Sam Mele MG 1.25 3.00
55 Ernie Banks 30.00 80.00
56 Hal Brown 1.25 3.00
57 Tim Harkness 2.50 6.00
58 Don Demeter 2.50 6.00
59 Ernie Broglio 1.25 3.00
60 Frank Malzone 2.50 6.00
61 B.Rodgers/E.Sadowski 2.50 6.00
62 Ted Savage 1.25 3.00
63 John Orsino 1.25 3.00
64 Ted Abernathy 1.25 3.00
65 Felipe Alou 2.50 6.00
66 Eddie Fisher 1.25 3.00
67 Detroit Tigers TC 2.50 6.00
68 Willie Davis 2.50 6.00
69 Clete Boyer 2.50 6.00
70 Joe Torre 3.00 8.00
71 Jack Spring 1.25 3.00
72 Chico Cardenas 2.50 6.00
73 Jimmie Hall RC 3.00 8.00
74 B.Priddy RC/T.Butters 1.25 3.00
75 Wayne Causey 1.25 3.00
76 Checklist 1 4.00 10.00
77 Jerry Walker 1.25 3.00
78 Merritt Ranew 1.25 3.00
79 Bob Heffner RC 1.25 3.00
80 Vada Pinson 3.00 8.00
81 N.Fox/H.Killebrew 5.00 12.00
82 Jim Davenport 2.50 6.00
83 Gus Triandos 2.50 6.00
84 Carl Willey 1.25 3.00
85 Pete Ward 1.25 3.00
86 Al Downing 2.50 6.00
87 St. Louis Cardinals TC 2.50 6.00
88 John Roseboro 2.50 6.00
89 Boog Powell 2.50 6.00
90 Earl Battey 1.25 3.00
91 Bob Bailey 2.50 6.00
92 Steve Ridzik 1.25 3.00
93 Gary Geiger 1.25 3.00
94 J.Britton RC/L.Maxie RC 1.25 3.00
95 George Altman 1.25 3.00
96 Bob Buhl 2.50 6.00
97 Jim Fregosi 2.50 6.00
98 Bill Bruton 1.25 3.00
99 Al Stanek RC 1.25 3.00
100 Elston Howard 2.50 6.00
101 Walt Alston MG 3.00 8.00
102 Checklist 2 4.00 10.00
103 Curt Flood 2.50 6.00
104 Art Mahaffey 2.50 6.00
105 Woody Held 1.25 3.00
106 Joe Nuxhall 2.50 6.00
107 B.Howard RC/F.Kruetzer RC 1.25 3.00
108 John Wyatt 1.25 3.00
109 Rusty Staub 2.50 6.00
110 Albie Pearson 2.50 6.00
111 Don Elston 1.25 3.00
112 Bob Tillman 1.25 3.00
113 Grover Powell RC 2.50 6.00
114 Don Lock 1.25 3.00
115 Frank Bolling 1.25 3.00
116 J.Ward RC/T.Oliva 10.00 25.00
117 Earl Francis 1.25 3.00
118 John Blanchard 2.50 6.00
119 Gary Kolb RC 1.25 3.00
120 Don Drysdale 10.00 25.00
121 Pete Runnels 2.50 6.00
122 Don McMahon 1.25 3.00
123 Jose Pagan 1.25 3.00
124 Orlando Pena 1.25 3.00
125 Pete Rose UER 125.00 300.00
126 Russ Snyder 1.25 3.00
127 A.Gatewood RC/D.Simpson 1.25 3.00
128 Mickey Lolich RC 10.00 25.00
129 Amado Samuel 1.25 3.00
130 Gary Peters 2.50 6.00
131 Steve Boros 1.25 3.00
132 Milwaukee Braves TC 2.50 6.00
133 Jim Grant 2.50 6.00
134 Don Zimmer 2.50 6.00
135 Johnny Callison 2.50 6.00
136 Sandy Koufax WS1 8.00 20.00
137 Willie Davis WS2 3.00 8.00
138 Ron Fairly WS3 3.00 8.00
139 Frank Howard WS4 3.00 8.00
140 Dodgers Celebrate WS 3.00 8.00
141 Danny Murtaugh MG 2.50 6.00
142 John Bateman 1.25 3.00
143 Bubba Phillips 1.25 3.00
144 Al Worthington 1.25 3.00
145 Norm Siebern 1.25 3.00
146 T.John RC/B.Chance RC 10.00 25.00
147 Ray Sadecki 1.25 3.00
148 J.C. Martin 1.25 3.00
149 Paul Foytack 1.25 3.00
150 Willie Mays 60.00 150.00
151 Kansas City Athletics TC 2.50 6.00
152 Denny Lemaster 1.25 3.00
153 Dick Williams 2.50 6.00
154 Dick Tracewski RC 2.50 6.00
155 Duke Snider 12.50 30.00
156 Bill Dailey 1.25 3.00
157 Gene Mauch MG 2.50 6.00
158 Ken Johnson 1.25 3.00
159 Charlie Dees RC 1.25 3.00
160 Ken Boyer 2.50 6.00
161 Dave McNally 2.50 6.00
162 D.Sisler/V.Pinson 2.50 6.00
163 Donn Clendenon 2.50 6.00
164 Bud Daley 1.25 3.00
165 Jerry Lumpe 1.25 3.00
166 Marty Keough 1.25 3.00
167 M.Brumley RC/L.Piniella RC 12.50 30.00
168 Al Weis 1.25 3.00
169 Del Crandall 2.50 6.00
170 Dick Radatz 2.50 6.00
171 Ty Cline 1.25 3.00
172 Cleveland Indians TC 2.50 6.00
173 Ryne Duren 2.50 6.00
174 Doc Edwards 1.25 3.00
175 Billy Williams 10.00 25.00
176 Tracy Stallard 1.25 3.00
177 Harmon Killebrew 12.00 30.00
178 Hank Bauer MG 2.50 6.00
179 Carl Warwick 1.25 3.00
180 Tommy Davis 2.50 6.00
181 Dave Wickersham 1.25 3.00
182 C.Yastrzemski/C.Schilling 6.00 15.00
183 Ron Taylor 1.25 3.00
184 Al Luplow 1.25 3.00
185 Jim O'Toole 2.50 6.00
186 Roman Mejias 1.25 3.00
187 Ed Roebuck 1.25 3.00
188 Checklist 3 4.00 10.00
189 Bob Hendley 1.25 3.00
190 Bobby Richardson 3.00 8.00
191 Clay Dalrymple 2.50 6.00
192 J.Boccabella RC/B.Cowan RC 1.25 3.00
193 Jerry Lynch 1.25 3.00
194 John Goryl 1.25 3.00
195 Floyd Robinson 1.25 3.00
196 Jim Gentile 1.25 3.00
197 Frank Lary 2.50 6.00
198 Len Gabrielson 1.50 4.00
199 Joe Azcue 1.50 4.00
200 Sandy Koufax 40.00 100.00
201 S.Bowens RC/W.Bunker RC 2.50 6.00
202 Galen Cisco 2.50 6.00
203 John Kennedy RC 2.50 6.00
204 Matty Alou 2.50 6.00
205 Nellie Fox 5.00 12.00
206 Steve Hamilton 2.50 6.00
207 Fred Hutchinson MG 2.50 6.00
208 Wes Covington 2.50 6.00
209 Bob Allen 1.50 4.00
210 Carl Yastrzemski 20.00 50.00
211 Jim Coker 1.50 4.00
212 Pete Lovrich 1.50 4.00
213 Los Angeles Angels TC 2.50 6.00
214 Ken McMullen 2.50 6.00
215 Ray Herbert 1.50 4.00
216 Mike de la Hoz 1.50 4.00
217 Jim King 1.50 4.00
218 Hank Fischer 1.50 4.00
219 A.Downing/J.Bouton 2.50 6.00
220 Dick Ellsworth 2.50 6.00
221 Bob Saverine 1.50 4.00
222 Billy Pierce 2.50 6.00
223 George Banks 1.50 4.00
224 Tommie Sisk 1.50 4.00
225 Roger Maris 30.00 80.00
226 J.Grote RC/L.Yellen RC 2.50 6.00
227 Barry Latman 1.50 4.00
228 Felix Mantilla 1.50 4.00
229 Charley Lau 2.50 6.00
230 Brooks Robinson 15.00 40.00
231 Dick Calmus RC 1.50 4.00
232 Al Lopez MG 3.00 8.00
233 Hal Smith 1.50 4.00
234 Gary Bell 1.50 4.00
235 Ron Hunt 1.50 4.00
236 Bill Faul 1.50 4.00
237 Chicago Cubs TC 2.50 6.00
238 Roy McMillan 2.50 6.00
239 Herm Starrette RC 1.50 4.00
240 Bill White 2.50 6.00
241 Jim Owens 1.50 4.00
242 Harvey Kuenn 2.50 6.00
243 R.Allen RC/J.Hernstein 12.50 30.00
244 Tony LaRussa RC 12.50 30.00
245 Dick Stigman 1.50 4.00
246 Manny Mota 2.50 6.00
247 Dave DeBusschere 2.50 6.00
248 Johnny Pesky MG 2.50 6.00
249 Doug Camilli 1.50 4.00
250 Al Kaline 15.00 40.00
251 Choo Choo Coleman 2.50 6.00
252 Ken Aspromonte 1.50 4.00
253 Wally Post 2.50 6.00
254 Don Hoak 2.50 6.00
255 Lee Thomas 2.50 6.00
256 Johnny Weekly 1.50 4.00
257 San Francisco Giants TC 2.50 6.00
258 Garry Roggenburk 1.50 4.00
259 Harry Bright 1.50 4.00
260 Frank Robinson 15.00 40.00
261 Jim Hannan 1.50 4.00
262 M.Shannon RC/H.Fanok 3.00 8.00
263 Chuck Estrada 1.50 4.00
264 Jim Landis 1.50 4.00
265 Jim Bunning 5.00 12.00
266 Gene Freese 1.50 4.00
267 Wilbur Wood RC 2.50 6.00
268 D.Murtaugh/B.Virdon 2.50 6.00
269 Ellis Burton 1.50 4.00
270 Rich Rollins 2.50 6.00
271 Bob Sadowski RC 1.50 4.00
272 Jake Wood 1.50 4.00
273 Mel Nelson 1.50 4.00
274 Checklist 4 4.00 10.00
275 John Tsitouris 1.50 4.00
276 Jose Tartabull 2.50 6.00
277 Ken Retzer 1.50 4.00
278 Bobby Shantz 2.50 6.00
279 Joe Koppe 1.50 4.00
280 Juan Marichal 12.00 30.00
281 J.,Gibbs/T.Metclaf RC 2.50 6.00
282 Bob Bruce 1.50 4.00
283 Tom McCraw RC 1.50 4.00
284 Dick Schofield 1.50 4.00
285 Robin Roberts 6.00 15.00
286 Don Landrum 1.50 4.00
287 T.Conig.RC/B.Spans.RC 20.00 50.00
288 Al Moran 1.50 4.00
289 Frank Funk 1.50 4.00
290 Bob Allison 2.50 6.00
291 Phil Ortega 1.50 4.00
292 Mike Roarke 1.50 4.00
293 Philadelphia Phillies TC 2.50 6.00
294 Ken L. Hunt 1.50 4.00
295 Roger Craig 2.50 6.00
296 Ed Kirkpatrick 1.50 4.00
297 Ken MacKenzie 1.50 4.00
298 Harry Craft MG 1.50 4.00
299 Bill Stafford 1.50 4.00
300 Hank Aaron 60.00 150.00
301 Larry Brown RC 1.50 4.00
302 Dan Pfister 1.50 4.00
303 Jim Campbell 1.50 4.00
304 Bob Johnson 1.50 4.00
305 Jack Lamabe 1.50 4.00
306 Willie Mays/O.Cepeda 15.00 40.00
307 Joe Gibbon 1.50 4.00
308 Gene Stephens 1.50 4.00
309 Paul Toth 1.50 4.00
310 Jim Gilliam 2.50 6.00
311 Tom W. Brown RC 2.50 6.00
312 F.Fisher RC/F.Gladding RC 1.50 4.00
313 Chuck Hiller 1.50 4.00
314 Jerry Buchek 1.50 4.00
315 Bo Belinsky 2.50 6.00
316 Gene Oliver 1.50 4.00
317 Al Smith 1.50 4.00
318 Minnesota Twins TC 2.50 6.00
319 Paul Brown 1.50 4.00
320 Rocky Colavito 5.00 12.00
321 Bob Lillis 1.50 4.00
322 George Brunet 1.50 4.00
323 John Buzhardt 1.50 4.00
324 Casey Stengel MG 6.00 15.00
325 Hector Lopez 2.50 6.00
326 Ron Brand RC 1.50 4.00
327 Don Blasingame 1.50 4.00
328 Bob Shaw 1.50 4.00
329 Russ Nixon 1.50 4.00
330 Tommy Harper 2.50 6.00
331 Maris/Cash/Mantle/Kaline 60.00 150.00
332 Ray Washburn 1.50 4.00
333 Billy Moran 1.50 4.00
334 Lew Krausse 1.50 4.00
335 Don Mossi 2.50 6.00
336 Andre Rodgers 1.50 4.00
337 A.Ferrara RC/J.Torborg RC 2.50 6.00
338 Jack Kralick 1.50 4.00
339 Walt Bond 1.50 4.00
340 Joe Cunningham 1.50 4.00
341 Jim Roland 1.50 4.00
342 Willie Stargell 20.00 50.00
343 Washington Senators TC 2.50 6.00
344 Phil Linz 2.50 6.00
345 Frank Thomas 3.00 8.00
346 Joey Jay 1.50 4.00
347 Bobby Wine 2.50 6.00
348 Ed Lopat MG 2.50 6.00
349 Art Fowler 1.50 4.00
350 Willie McCovey 12.00 30.00
351 Dan Schneider 1.50 4.00
352 Eddie Bressoud 1.50 4.00
353 Wally Moon 2.50 6.00
354 Dave Giusti 1.50 4.00
355 Vic Power 2.50 6.00

356 B.McCool RC/C.Ruiz	2.50	6.00
357 Charley James	1.50	4.00
358 Ron Kline	1.50	4.00
359 Jim Schaffer	1.50	4.00
360 Joe Pepitone	5.00	12.00
361 Jay Hook	1.50	4.00
362 Checklist 5	4.00	10.00
363 Dick McAuliffe	2.50	6.00
364 Joe Gaines	1.50	4.00
365 Cal McLish	2.50	6.00
366 Nelson Mathews	1.50	4.00
367 Fred Whitfield	1.50	4.00
368 F.Ackley RC/D.Buford RC	2.50	6.00
369 Jerry Zimmerman	1.50	4.00
370 Hal Woodeshick	1.50	4.00
371 Frank Howard	3.00	8.00
372 Howie Koplitz	3.00	8.00
373 Pittsburgh Pirates TC	5.00	12.00
374 Bobby Bolin	3.00	8.00
375 Ron Santo	4.00	10.00
376 Dave Morehead	3.00	8.00
377 Bob Skinner	3.00	8.00
378 W.Woodward RC/J.Smith	4.00	10.00
379 Tony Gonzalez	3.00	8.00
380 Whitey Ford	15.00	40.00
381 Bob Taylor	3.00	8.00
382 Wes Stock	3.00	8.00
383 Bill Rigney MG	3.00	8.00
384 Ron Hansen	3.00	8.00
385 Curt Simmons	4.00	10.00
386 Lenny Green	3.00	8.00
387 Terry Fox	3.00	8.00
388 J.O'Donoghue RC/G.Williams	4.00	10.00
389 Jim Umbricht	4.00	10.00
390 Orlando Cepeda	10.00	25.00
391 Sam McDowell	4.00	10.00
392 Jim Pagliaroni	3.00	8.00
393 C.Stengel/E.Kranepool	6.00	15.00
394 Bob Miller	3.00	8.00
395 Tom Tresh	4.00	10.00
396 Dennis Bennett	3.00	8.00
397 Chuck Cottier	3.00	8.00
398 B.Haas/D.Smith	4.00	10.00
399 Jackie Brandt	3.00	8.00
400 Warren Spahn	15.00	40.00
401 Charlie Maxwell	3.00	8.00
402 Tom Sturdivant	3.00	8.00
403 Cincinnati Reds TC	5.00	12.00
404 Tony Martinez	3.00	8.00
405 Ken McBride	3.00	8.00
406 Al Spangler	3.00	8.00
407 Bill Freehan	4.00	10.00
408 J.Stewart RC/F.Burdette RC	3.00	8.00
409 Bill Fischer	3.00	8.00
410 Dick Stuart	4.00	10.00
411 Lee Walls	3.00	8.00
412 Ray Culp	4.00	10.00
413 Johnny Keane MG	3.00	8.00
414 Jack Sanford	3.00	8.00
415 Tony Kubek	10.00	25.00
416 Lee Maye	3.00	8.00
417 Don Cardwell	3.00	8.00
418 D.Knowles RC/B.Narum RC	4.00	10.00
419 Ken Harrelson RC	6.00	15.00
420 Jim Maloney	4.00	10.00
421 Camilo Carreon	3.00	8.00
422 Jack Fisher	3.00	8.00
423 H.Aaron/W.Mays	40.00	100.00
424 Dick Bertell	3.00	8.00
425 Norm Cash	4.00	10.00
426 Bob Rodgers	3.00	8.00
427 Don Rudolph	3.00	8.00
428 A.Skeen RC/P.Smith RC	3.00	8.00
429 Tim McCarver	4.00	10.00
430 Juan Pizarro	3.00	8.00
431 George Alusik	3.00	8.00
432 Ruben Amaro	4.00	10.00
433 New York Yankees TC	15.00	40.00
434 Don Nottebart	3.00	8.00
435 Vic Davalillo	3.00	8.00
436 Charlie Neal	4.00	10.00
437 Ed Bailey	3.00	8.00
438 Checklist 6	6.00	15.00
439 Harvey Haddix	4.00	10.00
440 Roberto Clemente UER	75.00	200.00
441 Bob Duliba	3.00	8.00
442 Pumpsie Green	4.00	10.00
443 Chuck Dressen MG	4.00	10.00
444 Larry Jackson	3.00	8.00
445 Bill Skowron	4.00	10.00
446 Julian Javier	6.00	15.00
447 Ted Bowsfield	3.00	8.00
448 Cookie Rojas	4.00	10.00
449 Deron Johnson	4.00	10.00
450 Steve Barber	3.00	8.00
451 Joe Amalfitano	3.00	8.00
452 G.Garrido RC/J.Hart RC	4.00	10.00
453 Frank Baumann	3.00	8.00
454 Tommie Aaron	4.00	10.00
455 Bernie Allen	3.00	8.00
456 W.Parker RC/J.Werhas RC	4.00	10.00
457 Jesse Gonder	3.00	8.00
458 Ralph Terry	4.00	10.00
459 P.Charton RC/D.Jones RC	3.00	8.00
460 Bob Gibson	25.00	60.00
461 George Thomas	3.00	8.00
462 Birdie Tebbetts MG	3.00	8.00
463 Don Leppert	3.00	8.00
464 Dallas Green	6.00	15.00
465 Mike Hershberger	3.00	8.00
466 D.Green RC/A.Monteagudo RC	4.00	10.00
467 Bob Aspromonte	3.00	8.00
468 Gaylord Perry	15.00	40.00
469 F.Norman RC/S.Slaughter RC	4.00	10.00
470 Jim Bouton	5.00	12.00
471 Gates Brown RC	4.00	10.00
472 Vern Law	4.00	10.00
473 Baltimore Orioles TC	5.00	12.00
474 Larry Sherry	4.00	10.00
475 Ed Charles	3.00	8.00
476 R.Carty RC/D.Kelley RC	6.00	15.00
477 Mike Joyce	3.00	8.00
478 Dick Howser	4.00	10.00
479 D.Bakenhaster RC/J.Lewis RC	3.00	8.00
480 Bob Purkey	3.00	8.00
481 Chuck Schilling	3.00	8.00
482 J.Briggs RC/D.Cater RC	4.00	10.00
483 Fred Valentine RC	3.00	8.00
484 Bill Pleis	3.00	8.00
485 Tom Haller	3.00	8.00
486 Bob Kennedy MG	3.00	8.00
487 Mike McCormick	4.00	10.00
488 P.Mikkelsen RC/B.Meyer RC	6.00	15.00
489 Julio Navarro	3.00	8.00
490 Ron Fairly	4.00	10.00
491 Ed Rakow	3.00	8.00
492 J.Beauchamp RC/M.White RC	3.00	8.00
493 Don Lee	3.00	8.00
494 Al Jackson	3.00	8.00
495 Bill Virdon	4.00	10.00
496 Chicago White Sox TC	5.00	12.00
497 Jeoff Long RC	3.00	8.00
498 Dave Stenhouse	3.00	8.00
499 C.Slamon RC/G.Seyfried RC	3.00	8.00
500 Camilo Pascual	4.00	10.00
501 Bob Veale	4.00	10.00
502 B.Knoop RC/B.Lee RC	3.00	8.00
503 Earl Wilson	3.00	8.00
504 Claude Raymond	3.00	8.00
505 Stan Williams	3.00	8.00
506 Bobby Bragan MG	3.00	8.00
507 Johnny Edwards	3.00	8.00
508 Diego Segui	3.00	8.00
509 G.Alley RC/O.McFarlane RC	4.00	10.00
510 Lindy McDaniel	4.00	10.00
511 Lou Jackson	4.00	10.00
512 W.Horton RC/J.Sparma RC	6.00	15.00
513 Don Larsen	4.00	10.00
514 Jim Hickman	4.00	10.00
515 Johnny Romano	3.00	8.00
516 J.Arrigo RC/D.Siebler RC	3.00	8.00
517A Checklist 7 ERR	10.00	25.00
517B Checklist 7 COR	6.00	15.00
518 Carl Bouldin	3.00	8.00
519 Charlie Smith	3.00	8.00
520 Jack Baldschun	4.00	10.00
521 Tom Satriano	3.00	8.00
522 Bob Tiefenauer	3.00	8.00
523 Lou Burdette UER	8.00	20.00
524 J.Dickson RC/B.Klaus RC	6.00	15.00
525 Al McBean	6.00	15.00
526 Lou Clinton	6.00	15.00
527 Larry Bearnarth	6.00	15.00
528 D.Duncan RC/T.Reynolds RC	8.00	20.00
529 Alvin Dark MG	8.00	20.00
530 Leon Wagner	6.00	15.00
531 Los Angeles Dodgers TC	10.00	25.00
532 B.Bloomfield RC/J.Nossek RC	6.00	15.00
533 Johnny Klippstein	6.00	15.00
534 Gus Bell	6.00	15.00
535 Phil Regan	6.00	15.00
536 L.Elliot/J.Stephenson RC	6.00	15.00
537 Dan Osinski	6.00	15.00
538 Minnie Minoso	8.00	20.00
539 Roy Face	8.00	20.00
540 Luis Aparicio	15.00	40.00
541 P.Roof/P.Niekro RC	50.00	120.00
542 Don Mincher	6.00	15.00
543 Bob Uecker	20.00	50.00
544 S.Hertz RC/J.Hoerner RC	6.00	15.00
545 Max Alvis	6.00	15.00
546 Joe Christopher	6.00	15.00
547 Gil Hodges MG	12.50	30.00
548 W.Schurr RC/P.Speckenbach RC	8.00	20.00
549 Joe Moeller	6.00	15.00
550 Ken Hubbs MEM	15.00	40.00
551 Billy Hoeft	6.00	15.00
552 T.Kelley RC/S.Siebert RC	6.00	15.00
553 Jim Brewer	6.00	15.00
554 Hank Foiles	6.00	15.00
555 Lee Stange	6.00	15.00
556 S.Dillon RC/R.Locke RC	6.00	15.00
557 Leo Burke	6.00	15.00
558 Don Schwall	6.00	15.00
559 Dick Phillips	6.00	15.00
560 Dick Farrell	6.00	15.00
561 D.Bennett RC/R.Wise RC	8.00	20.00
562 Pedro Ramos	6.00	15.00
563 Dal Maxvill	8.00	20.00
564 J.McCabe RC/J.McNertney RC	8.00	20.00
565 Stu Miller	6.00	15.00
566 Ed Kranepool	8.00	20.00
567 Jim Kaat	8.00	20.00
568 P.Gagliano RC/C.Peterson RC	6.00	15.00
569 Fred Newman	6.00	15.00
570 Bill Mazeroski	15.00	40.00
571 Gene Conley	6.00	15.00
572 D.Gray RC/D.Egan	6.00	15.00
573 Jim Duffalo	6.00	15.00
574 Manny Jimenez	6.00	15.00
575 Tony Cloninger	6.00	15.00
576 J.Hinsley RC/B.Wakefield RC	6.00	15.00
577 Gordy Coleman	6.00	15.00
578 Glen Hobbie	6.00	15.00
579 Boston Red Sox TC	10.00	25.00
580 Johnny Podres	8.00	20.00
581 P.Gonzalez/A.Moore RC	8.00	20.00
582 Rod Kanehl	8.00	20.00
583 Tito Francona	6.00	15.00
584 Joel Horlen	6.00	15.00
585 Tony Taylor	8.00	20.00
586 Jimmy Piersall	8.00	20.00
587 Bennie Daniels	8.00	20.00

1964 Topps Coins

This set of 164 unnumbered coins issued in 1964 is sometimes divided into two sets -- the regular series (1-120) and the all-star series (121-164). Each metal coin is approximately 1 1/2" in diameter. The regular series features gold and silver coins with a full color photo of the player, including the background of the photo. The player's name, team and position are delineated on the coin front. The back includes the line "Collect the entire set of 120 all-stars". The all-star series (denoted AS in the checklist below) contains a full color cutout photo of the player on a solid background. The fronts feature the line "1964 All-stars" along with the name only of the player. The backs contain the line "Collect all 44 special stars". Mantle, Causey and Hinton appear in two variations each. The complete set price below includes all variations. Some dealers believe the following coins are short printed: Callison, Tresh, Rollins, Santo, Pappas, Freehan, Hendley, Staub, Bateman and O'Dell.

COMPLETE SET (167)	500.00	1,000.00
1 Don Zimmer	2.50	6.00
2 Jim Wynn	2.00	5.00
3 Johnny Orsino	1.50	4.00
4 Jim Bouton	2.00	5.00
5 Dick Groat	2.00	5.00
6 Leon Wagner	1.50	4.00
7 Frank Malzone	1.50	4.00
8 Steve Barber	1.50	4.00
9 Johnny Romano	1.50	4.00
10 Tom Tresh	2.50	6.00
11 Felipe Alou	2.00	5.00
12 Dick Stuart	2.00	5.00
13 Claude Osteen	1.50	4.00
14 Juan Pizarro	1.50	4.00
15 Donn Clendenon	1.50	4.00
16 Jimmie Hall	1.50	4.00
17 Al Jackson	1.50	4.00
18 Brooks Robinson	10.00	25.00
19 Bob Allison	2.00	5.00
20 Ed Roebuck	1.50	4.00
21 Pete Ward	1.50	4.00
22 Willie McCovey	4.00	10.00
23 Elston Howard	4.00	10.00
24 Diego Segui	1.50	4.00
25 Ken Boyer	2.50	6.00
26 Carl Yastrzemski	10.00	25.00
27 Bill Mazeroski	4.00	10.00
28 Jerry Lumpe	1.50	4.00
29 Woody Held	1.50	4.00
30 Dick Radatz	1.50	4.00
31 Luis Aparicio	2.50	6.00
32 Dave Nicholson	1.50	4.00
33 Eddie Mathews	10.00	25.00
34 Don Drysdale	8.00	20.00
35 Ray Culp	1.50	4.00
36 Juan Marichal	4.00	10.00
37 Frank Robinson	10.00	25.00
38 Chuck Hinton	1.50	4.00
39 Floyd Robinson	1.50	4.00
40 Tommy Harper	2.00	5.00
41 Ron Hansen	1.50	4.00
42 Ernie Banks	10.00	25.00
43 Jesse Gonder	1.50	4.00
44 Billy Williams	2.50	6.00
45 Vada Pinson	2.00	5.00
46 Rocky Colavito	5.00	12.00
47 Bill Monbouquette	1.50	4.00
48 Max Alvis	1.50	4.00
49 Norm Siebern	1.50	4.00
50 Johnny Callison	2.00	5.00
51 Rich Rollins	1.50	4.00
52 Ken McBride	1.50	4.00
53 Don Lock	1.50	4.00
54 Ron Fairly	2.00	5.00
55 Roberto Clemente	40.00	80.00
56 Dick Ellsworth	1.50	4.00
57 Tommy Davis	2.00	5.00
58 Tony Gonzalez	1.50	4.00
59 Bob Gibson	8.00	20.00
60 Jim Maloney	2.00	5.00
61 Frank Howard	2.00	5.00
62 Jim Pagliaroni	1.50	4.00
63 Orlando Cepeda	2.50	6.00
64 Ron Perranoski	1.50	4.00
65 Curt Flood	2.50	6.00
66 Alvin McBean	1.50	4.00
67 Dean Chance	1.50	4.00
68 Ron Santo	2.50	6.00
69 Jack Baldschun	1.50	4.00
70 Milt Pappas	2.00	5.00
71 Gary Peters	1.50	4.00
72 Bobby Richardson	2.50	6.00
73 Lee Thomas	1.50	4.00
74 Hank Aguirre	1.50	4.00
75 Carlton Willey	1.50	4.00
76 Camilo Pascual	2.00	5.00
77 Bob Friend	2.00	5.00
78 Bill White	2.00	5.00
79 Norm Cash	2.50	6.00
80 Willie Mays	30.00	60.00
81 Leon Carmel	1.50	4.00
82 Pete Rose	40.00	80.00
83 Hank Aaron	15.00	40.00
84 Bob Aspromonte	1.50	4.00
85 Jim O'Toole	1.50	4.00
86 Vic Davalillo	2.00	5.00
87 Bill Freehan	2.00	5.00
88 Warren Spahn	4.00	10.00
89 Ken Hunt	1.50	4.00
90 Denis Menke	1.50	4.00
91 Dick Farrell	1.50	4.00
92 Jim Hickman	2.00	5.00
93 Jim Bunning	2.50	6.00
94 Bob Hendley	1.50	4.00
95 Ernie Broglio	1.50	4.00
96 Rusty Staub	2.00	5.00
97 Lou Brock	4.00	10.00
98 Jim Fregosi	2.00	5.00
99 Jim Grant	1.50	4.00
100 Al Kaline	8.00	20.00
101 Earl Battey	2.00	5.00
102 Wayne Causey	1.50	4.00
103 Chuck Schilling	1.50	4.00
104 Boog Powell	2.50	6.00
105 Dave Wickersham	1.50	4.00
106 Sandy Koufax	10.00	25.00
107 John Bateman	2.00	5.00
108 Ed Brinkman	1.50	4.00
109 Al Downing	1.50	4.00
110 Joe Azcue	1.50	4.00
111 Albie Pearson	1.50	4.00
112 Harmon Killebrew	8.00	20.00
113 Tony Taylor	2.00	5.00
114 Larry Jackson	1.50	4.00
115 Billy O'Dell	2.00	5.00
116 Don Demeter	2.00	5.00
117 Ed Charles	1.50	4.00
118 Joe Torre	4.00	10.00
119 Don Nottebart	1.50	4.00
120 Mickey Mantle	50.00	100.00
121 Joe Pepitone AS	2.00	5.00
122 Dick Stuart AS	2.00	5.00
123 Bobby Richardson AS	2.50	6.00
124 Jerry Lumpe AS	1.50	4.00
125 Brooks Robinson AS	8.00	20.00
126 Frank Malzone AS	1.50	4.00
127 Luis Aparicio AS	2.50	6.00
128 Jim Fregosi AS	2.00	5.00
129 Al Kaline AS	6.00	15.00
130 Leon Wagner AS	1.50	4.00
131A Mickey Mantle AS Bat R	20.00	50.00
131B Mickey Mantle AS Bat L	20.00	50.00
132 Albie Pearson AS	1.50	4.00
133 Harmon Killebrew AS	6.00	15.00
134 Carl Yastrzemski AS	10.00	25.00
135 Elston Howard AS	2.50	6.00
136 Earl Battey AS	1.50	4.00
137 Camilo Pascual AS	1.50	4.00
138 Jim Bouton AS	2.00	5.00
139 Whitey Ford AS	8.00	20.00
140 Gary Peters AS	1.50	4.00
141 Bill White AS	2.00	5.00
142 Orlando Cepeda AS	2.50	6.00
143 Bill Mazeroski AS	4.00	10.00
144 Tony Taylor AS	1.50	4.00
145 Ken Boyer AS	2.50	6.00
146 Ron Santo AS	2.50	6.00
147 Dick Groat AS	2.00	5.00
148 Roy McMillan AS	1.50	4.00
149 Hank Aaron AS	10.00	25.00
150 Roberto Clemente AS	12.50	30.00
151 Willie Mays AS	12.50	30.00
152 Vada Pinson AS	2.00	5.00
153 Tommy Davis AS	2.00	5.00
154 Frank Robinson AS	8.00	20.00
155 Joe Torre AS	4.00	10.00
156 Tim McCarver AS	2.00	5.00
157 Juan Marichal AS	4.00	10.00
158 Jim Maloney AS	2.00	5.00
159 Sandy Koufax AS	10.00	25.00
160 Warren Spahn AS	4.00	10.00
161A Wayne Causey AS NL	6.00	15.00
161B Wayne Causey AS/American League	2.00	5.00
162A Chuck Hinton AS NL	8.00	20.00
162B Chuck Hinton AS/American League	2.00	5.00
163 Bob Aspromonte AS	1.50	4.00
164 Ron Hunt AS	1.50	4.00

1964 Topps Giants

The cards in this 60-card set measure approximately 3 1/8" by 5 1/4". The 1964 Topps Giants are postcard size cards containing color player photographs. They are numbered on the backs, which also contain biographical information presented in a newspaper format. These "giant size" cards were distributed in both cellophane and waxed gum packs apart from the Topps regular issue of 1964. The gum packs contain three cards. The Cards 3, 28, 42, 45, 47, 51 and 60 are more difficult to find and are indicated by SP in the checklist below.

COMPLETE SET (60)	150.00	300.00
COMMON CARD (1-60)	.60	1.50
COMMON SP'S	4.00	10.00
WRAPPER (5-CENT)	15.00	40.00
1 Gary Peters	.75	2.00
2 Ken Johnson	.60	1.50
3 Sandy Koufax SP	40.00	100.00
4 Bob Bailey	.60	1.50
5 Milt Pappas	.75	2.00
6 Ron Hunt	.60	1.50
7 Whitey Ford	8.00	20.00
8 Roy McMillan	.60	1.50
9 Rocky Colavito	2.00	5.00
10 Jim Bunning	1.25	3.00
11 Roberto Clemente	20.00	50.00
12 Al Kaline	6.00	15.00
13 Nellie Fox	4.00	10.00
14 Tony Gonzalez	.60	1.50
15 Jim Gentile	.75	2.00
16 Dean Chance	.75	2.00
17 Dick Ellsworth	.75	2.00
18 Jim Fregosi	.75	2.00
19 Dick Groat	.75	2.00
20 Chuck Hinton	.60	1.50
21 Elston Howard	.75	2.00
22 Dick Farrell	.60	1.50
23 Albie Pearson	.60	1.50
24 Frank Howard	.75	2.00
25 Mickey Mantle	40.00	100.00
26 Joe Torre	2.00	5.00
27 Eddie Brinkman	.60	1.50
28 Bob Friend SP	4.00	10.00
29 Frank Robinson	6.00	15.00
30 Bill Freehan	.75	2.00
31 Warren Spahn	5.00	12.00

32 Camilo Pascual	.75	2.00
33 Pete Ward	.60	1.50
34 Jim Maloney	.75	2.00
35 Dave Wickersham	.60	1.50
36 Johnny Callison	.75	2.00
37 Juan Marichal	1.25	3.00
38 Harmon Killebrew	6.00	15.00
39 Luis Aparicio	1.25	3.00
40 Dick Radatz	.60	1.50
41 Bob Gibson	12.00	30.00
42 Dick Stuart SP	6.00	15.00
43 Tommy Davis	.75	2.00
44 Tony Oliva	1.25	3.00
45 Wayne Causey SP	6.00	15.00
46 Max Alvis	.60	1.50
47 Galen Cisco SP	10.00	25.00
48 Carl Yastrzemski	8.00	20.00
49 Hank Aaron	20.00	50.00
50 Brooks Robinson	6.00	15.00
51 Willie Mays SP	30.00	80.00
52 Billy Williams	1.25	3.00
53 Juan Pizarro	.60	1.50
54 Leon Wagner	.60	1.50
55 Orlando Cepeda	1.25	3.00
56 Vada Pinson	.75	2.00
57 Ken Boyer	1.25	3.00
58 Ron Santo	1.25	3.00
59 John Romano	.60	1.50
60 Bill Skowron SP	12.00	30.00

1964 Topps Rookie All-Star Banquet

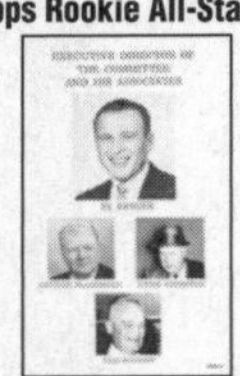

This 35-card set was actually the dinner program for the 1964 annual Topps Rookie All-Star Banquet and was housed in its own special presentation box. The first seven cards featured black and white photos of sport and media people and measured approximately 3" by 5 1/4". Cards 8-13 depicted the previous years' Rookie All-Star Teams each with black-and-white head shots of 10 players of that year on a light blue background. Cards 14-34A each displayed 3" by 3 1/4" black-and-white photos of one of the 1964 rookies being honored at the banquet or a photo of the PR Director for the team with a write-up of that team's rookie player.

COMPLETE SET (35)	600.00	1,200.00
1 Title Card	8.00	20.00
2 T. David	40.00	80.00
J. Torborg		
Santo		
Williams		
3 Aparicio	40.00	80.00
Bowens		
Tresh		
Gonzalez		
Bruce		
Bond		
Wh		
4 H. Greenberg HOF	40.00	80.00
F. Frisch HOF		
T. Cohane		
D. Gro		
5 J. Robinson HOF	75.00	150.00
J. McDermott		
J. McKenney AL DIR#		
6 Sy Berger	40.00	100.00
G. MacDonald		
H. Feimister		
T. Wright		
7 Joe Garagiola TRIB	30.00	60.00
8 1959 Rookie All-Star Team	50.00	100.00
McCovey		
Green		
Koppe/		
9 1960 Rookie All-Star Team	40.00	80.00
Gentile		
Javier		
Hansen		
10 1961 Rookie All-Star Team	50.00	100.00
Martin		
Wood		
Howser		
S		
11 1962 Rookie All-Star Team	20.00	50.00
Whitfield		
Allen		
Tresh		
12 1963 Rookie All-Star Team	250.00	500.00
Rose		
Staub		
Weis		
Ward		
13 64 Rookie AS Title Card	15.00	40.00
14 Ed Uhas DIR	15.00	40.00
15 Bob Chance	40.00	80.00
16 Garry Schumacher DIR	15.00	40.00
17 Hal Lanier	20.00	50.00
18 Larry Shenk DIR	15.00	40.00
19 Richie Allen	100.00	200.00
20 Jim Schaaf DIR	15.00	40.00
21 Bert Campaneris	60.00	120.00
22 Ernie Johnson DIR	15.00	40.00
23 Rico Carty	60.00	120.00
24 Bill Crowley DIR	15.00	40.00
25 Tony Conigliaro	100.00	200.00
26 Tom Mee DIR	15.00	40.00
27 Tony Oliva	125.00	250.00
28 Burt Hawkins DIR	15.00	40.00
29 Mike Brumley	40.00	80.00
30 Hank Zureick DIR	15.00	40.00
31 Billy McCool	40.00	80.00
32 Rob Brown DIR	15.00	40.00
33 Wally Bunker	40.00	80.00
34 Minor League POY Title Card	15.00	40.00
34A Luis Tiant	60.00	120.00

1964 Topps Stand-Ups

In 1964 Topps produced a die-cut "Stand-Up" card design for the first time since their Connie Mack and Current All Stars of 1951. These cards were issued in both one cent and five cent packs. The cards have full-length, color player photos set against a green and yellow background. Of the 77 cards in the set, 22 were single printed and these are marked in the checklist below with an SP. These unnumbered cards are standard-size (2 1/2" by 3 1/2"), blank backed, and have been numbered here for reference in alphabetical order of players. Interestingly there were four different wrapper designs used for this set. All the design variations are valued at the same price.

COMPLETE SET (77)	2,500.00	4,000.00
COMMON CARD (1-77)	4.00	10.00
COMMON CARD SP	15.00	40.00
WRAPPER (1-CENT)	75.00	150.00
WRAPPER (5-CENT)	175.00	350.00
1 Hank Aaron	75.00	200.00
2 Hank Aguirre	5.00	12.00
3 George Altman	8.00	20.00
4 Max Alvis	5.00	12.00
5 Bob Aspromonte	5.00	12.00
6 Jack Baldschun SP	20.00	50.00
7 Ernie Banks	50.00	100.00
8 Steve Barber	5.00	12.00
9 Earl Battey	5.00	12.00
10 Ken Boyer	10.00	25.00
11 Ernie Broglio	5.00	12.00
12 John Callison	8.00	20.00
13 Norm Cash SP	40.00	80.00
14 Wayne Causey	5.00	12.00
15 Orlando Cepeda	10.00	25.00
16 Ed Charles	8.00	20.00
17 Roberto Clemente	125.00	250.00
18 Donn Clendenon SP	20.00	50.00
19 Rocky Colavito	15.00	40.00
20 Ray Culp SP	30.00	60.00
21 Tommy Davis	8.00	20.00
22 Don Drysdale SP	75.00	150.00
23 Dick Ellsworth	5.00	12.00
24 Dick Farrell	5.00	12.00
25 Jim Fregosi	8.00	20.00
26 Bob Friend	5.00	12.00
27 Jim Gentile	8.00	20.00
28 Jesse Gonder SP	20.00	50.00
29 Tony Gonzalez SP	20.00	50.00
30 Dick Groat	10.00	25.00
31 Woody Held	5.00	12.00
32 Chuck Hinton	5.00	12.00
33 Elston Howard	10.00	25.00
34 Frank Howard SP	40.00	80.00
35 Ron Hunt	8.00	20.00
36 Al Jackson	5.00	12.00
37 Ken Johnson	5.00	12.00
38 Al Kaline	50.00	100.00
39 Harmon Killebrew	50.00	100.00
40 Sandy Koufax	100.00	200.00
41 Don Lock SP	20.00	50.00
42 Jerry Lumpe SP	20.00	50.00
43 Jim Maloney	8.00	20.00
44 Frank Malzone	5.00	12.00
45 Mickey Mantle	300.00	600.00
46 Juan Marichal SP	60.00	120.00
47 Eddie Mathews SP	75.00	150.00
48 Willie Mays	100.00	250.00
49 Bill Mazeroski	15.00	40.00
50 Ken McBride	5.00	12.00
51 Willie McCovey SP	60.00	120.00
52 Claude Osteen	8.00	20.00
53 Jim O'Toole	5.00	12.00
54 Camilo Pascual	8.00	20.00
55 Albie Pearson SP	30.00	60.00
56 Gary Peters	5.00	12.00
57 Vada Pinson	8.00	20.00
58 Juan Pizarro	5.00	12.00
59 Boog Powell	10.00	25.00
60 Bobby Richardson	10.00	25.00
61 Brooks Robinson	50.00	100.00
62 Floyd Robinson	5.00	12.00
63 Frank Robinson	50.00	100.00
64 Ed Roebuck SP	20.00	50.00
65 Rich Rollins	5.00	12.00
66 John Romano	5.00	12.00
67 Ron Santo SP	40.00	80.00
68 Norm Siebern	5.00	12.00
69 Warren Spahn SP	75.00	150.00
70 Dick Stuart SP	30.00	60.00
71 Lee Thomas	5.00	12.00
72 Joe Torre	10.00	25.00
73 Pete Ward	5.00	12.00
74 Bill White SP	30.00	60.00
75 Billy Williams SP	60.00	120.00
76 Hal Woodeshick SP	20.00	50.00
77 Carl Yastrzemski SP	250.00	500.00

1964 Topps Tattoos Inserts

These tattoos measure 1 9/16" by 3 1/2" and are printed in color on very thin paper. One side gives instructions for applying the tattoo. The picture side gives either the team logo and name (on tattoos numbered 1-20 below) or the player's face, name and team (21-75 below). The tattoos are unnumbered and are presented below in alphabetical order within type for convenience. This set was issued in one cent packs which came 120 to a box. The boxes had photos of Whitey Ford on them.

COMPLETE SET (75)	600.00	1,200.00
COMMON TATOO (1-20)	1.50	4.00
COMMON TATOO (21-75)	3.00	8.00
8 Detroit Tigers	2.00	5.00
11 Los Angeles Dodgers	5.00	12.00
14 New York Mets	2.00	5.00
15 New York Yankees	5.00	12.00
21 Hank Aaron	60.00	120.00
22 Max Alvis	3.00	8.00
23 Hank Aguirre	3.00	8.00
24 Ernie Banks	30.00	60.00
25 Steve Barber	3.00	8.00
26 Ken Boyer	5.00	12.00
27 John Callison	3.00	8.00
28 Norm Cash	4.00	10.00
29 Wayne Causey	3.00	8.00
30 Orlando Cepeda	8.00	20.00
31 Rocky Colavito	8.00	20.00
32 Ray Culp	3.00	8.00
33 Vic Davalillo	3.00	8.00
34 Moe Drabowsky	3.00	8.00
35 Dick Ellsworth	3.00	8.00
36 Curt Flood	5.00	12.00
37 Bill Freehan	4.00	10.00
38 Jim Fregosi	4.00	10.00
39 Bob Friend	3.00	8.00
40 Dick Groat	5.00	12.00
41 Woody Held	3.00	8.00
42 Frank Howard	5.00	12.00
43 Al Jackson	3.00	8.00
44 Larry Jackson	3.00	8.00
45 Ken Johnson	3.00	8.00
46 Al Kaline	30.00	60.00
47 Harmon Killebrew	15.00	40.00
48 Sandy Koufax	60.00	120.00
49 Don Lock	3.00	8.00
50 Frank Malzone	4.00	10.00
51 Mickey Mantle	150.00	300.00
52 Eddie Mathews	20.00	50.00
53 Willie Mays	60.00	120.00
54 Bill Mazeroski	6.00	15.00
55 Ken McBride	3.00	8.00
56 Bill Monbouquette	3.00	8.00
57 Dave Nicholson	3.00	8.00
58 Claude Osteen	3.00	8.00
59 Milt Pappas	4.00	10.00
60 Camilo Pascual	3.00	8.00
61 Albie Pearson	3.00	8.00
62 Ron Perranoski	3.00	8.00
63 Gary Peters	3.00	8.00
64 Boog Powell	5.00	12.00
65 Frank Robinson	20.00	50.00
66 Johnny Romano	3.00	8.00
67 Norm Siebern	3.00	8.00
68 Warren Spahn	20.00	50.00
69 Dick Stuart	4.00	10.00
70 Lee Thomas	3.00	8.00
71 Joe Torre	6.00	15.00
72 Pete Ward	3.00	8.00
73 Carlton Willey	3.00	8.00
74 Billy Williams	15.00	40.00
75 Carl Yastrzemski	30.00	60.00

1964 Topps Venezuelan

This set is a parallel version of the first 370 cards in the regular 1964 Topps set and is similar in design. The major difference is the black margin featured on the card back. The cards were issued for the Venezuelan market.

COMPLETE SET (370)	3,500.00	7,000.00
1 Sandy Koufax	60.00	120.00
Dick Ellsworth		
Bob Friend LL		
2 Gary Peters	10.00	25.00
Juan Pizarro		
Camilo Pascual LL		
3 Sandy Koufax	50.00	100.00
Juan Marichal		
Warren Spahn		
Jim Maloney LL		
4 Whitey Ford	20.00	50.00
Camilo Pascual		
Jim Bouton LL		
5 Sandy Koufax	40.00	80.00
Jim Maloney		
Don Drysdale LL		
6 Camilo Pascual	10.00	25.00
Jim Bunning		
Dick Stigman LL		
7 Tommy Davis	50.00	100.00
Bob Clemente		
Dick Groat		
Hank Aaron LL		
8 Carl Yastrzemski	30.00	60.00
Al Kaline		
Rich Rollins LL		
9 Hank Aaron	75.00	150.00
Willie McCovey		
Willie Mays		
Orlando Cepeda LL		
10 Harmon Killebrew/Dick Stuart	20.00	50.00
Bob Allison LL		
11 Hank Aaron	30.00	60.00
Ken Boyer		
Bill White LL		
12 Dick Stuart	20.00	50.00
Al Kaline		
Harmon Killebrew LL		
13 Hoyt Wilhelm	20.00	50.00
14 Dick Nen	8.00	20.00
Nick Willhite		
15 Zoilo Versalles	8.00	20.00
16 John Boozer	8.00	20.00
17 Willie Kirkland	8.00	20.00
18 Billy O'Dell	8.00	20.00
19 Don Wert	8.00	20.00
20 Bob Friend	8.00	20.00
21 Yogi Berra MG	75.00	150.00
22 Jerry Adair	8.00	20.00
23 Chris Zachary	8.00	20.00
24 Carl Sawatski	8.00	20.00
25 Bill Monbouquette	8.00	20.00
26 Gino Cimoli	8.00	20.00
27 New York Mets	12.50	30.00
Team Card		
28 Claude Osteen	8.00	20.00
29 Lou Brock	75.00	150.00
30 Ron Perranoski	8.00	20.00
31 Dave Nicholson	8.00	20.00
32 Dean Chance	8.00	20.00
33 Sammy Ellis	8.00	20.00
Mel Queen		
34 Jim Perry	8.00	20.00
35 Eddie Mathews	40.00	80.00
36 Hal Reniff	8.00	20.00
37 Smoky Burgess	8.00	20.00
38 Jim Wynn RC	12.50	30.00
39 Hank Aguirre	8.00	20.00
40 Dick Groat	8.00	20.00
41 Willie McCovey	12.50	30.00
Leon Wagner		
42 Moe Drabowsky	8.00	20.00
43 Roy Sievers	8.00	20.00
44 Duke Carmel	8.00	20.00
45 Milt Pappas	8.00	20.00
46 Ed Brinkman	8.00	20.00
47 Jesus Alou	8.00	20.00
Ron Herbel		
48 Bob Perry	8.00	20.00
49 Bill Henry	8.00	20.00
50 Mickey Mantle	750.00	1,500.00
51 Pete Richert	8.00	20.00
52 Chuck Hinton	8.00	20.00
53 Denis Menke	8.00	20.00
54 Sam Mele MG	8.00	20.00
55 Ernie Banks	75.00	150.00
56 Hal Brown	8.00	20.00
57 Tim Harkness	8.00	20.00
58 Don Demeter	8.00	20.00
59 Ernie Broglio	8.00	20.00
60 Frank Malzone	8.00	20.00
61 Bob Rodgers	8.00	20.00
Ed Sadowski		
62 Ted Savage	8.00	20.00
63 John Orsino	8.00	20.00
64 Ted Abernathy	8.00	20.00
65 Felipe Alou	12.50	30.00
66 Eddie Fisher	8.00	20.00
67 Tigers Team	12.50	30.00
68 Willie Davis	8.00	20.00
69 Clete Boyer	10.00	25.00
70 Joe Torre	15.00	40.00
71 Jack Spring	8.00	20.00
72 Chico Cardenas	8.00	20.00
73 Jimmie Hall	8.00	20.00
74 Bob Priddy	8.00	20.00
Tom Butters		
75 Wayne Causey	8.00	20.00
76 Checklist 1	15.00	40.00
77 Jerry Walker	8.00	20.00
78 Merritt Ranew	8.00	20.00
79 Bob Heffner	8.00	20.00
80 Vada Pinson	10.00	25.00
81 Nellie Fox	20.00	50.00
Harmon Killebrew		
82 Jim Davenport	8.00	20.00
83 Gus Triandos	8.00	20.00
84 Carl Willey	8.00	20.00
85 Pete Ward	8.00	20.00
86 Al Downing	10.00	25.00
87 St. Louis Cardinals	12.50	30.00
Team Card		
88 John Roseboro	8.00	20.00
89 Boog Powell	12.50	30.00
90 Earl Battey	8.00	20.00
91 Bob Bailey	8.00	20.00
92 Steve Ridzik	8.00	20.00
93 Gary Geiger	8.00	20.00
94 Jim Britton	8.00	20.00
Larry Maxie		
95 George Altman	8.00	20.00
96 Bob Buhl	8.00	20.00
97 Jim Fregosi	8.00	20.00
98 Bill Bruton	8.00	20.00
99 Al Stanek	8.00	20.00
100 Elston Howard	12.50	30.00
101 Walt Alston MG	12.50	30.00
102 Checklist 2	15.00	40.00
103 Curt Flood	10.00	25.00
104 Art Mahaffey	8.00	20.00
105 Woody Held	8.00	20.00
106 Joe Nuxhall	8.00	20.00
107 Bruce Howard	8.00	20.00
Frank Kreutzer		
108 John Wyatt	8.00	20.00
109 Rusty Staub	12.50	30.00
110 Albie Pearson	8.00	20.00
111 Don Elston	8.00	20.00
112 Bob Tillman	8.00	20.00
113 Grover Powell	8.00	20.00
114 Don Lock	8.00	20.00
115 Frank Bolling	8.00	20.00
116 Jay Ward	30.00	60.00
Tony Oliva		
117 Earl Francis	8.00	20.00
118 John Blanchard	8.00	20.00
119 Gary Kolb	8.00	20.00
120 Don Drysdale	50.00	100.00
121 Pete Runnels	8.00	20.00
122 Don McMahon	8.00	20.00
123 Jose Pagan	8.00	20.00
124 Orlando Pena	8.00	20.00
125 Pete Rose	500.00	1,000.00

Card	Low	High
126 Russ Snyder	8.00	20.00
127 Aubrey Gatewood	8.00	20.00
Dick Simpson		
128 Mickey Lolich RC	50.00	100.00
129 Amado Samuel	8.00	20.00
130 Gary Peters	8.00	20.00
131 Steve Boros	8.00	20.00
132 Braves Team	12.50	30.00
133 Jim Grant	8.00	20.00
134 Don Zimmer	8.00	20.00
135 Johnny Callison	8.00	20.00
136 Sandy Koufax WS	40.00	80.00
Strikes out 15		
137 Tommy Davis WS	10.00	25.00
138 Ron Fairly WS	10.00	25.00
139 Frank Howard WS	10.00	25.00
140 World Series Summary	10.00	25.00
Dodgers celebrate		
141 Danny Murtaugh MG	8.00	20.00
142 John Bateman	8.00	20.00
143 Bubba Phillips	8.00	20.00
144 Al Worthington	8.00	20.00
145 Norm Siebern	8.00	20.00
146 Tommy John	75.00	150.00
Bob Chance		
147 Ray Sadecki	8.00	20.00
148 J.C. Martin	8.00	20.00
149 Paul Foytack	8.00	20.00
150 Willie Mays	250.00	500.00
151 Athletics Team	12.50	30.00
152 Denny Lemaster	8.00	20.00
153 Dick Williams	10.00	25.00
154 Dick Tracewski	8.00	20.00
155 Duke Snider	75.00	150.00
156 Bill Dailey	8.00	20.00
157 Gene Mauch MG	8.00	20.00
158 Ken Johnson	8.00	20.00
159 Charlie Dees	8.00	20.00
160 Ken Boyer	12.50	30.00
161 Dave McNally	8.00	20.00
162 Dick Sisler CO	8.00	20.00
Vada Pinson		
163 Donn Clendenon	8.00	20.00
164 Bud Daley	8.00	20.00
165 Jerry Lumpe	8.00	20.00
166 Marty Keough	8.00	20.00
167 Mike Brumley	75.00	150.00
Lou Piniella		
168 Al Weis	8.00	20.00
169 Del Crandall	8.00	20.00
170 Dick Radatz	8.00	20.00
171 Ty Cline	8.00	20.00
172 Indians Team	12.50	30.00
173 Ryne Duren	8.00	20.00
174 Doc Edwards	8.00	20.00
175 Billy Williams	40.00	80.00
176 Tracy Stallard	8.00	20.00
177 Harmon Killebrew	50.00	100.00
178 Hank Bauer MG	8.00	20.00
179 Carl Warwick	8.00	20.00
180 Tommy Davis	10.00	25.00
181 Dave Wickersham	8.00	20.00
182 Carl Yastrzemski	40.00	80.00
Chuck Schilling		
183 Ron Taylor	8.00	20.00
184 Al Luplow	8.00	20.00
185 Jim O'Toole	8.00	20.00
186 Roman Mejias	8.00	20.00
187 Ed Roebuck	8.00	20.00
188 Checklist 3	15.00	40.00
189 Bob Hendley	8.00	20.00
190 Bobby Richardson	15.00	40.00
191 Clay Dalrymple	8.00	20.00
192 John Boccabella	8.00	20.00
Billy Cowan		
193 Jerry Lynch	8.00	20.00
194 John Goryl	8.00	20.00
195 Floyd Robinson	8.00	20.00
196 Jim Gentile	8.00	20.00
197 Frank Lary	8.00	20.00
198 Len Gabrielson	8.00	20.00
199 Joe Azcue	8.00	20.00
200 Sandy Koufax	250.00	500.00
201 Sam Bowens	8.00	20.00
Wally Bunker		
202 Galen Cisco	8.00	20.00
203 John Kennedy	8.00	20.00
204 Matty Alou	10.00	25.00
205 Nellie Fox	20.00	50.00
206 Steve Hamilton	8.00	20.00
207 Fred Hutchinson MG	8.00	20.00
208 Wes Covington	8.00	20.00
209 Bob Allen	8.00	20.00

Card	Low	High
210 Carl Yastrzemski	75.00	150.00
211 Jim Coker	8.00	20.00
212 Pete Lovrich	8.00	20.00
213 Angels Team	12.50	30.00
214 Ken McMullen	8.00	20.00
215 Ray Herbert	8.00	20.00
216 Mike de la Hoz	8.00	20.00
217 Jim King	8.00	20.00
218 Hank Fischer	8.00	20.00
219 Al Downing	8.00	20.00
Jim Bouton		
220 Dick Ellsworth	8.00	20.00
221 Bob Saverine	8.00	20.00
222 Billy Pierce	10.00	25.00
223 George Banks	8.00	20.00
224 Tommie Sisk	8.00	20.00
225 Roger Maris	125.00	250.00
226 Jerry Grote	10.00	25.00
Larry Yellen		
227 Barry Latman	8.00	20.00
228 Felix Mantilla	8.00	20.00
229 Charley Lau	8.00	20.00
230 Brooks Robinson	75.00	150.00
231 Dick Calmus	8.00	20.00
232 Al Lopez MG	12.50	30.00
233 Hal Smith	8.00	20.00
234 Gary Bell	8.00	20.00
235 Ron Hunt	8.00	20.00
236 Bill Faul	8.00	20.00
237 Cubs Team	12.50	30.00
238 Roy McMillan	8.00	20.00
239 Herm Starrette	8.00	20.00
240 Bill White	10.00	25.00
241 Jim Owens	8.00	20.00
242 Harvey Kuenn	8.00	20.00
243 Richie Allen	75.00	150.00
John Herrnstein		
244 Tony LaRussa	75.00	150.00
245 Dick Stigman	8.00	20.00
246 Manny Mota	10.00	25.00
247 Dave DeBusschere	12.50	30.00
248 Johnny Pesky MG	8.00	20.00
249 Doug Camilli	8.00	20.00
250 Al Kaline	100.00	200.00
251 Choo Choo Coleman	8.00	20.00
252 Ken Aspromonte	8.00	20.00
253 Wally Post	8.00	20.00
254 Don Hoak	8.00	20.00
255 Lee Thomas	8.00	20.00
256 Johnny Weekly	8.00	20.00
257 San Francisco Giants	12.50	30.00
Team Card		
258 Garry Roggenburk	8.00	20.00
259 Harry Bright	8.00	20.00
260 Frank Robinson	75.00	150.00
261 Jim Hannan	8.00	20.00
262 Mike Shannon	15.00	40.00
Harry Fanok		
263 Chuck Estrada	8.00	20.00
264 Jim Landis	8.00	20.00
265 Jim Bunning	40.00	80.00
266 Gene Freese	8.00	20.00
267 Wilbur Wood RC	12.50	30.00
268 Danny Murtaugh	8.00	20.00
Bill Virdon MG		
269 Ellis Burton	8.00	20.00
270 Rich Rollins	8.00	20.00
271 Bob Sadowski	8.00	20.00
272 Jake Wood	8.00	20.00
273 Mel Nelson	8.00	20.00
274 Checklist 4	15.00	40.00
275 John Tsitouris	8.00	20.00
276 Jose Tartabull	8.00	20.00
277 Ken Retzer	8.00	20.00
278 Bobby Shantz	8.00	20.00
279 Joe Koppe UER	8.00	20.00
Glove on wrong hand		
280 Juan Marichal	40.00	80.00
281 Jake Gibbs	8.00	20.00
Tom Metcalf		
282 Bob Bruce	8.00	20.00
283 Tom McCraw	8.00	20.00
284 Dick Schofield	8.00	20.00
285 Robin Roberts	40.00	80.00
286 Don Landrum	8.00	20.00
287 Tony Conigliaro	125.00	250.00
Bill Spanswick		
288 Al Moran	8.00	20.00
289 Frank Funk	8.00	20.00
290 Bob Allison	8.00	20.00
291 Phil Ortega	8.00	20.00
292 Mike Roarke	8.00	20.00
293 Phillies Team	12.50	30.00

Card	Low	High
294 Ken L. Hunt	8.00	20.00
295 Roger Craig	8.00	20.00
296 Ed Kirkpatrick	8.00	20.00
297 Ken MacKenzie	8.00	20.00
298 Harry Craft MG	8.00	20.00
299 Bill Stafford	8.00	20.00
300 Hank Aaron	200.00	400.00
301 Larry Brown	8.00	20.00
302 Dan Pfister	8.00	20.00
303 Jim Campbell	8.00	20.00
304 Bob Johnson	8.00	20.00
305 Jack Lamabe	8.00	20.00
306 Willie Mays	75.00	150.00
Orlando Cepeda		
307 Joe Gibbon	8.00	20.00
308 Gene Stephens	8.00	20.00
309 Paul Toth	8.00	20.00
310 Jim Gilliam	10.00	25.00
311 Tom Brown	8.00	20.00
312 Fritz Fisher	8.00	20.00
Fred Gladding		
313 Chuck Hiller	8.00	20.00
314 Jerry Buchek	8.00	20.00
315 Bo Belinsky	10.00	25.00
316 Gene Oliver	8.00	20.00
317 Al Smith	8.00	20.00
318 Minnesota Twins	12.50	30.00
Team Card		
319 Paul Brown	8.00	20.00
320 Rocky Colavito	40.00	80.00
321 Bob Lillis	8.00	20.00
322 George Brunet	8.00	20.00
323 John Buzhardt	8.00	20.00
324 Casey Stengel MG	40.00	80.00
325 Hector Lopez	8.00	20.00
326 Ron Brand	8.00	20.00
327 Don Blasingame	8.00	20.00
328 Bob Shaw	8.00	20.00
329 Russ Nixon	8.00	20.00
330 Tommy Harper	8.00	20.00
331 Roger Maris	500.00	1,000.00
Norm Cash		
Mickey Mantle		
Al Kaline		
332 Ray Washburn	8.00	20.00
333 Billy Moran	8.00	20.00
334 Lew Krausse	8.00	20.00
335 Don Mossi	8.00	20.00
336 Andre Rodgers	8.00	20.00
337 Al Ferrara	8.00	20.00
Jeff Torborg		
338 Jack Kralick	8.00	20.00
339 Walt Bond	8.00	20.00
340 Joe Cunningham	10.00	25.00
341 Jim Roland	8.00	20.00
342 Willie Stargell	75.00	150.00
343 Senators Team	12.50	30.00
344 Phil Linz	8.00	20.00
345 Frank Thomas	8.00	20.00
346 Joey Jay	8.00	20.00
347 Bobby Wine	8.00	20.00
348 Ed Lopat MG	8.00	20.00
349 Art Fowler	8.00	20.00
350 Willie McCovey	50.00	100.00
351 Dan Schneider	8.00	20.00
352 Eddie Bressoud	8.00	20.00
353 Wally Moon	8.00	20.00
354 Dave Giusti	8.00	20.00
355 Vic Power	8.00	20.00
356 Bill McCool	8.00	20.00
Chico Ruiz		
357 Charley James	8.00	20.00
358 Ron Kline	8.00	20.00
359 Jim Schaffer	8.00	20.00
360 Joe Pepitone	8.00	20.00
361 Jay Hook	8.00	20.00
362 Checklist 5	15.00	40.00
363 Dick McAuliffe	8.00	20.00
364 Joe Gaines	8.00	20.00
365 Cal McLish	8.00	20.00
366 Nelson Mathews	8.00	20.00
367 Fred Whitfield	8.00	20.00
368 Fritz Ackley	8.00	20.00
Don Buford		
369 Jerry Zimmerman	8.00	20.00
370 Hal Woodeshick	10.00	25.00

1965 Topps

The cards in this 598-card set measure 2 1/2" by 3 1/2". The cards comprising the 1965 Topps set have team names located within a distinctive pennant design below the picture. The cards have blue borders on the reverse and were issued by series. Within this last series (523-598) there are 44 cards that were printed in lesser quantities than the other cards in that series; these shorter-printed cards are marked by SP in the checklist below. Featured subsets within this set include League Leaders (1-12) and World Series cards (132-139). This was the last year Topps issued one-card penny packs. Card were also issued in five-card nickel packs. The key Rookie Cards in this set are Steve Carlton, Jim "Catfish" Hunter, Joe Morgan, Mansori Murakami and Tony Perez.

Card	Low	High
COMPLETE SET (598)	2,500.00	5,000.00
COMMON CARD (1-196)	.75	2.00
COMMON CARD (197-283)	1.00	2.50
COMMON CARD (284-370)	1.50	4.00
COMMON CARD (371-598)	3.00	8.00
WRAPPER (1-CENT)	60.00	120.00
WRAPPER (5-CENT)	50.00	100.00
1 Oliva/Howard/Brooks LL	8.00	20.00
2 Clemente/Aaron/Carty LL	20.00	50.00
3 Killebrew/Mantle/Powell LL	25.00	60.00
4 Mays/B.Will/Cepeda LL	10.00	25.00
5 Brooks/Kill/Mantle LL	25.00	60.00
6 Boyer/Mays Santo LL	8.00	20.00
7 D.Chance/J.Horlen LL	2.00	5.00
8 S.Koufax/D.Drysdale LL	8.00	20.00
9 Chance/Peters/Wick LL	2.00	5.00
10 Jackson/Sad/Marichal LL	2.00	5.00
11 Downing/Chance/Pascual LL	2.00	5.00
12 Veale/Drysdale/Gibson LL	4.00	10.00
13 Pedro Ramos	1.50	4.00
14 Len Gabrielson	.75	2.00
15 Robin Roberts	8.00	20.00
16 Joe Morgan RC DP	60.00	150.00
17 Johnny Romano	.75	2.00
18 Bill McCool	.75	2.00
19 Gates Brown	1.50	4.00
20 Jim Bunning	4.00	10.00
21 Don Blasingame	.75	2.00
22 Charlie Smith	.75	2.00
23 Bob Tiefenauer	.75	2.00
24 Minnesota Twins TC	2.50	6.00
25 Al McBean	.75	2.00
26 Bobby Knoop	.75	2.00
27 Dick Bertell	.75	2.00
28 Barney Schultz	.75	2.00
29 Felix Mantilla	.75	2.00
30 Jim Bouton	2.50	6.00
31 Mike White	.75	2.00
32 Herman Franks MG	.75	2.00
33 Jackie Brandt	.75	2.00
34 Cal Koonce	.75	2.00
35 Ed Charles	.75	2.00
36 Bobby Wine	.75	2.00
37 Fred Gladding	.75	2.00
38 Jim King	.75	2.00
39 Gerry Arrigo	.75	2.00
40 Frank Howard	2.50	6.00
41 B.Howard/M.Staehle RC	.75	2.00
42 Earl Wilson	1.50	4.00
43 Mike Shannon	1.50	4.00
44 Wade Blasingame RC	.75	2.00
45 Roy McMillan	1.50	4.00
46 Bob Lee	.75	2.00
47 Tommy Harper	1.50	4.00
48 Claude Raymond	1.50	4.00
49 C.Blefary RC/J.Miller	1.50	4.00
50 Juan Marichal	10.00	25.00
51 Bill Bryan	.75	2.00
52 Ed Roebuck	.75	2.00
53 Dick McAuliffe	1.50	4.00
54 Joe Gibbon	.75	2.00
55 Tony Conigliaro	6.00	15.00
56 Ron Kline	.75	2.00
57 St. Louis Cardinals TC	2.50	6.00
58 Fred Talbot RC	.75	2.00
59 Nate Oliver	.75	2.00
60 Jim O'Toole	1.50	4.00
61 Chris Cannizzaro	.75	2.00
62 Jim Kaat UER DP	2.50	6.00
63 Ty Cline	.75	2.00

Card	Low	High
64 Lou Burdette	1.50	4.00
65 Tony Kubek	4.00	10.00
66 Bill Rigney MG	.75	2.00
67 Harvey Haddix	1.50	4.00
68 Del Crandall	1.50	4.00
69 Bill Virdon	1.50	4.00
70 Bill Skowron	2.50	6.00
71 John O'Donoghue	.75	2.00
72 Tony Gonzalez	.75	2.00
73 Dennis Ribant RC	.75	2.00
74 R.Petrocelli RC/J.Steph RC	4.00	10.00
75 Deron Johnson	1.50	4.00
76 Sam McDowell	2.50	6.00
77 Doug Camilli	.75	2.00
78 Dal Maxvill	.75	2.00
79A Checklist 1 Cannizzaro	4.00	10.00
79B Checklist 1 C.Cannizzaro	4.00	10.00
80 Turk Farrell	.75	2.00
81 Don Buford	1.50	4.00
82 S.Alomar RC/J.Braun RC	2.50	6.00
83 George Thomas	.75	2.00
84 Ron Herbel	.75	2.00
85 Willie Smith RC	.75	2.00
86 Buster Narum	.75	2.00
87 Nelson Mathews	.75	2.00
88 Jack Lamabe	.75	2.00
89 Mike Hershberger	.75	2.00
90 Rich Rollins	1.50	4.00
91 Chicago Cubs TC	2.50	6.00
92 Dick Howser	1.50	4.00
93 Jack Fisher	.75	2.00
94 Charlie Lau	1.50	4.00
95 Bill Mazeroski DP	2.50	6.00
96 Sonny Siebert	1.50	4.00
97 Pedro Gonzalez	.75	2.00
98 Bob Miller	.75	2.00
99 Gil Hodges MG	2.50	6.00
100 Ken Boyer	4.00	10.00
101 Fred Newman	.75	2.00
102 Steve Boros	.75	2.00
103 Harvey Kuenn	1.50	4.00
104 Checklist 2	4.00	10.00
105 Chico Salmon	.75	2.00
106 Gene Oliver	.75	2.00
107 P.Corrales RC/C.Shockley RC	1.50	4.00
108 Don Mincher	.75	2.00
109 Walt Bond	.75	2.00
110 Ron Santo	2.50	6.00
111 Lee Thomas	1.50	4.00
112 Derrell Griffith RC	.75	2.00
113 Steve Barber	.75	2.00
114 Jim Hickman	1.50	4.00
115 Bobby Richardson	4.00	10.00
116 D.Dowling RC/B.Tolan RC	1.50	4.00
117 Wes Stock	.75	2.00
118 Hal Lanier RC	1.50	4.00
119 John Kennedy	.75	2.00
120 Frank Robinson	25.00	60.00
121 Gene Alley	1.50	4.00
122 Bill Pleis	.75	2.00
123 Frank Thomas	1.50	4.00
124 Tom Satriano	.75	2.00
125 Juan Pizarro	.75	2.00
126 Los Angeles Dodgers TC	2.50	6.00
127 Frank Lary	.75	2.00
128 Vic Davalillo	.75	2.00
129 Bennie Daniels	.75	2.00
130 Al Kaline	15.00	40.00
131 Johnny Keane MG	.75	2.00
132 Cards Take Opener WS1	4.00	10.00
133 Mel Stottlemyre WS2	2.50	6.00
134 Mickey Mantle WS3	30.00	80.00
135 Ken Boyer WS4	4.00	10.00
136 Tim McCarver WS5	2.50	6.00
137 Jim Bouton WS6	2.50	6.00
138 Bob Gibson WS7	5.00	12.00
139 Cards Celebrate WS	2.50	6.00
140 Dean Chance	1.50	4.00
141 Charlie James	.75	2.00
142 Bill Monbouquette	.75	2.00
143 J.Gelnar RC/J.May RC	.75	2.00
144 Ed Kranepool	1.50	4.00
145 Luis Tiant RC	12.00	30.00
146 Ron Hansen	.75	2.00
147 Dennis Bennett	.75	2.00
148 Willie Kirkland	.75	2.00
149 Wayne Schurr	.75	2.00
150 Brooks Robinson	20.00	50.00
151 Kansas City Athletics TC	2.50	6.00
152 Phil Ortega	.75	2.00
153 Norm Cash	10.00	25.00
154 Bob Humphreys RC	.75	2.00
155 Roger Maris	30.00	80.00

156 Bob Sadowski .75 2.00
157 Zoilo Versalles 1.50 4.00
158 Dick Sisler .75 2.00
159 Jim Duffalo .75 2.00
160 Roberto Clemente UER 60.00 150.00
161 Frank Baumann .75 2.00
162 Russ Nixon .75 2.00
163 Johnny Briggs .75 2.00
164 Al Spangler .75 2.00
165 Dick Ellsworth .75 2.00
166 G.Culver RC/T.Agee RC 1.50 4.00
167 Bill Wakefield .75 2.00
168 Dick Green .75 2.00
169 Dave Vineyard RC .75 2.00
170 Hank Aaron 75.00 200.00
171 Jim Roland .75 2.00
172 Jimmy Piersall 2.50 6.00
173 Detroit Tigers TC 2.50 6.00
174 Joey Jay .75 2.00
175 Bob Aspromonte .75 2.00
176 Willie McCovey 15.00 40.00
177 Pete Mikkelsen .75 2.00
178 Dalton Jones .75 2.00
179 Hal Woodeshick .75 2.00
180 Bob Allison 1.50 4.00
181 D.Loun RC/J.McCabe .75 2.00
182 Mike de la Hoz .75 2.00
183 Dave Nicholson .75 2.00
184 John Boozer .75 2.00
185 Max Alvis .75 2.00
186 Billy Cowan .75 2.00
187 Casey Stengel MG 10.00 25.00
188 Sam Bowens .75 2.00
189 Checklist 3 4.00 10.00
190 Bill White 2.50 6.00
191 Phil Regan 1.50 4.00
192 Jim Coker .75 2.00
193 Gaylord Perry 8.00 20.00
194 B.Kelso RC/R.Reichardt RC .75 2.00
195 Bob Veale 1.50 4.00
196 Ron Fairly 1.50 4.00
197 Diego Segui 1.00 2.50
198 Smoky Burgess 1.50 4.00
199 Bob Heffner 1.00 2.50
200 Joe Torre 2.50 6.00
201 S.Valdespino RC/C.Tovar RC 1.50 4.00
202 Leo Burke 1.00 2.50
203 Dallas Green 1.50 4.00
204 Russ Snyder 1.00 2.50
205 Warren Spahn 10.00 25.00
206 Willie Horton 1.50 4.00
207 Pete Rose 60.00 150.00
208 Tommy John 2.50 6.00
209 Pittsburgh Pirates TC 2.50 6.00
210 Jim Fregosi 1.50 4.00
211 Steve Ridzik 1.00 2.50
212 Ron Brand 1.00 2.50
213 Jim Davenport 1.00 2.50
214 Bob Purkey 1.00 2.50
215 Pete Ward 1.00 2.50
216 Al Worthington 1.00 2.50
217 Walter Alston MG 2.50 6.00
218 Dick Schofield 1.00 2.50
219 Bob Meyer 1.00 2.50
220 Billy Williams 4.00 10.00
221 John Tsitouris 1.00 2.50
222 Bob Tillman 1.00 2.50
223 Dan Osinski 1.00 2.50
224 Bob Chance 1.00 2.50
225 Bo Belinsky 1.50 4.00
226 E.Jimenez RC/J.Gibbs 2.50 6.00
227 Bobby Klaus 1.00 2.50
228 Jack Sanford 1.00 2.50
229 Lou Clinton 1.00 2.50
230 Ray Sadecki 1.00 2.50
231 Jerry Adair 1.00 2.50
232 Steve Blass RC 1.50 4.00
233 Don Zimmer 1.50 4.00
234 Chicago White Sox TC 2.50 6.00
235 Chuck Hinton 1.00 2.50
236 Denny McLain RC 15.00 40.00
237 Bernie Allen 1.00 2.50
238 Joe Moeller 1.00 2.50
239 Doc Edwards 1.00 2.50
240 Bob Bruce 1.00 2.50
241 Mack Jones 1.00 2.50
242 George Brunet 1.00 2.50
243 T.Davidson RC/T.Helms RC 1.50 4.00
244 Lindy McDaniel 1.50 4.00
245 Joe Pepitone 2.50 6.00
246 Tom Butters 1.50 4.00
247 Wally Moon 1.50 4.00
248 Gus Triandos 1.50 4.00
249 Dave McNally 1.50 4.00
250 Willie Mays 75.00 200.00
251 Billy Herman MG 1.50 4.00
252 Pete Richert 1.00 2.50
253 Danny Cater 1.00 2.50
254 Roland Sheldon 1.00 2.50
255 Camilo Pascual 1.50 4.00
256 Tito Francona 1.00 2.50
257 Jim Wynn 1.50 4.00
258 Larry Bearnarth 1.00 2.50
259 J.Northrup RC/R.Oyler RC 2.50 6.00
260 Don Drysdale 20.00 50.00
261 Duke Carmel 1.00 2.50
262 Bud Daley 1.00 2.50
263 Marty Keough 1.00 2.50
264 Bob Buhl 1.50 4.00
265 Jim Pagliaroni 1.00 2.50
266 Bert Campaneris RC 10.00 25.00
267 Washington Senators TC 2.50 6.00
268 Ken McBride 1.00 2.50
269 Frank Bolling 1.00 2.50
270 Milt Pappas 1.50 4.00
271 Don Wert 1.50 4.00
272 Chuck Schilling 1.00 2.50
273 Checklist 4 4.00 10.00
274 Lum Harris MG RC 1.00 2.50
275 Dick Groat 2.50 6.00
276 Hoyt Wilhelm 4.00 10.00
277 Johnny Lewis 1.00 2.50
278 Ken Retzer 1.00 2.50
279 Dick Tracewski 1.00 2.50
280 Dick Stuart 1.50 4.00
281 Bill Stafford 1.00 2.50
282 D.Est RC/M.Murakami RC 15.00 40.00
283 Fred Whitfield 1.00 2.50
284 Nick Willhite 1.50 4.00
285 Ron Hunt 1.50 4.00
286 J.Dickson/A.Monteagudo 1.50 4.00
287 Gary Kolb 1.50 4.00
288 Jack Hamilton 1.50 4.00
289 Gordy Coleman 2.50 6.00
290 Wally Bunker 2.50 6.00
291 Jerry Lynch 1.50 4.00
292 Larry Yellen 1.50 4.00
293 Los Angeles Angels TC 2.50 6.00
294 Tim McCarver 4.00 10.00
295 Dick Radatz 2.50 6.00
296 Tony Taylor 2.50 6.00
297 Dave DeBusschere 4.00 10.00
298 Jim Stewart 1.50 4.00
299 Jerry Zimmerman 1.50 4.00
300 Sandy Koufax 75.00 200.00
301 Birdie Tebbetts MG 2.50 6.00
302 Al Stanek 1.50 4.00
303 John Orsino 1.50 4.00
304 Dave Stenhouse 1.50 4.00
305 Rico Carty 2.50 6.00
306 Bubba Phillips 1.50 4.00
307 Barry Latman 1.50 4.00
308 C.Jones RC/T.Parsons 2.50 6.00
309 Steve Hamilton 2.50 6.00
310 Johnny Callison 2.50 6.00
311 Orlando Pena 1.50 4.00
312 Joe Nuxhall 1.50 4.00
313 Jim Schaffer 1.50 4.00
314 Sterling Slaughter 1.50 4.00
315 Frank Malzone 2.50 6.00
316 Cincinnati Reds TC 2.50 6.00
317 Don McMahon 1.50 4.00
318 Matty Alou 2.50 6.00
319 Ken McMullen 1.50 4.00
320 Bob Gibson 25.00 60.00
321 Rusty Staub 4.00 10.00
322 Rick Wise 2.50 6.00
323 Hank Bauer MG 2.50 6.00
324 Bobby Locke 1.50 4.00
325 Donn Clendenon 2.50 6.00
326 Dwight Siebler 1.50 4.00
327 Denis Menke 1.50 4.00
328 Eddie Fisher 1.50 4.00
329 Hawk Taylor 1.50 4.00
330 Whitey Ford 20.00 50.00
331 A.Ferrara/J.Purdin RC 2.50 6.00
332 Ted Abernathy 1.50 4.00
333 Tom Reynolds 1.50 4.00
334 Vic Roznovsky RC 1.50 4.00
335 Mickey Lolich 2.50 6.00
336 Woody Held 1.50 4.00
337 Mike Cuellar 2.50 6.00
338 Philadelphia Phillies TC 2.50 6.00
339 Ryne Duren 2.50 6.00
340 Tony Oliva 20.00 50.00
341 Bob Bolin 1.50 4.00
342 Bob Rodgers 2.50 6.00
343 Mike McCormick 2.50 6.00
344 Wes Parker 2.50 6.00
345 Floyd Robinson 1.50 4.00
346 Bobby Bragan MG 1.50 4.00
347 Roy Face 2.50 6.00
348 George Banks 1.50 4.00
349 Larry Miller RC 1.50 4.00
350 Mickey Mantle 400.00 800.00
351 Jim Perry 2.50 6.00
352 Alex Johnson RC 2.50 6.00
353 Jerry Lumpe 1.50 4.00
354 B.Ott RC/J.Warner RC 1.50 4.00
355 Vada Pinson 4.00 10.00
356 Bill Spanswick 1.50 4.00
357 Carl Warwick 1.50 4.00
358 Albie Pearson 2.50 6.00
359 Ken Johnson 1.50 4.00
360 Orlando Cepeda 6.00 15.00
361 Checklist 5 5.00 12.00
362 Don Schwall 1.50 4.00
363 Bob Johnson 1.50 4.00
364 Galen Cisco 1.50 4.00
365 Jim Gentile 2.50 6.00
366 Dan Schneider 1.50 4.00
367 Leon Wagner 1.50 4.00
368 K.Berry RC/J.Gibson RC 2.50 6.00
369 Phil Linz 2.50 6.00
370 Herman Thomas Davis 2.50 6.00
371 Frank Kreutzer 3.00 8.00
372 Clay Dalrymple 3.00 8.00
373 Curt Simmons 3.00 8.00
374 J.Cardenal RC/D.Simpson 3.00 8.00
375 Dave Wickersham 3.00 8.00
376 Jim Landis 3.00 8.00
377 Willie Stargell 15.00 40.00
378 Chuck Estrada 3.00 8.00
379 San Francisco Giants TC 3.00 8.00
380 Rocky Colavito 10.00 25.00
381 Al Jackson 3.00 8.00
382 J.C. Martin 3.00 8.00
383 Felipe Alou 6.00 15.00
384 Johnny Klippstein 3.00 8.00
385 Carl Yastrzemski 25.00 60.00
386 P.Jaeckel RC/F.Norman 3.00 8.00
387 Johnny Podres 6.00 15.00
388 John Blanchard 6.00 15.00
389 Don Larsen 6.00 15.00
390 Bill Freehan 6.00 15.00
391 Mel McGaha MG 3.00 8.00
392 Bob Friend 6.00 15.00
393 Ed Kirkpatrick 3.00 8.00
394 Jim Hannan 3.00 8.00
395 Jim Ray Hart 3.00 8.00
396 Frank Bertaina RC 3.00 8.00
397 Jerry Buchek 3.00 8.00
398 D.Neville RC/A.Shamsky RC 6.00 15.00
399 Ray Herbert 3.00 8.00
400 Harmon Killebrew 25.00 60.00
401 Carl Willey 3.00 8.00
402 Joe Amalfitano 3.00 8.00
403 Boston Red Sox TC 3.00 8.00
404 Stan Williams 3.00 8.00
405 John Roseboro 8.00 20.00
406 Ralph Terry 6.00 15.00
407 Lee Maye 3.00 8.00
408 Larry Sherry 3.00 8.00
409 J.Beauchamp RC/L.Dierker RC 6.00 15.00
410 Luis Aparicio 10.00 25.00
411 Roger Craig 6.00 15.00
412 Bob Bailey 3.00 8.00
413 Hal Reniff 3.00 8.00
414 Al Lopez MG 6.00 15.00
415 Curt Flood 8.00 20.00
416 Jim Brewer 3.00 8.00
417 Ed Brinkman 3.00 8.00
418 Johnny Edwards 3.00 8.00
419 Ruben Amaro 3.00 8.00
420 Larry Jackson 3.00 8.00
421 G.Dotter RC/J.Ward 3.00 8.00
422 Aubrey Gatewood 3.00 8.00
423 Jesse Gonder 3.00 8.00
424 Gary Bell 3.00 8.00
425 Wayne Causey 3.00 8.00
426 Milwaukee Braves TC 3.00 8.00
427 Bob Saverine 3.00 8.00
428 Bob Shaw 3.00 8.00
429 Don Demeter 3.00 8.00
430 Gary Peters 3.00 8.00
431 N.Briles RC/W.Spiezio RC 6.00 15.00
432 Jim Grant 6.00 15.00
433 John Bateman 3.00 8.00
434 Dave Morehead 3.00 8.00
435 Willie Davis 6.00 15.00
436 Don Elston 3.00 8.00
437 Chico Cardenas 6.00 15.00
438 Harry Walker MG 3.00 8.00
439 Moe Drabowsky 6.00 15.00
440 Tom Tresh 6.00 15.00
441 Denny Lemaster 3.00 8.00
442 Vic Power 3.00 8.00
443 Checklist 6 5.00 12.00
444 Bob Hendley 3.00 8.00
445 Don Lock 3.00 8.00
446 Art Mahaffey 3.00 8.00
447 Julian Javier 6.00 15.00
448 Lee Stange 3.00 8.00
449 J.Hinsley/G.Kroll RC 6.00 15.00
450 Elston Howard 6.00 15.00
451 Jim Owens 3.00 8.00
452 Gary Geiger 3.00 8.00
453 W.Crawford RC/J.Werhas 6.00 15.00
454 Ed Rakow 3.00 8.00
455 Norm Siebern 3.00 8.00
456 Bill Henry 3.00 8.00
457 Bob Kennedy MG 6.00 15.00
458 John Buzhardt 3.00 8.00
459 Frank Kostro 3.00 8.00
460 Richie Allen 15.00 40.00
461 C.Carroll RC/P.Niekro 25.00 60.00
462 Lew Krausse UER 3.00 8.00
463 Manny Mota 6.00 15.00
464 Ron Piche 3.00 8.00
465 Tom Haller 6.00 15.00
466 P.Craig RC/D.Nen 3.00 8.00
467 Ray Washburn 3.00 8.00
468 Larry Brown 3.00 8.00
469 Don Nottebart 3.00 8.00
470 Yogi Berra P/CO 25.00 60.00
471 Billy Hoeft 3.00 8.00
472 Don Pavletich 3.00 8.00
473 P.Blair RC/D.Johnson RC 6.00 15.00
474 Cookie Rojas 6.00 15.00
475 Clete Boyer 6.00 15.00
476 Billy O'Dell 3.00 8.00
477 Steve Carlton RC 75.00 200.00
478 Wilbur Wood 6.00 15.00
479 Ken Harrelson 6.00 15.00
480 Joel Horlen 3.00 8.00
481 Cleveland Indians TC 4.00 10.00
482 Bob Priddy 3.00 8.00
483 George Smith RC 3.00 8.00
484 Ron Perranoski 8.00 20.00
485 Nellie Fox P 6.00 15.00
CO
486 T.Egan/P.Rogan RC 3.00 8.00
487 Woody Woodward 6.00 15.00
488 Ted Wills 3.00 8.00
489 Gene Mauch MG 6.00 15.00
490 Earl Battey 3.00 8.00
491 Tracy Stallard 3.00 8.00
492 Gene Freese 3.00 8.00
493 B.Roman RC/B.Brubaker RC 3.00 8.00
494 Jay Ritchie RC 3.00 8.00
495 Joe Christopher 3.00 8.00
496 Joe Cunningham 3.00 8.00
497 K.Henderson RC/J.Hiatt RC 6.00 15.00
498 Gene Stephens 3.00 8.00
499 Stu Miller 6.00 15.00
500 Eddie Mathews 20.00 50.00
501 R.Gagliano RC/J.Rittwage RC 3.00 8.00
502 Don Cardwell 3.00 8.00
503 Phil Gagliano 3.00 8.00
504 Jerry Grote 6.00 15.00
505 Ray Culp 3.00 8.00
506 Sam Mele MG 3.00 8.00
507 Sammy Ellis 3.00 8.00
508 Checklist 7 5.00 12.00
509 B.Guindon RC/G.Vezendy RC 3.00 8.00
510 Ernie Banks 30.00 80.00
511 Ron Locke 3.00 8.00
512 Cap Peterson 3.00 8.00
513 New York Yankees TC 15.00 40.00
514 Joe Azcue 3.00 8.00
515 Vern Law 6.00 15.00
516 Al Weis 3.00 8.00
517 P.Schaal RC/J.Warner 3.00 8.00
518 Ken Rowe 3.00 8.00
519 Bob Uecker UER 20.00 50.00
520 Tony Cloninger 3.00 8.00
521 D.Bennett/M.Steevens RC 3.00 8.00
522 Hank Aguirre 3.00 8.00
523 Mike Brumley SP 5.00 12.00
524 Dave Giusti SP 5.00 12.00
525 Eddie Bressoud 3.00 8.00
526 J.Odom/J.Hunter SP RC 40.00 100.00
527 Jeff Torborg SP 5.00 12.00
528 George Altman 3.00 8.00
529 Jerry Fosnow SP RC 5.00 12.00
530 Jim Maloney 6.00 15.00
531 Chuck Hiller 3.00 8.00
532 Hector Lopez 6.00 15.00
533 R.Swob/T.McGraw SP RC 12.00 30.00
534 John Herrnstein 3.00 8.00
535 Jack Kralick SP 5.00 12.00
536 Andre Rodgers SP 5.00 12.00
537 Lopez/Roof/May RC 3.00 8.00
538 Chuck Dressen MG SP 5.00 12.00
539 Herm Starrette 3.00 8.00
540 Lou Brock SP 20.00 50.00
541 G.Bollo RC/B.Locker RC 3.00 8.00
542 Lou Klimchock 3.00 8.00
543 Ed Connolly SP RC 5.00 12.00
544 Howie Reed RC 3.00 8.00
545 Jesus Alou SP 6.00 15.00
546 Davis/Hed/Bark/Weav RC 3.00 8.00
547 Jake Wood SP 5.00 12.00
548 Dick Stigman 3.00 8.00
549 R.Pena RC/G.Beckert RC 8.00 20.00
550 Mel Stottlemyre SP RC 20.00 50.00
551 New York Mets TC SP 12.50 30.00
552 Julio Gotay 3.00 8.00
553 Coombs/Ratliff/McClure RC 3.00 8.00
554 Chico Ruiz SP 5.00 12.00
555 Jack Baldschun SP 5.00 12.00
556 R.Schoendienst SP 10.00 25.00
557 Jose Santiago RC 3.00 8.00
558 Tommie Sisk 3.00 8.00
559 Ed Bailey SP 5.00 12.00
560 Boog Powell SP 8.00 20.00
561 Dab/Kek/Valle/Lefebvre RC 6.00 15.00
562 Billy Moran 3.00 8.00
563 Julio Navarro 3.00 8.00
564 Mel Nelson 3.00 8.00
565 Ernie Broglio SP 5.00 12.00
566 Blanco/Moschitto/Lopez RC 5.00 12.00
567 Tommie Aaron 3.00 8.00
568 Ron Taylor SP 5.00 12.00
569 Gino Cimoli SP 5.00 12.00
570 Claude Osteen SP 6.00 15.00
571 Ossie Virgil SP 5.00 12.00
572 Baltimore Orioles TC SP 10.00 25.00
573 Jim Lonborg SP RC 10.00 25.00
574 Roy Sievers 6.00 15.00
575 Jose Pagan 3.00 8.00
576 Terry Fox SP 5.00 12.00
577 Knowles/Busch/Schein RC 5.00 12.00
578 Camilo Carreon SP 5.00 12.00
579 Dick Smith SP 5.00 12.00
580 Jimmie Hall SP 5.00 12.00
581 Tony Perez SP RC 40.00 100.00
582 Bob Schmidt SP 5.00 12.00
583 Wes Covington SP 5.00 12.00
584 Harry Bright 6.00 15.00
585 Hank Fischer 3.00 8.00
586 Tom McCraw SP UER 5.00 12.00
Name is spelled McGraw on the back
587 Joe Sparma 3.00 8.00
588 Lenny Green 3.00 8.00
589 F.Linzy RC/B.Schroder RC 5.00 12.00
590 John Wyatt 3.00 8.00
591 Bob Skinner SP 5.00 12.00
592 Frank Bork SP RC 5.00 12.00
593 J.Sullivan RC/J.Moore RC SP 5.00 12.00
594 Joe Gaines 3.00 8.00
595 Don Lee 3.00 8.00
596 Don Landrum SP 5.00 12.00
597 Nossek/Sevcik/Reese RC 3.00 8.00
598 Al Downing SP 10.00 25.00

1965 Topps Embossed

The cards in this 72-card set measure approximately 2 1/8" by 3 1/2". The 1965 Topps Embossed set contains gold foil cameo player portraits. Each league had 36 representatives set on blue backgrounds for the AL and red backgrounds for the NL. The Topps embossed set was distributed as inserts in packages of the regular 1965 baseball series.

COMPLETE SET (72) 150.00 300.00
1 Carl Yastrzemski 4.00 10.00
2 Ron Fairly .75 2.00
3 Max Alvis .75 2.00
4 Jim Ray Hart .75 2.00
5 Bill Skowron 1.25 3.00
6 Ed Kranepool .75 2.00
7 Tim McCarver 1.25 3.00
8 Sandy Koufax 8.00 20.00
9 Donn Clendenon .75 2.00
10 John Romano .75 2.00
11 Mickey Mantle 40.00 100.00
12 Joe Torre 2.00 5.00

13 Al Kaline	4.00	10.00
14 Al McBean	.75	2.00
15 Don Drysdale	2.00	5.00
16 Brooks Robinson	4.00	10.00
17 Jim Bunning	1.25	3.00
18 Gary Peters	.75	2.00
19 Roberto Clemente	20.00	50.00
20 Milt Pappas	.75	2.00
21 Wayne Causey	.75	2.00
22 Frank Robinson	2.00	5.00
23 Bill Mazeroski	2.00	5.00
24 Diego Segui	.75	2.00
25 Jim Bouton	1.25	3.00
26 Eddie Mathews	2.50	6.00
27 Willie Mays	10.00	25.00
28 Ron Santo	1.25	3.00
29 Boog Powell	1.25	3.00
30 Ken McBride	.75	2.00
31 Leon Wagner	.75	2.00
32 Johnny Callison	.75	2.00
33 Zoilo Versalles	.75	2.00
34 Jack Baldschun	.75	2.00
35 Ron Hunt	.75	2.00
36 Richie Allen	2.00	5.00
37 Frank Malzone	.75	2.00
38 Bob Allison	.75	2.00
39 Jim Fregosi	1.25	3.00
40 Billy Williams	1.25	3.00
41 Bill Freehan	1.25	3.00
42 Vada Pinson	1.25	3.00
43 Bill White	1.25	3.00
44 Roy McMillan	.75	2.00
45 Orlando Cepeda	1.25	3.00
46 Rocky Colavito	2.00	5.00
47 Ken Boyer	1.25	3.00
48 Dick Radatz	.75	2.00
49 Tommy Davis	1.25	3.00
50 Walt Bond	.75	2.00
51 John Orsino	.75	2.00
52 Joe Christopher	.75	2.00
53 Al Spangler	.75	2.00
54 Jim King	.75	2.00
55 Mickey Lolich	1.25	3.00
56 Harmon Killebrew	2.50	6.00
57 Bob Shaw	.75	2.00
58 Ernie Banks	4.00	10.00
59 Hank Aaron	15.00	40.00
60 Chuck Hinton	.75	2.00
61 Bob Aspromonte	.75	2.00
62 Lee Maye	.75	2.00
63 Joe Cunningham	.75	2.00
64 Pete Ward	.75	2.00
65 Bobby Richardson	1.25	3.00
66 Dean Chance	.75	2.00
67 Dick Ellsworth	.75	2.00
68 Jim Maloney	.75	2.00
69 Bob Gibson	2.00	5.00
70 Earl Battey	.75	2.00
71 Tony Kubek	1.25	3.00
72 Jack Kralick	.75	2.00

1965 Topps Transfers Inserts

The 1965 Topps transfers (2" by 3") were issued in series of 24 each as inserts in three of the regular 1965 Topps cards series. Thirty-six of the transfers feature blue bands at the top and bottom while 36 feature red bands at the top and bottom. The team name and position are listed in the top band while the player's name is listed in the bottom band. Transfers 1-36 have blue panels whereas 37-72 have red panels. These unnumbered transfers are ordered below alphabetically by player's name within each color group. Transfers of Bob Veale and Carl Yastrzemski are supposedly tougher to find than the others in the set; they are marked below by SP.

COMPLETE SET (72)	200.00	400.00
1 Bob Allison	1.00	2.50
2 Max Alvis	1.00	2.50
3 Luis Aparicio	2.50	6.00
4 Walt Bond	1.00	2.50
5 Jim Bouton	1.50	4.00
6 Jim Bunning	2.50	6.00
7 Rico Carty	1.50	4.00
8 Wayne Causey	1.00	2.50
9 Orlando Cepeda	2.50	6.00
10 Dean Chance	1.00	2.50
11 Tony Conigliaro	1.50	4.00
12 Bill Freehan	1.50	4.00
13 Jim Fregosi	1.50	4.00
14 Bob Gibson	4.00	10.00
15 Dick Groat	1.50	4.00
16 Tom Haller	1.00	2.50
17 Larry Jackson	1.00	2.50
18 Bobby Knoop	1.00	2.50
19 Jim Maloney	1.50	4.00
20 Juan Marichal	2.50	6.00
21 Lee Maye	1.00	2.50
22 Jim O'Toole	1.00	2.50
23 Camilo Pascual	1.00	2.50
24 Vada Pinson	1.50	4.00
25 Juan Pizarro	1.00	2.50
26 Bobby Richardson	2.50	6.00
27 Bob Rodgers	1.00	2.50
28 John Roseboro	1.00	2.50
29 Dick Stuart	1.50	4.00
30 Luis Tiant	1.50	4.00
31 Joe Torre	2.50	6.00
32 Bob Veale SP	5.00	12.00
33 Leon Wagner	1.00	2.50
34 Dave Wickersham	1.00	2.50
35 Billy Williams	2.50	6.00
36 Carl Yastrzemski SP	20.00	50.00
37 Hank Aaron	15.00	40.00
38 Richie Allen	4.00	10.00
39 Bob Aspromonte	1.00	2.50
40 Ken Boyer	2.50	6.00
41 Johnny Callison	1.50	4.00
42 Dean Chance	1.00	2.50
43 Joe Christopher	1.00	2.50
44 Roberto Clemente	30.00	60.00
45 Rocky Colavito	4.00	10.00
46 Tommy Davis	1.50	4.00
47 Don Drysdale	4.00	10.00
48 Chuck Hinton	1.00	2.50
49 Elston Howard	2.50	6.00
50 Ron Hunt	1.00	2.50
51 Al Kaline	8.00	20.00
52 Harmon Killebrew	5.00	12.00
53 Jim King	1.00	2.50
54 Ron Kline	1.00	2.50
55 Sandy Koufax	15.00	40.00
56 Ed Kranepool	1.00	2.50
57 Mickey Mantle	60.00	120.00
58 Willie Mays	15.00	40.00
59 Bill Mazeroski	4.00	10.00
60 Tony Oliva	2.50	6.00
61 Milt Pappas	1.00	2.50
62 Gary Peters	1.00	2.50
63 Boog Powell	2.50	6.00
64 Dick Radatz	1.00	2.50
65 Brooks Robinson	8.00	20.00
66 Frank Robinson	4.00	10.00
67 Ron Santo	2.50	6.00
68 Diego Segui	1.00	2.50
69 Bill Skowron	1.50	4.00
70 Al Spangler	1.00	2.50
71 Pete Ward	1.00	2.50
72 Bill White	1.50	4.00

1966 Topps

The cards in this 598-card set measure 2 1/2" by 3 1/2". There are the same number of cards as in the 1965 set. Once again, the seventh series cards (523 to 598) are considered more difficult to obtain than the cards of any other series in the set. Within this last series there are 43 cards that were printed in lesser quantities than the other cards in that series; these shorter-printed cards are marked by SP in the checklist below. Among other ways, cards were issued in five-card nickel wax packs, 12-card dime cello packs which came 36 packs to a box and 12 boxes to a case. These cards were also issued in 36-card rack packs which cost 29 cents. These rack packs were issued 48 to a case. The only featured subset within this set is League Leaders (215-226). Noteworthy Rookie Cards in the set include Jim Palmer (126), Ferguson Jenkins (254), and Don Sutton (288). Jim Palmer is described in the bio (on his card back) as a left-hander.

COMPLETE SET (598)	2,500.00	4,000.00
COMMON CARD (1-109)	.60	1.50
COMMON CARD (110-283)	.75	2.00
COMMON CARD (284-370)	1.25	3.00
COMMON CARD (371-446)	2.00	5.00
COMMON CARD (447-522)	4.00	10.00
COMMON CARD (523-598)	6.00	15.00
COMMON SP (523-598)	12.50	30.00
WRAPPER (5-CENT)	10.00	25.00
1 Willie Mays	100.00	250.00
2 Ted Abernathy	.60	1.50
3 Sam Mele MG	.60	1.50
4 Ray Culp	.60	1.50
5 Jim Fregosi	.75	2.00
6 Chuck Schilling	.60	1.50
7 Tracy Stallard	.60	1.50
8 Floyd Robinson	.60	1.50
9 Clete Boyer	.75	2.00
10 Tony Cloninger	.60	1.50
11 B.Alyea RC/P.Craig	.60	1.50
12 John Tsitouris	.60	1.50
13 Lou Johnson	.75	2.00
14 Norm Siebern	.60	1.50
15 Vern Law	.75	2.00
16 Larry Brown	.60	1.50
17 John Stephenson	.60	1.50
18 Roland Sheldon	.60	1.50
19 San Francisco Giants TC	2.00	5.00
20 Willie Horton	.75	2.00
21 Don Nottebart	.60	1.50
22 Joe Nossek	.60	1.50
23 Jack Sanford	.60	1.50
24 Don Kessinger RC	1.50	4.00
25 Pete Ward	.60	1.50
26 Ray Sadecki	.60	1.50
27 D.Knowles/A.Etchebarren RC	.60	1.50
28 Phil Niekro	8.00	20.00
29 Mike Brumley	.60	1.50
30 Pete Rose UER DP	40.00	100.00
31 Jack Cullen	.75	2.00
32 Adolfo Phillips RC	.60	1.50
33 Jim Pagliaroni	.60	1.50
34 Checklist 1	3.00	8.00
35 Ron Swoboda	1.50	4.00
36 Jim Hunter UER DP	8.00	20.00
37 Billy Herman MG	.75	2.00
38 Ron Nischwitz	.60	1.50
39 Ken Henderson	.60	1.50
40 Jim Grant	.60	1.50
41 Don LeJohn RC	.60	1.50
42 Aubrey Gatewood	.60	1.50
43A D.Landrum Dark Button	.75	2.00
43B D.Landrum Airbrush Button	8.00	20.00
43C D.Landrum No Button	.75	2.00
44 B.Davis/T.Kelley	.60	1.50
45 Jim Gentile	.75	2.00
46 Howie Koplitz	.60	1.50
47 J.C. Martin	.60	1.50
48 Paul Blair	.75	2.00
49 Woody Woodward	.75	2.00
50 Mickey Mantle DP	150.00	400.00
51 Gordon Richardson RC	.60	1.50
52 W.Covington/J.Callison	1.50	4.00
53 Bob Duliba	.60	1.50
54 Jose Pagan	.60	1.50
55 Ken Harrelson	.75	2.00
56 Sandy Valdespino	.60	1.50
57 Jim Lefebvre	.75	2.00
58 Dave Wickersham	.60	1.50
59 Cincinnati Reds TC	2.00	5.00
60 Curt Flood	1.50	4.00
61 Bob Bolin	.60	1.50
62A Merritt Ranew Sold Line	.75	2.00
62B Merritt Ranew NTR	12.50	30.00
63 Jim Stewart	.60	1.50
64 Bob Bruce	.60	1.50
65 Leon Wagner	.60	1.50
66 Al Weis	.60	1.50
67 C.Jones/D.Selma RC	1.50	4.00
68 Hal Reniff	.60	1.50
69 Ken Hamlin	.60	1.50
70 Carl Yastrzemski	25.00	60.00
71 Frank Carpin RC	.60	1.50
72 Tony Perez	20.00	50.00
73 Jerry Zimmerman	.60	1.50
74 Don Mossi	.75	2.00
75 Tommy Davis	.75	2.00
76 Red Schoendienst MG	1.50	4.00
77 John Orsino	.60	1.50
78 Frank Linzy	.60	1.50
79 Joe Pepitone	1.50	4.00
80 Richie Allen	2.50	6.00
81 Ray Oyler	.60	1.50
82 Bob Hendley	.60	1.50
83 Albie Pearson	.75	2.00
84 J.Beauchamp/D.Kelley	.60	1.50
85 Eddie Fisher	.60	1.50
86 John Bateman	.60	1.50
87 Dan Napoleon	.60	1.50
88 Fred Whitfield	.60	1.50
89 Ted Davidson	.60	1.50
90 Luis Aparicio	3.00	8.00
91A Bob Uecker TR	4.00	10.00
91B Bob Uecker NTR	15.00	40.00
92 New York Yankees TC	6.00	15.00
93 Jim Lonborg DP	.75	2.00
94 Matty Alou	.75	2.00
95 Pete Richert	.60	1.50
96 Felipe Alou	1.50	4.00
97 Jim Merritt RC	.60	1.50
98 Don Demeter	.60	1.50
99 W.Stargell/D.Clendenon	2.50	6.00
100 Sandy Koufax	50.00	100.00
101A Checklist 2 Spahn ERR	6.00	15.00
101B Cheklist 2 Henry COR	4.00	10.00
102 Ed Kirkpatrick	.60	1.50
103A Dick Groat TR	.75	2.00
103B Dick Groat NTR	15.00	40.00
104A Alex Johnson TR	.75	2.00
104B Alex Johnson NTR	12.50	30.00
105 Milt Pappas	.75	2.00
106 Rusty Staub	1.50	4.00
107 L.Stahl RC/R.Tompkins RC	.60	1.50
108 Bobby Klaus	.60	1.50
109 Ralph Terry	.75	2.00
110 Ernie Banks	25.00	60.00
111 Gary Peters	.75	2.00
112 Manny Mota	1.50	4.00
113 Hank Aguirre	.75	2.00
114 Jim Gosger	.75	2.00
115 Bill Henry	.75	2.00
116 Walter Alston MG	2.50	6.00
117 Jake Gibbs	.75	2.00
118 Mike McCormick	.75	2.00
119 Art Shamsky	.75	2.00
120 Harmon Killebrew	12.00	30.00
121 Ray Herbert	.75	2.00
122 Joe Gaines	.75	2.00
123 F.Bork/J.May	.75	2.00
124 Tug McGraw	1.50	4.00
125 Lou Brock	20.00	50.00
126 Jim Palmer UER RC	50.00	100.00
127 Ken Berry	.75	2.00
128 Jim Landis	.75	2.00
129 Jack Kralick	.75	2.00
130 Joe Torre	2.50	6.00
131 California Angels TC	2.00	5.00
132 Orlando Cepeda	3.00	8.00
133 Don McMahon	.75	2.00
134 Wes Parker	1.50	4.00
135 Dave Morehead	.75	2.00
136 Woody Held	.75	2.00
137 Pat Corrales	.75	2.00
138 Roger Repoz RC	.75	2.00
139 B.Browne RC/D.Young RC	.75	2.00
140 Jim Maloney	1.50	4.00
141 Tom McCraw	.75	2.00
142 Don Dennis RC	.75	2.00
143 Jose Tartabull	1.50	4.00
144 Don Schwall	.75	2.00
145 Bill Freehan	1.50	4.00
146 George Altman	.75	2.00
147 Lum Harris MG	.75	2.00
148 Bob Johnson	.75	2.00
149 Dick Nen	.75	2.00
150 Rocky Colavito	3.00	8.00
151 Gary Wagner RC	.75	2.00
152 Frank Malzone	1.50	4.00
153 Rico Carty	1.50	4.00
154 Chuck Hiller	.75	2.00
155 Marcelino Lopez	.75	2.00
156 D.Schofield/H.Lanier	.75	2.00
157 Rene Lachemann	.75	2.00
158 Jim Brewer	.75	2.00
159 Chico Ruiz	.75	2.00
160 Whitey Ford	20.00	50.00
161 Jerry Lumpe	.75	2.00
162 Lee Maye	.75	2.00
163 Tito Francona	.75	2.00
164 T.Agee/M.Staehle	1.50	4.00
165 Don Lock	.75	2.00
166 Chris Krug RC	.75	2.00
167 Boog Powell	2.50	6.00
168 Dan Osinski	.75	2.00
169 Duke Sims RC	.75	2.00
170 Cookie Rojas	1.50	4.00
171 Nick Willhite	.75	2.00
172 New York Mets TC	2.00	5.00
173 Al Spangler	.75	2.00
174 Ron Taylor	.75	2.00
175 Bert Campaneris	1.50	4.00
176 Jim Davenport	.75	2.00
177 Hector Lopez	.75	2.00
178 Bob Tillman	.75	2.00
179 D.Aust RC/B.Tolan	1.50	4.00
180 Vada Pinson	1.50	4.00
181 Al Worthington	.75	2.00
182 Jerry Lynch	.75	2.00
183A Checklist 3 Large Print	3.00	8.00
183B Checklist 3 Small Print	3.00	8.00
184 Denis Menke	.75	2.00
185 Bob Buhl	1.50	4.00
186 Ruben Amaro	.75	2.00
187 Chuck Dressen MG	1.50	4.00
188 Al Luplow	.75	2.00
189 John Roseboro	1.50	4.00
190 Jimmie Hall	.75	2.00
191 Darrell Sutherland RC	.75	2.00
192 Vic Power	1.50	4.00
193 Dave McNally	1.50	4.00
194 Washington Senators TC	2.00	5.00
195 Joe Morgan	25.00	60.00
196 Don Pavletich	.75	2.00
197 Sonny Siebert	.75	2.00
198 Mickey Stanley RC	2.50	6.00
199 Skowron/Romano/Robinson	1.50	4.00
200 Eddie Mathews	6.00	15.00
201 Jim Dickson	.75	2.00
202 Clay Dalrymple	.75	2.00
203 Jose Santiago	.75	2.00
204 Chicago Cubs TC	2.00	5.00
205 Tom Tresh	1.50	4.00
206 Al Jackson	.75	2.00
207 Frank Quilici RC	.75	2.00
208 Bob Miller	.75	2.00
209 F.Fisher/J.Hiller RC	1.50	4.00
210 Bill Mazeroski	3.00	8.00
211 Frank Kreutzer	.75	2.00
212 Ed Kranepool	1.50	4.00
213 Fred Newman	.75	2.00
214 Tommy Harper	1.50	4.00
215 Clemente/Aaron/Mays LL	30.00	80.00
216 Oliva/Yaz/Davalillo LL	2.00	5.00
217 Mays/McCovey/B.Will LL	10.00	25.00
218 Conigliaro/Cash/Horton LL	2.00	5.00
219 Johnson/F.Rob/Mays LL	10.00	25.00
220 Colavito/Horton/Oliva LL	2.00	5.00
221 Koufax/Marichal/Law LL	5.00	12.00
222 McDowell/Fisher/Siebert LL	2.00	5.00
223 Koufax/Clon/Drysdale LL	8.00	20.00
224 Grant/Stottlemyre/Kaat LL	2.00	5.00
225 Koufax/Veale/Gibson LL	12.00	30.00
226 McDowell/Lolich/McLain LL	2.00	5.00
227 Russ Nixon	.75	2.00
228 Larry Dierker	1.50	4.00
229 Hank Bauer MG	1.50	4.00
230 Johnny Callison	1.50	4.00
231 Floyd Weaver	.75	2.00
232 Glenn Beckert	1.50	4.00
233 Dom Zanni	.75	2.00
234 R.Beck RC/R.White RC	3.00	8.00
235 Don Cardwell	.75	2.00
236 Mike Hershberger	.75	2.00
237 Billy O'Dell	.75	2.00
238 Los Angeles Dodgers TC	2.00	5.00
239 Orlando Pena	.75	2.00
240 Earl Battey	.75	2.00
241 Dennis Ribant	.75	2.00
242 Jesus Alou	.75	2.00
243 Nelson Briles	1.50	4.00
244 C.Harrison RC//S.Jackson	.75	2.00
245 John Buzhardt	.75	2.00
246 Ed Bailey	.75	2.00
247 Carl Warwick	.75	2.00
248 Pete Mikkelsen	.75	2.00
249 Bill Rigney MG	.75	2.00
250 Sammy Ellis	.75	2.00
251 Ed Brinkman	.75	2.00
252 Denny Lemaster	.75	2.00
253 Don Wert	.75	2.00
254 Fergie Jenkins RC	30.00	80.00
255 Willie Stargell	15.00	40.00
256 Lew Krausse	.75	2.00
257 Jeff Torborg	1.50	4.00
258 Dave Giusti	.75	2.00
259 Boston Red Sox TC	2.00	5.00
260 Bob Shaw	.75	2.00
261 Ron Hansen	.75	2.00
262 Jack Hamilton	.75	2.00
263 Tom Egan	.75	2.00
264 A.Kosco RC/T.Uhlaender RC	.75	2.00
265 Stu Miller	1.50	4.00
266 Pedro Gonzalez UER	.75	2.00
267 Joe Sparma	.75	2.00
268 John Blanchard	.75	2.00

269 Don Heffner MG .75 2.00
270 Claude Osteen 1.50 4.00
271 Hal Lanier .75 2.00
272 Jack Baldschun .75 2.00
273 B.Aspromonte/R.Staub 1.50 4.00
274 Buster Narum .75 2.00
275 Tim McCarver 1.50 4.00
276 Jim Bouton 1.50 4.00
277 George Thomas .75 2.00
278 Cal Koonce .75 2.00
279A Checklist 4 Black Cap 3.00 8.00
279B Checklist 4 Red Cap 3.00 8.00
280 Bobby Knoop .75 2.00
281 Bruce Howard .75 2.00
282 Johnny Lewis .75 2.00
283 Jim Perry 1.50 4.00
284 Bobby Wine 1.25 3.00
285 Luis Tiant 2.00 5.00
286 Gary Geiger 1.25 3.00
287 Jack Aker RC 1.25 3.00
288 D.Sutton RC/B.Singer RC 25.00 60.00
289 Larry Sherry 1.25 3.00
290 Ron Santo 2.00 5.00
291 Moe Drabowsky 2.00 5.00
292 Jim Coker 1.25 3.00
293 Mike Shannon 2.00 5.00
294 Steve Ridzik 1.25 3.00
295 Jim Ray Hart 2.00 5.00
296 Johnny Keane MG 2.00 5.00
297 Jim Owens 1.25 3.00
298 Rico Petrocelli 2.00 5.00
299 Lew Burdette 2.00 5.00
300 Bob Clemente 60.00 150.00
301 Greg Bollo 1.25 3.00
302 Ernie Bowman 1.25 3.00
303 Cleveland Indians TC 2.00 5.00
304 John Herrnstein 1.25 3.00
305 Camilo Pascual 2.00 5.00
306 Ty Cline 1.25 3.00
307 Clay Carroll 2.00 5.00
308 Tom Haller 2.00 5.00
309 Diego Segui 1.25 3.00
310 Frank Robinson 15.00 40.00
311 T.Helms/D.Simpson 2.00 5.00
312 Bob Saverine 1.25 3.00
313 Chris Zachary 1.25 3.00
314 Hector Valle 1.25 3.00
315 Norm Cash 2.00 5.00
316 Jack Fisher 1.25 3.00
317 Dalton Jones 1.25 3.00
318 Harry Walker MG 1.25 3.00
319 Gene Freese 1.25 3.00
320 Bob Gibson 20.00 50.00
321 Rick Reichardt 1.25 3.00
322 Bill Faul 1.25 3.00
323 Ray Barker 1.25 3.00
324 John Boozer UER 1.25 3.00
1965 Record is incorrect
325 Vic Davalillo 1.25 3.00
326 Atlanta Braves TC 2.00 5.00
327 Bernie Allen 1.25 3.00
328 Jerry Grote 2.00 5.00
329 Pete Charton 1.25 3.00
330 Ron Fairly 2.00 5.00
331 Ron Herbel 1.25 3.00
332 Bill Bryan 1.25 3.00
333 J.Coleman RC/J.French RC 1.25 3.00
334 Marty Keough 1.25 3.00
335 Juan Pizarro 1.25 3.00
336 Gene Alley 2.00 5.00
337 Fred Gladding 1.25 3.00
338 Dal Maxvill 1.25 3.00
339 Del Crandall 2.00 5.00
340 Dean Chance 2.00 5.00
341 Wes Westrum MG 2.00 5.00
342 Bob Humphreys 1.25 3.00
343 Joe Christopher 1.25 3.00
344 Steve Blass 2.00 5.00
345 Bob Allison 2.00 5.00
346 Mike de la Hoz 1.25 3.00
347 Phil Regan 2.00 5.00
348 Baltimore Orioles TC 3.00 8.00
349 Cap Peterson 1.25 3.00
350 Mel Stottlemyre 3.00 8.00
351 Fred Valentine 1.25 3.00
352 Bob Aspromonte 1.25 3.00
353 Al McBean 1.25 3.00
354 Smoky Burgess 2.00 5.00
355 Wade Blasingame 1.25 3.00
356 O.Johnson RC/K.Sanders RC 1.25 3.00
357 Gerry Arrigo 1.25 3.00
358 Charlie Smith 1.25 3.00
359 Johnny Briggs 1.25 3.00
360 Ron Hunt 1.25 3.00
361 Tom Satriano 1.25 3.00
362 Gates Brown 2.00 5.00
363 Checklist 5 4.00 10.00
364 Nate Oliver 1.25 3.00
365 Roger Maris UER 40.00 100.00
366 Wayne Causey 1.25 3.00
367 Mel Nelson 1.25 3.00
368 Charlie Lau 2.00 5.00
369 Jim King 1.25 3.00
370 Chico Cardenas 1.25 3.00
371 Lee Stange 2.00 5.00
372 Harvey Kuenn 3.00 8.00
373 J.Hiatt/D.Estelle 3.00 8.00
374 Bob Locker 2.00 5.00
375 Donn Clendenon 3.00 8.00
376 Paul Schaal 2.00 5.00
377 Turk Farrell 2.00 5.00
378 Dick Tracewski 2.00 5.00
379 St. Louis Cardinals TC 4.00 10.00
380 Tony Conigliaro 4.00 10.00
381 Hank Fischer 2.00 5.00
382 Phil Roof 2.00 5.00
383 Jackie Brandt 2.00 5.00
384 Al Downing 3.00 8.00
385 Ken Boyer 4.00 10.00
386 Gil Hodges MG 3.00 8.00
387 Howie Reed 2.00 5.00
388 Don Mincher 2.00 5.00
389 Jim O'Toole 3.00 8.00
390 Brooks Robinson 20.00 50.00
391 Chuck Hinton 2.00 5.00
392 B.Hands RC/R.Hundley RC 3.00 8.00
393 George Brunet 2.00 5.00
394 Ron Brand 2.00 5.00
395 Len Gabrielson 2.00 5.00
396 Jerry Stephenson 2.00 5.00
397 Bill White 3.00 8.00
398 Danny Cater 2.00 5.00
399 Ray Washburn 2.00 5.00
400 Zoilo Versalles 3.00 8.00
401 Ken McMullen 2.00 5.00
402 Jim Hickman 2.00 5.00
403 Fred Talbot 2.00 5.00
404 Pittsburgh Pirates TC 4.00 10.00
405 Elston Howard 3.00 8.00
406 Joey Jay 2.00 5.00
407 John Kennedy 2.00 5.00
408 Lee Thomas 3.00 8.00
409 Billy Hoeft 2.00 5.00
410 Al Kaline 15.00 40.00
411 Gene Mauch MG 2.00 5.00
412 Sam Bowens 2.00 5.00
413 Johnny Romano 2.00 5.00
414 Dan Coombs 2.00 5.00
415 Max Alvis 2.00 5.00
416 Phil Ortega 2.00 5.00
417 J.McGlothlin RC/E.Sukla RC 2.00 5.00
418 Phil Gagliano 2.00 5.00
419 Mike Ryan 2.00 5.00
420 Juan Marichal 6.00 15.00
421 Roy McMillan 3.00 8.00
422 Ed Charles 2.00 5.00
423 Ernie Broglio 2.00 5.00
424 L.May RC/D.Osteen RC 4.00 10.00
425 Bob Veale 3.00 8.00
426 Chicago White Sox TC 4.00 10.00
427 John Miller 2.00 5.00
428 Sandy Alomar 2.00 5.00
429 Bill Monbouquette 2.00 5.00
430 Don Drysdale 12.00 30.00
431 Walt Bond 2.00 5.00
432 Bob Heffner 2.00 5.00
433 Alvin Dark MG 3.00 8.00
434 Willie Kirkland 2.00 5.00
435 Jim Bunning 6.00 15.00
436 Julian Javier 3.00 8.00
437 Al Stanek 2.00 5.00
438 Willie Smith 2.00 5.00
439 Pedro Ramos 2.00 5.00
440 Deron Johnson 3.00 8.00
441 Tommie Sisk 2.00 5.00
442 E.Barnowski RC/E.Watt RC 2.00 5.00
443 Bill Wakefield 2.00 5.00
444 Checklist 6 4.00 10.00
445 Jim Kaat 4.00 10.00
446 Mack Jones 2.00 5.00
447 D.Ellsw UER Hubbs 6.00 15.00
448 Eddie Stanky MG 4.00 10.00
449 Joe Moeller 4.00 10.00
450 Tony Oliva 6.00 15.00
451 Barry Latman 4.00 10.00
452 Joe Azcue 4.00 10.00
453 Ron Kline 4.00 10.00
454 Jerry Buchek 4.00 10.00
455 Mickey Lolich 6.00 15.00
456 D.Brandon RC/J.Foy RC 4.00 10.00
457 Joe Gibbon 4.00 10.00
458 Manny Jiminez 4.00 10.00
459 Bill McCool 4.00 10.00
460 Curt Blefary 4.00 10.00
461 Roy Face 6.00 15.00
462 Bob Rodgers 4.00 10.00
463 Philadelphia Phillies TC 6.00 15.00
464 Larry Bearnarth 4.00 10.00
465 Don Buford 4.00 10.00
466 Ken Johnson 4.00 10.00
467 Vic Roznovsky 4.00 10.00
468 Johnny Podres 6.00 15.00
469 B.Murcer RC/D.Womack RC 15.00 40.00
470 Sam McDowell 6.00 15.00
471 Bob Skinner 4.00 10.00
472 Terry Fox 4.00 10.00
473 Rich Rollins 4.00 10.00
474 Dick Schofield 4.00 10.00
475 Dick Radatz 4.00 10.00
476 Bobby Bragan MG 4.00 10.00
477 Steve Barber 4.00 10.00
478 Tony Gonzalez 4.00 10.00
479 Jim Hannan 4.00 10.00
480 Dick Stuart 4.00 10.00
481 Bob Lee 4.00 10.00
482 J.Boccabella/D.Dowling 4.00 10.00
483 Joe Nuxhall 4.00 10.00
484 Wes Covington 4.00 10.00
485 Bob Bailey 4.00 10.00
486 Tommy John 6.00 15.00
487 Al Ferrara 4.00 10.00
488 George Banks 4.00 10.00
489 Curt Simmons 4.00 10.00
490 Bobby Richardson 10.00 25.00
491 Dennis Bennett 4.00 10.00
492 Kansas City Athletics TC 6.00 15.00
493 Johnny Klippstein 4.00 10.00
494 Gordy Coleman 4.00 10.00
495 Dick McAuliffe 6.00 15.00
496 Lindy McDaniel 4.00 10.00
497 Chris Cannizzaro 4.00 10.00
498 L.Walker RC/W.Fryman RC 4.00 10.00
499 Wally Bunker 4.00 10.00
500 Hank Aaron 60.00 150.00
501 John O'Donoghue 4.00 10.00
502 Lenny Green UER 4.00 10.00
503 Steve Hamilton 6.00 15.00
504 Grady Hatton MG 4.00 10.00
505 Jose Cardenal 4.00 10.00
506 Bo Belinsky 6.00 15.00
507 Johnny Edwards 4.00 10.00
508 Steve Hargan RC 6.00 15.00
509 Jake Wood 4.00 10.00
510 Hoyt Wilhelm 10.00 25.00
511 B.Barton RC/T.Fuentes RC 4.00 10.00
512 Dick Stigman 4.00 10.00
513 Camilo Carreon 4.00 10.00
514 Hal Woodeshick 4.00 10.00
515 Frank Howard 6.00 15.00
516 Eddie Bressoud 4.00 10.00
517A Checklist 7 White Sox 6.00 15.00
517B Checklist 7 W.Sox 6.00 15.00
518 H.Hippauf RC/A.Umbach RC 4.00 10.00
519 Bob Friend 6.00 15.00
520 Jim Wynn 6.00 15.00
521 John Wyatt 4.00 10.00
522 Phil Linz 4.00 10.00
523 Bob Sadowski 4.00 10.00
524 O.Brown RC/D.Mason RC SP 20.00 50.00
525 Gary Bell SP 12.50 30.00
526 Minnesota Twins TC SP 50.00 100.00
527 Julio Navarro 6.00 15.00
528 Jesse Gonder SP 12.50 30.00
529 Elia/Higgins/Voss RC 6.00 15.00
530 Robin Roberts 20.00 50.00
531 Joe Cunningham 6.00 15.00
532 A.Monteagudo SP 12.50 30.00
533 Jerry Adair SP 12.50 30.00
534 D.Eilers RC/R.Gardner RC 6.00 15.00
535 Willie Davis SP 15.00 40.00
536 Dick Egan 6.00 15.00
537 Herman Franks MG 6.00 15.00
538 Bob Allen SP 12.50 30.00
539 B.Heath RC/C.Sembera RC 10.00 25.00
540 Denny McLain SP 40.00 100.00
541 Gene Oliver SP 12.50 30.00
542 George Smith 6.00 15.00
543 Roger Craig SP 12.50 30.00
544 Hoerner/Kernek/Williams RC SP 12.50 30.00
545 Dick Green SP 12.50 30.00
546 Dwight Siebler 10.00 25.00
547 Horace Clarke SP RC 50.00 120.00
548 Gary Kroll SP 12.50 30.00
549 A.Closter RC/C.Cox RC 6.00 15.00
550 Willie McCovey SP 50.00 100.00
551 Bob Purkey SP 12.50 30.00
552 B.Tebbetts MG SP 12.50 30.00
553 P.Garrett RC/J.Warner 6.00 15.00
554 Jim Northrup SP 12.50 30.00
555 Ron Perranoski SP 12.50 30.00
556 Mel Queen SP 12.50 30.00
557 Felix Mantilla SP 12.50 30.00
558 Grilli/Magrini/Scott RC 8.00 20.00
559 Roberto Pena SP 12.50 30.00
560 Joel Horlen 6.00 15.00
561 Choo Choo Coleman SP 50.00 120.00
562 Russ Snyder 10.00 25.00
563 P.Cimino RC/C.Tovar RC 6.00 15.00
564 Bob Chance SP 12.50 30.00
565 Jimmy Piersall SP 15.00 40.00
566 Mike Cuellar SP 12.50 30.00
567 Dick Howser SP 15.00 40.00
568 P.Lindblad RC/R.Stone RC 6.00 15.00
569 Orlando McFarlane SP 12.50 30.00
570 Art Mahaffey SP 12.50 30.00
571 Dave Roberts SP 12.50 30.00
572 Bob Priddy 6.00 15.00
573 Derrell Griffith 6.00 15.00
574 B.Hepler RC/B.Murphy RC 6.00 15.00
575 Earl Wilson 6.00 15.00
576 Dave Nicholson SP 12.50 30.00
577 Jack Lamabe SP 12.50 30.00
578 Chi Chi Olivo SP RC 12.50 30.00
579 Bertaina/Brabender/Johnson RC 8.00 20.00
580 Billy Williams SP 30.00 60.00
581 Tony Martinez 6.00 15.00
582 Garry Roggenburk 6.00 15.00
583 Tigers TC SP UER 60.00 120.00
584 F.Fernandez RC/F.Peterson RC 6.00 15.00
585 Tony Taylor 10.00 25.00
586 Claude Raymond SP 12.50 30.00
587 Dick Bertell 6.00 15.00
588 C.Dobson RC/K.Suarez RC 6.00 15.00
589 Lou Klimchock SP 12.50 30.00
590 Bill Skowron SP 15.00 40.00
591 B.Shirley RC/G.Jackson RC SP 100.00 250.00
592 Andre Rodgers 6.00 15.00
593 Doug Camilli SP 12.50 30.00
594 Chico Salmon 6.00 15.00
595 Larry Jackson 6.00 15.00
596 N.Colbert RC/G.Sims RC SP 12.50 30.00
597 John Sullivan 6.00 15.00
598 Gaylord Perry SP 60.00 150.00

1966 Topps Rub-Offs

There are 120 "rub-offs" in the Topps insert set of 1966, of which 100 depict players and the remaining 20 show team pennants. Each rub off measures 2 1/16" by 3". The color player photos are vertical while the team pennants are horizontal; both types of transfer have a large black printer's mark. These rub-offs were originally printed in rolls of 20 and are frequently still found this way. These rub-offs were issued one per wax pack and three per rack pack. Since these rub-offs are unnumbered, they are ordered below alphabetically within type, players (1-100) and team pennants (101-120).

COMPLETE SET (120) 200.00 400.00
COMMON RUB-OFF (1-120) .60 1.50
COMMON PEN. (101-120) .40 1.00
1 Hank Aaron 10.00 25.00
2 Jerry Adair .60 1.50
3 Richie Allen .75 2.00
4 Jesus Alou .75 2.00
5 Max Alvis .60 1.50
6 Bob Aspromonte .60 1.50
7 Ernie Banks 4.00 10.00
8 Earl Battey .60 1.50
9 Curt Blefary .60 1.50
10 Ken Boyer 1.25 3.00
11 Bob Bruce .60 1.50
12 Jim Bunning 1.25 3.00
13 Johnny Callison .75 2.00
14 Bert Campaneris .75 2.00
15 Jose Cardenal .60 1.50
16 Dean Chance .75 2.00
17 Ed Charles .60 1.50
18 Roberto Clemente 30.00 60.00
19 Tony Cloninger .60 1.50
20 Rocky Colavito 2.00 5.00
21 Tony Conigliaro .75 2.00
22 Vic Davalillo .60 1.50
23 Willie Davis .75 2.00
24 Don Drysdale 2.00 5.00
25 Sammy Ellis .60 1.50
26 Dick Ellsworth .60 1.50
27 Ron Fairly .75 2.00
28 Dick Farrell .60 1.50
29 Eddie Fisher .60 1.50
30 Jack Fisher .60 1.50
31 Curt Flood .75 2.00
32 Whitey Ford 2.00 5.00
33 Bill Freehan .75 2.00
34 Jim Fregosi .75 2.00
35 Bob Gibson 2.00 5.00
36 Jim Grant .60 1.50
37 Jimmie Hall .60 1.50
38 Ken Harrelson .75 2.00
39 Jim Ray Hart .60 1.50
40 Joel Horlen .60 1.50
41 Willie Horton .75 2.00
42 Frank Howard .75 2.00
43 Deron Johnson .60 1.50
44 Al Kaline 4.00 10.00
45 Harmon Killebrew 3.00 8.00
46 Bobby Knoop .60 1.50
47 Sandy Koufax 8.00 20.00
48 Ed Kranepool .60 1.50
49 Gary Kroll .60 1.50
50 Don Landrum .60 1.50
51 Vern Law .75 2.00
52 Johnny Lewis .60 1.50
53 Don Lock .60 1.50
54 Mickey Lolich .75 2.00
55 Jim Maloney .75 2.00
56 Felix Mantilla .60 1.50
57 Mickey Mantle 30.00 60.00
58 Juan Marichal 2.00 5.00
59 Eddie Mathews 3.00 8.00
60 Willie Mays 10.00 25.00
61 Bill Mazeroski 2.00 5.00
62 Dick McAuliffe .60 1.50
63 Tim McCarver .75 2.00
64 Willie McCovey 2.00 5.00
65 Sam McDowell .75 2.00
66 Ken McMullen .60 1.50
67 Denis Menke .60 1.50
68 Bill Monbouquette .60 1.50
69 Joe Morgan 2.00 5.00
70 Fred Newman .60 1.50
71 John O'Donoghue .60 1.50
72 Tony Oliva 1.25 3.00
73 Johnny Orsino .60 1.50
74 Phil Ortega .60 1.50
75 Milt Pappas .75 2.00
76 Dick Radatz .75 2.00
77 Bobby Richardson 1.25 3.00
78 Pete Richert .60 1.50
79 Brooks Robinson 4.00 10.00
80 Floyd Robinson .60 1.50
81 Frank Robinson 2.00 5.00
82 Cookie Rojas .60 1.50
83 Pete Rose 12.50 30.00
84 John Roseboro .75 2.00
85 Ron Santo 1.25 3.00
86 Bill Skowron .75 2.00
87 Willie Stargell 2.00 5.00
88 Mel Stottlemyre .75 2.00
89 Dick Stuart .60 1.50
90 Ron Swoboda .75 2.00
91 Fred Talbot .60 1.50
92 Ralph Terry .75 2.00
93 Joe Torre 2.00 5.00
94 Tom Tresh 1.25 3.00
95 Bob Veale .60 1.50
96 Pete Ward .60 1.50
97 Bill White .75 2.00
98 Billy Williams 1.25 3.00
99 Jim Wynn .75 2.00
100 Carl Yastrzemski 5.00 12.00
101 Baltimore Orioles 1.00 2.50
102 Boston Red Sox 1.00 2.50
103 California Angels .40 1.00
104 Chicago Cubs .40 1.00
105 Chicago White Sox .40 1.00
106 Cincinnati Reds .40 1.00
107 Cleveland Indians .40 1.00
108 Detroit Tigers 1.00 2.50

109 Houston Astros	.40	1.00
110 Kansas City Athletics	.40	1.00
111 Los Angeles Dodgers	1.00	2.50
112 Atlanta Braves	.40	1.00
113 Minnesota Twins	.40	1.00
114 New York Mets	1.00	2.50
115 New York Yankees	1.50	4.00
116 Philadelphia Phillies	.40	1.00
117 Pittsburgh Pirates	.40	1.00
118 San Francisco Giants	.40	1.00
119 St. Louis Cardinals	.40	1.00
120 Washington Senators	1.00	2.50

1966 Topps Venezuelan

This set is a parallel version of the first 370 cards of the regular 1966 Topps set and is similar in design. The cards were issued for the Venezuelan market. The backs of these cards are noticably darker than their American counterparts.

COMPLETE SET (370)	4,000.00	8,000.00
1 Willie Mays	500.00	1,000.00
2 Ted Abernathy	6.00	15.00
3 Sam Mele MG	6.00	15.00
4 Ray Culp	6.00	15.00
5 Jim Fregosi	6.00	15.00
6 Chuck Schilling	6.00	15.00
7 Tracy Stallard	6.00	15.00
8 Floyd Robinson	6.00	15.00
9 Clete Boyer	8.00	20.00
10 Tony Cloninger	6.00	15.00
11 Brant Alyea	6.00	15.00
Pete Craig		
12 John Tsitouris	6.00	15.00
13 Lou Johnson	6.00	15.00
14 Norm Siebern	6.00	15.00
15 Vern Law	6.00	15.00
16 Larry Brown	6.00	15.00
17 John Stephenson	6.00	15.00
18 Roland Sheldon	6.00	15.00
19 San Francisco Giants	10.00	25.00
Team Card		
20 Willie Horton	8.00	20.00
21 Don Nottebart	6.00	15.00
22 Joe Nossek	6.00	15.00
23 Jack Sanford	6.00	15.00
24 Don Kessinger	8.00	20.00
25 Pete Ward	6.00	15.00
26 Ray Sadecki	6.00	15.00
27 Darold Knowles	6.00	15.00
Andy Etchebarren		
28 Phil Niekro	60.00	120.00
29 Mike Brumley	6.00	15.00
30 Pete Rose	150.00	300.00
31 Jack Cullen	6.00	15.00
32 Dolfo Phillips	6.00	15.00
33 Jim Pagliaroni	6.00	15.00
34 Checklist 1	12.50	30.00
35 Ron Swoboda	6.00	15.00
36 Jim Hunter UER		
(Stats say 1963 and 1964, should b	60.00	120.00
37 Billy Herman MG	8.00	20.00
38 Ron Nischwitz	6.00	15.00
39 Ken Henderson	6.00	15.00
40 Jim Grant	6.00	15.00
41 Don LeJohn	6.00	15.00
42 Aubrey Gatewood	6.00	15.00
43 Don Landrum	6.00	15.00
44 Bill Davis	6.00	15.00
Tom Kelley		
45 Jim Gentile	6.00	15.00
46 Howie Koplitz	6.00	15.00
47 J.C. Martin	6.00	15.00
48 Paul Blair	6.00	15.00
49 Woody Woodward	6.00	15.00
50 Mickey Mantle	750.00	1,500.00
51 Gordon Richardson	6.00	15.00
52 Wes Covington	6.00	15.00
Johnny Callison		
53 Bob Duliba	6.00	15.00
54 Jose Pagan	6.00	15.00
55 Ken Harrelson	8.00	20.00
56 Sandy Valdespino	6.00	15.00
57 Jim Lefebvre	6.00	15.00
58 Dave Wickersham	6.00	15.00
59 Reds Team	10.00	25.00
60 Curt Flood	8.00	20.00
61 Bob Bolin	6.00	15.00
62 Merritt Ranew	6.00	15.00
63 Jim Stewart	6.00	15.00
64 Bob Bruce	6.00	15.00
65 Leon Wagner	6.00	15.00
66 Al Weis	6.00	15.00
67 Cleon Jones	6.00	15.00
Dick Selma		
68 Hal Reniff	6.00	15.00
69 Ken Hamlin	6.00	15.00
70 Carl Yastrzemski	75.00	150.00
71 Frank Carpin	6.00	15.00
72 Tony Perez	75.00	150.00
73 Jerry Zimmerman	6.00	15.00
74 Don Mossi	6.00	15.00
75 Tommy Davis	8.00	20.00
76 Red Schoendienst MG	8.00	20.00
77 John Orsino	6.00	15.00
78 Frank Linzy	6.00	15.00
79 Joe Pepitone	6.00	15.00
80 Richie Allen	12.50	30.00
81 Ray Oyler	6.00	15.00
82 Bob Hendley	6.00	15.00
83 Albie Pearson	6.00	15.00
84 Jim Beauchamp	6.00	15.00
Dick Kelley		
85 Eddie Fisher	6.00	15.00
86 John Bateman	6.00	15.00
87 Dan Napoleon	6.00	15.00
88 Fred Whitfield	6.00	15.00
89 Ted Davidson	6.00	15.00
90 Luis Aparicio	20.00	50.00
91 Bob Uecker	30.00	60.00
92 Yankees Team	40.00	80.00
93 Jim Lonborg	6.00	15.00
94 Matty Alou	8.00	20.00
95 Pete Richert	6.00	15.00
96 Felipe Alou	8.00	20.00
97 Jim Merritt	6.00	15.00
98 Don Demeter	6.00	15.00
99 Willie Stargell	12.50	30.00
Donn Clendenon		
100 Sandy Koufax	2,500.00	5,000.00
101 Checklist 2	15.00	40.00
102 Ed Kirkpatrick	6.00	15.00
103 Dick Groat	6.00	15.00
104 Alex Johnson	6.00	15.00
105 Milt Pappas	8.00	20.00
106 Rusty Staub	8.00	20.00
107 Larry Stahl	6.00	15.00
Ron Tompkins		
108 Bobby Klaus	6.00	15.00
109 Ralph Terry	6.00	15.00
110 Ernie Banks	100.00	200.00
111 Gary Peters	6.00	15.00
112 Manny Mota	8.00	20.00
113 Hank Aguirre	6.00	15.00
114 Jim Gosger	6.00	15.00
115 Bill Henry	6.00	15.00
116 Walt Alston MG	8.00	20.00
117 Jake Gibbs	6.00	15.00
118 Mike McCormick	6.00	15.00
119 Art Shamsky	6.00	15.00
120 Harmon Killebrew	50.00	100.00
121 Ray Herbert	6.00	15.00
122 Joe Gaines	6.00	15.00
123 Frank Bork	6.00	15.00
Jerry May		
124 Tug McGraw	8.00	20.00
125 Lou Brock	60.00	120.00
126 Jim Palmer UER		
(Described as a lefthander on card back)	300.00	600.00
127 Ken Berry	6.00	15.00
128 Jim Landis	6.00	15.00
129 Jack Kralick	6.00	15.00
130 Joe Torre	12.50	30.00
131 Angels Team	10.00	25.00
132 Orlando Cepeda	30.00	60.00
133 Don McMahon	6.00	15.00
134 Wes Parker	6.00	15.00
135 Dave Morehead	6.00	15.00
136 Woody Held	6.00	15.00
137 Pat Corrales	6.00	15.00
138 Roger Repoz	6.00	15.00
139 Byron Browne	6.00	15.00
Don Young		
140 Jim Maloney	6.00	15.00
141 Tom McCraw	6.00	15.00
142 Don Dennis	6.00	15.00
143 Jose Tartabull	6.00	15.00
144 Don Schwall	6.00	15.00
145 Bill Freehan	8.00	20.00
146 George Altman	6.00	15.00
147 Lum Harris MG	6.00	15.00
148 Bob Johnson	6.00	15.00
149 Dick Nen	6.00	15.00
150 Rocky Colavito	12.50	30.00
151 Gary Wagner	6.00	15.00
152 Frank Malzone	6.00	15.00
153 Rico Carty	8.00	20.00
154 Chuck Hiller	6.00	15.00
155 Marcelino Lopez	6.00	15.00
156 Dick Schofield	6.00	15.00
Hal Lanier		
157 Rene Lachemann	6.00	15.00
158 Jim Brewer	6.00	15.00
159 Chico Ruiz	6.00	15.00
160 Whitey Ford	75.00	150.00
161 Jerry Lumpe	6.00	15.00
162 Lee Maye	6.00	15.00
163 Tito Francona	6.00	15.00
164 Tommie Agee	6.00	15.00
Marv Staehle		
165 Don Lock	6.00	15.00
166 Chris Krug	6.00	15.00
167 Boog Powell	12.50	30.00
168 Dan Osinski	6.00	15.00
169 Duke Sims	6.00	15.00
170 Cookie Rojas	6.00	15.00
171 Nick Willhite	6.00	15.00
172 Mets Team	10.00	25.00
173 Al Spangler	6.00	15.00
174 Ron Taylor	6.00	15.00
175 Bert Campaneris	8.00	20.00
176 Jim Davenport	6.00	15.00
177 Hector Lopez	6.00	15.00
178 Bob Tillman	6.00	15.00
179 Dennis Aust	6.00	15.00
Bob Tolan		
180 Vada Pinson	8.00	20.00
181 Al Worthington	6.00	15.00
182 Jerry Lynch	6.00	15.00
183 Checklist 3	12.50	30.00
184 Denis Menke	6.00	15.00
185 Bob Buhl	6.00	15.00
186 Ruben Amaro	6.00	15.00
187 Chuck Dressen MG	6.00	15.00
188 Al Luplow	6.00	15.00
189 John Roseboro	6.00	15.00
190 Jimmie Hall	6.00	15.00
191 Darrell Sutherland	6.00	15.00
192 Vic Power	6.00	15.00
193 Dave McNally	6.00	15.00
194 Senators Team	6.00	15.00
195 Joe Morgan	50.00	100.00
196 Don Pavletich	6.00	15.00
197 Sonny Siebert	6.00	15.00
198 Mickey Stanley	6.00	15.00
199 Chisox Clubbers	6.00	15.00
200 Eddie Mathews	50.00	100.00
201 Jim Dickson	6.00	15.00
202 Clay Dalrymple	6.00	15.00
203 Jose Santiago	6.00	15.00
204 Cubs Team	10.00	25.00
205 Tom Tresh	8.00	20.00
206 Al Jackson	6.00	15.00
207 Frank Quilici	6.00	15.00
208 Bob Miller	6.00	15.00
209 Fritz Fisher	6.00	15.00
John Hiller		
210 Bill Mazeroski	40.00	80.00
211 Frank Kreutzer	6.00	15.00
212 Ed Kranepool	6.00	15.00
213 Fred Newman	6.00	15.00
214 Tommy Harper	6.00	15.00
215 NL Batting Leaders	150.00	300.00
Bob Clemente		
216 AL Batting Leaders	12.50	30.00
Tony Oliva		
Carl Yastrzemski/		
217 Willie Mays	60.00	120.00
Willie McCovey		
Billy Williams LL		
218 AL Home Run Leaders	10.00	25.00
Tony Conigliaro		
Norm Cash		
W		
219 NL RBI Leaders	15.00	40.00
Deron Johnson		
Frank Robinson		
Wil		
220 AL RBI Leaders	10.00	25.00
Rocky Colavito		
Willie Horton		
Ton		
221 NL ERA Leaders	30.00	60.00
Sandy Koufax		
Juan Marichal		
Vern		
222 AL ERA Leaders	10.00	25.00
Sam McDowell		
Eddie Fisher		
Sonny		
223 NL Pitching Leaders	30.00	60.00
Sandy Koufax		
Tony Cloninger#		
224 AL Pitching Leaders	10.00	25.00
Jim Grant		
Mel Stottlemyre		
J		
225 NL Strikeout Leaders	30.00	60.00
Sandy Koufax		
Bob Veale		
Bob		
226 AL Strikeout Leaders	10.00	25.00
Sam McDowell		
Mickey Lolich#		
227 Russ Nixon	6.00	15.00
228 Larry Dierker	6.00	15.00
229 Hank Bauer MG	6.00	15.00
230 Johnny Callison	6.00	15.00
231 Floyd Weaver	6.00	15.00
232 Glenn Beckert	6.00	15.00
233 Dom Zanni	6.00	15.00
234 Rich Beck	10.00	25.00
Roy White		
235 Don Cardwell	6.00	15.00
236 Mike Hershberger	6.00	15.00
237 Billy O'Dell	6.00	15.00
238 Dodgers Team	10.00	25.00
239 Orlando Pena	6.00	15.00
240 Earl Battey	6.00	15.00
241 Dennis Ribant	6.00	15.00
242 Jesus Alou	6.00	15.00
243 Nelson Briles	6.00	15.00
244 Chuck Harrison	6.00	15.00
Sonny Jackson		
245 John Buzhardt	6.00	15.00
246 Ed Bailey	6.00	15.00
247 Carl Warwick	6.00	15.00
248 Pete Mikkelsen	6.00	15.00
249 Bill Rigney MG	6.00	15.00
250 Sammy Ellis	6.00	15.00
251 Ed Brinkman	6.00	15.00
252 Denny Lemaster	6.00	15.00
253 Don Wert	6.00	15.00
254 Fergie Jenkins	250.00	500.00
Bill Sorrell		
255 Willie Stargell	60.00	120.00
256 Lew Krausse	6.00	15.00
257 Jeff Torborg	6.00	15.00
258 Dave Giusti	6.00	15.00
259 Boston Red Sox	10.00	25.00
Team Card		
260 Bob Shaw	6.00	15.00
261 Ron Hansen	6.00	15.00
262 Jack Hamilton	6.00	15.00
263 Tom Egan	6.00	15.00
264 Andy Kosco	6.00	15.00
Ted Uhlaender		
265 Stu Miller	6.00	15.00
266 Pedro Gonzalez UER	6.00	15.00
Misspelled Gonzales on card ba		
267 Joe Sparma	6.00	15.00
268 John Blanchard	6.00	15.00
269 Don Heffner MG	6.00	15.00
270 Claude Osteen	6.00	15.00
271 Hal Lanier	6.00	15.00
272 Jack Bladschun	6.00	15.00
273 Bob Aspromonte	6.00	15.00
Rusty Staub		
274 Buster Narum	6.00	15.00
275 Tim McCarver	10.00	25.00
276 Jim Bouton	8.00	20.00
277 George Thomas	6.00	15.00
278 Cal Koonce	6.00	15.00
279 Checklist 4	10.00	25.00
280 Bobby Knoop	6.00	15.00
281 Bruce Howard	6.00	15.00
282 Johnny Lewis	6.00	15.00
283 Jim Perry	8.00	20.00
284 Bobby Wine	6.00	15.00
285 Luis Tiant	10.00	25.00
286 Gary Geiger	6.00	15.00
287 Jack Aker	6.00	15.00
288 Bill Singer	125.00	250.00
Don Sutton		
289 Larry Sherry	6.00	15.00
290 Ron Santo	12.50	30.00
291 Moe Drabowsky	6.00	15.00
292 Jim Coker	6.00	15.00
293 Mike Shannon	6.00	15.00
294 Steve Ridzik	6.00	15.00
295 Jim Ray Hart	6.00	15.00
296 Johnny Keane MG	6.00	15.00
297 Jim Owens	6.00	15.00
298 Rico Petrocelli	6.00	15.00
299 Lou Burdette	8.00	20.00
300 Roberto Clemente	500.00	1,000.00
301 Greg Bollo	6.00	15.00
302 Ernie Bowman	6.00	15.00
303 Cleveland Indians	10.00	25.00
Team Card		
304 John Herrnstein	6.00	15.00
305 Camilo Pascual	6.00	15.00
306 Ty Cline	6.00	15.00
307 Clay Carroll	6.00	15.00
308 Tom Haller	6.00	15.00
309 Diego Segui	6.00	15.00
310 Frank Robinson	100.00	200.00
311 Tommy Helms	6.00	15.00
Dick Simpson		
312 Bob Saverine	6.00	15.00
313 Chris Zachary	6.00	15.00
314 Hector Valle	6.00	15.00
315 Norm Cash	10.00	25.00
316 Jack Fisher	6.00	15.00
317 Dalton Jones	6.00	15.00
318 Harry Walker MG	6.00	15.00
319 Gene Freese	6.00	15.00
320 Bob Gibson	75.00	150.00
321 Rick Reichardt	6.00	15.00
322 Bill Faul	6.00	15.00
323 Ray Barker	6.00	15.00
324 John Boozer	6.00	15.00
325 Vic Davalillo	6.00	15.00
326 Braves Team	10.00	25.00
327 Bernie Allen	6.00	15.00
328 Jerry Grote	6.00	15.00
329 Pete Charton	6.00	15.00
330 Ron Fairly	8.00	20.00
331 Ron Herbel	6.00	15.00
332 Bill Bryan	6.00	15.00
333 Joe Coleman	6.00	15.00
Jim French		
334 Marty Keough	6.00	15.00
335 Juan Pizarro	6.00	15.00
336 Gene Alley	6.00	15.00
337 Fred Gladding	6.00	15.00
338 Dal Maxvill	6.00	15.00
339 Del Crandall	6.00	15.00
340 Dean Chance	6.00	15.00
341 Wes Westrum MG	6.00	15.00
342 Bob Humphreys	6.00	15.00
343 Joe Christopher	6.00	15.00
344 Steve Blass	6.00	15.00
345 Bob Allison	6.00	15.00
346 Mike de la Hoz	6.00	15.00
347 Phil Regan	6.00	15.00
348 Orioles Team	12.50	30.00
349 Cap Peterson	6.00	15.00
350 Mel Stottlemyre	8.00	20.00
351 Fred Valentine	6.00	15.00
352 Bob Aspromonte	6.00	15.00
353 Al McBean	6.00	15.00
354 Smoky Burgess	6.00	15.00
355 Wade Blasingame	6.00	15.00
356 Owen Johnson	6.00	15.00
Ken Sanders		
357 Gerry Arrigo	6.00	15.00
358 Charlie Smith	6.00	15.00
359 Johnny Briggs	6.00	15.00
360 Ron Hunt	6.00	15.00
361 Tom Satriano	6.00	15.00
362 Gates Brown	6.00	15.00
363 Checklist 5	12.50	30.00
364 Nate Oliver	6.00	15.00
365 Roger Maris	100.00	200.00
366 Wayne Causey	6.00	15.00
367 Mel Nelson	6.00	15.00
368 Charlie Lau	6.00	15.00
369 Jim King	6.00	15.00
370 Chico Cardenas	6.00	15.00

1967 Topps

The cards in this 609-card set measure 2 1/2" by 3 1/2". The 1967 Topps series is considered by some collectors to be one of the company's finest accomplishments in baseball card production. Excellent color photographs are combined with easy-to-read backs. Cards 458 to 533 are slightly harder to find than numbers 1 to 457, and the inevitable high series (534 to 609) exists. Each checklist card features a small circular picture of a popular player included in that series.

Printing discrepancies resulted in some high series cards being in shorter supply. The checklist below identifies (by DP) 22 double-printed high numbers; of the 76 cards in the last series, 54 cards were short printed and the other 22 cards are much more plentiful. Featured subsets within this set include World Series cards (151-155) and League Leaders (233-244). A limited number of "proof" Roger Maris cards were produced. These cards are blank backed and Maris is listed as a New York Yankee on it. Some Bob Bolin cards: (number 252) have a white smear in between his names. Another tough variation that has been recently discovered involves card number 58 Paul Schaal. The tough version has a green bat above his name. The key Rookie Cards in the set are high number cards of Rod Carew and Tom Seaver. Confirmed methods of selling these cards include five-card nickel wax packs. Although rarely seen, there exists a salesman's sample panel of three cards that pictures Earl Battey, Manny Mota, and Gene Brabender with ad information on the back about the "new" Topps cards.

Card	Low	High
COMPLETE SET (609)	2,500.00	5,000.00
COMMON CARD (1-109)	.60	1.50
COMMON CARD (110-283)	.75	2.00
COMMON CARD (284-370)	1.00	2.50
COMMON CARD (371-457)	1.50	4.00
COMMON CARD (458-533)	2.50	6.00
COMMON CARD (534-609)	6.00	15.00
COMMON DP (534-609)	3.00	8.00
WRAPPER (5-CENT)	10.00	25.00
1 Robinson/Bauer/Robinson DP	15.00	40.00
2 Jack Hamilton	.60	1.50
3 Duke Sims	.60	1.50
4 Hal Lanier	.60	1.50
5 Whitey Ford UER	15.00	40.00
6 Dick Simpson	.60	1.50
7 Don McMahon	.60	1.50
8 Chuck Harrison	.60	1.50
9 Ron Hansen	.60	1.50
10 Matty Alou	1.50	4.00
11 Barry Moore RC	.60	1.50
12 J.Campanis RC/B.Singer	1.50	4.00
13 Joe Sparma	.60	1.50
14 Phil Linz	1.50	4.00
15 Earl Battey	.60	1.50
16 Bill Hands	.60	1.50
17 Jim Gosger	.60	1.50
18 Gene Oliver	.60	1.50
19 Jim McGlothlin	.60	1.50
20 Orlando Cepeda	12.00	30.00
21 Dave Bristol MG RC	.60	1.50
22 Gene Brabender	.60	1.50
23 Larry Elliot	.60	1.50
24 Bob Allen	.60	1.50
25 Elston Howard	1.50	4.00
26A Bob Priddy NTR	12.50	30.00
26B Bob Priddy TR	1.50	4.00
27 Bob Saverine	.60	1.50
28 Barry Latman	.60	1.50
29 Tom McCraw	.60	1.50
30 Al Kaline DP	12.00	30.00
31 Jim Brewer	.60	1.50
32 Bob Bailey	1.50	4.00
33 S.Bando RC/R.Schwartz RC	2.50	6.00
34 Pete Cimino	.60	1.50
35 Rico Carty	1.50	4.00
36 Bob Tillman	.60	1.50
37 Rick Wise	1.50	4.00
38 Bob Johnson	.60	1.50
39 Curt Simmons	1.50	4.00
40 Rick Reichardt	.60	1.50
41 Joe Hoerner	.60	1.50
42 New York Mets TC	4.00	10.00
43 Chico Salmon	.60	1.50
44 Joe Nuxhall	1.50	4.00
45 Roger Maris	25.00	60.00
45A R.Maris Yanks/Blank Back	900.00	1,500.00
46 Lindy McDaniel	1.50	4.00
47 Ken McMullen	.60	1.50
48 Bill Freehan	1.50	4.00
49 Roy Face	1.50	4.00
50 Tony Oliva	2.50	6.00
51 D.Adlesh RC/W.Bales RC	.60	1.50
52 Dennis Higgins	.60	1.50
53 Clay Dalrymple	.60	1.50
54 Dick Green	.60	1.50
55 Don Drysdale	15.00	40.00
56 Jose Tartabull	1.50	4.00
57 Pat Jarvis RC	1.50	4.00
58A Paul Schaal	8.00	20.00
Green Bat		
58B P.Schaal Normal Bat	.60	1.50
59 Ralph Terry	1.50	4.00
60 Luis Aparicio	3.00	8.00
61 Gordy Coleman	.60	1.50
62 Frank Robinson CL1	3.00	8.00
63 L.Brock/C.Flood	3.00	8.00
64 Fred Valentine	.60	1.50
65 Tom Haller	1.50	4.00
66 Manny Mota	1.50	4.00
67 Ken Berry	.60	1.50
68 Bob Buhl	1.50	4.00
69 Vic Davalillo	.60	1.50
70 Ron Santo	8.00	20.00
71 Camilo Pascual	1.50	4.00
72 G.Korince ERR RC/T.Matchick RC	.60	1.50
73 Rusty Staub	2.50	6.00
74 Wes Stock	.60	1.50
75 George Scott	1.50	4.00
76 Jim Barbieri RC	.60	1.50
77 Dooley Womack	1.50	4.00
78 Pat Corrales	.60	1.50
79 Bubba Morton	.60	1.50
80 Jim Maloney	1.50	4.00
81 Eddie Stanky MG	1.50	4.00
82 Steve Barber	.60	1.50
83 Ollie Brown	.60	1.50
84 Tommie Sisk	.60	1.50
85 Johnny Callison	1.50	4.00
86A Mike McCormick NTR	12.50	30.00
86B Mike McCormick TR	1.50	4.00
87 George Altman	.60	1.50
88 Mickey Lolich	1.50	4.00
89 Felix Millan RC	1.50	4.00
90 Jim Nash RC	.60	1.50
91 Johnny Lewis	.60	1.50
92 Ray Washburn	.60	1.50
93 S.Bahnsen RC/B.Murcer	1.50	4.00
94 Ron Fairly	1.50	4.00
95 Sonny Siebert	.60	1.50
96 Art Shamsky	.60	1.50
97 Mike Cuellar	1.50	4.00
98 Rich Rollins	.60	1.50
99 Lee Stange	.60	1.50
100 Frank Robinson DP	15.00	40.00
101 Ken Johnson	.60	1.50
102 Philadelphia Phillies TC	1.50	4.00
103A Mickey Mantle CL2 DP D.Mc	12.00	30.00
103B Mickey Mantle CL2 DP D Mc		
104 Minnie Rojas RC	.60	1.50
105 Ken Boyer	2.50	6.00
106 Randy Hundley	1.50	4.00
107 Joel Horlen	.60	1.50
108 Alex Johnson	1.50	4.00
109 R.Colavito/L.Wagner	2.50	6.00
110 Jack Aker	1.50	4.00
111 John Kennedy	.75	2.00
112 Dave Wickersham	.75	2.00
113 Dave Nicholson	.75	2.00
114 Jack Baldschun	.75	2.00
115 Paul Casanova RC	.75	2.00
116 Herman Franks MG	.75	2.00
117 Darrell Brandon	.75	2.00
118 Bernie Allen	.75	2.00
119 Wade Blasingame	.75	2.00
120 Floyd Robinson	.75	2.00
121 Eddie Bressoud	.75	2.00
122 George Brunet	.75	2.00
123 J.Price RC/L.Walker	1.50	4.00
124 Jim Stewart	.75	2.00
125 Moe Drabowsky	1.50	4.00
126 Tony Taylor	.75	2.00
127 John O'Donoghue	.75	2.00
128A Ed Spiezio	.75	2.00
128B Ed Spiezio		
Partial last name on front		
129 Phil Roof	.75	2.00
130 Phil Regan	1.50	4.00
131 New York Yankees TC	8.00	20.00
132 Ozzie Virgil	.75	2.00
133 Ron Kline	.75	2.00
134 Gates Brown	2.50	6.00
135 Deron Johnson	1.50	4.00
136 Carroll Sembera	.75	2.00
137 Rookie Stars	.75	2.00
Ron Clark RC		
Jim Ollum RC		
138 Dick Kelley	.75	2.00
139 Dalton Jones	1.50	4.00
140 Willie Stargell	12.00	30.00
141 John Miller	.75	2.00
142 Jackie Brandt	.75	2.00
143 P.Ward/D.Buford	.75	2.00
144 Bill Hepler	.75	2.00
145 Larry Brown	.75	2.00
146 Steve Carlton	20.00	50.00
147 Tom Egan	.75	2.00
148 Adolfo Phillips	.75	2.00
149 Joe Moeller	.75	2.00
150 Mickey Mantle	150.00	400.00
151 Moe Drabowsky WS1	2.00	5.00
152 Jim Palmer WS2	3.00	8.00
153 Paul Blair WS3	2.00	5.00
154 Robinson/McNally WS4	2.00	5.00
155 Orioles Celebrate WS	2.00	5.00
156 Ron Herbel	.75	2.00
157 Danny Cater	.75	2.00
158 Jimmie Coker	.75	2.00
159 Bruce Howard	.75	2.00
160 Willie Davis	1.50	4.00
161 Dick Williams MG	1.50	4.00
162 Billy O'Dell	.75	2.00
163 Vic Roznovsky	.75	2.00
164 Dwight Siebler UER	.75	2.00
165 Cleon Jones	1.50	4.00
166 Eddie Mathews	10.00	25.00
167 J.Coleman RC/T.Cullen RC	.75	2.00
168 Ray Culp	.75	2.00
169 Horace Clarke	1.50	4.00
170 Dick McAuliffe	1.50	4.00
171 Cal Koonce	.75	2.00
172 Bill Heath	.75	2.00
173 St. Louis Cardinals TC	1.50	4.00
174 Dick Radatz	1.50	4.00
175 Bobby Knoop	.75	2.00
176 Sammy Ellis	.75	2.00
177 Tito Fuentes	.60	1.50
178 John Buzhardt	.75	2.00
179 C.Vaughan RC/C.Epshaw RC	1.50	4.00
180 Curt Blefary	.75	2.00
181 Terry Fox	.75	2.00
182 Ed Charles	.75	2.00
183 Jim Pagliaroni	.75	2.00
184 George Thomas	.75	2.00
185 Ken Holtzman RC	1.50	4.00
186 E.Kranepool/R.Swoboda	1.50	4.00
187 Pedro Ramos	.75	2.00
188 Ken Harrelson	1.50	4.00
189 Chuck Hinton	.75	2.00
190 Turk Farrell	.75	2.00
191A W.Mays CL3 214 Tom	4.00	10.00
191B W.Mays CL3 214 Dick	5.00	12.00
192 Fred Gladding	.75	2.00
193 Jose Cardenal	1.50	4.00
194 Bob Allison	1.50	4.00
195 Al Jackson	.75	2.00
196 Johnny Romano	.75	2.00
197 Ron Perranoski	1.50	4.00
198 Chuck Hiller	.75	2.00
199 Billy Hitchcock MG	.75	2.00
200 Willie Mays UER	50.00	120.00
201 Hal Reniff	1.50	4.00
202 Johnny Edwards	.75	2.00
203 Al McBean	.75	2.00
204 M.Epstein RC/T.Phoebus RC	2.50	6.00
205 Dick Groat	1.50	4.00
206 Dennis Bennett	.75	2.00
207 John Orsino	.75	2.00
208 Jack Lamabe	.75	2.00
209 Joe Nossek	.75	2.00
210 Bob Gibson	15.00	40.00
211 Minnesota Twins TC	1.50	4.00
212 Chris Zachary	.75	2.00
213 Jay Johnstone RC	1.50	4.00
214 Tom Kelley	.75	2.00
215 Ernie Banks	25.00	60.00
216 A.Kaline/N.Cash	8.00	20.00
217 Rob Gardner	.75	2.00
218 Wes Parker	1.50	4.00
219 Clay Carroll	1.50	4.00
220 Jim Ray Hart	1.50	4.00
221 Woody Fryman	1.50	4.00
222 D.Osteen/L.May	1.50	4.00
223 Mike Ryan	1.50	4.00
224 Walt Bond	.75	2.00
225 Mel Stottlemyre	2.50	6.00
226 Julian Javier	1.50	4.00
227 Paul Lindblad	.75	2.00
228 Gil Hodges MG	2.50	6.00
229 Larry Jackson	.75	2.00
230 Boog Powell	2.50	6.00
231 John Bateman	.75	2.00
232 Don Buford	.75	2.00
233 Peters/Horlen/Hargan LL	1.50	4.00
234 Koufax/Cuellar/Marichal LL	10.00	25.00
235 Kaat/McLain/Wilson LL	2.50	6.00
236 Koufax/Mari/Gibs/Perry LL	10.00	25.00
237 McDowell/Kaat/Wilson LL	2.50	6.00
238 Koufax/Bunning/Veale LL	8.00	20.00
239 F.Rob/Oliva/Kaline LL	4.00	10.00
240 Alou/Alou/Carty LL	2.50	6.00
241 F.Rob/Killebrew/Powell LL	4.00	10.00
242 Aaron/Clemente/Allen LL	20.00	50.00
243 F.Rob/Killebrew/Powell LL	4.00	10.00
244 Aaron/Allen/Mays LL	12.00	30.00
245 Curt Flood	2.50	6.00
246 Jim Perry	1.50	4.00
247 Jerry Lumpe	.75	2.00
248 Gene Mauch MG	1.50	4.00
249 Nick Willhite	.75	2.00
250 Hank Aaron UER	40.00	100.00
251 Woody Held	.75	2.00
252 Bob Bolin	.75	2.00
253 B.Davis/G.Gil RC	.75	2.00
254 Milt Pappas	1.50	4.00
255 Frank Howard	1.50	4.00
256 Bob Hendley	.75	2.00
257 Charlie Smith	.75	2.00
258 Lee Maye	.75	2.00
259 Don Dennis	.75	2.00
260 Jim Lefebvre	1.50	4.00
261 John Wyatt	.75	2.00
262 Kansas City Athletics TC	1.50	4.00
263 Hank Aguirre	.75	2.00
264 Ron Swoboda	1.50	4.00
265 Lou Burdette	1.50	4.00
266 W.Stargell/D.Clendenon	1.50	4.00
267 Don Schwall	.75	2.00
268 Johnny Briggs	.75	2.00
269 Don Nottebart	.75	2.00
270 Zoilo Versalles	.75	2.00
271 Eddie Watt	.75	2.00
272 B.Connors RC/D.Dowling	1.50	4.00
273 Dick Lines RC	.75	2.00
274 Bob Aspromonte	.75	2.00
275 Fred Whitfield	.75	2.00
276 Bruce Brubaker	.75	2.00
277 Steve Whitaker RC	2.50	6.00
278 Jim Kaat CL4	3.00	8.00
279 Frank Linzy	.75	2.00
280 Tony Conigliaro	3.00	8.00
281 Bob Rodgers	.75	2.00
282 John Odom	.75	2.00
283 Gene Alley	1.50	4.00
284 Johnny Podres	1.50	4.00
285 Lou Brock	15.00	40.00
286 Wayne Causey	1.00	2.50
287 G.Goosen RC/B.Shirley	1.00	2.50
288 Denny Lemaster	1.00	2.50
289 Tom Tresh	2.00	5.00
290 Bill White	2.00	5.00
291 Jim Hannan	1.00	2.50
292 Don Pavletich	1.00	2.50
293 Ed Kirkpatrick	1.00	2.50
294 Walter Alston MG	3.00	8.00
295 Sam McDowell	2.00	5.00
296 Glenn Beckert	2.00	5.00
297 Dave Morehead	2.00	5.00
298 Ron Davis RC	1.00	2.50
299 Norm Siebern	1.00	2.50
300 Jim Kaat	2.00	5.00
301 Jesse Gonder	1.00	2.50
302 Baltimore Orioles TC	3.00	8.00
303 Gil Blanco	1.00	2.50
304 Phil Gagliano	1.00	2.50
305 Earl Wilson	2.00	5.00
306 Bud Harrelson RC	2.00	5.00
307 Jim Beauchamp	1.00	2.50
308 Al Downing	2.00	5.00
309 J.Callison/R.Allen	2.00	5.00
310 Gary Peters	1.00	2.50
311 Ed Brinkman	1.00	2.50
312 Don Mincher	1.00	2.50
313 Bob Lee	1.00	2.50
314 M.Andrews RC/R.Smith RC	3.00	8.00
315 Billy Williams	12.00	30.00
316 Jack Kralick	1.00	2.50
317 Cesar Tovar	1.00	2.50
318 Dave Giusti	1.00	2.50
319 Paul Blair	2.00	5.00
320 Gaylord Perry	6.00	15.00
321 Mayo Smith MG	1.00	2.50
322 Jose Pagan	1.00	2.50
323 Mike Hershberger	1.00	2.50
324 Hal Woodeshick	1.00	2.50
325 Chico Cardenas	2.00	5.00
326 Bob Uecker	10.00	25.00
327 California Angels TC	3.00	8.00
328 Clete Boyer UER	2.00	5.00
329 Charlie Lau	2.00	5.00
330 Claude Osteen	2.00	5.00
331 Joe Foy	2.00	5.00
332 Jesus Alou	1.00	2.50
333 Fergie Jenkins	10.00	25.00
334 H.Killebrew/B.Allison	4.00	10.00
335 Bob Veale	2.00	5.00
336 Joe Azcue	1.00	2.50
337 Joe Morgan	10.00	25.00
338 Bob Locker	1.00	2.50
339 Chico Ruiz	1.00	2.50
340 Joe Pepitone	3.00	8.00
341 D.Dietz RC/B.Sorrell	1.00	2.50
342 Hank Fischer	1.00	2.50
343 Tom Satriano	1.00	2.50
344 Ossie Chavarria RC	1.00	2.50
345 Stu Miller	2.00	5.00
346 Jim Hickman	1.00	2.50
347 Grady Hatton MG	1.00	2.50
348 Tug McGraw	2.00	5.00
349 Bob Chance	1.00	2.50
350 Joe Torre	10.00	25.00
351 Vern Law	2.00	5.00
352 Ray Oyler	1.00	2.50
353 Bill McCool	1.00	2.50
354 Chicago Cubs TC	3.00	8.00
355 Carl Yastrzemski	25.00	60.00
356 Larry Jaster RC	1.00	2.50
357 Bill Skowron	2.00	5.00
358 Ruben Amaro	1.00	2.50
359 Dick Ellsworth	1.00	2.50
360 Leon Wagner	1.00	2.50
361 Roberto Clemente CL5	8.00	20.00
362 Darold Knowles	1.00	2.50
363 Davey Johnson	2.00	5.00
364 Claude Raymond	1.00	2.50
365 John Roseboro	2.00	5.00
366 Andy Kosco	1.00	2.50
367 B.Kelso/D.Wallace RC	1.00	2.50
368 Jack Hiatt	1.00	2.50
369 Jim Hunter	10.00	25.00
370 Tommy Davis	2.00	5.00
371 Jim Lonborg	3.00	8.00
372 Mike de la Hoz	1.50	4.00
373 D.Josephson RC/F.Klages RC DP	1.50	4.00
374A Mel Queen ERR	8.00	20.00
374B Mel Queen COR DP	1.50	4.00
375 Jake Gibbs	3.00	8.00
376 Don Lock DP	1.50	4.00
377 Luis Tiant	3.00	8.00
378 Detroit Tigers TC UER	3.00	8.00
379 Jerry May DP	1.50	4.00
380 Dean Chance DP	1.50	4.00
381 Dick Schofield DP	1.50	4.00
382 Dave McNally	3.00	8.00
383 Ken Henderson DP	1.50	4.00
384 J.Cosman RC/D.Hughes RC	1.50	4.00
385 Jim Fregosi	3.00	8.00
386 Dick Selma DP	1.50	4.00
387 Cap Peterson DP	1.50	4.00
388 Arnold Earley DP	1.50	4.00
389 Alvin Dark MG DP	3.00	8.00
390 Jim Wynn DP	3.00	8.00
391 Wilbur Wood DP	3.00	8.00
392 Tommy Harper DP	3.00	8.00
393 Jim Bouton DP	3.00	8.00
394 Jake Wood DP	1.50	4.00
395 Chris Short RC	3.00	8.00
396 D.Menke/T.Cloninger	1.50	4.00
397 Willie Smith DP	1.50	4.00
398 Jeff Torborg	3.00	8.00
399 Al Worthington DP	1.50	4.00
400 Bob Clemente DP	60.00	120.00
401 Jim Coates	1.50	4.00
402A G.Jackson/B.Wilson Stat Line	8.00	20.00
402B G.Jackson/B.Wilson RC DP	3.00	8.00
403 Dick Nen	1.50	4.00
404 Nelson Briles	3.00	8.00
405 Russ Snyder	1.50	4.00
406 Lee Elia DP	1.50	4.00
407 Cincinnati Reds TC	3.00	8.00
408 Jim Northrup DP	3.00	8.00
409 Ray Sadecki	1.50	4.00
410 Lou Johnson DP	1.50	4.00
411 Dick Howser DP	1.50	4.00
412 N.Miller RC/D.Rader RC	3.00	8.00
413 Jerry Grote	1.50	4.00
414 Casey Cox	1.50	4.00
415 Sonny Jackson	1.50	4.00
416 Roger Repoz	1.50	4.00
417A Bob Bruce ERR	12.50	30.00
417B Bob Bruce COR DP	1.50	4.00
418 Sam Mele MG	1.50	4.00
419 Don Kessinger DP	3.00	8.00
420 Denny McLain	5.00	12.00
421 Dal Maxvill DP	1.50	4.00
422 Hoyt Wilhelm	6.00	15.00
423 W.Mays/W.McCovey DP	25.00	60.00

424 Pedro Gonzalez 1.50 4.00
425 Pete Mikkelsen 1.50 4.00
426 Lou Clinton 1.50 4.00
427A Ruben Gomez ERR 8.00 20.00
427B Ruben Gomez COR DP 1.50 4.00
428 T.Hutton RC/G.Michael RC DP 3.00 8.00
429 Garry Roggenburk DP 1.50 4.00
430 Pete Rose 50.00 100.00
431 Ted Uhlaender 1.50 4.00
432 Jimmie Hall DP 1.50 4.00
433 Al Luplow DP 1.50 4.00
434 Eddie Fisher DP 1.50 4.00
435 Mack Jones DP 1.50 4.00
436 Pete Ward 1.50 4.00
437 Washington Senators TC 3.00 8.00
438 Chuck Dobson 1.50 4.00
439 Byron Browne 1.50 4.00
440 Steve Hargan 1.50 4.00
441 Jim Davenport 1.50 4.00
442 B.Robinson RC/J.Verbanic RC DP 3.00 8.00
443 Tito Francona DP 1.50 4.00
444 George Smith 1.50 4.00
445 Don Sutton 10.00 25.00
446 Russ Nixon DP 1.50 4.00
447A Bo Belinsky ERR DP 1.50 4.00
447B Bo Belinsky COR 3.00 8.00
448 Harry Walker MG DP 1.50 4.00
449 Orlando Pena 1.50 4.00
450 Richie Allen 3.00 8.00
451 Fred Newman DP 1.50 4.00
452 Ed Kranepool 3.00 8.00
453 Aurelio Monteagudo DP 1.50 4.00
454A J.Marichal CL6 No Ear DP 5.00 12.00
454B Juan Marichal CL6 w/Ear DP 5.00 12.00
455 Tommie Agee 3.00 8.00
456 Phil Niekro UER 6.00 15.00
457 Andy Etchebarren DP 3.00 8.00
458 Lee Thomas 2.50 6.00
459 D.Bosman RC/P.Craig 2.50 6.00
460 Harmon Killebrew 15.00 40.00
461 Bob Miller 5.00 12.00
462 Bob Barton 2.50 6.00
463 S.McDowell/S.Siebert 5.00 12.00
464 Dan Coombs 2.50 6.00
465 Willie Horton 5.00 12.00
466 Bobby Wine 8.00 20.00
467 Jim O'Toole 2.50 6.00
468 Ralph Houk MG 2.50 6.00
469 Len Gabrielson 2.50 6.00
470 Bob Shaw 2.50 6.00
471 Rene Lachemann 2.50 6.00
472 J.Gelnar/G.Spriggs RC 2.50 6.00
473 Jose Santiago 2.50 6.00
474 Bob Tolan 4.00 10.00
475 Jim Palmer 20.00 50.00
476 Tony Perez SP 30.00 60.00
477 Atlanta Braves TC 6.00 15.00
478 Bob Humphreys 2.50 6.00
479 Gary Bell 2.50 6.00
480 Willie McCovey 15.00 40.00
481 Leo Durocher MG 8.00 20.00
482 Bill Monbouquette 2.50 6.00
483 Jim Landis 2.50 6.00
484 Jerry Adair 2.50 6.00
485 Tim McCarver 10.00 25.00
486 R.Reese RC/B.Whitby RC 2.50 6.00
487 Tommie Reynolds 2.50 6.00
488 Gerry Arrigo 2.50 6.00
489 Doug Clemens RC 2.50 6.00
490 Tony Cloninger 2.50 6.00
491 Sam Bowens 2.50 6.00
492 Pittsburgh Pirates TC 6.00 15.00
493 Phil Ortega 2.50 6.00
494 Bill Rigney MG 2.50 6.00
495 Fritz Peterson 2.50 6.00
496 Orlando McFarlane 2.50 6.00
497 Ron Campbell RC 2.50 6.00
498 Larry Dierker 5.00 12.00
499 G.Culver/J.Vidal RC 2.50 6.00
500 Juan Marichal 15.00 40.00
501 Jerry Zimmerman 2.50 6.00
502 Derrell Griffith 2.50 6.00
503 Los Angeles Dodgers TC 8.00 20.00
504 Orlando Martinez RC 2.50 6.00
505 Tommy Helms 5.00 12.00
506 Smoky Burgess 2.50 6.00
507 E.Barnowski/L.Haney RC 2.50 6.00
508 Dick Hall 2.50 6.00
509 Jim King 2.50 6.00
510 Bill Mazeroski 8.00 20.00
511 Don Wert 2.50 6.00
512 Red Schoendienst MG 10.00 25.00
513 Marcelino Lopez 2.50 6.00
514 John Werhas 2.50 6.00
515 Bert Campaneris 5.00 12.00
516 San Francisco Giants TC 6.00 15.00
517 Fred Talbot 5.00 12.00
518 Denis Menke 2.50 6.00
519 Ted Davidson 2.50 6.00
520 Max Alvis 2.50 6.00
521 B.Powell/C.Blefary 5.00 12.00
522 John Stephenson 2.50 6.00
523 Jim Merritt 2.50 6.00
524 Felix Mantilla 2.50 6.00
525 Ron Hunt 2.50 6.00
526 P.Dobson RC/G.Korince RC 2.50 6.00
527 Dennis Ribant 2.50 6.00
528 Rico Petrocelli 8.00 20.00
529 Gary Wagner 2.50 6.00
530 Felipe Alou 5.00 12.00
531 B.Robinson CL7 DP 6.00 15.00
532 Jim Hicks RC 2.50 6.00
533 Jack Fisher 2.50 6.00
534 Hank Bauer MG DP 3.00 8.00
535 Donn Clendenon 10.00 25.00
536 J.Niekro RC/P.Popovich RC 40.00 100.00
537 Chuck Estrada DP 3.00 8.00
538 J.C. Martin 6.00 15.00
539 Dick Egan DP 3.00 8.00
540 Norm Cash 25.00 60.00
541 Joe Gibbon 6.00 15.00
542 R.Monday RC/T.Pierce RC DP 10.00 25.00
543 Dan Schneider 6.00 15.00
544 Cleveland Indians TC 12.50 30.00
545 Jim Grant 10.00 25.00
546 Woody Woodward 10.00 25.00
547 R.Gibson RC/B.Rohr RC DP 3.00 8.00
548 Tony Gonzalez DP 3.00 8.00
549 Jack Sanford 6.00 15.00
550 Vada Pinson DP 4.00 10.00
551 Doug Camilli DP 3.00 8.00
552 Ted Savage 12.00 30.00
553 M.Hegan RC/T.Tillotson 15.00 40.00
554 Andre Rodgers DP 3.00 8.00
555 Don Cardwell 12.00 30.00
556 Al Weis DP 3.00 8.00
557 Al Ferrara 10.00 25.00
558 M.Belanger RC/B.Dillman RC 40.00 100.00
559 Dick Tracewski DP 3.00 8.00
560 Jim Bunning 40.00 100.00
561 Sandy Alomar 15.00 40.00
562 Steve Blass DP 3.00 8.00
563 Joe Adcock 15.00 40.00
564 A.Harris RC/A.Pointer RC DP 3.00 8.00
565 Lew Krausse 10.00 25.00
566 Gary Geiger DP 5.00 12.00
567 Steve Hamilton 15.00 40.00
568 John Sullivan 15.00 40.00
569 Rod Carew RC DP 250.00 500.00
570 Maury Wills 40.00 80.00
571 Larry Sherry 10.00 25.00
572 Don Demeter 10.00 25.00
573 Chicago White Sox TC 12.50 30.00
574 Jerry Buchek 10.00 25.00
575 Dave Boswell RC 6.00 15.00
576 R.Hernandez RC/N.Gigon RC 15.00 40.00
577 Bill Short 6.00 15.00
578 John Boccabella 6.00 15.00
579 Bill Henry 6.00 15.00
580 Rocky Colavito 75.00 150.00
581 Tom Seaver RC 500.00 1,200.00
582 Jim Owens DP 3.00 8.00
583 Ray Barker 15.00 40.00
584 Jimmy Piersall 15.00 40.00
585 Wally Bunker 10.00 25.00
586 Manny Jimenez 6.00 15.00
587 D.Shaw RC/G.Sutherland RC 15.00 40.00
588 Johnny Klippstein DP 3.00 8.00
589 Dave Ricketts DP 3.00 8.00
590 Pete Richert 6.00 15.00
591 Ty Cline 10.00 25.00
592 J.Shellenback RC/R.Willis RC 10.00 25.00
593 Wes Westrum MG 20.00 50.00
594 Dan Osinski 15.00 40.00
595 Cookie Rojas 10.00 25.00
596 Galen Cisco DP 3.00 8.00
597 Ted Abernathy 6.00 15.00
598 W.Williams RC/E.Stroud RC 10.00 25.00
599 Bob Duliba DP 3.00 8.00
600 Brooks Robinson 200.00 400.00
601 Bill Bryan DP 3.00 8.00
602 Juan Pizarro 15.00 40.00
603 T.Talton RC/R.Webster RC 10.00 25.00
604 Boston Red Sox TC 60.00 120.00
605 Mike Shannon 20.00 50.00
606 Ron Taylor 10.00 25.00
607 Mickey Stanley 20.00 50.00
608 R.Nye RC/J.Upham RC DP 3.00 8.00
609 Tommy John 30.00 80.00

1967 Topps Posters Inserts

The wrappers of the 1967 Topps cards have this 32-card set advertised as follows: 'Extra -- All Star Pin-Up Inside." Printed on (5" by 7") paper in full color, these "All-Star" inserts have fold lines which are generally not very noticeable when stored carefully. They are numbered, blank-backed, and carry a facsimile autograph.

COMPLETE SET (32) 50.00 100.00
1 Boog Powell 1.00 2.50
2 Bert Campaneris .75 2.00
3 Brooks Robinson 1.50 4.00
4 Tommie Agee .50 1.25
5 Carl Yastrzemski 2.00 5.00
6 Mickey Mantle 12.00 30.00
7 Frank Howard .75 2.00
8 Sam McDowell .75 2.00
9 Orlando Cepeda 1.25 3.00
10 Chico Cardenas .50 1.25
11 Roberto Clemente 4.00 10.00
12 Willie Mays 3.00 8.00
13 Cleon Jones .50 1.25
14 Johnny Callison .75 2.00
15 Hank Aaron 2.50 6.00
16 Don Drysdale 1.25 3.00
17 Bobby Knoop .50 1.25
18 Tony Oliva 1.00 2.50
19 Frank Robinson 1.25 3.00
20 Denny McLain 1.00 2.50
21 Al Kaline 1.50 4.00
22 Joe Pepitone .75 2.00
23 Harmon Killebrew 1.50 4.00
24 Leon Wagner .50 1.25
25 Joe Morgan 1.25 3.00
26 Ron Santo 1.00 2.50
27 Joe Torre 1.00 2.50
28 Juan Marichal 1.00 2.50
29 Matty Alou .50 1.25
30 Felipe Alou .75 2.00
31 Ron Hunt .50 1.25
32 Willie McCovey 1.25 3.00

1967 Topps Test Foil

This 24-card set of all-stars is know only in proof form and was intended to be pressed onto a pin-back button issue which never materialized. The set measures approximately 2 3/8" square and features a color player head photo in a 2 1/4" white circle on a silver foil background with the player's name and position printed in black across the neck. The word "Japan" is printed in tiny black letters at the top-left which meant that word was intended to be folded under the button's rim. The backs are blank. The cards are unnumbered and checklisted below in alphabetical order.

COMPLETE SET (23) 3,000.00 6,000.00
1 Hank Aaron 350.00 700.00
2 Johnny Callison 100.00 200.00
3 Bert Campaneris 125.00 250.00
4 Leo Cardenas 100.00 200.00
5 Orlando Cepeda 200.00 400.00
6 Roberto Clemente 500.00 1,000.00
7 Frank Howard 125.00 250.00
8 Cleon Jones 100.00 200.00
9 Bobby Knoop 100.00 200.00
10 Sandy Koufax 350.00 700.00
11 Mickey Mantle 600.00 1,200.00
12 Juan Marichal 200.00 400.00
13 Willie Mays 350.00 700.00
14 Sam McDowell 100.00 200.00
15 Denny McLain 125.00 250.00
16 Joe Morgan 200.00 400.00
17 Tony Oliva 125.00 250.00
18 Boog Powell 125.00 250.00
19 Brooks Robinson 200.00 400.00
20 Frank Robinson 200.00 400.00
21 John Romano 100.00 200.00
22 Ron Santo 150.00 300.00
23 Joe Torre 150.00 300.00
24 Carl Yastrzemski 200.00 400.00

1967 Topps Venezuelan

This set features color player photos in a white border on the fronts. The horizontal backs carry player information. The cards are printed in Spanish and were issued for the Venezuelan market. Cards from 139 through 188 feature retired players while the rest of the set features active players. The cards which feature the same photos as the 67 Topps cards seemed trimmed. However, by checking the back -- any collector should have confidence in what they are buying. The first 138 cards in this set feature players who were then playing in the Venezuelan Winter league. Those first 138 cards have red backs. Cards numbered 139 through 188 have green backs. The rest of the set (189-338) have a light blue back. Both Bobby Cox and Dave Concepcion have cards in this set which significantly predate their Topps Rookie Cards.

COMPLETE SET 7,500.00 15,000.00
COMMON CARD (1-138) 12.50 30.00
COMMON CARD (139-188) 15.00 40.00
COMMON CARD (189-338) 2.00 5.00
1 Regino Otero 12.50 30.00
2 Alejandro Carrasquel 12.50 30.00
3 Pompeyo Davalillo 12.50 30.00
4 Gonzalo Marquez 12.50 30.00
5 Cookie Rojas 15.00 40.00
6 Teodoro Obregon 12.50 30.00
7 Paul Schall 15.00 40.00
8 Juan Francia 12.50 30.00
9 Luis Tiant 20.00 50.00
10 Jose Tartabull 12.50 30.00
10A Jose Tartabull 12.50 30.00
11 Vic Davalillo 12.50 30.00
12 Cesar Tovar 12.50 30.00
13 Ron Klimkowski 12.50 30.00
14 Diego Segui 12.50 30.00
15 Luis Penalver 12.50 30.00
16 Urbano Lugo 12.50 30.00
17 Aurelio Monteagudo 12.50 30.00
18 Richard Underwood 12.50 30.00
19 Nelson Castellanos 12.50 30.00
20 Manuel Mendible 12.50 30.00
21 Fidel Garcia 12.50 30.00
22 Luis Cordoba 12.50 30.00
23 Jesus Padron 12.50 30.00
24 Lorenzo Fernandez 12.50 30.00
25 Leopoldo Tovar 12.50 30.00
26 Carlos Loreto 12.50 30.00
27 Ossie Blanco 12.50 30.00
28 Syd O'Brien 12.50 30.00
29 Cesar Gutierrez 12.50 30.00
30 Luis Garcia 12.50 30.00
31 Fred Klages 12.50 30.00
32 Isasis Chavez 12.50 30.00
33 Walt Williams 12.50 30.00
34 Jim Hicks 12.50 30.00
35 Gustavo Sposito 12.50 30.00
36 Cisco Carlos 12.50 30.00
37 Jim Mooring 12.50 30.00
38 Alonso Olivares 12.50 30.00
39 Gracilliano Parra 12.50 30.00
40 Merritt Ranew 12.50 30.00
41 Everest Contramaestre 12.50 30.00
42 Orlando Reyes 12.50 30.00
43 Edicto Arteaga 12.50 30.00
44 Francisco Diaz 12.50 30.00
45 Victor Diaz 12.50 30.00
46 Ramon Diaz 12.50 30.00
46A Francisco Diaz 12.50 30.00
Blue Back
47 Luis Aparicio 40.00 80.00
48 Reynaldo Cordeiro CO 12.50 30.00
49 Luis Aparicio 40.00 80.00
50 Ramon Webster 12.50 30.00
51 Remigio Hermoso 12.50 30.00
52 Mike de la Hoz 12.50 30.00
53 Enzo Hernandez 12.50 30.00
54 Ed Watt 12.50 30.00
55 Angel Bravo 12.50 30.00
56 Merv Rettenmund 12.50 30.00
57 Jose Herrera 12.50 30.00
58 Tom Fisher 12.50 30.00
59 Jim Weaver 12.50 30.00
60 Juan Quintana 12.50 30.00
60A Frank Fernandez 12.50 30.00
Blue Back
61 Hector Urbano 12.50 30.00
62A Hector Brito 12.50 30.00
Blue Back
63 Jesus Romero 12.50 30.00
64 Carlos Moreno 12.50 30.00
65 Nestor Mendible 12.50 30.00
66 Armando Ortiz 12.50 30.00
67 Graciano Ravelo 12.50 30.00
68 Paul Knechtges 12.50 30.00
69 Marcelino Lopez 12.50 30.00
70 Wilfredo Calvino 12.50 30.00
71 Jesus Avila 12.50 30.00
72 Carlos Pascual 12.50 30.00
73 Bob Burda 12.50 30.00
73A Bob Burda 12.50 30.00
74 Elio Chacon 12.50 30.00
75 Jacinto Hernandez 12.50 30.00
76 Jose Tovar 12.50 30.00
77 Bill Whitby 12.50 30.00
78 Enrique Izquierdo 12.50 30.00
79 Sandy Valdespino 12.50 30.00
80 John Lewis 12.50 30.00
81 Hector Martinez 12.50 30.00
82 Rene Paredes 12.50 30.00
83 Danny Morris 12.50 30.00
84 Pedro Ramos 12.50 30.00
85 Jose Ramon Lopez 12.50 30.00
86 Jesus Rizales 12.50 30.00
87 Winston Acosta 12.50 30.00
88 Pablo Bello 12.50 30.00
89 Dave Concepcion 50.00 100.00
90 Manuel Garcia 12.50 30.00
91 Anibal Longa 12.50 30.00
92 Francisco Moscoso 12.50 30.00
93 Mel McGaha MG 12.50 30.00
94 Aquiles Gomez 12.50 30.00
95 Alfonso Carrasquel UER 12.50 30.00
Card numbered 115
95A Alfonso Carrasquel 12.50 30.00
Blue Back
96 Tom Murray 12.50 30.00
97 Gus Gil 12.50 30.00
98 Damaso Blanco 12.50 30.00
99 Alberto Cambero 12.50 30.00
100 Don Bryant 12.50 30.00
101 George Culver 12.50 30.00
102 Teolindo Acosta 12.50 30.00
103 Aaron Pointer 12.50 30.00
104 Ed Kirkpatrick 12.50 30.00
106 Mike Daniel 12.50 30.00
108 Juan Quiroz 12.50 30.00
109 Juan Campos 12.50 30.00
110 Freddy Rivero 12.50 30.00
111 Dick Lemay 12.50 30.00
112 Raul Ortega 12.50 30.00
113 Bruno Estaba 12.50 30.00
114 Evangelista Nunez 12.50 30.00
115 Roberto Munoz 12.50 30.00
116 Tony Castanos 12.50 30.00
117 Domingo Barboza 12.50 30.00
118 Lucio Celis 12.50 30.00
119 Carlos Santeliz 12.50 30.00
120 Bart Shirley 12.50 30.00
121 Nuedo Morales 12.50 30.00
122 Bobby Cox 50.00 100.00
123 Cruz Amaya 12.50 30.00
Blue Back
124 Jim Campanis 12.50 30.00
125 Dave Roberts 12.50 30.00
126 Jerry Crider 12.50 30.00
127 Domingo Carrasquel 12.50 30.00
128 Leo Marentette 12.50 30.00
129 Frank Kreutzer 12.50 30.00
130 Jim Dickson 12.50 30.00
131 Bob Oliver 12.50 30.00
132 Pablo Torrealba 12.50 30.00
133 Pablo Torrealba 12.50 30.00
134 Iran Paz 12.50 30.00
135 Eliecer Bueno 12.50 30.00
136 Claudio Urdaneta 12.50 30.00
137 Faustino Zabala 12.50 30.00
138 Dario Chirinos 12.50 30.00
139 Walter Johnson 150.00 300.00
140 Bill Dickey 75.00 150.00
141 Lou Gehrig 300.00 600.00
142 Rogers Hornsby 150.00 300.00
143 Honus Wagner 200.00 400.00
144 Pie Traynor 75.00 150.00
145 Joe DiMaggio 300.00 600.00

146 Ty Cobb	300.00	600.00
147 Babe Ruth	400.00	800.00
148 Ted Williams	300.00	600.00
149 Mil Ott	75.00	150.00
150 Cy Young	150.00	300.00
151 Christy Mathewson	150.00	300.00
152 Warren Spahn	75.00	150.00
153 Mickey Cochrane	75.00	150.00
154 George Sisler	60.00	120.00
155 Jimmy Collins	50.00	100.00
156 Tris Speaker	125.00	250.00
157 Stan Musial	150.00	300.00
158 Luke Appling	60.00	120.00
159 Nap Lajoie	125.00	250.00
160 Bob Feller	150.00	300.00
161 Bill Terry	50.00	100.00
162 Sandy Koufax	200.00	400.00
163 Jimmy Foxx (Jimmie)	150.00	300.00
164 Joe Cronin	60.00	120.00
165 Frank Frisch	60.00	120.00
166 Paul Waner	75.00	150.00
167 Lloyd Waner	60.00	120.00
168 Lefty Grove	125.00	250.00
169 Bobby Doerr	50.00	100.00
170 Al Simmons	60.00	120.00
171 Grover Alexander	150.00	300.00
172 Carl Hubbell	150.00	300.00
173 Mordecai Brown	125.00	250.00
174 Ted Lyons	60.00	120.00
175 Johnny Vander Meer	50.00	100.00
176 Alex Carrasquel	40.00	80.00
177 Satchel Paige	250.00	500.00
178 Whitey Ford	125.00	250.00
179 Yogi Berra	125.00	250.00
180 Roy Campanella	125.00	250.00
181 Chico Carrasquel	40.00	80.00
182 Johnny Mize	60.00	120.00
183 Ted Kluszewski	40.00	80.00
Ray Herbert		
184 Jackie Robinson	300.00	600.00
185 Beto Avila	40.00	80.00
186 Phil Rizzuto	125.00	250.00
187 Minnie Minoso	50.00	100.00
188 Conrado Marrero	40.00	80.00
189 Luis Aparicio	6.00	15.00
190 Vic Davalillo	8.00	20.00
191 Cesar Tovar	8.00	20.00
192 Mickey Mantle	1,500.00	3,000.00
193 Carl Yastrzemski	250.00	500.00
194 Frank Robinson	75.00	150.00
195 Willie Horton	10.00	25.00
196 Gary Peters	8.00	20.00
197 Bert Campaneris	8.00	20.00
198 Norm Cash	12.50	30.00
199 Boog Powell	30.00	60.00
200 George Scott	8.00	20.00
201 Frank Howard	10.00	25.00
202 Rick Reichardt	8.00	20.00
203 Jose Cardenal	8.00	20.00
204 Rico Petrocelli	8.00	20.00
205 Lew Krausse	8.00	20.00
206 Harmon Killebrew	75.00	150.00
207 Leon Wagner	8.00	20.00
208 Joe Foy	8.00	20.00
209 Joe Pepitone	10.00	25.00
210 Al Kaline	75.00	150.00
211 Brooks Robinson	100.00	200.00
212 Bill Freehan	8.00	20.00
213 Willie Mays	400.00	800.00
214 Ed Mathews	75.00	150.00
215 Dick Green	8.00	20.00
216 Tom Tresh	8.00	20.00
217 Dean Chance	8.00	20.00
218 Paul Blair	8.00	20.00
219 Larry Brown	8.00	20.00
220 Fred Valentine	8.00	20.00
221 Al Downing	8.00	20.00
222 Earl Battey	8.00	20.00
223 Don Mincher	8.00	20.00
224 Tommie Agee	8.00	20.00
225 Jim McGlothlin	8.00	20.00
226 Zolio Versalles	8.00	20.00
227 Curt Blefary	8.00	20.00
228 Joel Horlen	8.00	20.00
229 Stu Miller	8.00	20.00
230 Tony Oliva	12.50	30.00
231 Paul Casanova	8.00	20.00
232 Orlando Pena	8.00	20.00
233 Ron Hansen	8.00	20.00
234 Earl Wilson	8.00	20.00
235 Ken Boyer	10.00	25.00
236 Jim Kaat	12.50	30.00
237 Dalton Jones	8.00	20.00
238 Pete Ward	8.00	20.00
239 Mickey Lolich	10.00	25.00
240 Jose Santiago	8.00	20.00
241 Dick McAuliffe	8.00	20.00
242 Mel Stottlemyre	10.00	25.00
243 Camilo Pascual	8.00	20.00
244 Jim Fregosi	10.00	25.00
245 Tony Conigliaro	50.00	100.00
246 Sonny Siebert	8.00	20.00
247 Jim Perry	8.00	20.00
248 Dave McNally	8.00	20.00
249 Fred Whitfield	8.00	20.00
250 Ken Berry	8.00	20.00
251 Jim Grant	8.00	20.00
252 Hank Aguirre	8.00	20.00
253 Don Wert	8.00	20.00
254 Wally Bunker	8.00	20.00
255 Elston Howard	12.50	30.00
256 Dave Johnson	8.00	20.00
257 Hoyt Wilhelm	50.00	100.00
258 Dick Buford	8.00	20.00
259 Sam McDowell	8.00	20.00
260 Bobby Knoop	8.00	20.00
261 Denny McLain	30.00	60.00
262 Steve Hargan	8.00	20.00
263 Jim Nash	8.00	20.00
264 Jerry Adair	8.00	20.00
265 Tony Gonzalez	8.00	20.00
266 Mike Shannon	8.00	20.00
267 Bob Gibson	100.00	200.00
268 John Roseboro	8.00	20.00
269 Bob Aspromonte	8.00	20.00
270 Pete Rose	400.00	800.00
271 Rico Carty	8.00	20.00
272 Juan Pizarro	8.00	20.00
273 Jim Lonborg	8.00	20.00
274 Jim Bunning	150.00	300.00
275 Ernie Banks	100.00	200.00
276 Curt Flood	10.00	25.00
277 Mack Jones	8.00	20.00
278 Roberto Clemente	500.00	1,000.00
279 Sammy Ellis	8.00	20.00
280 Willie Stargell	100.00	200.00
281 Felipe Alou	10.00	25.00
282 Ed Kranepool	8.00	20.00
283 Nelson Briles	8.00	20.00
284 Hank Aaron	400.00	800.00
285 Vada Pinson	10.00	25.00
286 Jim LeFebvre	8.00	20.00
287 Hal Lanier	8.00	20.00
288 Ron Swoboda	8.00	20.00
289 Mike McCormick	8.00	20.00
290 Lou Johnson	8.00	20.00
291 Orlando Cepeda	30.00	60.00
292 Rusty Staub	12.50	30.00
293 Manny Mota	10.00	25.00
294 Tommy Harper	8.00	20.00
295 Don Drysdale	75.00	150.00
296 Mel Queen	8.00	20.00
297 Red Schoendienst	40.00	80.00
298 Matty Alou	10.00	25.00
299 Johnny Callison	8.00	20.00
300 Jual Marichal	75.00	150.00
301 Al McBean	8.00	20.00
302 Claude Osteen	8.00	20.00
303 Willie McCovey	100.00	200.00
304 Jim Owens	8.00	20.00
305 Chico Ruiz	8.00	20.00
306 Fergie Jenkins	75.00	150.00
307 Lou Brock	100.00	200.00
308 Joe Morgan	75.00	150.00
309 Ron Santo	12.50	30.00
310 Chico Cardenas	8.00	20.00
311 Richie Allen	10.00	25.00
312 Gaylord Perry	75.00	150.00
313 Bill Mazeroski	40.00	80.00
314 Tony Taylor	8.00	20.00
315 Tommy Helms	8.00	20.00
316 Jim Wynn	10.00	25.00
317 Don Sutton	75.00	150.00
318 Mike Cueller	10.00	25.00
319 Willie Davis	8.00	20.00
320 Julian Javier	8.00	20.00
321 Maury Willis	10.00	25.00
322 Gene Alley	8.00	20.00
323 Ray Sadecki	8.00	20.00
324 Joe Torre	12.50	30.00
325 Jim Maloney	8.00	20.00
326 Jim Davenport	8.00	20.00
327 Tony Perez	60.00	120.00
328 Roger Maris	150.00	300.00
329 Chris Short	8.00	20.00
330 Jesus Alou	8.00	20.00
331 Deron Johnson	8.00	20.00
332 Tommy Davis	10.00	25.00
333 Bob Veale	8.00	20.00
334 Bill McCool	8.00	20.00
335 Jim Hart	8.00	20.00
336 Roy Face	10.00	25.00
337 Billy Williams	50.00	100.00
338 Dick Groat	10.00	25.00

1967 Topps Who Am I

These are just the "baseball" players issued by Topps in this set which features famous people. The front features a drawing of the person along with their name and claim to fame on the top. The back asks some questions about the person. We are just cataloguing the baseball players here. Cards with the player's name unscratched are worth 3x the listed prices.

COMPLETE SET (44)	250.00	500.00
1 George Washington		
2 Andrew Jackson		
3 James Monroe		
4 Joan of Arc		
5 Nero		
6 Franklin D. Roosevelt		
7 Henry VIII		
8 William Shakespeare		
9 Clara Barton		
10 Napoleon Bonaparte		
11 Harry Truman		
12 Babe Ruth	100.00	200.00
13 Thomas Jefferson		
14 Dolley Madison		
15 Julius Caesar		
16 Robert Louis Stevenson		
17 Woodrow Wilson		
18 Stonewall Jackson		
19 Charles de Gaulle		
20 John Quincy Adams		
21 Christopher Columbus		
22 Mickey Mantle	75.00	150.00
23 Albert Einstein		
24 Benjamin Franklin		
25 Abraham Lincoln		
26 Leif Ericsson		
27 Adm. Richard Byrd		
28 Capt. Kidd		
29 Thomas Edison		
30 Ulysses S. Grant		
31 Queen Elizabeth II		
32 Alexander Graham Bell		
33 Willie Mays	75.00	200.00
34 Theodore Roosevelt		
35 Genghis Khan		
36 Daniel Boone		
37 Winston Churchill		
38 Paul Revere		
39 Florence Nightingale		
40 Dwight Eisenhower		
41 Sandy Koufax	50.00	100.00
42 Jacqueline Kennedy		
43 Lady Bird Johnson		
44 Lyndon Johnson		

1968 Topps

The cards in this 598-card set measure 2 1/2" by 3 1/2". The 1968 Topps set includes Sporting News All-Star Selections as card numbers 361 to 380. Other subsets in the set include League Leaders (1-12) and World Series cards (151-158). The front of each checklist card features a picture of a popular player inside a circle. Higher numbers 458 to 598 are slightly more difficult to obtain. The first series looks different from the other series, as it has a lighter, wider mesh background on the card front. The later series all had a much darker, finer mesh pattern. Among other fashions, cards were issued in five-card nickel packs. Those five cent packs were issued 24 packs to a box. Thirty-six card rack packs with an SRP of 29 cents were also issued. The key Rookie Cards in the set are Johnny Bench and Nolan Ryan. Lastly, some cards were also issued along with the "Win-A-Card" board game from Milton Bradley that included cards from the 1965 Topps Hot Rods and 1967 Topps football card sets. This version of these cards is somewhat difficult to distinguish, but are often found with a slight touch of the 1967 football set white border on the front top or bottom edge as well as a brighter yellow card back instead of the darker yellow or gold color. The known cards from this product include card numbers 16, 20, 34, 45, 108, and 149.

COMPLETE SET (598)	1,500.00	3,000.00
COMMON CARD (1-457)	.75	2.00
COMMON CARD (458-598)	1.50	4.00
WRAPPER (5-CENT)	10.00	25.00
1 Clemente/Gonz/Alou LL	10.00	25.00
2 Yaz/F.Rob/Kaline LL	6.00	15.00
3 Cep/Clemente/Aaron LL	15.00	40.00
4 Yaz/Killebrew/F.Rob LL	6.00	15.00
5 Aaron/Santo/McCovey LL	8.00	20.00
6 Yaz/Killebrew/Howard LL	3.00	8.00
7 Niekro/Bunning/Short LL	1.50	4.00
8 Horlen/Peters/Siebert LL	1.50	4.00
9 McCor/Jenkins/Bunning LL	1.50	4.00
10A Lonb/Wils/Chance LL ERR	1.50	4.00
10B Lonb/Wils/Chance LL COR	1.50	4.00
11 Bunning/jenkins/Perry LL	2.50	6.00
12 Lonborg/McDow/Chance LL	1.50	4.00
13 Chuck Hartenstein RC	.75	2.00
14 Jerry McNertney	.75	2.00
15 Ron Hunt	.75	2.00
16 L.Piniella/R.Scheinblum	2.50	6.00
17 Dick Hall	.75	2.00
18 Mike Hershberger	.75	2.00
19 Juan Pizarro	.75	2.00
20 Brooks Robinson	12.00	30.00
21 Ron Davis	.75	2.00
22 Pat Dobson	1.50	4.00
23 Chico Cardenas	1.50	4.00
24 Bobby Locke	.75	2.00
25 Julian Javier	1.50	4.00
26 Darrell Brandon	.75	2.00
27 Gil Hodges MG	8.00	20.00
28 Ted Uhlaender	.75	2.00
29 Joe Verbanic	.75	2.00
30 Joe Torre	2.50	6.00
31 Ed Stroud	.75	2.00
32 Joe Gibbon	.75	2.00
33 Pete Ward	.75	2.00
34 Al Ferrara	.75	2.00
35 Steve Hargan	.75	2.00
36 B.Moose RC/B.Robertson RC	1.50	4.00
37 Billy Williams	3.00	8.00
38 Tony Pierce	.75	2.00
39 Cookie Rojas	.75	2.00
40 Denny McLain	3.00	8.00
41 Julio Gotay	.75	2.00
42 Larry Haney	.75	2.00
43 Gary Bell	.75	2.00
44 Frank Kostro	.75	2.00
45 Tom Seaver	30.00	80.00
46 Dave Ricketts	.75	2.00
47 Ralph Houk MG	1.50	4.00
48 Ted Davidson	.75	2.00
49A E.Brinkman White	.75	2.00
49B E.Brinkman Yellow Tm	20.00	50.00
50 Willie Mays	40.00	100.00
51 Bob Locker	.75	2.00
52 Hawk Taylor	.75	2.00
53 Gene Alley	1.50	4.00
54 Stan Williams	.75	2.00
55 Felipe Alou	1.50	4.00
56 D.Leonhard RC/D.May RC	.75	2.00
57 Dan Schneider	.75	2.00
58 Eddie Mathews	6.00	15.00
59 Don Lock	.75	2.00
60 Ken Holtzman	1.50	4.00
61 Reggie Smith	1.50	4.00
62 Chuck Dobson	.75	2.00
63 Dick Kenworthy RC	.75	2.00
64 Jim Merritt	.75	2.00
65 John Roseboro	1.50	4.00
66A Casey Cox White	.75	2.00
66B C.Cox Yellow Tm	50.00	100.00
67 Checklist 1/Kaat	2.50	6.00
68 Ron Willis	.75	2.00
69 Tom Tresh	1.50	4.00
70 Bob Veale	1.50	4.00
71 Vern Fuller RC	.75	2.00
72 Tommy John	2.50	6.00
73 Jim Ray Hart	1.50	4.00
74 Milt Pappas	1.50	4.00
75 Don Mincher	.75	2.00
76 J.Britton/R.Reed RC	1.50	4.00
77 Don Wilson RC	1.50	4.00
78 Jim Northrup	2.50	6.00
79 Ted Kubiak RC	.75	2.00
80 Rod Carew	20.00	50.00
81 Larry Jackson	.75	2.00
82 Sam Bowens	.75	2.00
83 John Stephenson	.75	2.00
84 Bob Tolan	.75	2.00
85 Gaylord Perry	3.00	8.00
86 Willie Stargell	10.00	25.00
87 Dick Williams MG	1.50	4.00
88 Phil Regan	1.50	4.00
89 Jake Gibbs	1.50	4.00
90 Vada Pinson	1.50	4.00
91 Jim Ollom	.75	2.00
92 Ed Kranepool	1.50	4.00
93 Tony Cloninger	.75	2.00
94 Lee Maye	.75	2.00
95 Bob Aspromonte	.75	2.00
96 F.Coggins RC/D.Nold	.75	2.00
97 Tom Phoebus	.75	2.00
98 Gary Sutherland	.75	2.00
99 Rocky Colavito	3.00	8.00
100 Bob Gibson	20.00	50.00
101 Glenn Beckert	1.50	4.00
102 Jose Cardenal	1.50	4.00
103 Don Sutton	3.00	8.00
104 Dick Dietz	.75	2.00
105 Al Downing	1.50	4.00
106 Dalton Jones	.75	2.00
107A Checklist 2/Marichal Wide	2.50	6.00
107B Checklist 2/J.Marichal Fine	2.50	6.00
108 Don Pavletich	.75	2.00
109 Bert Campaneris	1.50	4.00
110 Hank Aaron	40.00	100.00
111 Rich Reese	.75	2.00
112 Woody Fryman	.75	2.00
113 T.Matchick/D.Patterson RC	1.50	4.00
114 Ron Swoboda	1.50	4.00
115 Sam McDowell	1.50	4.00
116 Ken McMullen	.75	2.00
117 Larry Jaster	.75	2.00
118 Mark Belanger	1.50	4.00
119 Ted Savage	.75	2.00
120 Mel Stottlemyre	1.50	4.00
121 Jimmie Hall	.75	2.00
122 Gene Mauch MG	1.50	4.00
123 Jose Santiago	.75	2.00
124 Nate Oliver	.75	2.00
125 Joel Horlen	.75	2.00
126 Bobby Etheridge RC	.75	2.00
127 Paul Lindblad	.75	2.00
128 T.Dukes RC/A.Harris	.75	2.00
129 Mickey Stanley	2.50	6.00
130 Tony Perez	10.00	25.00
131 Frank Bertaina	.75	2.00
132 Bud Harrelson	1.50	4.00
133 Fred Whitfield	.75	2.00
134 Pat Jarvis	.75	2.00
135 Paul Blair	1.50	4.00
136 Randy Hundley	1.50	4.00
137 Minnesota Twins TC	1.50	4.00
138 Ruben Amaro	.75	2.00
139 Chris Short	.75	2.00
140 Tony Conigliaro	3.00	8.00
141 Dal Maxvill	.75	2.00
142 B.Bradford RC/B.Voss	.75	2.00
143 Pete Cimino	.75	2.00
144 Joe Morgan	8.00	20.00
145 Don Drysdale	10.00	25.00
146 Sal Bando	1.50	4.00
147 Frank Linzy	.75	2.00
148 Dave Bristol MG	.75	2.00
149 Bob Saverine	.75	2.00
150 Roberto Clemente	40.00	100.00
151 Lou Brock WS1	4.00	10.00
152 Carl Yastrzemski WS2	4.00	10.00
153 Nelson Briles WS3	2.00	5.00
154 Bob Gibson WS4	4.00	10.00
155 Jim Lonborg WS5	2.00	5.00
156 Rico Petrocelli WS6	2.00	5.00
157 St. Louis Wins It WS7	2.00	5.00
158 Cardinals Celebrate WS	2.00	5.00
159 Don Kessinger	1.50	4.00
160 Earl Wilson	1.50	4.00
161 Norm Miller	.75	2.00
162 H.Gilson RC/M.Torrez RC	1.50	4.00
163 Gene Brabender	.75	2.00
164 Ramon Webster	.75	2.00
165 Tony Oliva	2.50	6.00
166 Claude Raymond	.75	2.00

167 Elston Howard 2.50 6.00
168 Los Angeles Dodgers TC 1.50 4.00
169 Bob Bolin .75 2.00
170 Jim Fregosi 1.50 4.00
171 Don Nottebart .75 2.00
172 Walt Williams .75 2.00
173 John Boozer .75 2.00
174 Bob Tillman .75 2.00
175 Maury Wills 2.50 6.00
176 Bob Allen .75 2.00
177 N.Ryan RC/J.Koosman RC 400.00 1,000.00
178 Don Wert 1.50 4.00
179 Bill Stoneman RC .75 2.00
180 Curt Flood 2.50 6.00
181 Jerry Zimmerman .75 2.00
182 Dave Giusti .75 2.00
183 Bob Kennedy MG 1.50 4.00
184 Lou Johnson .75 2.00
185 Tom Haller .75 2.00
186 Eddie Watt .75 2.00
187 Sonny Jackson .75 2.00
188 Cap Peterson .75 2.00
189 Bill Landis RC .75 2.00
190 Bill White 1.50 4.00
191 Dan Frisella RC .75 2.00
192A Checklist 3/Yaz Ball 3.00 8.00
192B Checklist 3/Yaz Game 3.00 8.00
193 Jack Hamilton .75 2.00
194 Don Buford .75 2.00
195 Joe Pepitone 1.50 4.00
196 Gary Nolan RC 1.50 4.00
197 Larry Brown .75 2.00
198 Roy Face 1.50 4.00
199 R.Rodriguez RC/D.Osteen .75 2.00
200 Orlando Cepeda 10.00 25.00
201 Mike Marshall RC 1.50 4.00
202 Adolfo Phillips .75 2.00
203 Dick Kelley .75 2.00
204 Andy Etchebarren .75 2.00
205 Juan Marichal 3.00 8.00
206 Cal Ermer MG RC .75 2.00
207 Carroll Sembera .75 2.00
208 Willie Davis 1.50 4.00
209 Tim Cullen .75 2.00
210 Gary Peters .75 2.00
211 J.C. Martin .75 2.00
212 Dave Morehead .75 2.00
213 Chico Ruiz .75 2.00
214 S.Bahnsen/F.Fernandez 1.50 4.00
215 Jim Bunning 3.00 8.00
216 Bubba Morton .75 2.00
217 Dick Farrell .75 2.00
218 Ken Suarez .75 2.00
219 Rob Gardner .75 2.00
220 Harmon Killebrew 12.00 30.00
221 Atlanta Braves TC 1.50 4.00
222 Jim Hardin RC .75 2.00
223 Ollie Brown .75 2.00
224 Jack Aker .75 2.00
225 Richie Allen 2.50 6.00
226 Jimmie Price .75 2.00
227 Joe Hoerner .75 2.00
228 J.Billingham RC/J.Fairey RC 1.50 4.00
229 Fred Klages .75 2.00
230 Pete Rose 30.00 60.00
231 Dave Baldwin RC .75 2.00
232 Denis Menke .75 2.00
233 George Scott 1.50 4.00
234 Bill Monbouquette .75 2.00
235 Ron Santo 3.00 8.00
236 Tug McGraw 2.50 6.00
237 Alvin Dark MG 1.50 4.00
238 Tom Satriano .75 2.00
239 Bill Henry .75 2.00
240 Al Kaline 15.00 40.00
241 Felix Millan .75 2.00
242 Moe Drabowsky 1.50 4.00
243 Rich Rollins .75 2.00
244 John Donaldson RC .75 2.00
245 Tony Gonzalez .75 2.00
246 Fritz Peterson 1.50 4.00
247 Johnny Bench RC 100.00 250.00
248 Fred Valentine .75 2.00
249 Bill Singer .75 2.00
250 Carl Yastrzemski 15.00 40.00
251 Manny Sanguillen RC 2.50 6.00
252 California Angels TC 1.50 4.00
253 Dick Hughes .75 2.00
254 Cleon Jones 1.50 4.00
255 Dean Chance 1.50 4.00
256 Norm Cash 2.50 6.00
257 Phil Niekro 8.00 20.00
258 J.Arcia RC/B.Schlesinger .75 2.00
259 Ken Boyer 2.50 6.00
260 Jim Wynn 1.50 4.00
261 Dave Duncan 1.50 4.00
262 Rick Wise 1.50 4.00
263 Horace Clarke 1.50 4.00
264 Ted Abernathy .75 2.00
265 Tommy Davis 1.50 4.00
266 Paul Popovich .75 2.00
267 Herman Franks MG .75 2.00
268 Bob Humphreys .75 2.00
269 Bob Tiefenauer .75 2.00
270 Matty Alou 1.50 4.00
271 Bobby Knoop .75 2.00
272 Ray Culp .75 2.00
273 Dave Johnson 1.50 4.00
274 Mike Cuellar 1.50 4.00
275 Tim McCarver 2.50 6.00
276 Jim Roland .75 2.00
277 Jerry Buchek .75 2.00
278 Checklist 4/Cepeda 2.50 6.00
279 Bill Hands .75 2.00
280 Mickey Mantle 150.00 400.00
281 Jim Campanis .75 2.00
282 Rick Monday 1.50 4.00
283 Mel Queen .75 2.00
284 Johnny Briggs .75 2.00
285 Dick McAuliffe 2.50 6.00
286 Cecil Upshaw .75 2.00
287 M.Abarbanel RC/C.Carlos RC .75 2.00
288 Dave Wickersham .75 2.00
289 Woody Held .75 2.00
290 Willie McCovey 12.00 30.00
291 Dick Lines .75 2.00
292 Art Shamsky .75 2.00
293 Bruce Howard .75 2.00
294 Red Schoendienst MG 2.50 6.00
295 Sonny Siebert .75 2.00
296 Byron Browne .75 2.00
297 Russ Gibson .75 2.00
298 Jim Brewer .75 2.00
299 Gene Michael 1.50 4.00
300 Rusty Staub 1.50 4.00
301 G.Mitterwald RC/R.Renick RC .75 2.00
302 Gerry Arrigo .75 2.00
303 Dick Green 1.50 4.00
304 Sandy Valdespino .75 2.00
305 Minnie Rojas .75 2.00
306 Mike Ryan .75 2.00
307 John Hiller 1.50 4.00
308 Pittsburgh Pirates TC 1.50 4.00
309 Ken Henderson .75 2.00
310 Luis Aparicio 3.00 8.00
311 Jack Lamabe .75 2.00
312 Curt Blefary .75 2.00
313 Al Weis .75 2.00
314 B.Rohr/G.Spriggs .75 2.00
315 Zoilo Versalles .75 2.00
316 Steve Barber .75 2.00
317 Ron Brand .75 2.00
318 Chico Salmon .75 2.00
319 George Culver .75 2.00
320 Frank Howard 1.50 4.00
321 Leo Durocher MG 2.50 6.00
322 Dave Boswell .75 2.00
323 Deron Johnson 1.50 4.00
324 Jim Nash .75 2.00
325 Manny Mota 1.50 4.00
326 Dennis Ribant .75 2.00
327 Tony Taylor 1.50 4.00
328 C.Vinson RC/J.Weaver RC .75 2.00
329 Duane Josephson .75 2.00
330 Roger Maris 20.00 50.00
331 Dan Osinski .75 2.00
332 Doug Rader 1.50 4.00
333 Ron Herbel .75 2.00
334 Baltimore Orioles TC 1.50 4.00
335 Bob Allison 1.50 4.00
336 John Purdin .75 2.00
337 Bill Robinson 1.50 4.00
338 Bob Johnson .75 2.00
339 Rich Nye .75 2.00
340 Max Alvis .75 2.00
341 Jim Lemon MG .75 2.00
342 Ken Johnson .75 2.00
343 Jim Gosger .75 2.00
344 Donn Clendenon 1.50 4.00
345 Bob Hendley .75 2.00
346 Jerry Adair .75 2.00
347 George Brunet .75 2.00
348 L.Colton RC/D.Thoenen RC .75 2.00
349 Ed Spiezio 1.50 4.00
350 Hoyt Wilhelm 3.00 8.00
351 Bob Barton .75 2.00
352 Jackie Hernandez RC .75 2.00
353 Mack Jones .75 2.00
354 Pete Richert .75 2.00
355 Ernie Banks 20.00 50.00
356A Checklist 5/Holtzman Center 2.50 6.00
356B Checklist 5/Holtzman Right 2.50 6.00
357 Len Gabrielson .75 2.00
358 Mike Epstein .75 2.00
359 Joe Moeller .75 2.00
360 Willie Horton 2.50 6.00
361 Harmon Killebrew AS 8.00 20.00
362 Orlando Cepeda AS 2.50 6.00
363 Rod Carew AS 3.00 8.00
364 Joe Morgan AS 3.00 8.00
365 Brooks Robinson AS 3.00 8.00
366 Ron Santo AS 2.50 6.00
367 Jim Fregosi AS 1.50 4.00
368 Gene Alley AS 1.50 4.00
369 Carl Yastrzemski AS 10.00 25.00
370 Hank Aaron AS 20.00 50.00
371 Tony Oliva AS 2.50 6.00
372 Lou Brock AS 6.00 15.00
373 Frank Robinson AS 3.00 8.00
374 Roberto Clemente AS 20.00 50.00
375 Bill Freehan AS 1.50 4.00
376 Tim McCarver AS 1.50 4.00
377 Joel Horlen AS 1.50 4.00
378 Bob Gibson AS 3.00 8.00
379 Gary Peters AS 1.50 4.00
380 Ken Holtzman AS 1.50 4.00
381 Boog Powell 1.50 4.00
382 Ramon Hernandez .75 2.00
383 Steve Whitaker .75 2.00
384 B.Henry/H.McRae RC 2.50 6.00
385 Jim Hunter 4.00 10.00
386 Greg Goossen .75 2.00
387 Joe Foy .75 2.00
388 Ray Washburn .75 2.00
389 Jay Johnstone 1.50 4.00
390 Bill Mazeroski 3.00 8.00
391 Bob Priddy .75 2.00
392 Grady Hatton MG .75 2.00
393 Jim Perry 1.50 4.00
394 Tommie Aaron 2.50 6.00
395 Camilo Pascual 1.50 4.00
396 Bobby Wine .75 2.00
397 Vic Davalillo .75 2.00
398 Jim Grant .75 2.00
399 Ray Oyler 1.50 4.00
400A Mike McCormick YT 1.50 4.00
400B M.McCormick White Tm 400.00 800.00
401 Mets Team 1.50 4.00
402 Mike Hegan 1.50 4.00
403 John Buzhardt .75 2.00
404 Floyd Robinson .75 2.00
405 Tommy Helms 1.50 4.00
406 Dick Ellsworth .75 2.00
407 Gary Kolb .75 2.00
408 Steve Carlton 20.00 50.00
409 F.Peters RC/R.Stone .75 2.00
410 Ferguson Jenkins 4.00 10.00
411 Ron Hansen .75 2.00
412 Clay Carroll 1.50 4.00
413 Tom McCraw .75 2.00
414 Mickey Lolich 3.00 8.00
415 Johnny Callison 1.50 4.00
416 Bill Rigney MG .75 2.00
417 Willie Crawford .75 2.00
418 Eddie Fisher .75 2.00
419 Jack Hiatt .75 2.00
420 Cesar Tovar .75 2.00
421 Ron Taylor .75 2.00
422 Rene Lachemann .75 2.00
423 Fred Gladding .75 2.00
424 Chicago White Sox TC 1.50 4.00
425 Jim Maloney 1.50 4.00
426 Hank Allen .75 2.00
427 Dick Calmus .75 2.00
428 Vic Roznovsky .75 2.00
429 Tommie Sisk .75 2.00
430 Rico Petrocelli 1.50 4.00
431 Dooley Womack .75 2.00
432 B.Davis/J.Vidal .75 2.00
433 Bob Rodgers .75 2.00
434 Ricardo Joseph RC .75 2.00
435 Ron Perranoski 1.50 4.00
436 Hal Lanier .75 2.00
437 Don Cardwell .75 2.00
438 Lee Thomas 1.50 4.00
439 Lum Harris MG .75 2.00
440 Claude Osteen 1.50 4.00
441 Alex Johnson 1.50 4.00
442 Dick Bosman .75 2.00
443 Joe Azcue .75 2.00
444 Jack Fisher .75 2.00
445 Mike Shannon 1.50 4.00
446 Ron Kline .75 2.00
447 G.Korince/F.Lasher RC 1.50 4.00
448 Gary Wagner .75 2.00
449 Gene Oliver .75 2.00
450 Jim Kaat 2.50 6.00
451 Al Spangler .75 2.00
452 Jesus Alou .75 2.00
453 Sammy Ellis .75 2.00
454A Checklist 6/F.Rob Complete 3.00 8.00
454B Checklist 6/F.Rob Partial 3.00 8.00
455 Rico Carty 1.50 4.00
456 John O'Donoghue .75 2.00
457 Jim Lefebvre 1.50 4.00
458 Lew Krausse 2.50 6.00
459 Dick Simpson 1.50 4.00
460 Jim Lonborg 2.50 6.00
461 Chuck Hiller 1.50 4.00
462 Barry Moore 1.50 4.00
463 Jim Schaffer 1.50 4.00
464 Don McMahon 1.50 4.00
465 Tommie Agee 4.00 10.00
466 Bill Dillman 1.50 4.00
467 Dick Howser 4.00 10.00
468 Larry Sherry 1.50 4.00
469 Ty Cline 1.50 4.00
470 Bill Freehan 4.00 10.00
471 Orlando Pena 1.50 4.00
472 Walter Alston MG 2.50 6.00
473 Al Worthington 1.50 4.00
474 Paul Schaal 1.50 4.00
475 Joe Niekro 2.50 6.00
476 Woody Woodward 1.50 4.00
477 Philadelphia Phillies TC 3.00 8.00
478 Dave McNally 2.50 6.00
479 Phil Gagliano 2.50 6.00
480 Oliva/Chico/Clemente 25.00 60.00
481 John Wyatt 1.50 4.00
482 Jose Pagan 1.50 4.00
483 Darold Knowles 1.50 4.00
484 Phil Roof 1.50 4.00
485 Ken Berry 2.50 6.00
486 Cal Koonce 1.50 4.00
487 Lee May 4.00 10.00
488 Dick Tracewski 2.50 6.00
489 Wally Bunker 1.50 4.00
490 Kill/Mays/Mantle 75.00 200.00
491 Denny Lemaster 1.50 4.00
492 Jeff Torborg 2.50 6.00
493 Jim McGlothlin 1.50 4.00
494 Ray Sadecki 1.50 4.00
495 Leon Wagner 1.50 4.00
496 Steve Hamilton 2.50 6.00
497 St. Louis Cardinals TC 3.00 8.00
498 Bill Bryan 2.50 6.00
499 Steve Blass 2.50 6.00
500 Frank Robinson 12.50 30.00
501 John Odom 2.50 6.00
502 Mike Andrews 1.50 4.00
503 Al Jackson 2.50 6.00
504 Russ Snyder 1.50 4.00
505 Joe Sparma 4.00 10.00
506 Clarence Jones RC 1.50 4.00
507 Wade Blasingame 1.50 4.00
508 Duke Sims 1.50 4.00
509 Dennis Higgins 1.50 4.00
510 Ron Fairly 4.00 10.00
511 Bill Kelso 1.50 4.00
512 Grant Jackson 1.50 4.00
513 Hank Bauer MG 2.50 6.00
514 Al McBean 1.50 4.00
515 Russ Nixon 1.50 4.00
516 Pete Mikkelsen 1.50 4.00
517 Diego Segui 2.50 6.00
518A Checklist 7/Boyer ERR 5.00 12.00
518B Checklist 7/Boyer COR 5.00 12.00
519 Jerry Stephenson 1.50 4.00
520 Lou Brock 15.00 40.00
521 Don Shaw 1.50 4.00
522 Wayne Causey 1.50 4.00
523 John Tsitouris 1.50 4.00
524 Andy Kosco 2.50 6.00
525 Jim Davenport 1.50 4.00
526 Bill Denehy 1.50 4.00
527 Tito Francona 1.50 4.00
528 Detroit Tigers TC 30.00 60.00
529 Bruce Von Hoff RC 1.50 4.00
530 B.Robinson/F.Robinson 15.00 40.00
531 Chuck Hinton 1.50 4.00
532 Luis Tiant 5.00 12.00
533 Wes Parker 2.50 6.00
534 Bob Miller 2.50 6.00
535 Danny Cater 2.50 6.00
536 Bill Short 1.50 4.00
537 Norm Siebern 2.50 6.00
538 Manny Jimenez 2.50 6.00
539 J.Ray RC/M.Ferraro RC 1.50 4.00
540 Nelson Briles 2.50 6.00
541 Sandy Alomar 2.50 6.00
542 John Boccabella 1.50 4.00
543 Bob Lee 1.50 4.00
544 Mayo Smith MG 5.00 12.00
545 Lindy McDaniel 2.50 6.00
546 Roy White 2.50 6.00
547 Dan Coombs 1.50 4.00
548 Bernie Allen 1.50 4.00
549 C.Motton RC/R.Nelson RC 1.50 4.00
550 Clete Boyer 2.50 6.00
551 Darrell Sutherland 1.50 4.00
552 Ed Kirkpatrick 1.50 4.00
553 Hank Aguirre 1.50 4.00
554 Oakland Athletics TC 4.00 10.00
555 Jose Tartabull 2.50 6.00
556 Dick Selma 1.50 4.00
557 Frank Quilici 2.50 6.00
558 Johnny Edwards 1.50 4.00
559 C.Taylor RC/L.Walker 1.50 4.00
560 Paul Casanova 1.50 4.00
561 Lee Elia 1.50 4.00
562 Jim Bouton 4.00 10.00
563 Ed Charles 1.50 4.00
564 Eddie Stanky MG 2.50 6.00
565 Larry Dierker 2.50 6.00
566 Ken Harrelson 2.50 6.00
567 Clay Dalrymple 1.50 4.00
568 Willie Smith 1.50 4.00
569 I.Murrell RC/L.Rohr RC 1.50 4.00
570 Rick Reichardt 1.50 4.00
571 Tony LaRussa 5.00 12.00
572 Don Bosch RC 1.50 4.00
573 Joe Coleman 1.50 4.00
574 Cincinnati Reds TC 4.00 10.00
575 Jim Palmer 12.00 30.00
576 Dave Adlesh 1.50 4.00
577 Fred Talbot 1.50 4.00
578 Orlando Martinez 1.50 4.00
579 L.Hisle RC/M.Lum RC 4.00 10.00
580 Bob Bailey 1.50 4.00
581 Garry Roggenburk 1.50 4.00
582 Jerry Grote 4.00 10.00
583 Gates Brown 4.00 10.00
584 Larry Shepard MG RC 1.50 4.00
585 Wilbur Wood 2.50 6.00
586 Jim Pagliaroni 2.50 6.00
587 Roger Repoz 1.50 4.00
588 Dick Schofield 1.50 4.00
589 R.Clark/M.Ogier RC 1.50 4.00
590 Tommy Harper 2.50 6.00
591 Dick Nen 1.50 4.00
592 John Bateman 1.50 4.00
593 Lee Stange 1.50 4.00
594 Phil Linz 2.50 6.00
595 Phil Ortega 1.50 4.00
596 Charlie Smith 1.50 4.00
597 Bill McCool 1.50 4.00
598 Jerry May 2.50 6.00

1968 Topps Game

The cards in this 33-card set measure approximately 2 1/4" by 3 1/4". This "Game" card set of players, issued as inserts with the regular third series 1968 Topps baseball cards, was patterned directly after the Red Back and Blue Back sets of 1951. Each card has a color player photo set upon a white background, with a facsimile autograph underneath the picture. The cards have blue backs, and were also sold in boxed sets, which had an original cost of 15 cents on a limited basis.

COMPLETE SET (33) 60.00 120.00
COMP.FACT SET (33) 60.00 120.00
1 Matty Alou 1.00 2.50
2 Mickey Mantle 30.00 80.00
3 Carl Yastrzemski 3.00 8.00
4 Hank Aaron 10.00 25.00
5 Harmon Killebrew 8.00 20.00
6 Roberto Clemente 15.00 40.00
7 Frank Robinson 8.00 20.00
8 Willie Mays 15.00 40.00
9 Brooks Robinson 3.00 8.00
10 Tommy Davis .75 2.00
11 Bill Freehan 1.00 2.50
12 Claude Osteen .75 2.00
13 Gary Peters .75 2.00
14 Jim Lonborg .75 2.00
15 Steve Hargan .75 2.00
16 Dean Chance .75 2.00

17 Mike McCormick	.75	2.00
18 Tim McCarver	1.00	2.50
19 Ron Santo	1.25	3.00
20 Tony Gonzalez	.75	2.00
21 Frank Howard	1.00	2.50
22 George Scott	.75	2.00
23 Richie Allen	1.25	3.00
24 Jim Wynn	1.00	2.50
25 Gene Alley	.75	2.00
26 Rick Monday	.75	2.00
27 Al Kaline	3.00	8.00
28 Rusty Staub	1.00	2.50
29 Rod Carew	6.00	15.00
30 Pete Rose	15.00	40.00
31 Joe Torre	1.25	3.00
32 Orlando Cepeda	1.25	3.00
33 Jim Fregosi	1.00	2.50

1968 Topps Milton Bradley

These cards were included in a 1968 Milton Bradley Win-A-Card game. These cards, which are variations of some singles from the first two series, feature an "yellow" back rather than an orange back. These cards, along with some 1967 Topps Football cards and Topps Hot Rod cards were all part of the game. The key card in this set is a Nolan Ryan "Rookie".

COMPLETE SET (77)	400.00	800.00
7 Phil Niekro	1.50	4.00
Jim Bunning		
Chris Short LL		
8 AL ERA Leaders	1.50	4.00
Joel Horlen		
Gary Peters		
Sonny Siebert		
10 AL Pitching Leaders	1.50	4.00
Jim Lonborg ERR/(Misspelled Lonberg on card back)		
Earl Wilson		
Dean Chance		
13 Chuck Hartenstein	.75	2.00
16 Lou Piniella	1.50	4.00
Richie Scheinblum		
17 Dick Hall	.75	2.00
18 Mike Hershberger	.75	2.00
19 Juan Pizarro	.75	2.00
20 Brooks Robinson	10.00	25.00
24 Bobby Locke	.75	2.00
26 Darrell Brandon	.75	2.00
34 Al Ferrara	.75	2.00
36 Bob Moose	1.00	2.50
Bob Robertson		
38 Tony Pierce	.75	2.00
43 Gary Bell	.75	2.00
44 Frank Kostro	.75	2.00
45 Tom Seaver	20.00	50.00
48 Ted Davidson	.75	2.00
49 Eddie Brinkman	.75	2.00
Team Name Yellow		
53 Gene Alley	.75	2.00
57 Dan Schneider	.75	2.00
58 Eddie Mathews	6.00	15.00
60 Ken Holtzman	1.00	2.50
61 Reggie Smith	1.00	2.50
62 Chuck Dobson	.75	2.00
64 Jim Merritt	.75	2.00
66 Casey Cox	.75	2.00
Team Name Yellow		
68 Ron Willis	.75	2.00
72 Tommy John	1.25	3.00
74 Milt Pappas	1.00	2.50
77 Don Wilson	.75	2.00
78 Jim Northrup	1.25	3.00
80 Rod Carew	30.00	60.00
81 Larry Jackson	.75	2.00
85 Gaylord Perry	3.00	8.00
89 Jake Gibbs	1.00	2.50
94 Lee Maye	.75	2.00
98 Gary Sutherland	.75	2.00
99 Rocky Colavito	3.00	8.00
100 Bob Gibson	10.00	25.00
105 Al Downing	1.00	2.50
106 Dalton Jones	.75	2.00
107 Checklist 2 Juan Marichal (Tan Wide Mesh)	2.50	6.00
107 Juan Marichal CL	2.50	6.00
108 Don Pavletich	.75	2.00
110 Hank Aaron	30.00	60.00
112 Woody Fryman	.75	2.00
113 Tom Matchick	1.00	2.50
Daryl Patterson		
117 Larry Jaster	.75	2.00
118 Mark Belanger	.75	2.00
119 Ted Savage	.75	2.00
120 Mel Stottlemyre	1.00	2.50
121 Jimmie Hall	.75	2.00
124 Nate Oliver	.75	2.00
127 Paul Lindblad	.75	2.00
128 Tom Dukes	.75	2.00
Alonzo Harris		
129 Mickey Stanley	1.00	2.50
136 Randy Hundley	.75	2.00
139 Chris Short	.75	2.00
143 Pete Cimino	.75	2.00
146 Sal Bando	1.00	2.50
149 Bob Saverine	.75	2.00
155 Jim Lonborg WS	2.00	5.00
156 Rico Petrocelli WS	2.00	5.00
165 Tony Oliva	1.50	4.00
168 Dodgers Team	1.50	4.00
172 Walt Williams	.75	2.00
175 Maury Wills	1.50	4.00
176 Bob Allen	.75	2.00
177 Jerry Koosman	250.00	500.00
Nolan Ryan		
179 Bill Stoneman	.75	2.00
180 Curt Flood	1.25	3.00
185 Tom Haller	.75	2.00
189 Bill Landis	.75	2.00
191 Dan Frisella	.75	2.00
193 Jack Hamilton	.75	2.00
195 Joe Pepitone	1.25	3.00

1968 Topps 3-D

The cards in this 12-card set measure 2 1/4" by 3 1/2". Topps' experiment with "3-D" cards came two years before Kellogg's inaugural set. These cards are considered to be quite rare. This was a "test set" sold in a plain white wrapper with a sticker attached as a design, a device used by Topps for limited marketing. The cards employ a sharp foreground picture set against an indistinct background, covered by a layer of plastic to produce the "3-D" effect. The checklist below is ordered alphabetically. Test 3D cards of Sam McDowell and Brooks Robinson and were issued before this 12 card set was released. Those cards measures 2 1/4" by 3 1/4" and has the team name on the top but with no player identification. In addition, test cards of Tommy Davis, Rick Monday and John O'Donoghue were issued and recently discovered without either team identification or player identification.

COMPLETE SET (12)	6,000.00	12,000.00
WRAPPER (10-CENTS)	500.00	1,000.00
1 Roberto Clemente	2,500.00	5,000.00
2 Willie Davis	500.00	1,000.00
3 Ron Fairly	300.00	600.00
4 Curt Flood	500.00	1,000.00
5 Jim Lonborg	500.00	1,000.00
6 Jim Maloney	500.00	1,000.00
7 Tony Perez	750.00	1,500.00
8 Boog Powell	600.00	1,200.00
9 Bill Robinson	300.00	600.00
10 Rusty Staub	500.00	1,000.00
11 Mel Stottlemyre	500.00	1,000.00
12 Ron Swoboda	300.00	600.00

1968 Topps Action Stickers

This test issue is a set of 16 long stickers which is perforated and can be divided into three stickers. The middle sticker features a large sticker depicting only one player, whereas the top and bottom stickers feature three smaller stickers. These stickers are attractive and colorful. These cane packed 12 packs to a box with 24 boxes in a case.

COMPLETE SET (48)	2,000.00	4,000.00
COMMON INDIV. PANEL	6.00	15.00
COMMON TRIPLE PANEL	12.50	30.00
WRAPPER (10-CENT)	200.00	400.00
1A Horlen	6.00	15.00
Cepeda		
Mazeroski		
1B Carl Yastrzemski	125.00	250.00
1C Stottlemyre	15.00	40.00
Kaline		
Osteen		
2A Pete Ward	6.00	15.00
Mike McCormick		
Ron Swoboda		
2B Harmon Killebrew	60.00	120.00
2C Scott	12.50	30.00
Phoebus		
Drysdale		
3A Maloney	15.00	40.00
Pepitone		
Aaron		
3B Frank Robinson	75.00	150.00
3C Casanova	15.00	40.00
Reichardt		
Seaver		
4A F. Robin	12.50	30.00
Lefebvre		
Chance		
4B Ron Santo	15.00	40.00
4C Johnny Callison	6.00	15.00
Jim Lonborg		
Bob Aspromonte		
5A Bert Campaneris	6.00	15.00
Ron Santo		
Al Downing		
5B Willie Mays	150.00	300.00
5C Rose	75.00	150.00
Kranepool		
Horton		
6A Yaz	40.00	80.00
Alvis		
W. Williams		
6B Al Kaline	100.00	200.00
6C Banks	40.00	80.00
McCarver		
Staub		
7A McCovey	15.00	40.00
Monday		
Hargan		
7B Mickey Mantle	400.00	800.00
7C Carew	20.00	50.00
Gonzalez		
B. Williams		
8A Boyer	12.50	30.00
Mincher		
Bunning		
8B Joel Horlen	15.00	40.00
8C Tony Conigliaro	6.00	15.00
Ken McMullen		
Mike Cuellar		
9A Killebrew	12.50	30.00
Fregosi		
Wilson		
9B Orlando Cepeda	400.00	800.00
9C Clemente	125.00	250.00
Mays		
Short		
10A Mantle	100.00	200.00
Hunter		
Pinson		
10B Hank Aaron	150.00	300.00
10C Peters	12.50	30.00
Gibson		
Harrelson		
11A Tony Oliva	6.00	15.00
Bob Veale		
Bill Freehan		
11B Don Drysdale	60.00	120.00
11C Frank Howard	75.00	150.00
Fergie Jenkins		
Jim Wynn		
12A Joe Torre	6.00	15.00
Dick Allen		
Jim McGlothlin		
12B Roberto Clemente	200.00	400.00
12C B.Robinson	20.00	50.00
Perez		
McDow		
13A F.Robinson	15.00	40.00
Lefeb		
Chance		
13B Carl Yastrzemski	125.00	250.00
13C Phoebus	12.50	30.00
Scott		
Drysdale		
14A Horlen	6.00	15.00
Cepeda		
Mazeroski		
14B Harmon Killebrew	60.00	120.00
14C Casan	15.00	40.00
Reichardt		
Seaver		
15A Pete Ward	6.00	15.00
Mike McCormick		
Ron Swoboda		
15B Frank Robinson	100.00	200.00
15C Johnny Callison	6.00	15.00
Jim Lonborg		
Bob Aspromonte		
16A Maloney	15.00	40.00
Pepitone		
Aaron		
16B Ron Santo	15.00	40.00
16C Stottle	15.00	40.00
Kaline		
Osteen		

1968 Topps Giant Stand Ups

This test issue is quite scarce. The set features a color portrait photo of the player on a distinctive black background on heavy card stock. Each card measures 3 1/16" by 5 1/4" and is blank backed. The cards are numbered on the front in the lower left corner. Cards are found both with and without the stand up die cut.

COMPLETE SET (24)	25,000.00	50,000.00
1 Pete Rose	3,000.00	6,000.00
2 Gary Peters	300.00	600.00
3 Frank Robinson	600.00	1,200.00
4 Jim Lonborg	300.00	600.00
5 Ron Swoboda	300.00	600.00
6 Harmon Killebrew	600.00	1,200.00
7 Roberto Clemente	4,000.00	8,000.00
8 Mickey Mantle	6,000.00	12,000.00
9 Jim Fregosi	300.00	600.00
10 Al Kaline	600.00	1,200.00
11 Don Drysdale	600.00	1,200.00
12 Dean Chance	300.00	600.00
13 Orlando Cepeda	400.00	800.00
14 Tim McCarver	400.00	800.00
15 Frank Howard	400.00	800.00
16 Max Alvis	300.00	600.00
17 Rusty Staub	400.00	800.00
18 Richie Allen	400.00	800.00
19 Willie Mays	4,000.00	8,000.00
20 Hank Aaron	4,000.00	8,000.00
21 Carl Yastrzemski	2,500.00	5,000.00
22 Ron Santo	400.00	800.00
23 Jim Hunter	600.00	1,200.00
24 Jim Wynn	300.00	600.00

1968 Topps Plaks

These brown plastic "busts," measure roughly 1" by 2". One Checklist per pack was included with these plaks, which were issued three to a 10 cent pack (which came 12 to a box), which measured 2 1/8" by 4". The set is sequenced and therefore checklisted in alphabetical order within each league. Recent research appears to indicate that the following five plaks were never issued: Gary Peters, Frank Robinson, Hank Aaron, Don Drysdale and Willie Mays. We will keep searching to see if in fact these plaks were produced and if they were not, we will in the near future delete them from our checklist.

COMPLETE SET (26)	4,000.00	8,000.00
*WRAPPER (10-CENT)		
1 Max Alvis	40.00	80.00
2 Dean Chance	50.00	100.00
3 Jim Fregosi	50.00	100.00
4 Frank Howard	75.00	150.00
5 Jim Hunter	100.00	200.00
6 Al Kaline	200.00	400.00
7 Harmon Killebrew	125.00	250.00
8 Jim Lonborg	50.00	100.00
9 Mickey Mantle	750.00	1,500.00
10 Gary Peters	40.00	80.00
11 Frank Robinson	125.00	250.00
12 Carl Yastrzemski	150.00	300.00
13 Hank Aaron	400.00	800.00
14 Richie Allen	75.00	150.00
15 Orlando Cepeda	100.00	200.00
16 Roberto Clemente	500.00	1,000.00
17 Tommy Davis	50.00	100.00
18 Don Drysdale	125.00	250.00
19 Willie Mays	400.00	800.00
20 Tim McCarver	75.00	150.00
21 Pete Rose	400.00	800.00
22 Ron Santo	75.00	150.00
23 Rusty Staub	50.00	100.00
24 Jim Wynn	50.00	100.00
NNO Checklist Card 1-12	40.00	80.00
NNO Checklist Card 13-24	40.00	80.00

1968 Topps Plaks Checklists

These two cards, which measure 2 /18" by 4", were inserted one per 1968 Topps Plak pack. Each checklist card featured all the players each league that were available in the packs.

COMPLETE SET	750.00	1,500.00
1 Max Alvis	400.00	800.00
Dean Chance		
Jim Fregosi		
Frank Howard#		
2 Hank Aaron	400.00	800.00
Richie Allen		
Orlando Cepeda		
Roberto		

1968 Topps Posters

This 1968 color poster set is not an "insert" but was issued separately with a piece of gum and in its own wrapper. Each poster cost five cents and Mickey Mantle was the featured player on the box. The posters are numbered at the lower left and the player's name and team appear in a large star. The poster was folded six times to fit into the package, so fold lines are a factor in grading. Each poster measures 9 3/4" by 18 1/8".

COMPLETE SET (24)	150.00	300.00
WRAPPER (5-CENT)	12.50	30.00
1 Dean Chance	1.00	2.50
2 Max Alvis	1.00	2.50
3 Frank Howard	1.50	4.00
4 Jim Fregosi	1.00	2.50
5 Jim Hunter	4.00	10.00
6 Roberto Clemente	30.00	60.00
7 Don Drysdale	4.00	10.00
8 Jim Wynn	1.00	2.50
9 Al Kaline	6.00	15.00
10 Harmon Killebrew	5.00	12.00
11 Jim Lonborg	1.00	2.50
12 Orlando Cepeda	2.50	6.00
13 Gary Peters	1.00	2.50
14 Hank Aaron	8.00	20.00
15 Richie Allen	1.50	4.00
16 Carl Yastrzemski	6.00	15.00
17 Ron Swoboda	1.00	2.50
18 Mickey Mantle	40.00	80.00
19 Tim McCarver	1.50	4.00
20 Willie Mays	8.00	20.00
21 Ron Santo	1.50	4.00
22 Rusty Staub	1.50	4.00
23 Pete Rose	15.00	40.00
24 Frank Robinson	6.00	15.00

1968 Topps Venezuelan

This set is a parallel version of the first 370 cards of the regular 1968 Topps set and is similar in design. A major difference is that the Venezuelan cards are printed on a gray stock and have an orange background compared to the American Topps. There is also the "Hecho en Venezuela - C. A. Litoven" printed in faint white type at the bottom on the back of the card. However, not all of the cards have that expression printed on the bottom. Among the notable cards which do not is the Tom Seaver (number 45) card.

COMPLETE SET (376)	3,500.00	7,000.00
1 NL Batting Leaders	75.00	150.00
Bob Clemente		
Tony Gonzalez		
2 AL Batting Leaders	40.00	80.00
Carl Yastrzemski		
Frank Robins		
3 NL RBI Leaders	50.00	100.00
Orlando Cepeda		
Bob Clemente		
Hank		
4 AL RBI Leaders	30.00	60.00
Carl Yastrzemski		
Harmon Killebrew		
5 NL Home Run Leaders	15.00	40.00
Hank Aaron		
John Wynn		
Ron Sa		
6 AL Home Run Leaders	15.00	40.00
Carl Yastrzemski		
Harmon Kill		
7 NL ERA Leaders	8.00	20.00

Card	Low	High
Phil Neikro		
Jim Bunning		
Chris Sh		
8 AL ERA Leaders	8.00	20.00
Joel Horlen		
Gary Peters		
Sonny Si		
9 NL Pitching Leaders	8.00	20.00
Mike McCormick		
Ferguson Jenk		
10 AL Pitching Leaders	8.00	20.00
Jim Lonborg ERR/(Misspelled		
11 NL Strikeout Leaders	10.00	25.00
Jim Bunning		
Ferguson Jenkin		
12 AL Strikeout Leaders	10.00	25.00
Jim Lonborg UER/(Misspelled		
13 Chuck Hartenstein	5.00	12.00
14 Jerry McNertney	5.00	12.00
15 Ron Hunt	5.00	12.00
16 Lou Piniella	8.00	20.00
Richie Scheinblum		
17 Dick Hall	5.00	12.00
18 Mike Hershberger	5.00	12.00
19 Juan Pizarro	5.00	12.00
20 Brooks Robinson	75.00	150.00
21 Ron Davis	5.00	12.00
22 Pat Dobson	5.00	12.00
23 Chico Cardenas	5.00	12.00
24 Bobby Locke	5.00	12.00
25 Julian Javier	5.00	12.00
26 Darrell Brandon	5.00	12.00
27 Gil Hodges MG	20.00	50.00
28 Ted Uhlaender	5.00	12.00
29 Joe Verbanic	5.00	12.00
30 Joe Torre	10.00	25.00
31 Ed Stroud	5.00	12.00
32 Joe Gibbon	5.00	12.00
33 Pete Ward	5.00	12.00
34 Al Ferrara	5.00	12.00
35 Steve Hargan	5.00	12.00
36 Bob Moose	5.00	12.00
Bob Robertson		
37 Billy Williams	30.00	60.00
38 Tony Pierce	5.00	12.00
39 Cookie Rojas	5.00	12.00
40 Denny McLain	30.00	60.00
41 Julio Gotay	5.00	12.00
42 Larry Haney	5.00	12.00
43 Gary Bell	5.00	12.00
44 Frank Kostro	5.00	12.00
45 Tom Seaver	150.00	300.00
46 Dave Ricketts	5.00	12.00
47 Ralph Houk MG	5.00	12.00
48 Ted Davidson	5.00	12.00
49 Eddie Brinkman	5.00	12.00
50 Willie Mays	200.00	400.00
51 Bob Locker	5.00	12.00
52 Hawk Taylor	5.00	12.00
53 Gene Alley	5.00	12.00
54 Stan Williams	5.00	12.00
55 Felipe Alou	8.00	20.00
56 Dave Leonhard	5.00	12.00
Dave May		
57 Dan Schneider	5.00	12.00
58 Eddie Mathews	50.00	100.00
59 Don Lock	5.00	12.00
60 Ken Holtzman	5.00	12.00
61 Reggie Smith	6.00	15.00
62 Chuck Dobson	5.00	12.00
63 Dick Kenworthy	5.00	12.00
64 Jim Merritt	5.00	12.00
65 John Roseboro	5.00	12.00
66 Casey Cox	5.00	12.00
67 Checklist 1	10.00	25.00
Jim Kaat		
68 Ron Willis	5.00	12.00
69 Tom Tresh	6.00	15.00
70 Bob Veale	5.00	12.00
71 Vern Fuller	5.00	12.00
72 Tommy John	10.00	25.00
73 Jim Ray Hart	5.00	12.00
74 Milt Pappas	5.00	12.00
75 Don Wilson	5.00	12.00
76 Jim Britton	5.00	12.00
Ron Reed		
77 Don Wilson	5.00	12.00
78 Jim Northrup	5.00	12.00
79 Ted Kubiak	5.00	12.00
80 Rod Carew	150.00	300.00
81 Larry Jackson	5.00	12.00
83 John Stephenson	5.00	12.00
83 Sam Bowens	5.00	12.00
84 Bob Tolan	5.00	12.00
85 Gaylord Perry	20.00	50.00
86 Willie Stargell	20.00	50.00
87 Dick Williams MG	6.00	15.00
88 Phil Regan	5.00	12.00
89 Jake Gibbs	5.00	12.00
90 Vada Pinson	10.00	25.00
91 Jim Ollom	5.00	12.00
92 Ed Kranepool	6.00	15.00
93 Tony Cloninger	5.00	12.00
94 Lee Maye	5.00	12.00
95 Bob Aspromonte	5.00	12.00
96 Frank Coggins	5.00	12.00
Dick Nold		
97 Tom Phoebus	5.00	12.00
98 Gary Sutherland	5.00	12.00
99 Rocky Colavito	20.00	50.00
100 Bob Gibson	75.00	150.00
101 Glenn Beckert	5.00	12.00
102 Jose Cardenal	5.00	12.00
103 Don Sutton	15.00	40.00
104 Dick Dietz	5.00	12.00
105 Al Downing	5.00	12.00
106 Dalton Jones	5.00	12.00
107 Checklist 2	10.00	25.00
Juan Marichal		
108 Don Pavletich	5.00	12.00
109 Bert Campaneris	6.00	15.00
110 Hank Aaron	200.00	400.00
111 Rich Reese	5.00	12.00
112 Woody Fryman	5.00	12.00
113 Tom Matchick	5.00	12.00
Daryl Patterson		
114 Ron Swoboda	6.00	15.00
115 Sam McDowell	5.00	12.00
116 Ken McMullen	5.00	12.00
117 Larry Jaster	5.00	12.00
118 Mark Belanger	5.00	12.00
119 Ted Savage	5.00	12.00
120 Mel Stottlemyre	6.00	15.00
121 Jimmie Hall	5.00	12.00
122 Gene Mauch MG	5.00	12.00
123 Jose Santiago	5.00	12.00
124 Nate Oliver	5.00	12.00
125 Joe Horlen	5.00	12.00
126 Bobby Etheridge	5.00	12.00
127 Paul Lindblad	5.00	12.00
128 Tom Dukes	5.00	12.00
Alonzo Harris		
129 Mickey Stanley	5.00	12.00
130 Tony Perez	20.00	50.00
131 Frank Bertaina	5.00	12.00
132 Bud Harrelson	5.00	12.00
133 Fred Whitfield	5.00	12.00
134 Pat Jarvis	5.00	12.00
135 Paul Blair	5.00	12.00
136 Randy Hundley	5.00	12.00
137 Twins Team	8.00	20.00
138 Ruben Amaro	5.00	12.00
139 Chris Short	5.00	12.00
140 Tony Conigliaro	20.00	50.00
141 Dal Maxvill	5.00	12.00
142 Buddy Bradford	5.00	12.00
Bill Voss		
143 Pete Cimino	5.00	12.00
144 Joe Morgan	40.00	80.00
145 Don Drysdale	40.00	80.00
146 Sal Bando	5.00	12.00
147 Frank Linzy	5.00	12.00
148 Dave Bristol MG	5.00	12.00
149 Bob Saverine	5.00	12.00
150 Roberto Clemente	250.00	500.00
151 Lou Brock WS	30.00	60.00
152 Carl Yastrzemski WS	30.00	60.00
153 Nellie Briles WS	10.00	25.00
154 Bob Gibson WS	20.00	50.00
155 Jim Lonborg WS	10.00	25.00
156 Rico Petrocelli WS	10.00	25.00
157 World Series Game 7	10.00	25.00
St. Louis wins it		
158 World Series Summary	10.00	25.00
Cardinals celebrate		
159 Don Kessinger	5.00	12.00
160 Earl Wilson	5.00	12.00
161 Norm Miller	5.00	12.00
162 Hal Gibson	5.00	12.00
Mike Torrez		
163 Gene Brabender	5.00	12.00
164 Ramon Webster	5.00	12.00
165 Tony Oliva	10.00	25.00
166 Claude Raymond	5.00	12.00
167 Elston Howard	10.00	25.00
168 Dodgers Team	10.00	25.00
169 Bob Bolin	5.00	12.00
170 Jim Fregosi	6.00	15.00
171 Don Nottebart	5.00	12.00
172 Walt Williams	5.00	12.00
173 John Boozer	5.00	12.00
174 Bob Tillman	5.00	12.00
175 Maury Wills	10.00	25.00
176 Bob Allen	5.00	12.00
177 Jerry Koosman	4,000.00	8,000.00
Nolan Ryan		
178 Don Wert	5.00	12.00
179 Bill Stoneman	5.00	12.00
180 Curt Flood	8.00	20.00
181 Jerry Zimmerman	5.00	12.00
182 Dave Giusti	5.00	12.00
183 Bob Kennedy MG	5.00	12.00
184 Lou Johnson	5.00	12.00
185 Tom Haller	5.00	12.00
186 Eddie Watt	5.00	12.00
187 Sonny Jackson	5.00	12.00
188 Cap Peterson	5.00	12.00
189 Bill Landis	5.00	12.00
190 Bill White	10.00	25.00
191 Dan Frisella	5.00	12.00
192 Checklist 3	20.00	50.00
Carl Yastrzemski/(Special Baseball P		
193 Jack Hamilton	5.00	12.00
194 Don Buford	5.00	12.00
195 Joe Pepitone	5.00	12.00
196 Gary Nolan	5.00	12.00
197 Larry Brown	5.00	12.00
198 Roy Face	6.00	15.00
199 Roberto Rodriguez	5.00	12.00
Darrell fOsteen		
200 Orlando Cepeda	15.00	40.00
201 Mike Marshall	6.00	15.00
202 Adolfo Phillips	5.00	12.00
203 Dick Kelley	5.00	12.00
204 Andy Etchebarren	5.00	12.00
205 Juan Marichal	20.00	50.00
206 Cal Ermer MG	5.00	12.00
207 Carroll Sembera	5.00	12.00
208 Willie Davis	5.00	12.00
209 Tim Cullen	5.00	12.00
210 Gary Peters	5.00	12.00
211 J.C. Martin	5.00	12.00
212 Dave Morehead	5.00	12.00
213 Chico Ruiz	5.00	12.00
214 Stan Bahnsen	5.00	12.00
Frank Fernandez		
215 Jim Bunning	20.00	50.00
216 Bubba Morton	5.00	12.00
217 Dick Farrell	5.00	12.00
218 Ken Suarez	5.00	12.00
219 Rob Gardner	5.00	12.00
220 Harmon Killebrew	50.00	100.00
221 Braves Team	8.00	20.00
222 Jim Hardin	5.00	12.00
223 Ollie Brown	5.00	12.00
224 Jack Aker	5.00	12.00
225 Richie Allen	15.00	40.00
226 Jimmie Price	5.00	12.00
227 Joe Hoerner	5.00	12.00
228 Jack Billingham	5.00	12.00
Jim Fairey		
229 Fred Klages	5.00	12.00
230 Pete Rose	150.00	300.00
231 Dave Baldwin	5.00	12.00
232 Denis Menke	5.00	12.00
233 George Scott	5.00	12.00
234 Bill Monbouquette	5.00	12.00
235 Ron Santo	15.00	40.00
236 Tug McGraw	8.00	20.00
237 Alvin Dark MG	6.00	15.00
238 Tom Satriano	5.00	12.00
239 Bill Henry	5.00	12.00
240 Al Kaline	100.00	200.00
241 Felix Millan	5.00	12.00
242 Moe Drabowsky	5.00	12.00
243 Rich Rollins	5.00	12.00
244 John Donaldson	5.00	12.00
245 Tony Gonzalez	5.00	12.00
246 Fritz Peterson	5.00	12.00
247 Johnny Bench	400.00	800.00
Ron Tompkins		
248 Fred Valentine	5.00	12.00
249 Bill Singer	5.00	12.00
250 Carl Yastrzemski	75.00	150.00
251 Manny Sanguillen	10.00	25.00
252 Angels Team	8.00	20.00
253 Dick Hughes	5.00	12.00
254 Cleon Jones	5.00	12.00
255 Dean Chance	5.00	12.00
256 Norm Cash	15.00	40.00
257 Phil Niekro	20.00	50.00
258 Jose Arcia	5.00	12.00
Bill Schlesinger		
259 Ken Boyer	8.00	20.00
260 Jim Wynn	5.00	12.00
261 Dave Duncan	5.00	12.00
262 Rick Wise	5.00	12.00
263 Horace Clarke	5.00	12.00
264 Ted Abernathy	5.00	12.00
265 Tommy Davis	5.00	12.00
266 Paul Popovich	5.00	12.00
267 Herman Franks MG	5.00	12.00
268 Bob Humphreys	5.00	12.00
269 Bob Tiefenauer	5.00	12.00
270 Matty Alou	6.00	15.00
271 Bobby Knoop	5.00	12.00
272 Ray Culp	5.00	12.00
273 Dave Johnson	8.00	20.00
274 Mike Cuellar	6.00	15.00
275 Tim McCarver	10.00	25.00
276 Jim Roland	5.00	12.00
277 Jerry Buchek	5.00	12.00
278 Checklist 4	10.00	25.00
Orlando Cepeda		
279 Bill Hands	5.00	12.00
280 Mickey Mantle	750.00	1,500.00
281 Jim Campanis	5.00	12.00
282 Rick Monday	5.00	12.00
283 Mel Queen	5.00	12.00
284 Johnny Briggs	5.00	12.00
285 Dick McAuliffe	5.00	12.00
286 Cecil Upshaw	5.00	12.00
287 Mickey Abarbanel	5.00	12.00
Cisco Carlos		
288 Dave Wickersham	5.00	12.00
289 Woody Held	5.00	12.00
290 Willie McCovey	40.00	80.00
291 Dick Lines	5.00	12.00
292 Art Shamsky	5.00	12.00
293 Bruce Howard	5.00	12.00
294 Red Schoendienst MG	10.00	25.00
295 Sonny Siebert	5.00	12.00
296 Byron Browne	5.00	12.00
297 Russ Gibson	5.00	12.00
298 Jim Brewer	5.00	12.00
299 Gene Michael	5.00	12.00
300 Rusty Staub	8.00	20.00
301 George Mitterwald	5.00	12.00
Rick Renick		
302 Gerry Arrigo	5.00	12.00
303 Dick Green	5.00	12.00
304 Sandy Valdespino	5.00	12.00
305 Minnie Rojas	5.00	12.00
306 Mike Ryan	5.00	12.00
307 John Hiller	5.00	12.00
308 Pirates Team	8.00	20.00
309 Ken Henderson	5.00	12.00
310 Luis Aparicio	20.00	50.00
311 Jack Lamabe	5.00	12.00
312 Curt Blefary	5.00	12.00
313 Al Weis	5.00	12.00
314 Bill Rohr	5.00	12.00
George Spriggs		
315 Zoilo Versalles	5.00	12.00
316 Steve Barber	5.00	12.00
317 Ron Brand	5.00	12.00
318 Chico Salmon	5.00	12.00
319 George Culver	5.00	12.00
320 Frank Howard	6.00	15.00
321 Leo Durocher MG	10.00	25.00
322 Dave Boswell	5.00	12.00
323 Deron Johnson	5.00	12.00
324 Jim Nash	5.00	12.00
325 Manny Mota	6.00	15.00
326 Dennis Ribant	5.00	12.00
327 Tony Taylor	5.00	12.00
328 Chuck Vinson	5.00	12.00
Jim Weaver		
329 Duane Josephson	5.00	12.00
330 Roger Maris	125.00	250.00
331 Dan Osinski	5.00	12.00
332 Doug Rader	5.00	12.00
333 Ron Herbel	5.00	12.00
334 Orioles Team	8.00	20.00
335 Bob Allison	5.00	12.00
336 John Purdin	5.00	12.00
337 Bill Robinson	5.00	12.00
338 Bob Johnson	5.00	12.00
339 Rich Nye	5.00	12.00
340 Max Alvis	5.00	12.00
341 Jim Lemon MG	5.00	12.00
342 Ken Johnson	5.00	12.00
343 Jim Gosger	5.00	12.00
344 Donn Clendenon	5.00	12.00
345 Bob Hendley	5.00	12.00
346 Jerry Adair	5.00	12.00
347 George Brunet	5.00	12.00
348 Larry Colton	5.00	12.00
Dick Thoenen		
349 Ed Spiezio	5.00	12.00
350 Hoyt Wilhelm	15.00	40.00
351 Bob Barton	5.00	12.00
352 Jackie Hernandez	5.00	12.00
353 Mack Jones	5.00	12.00
354 Pete Richert	5.00	12.00
355 Ernie Banks	75.00	150.00
356 Checklist 5	10.00	25.00
Ken Holtzman/(Head centered within c		
357 Len Gabrielson	5.00	12.00
358 Mike Epstein	5.00	12.00
359 Joe Moeller	5.00	12.00
360 Willie Horton	8.00	20.00
361 Harmon Killebrew AS	15.00	40.00
362 Orlando Cepeda AS	10.00	25.00
363 Rod Carew AS	15.00	40.00
364 Joe Morgan AS	15.00	40.00
365 Brooks Robinson AS	15.00	40.00
366 Ron Santo AS	8.00	20.00
367 Jim Fregosi AS	5.00	12.00
368 Gene Alley AS	5.00	12.00
369 Carl Yastrzemski AS	30.00	60.00
370 Hank Aaron AS	60.00	120.00

1969 Topps

The cards in this 664-card set measure 2 1/2" by 3 1/2". The 1969 Topps set includes Sporting News All-Star Selections as card numbers 416 to 435. Other popular subsets within this set include League Leaders (1-12) and World Series cards (162-169). The fifth series contains several variations; the more difficult variety consists of cards with the player's first name, last name, and/or position in white letters instead of lettering in some other color. These are designated in the checklist below by WL (white letters). Each checklist card features a different popular player's picture inside a circle on the front of the checklist card. Two different team identifications of Clay Dalrymple and Donn Clendenon exist, as indicated in the checklist. The key Rookie Cards in this set are Rollie Fingers, Reggie Jackson, and Graig Nettles. This was the last year that Topps issued multi-player special star cards, ending a 13-year tradition, which they had begun in 1957. There were cropping differences in checklist cards 57, 214, and 412, due to their each being printed with two different series. The differences are difficult to explain and have not been greatly sought by collectors; hence they are not listed explicitly in the list below. The All-Star cards 426-435, when turned over and placed together, form a puzzle back of Pete Rose. This would turn out to be the final year that Topps issued cards in five-card nickel wax packs. Cards were also issued in thirty-six card rack packs which were sold for 29 cents.

Card	Low	High
COMP. MASTER SET (695)	2,500.00	5,000.00
COMPLETE SET (664)	1,500.00	3,000.00
COMMON (1-218/328-512)	.60	1.50
COMMON CARD (219-327)	1.00	2.50
COMMON CARD (513-588)	.75	2.00
COMMON CARD (589-664)	1.25	3.00
WRAPPER (5-CENT)	8.00	20.00
1 Yaz/Cater/Oliva LL	10.00	25.00
2 Rose/Alou/Alou LL	3.00	8.00
3 Harrelson/Howard/North LL	1.50	4.00
4 McCovey/Santo/B.Will LL	2.50	6.00
5 Howard/Horton/Harrelson LL	1.50	4.00
6 McCovey/Allen/Banks LL	2.50	6.00
7 Tiant/McDow/McNally LL	1.50	4.00
8 Gibson/Bolin/Veale LL	2.50	6.00
9 McLain/McNal/Tiant/Stott LL	1.50	4.00
10 Marichal/Gibson/Jenkins LL	3.00	8.00
11 McDowell/McLain/Tiant LL	1.50	4.00
12 Gibson/Jenkins/Singer LL	1.50	4.00
13 Mickey Stanley	1.00	2.50
14 Al McBean	.60	1.50
15 Boog Powell	1.50	4.00
16 C.Gutierrez RC/R.Robertson RC	.60	1.50
17 Mike Marshall	1.00	2.50
18 Dick Schofield	.60	1.50
19 Ken Suarez	.60	1.50
20 Ernie Banks	20.00	50.00

21 Jose Santiago .60 1.50
22 Jesus Alou 1.00 2.50
23 Lew Krausse .60 1.50
24 Walt Alston MG 1.50 4.00
25 Roy White 1.00 2.50
26 Clay Carroll 1.00 2.50
27 Bernie Allen .60 1.50
28 Mike Ryan .60 1.50
29 Dave Morehead .60 1.50
30 Bob Allison 1.00 2.50
31 G.Gentry RC/A.Otis RC 1.00 2.50
32 Sammy Ellis .60 1.50
33 Wayne Causey .60 1.50
34 Gary Peters .60 1.50
35 Joe Morgan 10.00 25.00
36 Luke Walker .60 1.50
37 Curt Motton .60 1.50
38 Zoilo Versalles 1.00 2.50
39 Dick Hughes .60 1.50
40 Mayo Smith MG .60 1.50
41 Bob Barton .60 1.50
42 Tommy Harper 1.00 2.50
43 Joe Niekro 1.00 2.50
44 Danny Cater .60 1.50
45 Maury Wills 1.00 2.50
46 Fritz Peterson 1.00 2.50
47A P.Popovich Thick Airbrush 1.00 2.50
47B P.Popovich Light Airbrush 1.00 2.50
47C P.Popovich C on Helmet 10.00 25.00
48 Brant Alyea .60 1.50
49A S.Jones/E.Rodriguez ERR 10.00 25.00
49B S.Jones RC/E.Rodriguez RC .60 1.50
50 Roberto Clemente UER 30.00 80.00
51 Woody Fryman 1.00 2.50
52 Mike Andrews .60 1.50
53 Sonny Jackson .60 1.50
54 Cisco Carlos .60 1.50
55 Jerry Grote 1.00 2.50
56 Rich Reese .60 1.50
57 Checklist 1/McLain 2.50 6.00
58 Fred Gladding .60 1.50
59 Jay Johnstone 1.00 2.50
60 Nelson Briles 1.00 2.50
61 Jimmie Hall .60 1.50
62 Chico Salmon .60 1.50
63 Jim Hickman 1.00 2.50
64 Bill Monbouquette .60 1.50
65 Willie Davis 1.00 2.50
66 M.Adamson RC/M.Rettenmund RC .60 1.50
67 Bill Stoneman 1.00 2.50
68 Dave Duncan 1.00 2.50
69 Steve Hamilton 1.00 2.50
70 Tommy Helms 1.00 2.50
71 Steve Whitaker 1.00 2.50
72 Ron Taylor .60 1.50
73 Johnny Briggs .60 1.50
74 Preston Gomez MG 1.00 2.50
75 Luis Aparicio 2.50 6.00
76 Norm Miller .60 1.50
77A R.Perranoski No LA .60 1.50
77B R.Perranoski LA Cap 10.00 25.00
78 Tom Satriano .60 1.50
79 Milt Pappas 1.00 2.50
80 Norm Cash 1.00 2.50
81 Mel Queen .60 1.50
82 R.Hebner RC/A.Oliver RC 3.00 8.00
83 Mike Ferraro 1.00 2.50
84 Bob Humphreys .60 1.50
85 Lou Brock 15.00 40.00
86 Pete Richert .60 1.50
87 Horace Clarke 1.00 2.50
88 Rich Nye .60 1.50
89 Russ Gibson .60 1.50
90 Jerry Koosman 1.00 2.50
91 Alvin Dark MG 1.00 2.50
92 Jack Billingham 1.00 2.50
93 Joe Foy 1.00 2.50
94 Hank Aguirre .60 1.50
95 Johnny Bench 60.00 150.00
96 Denny Lemaster .60 1.50
97 Buddy Bradford .60 1.50
98 Dave Giusti .60 1.50
99A D.Morris RC/G.Nettles RC 6.00 15.00
99B D.Morris/G.Nettles ERR 6.00 15.00
100 Hank Aaron 30.00 80.00
101 Daryl Patterson .60 1.50
102 Jim Davenport .60 1.50
103 Roger Repoz .60 1.50
104 Steve Blass .60 1.50
105 Rick Monday 1.00 2.50
106 Jim Hannan .60 1.50
107A Checklist 2/Gibson ERR 2.50 6.00
107B Checklist 2/Gibson COR 3.00 8.00
108 Tony Taylor 1.00 2.50
109 Jim Lonborg 1.00 2.50
110 Mike Shannon 1.00 2.50
111 John Morris RC .60 1.50
112 J.C. Martin 1.00 2.50
113 Dave May .60 1.50
114 A.Closter/J.Cumberland RC 1.00 2.50
115 Bill Hands .60 1.50
116 Chuck Harrison .60 1.50
117 Jim Fairey 1.00 2.50
118 Stan Williams .60 1.50
119 Doug Rader 1.00 2.50
120 Pete Rose 25.00 60.00
121 Joe Grzenda RC .60 1.50
122 Ron Fairly 1.00 2.50
123 Wilbur Wood 1.00 2.50
124 Hank Bauer MG 1.00 2.50
125 Ray Sadecki .60 1.50
126 Dick Tracewski .60 1.50
127 Kevin Collins 1.00 2.50
128 Tommie Aaron 1.00 2.50
129 Bill McCool .60 1.50
130 Carl Yastrzemski 20.00 50.00
131 Chris Cannizzaro .60 1.50
132 Dave Baldwin .60 1.50
133 Johnny Callison 1.00 2.50
134 Jim Weaver .60 1.50
135 Tommy Davis 1.00 2.50
136 S.Huntz RC/M.Torrez .60 1.50
137 Wally Bunker .60 1.50
138 John Bateman .60 1.50
139 Andy Kosco .60 1.50
140 Jim Lefebvre 1.00 2.50
141 Bill Dillman .60 1.50
142 Woody Woodward .60 1.50
143 Joe Nossek .60 1.50
144 Bob Hendley 1.00 2.50
145 Max Alvis .60 1.50
146 Jim Perry 1.00 2.50
147 Leo Durocher MG 1.50 4.00
148 Lee Stange .60 1.50
149 Ollie Brown 1.00 2.50
150 Denny McLain 1.50 4.00
151A C.Dalrymple Portrait .60 1.50
151B C.Dalrymple Catch 6.00 15.00
152 Tommie Sisk .60 1.50
153 Ed Brinkman .60 1.50
154 Jim Britton .60 1.50
155 Pete Ward .60 1.50
156 H.Gilson/L.McFadden RC .60 1.50
157 Bob Rodgers 1.00 2.50
158 Joe Gibbon .60 1.50
159 Jerry Adair .60 1.50
160 Vada Pinson 1.00 2.50
161 John Purdin .60 1.50
162 Bob Gibson WS1 3.00 8.00
163 Willie Horton WS2 2.50 6.00
164 T.McCarv w/Maris WS3 5.00 12.00
165 Lou Brock WS4 3.00 8.00
166 Al Kaline WS5 3.00 8.00
167 Jim Northrup WS6 2.50 6.00
168 M.Lolich/B.Gibson WS7 3.00 8.00
169 Tigers Celebrate WS 2.50 6.00
170 Frank Howard 1.00 2.50
171 Glenn Beckert 1.00 2.50
172 Jerry Stephenson .60 1.50
173 B.Christian RC/G.Nyman RC .60 1.50
174 Grant Jackson .60 1.50
175 Jim Bunning 2.50 6.00
176 Joe Azcue .60 1.50
177 Ron Reed .60 1.50
178 Ray Oyler 1.00 2.50
179 Don Pavletich .60 1.50
180 Willie Horton 1.00 2.50
181 Mel Nelson .60 1.50
182 Bill Rigney MG .60 1.50
183 Don Shaw 1.00 2.50
184 Roberto Pena .60 1.50
185 Tom Phoebus .60 1.50
186 Johnny Edwards .60 1.50
187 Leon Wagner .60 1.50
188 Rick Wise 1.00 2.50
189 J.Lahoud RC/J.Thibodeau RC .60 1.50
190 Willie Mays 40.00 100.00
191 Lindy McDaniel 1.00 2.50
192 Jose Pagan .60 1.50
193 Don Cardwell 1.00 2.50
194 Ted Uhlaender .60 1.50
195 John Odom .60 1.50
196 Lum Harris MG .60 1.50
197 Dick Selma .60 1.50
198 Willie Smith .60 1.50
199 Jim French .60 1.50
200 Bob Gibson 25.00 60.00
201 Russ Snyder .60 1.50
202 Don Wilson 1.00 2.50
203 Dave Johnson 1.00 2.50
204 Jack Hiatt .60 1.50
205 Rick Reichardt .60 1.50
206 L.Hisle/B.Lersch RC 1.00 2.50
207 Roy Face 1.00 2.50
208A D.Clendenon Houston 1.00 2.50
208B D.Clendenon Expos 6.00 15.00
209 Larry Haney UER .60 1.50
210 Felix Millan .60 1.50
211 Galen Cisco .60 1.50
212 Tom Tresh 1.00 2.50
213 Gerry Arrigo .60 1.50
214 Checklist 3 2.50 6.00
215 Rico Petrocelli 1.00 2.50
216 Don Sutton 2.50 6.00
217 John Donaldson .60 1.50
218 John Roseboro 1.00 2.50
219 Freddie Patek RC 1.50 4.00
220 Sam McDowell 1.50 4.00
221 Art Shamsky 1.50 4.00
222 Duane Josephson 1.00 2.50
223 Tom Dukes 1.50 4.00
224 B.Harrelson RC/S.Kealey RC 1.00 2.50
225 Don Kessinger 1.50 4.00
226 Bruce Howard 1.00 2.50
227 Frank Johnson RC 1.00 2.50
228 Dave Leonhard 1.00 2.50
229 Don Lock 1.00 2.50
230 Rusty Staub UER 1.50 4.00
231 Pat Dobson 1.50 4.00
232 Dave Ricketts 1.00 2.50
233 Steve Barber 1.50 4.00
234 Dave Bristol MG 1.00 2.50
235 Jim Hunter 4.00 10.00
236 Manny Mota 1.50 4.00
237 Bobby Cox RC 25.00 60.00
238 Ken Johnson 1.00 2.50
239 Bob Taylor 1.50 4.00
240 Ken Harrelson 1.50 4.00
241 Jim Brewer 1.00 2.50
242 Frank Kostro 1.00 2.50
243 Ron Kline 1.00 2.50
244 R.Fosse RC/G.Woodson RC 1.50 4.00
245 Ed Charles 1.50 4.00
246 Joe Coleman 1.00 2.50
247 Gene Oliver 1.00 2.50
248 Bob Priddy 1.00 2.50
249 Ed Spiezio 1.50 4.00
250 Frank Robinson 15.00 40.00
251 Ron Herbel 1.00 2.50
252 Chuck Cottier 1.00 2.50
253 Jerry Johnson RC 1.00 2.50
254 Joe Schultz MG RC 1.50 4.00
255 Steve Carlton 15.00 40.00
256 Gates Brown 1.50 4.00
257 Jim Ray 1.00 2.50
258 Jackie Hernandez 1.50 4.00
259 Bill Short 1.00 2.50
260 Reggie Jackson RC 150.00 300.00
261 Bob Johnson 1.00 2.50
262 Mike Kekich 1.50 4.00
263 Jerry May 1.00 2.50
264 Bill Landis 1.00 2.50
265 Chico Cardenas 1.50 4.00
266 T.Hutton/A.Foster RC 1.50 4.00
267 Vicente Romo RC 1.00 2.50
268 Al Spangler 1.00 2.50
269 Al Weis 1.50 4.00
270 Mickey Lolich 1.50 4.00
271 Larry Stahl 1.50 4.00
272 Ed Stroud 1.00 2.50
273 Ron Willis 1.00 2.50
274 Clyde King MG 1.00 2.50
275 Vic Davalillo 1.00 2.50
276 Gary Wagner 1.00 2.50
277 Elrod Hendricks RC 1.00 2.50
278 Gary Geiger UER 1.00 2.50
279 Roger Nelson 1.50 4.00
280 Alex Johnson 1.50 4.00
281 Ted Kubiak 1.00 2.50
282 Pat Jarvis 1.00 2.50
283 Sandy Alomar 1.50 4.00
284 J.Robertson RC/M.Wegener RC 1.50 4.00
285 Don Mincher 1.50 4.00
286 Dock Ellis RC 1.50 4.00
287 Jose Tartabull 1.50 4.00
288 Ken Holtzman 1.50 4.00
289 Bart Shirley 1.00 2.50
290 Jim Kaat 1.50 4.00
291 Vern Fuller 1.00 2.50
292 Al Downing 1.50 4.00
293 Dick Dietz 1.00 2.50
294 Jim Lemon MG 1.00 2.50
295 Tony Perez 12.00 30.00
296 Andy Messersmith RC 1.50 4.00
297 Deron Johnson 1.00 2.50
298 Dave Nicholson 1.50 4.00
299 Mark Belanger 1.50 4.00
300 Felipe Alou 1.50 4.00
301 Darrell Brandon 1.50 4.00
302 Jim Pagliaroni 1.00 2.50
303 Cal Koonce 1.50 4.00
304 B.Davis/C.Gaston RC 2.50 6.00
305 Dick McAuliffe 1.50 4.00
306 Jim Grant 1.50 4.00
307 Gary Kolb 1.00 2.50
308 Wade Blasingame 1.00 2.50
309 Walt Williams 1.00 2.50
310 Tom Haller 1.00 2.50
311 Sparky Lyle RC 4.00 10.00
312 Lee Elia 1.00 2.50
313 Bill Robinson 1.50 4.00
314 Checklist 4/Drysdale 2.50 6.00
315 Eddie Fisher 1.00 2.50
316 Hal Lanier 1.00 2.50
317 Bruce Look RC 1.00 2.50
318 Jack Fisher 1.00 2.50
319 Ken McMullen UER 1.00 2.50
320 Dal Maxvill 1.00 2.50
321 Jim McAndrew RC 1.50 4.00
322 Jose Vidal 1.50 4.00
323 Larry Miller 1.00 2.50
324 L.Cain RC/D.Campbell RC 1.50 4.00
325 Jose Cardenal 1.50 4.00
326 Gary Sutherland 1.50 4.00
327 Willie Crawford 1.00 2.50
328 Joel Horlen .60 1.50
329 Rick Joseph .60 1.50
330 Tony Conigliaro 1.50 4.00
331 G.Garrido/T.House RC 1.00 2.50
332 Fred Talbot .60 1.50
333 Ivan Murrell .60 1.50
334 Phil Roof .60 1.50
335 Bill Mazeroski 2.50 6.00
336 Jim Roland .60 1.50
337 Marty Martinez RC .60 1.50
338 Del Unser RC .60 1.50
339 S.Mingori RC/J.Pena RC .60 1.50
340 Dave McNally 1.00 2.50
341 Dave Adlesh .60 1.50
342 Bubba Morton .60 1.50
343 Dan Frisella .60 1.50
344 Tom Matchick .60 1.50
345 Frank Linzy .60 1.50
346 Wayne Comer RC .60 1.50
347 Randy Hundley 1.00 2.50
348 Steve Hargan .60 1.50
349 Dick Williams MG 1.00 2.50
350 Richie Allen 1.50 4.00
351 Carroll Sembera .60 1.50
352 Paul Schaal 1.00 2.50
353 Jeff Torborg 1.00 2.50
354 Nate Oliver .60 1.50
355 Phil Niekro 8.00 20.00
356 Frank Quilici .60 1.50
357 Carl Taylor .60 1.50
358 G.Lauzerique RC/R.Rodriguez .60 1.50
359 Dick Kelley .60 1.50
360 Jim Wynn 1.00 2.50
361 Gary Holman RC .60 1.50
362 Jim Maloney 1.00 2.50
363 Russ Nixon .60 1.50
364 Tommie Agee 1.50 4.00
365 Jim Fregosi 1.00 2.50
366 Bo Belinsky 1.00 2.50
367 Lou Johnson 1.00 2.50
368 Vic Roznovsky .60 1.50
369 Bob Skinner MG 1.00 2.50
370 Juan Marichal 3.00 8.00
371 Sal Bando 1.00 2.50
372 Adolfo Phillips .60 1.50
373 Fred Lasher .60 1.50
374 Bob Tillman .60 1.50
375 Harmon Killebrew 12.00 30.00
376 M.Fiore RC/J.Rooker RC .60 1.50
377 Gary Bell 1.00 2.50
378 Jose Herrera RC .60 1.50
379 Ken Boyer 1.00 2.50
380 Stan Bahnsen 1.00 2.50
381 Ed Kranepool 1.00 2.50
382 Pat Corrales 1.00 2.50
383 Casey Cox .60 1.50
384 Larry Shepard MG .60 1.50
385 Orlando Cepeda 2.50 6.00
386 Jim McGlothlin .60 1.50
387 Bobby Klaus .60 1.50
388 Tom McCraw .60 1.50
389 Dan Coombs .60 1.50
390 Bill Freehan 1.00 2.50
391 Ray Culp .60 1.50
392 Bob Burda RC .60 1.50
393 Gene Brabender 1.00 2.50
394 L.Piniella/M.Staehle 2.50 6.00
395 Chris Short .60 1.50
396 Jim Campanis .60 1.50
397 Chuck Dobson .60 1.50
398 Tito Francona .60 1.50
399 Bob Bailey 1.00 2.50
400 Don Drysdale 10.00 25.00
401 Jake Gibbs 1.00 2.50
402 Ken Boswell RC 1.00 2.50
403 Bob Miller .60 1.50
404 V.LaRose RC/G.Ross RC 1.00 2.50
405 Lee May 1.00 2.50
406 Phil Ortega .60 1.50
407 Tom Egan .60 1.50
408 Nate Colbert .60 1.50
409 Bob Moose .60 1.50
410 Al Kaline 10.00 25.00
411 Larry Dierker 1.00 2.50
412 Checklist 5/Mantle DP 12.00 30.00
413 Roland Sheldon 1.00 2.50
414 Duke Sims .60 1.50
415 Ray Washburn .60 1.50
416 Willie McCovey AS 3.00 8.00
417 Ken Harrelson AS 1.25 3.00
418 Tommy Helms AS 1.25 3.00
419 Rod Carew AS 4.00 10.00
420 Ron Santo AS 1.50 4.00
421 Brooks Robinson AS 3.00 8.00
422 Don Kessinger AS 1.25 3.00
423 Bert Campaneris AS 1.50 4.00
424 Pete Rose AS 10.00 25.00
425 Carl Yastrzemski AS 10.00 25.00
426 Curt Flood AS 1.50 4.00
427 Tony Oliva AS 1.50 4.00
428 Lou Brock AS 2.50 6.00
429 Willie Horton AS 1.25 3.00
430 Johnny Bench AS 20.00 50.00
431 Bill Freehan AS 1.50 4.00
432 Bob Gibson AS 6.00 15.00
433 Denny McLain AS 1.25 3.00
434 Jerry Koosman AS 1.25 3.00
435 Sam McDowell AS 1.00 2.50
436 Gene Alley 1.00 2.50
437 Luis Alcaraz RC .60 1.50
438 Gary Waslewski RC .60 1.50
439 E.Herrmann RC/D.Lazar RC .60 1.50
440A Willie McCovey 6.00 15.00
440B Willie McCovey WL 50.00 100.00
441A Dennis Higgins .60 1.50
441B Dennis Higgins WL 10.00 25.00
442 Ty Cline .60 1.50
443 Don Wert .60 1.50
444A Joe Moeller .60 1.50
444B Joe Moeller WL 10.00 25.00
445 Bobby Knoop .60 1.50
446 Claude Raymond .60 1.50
447A Ralph Houk MG 1.00 2.50
447B Ralph Houk MG WL 10.00 25.00
448 Bob Tolan 1.00 2.50
449 Paul Lindblad .60 1.50
450 Billy Williams 3.00 8.00
451A Rich Rollins 1.00 2.50
451B Rich Rollins WL 10.00 25.00
452A Al Ferrara .60 1.50
452B Al Ferrara WL 10.00 25.00
453 Mike Cuellar 1.00 2.50
454A L.Colton/D.Money RC 1.00 2.50
454B L.Colton/D.Money WL 10.00 25.00
455 Sonny Siebert .60 1.50
456 Bud Harrelson 1.00 2.50
457 Dalton Jones .60 1.50
458 Curt Blefary .60 1.50
459 Dave Boswell .60 1.50
460 Joe Torre 1.50 4.00
461A Mike Epstein .60 1.50
461B Mike Epstein WL 10.00 25.00
462 R.Schoendienst MG 1.00 2.50
463 Dennis Ribant .60 1.50
464A Dave Marshall RC .60 1.50
464B Dave Marshall WL 10.00 25.00
465 Tommy John 1.50 4.00
466 John Boccabella 1.00 2.50
467 Tommie Reynolds .60 1.50
468A B.Dal Canton RC/B.Robertson .60 1.50

468B B.Dal Canton/B.Robertson WL	10.00	25.00
469 Chico Ruiz	.60	1.50
470A Mel Stottlemyre	1.00	2.50
470B Mel Stottlemyre WL	12.50	30.00
471A Ted Savage	.60	1.50
471B Ted Savage WL	10.00	25.00
472 Jim Price	.60	1.50
473A Jose Arcia	.60	1.50
473B Jose Arcia WL	10.00	25.00
474 Tom Murphy RC	.60	1.50
475 Tim McCarver	1.50	4.00
476A K.Brett RC/G.Moses	1.00	2.50
476B K.Brett/G.Moses WL	12.50	30.00
477 Jeff James RC	.60	1.50
478 Don Buford	.60	1.50
479 Richie Scheinblum	.60	1.50
480 Tom Seaver	25.00	60.00
481 Bill Melton RC	1.00	2.50
482A Jim Gosger	.60	1.50
482B Jim Gosger WL	10.00	25.00
483 Ted Abernathy	.60	1.50
484 Joe Gordon MG	1.00	2.50
485A Gaylord Perry	4.00	10.00
485B Gaylord Perry WL	40.00	80.00
486A Paul Casanova	.60	1.50
486B Paul Casanova WL	10.00	25.00
487 Denis Menke	.60	1.50
488 Joe Sparma	.60	1.50
489 Clete Boyer	1.00	2.50
490 Matty Alou	1.00	2.50
491A J.Crider RC/G.Mitterwald	.60	1.50
491B J.Crider/G.Mitterwald WL	10.00	25.00
492 Tony Cloninger	.60	1.50
493A Wes Parker	1.00	2.50
493B Wes Parker WL	10.00	25.00
494 Ken Berry	.60	1.50
495 Bert Campaneris	1.00	2.50
496 Larry Jaster	.60	1.50
497 Julian Javier	1.00	2.50
498 Juan Pizarro	1.00	2.50
499 D.Bryant RC/S.Shea RC	.60	1.50
500A Mickey Mantle UER	150.00	400.00
500B Mickey Mantle UER WL	1,000.00	2,000.00
501A Tony Gonzalez	1.00	2.50
501B Tony Gonzalez WL	10.00	25.00
502 Minnie Rojas	.60	1.50
503 Larry Brown	.60	1.50
504 Checklist 6/B.Robinson	3.00	8.00
505A Bobby Bolin	.60	1.50
505B Bobby Bolin WL	10.00	25.00
506 Paul Blair	1.00	2.50
507 Cookie Rojas	1.00	2.50
508 Moe Drabowsky	1.00	2.50
509 Manny Sanguillen	1.00	2.50
510 Rod Carew	15.00	40.00
511A Diego Segui	1.00	2.50
511B Diego Segui WL	10.00	25.00
512 Cleon Jones	1.00	2.50
513 Camilo Pascual	1.25	3.00
514 Mike Lum	.75	2.00
515 Dick Green	.75	2.00
516 Earl Weaver MG RC	8.00	20.00
517 Mike McCormick	1.25	3.00
518 Fred Whitfield	.75	2.00
519 J.Kenney RC/L.Boehmer RC	.75	2.00
520 Bob Veale	1.25	3.00
521 George Thomas	.75	2.00
522 Joe Hoerner	.75	2.00
523 Bob Chance	.75	2.00
524 J.Laboy RC/F.Wicker RC	1.25	3.00
525 Earl Wilson	1.25	3.00
526 Hector Torres RC	.75	2.00
527 Al Lopez MG	2.00	5.00
528 Claude Osteen	1.25	3.00
529 Ed Kirkpatrick	1.25	3.00
530 Cesar Tovar	.75	2.00
531 Dick Farrell	.75	2.00
532 Phoeb/Hard/McNally/Cuellar	1.25	3.00
533 Nolan Ryan	100.00	250.00
534 Jerry McNertney	1.25	3.00
535 Phil Regan	1.25	3.00
536 D.Breeden RC/D.Roberts RC	.75	2.00
537 Mike Paul RC	.75	2.00
538 Charlie Smith	.75	2.00
539 T.Williams/M.Epstein	5.00	12.00
540 Curt Flood	1.25	3.00
541 Joe Verbanic	.75	2.00
542 Bob Aspromonte	.75	2.00
543 Fred Newman	.75	2.00
544 M.Kilkenny RC/R.Woods RC	.75	2.00
545 Willie Stargell	10.00	25.00
546 Jim Nash	.75	2.00
547 Billy Martin MG	2.00	5.00
548 Bob Locker	.75	2.00
549 Ron Brand	.75	2.00
550 Brooks Robinson	12.50	30.00
551 Wayne Granger RC	.75	2.00
552 T.Sizemore RC/B.Sudakis RC	1.25	3.00
553 Ron Davis	.75	2.00
554 Frank Bertaina	.75	2.00
555 Jim Ray Hart	1.25	3.00
556 Bando/Campaneris/Cater	1.25	3.00
557 Frank Fernandez	.75	2.00
558 Tom Burgmeier RC	1.25	3.00
559 J.Hague RC/J.Hicks	.75	2.00
560 Luis Tiant	1.25	3.00
561 Ron Clark	.75	2.00
562 Bob Watson RC	3.00	8.00
563 Marty Pattin RC	1.25	3.00
564 Gil Hodges MG	4.00	10.00
565 Hoyt Wilhelm	3.00	8.00
566 Ron Hansen	.75	2.00
567 E.Jimenez/J.Shellenback	.75	2.00
568 Cecil Upshaw	.75	2.00
569 Billy Harris	.60	1.50
570 Ron Santo	3.00	8.00
571 Cap Peterson	.75	2.00
572 W.McCovey/J.Marichal	6.00	15.00
573 Jim Palmer	12.00	30.00
574 George Scott	1.25	3.00
575 Bill Singer	1.25	3.00
576 R.Stone/B.Wilson	.75	2.00
577 Mike Hegan	1.25	3.00
578 Don Bosch	.75	2.00
579 Dave Nelson RC	.75	2.00
580 Jim Northrup	1.25	3.00
581 Gary Nolan	1.25	3.00
582A Checklist 7/Oliva White	2.50	6.00
582B Checklist 7/Oliva Red	3.00	8.00
583 Clyde Wright RC	.75	2.00
584 Don Mason	.75	2.00
585 Ron Swoboda	1.25	3.00
586 Tim Cullen	.75	2.00
587 Joe Rudi RC	3.00	8.00
588 Bill White	1.25	3.00
589 Joe Pepitone	2.00	5.00
590 Rico Carty	2.00	5.00
591 Mike Hedlund	1.25	3.00
592 R.Robles RC/A.Santorini RC	2.00	5.00
593 Don Nottebart	1.25	3.00
594 Dooley Womack	1.25	3.00
595 Lee Maye	1.25	3.00
596 Chuck Hartenstein	1.25	3.00
597 Rollie Fingers RC	30.00	80.00
598 Ruben Amaro	1.25	3.00
599 John Boozer	1.25	3.00
600 Tony Oliva	3.00	8.00
601 Tug McGraw	3.00	8.00
602 Distaso/Young/Qualls RC	2.00	5.00
603 Joe Keough RC	1.25	3.00
604 Bobby Etheridge	1.25	3.00
605 Dick Ellsworth	1.25	3.00
606 Gene Mauch MG	2.00	5.00
607 Dick Bosman	1.25	3.00
608 Dick Simpson	1.25	3.00
609 Phil Gagliano	1.25	3.00
610 Jim Hardin	1.25	3.00
611 Didier/Hriniak/Niebauer RC	2.00	5.00
612 Jack Aker	2.00	5.00
613 Jim Beauchamp	1.25	3.00
614 T.Griffin RC/S.Guinn RC	1.25	3.00
615 Len Gabrielson	1.25	3.00
616 Don McMahon	1.25	3.00
617 Jesse Gonder	1.25	3.00
618 Ramon Webster	1.25	3.00
619 Butler/Kelly/Rios RC	2.00	5.00
620 Dean Chance	2.00	5.00
621 Bill Voss	1.25	3.00
622 Dan Osinski	1.25	3.00
623 Hank Allen	1.25	3.00
624 Chaney/Dyer/Harmon RC	2.00	5.00
625 Mack Jones UER	2.00	5.00
626 Gene Michael	2.00	5.00
627 George Stone RC	1.25	3.00
628 Conigliaro/O'Brien/Wenz RC	2.00	5.00
629 Jack Hamilton	1.25	3.00
630 Bobby Bonds RC	15.00	40.00
631 John Kennedy	2.00	5.00
632 Jon Warden RC	1.25	3.00
633 Harry Walker MG	1.25	3.00
634 Andy Etchebarren	1.25	3.00
635 George Culver	1.25	3.00
636 Woody Held	1.25	3.00
637 DaVanon/Reberger/Kirby RC	2.00	5.00
638 Ed Sprague RC	1.25	3.00
639 Barry Moore	1.25	3.00
640 Ferguson Jenkins	8.00	20.00
641 Darwin/Miller/Dean RC	2.00	5.00
642 John Hiller	1.25	3.00
643 Billy Cowan	1.25	3.00
644 Chuck Hinton	1.25	3.00
645 George Brunet	1.25	3.00
646 D.McGinn RC/C.Morton RC	2.00	5.00
647 Dave Wickersham	1.25	3.00
648 Bobby Wine	2.00	5.00
649 Al Jackson	1.25	3.00
650 Ted Williams MG	8.00	20.00
651 Gus Gil	2.00	5.00
652 Eddie Watt	1.25	3.00
653 Aurelio Rodriguez UER RC	2.00	5.00
654 May/Secrist/Morales RC	2.00	5.00
655 Mike Hershberger	1.25	3.00
656 Dan Schneider	1.25	3.00
657 Bobby Murcer	3.00	8.00
658 Hall/Burbach/Miles RC	1.25	3.00
659 Johnny Podres	2.00	5.00
660 Reggie Smith	2.00	5.00
661 Jim Merritt	1.25	3.00
662 Drago/Spriggs/Oliver RC	2.00	5.00
663 Dick Radatz	2.00	5.00
664 Ron Hunt	2.00	5.00

1969 Topps Decals

The 1969 Topps Decal Inserts are a set of 48 unnumbered decals issued as inserts in packages of 1969 Topps regular issue cards. Each decal is approximately 1" by 1 1/2" although including the plain backing the measurement is 1 3/4" by 2 1/8". The decals appear to be miniature versions of the Topps regular issue of that year. The copyright notice on the side indicates that these decals were produced in the United Kingdom. Most of the players on the decals are stars.

COMPLETE SET (48)	250.00	500.00
1 Hank Aaron	20.00	50.00
2 Richie Allen	3.00	8.00
3 Felipe Alou	2.00	5.00
4 Matty Alou	2.00	5.00
5 Luis Aparicio	3.00	8.00
6 Roberto Clemente	30.00	60.00
7 Donn Clendenon	1.50	4.00
8 Tommy Davis	2.00	5.00
9 Don Drysdale	4.00	10.00
10 Joe Foy	1.50	4.00
11 Jim Fregosi	2.00	5.00
12 Bob Gibson	4.00	10.00
13 Tony Gonzalez	1.50	4.00
14 Tom Haller	1.50	4.00
15 Ken Harrelson	2.00	5.00
16 Tommy Helms	1.50	4.00
17 Willie Horton	2.00	5.00
18 Frank Howard	2.00	5.00
19 Reggie Jackson	20.00	50.00
20 Ferguson Jenkins	3.00	8.00
21 Harmon Killebrew	6.00	15.00
22 Jerry Koosman	2.00	5.00
23 Mickey Mantle	50.00	100.00
24 Willie Mays	10.00	25.00
25 Tim McCarver	2.00	5.00
26 Willie McCovey	4.00	10.00
27 Sam McDowell	2.00	5.00
28 Denny McLain	2.00	5.00
29 Dave McNally	2.00	5.00
30 Don Mincher	1.50	4.00
31 Rick Monday	2.00	5.00
32 Tony Oliva	3.00	8.00
33 Camilo Pascual	1.50	4.00
34 Rick Reichardt	1.50	4.00
35 Frank Robinson	4.00	10.00
36 Pete Rose	20.00	50.00
37 Ron Santo	3.00	8.00
38 Tom Seaver	12.50	30.00
39 Dick Selma	1.50	4.00
40 Chris Short	1.50	4.00
41 Rusty Staub	3.00	8.00
42 Mel Stottlemyre	2.00	5.00
43 Luis Tiant	2.00	5.00
44 Pete Ward	1.50	4.00
45 Hoyt Wilhelm	3.00	8.00
46 Maury Wills	3.00	8.00
47 Jim Wynn	2.00	5.00
48 Carl Yastrzemski	8.00	20.00

1969 Topps Deckle Edge

The cards in this 33-card set measure approximately 2 1/4" by 3 1/4". This unusual black and white insert set derives its name from the serrated border, or edge, of the cards. The cards were included as inserts in the regularly issued Topps baseball third series of 1969. Card number 11 is found with either Hoyt Wilhelm or Jim Wynn, and number 22 with either Rusty Staub or Joe Foy. The set price below does include all variations. The set numbering is arranged in team order by league except for cards 11 and 22.

COMPLETE SET (35)	50.00	100.00
1 Brooks Robinson	2.50	6.00
2 Boog Powell	1.25	3.00
3 Ken Harrelson	.60	1.50
4 Carl Yastrzemski	3.00	8.00
5 Jim Fregosi	.75	2.00
6 Luis Aparicio	1.25	3.00
7 Luis Tiant	.75	2.00
8 Denny McLain	1.25	3.00
9 Willie Horton	.75	2.00
10 Bill Freehan	.75	2.00
11A Hoyt Wilhelm	3.00	8.00
11B Jim Wynn	6.00	15.00
12 Rod Carew	1.50	4.00
13 Mel Stottlemyre	.75	2.00
14 Rick Monday	.60	1.50
15 Tommy Davis	.75	2.00
16 Frank Howard	.75	2.00
17 Felipe Alou	.75	2.00
18 Don Kessinger	.60	1.50
19 Ron Santo	1.25	3.00
20 Tommy Helms	.60	1.50
21 Pete Rose	5.00	12.00
22A Rusty Staub	.75	2.00
22B Joe Foy	10.00	25.00
23 Tom Haller	.60	1.50
24 Maury Wills	1.25	3.00
25 Jerry Kosman	.75	2.00
26 Richie Allen	1.50	4.00
27 Roberto Clemente	8.00	20.00
28 Curt Flood	1.25	3.00
29 Bob Gibson	1.50	4.00
30 Al Ferrara	.60	1.50
31 Willie McCovey	1.50	4.00
32 Juan Marichal	1.25	3.00
33 Willie Mays	5.00	12.00

1969 Topps Four-in-One

This was a test issue consisting of 25 sticker cards (blank back). Each card measures 2 1/2" by 3 1/2" and features four mini-stickers. These unnumbered stickers are ordered in the checklist below alphabetically by the upper left player's name on each card. Each mini-card featured is from the 1969 Topps second series. Five of the cards were double printed (technically 50 percent more were printed) compared to the others in the set; these are marked below by DP:

COMPLETE SET (25)	1,500.00	3,000.00
1 Adair	200.00	400.00
Wilson		
Mays		
Morris		
2 Gilson/McFad/Bubker/Gibbon/Cardwell	20.00	50.00
3 Clend/Woodw/TAaron/Britton	20.00	50.00
4 Tdavis/Pavl/WSG4/Pinson	40.00	80.00
5 Fairly	20.00	50.00
Wise		
Alvis		
Beckert		
6 French	20.00	50.00
Selma		
Callison		
Harris		
7 Gibson/WSG3?Reichardt/Haney	75.00	150.00
8 Kosco	30.00	60.00
Reed		
Bunning		
Brown		
9 Lefebvre	20.00	50.00
Purdin		
Dillman		
Roseboro		
10 Milan/Hands/McDan/Harrison	20.00	50.00
11 Nelson	30.00	60.00
Johnson		
Hiatt		
Sisk		
12 Odom	30.00	60.00
Durocher		
Wood		
Dalrymple		
13 Oyler	20.00	50.00
Bauer		
Collins		
Snyder		
14 Jperry/WSG7/Arrigo/RSRook	30.00	60.00
15 Rader	20.00	50.00
McCool		
Pena		
WSG2		
16 Rodgers	30.00	60.00
Horton		
Face		
Brink		
17 Sadecki/Bald/Martin/May	20.00	50.00
18 Shannon	30.00	60.00
WSG1		
Pagan		
Phoebus		
19 Stange/Sutton/Uhlae/Rose	450.00	900.00
20 Weaver/Trace/Gtzenda/Howard	20.00	50.00
21 WSRook/McLain/Jackson/Axcue	30.00	60.00
22 Williams/Edwards/Fairey/PhilRook	20.00	50.00
23 WSCele/Wagner/Bateman/Smith	20.00	50.00
24 YankRook/Canni/WSG5/Hendley	20.00	50.00
25 Yaz/Petro/Nossek/CardsRook	400.00	800.00

1969 Topps Bowie Kuhn

This one-card standard-size set was issued soon after Bowie Kuhn's elevation to Baseball Commissioner. The front features a superimposed photo of Kuhn in regal wear sitting on a base. The horizontal back features vital statistics as well as a brief biography.

1 Bowie Kuhn	20.00	50.00

1969 Topps Super

The cards in this 66-card set measure approximately 2 1/4" by 3 1/4". This beautiful Topps set was released independently of the regular baseball series of 1969. It is referred to as "Super Baseball" on the back of the card, a title which was also used for the postcard-size cards issued in 1970 and 1971. Complete sheets, and cards with square corners cut from these sheets, are sometimes encountered. The set numbering is in alphabetical order by teams within league. Cards from the far right of each row are usually found with a white line on the right edge. Although rarely seen, this set was issued in three-card cello packs. The set features Reggie Jackson in his Rookie Card year.

COMPLETE SET (66)	3,000.00	5,000.00
1 Dave McNally	8.00	20.00
2 Frank Robinson	100.00	200.00
3 Brooks Robinson	100.00	200.00
4 Ken Harrelson	10.00	25.00
5 Carl Yastrzemski	125.00	250.00
6 Ray Culp	8.00	20.00
7 Jim Fregosi	10.00	25.00
8 Rick Reichardt	8.00	20.00
9 Vic Davalillo	8.00	20.00
10 Luis Aparicio	40.00	80.00
11 Pete Ward	8.00	20.00
12 Joel Horlen	8.00	20.00
13 Luis Tiant	10.00	25.00
14 Sam McDowell	8.00	20.00
15 Jose Cardenal	8.00	20.00
16 Willie Horton	10.00	25.00
17 Denny McLain	12.50	30.00
18 Bill Freehan	10.00	25.00
19 Harmon Killebrew	75.00	150.00
20 Tony Oliva	15.00	40.00
21 Dean Chance	8.00	20.00
22 Joe Foy	8.00	20.00

Card	Low	High
23 Roger Nelson	8.00	20.00
24 Mickey Mantle	500.00	1,000.00
25 Mel Stottlemyre	10.00	25.00
26 Roy White	10.00	25.00
27 Rick Monday	8.00	20.00
28 Reggie Jackson	250.00	500.00
29 Bert Campaneris	10.00	25.00
30 Frank Howard	12.50	30.00
31 Camilo Pascual	8.00	20.00
32 Tommy Davis	10.00	25.00
33 Don Mincher	8.00	20.00
34 Hank Aaron	250.00	500.00
35 Felipe Alou	12.50	30.00
36 Joe Torre	20.00	50.00
37 Ferguson Jenkins	40.00	80.00
38 Ron Santo	15.00	40.00
39 Billy Williams	40.00	80.00
40 Tommy Helms	8.00	20.00
41 Pete Rose	200.00	400.00
42 Joe Morgan	60.00	120.00
43 Jim Wynn	8.00	20.00
44 Curt Blefary	8.00	20.00
45 Willie Davis	8.00	20.00
46 Don Drysdale	50.00	100.00
47 Tom Haller	8.00	20.00
48 Rusty Staub	12.50	30.00
49 Maury Wills	15.00	40.00
50 Cleon Jones	8.00	20.00
51 Jerry Koosman	12.50	30.00
52 Tom Seaver	200.00	400.00
53 Richie Allen	12.50	30.00
54 Chris Short	8.00	20.00
55 Cookie Rojas	8.00	20.00
56 Matty Alou	8.00	20.00
57 Steve Blass	8.00	20.00
58 Roberto Clemente	300.00	600.00
59 Curt Flood	12.50	30.00
60 Bob Gibson	75.00	150.00
61 Tim McCarver	15.00	40.00
62 Dick Selma	8.00	20.00
63 Ollie Brown	8.00	20.00
64 Juan Marichal	50.00	100.00
65 Willie Mays	250.00	500.00
66 Willie McCovey	50.00	100.00

1969 Topps Stamps

The 1969 Topps set of baseball player stamps contains 240 individual stamps and 24 separate albums, 10 stamps and one album per major league team. The stamps were issued in strips of 12 and have gummed backs. Each stamp measures 1" by 1 7/16". The eight-page albums are bright orange and have an autograph feature on the back cover. The stamps are numbered here alphabetically within each team and the teams are listed in alphabetical order within league, e.g., Atlanta Braves NL (1-10), Chicago Cubs (11-20), Cincinnati Reds (21-30), Houston Astros (31-40), Los Angeles Dodgers (41-50), Montreal Expos (51-60), New York Mets (61-70), Philadelphia Phillies (71-80), Pittsburgh Pirates (81-90), San Diego Padres (91-100), San Francisco Giants (101-110), St. Louis Cardinals (111-120), Baltimore Orioles AL (121-130), Boston Red Sox (131-140), California Angels (141-150), Chicago White Sox (151-160), Cleveland Indians (161-170), Detroit Tigers (171-180), Kansas City Royals (181-190), Minnesota Twins (191-200), New York Yankees (201-210), Oakland A's (211-220), Seattle Pilots (221-230) and Washington Senators (231-240). Stamps still in the original uncut sheets are at twice the listed prices below. These stamps were issued in five-cent wax packs which came 24 packs to a box.

Card	Low	High
COMPLETE SET (240)	125.00	250.00
WRAPPER (5-CENT)		
1 Hank Aaron	5.00	12.00
2 Felipe Alou	.30	.75
3 Clete Boyer	.20	.50
4 Tito Francona	.10	.25
5 Sonny Jackson	.10	.25
6 Pat Jarvis	.10	.25
7 Felix Millan	.10	.25
8 Milt Pappas	.20	.50
9 Ron Reed	.10	.25
10 Joe Torre	.60	1.50
11 Ernie Banks	1.50	4.00
12 Glenn Beckert	.10	.25
13 Bill Hands	.10	.25
14 Randy Hundley	.10	.25
15 Ferguson Jenkins	1.00	2.50
16 Don Kessinger	.20	.50
17 Adolfo Phillips	.10	.25
18 Phil Regan	.10	.25
19 Ron Santo	.60	1.50
20 Billy Williams	1.00	2.50
21 Ted Abernathy	.10	.25
22 Gerry Arrigo	.10	.25
23 Johnny Bench	2.00	5.00
24 Tommy Helms	.10	.25
25 Alex Johnson	.10	.25
26 Jim Maloney	.20	.50
27 Lee May	.20	.50
28 Tony Perez	1.00	2.50
29 Pete Rose	6.00	15.00
30 Bobby Tolan	.10	.25
31 Bob Aspromonte	.10	.25
32 Larry Dierker	.10	.25
33 Johnny Edwards	.10	.25
34 Denny Lemaster	.10	.25
35 Denis Menke	.10	.25
36 Joe Morgan	1.25	3.00
37 Doug Rader	.10	.25
38 Rusty Staub	.40	1.00
39 Don Wilson	.10	.25
40 Jim Wynn	.20	.50
41 Willie Davis	.20	.50
42 Don Drysdale	1.00	2.50
43 Ron Fairly	.10	.25
44 Len Gabrielson	.10	.25
45 Tom Haller	.10	.25
46 Jim LeFebvre	.10	.25
47 Claude Osteen	.20	.50
48 Paul Popovich	.10	.25
49 Bill Singer	.10	.25
50 Don Sutton	1.00	2.50
51 Jesus Alou	.10	.25
52 Bob Bailey	.10	.25
53 John Bateman	.10	.25
54 Donn Clendenon	.10	.25
55 Jim Grant	.10	.25
56 Larry Jaster	.10	.25
57 Mack Jones	.10	.25
58 Manny Mota	.20	.50
59 Gary Sutherland	.10	.25
60 Maury Wills	.40	1.00
61 Tommie Agee	.20	.50
62 Ed Charles	.10	.25
63 Jerry Grote	.10	.25
64 Bud Harrelson	.10	.25
65 Cleon Jones	.10	.25
66 Jerry Koosman	.20	.50
67 Ed Kranepool	.10	.25
68 Tom Seaver	3.00	8.00
69 Art Shamsky	.10	.25
70 Ron Swoboda	.10	.25
71 Richie Allen	.40	1.00
72 John Briggs	.10	.25
73 Johnny Callison	.20	.50
74 Clay Dalrymple	.10	.25
75 Woodie Fryman	.10	.25
76 Don Lock	.10	.25
77 Cookie Rojas	.20	.50
78 Chris Short	.10	.25
79 Tony Taylor	.10	.25
80 Rick Wise	.10	.25
81 Gene Alley	.10	.25
82 Matty Alou	.20	.50
83 Steve Blass	.10	.25
84 Jim Bunning	1.00	2.50
85 Roberto Clemente	8.00	20.00
86 Ron Kline	.10	.25
87 Jerry May	.10	.25
88 Bill Mazeroski	1.00	2.50
89 Willie Stargell	1.25	3.00
90 Bob Veale	.10	.25
91 Jose Arcia	.10	.25
92 Ollie Brown	.10	.25
93 Al Ferrara	.10	.25
94 Tony Gonzalez	.10	.25
95 Dave Giusti	.10	.25
96 Alvin McBean	.10	.25
97 Roberto Pena	.10	.25
98 Dick Selma	.10	.25
99 Larry Stahl	.10	.25
100 Zoilo Versalles	.10	.25
101 Bobby Bolin	.10	.25
102 Jim Davenport	.10	.25
103 Dick Dietz	.10	.25
104 Jim Ray Hart	.10	.25
105 Ron Hunt	.10	.25
106 Hal Lanier	.10	.25
107 Juan Marichal	1.25	3.00
108 Willie Mays	4.00	10.00
109 Willie McCovey	1.25	3.00
110 Gaylord Perry	1.00	2.50
111 Nelson Briles	.10	.25
112 Lou Brock	1.50	4.00
113 Orlando Cepeda	1.00	2.50
114 Curt Flood	.40	1.00
115 Bob Gibson	1.25	3.00
116 Julian Javier	.10	.25
117 Dal Maxvill	.10	.25
118 Tim McCarver	.40	1.00
119 Vada Pinson	.30	.75
120 Mike Shannon	.20	.50
121 Mark Belanger	.20	.50
122 Curt Blefary	.10	.25
123 Don Buford	.10	.25
124 Jim Hardin	.10	.25
125 Dave Johnson	.30	.75
126 Dave McNally	.20	.50
127 Tom Phoebus	.10	.25
128 Boog Powell	.40	1.00
129 Brooks Robinson	1.50	4.00
130 Frank Robinson	1.50	4.00
131 Mike Andrews	.10	.25
132 Ray Culp	.10	.25
133 Russ Gibson	.10	.25
134 Ken Harrelson	.30	.75
135 Jim Lonborg	.20	.50
136 Rico Petrocelli	.20	.50
137 Jose Santiago	.10	.25
138 George Scott	.20	.50
139 Reggie Smith	.30	.75
140 Carl Yastrzemski	2.00	5.00
141 George Brunet	.10	.25
142 Vic Davalillo	.10	.25
143 Eddie Fisher	.10	.25
144 Jim Fregosi	.20	.50
145 Bobby Knoop	.10	.25
146 Jim McGlothlin	.10	.25
147 Rick Reichardt	.10	.25
148 Roger Repoz	.10	.25
149 Bob Rodgers	.10	.25
150 Tom Satriano	.10	.25
151 Sandy Alomar	.10	.25
152 Luis Aparicio	1.00	2.50
153 Ken Berry	.10	.25
154 Joel Horlen	.10	.25
155 Tommy John	.60	1.50
156 Duane Josephson	.10	.25
157 Gary Peters	.10	.25
158 Leon Wagner	.10	.25
159 Pete Ward	.10	.25
160 Wilbur Wood	.10	.25
161 Max Alvis	.10	.25
162 Joe Azcue	.10	.25
163 Larry Brown	.10	.25
164 Jose Cardenal	.10	.25
165 Lee Maye	.10	.25
166 Sam McDowell	.20	.50
167 Sonny Siebert	.10	.25
168 Duke Sims	.10	.25
169 Luis Tiant	.40	1.00
170 Stan Williams	.10	.25
171 Norm Cash	.40	1.00
172 Bill Freehan	.20	.50
173 Willie Horton	.20	.50
174 Al Kaline	1.50	4.00
175 Mickey Lolich	.30	.75
176 Dick McAuliffe	.10	.25
177 Denny McLain	.40	1.00
178 Jim Northrup	.20	.50
179 Mickey Stanley	.20	.50
180 Don Wert	.10	.25
181 Jerry Adair	.10	.25
182 Wally Bunker	.10	.25
183 Moe Drabowsky	.10	.25
184 Joe Foy	.10	.25
185 Jackie Hernandez	.10	.25
186 Roger Nelson	.10	.25
187 Bob Oliver	.10	.25
188 Paul Schaal	.10	.25
189 Steve Whitaker	.10	.25
190 Hoyt Wilhelm	1.00	2.50
191 Bob Allison	.20	.50
192 Rod Carew	1.50	4.00
193 Dean Chance	.20	.50
194 Jim Kaat	.40	1.00
195 Harmon Killebrew	1.25	3.00
196 Tony Oliva	.60	1.50
197 Ron Perranoski	.10	.25
198 Johnny Roseboro	.10	.25
199 Cesar Tovar	.10	.25
200 Ted Uhlaender	.10	.25
201 Stan Bahnsen	.10	.25
202 Horace Clarke	.10	.25
203 Jake Gibbs	.10	.25
204 Andy Kosco	.10	.25
205 Mickey Mantle	15.00	40.00
206 Joe Pepitone	.20	.50
207 Bill Robinson	.10	.25
208 Mel Stottlemyre	.20	.50
209 Tom Tresh	.20	.50
210 Roy White	.20	.50
211 Sal Bando	.20	.50
212 Bert Campaneris	.20	.50
213 Danny Cater	.10	.25
214 Dave Duncan	.10	.25
215 Dick Green	.10	.25
216 Jim Hunter	1.00	2.50
217 Lew Krausse	.10	.25
218 Rick Monday	.20	.50
219 Jim Nash	.10	.25
220 John Odom	.10	.25
221 Jack Aker	.10	.25
222 Steve Barber	.10	.25
223 Gary Bell	.10	.25
224 Tommy Davis	.20	.50
225 Tommy Harper	.10	.25
226 Jerry McNertney	.10	.25
227 Don Mincher	.10	.25
228 Ray Oyler	.10	.25
229 Rich Rollins	.10	.25
230 Chico Salmon	.10	.25
231 Bernie Allen	.10	.25
232 Ed Brinkman	.10	.25
233 Paul Casanova	.10	.25
234 Joe Coleman	.10	.25
235 Mike Epstein	.10	.25
236 Jim Hannan	.10	.25
237 Dennis Higgins	.10	.25
238 Frank Howard	.40	1.00
239 Ken McMullen	.10	.25
240 Camilo Pascual	.10	.25

1969 Topps Stamp Albums

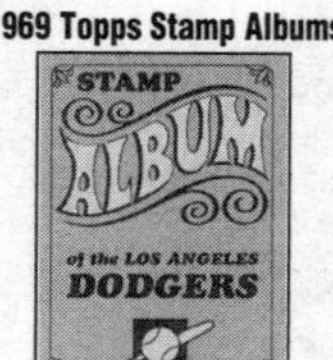

The 1969 Topps stamp set of baseball player stamps was intended to be mounted in 24 separate team albums, 10 stamps for that team's players going into that team's album. The eight-page albums are bright orange and have an autograph feature on the back cover. The albums measure approximately 2 1/2" by 3 1/2".

Album	Low	High
COMPLETE SET (24)	12.50	30.00
COMMON TEAM (1-24)	.60	1.50
23 Seattle Pilots	1.00	2.50

1969 Topps Team Posters

This set was issued as a separate set by Topps, but was apparently not widely distributed. It was folded many times to fit the packaging and hence is typically found with relatively heavy fold creases. Each team poster measures approximately 12" by 20". These posters are in full color with a blank back. Each team features nine or ten individual players; a complete list is listed in the checklist below. Each player photo is accompanied by a facsimile autograph. The posters are numbered in the bottom left corner. The unopened wax packs cost 10 cents in 1969.

Poster	Low	High
COMPLETE SET (24)	600.00	1,200.00
WRAPPER (10-CENT)		
1 Detroit Tigers	15.00	40.00
2 Atlanta Braves	30.00	60.00
3 Boston Red Sox	30.00	60.00
4 Chicago Cubs	20.00	50.00
5 Baltimore Orioles	30.00	60.00
6 Houston Astros	12.50	30.00
7 Kansas City Royals	10.00	25.00
8 Philadelphia Phillies	10.00	25.00
9 Seattle Pilots	15.00	40.00
10 Montreal Expos	10.00	25.00
11 Chicago White Sox	10.00	25.00
12 San Diego Padres	10.00	25.00
13 Cleveland Indians	10.00	25.00
14 San Francisco Giants	20.00	50.00
15 Minnesota Twins	12.50	30.00
16 Pittsburgh Pirates	60.00	120.00
17 California Angels	10.00	25.00
18 St. Louis Cardinals	15.00	40.00
19 New York Yankees	100.00	200.00
20 Cincinnati Reds	50.00	100.00
21 Oakland A's	50.00	100.00
22 Los Angeles Dodgers	12.50	30.00
23 Washington Senators	10.00	25.00
24 New York Mets	50.00	100.00

1970 Topps

The cards in this 720-card set measure 2 1/2" by 3 1/2". The Topps set for 1970 has color photos surrounded by white frame lines and gray borders. The backs have a blue biographical section and a yellow record section. All-Star selections are featured on cards 450 to 469. Other topical subsets within this set include League Leaders (61-72), Playoffs cards (195-202), and World Series cards (305-310). There are graduations of scarcity, terminating in the high series (634-720), which are outlined in the value summary. Cards were issued in ten-card dime packs as well as thirty-three card cello packs which sold for a quarter and were encased in a small Topps box, and in 54-card rack packs which sold for 39 cents. The key Rookie Card in this set is Thurman Munson.

Card	Low	High
COMPLETE SET (720)	1,000.00	2,000.00
COMMON CARD (1-132)	.30	.75
COMMON CARD (133-372)	.40	1.00
COMMON CARD (373-459)	.60	1.50
COMMON CARD (460-546)	.75	2.00
COMMON CARD (547-633)	1.50	4.00
COMMON CARD (634-720)	4.00	10.00
WRAPPER (10-CENT)	8.00	20.00
1 New York Mets TC	12.50	30.00
2 Diego Segui	.40	1.00
3 Darrel Chaney	.30	.75
4 Tom Egan	.30	.75
5 Wes Parker	.40	1.00
6 Grant Jackson	.30	.75
7 G.Boyd RC/R.Nagelson RC	.30	.75
8 Jose Martinez RC	.30	.75
9 Checklist 1	5.00	12.00
10 Carl Yastrzemski	8.00	20.00
11 Nate Colbert	.30	.75
12 John Hiller	.30	.75
13 Jack Hiatt	.30	.75
14 Hank Allen	.30	.75
15 Larry Dierker	.30	.75
16 Charlie Metro MG RC	.30	.75
17 Hoyt Wilhelm	1.50	4.00
18 Carlos May	.40	1.00
19 John Boccabella	.30	.75
20 Dave McNally	.40	1.00
21 V.Blue RC/G.Tenace RC	1.50	4.00
22 Ray Washburn	.30	.75
23 Bill Robinson	.40	1.00
24 Dick Selma	.30	.75
25 Cesar Tovar	.30	.75
26 Tug McGraw	.75	2.00
27 Chuck Hinton	.30	.75
28 Billy Wilson	.30	.75
29 Sandy Alomar	.40	1.00
30 Matty Alou	.40	1.00
31 Marty Pattin	.40	1.00
32 Harry Walker MG	.30	.75
33 Don Wert	.30	.75
34 Willie Crawford	.30	.75
35 Joel Horlen	.30	.75
36 D.Breeden/B.Carbo RC	.40	1.00
37 Dick Drago	.30	.75
38 Mack Jones	.30	.75
39 Mike Nagy RC	.30	.75
40 Rich Allen	.75	2.00
41 George Lauzerique	.30	.75
42 Tito Fuentes	.30	.75
43 Jack Aker	.30	.75
44 Roberto Pena	.30	.75
45 Dave Johnson	.40	1.00
46 Ken Rudolph RC	.30	.75
47 Bob Miller	.30	.75
48 Gil Garrido	.30	.75

Card	Low	High
49 Tim Cullen	.30	.75
50 Tommie Agee	.40	1.00
51 Bob Christian	.30	.75
52 Bruce Dal Canton	.30	.75
53 John Kennedy	.30	.75
54 Jeff Torborg	.40	1.00
55 John Odom	.30	.75
56 J.Lis RC/S.Reid RC	.30	.75
57 Pat Kelly	.30	.75
58 Dave Marshall	.30	.75
59 Dick Ellsworth	.30	.75
60 Jim Wynn	.40	1.00
61 Rose/Clemente/Jones LL	5.00	12.00
62 Carew/Smith/Oliva LL	.75	2.00
63 McCovey/Santo/Perez LL	.75	2.00
64 Kill/Powell/Jackson LL	1.50	4.00
65 McCovey/Aaron/May LL	5.00	12.00
66 Kill/Howard/Jackson LL	1.50	4.00
67 Marichal/Carlton/Gibson LL	1.50	4.00
68 Bosman/Palmer/Cuellar LL	.40	1.00
69 Seav/Niek/Jenk/Mari LL	1.50	4.00
70 McLain/Cuellar/Boswell LL	.40	1.00
71 Jenkins/Gibson/Singer LL	.75	2.00
72 McDowell/Lolich/Mess LL	.40	1.00
73 Wayne Granger	.30	.75
74 G.Washburn RC/W.Wolf	.30	.75
75 Jim Kaat	.40	1.00
76 Carl Taylor UER	.30	.75
Collecting is spelled incorrectly in the cartoon		
77 Frank Linzy	.30	.75
78 Joe Lahoud	.30	.75
79 Clay Kirby	.30	.75
80 Don Kessinger	.40	1.00
81 Dave May	.30	.75
82 Frank Fernandez	.30	.75
83 Don Cardwell	.30	.75
84 Paul Casanova	.30	.75
85 Max Alvis	.30	.75
86 Lum Harris MG	.30	.75
87 Steve Renko RC	.30	.75
88 M.Fuentes RC/D.Baney RC	.40	1.00
89 Juan Rios	.30	.75
90 Tim McCarver	.40	1.00
91 Rich Morales	.30	.75
92 George Culver	.30	.75
93 Rick Renick	.30	.75
94 Freddie Patek	.40	1.00
95 Earl Wilson	.40	1.00
96 L.Lee RC/J.Reuss RC	.40	1.00
97 Joe Moeller	.30	.75
98 Gates Brown	.40	1.00
99 Bobby Pfeil RC	.30	.75
100 Mel Stottlemyre	.40	1.00
101 Bobby Floyd	.30	.75
102 Joe Rudi	.40	1.00
103 Frank Reberger	.30	.75
104 Gerry Moses	.30	.75
105 Tony Gonzalez	.30	.75
106 Darold Knowles	.30	.75
107 Bobby Etheridge	.30	.75
108 Tom Burgmeier	.30	.75
109 G.Jestadt RC/C.Morton	.30	.75
110 Bob Moose	.30	.75
111 Mike Hegan	.40	1.00
112 Dave Nelson	.30	.75
113 Jim Ray	.30	.75
114 Gene Michael	.40	1.00
115 Alex Johnson	.40	1.00
116 Sparky Lyle	.40	1.00
117 Don Young	.30	.75
118 George Mitterwald	.30	.75
119 Chuck Taylor RC	.30	.75
120 Sal Bando	.40	1.00
121 F.Beene RC/T.Crowley RC	.30	.75
122 George Stone	.30	.75
123 Don Gutteridge MG RC	.30	.75
124 Larry Jaster	.30	.75
125 Deron Johnson	.30	.75
126 Marty Martinez	.30	.75
127 Joe Coleman	.30	.75
128A Checklist 2 R Perranoski	2.50	6.00
128B Checklist 2 R. Perranoski	2.50	6.00
129 Jimmie Price	.30	.75
130 Ollie Brown	.30	.75
131 R.Lamb RC/B.Stinson RC	.30	.75
132 Jim McGlothlin	.30	.75
133 Clay Carroll	.40	1.00
134 Danny Walton RC	.40	1.00
135 Dick Dietz	.40	1.00
136 Steve Hargan	.40	1.00
137 Art Shamsky	.40	1.00
138 Joe Foy	.40	1.00
139 Rich Nye	.40	1.00
140 Reggie Jackson	20.00	50.00
141 D.Cash RC/J.Jeter RC	.60	1.50
142 Fritz Peterson	.40	1.00
143 Phil Gagliano	.40	1.00
144 Ray Culp	.40	1.00
145 Rico Carty	.60	1.50
146 Danny Murphy	.40	1.00
147 Angel Hermoso RC	.40	1.00
148 Earl Weaver MG	1.25	3.00
149 Billy Champion RC	.40	1.00
150 Harmon Killebrew	3.00	8.00
151 Dave Roberts	.40	1.00
152 Ike Brown RC	.40	1.00
153 Gary Gentry	.40	1.00
154 J.Miles/J.Dukes RC	.40	1.00
155 Denis Menke	.40	1.00
156 Eddie Fisher	.40	1.00
157 Manny Mota	.60	1.50
158 Jerry McNertney	.60	1.50
159 Tommy Helms	.60	1.50
160 Phil Niekro	2.00	5.00
161 Richie Scheinblum	.40	1.00
162 Jerry Johnson	.40	1.00
163 Syd O'Brien	.40	1.00
164 Ty Cline	.40	1.00
165 Ed Kirkpatrick	.40	1.00
166 Al Oliver	1.25	3.00
167 Bill Burbach	.40	1.00
168 Dave Watkins RC	.40	1.00
169 Tom Hall	.40	1.00
170 Billy Williams	2.00	5.00
171 Jim Nash	.40	1.00
172 G.Hill RC/R.Garr RC	.60	1.50
173 Jim Hicks	.40	1.00
174 Ted Sizemore	.60	1.50
175 Dick Bosman	.40	1.00
176 Jim Ray Hart	.60	1.50
177 Jim Northrup	.60	1.50
178 Denny Lemaster	.40	1.00
179 Ivan Murrell	.40	1.00
180 Tommy John	.60	1.50
181 Sparky Anderson MG	2.00	5.00
182 Dick Hall	.40	1.00
183 Jerry Grote	.60	1.50
184 Ray Fosse	.40	1.00
185 Don Mincher	.60	1.50
186 Rick Joseph	.40	1.00
187 Mike Hedlund	.40	1.00
188 Manny Sanguillen	.60	1.50
189 Thurman Munson RC	40.00	100.00
190 Joe Torre	1.25	3.00
191 Vicente Romo	.40	1.00
192 Jim Qualls	.40	1.00
193 Mike Wegener	.40	1.00
194 Chuck Manuel RC	1.00	2.50
195 Tom Seaver NLCS1	6.00	15.00
196 Ken Boswell NLCS2	.75	2.00
197 Nolan Ryan NLCS3	12.50	30.00
198 Mets Celebrate/w/Ryan	6.00	15.00
199 Mike Cuellar ALCS1	.75	2.00
200 Boog Powell ALCS2	1.25	3.00
201 B.Powell/A.Etch ALCS3	.75	2.00
202 Orioles Celebrate ALCS	.75	2.00
203 Rudy May	.40	1.00
204 Len Gabrielson	.40	1.00
205 Bert Campaneris	.60	1.50
206 Clete Boyer	.60	1.50
207 N.McRae RC/B.Reed RC	.40	1.00
208 Fred Gladding	.40	1.00
209 Ken Suarez	.40	1.00
210 Juan Marichal	2.00	5.00
211 Ted Williams MG UER	8.00	20.00
212 Al Santorini	.40	1.00
213 Andy Etchebarren	.40	1.00
214 Ken Boswell	.40	1.00
215 Reggie Smith	.60	1.50
216 Chuck Hartenstein	.40	1.00
217 Ron Hansen	.40	1.00
218 Ron Stone	.40	1.00
219 Jerry Kenney	.40	1.00
220 Steve Carlton	8.00	20.00
221 Ron Brand	.40	1.00
222 Jim Rooker	.40	1.00
223 Nate Oliver	.40	1.00
224 Steve Barber	.60	1.50
225 Lee May	.60	1.50
226 Ron Perranoski	.40	1.00
227 J.Mayberry RC/B.Watkins RC	.60	1.50
228 Aurelio Rodriguez	.40	1.00
229 Rich Robertson	.40	1.00
230 Brooks Robinson	8.00	20.00
231 Luis Tiant	.60	1.50
232 Bob Didier	.40	1.00
233 Lew Krausse	.40	1.00
234 Tommy Dean	.40	1.00
235 Mike Epstein	.40	1.00
236 Bob Veale	.40	1.00
237 Russ Gibson	.40	1.00
238 Jose Laboy	.40	1.00
239 Ken Berry	.40	1.00
240 Ferguson Jenkins	2.00	5.00
241 A.Fitzmorris RC/S.Northey RC	.40	1.00
242 Walter Alston MG	1.25	3.00
243 Joe Sparma	.40	1.00
244A Checklist 3 Red Bat	2.50	6.00
244B Checklist 3 Brown Bat	2.50	6.00
245 Leo Cardenas	.40	1.00
246 Jim McAndrew	.40	1.00
247 Lou Klimchock	.40	1.00
248 Jesus Alou	.40	1.00
249 Bob Locker	.40	1.00
250 Willie McCovey UER	4.00	10.00
251 Dick Schofield	.40	1.00
252 Lowell Palmer RC	.40	1.00
253 Ron Woods	.40	1.00
254 Camilo Pascual	.40	1.00
255 Jim Spencer RC	.40	1.00
256 Vic Davalillo	.40	1.00
257 Dennis Higgins	.40	1.00
258 Paul Popovich	.40	1.00
259 Tommie Reynolds	.40	1.00
260 Claude Osteen	.40	1.00
261 Curt Motton	.40	1.00
262 J.Morales RC/J.Williams RC	.40	1.00
263 Duane Josephson	.40	1.00
264 Rich Hebner	.40	1.00
265 Randy Hundley	.40	1.00
266 Wally Bunker	.40	1.00
267 H.Hill RC/P.Ratliff	.40	1.00
268 Claude Raymond	.40	1.00
269 Cesar Gutierrez	.40	1.00
270 Chris Short	.40	1.00
271 Greg Goossen	.60	1.50
272 Hector Torres	.40	1.00
273 Ralph Houk MG	.60	1.50
274 Gerry Arrigo	.40	1.00
275 Duke Sims	.40	1.00
276 Ron Hunt	.40	1.00
277 Paul Doyle RC	.40	1.00
278 Tommie Aaron	.40	1.00
279 Bill Lee RC	.60	1.50
280 Donn Clendenon	.60	1.50
281 Casey Cox	.40	1.00
282 Steve Huntz	.40	1.00
283 Angel Bravo RC	.40	1.00
284 Jack Baldschun	.40	1.00
285 Paul Blair	.60	1.50
286 J.Jenkins RC/B.Buckner RC	6.00	15.00
287 Fred Talbot	.40	1.00
288 Larry Hisle	.60	1.50
289 Gene Brabender	.40	1.00
290 Rod Carew	10.00	25.00
291 Leo Durocher MG	1.25	3.00
292 Eddie Leon RC	.40	1.00
293 Bob Bailey	.60	1.50
294 Jose Azcue	.40	1.00
295 Cecil Upshaw	.40	1.00
296 Woody Woodward	.40	1.00
297 Curt Blefary	.40	1.00
298 Ken Henderson	.40	1.00
299 Buddy Bradford	.40	1.00
300 Tom Seaver	12.00	30.00
301 Chico Salmon	.40	1.00
302 Jeff James	.40	1.00
303 Brant Alyea	.40	1.00
304 Bill Russell RC	2.00	5.00
305 Don Buford WS1	1.50	4.00
306 Donn Clendenon WS2	1.50	4.00
307 Tommie Agee WS3	1.50	4.00
308 J.C. Martin WS4	1.50	4.00
309 Jerry Koosman WS5	1.50	4.00
310 Mets Celebrate WS	2.00	5.00
311 Dick Green	.40	1.00
312 Mike Torrez	.40	1.00
313 Mayo Smith MG	.40	1.00
314 Bill McCool	.40	1.00
315 Luis Aparicio	2.00	5.00
316 Skip Guinn	.40	1.00
317 B.Conigliaro/L.Alvarado RC	.60	1.50
318 Willie Smith	.40	1.00
319 Clay Dalrymple	.40	1.00
320 Jim Maloney	.60	1.50
321 Lou Piniella	.60	1.50
322 Luke Walker	.40	1.00
323 Wayne Comer	.40	1.00
324 Tony Taylor	.60	1.50
325 Dave Boswell	.40	1.00
326 Bill Voss	.40	1.00
327 Hal King RC	.40	1.00
328 George Brunet	.40	1.00
329 Chris Cannizzaro	.40	1.00
330 Lou Brock	8.00	20.00
331 Chuck Dobson	.40	1.00
332 Bobby Wine	.40	1.00
333 Bobby Murcer	.60	1.50
334 Phil Regan	.40	1.00
335 Bill Freehan	.60	1.50
336 Del Unser	.40	1.00
337 Mike McCormick	.60	1.50
338 Paul Schaal	.40	1.00
339 Johnny Edwards	.40	1.00
340 Tony Conigliaro	1.25	3.00
341 Bill Sudakis	.40	1.00
342 Wilbur Wood	.60	1.50
343A Checklist 4 Red Bat	2.50	6.00
343B Checklist 4 Brown Bat	2.50	6.00
344 Marcelino Lopez	.40	1.00
345 Al Ferrara	.40	1.00
346 Red Schoendienst MG	.60	1.50
347 Russ Snyder	.40	1.00
348 M.Jorgensen RC/J.Hudson RC	.60	1.50
349 Steve Hamilton	.40	1.00
350 Roberto Clemente	30.00	80.00
351 Tom Murphy	.40	1.00
352 Bob Barton	.40	1.00
353 Stan Williams	.40	1.00
354 Amos Otis	.60	1.50
355 Doug Rader	.40	1.00
356 Fred Lasher	.40	1.00
357 Bob Burda	.40	1.00
358 Pedro Borbon RC	.60	1.50
359 Phil Roof	.40	1.00
360 Curt Flood	.60	1.50
361 Ray Jarvis	.40	1.00
362 Joe Hague	.40	1.00
363 Tom Shopay RC	.40	1.00
364 Dan McGinn	.40	1.00
365 Zoilo Versalles	.40	1.00
366 Barry Moore	.40	1.00
367 Mike Lum	.40	1.00
368 Ed Herrmann	.40	1.00
369 Alan Foster	.40	1.00
370 Tommy Harper	.60	1.50
371 Rod Gaspar RC	.40	1.00
372 Dave Giusti	.40	1.00
373 Roy White	.75	2.00
374 Tommie Sisk	.60	1.50
375 Johnny Callison	.75	2.00
376 Lefty Phillips MG RC	.60	1.50
377 Bill Butler	.60	1.50
378 Jim Davenport	.60	1.50
379 Tom Tischinski RC	.60	1.50
380 Tony Perez	2.50	6.00
381 B.Brooks RC/M.Olivo RC	.60	1.50
382 Jack DiLauro RC	.60	1.50
383 Mickey Stanley	.75	2.00
384 Gary Neibauer	.60	1.50
385 George Scott	.75	2.00
386 Bill Dillman	.60	1.50
387 Baltimore Orioles TC	1.25	3.00
388 Byron Browne	.60	1.50
389 Jim Shellenback	.60	1.50
390 Willie Davis	.75	2.00
391 Larry Brown	.60	1.50
392 Walt Hriniak	.75	2.00
393 John Gelnar	.60	1.50
394 Gil Hodges MG	1.50	4.00
395 Walt Williams	.60	1.50
396 Steve Blass	.75	2.00
397 Roger Repoz	.60	1.50
398 Bill Stoneman	.60	1.50
399 New York Yankees TC	1.25	3.00
400 Denny McLain	1.50	4.00
401 J.Harrell RC/B.Williams RC	.60	1.50
402 Ellie Rodriguez	.60	1.50
403 Jim Bunning	2.50	6.00
404 Rich Reese	.60	1.50
405 Bill Hands	.60	1.50
406 Mike Andrews	.60	1.50
407 Bob Watson	.75	2.00
408 Paul Lindblad	.60	1.50
409 Bob Tolan	.60	1.50
410 Boog Powell	1.50	4.00
411 Los Angeles Dodgers TC	1.25	3.00
412 Larry Burchart	.60	1.50
413 Sonny Jackson	.60	1.50
414 Paul Edmondson RC	.60	1.50
415 Julian Javier	.75	2.00
416 Joe Verbanic	.60	1.50
417 John Bateman	.60	1.50
418 John Donaldson	.60	1.50
419 Ron Taylor	.60	1.50
420 Ken McMullen	.75	2.00
421 Pat Dobson	.75	2.00
422 Kansas City Royals TC	1.25	3.00
423 Jerry May	.60	1.50
424 Mike Kilkenny	.60	1.50
425 Bobby Bonds	2.50	6.00
426 Bill Rigney MG	.60	1.50
427 Fred Norman	.60	1.50
428 Don Buford	.60	1.50
429 R.Bobb RC/J.Cosman	.60	1.50
430 Andy Messersmith	.75	2.00
431 Ron Swoboda	.75	2.00
432A Checklist 5 Yellow Ltr	2.50	6.00
432B Checklist 5 White Ltr	2.50	6.00
433 Ron Bryant RC	.60	1.50
434 Felipe Alou	.75	2.00
435 Nelson Briles	.75	2.00
436 Philadelphia Phillies TC	1.25	3.00
437 Danny Cater	.60	1.50
438 Pat Jarvis	.60	1.50
439 Lee Maye	.60	1.50
440 Bill Mazeroski	2.50	6.00
441 John O'Donoghue	.60	1.50
442 Gene Mauch MG	.75	2.00
443 Al Jackson	.60	1.50
444 B.Farmer RC/J.Matias RC	.60	1.50
445 Vada Pinson	.75	2.00
446 Billy Grabarkewitz RC	.60	1.50
447 Lee Stange	.60	1.50
448 Houston Astros TC	1.25	3.00
449 Jim Palmer	5.00	12.00
450 Willie McCovey AS	8.00	20.00
451 Boog Powell AS	1.50	4.00
452 Felix Millan AS	.75	2.00
453 Rod Carew AS	2.50	6.00
454 Ron Santo AS	1.50	4.00
455 Brooks Robinson AS	2.50	6.00
456 Don Kessinger AS	.75	2.00
457 Rico Petrocelli AS	1.50	4.00
458 Pete Rose AS	12.00	30.00
459 Reggie Jackson AS	8.00	20.00
460 Matty Alou AS	1.25	3.00
461 Carl Yastrzemski AS	8.00	20.00
462 Hank Aaron AS	20.00	50.00
463 Frank Robinson AS	10.00	25.00
464 Johnny Bench AS	15.00	40.00
465 Bill Freehan AS	1.25	3.00
466 Juan Marichal AS	2.00	5.00
467 Denny McLain AS	1.25	3.00
468 Jerry Koosman AS	1.25	3.00
469 Sam McDowell AS	1.25	3.00
470 Willie Stargell	4.00	10.00
471 Chris Zachary	.75	2.00
472 Atlanta Braves TC	1.50	4.00
473 Don Bryant	.75	2.00
474 Dick Kelley	.75	2.00
475 Dick McAuliffe	1.25	3.00
476 Don Shaw	.75	2.00
477 A.Severinsen RC/R.Freed RC	.75	2.00
478 Bobby Heise RC	.75	2.00
479 Dick Woodson RC	.75	2.00
480 Glenn Beckert	1.25	3.00
481 Jose Tartabull	.75	2.00
482 Tom Hilgendorf RC	.75	2.00
483 Gail Hopkins RC	.75	2.00
484 Gary Nolan	1.25	3.00
485 Jay Johnstone	1.25	3.00
486 Terry Harmon	.75	2.00
487 Cisco Carlos	.75	2.00
488 J.C. Martin	.75	2.00
489 Eddie Kasko MG	.75	2.00
490 Bill Singer	1.25	3.00
491 Graig Nettles	2.00	5.00
492 K.Lampard RC/S.Spinks RC	.75	2.00
493 Lindy McDaniel	1.25	3.00
494 Larry Stahl	.75	2.00
495 Dave Morehead	.75	2.00
496 Steve Whitaker	.75	2.00
497 Eddie Watt	.75	2.00
498 Al Weis	.75	2.00
499 Skip Lockwood	1.25	3.00
500 Hank Aaron	25.00	60.00
501 Chicago White Sox TC	1.50	4.00
502 Rollie Fingers	10.00	25.00
503 Dal Maxvill	.75	2.00
504 Don Pavletich	.75	2.00
505 Ken Holtzman	1.25	3.00
506 Ed Stroud	.75	2.00
507 Pat Corrales	.75	2.00
508 Joe Niekro	1.25	3.00

509 Montreal Expos TC 1.50 4.00
510 Tony Oliva 2.00 5.00
511 Joe Hoerner .75 2.00
512 Billy Harris .75 2.00
513 Preston Gomez MG .75 2.00
514 Steve Hovley RC .75 2.00
515 Don Wilson 1.25 3.00
516 J.Ellis RC/J.Lyttle RC .75 2.00
517 Joe Gibbon .75 2.00
518 Bill Melton .75 2.00
519 Don McMahon .75 2.00
520 Willie Horton 1.25 3.00
521 Cal Koonce .75 2.00
522 California Angels TC 1.50 4.00
523 Jose Pena .75 2.00
524 Alvin Dark MG 1.25 3.00
525 Jerry Adair .75 2.00
526 Ron Herbel .75 2.00
527 Don Bosch .75 2.00
528 Elrod Hendricks .75 2.00
529 Bob Aspromonte .75 2.00
530 Bob Gibson 10.00 25.00
531 Ron Clark .75 2.00
532 Danny Murtaugh MG 1.25 3.00
533 Buzz Stephen RC .75 2.00
534 Minnesota Twins TC 1.50 4.00
535 Andy Kosco .75 2.00
536 Mike Kekich .75 2.00
537 Joe Morgan 8.00 20.00
538 Bob Humphreys .75 2.00
539 D.Doyle RC/L.Bowa RC 3.00 8.00
540 Gary Peters .75 2.00
541 Bill Heath .75 2.00
542A Checklist 6 Brown Bat 2.50 6.00
542B Checklist 6 Gray Bat 2.50 6.00
543 Clyde Wright .75 2.00
544 Cincinnati Reds TC 1.50 4.00
545 Ken Harrelson 1.25 3.00
546 Ron Reed .75 2.00
547 Rick Monday 2.50 6.00
548 Howie Reed 1.50 4.00
549 St. Louis Cardinals TC 2.50 6.00
550 Frank Howard 2.50 6.00
551 Dock Ellis 2.50 6.00
552 O'Riley/Paepke/Rico RC 1.50 4.00
553 Jim Lefebvre 2.50 6.00
554 Tom Timmermann RC 1.50 4.00
555 Orlando Cepeda 5.00 12.00
556 Dave Bristol MG 2.50 6.00
557 Ed Kranepool 2.50 6.00
558 Vern Fuller 1.50 4.00
559 Tommy Davis 2.50 6.00
560 Gaylord Perry 5.00 12.00
561 Tom McCraw 1.50 4.00
562 Ted Abernathy 1.50 4.00
563 Boston Red Sox TC 2.50 6.00
564 Johnny Briggs 1.50 4.00
565 Jim Hunter 8.00 20.00
566 Gene Alley 2.50 6.00
567 Bob Oliver 1.50 4.00
568 Stan Bahnsen 2.50 6.00
569 Cookie Rojas 2.50 6.00
570 Jim Fregosi 2.50 6.00
571 Jim Brewer 1.50 4.00
572 Frank Quilici 1.50 4.00
573 Corkins/Robles/Slocum RC 1.50 4.00
574 Bobby Bolin 2.50 6.00
575 Cleon Jones 2.50 6.00
576 Milt Pappas 2.50 6.00
577 Bernie Allen 1.50 4.00
578 Tom Griffin 1.50 4.00
579 Detroit Tigers TC 2.50 6.00
580 Pete Rose 30.00 60.00
581 Tom Satriano 1.50 4.00
582 Mike Paul 1.50 4.00
583 Hal Lanier 1.50 4.00
584 Al Downing 2.50 6.00
585 Rusty Staub 3.00 8.00
586 Rickey Clark RC 1.50 4.00
587 Jose Arcia 1.50 4.00
588A Checklist 7 Adolfo 3.00 8.00
588B Checklist 7 Adolpho 2.50 6.00
589 Joe Keough 1.50 4.00
590 Mike Cuellar 2.50 6.00
591 Mike Ryan UER 1.50 4.00
592 Daryl Patterson 1.50 4.00
593 Chicago Cubs TC 3.00 8.00
594 Jake Gibbs 1.50 4.00
595 Maury Wills 5.00 12.00
596 Mike Hershberger 2.50 6.00
597 Sonny Siebert 1.50 4.00
598 Joe Pepitone 2.50 6.00
599 Stelmaszek/Martin/Such RC 1.50 4.00
600 Willie Mays 30.00 80.00
601 Pete Richert 1.50 4.00
602 Ted Savage 1.50 4.00
603 Ray Oyler 1.50 4.00
604 Clarence Gaston 2.50 6.00
605 Rick Wise 2.50 6.00
606 Chico Ruiz 1.50 4.00
607 Gary Waslewski 1.50 4.00
608 Pittsburgh Pirates TC 2.50 6.00
609 Buck Martinez RC 2.50 6.00
610 Jerry Koosman 3.00 8.00
611 Norm Cash 2.50 6.00
612 Jim Hickman 2.50 6.00
613 Dave Baldwin 2.50 6.00
614 Mike Shannon 2.50 6.00
615 Mark Belanger 2.50 6.00
616 Jim Merritt 1.50 4.00
617 Jim French 1.50 4.00
618 Billy Wynne RC 1.50 4.00
619 Norm Miller 1.50 4.00
620 Jim Perry 2.50 6.00
621 McQueen/Evans/Kester RC 5.00 12.00
622 Don Sutton 5.00 12.00
623 Horace Clarke 2.50 6.00
624 Clyde King MG 1.50 4.00
625 Dean Chance 1.50 4.00
626 Dave Ricketts 1.50 4.00
627 Gary Wagner 1.50 4.00
628 Wayne Garrett RC 1.50 4.00
629 Merv Rettenmund 1.50 4.00
630 Ernie Banks 20.00 50.00
631 Oakland Athletics TC 2.50 6.00
632 Gary Sutherland 1.50 4.00
633 Roger Nelson 1.50 4.00
634 Bud Harrelson 6.00 15.00
635 Bob Allison 6.00 15.00
636 Jim Stewart 4.00 10.00
637 Cleveland Indians TC 5.00 12.00
638 Frank Bertaina 4.00 10.00
639 Dave Campbell 6.00 15.00
640 Al Kaline 15.00 40.00
641 Al McBean 4.00 10.00
642 Garrett/Lund/Tatum RC 4.00 10.00
643 Jose Pagan 4.00 10.00
644 Gerry Nyman 4.00 10.00
645 Don Money 6.00 15.00
646 Jim Britton 4.00 10.00
647 Tom Matchick 4.00 10.00
648 Larry Haney 4.00 10.00
649 Jimmie Hall 4.00 10.00
650 Sam McDowell 6.00 15.00
651 Jim Gosger 4.00 10.00
652 Rich Rollins 6.00 15.00
653 Moe Drabowsky 4.00 10.00
654 Gamble/Day/Mangual RC 8.00 20.00
655 John Roseboro 6.00 15.00
656 Jim Hardin 4.00 10.00
657 San Diego Padres TC 5.00 12.00
658 Ken Tatum RC 4.00 10.00
659 Pete Ward 4.00 10.00
660 Johnny Bench 60.00 150.00
661 Jerry Robertson 4.00 10.00
662 Frank Lucchesi MG RC 4.00 10.00
663 Tito Francona 4.00 10.00
664 Bob Robertson 4.00 10.00
665 Jim Lonborg 6.00 15.00
666 Adolpho Phillips 4.00 10.00
667 Bob Meyer 6.00 15.00
668 Bob Tillman 4.00 10.00
669 Johnson/Lazar/Scott RC 4.00 10.00
670 Ron Santo 10.00 25.00
671 Jim Campanis 4.00 10.00
672 Leon McFadden 4.00 10.00
673 Ted Uhlaender 4.00 10.00
674 Dave Leonhard 4.00 10.00
675 Jose Cardenal 6.00 15.00
676 Washington Senators TC 5.00 12.00
677 Woodie Fryman 4.00 10.00
678 Dave Duncan 6.00 15.00
679 Ray Sadecki 4.00 10.00
680 Rico Petrocelli 6.00 15.00
681 Bob Garibaldi RC 4.00 10.00
682 Dalton Jones 4.00 10.00
683 Geishart/McRae/Simpson RC 6.00 15.00
684 Jack Fisher 4.00 10.00
685 Tom Haller 4.00 10.00
686 Jackie Hernandez 4.00 10.00
687 Bob Priddy 4.00 10.00
688 Ted Kubiak 6.00 15.00
689 Frank Tepedino RC 6.00 15.00
690 Ron Fairly 6.00 15.00
691 Joe Grzenda 4.00 10.00
692 Duffy Dyer 4.00 10.00
693 Bob Johnson 4.00 10.00
694 Gary Ross 4.00 10.00
695 Bobby Knoop 4.00 10.00
696 San Francisco Giants TC 5.00 12.00
697 Jim Hannan 4.00 10.00
698 Tom Tresh 6.00 15.00
699 Hank Aguirre 4.00 10.00
700 Frank Robinson 25.00 60.00
701 Jack Billingham 4.00 10.00
702 Johnson/Klimkowski/Zepp RC 4.00 10.00
703 Lou Marone RC 4.00 10.00
704 Frank Baker RC 4.00 10.00
705 Tony Cloninger UER 4.00 10.00
706 John McNamara MG RC 4.00 10.00
707 Kevin Collins 4.00 10.00
708 Jose Santiago 4.00 10.00
709 Mike Fiore 4.00 10.00
710 Felix Millan 4.00 10.00
711 Ed Brinkman 4.00 10.00
712 Nolan Ryan 100.00 250.00
713 Seattle Pilots TC 10.00 25.00
714 Al Spangler 4.00 10.00
715 Mickey Lolich 6.00 15.00
716 Campisi/Cleveland/Guzman RC 6.00 15.00
717 Tom Phoebus 4.00 10.00
718 Ed Spiezio 4.00 10.00
719 Jim Roland 4.00 10.00
720 Rick Reichardt 6.00 15.00

1970 Topps Booklets

Inserted into packages of the 1970 Topps (and O-Pee-Chee) regular issue of cards, there are 24 miniature biographies of ballplayers in the set. Each numbered paper booklet, which features one player per team, contains six pages of comic book style story and a checklist of the booklet is available on the back page. These little booklets measure approximately 2 1/2" by 3 7/16".

COMPLETE SET (24) 15.00 40.00
COMMON CARD (1-16) .40 1.00
COMMON CARD (17-24) .40 1.00
1 Mike Cuellar .40 1.00
2 Rico Petrocelli .40 1.00
3 Jay Johnstone .40 1.00
4 Walt Williams .40 1.00
5 Vada Pinson .40 1.00
6 Bill Freehan .40 1.00
7 Wally Bunker .40 1.00
8 Tony Oliva .60 1.50
9 Bobby Murcer .40 1.00
10 Reggie Jackson 2.50 6.00
11 Tommy Harper .40 1.00
12 Mike Epstein .40 1.00
13 Orlando Cepeda .60 1.50
14 Ernie Banks 1.50 4.00
15 Pete Rose 2.50 6.00
16 Denis Menke .40 1.00
17 Bill Singer .40 1.00
18 Rusty Staub .60 1.50
19 Cleon Jones .40 1.00
20 Deron Johnson .40 1.00
21 Bob Moose .40 1.00
22 Bob Gibson 1.00 2.50
23 Al Ferrara .40 1.00
24 Willie Mays 3.00 8.00

1970 Topps Candy Lid

This 24-card set features color player portraits printed on the bottom of candy lids and measures approximately 1 7/8" in diameter. The lids are unnumbered and checklisted below in alphabetical order.

COMPLETE SET (24) 1,400.00 2,800.00
1 Hank Aaron 250.00 500.00
2 Rich Allen 175.00 350.00
3 Luis Aparicio 60.00 120.00
4 Johnny Bench 250.00 500.00
5 Ollie Brown 30.00 60.00
6 Willie Davis 30.00 60.00
7 Jim Fregosi 30.00 60.00
8 Mike Hegan 30.00 60.00
9 Frank Howard 40.00 80.00
10 Reggie Jackson 175.00 350.00
11 Fergie Jenkins 75.00 150.00
12 Harmon Killebrew 225.00 450.00
13 Bill Mazeroski 75.00 150.00
14 Juan Marichal 75.00 150.00
15 Tim McCarver 40.00 80.00
16 Sam McDowell 30.00 60.00
17 Denny McLain 30.00 60.00
18 Lou Piniella 30.00 60.00
19 Frank Robinson 100.00 200.00
20 Tom Seaver 200.00 400.00
21 Rusty Staub 30.00 60.00
22 Mel Stottlemyre 30.00 60.00
23 Jim Wynn 30.00 60.00
24 Carl Yastrzemski 225.00 450.00

1970 Topps Cloth Stickers

These stickers measure the standard size, and so far all found seem to be all from the 2nd series in 1970. These cards were intended to be pasted on jackets. Obviously this checklist is far from complete so any further information is greatly appreciated.

216 Chuck Hartenstein 250.00 500.00
226 Ron Perranoski 250.00 500.00
238 Coco Laboy 250.00 500.00
257 Dennis Higgins 250.00 500.00

1970 Topps Posters Inserts

In 1970 Topps raised its price per package of cards to ten cents, and a series of 24 color posters was included as a bonus to the collector. Each thin-paper poster is numbered and features a large portrait and a smaller black and white action pose. It was folded five times to fit in the packaging. Each poster measures 8 11/16" by 9 5/8".

COMPLETE SET (24) 30.00 60.00
1 Joe Horlen .60 1.50
2 Phil Niekro .75 2.00
3 Willie Davis .60 1.50
4 Lou Brock 2.00 5.00
5 Ron Santo 1.25 3.00
6 Ken Harrelson .60 1.50
7 Willie McCovey 2.00 5.00
8 Rick Wise .60 1.50
9 Andy Messersmith .60 1.50
10 Ron Fairly .60 1.50
11 Johnny Bench 4.00 10.00
12 Frank Robinson 2.00 5.00
13 Tommie Agee .60 1.50
14 Roy White .60 1.50
15 Larry Dierker .60 1.50
16 Rod Carew 2.00 5.00
17 Don Mincher .60 1.50
18 Ollie Brown .60 1.50
19 Ed Kirkpatrick .60 1.50
20 Reggie Smith .75 2.00
21 Roberto Clemente 8.00 20.00
22 Frank Howard .75 2.00
23 Bert Campaneris .75 2.00
24 Denny McLain .75 2.00

1970 Topps Scratchoffs

The 1970 Topps Scratch-off inserts are heavy cardboard, folded inserts issued with the regular card series of those years. Unfolded, they form a game board upon which a baseball game is played by means of rubbing off black ink from the playing squares to reveal moves. Inserts with white centers were issued in 1970 and inserts with red centers in 1971. Unfolded, these inserts measure 3 3/8" by 5". Obviously, a card which has been scratched off can be considered to be in no better than vg condition.

COMPLETE SET (24) 20.00 50.00
COMMON CARD (1-24) .40 1.00
1 Hank Aaron 3.00 8.00
2 Rich Allen .60 1.50
3 Luis Aparicio 1.00 2.50
4 Sal Bando .60 1.50
5 Glenn Beckert .40 1.00
6 Dick Bosman .40 1.00
7 Nate Colbert .40 1.00
8 Mike Hegan .40 1.00
9 Mack Jones .40 1.00
10 Al Kaline 2.00 5.00
11 Harmon Killebrew 2.00 5.00
12 Juan Marichal 1.00 2.50
13 Tim McCarver .60 1.50
14 Sam McDowell .60 1.50
15 Claude Osteen .40 1.00
16 Tony Perez 1.00 2.50
17 Lou Piniella .60 1.50
18 Boog Powell 1.00 2.50
19 Tom Seaver 2.00 5.00
20 Jim Spencer .40 1.00
21 Willie Stargell 1.50 4.00
22 Mel Stottlemyre .60 1.50
23 Jim Wynn .60 1.50
24 Carl Yastrzemski 2.50 6.00

1970 Topps Super

The cards in this 42-card set measure approximately 3 1/8" by 5 1/4". The 1970 Topps Super set was a separate Topps issue printed on heavy stock and marketed in its own wrapper with gum. The blue and yellow backs are identical to the respective player's backs in the 1970 Topps regular issue. Cards 38, Boog Powell, is the key card of the set; other short print run cards are listed in the checklist with SP. The obverse pictures are borderless and contain a facsimile autograph. The set was issued in three-card wax packs which came 24 packs to a box and 24 boxes to a case.

COMPLETE SET (42) 125.00 250.00
COMMON CARD (1-42) .75 2.00
WRAPPER (10-CENT)
COMMON SP 1.50 4.00
1 Claude Osteen SP 1.50 4.00
2 Sal Bando SP 1.50 4.00
3 Luis Aparicio SP 2.00 5.00
4 Harmon Killebrew 2.00 5.00
5 Tom Seaver SP 10.00 25.00
6 Larry Dierker 1.00 2.50
7 Bill Freehan 1.00 2.50
8 Johnny Bench 6.00 15.00
9 Tommy Harper .75 2.00
10 Sam McDowell .75 2.00
11 Lou Brock 2.00 5.00
12 Roberto Clemente 12.50 30.00
13 Willie McCovey 2.00 5.00
14 Rico Petrocelli .75 2.00
15 Phil Niekro 1.50 4.00
16 Frank Howard 1.00 2.50
17 Denny McLain 1.00 2.50
18 Willie Mays 8.00 20.00
19 Willie Stargell 2.00 5.00
20 Joel Horlen .75 2.00
21 Ron Santo 1.25 3.00
22 Dick Bosman .75 2.00
23 Tim McCarver 1.25 3.00
24 Hank Aaron 8.00 20.00
25 Andy Messersmith .75 2.00
26 Tony Oliva 1.25 3.00
27 Mel Stottlemyre 1.00 2.50
28 Reggie Jackson 6.00 15.00
29 Carl Yastrzemski 10.00 25.00
30 Jim Fregosi 1.00 2.50
31 Vada Pinson 1.00 2.50
32 Lou Piniella 1.25 3.00
33 Bob Gibson 2.00 5.00
34 Pete Rose 8.00 20.00
35 Jim Wynn 1.00 2.50
36 Ollie Brown SP 2.50 6.00
37 Frank Robinson SP 8.00 20.00
38 Boog Powell SP 20.00 50.00
39 Willie Davis SP 1.50 4.00
40 Billy Williams SP 4.00 10.00
41 Rusty Staub 1.25 3.00
42 Tommie Agee 1.00 2.50

1971 Topps

The cards in this 752-card set measure 2 1/2" by 3 1/2". The 1971 Topps set is a challenge to complete in strict mint condition because the black obverse border is easily scratched and damaged. An unusual feature of this set is that the player is also pictured in black and white on the back of the card. Featured subsets within this set include League Leaders (61-72), Playoffs cards (195-202), and World Series cards (327-332). Cards 524-643 and the last series (644-752) are somewhat scarce. The last series was printed in two sheets of 132. On the printing sheets 44 cards were printed in 50 percent greater quantity than the other 66 cards. These 66 (slightly) shorter-printed numbers are identified in the checklist below by SP. The key Rookie Cards in this set are the multi-player Rookie Card of Dusty Baker and Don Baylor and the individual cards of Bert Blyleven, Dave Concepcion, Steve Garvey, and Ted Simmons. The Jim Northrup and Jim Nash cards have been seen with our without printing "blotches" on the card. There is still debate on whether those two cards are just printing issues or legitimate variations. Among the ways these cards were issued were in 54-card rack packs which retailed for 39 cents.

COMPLETE SET (752) 1,250.00 2,500.00
COMMON CARD (1-393) .60 1.50
COMMON CARD (394-523) 1.00 2.50
COMMON CARD (524-643) 1.50 4.00
COMMON CARD (644-752) 3.00 8.00
COMMON SP (644-752) 5.00 12.00
WRAPPER (10-CENT) 6.00 15.00
1 Baltimore Orioles TC 8.00 20.00
2 Dock Ellis .60 1.50
3 Dick McAuliffe .75 2.00
4 Vic Davalillo .60 1.50
5 Thurman Munson 60.00 120.00
6 Ed Spiezio .60 1.50
7 Jim Holt RC .60 1.50
8 Mike McQueen 1.5
9 George Scott .75 2.00
10 Claude Osteen .75 2.00
11 Elliott Maddox RC .60 1.50
12 Johnny Callison .75 2.00
13 C.Brinkman RC/D.Moloney RC .60 1.50
14 Dave Concepcion RC 12.00 30.00
15 Andy Messersmith .75 2.00
16 Ken Singleton RC 1.50 4.00
17 Billy Sorrell .60 1.50
18 Norm Miller .60 1.50
19 Skip Pitlock RC .60 1.50
20 Reggie Jackson 20.00 50.00
21 Dan McGinn .60 1.50
22 Phil Roof .60 1.50
23 Oscar Gamble .60 1.50
24 Rich Hand RC .60 1.50
25 Clarence Gaston .75 2.00
26 Bert Blyleven RC 25.00 60.00
27 F.Cambria RC/G.Clines RC .60 1.50
28 Ron Klimkowski .60 1.50
29 Don Buford .60 1.50
30 Phil Niekro 6.00 15.00
31 Eddie Kasko MG .60 1.50
32 Jerry DaVanon .60 1.50
33 Del Unser .60 1.50
34 Sandy Vance RC .60 1.50
35 Lou Piniella .75 2.00
36 Dean Chance .75 2.00
37 Rich McKinney RC .60 1.50
38 Jim Colborn RC .60 1.50
39 L.LaGrow RC/G.Lamont RC .75 2.00
40 Lee May .75 2.00
41 Rick Austin RC .60 1.50
42 Boots Day .60 1.50
43 Steve Kealey .60 1.50
44 Johnny Edwards .60 1.50
45 Jim Hunter 6.00 15.00
46 Dave Campbell .75 2.00
47 Johnny Jeter .60 1.50
48 Dave Baldwin .60 1.50
49 Don Money .60 1.50
50 Willie McCovey 10.00 25.00
51 Steve Kline RC .60 1.50
52 O.Brown RC/E.Williams RC .60 1.50
53 Paul Blair .75 2.00
54 Checklist 1 4.00 10.00
55 Steve Carlton 10.00 25.00
56 Duane Josephson .60 1.50
57 Von Joshua RC .60 1.50
58 Bill Lee .75 2.00
59 Gene Mauch MG .75 2.00
60 Dick Bosman .60 1.50
61 Johnson/Yaz/Oliva LL 1.50 4.00
62 Carty/Torre/Sang LL .75 2.00
63 Howard/Conig/Powell LL 1.50 4.00
64 Bench/Perez/B.Will LL 2.50 6.00
65 Howard/Killebrew/Yaz LL 1.50 4.00
66 Bench/B.Will/Perez LL 2.50 6.00
67 Segui/Palmer/Wright LL 1.50 4.00
68 Seaver/Simp/Walk LL 1.50 4.00
69 Cuellar/McNally/Perry LL .75 2.00
70 Gibson/Perry/Jenkins LL 2.50 6.00
71 McDowell/Lolich/John LL .75 2.00
72 Seaver/Gibson/Jenkins LL 2.50 6.00
73 George Brunet .60 1.50
74 P.Hamm RC/J.Nettles RC .60 1.50
75 Gary Nolan .75 2.00
76 Ted Savage .60 1.50
77 Mike Compton RC .60 1.50
78 Jim Spencer .60 1.50
79 Wade Blasingame .60 1.50
80 Bill Melton .60 1.50
81 Felix Millan .60 1.50
82 Casey Cox .60 1.50
83 T.Foli RC/R.Bobb .75 2.00
84 Marcel Lachemann RC .60 1.50
85 Billy Grabarkewitz .60 1.50
86 Mike Kilkenny .60 1.50
87 Jack Heidemann RC .60 1.50
88 Hal King .60 1.50
89 Ken Brett .60 1.50
90 Joe Pepitone .75 2.00
91 Bob Lemon MG .75 2.00
92 Fred Wenz .60 1.50
93 N.McRae/D.Riddleberger .60 1.50
94 Don Hahn RC .60 1.50
95 Luis Tiant .75 2.00
96 Joe Hague .60 1.50
97 Floyd Wicker .60 1.50
98 Joe Decker RC .60 1.50
99 Mark Belanger .75 2.00
100 Pete Rose 25.00 60.00
101 Les Cain .60 1.50
102 K.Forsch RC/L.Howard RC .75 2.00
103 Rich Severson RC .60 1.50
104 Dan Frisella .60 1.50
105 Tony Conigliaro .75 2.00
106 Tom Dukes .60 1.50
107 Roy Foster RC .60 1.50
108 John Cumberland .60 1.50
109 Steve Hovley .60 1.50
110 Bill Mazeroski 2.50 6.00
111 L.Colson RC/B.Mitchell RC .60 1.50
112 Manny Mota .75 2.00
113 Jerry Crider .60 1.50
114 Billy Conigliaro .75 2.00
115 Donn Clendenon .75 2.00
116 Ken Sanders .60 1.50
117 Ted Simmons RC 50.00 120.00
118 Cookie Rojas .75 2.00
119 Frank Lucchesi MG .60 1.50
120 Willie Horton .75 2.00
121 J.Dunegan/R.Skidmore RC .60 1.50
122 Eddie Watt .60 1.50
123A Checklist 2 Right 4.00 10.00
123B Checklist 2 Centered 4.00 10.00
124 Don Gullett RC .75 2.00
125 Ray Fosse .60 1.50
126 Danny Coombs .60 1.50
127 Danny Thompson RC .75 2.00
128 Frank Johnson .60 1.50
129 Aurelio Monteagudo .60 1.50
130 Denis Menke .60 1.50
131 Curt Blefary .60 1.50
132 Jose Laboy .60 1.50
133 Mickey Lolich .75 2.00
134 Jose Arcia .60 1.50
135 Rick Monday .75 2.00
136 Duffy Dyer .60 1.50
137 Marcelino Lopez .60 1.50
138 J.Lis/W.Montanez RC .75 2.00
139 Paul Casanova .60 1.50
140 Gaylord Perry 2.50 6.00
141 Frank Quilici .60 1.50
142 Mack Jones .60 1.50
143 Steve Blass .75 2.00
144 Jackie Hernandez .60 1.50
145 Bill Singer .75 2.00
146 Ralph Houk MG .75 2.00
147 Bob Priddy .60 1.50
148 John Mayberry .75 2.00
149 Mike Hershberger .60 1.50
150 Sam McDowell .75 2.00
151 Tommy Davis .75 2.00
152 L.Allen RC/W.Llenas RC .60 1.50
153 Gary Ross .60 1.50
154 Cesar Gutierrez .60 1.50
155 Ken Henderson .60 1.50
156 Bart Johnson .60 1.50
157 Bob Bailey .75 2.00
158 Jerry Reuss .75 2.00
159 Jarvis Tatum .60 1.50
160 Tom Seaver 12.00 30.00
161 Coin Checklist 4.00 10.00
162 Jack Billingham .60 1.50
163 Buck Martinez .75 2.00
164 F.Duffy RC/M.Wilcox RC .75 2.00
165 Cesar Tovar .60 1.50
166 Joe Hoerner .60 1.50
167 Tom Grieve RC .75 2.00
168 Bruce Dal Canton .60 1.50
169 Ed Herrmann .60 1.50
170 Mike Cuellar .75 2.00
171 Bobby Wine .60 1.50
172 Duke Sims .60 1.50
173 Gil Garrido .60 1.50
174 Dave LaRoche RC .60 1.50
175 Jim Hickman .60 1.50
176 B.Montgomery RC/D.Griffin RC .75 2.00
177 Hal McRae .75 2.00
178 Dave Duncan .75 2.00
179 Mike Corkins .60 1.50
180 Al Kaline UER 12.00 30.00
181 Hal Lanier .60 1.50
182 Al Downing .75 2.00
183 Gil Hodges MG 1.50 4.00
184 Stan Bahnsen .60 1.50
185 Julian Javier .60 1.50
186 Bob Spence RC .60 1.50
187 Ted Abernathy .60 1.50
188 B.Valentine RC/M.Strahler RC 2.50 6.00
189 George Mitterwald .60 1.50
190 Bob Tolan .60 1.50
191 Mike Andrews .60 1.50
192 Billy Wilson .60 1.50
193 Bob Grich RC 1.50 4.00
194 Mike Lum .60 1.50
195 Boog Powell ALCS .75 2.00
196 Dave McNally ALCS .75 2.00
197 Jim Palmer ALCS 1.50 4.00
198 Orioles Celebrate ALCS .75 2.00
199 Ty Cline NLCS .75 2.00
200 Bobby Tolan NLCS .75 2.00
201 Ty Cline NLCS .75 2.00
202 Reds Celebrate NLCS .75 2.00
203 Larry Gura RC .75 2.00
204 B.Smith RC/G.Kopacz RC .60 1.50
205 Gerry Moses .60 1.50
206 Checklist 3 4.00 10.00
207 Alan Foster .60 1.50
208 Billy Martin MG 1.50 4.00
209 Steve Renko .60 1.50
210 Rod Carew 15.00 40.00
211 Phil Hennigan RC .60 1.50
212 Rich Hebner .75 2.00
213 Frank Baker RC .60 1.50
214 Al Ferrara .60 1.50
215 Diego Segui .60 1.50
216 R.Cleveland/L.Melendez RC .60 1.50
217 Ed Stroud .60 1.50
218 Tony Cloninger .60 1.50
219 Elrod Hendricks .60 1.50
220 Ron Santo 1.50 4.00
221 Dave Morehead .60 1.50
222 Bob Watson .75 2.00
223 Cecil Upshaw .60 1.50
224 Alan Gallagher RC .60 1.50
225 Gary Peters .60 1.50
226 Bill Russell .75 2.00
227 Floyd Weaver .60 1.50
228 Wayne Garrett .60 1.50
229 Jim Hannan .60 1.50
230 Willie Stargell 12.00 30.00
231 V.Colbert RC/J.Lowenstein RC .75 2.00
232 John Strohmayer RC .60 1.50
233 Larry Bowa .75 2.00
234 Jim Lyttle .60 1.50
235 Nate Colbert .60 1.50
236 Bob Humphreys .60 1.50
237 Cesar Cedeno RC .75 2.00
238 Chuck Dobson .60 1.50
239 Red Schoendienst MG .75 2.00
240 Clyde Wright .60 1.50
241 Dave Nelson .60 1.50
242 Jim Ray .60 1.50
243 Carlos May .60 1.50
244 Bob Tillman .60 1.50
245 Jim Kaat .75 2.00
246 Tony Taylor .60 1.50
247 J.Cram RC/P.Splittorff RC .75 2.00
248 Hoyt Wilhelm 2.50 6.00
249 Chico Salmon .60 1.50
250 Johnny Bench 25.00 60.00
251 Frank Reberger .60 1.50
252 Eddie Leon .60 1.50
253 Bill Sudakis .60 1.50
254 Cal Koonce .60 1.50
255 Bob Robertson .75 2.00
256 Tony Gonzalez .60 1.50
257 Nelson Briles .75 2.00
258 Dick Green .60 1.50
259 Dave Marshall .60 1.50
260 Tommy Harper .75 2.00
261 Darold Knowles .60 1.50
262 J.Williams/D.Robinson RC .60 1.50
263 John Ellis .60 1.50
264 Joe Morgan 3.00 8.00
265 Jim Northrup .75 2.00
266 Bill Stoneman .60 1.50
267 Rich Morales .60 1.50
268 Philadelphia Phillies TC 1.50 4.00
269 Gail Hopkins .60 1.50
270 Rico Carty .75 2.00
271 Bill Zepp .60 1.50
272 Tommy Helms .75 2.00
273 Pete Richert .60 1.50
274 Ron Slocum .60 1.50
275 Vada Pinson .75 2.00
276 M.Davison RC/G.Foster RC 3.00 8.00
277 Gary Waslewski .60 1.50
278 Jerry Grote .75 2.00
279 Lefty Phillips MG .60 1.50
280 Ferguson Jenkins 2.50 6.00
281 Danny Walton .60 1.50
282 Jose Pagan .60 1.50
283 Dick Such .60 1.50
284 Jim Gosger .60 1.50
285 Sal Bando .75 2.00
286 Jerry McNertney .60 1.50
287 Mike Fiore .60 1.50
288 Joe Moeller .60 1.50
289 Chicago White Sox TC 1.50 4.00
290 Tony Oliva 1.50 4.00
291 George Culver .60 1.50
292 Jay Johnstone .75 2.00
293 Pat Corrales .75 2.00
294 Steve Dunning RC .60 1.50
295 Bobby Bonds 1.50 4.00
296 Tom Timmermann .60 1.50
297 Johnny Briggs .60 1.50
298 Jim Nelson RC .60 1.50
299 Ed Kirkpatrick .60 1.50
300 Brooks Robinson 20.00 50.00
301 Earl Wilson .60 1.50
302 Phil Gagliano .60 1.50
303 Lindy McDaniel .75 2.00
304 Ron Brand .60 1.50
305 Reggie Smith .75 2.00
306 Jim Nash .60 1.50
307 Don Wert .60 1.50
308 St. Louis Cardinals TC 1.50 4.00
309 Dick Ellsworth .60 1.50
310 Tommie Agee .75 2.00
311 Lee Stange .60 1.50
312 Harry Walker MG .60 1.50
313 Tom Hall .60 1.50
314 Jeff Torborg .75 2.00
315 Ron Fairly .75 2.00
316 Fred Scherman RC .60 1.50
317 J.Driscoll RC/A.Mangual .60 1.50
318 Rudy May .60 1.50
319 Ty Cline .60 1.50
320 Dave McNally .75 2.00
321 Tom Matchick .60 1.50
322 Jim Beauchamp .60 1.50
323 Billy Champion .60 1.50
324 Graig Nettles .75 2.00
325 Juan Marichal 10.00 25.00
326 Richie Scheinblum .60 1.50
327 Boog Powell WS .75 2.00
328 Don Buford WS .75 2.00
329 Frank Robinson WS 1.50 4.00
330 Reds Stay Alive WS .75 2.00
331 Brooks Robinson WS 2.50 6.00
332 Orioles Celebrate WS .75 2.00
333 Clay Kirby .60 1.50
334 Roberto Pena .60 1.50
335 Jerry Koosman .75 2.00
336 Detroit Tigers TC 1.50 4.00
337 Jesus Alou .60 1.50
338 Gene Tenace .75 2.00
339 Wayne Simpson .60 1.50
340 Rico Petrocelli .75 2.00
341 Steve Garvey RC 25.00 60.00
342 Frank Tepedino .75 2.00
343 E.Acosta RC/M.May RC .75 2.00
344 Ellie Rodriguez .60 1.50
345 Joel Horlen .60 1.50
346 Lum Harris MG .60 1.50
347 Ted Uhlaender .60 1.50
348 Fred Norman .60 1.50
349 Rich Reese .60 1.50
350 Billy Williams 2.50 6.00
351 Jim Shellenback .60 1.50
352 Denny Doyle .60 1.50
353 Carl Taylor .60 1.50
354 Don McMahon .60 1.50
355 Bud Harrelson 1.50 4.00
Nolan Ryan in photo
356 Bob Locker .60 1.50
357 Cincinnati Reds TC 1.50 4.00
358 Danny Cater .60 1.50
359 Ron Reed .60 1.50
360 Jim Fregosi .75 2.00
361 Don Sutton 2.50 6.00
362 M.Adamson/R.Freed .60 1.50
363 Mike Nagy .60 1.50
364 Tommy Dean .60 1.50
365 Bob Johnson .60 1.50
366 Ron Stone .60 1.50
367 Dalton Jones .60 1.50
368 Bob Veale .75 2.00
369 Checklist 4 4.00 10.00
370 Joe Torre 1.50 4.00
371 Jack Hiatt .60 1.50
372 Lew Krausse .60 1.50
373 Tom McCraw .60 1.50
374 Clete Boyer .75 2.00
375 Steve Hargan .60 1.50
376 C.Mashore RC/E.McAnally RC .60 1.50
377 Greg Garrett .60 1.50
378 Tito Fuentes .60 1.50
379 Wayne Granger .60 1.50
380 Ted Williams MG 10.00 25.00
381 Fred Gladding .60 1.50
382 Jake Gibbs .60 1.50
383 Rod Gaspar .60 1.50
384 Rollie Fingers 2.50 6.00
385 Maury Wills 1.50 4.00
386 Boston Red Sox TC .75 2.00
387 Ron Herbel .60 1.50
388 Al Oliver 1.50 4.00
389 Ed Brinkman .60 1.50
390 Glenn Beckert .75 2.00
391 S.Brye RC/C.Nash RC .75 2.00
392 Grant Jackson .60 1.50
393 Merv Rettenmund .75 2.00
394 Clay Carroll 1.00 2.50
395 Roy White 1.50 4.00
396 Dick Schofield 1.00 2.50
397 Alvin Dark MG 1.50 4.00
398 Howie Reed 1.00 2.50
399 Jim French 1.00 2.50
400 Hank Aaron 30.00 80.00
401 Tom Murphy 1.00 2.50
402 Los Angeles Dodgers TC 2.50 6.00
403 Joe Coleman 1.00 2.50
404 B.Harris RC/R.Metzger RC 1.00 2.50
405 Leo Cardenas 1.00 2.50
406 Ray Sadecki 1.00 2.50
407 Joe Rudi 1.50 4.00
408 Rafael Robles 1.00 2.50
409 Don Pavletich 1.00 2.50
410 Ken Holtzman 1.50 4.00
411 George Spriggs 1.00 2.50
412 Jerry Johnson 1.00 2.50
413 Pat Kelly 1.00 2.50
414 Woodie Fryman 1.00 2.50
415 Mike Hegan 1.00 2.50
416 Gene Alley 1.00 2.50
417 Dick Hall 1.00 2.50
418 Adolfo Phillips 1.00 2.50
419 Ron Hansen 1.00 2.50
420 Jim Merritt 1.00 2.50
421 John Stephenson 1.00 2.50
422 Frank Bertaina 1.00 2.50
423 D.Saunders/T.Marting RC 1.00 2.50
424 Roberto Rodriguez 1.00 2.50
425 Doug Rader 1.50 4.00

426 Chris Cannizzaro 1.00 2.50
427 Bernie Allen 1.00 2.50
428 Jim McAndrew 1.00 2.50
429 Chuck Hinton 1.00 2.50
430 Wes Parker 1.50 4.00
431 Tom Burgmeier 1.00 2.50
432 Bob Didier 1.00 2.50
433 Skip Lockwood 1.00 2.50
434 Gary Sutherland 1.00 2.50
435 Jose Cardenal 1.50 4.00
436 Wilbur Wood 1.50 4.00
437 Danny Murtaugh MG 1.50 4.00
438 Mike McCormick 1.50 4.00
439 G.Luzinski RC/S.Reid 2.50 6.00
440 Bert Campaneris 1.50 4.00
441 Milt Pappas 1.50 4.00
442 California Angels TC 1.50 4.00
443 Rich Robertson 1.00 2.50
444 Jimmie Price 1.00 2.50
445 Art Shamsky 1.00 2.50
446 Bobby Bolin 1.00 2.50
447 Cesar Geronimo RC 1.50 4.00
448 Dave Roberts 1.00 2.50
449 Brant Alyea 1.00 2.50
450 Bob Gibson 20.00 50.00
451 Joe Keough 1.00 2.50
452 John Boccabella 1.00 2.50
453 Terry Crowley 1.00 2.50
454 Mike Paul 1.00 2.50
455 Don Kessinger 1.50 4.00
456 Bob Meyer 1.00 2.50
457 Willie Smith 1.00 2.50
458 R.Lolich RC/D.Lemonds RC 1.00 2.50
459 Jim Lefebvre 1.00 2.50
460 Fritz Peterson 1.00 2.50
461 Jim Ray Hart 1.00 2.50
462 Washington Senators TC 2.50 6.00
463 Tom Kelley 1.00 2.50
464 Aurelio Rodriguez 1.00 2.50
465 Tim McCarver 2.50 6.00
466 Ken Berry 1.00 2.50
467 Al Santorini 1.00 2.50
468 Frank Fernandez 1.00 2.50
469 Bob Aspromonte 1.00 2.50
470 Bob Oliver 1.00 2.50
471 Tom Griffin 1.00 2.50
472 Ken Rudolph 1.00 2.50
473 Gary Wagner 1.00 2.50
474 Jim Fairey 1.00 2.50
475 Ron Perranoski 1.00 2.50
476 Dal Maxvill 1.00 2.50
477 Earl Weaver MG 2.50 6.00
478 Bernie Carbo 1.00 2.50
479 Dennis Higgins 1.00 2.50
480 Manny Sanguillen 1.50 4.00
481 Daryl Patterson 1.00 2.50
482 San Diego Padres TC 2.50 6.00
483 Gene Michael 1.00 2.50
484 Don Wilson 1.00 2.50
485 Ken McMullen 1.00 2.50
486 Steve Huntz 1.00 2.50
487 Paul Schaal 1.00 2.50
488 Jerry Stephenson 1.00 2.50
489 Luis Alvarado 1.00 2.50
490 Deron Johnson 1.00 2.50
491 Jim Hardin 1.00 2.50
492 Ken Boswell 1.00 2.50
493 Dave May 1.00 2.50
494 R.Garr/R.Kester 1.50 4.00
495 Felipe Alou 1.50 4.00
496 Woody Woodward 1.00 2.50
497 Horacio Pina RC 1.00 2.50
498 John Kennedy 1.00 2.50
499 Checklist 5 4.00 10.00
500 Jim Perry 1.50 4.00
501 Andy Etchebarren 1.00 2.50
502 Chicago Cubs TC 2.50 6.00
503 Gates Brown 1.50 4.00
504 Ken Wright RC 1.00 2.50
505 Ollie Brown 1.00 2.50
506 Bobby Knoop 1.00 2.50
507 George Stone 1.00 2.50
508 Roger Repoz 1.00 2.50
509 Jim Grant 1.00 2.50
510 Ken Harrelson 1.50 4.00
511 Chris Short w/Rose 1.50 4.00
512 D.Mills RC/M.Garman RC 1.00 2.50
513 Nolan Ryan 50.00 120.00
514 Ron Woods 1.00 2.50
515 Carl Morton 1.00 2.50
516 Ted Kubiak 1.00 2.50
517 Charlie Fox MG RC 1.00 2.50
518 Joe Grzenda 1.00 2.50
519 Willie Crawford 1.00 2.50
520 Tommy John 2.50 6.00
521 Leron Lee 1.00 2.50
522 Minnesota Twins TC 2.50 6.00
523 John Odom 1.00 2.50
524 Mickey Stanley 2.50 6.00
525 Ernie Banks 30.00 80.00
526 Ray Jarvis 1.50 4.00
527 Cleon Jones 2.50 6.00
528 Wally Bunker 1.50 4.00
529 Hernandez/Bucker/Perez RC 2.50 6.00
530 Carl Yastrzemski 15.00 40.00
531 Mike Torrez 1.50 4.00
532 Bill Rigney MG 1.50 4.00
533 Mike Ryan 1.50 4.00
534 Luke Walker 1.50 4.00
535 Curt Flood 2.50 6.00
536 Claude Raymond 1.50 4.00
537 Tom Egan 1.50 4.00
538 Angel Bravo 1.50 4.00
539 Larry Brown 1.50 4.00
540 Larry Dierker 2.50 6.00
541 Bob Burda 1.50 4.00
542 Bob Miller 1.50 4.00
543 New York Yankees TC 4.00 10.00
544 Vida Blue 2.50 6.00
545 Dick Dietz 1.50 4.00
546 John Matias 1.50 4.00
547 Pat Dobson 2.50 6.00
548 Don Mason 1.50 4.00
549 Jim Brewer 2.50 6.00
550 Harmon Killebrew 12.00 30.00
551 Frank Linzy 1.50 4.00
552 Buddy Bradford 1.50 4.00
553 Kevin Collins 1.50 4.00
554 Lowell Palmer 1.50 4.00
555 Walt Williams 1.50 4.00
556 Jim McGlothlin 1.50 4.00
557 Tom Satriano 1.50 4.00
558 Hector Torres 1.50 4.00
559 Cox/Gogolewsk/Jones RC 1.50 4.00
560 Rusty Staub 2.50 6.00
561 Syd O'Brien 1.50 4.00
562 Dave Giusti 1.50 4.00
563 San Francisco Giants TC 3.00 8.00
564 Al Fitzmorris 1.50 4.00
565 Jim Wynn 2.50 6.00
566 Tim Cullen 1.50 4.00
567 Walt Alston MG 3.00 8.00
568 Sal Campisi 1.50 4.00
569 Ivan Murrell 1.50 4.00
570 Jim Palmer 10.00 25.00
571 Ted Sizemore 1.50 4.00
572 Jerry Kenney 1.50 4.00
573 Ed Kranepool 2.50 6.00
574 Jim Bunning 3.00 8.00
575 Bill Freehan 2.50 6.00
576 Garrett/Davis/Jestadt RC 1.50 4.00
577 Jim Lonborg 2.50 6.00
578 Ron Hunt 1.50 4.00
579 Marty Pattin 1.50 4.00
580 Tony Perez 20.00 50.00
581 Roger Nelson 1.50 4.00
582 Dave Cash 2.50 6.00
583 Ron Cook RC 1.50 4.00
584 Cleveland Indians TC 3.00 8.00
585 Willie Davis 2.50 6.00
586 Dick Woodson 1.50 4.00
587 Sonny Jackson 1.50 4.00
588 Tom Bradley RC 1.50 4.00
589 Bob Barton 1.50 4.00
590 Alex Johnson 2.50 6.00
591 Jackie Brown RC 1.50 4.00
592 Randy Hundley 2.50 6.00
593 Jack Aker 1.50 4.00
594 Chlupsa/Stinson/Hrabosky RC 2.50 6.00
595 Dave Johnson 2.50 6.00
596 Mike Jorgensen 1.50 4.00
597 Ken Suarez 1.50 4.00
598 Rick Wise 2.50 6.00
599 Norm Cash 2.50 6.00
600 Willie Mays 40.00 100.00
601 Ken Tatum 1.50 4.00
602 Marty Martinez 1.50 4.00
603 Pittsburgh Pirates TC 3.00 8.00
604 John Gelnar 1.50 4.00
605 Orlando Cepeda 3.00 8.00
606 Chuck Taylor 1.50 4.00
607 Paul Ratliff 1.50 4.00
608 Mike Wegener 1.50 4.00
609 Leo Durocher MG 3.00 8.00
610 Amos Otis 2.50 6.00
611 Tom Phoebus 1.50 4.00
612 Camilli/Ford/Mingori RC 1.50 4.00
613 Pedro Borbon 1.50 4.00
614 Billy Cowan 1.50 4.00
615 Mel Stottlemyre 2.50 6.00
616 Larry Hisle 2.50 6.00
617 Clay Dalrymple 1.50 4.00
618 Tug McGraw 2.50 6.00
619A Checklist 6 ERR w/o Copy 4.00 10.00
619B Checklist 6 COR w/Copy 2.50 6.00
620 Frank Howard 2.50 6.00
621 Ron Bryant 1.50 4.00
622 Joe Lahoud 1.50 4.00
623 Pat Jarvis 1.50 4.00
624 Oakland Athletics TC 3.00 8.00
625 Lou Brock 15.00 40.00
626 Freddie Patek 2.50 6.00
627 Steve Hamilton 1.50 4.00
628 John Bateman 1.50 4.00
629 John Hiller 2.50 6.00
630 Roberto Clemente 75.00 200.00
631 Eddie Fisher 1.50 4.00
632 Darrel Chaney 1.50 4.00
633 Brooks/Koegel/Northey RC 1.50 4.00
634 Phil Regan 1.50 4.00
635 Bobby Murcer 2.50 6.00
636 Denny Lemaster 1.50 4.00
637 Dave Bristol MG 1.50 4.00
638 Stan Williams 1.50 4.00
639 Tom Haller 1.50 4.00
640 Frank Robinson 15.00 40.00
641 New York Mets TC 6.00 15.00
642 Jim Roland 1.50 4.00
643 Rick Reichardt 1.50 4.00
644 Jim Stewart SP 5.00 12.00
645 Jim Maloney SP 6.00 15.00
646 Bobby Floyd SP 5.00 12.00
647 Juan Pizarro 3.00 8.00
648 Folkers/Martinez/Matlack SP RC 10.00 25.00
649 Sparky Lyle SP 15.00 40.00
650 Rich Allen SP 20.00 50.00
651 Jerry Robertson SP 5.00 12.00
652 Atlanta Braves TC 5.00 12.00
653 Russ Snyder SP 5.00 12.00
654 Don Shaw SP 5.00 12.00
655 Mike Epstein SP 5.00 12.00
656 Gerry Nyman SP 5.00 12.00
657 Jose Azcue 3.00 8.00
658 Paul Lindblad SP 5.00 12.00
659 Byron Browne SP 5.00 12.00
660 Ray Culp 3.00 8.00
661 Chuck Tanner MG SP 6.00 15.00
662 Mike Hedlund SP 5.00 12.00
663 Marv Staehle 3.00 8.00
664 Reynolds/Reynolds/Reynolds SP RC 5.00 12.00
665 Ron Swoboda SP 6.00 15.00
666 Gene Brabender SP 5.00 12.00
667 Pete Ward 3.00 8.00
668 Gary Neibauer 3.00 8.00
669 Ike Brown SP 5.00 12.00
670 Bill Hands 3.00 8.00
671 Bill Voss SP 5.00 12.00
672 Ed Crosby SP RC 5.00 12.00
673 Gerry Janeski SP RC 5.00 12.00
674 Montreal Expos TC 5.00 12.00
675 Dave Boswell 3.00 8.00
676 Tommie Reynolds 3.00 8.00
677 Jack DiLauro SP 5.00 12.00
678 George Thomas 3.00 8.00
679 Don O'Riley 3.00 8.00
680 Don Mincher SP 5.00 12.00
681 Bill Butler 3.00 8.00
682 Terry Harmon 3.00 8.00
683 Bill Burbach SP 5.00 12.00
684 Curt Motton 3.00 8.00
685 Moe Drabowsky 3.00 8.00
686 Chico Ruiz SP 5.00 12.00
687 Ron Taylor SP 5.00 12.00
688 S.Anderson MG SP 12.00 30.00
689 Frank Baker 3.00 8.00
690 Bob Moose 3.00 8.00
691 Bobby Heise 3.00 8.00
692 Haydel/Moret/Twitchell SP RC 5.00 12.00
693 Jose Pena SP 5.00 12.00
694 Rick Renick SP 5.00 12.00
695 Joe Niekro 5.00 12.00
696 Jerry Morales 3.00 8.00
697 Rickey Clark SP 5.00 12.00
698 Milwaukee Brewers TC SP 8.00 20.00
699 Jim Britton 3.00 8.00
700 Boog Powell SP 20.00 50.00
701 Bob Garibaldi 3.00 8.00
702 Milt Ramirez RC 3.00 8.00
703 Mike Kekich 3.00 8.00
704 J.C. Martin SP 5.00 12.00
705 Dick Selma SP 5.00 12.00
706 Joe Foy SP 5.00 12.00
707 Fred Lasher 3.00 8.00
708 Russ Nagelson SP 5.00 12.00
709 Baker/Baylor/Pac SP RC 40.00 100.00
710 Sonny Siebert 3.00 8.00
711 Larry Stahl SP 5.00 12.00
712 Jose Martinez 3.00 8.00
713 Mike Marshall SP 6.00 15.00
714 Dick Williams MG SP 6.00 15.00
715 Horace Clarke SP 6.00 15.00
716 Dave Leonhard 3.00 8.00
717 Tommie Aaron SP 5.00 12.00
718 Billy Wynne 3.00 8.00
719 Jerry May SP 5.00 12.00
720 Matty Alou 5.00 12.00
721 John Morris 3.00 8.00
722 Houston Astros TC SP 8.00 20.00
723 Vicente Romo SP 5.00 12.00
724 Tom Tischinski SP 5.00 12.00
725 Gary Gentry SP 5.00 12.00
726 Paul Popovich 3.00 8.00
727 Ray Lamb SP 5.00 12.00
728 Redmond/Lampard/Williams RC 3.00 8.00
729 Dick Billings RC 3.00 8.00
730 Jim Rooker 3.00 8.00
731 Jim Qualls SP 5.00 12.00
732 Bob Reed 3.00 8.00
733 Lee Maye SP 5.00 12.00
734 Rob Gardner SP 5.00 12.00
735 Mike Shannon SP 8.00 20.00
736 Mel Queen SP 5.00 12.00
737 Preston Gomez MG SP 5.00 12.00
738 Russ Gibson SP 5.00 12.00
739 Barry Lersch SP 5.00 12.00
740 Luis Aparicio SP 10.00 25.00
741 Skip Guinn 3.00 8.00
742 Kansas City Royals TC 5.00 12.00
743 John O'Donoghue SP 5.00 12.00
744 Chuck Manuel SP 5.00 12.00
745 Sandy Alomar SP 5.00 12.00
746 Andy Kosco 3.00 8.00
747 Severinsen/Spinks/Moore RC 3.00 8.00
748 John Purdin SP 5.00 12.00
749 Ken Szotkiewicz RC 3.00 8.00
750 Denny McLain SP 10.00 25.00
751 Al Weis SP 8.00 20.00
752 Dick Drago 5.00 12.00

1971 Topps Coins

This full-color set of 153 coins, which were inserted into packs, contains the photo of the player surrounded by a colored band, which contains the player's name, his team, his position and several stars. The backs contain the coin number, short biographical data and the line "Collect the entire set of 153 coins." The set was evidently produced in three groups of 51 as coins 1-51 have brass backs, coins 52-102 have chrome backs and coins 103-153 have blue backs. In fact it has been verified that the coins were printed in three sheets of 51 coins comprised of three rows of 17 coins. Each coin measures approximately 1 1/2" in diameter.

COMPLETE SET (153) 200.00 400.00
1 Clarence Gaston 1.00 2.50
2 Dave Johnson 1.00 2.50
3 Jim Bunning 2.00 5.00
4 Jim Spencer .75 2.00
5 Felix Millan .75 2.00
6 Gerry Moses .75 2.00
7 Ferguson Jenkins 2.00 5.00
8 Felipe Alou 1.00 2.50
9 Jim McGlothlin .75 2.00
10 Dick McAuliffe .75 2.00
11 Joe Torre 2.00 5.00
12 Jim Perry 1.00 2.50
13 Bobby Bonds 1.25 3.00
14 Danny Cater .75 2.00
15 Bill Mazeroski 2.00 5.00
16 Luis Aparicio 2.00 5.00
17 Doug Rader .75 2.00
18 Vada Pinson 1.25 3.00
19 John Bateman .75 2.00
20 Lew Krausse .75 2.00
21 Billy Grabarkewitz 1.00 2.50
22 Frank Howard 1.25 3.00
23 Jerry Koosman 1.25 3.00
24 Rod Carew 2.00 5.00
25 Al Ferrara .75 2.00
26 Dave McNally 1.00 2.50
27 Jim Hickman .75 2.00
28 Sandy Alomar 1.00 2.50
29 Lee May 1.00 2.50
30 Rico Petrocelli 1.00 2.50
31 Don Money .75 2.00
32 Jim Rooker .75 2.00
33 Dick Dietz .75 2.00
34 Roy White 1.00 2.50
35 Carl Morton .75 2.00
36 Walt Williams .75 2.00
37 Phil Niekro 2.00 5.00
38 Bill Freehan 1.00 2.50
39 Julian Javier .75 2.00
40 Rick Monday 1.00 2.50
41 Don Wilson .75 2.00
42 Ray Fosse 1.00 2.50
43 Art Shamsky .75 2.00
44 Ted Savage .75 2.00
45 Claude Osteen .75 2.00
46 Ed Brinkman .75 2.00
47 Matty Alou 1.00 2.50
48 Bob Oliver .75 2.00
49 Danny Coombs .75 2.00
50 Frank Robinson 2.00 5.00
51 Randy Hundley .75 2.00
52 Cesar Tovar 1.00 2.50
53 Wayne Simpson .75 2.00
54 Bobby Murcer 1.25 3.00
55 Carl Taylor .75 2.00
56 Tommy John 1.00 2.50
57 Willie McCovey 2.00 5.00
58 Carl Yastrzemski 5.00 12.00
59 Bob Bailey .75 2.00
60 Clyde Wright .75 2.00
61 Orlando Cepeda 2.00 5.00
62 Al Kaline 4.00 10.00
63 Bob Gibson 2.00 5.00
64 Bert Campaneris .75 2.00
65 Ted Sizemore .75 2.00
66 Duke Sims .75 2.00
67 Bud Harrelson 1.25 3.00
68 Gerald McNertney .75 2.00
69 Jim Wynn 1.00 2.50
70 Dick Bosman 1.00 2.50
71 Roberto Clemente 12.50 30.00
72 Rich Reese .75 2.00
73 Gaylord Perry 2.00 5.00
74 Boog Powell 1.00 2.50
75 Billy Williams 2.00 5.00
76 Bill Melton .75 2.00
77 Nate Colbert .75 2.00
78 Reggie Smith 1.00 2.50
79 Deron Johnson .75 2.00
80 Jim Hunter 2.00 5.00
81 Bobby Tolan 1.00 2.50
82 Jim Northrup .75 2.00
83 Ron Fairly 1.00 2.50
84 Alex Johnson .75 2.00
85 Pat Jarvis .75 2.00
86 Sam McDowell 1.00 2.50
87 Lou Brock 2.00 5.00
88 Danny Walton .75 2.00
89 Denis Menke .75 2.00
90 Jim Palmer 2.00 5.00
91 Tommy Agee 1.00 2.50
92 Duane Josephson .75 2.00
93 Willie Davis 1.00 2.50
94 Mel Stottlemyre 1.00 2.50
95 Ron Santo 1.00 2.50
96 Amos Otis 1.00 2.50
97 Ken Henderson .75 2.00
98 George Scott 1.00 2.50
99 Dock Ellis 1.00 2.50
100 Harmon Killebrew 4.00 10.00
101 Pete Rose 8.00 20.00
102 Rick Reichardt .75 2.00
103 Cleon Jones .75 2.00
104 Ron Perranoski .75 2.00
105 Tony Perez 2.00 5.00
106 Mickey Lolich 1.00 2.50
107 Tim McCarver 1.00 2.50
108 Reggie Jackson 6.00 15.00
109 Chris Cannizzaro .75 2.00
110 Steve Hargan .75 2.00
111 Rusty Staub 1.00 2.50
112 Andy Messersmith 1.00 2.50
113 Rico Carty 1.00 2.50
114 Brooks Robinson 4.00 10.00
115 Steve Carlton 2.00 5.00
116 Mike Hegan .75 2.00
117 Joe Morgan 2.00 5.00

118 Thurman Munson	5.00	12.00
119 Don Kessinger	.75	2.00
120 Joel Horlen	.75	2.00
121 Wes Parker	1.00	2.50
122 Sonny Siebert	.75	2.00
123 Willie Stargell	2.00	5.00
124 Ellie Rodgiuez	.75	2.00
125 Juan Marichal	2.00	5.00
126 Mike Epstein	.75	2.00
127 Tom Seaver	5.00	12.00
128 Tony Oliva	1.00	2.50
129 Jim Merritt	.75	2.00
130 Willie Horton	1.00	2.50
131 Rick Wise	.75	2.00
132 Sal Bando	1.00	2.50
133 Ollie Brown	.75	2.00
134 Ken Harrelson	1.00	2.50
135 Mack Jones	.75	2.00
136 Jim Fregosi	1.00	2.50
137 Hank Aaron	8.00	20.00
138 Fritz Peterson	.75	2.00
139 Joe Hague	.75	2.00
140 Tommy Harper	.75	2.00
141 Larry Dierker	.75	2.00
142 Tony Conigliaro	1.00	2.50
143 Glenn Beckert	.75	2.00
144 Carlos May	.75	2.00
145 Don Sutton	2.00	5.00
146 Paul Casanova	.75	2.00
147 Bob Moose	.75	2.00
148 Chico Cardenas	.75	2.00
149 Johnny Bench	6.00	15.00
150 Mike Cuellar	1.00	2.50
151 Donn Clendenon	.75	2.00
152 Lou Piniella	1.00	2.50
153 Willie Mays	10.00	25.00

1971 Topps Scratchoffs

These pack inserts featured the same players are the 1970 Topps Scratchoffs. However, the only difference is that the center of the game is red rather than black.

COMPLETE SET (24)	15.00	40.00
1 Hank Aaron	3.00	8.00
2 Rich Allen	.60	1.50
3 Luis Aparicio	1.50	4.00
4 Sal Bando	.40	1.00
5 Glenn Beckert	.40	1.00
6 Dick Bosman	.40	1.00
7 Nate Colbert	.40	1.00
8 Mike Hegan	.40	1.00
9 Mack Jones	.40	1.00
10 Al Kaline	2.00	5.00
11 Harmon Killebrew	2.00	5.00
12 Juan Marichal	1.50	4.00
13 Tim McCarver	.75	2.00
14 Sam McDowell	.50	1.25
15 Claude Osteen	.40	1.00
16 Tony Perez	1.25	3.00
17 Lou Piniella	.60	1.50
18 Boog Powell	.60	1.50
19 Tom Seaver	2.50	6.00
20 Jim Spencer	.40	1.00
21 Willie Stargell	2.00	5.00
22 Mel Stottlemyre	.50	1.25
23 Jim Wynn	.50	1.25
24 Carl Yastrzemski	2.00	5.00

1971 Topps Greatest Moments

The cards in this 55-card set measure 2 1/2" by 4 3/4". The 1971 Topps Greatest Moments set contains numbered cards depicting specific career highlights of current players. The obverses are black bordered and contain a small cameo picture of the left side; a deckle-bordered black and white action photo dominates the rest of the card. The backs are designed in newspaper style. Sometimes found in uncut sheets, this test set was retailed in gum packs on a very limited basis. Double prints (DP) are listed in our checklist; there were 22 double prints and 33 single prints.

COMPLETE SET (55)	750.00	1,500.00
COMMON CARD (1-55)	8.00	20.00
COMMON DP	3.00	8.00
1 Thurman Munson DP	15.00	40.00
2 Hoyt Wilhelm	10.00	25.00
3 Rico Carty	8.00	20.00
4 Carl Morton DP	3.00	8.00
5 Sal Bando DP	4.00	10.00
6 Bert Campaneris DP	4.00	10.00
7 Jim Kaat	10.00	25.00
8 Harmon Killebrew	40.00	80.00
9 Brooks Robinson	40.00	80.00
10 Jim Perry	8.00	20.00
11 Tony Oliva	12.50	30.00
12 Vada Pinson	10.00	25.00
13 Johnny Bench	60.00	120.00
14 Tony Perez	12.50	30.00
15 Pete Rose DP	40.00	80.00
16 Jim Fregosi DP	4.00	10.00
17 Alex Johnson DP	3.00	8.00
18 Clyde Wright DP	3.00	8.00
19 Al Kaline DP	15.00	40.00
20 Denny McLain	12.50	30.00
21 Jim Northrup	8.00	20.00
22 Bill Freehan	8.00	20.00
23 Mickey Lolich	10.00	25.00
24 Bob Gibson DP	12.50	30.00
25 Tim McCarver DP	3.00	8.00
26 Orlando Cepeda DP	8.00	20.00
27 Lou Brock DP	12.50	30.00
28 Nate Colbert DP	3.00	8.00
29 Maury Wills	12.50	30.00
30 Wes Parker	8.00	20.00
31 Jim Wynn	10.00	25.00
32 Larry Dierker	10.00	25.00
33 Bill Melton	8.00	20.00
34 Joe Morgan	12.50	30.00
35 Rusty Staub	10.00	25.00
36 Ernie Banks DP	15.00	40.00
37 Billy Williams	12.50	30.00
38 Lou Piniella	10.00	25.00
39 Rico Petrocelli DP	4.00	10.00
40 Carl Yastrzemski DP	20.00	50.00
41 Willie Mays DP	50.00	100.00
42 Tommy Harper	8.00	20.00
43 Jim Bunning DP	4.00	10.00
44 Fritz Peterson	10.00	25.00
45 Roy White	10.00	25.00
46 Bobby Murcer	12.50	30.00
47 Reggie Jackson	100.00	200.00
48 Frank Howard	10.00	25.00
49 Dick Bosman	8.00	20.00
50 Sam McDowell DP	4.00	10.00
51 Luis Aparicio DP	4.00	10.00
52 Willie McCovey DP	12.50	30.00
53 Joe Pepitone	10.00	25.00
54 Jerry Grote	10.00	25.00
55 Bud Harrelson	8.00	20.00

1971 Topps Super

The cards in this 63-card set measure 3 1/8" by 5 1/4". The obverse format of the Topps Super set of 1971 is identical to that of the 1970 set, that is, a borderless color photograph with a facsimile autograph printed on it. The backs are enlargements of the respective player's cards of the 1971 regular baseball issue. There are no reported scarcities in the set. Just as in 1970, this set was issued in three-card wax packs.

COMPLETE SET (63)	125.00	250.00
WRAPPER (10-CENT)		
1 Reggie Smith	.75	2.00
2 Gaylord Perry	1.50	4.00
3 Ted Savage	.60	1.50
4 Donn Clendenon	.60	1.50
5 Boog Powell	1.00	2.50
6 Tony Perez	1.50	4.00
7 Dick Bosman	.60	1.50
8 Alex Johnson	.60	1.50
9 Rusty Staub	1.00	2.50
10 Mel Stottlemyre	1.00	2.50
11 Tony Oliva	1.00	2.50
12 Bill Freehan	.75	2.00
13 Fritz Peterson	.60	1.50
14 Wes Parker	.75	2.00
15 Cesar Cedeno	.75	2.00
16 Sam McDowell	.75	2.00
17 Frank Howard	.75	2.00
18 Dave McNally	.75	2.00
19 Rico Petrocelli	.75	2.00
20 Pete Rose	10.00	25.00
21 Luke Walker	.60	1.50
22 Nate Colbert	.60	1.50
23 Luis Aparicio	1.50	4.00
24 Jim Perry	.75	2.00
25 Lou Brock	2.00	5.00
26 Roy White	.75	2.00
27 Claude Osteen	.60	1.50
28 Carl Morton	.60	1.50
29 Rico Carty	.75	2.00
30 Larry Dierker	.60	1.50
31 Bert Campaneris	.75	2.00
32 Johnny Bench	6.00	15.00
33 Felix Millan	.60	1.50
34 Tim McCarver	1.00	2.50
35 Ron Santo	1.00	2.50
36 Tommie Agee	.75	2.00
37 Roberto Clemente	12.50	30.00
38 Reggie Jackson	6.00	15.00
39 Clyde Wright	.60	1.50
40 Rich Allen	1.00	2.50
41 Curt Flood	.75	2.00
42 Ferguson Jenkins	1.50	4.00
43 Willie Stargell	1.50	4.00
44 Hank Aaron	20.00	50.00
45 Amos Otis	.75	2.00
46 Willie McCovey	2.00	5.00
47 Bill Melton	.60	1.50
48 Bob Gibson	2.00	5.00
49 Carl Yastrzemski	4.00	10.00
50 Glenn Beckert	.60	1.50
51 Ray Fosse	.60	1.50
52 Cito Gaston	.60	1.50
53 Tom Seaver	4.00	10.00
54 Al Kaline	3.00	8.00
55 Jim Northrup	.75	2.00
56 Willie Mays	8.00	20.00
57 Sal Bando	.75	2.00
58 Deron Johnson	.60	1.50
59 Brooks Robinson	3.00	8.00
60 Harmon Killebrew	2.00	5.00
61 Joe Torre	1.50	4.00
62 Lou Piniella	1.00	2.50
63 Tommy Harper	.60	1.50

1971 Topps Tattoos

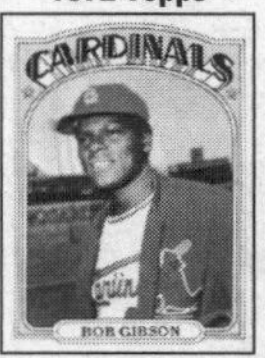

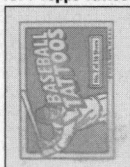

There are 16 different sheets (3 1/2" X 14 1/4") of baseball tattoos issued by Topps in 1971. Each contains two distinct sizes (1 3/4" by 2 3/8" and 1 3/16" by 1 3/4") of tattoos; those of players feature flesh-tone faces on red or yellow backgrounds; those of baseball figures, facsimile autographs (these are denoted by FAC in the checklist) and team pennants are one-half the player tattoo size. The "Baseball Tattoos" logo panel at the top of each sheet contains the sheet number; the sheet number is given (with an S prefix) in the checklist below after the name. The small baseball figures are not priced in the checklist. The complete tattoo panel prices can be figured as the sum of the individual (player, team and autograph) tatoos.

COMPLETE SET (134)	150.00	300.00
1 Sal Bando S1	.50	1.25
2 Dick Bosman S1	.40	1.00
3 Nate Colbert S1	.40	1.00
4 Cleon Jones S1	.40	1.00
5 Juan Marichal S1	2.00	5.00
6 Brooks Robinson S1	3.00	8.00
7 Brooks Robinson FAC S1	.75	2.00
8 Montreal Expos S1	.40	1.00
9 San Fran. Giants S1	.40	1.00
10 Glenn Beckert S2	.40	1.00
11 Tommy Harper S2	.40	1.00
12 Ken Henderson S2	.40	1.00
13 Carl Yastrzemski S2	3.00	8.00
14 Carl Yastrzemski FAC S2	.75	2.00
15 Boston Red Sox S2	.40	1.00
16 New York Mets S2	.40	1.00
17 Orlando Cepeda S3	.75	2.00
18 Jim Fregosi S3	.50	1.25
19 Jim Fregosi FAC S3	.40	1.00
20 Randy Hundley S3	.40	1.00
21 Reggie Jackson S3	4.00	10.00
22 Jerry Koosman S3	.60	1.50
23 Jim Palmer S3	2.00	5.00
24 Phila. Phillies S3	.40	1.00
25 New York Yankees S3	.50	1.25
26 Dick Dietz S4	.40	1.00
27 Clarence Gaston S4	.40	1.00
28 Dave Johnson S4	.60	1.50
29 Sam McDowell S4	.50	1.25
30 Sam McDowell FAC S4	.40	1.00
31 Gary Nolan S4	.40	1.00
32 Amos Otis S4	.50	1.25
33 Kansas City Royals S4	.40	1.00
34 Oakland A's S4	.40	1.00
35 Billy Grabarkewitz S5	.40	1.00
36 Al Kaline S5	3.00	8.00
37 Al Kaline FAC S5	.60	1.50
38 Lee May S5	.50	1.25
39 Tom Murphy S5	.40	1.00
40 Vada Pinson S5	.60	1.50
41 Manny Sanguillen S5	.40	1.00
42 Atlanta Braves S5	.40	1.00
43 Los Angeles Dodgers S5	.40	1.00
44 Luis Aparicio S6	2.00	5.00
45 Paul Blair S6	.40	1.00
46 Chris Cannizzaro S6	.40	1.00
47 Donn Clendenon S6	.40	1.00
48 Larry Dierker S6	.40	1.00
49 Harmon Killebrew S6	2.00	5.00
50 Harmon Killebrew FAC S6	.60	1.50
51 Chicago Cubs S6	.40	1.00
52 Cincinnati Reds S6	.40	1.00
53 Rich Allen S7	.75	2.00
54 Bert Campaneris S7	.50	1.25
55 Don Money S7	.40	1.00
56 Boog Powell S7	.75	2.00
57 Boog Powell FAC S7	.50	1.25
58 Ted Savage S7	.40	1.00
59 Rusty Staub S7	.60	1.50
60 Cleveland Indians S7	.40	1.00
61 Milwaukee Brewers S7	.40	1.00
62 Leo Cardenas S8	.40	1.00
63 Bill Hands S8	.40	1.00
64 Frank Howard S8	.60	1.50
65 Frank Howard FAC S8	.50	1.25
66 Wes Parker S8	.40	1.00
67 Reggie Smith S8	.50	1.25
68 Willie Stargell S8	2.00	5.00
69 Chicago White Sox S8	.40	1.00
70 San Diego Padres S8	.40	1.00
71 Hank Aaron S9	5.00	12.00
72 Hank Aaron FAC S9	.75	2.00
73 Tommy Agee S9	.40	1.00
74 Jim Hunter S9	2.00	5.00
75 Dick McAuliffe S9	.40	1.00
76 Tony Perez S9	1.50	4.00
77 Lou Piniella S9	.60	1.50
78 Detroit Tigers S9	.40	1.00
79 Roberto Clemente S10	8.00	20.00
80 Tony Conigliaro S10	.50	1.25
81 Fergie Jenkins S10	2.00	5.00
82 Fergie Jenkins FAC S10	.60	1.50
83 Thurman Munson S10	2.50	6.00
84 Gary Peters S10	.40	1.00
85 Joe Torre S10	.60	1.50
86 Baltimore Orioles S10	.40	1.00
87 Johnny Bench S11	3.00	8.00
88 Johnny Bench FAC S11	.60	1.50
89 Rico Carty S11	.50	1.25
90 Bill Mazeroski S11	1.50	4.00
91 Bob Oliver S11	.40	1.00
92 Rico Petrocelli S11	.50	1.25
93 Frank Robinson S11	2.50	6.00
94 Washington Senators S11	.40	1.00
95 Bill Freehan S12	.50	1.25
96 Dave McNally S12	.40	1.00
97 Felix Millan S12	.40	1.00
98 Mel Stottlemyre S12	.50	1.25
99 Bob Tolan S12	.40	1.00
100 Billy Williams S12	2.00	5.00
101 Billy Williams FAC S12	.60	1.50
102 Houston Astros S12	.40	1.00
103 Ray Culp S13	.40	1.00
104 Bud Harrelson S13	.40	1.00
105 Mickey Lolich S13	.60	1.50
106 Willie McCovey S13	2.00	5.00
107 Willie McCovey FAC S13	.60	1.50
108 Ron Santo S13	.75	2.00
109 Roy White S13	.50	1.25
110 Pittsburgh Pirates S13	.40	1.00
111 Bill Melton S14	.40	1.00
112 Jim Perry S14	.50	1.25
113 Pete Rose S14	5.00	12.00
114 Tom Seaver S14	4.00	10.00
115 Tom Seaver FAC S14	.75	2.00
116 Maury Wills S14	.60	1.50
117 Clyde Wright S14	.40	1.00
118 Minnesota Twins S14	.40	1.00
119 Rod Carew S15	3.00	8.00
120 Bob Gibson S15	3.00	8.00
121 Bob Gibson FAC S15	.60	1.50
122 Alex Johnson S15	.40	1.00
123 Don Kessinger S15	.40	1.00
124 Jim Merritt S15	.40	1.00
125 Rick Monday S15	.40	1.00
126 St. Louis Cardinals S15	.40	1.00
127 Larry Bowa S16	.50	1.25
128 Mike Cuellar S16	.50	1.25
129 Ray Fosse S16	.40	1.00
130 Willie Mays S16	6.00	15.00
131 Willie Mays FAC S16	.75	2.00
132 Carl Morton S16	.40	1.00
133 Tony Oliva S16	1.25	3.00
134 California Angels S16	.40	1.00

1972 Topps

The cards in this 787-card set measure 2 1/2" by 3 1/2". The 1972 Topps set contained the most cards ever for a Topps set to that point in time. Features appearing for the first time were "Boyhood Photos" (341-348/491-498), Awards and Trophy cards (621-626), "In Action" (distributed throughout the set), and "Traded Cards" (751-757). Other subsets included League Leaders (85-96), Playoffs cards (221-222), and World Series cards (223-230). The curved lines of the color picture are a departure from the rectangular designs of other years. There is a series of intermediate scarcity (526-656) and the usual high numbers (657-787). The backs of cards 692, 694, 696, 700, 706 and 710 form a picture back of Tom Seaver. The backs of cards 698, 702, 704, 708, 712, 714 form a picture back of Tony Oliva. As in previous years, cards were issued in a variety of ways including ten-card wax packs which cost a dime, 28-card cello packs which cost a quarter and 54-card rack packs which cost 39 cents. The 10 cents wax packs were issued 24 packs to a box while the cello packs were also issued 24 packs to a box. Rookie Cards in this set include Ron Cey and Carlton Fisk.

COMPLETE SET (787)	750.00	1,500.00
COMMON CARD (1-132)	.25	.60
COMMON CARD (133-263)	.40	1.00
COMMON CARD (264-394)	.50	1.25
COMMON CARD (395-525)	.60	1.50
COMMON CARD (526-656)	1.50	4.00
COMMON CARD (657-787)	5.00	12.00
WRAPPER (10-CENT)	6.00	15.00
1 Pittsburgh Pirates TC	3.00	8.00
2 Ray Culp	.25	.60
3 Bob Tolan	.25	.60
4 Checklist 1-132	2.50	6.00
5 John Bateman	.25	.60
6 Fred Scherman	.25	.60
7 Enzo Hernandez	.25	.60
8 Ron Swoboda	.50	1.25
9 Stan Williams	.25	.60
10 Amos Otis	.50	1.25
11 Bobby Valentine	.50	1.25
12 Jose Cardenal	.25	.60
13 Joe Grzenda	.25	.60
14 Koegel/Anderson/Twitchell RC	.25	.60
15 Walt Williams	.25	.60
16 Mike Jorgensen	.25	.60
17 Dave Duncan	.50	1.25
18A Juan Pizarro Yellow	.25	.60
18B Juan Pizarro Green	2.00	5.00
19 Billy Cowan	.25	.60
20 Don Wilson	.25	.60
21 Atlanta Braves TC	.60	1.50
22 Rob Gardner	.25	.60
23 Ted Kubiak	.25	.60
24 Ted Ford	.25	.60
25 Bill Singer	.25	.60
26 Andy Etchebarren	.25	.60
27 Bob Johnson	.25	.60
28 Gebhard/Brye Haydel RC	.25	.60
29A Bill Bonham Yellow RC	.25	.60
29B Bill Bonham Green	2.00	5.00
30 Rico Petrocelli	.50	1.25
31 Cleon Jones	.50	1.25
32 Cleon Jones IA	.25	.60
33 Billy Martin MG	1.50	4.00
34 Billy Martin IA	1.00	2.50

Card	Low	High
35 Jerry Johnson	.25	.60
36 Jerry Johnson IA	.25	.60
37 Carl Yastrzemski	10.00	25.00
38 Carl Yastrzemski IA	6.00	15.00
39 Bob Barton	.25	.60
40 Bob Barton IA	.25	.60
41 Tommy Davis	.50	1.25
42 Tommy Davis IA	.25	.60
43 Rick Wise	.50	1.25
44 Rick Wise IA	.25	.60
45A Glenn Beckert Yellow	.50	1.25
45B Glenn Beckert Green	2.00	5.00
46 Glenn Beckert IA	.25	.60
47 John Ellis	.25	.60
48 John Ellis IA	.25	.60
49 Willie Mays	20.00	50.00
50 Willie Mays IA	10.00	25.00
51 Harmon Killebrew	3.00	8.00
52 Harmon Killebrew IA	1.50	4.00
53 Bud Harrelson	.50	1.25
54 Bud Harrelson IA	.25	.60
55 Clyde Wright	.25	.60
56 Rich Chiles RC	.25	.60
57 Bob Oliver	.25	.60
58 Ernie McAnally	.25	.60
59 Fred Stanley RC	.25	.60
60 Manny Sanguillen	.50	1.25
61 Hooten/Hisler/Stephenson RC	.50	1.25
62 Angel Mangual	.25	.60
63 Duke Sims	.25	.60
64 Pete Broberg RC	.25	.60
65 Cesar Cedeno	.50	1.25
66 Ray Corbin RC	.25	.60
67 Red Schoendienst MG	1.00	2.50
68 Jim York RC	.25	.60
69 Roger Freed	.25	.60
70 Mike Cuellar	.50	1.25
71 California Angels TC	.60	1.50
72 Bruce Kison RC	.25	.60
73 Steve Huntz	.25	.60
74 Cecil Upshaw	.25	.60
75 Bert Campaneris	.50	1.25
76 Don Carrithers RC	.25	.60
77 Ron Theobald RC	.25	.60
78 Steve Arlin RC	.25	.60
79 C.Fisk RC/C.Cooper RC	20.00	50.00
80 Tony Perez	1.50	4.00
81 Mike Hedlund	.25	.60
82 Ron Woods	.25	.60
83 Dalton Jones	.25	.60
84 Vince Colbert	.25	.60
85 Torre/Garr/Beckert LL	1.00	2.50
86 Oliva/Murcer/Rett LL	1.00	2.50
87 Torre/Stargell/Aaron LL	5.00	12.00
88 Kill/F.Rob/Smith LL	1.50	4.00
89 Stargell/Aaron/May LL	4.00	10.00
90 Melton/Cash/Jackson LL	1.00	2.50
91 Seaver/Roberts/Wilson LL	1.00	2.50
92 Blue/Wood/Palmer LL	1.00	2.50
93 Jenkins/Carlton/Seaver LL	1.50	4.00
94 Lolich/Blue/Wood LL	1.00	2.50
95 Seaver/Jenkins/Stone LL	1.50	4.00
96 Lolich/Blue/Coleman LL	1.00	2.50
97 Tom Kelley	.25	.60
98 Chuck Tanner MG	.50	1.25
99 Ross Grimsley RC	.25	.60
100 Frank Robinson	3.00	8.00
101 Grief/Richard/Busse RC	1.00	2.50
102 Lloyd Allen	.25	.60
103 Checklist 133-263	2.50	6.00
104 Toby Harrah RC	.50	1.25
105 Gary Gentry	.25	.60
106 Milwaukee Brewers TC	.60	1.50
107 Jose Cruz RC	.50	1.25
108 Gary Waslewski	.25	.60
109 Jerry May	.25	.60
110 Ron Hunt	.25	.60
111 Jim Grant	.25	.60
112 Greg Luzinski	.50	1.25
113 Rogelio Moret	.25	.60
114 Bill Buckner	.50	1.25
115 Jim Fregosi	.50	1.25
116 Ed Farmer RC	.25	.60
117A Cleo James Yellow RC	.25	.60
117B Cleo James Green	2.00	5.00
118 Skip Lockwood	.25	.60
119 Marty Perez	.25	.60
120 Bill Freehan	.50	1.25
121 Ed Sprague	.25	.60
122 Larry Biittner RC	.25	.60
123 Ed Acosta	.25	.60
124 Closter/Torres/Hambright RC	.25	.60
125 Dave Cash	.50	1.25
126 Bart Johnson	.25	.60
127 Duffy Dyer	.25	.60
128 Eddie Watt	.25	.60
129 Charlie Fox MG	.25	.60
130 Bob Gibson	3.00	8.00
131 Jim Nettles	.25	.60
132 Joe Morgan	2.50	6.00
133 Joe Keough	.40	1.00
134 Carl Morton	.40	1.00
135 Vada Pinson	.75	2.00
136 Darrel Chaney	.40	1.00
137 Dick Williams MG	.75	2.00
138 Mike Kekich	.40	1.00
139 Tim McCarver	.75	2.00
140 Pat Dobson	.75	2.00
141 Capra/Stanton/Matlack RC	.75	2.00
142 Chris Chambliss RC	1.50	4.00
143 Garry Jestadt	.40	1.00
144 Marty Pattin	.40	1.00
145 Don Kessinger	.75	2.00
146 Steve Kealey	.40	1.00
147 Dave Kingman RC	6.00	15.00
148 Dick Billings	.40	1.00
149 Gary Neibauer	.40	1.00
150 Norm Cash	.75	2.00
151 Jim Brewer	.40	1.00
152 Gene Clines	.40	1.00
153 Rick Auerbach RC	.40	1.00
154 Ted Simmons	1.50	4.00
155 Larry Dierker	.40	1.00
156 Minnesota Twins TC	.75	2.00
157 Don Gullett	.40	1.00
158 Jerry Kenney	.40	1.00
159 John Boccabella	.40	1.00
160 Andy Messersmith	.75	2.00
161 Brock Davis	.40	1.00
162 Bell/Porter/Reynolds RC	.75	2.00
163 Tug McGraw	1.50	4.00
164 Tug McGraw IA	.75	2.00
165 Chris Speier RC	.75	2.00
166 Chris Speier IA	.40	1.00
167 Deron Johnson	.40	1.00
168 Deron Johnson IA	.40	1.00
169 Vida Blue	1.50	4.00
170 Vida Blue IA	.75	2.00
171 Darrell Evans	1.50	4.00
172 Darrell Evans IA	.75	2.00
173 Clay Kirby	.40	1.00
174 Clay Kirby IA	.40	1.00
175 Tom Haller	.40	1.00
176 Tom Haller IA	.40	1.00
177 Paul Schaal	.40	1.00
178 Paul Schaal IA	.40	1.00
179 Dock Ellis	.40	1.00
180 Dock Ellis IA	.40	1.00
181 Ed Kranepool	.75	2.00
182 Ed Kranepool IA	.40	1.00
183 Bill Melton	.40	1.00
184 Bill Melton IA	.40	1.00
185 Ron Bryant	.40	1.00
186 Ron Bryant IA	.40	1.00
187 Gates Brown	.40	1.00
188 Frank Lucchesi MG	.40	1.00
189 Gene Tenace	.75	2.00
190 Dave Giusti	.40	1.00
191 Jeff Burroughs RC	1.50	4.00
192 Chicago Cubs TC	.75	2.00
193 Kurt Bevacqua RC	.40	1.00
194 Fred Norman	.40	1.00
195 Orlando Cepeda	2.50	6.00
196 Mel Queen	.40	1.00
197 Johnny Briggs	.40	1.00
198 Hough/O'Brien/Strahler RC	2.50	6.00
199 Mike Fiore	.40	1.00
200 Lou Brock	3.00	8.00
201 Phil Roof	.40	1.00
202 Scipio Spinks	.40	1.00
203 Ron Blomberg RC	.40	1.00
204 Tommy Helms	.40	1.00
205 Dick Drago	.40	1.00
206 Dal Maxvill	.40	1.00
207 Tom Egan	.40	1.00
208 Milt Pappas	.75	2.00
209 Joe Rudi	.75	2.00
210 Denny McLain	.75	2.00
211 Gary Sutherland	.40	1.00
212 Grant Jackson	.40	1.00
213 Parker/Kusnyer/Silverio RC	.40	1.00
214 Mike McQueen	.40	1.00
215 Alex Johnson	.75	2.00
216 Joe Niekro	.75	2.00
217 Roger Metzger	.40	1.00
218 Eddie Kasko MG	.40	1.00
219 Rennie Stennett RC	.75	2.00
220 Jim Perry	.75	2.00
221 NL Playoffs Bucs	.75	2.00
222 AL Playoffs B.Robinson	1.50	4.00
223 Dave McNally WS	.75	2.00
224 D.Johnson/M.Belanger WS	.75	2.00
225 Manny Sanguillen WS	.75	2.00
226 Roberto Clemente WS	3.00	8.00
227 Nellie Briles WS	.75	2.00
228 F.Robinson/M.Sanguillen WS	.75	2.00
229 Steve Blass WS	.75	2.00
230 Pirates Celebrate WS	.75	2.00
231 Casey Cox	.40	1.00
232 Arnold/Barr/Rader RC	.40	1.00
233 Jay Johnstone	.75	2.00
234 Ron Taylor	.40	1.00
235 Merv Rettenmund	.40	1.00
236 Jim McGlothlin	.40	1.00
237 New York Yankees TC	.75	2.00
238 Leron Lee	.40	1.00
239 Tom Timmermann	.40	1.00
240 Rich Allen	.75	2.00
241 Rollie Fingers	2.50	6.00
242 Don Mincher	.40	1.00
243 Frank Linzy	.40	1.00
244 Steve Braun RC	.40	1.00
245 Tommie Agee	.75	2.00
246 Tom Burgmeier	.40	1.00
247 Milt May	.40	1.00
248 Tom Bradley	.40	1.00
249 Harry Walker MG	.40	1.00
250 Boog Powell	.75	2.00
251 Checklist 264-394	2.50	6.00
252 Ken Reynolds	.40	1.00
253 Sandy Alomar	.75	2.00
254 Boots Day	.40	1.00
255 Jim Lonborg	.75	2.00
256 George Foster	.75	2.00
257 Foor/Hosley/Jata RC	.40	1.00
258 Randy Hundley	.40	1.00
259 Sparky Lyle	.75	2.00
260 Ralph Garr	.75	2.00
261 Steve Mingori	.40	1.00
262 San Diego Padres TC	.75	2.00
263 Felipe Alou	.75	2.00
264 Tommy John	.75	2.00
265 Wes Parker	.75	2.00
266 Bobby Bolin	.50	1.25
267 Dave Concepcion	1.50	4.00
268 D.Anderson RC/C.Floethe RC	.50	1.25
269 Don Hahn	.50	1.25
270 Jim Palmer	6.00	15.00
271 Ken Rudolph	.50	1.25
272 Mickey Rivers RC	.75	2.00
273 Bobby Floyd	.50	1.25
274 Al Severinsen	.50	1.25
275 Cesar Tovar	.50	1.25
276 Gene Mauch MG	.75	2.00
277 Elliott Maddox	.50	1.25
278 Dennis Higgins	.50	1.25
279 Larry Brown	.50	1.25
280 Willie McCovey	2.50	6.00
281 Bill Parsons RC	.50	1.25
282 Houston Astros TC	.75	2.00
283 Darrell Brandon	.50	1.25
284 Ike Brown	.50	1.25
285 Gaylord Perry	2.50	6.00
286 Gene Alley	.50	1.25
287 Jim Hardin	.50	1.25
288 Johnny Jeter	.50	1.25
289 Syd O'Brien	.50	1.25
290 Sonny Siebert	.50	1.25
291 Hal McRae	.75	2.00
292 Hal McRae IA	.50	1.25
293 Dan Frisella	.50	1.25
294 Dan Frisella IA	.50	1.25
295 Dick Dietz	.50	1.25
296 Dick Dietz IA	.50	1.25
297 Claude Osteen	.75	2.00
298 Claude Osteen IA	.50	1.25
299 Hank Aaron	25.00	60.00
300 Hank Aaron IA	8.00	20.00
301 George Mitterwald	.50	1.25
302 George Mitterwald IA	.50	1.25
303 Joe Pepitone	.75	2.00
304 Joe Pepitone IA	.50	1.25
305 Ken Boswell	.50	1.25
306 Ken Boswell IA	.50	1.25
307 Steve Renko	.50	1.25
308 Steve Renko IA	.50	1.25
309 Roberto Clemente	30.00	80.00
310 Roberto Clemente IA	12.00	30.00
311 Clay Carroll	.50	1.25
312 Clay Carroll IA	.50	1.25
313 Luis Aparicio	2.50	6.00
314 Luis Aparicio IA	.75	2.00
315 Paul Splittorff	.50	1.25
316 Bibby/Roque/Guzman RC	.75	2.00
317 Rich Hand	.50	1.25
318 Sonny Jackson	.50	1.25
319 Aurelio Rodriguez	.50	1.25
320 Steve Blass	.75	2.00
321 Joe Lahoud	.50	1.25
322 Jose Pena	.50	1.25
323 Earl Weaver MG	1.50	4.00
324 Mike Ryan	.50	1.25
325 Mel Stottlemyre	.75	2.00
326 Pat Kelly	.50	1.25
327 Steve Stone RC	.75	2.00
328 Boston Red Sox TC	.75	2.00
329 Roy Foster	.50	1.25
330 Jim Hunter	2.50	6.00
331 Stan Swanson RC	.50	1.25
332 Buck Martinez	.50	1.25
333 Steve Barber	.50	1.25
334 Fahey/Mason Ragland RC	.50	1.25
335 Bill Hands	.50	1.25
336 Marty Martinez	.50	1.25
337 Mike Kilkenny	.50	1.25
338 Bob Grich	.75	2.00
339 Ron Cook	.50	1.25
340 Roy White	.75	2.00
341 Joe Torre KP	.50	1.25
342 Wilbur Wood KP	.50	1.25
343 Willie Stargell KP	.75	2.00
344 Dave McNally KP	.50	1.25
345 Rick Wise KP	.50	1.25
346 Jim Fregosi KP	.50	1.25
347 Tom Seaver KP	1.50	4.00
348 Sal Bando KP	.50	1.25
349 Al Fitzmorris	.50	1.25
350 Frank Howard	.75	2.00
351 House/Kester/Britton	.75	2.00
352 Dave LaRoche	.50	1.25
353 Art Shamsky	.50	1.25
354 Tom Murphy	.50	1.25
355 Bob Watson	.75	2.00
356 Gerry Moses	.50	1.25
357 Woody Fryman	.50	1.25
358 Sparky Anderson MG	1.50	4.00
359 Don Pavletich	.50	1.25
360 Dave Roberts	.50	1.25
361 Mike Andrews	.50	1.25
362 New York Mets TC	.75	2.00
363 Ron Klimkowski	.50	1.25
364 Johnny Callison	.75	2.00
365 Dick Bosman	.75	2.00
366 Jimmy Rosario RC	.50	1.25
367 Ron Perranoski	.50	1.25
368 Danny Thompson	.50	1.25
369 Jim Lefebvre	.75	2.00
370 Don Buford	.50	1.25
371 Denny Lemaster	.50	1.25
372 L.Clemons RC/M.Montgomery RC	.50	1.25
373 John Mayberry	.75	2.00
374 Jack Heidemann	.50	1.25
375 Reggie Cleveland	.50	1.25
376 Andy Kosco	.50	1.25
377 Terry Harmon	.50	1.25
378 Checklist 395-525	2.50	6.00
379 Ken Berry	.50	1.25
380 Earl Williams	.50	1.25
381 Chicago White Sox TC	.75	2.00
382 Joe Gibbon	.50	1.25
383 Brant Alyea	.50	1.25
384 Dave Campbell	.75	2.00
385 Mickey Stanley	.75	2.00
386 Jim Colborn	.50	1.25
387 Horace Clarke	.75	2.00
388 Charlie Williams RC	.50	1.25
389 Bill Rigney MG	.50	1.25
390 Willie Davis	.75	2.00
391 Ken Sanders	.50	1.25
392 F.Cambria/R.Zisk RC	.75	2.00
393 Curt Motton	.50	1.25
394 Ken Forsch	.75	2.00
395 Matty Alou	.75	2.00
396 Paul Lindblad	.60	1.50
397 Philadelphia Phillies TC	.75	2.00
398 Larry Hisle	.75	2.00
399 Milt Wilcox	.75	2.00
400 Tony Oliva	1.50	4.00
401 Jim Nash	.60	1.50
402 Bobby Heise	.60	1.50
403 John Cumberland	.60	1.50
404 Jeff Torborg	.75	2.00
405 Ron Fairly	.75	2.00
406 George Hendrick RC	.75	2.00
407 Chuck Taylor	.60	1.50
408 Jim Northrup	.75	2.00
409 Frank Baker	.60	1.50
410 Ferguson Jenkins	2.50	6.00
411 Bob Montgomery	.60	1.50
412 Dick Kelley	.60	1.50
413 D.Eddy RC/D.Lemonds	.60	1.50
414 Bob Miller	.60	1.50
415 Cookie Rojas	.75	2.00
416 Johnny Edwards	.60	1.50
417 Tom Hall	.60	1.50
418 Tom Shopay	.60	1.50
419 Jim Spencer	.60	1.50
420 Steve Carlton	8.00	20.00
421 Ellie Rodriguez	.60	1.50
422 Ray Lamb	.60	1.50
423 Oscar Gamble	.75	2.00
424 Bill Gogolewski	.60	1.50
425 Ken Singleton	.75	2.00
426 Ken Singleton IA	.60	1.50
427 Tito Fuentes	.60	1.50
428 Tito Fuentes IA	.60	1.50
429 Bob Robertson	.60	1.50
430 Bob Robertson IA	.60	1.50
431 Clarence Gaston	.75	2.00
432 Clarence Gaston IA	.75	2.00
433 Johnny Bench	15.00	40.00
434 Johnny Bench IA	8.00	20.00
435 Reggie Jackson	12.00	30.00
436 Reggie Jackson IA	6.00	15.00
437 Maury Wills	.75	2.00
438 Maury Wills IA	.75	2.00
439 Billy Williams	2.50	6.00
440 Billy Williams IA	1.50	4.00
441 Thurman Munson	12.00	30.00
442 Thurman Munson IA	3.00	8.00
443 Ken Henderson	.60	1.50
444 Ken Henderson IA	.60	1.50
445 Tom Seaver	15.00	40.00
446 Tom Seaver IA	5.00	12.00
447 Willie Stargell	3.00	8.00
448 Willie Stargell IA	1.50	4.00
449 Bob Lemon MG	.75	2.00
450 Mickey Lolich	.75	2.00
451 Tony LaRussa	1.50	4.00
452 Ed Herrmann	.60	1.50
453 Barry Lersch	.60	1.50
454 Oakland Athletics TC	.75	2.00
455 Tommy Harper	.75	2.00
456 Mark Belanger	.75	2.00
457 Fast/Thomas/Ivie RC	.60	1.50
458 Aurelio Monteagudo	.60	1.50
459 Rick Renick	.60	1.50
460 Al Downing	.60	1.50
461 Tim Cullen	.60	1.50
462 Rickey Clark	.60	1.50
463 Bernie Carbo	.60	1.50
464 Jim Roland	.60	1.50
465 Gil Hodges MG	1.50	4.00
466 Norm Miller	.60	1.50
467 Steve Kline	.60	1.50
468 Richie Scheinblum	.60	1.50
469 Ron Herbel	.60	1.50
470 Ray Fosse	.60	1.50
471 Luke Walker	.60	1.50
472 Phil Gagliano	.60	1.50
473 Dan McGinn	.60	1.50
474 Baylor/Harrison/Oates RC	6.00	15.00
475 Gary Nolan	.75	2.00
476 Lee Richard RC	.60	1.50
477 Tom Phoebus	.60	1.50
478 Checklist 526-656	2.50	6.00
479 Don Shaw	.60	1.50
480 Lee May	.75	2.00
481 Billy Conigliaro	.75	2.00
482 Joe Hoerner	.60	1.50
483 Ken Suarez	.60	1.50
484 Lum Harris MG	.60	1.50
485 Phil Regan	.75	2.00
486 John Lowenstein	.60	1.50
487 Detroit Tigers TC	.75	2.00
488 Mike Nagy	.60	1.50
489 T.Humphrey RC/K.Lampard	.60	1.50
490 Dave McNally	.75	2.00
491 Lou Piniella KP	.75	2.00
492 Mel Stottlemyre KP	.75	2.00
493 Bob Bailey KP	.75	2.00
494 Willie Horton KP	.75	2.00
495 Bill Melton KP	.75	2.00
496 Bud Harrelson KP	.75	2.00
497 Jim Perry KP	.75	2.00

498 Brooks Robinson KP 1.50 4.00
499 Vicente Romo .60 1.50
500 Joe Torre 1.50 4.00
501 Pete Hamm .60 1.50
502 Jackie Hernandez .60 1.50
503 Gary Peters .60 1.50
504 Ed Spiezio .60 1.50
505 Mike Marshall .75 2.00
506 Ley/Moyer/Tidrow RC .60 1.50
507 Fred Gladding .60 1.50
508 Elrod Hendricks .60 1.50
509 Don McMahon .60 1.50
510 Ted Williams MG 8.00 20.00
511 Tony Taylor .75 2.00
512 Paul Popovich .60 1.50
513 Lindy McDaniel .75 2.00
514 Ted Sizemore .60 1.50
515 Bert Blyleven 1.50 4.00
516 Oscar Brown .60 1.50
517 Ken Brett .60 1.50
518 Wayne Garrett .60 1.50
519 Ted Abernathy .60 1.50
520 Larry Bowa .75 2.00
521 Alan Foster .60 1.50
522 Los Angeles Dodgers TC .75 2.00
523 Chuck Dobson .60 1.50
524 E.Armbrister RC/M.Behney RC .60 1.50
525 Carlos May .75 2.00
526 Bob Bailey 2.50 6.00
527 Dave Leonhard 1.50 4.00
528 Ron Stone 1.50 4.00
529 Dave Nelson 2.50 6.00
530 Don Sutton 5.00 12.00
531 Freddie Patek 2.50 6.00
532 Fred Kendall RC 1.50 4.00
533 Ralph Houk MG 2.50 6.00
534 Jim Hickman 2.50 6.00
535 Ed Brinkman 1.50 4.00
536 Doug Rader 2.50 6.00
537 Bob Locker 1.50 4.00
538 Charlie Sands RC 1.50 4.00
539 Terry Forster RC 2.50 6.00
540 Felix Millan 1.50 4.00
541 Roger Repoz 1.50 4.00
542 Jack Billingham 1.50 4.00
543 Duane Josephson 1.50 4.00
544 Ted Martinez 1.50 4.00
545 Wayne Granger 1.50 4.00
546 Joe Hague 1.50 4.00
547 Cleveland Indians TC 3.00 8.00
548 Frank Reberger 1.50 4.00
549 Dave May 1.50 4.00
550 Brooks Robinson 8.00 20.00
551 Ollie Brown 1.50 4.00
552 Ollie Brown IA 1.50 4.00
553 Wilbur Wood 2.50 6.00
554 Wilbur Wood IA 1.50 4.00
555 Ron Santo 3.00 8.00
556 Ron Santo IA 2.50 6.00
557 John Odom 1.50 4.00
558 John Odom IA 1.50 4.00
559 Pete Rose 25.00 60.00
560 Pete Rose IA 10.00 25.00
561 Leo Cardenas 1.50 4.00
562 Leo Cardenas IA 1.50 4.00
563 Ray Sadecki 1.50 4.00
564 Ray Sadecki IA 1.50 4.00
565 Reggie Smith 2.50 6.00
566 Reggie Smith IA 1.50 4.00
567 Juan Marichal 6.00 15.00
568 Juan Marichal IA 2.50 6.00
569 Ed Kirkpatrick 1.50 4.00
570 Ed Kirkpatrick IA 1.50 4.00
571 Nate Colbert 1.50 4.00
572 Nate Colbert IA 1.50 4.00
573 Fritz Peterson 1.50 4.00
574 Fritz Peterson IA 1.50 4.00
575 Al Oliver 3.00 8.00
576 Leo Durocher MG 2.50 6.00
577 Mike Paul 2.50 6.00
578 Billy Grabarkewitz 1.50 4.00
579 Doyle Alexander RC 2.50 6.00
580 Lou Piniella 2.50 6.00
581 Wade Blasingame 1.50 4.00
582 Montreal Expos TC 3.00 8.00
583 Darold Knowles 1.50 4.00
584 Jerry McNertney 1.50 4.00
585 George Scott 2.50 6.00
586 Denis Menke 1.50 4.00
587 Billy Wilson 1.50 4.00
588 Jim Holt 1.50 4.00
589 Hal Lanier 1.50 4.00
590 Graig Nettles 3.00 8.00
591 Paul Casanova 1.50 4.00
592 Lew Krausse 1.50 4.00
593 Rich Morales 1.50 4.00
594 Jim Beauchamp 1.50 4.00
595 Nolan Ryan 40.00 100.00
596 Manny Mota 2.50 6.00
597 Jim Magnuson RC 1.50 4.00
598 Hal King 2.50 6.00
599 Billy Champion 1.50 4.00
600 Al Kaline 12.00 30.00
601 George Stone 1.50 4.00
602 Dave Bristol MG 1.50 4.00
603 Jim Ray 1.50 4.00
604A Checklist 657-787 Right Copy 5.00 12.00
604B Checklist 657-787 Left Copy 5.00 12.00
605 Nelson Briles 2.50 6.00
606 Luis Melendez 1.50 4.00
607 Frank Duffy 1.50 4.00
608 Mike Corkins 1.50 4.00
609 Tom Grieve 2.50 6.00
610 Bill Stoneman 2.50 6.00
611 Rich Reese 1.50 4.00
612 Joe Decker 1.50 4.00
613 Mike Ferraro 1.50 4.00
614 Ted Uhlaender 1.50 4.00
615 Steve Hargan 1.50 4.00
616 Joe Ferguson RC 2.50 6.00
617 Kansas City Royals TC 3.00 8.00
618 Rich Robertson 1.50 4.00
619 Rich McKinney 1.50 4.00
620 Phil Niekro 5.00 12.00
621 Commish Award 3.00 8.00
622 MVP Award 3.00 8.00
623 Cy Young Award 3.00 8.00
624 Minor Lg POY Award 3.00 8.00
625 Rookie of the Year 3.00 8.00
626 Babe Ruth Award 3.00 8.00
627 Moe Drabowsky 1.50 4.00
628 Terry Crowley 1.50 4.00
629 Paul Doyle 1.50 4.00
630 Rich Hebner 2.50 6.00
631 John Strohmayer 1.50 4.00
632 Mike Hegan 1.50 4.00
633 Jack Hiatt 1.50 4.00
634 Dick Woodson 1.50 4.00
635 Don Money 2.50 6.00
636 Bill Lee 2.50 6.00
637 Preston Gomez MG 1.50 4.00
638 Ken Wright 1.50 4.00
639 J.C. Martin 1.50 4.00
640 Joe Coleman 1.50 4.00
641 Mike Lum 1.50 4.00
642 Dennis Riddleberger RC 1.50 4.00
643 Russ Gibson 1.50 4.00
644 Bernie Allen 1.50 4.00
645 Jim Maloney 2.50 6.00
646 Chico Salmon 1.50 4.00
647 Bob Moose 1.50 4.00
648 Jim Lyttle 1.50 4.00
649 Pete Richert 1.50 4.00
650 Sal Bando 2.50 6.00
651 Cincinnati Reds TC 3.00 8.00
652 Marcelino Lopez 1.50 4.00
653 Jim Fairey 1.50 4.00
654 Horacio Pina 2.50 6.00
655 Jerry Grote 1.50 4.00
656 Rudy May 1.50 4.00
657 Bobby Wine 5.00 12.00
658 Steve Dunning 5.00 12.00
659 Bob Aspromonte 5.00 12.00
660 Paul Blair 6.00 15.00
661 Bill Virdon MG 5.00 12.00
662 Stan Bahnsen 5.00 12.00
663 Fran Healy RC 6.00 15.00
664 Bobby Knoop 5.00 12.00
665 Chris Short 5.00 12.00
666 Hector Torres 5.00 12.00
667 Ray Newman RC 5.00 12.00
668 Texas Rangers TC 12.50 30.00
669 Willie Crawford 5.00 12.00
670 Ken Holtzman 6.00 15.00
671 Donn Clendenon 6.00 15.00
672 Archie Reynolds 5.00 12.00
673 Dave Marshall 5.00 12.00
674 John Kennedy 5.00 12.00
675 Pat Jarvis 5.00 12.00
676 Danny Cater 5.00 12.00
677 Ivan Murrell 5.00 12.00
678 Steve Luebber RC 5.00 12.00
679 B.Fenwick RC/B.Stinson 5.00 12.00
680 Dave Johnson 6.00 15.00
681 Bobby Pfeil 5.00 12.00
682 Mike McCormick 6.00 15.00
683 Steve Hovley 5.00 12.00
684 Hal Breeden RC 5.00 12.00
685 Joel Horlen 5.00 12.00
686 Steve Garvey 20.00 50.00
687 Del Unser 5.00 12.00
688 St. Louis Cardinals TC 8.00 20.00
689 Eddie Fisher 5.00 12.00
690 Willie Montanez 6.00 15.00
691 Curt Blefary 5.00 12.00
692 Curt Blefary IA 5.00 12.00
693 Alan Gallagher 5.00 12.00
694 Alan Gallagher IA 5.00 12.00
695 Rod Carew 25.00 60.00
696 Rod Carew IA 12.00 30.00
697 Jerry Koosman 6.00 15.00
698 Jerry Kosman IA 6.00 15.00
699 Bobby Murcer 6.00 15.00
700 Bobby Murcer IA 6.00 15.00
701 Jose Pagan 5.00 12.00
702 Jose Pagan IA 5.00 12.00
703 Doug Griffin 5.00 12.00
704 Doug Griffin IA 5.00 12.00
705 Pat Corrales 6.00 15.00
706 Pat Corrales IA 5.00 12.00
707 Tim Foli 5.00 12.00
708 Tim Foli IA 5.00 12.00
709 Jim Kaat 6.00 15.00
710 Jim Kaat IA 6.00 15.00
711 Bobby Bonds 8.00 20.00
712 Bobby Bonds IA 6.00 15.00
713 Gene Michael 8.00 20.00
714 Gene Michael IA 6.00 15.00
715 Mike Epstein 5.00 12.00
716 Jesus Alou 5.00 12.00
717 Bruce Dal Canton 5.00 12.00
718 Del Rice MG 5.00 12.00
719 Cesar Geronimo 5.00 12.00
720 Sam McDowell 6.00 15.00
721 Eddie Leon 5.00 12.00
722 Bill Sudakis 5.00 12.00
723 Al Santorini 5.00 12.00
724 Curtis/Hinton/Scott RC 5.00 12.00
725 Dick McAuliffe 6.00 15.00
726 Dick Selma 5.00 12.00
727 Jose Laboy 5.00 12.00
728 Gail Hopkins 5.00 12.00
729 Bob Veale 6.00 15.00
730 Rick Monday 6.00 15.00
731 Baltimore Orioles TC 8.00 20.00
732 George Culver 5.00 12.00
733 Jim Ray Hart 6.00 15.00
734 Bob Burda 5.00 12.00
735 Diego Segui 5.00 12.00
736 Bill Russell 6.00 15.00
737 Len Randle RC 6.00 15.00
738 Jim Merritt 5.00 12.00
739 Don Mason 5.00 12.00
740 Rico Carty 6.00 15.00
741 Hutton/Milner/Miller RC 6.00 15.00
742 Jim Rooker 5.00 12.00
743 Cesar Gutierrez 5.00 12.00
744 Jim Slaton RC 5.00 12.00
745 Julian Javier 6.00 15.00
746 Lowell Palmer 5.00 12.00
747 Jim Stewart 5.00 12.00
748 Phil Hennigan 5.00 12.00
749 Walter Alston MG 8.00 20.00
750 Willie Horton 6.00 15.00
751 Steve Carlton TR 15.00 40.00
752 Joe Morgan TR 12.00 30.00
753 Denny McLain TR 8.00 20.00
754 Frank Robinson TR 10.00 25.00
755 Jim Fregosi TR 6.00 15.00
756 Rick Wise TR 6.00 15.00
757 Jose Cardenal TR 6.00 15.00
758 Gil Garrido 5.00 12.00
759 Chris Cannizzaro 5.00 12.00
760 Bill Mazeroski 10.00 25.00
761 Oglivie/Cey/Williams RC 20.00 50.00
762 Wayne Simpson 5.00 12.00
763 Ron Hansen 5.00 12.00
764 Dusty Baker 8.00 20.00
765 Ken McMullen 5.00 12.00
766 Steve Hamilton 5.00 12.00
767 Tom McCraw 6.00 15.00
768 Denny Doyle 5.00 12.00
769 Jack Aker 5.00 12.00
770 Jim Wynn 6.00 15.00
771 San Francisco Giants TC 8.00 20.00
772 Ken Tatum 5.00 12.00
773 Ron Brand 5.00 12.00
774 Luis Alvarado 5.00 12.00
775 Jerry Reuss 6.00 15.00
776 Bill Voss 5.00 12.00
777 Hoyt Wilhelm 10.00 25.00
778 Albury/Dempsey/Strickland RC 8.00 20.00
779 Tony Cloninger 5.00 12.00
780 Dick Green 5.00 12.00
781 Jim McAndrew 5.00 12.00
782 Larry Stahl 5.00 12.00
783 Les Cain 5.00 12.00
784 Ken Aspromonte 5.00 12.00
785 Vic Davalillo 5.00 12.00
786 Chuck Brinkman 5.00 12.00
787 Ron Reed 6.00 15.00

1972 Topps Candy Lids

A cross in design between the 1970 and the 1973 Topps Candy Lids. These lids do not have borders. Since the lids are unnumbered we have sequenced them alphabetically. Any further information on these lids are appreciated. These have been dated 1972 by Ray Fosse being listed as a member of the Cleveland Indians.

COMPLETE SET 1,250.00 2,500.00
1 Hank Aaron 250.00 500.00
2 Dick Allen 100.00 200.00
3 Carlton Fisk 400.00 800.00
4 Ray Fosse 50.00 100.00
5 Bob Gibson 100.00 200.00
6 Harmon Killebrew 10.00 25.00
7 Greg Luzinski 75.00 150.00
8 Thurman Munson 250.00 500.00
9 Gaylord Perry 100.00 200.00
10 Ellie Rodriguez 50.00 100.00

1972 Topps Posters

This giant (9 7/16" by 18"), full-color series of 24 paper-thin posters was issued as a separate set in 1972. The posters are individually numbered and unlike other Topps posters described in this book, are borderless. They are printed on thin paper and were folded five times to facilitate packaging. These posters were issued in one-poster, ten-cent packs which were issued 24 to a box. The box featured a photo of 1971 NL MVP Joe Torre.

COMPLETE SET (24) 400.00 800.00
WRAPPER (10-CENT)
1 Dave McNally 3.00 8.00
2 Carl Yastrzemski 40.00 80.00
3 Bill Melton 3.00 8.00
4 Ray Fosse 3.00 8.00
5 Mickey Lolich 4.00 10.00
6 Amos Otis 4.00 10.00
7 Tony Oliva 5.00 12.00
8 Vida Blue 4.00 10.00
9 Hank Aaron 50.00 100.00
10 Fergie Jenkins 8.00 20.00
11 Pete Rose 50.00 100.00
12 Willie Davis 4.00 10.00
13 Tom Seaver 40.00 80.00
14 Rick Wise 3.00 8.00
15 Willie Stargell 12.50 40.00
16 Joe Torre 5.00 12.00
17 Willie Mays 50.00 100.00
18 Andy Messersmith 4.00 10.00
19 Wilbur Wood 4.00 10.00
20 Harmon Killebrew 12.50 40.00
21 Billy Williams 12.50 40.00
22 Bud Harrelson 3.00 8.00
23 Roberto Clemente 75.00 150.00
24 Willie McCovey 12.50 40.00

1972 Topps Cloth Test

These "test" issue cards look like 1972 Topps cards except that they are on a "cloth sticker". Each card measures 2 1/2" by 3 1/2". The "cards" in this set are all taken from the third series of the 1972 Topps regular issue. Cards are blank backed and unnumbered. They are listed below in alphabetical order.

COMPLETE SET (33) 500.00 1,000.00
1 Hank Aaron 60.00 120.00
2 Luis Aparicio IA 12.50 40.00
3 Ike Brown 10.00 25.00
4 Johnny Callison 10.00 25.00
5 Checklist 264-319 10.00 25.00
6 Roberto Clemente 100.00 200.00
7 Dave Concepcion 12.50 30.00
8 Ron Cook 10.00 25.00
9 Willie Davis 10.00 25.00
10 Al Fitzmorris 10.00 25.00
11 Bobby Floyd 10.00 25.00
12 Roy Foster 10.00 25.00
13 Jim Fregosi KP 10.00 25.00
14 Danny Frisella IA 10.00 25.00
15 Woody Fryman 10.00 25.00
16 Terry Harmon 10.00 25.00
17 Frank Howard 10.00 25.00
18 Ron Klimkowski 10.00 25.00
19 Joe Lahoud 10.00 25.00
20 Jim Lefebvre 10.00 25.00
21 Elliott Maddox 10.00 25.00
22 Marty Martinez 10.00 25.00
23 Willie McCovey 40.00 80.00
24 Hal McRae 10.00 25.00
25 Syd O'Brien 10.00 25.00
26 Red Sox Team 10.00 25.00
27 Aurelio Rodriguez 10.00 25.00
28 Al Severinsen 10.00 25.00
29 Art Shamsky 10.00 25.00
30 Steve Stone 10.00 25.00
31 Stan Swanson 10.00 25.00
32 Bob Watson 10.00 25.00
33 Roy White 10.00 25.00

1972 Topps Test 53

These "test" issue cards were made to look like 1953 Topps cards as the cards show drawings rather than photos. The card number of the corresponding art from the 1953 Topps set is given in parentheses after the name of the player. For three of the cards in this set the player pictured in the art is not the same player as listed on the card; in these cases the actual player pictured is also listed parenthetically in the checklist below. Each card measures 2 1/2" by 3 1/2". Printing on the back is in blue ink on gray card stock.

COMPLETE SET (8) 600.00 1,200.00
1 Satchell Paige/(53 Topps 220) 125.00 250.00
2 Jackie Robinson/(53 Topps 1) 125.00 250.00
3 Carl Furillo/(53 Topps 272)/(picture actually 60.00
120.00
B
4 Al Rosen/(53 Topps 187)/(picture actually 60.00 120.00
Jim F
5 Hal Newhouser/(53 Topps 228) 75.00 150.00
6 Clyde McCullough/(53 Topps 222)/(picture actuall 40.00
80.00
7 Peanuts Lowrey/(53 Topps 16) 40.00 80.00
8 Johnny Mize/(53 Topps 77) 100.00 200.00

1973 Topps

The cards in this 660-card set measure 2 1/2" by 3 1/2". The 1973 Topps set marked the last year in which Topps marketed baseball cards in consecutive series. The last series (529-660) is more difficult to obtain. In some parts of the country, however, all five series were distributed together. Beginning in 1974, all Topps cards were printed at the same time, thus eliminating the "high number" factor. The set features team leader cards with small individual pictures of the coaching staff members and a larger picture of the manager. The "background" variations below with respect to these leader cards are subtle and are best understood after a side-by-side comparison of the two varieties. An "All-Time Leaders" series (471-478) appeared for the first time in this set. Kid Pictures appeared again for the second year in a row (341-346). Other topical subsets within the set included League Leaders (61-68), Playoffs cards (201-202), World Series cards (203-210), and Rookie Prospects (601-616). For the fourth and final time, cards were issued in ten-card dime packs which were issued 24 packs to a box, in addition, these cards were also released in 54-card rack packs which cost 39 cents upon release. The key Rookie Cards in this set are all in the Rookie Prospect series: Bob Boone, Dwight Evans, and Mike Schmidt.

Card	Low	High
COMPLETE SET (660)	350.00	700.00
COMMON CARD (1-264)	.20	.50
COMMON CARD (265-396)	.30	.75
COMMON CARD (397-528)	.50	1.25
COMMON CARD (529-660)	1.25	3.00
WRAPPER (10-CENT, BAT)	6.00	15.00
WRAPPER (10-CENT)	6.00	15.00
1 Ruth/Aaron/Mays HR	25.00	60.00
2 Rich Hebner	.60	1.50
3 Jim Lonborg	.60	1.50
4 John Milner	.20	.50
5 Ed Brinkman	.20	.50
6 Mac Scarce RC	.20	.50
7 Texas Rangers TC	.75	2.00
8 Tom Hall	.20	.50
9 Johnny Oates	.60	1.50
10 Don Sutton	1.50	4.00
11 Chris Chambliss UER	.60	1.50
12A Don Zimmer MG w/o Ear	1.25	3.00
12B Don Zimmer MG w/Ear	.30	.75
13 George Hendrick	.60	1.50
14 Sonny Siebert	.20	.50
15 Ralph Garr	.60	1.50
16 Steve Braun	.20	.50
17 Fred Gladding	.20	.50
18 Leroy Stanton	.20	.50
19 Tim Foli	.20	.50
20 Stan Bahnsen	.20	.50
21 Randy Hundley	.60	1.50
22 Ted Abernathy	.20	.50
23 Dave Kingman	.60	1.50
24 Al Santorini	.20	.50
25 Roy White	.60	1.50
26 Pittsburgh Pirates TC	.75	2.00
27 Bill Gogolewski	.20	.50
28 Hal McRae	.60	1.50
29 Tony Taylor	.60	1.50
30 Tug McGraw	.60	1.50
31 Buddy Bell RC	1.00	2.50
32 Fred Norman	.20	.50
33 Jim Breazeale RC	.20	.50
34 Pat Dobson	.20	.50
35 Willie Davis	.60	1.50
36 Steve Barber	.20	.50
37 Bill Robinson	.60	1.50
38 Mike Epstein	.20	.50
39 Dave Roberts	.20	.50
40 Reggie Smith	.60	1.50
41 Tom Walker RC	.20	.50
42 Mike Andrews	.20	.50
43 Randy Moffitt RC	.20	.50
44 Rick Monday	.60	1.50
45 Ellie Rodriguez UER	.20	.50
46 Lindy McDaniel	.60	1.50
47 Luis Melendez	.20	.50
48 Paul Splittorff	.20	.50
49A Frank Quilici MG Solid	1.25	3.00
49B Frank Quilici MG Natural	.30	.75
50 Roberto Clemente	25.00	60.00
51 Chuck Seelbach RC	.20	.50
52 Denis Menke	.20	.50
53 Steve Dunning	.20	.50
54 Checklist 1-132	1.25	3.00
55 Jon Matlack	.60	1.50
56 Merv Rettenmund	.20	.50
57 Derrel Thomas	.20	.50
58 Mike Paul	.20	.50
59 Steve Yeager RC	.60	1.50
60 Ken Holtzman	.60	1.50
61 B.Williams/R.Carew LL	1.00	2.50
62 J.Bench/D.Allen LL	1.00	2.50
63 J.Bench/D.Allen LL	1.00	2.50
64 L.Brock/Campaneris LL	.60	1.50
65 S.Carlton/L.Tiant LL	.60	1.50
66 Carlton/Perry/Wood LL	.60	1.50
67 S.Carlton/N.Ryan LL	5.00	12.00
68 C.Carroll/S.Lyle LL	.60	1.50
69 Phil Gagliano	.20	.50
70 Milt Pappas	.60	1.50
71 Johnny Briggs	.20	.50
72 Ron Reed	.20	.50
73 Ed Herrmann	.20	.50
74 Billy Champion	.20	.50
75 Vada Pinson	.60	1.50
76 Doug Rader	.20	.50
77 Mike Torrez	.60	1.50
78 Richie Scheinblum	.20	.50
79 Jim Willoughby RC	.20	.50
80 Tony Oliva UER	1.00	2.50
81A W.Lockman MG w/Banks Solid	.60	1.50
81B W.Lockman MG w/Banks Natural	.60	1.50
82 Fritz Peterson	.20	.50
83 Leron Lee	.20	.50
84 Rollie Fingers	1.50	4.00
85 Ted Simmons	.60	1.50
86 Tom McCraw	.20	.50
87 Ken Boswell	.20	.50
88 Mickey Stanley	.60	1.50
89 Jack Billingham	.20	.50
90 Brooks Robinson	3.00	8.00
91 Los Angeles Dodgers TC	.75	2.00
92 Jerry Bell	.20	.50
93 Jesus Alou	.20	.50
94 Dick Billings	.20	.50
95 Steve Blass	.60	1.50
96 Doug Griffin	.20	.50
97 Willie Montanez	.60	1.50
98 Dick Woodson	.20	.50
99 Carl Taylor	.20	.50
100 Hank Aaron	20.00	50.00
101 Ken Henderson	.20	.50
102 Rudy May	.20	.50
103 Celerino Sanchez RC	.20	.50
104 Reggie Cleveland	.20	.50
105 Carlos May	.20	.50
106 Terry Humphrey	.20	.50
107 Phil Hennigan	.20	.50
108 Bill Russell	.60	1.50
109 Doyle Alexander	.60	1.50
110 Bob Watson	.60	1.50
111 Dave Nelson	.20	.50
112 Gary Ross	.20	.50
113 Jerry Grote	.60	1.50
114 Lynn McGlothen RC	.20	.50
115 Ron Santo	.60	1.50
116A Ralph Houk MG Solid	1.25	3.00
116B Ralph Houk MG Natural	.30	.75
117 Ramon Hernandez	.20	.50
118 John Mayberry	.60	1.50
119 Larry Bowa	.60	1.50
120 Joe Coleman	.20	.50
121 Dave Rader	.20	.50
122 Jim Strickland	.20	.50
123 Sandy Alomar	.60	1.50
124 Jim Hardin	.20	.50
125 Ron Fairly	.60	1.50
126 Jim Brewer	.20	.50
127 Milwaukee Brewers TC	.75	2.00
128 Ted Sizemore	.20	.50
129 Terry Forster	.60	1.50
130 Pete Rose	12.00	30.00
131A Eddie Kasko MG w/oEar	1.25	3.00
131B Eddie Kasko MG w/Ear	.60	1.50
132 Matty Alou	.60	1.50
133 Dave Roberts RC	.20	.50
134 Milt Wilcox	.20	.50
135 Lee May UER	.60	1.50
136A Earl Weaver MG Orange	.60	1.50
136B Earl Weaver MG Pale	1.25	3.00
137 Jim Beauchamp	.20	.50
138 Horacio Pina	.20	.50
139 Carmen Fanzone RC	.20	.50
140 Lou Piniella	1.00	2.50
141 Bruce Kison	.20	.50
142 Thurman Munson	10.00	25.00
143 John Curtis	.20	.50
144 Marty Perez	.20	.50
145 Bobby Bonds	1.00	2.50
146 Woodie Fryman	.20	.50
147 Mike Anderson	.20	.50
148 Dave Goltz	.20	.50
149 Ron Hunt	.20	.50
150 Wilbur Wood	.60	1.50
151 Wes Parker	.60	1.50
152 Dave May	.20	.50
153 Al Hrabosky	.60	1.50
154 Jeff Torborg	.60	1.50
155 Sal Bando	.60	1.50
156 Cesar Geronimo	.20	.50
157 Denny Riddleberger	.20	.50
158 Houston Astros TC	.75	2.00
159 Clarence Gaston	.60	1.50
160 Jim Palmer	2.50	6.00
161 Ted Martinez	.20	.50
162 Pete Broberg	.20	.50
163 Vic Davalillo	.20	.50
164 Monty Montgomery	.20	.50
165 Luis Aparicio	1.50	4.00
166 Terry Harmon	.20	.50
167 Steve Stone	.60	1.50
168 Jim Northrup	.60	1.50
169 Ron Schueler RC	.60	1.50
170 Harmon Killebrew	6.00	15.00
171 Bernie Carbo	.20	.50
172 Steve Kline	.20	.50
173 Hal Breeden	.20	.50
174 Goose Gossage RC	15.00	40.00
175 Frank Robinson	8.00	20.00
176 Chuck Taylor	.20	.50
177 Bill Plummer RC	.20	.50
178 Don Rose RC	.20	.50
179A Dick Williams w/Ear	1.50	4.00
179B Dick Williams w/o Ear	.60	1.50
180 Ferguson Jenkins	1.50	4.00
181 Jack Brohamer RC	.20	.50
182 Mike Caldwell RC	.60	1.50
183 Don Buford	.20	.50
184 Jerry Koosman	.60	1.50
185 Jim Wynn	.60	1.50
186 Bill Fahey	.20	.50
187 Luke Walker	.20	.50
188 Cookie Rojas	.60	1.50
189 Greg Luzinski	1.00	2.50
190 Bob Gibson	8.00	20.00
191 Detroit Tigers TC	1.00	2.50
192 Pat Jarvis	.20	.50
193 Carlton Fisk	10.00	25.00
194 Jorge Orta RC	.20	.50
195 Clay Carroll	.20	.50
196 Ken McMullen	.20	.50
197 Ed Goodson RC	.20	.50
198 Horace Clarke	.20	.50
199 Bert Blyleven	1.00	2.50
200 Billy Williams	1.50	4.00
201 George Hendrick ALCS	.60	1.50
202 George Foster NLCS	.60	1.50
203 Gene Tenace WS	.60	1.50
204 A's Two Straight WS	.60	1.50
205 Tony Perez WS	1.00	2.50
206 Gene Tenace WS	.60	1.50
207 Blue Moon Odom WS	.60	1.50
208 Johnny Bench WS	2.00	5.00
209 Bert Campaneris WS	.60	1.50
210 A's Win WS	.20	.50
211 Balor Moore	.20	.50
212 Joe Lahoud	.20	.50
213 Steve Garvey	2.00	5.00
214 Dave Hamilton RC	.20	.50
215 Dusty Baker	1.00	2.50
216 Toby Harrah	.60	1.50
217 Don Wilson	.20	.50
218 Aurelio Rodriguez	.20	.50
219 St. Louis Cardinals TC	1.00	2.50
220 Nolan Ryan	15.00	40.00
221 Fred Kendall	.20	.50
222 Rob Gardner	.20	.50
223 Bud Harrelson	.60	1.50
224 Bill Lee	.60	1.50
225 Al Oliver	.60	1.50
226 Ray Fosse	.20	.50
227 Wayne Twitchell	.20	.50
228 Bobby Darwin	.20	.50
229 Roric Harrison	.20	.50
230 Joe Morgan	8.00	20.00
231 Bill Parsons	.20	.50
232 Ken Singleton	.60	1.50
233 Ed Kirkpatrick	.20	.50
234 Bill North RC	.20	.50
235 Jim Hunter	1.50	4.00
236 Tito Fuentes	.20	.50
237A Eddie Mathews MG w/Ear	.60	1.50
237B Eddie Mathews MG w/o Ear	1.25	3.00
238 Tony Muser RC	.20	.50
239 Pete Richert	.20	.50
240 Bobby Murcer	.60	1.50
241 Dwain Anderson	.20	.50
242 George Culver	.20	.50
243 California Angels TC	1.00	2.50
244 Ed Acosta	.20	.50
245 Carl Yastrzemski	10.00	25.00
246 Ken Sanders	.20	.50
247 Del Unser	.20	.50
248 Jerry Johnson	.20	.50
249 Larry Biittner	.20	.50
250 Manny Sanguillen	.60	1.50
251 Roger Nelson	.20	.50
252A Charlie Fox MG Orange	1.50	4.00
252B Charlie Fox MG Pale	.60	1.50
253 Mark Belanger	.60	1.50
254 Bill Stoneman	.20	.50
255 Reggie Jackson	8.00	20.00
256 Chris Zachary	.20	.50
257A Yogi Berra MG Orange	1.25	3.00
257B Yogi Berra MG Pale	2.00	5.00
258 Tommy John	.60	1.50
259 Jim Holt	.20	.50
260 Gary Nolan	.60	1.50
261 Pat Kelly	.20	.50
262 Jack Aker	.20	.50
263 George Scott	.60	1.50
264 Checklist 133-264	1.25	3.00
265 Gene Michael	.60	1.50
266 Mike Lum	.30	.75
267 Lloyd Allen	.30	.75
268 Jerry Morales	.30	.75
269 Tim McCarver	.60	1.50
270 Luis Tiant	.60	1.50
271 Tom Hutton	.30	.75
272 Ed Farmer	.30	.75
273 Chris Speier	.30	.75
274 Darold Knowles	.30	.75
275 Tony Perez	1.50	4.00
276 Joe Lovitto RC	.30	.75
277 Bob Miller	.30	.75
278 Baltimore Orioles TC	.60	1.50
279 Mike Strahler	.30	.75
280 Al Kaline	6.00	15.00
281 Mike Jorgensen	.30	.75
282 Steve Hovley	.30	.75
283 Ray Sadecki	.30	.75
284 Glenn Borgmann RC	.30	.75
285 Don Kessinger	.60	1.50
286 Frank Linzy	.30	.75
287 Eddie Leon	.30	.75
288 Gary Gentry	.30	.75
289 Bob Oliver	.30	.75
290 Cesar Cedeno	.60	1.50
291 Rogelio Moret	.30	.75
292 Jose Cruz	.60	1.50
293 Bernie Allen	.30	.75
294 Steve Arlin	.30	.75
295 Bert Campaneris	.60	1.50
296 Sparky Anderson MG	1.00	2.50
297 Walt Williams	.30	.75
298 Ron Bryant	.30	.75
299 Ted Ford	.30	.75
300 Steve Carlton	6.00	15.00
301 Billy Grabarkewitz	.30	.75
302 Terry Crowley	.30	.75
303 Nelson Briles	.30	.75
304 Duke Sims	.30	.75
305 Willie Mays	20.00	50.00
306 Tom Burgmeier	.30	.75
307 Boots Day	.30	.75
308 Skip Lockwood	.30	.75
309 Paul Popovich	.30	.75
310 Dick Allen	.60	1.50
311 Joe Decker	.30	.75
312 Oscar Brown	.30	.75
313 Jim Ray	.30	.75
314 Ron Swoboda	.60	1.50
315 John Odom	.30	.75
316 San Diego Padres TC	.60	1.50
317 Danny Cater	.30	.75
318 Jim McGlothlin	.30	.75
319 Jim Spencer	.30	.75
320 Lou Brock	3.00	8.00
321 Rich Hinton	.30	.75
322 Garry Maddox RC	.60	1.50
323 Billy Martin MG	.60	1.50
324 Al Downing	.30	.75
325 Boog Powell	.60	1.50
326 Darrell Brandon	.30	.75
327 John Lowenstein	.30	.75
328 Bill Bonham	.30	.75
329 Ed Kranepool	.60	1.50
330 Rod Carew	3.00	8.00
331 Carl Morton	.30	.75
332 John Felske RC	.30	.75
333 Gene Clines	.30	.75
334 Freddie Patek	.30	.75
335 Bob Tolan	.30	.75
336 Tom Bradley	.30	.75
337 Dave Duncan	.60	1.50
338 Checklist 265-396	1.25	3.00
339 Dick Tidrow	.30	.75
340 Nate Colbert	.30	.75
341 Jim Palmer KP	1.00	2.50
342 Sam McDowell KP	.30	.75
343 Bobby Murcer KP	.30	.75
344 Jim Hunter KP	1.00	2.50
345 Chris Speier KP	.30	.75
346 Gaylord Perry KP	.60	1.50
347 Kansas City Royals TC	.60	1.50
348 Rennie Stennett	.30	.75
349 Dick McAuliffe	.30	.75
350 Tom Seaver	10.00	25.00
351 Jimmy Stewart	.30	.75
352 Don Stanhouse RC	.30	.75
353 Steve Brye	.30	.75
354 Billy Parker	.30	.75
355 Mike Marshall	.60	1.50
356 Chuck Tanner MG	1.50	4.00
357 Ross Grimsley	.30	.75
358 Jim Nettles	.30	.75
359 Cecil Upshaw	.30	.75
360 Joe Rudi UER	.60	1.50
361 Fran Healy	.30	.75
362 Eddie Watt	.30	.75
363 Jackie Hernandez	.30	.75
364 Rick Wise	.30	.75
365 Rico Petrocelli	.60	1.50
366 Brock Davis	.30	.75
367 Burt Hooton	.60	1.50
368 Bill Buckner	.60	1.50
369 Lerrin LaGrow	.30	.75
370 Willie Stargell	2.00	5.00
371 Mike Kekich	.30	.75
372 Oscar Gamble	.30	.75
373 Clyde Wright	.30	.75
374 Darrell Evans	.60	1.50
375 Larry Dierker	.60	1.50
376 Frank Duffy	.30	.75
377 Gene Mauch MG	1.50	4.00
378 Len Randle	.30	.75
379 Cy Acosta RC	.30	.75
380 Johnny Bench	10.00	25.00
381 Vicente Romo	.30	.75
382 Mike Hegan	.30	.75
383 Diego Segui	.30	.75
384 Don Baylor	1.50	4.00
385 Jim Perry	.60	1.50
386 Don Money	.30	.75
387 Jim Barr	.30	.75
388 Ben Oglivie	.60	1.50
389 New York Mets TC	1.50	4.00
390 Mickey Lolich	.60	1.50
391 Lee Lacy RC	.60	1.50
392 Dick Drago	.30	.75
393 Jose Cardenal	.30	.75
394 Sparky Lyle	.60	1.50
395 Roger Metzger	.30	.75
396 Grant Jackson	.30	.75
397 Dave Cash	.50	1.25
398 Rich Hand	.50	1.25
399 George Foster	.75	2.00
400 Gaylord Perry	2.00	5.00
401 Clyde Mashore	.50	1.25
402 Jack Hiatt	.50	1.25
403 Sonny Jackson	.50	1.25
404 Chuck Brinkman	.50	1.25
405 Cesar Tovar	.50	1.25
406 Paul Lindblad	.50	1.25
407 Felix Millan	.50	1.25
408 Jim Colborn	.50	1.25
409 Ivan Murrell	.50	1.25
410 Willie McCovey	2.50	6.00
411 Ray Corbin	.50	1.25
412 Manny Mota	.75	2.00
413 Tom Timmermann	.50	1.25
414 Ken Rudolph	.50	1.25
415 Marty Pattin	.50	1.25
416 Paul Schaal	.50	1.25
417 Scipio Spinks	.50	1.25
418 Bob Grich	.75	2.00
419 Casey Cox	.50	1.25
420 Tommie Agee	.50	1.25
421A B.Winkles MG RC Orange	.60	1.50
421B Bobby Winkles MG Pale	1.25	3.00
422 Bob Robertson	.50	1.25
423 Johnny Jeter	.50	1.25
424 Denny Doyle	.50	1.25
425 Alex Johnson	.50	1.25
426 Dave LaRoche	.50	1.25
427 Rick Auerbach	.50	1.25
428 Wayne Simpson	.50	1.25
429 Jim Fairey	.50	1.25
430 Vida Blue	.75	2.00
431 Gerry Moses	.50	1.25
432 Dan Frisella	.50	1.25
433 Willie Horton	.75	2.00
434 San Francisco Giants TC	1.25	3.00
435 Rico Carty	.75	2.00
436 Jim McAndrew	.50	1.25
437 John Kennedy	.50	1.25
438 Enzo Hernandez	.50	1.25
439 Eddie Fisher	.50	1.25
440 Glenn Beckert	.50	1.25
441 Gail Hopkins	.50	1.25
442 Dick Dietz	.50	1.25

Card	Low	High
443 Danny Thompson	.50	1.25
444 Ken Brett	.50	1.25
445 Ken Berry	.50	1.25
446 Jerry Reuss	.75	2.00
447 Joe Hague	.50	1.25
448 John Hiller	.50	1.25
449A K.Aspro MG w/Spahn Point	1.50	4.00
449B K.Aspro MG w/Spahn Round	1.50	4.00
450 Joe Torre	1.25	3.00
451 John Vukovich RC	.50	1.25
452 Paul Casanova	.50	1.25
453 Checklist 397-528	1.25	3.00
454 Tom Haller	.50	1.25
455 Bill Melton	.50	1.25
456 Dick Green	.50	1.25
457 John Strohmayer	.50	1.25
458 Jim Mason	.50	1.25
459 Jimmy Howarth RC	.50	1.25
460 Bill Freehan	.75	2.00
461 Mike Corkins	.50	1.25
462 Ron Blomberg	.50	1.25
463 Ken Tatum	.50	1.25
464 Chicago Cubs TC	1.25	3.00
465 Dave Giusti	.50	1.25
466 Jose Arcia	.50	1.25
467 Mike Ryan	.50	1.25
468 Tom Griffin	.50	1.25
469 Dan Monzon RC	.50	1.25
470 Mike Cuellar	.75	2.00
471 Ty Cobb LDR	4.00	10.00
472 Lou Gehrig LDR	6.00	15.00
473 Hank Aaron LDR	8.00	20.00
474 Babe Ruth LDR	8.00	20.00
475 Ty Cobb LDR	6.00	15.00
476 Walter Johnson LDR	1.25	3.00
477 Cy Young LDR	1.25	3.00
478 Walter Johnson LDR	1.25	3.00
479 Hal Lanier	.50	1.25
480 Juan Marichal	2.00	5.00
481 Chicago White Sox TC	1.25	3.00
482 Rick Reuschel RC	1.25	3.00
483 Dal Maxvill	.50	1.25
484 Ernie McAnally	.50	1.25
485 Norm Cash	.75	2.00
486A D.Ozark MG RC Orange	.60	1.50
486B Danny Ozark MG Pale	1.25	3.00
487 Bruce Dal Canton	.50	1.25
488 Dave Campbell	.75	2.00
489 Jeff Burroughs	.75	2.00
490 Claude Osteen	.75	2.00
491 Bob Montgomery	.50	1.25
492 Pedro Borbon	.50	1.25
493 Duffy Dyer	.50	1.25
494 Rich Morales	.50	1.25
495 Tommy Helms	.50	1.25
496 Ray Lamb	.50	1.25
497A R.Schoen MG Orange	.75	2.00
497B R.Schoen MG Pale	1.25	3.00
498 Graig Nettles	1.25	3.00
499 Bob Moose	.50	1.25
500 Oakland Athletics TC	1.25	3.00
501 Larry Gura	.50	1.25
502 Bobby Valentine	1.25	3.00
503 Phil Niekro	2.00	5.00
504 Earl Williams	.50	1.25
505 Bob Bailey	.50	1.25
506 Bart Johnson	.50	1.25
507 Darrel Chaney	.50	1.25
508 Gates Brown	.50	1.25
509 Jim Nash	.50	1.25
510 Amos Otis	.75	2.00
511 Sam McDowell	.75	2.00
512 Dalton Jones	.50	1.25
513 Dave Marshall	.50	1.25
514 Jerry Kenney	.50	1.25
515 Andy Messersmith	.75	2.00
516 Danny Walton	.50	1.25
517A Bill Virdon MG w/o Ear	.60	1.50
517B Bill Virdon MG w/Ear	1.25	3.00
518 Bob Veale	.50	1.25
519 Johnny Edwards	.50	1.25
520 Mel Stottlemyre	.75	2.00
521 Atlanta Braves TC	1.25	3.00
522 Leo Cardenas	.50	1.25
523 Wayne Granger	.50	1.25
524 Gene Tenace	.75	2.00
525 Jim Fregosi	.75	2.00
526 Ollie Brown	.50	1.25
527 Dan McGinn	.50	1.25
528 Paul Blair	.50	1.25
529 Milt May	1.25	3.00
530 Jim Kaat	2.00	5.00
531 Ron Woods	1.25	3.00
532 Steve Mingori	1.25	3.00
533 Larry Stahl	1.25	3.00
534 Dave Lemonds	1.25	3.00
535 Johnny Callison	2.00	5.00
536 Philadelphia Phillies TC	2.50	6.00
537 Bill Slayback RC	1.25	3.00
538 Jim Ray Hart	2.00	5.00
539 Tom Murphy	1.25	3.00
540 Cleon Jones	2.00	5.00
541 Bob Bolin	1.25	3.00
542 Pat Corrales	2.00	5.00
543 Alan Foster	1.25	3.00
544 Von Joshua	1.25	3.00
545 Orlando Cepeda	3.00	8.00
546 Jim York	1.25	3.00
547 Bobby Heise	1.25	3.00
548 Don Durham RC	1.25	3.00
549 Whitey Herzog MG	2.00	5.00
550 Dave Johnson	2.00	5.00
551 Mike Kilkenny	1.25	3.00
552 J.C. Martin	1.25	3.00
553 Mickey Scott	1.25	3.00
554 Dave Concepcion	2.00	5.00
555 Bill Hands	1.25	3.00
556 New York Yankees TC	3.00	8.00
557 Bernie Williams	1.25	3.00
558 Jerry May	1.25	3.00
559 Barry Lersch	1.25	3.00
560 Frank Howard	2.00	5.00
561 Jim Geddes RC	1.25	3.00
562 Wayne Garrett	1.25	3.00
563 Larry Haney	1.25	3.00
564 Mike Thompson RC	1.25	3.00
565 Jim Hickman	1.25	3.00
566 Lew Krausse	1.25	3.00
567 Bob Fenwick	1.25	3.00
568 Ray Newman	1.25	3.00
569 Walt Alston MG	3.00	8.00
570 Bill Singer	2.00	5.00
571 Rusty Torres	1.25	3.00
572 Gary Sutherland	1.25	3.00
573 Fred Beene	1.25	3.00
574 Bob Didier	1.25	3.00
575 Dock Ellis	1.25	3.00
576 Montreal Expos TC	2.50	6.00
577 Eric Soderholm RC	1.25	3.00
578 Ken Wright	1.25	3.00
579 Tom Grieve	2.00	5.00
580 Joe Pepitone	2.00	5.00
581 Steve Kealey	1.25	3.00
582 Darrell Porter	2.00	5.00
583 Bill Greif	1.25	3.00
584 Chris Arnold	1.25	3.00
585 Joe Niekro	2.00	5.00
586 Bill Sudakis	1.25	3.00
587 Rich McKinney	1.25	3.00
588 Checklist 529-660	8.00	20.00
589 Ken Forsch	1.25	3.00
590 Deron Johnson	1.25	3.00
591 Mike Hedlund	1.25	3.00
592 John Boccabella	1.25	3.00
593 Jack McKeon MG RC	1.50	4.00
594 Vic Harris RC	1.25	3.00
595 Don Gullett	2.00	5.00
596 Boston Red Sox TC	2.50	6.00
597 Mickey Rivers	2.00	5.00
598 Phil Roof	1.25	3.00
599 Ed Crosby	1.25	3.00
600 Dave McNally	2.00	5.00
601 Robles/Pena/Stelmaszek RC	2.00	5.00
602 Behney/Garcia/Rau RC	2.00	5.00
603 Hughes/McNulty/Reitz RC	2.00	5.00
604 Jefferson/O'Toole/Stampe RC	2.00	5.00
605 Cabell/Bourque/Marquez RC	2.00	5.00
606 Matthews/Pac/Roque RC	2.00	5.00
607 Frias/Busse/Guerrero RC	2.00	5.00
608 Busby/Colpaert/Medich RC	2.00	5.00
609 Blanks/Garcia/Lopes RC	2.00	5.00
610 Freeman/Hough/Webb RC	2.00	5.00
611 Coggins/Wohlford/Zisk RC	2.00	5.00
612 Lawson/Reynolds/Strom RC	2.00	5.00
613 Boone/Jutze/Ivie RC	6.00	15.00
614 Bumbry/Evans/Spikes RC	10.00	25.00
615 Mike Schmidt RC	75.00	200.00
616 Angelini/Blateric/Garman RC	2.00	5.00
617 Rich Chiles	1.25	3.00
618 Andy Etchebarren	1.25	3.00
619 Billy Wilson	1.25	3.00
620 Tommy Harper	2.00	5.00
621 Joe Ferguson	2.00	5.00
622 Larry Hisle	2.00	5.00
623 Steve Renko	1.25	3.00
624 Leo Durocher MG	2.00	5.00
625 Angel Mangual	1.25	3.00
626 Bob Barton	1.25	3.00
627 Luis Alvarado	1.25	3.00
628 Jim Slaton	1.25	3.00
629 Cleveland Indians TC	2.50	6.00
630 Denny McLain	3.00	8.00
631 Tom Matchick	1.25	3.00
632 Dick Selma	1.25	3.00
633 Ike Brown	1.25	3.00
634 Alan Closter	1.25	3.00
635 Gene Alley	2.00	5.00
636 Rickey Clark	1.25	3.00
637 Norm Miller	1.25	3.00
638 Ken Reynolds	1.25	3.00
639 Willie Crawford	1.25	3.00
640 Dick Bosman	1.25	3.00
641 Cincinnati Reds TC	2.50	6.00
642 Jose Laboy	1.25	3.00
643 Al Fitzmorris	1.25	3.00
644 Jack Heidemann	1.25	3.00
645 Bob Locker	1.25	3.00
646 Del Crandall MG	1.50	4.00
647 George Stone	1.25	3.00
648 Tom Egan	1.25	3.00
649 Rich Folkers	1.25	3.00
650 Felipe Alou	2.00	5.00
651 Don Carrithers	1.25	3.00
652 Ted Kubiak	1.25	3.00
653 Joe Hoerner	1.25	3.00
654 Minnesota Twins TC	2.50	6.00
655 Clay Kirby	1.25	3.00
656 John Ellis	1.25	3.00
657 Bob Johnson	1.25	3.00
658 Elliott Maddox	1.25	3.00
659 Jose Pagan	1.25	3.00
660 Fred Scherman	2.00	5.00

1973 Topps Blue Team Checklists

This 24-card standard-size set is rather difficult to find. These blue-bordered team checklist cards are very similar in design to the mass produced red trim team checklist cards issued by Topps the next year. Reportedly these were inserts only found in the test packs that included all series. In addition, a collector could mail in 25 cents and receive a full uncut sheet of these cards. This offer was somewhat limited in terms of collectors mailing in for them.

Card	Low	High
COMPLETE SET (24)	75.00	150.00
COMMON TEAM (1-24)	3.00	8.00
16 New York Mets	4.00	10.00
17 New York Yankees	4.00	10.00

1973 Topps Pin-Ups

This test issue of 24 pin-ups is quite scarce. Each pin-up measures approximately 3 7/16" by 4 5/8" and is very colorful with a thick white border. The thin-paper pin-ups contain a facsimile autograph on the front of the card. The set shares the same checklist with the 1973 Topps Comics. The set is unnumbered and hence is ordered below alphabetically. The team insignia and logos on the cards have been airbrushed away, which is contra-indicative of a Topps issue.

Card	Low	High
COMPLETE SET (24)	4,000.00	8,000.00
1 Hank Aaron	400.00	800.00
2 Dick Allen	100.00	200.00
3 Johnny Bench	300.00	600.00
4 Steve Carlton	300.00	600.00
5 Nate Colbert	75.00	150.00
6 Willie Davis	75.00	150.00
7 Mike Epstein	75.00	150.00
8 Reggie Jackson	400.00	800.00
9 Harmon Killebrew	200.00	400.00
10 Mickey Lolich	100.00	200.00
11 Mike Marshall	75.00	150.00
12 Lee May	75.00	150.00
13 Willie McCovey	200.00	400.00
14 Bobby Murcer	100.00	200.00
15 Gaylord Perry	200.00	400.00
16 Lou Piniella	100.00	200.00
17 Brooks Robinson	300.00	600.00
18 Nolan Ryan	600.00	1,200.00
19 George Scott	75.00	150.00
20 Tom Seaver	400.00	800.00
21 Willie Stargell	200.00	400.00
22 Joe Torre	150.00	300.00
23 Billy Williams	200.00	400.00
24 Carl Yastrzemski	250.00	500.00

1973 Topps Candy Lids

One of Topps' most unusual test sets is this series of 55 color portraits of baseball players printed on the bottom of candy lids. These lids measure 1 7/8" in diameter. The product was called "Baseball Stars Bubble Gum" and consisted of a small tub of candy-coated gum kernels. The lids were issued in 10 cent containers which came 24 to a box. Issued in 1973, the lids are unnumbered and each has a small tab. Underneath the picture is a small ribbon design which contains the player's name, team and position. It is believed that this set was mainly tested on the east coast with some light testing in the midwest.

Card	Low	High
COMPLETE SET (55)	400.00	800.00
1 Hank Aaron	20.00	50.00
2 Dick Allen	2.00	5.00
3 Dusty Baker	2.00	5.00
4 Sal Bando	1.50	4.00
5 Johnny Bench	12.50	30.00
6 Bobby Bonds	2.00	5.00
7 Dick Bosman	1.50	4.00
8 Lou Brock	8.00	20.00
9 Rod Carew	8.00	20.00
10 Steve Carlton	8.00	20.00
11 Nate Colbert	1.50	4.00
12 Willie Davis	1.50	4.00
13 Larry Dierker	1.50	4.00
14 Mike Epstein	1.50	4.00
15 Carlton Fisk	12.50	40.00
16 Tim Foli	1.50	4.00
17 Ray Fosse	1.50	4.00
18 Bill Freehan	2.00	5.00
19 Bob Gibson	8.00	20.00
20 Bud Harrelson	1.50	4.00
21 Jim Hunter	5.00	12.00
22 Reggie Jackson	12.50	30.00
23 Ferguson Jenkins	5.00	12.00
24 Al Kaline	8.00	20.00
25 Harmon Killebrew	8.00	20.00
26 Clay Kirby	1.50	4.00
27 Mickey Lolich	2.00	5.00
28 Greg Luzinski	2.00	5.00
29 Willie McCovey	8.00	20.00
30 Mike Marshall	1.50	4.00
31 Lee May	1.50	4.00
32 John Mayberry	1.50	4.00
33 Willie Mays	20.00	50.00
34 Thurman Munson	5.00	12.00
35 Bobby Murcer	2.00	5.00
36 Gary Nolan	1.50	4.00
37 Amos Otis	1.50	4.00
38 Jim Palmer	8.00	20.00
39 Gaylord Perry	5.00	12.00
40 Lou Piniella	2.00	5.00
41 Brooks Robinson	8.00	20.00
42 Frank Robinson	8.00	20.00
43 Ellie Rodriguez	1.50	4.00
44 Pete Rose	20.00	50.00
45 Nolan Ryan	60.00	120.00
46 Manny Sanguillen	1.50	4.00
47 George Scott	1.50	4.00
48 Tom Seaver	12.50	30.00
49 Chris Speier	1.50	4.00
50 Willie Stargell	8.00	20.00
51 Don Sutton	5.00	12.00
52 Joe Torre	3.00	8.00
53 Billy Williams	5.00	12.00
54 Wilbur Wood	1.50	4.00
55 Carl Yastrzemski	12.50	30.00

1973 Topps Comics

This test issue of 24 comics is quite scarce. Each comic measures approximately 4 5/8" by 3 7/16" and is very colorful. The comics are subtitled "Career Highlights of ..." and feature six or seven panels of information about the particular player. The set shares the same checklist with the 1973 Topps Pin-Ups. The set is unnumbered and hence is ordered below alphabetically. The team insignia and logos on the cards have been airbrushed away, which is contra-indicative of a Topps issue.

Card	Low	High
COMPLETE SET (24)	1,500.00	3,000.00
1 Hank Aaron	300.00	600.00
2 Dick Allen	150.00	300.00
3 Johnny Bench	300.00	600.00
4 Steve Carlton	75.00	150.00
5 Nate Colbert	100.00	200.00
6 Willie Davis	100.00	200.00
7 Mike Epstein	125.00	250.00
8 Reggie Jackson	400.00	800.00
9 Harmon Killebrew	200.00	400.00
10 Mickey Lolich	125.00	250.00
11 Mike Marshall	100.00	200.00
12 Lee May	125.00	250.00
13 Willie McCovey	200.00	400.00
14 Bobby Murcer	125.00	250.00
15 Gaylord Perry	200.00	400.00
16 Lou Piniella	125.00	250.00
17 Brooks Robinson	250.00	500.00
18 Nolan Ryan	1,000.00	2,000.00
19 George Scott	100.00	200.00
20 Tom Seaver	300.00	600.00
21 Willie Stargell	200.00	400.00
22 Joe Torre	150.00	300.00
23 Billy Williams	200.00	400.00
24 Carl Yastrzemski	400.00	800.00

1974 Topps

The cards in this 660-card set measure 2 1/2" by 3 1/2". This year marked the first time Topps issued all the cards of its baseball set at the same time rather than in series. Among other methods, cards were issued in eight-card fifteen-cent wax packs and 42 card rack packs. The ten cent packs were issued 36 to a box. For the first time, factory sets were issued through the JC Penny's catalog. Sales were probably disappointing for it would be several years before factory sets were issued again. Some interesting variations were created by the rumored move of the San Diego Padres to Washington. Fifteen cards (13 players, the team card, and the rookie card (599) of the Padres were printed either as "San Diego" (SD) or "Washington." The latter are the scarcer variety and are denoted in the checklist below by WAS. Each team's manager and his coaches again have a combined card with small pictures of each coach below the larger photo of the team's manager. The first six cards in the set (1-6) feature Hank Aaron and his illustrious career. Other topical subsets included in the set are League Leaders (201-208), All-Star selections (331-339), Playoffs cards (470-471), World Series cards (472-479), and Rookie Prospects (596-608). The card backs for the All-Stars (331-339) have no statistics, but form a picture puzzle of Bobby Bonds, the 1973 All-Star Game MVP. The key Rookie Cards in this set are Ken Griffey Sr., Dave Parker and Dave Winfield.

Card	Low	High
COMPLETE SET (660)	200.00	400.00
COMP.FACT.SET (660)	300.00	600.00
WRAPPERS (10-CENTS)	4.00	10.00
1 Hank Aaron 715	15.00	40.00
2 Hank Aaron 54-57	5.00	12.00
3 Hank Aaron 58-61	5.00	12.00
4 Hank Aaron 62-65	5.00	12.00
5 Hank Aaron 66-69	5.00	12.00
6 Hank Aaron 70-73	5.00	12.00
7 Jim Hunter	1.50	4.00
8 George Theodore RC	.20	.50
9 Mickey Lolich	.40	1.00
10 Johnny Bench	8.00	20.00
11 Jim Bibby	.20	.50
12 Dave May	.20	.50
13 Tom Hilgendorf	.20	.50
14 Paul Popovich	.20	.50
15 Joe Torre	.75	2.00
16 Baltimore Orioles TC	.40	1.00
17 Doug Bird RC	.20	.50
18 Gary Thomasson RC	.20	.50
19 Gerry Moses	.20	.50
20 Nolan Ryan	12.00	30.00
21 Bob Gallagher RC	.20	.50
22 Cy Acosta	.20	.50
23 Craig Robinson RC	.20	.50
24 John Hiller	.40	1.00
25 Ken Singleton	.40	1.00
26 Bill Campbell RC	.20	.50
27 George Scott	.40	1.00
28 Manny Sanguillen	.40	1.00
29 Phil Niekro	1.25	3.00
30 Bobby Bonds	.75	2.00
31 Preston Gomez MG	.40	1.00
32A Johnny Grubb SD RC	.40	1.00
32B Johnny Grubb WASH	1.50	4.00

33 Don Newhauser RC .20 .50
34 Andy Kosco .20 .50
35 Gaylord Perry 1.25 3.00
36 St. Louis Cardinals TC .40 1.00
37 Dave Sells RC .20 .50
38 Don Kessinger .40 1.00
39 Ken Suarez .20 .50
40 Jim Palmer 6.00 15.00
41 Bobby Floyd .20 .50
42 Claude Osteen .40 1.00
43 Jim Wynn .40 1.00
44 Mel Stottlemyre .40 1.00
45 Dave Johnson .40 1.00
46 Pat Kelly .20 .50
47 Dick Ruthven RC .20 .50
48 Dick Sharon RC .20 .50
49 Steve Renko .20 .50
50 Rod Carew 3.00 8.00
51 Bobby Heise .20 .50
52 Al Oliver .40 1.00
53A Fred Kendall SD .40 1.00
53B Fred Kendall WASH 1.50 4.00
54 Elias Sosa RC .20 .50
55 Frank Robinson 3.00 8.00
56 New York Mets TC .40 1.00
57 Darold Knowles .20 .50
58 Charlie Spikes .20 .50
59 Ross Grimsley .20 .50
60 Lou Brock 2.50 6.00
61 Luis Aparicio 1.25 3.00
62 Bob Locker .20 .50
63 Bill Sudakis .20 .50
64 Doug Rau .20 .50
65 Amos Otis .40 1.00
66 Sparky Lyle .40 1.00
67 Tommy Helms .20 .50
68 Grant Jackson .20 .50
69 Del Unser .20 .50
70 Dick Allen .75 2.00
71 Dan Frisella .20 .50
72 Aurelio Rodriguez .20 .50
73 Mike Marshall .75 2.00
74 Minnesota Twins TC .40 1.00
75 Jim Colborn .20 .50
76 Mickey Rivers .40 1.00
77A Rich Troedson SD RC .40 1.00
77B Rich Troedson WASH 1.50 4.00
78 Charlie Fox MG .40 1.00
79 Gene Tenace .40 1.00
80 Tom Seaver 10.00 25.00
81 Frank Duffy .20 .50
82 Dave Giusti .20 .50
83 Orlando Cepeda 1.25 3.00
84 Rick Wise .20 .50
85 Joe Morgan 3.00 8.00
86 Joe Ferguson .40 1.00
87 Fergie Jenkins 1.25 3.00
88 Freddie Patek .40 1.00
89 Jackie Brown .20 .50
90 Bobby Murcer .40 1.00
91 Ken Forsch .20 .50
92 Paul Blair .40 1.00
93 Rod Gilbreath RC .20 .50
94 Detroit Tigers TC .40 1.00
95 Steve Carlton 3.00 8.00
96 Jerry Hairston RC .20 .50
97 Bob Bailey .20 .50
98 Bert Blyleven .75 2.00
99 Del Crandall MG .40 1.00
100 Willie Stargell 2.50 6.00
101 Bobby Valentine .40 1.00
102A Bill Greif SD .40 1.00
102B Bill Greif WASH 1.50 4.00
103 Sal Bando .40 1.00
104 Ron Bryant .20 .50
105 Carlton Fisk 5.00 12.00
106 Harry Parker RC .20 .50
107 Alex Johnson .20 .50
108 Al Hrabosky .40 1.00
109 Bob Grich .40 1.00
110 Billy Williams 1.25 3.00
111 Clay Carroll .20 .50
112 Dave Lopes .75 2.00
113 Dick Drago .20 .50
114 California Angels TC .40 1.00
115 Willie Horton .40 1.00
116 Jerry Reuss .40 1.00
117 Ron Blomberg .20 .50
118 Bill Lee .40 1.00
119 Danny Ozark MG .40 1.00
120 Wilbur Wood .20 .50
121 Larry Lintz RC .20 .50
122 Jim Holt .20 .50
123 Nelson Briles .40 1.00
124 Bobby Coluccio RC .20 .50
125A Nate Colbert SD .40 1.00
125B Nate Colbert WASH 1.50 4.00
126 Checklist 1-132 1.25 3.00
127 Tom Paciorek .40 1.00
128 John Ellis .20 .50
129 Chris Speier .20 .50
130 Reggie Jackson 8.00 20.00
131 Bob Boone .75 2.00
132 Felix Millan .20 .50
133 David Clyde RC .40 1.00
134 Denis Menke .20 .50
135 Roy White .40 1.00
136 Rick Reuschel .40 1.00
137 Al Bumbry .40 1.00
138 Eddie Brinkman .20 .50
139 Aurelio Monteagudo .20 .50
140 Darrell Evans .75 2.00
141 Pat Bourque .20 .50
142 Pedro Garcia .20 .50
143 Dick Woodson .20 .50
144 Walter Alston MG 1.25 3.00
145 Dock Ellis .20 .50
146 Ron Fairly .40 1.00
147 Bart Johnson .20 .50
148A Dave Hilton SD .40 1.00
148B Dave Hilton WASH 1.50 4.00
149 Mac Scarce .20 .50
150 John Mayberry .40 1.00
151 Diego Segui .20 .50
152 Oscar Gamble .40 1.00
153 Jon Matlack .40 1.00
154 Houston Astros TC .40 1.00
155 Bert Campaneris .40 1.00
156 Randy Moffitt .20 .50
157 Vic Harris .20 .50
158 Jack Billingham .20 .50
159 Jim Ray Hart .20 .50
160 Brooks Robinson 6.00 15.00
161 Ray Burris UER RC .40 1.00
162 Bill Freehan .40 1.00
163 Ken Berry .20 .50
164 Tom House .20 .50
165 Willie Davis .40 1.00
166 Jack McKeon MG .40 1.00
167 Luis Tiant .75 2.00
168 Danny Thompson .20 .50
169 Steve Rogers RC .75 2.00
170 Bill Melton .20 .50
171 Eduardo Rodriguez RC .20 .50
172 Gene Clines .20 .50
173A Randy Jones SD RC .75 2.00
173B Randy Jones WASH 2.00 5.00
174 Bill Robinson .40 1.00
175 Reggie Cleveland .20 .50
176 John Lowenstein .20 .50
177 Dave Roberts .20 .50
178 Garry Maddox .40 1.00
179 Yogi Berra MG 2.00 5.00
180 Ken Holtzman .40 1.00
181 Cesar Geronimo .40 1.00
182 Lindy McDaniel .40 1.00
183 Johnny Oates .40 1.00
184 Texas Rangers TC .40 1.00
185 Jose Cardenal .20 .50
186 Fred Scherman .20 .50
187 Don Baylor .75 2.00
188 Rudy Meoli RC .20 .50
189 Jim Brewer .20 .50
190 Tony Oliva .75 2.00
191 Al Fitzmorris .20 .50
192 Mario Guerrero .20 .50
193 Tom Walker .20 .50
194 Darrell Porter .40 1.00
195 Carlos May .20 .50
196 Jim Fregosi .40 1.00
197A Vicente Romo SD .40 1.00
197B Vicente Romo WASH 1.50 4.00
198 Dave Cash .20 .50
199 Mike Kekich .20 .50
200 Cesar Cedeno .40 1.00
201 R.Carew/P.Rose LL 2.50 6.00
202 R.Jackson/W.Stargell LL 2.00 5.00
203 R.Jackson/W.Stargell LL 2.00 5.00
204 T.Harper/L.Brock LL .75 2.00
205 W.Wood/R.Bryant LL .40 1.00
206 J.Palmer/T.Seaver LL 2.00 5.00
207 N.Ryan/T.Seaver LL 5.00 12.00
208 J.Hiller/M.Marshall LL .40 1.00
209 Ted Sizemore .20 .50
210 Bill Singer .20 .50
211 Chicago Cubs TC .40 1.00
212 Rollie Fingers 1.25 3.00
213 Dave Rader .20 .50
214 Billy Grabarkewitz .20 .50
215 Al Kaline UER 6.00 15.00
216 Ray Sadecki .20 .50
217 Tim Foli .20 .50
218 Johnny Briggs .20 .50
219 Doug Griffin .20 .50
220 Don Sutton 1.25 3.00
221 Chuck Tanner MG .40 1.00
222 Ramon Hernandez .20 .50
223 Jeff Burroughs .75 2.00
224 Roger Metzger .20 .50
225 Paul Splittorff .20 .50
226A San Diego Padres TC SD .75 2.00
226B San Diego Padres TC WASH 3.00 8.00
227 Mike Lum .20 .50
228 Ted Kubiak .20 .50
229 Fritz Peterson .20 .50
230 Tony Perez 1.50 4.00
231 Dick Tidrow .20 .50
232 Steve Brye .20 .50
233 Jim Barr .20 .50
234 John Milner .20 .50
235 Dave McNally .40 1.00
236 Red Schoendienst MG 1.25 3.00
237 Ken Brett .20 .50
238 F.Healy w/Munson .20 .50
239 Bill Russell .40 1.00
240 Joe Coleman .20 .50
241A Glenn Beckert SD .40 1.00
241B Glenn Beckert WASH 1.50 4.00
242 Bill Gogolewski .20 .50
243 Bob Oliver .20 .50
244 Carl Morton .20 .50
245 Cleon Jones .20 .50
246 Oakland Athletics TC .75 2.00
247 Rick Miller .20 .50
248 Tom Hall .20 .50
249 George Mitterwald .20 .50
250A Willie McCovey SD 3.00 8.00
250B Willie McCovey WASH 10.00 25.00
251 Graig Nettles .75 2.00
252 Dave Parker RC 10.00 25.00
253 John Boccabella .20 .50
254 Stan Bahnsen .20 .50
255 Larry Bowa .40 1.00
256 Tom Griffin .20 .50
257 Buddy Bell .75 2.00
258 Jerry Morales .20 .50
259 Bob Reynolds .20 .50
260 Ted Simmons .75 2.00
261 Jerry Bell .20 .50
262 Ed Kirkpatrick .20 .50
263 Checklist 133-264 1.25 3.00
264 Joe Rudi .40 1.00
265 Tug McGraw .75 2.00
266 Jim Northrup .40 1.00
267 Andy Messersmith .40 1.00
268 Tom Grieve .40 1.00
269 Bob Johnson .20 .50
270 Ron Santo .75 2.00
271 Bill Hands .20 .50
272 Paul Casanova .20 .50
273 Checklist 265-396 1.25 3.00
274 Fred Beene .20 .50
275 Ron Hunt .20 .50
276 Bobby Winkles MG .40 1.00
277 Gary Nolan .40 1.00
278 Cookie Rojas .40 1.00
279 Jim Crawford RC .20 .50
280 Carl Yastrzemski 6.00 15.00
281 San Francisco Giants TC .40 1.00
282 Doyle Alexander .40 1.00
283 Mike Schmidt 12.00 30.00
284 Dave Duncan .40 1.00
285 Reggie Smith .40 1.00
286 Tony Muser .20 .50
287 Clay Kirby .20 .50
288 Gorman Thomas RC .75 2.00
289 Rick Auerbach .20 .50
290 Vida Blue .40 1.00
291 Don Hahn .20 .50
292 Chuck Seelbach .20 .50
293 Milt May .20 .50
294 Steve Foucault RC .20 .50
295 Rick Monday .40 1.00
296 Ray Corbin .20 .50
297 Hal Breeden .20 .50
298 Roric Harrison .20 .50
299 Gene Michael .20 .50
300 Pete Rose 12.00 30.00
301 Bob Montgomery .20 .50
302 Rudy May .20 .50
303 George Hendrick .40 1.00
304 Don Wilson .20 .50
305 Tito Fuentes .20 .50
306 Earl Weaver MG 1.25 3.00
307 Luis Melendez .20 .50
308 Bruce Dal Canton .20 .50
309A Dave Roberts SD .40 1.00
309B Dave Roberts WASH 2.50 6.00
310 Terry Forster .40 1.00
311 Jerry Grote .40 1.00
312 Deron Johnson .20 .50
313 Barry Lersch .20 .50
314 Milwaukee Brewers TC .40 1.00
315 Ron Cey .75 2.00
316 Jim Perry .40 1.00
317 Richie Zisk .40 1.00
318 Jim Merritt .20 .50
319 Randy Hundley .20 .50
320 Dusty Baker .75 2.00
321 Steve Braun .20 .50
322 Ernie McAnally .20 .50
323 Richie Scheinblum .20 .50
324 Steve Kline .20 .50
325 Tommy Harper .40 1.00
326 Sparky Anderson MG 1.25 3.00
327 Tom Timmermann .20 .50
328 Skip Jutze .20 .50
329 Mark Belanger .40 1.00
330 Juan Marichal 2.00 5.00
331 C.Fisk/J.Bench AS 2.00 5.00
332 D.Allen/H.Aaron AS 3.00 8.00
333 R.Carew/J.Morgan AS 1.50 4.00
334 B.Robinson/R.Santo AS .75 2.00
335 B.Campaneris/C.Speier AS .40 1.00
336 B.Murcer/P.Rose AS 2.00 5.00
337 A.Otis/C.Cedeno AS .40 1.00
338 R.Jackson/B.Williams AS 2.00 5.00
339 J.Hunter/R.Wise AS 1.25 3.00
340 Thurman Munson 5.00 12.00
341 Dan Driessen RC .40 1.00
342 Jim Lonborg .40 1.00
343 Kansas City Royals TC .40 1.00
344 Mike Caldwell .20 .50
345 Bill North .20 .50
346 Ron Reed .20 .50
347 Sandy Alomar .40 1.00
348 Pete Richert .20 .50
349 John Vukovich .20 .50
350 Bob Gibson 3.00 8.00
351 Dwight Evans 1.25 3.00
352 Bill Stoneman .20 .50
353 Rich Coggins .20 .50
354 Whitey Lockman MG .40 1.00
355 Dave Nelson .20 .50
356 Jerry Koosman .40 1.00
357 Buddy Bradford .20 .50
358 Dal Maxvill .20 .50
359 Brent Strom .20 .50
360 Greg Luzinski .75 2.00
361 Don Carrithers .20 .50
362 Hal King .20 .50
363 New York Yankees TC .75 2.00
364A Cito Gaston SD .75 2.00
364B Cito Gaston WASH 3.00 8.00
365 Steve Busby .40 1.00
366 Larry Hisle .40 1.00
367 Norm Cash .75 2.00
368 Manny Mota .40 1.00
369 Paul Lindblad .20 .50
370 Bob Watson .40 1.00
371 Jim Slaton .20 .50
372 Ken Reitz .20 .50
373 John Curtis .20 .50
374 Marty Perez .20 .50
375 Earl Williams .20 .50
376 Jorge Orta .20 .50
377 Ron Woods .20 .50
378 Burt Hooton .40 1.00
379 Billy Martin MG .75 2.00
380 Bud Harrelson .40 1.00
381 Charlie Sands .20 .50
382 Bob Moose .20 .50
383 Philadelphia Phillies TC .40 1.00
384 Chris Chambliss .40 1.00
385 Don Gullett .40 1.00
386 Gary Matthews .75 2.00
387A Rich Morales SD .40 1.00
387B Rich Morales WASH 2.50 6.00
388 Phil Roof .20 .50
389 Gates Brown .20 .50
390 Lou Piniella .75 2.00
391 Billy Champion .20 .50
392 Dick Green .20 .50
393 Orlando Pena .20 .50
394 Ken Henderson .20 .50
395 Doug Rader .20 .50
396 Tommy Davis .40 1.00
397 George Stone .20 .50
398 Duke Sims .20 .50
399 Mike Paul .20 .50
400 Harmon Killebrew 2.50 6.00
401 Elliott Maddox .20 .50
402 Jim Rooker .20 .50
403 Darrell Johnson MG .40 1.00
404 Jim Howarth .20 .50
405 Ellie Rodriguez .20 .50
406 Steve Arlin .20 .50
407 Jim Wohlford .20 .50
408 Charlie Hough .40 1.00
409 Ike Brown .20 .50
410 Pedro Borbon .20 .50
411 Frank Baker .20 .50
412 Chuck Taylor .20 .50
413 Don Money .40 1.00
414 Checklist 397-528 1.25 3.00
415 Gary Gentry .20 .50
416 Chicago White Sox TC .40 1.00
417 Rich Folkers .20 .50
418 Walt Williams .20 .50
419 Wayne Twitchell .20 .50
420 Ray Fosse .20 .50
421 Dan Fife RC .20 .50
422 Gonzalo Marquez .20 .50
423 Fred Stanley .20 .50
424 Jim Beauchamp .20 .50
425 Pete Broberg .20 .50
426 Rennie Stennett .20 .50
427 Bobby Bolin .20 .50
428 Gary Sutherland .20 .50
429 Dick Lange RC .20 .50
430 Matty Alou .40 1.00
431 Gene Garber RC .40 1.00
432 Chris Arnold .20 .50
433 Lerrin LaGrow .20 .50
434 Ken McMullen .20 .50
435 Dave Concepcion .75 2.00
436 Don Hood RC .20 .50
437 Jim Lyttle .20 .50
438 Ed Herrmann .20 .50
439 Norm Miller .20 .50
440 Jim Kaat .75 2.00
441 Tom Ragland .20 .50
442 Alan Foster .20 .50
443 Tom Hutton .20 .50
444 Vic Davalillo .20 .50
445 George Medich .20 .50
446 Len Randle .20 .50
447 Frank Quilici MG .40 1.00
448 Ron Hodges RC .20 .50
449 Tom McCraw .20 .50
450 Rich Hebner .40 1.00
451 Tommy John .75 2.00
452 Gene Hiser .20 .50
453 Balor Moore .20 .50
454 Kurt Bevacqua .20 .50
455 Tom Bradley .20 .50
456 Dave Winfield RC 15.00 40.00
457 Chuck Goggin RC .20 .50
458 Jim Ray .20 .50
459 Cincinnati Reds TC .75 2.00
460 Boog Powell .75 2.00
461 John Odom .20 .50
462 Luis Alvarado .20 .50
463 Pat Dobson .20 .50
464 Jose Cruz .75 2.00
465 Dick Bosman .20 .50
466 Dick Billings .20 .50
467 Winston Llenas .20 .50
468 Pepe Frias .20 .50
469 Joe Decker .20 .50
470 Reggie Jackson ALCS 2.00 5.00
471 Jon Matlack NLCS .40 1.00
472 Darold Knowles WS1 .40 1.00
473 Willie Mays WS 6.00 15.00
474 Bert Campaneris WS3 .40 1.00
475 Rusty Staub WS4 .40 1.00
476 Cleon Jones WS5 .40 1.00
477 Reggie Jackson WS 2.00 5.00
478 Bert Campaneris WS7 .40 1.00
479 A's Celebrate WS .40 1.00
480 Willie Crawford .20 .50
481 Jerry Terrell RC .20 .50
482 Bob Didier .20 .50
483 Atlanta Braves TC .40 1.00
484 Carmen Fanzone .20 .50

Card	Low	High
485 Felipe Alou	.75	2.00
486 Steve Stone	.40	1.00
487 Ted Martinez	.20	.50
488 Andy Etchebarren	.20	.50
489 Danny Murtaugh MG	.40	1.00
490 Vada Pinson	.75	2.00
491 Roger Nelson	.20	.50
492 Mike Rogodzinski RC	.20	.50
493 Joe Hoerner	.20	.50
494 Ed Goodson	.20	.50
495 Dick McAuliffe	.40	1.00
496 Tom Murphy	.20	.50
497 Bobby Mitchell	.20	.50
498 Pat Corrales	.20	.50
499 Rusty Torres	.20	.50
500 Lee May	.40	1.00
501 Eddie Leon	.20	.50
502 Dave LaRoche	.20	.50
503 Eric Soderholm	.20	.50
504 Joe Niekro	.40	1.00
505 Bill Buckner	.40	1.00
506 Ed Farmer	.20	.50
507 Larry Stahl	.20	.50
508 Montreal Expos TC	.40	1.00
509 Jesse Jefferson	.20	.50
510 Wayne Garrett	.20	.50
511 Toby Harrah	.40	1.00
512 Joe Lahoud	.20	.50
513 Jim Campanis	.20	.50
514 Paul Schaal	.20	.50
515 Willie Montanez	.20	.50
516 Horacio Pina	.20	.50
517 Mike Hegan	.20	.50
518 Derrel Thomas	.20	.50
519 Bill Sharp RC	.20	.50
520 Tim McCarver	.75	2.00
521 Ken Aspromonte MG	.40	1.00
522 J.R. Richard	.75	2.00
523 Cecil Cooper	.75	2.00
524 Bill Plummer	.20	.50
525 Clyde Wright	.20	.50
526 Frank Tepedino	.40	1.00
527 Bobby Darwin	.20	.50
528 Bill Bonham	.20	.50
529 Horace Clarke	.40	1.00
530 Mickey Stanley	.40	1.00
531 Gene Mauch MG	.40	1.00
532 Skip Lockwood	.20	.50
533 Mike Phillips RC	.20	.50
534 Eddie Watt	.20	.50
535 Bob Tolan	.20	.50
536 Duffy Dyer	.20	.50
537 Steve Mingori	.20	.50
538 Cesar Tovar	.20	.50
539 Lloyd Allen	.20	.50
540 Bob Robertson	.20	.50
541 Cleveland Indians TC	.40	1.00
542 Goose Gossage	.75	2.00
543 Danny Cater	.20	.50
544 Ron Schueler	.20	.50
545 Billy Conigliaro	.40	1.00
546 Mike Corkins	.20	.50
547 Glenn Borgmann	.20	.50
548 Sonny Siebert	.20	.50
549 Mike Jorgensen	.20	.50
550 Sam McDowell	.40	1.00
551 Von Joshua	.20	.50
552 Denny Doyle	.20	.50
553 Jim Willoughby	.20	.50
554 Tim Johnson RC	.20	.50
555 Woodie Fryman	.20	.50
556 Dave Campbell	.40	1.00
557 Jim McGlothlin	.20	.50
558 Bill Fahey	.20	.50
559 Darrel Chaney	.20	.50
560 Mike Cuellar	.40	1.00
561 Ed Kranepool	.40	1.00
562 Jack Aker	.20	.50
563 Hal McRae	.40	1.00
564 Mike Ryan	.20	.50
565 Milt Wilcox	.20	.50
566 Jackie Hernandez	.20	.50
567 Boston Red Sox TC	.40	1.00
568 Mike Torrez	.40	1.00
569 Rick Dempsey	.40	1.00
570 Ralph Garr	.40	1.00
571 Rich Hand	.20	.50
572 Enzo Hernandez	.20	.50
573 Mike Adams RC	.20	.50
574 Bill Parsons	.20	.50
575 Steve Garvey	1.25	3.00
576 Scipio Spinks	.20	.50
577 Mike Sadek RC	.20	.50
578 Ralph Houk MG	.40	1.00
579 Cecil Upshaw	.20	.50
580 Jim Spencer	.20	.50
581 Fred Norman	.20	.50
582 Bucky Dent RC	2.00	5.00
583 Marty Pattin	.20	.50
584 Ken Rudolph	.20	.50
585 Merv Rettenmund	.20	.50
586 Jack Brohamer	.20	.50
587 Larry Christenson RC	.20	.50
588 Hal Lanier	.20	.50
589 Boots Day	.20	.50
590 Roger Moret	.20	.50
591 Sonny Jackson	.20	.50
592 Ed Bane RC	.20	.50
593 Steve Yeager	.40	1.00
594 Leroy Stanton	.20	.50
595 Steve Blass	.40	1.00
596 Gar/Hold/Lit/Pole RC	.20	.50
597 Chalk/Gam/Mac/Trillo RC	.40	1.00
598 Ken Griffey RC	8.00	20.00
599A Dior/Freis/Ric/Shan Wash	.75	2.00
599B Dior/Freis/Ric/Shan Lg	6.00	15.00
599C Dior/Freis/Ric/Shan Sm		
600 Cash/Cox/Madlock/Sand RC	2.00	5.00
601 Arm/Bladt/Downing/McBride RC	1.25	3.00
602 Abb/Henn/Swan/Voss RC	.40	1.00
603 Foote/Lund/Moore/Robles RC	.40	1.00
604 Hugh/Knox/Thornton/White RC	2.00	5.00
605 Alb/Frail/Kob/Tanana RC	1.50	4.00
606 Fuller/Howard/Smith/Velez RC	.40	1.00
607 Fost/Hein/Ros/Taveras RC	.40	1.00
608A Apod/Ban/D'Acq/Wall ERR	.75	2.00
608B Apod/Ban/D'Acq/Wall RC	.40	1.00
609 Rico Petrocelli	.40	1.00
610 Dave Kingman	.75	2.00
611 Rich Stelmaszek	.20	.50
612 Luke Walker	.20	.50
613 Dan Monzon	.20	.50
614 Adrian Devine RC	.20	.50
615 Johnny Jeter UER	.20	.50
616 Larry Gura	.20	.50
617 Ted Ford	.20	.50
618 Jim Mason	.20	.50
619 Mike Anderson	.20	.50
620 Al Downing	.20	.50
621 Bernie Carbo	.20	.50
622 Phil Gagliano	.20	.50
623 Celerino Sanchez	.20	.50
624 Bob Miller	.20	.50
625 Ollie Brown	.20	.50
626 Pittsburgh Pirates TC	.40	1.00
627 Carl Taylor	.20	.50
628 Ivan Murrell	.20	.50
629 Rusty Staub	.75	2.00
630 Tommie Agee	.40	1.00
631 Steve Barber	.20	.50
632 George Culver	.20	.50
633 Dave Hamilton	.20	.50
634 Eddie Mathews MG	1.25	3.00
635 Johnny Edwards	.20	.50
636 Dave Goltz	.20	.50
637 Checklist 529-660	1.25	3.00
638 Ken Sanders	.20	.50
639 Joe Lovitto	.20	.50
640 Milt Pappas	.40	1.00
641 Chuck Brinkman	.20	.50
642 Terry Harmon	.20	.50
643 Los Angeles Dodgers TC	.40	1.00
644 Wayne Granger	.20	.50
645 Ken Boswell	.20	.50
646 George Foster	.75	2.00
647 Juan Beniquez RC	.20	.50
648 Terry Crowley	.20	.50
649 Fernando Gonzalez RC	.20	.50
650 Mike Epstein	.20	.50
651 Leron Lee	.20	.50
652 Gail Hopkins	.20	.50
653 Bob Stinson	.20	.50
654A Jesus Alou NPOF	1.50	4.00
654B Jesus Alou COR	.40	1.00
655 Mike Tyson RC	.20	.50
656 Adrian Garrett	.20	.50
657 Jim Shellenback	.20	.50
658 Lee Lacy	.20	.50
659 Joe Lis	.20	.50
660 Larry Dierker	.75	2.00

1974 Topps Traded

The cards in this 44-card set measure 2 1/2" by 3 1/2". The 1974 Topps Traded set contains 43 player cards and one unnumbered checklist card. The fronts have the word "traded" in block letters and the backs are designed in newspaper style. Card numbers are the same as in the regular set except they are followed by a "T." No known scarcities exist for this set. The cards were inserted in all packs toward the end of the production run. They were produced in large enough quantity that they are no scarcer than the regular Topps cards.

Card	Low	High
COMPLETE SET (44)	8.00	20.00
23T Craig Robinson	.20	.50
42T Claude Osteen	.30	.75
43T Jim Wynn	.30	.75
51T Bobby Heise	.20	.50
59T Ross Grimsley	.20	.50
62T Bob Locker	.20	.50
63T Bill Sudakis	.20	.50
73T Mike Marshall	.30	.75
123T Nelson Briles	.30	.75
139T Aurelio Monteagudo	.20	.50
151T Diego Segui	.20	.50
165T Willie Davis	.30	.75
175T Reggie Cleveland	.20	.50
182T Lindy McDaniel	.30	.75
186T Fred Scherman	.20	.50
249T George Mitterwald	.20	.50
262T Ed Kirkpatrick	.20	.50
269T Bob Johnson	.20	.50
270T Ron Santo	.40	1.00
313T Barry Lersch	.20	.50
319T Randy Hundley	.30	.75
330T Juan Marichal	.75	2.00
348T Pete Richert	.20	.50
373T John Curtis	.20	.50
390T Lou Piniella	.40	1.00
428T Gary Sutherland	.20	.50
454T Kurt Bevacqua	.20	.50
458T Jim Ray	.20	.50
485T Felipe Alou	.40	1.00
486T Steve Stone	.30	.75
496T Tom Murphy	.20	.50
516T Horacio Pina	.20	.50
534T Eddie Watt	.20	.50
538T Cesar Tovar	.20	.50
544T Ron Schueler	.20	.50
579T Cecil Upshaw	.20	.50
585T Merv Rettenmund	.20	.50
612T Luke Walker	.20	.50
616T Larry Gura	.30	.75
618T Jim Mason	.20	.50
630T Tommie Agee	.30	.75
648T Terry Crowley	.20	.50
649T Fernando Gonzalez	.20	.50
NNO Traded Checklist	.60	1.50

1974 Topps Team Checklists

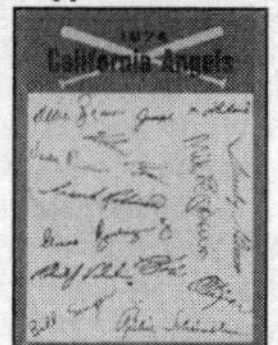

The cards in this 24-card set measure 2 1/2" by 3 1/2". The 1974 series of checklists was issued in packs with the regular cards for that year. The cards are unnumbered (arbitrarily numbered below alphabetically by team name) and have bright red borders. The year and team name appear in a green panel decorated by a crossed bats design, below which is a white area containing facsimile autographs of various players. The mustard-yellow and gray-colored backs list team members alphabetically, along with their card number, uniform number and position. Uncut sheets of these cards were also available through a wrapper mail-in offer. The uncut sheet value in NR/Mt or better condition is approximately $150.

Card	Low	High
COMPLETE SET (24)	8.00	20.00
COMMON TEAM (1-24)	.40	1.00

1974 Topps Deckle Edge

The cards in this 72-card set measure 2 7/8" by 5". Returning to a format first used in 1969, Topps produced a set of black and white photo cards in 1974 bearing an unusual serrated or "deckle" border. A facsimile autograph appears on the obverse while the backs contain the card number and a "newspaper-clipping" design detailing a milestone in the player's career. This was a test set and uncut sheets are sometimes found. Card backs are either white or gray; the white back cards are slightly tougher to obtain. The wrapper is also considered collectible. Wrappers featured Reggie Jackson and Tom Seaver and come with or without the phrase "With gum".

Card	Low	High
COMPLETE SET (72)	3,000.00	6,000.00
WRAPPER (With Gum)	8.00	20.00
WRAPPER (Without Gum)	8.00	20.00
1 Amos Otis	10.00	25.00
2 Darrell Evans	10.00	25.00
3 Bob Gibson	75.00	150.00
4 Dave Nelson	8.00	20.00
5 Steve Carlton	125.00	250.00
6 Jim Hunter	75.00	150.00
7 Thurman Munson	100.00	200.00
8 Bob Grich	10.00	25.00
9 Tom Seaver	150.00	300.00
10 Ted Simmons	10.00	25.00
11 Bobby Valentine	10.00	25.00
12 Don Sutton	40.00	80.00
13 Wilbur Wood	8.00	20.00
14 Doug Rader	8.00	20.00
15 Chris Chambliss	8.00	20.00
16 Pete Rose	150.00	300.00
17 John Hiller	8.00	20.00
18 Burt Hooton	8.00	20.00
19 Tim Foli	8.00	20.00
20 Lou Brock	75.00	150.00
21 Ron Bryant	8.00	20.00
22 Manny Sanguillen	8.00	20.00
23 Bob Tolan	8.00	20.00
24 Greg Luzinski	10.00	25.00
25 Brooks Robinson	125.00	250.00
26 Felix Millan	8.00	20.00
27 Luis Tiant	10.00	25.00
28 Willie McCovey	75.00	150.00
29 Chris Speier	8.00	20.00
30 George Scott	8.00	20.00
31 Willie Stargell	75.00	150.00
32 Rod Carew	100.00	200.00
33 Charlie Spikes	8.00	20.00
34 Nate Colbert	8.00	20.00
35 Rich Hebner	8.00	20.00
36 Bobby Bonds	10.00	25.00
37 Buddy Bell	10.00	25.00
38 Claude Osteen	8.00	20.00
39 Dick Allen	10.00	25.00
40 Bill Russell	8.00	20.00
41 Nolan Ryan	1,000.00	2,000.00
42 Willie Davis	8.00	20.00
43 Carl Yastrzemski	100.00	200.00
44 Jon Matlack	8.00	20.00
45 Jim Palmer	100.00	200.00
46 Bert Campaneris	8.00	20.00
47 Bert Blyleven	10.00	25.00
48 Jeff Burroughs	8.00	20.00
49 Jim Colborn	8.00	20.00
50 Dave Johnson	10.00	25.00
51 John Mayberry	8.00	20.00
52 Don Kessinger	8.00	20.00
53 Joe Coleman	8.00	20.00
54 Tony Perez	40.00	80.00
55 Jose Cardenal	8.00	20.00
56 Paul Splittorff	8.00	20.00
57 Hank Aaron	150.00	300.00
58 Dave May	8.00	20.00
59 Fergie Jenkins	75.00	150.00
60 Ron Blomberg	8.00	20.00
61 Reggie Jackson	150.00	300.00
62 Tony Oliva	10.00	25.00
63 Bobby Murcer	10.00	25.00
64 Carlton Fisk	100.00	200.00
65 Steve Rogers	8.00	20.00
66 Frank Robinson	100.00	200.00
67 Joe Ferguson	8.00	20.00
68 Bill Melton	8.00	20.00
69 Bob Watson	8.00	20.00
70 Larry Bowa	10.00	25.00
71 Johnny Bench	125.00	250.00
72 Willie Horton	8.00	20.00

1974 Topps Puzzles

This set of 12 jigsaw puzzles was supposedly distributed by Topps in 1974 as a test issue. Each puzzle measures approximately 5" by 7 1/8" and shows a colorful picture of the player inside a white border. Puzzles contained 40 pieces. The wrapper for the puzzles is also collectible as it shows a picture of Tom Seaver. The wrapper comes two ways: either with a pre-printed price of 29 cents or 25 cents. The puzzles are blank backed and unnumbered; they are listed below alphabetically.

Card	Low	High
COMPLETE SET (12)	1,000.00	2,000.00
WRAPPER/25 cents	50.00	100.00
WRAPPER/29 cents	4.00	10.00
1 Hank Aaron	75.00	150.00
2 Dick Allen	30.00	60.00
3 Johnny Bench	75.00	150.00
4 Bobby Bonds	20.00	50.00
5 Bob Gibson	40.00	80.00
6 Reggie Jackson	100.00	200.00
7 Bobby Murcer	20.00	50.00
8 Jim Palmer	40.00	80.00
9 Nolan Ryan	500.00	1,000.00
10 Tom Seaver	75.00	150.00
11 Willie Stargell	40.00	80.00
12 Carl Yastrzemski	60.00	120.00

1974 Topps Stamps

The 240 color portraits depicted on stamps in this 1974 Topps series have the player's name, team and position inside an oval below the picture area. Each stamp measures 1" by 1 1/2". The stamps were marketed in 12 stamp sheets, along with an album, in their own wrapper. The booklets have eight pages and measure 2 1/2" by 3 7/8". There are 24 albums, one for each team, designed to hold 10 stamps apiece. The stamps are numbered here alphabetically within each team and the teams are listed in alphabetical order within league, e.g., Atlanta Braves NL (1-10), Chicago Cubs (11-20), Cincinnati Reds (21-30), Houston Astros (31-40), Los Angeles Dodgers (41-50), Montreal Expos (51-60), New York Mets (61-70), Philadelphia Phillies (71-80), Pittsburgh Pirates (81-90), San Diego Padres (91-100), San Francisco Giants (101-110), St. Louis Cardinals (111-120), Baltimore Orioles AL (121-130), Boston Red Sox (131-140), California Angels (141-150), Chicago White Sox (151-160), Cleveland Indians (161-170), Detroit Tigers (171-180), Kansas City Royals (181-190), Milwaukee Brewers (191-200), Minnesota Twins (201-210), New York Yankees (211-220), Oakland A's (221-230) and Texas Rangers (231-240).

Card	Low	High
COMPLETE SET (240)	40.00	80.00
1 Hank Aaron	3.00	8.00
2 Dusty Baker	.10	.25
3 Darrell Evans	.10	.25
4 Ralph Garr	.08	.15
5 Roric Harrison	.08	.20
6 Dave Johnson	.20	.50
7 Mike Lum	.08	.20
8 Carl Morton	.08	.20
9 Phil Niekro	1.00	2.50
10 Johnny Oates	.08	.20
11 Glenn Beckert	.08	.20
12 Jose Cardenal	.08	.20
13 Vic Harris	.08	.20
14 Burt Hooton	.08	.20
15 Randy Hundley	.08	.20
16 Don Kessinger	.08	.15
17 Rick Monday	.08	.15
18 Rick Reuschel	.20	.50
19 Ron Santo	.40	1.00
20 Billy Williams	1.00	2.50
21 Johnny Bench	2.00	5.00
22 Jack Billingham	.08	.20
23 Pedro Borbon	.08	.20
24 Dave Concepcion	.20	.50
25 Dan Driessen	.08	.15
26 Cesar Geronimo	.08	.20

27 Don Gullett .08 .15
28 Joe Morgan 1.25 3.00
29 Tony Perez .60 1.50
30 Pete Rose 3.00 8.00
31 Cesar Cedeno .08 .15
32 Tommy Helms .08 .20
33 Lee May .08 .15
34 Roger Metzger .08 .20
35 Doug Rader .08 .20
36 J.R. Richard .08 .15
37 Dave Roberts .08 .20
38 Jerry Reuss .08 .15
39 Bob Watson .08 .15
40 Jim Wynn .08 .15
41 Bill Buckner .10 .25
42 Ron Cey .10 .25
43 Willie Crawford .08 .20
44 Willie Davis .08 .15
45 Joe Ferguson .08 .20
46 Davey Lopes .08 .15
47 Andy Messersmith .08 .15
48 Claude Osteen .08 .15
49 Bill Russell .08 .15
50 Don Sutton .60 1.50
51 Bob Bailey .08 .20
52 John Boccabella .08 .20
53 Ron Fairly .08 .15
54 Tim Foli .08 .20
55 Ron Hunt .08 .20
56 Mike Jorgensen .08 .20
57 Mike Marshall .08 .15
58 Steve Renko .08 .20
59 Steve Rogers .08 .15
60 Ken Singleton .10 .25
61 Wayne Garrett .08 .20
62 Jerry Grote .08 .20
63 Bud Harrelson .08 .15
64 Cleon Jones .08 .20
65 Jerry Koosman .20 .50
66 Jon Matlack .08 .15
67 Tug McGraw .20 .50
68 Felix Millan .08 .20
69 John Milner .08 .20
70 Tom Seaver 2.00 5.00
71 Bob Boone .20 .50
72 Larry Bowa .08 .15
73 Steve Carlton 2.00 5.00
74 Bill Grabarkewitz .08 .20
75 Jim Lonborg .08 .15
76 Greg Luzinski .10 .25
77 Willie Montanez .08 .20
78 Bill Robinson .08 .15
79 Wayne Twitchell .08 .20
80 Del Unser .08 .20
81 Nelson Briles .08 .15
82 Dock Ellis .08 .20
83 Dave Giusti .08 .20
84 Richie Hebner .08 .20
85 Al Oliver .10 .25
86 Dave Parker 1.00 2.50
87 Manny Sanguillen .08 .15
88 Willie Stargell 1.25 3.00
89 Rennie Stennett .08 .20
90 Richie Zisk .08 .15
91 Nate Colbert .08 .20
92 Bill Greif .08 .20
93 Johnny Grubb .08 .20
94 Randy Jones .08 .15
95 Fred Kendall .08 .20
96 Clay Kirby .08 .20
97 Willie McCovey 1.25 3.00
98 Jerry Morales .08 .20
99 Dave Roberts .08 .20
100 Dave Winfield 3.00 8.00
101 Bobby Bonds .20 .50
102 Tom Bradley .08 .20
103 Ron Bryant .08 .20
104 Tito Fuentes .08 .20
105 Ed Goodson .08 .20
106 Dave Kingman .40 1.00
107 Garry Maddox .08 .15
108 Dave Rader .08 .20
109 Elias Sosa .08 .20
110 Chris Speier .08 .15
111 Lou Brock 1.25 3.00
112 Reggie Cleveland .08 .20
113 Jose Cruz .10 .25
114 Bob Gibson 1.25 3.00
115 Tim McCarver .10 .25
116 Ted Simmons .10 .25
117 Ted Sizemore .08 .20
118 Reggie Smith .08 .15
119 Joe Torre .20 .50
120 Mike Tyson .08 .20
121 Don Baylor .20 .50
122 Mark Belanger .08 .15
123 Paul Blair .08 .20
124 Tommy Davis .08 .15
125 Bobby Grich .08 .15
126 Grant Jackson .08 .20
127 Dave McNally .08 .15
128 Jim Palmer 1.00 2.50
129 Brooks Robinson 1.50 4.00
130 Earl Williams .08 .20
131 Luis Aparicio 1.00 2.50
132 Orlando Cepeda .60 1.50
133 Carlton Fisk 1.50 4.00
134 Tommy Harper .08 .20
135 Bill Lee .08 .15
136 Rick Miller .08 .20
137 Roger Moret .08 .20
138 Luis Tiant .20 .50
139 Rick Wise .08 .20
140 Carl Yastrzemski 2.00 5.00
141 Sandy Alomar .08 .20
142 Mike Epstein .08 .20
143 Bob Oliver .08 .20
144 Vada Pinson .10 .25
145 Frank Robinson 1.50 4.00
146 Ellie Rodriguez .08 .20
147 Nolan Ryan 6.00 15.00
148 Richie Scheinblum .08 .20
149 Bill Singer .08 .20
150 Bobby Valentine .08 .15
151 Dick Allen .20 .50
152 Stan Bahnsen .08 .20
153 Terry Forster .08 .15
154 Ken Henderson .08 .20
155 Ed Herrmann .08 .20
156 Pat Kelly .08 .20
157 Carlos May .08 .20
158 Bill Melton .08 .20
159 Jorge Orta .08 .20
160 Wilbur Wood .08 .15
161 Buddy Bell .20 .50
162 Chris Chambliss .10 .25
163 Frank Duffy .08 .20
164 Dave Duncan .08 .20
165 John Ellis .08 .20
166 Oscar Gamble .08 .15
167 George Hendrick .08 .15
168 Gaylord Perry 1.00 2.50
169 Charlie Spikes .08 .20
170 Dick Tidrow .08 .20
171 Ed Brinkman .08 .20
172 Norm Cash .20 .50
173 Joe Coleman .08 .20
174 Bill Freehan .10 .25
175 John Hiller .08 .15
176 Willie Horton .08 .15
177 Al Kaline 2.00 5.00
178 Mickey Lolich .20 .50
179 Aurelio Rodriguez .08 .20
180 Mickey Stanley .08 .20
181 Steve Busby .08 .15
182 Fran Healy .08 .20
183 Ed Kirkpatrick .08 .20
184 John Mayberry .08 .15
185 Amos Otis .10 .25
186 Fred Patek .08 .20
187 Marty Pattin .08 .20
188 Lou Piniella .20 .50
189 Cookie Rojas .08 .20
190 Paul Splittorff .08 .20
191 Jerry Bell .08 .20
192 Johnny Briggs .08 .20
193 Jim Colborn .08 .20
194 Bob Collucio .08 .20
195 Pedro Garcia .08 .20
196 Dave May .08 .20
197 Don Money .08 .20
198 Darrell Porter .08 .15
199 George Scott .08 .15
200 Jim Slaton .08 .20
201 Bert Blyleven .20 .50
202 Steve Braun .08 .20
203 Rod Carew 2.00 5.00
204 Ray Corbin .08 .20
205 Bobby Darwin .08 .20
206 Joe Decker .08 .20
207 Jim Holt .08 .20
208 Harmon Killebrew 1.25 3.00
209 George Mitterwald .08 .20
210 Tony Oliva .20 .50
211 Ron Blomberg .08 .20
212 Sparky Lyle .10 .25
213 George Medich .08 .20
214 Gene Michael .08 .20
215 Thurman Munson 1.50 4.00
216 Bobby Murcer .10 .25
217 Graig Nettles .20 .50
218 Mel Stottlemyre .10 .25
219 Otto Velez .08 .20
220 Roy White .08 .15
221 Sal Bando .08 .15
222 Vida Blue .20 .50
223 Bert Campaneris .08 .15
224 Ken Holtzman .08 .15
225 Jim Hunter 1.00 2.50
226 Reggie Jackson 2.50 6.00
227 Deron Johnson .08 .20
228 Bill North .08 .20
229 Joe Rudi .08 .15
230 Gene Tenace .08 .15
231 Jim Bibby .08 .20
232 Jeff Burroughs .08 .15
233 David Clyde .08 .20
234 Jim Fregosi .10 .25
235 Toby Harrah .08 .15
236 Ferguson Jenkins 1.00 2.50
237 Alex Johnson .08 .20
238 Dave Nelson .08 .20
239 Jim Spencer .08 .20
240 Bill Sudakis .08 .20

1974 Topps Stamp Albums

The 1974 Topps stamp set of baseball player stamps was intended to be mounted in 24 separate team albums, 10 stamps for that team's players going into that team's album. The albums measure approximately 2 1/2" by 3 1/2".

COMPLETE SET (24) 200.00 400.00
COMMON TEAM (1-24) 10.00 25.00
17 New York Yankees 15.00 40.00

1975 Topps

The 1975 Topps set consists of 660 standard size cards. The design was radically different in appearance from sets of the preceding years. The most prominent change was the use of a two-color frame surrounding the picture area rather than a single, subdued color. A facsimile autograph appears on the picture, and the backs are printed in red and green on gray. Cards were released in ten-card wax packs, 18-card cello packs with a 25 cent SRP and were packaged 24 to a box and 15 boxes to a case, as well as in 42-card rack packs which cost 49 cents upon release. The cello packs were issued 24 to a box. Cards 189-212 depict the MVP's of both leagues from 1951 through 1974. The first seven cards (1-7) feature players (listed in alphabetical order) breaking records or achieving milestones during the previous season. Cards 306-313 picture league leaders in various statistical categories. Cards 459-466 depict the results of post-season action. Team cards feature a checklist back for players on that team and show a small inset photo of the manager on the front. The following players' regular issue cards are explicitly denoted as All-Stars, 1, 50, 80, 140, 170, 180, 260, 320, 350, 390, 400, 420, 440, 470, 530, 570, and 600. This set is quite popular with collectors, at least in part due to the fact that the Rookie Cards of George Brett, Gary Carter, Keith Hernandez, Fred Lynn, Jim Rice and Robin Yount are all in the set.

COMPLETE SET (660) 300.00 600.00
WRAPPER (15-CENT) 3.00 8.00
1 Hank Aaron HL 12.00 30.00
2 Lou Brock HL 1.25 3.00
3 Bob Gibson HL 1.25 3.00
4 Al Kaline HL 2.50 6.00
5 Nolan Ryan HL 6.00 15.00
6 Mike Marshall HL .40 1.00
7 Ryan 3.00 8.00
Busby
Bosman HL
8 Rogelio Moret .20 .50
9 Frank Tepedino .40 1.00
10 Willie Davis .40 1.00
11 Bill Melton .20 .50
12 David Clyde .20 .50
13 Gene Locklear RC .40 1.00
14 Milt Wilcox .20 .50
15 Jose Cardenal .40 1.00
16 Frank Tanana .75 2.00
17 Dave Concepcion .75 2.00
18 Detroit Tigers CL/Houk .75 2.00
19 Jerry Koosman .40 1.00
20 Thurman Munson 6.00 15.00
21 Rollie Fingers 1.25 3.00
22 Dave Cash .20 .50
23 Bill Russell .40 1.00
24 Al Fitzmorris .20 .50
25 Lee May .40 1.00
26 Dave McNally .40 1.00
27 Ken Reitz .20 .50
28 Tom Murphy .20 .50
29 Dave Parker 1.25 3.00
30 Bert Blyleven .75 2.00
31 Dave Rader .20 .50
32 Reggie Cleveland .20 .50
33 Dusty Baker .75 2.00
34 Steve Renko .20 .50
35 Ron Santo .40 1.00
36 Joe Lovitto .20 .50
37 Dave Freisleben .20 .50
38 Buddy Bell .75 2.00
39 Andre Thornton .40 1.00
40 Bill Singer .20 .50
41 Cesar Geronimo .40 1.00
42 Joe Coleman .20 .50
43 Cleon Jones .40 1.00
44 Pat Dobson .20 .50
45 Joe Rudi .40 1.00
46 Philadelphia Phillies CL/Ozark .75 2.00
47 Tommy John .75 2.00
48 Freddie Patek .40 1.00
49 Larry Dierker .40 1.00
50 Brooks Robinson 3.00 8.00
51 Bob Forsch RC .40 1.00
52 Darrell Porter .40 1.00
53 Dave Giusti .20 .50
54 Eric Soderholm .20 .50
55 Bobby Bonds .75 2.00
56 Rick Wise .40 1.00
57 Dave Johnson .40 1.00
58 Chuck Taylor .20 .50
59 Ken Henderson .20 .50
60 Fergie Jenkins 1.25 3.00
61 Dave Winfield 8.00 20.00
62 Fritz Peterson .20 .50
63 Steve Swisher RC .20 .50
64 Dave Chalk .20 .50
65 Don Gullett .40 1.00
66 Willie Horton .40 1.00
67 Tug McGraw .40 1.00
68 Ron Blomberg .20 .50
69 John Odom .20 .50
70 Mike Schmidt 6.00 15.00
71 Charlie Hough .40 1.00
72 Kansas City Royals CL/McKeon .75 2.00
73 J.R. Richard .40 1.00
74 Mark Belanger .40 1.00
75 Ted Simmons .75 2.00
76 Ed Sprague .20 .50
77 Richie Zisk .40 1.00
78 Ray Corbin .20 .50
79 Gary Matthews .40 1.00
80 Carlton Fisk 3.00 8.00
81 Ron Reed .20 .50
82 Pat Kelly .20 .50
83 Jim Merritt .20 .50
84 Enzo Hernandez .20 .50
85 Bill Bonham .20 .50
86 Joe Lis .20 .50
87 George Foster .75 2.00
88 Tom Egan .20 .50
89 Jim Ray .20 .50
90 Rusty Staub .75 2.00
91 Dick Green .20 .50
92 Cecil Upshaw .20 .50
93 Davey Lopes .75 2.00
94 Jim Lonborg .40 1.00
95 John Mayberry .40 1.00
96 Mike Cosgrove RC .20 .50
97 Earl Williams .20 .50
98 Rich Folkers .20 .50
99 Mike Hegan .20 .50
100 Willie Stargell 1.50 4.00
101 Montreal Expos CL/Mauch .75 2.00
102 Joe Decker .20 .50
103 Rick Miller .20 .50
104 Bill Madlock .75 2.00
105 Buzz Capra .20 .50
106 Mike Hargrove UER RC 1.25 3.00
107 Jim Barr .20 .50
108 Tom Hall .20 .50
109 George Hendrick .40 1.00
110 Wilbur Wood .20 .50
111 Wayne Garrett .20 .50
112 Larry Hardy RC .20 .50
113 Elliott Maddox .20 .50
114 Dick Lange .20 .50
115 Joe Ferguson .20 .50
116 Lerrin LaGrow .20 .50
117 Baltimore Orioles CL/Weaver 1.25 3.00
118 Mike Anderson .20 .50
119 Tommy Helms .20 .50
120 Steve Busby UER .40 1.00
121 Bill North .20 .50
122 Al Hrabosky .40 1.00
123 Johnny Briggs .20 .50
124 Jerry Reuss .40 1.00
125 Ken Singleton .40 1.00
126 Checklist 1-132 1.25 3.00
127 Glenn Borgmann .20 .50
128 Bill Lee .40 1.00
129 Rick Monday .40 1.00
130 Phil Niekro 1.25 3.00
131 Toby Harrah .40 1.00
132 Randy Moffitt .20 .50
133 Dan Driessen .40 1.00
134 Ron Hodges .20 .50
135 Charlie Spikes .20 .50
136 Jim Mason .20 .50
137 Terry Forster .40 1.00
138 Del Unser .20 .50
139 Horacio Pina .20 .50
140 Steve Garvey 1.25 3.00
141 Mickey Stanley .40 1.00
142 Bob Reynolds .20 .50
143 Cliff Johnson RC .40 1.00
144 Jim Wohlford .20 .50
145 Ken Holtzman .40 1.00
146 San Diego Padres CL/McNamara .75 2.00
147 Pedro Garcia .20 .50
148 Jim Rooker .20 .50
149 Tim Foli .20 .50
150 Bob Gibson 2.50 6.00
151 Steve Brye .20 .50
152 Mario Guerrero .20 .50
153 Rick Reuschel .40 1.00
154 Mike Lum .20 .50
155 Jim Bibby .20 .50
156 Dave Kingman .75 2.00
157 Pedro Borbon .40 1.00
158 Jerry Grote .20 .50
159 Steve Arlin .20 .50
160 Graig Nettles .75 2.00
161 Stan Bahnsen .20 .50
162 Willie Montanez .20 .50
163 Jim Brewer .20 .50
164 Mickey Rivers .40 1.00
165 Doug Rader .40 1.00
166 Woodie Fryman .20 .50
167 Rich Coggins .20 .50
168 Bill Greif .20 .50
169 Cookie Rojas .20 .50
170 Bert Campaneris .40 1.00
171 Ed Kirkpatrick .20 .50
172 Boston Red Sox CL/Johnson 1.25 3.00
173 Steve Rogers .40 1.00
174 Bake McBride .40 1.00
175 Don Money .40 1.00
176 Burt Hooton .40 1.00
177 Vic Correll RC .20 .50
178 Cesar Tovar .20 .50
179 Tom Bradley .20 .50
180 Joe Morgan 2.50 6.00
181 Fred Beene .20 .50
182 Don Hahn .20 .50
183 Mel Stottlemyre .40 1.00
184 Jorge Orta .20 .50
185 Steve Carlton 3.00 8.00
186 Willie Crawford .20 .50
187 Denny Doyle .20 .50
188 Tom Griffin .20 .50
189 Y.Berra/Campanella MVP 1.50 4.00
190 B.Shantz/H.Sauer MVP .75 2.00
191 Al Rosen/Campanella MVP .75 2.00
192 Y.Berra/W.Mays MVP 1.50 4.00
193 Y.Berra/Campanella MVP 1.25 3.00
194 M.Mantle/D.Newcombe MVP 4.00 10.00

195 M.Mantle/H.Aaron MVP 6.00 15.00
196 J.Jensen/E.Banks MVP 1.25 3.00
197 N.Fox/E.Banks MVP .75 2.00
198 R.Maris/D.Groat MVP .75 2.00
199 R.Maris/F.Robinson MVP 1.25 3.00
200 M.Mantle/M.Wills MVP 4.00 10.00
201 E.Howard/S.Koufax MVP .75 2.00
202 B.Robinson/K.Boyer MVP .40 1.00
203 Z.Versailes/W.Mays MVP .75 2.00
204 F.Robinson/B.Clemente MVP 2.50 6.00
205 C.Yastrzemski/O.Cepeda MVP .75 2.00
206 D.McLain/B.Gibson MVP .75 2.00
207 H.Killebrew/W.McCovey MVP .40 1.00
208 B.Powell/J.Bench MVP .75 2.00
209 V.Blue/J.Torre MVP .75 2.00
210 R.Allen/J.Bench MVP .75 2.00
211 R.Jackson/P.Rose MVP 2.00 5.00
212 J.Burroughs/S.Garvey MVP .75 2.00
213 Oscar Gamble .40 1.00
214 Harry Parker .20 .50
215 Bobby Valentine .40 1.00
216 San Francisco Giants CL/Westrum .75 2.00
217 Lou Piniella .75 2.00
218 Jerry Johnson .20 .50
219 Ed Herrmann .20 .50
220 Don Sutton 1.25 3.00
221 Aurelio Rodriguez .20 .50
222 Dan Spillner RC .20 .50
223 Robin Yount RC 20.00 50.00
224 Ramon Hernandez .20 .50
225 Bob Grich .40 1.00
226 Bill Campbell .20 .50
227 Bob Watson .40 1.00
228 George Brett RC 40.00 100.00
229 Barry Foote .20 .50
230 Jim Hunter 1.50 4.00
231 Mike Tyson .20 .50
232 Diego Segui .20 .50
233 Billy Grabarkewitz .20 .50
234 Tom Grieve .40 1.00
235 Jack Billingham .40 1.00
236 California Angels CL/Williams .75 2.00
237 Carl Morton .40 1.00
238 Dave Duncan .40 1.00
239 George Stone .20 .50
240 Garry Maddox .40 1.00
241 Dick Tidrow .20 .50
242 Jay Johnstone .40 1.00
243 Jim Kaat .75 2.00
244 Bill Buckner .40 1.00
245 Mickey Lolich .75 2.00
246 St. Louis Cardinals CL/Schoen .75 2.00
247 Enos Cabell .20 .50
248 Randy Jones .75 2.00
249 Danny Thompson .20 .50
250 Ken Brett .20 .50
251 Fran Healy .20 .50
252 Fred Scherman .20 .50
253 Jesus Alou .20 .50
254 Mike Torrez .40 1.00
255 Dwight Evans .75 2.00
256 Billy Champion .20 .50
257 Checklist: 133-264 1.25 3.00
258 Dave LaRoche .20 .50
259 Len Randle .20 .50
260 Johnny Bench 10.00 25.00
261 Andy Hassler RC .20 .50
262 Rowland Office RC .20 .50
263 Jim Perry .40 1.00
264 John Milner .20 .50
265 Ron Bryant .20 .50
266 Sandy Alomar .40 1.00
267 Dick Ruthven .20 .50
268 Hal McRae .40 1.00
269 Doug Rau .20 .50
270 Ron Fairly .40 1.00
271 Gerry Moses .20 .50
272 Lynn McGlothen .20 .50
273 Steve Braun .20 .50
274 Vicente Romo .20 .50
275 Paul Blair .40 1.00
276 Chicago White Sox CL/Tanner .75 2.00
277 Frank Taveras .20 .50
278 Paul Lindblad .20 .50
279 Milt May .20 .50
280 Carl Yastrzemski 5.00 12.00
281 Jim Slaton .20 .50
282 Jerry Morales .20 .50
283 Steve Foucault .20 .50
284 Ken Griffey Sr. 1.50 4.00
285 Ellie Rodriguez .20 .50
286 Mike Jorgensen .20 .50
287 Roric Harrison .20 .50
288 Bruce Ellingsen RC .20 .50
289 Ken Rudolph .20 .50
290 Jon Matlack .20 .50
291 Bill Sudakis .20 .50
292 Ron Schueler .20 .50
293 Dick Sharon .20 .50
294 Geoff Zahn RC .20 .50
295 Vada Pinson .75 2.00
296 Alan Foster .20 .50
297 Craig Kusick RC .20 .50
298 Johnny Grubb .20 .50
299 Bucky Dent .75 2.00
300 Reggie Jackson 5.00 12.00
301 Dave Roberts .20 .50
302 Rick Burleson RC .40 1.00
303 Grant Jackson .20 .50
304 Pittsburgh Pirates CL/Murtaugh .75 2.00
305 Jim Colborn .20 .50
306 R.Carew/R.Garr LL .75 2.00
307 D.Allen/M.Schmidt LL 1.50 4.00
308 J.Burroughs/J.Bench LL .75 2.00
309 B.North/L.Brock LL .75 2.00
310 Hunter/Jenk/Mess/Niek LL .75 2.00
311 J.Hunter/B.Capra LL .75 2.00
312 N.Ryan/S.Carlton LL 5.00 12.00
313 T.Forster/M.Marshall LL .40 1.00
314 Buck Martinez .20 .50
315 Don Kessinger .40 1.00
316 Jackie Brown .20 .50
317 Joe Lahoud .20 .50
318 Ernie McAnally .20 .50
319 Johnny Oates .40 1.00
320 Pete Rose 12.00 30.00
321 Rudy May .20 .50
322 Ed Goodson .20 .50
323 Fred Holdsworth .20 .50
324 Ed Kranepool .40 1.00
325 Tony Oliva .75 2.00
326 Wayne Twitchell .20 .50
327 Jerry Hairston .20 .50
328 Sonny Siebert .20 .50
329 Ted Kubiak .20 .50
330 Mike Marshall .40 1.00
331 Cleveland Indians CL/Robinson .75 2.00
332 Fred Kendall .20 .50
333 Dick Drago .20 .50
334 Greg Gross RC .20 .50
335 Jim Palmer 2.50 6.00
336 Rennie Stennett .20 .50
337 Kevin Kobel .20 .50
338 Rich Stelmaszek .20 .50
339 Jim Fregosi .40 1.00
340 Paul Splittorff .20 .50
341 Hal Breeden .20 .50
342 Leroy Stanton .20 .50
343 Danny Frisella .20 .50
344 Ben Oglivie .40 1.00
345 Clay Carroll .40 1.00
346 Bobby Darwin .20 .50
347 Mike Caldwell .20 .50
348 Tony Muser .20 .50
349 Ray Sadecki .20 .50
350 Bobby Murcer .40 1.00
351 Bob Boone .75 2.00
352 Darold Knowles .20 .50
353 Luis Melendez .20 .50
354 Dick Bosman .20 .50
355 Chris Cannizzaro .20 .50
356 Rico Petrocelli .40 1.00
357 Ken Forsch UER .20 .50
358 Al Bumbry .40 1.00
359 Paul Popovich .20 .50
360 George Scott .40 1.00
361 Los Angeles Dodgers CL/Alston .75 2.00
362 Steve Hargan .20 .50
363 Carmen Fanzone .20 .50
364 Doug Bird .20 .50
365 Bob Bailey .20 .50
366 Ken Sanders .20 .50
367 Craig Robinson .20 .50
368 Vic Albury .20 .50
369 Merv Rettenmund .20 .50
370 Tom Seaver 8.00 20.00
371 Gates Brown .20 .50
372 John D'Acquisto .20 .50
373 Bill Sharp .20 .50
374 Eddie Watt .20 .50
375 Roy White .40 1.00
376 Steve Yeager .40 1.00
377 Tom Hilgendorf .20 .50
378 Derrel Thomas .20 .50
379 Bernie Carbo .20 .50
380 Sal Bando .40 1.00
381 John Curtis .20 .50
382 Don Baylor .75 2.00
383 Jim York .20 .50
384 Milwaukee Brewers CL/Crandall .75 2.00
385 Dock Ellis .20 .50
386 Checklist: 265-396 UER 1.25 3.00
387 Jim Spencer .20 .50
388 Steve Stone .40 1.00
389 Tony Solaita RC .20 .50
390 Ron Cey .75 2.00
391 Don DeMola RC .20 .50
392 Bruce Bochte RC .40 1.00
393 Gary Gentry .20 .50
394 Larvell Blanks .20 .50
395 Bud Harrelson .40 1.00
396 Fred Norman .40 1.00
397 Bill Freehan .40 1.00
398 Elias Sosa .20 .50
399 Terry Harmon .20 .50
400 Dick Allen .75 2.00
401 Mike Wallace .20 .50
402 Bob Tolan .20 .50
403 Tom Buskey RC .20 .50
404 Ted Sizemore .20 .50
405 John Montague RC .20 .50
406 Bob Gallagher .20 .50
407 Herb Washington RC .75 2.00
408 Clyde Wright UER .20 .50
409 Bob Robertson .20 .50
410 Mike Cuellar UER .40 1.00
411 George Mitterwald .20 .50
412 Bill Hands .20 .50
413 Marty Pattin .20 .50
414 Manny Mota .40 1.00
415 John Hiller .40 1.00
416 Larry Lintz .20 .50
417 Skip Lockwood .20 .50
418 Leo Foster .20 .50
419 Dave Goltz .20 .50
420 Larry Bowa .75 2.00
421 New York Mets CL/Berra 1.25 3.00
422 Brian Downing .40 1.00
423 Clay Kirby .20 .50
424 John Lowenstein .20 .50
425 Tito Fuentes .20 .50
426 George Medich .20 .50
427 Clarence Gaston .40 1.00
428 Dave Hamilton .20 .50
429 Jim Dwyer RC .20 .50
430 Luis Tiant .75 2.00
431 Rod Gilbreath .20 .50
432 Ken Berry .20 .50
433 Larry Demery RC .20 .50
434 Bob Locker .20 .50
435 Dave Nelson .20 .50
436 Ken Frailing .20 .50
437 Al Cowens RC .40 1.00
438 Don Carrithers .20 .50
439 Ed Brinkman .20 .50
440 Andy Messersmith .40 1.00
441 Bobby Heise .20 .50
442 Maximino Leon RC .20 .50
443 Minnesota Twins CL/Quilici .75 2.00
444 Gene Garber .40 1.00
445 Felix Millan .20 .50
446 Bart Johnson .20 .50
447 Terry Crowley .20 .50
448 Frank Duffy .20 .50
449 Charlie Williams .20 .50
450 Willie McCovey 2.50 6.00
451 Rick Dempsey .40 1.00
452 Angel Mangual .20 .50
453 Claude Osteen .40 1.00
454 Doug Griffin .20 .50
455 Don Wilson .20 .50
456 Bob Coluccio .20 .50
457 Mario Mendoza RC .20 .50
458 Ross Grimsley .20 .50
459 1974 AL Championships .40 1.00
460 1974 NL Championships .75 2.00
461 Reggie Jackson WS1 2.00 5.00
462 W.Alston/J.Ferguson WS2 .40 1.00
463 Rollie Fingers WS3 .75 2.00
464 A's Batter WS4 .40 1.00
465 Joe Rudi WS5 .40 1.00
466 A's Do it Again WS .75 2.00
467 Ed Halicki RC .20 .50
468 Bobby Mitchell .20 .50
469 Tom Dettore RC .20 .50
470 Jeff Burroughs .40 1.00
471 Bob Stinson .20 .50
472 Bruce Dal Canton .20 .50
473 Ken McMullen .20 .50
474 Luke Walker .20 .50
475 Darrell Evans .40 1.00
476 Ed Figueroa RC .20 .50
477 Tom Hutton .20 .50
478 Tom Burgmeier .20 .50
479 Ken Boswell .20 .50
480 Carlos May .20 .50
481 Will McEnaney RC .40 1.00
482 Tom McCraw .20 .50
483 Steve Ontiveros .20 .50
484 Glenn Beckert .40 1.00
485 Sparky Lyle .40 1.00
486 Ray Fosse .20 .50
487 Houston Astros CL/Gomez .75 2.00
488 Bill Travers RC .20 .50
489 Cecil Cooper .75 2.00
490 Reggie Smith .40 1.00
491 Doyle Alexander .40 1.00
492 Rich Hebner .40 1.00
493 Don Stanhouse .20 .50
494 Pete LaCock RC .20 .50
495 Nelson Briles .40 1.00
496 Pepe Frias .20 .50
497 Jim Nettles .20 .50
498 Al Downing .20 .50
499 Marty Perez .20 .50
500 Nolan Ryan 20.00 50.00
501 Bill Robinson .40 1.00
502 Pat Bourque .20 .50
503 Fred Stanley .20 .50
504 Buddy Bradford .20 .50
505 Chris Speier .20 .50
506 Leron Lee .20 .50
507 Tom Carroll RC .20 .50
508 Bob Hansen RC .20 .50
509 Dave Hilton .20 .50
510 Vida Blue .40 1.00
511 Texas Rangers CL/Martin .75 2.00
512 Larry Milbourne RC .20 .50
513 Dick Pole .20 .50
514 Jose Cruz .75 2.00
515 Manny Sanguillen .40 1.00
516 Don Hood .20 .50
517 Checklist: 397-528 1.25 3.00
518 Leo Cardenas .20 .50
519 Jim Todd RC .20 .50
520 Amos Otis .40 1.00
521 Dennis Blair RC .20 .50
522 Gary Sutherland .20 .50
523 Tom Paciorek .40 1.00
524 John Doherty RC .20 .50
525 Tom House .20 .50
526 Larry Hisle .40 1.00
527 Mac Scarce .20 .50
528 Eddie Leon .20 .50
529 Gary Thomasson .20 .50
530 Gaylord Perry 1.25 3.00
531 Cincinnati Reds CL/Anderson 2.00 5.00
532 Gorman Thomas .40 1.00
533 Rudy Meoli .20 .50
534 Alex Johnson .20 .50
535 Gene Tenace .40 1.00
536 Bob Moose .20 .50
537 Tommy Harper .40 1.00
538 Duffy Dyer .20 .50
539 Jesse Jefferson .20 .50
540 Lou Brock 2.50 6.00
541 Roger Metzger .20 .50
542 Pete Broberg .20 .50
543 Larry Biittner .20 .50
544 Steve Mingori .20 .50
545 Billy Williams 1.25 3.00
546 John Knox .20 .50
547 Von Joshua .20 .50
548 Charlie Sands .20 .50
549 Bill Butler .20 .50
550 Ralph Garr .40 1.00
551 Larry Christenson .20 .50
552 Jack Brohamer .20 .50
553 John Boccabella .20 .50
554 Goose Gossage .75 2.00
555 Al Oliver .40 1.00
556 Tim Johnson .20 .50
557 Larry Gura .20 .50
558 Dave Roberts .20 .50
559 Bob Montgomery .20 .50
560 Tony Perez 1.50 4.00
561 Oakland Athletics CL/Dark .75 2.00
562 Gary Nolan .40 1.00
563 Wilbur Howard .20 .50
564 Tommy Davis .40 1.00
565 Joe Torre .75 2.00
566 Ray Burris .20 .50
567 Jim Sundberg RC .75 2.00
568 Dale Murray RC .20 .50
569 Frank White .40 1.00
570 Jim Wynn .40 1.00
571 Dave Lemanczyk RC .20 .50
572 Roger Nelson .20 .50
573 Orlando Pena .20 .50
574 Tony Taylor .20 .50
575 Gene Clines .20 .50
576 Phil Roof .20 .50
577 John Morris .20 .50
578 Dave Tomlin RC .20 .50
579 Skip Pitlock .20 .50
580 Frank Robinson 2.50 6.00
581 Darrel Chaney .20 .50
582 Eduardo Rodriguez .20 .50
583 Andy Etchebarren .20 .50
584 Mike Garman .20 .50
585 Chris Chambliss .40 1.00
586 Tim McCarver .75 2.00
587 Chris Ward RC .20 .50
588 Rick Auerbach .20 .50
589 Atlanta Braves CL/King .75 2.00
590 Cesar Cedeno .40 1.00
591 Glenn Abbott .20 .50
592 Balor Moore .20 .50
593 Gene Lamont .20 .50
594 Jim Fuller .20 .50
595 Joe Niekro .40 1.00
596 Ollie Brown .20 .50
597 Winston Llenas .20 .50
598 Bruce Kison .20 .50
599 Nate Colbert .20 .50
600 Rod Carew 3.00 8.00
601 Juan Beniquez .20 .50
602 John Vukovich .20 .50
603 Lew Krausse .20 .50
604 Oscar Zamora RC .20 .50
605 John Ellis .20 .50
606 Bruce Miller RC .20 .50
607 Jim Holt .20 .50
608 Gene Michael .20 .50
609 Elrod Hendricks .20 .50
610 Ron Hunt .20 .50
611 New York Yankees CL/Virdon .75 2.00
612 Terry Hughes .20 .50
613 Bill Parsons .20 .50
614 Kuc/Mill/Ruhle/Sieb RC .40 1.00
615 Darcy/Leonard/Und/Webb RC .75 2.00
616 Jim Rice RC 15.00 40.00
617 Cubb/DeCinces/Sand/Trillo RC .75 2.00
618 East/John/McGregor/Rhoden RC .40 1.00
619 Ayala/Nyman/Smith Turner RC .40 1.00
620 Gary Carter RC 12.00 30.00
621 Denny/Eastwick/Kern/Vein RC .75 2.00
622 Fred Lynn RC 6.00 15.00
623 K.Hern RC/P.Garner RC 4.00 10.00
624 Kon/Lavelle/Otten/Sol RC .40 1.00
625 Boog Powell .75 2.00
626 Larry Haney UER .20 .50
627 Tom Walker .20 .50
628 Ron LeFlore RC .40 1.00
629 Joe Hoerner .20 .50
630 Greg Luzinski .75 2.00
631 Lee Lacy .20 .50
632 Morris Nettles RC .20 .50
633 Paul Casanova .20 .50
634 Cy Acosta .20 .50
635 Chuck Dobson .20 .50
636 Charlie Moore .20 .50
637 Ted Martinez .20 .50
638 Chicago Cubs CL/Marshall .75 2.00
639 Steve Kline .20 .50
640 Harmon Killebrew 2.50 6.00
641 Jim Northrup .40 1.00
642 Mike Phillips .20 .50
643 Brent Strom .20 .50
644 Bill Fahey .20 .50
645 Danny Cater .20 .50
646 Checklist: 529-660 1.25 3.00
647 Claudell Washington RC .75 2.00
648 Dave Pagan RC .20 .50
649 Jack Heidemann .20 .50
650 Dave May .20 .50
651 John Morlan RC .20 .50
652 Lindy McDaniel .40 1.00
653 Lee Richard UER .20 .50
654 Jerry Terrell .20 .50
655 Rico Carty .40 1.00
656 Bill Plummer .20 .50
657 Bob Oliver .20 .50
658 Vic Harris .20 .50

659 Bob Apodaca .20 .50
660 Hank Aaron 20.00 50.00

1975 Topps Mini

COMPLETE SET (660) 300.00 600.00
*MINI VETS: .75X TO 1.5X BASIC CARDS
*MINI ROOKIES: .5X TO 1X BASIC RC

1975 Topps Team Checklist Sheet

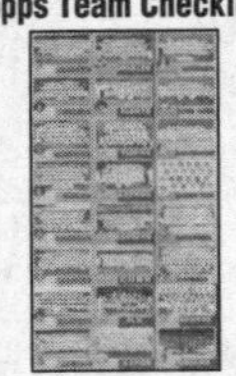

This uncut sheet of the 24 1975 Topps team checklists measures 10 1/2" by 20 1/8". The sheet was obtained by sending 40 cents plus one wrapper to Topps. When cut, each card measures the standard size.

1 Topps Team CL Sheet 20.00 50.00

1976 Topps

The 1976 Topps set of 660 standard-size cards is known for its sharp color photographs and interesting presentation of subjects. Cards were issued in ten-card wax packs which cost 15 cents upon release, 42-card rack packs as well as cello packs and other options. Team cards feature a checklist back for players on that team and show a small inset photo of the manager on the front. A "Father and Son" series (66-70) spotlights five Major Leaguers whose fathers also made the "Big Show." Other subseries include "All Time All Stars" (341-350), "Record Breakers" from the previous season (1-6), League Leaders (191-205), Post-season cards (461-462), and Rookie Prospects (589-599). The following players' regular issue cards are explicitly denoted as All-Stars, 10, 48, 60, 140, 150, 165, 169, 240, 300, 370, 380, 395, 400, 420, 475, 500, 580, and 650. The key Rookie Cards in this set are Dennis Eckersley, Ron Guidry, and Willie Randolph. We've heard recent reports that this set was also issued in seven-card wax packs which cost a dime. Confirmation of that information would be appreciated.

COMPLETE SET (660) 125.00 250.00
1 Hank Aaron RB 10.00 25.00
2 Bobby Bonds RB .60 1.50
3 Mickey Lolich RB .30 .75
4 Dave Lopes RB .30 .75
5 Tom Seaver RB 2.00 5.00
6 Rennie Stennett RB .30 .75
7 Jim Umbarger RC .15 .40
8 Tito Fuentes .15 .40
9 Paul Lindblad .15 .40
10 Lou Brock 2.00 5.00
11 Jim Hughes .15 .40
12 Richie Zisk .30 .75
13 John Wockenfuss RC .15 .40
14 Gene Garber .30 .75
15 George Scott .30 .75
16 Bob Apodaca .15 .40
17 New York Yankees CL/Martin .60 1.50
18 Dale Murray .15 .40
19 George Brett 12.50 30.00
20 Bob Watson .30 .75
21 Dave LaRoche .15 .40
22 Bill Russell .30 .75
23 Brian Downing .15 .40
24 Cesar Geronimo .30 .75
25 Mike Torrez .30 .75
26 Andre Thornton .30 .75
27 Ed Figueroa .15 .40
28 Dusty Baker .60 1.50
29 Rick Burleson .30 .75
30 John Montefusco RC .30 .75
31 Len Randle .15 .40
32 Danny Frisella .15 .40
33 Bill North .15 .40
34 Mike Garman .15 .40
35 Tony Oliva .60 1.50
36 Frank Taveras .15 .40
37 John Hiller .30 .75
38 Garry Maddox .30 .75
39 Pete Broberg .15 .40
40 Dave Kingman .60 1.50
41 Tippy Martinez RC .30 .75
42 Barry Foote .15 .40
43 Paul Splittorff .15 .40
44 Doug Rader .30 .75
45 Boog Powell .60 1.50
46 Los Angeles Dodgers CL/Alston .60 1.50
47 Jesse Jefferson .15 .40
48 Dave Concepcion .60 1.50
49 Dave Duncan .30 .75
50 Fred Lynn 2.00 5.00
51 Ray Burris .15 .40
52 Dave Chalk .15 .40
53 Mike Beard RC .15 .40
54 Dave Rader .15 .40
55 Gaylord Perry 1.00 2.50
56 Bob Tolan .15 .40
57 Phil Garner .30 .75
58 Ron Reed .15 .40
59 Larry Hisle .30 .75
60 Jerry Reuss .30 .75
61 Ron LeFlore .30 .75
62 Johnny Oates .30 .75
63 Bobby Darwin .15 .40
64 Jerry Koosman .30 .75
65 Chris Chambliss .30 .75
66 Gus/Buddy Bell FS .30 .75
67 Bob/Ray Boone FS .30 .75
68 Joe/Joe Jr. Coleman FS .15 .40
69 Jim/Mike Hegan FS .15 .40
70 Roy/Roy Jr. Smalley FS .30 .75
71 Steve Rogers .30 .75
72 Hal McRae .30 .75
73 Baltimore Orioles CL/Weaver .60 1.50
74 Oscar Gamble .30 .75
75 Larry Dierker .30 .75
76 Willie Crawford .15 .40
77 Pedro Borbon .30 .75
78 Cecil Cooper .30 .75
79 Jerry Morales .15 .40
80 Jim Kaat .60 1.50
81 Darrell Evans .30 .75
82 Von Joshua .15 .40
83 Jim Spencer .15 .40
84 Brent Strom .15 .40
85 Mickey Rivers .30 .75
86 Mike Tyson .15 .40
87 Tom Burgmeier .15 .40
88 Duffy Dyer .15 .40
89 Vern Ruhle .15 .40
90 Sal Bando .30 .75
91 Tom Hutton .15 .40
92 Eduardo Rodriguez .15 .40
93 Mike Phillips .15 .40
94 Jim Dwyer .15 .40
95 Brooks Robinson 2.50 6.00
96 Doug Bird .15 .40
97 Wilbur Howard .15 .40
98 Dennis Eckersley RC 15.00 40.00
99 Lee Lacy .15 .40
100 Jim Hunter 1.25 3.00
101 Pete LaCock .15 .40
102 Jim Willoughby .15 .40
103 Biff Pocoroba RC .15 .40
104 Cincinnati Reds CL/Anderson 1.00 2.50
105 Gary Lavelle .15 .40
106 Tom Grieve .30 .75
107 Dave Roberts .15 .40
108 Don Kirkwood RC .15 .40
109 Larry Lintz .15 .40
110 Carlos May .15 .40
111 Danny Thompson .15 .40
112 Kent Tekulve RC .60 1.50
113 Gary Sutherland .15 .40
114 Jay Johnstone .30 .75
115 Ken Holtzman .30 .75
116 Charlie Moore .15 .40
117 Mike Jorgensen .15 .40
118 Boston Red Sox CL/Johnson .60 1.50
119 Checklist 1-132 .60 1.50
120 Rusty Staub .30 .75
121 Tony Solaita .15 .40
122 Mike Cosgrove .15 .40
123 Walt Williams .15 .40
124 Doug Rau .15 .40
125 Don Baylor .60 1.50
126 Tom Dettore .15 .40
127 Larvell Blanks .15 .40
128 Ken Griffey Sr. 1.00 2.50
129 Andy Etchebarren .15 .40
130 Luis Tiant .60 1.50
131 Bill Stein RC .15 .40
132 Don Hood .15 .40
133 Gary Matthews .30 .75
134 Mike Ivie .15 .40
135 Bake McBride .30 .75
136 Dave Goltz .15 .40
137 Bill Robinson .30 .75
138 Lerrin LaGrow .15 .40
139 Gorman Thomas .30 .75
140 Vida Blue .30 .75
141 Larry Parrish RC .60 1.50
142 Dick Drago .15 .40
143 Jerry Grote .15 .40
144 Al Fitzmorris .15 .40
145 Larry Bowa .30 .75
146 George Medich .15 .40
147 Houston Astros CL/Virdon .60 1.50
148 Stan Thomas RC .15 .40
149 Tommy Davis .30 .75
150 Steve Garvey 1.00 2.50
151 Bill Bonham .15 .40
152 Leroy Stanton .15 .40
153 Buzz Capra .15 .40
154 Bucky Dent .30 .75
155 Jack Billingham .30 .75
156 Rico Carty .30 .75
157 Mike Caldwell .15 .40
158 Ken Reitz .15 .40
159 Jerry Terrell .15 .40
160 Dave Winfield 4.00 10.00
161 Bruce Kison .15 .40
162 Jack Pierce RC .15 .40
163 Jim Slaton .15 .40
164 Pepe Mangual .15 .40
165 Gene Tenace .30 .75
166 Skip Lockwood .15 .40
167 Freddie Patek .30 .75
168 Tom Hilgendorf .15 .40
169 Graig Nettles .60 1.50
170 Rick Wise .15 .40
171 Greg Gross .15 .40
172 Texas Rangers CL/Lucchesi .60 1.50
173 Steve Swisher .15 .40
174 Charlie Hough .30 .75
175 Ken Singleton .30 .75
176 Dick Lange .15 .40
177 Marty Perez .15 .40
178 Tom Buskey .15 .40
179 George Foster .60 1.50
180 Goose Gossage .60 1.50
181 Willie Montanez .15 .40
182 Harry Rasmussen .15 .40
183 Steve Braun .15 .40
184 Bill Greif .15 .40
185 Dave Parker .60 1.50
186 Tom Walker .15 .40
187 Pedro Garcia .15 .40
188 Fred Scherman .15 .40
189 Claudell Washington .30 .75
190 Jon Matlack .15 .40
191 Madlock/Simm/Mang LL .30 .75
192 Carew/Lynn/Munson LL 1.00 2.50
193 Schmidt/King/Luz LL 1.25 3.00
194 Reggie/Scott/Mayb LL 1.25 3.00
195 Luz/Bench/Perez LL .60 1.50
196 Scott/Mayb/Lynn LL .30 .75
197 Lopes/Morgan/Brock LL .60 1.50
198 Rivers/Wash/Otis LL .30 .75
199 Seaver/Jones/Mess LL 1.00 2.50
200 Hunter/Palmer/Blue LL .60 1.50
201 Jones/Mess/Seaver LL .60 1.50
202 Palmer/Hunter/Eck LL 1.25 3.00
203 Seaver/Mont/Mess LL 1.00 2.50
204 Tanana/Blyleven/Perry LL .30 .75
205 A.Hrabosky/G.Gossage LL .30 .75
206 Manny Trillo .15 .40
207 Andy Hassler .15 .40
208 Mike Lum .15 .40
209 Alan Ashby RC .15 .40
210 Lee May .30 .75
211 Clay Carroll .30 .75
212 Pat Kelly .15 .40
213 Dave Heaverlo RC .15 .40
214 Eric Soderholm .15 .40
215 Reggie Smith .30 .75
216 Montreal Expos CL/Kuehl .60 1.50
217 Dave Freisleben .15 .40
218 John Knox .15 .40
219 Tom Murphy .15 .40
220 Manny Sanguillen .30 .75
221 Jim Todd .15 .40
222 Wayne Garrett .15 .40
223 Ollie Brown .15 .40
224 Jim York .15 .40
225 Roy White .30 .75
226 Jim Sundberg .30 .75
227 Oscar Zamora .15 .40
228 John Hale RC .15 .40
229 Jerry Remy RC .15 .40
230 Carl Yastrzemski 8.00 20.00
231 Tom House .15 .40
232 Frank Duffy .15 .40
233 Grant Jackson .15 .40
234 Mike Sadek .15 .40
235 Bert Blyleven .60 1.50
236 Kansas City Royals CL/Herzog .60 1.50
237 Dave Hamilton .15 .40
238 Larry Biittner .15 .40
239 John Curtis .15 .40
240 Pete Rose 12.00 30.00
241 Hector Torres .15 .40
242 Dan Meyer .15 .40
243 Jim Rooker .15 .40
244 Bill Sharp .15 .40
245 Felix Millan .15 .40
246 Cesar Tovar .15 .40
247 Terry Harmon .15 .40
248 Dick Tidrow .15 .40
249 Cliff Johnson .30 .75
250 Fergie Jenkins 1.00 2.50
251 Rick Monday .30 .75
252 Tim Nordbrook RC .15 .40
253 Bill Buckner .30 .75
254 Rudy Meoli .15 .40
255 Fritz Peterson .15 .40
256 Rowland Office .15 .40
257 Ross Grimsley .15 .40
258 Nyls Nyman .15 .40
259 Darrel Chaney .15 .40
260 Steve Busby .15 .40
261 Gary Thomasson .15 .40
262 Checklist 133-264 .60 1.50
263 Lyman Bostock RC .60 1.50
264 Steve Renko .15 .40
265 Willie Davis .30 .75
266 Alan Foster .15 .40
267 Aurelio Rodriguez .15 .40
268 Del Unser .15 .40
269 Rick Austin .15 .40
270 Willie Stargell 1.25 3.00
271 Jim Lonborg .30 .75
272 Rick Dempsey .30 .75
273 Joe Niekro .30 .75
274 Tommy Harper .30 .75
275 Rick Manning RC .15 .40
276 Mickey Scott .15 .40
277 Chicago Cubs CL/Marshall .60 1.50
278 Bernie Carbo .15 .40
279 Roy Howell RC .15 .40
280 Burt Hooton .30 .75
281 Dave May .15 .40
282 Dan Osborn RC .15 .40
283 Merv Rettenmund .15 .40
284 Steve Ontiveros .15 .40
285 Mike Cuellar .30 .75
286 Jim Wohlford .15 .40
287 Pete Mackanin .15 .40
288 Bill Campbell .15 .40
289 Enzo Hernandez .15 .40
290 Ted Simmons .30 .75
291 Ken Sanders .15 .40
292 Leon Roberts .15 .40
293 Bill Castro RC .15 .40
294 Ed Kirkpatrick .15 .40
295 Dave Cash .15 .40
296 Pat Dobson .15 .40
297 Roger Metzger .15 .40
298 Dick Bosman .15 .40
299 Champ Summers RC .15 .40
300 Johnny Bench 10.00 25.00
301 Jackie Brown .15 .40
302 Rick Miller .15 .40
303 Steve Foucault .15 .40
304 California Angels CL/Williams .60 1.50
305 Andy Messersmith .30 .75
306 Rod Gilbreath .15 .40
307 Al Bumbry .30 .75
308 Jim Barr .15 .40
309 Bill Melton .15 .40
310 Randy Jones .30 .75
311 Cookie Rojas .15 .40
312 Don Carrithers .15 .40
313 Dan Ford RC .15 .40
314 Ed Kranepool .15 .40
315 Al Hrabosky .30 .75
316 Robin Yount 6.00 15.00
317 John Candelaria RC .60 1.50
318 Bob Boone .60 1.50
319 Larry Gura .15 .40
320 Willie Horton .30 .75
321 Jose Cruz .60 1.50
322 Glenn Abbott .15 .40
323 Rob Sperring RC .15 .40
324 Jim Bibby .15 .40
325 Tony Perez 1.25 3.00
326 Dick Pole .15 .40
327 Dave Moates RC .15 .40
328 Carl Morton .15 .40
329 Joe Ferguson .15 .40
330 Nolan Ryan 10.00 25.00
331 San Diego Padres CL/McNamara .60 1.50
332 Charlie Williams .15 .40
333 Bob Coluccio .15 .40
334 Dennis Leonard .30 .75
335 Bob Grich .30 .75
336 Vic Albury .15 .40
337 Bud Harrelson .30 .75
338 Bob Bailey .15 .40
339 John Denny .30 .75
340 Jim Rice 3.00 8.00
341 Lou Gehrig ATG 5.00 12.00
342 Rogers Hornsby ATG 1.25 3.00
343 Pie Traynor ATG .60 1.50
344 Honus Wagner ATG 2.00 5.00
345 Babe Ruth ATG 6.00 15.00
346 Ty Cobb ATG 5.00 12.00
347 Ted Williams ATG 5.00 12.00
348 Mickey Cochrane ATG .60 1.50
349 Walter Johnson ATG 2.00 5.00
350 Lefty Grove ATG .60 1.50
351 Randy Hundley .30 .75
352 Dave Giusti .15 .40
353 Sixto Lezcano RC .30 .75
354 Ron Blomberg .15 .40
355 Steve Carlton 2.50 6.00
356 Ted Martinez .15 .40
357 Ken Forsch .15 .40
358 Buddy Bell .30 .75
359 Rick Reuschel .30 .75
360 Jeff Burroughs .30 .75
361 Detroit Tigers CL/Houk .60 1.50
362 Will McEnaney .30 .75
363 Dave Collins RC .30 .75
364 Elias Sosa .15 .40
365 Carlton Fisk 2.50 6.00
366 Bobby Valentine .30 .75
367 Bruce Miller .15 .40
368 Wilbur Wood .15 .40
369 Frank White .30 .75
370 Ron Cey .30 .75
371 Elrod Hendricks .15 .40
372 Rick Baldwin RC .15 .40
373 Johnny Briggs .15 .40
374 Dan Warthen RC .15 .40
375 Ron Fairly .30 .75
376 Rich Hebner .30 .75
377 Mike Hegan .15 .40
378 Steve Stone .30 .75
379 Ken Boswell .15 .40
380 Bobby Bonds .60 1.50
381 Denny Doyle .15 .40
382 Matt Alexander RC .15 .40
383 John Ellis .15 .40
384 Philadelphia Phillies CL/Ozark .60 1.50
385 Mickey Lolich .30 .75
386 Ed Goodson .15 .40
387 Mike Miley RC .15 .40
388 Stan Perzanowski RC .15 .40
389 Glenn Adams RC .15 .40
390 Don Gullett .30 .75
391 Jerry Hairston .15 .40
392 Checklist 265-396 .60 1.50
393 Paul Mitchell RC .15 .40
394 Fran Healy .15 .40
395 Jim Wynn .30 .75
396 Bill Lee .15 .40
397 Tim Foli .15 .40
398 Dave Tomlin .15 .40
399 Luis Melendez .15 .40
400 Rod Carew 2.50 6.00
401 Ken Brett .15 .40
402 Don Money .30 .75
403 Geoff Zahn .15 .40
404 Enos Cabell .15 .40
405 Rollie Fingers 1.00 2.50
406 Ed Herrmann .15 .40
407 Tom Underwood .15 .40
408 Charlie Spikes .15 .40
409 Dave Lemanczyk .15 .40
410 Ralph Garr .30 .75
411 Bill Singer .15 .40
412 Toby Harrah .30 .75
413 Pete Varney RC .15 .40

414 Wayne Garland .15 .40
415 Vada Pinson .60 1.50
416 Tommy John .60 1.50
417 Gene Clines .15 .40
418 Jose Morales RC .15 .40
419 Reggie Cleveland .15 .40
420 Joe Morgan 2.00 5.00
421 Oakland Athletics CL .60 1.50
422 Johnny Grubb .15 .40
423 Ed Halicki .15 .40
424 Phil Roof .15 .40
425 Rennie Stennett .15 .40
426 Bob Forsch .15 .40
427 Kurt Bevacqua .15 .40
428 Jim Crawford .15 .40
429 Fred Stanley .15 .40
430 Jose Cardenal .30 .75
431 Dick Ruthven .15 .40
432 Tom Veryzer .15 .40
433 Rick Waits RC .15 .40
434 Morris Nettles .15 .40
435 Phil Niekro 1.00 2.50
436 Bill Fahey .15 .40
437 Terry Forster .15 .40
438 Doug DeCinces .30 .75
439 Rick Rhoden .30 .75
440 John Mayberry .30 .75
441 Gary Carter 3.00 8.00
442 Hank Webb .15 .40
443 San Francisco Giants CL .60 1.50
444 Gary Nolan .30 .75
445 Rico Petrocelli .30 .75
446 Larry Haney .15 .40
447 Gene Locklear .30 .75
448 Tom Johnson .15 .40
449 Bob Robertson .15 .40
450 Jim Palmer 2.00 5.00
451 Buddy Bradford .15 .40
452 Tom Hausman RC .15 .40
453 Lou Piniella .60 1.50
454 Tom Griffin .15 .40
455 Dick Allen .60 1.50
456 Joe Coleman .15 .40
457 Ed Crosby .15 .40
458 Earl Williams .15 .40
459 Jim Brewer .15 .40
460 Cesar Cedeno .30 .75
461 NL/AL Champs .30 .75
462 1975 WS/Reds Champs .30 .75
463 Steve Hargan .15 .40
464 Ken Henderson .15 .40
465 Mike Marshall .30 .75
466 Bob Stinson .15 .40
467 Woodie Fryman .15 .40
468 Jesus Alou .15 .40
469 Rawly Eastwick .30 .75
470 Bobby Murcer .30 .75
471 Jim Burton .15 .40
472 Bob Davis RC .15 .40
473 Paul Blair .30 .75
474 Ray Corbin .15 .40
475 Joe Rudi .30 .75
476 Bob Moose .15 .40
477 Cleveland Indians CL/Robinson .60 1.50
478 Lynn McGlothen .15 .40
479 Bobby Mitchell .15 .40
480 Mike Schmidt 8.00 20.00
481 Rudy May .15 .40
482 Tim Hosley .15 .40
483 Mickey Stanley .15 .40
484 Eric Raich RC .15 .40
485 Mike Hargrove .30 .75
486 Bruce Dal Canton .15 .40
487 Leron Lee .15 .40
488 Claude Osteen .30 .75
489 Skip Jutze .15 .40
490 Frank Tanana .30 .75
491 Terry Crowley .15 .40
492 Marty Pattin .15 .40
493 Derrel Thomas .15 .40
494 Craig Swan .30 .75
495 Nate Colbert .15 .40
496 Juan Beniquez .15 .40
497 Joe McIntosh RC .15 .40
498 Glenn Borgmann .15 .40
499 Mario Guerrero .15 .40
500 Reggie Jackson 6.00 15.00
501 Billy Champion .15 .40
502 Tim McCarver .60 1.50
503 Elliott Maddox .15 .40
504 Pittsburgh Pirates CL/Murtaugh .60 1.50
505 Mark Belanger .30 .75
506 George Mitterwald .15 .40
507 Ray Bare RC .15 .40
508 Duane Kuiper RC .15 .40
509 Bill Hands .15 .40
510 Amos Otis .30 .75
511 Jamie Easterley .15 .40
512 Ellie Rodriguez .15 .40
513 Bart Johnson .15 .40
514 Dan Driessen .30 .75
515 Steve Yeager .30 .75
516 Wayne Granger .15 .40
517 John Milner .15 .40
518 Doug Flynn RC .15 .40
519 Steve Brye .15 .40
520 Willie McCovey 2.00 5.00
521 Jim Colborn .15 .40
522 Ted Sizemore .15 .40
523 Bob Montgomery .15 .40
524 Pete Falcone RC .15 .40
525 Billy Williams 1.00 2.50
526 Checklist 397-528 .60 1.50
527 Mike Anderson .15 .40
528 Dock Ellis .15 .40
529 Deron Johnson .15 .40
530 Don Sutton 1.00 2.50
531 New York Mets CL/Frazier .60 1.50
532 Milt May .15 .40
533 Lee Richard .15 .40
534 Stan Bahnsen .15 .40
535 Dave Nelson .15 .40
536 Mike Thompson .15 .40
537 Tony Muser .15 .40
538 Pat Darcy .15 .40
539 John Balaz RC .15 .40
540 Bill Freehan .30 .75
541 Steve Mingori .15 .40
542 Keith Hernandez .30 .75
543 Wayne Twitchell .15 .40
544 Pepe Frias .15 .40
545 Sparky Lyle .30 .75
546 Dave Rosello .15 .40
547 Roric Harrison .15 .40
548 Manny Mota .30 .75
549 Randy Tate RC .15 .40
550 Hank Aaron 15.00 40.00
551 Jerry DaVanon .15 .40
552 Terry Humphrey .15 .40
553 Randy Moffitt .15 .40
554 Ray Fosse .15 .40
555 Dyar Miller .15 .40
556 Minnesota Twins CL/Mauch .60 1.50
557 Dan Spillner .15 .40
558 Clarence Gaston .30 .75
559 Clyde Wright .15 .40
560 Jorge Orta .15 .40
561 Tom Carroll .15 .40
562 Adrian Garrett .15 .40
563 Larry Demery .15 .40
564 Kurt Bevacqua GUM .60 1.50
565 Tug McGraw .30 .75
566 Ken McMullen .15 .40
567 George Stone .15 .40
568 Rob Andrews RC .15 .40
569 Nelson Briles .30 .75
570 George Hendrick .30 .75
571 Don DeMola .15 .40
572 Rich Coggins .15 .40
573 Bill Travers .15 .40
574 Don Kessinger .30 .75
575 Dwight Evans .60 1.50
576 Maximino Leon .15 .40
577 Marc Hill .15 .40
578 Ted Kubiak .15 .40
579 Clay Kirby .15 .40
580 Bert Campaneris .30 .75
581 St. Louis Cardinals CL/Schoendienst .60 1.50
582 Mike Kekich .15 .40
583 Tommy Helms .15 .40
584 Stan Wall RC .15 .40
585 Joe Torre .60 1.50
586 Ron Schueler .15 .40
587 Leo Cardenas .15 .40
588 Kevin Kobel .15 .40
589 Alc/Flanagan/Pac/Torr RC .60 1.50
590 Cruz/Lemon/Valen/Whit RC .30 .75
591 Grilli/Mitch/Sosa/Throop RC .30 .75
592 Randolph/McK/Roy/Sta RC 2.00 5.00
593 And/Crosby/Litell/Metzger RC .30 .75
594 Mer/Ott/Still/White RC .30 .75
595 DeFil/Lerch/Monge/Barr RC .30 .75
596 Rey/John/LeMas/Manuel RC .30 .75
597 Aase/Kucek/LaCorte/Pazik RC .30 .75
598 Cruz/Quirk/Turner/Wallis RC .30 .75
599 Dres/Guidry/McCl/Zach RC 3.00 8.00
600 Tom Seaver 6.00 15.00
601 Ken Rudolph .15 .40
602 Doug Konieczny .15 .40
603 Jim Holt .15 .40
604 Joe Lovitto .15 .40
605 Al Downing .15 .40
606 Milwaukee Brewers CL/Grammas .60 1.50
607 Rich Hinton .15 .40
608 Vic Correll .15 .40
609 Fred Norman .15 .40
610 Greg Luzinski .60 1.50
611 Rich Folkers .15 .40
612 Joe Lahoud .15 .40
613 Tim Johnson .15 .40
614 Fernando Arroyo RC .15 .40
615 Mike Cubbage .15 .40
616 Buck Martinez .15 .40
617 Darold Knowles .15 .40
618 Jack Brohamer .15 .40
619 Bill Butler .15 .40
620 Al Oliver .30 .75
621 Tom Hall .15 .40
622 Rick Auerbach .15 .40
623 Bob Allietta RC .15 .40
624 Tony Taylor .15 .40
625 J.R. Richard .30 .75
626 Bob Sheldon .15 .40
627 Bill Plummer .15 .40
628 John D'Acquisto .15 .40
629 Sandy Alomar .30 .75
630 Chris Speier .15 .40
631 Atlanta Braves CL/Bristol .60 1.50
632 Rogelio Moret .15 .40
633 John Stearns RC .30 .75
634 Larry Christenson .15 .40
635 Jim Fregosi .30 .75
636 Joe Decker .15 .40
637 Bruce Bochte .15 .40
638 Doyle Alexander .30 .75
639 Fred Kendall .15 .40
640 Bill Madlock .60 1.50
641 Tom Paciorek .30 .75
642 Dennis Blair .15 .40
643 Checklist 529-660 .60 1.50
644 Tom Bradley .15 .40
645 Darrell Porter .30 .75
646 John Lowenstein .15 .40
647 Ramon Hernandez .15 .40
648 Al Cowens .30 .75
649 Dave Roberts .15 .40
650 Thurman Munson 2.50 6.00
651 John Odom .15 .40
652 Ed Armbrister .15 .40
653 Mike Norris RC .30 .75
654 Doug Griffin .15 .40
655 Mike Vail RC .15 .40
656 Chicago White Sox CL/Tanner .60 1.50
657 Roy Smalley RC .30 .75
658 Jerry Johnson .15 .40
659 Ben Oglivie .30 .75
660 Davey Lopes .60 1.50

1976 Topps Traded

The cards in this 44-card set measure 2 1/2" by 3 1/2". The 1976 Topps Traded set contains 43 players and one unnumbered checklist card. The individuals pictured were traded after the Topps regular set was printed. A "Sports Extra" heading design is found on each picture and is also used to introduce the biographical section of the reverse. Each card is numbered according to the player's regular 1976 card with the addition of "T" to indicate his new status. As in 1974, the cards were inserted in all packs toward the end of the production run. According to published reports at the time, they were not released until April, 1976. Because they were produced in large quantities, they are no scarcer than the basic cards. Reports at the time indicated that a dealer could make approximately 35 sets from a vending case. The vending cases included both regular and traded cards.

COMPLETE SET (44) 12.50 30.00
27T Ed Figueroa .15 .40
28T Dusty Baker .60 1.50
44T Doug Rader .30 .75
58T Ron Reed .15 .40
74T Oscar Gamble .60 1.50
80T Jim Kaat .60 1.50
83T Jim Spencer .15 .40
85T Mickey Rivers .30 .75
99T Lee Lacy .15 .40
120T Rusty Staub .30 .75
127T Larvell Blanks .15 .40
146T George Medich .15 .40
158T Ken Reitz .15 .40
208T Mike Lum .15 .40
211T Clay Carroll .15 .40
231T Tom House .15 .40
250T Fergie Jenkins 1.25 3.00
259T Darrel Chaney .15 .40
292T Leon Roberts .15 .40
296T Pat Dobson .15 .40
309T Bill Melton .15 .40
338T Bob Bailey .15 .40
380T Bobby Bonds .60 1.50
383T John Ellis .15 .40
385T Mickey Lolich .30 .75
401T Ken Brett .15 .40
410T Ralph Garr .15 .40
411T Bill Singer .15 .40
428T Jim Crawford .15 .40
434T Morris Nettles .15 .40
464T Ken Henderson .15 .40
497T Joe McIntosh .15 .40
524T Pete Falcone .15 .40
527T Mike Anderson .15 .40
528T Dock Ellis .15 .40
532T Milt May .15 .40
554T Ray Fosse .15 .40
579T Clay Kirby .15 .40
583T Tommy Helms .15 .40
592T Willie Randolph 2.00 5.00
618T Jack Brohamer .15 .40
632T Rogelio Moret .15 .40
649T Dave Roberts .15 .40
NNO Traded Checklist .75 2.00

1976 Topps Team Checklist Sheet

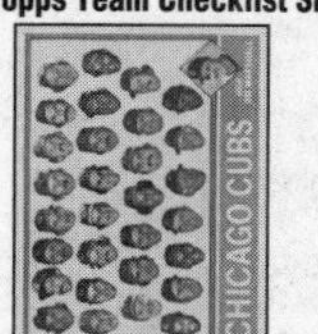

This uncut sheet of the 24 1976 Topps team checklists measures 10" by 21". The sheet was obtained by sending 50 cents plus one wrapper to Topps. When seperated, these cards measure the standard-size.

1 Topps Team CL Sheet 50.00 100.00

1976 Topps Cloth Sticker Test

Before releasing their 1977 Cloth Sticker set, Topps experimented and produced several type cards for a 1976 Cloth Sticker set. While these standard-size cards were never released to the public, a few have made their way into the secondary market. Any more information and additions to this checklist is appreciated.

1 Bob Apodaca 20.00 50.00
2 Duffy Dyer 20.00 50.00

1976 Topps Garagiola

This one-card set was produced by Topps in honor of catcher Joe Garagiola. The front features a color portrait of the player in a thin black fame with a white border. The back displays the player's name and business address in a black cut-out bubble with the player's information and statistics printed in the background.

1 Joe Garagiola 4.00 10.00

1977 Topps

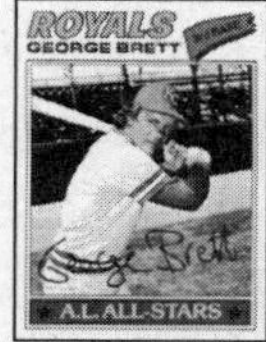

In 1977 for the fifth consecutive year, Topps produced a 660-card standard-size baseball set. Among other fashions, this set was released in 10-card wax packs as well as thirty-nine card rack packs. The player's name, team affiliation, and his position are compactly arranged over the picture area and a facsimile autograph appears on the photo. Team cards feature a checklist of that team's players in the set and a small picture of the manager on the front of the card. Appearing for the first time are the series "Brothers" (631-634) and "Turn Back the Clock" (433-437). Other subseries in the set are League Leaders (1-8), Record Breakers (231-234), Playoffs cards (276-277), World Series cards (411-413), and Rookie Prospects (472-479/487-494). The following players' regular issue cards are explicitly denoted as All-Stars, 30, 70, 100, 120, 170, 210, 240, 265, 301, 347, 400, 420, 450, 500, 521, 550, 560, and 580. The key Rookie Cards in the set are Jack Clark, Andre Dawson, Mark "The Bird" Fidrych, Dennis Martinez and Dale Murphy. Cards numbered 23 or lower, that feature Yankees and do not follow the numbering checklisted below, are not necessarily error cards. Those cards were issued in the NY area and distributed by Burger King. There was an aluminum version of the Dale Murphy rookie card number 476 produced (legally) in the early '80s; proceeds from the sales originally priced at 10.00) of this "card" went to the Huntington's Disease Foundation.

COMPLETE SET (660) 125.00 250.00
1 G.Brett/B.Madlock LL 3.00 8.00
2 G.Nettles/M.Schmidt LL 1.00 2.50
3 L.May/G.Foster LL .60 1.50
4 B.North/D.Lopes LL .30 .75
5 J.Palmer/R.Jones LL .60 1.50
6 N.Ryan/T.Seaver LL 6.00 15.00
7 M.Fidrych/J.Denny LL .30 .75
8 B.Campbell/R.Eastwick LL .30 .75
9 Doug Rader .12 .30
10 Reggie Jackson 6.00 15.00
11 Rob Dressler .12 .30
12 Larry Haney .12 .30
13 Luis Gomez RC .12 .30
14 Tommy Smith .12 .30
15 Don Gullett .30 .75
16 Bob Jones RC .12 .30
17 Steve Stone .30 .75
18 Cleveland Indians CL/Robinson .60 1.50
19 John D'Acquisto .12 .30
20 Graig Nettles .60 1.50
21 Ken Forsch .12 .30
22 Bill Freehan .30 .75
23 Dan Driessen .12 .30
24 Carl Morton .12 .30
25 Dwight Evans .60 1.50
26 Ray Sadecki .12 .30
27 Bill Buckner .30 .75
28 Woodie Fryman .12 .30
29 Bucky Dent .30 .75
30 Greg Luzinski .60 1.50
31 Jim Todd .12 .30
32 Checklist 1-132 .60 1.50
33 Wayne Garland .12 .30
34 California Angels CL/Sherry .60 1.50
35 Rennie Stennett .12 .30
36 John Ellis .12 .30
37 Steve Hargan .12 .30
38 Craig Kusick .12 .30
39 Tom Griffin .12 .30
40 Bobby Murcer .30 .75
41 Jim Kern .12 .30
42 Jose Cruz .30 .75
43 Ray Bare .12 .30
44 Bud Harrelson .30 .75
45 Rawly Eastwick .12 .30
46 Buck Martinez .12 .30
47 Lynn McGlothen .12 .30
48 Tom Paciorek .30 .75
49 Grant Jackson .12 .30
50 Ron Cey .30 .75
51 Milwaukee Brewers CL/Grammas .60 1.50
52 Ellis Valentine .12 .30
53 Paul Mitchell .12 .30
54 Sandy Alomar .30 .75
55 Jeff Burroughs .30 .75
56 Rudy May .12 .30
57 Marc Hill .12 .30
58 Chet Lemon .30 .75
59 Larry Christenson .12 .30
60 Jim Rice 1.50 4.00
61 Manny Sanguillen .30 .75
62 Eric Raich .12 .30
63 Tito Fuentes .12 .30
64 Larry Biittner .12 .30
65 Skip Lockwood .12 .30
66 Roy Smalley .30 .75
67 Joaquin Andujar RC .30 .75

Card	Low	High
68 Bruce Bochte	.12	.30
69 Jim Crawford	.12	.30
70 Johnny Bench	6.00	15.00
71 Dock Ellis	.12	.30
72 Mike Anderson	.12	.30
73 Charlie Williams	.12	.30
74 Oakland Athletics CL/McKeon	.60	1.50
75 Dennis Leonard	.30	.75
76 Tim Foli	.12	.30
77 Dyar Miller	.12	.30
78 Bob Davis	.12	.30
79 Don Money	.30	.75
80 Andy Messersmith	.30	.75
81 Juan Beniquez	.12	.30
82 Jim Rooker	.12	.30
83 Kevin Bell RC	.12	.30
84 Ollie Brown	.12	.30
85 Duane Kuiper	.12	.30
86 Pat Zachry	.12	.30
87 Glenn Borgmann	.12	.30
88 Stan Wall	.12	.30
89 Butch Hobson RC	.30	.75
90 Cesar Cedeno	.30	.75
91 John Verhoeven RC	.12	.30
92 Dave Rosello	.12	.30
93 Tom Poquette	.12	.30
94 Craig Swan	.12	.30
95 Keith Hernandez	.30	.75
96 Lou Piniella	.30	.75
97 Dave Heaverlo	.12	.30
98 Milt May	.12	.30
99 Tom Hausman	.12	.30
100 Joe Morgan	1.50	4.00
101 Dick Bosman	.12	.30
102 Jose Morales	.12	.30
103 Mike Bacsik RC	.12	.30
104 Omar Moreno RC	.30	.75
105 Steve Yeager	.30	.75
106 Mike Flanagan	.30	.75
107 Bill Melton	.12	.30
108 Alan Foster	.12	.30
109 Jorge Orta	.12	.30
110 Steve Carlton	2.00	5.00
111 Rico Petrocelli	.30	.75
112 Bill Greif	.12	.30
113 Toronto Blue Jays CL/Hartsfield	.60	1.50
114 Bruce Dal Canton	.12	.30
115 Rick Manning	.12	.30
116 Joe Niekro	.30	.75
117 Frank White	.30	.75
118 Rick Jones RC	.12	.30
119 John Stearns	.12	.30
120 Rod Carew	2.00	5.00
121 Gary Nolan	.12	.30
122 Ben Oglivie	.30	.75
123 Fred Stanley	.12	.30
124 George Mitterwald	.12	.30
125 Bill Travers	.12	.30
126 Rod Gilbreath	.12	.30
127 Ron Fairly	.30	.75
128 Tommy John	.60	1.50
129 Mike Sadek	.12	.30
130 Al Oliver	.30	.75
131 Orlando Ramirez RC	.12	.30
132 Chip Lang RC	.12	.30
133 Ralph Garr	.30	.75
134 San Diego Padres CL/McNamara	.60	1.50
135 Mark Belanger	.30	.75
136 Jerry Mumphrey RC	.30	.75
137 Jeff Terpko RC	.12	.30
138 Bob Stinson	.12	.30
139 Fred Norman	.12	.30
140 Mike Schmidt	5.00	12.00
141 Mark Littell	.12	.30
142 Steve Dillard RC	.12	.30
143 Ed Herrmann	.12	.30
144 Bruce Sutter RC	6.00	15.00
145 Tom Veryzer	.12	.30
146 Dusty Baker	.60	1.50
147 Jackie Brown	.12	.30
148 Fran Healy	.12	.30
149 Mike Cubbage	.12	.30
150 Tom Seaver	3.00	8.00
151 Johnny LeMaster	.12	.30
152 Gaylord Perry	1.00	2.50
153 Ron Jackson RC	.12	.30
154 Dave Giusti	.12	.30
155 Joe Rudi	.30	.75
156 Pete Mackanin	.12	.30
157 Ken Brett	.12	.30
158 Ted Kubiak	.12	.30
159 Bernie Carbo	.12	.30
160 Will McEnaney	.12	.30
161 Garry Templeton RC	.60	1.50
162 Mike Cuellar	.30	.75
163 Dave Hilton	.12	.30
164 Tug McGraw	.30	.75
165 Jim Wynn	.30	.75
166 Bill Campbell	.12	.30
167 Rich Hebner	.30	.75
168 Charlie Spikes	.12	.30
169 Darold Knowles	.12	.30
170 Thurman Munson	10.00	25.00
171 Ken Sanders	.12	.30
172 John Milner	.12	.30
173 Chuck Scrivener RC	.12	.30
174 Nelson Briles	.30	.75
175 Butch Wynegar RC	.30	.75
176 Bob Robertson	.12	.30
177 Bart Johnson	.12	.30
178 Bombo Rivera RC	.12	.30
179 Paul Hartzell RC	.12	.30
180 Dave Lopes	.30	.75
181 Ken McMullen	.12	.30
182 Dan Spillner	.12	.30
183 St.Louis Cardinals CL/V.Rapp	.60	1.50
184 Bo McLaughlin RC	.12	.30
185 Sixto Lezcano	.12	.30
186 Doug Flynn	.12	.30
187 Dick Pole	.12	.30
188 Bob Tolan	.12	.30
189 Rick Dempsey	.30	.75
190 Ray Burris	.12	.30
191 Doug Griffin	.12	.30
192 Clarence Gaston	.30	.75
193 Larry Gura	.12	.30
194 Gary Matthews	.30	.75
195 Ed Figueroa	.12	.30
196 Len Randle	.12	.30
197 Ed Ott	.12	.30
198 Wilbur Wood	.12	.30
199 Pepe Frias	.12	.30
200 Frank Tanana	.30	.75
201 Ed Kranepool	.12	.30
202 Tom Johnson	.12	.30
203 Ed Armbrister	.12	.30
204 Jeff Newman RC	.12	.30
205 Pete Falcone	.12	.30
206 Boog Powell	.60	1.50
207 Glenn Abbott	.12	.30
208 Checklist 133-264	.60	1.50
209 Rob Andrews	.12	.30
210 Fred Lynn	.75	2.00
211 San Francisco Giants CL/Altobelli	.60	1.50
212 Jim Mason	.12	.30
213 Maximino Leon	.12	.30
214 Darrell Porter	.30	.75
215 Butch Metzger	.12	.30
216 Doug DeCinces	.30	.75
217 Tom Underwood	.12	.30
218 John Wathan RC	.30	.75
219 Joe Coleman	.12	.30
220 Chris Chambliss	.30	.75
221 Bob Bailey	.12	.30
222 Francisco Barrios RC	.12	.30
223 Earl Williams	.12	.30
224 Rusty Torres	.12	.30
225 Bob Apodaca	.12	.30
226 Leroy Stanton	.30	.75
227 Joe Sambito RC	.12	.30
228 Minnesota Twins CL/Mauch	.60	1.50
229 Don Kessinger	.30	.75
230 Vida Blue	.30	.75
231 George Brett RB	3.00	8.00
232 Minnie Minoso RB	.30	.75
233 Jose Morales RB	.12	.30
234 Nolan Ryan RB	5.00	12.00
235 Cecil Cooper	.30	.75
236 Tom Buskey	.12	.30
237 Gene Clines	.12	.30
238 Tippy Martinez	.12	.30
239 Bill Plummer	.12	.30
240 Ron LeFlore	.30	.75
241 Dave Tomlin	.12	.30
242 Ken Henderson	.12	.30
243 Ron Reed	.12	.30
244 John Mayberry	.30	.75
245 Rick Rhoden	.30	.75
246 Mike Vail	.12	.30
247 Chris Knapp RC	.12	.30
248 Wilbur Howard	.12	.30
249 Pete Redfern RC	.12	.30
250 Bill Madlock	.30	.75
251 Tony Muser	.12	.30
252 Dale Murray	.12	.30
253 John Hale	.12	.30
254 Doyle Alexander	.12	.30
255 George Scott	.30	.75
256 Joe Hoerner	.12	.30
257 Mike Miley	.12	.30
258 Luis Tiant	.30	.75
259 New York Mets CL/Frazier	.60	1.50
260 J.R. Richard	.30	.75
261 Phil Garner	.30	.75
262 Al Cowens	.30	.75
263 Mike Marshall	.30	.75
264 Tom Hutton	.12	.30
265 Mark Fidrych RC	1.25	3.00
266 Derrel Thomas	.12	.30
267 Ray Fosse	.12	.30
268 Rick Sawyer RC	.12	.30
269 Joe Lis	.12	.30
270 Dave Parker	.60	1.50
271 Terry Forster	.12	.30
272 Lee Lacy	.12	.30
273 Eric Soderholm	.12	.30
274 Don Stanhouse	.12	.30
275 Mike Hargrove	.30	.75
276 Chris Chambliss ALCS	.60	1.50
277 Pete Rose NLCS	2.00	5.00
278 Danny Frisella	.12	.30
279 Joe Wallis	.12	.30
280 Jim Hunter	1.00	2.50
281 Roy Staiger	.12	.30
282 Sid Monge	.12	.30
283 Jerry DaVanon	.12	.30
284 Mike Norris	.12	.30
285 Brooks Robinson	2.00	5.00
286 Johnny Grubb	.12	.30
287 Cincinnati Reds CL/Anderson	.60	1.50
288 Bob Montgomery	.12	.30
289 Gene Garber	.30	.75
290 Amos Otis	.30	.75
291 Jason Thompson RC	.30	.75
292 Rogelio Moret	.12	.30
293 Jack Brohamer	.12	.30
294 George Medich	.12	.30
295 Gary Carter	1.50	4.00
296 Don Hood	.12	.30
297 Ken Reitz	.12	.30
298 Charlie Hough	.30	.75
299 Otto Velez	.30	.75
300 Jerry Koosman	.30	.75
301 Toby Harrah	.30	.75
302 Mike Garman	.12	.30
303 Gene Tenace	.30	.75
304 Jim Hughes	.12	.30
305 Mickey Rivers	.30	.75
306 Rick Waits	.12	.30
307 Gary Sutherland	.12	.30
308 Gene Pentz RC	.12	.30
309 Boston Red Sox CL/Zimmer	.60	1.50
310 Larry Bowa	.30	.75
311 Vern Ruhle	.12	.30
312 Rob Belloir RC	.12	.30
313 Paul Blair	.30	.75
314 Steve Mingori	.12	.30
315 Dave Chalk	.12	.30
316 Steve Rogers	.12	.30
317 Kurt Bevacqua	.12	.30
318 Duffy Dyer	.12	.30
319 Goose Gossage	.60	1.50
320 Ken Griffey Sr.	.60	1.50
321 Dave Goltz	.12	.30
322 Bill Russell	.30	.75
323 Larry Lintz	.12	.30
324 John Curtis	.12	.30
325 Mike Ivie	.12	.30
326 Jesse Jefferson	.12	.30
327 Houston Astros CL/Virdon	.60	1.50
328 Tommy Boggs RC	.12	.30
329 Ron Hodges	.12	.30
330 George Hendrick	.30	.75
331 Jim Colborn	.12	.30
332 Elliott Maddox	.12	.30
333 Paul Reuschel RC	.12	.30
334 Bill Stein	.12	.30
335 Bill Robinson	.30	.75
336 Denny Doyle	.12	.30
337 Ron Schueler	.12	.30
338 Dave Duncan	.30	.75
339 Adrian Devine	.12	.30
340 Hal McRae	.30	.75
341 Joe Kerrigan RC	.12	.30
342 Jerry Remy	.12	.30
343 Ed Halicki	.12	.30
344 Brian Downing	.30	.75
345 Reggie Smith	.30	.75
346 Bill Singer	.12	.30
347 George Foster	.60	1.50
348 Brent Strom	.12	.30
349 Jim Holt	.12	.30
350 Larry Dierker	.30	.75
351 Jim Sundberg	.30	.75
352 Mike Phillips	.12	.30
353 Stan Thomas	.12	.30
354 Pittsburgh Pirates CL/Tanner	.60	1.50
355 Lou Brock	1.50	4.00
356 Checklist 265-396	.60	1.50
357 Tim McCarver	.60	1.50
358 Tom House	.12	.30
359 Willie Randolph	.60	1.50
360 Rick Monday	.30	.75
361 Eduardo Rodriguez	.12	.30
362 Tommy Davis	.30	.75
363 Dave Roberts	.12	.30
364 Vic Correll	.12	.30
365 Mike Torrez	.30	.75
366 Ted Sizemore	.12	.30
367 Dave Hamilton	.12	.30
368 Mike Jorgensen	.12	.30
369 Terry Humphrey	.12	.30
370 John Montefusco	.12	.30
371 Kansas City Royals CL/Herzog	.60	1.50
372 Rich Folkers	.12	.30
373 Bert Campaneris	.30	.75
374 Kent Tekulve	.30	.75
375 Larry Hisle	.30	.75
376 Nino Espinosa RC	.12	.30
377 Dave McKay	.12	.30
378 Jim Umbarger	.12	.30
379 Larry Cox RC	.12	.30
380 Lee May	.30	.75
381 Bob Forsch	.12	.30
382 Charlie Moore	.12	.30
383 Stan Bahnsen	.12	.30
384 Darrel Chaney	.12	.30
385 Dave LaRoche	.12	.30
386 Manny Mota	.30	.75
387 New York Yankees CL/Martin	1.00	2.50
388 Terry Harmon	.12	.30
389 Ken Kravec RC	.12	.30
390 Dave Winfield	2.50	6.00
391 Dan Warthen	.12	.30
392 Phil Roof	.12	.30
393 John Lowenstein	.12	.30
394 Bill Laxton RC	.12	.30
395 Manny Trillo	.12	.30
396 Tom Murphy	.12	.30
397 Larry Herndon RC	.30	.75
398 Tom Burgmeier	.12	.30
399 Bruce Boisclair RC	.12	.30
400 Steve Garvey	1.00	2.50
401 Mickey Scott	.12	.30
402 Tommy Helms	.12	.30
403 Tom Grieve	.30	.75
404 Eric Rasmussen RC	.12	.30
405 Claudell Washington	.30	.75
406 Tim Johnson	.12	.30
407 Dave Freisleben	.12	.30
408 Cesar Tovar	.12	.30
409 Pete Broberg	.12	.30
410 Willie Montanez	.12	.30
411 J.Morgan/J.Bench WS	1.00	2.50
412 Johnny Bench WS	1.00	2.50
413 Cincy Wins WS	.30	.75
414 Tommy Harper	.30	.75
415 Jay Johnstone	.30	.75
416 Chuck Hartenstein	.12	.30
417 Wayne Garrett	.12	.30
418 Chicago White Sox CL/Lemon	.60	1.50
419 Steve Swisher	.12	.30
420 Rusty Staub	.60	1.50
421 Doug Rau	.12	.30
422 Freddie Patek	.30	.75
423 Gary Lavelle	.12	.30
424 Steve Brye	.12	.30
425 Joe Torre	.60	1.50
426 Dick Drago	.12	.30
427 Dave Rader	.12	.30
428 Texas Rangers CL/Lucchesi	.60	1.50
429 Ken Boswell	.12	.30
430 Fergie Jenkins	1.00	2.50
431 Dave Collins UER	.30	.75
432 Buzz Capra	.12	.30
433 Nate Colbert TBC	.12	.30
434 Carl Yastrzemski TBC	.60	1.50
435 Maury Wills TBC	.30	.75
436 Bob Keegan TBC	.12	.30
437 Ralph Kiner TBC	.60	1.50
438 Marty Perez	.12	.30
439 Gorman Thomas	.30	.75
440 Jon Matlack	.12	.30
441 Larvell Blanks	.12	.30
442 Atlanta Braves CL/Bristol	.60	1.50
443 Lamar Johnson	.12	.30
444 Wayne Twitchell	.12	.30
445 Ken Singleton	.30	.75
446 Bill Bonham	.12	.30
447 Jerry Turner	.12	.30
448 Ellie Rodriguez	.12	.30
449 Al Fitzmorris	.12	.30
450 Pete Rose	5.00	12.00
451 Checklist 397-528	.60	1.50
452 Mike Caldwell	.12	.30
453 Pedro Garcia	.12	.30
454 Andy Etchebarren	.12	.30
455 Rick Wise	.12	.30
456 Leon Roberts	.12	.30
457 Steve Luebber	.12	.30
458 Leo Foster	.12	.30
459 Steve Foucault	.12	.30
460 Willie Stargell	1.00	2.50
461 Dick Tidrow	.12	.30
462 Don Baylor	.60	1.50
463 Jamie Quirk	.12	.30
464 Randy Moffitt	.12	.30
465 Rico Carty	.30	.75
466 Fred Holdsworth	.12	.30
467 Philadelphia Phillies CL/Ozark	.60	1.50
468 Ramon Hernandez	.12	.30
469 Pat Kelly	.12	.30
470 Ted Simmons	.30	.75
471 Del Unser	.12	.30
472 Aase/McCl/Patt/Wehr RC	.12	.30
473 Andre Dawson RC	15.00	40.00
474 Bailor/Gar/Reyn/Tav RC	.30	.75
475 Batt/Camp/McGr/Sarm RC	.30	.75
476 Dale Murphy RC	12.00	30.00
477 Ault/Dauer/Gonz/Mank RC	.30	.75
478 Gid/Hoot/John/Lemong RC	.30	.75
479 Assel/Gross/Mej/Woods RC	.30	.75
480 Carl Yastrzemski	3.00	8.00
481 Roger Metzger	.12	.30
482 Tony Solaita	.12	.30
483 Richie Zisk	.12	.30
484 Burt Hooton	.30	.75
485 Roy White	.30	.75
486 Ed Bane	.12	.30
487 And/Glynn/Hend/Terl RC	.30	.75
488 J.Clark/L.Mazzilli RC	1.25	3.00
489 Barker/Ler/Mint/Overy RC	.30	.75
490 Almon/Klutts/McM/Wag RC	.30	.75
491 Dennis Martinez RC	1.25	3.00
492 Armas/Kemp/Lop/Woods RC	.30	.75
493 Krukow/Ott/Wheel/Will RC	.30	.75
494 J.Gantner/B.Wills RC	.60	1.50
495 Al Hrabosky	.30	.75
496 Gary Thomasson	.12	.30
497 Clay Carroll	.12	.30
498 Sal Bando	.30	.75
499 Pablo Torrealba	.12	.30
500 Dave Kingman	.60	1.50
501 Jim Bibby	.12	.30
502 Randy Hundley	.12	.30
503 Bill Lee	.12	.30
504 Los Angeles Dodgers CL/Lasorda	.60	1.50
505 Oscar Gamble	.30	.75
506 Steve Grilli	.12	.30
507 Mike Hegan	.12	.30
508 Dave Pagan	.12	.30
509 Cookie Rojas	.30	.75
510 John Candelaria	.12	.30
511 Bill Fahey	.12	.30
512 Jack Billingham	.12	.30
513 Jerry Terrell	.12	.30
514 Cliff Johnson	.12	.30
515 Chris Speier	.12	.30
516 Bake McBride	.30	.75
517 Pete Vuckovich RC	.30	.75
518 Chicago Cubs CL/Franks	.60	1.50
519 Don Kirkwood	.12	.30
520 Garry Maddox	.12	.30
521 Bob Grich	.30	.75
522 Enzo Hernandez	.12	.30
523 Rollie Fingers	1.00	2.50
524 Rowland Office	.12	.30
525 Dennis Eckersley	2.00	5.00
526 Larry Parrish	.30	.75
527 Dan Meyer	.30	.75
528 Bill Castro	.12	.30
529 Jim Essian RC	.12	.30
530 Rick Reuschel	.30	.75
531 Lyman Bostock	.30	.75
532 Jim Willoughby	.12	.30

533 Mickey Stanley .12 .30
534 Paul Splittorff .12 .30
535 Cesar Geronimo .12 .30
536 Vic Albury .12 .30
537 Dave Roberts .12 .30
538 Frank Taveras .12 .30
539 Mike Wallace .12 .30
540 Bob Watson .30 .75
541 John Denny .30 .75
542 Frank Duffy .12 .30
543 Ron Blomberg .12 .30
544 Gary Ross .10 .30
545 Bob Boone .30 .75
546 Baltimore Orioles CL/Weaver .60 1.50
547 Willie McCovey 1.50 4.00
548 Joel Youngblood RC .12 .30
549 Jerry Royster .12 .30
550 Randy Jones .12 .30
551 Bill North .12 .30
552 Pepe Mangual .12 .30
553 Jack Heidemann .12 .30
554 Bruce Kimm RC .12 .30
555 Dan Ford .12 .30
556 Doug Bird .12 .30
557 Jerry White .12 .30
558 Elias Sosa .12 .30
559 Alan Bannister RC .12 .30
560 Dave Concepcion .60 1.50
561 Pete LaCock .12 .30
562 Checklist 529-660 .60 1.50
563 Bruce Kison .12 .30
564 Alan Ashby .12 .30
565 Mickey Lolich .30 .75
566 Rick Miller .12 .30
567 Enos Cabell .12 .30
568 Carlos May .12 .30
569 Jim Lonborg .30 .75
570 Bobby Bonds .60 1.50
571 Darrell Evans .30 .75
572 Ross Grimsley .12 .30
573 Joe Ferguson .12 .30
574 Aurelio Rodriguez .12 .30
575 Dick Ruthven .12 .30
576 Fred Kendall .12 .30
577 Jerry Augustine RC .12 .30
578 Bob Randall RC .12 .30
579 Don Carrithers .12 .30
580 George Brett 8.00 20.00
581 Pedro Borbon .12 .30
582 Ed Kirkpatrick .12 .30
583 Paul Lindblad .12 .30
584 Ed Goodson .12 .30
585 Rick Burleson .30 .75
586 Steve Renko .12 .30
587 Rick Baldwin .12 .30
588 Dave Moates .12 .30
589 Mike Cosgrove .12 .30
590 Buddy Bell .30 .75
591 Chris Arnold .12 .30
592 Dan Briggs RC .12 .30
593 Dennis Blair .12 .30
594 Biff Pocoroba .12 .30
595 John Hiller .12 .30
596 Jerry Martin RC .12 .30
597 Seattle Mariners CL/Johnson .60 1.50
598 Sparky Lyle .30 .75
599 Mike Tyson .12 .30
600 Jim Palmer 1.50 4.00
601 Mike Lum .12 .30
602 Andy Hassler .12 .30
603 Willie Davis .30 .75
604 Jim Slaton .12 .30
605 Felix Millan .12 .30
606 Steve Braun .12 .30
607 Larry Demery .12 .30
608 Roy Howell .12 .30
609 Jim Barr .12 .30
610 Jose Cardenal .30 .75
611 Dave Lemanczyk .12 .30
612 Barry Foote .12 .30
613 Reggie Cleveland .12 .30
614 Greg Gross .12 .30
615 Phil Niekro 1.00 2.50
616 Tommy Sandt RC .12 .30
617 Bobby Darwin .12 .30
618 Pat Dobson .12 .30
619 Johnny Oates .30 .75
620 Don Sutton 1.00 2.50
621 Detroit Tigers CL/Houk .60 1.50
622 Jim Wohlford .12 .30
623 Jack Kucek .12 .30
624 Hector Cruz .12 .30
625 Ken Holtzman .30 .75
626 Al Bumbry .30 .75
627 Bob Myrick RC .12 .30
628 Mario Guerrero .12 .30
629 Bobby Valentine .30 .75
630 Bert Blyleven .60 1.50
631 Brett Brothers 2.50 6.00
632 Forsch Brothers .30 .75
633 May Brothers .30 .75
634 Reuschel Brothers UER .30 .75
635 Robin Yount 3.00 8.00
636 Santo Alcala .12 .30
637 Alex Johnson .12 .30
638 Jim Kaat .60 1.50
639 Jerry Morales .12 .30
640 Carlton Fisk 2.00 5.00
641 Dan Larson RC .12 .30
642 Willie Crawford .12 .30
643 Mike Pazik .12 .30
644 Matt Alexander .12 .30
645 Jerry Reuss .30 .75
646 Andres Mora RC .12 .30
647 Montreal Expos CL/Williams .60 1.50
648 Jim Spencer .12 .30
649 Dave Cash .12 .30
650 Nolan Ryan 10.00 25.00
651 Von Joshua .12 .30
652 Tom Walker .12 .30
653 Diego Segui .30 .75
654 Ron Pruitt RC .12 .30
655 Tony Perez 1.00 2.50
656 Ron Guidry .60 1.50
657 Mick Kelleher RC .12 .30
658 Marty Pattin .12 .30
659 Merv Rettenmund .12 .30
660 Willie Horton .60 1.50

1977 Topps Cloth Stickers

The "cards" in this 73-card set measure 2 1/2" by 3 1/2". The 1977 Cloth Stickers series was issued as a test set separately from the regular baseball series of that year. The packs of these cards contained two stickers as well as one "checklist puzzle" piece. The obverse pictures are identical to those appearing in the regular set, but the backs are completely different. There are 55 player cards and 18 unnumbered checklists, the latter bearing the title "Baseball Patches". The player cards are sequenced in alphabetical order. The checklists are puzzle pieces which, when properly arranged, form pictures of the A.L. and N.L. All-Star teams. Puzzle pieces are coded below by U (Upper), M (Middle), B (Bottom), L (left), C (Center), and R (Right). Cards marked with an SP in the checklist are in shorter supply than all others in the set. Even though we have assigned numbers 56 through 73 in our checklist for the puzzle cards, they are in fact all unnumbered. These cards came in 15 cent packs where were issued 36 packs to a box and 16 boxes to a case.

COMPLETE SET (73) 60.00 120.00
COMMON PLAYER (1-55) .10 .25
COMMON SP PLAYER (1-55) .40 1.00
COMMON PUZZLE (56-73) .08 .20
1 Alan Ashby .10 .25
2 Buddy Bell SP .50 1.25
3 Johnny Bench 1.50 4.00
4 Vida Blue .30 .75
5 Bert Blyleven .30 .75
6 Steve Braun SP .40 1.00
7 George Brett 4.00 10.00
8 Lou Brock 1.25 3.00
9 Jose Cardenal .10 .25
10 Rod Carew SP 2.50 6.00
11 Steve Carlton 1.50 4.00
12 Dave Cash .10 .25
13 Cesar Cedeno SP .50 1.25
14 Ron Cey .30 .75
15 Mark Fidrych 2.00 5.00
16 Dan Ford .10 .25
17 Wayne Garland .10 .25
18 Ralph Garr .10 .25
19 Steve Garvey 1.25 3.00
20 Mike Hargrove .30 .75
21 Jim Hunter .75 2.00
22 Reggie Jackson 1.50 4.00
23 Randy Jones .10 .25
24 Dave Kingman SP .50 1.25
25 Bill Madlock .30 .75
26 Lee May SP .50 1.25
27 John Mayberry .10 .25
28 John(Andy)Messersmith .10 .25
29 Willie Montanez .10 .25
30 John Montefusco SP .40 1.00
31 Joe Morgan .75 2.00
32 Thurman Munson .75 2.00
33 Bobby Murcer .30 .75
34 Al Oliver SP .50 1.25
35 Dave Pagan .10 .25
36 Jim Palmer SP 1.25 3.00
37 Tony Perez .75 2.00
38 Pete Rose SP 5.00 12.00
39 Joe Rudi .20 .50
40 Nolan Ryan SP 30.00 60.00
41 Mike Schmidt 4.00 10.00
42 Tom Seaver 2.00 5.00
43 Ted Simmons .30 .75
44 Bill Singer .10 .25
45 Willie Stargell 1.25 3.00
46 Rusty Staub .30 .75
47 Don Sutton .75 2.00
48 Luis Tiant .30 .75
49 Bill Travers .10 .25
50 Claudell Washington .30 .75
51 Bob Watson .30 .75
52 Dave Winfield 2.50 6.00
53 Carl Yastrzemski 1.50 4.00
54 Robin Yount 2.50 6.00
55 Richie Zisk .10 .25
56 AL Puzzle UL .08 .20
57 AL Puzzle UC .08 .20
58 AL Puzzle UR .08 .20
59 AL Puzzle ML .08 .20
60 AL Puzzle MC .08 .20
61 AL Puzzle MR .08 .20
62 AL Puzzle BL SP .08 .20
63 AL Puzzle BC SP .08 .20
64 AL Puzzle BR SP .08 .20
65 NL Puzzle UL .08 .20
66 NL Puzzle UC .08 .20
67 NL Puzzle UR .08 .20
68 NL Puzzle ML .08 .20
69 NL Puzzle MC .08 .20
70 NL Puzzle MR .08 .20
71 NL Puzzle BL .08 .20
72 NL Puzzle BC .08 .20
73 NL Puzzle BR .08 .20
CL Checklist .20 .50

1978 Topps

The cards in this 726-card set measure 2 1/2" by 3 1/2". As in previous years, this set was issued in many different ways: some of them include 14-card wax packs, 30-card supermarket packs which came 48 to a case and had an SRP of 20 cents and 39-card rack packs. The 1978 Topps set experienced an increase in number of cards from the previous five regular issue sets of 660. Card numbers 1 through 7 feature Record Breakers (RB) of the 1977 season. Other subsets within this set include League Leaders (201-208), Post-season cards (411-413), and Rookie Prospects (701-711). The key Rookie Cards in this set are the multi-player Rookie Card of Paul Molitor and Alan Trammell, Jack Morris, Eddie Murray, Lance Parrish, and Lou Whitaker. Many of the Molitor/Trammell cards are found with black printing smudges. The manager cards in the set feature a "then and now" format on the card front showing the manager as he looked during his playing days. While no scarcities exist, 66 of the cards are more abundant in supply, as they were "double printed." These 66 double-printed cards are noted in the checklist by DP. Team cards again feature a checklist of that team's players in the set on the back. Cards numbered 23 or lower, that feature Astros, Rangers, Tigers, or Yankees and do not follow the numbering checklisted below, are not necessarily error cards. They are undoubtedly Burger King cards, separate sets with their own pricing and mass distribution. The Bump Wills card has been seen with either no black mark or a major black mark on the front of the card. We will continue to investigate this card and see whether or not it should be considered a variation.

COMPLETE SET (726) 100.00 200.00
COMMON CARD (1-726) .10 .25
COMMON CARD DP .08 .20
1 Lou Brock RB 1.25 3.00
2 Sparky Lyle RB .25 .60
3 Willie McCovey RB 1.00 2.50
4 Brooks Robinson RB .50 1.25
5 Pete Rose RB 3.00 8.00
6 Nolan Ryan RB 6.00 15.00
7 Reggie Jackson RB 1.50 4.00
8 Mike Sadek .10 .25
9 Doug DeCinces .25 .60
10 Phil Niekro 1.00 2.50
11 Rick Manning .10 .25
12 Don Aase .10 .25
13 Art Howe RC .25 .60
14 Lerrin LaGrow .10 .25
15 Tony Perez DP .50 1.25
16 Roy White .25 .60
17 Mike Krukow .10 .25
18 Bob Grich .25 .60
19 Darrell Porter .25 .60
20 Pete Rose DP 5.00 12.00
21 Steve Kemp .10 .25
22 Charlie Hough .25 .60
23 Bump Wills .10 .25
24 Don Money DP .08 .20
25 Jon Matlack .10 .25
26 Rich Hebner .25 .60
27 Geoff Zahn .10 .25
28 Ed Ott .10 .25
29 Bob Lacey RC .10 .25
30 George Hendrick .25 .60
31 Glenn Abbott .10 .25
32 Garry Templeton .25 .60
33 Dave Lemanczyk .10 .25
34 Willie McCovey 1.25 3.00
35 Sparky Lyle .25 .60
36 Eddie Murray RC 12.00 30.00
37 Rick Waits .10 .25
38 Willie Montanez .10 .25
39 Floyd Bannister RC .10 .25
40 Carl Yastrzemski 2.50 6.00
41 Burt Hooton .25 .60
42 Jorge Orta .10 .25
43 Bill Atkinson RC .10 .25
44 Toby Harrah .25 .60
45 Mark Fidrych 1.00 2.50
46 Al Cowens .25 .60
47 Jack Billingham .10 .25
48 Don Baylor .50 1.25
49 Ed Kranepool .25 .60
50 Rick Reuschel .25 .60
51 Charlie Moore DP .08 .20
52 Jim Lonborg .25 .60
53 Phil Garner DP .10 .25
54 Tom Johnson .10 .25
55 Mitchell Page RC .10 .25
56 Randy Jones .10 .25
57 Dan Meyer .10 .25
58 Bob Forsch .10 .25
59 Otto Velez .10 .25
60 Thurman Munson 1.50 4.00
61 Larvell Blanks .10 .25
62 Jim Barr .10 .25
63 Don Zimmer MG .25 .60
64 Gene Pentz .10 .25
65 Ken Singleton .25 .60
66 Chicago White Sox CL .50 1.25
67 Claudell Washington .25 .60
68 Steve Foucault DP .08 .20
69 Mike Vail .10 .25
70 Goose Gossage .50 1.25
71 Terry Humphrey .10 .25
72 Andre Dawson 1.50 4.00
73 Andy Hassler .10 .25
74 Checklist 1-121 .50 1.25
75 Dick Ruthven .10 .25
76 Steve Ontiveros .10 .25
77 Ed Kirkpatrick .10 .25
78 Pablo Torrealba .10 .25
79 Darrell Johnson MG DP .08 .20
80 Ken Griffey Sr. .50 1.25
81 Pete Redfern .10 .25
82 San Francisco Giants CL .50 1.25
83 Bob Montgomery .10 .25
84 Kent Tekulve .25 .60
85 Ron Fairly .30 .75
86 Dave Tomlin .10 .25
87 John Lowenstein .10 .25
88 Mike Phillips .10 .25
89 Ken Clay RC .10 .25
90 Larry Bowa .50 1.25
91 Oscar Zamora .10 .25
92 Adrian Devine .10 .25
93 Bobby Cox DP .08 .20
94 Chuck Scrivener .10 .25
95 Jamie Quirk .10 .25
96 Baltimore Orioles CL .50 1.25
97 Stan Bahnsen .10 .25
98 Jim Essian .25 .60
99 Willie Hernandez RC .50 1.25
100 George Brett 4.00 10.00
101 Sid Monge .10 .25
102 Matt Alexander .10 .25
103 Tom Murphy .10 .25
104 Lee Lacy .10 .25
105 Reggie Cleveland .10 .25
106 Bill Plummer .10 .25
107 Ed Halicki .10 .25
108 Von Joshua .10 .25
109 Joe Torre MG .25 .60
110 Richie Zisk .10 .25
111 Mike Tyson .10 .25
112 Houston Astros CL .50 1.25
113 Don Carrithers .10 .25
114 Paul Blair .25 .60
115 Gary Nolan .10 .25
116 Tucker Ashford RC .10 .25
117 John Montague .10 .25
118 Terry Harmon .10 .25
119 Dennis Martinez 1.00 2.50
120 Gary Carter 1.00 2.50
121 Alvis Woods .10 .25
122 Dennis Eckersley 1.25 3.00
123 Manny Trillo .10 .25
124 Dave Rozema RC .10 .25
125 George Scott .25 .60
126 Paul Moskau RC .10 .25
127 Chet Lemon .25 .60
128 Bill Russell .25 .60
129 Jim Colborn .10 .25
130 Jeff Burroughs .25 .60
131 Bert Blyleven .50 1.25
132 Enos Cabell .10 .25
133 Jerry Augustine .10 .25
134 Steve Henderson RC .10 .25
135 Ron Guidry DP .50 1.25
136 Ted Sizemore .10 .25
137 Craig Kusick .10 .25
138 Larry Demery .10 .25
139 Wayne Gross .10 .25
140 Rollie Fingers 1.00 2.50
141 Ruppert Jones .10 .25
142 John Montefusco .10 .25
143 Keith Hernandez .25 .60
144 Jesse Jefferson .10 .25
145 Rick Monday .25 .60
146 Doyle Alexander .25 .60
147 Lee Mazzilli .10 .25
148 Andre Thornton .25 .60
149 Dale Murray .10 .25
150 Bobby Bonds .50 1.25
151 Milt Wilcox .10 .25
152 Ivan DeJesus RC .10 .25
153 Steve Stone .25 .60
154 Cecil Cooper DP .10 .25
155 Butch Hobson .10 .25
156 Andy Messersmith .25 .60
157 Pete LaCock DP .08 .20
158 Joaquin Andujar .25 .60
159 Lou Piniella .25 .60
160 Jim Palmer 1.25 3.00
161 Bob Boone .50 1.25
162 Paul Thormodsgard RC .10 .25
163 Bill North .10 .25
164 Bob Owchinko RC .10 .25
165 Rennie Stennett .10 .25
166 Carlos Lopez .10 .25
167 Tim Foli .10 .25
168 Reggie Smith .25 .60
169 Jerry Johnson .10 .25
170 Lou Brock 1.25 3.00
171 Pat Zachry .10 .25
172 Mike Hargrove .25 .60
173 Robin Yount UER 2.00 5.00
174 Wayne Garland .10 .25
175 Jerry Morales .10 .25
176 Milt May .10 .25
177 Gene Garber DP .10 .25
178 Dave Chalk .10 .25
179 Dick Tidrow .10 .25
180 Dave Concepcion .50 1.25
181 Ken Forsch .10 .25
182 Jim Spencer .10 .25
183 Doug Bird .10 .25
184 Checklist 122-242 .50 1.25
185 Ellis Valentine .10 .25
186 Bob Stanley DP RC .08 .20
187 Jerry Royster DP .08 .20
188 Al Bumbry .25 .60
189 Tom Lasorda MG DP 1.00 2.50
190 John Candelaria .25 .60
191 Rodney Scott RC .10 .25
192 San Diego Padres CL .50 1.25
193 Rich Chiles .10 .25
194 Derrel Thomas .10 .25
195 Larry Dierker .25 .60
196 Bob Bailor .10 .25
197 Nino Espinosa .10 .25
198 Ron Pruitt .10 .25

199 Craig Reynolds .10 .25
200 Reggie Jackson 3.00 8.00
201 D.Parker/R.Carew LL .50 1.25
202 G.Foster/J.Rice LL DP .25 .60
203 G.Foster/L.Hisle LL .25 .60
204 F.Taveras/F.Patek LL DP .10 .25
205 Carlton/Gol/Leon/Palm LL 1.00 2.50
206 P.Niekro/N.Ryan LL DP 2.50 6.00
207 J.Cand/F.Tanana LL DP .25 .60
208 R.Fingers/B.Campbell LL .50 1.25
209 Dock Ellis .10 .25
210 Jose Cardenal .10 .25
211 Earl Weaver MG DP .50 1.25
212 Mike Caldwell .10 .25
213 Alan Bannister .10 .25
214 California Angels CL .50 1.25
215 Darrell Evans .25 .60
216 Mike Paxton RC .10 .25
217 Rod Gilbreath .10 .25
218 Marty Pattin .10 .25
219 Mike Cubbage .10 .25
220 Pedro Borbon .10 .25
221 Chris Speier .10 .25
222 Jerry Martin .10 .25
223 Bruce Kison .10 .25
224 Jerry Tabb RC .10 .25
225 Don Gullett DP .10 .25
226 Joe Ferguson .10 .25
227 Al Fitzmorris .10 .25
228 Manny Mota DP .10 .25
229 Leo Foster .10 .25
230 Al Hrabosky .25 .60
231 Wayne Nordhagen RC .10 .25
232 Mickey Stanley .10 .25
233 Dick Pole .10 .25
234 Herman Franks MG .10 .25
235 Tim McCarver .25 .60
236 Terry Whitfield .10 .25
237 Rich Dauer .10 .25
238 Juan Beniquez .10 .25
239 Dyar Miller .10 .25
240 Gene Tenace .25 .60
241 Pete Vuckovich .25 .60
242 Barry Bonnell DP RC .08 .20
243 Bob McClure .10 .25
244 Montreal Expos CL DP .25 .60
245 Rick Burleson .25 .60
246 Dan Driessen .10 .25
247 Larry Christenson .10 .25
248 Frank White DP .25 .60
249 Dave Goltz DP .08 .20
250 Graig Nettles DP .25 .60
251 Don Kirkwood .10 .25
252 Steve Swisher DP .08 .20
253 Jim Kern .10 .25
254 Dave Collins .25 .60
255 Jerry Reuss .25 .60
256 Joe Altobelli MG RC .10 .25
257 Hector Cruz .10 .25
258 John Hiller .10 .25
259 Los Angeles Dodgers CL .50 1.25
260 Bert Campaneris .25 .60
261 Tim Hosley .10 .25
262 Rudy May .10 .25
263 Danny Walton .10 .25
264 Jamie Easterly .10 .25
265 Sal Bando DP .25 .60
266 Bob Shirley RC .10 .25
267 Doug Ault .10 .25
268 Gil Flores RC .10 .25
269 Wayne Twitchell .10 .25
270 Carlton Fisk 1.50 4.00
271 Randy Lerch DP .08 .20
272 Royle Stillman .10 .25
273 Fred Norman .10 .25
274 Freddie Patek .25 .60
275 Dan Ford .10 .25
276 Bill Bonham DP .08 .20
277 Bruce Boisclair .10 .25
278 Enrique Romo RC .10 .25
279 Bill Virdon MG .10 .25
280 Buddy Bell .25 .60
281 Eric Rasmussen DP .08 .20
282 New York Yankees CL 1.00 2.50
283 Omar Moreno .10 .25
284 Randy Moffitt .10 .25
285 Steve Yeager DP .25 .60
286 Ben Oglivie .25 .60
287 Kiko Garcia .10 .25
288 Dave Hamilton .10 .25
289 Checklist 243-363 .50 1.25
290 Willie Horton .25 .60
291 Gary Ross .10 .25
292 Gene Richards .10 .25
293 Mike Willis .10 .25
294 Larry Parrish .25 .60
295 Bill Lee .10 .25
296 Biff Pocoroba .10 .25
297 Warren Brusstar DP RC .08 .20
298 Tony Armas .25 .60
299 Whitey Herzog MG .25 .60
300 Joe Morgan 1.25 3.00
301 Buddy Schultz RC .10 .25
302 Chicago Cubs CL .50 1.25
303 Sam Hinds RC .10 .25
304 John Milner .10 .25
305 Rico Carty .25 .60
306 Joe Niekro .25 .60
307 Glenn Borgmann .10 .25
308 Jim Rooker .10 .25
309 Cliff Johnson .10 .25
310 Don Sutton 1.00 2.50
311 Jose Baez DP RC .08 .20
312 Greg Minton .10 .25
313 Andy Etchebarren .10 .25
314 Paul Lindblad .10 .25
315 Mark Belanger .25 .60
316 Henry Cruz DP .08 .20
317 Dave Johnson .10 .25
318 Tom Griffin .10 .25
319 Alan Ashby .10 .25
320 Fred Lynn .60 1.50
321 Santo Alcala .10 .25
322 Tom Paciorek .25 .60
323 Jim Fregosi DP .10 .25
324 Vern Rapp MG RC .10 .25
325 Bruce Sutter 1.25 3.00
326 Mike Lum DP .08 .20
327 Rick Langford DP RC .08 .20
328 Milwaukee Brewers CL .50 1.25
329 John Verhoeven .10 .25
330 Bob Watson .25 .60
331 Mark Littell .10 .25
332 Duane Kuiper .10 .25
333 Jim Todd .10 .25
334 John Stearns .10 .25
335 Bucky Dent .25 .60
336 Steve Busby .10 .25
337 Tom Grieve .25 .60
338 Dave Heaverlo .10 .25
339 Mario Guerrero .10 .25
340 Bake McBride .25 .60
341 Mike Flanagan .25 .60
342 Aurelio Rodriguez .10 .25
343 John Wathan DP .08 .20
344 Sam Ewing RC .10 .25
345 Luis Tiant .25 .60
346 Larry Biittner .10 .25
347 Terry Forster .10 .25
348 Del Unser .10 .25
349 Rick Camp DP .08 .20
350 Steve Garvey 1.00 2.50
351 Jeff Torborg .25 .60
352 Tony Scott RC .10 .25
353 Doug Bair RC .10 .25
354 Cesar Geronimo .10 .25
355 Bill Travers .10 .25
356 New York Mets CL .50 1.25
357 Tom Poquette .10 .25
358 Mark Lemongello .10 .25
359 Marc Hill .10 .25
360 Mike Schmidt 4.00 10.00
361 Chris Knapp .10 .25
362 Dave May .10 .25
363 Bob Randall .10 .25
364 Jerry Turner .10 .25
365 Ed Figueroa .10 .25
366 Larry Milbourne DP .08 .20
367 Rick Dempsey .25 .60
368 Balor Moore .10 .25
369 Tim Nordbrook .10 .25
370 Rusty Staub .50 1.25
371 Ray Burris .10 .25
372 Brian Asselstine .10 .25
373 Jim Willoughby .10 .25
374A Jose Morales .10 .25
Red stitching
374B Jose Morales
Black overprint stitching
375 Tommy John .50 1.25
376 Jim Wohlford .10 .25
377 Manny Sarmiento .10 .25
378 Bobby Winkles MG .10 .25
379 Skip Lockwood .10 .25
380 Ted Simmons .25 .60
381 Philadelphia Phillies CL .50 1.25
382 Joe Lahoud .10 .25
383 Mario Mendoza .10 .25
384 Jack Clark .50 1.25
385 Tito Fuentes .10 .25
386 Bob Gorinski RC .10 .25
387 Ken Holtzman .25 .60
388 Bill Fahey DP .08 .20
389 Julio Gonzalez RC .10 .25
390 Oscar Gamble .25 .60
391 Larry Haney .10 .25
392 Billy Almon .10 .25
393 Tippy Martinez .25 .60
394 Roy Howell DP .08 .20
395 Jim Hughes .10 .25
396 Bob Stinson DP .08 .20
397 Greg Gross .10 .25
398 Don Hood .10 .25
399 Pete Mackanin .10 .25
400 Nolan Ryan 10.00 25.00
401 Sparky Anderson MG .25 .60
402 Dave Campbell .10 .25
403 Bud Harrelson .25 .60
404 Detroit Tigers CL .50 1.25
405 Rawly Eastwick .10 .25
406 Mike Jorgensen .10 .25
407 Odell Jones RC .10 .25
408 Joe Zdeb RC .10 .25
409 Ron Schueler .10 .25
410 Bill Madlock .25 .60
411 Mickey Rivers ALCS .25 .60
412 Davey Lopes NLCS .25 .60
413 Reggie Jackson WS 1.50 4.00
414 Darold Knowles DP .08 .20
415 Ray Fosse .10 .25
416 Jack Brohamer .10 .25
417 Mike Garman DP .08 .20
418 Tony Muser .10 .25
419 Jerry Garvin RC .10 .25
420 Greg Luzinski .50 1.25
421 Junior Moore RC .10 .25
422 Steve Braun .10 .25
423 Dave Rosello .10 .25
424 Boston Red Sox CL .50 1.25
425 Steve Rogers DP .10 .25
426 Fred Kendall .10 .25
427 Mario Soto RC .25 .60
428 Joel Youngblood .10 .25
429 Mike Barlow RC .10 .25
430 Al Oliver .25 .60
431 Butch Metzger .10 .25
432 Terry Bulling RC .10 .25
433 Fernando Gonzalez .10 .25
434 Mike Norris .10 .25
435 Checklist 364-484 .50 1.25
436 Vic Harris DP .08 .20
437 Bo McLaughlin .10 .25
438 John Ellis .10 .25
439 Ken Kravec .10 .25
440 Dave Lopes .25 .60
441 Larry Gura .10 .25
442 Elliott Maddox .10 .25
443 Darrel Chaney .10 .25
444 Roy Hartsfield MG .10 .25
445 Mike Ivie .10 .25
446 Tug McGraw .25 .60
447 Leroy Stanton .10 .25
448 Bill Castro .10 .25
449 Tim Blackwell DP RC .08 .20
450 Tom Seaver 2.50 6.00
451 Minnesota Twins CL .50 1.25
452 Jerry Mumphrey .10 .25
453 Doug Flynn .10 .25
454 Dave LaRoche .10 .25
455 Bill Robinson .25 .60
456 Vern Ruhle .10 .25
457 Bob Bailey .10 .25
458 Jeff Newman .10 .25
459 Charlie Spikes .10 .25
460 Jim Hunter 1.00 2.50
461 Rob Andrews DP .08 .20
462 Rogelio Moret .10 .25
463 Kevin Bell .10 .25
464 Jerry Grote .10 .25
465 Hal McRae .25 .60
466 Dennis Blair .10 .25
467 Alvin Dark MG .25 .60
468 Warren Cromartie RC .25 .60
469 Rick Cerone .25 .60
470 J.R. Richard .25 .60
471 Roy Smalley .25 .60
472 Ron Reed .10 .25
473 Bill Buckner .25 .60
474 Jim Slaton .10 .25
475 Gary Matthews .25 .60
476 Bill Stein .10 .25
477 Doug Capilla RC .10 .25
478 Jerry Remy .10 .25
479 St. Louis Cardinals CL .50 1.25
480 Ron LeFlore .25 .60
481 Jackson Todd RC .10 .25
482 Rick Miller .10 .25
483 Ken Macha RC .10 .25
484 Jim Norris RC .10 .25
485 Chris Chambliss .25 .60
486 John Curtis .10 .25
487 Jim Tyrone .10 .25
488 Dan Spillner .10 .25
489 Rudy Meoli .10 .25
490 Amos Otis .25 .60
491 Scott McGregor .25 .60
492 Jim Sundberg .25 .60
493 Steve Renko .10 .25
494 Chuck Tanner MG .25 .60
495 Dave Cash .10 .25
496 Jim Clancy DP RC .08 .20
497 Glenn Adams .10 .25
498 Joe Sambito .10 .25
499 Seattle Mariners CL .50 1.25
500 George Foster .50 1.25
501 Dave Roberts .10 .25
502 Pat Rockett RC .10 .25
503 Ike Hampton RC .10 .25
504 Roger Freed .10 .25
505 Felix Millan .10 .25
506 Ron Blomberg .10 .25
507 Willie Crawford .10 .25
508 Johnny Oates .25 .60
509 Brent Strom .10 .25
510 Willie Stargell 1.00 2.50
511 Frank Duffy .10 .25
512 Larry Herndon .10 .25
513 Barry Foote .10 .25
514 Rob Sperring .10 .25
515 Tim Corcoran RC .10 .25
516 Gary Beare RC .10 .25
517 Andres Mora .10 .25
518 Tommy Boggs DP .08 .20
519 Brian Downing .25 .60
520 Larry Hisle .10 .25
521 Steve Staggs RC .10 .25
522 Dick Williams MG .25 .60
523 Donnie Moore RC .10 .25
524 Bernie Carbo .10 .25
525 Jerry Terrell .10 .25
526 Cincinnati Reds CL .50 1.25
527 Vic Correll .10 .25
528 Rob Picciolo RC .10 .25
529 Paul Hartzell .10 .25
530 Dave Winfield 1.50 4.00
531 Tom Underwood .10 .25
532 Skip Jutze .10 .25
533 Sandy Alomar .25 .60
534 Wilbur Howard .10 .25
535 Checklist 485-605 .50 1.25
536 Roric Harrison .10 .25
537 Bruce Bochte .10 .25
538 Johnny LeMaster .10 .25
539 Vic Davalillo DP .08 .20
540 Steve Carlton 1.50 4.00
541 Larry Cox .10 .25
542 Tim Johnson .10 .25
543 Larry Harlow DP RC .08 .20
544 Len Randle DP .08 .20
545 Bill Campbell .10 .25
546 Ted Martinez .10 .25
547 John Scott .10 .25
548 Billy Hunter MG DP .08 .20
549 Joe Kerrigan .10 .25
550 John Mayberry .25 .60
551 Atlanta Braves CL .50 1.25
552 Francisco Barrios .10 .25
553 Terry Puhl RC .25 .60
554 Joe Coleman .10 .25
555 Butch Wynegar .10 .25
556 Ed Armbrister .10 .25
557 Tony Solaita .10 .25
558 Paul Mitchell .10 .25
559 Phil Mankowski .10 .25
560 Dave Parker .50 1.25
561 Charlie Williams .10 .25
562 Glenn Burke RC .10 .25
563 Dave Rader .10 .25
564 Mick Kelleher .10 .25
565 Jerry Koosman .25 .60
566 Merv Rettenmund .10 .25
567 Dick Drago .10 .25
568 Tom Hutton .10 .25
569 Lary Sorensen RC .10 .25
570 Dave Kingman .50 1.25
571 Buck Martinez .10 .25
572 Rick Wise .10 .25
573 Luis Gomez .10 .25
574 Bob Lemon MG .50 1.25
575 Pat Dobson .10 .25
576 Sam Mejias .10 .25
577 Oakland Athletics CL .50 1.25
578 Buzz Capra .10 .25
579 Rance Mulliniks RC .10 .25
580 Rod Carew 1.50 4.00
581 Lynn McGlothen .10 .25
582 Fran Healy .10 .25
583 George Medich .10 .25
584 John Hale .10 .25
585 Woodie Fryman DP .08 .20
586 Ed Goodson .10 .25
587 John Urrea RC .10 .25
588 Jim Mason .10 .25
589 Bob Knepper RC .10 .25
590 Bobby Murcer .25 .60
591 George Zeber RC .10 .25
592 Bob Apodaca .10 .25
593 Dave Skaggs RC .10 .25
594 Dave Freisleben .10 .25
595 Sixto Lezcano .10 .25
596 Gary Wheelock .10 .25
597 Steve Dillard .10 .25
598 Eddie Solomon .10 .25
599 Gary Woods .10 .25
600 Frank Tanana .25 .60
601 Gene Mauch MG .25 .60
602 Eric Soderholm .10 .25
603 Will McEnaney .10 .25
604 Earl Williams .10 .25
605 Rick Rhoden .25 .60
606 Pittsburgh Pirates CL .50 1.25
607 Fernando Arroyo .10 .25
608 Johnny Grubb .10 .25
609 John Denny .10 .25
610 Garry Maddox .25 .60
611 Pat Scanlon RC .10 .25
612 Ken Henderson .10 .25
613 Marty Perez .10 .25
614 Joe Wallis .10 .25
615 Clay Carroll .10 .25
616 Pat Kelly .10 .25
617 Joe Nolan RC .10 .25
618 Tommy Helms .10 .25
619 Thad Bosley DP RC .08 .20
620 Willie Randolph .50 1.25
621 Craig Swan DP .08 .20
622 Champ Summers .10 .25
623 Eduardo Rodriguez .10 .25
624 Gary Alexander DP .08 .20
625 Jose Cruz .25 .60
626 Toronto Blue Jays CL DP .50 1.25
627 David Johnson .10 .25
628 Ralph Garr .25 .60
629 Don Stanhouse .10 .25
630 Ron Cey .50 1.25
631 Danny Ozark MG .10 .25
632 Rowland Office .10 .25
633 Tom Veryzer .10 .25
634 Len Barker .10 .25
635 Joe Rudi .25 .60
636 Jim Bibby .10 .25
637 Duffy Dyer .10 .25
638 Paul Splittorff .10 .25
639 Gene Clines .10 .25
640 Lee May DP .10 .25
641 Doug Rau .10 .25
642 Denny Doyle .10 .25
643 Tom House .10 .25
644 Jim Dwyer .10 .25
645 Mike Torrez .25 .60
646 Rick Auerbach DP .08 .20
647 Steve Dunning .10 .25
648 Gary Thomasson .10 .25
649 Moose Haas RC .10 .25
650 Cesar Cedeno .25 .60
651 Doug Rader .10 .25
652 Checklist 606-726 .50 1.25
653 Ron Hodges DP .08 .20
654 Pepe Frias .10 .25
655 Lyman Bostock .25 .60
656 Dave Garcia MG RC .10 .25
657 Bombo Rivera .10 .25
658 Manny Sanguillen .25 .60
659 Texas Rangers CL .50 1.25
660 Jason Thompson .25 .60

661 Grant Jackson .10 .25
662 Paul Dade RC .10 .25
663 Paul Reuschel .10 .25
664 Fred Stanley .10 .25
665 Dennis Leonard .25 .60
666 Billy Smith RC .10 .25
667 Jeff Byrd RC .10 .25
668 Dusty Baker .50 1.25
669 Pete Falcone .10 .25
670 Jim Rice 1.00 2.50
671 Gary Lavelle .10 .25
672 Don Kessinger .25 .60
673 Steve Brye .10 .25
674 Ray Knight RC 1.00 2.50
675 Jay Johnstone .25 .60
676 Bob Myrick .10 .25
677 Ed Herrmann .10 .25
678 Tom Burgmeier .10 .25
679 Wayne Garrett .10 .25
680 Vida Blue .25 .60
681 Rob Belloir .10 .25
682 Ken Brett .10 .25
683 Mike Champion .10 .25
684 Ralph Houk MG .25 .60
685 Frank Taveras .10 .25
686 Gaylord Perry 1.00 2.50
687 Julio Cruz RC .10 .25
688 George Mitterwald .10 .25
689 Cleveland Indians CL .50 1.25
690 Mickey Rivers .25 .60
691 Ross Grimsley .10 .25
692 Ken Reitz .10 .25
693 Lamar Johnson .10 .25
694 Elias Sosa .10 .25
695 Dwight Evans .50 1.25
696 Steve Mingori .10 .25
697 Roger Metzger .10 .25
698 Juan Bernhardt .10 .25
699 Jackie Brown .10 .25
700 Johnny Bench 3.00 8.00
701 Hume/Land/McC/Tay RC .25 .60
702 Nah/Pas/Sweet/Wer RC .25 .60
703 Jack Morris DP RC 6.00 15.00
704 Lou Whitaker RC 8.00 20.00
705 Berg/Milone/Hurdle/Nor RC .50 1.25
706 Cage/Cox/Put/Rev RC .25 .60
707 P.Molitor RC/A.Trammell RC 20.00 50.00
708 D.Murphy/L.Parrish RC 1.50 4.00
709 Burke/Keough/Rau/Schat RC .25 .60
710 Alston/Bos/Easler/Smith RC .50 1.25
711 Camp/Lamp/Mit/Tho DP RC .10 .25
712 Bobby Valentine .25 .60
713 Bob Davis .10 .25
714 Mike Anderson .10 .25
715 Jim Kaat .50 1.25
716 Clarence Gaston .25 .60
717 Nelson Briles .10 .25
718 Ron Jackson .10 .25
719 Randy Elliott RC .10 .25
720 Fergie Jenkins 1.00 2.50
721 Billy Martin MG .50 1.25
722 Pete Broberg .10 .25
723 John Wockenfuss .10 .25
724 Kansas City Royals CL .50 1.25
725 Kurt Bevacqua .10 .25
726 Wilbur Wood .50 1.25

1978 Topps Team Checklist Sheet

As part of a mail-away offer, Topps offered all 26 team checklist cards on an uncut sheet. These cards enabled the collector to have an easy reference for which card(s) he/she needed to finish their sets. When cut from the sheet, all cards measure the standard size.

1 Team Checklist Sheet 40.00 80.00

1978 Topps Zest

This set of five standard-size cards is very similar to the 1978 Topps regular issue. Although the cards were produced by Topps, they were used in a promotion for Zest Soap. The sponsor of the set, Zest Soap, is not mentioned anywhere on the cards. The card numbers are different and the backs are written in English and Spanish. By the choice of players in this small set, Zest appears to have been targeting the Hispanic community. Each player's card number in the regular 1978 Topps set is also given. A different photo was used for Montanez, showing his head and shoulders as a New York Met rather than as an Atlanta Brave in a batting stance as shown on Willie's Topps regular card.

COMPLETE SET (5) 2.50 6.00
1 Joaquin Andujar/78T-158 .60 1.50
2 Bert Campaneris/78T-260 .75 2.00
3 Ed Figueroa/78T-365 .40 1.00
4 Willie Montanez/78T-38 (different pose)/(New Yo .60 1.50
5 Manny Mota/78T-228 .60 1.50

1979 Topps

The cards in this 726-card set measure 2 1/2" by 3 1/2". Topps continued with the same number of cards as in 1978. As in previous years, this set was released in many different formats, among them are 12-card wax packs and 39-card rack packs which cost 59 cents upon release. Those rack packs came 24 packs to a box and three boxes to a case. Various series spotlight League Leaders (1-8), "Season and Career Record Holders" (411-418), "Record Breakers" (201-206), and one "Prospects" card for each team (701-726). Team cards feature a checklist on back of that team's players in the set and a small picture of the manager on the front of the card. There are 66 cards that were double printed and these are noted in the checklist by the abbreviation DP. Bump Wills (369) was initially depicted in a Ranger uniform but with a Blue Jays affiliation; later printings correctly labeled him with Texas. The set price includes either Wills card. The key Rookie Cards in this set are Pedro Guerrero, Carney Lansford, Ozzie Smith, Bob Welch and Willie Wilson. Cards numbered 23 or lower, which feature Phillies or Yankees and do not follow the numbering checklisted below, are not necessarily error cards. They are undoubtedly Burger King cards, separate sets for each team with their own pricing and mass distribution.

COMPLETE SET (726) 100.00 200.00
COMMON CARD (1-726) .10 .25
COMMON CARD DP .08 .20
1 R.Carew/D.Parker LL 1.00 2.50
2 J.Rice/G.Foster LL .60 1.50
3 J.Rice/G.Foster LL .60 1.50
4 R.LeFlore/O.Moreno LL .30 .75
5 R.Guidry/G.Perry LL .30 .75
6 N.Ryan/J.Richard LL 2.00 5.00
7 R.Guidry/C.Swan LL .30 .75
8 R.Gossage/R.Fingers LL .60 1.50
9 Dave Campbell .10 .25
10 Lee May .30 .75
11 Marc Hill .10 .25
12 Dick Drago .10 .25
13 Paul Dade .10 .25
14 Rafael Landestoy RC .10 .25
15 Ross Grimsley .10 .25
16 Fred Stanley .10 .25
17 Donnie Moore .10 .25
18 Tony Solaita .10 .25
19 Larry Gura DP .08 .20
20 Joe Morgan DP 1.00 2.50
21 Kevin Kobel .10 .25
22 Mike Jorgensen .10 .25
23 Terry Forster .10 .25
24 Paul Molitor 5.00 12.00
25 Steve Carlton 1.25 3.00
26 Jamie Quirk .10 .25
27 Dave Goltz .10 .25
28 Steve Brye .10 .25
29 Rick Langford .10 .25
30 Dave Winfield 1.50 4.00
31 Tom House DP .08 .20
32 Jerry Mumphrey .10 .25
33 Dave Rozema .10 .25
34 Rob Andrews .10 .25
35 Ed Figueroa .10 .25
36 Alan Ashby .10 .25
37 Joe Kerrigan DP .08 .20
38 Bernie Carbo .10 .25
39 Dale Murphy 1.25 3.00
40 Dennis Eckersley 1.00 2.50
41 Minnesota Twins CL/Mauch .60 1.50
42 Ron Blomberg .10 .25
43 Wayne Twitchell .10 .25
44 Kurt Bevacqua .10 .25
45 Al Hrabosky .30 .75
46 Ron Hodges .10 .25
47 Fred Norman .10 .25
48 Merv Rettenmund .10 .25
49 Vern Ruhle .10 .25
50 Steve Garvey DP .60 1.50
51 Ray Fosse DP .08 .20
52 Randy Lerch .10 .25
53 Mick Kelleher .10 .25
54 Dell Alston DP .08 .20
55 Willie Stargell 1.00 2.50
56 John Hale .10 .25
57 Eric Rasmussen .10 .25
58 Bob Randall DP .08 .20
59 John Denny DP .10 .25
60 Mickey Rivers .30 .75
61 Bo Diaz .10 .25
62 Randy Moffitt .10 .25
63 Jack Brohamer .10 .25
64 Tom Underwood .10 .25
65 Mark Belanger .30 .75
66 Detroit Tigers CL/Moss .60 1.50
67 Jim Mason DP .08 .20
68 Joe Niekro DP .10 .25
69 Elliott Maddox .10 .25
70 John Candelaria .30 .75
71 Brian Downing .30 .75
72 Steve Mingori .10 .25
73 Ken Henderson .10 .25
74 Shane Rawley RC .10 .25
75 Steve Yeager .30 .75
76 Warren Cromartie .30 .75
77 Dan Briggs DP .08 .20
78 Elias Sosa .10 .25
79 Ted Cox .10 .25
80 Jason Thompson .30 .75
81 Roger Erickson RC .10 .25
82 New York Mets CL/Torre .60 1.50
83 Fred Kendall .10 .25
84 Greg Minton .10 .25
85 Gary Matthews .30 .75
86 Rodney Scott .10 .25
87 Pete Falcone .10 .25
88 Bob Molinaro RC .10 .25
89 Dick Tidrow .10 .25
90 Bob Boone .60 1.50
91 Terry Crowley .10 .25
92 Jim Bibby .10 .25
93 Phil Mankowski .10 .25
94 Len Barker .10 .25
95 Robin Yount 2.00 5.00
96 Cleveland Indians CL/Torborg .60 1.50
97 Sam Mejias .10 .25
98 Ray Burris .10 .25
99 John Wathan .30 .75
100 Tom Seaver DP 1.50 4.00
101 Roy Howell .10 .25
102 Mike Anderson .10 .25
103 Jim Todd .10 .25
104 Johnny Oates DP .10 .25
105 Rick Camp DP .08 .20
106 Frank Duffy .10 .25
107 Jesus Alou DP .08 .20
108 Eduardo Rodriguez .10 .25
109 Joel Youngblood .10 .25
110 Vida Blue .30 .75
111 Roger Freed .10 .25
112 Philadelphia Phillies CL/Ozark .60 1.50
113 Pete Redfern .10 .25
114 Cliff Johnson .10 .25
115 Nolan Ryan 8.00 20.00
116 Ozzie Smith RC 20.00 50.00
117 Grant Jackson .10 .25
118 Bud Harrelson .30 .75
119 Don Stanhouse .10 .25
120 Jim Sundberg .30 .75
121 Checklist 1-121 DP .30 .75
122 Mike Paxton .10 .25
123 Lou Whitaker 1.00 2.50
124 Dan Schatzeder .10 .25
125 Rick Burleson .10 .25
126 Doug Bair .10 .25
127 Thad Bosley .10 .25
128 Ted Martinez .10 .25
129 Marty Pattin DP .08 .20
130 Bob Watson DP .10 .25
131 Jim Clancy .10 .25
132 Rowland Office .10 .25
133 Bill Castro .10 .25
134 Alan Bannister .10 .25
135 Bobby Murcer .30 .75
136 Jim Kaat .30 .75
137 Larry Wolfe DP RC .08 .20
138 Mark Lee RC .10 .25
139 Luis Pujols RC .10 .25
140 Don Gullett .30 .75
141 Tom Paciorek .30 .75
142 Charlie Williams .10 .25
143 Tony Scott .10 .25
144 Sandy Alomar .10 .25
145 Rick Rhoden .10 .25
146 Duane Kuiper .10 .25
147 Dave Hamilton .10 .25
148 Bruce Boisclair .10 .25
149 Manny Sarmiento .10 .25
150 Wayne Cage .10 .25
151 John Hiller .10 .25
152 Rick Cerone .10 .25
153 Dennis Lamp .10 .25
154 Jim Gantner DP .10 .25
155 Dwight Evans .60 1.50
156 Buddy Solomon .10 .25
157 U.L. Washington UER .10 .25
158 Joe Sambito .10 .25
159 Roy White .30 .75
160 Mike Flanagan .60 1.50
161 Barry Foote .10 .25
162 Tom Johnson .10 .25
163 Glenn Burke .10 .25
164 Mickey Lolich .30 .75
165 Frank Taveras .10 .25
166 Leon Roberts .10 .25
167 Roger Metzger DP .08 .20
168 Dave Freisleben .10 .25
169 Bill Nahorodny .10 .25
170 Don Sutton 1.00 2.50
171 Gene Clines .10 .25
172 Mike Bruhert RC .10 .25
173 John Lowenstein .10 .25
174 Rick Auerbach .10 .25
175 George Hendrick .60 1.50
176 Aurelio Rodriguez .10 .25
177 Ron Reed .10 .25
178 Alvis Woods .10 .25
179 Jim Beattie DP RC .08 .20
180 Larry Hisle .10 .25
181 Mike Garman .10 .25
182 Tim Johnson .10 .25
183 Paul Splittorff .10 .25
184 Darrel Chaney .10 .25
185 Mike Torrez .30 .75
186 Eric Soderholm .10 .25
187 Mark Lemongello .10 .25
188 Pat Kelly .10 .25
189 Ed Whitson RC .10 .25
190 Ron Cey .30 .75
191 Mike Norris .10 .25
192 St. Louis Cardinals CL/Boyer .60 1.50
193 Glenn Adams .10 .25
194 Randy Jones .10 .25
195 Bill Madlock .30 .75
196 Steve Kemp DP .10 .25
197 Bob Apodaca .10 .25
198 Johnny Grubb .10 .25
199 Larry Milbourne .10 .25
200 Johnny Bench DP 2.00 5.00
201 Mike Edwards RB .10 .25
202 Ron Guidry RB .30 .75
203 J.R. Richard RB .10 .25
204 Pete Rose RB 2.00 5.00
205 John Stearns RB .10 .25
206 Sammy Stewart RB .10 .25
207 Dave Lemanczyk .10 .25
208 Clarence Gaston .10 .25
209 Reggie Cleveland .10 .25
210 Larry Bowa .30 .75
211 Dennis Martinez 1.00 2.50
212 Carney Lansford RC .60 1.50
213 Bill Travers .10 .25
214 Boston Red Sox CL/Zimmer .60 1.50
215 Willie McCovey 1.00 2.50
216 Wilbur Wood .10 .25
217 Steve Dillard .10 .25
218 Dennis Leonard .30 .75
219 Roy Smalley .30 .75
220 Cesar Geronimo .10 .25
221 Jesse Jefferson .10 .25
222 Bob Beall RC .10 .25
223 Kent Tekulve .30 .75
224 Dave Revering .10 .25
225 Goose Gossage .60 1.50
226 Ron Pruitt .10 .25
227 Steve Stone .30 .75
228 Vic Davalillo .10 .25
229 Doug Flynn .10 .25
230 Bob Forsch .10 .25
231 John Wockenfuss .10 .25
232 Jimmy Sexton RC .10 .25
233 Paul Mitchell .10 .25
234 Toby Harrah .30 .75
235 Steve Rogers .10 .25
236 Jim Dwyer .10 .25
237 Billy Smith .10 .25
238 Balor Moore .10 .25
239 Willie Horton .30 .75
240 Rick Reuschel .30 .75
241 Checklist 122-242 DP .30 .75
242 Pablo Torrealba .10 .25
243 Buck Martinez DP .08 .20
244 Pittsburgh Pirates CL/Tanner .60 1.50
245 Jeff Burroughs .30 .75
246 Darrell Jackson RC .10 .25
247 Tucker Ashford DP .08 .20
248 Pete LaCock .10 .25
249 Paul Thormodsgard .10 .25
250 Willie Randolph .30 .75
251 Jack Morris 1.00 2.50
252 Bob Stinson .10 .25
253 Rick Wise .10 .25
254 Luis Gomez .10 .25
255 Tommy John .60 1.50
256 Mike Sadek .10 .25
257 Adrian Devine .10 .25
258 Mike Phillips .10 .25
259 Cincinnati Reds CL/Anderson .60 1.50
260 Richie Zisk .10 .25
261 Mario Guerrero .10 .25
262 Nelson Briles .10 .25
263 Oscar Gamble .30 .75
264 Don Robinson RC .10 .25
265 Don Money .10 .25
266 Jim Willoughby .10 .25
267 Joe Rudi .30 .75
268 Julio Gonzalez .10 .25
269 Woodie Fryman .10 .25
270 Butch Hobson .30 .75
271 Rawly Eastwick .10 .25
272 Tim Corcoran .10 .25
273 Jerry Terrell .10 .25
274 Willie Norwood .10 .25
275 Junior Moore .10 .25
276 Jim Colborn .10 .25
277 Tom Grieve .30 .75
278 Andy Messersmith .30 .75
279 Jerry Grote DP .08 .20
280 Andre Thornton .30 .75
281 Vic Correll DP .08 .20
282 Toronto Blue Jays CL/Hartsfield .30 .75
283 Ken Kravec .10 .25
284 Johnnie LeMaster .10 .25
285 Bobby Bonds .60 1.50
286 Duffy Dyer UER .10 .25
287 Andres Mora .10 .25
288 Milt Wilcox .10 .25
289 Jose Cruz .60 1.50
290 Dave Lopes .30 .75
291 Tom Griffin .10 .25
292 Don Reynolds RC .10 .25
293 Jerry Garvin .10 .25
294 Pepe Frias .10 .25
295 Mitchell Page .10 .25
296 Preston Hanna RC .10 .25
297 Ted Sizemore .10 .25
298 Rich Gale RC .10 .25
299 Steve Ontiveros .10 .25
300 Rod Carew 1.25 3.00
301 Tom Hume .10 .25
302 Atlanta Braves CL/Cox .60 1.50
303 Lary Sorensen DP .08 .20
304 Steve Swisher .10 .25
305 Willie Montanez .10 .25
306 Floyd Bannister .10 .25
307 Larvell Blanks .10 .25
308 Bert Blyleven .60 1.50
309 Ralph Garr .30 .75
310 Thurman Munson 1.25 3.00
311 Gary Lavelle .10 .25
312 Bob Robertson .10 .25
313 Dyar Miller .10 .25
314 Larry Harlow .10 .25
315 Jon Matlack .10 .25
316 Milt May .10 .25
317 Jose Cardenal .30 .75
318 Bob Welch RC 1.00 2.50
319 Wayne Garrett .10 .25
320 Carl Yastrzemski 2.00 5.00
321 Gaylord Perry 1.00 2.50
322 Danny Goodwin RC .10 .25
323 Lynn McGlothen .10 .25
324 Mike Tyson .10 .25
325 Cecil Cooper .30 .75
326 Pedro Borbon .10 .25

327 Art Howe DP .10 .25
328 Oakland Athletics CL/McKeon .60 1.50
329 Joe Coleman .10 .25
330 George Brett 4.00 10.00
331 Mickey Mahler .10 .25
332 Gary Alexander .10 .25
333 Chet Lemon .30 .75
334 Craig Swan .10 .25
335 Chris Chambliss .30 .75
336 Bobby Thompson RC .10 .25
337 John Montague .10 .25
338 Vic Harris .10 .25
339 Ron Jackson .10 .25
340 Jim Palmer 1.00 2.50
341 Willie Upshaw RC .30 .75
342 Dave Roberts .10 .25
343 Ed Glynn .10 .25
344 Jerry Royster .10 .25
345 Tug McGraw .30 .75
346 Bill Buckner .30 .75
347 Doug Rau .10 .25
348 Andre Dawson 1.25 3.00
349 Jim Wright RC .10 .25
350 Garry Templeton .30 .75
351 Wayne Nordhagen DP .08 .20
352 Steve Renko .10 .25
353 Checklist 243-363 .60 1.50
354 Bill Bonham .10 .25
355 Lee Mazzilli .10 .25
356 San Francisco Giants CL/Altobelli .60 1.50
357 Jerry Augustine .10 .25
358 Alan Trammell 1.25 3.00
359 Dan Spillner DP .08 .20
360 Amos Otis .30 .75
361 Tom Dixon RC .10 .25
362 Mike Cubbage .10 .25
363 Craig Skok RC .10 .25
364 Gene Richards .10 .25
365 Sparky Lyle .30 .75
366 Juan Bernhardt .10 .25
367 Dave Skaggs .10 .25
368 Don Aase .10 .25
369A Bump Wills ERR 1.25 3.00
369B Bump Wills COR .75 2.00
370 Dave Kingman .60 1.50
371 Jeff Holly RC .10 .25
372 Lamar Johnson .10 .25
373 Lance Rautzhan .10 .25
374 Ed Herrmann .10 .25
375 Bill Campbell .10 .25
376 Gorman Thomas .30 .75
377 Paul Moskau .10 .25
378 Rob Picciolo DP .08 .20
379 Dale Murray .10 .25
380 John Mayberry .30 .75
381 Houston Astros CL/Virdon .60 1.50
382 Jerry Martin .10 .25
383 Phil Garner .30 .75
384 Tommy Boggs .10 .25
385 Dan Ford .10 .25
386 Francisco Barrios .10 .25
387 Gary Thomasson .10 .25
388 Jack Billingham .10 .25
389 Joe Zdeb .10 .25
390 Rollie Fingers 1.00 2.50
391 Al Oliver .30 .75
392 Doug Ault .10 .25
393 Scott McGregor .30 .75
394 Randy Stein RC .10 .25
395 Dave Cash .10 .25
396 Bill Plummer .10 .25
397 Sergio Ferrer RC .10 .25
398 Ivan DeJesus .10 .25
399 David Clyde .10 .25
400 Jim Rice .75 2.00
401 Ray Knight .30 .75
402 Paul Hartzell .10 .25
403 Tim Foli .10 .25
404 Chicago White Sox CL/Kessinger .60 1.50
405 Butch Wynegar DP .08 .20
406 Joe Wallis DP .08 .20
407 Pete Vuckovich .30 .75
408 Charlie Moore DP .08 .20
409 Willie Wilson RC .60 1.50
410 Darrell Evans .60 1.50
411 G.Sisler/T.Cobb ATL 1.00 2.50
412 H.Wilson/H.Aaron ATL 1.00 2.50
413 R.Maris/H.Aaron ATL 1.50 4.00
414 R.Hornsby/T.Cobb ATL 1.00 2.50
415 L.Brock/L.Brock ATL .60 1.50
416 J.Chesbro/C.Young ATL .30 .75
417 N.Ryan/W.Johnson ATL DP 2.00 5.00
418 D.Leonard/W.Johnson ATL DP .10 .25
419 Dick Ruthven .10 .25
420 Ken Griffey Sr. .30 .75
421 Doug DeCinces .30 .75
422 Ruppert Jones .10 .25
423 Bob Montgomery .10 .25
424 California Angels CL/Fregosi .60 1.50
425 Rick Manning .10 .25
426 Chris Speier .10 .25
427 Andy Replogle RC .10 .25
428 Bobby Valentine .30 .75
429 John Urrea DP .08 .20
430 Dave Parker .30 .75
431 Glenn Borgmann .10 .25
432 Dave Heaverlo .10 .25
433 Larry Biittner .10 .25
434 Ken Clay .10 .25
435 Gene Tenace .30 .75
436 Hector Cruz .10 .25
437 Rick Williams RC .10 .25
438 Horace Speed RC .10 .25
439 Frank White .30 .75
440 Rusty Staub .60 1.50
441 Lee Lacy .10 .25
442 Doyle Alexander .10 .25
443 Bruce Bochte .10 .25
444 Aurelio Lopez RC .10 .25
445 Steve Henderson .10 .25
446 Jim Lonborg .30 .75
447 Manny Sanguillen .30 .75
448 Moose Haas .10 .25
449 Bombo Rivera .10 .25
450 Dave Concepcion .60 1.50
451 Kansas City Royals CL/Herzog .60 1.50
452 Jerry Morales .10 .25
453 Chris Knapp .10 .25
454 Len Randle .10 .25
455 Bill Lee DP .08 .20
456 Chuck Baker RC .10 .25
457 Bruce Sutter 1.00 2.50
458 Jim Essian .10 .25
459 Sid Monge .10 .25
460 Graig Nettles .60 1.50
461 Jim Barr DP .08 .20
462 Otto Velez .10 .25
463 Steve Comer RC .10 .25
464 Joe Nolan .10 .25
465 Reggie Smith .30 .75
466 Mark Littell .10 .25
467 Don Kessinger DP .10 .25
468 Stan Bahnsen DP .08 .20
469 Lance Parrish .60 1.50
470 Garry Maddox DP .10 .25
471 Joaquin Andujar .30 .75
472 Craig Kusick .10 .25
473 Dave Roberts .10 .25
474 Dick Davis RC .10 .25
475 Dan Driessen .10 .25
476 Tom Poquette .10 .25
477 Bob Grich .30 .75
478 Juan Beniquez .10 .25
479 San Diego Padres CL/Craig .60 1.50
480 Fred Lynn .40 1.00
481 Skip Lockwood .10 .25
482 Craig Reynolds .10 .25
483 Checklist 364-484 DP .30 .75
484 Rick Waits .10 .25
485 Bucky Dent .30 .75
486 Bob Knepper .10 .25
487 Miguel Dilone .10 .25
488 Bob Owchinko .10 .25
489 Larry Cox UER .10 .25
490 Al Cowens .30 .75
491 Tippy Martinez .10 .25
492 Bob Bailor .10 .25
493 Larry Christenson .10 .25
494 Jerry White .10 .25
495 Tony Perez 1.00 2.50
496 Barry Bonnell DP .08 .20
497 Glenn Abbott .10 .25
498 Rich Chiles .10 .25
499 Texas Rangers CL/Corrales .60 1.50
500 Ron Guidry .30 .75
501 Junior Kennedy RC .10 .25
502 Steve Braun .10 .25
503 Terry Humphrey .10 .25
504 Larry McWilliams RC .10 .25
505 Ed Kranepool .10 .25
506 John D'Acquisto .10 .25
507 Tony Armas .30 .75
508 Charlie Hough .30 .75
509 Mario Mendoza UER .10 .25
510 Ted Simmons .60 1.50
511 Paul Reuschel DP .08 .20
512 Jack Clark .30 .75
513 Dave Johnson .30 .75
514 Mike Proly RC .10 .25
515 Enos Cabell .10 .25
516 Champ Summers DP .08 .20
517 Al Bumbry .30 .75
518 Jim Umbarger .10 .25
519 Ben Oglivie .30 .75
520 Gary Carter .75 2.00
521 Sam Ewing .10 .25
522 Ken Holtzman .30 .75
523 John Milner .10 .25
524 Tom Burgmeier .10 .25
525 Freddie Patek .10 .25
526 Los Angeles Dodgers CL/Lasorda .60 1.50
527 Lerrin LaGrow .10 .25
528 Wayne Gross DP .08 .20
529 Brian Asselstine .10 .25
530 Frank Tanana .30 .75
531 Fernando Gonzalez .10 .25
532 Buddy Schultz .10 .25
533 Leroy Stanton .10 .25
534 Ken Forsch .10 .25
535 Ellis Valentine .10 .25
536 Jerry Reuss .30 .75
537 Tom Veryzer .10 .25
538 Mike Ivie DP .08 .20
539 John Ellis .10 .25
540 Greg Luzinski .30 .75
541 Jim Slaton .10 .25
542 Rick Bosetti .10 .25
543 Kiko Garcia .10 .25
544 Fergie Jenkins 1.00 2.50
545 John Stearns .10 .25
546 Bill Russell .30 .75
547 Clint Hurdle .10 .25
548 Enrique Romo .10 .25
549 Bob Bailey .10 .25
550 Sal Bando .30 .75
551 Chicago Cubs CL/Franks .60 1.50
552 Jose Morales .10 .25
553 Denny Walling .10 .25
554 Matt Keough .10 .25
555 Biff Pocoroba .10 .25
556 Mike Lum .10 .25
557 Ken Brett .10 .25
558 Jay Johnstone .30 .75
559 Greg Pryor RC .10 .25
560 John Montefusco .10 .25
561 Ed Ott .10 .25
562 Dusty Baker .60 1.50
563 Roy Thomas .10 .25
564 Jerry Turner .10 .25
565 Rico Carty .30 .75
566 Nino Espinosa .10 .25
567 Richie Hebner .30 .75
568 Carlos Lopez .10 .25
569 Bob Sykes .10 .25
570 Cesar Cedeno .30 .75
571 Darrell Porter .30 .75
572 Rod Gilbreath .10 .25
573 Jim Kern .10 .25
574 Claudell Washington .30 .75
575 Luis Tiant .30 .75
576 Mike Parrott RC .10 .25
577 Milwaukee Brewers CL/Bamberger .60 1.50
578 Pete Broberg .10 .25
579 Greg Gross .10 .25
580 Ron Fairly .30 .75
581 Darold Knowles .10 .25
582 Paul Blair .30 .75
583 Julio Cruz .10 .25
584 Jim Rooker .10 .25
585 Hal McRae .60 1.50
586 Bob Horner RC .60 1.50
587 Ken Reitz .10 .25
588 Tom Murphy .10 .25
589 Terry Whitfield .10 .25
590 J.R. Richard .30 .75
591 Mike Hargrove .30 .75
592 Mike Krukow .10 .25
593 Rick Dempsey .30 .75
594 Bob Shirley .10 .25
595 Phil Niekro 1.00 2.50
596 Jim Wohlford .10 .25
597 Bob Stanley .10 .25
598 Mark Wagner .10 .25
599 Jim Spencer .10 .25
600 George Foster .30 .75
601 Dave LaRoche .10 .25
602 Checklist 485-605 .60 1.50
603 Rudy May .10 .25
604 Jeff Newman .10 .25
605 Rick Monday DP .10 .25
606 Montreal Expos CL/Williams .60 1.50
607 Omar Moreno .10 .25
608 Dave McKay .10 .25
609 Silvio Martinez RC .10 .25
610 Mike Schmidt 3.00 8.00
611 Jim Norris .10 .25
612 Rick Honeycutt RC .30 .75
613 Mike Edwards RC .10 .25
614 Willie Hernandez .30 .75
615 Ken Singleton .30 .75
616 Billy Almon .10 .25
617 Terry Puhl .10 .25
618 Jerry Remy .10 .25
619 Ken Landreaux RC .30 .75
620 Bert Campaneris .30 .75
621 Pat Zachry .10 .25
622 Dave Collins .30 .75
623 Bob McClure .10 .25
624 Larry Herndon .10 .25
625 Mark Fidrych 1.00 2.50
626 New York Yankees CL/Lemon .60 1.50
627 Gary Serum RC .10 .25
628 Del Unser .10 .25
629 Gene Garber .30 .75
630 Bake McBride .30 .75
631 Jorge Orta .10 .25
632 Don Kirkwood .10 .25
633 Rob Wilfong DP RC .08 .20
634 Paul Lindblad .10 .25
635 Don Baylor .60 1.50
636 Wayne Garland .10 .25
637 Bill Robinson .30 .75
638 Al Fitzmorris .10 .25
639 Manny Trillo .10 .25
640 Eddie Murray 5.00 12.00
641 Bobby Castillo RC .10 .25
642 Wilbur Howard DP .08 .20
643 Tom Hausman .10 .25
644 Manny Mota .30 .75
645 George Scott DP .10 .25
646 Rick Sweet .10 .25
647 Bob Lacey .10 .25
648 Lou Piniella .30 .75
649 John Curtis .10 .25
650 Pete Rose 6.00 15.00
651 Mike Caldwell .10 .25
652 Stan Papi RC .10 .25
653 Warren Brusstar DP .08 .20
654 Rick Miller .10 .25
655 Jerry Koosman .30 .75
656 Hosken Powell RC .10 .25
657 George Medich .10 .25
658 Taylor Duncan RC .10 .25
659 Seattle Mariners CL/Johnson .60 1.50
660 Ron LeFlore DP .10 .25
661 Bruce Kison .10 .25
662 Kevin Bell .10 .25
663 Mike Vail .10 .25
664 Doug Bird .10 .25
665 Lou Brock 1.00 2.50
666 Rich Dauer .10 .25
667 Don Hood .10 .25
668 Bill North .10 .25
669 Checklist 606-726 .60 1.50
670 Jim Hunter DP .60 1.50
671 Joe Ferguson DP .08 .20
672 Ed Halicki .10 .25
673 Tom Hutton .10 .25
674 Dave Tomlin .10 .25
675 Tim McCarver .60 1.50
676 Johnny Sutton RC .10 .25
677 Larry Parrish .30 .75
678 Geoff Zahn .10 .25
679 Derrel Thomas .10 .25
680 Carlton Fisk 1.25 3.00
681 John Henry Johnson RC .10 .25
682 Dave Chalk .10 .25
683 Dan Meyer DP .08 .20
684 Jamie Easterly DP .08 .20
685 Sixto Lezcano .10 .25
686 Ron Schueler DP .08 .20
687 Rennie Stennett .10 .25
688 Mike Willis .10 .25
689 Baltimore Orioles CL/Weaver .60 1.50
690 Buddy Bell DP .10 .25
691 Dock Ellis DP .08 .20
692 Mickey Stanley .10 .25
693 Dave Rader .10 .25
694 Burt Hooton .30 .75
695 Keith Hernandez .30 .75
696 Andy Hassler .10 .25
697 Dave Bergman .10 .25
698 Bill Stein .10 .25
699 Hal Dues RC .10 .25
700 Reggie Jackson DP 2.00 5.00
701 Corey/Flinn/Stewart RC .30 .75
702 Finch/Hancock/Ripley RC .30 .75
703 Anderson/Frost/Slater RC .30 .75
704 Baumgarten/Colbern/Squires RC .30 .75
705 Griffin/Norrid/Oliver RC .60 1.50
706 Stegman/Tobik/Young RC .30 .75
707 Bass/Gaudet/McGilberry RC .60 1.50
708 Bass/Romero/Yost RC .60 1.50
709 Perlozzo/Sofield/Stanfield RC .30 .75
710 Doyle/Heath/Rajisch RC .30 .75
711 Murphy/Robinson/Wirth RC .60 1.50
712 Anderson/Biercevicz/McLaughlin RC .30 .75
713 Darwin/Putnam/Sample RC .60 1.50
714 Cruz/Kelly/Whitt RC .30 .75
715 Benedict/Hubbard/Whisenton RC .60 1.50
716 Geisel/Pagel/Thompson RC .30 .75
717 LaCoss/Oester/Spilman RC .30 .75
718 Bochy/Fischlin/Pisker RC 2.00 5.00
719 Guerrero/Law/Simpson RC .60 1.50
720 Fry/Pirtle/Sanderson RC .60 1.50
721 Berenguer/Bernard/Norman RC .30 .75
722 Morrison/Smith/Wright RC .60 1.50
723 Berra/Cotes/Wiltbank RC .30 .75
724 Bruno/Frazier/Kennedy RC .60 1.50
725 Beswick/Mura/Perkins RC .30 .75
726 Johnston/Strain/Tamargo RC .30 .75

1979 Topps Comics

This 33 card (comic) set, which measures approximately 3" by 3 1/4", is rather plentiful in spite of the fact that it was originally touted as a limited edition "test" issue. This flimsy set has never been very popular with collectors. These waxy comics are numbered and are blank backed. Each comic also features an "Inside Baseball" tip in the lower right corner.

COMPLETE SET (33) 6.00 15.00
1 Eddie Murray .50 1.25
2 Jim Rice .12 .30
3 Carl Yastrzemski .40 1.00
4 Nolan Ryan 1.50 4.00
5 Chet Lemon .08 .20
6 Andre Thornton .08 .20
7 Rusty Staub .08 .20
8 Ron LeFlore .08 .20
9 George Brett 1.25 3.00
10 Larry Hisle .08 .20
11 Rod Carew .40 1.00
12 Reggie Jackson .60 1.50
13 Ron Guidry .08 .20
14 Mitchell Page .08 .20
15 Leon Roberts .08 .20
16 Al Oliver .08 .20
17 John Mayberry .08 .20
18 Bob Horner .08 .20
19 Phil Niekro .40 1.00
20 Dave Kingman .12 .30
21 Johnny Bench .50 1.25
22 Tom Seaver .50 1.25
23 J.R. Richard .08 .20
24 Steve Garvey .12 .30
25 Reggie Smith .08 .20
26 Ross Grimsley .08 .20
27 Craig Swan .08 .20
28 Pete Rose .60 1.50
29 Dave Parker .08 .20
30 Ted Simmons .08 .20
31 Dave Winfield .40 1.00
32 Jack Clark .08 .20
33 Vida Blue .08 .20

1979 Topps Team Checklist Sheet

As part of a mail-away offer, Topps offered all 26 1979 team cards checklist cards on an uncut sheet. These cards enabled the collector to have an easy reference for which card(s) he/she needed to finish their sets. When cut from the sheet, all cards measure the standard size.

1 Team Checklist Sheet 30.00 60.00

1980 Topps

The cards in this 726-card set measure the standard size. In 1980 Topps released another set of the same size and number of cards as the previous two years. Distribution for these cards included 15-card wax packs as well as 42-card rack packs. The 15-card wax packs had an 25 cent SRP and came 36 packs to a box and 20 boxes to a case. A special experiment in 1980 was the issuance of a 28-card cello pack with a 59 cent SRP which had a three-pack of gum at the bottom so no cards would be damaged. As with those sets, Topps again produced 66 double-printed cards in the set; they are noted by DP in the checklist below. The player's name appears over the picture and his position and team are found in pennant design. Every card carries a facsimile autograph. Team cards feature a team checklist of players in the set on the back and the manager's name on the front. Cards 1-6 show Highlights (HL) of the 1979 season, cards 201-207 are League Leaders, and cards 661-686 feature American and National League rookie "Future Stars," one card for each team showing three young prospects. The key Rookie Card in this set is Rickey Henderson; other Rookie Cards included in this set are Dan Quisenberry, Dave Stieb and Rick Sutcliffe.

Card	Low	High
COMPLETE SET (726)	60.00	120.00
COMMON CARD (1-726)	.10	.25
COMMON DP	.08	.25
1 L.Brock/C.Yastrzemski HL	1.00	2.50
2 Willie McCovey HL	.30	.75
3 Manny Mota HL	.10	.25
4 Pete Rose HL	1.25	3.00
5 Garry Templeton HL	.10	.25
6 Del Unser HL	.10	.25
7 Mike Lum	.10	.25
8 Craig Swan	.10	.25
9 Steve Braun	.10	.25
10 Dennis Martinez	.30	.75
11 Jimmy Sexton	.10	.25
12 John Curtis DP	.10	.25
13 Ron Pruitt	.10	.25
14 Dave Cash	.30	.75
15 Bill Campbell	.10	.25
16 Jerry Narron RC	.10	.25
17 Bruce Sutter	.60	1.50
18 Ron Jackson	.10	.25
19 Balor Moore	.10	.25
20 Dan Ford	.10	.25
21 Manny Sarmiento	.10	.25
22 Pat Putnam	.10	.25
23 Derrel Thomas	.10	.25
24 Jim Slaton	.10	.25
25 Lee Mazzilli	.30	.75
26 Marty Pattin	.10	.25
27 Del Unser	.10	.25
28 Bruce Kison	.10	.25
29 Mark Wagner	.10	.25
30 Vida Blue	.30	.75
31 Jay Johnstone	.10	.25
32 Julio Cruz DP	.10	.25
33 Tony Scott	.10	.25
34 Jeff Newman DP	.10	.25
35 Luis Tiant	.30	.75
36 Rusty Torres	.10	.25
37 Kiko Garcia	.10	.25
38 Dan Spillner DP	.10	.25
39 Rowland Office	.10	.25
40 Carlton Fisk	1.00	2.50
41 Texas Rangers CL/Corrales	.30	.75
42 David Palmer RC	.10	.25
43 Bombo Rivera	.10	.25
44 Bill Fahey	.10	.25
45 Frank White	.30	.75
46 Rico Carty	.30	.75
47 Bill Bonham DP	.10	.25
48 Rick Miller	.10	.25
49 Mario Guerrero	.10	.25
50 J.R. Richard	.30	.75
51 Joe Ferguson DP	.10	.25
52 Warren Brusstar	.10	.25
53 Ben Oglivie	.30	.75
54 Dennis Lamp	.10	.25
55 Bill Madlock	.30	.75
56 Bobby Valentine	.30	.75
57 Pete Vuckovich	.10	.25
58 Doug Flynn	.10	.25
59 Eddy Putman RC	.10	.25
60 Bucky Dent	.30	.75
61 Gary Serum	.10	.25
62 Mike Ivie	.10	.25
63 Bob Stanley	.10	.25
64 Joe Nolan	.10	.25
65 Al Bumbry	.30	.75
66 Kansas City Royals CL/Frey	.30	.75
67 Doyle Alexander	.10	.25
68 Larry Harlow	.10	.25
69 Rick Williams	.10	.25
70 Gary Carter	.60	1.50
71 John Milner DP	.10	.25
72 Fred Howard DP RC	.10	.25
73 Dave Collins	.10	.25
74 Sid Monge	.10	.25
75 Bill Russell	.30	.75
76 John Stearns	.10	.25
77 Dave Stieb RC	.60	1.50
78 Ruppert Jones	.10	.25
79 Bob Owchinko	.10	.25
80 Ron LeFlore	.30	.75
81 Ted Sizemore	.10	.25
82 Houston Astros CL/Virdon	.30	.75
83 Steve Trout RC	.10	.25
84 Gary Lavelle	.10	.25
85 Ted Simmons	.30	.75
86 Dave Hamilton	.10	.25
87 Pepe Frias	.10	.25
88 Ken Landreaux	.10	.25
89 Don Hood	.10	.25
90 Manny Trillo	.30	.75
91 Rick Dempsey	.30	.75
92 Rick Rhoden	.10	.25
93 Dave Roberts DP	.10	.25
94 Neil Allen RC	.10	.25
95 Cecil Cooper	.30	.75
96 Oakland Athletics CL/Marshall	.30	.75
97 Bill Lee	.30	.75
98 Jerry Terrell	.10	.25
99 Victor Cruz	.10	.25
100 Johnny Bench	1.25	3.00
101 Aurelio Lopez	.10	.25
102 Rich Dauer	.10	.25
103 Bill Caudill RC	.10	.25
104 Manny Mota	.30	.75
105 Frank Tanana	.30	.75
106 Jeff Leonard RC	.60	1.50
107 Francisco Barrios	.10	.25
108 Bob Horner	.30	.75
109 Bill Travers	.10	.25
110 Fred Lynn DP	.20	.50
111 Bob Knepper	.10	.25
112 Chicago White Sox CL/LaRussa	.30	.75
113 Geoff Zahn	.10	.25
114 Juan Beniquez	.10	.25
115 Sparky Lyle	.30	.75
116 Larry Cox	.10	.25
117 Dock Ellis	.30	.75
118 Phil Garner	.30	.75
119 Sammy Stewart	.10	.25
120 Greg Luzinski	.30	.75
121 Checklist 1-121	.30	.75
122 Dave Rosello DP	.10	.25
123 Lynn Jones RC	.10	.25
124 Dave Lemanczyk	.10	.25
125 Tony Perez	.30	.75
126 Dave Tomlin	.10	.25
127 Gary Thomasson	.10	.25
128 Tom Burgmeier	.10	.25
129 Craig Reynolds	.10	.25
130 Amos Otis	.30	.75
131 Paul Mitchell	.10	.25
132 Biff Pocoroba	.10	.25
133 Jerry Turner	.10	.25
134 Matt Keough	.10	.25
135 Bill Buckner	.30	.75
136 Dick Ruthven	.10	.25
137 John Castino RC	.10	.25
138 Ross Baumgarten	.10	.25
139 Dane Iorg RC	.10	.25
140 Rich Gossage	.30	.75
141 Gary Alexander	.10	.25
142 Phil Huffman RC	.10	.25
143 Bruce Bochte DP	.10	.25
144 Steve Comer	.10	.25
145 Darrell Evans	.30	.75
146 Bob Welch	.30	.75
147 Terry Puhl	.10	.25
148 Manny Sanguillen	.30	.75
149 Tom Hume	.10	.25
150 Jason Thompson	.10	.25
151 Tom Hausman DP	.10	.25
152 John Fulgham RC	.10	.25
153 Tim Blackwell	.10	.25
154 Lary Sorensen	.10	.25
155 Jerry Remy	.10	.25
156 Tony Brizzolara RC	.10	.25
157 Willie Wilson DP	.20	.50
158 Rob Picciolo DP	.10	.25
159 Ken Clay	.10	.25
160 Eddie Murray	2.00	5.00
161 Larry Christenson	.10	.25
162 Bob Randall	.10	.25
163 Steve Swisher	.10	.25
164 Greg Pryor	.10	.25
165 Omar Moreno	.10	.25
166 Glenn Abbott	.10	.25
167 Jack Clark	.30	.75
168 Rick Waits	.10	.25
169 Luis Gomez	.10	.25
170 Burt Hooton	.30	.75
171 Fernando Gonzalez	.10	.25
172 Ron Hodges	.10	.25
173 John Henry Johnson	.10	.25
174 Ray Knight	.30	.75
175 Rick Reuschel	.30	.75
176 Champ Summers	.10	.25
177 Dave Heaverlo	.10	.25
178 Tim McCarver	.30	.75
179 Ron Davis RC	.10	.25
180 Warren Cromartie	.10	.25
181 Moose Haas	.10	.25
182 Ken Reitz	.10	.25
183 Jim Anderson DP	.10	.25
184 Steve Renko DP	.10	.25
185 Hal McRae	.30	.75
186 Junior Moore	.10	.25
187 Alan Ashby	.10	.25
188 Terry Crowley	.10	.25
189 Kevin Kobel	.10	.25
190 Buddy Bell	.30	.75
191 Ted Martinez	.10	.25
192 Atlanta Braves CL/Cox	.30	.75
193 Dave Goltz	.10	.25
194 Mike Easler	.10	.25
195 John Montefusco	.30	.75
196 Lance Parrish	.30	.75
197 Byron McLaughlin	.10	.25
198 Dell Alston DP	.10	.25
199 Mike LaCoss	.10	.25
200 Jim Rice	.30	.75
201 K.Hernandez/F.Lynn LL	.30	.75
202 D.Kingman/G.Thomas LL	.60	1.50
203 D.Winfield/D.Baylor LL	.60	1.50
204 O.Moreno/W.Wilson LL	.30	.75
205 Niekro/Niekro/Flan LL	.30	.75
206 J.Richard/N.Ryan LL	2.00	5.00
207 J.Richard/R.Guidry LL	.30	.75
208 Wayne Cage	.10	.25
209 Von Joshua	.10	.25
210 Steve Carlton	.60	1.50
211 Dave Skaggs DP	.10	.25
212 Dave Roberts	.10	.25
213 Mike Jorgensen DP	.10	.25
214 California Angels CL/Fregosi	.30	.75
215 Sixto Lezcano	.10	.25
216 Phil Mankowski	.10	.25
217 Ed Halicki	.10	.25
218 Jose Morales	.10	.25
219 Steve Mingori	.10	.25
220 Dave Concepcion	.30	.75
221 Joe Cannon RC	.10	.25
222 Ron Hassey RC	.10	.25
223 Bob Sykes	.10	.25
224 Willie Montanez	.10	.25
225 Lou Piniella	.30	.75
226 Bill Stein	.10	.25
227 Len Barker	.30	.75
228 Johnny Oates	.30	.75
229 Jim Bibby	.10	.25
230 Dave Winfield	.60	1.50
231 Steve McCatty	.10	.25
232 Alan Trammell	.60	1.50
233 LaRue Washington RC	.10	.25
234 Vern Ruhle	.10	.25
235 Andre Dawson	.60	1.50
236 Marc Hill	.10	.25
237 Scott McGregor	.30	.75
238 Rob Wilfong	.10	.25
239 Don Aase	.10	.25
240 Dave Kingman	.30	.75
241 Checklist 122-242	.30	.75
242 Lamar Johnson	.10	.25
243 Jerry Augustine	.10	.25
244 St. Louis Cardinals CL/Boyer	.30	.75
245 Phil Niekro	.30	.75
246 Tim Foli DP	.10	.25
247 Frank Riccelli	.10	.25
248 Jamie Quirk	.10	.25
249 Jim Clancy	.10	.25
250 Jim Kaat	.30	.75
251 Kip Young	.10	.25
252 Ted Cox	.10	.25
253 John Montague	.10	.25
254 Paul Dade DP	.10	.25
255 Dusty Baker DP	.20	.50
256 Roger Erickson	.10	.25
257 Larry Herndon	.10	.25
258 Paul Moskau	.10	.25
259 New York Mets CL/Torre	.60	1.50
260 Al Oliver	.30	.75
261 Dave Chalk	.10	.25
262 Benny Ayala	.10	.25
263 Dave LaRoche DP	.10	.25
264 Bill Robinson	.10	.25
265 Robin Yount	1.25	3.00
266 Bernie Carbo	.10	.25
267 Dan Schatzeder	.10	.25
268 Rafael Landestoy	.10	.25
269 Dave Tobik	.10	.25
270 Mike Schmidt DP	1.25	3.00
271 Dick Drago DP	.10	.25
272 Ralph Garr	.30	.75
273 Eduardo Rodriguez	.10	.25
274 Dale Murphy	1.00	2.50
275 Jerry Koosman	.30	.75
276 Tom Veryzer	.10	.25
277 Rick Bosetti	.10	.25
278 Jim Spencer	.10	.25
279 Rob Andrews	.10	.25
280 Gaylord Perry	.30	.75
281 Paul Blair	.30	.75
282 Seattle Mariners CL/Johnson	.30	.75
283 John Ellis	.10	.25
284 Larry Murray DP RC	.10	.25
285 Don Baylor	.30	.75
286 Darold Knowles DP	.10	.25
287 John Lowenstein	.10	.25
288 Dave Rozema	.10	.25
289 Bruce Bochy	.10	.25
290 Steve Garvey	.60	1.50
291 Randy Scarberry RC	.10	.25
292 Dale Berra	.10	.25
293 Elias Sosa	.10	.25
294 Charlie Spikes	.10	.25
295 Larry Gura	.10	.25
296 Dave Rader	.10	.25
297 Tim Johnson	.10	.25
298 Ken Holtzman	.30	.75
299 Steve Henderson	.10	.25
300 Ron Guidry	.30	.75
301 Mike Edwards	.10	.25
302 Los Angeles Dodgers CL/Lasorda	.60	1.50
303 Bill Castro	.10	.25
304 Butch Wynegar	.10	.25
305 Randy Jones	.30	.75
306 Denny Walling	.10	.25
307 Rick Honeycutt	.10	.25
308 Mike Hargrove	.30	.75
309 Larry McWilliams	.10	.25
310 Dave Parker	.30	.75
311 Roger Metzger	.10	.25
312 Mike Barlow	.10	.25
313 Johnny Grubb	.10	.25
314 Tim Stoddard RC	.10	.25
315 Steve Kemp	.30	.75
316 Bob Lacey	.10	.25
317 Mike Anderson DP	.10	.25
318 Jerry Reuss	.30	.75
319 Chris Speier	.10	.25
320 Dennis Eckersley	.60	1.50
321 Keith Hernandez	.30	.75
322 Claudell Washington	.10	.25
323 Mick Kelleher	.10	.25
324 Tom Underwood	.10	.25
325 Dan Driessen	.10	.25
326 Bo McLaughlin	.10	.25
327 Ray Fosse DP	.20	.50
328 Minnesota Twins CL/Mauch	.30	.75
329 Bert Roberge RC	.10	.25
330 Al Cowens	.30	.75
331 Richie Hebner	.10	.25
332 Enrique Romo	.10	.25
333 Jim Norris DP	.10	.25
334 Jim Beattie	.10	.25
335 Willie McCovey	.60	1.50
336 George Medich	.10	.25
337 Carney Lansford	.30	.75
338 John Wockenfuss	.10	.25
339 John D'Acquisto	.10	.25
340 Ken Singleton	.30	.75
341 Jim Essian	.10	.25
342 Odell Jones	.10	.25
343 Mike Vail	.10	.25
344 Randy Lerch	.10	.25
345 Larry Parrish	.30	.75
346 Buddy Solomon	.10	.25
347 Harry Chappas RC	.10	.25
348 Checklist 243-363	.30	.75
349 Jack Brohamer	.10	.25
350 George Hendrick	.30	.75
351 Bob Davis	.10	.25
352 Dan Briggs	.10	.25
353 Andy Hassler	.10	.25
354 Rick Auerbach	.10	.25
355 Gary Matthews	.30	.75
356 San Diego Padres CL/Coleman	.30	.75
357 Bob McClure	.10	.25
358 Lou Whitaker	.30	.75
359 Randy Moffitt	.10	.25
360 Darrell Porter DP	.20	.50
361 Wayne Garland	.10	.25
362 Danny Goodwin	.10	.25
363 Wayne Gross	.10	.25
364 Ray Burris	.10	.25
365 Bobby Murcer	.30	.75
366 Rob Dressler	.10	.25
367 Billy Smith	.10	.25
368 Willie Aikens RC	.10	.25
369 Jim Kern	.10	.25
370 Cesar Cedeno	.30	.75
371 Jack Morris	.30	.75
372 Joel Youngblood	.10	.25
373 Dan Petry DP RC	.30	.75
374 Jim Gantner	.30	.75
375 Ross Grimsley	.10	.25
376 Gary Allenson RC	.10	.25
377 Junior Kennedy	.10	.25
378 Jerry Mumphrey	.10	.25
379 Kevin Bell	.10	.25
380 Garry Maddox	.30	.75
381 Chicago Cubs CL/Gomez	.30	.75
382 Dave Freisleben	.10	.25
383 Ed Ott	.10	.25
384 Joey McLaughlin RC	.10	.25
385 Enos Cabell	.10	.25
386 Darrell Jackson	.10	.25
387A F.Stanley Yellow	.75	2.00
387B F.Stanley Red Name	.10	.25
388 Mike Paxton	.10	.25
389 Pete LaCock	.10	.25
390 Fergie Jenkins	.30	.75
391 Tony Armas DP	.20	.50
392 Milt Wilcox	.10	.25
393 Ozzie Smith	4.00	10.00
394 Reggie Cleveland	.10	.25
395 Ellis Valentine	.10	.25
396 Dan Meyer	.10	.25
397 Roy Thomas DP	.10	.25
398 Barry Foote	.10	.25
399 Mike Proly DP	.10	.25
400 George Foster	.30	.75
401 Pete Falcone	.10	.25
402 Merv Rettenmund	.10	.25
403 Pete Redfern DP	.10	.25
404 Baltimore Orioles CL/Weaver	.30	.75
405 Dwight Evans	.60	1.50
406 Paul Molitor	1.50	4.00
407 Tony Solaita	.10	.25
408 Bill North	.10	.25
409 Paul Splittorff	.10	.25
410 Bobby Bonds	.30	.75
411 Frank LaCorte	.10	.25
412 Thad Bosley	.10	.25
413 Allen Ripley	.10	.25
414 George Scott	.30	.75
415 Bill Atkinson	.10	.25
416 Tom Brookens RC	.10	.25
417 Craig Chamberlain DP RC	.10	.25
418 Roger Freed DP	.10	.25
419 Vic Correll	.10	.25
420 Butch Hobson	.10	.25
421 Doug Bird	.10	.25
422 Larry Milbourne	.10	.25
423 Dave Frost	.10	.25
424 New York Yankees CL/Howser	.30	.75
425 Mark Belanger	.30	.75
426 Grant Jackson	.10	.25
427 Tom Hutton DP	.10	.25
428 Pat Zachry	.10	.25
429 Duane Kuiper	.10	.25

430 Larry Hisle DP .10 .25
431 Mike Krukow .10 .25
432 Willie Norwood .10 .25
433 Rich Gale .10 .25
434 Johnnie LeMaster .10 .25
435 Don Gullett .30 .75
436 Billy Almon .10 .25
437 Joe Niekro .30 .75
438 Dave Revering .10 .25
439 Mike Phillips .10 .25
440 Don Sutton .30 .75
441 Eric Soderholm .10 .25
442 Jorge Orta .10 .25
443 Mike Parrott .10 .25
444 Alvis Woods .10 .25
445 Mark Fidrych .30 .75
446 Duffy Dyer .10 .25
447 Nino Espinosa .10 .25
448 Jim Wohlford .10 .25
449 Doug Bair .10 .25
450 George Brett 3.00 8.00
451 Cleveland Indians CL/Garcia .30 .75
452 Steve Dillard .10 .25
453 Mike Bacsik .10 .25
454 Tom Donohue RC .10 .25
455 Mike Torrez .30 .75
456 Frank Taveras .10 .25
457 Bert Blyleven .30 .75
458 Billy Sample .10 .25
459 Mickey Lolich DP .20 .50
460 Willie Randolph .30 .75
461 Dwayne Murphy .10 .25
462 Mike Sadek DP .10 .25
463 Jerry Royster .10 .25
464 John Denny .30 .75
465 Rick Monday .30 .75
466 Mike Squires .10 .25
467 Jesse Jefferson .10 .25
468 Aurelio Rodriguez .10 .25
469 Randy Niemann DP RC .10 .25
470 Bob Boone .30 .75
471 Hosken Powell DP .10 .25
472 Willie Hernandez .30 .75
473 Bump Wills .10 .25
474 Steve Busby .10 .25
475 Cesar Geronimo .30 .75
476 Bob Shirley .10 .25
477 Buck Martinez .10 .25
478 Gil Flores .10 .25
479 Montreal Expos CL/Williams .30 .75
480 Bob Watson .30 .75
481 Tom Paciorek .30 .75
482 Rickey Henderson RC 40.00 80.00
483 Bo Diaz .10 .25
484 Checklist 364-484 .30 .75
485 Mickey Rivers .30 .75
486 Mike Tyson DP .10 .25
487 Wayne Nordhagen .10 .25
488 Roy Howell .10 .25
489 Preston Hanna DP .10 .25
490 Lee May .30 .75
491 Steve Mura DP .10 .25
492 Todd Cruz RC .10 .25
493 Jerry Martin .10 .25
494 Craig Minetto RC .10 .25
495 Bake McBride .30 .75
496 Silvio Martinez .10 .25
497 Jim Mason .10 .25
498 Danny Darwin .10 .25
499 San Francisco Giants CL/Bristol .30 .75
500 Tom Seaver 1.25 3.00
501 Rennie Stennett .10 .25
502 Rich Wortham DP RC .10 .25
503 Mike Cubbage .10 .25
504 Gene Garber .10 .25
505 Bert Campaneris .30 .75
506 Tom Buskey .10 .25
507 Leon Roberts .10 .25
508 U.L. Washington .10 .25
509 Ed Glynn .10 .25
510 Ron Cey .30 .75
511 Eric Wilkins RC .10 .25
512 Jose Cardenal .10 .25
513 Tom Dixon DP .10 .25
514 Steve Ontiveros .10 .25
515 Mike Caldwell UER .10 .25
516 Hector Cruz .10 .25
517 Don Stanhouse .10 .25
518 Nelson Norman RC .10 .25
519 Steve Nicosia RC .10 .25
520 Steve Rogers .30 .75
521 Ken Brett .10 .25
522 Jim Morrison .10 .25
523 Ken Henderson .10 .25
524 Jim Wright DP .10 .25
525 Clint Hurdle .10 .25
526 Philadelphia Phillies CL/Green .30 .75
527 Doug Rau DP .10 .25
528 Adrian Devine .10 .25
529 Jim Barr .10 .25
530 Jim Sundberg DP .20 .50
531 Eric Rasmussen .10 .25
532 Willie Horton .30 .75
533 Checklist 485-605 .30 .75
534 Andre Thornton .30 .75
535 Bob Forsch .10 .25
536 Lee Lacy .10 .25
537 Alex Trevino RC .10 .25
538 Joe Strain .10 .25
539 Rudy May .10 .25
540 Pete Rose 3.00 8.00
541 Miguel Dilone .10 .25
542 Joe Coleman .10 .25
543 Pat Kelly .10 .25
544 Rick Sutcliffe RC .60 1.50
545 Jeff Burroughs .30 .75
546 Rick Langford .10 .25
547 John Wathan .10 .25
548 Dave Rajsich .10 .25
549 Larry Wolfe .10 .25
550 Ken Griffey Sr. .30 .75
551 Pittsburgh Pirates CL/Tanner .30 .75
552 Bill Nahorodny .10 .25
553 Dick Davis .10 .25
554 Art Howe .30 .75
555 Ed Figueroa .10 .25
556 Joe Rudi .30 .75
557 Mark Lee .10 .25
558 Alfredo Griffin .10 .25
559 Dale Murray .10 .25
560 Dave Lopes .30 .75
561 Eddie Whitson .10 .25
562 Joe Wallis .10 .25
563 Will McEnaney .10 .25
564 Rick Manning .10 .25
565 Dennis Leonard .10 .25
566 Bud Harrelson .30 .75
567 Skip Lockwood .10 .25
568 Gary Roenicke RC .10 .25
569 Terry Kennedy .10 .25
570 Roy Smalley .30 .75
571 Joe Sambito .10 .25
572 Jerry Morales DP .10 .25
573 Kent Tekulve .30 .75
574 Scot Thompson .10 .25
575 Ken Kravec .10 .25
576 Jim Dwyer .10 .25
577 Toronto Blue Jays CL/Matlick .30 .75
578 Scott Sanderson .10 .25
579 Charlie Moore .10 .25
580 Nolan Ryan 8.00 20.00
581 Bob Bailor .10 .25
582 Brian Doyle .10 .25
583 Bob Stinson .10 .25
584 Kurt Bevacqua .10 .25
585 Al Hrabosky .30 .75
586 Mitchell Page .10 .25
587 Garry Templeton .30 .75
588 Greg Minton .10 .25
589 Chet Lemon .30 .75
590 Jim Palmer .60 1.50
591 Rick Cerone .10 .25
592 Jon Matlack .30 .75
593 Jesus Alou .10 .25
594 Dick Tidrow .10 .25
595 Don Money .10 .25
596 Rick Matula RC .10 .25
597 Tom Poquette .10 .25
598 Fred Kendall DP .10 .25
599 Mike Norris .10 .25
600 Reggie Jackson 1.25 3.00
601 Buddy Schultz .10 .25
602 Brian Downing .30 .75
603 Jack Billingham DP .10 .25
604 Glenn Adams .10 .25
605 Terry Forster .30 .75
606 Cincinnati Reds CL/McNamara .30 .75
607 Woodie Fryman .10 .25
608 Alan Bannister .10 .25
609 Ron Reed .10 .25
610 Willie Stargell .60 1.50
611 Jerry Garvin DP .10 .25
612 Cliff Johnson .10 .25
613 Randy Stein .10 .25
614 John Hiller .10 .25
615 Doug DeCinces .30 .75
616 Gene Richards .10 .25
617 Joaquin Andujar .30 .75
618 Bob Montgomery DP .10 .25
619 Sergio Ferrer .10 .25
620 Richie Zisk .30 .75
621 Bob Grich .30 .75
622 Mario Soto .30 .75
623 Gorman Thomas .30 .75
624 Lerrin LaGrow .10 .25
625 Chris Chambliss .30 .75
626 Detroit Tigers CL/Anderson .30 .75
627 Pedro Borbon .10 .25
628 Doug Capilla .10 .25
629 Jim Todd .10 .25
630 Larry Bowa .30 .75
631 Mark Littell .10 .25
632 Barry Bonnell .10 .25
633 Bob Apodaca .10 .25
634 Glenn Borgmann DP .10 .25
635 John Candelaria .30 .75
636 Toby Harrah .30 .75
637 Joe Simpson .10 .25
638 Mark Clear RC .10 .25
639 Larry Biittner .10 .25
640 Mike Flanagan .30 .75
641 Ed Kranepool .30 .75
642 Ken Forsch DP .10 .25
643 John Mayberry .30 .75
644 Charlie Hough .30 .75
645 Rick Burleson .30 .75
646 Checklist 606-726 .30 .75
647 Milt May .10 .25
648 Roy White .30 .75
649 Tom Griffin .10 .25
650 Joe Morgan .60 1.50
651 Rollie Fingers .30 .75
652 Mario Mendoza .10 .25
653 Stan Bahnsen .10 .25
654 Bruce Boisclair DP .10 .25
655 Tug McGraw .30 .75
656 Larvell Blanks .10 .25
657 Dave Edwards RC .10 .25
658 Chris Knapp .10 .25
659 Milwaukee Brewers CL/Bamberger .30 .75
660 Rusty Staub .30 .75
661 Mark Corey .10 .25
Dave Ford RC
Wayne Krenchicki RC
662 Finch/O'Berry/Rainey RC .10 .25
663 Botting/Clark/Thon RC .30 .75
664 Colbern/Hoffman/Robinson RC .10 .25
665 Andersen/Cuellar/Wihtol RC .10 .25
666 Chris/Greene/Robbins RC .10 .25
667 Mart/Pasch/Quisenberry RC .30 .75
668 Boitano/Mueller/Sakata RC .10 .25
669 Graham/Sofield/Ward RC .30 .75
670 Brown/Gulden/Jones RC .10 .25
671 Bryant/Kingman/Morgan RC .30 .75
672 Beamon/Craig/Vasquez RC .10 .25
673 Allard/Gleaton/Mahlberg RC .10 .25
674 Edge/Kelly/Wilborn RC .10 .25
675 Benedict/Bradford/Miller RC .10 .25
676 Geisel/Macko/Pagel RC .10 .25
677 DeFreites/Pastore/Spilman RC .10 .25
678 Baldwin/Knicely/Ladd RC .10 .25
679 Beckwith/Hatcher/Patterson RC .30 .75
680 Bernazard/Miller/Tamargo RC .10 .25
681 Norman/Orosco/Scott RC .60 1.50
682 Aviles/Noles/Saucier RC .10 .25
683 Boyland/Lois/Saferight RC .10 .25
684 Frazier/Herr/O'Brien RC .30 .75
685 Flannery/Greer/Wilhelm RC .10 .25
686 Johnston/Littlejohn/Nastu RC .10 .25
687 Mike Heath DP .10 .25
688 Steve Stone .30 .75
689 Boston Red Sox CL/Zimmer .30 .75
690 Tommy John .30 .75
691 Ivan DeJesus .10 .25
692 Rawly Eastwick DP .20 .50
693 Craig Kusick .10 .25
694 Jim Rooker .10 .25
695 Reggie Smith .30 .75
696 Julio Gonzalez .10 .25
697 David Clyde .10 .25
698 Oscar Gamble .30 .75
699 Floyd Bannister .30 .75
700 Rod Carew DP .30 .75
701 Ken Oberkfell RC .10 .25
702 Ed Farmer .10 .25
703 Otto Velez .10 .25
704 Gene Tenace .30 .75
705 Freddie Patek .30 .75
706 Tippy Martinez .10 .25
707 Elliott Maddox .10 .25
708 Bob Tolan .10 .25
709 Pat Underwood RC .10 .25
710 Graig Nettles .30 .75
711 Bob Galasso RC .10 .25
712 Rodney Scott .10 .25
713 Terry Whitfield .10 .25
714 Fred Norman .10 .25
715 Sal Bando .30 .75
716 Lynn McGlothen .10 .25
717 Mickey Klutts DP .10 .25
718 Greg Gross .10 .25
719 Don Robinson .30 .75
720 Carl Yastrzemski DP .75 2.00
721 Paul Hartzell .10 .25
722 Jose Cruz .30 .75
723 Shane Rawley .10 .25
724 Jerry White .10 .25
725 Rick Wise .10 .25
726 Steve Yeager .30 .75

1980 Topps/O-Pee-Chee Retail Promotion Cards

This set features special promotional redemption cards from Mrs. Butterworth's Syrup and Kmart Stores that could be redeemed for an unopened pack of three standard Topps Baseball cards. A special "3000 or More Hits", "lifetime .300 hitters" or a "Major League Records" card came with the packs. Hunts bread did the same promotion up in Canada. The promotion was limited to certain states and to certain stores.

COMPLETE SET 8.00 20.00
1 Mrs. Butterworth's 2.00 5.00
2 Kmart 2.00 5.00
3 Squirt 2.00 5.00
4 Hunts Bread 2.00 5.00

1980 Topps Super

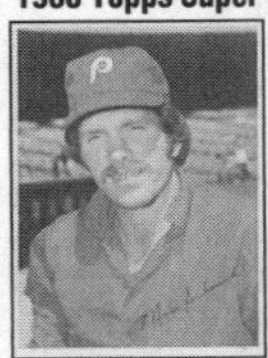

This 60-card set, measuring 4 7/8" by 6 7/8", consists primarily of star players. A player photo comprises the entire front with a facsimile signature at the lower portion of the photo. The backs contain a large Topps logo and the player's name. The cards were issued with either white or gray backs. The white backs have thicker card stock than the gray. White back cards were issued in three-card cellophane packs and gray back cards were issued through various promotional means. The prices below reflect those of the gray back. There are a number of cards that were Triple Printed. They are indicated by below (TP).

COMPLETE SET (60) 6.00 15.00
COMMON PLAYER (1-60) .05 .10
COMMON TP .13 .25
*WHITE BACKS: 2X GRAY BACKS
1 Willie Stargell .30 .75
2 Mike Schmidt TP .40 1.00
3 Johnny Bench .40 1.00
4 Jim Palmer .30 .75
5 Jim Rice .08 .25
6 Reggie Jackson TP .40 1.00
7 Ron Guidry .08 .25
8 Lee Mazzilli .02 .10
9 Don Baylor .20 .50
10 Fred Lynn .08 .25
11 Ken Singleton .08 .25
12 Rod Carew TP .30 .75
13 Steve Garvey TP .20 .50
14 George Brett TP .60 1.50
15 Tom Seaver .40 1.00
16 Dave Kingman .08 .25
17 Dave Parker TP .08 .25
18 Dave Winfield .30 .75
19 Pete Rose .30 .75
20 Nolan Ryan 1.25 3.00
21 Graig Nettles .08 .25
22 Carl Yastrzemski .30 .75
23 Tommy John .20 .50
24 George Foster .08 .25
25 J.R. Richard .02 .10
26 Keith Hernandez .08 .25
27 Bob Horner .02 .10
28 Eddie Murray .75 2.00
29 Steve Kemp .02 .10
30 Gorman Thomas .02 .10
31 Sixto Lezcano .02 .10
32 Bruce Sutter .40 1.00
33 Cecil Cooper .08 .25
34 Larry Bowa .08 .25
35 Al Oliver .20 .50
36 Ted Simmons .08 .25
37 Garry Templeton .02 .10
38 Jerry Koosman .08 .25
39 Darrell Porter .02 .10
40 Roy Smalley .02 .10
41 Craig Swan .02 .10
42 Jason Thompson .02 .10
43 Andre Thornton .02 .10
44 Rick Manning .02 .10
45 Kent Tekulve .02 .10
46 Phil Niekro .30 .75
47 Buddy Bell .08 .25
48 Randy Jones .02 .10
49 Brian Downing .02 .10
50 Amos Otis .02 .10
51 Rick Bosetti .02 .10
52 Gary Carter .40 1.00
53 Larry Parrish .08 .25
54 Jack Clark .08 .25
55 Bruce Bochte .02 .10
56 Cesar Cedeno .02 .10
57 Chet Lemon .02 .10
58 Dave Revering .02 .10
59 Vida Blue .08 .25
60 Dave Lopes .08 .25

1980 Topps Team Checklist Sheet

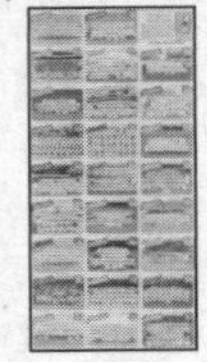

As part of a mail-away offer, Topps offered all 26 1980 team checklist cards on an uncut sheet. These cards enabled the collector to have an easy reference for which card(s) he/she needed to finish their sets. When cut from the sheet, all cards measure the standard size.

1 Team Checklist Sheet 20.00 50.00

1952 Topps Advertising Panels

These three card strips feature a regular 1952 Topps card and ad information on the back. These cards are not numbered in the traditional sense. Any additions to this list or any Advertising Panel list will be appreciated

COMPLETE SET 100.00 200.00
1 Bob Mahoney 75.00 150.00
Robin Roberts
Sid Hudson
2 Bob Wellman 50.00 100.00
Lou Kretlow
Ray Scarborough
3 Wally Westlake 50.00 100.00
Dizzy Trout
Irv Noren
4 Eddie Joost 50.00 100.00
Willie Jones
Gordon Goldsberry

1953 Topps Advertising Panels

These three card strips feature a regular 53 Topps card on the front and advertising information on the back.

COMPLETE SET 300.00 600.00
1 Johnny Mize 60.00 120.00
Clem Koshorek
Toby Atwell
2 Jim Hearn 50.00 100.00
Johnny Groth
Sherm Lollar

3 Mickey Mantle 250.00 500.00
Johnny Wyrostek
Sal Yvars

1954 Topps Advertising Panels

1 Granny Hamner 50.00 100.00
Richie Ashburn
Johnny Schmitz

1955 Topps Advertising Panels

These panels feature regular 1955 Topps cards on the front and advertising information on the back. These items have been seen with advertising for the 1955 Topps Double Header set affixed as well.

COMPLETE SET 150.00 300.00
1 Dave Jolly 25.00 50.00
Jim Pendleton
Karl Spooner
2 Danny Schell 25.00 50.00
Jake Thies
Howie Pollet
3 Jackie Robinson 125.00 250.00
Bill Taylor
Curt Roberts

1956 Topps Advertising Panels

These panels feature regular 1956 Topps cards on the front and advertising information on the back.

COMPLETE SET 25.00 50.00
1 Bob Grim 25.00 50.00
Dusty Rhodes
Each Card is printed twice
2 Johnny O'Brien 25.00 50.00
Harvey Haddix
Frank House

1957 Topps Advertising Panels

Issued in three card strips to promote the upcoming 1957 Topps set, these three card panels are somewhat different in that the backs of these cards were composites of other cards as well as an advertisment for Topps/Bazooka bubble gum.

COMPLETE SET 200.00 400.00
1 Dick Williams 30.00 60.00
Brooks Lawrence
Lou Skizas
2 Jim Piersall 75.00 150.00
Pee Wee Reese
Harvey Kuenn
3 Hector Lopez 40.00 80.00
Johnny Logan
Billy Martin
4 Tom Sturdivant 50.00 100.00
Elston Howard
Clem Labine
5 Brooks Lawrence 30.00 60.00
Lou Skizas
Bob Boyd

1959 Topps Advertising Panels

The fronts of these cards feature standard 1959 Topps cards while the backs feature cards of either Nellie Fox or Ted Kluszewski.

COMPLETE SET 400.00 800.00
1 Don McMahon 25.00 50.00
Red Wilson
Bob Boyd
2 Joe Pignatano 25.00 50.00
Sam Jones
Jack Urban
3 Billy Hunter 25.00 50.00
Chuck Stobbs
Carl Sawatski
4 Vito Valentinelli 25.00 50.00
Ken Lehman
Ed Bouchee
5 Mel Roach 50.00 100.00
Brooks Lawrence
Warren Spahn
6 Harvey Kuenn 25.00 50.00
Alex Grammas
Bob Cerv
7 Bob Cerv 250.00 500.00
Jim Bolger
Mickey Mantle

1960 Topps Advertising Panels

These panels were issued to promote the upcoming Topps set. The fronts feature standard 1960 Topps cards while the backs feature advertising information.

COMPLETE SET 200.00 400.00
1 Wayne Terwilliger 20.00 50.00
Kent Hadley
Faye Throneberry
2 Hank Foiles 20.00 50.00
Hobie Landrith
Hal Smith
3 Cal McLish 150.00 300.00
Hal Smith
Ernie Banks
Jim Grant
Al Kaline
Jerry Casale
Milt Pappas
Wally Moon

1961 Topps Advertising Panels

Used to promote the upcoming Topps sets; these fronts show standard 1961 Topps cards on the front with advertising information on the back.

COMPLETE SET 100.00 200.00
1 Dan Dobbek 20.00 50.00
Russ Nixon/1960 NL Pitching Leaders
2 Jack Kralick 20.00 50.00
Dick Stigman
Joe Christopher
3 Ed Roebuck 20.00 50.00
Bob Schmidt
Zoilo Versalles
4 Lindy Shows Larry 20.00 50.00
Johnny Blanchard
Johnny Kucks

1962 Topps Advertising Panels

These panels feature standard 1962 Topps cards on the front as well as a Roger Maris card back.

COMPLETE SET 75.00 150.00
1 AL Home Run Leaders 50.00 100.00
Barney Schultz
Carl Sawatski
2 NL Strikeout Leaders 50.00 100.00
Carroll Hardy
Carl Sawatski
3 Darrell Johnson 50.00 100.00
AL Strikeout Leaders
Jim Kaat
4 Norm Larker 50.00 100.00
Al Schroll
Jim King

1963 Topps Advertising Panels

These Panels features regular 1963 Topps cards on the front and a Stan Musial ad/endorsement on the back.

COMPLETE SET 75.00 150.00
1 Elston Howard 40.00 80.00
Bob Veale
Cal Koonce
2 Hoyt Wilhelm 50.00 100.00
Don Lock
Bob Duliba

1964 Topps Advertising Panels

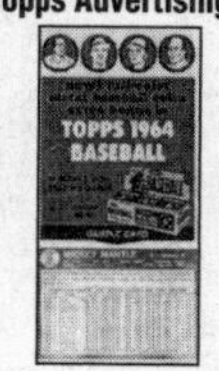

These panels, which were used to promote the 1964 Topps set; feature standard 1964 Topps cards on the front and a Mickey Mantle card back.

COMPLETE SET 150.00 300.00
1 Walt Alston 40.00 80.00
Bill Henry
Vada Pinson
2 Jimmie Hall 20.00 50.00
Ernie Broglio
A.L. ERA Leaders
3 Mickey Mantle 250.00 500.00
Jim Davenport
Boog Powell
4 Denis Menke 20.00 50.00
Dean Chance
Tim Harkness
5 Hoyt Wilhelm 40.00 80.00
Curt Flood
Bill Bruton
6 Carl Willey 20.00 50.00
White Sox Rookies
Bob Friend

1965 Topps Advertising Panels

This panel features three players on the front and an advertising for the upcoming Topps Embossed insert set.

1 Ron Herbel 20.00 50.00
Joe Gibbon
Ed Charles

1966 Topps Advertising Panels

This panel was issued to preview the 1966 Topps baseball set. As is traditional for these panels, they were issued in three card strips. The back of these inserts features information on the upcoming "rub-off" insert set

1 Sandy Koufax 125.00 250.00
Jim Fregosi
Don Mossi
2 Jim Lonborg 50.00 100.00
Howie Koplitz
Luis Aparicio

1967 Topps Advertising Panels

Described as a salesman's sample; the front of this panel features standard 1967 Topps cards on the front and advertising information on the back

COMPLETE SET 50.00 100.00
1 Earl Battey 20.00 50.00
Manny Mota
Gene Brabender
2 Ron Fairly 30.00 60.00
Bobby Murcer
Stan Bahnsen
Curt Simmo

1976 Towne Club Discs

This set, also is another version of the 76 Crane Discs. These discs have the Towne Club back and are a multiple of the Crane issue.

COMPLETE SET (70) 10.00 25.00
1 Hank Aaron 1.25 3.00
2 Johnny Bench .75 2.00
3 Vida Blue .12 .30
4 Larry Bowa .12 .30
5 Lou Brock .75 2.00
6 Jeff Burroughs .08 .20
7 John Candelaria .08 .20
8 Jose Cardenal .08 .20
9 Rod Carew .75 2.00
10 Steve Carlton .75 2.00
11 Dave Cash .08 .20
12 Cesar Cedeno .12 .30
13 Ron Cey .12 .30
14 Carlton Fisk 1.50 4.00
15 Tito Fuentes .08 .20
16 Steve Garvey .75 2.00
17 Ken Griffey .12 .30
18 Don Gullett .08 .20
19 Willie Horton .08 .20
20 Al Hrabosky .08 .20
21 Catfish Hunter 1.25 3.00
22A Reggie Jackson 4.00 10.00
Oakland Athletics
22B Reggie Jackson 1.25 3.00
Baltimore Orioles
23 Randy Jones .08 .20
24 Jim Kaat .25 .60
25 Don Kessinger .08 .20
26 Dave Kingman .25 .60
27 Jerry Koosman .12 .30
28 Mickey Lolich .12 .30
29 Greg Luzinski .25 .60
30 Fred Lynn .25 .60
31 Bill Madlock .12 .30
32A Carlos May .75 2.00
Chicago White Sox
32B Carlos May .08 .20
New York Yankees
33 John Mayberry .08 .20
34 Bake McBride .08 .20
35 Doc Medich .08 .20
36A Andy Messersmith .75 2.00
Los Angeles Dodgers
36B Andy Messersmith .08 .20
Atlanta Braves
37 Rick Monday .08 .20
38 John Montefusco .08 .20
39 Jerry Morales .08 .20
40 Joe Morgan 1.25 3.00
41 Thurman Munson .75 2.00
42 Bobby Murcer .25 .60
43 Al Oliver .25 .60
44 Jim Palmer 1.25 3.00
45 Dave Parker .40 1.00
46 Tony Perez .75 2.00
47 Jerry Reuss .08 .20
48 Brooks Robinson 1.25 3.00
49 Frank Robinson 1.25 3.00
50 Steve Rogers .08 .20
51 Pete Rose 1.50 4.00
52 Nolan Ryan 3.00 8.00
53 Manny Sanguillen .08 .20
54 Mike Schmidt 2.00 5.00
55 Tom Seaver 1.50 4.00
56 Ted Simmons .25 .60
57 Reggie Smith .12 .30
58 Willie Stargell 1.25 3.00
59 Rusty Staub .25 .60
60 Rennie Stennett .08 .20
61 Don Sutton 1.25 3.00
62A Andre Thornton .75 2.00
Chicago Cubs
62B Andre Thornton .08 .20
Montreal Expos
63 Luis Tiant .25 .60
64 Joe Torre .40 1.00
65 Mike Tyson .08 .20
66 Bob Watson .12 .30
67 Wilbur Wood .08 .20
68 Jimmy Wynn .08 .20
69 Carl Yastrzemski 1.25 3.00
70 Richie Zisk .08 .20

1969 Transogram Statues Cards

The reverse of the 1969 Transogram statue box contains a full color, blank-backed card corresponding to the statue inside. All prices are for just the cards. If a box is included, please use a 2X multiplier.

COMPLETE SET (60) 750.00 1,500.00
1 Joe Azcue 2.50 6.00
2 Willie Horton 3.00 8.00
3 Luis Tiant 4.00 10.00
4 Denny McLain 4.00 10.00
5 Jose Cardenal 2.50 6.00
6 Al Kaline 20.00 50.00
7 Tony Oliva 4.00 10.00
8 Blue Moon Odom 2.50 6.00
9 Cesar Tovar 2.50 6.00
10 Rick Monday 3.00 8.00
11 Harmon Killebrew 15.00 40.00
12 Danny Cater 2.50 6.00
13 Brooks Robinson 20.00 50.00
14 Jim Fregosi 4.00 10.00
15 Dave McNally 3.00 8.00
16 Frank Robinson 20.00 50.00
17 Bobby Knoop 2.50 6.00
18 Rick Reichardt 2.50 6.00
19 Carl Yastrzemski 20.00 50.00
20 Pete Ward 2.50 6.00
21 Rico Petrocelli 3.00 8.00
22 Tommy John 4.00 10.00
23 Ken Harrelson 4.00 10.00
24 Luis Aparicio 12.50 30.00
25 Mike Epstein 2.50 6.00
26 Roy White 3.00 8.00
27 Camilo Pascual 3.00 8.00
28 Mel Stottlemyre 3.00 8.00
29 Frank Howard 4.00 10.00
30 Mickey Mantle 150.00 300.00
31 Lou Brock 15.00 40.00
32 Juan Marichal 15.00 40.00
33 Bob Gibson 15.00 40.00
34 Willie Mays 75.00 150.00
35 Tim McCarver 6.00 15.00
36 Willie McCovey 15.00 40.00
37 Don Wilson 2.50 6.00
38 Billy Williams 12.50 30.00
39 Rusty Staub 4.00 10.00
40 Ernie Banks 20.00 50.00
41 Jim Wynn 3.00 8.00
42 Ron Santo 4.00 10.00
43 Tom Haller 3.00 8.00
44 Ron Swoboda 4.00 10.00
45 Willie Davis 2.50 6.00
46 Jerry Koosman 4.00 10.00
47 Jim Lefebvre 2.50 6.00
48 Tom Seaver 40.00 80.00
49 Joe Torre 4.00 10.00
50 Tony Perez 8.00 20.00
51 Felipe Alou 4.00 10.00
52 Lee May 3.00 8.00
53 Hank Aaron 60.00 120.00
54 Pete Rose 60.00 120.00
55 Cookie Rojas 2.50 6.00
56 Roberto Clemente 100.00 200.00
57 Richie Allen 6.00 15.00
58 Matty Alou 3.00 8.00
59 John Callison 3.00 8.00
60 Bill Mazeroski 6.00 15.00

1970 Mets Transogram Statues Cards

The reverse of each 1970 Transogram Mets box features blank backed, unnumbered cards issued in three card panels corresponding to the three small plastic statues honoring the 1969 Mets. The listed prices are for the single cards cut from the box. If the box is included, please use a 1.5X multiplier.

COMPLETE SET 200.00 400.00
21A Ed Kranepool 3.00 8.00
21B Al Weis 1.50 4.00
21C Tom Seaver 75.00 150.00
22A Ken Boswell 1.50 4.00
22B Jerry Koosman 4.00 10.00
22C Jerry Grote 2.00 5.00
23A Art Shamsky 1.50 4.00
23B Gary Gentry 1.50 4.00
23C Tommie Agee 2.00 5.00
24A Nolan Ryan 150.00 300.00
24B Tug McGraw 8.00 20.00
24C Cleon Jones 1.50 4.00
25A Ron Swoboda 1.50 4.00
25B Bud Harrelson 2.50 6.00
25C Donn Clendenon 1.50 4.00

1867 Troy Haymakers CdV's

These six cards represent one of the earliest known team sets. The Troy Haymakers were among the best known traveling squads of the tme. These photos were taken at a studio in Lansingburg, N.Y. Since these cards are unnumbered, we have sequenced them in alphabetical order.

COMPLETE SET 12,000.00 24,000.00
1 Thomas Abrams 2,000.00 4,000.00
2 William Craver 2,000.00 4,000.00
3 Steve King 2,000.00 4,000.00
4 Michael McAtee 2,000.00 4,000.00
5 Peter McKeon 2,000.00 4,000.00
6 Andrew McQuide 2,000.00 4,000.00

1910-11 Turkey Red T3

The cards in this 126-card set measure approximately 5 3/4" by 8". The 1911 Turkey Red set of color cabinet style cards, designated T3 in the American Card Catalog, is named after the brand of cigarettes with which it was offered as a premium. Cards 1-50 and 77-126 depict baseball players while the middle series (51-76) portrays boxers. The cards themselves are not numbered but were assigned numbers for ordering purposes by the manufacturer. This list appears on the backs of cards in the 77-126 sub-series and has been used in the checklist below. At one time the boxers (51-76) were assigned a separate catalog number (T9) but were later returned to the classification to which they properly belong. This attractive set has been reprinted in 2 1/2" by 3 1/2" form. A small number of proofs were found in the early 1970's. Approximately 70 of the cards in the set have been discovered in proof form.

1 Mordecai Brown 600.00 1,000.00
2 Bill Bergen 250.00 400.00
3 Fred Leach 250.00 400.00
4 Roger Bresnahan 350.00 600.00
5 Sam Crawford 500.00 800.00
6 Hal Chase 350.00 600.00
7 Howie Camnitz 250.00 400.00
8 Fred Clarke 500.00 800.00
9 Ty Cobb 3,500.00 6,000.00

10 Art Devlin	250.00	400.00
11 Bill Dahlen	250.00	400.00
12 Bill Donovan	250.00	400.00
13 Larry Doyle	250.00	400.00
14 Red Dooin	250.00	400.00
15 Kid Elberfeld	250.00	400.00
16 Johnny Evers	500.00	800.00
17 Clark Griffith	500.00	800.00
18 Hughie Jennings	500.00	800.00
19 Addie Joss	600.00	1,000.00
20 Tim Jordan	250.00	400.00
21 Red Kleinow	250.00	400.00
22 Harry Krause	250.00	400.00
23 Napoleon Lajoie	700.00	1,200.00
24 Mike Mitchell	250.00	400.00
25 Matty McIntyre	250.00	400.00
26 John McGraw	500.00	800.00
27 Christy Mathewson	2,500.00	4,000.00
28 Harry McIntire	250.00	400.00
29 Amby McConnell	250.00	400.00
30 George Mullin	250.00	400.00
31 Sherry Magee	300.00	500.00
32 Orval Overall	250.00	400.00
33 Jack Pfeister	250.00	400.00
34 Nap Rucker	250.00	400.00
35 Joe Tinker	500.00	800.00
36 Tris Speaker	900.00	1,500.00
37 Slim Sallee	250.00	400.00
38 Jake Stahl	250.00	400.00
39 Rube Waddell	500.00	800.00
40 Vic Willis	350.00	600.00
41 Hooks Wiltse	250.00	400.00
42 Cy Young	1,500.00	2,500.00
43 Out At Third	250.00	400.00
44 Trying to Catch Him Napping	250.00	400.00
45 Tim Jordan Buck Herzog	250.00	400.00
46 Safe At Third	250.00	400.00
47 Frank Chance At Bat	600.00	1,000.00
48 Jack Murray At Bat	300.00	500.00
49 Close Play At Second	300.00	500.00
50 Chief Myers At Bat UER	300.00	500.00
77 Red Ames	250.00	400.00
78 Frank Baker	500.00	800.00
79 George Bell	250.00	400.00
80 Chief Bender	500.00	800.00
81 Bob Bescher	250.00	400.00
82 Kitty Bransfield	250.00	400.00
83 Al Bridwell	250.00	400.00
84 George Browne	250.00	400.00
85 Bill Burns	250.00	400.00
86 Bill Carrigan	250.00	400.00
87 Eddie Collins	500.00	800.00
88 Harry Coveleski	250.00	400.00
89 Lou Criger	250.00	400.00
90 Mickey Doolan	250.00	400.00
91 Tom Downey	250.00	400.00
92 Jimmy Dygert	250.00	400.00
93 Art Fromme	250.00	400.00
94 George Gibson	250.00	400.00
95 Peaches Graham	250.00	400.00
96 Bob Groom	250.00	400.00
97 Bob Hoblitzel	300.00	500.00
98 Doc Hofman	250.00	400.00
99 Walter Johnson	1,500.00	2,500.00
100 Davy Jones	250.00	400.00
101 Willie Keeler	500.00	800.00
102 Johnny Kling	250.00	400.00
103 Ed Konetchy	250.00	400.00
104 Ed Lennox	250.00	400.00
105 Hans Lobert	250.00	400.00
106 Bris Lord	250.00	400.00
107 Rube Manning	250.00	400.00
108 Fred Merkle	250.00	400.00
109 Pat Moran	250.00	400.00
110 George McBride	250.00	400.00
111 Harry Niles	250.00	400.00
112 Dode Paskert	250.00	400.00
113 Bugs Raymond	250.00	400.00
114 Bob Rhoads	900.00	1,500.00
115 Admiral Schlei	250.00	400.00
116 Boss Schmidt	250.00	400.00
117 Frank Schulte	250.00	400.00
118 Charlie Smith	250.00	400.00
119 George Stone	250.00	400.00
120 Gabby Street	250.00	400.00
121 Billy Sullivan	250.00	400.00
122 Fred Tenney	700.00	1,200.00
123 Ira Thomas	250.00	400.00
124 Bobby Wallace	350.00	600.00
125 Ed Walsh	500.00	800.00
126 Chief Wilson	350.00	600.00
C1 Turkey Red Coupon 1-75 on back	20.00	50.00
C2 Turkey Red Coupon 1-76 on back	20.00	50.00
C3 Fez Coupon		
C4 Old Mill Coupon		

1961 Twins Universal Match Corp.

The Farmers and Mechanics Savings Bank of Minneapolis sponsored this issue produced by the Universal Match Corp. of Minneapolis, MN. Each cover carries a player photo on the outside and a brief bio for each player appears on the covers inside. Players are shown wearing Washington Senators hats. Complete matchbooks carry a fifty percent premium.

COMPLETE SET (13)	75.00	150.00
1 Bob Allison	6.00	15.00
2 Earl Battey	4.00	10.00
3 Reno Bertoia	4.00	10.00
4 Billy Gardner	4.00	10.00
5 Lenny Green	4.00	10.00
6 Jim Kaat/(With Twins cap)	8.00	20.00
7 Harmon Killebrew	10.00	25.00
8 Jack Kralick/(With Twins cap)	4.00	10.00
9 Cookie Lavagetto	6.00	15.00
10 Jim Lemon	4.00	10.00
11 Camilo Pascual	4.00	10.00
12 Pedro Ramos	4.00	10.00
13 Zoilo Versalles/(With Twins cap)	6.00	15.00

1961 Twins Peter's Meats

The cards in this 26 card set measure 3 1/2" by 4 5/8". The 1961 Peter's Meats set of full color numbered cards depicts Minnesota Twins players only. The individual cards served as partial packaging for various meat products and are blank backed and heavily waxed. Complete boxes are sometimes available and are valued approximately 50 percent more than single cards. The catalog designation is F173.

COMPLETE SET (26)	500.00	1,000.00
1 Zoilo Versalles	20.00	50.00
2 Ed Lopat	12.50	30.00
3 Pedro Ramos	10.00	25.00
4 Chuck Stobbs	10.00	25.00
5 Don Mincher	12.50	30.00
6 Jack Kralick	10.00	25.00
7 Jim Kaat	60.00	120.00
8 Hal Naragon	10.00	25.00
9 Don Lee	10.00	25.00
10 Cookie Lavagetto	12.50	30.00
11 Pete Whisenant	10.00	25.00
12 Elmer Valo	10.00	25.00
13 Ray Moore	10.00	25.00
14 Billy Gardner	10.00	25.00
15 Lenny Green	10.00	25.00
16 Sam Mele	10.00	25.00
17 Jim Lemon	10.00	25.00
18 Harmon Killebrew	150.00	300.00
19 Paul Giel	10.00	25.00
20 Reno Bertoia	10.00	25.00
21 Clyde McCullough	10.00	25.00
22 Earl Battey	10.00	25.00
23 Camilo Pascual	12.50	30.00
24 Dan Dobbek	10.00	25.00
25 Jose Valdivielso	10.00	25.00
26 Billy Consolo	10.00	25.00

1961 Twins Postcards

These postcards, most of which measure 4" by 5" and are in black and white and are blank-backed, feature members of the 1961 Minnesota Twins, the first year they were in Minnesota. These cards have black and white photograph along with a fascimile autograph. A couple of cards measure 5" by 4" instead. Since these cards are not numbered, we have sequenced them in alphabetical order. Some collectors refer to these as the type 1 postcards for the Twins.

COMPLETE SET	60.00	120.00
1 Bob Allison	1.50	4.00
2 Floyd Baker CO	1.50	4.00
3 Earl Battey	1.50	4.00
4 Reno Bertoia	1.50	4.00
5 Fred Bruckbauer	1.50	4.00
6 Billy Consolo	1.50	4.00
7 Dan Dobbek	1.50	4.00
8 Billy Gardner	1.50	4.00
9 Lenny Green	1.50	4.00
10 Calvin Griffith PRES	1.50	4.00
11 Ron Henry	1.50	4.00
12 Jim Kaat	3.00	8.00
13 Harmon Killebrew	6.00	15.00
14 Jack Kralick	1.50	4.00
15 Cookie Lavagetto MG	1.50	4.00
16 Don Lee	1.50	4.00
17 Jim Lemon	1.50	4.00
18 Ed Lopat CO	1.50	4.00
19 Clyde McCullough CO	1.50	4.00
20 Sam Mele CO	1.50	4.00
21 Don Mincher	1.50	4.00
22 Ray Moore	1.50	4.00
23 Hal Naragon	1.50	4.00
24 Ed Palmquist	1.50	4.00
25 Camilo Pascual	2.00	5.00
26 Bill Pleis	1.50	4.00
27 Pedro Ramos	1.50	4.00
28 Ted Sadowski	1.50	4.00
29 Lee Stange	1.50	4.00
30 Chuck Stobbs	1.50	4.00
31 Jose Valdivielso	1.50	4.00
32 Elmer Valo	1.50	4.00
33 Zoilo Versalles	2.00	5.00

1961-62 Twins Cloverleaf Dairy

These large (3 3/4" by 7 3/4") cards are unnumbered; they made up the side of a Cloverleaf Dairy milk carton. Cards still on the carton are valued double the listed price below. The last two digits of the year of issue for each player is given in parentheses. However those players appearing both (BOTH) years are indistinguishable (as to which year they were produced) when cut from the carton. There were 16 cards produced in 1961 and 24 cards produced in 1962. These unnumbered cards are sequenced in alphabetical order. The catalog designation for this set is F103.

COMPLETE SET (31)	1,250.00	2,500.00
1 Bernie Allen 62	40.00	80.00
2 George Banks 62	40.00	80.00
3 Earl Battey BOTH	30.00	60.00
4 Joe Bonikowski 62	40.00	80.00
5 Billy Gardner 61	50.00	100.00
6 Paul Giel 61	40.00	80.00
7 John Goryl 62	40.00	80.00
8 Lenny Green BOTH	30.00	60.00
9 Jim Kaat BOTH	60.00	120.00
10 Harmon Killebrew 61	200.00	400.00
11 Jack Kralick BOTH	30.00	60.00
12 Don Lee 61	40.00	80.00
13 Jim Lemon BOTH	30.00	60.00
14 Manager Coaches 62	40.00	80.00
15 Georges Maranda 62	40.00	80.00
16 Orlando Martinez 62	40.00	80.00
17 Don Mincher BOTH	40.00	80.00
18 Ray Moore 62	40.00	80.00
19 Hal Naragon 62	40.00	80.00
20 Camilo Pascual BOTH	40.00	80.00
21 Vic Power 62	40.00	80.00
22 Pedro Ramos 61	50.00	100.00
23 Rich Rollins 62	50.00	100.00
24 Theodore Sadowski 62	40.00	80.00
25 Albert Stange 62	40.00	80.00
26 Dick Stigman 62	40.00	80.00
27 Chuck Stobbs 61	50.00	100.00
28 Bill Tuttle BOTH	30.00	60.00
29 Jose Valdivielso 61	40.00	80.00
30 Zoilo Versalles BOTH	40.00	80.00
31 Gerald Zimmerman 62	40.00	80.00

1962 Twins Jay Publishing

This 12-card set of the Minnesota Twins measures approximately 5" by 7". The fronts feature black-and-white posed player photos with the player's and team name printed below in the white border. These cards were packaged 12 to a packet. The backs are blank. The cards are unnumbered and checklisted below in alphabetical order.

COMPLETE SET (12)	15.00	40.00
1 Bob Allison	1.50	4.00
2 Earl Battey	1.00	2.50
3 Lenny Green	1.00	2.50
4 Jim Kaat	2.00	5.00
5 Harmon Killebrew	5.00	12.00
6 John Kralick	1.00	2.50
7 Don Lee	1.00	2.50
8 Jim Lemon	1.00	2.50
9 Sam Mele MG	1.00	2.50
10 Camilo Pascual	1.25	3.00
11 Jose Valdivielso	1.00	2.50
12 Zoilo Versalles	1.50	4.00

1963 Twins Jay Publishing

This 12-card set of the Minnesota Twins measures approximately 5" by 7". The fronts feature black-and-white posed player photos with the player's and team name printed below in the white border. These cards were packaged 12 to a packet. The backs are blank. The cards are unnumbered and checklisted below in alphabetical order.

COMPLETE SET (12)	20.00	50.00
1 Bernie Allen	.75	2.00
2 Bob Allison	.75	2.00
3 Earl Battey	.75	2.00
4 Jim Kaat	1.50	4.00
5 Harmon Killebrew	5.00	12.00
6 Jack Kralick	.75	2.00
7 Jim Lemon	.75	2.00
8 Sam Mele MG	.75	2.00
9 Camilo Pascual	1.00	2.50
10 Vic Power	.75	2.00
11 Rich Rollins	1.00	2.50
12 Zoilo Versalles	1.00	2.50

1963 Twins Volpe

Sponsored by Western Oil and Fuel Company, these 24 portraits of the 1963 Minnesota Twins by noted artist Nicholas Volpe measure approximately 8 1/2" by 11". Each white-bordered color reproduction of pastel chalk on bordered color reproduction features a larger portrait and a smaller action drawing. The player's name appears in black lettering within the white margin at bottom, and also as a white fascimile autograph on the black background. The white back carries the player's name, position and biography at the top, followed below by career highlights and statistics. Artist information and the sponsor's logo at the bottom round out the backs. The drawings are unnumbered and checklisted in alphabetical order.

COMPLETE SET (24)	100.00	200.00
1 Bernie Allen	3.00	8.00
2 Bob Allison	4.00	10.00
3 George Banks	3.00	8.00
4 Earl Battey	4.00	10.00
5 Bill Dailey	3.00	8.00
6 John Goryl	3.00	8.00
7 Lenny Green	3.00	8.00
8 Jimmie Hall	3.00	8.00
9 Jim Kaat	6.00	15.00
10 Harmon Killebrew	10.00	25.00
11 Sam Mele MG	4.00	10.00
12 Don Mincher	4.00	10.00
13 Ray Moore	3.00	8.00
14 Camilio Pascual	4.00	10.00
15 Jim Perry	5.00	12.00
16 Bill Pleis	3.00	8.00
17 Vic Power	4.00	10.00
18 Gary Roggenburk	3.00	8.00
19 Jim Roland	3.00	8.00
20 Rich Rollins	4.00	10.00
21 Lee Stange	3.00	8.00
22 Dick Stigman		
23 Zoilo Versalles	4.00	10.00
24 Jerry Zimmerman	3.00	8.00

1964 Twins Jay Publishing

The 1964 Twins Jay set consists of 12 cards produced by Jay Publishing. The Henry and Oliva cards establish the year of the set, since 1964 was Henry's last year and Oliva's first year with the Twins. The cards measure approximately 5" by 7" and are printed on photographic paper stock. The white fronts feature a black-and-white player portrait with the player's name and the team name below. The backs are blank. The cards are packaged 12 to a packet. The cards are unnumbered and checklisted below in alphabetical order.

COMPLETE SET (12)	15.00	40.00
1 Bob Allison	1.25	3.00
2 Earl Battey	.75	2.00
3 Jim Grant	.75	2.00
4 Jimmie Hall	.75	2.00
5 Ron Henry	.75	2.00
6 Jim Kaat	1.50	4.00
7 Harmon Killebrew	5.00	12.00
8 Tony Oliva	1.50	4.00
9 Camilo Pascual	1.00	2.50
10 Rich Rollins	.75	2.00
11 Dick Stigman	.75	2.00
12 Zorro Versalles	1.00	2.50

1964 Twins Volpe

This 15 drawings, which measure 8" by 11", feature members of the 1964 Minnesota Twins. The fronts feature two drawings of the players while the backs have biographical information, a blurb about the player as well as career statistics. Since these are unnumbered, we have sequenced them in alphabetical order.

COMPLETE SET	75.00	150.00
1 Bernie Allen	3.00	8.00
2 Bob Allison	4.00	10.00
3 Earl Battey	3.00	8.00
4 Bill Dailey	3.00	8.00
5 Jim Hall	3.00	8.00
6 Jim Kaat	6.00	15.00
7 Harmon Killebrew	10.00	25.00
8 Don Mincher	4.00	10.00
9 Tony Oliva	8.00	20.00
10 Camilo Pascual	4.00	10.00
11 Bill Pleis	3.00	8.00
12 Jim Roland	3.00	8.00
13 Rich Rollins	3.00	8.00
14 Dick Stigman	3.00	8.00
15 Zoilo Versalles	3.00	8.00

1965 Twins Jay Publishing

This 12-card set of the Minnesota Twins measures approximately 5" by 7". The fronts feature black-and-white posed player photos with the player's and team name printed below in the white border. These cards were packaged 12 to a packet. The backs are blank. The cards are unnumbered and checklisted below in alphabetical order.

COMPLETE SET (12)	12.50	30.00
1 Bernie Allen	.75	2.00
2 Bob Allison	1.25	3.00
3 Earl Battey	.75	2.00
4 Bill Dailey	.75	2.00
5 Jim Kaat	1.50	4.00
6 Harmon Killebrew	5.00	12.00
7 Sam Mele MG	1.00	2.50
8 Camilo Pascual	1.25	3.00
9 Vic Power	.75	2.00
10 Rich Rollins	.75	2.00
11 Dick Stigman	.75	2.00
12 Zoilo Versalles	1.00	2.50

1965 Twins Postcards

This 10-card set of the Minnesota Twins features color player portraits measuring approximately 4 3/4" by 7" with the player's name in the wide bottom margin. The backs display a postcard format. The cards are unnumbered and checklisted below in alphabetical order.

COMPLETE SET (10)	50.00	100.00
1 Bob Allison	4.00	10.00
2 Earl Battey	3.00	8.00
3 Jimmie Hall	3.00	8.00
4 Jim Kaat	6.00	15.00
5 Harmon Killebrew	10.00	25.00
6 Sam Mele	3.00	8.00
7 Tony Oliva	6.00	15.00
8 Camilo Pascual	4.00	10.00
9 Rich Rollins	3.00	8.00
10 Zoilo Versalles	4.00	10.00

1966 Twins Fairway Grocery

This 17-card set features 8" by 10" color player portraits of the Minnesota Twins with player information and statistics on the backs. The cards are unnumbered and checklisted below in alphabetical order.

COMPLETE SET (17)	50.00	100.00
1 Bernie Allen	2.00	5.00
2 Bob Allison	3.00	8.00
3 Earl Battey	2.00	5.00
4 Jim Grant	2.50	6.00
5 Jimmie Hall	2.00	5.00
6 Jim Kaat	3.00	8.00
7 Harmon Killebrew	8.00	20.00
8 Jim Merritt	2.00	5.00
9 Don Mincher	2.00	5.00
10 Tony Oliva	4.00	10.00
11 Camilo Pascual	2.50	6.00
12 Jim Perry	2.50	6.00
13 Frank Quilici	2.00	5.00
14 Rich Rollins	2.50	6.00
15 Sandy Valdespino	2.00	5.00
16 Zoilo Versalles	2.50	6.00
17 Al Worthington	2.00	5.00

1967 Twins Team Issue

This 26-card set of the 1967 Minnesota Twins measures approximately 4" by 5" and features black-and-white facsimile autographed player portraits with white borders. The backs are blank. The cards are unnumbered and checklisted below in alphabetical order. A card of Rod Carew is featured in his Rookie Card year.

COMPLETE SET (26)	30.00	60.00
1 Bob Allison	1.00	2.50
2 Earl Battey	.75	2.00
3 Rod Carew	6.00	15.00
4 Dean Chance Pitching	1.00	2.50
5 Dean Chance Portrait	1.00	2.50
6 Ron Clark	.75	2.00
7 Harmon Killebrew	4.00	10.00
8 Ron Kline	.75	2.00
9 Jim Lemon CO	.75	2.00
10 Billy Martin CO	1.50	4.00
11 Jim Merritt	.75	2.00
12 Tony Oliva Portrait	1.50	4.00
13 Tony Oliva Batting)	1.50	4.00
14 Jim Ollom	.75	2.00
15 Jim Perry	1.00	2.50
16 Frank Quilici	.75	2.00
17 Rich Reese	.75	2.00
18 Jim Roland	.75	2.00
19 Rich Rollins	.75	2.00
20 Cesar Tovar	.75	2.00
21 Cesar Tovar Closeup	.75	2.00
22 Ted Uhlaender	.75	2.00
23 Sandy Valdespino	.75	2.00
24 Zoilo Versalles	1.00	2.50
25 Early Wynn CO	1.50	4.00
26 Jerry Zimmerman	.75	2.00

1969 Twins Team Issue Color

This 13-card set of the Minnesota Twins measures approximately 7" by 8 3/4" with the fronts featuring white-bordered color player photos. The player's name and team is printed in black in the white margin below the picture. The backs are blank. The cards are unnumbered and checklisted below in alphabetical order.

COMPLETE SET (13)	30.00	60.00
1 Bob Allison	1.50	4.00
2 Leo Cardenas	1.50	4.00
3 Rod Carew	4.00	10.00
4 Dean Chance	1.50	4.00
5 Jim Kaat	2.00	5.00
6 Harmon Killebrew	3.00	8.00
7 Billy Martin MG	3.00	8.00
8 Tony Oliva	2.50	6.00
9 Ron Perranoski	1.25	3.00
10 Jim Perry	1.50	4.00
11 Rich Reese	1.25	3.00
12 Cesar Tovar	1.50	4.00
13 Ted Uhlaender	1.25	3.00

1970 Twins Super Valu

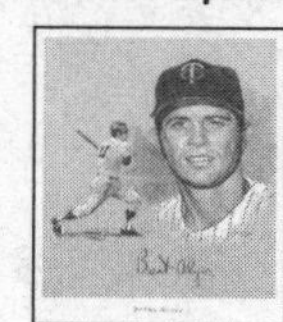

This 12-card set features color player drawings in white borders and measures approximately 7 3/4" by 9 3/8". The cards feature both an action player drawing and a head drawing with a facsimile autograph. The player's name is printed in the bottom margin. The backs are blank. The cards are unnumbered and checklisted below in alphabetical order.

COMPLETE SET (12)	20.00	50.00
1 Brant Alyea	1.25	3.00
2 Leo Cardenas	1.25	3.00
3 Rod Carew	6.00	15.00
4 Jim Kaat	1.50	4.00
5 Harmon Killebrew	4.00	10.00
6 George Mitterwald	1.25	3.00
7 Tony Oliva	2.50	6.00
8 Ron Perranoski	1.50	4.00
9 Jim Perry	2.00	5.00
10 Rich Reese	1.25	3.00
11 Luis Tiant	2.50	6.00
12 Cesar Tovar	1.25	3.00

1970 Twins Team Issue

This 14-card set features black-and-white player portraits with white borders and a facsimile autograph printed on the front. The backs are blank. The cards are unnumbered and checklisted below in alphabetical order.

COMPLETE SET (14)	6.00	15.00
1 Brant Alyea	.40	1.00
2 Steve Barber	.40	1.00
3 Frank Crosetti CO	.75	2.00
4 Marv Grissom	.40	1.00
5 Minnie Mendoza	.40	1.00
6 Paul Ratliff	.40	1.00
7 Rich Reese	.40	1.00
8 Bill Rigney MG	.40	1.00
9 Bob Rodgers Co	.40	1.00
10 Luis Tiant	1.00	2.50
11 Cesar Tovar	.40	1.00
12 Stan Williams	.40	1.00
13 Bill Zepp	.40	1.00
14 Metropolitan Stadium	.40	1.00

1972 Twins Team Issue

This 25-card set of the Minnesota Twins features black-and-white player portraits in white borders with facsimile autographs and measures approximately 4" by 5 1/8". The backs are blank. The cards are unnumbered and checklisted below in alphabetical order.

COMPLETE SET (25)	40.00	80.00
1 Bert Blyleven	2.50	6.00
2 Steve Braun	1.25	3.00
3 Ray Corbin	1.25	3.00
4 Rick Dempsey	2.00	5.00
5 Bob Gebhard	1.25	3.00
6 Wayne Granger	1.25	3.00
7 Jim Kaat	2.50	6.00
8 Harmon Killebrew	4.00	10.00
9 Dave Laroche	1.25	3.00
10 George Mitterwald	1.25	3.00
11 Dan Monzon	1.25	3.00
12 Vern Morgan	1.25	3.00
13 Jim Nettles	1.25	3.00
14 Tom Norton	1.25	3.00
15 Tony Oliva	2.50	6.00
16 Jim Perry	2.00	5.00
17 Frank Quilici	1.25	3.00
18 Rich Reese	1.25	3.00
19 Phil Roof	1.25	3.00
20 Ralph Rowe CO	1.25	3.00
21 Eric Soderholm	1.25	3.00
22 Danny Thompson	1.25	3.00
23 Cesar Tovar	1.50	4.00
24 Dick Woodson	1.25	3.00
25 Al Worthington CO	1.25	3.00

1975 Twins Postcards

This 24-card set of the Minnesota Twins features player photos on postcard-size cards. The cards are unnumbered and checklisted below in alphabetical order.

COMPLETE SET (24)	5.00	12.00
1 Vic Albury	.20	.50
2 Bert Blyleven	.60	1.50
3 Glenn Borgmann	.20	.50
4 Steve Braun	.20	.50
5 Steve Brye	.20	.50
6 Bill Campbell	.20	.50
7 Rod Carew	1.50	4.00
8 Ray Corbin	.20	.50
9 Bobby Darwin	.20	.50
10 Joe Decker	.20	.50
11 Dan Ford	.20	.50
12 Dave Goltz	.20	.50
13 Luis Gomez	.20	.50
14 Larry Hisle	.30	.75
15 Craig Kusick	.20	.50
16 Tom Lundstedt	.20	.50
17 Vern Morgan CO	.20	.50
18 Tony Oliva	.40	1.00
19 Frank Quilici MG	.20	.50
20 Phil Roof	.20	.50
21 Ralph Rowe CO	.20	.50
22 Eric Soderholm	.20	.50
23 Lee Stange CO	.20	.50
24 Jerry Terrell	.20	.50

1975 Twins Team Issue

These photos feature members of the 1975 Minnesota Twins. They are unnumbered and we have sequenced them in alphabetical order.

COMPLETE SET	10.00	25.00
1 Vic Albury	.40	1.00
2 Bert Blyleven	1.00	2.50
3 Glen Borgmann	.40	1.00
4 Lyman Bostock	1.00	2.50
5 Steve Braun	.40	1.00
6 John Briggs	.40	1.00
7 Steve Brye	.40	1.00
8 Tom Burgmeier	.40	1.00
9 Bill Butler	.40	1.00
10 Bill Campbell	.40	1.00
11 Ray Corbin	.40	1.00
12 Joe Decker	.40	1.00
13 Dan Ford	.40	1.00
14 Dave Goltz	.40	1.00
15 Luis Gomez	.40	1.00
16 Larry Hisle	.40	1.00
17 Jim Hughes	.40	1.00
18 Tom Johnson	.40	1.00
19 Craig Kusick	.40	1.00
20 Tom Lundstedt	.40	1.00
21 Tony Oliva	1.00	2.50
22 Frank Quilici MG	.40	1.00
23 Phil Roof	.40	1.00
24 Eric Soderholm	.40	1.00
25 Lee Strange	.40	1.00
26 Jerry Terrell	.40	1.00
27 Danny Thompson	.40	1.00
28 Mark Wiley	.40	1.00

1976 Twins Postcards

This 18-card set of the Minnesota Twins features player photos on postcard-size cards. The cards are unnumbered and checklisted below in alphabetical order.

COMPLETE SET (18)	4.00	10.00
1 Bert Blyleven	.60	1.50
2 Lyman Bostock	.40	1.00
3 Steve Brye	.20	.50
4 Bill Campbell	.20	.50
5 Rod Carew	1.50	4.00
6 Mike Cubbage	.20	.50
7 Dan Ford	.20	.50
8 Dave Goltz	.20	.50
9 Larry Hisle	.20	.50
10 Craig Kusick	.20	.50
11 Dave McKay	.20	.50
12 Bob Randall	.20	.50
13 Pete Redfern	.20	.50
14 Phil Roof	.20	.50
15 Bill Singer	.20	.50
16 Roy Smalley	.30	.75
17 Jerry Terrell	.20	.50
18 Danny Thompson	.20	.50

1977 Twins Postcards

These black and white postcards, which measure approximately 4" by 5" feature members of the 1977 Minnesota Twins. As these postcards were issued over a series of years, most of these years look alike and this grouping appears to be players who were fairly new to the Twins in 1977. Since these photos are not numbered, we have sequenced them in alphabetical order.

COMPLETE SET (17)	4.00	10.00
1 Glenn Adams	.20	.50
2 Rich Chiles	.20	.50
3 Mike Cubbage	.20	.50
4 Bob Gorinski	.20	.50
5 Jeff Holly	.20	.50
6 Dave Johnson	.20	.50
7 Tom Johnson	.20	.50
8 Karl Kuehl CO	.20	.50
9 Don McMahon CO	.20	.50
10 Willie Norwood	.20	.50
11 Tony Oliva CO	1.00	2.50
12 Ron Schueler	.20	.50
13 Roy Smalley	.40	1.00
14 Paul Thormodsgard	.20	.50
15 Rob Wilfong	.20	.50
16 Geoff Zahn	.20	.50
17 Jerry Zimmerman CO	.20	.50

1978 Twins Frisz

Manufactured by Barry R. Frisz and issued by the Twins in two 25-card series, these cards measure approximately 2 1/2" by 3 3/4" and feature on their fronts white-bordered posed color photos of retired Twins players. The white and gray horizontal back carries the player's name, biography, position, statistics, and career highlights. The cards are numbered on the back.

COMPLETE SET (50)	10.00	25.00
1 Bob Allison	.60	1.50
2 Earl Battey	.20	.50
3 Dave Boswell	.20	.50
4 Dean Chance	.60	1.50
5 Jim Grant	.40	1.00
6 Calvin Griffith PRES	.20	.50
7 Jimmie Hall	.20	.50
8 Harmon Killebrew	1.00	2.50
9 Jim Lemon	.20	.50
10 Billy Martin MG	.60	1.50
11 Gene Mauch MG	.30	.75
12 Sam Mele MG	.20	.50
13 Metropolitan Stadium	.60	1.50
14 Don Mincher	.20	.50
15 Tony Oliva	.40	1.00
16 Camilo Pascual	.30	.75
17 Jim Perry	.20	.50
18 Frank Quilici MG	.20	.50
19 Rich Reese	.20	.50
20 Bill Rigney MG	.20	.50
21 Cesar Tovar	.30	.75
22 Zoilo Versalles	.30	.75
23 Al Worthington	.20	.50
24 Jerry Zimmerman	.20	.50
25 Checklist 1-25	.20	.50
26 Bernie Allen	.20	.50
27 Leo Cardenas	.40	1.00
28 Ray Corbin	.20	.50
29 Joe Decker	.20	.50
30 Johnny Goryl	.20	.50
31 Tom Hall	.20	.50
32 Bill Hands	.20	.50
33 Jim Holt	.20	.50
34 Randy Hundley	.40	1.00
35 Jerry Kindall	.20	.50
36 Johnny Klippstein	.20	.50
37 Jack Kralick	.20	.50
38 Jim Merritt	.20	.50
39 Joe Nossek	.20	.50
40 Ron Perranoski	.30	.75
41 Bill Pleis	.20	.50
42 Rick Renick	.20	.50
43 Jim Roland	.20	.50
44 Lee Stange	.20	.50
45 Dick Stigman	.20	.50
46 Danny Thompson	.20	.50
47 Ted Uhlaender	.20	.50
48 Sandy Valdespino	.30	.75
49 Dick Woodson	.20	.50
50 Checklist 25-50	.20	.50

1978 Twins Frisz Postcards

Manufactured by Barry R. Frisz and issued by the Twins, these 25 postcards measure 3 1/2" by 5 1/2" and feature on their fronts borderless color posed-on-field photos of then-current Twins. The back carries the player's name, position, and height and weight at the upper left. Below is a ghosted cartoon logo that carries the words "Win, Twins." The year of the set appears in the vertical lettering bisecting the postcard. The postcards are unnumbered and checklisted below in alphabetical order.

COMPLETE SET (25)	8.00	20.00
1 Glenn Adams	.30	.75
2 Glenn Borgmann	.30	.75
3 Rod Carew	1.50	4.00
4 Rich Chiles	.30	.75
5 Mike Cubbage	.30	.75
6 Roger Erickson	.30	.75
7 Dan Ford	.30	.75
8 Dave Goltz	.30	.75
9 Dave Johnson	.30	.75
10 Tom Johnson	.30	.75
11 Craig Kusick	.30	.75
12 Jose Morales	.30	.75
13 Willie Norwood	.30	.75
14 Hosken Powell	.30	.75
15 Bob Randall	.30	.75
16 Pete Redfern	.30	.75
17 Bombo Rivera	.30	.75
18 Gary Serum	.30	.75
19 Roy Smalley	.60	1.50
20 Greg Thayer	.30	.75
21 Paul Thormodsgard	.30	.75
22 Rob Wilfong	.30	.75
23 Larry Wolfe	.30	.75
24 Butch Wynegar	.30	.75
25 Geoff Zahn	.30	.75

1979 Twins Frisz Postcards

Manufactured by Barry R. Frisz and issued by the Twins,

these 30 postcards measure 3 1/2" by 5 1/2" and feature on their fronts borderless color posed-on-field photos of then-current Twins. The back carries the player's name, position, and height and weight at the upper left. Below is a ghosted cartoon logo that carries the words "Win, Twins." The year of the set appears in the vertical lettering bisecting the postcard. The postcards are unnumbered and checklisted below in alphabetical order.

COMPLETE SET (30)	6.00	15.00
1 Glenn Adams	.20	.50
2 Glenn Borgmann	.20	.50
3 John Castino	.20	.50
4 Mike Cubbage	.20	.50
5 Dave Edwards	.20	.50
6 Roger Erickson	.20	.50
7 Dave Goltz	.20	.50
8 John Goryl CO	.20	.50
9 Paul Hartzell	.20	.50
10 Jeff Holly	.20	.50
11 Ron Jackson	.20	.50
12 Jerry Koosman	.60	1.50
13 Karl Kuehl CO	.20	.50
14 Craig Kusick	.20	.50
15 Ken Landreaux	.20	.50
16 Mike Marshall	.40	1.00
17 Gene Mauch MG	.40	1.00
18 Jose Morales	.20	.50
19 Willie Norwood	.20	.50
20 Camilo Pascual CO	.40	1.00
21 Hosken Powell	.20	.50
22 Bobby Randall	.20	.50
23 Pete Redfern	.20	.50
24 Bombo Rivera	.20	.50
25 Gary Serum	.20	.50
26 Roy Smalley	.40	1.00
27 Rob Wilfong	.20	.50
28 Butch Wynegar	.20	.50
29 Geoff Zahn	.20	.50
30 Jerry Zimmerman CO	.20	.50

1980 Twins Postcards

This 33-card set features photos of the 1980 Minnesota Twins on postcard-size cards. A facsimile autograph is printed on some of the cards. The cards are unnumbered and checklisted below in alphabetical order.

COMPLETE SET (33)	6.00	15.00
1 Glenn Adams	.20	.50
2 Sal Butera	.20	.50
3 John Castino	.20	.50
4 Doug Corbett	.20	.50
5 Mike Cubbage	.20	.50
6 Dave Edwards	.20	.50
7 Roger Erickson	.20	.50
8 Terry Felton	.20	.50
9 Danny Goodwin	.20	.50
10 Johnny Goryl CO	.20	.50
11 Darrell Jackson	.20	.50
12 Ron Jackson	.20	.50
13 Harmon Killebrew CO	1.25	3.00
14 Jerry Koosman	.40	1.00
15 Karl Kuehl CO	.20	.50
16 Ken Landreaux	.20	.50
17 Pete Mackanin	.20	.50
18 Mike Marshall	.30	.75
19 Gene Mauch MG	.20	.50
20 Jose Morales	.20	.50
21 Willie Norwood	.20	.50
22 Camilo Pascual CO	.30	.75
23 Hosken Powell	.20	.50
24 Bobby Randall CO	.20	.50
25 Pete Redfern	.20	.50
26 Bombo Rivera	.20	.50
27 Roy Smalley	.20	.50
28 Rich Sofield	.20	.50
29 John Verhoeven	.20	.50
30 Rob Wilfong	.20	.50
31 Butch Wynegar	.20	.50
32 Geoff Zahn	.20	.50
33 Jerry Zimmerman CO	.20	.50

1932 U.S. Caramel

The cards in this 32-card set measure 2 1/2" by 3". The U.S. Caramel set of "Famous Athletes" was issued in 1932. The cards contain black and white bust shots set against an attractive red background. Boxers and golfers are included in the set. The existence of card number 16, Fred Lindstrom has only recently been verified. The set price does not include the Lindstrom card.

1 Eddie Collins	200.00	400.00
2 Paul Waner	200.00	400.00
4 Bill Terry	200.00	400.00
5 Earl Combs	200.00	400.00
6 Bill Dickey	200.00	400.00
7 Joe Cronin	200.00	400.00
8 Chick Hafey	150.00	300.00
10 Rabbit Maranville	150.00	300.00
11 Rogers Hornsby	250.00	500.00
12 Mickey Cochrane	200.00	400.00
13 Lloyd Waner	150.00	300.00
14 Ty Cobb	500.00	1,000.00
16 Fred Lindstrom	75,000.00	125,000.00
17 Al Simmons	200.00	400.00
18 Tony Lazzeri	150.00	300.00
19 Wally Berger	125.00	250.00
20 Red Ruffing	150.00	300.00
21 Chuck Klein	200.00	400.00
23 Jimmie Foxx	1,500.00	2,500.00
24 Lefty O'Doul	100.00	200.00
26 Lou Gehrig	5,000.00	10,000.00
27 Lefty Grove	250.00	500.00
28 Edward Brandt	100.00	200.00
29 George Earnshaw	100.00	200.00
30 Frankie Frisch	200.00	400.00
31 Lefty Gomez	200.00	400.00
32 Babe Ruth	8,000.00	12,000.00

1925 Universal Toy and Novelty W-504

Issued in uncut sheet form, by Universal Toy and Novelty, this "Strip card" series appears to have been issued early in the 1925 season. Presently, examples of individual players representing four teams are accounted for. Three of the checklists appear to be complete (Brooklyn, Giants, Yankees - as listed below). The cards are numbered on the fronts, although the number is sometimes cut off when being separated from the sheet. The backs are blank. Like all "Strip cards" these were cut down by hand, after they were marketed. As such, size variances may very well exist. Approximate size is 1 3/8" x 2 1/4".

COMPLETE SET (58)	750.00	1,500.00
101 Eddie Brown	10.00	20.00
102 Hank DeBerry	10.00	20.00
103 Bill Doak	10.00	20.00
104 Rube Ehrhardt	10.00	20.00
105 Jake Fournier	12.50	25.00
106 Tommy Griffith	10.00	20.00
107 Burleigh Grimes	20.00	40.00
108 Charlie Hargreaves	10.00	20.00
109 Andy High	10.00	20.00
110 Jimmy Johnston	10.00	20.00
111 John Mitchell	10.00	20.00
112 Tiny Osborne	10.00	20.00
113 Milt Stock	10.00	20.00
114 Zack Taylor	10.00	20.00
115 Dazzy Vance	20.00	40.00
116 Zach Wheat	20.00	40.00
117 Bennie Bengough	10.00	20.00
118 Joe Dugan	10.00	20.00
119 Waite Hoyt	20.00	40.00
120 Sam Jones	12.50	25.00
121 Bob Meusel	15.00	30.00
122 Wally Pipp	10.00	20.00
123 Babe Ruth	50.00	150.00
124 Wally Schang	10.00	20.00
125 Bob Shawkey	12.50	25.00
126 Everett Scott	10.00	20.00
127 Urban Shocker	10.00	20.00
128 Aaron Ward	10.00	20.00
129 Whitey Witt	10.00	20.00
130 Carl Mays	10.00	20.00
131 Miller Huggins	20.00	40.00
132 Ben. Paschal	10.00	20.00
133 Virgil Barnes	10.00	20.00
134 Jack Bentley	10.00	20.00
135 Frank Frisch	20.00	40.00
136 Hank Gowdy	10.00	20.00
137 Heinie Groh	12.50	25.00
138 Travis Jackson	20.00	40.00
139 George Kelly	20.00	40.00
140 Emil Meusel	10.00	20.00
141 Hugh McQuillan	10.00	20.00
142 Arthur Nehf	10.00	20.00
143 Rosy Ryan	10.00	20.00
144 Pancho Snyder	10.00	20.00
145 Hack Wilson	20.00	40.00
146 Ross Youngs	20.00	40.00
147 Hugh Jennings	20.00	40.00
148 John J. McGraw	25.00	50.00
149 Joe Judge	12.50	25.00
151 R. Peckinpaugh	12.50	25.00
152 Ossie Bluege	10.00	20.00
153 Mike McNally	10.00	20.00
154 Sam Rice	20.00	40.00
159 Pinky Hargrave	10.00	20.00
162 Muddy Ruel	10.00	20.00
164 George Mogridge	10.00	20.00
NNO Brooklyn Dodgers Team Photo	20.00	40.00
NNO New York Yankees Team Photo	20.00	40.00
NNO New York Giants Team Photo	20.00	40.00

1933 Uncle Jack

These blank-backed cards, which measure approximately 1 7/8" by 2 7/8" feauture the leading players in baseball at this time. The fronts feature a blue duotone photo with the players name on the bottom. Since the cards are unnumbered, they are sequenced in alphabetical order. The cards were issued in one-card packs along with a coupon for a "World Series trip" contest and a piece of gum.

COMPLETE SET (30)	1,800.00	3,600.00
1 Earl Averill	200.00	400.00
2 James Bottomley	200.00	400.00
3 Ed Brandt	100.00	200.00
4 Ben Chapman	100.00	200.00
5 Gordon Cochrane	200.00	400.00
6 Joe Cronin	200.00	400.00
7 Kiki Cuyler	200.00	400.00
8 George Earnshaw	100.00	200.00
9 Wes Ferrell	150.00	300.00
10 Jimmie Foxx	300.00	600.00
11 Frank Frisch	200.00	400.00
12 Burleigh Grimes	200.00	400.00
13 Lefty Grove	300.00	600.00
14 Wild Bill Hallahan	125.00	250.00
15 Gabby Hartnett	200.00	400.00
16 Babe Herman	150.00	300.00
17 Rogers Hornsby	500.00	1,000.00
18 Charles Klein	200.00	400.00
19 Tony Lazzeri	200.00	400.00
20 Fred Lindstrom	200.00	400.00
21 Ted Lyons	200.00	400.00
22 Pepper Martin	150.00	300.00
23 Herb Pennock	200.00	400.00
24 Babe Ruth	750.00	1,500.00
25 Al Simmons	200.00	400.00
26 Bill Terry	200.00	400.00
27 Dazzy Vance	200.00	400.00
28 Lloyd Waner	200.00	400.00
29 Paul Waner	200.00	400.00
30 Hack Wilson	200.00	400.00

1912 Vassar Sweaters

This oversized set measures approximately 4" by 6 1/2" and features black-and-white photos of players in sweaters with white borders. The only known players in the set are listed below in alphabetical order. Other cards may exist and any confirmed additions are welcomed.

COMPLETE SET	1,250.00	2,500.00
1 Ty Cobb	2,000.00	4,000.00
2 Sam Crawford	600.00	1,200.00
3 Walter Johnson	1,250.00	2,500.00
4 Larry Lajoie	1,250.00	2,500.00
5 Smokey Joe Wood	500.00	1,000.00

1915 Victory T214

The cards in this set measure 1 1/2" by 2 5/8". The set is easily distinguished by the presence of the reference to Victory Tobacco on the card backs. The players in this unnumbered set have been alphabetized and numbered for reference in the checklist below. The set can be dated to 1915 with Chief Bender's appearence as a Baltimore Federal.

1 Red Ames	1,500.00	2,500.00
2 Chief Bender	3,000.00	5,000.00
3 Roger Bresnahan	3,000.00	5,000.00
4 Al Bridwell	1,500.00	2,500.00
5 Howie Camnitz	1,500.00	2,500.00
6 Hal Chase Portrait	1,500.00	2,500.00
7 Hal Chase Throwing	1,500.00	2,500.00
8 Ty Cobb	8,000.00	12,000.00
9 Doc Crandall	1,500.00	2,500.00
10 Birdie Cree	1,500.00	2,500.00
11 Josh Devore	1,500.00	2,500.00
12 Ray Demmitt	1,500.00	2,500.00
13 Mickey Doolan	1,500.00	2,500.00
14 Mike Donlin	1,500.00	2,500.00
15 Tom Downey	1,500.00	2,500.00
16 Larry Doyle	1,500.00	2,500.00
17 Kid Elberfeld	1,500.00	2,500.00
18 Johnny Evers	3,000.00	5,000.00
19 Russ Ford	1,500.00	2,500.00
20 Art Fromme	1,500.00	2,500.00
21 Chick Gandil	1,500.00	2,500.00
22 Rube Geyer	1,500.00	2,500.00
23 Clark Griffith MG	3,000.00	5,000.00
24 Bob Groom	1,500.00	2,500.00
25 Buck Herzog	1,500.00	2,500.00
26 Hugh Jennings MG	3,000.00	5,000.00
27 Walter Johnson	5,000.00	8,000.00
28 Joe Kelley	3,000.00	5,000.00
29 Ed Konetchy	1,500.00	2,500.00
30 Nap Lajoie	3,000.00	5,000.00
31 Ed Lennox	1,500.00	2,500.00
32 Sherry Magee	1,500.00	2,500.00
33 Rube Marquard	1,500.00	2,500.00
34 John McGraw MG	3,000.00	5,000.00
35 George McQuillan	1,500.00	2,500.00
36 Chief Meyers Catching	1,500.00	2,500.00
37 Chief Meyers Portrait	1,500.00	2,500.00
38 George Mullin	1,500.00	2,500.00
39 Red Murray	1,500.00	2,500.00
40 Tom Needham	1,500.00	2,500.00
41 Rebel Oakes	1,500.00	2,500.00
43 Jack Quinn	1,500.00	2,500.00
42 Dode Paskert	1,500.00	2,500.00
44 Nap Rucker	1,500.00	2,500.00
46 Frank Schulte	1,500.00	2,500.00
45 Germany Schaefer	1,500.00	2,500.00
47 Frank Smith	1,500.00	2,500.00
49 George Stovall	1,500.00	2,500.00
48 Tris Speaker	3,500.00	6,000.00
50 Ed Summers	1,500.00	2,500.00
52 Ed Sweeney	1,500.00	2,500.00
51 Bill Sweeney	1,500.00	2,500.00
54 Joe Tinker	3,000.00	5,000.00
53 Ira Thomas	1,500.00	2,500.00
55 Heinie Wagner	1,500.00	2,500.00
56 Zack Wheat	3,000.00	5,000.00
58 Hooks Wiltse	1,500.00	2,500.00
57 Kaiser Wilhelm	1,500.00	2,500.00

1909 W.W. Smith Postcards

In 1909 W.W. Smith of Pittsburgh produced a set of Postcards for the 1909 World Series between the Pittsburgh Pirates and Detroit Tigers. One card is titled "World's Series Souvenir" titled two of a kind featuring the stars of each team, Ty Cobb of the Tigers and Honus Wagner of the Pirates featuring caracitures of the two stars. The other known card titled "The Mighty Honus" shows a caracature of Wagner. It is possible that a caracature of Cobb exists as well as some of the other prominent players from both teams but they have yet to be identified.

COMPLETE SET (2)	350.00	700.00
1 T.Cobb/H.Wagner WS Souvenir	500.00	1,000.00
2 Honus Wagner The Mighty Honus	250.00	500.00

1922 W501

This 120-card set, referenced by the catalog designation W501, measures approximately 1 15/16" by 3 1/2". The cards have white borders which frame a posed black and white photo. The cards are blank backed and have the number in the upper right hand corner. The cards are thought to have been issued about 1922. All these pictures are the same as the ones in E-121. All photos are all identified by a G-4-22, which is the best guess to how the set is dated as 1922.

COMPLETE SET (120)	2,000.00	4,000.00
1 Ed Rommel	25.00	50.00
2 Urban Shocker	30.00	60.00
3 Frank Davis	50.00	100.00
4 George Sisler	100.00	200.00
5 Bobby Veach	25.00	50.00
6 Harry Heilmann	75.00	150.00
7 Ira Flagstead	25.00	50.00
8 Ty Cobb	300.00	600.00
9 Oscar Vitt	25.00	50.00
10 Muddy Ruel	25.00	50.00
11 Del Pratt	25.00	50.00
12 Joe Gharrity	25.00	50.00
13 Joe Judge	30.00	60.00
14 Sam Rice	50.00	100.00
15 Clyde Milan	30.00	60.00
16 Joe Sewell	50.00	100.00
17 Walter Johnson	200.00	400.00
18 Stuffy McInnis	30.00	60.00
19 Tris Speaker	125.00	250.00
20 Jim Bagby	25.00	50.00
21 Stan Coveleski	50.00	100.00
22 Bill Wambsganss	30.00	60.00
23 John Mails	25.00	50.00
24 Larry Gardner	25.00	50.00
25 Aaron Ward	25.00	50.00
26 Miller Huggins MG	50.00	100.00
27 Wally Schang	30.00	60.00
28 Thomas Rogers	25.00	50.00
29 Carl Mays	30.00	60.00
30 Everett Scott	25.00	50.00
31 Bob Shawkey	30.00	60.00
32 Waite Hoyt	75.00	150.00
33 Mike McNally	25.00	50.00
34 Joe Bush	25.00	50.00
35 Bob Meusel	40.00	80.00
36 Irish Meusel	25.00	50.00
37 Dickie Kerr	25.00	50.00
38 Eddie Collins	75.00	150.00
39 Kid Gleason MG	30.00	60.00
40 Johnny Mostil	25.00	50.00
41 Bibb Falk	25.00	50.00
42 Clarence Hodge	25.00	50.00
43 Ray Schalk	50.00	100.00
44 Amos Strunk	25.00	50.00
45 Edward Mulligan	25.00	50.00
46 Earl Sheely	25.00	50.00
47 Harry Hooper	75.00	150.00
48 Red Faber	50.00	100.00
49 Babe Ruth	500.00	1,000.00
50 Ivy Wingo	25.00	50.00
51 Greasy Neale	30.00	60.00
52 Jake Daubert	25.00	50.00
53 Edd Roush	75.00	150.00
54 Eppa Rixey	50.00	100.00
55 Speed Martin	25.00	50.00
56 Bill Killifer	25.00	50.00
57 Charlie Hollocher	25.00	50.00
58 Zeb Terry	25.00	50.00
59 Grover Alexander	100.00	200.00
60 Turner Barber	25.00	50.00
61 Johnny Rawlings	25.00	50.00
62 Frankie Frisch	125.00	250.00
63 Red Shea	25.00	50.00
64 Dave Bancroft	50.00	100.00
65 Red Causey	25.00	50.00
66 Pancho Snyder	25.00	50.00
67 Heinie Groh	30.00	60.00
68 Ross Youngs	50.00	100.00
69 Fred Toney	25.00	50.00
70 Art Nehf	25.00	50.00
71 Earl Smith	25.00	50.00
72 George Kelly	50.00	100.00
73 John McGraw MG	75.00	150.00
74 Phil Douglas	25.00	50.00
75 Rosy Ryan	25.00	50.00
76 Jesse Haines	50.00	100.00
77 Milt Stock	25.00	50.00
78 Bill Doak	25.00	50.00
79 Specs Toporcer	25.00	50.00
80 Wilbur Cooper	25.00	50.00
81 Possum Whitted	25.00	50.00
82 Charlie Grimm	30.00	60.00
83 Rabbit Maranville	50.00	100.00
84 Babe Adams	30.00	60.00
85 Carson Bigbee	25.00	50.00
86 Max Carey	75.00	150.00
87 Whitey Glazner	25.00	50.00
88 George Gibson	25.00	50.00

89 Billy Southworth	30.00	60.00
90 Hank Gowdy	25.00	50.00
91 Walter Holke	25.00	50.00
92 Joe Oeschger	25.00	50.00
93 Pete Kilduff	25.00	50.00
94 Chief Meyers	30.00	60.00
95 Otto Miller	25.00	50.00
96 Wilbert Robinson MG	50.00	100.00
97 Zack Wheat	50.00	100.00
98 Dutch Ruether	25.00	50.00
99 Tilly Walker	25.00	50.00
100 Cy Williams	30.00	60.00
101 Dave Danforth	25.00	50.00
102 Ed Rommell	25.00	50.00
103 John McGraw MG	75.00	150.00
104 Frank Frisch	75.00	150.00
105 Al DeVormer	25.00	50.00
106 Tommy Griffith	25.00	50.00
107 George Harper	25.00	50.00
108 Doc Lavan	25.00	50.00
109 Elmer Smith	25.00	50.00
110 Hooks Dauss	25.00	50.00
111 Alex Gaston	25.00	50.00
112 Jack Graney	25.00	50.00
113 Irish Meusel	25.00	50.00
114 Rogers Hornsby	125.00	250.00
115 Les Nunamaker	25.00	50.00
116 Steve O'Neill	30.00	60.00
117 Max Flack	25.00	50.00
118 Billy Southworth	25.00	50.00
119 Art Nehf	25.00	50.00
120 Chick Fewster	25.00	50.00

1928 W502

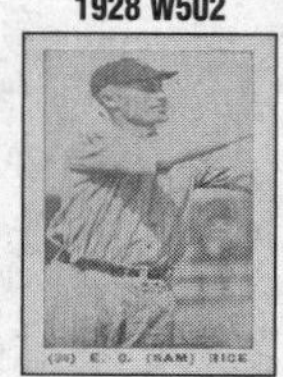

This 60-card set, referenced by the catalog designation W502, measures approximately 1 5/16" by 2 1/2". The photo is a black and white action-posed photo, while the back reads "One Bagger. Hold what you've got." The cards are thought to have been issued about 1928.

COMPLETE SET (60)	3,000.00	6,000.00
1 Burleigh Grimes	50.00	100.00
2 Walter Reuther	25.00	50.00
3 Joe Dugan	30.00	60.00
4 Red Faber	50.00	100.00
5 Gabby Hartnett	50.00	100.00
6 Babe Ruth	400.00	800.00
7 Bob Meusel	40.00	80.00
8 Herb Pennock	50.00	100.00
9 George Burns	25.00	50.00
10 Joe Sewell	50.00	100.00
11 George Uhle	25.00	50.00
12 Bob O'Farrell	25.00	50.00
13 Rogers Hornsby	100.00	200.00
14 Pie Traynor	50.00	100.00
15 Clarence Mitchell	25.00	50.00
16 Eppa Rixey	50.00	100.00
17 Carl Mays	25.00	50.00
18 Adolfo Luque	30.00	60.00
19 Dave Bancroft	50.00	100.00
20 George Kelly	50.00	100.00
21 Earle Combs	50.00	100.00
22 Harry Heilmann	50.00	100.00
23 Ray W. Schalk	50.00	100.00
24 Johnny Mostil	25.00	50.00
25 Hack Wilson	50.00	100.00
26 Lou Gehrig	250.00	500.00
27 Ty Cobb	250.00	500.00
28 Tris Speaker	100.00	200.00
29 Tony Lazzeri	50.00	100.00
30 Waite Hoyt	50.00	100.00
31 Sherwood Smith	25.00	50.00
32 Max Carey	50.00	100.00
33 Eugene Hargrave	25.00	50.00
34 Miguel J. Gonzalez	25.00	50.00
35 Joe Judge	30.00	60.00
36 E.C. (Sam) Rice	50.00	100.00
37 Earl Sheely	25.00	50.00
38 Sam Jones	25.00	50.00
39 Bob A. Falk	25.00	50.00
40 Willie Kamm	30.00	60.00
41 Bucky Harris	50.00	100.00
42 John J. McGraw	50.00	100.00
43 Artie Nehf	25.00	50.00
44 Grover Alexander	100.00	200.00
45 Paul Waner	50.00	100.00
46 William H. Terry	50.00	100.00
47 Glenn Wright	25.00	50.00
48 Earl Smith	25.00	50.00
49 Leon (Goose) Goslin	50.00	100.00
50 Frank Frisch	50.00	100.00
51 Joe Harris	25.00	50.00
52 Fred (Cy) Wiliams	30.00	60.00
53 Ed Roush	50.00	100.00
54 George Sisler	50.00	100.00
55 Ed Rommel	25.00	50.00
56 Roger Peckinpaugh	25.00	50.00
57 Stanley Coveleski	50.00	100.00
58 Lester Bell	25.00	50.00
59 Lloyd Waner	50.00	100.00
60 John P. McInnis	30.00	60.00

1923 W503

This 64-card set, referenced by the catalog designation W503, measures approximately 1 3/4" by 2 3/4". The cards have white borders which frame a black-and-white player portrait or action photo and the card number. The backs are blank, and there is no evidence of a manufacturer. The set is thought to have been issued in early 1923.

COMPLETE SET (64)	15,000.00	30,000.00
1 Joe Bush	200.00	400.00
2 Wally Schang	200.00	400.00
3 Dave Robertson	150.00	300.00
4 Wally Pipp	150.00	300.00
5 Bill Ryan	150.00	300.00
6 George Kelly	300.00	600.00
7 Frank Snyder	150.00	300.00
8 Jimmy O'Connell	150.00	300.00
9 Bill Cunningham	150.00	300.00
10 Norman McMillan	150.00	300.00
11 Waite Hoyt	300.00	600.00
12 Art Nehf	150.00	300.00
13 George Sisler	400.00	800.00
14 Al Devormer	150.00	300.00
15 Casey Stengel	500.00	1,000.00
16 Ken Williams	200.00	400.00
17 Joe Dugan	200.00	400.00
18 Irish Muesel	150.00	300.00
19 Bob Meusel	250.00	500.00
20 Carl Mays	150.00	300.00
21 Frank Frisch	300.00	600.00
22 Jess Barnes	150.00	300.00
23 Walter Johnson	600.00	1,200.00
24 Claude Jonnard	150.00	300.00
25 Dave Bancroft	300.00	600.00
26 Johnny Rawlings	150.00	300.00
27 Pep Young	150.00	300.00
28 Earl Smith	150.00	300.00
29 Willie Kamm	150.00	300.00
30 Art Fletcher	150.00	300.00
31 Kid Gleason	150.00	300.00
32 Babe Ruth	2,000.00	4,000.00
33 Guy Morton	150.00	300.00
34 Heinie Groh	150.00	300.00
35 Leon Cadore	150.00	300.00
36 Joe Tobin	150.00	300.00
37 Rube Marquard	150.00	300.00
38 Grover Alexander	500.00	1,000.00
39 George Burns	150.00	300.00
40 Joe Oeschger	150.00	300.00
41 Chick Shorten	150.00	300.00
42 Roger Hornsby UER misspelled Rogers	600.00	1,200.00
43 Adolfo Luque	200.00	400.00
44 Zack Wheat	300.00	600.00
45 Her Pruett UER misspelled Hub	150.00	300.00
46 Rabbit Maranville	300.00	600.00
47 Jimmy Ring	150.00	300.00
48 Sherrod Smith	150.00	300.00
49 Lea Meadows UER misspelled Lee	150.00	300.00
50 Aaron Ward	150.00	300.00
51 Herb Pennock	300.00	600.00
52 Carlson Bigbee UER misspelled Carson	150.00	300.00
53 Max Carey	300.00	600.00
54 Charels Robertson	150.00	300.00
55 Urban Shocker	200.00	400.00
56 Dutch Ruether	150.00	300.00
57 Jake Daubert	200.00	400.00
58 Louis Guisto	150.00	300.00
59 Ivy Wingo	150.00	300.00
60 Bill Pertica	150.00	300.00
61 Luke Sewell	150.00	300.00
62 Hank Gowdy	150.00	300.00
63 Jack Scott	150.00	300.00
64 Stan Coveleskie UER misspelled Coveleski	300.00	600.00

1926-27 W512

This set, referenced by the catalog designation W512, measures approximately 1 3/16" by 2 3/16" and features crude color drawings of the noted athlete. The cards are blank backed and the set includes actors and actresses as well as some of the athletes that made the 1920s "The Golden Age of Sports," Babe Ruth, Bill Tilden, Johnny Weismuller, Walter Hagen, and Jack Dempsey. The cards are thought to have been issued between 1926-1927 and are often referred to as strip cards since they were commonly issued in panels or strips of multiple cards. The set is sometimes titled as "Athletes, Aviators, Movie Stars and Boxers."

COMPLETE SET (50)	187.50	375.00
1 Dave Bancroft	7.50	15.00
2 Grover Alexander	15.00	30.00
3 Ty Cobb	30.00	60.00
4 Tris Speaker	15.00	30.00
5 Glenn Wright	4.00	8.00
6 Babe Ruth	60.00	120.00
7 Everett Scott	5.00	10.00
8 Frank Frisch	7.50	15.00
9 Rogers Hornsby	15.00	30.00
10 Dazzy Vance	7.50	15.00

1928 W513

This set, referenced by the catalog designation W513, continues the numbering sequence started with W512. This set contains drawings and the cards which measure approximately 1 3/16" by 2 3/16" are blank backed. The most famous athletes outside the baseball players are Jack Sharkey, the heavyweight champion and Rene LaCoste, the famed tennis player and entrepeneur. The cards are thought to have been issued about 1928. The set is sometimes titled as "Athletes, Aviators, Movie Stars and Boxers."

COMPLETE SET (42)	2,250.00	4,500.00
61 Eddie Roush	10.00	20.00
62 Waite Hoyt	10.00	20.00
63 Gink Hundrick	5.00	10.00
64 Jumbo Elliott	5.00	10.00
65 John Miljus	5.00	10.00
66 Jumping Joe Dugan	5.00	10.00
67 Smiling Bill Terry	10.00	20.00
68 Herb Pennock	10.00	20.00
69 Rube Benton	5.00	10.00
70 Paul Waner	10.00	20.00
71 Adolfo Luque	5.00	10.00
72 Burleigh Grimes	10.00	20.00
73 Lloyd Waner	10.00	20.00
74 Hack Wilson	10.00	20.00
75 Hal Carlson	5.00	10.00
76 L. Grantham	5.00	10.00
77 Wilcey Moore	5.00	10.00
78 Jess Haines	10.00	20.00
79 Tony Lazzeri	10.00	20.00
80 Al DeVormer	5.00	10.00
81 Joe Harris	5.00	10.00
82 Pie Traynor	10.00	20.00
83 Mark Koenig	5.00	10.00
84 Babe Herman	6.00	12.00
85 George Harper	5.00	10.00
86 Earle Combs	10.00	20.00
92 Babe Herman	4.00	8.00

1919-21 W514

This 120-card set measures approximately 1 7/16" by 2 1/2" and are numbered in the lower right. The cards portray drawings of the athletes portrayed. The cards are thought to have been issued about 1919. Variations on team names are known to exist. This might suggest that these cards were actually issued over a period of years. Any further information on this fact would be appreciated.

COMPLETE SET (120)	4,000.00	8,000.00
1 Ira Flagstead	25.00	50.00
2 Babe Ruth	500.00	1,000.00
3 Happy Felsch	50.00	100.00
4 Doc Lavan	25.00	50.00
5 Phil Douglas	25.00	50.00
6 Earl Neale	30.00	60.00
7 Leslie Nunamaker	25.00	50.00
8 Sam Jones	30.00	60.00
9 Claude Hendrix	25.00	50.00
10 Frank Schulte	25.00	50.00
11 Cactus Cravath	25.00	50.00
12 Pat Moran	25.00	50.00
13 Dick Rudolph	25.00	50.00
14 Arthur Fletcher	25.00	50.00
15 Joe Jackson	750.00	1,500.00
16 Bill Southworth	30.00	60.00
17 Ad Luque	30.00	60.00
18 Charlie Deal	25.00	50.00
19 Al Mamaux	25.00	50.00
20 Stuffy McInnis	30.00	60.00
21 Rabbit Maranville	50.00	100.00
22 Max Carey	50.00	100.00
23 Dick Kerr	30.00	60.00
24 George Burns	25.00	50.00
25 Eddie Collins	50.00	100.00
26 Steve O'Neil	25.00	50.00
27 Bill Fisher	25.00	50.00
28 Rube Bressler	25.00	50.00
29 Bob Shawkey	30.00	60.00
30 Donie Bush	25.00	50.00
31 Chick Gandil	50.00	100.00
32 Ollie Zeider	25.00	50.00
33 Vean Gregg	25.00	50.00
34 Miller Huggins	50.00	100.00
35 Lefty Williams	50.00	100.00
36 Tub Spencer	25.00	50.00
37 Lew McCarthy	25.00	50.00
38 Hod Eller	25.00	50.00
39 Joe Gedeon	25.00	50.00
40 Dave Bancroft	50.00	100.00
41 Clark Griffith	50.00	100.00
42 Wilbur Cooper	25.00	50.00
43 Ty Cobb	250.00	500.00
44 Roger Peckinpaugh	30.00	60.00
45 Nic Carter	25.00	50.00
46 Heinie Groh	25.00	50.00
47 Bob Roth	25.00	50.00
48 Frank Davis	25.00	50.00
49 Leslie Mann	25.00	50.00
50 Fielder Jones	25.00	50.00
51 Bill Doak	25.00	50.00
52 John J. McGraw MG	50.00	100.00
53 Charles Hollocher	25.00	50.00
54 Babe Adams	30.00	60.00
55 Dode Paskert	25.00	50.00
56 Rogers Hornsby	100.00	200.00
57 Max Rath	25.00	50.00
58 Jeff Pfeffer	25.00	50.00
59 Nick Cullop	25.00	50.00
60 Ray Schalk	50.00	100.00
61 Bill Jacobson	25.00	50.00
62 Nap Lajoie	50.00	100.00
63 George Gibson MG	25.00	50.00
64 Harry Hooper	50.00	100.00
65 Grover Alexander	50.00	100.00
66 Ping Bodie	25.00	50.00
67 Hank Gowdy	25.00	50.00
68 Jake Daubert	30.00	60.00
69 Red Faber	50.00	100.00
70 Ivan Olson	25.00	50.00
71 Pickles Dilhoefer	25.00	50.00
72 Christy Mathewson	100.00	200.00
73 Ira Wingo	25.00	50.00
74 Fred Merkle	30.00	60.00
75 Frank Baker	50.00	100.00
76 Bert Gallia	25.00	50.00
77 Milton Watson	25.00	50.00
78 Bert Shotten	25.00	50.00
79 Sam Rice	50.00	100.00
80 Dan Greiner	25.00	50.00
81 Larry Doyle	30.00	60.00
82 Eddie Cicotte	50.00	100.00
83 Hugo Bezdek MG	25.00	50.00
84 Wally Pipp	30.00	60.00
85 Eddie Roush	50.00	100.00
86 Slim Sallee	25.00	50.00
87 Bill Killifer	25.00	50.00
88 Bob Veach	25.00	50.00
89 Jim Burke	25.00	50.00
90 Everett Scott	25.00	50.00
91 Buck Weaver	50.00	100.00
92 George Whitted	25.00	50.00
93 Ed Konetchy	25.00	50.00
94 Walter Johnson	100.00	200.00
95 Sam Crawford	50.00	100.00
96 Fred Mitchell	25.00	50.00
97 Ira Thomas	25.00	50.00
98 Jimmy Ring	25.00	50.00
99 Wally Schang	25.00	50.00
100 Benny Kauff	25.00	50.00
101 George Sisler	50.00	100.00
102 Tris Speaker	50.00	100.00
103 Carl Mays	25.00	50.00
104 Buck Herzog	25.00	50.00
105 Swede Risberg	50.00	100.00
106 Hugh Jennings CO	50.00	100.00
107 Pep Young	25.00	50.00
108 Walter Reuther	25.00	50.00
109 Joe Gharrity	25.00	50.00
110 Zack Wheat	50.00	100.00
111 Jim Vaughn	25.00	50.00
112 Kid Gleason MG	40.00	80.00
113 Casey Stengel	100.00	200.00
114 Hal Chase	30.00	60.00
115 Oscar Stanage	25.00	50.00
116 Larry Shean	25.00	50.00
117 Steve Pendergast	25.00	50.00
118 Larry Kopf	25.00	50.00
119 Charles Whiteman	25.00	50.00
120 Jesse Barnes	25.00	50.00

1923 W515-1

This 60-card set, referenced by the catalog designation W515, measures approximately 1 5/16" by 2 3/16". The cards are blank backed and feature drawings on the front with the name of the player, his position, and his team on the bottom of the card.

COMPLETE SET (60)	600.00	1,200.00
1 Bill Cunningham	20.00	40.00
2 Al Mamaux	20.00	40.00
3 Babe Ruth	400.00	800.00
4 Dave Bancroft	40.00	80.00
5 Ed Rommell	20.00	40.00
6 Babe Adams	25.00	50.00
7 Clarence Walker	20.00	40.00
8 Waite Hoyt	40.00	80.00
9 Bob Shawkey	25.00	50.00
10 Ty Cobb	200.00	400.00
11 George Sisler	60.00	120.00
12 Jack Bentley	20.00	40.00
13 Jim O'Connell	20.00	40.00
14 Frank Frisch	60.00	120.00
15 Frank Baker	40.00	80.00
16 Burleigh Grimes	40.00	80.00
17 Wally Schang	25.00	50.00
18 Harry Heilman	40.00	80.00
19 Aaron Ward	20.00	40.00
20 Carl Mays	20.00	40.00
21 The Meusel Bros.	30.00	60.00
22 Arthur Nehf	20.00	40.00
23 Lee Meadows	20.00	40.00
24 Casey Stengel	100.00	200.00
25 Jack Scott	20.00	40.00
26 Kenneth Williams	25.00	50.00
27 Joe Bush	20.00	40.00
28 Tris Speaker	60.00	120.00
29 Ross Youngs	40.00	80.00
30 Joe Dugan	25.00	50.00
31 The Barnes Bros.	25.00	50.00
32 George Kelly	40.00	80.00
33 Hugh McQuillen	20.00	40.00
34 Hugh Jennings MG	40.00	80.00
35 Tom Griffith	20.00	40.00
36 Miller Huggins MG	40.00	80.00
37 Whitey Witt	20.00	40.00
38 Walter Johnson	100.00	200.00
39 Wally Pipp	25.00	50.00
40 Dutch Reuther	20.00	40.00
41 Jim Johnston	20.00	40.00
42 Willie Kamm	25.00	50.00
43 Sam Jones	20.00	40.00
44 Frank Snyder	20.00	40.00
45 John McGraw MG	40.00	80.00
46 Everett Scott	20.00	40.00
47 Babe Ruth	400.00	800.00
48 Urban Shocker	25.00	50.00
49 Grover Alexander	60.00	120.00
50 Rabbit Maranville	40.00	80.00
51 Ray Schalk	40.00	80.00
52 Heinie Groh	25.00	50.00
53 Wilbert Robinson MG	40.00	80.00
54 George Burns	20.00	40.00

55 Rogers Hornsby 100.00 200.00
56 Zack Wheat 40.00 80.00
57 Eddie Roush 40.00 80.00
58 Eddie Collins 40.00 80.00
59 Charlie Hollocher 20.00 40.00
60 Red Faber 40.00 80.00

1920 W516-1

This 30-card set, referenced by the catalog designation W516, measures approximately 1 7/16" by 2 5/16". The cards have colorful photos with a blank back. The copyright is reversed on the front of the card. There is also the name of the player and position on the bottom of the card.

COMPLETE SET (30) 3,000.00 6,000.00
1 Babe Ruth 750.00 1,500.00
2 Heine Groh 60.00 120.00
3 Ping Bodie 50.00 100.00
4 Ray Shalk (Schalk) 100.00 200.00
5 Tris Speaker 200.00 400.00
6 Ty Cobb 400.00 800.00
7 Roger Hornsby (Rogers) 300.00 600.00
8 Walter Johnson 300.00 600.00
9 Grover Alexander 200.00 400.00
10 George Burns 50.00 100.00
11 Jimmy Ring 50.00 100.00
12 Jess Barnes 50.00 100.00
13 Larry Doyle 60.00 120.00
14 Arty Fletcher 50.00 100.00
15 Dick Rudolph 50.00 100.00
16 Benny Kauf (Kauff) 50.00 100.00
17 Art Nehf 50.00 100.00
18 Babe Adams 60.00 120.00
19 Will Cooper 50.00 100.00
20 R.Peckingpaugh 50.00 100.00
21 Eddie Cicotte 100.00 200.00
22 Hank Gowdy 50.00 100.00
23 Eddie Collins 100.00 200.00
24 Christy Mathewson 300.00 600.00
25 Clyde Milan 60.00 120.00
26 M. Kelley (G.) 50.00 100.00
27 Ed Hooper (Harry) 50.00 100.00
28 Pep Young 100.00 200.00
29 Eddie Rousch (Roush) 100.00 200.00
30 George Bancroft (Dave) 50.00 100.00

1921 W516-2-1

1 George Burns
2 Grover Alexander
3 Walter Johnson
4 Roger Hornsby (Rogers)
5 Ty Cobb
6 Tris Speaker
7 Ray Shalk (Schalk)
8 Ping Bodie
9 Heinie Groh
10 Babe Ruth
11 R.Peckingpaugh
12 Will Cooper
13 Babe Adams
14 Art Nehf
15 Benny Kauf (Kauff)
16 Dick Rudolph
17 Arty Fletcher
18 Larry Doyle
19 Jess Barnes
20 Jimmy Ring
21 George Bancroft (Dave)
22 Eddie Rousch (Roush)
23 Pep Young
24 Ed Hooper (Harry)
25 M. Kelly (G.)
26 Clyde Milan
27 Christy Mathewson
28 Eddie Collins
29 Hank Gowdy
30 Eddie Cicotte

1931 W517

The cards in this 54-card set measure approximately 3" by 4". This 1931 set of numbered, blank-backed cards was placed in the "W~ category in the original American Card Catalog because (1) its producer was unknown and (2) it was issued in strips of three. The photo is black and white but the entire obverse of each card is generally found tinted in tones of sepia, blue, green, yellow, rose, black or gray. The cards are numbered in a small circle on the front. A solid dark line at one end of a card entitled the purchaser to another piece of candy as a prize. There are two different cards of both Babe Ruth and Mickey Cochrane. There may be other variations in this set: such as cards without numbers (e.g., Paul Waner and Dazzy Vance) as well as Chalmer Cissell with both Chicago and Cleveland, Chick Hafey with both the Cardinals and Cincinnati, and George Kelly and Lefty O'Doul with Brooklyn.

COMPLETE SET (54) 3,750.00 7,500.00
1 Earle Combs 40.00 80.00
2 Pie Traynor 50.00 100.00
3 Eddie Roush/(Wearing Cincinnati uniform& but lis 50.00 100.00
4 Babe Ruth/(Throwing) 750.00 1,500.00
5 Chalmer Cissell 20.00 40.00
6 Bill Sherdel 20.00 40.00
7 Bill Shore 20.00 40.00
8 George Earnshaw 20.00 40.00
9 Bucky Harris 40.00 80.00
10 Chuck Klein 50.00 100.00
11 George Kelly 40.00 80.00
12 Travis Jackson 40.00 80.00
13 Willie Kamm 20.00 40.00
14 Harry Heilmann 50.00 100.00
15 Grover Alexander 75.00 150.00
16 Frank Frisch 50.00 100.00
17 Jack Quinn 30.00 60.00
18 Cy Williams 30.00 60.00
19 Kiki Cuyler 40.00 80.00
20 Babe Ruth/(Portrait) 1,000.00 2,000.00
21 Jimmy Foxx 125.00 250.00
(Jimmie)
22 Jimmy Dykes 30.00 60.00
23 Bill Terry 60.00 120.00
24 Freddy Lindstrom 40.00 80.00
25 Hugh Critz 20.00 40.00
26 Pete Donahue 20.00 40.00
27 Tony Lazzeri 50.00 100.00
28 Heinie Manush 40.00 80.00
29 Chick Hafey 40.00 80.00
St.Louis
30 Melvin Ott 100.00 200.00
31 Bing Miller 20.00 40.00
32 Mule Haas 20.00 40.00
33 Lefty O'Doul 30.00 60.00
34 Paul Waner 40.00 80.00
35 Lou Gehrig 500.00 1,000.00
36 Dazzy Vance 40.00 80.00
37 Mickey Cochrane/(Catching pose) 50.00 100.00
38 Rogers Hornsby 125.00 250.00
39 Lefty Grove 100.00 200.00
40 Al Simmons 50.00 100.00
41 Rube Walberg 20.00 40.00
42 Hack Wilson 50.00 100.00
43 Art Shires 20.00 40.00
44 Sammy Hale 20.00 40.00
45 Ted Lyons 40.00 80.00
46 Joe Sewell 40.00 80.00
47 Goose Goslin 40.00 80.00
48 Lou Fonseca 20.00 40.00
49 Bob Meusel 30.00 60.00
50 Lu Blue 20.00 40.00
51 Earl Averill 40.00 80.00
52 Eddie Collins 50.00 100.00
53 Joe Judge 20.00 40.00
54 Mickey Cochrane/(Portrait) 50.00 100.00

1920 W519 Un-Numbered

This 10-card unnumbered blank-backed strip-card set has a blue photo of the featured player along with his name on the bottom in block letters. Since these cards are unnumbered, we have sequenced them in alphabetical order.

COMPLETE SET 500.00 1,000.00
1 Eddie Cicotte 60.00 120.00
2 Eddie Collins 60.00 120.00
3 Gavvy Cravath 40.00 80.00
4 Frank Frisch 30.00 60.00
5 Kid Gleason MG 40.00 80.00
6 Ernie Krueger 20.00 40.00
7 Rube Marquard 30.00 60.00
8 Guy Morton 20.00 40.00
9 Joe Murphy 20.00 40.00
10 Babe Ruth 400.00 800.00

1920 W519 Numbered

Apparently some of the W519 cards were issued with numbers on the side. This list is far from complete and any further information is appreciated.

COMPLETE SET 25.00 50.00

1920 W520

These cards which measure 1 3/"" by 2 1/4" are numbered in the lower right hand corner. For some unexplicable reason, there are two Mike Gonzales cards in this set.

COMPLETE SET (20) 400.00 800.00
1 Dave Bancroft 50.00 100.00
2 Christy Mathewson 200.00 400.00
3 Larry Doyle 30.00 60.00
4 Jess Barnes 25.00 50.00
5 Art Fletcher 25.00 50.00
6 Wilbur Cooper 25.00 50.00
7 Mike Gonzalez 25.00 50.00
8 Zach Wheat 50.00 100.00
9 Tris Speaker 125.00 250.00
10 Benny Kauff 25.00 50.00
11 Zach Wheat 50.00 100.00
12 Phil Douglas 25.00 50.00
13 Babe Ruth 400.00 800.00
14 Stan Coveleski 50.00 100.00
Spelled Koveleski
15 Goldie Rapp 25.00 50.00
16 Pol Perritt 25.00 50.00
17 Otto Miller 25.00 50.00
18 George Kelly 50.00 100.00
19 Mike Gonzalez 25.00 50.00
20 Les Nunamaker 25.00 50.00

1921 W551

This 10-card set features color drawings of players that measure approximately 1 3/8" by 3 1/4" and were printed in strips. The players name and team name are printed in the bottom margin. The backs are blank. The cards are unnumbered and checklisted below in alphabetical order.

COMPLETE SET (10) 500.00 1,000.00
1 Frank Baker 75.00 150.00
2 Dave Bancroft 50.00 100.00
3 Jess Barnes 25.00 50.00
4 Ty Cobb 400.00 800.00
5 Walter Johnson 300.00 600.00
6 Wally Pipp 25.00 50.00
7 Babe Ruth 500.00 1,000.00
8 George Sisler 125.00 250.00
9 Tris Speaker 200.00 400.00
10 Casey Stengel 200.00 400.00

1929 W553

These cards, which measure 1 3/4" by 2 3/4", are very obscure and feature star players from the late 1920's. These blank-backed cards are known to exist in either green, red or B&W. The photos are framed with ornate picture frame style borders. Verified cards are listed below and more may exist so any additions to this checklist are appreciated.

COMPLETE SET 1,000.00 4,000.00
1 Lu Blue 50.00 100.00
2 Mickey Cochrane 125.00 250.00
3 Jimmy Foxx 300
(Jimmie)
4 Frank Frisch 125.00 250.00
5 Lou Gehrig 250.00 500.00
6 Goose Goslin 125.00 250.00
7 Burleigh Grimes 125.00 250.00
8 Lefty Grove 150.00 300.00
9 Rogers Hornsby 150.00 300.00
10 Rabbit Maranville 125.00 250.00
11 Bing Miller 75.00 150.00
12 Lefty O'Doul 75.00 150.00
13 Babe Ruth 400.00 800.00
14 Al Simmons 125.00 250.00
15 Pie Traynor 125.00 250.00

1930 W554

This set corresponds to the poses in R316 and R306. The cards measure 5" by 7" and are reasonably available within the Hobby.

COMPLETE SET (18) 150.00 300.00
1 Gordon S. (Mickey) Cochrane 40.00 80.00
2 Lewis A. Fonseca 25.00 50.00
3 Jimmy Foxx 75.00 150.00
(Jimmie)
4 Lou Gehrig 250.00 500.00
5 Burleigh Grimes 50.00 100.00
6 Robert M. Grove 60.00 120.00
7 Waite Hoyt 50.00 100.00
8 Joe Judge 30.00 60.00
9 Charles(Chuck)Klein 50.00 100.00
10 Douglas McWeeny 25.00 50.00
11 Frank O'Doul 30.00 60.00
12 Melvin Ott 75.00 150.00
13 Herbert Pennock 50.00 100.00
14 Eddie Rommel 30.00 60.00
15 Babe Ruth 400.00 800.00
16 Al Simmons 60.00 120.00
17 Lloyd Waner 50.00 100.00
18 Hack Wilson 50.00 100.00

1910 W555

This 66 card set measures 1 1/8" by 1 3/16" and have sepia pictures surrounded by a black border, which is framed by a white line. Eight cards: Bates, Bescher, Byrne, Collins, Crawford, Devlin, Lake and Mowery are frequently found on want lists. The Eddie Cicotte card was the most recent discovery and is also assumed to be one of the tougher cards. A recent discovery shows that these cards were included in box tops from the Jay S Meyer company in which a child could pretend he was taking the photo to match the actual photo on the box top. These cards came four to a box and were all in seperate parts of the cover.

COMPLETE SET (66) 5,500.00 11,000.00
1 Red Ames 50.00 100.00
2 Jimmy Austin 50.00 100.00
3 Johnny Bates 50.00 100.00
4 Chief Bender 125.00 250.00
5 Bob Bescher 50.00 100.00
6 Joe Birmingham 50.00 100.00
7 Bill Bradley 50.00 100.00
8 Kitty Bransfield 50.00 100.00
9 Mordecai Brown 125.00 250.00
10 Bobby Byrne 50.00 100.00
11 Frank Chance 125.00 250.00
12 Hal Chase 75.00 150.00
13 Eddie Cicotte 125.00 250.00
14 Fred Clarke 125.00 250.00
15 Ty Cobb 750.00 1,500.00
16 Eddie Collins 250.00 500.00
dark uniform
17 Eddie Collins 250.00 500.00
light uniform
18 Harry Covelskie 50.00 100.00
19 Sam Crawford 125.00 250.00
20 Harry Davis 50.00 100.00
21 Jim Delahanty 50.00 100.00
22 Art Devlin 50.00 100.00
23 Josh Devore 50.00 100.00
24 Bill Donovan 50.00 100.00
25 Red Dooin 50.00 100.00
26 Mickey Doolan 50.00 100.00
27 Bull Durham 50.00 100.00
28 Jimmy Dygert 50.00 100.00
29 Johnny Evers 125.00 250.00
30 Russ Ford 50.00 100.00
31 George Gibson 50.00 100.00
32 Clark Griffith 125.00 250.00
33 Topsy Hartsell 50.00 100.00
34 Bill Hinchman 50.00 100.00
Sic, Heinchman
35 Charlie Hemphill 50.00 100.00
36 Hugh Jennings MG 125.00 250.00
37 Davy Jones 50.00 100.00
38 Addie Joss 150.00 300.00
39 Willie Keeler 125.00 250.00
40 Red Kleinow 50.00 100.00
41 Nap Lajoie 250.00 500.00
42 Joe Lake 50.00 100.00
43 Tommy Leach 50.00 100.00
44 Sherry Magee 50.00 100.00
45 Christy Mathewson 250.00 500.00
46 Ambrose McConnell 50.00 100.00
47 John McGraw MG 125.00 250.00
48 Chief Meyers 50.00 100.00
49 Earl Moore 50.00 100.00
50 Mike Mowrey 50.00 100.00
51 George Mullin 50.00 100.00
52 Red Murray 50.00 100.00
53 Simon Nicholls 50.00 100.00
54 Jim Pastorius 50.00 100.00
55 Deacon Phillipe 50.00 100.00
56 Eddie Plank 150.00 300.00
57 Fred Snodgrass 50.00 100.00
58 Harry Steinfeldt 50.00 100.00
59 Joe Tinker 125.00 250.00
60 Hippo Vaughn 50.00 100.00
61 Honus Wagner 500.00 1,000.00
62 Rube Waddell 125.00 250.00
63 Hooks Wiltse 50.00 100.00
64 Cy Young 300.00 600.00
Cleveland Amer.
65 Cy Young 300.00 600.00
Same pose as E93
66 Cy Young 300.00 600.00
Same pose as E97-8

1927 W560 Black

Cards in this set feature athletes from baseball and college football, along with an assortment of other sports and non-sports. The cards were issued in strips and full sheets and follow a standard playing card design. Quite a few Joker cards were produced. We've numbered the cards below according to the suit and playing card number (face cards were assigned numbers as well). It is thought there were at least three different printings and that the baseball and football players were added in the second printing replacing other subjects. All are baseball players below unless otherwise noted. Many cards were printed in a single color red, single color black, and a black/red dual color printing, thereby creating up to three versions. The full set, with just one of each different subject, contains 88-different cards. It is thought that the two-color cards are slightly tougher to find than the single color version.

COMPLETE SET (63) 900.00 1,500.00
*RED: .4X TO 1X BLACK
*BLACK/RED: .5X TO 1.2X BLACK
C1 Kiki Cuyler 20.00 40.00
C2 Fred McGuire 4.00 8.00
C3 Lou Gehrig 250.00 400.00
C4 Max Bishop 4.00 8.00
C5 Jim Bottomley 12.50 25.00
C6 Buddy Myer 4.00 8.00

C7 Taylor Douthit	4.00	8.00
C8 Bill Sherdel	4.00	8.00
C9 Remy Kremer	4.00	8.00
C10 Goose Goslin	12.50	25.00
C11 Al Simmons	25.00	50.00
C12 Vic Aldridge	4.00	8.00
C13 Lefty Grove	30.00	60.00
D3 Paul Waner	20.00	40.00
D5 George Uhle	4.00	8.00
D8 Fred Lindstrom	12.50	25.00
D9 Larry Benton	4.00	8.00
D11 Cy Williams	4.00	8.00
D12 Lloyd Waner	12.50	25.00
D13 Fred Fitzsimmons	7.50	15.00
H1 Watty Clark	4.00	8.00
H2 Hugh Critz	4.00	8.00
H3 Willie Kamm	4.00	8.00
H4 Rogers Hornsby	40.00	75.00
H5 Luke Sewell	5.00	10.00
H7 Babe Herman	7.50	15.00
H10 Sam Gray	4.00	8.00
H11 Waite Hoyt	12.50	25.00
H13 Andy Cohen	4.00	8.00
S1 Glen Wright	4.00	8.00
S2 Walter Johnson	50.00	100.00
S3 Flint Rhem	4.00	8.00
S4 George Pipgras	4.00	8.00
S5 Jim Wilson	4.00	8.00
S6 Dazzy Vance	20.00	40.00
S7 Fred Marberry	4.00	8.00
S8 Thomas Thevenow	4.00	8.00
S9 Fresco Thompson	4.00	8.00
S10 Jesse Haines	12.50	25.00
S11 Guy Bush	4.00	8.00
S12 Johnny Mostil	4.00	8.00
S13 Del Bissonette	4.00	8.00
JOK Lester Bell	4.00	8.00
JOK Mickey Cochrane	20.00	40.00
JOK Jimmie Foxx	60.00	120.00
JOK Henry Johnson	4.00	8.00
JOK Herb Pennock	7.50	15.00
JOK Babe Ruth	175.00	300.00
JOK Rube Walberg	5.00	10.00

1922 W572

This 119-card set was issued in 1922 in ten-card strips along with strips of boxer cards. The cards measure approximately 1 5/16" by 2 1/2" and are blank backed. Most of the player photos on the fronts are black and white, although a few photos are sepia-toned. The pictures are the same ones used in the E120 set, but they have been cropped to fit on the smaller format. The player's signature and team appear at the bottom of the pictures, along with an IFS (International Feature Service) copyright notice. The cards are unnumbered and checklisted below in alphabetical order.

COMPLETE SET (119)	2,500.00	5,000.00
1 Eddie Ainsmith	20.00	40.00
2 Vic Aldridge	20.00	40.00
3 Grover C. Alexander	125.00	250.00
4 Dave Bancroft	40.00	80.00
5 Jesse Barnes	20.00	40.00
6 John Bassler	20.00	40.00
7 Lu Blue	20.00	40.00
8 Norm Boeckel	20.00	40.00
9 George Burns	20.00	40.00
10 Joe Bush	25.00	50.00
11 Leon Cadore	20.00	40.00
12 Virgil Cheevers	20.00	40.00
13 Ty Cobb	600.00	1,200.00
14 Eddie Collins	50.00	100.00
15 John Collins	20.00	40.00
16 Wilbur Cooper	20.00	40.00
17 Stanley Coveleski	40.00	80.00
18 Walton Cruise	20.00	40.00
19 Dave Danforth	20.00	40.00
20 Jake Daubert	25.00	50.00
21 Hank DeBerry	20.00	40.00
22 Lou DeVormer	20.00	40.00
23 Bill Doak	20.00	40.00
24 Pete Donohue	20.00	40.00
25 Pat Duncan	20.00	40.00
26 Jimmy Dykes	25.00	50.00
27 Urban Faber	40.00	80.00
28 Bibb Falk	20.00	40.00
29 Frank Frisch	60.00	120.00
30 Chick Galloway	20.00	40.00
31 Ed Gharrity	20.00	40.00
32 Charles Glazner	20.00	40.00
33 Hank Gowdy	25.00	50.00
34 Tom Griffith	20.00	40.00
35 Burleigh Grimes	40.00	80.00
36 Ray Grimes	20.00	40.00
37 Heinie Groh	25.00	50.00
38 Joe Harris	20.00	40.00
39 Bucky Harris	40.00	80.00
40 Joe Hauser	20.00	40.00
41 Harry Heilmann	40.00	80.00
42 Walter Henline	20.00	40.00
43 Charles Hollocher	20.00	40.00
44 Harry Hooper	40.00	80.00
45 Rogers Hornsby	150.00	300.00
46 Waite Hoyt	40.00	80.00
47 Wilbur Hubbell	20.00	40.00
48 William Jacobson	20.00	40.00
49 Charles Jamieson	20.00	40.00
50 Syl Johnson	20.00	40.00
51 Walter Johnson	250.00	500.00
52 Jimmy Johnston	20.00	40.00
53 Joe Judge	25.00	50.00
54 George Kelly	40.00	80.00
55 Lee King	20.00	40.00
56 Larry Kopf	20.00	40.00
57 George Leverette	20.00	40.00
58 Al Mamaux	20.00	40.00
59 Rabbit Maranville	40.00	80.00
60 Rube Marquard	40.00	80.00
61 Martin McManus	20.00	40.00
62 Lee Meadows	20.00	40.00
63 Mike Menosky	20.00	40.00
64 Bob Meusel	30.00	60.00
65 Emil Meusel	20.00	40.00
66 George Mogridge	20.00	40.00
67 John Morrison	20.00	40.00
68 Johnny Mostil	20.00	40.00
69 Roleine Naylor	20.00	40.00
70 Art Nehf	20.00	40.00
71 Joe Oeschger	20.00	40.00
72 Bob O'Farrell	20.00	40.00
73 Steve O'Neill	25.00	50.00
74 Frank Parkinson	20.00	40.00
75 Ralph Perkins	20.00	40.00
76 Herman Pillette	20.00	40.00
77 Babe Pinelli	25.00	50.00
78 Wallie Pipp	30.00	60.00
79 Ray Powell	20.00	40.00
80 Jack Quinn	20.00	40.00
81 Goldie Rapp	20.00	40.00
82 Walt Reuther	20.00	40.00
83 Sam Rice	40.00	80.00
84 Emory Rigney	20.00	40.00
85 Eppa Rixey	40.00	80.00
86 Ed Rommel	25.00	50.00
87 Eddie Roush	60.00	120.00
88 Babe Ruth	1,250.00	2,500.00
89 Ray Schalk	40.00	80.00
90 Wally Schang	25.00	50.00
91 Walter Schmidt	20.00	40.00
92 Joe Schultz	20.00	40.00
93 Hank Severeid	20.00	40.00
94 Joe Sewell	40.00	80.00
95 Bob Shawkey	25.00	50.00
96 Earl Sheely	20.00	40.00
97 Will Sherdel	20.00	40.00
98 Urban Shocker	25.00	50.00
99 George Sisler	100.00	200.00
100 Earl Smith	20.00	40.00
101 Elmer Smith	20.00	40.00
102 Jack Smith	20.00	40.00
103 Bill Southworth	25.00	50.00
104 Tris Speaker	125.00	250.00
105 Jigger Statz	20.00	40.00
106 Milton Stock	20.00	40.00
107 Jim Tierney	20.00	40.00
108 Harold Traynor	50.00	100.00
109 George Uhle	20.00	40.00
110 Bob Veach	20.00	40.00
111 Clarence Walker	20.00	40.00
112 Curtis Walker	20.00	40.00
113 Bill Wambsganss	25.00	50.00
114 Aaron Ward	20.00	40.00
115 Zach Wheat	40.00	80.00
116 Fred Williams	20.00	40.00
117 Ken Williams	30.00	60.00
118 Ivy Wingo	20.00	40.00
119 Joe Wood	30.00	60.00
120 Tom Zachary	20.00	40.00

1922 W573

This set's design is similar to the E120 American Caramel set. The backs are blank. These cards have been described as a "small strip card type of E120. Albums for these cards exist. They are made of black construction paper and the inside has pages for each team and specific places for each player.

COMPLETE SET (143)	1,500.00	3,000.00
1 Babe Adams	30.00	60.00
2 Eddie Ainsmith	25.00	50.00
3 Vic Aldridge	25.00	50.00
4 Grover C. Alexander	150.00	300.00
5 Frank Baker	50.00	100.00
6 Dave Bancroft	50.00	100.00
7 Turner Barber	25.00	50.00
8 Jesse Barnes	25.00	50.00
9 Johnny Bassler	25.00	50.00
10 Carson Bigbee	25.00	50.00
11 Lu Blue	25.00	50.00
12 Tony Boeckel	25.00	50.00
13 George H. Burns	25.00	50.00
14 George J. Burns	25.00	50.00
15 Marty Callaghan	25.00	50.00
16 Max Carey	50.00	100.00
17 Ike Caveney	25.00	50.00
18 Virgil Cheeves	25.00	50.00
19 Verne Clemons	25.00	50.00
20 Ty Cobb	300.00	600.00
21 Al Cole	25.00	50.00
22 Eddie Collins	50.00	100.00
23 Pat Collins	25.00	50.00
24 Wilbur Cooper	25.00	50.00
25 Dick Cox	25.00	50.00
26 Bill Cunningham	25.00	50.00
27 George Cutshaw	25.00	50.00
28 Dave Danforth	25.00	50.00
29 Hooks Dauss	25.00	50.00
30 Dixie Davis	25.00	50.00
31 Hank DeBerry	25.00	50.00
32 Al DeVormer	25.00	50.00
33 Bill Doak	25.00	50.00
34 Joe Dugan	30.00	60.00
35 Howard Ehmke	30.00	60.00
36 Frank Ellerbe	25.00	50.00
37 Red Faber	50.00	100.00
38 Bibb Falk	25.00	50.00
39 Max Flack	25.00	50.00
40 Ira Flagstead	25.00	50.00
41 Art Fletcher	25.00	50.00
42 Hod Ford	25.00	50.00
43 Jacques Fournier	25.00	50.00
44 Frank Frisch	75.00	150.00
45 Ollie Fuhrman	25.00	50.00
46 Chick Galloway	25.00	50.00
47 Wally Gerber	25.00	50.00
48 Patsy Gharrity	25.00	50.00
49 Whitey Glazner	25.00	50.00
50 Goose Goslin	50.00	100.00
51 Hank Gowdy	30.00	60.00
52 Jack Graney	25.00	50.00
53 Burleigh Grimes	50.00	100.00
54 Heinie Groh	30.00	60.00
55 Jesse Haines	50.00	100.00
56 Bubbles Hargrave	25.00	50.00
57 Joe Harris	25.00	50.00
58 Earl Hamilton	25.00	50.00
59 Cliff Heathcote	25.00	50.00
60 Harry Heilmann	50.00	100.00
61 Clarence Hodge	25.00	50.00
62 Charlie Hollocher	25.00	50.00
63 Harry Hooper	50.00	100.00
64 Rogers Hornsby	150.00	300.00
65 Waite Hoyt	50.00	100.00
66 Ernie Johnson	25.00	50.00
67 Syl Johnson	25.00	50.00
68 Walter Johnson	150.00	300.00
69 Paul Johnson	25.00	50.00
70 Sam Jones	30.00	60.00
71 Benjamin Karr	25.00	50.00
72 Doc Lavan	25.00	50.00
73 Dixie Levrette	25.00	50.00
74 Rabbit Maranville	50.00	100.00
75 Cliff Markle	25.00	50.00
76 Carl Mays	25.00	50.00
77 Harvey McClellan	25.00	50.00
78 Marty McManus	25.00	50.00
79 Lee Meadows	25.00	50.00
80 Mike Menosky	25.00	50.00
81 Irish Meusel	25.00	50.00
82 Clyde Milan	30.00	60.00
83 Bing Miller	25.00	50.00
84 Elmer Miller	25.00	50.00
85 Ralph Miller	25.00	50.00
86 Hack Miller	25.00	50.00
87 Clarence Mitchell	25.00	50.00
88 George Mogridge	25.00	50.00
89 John Morrison	25.00	50.00
90 Johnny Mostil	25.00	50.00
91 Elmer Myers	25.00	50.00
92 Roleine Naylor	25.00	50.00
93 Les Nunamaker	25.00	50.00
94 Bob O'Farrell	25.00	50.00
95 Steve O'Neill	30.00	60.00
96 Herb Pennock	50.00	100.00
97 Cy Perkins	25.00	50.00
98 Thomas Phillips	25.00	50.00
99 Val Picinich	25.00	50.00
100 Herman Pillette	25.00	50.00
101 Babe Pinelli	25.00	50.00
102 Wally Pipp	30.00	60.00
103 Clark Pittenger	25.00	50.00
104 Del Pratt	25.00	50.00
105 Goldie Rapp	25.00	50.00
106 Johnny Rawlings	25.00	50.00
107 Topper Rigney	25.00	50.00
108 Charlie Robertson	25.00	50.00
109 Ed Rommel	25.00	50.00
110 Muddy Ruel	25.00	50.00
111 Dutch Ruether	25.00	50.00
112 Babe Ruth	500.00	1,000.00
113 Ray Schalk	50.00	100.00
114 Wally Schang	30.00	60.00
115 Ray Schmandt	25.00	50.00
116 Walter Schmidt	25.00	50.00
117 Germany Schultz	25.00	50.00
118 Henry Severeid	25.00	50.00
119 Joe Sewell	50.00	100.00
120 Bob Shawkey	40.00	80.00
121 Earl Sheely	25.00	50.00
122 Ralph Shinners	25.00	50.00
123 Urban Shocker	25.00	50.00
124 George Sisler	75.00	150.00
125 Earl L. Smith	25.00	50.00
126 Earl S. Smith	25.00	50.00
127 Jack Smith	25.00	50.00
128 Allen Sothoron	25.00	50.00
129 Tris Speaker	125.00	250.00
130 Amos Strunk	25.00	50.00
131 Cotton Tierney	25.00	50.00
132 Jack Tobin	25.00	50.00
133 Specs Toporcer	25.00	50.00
134 George Uhle	25.00	50.00
135 Bobby Veach	25.00	50.00
136 John Watson	25.00	50.00
137 Zack Wheat	50.00	100.00
138 Ken Williams	30.00	60.00
139 Cy Williams	25.00	50.00
140 Charles Woodall	25.00	50.00
141 Russell Wrightstone	25.00	50.00
142 Ross Youngs	50.00	100.00
143 Tom Zachary	25.00	50.00

1932 W574

This white-bordered blank-backed set, which measures approximately 2 1/8" by 2 3/4" and features a black and white photo with the player's name on the side and the team name on the bottom. Since these cards are unnumbered, we have sequenced them in alphabetical order.

COMPLETE SET (29)	600.00	1,200.00
1 Dale Alexander	25.00	50.00
2 Paul Andrews	25.00	50.00
3 Luke Appling	50.00	100.00
4 Earl Averill	50.00	100.00
5 Irving Burns	25.00	50.00
6 George Blaeholder	25.00	50.00
7 Pat Caraway	25.00	50.00
8 Bud Cissell	25.00	50.00
9 Harry Davis	25.00	50.00
10 Jimmy Dykes	25.00	50.00
11 George Earnshaw	30.00	60.00
12 Red Faber	50.00	100.00
13 Lew Fonseca	25.00	50.00
14 Jimmie Foxx	125.00	250.00
15 Vic Frasier	25.00	50.00
16 Lefty Grove	100.00	200.00
17 Frank Grube	25.00	50.00
18 Bump Hadley	25.00	50.00
19 Willie Kamm	25.00	50.00
20 Bill Killefer	25.00	50.00
21 Red Kress	25.00	50.00
22 Firpo Marberry	25.00	50.00
23 Roger Peckinpaugh	30.00	60.00
24 Frank Reiber	25.00	50.00
25 Carl Reynolds	25.00	50.00
26 Al Simmons	75.00	150.00
27 Joe Vosmik	25.00	50.00
28 Gee Walker	25.00	50.00
29 Whit Wyatt	25.00	50.00

1922 W575

This 154-card set, referenced by the catalog designation W575, measures approximately 1 15/16" by 3 3/16". The cards have a black and white action posed photo are blank backed. The players name and position are under the photo on the front. Cards that are part of the "autograph on shoulder" series are marked with an asterisk in the checklist below and are worth a little more.

COMPLETE SET (154)	2,000.00	4,000.00
1 Babe Adams	25.00	50.00
2 Grover C. Alexander (2)	100.00	200.00
3 Jim Bagby	25.00	50.00
4 Frank Baker	50.00	100.00
5 Dave Bancroft (2)	100.00	200.00
6 Jesse Barnes	25.00	50.00
7 Johnny Bassler	40.00	80.00
8 Joe Berry	25.00	50.00
9 Carson Bigbee	25.00	50.00
10 Ping Bodie	25.00	50.00
11 Eddie Brown	25.00	50.00
12 Jesse Burkett CO	50.00	100.00
13 George H. Burns	25.00	50.00
14 Donie Bush	40.00	80.00
15 Joe Bush	25.00	50.00
16 Max Carey (2)	50.00	100.00
17 Ty Cobb	300.00	600.00
18 Eddie Collins*	50.00	100.00
19 Rip Collins	25.00	50.00
20 Stan Coveleski*	50.00	100.00
21 Bill Cunningham	25.00	50.00
22 Jake Daubert	40.00	80.00
23 Hooks Dauss (2)	25.00	50.00
24 Dixie Davis	25.00	50.00
25 Charlie Deal (2)	25.00	50.00
26 Al Devormer	25.00	50.00
27 Bill Doak	25.00	50.00
28 Bill Donovan MG	25.00	50.00
29 Phil Douglas	25.00	50.00
30 Joe Dugan	40.00	80.00
31 Johnny Evers MG (2)	50.00	100.00
32 Red Faber	50.00	100.00
33 Bibb Falk	25.00	50.00
34 Alex Ferguson	25.00	50.00
35 Chick Fewster	25.00	50.00
36 Eddie Foster	25.00	50.00
37 Frank Frisch	100.00	200.00
38 Larry Gardner	25.00	50.00
39 Alex Gaston	25.00	50.00
40 Wally Gerber	40.00	80.00
41 Patsy Gharrity	25.00	50.00
42 Whitey Glazner	25.00	50.00
43 Kid Gleason MG	30.00	60.00
44 Mike Gonzales	25.00	50.00
45 Hank Gowdy	30.00	60.00
46 Jack Graney (2)	25.00	50.00
47 Tommy Griffith	25.00	50.00
48 Charlie Grimm	30.00	60.00
49 Heinie Groh New York NL	30.00	60.00
50 Henie Groh Cincinnati NL	30.00	60.00
51 Jesse Haines	50.00	100.00
52 Harry Harper	25.00	50.00
53 Chicken Hawks	25.00	50.00
54 Harry Heilmann	50.00	100.00

1922 W575

55 Fred Hoffman	25.00	50.00
56 Walter Holke (3)	25.00	50.00
57 Charlie Hollocher (2)	25.00	50.00
58 Harry Hooper	50.00	100.00
59 Rogers Hornsby	100.00	200.00
60 Waite Hoyt	50.00	100.00
61 Miller Huggins MG	50.00	100.00
62 Baby Doll Jacobson	25.00	50.00
63 Hugh Jennings CO	50.00	100.00
64 Walter Johnson (2)	200.00	400.00
65 Jimmy Johnston	25.00	50.00
66 Joe Judge	40.00	80.00
67 George Kelly (2)	50.00	100.00
68 Dickie Kerr	30.00	60.00
69 Pete Kilduff	25.00	50.00
70 Doc Lavan	25.00	50.00
71 Nemo Leibold	25.00	50.00
72 Duffy Lewis	30.00	60.00
73 Al Mamaux	25.00	50.00
74 Rabbit Maranville*	50.00	100.00
75 Rube Marquard	50.00	100.00
76 Carl Mays (2)	30.00	60.00
77 John McGraw MG	100.00	200.00
78 Stuffy McInnis	30.00	60.00
79 Mike McNally	25.00	50.00
80 Bob Meusel	40.00	80.00
81 Irish Meusel	25.00	50.00
82 Clyde Milan	30.00	60.00
83 Elmer Miller	25.00	50.00
84 Otto Miller	25.00	50.00
85 Johnny Mitchell	25.00	50.00
86 Guy Morton	40.00	80.00
87 Eddie Mulligan	25.00	50.00
88 Eddie Murphy	25.00	50.00
89 Hy Myers (3)	25.00	50.00
90 Greasy Neale	30.00	60.00
91 Art Nehf	40.00	80.00
92 Joe Oeschger	25.00	50.00
93 Charley O'Leary CO	25.00	50.00
94 Steve O'Neill	30.00	60.00
95 Roger Peckinpaugh (2)	30.00	60.00
96 Bill Piercy	25.00	50.00
97 Jeff Pfeffer Brook. NL	25.00	50.00
98 Jeff Pfeffer St. L. NL	25.00	50.00
99 Wally Pipp	30.00	60.00
100 Jack Quinn	25.00	50.00
101 Johnny Rawlings (2)	25.00	50.00
102 Sam Rice (2)	50.00	100.00
103 Jimmy Ring	40.00	80.00
104 Eppa Rixey	50.00	100.00
105 Charlie Robertson*	40.00	80.00
106 Wilbert Robinson MG	50.00	100.00
107 Tom Rogers	25.00	50.00
108 Ed Rommel#(sic.Rounnel	40.00	80.00
109 Braggo Roth	25.00	50.00
110 Edd Roush (2)	50.00	100.00
111 Muddy Ruel	25.00	50.00
112 Babe Ruth (2)	500.00	1,000.00
113 Rosy Ryan (2)	25.00	50.00
114 Slim Sallee (2)	25.00	50.00
115 Ray Schalk (2)	50.00	100.00
116 Wally Schang* (2)	40.00	80.00
117 Ferd Schupp (2)	25.00	50.00
118 Everett Scott Boston AL	40.00	80.00
119 Everett Scott New York AL	25.00	50.00
120 Hank Severeid	40.00	80.00
121 Joe Sewell*	50.00	100.00
122 Bob Shawkey	40.00	80.00
123 Red Shea	25.00	50.00
124 Earl Sheely	25.00	50.00
125 Urban Shocker	30.00	60.00
126 George Sisler* (2)	100.00	200.00
127 Elmer Smith	25.00	50.00
128 Earl Smith	25.00	50.00
129 Pancho Snyder	25.00	50.00
130 Tris Speaker* (2)	100.00	200.00
131 Casey Stengel New York NL	100.00	200.00
132 Casey Stengel Phila. NL	100.00	200.00
133 Riggs Stephenson	40.00	80.00
134 Milt Stock	25.00	50.00
135 Amos Strunk (2)	25.00	50.00
136 Zeb Terry	25.00	50.00
137 Pinch Thomas	25.00	50.00
138 Fred Toney (2)	25.00	50.00
139 Specs Torporcer	25.00	50.00
140 Lefty Tyler	25.00	50.00
141 Hippo Vaughn (2)	30.00	60.00
142 Bobby Veach (3)	40.00	80.00
143 Ossie Vitt	25.00	50.00
144 Frank Walker	40.00	80.00
145 Curt Walker	40.00	80.00
146 Bill Wambsganss (2)	30.00	60.00
147 Zack Wheat	50.00	100.00
148 Possum Whitted	25.00	50.00
149 Williams Chicago AL *	40.00	80.00
150 Cy Williams	25.00	50.00
151 Ivy Wingo	25.00	50.00
152 Joe Wood	40.00	80.00
153 Ralph Young	25.00	50.00
154 Ross Youngs	100.00	200.00

1925-31 W590 Athletes

Issued over a period of years, this set (which measure approximately 1 3/8" by 2 1/2") features some of the leading athletes from the 1920's. The fronts have a B&W photo with the players name, position and team on the bottom for the baseball players and sport and additional short bio info on the other athletes. The backs are blank and as these cards are unnumbered we have sequenced them in alphabetical order within sport. They were initally issued in strips and panels and can often be found intact. A number of the baseball players were re-issued from year-to-year with updated team information.

1 Grover Cleveland Alexander	100.00	200.00
2 Dave Bancroft	40.00	80.00
3 Jess Barnes	20.00	40.00
4 Ray Blades	20.00	40.00
5 Ozzie Bluege	20.00	40.00
6A George Burns NY NL	25.00	50.00
6B George Burns Phi NL	25.00	50.00
6C George Burns Cleveland	25.00	50.00
7 Max Carey	40.00	80.00
8 Jimmy Caveney	20.00	40.00
9 Ty Cobb	150.00	300.00
10 Eddie Collins	100.00	200.00
11 George Dauss	20.00	40.00
12 Red Faber	40.00	80.00
13 Frankie Frisch	60.00	120.00
14 Lou Gehrig	200.00	400.00
15 Sam Gray	20.00	40.00
16 Hank Gowdy	20.00	40.00
17 Charley Grimm	25.00	50.00
18 Bucky Harris	40.00	80.00
19A Rogers Hornsby St Louis	125.00	250.00
19B Rogers Hornsby Boston	125.00	250.00
20 Travis Jackson	40.00	80.00
21 Walter Johnson	125.00	250.00
22 George Kelly	25.00	50.00
23 Fred Lindstrom	40.00	80.00
24 Rabbit Maranville	40.00	80.00
25 Bob Meusel	30.00	60.00
26 Jack Quinn	25.00	50.00
27 Eppa Rixey	25.00	50.00
28 Ed Rommel	20.00	40.00
29 Babe Ruth	300.00	600.00
30 Heinie Sand	20.00	40.00
31 George Sissler UER Sisler	40.00	80.00
32 Earl Smith	20.00	40.00
33 Tris Speaker	100.00	200.00
34 Roy Spencer	20.00	40.00
35 Milt Stock	20.00	40.00
36A Phil Todt Phi AL	20.00	40.00
36B Phil Todt Bos AL	20.00	40.00
37 Dazzy Vance	40.00	80.00
38 Zack Wheat	40.00	80.00
39A Ken Williams St Louis AL	25.00	50.00
39B Ken Williams Bos AL	25.00	50.00
40A Ross Youngs Right Fielder	40.00	80.00
40B Ross Youngs Former Right Fielder	40.00	80.00

1921 W9316

1 Bobby Veach
2 Frank Baker
3 Wilbert Robinson MG
4 Tommy Griffith
5 Jimmie Johnston
6 Wally Schang
7 Leon Cadore
8 George Sisler
9 Ray Schalk
10 Jesse Barnes

1963 Wagner Otto Milk Carton

This is the only baseball player featured in this set which honored promiment Western Pennsylvanians. The side panel of the milk carton inlcuded a drawing of Wagner as well as some brief biographical informaion as well as a biography.

1 Honus Wagner	40.00	80.00

1924 Walter Mails WG7

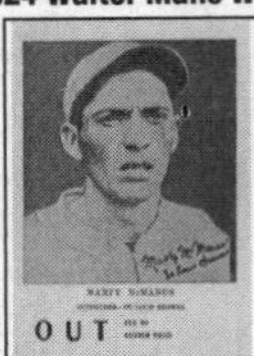

These cards were distributed as part of a baseball game produced in 1924. The cards each measure approximately 2 5/16" by 3 1/4" and have rounded corners. The card fronts show a black and white photo of the player, his name, position, his team, and the game outcome associated with that particular card. The card backs are all the same, each showing an ornate red and white design with "Walter Mails" inside a red circle in the middle all surrounded by a thin white outer border. Since the cards are unnumbered, they are listed below in alphabetical order.

COMPLETE SET	1,800.00	3,500.00
1 Buzz Arlett	50.00	100.00
2 Jim Bagby	50.00	100.00
3 Dave Bancroft	125.00	250.00
4 Johnny Bassler Sic, Basseler	50.00	100.00
5 Jack Bentley	50.00	100.00
6 Rube Benton	50.00	100.00
7 George Burns	50.00	100.00
8 Joe Bush	50.00	100.00
9 Harold P. Chavez	50.00	100.00
10 Hugh Critz	50.00	100.00
11 Jake Daubert	100.00	200.00
12 Wheezer Dell	50.00	100.00
13 Joe Dugan	75.00	150.00
14 Pat Duncan	50.00	100.00
15 Howard Ehmke	50.00	100.00
16 Lew Fonseca	50.00	100.00
17 Ray French	50.00	100.00
18 Ed Gharity Sic, Gharitty	50.00	100.00
19 Heinie Groh	75.00	150.00
20 George Grove	50.00	100.00
21 Bubbles Hargrave	50.00	100.00
22 Elmer Jacobs	50.00	100.00
23 Walter Johnson	500.00	1,000.00
24 Duke Kenworthy	50.00	100.00
25 Harry Krause	50.00	100.00
26 Ray Kremer	50.00	100.00
27 Walter Mails	50.00	100.00
28 Rabbit Maranville	125.00	250.00
29 Stuffy McInnis	75.00	150.00
30 Marty McManus	50.00	100.00
31 Bob Meusel	100.00	200.00
32 Hack Miller	50.00	100.00
33 Pat J. Moran	75.00	150.00
34 Guy Morton	50.00	100.00
35 Johnny Mostil	50.00	100.00
36 Red Murphy	50.00	100.00
37 Jimmy O'Connell	50.00	100.00
38 Joe Oeschger	50.00	100.00
39 Steve O'Neil	75.00	150.00
40 Roger Peckinpaugh	75.00	150.00
41 Babe Pinelli	50.00	100.00
42 Wally Pipp	100.00	200.00
43 Elmer Ponder	50.00	100.00
44 Sam Rice	125.00	250.00
45 Ed Rommell	50.00	100.00
46 Walter Schmidt	50.00	100.00
47 Joe Sewell	125.00	250.00
48 Pat Shea	50.00	100.00
49 Wilford Shupe	50.00	100.00
50 Paddy Siglin	50.00	100.00
51 George Sisler	150.00	300.00
52 Bill Skiff	50.00	100.00
53 Jack Smith	50.00	100.00
54 Suds Sutherland	50.00	100.00
55 Cotton Tierney	50.00	100.00
56 George Uhle	50.00	100.00

1910 Washington Times

This very rare and obscure issue was apparently a supplement for the Washington Times newspaper. The cards measure approximately 2 1/2" by 3 1/2" and feature black-and-white player photos with blank backs. The cards are unnumbered and checklisted below in alphabetical order. The Walter Johnson card is rumored as being in the set. The checklist is probably incomplete and any confirmed additions are welcomed.

1 Ty Cobb	5,000.00	10,000.00
2 Eddie Collins	1,500.00	3,000.00
3 Wid Conroy	500.00	1,000.00
4 Sam Crawford	1,500.00	3,000.00
5 Walter Johnson	2,500.00	5,000.00
6 Nap Lajoie	1,500.00	3,000.00
7 George McBride	500.00	1,000.00
8 Clyde Milan	600.00	1,200.00
9 Frank Oberlin	500.00	1,000.00
10 Jack O'Connor	500.00	1,000.00
11 Gabby Street	500.00	1,000.00
12 Lee Tannehill	500.00	1,000.00
13 Bob Unglaub	500.00	1,000.00
14 Dixie Walker	500.00	1,000.00
15 Ed Walsh	1,000.00	2,000.00
16 Joe Wood	750.00	1,500.00
17 Cy Young	2,500.00	5,000.00

1888 WG1 Card Game

These cards were distributed as part of a baseball game. The cards each measure approximately 2 1/2" by 3 1/2" and have rounded corners. The card fronts show a color drawing of the player, his name, his position, and the game outcome associated with that particular card. The card backs are all the same, each showing a geometric graphic design in blue. Since the cards are unnumbered, they are listed below in alphabetical order within each of the eight teams. The box features a photo of King Kelly on the front along with the words, "Patented Feb. 28, 1888".

COMPLETE SET (72)	25,000.00	50,000.00
1 Tom Brown	300.00	600.00
2 John Clarkson	750.00	1,500.00
3 Joe Hornung	300.00	600.00
4 Dick Johnston	300.00	600.00
5 King Kelly	1,250.00	2,500.00
6 John Morrill	300.00	600.00
7 Billy Nash	300.00	600.00
8 Ezra Sutton	300.00	600.00
9 Sam Wise	300.00	600.00
10 Cap Anson	2,500.00	5,000.00
11 Tom Burns	300.00	600.00
12 Silver Flint	300.00	600.00
13 Bob Pettit	300.00	600.00
14 Fred Pfeffer	300.00	600.00
15 Jimmy Ryan	300.00	600.00
16 Marty Sullivan	600.00	1,200.00
17 George Van Haltren	300.00	600.00
18 Ned Williamson	400.00	800.00
19 Charlie Bennett	400.00	800.00
20 Dan Brouthers	1,000.00	2,000.00
21 Charlie Getzein	300.00	600.00
22 Ned Hanlon	600.00	1,200.00
23 Hardy Richardson	300.00	600.00
24 Jack Rowet	300.00	600.00
25 Sam Thompson	600.00	1,200.00
26 Larry Twitchell	300.00	600.00
27 Deacon White	400.00	800.00
28 Charley Bassett	300.00	600.00
29 Henry Boyle	300.00	600.00
30 Jerry Denny	300.00	600.00
31 Dude Esterbrook	300.00	600.00
32 Jack Glasscock	600.00	1,200.00
33 Paul Hines	300.00	600.00
34 George Meyers	300.00	600.00
35 Emmett Seery	300.00	600.00
36 Jumbo Shoeneck	300.00	600.00
37 Roger Connor	600.00	1,200.00
38 Buck Ewing	1,000.00	2,000.00
39 Elmer Foster	300.00	600.00
40 George Gore	300.00	600.00
41 Tim Keefe	600.00	1,200.00
42 Jim O'Rourke	600.00	1,200.00
43 Danny Richardson	300.00	600.00
44 Mike Tiernan	300.00	600.00
45 John Ward	1,000.00	2,000.00
46 Ed Andrews	300.00	600.00
47 Charlie Bastian	300.00	600.00
48 Don Casey	300.00	600.00
49 Jack Clements	300.00	600.00
50 Sid Farrar	400.00	800.00
51 Jim Fogarty	300.00	600.00
52 Arthur Irwin	300.00	600.00
53 Joe Mulvey	300.00	600.00
54 George Wood	300.00	600.00
55 Fred Carroll	300.00	600.00
56 John Coleman	300.00	600.00
57 Abner Dalrymple	300.00	600.00
58 Fred Dunlap	300.00	600.00
59 Pud Galvin	600.00	1,200.00
60 Willie Kuehne	300.00	600.00
61 Al Maul	300.00	600.00
62 Pop Smith	300.00	600.00
63 Billy Sunday	600.00	1,200.00
64 Jim Donelly	300.00	600.00
65 Dummy Hoy	600.00	1,200.00
66 John Irwin	300.00	600.00
67 Connie Mack	1,500.00	3,000.00
68 Al Myers	300.00	600.00
69 Billy O'Brien	300.00	600.00
70 George Shoch	300.00	600.00
71 Jim Whitney	300.00	600.00
72 Walt Wilmot	300.00	600.00

1935 Wheaties BB1

This set is referred to as "Fancy Frame with Script Signature". These cards (which made up the back of the Wheaties cereal box) measure 6" by 6 1/4" with the frame and about 5" by 5 1/2" if the frame is trimmed off. The player photo appears in blue on a blue-tinted field with a solid orange background behind the player. The player's facsimile autograph is displayed at the bottom of the card.

COMPLETE SET (27)	750.00	1,500.00
1 Jack Armstrong batting pose fictional character	15.00	30.00
2 Jack Armstrong throwing your friend fictional character	15.00	30.00
3 Wally Berger batting follow through Sincerely Yours	15.00	30.00
4 Tommy Bridges pitching	15.00	30.00
5A Mickey Cochrane squatting wearing black hat and uniform with stripes	30.00	60.00
5B Mickey Cochrane squatting wearing white hat and uniform with no stripes	100.00	200.00
6 James Rip Collins jumping	15.00	30.00
7 Dizzy Dean pitching follow through	60.00	120.00
8 Dizzy Dean and Paul Dean squatting	40.00	80.00
9 Paul Dean pitching	20.00	40.00
10 William Delancey catching	15.00	30.00
11 Jimmie Foxx facing camera knee up	50.00	100.00
12 Frank Frisch stooping to field	30.00	60.00
13 Lou Gehrig batting follow through	200.00	400.00
14 Goose Goslin batting	30.00	60.00
15 Lefty Grove holding trophy	50.00	100.00
16 Carl Hubbell pitching	30.00	60.00
17 Travis C. Jackson stooping to field	20.00	40.00
18 Chuck Klein with four bats	30.00	60.00
19 Gus Mancuso catching	15.00	30.00
20A Pepper Martin batting	15.00	30.00

20B Pepper Martin portrait Sincerely Yours 15.00 30.00
21 Joe Medwick batting follow through 30.00 60.00
22 Mel Ott batting follow through 50.00 100.00
23 Harold Schumacher pitching 15.00 30.00
24 Al Simmons batting follow through Sincerely Yours 30.00 60.00
25 Jo Jo White batting follow through 15.00 30.00

1936 Wheaties BB3

This set is referred to as "Fancy Frame with Printed Name and Data." These cards (which made up the back of the Wheaties cereal box) measure 6" by 6 1/4" with the frame and about 5" by 5 1/2" if the frame is trimmed off. This set is distinguished from BB1 (above) in that this set also shows the player's name and some fact about him. The player's facsimile autograph is displayed at the bottom of the card. In the checklist below, the first few words of the printed data found on the card is also provided.

COMPLETE SET (12) 350.00 700.00
1 Earl Averill batting Star Outfielder 25.00 50.00
2 Mickey Cochrane catching Manager World Champion Detroit 40.00 80.00
3 Jimmie Foxx batting All Around Star 50.00 100.00
4 Lou Gehrig stooping to field Iron Man 150.00 300.00
5 Hank Greenberg jumping Home Run Champion 40.00 80.00
6 Gabby Hartnett squatting Catcher Voted Most Valuable 30.00 60.00
7 Carl Hubbell ready to throw Star Pitcher 30.00 60.00
8 Pepper Martin jumping Heavy Hitter 15.00 30.00
9 Van L. Mungo pitching Star Pitcher 15.00 30.00
10 Buck Newsom pitching Star Pitcher 15.00 30.00
11 Arky Vaughan batting Batting Champion 25.00 50.00
12 Jimmy Wilson squatting Manager and Star Catcher 15.00 30.00

1936 Wheaties BB4

This set is refered to as "Thin Orange Border / Figures in Border." These unnumbered cards (which made up the back of the Wheaties cereal box) mwasure 6" by 8 1/2". The set is the first in this larger size. The figures in the border include drawings of men and women competing baseball, football, hockey, track, golf, tennis, skiing and swimming. A train and an airplane also appear. The rectangular photo of the player appears in a box above an endorsment for Wheaties. The player's name is in script below the endorsment, A printed name, team and other information is near the top in the solid orange background.

COMPLETE SET (12) 300.00 600.00
1 Curt Davis Philadelphia Phillies 15.00 30.00
2 Lou Gehrig New York Yankees 150.00 300.00
3 Charlie Gehringer Detroit Tigers 30.00 60.00
4 Lefty Grove Boston Red Sox 40.00 80.00
5 Rollie Hemsley St. Louis Browns 15.00 30.00
6 Billy Herman Chicago Cubs 25.00 50.00
7 Joe Medwick St. Louis Cardinals 30.00 60.00
8 Mel Ott New York Giants 40.00 80.00
9 Schoolboy Rowe Detroit Tigers 15.00 30.00
10 Arky Vaughan Detroit Tigers 25.00 50.00
11 Joe Vosmik Cleveland Indians 15.00 30.00
12 Lon Warneke Chicago Cubs 15.00 30.00

1936 Wheaties BB5

This set is referred to as "How to Play Winning Baseball." These cards, which made up the back of the Wheaties box. measure 6" X 8 1/2" These panels combine a photo of the player with a series of blue and white drawings illustrating playing instrustions. All of the players are shown in full length poses, except Earl Averill, who is pictured to the thighs. The players appear aganist a solid orange background. In addition to the numbers 1 thru 12, these panels are also found with a small number 28 combined with captial letters "A" thru "L." However, panels are know without these letter-number combinations. This set is sometimes refered to as the "28 Series."

COMPLETE SET (13) 250.00 500.00
1 Lefty Gomez 25.00 50.00
2 Billy Herman 20.00 40.00
3 Luke Appling 20.00 40.00
4 Jimmie Foxx 30.00 60.00
5 Joe Medwick 25.00 50.00
6 Charlie Gehringer 30.00 60.00
7A Mel Ott (large figure) 30.00 60.00
7B Mel Ott (small figure) 30.00 60.00
8 Odell Hale 15.00 30.00
9 Bill Dickey 30.00 60.00
10 Lefty Grove 30.00 60.00
11 Carl Hubbell 25.00 50.00
12 Earl Averill 20.00 40.00

1937 Wheaties BB6

This set is refered to as "How to Star in Baseball." These numbered cards, which made up the back of the cereal box, measure 6" X 8 1/4". This series is very similar to BB5. Both are instructional series' and the text and drawings used to illuatrate the tips are similar and in some cases identical. Each panel is a full length photo, The players name, team and script signature also appears on the card.

COMPLETE SET (12) 350.00 700.00
1 Bill Dickey How to Catch 40.00 80.00
2 Red Ruffing Pitching the Fast Ball 25.00 50.00
3 Zeke Bonura First Base - Make More Outs 15.00 30.00
4 Charlie Gehringer/Second Base as the Stars Pla 40.00 80.00
5 Arky Vaughan Shortstop, Play It Right 25.00 50.00
6 Carl Hubbell Pitching the Slow Ball 30.00 60.00
7 John Lewis Third Base, Field Those Hot Ones 15.00 30.00
8 Heinie Manush Fielding for Extra Outs 25.00 50.00
9 Lefty Grove Pitching the Outdrop Ball 40.00 80.00
10 Billy Herman How to Score/(baserunning) 25.00 50.00
11 Joe DiMaggio Bat Like a Home Run King 150.00 300.00
12 Joe Medwick Batting for Extra Bases 25.00 50.00

1937 Wheaties BB7

This set is refered to as the "29 Series" These numbered cards which make up the back of the box measure 6" X 8 1/4". The players name, position, team and some information about him are printed near the top. His signature appears on the lower part of the panel near a printed endorsment for the cereal. This set contains several different card designs. One design shows the player outlined aganist an orange (nearly red) background. A two or three line endorsment is at the bottom. DiMaggio, Bonura and Bridges appear in this form. Another design shows a player against a solid white background , but the panel is rimmed by a red, white and blue border. Players shown in this fashion are Moore, Radcliff and Martin. A third style offers a panel with an orange border and a large orange circle behind the player. The rest of the background is white. Lombardi, Travis and Mungo appear in this design. The final style is a titled, orange background picture of the player with white and blue framing the photo. Trosky, Demaree and Vaughan show up in this design. The set also has three known Pacific Coast League players. One number, 29N, which could be a PCL player, is unknown.

COMPLETE SET (15) 400.00 800.00
29A Zeke Bonura/(batting) 15.00 30.00
29B Cecil Travis/(reaching left) 15.00 30.00
29C Frank Demaree/(batting) 15.00 30.00
29D Joe Moore/(batting) 15.00 30.00
29E Ernie Lombardi/(crouch) 25.00 50.00
29F Pepper Martin/(reaching) 15.00 30.00
29G Harold Trosky/(batting) 15.00 30.00
29H Ray Radcliff/(batting) 15.00 30.00
29I Joe DiMaggio/(batting) 150.00 300.00
29J Tommy Bridges/(hands over head) 15.00 30.00
29K Van L. Mungo/(pitching) 15.00 30.00
29L Arky Vaughan/(batting) 25.00 50.00
29M Arnold Statz (PCL) 60.00 120.00
29N Unknown
29O Fred Muller (PCL) 60.00 120.00
29P Gene Lillard (PCL) 60.00 120.00

1937 Wheaties BB8

This set is refered to as the "Speckled Orange, White and Blue Series." These unnumbered cards which made up the back of the Wheaties box measure 6" X 8 1/2". The set contains several different card designs. One design (DiMaggio and Feller) shows the player surrounded by orange sprekles on a white backgroung with a group of four blue and white drawings of players in action along the panel's right side. Another design shows the panel divided into four rectangles -- white at upper right and lower left and orange on the other two. -- with the players (Appling and Averill) leaping to catch the ball. Blue circles surrounded by orange and white speckles appear on the pictures of Hubbel and Grove. Medwick and Gehringer appear on white panels with a cloud of orange speckles behind them. The player's name in script style appears along with printed data about his 1936 season and a brief endorsement for the cereal.

COMPLETE SET (8) 450.00 900.00
1 Luke Appling/(reaching) 30.00 60.00
2 Earl Averill/(reaching) 30.00 60.00
3 Joe DiMaggio/(batting) 250.00 500.00
4 Bob Feller/(throwing) 75.00 150.00
5 Charlie Gehringer/(batting) 60.00 120.00
6 Lefty Grove/(throwing) 60.00 120.00
7 Carl Hubbell/(throwing) 60.00 120.00
8 Joe Medwick/(fielding) 30.00 60.00

1937 Wheaties BB9

This set is refered to as the "Color Series." These unnumbered cards measure 6" X 8 1/2" Photos of the players appear in circles. "V" shapes and rectangles, and stars among others. A player from every major League team is included. The player's name is in script with the team name below. The name , endorsment and player's 1936 highlights are printed near the bottom. John Moore and Harland Cliff have been reported on paper stock. Whether they were part of a store display is unknown.

COMPLETE SET (16) 400.00 800.00
1 Zeke Bonura Chicago White Sox fielding crossed bats glove ball at upper left 15.00 30.00
2 Tom Bridges Detroit Tigers pitching figure in large orange circle 15.00 30.00
3 Harland Clift St. Louis Browns batting large baseball behind him 15.00 30.00
4 Kiki Cuyler Cincinnati Reds batting on green background 25.00 50.00
5 Joe DiMaggio New York Yankees leaping green and white circle behind 150.00 300.00
6 Bob Feller Cleveland Indians pitching blue circle on left knee 50.00 100.00
7 Lefty Grove Boston Red Sox pitching red orange home plate 40.00 80.00
8 Billy Herman Chicago Cubs throwing yellow star behind him 25.00 50.00
9 Carl Hubbell New York Giants pitching orange yellow V's behind 30.00 60.00
10 Buck Jordan Boston Bees batting dark orange rectangle blue sides 15.00 30.00
11 Pepper Martin St. Louis Cardinals reaching orange rectangle 20.00 40.00
12 John Moore Philadelphia Phillies batting blue background stands on green 15.00 30.00
13 Wally Moses Philadelphia A's leaping dark orange background yellow and blue 15.00 30.00
14 Van L. Mungo Brooklyn Dodgers pitching green background orange and blue 20.00 40.00
15 Cecil Travis Washington Senators batting orange lightning 15.00 30.00
16 Arky Vaughan Pittsburgh Pirates batting blue diamond green frame 25.00 50.00

1937 Wheaties BB14

This set is referred to as the "Small Panels with Orange Background Series." These numbered (and unnumbered) cards, which made up the back of the Wheaties individual serving cereal box, measure about 2 5/8" by 3 7/8". These small panels have orange backgrounds and some, but not all, use poses that appear in some of the regular sized panels. Joe DiMaggio, for example, is the same pose as in the large Wheaties BB7 set and the Mel Ott is similar to the BB5 pose, but cropped a little differently. Some panels have been seen with and without the number 29 in combination with a letter, so apparently there were several printings. The player's name is in all capitals with his position and team in smaller caps. A printed block of data about him is on the main part of the card with a Wheaties endorsement in a white strip at the bottom.

COMPLETE SET (17) 700.00 1,400.00
1 Zeke Bonura 29A Led all A.L. First Basemen BB7 pose 40.00 80.00
2 Tommy Bridges 29J Struck Out Most Batters 173 ... not BB7 pose 40.00 80.00
3 Dolph Camilli Most Put Outs 1446 ... unnumbered 50.00 100.00
4 Frank Demaree 40.00 80.00
5 Joe DiMaggio 29I Outstanding Rookie 1936 ... BB7 pose 250.00 500.00
6 Billy Herman Lifetime .300 Hitter ... unnumbered 60.00 120.00
7 Carl Hubbell Won Most Games 26 ... unnumbered 100.00 200.00
8 Ernie Lombardi 60.00 120.00
9 Pepper Martin 50.00 100.00
10 Joe Moore 40.00 80.00
11 Van L. Mungo 50.00 100.00
12 Mel Ott 100.00 200.00
13 Raymond Radcliff 29H most one-base hits BB7 pose 40.00 80.00
14 Cecil Travis 29B One of the Leading Bats in ... BB7 pose 40.00 80.00
15 Harold Trosky 40.00 80.00
16A Arky Vaughan unnumbered 75.00 150.00
16B Arky Vaughan 29L Lifetime .300 Hitter who ... BB7 pose 75.00 150.00

1938 Wheaties BB10

This set is refered to as the "Biggest Thrills in Baseball." These numbered cards which make up the back of the cereal box measure 6" X 8 1/2." A player from every Major League team is included. Each panel describes the player's greatest thrill playing the game. The thrill is announced in large banner headline type and described in a block of copy over the players script signature, His team name and position are printed below the name. All sixteen are known to exist on both paper stock as well as heavy cardboard.

COMPLETE SET (16)	500.00	1,000.00
1 Bob Feller	75.00	150.00
Cleveland Indians/(Two Hits in One		
I		
2 Cecil Travis	20.00	50.00
Washington Nationals/(Clicks in Fir		
3 Joe Medwick	40.00	80.00
St. Louis Cardinals/(Goes on Batting		
4 Gerald Walker	20.00	50.00
Chicago White Sox/(World Series Ga		
5 Carl Hubbell	50.00	100.00
New York Giants/(Strikes Out		
Murde		
6 Bob Johnson	20.00	50.00
Philadelphia A's/(Setting New		
A.L.		
7 Beau Bell	20.00	50.00
St. Louis Browns/(Smacks First Major/		
8 Ernie Lombardi	30.00	60.00
Cincinnati Reds/(Sold to Majors)		
9 Lefty Grove	60.00	120.00
Boston Red Sox/(Fans Babe Ruth)		
10 Lou Fette	20.00	50.00
Boston Bees/(Wins 20 Games)		
11 Joe DiMaggio	200.00	400.00
New York Yankees/(Home Run King Get		
12 Pinky Whitney	20.00	50.00
Philadelphia Phillies/(Hits Three		
13 Dizzy Dean	60.00	120.00
Chicago Cubs/(11-0 Victory		
Clinches		
14 Charlie Gehringer	50.00	100.00
Detroit Tigers/(Homers Off		
Di		
15 Paul Waner	40.00	80.00
Pittsburgh Pirates/(Four Perfect Sixe		
16 Dolph Camilli	30.00	60.00

1938 Wheaties BB11

This set is refered to as the "Dress Clothes or Civies Series." The cards are unnumbered and measure 6" 8 1/4" The panels feature the players and their friends in blue photos. The remainder of the panel uses the traditional orange, blue and white Wheaties colors.

COMPLETE SET (8)	150.00	300.00
1 Lou Fette/(pouring milk	15.00	30.00
over his Wheaties)		
2 Jimmie Foxx/(slices banana for	30.00	60.00
his son's Wheatie		
3 Charlie Gehringer/(and his young fan)	25.00	50.00
4 Lefty Grove/(watches waitress	25.00	50.00
pour Wheaties)		
5 Hank Greenberg	30.00	60.00
and Roxie Lawson/(eat breakfast)		
6 Ernie Lombardi	15.00	30.00
and Lee Grissom/(prepare to eat)		
7 Joe Medwick/(pours milk	20.00	40.00
over cereal)		
8 Lon Warneke/(smiles in anticip-	15.00	30.00
ation of Wheatie		

1938 Wheaties BB15

This set is referred to as the "Small Panels with Orange, Blue and White Background Series." These numbered (and unnumbered) cards, which made up the back of the Wheaties individual serving cereal box, measure about 2 5/8" by 3 7/8". These small panels have orange, blue and white backgrounds and some, but not all, use poses that appear in some of the regular, larger-sized panels. Greenberg and Lewis are featured with a horizontal (HOR) pose.

COMPLETE SET (11)	500.00	1,000.00
1 Zeke Bonura/(batted .345)	25.00	50.00
2 Joe DiMaggio/(46 home runs)	200.00	400.00
3A Charlie Gehringer (Leaping)	50.00	100.00
3B Charlie Gehringer (batting)	50.00	100.00
4 Hank Greenberg HOR/(second in home	60.00	120.00
runs)		
5 Lefty Grove/(17-9 won-lost	60.00	120.00
record)		
6 Carl Hubbell/(star pitcher,/1937 Giants)	50.00	100.00
7 John (Buddy) Lewis/(batted .314) HOR	25.00	50.00
8 Heinie Manush/(batted .332)	40.00	80.00
9 Joe Medwick	40.00	80.00
10 Arky Vaughan	40.00	80.00

1939 Wheaties BB12

This set is refered to as the "Personal Pointers Series." These numbered cards measure 6" X 8 1/4'. The panels feature an instructional format similar to both the BB5 and BB6 Wheaties sets. Drawings again illustrate the tips on batting and pitching. The colors are orange, blue and white and the players appear in photographs.

COMPLETE SET (9)	250.00	500.00
1 Ernie Lombardi	30.00	60.00
How to Place Hits		
For Scores		
2 Johnny Allen	20.00	40.00
It's Windup That		
Counts		
3 Lefty Gomez	40.00	80.00
Delivery That		
Keeps 'Em Guessing		
4 Bill Lee	20.00	40.00
Follow Through		
For Stops		
5 Jimmie Foxx	50.00	100.00
Stance Helps		
Sluggers		
6 Joe Medwick	30.00	60.00
Power-Drive Grip		
7 Hank Greenberg	50.00	100.00
Smooth Swing		
8 Mel Ott	40.00	80.00
Study That		
Pitcher		
9 Arky Vaughan	30.00	60.00
Beat 'Em With		
Bunts		

1939 Wheaties BB13

This set is referred to as the "100 Years of Baseball or Baseball Centennial Series." These numbered cards which make up the back of the Wheaties box measure 6" X 6 3/4". Each panel has a drawing that depicts various aspects and events in baseball in the traditional orange, blue and white Wheaties colors.

COMPLETE SET (8)	100.00	200.00
1 Design of First	25.00	50.00
Diamond with		
Picture of Abner		
D		
2 Lincoln Gets News	25.00	50.00
3 Crowd Boos First	15.00	30.00
Baseball Glove/(pictures of		
gl		
4 Curve Ball	15.00	30.00
5 Fencer's Mask	15.00	30.00
6 Baseball Gets Dressed Up	15.00	30.00
7 Modern Bludgeon	15.00	30.00
Enters Game/(pictures of		
bats)		
8 Casey at the Bat	25.00	50.00

1940 Wheaties M4

This set is referred to as the "Champs in the USA" The cards measure about 6" 8 1'4" and are numbered. The drawing portion (inside the dotted lines) measures approximately 6" X 6". There is a Baseball player on each card and they are joined by football players, football coaches, race car drivers, airline pilots, a circus clown, ice skater, hockey star and golfers. Each athlete appears in what looks like a stamp with a serrated edge. The stamps appear one above the other with a brief block of copy describing his or her achievements. There appears to have been three printings, resulting in some variation panels. The full panels tell the cereal buyer to look for either 27, 39, or 63 champ stamps. The first nine panels apparently were printed more than once, since all the unknown variations occur with those numbers.

COMPLETE SET (20)	400.00	800.00
1A R. Ruffing/B. Feller	40.00	80.00
1B R. Ruffing/L. Durocher	30.00	50.00
2A J. DiMaggio/H. Greenberg	100.00	200.00
2B J. DiMaggio/M. Ott	100.00	200.00
3 J. Foxx/B. Dickey	35.00	60.00
5 Joe Medwick	15.00	25.00
Matty Bell		
Ab Jenkins		
6A J. Mize/D. O'Brien/Ralph		
Guldahl/(27 stamp	15.00	25.00
6B Mize/Feller/York/(39 stamp series	40.00	80.00
6C G. Hartnett/D. O'Brien		
Ralph Guldahl/(unk	15.00	25.00
7A J. Cronin/Byron Nelson/(27 stamp	15.00	25.00
7B J. Cronin/H. Greenberg	25.00	50.00
7C P. Derringer/Byron Nelson/(unkno	15.00	25.00
8A J. Manders/E. Lombardi		
George I. Myers/(27	15.00	25.00
8B P. Derringer/E. Lombardi		
George I. Myers/(	15.00	25.00
10 A. Inge/B. Herman	15.00	25.00
11 Dolph Camilli	15.00	25.00
Antoinette Concello		
Wallace Wade		
12 L. Appling/S. Hack	15.00	25.00
13 F. Adler/H. Trosky/Mabel Vinson	15.00	25.00

1941 Wheaties M5

This set is also referred to as "Champs of the U.S.A." These numbered cards made up the back of the Wheaties box; the whole panel measures 6" X 8 1/4" but the drawing portion (inside the dotted lines) is apparently 6" X 6". Each athlete appears in what looks like a stamp with a serrated edge. The stamps appear one above the other with a brief block of copy describing his or her achievements. The format is the same as the previous M4 set -- even the numbering system continues where the M4 set stops.

COMPLETE SET (8)	175.00	350.00
14 Jimmie Foxx	25.00	50.00
Felix Adler		
Capt. R.G. Hanson		
15 B. Bierman/B. Feller/Jessie McLeod	20.00	40.00
16 Hank Greenberg	20.00	40.00
Lowell Red Dawson		
J.W. Stoker		
17 J. DiMaggio/B. Nelson		
Antoniette Concello	100.00	200.00
18 Pee Wee Reese	25.00	50.00
20 B. Walters/Barney McCosky	12.50	25.00
21 J. Gordon/S. Hack	12.50	25.00

1951 Wheaties

The cards in this six-card set measure approximately 2 1/2" by 3 1/4". Cards of the 1951 Wheaties set are actually the backs of small individual boxes of Wheaties. The cards are waxed and depict three baseball players, one football player, one basketball player, and one golfer. They are occasionally found as complete boxes, which are worth 50 percent more than the prices listed below. The catalog designation for this set is F272-3. The cards are blank-backed and unnumbered; they are numbered below in alphabetical order for convenience.

COMPLETE SET (6)	300.00	600.00
1 Bob Feller	40.00	80.00
4 Stan Musial	60.00	120.00
6 Ted Williams	75.00	150.00

1952 Wheaties

The cards in this 60-card set measure 2" by 2 3/4". The 1952 Wheaties set of orange, blue and white, unnumbered cards was issued in panels of eight or ten cards on the backs of Wheaties cereal boxes. Each player appears in an action pose, designated in the checklist with an "A", and as a portrait, listed in the checklist with a "B". The catalog designation is F272-4. The cards are blank-backed and unnumbered, but have been assigned numbers below using a sport prefix (BB- baseball, BK- basketball, FB- football, G-Golf, OT- other).

COMPLETE SET (60)	600.00	1,000.00
BB1A Yogi Berra	20.00	40.00
Action		
BB1B Yogi Berra	20.00	40.00
Portrait		
BB2A Roy Campanella	25.00	50.00
Action		
BB2B Roy Campanella	25.00	50.00
Portrait		
BB3A Bob Feller	20.00	40.00
Action		
BB3B Bob Feller	20.00	40.00
Portrait		
BB4A George Kell	12.50	25.00
Action		
BB4B George Kell	12.50	25.00
Portrait		
BB5A Ralph Kiner	12.50	25.00
Action		
BB5B Ralph Kiner	12.50	25.00
Portrait		
BB6A Bob Lemon	12.50	25.00
Action		
BB6B Bob Lemon	12.50	25.00
Portrait		
BB7A Stan Musial	40.00	80.00
Action		
BB7B Stan Musial	40.00	80.00
Portrait		
BB8A Phil Rizzuto	15.00	30.00
Action		
BB8B Phil Rizzuto	15.00	30.00
Portrait		
BB9A Preacher Roe	5.00	10.00
Action		
BB9B Preacher Roe	5.00	10.00
Portrait		
BB10A Ted Williams	50.00	100.00
Action		
BB10B Ted Williams	50.00	100.00
Portrait		

1964 Wheaties Stamps

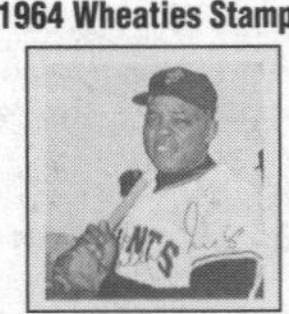

In 1964 General Mills issued the Wheaties Major League All-Star Baseball Player Stamp Album. The album is orange, blue and white and measures approximately 8 3/8" by 11"; it contains 48 pages with places for one or two stamps per page. The individual stamps are in full color with a thick white border and measure approximately 2 9/16" by 2 3/4". The stamps are unnumbered so they listed below in alphabetical order.

COMPLETE SET (50)	250.00	500.00
1 Hank Aaron	20.00	50.00
2 Bob Allison	1.50	4.00
3 Luis Aparicio	5.00	12.00
4 Ed Bailey	1.50	4.00
5 Steve Barber	1.50	4.00
6 Earl Battey	1.50	4.00
7 Jim Bouton	1.50	4.00
8 Ken Boyer	2.00	5.00
9 Jim Bunning	5.00	12.00
10 Orlando Cepeda	5.00	12.00
11 Roberto Clemente	40.00	80.00
12 Ray Culp	1.50	4.00
13 Tommy Davis	1.50	4.00
14 John Edwards	1.50	4.00
15 Whitey Ford	8.00	20.00
16 Nelson Fox	5.00	12.00
17 Bob Friend	1.50	4.00
18 Jim Gilliam	2.00	5.00
19 Jim Grant	1.50	4.00
20 Dick Groat	1.50	4.00
21 Elston Howard	2.00	5.00
22 Larry Jackson	1.50	4.00
23 Julian Javier	1.50	4.00
24 Al Kaline	10.00	25.00
25 Harmon Killebrew	8.00	20.00
26 Don Leppert	1.50	4.00
27 Frank Malzone	1.50	4.00
28 Juan Marichal	6.00	15.00
29 Willie Mays	20.00	50.00
30 Ken McBride	1.50	4.00
31 Willie McCovey	6.00	15.00
32 Jim O'Toole	1.50	4.00
33 Albie Pearson	1.50	4.00
34 Joe Pepitone	1.50	4.00
35 Ron Perranoski	1.50	4.00
36 Juan Pizarro	1.50	4.00
37 Dick Radatz	1.50	4.00
38 Bobby Richardson	2.50	6.00
39 Brooks Robinson	10.00	25.00
40 Ron Santo	2.50	6.00
41 Norm Siebern	1.50	4.00
42 Duke Snider	10.00	25.00
43 Warren Spahn	10.00	25.00
44 Joe Torre	2.50	6.00
45 Tom Tresh	1.50	4.00
46 Zoilo Versalles	1.50	4.00
47 Leon Wagner	1.50	4.00
48 Bill White	1.50	4.00
49 Hal Woodeshick	1.50	4.00
50 Carl Yastrzemski	8.00	20.00

1907 White Sox George W. Hull

This 12 card set measures 3 1/2" by 5 1/2" and contains World Champion White Sox players only. Each postcard contains club president Charles Comiskey's picture in a circle on the lower left on the front; assorted White Sox players pictures in ovals on socks in a clothesline; and the subject player's picture on the right side of the card. The George W. Hall identification is also pictured on the front.

COMPLETE SET (12)	800.00	1,600.00
1 Nick Altrock	300.00	600.00
2 George Davis	500.00	1,000.00
3 Jiggs Donohue	250.00	500.00
4 Pat Dougherty	250.00	500.00
5 Eddie Hahn	250.00	500.00
6 Frank Isbell	250.00	500.00
7 Fielder Jones	250.00	500.00
8 Ed McFarland	250.00	500.00
9 Frank Owens	250.00	500.00
10 Ray Patterson	250.00	500.00
11 George Rohe	250.00	500.00
12 Frank Smith	250.00	500.00
13 Billy Sullivan	250.00	500.00
14 Lee Tannehill	250.00	500.00
15 Ed Walsh	500.00	1,000.00
16 Doc White	250.00	500.00

1917 White Sox Team Issue

These cards which measure 1 3/4" by 2 3/4" were issued in a box labeled "Davis Printing Works". The fronts feature clear photos and glossy photographs. The cards are unnumbered and we have sequenced them in alphabetical order.

COMPLETE SET (25)	14,000.00	28,000.00
1 Charles Comiskey OWN	600.00	1,200.00
2 Joe Benz	200.00	400.00
3 Eddie Cicotte	1,000.00	2,000.00
4 Eddie Collins	1,000.00	2,000.00
5 Shano Collins	200.00	400.00
6 Dave Danforth	200.00	400.00
7 Red Faber	600.00	1,200.00
8 Happy Felsch	600.00	1,200.00
9 Chick Gandil	600.00	1,200.00
10 Kid Gleason CO	400.00	800.00
11 Joe Jackson	4,000.00	8,000.00
12 Joe Jenkins	200.00	400.00
13 Ted Jourdan	200.00	400.00
14 Nemo Leibold	200.00	400.00
15 Byrd Lynn	200.00	400.00
16 Fred McMullen	400.00	800.00
17 Eddie Murphy	200.00	400.00
18 Swede Risberg	400.00	800.00
19 Pants Rowland MG	200.00	400.00
20 Reb Russell	200.00	400.00
21 Ray Schalk	1,000.00	2,000.00
22 James Scott	200.00	400.00
23 Buck Weaver	1,000.00	2,000.00
24 Claude Williams	600.00	1,200.00
25 Meldon Wolfgang	200.00	400.00

1930 White Sox Blue Ribbon Malt

In addition to the smaller photos which were cut out of the team panorama, Blue Ribbon Malt also issued larger sized photos of members of the 1930 Chicago White Sox. These photos measure approximately 5" by 7" and are attached to grey mounts in a similar fashion to the Cubs issue. This checklist is probably incomplete and any additions are welcome.

COMPLETE SET	30.00	60.00
1 Jimmie Burke	25.00	50.00
2 Donie Bush MG	25.00	50.00
3 Bill Cissell	25.00	50.00

4 Red Faber	50.00	100.00
5 Lew Fonseca	25.00	50.00
6 Vic Frasier	25.00	50.00
7 Smead Jolley	30.00	60.00
8 Willie Kamm	30.00	60.00
9 Ted Lyons	60.00	120.00
10 Carl Reynolds	25.00	50.00
11 Art Shires	25.00	50.00
12 Tommy Thomas	25.00	50.00
13 Hal Totten ANN	25.00	50.00
14 Johnny Watwood	25.00	50.00

1930 White Sox Team Issue

These cards, which measure between 1 7/16 to 2 7/8" by 3 1/2" are actually photos cut out of a 1930 White Sox Team Panorama, which originally measured 11" by 37", and was issued by Blue Ribbon Malt.

COMPLETE SET (27)	150.00	300.00
1 Chick Autry	7.50	15.00
2 Red Barnes	7.50	15.00
3 Moe Berg	20.00	40.00
4 Garland Braxton	7.50	15.00
5 Donie Bush MG	10.00	20.00
6 Pat Caraway	7.50	15.00
7 Bill Cissell	7.50	15.00
8 Bud Clancy	7.50	15.00
9 Clyde Crouse	7.50	15.00
10 Red Faber	20.00	40.00
11 Bob Fothergill	10.00	20.00
12 Dutch Henry	7.50	15.00
13 Smead Jolley	10.00	20.00
14 Willie Kamm	10.00	20.00
15 Mike Kelly	7.50	15.00
16 Johnny Kerr	7.50	15.00
17 Ted Lyons	20.00	40.00
18 Harold McKain	7.50	15.00
19 Jim Moore	7.50	15.00
20 Greg Mulleavy	7.50	15.00
21 Carl Reynolds	10.00	20.00
22 Blondy Ryan	7.50	15.00
23 Benny Tate	7.50	15.00
24 Tommy Thomas	7.50	15.00
25 Ed Walsh Jr.	10.00	20.00
26 Johnny Watwood	7.50	15.00
27 Bob Weiland	7.50	15.00

1939 White Sox Team Issue

These 23 photos measure approximately 5 1/4" by 6 3/4". They feature player photos and a fascimile autograph. The backs are blank and we have sequenced them in alphabetical order.

COMPLETE SET (23)	200.00	400.00
1 Pete Appleton	7.50	15.00
2 Luke Appling	25.00	50.00
3 Clint Brown	7.50	15.00
4 Bill Dietrich	7.50	15.00
5 Mule Haas	7.50	15.00
6 Jack Hayes	7.50	15.00
7 Bob Kennedy	7.50	15.00
8 Jack Knott	7.50	15.00
9 Mike Kreevich	7.50	15.00
10 Joe Kuhel	7.50	15.00
11 Thornton Lee	15.00	30.00
12 Ted Lyons	25.00	50.00
13 Eric McNair	7.50	15.00
14 John Rigney	7.50	15.00
15 Larry Rosenthal	7.50	15.00
16 Ken Silvestri	7.50	15.00
17 Eddie Smith	7.50	15.00
18 Moose Solters	7.50	15.00
19 Monty Stratton	15.00	30.00
20 Mike Tresh	7.50	15.00
21 Skeeter Webb	7.50	15.00
22 Ed Weiland	7.50	15.00
23 Taft Wright	7.50	15.00

1948 White Sox Team Issue

These 30 photos represent members of the 1948 Chicago White Sox. They measure approximately 6 1/2" by 9" are black and white and have blank backs. We have sequenced this set in alphabetical order.

COMPLETE SET (30)	200.00	400.00
1 Luke Appling	20.00	40.00
2 Floyd Baker	5.00	10.00
3 Fred Bradley	5.00	10.00
4 Earl Caldwell	5.00	10.00
5 Red Faber CO	15.00	30.00
6 Bob Gillespie	5.00	10.00
7 Jim Goodwin	5.00	10.00
8 Orval Grove	5.00	10.00
9 Earl Harrist	5.00	10.00
10 Joe Haynes	5.00	10.00
11 Ralph Hodgin	5.00	10.00
12 Howie Judson	5.00	10.00
13 Bob Kennedy	6.00	12.00
14 Don Kolloway	5.00	10.00
15 Tony Lupien	5.00	10.00
16 Ted Lyons MG	15.00	30.00
17 Cass Michaels	5.00	10.00
18 Bing Miller CO	5.00	10.00
19 Buster Mills CO	5.00	10.00
20 Glen Moulder	5.00	10.00
21 Frank Papish	5.00	10.00
22 Ike Pearson	5.00	10.00
23 Dave Philley	5.00	10.00
24 Aaron Robinson	5.00	10.00
25 Mike Tresh	5.00	10.00
26 Jack Wallaesa	5.00	10.00
27 Ralph Weigel	5.00	10.00
28 Bill Wight	5.00	10.00
29 Taft Wright	5.00	10.00
30 Team Photo	25.00	50.00

1958 White Sox Jay Publishing

This 12-card set of the Chicago White Sox measures approximately 5" by 7" and features black-and-white player photos in a white border. These cards were packaged 12 to a packet. The backs are blank. The cards are unnumbered and checklisted below in alphabetical order.

COMPLETE SET (12)	25.00	50.00
1 Luis Aparicio	5.00	10.00
2 Dick Donovan	1.50	3.00
3 Nelson Fox	5.00	10.00
4 Tito Francona	1.50	3.00
5 Bill Goodman	1.50	3.00
6 Sherman Lollar	1.50	3.00
7 Ray Moore	1.50	3.00
8 Billy Pierce	2.50	5.00
9 Jim Rivera	1.50	3.00
10 Al Smith	1.50	3.00
11 Jim Wilson	1.50	3.00
12 Early Wynn	5.00	10.00

1959 White Sox Jay Publishing

This 12-card set of the Chicago White Sox measures approximately 5" by 7" and features black-and-white player photos in a white border. These cards were packaged 12 to a packet. The backs are blank. The cards are unnumbered and checklisted below in alphabetical order.

COMPLETE SET	30.00	60.00
1 Luis Aparicio	5.00	10.00
2 Johnny Callison	3.00	6.00
3 Dick Donovan	1.50	3.00
4 Nellie Fox	5.00	10.00
5 Billy Goodman	2.00	4.00
6 Jim Landis	1.50	3.00
7 Sherm Lollar	1.50	3.00
8 Al Lopez MG	3.00	6.00
9 Bubba Phillips	1.50	3.00
10 Billy Pierce	3.00	6.00
11 Al Smith	1.50	3.00
12 Early Wynn	5.00	10.00

1960 White Sox Jay Publishing

This 12-card set of the Chicago White Sox measures approximately 5" by 7" and features black-and-white player photos in a white border. These cards were packaged 12 to a packet. The backs are blank. The cards are unnumbered and checklisted below in alphabetical order.

COMPLETE SET (12)	20.00	50.00
1 Luis Aparicio	4.00	10.00
2 Nelson Fox	4.00	10.00
3 Gene Freese	.75	2.00
4 Ted Kluszewski	1.50	4.00
5 Jim Landis	.75	2.00
6 Sherman Lollar	.75	2.00
7 Al Lopez MG	1.50	4.00
8 Minnie Minoso	1.50	4.00
9 Bob Shaw	.75	2.00
10 Roy Sievers	1.00	2.50
11 Al Smith	.75	2.00
12 Early Wynn	4.00	10.00

1960 White Sox Ticket Stubs

This set was the brainchild of famed owner Bill Veeck. Player's photos were put on a ticket stub so they could be collected. The players marked UNC below in the checklist are unconfirmed at this time and may not exist. These tickets come in mulitple colors. No extra value is attached for any color.

COMPLETE SET	50.00	100.00
1 Luis Aparicio	3.00	8.00
2 Earl Battey UNC	1.50	4.00
3 Frank Baumann	1.50	4.00
4 Dick Donovan	1.50	4.00
5 Nelson Fox	6.00	15.00
6 Gene Freese	1.50	4.00
7 Billy Goodman UNC	1.50	4.00
8 Ted Kluzewski	3.00	8.00
9 Jim Landis	1.50	4.00
10 Barry Latman	1.50	4.00
11 Sherman Lollar	1.50	4.00
12 Al Lopez MG	2.50	6.00
13 Turk Lown	1.50	4.00
14 Minnie Minoso	3.00	8.00
15 Billy Pierce	2.50	6.00
16 Jim Rivera	1.50	4.00
17 Bob Shaw	1.50	4.00
18 Roy Sievers	2.00	5.00
19 Al Smith	1.50	4.00
20 Gerry Staley	1.50	4.00
21 Earl Torgeson UNC	1.50	4.00
22 Early Wynn	3.00	8.00

1961 White Sox Jay Publishing

This 12-card set of the Chicago White Sox measures approximately 5" by 7". The fronts feature black-and-white posed player photos with the player's and team name printed below in the white border. These cards were packaged 12 in a packet. The backs are blank. The cards are unnumbered and checklisted below in alphabetical order.

COMPLETE SET (12)	4.00	10.00
1 Luis Aparicio	2.00	5.00
2 Frank Baumann	.60	1.50
3 Nellie Fox	2.00	5.00
4 Jim Landis	.60	1.50
5 Al Lopez MG	1.25	3.00
6 Sherm Lollar	.60	1.50
7 Minnie Minoso	1.25	3.00
8 Billy Pierce	1.00	2.50
9 Roy Sievers	.75	2.00
10 Al Smith	.60	1.50
11 Gerry Staley	.60	1.50
12 Early Wynn	2.00	5.00

1961 White Sox Rainbow Orchard Laundry Cleaners

This Pizzaro card is assumed to be part of a 20 card set. When unfolded the card measures 19 1/2" by 2 1/2" and has the player's photo on it as well as the 1961 White Sox home schedule. Since it is assumed this is part of a set any additions to this checklist is appreciated

9 Juan Pizzaro	20.00	50.00

1961 White Sox Ticket Stubs

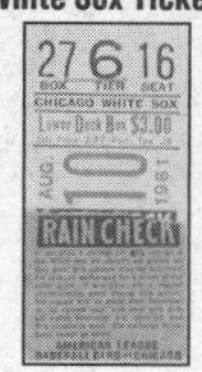

For the second year, the White Sox placed player photos on ticket stubs to promote interest in their players.

COMPLETE SET	40.00	80.00
1 Luis Aparicio	2.50	6.00
2 Frank Baumann	1.25	3.00
3 Cam Carreon	1.25	3.00
4 Sam Esposito	1.25	3.00
5 Nelson Fox	4.00	10.00
6 Jim Landis	1.25	3.00
7 Sherm Lollar	1.25	3.00
8 Al Lopez MG	2.00	5.00
9 Cal McLish	1.25	3.00
10 J.C. Martin	1.25	3.00
11 Minnie Minoso	2.50	6.00
12 Billy Pierce	2.00	5.00
13 Juan Pizarro	1.25	3.00
14 Bob Roselli	1.25	3.00
15 Herb Score	2.00	5.00
16 Bob Shaw	1.25	3.00
17 Roy Sievers	1.50	4.00
18 Al Smith	1.25	3.00
19 Gerry Staley	1.25	3.00
20 Early Wynn	3.00	8.00

1962 White Sox Jay Publishing

This 12-card set of the Chicago White Sox measures approximately 5" by 7". The fronts feature black-and-white posed player photos with the player's and team name printed below in the white border. These cards were packaged 12 to a packet. The backs are blank. The cards are unnumbered and checklisted below in alphabetical order.

COMPLETE SET (12)	20.00	50.00
1 Luis Aparicio	4.00	10.00
2 Frank Baumann	1.00	2.50
3 Nellie Fox	4.00	10.00
4 Russ Kemmerer	1.00	2.50
5 Jim Landis	1.00	2.50
6 Sherm Lollar	1.00	2.50
7 Al Lopez MG	2.00	5.00
8 Joe Martin	1.00	2.50
9 Juan Pizzaro	1.00	2.50
10 Floyd Robinson	1.00	2.50
11 Al Smith	1.00	2.50
12 Early Wynn	4.00	10.00

1962 White Sox Ticket Stubs

This stubs featured White Sox players. The stubs had the player photo imprinted so fans could have more keepsakes of their favorite players.

COMPLETE SET	50.00	100.00
1 Luis Aparicio	3.00	8.00
2 Frank Baumann	1.50	4.00
3 John Buzhardt	1.50	4.00
4 Camilo Carreon	1.50	4.00
5 Joe Cunningham	2.00	5.00
6 Bob Farley	1.50	4.00
7 Eddie Fisher	1.50	4.00
8 Nelson Fox	3.00	8.00
9 Jim Landis	1.50	4.00
10 Sherm Lollar	2.00	5.00
11 Al Lopez MG	2.50	6.00
12 Turk Lown	1.50	4.00
13 J.C. Martin	1.50	4.00
14 Cal McLish	1.50	4.00
15 Gary Peters	2.00	5.00
16 Juan Pizarro	1.50	4.00
17 Floyd Robinson	1.50	4.00
18 Bob Roselli	1.50	4.00
19 Herb Score	2.50	6.00
20 Al Smith	1.50	4.00
21 Charles Smith	1.50	4.00
22 Early Wynn	3.00	8.00

1963 White Sox Jay Publishing

This 12-card set of the Chicago White Sox measures approximately 5" by 7". The fronts feature black-and-white posed player photos with the player's and team name printed below in the white border. These cards were packaged 12 to a packet. The backs are blank. The cards are unnumbered and checklisted below in alphabetical order.

COMPLETE SET (12)	12.50	30.00
1 Frank Baumann	.75	2.00
2 Camilio Carreon	.75	2.00
3 Joe Cunningham	.75	2.00
4 Sam Esposito	.75	2.00
5 Nellie Fox	3.00	8.00
6 Ray Herbert	.75	2.00
7 Joel Horlen	1.00	2.50
8 Jim Landis	.75	2.00
9 Sherm Lollar	.75	2.00
10 Al Lopez MG	1.50	4.00
11 Juan Pizarro	.75	2.00
12 Floyd Robinson	.75	2.00

1963 White Sox Ticket Stubs

Again, the White Sox featured player photos on their ticket stubs. These photos were originally the idea of Hall of Famer Bill Vecck, but the promotion continued even after he had sold all his interest in the White Sox.

COMPLETE SET	40.00	80.00
1 Frank Baumann	1.25	3.00
2 John Buzhardt	1.25	3.00
3 Camilo Carreon	1.25	3.00
4 Joe Cunningham	1.50	4.00
5 Dave DeBusschere	2.00	5.00
6 Eddie Fisher	1.25	3.00
7 Nelson Fox	4.00	10.00
8 Ron Hansen	1.25	3.00
9 Ray Herbert	1.25	3.00
10 Mike Hershberger	1.25	3.00
11 Joel Horlen	1.50	4.00
12 Grover Jones	1.25	3.00
13 Mike Joyce	1.25	3.00
14 Frank Kreutzer	1.25	3.00
15 Jim Landis	1.25	3.00
16 Sherm Lollar	1.25	3.00
17 Al Lopez MG	2.50	6.00
18 J.C. Martin	1.25	3.00
19 Charlie Maxwell	1.25	3.00
20 Dave Nicholson	1.25	3.00
21 Juan Pizarro	1.25	3.00
22 Floyd Robinson	1.25	3.00
23 Charlie Smith	1.25	3.00
24 Pete Ward	1.25	3.00
25 Al Weis	1.25	3.00
26 Hoyt Wilhelm	4.00	10.00
27 Dom Zanni	1.25	3.00

1964 White Sox Iron-Ons

This 27-card set of the Chicago White Sox features head player drawings that could be ironed on various items and articles of clothing. The set was distributed in packages of three sheets with nine players to a sheet. One sheet displayed blue heads, another red, and another black. The cards are unnumbered and checklisted below in alphabetical order.

COMPLETE SET (27)	10.00	25.00
1 Fritz Ackley	.40	1.00
2 Frank Bauman	.40	1.00
3 Jim Brosnan	.75	2.00
4 Don Buford	.40	1.00

5 John Buzhardt	.40	1.00
6 Camilo Carreon	.40	1.00
7 Joe Cunningham	.40	1.00
8 Dave DeBusschere	1.50	4.00
9 Ed Fisher	.40	1.00
10 Jim Golden	.40	1.00
11 Ron Hansen	.40	1.00
12 Ray Herbert	.40	1.00
13 Mike Hershberger	.40	1.00
14 Joel Horlen	.40	1.00
15 Mike Joyce	.40	1.00
16 Jim Landis	.40	1.00
17 J.C. Martin	.40	1.00
18 Charlie Maxwell	.40	1.00
19 Tom McGraw	.40	1.00
20 Dave Nicholson	.40	1.00
21 Gary Peters	.40	1.00
22 Floyd Robinson	.40	1.00
23 Gene Stephens	.40	1.00
24 Pete Ward	.40	1.00
25 Al Weis	.40	1.00
26 Hoyt Wilhelm	2.50	6.00
27 Team Logo	.40	1.00

1964 White Sox Jay Publishing

This 12-card set of the Chicago White Sox measures approximately 5" by 7". The fronts feature black-and-white posed player photos with the player's and team name printed below in the white border. These cards were packaged 12 to a packet. The backs are blank. The cards are unnumbered and checklisted below in alphabetical order.

COMPLETE SET (12)	15.00	40.00
1 Camilio Carreon	1.00	2.50
2 Joe Cunningham	1.25	3.00
3 Ron Hansen	1.00	2.50
4 Ray Herbert	1.00	2.50
5 Mike Hershberger	1.00	2.50
6 Joel Horlen	1.00	2.50
7 Jim Landis	1.00	2.50
8 Al Lopez MG	2.00	5.00
9 Dave Nicholson	1.00	2.50
10 Gary Peters	1.25	3.00
11 Juan Pizarro	1.25	3.00
12 Pete Ward	1.00	2.50

1964 White Sox Ticket Stubs

For the fifth consecutive year, White Sox players were featured on these collector strips. These stubs were issued so fans could have another way of collecting memorabilia of their favorite players.

COMPLETE SET	40.00	80.00
1 Fritz Ackley	1.25	3.00
2 Frank Baumann	1.25	3.00
3 Don Buford	1.25	3.00
4 John Buzhardt	1.25	3.00
5 Camilo Carreon	1.25	3.00
6 Joe Cunningham	1.25	3.00
7 Dave DeBusschere	2.00	5.00
8 Eddie Fisher	1.25	3.00
9 Jim Golden	1.25	3.00
10 Ron Hansen	1.25	3.00
11 Ray Herbert	1.25	3.00
12 Mike Hershberger	1.25	3.00
13 Joe Horlen	1.25	3.00
14 Jim Landis	1.25	3.00
15 Al Lopez MG	2.50	6.00
16 J.C. Martin	1.25	3.00
17 Dave Nicholson	1.25	3.00
18 Gary Peters	1.50	4.00
19 Juan Pizarro	1.25	3.00
20 Floyd Robinson	1.25	3.00
21 Gene Stephens	1.25	3.00
22 Pete Ward	1.50	4.00
23 Hoyt Wilhelm	3.00	8.00

1965 White Sox Jay Publishing

This 12-card set of the Chicago White Sox measures approximately 5" by 7". The fronts feature black-and-white posed player photos with the player's and team name printed below in the white border. These cards were packaged 12 to a packet. The backs are blank. The cards are unnumbered and checklisted below in alphabetical order.

COMPLETE SET (12)	15.00	40.00
1 Ron Hansen	1.00	2.50
2 Al Lopez MG	2.00	5.00
3 J.C. Martin	1.00	2.50
4 Tom McCraw	1.00	2.50
5 Dave Nicholson	1.00	2.50
6 Gary Peters	1.25	3.00
7 Juan Pizarro	1.00	2.50
8 Floyd Robinson	1.00	2.50
9 John Romano	1.00	2.50
10 Bill Skowron	1.25	3.00
11 Pete Ward	1.00	2.50
12 Hoyt Wilhelm	4.00	10.00

1966 White Sox Team Issue

This 12-card set of the Chicago White Sox measures 4 7/8" by 7" and features black-and-white player photos in a white border with blank backs. These cards were originally packaged 12 to a packet. The cards are unnumbered and checklisted below in alphabetical order.

COMPLETE SET (12)	10.00	25.00
1 Tommy Agee	1.00	2.50
2 John Buzhardt	.75	2.00
3 Don Buford	.75	2.00
4 Joel Horlen	.75	2.00
5 Tommy John	1.50	4.00
6 Bob Locker	.75	2.00
7 Gary Peters	.75	2.00
8 Juan Pizarro	.75	2.00
9 Floyd Robinson	.75	2.00
10 Johnny Romano	.75	2.00
11 Bill Skowron	1.25	3.00
12 Eddie Stanky MG	.75	2.00

1967 White Sox Team Issue

This 12-card set of the Chicago White Sox measures 4 7/8" by 7" and features black-and-white player photos in a white border with blank backs. These cards were originally packaged 12 to a packet. The cards are unnumbered and checklisted below in alphabetical order.

COMPLETE SET (12)	10.00	25.00
1 Jerry Adair	.75	2.00
2 Tom Agee	.75	2.00
3 Ken Berry	.75	2.00
4 Don Buford	.75	2.00
5 Ron Hansen	.75	2.00
6 Joe Horlen	.75	2.00
7 Tommy John	1.50	4.00
8 Duane Josephson	.75	2.00
9 Tom McCraw	.75	2.00
10 Gary Peters	.75	2.00
11 Ed Stanky MG	.75	2.00
12 Pete Ward	.75	2.00

1969 White Sox Team Issue Black and White

This 12-card set of the Chicago White Sox measures approximately 4 1/4" by 7". The fronts display black-and-white player portraits bordered in white. The player's name and team are printed in the top margin. The backs are blank. The cards are unnumbered and checklisted below in alphabetical order.

COMPLETE SET (12)	8.00	20.00
1 Sandy Alomar	.75	2.00
2 Luis Aparicio	1.50	4.00
3 Ken Berry	.60	1.50
4 Charles Bradford	.60	1.50
5 Joe Horlen	.60	1.50
6 Tommy John	1.00	2.50
7 Duane Josephson	.60	1.50
8 Al Lopez	1.25	3.00
9 Carlos May	.60	1.50
10 Bill Melton	.60	1.50
11 Gary Peters	.75	2.00
12 Pete Ward	.60	1.50

1969 White Sox Team Issue Color

Similar to the Jewel food store issues, these color photos measure approximately 5" by 7" and feature members of the 1969 Chicago White Sox. Since these are unnumbered, we have sequenced them in alphabetical order.

COMPLETE SET	12.50	30.00
1 Luis Aparicio	2.50	6.00
2 Ken Berry	.75	2.00
3 Buddy Bradford	.75	2.00
4 Kerby Farrell CO	.75	2.00
5 Don Gutteridge MG	.75	2.00
6 Ed Herrmann	.75	2.00
7 Gail Hopkins	.75	2.00
8 Joel Horlen	.75	2.00
9 Tommy John	1.50	4.00
10 Duane Josephson	.75	2.00
11 Carlos May	.75	2.00
12 Rich Morales	.75	2.00
13 Bill Melton	.75	2.00
14 Dan Osinski	.75	2.00
15 Gary Peters	1.00	2.50
16 Wilbur Wood	1.00	2.50

1970 White Sox Team Issue

This 12-card set of the Chicago White Sox measures approximately 4 1/4" by 7" and features black-and-white player photos in a white border. Packaged 12 to a packet with blank backs, the cards are unnumbered and checklisted below in alphabetical order.

COMPLETE SET (12)	10.00	25.00
1 Luis Aparicio	2.50	6.00
2 Ken Berry	.75	2.00
3 Charles Bradford	.75	2.00
4 Don Gutteridge MG	.75	2.00
5 Gail Hopkins	.75	2.00
6 Joe Horlen	.75	2.00
7 Tommy John	1.50	4.00
8 Duane Josephson	.75	2.00
9 Bobby Knoop	.75	2.00
10 Carlos May	.75	2.00
11 Bill Melton	.75	2.00
12 Walter Williams	.75	2.00

1972 White Sox

The 1972 Chicago White Sox are featured in this set of 12 approximately 7 1/2" by 9 3/8" glossy color player photos. The photos are bordered in white, and the player's name is given below the picture. The backs are blank and the photos are checklisted below in alphabetical order.

COMPLETE SET (12)	15.00	40.00
1 Dick Allen	2.00	5.00
2 Stan Bahnsen	1.25	3.00
3 Terry Forster	1.50	4.00
4 Ken Henderson	1.25	3.00
5 Ed Herrmann	1.25	3.00
6 Pat Kelly	1.25	3.00
7 Eddie Leon	1.25	3.00
8 Carlos May	1.25	3.00
9 Bill Melton	1.50	4.00
10 Jorge Orta	1.25	3.00
11 Steve Stone	1.50	4.00
12 Wilbur Wood	1.50	4.00

1972 White Sox Chi-Foursome

These drawings feature members of the Chicago White Sox. These drawings measure 11" by 14" and also have the player's fascimile signature. The backs are blank and we have sequenced this set in alphabetical order.

COMPLETE SET (7)	15.00	40.00
1 Mike Andrews	2.00	5.00
2 Ed Herrmann	2.00	5.00
3 Pat Kelly	2.00	5.00
4 Carlos May	2.50	6.00
5 Bill Melton	2.50	6.00
6 Chuck Tanner MG	2.50	6.00
7 Wilbur Wood	3.00	8.00

1972 White Sox Durochrome Stickers

These stickers measure 3 1/2" by 4 1/2". They are unnumbered and we have sequenced them in alphabetical order.

COMPLETE SET (6)	5.00	12.00
1 Dick Allen	1.50	4.00
2 Ed Herrmann	.60	1.50
3 Bart Johnson	.60	1.50
4 Carlos May	.60	1.50
5 Bill Melton	.75	2.00
6 Wilbur Wood	1.25	3.00

1972 White Sox Team Issue

These cards measure 4 1/4" by 7" and were issued in groups of 12. The fronts feature a player photo against a white border along with the player's name and team on the bottom. The backs are blank. These cards were issued continually throughout the year so there is not an exact number divisible by 12.

COMPLETE SET	20.00	50.00
1 Dick Allen	2.50	6.00
2 Mike Andrews	1.25	3.00
3 Stan Bahnsen	1.50	4.00
4 Tom Bradley	1.25	3.00
5 Tom Egan	1.25	3.00
6 Terry Forster	1.50	4.00
7 Ed Herrmann	1.25	3.00
8 Jay Johnstone	1.50	4.00
9 Pat Kelly	1.25	3.00
10 Carlos May	1.25	3.00
10 Rick Reichardt	1.25	3.00
11 Bill Melton	1.50	4.00
12 Jorge Orta	1.25	3.00
13 Chuck Tanner MG	1.25	3.00
14 Walt Williams	1.25	3.00
15A Wilbur Wood UER/(Says Wilber on card)	2.00	5.00
15B Wilbur Wood COR	2.00	5.00

1973 White Sox Jewel

These 6 1/2" by 9 1/2" blank-backed, white bordered, full-color photos were issued as a premium by Jewel Foods. The photos have a fascimile autograph and since they are unnumbered we have sequenced them in alphabetical order.

COMPLETE SET	8.00	20.00
1 Dick Allen	1.25	3.00
2 Mike Andrews	.60	1.50
3 Stan Bahnsen	.60	1.50
4 Eddie Fisher	.60	1.50
5 Terry Forster	.60	1.50
6 Ken Henderson	.60	1.50
7 Ed Herrmann	.60	1.50
8 Johnny Jeter	.60	1.50
9 Pat Kelly	.60	1.50
10 Eddie Leon	.60	1.50
11 Carlos May	.60	1.50
12 Bill Melton	.60	1.50
13 Tony Muser	.60	1.50
14 Jorge Orta	.60	1.50
15 Rick Reichardt	.60	1.50
16 Wilbur Wood	.75	2.00

1973 White Sox Team Issue

Measuring approximately 7" by 8 3/4" these blank-backed photos were issued to promote some of the leading players of the White Sox. The full-color photos are surrounded by white borders with the player's name and team on the bottom. Since these photos are unnumbered, we have sequenced them in alphabetical order.

COMPLETE SET	4.00	10.00
1 Dick Allen	1.25	3.00
2 Stan Bahnsen	.60	1.50
3 Pat Kelly	.60	1.50
4 Carlos May	.60	1.50
5 Bill Melton	.60	1.50
6 Wilbur Wood UER Spelled Wilber	.75	2.00

1975 White Sox 1919 TCMA

This 28-card set features the 1919 Chicago White Sox Team. The fronts display black-and-white player photos while the backs carry player statistics. The set includes one team picture jumbo card which measures approximately 3 1/2" by 4 3/4". The cards are unnumbered and checklisted below in alphabetical order.

COMPLETE SET (28)	10.00	25.00
1 Joe Benz	.20	.50
2 Eddie Cicotte	.75	2.00
3 Eddie Collins	1.25	3.00
4 Shano Collins	.20	.50
5 Dave Danforth	.20	.50
6 Red Faber	.75	2.00
7 Happy Felsch	.60	1.50
8 Charles Chick Gandil	.60	1.50
9 Kid Gleason MG	.40	1.00
10 Joe Jackson	2.00	5.00
11 Bill James	.20	.50
12 Dickie Kerr	.40	1.00
13 Nemo Leibold	.20	.50
14 Byrd Lynn	.20	.50
15 Erskine Mayer	.20	.50
16 Harvey McClellan	.20	.50
17 Fred McMullin	.40	1.00

18 Eddie Murphy	.20	.50
19 Pat Ragan	.20	.50
20 Swede Risberg	.40	1.00
21 Charlie Robertson	.20	.50
22 Red Russell	.20	.50
23 Ray Schalk	.75	2.00
24 Frank Shellenback Grover Lowdermilk	.20	.50
25 Buck Weaver	.75	2.00
26 Roy Wilkinson	.20	.50
27 Lefty Williams	.60	1.50
28 Team Picture	.40	1.00

1976 White Sox TCMA All-Time Greats

This 12-card set of the All-Time Chicago White Sox Team features black-and-white player photos bordered in white with the player's name and position printed in red in the bottom margin. The white backs carry the roster of the team. The cards are unnumbered and checklisted below in alphabetical order.

COMPLETE SET (12)	4.00	10.00
1 Luke Appling	.40	1.00
2 Eddie Collins	.60	1.50
3 Harry Hooper	.40	1.00
4 Willie Kamm	.20	.50
5 Al Lopez MG	.30	.75
6 Ted Lyons	.40	1.00
7 Johnny Mostil	.20	.50
8 Billy Pierce	.30	.75
9 Eddie Robinson	.20	.50
10 Ray Schalk	.30	.75
11 Al Simmons	.60	1.50
12 Gerry Staley	.20	.50

1977 White Sox Jewel Tea

This 16-card set of the Chicago White Sox measures approximately 5 7/8" by 9". The white-bordered fronts feature color player head photos with a facsimile autograph below. The backs are blank. The cards are unnumbered and checklisted below in alphabetical order.

COMPLETE SET (16)	6.00	15.00
1 Alan Bannister	.40	1.00
2 Francisco Barrios	.40	1.00
3 Jim Essian	.40	1.00
4 Oscar Gamble	.60	1.50
5 Ralph Garr	.60	1.50
6 Lamar Johnson	.40	1.00
7 Chris Knapp	.40	1.00
8 Ken Kravec	.40	1.00
9 Lerrin LaGrow	.40	1.00
10 Chet Lemon	.60	1.50
11 Jorge Orta	.40	1.00
12 Eric Soderholm	.40	1.00
13 Jim Spencer	.40	1.00
14 Steve Stone	.60	1.50
15 Wilbur Wood	.40	1.00
16 Richie Zisk	.60	1.50

1977 White Sox Tribune

These portraits were issued as inserts in the Chicago Tribune newpaper and were issued two at a time. One player pictured was a Chicago Cub and another was a Chicago White Sox. The photos are black and white and are posed head shots, the bottom of the photo features statistics up to that time. The photos are unnumbered so we have sequenced them in alphabetical order.

COMPLETE SET	10.00	25.00
1 Alan Bannister	.40	1.00
2 Francisco Barrios	.40	1.00
3 Kevin Bell	.40	1.00
4 Jack Brohamer	.40	1.00
5 Bruce Dal Canton	.40	1.00
6 Brian Downing	.60	1.50
7 Jim Essian	.40	1.00
8 Oscar Gamble	.60	1.50
9 Ralph Garr	.40	1.00
10 Dave Hamilton	.40	1.00
11 Bart Johnson	.40	1.00
12 Lamar Johnson	.40	1.00
13 Don Kirkwood	.40	1.00
14 Chris Knapp	.40	1.00
15 Ken Kravec	.40	1.00
16 Jack Kucek	.40	1.00
17 Lerrin LaGrow	.40	1.00
18 Chet Lemon	.40	1.00
19 Tim Nordbrook	.40	1.00
20 Wayne Nordhagen	.40	1.00
21 Jorge Orta	.40	1.00
22 Eric Soderholm	.40	1.00
23 Jim Spencer	.40	1.00
24 Royle Stillman	.40	1.00
25 Steve Stone	.60	1.50
26 Wilbur Wood	.60	1.50
27 Richie Zisk	.40	1.00

1980 White Sox Greats TCMA

This 12-card standard-size set features various all-time White Sox greats. The fronts display a player photo, while the backs carry information about the player.

COMPLETE SET (12)	2.00	5.00
1 Ted Lyons	.30	.75
2 Eddie Collins	.40	1.00
3 Al Lopez MG	.20	.50
4 Luke Appling	.40	1.00
5 Billy Pierce	.20	.50
6 Willie Kamm	.08	.25
7 Johnny Mostil	.08	.25
8 Al Simmons	.30	.75
9 Ray Schalk	.30	.75
10 Gerry Staley	.08	.25
11 Harry Hooper	.30	.75
12 Eddie Robinson	.08	.25

1978 Wiffle Ball Discs

These discs were on the side of Wiffle Ball boxes. Even though the copyright date on the discs are 1976, the player selection implies that this set was issued early in 1978. For some reason, Thurman Munson discs seem to be available in significantly higher quantities and we have labeled Munson as a DP. These discs are ununumbered and we have sequenced this set in alphabetical order.

COMPLETE SET	175.00	350.00
COMMON PLAYER	.75	2.00
1 Sal Bando	1.00	2.50
2 Buddy Bell	1.25	3.00
3 Johnny Bench	3.00	8.00
4 Vida Blue	1.00	2.50
5 Bert Blyleven	1.25	3.00
6 Bobby Bonds	1.00	2.50
7 George Brett	10.00	25.00
8 Lou Brock	2.50	6.00
9 Bill Buckner	1.00	2.50
10 Ray Burris	.75	2.00
11 Jeff Burroughs	.75	2.00
12 Campy Campaneris	1.00	2.50
13 Rod Carew	2.50	6.00
14 Steve Carlton	2.50	6.00
15 Dave Cash	.75	2.00
16 Cesar Cedeno	1.00	2.50
17 Ron Cey	1.25	3.00
18 Chris Chambliss	.75	2.00
19 Dave Concepcion	1.25	3.00
20 Dennis Eckersley	2.50	6.00
21 Mark Fidrych	2.00	5.00
22 Rollie Fingers	2.50	6.00
23 Carlton Fisk	4.00	10.00
24 George Foster	1.00	2.50
25 Wayne Garland	.75	2.00
26 Ralph Garr	.75	2.00
27 Steve Garvey	2.00	5.00
28 Don Gullett	.75	2.00
29 Larry Hisle	.75	2.00
30 Al Hrabosky	.75	2.00
31 Catfish Hunter	2.50	6.00
32 Reggie Jackson	5.00	12.00
33 Randy Jones	.75	2.00
34 Dave Kingman	1.50	4.00
35 Jerry Koosman	1.25	3.00
36 Ed Kranepool	.75	2.00
37 Ron LeFlore	1.00	2.50
38 Sixto Lezcano	.75	2.00
39 Davey Lopes	1.00	2.50
40 Greg Luzinski	1.25	3.00
41 Fred Lynn	1.00	2.50
42 Garry Maddox	.75	2.00
43 Jon Matlack	.75	2.00
44 Gary Matthews	1.00	2.50
45 Lee May	1.00	2.50
46 John Mayberry	.75	2.00
47 Bake McBride	.75	2.00
48 Tug McGraw	1.25	3.00
49 Hal McRae	1.00	2.50
50 Andy Messersmith	.75	2.00
51 Randy Moffitt	.75	2.00
52 John Montefusco	.75	2.00
53 Joe Morgan	2.50	6.00
54 Thurman Munson DP	4.00	10.00
55 Graig Nettles	1.25	3.00
56 Al Oliver	1.00	2.50
57 Jorge Orta	.75	2.00
58 Jim Palmer	2.50	6.00
59 Dave Parker	1.50	4.00
60 Tony Perez	2.00	5.00
61 Gaylord Perry	2.50	6.00
62 Jim Rice	1.50	4.00
63 Steve Rogers	.75	2.00
64 Pete Rose	15.00	40.00
65 Joe Rudi	.75	2.00
66 Nolan Ryan	15.00	40.00
67 Manny Sanguillen	.75	2.00
68 Mike Schmidt	5.00	12.00
69 Tom Seaver	5.00	12.00
70 Ted Simmons	1.25	3.00
71 Reggie Smith	1.00	2.50
72 Willie Stargell	5.00	12.00
73 Rusty Staub	1.25	3.00
74 Rennie Stennett	.75	2.00
75 Frank Tanana	1.00	2.50
76 Gene Tenace	.75	2.00
77 Luis Tiant	1.25	3.00
78 Manny Trillo	.75	2.00
79 Bob Watson	1.00	2.50
80 Carl Yastrzemski	8.00	20.00
81 Richie Zisk	1.00	2.50

1963 Wilhelm Motel

This one card postcard set was issued on November 2, 1963 to commemorate the opening of a motel in Georgia that Wilhelm had a stake in. The front of the postcard shows a photo of Wilhelm warming up in front of the White Sox dugout while the back has an ad for the motel.

1 Hoyt Wilhelm	4.00	10.00

1923 Willard's Chocolates V100

Issued in Canada by Willards Chocolates, these 180 blank-backed cards measure approximately 2" by 3 1/4". The catalog designation for this set is V100. The white-bordered fronts feature sepia-tone player photos. The player's facsimile autograph appears on the card face. The cards are unnumbered and checklisted below in alphabetical order.

COMPLETE SET (180)	5,250.00	10,500.00
1 Babe Adams	40.00	80.00
2 Grover C. Alexander	100.00	200.00
3 James Austin MG	30.00	60.00
4 Jim Bagby	30.00	60.00
5 Frank Baker	60.00	120.00
6 Dave Bancroft	60.00	120.00
7 Turner Barber	30.00	60.00
8 Jesse L. Barnes	30.00	60.00
9 John Bassler	30.00	60.00
10 Lu Blue	30.00	60.00
11 Norman Boekel	30.00	60.00
12 Frank Brazill	30.00	60.00
13 George H. Burns	30.00	60.00
14 George J. Burns	30.00	60.00
15 Leon Cadore	40.00	80.00
16 Max Carey	60.00	120.00
17 Harold G. Carlson	30.00	60.00
18 Lloyd Christenberry	30.00	60.00
19 Vernon J. Clemons	30.00	60.00
20 Ty Cobb	500.00	1,000.00
21 Bert Cole	30.00	60.00
22 John F. Collins	30.00	60.00
23 Stan Coveleski	60.00	120.00
24 Walton E. Cruise	30.00	60.00
25 George W. Cutshaw	30.00	60.00
26 Jake Daubert	40.00	80.00
27 George Dauss	30.00	60.00
28 Frank Davis	30.00	60.00
29 Charles A. Deal	30.00	60.00
30 William L. Doak	30.00	60.00
31 Wild Bill Donovan MG	30.00	60.00
32 Hugh Duffy MG	60.00	120.00
33 Joe Dugan	40.00	80.00
34 Louis B. Duncan	30.00	60.00
35 Jimmy Dykes	40.00	80.00
36 Howard Ehmke	40.00	80.00
37 Francis R. Ellerbe	30.00	60.00
38 Eric G. Erickson	30.00	60.00
39 Johnny Evers MG	60.00	120.00
40 Urban Faber	60.00	120.00
41 Bibb Falk	30.00	60.00
42 Max Flack	30.00	60.00
43 Lee Fohl MG	30.00	60.00
44 Jack Fournier	30.00	60.00
45 Frank Frisch	60.00	120.00
46 C.E. Galloway	30.00	60.00
47 Billy Gardner	30.00	60.00
48 Edward Gharrity	30.00	60.00
49 George Gibson	30.00	60.00
50 Kid Gleason MG	50.00	100.00
51 William Gleason	30.00	60.00
52 Hank Gowdy	40.00	80.00
53 I.M. Griffin	30.00	60.00
54 Thomas Griffith	30.00	60.00
55 Burleigh Grimes	60.00	120.00
56 Charlie Grimm	40.00	80.00
57 Jesse Haines	60.00	120.00
58 Bill Harris	30.00	60.00
59 Bucky Harris	60.00	120.00
60 Robert Hasty	30.00	60.00
61 Harry Heilmann	60.00	120.00
62 Walter Henline	30.00	60.00
63 Walter Holke	30.00	60.00
64 Charles Hollocher	30.00	60.00
65 Harry Hooper	60.00	120.00
66 Rogers Hornsby	150.00	300.00
67 Waite Hoyt	60.00	120.00
68 Miller Huggins MG	60.00	120.00
69 W.C. Jacobson	30.00	60.00
70 Charlie Jamieson	30.00	60.00
71 E. Johnson	30.00	60.00
72 Walter Johnson	250.00	500.00
73 James H. Johnston	30.00	60.00
74 Bob Jones	30.00	60.00
75 Sam Jones	40.00	80.00
76 Joe Judge	40.00	80.00
77 James W. Keenan	30.00	60.00
78 Geo. L. Kelly	60.00	120.00
79 Peter J. Kilduff	30.00	60.00
80 William Killefer	30.00	60.00
81 Lee King	30.00	60.00
82 Ray Kolp	30.00	60.00
83 John Lavan	30.00	60.00
84 Nemo Leibold	30.00	60.00
85 Connie Mack MG	100.00	200.00
86 Duster Mails	30.00	60.00
87 Walter Maranville	60.00	120.00
88 Richard W. Marquard	60.00	120.00
89 Carl W. Mays	40.00	80.00
90 Geo. F. McBride	30.00	60.00
91 Harvey McClellan	30.00	60.00
92 John J. McGraw MG	75.00	150.00
93 Austin B. McHenry	30.00	60.00
94 Snuffy McInnis	40.00	80.00
95 Douglas McWeeny	30.00	60.00
96 Mike Menosky	30.00	60.00
97 Emil F. Meusel	30.00	60.00
98 Bob Meusel	40.00	80.00
99 Henry W. Meyers	30.00	60.00
100 Clyde Milan MG	40.00	80.00
101 John K. Miljus	30.00	60.00
102 Edmund J. Miller	40.00	80.00
103 Elmer Miller	30.00	60.00
104 Otto L. Miller	30.00	60.00
105 Fred Mitchell MG	30.00	60.00
106 Geo. Mogridge	30.00	60.00
107 Patrick J. Moran MG	30.00	60.00
108 John D. Morrison	30.00	60.00
109 Johnny Mostil	30.00	60.00
110 Clarence F. Mueller	30.00	60.00
111 Greasy Neale	50.00	100.00
112 Joseph Oeschger	30.00	60.00
113 Robert J. O'Farrell	30.00	60.00
114 John Oldham	30.00	60.00
115 Ivy Olson	30.00	60.00
116 Geo. M. O'Neil	30.00	60.00
117 Steve O'Neill	40.00	80.00
118 Frank J. Parkinson	30.00	60.00
119 Dode Paskert	30.00	60.00
120 Roger Peckinpaugh	40.00	80.00
121 Herb Pennock	60.00	120.00
122 Ralph Perkins	30.00	60.00
123 Jeff Pfeffer	30.00	60.00
124 Wally Pipp	40.00	80.00
125 Charles Ponder	30.00	60.00
126 Raymond R. Powell	30.00	60.00
127 Del Pratt	30.00	60.00
128 Joseph Rapp	30.00	60.00
129 John H. Rawlings	30.00	60.00
130 Edgar Rice	60.00	120.00
131 Branch Rickey MG	75.00	150.00
132 James J. Ring	30.00	60.00
133 Eppa J. Rixey	60.00	120.00
134 Davis A. Robertson	30.00	60.00
135 Edwin Rommel	40.00	80.00
136 Edd J. Roush	60.00	120.00
137 Harold Ruel	30.00	60.00
138 Allen Russell	30.00	60.00
139 Babe Ruth	750.00	1,500.00
140 Wilfred D. Ryan	30.00	60.00
141 Henry F. Sallee	30.00	60.00
142 Wally Schang	40.00	80.00
143 Raymond H. Schmandt	30.00	60.00
144 Everett Scott	40.00	80.00
145 Henry Severeid	30.00	60.00
146 Joseph W. Sewell	60.00	120.00
147 Howard S. Shanks	30.00	60.00
148 Earl Sheely	30.00	60.00
149 Ralph Shinners	30.00	60.00
150 Urban J. Shocker	40.00	80.00
151 George H. Sisler	75.00	150.00
152 Earl L. Smith	30.00	60.00
153 Earl S. Smith	30.00	60.00
154 George A. Smith	30.00	60.00
155 John Smith	30.00	60.00
156 Tris Speaker MG	100.00	200.00
157 Arnold Staatz	30.00	60.00
158 Riggs Stephenson	50.00	100.00
159 Milton J. Stock	30.00	60.00
160 John L. Sullivan	30.00	60.00
161 Herb Thormahlen	30.00	60.00
162 James A. Tierney	30.00	60.00
163 John Tobin	30.00	60.00
164 James L. Vaughn	30.00	60.00
165 Bobby Veach	30.00	60.00
166 Tilly Walker	30.00	60.00
167 Aaron Ward	30.00	60.00
168 Zack D. Wheat	60.00	120.00
169 George B. Whitted	30.00	60.00
170 Irvin K. Wilhelm	30.00	60.00
171 Roy H. Wilkinson	30.00	60.00
172 Fred C. Williams	40.00	80.00
173 Ken Williams	40.00	80.00
174 Samuel W. Wilson	30.00	60.00
175 Ivy B. Wingo	30.00	60.00
176 Whitey Witt	40.00	80.00
177 Joseph Wood	50.00	100.00
178 Clarence Yaryan	30.00	60.00
179 Ralph Young	30.00	60.00
180 Ross Youngs	60.00	120.00

1924 Willard's Chocolates Sports Champions V122

2 Eddie Collins
5 Babe Ruth
39 Ty Cobb

1922 William Paterson V89

This 50-card set was inserted in packages of caramel candy. The cards measure approximately 2" by 3 1/4". the fronts feature sepia-toned player photos framed by white borders. The following information appears in the bottom border beneath the picture: card number, player's name, team name and imprint information (Wm. Paterson, Limited; Brantford, Canada). The backs are blank.

COMPLETE SET (50)	3,000.00	6,000.00
1 Ed Roush	200.00	400.00
2 Rube Marquard	200.00	400.00

3 Del Gainer	100.00	200.00
4 George Sisler	200.00	400.00
5 Joe Bush	125.00	250.00
6 Joe Oeschger	100.00	200.00
7 Willie Kamm	100.00	200.00
8 John Watson	100.00	200.00
9 Adolfo Luque	125.00	250.00
10 Miller Huggins MG	200.00	400.00
11 Wally Schang	125.00	250.00
12 Bob Shawkey	125.00	250.00
13 Tris Speaker MG	200.00	400.00
14 Hugh McQuillen	100.00	200.00
15 George Kelly	200.00	400.00
16 Ray Schalk	200.00	400.00
17 Sam Jones	125.00	250.00
18 Grover Alexander	400.00	800.00
19 Bob Meusel	150.00	300.00
20 Emil Meusel	100.00	200.00
21 Rogers Hornsby	500.00	1,000.00
22 Harry Heilmann	200.00	400.00
23 Heinie Groh	125.00	250.00
24 Frankie Frisch	200.00	400.00
25 Babe Ruth	3,000.00	6,000.00
26 Jack Bentley	100.00	200.00
27 Everett Scott	100.00	200.00
28 Max Carey	200.00	400.00
29 Chick Fewster	100.00	200.00
30 Cy Williams	125.00	250.00
31 Burleigh Grimes	200.00	400.00
32 Waite Hoyt	200.00	400.00
33 Frank Snyder	100.00	200.00
34 Clyde Milan MG	100.00	200.00
35 Eddie Collins	200.00	400.00
36 Travis Jackson	200.00	400.00
37 Ken Williams	125.00	250.00
38 Dave Bancroft	200.00	400.00
39 Mike McNally	100.00	200.00
40 John McGraw MG	400.00	800.00
41 Art Nehf	125.00	250.00
42 Rabbit Maranville	200.00	400.00
43 Charlie Grimm	125.00	250.00
44 Joe Judge	125.00	250.00
45 Wally Pipp	125.00	250.00
46 Ty Cobb	1,500.00	3,000.00
47 Walter Johnson	600.00	1,200.00
48 Jake Daubert	100.00	200.00
49 Zach Wheat	200.00	400.00
50 Herb Pennock	200.00	400.00

1910 Williams Caramel E103

The cards in this 30-card set measure 1 1/2" by 2 3/4". E103 is distinctive for its black and white player portraits set onto a solid red background. Player names and teams are listed below each photo, with "Williams", the manufacturer's name, in the line below. Printed on thin cardboard, the blank back Williams set was released to the public about 1910. Since the cards are unnumbered, they are ordered below alphabetically

COMPLETE SET (30)	60,000.00	120,000.00
1 Chas. Bender	2,000.00	4,000.00
2 Roger Bresnahan	2,000.00	4,000.00
3 Mordecai Brown	2,000.00	4,000.00
4 Frank Chance	2,000.00	4,000.00
5 Hal Chase	1,500.00	3,000.00
6 Ty Cobb	15,000.00	30,000.00
7 Eddie Collins	2,500.00	5,000.00
8 Sam Crawford	2,000.00	4,000.00
9 Harry Davis	1,000.00	2,000.00
10 Arthur Devlin	1,000.00	2,000.00
11 William Donovan	1,000.00	2,000.00
12 Chas. Dooin	1,000.00	2,000.00
13 Larry Doyle	1,500.00	3,000.00
14 John Ewing	1,000.00	2,000.00
15 George Gibson	1,000.00	2,000.00
16 Hugh Jennings	2,000.00	4,000.00
17 David Jones	1,000.00	2,000.00
18 Tim Jordon	1,000.00	2,000.00
19 Nap Lajoie	4,000.00	8,000.00
20 Thomas Leach	1,000.00	2,000.00
21 Harry Lord	1,000.00	2,000.00
22 Christy Mathewson	6,000.00	12,000.00
23 John McLean	1,000.00	2,000.00
24 George McQuillan	1,000.00	2,000.00
25 Jim Pastorious	1,000.00	2,000.00
26 Nap Rucker	1,250.00	2,500.00
27 Fred Tenney	1,000.00	2,000.00
28 Ira Thomas	1,000.00	2,000.00
29 Honus Wagner	7,500.00	15,000.00
30 Robert Wood	1,500.00	3,000.00

1912 Gus Williams Lemon Drop

Measuring approximately 2 1/4" by 4" this card feature a photo of Gus Williams taken by Johnston and Co. The front has a photo of Wiliams in street clothes while the back has the words "Compliments of W.T. Crane's Lemon Drop Package". It is possible that other players were created for this set.

1 Gus Williams	60.00	120.00

1929 Hack Wilson All-Weather Tire

This one card blank-backed photo set, measuring approximately 7" by 9" features Cub slugger Hack Wilson as a promotion for All-Weather Tire Co. on July 2, 1929.

1 Hack Wilson		100

1954 Wilson Franks

The cards in this 20-card set measure approximately 2 5/8" by 3 3/4". The 1954 "Wilson Wieners" set contains 20 full color, unnumbered cards. The obverse design of a package of hot dogs appearing to fly through the air is a distinctive feature of this set. Uncut sheets have been seen. Cards are numbered below alphabetically by player's name.

COMPLETE SET (20)	7,500.00	15,000.00
1 Roy Campanella	750.00	1,500.00
2 Del Ennis	200.00	400.00
3 Carl Erskine	250.00	500.00
4 Ferris Fain	150.00	300.00
5 Bob Feller	600.00	1,200.00
6 Nellie Fox	300.00	600.00
7 Johnny Groth	150.00	300.00
8 Stan Hack MG	150.00	300.00
9 Gil Hodges	300.00	600.00
10 Ray Jablonski	150.00	300.00
11 Harvey Kuenn	200.00	400.00
12 Roy McMillan	150.00	300.00
13 Andy Pafko	150.00	300.00
14 Paul Richards MG	150.00	300.00
15 Hank Sauer	150.00	300.00
16 Red Schoendienst	300.00	600.00
17 Enos Slaughter	300.00	600.00
18 Vern Stephens	150.00	300.00
19 Sammy White	150.00	300.00
20 Ted Williams	3,000.00	6,000.00

1959-61 Wilson Sporting Goods

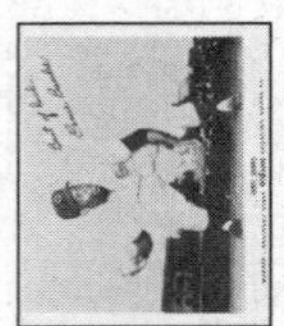

This seven-card set measures approximately 8" by 10" and features white-bordered black-and-white player photos with a facsimile autograph. The player's and sponsor's names are printed in the bottom margin. The backs are blank. The cards are unnumbered and checklisted below in alphabetical order.

COMPLETE SET (8)	100.00	200.00
1 Luis Aparicio	12.50	25.00
2 Ernie Banks	40.00	80.00
3 Nellie Fox	40.00	80.00
4 Harmon Killebrew	40.00	80.00
5 Billy Pierce	7.50	15.00
6 Pete Runnels	5.00	10.00
7 Larry Sherry	5.00	10.00
8 Early Wynn	10.00	20.00

1961 Wilson Sporting Goods H828

This three-card set features black-and-white player images on a gray background with a black border and looks as if the cards were cut from boxes. A player facsimile autograph is printed at the bottom. The cards measure approximately 1 7/8" by 5 1/4" and the catalog number is H828. The cards are unnumbered and checklisted below in alphabetical order.

COMPLETE SET (3)	150.00	300.00
1 Don Hoak	50.00	100.00
2 Harvey Kuenn	50.00	100.00
3 Jim Piersall	50.00	100.00

1961 Wilson Sporting Goods H828-1

This six card set measures approximately 2 1/4" by 4" and features black and white blank backed photos containing a blue facsimile autograph and "Member - Advisory Staff Wilson Sporting Goods Co." across the bottom of the card. According to old hobby experts, this set may very well have more than six players. All additions to this checklist are appreciated. The catalog designation for this set is H828-1.

COMPLETE SET (6)	30.00	60.00
1 Dick Ellsworth	4.00	10.00
2 Don Hoak	4.00	10.00
3 Harvey Kuenn	4.00	10.00
4 Roy McMillan	4.00	10.00
5 Jim Piersall	6.00	15.00
6 Ron Santo	8.00	20.00

1951-53 Wisconsin Hall of Fame Postcards

These 12 postcards were issued by the Wisconsin Hall of Fame and feature some of the leading athletes out of Milwaukee. The sepia illustrations have a relief of the player as well as some information about them. Since these cards are unnumbered, we have sequenced them in alphabetical order.

COMPLETE SET (12)	175.00	350.00
1 Addie Joss BB	30.00	60.00
4 George McBride BB	7.50	15.00
7 Kid Nichols BB	25.00	50.00
10 Al Simmons BB	30.00	60.00
11 Billy Sullivan BB	10.00	20.00

1910 World Series Photo Pack

These 12 pictures, which measure 4 1/2" by 6" are blank-backed and may have been cut from a larger album which featured all these cards. Since these cards are unnumbered, we are listing them in alphabetical order.

COMPLETE SET	1,000.00	2,000.00
1 Harry Davis Eddie Collins	150.00	300.00
2 Rube Oldring Topsy Hartsell	50.00	100.00
3 Lew Richie Harry McIntyre	50.00	100.00
4 Ginger Beaumont Solly Hofman	50.00	100.00
5 King Cole Jimmy Archer	50.00	100.00
6 Frank Chance Johnny Evers	200.00	400.00
7 John Kane Ed Reulbach	50.00	100.00
8 Joe Tinker Harry Steinfeldt	125.00	250.00
9 Orvie Overall Tom Needham	50.00	100.00
10 Mordecai Brown Johnny Kling	150.00	300.00
11 Frank Schulte Jimmy Sheckard	50.00	100.00
12 Jack Pfeister Heinie Zimmerman	75.00	150.00

1936 World Wide Gum

The cards in this 135-card set measure approximately 2 1/2" by 3". The 1936 Canadian Goudey set was issued by World Wide Gum Company and contains black and white cards. This issue is the most difficult to obtain of the Canadian Goudeys. The fronts feature player photos with white borders. The bilingual (French and English) backs carry player biography and career highlights. The World Wide Gum Company has its location listed as Granby, Quebec on these cards (as opposed to Montreal on earlier issues). The cards are numbered on both sides. The Phil Weintraub card (number 135) is very scarce and on many collectors wantlists.

COMPLETE SET (135)	10,000.00	20,000.00
1 Jimmy Dykes	60.00	120.00
2 Paul Waner	100.00	200.00
3 Cy Blanton	50.00	100.00
4 Sam Leslie	50.00	100.00
5 Johnny Vergez	50.00	100.00
6 Arky Vaughan	100.00	200.00
7 Bill Terry	100.00	200.00
8 Joe Moore	50.00	100.00
9 Gus Mancuso	50.00	100.00
10 Fred Marberry	50.00	100.00
11 George Selkirk	60.00	120.00
12 Spud Davis	50.00	100.00
13 Chuck Klein	100.00	200.00
14 Fred Fitzsimmons	60.00	120.00
15 Bill DeLancey	50.00	100.00
16 Billy Herman	100.00	200.00
17 George Davis	50.00	100.00
18 Rip Collins	50.00	100.00
19 Dizzy Dean		500
20 Roy Parmelee	50.00	100.00
21 Vic Sorrell	50.00	100.00
22 Harry Danning	50.00	100.00
23 Hal Schumacher	60.00	120.00
24 Cy Perkins	50.00	100.00
25 Leo Durocher		300
26 Glenn Myatt	50.00	100.00
27 Bob Seeds	50.00	100.00
28 Jimmy Ripple	50.00	100.00
29 Al Schacht	60.00	120.00
30 Pete Fox	50.00	100.00
31 Del Baker	50.00	100.00
32 Herman(Flea) Clifton	50.00	100.00
33 Tommy Bridges	60.00	120.00
34 Bill Dickey		300
35 Wally Berger	60.00	120.00
36 Slick Castleman	50.00	100.00
37 Dick Bartell	60.00	120.00
38 Red Rolfe	60.00	120.00
39 Waite Hoyt	100.00	200.00
40 Wes Ferrell	75.00	150.00
41 Hank Greenberg		300
42 Charlie Gehringer	100.00	200.00
43 Goose Goslin	100.00	200.00
44 Schoolboy Rowe	60.00	120.00
45 Mickey Cochrane MG	100.00	200.00
46 Joe Cronin	100.00	200.00
47 Jimmie Foxx		500
48 Jerry Walker	50.00	100.00
49 Charlie Gelbert	50.00	100.00
50 Ray Hayworth	50.00	100.00
51 Joe DiMaggio		5000
52 Billy Rogell	50.00	100.00
53 John McCarthy	50.00	100.00
54 Phil Cavarretta	60.00	120.00
55 KiKi Cuyler	100.00	200.00
56 Lefty Gomez	100.00	200.00
57 Gabby Hartnett	100.00	200.00
58 John Marcum	50.00	100.00
59 Burgess Whitehead	50.00	100.00
60 Whitey Whitehill	50.00	100.00
61 Bucky Walters	60.00	120.00
62 Luke Sewell	60.00	120.00
63 Joe Kuhel	50.00	100.00
64 Lou Finney	50.00	100.00
65 Fred Lindstrom	100.00	200.00
66 Paul Derringer	60.00	120.00
67 Steve O'Neill MG	60.00	120.00
68 Mule Haas	50.00	100.00
69 Marv Owen	50.00	100.00
70 Bill Hallahan	50.00	100.00
71 Billy Urbanski	50.00	100.00
72 Dan Taylor	50.00	100.00
73 Heinie Manush	100.00	200.00
74 Jo Jo White	50.00	100.00
75 Joe Medwick	100.00	200.00
76 Joe Vosmik	50.00	100.00
77 Al Simmons	100.00	200.00
78 Frank Shaughnessy	50.00	100.00
79 Harry Smythe	50.00	100.00
80 Bennie Tate	50.00	100.00
81 Billy Rheil	50.00	100.00
82 Lauri Myllykangas	50.00	100.00
83 Ben Sankey	50.00	100.00
84 Crip Polli	50.00	100.00
85 Jim Bottomley	100.00	200.00
86 Watson Clark	50.00	100.00
87 Ossie Bluege	60.00	120.00
88 Lefty Grove		300
89 Charlie Grimm MG	60.00	120.00
90 Ben Chapman	60.00	120.00
91 Frank Crosetti Not him pictured on card	75.00	150.00
92 John Pomorski	50.00	100.00
93 Jess Haines	100.00	200.00
94 Chick Hafey	100.00	200.00
95 Tony Piet	50.00	100.00
96 Lou Gehrig	2,000.00	4,000.00
97 Billy Jurges	60.00	120.00
98 Smead Jolley	60.00	120.00
99 Jimmy Wilson	60.00	120.00
100 Lon Warneke	60.00	120.00
101 Vito Tamulis	50.00	100.00
102 Red Ruffing	100.00	200.00
103 Earl Grace	50.00	100.00
104 Rox Lawson	50.00	100.00
105 Stan Hack	60.00	120.00
106 Augie Galan	50.00	100.00
107 Frank Frisch MG	100.00	200.00
108 Bill McKechnie MG	100.00	200.00
109 Bill Lee	60.00	120.00
110 Connie Mack MG	100.00	200.00
111 Frank Reiber	50.00	100.00
112 Zeke Bonura	60.00	120.00
113 Luke Appling	100.00	200.00
114 Monte Pearson	50.00	100.00
115 Bob O'Farrell	60.00	120.00
116 Marvin Duke	50.00	100.00
117 Paul Florence	50.00	100.00
118 John Berley	50.00	100.00
119 Tom Oliver	50.00	100.00
120 Norman Kies	50.00	100.00
121 Hal King	50.00	100.00
122 Tom Abernathy	50.00	100.00
123 Phil Hensich	50.00	100.00
124 Ray Schalk	100.00	200.00
125 Paul Dunlap	50.00	100.00
126 Benny Bates	50.00	100.00
127 George Puccinelli	50.00	100.00
128 Stevie Stevenson	50.00	100.00
129 Rabbit Maranville MG	100.00	200.00
130 Bucky Harris MG	100.00	200.00
131 Al Lopez	100.00	200.00
132 Buddy Myer	60.00	120.00
133 Cliff Bolton	50.00	100.00
134 Estel Crabtree	50.00	100.00
135 Phil Weintraub	400.00	800.00

1939 World Wide Gum V351A

These 25 photos measure approximately 4" by 5 3/4" and feature on their fronts white-bordered sepia-toned posed player photos. The player's facsimile autograph appears across the picture. The backs carry tips printed in brown ink on how to play baseball. The photos are unnumbered and checklisted below in alphabetical order.

COMPLETE SET (25)	2,000.00	4,000.00
1 Morris Arnovich	30.00	60.00
2 Sam Bell	30.00	60.00
3 Zeke Bonura	40.00	80.00
4 Earl Caldwell	30.00	60.00
5 Flea Clifton	30.00	60.00
6 Frank Crosetti	50.00	100.00
7 Harry Danning	30.00	60.00
8 Dizzy Dean	150.00	300.00
9 Emile De Jonghe	30.00	60.00
10 Paul Derringer	30.00	60.00
11 Joe DiMaggio	600.00	1,200.00
12 Vince DiMaggio	60.00	120.00
13 Charles Gehringer	150.00	300.00
14 Gene Hasson	30.00	60.00
15 Tommy Henrich	60.00	120.00
16 Fred Hutchinson	50.00	100.00
17 Phil Marchildon	40.00	80.00
18 Mike Meola	30.00	60.00
19 Arnold Moser	30.00	60.00
20 Frank Pytlak	30.00	60.00
21 Frank Reiber	30.00	60.00
22 Lee Rogers	30.00	60.00
23 Cecil Travis	40.00	80.00
24 Hal Trosky	40.00	80.00
25 Ted Williams	600.00	1,200.00

1939 World Wide Gum Trimmed Premiums V351B

These 48 photos measure approximately 4" by 5 3/4" and feature on their fronts white-bordered sepia-toned posed player photos. The set is essentially a re-issue of the R303A set. The white borders at the top and bottom were trimmed (during the manufacturing process) to the same size as the Series A photos. The player's facsimile autograph appears across the photo. The backs carry tips printed in brown ink on how to play baseball. The photos are unnumbered and checklisted below in alphabetical order.

COMPLETE SET (48)	2,500.00	5,000.00
1 Luke Appling	60.00	120.00
2 Earl Averill	60.00	120.00
3 Wally Berger	40.00	80.00
4 Darrell Blanton	30.00	60.00
5 Zeke Bonura	40.00	80.00
6 Mace Brown	30.00	60.00
7 George Case	40.00	80.00
8 Ben Chapman	30.00	60.00
9 Joe Cronin	60.00	120.00
10 Frank Crosetti	50.00	100.00
11 Paul Derringer	40.00	80.00
12 Bill Dickey	60.00	120.00
13 Joe DiMaggio	400.00	800.00
14 Bob Feller	125.00	250.00
15 Jimmy Foxx (Jimmie)	100.00	200.00
16 Charlie Gehringer	60.00	120.00
17 Lefty Gomez	60.00	120.00
18 Ival Goodman	30.00	60.00
19 Joe Gordon	50.00	100.00
20 Hank Greenberg	60.00	120.00
21 Buddy Hassett	30.00	60.00
22 Jeff Heath	30.00	60.00
23 Tommy Henrich	50.00	100.00
24 Billy Herman	60.00	120.00
25 Frank Higgins	30.00	60.00
26 Fred Hutchinson	40.00	80.00
27 Bob Johnson	40.00	80.00
28 Ken Keltner	40.00	80.00
29 Mike Kreevich	30.00	60.00
30 Ernie Lombardi	60.00	120.00
31 Gus Mancuso	30.00	60.00
32 Eric McNair	30.00	60.00
33 Van Mungo	40.00	80.00
34 Buck Newsom	40.00	80.00
35 Mel Ott	60.00	120.00
36 Marvin Owen	30.00	60.00
37 Frankie Pytlak	30.00	60.00
38 Woody Rich	30.00	60.00
39 Charlie Root	40.00	80.00
40 Al Simmons	60.00	120.00
41 Jim Tabor	30.00	60.00
42 Cecil Travis	30.00	60.00
43 Hal Trosky	30.00	60.00
44 Arky Vaughan	60.00	120.00
45 Joe Vosmik	30.00	60.00
46 Lon Warneke	30.00	60.00
47 Ted Williams	400.00	800.00
48 Rudy York	40.00	80.00

1933 Worch Cigar

These 3 7/16" by 5 7/16" photos were issued by Worch Cigars. They feature both major and minor leaguers and according to documentation issued by Worch in 1933 the players issued were the players they figured to be in the most demand and had negatives on hand to make. Interesting to note that just as many minor leaguers as major leaguers were produced.

COMPLETE SET	3,000.00	6,000.00
1 Sparky Adams	25.00	50.00
2 Dale Alexander	25.00	50.00
3 Ivy Paul Andrews	25.00	50.00
4 Earl Averill Name at left)	50.00	100.00
5 Earl Averill Name at right)	50.00	100.00
6 Richard Bartell	30.00	60.00
7 Walter Berger Bos NL	30.00	60.00
8 Walter Berger No team name	30.00	60.00
9 Huck Betts	25.00	50.00
10 Max Bishop	25.00	50.00
11 Jim Bottomley	50.00	100.00
12 Tom Bridges	25.00	50.00
13 Clint Brown	25.00	50.00
14 Max Carey	50.00	100.00
15 Tex Carleton	25.00	50.00
16 Ben Chapman Name not in box	25.00	50.00
17 Ben Chapman Name in box	25.00	50.00
18 Chalmer Cissell	25.00	50.00
19 Mickey Cochrane	75.00	150.00
20 Mickey Cochrane Name spelled Cochran	75.00	150.00
21 Earle Combs	50.00	100.00
22 Rip Collins	25.00	50.00
23 Adam Comorosky	25.00	50.00
24 Crabtree	25.00	50.00
25 Roger Cramer	30.00	60.00
26 Pat Crawford	25.00	50.00
27 Hugh Critz	25.00	50.00
28 Joe Cronin	75.00	150.00
29 Frank Crosetti	40.00	80.00
30 Alvin Crowder	25.00	50.00
31 Tony Cuccinello	25.00	50.00
32 Kiki Cuyler	50.00	100.00
33 Geo. Davis	25.00	50.00
34 Dizzy Dean	125.00	250.00
35 Bill Dickey Name not in box	100.00	200.00
36 Bill Dickey Name in Box	100.00	200.00
37 Leo Durocher	100.00	200.00
38 James Dykes	40.00	80.00
39 George Earnshaw	25.00	50.00
40 Woody English	30.00	60.00
41 Richard Ferrel Name Spelled incorrectly	50.00	100.00
42 Richard Ferrell	50.00	100.00
43 Wesley Ferrell	30.00	60.00
44 James Foxx (Jimmie)	250.00	500.00
45 Fred Frankhouse	25.00	50.00
46 Frank Frisch Large cropping)	20.00	40.00
47 Frank Frisch Small cropping)	20.00	40.00
48 George Gantham	25.00	50.00
49 Lou Gehrig Box on Card	750.00	1,500.00
50 Lou Gehrig No Box on Card	750.00	1,500.00
51 Charlie Gehringer	100.00	200.00
52 Geo. Gibson MG	25.00	50.00
53 Lefty Gomez No Box	125.00	250.00
54 Vernon Gomez Box on Card	125.00	250.00
55 Leon Goslin Name spelled Gaslin	50.00	100.00
56 Leon Goslin Name correctly spelled	50.00	100.00
57 Charlie Grimm	40.00	80.00
58 Robert Grove Name in box	125.00	250.00
59 Robert Grove Name not in box	125.00	250.00
60 Chic Hafey No Background on card	50.00	100.00
61 Chic Hafey Photo Background on Card	50.00	100.00
62 Bill Hallahan	30.00	60.00
63 Mel Harder	30.00	60.00
64 Gabby Hartnett	50.00	100.00
65 Dutch Henry	25.00	50.00
66 Babe Herman	40.00	80.00
67 Bill Herman	50.00	100.00
68 Oral Hildebrand Box on Card	25.00	50.00
69 Oral Hildebrand No Box on Card	25.00	50.00
70 Rogers Hornsby St Louis AL	125.00	250.00
71 Rogers Hornsby St Louis Cards NL	125.00	250.00
72 Carl Hubbell	100.00	200.00
73 Travis Jackson New York N.L.	50.00	100.00
74 Travis Jackson No team name	50.00	100.00
75 Charles Klein Philadelphia N.L., No Background	50.00	100.00
76 Chuck Klein Chicago NL, no background	50.00	100.00
77 Chuck Klein Philadelphia NL, background	50.00	100.00
78 Joe Kuhel	25.00	50.00
79 Tony Lazzeri New York A.L.	50.00	100.00
80 Tony Lazzeri N.Y. A.L.	50.00	100.00
81 Ernie Lombardi	50.00	100.00
82 Al Lopez	50.00	100.00
83 Red Lucas	25.00	50.00
84 Henry Manush	50.00	100.00
85 Fred Marberry	25.00	50.00
86 Pepper Martin Has Background	30.00	60.00
87 Pepper Martin No background	30.00	60.00
88 Joe Medwick	50.00	100.00
89 Joe Moore	25.00	50.00
90 Van Mungo	30.00	60.00
91 Buddy Myer	25.00	50.00
92 Bob O'Farrell	25.00	50.00
93 Lefty O'Doul New York N.L>	40.00	80.00
94 Lefty O'Doul No team name)	40.00	80.00
95 Ernie Orsatti standing)	25.00	50.00
96 Ernie Orsatti batting)	25.00	50.00
97 Melvin Ott	75.00	150.00
98 Homer Peel	25.00	50.00
99 Charles Ruffing	50.00	100.00
100 Jack Russell	25.00	50.00
101 Babe Ruth Box on Card	1,250.00	2,500.00
102 Babe Ruth No Box on Card	1,250.00	2,500.00
103 Blondy Ryan	25.00	50.00
104 Wilfred Ryan	25.00	50.00
105 Hal Schumacher	25.00	50.00
106 Luke Sewel	25.00	50.00
107 Luke Sewell No Box Around Name	25.00	50.00
108 Al Simmons Name at left)	75.00	150.00
109 Al Simmons Name at right)	75.00	150.00
110 Ray Spencer	25.00	50.00
111 Gus Suhr	25.00	50.00
112 Bill Terry	75.00	150.00
113 Pie Traynor	100.00	200.00
114 Dazzy Vance	50.00	100.00
115 Gerald Walker	25.00	50.00
116 Lloyd Waner With background)	50.00	100.00
117 Lloyd Waner Without background)	50.00	100.00
118 Paul Waner With background)	60.00	120.00
119 Paul Waner Without background)	60.00	120.00
120 Lon Warneke Brown background)	25.00	50.00
121 Lon Warneke White background)	25.00	50.00
122 Monte Weaver	25.00	50.00
123 Sam West	25.00	50.00
124 Burgess Whitehead	25.00	50.00
125 Hack Wilson	50.00	100.00
126 Jimmy Wilson	25.00	50.00

1944 Yankees Stamps

This stamp set commemorates the New York Yankees and their World Series victory in 1943. The stamps were perforated together in a sheet with five rows of six stamps across. The stamps are ordered alphabetically on the stamp sheet left to right. Each stamp measures approximately 1 3/4" by 2 3/8" and is in full color. The player's name is printed in white on a red background at the bottom of each stamp. An album for the set was issued but it is more difficult to find than the stamps. The catalog designation for this set is ST101.

COMPLETE SET (30)	40.00	80.00
1 Ernie Bonham	2.50	5.00
2 Hank Borowy	2.50	5.00
3 Marvin Breuer	2.00	4.00
4 Tommy Byrne	2.50	5.00
5 Spud Chandler	3.00	6.00
6 Earle Combs CO	3.00	5.00
7 Frank Crosetti	3.00	6.00
8 Bill Dickey	10.00	20.00
9 Atley Donald	2.00	4.00
10 Nick Etten	2.00	4.00
11 Art Fletcher CO	2.00	4.00
12 Joe Gordon	3.00	6.00
13 Oscar Grimes	2.00	4.00
14 Rollie Hemsley	2.00	4.00
15 Bill Johnson	2.00	4.00
16 Charlie Keller	3.00	6.00
17 John Lindell	2.50	5.00
18 Joe McCarthy MG	5.00	10.00
19 Bud Metheny	2.00	4.00
20 Johnny Murphy	2.50	5.00
21 Pat O'Dougherty	2.00	4.00
22 Marius Russo	2.00	4.00
23 John Schulte	2.00	4.00
24 Ken Sears	2.00	4.00
25 Tuck Stainback	2.00	4.00
26 George Stirnweiss	2.50	5.00
27 Jim Turner	2.50	5.00
28 Roy Weatherly	2.00	4.00
29 Charley Wensloff	2.00	4.00
30 Bill Zuber	2.00	4.00
NNO Album	20.00	50.00

1947 Yankees Team Issue

This 25-card set of the New York Yankees measures approximately 6 1/2" by 9" and features black-and-white player portraits with white borders and facsimile autographs. The backs are blank. The cards are unnumbered and checklisted below in alphabetical order. This set was available from the Yankees at time of issue for 50 cents.

COMPLETE SET (25)	100.00	250.00
1 Yogi Berra	10.00	50.00
2 Bill Bevans	2.50	5.00
3 Bobby Brown	5.00	10.00
4 Spud Chandler	2.50	5.00
5 Gerry Coleman	2.50	5.00
6 John Corriden CO	2.50	5.00
7 Frank Crosetti	2.50	5.00
8 Joe DiMaggio	40.00	80.00
9 Chuck Dressen CO	4.00	8.00
10 Randy Gumpert	2.50	5.00
11 Bucky Harris MG	5.00	10.00
12 Tommy Henrich	4.00	8.00
13 Ralph Houk	3.00	6.00
14 Don Johnson	2.50	5.00
15 Bill Johnson	2.50	5.00
16 Charlie Keller	2.50	5.00
17 John Lindell	2.50	5.00
18 George McQuinn	2.50	5.00
19 Joe Page	2.50	5.00
20 Allie Reynolds	4.00	8.00
21 Phil Rizzuto	10.00	20.00
22 Aaron Robinson	2.50	5.00
23 Frank Shea	2.50	5.00
24 Ken Silvestri	2.50	5.00
25 George Stirnweiss	2.50	5.00

1948 Yankees Team Issue

These 26 photos measure approximately 6 1/2" by 9". They feature members of the 1948 New York Yankees. These black and white photos also feature a facsimile signature and are framed by white borders. The photos are unnumbered and we have sequenced them in alphabetical order.

COMPLETE SET (26)	137.50	275.00
1 Mel Allen ANN	5.00	10.00
2 Yogi Berra	15.00	40.00
3 Bobby Brown	3.00	6.00
4 Red Corriden CO	2.50	5.00
5 Frank Crosetti	4.00	8.00
6 Joe DiMaggio	40.00	80.00
7 Chuck Dressen CO	3.00	6.00
8 Karl Drews	2.50	5.00
9 Red Embree	2.50	5.00
10 Randy Gumpert	2.50	5.00
11 Bucky Harris MG	5.00	10.00
12 Tommy Henrich	4.00	8.00
13 Frank Hiller	2.50	5.00
14 Bill Johnson	2.50	5.00
15 Charlie Keller	3.00	6.00
16 Ed Lopat	4.00	8.00
17 John Lindell	2.50	5.00
18 Cliff Mapes	2.50	5.00
19 Gus Niarhos	2.50	5.00
20 George McQuinn	2.50	5.00
21 Joe Page	3.00	6.00
22 Vic Raschi	4.00	8.00
23 Allie Reynolds	4.00	8.00
24 Phil Rizzuto	12.50	30.00
25 Frank Shea	2.50	5.00
26 Snuffy Stirnweiss	3.00	6.00

1949 Yankees Team Issue

This 25-card set of the New York Yankees measures approximately 6 1/2" by 9" and features black-and-white player portraits with white borders. The backs are blank. The cards are unnumbered and checklisted below in alphabetical order.

COMPLETE SET (25)	150.00	300.00
1 Mel Allen ANN	5.00	10.00
2 Larry Berra	12.50	40.00
3 Bobby Brown	5.00	10.00
4 Tommy Byrne	2.50	5.00
5 Jerry Coleman	4.00	8.00
6 Frank Crosetti CO	4.00	8.00
7 Bill Dickey CO	10.00	20.00
8 Joe DiMaggio	40.00	80.00
9 Tom Henrich	4.00	8.00
10 Bill Johnson	2.50	5.00
11 Charlie Keller	2.50	5.00
12 John Lindell	2.50	5.00
13 Ed Lopat	4.00	8.00
14 Gus Niarhos	2.50	5.00
15 Joe Page	2.50	5.00
16 Bob Porterfield	2.50	5.00
17 Vic Raschi	4.00	8.00
18 Allie Reynolds	4.00	8.00
19 Phil Rizzuto	10.00	30.00
20 Fred Sanford	2.50	5.00
21 Frank Shea	2.50	5.00
22 Casey Stengel MG	10.00	25.00
23 George Stirnweiss	2.50	5.00
24 Jim Turner CO	2.50	5.00
25 Gene Woodling	3.00	6.00

1950 Yankees Team Issue

This 25-card set of the New York Yankees measures approximately 6 1/2" by 9" and features black-and-white player portraits with white borders. The backs are blank. The cards are unnumbered and checklisted below in alphabetical order.

COMPLETE SET (25)	150.00	300.00
1 Mel Allen ANN	5.00	10.00
2 Hank Bauer	5.00	10.00
3 Larry Berra	10.00	40.00
4 Bobby Brown	5.00	10.00
5 Tommy Byrne	2.50	5.00
6 Jerry Coleman	4.00	8.00
7 Frank Crosetti CO	4.00	8.00
8 Bill Dickey CO	10.00	20.00
9 Joe DiMaggio	40.00	80.00
10 Tom Henrich	4.00	8.00
11 Jack Jensen	7.50	20.00
12 Bill Johnson	2.50	5.00
13 Ed Lopat	2.50	5.00

14 Cliff Mapes	2.50	5.00
15 Joe Page	2.50	5.00
16 Bob Porterfield	2.50	5.00
17 Vic Raschi	4.00	8.00
18 Allie Reynolds	4.00	8.00
19 Phil Rizzuto	10.00	30.00
20 Fred Sanford	2.50	5.00
21 Charlie Silvera	2.50	5.00
22 Casey Stengel MG	10.00	25.00
23 George Stirnweiss	2.50	5.00
24 Jim Turner CO	2.50	5.00
25 Gene Woodling	3.00	6.00

1953 Yankees Photos

Issued by one of the "stores" across the street from Yankee Stadium, these photos feature portrait photos of the Yankees on the front and the backs have the name, address and phone number of the store used to distribute the photos. It is possible that there might be more photos so any additions are appreciated. Since the cards are unnumbered, we have sequenced them in alphabetical order.

COMPLETE SET	50.00	100.00
1 Hank Bauer	5.00	10.00
2 Yogi Berra	10.00	20.00
3 Joe Collins	2.50	5.00
4 Whitey Ford	10.00	20.00
5 Billy Martin	7.50	15.00
6 Gil McDougald	4.00	8.00
7 Johnny Mize	6.00	12.00
8 Vic Raschi	4.00	8.00
9 Phil Rizzuto	7.50	15.00
10 Gene Woodling	3.00	6.00

1956 Yankees Jay Publishing

This 12-card set of the New York Yankees measures approximately 5 1/8" by 7". The fronts feature black-and-white posed player photos with the player's and team name printed below in the white border. These cards were packaged 12 to a packet and originally sold for 25 cents. The backs are blank. The cards are unnumbered and checklisted below in alphabetical order.

COMPLETE SET (12)	60.00	120.00
1 Hank Bauer	3.00	6.00
2 Larry Berra	7.50	15.00
3 Tommy Byrne	2.00	4.00
4 Andy Carey	2.00	4.00
5 Joe Collins	2.00	4.00
6 Whitey Ford	7.50	15.00
7 Elston Howard	4.00	8.00
8 Mickey Mantle	20.00	50.00
9 Billy Martin	6.00	12.00
10 Gil McDougald	3.00	6.00
11 Casey Stengel MG	7.50	15.00
12 Bob Turley	2.00	4.00

1956 Yankees Team Issue

This 24-card set of the New York Yankees features black-and-white player photos measuring approximately 6" by 9" with the player's name printed at the bottom. The cards are unnumbered and checklisted below in alphabetical order.

COMPLETE SET (24)	125.00	250.00
1 Hank Bauer	6.00	12.00
2 Yogi Berra	10.00	20.00
3 Tommy Byrne	4.00	8.00
4 Andy Carey	4.00	8.00
5 Bob Cerv	4.00	8.00
6 Gerry Coleman	4.00	8.00
7 Joe Collins	4.00	8.00
8 Whitey Ford	10.00	20.00
9 Bob Grim	4.00	8.00
10 Elston Howard	7.50	15.00
11 Johnny Kucks	4.00	8.00
12 Don Larsen	6.00	12.00
13 Jerry Lumpe	4.00	8.00
14 Mickey Mantle	25.00	50.00
15 Billy Martin	7.50	15.00
16 Mickey McDermott	4.00	8.00
17 Gil McDougald	5.00	10.00
18 Tom Morgan	4.00	8.00
19 Irv Noren	4.00	8.00
20 Phil Rizzuto	10.00	20.00
21 Eddie Robinson	4.00	8.00
22 Charley Silvera	4.00	8.00
23 Bill Skowron	6.00	12.00
24 Bob Turley	5.00	10.00

1957 Yankees Jay Publishing

This 16-card set of the New York Yankees measures approximately 5" X 7". Since personnel changes were made during the season, there were more than just 12 cards issued. The fronts feature black-and-white posed player photos with the player's and team name printed below in the white border. These cards were packaged 12 to a packet and originally sold for 25 cents. The backs are blank. The cards are unnumbered and checklisted below in alphabetical order.

COMPLETE SET (12)	87.50	175.00
1 Hank Bauer	3.00	6.00
2 Larry Berra	12.50	25.00
3 Tommy Byrne	2.00	4.00
4 Jerry Coleman	2.00	4.00
5 Ed (Whitey) Ford	12.50	25.00
6 Elston Howard	4.00	8.00
7 Johnny Kucks	2.00	4.00
8 Don Larsen	2.50	5.00
9 Sal Maglie	2.50	5.00
10 Mickey Mantle	25.00	50.00
11 Billy Martin	4.00	8.00
12 Gil McDougald	2.50	5.00
13 Bill Skowron	3.00	6.00
14 Enos Slaughter	5.00	10.00
15 Casey Stengel MG	7.50	15.00
16 Tom Sturdivant	2.00	4.00

1957 Yankee Team Issue

These photos, which measure approximately 7 1/2" by 10" feature members of the 1957 New York Yankees. Since these photos are unnumbered, we have sequenced them in alphabetical order.

COMPLETE SET	100.00	200.00
1 Hank Bauer	8.00	15.00
2 Yogi Berra	10.00	20.00
3 Andy Carey	4.00	8.00
4 Joe Collins	4.00	8.00
5 Whitey Ford	10.00	20.00
6 Elston Howard	8.00	15.00
7 Don Larsen	5.00	10.00
8 Mickey Mantle	25.00	50.00
9 Gil McDougald	5.00	10.00
10 Bill Skowron	8.00	15.00
11 Casey Stengel MG	10.00	20.00
12 Bob Turley	5.00	10.00

1958 Yankees Jay Publishing

This 16-card set of the New York Yankees measures approximately 5" by 7" and features black-and-white player photos in a white border. These cards were packaged 12 to a packet. The backs are blank. The cards are unnumbered and checklisted below in alphabetical order. More than 12 cards are included in this set as they were released at different times during the season

COMPLETE SET	37.50	150.00
1 Hank Bauer	3.00	6.00
2 Yogi Berra	6.00	15.00
3 Andy Carey	2.00	4.00
4 Whitey Ford	6.00	15.00
5 Elston Howard	4.00	8.00
6 Tony Kubek	4.00	8.00
7 Don Larsen	2.50	5.00
8 Jerry Lumpe	2.00	4.00
9 Mickey Mantle	12.50	50.00
10 Gil McDougald	2.00	4.00
11 Bobby Shantz	2.50	5.00
12 Bill Skowron	3.00	6.00
13 Casey Stengel MG		15
14 Tom Sturdivant	2.00	4.00
15 Bob Turley	2.00	4.00
16 Jim Turner CO	4.00	8.00
Bill Dickey CO		
Frank Crosetti CO/		

1959 Yankees Team Issue

These 12 black and white blank-backed photos measure 8" by 10" and feature a photo surrounded by white borders with the player's name printed in the lower left hand corner. As the photos are unnumbered, we have sequenced them in alphabetical order.

COMPLETE SET	60.00	120.00
1 Yogi Berra	5.00	15.00
2 Ryne Duren	2.00	4.00
3 Whitey Ford	5.00	15.00
4 Elston Howard	4.00	8.00
5 Tony Kubek	4.00	8.00
6 Mickey Mantle	12.50	50.00
7 Gil McDougald	2.50	5.00
8 Bobby Richardson	4.00	8.00
9 Bobby Shantz	2.00	4.00
10 Bill Skowron	3.00	6.00
11 Casey Stengel MG	4.00	10.00
12 Bob Turley	2.50	5.00

1959 Yankees Yoo-Hoo

These cards are black and white, with no printing on the back. They feature New York Yankee ballplayers, and were distributed as a premium in the New York area with a six-pack of Yoo-Hoo. There were six cards issued in the set. A facsimile signature of the player, along with the phrase "Me for Yoo-Hoo" appears on the front. The cards have a 15/16" tab at the bottom. The cards measure approximately 2 7/16" by 3 9/16" without the tab and 2 7/16" by 4 1/2" with the tab. The cards are valued below as being with tabs intact. The Mantle card is actually an advertising piece for Yoo-Hoo and is blank-backed. Cards without tabs are valued between 50 and 75 percent of the full card.

COMPLETE SET (6)	2,000.00	4,000.00
1 Yogi Berra	500.00	1,000.00
2 Whitey Ford	200.00	400.00
3 Tony Kubek	125.00	250.00
4 Mickey Mantle SP	1,000.00	2,000.00
5 Gil McDougald	100.00	200.00
6 Moose Skowron	125.00	250.00

1960 Yankees Jay Publishing

This 12-card set of the New York Yankees measures approximately 5" by 7" and features black-and-white player photos in a white border. These cards were packaged 12 to a packet. The backs are blank. The cards are unnumbered and checklisted below in alphabetical order.

COMPLETE SET (12)	50.00	100.00
1 Yogi Berra	6.00	15.00
2 Andy Carey	1.00	2.50
3 Whitey Ford	6.00	15.00
4 Elston Howard	2.00	5.00
5 Tony Kubek	2.00	5.00
6 Hector Lopez	1.00	2.50
7 Mickey Mantle	15.00	40.00
8 Roger Maris	5.00	12.00
9 Gil McDougald	1.00	2.50
10 Bill Skowron	1.25	3.00
11 Casey Stengel MG	4.00	10.00
12 Bob Turley	1.00	2.50

1960 Yankees Team Issue

These black and white cards, which measure approximately 6" by 8 1/2" featured members of the 1960 New York Yankees. Since these cards are unnumbered, we have sequenced them in alphabetical order.

COMPLETE SET	75.00	150.00
1 Yogi Berra	8.00	20.00
2 Andy Carey	2.00	5.00
3 Art Ditmar	2.00	5.00
4 Ryne Duren	2.00	5.00
5 Whitey Ford	8.00	20.00
6 Elston Howard	4.00	10.00
7 Tony Kubek	4.00	10.00
8 Mickey Mantle	15.00	40.00
9 Gil McDougald	2.50	6.00
10 Bobby Richardson	4.00	10.00
11 Bobby Shantz	2.00	5.00
12 Bill Skowron	4.00	10.00
13 Casey Stengel MG	5.00	12.00
14 Bob Turley	2.50	6.00

1961 Yankees Jay Publishing

This 12-card set of the New York Yankees measures approximately 5" by 7". The fronts feature black-and-white posed player photos with the player's and team name printed below in the white border. These cards were packaged 12 to a packet. The backs are blank. The cards are unnumbered and checklisted below in alphabetical order.

COMPLETE SET (12)	60.00	120.00
1 Yogi Berra	8.00	20.00
2 Clete Boyer	1.50	4.00
3 Art Ditmar	1.00	2.50
4 Whitey Ford	8.00	20.00
5 Ralph Houk MG	1.25	3.00
6 Elston Howard	2.00	5.00
7 Tony Kubek	2.00	5.00
8 Mickey Mantle	15.00	40.00
9 Roger Maris	8.00	20.00
10 Bobby Richardson	2.00	5.00
11 Bill Skowron	1.50	4.00
12 Bob Turley	1.00	2.50

1961 Yankees Team Issue

These 8" by 10" photos were issued to members of the press by the New York Yankees. These photos feature the player photo surrounded by white borders. Since these cards are not numbered, we have checklisted these cards in alphabetical order.

COMPLETE SET	75.00	150.00
1 Luis Arroyo	2.00	5.00
2 Yogi Berra	8.00	20.00
3 Jim Coates	2.00	5.00
4 Joe DeMaestri	2.00	5.00
5 Art Ditmar	2.00	5.00
6 Whitey Ford	8.00	20.00
7 Jesse Gonder	2.00	5.00
8 Ralph Houk MG	2.50	6.00
9 Deron Johnson	2.00	5.00
10 Tony Kubek	4.00	10.00
11 Mickey Mantle	15.00	40.00
12 Roger Maris	12.50	30.00
13 Bobby Richardson	4.00	10.00
14 Bill Skowron	3.00	8.00
15 Ralph Terry	2.00	5.00
16 Bob Turley	2.00	5.00

1962 Yankees Jay Publishing

This 12-card set of the New York Yankees measures approximately 5" by 7". The fronts feature black-and-white posed player photos with the player's and team name printed below in the white border. These cards were packaged 12 to a packet. The backs are blank. The cards are unnumbered and checklisted below in alphabetical order.

COMPLETE SET (12)	50.00	100.00
1 Luis Arroyo	1.00	2.50
2 Yogi Berra	8.00	20.00
3 John Blanchard	1.00	2.50
4 Cletis Boyer	1.50	4.00
5 Bud Daley	1.00	2.50
6 Whitey Ford	8.00	20.00
7 Ralph Houk MG	1.25	3.00
8 Elston Howard	2.00	5.00
9 Mickey Mantle	15.00	40.00
10 Roger Maris	8.00	20.00
11 Bobby Richardson	2.00	5.00
12 Bill Skowron	1.50	4.00

1962 Yankees Team Issue

These 5" by 7" blank backed photos feature members of the 1962 New York Yankees. The fronts feature black and white photos along with the players name printed in blank ink on the bottom. Since these photos are unnumbered we have sequenced them in alphabetical order

COMPLETE SET	60.00	120.00
1 Luis Arroyo	1.50	4.00
2 Yogi Berra	6.00	15.00
3 John Blanchard	1.50	4.00
4 Clete Boyer	2.00	5.00
5 Bob Cerv	1.50	4.00
6 Whitey Ford	6.00	15.00
7 Elston Howard	3.00	8.00
8 Tony Kubek	3.00	8.00
9 Hector Lopez	1.50	4.00
10 Mickey Mantle	15.00	40.00
11 Roger Maris	8.00	20.00
12 Bobby Richardson	3.00	8.00
13 Bill Skowron	2.00	5.00
14 Bob Turley	1.50	4.00

1963 Yankee Emblems

These seven patches which measure 3 1/2" by 4 1/2" feature members of the early 1960's Yankees. These patches have a player photo on the front and were issued in plastic-wrapped cardboard displays. Since these are unnumbered, we have sequenced them in alphabetical order.

COMPLETE SET	125.00	250.00
1 Yogi Berra	20.00	50.00
2 Clete Boyer	6.00	15.00
3 Elston Howard	12.50	30.00
4 Tony Kubek	12.50	30.00
5 Mickey Mantle	50.00	100.00
6 Roger Maris	40.00	80.00
7 Joe Pepitone	8.00	20.00
8 Bobby Richardson	12.50	30.00

1963 Yankees Jay Publishing

This 12-card set of the New York Yankees measures approximately 5" by 7". The fronts feature black-and-white posed player photos with the player's and team name printed below in the white border. These cards were packaged 12 to a packet. The backs are blank. The cards are unnumbered and checklisted below in alphabetical order.

COMPLETE SET (12)	50.00	100.00
1 Yogi Berra	6.00	15.00
2 Clete Boyer	1.50	4.00
3 Whitey Ford	6.00	15.00
4 Ralph Houk MG	1.25	3.00
5 Elston Howard	2.00	5.00
6 Tony Kubek	2.00	5.00
7 Mickey Mantle	15.00	40.00
8 Roger Maris	8.00	20.00
9 Joe Pepitone	2.00	5.00
10 Bobby Richardson	2.00	5.00
11 Ralph Terry	1.00	2.50
12 Tom Tresh	2.00	5.00

1963-67 Yankees Requena K Postcards

Issued over a period of several years this set features New York Yankee players only.The set features two types -- one in color, the other in black and white. Bridges only appears in black and white. We have sequenced this set in alphabetical order. Similar to the Dormand and Bill and Bob postcard, Requena postcards feature a K in the lower left of the reverse.

COMPLETE SET	250.00	500.00
1 Steve Barber	6.00	15.00
2A Yogi Berra Facsimile sig at top	20.00	50.00
2B Yogi Berra Facsimile Sig at bottom	20.00	50.00
2C Yogi Berra No signature	20.00	50.00
3 Johnny Blanchard	6.00	15.00
4 Jim Bouton	10.00	25.00
5 Clete Boyer	8.00	20.00
6 Marshall Bridges	6.00	15.00
7 Whitey Ford (2)	20.00	50.00
8 Elston Howard	12.50	30.00
9 Tony Kubek	12.50	30.00
10 Phil Linz	6.00	15.00
11 Fritz Peterson	6.00	15.00
12 Joe Pepitone	10.00	25.00
13 Pedro Ramos	6.00	15.00
14 Bobby Richardson	12.50	30.00
15 Bill Stafford	6.00	15.00
16 Mel Stottlemyre	10.00	25.00

18 Ralph Terry 6.00 15.00
19 Tom Tresh (2) 8.00 20.00

1964 Yankees Jay Publishing

This 12-card set of the New York Yankees measures approximately 5" by 7". The fronts feature black-and-white posed player photos with the player's and team name printed below in the white border. These cards were packaged 12 to a packet. The backs are blank. The cards are unnumbered and checklisted below in alphabetical order.

COMPLETE SET (12) 50.00 100.00
1 Yogi Berra MG 6.00 15.00
2 Clete Boyer 1.25 3.00
3 Al Downing 1.00 2.50
4 Whitey Ford 3.00 8.00
5 Elston Howard 2.00 5.00
6 Tony Kubek 2.00 5.00
7 Mickey Mantle 15.00 40.00
8 Roger Maris 8.00 20.00
9 Joe Pepitone 1.50 4.00
10 Bobby Richardson 2.00 5.00
11 Ralph Terry 1.00 2.50
12 Tom Tresh 1.50 4.00

1965 Yankees Jay Publishing

This 12-card set of the New York Yankees measures approximately 5" by 7". The fronts feature black-and-white posed player photos with the player's and team name printed below in the white border. These cards were packaged 12 to a packet. The backs are blank. The cards are unnumbered and checklisted below in alphabetical order.

COMPLETE SET (12) 50.00 100.00
1 Jim Bouton 2.00 5.00
2 Clete Boyer 1.50 4.00
3 Al Downing 1.00 2.50
4 Whitey Ford 6.00 15.00
5 Elston Howard 2.00 5.00
6 Tony Kubek 2.00 5.00
7 Mickey Mantle 15.00 40.00
8 Roger Maris 8.00 20.00
9 Joe Pepitone 1.50 4.00
10 Bobby Richardson 2.00 5.00
11 Mel Stottlemyre 1.50 4.00
12 Tom Tresh 1.50 4.00

1966 Yankees Team Issue

This 12-card set of the New York Yankees measures 4 7/8" by 7" and features black-and-white player photos in a white border with blank backs. These cards were originally packaged 12 to a packet with a price of 25 cents. The cards are unnumbered and checklisted below in alphabetical order. Changes in personnel are responsible for this checklist having more than 12 names.

COMPLETE SET (12) 40.00 80.00
1 Jim Bouton 1.50 4.00
2 Clete Boyer 1.25 3.00
3 Al Downing .75 2.00
4 Whitey Ford 6.00 15.00
5 Ralph Houk MG .75 2.00
6 Elston Howard 2.00 5.00
7 Johnny Keane MG .75 2.00
8 Hector Lopez .75 2.00
9 Mickey Mantle 12.50 30.00
10 Roger Maris 6.00 15.00
11 Joe Pepitone 1.50 4.00
12 Bobby Richardson 2.00 5.00
13 Mel Stottlemyre 1.50 4.00
14 Tom Tresh 1.50 4.00

1967 Yankees Photos SCFC

This 12-card set of the New York Yankees measures approximately 4" by 5" and features black-and-white player photos with white borders. The cards are listed below according to the numbers stamped on their white backs.

COMPLETE SET (12) 8.00 20.00
88 Team Photo 1.50 4.00
89 Ruben Amaro .75 2.00
90 Steve Barber .75 2.00
91 Steve Hamilton .75 2.00
92 Bill Monbouquette .75 2.00
93 Hal Reniff .75 2.00
94 Tom Shopay .75 2.00
95 Charlie Smith .75 2.00
96 Thad Tillotson .75 2.00
97 Dooley Womack .75 2.00
98 Yankee Stadium 1.50 4.00
99 Jerry Coleman ANN 1.00 2.50

1968 Yankees Photos SCFC

This 29-card set of the New York Yankees measures approximately 4" by 5" and features black-and-white player photos with white borders. The cards are listed below according to the numbers stamped on their white backs.

COMPLETE SET (29) 30.00 60.00
59 Ruben Amaro .75 2.00
60 Stan Bahnsen .75 2.00
61 Steve Barber .75 2.00
62 Horace Clarke .75 2.00
63 Rocky Colavito 4.00 10.00
64 Al Downing .75 2.00
65 Frank Fernandez .75 2.00
66 Jake Gibbs .75 2.00
67 Steve Hamilton .75 2.00
68 Dick Howser .75 2.00
69 Andy Kosco .75 2.00
70 Lindy McDaniel .75 2.00
71 Gene Michael .75 2.00
72 Bill Monbouquette .75 2.00
73 Joe Pepitone 1.25 3.00
74 Fritz Peterson/(Autographed) .75 2.00
75 Fritz Peterson/(Closer Portrait) .75 2.00
76 Bill Robinson .75 2.00
77 Charlie Smith .75 2.00
78 Fred Talbot .75 2.00
79 Joe Verbanic .75 2.00
80 Steve Whitaker .75 2.00
81 Roy White 1.25 3.00
82 Dooley Womack .75 2.00
83 Bobby Cox 3.00 8.00
84 Bill Dickey CO 1.50 4.00
85 Frank Fernandez .75 2.00
86 Tom Tresh 1.25 3.00
87 Jim Turner CO 1.25 3.00

1969 Yankees Malanga

This 12-card set was issued in four strips of three cards each measuring approximately 8 1/2" by 3 3/4" and could be obtained from the artist. The fronts carry very crude black-and-white drawings of New York Yankee players by Rocco Malanga. The backs are blank. The cards are unnumbered and checklisted below in alphabetical order.

COMPLETE SET (12) 8.00 20.00
1 Horace Clarke .60 1.50
2 Jake Gibbs .60 1.50
3 Steve Hamiltom UER
(misspelled Hamilton) .60 1.50
4 Ralph Houk MG .75 2.00
5 Mickey Mantle 4.00 10.00
6 Joe Pepitone 1.00 2.50
7 Bill Robinson .60 1.50
8 Mel Stottlemyre UER
(misspelled Stottlemyre) 1.00 2.50
9 Fred Talbot .60 1.50
10 Tom Tresh 1.00 2.50
11 Joe Verbanic .60 1.50
12 Roy White 1.00 2.50

1969 Yankees Photos SCFC

This 22-card set of the New York Yankees measures approximately 4" by 5" and features black-and-white player photos with white borders. The cards are listed below according to the numbers stamped on their white backs.

COMPLETE SET (22) 40.00 80.00
37 Len Boehmer 1.25 3.00
38 Bill Burbach 1.25 3.00
39 Bobby Cox 2.50 6.00
40 Jimmie Hall 1.25 3.00
41 Steve Hamilton 1.25 3.00
42 Jack Kennedy 1.25 3.00
43 Jerry Kenney 1.25 3.00
44 Lindy McDaniel 1.25 3.00
45 Bobby Murcer 2.50 6.00
46 Joe Pepitone 2.00 5.00
47 Fritz Peterson 1.25 3.00
48 Bill Robinson 1.25 3.00
49 Dick Simpson 1.25 3.00
50 Mel Stottlemyre 2.00 5.00
51 Fred Talbot 1.25 3.00
52 Joe Verbanic 1.25 3.00
53 Ron Woods 1.25 3.00
54 Jack Aker 1.25 3.00
55 Horace Clarke 1.25 3.00
56 Billy Cowan 1.25 3.00
57 John Ellis 1.25 3.00
58 Mike Kekich 1.25 3.00

1970 Yankees Clinic Day Postcards

During the 1970 season, The New York Yankees had a promotion where fans could meet their favorite players before a game. These postcards were issued so the fans could have something to sign. These cards are sequenced in order of the player's appearance. Some cards are known to be in much shorter supply. The card of Roy White is extremely difficult since the game was rained out. The Murcer card was issued early in the season is difficult as well. Both cards are noted with a SP in the listings.

COMPLETE SET 20.00 50.00
COMMON PLAYER .40 1.00
COMMON SP 2.00 5.00
1 Bobby Murcer SP 2.00 5.00
2 Roy White SP 10.00 25.00
3 Curt Blefary .40 1.00
4 Fritz Peterson .40 1.00
5 Danny Cater .40 1.00
6 Horace Clarke .40 1.00
7 Gene Michael .40 1.00
8 Stan Bahnsen .40 1.00
9 Thurman Munson 4.00 10.00
10 John Ellis .40 1.00
11 Jerry Kenney .40 1.00
12 Mel Stottlemyre .60 1.50
13 Joe DiMaggio 4.00 10.00
Mickey Mantle

1970 Yankees Photos SCFC

This 36-card set of the New York Yankees measures approximately 4" by 5" and features black-and-white player photos with white borders. The cards are listed below according to the numbers stamped on their white backs.

COMPLETE SET (36) 20.00 50.00
1 Jack Aker .60 1.50
2 Stan Bahnsen .60 1.50
3 Frank Baker .60 1.50
4 Curt Blefary .60 1.50
5 Ron Blomberg .60 1.50
6 Bill Burbach .60 1.50
7 Danny Cater .60 1.50
8 Horace Clarke .60 1.50
9 John Cumberland .60 1.50
10 John Ellis .60 1.50
11 Jake Gibbs .60 1.50
12 Steve Hamilton .60 1.50
13 Ron Hansen .60 1.50
14 Mike Hegan .60 1.50
15 Ralph Houk MG .60 1.50
16 Elston Howard CO 1.00 2.50
17 Dick Howser CO .60 1.50
18 Mike Kekich .60 1.50
19 Jerry Kenney .60 1.50
20 Ron Klimkowski .60 1.50
21 Steve Kline .60 1.50
22 Jim Lyttle .60 1.50
23 Mickey Mantle CO 4.00 10.00
24 Mike McCormick .60 1.50
25 Lindy McDaniel .60 1.50
26 Gene Michael .75 2.00
27 Thurman Munson 2.00 5.00
28 Bobby Murcer 1.00 2.50
29 Fritz Peterson .60 1.50
30 Mel Stottlemyre 1.00 2.50
31 Frank Tepedino .75 2.00
32 Joe Verbanic .60 1.50
33 Pete Ward .60 1.50
34 Gary Waslewski .60 1.50
35 Roy White .75 2.00
36 Ron Woods .60 1.50

1971 Yankees Arco Oil

Sponsored by Arco Oil, these 12 pictures of the 1971 New York Yankees measure approximately 8" by 10" and feature on their fronts white-bordered posed color player photos. The player's name is shown in black lettering within the white margin below the photo. His facsimile autograph appears across the picture. The white back carries the team's and player's names at the top, followed below by position, biography, career highlights, and statistics. An ad at the bottom for picture frames rounds out the back. The cards are unnumbered and checklisted below in alphabetical order.

COMPLETE SET (12) 30.00 60.00
1 Jack Aker 1.50 4.00
2 Stan Bahnsen 1.50 4.00
3 Frank Baker 1.50 4.00
4 Danny Cater 1.50 4.00
5 Horace Clarke 2.50 6.00
6 John Ellis 1.50 4.00
7 Gene Michael 2.50 6.00
8 Thurman Munson 5.00 12.00
9 Bobby Murcer 3.00 8.00
10 Fritz Peterson 1.50 4.00
11 Mel Stottlemyre 3.00 8.00
12 Roy White 2.50 6.00

1971 Yankees Clinic Day Postcards

Similar to the 1970 promotion, the New York Yankees again had days where the fans could meet their favorite players before selected home games. These cards were issued so fans could have an item for the player to sign. We have sequenced this set in alphabetical order. These postcards were produced by Dexter Press.

COMPLETE SET (16) 20.00 50.00
1 Stan Bahnsen .40 1.00
2 Curt Blefary .40 1.00
3 Danny Cater .40 1.00
4 Horace Clarke .40 1.00
Gene Michael
5 John Ellis .40 1.00
6 Jake Gibbs .40 1.00
7 Ralph Houk MG .40 1.00
8 Jerry Kenney .40 1.00
Frank Baker
9 Jim Lyttle .40 1.00
Felipe Alou
10 Mickey Mantle 10.00 25.00
11 Lindy McDaniel .40 1.00
12 Thurman Munson 4.00 10.00
13 Bobby Murcer 1.25 3.00
14 Fritz Peterson .40 1.00
15 Mel Stottlemyre .75 2.00
16 Roy White 1.25 3.00

1972 Yankees Schedules

This eight card set was issued in very limited quantities. These cards have 1972 Yankees schedules on the back and are very difficult to obtain. These cards are unnumbered and we have sequenced them in alphabetical order.

COMPLETE SET (8) 300.00 600.00
1 Felipe Alou 50.00 100.00
2 Ron Blomberg 10.00 25.00
3 Thurman Munson 100.00 200.00
4 Bobby Murcer 50.00 100.00
5 Mel Stottlemyre 40.00 80.00
6 Ron Swoboda 20.00 50.00
7 Roy White 40.00 80.00
8 Bill White ANN 50.00 100.00
Phil Rizzuto
Frank Messer

1972 Yankees Team Issue

This six-card set of the 1972 New York Yankees measures approximately 4" by 6" and features color player photos with white borders. The backs are blank. The cards are unnumbered and checklisted below in alphabetical order.

COMPLETE SET (6) 10.00 25.00
1 Danny Cater 1.25 3.00
2 John Ellis 1.25 3.00
3 Thurman Munson 4.00 10.00
4 Bobby Murcer 2.00 5.00
5 Fritz Peterson 1.25 3.00
6 Roy White 2.00 5.00

1973 Yankees TCMA All-Time Team

These cards measure 3.5 x 5.5 and feature black and white photos of twelve Yankee greats. The player's name appears on the front of the card beneath their photo, while the cardbacks lists the checklist. The unnumbered cards have been checklisted alphabetically.

COMPLETE SET (12) 12.50 30.00
1 Bill Dickey .60 1.50
2 Joe DiMaggio 4.00 10.00
3 Whitey Ford 1.00 2.50
4 Lou Gehrig 2.50 6.00
5 Tony Lazzeri .40 1.00
6 Mickey Mantle 2.50 6.00
7 Johnny Murphy .40 1.00
8 Phil Rizzuto .60 1.50
9 Red Rolfe .40 1.00
10 Red Ruffing .40 1.00
11 Babe Ruth 4.00 10.00
12 Casey Stengel MG 1.00 2.50

1973 Yankees Team Issue

This six-card set of the New York Yankees measures approximately 7" by 8 3/4" and features color player photos in a white border. The player's name and team are printed in the wide bottom margin. The backs are blank. The cards are unnumbered and checklisted in alphabetical order.

COMPLETE SET (6) 10.00 25.00
1 Ron Blomberg 1.25 3.00

2 Sparky Lyle	2.00	5.00
3 Bobby Murcer	2.00	5.00
4 Graig Nettles	2.00	5.00
5 Fritz Peterson	1.25	3.00
6 Roy White	1.50	4.00

1975 Yankees 1927 TCMA

This 30-card set of the 1927 New York Yankees features black-and-white player photos in white borders. The backs carry player information and statistics. The cards are unnumbered and checklisted below in alphabetical order.

COMPLETE SET (30)	20.00	50.00
1 Walter Beall	.40	1.00
2 Benny Bengough	.60	1.50
3 Pat Collins	.40	1.00
4 Earle Combs	1.00	2.50
5 Joe Dugan	.40	1.00
6 Cedric Durst	.40	1.00
7 Mike Gazella	.40	1.00
8 Lou Gehrig	2.00	5.00
9 Joe Giard	.40	1.00
10 Johnny Grabowski	.40	1.00
11 Waite Hoyt	1.00	2.50
12 Miller Huggins MG	1.00	2.50
13 Mark Koenig	.60	1.50
14 Tony Lazzeri	1.00	2.50
15 Bob Meusel	.75	2.00
16 Wiley Moore	.40	1.00
17 Ray Morehart	.40	1.00
18 Ben Paschal	.40	1.00
19 Herb Pennock	1.00	2.50
20 George Pipgras	.40	1.00
21 Dutch Ruether	.40	1.00
22 Jacob Ruppert OWN	.60	1.50
23 Babe Ruth	3.00	8.00
24 Bob Shawkey	.60	1.50
25 Urban Shocker	.40	1.00
26 Myles Thomas	.40	1.00
27 Julie Wera	.40	1.00
28 Yankee Stadium	.40	1.00
29 Miller Huggins MG Charlie O'Leary CO Art Fletche	.60	1.50
30 Lou Gehrig Tony Lazzeri Mark Koenig Joe Dugan/	1.25	3.00

1975 Yankees All-Time Team TCMA

This 12-card set features two different photo variations of all-time great New York Yankees: blue-and-white and black and white. The cards measure approximately 2 1/2" by 3 3/4". The cardbacks carry the checklist of the set. The cards are unnumbered and checklisted below in alphabetical order.

COMPLETE SET (12)	10.00	25.00
1 Bill Dickey	1.00	2.50
2 Joe DiMaggio	2.00	5.00
3 Whitey Ford	1.00	2.50
4 Lou Gehrig	2.00	5.00
5 Tony Lazzeri	1.00	2.50
6 Mickey Mantle	2.00	5.00
7 Johnny Murphy	.40	1.00
8 Phil Rizzuto	1.00	2.50
9 Red Rolfe	.40	1.00
10 Red Ruffing	.75	2.00
11 Babe Ruth	3.00	8.00
12 Casey Stengel MG	1.00	2.50

1975 Yankees Dynasty 1936-39 TCMA

The first 49 cards in this set measure 2 3/4" by 4" and feature black-and-white player photos with white borders. The final five cards are 4" by 5 1/2" and feature photos of Yankees from 1936-39. The player's name and position are printed in blue below the picture. The phrase "1936-1939 Yankee Dynasty" is at the top except for card numbers 50-53, which have "World Champions -- 19XX" printed at the top. The backs carry statistics printed in blue. The cards are unnumbered and checklisted below in alphabetical order. This set can be distinguished from the 1983 reprint by two major characteristics: The first one is the printing of these cards in blue and the second one is that neither Joe Gallagher or Lee Stine is in the 1975 set.

COMPLETE SET (54)	15.00	40.00
1 Ivy Paul Andrews	.20	.50
2 Joe Beggs	.20	.50
3 Marv Breuer	.20	.50
4 Johnny Broaca	.20	.50
5 Jumbo Brown	.20	.50
6 Spud Chandler	.30	.75
7 Ben Chapman	.20	.50
8 Earl Combs CO	.60	1.50
9 Frankie Crosetti	.40	1.00
10 Babe Dahlgren	.20	.50
11 Joe DiMaggio	2.50	6.00
12 Bill Dickey	.60	1.50
13 Atley Donald	.20	.50
14 Wes Farrell	.30	.75
15 Artie Fletcher CO	.20	.50
16 Lou Gehrig	2.50	6.00
17 Joe Glenn	.20	.50
18 Lefty Gomez	.60	1.50
19 Joe Gordon	.40	1.00
20 Bump Hadley	.20	.50
21 Don Heffner	.20	.50
22 Tommy Henrich	.40	1.00
23 Oral Hildebrand	.20	.50
24 Myril Hoag	.20	.50
25 Roy Johnson	.20	.50
26 Art Jorgens	.20	.50
27 Charlie Keller	.30	.75
28 Ted Kleinhans	.20	.50
29 Billy Knickerbocker	.20	.50
30 Tony Lazzeri	.60	1.50
31 Frank Makosky	.20	.50
32 Pat Malone	.20	.50
33 Joe McCarthy MG Jacob Ruppert OWN	.40	1.00
34 Johnny Murphy	.30	.75
35 Monty Pearson	.20	.50
36 Jake Powell	.20	.50
37 Red Rolfe	.30	.75
38 Buddy Rosar	.20	.50
39 Red Ruffing	.60	1.50
40 Marius Russo	.20	.50
41 Jack Saltzgaver	.20	.50
42 Paul Schreiber	.20	.50
43 Johnny Schulte	.20	.50
44 Bob Seeds	.20	.50
45 Twinkletoes Selkirk	.30	.75
46 Steve Sundra	.20	.50
47 Sandy Vance	.20	.50
48 Dixie Walker	.30	.75
49 Kemp Wicker	.20	.50
50 World Champions 1936 (Team celebrating)	1.50	4.00
51 World Champions 1937 Joe DiMaggio Frankie Croset	1.50	4.00
52 World Champions 1938 Red Rolfe Tony Lazzeri Lou	.60	1.50
53 World Champions 1939 Lou Gehrig Joe DiMaggio	1.50	4.00
54 Lou Gehrig Hits Another	1.50	4.00

1975 Yankees SSPC

This 23-card standard-size set of New York Yankees features white-bordered posed color player photos on their fronts, which are free of any other markings. The white back carries the player's name in red lettering above his blue-lettered biography and career highlights. The cards are numbered on the back within a circle formed by the player's team name. A similar set of New York Mets was produced at the same time. This set is dated 1975 because that was Ed Brinkman's only season with the Yankees.

COMPLETE SET (23)	8.00	20.00
1 Jim Hunter	1.50	4.00
2 Bobby Bonds	.40	1.00
3 Ed Brinkman	.10	.25
4 Ron Blomberg	.20	.50
5 Thurman Munson	2.00	5.00
6 Roy White	.30	.75
7 Larry Gura	.10	.25
8 Ed Herrmann	.10	.25
9 Bill Virdon MG	.20	.50
10 Elliott Maddox	.20	.50
11 Lou Piniella	.40	1.00
12 Rick Dempsey	.30	.75
13 Fred Stanley	.10	.25
14 Chris Chambliss	.40	1.00
15 George Medich	.10	.25
16 Pat Dobson	.20	.50
17 Alex Johnson	.20	.50
18 Jim Mason	.10	.25
19 Sandy Alomar	.10	.25
20 Graig Nettles	.40	1.00
21 Walt Williams	.10	.25
22 Sparky Lyle	.30	.75
23 Dick Tidrow	.10	.25

1977 Yankees Burger King

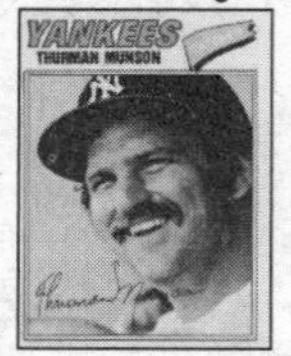

The cards in this 24-card set measure 2 1/2" by 3 1/2". The cards in this set marked with an asterisk have different poses than those cards in the regular 1977 Topps set. The checklist card is unnumbered and the Piniella card was issued subsequent to the original printing. The complete set price below refers to all 24 cards listed, including Piniella.

COMPLETE SET (24)	15.00	40.00
1 Yankees Team Billy Martin MG	.40	1.00
2 Thurman Munson * UER (Facsimile autograph misspe	3.00	8.00
3 Fran Healy	.10	.25
4 Jim Hunter	1.00	2.50
5 Ed Figueroa	.10	.25
6 Don Gullett */(Mouth closed)	.20	.50
7 Mike Torrez */(Shown as A's in 1977 Topps)	.20	.50
8 Ken Holtzman	.20	.50
9 Dick Tidrow	.10	.25
10 Sparky Lyle	.20	.50
11 Ron Guidry	.30	.75
12 Chris Chambliss	.20	.50
13 Willie Randolph* No rookie trophy	.30	.75
14 Bucky Dent* Shown as White Sox in 1977 Topps	.20	.50
15 Graig Nettles */(Closer photo than in 1977 Topps	.40	1.00
16 Fred Stanley	.10	.25
17 Reggie Jackson* Looking up with bat	5.00	12.00
18 Mickey Rivers	.30	.75
19 Roy White	.20	.50
20 Jim Wynn* Shown as Brave in 1977 Topps	.30	.75
21 Paul Blair*	.30	.75
Shown as Oriole in 1977 Topps		
22 Carlos May */(Shown as White Sox in 1977 Topps)	.20	.50
23 Lou Piniella SP	8.00	20.00
NNO Checklist Card TP	.10	.25

1978 Yankees Burger King

The cards in this 23-card set measure 2 1/2" by 3 1/2". These cards were distributed in packs of three players plus a checklist at Burger King's New York area outlets. Cards with an asterisk have different poses than those in the Topps regular issue.

COMPLETE SET (23)	6.00	15.00
1 Billy Martin MG	.40	1.00
2 Thurman Munson	1.50	4.00
3 Cliff Johnson	.10	.25
4 Ron Guidry	.40	1.00
5 Ed Figueroa	.10	.25
6 Dick Tidrow	.10	.25
7 Jim Hunter	1.00	2.50
8 Don Gullett	.10	.25
9 Sparky Lyle	.30	.75
10 Goose Gossage *	.40	1.00
11 Rawly Eastwick *	.10	.25
12 Chris Chambliss	.30	.75
13 Willie Randolph	.30	.75
14 Graig Nettles	.40	1.00
15 Bucky Dent	.30	.75
16 Jim Spencer *	.10	.25
17 Fred Stanley	.10	.25
18 Lou Piniella	.40	1.00
19 Roy White	.30	.75
20 Mickey Rivers	.30	.75
21 Reggie Jackson	1.50	4.00
22 Paul Blair	.10	.25
NNO Checklist Card TP	.08	.20

1978 Yankees Photo Album

This 27-card set of the New York Yankees measures approximately 8" square and features a color player portrait in a white border with a facsimile autograph. The backs are blank. The cards are unnumbered and checklisted below in alphabetical order.

COMPLETE SET (27)	6.00	15.00
1 Jim Beattie Brian Doyle Paul Lindblad Larry McC	.10	.25
2 Yogi Berra Art Fowler Elston Howard Dick Howser	.40	1.00
3 Paul Blair	.10	.25
4 Chris Chambliss	.30	.75
5 Kenny Clay	.10	.25
6 Bucky Dent	.30	.75
7 Ed Figueroa	.10	.25
8 Goose(Rich) Gossage	.40	1.00
9 Ron Guidry	.40	1.00
10 Don Gullett	.20	.50
11 Mike Heath	.10	.25
12 Catfish(Jim) Hunter	.60	1.50
13 Reggie Jackson	1.50	4.00
14 Cliff Johnson	.10	.25
15 Jay Johnstone	.20	.50
16 Bob Lemon MG	.40	1.00
17 Sparky Lyle	.20	.50
18 Thurman Munson	.75	2.00
19 Graig Nettles	.40	1.00
20 Lou Piniella	.40	1.00
21 Willie Randolph	.30	.75
22 Mickey Rivers	.20	.50
23 Jim Spencer	.10	.25
24 Fred Stanley	.10	.25
25 Gary Thomasson	.10	.25
26 Dick Tidrow	.10	.25
27 Roy White	.20	.50

1978 Yankees SSPC Diary

This 27 card standard-size set was inserted into the 1978 Yankees Yearbook and Diary of a Champion Yankee. These cards are full bleed and the backs have 1977 seasonal highlights.

COMPLETE SET (27)	4.00	10.00
1 Thurman Munson	1.25	3.00
2 Cliff Johnson	.08	.20
3 Lou Piniella	.30	.75
4 Dell Alston	.08	.20
5 Yankee Stadium	.08	.20
6 Ken Holtzman	.08	.20
7 Chris Chambliss	.10	.25
8 Roy White	.08	.20
9 Ed Figueroa	.08	.20
10 Dick Tidrow	.08	.20
11 Sparky Lyle	.10	.25
12 Fred Stanley	.08	.20
13 Mickey Rivers	.08	.20
14 Billy Martin MG	.10	.25
15 George Zeber	.08	.20
16 Ken Clay	.08	.20
17 Ron Guidry	.30	.75
18 Don Gullett	.08	.20
19 Fran Healy	.08	.20
20 Paul Blair	.08	.20
21 Mickey Klutts	.08	.20
22 Yankee Team	.08	.20
23 Catfish Hunter	.75	2.00
24 Bucky Dent	.10	.25
25 Graig Nettles	.30	.75
26 Reggie Jackson	1.25	3.00
27 Willie Randolph	.30	.75

1979 Yankees Burger King

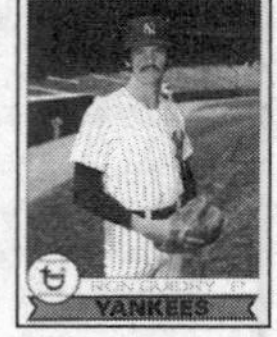

The cards in this 23-card set measure 2 1/2" by 3 1/2". There are 22 numbered cards and one unnumbered checklist in the 1979 Burger King Yankee set. The poses of Guidry, Tiant, John and Beniquez, each marked with an asterisk below, are different from their poses appearing in the regular Topps issue. The team card has the team leaders noted on the back.

COMPLETE SET (23)	5.00	12.00
1 Yankees Team: Bob Lemon MG	.40	1.00
2 Thurman Munson	1.50	4.00
3 Cliff Johnson	.10	.25
4 Ron Guidry *	.30	.75
5 Jay Johnstone	.20	.50
6 Jim Hunter	1.00	2.50
7 Jim Beattie	.20	.50
8 Luis Tiant */(Shown as Red Sox in 1979 Topps)	.40	1.00
9 Tommy John */(Shown as Dodgers in 1979 Topps)	.40	1.00
10 Goose Gossage	.40	1.00
11 Ed Figueroa	.10	.25
12 Chris Chambliss	.30	.75
13 Willie Randolph	.40	1.00
14 Bucky Dent	.30	.75
15 Graig Nettles	.40	1.00
16 Fred Stanley	.10	.25
17 Jim Spencer	.10	.25
18 Lou Piniella	.40	1.00
19 Roy White	.30	.75
20 Mickey Rivers	.30	.75
21 Reggie Jackson	1.50	4.00
22 Juan Beniquez *	.20	.50
NNO Checklist Card TP	.08	.15

1979 Yankees 1927 TCMA

This 32-card set features sepia tone pictures of the 1927 New York Yankees team. The fronts feature the player photo while the back has information about the featured player.

COMPLETE SET (32)	8.00	20.00
1 Babe Ruth	3.00	8.00
2 Lou Gehrig	2.00	5.00

3 Tony Lazzeri .40 1.00
4 Mark Koenig .20 .50
5 Julie Wera .10 .25
6 Ray Morehart .10 .25
7 Art Fletcher CO .10 .25
8 Joe Dugan .20 .50
9 Charlie O'Leary CO .10 .25
10 Bob Meusel .30 .75
11 Earle Combs .40 1.00
12 Cedric Durst .10 .25
13 John Grabowski .10 .25
14 Mike Gazella .10 .25
15 Pat Collins .10 .25
16 Waite Hoyt .40 1.00
17 Myles Thomas .10 .25
18 Benny Bengough .20 .50
19 Herb Pennock .40 1.00
20 Wilcy Moore .10 .25
21 Urban Shocker .10 .25
22 Dutch Reuther .10 .25
23 George Pipgras .10 .25
24 Jacob Ruppert OWN .20 .50
25 Eddie Bennett BB .10 .25
26 Ed Barrow GM .20 .50
27 Ben Paschal .10 .25
28 Miller Huggins MG .40 1.00
29 Joe Giard .10 .25
30 Bob Shawkey .20 .50
31 Walter Beall .10 .25
32 Don Miller .10 .25

1979 Yankees Picture Album

This 32-page Picture Album of the 1979 New York Yankees measures approximately 8" by 8" and features posed color player photos in white borders with a facsimile autograph across the bottom. The backs are blank. The cards are unnumbered and checklisted below in alphabetical order. This set was issued late during the 1979 season as Thurman Munson is memorialized in his photo.

COMPLETE SET (34) 8.00 20.00
1 Jim Beattie .20 .50
2 Juan Beniquez .10 .25
3 Yogi Berra CO .75 2.00
4 Bobby Brown .10 .25
5 Ray Burris .10 .25
6 Chris Chambliss .20 .50
7 Ken Clay .10 .25
8 Ron Davis .10 .25
9 Bucky Dent .20 .50
10 Brian Doyle .10 .25
11 Mike Ferraro .10 .25
12 Ed Figueroa .10 .25
13 Art Fowler CO .10 .25
14 Goose Gossage .40 1.00
15 Ron Guidry .40 1.00
16 Don Gullett .10 .25
17 Jim Hegan CO .10 .25
18 Don Hood .10 .25
19 Jim Hunter .50 1.25
20 Reggie Jackson 1.25 3.00
21 Tommy John .40 1.00
22 Jim Kaat .30 .75
23 Charley Lau CO .10 .25
24 Billy Martin MG .40 1.00
25 Thurman Munson .75 2.00
26 Bobby Murcer .30 .75
27 Jerry Narron .10 .25
28 Graig Nettles .40 1.00
29 Lou Piniella .30 .75
30 Willie Randolph .40 1.00
31 Jim Spencer .10 .25
32 Fred Stanley .10 .25
33 Luis Tiant .30 .75
34 Roy White .20 .50

1980 Yankees Greats TCMA

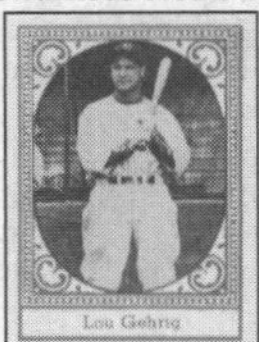

These 12 standard-size cards feature all-time Yankee greats. The fronts have a player photo and the backs display a checklist of who is in the set.

COMPLETE SET (12) 4.00 10.00
1 Lou Gehrig 1.25 3.00
2 Tony Lazzeri .30 .75
3 Red Rolfe .20 .50
4 Phil Rizzuto .60 1.50
5 Babe Ruth 1.50 4.00
6 Mickey Mantle 1.50 4.00
7 Joe DiMaggio 1.25 3.00
8 Bill Dickey .40 1.00
9 Red Ruffing .40 1.00
10 Whitey Ford .60 1.50
11 Johnny Murphy .20 .50
12 Casey Stengel MG .40 1.00

1980 Yankees Photo Album

This 27-card set of the New York Yankees was distributed in a booklet measuring approximately 8" by 7 7/8". The fronts feature a color player portrait in a white border with a facsimile autograph. The backs are blank. The cards are unnumbered and checklisted below in alphabetical order.

COMPLETE SET (27) 5.00 12.00
1 Yogi Berra .40 1.00
Mike Ferraro
Jim Hegan
Charley Lau/
2 Bobby Brown .08 .25
3 Rick Cerone .08 .25
4 Ron Davis .08 .25
5 Bucky Dent .30 .75
6 Ed Figueroa .08 .25
7 Oscar Gamble .20 .50
8 Goose(Rich) Gossage .40 1.00
9 Ron Guidry .40 1.00
10 Don Gullett .08 .25
Johnny Oates
11 Dick Howser MG .08 .25
12 Reggie Jackson .75 2.00
13 Tommy John .40 1.00
14 Ruppert Jones .08 .25
15 Joe Lefebvre .08 .25
16 Rudy May .08 .25
17 Bobby Murcer .40 1.00
18 Graig Nettles .40 1.00
19 Lou Piniella .40 1.00
20 Willie Randolph .40 1.00
21 Eric Soderholm .08 .25
22 Jim Spencer .08 .25
23 Fred Stanley .08 .25
24 Luis Tiant .20 .50
25 Tom Underwood .08 .25
26 Bob Watson .20 .50
27 Dennis Werth .08 .25

1958 Yoo-Hoo Match Book Covers

This yellow match book cover was issued by the Yoo-Hoo chocolate drink company and featured a photo of Yogi Berra on the back. The sepia, head shot photo is encircled with a bottle cap design and above and below the cap are the words "Me for Yoo-Hoo". Yogi Berra's name is printed on the lower portion of the picture. The inner portion of the match book cover carries an offer to mail in the empty cover with $2.50 and receive a book entitled "The Story of Yogi Berra". A matchbook was also made of Yankee great Mickey Mantle and that had offers inside for memorabilia from assorted New York Yankee.

COMPLETE SET 62.50 125.00
1 Yogi Berra 12.50 25.00
2 Mickey Mantle 50.00 100.00

1927 York Caramel Type 1 E210

The cards in this 60-card set measure 1 3/8" by 2 1/2". This set contains numbered cards with black and white photos of baseball players in the series of "most prominent baseball stars" issued by the York Caramel Company. They were released to the public in 1927. Number 12 has been found with two spellings; number 58 appears with either Bell or Galloway; and numbers 9, 25, 31 and 46 have incorrect photos of players with the same last names. An interesting feature is the caption which appears under the player's's name on back, e.g., Burleigh Grimes is dubbed "A Sterling National League Pitcher." The complete set price includes all variation cards listed in the checklist below.

COMPLETE SET (64) 20,000.00 40,000.00
1 Burleigh Grimes 250.00 500.00
2 Walter Reuther/(sic& Ruether) 150.00 300.00
3A Joe Duggan ERR/(sic& Dugan) 200.00 400.00
3B Joe Dugan COR 200.00 400.00
4 Red Faber 250.00 500.00
5 Gabby Hartnett 300.00 600.00
6 Babe Ruth 4,000.00 8,000.00
7 Bob Meusel 200.00 400.00
8 Herb Pennock 250.00 500.00
9 George (H.) Burns/(photo actually George J. Burn 150.00 300.00
10 Joe Sewell 250.00 500.00
11 George Uhle 150.00 300.00
12A Bob O'Farrel ERR 200.00 400.00
12B Bob O'Farrell COR 200.00 400.00
13 Rogers Hornsby 750.00 1,500.00
14 Pie Traynor 300.00 600.00
15 Clarence Mitchell 150.00 300.00
16 Eppa Rixey 250.00 500.00
17 Carl Mays 200.00 400.00
18 Dolf Luque 150.00 300.00
19 Dave Bancroft 250.00 500.00
20 George Kelly 250.00 500.00
21 Ira Flagstead 150.00 300.00
22 Harry Heilmann 300.00 600.00
23 Ray Schalk 250.00 500.00
24 Johnny Mostil 150.00 300.00
25 Hack Wilson/(photo actually Art Wilson) 500.00 1,000.00
26 Tom Zachary 150.00 300.00
27 Ty Cobb 2,500.00 5,000.00
28 Tris Speaker 750.00 1,500.00
29 Ralph Perkins 150.00 300.00
30 Jess Haines/(sic& Jesse) 250.00 500.00
31 Sherwood Smith/(photo actually Jack Coombs) 150.00 300.00
32 Max Carey 250.00 500.00
33 Eugene Hargraves 150.00 300.00
34 Miguel L. Gonzales 150.00 300.00
35A Clifton Heathcot ERR 200.00 400.00
35B Clifton Heathcote COR 200.00 400.00
36 Sam Rice 250.00 500.00
37 Earl Sheely 150.00 300.00
38 Emory E. Rigney 150.00 300.00
39 Bib Falk 150.00 300.00
40 Nick Altrock 150.00 300.00
41 Bucky Harris 250.00 500.00
42 John J. McGraw MG 500.00 1,000.00
43 Wilbert Robinson MG 300.00 600.00
44 Grover C. Alexander 750.00 1,500.00
45 Walter Johnson 1,000.00 2,000.00
46 William H. Terry/(photo actually Zeb Terry) 300.00 600.00
47 Eddie Collins 300.00 600.00
48 Marty McManus 150.00 300.00
49 Goose Goslin 300.00 600.00
50 Frankie Frisch 500.00 1,000.00
51 Jimmy Dykes 200.00 400.00
52 Cy Williams 200.00 400.00
53 Ed Roush 300.00 600.00
54 George Sisler 500.00 1,000.00
55 Ed Rommel 200.00 400.00
56 Rogers Peckinpaugh/(sic& Roger) 200.00 400.00
57 Stan Coveleskie 250.00 500.00
58A Clarence Galloway 200.00 400.00
58B Lester Bell 200.00 400.00
59 Bob Shawkey 200.00 400.00
60 John P. McInnis 200.00 400.00

1974 Cy Young Museum Postcard

This one card postcard set was issued by TCMA to promote the Cy Young Museum in Newcomerstown, Ohio. The front has a picture of Young surrounded by the words "Cy Young Museum" on top and its location on the bottom. The back has some information about Young's career.

1 Cy Young 2.00 5.00

1928 Yuengling's Ice Cream

The cards in this 60-card set measure approximately 1 3/8" by 2 9/16". This black and white, numbered set contains many Hall of Famers. The card backs are the same as those found in sets of E210 and W502. The Paul Waner card, number 45, actually contains a picture of Clyde Barnhardt. Each back contains an offer to redeem pictures of Babe Ruth for ice cream. The catalog designation for this set is F50.

COMPLETE SET (60) 1,500.00 3,000.00
1 Burleigh Grimes 50.00 100.00
2 Walter Reuther 20.00 50.00
3 Joe Dugan 30.00 60.00
4 Red Faber 50.00 100.00
5 Gabby Hartnett 50.00 100.00
6 Babe Ruth 1,250.00 2,500.00
7 Bob Meusel 40.00 80.00
8 Herb Pennock 50.00 100.00
9 George Burns 20.00 50.00
10 Joe Sewell 50.00 100.00
11 George Uhle 20.00 50.00
12 Bob O'Farrell 7.50 15.00
13 Rogers Hornsby 150.00 300.00
14 Pie Traynor 50.00 100.00
15 Clarence Mitchell 20.00 50.00
16 Eppa Rixey 50.00 100.00
17 Carl Mays 30.00 60.00
18 Adolfo Luque 30.00 60.00
19 Dave Bancroft 50.00 100.00
20 George Kelly 50.00 100.00
21 Earle Combs 50.00 100.00
22 Harry Heilmann 50.00 100.00
23 Ray Schalk 50.00 100.00
24 John Mostil 20.00 50.00
25 Hack Wilson 75.00 150.00
26 Lou Gehrig 750.00 1,500.00
27 Ty Cobb 750.00 1,500.00
28 Tris Speaker 125.00 250.00
29 Tony Lazzeri 50.00 100.00
30 Waite Hoyt 50.00 100.00
31 Sherwood Smith 20.00 50.00
32 Max Carey 50.00 100.00
33 Gene Hargrave 20.00 50.00
34 Miguel Gonzalez 30.00 60.00
35 Joe Judge 30.00 60.00
36 Sam Rice 50.00 100.00
37 Earl Sheely 20.00 50.00
38 Sam Jones 30.00 60.00
39 Bibb Falk 20.00 50.00
40 Willie Kamm 20.00 50.00
41 Bucky Harris 50.00 100.00
42 John McGraw MG 75.00 150.00
43 Art Nehf 30.00 60.00
44 Grover C. Alexander 150.00 300.00
45 Paul Waner 50.00 100.00
46 Bill Terry 100.00 200.00
47 Glenn Wright 20.00 50.00
48 Earl Smith 20.00 50.00
49 Goose Goslin 50.00 100.00
50 Frank Frisch 75.00 150.00
51 Joe Harris 20.00 50.00
52 Cy Williams 30.00 60.00
53 Eddie Roush 50.00 100.00
54 George Sisler 100.00 200.00
55 Ed Rommel 30.00 60.00
56 Roger Peckinpaugh 30.00 60.00
57 Stanley Coveleskie 50.00 100.00
58 Lester Bell 20.00 50.00
59 Lloyd Waner 50.00 100.00
60 John McInnis 30.00 60.00

1960 Bill Zuber Restaurant

These items features retired Yankee Bill Zuber. The postcard is black-and-white borderless portrait in his New York Yankees uniform with a facsimile autograph. The back displays a postcard format with an advertisement for his restaurant in Homestead, Iowa. The matchbook has a small photo of Zuber and then complete informaiton about the restaurant as well as some details about his career.

COMPLETE SET (2) 12.50 30.00
1 Bill Zuber Postcard 6.00 15.00
2 Bill Zuber Matchbook 6.00 15.00

1883 California League Cabinets

These cabinets were recently discovered and feature members of the Haverlys, which played their games in San Francisco. The cabinets have the player photographed in their team uniforms with the player adding a fascimile signature on the bottom. Since these items are unnumbered we have sequenced them in alphabetical order. Any additions to this checklist are appreciated.

COMPLETE SET 1,500.00 3,000.00
1 Patsy Cahill 500.00 1,000.00
2 Frank Carrol 500.00 1,000.00
3 Peter Meegan 500.00 1,000.00
4 Tom McCord 500.00 1,000.00
5 A. Sohn 500.00 1,000.00

VINTAGE MINOR LEAGUES

1886 Syracuse Stars Hancock

This three card set was issued by Hancock's Gents Furnishing Store and featured members of the 1886 Syracuse Stars. The fronts have a street clothes portrait of the featured player while the back has an advertisment for Hancock's. Interestingly the Photographer is noted as Goodwin, who would later in the decade produce more famous card sets. Since these cards are unnumbered, we have sequenced them in alphabetical order. It is possible that more cards exist so if there is any additional information we would appreciate it.

COMPLETE SET 15000
1 Richard Buckley 6,000.00 12,000.00
2 Douglas Crothers 6,000.00 12,000.00
3 Philip Tomney 6,000.00 12,000.00

1888 S.F. Hess and Co. Creole N321

It is not known why S.F. Hess based in Rochester, N.Y., produced this set of regional ballplayers from the California League. Each card has a color drawing of a ballplayer and is copyrighted 1888. The teams represented are G and M's, Haverlys, Pioneers and Stocktons. There are 40 cards known (37 players, three of whom are pictured on two separate cards) and all carry advertising for Creole cigarettes.

COMPLETE SET 40,000.00 80,000.00
1 Eddie Bennett (Haverly's) 1,500.00 3,000.00
2 George Borchers (G and M's) 1,500.00 3,000.00
3 Tom Buckley (Haverly's) 1,500.00 3,000.00
4 Turk Burke Batting (Stockton's) 1,500.00 3,000.00
5 Turk Burke Ready to Pitch (Stockton's) 1,500.00 3,000.00
6 Frank Carroll (Pioneers) 1,500.00 3,000.00
7 John Donohue (Pioneers) 1,500.00 3,000.00
8 Jack Donovan (G and M's) 1,500.00 3,000.00
9 Michael Finn (Pioneers) 1,500.00 3,000.00
10 Charles Gagus (Haverly's) 1,500.00 3,000.00
11 William Gurnett (G and M's) 1,500.00 3,000.00
12 George Hanley (Haverly's) 1,500.00 3,000.00
13 Pop Hardie Catching (G and M's) 1,500.00 3,000.00
14 Pop Hardie with Bat (G and M's) 1,500.00 3,000.00
15 Jack Hayes (Stockton's) 1,500.00 3,000.00
16 Jack Lawton (Haverly's) 1,500.00 3,000.00
17 Rube Levy (Haverly's) 4,000.00 8,000.00
18 Daniel Long (G and M's) 1,500.00 3,000.00
19 Tom McCord (G and M's) 1,500.00 3,000.00
20 Peter Meegan (Haverly's) 1,500.00 3,000.00
21 Henry Moore (Stockton's) 1,500.00 3,000.00
22 James Mullee (Pioneers) 1,500.00 3,000.00
23 Billy Newhart (G and M's) 1,500.00 3,000.00
24 Joseph Noonan (Pioneers) 1,500.00 3,000.00
25 Harry O'Day (Stockton's) 1,500.00 3,000.00
26 Hip Perrier (Pioneers) 1,500.00 3,000.00
27 Thomas Powers Catching (Haverly's) 1,500.00 3,000.00
28 Thomas Powers with Bat (Haverly's) 1,500.00 3,000.00
29 Jack Ryan (G and M's) 1,500.00 3,000.00
30 Charles Selna (Stockton's) 1,500.00 3,000.00
31 Joseph Shea (G and M's) 1,500.00 3,000.00
32 Jack Sheridan (Umpire) 1,500.00 3,000.00
33 Big Smith (Pioneers) 1,500.00 3,000.00
34 Hugh Smith (Pioneers) 1,500.00 3,000.00
35 John Smith (Pioneers) 1,500.00 3,000.00
36 Leonard Stockwell Catching (Stockton's) 1,500.00 3,000.00
37 Leonard Stockwell Batting (Stockton's) 1,500.003,000.00
38 Charles Sweeney (Haverly's) 1,500.00 3,000.00
39 Pop Swett (Haverly's) 1,500.00 3,000.00
40 Milton Whitehead (Stockton's) 1,500.00 3,000.00

1905 Providence Clamdiggers Postcard

Little is known about these items. The front features a posed action shot of the featured player and the photo is credited to a photographer from the Providence Tribune. The back featured a baseball opinion. Any additional information would be appreciated.

1 Jack Cronin	50.00	100.00
2 Bob Peterson	50.00	100.00

1907 Newark Evening World Supplements

These fifteen 7 1/2" by 10 15/16" photos were printed as supplements to the Newark Evening World Newspaper. They feature players from the 1907 Newark franchise.

COMPLETE SET (15)	2,250.00	4,500.00
1 William Carrick	150.00	300.00
2 James Cockman	150.00	300.00
3 Clyde Engle	250.00	500.00
4 James Jones	150.00	300.00
5 Paul Krichell	250.00	500.00
6 Henry LaBelle	150.00	300.00
7 William Mahling	150.00	300.00
8 Chas. McCafferty	150.00	300.00
9 Thomas McCarthy	150.00	300.00
10 James Mullin Sic, Mullen	150.00	300.00
11 Al Pardee	150.00	300.00
12 Bayard Sharpe	150.00	300.00
13 John E. Shea	150.00	300.00
14 Oscar Stanage	200.00	400.00
15 Elmer Zacher	200.00	400.00

1908 Buffalo Bisons F.J. Offerman

This set was issued in 1908 by F.J. Offerman and bears remarkable similarities to the PC American League Publishing set. Like the PC 770 set, this set features a large action shot of the player plus a smaller street clothes shot enclosed in an oval on the front of the card. The set features Buffalo players only.

COMPLETE SET(19)	2,000.00	4,000.00
1 James Archer	150.00	300.00
2 James Cleary	125.00	250.00
3 Larry Hestefer	125.00	250.00
4 Hunter Hill	125.00	250.00
5 William H. Kester	125.00	250.00
6 Charles Kisinger	125.00	250.00
7 Leri Knapp	125.00	250.00
8 Lew McAllister	125.00	250.00
9 George N. McConnell	125.00	250.00
10 William J. Mulligan	125.00	250.00
11 James Murray	125.00	250.00
12 William H. Nattress	125.00	250.00
13 Ralph Parrott	125.00	250.00
14 John B. Ryan	125.00	250.00
15 George Schirm	125.00	250.00
16 George Smith	125.00	250.00
17 John H. Vowinkle	125.00	250.00
18 John White	125.00	250.00
19 Merton Whitney	125.00	250.00

1908 Indianapolis Postcards

These postcards feature members of the Indianapolis Team of the American Association. The fronts feature posed action shots while the backs have standard postcard backs. An extremely early card of Hall of Famer Rube Marquard is in this set.

COMPLETE SET (20)	1,000.00	2,000.00
1 Bert Briggs	50.00	100.00
2 Owen Bush	75.00	150.00
3 Charles Carr MG	50.00	100.00
4 James Cook	50.00	100.00
5 Chirs Coulter	50.00	100.00
6 Paul Davidson	50.00	100.00
7 Carl Druhot	50.00	100.00
8 Louis Durham	62.50	125.00
9 Claude Elliott	50.00	100.00
10 John Eubanks	50.00	100.00
11 John Hayden	50.00	100.00
12 William Hopke	50.00	100.00
13 Daniel Howley	62.50	125.00
14 Chris Lindsey	50.00	100.00
15 Patrick Livingston	50.00	100.00
16 Rube Marquard	250.00	500.00
17 Ed Siever	50.00	100.00
18 Walter Slagle	50.00	100.00
19 Perry Werden	50.00	100.00
20 Otto Williams	50.00	100.00

1909 Atlanta Crackers Postcard

These postcards, which measure approximately 4" by 6" features members of the 1909 Altlanta Crackers. The ornate front has "Atlanta-1909" on top and the player photo in an oval in the middle with his name and position on the bottom. These card were actually issued with rounded corners.

1 Dick Bayless	50.00	100.00
2 Roy Castleton	50.00	100.00

1909 Clement Brothers D380-1

These eight black and white cards, which measure approximately 1 1/2" by 2 1/2" feature members of the 1909 Rochester Eastern League Team. Since these cards are unnumbered, we have sequenced them in alphabetical order.

COMPLETE SET (8)		
1 Ed Anderson	1,500.00	3,000.00
2 Emil Batch	1,500.00	3,000.00
3 John Butler	1,500.00	3,000.00
4 Ed Holly	1,500.00	3,000.00
5 Jim Holmes	1,500.00	3,000.00
6 George McConnell	1,500.00	3,000.00
7 Fred Osborn	1,500.00	3,000.00
8 Harry Pattee	1,500.00	3,000.00

1909-11 Obak T212

The catalog designation T212 actually encompasses three separate minor league sets (listed in sequence in the checklist below). Each card measures 1 7/16" by 2 5/8". Set 1 (1-76) features 76 colored player cards representing six PCL teams and was issued in 1909. The obverse captions are stylized (slanted), and the word "Obak" on the reverse is inscribed in "Old English" letters. Set 2 contains 175 colored cards (77-251) of players from six PCL and four NWL teams. The captions are not slanted, and "Obak" appears in large block letters on the back. Reverses advertise either "150" or "175" subjects, and some 35 different slogans exist. The backs of sets 1 and 2 are printed in blue. In contrast, the 1911 set of 175 colored cards has red-printed backs which contain a short biography and some statistics (252-426). The PCL and NWL are each represented by six teams in this set. Note that there is a Portland club in each league. The Obak brand was produced and distributed in California by a branch of the American Tobacco Company. Cards are ordered below alphabetically within team. Type 1 consists of Los Angeles (1-6), Oakland (9-22), Portland (23-33), Sacramento (34-46), San Francisco (47-62) and Vernon (63-76). Type 2 consists of Los Angeles (77-96), Oakland (97-113), Portland (114-132), Sacramento (133-151), San Francisco (152-172), Vernon (173-188), Seattle NWL (189-204), Spokane NWL (205-219), Tacoma NWL (220-235) and Vancouver NWL (236-251). Type 3 consists of Los Angeles (252-268), Oakland (269-287), Portland PCL (288-303), Sacramento (304-320), San Francisco (321-339), Vernon (340-358), Portland NWL (359-368), Seattle NWL (369-380), Spokane NWL (381-392), Tacoma NWL (393-403), Vancouver NWL (404-415), and Victoria NWL (416-426). While it is possible that it is unique; an album featuring 175 cards has surfaced.

COMPLETE SET	50,000.00	100,000.00
COMMON PLAYER (1-76)	250.00	500.00
COMMON PLAYER (77-251)	100.00	200.00
COMMON PLAYER (252-426)	100.00	200.00
1 Beall (Los Angeles) 1	250.00	500.00
2 Delmas (Los Angeles) 1	250.00	500.00
3 Dillon (Los Angeles) 1	250.00	500.00
4 Howard (Los Angeles) 1	250.00	500.00
5 Nagle (Los Angeles) 1	250.00	500.00
6 Orendorff (Los Angeles) 1	250.00	500.00
7 Smith, Jud (Los Angeles) 1	250.00	500.00
8 Wheeler (Los Angeles) 1	250.00	500.00
9 Boice (Oakland) 1	250.00	500.00
10 Cameron (Oakland) 1	250.00	500.00
11 Carroll (Oakland) 1	250.00	500.00
12 Christian (Oakland) 1	250.00	500.00
13 Hogan (Oakland) 1	250.00	500.00
14 LaLonge (Oakland) 1	250.00	500.00
15 Lewis, George (Oakland) 1	250.00	500.00
16 Lewis, D. (Oakland) 1	250.00	500.00
17 McKune (Oakland) 1	250.00	500.00
18 Murphy (Oakland) 1	250.00	500.00
19 Nelson (Oakland) 1	250.00	500.00
20 Ragan (Oakland) 1	250.00	500.00
21 Reidy (Oakland) 1	250.00	500.00
22 Wiggs (Oakland) 1	250.00	500.00
23 Breen (Portland) 1	250.00	500.00
24 Carson (Portland) 1	250.00	500.00
25 Fisher (Portland) 1	250.00	500.00
26 Garrett (Portland) 1	250.00	500.00
27 Graney (Portland) 1	300.00	600.00
28 Guyn (Portland) 1	250.00	500.00
29 McCredie (Portland) 1	250.00	500.00
30 Olson (Portland) 1	300.00	600.00
31 Ort (Portland) 1	250.00	500.00
32 Ryan, Bud (Portland) 1	250.00	500.00
33 Speas (Portland) 1	250.00	500.00
34 Baum (Sacramento) 1	250.00	500.00
35 Brown (Sacramento) 1	250.00	500.00
36 Byrnes (Sacramento) 1	250.00	500.00
37 Ehman (Sacramento) 1	250.00	500.00
38 Fitzgerald (Sacramento) 1	250.00	500.00
39 Flannagan (Sacramento) 1	250.00	500.00
40 Gandil (Sacramento) 1	600.00	1,200.00
41 Graham (Sacramento) 1	250.00	500.00
42 Howse (Sacramento) 1	250.00	500.00
43 Jansing (Sacramento) 1	250.00	500.00
44 Raymer (Sacramento)1	250.00	500.00
45 James Shinn	250.00	500.00
46 Whalen (Sacramento) 1	250.00	500.00
47 Berry (San Francisco) 1	250.00	500.00
48 Bodie (San Francisco) 1	300.00	600.00
49 Browning (San Francisco) 1	250.00	500.00
50 Eastley (San Francisco) 1	250.00	500.00
51 Griffin (San Francisco) 1	250.00	500.00
52 Henley (San Francisco) 1	250.00	500.00
53 Lewis (San Francisco) 1	250.00	500.00
54 McArdle (San Francisco) 1	250.00	500.00
55 Melchior (San Francisco) 1	250.00	500.00
56 Mohler (San Francisco) 1	250.00	500.00
57 Mundorff (San Francisco) 1	250.00	500.00
58 Tennant (San Francisco) 1	250.00	500.00
59 Williams, F. (San Francisco) 1	250.00	500.00
60 Williams, Nick (San Francisco) 1	250.00	500.00
61 Willis (San Francisco) 1	250.00	500.00
62 Zeider (San Francisco) 1	300.00	600.00
63 Bernard (Vernon) 1	250.00	500.00
64 Breckenridge (Vernon) 1	250.00	500.00
65 Brashear, Norman (Vernon) 1	250.00	500.00
66 Brown (Vernon) 1	250.00	500.00
67 Coy (Vernon) 1	250.00	500.00
68 Eagan (Vernon) 1	250.00	500.00
69 Haley (Vernon) 1	250.00	500.00
70 Harkins (Vernon) 1	250.00	500.00
71 Hitt (Vernon) 1	250.00	500.00
72 Hogan (Vernon) 1	250.00	500.00
73 Martinke (Vernon) 1	250.00	500.00
74 Mott (Vernon) 1	250.00	500.00
75 Stovall (Vernon) 1	250.00	500.00
76 Willett (Vernon) 1	250.00	500.00
77 Agnew (Los Angeles) 2	100.00	200.00
78 Bernard, Claude (Los Angeles) 2	100.00	200.00
79 Briswalter (Los Angeles) 2	100.00	200.00
80 Castleton (Los Angeles) 2	100.00	200.00
81 Criger (Los Angeles) 2	100.00	200.00
82 Daley (Los Angeles) 2	100.00	200.00
83 Delhi (Los Angeles) 2	100.00	200.00
84 Delmas (Los Angeles) 2	100.00	200.00
85 Dillon (Los Angeles) 2	100.00	200.00
86 Howard (Los Angeles) 2	100.00	200.00
87 Klein (Los Angeles) 2	100.00	200.00
88 Murphy (Los Angeles) 2	100.00	200.00
89 Nagle (Los Angeles) 2	100.00	200.00
90 Orendorff (Los Angeles) 2	100.00	200.00
91 Roth (Los Angeles) 2	100.00	200.00
92 Smith, Hugh (Los Angeles) 2	100.00	200.00
93 Smith, Jud (Los Angeles) 2	100.00	200.00
94 Thorsen (Los Angeles) 2	100.00	200.00
95 Tozer (Los Angeles) 2	100.00	200.00
96 Waring (Los Angeles) 2	100.00	200.00
97 Cameron (Oakland) 2	100.00	200.00
98 Carroll (Oakland) 2	100.00	200.00
99 Christian (Oakland) 2	100.00	200.00
100 Cutshaw (Oakland) 2	125.00	250.00
101 Harkins (Oakland) 2	100.00	200.00
102 Logan (Oakland) 2	100.00	200.00
103 Lively (Oakland) 2	100.00	200.00
104 Manush (Oakland) 2	125.00	300.00
105 Mitze (Oakland) 2	100.00	200.00
106 Moser (Oakland) 2	100.00	200.00
107 Nelson (Oakland) 2	100.00	200.00
108 Spiesman (Oakland) 2	100.00	200.00
109 Swander (Oakland) 2	100.00	200.00
110 Thomas (Oakland) 2	100.00	200.00
111 Tonnesen (Oakland) 2	100.00	200.00
112 Wares (Oakland) 2	100.00	200.00
113 Wolverton (Oakland) 2	100.00	200.00
114 Armbruster (Portland) 2	100.00	200.00
115 Casey (Portland) 2	100.00	200.00
116 Fisher (Portland) 2	100.00	200.00
117 Garrett (Portland) 2	100.00	200.00
118 Greggs (Portland) 2	125.00	250.00
119 Hetling (Portland) 2	100.00	200.00
120 Krapp (Portland) 2	100.00	200.00
121 McCredie (Portland) 2	100.00	200.00
122 Netzel (Portland) 2	100.00	200.00
123 Olson (Portland) 2	125.00	250.00
124 Ort (Portland) 2	100.00	200.00
125 Perrine (Portland) 2	100.00	200.00
126 Rapps (Portland) 2	100.00	200.00
127 Ryan, Dan (Portland) 2	100.00	200.00
128 Ryan, Bud (Portland) 2	100.00	200.00
129 Seaton (Portland) 2	100.00	200.00
130 Smith (Portland) 2	100.00	200.00
131 Speas (Portland) 2	100.00	200.00
132 Steen (Portland) 2	100.00	200.00
133 Baum (Sacramento) 2	100.00	200.00
134 Boardman (Sacramento) 2	100.00	200.00
135 Briggs (Sacramento) 2	100.00	200.00
136 Brown (Sacramento) 2	100.00	200.00
137 Danzig (Sacramento) 2	100.00	200.00
138 Daringer (Sacramento) 2	100.00	200.00
139 Fitzgerald (Sacramento) 2	100.00	200.00
140 Fournier (Sacramento) 2	100.00	200.00
141 Hiester (Sacramento) 2	100.00	200.00
142 Hollis (Sacramento) 2	100.00	200.00
143 Hunt (Sacramento) 2	100.00	200.00
144 LaLonge (Sacramento) 2	100.00	200.00
145 Nourse (Sacramento) 2	100.00	200.00
146 Perry (Sacramento) 2	100.00	200.00
147 Persons (Sacramento) 2	100.00	200.00
148 Raymer (Sacramento) 2	100.00	200.00
149 Shinn (Sacramento) 2	100.00	200.00
150 Van Buren (Sacramento) 2	100.00	200.00
151 Whalen (Sacramento) 2	100.00	200.00
152 Ames (San Francisco) 2	100.00	200.00
153 Berry (San Francisco) 2	100.00	200.00
154 Bodie (San Francisco) 2	125.00	250.00
155 Browning (San Francisco) 2	100.00	200.00
156 Byrd (San Francisco) 2	100.00	200.00
157 Eastley (San Francisco) 2	100.00	200.00
158A Griffin 175 (San Francisco) 2	100.00	200.00
158B Griffin 150 (San Francisco) 2	100.00	200.00
159 Henley (San Francisco) 2	100.00	200.00
160 Lewis (San Francisco) 2	100.00	200.00
161 McArdle (San Francisco) 2	100.00	200.00
162 Melchoir (San Francisco) 2	100.00	200.00
163 Miller (San Francisco) 2	100.00	200.00
164 Mohler (San Francisco) 2	100.00	200.00
165 Mundorff (San Francisco) 2	250.00	500.00
166 Shaw (San Francisco) 2	100.00	200.00
167 Stewart (San Francisco) 2	100.00	200.00
168 Sutor (San Francisco) 2	100.00	200.00
169 Tennant (San Francisco) 2	100.00	200.00
170 Vitt (San Francisco) 2	125.00	250.00
171 Williams, John (San Francisco) 2	100.00	200.00
172 Willis (San Francisco) 2	100.00	200.00
173 Breckenridge (Vernon) 2	100.00	200.00
174 Brashear, Norman (Vernon) 2	100.00	200.00
175 Brashear, Roy (Vernon) 2	100.00	200.00
176 Brown (Vernon) 2	100.00	200.00
177 Burrell (Vernon) 2	100.00	200.00
178 Carlisle (Vernon) 2	100.00	200.00
179 Coy (Vernon) 2	100.00	200.00
180 Fisher (Vernon) 2	100.00	200.00
181 Hensling (Vernon) 2	100.00	200.00
182 Hitt (Vernon) 2	100.00	200.00
183 Hogan (Vernon) 2	100.00	200.00
184 Lindsay (Vernon) 2	100.00	200.00
185 Martinke (Vernon) 2	100.00	200.00
186 Schafer (Vernon) 2	100.00	200.00
187 Stovall (Vernon) 2	100.00	200.00
188 Willett (Vernon) 2	100.00	200.00
189 Akin (Seattle) 2	100.00	200.00
190 Bennett (Seattle) 2	100.00	200.00
191 Custer (Seattle) 2	100.00	200.00
192 Dretchko (Seattle) 2	100.00	200.00
193 Frisk (Seattle) 2	100.00	200.00
194 Hall (Seattle) 2	100.00	200.00
195 Hendrix (Seattle) 2	100.00	200.00
196 Johnston (Seattle) 2	100.00	200.00
197 Lynch (Seattle) 2	100.00	200.00
198 Miller (Seattle) 2	100.00	200.00
199 Pennington (Seattle) 2	100.00	200.00
200 Raymond (Seattle) 2	100.00	200.00
201 Seaton (Seattle) 2	100.00	200.00
202 Shea (Seattle) 2	100.00	200.00
203 Thompson (Seattle) 2	100.00	200.00
204 Zackert (Seattle) 2	100.00	200.00
205 Baker (Spokane) 2	100.00	200.00
206 Bonner (Spokane) 2	100.00	200.00
207 Brooks (Spokane) 2	100.00	200.00
208 Cartwright (Spokane) 2	100.00	200.00
209 Cooney (Spokane) 2	100.00	200.00
210 Davis (Spokane) 2	100.00	200.00
211 Flood (Spokane) 2	100.00	200.00
212 Hickey (Spokane) 2	100.00	200.00
213 Holm (Spokane) 2	100.00	200.00
214 Keener (Spokane) 2	100.00	200.00
215 Killilay (Spokane) 2	100.00	200.00
216 Kippert (Spokane) 2	100.00	200.00
217 Nordyke (Spokane) 2	100.00	200.00
218 Ostdiek (Spokane) 2	100.00	200.00
219 Weed (Spokane) 2	100.00	200.00
220 Annis (Tacoma) 2	100.00	200.00
221 Bassey (Tacoma) 2	100.00	200.00
222 Blankenship (Tacoma) 2	100.00	200.00
223 Byrnes (Tacoma) 2	100.00	200.00
224 Coleman (Tacoma) 2	100.00	200.00
225 Gaddy (Tacoma) 2	100.00	200.00
226 Gurney (Tacoma) 2	100.00	200.00
227 Hall (Tacoma) 2	100.00	200.00
228 Hartman (Tacoma) 2	100.00	200.00
229 Jansing (Tacoma) 2	100.00	200.00
230 Mott (Tacoma) 2	100.00	200.00
231 Rockenfield (Tacoma) 2	125.00	250.00
232 Schmutz (Tacoma) 2	100.00	200.00
233 Starkell (Tacoma) 2	100.00	200.00
234 Stevens (Tacoma) 2	100.00	200.00
235 Warren (Tacoma) 2	100.00	200.00
236 Breen (Vancouver) 2	100.00	200.00
237 Brinker (Vancouver) 2	100.00	200.00
238 Brown (Vancouver) 2	100.00	200.00
239 Capron (Vancouver) 2	100.00	200.00
240 Chenault (Vancouver) 2	100.00	200.00
241 Erickson (Vancouver) 2	100.00	200.00
242 Flannagan (Vancouver) 2	100.00	200.00
243 Gardner (Vancouver) 2	100.00	200.00
244 James (Vancouver) 2	100.00	200.00
245 Jensen (Vancouver) 2	100.00	200.00
246 Kusel (Vancouver) 2	100.00	200.00
247 Lewis (Vancouver) 2	100.00	200.00
248 Scharnweber (Vancouver) 2	100.00	200.00
249 Streib (Vancouver) 2	100.00	200.00
250 Sugden (Vancouver) 2	100.00	200.00
251 Swain (Vancouver) 2	100.00	200.00
252 Abbott (Los Angeles) 3	100.00	200.00
253 Agnew (Los Angeles) 3	100.00	200.00
254 Akin (Los Angeles) 3	100.00	200.00
255 Bernard, Curtis (Los Angeles) 3	100.00	200.00
256 Criger (Los Angeles) 3	100.00	200.00
257 Daley (Los Angeles) 3	100.00	200.00
258 Delhi (Los Angeles) 3	100.00	200.00
259 Delmas (Los Angeles) 3	100.00	200.00
260 Dillon (Los Angeles) 3	100.00	200.00
261 Grindle (Los Angeles) 3	100.00	200.00
262 Howard (Los Angeles) 3	100.00	200.00
263 Metzger (Los Angeles) 3	100.00	200.00
264 Moore (Los Angeles) 3	100.00	200.00
265 Smith, Hugh (Los Angeles) 3	100.00	200.00
266 Thorsen (Los Angeles) 3	100.00	200.00
267 Tozer (Los Angeles) 3	100.00	200.00
268 Wheeler (Los Angeles) 3	100.00	200.00
269 Ables (Oakland) 3	100.00	200.00
270 Christian (Oakland) 3	100.00	200.00
271 Coy (Oakland) 3	100.00	200.00
272 Cutshaw (Oakland) 3	125.00	250.00
273 Flater (Oakland) 3	100.00	200.00
274 Hetling (Oakland) 3	100.00	200.00
275 Hoffman (Oakland) 3	100.00	200.00

Card	Low	High
276 Knight (Oakland) 3	100.00	200.00
277 Maggert (Oakland) 3	100.00	200.00
278 Miller (Oakland) 3	100.00	200.00
279 Mitze (Oakland) 3	100.00	200.00
280 Pearce (Oakland) 3	100.00	200.00
281 Pernoll (Oakland) 3	100.00	200.00
282 Pfyl (Oakland) 3	100.00	200.00
283 Tiedeman (Oakland) 3	100.00	200.00
284 Wares (Oakland) 3	100.00	200.00
285 Wiggs (Oakland) 3	100.00	200.00
286 Wolverton (Oakland) 3	100.00	200.00
287 Zacher (Oakland) 3	100.00	200.00
288 Barry (Portland) 3	100.00	200.00
289 Chadbourne (Portland) 3	100.00	200.00
290 Fullerton (Portland) 3	100.00	200.00
291 Henderson (Portland) 3	100.00	200.00
292 Koestner (Portland) 3	100.00	200.00
293 Krueger (Portland) 3	100.00	200.00
294 Kuhn (Portland) 3	100.00	200.00
295 McCredie (Portland) 3	100.00	200.00
296 Murray (Portland) 3	100.00	200.00
297 Peckinpaugh (Portland) 3	150.00	300.00
298 Rapps (Portland) 3	100.00	200.00
299 Rodgers (Portland) 3	100.00	200.00
300 Ryan, Bud (Portland) 3	100.00	200.00
301 Seaton (Portland) 3	100.00	200.00
302 Sheehan (Portland) 3	125.00	250.00
303 Steen (Portland) 3	100.00	200.00
304 Arrelanes (Sacramento) 3	100.00	200.00
305 Baum (Sacramento) 3	100.00	200.00
306 Byram (Sacramento) 3	100.00	200.00
307 Danzig (Sacramento) 3	100.00	200.00
308 Fitzgerald (Sacramento) 3	100.00	200.00
309 Hiester (Sacramento) 3	100.00	200.00
310 Hunt (Sacramento) 3	100.00	200.00
311 LaLonge (Sacramento) 3	100.00	200.00
312 Lerchen (Sacramento) 3	100.00	200.00
313 Mahoney (Sacramento) 3	100.00	200.00
314 Nourse (Sacramento) 3	100.00	200.00
315 O'Rourke (Sacramento) 3	100.00	200.00
316 Shinn (Sacramento) 3	100.00	200.00
317 Thomas (Sacramento) 3	100.00	200.00
318 Thompson (Sacramento) 3	100.00	200.00
319 Thornton (Sacramento) 3	100.00	200.00
320 Van Buren (Sacramento) 3	100.00	200.00
321 Berry (San Francisco) 3	100.00	200.00
322 Browning (San Francisco) 3	100.00	200.00
323 Henley (San Francisco) 3	100.00	200.00
324 Madden (San Francisco) 3	100.00	200.00
325 McArdle (San Francisco) 3	100.00	200.00
326 Meikle (San Francisco) 3	100.00	200.00
327 Melchoir (San Francisco) 3	100.00	200.00
328 Miller (San Francisco) 3	100.00	200.00
329 Mohler (San Francisco) 3	100.00	200.00
330 Moskiman (San Francisco) 3	100.00	200.00
331 Powell (San Francisco) 3	100.00	200.00
332 Ryan (San Francisco) 3	100.00	200.00
333 Schmidt (San Francisco) 3	100.00	200.00
334 Shaw (San Francisco) 3	100.00	200.00
335 Sutor (San Francisco) 3	100.00	200.00
336 Tennant (San Francisco) 3	100.00	200.00
337 Vitt (San Francisco) 3	125.00	250.00
338 Weaver (San Francisco) 3	1,250.00	2,500.00
339 Zamlock (San Francisco) 3	100.00	200.00
340 Brackenridge (Vernon) 3	100.00	200.00
341 Brashear, Roy (Vernon) 3	100.00	200.00
342 Brown (Vernon) 3	100.00	200.00
343 Burrell (Vernon) 3	100.00	200.00
344 Carlisle (Vernon) 3	100.00	200.00
345 Carson (Vernon) 3	100.00	200.00
346 Castleton (Vernon) 3	100.00	200.00
347 Hitt (Vernon) 3	100.00	200.00
348 Hogan (Vernon) 3	100.00	200.00
349 Hosp (Vernon) 3	100.00	200.00
350 Kane (Vernon) 3	100.00	200.00
351 McDonnell (Vernon) 3	100.00	200.00
352 Patterson (Vernon) 3	100.00	200.00
353 Raleigh (Vernon) 3	100.00	200.00
354 Ross (Vernon) 3	100.00	200.00
355 Sheehan (Vernon) 3	100.00	200.00
356 Stewart (Vernon) 3	100.00	200.00
357 Stinson (Vernon) 3	100.00	200.00
358 Willett (Vernon) 3	100.00	200.00
359 Bloomfield (Portland) 3	100.00	200.00
360 Casey (Portland) 3	100.00	200.00
361 Garrett (Portland) 3	100.00	200.00
362 Harris (Portland) 3	100.00	200.00
363 Lamline (Portland) 3	100.00	200.00
364 Mensor (Portland) 3	100.00	200.00
365 Mundorff (Portland) 3	100.00	200.00
366 Speas (Portland) 3	100.00	200.00
367 Stovall (Portland) 3	125.00	250.00
368 Williams (Portland) 3	100.00	200.00
369 Bues (Seattle) 3	100.00	200.00
370 Butler (Seattle) 3	100.00	200.00
371 Crukshank (Seattle) 3	100.00	200.00
372 Kading (Seattle) 3	100.00	200.00
373 Leard (Seattle) 3	100.00	200.00
374 Raymond (Seattle) 3	100.00	200.00
375 Seaton (Seattle) 3	100.00	200.00
376 Shea (Seattle) 3	100.00	200.00
377 Skeels (Seattle) 3	100.00	200.00
378 Spencer (Seattle) 3	100.00	200.00
379 Weed (Seattle) 3	100.00	200.00
380 Zackert (Seattle) 3	100.00	200.00
381 Bonner (Spokane) 3	100.00	200.00
382 Cartwright (Spokane) 3	100.00	200.00
383 Cooney (Spokane) 3	100.00	200.00
384 Frisk (Spokane) 3	100.00	200.00
385 Hasty (Spokane) 3	100.00	200.00
386 Holm (Spokane) 3	100.00	200.00
387 Kippert (Spokane) 3	100.00	200.00
388 Netzel (Spokane) 3	100.00	200.00
389 Nordyke (Spokane) 3	100.00	200.00
390 Ostdiek (Spokane) 3	100.00	200.00
391 Strand (Spokane) 3	100.00	200.00
392 Zimmerman	100.00	200.00
393 Annis (Tacoma) 3	100.00	200.00
394 Bassey (Tacoma) 3	100.00	200.00
395 Burns (Tacoma) 3	100.00	200.00
396 Coleman (Tacoma) 3	100.00	200.00
397 Gordon (Tacoma) 3	100.00	200.00
398 Hall (Tacoma) 3	100.00	200.00
399 Higgins (Tacoma) 3	100.00	200.00
400 Morse (Tacoma) 3	100.00	200.00
401 Rockenfield (Tacoma) 3	125.00	250.00
402 Schmutz (Tacoma) 3	100.00	200.00
403 Warren (Tacoma) 3	100.00	200.00
404 Adams (Vancouver) 3	100.00	200.00
405 Bennett (Vancouver) 3	100.00	200.00
406 Brashear (Vancouver) 3	100.00	200.00
407 Brinker (Vancouver) 3	100.00	200.00
408 Engel (Vancouver) 3	100.00	200.00
409 Erickson (Vancouver) 3	100.00	200.00
410 James (Vancouver) 3	100.00	200.00
411 Jensen (Vancouver) 3	100.00	200.00
412 Lewis (Vancouver) 3	100.00	200.00
413 Scharnweber (Vancouver) 3	100.00	200.00
414 Spiesman (Vancouver) 3	100.00	200.00
415 Swain (Vancouver) 3	100.00	200.00
416 Dashwood (Victoria) 3	100.00	200.00
417 Davis (Victoria) 3	100.00	200.00
418 Goodman (Victoria) 3	100.00	200.00
419 Householder (Victoria) 3	100.00	200.00
420 Raymer (Victoria) 3	100.00	200.00
421 Reddick (Victoria) 3	100.00	200.00
422 Roche (Victoria) 3	100.00	200.00
423 Starkel (Victoria) 3	100.00	200.00
424 Ten Million (Victoria) 3	125.00	250.00
425 Thomas (Victoria) 3	100.00	200.00
426 Ward (Victoria) 3	100.00	200.00

1910 Bishop Coast League E99

The cards in this 30-card set measure 1 1/2" by 2 3/4". Although there is no manufacturer's name to be found on the cards of this series, the similarities to set E100 almost certainly mark it as a product of Bishop and Co. The subjects are Coast League players, portrayed in black and white photos on solid color backgrounds. The cards are unnumbered but are back listed (starting with "Knapp"). The set was issued about 1910, and some players are found with more than one background color. The cards have been alphabetized and assigned numbers in the checklist below.

Card	Low	High
COMPLETE SET (30)	14,000.00	28,000.00
1 Ping Bodie	700.00	1,400.00
2 Norman Brashear	600.00	1,200.00
3 Hap Briggs	600.00	1,200.00
4 Jimmy Byones sic, Byrnes	600.00	1,200.00
5 Don Cameron	600.00	1,200.00
6 Pearl Casey	600.00	1,200.00
7 George Cutshaw	600.00	1,200.00
8 Bert Delmas	600.00	1,200.00
9 Frank Dillon	600.00	1,200.00
10 Tom Hasty	600.00	1,200.00
11 Roy Hitt	600.00	1,200.00
12 Wallace Hap. Hogan	600.00	1,200.00
13 Ben Hunt	600.00	1,200.00
14 Gene Krapp	600.00	1,200.00
15 John Lindsay	600.00	1,200.00
16 Harl Maggert	600.00	1,200.00
17 Harry McArdle	600.00	1,200.00
18 Walter McCredie sic, McCreedie	600.00	1,200.00
19 Henry Melchoir	600.00	1,200.00
20 Ernest Mohler	600.00	1,200.00
21 Walter Nagle	600.00	1,200.00
22 Slim Nelson	600.00	1,200.00
23 Chester Nourse	600.00	1,200.00
24 Ivy Olsen	600.00	1,200.00
25 Fred Raymer	600.00	1,200.00
26 Smith	600.00	1,200.00
27 Thomas Tennent sic, Tennant	600.00	1,200.00
28 Bill Thorsen	600.00	1,200.00
29 Edward Van Buren	600.00	1,200.00
30 Harry Wolverton	600.00	1,200.00

1910 Contentnea T209

These baseball cards (each measuring 1 1/2" by 2 5/8") found as inserts in packs of Contentnea Cigarettes were released to the public in 1909 and 1910. Although both sets depict players from the Virginia, Carolina Association and Eastern Carolina leagues, they are otherwise dissimilar. The 16-card color series, known as Type I, is much tougher and more valuable. The obverse captions are printed in blue and are located in the white border at the bottom. The reverse is marked "First Series", but no subsequent printings are known. There are also 219 of the Type II black and white "Photo Series" listed below, although more are believed to exist. The captions on this type are printed in black and are found within a white panel inside the picture area. Both types are unnumbered. Type I cards are alphabetized below. while Type II cards are arranged in alphabetical order within team. Teams in Type II are Anderson (17-27), Charlotte (28-40), Danville (41-50), Fayetteville (51-58), Goldsboro (59-73), Greensboro (74-86), Greenville (87-99), Lynchburg (100-111), Norfolk (112-124), Portsmouth (125-135), Raleigh (136-154), Richmond (155-168), Roanoke (169-181), Rocky Mount (182-188), Spartanburg (189-200), Wilmington (201-211), Wilson (212-223), and Winston-Salem (224-236).

Card	Low	High
COMMON TYPE I (1-16)	250.00	500.00
COMMON TYPE II (17-236)	200.00	400.00
1 Armstrong (Wilson) 1	250.00	500.00
2 Booles (Raleigh) 1	250.00	500.00
3 Bourquise (Rocky Mount) 1	250.00	500.00
4 Cooper (Wilson) 1	250.00	500.00
5 Cowell (Wilson) 1	250.00	500.00
6 Crockett (Goldsboro) 1	250.00	500.00
7 Fullenwider (Raleigh) 1	250.00	500.00
8 Gilmore (Winston-Salem) 1	250.00	500.00
9 Hoffman (Raleigh) 1	250.00	500.00
10 Lane (Wilson) 1	250.00	500.00
12 McGeehan (Wilson) 1	250.00	500.00
13 Pope (Raleigh) 1	250.00	500.00
14 Sisson (Greensboro) 1	250.00	500.00
15 Stubbe (Goldsboro) 1	250.00	500.00
16 Walsh (Goldsboro) 1	250.00	500.00
17 Byrd (Anderson) 2	200.00	400.00
18 Corbett (Anderson) 2	200.00	400.00
19 Farmer (Anderson) 2	200.00	400.00
20 Gorham (Anderson) 2	200.00	400.00
21 Harley (Anderson) 2	200.00	400.00
22 Kelly (Anderson) 2	200.00	400.00
23 McCarthy, A. (Anderson) 2	200.00	400.00
24 McCarthy, J. (Anderson) 2	200.00	400.00
25 Peloguin (Anderson) 2	200.00	400.00
26 Roth (Anderson) 2	200.00	400.00
27 Wehrell (Anderson) 2	200.00	400.00
28 Bausewein (Charlotte) 2	200.00	400.00
29 Brazelle (Charlotte) 2	200.00	400.00
30 Coutts (Charlotte) 2	200.00	400.00
31 Cross (Charlotte) 2	200.00	400.00
32 Dobard (Charlotte) 2	200.00	400.00
33 Duvie (Charlotte) 2	200.00	400.00
34 Francisco (Charlotte) 2	200.00	400.00
35 Garman (Charlotte) 2	200.00	400.00
36 Hargrave (Charlotte) 2	200.00	400.00
37 Hemphrey (Charlotte) 2	200.00	400.00
38 McHugh (Charlotte) 2	200.00	400.00
39 Taxis (Charlotte) 2	200.00	400.00
40 Williams (Charlotte) 2	200.00	400.00
41 Bussey (Danville) 2	200.00	400.00
42 Callahan (Danville) 2	200.00	400.00
43 Griffin (Danville) 2	200.00	400.00
44 Hooker (Danville) 2	200.00	400.00
45 Mayberry (Danville) 2	200.00	400.00
46 Mullinix (Danville) 2	200.00	400.00
47 Priest (Danville) 2	200.00	400.00
48 Rickert (Danville) 2	200.00	400.00
49 Schrader (Danville) 2	200.00	400.00
50 Sullivan (Danville) 2	200.00	400.00
51 Boyle (Fayetteville) 2	200.00	400.00
52 Crockett (Fayetteville) 2	200.00	400.00
53 Dobson (Fayetteville) 2	200.00	400.00
54 Galvin (Fayetteville) 2	200.00	400.00
55 Lavoia (Fayetteville) 2	200.00	400.00
56 Luyster (Fayetteville) 2	200.00	400.00
57 Schumaker (Fayetteville) 2	200.00	400.00
58 Waters (Fayetteville) 2	200.00	400.00
59 Wamack (Goldsboro) 2	200.00	400.00
60 Dailey (Goldsboro) 2	200.00	400.00
61 Evans (Goldsboro) 2	200.00	400.00
62 Fulton (Goldsboro) 2	200.00	400.00
63 Gates (Goldsboro) 2	200.00	400.00
64 Gunderson (Goldsboro) 2	200.00	400.00
65 Handiboe (Goldsboro) 2	200.00	400.00
66 Kelly (Goldsboro) 2	200.00	400.00
67 Malcolm (Goldsboro) 2	200.00	400.00
68 Merchant (Goldsboro) 2	200.00	400.00
69 Morgan (Goldsboro) 2	200.00	400.00
70 Sharp (Goldsboro) 2	200.00	400.00
71 Stoehr (Goldsboro) 2	200.00	400.00
72 Webb (Goldsboro) 2	200.00	400.00
73 Wolf (Goldsboro) 2	200.00	400.00
74 Bentley (Greensboro) 2	200.00	400.00
75 Beusse (Greensboro) 2	200.00	400.00
76 Doak (Greensboro) 2	200.00	400.00
77 Eldridge (Greensboro) 2	200.00	400.00
78 Hammersley (Greensboro) 2	200.00	400.00
79 Hicks (Greensboro) 2	200.00	400.00
80 Jackson (Greensboro) 2	200.00	400.00
81 Martin (Greensboro) 2	200.00	400.00
82 Pickard (Greensboro) 2	200.00	400.00
83 Ridgeway (Greensboro) 2	200.00	400.00
84 Springs (Greensboro) 2	200.00	400.00
85 Walters (Greensboro) 2	200.00	400.00
86 Weldon (Greensboro) 2	200.00	400.00
87 Blackstone (Greenville) 2	200.00	400.00
88 Derrck (Greenville) 2 ERR Correct spelling is Derrick	200.00	400.00
89 Derrick (Greenville) 2 COR	200.00	400.00
90 Drumm (Greenville) 2	200.00	400.00
91 Flowers (Greenville) 2	200.00	400.00
92 Jenkins (Greenville) 2	200.00	400.00
93 McFarlin (Greenville) 2	200.00	400.00
94 Noojin (Greenville) 2	200.00	400.00
95 Ochs (Greenville) 2	200.00	400.00
96 Redfern (Greenville) 2	200.00	400.00
97 Stouch (Greenville) 2	200.00	400.00
98 Wingo (Greenville) 2	200.00	400.00
99 Workman (Greenville) 2	200.00	400.00
100 Brandon (Lynchburg) 2	200.00	400.00
101 Griffin (Lynchburg) 2	200.00	400.00
102 Hoffman (Lynchburg) 2	200.00	400.00
103 Howedel (Lynchburg) 2	200.00	400.00
104 Levy (Lynchburg) 2	200.00	400.00
105 Lloyd (Lynchburg) 2	200.00	400.00
106 Lucia (Lynchburg) 2	200.00	400.00
107 Rawe (Lynchburg) 2	200.00	400.00
108 Sexton (Lynchburg) 2	200.00	400.00
109 Smith, A. (Lynchburg) 2	200.00	400.00
110 Smith, D. (Lynchburg) 2	200.00	400.00
111 Woolums (Lynchburg) 2	200.00	400.00
112 Armstrong (Norfolk) 2	200.00	400.00
113 Banner (Norfolk) 2	200.00	400.00
114 Busch (Norfolk) 2	200.00	400.00
115 Chandler (Norfolk) 2	200.00	400.00
116 Clark (Norfolk) 2	200.00	400.00
117 Johnson (Norfolk) 2	200.00	400.00
118 Mullany (Norfolk) 2	200.00	400.00
119 Munsen (Norfolk) 2	200.00	400.00
120 Murdock (Norfolk) 2	200.00	400.00
121 Reggy (Norfolk) 2	200.00	400.00
122 Tiedmann (Norfolk) 2	200.00	400.00
123 Walker (Norfolk) 2	200.00	400.00
124 Walsh (Norfolk) 2	200.00	400.00
125 Bowen (Portsmouth) 2	200.00	400.00
126 Clunk (Portsmouth) 2	200.00	400.00
127 Guiheen (Portsmouth) 2	200.00	400.00
128 Hamilton (Portsmouth) 2	200.00	400.00
129 Hannifen (Portsmouth) 2	200.00	400.00
130 Kunkle (Portsmouth) 2	200.00	400.00
131 McFarland (Portsmouth) 2	200.00	400.00
132 Smith (Portsmouth) 2	200.00	400.00
133 Toner (Portsmouth) 2	200.00	400.00
134 Vail (Portsmouth) 2	200.00	400.00
135 Welsher (Portsmouth) 2	200.00	400.00
136 Beatty (Raleigh) 2	200.00	400.00
137 Biel (Raleigh) 2	200.00	400.00
138 Bigbie (Raleigh) 2	200.00	400.00
139 Clemens (Raleigh) 2	200.00	400.00
140 Hart (Raleigh) 2	200.00	400.00
141 Hawkins (Raleigh) 2	200.00	400.00
142 Hobbs (Raleigh) 2	200.00	400.00
143 Jobson (Raleigh) 2	200.00	400.00
144 Keating (Raleigh) 2	200.00	400.00
145 Kelly (Raleigh) 2	200.00	400.00
146 Lathrop (Raleigh) 2	200.00	400.00
147 McCormick (Raleigh) 2	200.00	400.00
148 Mundell (Raleigh) 2	200.00	400.00
149 Phoenix (Raleigh) 2	200.00	400.00
150 Prim (Raleigh) 2	200.00	400.00
151 Richardson (Raleigh) 2	200.00	400.00
152 Simmons (Raleigh) 2	200.00	400.00
153 Turner (Raleigh) 2	200.00	400.00
154 Wright (Raleigh) 2	200.00	400.00
155 Baker (Richmond) 2	200.00	400.00
156 Bigbie (Richmond) 2	200.00	400.00
157 Brown (Richmond) 2	200.00	400.00
158 Cowan (Richmond) 2	200.00	400.00
159 Hale (Richmond) 2	200.00	400.00
160 Irvine (Richmond) 2	200.00	400.00
161 Landgraff (Richmond) 2	200.00	400.00
162 Missitt (Richmond) 2	200.00	400.00
163 Morrissey (Richmond) 2	200.00	400.00
164 Salve (Richmond) 2	200.00	400.00
165 Shaw (Richmond) 2	200.00	400.00
166 Titman (Richmond) 2	200.00	400.00
167 Verbout (Richmond) 2	200.00	400.00
168 Wallace (Richmond) 2	200.00	400.00
169 Andrada (Roanoke) 2	200.00	400.00
170 Cafalu (Roanoke) 2	200.00	400.00
171 Doyle (Roanoke) 2	200.00	400.00
172 Fisher (Roanoke) 2	200.00	400.00
173 Halland (Roanoke) 2	200.00	400.00
174 Jenkins (Roanoke) 2	200.00	400.00
175 Newton (Roanoke) 2	200.00	400.00
176 Powell (Roanoke) 2	200.00	400.00
177 Presley and Pritchard (Roanoke) 2 UER Correct spelling is Pressley	200.00	400.00
178 Pritchard (Roanoke) 2	200.00	400.00
179 Schmidt (Roanoke) 2	200.00	400.00
180 Shanghnessy (Roanoke) 2	200.00	400.00
181 Spratt (Roanoke) 2	200.00	400.00
182 Bonner (Rocky Mount) 2	200.00	400.00
183 Creagan (Rocky Mount) 2	200.00	400.00
184 Forque (Rocky Mount) 2	200.00	400.00
185 Gatmeyer (Rocky Mount) 2	200.00	400.00
186 Gillespie (Rocky Mount) 2	200.00	400.00
187 Novak (Rocky Mount) 2	200.00	400.00
188 Phealean (Rocky Mount) 2	200.00	400.00
189 Abercrombie (Spartanburg) 2	200.00	400.00
190 Averett (Spartanburg) 2	200.00	400.00
191 Fairbanks (Spartanburg) 2	200.00	400.00
192 Gardin (Spartanburg) 2	200.00	400.00
193 Harrington (Spartanburg) 2	200.00	400.00
194 Harris (Spartanburg) 2	200.00	400.00
195 Jackson (Spartanburg) 2	200.00	400.00
196 Thompson (Spartanburg) 2	200.00	400.00
197 Vickery (Spartanburg) 2	200.00	400.00
198 Walker (Spartanburg) 2	200.00	400.00
199 Wood (Spartanburg) 2	200.00	400.00
200 Wynne (Spartanburg) 2	200.00	400.00
201 Bourquin (Wilmington) 2	200.00	400.00
202 Cooper (Wilmington) 2	200.00	400.00
203 Doak (Wilmington) 2	200.00	400.00
204 Ebinger (Wilmington) 2	200.00	400.00
205 Foltz (Wilmington) 2	200.00	400.00
206 Gehring (Wilmington) 2	200.00	400.00
207 Howard (Wilmington) 2	200.00	400.00
208 Hyames (Wilmington) 2	200.00	400.00
209 Kelley (Wilmington) 2	200.00	400.00
210 Kite (Wilmington) 2	200.00	400.00
211 Tydeman (Wilmington) 2	200.00	400.00
212 Charles Clapp (Wilson) 2	200.00	400.00
213 Cowells (Wilson) 2	200.00	400.00
214 Foreman (Wilson) 2	200.00	400.00
215 Hearne (Wilson) 2	200.00	400.00
216 Hudson (Wilson) 2	200.00	400.00
217 Lane (Wilson) 2	200.00	400.00
218 McGeehan, C. (Wilson) 2	200.00	400.00
219 McGeehan, D. (Wilson) 2	200.00	400.00
220 Miller (Wilson) 2	200.00	400.00
221 Stewart (Wilson) 2	200.00	400.00
222 Thompson (Wilson) 2	300.00	600.00
223 Westlake (Wilson) 2	200.00	400.00
224 Brent (Winston-Salem) 2	200.00	400.00
225 Cote (Winston-Salem) 2	200.00	400.00

226 Ferrell (Winston-Salem) 2 200.00 400.00
227 Fogarty (Winston-Salem) 2 200.00 400.00
228 King (Winston-Salem) 2 200.00 400.00
229 Loval (Winston-Salem) 2 200.00 400.00
230 MacConachie (Winston-Salem) 2 200.00 400.00
231 McKeavitt (Winston-Salem) 2 200.00 400.00
232 Midkiff (Winston-Salem) 2 200.00 400.00
233 Painter (Winston-Salem) 2 200.00 400.00
234 Swindell (Winston-Salem) 2 200.00 400.00
235 Templin (Winston-Salem) 2 200.00 400.00
236 Willis (Winston-Salem) 2 200.00 400.00

1910 Old Mill T210

At 640 cards, this is the largest 20th Century tobacco-issued baseball series, and it presents a formidable challenge to the collector. Each card measures 1 1/2" by 2 5/8". Eight minor leagues are each represented by a specific numbered series indicated on the reverse of each card. Each player's name and team are printed in black within the bottom white picture area. The list below is ordered alphabetically by player's name within team within series. Series 1 (South Atlantic League) teams are Augusta (1-13), Columbia (14-26), Columbus (27-39), Jacksonville (40-51), Macon (52-63) and Savannah (64-75). Series 2 (Virginia League) teams are Danville (76-88), Lynchburg (89-105), Norfolk (106-117), Portsmouth (118-132), Richmond (133-151), and Roanoke (152-162). Series 3 (Texas League) teams are Dallas (163-181), Ft. Worth (182-197), Galveston (198-204), Houston (205-216), Oklahoma City (217-221), San Antonio (222-230), Shreveport (231-243) and Waco (244-257). Series 4 (Virginia Valley League) teams are Charleston (258-272), Huntington (273-285), Montgomery (286-296) and Mt. Pleasant (297-306). Series 5 (Carolina Association) teams are Anderson (307-320), Charlotte (321-335), Greensboro (336-348), Greenville (349-364), Spartanburg (365-379) and Winston-Salem (380-393). Series 6 (Blue Grass League) teams are Frankfort (394-401), Lexington (402-414), Maysville (415-422), Paris (423-433), Richmond (434-443), Shelbyville (444-446) and Winchester (447-459). Series 7 (Eastern Carolina League) teams are Fayetteville (460-468), Goldsboro (469-490), Raleigh (491-504), Rocky Mount (505-519), Wilmington (520) and Wilson (521-526). Series 8 (Southern Association) teams are Atlanta (527-539), Birmingham (540-556), Chattanooga (557-566), Memphis (567-580), Mobile (581-592), Montgomery (593-608), Nashville (609-625) and New Orleans (626-640). The two key cards in the set are Casey Stengel and Joe Jackson.

COMMON SERIES 1 (1-75) 100.00 200.00
COMMON SERIES 2 (76-162) 100.00 200.00
COMMON SERIES 3 (163-257) 100.00 200.00
COMMON SERIES 4 (258-306) 100.00 200.00
COMMON SERIES 5 (307-393) 175.00 350.00
COMMON SERIES 6 (394-459) 175.00 350.00
COMMON SERIES 7 (460-526) 350.00 700.00
COMMON SERIES 8 (527-640) 350.00 700.00
1 Bagwell 100.00 200.00
2 Bierkorttle (Augusta) 1 100.00 200.00
3 Dudley (Augusta) 1 100.00 200.00
4 Edwards (Augusta) 1 100.00 200.00
5 Hannifan (Augusta) 1 100.00 200.00
6 Hauser (Augusta) 1 100.00 200.00
7 McMahon (Augusta) 1 100.00 200.00
8 Norcum (Augusta) 1 100.00 200.00
9 Pierce (Augusta) 1 100.00 200.00
10 Shields (Augusta) 1 100.00 200.00
11 Smith (Augusta) 1 100.00 200.00
12 Viola (Augusta) 1 100.00 200.00
13 Wagner (Augusta) 1 100.00 200.00
14 Breitenstein (Columbia) 1 100.00 200.00
15 Cavender (Columbia) 1 100.00 200.00
16 Collins (Columbia) 1 100.00 200.00
17 Dwyer (Columbia) 1 100.00 200.00
18 Jones (Columbia) 1 100.00 200.00
19 Lewis (Columbia) 1 100.00 200.00
20 Marshall (Columbia) 1 100.00 200.00
21 Martin (Columbia) 1 100.00 200.00
22 Massing (Columbia) 1 100.00 200.00
23 Mulldowney (Columbia) 1 100.00 200.00
24 Redfern (Columbia) 1 100.00 200.00
25 Schwietzka (Columbia) 1 100.00 200.00
26 Wohlleben (Columbia) 1 100.00 200.00
27 Becker (Columbus) 1 100.00 200.00
28 Bensen (Columbus) 1 100.00 200.00
29 Fox (Columbus) 1 100.00 200.00
30 Harley (Columbus) 1 100.00 200.00
31 Hille (Columbus) 1 100.00 200.00
32 Krebs (Columbus) 1 100.00 200.00
33 Lewis (Columbus) 1 100.00 200.00
34 Long (Columbus) 1 100.00 200.00
35 McLeod (Columbus) 1 100.00 200.00
36 Radebaugh (Columbus) 1 100.00 200.00
37 Reynolds (Columbus) 1 100.00 200.00
38 Sisson (Columbus) 1 100.00 200.00
39 Toren (Columbus) 1 100.00 200.00
40 Bierman (Jacksonville) 1 100.00 200.00
41 Bremmerhoff (Jacksonville) 1 100.00 200.00
42 Carter (Jacksonville) 1 100.00 200.00
43 DeFraites (Jacksonville) 1 100.00 200.00
44 Hoyt (Jacksonville) 1 100.00 200.00
45 Huber (Jacksonville) 1 100.00 200.00
46 Lee (Jacksonville) 1 100.00 200.00
47 Manion (Jacksonville) 1 100.00 200.00
48 Mullaney (Jacksonville) 1 100.00 200.00
49 Pope (Jacksonville) 1 100.00 200.00
50 Taffee (Jacksonville) 1 100.00 200.00
51 Sahl (Jacksonville) 1 100.00 200.00
52 Benton (Macon) 1 100.00 200.00
53 Enbanks (Macon) 1 100.00 200.00
54 Eubank (Macon) 1 100.00 200.00
55 Ison (Macon) 1 100.00 200.00
56 Kalkhoff (Macon) 1 100.00 200.00
57 Lawrence (Macon) 1 100.00 200.00
58 Lee (Macon) 1 100.00 200.00
59 Lipe Portrait (Macon) 1 100.00 200.00
60 Lipe Batting (Macon) 1 100.00 200.00
61 Morse (Macon) 1 100.00 200.00
62 Schulze (Macon) 1 100.00 200.00
63 Weems (Macon) 1 100.00 200.00
64 Balenti (Savannah) 1 100.00 200.00
65 Howard (Savannah) 1 100.00 200.00
66 Magoon (Savannah) 1 100.00 200.00
67 Martina (Savannah) 1 100.00 200.00
68 Murch (Savannah) 1 100.00 200.00
69 Pelkey (Savannah) 1 100.00 200.00
70 Petit (Savannah) 1 100.00 200.00
71 Regan (Savannah) 1 100.00 200.00
72 Reynolds (Savannah) 1 100.00 200.00
73 Schulze (Savannah) 1 100.00 200.00
74 Sweeney (Savannah) 1 100.00 200.00
75 Wells (Savannah) 1 100.00 200.00
76 Bussey (Danville) 2 100.00 200.00
77 Gaston (Danville) 2 100.00 200.00
78 Griffin (Danville) 2 100.00 200.00
79 Hanks (Danville) 2 100.00 200.00
80 Hooker (Danville) 2 100.00 200.00
81 Kinkel (Danville) 2 100.00 200.00
82 Larkins (Danville) 2 100.00 200.00
83 Laughlin (Danville) 2 100.00 200.00
84 Lloyd (Danville) 2 100.00 200.00
85 Loos (Danville) 2 100.00 200.00
86 Mayberry (Danville) 2 100.00 200.00
87 Schrader (Danville) 2 100.00 200.00
88 Tydeman (Danville) 2 100.00 200.00
89 Beham (Lynchburg) 2 100.00 200.00
90 Brandon (Lynchburg) 2 100.00 200.00
91 Breivogel (Lynchburg) 2 100.00 200.00
92 Eddowes (Lynchburg) 2 100.00 200.00
93 Gehring (Lynchburg) 2 100.00 200.00
94 Griffen (Lynchburg) 2 100.00 200.00
95 Hoffman (Lynchburg) 2 100.00 200.00
96 Jackson (Lynchburg) 2 100.00 200.00
97 Levy (Lynchburg) 2 100.00 200.00
98 Lucia (Lynchburg) 2 100.00 200.00
99 Michaels (Lynchburg) 2 100.00 200.00
100 Rowe (Lynchburg) 2 100.00 200.00
101 Sharp (Lynchburg) 2 100.00 200.00
102 Smith Batting (Lynchburg) 2 100.00 200.00
103 Smith Catching (Lynchburg) 2 100.00 200.00
104 Woolums (Lynchburg) 2 100.00 200.00
105 Zimmerman (Lynchburg) 2 100.00 200.00
106 Bonner (Norfolk) 2 100.00 200.00
107 Busch (Norfolk) 2 100.00 200.00
108 Chandler (Norfolk) 2 100.00 200.00
109 Clarke (Norfolk) 2 100.00 200.00
110 Fox (Norfolk) 2 100.00 200.00
111 Jackson (Norfolk) 2 100.00 200.00
112 Lovell (Norfolk) 2 100.00 200.00
113 MacConachie (Norfolk) 2 100.00 200.00
114 Mullaney (Norfolk) 2 100.00 200.00
115 Munson (Norfolk) 2 100.00 200.00
116 Nimmo (Norfolk) 2 100.00 200.00
117 Walker (Norfolk) 2 100.00 200.00
118 Bowen (Portsmouth) 2 100.00 200.00
119 Clunk (Portsmouth) 2 100.00 200.00
120 Cote (Portsmouth) 2 100.00 200.00
121 Cowan (Portsmouth) 2 100.00 200.00
122 Foxen (Portsmouth) 2 100.00 200.00
123 Hamilton (Portsmouth) 2 100.00 200.00
124 Hannifan (Portsmouth) 2 100.00 200.00
125 Jackson (Portsmouth) 2 100.00 200.00
126 Kirkpatrick (Portsmouth) 2 100.00 200.00
127 McFarland (Portsmouth) 2 100.00 200.00
128 Norris (Portsmouth) 2 100.00 200.00
129 Smith (Portsmouth) 2 100.00 200.00
130 Spicer (Portsmouth) 2 100.00 200.00
131 Toner (Portsmouth) 2 100.00 200.00
132 Vail (Portsmouth) 2 100.00 200.00
133 Archer (Richmond) 2 100.00 200.00
134 Baker (Richmond) 2 100.00 200.00
135 Brooks (Richmond) 2 100.00 200.00
136 Brown (Richmond) 2 100.00 200.00
137 Decker (Richmond) 2 100.00 200.00
138 Hale (Richmond) 2 100.00 200.00
139 Irvine (Richmond) 2 100.00 200.00
140 Jackson (Richmond) 2 100.00 200.00
141 Keifel (Richmond) 2 100.00 200.00
142 Landgradd (Richmond) 2 100.00 200.00
143 Lawlor (Richmond) 2 100.00 200.00
144 Messitt (Richmond) 2 100.00 200.00
145 Peterson (Richmond) 2 100.00 200.00
146 Revelle (Richmond) 2 100.00 200.00
147 Shaw (Richmond) 2 100.00 200.00
148 Titman (Richmond) 2 100.00 200.00
149 Verbout (Richmond) 2 100.00 200.00
150 Wallace (Richmond) 2 100.00 200.00
151 Waymack (Richmond) 2 100.00 200.00
152 Andrada (Roanoke) 2 100.00 200.00
153 Cefalu (Roanoke) 2 100.00 200.00
154 Doyle (Roanoke) 2 100.00 200.00
155 Fisher (Roanoke) 2 100.00 200.00
156 Holland (Roanoke) 2 100.00 200.00
157 Jenkins (Roanoke) 2 100.00 200.00
158 Neuton (Roanoke) 2 100.00 200.00
159 Powell (Roanoke) 2 100.00 200.00
160 Pressley (Roanoke) 2 100.00 200.00
161 Pritchard (Roanoke) 2 100.00 200.00
162 Schmidt (Roanoke) 2 100.00 200.00
163 Berlick (Dallas) 3 100.00 200.00
164 Dale (Dallas) 3 100.00 200.00
165 Doyle (Dallas) 3 100.00 200.00
166 Enos (Dallas) 3 100.00 200.00
167 Evans (Dallas) 3 100.00 200.00
168 Glawe (Dallas) 3 100.00 200.00
169 Gowdy (Dallas) 3 100.00 200.00
170 Hicks (Dallas) 3 100.00 200.00
171 Hirsch (Dallas) 3 100.00 200.00
172 Maloney (Dallas) 3 100.00 200.00
173 Meagher (Dallas) 3 100.00 200.00
174 Mullen (Dallas) 3 100.00 200.00
175 Ogle (Dallas) 3 100.00 200.00
176 Onslow (Dallas) 3 100.00 200.00
177 Robertson (Dallas) 3 100.00 200.00
178 Shindel (Dallas) 3 100.00 200.00
179 Shontz (Dallas) 3 100.00 200.00
180 Storch (Dallas) 3 100.00 200.00
181 Woodburn (Dallas) 3 100.00 200.00
182 Ash (Fort Worth) 3 100.00 200.00
183 Belew (Fort Worth) 3 100.00 200.00
184 Burke (Fort Worth) 3 100.00 200.00
185 Coyle (Fort Worth) 3 100.00 200.00
186 Deardoff (Fort Worth) 3 100.00 200.00
187 Fillman (Fort Worth) 3 100.00 200.00
188 Francis (Fort Worth) 3 100.00 200.00
189 Jolley (Fort Worth) 3 100.00 200.00
190 McKay (Fort Worth) 3 100.00 200.00
191 Morris (Fort Worth) 3 100.00 200.00
192 Pendelton (Fort Worth) 3 100.00 200.00
193 Powell (Fort Worth) 3 100.00 200.00
194 Salazor (Fort Worth) 3 100.00 200.00
195 Weber (Fort Worth) 3 100.00 200.00
196 Weeks (Fort Worth) 3 100.00 200.00
197 Wertherford (Fort Worth) 3 100.00 200.00
198 Cable (Galveston) 3 100.00 200.00
199 Donnelley (Galveston) 3 100.00 200.00
200 Hise (Galveston) 3 100.00 200.00
201 Kaphan (Galveston) 3 100.00 200.00
202 Riley (Galveston) 3 100.00 200.00
203 Spangler (Galveston) 3 100.00 200.00
204 Stringer (Galveston) 3 100.00 200.00
205 Bell (Houston) 3 100.00 200.00
206 Burch (Houston) 3 100.00 200.00
207 Carlin (Houston) 3 100.00 200.00
208 Corkhill (Houston) 3 100.00 200.00
209 Hill (Houston) 3 100.00 200.00
210 Hornsby (Houston) 3 100.00 200.00
211 Malloy (Houston) 3 100.00 200.00
212 Merritt (Houston) 3 100.00 200.00
213 Norten (Houston) 3 100.00 200.00
214 Rose (Houston) 3 100.00 200.00
215 Watson (Houston) 3 100.00 200.00
216 Wickenhorf (Houston) 3 100.00 200.00
217 Bandy (Oklahoma City) 3 100.00 200.00
218 Davis (Oklahoma City) 3 100.00 200.00
219 Jones (Oklahoma City) 3 100.00 200.00
220 Nagel (Oklahoma City) 3 100.00 200.00
221 Walsh (Oklahoma City) 3 100.00 200.00
222 Alexander (San Antonio) 3 100.00 200.00
223 Billiard (San Antonio) 3 100.00 200.00
224 Blanding (San Antonio) 3 100.00 200.00
225 Firestone (San Antonio) 3 100.00 200.00
226 Kipp (San Antonio) 3 100.00 200.00
227 Leidy (San Antonio) 3 100.00 200.00
228 Slaven (San Antonio) 3 100.00 200.00
229 Stinson (San Antonio) 3 100.00 200.00
230 Yantz (San Antonio) 3 100.00 200.00
231 Barenkamp (Shreveport) 3 100.00 200.00
232 Cowans (Shreveport) 3 100.00 200.00
233 Galloway (Shreveport) 3 100.00 200.00
234 Gardner (Shreveport) 3 100.00 200.00
235 Gear (Shreveport) 3 100.00 200.00
236 Harper (Shreveport) 3 100.00 200.00
237 Hinninger (Shreveport) 3 100.00 200.00
238 Howell (Shreveport) 3 100.00 200.00
239 Mills (Shreveport) 3 100.00 200.00
240 Smith Bat over Shoulder (Shreveport) 3 100.00 200.00
241 Smith Bat at Hip (Shreveport) 3 100.00 200.00
242 Stadeli (Shreveport) 3 100.00 200.00
243 Tesreau (Shreveport) 3 100.00 200.00
244 Bennett (Waco) 3 100.00 200.00
245 Blue (Waco) 3 100.00 200.00
246 Conoway (Waco) 3 100.00 200.00
247 Curry (Waco) 3 100.00 200.00
248 Drucke (Waco) 3 100.00 200.00
249 Dugey (Waco) 3 100.00 200.00
250 Gordon (Waco) 3 100.00 200.00
251 Harbison (Waco) 3 100.00 200.00
252 Hooks (Waco) 3 100.00 200.00
253 Johnston (Waco) 3 100.00 200.00
254 Munsell (Waco) 3 100.00 200.00
255 Thebo (Waco) 3 100.00 200.00
256 Tullas (Waco) 3 100.00 200.00
257 Williams (Waco) 3 100.00 200.00
258 Benny (Charleston) 4 100.00 200.00
259 Carney (Charleston) 4 100.00 200.00
260 Conolly (Charleston) 4 100.00 200.00
261 Donnel (Charleston) 4 100.00 200.00
262 Erlewein (Charleston) 4 100.00 200.00
263 Ferrell (Charleston) 4 100.00 200.00
264 Heady (Charleston) 4 100.00 200.00
265 Hollis (Charleston) 4 100.00 200.00
266 Johnson (Charleston) 4 100.00 200.00
267 Moore (Charleston) 4 100.00 200.00
268 Pick (Charleston) 4 100.00 200.00
269 Stanley (Charleston) 4 100.00 200.00
270 Stockum (Charleston) 4 100.00 200.00
271 Willis (Charleston) 4 100.00 200.00
272 Zurlage (Charleston) 4 100.00 200.00
273 Bonno (Huntington) 4 100.00 200.00
274 Brumfield (Huntington) 4 100.00 200.00
275 Campbell (Huntington) 4 100.00 200.00
276 Canepa (Huntington) 4 100.00 200.00
277 Carter (Huntington) 4 100.00 200.00
278 Collier (Huntington) 4 100.00 200.00
279 Halterman (Huntington) 4 100.00 200.00
280 Kane (Huntington) 4 100.00 200.00
281 Leonard (Huntington) 4 100.00 200.00
282 McClain (Huntington) 4 100.00 200.00
283 Seaman (Huntington) 4 100.00 200.00
284 Titlow (Huntington) 4 100.00 200.00
285 Young (Huntington) 4 100.00 200.00
286 Aylor (Montgomery) 4 100.00 200.00
287 Cochrane (Montgomery) 4 100.00 200.00
288 Davis (Montgomery) 4 100.00 200.00
289 Geary (Montgomery) 4 100.00 200.00
290 Lux (Montgomery) 4 100.00 200.00
291 Moye (Montgomery) 4 100.00 200.00
292 O'Connor (Montgomery) 4 100.00 200.00
293 Orcutt (Montgomery) 4 100.00 200.00
294 Spicer (Montgomery) 4 100.00 200.00
295 Waldron (Montgomery) 4 100.00 200.00
296 Womach (Montgomery) 4 100.00 200.00
297 Best (Mt. Pleasant) 4 100.00 200.00
298 Boshmer (Mt. Pleasant) 4 100.00 200.00
299 Brown (Mt. Pleasant) 4 100.00 200.00
300 Dougherty (Mt. Pleasant) 4 100.00 200.00
301 Hunter (Mt. Pleasant) 4 100.00 200.00
302 Kuehn (Mt. Pleasant) 4 100.00 200.00
303 Mollenkamp (Mt. Pleasant) 4 100.00 200.00
304 Pickels (Mt. Pleasant) 4 100.00 200.00
305 Schafer (Mt. Pleasant) 4 100.00 200.00
306 Witter (Mt. Pleasant) 4 100.00 200.00
307 Brannon (Anderson) 5 175.00 350.00
308 Corbett 3/4 View (Anderson) 5 175.00 350.00
309 Corbett Full View (Anderson) 5 175.00 350.00
310 Farmer (Anderson) 5 175.00 350.00
311 Finn (Anderson) 5 175.00 350.00
312 Gorham (Anderson) 5 175.00 350.00
313 Harley (Anderson) 5 175.00 350.00
314 Kelly (Anderson) 5 175.00 350.00
315 Lothrop (Anderson) 5 175.00 350.00
316 McCarthy (Anderson) 5 175.00 350.00
317 McCarthy J. (Anderson) 5 175.00 350.00
318 McEnvoe (Anderson) 5 175.00 350.00
319 Mangum (Anderson) 5 175.00 350.00
320 Wehrell (Anderson) 5 175.00 350.00
321 Bausewein (Charlotte) 5 175.00 350.00
322 Brazell (Charlotte) 5 175.00 350.00
323 Cross (Charlotte) 5 175.00 350.00
324 Coutts (Charlotte) 5 175.00 350.00
325 Dobard (Charlotte) 5 175.00 350.00
326 Duvie (Charlotte) 5 175.00 350.00
327 Francisco (Charlotte) 5 175.00 350.00
328 Gorman (Charlotte) 5 175.00 350.00
329 Hargrave (Charlotte) 5 175.00 350.00
330 Hayes (Charlotte) 5 175.00 350.00
331 Humphrey (Charlotte) 5 175.00 350.00
332 Johnson (Charlotte) 5 175.00 350.00
333 McHugh (Charlotte) 5 175.00 350.00
334 Taxis (Charlotte) 5 175.00 350.00
335 Williams (Charlotte) 5 175.00 350.00
336 Bentley (Greensboro) 5 175.00 350.00
337 Beusse C. (Greensboro) 5 175.00 350.00
338 Beusse F. (Greensboro) 5 175.00 350.00
339 Eldridge (Greensboro) 5 175.00 350.00
340 Hammersley (Greensboro) 5 175.00 350.00
341 Hicks (Greensboro) 5 175.00 350.00
342 Jackson (Greensboro) 5 175.00 350.00
343 James (Greensboro) 5 175.00 350.00
344 Rickard (Greensboro) 5 175.00 350.00
345 Smith (Greensboro) 5 175.00 350.00
346 Thrasher (Greensboro) 5 175.00 350.00
347 Walters (Greensboro) 5 175.00 350.00
348 Weldon (Greensboro) 5 175.00 350.00
349 Blackstone (Greenville) 5 175.00 350.00
350 Cashion (Greenville) 5 175.00 350.00
351 Derrick C. (Greenville) 5 175.00 350.00
352 Derrick (Greenville) 5 175.00 350.00
353 Drumm (Greenville) 5 175.00 350.00
354 Flowers (Greenville) 5 175.00 350.00
355 Jenkins (Greenville) 5 175.00 350.00
356 McFarlin (Greenville) 5 175.00 350.00
357 Noojin (Greenville) 5 175.00 350.00
358 Ochs (Greenville) 5 175.00 350.00
359 Redfern (Greenville) 5 175.00 350.00
360 Stouch (Greenville) 5 175.00 350.00
361 Trammell (Greenville) 5 175.00 350.00
362 Wingo (Greenville) 5 175.00 350.00
363 Workman (Greenville) 5 175.00 350.00
364 Wysong (Greenville) 5 175.00 350.00
365 Abercrombie (Spartanburg) 5 175.00 350.00
366 Avarett (Spartanburg) 5 175.00 350.00
367 Bigbee (Spartanburg) 5 175.00 350.00
368 Bullock (Spartanburg) 5 175.00 350.00
369 Crouch (Spartanburg) 5 175.00 350.00
370 Ehrhardt (Spartanburg) 5 175.00 350.00
371 Fairbanks (Spartanburg) 5 175.00 350.00
372 Gardin (Spartanburg) 5 175.00 350.00
373 Harrington (Spartanburg) 5 175.00 350.00
374 Harris (Spartanburg) 5 175.00 350.00
375 Roth At Bat (Spartanburg) 5 175.00 350.00
376 Roth Fielding (Spartanburg) 5 175.00 350.00
377 Springs (Spartanburg) 5 175.00 350.00
378 Walker (Spartanburg) 5 175.00 350.00
379 Wynne (Spartanburg) 5 175.00 350.00
380 Bievens (Winston-Salem) 5 175.00 350.00
381 Brent (Winston-Salem) 5 175.00 350.00
382 Ferrell (Winston-Salem) 5 175.00 350.00
383 Fogarty (Winston-Salem) 5 175.00 350.00
384 Gilmore (Winston-Salem) 5 175.00 350.00
385 Guss (Winston-Salem) 5 175.00 350.00
386 Laval (Winston-Salem) 5 175.00 350.00
387 MacConachie (Winston-Salem) 5 175.00 350.00
388 McKevitt (Winston-Salem) 5 175.00 350.00
389 Midkiff (Winston-Salem) 5 175.00 350.00
390 Moore (Winston-Salem) 5 175.00 350.00
391 Painter (Winston-Salem) 5 175.00 350.00
392 Reis (Winston-Salem) 5 175.00 350.00
393 Templin (Winston-Salem) 5 175.00 350.00
394 Angermeier Fielding (Frankfort) 6 (Angermeir) 175.00 350.00
395 Angermeir Portrait (Frankfort) 6 175.00 350.00
396 Beard (Frankfort) 6 175.00 350.00
397 Bohannon (Frankfort) 6 175.00 350.00
398 Cornell (Frankfort) 6 175.00 350.00
399 Hicks (Frankfort) 6 175.00 350.00
400 Hoffman (Frankfort) 6 175.00 350.00
401 McIlvain (Frankfort) 6 175.00 350.00

Card	Low	High
402 Badger (Lexington) 6	175.00	350.00
403 Ellis (Lexington) 6	175.00	350.00
404 Endington (Lexington) 6	175.00	350.00
405 Haines (Lexington) 6	175.00	350.00
406 Heveron (Lexington) 6	175.00	350.00
407 Keifel (Lexington) 6	175.00	350.00
408 Kinbrough (Lexington) 6	175.00	350.00
409 L'Heuveux (Lexington) 6	175.00	350.00
410 Meyers (Lexington) 6	175.00	350.00
411 Sinex (Lexington) 6	175.00	350.00
412 Van Landingham (Lexington) 6	175.00	350.00
413 Viox (Lexington) 6	175.00	350.00
414 Yancey (Lexington) 6	175.00	350.00
415 Chase (Maysville) 6	175.00	350.00
416 Dailey (Maysville) 6	175.00	350.00
417 Everden (Maysville) 6	175.00	350.00
418 Gisler (Maysville) 6	175.00	350.00
419 Oyler (Maysville) 6	175.00	350.00
420 Ross (Maysville) 6	175.00	350.00
421 Schultz (Maysville) 6	175.00	350.00
422 Stengel (Maysville) 6	30,000.00	60,000.00
423 Barnett (Paris) 6	175.00	350.00
424 Chapman (Paris) 6	175.00	350.00
425 Goodman (Paris) 6	175.00	350.00
426 Harold (Paris) 6	175.00	350.00
427 Kaiser (Paris) 6	175.00	350.00
428 Kuhlman 3/4 Length (Paris) 6 (Kuhlmann)	175.00	350.00
429 Kuhlmann Portrait (Paris) 6	175.00	350.00
430 McKernon (Paris) 6	175.00	350.00
431 Scheneberg Portrait (Paris) 6	175.00	350.00
432 Scheneberg Fielding (Paris) 6	175.00	350.00
433 Scott (Paris) 6	175.00	350.00
434 Creager (Richmond) 6	175.00	350.00
435 Elgin (Richmond) 6	175.00	350.00
436 Moloney (Richmond) 6	175.00	350.00
437 Olson (Richmond) 6	175.00	350.00
438 Thoss (Richmond) 6	175.00	350.00
439 Tilford (Richmond) 6	175.00	350.00
440 Walden (Richmond) 6	175.00	350.00
441 Whitaker (Richmond) 6	175.00	350.00
442 Willis (Richmond) 6	175.00	350.00
443 Wright (Richmond) 6	175.00	350.00
444 Kircher (Shelbyville) 6	175.00	350.00
445 Van Landingham (Shelbyville) 6	175.00	350.00
446 Womble (Shelbyville) 6	175.00	350.00
447 Atwell (Winchester) 6	175.00	350.00
448 Barney (Winchester) 6	175.00	350.00
449 Callahan (Winchester) 6	175.00	350.00
450 Coleman (Winchester) 6	175.00	350.00
451 Cornell (Winchester) 6	175.00	350.00
452 Goosetree Leaning on Bat (Winchester) 6	175.00	350.00
453 Goosetree Hands Behind Back (Winchester) 6	175.00	350.00
454 Horn (Winchester) 6	175.00	350.00
455 Kircher (Winchester) 6	175.00	350.00
456 Mullin (Winchester) 6	175.00	350.00
457 Reed (Winchester) 6	175.00	350.00
458 Toney (Winchester) 6	175.00	350.00
459 Yeager (Winchester) 6	350.00	700.00
460 Brandt (Fayetteville) 7	350.00	700.00
461 Cantwell (Fayetteville) 7	350.00	700.00
462 Dwyer (Fayetteville) 7	350.00	700.00
463 Galvin (Fayetteville) 7	350.00	700.00
464 Hartley (Fayetteville) 7	350.00	700.00
465 Luyster (Fayetteville) 7	350.00	700.00
466 Mayer (Fayetteville) 7	350.00	700.00
467 O'Halloran (Fayetteville) 7	350.00	700.00
468 Schumaker (Fayetteville) 7	350.00	700.00
469 Brown (Goldsboro) 7	350.00	700.00
470 Crockett (Goldsboro) 7	350.00	700.00
471 Dailey (Goldsboro) 7	350.00	700.00
472 Evans (Goldsboro) 7	350.00	700.00
473 Fulton (Goldsboro) 7	350.00	700.00
474 Gates (Goldsboro) 7	350.00	700.00
475 Gunderson (Goldsboro) 7	350.00	700.00
476 Handibe (Goldsboro) 7	350.00	700.00
477 Irving (Goldsboro) 7	350.00	700.00
478 Kaiser (Goldsboro) 7	350.00	700.00
479 Kelly (Goldsboro) 7	350.00	700.00
480 Kelly Mascot (Goldsboro) 7	600.00	1,200.00
481 MacDonald (Goldsboro) 7	350.00	700.00
482 Malcolm (Goldsboro) 7	350.00	700.00
483 Merchant (Goldsboro) 7	350.00	700.00
484 Morgan (Goldsboro) 7	350.00	700.00
485 Sharp (Goldsboro) 7	350.00	700.00
486 Steinback (Goldsboro) 7	350.00	700.00
487 Stoehr (Goldsboro) 7	350.00	700.00
488 Taylor (Goldsboro) 7	350.00	700.00
489 Webb (Goldsboro) 7	350.00	700.00
490 Wolf (Goldsboro) 7	350.00	700.00
491 Beatty (Raleigh) 7	350.00	700.00
492 Biel (Raleigh) 7	350.00	700.00
493 Carrol (Raleigh) 7	350.00	700.00
494 Ham (Raleigh) 7	350.00	700.00
495 Hart (Raleigh) 7	350.00	700.00
496 Hobbs (Raleigh) 7	350.00	700.00
497 Kelly (Raleigh) 7	350.00	700.00
498 McCormac (Raleigh) 7	350.00	700.00
499 Newman (Raleigh) 7	350.00	700.00
500 Prim (Raleigh) 7	350.00	700.00
501 Richardson (Raleigh) 7	350.00	700.00
502 Sherrill (Raleigh) 7	350.00	700.00
503 Simmons (Raleigh) 7	350.00	700.00
504 Wright (Raleigh) 7	350.00	700.00
505 Bonner (Rocky Mount) 7	350.00	700.00
506 Creagan (Rocky Mount) 7	350.00	700.00
507 Cooney (Rocky Mount) 7	350.00	700.00
508 Dobbs (Rocky Mount) 7	350.00	700.00
509 Dussault (Rocky Mount) 7	350.00	700.00
510 Forgue (Rocky Mount) 7	350.00	700.00
511 Gastmeyer Batting (Rocky Mount) 7	350.00	700.00
512 Gastmeyer Fielding (Rocky Mount) 7	350.00	700.00
513 Gillespie (Rocky Mount) 7	350.00	700.00
514 Griffin (Rocky Mount) 7	350.00	700.00
515 Morris (Rocky Mount) 7	350.00	700.00
516 Munson (Rocky Mount) 7	350.00	700.00
517 Noval (Rocky Mount) 7	350.00	700.00
518 Phelan (Rocky Mount) 7	350.00	700.00
519 Reeves (Rocky Mount) 7	350.00	700.00
520 Hyames (Wilmington) 7	350.00	700.00
521 Armstrong (Wilson) 7	350.00	700.00
522 Cooper (Wilson) 7	350.00	700.00
523 Cowell (Wilson) 7	350.00	700.00
524 McGeehan (Wilson) 7	350.00	700.00
525 Mills (Wilson) 7	350.00	700.00
526 Whelan (Wilson) 7	350.00	700.00
527 Bartley (Atlanta) 8	350.00	700.00
528 Bayless (Atlanta) 8	350.00	700.00
529 Fisher (Atlanta) 8	350.00	700.00
530 Griffin (Atlanta) 8	350.00	700.00
531 Hanks (Atlanta) 8	350.00	700.00
532 Hohnhorst (Atlanta) 8	350.00	700.00
533 Jordan (Atlanta) 8	350.00	700.00
534 Moran (Atlanta) 8	350.00	700.00
535 Rogers (Atlanta) 8	350.00	700.00
536 Seitz (Atlanta) 8	350.00	700.00
537 Smith (Atlanta) 8	350.00	700.00
538 Sweeney (Atlanta) 8	350.00	700.00
539 Walker (Atlanta) 8	350.00	700.00
540 Bauer (Birmingham) 8	350.00	700.00
541 Elliott (Birmingham) 8	350.00	700.00
542 Emery (Birmingham) 8	350.00	700.00
543 Fleharty (Birmingham) 8	350.00	700.00
544 Gygli (Birmingham) 8	350.00	700.00
545 Kane (Birmingham) 8	350.00	700.00
546 Larsen (Birmingham) 8	350.00	700.00
547 Manuel (Birmingham) 8	350.00	700.00
548 Marcan (Birmingham) 8	350.00	700.00
549 McBride (Birmingham) 8	350.00	700.00
550 McGilvray (Birmingham) 8	350.00	700.00
551 McTigue (Birmingham) 8	350.00	700.00
552 Molesworth (Birmingham) 8	350.00	700.00
553 Newton (Birmingham) 8	350.00	700.00
554 Owen (Birmingham) 8	350.00	700.00
555 Schopp (Birmingham) 8	350.00	700.00
556 Wagner (Birmingham) 8	350.00	700.00
557 Carson (Chattanooga) 8	350.00	700.00
558 Collins (Chattanooga) 8	350.00	700.00
559 Demaree (Chattanooga) 8	350.00	700.00
560 Dobbs (Chattanooga) 8	350.00	700.00
561 McLaurin (Chattanooga) 8	350.00	700.00
562 Miller (Chattanooga) 8	350.00	700.00
563 Patterson (Chattanooga) 8	350.00	700.00
564 Rhodes (Chattanooga) 8	350.00	700.00
565 Schlitzer (Chattanooga) 8	350.00	700.00
566 Yerkes (Chattanooga) 8	350.00	700.00
567 Allen (Memphis) 8	350.00	700.00
568 Babb (Memphis) 8	350.00	700.00
569 Crandall (Memphis) 8	350.00	700.00
570 Cross (Memphis) 8	350.00	700.00
571 Davis (Memphis) 8	350.00	700.00
572 Dick (Memphis) 8	350.00	700.00
573 Dudley (Memphis) 8	350.00	700.00
574 Farrell (Memphis) 8	350.00	700.00
575 Fritz (Memphis) 8	350.00	700.00
576 Peters (Memphis) 8	350.00	700.00
577 Rementer (Memphis) 8	350.00	700.00
578 Steele (Memphis) 8	350.00	700.00
579 Wanner (Memphis) 8	350.00	700.00
580 Whitney (Memphis) 8	350.00	700.00
581 Allen (Mobile) 8	350.00	700.00
582 Berger (Mobile) 8	350.00	700.00
583 Bittroff (Mobile) 8	350.00	700.00
584 Chappelle (Mobile) 8	350.00	700.00
585 Dunn (Mobile) 8	350.00	700.00
586 Hickman (Mobile) 8	350.00	700.00
587 Huelsman (Mobile) 8	350.00	700.00
588 Kerwin (Mobile) 8	350.00	700.00
589 Rhoton (Mobile) 8	350.00	700.00
590 Swacina (Mobile) 8	350.00	700.00
591 Wagner (Mobile) 8	350.00	700.00
592 Wilder (Mobile) 8	350.00	700.00
593 Burnett (Montgomery) 8	350.00	700.00
594 Daly (Montgomery) 8	350.00	700.00
595 Graninger (Montgomery) 8	350.00	700.00
596 Gribbin (Montgomery) 8	350.00	700.00
597 Hart (Montgomery) 8	350.00	700.00
598 McCreery (Montgomery) 8	350.00	700.00
599 Miller (Montgomery) 8	350.00	700.00
600 Nolley (Montgomery) 8	350.00	700.00
601 Osteen (Montgomery) 8	350.00	700.00
602 Pepe (Montgomery) 8	350.00	700.00
603 Phillips (Montgomery) 8	350.00	700.00
604 Pratt (Montgomery) 8	350.00	700.00
605 Smith (Montgomery) 8	350.00	700.00
606 Thomas Portrait (Montgomery) 8	350.00	700.00
607 Thomas Fielding (Montgomery) 8	350.00	700.00
608 Whiteman (Montgomery) 8	350.00	700.00
609 Anderson (Nashville) 8	350.00	700.00
610 Bay (Nashville) 8	350.00	700.00
611 Bernard (Nashville) 8	350.00	700.00
612 Bronkie (Nashville) 8	350.00	700.00
613 Case (Nashville) 8	350.00	700.00
614 Cohen (Nashville) 8	350.00	700.00
615 Erloff (Nashville) 8	350.00	700.00
616 Flood (Nashville) 8	350.00	700.00
617 Kelly (Nashville) 8	350.00	700.00
618 Keupper (Nashville) 8	350.00	700.00
619 Lynch (Nashville) 8	350.00	700.00
620 Perdue (Nashville) 8	350.00	700.00
621 Seabough (Nashville) 8	350.00	700.00
622 Siegle (Nashville) 8	350.00	700.00
623 Vinson (Nashville) 8	350.00	700.00
624 Weif (Nashville) 8	350.00	700.00
625 Wiseman (Nashville) 8	350.00	700.00
626 Breitenstein (New Orleans) 8	350.00	700.00
627 Brooks (New Orleans) 8	350.00	700.00
628 Cafalu (New Orleans) 8	350.00	700.00
629 DeMontreville (New Orleans) 8	350.00	700.00
630 DeMontreville E. (New Orleans) 8	350.00	700.00
631 Doster (New Orleans) 8	350.00	700.00
632 Hess (New Orleans) 8	350.00	700.00
633 Joe Jackson (New Orleans) 8	100,000.00	200,000.00
634 LaFitte (New Orleans) 8	350.00	700.00
635 Lindsay (New Orleans) 8	350.00	700.00
636 Manush (New Orleans) 8	350.00	700.00
637 Maxwell (New Orleans) 8	350.00	700.00
638 Paige (New Orleans) 8	350.00	700.00
639 Robertson (New Orleans) 8	350.00	700.00
640 Rohe (New Orleans) 8	350.00	700.00

1910 Red Sun T211

The green-bordered cards in this 75-card set measure approximately 1 1/2" by 2 5/8". The obverse design of this 1910 issue resembles that of the the T210 set except for the green borders surrounding the black and white picture area. All players in the set are from the Southern Association and all also appear in the T210 Series 8. The players have been alphabetized within team and numbered for reference in the checklist below. The teams are also ordered alphabetically: Atlanta (1-13), Birmingham (14-16), Memphis (17-22), Mobile (23-34), Montgomery (35-45), Nashville (46-62) and New Orleans (63-75).

Card	Low	High
1 Bartley	500.00	1,000.00
2 Bayless	400.00	800.00
3 Fisher	400.00	800.00
4 Griffin	400.00	800.00
5 Gornhorst	400.00	800.00
6 Hanks	400.00	800.00
7 Jordan	400.00	800.00
8 Moran	400.00	800.00
9 Rogers	400.00	800.00
10 Seitz	400.00	800.00
11 Sid Smith	400.00	800.00
12 Sweeney	400.00	800.00
13 Walker	400.00	800.00
14 Gygli	400.00	800.00
15 Kane	400.00	800.00
16 Molesworth	400.00	800.00
17 Babb	400.00	800.00
18 Cross	400.00	800.00
19 Davis	400.00	800.00
20 Dick	400.00	800.00
21 Fritz	400.00	800.00
22 Steele	400.00	800.00
23 Allen	400.00	800.00
24 Berger	400.00	800.00
25 Bittroff	400.00	800.00
26 Chappelle	400.00	800.00
27 Dunn	400.00	800.00
28 Hickman	400.00	800.00
29 Huelsman	400.00	800.00
30 Kerwin	400.00	800.00
31 Rhoton	400.00	800.00
32 Swacina	400.00	800.00
33 Wagner	400.00	800.00
34 Wilder	400.00	800.00
35 Jud Daly	400.00	800.00
36 Greminger	400.00	800.00
37 Gribbin	400.00	800.00
38 Hart	400.00	800.00
39 McCreary	400.00	800.00
40 Miller	400.00	800.00
41 Nolley	400.00	800.00
42 Pepe	400.00	800.00
43 Pratt	400.00	800.00
44 Smith	400.00	800.00
45 Thomas	400.00	800.00
46 Anderson	400.00	800.00
47 Bay	400.00	800.00
48 Bernard	400.00	800.00
49 Bronkie	400.00	800.00
50 Case	400.00	800.00
51 Cohen	400.00	800.00
52 Erloff	400.00	800.00
53 Flood	400.00	800.00
54 Kelly	400.00	800.00
55 Keupper	400.00	800.00
56 Lynch	400.00	800.00
57 Perdue	400.00	800.00
58 Seabrough	400.00	800.00
59 Siegel	400.00	800.00
60 Vinson	400.00	800.00
61 Wiseman	400.00	800.00
62 Welf	400.00	800.00
63 Breitenstein	400.00	800.00
64 Brooks	400.00	800.00
65 Cafalu	400.00	800.00
66 DeMontreville	400.00	800.00
67 E. DeMontreville	400.00	800.00
68 Foster	400.00	800.00
69 Hess	400.00	800.00
70 LaFitte	400.00	800.00
71 Lindsay	400.00	800.00
72 Manush	400.00	800.00
73 Paige	400.00	800.00
74 Robertson	400.00	800.00
75 Rohe	400.00	800.00

1911 Big Eater E-Unc.

This 20-card set of the Pacific Coast League's team, the Sacramento Senators, features black-and-white player photos which measure approximately 2 1/8" by 4". Each card has a three line capiton giving the name of the player, the team as "SAC'TO" and the words, "HE EATS 'BIG EATER' " which is presumed to be the name of a candy. These cards are rarely found in a better condition than g-vg. There is speculation that these were issued by a candy company -- therefore the cards are listed with the "E" designation.

Card	Low	High
COMPLETE SET (20)	10,000.00	20,000.00
1 Frank Arellanes	2,500.00	5,000.00
2 Charles Baum	2,500.00	5,000.00
3 Herbert Byram	2,500.00	5,000.00
4 Hal Danzig	2,500.00	5,000.00
5 John Fitzgerald	2,500.00	5,000.00
6 Gaddy/(unidentified player)	2,500.00	5,000.00
7 Elwood Heister	2,500.00	5,000.00
8 Hunt	2,500.00	5,000.00
9 Henry Kerns	2,500.00	5,000.00
10 Louis LaLonge	2,500.00	5,000.00
11 Bertram Lerchen	2,500.00	5,000.00
12 Jim Lewis	2,500.00	5,000.00
13 Christopher Mahoney	2,500.00	5,000.00
14 Richard Nebinger	2,500.00	5,000.00
15 Joseph L. O'Rourke	2,500.00	5,000.00
16 James Shinn	2,500.00	5,000.00
17 Chester Thomas	2,500.00	5,000.00
18 Cecil Thompson	2,500.00	5,000.00
19 Frank Thornton	2,500.00	5,000.00
20 Edward Van Buren	2,500.00	5,000.00

1911 Bishop Coast League E100

The cards in this 30-card set measure 1 1/2" by 2 3/4". Each of the cards of this Pacific Coast League set have the inscription "Bishop and Co." printed on the reverse at the bottom. Otherwise, the style of the cards is similar to set E99. They have black and white photos set on solid color backgrounds, they are backlisted (starts with "Seaton"), and they are unnumbered. There are color variations for many players. Subjects marked by an asterisk are found also in a blank-backed, slightly larger (photo on) card with a green or orange backgound. These blank-backed (Type II) cards are valued double the prices below. According to some hobbyists, there has never been a type two found in better than vg/ex condition. The cards in the set have been alphabetized and numbered in the checklist below. The set was produced around 1910.

Card	Low	High
COMPLETE SET (30)	4,000.00	8,000.00
1 Spider Baum	400.00	800.00
2 Len Burrell *	400.00	800.00
3 Walt Carlisle	400.00	800.00
4 George Cutshaw	400.00	800.00
5 Pete Daley	400.00	800.00
6 Babe Danzig *	400.00	800.00
7 Flame Delhi	400.00	800.00
8 Bert Delmas	400.00	800.00
9 Roy Hitt *	400.00	800.00
10 Happy Hogan	400.00	800.00
11 Dutch Lerchen	400.00	800.00
12 Walt McCreedie	400.00	800.00
13 Kid Mohler	400.00	800.00
14 Charlie Moore	400.00	800.00
15 Slim Nelson	400.00	800.00
16 Patsy O'Rourke	400.00	800.00
17 Ham Patterson	400.00	800.00
18 Ducky Pearce *	400.00	800.00
19 Roger Peckinpaugh	500.00	1,000.00
20 Monte Pfyle sic, Pfyl *	400.00	800.00
21 Watt Powell	400.00	800.00
22 Bill Rapps	400.00	800.00
23 Tom Seaton *	400.00	800.00
24 Bill Steen	400.00	800.00
25 Harry Sutor	400.00	800.00
26 Tom Tennant	400.00	800.00
27 Pinch Thomas	400.00	800.00
28 Bill Tozer	400.00	800.00
29 Clyde Wares	400.00	800.00
30 Buck Weaver	1,500.00	3,000.00

1911 Mono T217

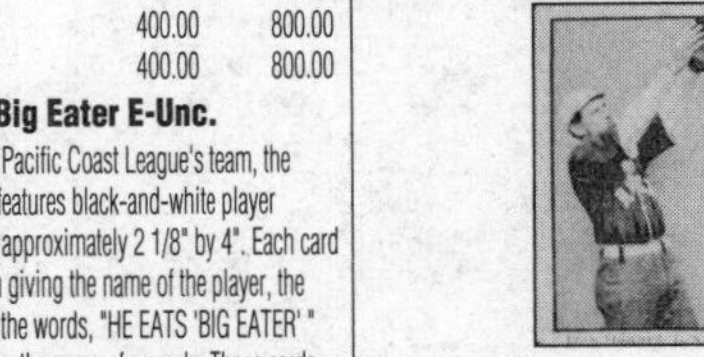

These 25 cards, which were issued as part of a far more inclusive set, including many famous actresses, feature players from the PCL. Since these cards are unnumbered, we have sequenced them in alphabetical order.

Card	Low	High
COMPLETE SET	35,000.00	70,000.00
1 Roy Akin	2,500.00	5,000.00
2 Curtis Bernard	2,500.00	5,000.00
3 Len Burrell	2,500.00	5,000.00
4 Chet Chadbourne	2,500.00	5,000.00
5 Bob Couchman	2,500.00	5,000.00
6 Elmer Criger	2,500.00	5,000.00
7 Pete Daley	2,500.00	5,000.00
8 Flame Delhi Eyes Closed	2,500.00	5,000.00
9 Flame Delhi Eyes Opened	2,500.00	5,000.00
10 Bert Delmas	2,500.00	5,000.00
11 Ivan Howard	2,500.00	5,000.00
12 Kitty Knight	2,500.00	5,000.00
13 Gene Krapp Sic, Knapp	2,500.00	5,000.00
14 George Metzger	2,500.00	5,000.00
15 Carl Mitze	2,500.00	5,000.00
16 Patsy O'Rourke	2,500.00	5,000.00
17 Roger Peckinpaugh	3,000.00	6,000.00

18 Walter Schmidt	2,500.00	5,000.00
19 Hugh Smith Batting	2,500.00	5,000.00
20 Hugh Smith Fielding	2,500.00	5,000.00
21 William Stein	2,500.00	5,000.00
22 Elmer Thorsen	2,500.00	5,000.00
23 Oscar Vitt	3,000.00	6,000.00
24 Clyde Wares	2,500.00	5,000.00
25 George Wheeler	2,500.00	5,000.00

1911 Pacific Coast Biscuit D310

These cards, which measure approximately 2 1/2" by 4 1/2" feature players from the Pacific Coast League . Most of the cards were issued in black and white but a few were issued with a greenish sepia black and white.

COMPLETE SET	7,500.00	15,000.00
1 Harry Ables	200.00	400.00
2 James Agnew	200.00	400.00
3 Roy Akin	200.00	400.00
4 Frank Arelanes	200.00	400.00
5 Charles Baum	200.00	400.00
6 Curtis Bernard	200.00	400.00
7 Claude Berry	200.00	400.00
8 Roy Brashear	200.00	400.00
9 Frank Browning	200.00	400.00
10 Leland Burrell	200.00	400.00
11 Herbert Byram	200.00	400.00
12 Walter Carlisle	200.00	400.00
13 Chester Chadbourne	200.00	400.00
14 Tyler Christian	200.00	400.00
15 George Cutshaw	200.00	400.00
16 Thomas Daley	200.00	400.00
17 Harold Danzig	200.00	400.00
18 Lee Delhi	200.00	400.00
19 Bert Delmas	200.00	400.00
20 Frank Dillon	200.00	400.00
21 Joseph Fitzgerald	200.00	400.00
22 Alva Gipe	200.00	400.00
23 Woody Heister	200.00	400.00
24 Ben Henderson	200.00	400.00
25 Clarence Henley	200.00	400.00
26 Roy Hitt	200.00	400.00
27 Harry Hoffman	200.00	400.00
28 Wallace Hogan	200.00	400.00
29 Joseph Holland	200.00	400.00
30 Franz Hosp	200.00	400.00
31 Ivon Howard	200.00	400.00
32 Elmer Kostner	200.00	400.00
33 Walter Kuhn	200.00	400.00
34 L.W. LaLonge	200.00	400.00
35 James Lewis	200.00	400.00
36 Thomas Madden	200.00	400.00
37 Harl Maggart	200.00	400.00
38 Harry McArdle	200.00	400.00
39 Walt McCredie	200.00	400.00
40 C. McDonnell	200.00	400.00
41 George Metzger	200.00	400.00
42 Carl Mitze	200.00	400.00
43 Ernest Mohler	200.00	400.00
44 Charles Moore	200.00	400.00
45 Daniel Murray	200.00	400.00
46 Chester Nourse	200.00	400.00
47 Joe O'Rourke	200.00	400.00
47 Ham Patterson	200.00	400.00
49 Roger Peckinpaugh	500.00	1,000.00
50 Hub Pernoll	200.00	400.00
51 M.C. Pfyl	200.00	400.00
52 John Raleigh	200.00	400.00
53 William Rapps	200.00	400.00
54 Arthur Ross	200.00	400.00
55 John Ryan	200.00	400.00
56 Tom Seaton	200.00	400.00
57 Tom Sheehan	200.00	400.00
58 Arthur Smith	200.00	400.00
59 Hughie Smith	200.00	400.00
60 William Steen	200.00	400.00
61 George Stinson	200.00	400.00
62 Harry Sutor	200.00	400.00
63 Thomas Tennant	200.00	400.00
64 Fuller Thompson	200.00	400.00
65 John Tiedeman	200.00	400.00
66 William Tozer	200.00	400.00
67 Edward Van Buren	200.00	400.00
68 Oscar Vitt	250.00	500.00
69 Clyde Wares	200.00	400.00
70 Buck Weaver	1,000.00	2,000.00
71 Harry Wolverton	200.00	400.00
72 Elmer Zacher	200.00	400.00

1911 Pacific Coast Biscuit D311

These color cards, which measure approximately 1 1/2" by 2 1/2" feature players from the Pacific Coast League. The fronts have feature the player photo with his last name and team on the bottom. The backs list the 12 players featured from each team. Since these cards are unnumbered, we have sequenced them in alphabetical order.

1 Jimmy Agnew	250.00	500.00
2 Roy Akin	250.00	500.00
3 Frank Arellanes	250.00	500.00
4 Spider Baum	250.00	500.00
5 Curt Bernard	250.00	500.00
6 Claude Berry	250.00	500.00
7 Roy Brashear	250.00	500.00
8 Drummond Brown	250.00	500.00
9 Frank Browning	250.00	500.00
10 Len Burrell	250.00	500.00
11 Herb Byram	250.00	500.00
12 Roy Castleton	250.00	500.00
13 Chet Chadbourne	250.00	500.00
14 Tyler Christian	250.00	500.00
15 George Cutshaw	250.00	500.00
16 Pete Daley	250.00	500.00
17 Babe Danzig	250.00	500.00
18 Flame Delhi	250.00	500.00
19 Bert Delmas	250.00	500.00
20 Cap Dillon	250.00	500.00
21 Jack Fitzgerald	250.00	500.00
22 Jake Gipe	250.00	500.00
23 Howie Gregory	250.00	500.00
24 Spec Harkness	250.00	500.00
25 Elwood Heister	250.00	500.00
26 Ben Henderson	250.00	500.00
27 Izzy Hoffman	250.00	500.00
28 Happy Hogan	250.00	500.00
29 Joe Holland	250.00	500.00
30 Franz Hosp	250.00	500.00
31 Ivan Howard	250.00	500.00
32 Red Kuhn	250.00	500.00
33 Mickey LaLonge	250.00	500.00
34 Jimmy Lewis	250.00	500.00
35 Harl Maggert	250.00	500.00
36 Roy McArdle	250.00	500.00
37 Walt McCredie	250.00	500.00
38 Speed McDonnell	250.00	500.00
39 Williard Meikle	250.00	500.00
40 Harry Melchior	250.00	500.00
41 George Metzger	250.00	500.00
42 Honus Mitze	250.00	500.00
43 Kid Mohler	250.00	500.00
44 Charlie Moore	250.00	500.00
45 Tommy Murray	250.00	500.00
46 Chet Nourse	250.00	500.00
47 Patsy O'Rourke	250.00	500.00
48 Ham Patterson	250.00	500.00
49 Ducky Pearce	250.00	500.00
50 Roger Peckinpaugh	600.00	1,200.00
51 Hub Pernoll	250.00	500.00
52 Monte Pfyl	250.00	500.00
53 John Raleigh	250.00	500.00
54 Bill Rapps	250.00	500.00
55 Buddy Ryan	250.00	500.00
56 Walt Schmidt	250.00	500.00
57 Tom Seaton	250.00	500.00
58 Tommy Sheehan	300.00	600.00
59 Art Smith	250.00	500.00
60 Hugh Smith	250.00	500.00
61 Scott Stanfield	250.00	500.00
62 Bill Steen	250.00	500.00
63 George Stinson	250.00	500.00
64 Harry Sutor	250.00	500.00
65 Tom Tennant	250.00	500.00
66 Chester Thompson	250.00	500.00
67 John Tiedeman	250.00	500.00
68 Bill Tozer	250.00	500.00
69 Deacon Van Buren	250.00	500.00
70 Ossie Vitt	450.00	900.00
71 Buzzy Wares	250.00	500.00
72 Harry Wolverton	250.00	500.00

1911 Western Playground Assocation

These cards, which were issued as part of a redemption to help school kids, measure approximately 2 1/4" by 3 1/2". Each of these cards have the brown borders surrounding the player's photo. The backs of these cards feature certificates which could be used to recieive playground equipment. These cards were produced by Mysell-Rollins (a leading San Francisco turn of the century printer) and were used as give aways with students purchasing composition notebooks. The cards were then designed to be returned to teachers who would return them to the manufacturer for either playground equipment or other school supplies. These cards are unnumbered, so we have sequenced them in alphabetical order.

COMPLETE SET	20,000.00	40,000.00
1 Claude Berry	2,500.00	5,000.00
2 Kitty Brashear	2,500.00	5,000.00
3 Herb Byram	2,500.00	5,000.00
4 Walt Carlisle	2,500.00	5,000.00
5 Roy Castleton	2,500.00	5,000.00
6 Chet Chadbourne	2,500.00	5,000.00
7 Tyler Christian	2,500.00	5,000.00
8 Bert Coy	2,500.00	5,000.00
9 Pete Daley	2,500.00	5,000.00
10 Cap Dillon	2,500.00	5,000.00
11 Joe French	2,500.00	5,000.00
12 Howie Gregory	2,500.00	5,000.00
13 Spec Harkness	2,500.00	5,000.00
14 Henie Heitmuller	2,500.00	5,000.00
15 Ben Henderson	2,500.00	5,000.00
16 Cack Henley	2,500.00	5,000.00
17 Izzy Hoffman	2,500.00	5,000.00
18 Happy Hogan	2,500.00	5,000.00
19 Johnny Kane	2,500.00	5,000.00
20 Jimmy Lewis	2,500.00	5,000.00
21 Tom Madden	2,500.00	5,000.00
22 Chris Mahoney	2,500.00	5,000.00
23 George Metzger	2,500.00	5,000.00
24 Frank Miller	2,500.00	5,000.00
25 Kid Mohler	2,500.00	5,000.00
26 Walter Nagle	2,500.00	5,000.00
27 Patsy O'Rourke	2,500.00	5,000.00
28 Ham Patterson	2,500.00	5,000.00
29 Roger Peckinpaugh	3,000.00	6,000.00
30 Bill Rapps	2,500.00	5,000.00
31 Bill Rodgers Sic, Rogers	2,500.00	5,000.00
32 Buddy Ryan	2,500.00	5,000.00
33 Walter Schmidt Sic, Schmitt	2,500.00	5,000.00
34 Tom Seaton	2,500.00	5,000.00
35 Tommy Sheehan	2,500.00	5,000.00
36 Harry Stewart	2,500.00	5,000.00
37 George Stinson	2,500.00	5,000.00
38 Harry Sutor Sic, Suter	2,500.00	5,000.00
39 Harry Wolverton	2,500.00	5,000.00
40 Elmer Zacher	2,500.00	5,000.00

1911 Zeenuts

Zee-Nut cards were issued over a 28 year period. The cards measure a different size depending on when issued. 1911, 12 and Home Run Kisses have similar sizes. 1913, 14 and 15 have similar sizes. 1916 through 1918 are somewhat similar. 1919 through 1923 are somewhat similar. And 1924 through 1937 is somewhat similar. 1937's came with a coupon attached while 1938 came with a separate coupon. But once the coupon is taken off a 37 it is identical to a 38. Cards were issued one to a box in one of three 5 cent products; ZeeNuts, Rufneck and Home Run Kisses. These cards were made by Collins-McCarthy Candy Co. (And their successors). Most of the cards were marketed within a 100 mile radius of San Francisco. Cards are usually blank backed. Cards have also been seen, however, with printing on both sides. In this set, Included in the 1911 set is a very early card of Buck Weaver. There is also a premium for Roger Peckinpaugh. Cards are priced without the coupon. There is currently an 100 percent premium for most cards if the coupon is attached. Complete set for each Zeenut yearly series is provided although completing almost any year set is a daunting task. Dimensions are provided for each set; however all dimensions are approximate and cards can vary since printing was not as scientific pre-1940 as it is today. The 1911's measure approximately 2 1/8" by 4"

COMPLETE SET (122)	8,000.00	16,000.00
1 Frederick Abbott	75.00	150.00
2 James Agnew	75.00	150.00
3 Roy Akin	75.00	150.00
4 Curtis Bernard	75.00	150.00
5 Robert Couchman	75.00	150.00
6 Elmer Criger	75.00	150.00
7 Thomas Daley	75.00	150.00
8 Lee W. Delhi	75.00	150.00
9 Bert C. Delmas	75.00	150.00
10 Frank E. Dillon	75.00	150.00
11 Milton Driscoll	75.00	150.00
12 John A. Halla	75.00	150.00
13 William Heitmuller	75.00	150.00
14 Ivan Howard	75.00	150.00
15 Walter Leverenz	75.00	150.00
16 Elmer Lober	75.00	150.00
17 George Metzger	75.00	150.00
18 Charles W. Moore	75.00	150.00
19A Hugh Smith small	75.00	150.00
19B Hugh Smith Large	75.00	150.00
20 Harry Ables	75.00	150.00
21 Alex Arlett	75.00	150.00
22 Leo Bohen	75.00	150.00
23 J. Tyler Christian	75.00	150.00
24 Bert Coy	75.00	150.00
25 George Cutshaw	75.00	150.00
26 John Flater	75.00	150.00
27 William Gleason	75.00	150.00
28 Howard Gregory	75.00	150.00
29 August Hetling	75.00	150.00
30 Harry C. Hoffman	75.00	150.00
31 Orville Kilroy	75.00	150.00
32 Grover Knight	75.00	150.00
33 Harl Maggart	75.00	150.00
34 Elmer Martinoni	75.00	150.00
35 Carl Mitze	75.00	150.00
36 Lorenzo Patterson	75.00	150.00
37 William C. Pearce	75.00	150.00
38 Henry Pernoll	75.00	150.00
39 Meinhard Pfyl	75.00	150.00
40 John C. Tiedeman	75.00	150.00
41 Clyde Wares	75.00	150.00
42 Harry Wolverton MG	75.00	150.00
43 Elmer Zacher	75.00	150.00
44 John C. Barry	75.00	150.00
45 Chester Chadbourne	75.00	150.00
46 Charles Fullerton	75.00	150.00
47 Frederick Harkness	75.00	150.00
48 Elmer Koestner	75.00	150.00
49 Arthur Krueger	75.00	150.00
50 Walter Kuhn	75.00	150.00
51 William G. Lindsay	75.00	150.00
52 Walter McCredie	75.00	150.00
53 Terry W. McKune	75.00	150.00
54 Thomas J. Murray	75.00	150.00
55 Roger Peckinpaugh	100.00	200.00
56 William H. Rapps	75.00	150.00
57 Wilbur Rodgers	75.00	150.00
58 John B. Ryan	75.00	150.00
59 Thomas G. Seaton	75.00	150.00
60 Thomas H. Sheehan	100.00	200.00
61 William J. Steen	75.00	150.00
62 Frank Arellanes	75.00	150.00
63 Charles A. Baum	75.00	150.00
64 Herbert F. Byram	75.00	150.00
65 Harold Danzig	75.00	150.00
66 James Dulin	75.00	150.00
67 John P. Fitzgerald	75.00	150.00
68 Elwood Heister	75.00	150.00
69 Henry B. Kerns	75.00	150.00
70 Louis LaLonge	75.00	150.00
71 Bertram Lerchen	75.00	150.00
72 James J. Lewis	75.00	150.00
73 Christopher Mahoney	75.00	150.00
74 Richard Nebinger	75.00	150.00
75 Chester L. Nourse	75.00	150.00
76 Joseph L. O'Rourke	75.00	150.00
77 James E. Shinn	75.00	150.00
78 Chester Thomas	75.00	150.00
79 Cecil A. Thompson	75.00	150.00
80 Frank J. Thornton	75.00	150.00
81 Edward E. Van Buren	75.00	150.00
82 Claude E. Berry	75.00	150.00
83 Frank Browning	75.00	150.00
84 Fred Carman	75.00	150.00
85 Charles H. Fanning	75.00	150.00
86 Asa A. French	75.00	150.00
87 Clarence Henley	75.00	150.00
88 Joe G. Holland	75.00	150.00
89 Thomas J. Madden	75.00	150.00
90 Harry McArdle	75.00	150.00
91 Willard Meikle	75.00	150.00
92 Henry Melchoir	75.00	150.00
93 Frank L. Miller	75.00	150.00
94 Ernest F. Mohler	75.00	150.00
95 William B. Moskiman	75.00	150.00
96 Arthur E. Naylor	75.00	150.00
97 Winfield C. Noyes	75.00	150.00
98 Watt B. Powell	75.00	150.00
99 William Ryan	75.00	150.00
100 Royal N. Shaw	75.00	150.00
101 Arthur S. Smith	75.00	150.00
102 Harry R. Suter	75.00	150.00
103 Thomas F. Tennant	75.00	150.00
104 Oscar J. Vitt	100.00	200.00
105 George D. Weaver	1,500.00	3,000.00
106 Carl E. Zamloch	75.00	150.00
107 John Brackenridge	75.00	150.00
108 Roy P. Brashear	75.00	150.00
109A Drummond Brown small	75.00	150.00
109B Drummond Brown Medium	75.00	150.00
109C Drummond Brown Large	75.00	150.00
110 Leonard Burrell	75.00	150.00
111 Walter G. Carlisle	75.00	150.00
112A Alexander J. Carson Small	75.00	150.00
112B Albert Carson Medium	75.00	150.00
112C Albert Carson Large	75.00	150.00
113 Royal E. Castleton	75.00	150.00
114 Roy W. Hitt	75.00	150.00
115 Wallace L. Hogan	75.00	150.00
116 Franz P. Hosp	75.00	150.00
117 John F. Kane	75.00	150.00
118 Clarence M. McDonnell	75.00	150.00
119 Hamilton Patterson	75.00	150.00
120 John A. Raleigh	75.00	150.00
121 Harry L. Stewart	75.00	150.00
122A George C. Stinson Small	75.00	150.00
122B George Stinson Medium	75.00	150.00
122C George Stinson Large	75.00	150.00

1911-12 Obak Premiums T4

Similar to the Pinkerton cabinets issued around the same time; this checklist is presented without prices. These cards are very scarce within the hobby as it originally took 50 coupons to receive one of these premiums. These cabinets measure approximately 5" by 7" are usually have a pencil marking in the back which correspond to the Obak listings of the 1911 set. In addition, subtle differences are known in every photo since they were enlarged from the original photo. It is believed that by 1913 only 25 coupons were needed for these and possibly less later in the decade. While there is not a lot of activity on these cards, a price of approximately $2500 for known copies in ex/mt condition is a good base to use for pricing. A nice grouping of these cards were auctioned off in the December, 2006 SCP/Sotheby's with the prices being in range with the base pricing we discussed a sentence earlier.

COMPLETE SET (175)

1912 Home Run Kisses E136-1

The cards in this 90-card set measure 2" by 4". This is perhaps the most distinctive of all the baseball series issued by the Collins-McCarthy company because of the clever product name and the distinctive ornate frame surrounding the picture area of the card. The players are from six different Pacific Coast League teams in the set. The name "Home Run Kisses" and the player's name and team are printed within the picture area; the picture itself is sepia. Some cards are found with premium advertising on the reverse but the great majority have only a simple easel design on the back. The cards have been alphabetized and numbered in the checklist below. These cards have been found with two different backs: Bardell Sepia Logo and a Premium Offer.

1 Walter Boles	350.00	700.00
2 Harvey Brooks	350.00	700.00
3 Charles Check	350.00	700.00
4 John Core	350.00	700.00
5 Thomas Daley	350.00	700.00
6 Frank Dillon MG	350.00	700.00
7 Milton Driscoll	400.00	800.00
8 John Flater	350.00	700.00
9 William Heitmuller	400.00	800.00
10 Walter Leverenz	400.00	800.00
11 Elmer Lober	350.00	700.00
12 George Metzger	400.00	800.00
13 Walter Nagle	350.00	700.00
14 William Page	350.00	700.00
15 Walter Slage	350.00	700.00
16 Hugh Smith	350.00	700.00
17 William Tozer	350.00	700.00
18 Harry Ables	350.00	700.00
19 Harvey Brooks	350.00	700.00
20 Bert Coy	350.00	700.00
21 Howard Gregory	350.00	700.00
22 Harry Hoffman	350.00	700.00
23 William Leard	350.00	700.00
24 William Malarkey	350.00	700.00
25 Elmer Martinoni	350.00	700.00
26 Henry Olmstead	350.00	700.00
27 Roy Parkins	350.00	700.00
28 Lorenzo Patterson	350.00	700.00
29 Henry Pernoll	350.00	700.00
30 John Tiedeman	350.00	700.00
31 Elmer Zacher	400.00	800.00
32 David Bancroft	600.00	1,200.00
33 Willie Butler	350.00	700.00
34 Chester Chadbourne	350.00	700.00
35 Walter Doane	350.00	700.00
36 August Fisher	350.00	700.00
37 David Gregg	350.00	700.00
38 Frederick Harkness	350.00	700.00
39 Daniel Howley	400.00	800.00
40 Albert Klawitter	350.00	700.00
41 Arthur Krueger	350.00	700.00
42 William Lindsay	350.00	700.00
43 Ward McDowell	350.00	700.00
44 Wilbur Rodgers	350.00	700.00
45 George Stone	350.00	700.00
46 Frank Arrelanes	350.00	700.00
47 George Gaddy	350.00	700.00
48 Elwood Heister	350.00	700.00
49 Harold Ireland	350.00	700.00
50 Ralph Kreitz	350.00	700.00
51 James Lewis	350.00	700.00
52 Joseph O'Rourke MG	350.00	700.00
53 Harry Price	350.00	700.00
54 Rudolph Schwenck	350.00	700.00
55 Thomas Sheehan	400.00	800.00
56 James Shinn	350.00	700.00
57 Charles Swain	350.00	700.00
58 Edward Van Buren	350.00	700.00
59 John Williams	450.00	900.00
60 Joseph Altman	350.00	700.00
61 Otto Auer	350.00	700.00
62 Claude Berry	350.00	700.00
63 Roy Corhan	350.00	700.00
64 Clarence Henley	350.00	700.00
65 William Johnson	350.00	700.00
66 Harry McArdle	350.00	700.00
67 William McCorry	350.00	700.00
68 Edward McIver	350.00	700.00
69 Frank Miller	350.00	700.00
70 Howard Mundorf	350.00	700.00
71 Winfield Noyes	350.00	700.00
72 Watt Powell	350.00	700.00
73 Thomas Raftery	350.00	700.00
74 Walter Schmidt	350.00	700.00
75 Willy Taylor	350.00	700.00
76 Thomas Toner	350.00	700.00
77 Samuel Agnew	350.00	700.00
78 Harry Bayless	350.00	700.00
79 Roy Brashear	350.00	700.00
80 Drummond Brown	350.00	700.00
81 Lenny Burrell	350.00	700.00
82 Walter Carlisle	400.00	800.00
83 Alexander Carson	350.00	700.00
84 Royal Castleton	350.00	700.00
85 Wallace Hogan MG	350.00	700.00
86 Frank Hosp	350.00	700.00
87 John Kane	350.00	700.00
88 Louis Litschi	350.00	700.00
89 Hamilton Patterson	350.00	700.00
90 John Raleigh	350.00	700.00

1912 Imperial Tobacco C46

The cards in this 90-card set measure approximately 1 1/2" by 2 3/4". The 1912 C46 set features numbered cards which were issued with unidentified brands of cigarettes although there is speculation that Imperial Tobacco was the sponsor of the set. The set features International League players and is styled with a brown wood-grain look. Card backs feature brief biographical information.

COMPLETE SET (90)	4,000.00	8,000.00
1 William O'Hara	150.00	300.00
2 James McGinley	50.00	100.00
3 Geo.Frenchy LeClaire	50.00	100.00
4 John White	50.00	100.00
5 James Murray	50.00	100.00
6 Joe Ward	50.00	100.00
7 Whitey Alperman	50.00	100.00
8 Natty Nattress	50.00	100.00
9 Fred Sline	50.00	100.00
10 Royal Rock	50.00	100.00
11 Ray Demmitt	60.00	120.00
12 Butcher Boy Schmidt	50.00	100.00
13 Samuel Frock	50.00	100.00
14 Fred Burchell	50.00	100.00
15 Jack Kelley	50.00	100.00
16 Frank Barberich	50.00	100.00
17 Frank Corridon	50.00	100.00
18 Doc Adkins	50.00	100.00
19 Jack Dunn MG	60.00	120.00
20 James Walsh	50.00	100.00
21 Charles Handford	50.00	100.00
22 Dick Rudolph	60.00	120.00
23 Curt Elston	50.00	100.00
24 Carl Sitton	50.00	100.00
25 Charlie French	50.00	100.00
26 John Ganzel	50.00	100.00
27 Joe Kelley	200.00	400.00
28 Benny Meyers	50.00	100.00
29 George Schirm	50.00	100.00
30 William Purtell	50.00	100.00
31 Bayard Sharpe	50.00	100.00
32 Tony Smith	50.00	100.00
33 John Lush	50.00	100.00
34 William Collins	50.00	100.00
35 Art Phelan	50.00	100.00
36 Edward Phelps	50.00	100.00
37 Rube Vickers	60.00	120.00
38 Cy Seymour	75.00	150.00
39 Shadow Carroll	50.00	100.00
40 Jake Gettman	50.00	100.00
41 Luther Taylor	60.00	120.00
42 Walter Justis	50.00	100.00
43 Robert Fisher	50.00	100.00
44 Fred Parent	60.00	120.00
45 James Dygert	50.00	100.00
46 Johnnie Butler	50.00	100.00
47 Fred Mitchell	50.00	100.00
48 Heine Batch	50.00	100.00
49 Michael Corcoran	50.00	100.00
50 Edward Doescher	50.00	100.00
51 George Wheeler	50.00	100.00
52 Elijah Jones	50.00	100.00
53 Fred Truesdale	50.00	100.00
54 Fred Beebe	50.00	100.00
55 Louis Brockett	50.00	100.00
56 Robert Wells	50.00	100.00
57 Lew McAllister	50.00	100.00
58 Ralph Stroud	50.00	100.00
59 Vernon Manser	50.00	100.00
60 Ducky Holmes	50.00	100.00
61 Rube Dessau	50.00	100.00
62 Fred Jacklitsch	50.00	100.00
63 George Graham	50.00	100.00
64 Noah Henline	50.00	100.00
65 Chick Gandil	300.00	600.00
66 Tom Hughes	75.00	150.00
67 Joseph Delehanty	60.00	120.00
68 George Pierce	50.00	100.00
69 Gantt	50.00	100.00
70 Edward Fitzpatrick	50.00	100.00
71 Wyatt Lee	50.00	100.00
72 John Kissinger	50.00	100.00
73 William Malarkey	50.00	100.00
74 William Byers	50.00	100.00
75 George Simmons	50.00	100.00
76 Daniel Moeller	50.00	100.00
77 Joseph McGinnity	200.00	400.00
78 Alex Hardy	50.00	100.00
79 Bob Holmes	50.00	100.00
80 William Baxter	50.00	100.00
81 Edward Spencer	50.00	100.00
82 Bradley Kocher	50.00	100.00
83 Robert Shaw	50.00	100.00
84 Joseph Yeager	50.00	100.00
85 Carlo	50.00	100.00
86 William Abstein	60.00	120.00
87 Tim Jordan	50.00	100.00
88 Dick Breen	50.00	100.00
89 Tom McCarty	50.00	100.00
90 Ed Curtis	50.00	100.00

1912 Zeenuts

Counterfeit copies of certain Zeenuts have been produced in the last 10 years. A very early card of Dave "Beauty" Bancroft is in this set. Honolulu John Williams also has his first card in the set. Williams was the first player from Hawaii to play in the majors. The 1912's measure 2 1/8" by 4 1/16". Four different backs are known for this set: Bardell Sepia Logo -- small; Bardell Sepia Logo -- large; Premium Offer; Blank Back.

COMPLETE SET (158)	5,000.00	10,000.00
1 Joseph Berger	50.00	100.00
2 Walter Boles	50.00	100.00
3 Clarence Brooks	50.00	100.00
4 Charles Check	50.00	100.00
5 John Core	50.00	100.00
6 Thomas Daley	50.00	100.00
7 Frank Dillon	50.00	100.00
8 Milton Driscoll	50.00	100.00
9 John Flater	50.00	100.00
10 John Halla	50.00	100.00
11 William Heitmuller	50.00	100.00
12 Ivon Howard	50.00	100.00
13 Walter Leverenz	50.00	100.00
14 Elmer Lober	50.00	100.00
15 George Metzger	50.00	100.00
16 Charles Moore	50.00	100.00
17 Walter Nagle	50.00	100.00
18 William Page	50.00	100.00
19 Walter Slagle	50.00	100.00
20 Hugh Smith	50.00	100.00
21 William Tozer	50.00	100.00
22 Ody Abbott	50.00	100.00
23 Harry Ables	50.00	100.00
24 Leo Bohen	50.00	100.00
25 Harvey Brooks	50.00	100.00
26 Tyler Christian	50.00	100.00
27 Al Cook	50.00	100.00
28 Bert Coy	50.00	100.00
29 Blaine Durbin	50.00	100.00
30 James Frick	50.00	100.00
31 Howard Gregory	50.00	100.00
32 Joseph Hamilton	50.00	100.00
33 August Hetling	50.00	100.00
34 August Hetling	50.00	100.00
35 Harry Hoffman	50.00	100.00
36 John Killilay	50.00	100.00
37 William Leard	50.00	100.00
38 William Malarkey	50.00	100.00
39 Elmer Martinoni	50.00	100.00
40 Carl Mitze	50.00	100.00
41 Henry Olmstead	50.00	100.00
42 Roy Parkins	50.00	100.00
43 Lorenzo Patterson	50.00	100.00
44 Henry Pernoll	50.00	100.00
45 Ashley Pope	50.00	100.00
46 William Rohrer	50.00	100.00
47 Bayard Sharpe	50.00	100.00
48 John Tiedeman	50.00	100.00
49 Elmer Zacher	50.00	100.00
50 David Bancroft	375.00	750.00
51 John Burch	50.00	100.00
52 Henry Butcher	50.00	100.00
53 Willie Butler	50.00	100.00
54 Chester Chadbourne	50.00	100.00
55 Walter Doane	50.00	100.00
56 August Fisher	50.00	100.00
57 John Gilligan	50.00	100.00
58 Leo Girot	50.00	100.00
59 David Gregg	50.00	100.00
60 Frederick Harkness	50.00	100.00
61 Irving Higginbotham	50.00	100.00
62 Daniel Howley	50.00	100.00
63 Albert Klawitter	50.00	100.00
64 Elmer Koestner	50.00	100.00
65 Elmer Koestner	50.00	100.00
66 Arthur Krueger	50.00	100.00
67 Louis LaLonge	50.00	100.00
68 William Lindsay	50.00	100.00
69 Walter McCredie	50.00	100.00
70 Ward McDowell	50.00	100.00
71 William Rapps	50.00	100.00
72 William Rapps	50.00	100.00
73 Wilbur Rodgers	50.00	100.00
74 George Stone	50.00	100.00
75 Frank Arellanes	50.00	100.00
76 Charles Baum	50.00	100.00
77 Herbert Byram	50.00	100.00
78 Harry Cheek	50.00	100.00
79 John Fitzgerald	50.00	100.00
80 George Gaddy	50.00	100.00
81 Elwood Heister	50.00	100.00
82 Harold Ireland	50.00	100.00
83 Grover Knight	50.00	100.00
84 Ralph Kreitz	50.00	100.00
85 James Lewis	50.00	100.00
86 Thomas Madden	50.00	100.00
87 Christopher Mahoney	50.00	100.00
88 Hugh Miller	50.00	100.00
89 Joseph O'Rourke	50.00	100.00
90 William Orr	50.00	100.00
91 Harry Price	50.00	100.00
92 Rudolph Schwenck	50.00	100.00
93 Thomas Sheehan	50.00	100.00
94 James Shinn	50.00	100.00
95 Charles Swain	50.00	100.00
96 Edward Van Buren	50.00	100.00
97 John Williams	75.00	150.00
98 Joe Williams	50.00	100.00
99 Joseph Altman	50.00	100.00
100 Otto Auer	50.00	100.00
101 Jesse Baker	50.00	100.00
102 Jesse Baker	50.00	100.00
103 Claude Berry	50.00	100.00
104 Al Bonner	50.00	100.00
105 Breen	50.00	100.00
106 Roy Corhan	50.00	100.00
107 Lee Delhi	50.00	100.00
108 Charles Fanning	50.00	100.00
109 Albert Felts	50.00	100.00
110 Elmer Gedeon	50.00	100.00
111 Don Hamilton	50.00	100.00
112 Walter Hartley	50.00	100.00
113 Clarence Henley	50.00	100.00
114 William Jackson	50.00	100.00
115 William Johnson	50.00	100.00
116 Harry McArdle	50.00	100.00
117 George McAvoy	50.00	100.00
118 William McCorry	50.00	100.00
119 Edward McIver	50.00	100.00
120 Willard Meikle	50.00	100.00
121 Frank Miller	50.00	100.00
122 Ernest Mohler	50.00	100.00
123 Howard Mundorf	50.00	100.00
124 Howard Mundorf	50.00	100.00
125 Winfield Noyes	50.00	100.00
126 Watt Powell	50.00	100.00
127 Thomas Raftery	50.00	100.00
128 William Reidy	50.00	100.00
129 Walter Schmidt	50.00	100.00
130 Willy Taylor	50.00	100.00
131 Thomas Toner	50.00	100.00
132 Joseph Wagner	50.00	100.00
133 L. Williams	50.00	100.00
134 John Wuffli	50.00	100.00
135 Everette Zimmerman	50.00	100.00
136 Samuel Agnew	50.00	100.00
137 Harry Bayless	50.00	100.00
138 John Brackenridge	50.00	100.00
139 Roy Brashear	50.00	100.00
140 Drummond Brown	50.00	100.00
141 Leonard Burrell	50.00	100.00
142 Walter Carlisle	50.00	100.00
143 Alexander Carson	50.00	100.00
144 Royal Castleton	50.00	100.00
145 William Gray	50.00	100.00
146 Roy Hitt	50.00	100.00
147 Wallace Hogan	50.00	100.00
148 Franz Hosp	50.00	100.00
149 John Kane	50.00	100.00
150 Louis Litschi	50.00	100.00
151 Clarence McDonnell	50.00	100.00
152 Hamilton Patterson	50.00	100.00
153 John Raleigh	50.00	100.00
154 Harry Stewart	50.00	100.00
155 George Stinson	50.00	100.00
156 John Sullivan	50.00	100.00
157 William Temple	50.00	100.00
158 James Whalen	50.00	100.00

1913 Oakland Oaks Team Issue

This 20 card set, which measure approximately 2" by 3 5/8" features members of the 1913 Oakland Oaks. These blank-backed cards are sepia toned and have the player's last name and oakland on the bottom of the card. These cards are usually found with some trimming at either the top or the bottom.

COMPLETE SET	10,000.00	20,000.00
1 O.C. Abbott	800.00	1,200.00
2 Harry Ables	800.00	1,200.00
3 Jesse Becker	800.00	1,200.00
4 W.W. Cook	800.00	1,200.00
5 Bert Coy	800.00	1,200.00
6 Rube Gardner	800.00	1,200.00
7 Howard Gregory	800.00	1,200.00
8 Gus Hetling	800.00	1,200.00
9 Jack Killilay	800.00	1,200.00
10 Bill Leard	800.00	1,200.00
11 William John Malarkey	800.00	1,200.00
12 Carl Mitze	800.00	1,200.00
13 John Ness	800.00	1,200.00
14 Henry Olmstead	800.00	1,200.00
15 Cy Parkin	800.00	1,200.00
16 W.J. Pearce	800.00	1,200.00
17 Heine Pernoll	800.00	1,200.00
18 Ashley Pope	800.00	1,200.00
19 George Schirm	800.00	1,200.00
20 Elmer Zacher	800.00	1,200.00

1913 Zeenuts

Harry Heilmann has a very early card in this set. From 1913 through 1933 all measurements are given with coupons. These cards measure approximately 1 11/16" by 3 3/4".

COMPLETE SET (148)	4,500.00	9,000.00
1 Walter Boles	50.00	100.00
2 Clarence Brooks	50.00	100.00
3 James Byrnes	50.00	100.00
4 James Crabb	50.00	100.00
5 Frank Dillon	50.00	100.00
6 Milton Driscoll	50.00	100.00
7 George Ellis	50.00	100.00
8 Warren Gill	50.00	100.00
9 Claire Goodwin	50.00	100.00
10 John Halla	50.00	100.00
11 Ivon Howard	50.00	100.00
12 Charles Jackson	50.00	100.00
13 Ernest Johnson	50.00	100.00
14 Harl Maggart	50.00	100.00
15 George Metzger	50.00	100.00

16 Charles Moore 50.00 100.00
17 William Page 50.00 100.00
18 Madison Perritt 50.00 100.00
19 Brown Rogers 50.00 100.00
20 Jack Ryan 50.00 100.00
21 William Tozer 50.00 100.00
22 Michael Wotell 50.00 100.00
23 Ody Abbott 50.00 100.00
24 Harry Ables 50.00 100.00
25 Jesse Becker 50.00 100.00
26 Tyler Christian 50.00 100.00
27 Robert Clemons 50.00 100.00
28 Al Cook 50.00 100.00
29 Bert Coy 50.00 100.00
30 Joseph Crisp 50.00 100.00
31 L. Gardner 50.00 100.00
32 Howard Gregory 50.00 100.00
33 William Grey 50.00 100.00
34 Arthur Guest 50.00 100.00
35 August Hetling 50.00 100.00
36 Teddy Kaylor 50.00 100.00
37 John Killilay 50.00 100.00
38 William Leard 50.00 100.00
39 Claude Lohman 50.00 100.00
40 William Malarkey 50.00 100.00
41 Carl Mitze 50.00 100.00
42 John Ness 50.00 100.00
43 Roy Parkin 50.00 100.00
44 William Pearce 50.00 100.00
45 Henry Pernoll 50.00 100.00
46 Ashley Pope 50.00 100.00
47 Charles Pruitt 50.00 100.00
48 William Rohrer 50.00 100.00
49 George Schirm 50.00 100.00
50 Elmer Zacher 50.00 100.00
51 Claude Berry 50.00 100.00
52 Alexander Carson 50.00 100.00
53 Chester Chadbourne 50.00 100.00
54 Fred Derrick 50.00 100.00
55 Walter Doane 50.00 100.00
56 August Fisher 50.00 100.00
57 Justin Fitzgerald 50.00 100.00
58 Zeriah Hagerman 50.00 100.00
59 Harry Heilmann 500.00 1,000.00
Actually playing with Portland in
60 Irving Higginbotham 50.00 100.00
61 William James 50.00 100.00
62 Arthur Kores 50.00 100.00
63 Eugene Krapp 50.00 100.00
64 Harry Krause 50.00 100.00
65 Arthur Krueger 50.00 100.00
66 William Lindsay 50.00 100.00
67 Elmer Lober 50.00 100.00
68 Michael McCormick 50.00 100.00
69 Walter McCredie 50.00 100.00
70 James Riordan 50.00 100.00
71 Wilbur Rodgers 50.00 100.00
72 John Stanley 50.00 100.00
73 Harry Todd 50.00 100.00
74 James West 50.00 100.00
75 Frank Arellanes 50.00 100.00
76 John Bliss 50.00 100.00
77 Harry Cheek 50.00 100.00
78 Louis Drucke 50.00 100.00
79 Edward Hallinan 50.00 100.00
80 William Kenworthy 50.00 100.00
81 Albert Klawitter 50.00 100.00
82 James Lewis 50.00 100.00
83 Henry Lively 50.00 100.00
84A Hugh Miller 50.00 100.00
Full Glove
84B Hugh Miller 50.00 100.00
Part Glove
85 Roy Moran 50.00 100.00
86 Emmett Munsell 50.00 100.00
87 Paul Reitmyer 50.00 100.00
88 Joseph Schulz 50.00 100.00
89 James Shinn 50.00 100.00
90 Monroe Stark 50.00 100.00
91 Ralph Stroud 50.00 100.00
92 Thomas Tennant 50.00 100.00
93 Edward Van Buren 50.00 100.00
94 John Williams 75.00 150.00
95 Harry Wolverton 50.00 100.00
96 Ralph Young 50.00 100.00
97 Alex Arlett 50.00 100.00
98 Jesse Baker 50.00 100.00
99 William Cadreau 50.00 100.00
100 Walter Cartwright 50.00 100.00
101 Raymond Charles 50.00 100.00
102 Jay Clarke 50.00 100.00
103 Roy Corhan 50.00 100.00
104 Frank DeCanniere 50.00 100.00
105 Phillip Douglass 50.00 100.00
106 Jerome Downs 50.00 100.00
107 Charles Fanning 50.00 100.00
108 Clarence Henley 50.00 100.00
109 Harry Hoffman 50.00 100.00
110 William Hogan 50.00 100.00
111 George Howard 50.00 100.00
112 Harry Hughes 50.00 100.00
113 James Johnston 50.00 100.00
114 Albert Leifield 50.00 100.00
115 Harry McArdle 50.00 100.00
116 George McCarl 50.00 100.00
117 William McCorry 50.00 100.00
118 Howard Mundorf 50.00 100.00
119 Orval Overall 60.00 120.00
120 Walter Schaller 50.00 100.00
121 Walter Schmidt 50.00 100.00
122 Louis Sepulveda 50.00 100.00
123 Edward Spenger 50.00 100.00
124 Alfred Stanridge 50.00 100.00
125 Forrest Thomas 50.00 100.00
126 Charles Tonneman 50.00 100.00
127 Joseph Wagner 50.00 100.00
128 John Wuffli 50.00 100.00
129 Everette Zimmerman 50.00 100.00
130 Charles Baum 50.00 100.00
131 Harry Bayless 50.00 100.00
132 John Brackenridge 50.00 100.00
133 Roy Brashear 50.00 100.00
134 Walter Carlisle 50.00 100.00
135 Harold Elliott 50.00 100.00
136 Roy Hitt 50.00 100.00
137 Wallace Hogan 50.00 100.00
138 Franz Hosp 50.00 100.00
139 John Kane 50.00 100.00
140 Elmer Koestner 50.00 100.00
141 Ralph Kreitz 50.00 100.00
142 Louis Litschi 50.00 100.00
143 Clarence McDonnell 50.00 100.00
144 Paul Meloan 50.00 100.00
145 Joseph O'Rourke 50.00 100.00
146 Hamilton Patterson 50.00 100.00
147 John Raleigh 50.00 100.00
148 Charles Sterritt 50.00 100.00

1914 Baltimore News

These schedule/cards were issued during Babe Ruth's first season in professional baseball. The front has a picture of the Babe with his name and position in the lower left corner. The back has the 1914 Baltimore Orioles schedule. This list may be incomplete and any further additions are appreciated.

COMPLETE SET 250,000.00 500,000.00
1 Neal Ball 1,500.00 3,000.00
2 Ensign Cottrell 1,250.00 2,500.00
3 Birdie Cree 1,250.00 2,500.00
4 Davidson 1,250.00 2,500.00
5 Mike Doolan 1,250.00 2,500.00
6 Jack Dunn OWN 2,000.00 4,000.00
7 Babe Ruth 250,000.00 500,000.00
8 George Suggs 1,250.00 2,500.00
9 George Twombley 1,250.00 2,500.00
10 Ducky Yount 1,250.00 2,500.00
11 Guy Zinn 1,250.00 2,500.00

1914 Zeenuts

Jacinto Calvo has a card in this set. He was one of the early Cuban players in Professional Baseball. These cards measure approximately 2" by 4 1/16".

COMPLETE SET (146) 4,500.00 9,000.00
1 William Abstein 50.00 100.00
2 Carroll Barton 50.00 100.00
3 Walter Boles 50.00 100.00
4 Clarence Brooks 50.00 100.00
5 Jacinto Calvo 100.00 200.00
6 Charles Chech 50.00 100.00
7 James Crabb 50.00 100.00
8 Frank Dillon 50.00 100.00
9 Howard Ehmke 75.00 150.00
10 George Ellis 50.00 100.00
11 Elmer Gedeon 50.00 100.00
12 Thomas Hughes 50.00 100.00
13 Ernest Johnson 50.00 100.00
14 Edward Love 50.00 100.00
15 Harl Maggart 50.00 100.00
16 Herman Meek 50.00 100.00
17 George Metzger 50.00 100.00
18 Charles Moore 50.00 100.00
19 Paul Musser 50.00 100.00
20 William Page 50.00 100.00
21 Madison Perritt 50.00 100.00
22 Brown Rogers 50.00 100.00
23 Jack Ryan 50.00 100.00
24 Carl Sawyer 50.00 100.00
25 Harry Wolter 50.00 100.00
26 Harry Ables 50.00 100.00
27 Walter Alexander 50.00 100.00
28 Carl Arbogast 50.00 100.00
29 William Barrenkamp 50.00 100.00
30 Tyler Christian 50.00 100.00
31 Al Cook 50.00 100.00
32 Arthur Devlin 60.00 120.00
33 L. Gardner 50.00 100.00
34 Jacob Geyer 50.00 100.00
35 Arthur Guest 50.00 100.00
36 August Hettling 50.00 100.00
37 Teddy Kaylor 50.00 100.00
38 John Killilay 50.00 100.00
39 Albert Loomis 50.00 100.00
40 William Malarkey 50.00 100.00
41 William Menges 50.00 100.00
42 Robert Middleton 50.00 100.00
43 Carl Mitze 50.00 100.00
44 Rod Murphy 50.00 100.00
45 John Ness 50.00 100.00
46 Herschel Prough 50.00 100.00
47 Charles Pruiett 50.00 100.00
48A Thomas Quinlan 50.00 100.00
Small
48B Thomas Quinlan 50.00 100.00
Large
49 L. M. Ramey 50.00 100.00
50 Elmer Zacher 50.00 100.00
51 David Bancroft 375.00 750.00
52 Roy Brashear 50.00 100.00
53 Olaf Brenegan 50.00 100.00
54 Everett Brown 50.00 100.00
55 Robert Davis 50.00 100.00
56 Fred Derrick 50.00 100.00
57 Walter Doane 50.00 100.00
58 Evan Evans 50.00 100.00
59 August Fisher 50.00 100.00
60 Fred Frambach 50.00 100.00
61 Homer Haworth 50.00 100.00
62 Homer Haworth 50.00 100.00
63 Irving Higginbotham 50.00 100.00
64 Arthur Kores 50.00 100.00
65 Harry Krause 50.00 100.00
66 Elmer Lober 50.00 100.00
67 Elmer Martinoni 50.00 100.00
68 Walter McCredie 50.00 100.00
69 Lawrence Pape 50.00 100.00
70 Harold Peet 50.00 100.00
71A Floyd Perkins 50.00 100.00
Small
71B Floyd Perkins 50.00 100.00
Large
72 Elmer Rieger 50.00 100.00
73A Wilbur Rodgers 50.00 100.00
Small
73B Wilbur Rogers 50.00 100.00
Large
74 John Ryan 50.00 100.00
75 William Speas 50.00 100.00
76 James West 50.00 100.00
77 George Yantz 50.00 100.00
78 Frank Arellanes 50.00 100.00
79 Bert Coy 50.00 100.00
80 Joseph Gianini 50.00 100.00
81 Howard Gregory 50.00 100.00
82 Edward Hallinan 50.00 100.00
83 James Hannah 50.00 100.00
84 Sam Hern 50.00 100.00
85 Albert Klawitter 50.00 100.00
86 Remy Kramer 60.00 120.00
87 Byrd Lynn 50.00 100.00
88 Ernest Mohler 50.00 100.00
89 Roy Moran 50.00 100.00
90 William Orr 50.00 100.00
91 William Rohrer 50.00 100.00
92 James Shinn 50.00 100.00
93 Walter Slagle 50.00 100.00
94 Ralph Stroud 50.00 100.00
95 Thomas Tennant 50.00 100.00
96 Edward Van Buren 50.00 100.00
97 Harry Wolverton 50.00 100.00
98 Ralph Young 50.00 100.00
99 Alex Arlett 50.00 100.00
100 Wayne Barham 50.00 100.00
101 Charles Baum 50.00 100.00
102 Willie Butler 50.00 100.00
103 Walter Cartwright 50.00 100.00
104 Raymond Charles 50.00 100.00
105 Jay Clarke 50.00 100.00
106 Edward Colligan 50.00 100.00
107 Roy Corhan 50.00 100.00
108 Jerome Downs 50.00 100.00
109 Charles Fanning 50.00 100.00
110 Justin Fitzgerald 50.00 100.00
111 Ben Henderson 50.00 100.00
112 George Howard 50.00 100.00
113 Harry Hughes 50.00 100.00
114 Albert Liefield 50.00 100.00
115 Howard Mundorf 50.00 100.00
116 Charles O'Leary 60.00 120.00
117 Roy Parkin 50.00 100.00
118 Henry Pernoll 50.00 100.00
119 Walter Schaller 50.00 100.00
120 Walter Schmidt 50.00 100.00
121 Louis Sepulveda 50.00 100.00
122 Alfred Stanridge 50.00 100.00
123 Joseph Tobin 50.00 100.00
124 William Tozer 50.00 100.00
125 Zumwalt 50.00 100.00
126 Harry Bayless 50.00 100.00
127 John Bliss 50.00 100.00
128 William Borton 50.00 100.00
129 Walter Carlisle 50.00 100.00
130 Frank DeCannier 50.00 100.00
131 Earle Fleharty 50.00 100.00
132 Frederick Harkness 50.00 100.00
133 Clarence Henley 50.00 100.00
134 Roy Hitt 50.00 100.00
135 Wallace Hogan 50.00 100.00
136 Franz Hosp 50.00 100.00
137 John Kane 50.00 100.00
138 Edward Klepfer 50.00 100.00
139 William Leard 50.00 100.00
140 Louis Litschi 50.00 100.00
141 Harry McArdle 50.00 100.00
142 Clarence McDonald 50.00 100.00
143 Paul Meloan 50.00 100.00
144 Red Powell 50.00 100.00
Small
144 Red Powell 50.00 100.00
Large
145 Guy White 50.00 100.00
146 Harold Elliott 50.00 100.00

1915 Zeenuts

Up to four variations per card are presently accounted for. These variations are in the sepia overlay. Cards were printed in black and white and the sepia overlay is where the variation is. Early cards of Fred McMullin (Only known card during his career), Swede Risberg, Lefty Williams and "Sleepy" Bill Burns are in this set. All four of those people had roles in the Black Sox Scandal of 1919. These cards measure approximately 2 by 3 3/4".

COMPLETE SET (133) 7,000.00 14,000.00
1 William Abstein 50.00 100.00
2 Justin Beatty 50.00 100.00
3 Albert Beumiller 50.00 100.00
4 Walter Boles 50.00 100.00
5 Clarence Brooks 50.00 100.00
6 William Burns 75.00 150.00
7 Frank Dillon 50.00 100.00
8 George Ellis 50.00 100.00
9 Howard Harper 50.00 100.00
10 Thomas Hughes 50.00 100.00
11 Edward Love 50.00 100.00
12 Clarence McDonnell 50.00 100.00
13 Frederick McMullen 2,500.00 5,000.00
14 Harl Maggart 50.00 100.00
15 Herman Meek 50.00 100.00
16 George Metzger 50.00 100.00
17 Madison Perritt 50.00 100.00
18 Jack Ryan 50.00 100.00
19 Lynn Scoggins 50.00 100.00
20 Zebulon Terry 50.00 100.00
21 Harry Wolter 50.00 100.00
22 Harry Ables 50.00 100.00
23 John Alcock 50.00 100.00
24 Carl Arbogast 50.00 100.00
25 Samuel Beer 50.00 100.00
26 Raymond Boyd 50.00 100.00
27 Jack Bromley 50.00 100.00
28 Tyler Christian 50.00 100.00
29 William Daniels 50.00 100.00
30 Frank Elliott 50.00 100.00
31 Frank Elliott 50.00 100.00
32 L. Gardiner 50.00 100.00
33 Arthur Guest 50.00 100.00
34 George Howard 50.00 100.00
35 James Johnston 50.00 100.00
36 Albert Klawitter 50.00 100.00
37 Philip Koerner 50.00 100.00
38 Walter Kuhn 50.00 100.00
39 William Lindsay 50.00 100.00
40 Louis Litschi 50.00 100.00
41 Charles McAvoy 50.00 100.00
42 William Malarkey 50.00 100.00
43 Carl Manda 50.00 100.00
44 Arthur Marcan 50.00 100.00
45 Elmer Martinoni 50.00 100.00
46 Robert Middleton 50.00 100.00
47 Howard Mundorf 50.00 100.00
48 John Ness 50.00 100.00
49 Harry Price 50.00 100.00
50 Herschel Prough 50.00 100.00
51 Charles Prueitt 50.00 100.00
52 Alexander Remneas 50.00 100.00
53 John Russell 50.00 100.00
54 Ray Bates 50.00 100.00
55 Frederick Carrisch 50.00 100.00
56 Stanley Covaleski 500.00 1,000.00
57 Bob Davis 50.00 100.00
58 Fred Derrick 50.00 100.00
59 Walter Doane 50.00 100.00
60 Evan Evans 50.00 100.00
61 August Fisher 50.00 100.00
62 Irving Higginbotham 50.00 100.00
63 David Hilliard 50.00 100.00
64 George Kahler 50.00 100.00
65 Harry Krause 50.00 100.00
66 Elmer Lober 50.00 100.00
67 John Lush 50.00 100.00
68 Herbert Murphy 50.00 100.00
69 Walter McCredie 50.00 100.00
70 Milton Reed 50.00 100.00
71 William Speas 50.00 100.00
72 Bill Stumpf 50.00 100.00
73 Louis Barbour 50.00 100.00
74 Clifford Blankenship 50.00 100.00
75 Eddie Faye 50.00 100.00
76 Paul Fittery 50.00 100.00
77 Elmer Gedeon 50.00 100.00
78 Howard Gregory 50.00 100.00
79 Herbert Hall 50.00 100.00
80 John Halla 50.00 100.00
81 Edward Hallinan 50.00 100.00
82 James Hannah 50.00 100.00
83 Louis LaRoy 50.00 100.00
84 Willis Morgan 50.00 100.00
85 John Nutt 50.00 100.00
86 William Orr 50.00 100.00
87 William Rohrer 50.00 100.00
88 John Ryan 50.00 100.00
89 James Shinn 50.00 100.00
90 Thomas Tennant 50.00 100.00
91 Claude Williams 500.00 1,000.00
92 John Williams 75.00 150.00
93 Elmer Zacher 50.00 100.00
94 Rudolf Baerwald 50.00 100.00
95 Charles Baum 50.00 100.00
96 Arthur Benham 50.00 100.00
97 George Block 50.00 100.00
98 Frank Bodie 50.00 100.00
99 Charles Brown 50.00 100.00
100 Raymond Charles 50.00 100.00
101 Jay Clarke 50.00 100.00
102 John Couch 50.00 100.00
103 Elliott Dent 50.00 100.00
104 Jerome Downs 50.00 100.00
105 Charles Fanning 50.00 100.00
106 Justin Fitzgerald 50.00 100.00
107 Harry Heilmann 500.00 1,000.00
108 Robert Jones 50.00 100.00
109 Benjamin Karr 50.00 100.00

110 Jack Killilay	50.00	100.00
111 William Leard	50.00	100.00
112 Paul Meloan	50.00	100.00
113 Henry Pernoll	50.00	100.00
114 Jacob Reisigl	50.00	100.00
115 Walter Schaller	50.00	100.00
116 Walter Schmidt	50.00	100.00
117 Louis Sepulveda	50.00	100.00
118 Luther Smith	50.00	100.00
119 Joseph Tobin	50.00	100.00
120 Harry Wolverton	50.00	100.00
121 Harry Bayless	50.00	100.00
122 Joseph Berger	50.00	100.00
123 Walter Carlisle	50.00	100.00
124 Frank DeCanniere	50.00	100.00
125 Gustave Gleischmann	50.00	100.00
126 Clarence Henley	50.00	100.00
127 August Hetling	50.00	100.00
128 Roy Hitt	50.00	100.00
129 Roy Hitt	50.00	100.00
130 Wallace Hogan	50.00	100.00
131 Franz Hosp	50.00	100.00
132 John Kane	50.00	100.00
133 Carl Mitze	50.00	100.00
134 William Piercey	50.00	100.00
135 William Purtell	50.00	100.00
136 Charles Risberg	500.00	1,000.00
137 Charlie Chech	50.00	100.00
138 Arthur Fromme	50.00	100.00
139 Albert Mitchell	50.00	100.00
140 Edward Spencer	50.00	100.00
141 James West	50.00	100.00
142 Guy White	50.00	100.00

1916 Zeenuts

Jimmy Claxton in this set. That was the first regular card depicting a person of color marketed in the United States with a product. These cards measure 1 15/16" by 3 11/16".

COMPLETE SET (143)	5,500.00	11,000.00
1 John Bassler	40.00	80.00
2 Walter Boles	40.00	80.00
3 John Butler	40.00	80.00
4 Frank Chance	500.00	1,000.00
5 George Ellis	40.00	80.00
6 James Galloway	40.00	80.00
7 Carter Hogg	40.00	80.00
8 Oscar Horstman	40.00	80.00
9 George Kahler	40.00	80.00
10 John Kane	40.00	80.00
11 Philip Koerner	40.00	80.00
12 Frank Larsen	40.00	80.00
13 Howard McLarry	40.00	80.00
14 Harl Maggert	40.00	80.00
15 Jack Ryan	40.00	80.00
16 Lynn Scoggins	40.00	80.00
17 Alfred Stanridge	40.00	80.00
18 George Zabel	40.00	80.00
19 William Barbeau	40.00	80.00
20 Malcomb Barry	40.00	80.00
21 Samuel Beer	40.00	80.00
22 Joseph Berg	40.00	80.00
23 Joseph Berger	40.00	80.00
24 Raymond Boyd	40.00	80.00
25 James Claxton	2,500.00	5,000.00
26 Luther Cook	40.00	80.00
27 James Crandall	40.00	80.00
28 Robert Davis	40.00	80.00
29 Frank Elliott	40.00	80.00
30 Harold Elliott	40.00	80.00
31 L. Gardner	40.00	80.00
32 David Griffith	40.00	80.00
33 Irving Higginbotham	40.00	80.00
34 George Howard	40.00	80.00
35 William Kenworthy	40.00	80.00
36 Albert Klawitter	40.00	80.00
37 Edward Klein	40.00	80.00
38 Walter Kuhn	40.00	80.00
39 William Lane	40.00	80.00
40 James Manser	40.00	80.00
41 Elwood Martin	40.00	80.00
42 Robert Middleton	40.00	80.00
43 Herschel Prough	40.00	80.00
44 Charles Prueitt	40.00	80.00
45 Newton Randall	40.00	80.00
46 William Zimmerman	40.00	80.00
47 Frederick Carrisch	40.00	80.00
48 Fred Derrick	40.00	80.00
49 August Fisher	40.00	80.00
50 Louis Guisto	40.00	80.00
51 Zeriah Hagerman	40.00	80.00
52 Oscar Harstadt	40.00	80.00
53 Homer Haworth	40.00	80.00
54 Charles Hollocher	60.00	120.00
55 Byron Houck	40.00	80.00
56 Herbert Kelly	40.00	80.00
57 Harry Krause	40.00	80.00
58 John Lush	40.00	80.00
59 Walter McCredie	40.00	80.00
60 William Nixon	40.00	80.00
61 Winfield Noyes	40.00	80.00
62 Owen Quinn	40.00	80.00
63 John Roche	40.00	80.00
64 Clarence Smith	40.00	80.00
65 Allen Sothoron	40.00	80.00
66 William Southworth	60.00	120.00
67 Bill Speas	40.00	80.00
68 William Stumpf	40.00	80.00
69 Robert Vaughn	40.00	80.00
70 Charles Ward	40.00	80.00
71 Denny Wilie	40.00	80.00
72 Kenneth Williams	60.00	120.00
73 Harry Bayless	40.00	80.00
74 Clifford Blankenship	40.00	80.00
75 Anthony Brief	40.00	80.00
76 Stanley Dugan	40.00	80.00
77 Ross Eldred	40.00	80.00
78 Paul Fittery	40.00	80.00
79 Herbert Hall	40.00	80.00
80 Edward Hallinan	40.00	80.00
81 James Hannah	40.00	80.00
82 Thomas Hughes	40.00	80.00
83 William Menges	40.00	80.00
84 Emmett Munsell	40.00	80.00
85 Herbert Murphy	40.00	80.00
86 John Nutt	40.00	80.00
87 William Orr	40.00	80.00
88 Thomas Quinlan	40.00	80.00
89 Morris Rath	50.00	100.00
90 Jacob Reisegl	40.00	80.00
91 Walter Reuther	50.00	100.00
92 John Ryan	40.00	80.00
93 James Shinn	40.00	80.00
94 John Vann	40.00	80.00
95 Elmer Zacher	40.00	80.00
96 William Autrey	40.00	80.00
97 Charles Baum	40.00	80.00
98 George Block	40.00	80.00
99 Frank Bodie	60.00	120.00
100 Samuel Bohne	40.00	80.00
101 Clarence Brooks	40.00	80.00
102 Charles Brown	40.00	80.00
103 John Coffey	40.00	80.00
104 Joseph Corbett	40.00	80.00
105 John Couch	40.00	80.00
106 Talbot Dalton	40.00	80.00
107 Jerome Downs	40.00	80.00
108 Eric Erickson	40.00	80.00
109 Charles Fanning	40.00	80.00
110 Justin Fitzgerald	40.00	80.00
111 Frank Gay	40.00	80.00
112 Robert Jones	40.00	80.00
113 A.D. Machold	40.00	80.00
114 Frank O'Brien	40.00	80.00
115 John Oldham	40.00	80.00
116 Madison Perritt	40.00	80.00
117 Walter Schaller	40.00	80.00
118 Louis Sepulveda	40.00	80.00
119 Leslie Sheehan	40.00	80.00
120 William Steen	40.00	80.00
121 Harry Wolverton	40.00	80.00
122 John Wuffli	40.00	80.00
123 Donald Rader	40.00	80.00
124 Raymond Bates	40.00	80.00
125 C.H. Callahan	40.00	80.00
126 Frank DeCanniere	40.00	80.00
127 Walter Doane	40.00	80.00
128 Arthur Fromme	50.00	100.00
129 Gustave Gleischmann	40.00	80.00
130 Art Griggs	40.00	80.00
131 Otto Hess	40.00	80.00
132 Roy Hitt	40.00	80.00
133 Ellis Johnston	40.00	80.00
134 George Johnston	40.00	80.00
135 Mark McGaffigan	40.00	80.00
136 Walter Mattick	40.00	80.00
137 Albert Mitchell	40.00	80.00
138 Carl Mitze	40.00	80.00
139 Hamilton Patterson	40.00	80.00
140 John Quinn	60.00	120.00
141 Donald Rader	40.00	80.00
142 Charles Risberg	375.00	750.00
143 Edward Spencer	40.00	80.00
144 Albert Whalling	40.00	80.00
145 Dennis Wilie	40.00	80.00

1917 Zeenuts

These cards measure approximately 1 3/4" by 3 3/4".

COMPLETE SET (121)	3,400.00	6,800.00
1 John Bassler	50.00	100.00
2 Walter Boles	40.00	80.00
3 Charles Brown	40.00	80.00
4 Frank Chance	500.00	1,000.00
5 James Crandall	40.00	80.00
6 Robert Davis	40.00	80.00
7 Jacques Fournier	60.00	120.00
8 Frank Groehling	40.00	80.00
9 Charles Hall	40.00	80.00
10 Wade Killiffer	40.00	80.00
11 Peter Lapan	40.00	80.00
12 Harl Maggert	40.00	80.00
13 Emil Meusel	60.00	120.00
14 Jack Ryan	40.00	80.00
15 Joseph Schultz	40.00	80.00
16 Alfred Stanrdige	40.00	80.00
17 Zebulon Terry	40.00	80.00
18 Robert Vaughan	40.00	80.00
19 Alex Arlett	40.00	80.00
20 Samuel Beer	40.00	80.00
21 William Burns	40.00	80.00
22 F. Callan	40.00	80.00
23 Chester Chadbourne	40.00	80.00
24 Robert Coltrin	40.00	80.00
25 Richard Goodbred	40.00	80.00
26 George Howard	40.00	80.00
27 Joseph Kilhullen	40.00	80.00
28 Harry Krause	40.00	80.00
29 William Lane	40.00	80.00
30 William Lee	40.00	80.00
31 Edward Mensor	40.00	80.00
32 Robert Middleton	40.00	80.00
33 Lawrence Miller	40.00	80.00
34 Lawrence Miller	40.00	80.00
35 Rod Murphy	40.00	80.00
36 Daniel Murray	40.00	80.00
37 Oliver O'Mara	40.00	80.00
38 Herschel Prough	40.00	80.00
39 Charles Pruiett	40.00	80.00
40 John Roche	40.00	80.00
41 John Sheehan	40.00	80.00
42 Earl Baldwin	40.00	80.00
43 Lynn Brenton	40.00	80.00
44 Floyd Farmer	40.00	80.00
45 William Fincher	40.00	80.00
46 August Fisher	40.00	80.00
47 Oscar Harstad	40.00	80.00
48 Allan Helfrich	40.00	80.00
49 Charles Hollacher	50.00	100.00
50 Byron Houck	40.00	80.00
51 Albert Leake	40.00	80.00
52 Walter McCreedie	40.00	80.00
53 Frank O'Brien	40.00	80.00
54 Ralph Penelli	75.00	150.00
55 Kenneth Penner	40.00	80.00
56 Wesley Siglin	40.00	80.00
57 William Stumpf	40.00	80.00
58 Dennis Wilie	40.00	80.00
59 William Bernhard	40.00	80.00
60 Roy Bliss	40.00	80.00
61 Anthony Brief	40.00	80.00
62 Karl Crandall	40.00	80.00
63 Robert Cress	40.00	80.00
64 Stanley Dougan	40.00	80.00
65 Jean Dubuc	40.00	80.00
66 Evan Evans	40.00	80.00
67 Garde Gislason	40.00	80.00
68 James Hannah	40.00	80.00
69 Chester Hoff	40.00	80.00
70 Thomas Hughes	40.00	80.00
71 Walter Leverenz	40.00	80.00
72 William Orr	40.00	80.00
73 Thomas Quinlan	40.00	80.00
74 Morris Rath	50.00	100.00
75 John Ryan	40.00	80.00
76 Adolph Schinkle	40.00	80.00
77 Earl Sheeley	40.00	80.00
78 James Shinn	40.00	80.00
79 John Tobin	40.00	80.00
80 Delmer Baker	50.00	100.00
81 Delmer Baker	50.00	100.00
82 Charles Baum	40.00	80.00
83 Jacinto Calvo	125.00	250.00
84 Roy Corhan	40.00	80.00
85 Patrick Dougherty	40.00	80.00
86 Jerome Downs	40.00	80.00
87 George Ellis	40.00	80.00
88 Eric Erickson	40.00	80.00
89 Justin Fitzgerald	40.00	80.00
90 F. F. Hall	40.00	80.00
91 Leonard Hollywood	40.00	80.00
92 Philip Koerner	40.00	80.00
93 George Maisel	40.00	80.00
94 John Oldham	40.00	80.00
95 Charles Pick	40.00	80.00
96 Walter Schaller	40.00	80.00
97 Luther Smith	40.00	80.00
98 William Steen	40.00	80.00
99 Harry Wolverton	40.00	80.00
100 Frank Arellanes	40.00	80.00
101 C. H. Callahan	40.00	80.00
102 Barney Connifer	40.00	80.00
103 Frank DeCanniere	40.00	80.00
104 Walter Doane	40.00	80.00
105 Arthur Fromme	50.00	100.00
106 James Galloway	40.00	80.00
107 Art Griggs	40.00	80.00
108 Otto Hess	40.00	80.00
109 Roy Hitt	40.00	80.00
110 George Johnson	40.00	80.00
111 Howard McLarry	40.00	80.00
112 Walter Mattick	40.00	80.00
113 Albert Mitchell	40.00	80.00
114 Carl Mitze	40.00	80.00
115 John Quinn	60.00	120.00
116 Michael Simon	40.00	80.00
117 Robert Snyder	40.00	80.00
118 George Stovall	40.00	80.00
119 Joseph Sullivan	40.00	80.00
120 Ralph Valencia	40.00	80.00
121 Albert Whalling	40.00	80.00

1918 Zeenuts

These cards measure approximately 1 13/16" by 3 5/8".

COMPLETE SET (104)	3,500.00	7,000.00
1 Walter Boles	50.00	100.00
2 Charles Brown	50.00	100.00
3 Claude Cooper	50.00	100.00
4 James Crandall	50.00	100.00
5 Samuel Crawford	500.00	1,000.00
6 George Ellis	50.00	100.00
7 Paul Fittery	50.00	100.00
8 Jacques Fournier	60.00	120.00
9 Wade Killifer	50.00	100.00
10 Peter Lapan	50.00	100.00
11 Harold Leathers	50.00	100.00
12 Joseph Pepe	50.00	100.00
13 William Pertica	50.00	100.00
14 Alfred Stanbridge	50.00	100.00
15 Zebulon Terry	50.00	100.00
16 Ralph Valencia	50.00	100.00
17 Alex Arlett	50.00	100.00
18 Eugene Caldera	50.00	100.00
19 Paul Codington	50.00	100.00
20 Ralph Croll	50.00	100.00
21 L. Gardner	50.00	100.00
22 Nelson Hawkes	50.00	100.00
23 William Hollander	50.00	100.00
24 George Howard	50.00	100.00
25 Remy Kremer	60.00	120.00
26 Elmer Leifer	50.00	100.00
27 Elwood Martin	50.00	100.00
28 Edward Mensor	50.00	100.00
29 Robert Middleton	50.00	100.00
30 Lawrence Miller	50.00	100.00
31 Carl Mitze	50.00	100.00
32 Daniel Murray	50.00	100.00
33 Herschel Prough	50.00	100.00
34 George Shader	50.00	100.00
35 Robert Smale	50.00	100.00
36 Lynn Brenton	50.00	100.00
37 Jack Bromley	50.00	100.00
38 William Camm	50.00	100.00
39 D.K. Davis	50.00	100.00
40 Theodore Easterly	50.00	100.00
41 Ross Eldred	50.00	100.00
42 Carter Elliot	50.00	100.00
43 August Fisher	50.00	100.00
44 Frank Forsythe	50.00	100.00
45 Harry Gardner	50.00	100.00
46 Art Griggs	50.00	100.00
47 Albert Leake	50.00	100.00
48 J.M. McNulty	50.00	100.00
49 Babe Pinelli	100.00	200.00
50 Elton Prentice	50.00	100.00
51 Wilbur Rogers	50.00	100.00
52 James West	50.00	100.00
53 Dennis Wilie	50.00	100.00
54 Levi Arkenburg	50.00	100.00
55 Laverne Chappell	50.00	100.00
56 Allen Conwright	50.00	100.00
57 Elmer Cox	50.00	100.00
58 Karl Crandall	50.00	100.00
59 Jean Dubuc	50.00	100.00
60 John Dunn	50.00	100.00
61 Floyd Farmer	50.00	100.00
62 Michael Konnick	50.00	100.00
63 Walter Leverenz	50.00	100.00
64 Timothy McCabe	50.00	100.00
65 Walter McCredie	50.00	100.00
66 Ward Miller	50.00	100.00
67 Harry Morton	50.00	100.00
68 William Orr	50.00	100.00
69 Thomas Quinlan	50.00	100.00
70 John Ryan MG	50.00	100.00
71 John Sand	50.00	100.00
72 Earl Sheely	50.00	100.00
73 Wesley Siglin	50.00	100.00
74 Wallace Smith	50.00	100.00
75 Charles Baum	50.00	100.00
76 Clarence Brooks	50.00	100.00
77 Victor Dobbs	50.00	100.00
78 Jerome Downs	50.00	100.00
79 Jack Goldie	50.00	100.00
80 John Hummel	50.00	100.00
81 Herbert Hunter	50.00	100.00
82 George Johnson	50.00	100.00
83 George Johnson	50.00	100.00
84 Erving Kantlehner	50.00	100.00
85 Philip Koerner	50.00	100.00
86 William Llewlyn	50.00	100.00
87 Raymond McKee	50.00	100.00
88 Francis O'Doul	500.00	1,000.00
89 Andrew Phillips	50.00	100.00
90 Charles Pick	50.00	100.00
91 Peter Ritchie	50.00	100.00
92 Luther Smith	50.00	100.00
93 David Williams	50.00	100.00
94 John Alcock	50.00	100.00
95 William Borton	50.00	100.00
96 Albert DeVormer	60.00	120.00
97 Chester Chadbourne	50.00	100.00
98 William Essick	50.00	100.00
99 Arthur Fromme	60.00	120.00
100 Franz Hosp	50.00	100.00
101 John Mitchell	50.00	100.00
102 Roy Mitchell	50.00	100.00
103 Henry Moore	50.00	100.00
104 George Wisterzill	50.00	100.00

1919 Zeenuts

Some cards have been seen without sepia overlay. Fatty Arbuckle, the famous silent movie comedian has a card in this set. He was part owner of the Vernon Tigers which is how he ended up with a card. This card is considered among the keys in collecting Zeenuts. These cards measure approximately 1 3/4" by 3 5/8".

COMPLETE SET (144)	4,500.00	9,000.00
1 Walter Boles	40.00	80.00
2 Charles Brown	40.00	80.00
3 Claude Cooper	40.00	80.00
4 James Crandall	40.00	80.00
5 John Paddy Driscoll	600.00	1,000.00
6 George Ellis	40.00	80.00
7 Jacques Fournier	50.00	100.00
8 Fred Haney	50.00	100.00
9 William Kenworthy	40.00	80.00
10 Wade Killeffer	40.00	80.00
11 Peter Lapan	40.00	80.00
12 John Niehoff	40.00	80.00
13 Alex Arlett	40.00	80.00
14 Russ Buzz Arlett	60.00	120.00
15 Samuel Bohne	40.00	80.00
16 Claude Cooper	40.00	80.00

1919 Zeenuts

17 Ralph Croll 40.00 80.00
18 Harold Elliott 40.00 80.00
19 Carl Holling 40.00 80.00
20 George Howard MG 40.00 80.00
21 Remy Kramer 50.00 100.00
22 William Lane 40.00 80.00
23 William Lee 40.00 80.00
24 Carl Mitze MG 40.00 80.00
25 Rod Murphy 40.00 80.00
26 Chester Norse 40.00 80.00
27 John Roach 40.00 80.00
28 William Stumpf 40.00 80.00
29 Clyde Ware 40.00 80.00
30 Harry Weaver 40.00 80.00
31 Dennis Wilie 40.00 80.00
32 Delmer Baker 50.00 100.00
33 Luzurne Blue 50.00 100.00
34 Guy Cooper 40.00 80.00
35 Elmer Cox 40.00 80.00
36 Ernest Fallentine 40.00 80.00
37 Arthur Koehler 40.00 80.00
38 Walter McCreddie 40.00 80.00
39 George Maisel 40.00 80.00
40 John Oldham 40.00 80.00
41 Kenneth Penner 40.00 80.00
42 George Pennington 40.00 80.00
43 Donald Rader 40.00 80.00
44 Wesley Siglin 40.00 80.00
45 William Speas 40.00 80.00
46 Harvey Sutherland 40.00 80.00
47 Charles Walker 40.00 80.00
48 George Westerzil 40.00 80.00
49 Albert Zweifel 40.00 80.00
50 Ross Eldred 40.00 80.00
51 August Fisher 40.00 80.00
52 Art Griggs 40.00 80.00
53 Earl Larkin 40.00 80.00
54 Mark McGaffigan 40.00 80.00
55 Frank McHenry 40.00 80.00
56 J.M. McNulty 40.00 80.00
57 Robert Middleton 40.00 80.00
58 Daniel Murray 40.00 80.00
59 William Orr 40.00 80.00
60 William Piercy 40.00 80.00
61 Ralph Pinelli 60.00 120.00
62 Herschel Prough 40.00 80.00
63 Wilbur Rodgers 40.00 80.00
64 Clarence Vance 375.00 750.00
65 Ally 40.00 80.00
66 Charles Byler 40.00 80.00
67 Eugene Caldera 40.00 80.00
68 Allen Conkwright 40.00 80.00
69 Raymond French 40.00 80.00
70 C.W. Henkle 40.00 80.00
71 Edward Herr 40.00 80.00
72 A.V. King 40.00 80.00
73 Emmet Mulory 40.00 80.00
74 William Rumler 40.00 80.00
75 John Sands 40.00 80.00
76 Earl Sheely 50.00 100.00
77 Kirby Sprangler 40.00 80.00
78 Edward Spencer 40.00 80.00
79 Pete Starasenich 40.00 80.00
80 Robert Willets 40.00 80.00
81 Earl Baldwin 40.00 80.00
82 Charles Baum 40.00 80.00
83 Clarence Brooks 40.00 80.00
84 James Cavaney 40.00 80.00
85 James Church 40.00 80.00
86 Jerry Coleman 40.00 80.00
87 Joseph Connolly 40.00 80.00
88 Roy Corhan 40.00 80.00
89 John Couch 40.00 80.00
90 Karl Crandall 40.00 80.00
91 Dell Crespi 40.00 80.00
92 Justin Fitzgerald 40.00 80.00
93 R. Flannigan 40.00 80.00
94 George Gibson 50.00 100.00
95 Howard Harper 40.00 80.00
96 Thomas Hickey 40.00 80.00
97 William Kamm 60.00 120.00
98 Philip Koerner 40.00 80.00
99 Remy Kramer 50.00 100.00
100 Maurice Schick 40.00 80.00
101 James Scott 40.00 80.00
102 Thomas Seaton 40.00 80.00
103 Bill Smith 40.00 80.00
104 Luther Smith 40.00 80.00
105 Snell 40.00 80.00
106 Carl Zamloch 40.00 80.00
107 Lyle Bigbee 40.00 80.00
108 Alvah Bowman 40.00 80.00
109 William Clymer 40.00 80.00
110 Pete Compton 40.00 80.00
111 William Cunningham 50.00 100.00
112 Frank Eastley 40.00 80.00
113 Albert Fabrique 40.00 80.00
114 Frederick Falkenberg 40.00 80.00
115 Grover Land 40.00 80.00
116 John Mails 50.00 100.00
117 Miles Mains 40.00 80.00
118 John Niehoff 40.00 80.00
119 Peter Ritchie 40.00 80.00
120 Wallace Schultz 40.00 80.00
121 James Walsh 40.00 80.00
122 Joseph Wilhoit 40.00 80.00
123 Roscoe Arbuckle 1,250.00 2,500.00
124 Zinn Beck 40.00 80.00
125 William Borton 40.00 80.00
126 Chester Chadbourne 40.00 80.00
127 Charles Chech 40.00 80.00
128 Lester Cook 40.00 80.00
129 Rexford Dawson 40.00 80.00
130 William Dell 40.00 80.00
131 Albert DeVormer 50.00 100.00
132 Jacob Edington 40.00 80.00
133 William Essick 50.00 100.00
134 Joseph Finneran 40.00 80.00
135 Robert Fisher 40.00 80.00
136 Arthur Fromme 50.00 100.00
137 Hugh High 40.00 80.00
138 Franz Hosp 40.00 80.00
139 Byron Houck 40.00 80.00
140 Thomas Long 40.00 80.00
141 Joseph Mathes 40.00 80.00
142 Bob Meusel 75.00 150.00
143 John Mitchell 40.00 80.00
144 Elmer Reigher 40.00 80.00

1920 Zeenuts

Some cards have been seen without grandstand. These cards measure approximately 1 3/4" by 3 5/8".

COMPLETE SET (151) 3,750.00 7,500.00
1 Victor Aldridge 50.00 100.00
2 Raymond Andrews 40.00 80.00
3 John Bassler 50.00 100.00
4 Charles Brown 40.00 80.00
5 James Crandall 40.00 80.00
6 Karl Crandall 40.00 80.00
7 Samuel Crawford 125.00 250.00
8 Nicholas Dumovich 40.00 80.00
9 George Ellis 40.00 80.00
10 Art Griggs 40.00 80.00
11 Fred Hanicy 40.00 80.00
12 Raymond Keating 40.00 80.00
13 Wade Killefer 40.00 80.00
14 James McAuley 40.00 80.00
15 John Niehoff 40.00 80.00
16 William Pertica 40.00 80.00
17 Alex Arlett 50.00 100.00
18 Russell Arlett 60.00 120.00
19 George Cunningham 40.00 80.00
20 Charles Dorman 40.00 80.00
21 Henry Ginglardi 40.00 80.00
22 Louis Guisto 40.00 80.00
23 William Hamilton 40.00 80.00
24 George Howard MG 40.00 80.00
25 John Knight 40.00 80.00
26 Remy Kremer 50.00 100.00
27 Don Lambert 40.00 80.00
28 William Lane 40.00 80.00
29 Lawrence Miller 40.00 80.00
30 Claude Mitchell 40.00 80.00
31 Carl Mitze 40.00 80.00
32 William Paull 40.00 80.00
33 George Petterson 40.00 80.00
34 Don Reagan 40.00 80.00
35 John Russell 40.00 80.00
36 Ed Spellman 40.00 80.00
37 Harry Weaver 40.00 80.00
38 Dennis Wilie 40.00 80.00
39 George Winn 40.00 80.00
40 Rollie Zeider 40.00 80.00
41 Delmer Baker 50.00 100.00
42 Luzurne Blue 50.00 100.00
43 Elmer Cox 40.00 80.00
44 Sylvester Johnson 50.00 100.00
45 Carroll Jones 40.00 80.00
46 Frank Juney 40.00 80.00
47 Rudolph Kallio 40.00 80.00
48 Wescott Kingdon 40.00 80.00
49 Arthur Koehler 40.00 80.00
50 Walter McCredie 40.00 80.00
51 George Maisel 40.00 80.00
52 Harold Polson 40.00 80.00
53 Samuel Ross 40.00 80.00
54 Walter Schaller 40.00 80.00
55 Clyde Schroeder 40.00 80.00
56 Wesley Siglin 40.00 80.00
57 Carl Spranger 40.00 80.00
58 Harvey Sutherland 40.00 80.00
59 George Wisterzill 40.00 80.00
60 Willie Butler 40.00 80.00
61 Pete Compton 40.00 80.00
62 Lester Cook 40.00 80.00
63 Ross Eldred 40.00 80.00
64 Guy Hodges 40.00 80.00
65 Jack Killeen 40.00 80.00
66 Earl Kunz 40.00 80.00
67 Earl Larkin 40.00 80.00
68 Mark McGaffigan 40.00 80.00
69 Walter Mails 50.00 100.00
70 Fred Mollwitz 40.00 80.00
71 Billy Orr 40.00 80.00
72 Kenneth Penner 40.00 80.00
73 Herschel Prough 40.00 80.00
74 Bill Rodgers MG 40.00 80.00
75 Robert Schang 40.00 80.00
76 William Stumpf 40.00 80.00
77 Charles Baum 40.00 80.00
78 Jack Bromley dark hat 40.00 80.00
79 Jack Bromley light hat 40.00 80.00
80 Norman Cullop 40.00 80.00
81 Charles Dylar 40.00 80.00
82 Russell James 40.00 80.00
83 Joe Jenkins 40.00 80.00
84 Ernest Johnson 40.00 80.00
85 Martin Krug 40.00 80.00
86 Walter Leverenz 40.00 80.00
87 Frank McHenry 40.00 80.00
88 Harl Maggart 40.00 80.00
89 Henry Matterson 40.00 80.00
90 Eddie Matteson 40.00 80.00
91 Elmer O'Shaughnessy 40.00 80.00
92 Elmer Reiger 40.00 80.00
93 Alex Reilly 40.00 80.00
94 Bill Rumler 40.00 80.00
95 John Sands 40.00 80.00
96 Earl Sheely 50.00 100.00
97 Ralph Stroud 40.00 80.00
98 Hollis Thurston dark hat 50.00 100.00
99 Hollis Thurston light hat 50.00 100.00
100 J.W. Worth 40.00 80.00
101 Samuel Agnew 40.00 80.00
102 Edward Anfinson 40.00 80.00
103 James Caveney 40.00 80.00
104 Joseph Connolly 40.00 80.00
105 Roy Corhan 40.00 80.00
106 Mario DeVitalus 40.00 80.00
107 Joseph Dooley 40.00 80.00
108 Justin Fitzgerald 40.00 80.00
109 John Gough 40.00 80.00
110 Bill Kamm 50.00 100.00
111 Phillip Koerner 40.00 80.00
112 Edward Love 40.00 80.00
113 Herbert McQuaid 40.00 80.00
114 Maurice Schick 40.00 80.00
115 James Scott 40.00 80.00
116 Thomas Seaton 40.00 80.00
117 Luther Smith 40.00 80.00
118 Michael Walsh 40.00 80.00
119 Archie Yelle 40.00 80.00
120 John Adams 40.00 80.00
121 Earl Baldwin 40.00 80.00
122 Samuel Bohne 40.00 80.00
123 Lynn Brenton 40.00 80.00
124 Harry Gardner 40.00 80.00
125 Bruce Hartford 40.00 80.00
126 William Kenworthy 40.00 80.00
127 Merlin Kopp 40.00 80.00
128 Rod Murphy 40.00 80.00
129 Robert Nixon 40.00 80.00
130 Arthur Rheinhart 40.00 80.00
131 Charles Schorr 40.00 80.00
132 Harry Siebold 40.00 80.00
133 Clyde Wares 40.00 80.00
134 Carl Zamlock 40.00 80.00
135 John Alcock 40.00 80.00
136 Chester Chadbourne 40.00 80.00
137 Albert DeVormer 50.00 100.00
138 Jacob Edington 40.00 80.00
139 William Essick 50.00 100.00
140 Robert Fisher 40.00 80.00
141 Arthur Fromme 50.00 100.00
142 Hugh High 40.00 80.00
143 Elmer Hill 40.00 80.00
144 Thomas Long 40.00 80.00
145 John Mitchell 40.00 80.00
146 Willie Mitchell 40.00 80.00
147 Moffitt 40.00 80.00
148 Harry Morse 40.00 80.00
149 Frank Schellenback 50.00 100.00
150 James Smith 40.00 80.00
151 James Sullivan 40.00 80.00

1921 Zeenuts

These cards measure 1 3/4" by 3 3/4".

COMPLETE SET (167) 4,000.00 8,000.00
1 Victor Aldridge 50.00 100.00
2 Earl Baldwin 40.00 80.00
3 Dorsey Carroll 40.00 80.00
4 Thomas Casey 40.00 80.00
5 Otis Crandall 40.00 80.00
6 Sam Crawford 125.00 250.00
7 Ken Douglas 40.00 80.00
8 Nick Dumovich 40.00 80.00
9 George Ellis 40.00 80.00
10 Arthur Griggs 40.00 80.00
11 Tom Hughes 40.00 80.00
12 Wade Killefer 40.00 80.00
13 Howard Lindimore 40.00 80.00
14 George Lyons 40.00 80.00
15 Jim McAuley 40.00 80.00
16 Bert Niehoff 40.00 80.00
17 Arthur Reinhardt 40.00 80.00
18 Oscar Stanage 40.00 80.00
19 Arnold Statz 60.00 120.00
20 Claude Thomas 40.00 80.00
21 Rollie Zeider 40.00 80.00
22 Allen Alton 40.00 80.00
23 Alex Arlett 50.00 100.00
24 Ray Brubaker 40.00 80.00
25 Ted Cather 40.00 80.00
26 Claude Cooper 40.00 80.00
27 Bernard Kearns 40.00 80.00
28 Eugene Kersten 40.00 80.00
29 Jack Knight 40.00 80.00
30 Arthur Koehler 40.00 80.00
31 Harry Krause 40.00 80.00
32 Ray Kremer 50.00 100.00
33 Lawrence Miller 40.00 80.00
34 Carl Mitze 40.00 80.00
35 Ralph Pinelli 60.00 120.00
36 Addison Read 40.00 80.00
37 Lane Shultis 40.00 80.00
38 Harry Siebold 40.00 80.00
39 Al White 40.00 80.00
40 Dennis Wilie 40.00 80.00
41 George Winn 40.00 80.00
42 Dale Baker 40.00 80.00
43 Art Bourg 40.00 80.00
44 Willie Butler 40.00 80.00
45 Fred Connel 40.00 80.00
46 Dick Cox 40.00 80.00
47 Gus Fisher 40.00 80.00
48 Walt Gennin 40.00 80.00
49 Sam Hale 40.00 80.00
50 Sylvester Johnson 50.00 100.00
51 Rudy Kallio 40.00 80.00
52 A.V. King 40.00 80.00
53 Wesley Kingdon 40.00 80.00
54 M.J. Krug 40.00 80.00
55 Walt McCredie 40.00 80.00
56 J.C. Notziger 40.00 80.00
57 O'Malia 40.00 80.00
58 Hazen Paton 40.00 80.00
59 Herman Pillette 50.00 100.00
60 H.G. Polson 40.00 80.00
61 J.R. Poole 40.00 80.00
62 Sam Ross 40.00 80.00
63 M.J. Wolfer 40.00 80.00
64 Clyde Young 40.00 80.00
65 Ray Blossom 40.00 80.00
66 Pete Compton 40.00 80.00
67 Les Cook 40.00 80.00
68 Howard Elliott 40.00 80.00
69 Tony Faeth 40.00 80.00
70 Paul Fittery 40.00 80.00
71 Carroll Jones 40.00 80.00
72 Merlin Kopp 40.00 80.00
73 Earl Kunz 40.00 80.00
74 Mark McGaffigan 40.00 80.00
75 Fred Mollwitz 40.00 80.00
76 Dick Niehaus 40.00 80.00
77 Bill Orr 40.00 80.00
78 Ken Penner 40.00 80.00
79 Charley Pick 40.00 80.00
80 H.C. Prough 40.00 80.00
81 Wilbur Rodgers MG 40.00 80.00
82 Pete Rose 40.00 80.00
83 Sid Ross 40.00 80.00
84 Buddy Ryan 40.00 80.00
85 Bob Shang 40.00 80.00
86 Les Sheehan 40.00 80.00
87 Rich Berry 40.00 80.00
88 Harry Blacholder 40.00 80.00
89 Earl Brinley 40.00 80.00
90 John Bromley 40.00 80.00
91 Brown 40.00 80.00
92 C.A. Byler 40.00 80.00
93 Gavvy Cravath 60.00 120.00
94 A.F. Gould 40.00 80.00
95 A.J. Hesse 40.00 80.00
96 W.P. Jackson 40.00 80.00
97 P.W. Jacobs 40.00 80.00
98 Joe Jenkins 40.00 80.00
99 Ted Jourden 40.00 80.00
100 Jack Kifer 40.00 80.00
101 Walter Leverenz 40.00 80.00
102 Byrd Lynn 40.00 80.00
103 Mustain 40.00 80.00
104 Nickels 40.00 80.00
105 Harry Oliver 40.00 80.00
106 Elmer Rieger 40.00 80.00
107 Peter Rose 40.00 80.00
108 Heinie Sand 40.00 80.00
109 Paddy Siglin 40.00 80.00
110 Hollis Thurston 50.00 100.00
111 Hilliard Tyrell 40.00 80.00
112 Ed Van Osdoll 40.00 80.00
113 J.W. Wilhoit 40.00 80.00
114 Edwin Anfinson 40.00 80.00
115 Jim Caveney 40.00 80.00
116 Jack Couch 40.00 80.00
117 Roy Crumpler 40.00 80.00
118 Bert Ellison 40.00 80.00
119 Justin Fitzgerald 40.00 80.00
120 Ed Flaherty 40.00 80.00
121 Elmer Hansen 40.00 80.00
122 Bill Kamm 50.00 100.00
123 Joe Kelly 40.00 80.00
124 Sam Lewis 40.00 80.00
125 Willie Ludolph 40.00 80.00
126 Herb McQuaid 40.00 80.00
127 John Merritt 40.00 80.00
128 Jim O'Connell 40.00 80.00
129 Frank O'Doul 250.00 500.00
130 Morris Rath 50.00 100.00
131 Maurice Schick 40.00 80.00
132 Jim Scott 40.00 80.00
133 Shore 40.00 80.00
134 Tom Walsh 40.00 80.00
135 Archie Yelle 40.00 80.00
136 J.B. Adams 40.00 80.00
137 Ray Bates 40.00 80.00
138 Bill Cunningham 50.00 100.00
139 Joe Daley 40.00 80.00
140 Al Demaree 50.00 100.00
141 Ray Francis 40.00 80.00
142 Harry Gardner 40.00 80.00
143 Bob Geary 40.00 80.00
144 Elmer Jacobs 40.00 80.00
145 Bill Lane 40.00 80.00
146 Bob Middelton 40.00 80.00
147 Rod Murphy 40.00 80.00
148 Rube Oldring 50.00 100.00
149 Ernie Shorr 50.00 100.00
150 Ed Spencer 40.00 80.00
151 William Wtumpf 40.00 80.00
152 Forbes Alcock 40.00 80.00
153 Chester Chadbourne 40.00 80.00
154 Wheezer Dell 40.00 80.00
155 Bill Essick 50.00 100.00
156 Ray French 40.00 80.00
157 Arthur Fromme 50.00 100.00

158 Charles Gorman	40.00	80.00
159 James Hannah	40.00	80.00
160 Hugh High	40.00	80.00
161 Ham Hyatt	40.00	80.00
162 Ed Love	40.00	80.00
163 Bob McGraw	40.00	80.00
164 Willie Mitchell	40.00	80.00
165 Harry Morse	40.00	80.00
166 Dennis Murphy	40.00	80.00
167 Pete Schneider	40.00	80.00
168 Walter Smallwood	40.00	80.00
169 J.C. Smith	40.00	80.00

1922 Zeenuts

Cards seen with variations in Sepia tone overlay. A very early card of Hall of Famer Tony Lazzeri is in this set along with a card of Jim Thorpe. This is one of the few cards picturing Thorpe as a baseball player during his professional career. These cards measure 1 13/16" by 3 9/16".

COMPLETE SET (162)	7,000.00	14,000.00
1 Earle Baldwin	40.00	80.00
2 Dorsey Carroll	40.00	80.00
3 Otis Crandall	40.00	80.00
4 Tom Daly	40.00	80.00
5 Charles Deal	40.00	80.00
6 Nick Dumovich	40.00	80.00
7 Art Griggs	40.00	80.00
8 Tom Hughes	40.00	80.00
9 Wade Killefer	40.00	80.00
10 Howard Lindimore	40.00	80.00
11 George Lyons	40.00	80.00
12 Jim McAuley	40.00	80.00
13 Bill McCabe	40.00	80.00
14 Elmer Ponder	40.00	80.00
15 Harry Sullivan	40.00	80.00
16 Claude Thomas	40.00	80.00
17 Clarence Twombly	40.00	80.00
18 Bernie Viveros	40.00	80.00
19 Robert Wallace	40.00	80.00
20 Mark Wheat	40.00	80.00
21 Russ Arlett	50.00	100.00
22 Lynn Brenton	40.00	80.00
23 Don Brown	40.00	80.00
24 Ray Brubaker	40.00	80.00
25 Claude Cooper	40.00	80.00
26 Hod Eller	60.00	120.00
27 Ivan Howard	40.00	80.00
28 Gordon Jones	40.00	80.00
29 Earl Keiser	40.00	80.00
30 Jack Knight	40.00	80.00
31 Art Koehler	40.00	80.00
32 Ray Kremer	60.00	120.00
33 George Lafayette	40.00	80.00
34 Bill Marriott	40.00	80.00
35 Carl Mitze	40.00	80.00
36 Pat Monahan	40.00	80.00
37 Addison Read	40.00	80.00
38 Frank Schulte	50.00	100.00
39 Dennis Wilie	40.00	80.00
40 Dick Cox	40.00	80.00
41 Roy Crumpler	40.00	80.00
42 Howard Elliott	40.00	80.00
43 Harvey Freeman	40.00	80.00
44 Leroy Gressett	40.00	80.00
45 Charley High	40.00	80.00
46 Harry Kenworthy	40.00	80.00
47 Joseph Killhullen	40.00	80.00
48 A.V. King	40.00	80.00
49 Emmett McCann	40.00	80.00
50 J.R. Poole	40.00	80.00
51 Samuel Ross	40.00	80.00
52 J.A. Sargent	40.00	80.00
53 Harvey Sutherland	40.00	80.00
54 Jim Thorpe	5,000.00	10,000.00
55 Tom Turner	40.00	80.00
56 Carroll Canfield	40.00	80.00
57 Pete Compton	40.00	80.00
58 Les Cook	40.00	80.00
59 Paul Fittery	40.00	80.00
60 George Gibson	40.00	80.00
61 Hampton	40.00	80.00
62 Earl Kunz	40.00	80.00
63 Henry Hampton	40.00	80.00
64 Frederick Mollwitz	40.00	80.00
65 Dick Niehaus	40.00	80.00
66 Billy Orr	40.00	80.00
67 Walt Pearce	40.00	80.00
68 Charles Pick	40.00	80.00
69 Bill Prough	40.00	80.00
70 Buddy Ryan	40.00	80.00
71 Bob Schang	40.00	80.00
72 Elmer Shea	40.00	80.00
73 Les Sheehan	40.00	80.00
74 Oscar Stanage	40.00	80.00
75 Harry Blaeholder	40.00	80.00
76 Jack Bromley	40.00	80.00
77 C.A. Byler	40.00	80.00
78 Joseph Cartwright	40.00	80.00
79 A.F. Gould	40.00	80.00
80 Joe Jenkins	40.00	80.00
81 Rudy Kallio	40.00	80.00
82 Tony Lazzeri	375.00	750.00
83 Duffy Lewis	75.00	150.00
84 Sam Lewis	40.00	80.00
85 Lem Owen	40.00	80.00
86 Elmer Rieger	40.00	80.00
87 Heinie Sand	60.00	120.00
88 Maurice Schick	40.00	80.00
89 Paddy Siglin	40.00	80.00
90 Frank Soria	40.00	80.00
91 Paul Strand	40.00	80.00
92 Hollis Thurston	60.00	120.00
93 J.W. Wilhoit	40.00	80.00
94 Sam Agnew	60.00	120.00
95 Ed Anfinson	40.00	80.00
96 Fritz Coumbe	40.00	80.00
97 Bert Ellison	40.00	80.00
98 Justin Fitzgerald	40.00	80.00
99 Bob Geary	40.00	80.00
100 Bill Kamm	60.00	120.00
101 Pete Kilduff	60.00	120.00
102 Ross Lefevre	40.00	80.00
103 Herb McQuaid	40.00	80.00
104 John Miller	40.00	80.00
105 Oliver Mitchell	40.00	80.00
106 Jim O'Connell	60.00	120.00
107 Jim Scott	40.00	80.00
108 Charley See	40.00	80.00
109 Gene Valla	40.00	80.00
110 Andy Vargas	40.00	80.00
111 Tom Walsh	40.00	80.00
112 Lyle Wells	40.00	80.00
113 Richard Williams	40.00	80.00
114 Archie Yelle	40.00	80.00
115 Jack Adams	40.00	80.00
116 Spencer Adams	40.00	80.00
117 Ed Barney	40.00	80.00
118 L.T. Bell	40.00	80.00
119 George Brovold	40.00	80.00
120 George Burger	40.00	80.00
121 Thomas Connolly	40.00	80.00
122 Manuel Cueto	40.00	80.00
123 Joe Dailey	40.00	80.00
124 R.C. Eldred	40.00	80.00
125 Joe Finneran	40.00	80.00
126 Harry Gardner	40.00	80.00
127 Vean Gregg	60.00	120.00
128 Henry Henke	40.00	80.00
129 Elmer Jacobs	40.00	80.00
130 Reynolds Kelly	40.00	80.00
131 Bill Lane	40.00	80.00
132 Walter McCredie MG	40.00	80.00
133 Frank Mack	40.00	80.00
134 Herb May	40.00	80.00
135 Rod Murphy	40.00	80.00
136 James Richardson	40.00	80.00
137 Pete Ritchie	40.00	80.00
138 Ernie Schorr	40.00	80.00
139 Frank Schulte	50.00	100.00
140 Ed Spencer	40.00	80.00
141 William Stumpf	40.00	80.00
142 Frank Tobin	40.00	80.00
143 George Westersil	40.00	80.00
144 Ping Bodie	75.00	150.00
145 Chester Chadbourne	40.00	80.00
146 Wheezer Dell	40.00	80.00
147 Jesse Doyle	40.00	80.00
148 Bill Essick MG	60.00	120.00
149 Ray French	40.00	80.00
150 Ray Gilder	40.00	80.00
151 Harry Hannah	40.00	80.00
152 Nelson Hawks	40.00	80.00
153 Hugh High	40.00	80.00
154 Byron Houck	40.00	80.00
155 Ham Hyatt	40.00	80.00
156 William James	40.00	80.00
157 Dallas Locker	40.00	80.00
158 Dennis Murphy	40.00	80.00
159 Carl Sawyer	40.00	80.00
160 Pete Schneider	40.00	80.00
161 Red Smith	40.00	80.00
162 Rollie Zeider	40.00	80.00

1923 Kansas City Blues Baltimore Shirt

This 20 card set was issued as part of an "accordian-style" booklet. This set honored the pennant winning Kansas City Blues team as it was issued in an envelope from the Baltimore Shirt Co which then had four stores in the Kansas City area. Please note that since these cards are unnumbered, we have sequenced them in alphabetical order.

COMPLETE SET	300.00	600.00
1 George Armstrong	20.00	40.00
2 Beals Becker	20.00	40.00
3 Lena Blackburne	20.00	40.00
4 Bunny Brief	20.00	40.00
5 Dudley Branom	20.00	40.00
6 Ray Caldwell	20.00	40.00
7 Nick Carter	20.00	40.00
8 Joe Dawson	20.00	40.00
9 Wilbur Good MG	20.00	40.00
10 Walter Hammond	20.00	40.00
11 Lew McCarty	20.00	40.00
12 George Muehlebach PRES	20.00	40.00
13 John Saladna	20.00	40.00
14 Ferd Schupp	20.00	40.00
15 Pete Scott	20.00	40.00
16 Bill Skiff	20.00	40.00
17 Herb Thormahlen	20.00	40.00
18 Roy Wilkinson	20.00	40.00
19 Glenn Wright	25.00	50.00
20 Jimmie Zinn	20.00	40.00
21 Dutch Zwilling	20.00	40.00

1923 Zeenuts

An early card of Hall of Famer Paul Waner is in this set. These cards measure approximately 1 7/8" by 3 9/16". Two different expiration dates have been noted for these cards. Cards with a sepia tint which were reissued from 1922 have an expiration date of April 1, 1923 while the regular black and white cards have an expiration date of April 1, 1924.

COMPLETE SET (198)	5,000.00	10,000.00
1 Earl Baldwin	40.00	80.00
2 Dorsey Carroll	40.00	80.00
3 Otis Crandall	40.00	80.00
4 Tom Daly	40.00	80.00
5 Charles Deal	40.00	80.00
6 Walter Golvin	40.00	80.00
7 Art Griggs	40.00	80.00
8 Roy Hannah	40.00	80.00
9 Wallace Hood	40.00	80.00
10 Percy Jones	40.00	80.00
11 Wade Killifer	40.00	80.00
12 Martin Krug	40.00	80.00
13 Howard Lindimore	40.00	80.00
14 George Lyons	40.00	80.00
15 Jim McAuley	40.00	80.00
16 James McAuliffe	40.00	80.00
17 Bill McCabe	40.00	80.00
18 Elmer Ponder	40.00	80.00
19 Lawrence Robertson	40.00	80.00
20 Claude Thomas	40.00	80.00
21 Clarence Twombly	40.00	80.00
22 Bob Wallace	50.00	100.00
23 Russ Arlett	60.00	120.00
24 Dale Baker	40.00	80.00
25 Lynn Brenton	40.00	80.00
26 Don Brown	40.00	80.00
27 Roy Brubaker	40.00	80.00
28 Ted Cather	40.00	80.00
29 Harold Chavez	40.00	80.00
30 Ira Colwell	40.00	80.00
31 Claude Cooper	40.00	80.00
32 Claude Cooper	40.00	80.00
33 Orville Eley	40.00	80.00
34 Horace Eller	50.00	100.00
35 Ivan Howard	40.00	80.00
36 Ivan Howard	40.00	80.00
37 Del Howard	40.00	80.00
38 Osborne Johnson	40.00	80.00
39 Gordon Jones	40.00	80.00
40 Earl Keiser	40.00	80.00
41 Jack Knight	40.00	80.00
42 Jack Knight	40.00	80.00
43 Art Koehler	40.00	80.00
44 Harry Krause	40.00	80.00
45 Ray Kremer	50.00	100.00
46 George Lafayette	40.00	80.00
47 George Lafayette	40.00	80.00
48 Mark McGaffigan	40.00	80.00
49 A.J. Maderas	40.00	80.00
50 Walt Mails	50.00	100.00
51 William Marriott	40.00	80.00
52 Carl Mitze	40.00	80.00
53 George Murchio	40.00	80.00
54 Addison Read	40.00	80.00
55 Addison Read	40.00	80.00
56 Marvin Smith	40.00	80.00
57 Chet Thomas	40.00	80.00
58 Lyle Wells	40.00	80.00
59 Dennis Wilie	40.00	80.00
60 Dennis Wilie	40.00	80.00
61 Frank Wetzel	40.00	80.00
62 Frank Brazil	40.00	80.00
63 Roy Crumpler	40.00	80.00
64 Tom Daly	40.00	80.00
65 Chas Eckert	40.00	80.00
66 Leroy Gressett	40.00	80.00
67 Charley High	40.00	80.00
68 John Jones	40.00	80.00
69 Lee King	40.00	80.00
70 Walt Leverenz	40.00	80.00
71 Emmett McCann	40.00	80.00
72 J.B. Middleton	40.00	80.00
73 Jack Onslow	40.00	80.00
74 Jim Poole	40.00	80.00
75 C.M. Schroeder	40.00	80.00
76 William Stumpf	40.00	80.00
77 Harvey Sutherland	40.00	80.00
78 M.J. Wolfer	40.00	80.00
79 B.W. Yarrison	40.00	80.00
80 Rollie Zeider	40.00	80.00
81 Harry Brown	40.00	80.00
82 Carroll Canfield	40.00	80.00
83 Charles Cochrane	40.00	80.00
84 Les Cook	40.00	80.00
85 Paul Fittery	40.00	80.00
86 Ed Hemingway	40.00	80.00
87 Hughes Houghs	40.00	80.00
88 Art Koehler	40.00	80.00
89 Merlin Kopp	40.00	80.00
90 George McGinnis	40.00	80.00
91 Earl McNeilly	40.00	80.00
92 Ken Penner	40.00	80.00
93 Charles Pick	40.00	80.00
94 Claude Rohwer	40.00	80.00
95 Buddy Ryan	40.00	80.00
96 Bob Schang	40.00	80.00
97 Merv Shea	40.00	80.00
98 Elmer Shea	40.00	80.00
99 Paddy Siglin	40.00	80.00
100 Moses Yellowhorse	125.00	250.00
101 Ed Anfinson	40.00	80.00
102 Fritz Coumbe	40.00	80.00
103 James Duchalsky	40.00	80.00
104 John Frederick	40.00	80.00
105 A.P. Gould	40.00	80.00
106 Rudy Kallio	40.00	80.00
107 Bernard Kearns	40.00	80.00
108 Lloyd Keller	40.00	80.00
109 Roy Leslie	40.00	80.00
110 Duffy Lewis	60.00	120.00
111 R.J. McCabe	40.00	80.00
112 Charles Matzen	40.00	80.00
113 Walt Pearce	40.00	80.00
114 John Peters	40.00	80.00
115 Les Sheehan	40.00	80.00
116 John Singleton	40.00	80.00
117 Paul Strand	40.00	80.00
118 Oscar Vitt	50.00	100.00
119 J.W. Wilhoit	40.00	80.00
120 Sam Agnew	40.00	80.00
121 Sam Agnew	40.00	80.00
122 Ernest Alten	40.00	80.00
123 Ed Anfinson	40.00	80.00
124 Timothy Buckley	40.00	80.00
125 Pete Compton	40.00	80.00
126 Henry Courtney	40.00	80.00
127 Bert Ellison	40.00	80.00
128 Bert Ellison	40.00	80.00
129 Ray Flashkamper	40.00	80.00
130 Robert Geary	40.00	80.00
131 Robert Geary	40.00	80.00
132 Timothy Hendryx	40.00	80.00
133 C.C. Hodge	40.00	80.00
134 Joe Kelly	40.00	80.00
135 Pete Kilduff	40.00	80.00
136 Alfred Lefevre	40.00	80.00
137 Doug McWeeney	40.00	80.00
138 John Miller	40.00	80.00
139 Oliver Mitchell	40.00	80.00
140 Oliver Mitchell	40.00	80.00
141 Edward Mulligan	40.00	80.00
142 Gus Noack	40.00	80.00
143 Hal Rhyne	40.00	80.00
144 Jim Scott	40.00	80.00
145 Charley See	40.00	80.00
146 Pat Shea	40.00	80.00
147 George Stanton	40.00	80.00
148 Gene Valla	40.00	80.00
149 Andy Vargas	40.00	80.00
150 Tom Dee Walsh	40.00	80.00
151 Paul Waner	500.00	1,000.00
152 Lyle Wells	40.00	80.00
153 Archie Yelle	40.00	80.00
154 Archie Yelle	40.00	80.00
155 Anderson	40.00	80.00
156 Ed Barney	40.00	80.00
157 Fred Blake	40.00	80.00
158 Sam Crane	40.00	80.00
159 Alvin Crowder	60.00	120.00
160 R.C. Eldred	40.00	80.00
161 Elmer Jacobs	40.00	80.00
162 Wheeler Johnston	40.00	80.00
163 Reynolds Kelly	40.00	80.00
164 Bill Lane	40.00	80.00
165 Alfred Levere	40.00	80.00
166 Bill Orr	40.00	80.00
167 Vic Pigg	40.00	80.00
168 William Plummer	40.00	80.00
169 W.C. Ramage	40.00	80.00
170 Pete Ritchie	40.00	80.00
171 Ray Rohwer	40.00	80.00
172 John Tesar	40.00	80.00
173 Frank Tobin	40.00	80.00
174 Tommy Walsh	40.00	80.00
175 Jim Welsh	40.00	80.00
176 Carl Williams	40.00	80.00
177 Harry Wolverton	40.00	80.00
178 Clarence Yaryan	40.00	80.00
179 Frank Bodie	60.00	120.00
180 Chester Chadbourne	40.00	80.00
181 Jesse Doyle	40.00	80.00
182 Bill Essick MG	50.00	100.00
183 Ray French	40.00	80.00
184 Ray Gilder	40.00	80.00
185 Charles Gorman	40.00	80.00
186 Harry Hannah	40.00	80.00
187 Hugh High	40.00	80.00
188 William James	40.00	80.00
189 James Jolly	40.00	80.00
190 Ed Kenna	40.00	80.00
191 Dallas Locker	40.00	80.00
192 Dennis Murphy	40.00	80.00
193 Rod Murphy	40.00	80.00
194 Perry O'Brien	40.00	80.00
195 Carl Sawyer	40.00	80.00
196 Pete Schneider	40.00	80.00
197 Frank Shellenback	50.00	100.00
198 Carlisle Smith	40.00	80.00

1924 Zeenuts

An early card of Hall of Famer Mickey Cochrane is in this set. These cards measure approximately 1 3/4" by 3 7/16".

COMPLETE SET (144)	2,750.00	5,500.00
1 Clyde Beck	25.00	50.00
2 Lyle Bigbee	25.00	50.00
3 John Billings	25.00	50.00
4 C.A. Byler	25.00	50.00
5 Otis Crandall	25.00	50.00
6 Ced Durst	25.00	50.00
7 Walt Golvin	25.00	50.00
8 Fred Gunther	25.00	50.00

9 Wally Hood	25.00	50.00
10 Tom Hughes	25.00	50.00
11 Ray Jacobs	25.00	50.00
12 Marty Krug	25.00	50.00
13 Jim McAuley	25.00	50.00
14 Elmer Meyers	25.00	50.00
15 Charley Root	50.00	100.00
16 C.E. Twombley	25.00	50.00
17 Robert Wallace	25.00	50.00
18 Bill Whaley	25.00	50.00
19 Spencer Adams	25.00	50.00
20 Russ Arlett	40.00	80.00
21 Del Baker	25.00	50.00
22 Ray Brubaker	25.00	50.00
23 Ted Cather	25.00	50.00
24 Claude Cooper	25.00	50.00
25 George Foster	25.00	50.00
26 Ed Goebel	25.00	50.00
27 Lou Guisto	25.00	50.00
28 Ivan Howard	25.00	50.00
29 Osborne Johnson	25.00	50.00
30 Harry Krause	25.00	50.00
31 Earl Kunz	25.00	50.00
32 George Lafayette	25.00	50.00
33 Leptich	25.00	50.00
34 Al Maderas	25.00	50.00
35 Walt Mails	25.00	50.00
36 Addison Read	25.00	50.00
37 Harry Siebold	25.00	50.00
38 Stan Benton	25.00	50.00
39 Frank Brazil	25.00	50.00
40 Mickey Cochrane	500.00	1,000.00
41 Dick Cox	25.00	50.00
42 Tom Daly	25.00	50.00
43 George Distel	25.00	50.00
44 Charley Eckert	25.00	50.00
45 LeRoy Gressett	25.00	50.00
46 Charley High	25.00	50.00
47 John Jones	25.00	50.00
48 Bill Kenworthy	25.00	50.00
49 Ed Lennon	25.00	50.00
50 Walt Leverenz	25.00	50.00
51 Emmett McCann	25.00	50.00
52 Jake Miller	25.00	50.00
53 Ted Pillette	25.00	50.00
54 Jim Poole	25.00	50.00
55 Wray Querry	25.00	50.00
56 C.M. Schroeder	25.00	50.00
57 Frank Wetzel	25.00	50.00
58 M.J. Wolfer	25.00	50.00
59 Harry Brown	25.00	50.00
60 Charles Cochrane	25.00	50.00
61 Sea Lion Hall	25.00	50.00
62 William Hughes	25.00	50.00
63 William James	25.00	50.00
64 Merlin Kopp	25.00	50.00
65 Earl McNeely	40.00	80.00
66 Harlan Peters	25.00	50.00
67 Charley Pick	25.00	50.00
68 Bill Prough	25.00	50.00
69 Claude Rowher	25.00	50.00
70 Bob Schang	25.00	50.00
71 Speck Shay	25.00	50.00
72 Merv Shea	40.00	80.00
73 Paddy Siglin	25.00	50.00
74 Art Smith	25.00	50.00
75 Moses Yellowhorse	50.00	100.00
76 Fred Coumbe	25.00	50.00
77 John Fredericks	25.00	50.00
78 Al Gould	25.00	50.00
79 Joe Jenkins	25.00	50.00
80 Roy Leslie	25.00	50.00
81 Duffy Lewis	50.00	100.00
82 John Peters	25.00	50.00
83 Oscar Vitt	30.00	60.00
84 Joseph Wilhoit	25.00	50.00
85 Sam Agnew	25.00	50.00
86 Timothy Buckley	25.00	50.00
87 George Burger	25.00	50.00
88 Bert Ellison	25.00	50.00
89 Raymond Flaskamper	25.00	50.00
90 Bob Geary	25.00	50.00
91 Martin Griffin	25.00	50.00
92 Tim Hendryx	25.00	50.00
93 C.C. Hodge	25.00	50.00
94 Joe Kelly	25.00	50.00
95 Pete Kilduff	40.00	80.00
96 Oliver Mitchell	25.00	50.00
97 Ed Mulligan	25.00	50.00
98 Norb Paynter	25.00	50.00
99 Hal Rhyne	25.00	50.00
100 Pete Ritchie	25.00	50.00
101 Charles Schorr	25.00	50.00
102 Jim Scott	25.00	50.00
103 Pat Shea	25.00	50.00
104 James Smith	25.00	50.00
105 George Stanton	25.00	50.00
106 Phillip Tanner	25.00	50.00
107 Gene Valla	25.00	50.00
108 Andy Vargas	25.00	50.00
109 Tom Dee Walsh	25.00	50.00
110 Paul Waner	375.00	750.00
111 Guy Williams	25.00	50.00
112 Archie Yelle	25.00	50.00
113 Earl Baldwin	25.00	50.00
114 Ted Baldwin	25.00	50.00
115 Cliff Brady	25.00	50.00
116 R.C. Eldred	25.00	50.00
117 Wade Killifer	25.00	50.00
118 Frank Osborne	25.00	50.00
119 Jim Welsh	25.00	50.00
120 Carl Williams	25.00	50.00
121 Andrew Bernard	25.00	50.00
122 Jim Blakesly	25.00	50.00
123 Leon Cadore	40.00	80.00
124 Chester Chadbourne	25.00	50.00
125 C.V. Christian	25.00	50.00
126 Charley Deal	25.00	50.00
127 Bill Essick	40.00	80.00
128 Charles Gorman	25.00	50.00
129 Wes Griffin	25.00	50.00
130 Harry Hannah	25.00	50.00
131 Frank Keck	25.00	50.00
132 Walt Kimmick	25.00	50.00
133 James McDowell	25.00	50.00
134 Mike Menosky	25.00	50.00
135 Dennis Murphy	25.00	50.00
136 Rod Murphy	25.00	50.00
137 Ken Penner	25.00	50.00
138 Pete Schneider	25.00	50.00
139 Alvy Sellers	25.00	50.00
140 Frank Shellenback	40.00	80.00
141 Oski Slade	25.00	50.00
142 Robert Vines	25.00	50.00
143 John Warner fielding	25.00	50.00
144 John Warner throwing	25.00	50.00

1925 Zeenuts

An early card of Hall of Famer Lloyd Waner is in this set. These cards measure approximately 1 3/4" by 3 7/16".

COMPLETE SET (162)	3,400.00	6,800.00
1 Clyde Beck	25.00	50.00
2 Otis Crandall	25.00	50.00
3 Russ Ennis	25.00	50.00
4 Ray Grimes	25.00	50.00
5 Wally Hood	25.00	50.00
6 Joe Horan	25.00	50.00
7 Ray Jacobs	25.00	50.00
8 Marty Krug	25.00	50.00
9 George Milstead	25.00	50.00
10 Elmer Phillips	25.00	50.00
11 Gus Sandberg	25.00	50.00
12 Ed Spencer	25.00	50.00
13 C.E. Twombly	25.00	50.00
14 Philip Weinert	25.00	50.00
15 Bill Whaley	25.00	50.00
16 Russ Arlett	40.00	80.00
17 Dale Baker	25.00	50.00
18 George Boehler	25.00	50.00
19 Joe Bratcher	25.00	50.00
20 Ray Brubaker	25.00	50.00
21 Ted Cather	25.00	50.00
22 Harold Chavez	25.00	50.00
23 Claude Cooper	25.00	50.00
24 Art Delaney	25.00	50.00
25 Mike Dempsey	25.00	50.00
26 Jake Flowers	40.00	80.00
27 Lon Guisto	25.00	50.00
28 Ivan Howard	25.00	50.00
29 Harry Krause	25.00	50.00
30 Earl Kunz	25.00	50.00
31 George Lafayette	25.00	50.00
32 William McCarren	25.00	50.00
33 Ron McDonald	25.00	50.00
34 George Makin	25.00	50.00
35 Urbane Pickering	25.00	50.00
36 Hub Pruett	25.00	50.00
37 Addison Read	25.00	50.00
38 Jim Reese	125.00	250.00
39 W.L. Crosby	25.00	50.00
40 Charles Deal	25.00	50.00
41 Charley High	25.00	50.00
42 Bill Hunnefield	25.00	50.00
43 Dave Keefe	25.00	50.00
44 Walt Leverenz	25.00	50.00
45 Duffy Lewis	50.00	100.00
46 Martin	25.00	50.00
47 Emmett McCann	25.00	50.00
48 George McGinnis	25.00	50.00
49 Fred Ortman	25.00	50.00
50 Ted Pillette	25.00	50.00
51 Reggie Rawlings	25.00	50.00
52 Harry Riconda	25.00	50.00
53 Ray Rohwer	25.00	50.00
54 Charles Rowland	25.00	50.00
55 Edward Sherling	25.00	50.00
56 Charles Thomas	25.00	50.00
57 Jess Winters	25.00	50.00
58 Arthur Woodring	25.00	50.00
59 Harry Brown	25.00	50.00
60 Carroll Canfield	25.00	50.00
61 Wallace Canfield	25.00	50.00
62 Charles Cockran	25.00	50.00
63 Wilbur Davis	25.00	50.00
64 E.M. Gorman	25.00	50.00
65 Clarence Hoffman	25.00	50.00
66 Vince Horton	25.00	50.00
67 William Hughes	25.00	50.00
68 W.J. James	25.00	50.00
69 Ray Keating	25.00	50.00
70 Art Koehler	25.00	50.00
71 Merlin Kopp	25.00	50.00
72 George McGinnis	25.00	50.00
73 Jim McLaughlin	25.00	50.00
74 Elwood Martin	25.00	50.00
75 Buddy Ryan	25.00	50.00
76 Bob Schang	25.00	50.00
77 Elmer Shea	25.00	50.00
78 Mervin Shea	40.00	80.00
79 Frank Shellenbach	40.00	80.00
80 Paddy Siglin	25.00	50.00
81 Harry Thompson	25.00	50.00
82 Lauri Vinci	25.00	50.00
83 Gene Wachenfeld	25.00	50.00
84 J.W. Watson	25.00	50.00
85 Chris Bahr	25.00	50.00
86 Joe Connolly	25.00	50.00
87 Les Cook	25.00	50.00
88 Fred Coumbe	25.00	50.00
89 John Frederick	25.00	50.00
90 Hensel Hulvey	25.00	50.00
91 Tony Lazzeri	375.00	750.00
92 Roy Leslie	25.00	50.00
93 Howard Lindemore	25.00	50.00
94 Rich McCabe	25.00	50.00
95 Mulcahy	25.00	50.00
96 Frank O'Doul	200.00	400.00
97 J.H. O'Neil	25.00	50.00
98 George Peery	25.00	50.00
99 Bill Piercey	25.00	50.00
100 Elmer Ponder	25.00	50.00
101 G.G. Steward	25.00	50.00
102 Oscar Vitt	40.00	80.00
103 James Aydelott	25.00	50.00
104 Sam Agnew	25.00	50.00
105 Frank Brower	25.00	50.00
106 J.W. Crockett	25.00	50.00
107 Bert Ellison	25.00	50.00
108 Bob Geary	25.00	50.00
109 Martin Griffin	25.00	50.00
110 Haughy	25.00	50.00
111 Tim Hendryx	25.00	50.00
112 Joe Kelly	25.00	50.00
113 Pete Kilduff	25.00	50.00
114 Oliver Mitchell	25.00	50.00
115 M.J. Moudy	25.00	50.00
116 Ed Mulligan	25.00	50.00
117 Norbi Paynter	25.00	50.00
118 Jeff Pfeffer	25.00	50.00
119 Hal Rhyne	25.00	50.00
120 Pete Ritchie	25.00	50.00
121 Vernon Stivers	25.00	50.00
122 Gus Suhr	40.00	80.00
123 Gene Valla	25.00	50.00
124 Paul Waner	375.00	750.00
125 Lloyd Waner	375.00	750.00
126 Guy Williams	25.00	50.00
127 Archie Yelle	25.00	50.00
128 Jim Bagby	50.00	100.00
129 Earl Baldwin	25.00	50.00
130 Cliff Brady	25.00	50.00
131 Ed Brandt	25.00	50.00
132 Frank Brazil	25.00	50.00
133 Sam Crane	25.00	50.00
134 George Cutshaw	25.00	50.00
135 Tom Daly	25.00	50.00
136 Nick Dumovich	25.00	50.00
137 R.C. Eldred	25.00	50.00
138 A.C. Elliott	25.00	50.00
139 Frank Emmer	25.00	50.00
140 Fred Fussell	25.00	50.00
141 Floyd Herman	50.00	100.00
142 Tom Daley	25.00	50.00
143 W.L. Plummer	25.00	50.00
144 Harvey Sutherland	25.00	50.00
145 Frank Tobin	25.00	50.00
146 James Yeargin	25.00	50.00
147 Clyde Barfoot	25.00	50.00
148 Beals Becker	25.00	50.00
149 Jim Blakesley	25.00	50.00
150 Ed Bryan	25.00	50.00
151 Carl Christain	25.00	50.00
152 Charles Eckert	25.00	50.00
153 William Essick	40.00	80.00
154 Neal Finn	25.00	50.00
155 Wes Griffin	25.00	50.00
156 Harry Hannah	25.00	50.00
157 Ed Hemingway	25.00	50.00
158 Willie Ludolph	25.00	50.00
159 Ken Penner	25.00	50.00
160 Gordon Slade	25.00	50.00
161 C.A. Thomas	25.00	50.00
162 Jack Warner	25.00	50.00
163 Rod Whitney	25.00	50.00
164 M.J. Wolfer	25.00	50.00

1926 Zeenuts

An early card of Hall of Famer Earl Averill is in this set. These cards measure approximately 1 3/4" by 3 7/16".

COMPLETE SET (172)	3,300.00	6,600.00
1 Joseph Connolly	25.00	50.00
2 Les Cook	25.00	50.00
3 Fred Coumbe	25.00	50.00
4 John Frederick	40.00	80.00
5 Malcolm Hillis	25.00	50.00
6 George Hollerson	25.00	50.00
7 Hensel Hulvey	25.00	50.00
8 John Kerr	25.00	50.00
9 Roy Leslie	25.00	50.00
10 Howard Lindemore	25.00	50.00
11 Walter McPhee	25.00	50.00
12 Phil Mulcahy	25.00	50.00
13 Frank O'Doul	200.00	400.00
14 Joseph O'Neill	25.00	50.00
15 John Peters	25.00	50.00
16 Augustus Redman	25.00	50.00
17 Leslie Sheehan	25.00	50.00
18 Frank Shellenbach	25.00	50.00
19 Ralph Stroud	25.00	50.00
20 Frank Zoellers	25.00	50.00
21 Frank Brazil	25.00	50.00
22 Charles Glazner	25.00	50.00
23 Earl Hamilton	25.00	50.00
24 Harry Hannah	25.00	50.00
25 Edson Hemingway	25.00	50.00
26 Lester Holmes	25.00	50.00
27 Wallace Hood	25.00	50.00
28 Ray Jacobs	25.00	50.00
29 Arthur Jahn	25.00	50.00
30 Martin Krug	25.00	50.00
31 John Mitchell	25.00	50.00
32 Gustave Sandberg	25.00	50.00
33 Herbert Sanders	25.00	50.00
34 George Staley	25.00	50.00
35 Arnold Statz	50.00	100.00
36 Arthur Weis	25.00	50.00
37 Wayne Wright	25.00	50.00
38 Byron Yarrison	25.00	50.00
39 Eugene Allen	25.00	50.00
40 Isaac Boone	50.00	100.00
41 Edwin Bryan	25.00	50.00
42 Clayton Carson	25.00	50.00
43 Carl Christian	25.00	50.00
44 Albert Cole	25.00	50.00
45 Ike Danning	25.00	50.00
46 Charles Eckert	25.00	50.00
47 Cornelius Finn	25.00	50.00
48 Bob Gillespie	25.00	50.00
49 Wes Griffin	25.00	50.00
50 Ducky Jones	25.00	50.00
51 William Ludolph	25.00	50.00
52 Walter McCredie MG	25.00	50.00
53 James McDowell	25.00	50.00
54 Denny Murphy	25.00	50.00
55 Joseph Oeschger	40.00	80.00
56 Thomas Oliver	40.00	80.00
57 Herman Pillette	25.00	50.00
58 William Rodda	25.00	50.00
59 Paddy Siglin	25.00	50.00
60 Gordon Slade	25.00	50.00
61 Evar Swanson	40.00	80.00
62 C.B. Thompson	25.00	50.00
63 Al Walters	25.00	50.00
64 Robert Whitney	25.00	50.00
65 Del Baker	40.00	80.00
66 Albert Bool	25.00	50.00
67 Ray Brubaker	25.00	50.00
68 Peter Daglia	25.00	50.00
69 Arthur Delaney	25.00	50.00
70 John Fenton	25.00	50.00
71 Jesse Fowler	25.00	50.00
72 Alex Freeman	25.00	50.00
73 Albert Gould	25.00	50.00
74 Antone Governor	25.00	50.00
75 Louis Guisto	25.00	50.00
76 Rex Hickok	25.00	50.00
77 Ivan Howard	25.00	50.00
78 Harry Krause	25.00	50.00
79 Earl Kunz	25.00	50.00
80 Lynford Lary	40.00	80.00
81 Frank McKenry	25.00	50.00
82 Earl McNally	25.00	50.00
83 George Makin	25.00	50.00
84 Lawrence Miller	25.00	50.00
85 Hubert Pruett	40.00	80.00
86 Addison Read	25.00	50.00
87 Jim Reese	125.00	250.00
88 John Stuart	25.00	50.00
89 William Bagwell	25.00	50.00
90 Charles Berry	25.00	50.00
91 Dennis Burns	25.00	50.00
92 John Couch	25.00	50.00
93 Eugene Elsh	25.00	50.00
94 Ernie Johnson	25.00	50.00
95 George Lafayette	25.00	50.00
96 Leo Mangum	25.00	50.00
97 Charles Meeker	25.00	50.00
98 Leonard Metz	25.00	50.00
99 Frederick Ortman	25.00	50.00
100 James Prothro	25.00	50.00
101 Max Rachac	25.00	50.00
102 Ray Rohwer	25.00	50.00
103 Elmer Smith	25.00	50.00
104 Marvin Smith	25.00	50.00
105 Charles Thomas	25.00	50.00
106 Frank Tobin	25.00	50.00
107 Daniel Alley	25.00	50.00
108 Carroll Canfield	25.00	50.00
109 William Canfield	25.00	50.00
110 Bill Cunningham	40.00	80.00
111 Wilbur Davis	25.00	50.00
112 Ray French	25.00	50.00
113 Dutch Hoffman	25.00	50.00
114 William Hughes	25.00	50.00
115 Rudolph Kallio	25.00	50.00
116 Raymond Keating	25.00	50.00
117 J.W. Knight	25.00	50.00
118 Arthur Koehler	25.00	50.00
119 Merlin Kopp	25.00	50.00
120 J.R. McLoughlin	25.00	50.00
121 Elwood Martin	25.00	50.00
122 John Monroe	25.00	50.00
123 Frank Osborn	25.00	50.00
124 Fred Pfahler	25.00	50.00
125 John Ryan	25.00	50.00
126 Elmer Shea	25.00	50.00
127 Mervin Shea	40.00	80.00
128 Bill Sweeney	25.00	50.00
129 Louri Vinci	25.00	50.00
130 Sam Agnew	25.00	50.00
131 Earl Averill	375.00	750.00
132 Francis Brower	25.00	50.00
133 James Crockett	25.00	50.00
134 Herbert Ellison	25.00	50.00
135 Raymond Flashkamper	25.00	50.00
136 Robert Geary	25.00	50.00
137 Martin Griffin	25.00	50.00
138 Sydney Hansen	25.00	50.00
139 Timothy Hendryx	25.00	50.00
140 Robert Hurst	25.00	50.00
141 James Jolly	25.00	50.00
142 Dick Kerr	50.00	100.00
143 Peter Kilduff	25.00	50.00
144 Bert Lang	25.00	50.00
145 Oliver Mitchell	25.00	50.00
146 Marvin Moudy	25.00	50.00

147 Edward Mulligan	25.00	50.00
148 Norbert Paynter	25.00	50.00
149 Edwin Rathjen	25.00	50.00
150 August Suhr	40.00	80.00
151 John Tadevich	25.00	50.00
152 Eugene Valla	25.00	50.00
153 Andrew Vargas	25.00	50.00
154 Lloyd Waner	375.00	750.00
155 Guy Williams	25.00	50.00
156 Archie Yelle	25.00	50.00
157 John Zaeffel	25.00	50.00
158 Ted Baldwin	25.00	50.00
159 Clifford Boyd	25.00	50.00
160 Cliff Brady	25.00	50.00
161 George Cutshaw	30.00	60.00
162 Ross Eldred	25.00	50.00
163 Jim Elliott	25.00	50.00
164 Floyd Ellsworth	25.00	50.00
165 Bob Hasty	25.00	50.00
166 Fuzzy Hufft	25.00	50.00
167 Joseph Jenkins	25.00	50.00
168 Wade Killifer	25.00	50.00
169 William Lane	25.00	50.00
170 William Plummer	25.00	50.00
171 C.A. Ramsey	25.00	50.00
172 Jack Sherlock	25.00	50.00

1927 Zeenuts

These cards measure approximately 1 3/4" by 3 3/8".

COMPLETE SET (144)	3,000.00	6,000.00
1 Les Cook	25.00	50.00
2 John Frederick	30.00	60.00
3 Curtis Fullerton	25.00	50.00
4 Charles Gooch	25.00	50.00
5 Rich McCabe	25.00	50.00
6 D.J. Murphy	25.00	50.00
7 Les Sheehan	25.00	50.00
8 James Tierney	25.00	50.00
9 Oscar Vitt	40.00	80.00
10 Dick Cox	25.00	50.00
11 Bruce Cunningham	25.00	50.00
12 Harry Hannah	25.00	50.00
13 Ed Hemingway	25.00	50.00
14 Wally Hood	25.00	50.00
15 Art Jahn	25.00	50.00
16 Martin Krug	25.00	50.00
17 Gustave Sandberg	25.00	50.00
18 Herbert Sanders	25.00	50.00
19 Arthur Weis	25.00	50.00
20 Wayne Wright	25.00	50.00
21 Eddie Bryan	25.00	50.00
22 Carl Christian	25.00	50.00
23 Nick Dumovitch	25.00	50.00
24 Charles Eckert	25.00	50.00
25 Cornelius Finn	25.00	50.00
26 Bob Gillespie	25.00	50.00
27 Harry Hooper	375.00	750.00
28 Ducky Jones	25.00	50.00
29 William Leard	25.00	50.00
30 Willie Ludolph	25.00	50.00
31 Osborne McDaniel	25.00	50.00
32 Tom Oliver	40.00	80.00
33 S.R. Parker bat	25.00	50.00
34 S.R. Parker throw	25.00	50.00
35 Herman Pillette	40.00	80.00
36 William Rodda	25.00	50.00
37 Edward Rose	25.00	50.00
38 Gordon Slade	25.00	50.00
39 Evar Swanson	40.00	80.00
40 Phil Weinert	25.00	50.00
41 Rodney Whitney	25.00	50.00
42 Russ Arlett	40.00	80.00
43 Delmer Baker	25.00	50.00
44 George Boehler	25.00	50.00
45 Albert Bool	25.00	50.00
46 Joseph Bratcher	25.00	50.00
47 Ray Brubaker	25.00	50.00
48 James Caveney	25.00	50.00
49 Wilbur Cooper	40.00	80.00
50 Pete Daglia	25.00	50.00
51 Leo Dickerman	25.00	50.00
52 John Fenton	25.00	50.00
53 Albert Gould	25.00	50.00
54 Antone Governor	25.00	50.00
55 Louis Guisto	25.00	50.00
56 Robert Hasty	25.00	50.00
57 Harry Krause	25.00	50.00
58 Lynford Lary	40.00	80.00
59 George Makin	25.00	50.00
60 Addison Read	25.00	50.00
61 Jim Reese	125.00	250.00
62A Shinners '27	25.00	50.00
62B Shinners 1927	25.00	50.00
63 Herman Sparks	25.00	50.00
64 Eugene Valla	25.00	50.00
65 William Bagwell	25.00	50.00
66 Stanwood Baumgartner	25.00	50.00
67 Bill Cissell	40.00	80.00
68 Bill Fischer	25.00	50.00
69 William Hughes	25.00	50.00
70 Ernie Johnson	25.00	50.00
71 Walter Kinney	25.00	50.00
72 Ray Lingrel	25.00	50.00
73 Al McCurdy	25.00	50.00
74 Leonard Metz	25.00	50.00
75 Parry O'Brien	25.00	50.00
76 Arthur Parker	25.00	50.00
77 Charles Ponder	25.00	50.00
78 James Prothro	30.00	60.00
79 Elmer Smith	25.00	50.00
80 Joe Storti	25.00	50.00
81 Lindo Storti	25.00	50.00
82 Paul Strand	25.00	50.00
83 Louis Wendell	25.00	50.00
84 Archie Yelle	25.00	50.00
85 Leonard Backer	25.00	50.00
86 Roy Brown	25.00	50.00
87 Claude Cooper	25.00	50.00
88 Ray French	25.00	50.00
89 Clarence Hoffman	25.00	50.00
90 Rudolph Kallio	25.00	50.00
91 Raymond Keating	25.00	50.00
92 David Keefe	25.00	50.00
93 J.W. Knight	25.00	50.00
94 Arthur Koehler	25.00	50.00
95 Merlin Kopp	25.00	50.00
96 Francis McGee	25.00	50.00
97 James McLaughlin	25.00	50.00
98 John Monroe	25.00	50.00
99 Frank Osborn	25.00	50.00
100 Max Rachac	25.00	50.00
101 Ray Rohwer	25.00	50.00
102 John Ryan MG	25.00	50.00
103 Henry Severeid	25.00	50.00
104 Elmer Shea	25.00	50.00
105 John Singleton	25.00	50.00
106 Peter Sunseri	25.00	50.00
107 Sam Agnew	25.00	50.00
108 Earl Averill	375.00	750.00
109 Loris Baker	25.00	50.00
110 Herbert Ellison	25.00	50.00
111 Robert Geary	25.00	50.00
112 Roy Johnson	25.00	50.00
113 James Jolly	25.00	50.00
114 Earl Kunz	25.00	50.00
115 Orville McMurtry	25.00	50.00
116 John Mails	25.00	50.00
117 Herb May	25.00	50.00
118 Oliver Mitchell	25.00	50.00
119 Marvin Moudy	25.00	50.00
120 Edward Mulligan	25.00	50.00
121 Frank O'Doul	200.00	400.00
122 John Sheehan	25.00	50.00
123 Al Stokes	25.00	50.00
124 August Suhr	40.00	80.00
125 Andrew Vargas	25.00	50.00
126 Nick Williams	25.00	50.00
127 Guy Williams	25.00	50.00
128 Burquist Woodson	25.00	50.00
129 Pellham Ballenger	25.00	50.00
130 Carson Bigbee	30.00	60.00
131 Charles Borreani	25.00	50.00
132 Clifford Brady	25.00	50.00
133 Herbert Brett	25.00	50.00
134 Martin Callaghan	25.00	50.00
135 Ross Eldred	25.00	50.00
136 James Hudgens	25.00	50.00
137 Irvin Hufft	25.00	50.00
138 Wade Killifer	25.00	50.00
139 Walter Kimmick	25.00	50.00
140 Sid Martin	25.00	50.00
141 John Miljus	40.00	80.00
142 Wilber Peters	25.00	50.00
143 C.A. Ramsey	25.00	50.00
144 Jack Sherlock	25.00	50.00

1928 Exhibits PCL

Exhibit card collectors speculate that this 32-card set, produced in 1928, was distributed regionally, in California only, in conjunction with the Exhibit Company's regular series of major league players. The cards are blue in color (as are the major league cards) and contain pictures of ball players from the six California teams of the PCL. There are no cards known for Portland and Seattle (and given that 32 cards is the exact length of a one-half sheet printing, none can be expected to appear). The cards have plain backs and carry a divided legend (two lines on each side) on the front. Several names are misspelled, several more are wrongly assigned ("Carl" instead of "Walter" Berger), and the Hollywood team name should read "Sheiks". Several of the cards are oriented horizontally (HOR). Each card measures 3 3/8" by 5 3/8". The catalog designation for this set is W465.

COMPLETE SET (32)	2,500.00	5,000.00
1 Buzz Arlett	200.00	400.00
2 Earl Averill	300.00	600.00
3 Carl Berger Walter, sic	200.00	400.00
4 Ping Bodie	200.00	400.00
5 Carl Dittmar HOR	150.00	300.00
6 Jack Penton	150.00	300.00
7 Neal Mickey Finn Cornelius, sic	200.00	400.00
8 Tony Governor	150.00	300.00
9 Truck Hannah HOR	200.00	400.00
10 Mickey Heath HOR	150.00	300.00
11 Wally Hood	150.00	300.00
12 Fuzzy Hufft	150.00	300.00
13 Snead Jolly (Smead Jolley, sic)	200.00	400.00
14 Ducky Jones	150.00	300.00
15 Rudy Kallio	150.00	300.00
16 Johnny Kerr HOR	150.00	300.00
17 Harry Krause	150.00	300.00
18 Lynford H. Larry/(sic, Lary)	200.00	400.00
19 Dudley Lee	150.00	300.00
20 Walter Duster Mails	200.00	400.00
21 Jimmy Reese	250.00	500.00
22 Dusty Rhodes	150.00	300.00
23 Hal Rhyne	150.00	300.00
24 Hank Severied Severeid, sic	150.00	300.00
25 Earl Sheely	200.00	400.00
26 Frank Shellenback	200.00	400.00
27 Gordon Slade	150.00	300.00
28 Hollis Thurston	200.00	400.00
29 Babe Twombly	150.00	300.00
30 Earl Tex Weathersby	150.00	300.00
31 Ray French	150.00	300.00
32 Ray Keating	150.00	300.00

1928 Zeenuts

An early card of Ernie Lombardi is in this set. These cards measure approximately 1 3/4" by 3 3/8".

COMPLETE SET (168)	3,200.00	6,400.00
1 Samuel Agnew	25.00	50.00
2 John Bassler	40.00	80.00
3 Les Cook	25.00	50.00
4 Leo Fitterer	25.00	50.00
5 Curtis Fullerton	25.00	50.00
6 Charles Gooch	25.00	50.00
7 Mickey Heath	25.00	50.00
8 James Hulvey	25.00	50.00
9 Arthur Jacobs	25.00	50.00
10 John Kerr	25.00	50.00
11 Walter Kinney	25.00	50.00
12 Dudley Lee	25.00	50.00
13 Rich McCabe	25.00	50.00
14 Pat McNulty	25.00	50.00
15 Philip Mulcahy	25.00	50.00
16 Bill Murphy	25.00	50.00
17 Gordon Rhodes	25.00	50.00
18 Bob Roth	25.00	50.00
19 Frank Shellenback	40.00	80.00
20 James Sweeney	25.00	50.00
21 Clarence Twombly	25.00	50.00
22 Oscar Vitt MG	40.00	80.00
23 Julian Wera	25.00	50.00
24 Clyde Barfoot	25.00	50.00
25 Wally Berger	50.00	100.00
26 Carson Bigbee	30.00	60.00
27 Howard Burkett	25.00	50.00
28 Bruce Cunningham	25.00	50.00
29 Carl Dittmar	25.00	50.00
30 Glen Gabler	25.00	50.00
31 James Hannah	25.00	50.00
32 Wally Hood	25.00	50.00
33 Ducky Jones (bat)	25.00	50.00
34 Ducky Jones (throw)	25.00	50.00
35 Martin Krug MG	25.00	50.00
36 Bob Osborne	25.00	50.00
37 Wilbert Peters	25.00	50.00
38 Norman Plitt	25.00	50.00
39 Gustave Sandberg	25.00	50.00
40 Edward Schulmerich	25.00	50.00
41 Alfred Smith	25.00	50.00
42 George Staley	25.00	50.00
43 Earl Weathersby	25.00	50.00
44 Earl Baldwin	25.00	50.00
45 William Brenzel	25.00	50.00
46 Ed Bryan	25.00	50.00
47 Paul Downs	25.00	50.00
48 Charles Eckert	25.00	50.00
49 Cornelius Finn	40.00	80.00
50 Eugene Gomes	25.00	50.00
51 Carl Holling	25.00	50.00
52 William Hughes	25.00	50.00
53 Wade Killifer	25.00	50.00
54 Osborne McDaniel	25.00	50.00
55 Louis Martin	25.00	50.00
56 Merton Nelson	25.00	50.00
57 Herman Pillette	40.00	80.00
58 Bill Rodda	25.00	50.00
59 Edward Rose	25.00	50.00
60 Gordon Slade	25.00	50.00
61 Ernest Swanson	40.00	80.00
62 Arthur Weiss	25.00	50.00
63 Rodney Whitney	25.00	50.00
64 Del Baker	40.00	80.00
65 George Boehler	25.00	50.00
66 Albert Bool	25.00	50.00
67 Joseph Bratcher	25.00	50.00
68 Ray Brubaker	25.00	50.00
69 James Caveney	25.00	50.00
70 Wilburn Cooper	40.00	80.00
71 Howard Craghead	25.00	50.00
72 Peter Daglia	25.00	50.00
73 Monroe Dean	25.00	50.00
74 Cecil Duff	25.00	50.00
75 John Fenton	25.00	50.00
76 Foy Frazier	25.00	50.00
77 Al Gould	25.00	50.00
78 Antone Governor	25.00	50.00
79 Louis Guisto	25.00	50.00
80 Robert Hasty	25.00	50.00
81 Ivan Howard MG	25.00	50.00
82 Harry Krause	25.00	50.00
83 Lynford Lary	40.00	80.00
84 Ernie Lombardi	375.00	750.00
85 Emil Muesel	40.00	80.00
86 Addison Read	25.00	50.00
87 Jim Reese	125.00	250.00
88 Carson Bigbee	25.00	50.00
89 Isaac Boone	50.00	100.00
90 Ike Davis	25.00	50.00
91 Larry French	50.00	100.00
92 Ernie Johnson MG	25.00	50.00
93 James Keesey	25.00	50.00
94 W. E. Knothe	25.00	50.00
95 DeWitt LeBourveau	25.00	50.00
96 Joe Mellana	25.00	50.00
97 Charles Ponder	25.00	50.00
98 Tony Rego	40.00	80.00
99 Francis Sigafoos	25.00	50.00
100 John Warhop	25.00	50.00
101 Charles Wetzel	25.00	50.00
102 Carroll Yerkes	25.00	50.00
103 Leonard Backer	25.00	50.00
104 Wallace Canfield	25.00	50.00
105 Tom Flynn	25.00	50.00
106 Ray French	25.00	50.00
107 Andrew Harris	25.00	50.00
108 Dutch Hoffman	25.00	50.00
109 Rudolph Kallio	25.00	50.00
110 Ray Keating	25.00	50.00
111 David Keefe	25.00	50.00
112 Arthur Koehler	25.00	50.00
113 Merlin Kopp	25.00	50.00
114 Jim McLaughlin	25.00	50.00
115 John Monroe	25.00	50.00
116 Frank Osborn	25.00	50.00
117 Max Rachac	25.00	50.00
118 Ray Rohwer	25.00	50.00
119 John Ryan MG	25.00	50.00
120 Henry Severeid	25.00	50.00
121 Elmer Shea	25.00	50.00
122 Earl Sheely	25.00	50.00
123 John Singleton	25.00	50.00
124 Louri Vinci	25.00	50.00
125 Earl Averill	375.00	750.00
126 Frank Bodie	50.00	100.00
127 Adolph Camilli	50.00	100.00
128 Sid Cohen	25.00	50.00
129 Frank Crosetti	50.00	100.00
130 Jerry Donovan	25.00	50.00
131 Sydney Hansen	25.00	50.00
132 Roy Johnson	25.00	50.00
133 Smead Jolley	50.00	100.00
134 Francis McCrea	25.00	50.00
135 John Mails	25.00	50.00
136 William May	25.00	50.00
137 Solly Mishkin	25.00	50.00
138 Oliver Mitchell	25.00	50.00
139 Marvin Moudy	25.00	50.00
140 Edward Mulligan	25.00	50.00
141 Ralph Pinelli	50.00	100.00
142 Robert Reed	25.00	50.00
143 Hal Rhyne	25.00	50.00
144 Joe Sprinz	25.00	50.00
145 August Suhr	40.00	80.00
146 Andy Vargas	25.00	50.00
147 Frank Welch	25.00	50.00
148 Nick Williams MG	25.00	50.00
149 Charles Borreani	25.00	50.00
150 Ross Eldred	25.00	50.00
151 Fred Ellsworth	25.00	50.00
152 Kyle Graham	25.00	50.00
153 Kyle Graham	25.00	50.00
154 Andy House	25.00	50.00
155 James Hudgens	25.00	50.00
156 Irving Hufft	25.00	50.00
157 E. R. Knight	25.00	50.00
158 Elwood Martin	25.00	50.00
159 Jim Middleton	25.00	50.00
160 Fred Muller	25.00	50.00
161 Clyde Nance	25.00	50.00
162 Roy Parker	25.00	50.00
163 William Ruble	25.00	50.00
164 Jack Sherlock	25.00	50.00
165 Peter Sunseri	25.00	50.00
166 Arthur Teachout	25.00	50.00
167 Gomer Wilson	25.00	50.00
168 Merle Wolfer	25.00	50.00

1928-32 La Presse

These color retouched photos of Canadian ballplayers of the late '20s and early '30s were published in La Presse, a French-language newspaper of Montreal. The pictures measure approximately 10" by 16"; the player's name, followed by career highlights, appear within a rectangle below. The drawings are unnumbered and checklisted below in chronological order of publication. This checklist may be incomplete and any further additions are welcomed.

COMPLETE SET	1,000.00	2,000.00
1 Lachine Club 9-Jun-28	25.00	50.00
2 Buckalew Dunagan Smith Radwan Fowler Gulley/	25.00	50.00
3 Seymour Bailey 23-Jun-28	25.00	50.00
4 Wilson Fewster 30-Jun-28	25.00	50.00
5 Tom Daly 14-Jul-28	25.00	50.00
6 Red Holt 11-Aug-28	25.00	50.00

Card	Low	High
7 Babe Ruth	125.00	250.00
13-Oct-28		
8 Johnny Prud'homme	25.00	50.00
3-Nov-28		
9 Walter Gautreau	25.00	50.00
13-Apr-29		
10 Herb Thormahlen	25.00	50.00
27-Apr-29		
11 Elon Hogsett	30.00	60.00
13-Jul-29		
12 Lefty Grove	75.00	150.00
19-Oct-29		
13 Philadelphia A's Montage	50.00	100.00
16-Nov-29		
14 Art Smith/Herb Thormalen/Mart Griffin/John Leon Pomorski/(May 31& 1930	25.00	50.00
15 Del Bissonette	30.00	60.00
28-Jun-30		
16 Jimmy Ripple	25.00	50.00
4-Jul-30		
17 Joe Hauser	50.00	100.00
12-Jul-30		
18 Sol Mishkin	25.00	50.00
18-Jul-30		
19 Gowell Classet	25.00	50.00
13-Sep-30		
20 Chuck Klein	50.00	100.00
30-May-31		
21 Jocko Conlan	50.00	100.00
6-Jun-31		
22 Walter Brown	25.00	50.00
15-Aug-31		
23 Pepper Martin	50.00	100.00
21-Nov-31		
24 Johnny Grabowski	25.00	50.00
28-May-32		
25 John Clancy	25.00	50.00
25-Jun-32		
26 Buck Walters	50.00	100.00
2-Jul-32		
27 Bill McAfee	25.00	50.00
9-Jul-32		
28 George Puccinelli	25.00	50.00
16-Jul-32		
29 Buck Crouse	25.00	50.00
6-Aug-32		
30 Olie Carnegie	25.00	50.00
13-Aug-32		
31 Leo Mangum	25.00	50.00
20-Aug-32		
32 Roy Parmalee	30.00	60.00
19-Oct-32		

1929 Zeenuts

Early cards of Ernie Nevers (Football Hall of Famer) and Lefty Gomez are in this set. These cards measure approximately 1 3/4" by 3 1/2".

Card	Low	High
COMPLETE SET (168)	3,400.00	6,800.00
1 William Albert	25.00	50.00
2 John Bassler	40.00	80.00
3 Cleo Carlyle	25.00	50.00
4 Minor Heath	25.00	50.00
5 Martin Krug MG	25.00	50.00
6 Dudley Lee	25.00	50.00
7 Rich McCabe	25.00	50.00
8 Mike Maloney	25.00	50.00
9 Leo Ostenberg	25.00	50.00
10 Wallace Ritter	25.00	50.00
11 Russ Rollings	25.00	50.00
12 William Rumler	25.00	50.00
13 Clyde Barfoot	25.00	50.00
14 Wally Berger	50.00	100.00
15 Howard Burkett	25.00	50.00
16 John Butler	25.00	50.00
17 Harry Childs	25.00	50.00
18 Carl Dittmar	25.00	50.00
19 Glen Gabler	25.00	50.00
20 James Hannah MG	25.00	50.00
21 Carl Holling	25.00	50.00
22 Ray Jacobs	25.00	50.00
23 Ducky Jones	25.00	50.00
24 Martin Krug MG	25.00	50.00
25 Russ Miller	25.00	50.00
26 W.A. Peters	25.00	50.00
27 Norman Plitt	25.00	50.00
28 Vaughn Roberts	25.00	50.00
29 Gustave Sandberg	25.00	50.00
30 Edward Schulmerich	25.00	50.00
31 Arnold Statz	50.00	100.00
32 Martin Tierney	25.00	50.00
33 Charles Tolson	25.00	50.00
34 August Walsh	25.00	50.00
35 Dallas Warren	25.00	50.00
36 Earl Webb	40.00	80.00
37 Earl Baldwin	25.00	50.00
38 Ike Boone	50.00	100.00
39 William Brenzel	25.00	50.00
40 Walter Christensen	25.00	50.00
41 Bert Cole	25.00	50.00
42 Neal Finn	25.00	50.00
43 Fred Hoffman	25.00	50.00
44 W. W. Hubbell	25.00	50.00
45 Irving Hufft	25.00	50.00
46 John Keane	25.00	50.00
47 Wade Killifer MG	25.00	50.00
48 John Knott	25.00	50.00
49 Harry Krause	25.00	50.00
50 Herbert McQuaid	25.00	50.00
51 Ed Mulligan	25.00	50.00
52 Clyde Nance	25.00	50.00
53 M. A. Nelson	25.00	50.00
54 Ernie Nevers	375.00	750.00
55 Herman Pillette	40.00	80.00
56 William Rodda	25.00	50.00
57 Pete Scott	25.00	50.00
58 Jack Sherlock	25.00	50.00
59 Gordon Slade	25.00	50.00
60 Leroy Anton	25.00	50.00
61 George Boehler	25.00	50.00
62 Mandy Brooks	25.00	50.00
63 Ray Brubaker	25.00	50.00
64 Joe Burns	25.00	50.00
65 Roy Carlyle	25.00	50.00
66 Howard Craghead	25.00	50.00
67 Peter Daglia	25.00	50.00
68 Monroe Dean	25.00	50.00
69 Martin Dumovich	25.00	50.00
70 John Fenton	25.00	50.00
71 Foy Frazier	25.00	50.00
72 Antone Governor	25.00	50.00
73 Ivan Howard MG	25.00	50.00
74 Bob Hurst	25.00	50.00
75 Charles Jeffcoat	25.00	50.00
76 Charles Kasich	25.00	50.00
77 Ernie Lombardi	375.00	750.00
78 Lou McEvoy	25.00	50.00
79 Gus McIsaacs	25.00	50.00
80 Addison Read	25.00	50.00
81 James Reese	125.00	250.00
82 John Vergez	25.00	50.00
83 Charles Bates	25.00	50.00
84 Leslie Bush	25.00	50.00
85 Joseph Cascarella	25.00	50.00
86 Guy Cooper	25.00	50.00
87 Jim Cronin	25.00	50.00
88 Ernest Hepting	25.00	50.00
89 Malcolm Hillis	25.00	50.00
90 Arthur Jahn	25.00	50.00
91 James Keesey	25.00	50.00
92 Jack Knight	25.00	50.00
93 W. E. Knothe	25.00	50.00
94 Leroy Mahaffey	40.00	80.00
95 Frederick Ortman	25.00	50.00
96 Tony Rego	50.00	100.00
97 Bill Rodgers MG	25.00	50.00
98 Robert Shanklin	25.00	50.00
99 Gale Staley	25.00	50.00
100 Edwin Tomlin	25.00	50.00
101 Raymond Volkman	25.00	50.00
102 George Weustling	25.00	50.00
103 Leonard Backer	25.00	50.00
104 Ed Bryan	25.00	50.00
105 William Burke	25.00	50.00
106 Adolph Camilli	50.00	100.00
107 J. O. Crandall	25.00	50.00
108 Tom Flynn	25.00	50.00
109 Antonio Freitas	30.00	60.00
110 Ray French	25.00	50.00
111 Albert Gould	25.00	50.00
112 Andrew Harris	25.00	50.00
113 Raymond Keating	25.00	50.00
114 Art Koehler	25.00	50.00
115 Anthony Krasovich	25.00	50.00
116 Earl Kunz	25.00	50.00
117 John Monroe	25.00	50.00
118 Frank Osborne	25.00	50.00
119 Max Rachac	25.00	50.00
120 Ray Rohwer	25.00	50.00
121 John Ryan	25.00	50.00
122 Henry Severeid	25.00	50.00
123 Louri Vinci	25.00	50.00
124 Loris Baker	25.00	50.00
125 James Caveney	25.00	50.00
126 John Couch	25.00	50.00
127 Frank Crosetti	50.00	100.00
128 Curt Davis	40.00	80.00
129 Jerry Donovan	25.00	50.00
130 Val Glynn	25.00	50.00
131 Lefty Gomez	375.00	750.00
132 Harvey Hand	25.00	50.00
133 Elmer Jacobs	25.00	50.00
134 Smead Jolley	30.00	60.00
135 Gordon Jones	25.00	50.00
136 Elton Langford	25.00	50.00
137 John Mails	25.00	50.00
138 Henry Oana	100.00	200.00
139 Ralph Pinelli	50.00	100.00
140 Fred Polvogt	25.00	50.00
141 Bob Reed	25.00	50.00
142 Stanley Schino	25.00	50.00
143 Walton Schmidt	25.00	50.00
144 August Suhr	40.00	80.00
145 Hollis Thurston	40.00	80.00
146 Nick Williams MG	25.00	50.00
147 Ab Wingo	25.00	50.00
148 Luis Almada	25.00	50.00
149 Andy Anderson	25.00	50.00
150 Dave Barbee	25.00	50.00
151 Charles Borreani	25.00	50.00
152 Earl Collard	25.00	50.00
153 Frank Cox	25.00	50.00
154 Oscar Eckhardt	50.00	100.00
155 Floyd Ellsworth	25.00	50.00
156 Elbert Fisch	25.00	50.00
157 Kyle Graham	25.00	50.00
158 Kyle Heatherly	25.00	50.00
159 Wally Hood	25.00	50.00
160 Andy House	25.00	50.00
161 Ernie Johnson MG	25.00	50.00
162 Rudolph Kallio	25.00	50.00
163 Osborne McDaniel	25.00	50.00
164 Fred Muller	25.00	50.00
165 Walter Olney	25.00	50.00
166 Fred Pipgras	25.00	50.00
167 William Steinecke	25.00	50.00
168 Harry Taylor	25.00	50.00

1930 Zeenuts

These cards measure approximately 1 13/16" by 3 1/2". Most of these cards have an expiration date of April 1, 1931; however, some have no expiration date featured on the coupons.

Card	Low	High
COMPLETE SET (186)	3,400.00	6,800.00
1 John Bassler	40.00	80.00
2 Otis Brannon	25.00	50.00
3 Howard Burkett	25.00	50.00
4 Cleo Carlyle	25.00	50.00
5 Michael Gazella	40.00	80.00
6 Ernest Kelly	25.00	50.00
7 Minor Heath	25.00	50.00
8 George Hollerson	25.00	50.00
9 Augustus Johns	25.00	50.00
10 Dudley Lee	25.00	50.00
11 Edwin Leishman	25.00	50.00
12 Mike Maloney	25.00	50.00
13 Vance Page	25.00	50.00
14 Walter Rehg	25.00	50.00
15 William Rumler	25.00	50.00
16 Henry Severeid	25.00	50.00
17 Jim Turner	50.00	100.00
18 Oscar Vitt MG	40.00	80.00
19 Frank Wetzel	25.00	50.00
20 Charles Wetzell	25.00	50.00
21 Edward Baecht	25.00	50.00
22 Noble Ballou	25.00	50.00
23 Clyde Barfoot	25.00	50.00
24 John Butler	25.00	50.00
25 Harry Childs	25.00	50.00
26 Carl Dittmar	25.00	50.00
27 Glen Gabler	25.00	50.00
28 Fred Haney	40.00	80.00
29 Roy Hannah	25.00	50.00
30 George Harper	25.00	50.00
31 Carl Holling	25.00	50.00
32 Berlyn Horn	25.00	50.00
33 Ray Jacobs	25.00	50.00
34 John Lelivelt	25.00	50.00
35 Johnny Moore	25.00	50.00
36 Art Parker	25.00	50.00
37 Wilbert Peters	25.00	50.00
38 Vaughn Roberts	25.00	50.00
39 Francis Sigafoos	25.00	50.00
40 Arnold Statz	50.00	100.00
41 August Walsh	25.00	50.00
42 Dallas Warren	25.00	50.00
43 Earl Webb	25.00	50.00
44 Earl Baldwin	25.00	50.00
45 Ike Boone	40.00	80.00
46 William Brenzel	25.00	50.00
47 George Burns	40.00	80.00
48 George Caster	25.00	50.00
49 Walter Christensen	25.00	50.00
50 Edwin Church	25.00	50.00
51 Bert Cole	25.00	50.00
52 Joe Coscarart	25.00	50.00
53 Ken Douglas	25.00	50.00
54 Fred Hoffman	25.00	50.00
55 Irving Hufft	25.00	50.00
56 Ernest Kelly	25.00	50.00
57 Wade Killifer MG	25.00	50.00
58 Charles Lieber	25.00	50.00
59 Herb McQuaide	25.00	50.00
60 John Monroe	25.00	50.00
61 Ed Mulligan	25.00	50.00
62 Merton Nelson	25.00	50.00
63 Ernie Nevers	375.00	750.00
64 Herman Pillette	25.00	50.00
65 Edward Pillette	25.00	50.00
66 William Rodda	25.00	50.00
67 Harry Rosenberg	50.00	100.00
68 Robert Shanklin	25.00	50.00
69 Charles Wallgren	25.00	50.00
70 Paul Andrews	25.00	50.00
71 Leroy Anton	25.00	50.00
72 Russ Arlett	50.00	100.00
73 Ray Brubaker	25.00	50.00
74 Harold Chamberlain	25.00	50.00
75 Howard Craghead	25.00	50.00
76 Pete Daglia	25.00	50.00
77 Monroe Dean	25.00	50.00
78 Bernard DeViveiros	25.00	50.00
79 Martin Dumovich	25.00	50.00
80 Jim Edwards	25.00	50.00
81 Antone Governor	25.00	50.00
82 Francis Griffin	25.00	50.00
83 Bob Hurst	25.00	50.00
84 Jack Jacobs	25.00	50.00
85 Charles Jeffcoat	25.00	50.00
86 Roy Joiner	25.00	50.00
87 Charles Kasich	25.00	50.00
88 Ernie Lombardi	375.00	750.00
89 Louis Martin	25.00	50.00
90 Joe Mellana	25.00	50.00
91 Monte Pearson	40.00	80.00
92 Walter Porter	25.00	50.00
93 Addison Read	25.00	50.00
94 Peter Ricci	25.00	50.00
95 Stanley Schino	25.00	50.00
96 Robert Stevenson	25.00	50.00
97 Bernard Uhalt	25.00	50.00
98 John Vergez	25.00	50.00
99 Carl Zamlach MG	25.00	50.00
100 Charles Bates	25.00	50.00
101 John Beck	25.00	50.00
102 Joe Bowman	25.00	50.00
103 Charles Chatham	25.00	50.00
104 Jim Cronin	25.00	50.00
105 Wally French	25.00	50.00
106 Malcolm Hillis	25.00	50.00
107 Bob Johnson	40.00	80.00
108 Frank Mulana	25.00	50.00
109 Ray Odell	25.00	50.00
110 Joseph Palmisano	25.00	50.00
111 Bill Pasedel	40.00	80.00
112 Joseph Trembly	25.00	50.00
113 Charles Woodall	25.00	50.00
114 Leonard Backer	25.00	50.00
115 Harry Brown	25.00	50.00
116 Ed Bryan	25.00	50.00
117 Dolph Camilli	50.00	100.00
118 Clem Coyle	25.00	50.00
119 Tom Flynn	25.00	50.00
120 Antonio Freitas	40.00	80.00
121 Ray French	25.00	50.00
122 Al Gould	25.00	50.00
123 Myril Hoag	40.00	80.00
124 Wally Hood	25.00	50.00
125 Ray Keating	25.00	50.00
126 Art Koehler	25.00	50.00
127 Jim McLaughlin	25.00	50.00
128 Frank Osborne	25.00	50.00
129 Ray Rohwer	25.00	50.00
130 John Ryan MG	25.00	50.00
131 Henry Steinbacker	25.00	50.00
132 Fay Thomas	25.00	50.00
133 Louri Vinci	25.00	50.00
134 Aaron Ward	40.00	80.00
135 Elwood Wirts	25.00	50.00
136 Loris Baker	25.00	50.00
137 James Caveney	25.00	50.00
138 Ed Coleman	25.00	50.00
139 Frank Crosetti	50.00	100.00
140 Curt Davis	40.00	80.00
141 Jerry Donovan	25.00	50.00
142 Alex Gaston	25.00	50.00
143 Elmer Jacobs	25.00	50.00
144 Arthur Jahn	25.00	50.00
145 E. R. Knight	25.00	50.00
146 Art McDougal	25.00	50.00
147 John Mails	40.00	80.00
148 John Miljus	40.00	80.00
149 John Miljus	40.00	80.00
150 Al Montgomery	25.00	50.00
151 Adolph Penebskey	25.00	50.00
152 Clyde Perry	25.00	50.00
153 Mel Petterson	25.00	50.00
154 Ralph Pinelli	50.00	100.00
155 George Powles	25.00	50.00
156 Bob Reed	25.00	50.00
157 Earl Sheely	25.00	50.00
158 Ernest Sulik	25.00	50.00
159 Milt Thomas	25.00	50.00
160 Hal Turpin	25.00	50.00
161 Nick Williams MG	25.00	50.00
162 Ab Wingo	25.00	50.00
163 James Zinn	25.00	50.00
164 William Allington	25.00	50.00
165 Luis Almada	25.00	50.00
166 David Barbee	25.00	50.00
167 Earl Brucker	25.00	50.00
168 Pat Collins	25.00	50.00
169 Frank Cox	25.00	50.00
170 Floyd Ellsworth	25.00	50.00
171 Charles Falk	25.00	50.00
172 Gilbert Fisch	25.00	50.00
173 Bob Holland	25.00	50.00
174 Andy House	25.00	50.00
175 W. W. Hubbell	25.00	50.00
176 Ernie Johnson MG	25.00	50.00
177 Rudolph Kallio	25.00	50.00
178 W. E. Knothe	25.00	50.00
179 Earl Kunz	25.00	50.00
180 Frank Lamanski	25.00	50.00
181 Bill Lawrence	25.00	50.00
182 Frederick Muller	25.00	50.00
183 Walter Olney	25.00	50.00
184 Fred Pipgrass	25.00	50.00
185 Harry Taylor	25.00	50.00
186 Gomer Wilson	25.00	50.00

1931 Zeenuts

These cards measure approximately 1 3/4" by 3 1/2".

Card	Low	High
COMPLETE SET (120)	3,000.00	6,000.00
1 David Barbee	20.00	50.00
2 John Bassler	30.00	60.00
3 Cleo Carlyle	20.00	50.00
4 Michael Gazella	30.00	60.00
5 Dudley Lee	20.00	50.00
6 Henry Severeid	20.00	50.00
7 Frank Shellenback	30.00	60.00
8 Jim Turner	40.00	80.00
9 Oscar Vitt	30.00	60.00
10 Charles Wetzel	20.00	50.00
11 Louis Baker	20.00	50.00
12 Vince Barton	20.00	50.00
13 Gilly Campbell	20.00	50.00
14 Eddie Farrell	20.00	50.00
15 Glen Gabler	20.00	50.00
16 Fred Haney	30.00	60.00
17 Roy Hannah	20.00	50.00
18 George Harper	20.00	50.00

19 Leroy Herrmann	20.00	50.00
20 John Lelivelt MG	20.00	50.00
21 Malcolm Moss	20.00	50.00
22 Art Parker	20.00	50.00
23 John Schulte	20.00	50.00
24 Carroll Yerkes	20.00	50.00
25 Fred Berger	20.00	50.00
26 Charles Biggs	20.00	50.00
27 William Brenzel	20.00	50.00
28 George Burns MG	30.00	60.00
29 Bert Cole	20.00	50.00
30 Joe Coscarart	20.00	50.00
31 Fred Hoffman	20.00	50.00
32 Carl Holling	20.00	50.00
33 Irving Hufft	20.00	50.00
34 John Knott	20.00	50.00
35 Charles Lieber	20.00	50.00
36 John Monroe	20.00	50.00
37 Ed Mulligan	20.00	50.00
38 Herman Pillette	20.00	50.00
39 Ted Pillette	20.00	50.00
40 William Sharpe	20.00	50.00
41 Augie Walsh	20.00	50.00
42 Paul Andrews	20.00	50.00
43 Leroy Anton	20.00	50.00
44 Monroe Dean	20.00	50.00
45 Hank DeBerry	30.00	60.00
46 Leonard Dondero	20.00	50.00
47 Bob Hurst	20.00	50.00
48 Fred Ortman	20.00	50.00
49 Harlen Pool	20.00	50.00
50 Ellis Powers	20.00	50.00
51 Addison Read	20.00	50.00
52 Andy Reese	20.00	50.00
53 Peter Ricci	20.00	50.00
54 Stanley Schino	20.00	50.00
55 Frank Tubbs	20.00	50.00
56 Bernard Uhalt	20.00	50.00
57 Charles Wade	20.00	50.00
58 Carl Zamlock	20.00	50.00
59 Spencer Abbott MG	20.00	50.00
60 Fred Berger	20.00	50.00
61 Joe Bowman	20.00	50.00
62 Ed Coleman	20.00	50.00
63 John Fenton	20.00	50.00
64 John Fitzpatrick	20.00	50.00
65 Ira Flagstead	20.00	50.00
66 Sam Hale	20.00	50.00
67 Rudy Kallio	20.00	50.00
68 Ray Keating	20.00	50.00
69 Edward Lipanovic	20.00	50.00
70 Hank McDonald	20.00	50.00
71 Oswald Orwoll	20.00	50.00
72 Bill Posedel	30.00	60.00
73 William Rhiel	20.00	50.00
74 Homer Summa	30.00	60.00
75 John Walters	20.00	50.00
76 Ken Williams	30.00	60.00
77 George Wise	20.00	50.00
78 Charles Woodall	20.00	50.00
79 Leonard Backer	20.00	50.00
80 Ed Bryan	20.00	50.00
81 Dolf Camilli	40.00	80.00
82 Roy Chesterfield	20.00	50.00
83 Frank Demaree	30.00	60.00
84 Tom Flynn	20.00	50.00
85 Tony Freitas	20.00	50.00
86 Ray French	20.00	50.00
87 Curtis Fullerton	20.00	50.00
88 Clarence Hamilton	20.00	50.00
89 W.W. Hubbell	20.00	50.00
90 Art Koehler	20.00	50.00
91 Jim McLaughlin	20.00	50.00
92 Ray Rohwer	20.00	50.00
93 John Ryan MG	20.00	50.00
94 William Simas	20.00	50.00
95 Henry Steinbacker	20.00	50.00
96 Louri Vinci	20.00	50.00
97 Elwood Wirts	20.00	50.00
98 Earl Baldwin	20.00	50.00
99 James Cavaney	20.00	50.00
100 Frank Crosetti	40.00	80.00
101 Curtis Davis	30.00	60.00
102 Art Delaney	20.00	50.00
103 Jerry Donovan	20.00	50.00
104 Ken Douglas	20.00	50.00
105 Foy Frazier	20.00	50.00
106 William Henderson	20.00	50.00
107 Elmer Jacobs	20.00	50.00
108 James Keesey	20.00	50.00
109 Art McDougall	20.00	50.00
110 Adolph Penebskey	20.00	50.00
111 Ralph Pinelli	40.00	80.00
112 Hal Turpin	20.00	50.00
113 Julian Wera	20.00	50.00
114 Nick Williams MG	20.00	50.00
115 Al Wingo	20.00	50.00
116 Jimmy Zinn	20.00	50.00
117 Floyd Ellsworth	20.00	50.00
118 Bob Holland	20.00	50.00
119 Fritz Knothe	20.00	50.00
120 Frank Lamanski	20.00	50.00

1932 Minneapolis Millers Wheaties

These blank backed cards, which measure approximately 5 7/16" by 3 7/16" feature members of the 1932 Minneapolis Millers. The cards feature player photos on the front in either black and white or sepia toned. Many players are not identified so one must tell who the player is from the signature.

COMPLETE SET	1,000.00	2,000.00
1 Dave Bancroft	75.00	150.00
2 Rube Benton	40.00	80.00
3 Donie Bush MG	40.00	80.00
4 Andy Cohen	40.00	80.00
5 Pea Ridge Day	40.00	80.00
6 Ray Fitzgerald	40.00	80.00
7 Fabian Gaffke	40.00	80.00
8 Babe Ganzel	40.00	80.00
9 Wes Griffin	40.00	80.00
10 Spencer Harris	40.00	80.00
11 Joe Hauser	50.00	100.00
12 Phil Hensick	40.00	80.00
13 Dutch Henry Minneapolis	40.00	80.00
14 Dutch Henry Chicago White Sox	40.00	80.00
15 Bunker Hill	40.00	80.00
16 Joe Mowry	40.00	80.00
17 Jess Petty	40.00	80.00
18 Bill Rodda	40.00	80.00
19 Harry Rice	40.00	80.00
20 Paul Richards	60.00	120.00
21 Art Ruble	40.00	80.00
22 Rosy Ryan	40.00	80.00
23 Al Sheehan ANN	40.00	80.00
24 Eddie Sicking	40.00	80.00
25 Ernie Smith	40.00	80.00
26 E.R. Vangilder	40.00	80.00
27 Wally Tauscher	40.00	80.00
28 Hy VanDenburg	40.00	80.00

1932 Zeenuts

These cards measure approximately 1 3/4" by 3 1/2".

COMPLETE SET (120)	3,000.00	6,000.00
1 John Bassler	30.00	60.00
2 Otis Brannon	25.00	50.00
3 Martin Callaghan	25.00	50.00
4 Cleo Carlyle	25.00	50.00
5 Les Cook	25.00	50.00
6 Mike Gazella	30.00	60.00
7 Robert Hipps	25.00	50.00
8 Augustus Johns	25.00	50.00
9 Dudley Lee	25.00	50.00
10 Al McNeely	25.00	50.00
11 John Miljus	30.00	60.00
12 Vance Page	25.00	50.00
13 George Quellich	25.00	50.00
14 Tom Sheehan	25.00	50.00
15 Frank Shellenback	30.00	60.00
16 Jack Sherlock	25.00	50.00
17 Oscar Vitt MG	30.00	60.00
18 Emil Yde	30.00	60.00
19 Loris Baker	25.00	50.00
20 Noble Ballou	25.00	50.00
21 Gilly Campbell	25.00	50.00
22 Carl Dittmar	25.00	50.00
23 Fred Haney	30.00	60.00
24 James Hannah	25.00	50.00
25 Leroy Herrmann	25.00	50.00
26 Malcolm Moss	25.00	50.00
27 Arnold Statz	40.00	80.00
28 Homer Summa	25.00	50.00
29 Charles Briggs	25.00	50.00
30 George Caster	25.00	50.00
31 Bert Cole	25.00	50.00
32 Joe Coscarart	25.00	50.00
33 Babe Dahlgren	40.00	80.00
34 Joe Devine MG	25.00	50.00
35 Dan Hafey	25.00	50.00
36 Fred Hofman	25.00	50.00
37 Lloyd Johnson	25.00	50.00
38 Ernest Kelly	25.00	50.00
39 Charles Lieber	25.00	50.00
40 Jim Mosolf	25.00	50.00
41 Ed Mulligan	25.00	50.00
42 Herman Pillette	30.00	60.00
43 Peter Ricci	25.00	50.00
44 Ben Sankey	25.00	50.00
45 Vince Sherlock	25.00	50.00
46 Angie Walsh	25.00	50.00
47 Jim Welsh	25.00	50.00
48 Paul Zahniser	25.00	50.00
49 Leroy Anton	25.00	50.00
50 George Blackerby	25.00	50.00
51 Ray Brubaker	25.00	50.00
52 Pete Daglia	25.00	50.00
53 Monroe Dean	25.00	50.00
54 Arthur Delaney	25.00	50.00
55 Andy House	25.00	50.00
56 Irving Hufft	25.00	50.00
57 Robert Hurst	25.00	50.00
58 Roy Joiner	25.00	50.00
59 Charles Kasich	25.00	50.00
60 Arthur Koehler	25.00	50.00
61 Emil Mailho	25.00	50.00
62 Louis Martin	25.00	50.00
63 Ralph Pinelli	40.00	80.00
64 Harlin Poole	25.00	50.00
65 Addison Read	25.00	50.00
66 Fay Thomas	25.00	50.00
67 Bernard Uhalt	25.00	50.00
68 Ed Walsh	25.00	50.00
69 Carl Zamloch	25.00	50.00
70 Spencer Abbott MG	25.00	50.00
71 Fred Berger	25.00	50.00
72 John Fitzpatrick	25.00	50.00
73 Bob Johnson	40.00	80.00
74 John Monroe	25.00	50.00
75 Walter Shores	25.00	50.00
76 Ken Williams	30.00	60.00
77 George Wise	25.00	50.00
78 Leonard Backer	25.00	50.00
79 Stan Bordagaray	30.00	60.00
80 Adolph Camilli	40.00	80.00
81 Earl Collard	25.00	50.00
82 Jim Cronin	25.00	50.00
83 Frank Demaree	40.00	80.00
84 Bernard DeViveiros	25.00	50.00
85 Tony Freitas	30.00	60.00
86 Lawrence Gillick	25.00	50.00
87 Frank Osborn	25.00	50.00
88 Manuel Salvo	25.00	50.00
89 William Simas	25.00	50.00
90 Henry Steinbacker	25.00	50.00
91 Louri Vinci	25.00	50.00
92 Elwood Wirts	25.00	50.00
93 Charles Woodall	25.00	50.00
94 John Babich	30.00	60.00
95 James Caveney MG	25.00	50.00
96 Joseph Chamberlain	25.00	50.00
97 Curt Davis	30.00	60.00
98 Jerry Donovan	25.00	50.00
99 Foy Frazier	25.00	50.00
100 Art Garibaldi	25.00	50.00
101 William Henderson	25.00	50.00
102 Art Hunt	25.00	50.00
103 Elmer Jacobs	30.00	60.00
104 Jim Keesey	25.00	50.00
105 Heber Martin	25.00	50.00
106 Henry Oana	75.00	150.00
107 Adolph Penebsky	25.00	50.00
108 Ernie Sulik	25.00	50.00
109 Joe Ward	25.00	50.00
110 Julian Wera	25.00	50.00
111 Claude Willoughby	30.00	60.00
112 Luis Almada	25.00	50.00
113 Frank Cox	25.00	50.00
114 Floyd Ellsworth	25.00	50.00
115 Alex Gaston	30.00	60.00
116 Bob Holland	25.00	50.00
117 Ernie Johnson MG	25.00	50.00
118 Rudolph Kallio	25.00	50.00
119 Fred Muller	25.00	50.00
120 John Walters	25.00	50.00

1933 Minneapolis Millers Wheaties

These cards, which measure approximately 5 3/4" by 4" feature members of the 1933 Millers. The fronts have a player photo with his name and position on the bottom, while the postcard backs feature an advertisment for Wheaties. Since these cards are unnumbered, we have sequenced them in alphabetical order.

COMPLETE SET	4,000.00	8,000.00
1 Dave Bancroft MG	400.00	800.00
2 Rube Benton	200.00	400.00
3 Andy Cohen	200.00	400.00
4 Bob Fothergill	200.00	400.00
5 Babe Ganzel	200.00	400.00
6 Joe Glenn	200.00	400.00
7 Wes Griffin CO	200.00	400.00
8 Jack Hallett	200.00	400.00
9 Jerry Harrington ANN	200.00	400.00
10 Spencer Harris	200.00	400.00
11 Joe Hauser	250.00	500.00
12 Butch Henline	200.00	400.00
13 Walter Hilcher	200.00	400.00
14 Dutch Holland	200.00	400.00
15 Harry Holsclaw	200.00	400.00
16 Wes Kingdon	200.00	400.00
17 George Murray	200.00	400.00
18 Leo Norris	200.00	400.00
19 Jess Petty	200.00	400.00
20 Art Ruble	200.00	400.00
21 Al Sheehan ANN	200.00	400.00
22 Ernie Smith	200.00	400.00
23 Wally Tauscher	200.00	400.00
24 Hy VanDenburg	200.00	400.00

1933 Worch Cigar Minors

This is the companion set to the major league Worch issue. Please see that set for further details.

COMPLETE SET (103)	500.00	1,000.00
1 Buzz Arlett	30.00	60.00
2 Dave Bancroft With background	50.00	100.00
3 Dave Bancroft Without background	50.00	100.00
4 Clyde Beck	25.00	50.00
5 Rube Benton Throwing	25.00	50.00
6 Otto Bluege	25.00	50.00
7 Bob Boken	25.00	50.00
8 Dudley Bramon	25.00	50.00
9 James Brown	25.00	50.00
10 Donie Bush Printed name	30.00	60.00
11 Donie Bush In business suit	30.00	60.00
12 Spurgeon Chandler	50.00	100.00
13 Tiny Chaplin	25.00	50.00
14 Gowell Claset	25.00	50.00
15 Andy Cohen Fielding	30.00	60.00
16 Bob Coleman MG	25.00	50.00
17 Nick Cullop	25.00	50.00
18 Robert Fenner	25.00	50.00
19 Lou Fetter	25.00	50.00
20 Bob Fothergill	40.00	80.00
21 Fabian Gaffke	25.00	50.00
22 Denny Galehouse	25.00	50.00
23 Babe Ganzel Batting with background)	25.00	50.00
24 Babe Ganzel Batting without background)	25.00	50.00
25 Lou Garland	25.00	50.00
26 Johnny Gill	25.00	50.00
27 Joe Glenn	25.00	50.00
28 Berley Grimes	25.00	50.00
29 Pinky Hargrave	25.00	50.00
30 Bryan Harriss	25.00	50.00
31 Spencer Harris Batting	25.00	50.00
32 Joe Hauser Batting	30.00	60.00
33 Joe Hauser Not batting	30.00	60.00
34 Butch Henline	25.00	50.00
35 Phil Hensick Throwing	25.00	50.00
36 Walter Hilcher	25.00	50.00
37 Jess Hill	25.00	50.00
38 Robert Holland	25.00	50.00
39 Harry Holsclaw	25.00	50.00
40 Meredith Hopkins	25.00	50.00
41 Irvine Jeffries	25.00	50.00
41 Spike Hunter	25.00	50.00
42 Monk Joyner	25.00	50.00
43 Ralph Judd	25.00	50.00
44 Ray Kolp	25.00	50.00
45 Eddie Leishman	25.00	50.00
46 Leitz	25.00	50.00
47 Chuck Morrow	25.00	50.00
48 Emmett McCann	25.00	50.00
49 Marty McManus	25.00	50.00
50 Bill McWilliams	25.00	50.00
51 Howard Mills	25.00	50.00
52 Joe Mowry Batting)	25.00	50.00
53 Leslie Munns	25.00	50.00
54 Floyd Newkirk	25.00	50.00
55 Leo Norris	25.00	50.00
56 Ben Paschal	25.00	50.00
57 Bill Perrin	25.00	50.00
58 Jess Petty Throwing, outfield wall visible	25.00	50.00
59 Jess Petty Throwing, clear background	25.00	50.00
60 Ray Radcliff	25.00	50.00
61 Joe Rezotko	25.00	50.00
62 John Rigney	25.00	50.00
63 Lawrence Rosenthal	25.00	50.00
64 Art Ruble Batting with background)	25.00	50.00
65 Art Ruble Batting without background)	25.00	50.00
66 Ivy Shiver	25.00	50.00
67 Ernie Smith Batting with background)	25.00	50.00
68 Ernie Smith Batting without background)	25.00	50.00
69 Ray Starr	25.00	50.00
70 Lee Stine	25.00	50.00
71 Monty Stratton	50.00	100.00
72 Steve Sundra	25.00	50.00
73 Walt Tauscher	25.00	50.00
74 Miles Thomas	25.00	50.00
75 Phil Todt	25.00	50.00
76 Gene Trow	25.00	50.00
77 Russell Vanatta	25.00	50.00
78 Hy VanDenberg Pitching, clear background	25.00	50.00
79 Hy Vandenburg Pitching, wall visible	25.00	50.00
80 Elam Vangilder Pitching	25.00	50.00
81 Jack Warner	25.00	50.00
82 Wolcyn	25.00	50.00
83 A.B. Wright	25.00	50.00
84 Russ Young	25.00	50.00

1933 Zeenuts (Sepia)

These cards measure 1 3/4" by 3 1/2".

COMPLETE SET (48)	1,200.00	2,500.00
1 John Bassler	30.00	60.00
2 Otis Brannan	25.00	50.00
3 Frank Shellenback	30.00	60.00
4 John Sherlock	25.00	50.00
5 Alan Strange	25.00	50.00
6 Oscar Vitt	30.00	60.00
7 William Cronin	25.00	50.00
8 John Lelivelt MG	25.00	50.00
9 Charles Moncrief	25.00	50.00
10 Lester Sweetland	25.00	50.00
11 Charles Wetzel	25.00	50.00
12 Louis Almada	25.00	50.00

Card	Low	High
13 Albert Cole	25.00	50.00
14 Ellsworth Dahlgren	40.00	80.00
15 Fred Hofmann	25.00	50.00
16 Paul Kelman	25.00	50.00
17 Wayne Osborne	25.00	50.00
18 Vincent Sherlock	25.00	50.00
19 Leroy Anton	25.00	50.00
20 Ray Brubaker	25.00	50.00
21 Myer Chozen	25.00	50.00
22 William Ludolph	25.00	50.00
23 Floyd Scott	25.00	50.00
24 Bernard Uhalt	25.00	50.00
25 Henry McDonald	25.00	50.00
26 James Petersen	25.00	50.00
27 Robert Reeves	25.00	50.00
28 Stanley Bordagary	30.00	60.00
29 Edwin Bryan	25.00	50.00
30 Adolph Camilli	40.00	80.00
31 Thomas Flynn	25.00	50.00
32 Raymond French	25.00	50.00
33 George McNeely MG	25.00	50.00
34 Herbert McQuaid	25.00	50.00
35 Henry Steinbacker	25.00	50.00
36 Louri Vinci	25.00	50.00
37 Charles Woodall	25.00	50.00
38 Gerald Donovan	25.00	50.00
39 Kenneth Douglas	25.00	50.00
40 August Galan	30.00	60.00
41 Lee Stine	25.00	50.00
42 Ernest Sulik	25.00	50.00
43 James Zinn	25.00	50.00
44 Richard Bonnelly	25.00	50.00
45 John Bottarini	25.00	50.00
46 George Burns MG	30.00	60.00
47 Richard Frietas	25.00	50.00
48 Lynn Nelson	25.00	50.00

1933-36 Zeenuts PCL

Set includes: 1933, 1934, 1935, 1936. The reason they are grouped together is that once the coupon is removed there is no way to distinguish these cards. 1933 the coupons expiration date is April 1st, 1934. The 1934 cards coupons expire April 1st, 1935. The 1935 cards coupons expire April 1st, 1936. The 1936 cards have an expiration date of October 1st, 1936. However -- you need the coupons attached to be sure of what year your card is. If a player's name appears on 2 straight lines with the same card number it means the card was issued in 2 different sizes. These cards measure approximately 1 3/4" by 3 1/2".

Card	Low	High
COMPLETE SET (161)	10,000.00	20,000.00
1 Cleo Carlyle	25.00	50.00
2 Cedric Durst	30.00	60.00
3 Fred Haney	30.00	60.00
4 Gus Johns	25.00	50.00
5 Smead Jolley	40.00	80.00
6 Vance Page	25.00	50.00
7 Oscar Vitt MG	30.00	60.00
8 Carl Dittmar	25.00	50.00
9 Jim Oglesby	25.00	50.00
10 J.Reese	125.00	250.00
J.Reese		
11 Arnold Statz	40.00	80.00
12 Hal Stitzel	25.00	50.00
13 Louis Almada	25.00	50.00
Louis Almada		
14 John Babich	30.00	60.00
John Babich		
15 Clyde Beck	25.00	50.00
16 Clyde Beck	25.00	50.00
17 Walter Beck	30.00	60.00
18 Lincoln Blakely	25.00	50.00
19 Italo Chelini	25.00	50.00
20 Joseph Coscarart	25.00	50.00
21A M.Duggan	25.00	50.00
Small		
21B M. Duggan	25.00	50.00
Medium		
21C M.Duggan	25.00	50.00
Large		
22 O.Eckhardt	40.00	80.00
O.Eckhardt		
23 John Fitzpatrick	25.00	50.00
24 Mitchell Frankovich	25.00	50.00
25 Dan Hafey	25.00	50.00
Dan Hafey		
26 Don Johnson	25.00	50.00
27 Lloyd Johnson	25.00	50.00
28 Edwin Joost	30.00	60.00
29 William Kamm MG	30.00	60.00
30 Charles Lieber	25.00	50.00
31 Clarence Mitchell	25.00	50.00
32 Roy Mort (throwing)	25.00	50.00
33 Roy Mort (batting)	25.00	50.00
34 Otho Nicholas	25.00	50.00
35 Otho Nitcholas	25.00	50.00
36 William Outen (throwing)	25.00	50.00
37 William Outen (batting)	25.00	50.00
38 Art Parker	25.00	50.00
39A Ted Pillette	25.00	50.00
Small		
39B Ted Pillette#[Large	25.00	50.00
40 Harry Rosenberg	40.00	80.00
41 Joe Sprinz	25.00	50.00
42 Walter Stewart	25.00	50.00
43 Hal Stitzel	25.00	50.00
44 John Stoneham	25.00	50.00
45 Charles Street MG	25.00	50.00
46 Hollis Thurston	30.00	60.00
47 Hollis Thurston	30.00	60.00
48 Bill Walters	25.00	50.00
49 Max West	30.00	60.00
50 Albert Wright	25.00	50.00
51 Albert Wright	25.00	50.00
52 Leroy Anton	25.00	50.00
Leroy Anton		
53 Merv Connors	30.00	60.00
54 Bernard DeViveiros	25.00	50.00
55 Ken Douglas	25.00	50.00
56 Henry Glaister	25.00	50.00
57 Hal Haid	25.00	50.00
58 Roy Joiner	25.00	50.00
59 Ernest Kelly	25.00	50.00
60 L.Kintana	25.00	50.00
L.Kintana		
61 Willie Ludolph	25.00	50.00
62 L.McEvoy	25.00	50.00
L.McEvoy		
63 Gene McIsaacs	25.00	50.00
64 Hugh McMullen	25.00	50.00
65 Emil Mailho	25.00	50.00
66 Fred Muller	25.00	50.00
Fred Muller		
67 Ed Mulligan	25.00	50.00
68 Ed Mulligan	25.00	50.00
69 Raymond Phebus	25.00	50.00
70 Harlin Poole	25.00	50.00
71 George Quellich	25.00	50.00
72 Albert Raimondi	25.00	50.00
Albert Raimondi		
73 Jimmy Rego	40.00	80.00
74 Michael Salinsen	25.00	50.00
75 Oscar Vitt MG	30.00	60.00
76 Ed Walsh	25.00	50.00
77 George Blackerby	25.00	50.00
78 Harold Brundin	25.00	50.00
79 Frank Cox	25.00	50.00
80 Arthur Jacobs	25.00	50.00
81 Rudy Kallio	25.00	50.00
82 Joe Palmisano	25.00	50.00
83 E.Sheely	25.00	50.00
E.Sheely		
84 Tony Borja	25.00	50.00
85 Jerry Donovan	25.00	50.00
86 Floyd Ellsworth	25.00	50.00
87 Daniel Hafey	25.00	50.00
88 William Hartwig	25.00	50.00
Willam Hartwig		
89 Berlyn.Horne	25.00	50.00
90 Andy House	25.00	50.00
91 Alex Kampouris	30.00	60.00
92 Cal Lahman	25.00	50.00
93 Leo Ostenberg	25.00	50.00
94 Manuel Salvo	25.00	50.00
95 Henry Steinbacker	25.00	50.00
Henry Steinbacker		
96 James Stroner	25.00	50.00
97 Elwood Wirts	25.00	50.00
Elwood Wirts		
98 Leo Backer	25.00	50.00
99 William Ballou	25.00	50.00
William Ballou		
100 William Ballou	25.00	50.00
101 Steve Barath	25.00	50.00
102 Joe Becker	25.00	50.00
103 Tony Borja	25.00	50.00
104 James Cavaney MG	25.00	50.00
James Cavaney		
105 Albert Cole	25.00	50.00
106 Albert Cole	25.00	50.00
107 Curt Davis	30.00	60.00
108 Joe DiMaggio	3,750.00	7,500.00
109 Joe DiMaggio BAT	4,500.00	9,000.00
110 Vincent DeMaggio	300.00	600.00
111 James Densmore	25.00	50.00
112 Ken Douglas	25.00	50.00
113 John Fenton	25.00	50.00
114 Elias Funk	25.00	50.00
115 A.Garibaldi	25.00	50.00
A.Garibaldi		
116 Sam Gibson	25.00	50.00
117 Sam Gibson	25.00	50.00
118 Gira	25.00	50.00
119 R. J. Graves	25.00	50.00
120 William Hartwig	25.00	50.00
121 Bill Henderson	25.00	50.00
122 Leroy Herrmann	25.00	50.00
123 Brooks Holder	25.00	50.00
124 Art Hunt	25.00	50.00
125 Karl Jorgensen	25.00	50.00
126 Ed Kenna	25.00	50.00
127 Hugh McMullen	25.00	50.00
128 W.Mails	30.00	60.00
W.Mails		
129 Joseph Marty	25.00	50.00
White Sleeves		
130 Joseph Marty	25.00	50.00
Black Sleeves		
131 Tony Massuci	25.00	50.00
132 Tony Massuci	25.00	50.00
133 V.Monzo	25.00	50.00
V.Monzo		
134 Floyd Newkirk	25.00	50.00
135 T.Norbert	25.00	50.00
T.Norbert		
136 Frank O'Doul MG	125.00	250.00
White Sleeves		
137 Frank O'Doul MG	125.00	250.00
Black Sleeves		
138 Les Powers	25.00	50.00
139A Harold Rhyne	25.00	50.00
Small		
139B Harold Rhyne	25.00	50.00
Large		
140 Harold Rhyne	25.00	50.00
141 Bill Salkeld	30.00	60.00
142 Carl Sever	25.00	50.00
143 Ken Sheehan	25.00	50.00
144 Ken Sheehan	25.00	50.00
145 Caesar Sinibaldi	25.00	50.00
146 Starritt	25.00	50.00
147 Hal Stitzel	25.00	50.00
148A Edward Stutz	25.00	50.00
Small		
148B Edward Stutz	25.00	50.00
Large		
149 Ernie Sulik	25.00	50.00
150 Charles Wallgren	25.00	50.00
151 Larry Woodall	25.00	50.00
Larry Woodall		
152 Larry Woodall	25.00	50.00
153 James Zinn	25.00	50.00
154 Nino Biongovanni	25.00	50.00
155 Joe Coscarart	25.00	50.00
156 Hal Haid	25.00	50.00
157 Bob Holland	25.00	50.00
158 Ernest Kelly	25.00	50.00
159 Fred Muller	25.00	50.00
160 Phil Page	25.00	50.00
161 William Radonitz	25.00	50.00

1935 Pebble Beach

This seven-card extremely rare set features sepia tinted photos with autographs of players from the San Francisco-Oakland Bay Area Coast League minor league teams printed on postcard size cards. The set was offered on an evening sports show on radio station KYA in Oakland, sponsored by Pebble Beach clothier. The cards were issued periodically, and a collector could obtain them by sending in his name to the station when each new card was announced. The cards are unnumbered and checklisted below in alphabetical order. All cards seen in the marketplace have been signed in fountain pen ink.

Card	Low	High
COMPLETE SET (7)	5,000.00	10,000.00
1 Leroy Anton	250.00	500.00
2 Joe DiMaggio	4,000.00	8,000.00
3 Wee Ludolph	250.00	500.00
4 Walter Mails	300.00	600.00
5 Lefty O'Doul	500.00	1,000.00
6 Gabby Street MG	300.00	600.00
7 Oscar Vitt MG	300.00	600.00

1937-38 Zeenuts

Set includes: 1937, 1938. 37's were issued with coupons. 38's with separate same size card that was a coupon. 37's and 38's are grouped together for when the coupon is cut off the 37's they measure the same as the 38's. When found, these cards along with 1911's are usually in better condition than other Zeenuts. 1937's without coupons measure approximately 1 11/16" by 3 1/2"; 1938's without coupons measure approximately 1 3/4" by 2 13/16".

Card	Low	High
COMPLETE SET (94)	2,100.00	4,200.00
1 Joe Coscarart	40.00	80.00
2 Harry Marble	40.00	80.00
3 Robert Mort	40.00	80.00
4 William Outen	40.00	80.00
5 Gordon Slade	40.00	80.00
6 Lou Tost	40.00	80.00
7 Joseph Vitter	40.00	80.00
8 Marv Gudat	40.00	80.00
9 Harry Hannah MG	40.00	80.00
10 Arnold Statz	75.00	150.00
11 Joe Annunzio	40.00	80.00
12 Walter Beck	50.00	100.00
13 Stewart Bolin	40.00	80.00
14 Mitchell Frankovich	40.00	80.00
15 Leroy Herrmann	40.00	80.00
16 Mark Koenig	60.00	120.00
17 Frank Lamanski	40.00	80.00
18 Harry Marble	40.00	80.00
19 Robert Mort	40.00	80.00
20 Otho Nitcholas	40.00	80.00
21 Wayne Osborne	40.00	80.00
22 William Outen	40.00	80.00
23 Willaim Outen	40.00	80.00
24 Albert Raimondi	40.00	80.00
25 Harry Rosenberg	75.00	150.00
26 Gordon Slade	40.00	80.00
27 Joseph Sprinz	40.00	80.00
28 Louis Tost	40.00	80.00
29 Max West	50.00	100.00
30 William Baker	40.00	80.00
31 C. Beck	40.00	80.00
32 Ken Douglas	40.00	80.00
33 Leonard Gabrielson	40.00	80.00
34 Hal Haid	40.00	80.00
35 Walt Judnich	50.00	100.00
36 Ed Leishman	40.00	80.00
37 Floyd Olds	40.00	80.00
38 Albert Raimondi	40.00	80.00
39 Ernie Koy	60.00	120.00
40 William Raimondi	40.00	80.00
41 Ken Sheehan	40.00	80.00
42 Sawyer	40.00	80.00
43 Anthony Bongiavanni	40.00	80.00
44 Harold Carson	40.00	80.00
45 Moose Clabaugh	40.00	80.00
46 William Cronin	40.00	80.00
47 John Fredericks	40.00	80.00
48 Bill Radonitz	40.00	80.00
49 Harry Rosenberg	75.00	150.00
50 Bill Sweeney	40.00	80.00
51 William Wilson	40.00	80.00
52 Henry Cullop	40.00	80.00
53 Tony Freitas	50.00	100.00
54 Art Garibaldi	40.00	80.00
55 Bob Klinger	40.00	80.00
56 George Murray	40.00	80.00
57 H. H. Newsome	40.00	80.00
58 Joe Orengo	40.00	80.00
59 Harry Pippin	40.00	80.00
60 Tom Seats	40.00	80.00
61 Sidney Stringfellow	40.00	80.00
62 John Vergez	40.00	80.00
63 Louis Vezelich	40.00	80.00
64 William Ballou	40.00	80.00
65 Harley Boss	40.00	80.00
66 Robert Cole	40.00	80.00
67 Neal Clifford	40.00	80.00
68 Pete Daglia	40.00	80.00
69 Dominic DiMaggio	375.00	750.00
70 Keith Frazier	40.00	80.00
71 Sam Gibson	40.00	80.00
72 John Gill	40.00	80.00
73 Graves	40.00	80.00
74 Larry Guay	40.00	80.00
75 Frank Hawkins	40.00	80.00
76 Brooks Holder	40.00	80.00
77 Ted Jennings	40.00	80.00
78 Lou Koupal	40.00	80.00
79 Gene Lillard	50.00	100.00
80 Gordon Mann	40.00	80.00
81 Oscar Miller	40.00	80.00
82 Pinckney Mills	40.00	80.00
83 Vincent Monzo	40.00	80.00
84 Lawrence Powell	40.00	80.00
85 Ernest Raimondi	40.00	80.00
86 Harold Rhyne	40.00	80.00
87 Ken Sheehan	40.00	80.00
88 William Shores	40.00	80.00
89 Joseph Sprinz	40.00	80.00
90 Harvey Storey	40.00	80.00
91 Ed Stutz	40.00	80.00
92 Francis Thomson	40.00	80.00
93 Joseph Vitter	40.00	80.00
94 Larry Woodall	40.00	80.00
95 Al Wright	40.00	80.00
96 Leonard Gabrielson	40.00	80.00
97 Ed Leishman	40.00	80.00
98 Fred Muller	40.00	80.00
99 Henry Ulrich	40.00	80.00

1938 Oakland Oaks Signal Oil Stamps

These stamps, which measure approximately 1 5/8" by 2 1/2" feature members of the 1938 Oakland Oaks. The white bordered stamps have black and white photos with the player's name on the bottom. Since these stamps are unnumbered, we have sequenced them in alphabetical order.

Card	Low	High
COMPLETE SET		400
1 Joe Abreu	12.50	25.00
2 Pat Ambrose	12.50	25.00
3 Al Browne	12.50	25.00
4 Bill Conroy	12.50	25.00
5 Jerry Donovan	12.50	25.00
6 Ken Douglas	12.50	25.00
7 Bob Gibson	12.50	25.00
8 Jesse Hill	12.50	25.00
9 Delbert Holmes	12.50	25.00
10 Bob Joyce	12.50	25.00
11 Hugh Luby	12.50	25.00
12 Harry Martinez	12.50	25.00
13 Wilcy Moore		40
14 Floyd Newkirk	12.50	25.00
15 Floyd Olds	12.50	25.00
16 Bill Raimondi	12.50	25.00
17 Ken Sheehan	12.50	25.00
18 Holllis Thurston		30
19 George Turbeville	12.50	25.00
20 Lauri Vinci	12.50	25.00
21 Frank Volpi	12.50	25.00
22 Jackie Warner	12.50	25.00
23 Ed Yount	12.50	25.00
24 Dutch Zwilling		30
XX Album		

1940 Binghampton Crowley's Milk

These 3" by 5" blank-backed cards were issued to feature players on the Binghampton Eastern League team. The front have a blue-tinted player photo surrounded by a red-tinted illustrated baseball-scene border. The front also includes a facsimile player signature with their endorsement for Crowley's milk. Some backs with a stamped postcard back which are much tougher than the blank backs. This checklist could be incomplete so any additions are greatly appreciated.

1 Jimmy Adlam	150.00	300.00
2 Russ Bergman	150.00	300.00
3 Bruno Betzel	150.00	300.00
4 Vince DiBiassi	150.00	300.00
5 Jack Graham	150.00	300.00
6 Randy Gumpert	150.00	300.00
7 Mike Milosevich	150.00	300.00
8 Earl Reid	150.00	300.00
9 Frankie Slivanic	150.00	300.00
10 Pete Suder	150.00	300.00
11 Herb White	150.00	300.00

1940 San Francisco Seals Associated Station Stamps

These stamps, which measure approximately 2 1/4" by 1 3/4", and were in a blue on cream color, featured members of the 1940 San Francisco Seals. Since these stamps are unnumbered, we have sequenced them in alphabetical order.

COMPLETE SET		500
1 Win Ballou	8.00	20.00
2 John Barrett	8.00	20.00
3 Ed Botelho	8.00	20.00
4 Jack Burns	8.00	20.00
5 Frank Dasso	8.00	20.00
6 Al Epperly	8.00	20.00
7 Ferris Fain	15.00	40.00
8 Sam Gibson	8.00	20.00
9 Larry Guay	8.00	20.00
10 Brooks Holder	8.00	20.00
11 Ted Jennings	8.00	20.00
12 Bob Jensen	8.00	20.00
13 Orville Jorgens	8.00	20.00
14 Gene Kiley	8.00	20.00
15 Wilfred Lefebre	8.00	20.00
16 Wil Leonard	8.00	20.00
17 Ted Norbert	8.00	20.00
18 Lefty O'Doul MG	15.00	40.00
19 Larry Powell	8.00	20.00
20 Bob Price	8.00	20.00
21 Joe Sprinz	8.00	20.00
22 Harvey Storey	8.00	20.00
23 Ed Stutz	8.00	20.00
24 Jack Warner	8.00	20.00
25 Larry Woodall	8.00	20.00
26 Al Wright	8.00	20.00

1940 Solons Hughes

This unnumbered set features 20 members of the Sacramento Solons of the Pacific Coast League. The cards measure approximately 2" by 3" and are printed in black and white on rather thick card stock. Each card has a facsimile autograph on the front and a 1940 season home game schedule for the Sacramento Solons. The bottom of the reverse shows "Courtesy of Hughes Frozen Confections" and a tiny union label.

COMPLETE SET (20)	1,500.00	3,000.00
1 Mel Almada	100.00	200.00
2 Frank Asbell	100.00	200.00
3 Larry Barton	100.00	200.00
4 Robert Blattner	100.00	200.00
5 Bennie Borgmann	100.00	200.00
6 Tony Freitas	100.00	200.00
7 Art Garibaldi	100.00	200.00
8 Jim Grilk	100.00	200.00
9 Gene Handley	100.00	200.00
10 Oscar Judd	100.00	200.00
11 Lynn King	100.00	200.00
12 Norbert Kleinke	100.00	200.00
13 Max Marshall	100.00	200.00
14 Wm. McLaughlin	100.00	200.00
15 Bruce Ogrodowski	100.00	200.00
16 Franich Riel	100.00	200.00
17 Bill Schmidt	100.00	200.00
18 Melvin Wasley	100.00	200.00
19 Chet Wieczorek	100.00	200.00
20 Deb Williams	100.00	200.00

1943 Centennial Flour

This set of 25 black and white cards features members of the Seattle Rainiers of the Pacific Coast League. The cards measure approximately 4" by 5" and contain a brief biographical sketch on the back. The cards are unnumbered and hence they are listed below alphabetically. This set can be distinguished from the other Centennial sets by looking at the obverse; Compliments of Centennial Flouring Mills is printed at the bottom.

COMPLETE SET (25)	900.00	1,800.00
1 John Babich	40.00	80.00
2 Nick Bonarigo	40.00	80.00
3 Eddie Carnett	40.00	80.00
4 Loyd Christopher	40.00	80.00
5 Joe Demoran	40.00	80.00
6 Joe Dobbins	40.00	80.00
7 Glenn Elliott	40.00	80.00
8 Carl Fischer	40.00	80.00
9 Leonard Gabrielson	40.00	80.00
10 Stanley Gray	40.00	80.00
11 Dick Gyselman	40.00	80.00
12 Jim Jewell	40.00	80.00
13 Sylvester Johnson	50.00	100.00
14 Pete Jonas	40.00	80.00
15 Bill Kats	40.00	80.00
16 Lynn King	40.00	80.00
17 Bill Lawrence	40.00	80.00
18 Clarence Marshall	40.00	80.00
19 Bill Matheson	40.00	80.00
20 Ford Mullen	40.00	80.00
21 Bill Skiff	40.00	80.00
22 Byron Speece	40.00	80.00
23 Hal Sueme	40.00	80.00
24 Hal Turpin	40.00	80.00
25 John Yelovic	40.00	80.00

1943 Milwaukee Brewers Team Issue

These 22 postcard-sized blank-backed photos, measuring 3 1/2" by 5" featuring members of the 1943 Milwaukee Brewers, were taken by Grand Studio and issued in a brown envelope as a complete team set. Since the cards are not numbered, we are sequencing them alphabetically.

COMPLETE SET (22)	400.00	800.00
1 Bob Bowman	20.00	40.00
2 Joe Berry	20.00	40.00
3 Earl Caldwell	20.00	40.00
4 Greg Clarke	20.00	40.00
5 Merv Connors	20.00	40.00
6 Paul Erickson	20.00	40.00
7 Charlie Grimm MG	40.00	80.00
8 Hank Helf	20.00	40.00
9 Don Johnson	20.00	40.00
10 Wes Livengood	20.00	40.00
11 Herschel Martin	20.00	40.00
12 Tommy Nelson	20.00	40.00
13 Bill Norman	20.00	40.00
14 Ted Norbert	20.00	40.00
15 Henry Oana	25.00	50.00
16 Jimmy Pruett	20.00	40.00
17 Bill Sahlin	20.00	40.00
18 Frank Secory	20.00	40.00
19 Red Smith	20.00	40.00
20 Charlie Sproull	20.00	40.00
21 Hugh Todd	20.00	40.00
22 Tony York	20.00	40.00

1943 Wilkes-Barre Barons

These six black and white blank-backed photos feature members of the Wilkes-Barre Barons. The photos were issued compliments of Golden Quality Ice Cream. The cards are unnumbered and we have sequenced them in alphabetical order. There may be more photos so any additions are appreciated.

COMPLETE SET	250.00	500.00
1 Alex Damaliton	40.00	80.00
2 Tony Lazzeri MG Batting Pose	60.00	120.00
3 Tony Lazzeri MG Hands on Knee	60.00	120.00
4 Jim McDonell	40.00	80.00
5 Joe Pennington	40.00	80.00
6 Ned Tryon	40.00	80.00

1944 Centennial Flour

This set of 25 black and white cards features members of the Seattle Rainiers of the Pacific Coast League. The cards measure approximately 4" by 5" and contain a brief biographical sketch on the back. The cards are unnumbered and hence they are listed below alphabetically. This set can be distinguished from the other Centennial sets by looking at the obverse; Compliments of Centennial Hotcake and Waffle Flour is printed at the bottom.

COMPLETE SET (25)	900.00	1,800.00
1 John Babich	40.00	80.00
2 Paul Carpenter	40.00	80.00
3 Loyd Christopher	40.00	80.00
4 Joe Demoran	40.00	80.00
5 Joe Dobbins	40.00	80.00
6 Glenn Elliott	40.00	80.00
7 Carl Fischer	40.00	80.00
8 Bob Garbould	40.00	80.00
9 Stanley Gray	40.00	80.00
10 Dick Gyselman	40.00	80.00
11 Gene Holt	40.00	80.00
12 Roy Johnson	40.00	80.00
13 Sylvester Johnson	50.00	100.00
14 Al Libke	40.00	80.00
15 Billy Lyman	40.00	80.00
16 Bill Matheson	40.00	80.00
17 Jack McClure	40.00	80.00
18 Jimmy Ripple	50.00	100.00
19 Sicks Stadium	40.00	80.00
20 Bill Skiff MG	40.00	80.00
21 Byron Speece	40.00	80.00
22 Hal Sueme	40.00	80.00
23 Frank Tincup	40.00	80.00
24 Jack Treece	40.00	80.00
25 Hal Turpin	40.00	80.00

1944 Milwaukee Brewers Team Issue

For the second straight year during World War II, these photos, which measure 3 1/2" by 5" were issued by the Triple AAA Milwaukee Brewers. These photos are unnumbered and are sequenced in alphabetical order.

COMPLETE SET	500.00	1,000.00
1 Julio Acosto	20.00	40.00
2 Heinz Becker	20.00	40.00
3 George Binks	20.00	40.00
4 Bob Bowman	20.00	40.00
5 Earl Caldwell	20.00	40.00
6 Dick Culler	20.00	40.00
7 Roy Eastwood	20.00	40.00
8 Jack Farmer	20.00	40.00
9 Charles Gassaway	20.00	40.00
10 Dick Hearn	20.00	40.00
11 Don Hendrickson	20.00	40.00
12 Ed Levy	20.00	40.00
13 Herschel Martin	20.00	40.00
14 Bill Nagel	20.00	40.00
15 Tommy Nelson	20.00	40.00
16 Bill Norman	20.00	40.00
17 Hal Peck	20.00	40.00
18 Jimmy Pruitt	20.00	40.00
19 Ken Raddant	20.00	40.00
20 Owen Scheetz	20.00	40.00
21 Eddie Scheive	20.00	40.00
22 Frank Secory	20.00	40.00
23 Red Smith	20.00	40.00
24 Floyd Speer	20.00	40.00
25 Charlie Sproull	20.00	40.00
26 Casey Stengel MG	60.00	120.00

1945 Centennial Flour

This set of 27 black and white cards features members of the Seattle Rainiers of the Pacific Coast League. The cards measure approximately 3 7/8" by 5 1/16" and contain a brief biographical sketch on the back. The picture of the player on the front is borderless and contains the player's name and team in a black strip at the bottom. The cards are unnumbered and hence they are listed below alphabetically.

COMPLETE SET (27)	500.00	1,000.00
1 Charley Aleno	20.00	40.00
2 Dick Briskey	20.00	40.00
3 John Carpenter	20.00	40.00
4 Joe Demoran	20.00	40.00
5 Joe Dobbins	20.00	40.00
6 Glenn Elliott	20.00	40.00
7 Bob Finley	20.00	40.00
8 Carl Fischer	20.00	40.00
9 Keith Frazier	20.00	40.00
10 Johnny Gill	20.00	40.00
11 Bob Gorbould	20.00	40.00
12 Chet Johnson	20.00	40.00
13 Sylvester Johnson	25.00	50.00
14 Bill Kats	20.00	40.00
15 Billy Lyman	20.00	40.00
16 Bill Matheson	20.00	40.00
17 George McDonald	20.00	40.00
18 Ted Norbert	20.00	40.00
19 Alex Palica	20.00	40.00
20 Joe Passero	20.00	40.00
21 Hal Patchett	20.00	40.00
22 Bill Skiff MG	20.00	40.00
23 Byron Speece	20.00	40.00
24 Hal Sueme	20.00	40.00
25 Eddie Taylor	20.00	40.00
26 Hal Turpin	20.00	40.00
27 Jack Whipple	20.00	40.00

1945 Milwaukee Brewers Team Issue

For the third and final season, the Brewers issued these 3 1/2" by 5" photos. These photos have blank-backed and are sequenced in alphabetical order.

COMPLETE SET	300.00	600.00
1 Julio Acosta	20.00	40.00
2 Arky Biggs	20.00	40.00
3 Bill Burgu	20.00	40.00
4 Nick Cullop MG	20.00	40.00
5 Peaches Davis	20.00	40.00
6 Otto Denning	20.00	40.00
7 Lew Flick	20.00	40.00
8 Don Hendrickson	20.00	40.00
9 Ed Kobesky	20.00	40.00
10 Carl Lindquist	20.00	40.00
11 Jack McGillen	20.00	40.00
12 Gene Nance	20.00	40.00
13 Bill Norman	20.00	40.00
14 Joe Rullo	20.00	40.00
15 Owen Scheetz	20.00	40.00
16 Floyd Speer	20.00	40.00

1946 Remar Bread

The 1946 Remar Bread set of 23 black and white cards was issued one player per week in stores carrying Remar Bread. The cards are easily identified by the "red loaf" of Remar bread on the back. The first cards issued were not numbered, but the rest were, beginning with No. 5. Raimondi was the first card issued and is scarce. The set depicts Oakland Oaks players only. Even though we have numbered the last five cards, they are actually unnumbered. The catalog designation is D317-1. Cards in this set measure approximately 2" by 3".

COMPLETE SET (23)	250.00	500.00
5 Herschel Martin	10.00	20.00
6 Bill Hart	10.00	20.00
7 Chuck Gassaway	10.00	20.00
8 Wally Westlake	10.00	20.00
9 Ora Burnett	10.00	20.00
10 Casey Stengel MG	60.00	120.00
11 Charles Metro	10.00	20.00
12 Tom Hafey	10.00	20.00
13 Tony Sabol	10.00	20.00
14 Ed Kearse	10.00	20.00
15 Bud Foster ANN	10.00	20.00
16 Johnny Price	10.00	20.00
17 Gene Bearden	10.00	20.00
18 Floyd Speer	10.00	20.00
19 Bryan Stephens	10.00	20.00
20 Rinaldo Ardizola	10.00	20.00
21 Ralph Buxton	10.00	20.00
22 Ambrose Palica	10.00	20.00
23 Brooks Holder	10.00	20.00
24 Henry Pippen	10.00	20.00
25 Bill Raimondi	30.00	60.00
26 Les Scarsella	10.00	20.00
27 Glen Stewart	10.00	20.00

1946 Sunbeam Bread

The 1946 Sunbeam Bread set of 21 black and white, unnumbered cards features the Sacramento Solons only. There is a reference to the "1946 Solons" on the fronts of the cards and small yellow and red bread loafs on the backs of the cards. The backs are in blue print and give a brief biography and a Sunbeam Bread ad. The catalog designation is D315-1. Cards in this set measure approximately 2" by 3".

COMPLETE SET (21)	500.00	1,000.00
1 Bud Beasley	25.00	50.00
2 Jack Calvey	25.00	50.00
3 Gene Corbett	25.00	50.00
4 Bill Conroy	25.00	50.00
5 Guy Fletcher	25.00	50.00
6 Tony Freitas	25.00	50.00
7 Ted Greenhalgh	25.00	50.00
8 Al Jarlett	25.00	50.00
9 Landrum	25.00	50.00
10 Gene Lillard	25.00	50.00
11 Garth Mann	25.00	50.00
12 Lilo Marcucci	25.00	50.00
13 Joe Marty	100.00	200.00
14 Steve Mesner	25.00	50.00
15 Herm Pillette	25.00	50.00
16 Earl Sheely	25.00	50.00
17 Al Smith	25.00	50.00
18 Gerald Staley	25.00	50.00
19 Averett Thompson	25.00	50.00
20 Jo Jo White	25.00	50.00
21 Bud Zipay	25.00	50.00

1947 Centennial Flour

This set of 32 black and white cards features members of the Seattle Rainiers of the Pacific Coast League. The cards measure approximately 3 7/8" by 5 1/8" and contain a brief biographical sketch on the back. The picture of the player on the front is borderless and contains the player's name and team in a black strip at the bottom. The cards are unnumbered and hence they are listed below alphabetically. This set can be distinguished from the other Centennial sets by looking at the obverse; Compliments of Centennial Pancake and Waffle Flour is printed at the bottom.

COMPLETE SET (32)	450.00	900.00
1 Dick Barrett	25.00	50.00
2 Joe Buzas	15.00	30.00
3 Paul Carpenter	15.00	30.00
4 Rex Cecil	15.00	30.00
5 Tony Criscola	15.00	30.00
6 Walter Dubiel	15.00	30.00

7 Doug Ford	15.00	30.00
8 Rollie Hemsley	25.00	50.00
9 Jim Hill	15.00	30.00
10 Jim Hopper	15.00	30.00
11 Sigmund Jakucki	25.00	50.00
12 Bob Johnson	25.00	50.00
13 Pete Jonas	15.00	30.00
14 Joe Kaney	15.00	30.00
15 Hillis Layne	15.00	30.00
16 Lou Novikoff	25.00	50.00
17 Johnny O'Neil	15.00	30.00
18 John Orphal	15.00	30.00
19 Ike Pearson	15.00	30.00
20 Bill Posedel	25.00	50.00
21 Don Pulford	15.00	30.00
22 Tom Reis	15.00	30.00
23 Charley Ripple	15.00	30.00
24 Mickey Rocco	15.00	30.00
25 Johnny Rucker	15.00	30.00
26 Earl Sheely	15.00	30.00
27 Bob Stagg	15.00	30.00
28 Hal Sueme	15.00	30.00
29 Eddie Taylor	15.00	30.00
30 Edo Vanni	15.00	30.00
31 Jo Jo White	25.00	50.00
32 Tony York	15.00	30.00

1947 Padres Team Issue

This 24-card set of the San Diego Padres features black-and-white full-length player pictures with white borders. The set measures approximately 4 1/2" by 6 1/2" and was printed on linen finish paper. The backs are blank. The cards are unnumbered and checklisted below in alphabetical order.

COMPLETE SET (24)	125.00	250.00
1 John Barrett	5.00	10.00
2 Jim Brillheart CO	5.00	10.00
3 Dwain Clay	5.00	10.00
4 Jim(Rip) Collins MG	10.00	20.00
5 Pete Coscarart	5.00	10.00
6 Charles Eisenman	5.00	10.00
7 Dick Gyselman	5.00	10.00
8 Bob Hamilton	5.00	10.00
9 John Jensen	5.00	10.00
10 Vern Kennedy	7.50	15.00
11 Frank Kerr	5.00	10.00
12 Bob Kerrigan	5.00	10.00
13 Larry Lee	5.00	10.00
14 Jim McDonnell	5.00	10.00
15 John Olsen	5.00	10.00
16 Len Rice	5.00	10.00
17 Manuel Salvo	5.00	10.00
18 Tom Seats	5.00	10.00
19 Vince Shupe	5.00	10.00
20 Ray Tran	5.00	10.00
21 Al Triechel	5.00	10.00
22 Jim Triner	5.00	10.00
23 Ed Vitalich	5.00	10.00
24 Max West	7.50	15.00

1947 Remar Bread

The 1947 Remar Bread set of 25 black and white, numbered cards features Oakland Oaks players only. Many cards are identical to the 1946 issue on the front except for the numbering. These cards are listed with an asterisk in the checklist. The backs are distinguishable from the 1946 issue by a "blue loaf" of Remar Bread. The backs are printed in blue and include player biographies and an ad for the Oakland Oaks radio station. The cards are on very thin stock. The catalog designation is D317-2. Cards in this set measure approximately 2" by 3".

COMPLETE SET	300.00	600.00
1 Bill Raimondi	10.00	20.00
2 Les Scarsella	10.00	20.00
3 Brooks Holder	10.00	20.00
4 Chuck Gassaway	10.00	20.00
5 Ora Burnett	10.00	20.00
6 Ralph Buxton	10.00	20.00
7 Ed Kearse	10.00	20.00
8 Casey Stengel MG	75.00	150.00
9 Bud Foster ANN	10.00	20.00
10 Ambrose Palica	10.00	20.00
11 Tom Hafey	10.00	20.00
12 Herschel Martin	10.00	20.00
13 Henry Pippen	10.00	20.00
14 Floyd Speer	10.00	20.00
15 Tony Sabol	10.00	20.00
16 Will Hafey	10.00	20.00
17 Ray Hamrick	10.00	20.00
18 Maurice Van Robays	10.00	20.00
19 Dario Lodigiani	10.00	20.00
20 Mel Duezabou	10.00	20.00
21 Damon Hayes	10.00	20.00
22 Gene Lillard	10.00	20.00
23 Al Wilkie	10.00	20.00
24 Tony Soriano	10.00	20.00
25 Glenn Crawford	10.00	20.00

1947 Royals Montreal

These cards measure approximately 4" by 6" and are printed on thick cardboard stock. The fronts feature black-and-white posed action photos bordered in white. Player information, including a brief biography, is printed in the wider bottom border. The backs are blank. The cards are unnumbered and checklisted below in alphabetical order.

COMPLETE SET (3)	12.50	25.00
1 Claude Corbitt	5.00	10.00
2 Roy Hughes	5.00	10.00
3 Don Ross	5.00	10.00

1947 Signal Oil

The 1947 Signal Oil set of 89 black and white, unnumbered drawings, by Al DeMaree, features Pacific Coast League players from five teams -- Hollywood Stars (1-20), Los Angeles Angels (21-38), Oakland Oaks (39-57), Sacramento Solons (58-73) and Seattle Rainiers (74-89). Numbers are assigned alphabetically within teams. The Sacramento player cards and to a greater extent the Seattle player cards are more difficult to obtain. The highlights of the careers of the players appear on the backgrounds of the cards as cartoons. Four players appear with two teams -- Frank Dasso, Guy Fletcher, Red Mann and Bill Ramsey. Woody Williams is considered quite scarce and Charles Ripple is somewhat less scarce. The catalog designation is U011. Cards in this set measure approximately 5 1/2" by 3 1/2".

COMPLETE SET (89)	2,500.00	5,000.00
COMMON PLAYER (39-57)	10.00	20.00
COMMON PLAYER (58-73)	25.00	50.00
COMMON PLAYER (74-89)	50.00	100.00
1 Ed Albosta	15.00	30.00
2 Carl Cox	15.00	30.00
3 Frank Dasso	15.00	30.00
4 Tod Davis	15.00	30.00
5 Jimmy Delsing	20.00	40.00
6 Jimmy Dykes MG	30.00	60.00
7 Paul Gregory	15.00	30.00
8 Fred Haney GM	20.00	40.00
9 Francis Kelleher	15.00	30.00
10 Joe Krakauskas	15.00	30.00
11 Al Libke	15.00	30.00
12 Tony Lupien	20.00	40.00
13 Xavier Rescigno	15.00	30.00
14 Jack Sherman	15.00	30.00
15 Andy Skurski	15.00	30.00
16 Glen Stewart	15.00	30.00
17 Al Unser	20.00	40.00
18 Fred Vaughn	15.00	30.00
19 Woody Williams	400.00	800.00
20 Dutch Zernial	25.00	50.00
21 Red Adams	15.00	30.00
22 Larry Barton	15.00	30.00
23 Cliff Chambers	20.00	40.00
24 Loyd Christopher	15.00	30.00
25 Cece Garriott	15.00	30.00
26 Al Glossops	15.00	30.00
27 Bill Kelly	15.00	30.00
28 Red Lynn	15.00	30.00
29 Eddie Malone	15.00	30.00
30 Dutch McCall	15.00	30.00
31 Don Osborn	15.00	30.00
32 John Ostrowski	15.00	30.00
33 Reggie Otero	15.00	30.00
34 Ray Prim	15.00	30.00
35 Ed Sauer	15.00	30.00
36 Bill Schuster	15.00	30.00
37 Tuck Stainback	20.00	40.00
38 Lou Stringer	15.00	30.00
39 Vic Buccola	10.00	20.00
40 Mickey Burnett	10.00	20.00
41 Ralph Buxton	10.00	20.00
42 Vince DiMaggio	50.00	100.00
43 Dizz Duezabou	10.00	20.00
44 Bud Foster ANN	10.00	20.00
45 Sherriff Gassaway	10.00	20.00
46 Tom Hafey	10.00	20.00
47 Brooks Holder	10.00	20.00
48 Gene Lillard	10.00	20.00
49 Dario Lodigiani	10.00	20.00
50 Hershel Martin	10.00	20.00
51 Cotton Pippen	10.00	20.00
52 Bill Raimondi	10.00	20.00
53 Tony Sabol	10.00	20.00
54 Les Scarsella	10.00	20.00
55 Floyd Speer	10.00	20.00
56 Casey Stengel MG	100.00	200.00
57 Maurice Van Robays	10.00	20.00
58 Bud Beasley	25.00	50.00
59 Frank Dasso	25.00	50.00
60 Ed Fitzgerald	25.00	50.00
61 Guy Fletcher	25.00	50.00
62 Tony Freitas	25.00	50.00
63 Red Mann	25.00	50.00
64 Joe Marty	25.00	50.00
65 Steve Mesner	25.00	50.00
66 Bill Ramsey	25.00	50.00
67 Chas. Ripple	200.00	400.00
68 John Rizzo	25.00	50.00
69 Al Smith	30.00	60.00
70 Ronnie Smith	25.00	50.00
71 Tommy Thompson	25.00	50.00
72 Jim Warner	30.00	60.00
73 Ed Zipay	25.00	50.00
74 Kewpie Barrett	60.00	120.00
75 Herman Besse	50.00	100.00
76 Guy Fletcher	50.00	100.00
77 Jack Jakucki	60.00	120.00
78 Bob Johnson	60.00	120.00
79 Pete Jonas	50.00	100.00
80 Hillis Layne	50.00	100.00
81 Red Mann	50.00	100.00
82 Lou Novikoff	60.00	120.00
83 John O'Neill	50.00	100.00
84 Bill Ramsey	50.00	100.00
85 Mickey Rocco	50.00	100.00
86 Geo. Scharein	50.00	100.00
87 Hal Sueme	50.00	100.00
88 Jo Jo White	60.00	120.00
89 Tony York	50.00	100.00

1947 Smith's Clothing

The 1947 Smith's Clothing set of 25 black and white, numbered cards features players from the Oakland Oaks only and is similar to the Remar Bread set. The backs give brief player biographies and a Smith's ad. The set is on very thin stock paper. The Max Marshall card is quite scarce, while the Gillespie, Hayes and Faria cards are tougher to find. The catalog designation is H801-3A. Cards in this set measure approximately 2" by 3".

COMPLETE SET (25)	400.00	800.00
1 Casey Stengel MG	100.00	200.00
2 Billy Raimondi	12.50	25.00
3 Les Scarsella	12.50	25.00
4 Brooks Holder	12.50	25.00
5 Ray Hamrick	12.50	25.00
6 Gene Lillard	12.50	25.00
7 Maurice Van Robays	12.50	25.00
8 Charlie Gassaway	12.50	25.00
9 Henry Pippen	12.50	25.00
10 James Arnold	12.50	25.00
11 Ralph Buxton	12.50	25.00
12 Ambrose Palica	12.50	25.00
13 Tony Sabol	12.50	25.00
14 Ed Kearse	12.50	25.00
15 Bill Hart	12.50	25.00
16 Snuffy Smith	12.50	25.00
17 Mickey Burnett	12.50	25.00
18 Tom Hafey	12.50	25.00
19 Will Hafey	12.50	25.00
20 Paul Gillespie	25.00	50.00
21 Damon Hayes	25.00	50.00
22 Max Marshall	60.00	120.00
23 Mel Duezabou	12.50	25.00
24 Mel Reeves	12.50	25.00
25 Joe Faria	25.00	50.00

1947 Sunbeam Bread Solons

The 1947 Sunbeam Bread set of 26 black and white, unnumbered cards features the Sacramento Solons only. This set is distinguishable from the 1946 set by a reference to the "1947 Solons" on the fronts of the cards and a colored Sunbeam Bread loaf filling the entire back of the card. This issue is printed on very thin paper stock. The catalog designation is D315-2. Cards in this set measure approximately 2" by 3".

COMPLETE SET (26)	500.00	1,000.00
1 Gene Babbit	25.00	50.00
2 Bob Barthelson	25.00	50.00
3 Bud Beasley	25.00	50.00
4 Chuck Cronin	25.00	50.00
5 Eddie Fernandes	25.00	50.00
6 Ed Fitzgerald	25.00	50.00
7 Van Fletcher	25.00	50.00
8 Tony Freitas	25.00	50.00
9 Garth Mann	25.00	50.00
10 Joe Marty	50.00	100.00
11 Lou McCollum	25.00	50.00
12 Steve Mesner	25.00	50.00
13 Frank Nelson	25.00	50.00
14 Tommy Nelson	25.00	50.00
15 Joe Orengo	25.00	50.00
16 Hugh Orhan	25.00	50.00
17 Nick Pesut	25.00	50.00
18 Bill Ramsey	25.00	50.00
19 Johnny Rizzo	30.00	60.00
20 Mike Schemer	25.00	50.00
21 Al Smith	40.00	80.00
22 Tommy Thompson	25.00	50.00
23 Jim Warner	40.00	80.00
24 Mel Wasley	40.00	80.00
25 Leo Wells	20.00	50.00
26 Eddie Zipay	25.00	50.00

1948 Angels Team Issue

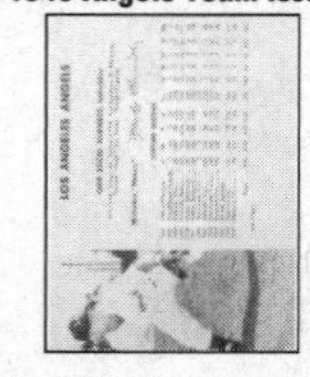

This 25-card set of the Los Angeles Angels features glossy black-and-white player photos printed on horizontal cards measuring approximately 6 3/4" by 4 3/4" with the player's autograph and complete playing record. The cards are unnumbered and checklisted below in alphabetical order.

COMPLETE SET (26)	300.00	600.00
1 Cliff Aberson	12.50	25.00
2 Charles Adams	12.50	25.00
3 John Adkins	12.50	25.00
4 Omer Anthony	12.50	25.00
5 Russell Bauers	12.50	25.00
6 Ora Escdal Burnett	12.50	25.00
7 Donald Carleen	12.50	25.00
8 Dom Dallessandro	15.00	30.00
9 Virgil Garriott	12.50	25.00
10 Paul Gillespie	12.50	25.00
11 Alban Glossop	12.50	25.00
12 Thomas Hafey	12.50	25.00
13 Donald Johnson	12.50	25.00
14 William Kelly MG	12.50	25.00
15 Harold Kleine	12.50	25.00
16 Walter Lanfranconi	12.50	25.00
17 Edward Lukon	12.50	25.00
18 Japhet Lynn	12.50	25.00
19 Edward Malone	12.50	25.00
20 Leonard Merullo	15.00	30.00
21 Ralph Novotney	12.50	25.00
22 John Ostrowski	15.00	30.00
23 John Sanford	12.50	25.00
24 Ed Sauer	12.50	25.00
25 William Schuster	12.50	25.00
26 John Warner CO	12.50	25.00

1948 Signal Oil

This set of 24 color photos of Oakland Oaks (Pacific Coast League) was given away at local gas stations. The cards are not numbered and are found with either blue or black printing on the back. Nicholas Etten and Brooks Holder are considered to be harder to find than the other cards in this set; they are notated with SP below. The catalog designation is U010. The cards are listed below in alphabetical order. The cards in this set measure approximately 2 3/8" by 3 1/2".

COMPLETE SET (24)	750.00	1,500.00
COMMON PLAYER (1-24)	25.00	50.00
COMMON SP	25.00	50.00
1 John Babich	25.00	50.00
2 Ralph Buxton	25.00	50.00
3 Loyd Christopher	25.00	50.00
4 Merrill Combs	25.00	50.00
5 Melvin Duezabou	25.00	50.00
6 Nicholas Etten SP	60.00	120.00
7 Bud Foster ANN	25.00	50.00
8 Charles Gassaway	25.00	50.00
9 Will Hafey	25.00	50.00
10 Ray Hamrick	25.00	50.00
11 Brooks Holder SP	50.00	100.00
12 Earl Jones	25.00	50.00
13 Cookie Lavagetto	50.00	100.00
14 Robert Lillard	25.00	50.00
15 Dario Lodigiani	25.00	50.00
16 Ernie Lombardi	100.00	200.00
17 Alfred Martin	150.00	300.00
18 George Metkovich	30.00	60.00
19 William Raimondi	25.00	50.00
20 Les Scarsella	25.00	50.00
21 Floyd Speer	25.00	50.00
22 Casey Stengel MG	200.00	400.00
23 Maurice Van Robays	25.00	50.00
24 Aldon Wilkie	25.00	50.00

1948 Smith's Clothing

The 1948 Smith's Clothing set of 25 black and white numbered cards features Oakland Oaks players only and is printed on a much heavier stock than the 1947 Smith's set. The cards have a glossy finish. All cards feature full body shots showing players in either fielding, batting or pitching positions. The catalog designation is H801-3B. Cards in this set measure approximately 2" by 3".

COMPLETE SET (25)	500.00	1,000.00
1 Billy Raimondi	20.00	40.00
2 Brooks Holder	20.00	40.00
3 Will Hafey	30.00	60.00
4 Nick Etten	30.00	60.00
5 Loyd Christopher	20.00	40.00
6 Les Scarsella	20.00	40.00
7 Ray Hamrick	20.00	40.00
8 Gene Lillard	20.00	40.00
9 Maurice Van Robays	20.00	40.00
10 Charlie Gassaway	20.00	40.00
11 Ralph Buxton	20.00	40.00
12 Tom Hafey	20.00	40.00
13 Damon Hayes	20.00	40.00
14 Mel Dizz Duezabou	20.00	40.00
15 Dario Lodigiani	20.00	40.00
16 Vic Buccola	20.00	40.00
17 Billy Martin	125.00	250.00
18 Floyd Speer	20.00	40.00
19 Eddie Samcoff	20.00	40.00
20 Casey Stengel MG	150.00	300.00
21 Floyd Hittle	20.00	40.00
22 John Babich	20.00	40.00
23 Merrill Combs	20.00	40.00
24 Eddie Murphy	30.00	60.00
25 Bob Klinger	30.00	60.00

1948 Sommer and Kaufmann

The 1948 Sommer and Kaufmann set of 30 numbered, black and white cards features players from the San Francisco Seals of the Pacific Coast League. The catalog designation is H801-4A. According to a recently rediscovered header card, these cards were given out three per week at the participating Sommer and Kaufmann Shoe Stores. The backs give brief player biographies and a Sommer and Kaufmann ad. The 1948 set can be distinguished from the 1949 set by the script writing of "Sommer and Kaufmann". The 1949 set has "Sommer and Kaufmann" in fancy print. Cards in this set measure approximately 2" by 3".

COMPLETE SET (30)	1,000.00	2,000.00
1 Lefty O'Doul MG	75.00	150.00
2 Jack Brewer	40.00	80.00
3 Cornelius Dempsey	50.00	100.00
4 Tommy Fine	40.00	80.00
5 Kenneth Gables	40.00	80.00
6 Robert Joyce	40.00	80.00
7 Alfred Lien	40.00	80.00
8 Cliff Melton	50.00	100.00
9 Frank S. Shofner	40.00	80.00
10 Don Trower	40.00	80.00
11 Joe Brovia	40.00	80.00
12 Dino Restelli	50.00	100.00
13 Gene Woodling	60.00	120.00
14 Benjamin Guintini	40.00	80.00
15 Felix Mackiewicz	40.00	80.00
16 John Patrick Tobin	40.00	80.00
17 Manuel Perez Jr.	40.00	80.00
18 William Werle	40.00	80.00
19 Homer E. Howell Jr.	40.00	80.00
20 Wilfred Leonard	40.00	80.00
21 Bruce Ogrodowski	40.00	80.00
22 R. Dick Lajeskie	40.00	80.00
23 Hugh Luby	40.00	80.00
24 Roy Melvin Nicely	40.00	80.00
25 Raymond Orteig	40.00	80.00
26 Michael D. Rocco	40.00	80.00
27 Del Edward Young	40.00	80.00
28 Joe Sprinz	40.00	80.00
29 Leo Doc Hughes TR	40.00	80.00
30 Don Rode BB	40.00	80.00
Albert Bero BB		
Charlie Barnes BB		
NNO Header Card		
Salmon colored		

1949 Angels Team Issue

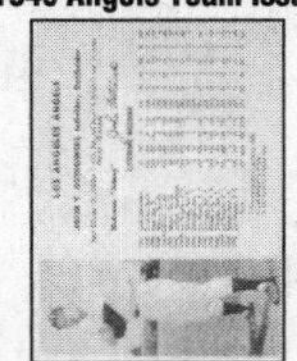

This 39-card set of the Los Angeles Angeles is similar to the 1948 Angels Team Issue set. The cards are unnumbered and checklisted below in alphabetical order. The blank-backed cards feature a player photo on the left and his career stats on the right side. This set was available at time of issue from the team for $1.

COMPLETE SET (39)	400.00	800.00
1 Clifford Aberson	12.50	25.00
2 Donald Alfano	12.50	25.00
3 Quentin Altizer	12.50	25.00
4 Omer Anthony	12.50	25.00
5 Nelson Burbrink	12.50	25.00
6 Forrest Burgess	20.00	40.00
7 Donald Carlsen	12.50	25.00
8 Joseph Damato	12.50	25.00
9 William Emmerich	12.50	25.00
10 Kenneth Gables	12.50	25.00
11 Virgil Garriott	12.50	25.00
12 Gordon Goldsberry	12.50	25.00
13 Alban Glossop	12.50	25.00
14 Frank Gustine	12.50	25.00
15 Lee Handley	12.50	25.00
16 Alan Ihde	12.50	25.00
17 Robert John Kelley ANN	12.50	25.00
18 Robert Edward Kelly	12.50	25.00
19 William Kelly MG	12.50	25.00
20 Walter Lanfranconi	12.50	25.00
21 Japhet Lynn	12.50	25.00
22 Clarence Maddern	12.50	25.00
23 Edward Malone	12.50	25.00
24 Carmen Mauro	12.50	25.00
25 Booker McDaniels	12.50	25.00
26 Calvin McLish	15.00	30.00
27 Cyril Moran	12.50	25.00
28 Ralph Novotney	12.50	25.00
29 John Ostrowski	12.50	25.00
30 Robert Rhawn	12.50	25.00
31 William Schuster	12.50	25.00
32 James Seerey	12.50	25.00
33 Bryan Stephens	12.50	25.00
34 Robert Sturgeon	12.50	25.00
35 W. Wayne Terwilliger	15.00	30.00
36 Gordon Van Dyke	12.50	25.00
37 John Warner CO	12.50	25.00
38 Don Watkins	12.50	25.00
39 The Trainers and Bat Boys	12.50	25.00

1949 Bowman PCL

The 1949 Bowman Pacific Coast League set is recognized as one of the scarcest sets of the post-war period. Each card measures 2 1/16" by 2 1/2". Marketed regionally on the West Coast, it is thought that it may have been sold in sheets in candy and variety stores rather than in gum packs. The format of tinted photographs on colored backgrounds is identical to the regular 1949 Bowman issue.

COMPLETE SET (36)	4,500.00	9,000.00
1 Lee Anthony	200.00	400.00
2 George Metkovich	250.00	500.00
3 Ralph Hodgin	200.00	400.00
4 George Woods	200.00	400.00
5 Xavier Rescigno	200.00	400.00
6 Mickey Grasso	200.00	400.00
7 Johnny Rucker	200.00	400.00
8 Jack Brewer	200.00	400.00
9 Dom D'Allessandro	200.00	400.00
10 Charlie Gassaway	200.00	400.00
11 Tony Freitas	200.00	400.00
12 Gordon Maltzberger	200.00	400.00
13 John Jensen	200.00	400.00
14 Joyner White	200.00	400.00
15 Harvey Storey	200.00	400.00
16 Dick Lajeski	200.00	400.00
17 Albie Glossup	200.00	400.00
18 Bill Raimondi	200.00	400.00
19 Ken Holcombe	200.00	400.00
20 Don Ross	200.00	400.00
21 Pete Coscarart	200.00	400.00
22 Tony York	200.00	400.00
23 Jake Mooty	200.00	400.00
24 Charles Adams	200.00	400.00
25 Les Scarsella	200.00	400.00
26 Joe Marty	200.00	400.00
27 Frank Kelleher	200.00	400.00
28 Lee Handley	200.00	400.00
29 Herman Besse	200.00	400.00
30 John Lazor	200.00	400.00
31 Eddie Malone	200.00	400.00
32 Maurice Van Robays	200.00	400.00
33 Jim Tabor	200.00	400.00
34 Gene Handley	200.00	400.00
35 Tom Seats	200.00	400.00
36 Ora Burnett	200.00	400.00

1949 Fort Worth Cats

This 18 card set which was issued on heavy card stock and measures approximately 8" by 10" featured members of the 1949 Ft Worth Cats, which was a farm team of the Brooklyn Dodgers. Other than card numbers 1 and 9 -- this set is sequenced in alphabetical order.

COMPLETE SET	100.00	200.00
1 Sam DiBlasi	10.00	20.00
Joe Landrum		
2 Cal Abrams	12.50	25.00
3 Bob Austin	10.00	20.00
4 Carroll Berringer	12.50	25.00
5 Bobby Bragan	15.00	30.00
6 Bob Bundy	10.00	20.00
7 Eddie Chandler	10.00	20.00
8 Chris Van Cuyk	10.00	20.00
9 Sam DiBlasi	10.00	20.00
Joe Landrum		
10 George Dockins	10.00	20.00
11 Carl Erskine	20.00	40.00
12 Wally Fieta	10.00	20.00
13 Jack Lindsey	10.00	20.00
14 Bob Milliken	12.50	25.00
15 Walter Sessi	10.00	20.00
16 Ken Staples	10.00	20.00
17 Preston Ward	10.00	20.00
18 Dick Williams	20.00	40.00

1949 Hollywood Stars

This 24 card set measures 7" by 4 3/4". The set was published by "Fan Pix" and the cards are set out in an horizontal format. The cards also had complete playing records and a space for autographs. This set was available for 60 cents from the Hollywood Stars at the time of issue.

COMPLETE SET	200.00	400.00
1 Jim Baxes	10.00	20.00
2 George Fallon	10.00	20.00
3 John Fitzpatrick	10.00	20.00
4 George Genovese	10.00	20.00
5 Hubert Gorman	10.00	20.00
6 Gene Handley	10.00	20.00
7 Fred Haney MG	10.00	20.00
8 James R. Hughes	10.00	20.00
9 Frank Kellerher	10.00	20.00
10 Gordon Maltzberger	10.00	20.00
11 Glen Moulder	10.00	20.00
12 Irv Noren	12.50	25.00
13 Edward Oliver	10.00	20.00
14 John O'Neil	10.00	20.00
15 Walter Olsen	10.00	20.00
16 Jack Paepke	10.00	20.00
17 Willard Ramsdell	10.00	20.00
18 Jack Salveson	10.00	20.00
19 Mike Sandlock	10.00	20.00
20 Art Schallock	10.00	20.00
21 Andy Skurski	10.00	20.00
22 Chuck Stevens	10.00	20.00
23 Al Unser	10.00	20.00
24 George Woods	10.00	20.00

1949 Remar Bread

The 1949 Remar Bread set of 32 black and white picture cards depicts Oakland Oaks players only. The backs, in blue print on white stock, give vital statistics, 1948 records and show a Sunbeam bread loaf. Some cards were printed in limited quantities and the players have been placed in alphabetical order and numbered in the checklist, although the cards themselves are not numbered. The catalog designation is D317-4. Cards in this set measure approximately 2" by 3".

COMPLETE SET (32)	500.00	1,000.00
1 Ralph Buxton	10.00	20.00
2 Mario Candini	25.00	50.00
3 Rex Cecil	25.00	50.00
4 Loyd Christopher	10.00	20.00
5 Mel Duezabou	10.00	20.00
6 Chuck Dressen MG	25.00	50.00
7 Bud Foster ANN	10.00	20.00
8 Clarence Gassaway	10.00	20.00
9 Ray Hamrick	10.00	20.00
10 Jackie Jensen	50.00	100.00
11 Earl Jones	10.00	20.00
12 George Kelly	25.00	50.00
13 Frank Kerr	25.00	50.00
14 Dick Kryhoski	25.00	50.00
15 Cookie Lavagetto	40.00	80.00
16 Dario Lodigiani	10.00	20.00
17 Billy Martin	100.00	200.00
18 George Metkovich	10.00	20.00
19 Frank Nelson	10.00	20.00
20 Don Padgett	10.00	20.00
21 Alonzo Perry	25.00	50.00
22 Bill Raimondi	10.00	20.00
23 Earl Rapp	10.00	20.00
24 Ed Samcoff	10.00	20.00
25 Les Scarsella	10.00	20.00
26 Forest Thompson	25.00	50.00
27 Earl Toolson	25.00	50.00
28 Louis Tost	25.00	50.00
29 Maurice Van Robays	10.00	20.00
30 Jim Wallace	10.00	20.00
31 Artie Wilson	10.00	20.00
32 Parnell Woods	25.00	50.00

1949 Solon Sunbeam/Pureta PC759

This set was co-issued by Sunbeam Bread and Pureta Sausage and features Sacramento Solons. The fronts feature the player and an microphone insert with station call letters printed on it. The backs feature ads for both Sunbeam Bread and Pureta Sausage. This is considered the toughest of the Remar-Sunbeam sets for these postcards were issued weekly and only through a special radio promotion.

COMPLETE SET (12)	700.00	1,400.00
1 Del Baker MG	75.00	150.00
2 Frankie Dasso	75.00	150.00
3 Walt Dropo	125.00	250.00
4 Joe Grace	75.00	150.00
5 Bob Gillespie	75.00	150.00
6 Ralph Hodgin	75.00	150.00
7 Freddie Marsh	75.00	150.00
8 Joe Marty	75.00	150.00
9 Len Ratto	75.00	150.00
10 Jim Tabor	75.00	150.00
11 Al White	75.00	150.00
12 Bill Wilson	75.00	150.00

1949 Sommer and Kaufmann

The 1949 Sommer and Kaufmann set of 28 numbered, black and white cards features players of the San Francisco Seals of the Pacific Coast League. Card No. 24 is not known to exist. The catalog designation is H801-4B. Cards in this set measure approximately 2" by 3".

COMPLETE SET (28)	1,000.00	2,000.00
1 Lefty O'Doul MG	75.00	150.00
2 Jack Brewer	40.00	80.00
3 Kenneth H. Gables	40.00	80.00
4 Con Dempsey	50.00	100.00
5 Alfred Lien	40.00	80.00
6 Cliff Melton	50.00	100.00
7 Steve Nagy	40.00	80.00
8 Manny Perez	40.00	80.00
9 Roy Jarvis	40.00	80.00
10 Roy Partee	40.00	80.00
11 Reno Cheso	40.00	80.00
12 Dick Lajeskie	40.00	80.00
13 Roy M. Nicely	40.00	80.00
14 Mickey Rocco	40.00	80.00
15 Frank Shofner	40.00	80.00
16 Richard Holder	40.00	80.00
17 Dino Restelli	50.00	100.00
18 Arky Vaughan	75.00	150.00
19 Jackie Baccioccu	40.00	80.00
20 Robert F. Drilling	40.00	80.00
21 Del E. Young	40.00	80.00
22 Joseph D. Sprinz	40.00	80.00
23 Leo E.Doc Hughes TR	40.00	80.00
25 Bert Singleton	40.00	80.00
26 John Gene Brocker	40.00	80.00
27 Jack Tobin	40.00	80.00
28 Walter Judnich	50.00	100.00
29 Harry (Hal) Foldman	40.00	80.00

1949 Stockton Ports

These cards, which measure 2" by 3" feature members of the 1949 Stockton Ports of the Pacific Coast League. These cards are either black and white or blue and white and since they are unnumbered, we have sequenced them in alphabetical order.

COMPLETE SET	750.00	1,500.00
1 Nino Bongiovanni	75.00	150.00
2 Lou Bronzan	75.00	150.00
3 Jimmie Brown	75.00	150.00
4 Rocco Cardinale	75.00	150.00
5 Harry Clements	75.00	150.00
6 Norm Grabar	75.00	150.00
7 Bud Guldborg	75.00	150.00
8 Carl Hoberg	75.00	150.00
9 Eddie Murphy	75.00	150.00
10 Sandy Sandel	75.00	150.00
11 Dick Stone	75.00	150.00
12 Matt Zidich	75.00	150.00

1950 Ft Worth Cats

This set is similar to the 1949 Ft Worth Cats sets and feature players from the 1950 Ft Worth Cats. These cards are sequenced in alphabetical order. The Austin, Berringer, Van Cuyk and Landrum photos are the same ones used in 1949

COMPLETE SET	100.00	200.00
1 Bob Austin	10.00	20.00
2 Carroll Berringer	12.50	25.00
3 Frank Brown	10.00	20.00
4 Gene Clough	10.00	20.00
5 Chris Van Cuyk	10.00	20.00
6 Don Hoak	12.50	25.00
7 Wallace Jay	10.00	20.00
8 Jay Kelchner	10.00	20.00
9 Joe Landrum	10.00	20.00
10 Mike Lemish	10.00	20.00
11 Jack Lindsay	10.00	20.00
12 Ray Moore	10.00	20.00
13 John Reeves	10.00	20.00
14 Russ Rose	10.00	20.00
15 John Rutherford	10.00	20.00
16 Ken Staples	10.00	20.00
17 Fred Storck	10.00	20.00
18 Tommy Tatum	10.00	20.00
19 Joe Torpay	10.00	20.00
20 Mel Waters	10.00	20.00

1950 Hollywood Stars

This set is very similar to the 1949 Hollywood Stars issue. The major difference is that there are fascimile autographs on the front. The photos are also totally different from the 1949 issue. This set was also issued by "Fan Pix".

COMPLETE SET	300.00	600.00
1 Lee Anthony	10.00	20.00
2 Bill Antonelle	10.00	20.00
3 Dick Barrett	10.00	20.00
5 Clint Conatser	10.00	20.00
6 Clifford Dapper	10.00	20.00
7 George Fallen	10.00	20.00
8 John Fitzpatrick	10.00	20.00
9 Murray Franklin	10.00	20.00
10 Herbert Gorman	10.00	20.00
11 Gene Handley	10.00	20.00
13 Clarence Hicks	10.00	20.00
14 Herb Karpel	10.00	20.00
15 Gene Kelleher	10.00	20.00
16 Ken Lehman	10.00	20.00
17 John Lindell	12.50	25.00
18 Gordon Maltzberger	10.00	20.00
19 Daniel Menendez	10.00	20.00
20 Larry Mondroff	10.00	20.00
21 Glenn Moulder	10.00	20.00
22 John O'Neil	10.00	20.00
23 Jack Paepke	10.00	20.00
24 Jean Pierre Roy	10.00	20.00
25 John Salveson, Jr.	10.00	20.00
26 Mike Sandlock	10.00	20.00
27 Edward Dauer	10.00	20.00
28 Art Schallock	10.00	20.00
29 George Schmees	10.00	20.00
30 Chuck Stevens	10.00	20.00
31 Ben Wade	10.00	20.00
32 George Woods	10.00	20.00

1950 Indianapolis Indians Team Issue

COMPLETE SET	60.00	120.00
1 Ted Beard	10.00	20.00
2 Gus Bell	20.00	40.00
3 Al Lopez MG	25.00	50.00
4 Paul LaPalme	10.00	20.00

1950 Remar Bread

The 1950 Remar Bread set of 27 black and white, unnumbered cards features Oakland Oaks players only. The format is identical to the 1949 set except that the backs include 1949 records. The catalog designation is D317-5.

The cards are listed below in alphabetical order. Cards in this set measure approximately 2" by 3".

COMPLETE SET (27)	150.00	300.00
1 George Bamberger	12.50	25.00
2 Hank Behrman	5.00	10.00
3 Loyd Christopher	5.00	10.00
4 Chuck Dressen	10.00	20.00
5 Mel Duezabou	5.00	10.00
6 Augie Galan	6.00	12.00
7 Clarence Gassaway	5.00	10.00
8 Allen Gettel	5.00	10.00
9 Ernie Groth	6.00	12.00
10 Ray Hamrick	5.00	10.00
11 Earl Harrist	5.00	10.00
12 Billy Herman	20.00	40.00
13 Bob Hofman	5.00	10.00
14 George Kelly	20.00	40.00
15 Cookie Lavagetto	10.00	20.00
16 Eddie Malone	5.00	10.00
17 George Metkovich	5.00	10.00
18 Frank Nelson	5.00	10.00
19 Ray Noble	5.00	10.00
20 Don Padgett	5.00	10.00
21 Earl Rapp	5.00	10.00
22 Clyde Shoun	5.00	10.00
23 Forest Thompson	5.00	10.00
24 Louis Tost	5.00	10.00
25 Dick Wakefield	10.00	20.00
26 Artie Wilson	6.00	12.00
27 Roy Zimmerman	5.00	10.00

1950 San Francisco Seals Popcorn

This extremely difficult regional set, which measures 3 1/4" by 4 1/2" and are blank-backed was issued in special caramel corn bags at Seals games in 1950. Since these cards are unnumbered, we have sequenced them in alphabetical order. Since these photos are unnumbered, we have sequenced them in alphabetical order.

COMPLETE SET	500.00	1,000.00
1 Tom Bridges	50.00	100.00
2 Dick Briskey	40.00	80.00
3 Ralph Buxton	40.00	80.00
4 Con Dempsey	40.00	80.00
5 Harry Feldman	40.00	80.00
6 Les Fleming	40.00	80.00
7 Joe Grace	40.00	80.00
8 Chet Johnson	40.00	80.00
9 Al Lien	40.00	80.00
10 Dario Lodigiani	40.00	80.00
11 Cliff Melton	50.00	100.00
12 Roy Nicely	40.00	80.00
13 Roy Partee	40.00	80.00
14 Manny Perez	40.00	80.00
15 Neil Sheridan	40.00	80.00
16 Elmer Singleton	40.00	80.00
17 Jack Tobin	40.00	80.00

1950 World Wide Gum V362

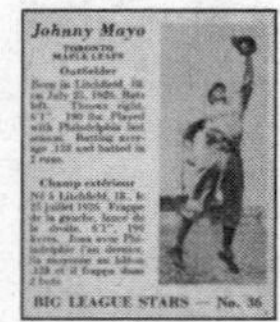

The cards in this 48-card set measure approximately 2 1/2" by 3 1/4". In 1950, long after its former parent company had disappeared from the card market, the World Wide Gum Company issued a set of blue printed cards depicting players from the International League. The fronts feature player photos with bilingual (French and English) biographies. The backs are blank. The series was entitled "Big League Stars". The catalog designation for this set is V362. The cards are numbered on the front. There is an early card of Hall of Fame manager Tommy Lasorda in this set.

COMPLETE SET (48)	2,000.00	4,000.00
1 Rocky Bridges	50.00	100.00
2 Chuck Connors	200.00	400.00
3 Jake Wade	40.00	80.00
4 Al Cihocki	40.00	80.00
5 John Simmons	40.00	80.00
6 Frank Trechock	40.00	80.00
7 Steve Lembo	40.00	80.00
8 Johnny Welaj	40.00	80.00
9 Seymour Block	40.00	80.00
10 Pat McGlothlin	40.00	80.00
11 Bryan Stephens	40.00	80.00
12 Clarence Podbielan	50.00	100.00
13 Clem Hausmann	40.00	80.00
14 Turk Lown	50.00	100.00
15 Joe Payne	40.00	80.00
16 Coaker Triplett	50.00	100.00
17 Nick Strincevich	40.00	80.00
18 Charlie Thompson	40.00	80.00
19 Eric Silverman	40.00	80.00
20 George Schmees	40.00	80.00
21 George Binks	40.00	80.00
22 Gino Cimoli	50.00	100.00
23 Marty Tabacheck	40.00	80.00
24 Al Gionfriddo	50.00	100.00
25 Ronnie Lee	40.00	80.00
26 Clyde King	50.00	100.00
27 Harry Heslet	40.00	80.00
28 Jerry Scala	40.00	80.00
29 Boris Woyt	40.00	80.00
30 Jack Collum	40.00	80.00
31 Chet Laabs	50.00	100.00
32 Carden Gillenwater	40.00	80.00
33 Irving Medlinger	40.00	80.00
34 Toby Atwell	40.00	80.00
35 Charlie Marshall	40.00	80.00
36 Johnny Mayo	40.00	80.00
37 Gene Markland	40.00	80.00
38 Russ Kerns	40.00	80.00
39 Jim Prendergast	40.00	80.00
40 Lou Welaj	40.00	80.00
41 Clyde Kluttz	50.00	100.00
42 Bill Glynn	40.00	80.00
43 Don Richmond	40.00	80.00
44 Hank Biasatti	40.00	80.00
45 Tommy Lasorda	250.00	500.00
46 Al Roberge	40.00	80.00
47 George Byam	40.00	80.00
48 Dutch Mele	50.00	100.00

1952 Dallas Eagles Team Issue

These cards, which measure approximately 2 1/2" by 3 1/2" feature members of the 1952 Dallas Eagles team. These black and white cards feature posed action shots surrounded by a white border which measured 1/8" all around. Since these photos are unnumbered, we have sequenced them in alphabetical order. There might be more cards in this set so all additions are appreciated.

COMPLETE SET	75.00	150.00
1 Ralph Albers	10.00	20.00
2 Bob Bundy	10.00	20.00
3 Dave Hoskins	10.00	20.00
4 Eddie Knoblauch	10.00	20.00
5 Walt Lanfranconi	10.00	20.00
6 Don Mossi	15.00	30.00
7 Clyde Perry	10.00	20.00
8 Harry Sullivan	10.00	20.00

1952 Fort Worth Cats Globe

Measuring approximately 2 1/4" by 3 3/8" and printed by Globe Printing Co, these blank-backed black and white cards feature members of the 1952 Fort Worth Cats, which was a Brooklyn Dodger farm team. It is possible that this checklist is incomplete, so any additions are appreciated.

COMPLETE SET	150.00	300.00
1 Wayne Belardi	10.00	20.00
2 Bobby Bragan MG	12.50	25.00
3 Al Brancato	10.00	20.00
4 Ralph Butler	10.00	20.00
5 Ted Del Guercio	10.00	20.00
6 Elroy Face	20.00	40.00
7 Al Gionfriddo	12.50	25.00
8 Bill Glane	10.00	20.00
9 Bert Hamric	10.00	20.00
10 Kenny Hemphill	10.00	20.00
11 Billy Hunter	10.00	20.00
12 Joe Landrum	10.00	20.00
13 Steve Lembo	10.00	20.00
14 Jack Lindsay	10.00	20.00
15 Jim Melton	10.00	20.00
16 Pete Mondorff	10.00	20.00
17 Joe Torpey	10.00	20.00
18 Pete Wojey	10.00	20.00

1952 La Patrie

These posed color photos of Canadian baseball players of 1952 comprised an "Album Sportif" in La Patrie, a French-language Montreal newspaper. They are bordered in red, white and blue and measure approximately 11" by 15 1/4". The player's name appears at the upper right. The photos are unnumbered and checklisted below in alphabetical order.

COMPLETE SET (19)	300.00	600.00
1 Bob Alexander	10.00	20.00
2 Georges Carpentier	10.00	20.00
3 Hampton Coleman	10.00	20.00
4 Walter Fiala	10.00	20.00
5 Jim Gilliam UER/(Gilliams printed on front)	50.00	100.00
6 Tom Hackett	10.00	20.00
7 Don Hoak	20.00	40.00
8 Tom Lasorda	100.00	200.00
9 Herbie Lash	10.00	20.00
10 Mal Mallatte	10.00	20.00
11 Georges Maranda	10.00	20.00
12 Carmen Mauro	10.00	20.00
13 Solly Mohn	10.00	20.00
14 Jacques Monette	10.00	20.00
15 Johnny Podres	50.00	100.00
16 Ed Roebuck	15.00	30.00
17 Charlie Thompson	10.00	20.00
18 Don Thompson	10.00	20.00
19 John Wingo	10.00	20.00

1952 Laval Provinciale

Issued by Laval Dairies of Quebec, these 114 blank-backed cards measure approximately 1 1/4" by 2 1/2" and feature white-bordered black-and-white posed player photos. The player's name, team, position, birthplace and birthdate appear in the white margin below the photo. All text is in French. The cards are numbered on the front.

COMPLETE SET (114)	1,250.00	2,500.00
1 Georges McQuinn	25.00	50.00
2 Cliff Statham	12.50	25.00
3 Frank Wilson	12.50	25.00
4 Frank Neri	12.50	25.00
5 Georges Maranda	20.00	40.00
6 Richard Cordeiro	12.50	25.00
7 Roger McCardell	12.50	25.00
8 Joseph Janiak	12.50	25.00
9 Herbert Shankman	12.50	25.00
10 Joe Subbiondo	12.50	25.00
11 Jack Brenner	12.50	25.00
12 Donald Buchanan	12.50	25.00
13 Bob Smith	20.00	40.00
14 Raymond Lague	12.50	25.00
15 Mike Fandozzi	12.50	25.00
16 Dick Moler	12.50	25.00
17 Edward Bazydlo	12.50	25.00
18 Danny Mazurek	12.50	25.00
19 Edwin Charles	20.00	40.00
20 Jack Mullaney	12.50	25.00
21 Bob Bolan	12.50	25.00
22 Bob Long	12.50	25.00
23 Cleo Lewright	12.50	25.00
24 Herb Taylor	12.50	25.00
25 Frank Gaeta	12.50	25.00
26 Bill Truitt	12.50	25.00
27 Jean Prats	12.50	25.00
28 Tex Taylor	12.50	25.00
29 Ronnie Delbianco	12.50	25.00
30 Joe Dilorenzo	12.50	25.00
31 John Paszek	12.50	25.00
32 Ken Suess	12.50	25.00
33 Harry Sims	12.50	25.00
34 William Jackson	12.50	25.00
35 Jerry Mayers	12.50	25.00
36 Gordon Maltzberger	20.00	40.00
37 Gerry Cabana	12.50	25.00
38 Gary Rutkay	12.50	25.00
39 Ken Hatcher	12.50	25.00
40 Vincent Cosenza	12.50	25.00
41 Edward Yaeger	12.50	25.00
42 Jimmy Orr	12.50	25.00
43 John Dimartino	12.50	25.00
44 Len Wisnaski	12.50	25.00
45 Pete Caniglia	12.50	25.00
46 Guy Coleman	12.50	25.00
47 Herb Fleischer	12.50	25.00
48 Charles Yahrling	12.50	25.00
49 Roger Bedard	12.50	25.00
50 Al Barillari	12.50	25.00
51 Hugh Mulcahy	20.00	40.00
52 Vincent Canepa	12.50	25.00
53 Bob Loranger	12.50	25.00
54 Georges Carpentier	12.50	25.00
55 Bill Hamilton	12.50	25.00
56 Hector Lopez	25.00	50.00
57 Joe Taylor	12.50	25.00
58 Alonso Brathwaite	12.50	25.00
59 Carl McQuillen	12.50	25.00
60 Robert Trice	20.00	40.00
61 John Dworak	12.50	25.00
62 Lal Pinkston	12.50	25.00
63 William Shannon	12.50	25.00
64 Stanley Watychowics	12.50	25.00
65 Roger Hebert	12.50	25.00
66 Troy Spencer	12.50	25.00
67 Johnny Rahan	12.50	25.00
68 John Sosh	12.50	25.00
69 Raymond Mason	12.50	25.00
70 Tom Smith	12.50	25.00
71 Douglas McBean	12.50	25.00
72 Bill Babik	12.50	25.00
73 Dante Cozzi	12.50	25.00
74 Melvil Doxtator	12.50	25.00
75 William(Bill) Gilday	12.50	25.00
76 Armando Diaz	12.50	25.00
77 Ackroyd Smith	12.50	25.00
78 Germain Pizarro	12.50	25.00
79 James Heap	12.50	25.00
80 Herbert B. Crompton	12.50	25.00
81 Howard J. Bodell	12.50	25.00
82 Andre Schreiser	12.50	25.00
83 John Wingo	12.50	25.00
84 Salvatore Arduini	12.50	25.00
85 Fred Paccito	12.50	25.00
86 Aaron Osofsky	12.50	25.00
87 Jack Digrace	12.50	25.00
88 Alfonzo Gerard	12.50	25.00
89 Manuel Trabous	12.50	25.00
90 Tom Barnes	12.50	25.00
91 Humberto Robinson	20.00	40.00
92 Jack Buxowatz	12.50	25.00
93 Marco Mainini	12.50	25.00
94 Claude St-Vincent	12.50	25.00
95 Fernand Brousseau	12.50	25.00
96 John Malangone	12.50	25.00
97 Pierre Nantel	12.50	25.00
98 Donald Stevens	12.50	25.00
99 Jim Prappas	12.50	25.00
100 Richard Fitzgerald	12.50	25.00
101 Yves Aubin	12.50	25.00
102 Frank Novosel	12.50	25.00
103 Tony Campos	12.50	25.00
104 Gelso Oviedo	12.50	25.00
105 July Becker	12.50	25.00
106 Aurelio Ala	12.50	25.00
107 Orlando Andux	12.50	25.00
108 Tom Hackett	12.50	25.00
109 Guillaume Vargas	12.50	25.00
110 Francisco Salfran	12.50	25.00
111 Jean-Marc Blais	12.50	25.00
112 Vince Pizzitola	12.50	25.00
113 John Olsen	12.50	25.00
114 Jacques Monette	12.50	25.00

1952 Miami Beach Flamingos Team Issue

This 18 card set, which measures approximately 2 1/4" by 3 1/2" feature members of the 1952 Miami Beach Flamingos of the Florida International League. These cards were issued in an souvenir album. Since these cards are unnumbered, we have sequenced them in alphabetical order.

COMPLETE SET (18)	150.00	300.00
1 Billy Barrett	10.00	20.00
2 Art Bosch	10.00	20.00
3 Jack Caro	10.00	20.00
4 George Handy	10.00	20.00
5 Clark Henry	10.00	20.00
6 Dario Jiminez	10.00	20.00
7 Jesse Levan	10.00	20.00
8 Bobby Lyons	10.00	20.00
9 Pepper Martin MG	20.00	40.00
10 Dick McMillin	10.00	20.00
11 Chico Morilla	10.00	20.00
12 Walt Nothe	10.00	20.00
13 Johnny Podgajny	10.00	20.00
14 Whitey Platt	10.00	20.00
15 Knobby Rosa	10.00	20.00
16 Mort Smith	10.00	20.00
17 Tommy Venn	10.00	20.00
18 Ray Williams	10.00	20.00

1952 Mother's Cookies

The cards in this 64-card set measure 2 3/16" by 3 1/2". The 1952 Mother's Cookies set contains numbered, full-color cards. They feature PCL players only and were distributed on the West Coast in bags of Mothers Cookies. Reported scarcities are 29 Peterson, 43 Erautt, 37 Welmaker, 11 MacCawley and 16 Talbot. Chuck Connors (4), the "Rifleman," is not scarce but is widely sought after. The catalog designation is D357-1. Johnny Lindell (#1) and Fred Haney (#13) are also known to exist with schedule backs. These backs are very scarce and are worth approximately 10 times the value of the regular cards.

COMPLETE SET (64)	2,000.00	4,000.00
COMMON PLAYER (1-64)	12.50	25.00
COMMON SP		50
1 Johnny Lindell	30.00	60.00
2 Jim Davis	25.00	50.00
3 Al Gettel	25.00	50.00
4 Chuck Connors	250.00	500.00
5 Joe Grace	25.00	50.00
6 Eddie Basinski	25.00	50.00
7 Gene Handley	25.00	50.00
8 Walt Judnich	25.00	50.00
9 Jim Marshall	25.00	50.00
10 Max West	25.00	50.00
11 Bill MacCawley SP	50.00	100.00
12 Moreno Pieretti	25.00	50.00
13 Fred Haney MG	30.00	60.00
14 Earl Johnson	25.00	50.00
15 Dave Dahle	25.00	50.00
16 Bob Talbot SP	50.00	100.00
17 Smokey Singleton	25.00	50.00
18 Frank Austin	25.00	50.00
19 Joe Gordon MG	40.00	80.00
20 Joe Marty	25.00	50.00
21 Bob Gillespie	25.00	50.00
22 Red Embree	25.00	50.00
23 Lefty Olsen	25.00	50.00
24 Whitey Wietelmann	25.00	50.00
25 Lefty O'Doul MG	40.00	80.00
26 Memo Luna	25.00	50.00
27 John Davis	25.00	50.00
28 Dick Faber	25.00	50.00
29 Buddy Peterson SP	150.00	300.00
30 Hank Schenz	25.00	50.00
31 Tookie Gilbert	25.00	50.00
32 Mel Ott MG	100.00	200.00
33 Sam Chapman	30.00	60.00
34 John Ragni	25.00	50.00
35 Dick Cole	25.00	50.00
36 Tom Saffel	25.00	50.00
37 Roy Welmaker SP	100.00	200.00
38 Lou Stringer	25.00	50.00
39 Chuck Stevens	25.00	50.00
40 Artie Wilson	30.00	60.00
41 Charlie Schanz	25.00	50.00
42 Al Lyons	25.00	50.00
43 Joe Erautt SP	150.00	300.00
44 Clarence Maddern	25.00	50.00
45 Gene Baker	30.00	60.00
46 Tom Heath	25.00	50.00
47 Al Lien	25.00	50.00
48 Bill Reeder	25.00	50.00
49 Bob Thurman	30.00	60.00
50 Ray Orteig	25.00	50.00
51 Joe Brovia	25.00	50.00
52 Jim Russell	25.00	50.00
53 Fred Sanford	25.00	50.00
54 Jim Gladd	25.00	50.00
55 Clay Hopper MG	25.00	50.00
56 Bill Glynn	25.00	50.00
57 Mike McCormick	25.00	50.00
58 Richie Myers	25.00	50.00
59 Vinnie Smith	25.00	50.00
60 Stan Hack MG	30.00	60.00

61 Bob Spicer	25.00	50.00
62 Jack Hollis	25.00	50.00
63 Ed Chandler	25.00	50.00
64 Bill Moisan	25.00	50.00

1952 Ogden Reds Globe

Measuring approximately 2 1/4" by 3 3/8" and printed by Globe Printing Co, these blank-backed black and white cards feature members of the 1952 Ogden Reds, which was a Cincinnati Reds farm team. It is possible that this checklist is incomplete, so any additions are appreciated. The best known player in this set is Dave Bristol, who later became a major league manager for several teams. Since this checklist is unnumbered, we have sequenced the list in alphabetical order.

COMPLETE SET	100.00	200.00
1 Bill Bowman	10.00	20.00
2 Dave Bristol	15.00	30.00
3 Vince Capece	10.00	20.00
4 Gerald Davis	10.00	20.00
5 Bob Flowers	10.00	20.00
6 Howard Leister	10.00	20.00
7 Dee Moore	10.00	20.00
8 Augie Navarro ANN	10.00	20.00
9 Grady Watts	10.00	20.00
10 Carl Wells	10.00	20.00

1952 Parkhurst

The 100 cards comprising the 1952 Parkhurst/Frostade set measure approximately 2" by 2 1/2" and depict players from three Canadian International League teams: Montreal Royals (49-76), Ottawa Athletics (77-100) and Toronto Maple Leafs (1-26). The fronts feature white-bordered black-and-white player photos. The plain backs have red print and carry the player's name, team, position and biography at the top; an ad for Frostade follows below. The set also includes a number of playing tip and play diagram cards (27-48). The catalog designation for this set is V338-1. Cards oriented horizontally are indicated below by HOR. These cards were issued in five-card packs which cost five cents upon release.

COMPLETE SET (100)	825.00	1,650.00
COMMON PLAYER (1-25)	7.50	15.00
COMMON CARD (26-48)	5.00	10.00
COMMON PLAYER (49-100)	7.50	15.00
1 Joe Becker MG	10.00	20.00
2 Aaron Silverman	7.50	15.00
3 Bobby Rhawn HOR	7.50	15.00
4 Russ Bauers HOR	7.50	15.00
5 William Jennings HOR	7.50	15.00
6 Grover Bowers	7.50	15.00
7 Vic Lombardi	10.00	20.00
8 Billy DeMars	10.00	20.00
9 Frank Colman	7.50	15.00
10 Charles Grant	7.50	15.00
11 Irving Medlinger	7.50	15.00
12 Burke McLaughlin	7.50	15.00
13 Lew Morton	7.50	15.00
14 Red Barrett	10.00	20.00
15 Leon Foulk	7.50	15.00
16 Neil Sheridan	7.50	15.00
17 Ferrell(Andy) Anderson	7.50	15.00
18 Ray Shore	7.50	15.00
19 Duke Markell	7.50	15.00
20 Robert Balcena	7.50	15.00
21 Wilmer Fields	7.50	15.00
22 Charles White HOR	7.50	15.00
23 Gerald Fahr	7.50	15.00
24 Jose Bracho HOR	7.50	15.00
25 Edward Stevens HOR	10.00	20.00
26 Maple Leaf Stadium HOR	10.00	20.00
27 Throwing Home HOR	5.00	10.00
28 Regulation Baseball Diamond HOR	5.00	10.00
29 Gripping The Bat	5.00	10.00
30 Hiding Kind of Pitch	5.00	10.00
31 Catcher's Stance	5.00	10.00
32 Quiz Question How long does a batter have to see	5.00	10.00
33 Finger and Arm Exercises HOR	5.00	10.00
34 First Baseman	5.00	10.00
35 Pitcher's Stance	5.00	10.00
36 Swinging Bats	5.00	10.00
37 Quiz Question HOR Can a player advance a base wh	5.00	10.00
38 Watch the Ball HOR	5.00	10.00
39 Quiz Question HOR Can a team ever win a game wit	5.00	10.00
40 Quiz Question Can a player put his own teammate	5.00	10.00
41 How to Bunt	5.00	10.00
42 Wrist Snap	5.00	10.00
43 Pitching Practice	5.00	10.00
44 Stealing Bases	5.00	10.00
45 Pitching I	5.00	10.00
46 Pitching II	5.00	10.00
47 Signals	5.00	10.00
48 Regulation Baseballs	5.00	10.00
49 Albert Ronning	5.00	10.00
50 William C. Lane	7.50	15.00
51 William Samson	7.50	15.00
52 Charles Thompson	7.50	15.00
53 Ezra McGlothin	7.50	15.00
54 Forrest Jacobs	10.00	20.00
55 Arthur Fabbro	7.50	15.00
56 James Hughes	10.00	20.00
57 Don Hoak	12.50	25.00
58 Tommy Lasorda	100.00	200.00
59 Gilbert Mills	7.50	15.00
60 Malcolm Mallette	7.50	15.00
61 Rocky Nelson	7.50	15.00
62 John Simmons	7.50	15.00
63 R.S. Alex Alexander	7.50	15.00
64 Dan Bankhead	10.00	20.00
65 Solomon Coleman	7.50	15.00
66 Walter Alston MG	50.00	100.00
67 Walter Fiala	7.50	15.00
68 Jim Gilliam	30.00	60.00
69 Jim Pendleton	10.00	20.00
70 Gino Cimoli	10.00	20.00
71 Carmen Mauro	7.50	15.00
72 Walt Moryn	10.00	20.00
73 James Romano	7.50	15.00
74 Rollin Lutz	7.50	15.00
75 Ed Roebuck	10.00	20.00
76 John Podres	25.00	50.00
77 Walter Novick	7.50	15.00
78 Lefty Gohl	7.50	15.00
79 Thomas Kirk	7.50	15.00
80 Robert Betz	7.50	15.00
81 Bill Hockenbury	7.50	15.00
82 Albert Rubeling HOR	7.50	15.00
83 Julius Watlington	7.50	15.00
84 Frank Fanovich	7.50	15.00
85 Hank Foiles	10.00	20.00
86 Lou Limmer HOR	10.00	20.00
87 Edward Hrabcsak	7.50	15.00
88 Bob Gardner	7.50	15.00
89 John Metkovich	7.50	15.00
90 Jean-Pierre Roy	7.50	15.00
91 Frank Skaff MG	7.50	15.00
92 Harry Desert	7.50	15.00
93 Stan Jok	10.00	20.00
94 Russ Swingle	7.50	15.00
95 Bob Wellman	7.50	15.00
96 John Conway HOR	7.50	15.00
97 George Maskovich HOR	7.50	15.00
98 Charles Bishop	7.50	15.00
99 Joseph Murray	7.50	15.00
100 Mike Kume	10.00	20.00

1952 Sioux City Soos Team Issue

This 22 card set, which measures 2 3/16" by 3 3/8" features members of the 1952 Sioux City Soos team. These cards are very similar in design to a set issued in 1953 and thus complete or near-complete sets are needed to indentify which year these cards belong to. Since these cards are unnumbered we have sequenced them in alphabetical order.

COMPLETE SET (22)	100.00	200.00
7 Bob Giddings	5.00	10.00
8 Dick Hamlin	5.00	10.00
9 Gail Harris	7.50	15.00
10 Chico Ibanez	5.00	10.00
11 Ray Johnson	5.00	10.00
12 Denny Landry	5.00	10.00
13 Vince LaSala	5.00	10.00
14 Bob Lee	5.00	10.00
15 Bill McMillian	5.00	10.00
16 Dick Messner	5.00	10.00
17 Ray Mueller	5.00	10.00
18 Roy Pardue	5.00	10.00
19 Mario Picone	5.00	10.00
20 Jim Singleton	5.00	10.00
21 John Uber	5.00	10.00
22 Ernie Yelen	5.00	10.00

1953 Fargo Moorehead

Roger Maris (spelled Maras) has an very early card in this set. Some players, including Maris, have two different cards. This checklist may be incomplete, so any additions are appreciated.

COMPLETE SET (16)	600.00	1,200.00
1 Ken Braeseke	20.00	40.00
2 Zeke Bonura MG	30.00	60.00
3 Bob Borovica	20.00	40.00
4 Joe Camacho	20.00	40.00
5 Frank Gravino Hands at knees	20.00	40.00
6 Frank Gravino Hands at waist	20.00	40.00
7 Santo Luberto	20.00	40.00
8 Roger Maris Spelled Maras Fielding	500.00	1,000.00
9 Roger Maris Spelled Maras Batting	500.00	1,000.00
10 Jerry Mehlish	20.00	40.00
11 Ray Mendoza Hands outstretched for throw	20.00	40.00
12 Ray Mendoza Stretching for throw	20.00	40.00
13 Don Nance	20.00	40.00
14 Ray Seif	20.00	40.00
15 Will Sirois	20.00	40.00
16 Don Wolf	20.00	40.00

1953 Mother's Cookies

The cards in this 63-card set measure 2 3/16" by 3 1/2". The 1953 Mother's Cookies set features PCL players only. The cards are numbered and the corners are rounded in "playing-card" style. The set has different numbers than the 1952 series and carries a "trading card album" offer on the back. Eleven cards are marked with DP in the checklist below as they essentially were double printed and are much more plentiful than the other numbers in the set. The catalog designation of the set is D357-2.

COMPLETE SET (63)	750.00	1,500.00
COMMON PLAYER (1-63)	7.50	15.00
COMMON PLAYER DP	4.00	8.00
1 Lee Winters	25.00	50.00
2 Joe Ostrowski	15.00	30.00
3 Willie Ramsdell	15.00	30.00
4 Bobby Bragan	25.00	50.00
5 Fletcher Robbe	15.00	30.00
6 Aaron Robinson	20.00	40.00
7 Augie Galan	20.00	40.00
8 Buddy Peterson	15.00	30.00
9 Lefty O'Doul	50.00	100.00
10 Walt Poceday	15.00	30.00
11 Nine Tornay	15.00	30.00
12 Jim Moran	15.00	30.00
13 George Schmees	15.00	30.00
14 Al Widmar	15.00	30.00
15 Richie Myers	15.00	30.00
16 Bill Howerton	15.00	30.00
17 Chuck Stevens	15.00	30.00
18 Joe Brovia	15.00	30.00
19 Max West	20.00	40.00
20 Eddie Malone	15.00	30.00
21 Gene Handley	15.00	30.00
22 William D. McCawley	15.00	30.00
23 Bill Sweeney	15.00	30.00
24 Tom Alston	20.00	40.00
25 George Vico	15.00	30.00
26 Hank Arft	15.00	30.00
27 Al Benton	20.00	40.00
28 Pete Milne	15.00	30.00
29 Jim Gladd	15.00	30.00
30 Earl Rapp	15.00	30.00
31 Ray Orteig	15.00	30.00
32 Eddie Basinski	15.00	30.00
33 Reno Cheso	15.00	30.00
34 Clarence Maddern	15.00	30.00
35 Marino Pieretti	15.00	30.00
36 Bill Raimondi	15.00	30.00
37 Frank Kelleher	15.00	30.00
38 George Bamberger	30.00	60.00
39 Dick Smith	15.00	30.00
40 Charley Schanz	15.00	30.00
41 John Van Cuyk	15.00	30.00
42 Lloyd Hittle	15.00	30.00
43 Tommy Heath	15.00	30.00
44 Frank Kalin	15.00	30.00
45 Jack Tobin DP	7.50	15.00
46 Jim Davis	15.00	30.00
47 Claude Christy	15.00	30.00
48 Elvin Tappe	15.00	30.00
49 Stan Hack	20.00	40.00
50 Fred Richards DP	7.50	15.00
51 Clay Hopper DP	7.50	15.00
52 Roy Welmaker	15.00	30.00
53 Red Adams DP	7.50	15.00
54 Piper Davis DP	7.50	15.00
55 Spider Jorgensen	20.00	40.00
56 Lee Walls	20.00	40.00
57 Jack Phillips DP	7.50	15.00
58 Red Lynn DP	7.50	15.00
59 Eddie Robinson DP	10.00	20.00
60 Gene Desautels DP	7.50	15.00
61 Bob Dillinger DP	15.00	30.00
62 Al Federoff	15.00	30.00
63 Bill Boemler DP	7.50	15.00

1953 San Francisco Seals Team Issue

This 24-card set measuring approximately 4" by 5" was issued by the club and features black-and-white player portraits with white borders. The player's autograph is printed on the picture. The backs are blank. The cards are unnumbered and checklisted below in alphabetical order. The Dave Melton card is known to exist on standard stock as well as an heavier paper stock.

COMPLETE SET (24)	250.00	500.00
1 Bill Boemler	10.00	20.00
2 Bill Bradford	10.00	20.00
3 Reno Cheso	10.00	20.00
4 Harland Clift CO	12.50	25.00
5 Walt Clough	10.00	20.00
6 Cliff Coggin	10.00	20.00
7 Tommy Heath MG	12.50	25.00
8 Leo Hughes TR	10.00	20.00
9 Frank Kalin	10.00	20.00
10 Al Lien	10.00	20.00
11 Al Lyons	10.00	20.00
12 John McCall	10.00	20.00
13 Bill McCawley	10.00	20.00
14 Jim Moran	10.00	20.00
15 Bob Muncrief	10.00	20.00
16 Leo Righetti	15.00	30.00
17 Ted Shandor	10.00	20.00
18 Elmer Singleton	10.00	20.00
19 Sal Taormina	10.00	20.00
20 Will Tiesiera	10.00	20.00
21 Nini Tornay	10.00	20.00
22 Lou Stringer	10.00	20.00
23 George Vico	10.00	20.00
24 Jerry Zuvela	10.00	20.00
25 Dave Melton	10.00	20.00

1954 Charleston Senators Blossom Dairy

These blank-backed cards which measure 2 1/4" by 3 3/16" were sponsored by Blossom Dairy and featured members of the 1954 Charleston Senators. Since these cards are unnumbered, we have sequenced them in alphabetical order. There was also an album specially created for this set.

COMPLETE SET	1,000.00	2,000.00
1 Al Baro	40.00	100.00
2 Joe Becker	40.00	100.00
3 Joe Carroll	40.00	100.00
4 Gerald Red Fahr	40.00	100.00
5 Dick Fowler	40.00	100.00
6 Alex Garbowski	40.00	100.00
7 Gordon Goldsberry	40.00	100.00
8 Ross Grimsley	40.00	100.00
9 Sam Hairston	50.00	125.00
10 Phil Haugstad	40.00	100.00
11 Tom Hurd	40.00	100.00
12 Bob Killinger	40.00	100.00
13 John Kropf	40.00	100.00
14 Bob Masser	40.00	100.00
15 Danny Melendez	40.00	100.00
16 Bill Paolisso	40.00	100.00
17 Bill Pope	40.00	100.00
18 Lou Sleater	40.00	100.00
19 Dick Strahs	40.00	100.00
20 Joe Torpey	40.00	100.00
21 Bill Voiselle	50.00	125.00
22 Al Ware	40.00	100.00
XX Album		

1954 Lincoln Chiefs Weaver's Wafers

1 Ted Laguna
2 Vance Carlson
3 Noel Oquendo
4 Andy Bush
5 Billy Smith
6 Red McQuillen
7 Whitey Wietelman MG
8 Jim Lightbody Trainer
9 Tom Neill
10 TBD
11 Andy Anderson
12 Burt Greenstein
13 Johnny Jones
14 Frank Stewart
15 Norm Brown
16 Walt Linden
17 Roger Wright
18 Charlie Grant
19 TBD
20 Bill King Announcer

1954 Seattle Popcorn

This 28-card set of the Seattle ballclub of the Pacific Coast League was distributed to the public as inserts in boxes of popcorn sold at Sicks' Stadium in Seattle. Only one card was inserted per box and measured approximately 2" by 3". The sets were produced by the Seattle ballclub and issued each season from 1954 through 1968. The fronts feature a black-and-white player photo with the player's name and position printed at the bottom. The backs are blank. All of the cards seem to have been cropped from a "premium" 8" by 10". All Popcorn cards may have part of a "premium". The cards are unnumbered and checklisted below in alphabetical order. Uncut sheets of these cards of any year of Seattle Popcorn should go for 1.5X to 2X the sum of any listed cards. All 1954 through 1968 Seattle Popcorn cards are expected to exist in a 8' by 10' "premium" form. All the photos are the same for the players each year but they may be cropped differently. These 8" by 10" single player photos of commons are currently valued at 1.5X to 2X the smaller player photos.

COMPLETE SET (23)	700.00	1,400.00
1 Gene Bearden	50.00	100.00
2 Al Brightman CO	30.00	60.00
3 Jack Burkowatz	30.00	60.00
4 Tommy Byrne	50.00	100.00
5 Merrill Combs	30.00	60.00
6 Joe Erautt	30.00	60.00
7 Bill Evans	30.00	60.00
8 Nanny Fernandez	30.00	60.00
9 Van Fletcher	30.00	60.00
10 Bob Hall	30.00	60.00
11 Pete Hernandez	30.00	60.00
12 Lloyd Jenney	30.00	60.00
13 Joe Joshua	30.00	60.00
14 Vern Kindsfather	30.00	60.00
15 Tom Lovrich	30.00	60.00
16 Clarence Maddern	30.00	60.00
17 Don Mallott	30.00	60.00

18 Loren Meyers	30.00	60.00
19 Steve Nagy	30.00	60.00
20 Ray Orteig	30.00	60.00
21 Gerry Priddy P MG	50.00	100.00
22 George Schmees	30.00	60.00
23 Bill Schuster CO	30.00	60.00
24 Leo Thomas	30.00	60.00
25 Jack Tobin	30.00	60.00
26 Al Widmar	30.00	60.00
27 Artie Wilson	60.00	120.00
28 Al Zarilla	50.00	100.00

1955 Des Moines Homestead Bruins

This 21-card set features player portraits on cards measuring approximately 2 5/8" by 3 3/4" and was issued by the Iowa Packing Co. The cards were either distributed in packages of Old Homestead Franks or at Bruins ball games. The backs carry an ad for Old Homestead products. The cards are unnumbered and checklisted below alphabetically.

COMPLETE SET (21)	2,000.00	4,000.00
1 Bob Anderson	125.00	250.00
2 Ray Bellino	125.00	250.00
3 Don Biebel	125.00	250.00
4 Bobby Cooke	125.00	250.00
5 Dave Cunningham	125.00	250.00
6 Bert Flammini	125.00	250.00
7 Gene Fodge	125.00	250.00
8 Eddie Haas	125.00	250.00
9 Paul Hoffmeister	125.00	250.00
10 Pepper Martin MG	200.00	400.00
11 Jim McDaniel	125.00	250.00
12 Bob McKee	125.00	250.00
13 Paul Menking	125.00	250.00
14 Vern Morgan	125.00	250.00
15 Joe Pearson	125.00	250.00
16 John Pramesca	125.00	250.00
17 Joe Stanks	125.00	250.00
18 Jim Stoddard	125.00	250.00
19 Bob Thorpe	125.00	250.00
20 Burdy Thurlby	125.00	250.00
21 Don Watkins	125.00	250.00

1955 Seattle Popcorn

This 20-card set of the Seattle ballclub of the Pacific Coast League was distributed to the public as inserts in boxes of popcorn sold at Sicks' Stadium in Seattle. Only one card was inserted per box and measured approximately 2" by 3". The sets were produced by the Seattle ballclub and issued each season from 1954 through 1968. The fronts feature a black-and-white player photo with the player's name and position printed at the bottom. The backs are blank. No significant variations in these cards have been discovered. The cards are unnumbered and checklisted below in alphabetical order.

COMPLETE SET (20)	550.00	1,100.00
1 Bob Balcena	30.00	60.00
2 Monty Basgall	40.00	80.00
3 Ewell Blackwell	50.00	100.00
4 Bill Brenner	30.00	60.00
5 Jack Bukowatz	30.00	60.00
6 Van Fletcher	30.00	60.00
7 Joe Ginsberg	30.00	60.00
8 Jehosie Heard	30.00	60.00
9 Fred Hutchinson MG	100.00	200.00
10 Larry Jansen	50.00	100.00
11 Bob Kelly	30.00	60.00
12 Bill Kennedy	40.00	80.00
13 Lou Kretlow	30.00	60.00
14 Rocco Krsnich	30.00	60.00
15 Carmen Mauro	30.00	60.00
16 John Oldham	30.00	60.00
17 George Schmees	30.00	60.00
18 Elmer Singleton	30.00	60.00
19 Alan Strange CO	30.00	60.00
20 Gene Verble	30.00	60.00
21 Marv Williams	30.00	60.00
22 Harvey Zernia	30.00	60.00

1956 Lincon Chiefs Stuart Mutual Savings

This postcard sized card features slugging outfielder Dick Stuart, who was on his way to slugging 66 homers during the 1956 season. The top of the card has a posed action shot of Stuart while the bottom has information on who sponsored the photo as well the player's name and position

1 Dick Stuart	25.00	50.00

1956 Seattle Popcorn

This 27-card set of the Seattle Rainiers ballclub of the Pacific Coast League was distributed to the public as inserts in boxes of popcorn sold at Sicks' Stadium in Seattle. Only one card was inserted per box and measured approximately 2" by 3". The sets were produced by the ballclub and issued each season from 1954 through 1968. The fronts feature a black-and-white player photo with the player's name and position printed at the bottom. The backs are blank. The 1956's come either in blank back form or with 2 Gil's locations. The cards are unnumbered and checklisted below in alphabetical order.

COMPLETE SET (27)	650.00	1,300.00
1 Fred Baczewski	30.00	60.00
2 Bob Balcena	30.00	60.00
3 Bill Brenner	30.00	60.00
4 Sherry Dixon	30.00	60.00
5 Don Fracchia	30.00	60.00
6 Bill Glynn	30.00	60.00
7 Larry Jansen	50.00	100.00
8 Howie Judson	30.00	60.00
9 Bill Kennedy	30.00	60.00
10 Jack Lohrke	40.00	80.00
11 Vic Lombardi	40.00	80.00
12 Carmen Mauro	30.00	60.00
13 Raoy Orteig	30.00	60.00
14 Bud Podbielan	30.00	60.00
15 Leo Righetti	40.00	80.00
16 Jim Robertson	30.00	60.00
17 Art Shallock UER/(misspelled Schallock)	30.00	60.00
18 Art Schult	30.00	60.00
19 Luke Sewell MG	50.00	100.00
20 Elmer Singleton	30.00	60.00
21 Milt Smith/(Action)	30.00	60.00
22 Milt Smith/(Head)	30.00	60.00
23 Vern Stephens	40.00	80.00
24 Alan Strange CO	30.00	60.00
25 Joe Taylor	30.00	60.00
26 Artie Wilson	60.00	120.00
27 Harvey Zernia	30.00	60.00

1957 Chattanooga Lookouts Team Issue

These 8 1/2" by 11" blank-backed black and white photos feature members of the 1957 Chattanooga Lookouts. The players are in posed shots and the photos were taken by Hoss Photo Service in NY. Since these photos are unnumbered we have sequenced them in alphabetical order. An very early Harmon Killebrew card is in this set as well. It is possible that there are additional players so any additional information is appreciated.

COMPLETE SET	125.00	250.00
1 Bobby Brown	10.00	20.00
2 Hal Griggs	10.00	20.00
3 Harmon Killebrew	50.00	100.00
4 Jesse Levan	10.00	20.00
5 Ernie Oravetz	10.00	20.00
6 Tony Roig	10.00	20.00
7 Stan Roseboro	10.00	20.00
8 Bunky Stewart	10.00	20.00
9 Chattanooga Lookouts	10.00	20.00

1957 Hygrade Meats

This 12-card set features Seattle Rainiers of the Pacific Coast League (PCL) only. The cards measure 3 3/4" by 4 1/2" and they are unnumbered. The catalog designation for this scarce set is F178. These cards, along with Milwaukee Sausage and the Henry House issues were in direct contact with hot dog meats. Therefore, these cards are usually found in vg or less condition in these sets and a significant premium is attached for nm/mt cards or better.

COMPLETE SET (12)	1,250.00	2,500.00
1 Dick Aylward	100.00	200.00
2 Bob Balcena	100.00	200.00
3 Jim Dyck	100.00	200.00
4 Marion Fricano	100.00	200.00
5 Billy Glynn	100.00	200.00
6 Larry Jansen	125.00	250.00
7 Bill Kennedy	100.00	200.00
8 Jack Wayne (Lucky) Lohrke	100.00	200.00
9 Lefty O'Doul MG	150.00	300.00
10 Ray Orteig	100.00	200.00
11 Joe Taylor	100.00	200.00
12 Morrie Wills sic, Maury	200.00	400.00

1957 San Francisco Seals Golden State Dairy Stamps

These stamps, which measure approximately 2" by 2 1/2", which were in rust brown on orange, were designed to be glued into an album. The album is an attractive yellow and red piece. Since these stamps are unnumbered, we have sequenced them in alphabetical order.

COMPLETE SET	250.00	500.00
1 Bill Abernathie	12.50	25.00
2 Ken Aspromonte	12.50	25.00
3 Harry Dorish	12.50	25.00
4 Joe Gordon MG	20.00	40.00
5 Grady Hatton	12.50	25.00
6 Tommy Hurd	12.50	25.00
7 Frank Kellert	12.50	25.00
8 Leo Kiely	12.50	25.00
9 Harry Malmberg	12.50	25.00
10 John McCall	12.50	25.00
11 Albie Pearson	15.00	30.00
12 Jack Phillips	12.50	25.00
13 Bill Renna	12.50	25.00
14 Ed Sadowski	12.50	25.00
15 Robert Smith	12.50	25.00
16 Jack Spring	12.50	25.00
17 Joe Tanner	12.50	25.00
18 Sal Taormina	12.50	25.00
19 Bert Thiel	12.50	25.00
20 Nini Tornay	12.50	25.00
21 Tommy Umphlett	12.50	25.00
22 Glenn Wright	12.50	25.00

1957 Seattle Popcorn

This 24-card set of the Seattle Rainiers ballclub of the Pacific Coast League was distributed to the public as inserts in boxes of popcorn sold at Sicks' Stadium in Seattle. Only one card was inserted per box and measured approximately 2" by 3". The sets were produced by the ballclub and issued each season from 1954 through 1968. The fronts feature a black-and-white player photo with the player's name and position printed at the bottom. The backs are either blank or note Gil's three drive in locations. The cards are unnumbered and checklisted below in alphabetical order.

COMPLETE SET (24)	700.00	1,400.00
1 Dick Aylward	30.00	60.00
2 Bob Balcena	30.00	60.00
3 Eddie Basinski	30.00	60.00
4 Hal Bevan	30.00	60.00
5 Joe Black	60.00	120.00
6 Juan Delis	30.00	60.00
7 Jim Dyck	30.00	60.00
8 Marion Fricano	30.00	60.00
9 Bill Glynn	30.00	60.00
10 Larry Jansen	40.00	80.00
11 Howie Judson	30.00	60.00
12 Bill Kennedy	30.00	60.00
13 Jack Lohrke	30.00	60.00
14 Carmen Mauro	30.00	60.00
15 George Munger	30.00	60.00
16 Lefty O'Doul MG	100.00	200.00
17 Ray Orteig	30.00	60.00
18 Duane Pillette	30.00	60.00
19 Bud Podbielan	30.00	60.00
20 Charley Rabe	30.00	60.00
21 Leo Righetti	40.00	80.00
22 Joe Taylor	30.00	60.00
23 Edo Vanni CO	30.00	60.00
24 Maury Willis UER misspelled Morrie	150.00	300.00

1958 Buffalo Bisons Bond Bread

This standard-size set black and white set features members of the 1958 Buffalo Bisons. This set has the ACC designation of D301 and the cards feature an advertisment for the TV show "Casey Jones" at the bottom and a player bio with a blurb along with an ad for Bond Bread on the back.

COMPLETE SET (9)	150.00	300.00
1 Al Aber	15.00	30.00
2 Joe Caffie	15.00	30.00
3 Phil Cavarretta MG	30.00	60.00
4 Rip Coleman	15.00	30.00
5 Luke Easter	30.00	60.00
6 Ken Johnson	20.00	40.00
7 Lou Ortiz	15.00	30.00
8 Jack Phillips	15.00	30.00
9 Jim Small	15.00	30.00

1958 Omaha Cardinals Team Issue

This 24 card black and white blank-backed set, which measures approximately 3 3/*" by 4 3/8" features members of the Omaha Cardinals, who were a St Louis Cardinals farm club at that time. These cards are not numbered, so we have sequenced them in alphabetical order. This set features a Bob Gibson card, which pre-dates his Topps Rookie Card.

COMPLETE SET	500.00	1,000.00
1 Antonio Alomar	15.00	30.00
2 Dave Benedict	15.00	30.00
3 Bill Bergesch	15.00	30.00
4 Bob Blaylock	15.00	30.00
5 Pidge Browne	15.00	30.00
6 Chris Cannizzaro	20.00	40.00
7 Nels Chittum	15.00	30.00
8 Don Choate	15.00	30.00
9 Phil Clark	15.00	30.00
10 Jim Frey	20.00	40.00
11 Bob Gibson	150.00	300.00
12 Ev Joyner	15.00	30.00
13 Johnny Keane MG	15.00	30.00
14 Paul Kippels	15.00	30.00
15 Boyd Linker	15.00	30.00
16 Bob Mabe	15.00	30.00
17 Bernie Mateosky	15.00	30.00
18 Ron Plaza	15.00	30.00
19 Bill Queen	15.00	30.00
20 Bill Smith	15.00	30.00
21 Bobby Gene Smith	15.00	30.00
22 Lee Tate	15.00	30.00
23 Benny Valenzuela	15.00	30.00
24 Header Card	15.00	30.00

1958 Seattle Popcorn

This set is similar to the other Seattle Popcorn sets. The backs carry an advertisement for Ralph's Thriftway. Also mentioned was an offer of a free 8" by 10" player picture of the collector's choice for any nine cards. The nine cards were punched and returned to the collector along with the chosen 8" by 10" photo. The large photos were referred to as "Seattle Premiums." The cards are unnumbered and checklisted below in alphabetical order. Ralph's Thriftway took the place of Gil's Drive-In used in 1956 and 1957 for this promotion. No blank back Seattle cards were issued in 1958.

COMPLETE SET (19)	500.00	1,000.00
1 Bob Balcena	30.00	60.00
2 Eddie Basinski	30.00	60.00
3 Hal Bevan	30.00	60.00
4 Jack Bloomfield	30.00	60.00
5 Juan Delis	30.00	60.00
6 Dutch Dotterer	30.00	60.00
7 Jim Dyck	30.00	60.00
8 Al Federoff	30.00	60.00
9 Art Fowler	40.00	80.00
10 Bill Kennedy	30.00	60.00
11 Marty Kutyna	30.00	60.00
12 Ray Orteig	30.00	60.00
13 Duane Pillette	30.00	60.00
14 Vada Pinson	150.00	300.00
15 Connie Ryan MG	40.00	80.00
16 Phil Shartzer	30.00	60.00
17 Max Surkont	30.00	60.00
18 Gale Wade	30.00	60.00
19 Ted Wieand	30.00	60.00

1958 Union Oil

The 1958 Union Olil set of ten black and white, unnumbered cards depicts members of the Sacramento Solons. Each card has a white strip containing the player's name, team and position below the picture. The back has a pennant design advertising the "76 Sports Club" and states that the card is redeemable for free admission to a specific Solons game. The cards measure approximately 2 1/2" by 3 1/2".

COMPLETE SET (10)	250.00	500.00
1 Marshall Bridges	75.00	150.00
2 Dick Cole	25.00	50.00
3 Jim Greengrass	30.00	60.00
4 Al Heist	30.00	60.00
5 Nippy Jones	30.00	60.00
6 Carlos Paula	30.00	60.00
7 Kal Segrist	25.00	50.00
8 Sibbi Sisti	30.00	60.00
9 Joe Stanka	25.00	50.00
10 Bud Watkins	50.00	100.00

1959 Darigold Farms

The cards in this 22-card set measure 2 1/2" by 2 3/8". Darigold Farms produced this 1959 set to spotlight the Spokane Indians baseball team. The cards are unnumbered and contain black and white photos set against colored backgrounds (1-8 have yellow, 9-16 have red and 17-22 have blue). The cards were attached to milk cartons by tabs and carry the catalog number F115-1. The cards have been alphabetized and assigned numbers in the checklist below.

COMPLETE SET (22)	1,300.00	2,600.00
1 Facundo Barragan	75.00	150.00
2 Steve Bilko	100.00	200.00
3 Bobby Bragan MG	100.00	200.00
4 Chuck Churn	75.00	150.00
5 Tommy Davis	150.00	300.00
6 Dom Domenichelli	75.00	150.00
7 Bob Giallombardo	75.00	150.00
8 Connie Grob	75.00	150.00
9 Fred Hatfield	75.00	150.00
10 Bob Lillis	100.00	200.00
11 Lloyd Merritt	75.00	150.00
12 Larry Miller	75.00	150.00
13 Chris Nicolosi	75.00	150.00
14 Allen Norris	75.00	150.00
15 Phil Ortega	75.00	150.00
16 Phillips Paine	75.00	150.00
17 Bill Parsons	75.00	150.00
18 Hisel Patrick	75.00	150.00
19 Tony Roig	75.00	150.00
20 Tom Saffell	75.00	150.00
21 Norm Sherry	100.00	200.00
22 Ben Wade	75.00	150.00

1959 Montreal Royals O'Keefe Ale

These 24 black and white photo stamps were issued by O'Keefe Ale and feature members of the 1959 Montreal Royals. The photos measure 3" by 4" and the stamps have a player photo. The bottom of the stamp has the players name and the position which is printed in English and French. Each of these stamps were designed to be mounted into an album.

COMPLETE SET (24)	350.00	700.00
COMMON CARD (1-22)	20.00	40.00
COMMON STAT CARD	10.00	20.00
1 Edmundo Amoros	30.00	60.00
2 Bob Aspromonte	25.00	50.00
3 Babe Birrer	20.00	40.00
4 Mike Brumley	20.00	40.00
5 Clay Bryant MG	20.00	40.00
6 Yvon Dunn TR	20.00	40.00
7 Bill George	20.00	40.00
8 Mike Goliat	20.00	40.00
9 John Gray	20.00	40.00
10 Billy Harris	20.00	40.00
11 Jim Koranda	20.00	40.00
12 Paul LaPalme	20.00	40.00
13 Tom Lasorda	60.00	120.00
14 Bob Lennon	20.00	40.00
15 Clyde Parris	20.00	40.00
16 Ed Rakow	20.00	40.00
17 Curt Roberts	20.00	40.00
18 Freddy Rodriguez	20.00	40.00
19 Harry Schwegman	20.00	40.00
20 Angel Scull	20.00	40.00
21 Dick Teed	20.00	40.00
22 Rene Valdes	20.00	40.00
23 Mid-Season Batting Averages	10.00	20.00
24 Mid-Season Pitching Averages	10.00	20.00
XX Album		

1959 Seattle Popcorn

This 38-card set of the Seattle Rainiers ballclub of the Pacific Coast League was distributed to the public as inserts in boxes of popcorn sold at Sicks' Stadium in Seattle. Only one card was inserted per box and measured approximately 2" by 3". The sets were produced by the ballclub and issued each season from 1954 through 1968. The fronts feature a black-and-white player photo with the player's name and position printed at the bottom. The backs are blank. Two separate releases were issued in 1959--one in the Spring in April using 1958 photos (1-13), and one in the Summer using 1959 photos (14-38). The cards are unnumbered and checklisted below in alphabetical order within the Spring or Summer season issues.

COMPLETE SET (38)	900.00	1,800.00
1 Frank Amaya	30.00	60.00

2 Hal Bevan 30.00 60.00
3 Jack Bloomfield 30.00 60.00
4 Clarence Churn 30.00 60.00
5 Eddie Kazak 30.00 60.00
6 Bill Kennedy 30.00 60.00
7 Harry Malmbeg 30.00 60.00
8 Claude Osteen 50.00 100.00
9 Charley Rabe 30.00 60.00
10 Max Surkont 30.00 60.00
11 Ted Tappe 30.00 60.00
12 Gale Wade 30.00 60.00
13 Bill Wight 30.00 60.00
14 Bobby Adams 30.00 60.00
15 Jack Dittmer 30.00 60.00
16 Jim Dyck 30.00 60.00
17 Dee Fondy 30.00 60.00
18 Mark Freeman 30.00 60.00
19 Dick Hanlon 30.00 60.00
20 Carroll Hardy 30.00 60.00
21 Bobby Henrich 30.00 60.00
22 Jay Hook 30.00 60.00
23 Fred Hutchinson MG 75.00 150.00
24 Jake Jenkins 30.00 60.00
25 Harry Lowren 30.00 60.00
26 Bob Mape UER/(misspelled Mabe) 30.00 60.00
27 Harry Malmbeg UER/(misspelled Malmberg 30.00
60.00
28 Darrell Martin 30.00 60.00
29 John McCall 30.00 60.00
30 Paul Pettit 50.00 100.00
31 Rudy Regalado 30.00 60.00
32 Eric Rodin 30.00 60.00
33 Don Rudolph 30.00 60.00
34 Lou Skizas 30.00 60.00
35 Dave Stenhouse 30.00 60.00
36 Alan Strange MG 30.00 60.00
37 Elmer Valo 50.00 100.00
38 Ed Winceniak 30.00 60.00

1960 Darigold Farms

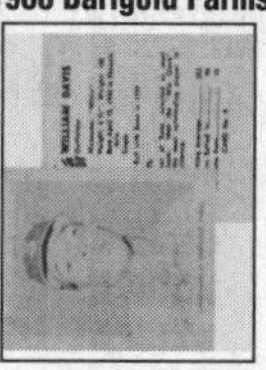

The cards in this 24-card set measure 2 3/8" by 2 9/16". The 1960 Darigold edition of the Spokane Indians has several distinguishing features which allow it to be separated from the similar set produced the year before. These cards are also cut similar to what a matchbook cover would be like. While the top half is basically just a white square, the bottom is where the picture is. In addition and most importantly, the cards are numbered and there are 24 in the set. The sequential use of color background was retained; with cards number 1-8 having a yellow background, cards 9-16 have a green background and 17-24 have a red background. A facsimile autograph was added to the front of each card. The catalog designation is F115-2.

COMPLETE SET (24) 500.00 1,000.00
1 Chris Nicolosi 40.00 80.00
2 Jim Pagliaroni 60.00 120.00
3 Roy Smalley 60.00 120.00
4 Bill Bethee 40.00 80.00
5 Joe Liscio TR 40.00 80.00
6 Curt Roberts 40.00 80.00
7 Ed Palmquist 40.00 80.00
8 Willie Davis 75.00 150.00
9 Bob Giallombardo 40.00 80.00
10 Pedro Gomez MG 60.00 120.00
11 Mel Nelson 40.00 80.00
12 Charlie Smith 50.00 100.00
13 Clarence Churn 40.00 80.00
14 Ramon Conde 40.00 80.00
15 George O'Donnell 40.00 80.00
16 Tony Roig 40.00 80.00
17 Frank Howard 75.00 150.00
18 Billy Harris 40.00 80.00
19 Mike Brumley 40.00 80.00
20 Earl Robinson 40.00 80.00
21 Ron Fairly 75.00 150.00
22 Joe Frazier 40.00 80.00
23 Allen Norris 40.00 80.00
24 Ford Young 40.00 80.00

1960 Henry House Wieners

This 18-card set features Seattle Rainiers of the Pacific Coast League (PCL) only. The cards measure 3 3/4" by 4 1/2" and they are skip-numbered by uniform number. Cards are printed on stiff cardboard with red ink. The catalog designation for this scarce set is F171.

COMPLETE SET (18) 2,000.00 4,000.00
2 Harry Malmberg 125.00 250.00
3 Francisco Obregon 125.00 250.00
4 Johnny O'Brien 150.00 300.00
5 Gordon Coleman 150.00 300.00
6 Bill Hain 125.00 250.00
8 Dick Sisler 150.00 300.00
9 Jerry Zimmerman 125.00 250.00
10 Hal Bevan 125.00 250.00
14 Rudy Regalado 125.00 250.00
15 Paul Pettit 150.00 300.00
16 Buddy Gilbert 125.00 250.00
21 Erv Palica 125.00 250.00
22 Joe Taylor 125.00 250.00
25 Bill Kennedy 125.00 250.00
26 Dave Stenhouse 125.00 250.00
28 Ray Ripplemeyer 150.00 300.00
30 Charlie Beamon 125.00 250.00
33 Don Rudolph 125.00 250.00

1960 Maple Leafs Shopsy's Frankfurters

These 23 blank-backed cards measure approximately 2 3/16" by 3 1/4" and feature players from the Toronto Maple Leafs of the International League. The white-bordered cards carry posed black-and-white player photos. The player's name and position appear in black lettering within the bottom white margin; the words "Shopsy's Player Photo" appear in black lettering within the top white margin. The catalog designation for this set is FC35. The cards are unnumbered and checklisted below in alphabetical order.

COMPLETE SET (23) 500.00 1,000.00
1 Sparky Anderson 75.00 150.00
2 Bob Chakales 15.00 40.00
3 Al Cicotte 15.00 40.00
4 Rip Coleman 15.00 40.00
5 Steve Demeter 15.00 40.00
6 Don Dillard 15.00 40.00
7 Frank Funk 15.00 40.00
8 Russ Heman 15.00 40.00
9 Earl Hersh 15.00 40.00
10 Allen Jones 15.00 40.00
11 Jim King 15.00 40.00
12 Jack Kubiszyn 15.00 40.00
13 Mel McGaha CO 15.00 40.00
14 Bill Moran 15.00 40.00
15 Ron Negray 15.00 40.00
16 Herb Plews 15.00 40.00
17 Steve Ridzik 15.00 40.00
18 Pat Scantlebury 15.00 40.00
19 Bill Smith 15.00 40.00
20 Bob Smith 15.00 40.00
21 Tim Thompson 15.00 40.00
22 Jack Waters 15.00 40.00
23 Archie Wilson 15.00 40.00

1960 Seattle Popcorn

This 18-card set of the Seattle Rainiers ballclub of the Pacific Coast League was distributed to the public as inserts in boxes of popcorn sold at Sicks' Stadium in Seattle. Only one card was inserted per box and measured approximately 2" by 3". The sets were produced by the ballclub and issued each season from 1954 through 1968. The fronts feature a black-and-white player photo with the player's name and position printed at the bottom. The backs are blank. The cards are unnumbered and checklisted below in alphabetical order.

COMPLETE SET (18) 400.00 800.00
1 Charlie Beamon 30.00 60.00
2 Hal Bevan 30.00 60.00
3 Whammy Douglas 30.00 60.00
4 Buddy Gilbert 30.00 60.00
5 Hal Jeffcoat CO 30.00 60.00
6 Leigh Lawrence 30.00 60.00
7 Darrell Martin 30.00 60.00
8 Francisco Obregon 30.00 60.00
9 Johnny O'Brien 50.00 100.00
10 Paul Pettit 30.00 60.00
11 Ray Rippelmeyer 30.00 60.00
12 Don Rudolph 30.00 60.00
13 Willard Schmidt 30.00 60.00
14 Dick Sisler MG 50.00 100.00
15 Lou Skizas 30.00 60.00
16 Joe Taylor 30.00 60.00
17 Bob Thurman 30.00 60.00
18 Gerald Zimmerman 30.00 60.00

1960 Tacoma Bank

The Tacoma National Bank of Washington set features 21 large cards each measuring 3" by 5". The set exclusively features players from the Tacoma Giants of the Pacific Coast League (PCL). Several of the players went on to later play for the big league Giants. The catalog designation is H801-14. A pre-Rookie Card of Juan Marichal is in this set.

COMPLETE SET (21) 600.00 1,200.00
1 Matty Alou 50.00 100.00
2 Ossie Alvarez 30.00 60.00
3 Don Choate 30.00 60.00
4 Red Davis 30.00 60.00
5 Bob Farley 30.00 60.00
6 Eddie Fisher 40.00 80.00
7 Tom Haller 40.00 80.00
8 Sherman Jones 30.00 60.00
9 Juan Marichal 150.00 300.00
10 Ramon Monzant 30.00 60.00
11 Danny O'Connell 50.00 100.00
12 Jose Pagan 40.00 80.00
13 Bob Perry 30.00 60.00
14 Dick Phillips 30.00 60.00
15 Bobby Prescott 30.00 60.00
16 Marshall Renfroe 30.00 60.00
17 Frank Reveira 30.00 60.00
18 Dusty Rhodes 50.00 100.00
19 Sal Taormina 30.00 60.00
20 Verle Tiefenthaler 30.00 60.00
21 Dom Zanni 30.00 60.00

1960 Union Oil

The 1960 Union Oil set consists of nine full-color, skip-numbered cards spotlighting the Seattle Rainers. These cards were given away by Union Oil stations in the Seattle area. The fronts contain full-length action photos taken at Sicks Stadium. Ripplemeyer and Obregon are considered the "scarcities" of the set. The biographical material on the back is entitled "Thumb Nail Sketches". Cards in this set measure approximately 3 1/8" by 4".

COMPLETE SET (9) 125.00 250.00
4 Francisco Obregon 10.00 25.00
6 Drew Gilbert 5.00 12.00
7 Bill Hain 5.00 12.00
10 Ray Ripplemeyer 60.00 120.00
13 Joe Taylor 5.00 12.00
15 Lou Skizas 5.00 12.00
17 Don Rudolph 6.00 15.00
19 Gordy Coleman 8.00 20.00
22 Hal Bevan 5.00 12.00

1961 Maple Leafs Bee Hive

These 24 blank-backed cards measure approximately 2 3/16" by 3 3/16" and are printed on thin stock. The set features white-bordered black-and-white photos of the 1961 Toronto Maple Leafs of the International League. The player's name and position appear in black lettering within the lower white margin. The catalog designation for this set is FC36. The cards are unnumbered and checklisted below in alphabetical order.

COMPLETE SET (24) 600.00 1,200.00
1 Sparky Anderson 125.00 250.00
2 Fritzie Brickell 30.00 60.00
3 Ellis Burton 30.00 60.00
4 Bob Chakales 30.00 60.00
5 Rip Coleman 30.00 60.00
6 Steve Demeter 30.00 60.00
7 Joe Hannah 30.00 60.00
8 Earl Hersh 30.00 60.00
9 Lou Jackson 30.00 60.00
10 Ken Johnson 40.00 80.00
11 Lou Johnson 40.00 80.00
12 John Lipon 30.00 60.00
13 Carl Mathias 30.00 60.00
14 Bill Moran 30.00 60.00
15 Ron Negray 30.00 60.00
16 Herb Plews 30.00 60.00
17 Dave Pope 30.00 60.00
18 Steve Ridzik 30.00 60.00
19 Raul Sanchez 30.00 60.00
20 Pat Scantlebury 30.00 60.00
21 Bill Smith 30.00 60.00
22 Bob Smith 30.00 60.00
23 Chuck Tanner 50.00 100.00
24 Tim Thompson 30.00 60.00

1961 Seattle Popcorn

This 29-card set of the Seattle Rainiers ballclub of the Pacific Coast League was distributed to the public as inserts in boxes of popcorn sold at Sicks' Stadium in Seattle. Only one card was inserted per box and measured approximately 2" by 3". The sets were produced by the ballclub and issued each season from 1954 through 1968. The fronts feature a black-and-white player photo with the player's name and position printed at the bottom. The backs are blank. The cards are unnumbered and checklisted below in alphabetical order.

COMPLETE SET (29) 300.00 600.00
1 Galen Cisco 10.00 25.00
2 Marlin Coughtry 8.00 20.00
3 Marlin Coughtry Batting 8.00 20.00
4 Pete Cronin 8.00 20.00
5 Arnold Earley 8.00 20.00
6 Bob Heffner 8.00 20.00
7 Bob Heffner Close-up 8.00 20.00
8 Curt Jenson 8.00 20.00
9 Curt Jenson Close-up 8.00 20.00
10 Harry Malmberg P CO 8.00 20.00
11 Harry Malmberg CO Close-up 8.00 20.00
12 Dave Mann 8.00 20.00
13 Darrell Martin 8.00 20.00
14 Erv Palica 8.00 20.00
15 Ervin Palica 8.00 20.00
16 Johnny Pesky MG 15.00 40.00
17 Johnny Pesky MG Close-up 15.00 40.00
18 Dick Radatz 12.50 30.00
19 Ted Schreiber 8.00 20.00
20 Ted Shreiber UER misspelled Schreiber Batting 8.00 20.00
21 Paul Smith 8.00 20.00
22 Paul Smith Close-up 8.00 20.00
23 Bob Tillman Marked as an infielder He played catcher Card says John Tillman 8.00 20.00
24 Bob Tillman Catcher 8.00 20.00
25 Bo Toft 8.00 20.00
26 Tom Umphlett 8.00 20.00
27 Tom Umphlett Close-up 8.00 20.00
28 Earl Wilson 12.50 30.00
29 Ken Wolfe 8.00 20.00

1961 Syracuse Chiefs Team Issue

These 5" by 7" cards photos were issued by the team to promote the players on the 1961 Syracuse Chiefs team. Since these photos are unnumbered, we have entered them in alphabetical order.

COMPLETE SET 60.00 120.00
1 Joe Bonikowski 4.00 10.00
2 Mike Cuellar 8.00 20.00
3 Ralph Lumenti 4.00 10.00
4 Dan Motta 4.00 10.00
5 Willie Miranda 4.00 10.00
6 Rip Repulski 5.00 12.00
7 Ted Sadowski 4.00 10.00
8 Woody Smith 4.00 10.00
9 Lee Stange 5.00 12.00
10 Ron Stillwell 4.00 10.00
11 Sandy Valdespino 4.00 10.00

1961 Tacoma Bank

The Tacoma National Bank of Washington set again consists of 21 large (3" by 5") cards. The set exclusively features players from the Tacoma Giants of the Pacific Coast League (PCL). Several of the players went on to later play for the big league Giants. The catalog designation is H801-15. A pre-Rookie Card of Gaylord Perry is in this set.

COMPLETE SET (21) 150.00 300.00
1 Rafael Alomar 6.00 15.00
2 Ernie Bowman 6.00 15.00
3 Bud Byerly 6.00 15.00
4 Ray Daviault 6.00 15.00
5 Red Davis 6.00 15.00
6 Bob Farley 6.00 15.00
7 Gil Garrido 6.00 15.00
8 John Goetz 6.00 15.00
9 Bill Hain 6.00 15.00
10 Ronald Herbel 6.00 15.00
11 Lynn Lovenguth 6.00 15.00
12 Georges H. Maranda 6.00 15.00
13 Manny Mota 8.00 20.00
14 John Orsino 6.00 15.00
15 Gaylord Perry 20.00 50.00
16 Bob Perry 6.00 15.00
17 Dick Phillips 6.00 15.00
18 Frank Reveira 6.00 15.00
19 Dusty Rhodes 8.00 20.00
20 Verle Tiefenthaler 6.00 15.00
21 Dom Zanni 6.00 15.00

1961 Union Oil

The cards in thie 67-card set measure 3" by 4". The 1961 Union Oil set of sepia, unnumbered cards contains players from six Pacific Coast League teams. Individual player cards were available only in their respective cities at Union 76 stations. The backs are in blue print and give player biographies and depict the Union 76 logo. Spokane players are more difficult to obtain than players from other teams. The Gomez and Prescott cards are scarce. The Mike Hershberger card actually depicts Bobby Knoop. Cards are numbered alphabetically with team (except Tacoma's uniform numbering) and have a prefix before the number indicating the team, i.e. Hawaii (H), Portland (P), San Diego (SD), Sacramento (S), Spokane (SP) and Tacoma (T). Later on in the 1961 season, some exhibition games were played between the Taiyo Whales of Japan and the Hawaii team. We are listing those cards at the end of our listing for this set.

COMPLETE SET (67) 600.00 1,200.00
COMMON PLAYER (SD/T) 5.00 12.00
COMMON CARDS SD/T 6.00 15.00
H1 Ray Jablonski 12.50 30.00
H2 Jim McManus 10.00 25.00
H3 George Prescott 50.00 100.00
H4 Diego Segui 12.50 30.00
H5 Rachel Slider 10.00 25.00
H6 Jim Small 10.00 25.00
H7 Milt Smith 10.00 25.00
H8 Dave Thies 10.00 25.00
H9 Jay Ward 10.00 25.00
H10 Bill Werle 10.00 25.00
P1 Ed Bauta 5.00 12.00
P2 Vern Benson 5.00 12.00
P3 Jerry Buchek 5.00 12.00
P4 Bob Burda 5.00 12.00
P5 Duke Carmel 5.00 12.00
P6 Don Choate 5.00 12.00
P7 Phil Gagliano 5.00 12.00
P8 Jim Hickman 6.00 15.00
P9 Ray Katt 5.00 12.00
P10 Mel Nelson 5.00 12.00
P11 Jim Schaffer 5.00 12.00
P12 Mike Shannon 10.00 25.00
P13 Clint Stark 5.00 12.00
S1 Galen Cisco 5.00 12.00
S2 Lou Clinton 5.00 12.00
S3 Marlan Coughtry 5.00 12.00
S4 Harry Malmberg 5.00 12.00
S5 Dave Mann 5.00 12.00
S6 Derrell Martin 5.00 12.00
S7 Erv Palica 5.00 12.00
S8 John Pesky 8.00 20.00
S9 Bob Tillman 5.00 12.00
S10 Marv Toft 5.00 12.00
S11 Tom Umphlett 5.00 12.00
T10 Red Davis 5.00 12.00
T12 Dick Phillips 5.00 12.00
T17 Gil Garrido 5.00 12.00
T20 Georges Maranda 5.00 12.00
T25 John Orsino 5.00 12.00
T26 Dusty Rhodes 10.00 25.00

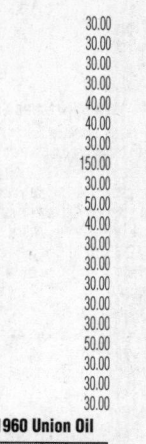

T28 Ron Herbel	5.00	12.00
T29 Gaylord Perry	75.00	150.00
T30 Rafael Alomar	5.00	12.00
T34 Bob Farley	5.00	12.00
SD1 Dick Barone	5.00	12.00
SD2 Jim Bolger	5.00	12.00
SD3 Kent Hadley	5.00	12.00
SD4 Mike Hershberger	5.00	12.00
SD5 Stan Johnson	5.00	12.00
SD6 Dick Lines	5.00	12.00
SD7 Jim Napier	5.00	12.00
SD8 Tony Roig	5.00	12.00
SD9 Herb Score	20.00	50.00
SD10 Harry Simpson	6.00	15.00
SD11 Joe Taylor	5.00	12.00
SD12 Ben Wade	5.00	12.00
SP1 Doug Camilli	10.00	25.00
SP2 Ramon Conde	10.00	25.00
SP3 Bob Giallombardo	10.00	25.00
SP4 Mike Goliat	10.00	25.00
SP5 Preston Gomez	50.00	100.00
SP6 Rod Graber	10.00	25.00
SP7 Tim Harkness	10.00	25.00
SP8 Jim Harwell	10.00	25.00
SP9 Howie Reed	10.00	25.00
SP10 Curt Roberts	10.00	25.00
SP11 Rene Valdes	10.00	25.00
TW1 Akihito Kondo		
TW2 Gentaro Shimada		
TW3 Taiyo Whales		

1962 Kahn's Atlanta

The cards in this 24-card set measure 3 1/4" X 4". The 1962 Kahn's Wieners Atlanta set features unnumbered, black and white cards of the Atlanta Crackers of the International League. The backs contain player statistical information as well as instructions on how to obtain free tickets. The catalog designation is F155-9. The cards are listed and numbered below in alphabetical order by the subject's name.

COMPLETE SET (24)	300.00	600.00
1 Jim Beauchamp	12.50	30.00
2 Gerry Buchek	10.00	25.00
3 Bob Burda	10.00	25.00
4 Dick Dietz	12.50	30.00
5 Bob Duliba	10.00	25.00
6 Harry Fanok	10.00	25.00
7 Phil Gagliano	12.50	30.00
8 John Glenn	10.00	25.00
9 Leroy Gregory	10.00	25.00
10 Dick Hughes	10.00	25.00
11 Johnny Kucks	12.50	30.00
12 Johnny Lewis	12.50	30.00
13 Tim McCarver	75.00	150.00
14 Bob Milliken	10.00	25.00
15 Joe M. Morgan	12.50	30.00
16 Ron Plaza	10.00	25.00
17 Bob Sadowski	10.00	25.00
18 Jim Saul	10.00	25.00
19 Willard Schmidt	10.00	25.00
20 Joe Schultz MG	12.50	30.00
21 Mike Shannon	30.00	60.00
22 Paul Toth	10.00	25.00
23 Lou Vickery	10.00	25.00
24 Fred Whitfield	12.50	30.00

1962 Omaha Dodgers Team Issue

This 22 card blank backed set, which measured approximately 3 3/" by 4 1/4" was issued by the team and featured members of the 1962 Omaha Dodgers. Each black and white photo features a facsimile autograph. Since these cards are unnumbered, we have sequenced them in alphabetical order.

COMPLETE SET	150.00	300.00
1 Joe Altobelli MG	8.00	20.00
2 Jim Barbieri	8.00	20.00
3 Scott Breeden	8.00	20.00
4 Mike Brumley	8.00	20.00
5 Jose Ceasar	8.00	20.00
6 Billy Hunter	8.00	20.00
7 Don LeJohn	8.00	20.00
8 Jack Lutz	8.00	20.00
9 Ken McMullen	10.00	25.00
10 Danny Ozark CO	8.00	20.00
11 Curt Roberts	8.00	20.00
12 Ernie Rodriguez	8.00	20.00
13 Dick Scarborough	8.00	20.00
14 Bart Shirley	8.00	20.00
15 Dick Smith	8.00	20.00
16 Jack Smith	8.00	20.00
17 Nate Smith	8.00	20.00
18 Gene Snyder	8.00	20.00
19 Burbon Wheeler	8.00	20.00
20 Nick Willhite	8.00	20.00
21 Jim Williams	8.00	20.00
22 Larry Williams	8.00	20.00

1962 Seattle Popcorn

This 19-card set of the Seattle Rainiers ballclub of the Pacific Coast League was distributed to the public as inserts in boxes of popcorn sold at Sicks' Stadium in Seattle. Only one card was inserted per box and measured approximately 2" by 3". The sets were produced by the ballclub and issued each season from 1954 through 1968. The fronts feature a black-and-white player photo with the player's name and position printed at the bottom. The backs are blank. The cards are unnumbered and checklisted below in alphabetical order.

COMPLETE SET (18)	400.00	800.00
1 Dave Hall	30.00	60.00
2 Billy Harrell	30.00	60.00
3 Curt Jenson UER misspelled Jensen	30.00	60.00
4 Stew MacDonald	30.00	60.00
5 Bill MacLeod	30.00	60.00
6 Dave Mann	30.00	60.00
7 Dave Mann Sliding	30.00	60.00
8 Dave Morehead	30.00	60.00
9 John Pesky MG	50.00	100.00
10 Ted Schreiber Position says Infielder	30.00	60.00
11 Ted Schreiber Position says Second Base	30.00	60.00
12 Elmer Singleton	30.00	60.00
13 Archie Skeen	30.00	60.00
14 Pete Smith	30.00	60.00
15 George Spencer	30.00	60.00
16 Bo Toft	30.00	60.00
17 Tom Umphlett	30.00	60.00
18 Ken Wolfe	30.00	60.00

1962 Tulsa Oilers Pepsi

Issued by Pepsi Cola to spotlight the 1962 Tulsa Oilers, these cards were originally distributed in two-card panels with a ring tab for attachment to a carton of soda. The cards are not numbered so we have sequenced them alphabetically and this set has a catalog number of F230-1. If a pair for any of the 1962, 63 or 66 sets is seen with the ring tab complete, add 25 percent to the combined values of the two players.

COMPLETE SET (24)	100.00	200.00
1 Bob Blaylock	3.00	8.00
2 Bud Bloomfield	3.00	8.00
3 Dick Hughes	3.00	8.00
4 Gary Kolb	3.00	8.00
5 Chris Krug	3.00	8.00
6 Hank Kuhlmann	3.00	8.00
7 Whitey Kurowski	5.00	12.00
8 Johnny Lewis	3.00	8.00
9 Elmer Lindsey	3.00	8.00
10 Jeoff Long	3.00	8.00
11 Pepper Martin	6.00	15.00
12 Jerry Marx	3.00	8.00
13 Weldon Mauldin	3.00	8.00
14 Dal Maxvill	3.00	8.00
15 Bill McNamee	3.00	8.00
16 Joe Patterson	3.00	8.00
17 Gordon Richardson	3.00	8.00
18 Daryl Robertson	3.00	8.00
19 Tommy Schwaner	3.00	8.00
20 Joe Shipley	3.00	8.00
21 Jon Smith Batboy	3.00	8.00
22 Clint Stark	3.00	8.00
23 Terry Tucker Batboy	3.00	8.00
24 Bill Wakefield	3.00	8.00

1963 Milwaukee Sausage

This 11-card set features Seattle Rainiers of the Pacific Coast League (PCL) only. The cards measure approximately 4 1/2" by 4 9/16" and they are unnumbered. Cards are printed on stiff cardboard with blue ink. The Milwaukee brand logo is featured in the upper right corner in red and yellow. The catalog designation for this scarce set is F180.

COMPLETE SET (11)	1,250.00	2,500.00
1 Dave Hall	125.00	250.00
2 Bill Harrell	125.00	250.00
3 Pete Jernigan	125.00	250.00
4 Bill McLeod	125.00	250.00
5 Mel Parnell	150.00	300.00
6 Elmer Singleton	125.00	250.00
7 Archie Skeen	125.00	250.00
8 Paul Smith	150.00	300.00
9 Pete Smith	125.00	250.00
10 Bill Spanswick	125.00	250.00
11 George Spencer	125.00	250.00

1963 Rochester Red Wings Schieble Press W745

These ten cards measure approximately 6" by 3 3/4". The full-color borderless fronts feature a player photo along with a fascimile autograph. The horizontal backs feature player information along with a brief biography. The cards were produced by Scheible Press and their logo is listed on the bottom of the card. The Chittum card is made out of a thicker cardboard stock. The others are more of a thin paper stock. The cards were packaged in a envelope with nine cards indicating that there was a change in player selection later in the season.

COMPLETE SET (10)	75.00	150.00
1 Joe Altobelli HOR	10.00	25.00
2 Steve Bilko	8.00	20.00
3 Sam Bowens HOR	6.00	15.00
4 Don Brummer	6.00	15.00
5 Nelson Chittum	6.00	15.00
6 Luke Easter	12.50	30.00
7 Darrell Johnson MG Chris Krug	6.00	15.00
8 Fred Valentine	6.00	15.00
9 Ozzie Virgil	6.00	15.00
10 Ray Youngdahl	6.00	15.00

1963-64 San Diego Padres Team Issue

These 8" by 10" blank-backed black and white photos feature members of the San Diego Padres, which were at that time a farm team for the Cincinnati Reds. The highlight of these photos is a pre-rookie photo of Hall of Famer Tony Perez. Since these photos are unnumbered, we have sequenced them in alphabetical order. It is possible that there are more photos so any additions are greatly appreciated.

COMPLETE SET	60.00	120.00
1 Don Heffner MG	6.00	15.00
2 Tommy Helms	8.00	20.00
3 Tony Perez	40.00	80.00
4 Ray Rippelmeyer	6.00	15.00

1963 Seattle Popcorn

This 15-card set of the Seattle Rainiers ballclub of the Pacific Coast League was distributed to the public as inserts in boxes of popcorn sold at Sicks' Stadium in Seattle. Only one card was inserted per box and measured approximately 2" by 3". The sets were produced by the ballclub and issued each season from 1954 through 1968. The fronts feature a black-and-white player photo with the player's name printed at the bottom. The backs are blank. The cards are unnumbered and checklisted below in alphabetical order.

COMPLETE SET (15)	350.00	700.00
1 Don Gile	30.00	60.00
2 Dave Hall	30.00	60.00
3 Billy Harrell	30.00	60.00
4 Pete Jernigan	30.00	60.00
5 Stan Johnson	30.00	60.00
6 Dalton Jones	30.00	60.00
7 Mel Parnell MG	40.00	80.00
8 Joe Pedrazzini	30.00	60.00
9 Elmer Singleton CO	30.00	60.00
10 Archie Skeen	30.00	60.00
11 Rac Slider	30.00	60.00
12 Pete Smith	30.00	60.00
13 Bill Spanswick	30.00	60.00
14 George Spencer	30.00	60.00
15 Wilbur Wood	50.00	100.00

1963 Tulsa Oilers Pepsi

These sepia tone cards are unnumbered, as in the previous year, and depict Tulsa Oilers only. They are easily distinguished from the 1962 set by the Pepsi logo on the bottom right, which has "Pepsi-Cola" written over the bottle cap. The ring tab contains contest rules and an offer of free admission to an Oilers game. The catalog designation is F230-2.

COMPLETE SET (24)	100.00	200.00
1 Dennis Aust	3.00	8.00
2 Jim Beauchamp	3.00	8.00
3 Bud Bloomfield	3.00	8.00
4 Felix DeLeon	3.00	8.00
5 Don Dennis	3.00	8.00
6 Lamar Drummonds	3.00	8.00
7 Tom Hilgendorf	3.00	8.00
8 Gary Kolb	3.00	8.00
9 Chris Krug	3.00	8.00
10 Bee Lindsey	3.00	8.00
11 Roy Majtyka	3.00	8.00
12 Pepper Martin CO	6.00	15.00
13 Jerry Marx	3.00	8.00
14 Hunkey Mauldin	3.00	8.00
15 Joe Patterson	3.00	8.00
16 Grover Resinger	3.00	8.00
17 Gordon Richardson	3.00	8.00
18 Jon Smith BB	3.00	8.00
19 Chuck Taylor	3.00	8.00
20 Terry Tucker BB	3.00	8.00
21 Lou Vickery	3.00	8.00
22 Bill Wakefield	3.00	8.00
23 Harry Watts	3.00	8.00
24 Jerry Wild	3.00	8.00

1964 Seattle Popcorn

This 18-card set of the Seattle Rainiers ballclub of the Pacific Coast League was distributed to the public as inserts in boxes of popcorn sold at Sicks' Stadium in Seattle. Only one card was inserted per box and measured approximately 2" by 3". The sets were produced by the ballclub and issued each season from 1954 through 1968. The fronts feature a black-and-white player photo with the player's name printed at the bottom. The backs are blank. The cards are unnumbered and checklisted below in alphabetical order.

COMPLETE SET (18)	500.00	1,000.00
1 Earl Averill	50.00	100.00
2 Billy Gardner	50.00	100.00
3 Russ Gibson	30.00	60.00
4 Guido Grilli	30.00	60.00
5 Bob Guindon	30.00	60.00
6 Billy Harrell	30.00	60.00
7 Fred Holmes	30.00	60.00
8 Stan Johnson	30.00	60.00
9 Hal Kolstad	30.00	60.00
10 Gary Modrell	30.00	60.00
11 Felix Maldonado	30.00	60.00
12 Merlin Nippert	30.00	60.00
13 Rico Petrocelli	60.00	120.00
14 Jay Ritchie	30.00	60.00
15 Barry Shetrone	30.00	60.00
16 Pete Smith	30.00	60.00
17 Bill Tuttle	40.00	80.00
18 Edo Vanni MG	30.00	60.00

1964 Tulsa Oilers Pepsi

This eight-card set measures approximately 9" by 2 3/16" and was distributed by Pepsi-Cola. The fronts feature a facsimile player's autograph inside a baseball with player information printed below. These cards allowed a child under 12, when accompanied by an adult, free admission to Oiler Park on Pepsi-Oiler nights which were each Tuesday the Oilers were Home. The cards are unnumbered and checklisted below in alphabetical order.

COMPLETE SET	40.00	80.00
1 Bob Blaylock CO	2.00	5.00
2 Nelson Briles	4.00	10.00
3 Don Dennis	2.00	5.00
4 Bobby Dews	2.00	5.00
5 Dave Dowling	2.00	5.00
6 George Kernek	2.00	5.00
7 Chris Krug	2.00	5.00
8 Otto Meischner	2.00	5.00
9 Roy Majtyka	2.00	5.00
10 Grover Resinger MG	2.00	5.00
11 Rogers Robinson	2.00	5.00
12 Bobby Tolan	4.00	10.00
13 Lou Vickery	2.00	5.00
14 Harry Watts	2.00	5.00
15 Jerry Wild	2.00	5.00

1965 Seattle Popcorn

This 25-card set of the Seattle ballclub of the Pacific Coast League was distributed to the public as inserts in boxes of popcorn sold at Sicks' Stadium in Seattle. Only one card was inserted per box and measured approximately 2" by 3". The sets were produced by the ballclub and issued each season from 1954 through 1968. Since Seattle's major league affiliation switched from the Boston Red Sox to the California Angels, their name was changed from the "Rainiers" to the "Angels" for 1965. The fronts feature a black-and-white player photo with the player's name printed at the bottom. The backs carry an advertisement for radio station KVI 570 which carried Seattle's games. Since KVI is the only sponsor, this is how a collector can tell it is a 1965 card. Some cards are currently only known to exist in blank-back form. The cards are unnumbered and checklisted below in alphabetical order.

COMPLETE SET (24)	200.00	400.00
1 Earl Averill	8.00	20.00
2 Tom Burgmeier	6.00	15.00
3 Chuck Estrada Blank Back Same pose and crop as 6	6.00	15.00
4 Bob Guindon	6.00	15.00
5 Jack Hernandez	6.00	15.00
6 Fred Holmes	6.00	15.00
7 Ed Kirkpatrick	6.00	15.00
8 Hal Kolstad	6.00	15.00
9 Joe Koppe	6.00	15.00
10 Les Kuhnz	6.00	15.00
11 Bob Lemon MG	12.50	30.00
12 Bobby Locke	6.00	15.00
13 Jim McGlothlin	6.00	15.00
14 Bob Radovich Blankback	6.00	15.00
15 Bob Radovich	6.00	15.00
16 Merritt Ranew	6.00	15.00
17 Jimmie Reese Blank-Back	12.50	30.00
18 Rick Reichardt Blankback	6.00	15.00
19 Rick Reichardt	6.00	15.00
20 Tom Satriano	6.00	15.00
21 Dick Simpson	6.00	15.00
22 Jack Spring Blankback	6.00	15.00
23 Ed Sukla	6.00	15.00
24 Jackie Warner	6.00	15.00
25 Stan Williams	8.00	20.00

1966 Columbus Yankees Royal Crown

These cards, which measure the standard size when the coupon was detached, was issued by Royal Crown Cola in 1966. The black and white photos are only a small part of the card as the rest of the card is devoted to information about a contest in which a collector who completed the set was eligible for various prizes. Since this set is unnumbered, we have sequenced them in alphabetical order. Cards with tabs attached are worth 1.5X listed price. According to the tab, an album was also made for this set.

COMPLETE SET (20)	200.00	400.00
1 Gil Blanco	8.00	20.00
2 Ron Boyer	8.00	20.00
3 Jim Brenneman	8.00	20.00
4 Butch Cretara	8.00	20.00
5 Bill Henry	8.00	20.00
6 Joe Jeran	8.00	20.00
7 Jerry Kenney	8.00	20.00

8 Ron Kirk	8.00	20.00
9 Tom Kowalowski	8.00	20.00
10 Jim Marrujo	8.00	20.00
11 Dave McDonald	8.00	20.00
12 Ed Merritt	8.00	20.00
13 Jim Palma	8.00	20.00
14 Cecil Parkins	8.00	20.00
15 Jack Reed	8.00	20.00
16 Ellie Rodriguez	8.00	20.00
17 John Schroetpel	8.00	20.00
18 Dave Truelock	8.00	20.00
19 Steve Whitaker	8.00	20.00
20 Earl Willoughby	8.00	20.00
XX Album		

1966 Seattle Popcorn

This 30-card set of the Seattle Angels ballclub of the Pacific Coast League was distributed to the public as inserts in boxes of popcorn sold at Sicks' Stadium in Seattle. Only one card was inserted per box and measured approximately 2" by 3". The sets were produced by the ballclub and issued each season from 1954 through 1968. The fronts feature a black-and-white player photo with the player's name printed at the bottom. The backs carry an advertisement for radio station KVI 570 which carried Seattle's games. The 1966 cards list four other sponsors on the card. The cards are unnumbered and checklisted below in alphabetical order. John Olerud, father of future major league first baseman John Olerud, is believed to only have been released in a very scarce uncut sheet version. It is thought that less than five copies are known in the secondary market. Therefore, we are listing this card and not pricing it.

COMPLETE SET (29)	200.00	400.00
1 Del Bates	6.00	15.00
2 Tom Burgmeier	6.00	15.00
3 Jim Campanis	6.00	15.00
4 Jim Coates	6.00	15.00
5 Tony Cortopassi	6.00	15.00
6 Chuck Estrada	8.00	20.00
7 Ray Hernandez	6.00	15.00
8 Jay Johnstone	12.50	30.00
9 Bill Kelso	6.00	15.00
10 Vic LaRose	6.00	15.00
11 Bobby Locke	6.00	15.00
12 Rudy May	12.50	30.00
13 Andy Messersmith	12.50	30.00
14 Bubba Morton	6.00	15.00
15 Cotton Nash	10.00	25.00
16 John Olerud		
17 Marty Pattin	6.00	15.00
18 Merritt Ranew	6.00	15.00
19 Minnie Rojas Blank-Back	6.00	15.00
20 Minnie Rojas	6.00	15.00
21 George Rubio	6.00	15.00
22 Al Spangler	6.00	15.00
23 Ed Sukla	6.00	15.00
24 Felix Torres	6.00	15.00
25 Hector Torres	6.00	15.00
26 Ken Turner	6.00	15.00
27 Chuck Vinson	6.00	15.00
28 Don Wallace	6.00	15.00
29 Jack Warner	6.00	15.00
30 Mike White	6.00	15.00

1966 St. Petersburg Cardinals Team Issue

This 20-card set of the 1966 St. Petersburg Cardinals was sponsored by Foremost Milk and features black-and-white player portraits in white borders. The cards measure approximately 3 1/2" by 5". The backs are blank. The cards are unnumbered and checklisted below in alphabetical order.

COMPLETE SET (20)	40.00	80.00
1 Sparky Anderson	40.00	80.00
2 Dave Bakenhaster	.40	1.00
3 Leonard Boyer	.40	1.00
4 Ron Braddock	.40	1.00
5 Thomas Chip Coulter	.40	1.00
6 Ernest Sweet Pea Davis	.40	1.00
7 Phil Knuckles	.40	1.00
8 Doug Lukens	.40	1.00
9 Terry Milani	.40	1.00
10 Tim Morgan	.40	1.00
11 Harry Parker	.40	1.00
12 Jerry Robertson	.40	1.00
13 Francisco Rodriguez	.40	1.00
14 John Sonny Ruberto	.40	1.00
15 Charlie Stewart	.40	1.00
16 Gary L. Stone	.40	1.00
17 Charles Tim Thompson	.40	1.00
18 Jose Villar	.40	1.00
19 Archie L. Wade	.40	1.00
20 Jim Williamson	.40	1.00

1966 Toledo Mud Hens Team Issue

This 25-card set of the Toledo Mud Hens measures approximately 3 3/16" by 5" and features borderless black-and-white player photos. The backs are blank. The cards are unnumbered and checklisted below in alphabetical order.

COMPLETE SET (25)	250.00	500.00
1 Loren Babe MG	8.00	20.00
2 Jean Bahnsen	8.00	20.00
3 Bill Bethea	8.00	20.00
4 Wayne Comer	8.00	20.00
5 Jack Cullen	8.00	20.00
6 Jack Curtis	8.00	20.00
7 Jim Downs	8.00	20.00
8 Joe Faraci	8.00	20.00
9 Frank Fernandez	8.00	20.00
10 Mike Ferraro	8.00	20.00
11 Doc Foley	8.00	20.00
12 Mike Hegan	8.00	20.00
13 Jim Horsford	8.00	20.00
14 Dick Hughes	8.00	20.00
15 Elvis Jimenez	8.00	20.00
16 Tom Martz	8.00	20.00
17 Ed Merritt	8.00	20.00
18 Archie Moore	8.00	20.00
19 Bobby Murcer	50.00	100.00
20 Tony Przybycien	8.00	20.00
21 Bob Schmidt	8.00	20.00
22 Bill Shantz CO Charles Senger GM Loren Babe MG	8.00	20.00
23 Bill Shantz CO	8.00	20.00
24 Paul Toth	8.00	20.00
25 Jerry Walker	8.00	20.00

1966 Tulsa Oilers Pepsi

This set has 24 sepia tone, unnumbered Oilers cards, similar to previous issues but printed on thinner stock. Eight players were double printed (they are notated with a DP next to their names) and 16 two-card panels exist. Panel prices are 50 percent more than the sum of the individual prices.

COMPLETE SET (24)	125.00	250.00
COMMON CARD (1-24)	5.00	12.00
COMMON DP	3.00	8.00
1 Fritz Ackley	5.00	12.00
2 Dennis Aust	5.00	12.00
3 Elio Chacon DP	3.00	8.00
4 Jim Cosman	5.00	12.00
5 Mack Creager	5.00	12.00
6 Bobby Dews DP	3.00	8.00
7 Hal Gilson	5.00	12.00
8 Larry Jaster	5.00	12.00
9 Alex Johnson	6.00	15.00
10 George Kernek DP	3.00	8.00
11 Coco Laboy	5.00	12.00
12 Dick LeMay	5.00	12.00
13 Charlie Metro MG	5.00	12.00
14 Dave Pavlesic	5.00	12.00
15 Bobby Pfeil DP	3.00	8.00
16 Ron Piche	5.00	12.00
17 Bob Radovich	5.00	12.00
18 Dave Ricketts DP	3.00	8.00
19 Ted Savage DP	3.00	8.00
20 George Schultz	5.00	12.00
21 Ed Spiezio DP	3.00	8.00
22 Clint Stark	5.00	12.00
23 Bobby Tolan	6.00	15.00
24 Walt Williams	5.00	12.00

1967 Buffalo Bisons Jones Dairy

This one-card set was distributed by Jones Dairy on its milk cartons and features a 2 1/2" by 3" color photo of Duke Carmel of the Buffalo Bisons. The 1967 home schedule for the Bisons was also printed on the cartons.

1 Duke Carmel	20.00	50.00

1967 Seattle Popcorn

This 19-card set of the Seattle ballclub of the Pacific Coast League was distributed to the public as inserts in boxes of popcorn sold at Sicks' Stadium in Seattle. Only one card was inserted per box and measured approximately 2" by 3". The sets were produced by the ballclub and issued each season from 1954 through 1968. Since Seattle's major league affiliation switched from the Boston Red Sox to the California Angels, their name was changed from the "Rainiers" to the "Angels" for 1965. The fronts feature a black-and-white player photo with the player's name printed at the bottom. The backs carry an advertisement for radio station KVI 570 which carried Seattle's games. The 1967 cards have five listed sponsors. The cards are unnumbered and checklisted below in alphabetical order.

COMPLETE SET (19)	125.00	250.00
1 George Banks	6.00	15.00
2 Tom Burgmeier	6.00	15.00
3 Jim Coates	6.00	15.00
4 Chuck Cottier	6.00	15.00
5 Tony Curry	6.00	15.00
6 Vern Geishert	6.00	15.00
7 Jesse Hickman	6.00	15.00
8 Bill Kelso	6.00	15.00
9 Ed Kirkpatrick	6.00	15.00
10 Chris Krug	6.00	15.00
11 Bobby Locke	6.00	15.00
12 Bill Murphy	6.00	15.00
13 Marty Pattin	6.00	15.00
14 Merrit Ranew	6.00	15.00
15 Bob Sadowski	6.00	15.00
16 Ed Sukla	6.00	15.00
17 Hector Torres	6.00	15.00
18 Chuck Vinson	6.00	15.00
19 Don Wallace	6.00	15.00

1967 Tacoma Cubs Team Issue

These black and white photos, which measure approximatel 3 1/2" by 3 1/4" were issued as part of the 1967 Clay Huntington's Pictorial Yearbook. These photos were given out a selected Tacoma Cubs game during the 1967 season. Since these photos are unnumbered, we have sequenced them in alphabetical order.

COMPLETE SET (23)	150.00	300.00
1 George Altman	8.00	20.00
2 Bob Barton	6.00	15.00
3 John Boccabella	8.00	20.00
4 Marv Breeding	6.00	15.00
5 Dick Calmus	6.00	15.00
6 Ron Campbell	6.00	15.00
7 Len Church	6.00	15.00
8 Billy Connors	8.00	20.00
9 Lee Elia	8.00	20.00
10 Chico Fernandez	6.00	15.00
11 Tom Fletcher	6.00	15.00
12 Dick James	6.00	15.00
14 Whitey Lockman MG	8.00	20.00
15 Tom Mandile	6.00	15.00
16 Bobby Mitchell	6.00	15.00
17 Joe Proski TR	6.00	15.00
18 Dick Radatz	8.00	20.00
19 Shorty Raudman	6.00	15.00
20 Gary Ross	6.00	15.00
21 Bob Scott	6.00	15.00
21 Elmer Singleton	6.00	15.00
22 Bobby Gene Smith	6.00	15.00
23 Gene Stephens	6.00	15.00

1967 Vancouver Mounties Standard Oil

This 27-card set measures approximately 2" by 3" and features glossy black-and-white photos of the 1967 Pacific Coast League's Vancouver Mounties. The set was co-produced by Standard Oil (Chevron) and Uniroyal tires. This limited edition set is thought to have been distributed at participating service stations upon request with a fill-up.

COMPLETE SET (27)	50.00	100.00
1 Sal Bando	10.00	25.00
2 Frank Bastrire TR	1.50	4.00
3 Ossie Chavarria	1.50	4.00
4 Jim Dickson	1.50	4.00
5 John Donaldson	1.50	4.00
6 Jim Driscoll	1.50	4.00
7 Bob Duliba	1.50	4.00
8 Bill Edgerton	1.50	4.00
9 Larry Elliot	1.50	4.00
10 Ernie Foli	1.50	4.00
11 Joe Gaines	1.50	4.00
12 Vern Handrahan	1.50	4.00
13 Jim Hughes	1.50	4.00
14 Woody Huyke	1.50	4.00
15 Rene Lachemann	2.50	6.00
16 Bob Meyer	1.50	4.00
17 Wayne Norton	1.50	4.00
18 Gerry Reimer	1.50	4.00
19 Roberto Rodriquez	1.50	4.00
20 Ken Sanders	1.50	4.00
21 Randy Schwartz	1.50	4.00
22 Diego Segui	1.50	4.00
23 Paul Seitz	1.50	4.00
24 Ron Tompkins	1.50	4.00
25 Mickey Vernon MG	5.00	12.00
26 Jim Ward	1.50	4.00
27 Don Yingling	1.50	4.00

1968 Memphis Blues Red Barn

This set was issued by the Red Barn restaurant chain and featured members of the 1968 Memphis Blues. The fronts have the players photo located inside a "red barn" and the bottom has the player name and some biographical and career information. These cards are sequenced by uniform number and any additions to this checklist is appreciated. The Red Barn chain closed shortly after this set was issued.

COMPLETE SET	150.00	300.00
3 Mike Jorgensen	30.00	60.00
6 Joe Moock	20.00	50.00
9 Rod Gaspar	20.00	50.00
16 Barry Raziano	20.00	50.00
17 Curtis Brown	20.00	50.00
19 Ron Paul	20.00	50.00
24 Steve Christopher	20.00	50.00

1968 Seattle Popcorn

This 18-card set of the Seattle Angels ballclub of the Pacific Coast League was distributed to the public as inserts in boxes of popcorn sold at Sicks' Stadium in Seattle. Only one card was inserted per box and measured approximately 2" by 3". The sets were produced by the ballclub and issued each season from 1954 through 1968. The fronts feature a black-and-white player photo with the player's name printed at the bottom. The backs are blank. The cards are unnumbered and checklisted below in alphabetical order. The Overton is currently known to exist only in an uncut sheet. It is also not priced currently.

COMPLETE SET (18)	125.00	250.00
1 Ethan Blackaby	6.00	15.00
2 Jim Coates	6.00	15.00
3 Tom Egan	6.00	15.00
4 Larry Elliott	6.00	15.00
5 Jim Engelhardt	6.00	15.00
6 Gus Gil	6.00	15.00
7 Bill Harrelson	6.00	15.00
8 Steve Hovley	6.00	15.00
9 Jim Mahoney	6.00	15.00
10 Mickey McGuire	6.00	15.00
11 Joe Overton		
12 Marty Pattin	6.00	15.00
13 Larry Sherry	10.00	25.00
14 Marv Staehle	6.00	15.00
15 Ed Sukla	6.00	15.00
16 Jarvis Tatum	6.00	15.00
17 Hawk Taylor	6.00	15.00
18 Chuck Vinson	6.00	15.00

1970 Wichita Aeros McDonald's

This 18-card set features black-and-white photos of the Wichita Aeros printed on 2 1/2" by 3 1/4" cards with blank backs. The set was issued by McDonald's Restaurant. The cards are unnumbered and checklisted below in alphabetical order.

COMPLETE SET (18)	30.00	60.00
1 Ken Aspromonte MG	2.00	5.00
2 Frank Baker	1.50	4.00
3 Larry Burchart	1.50	4.00
4 Lou Camilli	1.50	4.00
5 Mike Carruthers	1.50	4.00
6 Chris Chambliss	6.00	15.00
7 Ed Farmer	1.50	4.00
8 Pedro Gonzales	1.50	4.00
9 Jerry Hinsley	1.50	4.00
10 Luis Isaac	1.50	4.00
11 John Lowenstein	2.00	5.00
12 Cap Peterson	1.50	4.00
13 Jim Rittwage	1.50	4.00
14 Bill Rohr	1.50	4.00
15 Richie Scheinblum	2.00	5.00
16 John Scruggs	1.50	4.00
17 Ken Suarez	1.50	4.00
18 Dick Tidrow	2.00	5.00

1971 Richmond Braves Team Issue

This 18-card black and white set was sponsored by Currie Press. The cards measure 3-3/8" X 5-5/16. A pre-Rookie Card of Dusty Baker is in this set.

COMPLETE SET (18)	40.00	80.00
1 Tommie Aaron	2.00	5.00
2 Sam Ayoub TR	1.25	3.00
3 Dusty Baker	8.00	20.00
4 Jim Breazeale	1.25	3.00
5 Jack Crist	1.25	3.00
6 Shaun Fitzmaurice	1.25	3.00
7 Jim French	1.25	3.00
8 Larry Jaster	2.50	6.00
9 Van Kelly	1.25	3.00
10 Rick Kester	1.25	3.00
11 Clyde King MG	2.00	5.00
12 Dave Lobb	1.25	3.00
13 Larry Maxie	1.25	3.00
14 Hank McGraw	1.25	3.00
15 Gary Neibauer	1.25	3.00
16 Guy Rose	1.25	3.00
17 Fred Velazquez	1.25	3.00
18 Bobby Young	1.25	3.00

1971 Syracuse Chiefs Postcards

These eight postcards were produced by long time hobbyist and photographer Jeffrey Morey. These cards feature members of the 1971 Syracuse Chiefs and have the players photo along with his name on the front. The backs are in the standard postcard format.

COMPLETE SET (8)	15.00	40.00
1 Len Boehmer	2.00	5.00
2 Ozzie Chavarria	2.00	5.00
3 Alan Closter	2.00	5.00
4 Fred Frazier	2.00	5.00
5 Rob Gardner	2.00	5.00
6 George Pena	2.00	5.00
7 Rusty Torres	2.00	5.00
8 Danny Walton	2.00	5.00

1972 Cedar Rapids Cardinals TCMA

COMPLETE SET (29)	125.00	250.00
COM.SET W/TEAM CARD (30)	200.00	400.00

1972 San Francisco Seals 1954 Aldama

COMPLETE SET	10.00	25.00

1972 Seattle Rainers Team Issue

Theser cards, issued in sheets of four players, were inserted in Seattle Rainier game programs. These sheets were issued on an irregular basis and since these cards are unnumbered, we have sequenced them in alphabetical order.

COMPLETE SET	12.50	30.00
1 Willy Adams	.75	2.00
2 Rafael Aniama	.75	2.00
3 Greg Brust	.75	2.00
4 Wade Carpenter	.75	2.00
5 Wes Dixon	.75	2.00
6 Ray Ewing	.75	2.00
7 Jose Gomez	.75	2.00
8 Rocky Hernandez	.75	2.00
9 Bill Kindall	.75	2.00
10 Kevin Kooyman	.75	2.00
11 Gene Lanthorn	.75	2.00
12 Jeff McKay	.75	2.00
13 Steve Mezich CO	.75	2.00
14 John Owens	.75	2.00
15 Tony Pepper	.75	2.00
16 Mike Peters	.75	2.00
17 Roger Rasmussen	.75	2.00
18 Ken Roll TR	.75	2.00
19 Rich Thompson	.75	2.00
20 Jesse Winchester	.75	2.00

1972 Tacoma Twins Team Issue

These cards, issued in the style of the Seattle "Popcorn" cards feature members of the 1972 Tacoma Twins. The fronts have a player photo with their name, position and some personal data on the bottom. Jim Strickland, Glenn Borgmann, Jerry Terrell and Ron Herbel are believed to be more difficult to obtain. We have notated those cards with an SP in our checklist. Since these cards are unnumbered, we have sequenced them in alphabetical order.

COMPLETE SET	15.00	40.00
SP COMMONS	2.00	5.00
1 Mike Adams	.75	2.00
2 Glenn Borgmann SP	2.00	5.00
3 Mike Brooks	.75	2.00
4 Ezell Carter	.75	2.00
5 Mike Derrick	.75	2.00
6 Glen Ezell	.75	2.00
7 Ken Gill	.75	2.00
8 Hal Haydel	.75	2.00
9 Ron Herbel SP	2.00	5.00
10 Jim Holt	.75	2.00
11 Tom Kelly	1.50	4.00
12 Steve Luebber	.75	2.00
13 Cap Peterson	.75	2.00
14 Dennis Saunders	.75	2.00
15 Jim Strickland SP	2.00	5.00
16 Jerry Terrell SP	2.00	5.00

Basketball Card Price Guide

1970-71 ABA All-Star 5x7 Picture Pack

This 12-card set featues black and white photos of ABA All-Stars from 1970-71. Each photo measures 5" by 7". The backs are blank and checklisted below in alphabetical order.

COMPLETE SET (12)	75.00	150.00
1 Rick Barry	20.00	40.00
2 John Brisker	5.00	10.00
3 George Carter	5.00	10.00
4 Mack Calvin	6.00	12.00
5 Joe Caldwell	6.00	12.00
6 Warren Jabali	7.50	15.00
7 Larry Jones	5.00	10.00
8 George Lehmann	5.00	10.00
9 Jim McDaniel	5.00	10.00
10 Bill Melchionni	7.50	15.00
11 John Roche	5.00	10.00
12 George Thompson	5.00	10.00

1956 Adventure R749

The Adventure series produced by Gum Products in 1956, contains a wide variety of subject matter. Cards in the set measure the standard size. The color drawings are printed on a heavy thickness of cardboard and have large white borders. The backs contain the card number, the caption, and a short text. The most expensive cards in the series of 100 are those associated with sports (Louis, Tunney, etc.). In addition, card number 86 (Schmelling) is notorious and sold at a premium price because of the Nazi symbol printed on the card. Although this set is considered by many to be a topical or non-sport set, several boxers are featured (cards 11, 22, 31-35, 41-44, 76-80, 86-90). One of the few cards of Boston-area legend Harry Agannis is in this set. The sports-related cards are in greater demand than the non-sport cards. These cards came in one-card penny packs where were packed 240 to a box.

COMPLETE SET (100)	225.00	450.00
8 Baskets and Rebounds Makes Points	12.50	25.00

1979 Arizona Sports Collectors Show

COMPLETE SET (10)	7.50	15.00
8 Dick Van Arsdale	2.00	5.00
9 Tom Van Arsdale	2.00	5.00

1955 Ashland/Aetna Oil

The 1955 Ashland/Aetna Oil Basketball set contains 96 black and white, unnumbered cards each measuring 2 5/8" by 3 3/4". There are two different backs for each card front, one with an Ashland Oil ad, the other with an Aetna Oil ad. Aetna cards are considered to be worth an additional premium of 25 percent above the prices listed below. The backs contain a player's vital statistics, his home town, and his graduation class. These thin-stocked cards are difficult to obtain and have been numbered in the checklist below, by team and alphabetically within each team. The cards were distributed one at a time at Ashland (Kentucky and West Virginia) or Aetna (Ohio) gas stations in the region of the particular college. The set contains 12 players each from eight colleges: Eastern Kentucky 1-12, Kentucky 13-24, Louisville 25-36, Marshall 37-48, Morehead 49-60, Murray 61-72, Western Kentucky 73-84, and West Virginia 85-96. The cards of smaller school players within this set seem to be in shorter supply than the cards of the larger schools. However, the prices below reflect the smaller demand for the cards of players from the smaller schools. The key cards in the set are the first cards of Adolph Rupp, Hall of Famer and legendary coach of the Kentucky Wildcats, Ed Diddle, and Laker player/announcer Hot Rod Hundley. The catalog designation for this set is UO18.

COMPLETE SET (96)	5,000.00	8,500.00
COMMON CARD (1-36/73-84)	35.00	700.00
COMMON CARD (37-60)	35.00	70.00
COMMON CARD (61-72)	45.00	90.00
COMMON CARD (85-96)	50.00	100.00
1 Jack Adams	35.00	70.00
2 William Baxter	35.00	70.00
3 Jeffrey Brock	35.00	70.00
4 Paul Collins	35.00	70.00
5 Richard Culbertson	35.00	70.00
6 James Floyd	35.00	70.00
7 Harold Fraler	35.00	70.00
8 George Francis Jr.	35.00	70.00
9 Paul McBrayer CO	50.00	100.00
10 James Mitchell	35.00	70.00
11 Ronald Pellegrinon	35.00	70.00
12 Guy Strong	35.00	70.00
13 Earl Adkins	35.00	70.00
14 William Bibb	35.00	70.00
15 Jerry Bird	35.00	70.00
16 John Brewer	35.00	70.00
17 Robert Burrow	35.00	70.00
18 Gerry Calvert	35.00	70.00
19 William Evans	40.00	80.00
20 Phillip Grawemeyer	35.00	70.00
21 Ray Mills	35.00	70.00
22 Linville Puckett	35.00	70.00
23 Gayle Rose	40.00	80.00
24 Adolph Rupp CO	250.00	500.00
25 William Darragh	35.00	70.00
26 Vladimir Gastevich	35.00	70.00
27 Allan Glaza	35.00	70.00
28 Herbert Harrah	35.00	70.00
29 Bernard Peck Hickman CO	50.00	100.00
30 Richard Keffer	35.00	70.00
31 Gerald Moreman	35.00	70.00
32 James Morgan	35.00	70.00
33 John Prudhoe	35.00	70.00
34 Phillip Rollins	35.00	70.00
35 Roscoe Shackelford	35.00	70.00
36 Charles Tyra	50.00	100.00
37 Robert Ashley	35.00	70.00
38 Lewis Burns	35.00	70.00
39 Francis Crum	35.00	70.00
40 Raymond Frazier	35.00	70.00
41 Cam Henderson CO	40.00	80.00
42 Joseph Hunnicutt	35.00	70.00
43 Clarence Parkins	35.00	70.00
44 Jerry Pierson	35.00	70.00
45 David Robinson	35.00	70.00
46 Paul Underwood	35.00	70.00
47 Cebert Price	35.00	70.00
48 Charles Slack	35.00	70.00
49 David Breeze	35.00	70.00
50 Leonard Carpenter	35.00	70.00
51 Omar Fannin	35.00	70.00
52 Donnie Gaunce	35.00	70.00
53 Steve Hamilton	75.00	130.00
54 Bobby Laughlin CO	35.00	70.00
55 Jesse Mayabb	35.00	70.00
56 Jerry Riddle	35.00	70.00
57 Howard Shumate	35.00	70.00
58 Dan Swartz	35.00	70.00
59 Harlan Tolle	35.00	70.00
60 Donald Whitehouse	35.00	70.00
61 Rex Alexander CO	45.00	90.00
62 Jorgen Anderson	45.00	90.00
63 Jack Clutter	45.00	90.00
64 Howard Crittenden	45.00	90.00
65 James Gainey	45.00	90.00
66 Richard Kinder	45.00	90.00
67 Theo. Koenigsmark	45.00	90.00
68 Joseph Mikez	45.00	90.00
69 John Powless	50.00	100.00
70 Dolph Regelsky	45.00	90.00
71 Reinhard Tauck	45.00	90.00
72 Francis Watrous	45.00	90.00
73 Forrest Able	35.00	70.00
74 Tom Benbrook	35.00	70.00
75 Ronald Clark	35.00	70.00
76 Lynn Cole	35.00	70.00
77 Robert Daniels	35.00	70.00
78 Ed Diddle CO	125.00	250.00
79 Victor Harned	35.00	70.00
80 Dencil Miller	35.00	70.00
81 Ferrel Miller	35.00	70.00
82 George Orr	35.00	70.00
83 Jerry Weber	35.00	70.00
84 Jerry Whitsell	35.00	70.00
85 William Bergines	50.00	100.00
86 James Brennan	50.00	100.00
87 Marc Constantine	50.00	100.00
88 Michael Holt	50.00	100.00
89 Hot Rod Hundley	250.00	500.00
90 Clayce Kishbaugh	50.00	100.00
91 Ronald LaNeve	50.00	100.00
92 Gary Mullins	50.00	100.00
93 Fred Schaus CO	150.00	275.00
94 Frank Spadafore	50.00	100.00
95 Peter White	50.00	100.00
96 Paul Witting	50.00	100.00

1951 Berk Ross

The 1951 Berk Ross set consists of 72 cards (each measuring approximately 2 1/16" by 2 1/2") with tinted photographs, divided evenly into four series (designated in the checklist as 1, 2, 3 and 4). The cards were marketed in boxes containing two card panels, without gum, and the set includes stars of other sports as well as baseball players. The set is sometimes still found in the original packaging. Intact panels command a premium over the listed prices. The catalog designation for this set is W532-1. In every series the first ten cards are baseball players; the set has a heavy emphasis on Yankees and Phillies players as they were in the World Series the year before. The set includes the first card of Bob Cousy as well as a card of Whitey Ford in his Rookie Card year.

COMPLETE SET (72)	900.00	1,500.00
11-Jan Bob Cousy Basketball	100.00	200.00
12-Jan Dick Schnittker Basketball	5.00	10.00
11-Feb Sherman White Basketball	5.00	10.00
11-Mar Paul Unruh Basketball	5.00	10.00
11-Apr Bill Sharman Basketball	20.00	40.00

1948 Bowman

The 1948 Bowman set of 72 cards was the company's only basketball issue. Five cards were issued in each pack. It was also the only major basketball issue until 1957-58 when Topps released a set. Cards in the set measure 2 1/16" by 2 1/2". The set is in color and features both player cards and diagram cards. The player cards in the second series are sometimes found without the red or blue printing on the card front, leaving only a gray background. These gray versions are more difficult to find, as they are printing errors where the printer apparently ran out of red or blue ink that was supposed to print on the player's uniform. The key Rookie Card in this set is George Mikan. Other Rookie Cards include Carl Braun, Joe Fulks, William Red Holzman, Jim Pollard, and Max Zaslofsky.

COMPLETE SET (72)	4,000.00	6,000.00
CARDS PRICED IN EX-MT CONDITION		
1 Ernie Calverley RC	60.00	120.00
2 Ralph Hamilton	25.00	60.00
3 Gale Bishop	25.00	60.00
4 Fred Lewis RC	25.00	60.00
5 Basketball Play Single cut off post	30.00	50.00
6 Bob Feerick RC	30.00	80.00
7 John Logan	30.00	80.00
8 Mel Riebe	25.00	60.00
9 Andy Phillip RC	40.00	100.00
10 Bob Davies RC	60.00	120.00
11 Basketball Play Single cut with return pass to post	30.00	50.00
12 Kenny Sailors RC	30.00	80.00
13 Paul Armstrong	25.00	60.00
14 Howard Dallmar RC	30.00	80.00
15 Bruce Hale RC	30.00	80.00
16 Sid Hertzberg	30.00	80.00
17 Basketball Play Single cut	30.00	50.00
18 Red Rocha	25.00	60.00
19 Eddie Ehlers	25.00	60.00
20 Ellis(Gene) Vance	25.00	60.00
21 Fuzzy Levane RC	30.00	80.00
22 Earl Shannon	25.00	60.00
23 Basketball Play Double cut off post	30.00	50.00
24 Leo (Crystal) Klier	25.00	60.00
25 George Senesky	25.00	60.00
26 Price Brookfield	25.00	60.00
27 John Norlander	25.00	60.00
28 Don Putman	25.00	60.00
29 Basketball Play Double post	30.00	50.00
30 Jack Garfinkel	25.00	60.00
31 Chuck Gilmur	25.00	60.00
32 Red Holzman RC	125.00	225.00
33 Jack Smiley	25.00	60.00
34 Joe Fulks RC	60.00	150.00
35 Basketball Play Screen play	30.00	50.00
36 Hal Tidrick	25.00	60.00
37 Don (Swede) Carlson	30.00	80.00
38 Buddy Jeanette CO RC	50.00	120.00
39 Ray Kuka	30.00	80.00
40 Stan Miasek	30.00	80.00
41 Basketball Play Double screen	50.00	75.00
42 George Nostrand	30.00	80.00
43 Chuck Halbert RC	75.00	125.00
44 Arnie Johnson	30.00	80.00
45 Bob Doll	30.00	80.00
46 Bones McKinney RC	80.00	135.00
47 Basketball Play Out of bounds	50.00	75.00
48 Ed Sadowski	50.00	120.00
49 Bob Kinney	30.00	80.00
50 Charles (Hawk) Black	30.00	80.00
51 Jack Dwan	50.00	120.00
52 Connie Simmons RC	75.00	200.00
53 Basketball Play Out of bounds	50.00	75.00
54 Bud Palmer RC	100.00	150.00
55 Max Zaslofsky RC	125.00	200.00
56 Lee Roy Robbins	40.00	100.00
57 Arthur Spector	40.00	100.00
58 Arnie Risen RC	75.00	200.00
59 Basketball Play Out of bounds play	50.00	75.00
60 Ariel Maughan	30.00	80.00
61 Dick O'Keefe	50.00	120.00
62 Herman Schaefer	30.00	80.00
63 John Mahnken	30.00	80.00
64 Tommy Byrnes	30.00	80.00
65 Basketball Play Held ball	50.00	75.00
66 Jim Pollard RC	125.00	250.00
67 Lee Mogus	30.00	80.00
68 Lee Knorek	30.00	80.00
69 George Mikan RC	2,000.00	5,000.00
70 Walter Budko	30.00	80.00
71 Basketball Play Guards Play	50.00	75.00
72 Carl Braun RC	200.00	400.00

1974-75 Braves Buffalo Linnett

These three charcoal drawings are skillfully executed facial portraits of Buffalo Braves players. They were drawn by noted sports artist Charles Linnett and measure approximately 8 1/2" by 11". In the lower right corner, a facsimile autograph of the player is written across the portrait. The backs are blank. The drawings are unnumbered and are checklisted below in alphabetical order.

COMPLETE SET (3)	10.00	20.00
1 Ernie DiGregorio	5.00	10.00
2 Garfield Heard	2.50	6.00
3 Jim McMillian	2.50	6.00

1976-77 Braves Team Issue

These 8" by 10" blank-backed black and white glossy photos feature members of the 1976-77 Buffalo Braves. Since these photos are unnumbered, we have sequenced them in alphabetical order.

COMPLETE SET (14)	15.00	30.00
1 Don Adams	.75	2.00
2 Bird Averitt	.75	2.00
3 Gary Brewster	.75	2.00
4 Fred Foster	.75	2.00
5 George Jackson	.75	2.00
6 Greg Jackson	.75	2.00
7 Bob McAdoo	5.00	10.00
8 John Neumann	.75	2.00
9 Dale Schlueter	.75	2.00
10 Randy Smith	2.50	6.00
11 John Shumate	1.00	2.50
12 Claude Terry	.75	2.00
13 Bob MacKinnon GM Tates Locke CO	.75	2.00
14 Charlie Harrison ACO Ray Melchiorre TR	.75	2.00

1951 Bread For Energy

The 1951 Bread for Energy bread end labels set contains 11 known labels of players in the National Football League, professional basketball, pro boxing, and famous actors. Each measures approximately 2 3/4" by 2 3/4" with the corners cut out in typical bread label style. These labels are not usually found in top condition due to the difficulty in removing them from the bread package. While all the bakeries who issued this set are not presently known, Junge's Brand Bread in the New England area is one bakery that has been confirmed. As with many of the bread label sets of the early 1950's, an album to house the set was probably issued. Each label was printed with a red, yellow, and blue background. The cards are unnumbered but are arranged alphabetically within subject below.

28 Bob Davies BK	600.00	1,000.00
29 Joe Fulks BK	1,000.00	1,500.00
30 Dick McGuire BK	600.00	1,000.00
31 George Mikan BK	6,000.00	8,000.00

1950-51 Bread for Health

The 1950-51 Bread for Health basketball set consists of 32 bread end labels (each measuring approximately 2 3/4" by 2 3/4") of players in the National Basketball Association. While all the bakeries who issued this set are not at present known, Fisher's Bread in the New Jersey, New York and Pennsylvania area and NBC Bread in the Michigan area are two of the bakeries that have been confirmed to date. As with many of the bread label sets of the early '50s, an album to house the set was probably issued. Each label contains the

B.E.B. copyright found on so many of the labels of this period. Labels which contain "Bread for Energy" at the bottom are not a part of the set but part of a series of movie, western and sports stars issued during the same approximate time period. The American Card Catalog does not designate a number to this series; however, based on its similarity to a corresponding football issue, it is referenced as D290-15A. The set is dated by the fact that 1949-50 was Buddy Jeanette and Bob Kinney's last active year and Vince Boryla, Tony Lavelli, and Vern Mikkelsen's first active year.

COMPLETE SET (32)	18,000.00	22,000.00
1 Paul Armstrong	250.00	450.00
2 Ralph Beard	400.00	750.00
3 Vince Boryla	300.00	600.00
4 Walter Budko	250.00	450.00
5 Al Cervi	250.00	450.00
6 Bob Davies	600.00	950.00
7 Dwight Eddleman	300.00	600.00
8 Arnold Ferrin	300.00	600.00
9 Joe Fulks	800.00	1,200.00
10 Harry Gallatin	400.00	650.00
11 Chuck Gilmur	250.00	450.00
12 Alex Groza	400.00	750.00
13 Bruce Hale	300.00	600.00
14 Paul Hoffman	250.00	450.00
15 Buddy Jeanette	400.00	750.00
16 Bob Kinney	250.00	450.00
17 Tony Lavelli	250.00	450.00
18 Ron Livingstone	250.00	450.00
19 Horace McKinney	400.00	700.00
20 Stan Miasek	250.00	450.00
21 George Mikan	2,500.00	3,500.00
22 Andy Phillip	300.00	600.00
23 Arnie Risen	400.00	750.00
24 Fred Schaus	400.00	700.00
25 Dolph Schayes	1,100.00	1,500.00
26 Fred Scolari	250.00	450.00
27 George Senesky	250.00	450.00
28 Paul Seymour	300.00	600.00
29 Cornelius Simmons	300.00	600.00
30 Gene Vance	250.00	450.00
31 Brady Walker	250.00	450.00
32 Max Zaslofsky	350.00	700.00

1976 Buckmans Discs

The 1976 Buckmans Discs set contains 20 unnumbered discs measuring approximately 3 3/8" in diameter. The discs have various color borders containing brief biographical information and feature black and white drawings of the players with fascimile signatures. This set was distributed through Buckmans Ice Cream Village in Rochester, New York. The discs can be found with Buckmans backs or blank backs with the Buckmans backs being harder to find and carrying a 50 percent premium above the prices listed below. The cards are listed alphabetically in the checklist below. The set was also issued with Crane Potato Chips; the Crane Potato Chips advertisement on the backs is printed in red and blue on a white background. The Crane variations show Crane at the top of the disc rather than four stars; the Crane discs are harder to find and are valued at approximately six times the Buckmans prices listed below.

COMPLETE SET (20)	25.00	50.00
1 Kareem Abdul-Jabbar	4.00	10.00
2 Nate Archibald	2.00	5.00
3 Rick Barry	2.00	5.00
4 Tom Boerwinkle	.75	2.00
5 Bill Bradley	2.00	5.00
6 Dave Cowens	2.50	6.00
7 Bob Dandridge	1.00	2.50
8 Walt Frazier	2.50	6.00
9 Gail Goodrich	2.50	6.00
10 John Havlicek	3.00	8.00
11 Connie Hawkins	2.50	6.00
12 Lou Hudson	1.25	3.00
13 Sam Lacey	.75	2.00
14 Bob Lanier	2.00	5.00
15 Bob Love	1.50	4.00
16 Bob McAdoo	2.00	5.00
17 Earl Monroe	2.00	5.00
18 Jerry Sloan	2.00	5.00
19 Norm Van Lier	1.25	3.00
20 Jo Jo White	1.25	3.00

1977-78 Bucks Action Photos

These glossy action photos featuring members of the Milwaukee Bucks measure approximately 5" by 7" and are printed on very thin paper. The photos are in full color and borderless. The players are identified only by their facsimile autographs inscribed across the picture. The backs are blank.

COMPLETE SET (10)	6.00	15.00
1 Kent Benson	.75	2.00
2 Junior Bridgeman	.75	2.00
3 Quinn Buckner	1.00	2.50
4 Alex English	3.00	8.00
5 John Gianelli	.60	1.50
6 Ernie Grunfeld	1.00	2.50
7 Marques Johnson	2.00	5.00
8 Dave Meyers	.75	2.00
9 Lloyd Walton	.60	1.50
10 Brian Winters	1.00	2.50

1973-74 Bucks Linnett

Measuring 8 1/2" by 11", these six charcoal drawings are facial portraits by noted sports artist Charles Linnett. The player's facsimile autograph is inscribed across the lower right corner. The backs are blank. Three portraits were included in each package, with a suggested retail price of 99 cents. The portraits are unnumbered and checklisted below in alphabetical order. The set is dated by the fact that 1973-74 is Oscar Robertson's last year with the Bucks and Terry Driscoll's first year with the Bucks.

COMPLETE SET (6)	20.00	40.00
1 Kareem Abdul-Jabbar	12.50	25.00
2 Lucius Allen	1.50	4.00
3 Terry Driscoll	1.25	3.00
4 Russell Lee	1.25	3.00
5 Curtis Perry	1.25	3.00
6 Oscar Robertson	10.00	20.00

1974-75 Bucks Linnett

These ten charcoal drawings are skillfully executed facial portraits of Milwaukee Bucks players. They were drawn by noted sports artist Charles Linnett and measure approximately 8 1/2" by 11". In the lower right corner, a facsimile autograph of the player is written across the portrait. The backs are blank. The drawings are unnumbered and we have checklisted them below in alphabetical order. The set is dated by the fact that 1974-75 was Gary Brokaw and Kevin Restani's first active year and Steve Kuberski and George Thompson's only year with the Bucks.

COMPLETE SET (10)	25.00	50.00
1 Kareem Abdul-Jabbar	12.50	25.00
2 Gary Brokaw	1.25	3.00
3 Bob Dandridge	1.50	4.00
4 Mickey Davis	1.00	2.50
5 Steve Kuberski	1.00	2.50
6 Jon McGlocklin	1.50	4.00
7 Jim Price	1.00	2.50
8 Kevin Restani	1.00	2.50
9 George Thompson	1.00	2.50
10 Cornell Warner	1.00	2.50

1976-77 Bucks Playing Cards

The 55-card deck of playing cards was co-sponsored by White Hen Pantry and Coca-Cola. The cards measure approximately 2 1/4" by 3 1/2" and have rounded corners. The fronts feature black-and-white action shots with coach or player identification, player background and statistics below the picture. The backs have a brown, red and yellow design with a basketball in the center. The two sponsors logos appear twice at opposite diagonal corners of the card. The set is checklisted below as if it was a playing card set. In the checklist, C means Clubs, D means Diamonds, H means Hearts and S means Spades. The cards are checklisted in playing card order by suits and numbers are assigned to Aces (1), Jacks (11), Queens (12), and Kings (13). Two coaches cards that could be used as jokers and a filler card with a color Bucks logo and White Hen Pantry ad are listed at the end. Key cards include the first ever of Quinn Buckner and Alex English.

COMP.FACT SET (55)	35.00	70.00
C1 Bucks Logo	.30	.75
C2 Brian Winters	1.25	3.00
C3 Lloyd Walton	.30	.75
C4 Junior Bridgeman	.75	2.00
C5 Alex English	5.00	10.00
C6 Quinn Buckner	1.25	3.00
C7 David Meyers	.75	2.00
C8 Swen Nater	.75	2.00
C9 Scott Lloyd	.30	.75
C10 Bob Dandridge	1.00	2.50
C11 Kevin Restani	.40	1.00
C12 Rowland Garrett	.30	.75
C13 Fred Carter	1.25	3.00
D1 Bucks Logo	.30	.75
D2 Fred Carter	.75	2.00
D3 Rowland Garrett	.30	.75
D4 Kevin Restani	.40	1.00
D5 Bob Dandridge	1.00	2.50
D6 Scott Lloyd	.30	.75
D7 Swen Nater	.75	2.00
D8 David Meyers	.75	2.00
D9 Quinn Buckner	1.25	3.00
D10 Alex English	5.00	10.00
D11 Junior Bridgeman	1.00	2.50
D12 Lloyd Walton	.75	2.00
D13 Brian Winters	1.00	2.50
H1 Bucks Logo	.30	.75
H2 Fred Carter	.60	1.50
H3 Rowland Garrett	.30	.75
H4 Kevin Restani	.40	1.00
H5 Bob Dandridge	1.00	2.50
H6 Scott Lloyd	.30	.75
H7 Swen Nater	.75	2.00
H8 David Meyers	.75	2.00
H9 Quinn Buckner	1.25	3.00
H10 Alex English	5.00	10.00
H11 Junior Bridgeman	1.00	2.50
H12 Lloyd Walton	.30	.75
H13 Brian Winters	1.25	3.00
S1 Bucks Logo	.30	.75
S2 Brian Winters	1.25	3.00
S3 Lloyd Walton	.30	.75
S4 Junior Bridgeman	1.00	2.50
S5 Alex English	5.00	10.00
S6 Quinn Buckner	1.25	3.00
S7 David Meyers	.75	2.00
S8 Swen Nater	.75	2.00
S9 Scott Lloyd	.30	.75
S10 Bob Dandridge	1.00	2.50
S11 Kevin Restani	.40	1.00
S12 Rowland Garrett	.30	.75
S13 Fred Carter	.75	2.00
NNO K.C. Jones ACO	2.00	5.00
NNO Don Nelson CO	2.50	6.00
NNO Bucks Logo White Hen Pantry Ad	.30	.75

1979-80 Bucks Police/Spic'n'Span

This set contains 12 standard-size cards measuring featuring the Milwaukee Bucks. Card backs contain safety tips ("Game Plan Tip"). The cards are numbered on the back next to the facsimile autograph. The cards feature full-color fronts and black printing on a white card stock back. The set was sponsored by Spic'N'Span. The cards were available one per cleaning order or were available (originally) for sale as a set from the Wisconsin Sports Collectors Association for 2.25 postpaid. A coupon card was also available which was good for 1.00 discount on cleaning.

COMPLETE SET (13)	40.00	80.00
2 Junior Bridgeman	3.00	8.00
4 Sidney Moncrief	12.50	25.00
6 Pat Cummings	2.00	5.00
7 Dave Meyers	3.00	8.00
8 Marques Johnson	8.00	20.00
11 Lloyd Walton	1.50	4.00
21 Quinn Buckner	2.50	6.00
31 Richard Washington	2.50	6.00
32 Brian Winters	3.00	8.00
42 Harvey Catchings	2.00	5.00
54 Kent Benson	2.50	6.00
NNO Don Nelson CO and John Killilea ACO	5.00	10.00
NNO Coupon Card	10.00	25.00

1972-73 Bucks Ruler

This standard 12" ruler features a head shot of the players from the 1972-3 Milwaukee Bucks. Similar to the ruler, we have identified the rulers using the left to right method.

1 Kareem Abdul-Jabbar Jon McGlocklin Curtis Perry Dick Cunningham Russell Lee Oscar Robertson Mickey Davis Lucius Allen Terry Driscoll Bob Dandridge Bill Bates TR Hubie Brown ACO Larry Costello CO	5.00	10.00

1970-71 Bucks Team Issue

Each of these team-issued photos measure approximately 5" by 7" and feature black and white player portraits. The player's name is listed below the photo. The backs are blank. The photos are unnumbered and listed below alphabetically.

COMPLETE SET (10)	25.00	50.00
1 Lew Alcindor	12.50	25.00
2 Lucius Allen	2.00	5.00
3 Bob Boozer	1.50	4.00
4 Larry Costello CO	1.25	3.00
5 Dick Cunningham	.75	2.00
6 Bob Dandridge	2.00	5.00
7 Bob Greacen	.75	2.00
8 Jon McGlocklin	1.50	4.00
9 Oscar Robertson	10.00	20.00
10 Greg Smith	.75	2.00

1971-72 Bucks Team Issue

Each of these team-issued photos measure approximately 5" by 6 3/4" and feature black and white player portraits. The player's name is listed below the photo. The backs are blank. The photos are unnumbered and listed below alphabetically.

COMPLETE SET (12)	25.00	50.00
1 Kareem Abdul-Jabbar	10.00	20.00
2 Lucius Allen	1.50	4.00
3 John Block	.75	2.00
4 Larry Costello CO	1.00	2.50
5 Bob Dandridge	1.50	4.00
6 Toby Kimball	.75	2.00
7 Jon McGlocklin	1.25	3.00
8 McCoy McLemore	.75	2.00
9 Barry Nelson	.75	2.00
10 Oscar Robertson	8.00	20.00
11 Greg Smith	.75	2.00
12 Jeff Webb	.75	2.00

1954-55 Bullets Gunther Beer

This 11-card set of Baltimore Bullets was sponsored by Gunther Beer. These black and white cards measure approximately 2 5/8" by 3 5/8". The fronts feature a black and white posed player photo. The question "What's the good word," is written across the card top. A Gunther Beer bottle cap and the player's name are superimposed on the player's chest. The back has the words "Follow the Bullets with Gunther Beer" at the top, with biographical information and career summary below. A radio and TV notice on the bottom round out the card back. The cards are unnumbered and are checklisted below in alphabetical order. The cards are frequently found personally autographed. The catalog designation for this set is H805.

COMPLETE SET (11)	2,000.00	3,500.00
1 Leo Barnhorst	150.00	300.00
2 Clair Bee CO	400.00	800.00
3 Bill Bolger	150.00	300.00
4 Ray Felix	250.00	500.00
5 Jim Fritsche	150.00	300.00
6 Rollen Hans	150.00	300.00
7 Paul Hoffman	200.00	400.00
8 Bob Houbregs	250.00	500.00
9 Ed Miller	150.00	300.00
10 Al Roges	150.00	300.00
11 Harold Uplinger	150.00	300.00

1973-74 Bullets Standups

These 12 player cards were issued by Johnny Pro Enterprises in an album, with six players per 11 1/4" by 14" sheet. Reportedly 6,000 albums were produced for distribution in a promotion at the Bullets' February 16th game at the Capital Centre. After perforation, the cards measure approximately 3 3/4" by 7 1/16". The cards are die cut, allowing the player pictures and bases to be pushed out and displayed as stand-ups. The fronts feature a color photo of the player, either dribbling or shooting the ball. The backs are blank. The cards are unnumbered and are checklisted below in alphabetical order. A card set, still intact in the album, would be valued at double the values listed below.

COMPLETE SET (12)	25.00	50.00
1 Phil Chenier	2.00	5.00
2 Archie Clark	2.00	5.00
3 Elvin Hayes	10.00	20.00
4 Tom Kozelko	1.25	3.00
5 Manny Leaks	1.25	3.00
6 Louie Nelson	1.25	3.00
7 Kevin Porter	1.50	4.00
8 Mike Riordan	1.50	4.00
9 Dave Stallworth	1.50	4.00
10 Wes Unseld	7.50	15.00
11 Nick Weatherspoon	1.25	3.00
12 Walt Wesley	1.25	3.00

1977-78 Bullets Standups

These 11 player cards were issued by Johnny Pro Enterprises in conjunction with Dart Drugs. The cards were issued in a four-page colorful album and were given out at the Bullets game on March 25, 1978. The cards are die cut, allowing the player pictures and bases to be pushed out and displayed as stand-ups. The backs are blank. The cards are unnumbered and are checklisted below in alphabetical order. A card set, still intact in the album, would be valued at double the values listed below.

COMPLETE SET (11)	15.00	30.00
1 Greg Ballard	.75	2.00
2 Phil Chenier	1.50	4.00
3 Bob Dandridge	1.25	3.00
4 Kevin Grevey	1.25	3.00
5 Elvin Hayes	7.50	15.00
6 Tom Henderson	.75	2.00
7 Mitch Kupchak	1.50	4.00
8 Joe Pace	.75	2.00
9 Wes Unseld	5.00	10.00
10 Phil Walker	.75	2.00
11 Larry Wright	.75	2.00

1964-65 Bullets Team Issue

These blank-backed photos, which measure 8" by 11" and have blank backs, Since these photos are unnumbered, we have sequenced them in alphabetical order.

COMPLETE SET (7)	75.00	150.00
1 Gary Bradds	10.00	20.00
2 Bob Ferry	12.50	25.00
3 Sl Green	10.00	20.00
4 Les Hunter	10.00	20.00
5 Wally Jones	12.50	25.00
6 Kevin Loughery	20.00	40.00
7 Don Ohl	10.00	20.00

1968-69 Bullets Team Issue

This set is complete at 12 pieces and is measured at 8 1/2 by 11 1/2. The items were printed on thin paper stock (newsprint type quality, but thicker than ordinary writing paper) in black and white and feature a facsimile signature on the front with a blank back.

COMPLETE SET (12)	150.00	300.00
1 Leroy Ellis	15.00	30.00
2 Bob Ferry	15.00	30.00
3 Gus Johnson	15.00	30.00
4 Kevin Loughery	15.00	30.00
5 Jack Matin	15.00	30.00
6 Earl Monroe	25.00	50.00
7 Barry Orms	15.00	30.00
8 Bob Quick	15.00	30.00
9 Ray Scott	15.00	30.00
10 Gene Shue	15.00	30.00
11 Wes Unseld	20.00	50.00
12 Tom Workman	15.00	30.00

1969-70 Bullets Team Issue

Each of these team-issued photos measure approximately 8" by 10" and feature black and white player portraits. The player's name is listed below the photo. Each photo also contains a facsimile autograph. The backs are blank. The photos are unnumbered and listed below alphabetically.

COMPLETE SET (12)	25.00	50.00
1 Mike Davis	.75	2.00
2 Fred Carter	2.00	5.00
3 Leroy Ellis	1.25	3.00
4 Gus Johnson	2.00	5.00
5 Kevin Loughery	2.00	5.00
6 Ed Manning	1.25	3.00
7 Jack Marin	.75	2.00
8 Earl Monroe	7.50	15.00
9 Bob Quick	.75	2.00
10 Ray Scott	.75	2.00
11 Gene Shue CO	2.00	5.00
12 Wes Unseld	6.00	12.00

1975-76 Bullets Team Issue

Each of these 11 team-issued photos measure approximately 5" by 7" and feature black and white player portraits. The backs are blank. The photos are unnumbered and listed below alphabetically.

COMPLETE SET (11)	20.00	35.00
1 Dave Bing	2.50	6.00
2 Bernie Bickerstaff ACO	2.00	5.00
3 Clem Haskins	1.25	3.00
4 Elvin Hayes	6.00	12.00
5 Jimmy Jones	.75	2.00
6 K.C. Jones CO	1.25	3.00
7 Tom Kozelko	.75	2.00
8 Mike Riordan	1.00	2.50
9 Leonard Robinson	1.25	3.00
10 Nick Weatherspoon	.75	2.00
11 Wes Unseld	2.50	6.00

1976-77 Bullets Team Issue

Each of these team-issued photos measure approximately 5" by 7" and feature black and white player portraits. The player's name is listed below the photo. The backs are blank. The photos are unnumbered and listed below alphabetically.

COMPLETE SET (15)	20.00	40.00
1 Bernie Bickerstaff ACO	.75	2.00
2 Dave Bing	1.50	4.00
3 Phil Chenier	1.25	3.00
4 Leonard Gray	.60	1.50
5 Kevin Grevey	1.25	3.00
6 Elvin Hayes	5.00	10.00
7 Jimmy Jones	.60	1.50
8 Mitch Kupchak	1.50	4.00
9 Dick Motta CO	.75	2.00
10 Joe Pace	.60	1.50
11 Mike Riordan	.75	2.00
12 Len Robinson	.75	2.00
13 Wes Unseld	2.00	5.00
14 Bob Weiss	.75	2.00
15 Larry Wright	.60	1.50

1977-78 Bullets Team Issue 5x7

This 5" x7" set was produced for the Washington Bullets during the 1977-78 season. The set features 12 black and white cards of the team's players and coaches.

COMPLETE SET (12)	20.00	40.00
1 Greg Ballard	1.25	3.00
2 Bernie Bickerstaff ACO	1.25	3.00
3 Phil Chenier	1.50	4.00
4 Bob Dandridge	2.00	5.00
5 Elvin Hayes	2.50	6.00
6 Tom Henderson	1.25	3.00
7 Mitch Kupchak	1.25	3.00
8 Dick Motta CO	1.50	4.00
9 Joe Pace	1.25	3.00
10 Wes Unseld	2.00	5.00
11 Phil Walker	1.25	3.00
12 Larry Wright	1.25	3.00

1977-78 Bullets Team Issue

These black and white glossy blank-backed photos, which measure 8" by 10" feature members of the World Championship Washington Bullets team. Since these photos are unnumbered, we have sequenced them in alphabetical order.

COMPLETE SET (13)	15.00	30.00
1 Greg Ballard	.75	2.00
2 Dave Corzine	.75	2.00
3 Bob Dandridge	1.00	2.50
4 Kevin Grevey	1.00	2.50
5 Elvin Hayes	2.50	6.00
6 Tom Henderson	.75	2.00
7 Charles Johnson	.75	2.00
8 Mitch Kupchak	1.00	2.50
9 Dick Motta CO	1.00	2.50
10 Roger Phegley	.75	2.00
11 Wes Unseld	2.00	5.00
12 Larry Wright	.75	2.00
13 Bernie Bickerstaff ACO John Lally TR	1.00	2.50

1970-71 Bulls Hawthorne Milk

This six-card set was issued on the side panels of Hawthorne Milk cartons. The cards were intended to be cut from the carton and measure approximately 3 1/4" by 3 3/8" and feature on the front a posed head shot of the player within a circular picture frame. The second Weiss card measures 4 11/16" by 2 7/8". The backs are blank. The cards are unnumbered and are checklisted below in alphabetical order. The player photo is printed in blue but the outer border of the card is bright red.

COMPLETE SET (6)	1,000.00	1,800.00
1 Bob Love	250.00	450.00
2 Jerry Sloan	250.00	450.00
3 Jerry Sloan	250.00	450.00
4 Chet Walker	200.00	350.00
5 Bob Weiss	125.00	225.00
6 Bob Weiss	125.00	250.00

1969-70 Bulls Pepsi

Sponsored by Pepsi, this 13-card set measures 8" by 10" and features members of the 1969-70 Chicago Bulls. The fronts have black-and-white player portraits with white borders. The player's name and height appear under the photo, along with team and sponsor logos, and the slogan "You've got a lot to live. Pepsi's got a lot to give." The backs are blank. The cards are unnumbered and checklisted below in alphabetical order.

COMPLETE SET (13)	75.00	150.00
1 Tom Boerwinkle	6.00	12.00
2 Shaler Halimon	2.50	6.00
3 Clem Haskins	5.00	10.00
4 Bob Kauffman	2.50	6.00
5 Bob Love	20.00	40.00
6 Ed Manning	3.00	8.00
7 Dick Motta CO	5.00	10.00
8 Loy Petersen	2.50	6.00
9 Jerry Sloan	15.00	40.00
10 Al Tucker	2.50	6.00
11 Chet Walker	12.50	25.00
12 Bob Weiss	5.00	12.00
13 Walt Wesley	3.00	8.00

1979-80 Bulls Police

This set contains 16 cards measuring approximately 2 5/8" by 4 1/8" featuring the Chicago Bulls. Cards in the set have either rounded or squred corners. Backs contain safety tips and are written in black ink with blue accent. The set was also sponsored by La Margarita Mexican Restaurants and Azteca Tortillas. The card backs are subtitled Kiwanis Cue Cards. Cards are unnumbered except for uniform number; they are checklisted below by uniform number. The cards of Coby Dietrick and (especially) Reggie Theus are considered more difficult to find and are marked as SP in the listings below.

COMPLETE SET (16)	40.00	70.00
1 Delmer Beshore	.75	2.00
13 Dwight Jones	.75	2.00
15 John Mengelt	.75	2.00
17 Scott May	1.25	3.00
20 Dennis Awtrey	1.00	2.50
24 Reggie Theus SP	15.00	30.00
26 Coby Dietrick SP	7.50	15.00
27 Ollie Johnson	.75	2.00
28 Sam Smith	.75	2.00
34 David Greenwood	2.00	5.00
40 Ricky Sobers	1.25	3.00
53 Artis Gilmore	2.50	6.00
54 Mark Landsberger	1.25	3.00
NNO Jerry Sloan CO	2.50	6.00
NNO Phil Johnson ACO	1.25	3.00
NNO Luv-A-Bull	.75	2.00

1976-77 Bulls Team Issue

These black and white blank-backed glossy photos, which measure 8" by 10", feature members of the 1976-77 Chicago Bulls. Since these photos are unnumbered, we have sequenced them in alphabetical order.

COMPLETE SET (17)	17.50	35.00
1 Ed Badger CO	1.00	2.50
2 Leon Benbow	.75	2.00
3 Tom Boerwinkle	1.00	2.50
4 Eric Fernsten	.75	2.00
5 Mickey Johnson	.75	2.00
6 Tom Kropp	.75	2.00
7 John Laskowski	.75	2.00
8 Bob Love	1.25	3.00
9 Jack Marin	1.00	2.50
10 Scott May	1.00	2.50
11 Cliff Pondexter	.75	2.00
12 Jerry Sloan	1.50	4.00
13 Willie Smith	.75	2.00
14 Keith Starr	.75	2.00
15 Norm Van Lier	1.00	2.50
16 Bob Wilson	.75	2.00
17 Doug Atkinson TR Gene Tormohlen ACO	.75	2.00

1977-78 Bulls White Hen Pantry

These high gloss player photos are printed on very thin paper and measure approximately 5" by 7". The fronts feature borderless color game action photos with a facsimile autograph; the backs are blank. The photos are unnumbered and we have checklisted them below in alphabetical order.

COMPLETE SET (7)	6.00	12.00
1 Tom Boerwinkle	.75	2.00
2 Artis Gilmore	2.00	5.00
3 Wilbur Holland	.60	1.50
4 Mickey Johnson	.75	2.00
5 Scott May	1.00	2.50
6 John Mengelt	.60	1.50
7 Norm Van Lier	1.00	2.50

1932 Briggs Chocolate

This set was issued by C.A. Brigss Chocolate company in 1932. The cards feature 31-different sports with each card including an artist's rendering of a sporting event. Although players are not named, it is thought that most were modeled after famous athletes of the time. The cardbacks include a written portion about the sport and an offer from Briggs for free baseball equipment for building a compete set of cards.

8 Basketball	125.00	250.00

1975 Carvel Discs

The 1975 Carvel NBA Basketball Discs set contains 36 unnumbered discs measuring approximately 3 3/8" in diameter. The blank-backed discs have various (five different colors) color borders, and feature black and white drawings of the players with fascimile signatures. There are also white (colorless) border variations, which can be found with or without Carvel at the top, which are very difficult to find. A poster was produced which provided circular places for each of the 36 discs to be taped or glued onto. Since the discs are unnumbered, they are checklisted below in alphabetical order. The set is dated by the fact that 1974-75 was Happy Hairston and Chet Walker's last active year in the NBA.

COMPLETE SET (36)	40.00	80.00
1 Kareem Abdul-Jabbar	4.00	10.00
2 Nate Archibald	2.00	5.00
3 Bill Bradley	2.00	5.00
4 Don Chaney	1.25	3.00
5 Dave Cowens	2.00	5.00
6 Bob Dandridge	1.00	2.50
7 Ernie DiGregorio	1.25	3.00
8 Walt Frazier	2.00	5.00
9 John Gianelli	.75	2.00
10 Gail Goodrich	2.00	5.00
11 Happy Hairston	1.25	3.00
12 John Havlicek	3.00	8.00
13 Spencer Haywood	1.25	3.00
14 Garfield Heard	.75	2.00
15 Lou Hudson	1.00	2.50
16 Phil Jackson	2.00	5.00
17 Sam Lacey	.75	2.00
18 Bob Lanier	2.00	5.00
19 Bob Love	1.50	4.00
20 Bob McAdoo	2.00	5.00
21 Jim McMillian	1.25	3.00
22 Dean Meminger	.75	2.00
23 Earl Monroe	2.00	5.00
24 Don Nelson	1.50	4.00
25 Jim Price	.75	2.00
26 Clifford Ray	.75	2.00
27 Charlie Scott	1.00	2.50
28 Paul Silas	1.50	4.00
29 Jerry Sloan	2.00	5.00
30 Randy Smith	1.25	3.00
31 Dick Van Arsdale	1.25	3.00
32 Norm Van Lier	1.25	3.00
33 Chet Walker	1.25	3.00
34 Paul Westphal	2.00	5.00
35 Jo Jo White	1.25	3.00
36 Hawthorne Wingo	.75	2.00

1973-74 Cavaliers Postcards

This eight-card set was released during the 1973-74 season, and features many of the Cleveland Cavalier players from that year. Please note that these postcards measure 3 1/2"x5 1/4".

COMPLETE SET (8)	20.00	40.00
1 Lenny Wilkens CO	2.50	6.00
2 Austin Carr	1.50	4.00
3 Barry Clemens	1.25	3.00
4 Bobby Smith	1.25	3.00
5 Jim Brewer	1.25	3.00
6 Dwight Davis	1.25	3.00
7 Steve Patterson	1.25	3.00
8 Fred Foster	1.25	3.00
9 Jim Cleamons	1.50	4.00
10 Luke Witte	1.25	3.00
11 Bob Rule	1.25	3.00
12 John Warren	1.25	3.00

1976 Cavaliers Royal Crown Cola Cans

The 1976 Royal Crown Cola Cleveland Cavaliers Cans team issue contains at least seven standard-sized cans. Each can contains a facsimile autograph, except one - Dick Snyder has cans with and without an autograph. There is no number given, thus the set is listed below alphabetically. Cans opened from the bottom command up to a 25 percent premium over the prices below. The checklist below is thought to be incomplete--any additional input on this series would be appreciated.

COMPLETE SET (7)	20.00	40.00
1 Jim Brewer	2.00	5.00
2 Austin Carr	3.00	8.00
3 Bill Fitch CO	2.50	6.00
4 Jim Chones	2.50	6.00
5 Jim Cleamons	2.50	6.00
6 Dick Snyder with autograph	2.00	5.00
6A Dick Snyder without autograph	2.00	5.00
7 Bingo Smith	2.50	6.00

1980-81 Cavaliers Team Issue

This 5 1/2"x 8 1/2" set was produced for the Cleveland Cavaliers during the 1980-81 season. The set features 10 black and white cards of the team's players.

COMPLETE SET (10)	15.00	30.00
1 Kenny Carr	1.25	3.00
2 Mack Calvin	1.50	4.00
3 Mike Bratz	1.25	3.00
4 Geoff Huston	1.25	3.00
5 Walter Jordan	1.25	3.00
6 Bill Laimbeer	2.50	6.00
7 Don Ford	1.25	3.00
8 Mike Mitchell	1.50	4.00
9 Roger Phegley	1.25	3.00
10 Randy Smith	1.50	4.00

1977-78 Celtics Citgo

Sponsored by Citgo Gas, the 17 photos in this set each measure approximately 8 1/2" by 11". The fronts feature full bleed glossy color action pictures. Most card backs carry player information for the featured player including biography, career summary, amd complete statistics. The back of card number 5 exhibits a chart titled "Celtics vs. NBA Opponents Over The Years" (1946-1977), while the back of card number 6 lists the Celtics' roster for the 1977-78 season. Only the Kermit Washington photo is a non-action, portrait shot, suggesting that he may have been added to the set later. The photos are unnumbered and ordered below in alphabetical order.

COMPLETE SET (17)	40.00	75.00
1 Dave Bing	2.50	6.00
2 Tommy Boswell	1.25	3.00
3 Don Chaney	2.00	5.00
4 Dave Cowens	3.00	8.00
5 Dave Cowens	3.00	8.00
6 Dave Cowens	3.00	8.00
7 John Havlicek	7.50	15.00
8 Sam Jones	2.50	6.00
9 Cedric Maxwell	1.50	4.00
10 Curtis Rowe	2.00	5.00
11 Tom Sanders CO	1.50	4.00
12 Fred Saunders	1.25	3.00
13 Kevin Stacom	1.25	3.00
14 Kermit Washington	1.25	3.00
15 Jo Jo White	2.50	6.00
16 Sidney Wicks	2.50	6.00
17 Ballboy Contest	1.25	3.00

1974-75 Celtics Linnett

These charcoal drawings are skillfully executed facial portraits of Boston Celtic players. They were drawn by noted sports artist Charles Linnett and measure approximately 8 1/2" by 11". A facsimile autograph of the player is written across the lower right, the Celtics' logo appears in the lower left, and the backs are blank. The drawings are unnumbered and checklisted below in alphabetical order. The set is very similar to the Linnett Milwaukee Bucks set of the same year. A 1969 NBA Properties copyright is printed in the lower left corner of the card and a 1973 NBAPA copyright is printed on the wrapper of the two-card package in which they were sold. The set is dated by the fact that Steve Downing and Phil Hankinson's first year with the Boston Celtics was 1973-74.

COMPLETE SET (9)	30.00	60.00
1 Don Chaney	2.50	6.00
2 Dave Cowens	7.50	15.00
3 Steve Downing	2.00	5.00
4 Henry Finkel	2.50	6.00
5 Phil Hankinson	2.00	5.00
6 John Havlicek	10.00	20.00
7 Don Nelson	5.00	10.00
8 Paul Silas	3.00	8.00
9 Jo Jo White	3.00	8.00

1975-76 Celtics Linnett Green Borders

Packaged in cello wrap, these three cards measure approximately 4" by 6" and feature artwork by Charles Linnett. The fronts feature a charcoal portrait of the player surrounded by a green border displaying players from various sports. The team logo, player's name, and facsimile autograph appear across the lower portion of the front. The backs are blank. The cards are unnumbered and checklisted below in alphabetical order.

COMPLETE SET (3)	8.00	20.00
1 Dave Cowens	3.00	8.00
2 John Havlicek	4.00	10.00
3 Jo Jo White	2.50	6.00

1956-57 Celtics Photos

This ten card oversized blank backed set was released during the 1956-57 season, and features such Celtics stars as Bob Cousy and Bill Sharman. Please note that these black and white cards measure 6.5"x 8".

COMPLETE SET (10)	1,000.00	2,000.00
1 Bob Cousy	250.00	500.00
2 Tom Heinsohn	200.00	400.00
3 Dick Hemric	75.00	150.00
4 Jim Loscutoff	100.00	200.00
5 Jack Nichols	75.00	150.00
6 Togo Palazzi	75.00	150.00
7 Andy Phillip	100.00	200.00
8 Arnie Risen	100.00	200.00
9 Bill Sharman	150.00	300.00
10 Lou Tsioropoulos	75.00	150.00

1976-77 Celtics Team Issue

These black and white blank-backed photos, which measure 8" by 10" feature members of the 1976-77 Boston Celtics. Since these photos are unnumbered, we have sequenced them in alphabetical order.

COMPLETE SET (12)	15.00	30.00
1 Jerome Anderson	.75	2.00
2 Jim Ard	.75	2.00
3 Tom Boswell	.75	2.00
4 Norm Cook	.75	2.00
5 John Havlicek	3.00	8.00
6 Steve Kuberski	.75	2.00
7 Glenn McDonald	.75	2.00
8 Curtis Rowe	1.00	2.50
9 Fred Saunders	.75	2.00
10 Paul Silas	1.50	4.00
11 Kevin Stacom	.75	2.00
12 Sidney Wicks	1.00	2.50

1978-79 Clippers Handyman

The 1978-79 San Diego Clippers Handyman set contains nine cards measuring approximately 2" by 4 1/4". The cards are "3-D" and are similar to the 1970s Kelloggs baseball sets. Each card has a coupon tab attached (included in the dimensions given above). Coach Gene Shue's card was apparently not distributed (as it was the grand prize winner of the contest) with the other cards but it does exist. Some veteran collectors and dealers also consider Kunnert to be somewhat tougher to find. In addition there is a second version of the Lloyd Free card with a signature variation. The set price below does not include the Gene Shue card.

COMPLETE SET (9)	25.00	50.00
1 Randy Smith 9	2.50	6.00
2 Nick Weatherspoon 12	2.00	5.00
3 Freeman Williams 20	1.50	4.00
4 Sidney Wicks 21	3.00	8.00
5A Lloyd Free 24	2.50	6.00
5B Lloyd Free 24 (Signature variation)	10.00	20.00
6 Swen Nater 31	2.00	5.00
7 Jerome Whitehead 33	1.25	3.00
8 Kermit Washington 42	1.50	4.00
9 Kevin Kunnert 44	10.00	20.00
NNO Gene Shue CO SP	750.00	1,200.00

1971-72 Colonels Volpe Marathon Oil

This set of Marathon Oil Pro Star Portraits consists of colorful portraits by distinguished artist Nicholas Volpe. Each (ABA Kentucky Colonels) portrait measures approximately 7 1/2" by 9 7/8" and features a painting of the player's face on a black background, with an action painting superimposed to the side. A facsimile autograph in white appears at the bottom of the portrait. At the bottom of each portrait is a postcard measuring 7 1/2" by 4" after perforation. While the back of the portrait has offers for a basketball photo album, autographed tumblers, and a poster, the postcard itself could also be used to apply for a Marathon credit card. The portraits are unnumbered and checklisted below in alphabetical order. Tumblers featuring these drawings are valued at 3x the listed prices. The key card in the set is Dan Issel during his Rookie Card year.

COMPLETE SET (11)	50.00	100.00
1 Darrell Carrier	5.00	10.00
2 Bobby Croft	3.00	8.00
3 Louie Dampier	10.00	25.00
4 Les Hunter	3.00	8.00
5 Dan Issel	20.00	40.00
6 Jim Ligon	3.00	8.00
7 Cincy Powell	5.00	12.00
8 Mike Pratt	5.00	10.00
9 Walt Simon	3.00	8.00
10 Sam Smith	3.00	8.00
11 Howard Wright	3.00	8.00

1959 Comet Sweets Olympic Achievements

Celebrating various Olympic events, ceremonies, and their history, this 25-card set was issued by Comet Sweets. The cards are printed on thin cardboard stock and measure 1 7/16" by 2 9/16". Inside white borders, the fronts display water color paintings of various Olympic events. Some cards are horizontally oriented; others are vertically oriented. The set title "Olympic Achievements" appears at the top on the backs, with a discussion of the event below. This set is the first series; the cards are numbered "X to 25."

COMPLETE SET (25)	30.00	60.00
12 Basketball	2.50	5.00

1972-73 Comspec

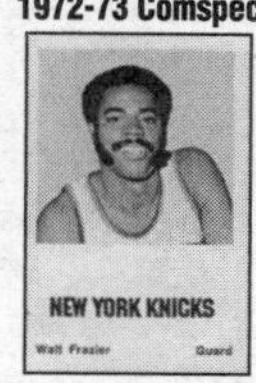

This 36-card set is printed on thin card stock, and each card measures approximately 2 1/4" by 3 1/2". The fronts display posed color player photos bordered in white. The photos have different color backgrounds (blue, green, orange, pink, red, or yellow). The only card that contains a genuine action shot from a game is that of Chet Walker. The team name, player's name, and his position appear in the white border beneath each picture. The horizontally oriented backs have biography and career statistics. The cards are unnumbered and checklisted below in alphabetical order.

COMPLETE SET (36)	2,200.00	2,800.00
1 Kareem Abdul-Jabbar	150.00	300.00
2 Rick Adelman	20.00	50.00
3 Nate Archibald	40.00	80.00
4 Rick Barry	40.00	80.00
5 Walt Bellamy	20.00	50.00
6 Dave Bing	30.00	75.00
7 Austin Carr	15.00	40.00
8 Wilt Chamberlain	250.00	500.00
9 Dave Cowens	40.00	80.00
10 Walt Frazier	40.00	80.00
11 Gail Goodrich	30.00	75.00
12 John Havlicek	125.00	250.00
13 Connie Hawkins	45.00	90.00
14 Elvin Hayes	30.00	75.00
15 Spencer Haywood	15.00	40.00
16 John Hummer	12.50	30.00
17 Don Kojis	15.00	40.00
18 Bob Lanier	40.00	80.00
19 Kevin Loughery	15.00	40.00
20 Jerry Lucas	30.00	75.00
21 Pete Maravich	300.00	600.00
22 Jack Marin	15.00	40.00
23 Calvin Murphy	30.00	60.00
24 Geoff Petrie	25.00	50.00
25 Willis Reed	40.00	80.00
26 Oscar Robertson	100.00	225.00
27 Cazzie Russell	20.00	40.00
28 Elmore Smith	15.00	40.00
29 Dick Snyder	15.00	40.00
30 Wes Unseld	40.00	80.00
31 Dick Van Arsdale	25.00	50.00
32 Tom Van Arsdale	15.00	40.00
33 Norm Van Lier	30.00	60.00
34 Chet Walker	30.00	60.00
35 Jerry West	150.00	300.00
36 Lenny Wilkens	45.00	90.00

1971-72 Condors Pittsburgh Team Issue

This set of 11 photos features the Pittsburgh Condors of the American Basketball Association. The cards measure approximately 5 1/2" by 7". The fronts carry black-and-white posed action photos with a white border. The player's name and the team name appear under the picture. The backs are blank. The photos are unnumbered and checklisted below in alphabetical order.

COMPLETE SET (11)	35.00	70.00
1 John Brisker	5.00	10.00
2 George Carter	3.00	8.00
3 Mickey Davis	2.50	6.00
4 Stew Johnson	2.50	6.00
5 Arvesta Kelly	2.50	6.00
6 Dave Lattin	5.00	12.00
7 Mike Lewis	2.50	6.00
8 Jimmy O'Brien	4.00	10.00
9 Paul Ruffner	2.50	6.00
10 Skeeter Swift	3.00	8.00
11 George Thompson	5.00	10.00

1971-72 Condors Pittsburgh Team Photo

Each of these team-issued photos measure approximately 8" by 10" and feature black and white player portraits on two different sheets. The player's name is listed below the photo. Each sheet contains eight player portraits. The backs are blank. The photos are unnumbered and listed below alphabetically.

COMPLETE SET (2)	20.00	40.00
1 John Brisker George Carter Mickey Davis Mike Lewis Jimmy O'Brien Paul Ruffner Skeeter Swift George Thompson	12.50	25.00
2 Don Bezahler Mark Binstein Stew Johnson Arvesta Kelly David Lattin Jack McMahon Ray Melchiorre Walt Szczerbiak	10.00	20.00

1969-70 Converse Staff

This ten-card set was sponsored by Converse Shoes. The cards measure approximately 2 1/4" by 2 3/4". The fronts feature a drawn player portrait and basketball tip. The backs are blank. The cards are unnumbered and are checklisted below in alphabetical order.

COMPLETE SET (10)	175.00	350.00
1 Bob Davies	40.00	80.00
2 Joe Dean	12.00	30.00
3 Gib Ford	10.00	25.00
4 Bob Houbregs	15.00	40.00
5 Rod Hundley	40.00	80.00
6 Stu Inman	15.00	40.00
7 Bunny Levitt	15.00	40.00
8 Earl Lloyd	15.00	40.00
9 John Norlander	12.00	30.00
10 Phil Rollins	10.00	25.00

1969-70 Cougars Carolina Team Issue

Each of these team-issued photos measure approximately 8" by 10" and feature black and white player portraits. The player's name is listed below the photo and the fronts feature a facsimile autograph. The backs are blank. The photos are unnumbered and listed below alphabetically.

COMPLETE SET (15)	50.00	100.00
1 Carolina Cougars Team Photo	5.00	10.00
2 Bill Bunting	2.50	6.00
3 Cal Fowler	2.50	6.00
4 Steve Kramer	2.50	6.00
5 Gene Littles	3.00	8.00
6 Randy Mahaffey	2.50	6.00
7 Bones McKinney CO	5.00	10.00
8 Larry Miller	3.00	8.00
9 Doug Moe	5.00	10.00
10 Rich Niemann	2.50	6.00
11 George Peeples	2.50	6.00
12 Ron Perry	2.50	6.00
13 George Sutor	2.50	6.00
14 Bob Verga	3.00	8.00
15 Hank Whitney	2.50	6.00

1970-71 Cougars Team Issue

These photos were issued by the Carolina Cougars. They feature members of the 1970-71 Cougars team. This list may not be complete so any additions are appreciated. Jim McDaniel was signed out of college and was going to be the star rookie the next season. Also please note the Larry Steele never played for the Cougars.

COMPLETE SET	12.50	25.00
1 Gary Bradds	2.00	5.00
2 Jim McDaniels	2.50	6.00
3 Dave Newmark	2.00	5.00
4 George Peeples	2.00	5.00
5 Larry Steele	3.00	8.00

1977-78 Dell Flipbooks

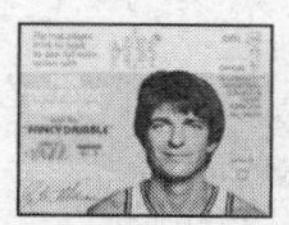

This set of flipbooks was produced by Pocket Money Basketball Co. and were sold in most retail outlets and toy stores. The retail display featured eight complete sets of six booklets or 48 books individually for sale at a suggested retail price of 50 cents. These flipbooks measure approximately 4" by 3 1/8" and are 24 pages in length. They have color action player photos and career statistics. The booklets are unnumbered and are checklisted below in alphabetical order by subject. The front has a white stripe at the top, and a color head and shoulders shot of the player on a color background. The inside front cover has a table of contents, while the inside back cover has the logos of all 22 NBA teams. Each flipbook features a different play or move by the player; e.g., the Maravich flipbook is titled, "Pete The Pistol Maravich and his Fancy Dribble." When the odd-numbered pages are flipped in a smooth movement from front to back, they form a color "motion picture~ of Maravich crossing over his dribble through his legs. The even-numbered pages present a variety of information on Maravich, his team (New Orleans Jazz), and the 1976-77 NBA season.

COMPLETE SET (6)	40.00	80.00
1 Kareem Abdul-Jabbar	7.50	15.00
2 Dave Cowens	6.00	12.00
3 Julius Erving	7.50	15.00
4 Pete Maravich	20.00	40.00
5 David Thompson	6.00	12.00
6 Bill Walton	6.00	12.00

1970 Detroit Free Press

These color clippings came from the Detroit Free Press News in 1970. The set features six known players (as listed below), but it is assumed that there are more players in the set. We are still looking for additional players to add to the checklist, thus if you know of any, please contact us. The clippings are not numbered and checklisted below in alphabetical order.

COMPLETE SET (6)	30.00	60.00
1 Dave Bing	12.50	25.00
2 Howard Komives	3.00	8.00
3 Eddie Miles	3.00	8.00
4 Ralph Simpson	6.00	12.00
5 Rudy Tomjanovich	10.00	20.00
6 Jimmy Walker	5.00	10.00

1967-73 Equitable Sports Hall of Fame

This set consists of copies of art work found over a number of years in many national magazines, especially "Sports Illustrated," honoring sports heroes that Equitable Life Assurance Society selected to be in its very own Sports Hall of Fame. The cards consists of charcoal-type drawings on white backgrounds by artists, George Loh and Robert Riger, and measure approximately 11" by 7 3/4". The unnumbered cards have been assigned numbers below using a sport prefix (BB- baseball, BK- basketball, FB- football, HK- hockey, OT-other).

COMPLETE SET (95)	250.00	500.00
BK1 Elgin Baylor	3.00	6.00
BK2 Wilt Chamberlain	5.00	10.00
BK3 Bob Cousy	3.00	6.00
BK4 Hal Grier	2.00	4.00
BK5 Jerry Lucas	2.00	4.00
BK6 George Mikan	3.00	6.00
BK7 Bob Pettit	3.00	6.00
BK8 Willis Reed	2.00	4.00
BK9 Bill Russell	5.00	10.00
BK10 Dolph Schayes	2.00	4.00

1961-62 Fleer

The 1961-62 Fleer set was the company's only major basketball issue until the 1986-87 season. The cards were issued in five-cent wax packs with 24 packs in a box. The cards in the set measure the standard 2 1/2" by 3 1/2". Cards numbered 45 to 66 are action shots (designated IA) of players elsewhere in the set. Both the regular cards and the IA cards are numbered alphabetically within that particular subset. No known scarcities exist, although the set is quite popular since it contains the first mainstream basketball cards of many of the game's all-time greats including Elgin Baylor, Wilt Chamberlain, Oscar Robertson and Jerry West. Most cards are frequently found with centering problems

COMPLETE SET (66)	2,800.00	4,000.00
CONDITION SENSITIVE SET		
CARDS PRICED IN NM CONDITION		
1 Al Attles RC	30.00	80.00
2 Paul Arizin	25.00	60.00
3 Elgin Baylor RC	125.00	300.00
4 Walt Bellamy RC	30.00	80.00
5 Arlen Bockhorn	8.00	20.00
6 Bob Boozer RC	10.00	25.00
7 Carl Braun	10.00	25.00
8 Wilt Chamberlain RC	600.00	1,200.00
9 Larry Costello	6.00	15.00
10 Bob Cousy	75.00	200.00
11 Walter Dukes	6.00	15.00
12 Wayne Embry RC	20.00	50.00
13 Dave Gambee	6.00	15.00
14 Tom Gola	12.00	30.00
15 Sihugo Green RC	10.00	25.00
16 Hal Greer RC	40.00	100.00
17 Richie Guerin RC	15.00	40.00
18 Cliff Hagan	15.00	40.00
19 Tom Heinsohn	30.00	80.00
20 Bailey Howell RC	25.00	60.00
21 Rod Hundley	25.00	60.00
22 K.C. Jones RC	40.00	100.00
23 Sam Jones RC	40.00	100.00
24 Phil Jordan	8.00	20.00
25 John Kerr	15.00	40.00
26 Rudy LaRusso RC	15.00	40.00
27 George Lee	6.00	15.00
28 Bob Leonard	8.00	20.00
29 Clyde Lovellette	20.00	50.00
30 John McCarthy	6.00	15.00
31 Tom Meschery RC	10.00	25.00
32 Willie Naulls	10.00	25.00
33 Don Ohl RC	12.00	30.00
34 Bob Pettit	30.00	80.00
35 Frank Ramsey	12.00	30.00
36 Oscar Robertson RC	200.00	500.00
37 Guy Rodgers RC	12.00	30.00
38 Bill Russell !	150.00	400.00
39 Dolph Schayes	25.00	60.00
40 Frank Selvy	8.00	20.00
41 Gene Shue	8.00	20.00
42 Jack Twyman	12.00	30.00
43 Jerry West RC	300.00	600.00
44 Len Wilkens UER RC	60.00	150.00
45 Paul Arizin IA	10.00	25.00
46 Elgin Baylor IA	50.00	125.00
47 Wilt Chamberlain IA !	150.00	300.00
48 Larry Costello IA	8.00	20.00
49 Bob Cousy IA	50.00	125.00
50 Walter Dukes IA	6.00	15.00
51 Tom Gola IA	10.00	25.00
52 Richie Guerin IA	8.00	20.00
53 Cliff Hagan IA	10.00	25.00
54 Tom Heinsohn IA	20.00	50.00
55 Bailey Howell IA	10.00	25.00
56 John Kerr IA	12.00	30.00
57 Rudy LaRusso IA	8.00	20.00
58 Clyde Lovellette IA	12.00	30.00
59 Bob Pettit IA	20.00	50.00
60 Frank Ramsey IA	10.00	25.00
61 Oscar Robertson IA !	60.00	150.00
62 Bill Russell IA !	100.00	250.00
63 Dolph Schayes IA	15.00	40.00
64 Gene Shue IA	8.00	20.00
65 Jack Twyman IA	10.00	25.00
66 Jerry West IA !	75.00	200.00

1973-74 Fleer The Shots

This 21-card set was produced by artist R.G. Laughlin for Fleer. The cards measure approximately 2 1/2" by 4". The cards were distributed in packs with one "Shots" card along with two team logo cloth patches and one stick of gum. The fronts feature an illustration of the shot depicted on the card. The illustration is in color, although crudely drawn. The back has a discussion of the shot.

COMPLETE SET (21)	40.00	80.00
COMMON CARD (1-21)	1.50	4.00
21 The Good Shot	2.00	5.00

1974 Fleer Team Patches/Stickers

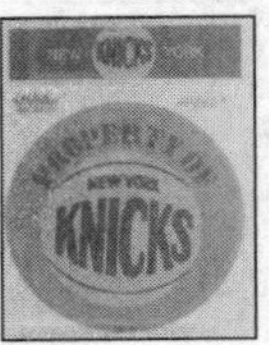

These cloth patches, each measuring 2 1/2" by 3 3/8", were sold in wax packs. There were two forms of distribution. One entailed packs including one patch, one sticker, one Fleer "The Shots" card, and a stick of gum. The other had two patches instead of a sticker. The team name appears in a color bar across the top of the patch. The team logo is printed inside a round-cut out area in the patch; the words "Property Of" are printed immediately above some of the logos and follow the curve of the logo. The backs are blank. The stickers have the team name across the top and the team logo below. In addition to a NBA logo and sticker, one cloth patch and one sticker were issued for each NBA team. The patches are unnumbered and checklisted below in alphabetical order, with the NBA cloth patches listed first.

COMPLETE SET (38)	40.00	80.00
1 NBA Logo	1.00	2.50
2 Atlanta Hawks	.75	2.00
3 Boston Celtics	1.00	2.50
4 Buffalo Braves	1.00	2.50
5 Chicago Bulls	.75	2.00
6 Cleveland Cavaliers	.75	2.00
7 Detroit Pistons	.75	2.00
8 Golden State Warriors	1.00	2.50
9 Houston Rockets	.75	2.00
10 Kansas City Kings	.75	2.00
11 Los Angeles Lakers	1.00	2.50
12 Milwaukee Bucks	.75	2.00
13 New Orleans Jazz	1.00	2.50
14 New York Knicks	1.00	2.50
15 Philadelphia 76ers	.75	2.00
16 Phoenix Suns	.75	2.00
17 Portland Trail Blazers	.75	2.00
18 Seattle Supersonics	.75	2.00
19 Washington Bullets	.75	2.00
20 NBA Logo	1.25	3.00
21 Atlanta Hawks	1.00	2.50
22 Boston Celtics	1.25	3.00
23 Buffalo Braves	1.25	3.00
24 Chicago Bulls	1.00	2.50
25 Cleveland Cavaliers	1.00	2.50
26 Detroit Pistons	1.00	2.50
27 Golden State Warriors	1.00	2.50
28 Houston Rockets	1.00	2.50
29 Kansas City Kings	1.25	3.00
30 Los Angeles Lakers	1.25	3.00
31 Milwaukee Bucks	1.00	2.50
32 New Orleans Jazz	1.25	3.00
33 New York Knicks	1.25	3.00
34 Philadelphia 76ers	1.00	2.50
35 Phoenix Suns	1.00	2.50
36 Portland Trail Blazers	1.00	2.50
37 Seattle Supersonics	1.00	2.50
38 Washington Bullets	1.00	2.50

1977-78 Fleer Team Stickers

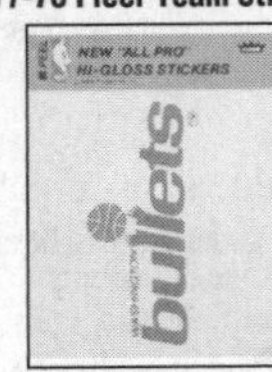

Each measuring 2 1/2" by 3 3/16", this set features one sticker for all twenty-two NBA teams. A color stripe across the top carries the NBA logo and the words "New 'All Pro' Hi-Gloss Stickers." The sticker itself consists of the team name and logo on a white background. Though all 22 NBA teams are represented in this set, there are 71 color variations in the set. The backs are blank. The team stickers are unnumbered and checklisted below in alphabetical order.

COMPLETE SET (22)	7.50	15.00
1 Atlanta Hawks	.30	.75
2 Boston Celtics	.40	1.00
3 Buffalo Braves	.40	1.00
4 Chicago Bulls	.30	.75
5 Cleveland Cavaliers	.30	.75
6 Denver Nuggets	.30	.75
7 Detroit Pistons	.30	.75
8 Golden State Warriors	.30	.75
9 Houston Rockets	.30	.75
10 Indiana Pacers	.30	.75
11 Kansas City Kings	.40	1.00
12 Los Angeles Lakers	.40	1.00
13 Milwaukee Bucks	.30	.75
14 New Jersey Nets	.30	.75
15 New Orleans Jazz	.40	1.00
16 New York Knicks	.40	1.00
17 Philadelphia 76ers	.30	.75
18 Phoenix Suns	.30	.75
19 Portland Trail Blazers	.30	.75
20 San Antonio Spurs	.30	.75
21 Seattle Supersonics	.30	.75
22 Washington Bullets	.30	.75

1971-72 Floridians McDonald's

This ten-card set of ABA Miami Floridians was sponsored by McDonald's. The cards measure approximately 2 1/2" by 4", including a 1/2" tear-off tab at the bottom. The bottom tab admitted one 14-or-under child to the game with each regular price adult ticket. Prices below refer to cards with tabs intact. The fronts feature color action player photos with rounded corners and black borders. The backs have player information, rules governing the free youth tickets, and an offer to receive an ABA basketball in exchange for a set of ten different Floridian tickets. The cards are unnumbered and are checklisted below in alphabetical order.

COMPLETE SET (10)	300.00	600.00
1 Warren Armstrong	40.00	80.00
2 Mack Calvin	40.00	80.00
3 Ron Franz	30.00	60.00
4 Ira Harge	30.00	60.00
5 Larry Jones	30.00	60.00
6 Willie Long	30.00	60.00
7 Sam Robinson	30.00	60.00
8 Al Tucker	30.00	60.00
9 George Tinsley	30.00	60.00
10 Lonnie Wright	30.00	60.00

1963 Gad Fun Cards

This set of 1963 Fun Cards were issued by a sports illustrator by the name of Gad from Minneapolis, Minnesota. The cards are printed on cardboard stock paper. The borderless fronts have black and white line drawings. A fun sport's fact or player career statistic is depicted in the drawing. The backs of the first six cards display numbers used to play the game explained on card number 6. The other backs carry a cartoon with a joke or riddle. Copyright information is listed on the lower portion of the card.

COMPLETE SET (84)	37.50	75.00
76 Buffalo Germans Basketball Squad	.25	.50

1971-72 Globetrotters Cocoa Puffs 28

This 1971-72 Harlem Globetrotters set was produced for Cocoa Puffs cereal by Fleer and contains 28 standard size cards. The cards were issued inside specially marked cereal boxes with four consecutively numbered cards per box. The card fronts have full color pictures with facsimile autographs. The card backs are subtitled "Cocoa Puffs presents the magicians of basketball and have black printing on gray card stock and feature biographical sketches and other interesting information about the Globetrotters. The cards are numbered on back X of 28.

COMPLETE SET (28)	90.00	180.00
1 Geese Ausbie and Curly Neal	8.00	20.00
2 Neal and Meadowlark	5.00	12.00
3 Meadowlark is Safe	4.00	10.00
4 Meadowlark Lemon Curly Neal and Geese Ausbie	3.00	8.00
5 Mel Davis and Bill Meggett	2.00	5.00
6 Geese Ausbie Meadowlark Lemon and Curly Neal	3.00	8.00
7 Geese Ausbie Meadowlark Lemon and Curly Neal	3.00	8.00
8 Mel Davis and Curly Neal	2.50	6.00
9 Meadowlark Lemon Curly Neal and Geese Ausbie	3.00	8.00
10 Curly Neal Meadowlark Lemon and Mel Davis	3.00	8.00
11 Football Routine	2.00	5.00
12 1970-71 Highlights	2.00	5.00
13 Pabs Robertson	2.00	5.00
14 Bobby Joe Mason	2.00	5.00
15 Pabs Robertson	2.00	5.00
16 Clarence Smith	2.00	5.00
17 Clarence Smith	2.00	5.00
18 Hubert (Geese) Ausbie	2.50	6.00
19 Hubert(Geese) Ausbie (Two balls)	2.50	6.00
20 Bobby Hunter	2.00	5.00
21 Bobby Hunter (One leg up)	2.00	5.00
22 Meadowlark Lemon (Three balls)	3.00	8.00
23 Meadowlark Lemon	4.00	10.00
24 Freddie (Curly) Neal	3.00	8.00
25 Freddie (Curly) Neal (Three paint brushes)	3.00	8.00
26 Meadowlark Lemon (Palming two balls)	4.00	10.00
27 Mel Davis (Leaning over with ball)	2.00	5.00
28 Freddie Curly Neal	7.50	15.00

1971-72 Globetrotters 84

The 1971-72 Harlem Globetrotters set was produced by Fleer and sold in wax packs. The set contains 84 standard size cards. The card fronts have full color pictures. The card backs have black printing on gray card stock and feature biographical sketches and other interesting information about the Globetrotters. The cards are numbered on back "X" of 84. A Globetrotter Emblem sticker was inserted in each wax pack.

COMPLETE SET (85)	75.00	150.00
1 Bob Showboat Hall	5.00	12.00
2 Bob Showboat Hall (kicking ball)	.75	2.00
3 Bob Showboat Hall (passing behind back)	.75	2.00
4 Pabs Robertson	.75	2.00
5 Pabs Robertson	.75	2.00
6 Pabs Robertson	.75	2.00
7 Pabs Robertson	.75	2.00
8 Pabs Robertson	.75	2.00
9 Meadowlark Lemon (kicking behind back)	2.50	6.00
10 Meadowlark Lemon (rolling ball on arm)	2.50	6.00
11 Meadowlark Lemon (palming two balls)	2.50	6.00
12 Meadowlark Lemon (ball on neck)	2.50	6.00
13 Meadowlark Lemon (three balls)	2.50	6.00
14 Meadowlark Lemon (three balls in front)	2.50	6.00
15 Meadowlark Lemon (three balls)	2.50	6.00
16 Meadowlark Lemon (dribbling two balls)	2.50	6.00
17 Meadowlark Lemon (with cap)	2.50	6.00
18 Curley Neal Meadowlark Lemon and Mel Davis	2.50	6.00
19 Football Play (Meadowlark centering)	2.50	6.00
20 Meadowlark Lemon (hooking)	2.50	6.00
21 Hubert Geese Ausbie (balls between legs)	1.00	2.50
22 Hubert Geese Ausbie (ball under arm)	1.00	2.50
23 Hubert Geese Ausbie (ball on finger)	1.00	2.50
24 Hubert Geese Ausbie (ball behind back)	1.00	2.50
25 Hubert Geese Ausbie (no ball)	1.00	2.50
26 Geese Ausbie and (Curly Neal with confetti)	2.00	5.00
27 Freddie Curly Neal (artist)	2.50	6.00
28 Freddie Curly Neal (sitting on ball)	2.50	6.00
29 Freddie Curly Neal (two balls on head)	2.50	6.00
30 Mel Davis and Freddie Curly Neal	1.50	4.00
31 Freddie Curly Neall (smiling)	2.50	6.00
32 Freddie CurlyNeal (looking to side)	2.50	6.00
33 Mel Davis (looking down)	.75	2.00
34 Mel Davis (ready to shoot)	.75	2.00
35 Mel Davis (ball in hand)	.75	2.00
36 Mel Davis (ball over head)	.75	2.00
37 Mel Davis and Bill Meggett (leap frog)	.75	2.00
38 Mel Davis (ball on knee)	.75	2.00
39 Bobby Joe Mason (ball under arm)	.75	2.00
40 Bobby Joe Mason (ball between legs)	.75	2.00
41 Bobby Joe Mason (passing behind back)	.75	2.00
42 Bobby Joe Mason and (Frank Stephens	.75	2.00
43 Bobby Joe Mason (ball to side)	.75	2.00
44 Bobby Joe Mason (ready to shoot)	.75	2.00
45 Clarence Smith (three balls between legs)	.75	2.00
46 Clarence Smith (on bike)	.75	2.00
47 Clarence Smith (ball at ear)	.75	2.00
48 Clarence Smith (dribbling on side)	.75	2.00
49 Jerry Venable	.75	2.00
50 Frank Stephens (hands in front)	.75	2.00
51 Frank Stephens (ball on finger)	.75	2.00
52 Frank Stephens	.75	2.00

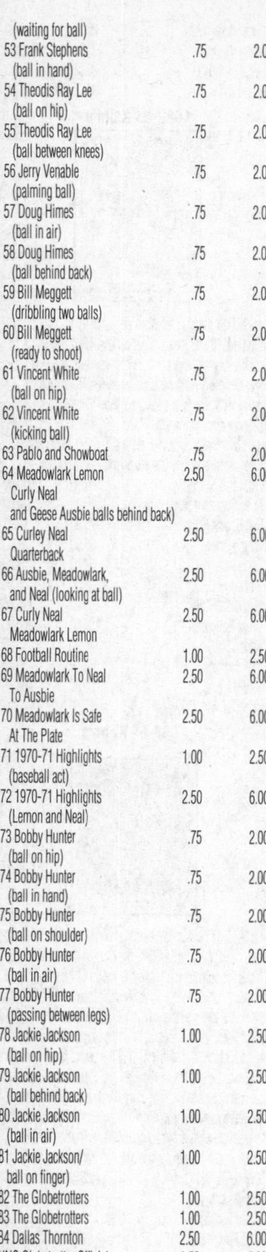

(waiting for ball)		
53 Frank Stephens (ball in hand)	.75	2.00
54 Theodis Ray Lee (ball on hip)	.75	2.00
55 Theodis Ray Lee (ball between knees)	.75	2.00
56 Jerry Venable (palming ball)	.75	2.00
57 Doug Himes (ball in air)	.75	2.00
58 Doug Himes (ball behind back)	.75	2.00
59 Bill Meggett (dribbling two balls)	.75	2.00
60 Bill Meggett (ready to shoot)	.75	2.00
61 Vincent White (ball on hip)	.75	2.00
62 Vincent White (kicking ball)	.75	2.00
63 Pablo and Showboat	.75	2.00
64 Meadowlark Lemon Curly Neal and Geese Ausbie balls behind back)	2.50	6.00
65 Curley Neal Quarterback	2.50	6.00
66 Ausbie, Meadowlark, and Neal (looking at ball)	2.50	6.00
67 Curly Neal Meadowlark Lemon	2.50	6.00
68 Football Routine	1.00	2.50
69 Meadowlark To Neal To Ausbie	2.50	6.00
70 Meadowlark Is Safe At The Plate	2.50	6.00
71 1970-71 Highlights (baseball act)	1.00	2.50
72 1970-71 Highlights (Lemon and Neal)	2.50	6.00
73 Bobby Hunter (ball on hip)	.75	2.00
74 Bobby Hunter (ball in hand)	.75	2.00
75 Bobby Hunter (ball on shoulder)	.75	2.00
76 Bobby Hunter (ball in air)	.75	2.00
77 Bobby Hunter (passing between legs)	.75	2.00
78 Jackie Jackson (ball on hip)	1.00	2.50
79 Jackie Jackson (ball behind back)	1.00	2.50
80 Jackie Jackson (ball in air)	1.00	2.50
81 Jackie Jackson/ ball on finger)	1.00	2.50
82 The Globetrotters	1.00	2.50
83 The Globetrotters	1.00	2.50
84 Dallas Thornton	2.50	6.00
NNO Globetrotter Official Peel-off Team Emblem Sticker	1.50	4.00

1971-72 Globetrotters Phoenix Candy

This eight-card set was issued as unnumbered cards on the back panels of Phoenix Candy boxes. The cards measure approximately 4 7/8" by 2 1/2" whereas the box measures approximately 3 1/4" by 6 1/2". The year of issue is assumed from the 71 over 72 inside a "clock face" on the box flap. Complete boxes are valued at 1.5 times the prices listed below.

COMPLETE SET (8)	175.00	350.00
1 J.C. Gipson	20.00	40.00
2 Bob Showboat Hall	20.00	40.00
3 Leon Hillard	20.00	40.00
4 Meadowlark Lemon	50.00	100.00
5 Freddie(Curly) Neal	40.00	80.00
6 Pablo Robertson	20.00	40.00
7 National Unit (Team picture)	25.00	50.00
8 International Unit (Team picture)	25.00	50.00

1974 Globetrotters Wonder Bread

Six of the twenty-five cards in this set depict Harlem Globetrotters. All cards were randomly inserted inside loaves of Wonder Bread and feature Hanna-Barbera TV cartoon show characters. The fronts feature a multi-color Globetrotter cartoon. The backs carry a lesson in how to do a magic trick. The cards are numbered on the back "X in a series of 25."

COMPLETE SET (25)	25.00	50.00
3 Curley Neal B.J. Mason	7.50	15.00
4 Curley Neal Geese Ausbie	7.50	15.00
5 J.C. Gipson	2.50	6.00
14 Pablo Robertson	2.50	6.00
16 Meadowlark and Granny	5.00	10.00
20 J.C. Gipson and Granny	2.50	6.00

1980 Globetrotters

This six photo set features black and white glossy 8" x10" s. The photo backs are blank, and the set is not numbered, therefore appear alphabetically.

COMPLETE SET (6)	10.00	20.00
1 Geese Ausbie	1.50	4.00
2 Geese Ausbie Curly Neal Nate Branch	2.00	5.00
3 Nate Branch	1.25	3.00
4 Billy Ray Hobley	1.25	3.00
5 Curly Neal	2.50	6.00
6 Dallas Thornton Fred Neal Hubert Ausbie Nate Branch General Lee Holman Billy Ray Hobley Robert Paige Lionel Garrett Reggie Franklin Eddie Fields	1.50	4.00

1968-74 Hall of Fame Bookmarks

These bookmarks commemorate individuals who were elected to the Basketball Hall of Fame. The cards were probably issued year after year (with additions) by the Hall of Fame book store. They measure approximately 2 7/16" by 6 3/8". The top of the front has a blue-tinted 2 1/8" by 2 5/16 "mug shot" of the individual on paper stock. In blue lettering the individual's name and a brief biography are printed below the picture. The backs are blank and the cards are unnumbered. The last seven cards listed below were inducted in 1969 (47-48), 1970 (49-51), 1972 (52), and 1974 (53); there are some slight style and size differences in these later issue cards compared to the first 46 cards in the set.

COMPLETE SET (53)	150.00	300.00
1 Forrest C. Allen	.60	1.50
2 Arnold J. Auerbach	1.25	3.00
3 Clair F. Bee	.60	1.50
4 Bernhard Borgmann	.20	.50
5 Walter A. Brown	.20	.50
6 John W. Bunn	.20	.50
7 Howard G. Cann	.20	.50
8 H. Clifford Carlson	.20	.50
9 Everett S. Dean	.20	.50
10 Forrest S. DeBernardi	.20	.50
11 Henry G. Dehnert	.20	.50
12 Harold E. Foster	.20	.50
13 Amory T. Gill	.20	.50
14 Victor A. Hanson	.20	.50
15 Edward J. Hickox	.20	.50
16 Paul D. Hinkle	.20	.50
17 Howard A. Hobson	.20	.50
18 Nat Holman	.75	2.00
19 Charles D. Hyatt	.20	.50
20 Henry P. Iba	.60	1.50
21 Edward S. Irish	.25	.60
22 Alvin F. Julian	.20	.50
23 Matthew P. Kennedy	.20	.50
24 Robert A. Kurland	.40	1.00
25 Ward L. Lambert	.60	1.50
26 Joe Lapchick	.40	1.00
27 Kenneth D. Loeffler	.20	.50
28 Angelo Luisetti	.50	1.25
29 Ed Macauley	.50	1.25
30 Branch McCracken	.25	.60
31 George Mikan	2.00	5.00
32 William G. Mokray	.20	.50
33 Charles C. Murphy	.60	1.50
34 James Naismith	1.25	3.00
35 Andy Phillip	.40	1.00
36 John S. Roosma	.20	.50
37 Adolph F. Rupp	1.50	4.00
38 John D. Russell	.20	.50
39 Arthur A. Schabinger	.20	.50
40 Amos Alonzo Stagg	1.25	3.00
41 Charles H. Taylor	.20	.50
42 John A. Thompson	.20	.50
43 David Tobey	.20	.50
44 Oswald Tower	.20	.50
45 David H. Walsh	.20	.50
46 John R. Wooden	2.00	5.00
47 Bernard Carnevale	8.00	20.00
48 Bob Davies	12.00	30.00
49 Bob Cousy	25.00	60.00
50 Bob Pettit	15.00	40.00
51 Abraham M. Saperstein	20.00	50.00
52 Adolph Schayes	15.00	40.00
53 Bill Russell	40.00	100.00

1959-60 Hawks Busch Bavarian

These black and white photo-like cards were sponsored by Busch Bavarian Beer and feature members of the St. Louis Hawks. The cards are blank backed and measure approximately 4" by 5". The cards show a facsimile autograph of the player on a drop-out background. The set is dated by the fact that 1959-60 was John McCarthy's first year with the St. Louis Hawks.

COMPLETE SET (5)	400.00	800.00
1 Sihugo Green	100.00	200.00
2 Cliff Hagan	125.00	250.00
3 Clyde Lovellette	125.00	250.00
4 John McCarthy	75.00	150.00
5 Bob Pettit	250.00	450.00

1978-79 Hawks Coke/WPLO

This rather unattractive 14-card set was sponsored by V-103/WPLO radio and Coca-Cola, and they were given out at 7-Eleven stores. The cards are printed on thin cardboard stock and measure approximately 3 by 4 1/4". The fronts feature a black and white pen and ink drawing of the player's head, with the Hawks' and Coke logos in the lower corners in red. The back has a career summary and the sponsor's "V-103 Disco Stereo" at the bottom. The cards are unnumbered and are checklisted below in alphabetical order.

COMPLETE SET (14)	25.00	50.00
1 Hubie Brown CO	5.00	12.00
2 Charlie Criss	2.00	5.00
3 John Drew	2.00	5.00
4 Mike Fratello CO	3.00	8.00
5 Jack Givens	3.00	8.00
6 Steve Hawes	1.25	3.00
7 Armond Hill	1.50	4.00
8 Eddie Johnson	2.00	5.00
9 Frank Layden CO	3.00	8.00
10 Butch Lee	1.25	3.00
11 Tom McMillen	2.50	6.00
12 Tree Rollins	2.50	6.00
13 Dan Roundfield	1.50	4.00
14 Rick Wilson	1.25	3.00

1961 Hawks Essex Meats

The 1961 Essex Meats set contains 14 standard-size cards featuring the St. Louis Hawks. The fronts picture a posed black and white photo of the player with his name at the bottom of the card in bold-faced type. The backs of this white-stock card feature the player's name, brief physical data and biographical information. The cards are unnumbered and give no indication of the producer on the card. The cards were distributed by Bonnie Brands. The catalog designation for the set is F175. The Sihugo Green was reportedly short printed.

COMP.SET w/o SP (13)	200.00	400.00
1 Barney Cable	6.00	15.00
2 Al Ferrari	6.00	15.00
3 Larry Foust	6.00	15.00
4 Cliff Hagan	25.00	45.00
5 Sihugo Green SP	60.00	150.00
6 Vern Hatton	10.00	20.00
7 Cleo Hill	6.00	15.00
8 Fred LaCour	6.00	15.00
9 Fuzzy Levane CO	8.00	20.00
10 Clyde Lovellette	25.00	45.00
11 John McCarthy	6.00	15.00
12 Shellie McMillon	6.00	15.00
13 Bob Pettit	45.00	90.00
14 Bobby Sims	6.00	15.00

1979-80 Hawks Majik Market

The 1979-80 Majik Market/Coca-Cola Atlanta Hawks set contains 15 cards on thin white stock. Cards are approximately 3" by 4 1/4". The fronts of the cards include a crude, black line drawing of the player, the player's name and, in red, a Coke logo and a stylized Hawks logo. The backs contain biographical data and a summary of the player's activity during the 1978-79 season. The Majik Market logo and the call letters V-103/WPLO are printed in red on the back of the cards. Most collectors consider the set quite unattractive and poorly produced. The cards are unnumbered and are checklisted below in alphabetical order.

COMPLETE SET (15)	25.00	50.00
1 Hubie Brown CO	3.00	8.00
2 John Brown	1.25	3.00
3 Charlie Criss	2.00	5.00
4 John Drew	2.00	5.00
5 Mike Fratello ACO	2.50	6.00
6 Jack Givens	2.50	6.00
7 Steve Hawes	1.50	4.00
8 Armond Hill	1.50	4.00
9 Eddie Johnson	2.00	5.00
10 Jimmy McElroy	1.25	3.00
11 Tom McMillen	2.50	6.00
12 Sam Pellom	1.25	3.00
13 Tree Rollins	2.50	6.00
14 Dan Roundfield	2.00	5.00
15 Brendan Suhr ACO	1.50	4.00

1968-69 Hawks Team Issue

Measuring 8" by 10", this seven photo set was released featuring the 1968-69 Atlanta Hawks. Each photo features a posed shot with the player's name in the lower left-hand corner and the team name in the lower right. Each photo is in black and white with blank backs. The photos are not numbered and listed below in alphabetical order.

COMPLETE SET (7)	20.00	40.00
1 Zelmo Beaty	5.00	10.00
2 Joe Caldwell	3.00	8.00
3 Jim Davis	2.50	6.00
4 Dennis Hamilton	2.50	6.00
5 Skip Harlicka	2.50	6.00
6 George Lehmann	3.00	8.00
7 Don Ohl	3.00	8.00

1969-70 Hawks Team Issue

This 10-photo team issue set was released to the press for the Atlanta Hawks' 1969-70 season. The photos measure 8" x 10", are black and white and are blank-backed. All that appears on the photo is a player close-up or action shot set against a white background and the player's name and "Atlanta Hawks" at the bottom. The photos are checklisted below in alphabetical order.

COMPLETE SET (10)	30.00	60.00
1 Butch Beard	3.00	8.00
2 Bill Bridges	2.50	6.00
3 Joe Caldwell	2.50	6.00
4 Jim Davis	2.00	5.00
5 Gary Gregor	2.00	5.00
6 Richie Guerin CO	2.50	6.00
7 Walt Hazzard	5.00	10.00
8 Lou Hudson	6.00	12.00
9 Don Ohl	2.00	5.00
10 Grady O'Malley	2.00	5.00

1972-73 Hawks Team Issue

Measuring 8" by 10", this 9-photo set features members of the 1972-73 Atlanta Hawks. Half of the set features a two-shot front and the other half features one large posed shot. All of the photos are in black and white. The backs are blank and not numbered, thus, listed below in alphabetical order.

COMPLETE SET (9)	17.50	35.00
1 Don Adams	1.50	4.00
2 Walt Bellamy	3.00	8.00
3 Bob Christian	1.25	3.00
4 Herm Gilliam	1.25	3.00
5 Jeff Halliburton	1.25	3.00
6 Lou Hudson	3.00	8.00
7 Tom Payne	1.50	4.00
8 George Trapp	1.25	3.00
9 Jim Washington	1.25	3.00

1977-78 Hawks Team Issue

These 12 photos, which are black and white glossies and measure 8" by 10" feature members of the 1977-78 Atlanta Hawks. Since these photos are unnumbered, we have sequenced them in alphabetical order.

COMPLETE SET (12)	12.50	25.00
1 Hubie Brown HEAD CO	1.50	4.00
2 John Brown	.75	2.00
3 Charles Criss	1.00	2.50
4 John Drew	1.00	2.50
5 Steve Hawes	.75	2.00
6 Armond Hill	1.00	2.50
7 Eddie Johnson	.75	2.00
8 Ollie Johnson	.75	2.00
9 Tom McMillen	1.50	4.00
10 Tony Robertson	.75	2.00
11 Wayne Rollins	1.00	2.50
12 Mike Fratello ACO Frank Layden ACO	1.50	4.00

1978-79 Hawks Team Issue

This 4 1/2" x 6" set was produced for the Atlanta Hawks during the 1978-79 season. The set features 11 full-colored cards of the team's players.

COMPLETE SET (11)	20.00	50.00
1 John Drew	2.50	6.00
2 Eddie Johnson	2.50	6.00
3 Dan Roundfield	3.00	8.00
4 Tree Rollins	3.00	8.00
5 Butch Lee	3.00	8.00
6 Jack Givens	3.00	8.00
7 Tom McMillen	3.00	8.00
8 Armond Hill	2.00	5.00
9 Steve Hawes	2.00	5.00
10 Charlie Criss	2.00	5.00
11 Rick Wilson	2.00	5.00

1910 Helmar Premiums

These premiums were drawn by reknowned artist Hamilton King who originally illustrated advertistments for Coca Cola around 1900. These images are known as the "Women in Athletic Costumes" series. Smokers could redeem coupons for these lithographs either on card stock, on satin or on bookbinding leather. There was also a gift slip which checklisted all the premiums available from the tobacco company, which also listed the number of coupons required for each specific type of premum.

COMPLETE SET	2,500.00	5,000.00
1 Card Stock	200.00	400.00
2 Individual Satin	400.00	800.00
3 Leather	1,000.00	2,000.00
4 Satin Pillow Top	1,500.00	3,000.00
Eight Women shown including Basketball Girl		

1980-81 Hustle Chicago/La-Z-Boy Team Issue

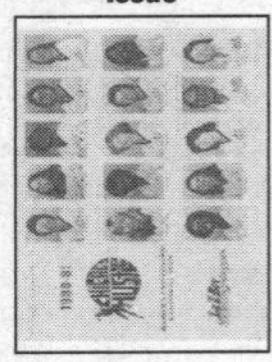

This team-issued photo measures approximately 8 3/4" by 11" and feature black and white player portraits on one sheet. The player's name is listed below the photo. The sheet contains portraits of the Chicago Hustle from the Women's Professional Basketball Team Association. The backs contains a La-Z-Boy advertisement.The photo is unnumbered.

1 B.Caldwell	12.50	25.00
B.Candler		
S.Digitale		
R.Easterling		
J.Fincher		
D.Geils		
B.Gleason CO		
P.Hodgson		
P.Kilday		
L.Matthews		
P.Mayo		
C.McWhorter		
I.Nissen		
C.Steele TR		
E.White		

1972-73 Icee Bear

The 1972-73 Icee Bear set contains 20 player cards each measuring approximately 3" by 5". The cards are printed on thin stock. The fronts feature color facial pictures, and the backs show brief biographical information. The set may have been printed in 1973-74 or perhaps later as they were available in the Seattle area as late as summer 1974. The cards were reportedly distributed one card with each Icee Bear Slurpee purchased. There are four cards that are more difficult to find than the other 16; these four are listed as SP's in the checklist below.

COMPLETE SET (20)	75.00	200.00
1 Kareem Abdul-Jabbar	15.00	40.00
2 Dennis Awtrey	1.25	3.00
3 Tom Boerwinkle	2.00	5.00
4 Austin Carr SP	3.00	8.00
5 Wilt Chamberlain	20.00	50.00
6 Archie Clark SP	15.00	40.00
7 Dave DeBusschere	3.00	8.00
8 Walt Frazier SP	6.00	15.00
9 John Havlicek	12.00	30.00
10 Connie Hawkins	5.00	10.00
11 Bob Love	2.00	5.00
12 Jerry Lucas	4.00	10.00
13 Pete Maravich SP	25.00	60.00
14 Calvin Murphy	2.00	5.00
15 Oscar Robertson	12.00	30.00
16 Jerry Sloan	3.00	8.00
17 Wes Unseld	2.50	6.00
18 Dick Van Arsdale	1.25	3.00
19 Jerry West	15.00	40.00
20 Sidney Wicks	3.00	8.00

1950-70 J.D. McCarthy Postcards

This 15-postcard set was released by J.D. McCarthy in the 1950-70's. Each card was produced in black and white and measured 3.25x5.5. Please note that these postcards have blank backs, and are listed below in alphabetical order. This list may be far from complete and because of the wide disparity of years, please note no pricing is provided. Any further information on cards or pricing would be appreciated.

COMPLETE SET (15)
1 Rick Barry
2 Rick Barry
3 Dave Bing
4 Dave DeBusschere
5 Archie Dees
6 Terry Dischinger
7 Walter Dukes
8 Bailey Howell
9 Bob Lanier
10 Lloyd Love
11 Dick McGuire
12 Eddie Miles
13 Jackie Moreland
14 Gene Shue
15 John Tresvant

1975-76 Jazz Team Issue

This 8"x10" set was produced for the New Orleans Jazz during the 1975-76 season. The set features nine black and white cards of the team's players.

COMPLETE SET (9)	12.50	25.00
1 Ron Behagen	1.25	3.00
2 Fred Boyd	1.25	3.00
3 E.C. Coleman	1.25	3.00
4 Aaron James	1.25	3.00
5 Rich Kelley	1.25	3.00
6 Jim McElroy	1.25	3.00
7 Louie Nelson	1.25	3.00
8 Bud Stallworth	1.25	3.00
9 Nate Williams	1.25	3.00

1973-74 Jets Allentown CBA

This crude eight-card set was produced by G.S. Gallery of Allentown, Pennsylvania, whose name and address are listed at the bottom of each card. The cards feature members of the Allentown Jets of the CBA and measure approximately 2 5/8" by 4 1/4". Uncut sheets are available as well. The card fronts are printed in black ink on light-blue construction-paper stock; the card backs are blank. These sets were originally available from the producer for less than 50 cents each in quantity.

COMPLETE SET (8)	15.00	40.00
1 Tony Johnson	2.00	5.00
2 Allie McGuire	3.00	8.00
3 Frank Card	2.00	5.00
4 George Lehmann	2.50	6.00
5 Dennis Bell	2.00	5.00
6 Ken Wilburn	2.00	5.00
7 George Bruns	2.00	5.00
8 Ed Mast	2.50	6.00

1963 Jewish Sports Champions

The 16 cards in this set, measuring roughly 2 2/3" x 3", are cut out of an "Activity Funbook" entitled Jewish Sports Champions. The set pays tribute to famous Jewish athletes from baseball, football, bull fighting to chess. The cards have a green border with a yellow background and a player close-up illustration. Cards that are still attached carry a premium over those that have been cut-out. The cards are unnumbered and listed below in alphabetical order with an assigned sport prefix (BB-baseball, BK- basketball, BX- boxing, FB- football, OT- other).

COMPLETE SET (16)	100.00	200.00
BK1 Nat Holman BK	12.50	25.00
BK2 Dolph Schayes BK	10.00	20.00

1973 Jewish Sports Champions

The 16 cards in this set, measuring roughly 2 2/3" x 3", are cut out of a sequel to the 1968 Activity Funbook. This time, the cards come from a funbook entitled "More Jewish Sports Champions". There are two variations to each card that are valued equally. One has a pink border with a yellow background and blue ink on the player close-up illustration. The other has a blue background and black ink on the player illustration. Cards that are still attached carry a premium over those that have been cut-out. The cards are unnumbered and listed below in alphabetical order.

COMPLETE SET (16)	65.00	125.00
1 Arnold (Red) Auerbach BK	15.00	30.00

1957-58 Kahn's

The 1957-58 Kahn's Basketball set contains 11 black and white cards. Cards are approximately 3 3/16" by 3 15/16". The backs contain "How To" articles and instructional text. Only Cincinnati Royals players are depicted.

COMPLETE SET (11)	2,000.00	3,000.00
1 Richard Duckett	75.00	150.00
2 George King	75.00	150.00
3 Clyde Lovellette	300.00	550.00
4 Tom Marshall	75.00	150.00
5 Jim Paxson UER	150.00	275.00
6 Dave Piontek	75.00	150.00
7 Richard Regan	75.00	150.00
8 Dick Ricketts	175.00	275.00
9 Maurice Stokes	300.00	600.00
10 Jack Twyman	300.00	500.00
11 Bobby Wanzer	150.00	275.00

1958-59 Kahn's

The 1958-59 Kahn's Basketball set contains 10 black and white cards. Cards measure approximately 3 1/4" by 3 15/16". The backs feature a short narrative entitled "My Greatest Thrill in Basketball" allegedly written by the player depicted on the front. Only Cincinnati Royals players are depicted. The Sihugo Green card is supposedly a little tougher to find than the other cards in the set.

COMPLETE SET (10)	1,000.00	1,500.00
1 Arlen Bockhorn	60.00	125.00
2 Archie Dees	60.00	125.00
3 Sihugo Green	100.00	175.00
4 Vern Hatton	80.00	160.00
5 Tom Marshall	60.00	125.00
6 Jack Parr	80.00	160.00
7 Jim Palmer	60.00	125.00
Card lists him as George, his middle name		
8 Jim Palmer	60.00	125.00
9 Dave Piontek	60.00	125.00
10 Jack Twyman	200.00	325.00

1959-60 Kahn's

The 1959-60 Kahn's Basketball set features 10 black and white cards. Cards are approximately 3 1/4" by 4". The backs feature descriptive narratives allegedly written by the player depicted on the front. No statistics are featured on the backs. Only Cincinnati Royals players are depicted.

COMPLETE SET (10)	500.00	900.00
1 Arlen Bockhorn	50.00	100.00
2 Wayne Embry	75.00	150.00
3 Tom Marshall	50.00	100.00
4 Med Park	60.00	120.00
5 Dave Piontek	50.00	100.00
6 Hub Reed	50.00	100.00
7 Phil Rollins	50.00	100.00
8 Larry Staverman	50.00	100.00
9 Jack Twyman	100.00	225.00
10 Win Wilfong	50.00	100.00

1960-61 Kahn's

The 1960-61 Kahn's Basketball set features 12 black and white cards. Cards are approximately 3 1/4" by 3 15/16". The backs contain statistical season-by-season records up through the 1959-60 season, player vital statistics, and a short biography of the player's career. The key cards in the set are the first professional cards of Hall of Famers Oscar Robertson and Jerry West. The Lakers' Jerry West is the only non-Cincinnati Royals player depicted and his card does not have any statistical breakdown.

COMPLETE SET (12)	2,000.00	3,200.00
1 Arlen Bockhorn	30.00	60.00
2 Bob Boozer	45.00	90.00
3 Ralph E. Davis	25.00	60.00
4 Wayne Embry	50.00	100.00
5 Mike Farmer	25.00	60.00
6 Phil Jordan	30.00	60.00
7 Hub Reed	25.00	60.00
8 Oscar Robertson	700.00	1,300.00
9 Larry Staverman	25.00	60.00
10 Jack Twyman	75.00	150.00
11 Jerry West	900.00	1,500.00
12 Win Wilfong	25.00	60.00

1961-62 Kahn's

The 1961-62 Kahn's Basketball set consists of 13 black and white cards. Cards measure approximately 3 3/16" by 4 1/16". The Lakers' Jerry West is the only non-Cincinnati Royals player depicted and there is also a card of coach Charley Wolf. The backs of the cards are blank; this was the only year the Kahn's basketball cards were blank backed.

COMPLETE SET (13)	1,100.00	1,600.00
1 Arlen Bockhorn	20.00	50.00
2 Bob Boozer	35.00	75.00
3 Joe Buckhalter	25.00	50.00
4 Wayne Embry	30.00	60.00
5 Bob Nordmann	25.00	50.00
6 Hub Reed	25.00	50.00
7 Oscar Robertson	300.00	600.00
8 Adrian Smith	35.00	75.00
9 Jack Twyman	65.00	125.00
10 Bob Wesenhahn	25.00	50.00
11 Jerry West	400.00	800.00
12 Charley Wolf CO	20.00	50.00
13 Dave Zeller	25.00	50.00

1962-63 Kahn's

The 1962-63 Kahn's Basketball set contains 11 black and white cards. Cards measure approximately 3 1/4" by 4 3/16". Jerry West of the Lakers is the only non-Cincinnati Royals player depicted and there is also a card of Royals' coach Charley Wolf. The backs feature a short biography of the player depicted on the front of the card. The Jerry West card has a picture with no border around it. Cards of Bockhorn, Boozer, Reed, and Twyman are oriented horizontally.

COMPLETE SET (11)	500.00	1,000.00
1 Arlen Bockhorn HOR	15.00	40.00
2 Bob Boozer HOR	25.00	50.00
3 Wayne Embry	30.00	55.00
4 Tom Hawkins	30.00	65.00
5 Bud Olsen	15.00	40.00
6 Hub Reed HOR	15.00	40.00
7 Oscar Robertson	150.00	300.00
8 Adrian Smith	25.00	50.00
9 Jack Twyman HOR	40.00	80.00
10 Jerry West	200.00	400.00
11 Charley Wolf CO	15.00	40.00

1963-64 Kahn's

The 1963-64 Kahn's Basketball set contains 13 black and white cards. Cards measure approximately 3 1/4" by 4 3/16". This is the only Kahn's basketball set on which there is a distinctive white border on the fronts of the cards; in this respect the set is similar to the 1963 Kahn's baseball and football sets. A brief biography of the player is contained on the back of the card. Jerry West of the Lakers is the only non-Cincinnati Royals player depicted and there is also a card of coach Jack McMahon. The Jerry West card is identical to that of the previous year except set in smaller type and with the distinctive white border on the front. The cards of Bob Boozer and Jack Twyman are oriented horizontally.

COMPLETE SET (13)	400.00	800.00
1 Jay Arnette	15.00	30.00
2 Arlen Bockhorn	15.00	30.00
3 Bob Boozer HOR	20.00	45.00
4 Wayne Embry	20.00	45.00
5 Tom Hawkins	35.00	55.00
6 Jerry Lucas	60.00	120.00
7 Jack McMahon CO	15.00	30.00
8 Bud Olsen	15.00	30.00
9 Oscar Robertson	100.00	200.00
10 Adrian Smith	15.00	40.00
11 Tom Thacker	15.00	30.00
12 Jack Twyman HOR	30.00	65.00
13 Jerry West	125.00	250.00

1964-65 Kahn's

The 1964-65 Kahn's Basketball set contains 12 full-color subjects on 14 distinct cards. Cards measure approximately 3" by 3 5/8". These cards come in two types distinguishable by the color of the printing on the backs. Type I cards (1-3) have light maroon printing on the backs, while type II (4-12) have black printing on the backs. The fronts are completely devoid of any written material. There are two poses each of Jerry Lucas and Oscar Robertson.

COMPLETE SET (14)	325.00	650.00
1 Happy Hairston	35.00	70.00
2 Jack McMahon CO	15.00	40.00

3 George Wilson	15.00	30.00
4 Jay Arnette	15.00	30.00
5 Arlen Bockhorn	15.00	30.00
6 Wayne Embry	20.00	45.00
7 Tom Hawkins	20.00	50.00
8A Jerry Lucas	40.00	80.00
8B Jerry Lucas	40.00	80.00
9 Bud Olsen	15.00	30.00
10A Oscar Robertson	75.00	150.00
10B Oscar Robertson	75.00	150.00
11 Adrian Smith	15.00	40.00
12 Jack Twyman	30.00	60.00

1965-66 Kahn's

The 1965-66 Kahn's Basketball set contains four full-color cards featuring players of the Cincinnati Royals. Cards in this set measure approximately 3" by 3 9/16". This was the last of the Kahn's Basketball issues and the second in full color. The fronts are devoid of all written material, and the backs are printed in red ink. The "Compliments of Kahn's, The Wiener the World Awaited" slogan appears on the backs of the cards. The set is presumed complete with the following cards.

COMPLETE SET (4)	150.00	300.00
1 Wayne Embry	20.00	40.00
2 Jerry Lucas	40.00	80.00
3 Oscar Robertson	75.00	150.00
4 Jack Twyman	30.00	60.00

1971 Keds KedKards

This set is composed of crude artistic renditions of popular subjects from various sports from 1971 who were apparently celebrity endorsers of Keds shoes. The cards actually form a complete panel on the Keds tennis shoes box. The three different panels are actually different sizes; the Bing panel contains smaller cards. The smaller Bubba Smith shows him without beard and standing straight; the large Bubba shows him leaning over, with beard, and jersey number partially visible. The individual player card portions of the card panels measure approximately 2 15/16" by 2 3/4" and 2 5/16" by 2 3/16" respectively, although it should noted that there are slight size differences among the individual cards even on the same panel. The panel background is colored in black and yellow. On the Bench/Reed card (number 3 below) each player measures approximately 5 1/4" by 3 1/2". A facsimile autograph appears in the upper left corner of each player's drawing. The Bench/Reed was issued with the Keds Champion boys basketball shoe box, printed on the box top with a black broken line around the card to follow when cutting the card out.

COMPLETE SET (3)	112.50	225.00
1BK Dave Bing	30.00	60.00
2BK Willis Reed	30.00	60.00
3BK Willis Reed	30.00	60.00

1948 Kellogg's Pep

These small cards measure approximately 1 7/16" by 1 5/8". The card front presents a black and white head-and-shoulders shot of the player, with a white border. The back has the player's name and a brief description of his accomplishments. The cards are unnumbered, but have been assigned numbers below using a sport (BB- baseball, FB- football, BK- basketball, OT- other) prefix. Other Movie Star Kellogg's Pep cards exist, but they are not listed below. The catalog designation for this set is F273-19. An album was also produced to house the set.

COMPLETE SET (20)	700.00	1,400.00
BK1 George Mikan	200.00	400.00

1973-74 Kings Linnett

Measuring 8 1/2" by 11", these nine charcoal drawings are facial portraits by noted sports artist Charles Linnett. The player's facsimile autograph is inscribed across the lower right corner. The backs are blank. Three portraits were included in each package, with a suggested retail price of 99 cents. The portraits are unnumbered and checklisted below in alphabetical order. The set is dated by the fact that 1973-74 was John Block's and Ken Durrett's last year with the Kings but Ron Behagen's and Jimmy Walker's first year with the team.

COMPLETE SET (9)	20.00	40.00
1 Nate Archibald	7.50	15.00
2 Ron Behagen	1.00	2.50
3 John Block	2.00	5.00
4 Mike D'Antoni	2.00	5.00
5 Ken Durrett	1.00	2.50
6 Sam Lacey	3.00	8.00
7 Larry McNeill	1.00	2.50
8 Jimmy Walker	3.00	8.00
9 Nate Williams	1.00	2.50

1975-76 Kings Team Issue

This oversized set was produced for the Kansas City Kings during the 1975-76 season. The set features 10 cards of the team's players and coaches

COMPLETE SET (10)	12.50	25.00
1 Bob Bigelow	1.25	3.00
2 Glenn Hansen	1.25	3.00
3 Ollie Johnson	1.25	3.00
4 Larry McNeill	1.25	3.00
5 Bill Robinzine	1.25	3.00
6 Jimmy Walker	1.50	4.00
7 Lee Winfield	1.25	3.00
8 Richard Washington	1.25	3.00
9 Dan Sparks ACO	1.25	3.00
10 Phil Johnson CO	1.25	3.00

1970-71 Knicks Photos

This six card oversized set was released during the 1970-71 season, and features such Knick stars as Bill Bradley and Walt Frazier. Please note that these black and white cards measure 8"x10", and have blank backs.

COMPLETE SET (6)	75.00	150.00
1 Dick Barnett	5.00	10.00
2 Bill Bradley	12.00	30.00
3 Dave DeBusschere	15.00	30.00
4 Walt Frazier	20.00	40.00
5 Willis Reed	15.00	30.00
6 Danny Whelan TR	5.00	10.00

1962-63 Knicks Photos

This six card oversized glossy set was released during the 1962-63 season, and features such Knick stars as Willie Naulls. Please note that these black and white cards measure 8"x10", and have the player names stamped on back. Obviously, this checklist is incomplete and all additional information is welcome.

COMPLETE SET (6)	75.00	150.00
1 Dave Budd	10.00	20.00
2 Donnis Butcher	10.00	20.00
3 Knicks Team Photo	20.00	40.00
4 Whitey Martin	10.00	20.00
5 Willie Naulls	25.00	50.00
6 Unknown		

1972-73 Knicks Photos

This two card oversized set was released during the 1972-73 season, and features such Knicks stars as Bill Bradley and Phil Jackson. Please note that these black and white cards measure 8"x10", and have blank backs.

COMPLETE SET (2)	12.50	25.00
1 Dick Barnett	7.50	15.00
Henry Bibby		
Bill Bradley		
Dave DeBusschere		
Walt Frazier		
John Gianelli		
Phil Jackson		
2 Jerry Lucas	5.00	10.00
Dean Meminger		
Earl Monroe		
Willis Reed		
Tom Riker		
Red Holzman CO		

1970-71 Knicks Portraits

Each of these black and white illustrated portraits measure approximately 9" by 12". The player's name and facsimile autograph are also contained on the front. The backs are blank. The photos are unnumbered and listed below alphabetically.

COMPLETE SET (8)	75.00	150.00
1 Dick Barnett	5.00	10.00
2 Dave DeBusschere	12.50	25.00
3 Walt Frazier	20.00	40.00
4 Red Holzman CO	10.00	20.00
5 Willis Reed	15.00	30.00
6 Mike Riordan	5.00	10.00
7 Cazzie Russell	10.00	20.00
8 Dave Stallworth	5.00	10.00

1960-61 Lakers Bell Brand

This card measures approximately 6" by 3 1/2" and features Frank Selvy of the Los Angeles Lakers basketball team. The card was inserted one per bag of Bell Brand Potato Chips reportedly midway through the 1960-61 season. The left half of the card features the player whereas the the right side features a 1961 Los Angeles Lakers schedule. The reverse carries a Bell Brand ad along with a coupon offer of a free game ticket with purchase of potato chips. The card is printed in blue ink on heavy white paper stock. The catalog designation is F391-1.

NNO Frank Selvy	400.00	700.00

1961-62 Lakers Bell Brand

The unattractive cards within this ten-card set measure approximately 6" by 3 1/2" and feature members of the Los Angeles Lakers basketball team. The cards were inserted one per bag of Bell Brand Potato Chips. Each player has two versions of his card, once in blue ink on white stock and again in brown ink on cream-tinted stock. The blue-tint versions show a schedule starting with October 27, whereas the brown-tint versions have a schedule starting with December 2. Some veteran collectors feel that the blue-tint versions are touygher to find. The left half of the card features the player whereas the right side features a Bell Brand ad. The reverse has the Los Angeles Lakers schedule behind the player photo and the free ticket offer behind the ad. The catalog designation is F391-2. The key cards in the set are Elgin Baylor and Jerry West.

COMPLETE SET (10)	5,000.00	8,000.00
1 Elgin Baylor	1,500.00	2,500.00
2 Ray Felix	200.00	400.00
3 Tom Hawkins	300.00	600.00
4 Rod Hundley	400.00	800.00
5 Howard Joliff	175.00	350.00
6 Rudy LaRusso	250.00	500.00
7 Fred Schaus CO	200.00	600.00
8 Frank Selvy	250.00	450.00
9 Jerry West	2,400.00	3,000.00
10 Wayne Yates	150.00	300.00

1974-75 Lakers Datsun

These 16 blank backed 8 1/4" x 10 1/4" black and white photos were issued during the 1975-75 season to Southern California Datsun dealers. The photos were given out to customers as a promotional offer as well as a Laker game as a complete set with an accompying envelope.

COMPLETE SET (16)	25.00	50.00
1 B.Sharman/J.Barnhill	2.00	5.00
2 P.Newell/L.Creger	1.25	3.00
3 C.Hearn/L.Shackelford	3.00	8.00
4 Lucius Allen	1.25	3.00
5 Zelmo Beaty	1.25	3.00
6 Corky Calhoun	1.25	3.00
7 Gail Goodrich	2.00	5.00
8 Happy Hairston	1.25	3.00
9 Connie Hawkins	2.00	5.00
10 Stu Lantz	1.25	3.00
11 Stan Love	1.25	3.00
12 Pat Riley	3.00	8.00
13 Cazzie Russell	1.50	4.00
14 Elmore Smith	1.25	3.00
15 Kermit Washington	1.25	3.00
16 Brian Winters	1.25	3.00

1972-73 Lakers Lunch Bags

Measuring 6" by 11", these five paper lunch bags were manufacturered by Mason Hamlin Ind. in 1972. The bags feature blue pencil drawings with the player's name and "Los Angeles" at the bottom of the bag. There are no backs. The bags are not numbered and listed below in alphabetical order.

COMPLETE SET (5)	25.00	50.00
1 Wilt Chamberlain	10.00	20.00
2 Happy Hairston	3.00	8.00
3 Gail Goodrich	5.00	10.00
4 Jim McMillian	2.50	6.00
5 Jerry West	6.00	12.00

1950-51 Lakers Scott's

This 13-card set was sponsored by Scott's Potato Chips as indicated by its logo appearing on the card face. The cards were printed on heavy stock. A complete set was redeemable for tickets to Minneapolis Lakers games and Minneapolis Lakers player photos. The cards measure approximately 2" by 4 1/2" and were distributed in potato chip and cheese potato boxes. The fronts have a cartoon-like drawing of the player in an action pose, with a facsimile autograph below the drawing. The cards are unnumbered and checklisted below in alphabetical order. The Bud Grant in the set also was active as a player in the CFL and later went on to fame as coach of the Minnesota Vikings.

COMPLETE SET (13)	14,000.00	21,000.00
1 Bobby Doll	300.00	600.00
2 Arnie Ferrin	400.00	800.00
3 Bud Grant	2,000.00	2,500.00
4 Bob Harrison	400.00	800.00
5 Joey Hutton	300.00	600.00
6 Tony Jaros	300.00	600.00
7 John Kundla CO	400.00	800.00
8 Slater Martin	900.00	1,400.00
9 George Mikan	6,000.00	12,000.00
10 Vern Mikkelsen	1,000.00	1,600.00
11 Kevin O'Shea	300.00	600.00
12 Jim Pollard	1,000.00	1,600.00
13 Herm Schaeffer	300.00	600.00

1969-70 Lakers Tickets

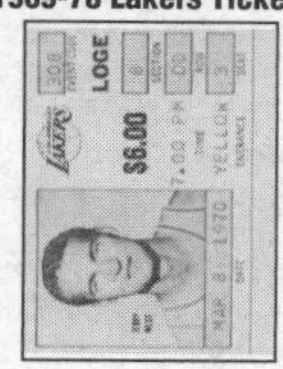

Issued as part of the regular admission tickets to Los Angeles Laker home games, there feature players from the Western Conference Champion Los Angeles Lakers. The tickets are not numbered and listed in alphabetical order below.

COMPLETE SET	40.00	80.00
1 Elgin Baylor	12.50	25.00
2 Wilt Chamberlain	15.00	30.00
3 Keith Erickson	5.00	10.00
4 Jerry West	15.00	30.00

1979-80 Lakers/Kings Alta-Dena

This eight-card set was sponsored by Alta-Dena Dairy, and its logo adorns the bottom of both sides of the card. The cards measure approximately 2 3/4" by 4" and feature color action player photos on the fronts. While the sides of the picture have no borders, green and red-orange stripes border the picture on its top and bottom. The player's name appears in black lettering in the top red-orange stripe. The team logo appears in the bottom red-orange stripe. The back has an offer for youngsters 14-and-under, who could present the complete eight-card set in the souvenir folder to the Forum Box Office and receive a half-price discount on certain tickets to any one of the Lakers and Kings games listed on the reverse of the card. The cards are unnumbered and are checklisted below in alphabetical order. This small set features Los Angeles Kings and Los Angeles Lakers as they were both owned by Jerry Buss. Cards 1-4 are Los Angeles Lakers (NBA) and Cards 5-8 are Los Angeles Kings (NHL). The set must have been planned and produced in the late summer of 1979 since Adrian Dantley was traded to Utah for Spencer Haywood on September 13

COMPLETE SET (8)	10.00	20.00
1 Adrian Dantley	1.25	3.00
2 Don Ford	.40	1.00
3 Kareem Abdul-Jabbar	5.00	12.00
4 Norm Nixon	.75	2.00

1973-74 Linnett Portraits

Measuring 8 1/2" by 11", these 112 charcoal drawings are facial portraits by noted sports artist Charles Linnett. The player's facsimile autograph is inscribed across the lower right corner. The backs are blank. Three portraits of players from the same team were included in each clear plastic packet. A checklist was also included in each packet, with an offer to order individual player portraits for 50 cents each. Originally, the suggested retail price was 99 cents. In later issues, the price was raised to $1.19. The portraits are unnumbered and listed alphabetically according to teams as follows: Atlanta Hawks (1-10), Boston Celtics (11-22), Buffalo Braves (23-33), Capitol Bullets (34-36), Chicago Bulls (37-43), Cleveland Cavaliers (44-45), Detroit Pistons (46), Golden State Warriors (47-56), Houston Rockets (57-59), Kansas City-Omaha Kings (60-67), Los Angeles Lakers (68-76), Milwaukee Bucks (77-85), New York Knicks (86-96), Philadelphia 76ers (97), Phoenix Suns (98-105), Portland Trail Blazers (106-107), and Seattle Supersonics (108). This listing concludes with four Harlem Globetrotter portraits (109-112).

COMPLETE SET (112)	350.00	700.00
1 Walt Bellamy	2.50	6.00
2 Steve Bracey	2.00	5.00
3 John Brown	2.00	5.00
4 Bob Christian	2.00	5.00
5 Herm Gilliam	2.00	5.00
6 Lou Hudson	2.50	6.00
7 Dwight Jones	2.00	5.00
8 Pete Maravich	12.50	25.00
9 Dale Schlueter	2.00	5.00
10 Jim Washington	2.00	5.00
11 Don Chaney	2.50	6.00
12 Dave Cowens	5.00	10.00
13 Steve Downing	2.00	5.00
14 Hank Finkel	2.00	5.00
15 Phil Hankinson	2.00	5.00
16 John Havlicek	7.50	15.00
17 Steve Kuberski	2.00	5.00
18 Don Nelson	3.00	8.00
19 Paul Silas	2.50	6.00
20 Paul Westphal	5.00	10.00
21 Jo Jo White	2.50	6.00
22 Art Williams	2.00	5.00
23 Ken Charles	2.00	5.00
24 Ernie DiGregorio (Wearing a turtle neck)	3.00	8.00
25 Ernie DiGregorio (Wearing a t-shirt)	3.00	8.00
26 Garfield Heard	2.50	6.00
27 Bob Kauffman	2.00	5.00
28 Mike Macaluso	2.00	5.00
29 Bob McAdoo	6.00	12.00
30 Jim McMillian	2.50	6.00
31 Paul Ruffner	2.00	5.00
32 Randy Smith	2.50	6.00
33 Dave Wohl	2.00	5.00
34 Archie Clark	2.50	6.00
35 Elvin Hayes	6.00	12.00
36 Howard Porter	2.50	6.00
37 Dennis Awtrey	2.00	5.00
38 Tom Boerwinkle	2.50	6.00
39 Bob Love	2.50	6.00
40 Jerry Sloan	3.00	8.00
41 Norm Van Lier	2.50	6.00
42 Chet Walker	2.50	6.00
43 Bob Weiss	2.50	6.00
44 Austin Carr	2.50	6.00
45 Lenny Wilkens	3.00	8.00
46 Bob Lanier	5.00	10.00
47 Jim Barnett	2.00	5.00
48 Rick Barry	5.00	10.00
49 Butch Beard	2.50	6.00
50 Derrek Dickey	2.50	6.00
51 Charlie Johnson	2.00	5.00
52 Clyde Lee	2.00	5.00
53 Jeff Mullins	2.50	6.00
54 Clifford Ray	2.00	5.00
55 Cazzie Russell	2.50	6.00
56 Nate Thurmond	3.00	8.00
57 Kevin Kunnert	2.00	5.00
58 Calvin Murphy	3.00	8.00
59 Jimmy Walker	2.50	6.00
60 Nate Archibald	3.00	8.00
61 Ron Behagen	2.00	5.00
62 John Block	2.00	5.00
63 Mike D'Antoni	2.00	5.00
64 Ken Durrett	2.00	5.00
65 Sam Lacey	2.00	5.00
66 Larry McNeill	2.00	5.00
67 Nate Williams	2.00	5.00
68 Bill Bridges	2.00	5.00
69 Mel Counts	2.00	5.00
70 Keith Erickson	2.00	5.00
71 Gail Goodrich	3.00	8.00
72 Happy Hairston	2.50	6.00

73 Jim Price 2.00 5.00
74 Pat Riley 6.00 12.00
75 Elmore Smith 2.00 5.00
76 Jerry West 6.00 12.00
77 Kareem Abdul-Jabbar 10.00 20.00
78 Lucius Allen 2.00 5.00
79 Bob Dandridge 2.50 6.00
80 Mickey Davis 2.00 5.00
81 Terry Driscoll 2.00 5.00
82 Russell Lee 2.00 5.00
83 Jon McGlocklin 2.00 5.00
84 Curtis Perry 2.00 5.00
85 Oscar Robertson 5.00 10.00
86 Henry Bibby 2.50 6.00
87 Bill Bradley 6.00 12.00
88 Dave DeBusschere 3.00 8.00
89 Walt Frazier 5.00 10.00
90 John Gianelli 2.00 5.00
91 Phil Jackson 5.00 10.00
92 Jerry Lucas 3.00 8.00
93 Dean Meminger 2.00 5.00
94 Earl Monroe 3.00 8.00
95 Willis Reed 3.00 8.00
96 Harthorne Wingo 2.00 5.00
97 Tom Van Arsdale 2.50 6.00
98 Mike Bantom 2.00 5.00
99 Corky Calhoun 2.00 5.00
100 Lamar Green 2.00 5.00
101 Clem Haskins 2.00 5.00
102 Connie Hawkins 5.00 10.00
103 Charlie Scott 2.50 6.00
104 Dick Van Arsdale 2.50 6.00
105 Neal Walk 2.00 5.00
106 Geoff Petrie 2.50 6.00
107 Sidney Wicks 3.00 8.00
108 Spencer Haywood 3.00 8.00
109 Geese Ausbie 2.50 6.00
110 Marques Haynes 3.00 8.00
111 Meadowlark Lemon 3.00 8.00
112 Curly Neal 3.00 8.00

1971 Mattel Mini-Records

This set was designed to be played on a special Mattel mini-record player, which is not included in the complete set price. Each black plastic disc, approximately 2 1/2" in diameter, features a recording on one side and a color drawing of the player on the other. The picture appears on a paper disk that is glued onto the smooth unrecorded side of the mini-record. On the recorded side, the player's name and the set's subtitle appear in arcs stamped in the central portion of the mini-record. The hand-engraved player's name appears again along with a production number, copyright symbol, and the Mattel name and year of production in the ring between the central portion of the record and the grooves. The ivory discs are the ones which are double sided and are considered to be tougher than the black discs. They were also known as "Mattel Show 'N Tell". The discs are unnumbered and checklisted below in alphabetical order according to sport

COMPLETE SET (18) 200.00 400.00
BK1 Lew Alcindor 8.00 20.00
BK2 Elgin Baylor 4.00 10.00
BK3 Wilt Chamberlain 6.00 15.00
BK4 Jerry Lucas 2.50 6.00
BK5 Pete Maravich 8.00 20.00
BK6 John Havlicek 4.00 10.00
BK7 Willis Reed 2.50 6.00
BK8 Oscar Robertson 4.00 10.00
BK9 Bill Russell SP 50.00 100.00
BK10 Jerry West 5.00 12.00

1976-77 MSA Drinking Cups

This set of MSA (Michael Schacter Associates) Drinking Cups was released in 1976. According to our information, there are relatively few cups that have the MSA credit ONLY. The oval bands that surround the player photo are blue and maize and they are reportedly far rarer than the already rare MSA Circle K variety. This set features some of the top players in the game. Please note that these cups are not numbered and are listed below in alphabetical order.

1 Kareem Abdul-Jabbar 25.00 50.00
2 Alvan Adams 10.00 20.00
3 Nate Archibald 15.00 30.00
4 Dennis Awtrey 10.00 20.00
5 Rick Barry 15.00 30.00
6 Otis Birdsong 10.00 20.00
7 Mike Bratz 10.00 20.00
8 Allan Bristow 10.00 20.00
9 Fred Brown 10.00 20.00
10 Louis Dampier 10.00 20.00
11 Adrian Dantley 15.00 30.00
12 Walter Davis 10.00 20.00
13 John Drew 10.00 20.00
14 Julius Erving 25.00 50.00
15 Walt Frazier 15.00 30.00
16 George Gervin 20.00 40.00
17 Artis Gilmore 15.00 30.00
18 Bob Gross 10.00 20.00
19 John Havlicek 20.00 40.00
20 Elvin Hayes 20.00 40.00
21 Spencer Haywood 15.00 30.00
22 Garfield Heard 10.00 20.00
23 Lionel Hollins 10.00 20.00
24 Dan Issel 15.00 30.00
25 Marques Johnson 10.00 20.00
26 Bernard King 10.00 20.00
27 Billy Knight 10.00 20.00
28 Bob Lanier 15.00 30.00
29 Ron Lee 10.00 20.00
30 Maurice Lucas 10.00 20.00
31 Pete Maravich 30.00 60.00
32 Bob McAdoo 15.00 30.00
33 Earl Monroe 15.00 30.00
34 Calvin Murphy 15.00 30.00
35 Mark Olberding 10.00 20.00
36 Curtis Perry 10.00 20.00
37 Charlie Scott 10.00 20.00
38 Phil Smith 10.00 20.00
39 Ricky Sobers 10.00 20.00
40 David Thompson 15.00 30.00
41 Rudy Tomjanovich 15.00 30.00
42 Dave Twardzik 10.00 20.00
43 Norm Van Lier 10.00 20.00
44 Bill Walton 15.00 30.00
45 Marvin Webster 10.00 20.00
46 Paul Westphal 10.00 20.00

1911 Murad College Series T51

These colorful cigarette cards featured several colleges and a variety of sports and recreations of the day and were issued in packs of Murad Cigarettes. The cards measure approximately 2" by 3". Two variations of each of the first 50 cards were produced; one variation says "College Series" on back, the other, "2nd Series". The drawings on cards of the 2nd Series are slightly different from those of the College Series. There are 6 different series of 25 in the College Series and they are listed here in the order that they appear on the checklist on the cardbacks. There is also a larger version (5" x 8") that was available for the first 25 cards as a premium (catalog designation T6) that could be obtained in exchange for 15 Murad cigarette coupons; the offers expired June 30, 1911.

*2ND SERIES: .4X TO 1X COLLEGE SERIES
24 Williams College Basketball 40.00 80.00
35 Northwestern Basketball 40.00 80.00
120 Luther Basketball 40.00 80.00
150 Xavier Basketball 40.00 80.00

1911 Murad College Series Premiums T6

24 Williams College Basketball 300.00 500.00

1974 Nabisco Sugar Daddy

This set of 25 tiny (approximately 1 1/16" by 2 3/4") cards features athletes from a variety of popular pro sports. One card was included in specially marked Sugar Daddy and Sugar Mama candy bars. The cards were designed to be placed on a 18" by 24" poster, which could only be obtained through a mail-in offer direct from Nabisco. The set is referred to as "Pro Faces" as the cards show an enlarged head photo with a small caricature body. Cards 1-10 are football players, cards 11-16 and 22 are hockey players, and cards 17-21 and 23-25 are basketball players. Each card was produced in two printings. The first printing has a copyright date of 1973 printed on the backs (although the cards are thought to have been released in early 1974) and the second printing is missing a copyright date altogether.

COMPLETE SET (25) 75.00 150.00
17 Oscar Robertson 10.00 20.00
18 Spencer Haywood 2.50 5.00
19 Jo Jo White 2.50 5.00
20 Connie Hawkins 5.00 10.00
21 Nate Thurmond 2.50 6.00
23 Chet Walker 2.50 6.00
24 Calvin Murphy 2.50 5.00
25 Kareem Abdul-Jabbar 12.50 25.00

1975 Nabisco Sugar Daddy

This set of 25 tiny (approximately 1 1/16" by 2 3/4") cards features athletes from a variety of popular pro sports. One card was included in specially marked Sugar Daddy and Sugar Mama candy bars. The cards were designed to be placed on a 18" by 24" poster, which could only be obtained through a mail-in offer direct from Nabisco. The set is referred to as "Sugar Daddy All-Stars". As with the set of the previous year, the cards show an enlarged head photo with a small caricature body with a flag background of stars and stripes. This set is referred on the back as Series No. 2 and has a red, white, and blue background behind the picture on the front of the card. Cards 1-10 are pro football players and the remainder are pro basketball (17-21, 23-25) and hockey (11-16, 22) players.

COMPLETE SET (25) 75.00 150.00
17 Jerry Sloan 2.50 6.00
18 Spencer Haywood 2.50 6.00
19 Bob Lanier 3.00 8.00
20 Connie Hawkins 4.00 10.00
21 Geoff Petrie 1.50 4.00
23 Chet Walker 2.00 5.00
24 Bob McAdoo 3.00 8.00
25 Kareem Abdul-Jabbar 10.00 25.00

1976 Nabisco Sugar Daddy 1

This set of 25 tiny (approximately 1 1/16" by 2 3/4") cards features action scenes from a variety of popular sports from around the world. One card was included in specially marked Sugar Daddy and Sugar Mama candy bars. The set is referred to as "Sugar Daddy Sports World - Series 1" on the backs of the cards. The cards are in color with a relatively wide white border around the front of the cards.

COMPLETE SET (25) 40.00 80.00
11 Basketball 5.00 10.00

1976 Nabisco Sugar Daddy 2

This set of 25 tiny (approximately 1 1/16" by 2 3/4") cards features action scenes from a variety of popular sports from around the world. One card was included in specially marked Sugar Daddy and Sugar Mama candy bars. The set is referred to as "Sugar Daddy Sports World - Series 2" on the backs of the cards. The cards are in color with a relatively wide white border around the front of the cards.

COMPLETE SET (25) 40.00 80.00
13 Basketball 5.00 10.00

1973-74 NBA Players Association

This set contains 40 full-color postcard format cards measuring approximately 3 3/8" by 5 5/8". The front features a borderless posed "action" shot of the player. The back has the player's name at the top, and the NBA Players Association logo. The cards are unnumbered and are checklisted below in alphabetical order. There are ten tougher cards which are marked as SP in the checklist below. The two toughest of these are Mike Newlin and Paul Silas. Walt Bellamy was listed on the checklist, but was never issued, having been replaced by Lou Hudson.

COMPLETE SET (40) 300.00 600.00
1 Lucius Allen 1.50 4.00
2 Dave Bing SP 8.00 20.00
3 Bill Bradley 4.00 10.00
4 Fred Carter SP 7.50 15.00
5 Austin Carr 1.50 4.00
6 Dave Cowens 5.00 10.00
7 Dave DeBusschere 5.00 10.00
8 Ernie DiGregorio 2.50 6.00
9 Gail Goodrich 5.00 10.00
10 Hal Greer 3.00 8.00
11 John Havlicek 7.50 15.00
12 Connie Hawkins 5.00 10.00
13 Spencer Haywood 2.00 5.00
14 Lou Hudson 2.00 5.00
15 Bob Kauffman 1.25 3.00
16 Bob Lanier 4.00 10.00
17 Bob Love 3.00 8.00
18 Jack Marin 2.00 5.00
19 Jim McMillian 2.00 5.00
20 Earl Monroe SP 12.50 25.00
21 Calvin Murphy 3.00 8.00
22 Mike Newlin SP 50.00 100.00
23 Geoff Petrie 2.50 6.00
24 Willis Reed SP 12.50 25.00
25 Rich Rinaldi 1.50 4.00
26 Mike Riordan SP 7.50 15.00
27 Oscar Robertson SP 20.00 40.00
28 Cazzie Russell 2.00 5.00
29 Paul Silas SP 50.00 100.00
30 Jerry Sloan 3.00 8.00
31 Elmore Smith 1.50 4.00
32 Dick Snyder 1.50 4.00
33 Nate Thurmond 3.00 8.00
34 Rudy Tomjanovich 4.00 10.00
35 Wes Unseld 5.00 10.00
36 Dick Van Arsdale SP 10.00 20.00
37 Tom Van Arsdale 1.50 4.00
38 Chet Walker SP 10.00 25.00
39 Jo Jo White 2.50 6.00
40 Len Wilkens 5.00 10.00

1973-74 NBA Players Association 8x10

These ten (approximately) 8" by 10" cards feature full-bleed color posed "action" player photos on the matte-finished fronts. The backs carry the NBA Players Association logo. The cards are unnumbered and checklisted below according to the order sheet. On an order sheet concerning the reprinting of the 1973-74 NBA Players Assn. set, these large photos are mentioned as individual mat finish 8" by 10" pictures.

COMPLETE SET (10) 100.00 200.00
A Dave DeBusschere 10.00 20.00
B John Havlicek 20.00 40.00
C Willis Reed 10.00 20.00
D Ernie DiGregorio 5.00 10.00
E Dave Cowens 10.00 20.00
F Oscar Robertson 20.00 40.00
G Bill Bradley 12.50 25.00
H Jo Jo White 5.00 10.00
I Nate Thurmond 7.50 15.00
J Gail Goodrich 10.00 20.00

1971-72 NBA Stickers

This sticker sheet was released during the 1971-72 season, and features team logo stickers of 17 teams. This sheet measures 5.5x9.25 and was done in full color. Please note that this sticker sheet has a blank back.

1 Team Logos 2.00 5.00

1969 NBAP Members

These rather unattractive cards, which definitely vary somewhat in size, measure approximately 2 3/4" by 4 1/2". The blank-backed cards feature borderless black-and-white photos and have light blue bottoms. These cards must not have been licensed by the NBA because the red, white and blue NBA logos have been airbrushed out. The cards may have been made from boxes of basketball shoes, possibly Converse. There may also be other cards in the set. Small and large versions of the logo card exist, both of which are almost square and are red, white, and blue. The cards are unnumbered and are listed below,in alphabetical order. With some recent discoveries, it is believed that this set was issued into the 1970's as there was a recently discovered Kareem Abdul-Jabbar card. However, with the inclusion of Bill Russell, it becomes obvious that this set was issued over a number of years as Russell retired after the 1968-69 season.

COMPLETE SET (20) 3,500.00 5,000.00
1 Kareem Abdul-Jabbar 300.00 600.00
2 Elgin Baylor 200.00 400.00
3 Zelmo Beaty 75.00 150.00
4 Bob Boozer 75.00 150.00
5 Bill Bradley 100.00 200.00
6 Wilt Chamberlain 400.00 800.00
7 John Havlicek 200.00 500.00
8 Don Kojis 75.00 150.00
9 Jerry Lucas 100.00 200.00
10 Eddie Miles 75.00 150.00
11 Jeff Mullins 75.00 150.00
12 Willis Reed 100.00 200.00
13 Oscar Robertson 250.00 500.00
14 Bill Russell 400.00 800.00
15 Wes Unseld 100.00 200.00
16 Dick Van Arsdale 75.00 150.00
17 Chet Walker 75.00 150.00
18 Jerry West 400.00 800.00
19 Len Wilkens 100.00 200.00
20 NBAP Logo 75.00 150.00

1971-72 Nets New York Team Issue

Each of these team-issued photos measure approximately 8" by 10" and feature black and white player portraits on two sheets. The player's name is listed below the photo. Each sheet contains either six or eight player portraits. The backs are blank. The photos are unnumbered and listed below alphabetically.

COMPLETE SET (2) 12.50 25.00
1 Jim Ard 7.50 15.00
Rick Barry
Jeff Congdon
Joe Depre
Sonny Dove
Jarrett Durham
Manny Leaks
Bill Melchionni
2 Roy Boe PRES 5.00 10.00
Lou Carnesecca CO
Billy Paultz
John Roche
Ollie Taylor
Tom Washington

1974 New York News This Day in Sports

These cards are newspaper clippings of drawings by Hollreiser and are accompanied by textual description highlighting a player's unique sports feat. Cards are approximately 2" X 4 1/4". These are multisport cards and aranged in chronological order.

COMPLETE SET 50.00 120.00
36 Wilt Chamberlain 2.00 4.00
Dec. 6, 1963

1977-78 Nuggets Iron-On

This six item iron-on set was sponsored by Pepsi-Cola, and was released during the 1977-78 season, and features some of the Denver Nugget players and coaches. The iron-ons measure 6 1/4"x11".

COMPLETE SET (6) 20.00 40.00
1 Dan Issel 5.00 10.00
2 Brian Taylor 2.00 5.00
3 Bobby Wilkerson 2.00 5.00
4 Bobby Jones 5.00 10.00
5 Larry Brown CO 3.00 8.00
6 David Thompson 5.00 10.00

1975-76 Nuggets Pepsi Cans

The 1975-76 Nuggets Pepsi Cans feature 15 players, coaches and front office personnel of the Denver Nuggets. The top of the panel that features the player contains the salutation "Congratulations Denver Nuggets", which contains below it a sketch of the player, as well as a facsimile signature and a short biography. These standard-sized aluminum cans then have below the player sketch "75-76 ABA Regular Season Champions". The cans contain no numbering other than jersey numbers, thus the set is listed alphabetically below. Cans opened from the bottom command up to a 25% premium over the prices below.

COMPLETE SET (15) 80.00 160.00
1 Byron Beck 5.00 10.00
2 Larry Brown CO 7.50 15.00
3 Jimmy Foster 3.00 8.00
4 Gus Gerard 3.00 8.00
5 George Irvine 3.00 8.00
6 Dan Issel 12.50 25.00
7 Bobby Jones 10.00 20.00
8 Doug Moe ACO 7.50 15.00
9 Carl Scheer GM 3.00 8.00
10 Ralph Simpson 5.00 10.00
11 Claude Terry 3.00 8.00
12 David Thompson 12.50 25.00
13 Monte Towe 5.00 10.00
14 Marvin Webster 3.00 8.00
15 Chuck Williams 3.00 8.00

1976-77 Nuggets Pepsi Cans

The 1976-77 Nuggets Pepsi Can Issue contains 17 standard-sized aluminum cans which portray players, coaches, and the team trainer. The cans state "Congratulations Denver Nuggets" and have a sketched drawing of the player with a facsimile signature and short biography next to the drawing. Below the drawing the can states "76-77 Midwest Division Champions" and has the NBA logo beside it. The cans contain no number except for players' uniform numbers--they are checklisted alphabetically below. Cans opened from the bottom command up to a 25% premium over the prices below.

COMPLETE SET (17) 60.00 120.00
1 Byron Beck 3.00 8.00
2 Larry Brown CO 5.00 10.00
3 Mack Calvin 3.00 8.00
4 Frank Hamblen ACO 2.00 5.00
5 George Irvine ACO 2.00 5.00
6 Dan Issel 10.00 20.00
7 Bobby Jones 7.50 15.00
8 Ted McClain 2.00 5.00
9 Jim Price 2.00 5.00
10 Carl Scheer GM 2.00 5.00
11 Paul Silas 3.00 8.00

12 Roland Taylor	2.00	5.00
13 David Thompson	10.00	20.00
14 Monte Towe	3.00	8.00
15 Bob Travaglini TR	2.00	5.00
16 Marvin Webster	2.00	5.00
17 Willie Wise	3.00	8.00

1979 Open Pantry

This set is an unnumbered, 12-card issue featuring players from Milwaukee area professional sports teams with five Brewers baseball (1-5), five Bucks basketball (6-10), and two Packers football (11-12). Cards are black and white with red trim and measure approximately 5" by 6". Cards were sponsored by Open Pantry, Lake to Lake, and MACC (Milwaukee Athletes against Childhood Cancer). The cards are unnumbered and hence are listed and numbered below alphabetically within sport.

COMPLETE SET (12)	12.50	25.00
6 Kent Benson	2.00	4.00
7 Junior Bridgeman	2.00	4.00
8 Quinn Buckner	2.50	5.00
9 Marques Johnson	3.00	6.00
10 Jon McGlocklin	2.00	4.00

1971-72 Pacers Volpe Tumblers

This set of Pacers Drinking Cups consists of colorful portraits by distinguished artist Nicholas Volpe. The set features six clear plastic cups that has a paper portrait inserted between the layers of clear plastic. Please note that these cups are not numbered, and are listed below in alphabetical order.

COMPLETE SET (6)	50.00	100.00
1 Mel Daniels	10.00	25.00
2 Bill Keller	6.00	15.00
3 Art Becker	6.00	15.00
4 Bob Netolicky	8.00	20.00
5 Roger Brown	10.00	25.00
6 Rick Mount	8.00	20.00

1971-72 Pacers Volpe Marathon Oil

This set of Marathon Oil Pro Star Portraits consists of colorful portraits by distinguished artist Nicholas Volpe. The cards were part of a gas station promotion. Each portrait measures approximately 7 1/2" by 9 7/8" and features a painting of the player's face on a black background, with an action painting superimposed to the side. A facsimile autograph in white appears at the bottom of the portrait. At the bottom of each portrait is a postcard measuring 7 1/2" by 4" after perforation. While the back of the portrait has offers for a basketball photo album, autographed tumblers, and a poster, the postcard itself may be used to apply for a Marathon credit card. The portraits are unnumbered and checklisted below according to alphabetical order.

COMPLETE SET (12)	40.00	80.00
1 Warren Armstrong	2.50	6.00
2 John Barnhill	2.00	5.00
3 Art Becker	3.00	8.00
4 Roger Brown	3.00	8.00
5A Mel Daniels Releasing ball from both hands	5.00	12.00
5B Mel Daniels Releasing ball from right hand	5.00	12.00
6 Earle Higgins	2.00	5.00
7 Bill Keller	4.00	10.00
8 Bob Leonard CO	4.00	10.00
9 Freddie Lewis	3.00	8.00
10 Rick Mount	6.00	15.00
11 Bob Netolicky	3.00	8.00

1971-72 Pacers Team Issue

Each of these team-issued photos measure approximately 8" by 10" and feature black and white player portraits on sheets. Each sheet contains either seven or eight player portraits. The player's name is listed below the photo. The backs are blank. The photos are unnumbered and listed below alphabetically. George McGinnis is featured in his rookie year.

COMPLETE SET (2)	12.50	25.00
1 Roger Brown Wayne Chapman Mel Daniels Earle Higgins Darnell Hillman Bill Keller Freddie Lewis George McGinnis	8.00	20.00
2 Bob Hooper ACO Bob Leonard CO Rick Mount Bob Netolicky Don Sidle John Weissert GM Marv Winkler	5.00	12.00

1968-70 Partridge Meats

These black and white (with some red trim and text) photo-like cards feature players from all three Cincinnati major league sports teams of that time: Cincinnati Reds baseball (BB1-BB20), Cincinnati Bengals football (FB1-FB5), and Cincinnati Royals basketball (BK1-BK2). The cards measure approximately 4" by 5" or 3-3/4" by 5-1/2" and were issued over a period of years. The cards are blank backed and a "Mr. Whopper" card was also issued in honor of the 7'-3" company spokesperson. The Tom Rhoads football card was only recently discovered, in 2012, adding to the prevailing thought that these cards were issued over a period of years since its format matches some of the baseball cards and not the other four more well-known football cards in the set. Joe Morgan was also recently added to the checklist indicating that more cards could turn up in the future. This card follows the same format as Gullett, May, Perez, and Tolan (all measuring 3-3/4" by 5-1/2") missing the team's logo on the cap, missing the team's nickname in the text, and missing the company's slogan below the image. Some collectors believe this style to be consistent with a 1972 release.

COMPLETE SET (14)	400.00	800.00
BK1 Adrian Smith SP	30.00	60.00
BK2 Tom Van Arsdale SP	30.00	60.00

1977-78 Pepsi All-Stars

This set of eight photos was sponsored by Pepsi. The borderless color player photos measure approximately 8" by 10" and are printed on thick cardboard stock. All the photos depict players either shooting or dunking the ball. The Pepsi logo and the player's name appear in the upper right corner. In blue print the back presents various statistics. The photos are unnumbered and are checklisted below in alphabetical order.

COMPLETE SET (8)	350.00	550.00
1 Rick Barry	15.00	40.00
2 Dave Cowens	15.00	40.00
3 Julius Erving	40.00	75.00
4 Kareem Abdul-Jabbar	40.00	75.00
5 Pete Maravich	150.00	300.00
6 Bob McAdoo	20.00	50.00
7 David Thompson	15.00	40.00
8 Bill Walton	40.00	75.00

1974-75 Picture Buttons

These 11 buttons were issued in 1974, and feature many of the superstar calliber players of the time. Please note that each button was done in full color.

COMPLETE SET (11)	300.00	600.00
1 Kareem Abdul-Jabbar	50.00	100.00
2 Bill Bradley	40.00	80.00
3 Dave DeBusschere	25.00	50.00
4 Walt Frazier	40.00	80.00
5 John Havlicek	50.00	100.00
6 Bob Lanier	25.00	50.00
7 Jerry Lucas	12.50	25.00
8 Pete Maravich	75.00	125.00
9 Willis Reed	40.00	80.00
10 Jerry West	50.00	100.00
11 JoJo White	12.50	25.00

1968-69 Pipers Minnesota Team Issue

Each of these team-issued photos measure approximately 4 1/4" by 5 1/2" and feature black and white player portraits. The player's name is listed below the photo. The backs are blank. The photos are unnumbered and listed below alphabetically.

COMPLETE SET (10)	35.00	75.00
1 Frank Card	2.00	5.00
2 Connie Hawkins	15.00	40.00
3 Art Heyman	3.00	8.00
4 Arvesta Kelly	2.50	6.00
5 Mike Lewis	2.50	6.00
6 George Sutor	2.00	5.00
7 Steve Vacendak	2.00	5.00
8 Chico Vaughn	2.00	5.00
9 Tom Washington	3.00	8.00
10 Charlie Williams	3.00	8.00

1977-78 Pistons Team Issue

These blank-backed black and white photos, which measure 8" by 10" feature members of the 1977-78 Detroit Pistons. Since these photos are unnumbered, we have sequenced them in alphabetical order.

COMPLETE SET (11)	20.00	35.00
1 Roger Brown	1.25	3.00
2 M.L. Carr	3.00	8.00
3 Leon Douglas	1.25	3.00
4 Al Eberhard	1.25	3.00
5 Chris Ford	2.50	6.00
6 Larry Jones	1.25	3.00
7 Al Menendez	1.25	3.00
8 Eric Money	1.25	3.00
9 Willie Norwood	1.25	3.00
10 Howard Porter	1.50	4.00
11 Ralph Simpson	1.50	4.00

1978-79 Pistons Team Issue

These 8" by 10" blank-backed black and white photos feature members of the 1978-79 Detroit Pistons. Since these photos are unnumbered, we have sequenced them in alphabetical order.

COMPLETE SET (13)	20.00	35.00
1 M.L. Carr	1.00	2.50
2 Leon Douglas	.75	2.00
3 Chris Ford	1.50	4.00
4 Gus Gerard	.75	2.00
5 Bubbles Hawkins	.75	2.00
6 Bob Lanier	3.00	8.00
7 John Long	.75	2.00
8 Ben Poquette	.75	2.00
9 Kevin Porter	1.00	2.50
10 Terry Tyler	.75	2.00
11 Dick Vitale CO	5.00	10.00
12 Al Menendez ACO Mike Abdenor TR	.75	2.00
13 Mike Brunker ACO Richie Adubato ACO	.75	2.00

1977-78 Post Auerbach Tips

These 12 cereal-box cards measure approximately 7 3/16" by 1 3/16" and were available (they formed the back panel of the cereal box) on 15-ounce (cards 1-6) and 20-ounce (cards 7-12) boxes of Post Raisin Bran and Post Grape Nuts. The blank-backed cards feature "NBA" Tips from legendary Boston Celtics coach Red Auerbach. A drawing of him accompanies his description of each line-illustrated play. The cards are numbered on the front.

COMPLETE SET (12)	60.00	120.00
COMMON TIP (1-12)	6.00	12.00

1960 Post Cereal

These large cards measure approximately 7" by 8 3/4". The 1960 Post Cereal Sports Stars set contains nine cards depicting current baseball, football and basketball players. Each card comprised the entire back of a Grape Nuts Flakes Box and is blank backed. The color player photos are set on a colored background surrounded by a wooden frame design, and they are unnumbered (assigned numbers below for reference according to sport). The catalog designation is F278-26.

COMPLETE SET (9)	3,000.00	5,000.00
BK1 Bob Cousy	200.00	400.00
BK2 Bob Pettit	150.00	300.00

1980-81 Pride New Orleans WBL

This 11-card set features the 1980-81 New Orleans Pride of the Women's Basketball League. It's believed that 13 cards actually exist, but we only have 11 cards that have been verified at this point in time. According to the backs, these cards were available at Dome Souvenir Stands or at the Pride office. Inside white borders, the fronts display blue-tinted posed action shots. The player's uniform number and autograph are printed on the picture. In blue print on a white background, the backs carry biography, player profile, and a "Trade 'em and win!" contest.

COMPLETE SET (11)	50.00	100.00
1 Kathy Andrykowski	4.00	10.00
2 Sybil Blalock	4.00	10.00
3 Cindy Brogden	7.50	15.00
4 Vicky Chapman	4.00	10.00
5 Beverly Crusoe	4.00	10.00
6 Sharon Farrah	4.00	10.00
7 Eileen Feeney	4.00	10.00
8 Augusta Forest	4.00	10.00
9 Bertha Hardy	4.00	10.00
10 Sue Peters	4.00	10.00
11 Heidi Wayment	4.00	10.00

1979-80 Quaker Iron-Ons

This 10-card set was sponsored by the Quaker Company and was offically licensed by the NBA. Each iron-on measures 4 3/8" by 6 1/8". Card fronts contain a head shot of the player with directions for the iron-on. The backs are blank.

COMPLETE SET (9)	125.00	250.00
1 Kareem Abdul-Jabbar	20.00	40.00
2 Rick Barry	10.00	25.00
3 Julius Erving	25.00	50.00
4 George Gervin	15.00	40.00
5 Elvin Hayes	10.00	20.00
6 Maurice Lucas	5.00	12.00
7 Pete Maravich	45.00	90.00
8 David Thompson	10.00	20.00
9 Paul Westphal	6.00	12.00

1954 Quaker Sports Oddities

This 27-card set features strange moments in sports and was issued as an insert inside Quaker Puffed Rice cereal boxes. Fronts of the cards are drawings depicting the person or the event. In a stripe at the top of the card face appear the words "Sports Oddities." Two colorful drawings fill the remaining space: the left half is a portrait, while the right half is action-oriented. A variety of sports are included. The cards measure approximately 2 1/4" by 3 1/2" and have rounded corners. The last line on the back of each card declares, "It's Odd but True." A person could also buy the complete set for fifteen cents and two box tops from Quaker Puffed Wheat or Quaker Rice. If a collector did send in their material to Quaker Oats the set came back in a specially marked box with the cards in cellophane wrapping. Sets in original wrapping are valued at 1.25x to 1.5X the high column listings in our checklist.

COMPLETE SET (27)	125.00	250.00
5 Harold(Bunny) Levitt	15.00	30.00
12 Dartmouth College BK	7.50	15.00
23 Harlem Globetrotters	20.00	40.00
24 Everett Dean BK	12.50	25.00

1961-64 Rawlings

These photos were released during the 1960's by Rawlings to promote their products. Please note that these photos were done in black and white, and have blank backs.

COMPLETE SET (7)	125.00	250.00
1 Richie Guerin	10.00	25.00
2 Cliff Hagan	17.50	35.00
3 John Havlicek	40.00	70.00
4 Gus Johnson	10.00	25.00
5 Bob Pettit	40.00	70.00
6 Frank Ramsey	10.00	25.00
7 Len Wilkens	25.00	60.00

1971-72 Rockets Carnation Milk

Issued on the side of Carnation Milk cartons, the side panels were used to picture members of the 1971-72 Houston Rockets. Since these were unnumbered, the cards are sequenced in alphabetical order.

COMPLETE SET	300.00	600.00
1 Dick Cunningham	30.00	60.00
2 Dick Gibbs	30.00	60.00
3 Elvin Hayes	75.00	150.00
4 Stu Lantz	50.00	100.00
5 Cliff Meely	30.00	60.00
6 Calvin Murphy	50.00	100.00
7 Mike Newlin	40.00	75.00
8 Rudy Tomjanovich	60.00	120.00

1969-70 Rockets Coca-Cola

Measuring 8 1/2" by 11", this 9-card set features members from the 1969-70 San Diego Rockets. The fronts feature color close-up shots, with the player's name, weight, age and college. The team logo is located in the lower left corner, with a Coca-Cola logo in the lower right. The backs feature text; the Coca-Cola logo and "Rockets Cage Club", and are not numbered. The photos are listed below in alphabetical order.

COMPLETE SET (9)	75.00	150.00
1 Rick Adelman	8.00	20.00
2 Jim Barnett	5.00	10.00
3 John Block	5.00	10.00
4 Elvin Hayes	12.50	25.00
5 Toby Kimball	5.00	10.00
6 Stu Lantz	8.00	20.00
7 Pat Riley	15.00	40.00
8 John Trapp	5.00	10.00
9 Art Williams	5.00	10.00

1971-72 Rockets Denver Team Issue

Each of these team-issued photos measure approximately 8" by 10" and feature black and white player portraits. The player's name is listed below the photo. Each sheet contains eight photos. The backs are blank. The photos are unnumbered and listed below alphabetically.

COMPLETE SET (2)	15.00	30.00
1 Byron Beck Art Becker Julian Hammond Marv Roberts Ralph Simpson Dwight Waller Chuck Williams Steve Wilson	7.50	15.00
2 Stan Albeck ACO Larry Brown Alex Hannum CO Julius Keye	10.00	20.00

Del Klone GM		
Dave Robisch		
Al Smith		
Lloyd Williams TR		

1968-69 Rockets Jack in the Box

This 14-card set of San Diego Rockets was sponsored by Jack-in-the-Box and available at their restaurants in the greater San Diego area. There is evidence that this set was substantially reissued the following year with cards of Bobby Smith and Bernie Williams replacing the cards of Harry Barnes and Henry Finkel. Bobby Smith's only season with the San Diego Rockets was 1969-70 and Harry Barnes' only season with the San Diego Rockets was 1968-69. The cards only measure approximately 2" by 3" and have the appearance of wallet-size photos. The fronts have posed color head and shoulders shots, with the player's name, team name, team logo, and sponsor's logo below the picture. The backs are blank. The cards are unnumbered and are checklisted below in alphabetical order. The two cards in the set that are more difficult to find are marked by SP in the checklist below. The set features the first professional cards of Rick Adelman, Elvin Hayes, and Pat Riley among others.

COMPLETE SET (14)	50.00	90.00
1 Rick Adelman	2.50	6.00
2 Harry Barnes SP	20.00	50.00
3 Jim Barnett	.75	2.00
4 John Block	.60	1.50
5 Henry Finkel SP	20.00	50.00
6 Elvin Hayes	3.00	8.00
7 Toby Kimball	.60	1.50
8 Don Kojis	.60	1.50
9 Stu Lantz	1.25	3.00
10 Pat Riley	4.00	10.00
11 Bobby Smith	1.50	4.00
12 John Trapp	.60	1.50
13 Art Williams	.60	1.50
14 Bernie Williams	1.00	2.50

1978-79 Rockets Photos

This six card oversized glossy set was released during the 1978-79 season, and features such Rockets stars as Rudy Tomjanovich and Moses Malone. Please note that these black and white cards measure 8"x10", and have blank backs.

COMPLETE SET	15.00	30.00
1 Rick Barry	3.00	8.00
2 Alonzo Bradley	1.00	2.50
3 Jacky Dorsey	1.00	2.50
4 Mike Dunleavy	1.50	4.00
5 Moses Malone	2.50	6.00
6 Calvin Murphy	2.00	5.00
7 Mike Newlin	1.25	3.00
8 Jackie Robinson	1.00	2.50
9 Rudy Tomjanovich	2.00	5.00
10 Slick Watts	1.25	3.00

1975-76 Rockets Team Issue

This 8"x10" set was produced for the Houston Rockets during the 1975-76 season. The set features eight cards of the team's players and coaches Please note that the card of Tom Nissalke was done as a 5"x7" card.

COMPLETE SET (8)	12.50	25.00
1 John Johnson	1.50	4.00
2 Kevin Kunnert	1.25	3.00
3 Mike Newlin	1.50	4.00
4 Ed Ratleff	1.25	3.00
5 Ron Riley	1.25	3.00
6 Rudy White	1.25	3.00
7 Dave Wohl	1.25	3.00
8 Tom Nissalke CO	1.25	3.00

1977-78 Rockets Team Issue

These eight photos featured members of the 1976-77 Houston Rockets. Since they are unnumbered we have sequenced them in alphabetical order.

COMPLETE SET	10.00	20.00
1 John Johnson	1.50	4.00
2 Kevin Kunnert	1.25	3.00
3 Mike Newlin	1.50	4.00
4 Tom Nissalke CO	1.25	3.00
5 Ed Ratleff	1.25	3.00
6 Ron Riley	1.25	3.00
7 Rudy White	1.25	3.00
8 Dave Wohl	1.50	4.00

1971-72 Rockets Team Photo

This black and white press photo, measuring 7 3/4" x 10", was issued for the Houston Rockets' first NBA season. The photo is made up of twelve pictures divided up into three rows. Each individual shot is a close-up of each player. The Houston Rockets' debut logo appears at the bottom middle.

1 Team Photo	6.00	12.00
Curtis Perry		
Elvin Hayes		
Dick Cunningham		
John Egan		
Dick Gibbs		
Rudy Tomjanovich		
Mike Newlin		
Jim Davis		
Cliff Meely		
Calvin Murphy		
Stu Lantz		
John Vallely		

1978-79 Royal Crown Cola

This set was sponsored by RC Cola, and its logo appears at the top of the card face. The cards were supposedly primarily issued in the southern New England area. The cards were intended to be placed in six-packs of Royal Crown Cola, one per six-pack. The cards measure 3" by 6". The front features a black-and-white head shot framed by a basketball hoop net on red and blue panels. The backs carry a mail-in offer to purchase a Spalding basketball for $6.99. The cards are unnumbered and are checklisted below in alphabetical order. The cards were apparently only licensed by the NBA Players Association since there are no team logos or team markings anywhere on the cards. The set features early professional cards of Walter Davis and Bernard King. Variations of Nate Archibald, Julius Erving, and Walt Frazier cards are reported. They measure 2 1/4" by 9 1/2", have the mail-in offer beneath the picture, and are blank-backed. They are also distinguished by a NBA Players logo, a 1978 MSA (Michael Schlecter Associates) copyright. and a 1978 RC Cola Co. copyright at the bottom.

COMPLETE SET	1,500.00	3,000.00
1 Kareem Abdul-Jabbar	150.00	300.00
2 Nate Archibald	50.00	100.00
3 Rick Barry	50.00	100.00
4 Jim Chones	25.00	50.00
5 Doug Collins	40.00	80.00
6 Dave Cowens	50.00	100.00
7 Adrian Dantley	45.00	90.00
8 Walter Davis	45.00	85.00
9 John Drew	20.00	45.00
10 Julius Erving	175.00	350.00
11 Walt Frazier	50.00	100.00
12 George Gervin	60.00	120.00
13 Artis Gilmore	45.00	90.00
14 Elvin Hayes	45.00	90.00
15 Dan Issel	45.00	90.00
16 Marques Johnson	35.00	70.00
17 Mickey Johnson	20.00	45.00
18 Bernard King	50.00	100.00
19 Bob Lanier	50.00	100.00
20 Maurice Lucas	35.00	65.00
21 Pete Maravich	300.00	475.00
22 Bob McAdoo	45.00	90.00
23 George McGinnis	30.00	60.00
24 Eric Money	25.00	45.00
25 Earl Monroe	45.00	90.00
26 Calvin Murphy	35.00	75.00
27 Robert Parish	60.00	120.00
28 Billy Paultz	25.00	45.00
29 Jack Sikma	35.00	65.00
30 Ricky Sobers	25.00	45.00
31 David Thompson	60.00	120.00
32 Rudy Tomjanovich	45.00	90.00
33 Wes Unseld	45.00	90.00
34 Norm Van Lier	30.00	60.00
35 Bill Walton	75.00	150.00
36 Marvin Webster	25.00	45.00
37 Scott Wedman	25.00	45.00
38 Paul Westphal	40.00	75.00
39 Jo Jo White	35.00	70.00
40 John Williamson	25.00	45.00
41 Brian Winters	40.00	80.00

1979-80 Royal Crown Cola Cans

The 1979 Royal Crown Cola Cans contain 35 standard-sized cans. The cans were made from steel, and thus are susceptible to rust if they have been in a moisture filled environment. The players head is in an oval picture shaped like a basketball and contains a short biographies below the picture. Each can is numbered "X" of 35. Cans opened from the bottom command up to a 25% premium over the prices listed below.

COMPLETE SET (35)	225.00	450.00
1 Dave Cowens	7.50	15.00
2 Nate Archibald	5.00	10.00
3 Artis Gilmore	7.50	15.00
4 David Thompson	7.50	15.00
5 Bob Lanier	5.00	10.00
6 Rick Barry	10.00	20.00
7 Rudy Tomjanovich	5.00	10.00
8 Kareem Abdul-Jabbar	20.00	40.00
9 Brian Winters	2.00	5.00
10 Bernard King	3.00	8.00
11 Pete Maravich	25.00	50.00
12 Bob McAdoo	5.00	10.00
13 Doug Collins	5.00	10.00
14 George McGinnis	5.00	10.00
15 Walter Davis	2.00	5.00
16 Paul Westphal	5.00	10.00
17 Robert Parish	7.50	15.00
18 Bill Walton	12.50	25.00
19 George Gervin	12.50	25.00
20 Elvin Hayes	7.50	15.00
21 Norm Van Lier	2.00	5.00
22 Dan Issel	7.50	15.00
23 Julius Erving	20.00	40.00
24 Jim Chones	2.00	5.00
25 Jo Jo White	3.00	8.00
26 Calvin Murphy	6.00	12.00
27 Earl Monroe	7.50	15.00
28 Billy Paultz	2.00	5.00
29 John Drew	2.00	5.00
30 John Williamson	2.00	5.00
31 Jack Sikma	3.00	8.00
32 Scott Wedman	2.00	5.00
33 Ricky Sobers	2.00	5.00
34 Maurice Lucas	3.00	8.00
35 Marvin Webster	2.00	5.00

1952 Royal Desserts

The 1952 Royal Desserts Stars of Basketball set contains eight horizontally oriented cards. The cards formed the backs of Royal Desserts packages of the period; consequently many cards are found with uneven edges stemming from the method of cutting the cards off the box. Each card has its number and the statement "Royal Stars of Basketball" in a red rectangle at the top. The cards measure approximately 2 5/8" by 3 1/4". The cards fronts have a stripe at the top and are divided into halves. The left half has a light-blue tinted head shot of the player and a facsimile autograph, while the right half has career summary. The blue tinted picture contains a facsimile autograph of the player. An album was presumably available as it is advertised on the card. The catalog designation for this scarce set is F219-2. The key card in the set is George Mikan.

COMPLETE SET (8)	7,000.00	9,500.00
1 Fred Schaus	350.00	700.00
2 Dick McGuire	400.00	850.00
3 Jack Nichols	250.00	500.00
4 Frank Brian	250.00	500.00
5 Joe Fulks	700.00	1,200.00
6 George Mikan	3,000.00	4,000.00
7 Jim Pollard	700.00	1,200.00
8 Buddy Jeanette	400.00	800.00

1970-71 Royals Cincinnati Team Issue

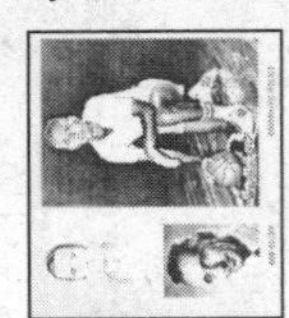

Measuring 8 1/2" by 11", this 12-photo set features members of the 1970-71 Cincinnati Royals. The fronts feature three photos - one drawing, one head shot and one in-action shot, with the player's name in the lower left and the team name in the lower right. The player's facsimile autograph is located on the in-action shot. The photos are black and white. The backs are black and listed below in alphabetical order.

COMPLETE SET (12)	50.00	100.00
1 Nate Archibald	8.00	20.00
2 Bob Arnzen	2.00	5.00
3 Moe Barr	2.00	5.00
4 Bob Cousy	12.50	25.00
5 Johnny Green	3.00	8.00
6 Greg Hyder	2.00	5.00
7 Darrall Imhoff	3.00	8.00
8 Sam Lacey	3.00	8.00
9 Charlie Paulk	2.00	5.00
10 Flynn Robinson	3.00	8.00
11 Tom Van Arsdale	3.00	8.00
12 Norm Van Lier	5.00	10.00

1972 7-11 Cups

Distributed through 7-11 in 1972, these cups feature color portraits of NBA players. They also feature a facsimile autograph and the player's name and team underneath the photo. The "back" side of the cup features statistics and a brief summary on the player. It also contains the 7-11 and NBA Players Association logos. The cups are not numbered and listed below in alphabetical order.

COMPLETE SET	300.00	600.00
1 Kareem Abdul-Jabbar	20.00	40.00
2 Mahdi Abdul-Rahman	5.00	10.00
3 Nate Archibald	8.00	20.00
4 Rick Barry	8.00	20.00
5 Dave Bing	6.00	15.00
6 Austin Carr	5.00	10.00
7 Wilt Chamberlain	25.00	50.00
8 Dave DeBusschere	8.00	20.00
9 Walt Frazier	10.00	20.00
10 Gail Goodrich	6.00	15.00
11 Hal Greer	6.00	15.00
12 Happy Hairston	5.00	10.00
13 John Havlicek	10.00	25.00
14 Connie Hawkins	8.00	20.00
15 Elvin Hayes	10.00	20.00
16 Spencer Haywood	5.00	10.00
17 Lou Hudson	5.00	10.00
18 John Johnson	5.00	10.00
19 Don Kojis	5.00	10.00
20 Bob Lanier	7.50	15.00
21 Kevin Loughery	5.00	10.00
22 Jerry Lucas	6.00	15.00
23 Pete Maravich	50.00	100.00
24 Jack Marin	5.00	10.00
25 Jim McMillian	5.00	10.00
26 Jeff Mullins	5.00	10.00
27 Geoff Petrie	5.00	10.00
28 Willis Reed	8.00	20.00
29 Oscar Robertson	15.00	30.00
30 Paul Silas	6.00	15.00
31 Jerry Sloan	8.00	20.00
32 Elmore Smith	5.00	10.00
33 Nate Thurmond	6.00	15.00
34 Wes Unseld	6.00	15.00
35 Dick Van Arsdale	6.00	12.00
36 Tom Van Arsdale	6.00	12.00
37 Chet Walker	6.00	12.00
38 John Warren	5.00	10.00
39 Jerry West	25.00	50.00
40 Jo Jo White	6.00	15.00

1976-77 76ers Canada Dry Cans

The 1976-77 Canada Dry Philadelphia 76ers Cans team issue contains at least 14 standard-sized cans which paid tribute to the "Team of the Year 1976-77". Under this caption, the cans contain a 76ers logo and a black and white headshot of the player with the name, uniform number and position below the picture.There is no number given other than the jersey number, thus the set is listed below alphabetically. Cans opened from the bottom command up to a 25% premium over the prices below.The checklist below is thought to be incomplete--any additional input on this series would be appreciated.

COMPLETE SET (14)	37.50	75.00
1 Henry Bibby	2.50	6.00
2 Joe Bryant	2.50	6.00
3 Harvey Catchings	1.50	4.00
4 Darryl Dawkins	5.00	10.00
5 Al Domenico TR	1.50	4.00
6 Mike Dunleavy	3.00	8.00
7 Julius Erving	15.00	30.00
8 Lloyd Free	2.50	6.00
9 Terry Furlow	1.50	4.00
10 Caldwell Jones	2.50	6.00
11 George McGinnis	5.00	10.00
12 Jack McMahon ACO	1.50	4.00
13 Steve Mix	1.50	4.00
14 Gene Shue CO	3.00	8.00

1975-76 76ers McDonald's Standups

The 1975-76 McDonalds Philadelphia 76ers set contains six blank-backed cards measuring approximately 3 3/4" by 7". The cards were produced by Johnny Pro Enterprises. The cards are die cut, allowing the player pictures to be punched out and displayed. Johnny Pro Enterprises originally sold the sets directly to consumers for $1.25 postpaid. The cards are unnumbered and checklisted below in alphabetical order.

COMPLETE SET (6)	6.00	15.00
1 Fred Carter	1.25	3.00
2 Harvey Catchings	1.25	3.00
3 Doug Collins	3.00	8.00
4 Billy Cunningham	3.00	8.00
5 George McGinnis	2.00	5.00
6 Steve Mix	1.25	3.00

1979-80 76ers Stand-ups

This set was released during the 1979-80 season, and features twelve of the 76er's top players. These full-color player figures were produced on very thick stock, and stand about ten inches tall. Please note that these stand-ups are not numbered and are listed below in alphabetical order.

COMPLETE SET (12)	60.00	120.00
1 Henry Bibby	3.00	8.00
2 Joe Bryant	3.00	8.00
3 Harvey Catchings	2.50	6.00
4 Doug Collins	7.50	15.00
5 Darryl Dawkins	6.00	12.00
6 Mike Dunleavy	5.00	12.00
7 Julius Erving	30.00	55.00
8 Lloyd Free	5.00	10.00
9 Terry Furlow	2.50	6.00
10 Caldwell Jones	2.50	6.00
11 George McGinnis	5.00	10.00
12 Steve Mix	2.50	6.00

1969-70 76ers Team Issue

Each of these team-issued photos measure approximately 5 3/4" by 7 1/4" and feature black and white player portraits. The player's name is listed below the photo. The backs are blank. The photos are unnumbered and listed below alphabetically.

COMPLETE SET (11)	25.00	50.00
1 Archie Clark	2.00	5.00
2 Bill Cunningham	5.00	10.00
3 Hal Greer	3.00	8.00
4 Matt Guokas	2.50	6.00
5 Fred Hetzel	1.25	3.00
6 Darrall Imhoff	1.25	3.00
7 Luke Jackson	2.00	5.00
8 Wally Jones	2.00	5.00
9 Bud Ogden	1.25	3.00

10 Jack Ramsay CO 2.50 6.00
11 George Wilson 1.25 3.00

1970-71 76ers Team Issue

Measuring 5 1/2" by 7", this 13-photo set was issued for the 1970-71 season. The front photos feature a black and white posed shot with the player's name and team directly underneath. The backs are blank, unnumbered, and listed below in alphabetical order.

COMPLETE SET (13) 20.00 40.00
1 Dennis Awtrey 1.00 2.50
2 Archie Clark 1.50 4.00
3 Billy Cunningham 3.00 8.00
4 Connie Dierking 1.25 3.00
5 Fred Foster 1.00 2.50
6 Hal Greer 2.00 5.00
7 Al Henry 1.00 2.50
8 Bailey Howell 1.25 3.00
9 Luke Jackson 1.25 3.00
10 Wally Jones 1.50 4.00
11 Bud Ogden 1.00 2.50
12 Jack Ramsay CO 2.00 5.00
13 Jim Washington 1.25 3.00

1976-77 76ers Team Issue Black and White

This 8"x10" set was produced for the Philadelphia 76ers during the 1976-77 season. The set features 12 black and white cards of the team's players and coaches.

COMPLETE SET (12) 15.00 30.00
1 Henry Bibby 1.50 4.00
2 Joe Bryant 1.50 4.00
3 Fred Carter 1.25 3.00
4 Harvey Catchings 1.25 3.00
5 Lloyd Free 2.00 5.00
6 Steve Mix 1.25 3.00
7 Coniel Norman 1.25 3.00
8 F. Eugene Dixon Jr. PRES 1.25 3.00
9 Al Domenico TR 1.25 3.00
10 Jack McMahon CO 1.25 3.00
11 Gene Shue CO 1.50 4.00
12 Pat Williams VP 1.25 3.00

1976-77 76ers Team Issue Color

These 12 color blank-backed photos, which measure 4 3/4" by 6 1/2" feature members of the Eastern Conference Champions Philadelphia 76ers. These photos were sold in a 12-pack.

COMPLETE SET (12) 20.00 50.00
1 Henry Bibby 1.25 3.00
2 Joe Bryant 1.50 4.00
3 Harvey Catchings .75 2.00
4 Doug Collins 3.00 8.00
5 Darryl Dawkins 2.50 6.00
6 Mike Dunleavy 2.00 5.00
7 Julius Erving 12.00 30.00
8 Lloyd Free 2.00 5.00
9 Terry Furlow .75 2.00
10 Caldwell Jones 1.25 3.00
11 George McGinnis 1.50 4.00
12 Steve Mix .75 2.00

1948-1950 Safe-T-Card

Cards from this set were issued in the Washington D.C. area in the late 1940s and early 1950s. Each card was printed in either black or red and features an artist's rendering of a famous area athlete or personality from a variety of sports. The card backs feature an ad for Jim Gibbons Cartoon-A-Quiz television show along with an ad from a local business. The player's facsimile autograph and team or sport affiliation is included on the fronts.

4 Red Auerbach 50.00 100.00
25 Bob Feerick BK 15.00 30.00
36 Kleggie Hermsen BK 15.00 30.00

1972-73 Spalding

Each of these seven photos measures 8 1/2" by 11". The fronts feature black-and-white action or posed player photos with a brown outer border that looks like a picture frame and a white inner border. The player's name and the words "Spalding Advisory Staff" appear in a gold bar under the photo. The backs are blank. The cards are unnumbered and checklisted below in alphabetical order.

COMPLETE SET (7) 150.00 300.00
1 Rick Barry 25.00 60.00
2 Rick Barry (Action Shot) 25.00 60.00
3 Wilt Chamberlain (Philadelphia) 50.00 120.00
4 Wilt Chamberlain (San Francisco) 50.00 120.00
5 Julius Erving 40.00 100.00
6 Gail Goodrich 20.00 50.00
7 Luke Jackson 10.00 25.00

1953 Sport Magazine Premiums

This 10-card set features 5 1/2" by 7" color portraits and was issued as a subscription premium by Sport Magazine. These photos were taken by noted sports photographer Ozzie Sweet. Each features a top player from a number of different sports. The photo backs are blank and unnumbered. We've checklisted the set below in alphabetical order.

COMPLETE SET (10) 30.00 60.00
2 Bob Cousy BK 7.50 15.00

1933 Sport Kings

The cards in this 48-card set measure 2 3/8" by 2 7/8". The 1933 Sport Kings set, issued by the Goudey Gum Company, contains cards for the most famous athletic heroes of the times. No less than 18 different sports are represented in the set. The baseball cards of Cobb, Hubbell, and Ruth, and the football cards of Rockne, Grange and Thorpe command premium prices. The cards were issued in one-card penny packs which came 100 packs to a box along with a piece of gum. The catalog designation for this set is R338.

COMPLETE SET 10,000.00 16,000.00
3 Nat Holman BK 200.00 350.00
5 Ed Wachter BK 75.00 125.00
32 Joe Lapchick BK 250.00 400.00
33 Eddie Burke BK 125.00 250.00

1978 Sports I.D. Patches

This patch set was issued in 1978, and featured many of the NBA's top players or teams. Each patch was done in full color, and measured 3" x 5". Each patch is unnumbered and is listed below in alphabetical order.

COMPLETE SET (6) 60.00 120.00
1 Darryl Dawkins 5.00 10.00
2 Julius Erving 20.00 40.00
3 Dan Issel 12.50 25.00
4 Bobby Jones 7.50 15.00
5 Nuggets Team Photo 7.50 15.00
6 Spurs Team Photo 7.50 15.00
7 David Thompson 7.50 15.00

1977-79 Sportscaster Series 1

COMPLETE SET (24) 17.50 35.00
124 Pete Maravich 3.00 8.00

1977-79 Sportscaster Series 2

COMPLETE SET (24) 30.00 60.00
203 Kareem Abdul-Jabbar 2.00 4.00
209 USA-USSR 1.00 2.00

1977-79 Sportscaster Series 3

COMPLETE SET (24) 15.00 30.00
315 Julius Erving 3.00 6.00

1977-79 Sportscaster Series 4

COMPLETE SET (24) 15.00 30.00
412 Bill Russell 3.00 6.00
414 Dave Cowens 1.00 2.00
415 Rick Barry 1.00 2.00

1977-79 Sportscaster Series 5

COMPLETE SET (24) 12.50 25.00
510 Referee's Signals .75 1.50
519 The 1969-70 1.00 2.00

1977-79 Sportscaster Series 6

COMPLETE SET (24) 12.50 25.00
608 The UCLA Dynasty 1.50 3.00
621 George McGinnis .75 1.50

1977-79 Sportscaster Series 7

COMPLETE SET (24) 15.00 30.00
712 A Laboratory Sport 1.00 2.00
713 Walt Frazier 1.50 3.00
720 Wilt Chamberlain 5.00 10.00

1977-79 Sportscaster Series 8

COMPLETE SET (24) 12.50 25.00
810 Jerry West 2.50 5.00

1977-79 Sportscaster Series 9

COMPLETE SET (24) 15.00 30.00
912 Nate Archibald 1.00 2.00
916 A Game for Giants 1.25 2.50

1977-79 Sportscaster Series 10

COMPLETE SET (24) 17.50 35.00
1018 John Havlicek 1.50 4.00

1977-79 Sportscaster Series 11

COMPLETE SET (25) 20.00 40.00
1124A UCLA vs Houston ERR Bill Walton 10.00 20.00
1124B UCLA vs. Houston 5.00 10.00

1977-79 Sportscaster Series 12

COMPLETE SET (24) 12.50 25.00
1213 Wes Unseld 1.00 2.50

1977-79 Sportscaster Series 13

COMPLETE SET (24) 12.50 25.00
1304 The European Championship Cup .50 1.00
1310 Lakers Win 33 In 2.00 4.00

1977-79 Sportscaster Series 14

COMPLETE SET (24) 17.50 35.00
1412 Emil Zatopek .50 1.00
1418 Oscar Robertson 2.00 4.00

1977-79 Sportscaster Series 16

COMPLETE SET (24) 15.00 30.00
1614 Elgin Baylor 1.25 2.50
1624 Dick Button 1.00 2.00

1977-79 Sportscaster Series 18

COMPLETE SET (24) 12.50 25.00
1820 Jackie Chazalon .50 1.00

1977-79 Sportscaster Series 19

COMPLETE SET (24) 25.00 50.00
1914 Bob Pettit 1.00 2.00

1977-79 Sportscaster Series 20

COMPLETE SET (24) 7.50 15.00
2021 24-Second Clock .75 1.50

1977-79 Sportscaster Series 21

COMPLETE SET (24) 15.00 30.00
2114 Clarence(Bevo) .50 1.00

1977-79 Sportscaster Series 22

COMPLETE SET (24) 15.00 30.00
2208 Milwaukee Bucks 1.50 3.00

1977-79 Sportscaster Series 23

COMPLETE SET (24) 20.00 40.00
2303 Lingo 1.50 3.00

1977-79 Sportscaster Series 26

COMPLETE SET (24) 15.00 30.00
2624 Villeurbanne .25 .50

1977-79 Sportscaster Series 30

COMPLETE SET (24) 12.50 25.00
3010 Fouls and Penalties .50 1.00
3012 Podoloff Cup 1.50 3.00
3013 NBA All-Star Game 1.00 2.00

1977-79 Sportscaster Series 33

COMPLETE SET (24) 10.00 20.00
3304 Pivot Play 2.50 5.00

1977-79 Sportscaster Series 34

COMPLETE SET (24) 15.00 30.00
3414 Defenses .50 1.00

1977-79 Sportscaster Series 35

COMPLETE SET (24) 15.00 30.00
3506 The Highest Scoring 3.00 6.00

1977-79 Sportscaster Series 36

COMPLETE SET (24) 15.00 30.00
3608A Artis Gilmore UER 1.50 3.00
3608B Artis Gilmore COR Basketball 1.50 3.00
3612A The Four Corner UER 1.50 3.00
3612B Phil Ford COR Basketball 1.50 3.00
3622 The NCAA Tournament 2.50 5.00

1977-79 Sportscaster Series 38

COMPLETE SET (24) 20.00 40.00
3811 Paul Westphal 1.00 2.00
3812 Biddy-Basket .50 1.00

1977-79 Sportscaster Series 39

COMPLETE SET (24) 7.50 15.00
3910 Maccabi of Tel Aviv .50 1.00
3915 Doug Collins 1.50 3.00

1977-79 Sportscaster Series 40

COMPLETE SET (24) 10.00 20.00
4007 Marques Johnson 2.00 4.00
4009 Walter Davis 2.00 4.00

1977-79 Sportscaster Series 42

COMPLETE SET (24) 15.00 30.00
4202 Bernard King 1.00 2.00

1977-79 Sportscaster Series 43

COMPLETE SET (24) 12.50 25.00
4301 The Washington 1.00 2.00
4318 Power Forward 1.25 2.50

1977-79 Sportscaster Series 44

COMPLETE SET (24) 12.50 25.00
4416 Butch Lee .75 1.50
4421 3-Guard Offense 1.00 2.00

1977-79 Sportscaster Series 52

COMPLETE SET (24) 10.00 20.00
5224 Hank Luisetti 1.25 2.50

1977-79 Sportscaster Series 53

COMPLETE SET (24) 15.00 30.00
5322 Jack Sikma 1.25 2.50
5323 John Walker .75 1.50

1977-79 Sportscaster Series 54

COMPLETE SET (24) 15.00 30.00
5415 George Mikan 5.00 10.00
5423 Manuel Raga .75 1.50

1977-79 Sportscaster Series 55

COMPLETE SET (24) 12.50 25.00
5518 Leonard Robinson .75 1.50

1977-79 Sportscaster Series 56

COMPLETE SET (24) 37.50 75.00
5611 Marvin Webster 2.00 4.00

1977-79 Sportscaster Series 59

COMPLETE SET (24) 50.00 100.00
5905 David Thompson 4.00 8.00

1977-79 Sportscaster Series 60

COMPLETE SET (24) 37.50 75.00
6008 Carol Blazejowski 3.00 6.00

1977-79 Sportscaster Series 61

COMPLETE SET (24) 50.00 100.00
6110 Bill Bradley 5.00 12.00

1977-79 Sportscaster Series 62

COMPLETE SET (24) 40.00 80.00
6209 Calvin Murphy 2.50 5.00

1977-79 Sportscaster Series 63

COMPLETE SET (24) 30.00 60.00
6305 First TV Game 1.00 2.00
6320 Austin Carr 2.00 4.00

1977-79 Sportscaster Series 64

COMPLETE SET (24) 25.00 50.00
6404 Chinese Tour 1.00 2.00
6405 Olympic Games 2.50 5.00
6424 Three Officials 1.00 2.00

1977-79 Sportscaster Series 65

COMPLETE SET (24) 40.00 80.00
6502 Wilt Chamberlain 6.00 12.00
6515 20000 Point Club 2.50 5.00

1977-79 Sportscaster Series 66

COMPLETE SET (24) 37.50 75.00
6611 Hall of Fame 2.00 4.00

1977-79 Sportscaster Series 67

COMPLETE SET (24) 40.00 80.00
6702 Nancy Lieberman 5.00 10.00
6711 Bob Morse 2.00 4.00

1977-79 Sportscaster Series 70

COMPLETE SET (24) 30.00 60.00
7021 Kurt Thomas 3.00 6.00

1977-79 Sportscaster Series 73

COMPLETE SET (24) 40.00 80.00
7303 Rudy Tomjanovich 5.00 10.00

1977-79 Sportscaster Series 74

COMPLETE SET (24) 200.00 400.00
7407 A Pro Oddity 2.00 4.00
7418 Larry Bird 125.00 250.00

1977-79 Sportscaster Series 76

COMPLETE SET (24) 30.00 60.00
7608 The Longest Shot 1.00 2.00
7614 Inge Nissen 2.00 4.00

1977-79 Sportscaster Series 77

COMPLETE SET (24) 150.00 300.00
7705 Kevin Porter 2.50 5.00
7721 Nat Holman 4.00 8.00

1977-79 Sportscaster Series 78

COMPLETE SET (24) 150.00 300.00
7802 Earvin Johnson 100.00 200.00
7824 Dave Bing 4.00 8.00

1977-79 Sportscaster Series 79

COMPLETE SET (24) 60.00 120.00
7910 Ouliana Semenova 4.00 8.00
7915 Phil Ford 2.50 5.00
7919 Women's Basketball 2.00 4.00

1977-79 Sportscaster Series 81

COMPLETE SET (24) 62.50 125.00
8102 Lenny Wilkens 7.50 15.00

1977-79 Sportscaster Series 82

COMPLETE SET (24) 50.00 100.00
8202 Moses Malone 7.50 15.00
8215 Academic Basketball 3.00 6.00

1977-79 Sportscaster Series 83

COMPLETE SET (24) 62.50 125.00
8307 Three-Point Field 3.00 6.00
8317 Dutch Dehnert 3.00 6.00

1977-79 Sportscaster Series 84

COMPLETE SET (24) 60.00 120.00
8409 United Basketball 3.00 6.00

1977-79 Sportscaster Series 85

COMPLETE SET (24) 62.50 125.00
8515 Women's Draft 2.00 4.00
8522 F.P. Naismith Award 3.00 6.00

1977-79 Sportscaster Series 86

COMPLETE SET (24) 50.00 100.00
8608 Danny Ainge 15.00 40.00

1977-79 Sportscaster Series 102

COMPLETE SET (24) 75.00 150.00
10202 Ray Meyer 7.50 15.00

1977-79 Sportscaster Series 103

COMPLETE SET (24) 87.50 175.00
10304 Ann Meyers 10.00 20.00

1972 Sportscope Arena Great Moments in Basketball

Issued in 1972 by Sportscope, Inc. these items have been described as arena card booklets. We are not sure if the checklist is complete and will continue to add as we find other players.

1 Lew Alcindor/Wilt Chamberlain 40.00 75.00
2 Lew Alcindor/Bob Lanier 40.00 75.00
3 Lew Alcindor/Willis Reed/Bill Bradley 40.00 75.00
4 Dave Bing/Oscar Robertson 25.00 50.00
5 Austin Carr 15.00 30.00
6 Wilt Chamberlain/Lew Alcindor 50.00 100.00
7 Wilt Chamberlain/Jerry Lucas 75.00 150.00
8 Dave Cowens 25.00 50.00
9 Billy Cunningham/Phil Jackson 25.00 50.00
10 Dave DeBusschere 25.00 50.00
11 Walt Frazier 25.00 50.00
12 Gail Goodrich 20.00 40.00
13 John Havlicek 25.00 50.00
14 Pete Maravich 75.00 150.00
15 Jack Marin 15.00 30.00
16 Jack Newman 15.00 30.00
17 Unidentified Chicago Bulls #18 15.00 30.00
18 Dick VanArsdale/Walt Frazier 20.00 40.00
19 Lenny Wilkens 25.00 50.00

1976 Sportstix

This blank-backed irregularly shaped sticker features a borderless color player action photo. The team markings were crudely obliterated from the photo. The one basketball sticker is part of a larger multi-sport release. The stickers came in packs of five.

1 Dave DeBusschere 7.50 15.00

1979-80 Spurs Police

This set contains 15 cards measuring approximately 2 5/8" by 4 1/8" featuring the San Antonio Spurs. Backs contain safety tips, "Tips from the Spurs." The set was also sponsored by Handy Dan and were put out by Express News and Handy Dan in conjunction with the Police Department.

COMPLETE SET (15)	3.00	6.00
1 Bob Bass	.25	.60
2 Mike Evans	.25	.60
3 Mike Gale	.25	.60
4 George Gervin	1.50	4.00
5 Paul Griffin	.25	.60
6 George Karl ACO	.40	1.00
7 Larry Kenon	.30	.75
8 Irv Kiffin	.25	.60
9 Bernie LaReau	.25	.60
10 Doug Moe CO	.40	1.00
11 Mark Olberding	.25	.60
12 Billy Paultz	.30	.75
13 Wiley Peck	.25	.60
14 Kevin Restani	.25	.60
15 James Silas	.30	.75

1976-77 Spurs Team Issue

This 8" x 10" set was produced for the San Antonio Spurs during the 1976-77 season. The set features eight black and white cards of the team's players.

COMPLETE SET (8)	12.50	25.00
1 Mike D'Antoni	2.00	5.00
2 Louie Dampier	2.00	5.00
3 Coby Dietrick	1.25	3.00
4 Mike Gale	1.25	3.00
5 Billy Paultz	1.50	4.00
6 James Silas	1.50	4.00
7 Ken Smith	1.25	3.00
8 Henry Ward	1.25	3.00

1971-72 Squires Virginia Team Issue

Each of these team-issued photos measure approximately 8" by 10" and feature black and white player portraits on two sheets. The player's name and vitals are listed below the photo. Each sheet contains either seven or eight player portraits. The backs are blank. The photos are unnumbered and listed below alphabetically. Julius Erving is featured in his rookie season.

COMPLETE SET (2)	25.00	50.00
1 Bill Bunting	20.00	40.00
Jim Eakins		
Julius Erving		
George Irvine		
Neil Johnson		
Mike Maloy		
Doug Moe		
Dana Pagett		
2 Al Bianchi CO	7.50	15.00
Earl M. Foreman PRES		
Charlie Scott		
Ray Scott		
Willie Sojourner		
Adrian Smith		
Roland Taylor		

1976-77 Suns 8 x 10

This 8x10 set was produced for the Phoenix Suns during the 1976-77 season. The set features nice black and white cards of the team's players and coaches.

COMPLETE SET (9)	25.00	50.00
1 Dennis Awtrey	1.25	3.00
2 Al Bianchi CO	1.50	4.00
3 Jerry Colangelo GM	1.25	3.00
4 Keith Erickson	1.25	3.00
5 Butch Feher	1.25	3.00
6 Garfield Heard	2.00	5.00
7 Ron Lee	1.25	3.00
8 John McLeod CO	1.25	3.00
9 Curtis Perry	1.25	3.00
10 Joe Proski TR	1.25	3.00
11 Ricky Sobers	1.25	3.00
12 Ira Terrell	1.25	3.00
13 Dick Van Arsdale	2.00	5.00
14 Tom Van Arsdale	1.50	4.00
15 Dick Van Arsdale Tom Van Arsdale	2.00	5.00
16 Paul Westphal	2.50	6.00

1970-71 Suns A1 Premium Beer

These scarce cards are black and white and come with unperforated tabs. The cards were actually the advertising-oriented price tabs for six-packs of A1 Premium Beer. The set features members of the Phoenix Suns. There are three variations primarily based on the price marked on the tab; they are 95 cents (most common), 98 cents (tougher to find), and no price listed. Those not specifically identified in the checklist below are the 95 cents varieties. In terms of size, they resemble bookmarks, each measuring approximately 2 1/4" by 8 3/4". The top of each ad has a circular A-1 Premium Beer emblem. Immediately below the price for the six-pack appears; this can be either 95 or 98 cents, or on some ads no price was given. The black-and-white photo itself measures approximately 2 1/4" by 3 3/8" and features a posed action shot of the player. The backs are blank. The cards are unnumbered and are checklisted below in alphabetical order.

COMPLETE SET (13)	900.00	1,700.00
1A Mel Counts (95 cents)	50.00	100.00
1B Mel Counts (98 cents)	60.00	120.00
2 Lamar Green	40.00	85.00
3 Clem Haskins	75.00	150.00
4 Connie Hawkins (98 cents)	250.00	450.00
5 Greg Howard	40.00	85.00
6 Paul Silas	125.00	225.00
7 Fred Taylor CO	40.00	85.00
8A Dick Van Arsdale ERR	100.00	175.00
8B Dick Van Arsdale COR	75.00	150.00
9A Neal Walk (95 cents)	50.00	100.00
9B Neal Walk (No price)	60.00	120.00
10 John Wetzel (No price)	50.00	100.00

1968-69 Suns Carnation Milk

This 12-card set of Phoenix Suns was sponsored by Carnation Milk and was issued as panels on the sides of milk cartons. The fronts feature a player pose and brief biographical information near the photo. The bottom of the panels indicate "WIN, 440 Home Game tickets to be given away." The cards measure approximately 3 1/2" by 7 1/2" and are blank backed. The cards are unnumbered and are checklisted below in alphabetical order. Bob Warlick was only with the Phoenix Suns during the last half of the 1968-69 season. The set features the first professional card of Gail Goodrich.

COMPLETE SET (12)	800.00	1,400.00
1 Jim Fox	60.00	125.00
2 Gail Goodrich	200.00	400.00
3 Gary Gregor	50.00	100.00
4 Neil Johnson	60.00	125.00
5 John Kerr CO	90.00	170.00
6 Dave Lattin	60.00	125.00
7 Stan McKenzie	40.00	80.00
8 McCoy McLemore	40.00	80.00
9 Dick Snyder	40.00	80.00
10 Dick Van Arsdale	75.00	150.00
11 Bob Warlick	60.00	125.00
12 George Wilson	40.00	80.00

1969-70 Suns Carnation Milk

This ten-card set features members of the Phoenix Suns and was produced by Carnation Milk. The cards show white backgrounds with blue and white drawings of the players. Playing tips (in red type) are found at the bottom of each card. Player statistics were on the opposite milk carton panel and hence were not saved in most cases. The cards measure approximately 3 1/2" by 7 1/2". The backs are blank. The cards are unnumbered and are checklisted below in alphabetical order. The set features the first professional card of Connie Hawkins.

COMPLETE SET (10)	700.00	1,100.00
1 Jerry Chambers	35.00	70.00
2 Jim Fox	35.00	70.00
3 Gail Goodrich	100.00	200.00
4 Connie Hawkins	200.00	400.00
5 Stan McKenzie	35.00	70.00
6 Paul Silas	100.00	200.00
7 Dick Snyder	35.00	70.00
8 Dick Van Arsdale	50.00	100.00
9 Neal Walk	60.00	120.00
10 Gene Williams	35.00	70.00

1970-71 Suns Carnation Milk

This ten-card set features members of the Phoenix Suns and was produced by Carnation Milk. The cards have solid red backgrounds or orange backgrounds if the cards were from diet milk cartons. Apparently the entire set was issued in both color backgrounds. The cards measure approximately 3 1/2" by 7 1/2". The backs are blank. The cards are unnumbered and are checklisted below in alphabetical order.

COMPLETE SET (10)	400.00	800.00
1 Mel Counts	30.00	60.00
2 Lamar Green	25.00	50.00
3 Art Harris	25.00	50.00
4 Clem Haskins	40.00	80.00
5 Connie Hawkins	125.00	250.00
6 Gus Johnson	60.00	120.00
7 Otto Moore	25.00	50.00
8 Paul Silas	60.00	120.00
9 Dick Van Arsdale	40.00	80.00
10 Neal Walk	30.00	60.00

1971-72 Suns Carnation Milk

This five-card set features members of the Phoenix Suns and was produced by Carnation Milk and issued as panels on the sides of milk cartons. The cards measure approximately 3 1/2" by 7 1/2". The backs are blank. The cards are unnumbered and are checklisted below in alphabetical order.

COMPLETE SET (5)	200.00	400.00
1 Connie Hawkins	100.00	200.00
2 Otto Moore	25.00	50.00
3 Fred Taylor CO	25.00	50.00
4 Neal Walk	30.00	60.00
5 John Wetzel	30.00	60.00

1972-73 Suns Carnation Milk

This 12-card set features members of the Phoenix Suns and was produced by Carnation Milk and issued as panels on the sides of milk cartons. The picture and text are in the team's colors, purple and orange. The cards measure approximately 3 1/2" by 7 1/2". The backs are blank. The cards are unnumbered and are checklisted below in alphabetical order.

COMPLETE SET (12)	400.00	800.00
1 Mel Counts	30.00	60.00
2 Lamar Green	25.00	50.00
3 Clem Haskins	40.00	80.00
4 Connie Hawkins	100.00	200.00
5 Gus Johnson	50.00	100.00
6 Dennis Layton	30.00	60.00
7 Otto Moore	25.00	50.00
8 Fred Taylor CO	25.00	50.00
9 Dick Van Arsdale	40.00	80.00
10 Bill VanBredaKolff CO	25.00	50.00
11 Neal Walk	30.00	60.00
12 John Wetzel	30.00	60.00

1975-76 Suns Fan Grabber

The 1975-76 Phoenix Suns set contains 16 cards, including 12 player cards. The fronts feature black and white pictures, and the backs are blank. The dimensions are approximately 3 1/2" by 4 3/8". The set commemorates the Suns' Western Conference Championship. The cards are unnumbered and are checklisted below in alphabetical order. The set features Alvan Adams' first professional card. These cards were available through at the Fan Grabber concession stands at all Suns playoff games.

COMPLETE SET (16)	10.00	25.00
1 Alvan Adams	2.00	5.00
2 Dennis Awtrey	.60	1.50
3 Al Bianchi GM	.60	1.50
4 Jerry Colangelo VP	1.00	2.50
5 Keith Erickson	1.25	3.00
6 Nate Hawthorne	.60	1.50
7 Garfield Heard	1.00	2.50
8 Phil Lumpkin	.60	1.50
9 John MacLeod CO	.75	2.00
10 Curtis Perry	.75	2.00
11 Joe Proski TR	.60	1.50
12 Pat Riley	7.50	15.00
13 Ricky Sobers	1.00	2.50
14 Dick Van Arsdale	1.25	3.00
15 Paul Westphal	3.00	8.00
16 John Wetzel	.40	1.00

1972-73 Suns Holsum

Sponsored by Holsum Bread in Phoenix, Arizona, these inserts were available in loaves of bread. Each one measures approximately 2 1/2" by 4", is printed on glossy paper, and is devoted to a different Sun player and basketball topic. While the front displays a player portrait, the back carries a Holsum bread advertisement. The trifold insert unfolds to reveal player biography, basketball tips, and records and facts. All print is in light blue lettering; the fronts and backs are accented with red-orange as well. The inserts are unnumbered and checklisted below in alphabetical order.

COMPLETE SET (9)	100.00	175.00
1 Corky Calhoun	8.00	20.00
2 Lamar Green	8.00	20.00
3 Clem Haskins	15.00	30.00
4 Connie Hawkins	60.00	120.00
5 Dennis Layton	8.00	20.00
6 Charlie Scott	25.00	50.00
7 Dick Van Arsdale	15.00	30.00
8 Neal Walk	10.00	20.00
9 Walt Wesley	8.00	20.00

1977-78 Suns Humpty Dumpty Discs

The 1977-78 Humpty Dumpty Phoenix Suns set contains 12 discs measuring approximately 3 1/4" in diameter. The blankbacked discs are printed on thick stock. The fronts feature small black and white facial photos surrounded by a purple border with orange trim. Players are numbered below in alphabetical order by subject. The set features Walter Davis' first professional card.

COMPLETE SET (12)	15.00	30.00
1 Alvan Adams	1.25	3.00
2 Dennis Awtrey	.75	2.00
3 Mike Bratz	1.00	2.50
4 Don Buse	1.00	2.50
5 Walter Davis	7.50	15.00
6 Bayard Forrest	.75	2.00
7 Garfield Heard	1.25	3.00
8 Ron Lee	.75	2.00
9 Curtis Perry	.75	2.00
10 Alvin Scott	.75	2.00
11 Ira Terrell	1.00	2.50
12 Paul Westphal	2.50	6.00

1980-81 Suns Pepsi

The 1980-81 Pepsi Phoenix Suns set contains 12 numbered cards attached to a bumper sticker-sized promotional flyer/entry blank. The cards were part of a promotion featuring the fans' selection of their Suns' dream team. The entire strip measures approximately 2 7/8" by 11" whereas the cards themselves are standard size, 2 1/2" by 3 1/2". The strips were perforated twice to allow for the card and two ads. The strips were found in six-packs and eight-packs of Pepsi-Cola in the Phoenix area. The fronts feature color photos, and the backs include statistics and biographical information.

COMPLETE SET (12)	5.00	10.00
1 Walter Davis	1.25	3.00
2 Alvin Scott	.30	.75
3 Johnny High	.30	.75
4 Dennis Johnson	1.25	3.00
5 Alvan Adams	.75	2.00
6 Rich Kelley	.30	.75
7 Truck Robinson	.60	1.50
8 Joel Kramer	.50	1.25
9 Jeff Cook	.30	.75
10 Mike Niles	.30	.75
11 Kyle Macy	.60	1.50
12 John MacLeod CO	.30	.75

1972-73 Suns Team Issue

Each of these team-issued photos measure approximately 8" by 10" and feature two black and white player photos - one a portrait and the other a posed action shot. The player's name is listed below the portrait. The backs are blank. The photos are unnumbered and listed below alphabetically.

COMPLETE SET (10)	25.00	50.00
1 Corky Calhoun	1.25	3.00
2 Mel Counts	1.25	3.00
3 Lamar Green	1.25	3.00
4 Clem Haskins	2.50	6.00
5 Connie Hawkins	7.50	15.00
6 Gus Johnson	2.00	5.00
7 Dennis Mo Layton	1.25	3.00
8 Charlie Scott	3.00	8.00
9 Dick Van Arsdale	2.00	5.00
10 Neal Walk	1.50	4.00

1973-74 Suns Team Issue

Measuring approximately 8" by 10", these photos feature members of the 1973-74 Phoenix Suns.

COMPLETE SET	15.00	30.00
1 Dick Van Arsdale	1.50	4.00
2 Neal Walk	1.25	3.00
3 Dennis Scott	1.50	4.00
4 Lamar Green	1.25	3.00
5 Clem Haskins	1.25	3.00
6 Mike Bantom	1.25	3.00
7 Jim Owens	1.25	3.00
8 Bob Christian	1.25	3.00
9 Corky Calhoun	1.25	3.00
10 Gary Melchionni	1.25	3.00
11 Keith Erickson	1.25	3.00
12 Bill Chamberlain	1.25	3.00

1974-75 Suns Team Issue

This set of 11 oversized cards picture a face shot of the player to the left, a posed shot to the right and career statistics at the bottom left. The set is black and white. The cards are not numbered and checklisted below in alphabetical order.

COMPLETE SET (11)	17.50	35.00
1 Dennis Awtrey	1.25	3.00
2 Mike Bantom	1.25	3.00
3 Keith Erickson	1.50	4.00
4 Nate Hawthorne	1.25	3.00
5 Gary Melchionni	1.25	3.00
6 Jim Owens	1.25	3.00
7 Curtis Perry	1.25	3.00
8 Fred Saunders	1.25	3.00
9 Charlie Scott	2.50	6.00
10 Dick Van Arsdale	1.50	4.00
11 Earl Williams	1.25	3.00

1975-76 Suns Team Issue

Measuring 8" by 10", this 14-card set features members of the Phoenix Suns. The set features black and white photos with the backs being blank. The cards are not numbered and checklisted below in alphabetical order.

COMPLETE SET (14)	12.00	30.00
1 Alvan Adams	1.50	4.00
2 Dennis Awtrey	.75	2.00
3 Keith Erickson	1.25	3.00
4 Nate Hawthorne	.75	2.00
5 Phil Lumpkin	.75	2.00
6 John MacLeod CO	1.25	3.00
7 Curtis Perry	.75	2.00
8 Joe Proski TR	.75	2.00
9 Pat Riley	5.00	10.00
10 Fred Saunders	.75	2.00
11 John Shumate	1.25	3.00
12 Ricky Sobers	.75	2.00
13 Paul Westphal	2.00	5.00
14 John Wetzel	.75	2.00

1977-78 Suns Team Issue

This 12-card set was released during the 1977-78 season, and features all of the Phoenix Suns players from that year. Please note that these cards are slightly oversized at 3x5, and the card backs are blank.

COMPLETE SET (12)	20.00	40.00
1 Alvan Adams	2.00	5.00
2 Dennis Awtrey	1.25	3.00
3 Mike Bratz	1.25	3.00
4 Don Buse	1.25	3.00
5 Walter Davis	3.00	8.00
6 Bayard Forrest	1.25	3.00
7 Greg Griffin	1.25	3.00
8 Garfield Heard	1.50	4.00
9 Ron Lee	1.25	3.00
10 Curtis Perry	1.25	3.00
11 Alvin Scott	1.25	3.00
12 Paul Westphal	2.00	5.00

1976-77 Suns

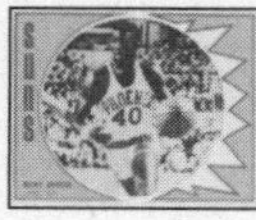

The 1976-77 Phoenix Suns set contains 12 horizontal player cards measuring 3 1/2" by 4 3/8". The fronts have circular black and white photos framed by the Suns' orange and purple logo. The backs are blank.

COMPLETE SET (12)	6.00	15.00
1 Alvan Adams	1.25	3.00
2 Dennis Awtrey	.60	1.50
3 Keith Erickson	1.25	3.00
4 Butch Feher	.60	1.50
5 Garfield Heard	1.00	2.50
6 Ron Lee	.60	1.50
7 Curtis Perry	.60	1.50
8 Ricky Sobers	1.00	2.50
9 Ira Terrell	.75	2.00
10 Dick Van Arsdale	1.25	3.00
11 Tom Van Arsdale	1.25	3.00
12 Paul Westphal	2.00	5.00

1974-75 Supersonics KTW-1250 Milk Cartons

These cards measure approximately 3 1/4" by 2 5/8" and feature drawings of the featured person in navy blue on a yellow background. A brief profile of the person appears in navy below the drawing. The cards are unnumbered and checklisted below in alphabetical order.

COMPLETE SET (2)	60.00	120.00
1 Wayne Cody ANN	10.00	20.00
2 Bill Russell GM	50.00	100.00

1978-79 Supersonics Police

This set contains 16 unnumbered cards measuring 2 5/8" by 4 1/8" featuring the Seattle Supersonics. The set was sponsored by the Washington State Crime Prevention Association, Kiwanis Club, and local law enforcement agencies. The year of issue is printed in the lower right corner of the reverse. Backs contain safety tips ("Tips from the Sonics") and are written in black ink with blue accent. The cards are listed below in alphabetical order. The set features early professional cards of Dennis Johnson and Jack Sikma.

COMPLETE SET (16)	10.00	20.00
1 Fred Brown	.75	2.00
2 Joe Hassett	.30	.75
3 Dennis Johnson	1.50	4.00
4 John Johnson	.30	.75
5 Tom LaGarde	.40	1.00
6 Lonnie Shelton	.50	1.25
7 Jack Sikma	1.00	2.50
8 Paul Silas	1.00	2.50
9 Dick Snyder	.30	.75
10 Wally Walker	.30	.75
11 Gus Williams	.75	2.00
12 Len Wilkens CO	1.50	4.00
13 Les Habegger ACO	.30	.75
14 Frank Furtado TR	.30	.75
15 T. Wheedle mascot	.30	.75
16 Team Photo	.75	2.00

1979-80 Supersonics Police

This set contains 16 numbered cards measuring 2 5/8" by 4 1/8" featuring the Seattle Supersonics. Backs contain safety tips ("Tips for the Sonics") and are written in blue ink with red accent. The cards are numbered and dated in the lower right corner of the obverse. The set was sponsored by the Washington State Crime Prevention Association, Kiwanis, Coca Cola, Rainier Bank, and local area law enforcement agencies. The set features the first professional card of Vinnie Johnson.

COMPLETE SET (16)	7.50	15.00
1 Gus Williams	.60	1.50
2 James Bailey	.30	.75
3 Jack Sikma	.60	1.50
4 Tom LaGarde	.30	.75
5 Paul Silas	.75	2.00
6 Lonnie Shelton	.40	1.00
7 T. Wheedle (Mascot)	.20	.50
8 Vinnie Johnson	1.25	3.00
9 Dennis Johnson	1.00	2.50
10 Wally Walker	.40	1.00
11 Les Habegger ACO	.25	.60
12 Frank Furtado TR	.25	.60
13 Fred Brown	.60	1.50
14 John Johnson	.30	.75
15 Team Photo	1.00	2.50
16 Len Wilkens CO	1.00	2.50

1979-80 Supersonics Portfolio

These limited collector prints of Seattle Supersonics were produced by artist Bill Vanderdasson and measure 11" by 14". Each print depicts a player in game action. While ten of the prints are in black and white on a gray background, the Sikma print is in full color. Each print has a hand-drawn border with rounded corners. The backs are blank. Dennis Awtrey was acquired from Boston on January 17, 1979 and left the SuperSonics via free agency on August 14, 1980. Dennis Johnson was traded to the Phoenix Suns on June 4, 1980.

COMPLETE SET (11)	22.50	45.00
1 Dennis Awtrey	1.25	3.00
2 Fred Brown	3.00	8.00
3 Dennis Johnson	5.00	10.00
4 John Johnson	1.25	3.00
5 Tom LaGarde	1.25	3.00
6 Lonnie Shelton	1.50	4.00
7 Jack Sikma	3.00	8.00
8 Paul Silas	3.00	8.00
9 Dick Snyder	1.25	3.00
10 Wally Walker	1.50	4.00
11 Gus Williams	2.50	6.00

1971-72 Supersonics Reed

These 13 pencil drawings of the 1971-72 Supersonics were drawn by Ashby Reed during the 1971-72 season. Each photo measures approximately 8 1/2" x 10". Each photo is black and white with a blank back.

COMPLETE SET (13)	25.00	50.00
1 Fred Brown	2.50	6.00
2 Barry Clemens	1.25	3.00
3 Pete Cross	1.25	3.00
4 Jake Ford	1.25	3.00
5 Spencer Haywood	3.00	8.00
6 Garfield Heard	1.50	4.00
7 Don Kojis	1.25	3.00
8 Bob Rule	1.25	3.00
9 Don Smith	1.25	3.00
10 Dick Snyder	1.25	3.00
11 Rod Thorn ACO	1.50	4.00
12 Lenny Wilkens	5.00	10.00
13 Lee Winfield	1.25	3.00

1973-74 Supersonics Shur-Fresh

The 1973-74 Shur-Fresh Seattle Supersonics set contains 12 cards measuring approximately 2 3/4" square. There are ten player cards and two coach cards. The cards have plastic bread ties attached to them. The fronts have color photos and the backs have biographical information. Cards are unnumbered so they are listed below in alphabetical order. The set features one of the few cards of Hall of Famer Bill Russell. Bill Russell's card may be slightly more difficult as a consumer could earn tickets to a Sonics game for five different cards of which one needed to be Russell's.

COMPLETE SET (12)	50.00	100.00
1 John Brisker	5.00	10.00
2 Fred Brown	10.00	20.00
3 Emmette Bryant ACO	3.00	8.00
4 Jim Fox	5.00	10.00
5 Dick Gibbs	3.00	8.00
6 Spencer Haywood	6.00	15.00
7 Bill Russell CO	30.00	60.00
8 Jim McDaniels	6.00	12.00
9 Kennedy McIntosh	3.00	8.00
10 Dick Snyder	3.00	8.00
11 Bud Stallworth	3.00	8.00
12 Lee Winfield	3.00	8.00

1969-70 Supersonics Sunbeam Bread

This 11-card set consists of cards measuring approximately 2 3/4" by 2 3/4". The cards were attached to plastic bread ties and issued on loaves of Sunbeam Bread. The cards of either Tom Meschery or Len Wilkens along with any four other player cards could be redeemed by a fan 16 years of age or younger for a free ticket to a 1969-70 Seattle Supersonics game. The card fronts feature a color posed photo of each player shot from the waist up. The team and player name are given in white lettering in the picture. The photo has a thin red border, with the words "Sunbeam Enriched Bread" across the top of the card face. The words "Sonic Stars" are written vertically along the right side of the picture. Cards show the team's schedule for the 1969-70 season. Cards are unnumbered so they are listed below in alphabetical order.

COMPLETE SET (11)	50.00	100.00
1 Lucius Allen	10.00	20.00
2 Bob Boozer	6.00	12.00
3 Barry Clemens	5.00	10.00
4 Art Harris	5.00	10.00
5 Tom Meschery SP	7.50	15.00
6 Erwin Mueller	5.00	10.00
7 Dorie Murrey	5.00	10.00
8 Bob Rule	6.00	12.00
9 John Tresvant	5.00	10.00
10 Len Wilkens P/CO SP	20.00	40.00
11 Seattle Coliseum DP	5.00	10.00

1970-71 Supersonics Sunbeam Bread

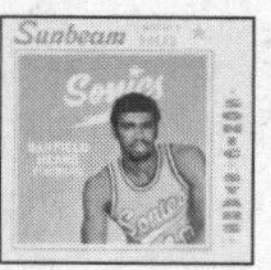

This 11-card set consists of cards measuring approximately 2 3/4" by 2 3/4". The cards were attached to plastic bread ties and issued on loafs of Sunbeam Bread. The front features a color posed photo of each player shot from the waist up. The team and player name are given in white lettering in the picture. The photo has a thin red border, with the words "Sunbeam Enriched Bread" across the top of the card face. The words "Sonic Stars" are written vertically along the right side of the picture. The back has a career summary of the player and an offer for fans 16 years of age or younger to complete and send in a set of five different Sonic players (including Tom Meschery or Len Wilkens) for a complimentary ticket to a 1970-71 Seattle Supersonics home game. Cards are unnumbered so they are listed below in alphabetical order.

COMPLETE SET (11)	50.00	100.00
1 Tom Black	5.00	10.00
2 Barry Clemens	5.00	10.00
3 Pete Cross	5.00	10.00
4 Jake Ford	5.00	10.00
5 Garfield Heard	6.00	15.00
6 Don Kojis	6.00	12.00
7 Tom Meschery SP	6.00	15.00
8 Dick Snyder	5.00	10.00
9 Len Wilkens P/CO SP	20.00	40.00
10 Lee Winfield	5.00	10.00
11 Seattle Coliseum	5.00	10.00

1971-72 Supersonics Sunbeam Bread

This 11-card set consists of cards measuring approximately 2 3/4" by 2 3/4". The cards were attached to plastic bread ties and issued on loafs of Sunbeam Bread. The front features a color posed photo of each player shot from the waist up. The team and player name are given in white lettering in the picture. The photo has a thin red border, with the words "Sunbeam Enriched Bread" across the top of the card face. The words "Sonic Stars" are written vertically along the right side of the picture. Cards are unnumbered so they are listed below in alphabetical order.

COMPLETE SET (11)	50.00	100.00
1 Pete Cross	5.00	10.00
2 Jake Ford	5.00	10.00
3 Spencer Haywood	10.00	20.00
4 Garfield Heard	7.50	15.00
5 Don Kojis	6.00	12.00
6 Bob Rule	6.00	12.00
7 Don Smith	5.00	10.00
8 Dick Snyder	5.00	10.00
9 Len Wilkens P/CO	15.00	30.00
10 Lee Winfield	5.00	10.00
11 Sonics Coliseum	5.00	10.00

1967-68 Supersonics Team Issue

Each of these team issued photos measure approximately 4" by 5" and feature black and white close-up player portraits. The backs are blank. The photos are not numbered and listed below alphabetically.

COMPLETE SET (12)	100.00	200.00
1 Henry Akin	7.50	15.00
2 Walt Hazzard	15.00	30.00
3 Tommy Kron	7.50	15.00
4 Plummer Lott	7.50	15.00
5 Tom Meschery	10.00	20.00
6 Dorie Murrey	7.50	15.00
7 Bud Olsen	7.50	15.00
8 Bob Rule	10.00	20.00
9 Rod Thorn	10.00	20.00
10 Al Tucker	7.50	15.00
11 Bob Weiss	10.00	20.00
12 George Wilson	7.50	15.00

1968-69 Supersonics Team Issue

This 5x7 set was produced for the Seattle Supersonics during the 1968-69 season. The set features 12 black and white cards of the team's players.

COMPLETE SET (12)	60.00	120.00
1 Dorie Murrey	5.00	10.00
2 Tom Meschery	6.00	12.00
3 Len Wilkens	12.50	25.00
4 Al Hairston	5.00	10.00
5 Art Harris	5.00	10.00
6 Bob Kauffman	5.00	10.00
7 Rod Thorn	6.00	12.00
8 Al Tucker	5.00	10.00
9 Bob Rule	6.00	12.00
10 Plummer Lott	5.00	10.00
11 Tommy Kron	5.00	10.00
12 Joe Kennedy	5.00	10.00

1975-76 Supersonics Team Issue

This 8" x10" set was produced for the Seattle Supersonics during the 1975-76 season. The set features eight black and white cards of the team's players.

COMPLETE SET (8)	10.00	20.00
1 Mike Bantom	1.25	3.00
2 Rod Derline	1.25	3.00
3 Herm Gilliam	1.25	3.00
4 Leonard Gray	1.25	3.00
5 Willie Norwood	1.25	3.00
6 Frank Oleynick	1.25	3.00
7 Bruce Seals	1.25	3.00
8 Talvin Skinner	1.25	3.00

1976-77 Supersonics Team Issue

This 8" x10" set was produced for the Seattle Supersonics during the 1976-77 season. The set features nine black and white cards of the team's players and coaches.

COMPLETE SET (9)	12.50	25.00
1 Mike Bantom	1.25	3.00
2 Tommy Burleson	1.50	4.00
3 Leonard Gray	1.25	3.00

4 Mike Green	1.25	3.00
5 Willie Norwood	1.25	3.00
6 Frank Oleynick	1.25	3.00
7 Bruce Seals	1.25	3.00
8 Slick Watts	1.25	3.00
9 Bob Wilkerson	1.50	4.00

1978-79 Supersonics Team Issue

Each of these team-issued photos measure approximately 5 7/8" by 9" and feature color close-up player portraits with white borders. A facsimile autograph appears at the bottom. The backs are blank. The photos are unnumbered and listed below alphabetically.

COMPLETE SET (11)	17.50	35.00
1 Fred Brown	2.50	6.00
2 Al Fleming	.75	2.00
3 Joe Hassett	.75	2.00
4 Dennis Johnson	3.00	8.00
5 John Johnson	.75	2.00
6 Jack Sikma	2.50	6.00
7 Paul Silas	2.50	6.00
8 Wally Walker	1.00	2.50
9 Marvin Webster	1.25	3.00
10 Gus Williams	2.00	5.00
11 Cover Photo (Smaller versions of all ten photos)	2.00	5.00

1978-79 Supersonics Team Issue 8 X 10

This seven photo set was released during the 1978-79 season. The set features many of the players on that years team. Please note that these cards measure 8" x 10" and are listed below in alphabetical order.

COMPLETE SET (7)	12.50	25.00
1 Fred Brown	2.00	5.00
2 Dennis Johnson	2.00	5.00
3 John Johnson	1.50	4.00
4 Lonnie Shelton	1.25	3.00
5 Jack Sikma	2.00	5.00
6 Wally Walker	1.50	4.00
7 Gus Williams	1.25	3.00

1980 Superstar Matchbook

These collector issued matchbooks were issued in the New England area in 1980 and featured superstars from all sports but with an emphasis on players who made their fame in New England. Since these are unnumbered, we have sequenced them in alphabetical order.

COMPLETE SET	30.00	60.00
2 Larry Bird	5.00	10.00

1975 SuperStar Sock Wrappers

1 Kareem Abdul-Jabbar	200.00	400.00
2 Lucius Allen	100.00	200.00
3 Nate Archibald	125.00	250.00
4 Rick Barry	125.00	250.00
5 Doug Collins	125.00	250.00
6 Elvin Hayes	150.00	300.00
7 Spencer Haywood	100.00	200.00
8 Bob Lanier	150.00	300.00
9 Pete Maravich	500.00	1,000.00

1951 Syracuse National Glasses

These glasses were given out to a select few fans at a Syracuse National game in 1951. The glasses have a silhouette of the player on them along with their name. Since they are unnumbered we have sequenced them in alphabetical order.

COMPLETE SET (9)	500.00	850.00
1 Al Cervi	50.00	100.00
2 Billy Gabor	25.00	50.00
3 Alex Hannum	60.00	120.00
4 Noble Jorgensen	25.00	50.00
5 George Ratkovicz	25.00	50.00
6 Dolph Schayes	250.00	400.00
7 Paul Seymour	60.00	120.00
8 Front Office Personnel	25.00	50.00
9 Onodoga Cty War Memorial	25.00	50.00

1958-59 Syracuse Nationals

This set consists of 8" by 10" glossy photos of the 1955-56 Syracuse Nationals. Originally the photos sold for 25 cents each, or the entire set for $2.00. The order blank also included an offer for a 32-page record book that could be purchased for 50 cents. The photos are unnumbered and checklisted below in alphabetical order. We have dated this set 1958-59 as it was Hal Greer's and Connie Dierking's rookie NBA season and Togo Palazzi's last full NBA season.

COMPLETE SET (11)	800.00	1,600.00
1 Al Bianchi	75.00	150.00
2 Ed Conlin	65.00	125.00
3 Larry Costello	75.00	150.00
4 Connie Dierking	75.00	150.00
5 Hal Greer	100.00	200.00
6 Bob Hopkins	65.00	125.00
7 John Kerr	100.00	200.00
8 Togo Palazzi	65.00	125.00
9 Dolph Schayes	150.00	300.00
10 Paul Seymour	65.00	125.00
11 Team Photo	75.00	150.00

1962-63 Syracuse Nationals

These photos, which measure 8" by 10", feature members of the Syracuse Nationals. Since these photos are unnumbered, we have sequenced them in alphabetical order.

COMPLETE SET	400.00	800.00
1 Al Bianchi	30.00	60.00
2 Len Chappell	25.00	50.00
3 Larry Costello	40.00	80.00
4 Dave Gambee	25.00	50.00
5 Hal Greer	60.00	120.00
6 Alex Hannum	30.00	60.00
7 Swede Halbrook	25.00	50.00
8 John Kerr	50.00	100.00
9 Paul Neuman	25.00	50.00
10 Joe Roberts	25.00	50.00
11 Dolph Schayes	75.00	150.00
12 Lee Shaffer	25.00	50.00

1980-81 TCMA CBA

The 1980-81 Continental Basketball Association set, produced by TCMA, features 45 black and white photos of the players along with the team name in red along the side of the front of the card. The sets were originally available direct from the CBA for 5.50. The backs contain brief biographical data and statistics, the CBA logo, the team logo and the card number. A 1981 TCMA copyright date also appears on the back. The standard-size cards are printed on white cardboard backs.

COMPLETE SET (45)	40.00	80.00
1 Chubby Cox	1.25	3.00
2 Sylvester Cuyler	1.00	2.50
3 Harry Davis	.75	2.00
4 Danny Salisbury	.75	2.00
5 Cazzie Russell	4.00	10.00
6 Al Green	1.00	2.50
7 Rick Wilson	.75	2.00
8 Jim Brogan	.75	2.00
9 Andre McCarter	2.50	6.00
10 Jerry Baskerville	1.25	3.00
11 James Woods	.75	2.00
12 Geoff Crompton	1.25	3.00
13 Korky Nelson	.75	2.00
14 George Karl CO	7.50	15.00
15 Stan Pietkiewicz	1.25	3.00
16 Raymond Townsend	2.00	5.00
17 Lenny Horton	.75	2.00
18 Carl Bailey	.75	2.00
19 Ken Jones	.75	2.00
20 Rory Sparrow	3.00	8.00
21 Mauro Panaggio CO	1.50	4.00
22 Glenn Hagan	1.25	3.00
23 Larry Fogle	1.25	3.00
24 Wayne Abrams	.75	2.00
25 Jerry Christian	.75	2.00
26 Edgar Jones	1.50	4.00
27 Jerry Radocha	.75	2.00
28 Greg Jackson	1.00	2.50
29 Eddie Mast P/CO	1.25	3.00
30 Ron Davis	1.25	3.00
31 Tico Brown	1.00	2.50
32 Freeman Blade	1.00	2.50
33 Bill Klucas CO	1.00	2.50
34 Melvin Davis	1.00	2.50
35 James Hardy	.75	2.00
36 Brad Davis	4.00	10.00
37 Andre Wakefield	.75	2.00
38 Brett Vroman	1.25	3.00
39 Larry Knight	.75	2.00
40 Mel Bennett	.75	2.00
41 Stan Eckwood	.75	2.00
42 Andrew Parker	.75	2.00
43 Billy Ray (Dunk) Bates	1.50	4.00
44 Matt Teahan	.75	2.00
45 Carlton Green	.75	2.00

1957-58 Topps

The 1957-58 Topps basketball set of 80 cards was Topps first basketball issue. Topps did not produce another basketball set until it released a test issue in 1968. A major set followed in 1969. Cards were issued in 5-cent packs (six cards per pack, 24 per box) and measure the standard size. A number of cards in the set were double printed (indicated by DP in checklist below). The set contains 49 double prints, 30 single prints and one quadruple print (No. 24 Bob Pettit). Card backs give statistical information from the 1956-57 NBA season. Bill Russell's Rookie Card is part of the set. Other Rookie Cards include Paul Arizin, Nat "Sweetwater" Clifton, Bob Cousy, Cliff Hagan, Tom Heinsohn, Rod Hundley, Red Kerr, Clyde Lovellette, Pettit, Dolph Schayes, Bill Sharman and Jack Twyman. The set contains the only card of Maurice Stokes. Topps also produced a three-card advertising panel featuring the fronts of Walt Davis, Joe Graboski and Cousy with an advertisement for the upcoming Topps basketball set on the combined reverse.

COMPLETE SET (80)	3,000.00	6,000.00
CONDITION SENSITIVE SET		
CARDS PRICED IN EX-MT CONDITION		
1 Nat Clifton DP RC	60.00	150.00
2 George Yardley DP RC	25.00	60.00
3 Neil Johnston DP RC	20.00	50.00
4 Carl Braun DP	30.00	50.00
5 Bill Sharman DP RC	60.00	150.00
6 George King DP RC	15.00	40.00
7 Kenny Sears DP RC	15.00	40.00
8 Dick Ricketts DP RC	15.00	40.00
9 Jack Nichols DP	15.00	40.00
10 Paul Arizin DP RC	30.00	80.00
11 Chuck Noble DP	10.00	25.00
12 Slater Martin DP RC	30.00	60.00
13 Dolph Schayes DP RC	25.00	60.00
14 Dick Atha DP	10.00	25.00
15 Frank Ramsey DP RC	40.00	100.00
16 Dick McGuire DP RC	20.00	50.00
17 Bob Cousy DP RC	150.00	400.00
18 Larry Foust DP RC	15.00	40.00
19 Tom Heinsohn RC	100.00	250.00
20 Bill Thieben DP	10.00	25.00
21 Don Meineke DP RC	15.00	40.00
22 Tom Marshall	15.00	40.00
23 Dick Garmaker	15.00	40.00
24 Bob Pettit QP RC	60.00	150.00
25 Jim Krebs DP RC	15.00	40.00
26 Gene Shue DP RC	25.00	60.00
27 Ed Macauley DP RC	25.00	60.00
28 Vern Mikkelsen RC	40.00	100.00
29 Willie Naulls RC	25.00	60.00
30 Walter Dukes DP RC	15.00	40.00
31 Dave Piontek DP	10.00	25.00
32 Johnny Red Kerr RC	50.00	120.00
33 Larry Costello DP RC	25.00	60.00
34 Woody Sauldsberry DP RC	15.00	40.00
35 Ray Felix RC	20.00	50.00
36 Ernie Beck	15.00	40.00
37 Cliff Hagan RC	60.00	150.00
38 Guy Sparrow DP	10.00	25.00
39 Jim Loscutoff RC	40.00	100.00
40 Arnie Risen DP	50.00	120.00
41 Joe Graboski	15.00	40.00
42 M.Stokes DP UER RC	60.00	150.00
43 Rod Hundley DP RC	40.00	100.00
44 Tom Gola DP RC	40.00	100.00
45 Med Park RC	20.00	50.00
46 Mel Hutchins DP	10.00	25.00
47 Larry Friend DP	12.00	30.00
48 Lennie Rosenbluth DP RC	40.00	100.00
49 Walt Davis	15.00	40.00
50 Richie Regan RC	15.00	40.00
51 Frank Selvy DP RC	25.00	60.00
52 Art Spoelstra DP	10.00	25.00
53 Bob Hopkins RC	15.00	40.00
54 Earl Lloyd RC	30.00	80.00
55 Phil Jordan DP	10.00	25.00
56 Bob Houbregs DP RC	15.00	40.00
57 Lou Tsioropoulos DP	10.00	25.00
58 Ed Conlin RC	15.00	40.00
59 Al Bianchi RC	30.00	80.00
60 George Dempsey RC	15.00	40.00
61 Chuck Share	15.00	40.00
62 Harry Gallatin DP RC	20.00	50.00
63 Bob Harrison	15.00	40.00
64 Bob Burrow DP	10.00	25.00
65 Win Wilfong DP	10.00	25.00
66 Jack McMahon DP RC	15.00	40.00
67 Jack George	15.00	40.00
68 Charlie Tyra DP	10.00	25.00
69 Ron Sobie	15.00	40.00
70 Jack Coleman	15.00	40.00
71 Jack Twyman DP RC	50.00	120.00
72 Paul Seymour RC	15.00	40.00
73 Jim Paxson DP RC	20.00	50.00
74 Bob Leonard RC	20.00	50.00
75 Andy Phillip	25.00	60.00
76 Joe Holup	15.00	40.00
77 Bill Russell RC	1,000.00	3,000.00
78 Clyde Lovellette DP RC	40.00	100.00
79 Ed Fleming DP	10.00	25.00
80 Dick Schnittker RC	40.00	100.00

1968-69 Topps Test

This set was apparently a limited test issue produced by Topps. The cards measure the standard size. The fronts feature a black and white "action" pose of the player, on white card stock. The player's name, team, and height are given below the picture. The horizontally oriented card backs form a composite of Wilt Chamberlain. The set is dated as 1968-69 since Earl Monroe's first season was 1967-68. The set features the first professional cards of Dave Bing, Bill Bradley, Dave DeBusschere, John Havlicek, Earl Monroe, and Willis Reed, among others.

COMPLETE SET (22)	18,000.00	24,000.00
1 Wilt Chamberlain	3,000.00	4,000.00
2 Hal Greer	400.00	800.00
3 Chet Walker	250.00	500.00
4 Bill Russell	3,000.00	4,000.00
5 John Havlicek UER	1,600.00	2,200.00
6 Cazzie Russell	300.00	600.00
7 Willis Reed	500.00	850.00
8 Bill Bradley	500.00	850.00
9 Odie Smith	200.00	450.00
10 Dave Bing	500.00	850.00
11 Dave DeBusschere	500.00	850.00
12 Earl Monroe	500.00	850.00
13 Nate Thurmond	400.00	800.00
14 Jim King	200.00	450.00
15 Len Wilkens	500.00	900.00
16 Bill Bridges	250.00	500.00
17 Zelmo Beaty	300.00	600.00
18 Elgin Baylor	1,400.00	2,000.00
19 Jerry West	2,400.00	3,000.00
20 Jerry Sloan	600.00	900.00
21 Jerry Lucas	500.00	850.00
22 Oscar Robertson	1,500.00	2,000.00

1969-70 Topps

The 1969-70 Topps set of 99 cards was Topps' first major basketball issue since 1957. Cards were issued in 10-cent packs (10 cards per pack, 24 packs per box) and measure 2 1/2" by 4 11/16". The set features the first card of Lew Alcindor (later Kareem Abdul-Jabbar). Other notable Rookie Cards in the set are Dave Bing, Bill Bradley, Billy Cunningham, Dave DeBusschere, Walt Frazier, John Havlicek, Connie Hawkins, Elvin Hayes, Jerry Lucas, Earl Monroe, Don Nelson, Willis Reed, Nate Thurmond and Wes Unseld. The set was printed on a sheet of 99 cards (nine rows of eleven across) with the checklist card occupying the lower right corner of the sheet. As a result, the checklist is prone to wear and very difficult to obtain in Near Mint or better condition.

COMPLETE SET (99)	1,000.00	1,800.00
CONDITION SENSITIVE SET		
CARDS PRICED IN NM CONDITION		
1 Wilt Chamberlain	50.00	120.00
2 Gail Goodrich RC	15.00	40.00
3 Cazzie Russell RC	8.00	20.00
4 Darrall Imhoff RC	2.50	6.00
5 Bailey Howell	3.00	8.00
6 Lucius Allen RC	5.00	12.00
7 Tom Boerwinkle RC	3.00	8.00
8 Jimmy Walker RC	3.00	8.00
9 John Block RC	2.50	6.00
10 Nate Thurmond RC	12.00	30.00
11 Gary Gregor	1.50	4.00
12 Gus Johnson RC	6.00	15.00
13 Luther Rackley	1.50	4.00
14 Jon McGlocklin RC	12.00	30.00
15 Connie Hawkins RC	15.00	40.00
16 Johnny Egan	1.50	4.00
17 Jim Washington	1.50	4.00
18 Dick Barnett RC	3.00	8.00
19 Tom Meschery	3.00	8.00
20 John Havlicek RC	30.00	80.00
21 Eddie Miles	1.50	4.00
22 Walt Wesley	2.50	6.00
23 Rick Adelman RC	5.00	12.00
24 Al Attles	3.00	8.00
25 Lew Alcindor RC	125.00	300.00
26 Jack Marin RC	3.00	8.00
27 Walt Hazzard RC	4.00	10.00
28 Connie Dierking	1.50	4.00
29 Keith Erickson RC	4.00	10.00
30 Bob Rule RC	4.00	10.00
31 Dick Van Arsdale RC	4.00	10.00
32 Archie Clark RC	4.00	10.00
33 Terry Dischinger RC	1.50	4.00
34 Henry Finkel RC	1.50	4.00
35 Elgin Baylor	10.00	25.00
36 Ron Williams	1.50	4.00
37 Loy Petersen	1.50	4.00
38 Guy Rodgers	3.00	8.00
39 Toby Kimball	1.50	4.00
40 Billy Cunningham RC	10.00	25.00
41 Joe Caldwell RC	3.00	8.00
42 Leroy Ellis RC	2.50	6.00
43 Bill Bradley RC	15.00	40.00
44 Len Wilkens UER	10.00	25.00
45 Jerry Lucas RC	10.00	25.00
46 Neal Walk RC	2.50	6.00
47 Emmette Bryant RC	2.50	6.00
48 Bob Kauffman RC	1.50	4.00
49 Mel Counts RC	2.50	6.00
50 Oscar Robertson	15.00	40.00
51 Jim Barnett RC	3.00	8.00
52 Don Smith	1.50	4.00
53 Jim Davis	1.50	4.00
54 Wally Jones RC	2.50	6.00
55 Dave Bing RC	12.00	30.00
56 Wes Unseld RC	12.00	30.00
57 Joe Ellis	1.50	4.00
58 John Tresvant	1.50	4.00
59 Larry Siegfried RC	2.50	6.00
60 Willis Reed RC	15.00	40.00
61 Paul Silas RC	6.00	15.00
62 Bob Weiss RC	3.00	8.00
63 Willie McCarter	1.50	4.00
64 Don Kojis RC	1.50	4.00
65 Lou Hudson RC	8.00	20.00
66 Jim King	1.50	4.00
67 Luke Jackson RC	2.50	6.00
68 Len Chappell RC	1.50	4.00
69 Ray Scott	1.50	4.00
70 Jeff Mullins RC	4.00	10.00
71 Howie Komives	1.50	4.00
72 Tom Sanders RC	5.00	12.00
73 Dick Snyder	1.50	4.00
74 Dave Stallworth RC	2.50	6.00
75 Elvin Hayes RC	15.00	40.00
76 Art Harris	1.50	4.00
77 Don Ohl	2.50	6.00
78 Bob Love RC	12.00	30.00
79 Tom Van Arsdale RC	5.00	12.00
80 Earl Monroe RC	12.00	30.00
81 Greg Smith	1.50	4.00
82 Don Nelson RC	12.00	30.00
83 Happy Hairston RC	3.00	8.00
84 Hal Greer	5.00	12.00
85 Dave DeBusschere RC	12.00	30.00
86 Bill Bridges RC	3.00	8.00
87 Herm Gilliam RC	2.50	6.00
88 Jim Fox	1.50	4.00
89 Bob Boozer	2.50	6.00
90 Jerry West	20.00	50.00
91 Chet Walker RC	6.00	15.00
92 Flynn Robinson RC	3.00	8.00
93 Clyde Lee	1.50	4.00
94 Kevin Loughery RC	5.00	12.00
95 Walt Bellamy	4.00	10.00

96 Art Williams 1.50 4.00
97 Adrian Smith RC 2.50 6.00
98 Walt Frazier RC 20.00 50.00
99 Checklist 1-99 50.00 120.00

1969-70 Topps Rulers

The 1969-70 Topps basketball cartoon poster inserts are clever color cartoon drawings of NBA players, with "ruler" markings on the left edge of the insert. These paper-thin posters measure approximately 2 1/2" by 9 7/8". The player's height is indicated in an arrow pointing towards the ruler, and the top of the player's head corresponds to this line on the ruler. The inserts are numbered and contain the player's name and team in an oval near the bottom of the insert. As might be expected, these inserts make the players look both taller and thinner than they actually are. Insert number 5 was never issued; it was intended to be Bill Russell. The inserts came with gum packs (one per pack) of Topps regular issue basketball cards of that year.

COMPLETE SET (23) 200.00 400.00
1 Walt Bellamy 3.00 8.00
2 Jerry West 20.00 50.00
3 Bailey Howell 3.00 8.00
4 Elvin Hayes 8.00 20.00
6 Bob Rule 5.00 12.00
7 Gail Goodrich 5.00 12.00
8 Jeff Mullins 4.00 10.00
9 John Havlicek 15.00 40.00
10 Lew Alcindor 40.00 100.00
11 Wilt Chamberlain 30.00 80.00
12 Nate Thurmond 6.00 15.00
13 Hal Greer 6.00 15.00
14 Lou Hudson 3.00 8.00
15 Jerry Lucas 6.00 15.00
16 Dave Bing 6.00 15.00
17 Walt Frazier 8.00 20.00
18 Gus Johnson 3.00 8.00
19 Willis Reed 8.00 20.00
20 Earl Monroe 8.00 20.00
21 Billy Cunningham 6.00 15.00
22 Wes Unseld 5.00 12.00
23 Bob Boozer 3.00 8.00
24 Oscar Robertson 12.00 30.00

1970-71 Topps

The 1970-71 Topps basketball card set of 175 color cards continued the larger-size (2 1/2" by 4 11/16") format established the previous year. Cards were issued in 10-cent wax packs with 10 cards per pack and 24 packs per box. Cards numbered 106 to 115 contain the previous season's NBA first and second team All-Star selections. The first six cards in the set (1-6) feature the statistical league leaders from the previous season. The last eight cards in the set (168-175) summarize the results of the previous season's NBA championship playoff series won by the Knicks over the Lakers. The key Rookie Cards in this set are Pete Maravich, Calvin Murphy and Pat Riley. There are 22 short-printed cards in the first series which are marked SP in the checklist below.

COMPLETE SET (175) 700.00 1,200.00
1 Alcind/West/Hayes LL ! 12.00 30.00
2 West/Alcin/Hayes LL SP 15.00 40.00
3 Green/Imhoff/Hudson LL 2.00 5.00
4 Rob/Walker/Mull LL SP ! 5.00 10.00
5 Hayes/Uns/Alcindor LL 12.00 30.00
6 Wilkens/Fraz/Hask LL SP 6.00 12.00
7 Bill Bradley 10.00 25.00
8 Ron Williams 1.00 2.50
9 Otto Moore 1.00 2.50
10 John Havlicek SP ! 25.00 60.00
11 George Wilson RC 1.00 2.50
12 John Trapp 1.00 2.50
13 Pat Riley RC 15.00 40.00
14 Jim Washington 1.00 2.50
15 Bob Rule 1.50 4.00
16 Bob Weiss 1.50 4.00
17 Neil Johnson 1.00 2.50
18 Walt Bellamy 2.50 6.00
19 McCoy McLemore 1.00 2.50
20 Earl Monroe 6.00 15.00
21 Wally Anderzunas 1.00 2.50
22 Guy Rodgers 1.50 4.00
23 Rick Roberson 1.00 2.50
24 Checklist 1-110 15.00 40.00
25 Jimmy Walker 1.50 4.00
26 Mike Riordan RC 2.50 6.00
27 Henry Finkel 1.00 2.50
28 Joe Ellis 1.00 2.50
29 Mike Davis 1.00 2.50
30 Lou Hudson 2.50 6.00
31 Lucius Allen SP 4.00 10.00
32 Toby Kimball SP 4.00 10.00
33 Luke Jackson SP 4.00 10.00
34 Johnny Egan 3.00 8.00
35 Leroy Ellis SP 4.00 10.00
36 Jack Marin SP 4.00 10.00
37 Joe Caldwell SP 4.00 10.00
38 Keith Erickson 2.50 6.00
39 Don Smith 1.00 2.50
40 Flynn Robinson 1.50 4.00
41 Bob Boozer 1.00 2.50
42 Howie Komives 1.00 2.50
43 Dick Barnett 1.50 4.00
44 Stu Lantz RC 1.50 4.00
45 Dick Van Arsdale 2.50 6.00
46 Jerry Lucas 4.00 10.00
47 Don Chaney RC 5.00 12.00
48 Ray Scott 1.00 2.50
49 Dick Cunningham SP 4.00 10.00
50 Wilt Chamberlain 20.00 50.00
51 Kevin Loughery 1.50 4.00
52 Stan McKenzie 1.00 2.50
53 Fred Foster 1.00 2.50
54 Jim Davis 1.00 2.50
55 Walt Wesley 1.00 2.50
56 Bill Hewitt 1.00 2.50
57 Darrall Imhoff 1.00 2.50
58 John Block 1.00 2.50
59 Al Attles SP 5.00 12.00
60 Chet Walker 2.50 6.00
61 Luther Rackley 1.00 2.50
62 Jerry Chambers SP RC 4.00 10.00
63 Bob Dandridge RC 3.00 8.00
64 Dick Snyder 1.00 2.50
65 Elgin Baylor 12.00 30.00
66 Connie Dierking 1.00 2.50
67 Steve Kuberski RC 1.00 2.50
68 Tom Boerwinkle 1.00 2.50
69 Paul Silas 2.50 6.00
70 Elvin Hayes 12.00 30.00
71 Bill Bridges 1.50 4.00
72 Wes Unseld 6.00 15.00
73 Herm Gilliam 1.00 2.50
74 Bobby Smith SP RC 4.00 10.00
75 Lew Alcindor 20.00 50.00
76 Jeff Mullins 1.50 4.00
77 Happy Hairston 1.50 4.00
78 Dave Stallworth SP 3.00 8.00
79 Fred Hetzel 1.00 2.50
80 Len Wilkens SP 10.00 25.00
81 Johnny Green RC 2.50 6.00
82 Erwin Mueller 1.00 2.50
83 Wally Jones 1.50 4.00
84 Bob Love 3.00 8.00
85 Dick Garrett RC 1.00 2.50
86 Don Nelson SP 10.00 25.00
87 Neal Walk SP 3.00 8.00
88 Larry Siegfried 1.00 2.50
89 Gary Gregor 1.00 2.50
90 Nate Thurmond 3.00 8.00
91 John Warren 1.00 2.50
92 Gus Johnson 2.50 6.00
93 Gail Goodrich 6.00 15.00
94 Dorie Murrey 1.00 2.50
95 Cazzie Russell SP 5.00 12.00
96 Terry Dischinger 1.00 2.50
97 Norm Van Lier SP RC 8.00 20.00
98 Jim Fox 1.00 2.50
99 Tom Meschery 1.00 2.50
100 Oscar Robertson 12.00 30.00
101A Checklist 111-175 12.00 30.00
101B Checklist 111-175 12.00 30.00
102 Rich Johnson 1.00 2.50
103 Mel Counts 1.50 4.00
104 Bill Hosket SP RC 3.00 8.00
105 Archie Clark 1.50 4.00
106 Walt Frazier AS 4.00 10.00
107 Jerry West AS 10.00 25.00
108 Billy Cunningham AS SP 5.00 12.00
109 Connie Hawkins AS 3.00 8.00
110 Willis Reed AS 3.00 8.00
111 Nate Thurmond AS 2.00 5.00
112 John Havlicek AS 12.00 30.00
113 Elgin Baylor AS 8.00 20.00
114 Oscar Robertson AS 8.00 20.00
115 Lou Hudson AS 1.25 3.00
116 Emmette Bryant 1.25 3.00
117 Greg Howard 1.25 3.00
118 Rick Adelman 2.50 6.00
119 Barry Clemens 1.25 3.00
120 Walt Frazier 12.00 30.00
121 Jim Barnes RC 1.25 3.00
122 Bernie Williams 1.25 3.00
123 Pete Maravich RC 150.00 400.00
124 Matt Guokas RC 3.00 8.00
125 Dave Bing 6.00 15.00
126 John Tresvant 1.25 3.00
127 Shaler Halimon 1.25 3.00
128 Don Ohl 1.25 3.00
129 Fred Carter RC 2.50 6.00
130 Connie Hawkins 8.00 20.00
131 Jim King 1.25 3.00
132 Ed Manning RC 2.50 6.00
133 Adrian Smith 1.25 3.00
134 Walt Hazzard 2.50 6.00
135 Dave DeBusschere 6.00 15.00
136 Don Kojis 1.25 3.00
137 Calvin Murphy RC 15.00 40.00
138 Nate Bowman 1.25 3.00
139 Jon McGlocklin 2.00 5.00
140 Billy Cunningham 8.00 20.00
141 Willie McCarter 1.25 3.00
142 Jim Barnett 1.25 3.00
143 Jo Jo White RC 8.00 20.00
144 Clyde Lee 1.25 3.00
145 Tom Van Arsdale 2.50 6.00
146 Len Chappell 1.25 3.00
147 Lee Winfield 1.25 3.00
148 Jerry Sloan RC 10.00 25.00
149 Art Harris 1.25 3.00
150 Willis Reed 8.00 20.00
151 Art Williams 1.25 3.00
152 Don May 1.25 3.00
153 Loy Petersen 1.25 3.00
154 Dave Gambee 1.25 3.00
155 Hal Greer 2.50 6.00
156 Dave Newmark 1.25 3.00
157 Jimmy Collins 1.25 3.00
158 Bill Turner 1.25 3.00
159 Eddie Miles 1.25 3.00
160 Jerry West 20.00 50.00
161 Bob Quick 1.25 3.00
162 Fred Crawford 1.25 3.00
163 Tom Sanders 2.50 6.00
164 Dale Schlueter 1.25 3.00
165 Clem Haskins RC 4.00 10.00
166 Greg Smith 1.25 3.00
167 Rod Thorn RC 3.00 8.00
168 Willis Reed PO 4.00 10.00
169 Dick Garnett PO 2.00 5.00
170 Dave DeBusschere PO 5.00 12.00
171 Jerry West PO 8.00 20.00
172 Bill Bradley PO 8.00 20.00
173 Wilt Chamberlain PO 8.00 20.00
174 Walt Frazier PO 5.00 12.00
175 Knicks Celebrate 8.00 20.00

1970-71 Topps Poster

This set of 24 large (8" by 10") thin paper posters was issued as an insert in second series wax packs along with the 1970-71 Topps regular basketball cards. The posters are in full color and contain the player's name and his team near the upper left of the poster. The number appears in the border at the lower right, and a Topps copyright date and a 1968 National Basketball Player's Association copyright date appears in the border at the left.

COMPLETE SET (24) 100.00 250.00
1 Walt Frazier 5.00 12.00
2 Joe Caldwell 3.00 8.00
3 Willis Reed 5.00 12.00
4 Elvin Hayes 8.00 20.00
5 Jeff Mullins 3.00 8.00
6 Oscar Robertson 12.00 30.00
7 Dave Bing 4.00 10.00
8 Jerry Sloan 4.00 10.00
9 Leroy Ellis 4.00 10.00
10 Hal Greer 3.00 8.00
11 Emmette Bryant 3.00 8.00
12 Bob Rule 5.00 12.00
13 Lew Alcindor 20.00 50.00
14 Chet Walker 4.00 10.00
15 Jerry West 15.00 40.00
16 Billy Cunningham 5.00 12.00
17 Wilt Chamberlain 15.00 40.00
18 John Havlicek 12.00 30.00
19 Lou Hudson 3.00 8.00
20 Earl Monroe 6.00 15.00
21 Wes Unseld 5.00 12.00
22 Connie Hawkins 5.00 12.00
23 Tom Van Arsdale 4.00 10.00
24 Len Chappell 4.00 10.00

1971-72 Topps

The 1971-72 Topps basketball set of 233 witnessed a return to the standard-sized card, i.e., 2 1/2" by 3 1/2". Cards were issued in 10-card, 10 cent packs with 24 packs per box. National Basketball Association players are depicted on cards 1 to 144 and American Basketball Association players are depicted on cards 145 to 233. The set was produced on two sheets. The second production sheet contained the ABA players (145-233) as well as 31 double-printed cards (NBA players) from the first sheet. These DP's are indicated in the checklist below. Subsets include NBA Playoffs (133-137), NBA Statistical Leaders (138-143) and ABA Statistical Leaders (146-151). The key Rookie Cards in this set are Nate Archibald, Rick Barry, Larry Brown, Dave Cowens, Spencer Haywood, Dan Issel, Bob Lanier, Rudy Tomjanovich and Doug Moe.

COMPLETE SET (233) 500.00 750.00
CARDS PRICED IN NM CONDITION
1 Oscar Robertson ! 8.00 20.00
2 Bill Bradley 6.00 15.00
3 Jim Fox .60 1.50
4 John Johnson RC .75 2.00
5 Luke Jackson .75 2.00
6 Don May DP .60 1.50
7 Kevin Loughery .75 2.00
8 Terry Dischinger .60 1.50
9 Neal Walk .75 2.00
10 Elgin Baylor 6.00 15.00
11 Rick Adelman .75 2.00
12 Clyde Lee .60 1.50
13 Jerry Chambers .60 1.50
14 Fred Carter .75 2.00
15 Tom Boerwinkle DP .60 1.50
16 John Block .60 1.50
17 Dick Barnett .75 2.00
18 Henry Finkel .60 1.50
19 Norm Van Lier 1.50 4.00
20 Spencer Haywood RC 8.00 20.00
21 George Johnson .60 1.50
22 Bobby Lewis .60 1.50
23 Bill Hewitt .60 1.50
24 Walt Hazzard DP 1.50 4.00
25 Happy Hairston .75 2.00
26 George Wilson .60 1.50
27 Lucius Allen .75 2.00
28 Jim Washington .60 1.50
29 Nate Archibald RC 8.00 20.00
30 Willis Reed 3.00 8.00
31 Erwin Mueller .60 1.50
32 Art Harris .60 1.50
33 Pete Cross .75 2.00
34 Geoff Petrie RC 2.00 5.00
35 John Havlicek 6.00 15.00
36 Larry Siegfried .60 1.50
37 John Tresvant DP .60 1.50
38 Ron Williams .60 1.50
39 Lamar Green DP .60 1.50
40 Bob Rule DP .75 2.00
41 Jim McMillian RC .75 2.00
42 Wally Jones .75 2.00
43 Bob Boozer .60 1.50
44 Eddie Miles .60 1.50
45 Bob Love DP 2.00 5.00
46 Claude English .60 1.50
47 Dave Cowens RC 10.00 25.00
48 Emmette Bryant .60 1.50
49 Dave Stallworth .75 2.00
50 Jerry West 8.00 20.00
51 Joe Ellis .60 1.50
52 Walt Wesley DP .60 1.50
53 Howie Komives .60 1.50
54 Paul Silas 1.50 4.00
55 Pete Maravich DP 10.00 25.00
56 Gary Gregor .60 1.50
57 Sam Lacey RC 1.50 4.00
58 Calvin Murphy DP 2.50 6.00
59 Bob Dandridge .75 2.00
60 Hal Greer 1.50 4.00
61 Keith Erickson 1.50 4.00
62 Joe Cooke .60 1.50
63 Bob Lanier RC 12.00 30.00
64 Don Kojis .60 1.50
65 Walt Frazier 5.00 12.00
66 Chet Walker DP 1.50 4.00
67 Dick Garrett .60 1.50
68 John Trapp .75 2.00
69 Jo Jo White 3.00 8.00
70 Wilt Chamberlain 15.00 40.00
71 Dave Sorenson .60 1.50
72 Jim King .60 1.50
73 Cazzie Russell 1.50 4.00
74 Jon McGlocklin .75 2.00
75 Tom Van Arsdale .75 2.00
76 Dale Schlueter .60 1.50
77 Gus Johnson DP 1.50 4.00
78 Dave Bing 3.00 8.00
79 Billy Cunningham 3.00 8.00
80 Len Wilkens 3.00 8.00
81 Jerry Lucas DP 2.00 5.00
82 Don Chaney 1.50 4.00
83 McCoy McLemore .60 1.50
84 Bob Kauffman DP .60 1.50
85 Dick Van Arsdale 1.50 4.00
86 Johnny Green .75 2.00
87 Jerry Sloan 2.00 5.00
88 Luther Rackley DP .60 1.50
89 Shaler Halimon .60 1.50
90 Jimmy Walker .75 2.00
91 Rudy Tomjanovich RC 6.00 15.00
92 Levi Fontaine .60 1.50
93 Bobby Smith .75 2.00
94 Bob Arnzen .60 1.50
95 Wes Unseld DP 3.00 8.00
96 Clem Haskins DP 1.50 4.00
97 Jim Davis .60 1.50
98 Steve Kuberski .60 1.50
99 Mike Davis DP .60 1.50
100 Lew Alcindor 12.00 30.00
101 Willie McCarter .60 1.50
102 Charlie Paulk .60 1.50
103 Lee Winfield .60 1.50
104 Jim Barnett .60 1.50
105 Connie Hawkins DP 2.50 6.00
106 Archie Clark DP .75 2.00
107 Dave DeBusschere 2.50 6.00
108 Stu Lantz DP .75 2.00
109 Don Smith .60 1.50
110 Lou Hudson 1.50 4.00
111 Leroy Ellis .60 1.50
112 Jack Marin .75 2.00
113 Matt Guokas .75 2.00
114 Don Nelson 3.00 8.00
115 Jeff Mullins DP .75 2.00
116 Walt Bellamy 2.50 6.00
117 Bob Quick .60 1.50
118 John Warren .60 1.50
119 Barry Clemens .60 1.50
120 Elvin Hayes DP 3.00 8.00
121 Gail Goodrich 3.00 8.00
122 Ed Manning .75 2.00
123 Herm Gilliam DP .60 1.50
124 Dennis Awtrey RC .75 2.00
125 John Hummer DP .60 1.50
126 Mike Riordan .75 2.00
127 Mel Counts .60 1.50
128 Bob Weiss DP .60 1.50
129 Greg Smith DP .60 1.50
130 Earl Monroe 3.00 8.00
131 Nate Thurmond DP 1.50 4.00
132 Bill Bridges DP .75 2.00
133 Lew Alcindor PO 3.00 8.00
134 NBA Playoffs G2 1.50 4.00
135 Bob Dandridge PO 1.50 4.00
136 Oscar Robertson PO 2.50 6.00
137 Oscar Robertson PO 5.00 12.00
138 Alcind/Hayes/Havl LL 5.00 12.00
139 Alcind/Havl/Hayes LL 5.00 12.00
140 Green/Alcind/Wilt LL 4.00 10.00
141 Walker/Oscar/Williams LL 2.00 5.00
142 Wilt/Hayes/Alcind LL 8.00 20.00
143 Van Lier/Oscar/West LL 3.00 8.00
144A NBA Checklist 1-144 6.00 15.00
144B NBA Checklist 1-144 6.00 15.00
145 ABA Checklist 145-233 6.00 15.00
146 Issel/Brisker/Scott LL 2.50 6.00
147 Issel/Barry/Brisker LL 4.00 10.00
148 ABA 2pt FG Pct Leaders 1.50 4.00
149 Barry/Carrier/Keller LL 3.00 8.00
150 ABA Rebound Leaders 1.50 4.00

151 ABA Assist Leaders 1.50 4.00
152 Larry Brown RC 6.00 15.00
153 Bob Bedell .75 2.00
154 Merv Jackson .75 2.00
155 Joe Caldwell 1.00 2.50
156 Billy Paultz RC 2.00 5.00
157 Les Hunter 1.00 2.50
158 Charlie Williams .75 2.00
159 Stew Johnson .75 2.00
160 Mack Calvin RC 2.00 5.00
161 Don Sidle .75 2.00
162 Mike Barrett .75 2.00
163 Tom Workman .75 2.00
164 Joe Hamilton 1.00 2.50
165 Zelmo Beaty RC 2.50 6.00
166 Dan Hester .75 2.00
167 Bob Verga .75 2.00
168 Wilbert Jones .75 2.00
169 Skeeter Swift .75 2.00
170 Rick Barry RC 15.00 40.00
171 Billy Keller RC 1.50 4.00
172 Ron Franz .75 2.00
173 Roland Taylor RC 1.00 2.50
174 Julian Hammond .75 2.00
175 Steve Jones RC 2.50 6.00
176 Gerald Govan 1.00 2.50
177 Darrell Carrier RC 1.00 2.50
178 Ron Boone RC 2.50 6.00
179 George Peeples .75 2.00
180 John Brisker 1.00 2.50
181 Doug Moe RC 2.50 6.00
182 Ollie Taylor .75 2.00
183 Bob Netolicky RC 1.00 2.50
184 Sam Robinson .75 2.00
185 James Jones 1.00 2.50
186 Julius Keye 1.00 2.50
187 Wayne Hightower .75 2.00
188 Warren Armstrong RC 1.00 2.50
189 Mike Lewis .75 2.00
190 Charlie Scott RC 4.00 10.00
191 Jim Ard .75 2.00
192 George Lehmann .75 2.00
193 Ira Harge .75 2.00
194 Willie Wise RC 2.00 5.00
195 Mel Daniels RC 4.00 10.00
196 Larry Cannon .75 2.00
197 Jim Eakins 1.00 2.50
198 Rich Jones 1.00 2.50
199 Bill Melchionni RC 1.50 4.00
200 Dan Issel RC 8.00 20.00
201 George Stone .75 2.00
202 George Thompson .75 2.00
203 Craig Raymond .75 2.00
204 Freddie Lewis RC 1.00 2.50
205 George Carter 1.00 2.50
206 Lonnie Wright .75 2.00
207 Cincy Powell 1.00 2.50
208 Larry Miller 1.00 2.50
209 Sonny Dove .75 2.00
210 Byron Beck RC 1.00 2.50
211 John Beasley .75 2.00
212 Lee Davis .75 2.00
213 Rick Mount RC 2.50 6.00
214 Walt Simon .75 2.00
215 Glen Combs .75 2.00
216 Neil Johnson .75 2.00
217 Manny Leaks .75 2.00
218 Chuck Williams 1.00 2.50
219 Warren Davis .75 2.00
220 Donnie Freeman RC 1.00 2.50
221 Randy Mahaffey .75 2.00
222 John Barnhill .75 2.00
223 Al Cueto .75 2.00
224 Louie Dampier RC 4.00 10.00
225 Roger Brown RC 2.50 6.00
226 Joe DePre .75 2.00
227 Ray Scott .75 2.00
228 Arvesta Kelly .75 2.00
229 Vann Williford .75 2.00
230 Larry Jones 1.00 2.50
231 Gene Moore .75 2.00
232 Ralph Simpson RC 1.50 4.00
233 Red Robbins RC 2.00 5.00

1971-72 Topps Trios

The 1971-72 Topps Trios (insert sticker panels) set contains 26 standard card-sized panels each with three player stickers. There are also three logo sticker panels. Each player sticker has a black border surrounding a color photo with a yellow player's name, and white team name. The NBA players are numbered by the number indicated; stickers of ABA players have the suffix "A" added to their numbers in order to differentiate them. The stickers were printed on a sheet of 77 (7 rows and 11 columns). There are a number of oddities with respect to the distribution on the sheet and hence also to the availability of respective cards in the set. The most difficult cards in the set (34, 37, 40, 43, 1A, 4A, 7A, 10A, 13A, 16A, 19A, 23A, and 24A) appeared on the sheet only twice; they are designated as short prints (SP) in the checklist below. Cards 1, 4, 7, 10, 13, 16, 19, 22, 25, 28, and 31 were all printed three times on the sheet and are hence 50 percent more available than the SP's. The rest of the sheet is comprised of 4 copies of card 22A and 14 copies of card 46; they are referenced as DP and QP respectively. The logo stickers are hard to find in good shape.

COMPLETE SET (26) 200.00 400.00
1 Hudson/Rule/Murphy 4.00 10.00
1A Jones/Wise/Issel SP 8.00 20.00
4 Wesley/White/Dand 3.00 8.00
4A Calvin/Brown/Verga SP 4.00 10.00
7 Thurm/Monroe/Hay 5.00 10.00
7A Melch/Daniels/Freem SP 4.00 10.00
10 DeBuss/Lanier/Van Ars 6.00 15.00
10A Cald/Dampier/Lewis SP 4.00 10.00
13 Greer/Green/Hayes 5.00 12.00
13A Barry/Jones/Keye SP 10.00 25.00
16 Walker/May/Clark 1.50 4.00
16A Cannon/Beaty/Scott SP 3.00 8.00
19 Hairston/Ellis/Sloan 4.00 10.00
19A Jones/Carter/Brisk SP 4.00 10.00
22 Maravich/Kauf/Hav 30.00 80.00
22A ABA Team DP 1.50 4.00
23A ABA Team SP 15.00 40.00
24A ABA Team SP 15.00 40.00
25 Frazier/Van Arsd/Bing 6.00 15.00
28 Love/Williams/Cowens 6.00 15.00
31 West/Reed/Walker 25.00 60.00
34 Rober/Unsel/Smith SP 15.00 40.00
37 Hawk/Mullins/Alcin 30.00 80.00
40 Cunn/Bellamy/Petrie SP 6.00 15.00
43 Cham/Johns/Van L SP 25.00 60.00
46 NBA Team QP 1.25 3.00

1972-73 Topps

The 1972-73 Topps set of 264 standard size cards contains NBA players (1-176) and ABA players (177-264). Cards were issued in 10-card packs with 24 packs per box. All-Star selections are depicted for the NBA on cards 161-170 and for the ABA on cards 249-258. Subsets include NBA Playoffs (154-159), NBA Statistical Leaders (171-176), ABA Playoffs (241-247) and ABA Statistical Leaders (259-264). The key Rookie Card is Julius Erving. Other Rookie Cards include Artis Gilmore and Phil Jackson.

COMPLETE SET (264) 350.00 700.00
CARDS PRICED IN NM CONDITION
1 Wilt Chamberlain ! 25.00 60.00
2 Stan Love .40 1.00
3 Geoff Petrie .60 1.50
4 Curtis Perry RC .40 1.00
5 Pete Maravich 15.00 40.00
6 Gus Johnson 1.25 3.00
7 Dave Cowens 6.00 15.00
8 Randy Smith RC 1.50 4.00
9 Matt Guokas .60 1.50
10 Spencer Haywood 1.50 4.00
11 Jerry Sloan 1.25 3.00
12 Dave Sorenson .40 1.00
13 Howie Komives .40 1.00
14 Joe Ellis .40 1.00
15 Jerry Lucas 2.00 5.00
16 Stu Lantz .60 1.50
17 Bill Bridges .60 1.50
18 Leroy Ellis .40 1.00
19 Art Williams .40 1.00
20 Sidney Wicks RC 3.00 8.00
21 Wes Unseld 2.50 6.00
22 Jim Washington .40 1.00
23 Fred Hilton .40 1.00
24 Curtis Rowe RC .60 1.50
25 Oscar Robertson 10.00 25.00
26 Larry Steele RC .60 1.50
27 Charlie Davis .40 1.00
28 Nate Thurmond 2.00 5.00
29 Fred Carter .60 1.50
30 Connie Hawkins 3.00 8.00
31 Calvin Murphy 2.00 5.00
32 Phil Jackson RC 15.00 40.00
33 Lee Winfield .40 1.00
34 Jim Fox .40 1.00
35 Dave Bing 2.50 6.00
36 Gary Gregor .40 1.00
37 Mike Riordan .60 1.50
38 George Trapp .40 1.00
39 Mike Davis .40 1.00
40 Bob Rule .60 1.50
41 John Block .40 1.00
42 Bob Dandridge .60 1.50
43 John Johnson .60 1.50
44 Rick Barry 8.00 20.00
45 Jo Jo White 1.50 4.00
46 Cliff Meely .40 1.00
47 Charlie Scott 1.25 3.00
48 Johnny Green .60 1.50
49 Pete Cross .40 1.00
50 Gail Goodrich 2.50 6.00
51 Jim Davis .40 1.00
52 Dick Barnett .60 1.50
53 Bob Christian .40 1.00
54 Jon McGlocklin .60 1.50
55 Paul Silas 1.25 3.00
56 Hal Greer 1.50 4.00
57 Barry Clemens .40 1.00
58 Nick Jones .40 1.00
59 Cornell Warner .40 1.00
60 Walt Frazier 4.00 10.00
61 Dorie Murrey .40 1.00
62 Dick Cunningham .40 1.00
63 Sam Lacey .60 1.50
64 John Warren .40 1.00
65 Tom Boerwinkle .40 1.00
66 Fred Foster .40 1.00
67 Mel Counts .40 1.00
68 Toby Kimball .40 1.00
69 Dale Schlueter .40 1.00
70 Jack Marin .60 1.50
71 Jim Barnett .40 1.00
72 Clem Haskins 1.25 3.00
73 Earl Monroe 2.50 6.00
74 Tom Sanders .60 1.50
75 Jerry West 10.00 25.00
76 Elmore Smith RC .60 1.50
77 Don Adams .40 1.00
78 Wally Jones .60 1.50
79 Tom Van Arsdale .60 1.50
80 Bob Lanier 8.00 20.00
81 Len Wilkens 3.00 8.00
82 Neal Walk .60 1.50
83 Kevin Loughery .60 1.50
84 Stan McKenzie .60 1.50
85 Jeff Mullins .60 1.50
86 Otto Moore .40 1.00
87 John Tresvant .40 1.00
88 Dean Meminger RC .40 1.00
89 Jim McMillian .60 1.50
90 Austin Carr RC 3.00 8.00
91 Clifford Ray RC .60 1.50
92 Don Nelson 1.50 4.00
93 Mahdi Abdul-Rahman .60 1.50
94 Willie Norwood .40 1.00
95 Dick Van Arsdale .60 1.50
96 Don May .40 1.00
97 Walt Bellamy 1.50 4.00
98 Garfield Heard RC 1.50 4.00
99 Dave Wohl .40 1.00
100 Kareem Abdul-Jabbar 12.00 30.00
101 Ron Knight .40 1.00
102 Phil Chenier RC 1.50 4.00
103 Rudy Tomjanovich 3.00 8.00
104 Flynn Robinson .40 1.00
105 Dave DeBusschere 2.50 6.00
106 Dennis Layton .40 1.00
107 Bill Hewitt .40 1.00
108 Dick Garrett .40 1.00
109 Walt Wesley .40 1.00
110 John Havlicek 10.00 25.00
111 Norm Van Lier .60 1.50
112 Cazzie Russell 1.25 3.00
113 Herm Gilliam .40 1.00
114 Greg Smith .40 1.00
115 Nate Archibald 2.50 6.00
116 Don Kojis .40 1.00
117 Rick Adelman .60 1.50
118 Luke Jackson .60 1.50
119 Lamar Green .40 1.00
120 Archie Clark .60 1.50
121 Happy Hairston .60 1.50
122 Bill Bradley 6.00 15.00
123 Ron Williams .40 1.00
124 Jimmy Walker .60 1.50
125 Bob Kauffman .40 1.00
126 Rick Roberson .60 1.50
127 Howard Porter RC .60 1.50
128 Mike Newlin RC .60 1.50
129 Willis Reed 3.00 8.00
130 Lou Hudson 1.25 3.00
131 Don Chaney 1.25 3.00
132 Dave Stallworth .40 1.00
133 Charlie Yelverton .40 1.00
134 Ken Durrett .40 1.00
135 John Brisker .60 1.50
136 Dick Snyder .40 1.00
137 Jim McDaniels .40 1.00
138 Clyde Lee .40 1.00
139 Dennis Awtrey UER .60 1.50
140 Keith Erickson .60 1.50
141 Bob Weiss .60 1.50
142 Butch Beard RC 1.25 3.00
143 Terry Dischinger .40 1.00
144 Pat Riley 8.00 20.00
145 Lucius Allen .60 1.50
146 John Mengelt RC .40 1.00
147 John Hummer .40 1.00
148 Bob Love 2.00 5.00
149 Bobby Smith .60 1.50
150 Elvin Hayes 4.00 10.00
151 Nate Williams .40 1.00
152 Chet Walker 1.25 3.00
153 Steve Kuberski .40 1.00
154 Earl Monroe PO 1.25 3.00
155 NBA Playoffs G2 1.25 3.00
156 NBA Playoffs G3 1.25 3.00
157 NBA Playoffs G4 1.25 3.00
158 Jerry West PO 3.00 8.00
159 Wilt Chamberlain PO 5.00 12.00
160 NBA Checklist 1-176 6.00 15.00
161 John Havlicek AS 5.00 12.00
162 Spencer Haywood AS 1.25 3.00
163 Kareem Abdul-Jabbar AS 10.00 25.00
164 Jerry West AS 8.00 20.00
165 Walt Frazier AS 2.00 5.00
166 Bob Love AS 1.25 3.00
167 Billy Cunningham AS 1.50 4.00
168 Wilt Chamberlain AS 10.00 25.00
169 Nate Archibald AS 2.00 5.00
170 Archie Clark AS 1.25 3.00
171 Jabbar/Havl/Arch LL 6.00 15.00
172 Jabbar/Arch/Havl LL 6.00 15.00
173 Wilt/Jabbar/Bell LL 6.00 15.00
174 Marin/Murphy/Goodr LL 1.25 3.00
175 Wilt/Jabbar/Unseld LL 6.00 15.00
176 Wilkens/West/Arch LL 5.00 12.00
177 Roland Taylor .60 1.50
178 Art Becker .60 1.50
179 Mack Calvin .75 2.00
180 Artis Gilmore RC 12.00 30.00
181 Collis Jones .60 1.50
182 John Roche RC .75 2.00
183 George McGinnis RC 6.00 15.00
184 Johnny Neumann .75 2.00
185 Willie Wise .75 2.00
186 Bernie Williams .60 1.50
187 Byron Beck .75 2.00
188 Larry Miller .75 2.00
189 Cincy Powell .60 1.50
190 Donnie Freeman .75 2.00
191 John Baum .60 1.50
192 Billy Keller .75 2.00
193 Wilbert Jones .60 1.50
194 Glen Combs .60 1.50
195 Julius Erving RC 75.00 200.00
196 Al Smith .60 1.50
197 George Carter .60 1.50
198 Louie Dampier 1.25 3.00
199 Rich Jones .60 1.50
200 Mel Daniels 1.25 3.00
201 Gene Moore .60 1.50
202 Randy Denton .60 1.50
203 Larry Jones .60 1.50
204 Jim Ligon .60 1.50
205 Warren Jabali .75 2.00
206 Joe Caldwell .75 2.00
207 Darrell Carrier .75 2.00
208 Gene Kennedy .60 1.50
209 Ollie Taylor .60 1.50
210 Roger Brown .75 2.00
211 George Lehmann .60 1.50
212 Red Robbins .75 2.00
213 Jim Eakins .75 2.00
214 Willie Long .60 1.50
215 Billy Cunningham 3.00 8.00
216 Steve Jones .75 2.00
217 Les Hunter .60 1.50
218 Billy Paultz .75 2.00
219 Freddie Lewis .75 2.00
220 Zelmo Beaty .75 2.00
221 George Thompson .60 1.50
222 Neil Johnson .60 1.50
223 Dave Robisch RC .75 2.00
224 Walt Simon .60 1.50
225 Bill Melchionni .75 2.00
226 Wendell Ladner RC .75 2.00
227 Joe Hamilton .60 1.50
228 Bob Netolicky .75 2.00
229 James Jones .75 2.00
230 Dan Issel 4.00 10.00
231 Charlie Williams .60 1.50
232 Willie Sojourner .60 1.50
233 Merv Jackson .60 1.50
234 Mike Lewis .60 1.50
235 Ralph Simpson .75 2.00
236 Darnell Hillman .75 2.00
237 Rick Mount 1.25 3.00
238 Gerald Govan .60 1.50
239 Ron Boone .75 2.00
240 Tom Washington .60 1.50
241 ABA Playoffs G1 1.25 3.00
242 Rick Barry PO 2.00 5.00
243 George McGinnis PO 1.50 4.00
244 Rick Barry PO 2.00 5.00
245 Billy Keller PO 1.25 3.00
246 ABA Playoffs G6 1.25 3.00
Tight Defense
247 ABA Champs: Pacers 1.25 3.00
248 ABA Checklist 177-264 6.00 15.00
249 Dan Issel AS 2.50 6.00
250 Rick Barry AS 3.00 8.00
251 Artis Gilmore AS 2.50 6.00
252 Donnie Freeman AS 1.25 3.00
253 Bill Melchionni AS 1.25 3.00
254 Willie Wise AS 1.25 3.00
255 Julius Erving AS 15.00 40.00
256 Zelmo Beaty AS 1.25 3.00
257 Ralph Simpson AS 1.25 3.00
258 Charlie Scott AS 1.25 3.00
259 Scott/Barry/Issel LL 3.00 8.00
260 Gilmore/Wash/Jones LL 1.50 4.00
261 Combs/Damp/Jabali LL 1.25 3.00
262 Barry/Calvin/Jones LL 1.50 4.00
263 Gilmore/Erving/Dan LL 8.00 20.00
264 Melch/Brown/Damp LL! 2.50 6.00

1973-74 Topps

The 1973-74 Topps set of 264 standard-size cards contains NBA players on cards numbered 1 to 176 and ABA players on cards numbered 177 to 264. Cards were issued in 10-card packs with 24 packs per box. All-Star selections (first and second team) for both leagues are noted on the respective player's regular cards. Card backs are printed in red and green on gray card stock. The backs feature year-by-year ABA and NBA statistics. Subsets include NBA Playoffs (62-68), NBA League Leaders (153-158), ABA Playoffs (202-208) and ABA League Leaders (234-239). The only notable Rookie Cards in this set are Chris Ford, Bob McAdoo, and Paul Westphal.

COMPLETE SET (264) 200.00 325.00
CONDITION SENSITIVE SET
CARDS PRICED IN NM CONDITION
1 Nate Archibald ! 4.00 10.00
2 Steve Kuberski .20 .50
3 John Mengelt .20 .50
4 Jim McMillian .40 1.00
5 Nate Thurmond 1.50 4.00
6 Dave Wohl .20 .50
7 John Brisker .20 .50
8 Charlie Davis .20 .50
9 Lamar Green .20 .50
10 Walt Frazier AS2 2.50 6.00
11 Bob Christian .20 .50
12 Cornell Warner .20 .50
13 Calvin Murphy 1.50 4.00
14 Dave Sorenson .20 .50
15 Archie Clark .40 1.00
16 Clifford Ray .40 1.00
17 Terry Driscoll .20 .50
18 Matt Guokas .60 1.50
19 Elmore Smith .40 1.00
20 John Havlicek AS1 6.00 15.00
21 Pat Riley 3.00 8.00
22 George Trapp .20 .50
23 Ron Williams .20 .50

24 Jim Fox .20 .50
25 Dick Van Arsdale .40 1.00
26 John Trevsant .20 .50
27 Rick Adelman .40 1.00
28 Eddie Mast .20 .50
29 Jim Cleamons .40 1.00
30 Dave DeBusschere AS2 2.00 5.00
31 Norm Van Lier .40 1.00
32 Stan McKenzie .20 .50
33 Bob Dandridge .40 1.00
34 Leroy Ellis .40 1.00
35 Mike Riordan .40 1.00
36 Fred Hilton .20 .50
37 Toby Kimball .20 .50
38 Jim Price .20 .50
39 Willie Norwood .20 .50
40 Dave Cowens AS2 5.00 10.00
41 Cazzie Russell .40 1.00
42 Lee Winfield .20 .50
43 Connie Hawkins 2.00 5.00
44 Mike Newlin .40 1.00
45 Chet Walker .40 1.00
46 Walt Bellamy 1.50 4.00
47 John Johnson .40 1.00
48 Henry Bibby RC 2.50 6.00
49 Bobby Smith .40 1.00
50 Kareem Abdul-Jabbar AS1 10.00 25.00
51 Mike Price .20 .50
52 John Hummer .20 .50
53 Kevin Porter RC 2.00 5.00
54 Nate Williams .20 .50
55 Gail Goodrich 1.50 4.00
56 Fred Foster .20 .50
57 Don Chaney .40 1.00
58 Bud Stallworth .20 .50
59 Clem Haskins .60 1.50
60 Bob Love AS2 1.25 3.00
61 Jimmy Walker .40 1.00
62 NBA Eastern Semis .40 1.00
63 NBA Eastern Semis .40 1.00
64 Wilt Chamberlain PO 3.00 8.00
65 NBA Western Semis .40 1.00
66 Willis Reed/H.Finkel PO 1.25 3.00
67 NBA Western Finals .40 1.00
68 W.Frazier/Erickson Champ 1.50 4.00
69 Larry Steele .40 1.00
70 Oscar Robertson 6.00 15.00
71 Phil Jackson 6.00 15.00
72 John Wetzel .20 .50
73 Steve Patterson RC .40 1.00
74 Manny Leaks .20 .50
75 Jeff Mullins .40 1.00
76 Stan Love .20 .50
77 Dick Garrett .20 .50
78 Don Nelson 1.50 4.00
79 Chris Ford RC 1.25 3.00
80 Wilt Chamberlain 12.00 30.00
81 Dennis Layton .20 .50
82 Bill Bradley 6.00 15.00
83 Jerry Sloan .40 1.00
84 Cliff Meely .20 .50
85 Sam Lacey .20 .50
86 Dick Snyder .20 .50
87 Jim Washington .20 .50
88 Lucius Allen .40 1.00
89 LaRue Martin RC .20 .50
90 Rick Barry 3.00 8.00
91 Fred Boyd .20 .50
92 Barry Clemens .20 .50
93 Dean Meminger .20 .50
94 Henry Finkel .20 .50
95 Elvin Hayes 2.50 6.00
96 Stu Lantz .40 1.00
97 Bill Hewitt .20 .50
98 Neal Walk .20 .50
99 Garfield Heard .40 1.00
100 Jerry West AS1 8.00 20.00
101 Otto Moore .20 .50
102 Don Kojis .20 .50
103 Fred Brown RC 2.50 6.00
104 Dwight Davis .20 .50
105 Willis Reed 2.50 6.00
106 Herm Gilliam .20 .50
107 Mickey Davis .40 1.00
108 Jim Barnett .20 .50
109 Ollie Johnson .20 .50
110 Bob Lanier 2.50 6.00
111 Fred Carter .40 1.00
112 Paul Silas 1.25 3.00
113 Phil Chenier .40 1.00
114 Dennis Awtrey .20 .50
115 Austin Carr .40 1.00
116 Bob Kauffman .20 .50
117 Keith Erickson .40 1.00
118 Walt Wesley .20 .50
119 Steve Bracey .20 .50
120 Spencer Haywood AS1 1.25 3.00
121 NBA Checklist 1-176 5.00 12.00
122 Jack Marin .40 1.00
123 Jon McGlocklin .20 .50
124 Johnny Green .40 1.00
125 Jerry Lucas 1.25 3.00
126 Paul Westphal RC 8.00 20.00
127 Curtis Rowe .40 1.00
128 Mahdi Abdul-Rahman .40 1.00
129 Lloyd Neal RC .40 1.00
130 Pete Maravich AS1 12.00 30.00
131 Don May .20 .50
132 Bob Weiss .40 1.00
133 Dave Stallworth .20 .50
134 Dick Cunningham .20 .50
135 Bob McAdoo RC 8.00 20.00
136 Butch Beard .40 1.00
137 Happy Hairston .40 1.00
138 Bob Rule .60 1.50
139 Don Adams .20 .50
140 Charlie Scott .40 1.00
141 Ron Riley .20 .50
142 Earl Monroe 1.50 4.00
143 Clyde Lee .20 .50
144 Rick Roberson .20 .50
145 Rudy Tomjanovich 2.50 6.00
146 Tom Van Arsdale .40 1.00
147 Art Williams .20 .50
148 Curtis Perry .20 .50
149 Rich Rinaldi .20 .50
150 Lou Hudson .40 1.00
151 Mel Counts .20 .50
152 Jim McDaniels .20 .50
153 Arch/Jabbar/Hayw LL 3.00 8.00
154 Arch/Jabbar/Hayw LL 3.00 8.00
155 Wilt/Guokas/Jabbar LL 5.00 12.00
156 Barry/Murphy/Newlin LL 1.50 4.00
157 Wilt/Thurm/Cowens LL 3.00 8.00
158 Arch/Wilkens/Bing LL 1.50 4.00
159 Don Smith .20 .50
160 Sidney Wicks 1.25 3.00
161 Howie Komives .20 .50
162 John Gianelli .20 .50
163 Jeff Halliburton .20 .50
164 Kennedy McIntosh .20 .50
165 Len Wilkens 3.00 8.00
166 Corky Calhoun .20 .50
167 Howard Porter .40 1.00
168 Jo Jo White 1.25 3.00
169 John Block .20 .50
170 Dave Bing 1.50 4.00
171 Joe Ellis .20 .50
172 Chuck Terry .20 .50
173 Randy Smith .40 1.00
174 Bill Bridges .40 1.00
175 Geoff Petrie .40 1.00
176 Wes Unseld 1.50 4.00
177 Skeeter Swift .40 1.00
178 Jim Eakins .60 1.50
179 Steve Jones .60 1.50
180 George McGinnis AS1 1.25 3.00
181 Al Smith .40 1.00
182 Tom Washington .40 1.00
183 Louie Dampier .60 1.50
184 Simmie Hill .40 1.00
185 George Thompson .40 1.00
186 Cincy Powell .60 1.50
187 Larry Jones .40 1.00
188 Neil Johnson .40 1.00
189 Tom Owens .40 1.00
190 Ralph Simpson AS2 .60 1.50
191 George Carter .60 1.50
192 Rick Mount .60 1.50
193 Red Robbins .60 1.50
194 George Lehmann .40 1.00
195 Mel Daniels AS2 .60 1.50
196 Bob Warren .40 1.00
197 Gene Kennedy .40 1.00
198 Mike Barr .40 1.00
199 Dave Robisch .40 1.00
200 Billy Cunningham AS1 2.00 5.00
201 John Roche .60 1.50
202 ABA Western Semis 1.25 3.00
203 ABA Western Semis 1.25 3.00
204 Dan Issel PO 1.25 3.00
205 ABA Eastern Semis 1.25 3.00
206 ABA Western Finals 1.25 3.00
207 Artis Gilmore PO 1.25 3.00
208 George McGinnis PO 1.25 3.00
209 Glen Combs .40 1.00
210 Dan Issel AS2 2.50 6.00
211 Randy Denton .40 1.00
212 Freddie Lewis .60 1.50
213 Stew Johnson .40 1.00
214 Roland Taylor .40 1.00
215 Rich Jones .40 1.00
216 Billy Paultz .60 1.50
217 Ron Boone .60 1.50
218 Walt Simon .40 1.00
219 Mike Lewis .40 1.00
220 Warren Jabali AS1 .60 1.50
221 Wilbert Jones .40 1.00
222 Don Buse RC .60 1.50
223 Gene Moore .40 1.00
224 Joe Hamilton .60 1.50
225 Zelmo Beaty .60 1.50
226 Brian Taylor RC .60 1.50
227 Julius Keye .40 1.00
228 Mike Gale RC .60 1.50
229 Warren Davis .40 1.00
230 Mack Calvin AS2 .60 1.50
231 Roger Brown .60 1.50
232 Chuck Williams .60 1.50
233 Gerald Govan .60 1.50
234 Erving/McG/Issel LL 4.00 10.00
235 Gil/Kenn/Owens LL 1.25 3.00
236 Comb/Brwn/Damp LL 1.25 3.00
237 Kellr/Boone/War LL 1.25 3.00
238 Gilmore/Daniels/Paultz LL 1.25 3.00
239 Mel/Will/Jabali LL 1.25 3.00
240 Julius Erving AS2 12.00 30.00
241 Jimmy O'Brien .40 1.00
242 ABA Checklist 177-264 6.00 12.00
243 Johnny Neumann .40 1.00
244 Darnell Hillman .60 1.50
245 Willie Wise .60 1.50
246 Collis Jones .40 1.00
247 Ted McClain .40 1.00
248 George Irvine RC .40 1.00
249 Bill Melchionni .60 1.50
250 Artis Gilmore AS1 2.50 6.00
251 Willie Long .40 1.00
252 Larry Miller .40 1.00
253 Lee Davis .40 1.00
254 Donnie Freeman .60 1.50
255 Joe Caldwell .60 1.50
256 Bob Netolicky .60 1.50
257 Bernie Williams .40 1.00
258 Byron Beck .60 1.50
259 Jim Chones RC 1.25 3.00
260 James Jones AS1 .60 1.50
261 Wendell Ladner .40 1.00
262 Ollie Taylor .40 1.00
263 Les Hunter .40 1.00
264 Billy Keller ! 1.25 3.00

1973-74 Topps Team Stickers

Measuring 2 1/2" by 3 1/2", these ABA and NBA team stickers were inserted one per wax pack. Two teams are represented on each color sticker. The larger (2 1/2" by 2 1/2") top sticker carries the team logo, while the smaller (1" by 2 1/2") bottom sticker displays only the team name on a banner. Only one of each ABA sticker was produced, while some NBA stickers exhibit two team combinations. The stickers are unnumbered and checklisted below in alphabetical order according to the top sticker for the ABA (1-10) and the NBA (11-33). The team represented on the bottom sticker is listed immediately below each entry.

COMPLETE SET (33) 60.00 125.00
1 Carolina Cougars 2.00 5.00
Stars
2 Denver Rockets 2.00 5.00
Spurs
3 Indiana Pacers 2.50 6.00
Squires
4 Kentucky Colonels 2.50 6.00
Tams
5 Memphis Tams 2.50 6.00
Cougars
6 New York Nets 2.50 6.00
Conquistadors
7 San Antonio Spurs 2.00 5.00
Nets
8 San Diego Conquistadors 2.00 5.00
Pacers
9 Utah Stars 2.00 5.00
Colonels
10 Virginia Squires 2.00 5.00
Rockets
11 Atlanta Hawks 1.25 3.00
Celtics
12 Atlanta Hawks 1.25 3.00
Supersonics
13 Boston Celtics 1.50 4.00
Braves
14 Boston Celtics/76ers 1.50 4.00
15 Buffalo Braves 1.50 4.00
Lakers
16 Buffalo Braves 1.50 4.00
Trail Blazers
17 Capitol Bullets 1.25 3.00
Knicks
18 Chicago Bulls 1.25 3.00
Pistons
19 Cleveland Cavaliers 1.25 3.00
Hawks
20 Detroit Pistons 1.25 3.00
Warriors
21 Golden State Warriors 1.25 3.00
Bucks
22 Golden State Warriors 1.25 3.00
Kings
23 Houston Rockets 1.25 3.00
Braves
24 Kansas City Kings 1.25 3.00
Lakers/76ers
25 Los Angeles Lakers 1.50 4.00
Bullets
26 Los Angeles Lakers 1.50 4.00
Celtics
27 Milwaukee Bucks 1.25 3.00
Knicks
28 New York Knicks 1.25 3.00
Bulls
29 New York Knicks 1.25 3.00
Warriors
30 Philadelphia 76ers 1.25 3.00
Hawks
31 Phoenix Suns 1.25 3.00
Cavaliers
32 Portland Trail Blazers 1.25 3.00
Rockets
33 Seattle Supersonics 1.25 3.00
Suns

1974-75 Topps

The 1974-75 Topps set of 264 standard-size cards contains NBA players on cards numbered 1 to 176 and ABA players on cards numbered 177 to 264. For the first time Team Leader (TL) cards are provided for each team. The cards were issued in 10-card packs with 24 packs per box. All-Star selections (first and second team) for both leagues are noted on the respective player's regular cards. The card backs are printed in blue and red on gray card stock. Subsets include NBA Team Leaders (81-98), NBA Statistical Leaders (144-149), NBA Playoffs (161-164), ABA Statistical Leaders (207-212), ABA Team Leaders (221-230) and ABA Playoffs (246-249). The key Rookie Cards in this set are Doug Collins, George Gervin and Bill Walton.

COMPLETE SET (264) 200.00 325.00
CARDS PRICED IN NM CONDITION
1 Kareem Abdul-Jabbar ! 10.00 25.00
2 Don May .20 .50
3 Bernie Fryer RC .40 1.00
4 Don Adams .20 .50
5 Herm Gilliam .20 .50
6 Jim Chones .40 1.00
7 Rick Adelman .40 1.00
8 Randy Smith .40 1.00
9 Paul Silas 1.25 3.00
10 Pete Maravich 8.00 20.00
11 Ron Behagen .20 .50
12 Kevin Porter .40 1.00
13 Bill Bridges .40 1.00
14 Charles Johnson RC .20 .50
15 Bob Love .40 1.00
16 Henry Bibby .40 1.00
17 Neal Walk .20 .50
18 John Brisker .20 .50
19 Lucius Allen .20 .50
20 Tom Van Arsdale .40 1.00
21 Larry Steele .20 .50
22 Curtis Rowe .40 1.00
23 Dean Meminger .20 .50
24 Steve Patterson .20 .50
25 Earl Monroe 1.25 3.00
26 Jack Marin .20 .50
27 Jo Jo White 1.25 3.00
28 Rudy Tomjanovich 2.50 6.00
29 Otto Moore .20 .50
30 Elvin Hayes AS2 2.00 5.00
31 Pat Riley 3.00 8.00
32 Clyde Lee .20 .50
33 Bob Weiss .20 .50
34 Jim Fox .20 .50
35 Charlie Scott .40 1.00
36 Cliff Meely .20 .50
37 Jon McGlocklin .20 .50
38 Jim McMillian .40 1.00
39 Bill Walton RC 20.00 50.00
40 Dave Bing AS2 1.25 3.00
41 Jim Washington .20 .50
42 Jim Cleamons .40 1.00
43 Mel Davis .20 .50
44 Garfield Heard .40 1.00
45 Jimmy Walker .40 1.00
46 Don Nelson .40 1.00
47 Jim Barnett .20 .50
48 Manny Leaks .20 .50
49 Elmore Smith .40 1.00
50 Rick Barry AS1 2.50 6.00
51 Jerry Sloan 1.25 3.00
52 John Hummer .20 .50
53 Keith Erickson .40 1.00
54 George E. Johnson .20 .50
55 Oscar Robertson 5.00 12.00
56 Steve Mix RC .40 1.00
57 Rick Roberson .20 .50
58 John Mengelt .20 .50
59 Dwight Jones RC .40 1.00
60 Austin Carr .40 1.00
61 Nick Weatherspoon RC .40 1.00
62 Clem Haskins .40 1.00
63 Don Kojis .20 .50
64 Paul Westphal 1.25 3.00
65 Walt Bellamy 1.50 4.00
66 John Johnson .40 1.00
67 Butch Beard .40 1.00
68 Happy Hairston .40 1.00
69 Tom Boerwinkle .20 .50
70 Spencer Haywood AS2 1.25 3.00
71 Gary Melchionni .20 .50
72 Ed Ratleff RC .40 1.00
73 Mickey Davis .20 .50
74 Dennis Awtrey .20 .50
75 Fred Carter .40 1.00
76 George Trapp .20 .50
77 John Wetzel .20 .50
78 Bobby Smith .40 1.00
79 John Gianelli .20 .50
80 Bob McAdoo AS2 2.50 6.00
81 Hawks TL/Maravich/Bell 2.50 6.00
82 Celtics TL/John Havlicek 2.00 5.00
83 Buffalo Braves TL .40 1.00
84 Bulls TL/Love/Walker 1.25 3.00
85 Cleveland Cavs TL .40 1.00
86 Detroit Pistons TL .40 1.00
87 Warriors TL/Rick Barry 1.25 3.00
88 Houston Rockets TL .40 1.00
89 Kansas City Omaha TL .40 1.00
90 Lakers TL/Gail Goodrich .40 1.00
91 Bucks TL/Jabbar/Oscar 5.00 12.00
92 New Orleans Jazz .40 1.00
93 Knicks TL/Fraz/Brad/DeB 2.00 5.00
94 Philadelphia 76ers TL .40 1.00
95 Phoenix Suns TL .40 1.00
96 Trail Blazers TL .40 1.00
97 Seattle Supersonics TL .40 1.00
98 Capitol Bullets TL .40 1.00
99 Sam Lacey .20 .50
100 John Havlicek AS1 4.00 10.00
101 Stu Lantz .40 1.00
102 Mike Riordan .20 .50
103 Larry Jones .20 .50
104 Connie Hawkins 1.50 4.00
105 Nate Thurmond 1.25 3.00
106 Dick Gibbs .20 .50
107 Corky Calhoun .20 .50
108 Dave Wohl .20 .50
109 Cornell Warner .20 .50
110 Geoff Petrie UER .40 1.00
111 Leroy Ellis .40 1.00
112 Chris Ford .40 1.00

113 Bill Bradley 4.00 10.00
114 Clifford Ray .40 1.00
115 Dick Snyder .20 .50
116 Nate Williams .20 .50
117 Matt Guokas .40 1.00
118 Henry Finkel .20 .50
119 Curtis Perry .20 .50
120 Gail Goodrich AS1 1.25 3.00
121 Wes Unseld 1.25 3.00
122 Howard Porter .40 1.00
123 Jeff Mullins .20 .50
124 Mike Bantom RC .40 1.00
125 Fred Brown .40 1.00
126 Bob Dandridge .40 1.00
127 Mike Newlin .40 1.00
128 Greg Smith .20 .50
129 Doug Collins RC 6.00 15.00
130 Lou Hudson .40 1.00
131 Bob Lanier 2.00 5.00
132 Phil Jackson 4.00 10.00
133 Don Chaney .40 1.00
134 Jim Brewer RC .40 1.00
135 Ernie DiGregorio RC 1.25 3.00
136 Steve Kuberski .20 .50
137 Jim Price .20 .50
138 Mike D'Antoni .20 .50
139 John Brown .20 .50
140 Norm Van Lier AS2 .40 1.00
141 NBA Checklist 1-176 5.00 10.00
142 Slick Watts RC .40 1.00
143 Walt Wesley .20 .50
144 McAd/Jabbar/Marav LL 5.00 12.00
145 McAd/Marav/Jabbar LL 5.00 12.00
146 McAd/Jabbar/Tomjan LL 4.00 10.00
147 NBA F.T. Pct. Leaders .40 1.00
148 Hayes/Cowens/McAd LL 1.50 4.00
149 NBA Assist Leaders .40 1.00
150 Walt Frazier AS1 2.00 5.00
151 Cazzie Russell .40 1.00
152 Calvin Murphy 1.25 3.00
153 Bob Kauffman .20 .50
154 Fred Boyd .20 .50
155 Dave Cowens 2.50 6.00
156 Willie Norwood .20 .50
157 Lee Winfield .20 .50
158 Dwight Davis .20 .50
159 George T. Johnson .20 .50
160 Dick Van Arsdale .40 1.00
161 NBA Eastern Semis .40 1.00
162 NBA Western Semis .40 1.00
163 NBA Div. Finals .40 1.00
164 NBA Championship .60 1.50
165 Phil Chenier .40 1.00
166 Kermit Washington RC .40 1.00
167 Dale Schlueter .20 .50
168 John Block .20 .50
169 Don Smith .20 .50
170 Nate Archibald 1.50 4.00
171 Chet Walker .40 1.00
172 Archie Clark .40 1.00
173 Kennedy McIntosh .20 .50
174 George Thompson .20 .50
175 Sidney Wicks 1.25 3.00
176 Jerry West 8.00 20.00
177 Dwight Lamar .40 1.00
178 George Carter .60 1.50
179 Wil Robinson .40 1.00
180 Artis Gilmore AS1 1.50 4.00
181 Brian Taylor .60 1.50
182 Darnell Hillman .60 1.50
183 Dave Robisch .60 1.50
184 Gene Littles RC .60 1.50
185 Willie Wise AS2 .60 1.50
186 James Silas RC 1.25 3.00
187 Caldwell Jones RC 1.25 3.00
188 Roland Taylor .40 1.00
189 Randy Denton .40 1.00
190 Dan Issel AS2 2.00 5.00
191 Mike Gale .40 1.00
192 Mel Daniels .60 1.50
193 Steve Jones .60 1.50
194 Marv Roberts .40 1.00
195 Ron Boone AS2 .60 1.50
196 George Gervin RC 15.00 40.00
197 Flynn Robinson .40 1.00
198 Cincy Powell .60 1.50
199 Glen Combs .40 1.00
200 Julius Erving UER 15.00 40.00
201 Billy Keller .60 1.50
202 Willie Long .40 1.00
203 ABA Checklist 177-264 5.00 10.00
204 Joe Caldwell .60 1.50
205 Swen Nater RC .60 1.50
206 Rick Mount .60 1.50
207 Erving/McG/Issel LL 4.00 10.00
208 ABA Two-Point Field 1.25 3.00
209 ABA Three-Point Field 1.25 3.00
210 ABA Free Throw 1.25 3.00
211 Gil/McGinn/Jones LL 1.25 3.00
212 ABA Assist Leaders 1.25 3.00
213 Larry Miller .40 1.00
214 Stew Johnson .40 1.00
215 Larry Finch RC 1.25 3.00
216 Larry Kenon RC 1.25 3.00
217 Joe Hamilton .60 1.50
218 Gerald Govan .60 1.50
219 Ralph Simpson .60 1.50
220 George McGinnis AS1 1.25 3.00
221 Carolina Cougars TL 1.25 3.00
222 Denver Nuggets TL 1.25 3.00
223 Indiana Pacers TL 1.25 3.00
224 Colonels TL/Dan Issel 1.25 3.00
225 Memphis Sounds TL 1.25 3.00
226 Nets TL/Erving 4.00 10.00
227 Spurs TL/George Gervin 2.50 6.00
228 San Diego Conq. TL 1.25 3.00
229 Utah Stars TL 1.25 3.00
230 Virginia Squires TL 1.25 3.00
231 Bird Averitt .40 1.00
232 John Roche .40 1.00
233 George Irvine .40 1.00
234 John Williamson RC .60 1.50
235 Billy Cunningham 1.50 4.00
236 Jimmy O'Brien .40 1.00
237 Wilbert Jones .40 1.00
238 Johnny Neumann .40 1.00
239 Al Smith .40 1.00
240 Roger Brown .60 1.50
241 Chuck Williams .60 1.50
242 Rich Jones .40 1.00
243 Dave Twardzik RC .60 1.50
244 Wendell Ladner .60 1.50
245 Mack Calvin AS1 .60 1.50
246 ABA Eastern Semis 1.25 3.00
247 ABA Western Semis 1.25 3.00
248 ABA Div. Finals 1.25 3.00
249 Julius Erving PO 5.00 12.00
250 Wilt Chamberlain CO 12.00 30.00
251 Ron Robinson .40 1.00
252 Zelmo Beaty .60 1.50
253 Donnie Freeman .60 1.50
254 Mike Green .40 1.00
255 Louie Dampier AS2 .60 1.50
256 Tom Owens .40 1.00
257 George Karl RC 4.00 10.00
258 Jim Eakins .60 1.50
259 Travis Grant .60 1.50
260 James Jones AS1 .60 1.50
261 Mike Jackson .40 1.00
262 Billy Paultz .60 1.50
263 Freddie Lewis .60 1.50
264 Byron Beck ! 1.25 3.00

1975-76 Topps

The 1975-76 Topps basketball card set of 330 standard-size cards was the largest basketball set ever produced up to that time. Cards were issued in 10-card which cost 15 cents per pack and had 24 packs per box. NBA players are depicted on cards 1-220 and ABA players on cards 221-330. Team Leaders (TL) cards are 116-133 (NBA teams) and 278-287 (ABA). Other subsets include NBA Statistical Leaders (1-6), NBA Playoffs (188-189), NBA Team Checklists (203-220), ABA Statistical Leaders (221-226), ABA Playoffs (309-310) and ABA Team Checklists (321-330). All-Star selections (first and second team) for both leagues are noted on the respective player's regular cards. Card backs are printed in blue and green on gray card stock. The set is particularly hard to sort numerically, as the small card number on the back is printed in blue on a dark green background. The set was printed on three large sheets each containing 110 different cards. Investigation of the second (series) sheet reveals that 22 of the cards were double printed; they are marked DP in the checklist below. Rookie Cards in this set include Bobby Jones, Maurice Lucas, Moses Malone and Keith (Jamaal) Wilkes.

COMPLETE SET (330) 250.00 400.00
CARDS PRICED IN NM CONDITION
1 McAd/Barry/Jabbar LL ! 6.00 12.00
2 Nelson/Beard/Tomj LL 1.50 4.00
3 Barry/Murphy/Bradley LL 2.00 5.00
4 Unseld/Cowens/Lacey LL 1.25 3.00
5 Porter/Bing/Arch LL 1.25 3.00
6 Barry/Frazier/Steele LL 1.50 4.00
7 Tom Van Arsdale .50 1.25
8 Paul Silas .50 1.25
9 Jerry Sloan 1.25 3.00
10 Bob McAdoo AS1 2.50 6.00
11 Dwight Davis .30 .75
12 John Mengelt .50 1.25
13 George Johnson .30 .75
14 Ed Ratleff .30 .75
15 Nate Archibald AS1 1.50 4.00
16 Elmore Smith .30 .75
17 Bob Dandridge .50 1.25
18 Louie Nelson RC .30 .75
19 Neal Walk .30 .75
20 Billy Cunningham 1.50 4.00
21 Gary Melchionni .30 .75
22 Barry Clemens .30 .75
23 Jimmy Jones .30 .75
24 Tom Burleson RC .50 1.25
25 Lou Hudson .50 1.25
26 Henry Finkel .30 .75
27 Jim McMillian .50 1.25
28 Matt Guokas .50 1.25
29 Fred Foster DP .30 .75
30 Bob Lanier 2.00 5.00
31 Jimmy Walker .50 1.25
32 Cliff Meely .30 .75
33 Butch Beard .75 2.00
34 Cazzie Russell .50 1.25
35 Jon McGlocklin .30 .75
36 Bernie Fryer .30 .75
37 Bill Bradley 5.00 10.00
38 Fred Carter .50 1.25
39 Dennis Awtrey DP .30 .75
40 Sidney Wicks .50 1.25
41 Fred Brown .50 1.25
42 Rowland Garrett .30 .75
43 Herm Gilliam .30 .75
44 Don Nelson .50 1.25
45 Ernie DiGregorio .75 2.00
46 Jim Brewer .30 .75
47 Chris Ford .75 2.00
48 Nick Weatherspoon .50 1.25
49 Zaid Abdul-Aziz .30 .75
50 Keith Wilkes RC 4.00 10.00
51 Ollie Johnson DP .30 .75
52 Lucius Allen .50 1.25
53 Mickey Davis .30 .75
54 Otto Moore .30 .75
55 Walt Frazier AS1 2.00 5.00
56 Steve Mix .50 1.25
57 Nate Hawthorne .30 .75
58 Lloyd Neal .30 .75
59 Slick Watts .50 1.25
60 Elvin Hayes 2.00 5.00
61 Checklist 1-110 3.00 8.00
62 Mike Sojourner .30 .75
63 Randy Smith .50 1.25
64 John Block DP .30 .75
65 Charlie Scott .50 1.25
66 Jim Chones .50 1.25
67 Rick Adelman .50 1.25
68 Curtis Rowe .30 .75
69 Derrek Dickey RC .50 1.25
70 Rudy Tomjanovich 2.00 5.00
71 Pat Riley 2.50 6.00
72 Cornell Warner .30 .75
73 Earl Monroe 1.25 3.00
74 Allan Bristow RC 1.25 3.00
75 Pete Maravich DP 8.00 20.00
76 Curtis Perry .30 .75
77 Bill Walton 8.00 20.00
78 Leonard Gray .30 .75
79 Kevin Porter .50 1.25
80 John Havlicek AS2 5.00 10.00
81 Dwight Jones .30 .75
82 Jack Marin .30 .75
83 Dick Snyder .30 .75
84 George Trapp .30 .75
85 Nate Thurmond 1.25 3.00
86 Charles Johnson .30 .75
87 Ron Riley .30 .75
88 Stu Lantz .50 1.25
89 Scott Wedman RC .60 1.50
90 Kareem Abdul-Jabbar 8.00 20.00
91 Aaron James .30 .75
92 Jim Barnett .30 .75
93 Clyde Lee .30 .75
94 Larry Steele .50 1.25
95 Mike Riordan .30 .75
96 Archie Clark .50 1.25
97 Mike Bantom .30 .75
98 Bob Kauffman .30 .75
99 Kevin Stacom RC .30 .75
100 Rick Barry AS1 2.50 6.00
101 Ken Charles .30 .75
102 Tom Boerwinkle .30 .75
103 Mike Newlin .50 1.25
104 Leroy Ellis .50 1.25
105 Austin Carr .50 1.25
106 Ron Behagen .30 .75
107 Jim Price .30 .75
108 Bud Stallworth .30 .75
109 Earl Williams .30 .75
110 Gail Goodrich 1.25 3.00
111 Phil Jackson 2.50 6.00
112 Rod Derline .30 .75
113 Keith Erickson .30 .75
114 Phil Lumpkin .30 .75
115 Wes Unseld 1.25 3.00
116 Atlanta Hawks TL .60 1.50
117 Cowens/White TL 1.25 3.00
118 Buffalo Braves TL 1.25 3.00
119 Love/Walk/Thur TL 1.25 3.00
120 Cleveland Cavs TL .60 1.50
121 Lanier/Bing TL 1.25 3.00
122 Rick Barry TL 1.25 3.00
123 Houston Rockets TL .75 2.00
124 Kansas City Kings TL .75 2.00
125 Los Angeles Lakers TL .60 1.50
126 K.Abdul-Jabbar TL 3.00 8.00
127 Pete Maravich TL 5.00 10.00
128 Frazier/Bradley TL DP 1.25 3.00
129 Car/Coll/Cunn TL DP .75 2.00
130 Phoenix Suns TL DP .60 1.50
131 Portland Blazers TL DP .60 1.50
132 Seattle Sonics TL .75 2.00
133 Hayes/Unseld TL 1.25 3.00
134 John Drew RC .50 1.25
135 Jo Jo White AS2 .75 2.00
136 Garfield Heard .50 1.25
137 Jim Cleamons .30 .75
138 Howard Porter .50 1.25
139 Phil Smith RC .50 1.25
140 Bob Love .50 1.25
141 John Gianelli DP .30 .75
142 Larry McNeill RC .30 .75
143 Brian Winters RC 1.25 3.00
144 George Thompson .30 .75
145 Kevin Kunnert .30 .75
146 Henry Bibby .50 1.25
147 John Johnson .30 .75
148 Doug Collins 1.50 4.00
149 John Brisker .30 .75
150 Dick Van Arsdale .50 1.25
151 Leonard Robinson RC 1.25 3.00
152 Dean Meminger .30 .75
153 Phil Hankinson .30 .75
154 Dale Schlueter .30 .75
155 Norm Van Lier .50 1.25
156 Campy Russell RC 1.50 4.00
157 Jeff Mullins .50 1.25
158 Sam Lacey .30 .75
159 Happy Hairston .50 1.25
160 Dave Bing DP 1.25 3.00
161 Kevin Restani RC .30 .75
162 Dave Wohl .30 .75
163 E.C. Coleman .30 .75
164 Jim Fox .30 .75
165 Geoff Petrie .50 1.25
166 Hawthorne Wingo DP UER .30 .75
167 Fred Boyd .30 .75
168 Willie Norwood .30 .75
169 Bob Wilson .30 .75
170 Dave Cowens 2.50 6.00
171 Tom Henderson RC .30 .75
172 Jim Washington .30 .75
173 Clem Haskins .50 1.25
174 Jim Davis .30 .75
175 Bobby Smith DP .30 .75
176 Mike D'Antoni .30 .75
177 Zelmo Beaty .50 1.25
178 Gary Brokaw RC .30 .75
179 Mel Davis .30 .75
180 Calvin Murphy 1.25 3.00
181 Checklist 111-220 DP 3.00 8.00
182 Nate Williams .30 .75
183 LaRue Martin .30 .75
184 George McGinnis 1.25 3.00
185 Clifford Ray .30 .75
186 Paul Westphal 1.50 4.00
187 Talvin Skinner .30 .75
188 NBA Playoff Semis DP 1.25 3.00
189 Clifford Ray PO 1.25 3.00
190 Phil Chenier AS2 DP .50 1.25
191 John Brown .30 .75
192 Lee Winfield .30 .75
193 Steve Patterson .30 .75
194 Charles Dudley .30 .75
195 Connie Hawkins DP 1.25 3.00
196 Leon Benbow .30 .75
197 Don Kojis .30 .75
198 Ron Williams .30 .75
199 Mel Counts .30 .75
200 Spencer Haywood AS2 1.25 3.00
201 Greg Jackson .30 .75
202 Tom Kozelko DP .30 .75
203 Atlanta Hawks CL .60 1.50
204 Boston Celtics CL 1.25 3.00
205 Buffalo Braves CL .60 1.50
206 Chicago Bulls CL 1.25 3.00
207 Cleveland Cavs CL .60 1.50
208 Detroit Pistons CL .60 1.50
209 Golden State CL .60 1.50
210 Houston Rockets CL .60 1.50
211 Kansas City Kings CL DP .60 1.50
212 Los Angeles Lakers CL DP .60 1.50
213 Milwaukee Bucks CL .60 1.50
214 New Orleans Jazz CL .60 1.50
215 New York Knicks CL .60 1.50
216 Philadelphia 76ers CL .60 1.50
217 Phoenix Suns CL DP .60 1.50
218 Portland Blazers CL .60 1.50
219 Sonics/B.Russell DP 5.00 10.00
220 Washington Bullets CL .60 1.50
221 McGin/Erving/Boone LL 3.00 8.00
222 Jones/Gilmore/Malone LL 3.00 8.00
223 ABA 3 Pt. Field Goal .75 2.00
224 ABA Free Throw .75 2.00
225 ABA Rebounds Leaders .75 2.00
226 ABA Assists Leaders .75 2.00
227 Mack Calvin AS1 .75 2.00
228 Billy Knight RC 1.25 3.00
229 Bird Averitt .60 1.50
230 George Carter .60 1.50
231 Swen Nater AS2 .75 2.00
232 Steve Jones .75 2.00
233 George Gervin 8.00 20.00
234 Lee Davis .60 1.50
235 Ron Boone AS1 .75 2.00
236 Mike Jackson .60 1.50
237 Kevin Joyce RC .60 1.50
238 Marv Roberts .60 1.50
239 Tom Owens .60 1.50
240 Ralph Simpson .75 2.00
241 Gus Gerard .60 1.50
242 Brian Taylor AS2 .75 2.00
243 Rich Jones .60 1.50
244 John Roche .60 1.50
245 Travis Grant .75 2.00
246 Dave Twardzik .75 2.00
247 Mike Green .60 1.50
248 Billy Keller .75 2.00
249 Stew Johnson .60 1.50
250 Artis Gilmore AS1 2.00 5.00
251 John Williamson .75 2.00
252 Marvin Barnes RC 1.50 4.00
253 James Silas AS2 .75 2.00
254 Moses Malone RC 15.00 40.00
255 Willie Wise .75 2.00
256 Dwight Lamar .60 1.50
257 Checklist 221-330 3.00 8.00
258 Byron Beck .75 2.00
259 Len Elmore RC 1.25 3.00
260 Dan Issel 2.00 5.00
261 Rick Mount .60 1.50
262 Billy Paultz .75 2.00
263 Donnie Freeman .60 1.50
264 George Adams .60 1.50
265 Don Chaney .75 2.00
266 Randy Denton .60 1.50
267 Don Washington .60 1.50
268 Roland Taylor .60 1.50
269 Charlie Edge .60 1.50
270 Louie Dampier .75 2.00
271 Collis Jones .60 1.50
272 Al Skinner RC .60 1.50
273 Coby Dietrick .60 1.50
274 Tim Bassett .60 1.50
275 Freddie Lewis .75 2.00
276 Gerald Govan .60 1.50
277 Ron Thomas .60 1.50
278 Denver Nuggets TL .75 2.00
279 McGinnis/Keller TL 1.00 2.50
280 Gilmore/Dampier TL 1.00 2.50

Card	Low	High
281 Memphis Sounds TL	.75	2.00
282 Julius Erving TL	6.00	15.00
283 Barnes/Lewis TL	1.00	2.50
284 George Gervin TL	2.00	5.00
285 San Diego Sails TL	.75	2.00
286 Malone/Boone TL	3.00	8.00
287 Virginia Squires TL	.75	2.00
288 Claude Terry	.60	1.50
289 Wilbert Jones	.60	1.50
290 Darnell Hillman	.75	2.00
291 Bill Melchionni	.75	2.00
292 Mel Daniels	.75	2.00
293 Fly Williams RC	.75	2.00
294 Larry Kenon	.75	2.00
295 Red Robbins	.75	2.00
296 Warren Jabali	.75	2.00
297 Jim Eakins	.75	2.00
298 Bobby Jones RC	5.00	12.00
299 Don Buse	.75	2.00
300 Julius Erving AS1	12.00	30.00
301 Billy Shepherd	.60	1.50
302 Maurice Lucas RC	2.50	6.00
303 George Karl	2.00	5.00
304 Jim Bradley	.60	1.50
305 Caldwell Jones	.75	2.00
306 Al Smith	.60	1.50
307 Jan Van Breda Kolff RC	.75	2.00
308 Darrell Elston	.60	1.50
309 ABA Playoff Semifinals	.75	2.00
310 Artis Gilmore PO	1.00	2.50
311 Ted McClain	.60	1.50
312 Willie Sojourner	.60	1.50
313 Bob Warren	.60	1.50
314 Bob Netolicky	.75	2.00
315 Chuck Williams	.60	1.50
316 Gene Kennedy	.60	1.50
317 Jimmy O'Brien	.60	1.50
318 Dave Robisch	.60	1.50
319 Wali Jones	.60	1.50
320 George Irvine	.60	1.50
321 Denver Nuggets CL	.75	2.00
322 Indiana Pacers CL	.75	2.00
323 Kentucky Colonels CL	.75	2.00
324 Memphis Sounds CL	.75	2.00
325 New York Nets CL	.75	2.00
326 St. Louis Spirits CL (Spirits of St. Louis on card back)	.75	2.00
327 San Antonio Spurs CL	.75	2.00
328 San Diego Sails CL	.75	2.00
329 Utah Stars CL	.75	2.00
330 Virginia Squires CL !	1.50	4.00

1975-76 Topps Team Checklist

These team checklists were issued in three panels, with nine teams per panel. The panels were available as a complete set via a mail-in offer. Each panel measures approximately 7 1/2" by 10 1/2" and are joined together to form one continuous sheet. The checklists are printed in blue and green on white card stock and list all NBA and ABA teams. They are numbered on the front and listed alphabetically according to the city names. The backs are blank. Since there was only room for 27 teams on the three-part sheet, Topps apparently left off card 324 (Memphis Sounds), which is in the regular set.

Card	Low	High
COMPLETE SET (27)	75.00	150.00
203 Atlanta Hawks	2.50	6.00
204 Boston Celtics	5.00	10.00
205 Buffalo Braves	2.50	6.00
206 Chicago Bulls	2.50	6.00
207 Cleveland Cavaliers	2.50	6.00
208 Detroit Pistons	2.50	6.00
209 Golden State Warriors	2.50	6.00
210 Houston Rockets	2.50	6.00
211 Kansas City Kings	2.50	6.00
212 Los Angeles Lakers	5.00	10.00
213 Milwaukee Bucks	2.50	6.00
214 New Orleans Jazz	2.50	6.00
215 New York Knicks	3.00	8.00
216 Philadelphia 76ers	2.50	6.00
217 Phoenix Suns	2.50	6.00
218 Portland Trail Blazers	3.00	8.00
219 Seattle SuperSonics	2.50	6.00
220 Washington Bullets	2.50	6.00
321 Denver Nuggets	3.00	8.00
322 Indiana Pacers	3.00	8.00
323 Kentucky Colonels	3.00	8.00
325 New York Nets	3.00	8.00
326 Spirits of St. Louis	3.00	8.00
327 San Antonio Spurs	3.00	8.00
328 San Diego Sails	3.00	8.00
329 Utah Stars	3.00	8.00
330 Virginia Squires	2.50	6.00

1976-77 Topps

Perhaps the most popular set of the seventies, the 144-card 1976-77 Topps set witnessed a return to the larger-size at 3 1/8" by 5 1/4". The larger size and excellent photo quality are appealing to collectors. Also, because of the size, they are attractive to autograph collectors. Cards were issued in 10-card packs which cost 15 cents with 24 packs per box. The fronts have a large color photo with the team name vertical on the left border. The player's name and position are at the bottom. Backs have statistical and biographical data. Cards numbered 126-135 are the previous season's NBA All-Star selections. The cards were printed on two large sheets, each with eight rows and nine columns. The checklist card was located in the lower right corner of the second sheet. Card No. 1, Julius Erving, is rarely found centered. Rookie Cards include Alvan Adams, Lloyd Free, Gus Williams and David Thompson.

COMPLETE SET (144) 175.00 375.00
CONDITION SENSITIVE SET
CARDS PRICED IN NM CONDITION

Card	Low	High
1 Julius Erving !	15.00	40.00
2 Dick Snyder	.75	2.00
3 Paul Silas	1.00	2.50
4 Keith Erickson	.75	2.00
5 Wes Unseld	2.00	5.00
6 Butch Beard	1.00	2.50
7 Lloyd Neal	.75	2.00
8 Tom Henderson	.75	2.00
9 Jim McMillian	1.00	2.50
10 Bob Lanier	2.50	6.00
11 Junior Bridgeman RC	1.00	2.50
12 Corky Calhoun	.75	2.00
13 Billy Keller	1.00	2.50
14 Mickey Johnson RC	.75	2.00
15 Fred Brown	1.00	2.50
16 Keith Wilkes	1.00	2.50
17 Louie Nelson	.75	2.00
18 Ed Ratleff	.75	2.00
19 Billy Paultz	1.00	2.50
20 Nate Archibald	2.00	5.00
21 Steve Mix	1.00	2.50
22 Ralph Simpson	.75	2.00
23 Campy Russell	1.00	2.50
24 Charlie Scott	1.00	2.50
25 Artis Gilmore	2.00	5.00
26 Dick Van Arsdale	1.00	2.50
27 Phil Chenier	1.00	2.50
28 Spencer Haywood	2.00	5.00
29 Chris Ford	1.00	2.50
30 Dave Cowens	5.00	12.00
31 Sidney Wicks	1.00	2.50
32 Jim Price	.75	2.00
33 Dwight Jones	.75	2.00
34 Lucius Allen	.75	2.00
35 Marvin Barnes	1.00	2.50
36 Henry Bibby	1.00	2.50
37 Joe Meriweather RC	.75	2.00
38 Doug Collins	2.50	6.00
39 Garfield Heard	1.00	2.50
40 Randy Smith	1.00	2.50
41 Tom Burleson	1.00	2.50
42 Dave Twardzik	1.00	2.50
43 Bill Bradley	6.00	12.00
44 Calvin Murphy	2.00	5.00
45 Bob Love	1.00	2.50
46 Brian Winters	1.00	2.50
47 Glenn McDonald	.75	2.00
48 Checklist 1-144	10.00	25.00
49 Bird Averitt	.75	2.00
50 Rick Barry	5.00	12.00
51 Ticky Burden RC	.75	2.00
52 Rich Jones	.75	2.00
53 Austin Carr	1.00	2.50
54 Steve Kuberski	.75	2.00
55 Paul Westphal	1.00	2.50
56 Mike Riordan	.75	2.00
57 Bill Walton	10.00	25.00
58 Eric Money RC	.75	2.00
59 John Drew	1.00	2.50
60 Pete Maravich	12.00	30.00
61 John Shumate RC	1.00	2.50
62 Mack Calvin	1.00	2.50
63 Bruce Seals	.75	2.00
64 Walt Frazier	3.00	8.00
65 Elmore Smith	.75	2.00
66 Rudy Tomjanovich	2.50	6.00
67 Sam Lacey	.75	2.00
68 George Gervin	10.00	25.00
69 Gus Williams RC	2.00	5.00
70 George McGinnis	1.00	2.50
71 Len Elmore	.75	2.00
72 Jack Marin	.75	2.00
73 Brian Taylor	.75	2.00
74 Jim Brewer	.75	2.00
75 Alvan Adams RC	2.50	6.00
76 Dave Bing	2.00	5.00
77 Phil Jackson	5.00	10.00
78 Geoff Petrie	1.00	2.50
79 Mike Sojourner	.75	2.00
80 James Silas	1.00	2.50
81 Bob Dandridge	1.00	2.50
82 Ernie DiGregorio	1.00	2.50
83 Cazzie Russell	1.00	2.50
84 Kevin Porter	1.00	2.50
85 Tom Boerwinkle	.75	2.00
86 Darnell Hillman	1.00	2.50
87 Herm Gilliam	.75	2.00
88 Nate Williams	.75	2.00
89 Phil Smith	1.00	2.50
90 John Havlicek	6.00	15.00
91 Kevin Kunnert	.75	2.00
92 Jimmy Walker	1.00	2.50
93 Billy Cunningham	2.00	5.00
94 Dan Issel	2.50	6.00
95 Ron Boone	1.00	2.50
96 Lou Hudson	1.00	2.50
97 Jim Chones	1.00	2.50
98 Earl Monroe	2.50	6.00
99 Tom Van Arsdale	1.00	2.50
100 Kareem Abdul-Jabbar	15.00	40.00
101 Moses Malone	10.00	25.00
102 Ricky Sobers RC	.75	2.00
103 Swen Nater	1.00	2.50
104 Leonard Robinson	1.00	2.50
105 Slick Watts	1.00	2.50
106 Otto Moore	.75	2.00
107 Maurice Lucas	1.00	2.50
108 Norm Van Lier	1.00	2.50
109 Clifford Ray	.75	2.00
110 David Thompson RC	15.00	40.00
111 Fred Carter	1.00	2.50
112 Caldwell Jones	1.00	2.50
113 John Williamson	1.00	2.50
114 Bobby Smith	1.00	2.50
115 Jo Jo White	1.00	2.50
116 Curtis Perry	.75	2.00
117 John Gianelli	.75	2.00
118 Curtis Rowe	.75	2.00
119 Lionel Hollins RC	1.00	2.50
120 Elvin Hayes	2.50	6.00
121 Ken Charles	.75	2.00
122 Dave Meyers RC	1.00	2.50
123 Jerry Sloan	1.00	2.50
124 Billy Knight	1.00	2.50
125 Gail Goodrich	1.00	2.50
126 K. Abdul-Jabbar AS	10.00	25.00
127 Julius Erving AS	10.00	25.00
128 George McGinnis AS	1.00	2.50
129 Nate Archibald AS	1.00	2.50
130 Pete Maravich AS	10.00	25.00
131 Dave Cowens AS	2.00	5.00
132 Rick Barry AS	2.00	5.00
133 Elvin Hayes AS	2.00	5.00
134 James Silas AS	.75	2.00
135 Randy Smith AS	.75	2.00
136 Leonard Gray	.75	2.00
137 Charles Johnson	.75	2.00
138 Ron Behagen	.75	2.00
139 Mike Newlin	1.00	2.50
140 Bob McAdoo	2.50	6.00
141 Mike Gale	.75	2.00
142 Scott Wedman	1.00	2.50
143 Lloyd Free RC	3.00	8.00
144 Bobby Jones !	3.00	8.00

1977-78 Topps

The 1977-78 Topps basketball card set consists of 132 standard-size cards. Cards were issued in 10-card packs with 24 packs per box. Fronts feature team and player name at the bottom with the player's position in a basketball at bottom left of the photo. Card backs are printed in green and black on either white or gray card stock. The white card stock is considered more desirable by most collectors and may even be a little tougher to find. However, there is no difference in value for either card stock. Rookie Cards include Adrian Dantley, Darryl Dawkins, John Lucas, Tom McMillen and Robert Parish.

Card	Low	High
COMPLETE SET (132)	50.00	100.00
1 Kareem Abdul-Jabbar !	8.00	20.00
2 Henry Bibby	.15	.40
3 Curtis Rowe	.10	.30
4 Norm Van Lier	.15	.40
5 Darnell Hillman	.15	.40
6 Earl Monroe	.60	1.50
7 Leonard Gray	.10	.30
8 Bird Averitt	.10	.30
9 Jim Brewer	.10	.30
10 Paul Westphal	.40	1.00
11 Bob Gross RC	.15	.40
12 Phil Smith	.10	.30
13 Dan Roundfield RC	.25	.60
14 Brian Taylor	.10	.30
15 Rudy Tomjanovich	.75	2.00
16 Kevin Porter	.15	.40
17 Scott Wedman	.15	.40
18 Lloyd Free	.25	.60
19 Tom Boswell RC	.10	.30
20 Pete Maravich	6.00	15.00
21 Cliff Pondexter	.10	.30
22 Bubbles Hawkins	.15	.40
23 Kevin Grevey RC	.50	1.25
24 Ken Charles	.10	.30
25 Bob Dandridge	.15	.40
26 Lonnie Shelton RC	.15	.40
27 Don Chaney	.15	.40
28 Larry Kenon	.15	.40
29 Checklist 1-132	1.25	3.00
30 Fred Brown	.15	.40
31 John Gianelli UER	.10	.30
32 Austin Carr	.15	.40
33 Keith Wilkes	.25	.60
34 Caldwell Jones	.15	.40
35 Jo Jo White	.40	1.00
36 Scott May RC	.60	1.50
37 Mike Newlin	.10	.30
38 Mel Davis	.10	.30
39 Lionel Hollins	.25	.60
40 Elvin Hayes	1.00	2.50
41 Dan Issel	.75	2.00
42 Ricky Sobers	.10	.30
43 Don Ford	.10	.30
44 John Williamson	.10	.30
45 Bob McAdoo	.75	2.00
46 Geoff Petrie	.15	.40
47 M.L. Carr RC	.75	2.00
48 Brian Winters	.20	.60
49 Sam Lacey	.10	.30
50 George McGinnis	.25	.60
51 Slick Watts	.15	.40
52 Sidney Wicks	.25	.60
53 Wilbur Holland	.10	.30
54 Tim Bassett	.15	.40
55 Phil Chenier	.15	.40
56 Adrian Dantley RC	3.00	8.00
57 Jim Chones	.15	.40
58 John Lucas RC	1.00	2.50
59 Cazzie Russell	.15	.40
60 David Thompson	2.00	5.00
61 Bob Lanier	.75	2.00
62 Dave Twardzik	.15	.40
63 Wilbert Jones	.10	.30
64 Clifford Ray	.10	.30
65 Doug Collins	.60	1.50
66 Tom McMillen RC	1.00	2.50
67 Rich Kelley RC	.10	.30
68 Mike Bantom	.10	.30
69 Tom Boerwinkle	.10	.30
70 John Havlicek	2.50	6.00
71 Marvin Webster RC	.25	.60
72 Curtis Perry	.10	.30
73 George Gervin	3.00	8.00
74 Leonard Robinson	.25	.60
75 Wes Unseld	.60	1.50
76 Dave Meyers	.15	.40
77 Gail Goodrich	.25	.60
78 Richard Washington RC	.25	.60
79 Mike Gale	.10	.30
80 Maurice Lucas	.25	.60
81 Harvey Catchings RC	.15	.40
82 Randy Smith	.10	.30
83 Campy Russell	.15	.40
84 Kevin Kunnert	.10	.30
85 Lou Hudson	.15	.40
86 Mickey Johnson	.10	.30
87 Lucius Allen	.10	.30
88 Spencer Haywood	.40	1.00
89 Gus Williams	.25	.60
90 Dave Cowens	1.25	3.00
91 Al Skinner	.10	.30
92 Swen Nater	.10	.30
93 Tom Henderson	.10	.30
94 Don Buse	.15	.40
95 Alvan Adams	.25	.60
96 Mack Calvin	.15	.40
97 Tom Burleson	.10	.30
98 John Drew	.15	.40
99 Mike Green	.10	.30
100 Julius Erving	6.00	15.00
101 John Mengelt	.10	.30
102 Howard Porter	.15	.40
103 Billy Paultz	.15	.40
104 John Shumate	.15	.40
105 Calvin Murphy	.60	1.50
106 Elmore Smith	.10	.30
107 Jim McMillian	.10	.30
108 Kevin Stacom	.10	.30
109 Jan Van Breda Kolff	.10	.30
110 Billy Knight	.25	.60
111 Robert Parish	10.00	25.00
112 Larry Wright	.10	.30
113 Bruce Seals	.10	.30
114 Junior Bridgeman	.15	.40
115 Artis Gilmore	.60	1.50
116 Steve Mix	.15	.40
117 Ron Lee	.15	.40
118 Bobby Jones	.40	1.00
119 Ron Boone	.15	.40
120 Bill Walton	4.00	10.00
121 Chris Ford	.15	.40
122 Earl Tatum	.10	.30
123 E.C. Coleman	.10	.30
124 Moses Malone	2.50	6.00
125 Charlie Scott	.25	.60
126 Bobby Smith	.10	.30
127 Nate Archibald	.75	2.00
128 Mitch Kupchak RC	.50	1.25
129 Walt Frazier	1.00	2.50
130 Rick Barry	1.25	3.00
131 Ernie DiGregorio	.15	.40
132 Darryl Dawkins RC	5.00	12.00

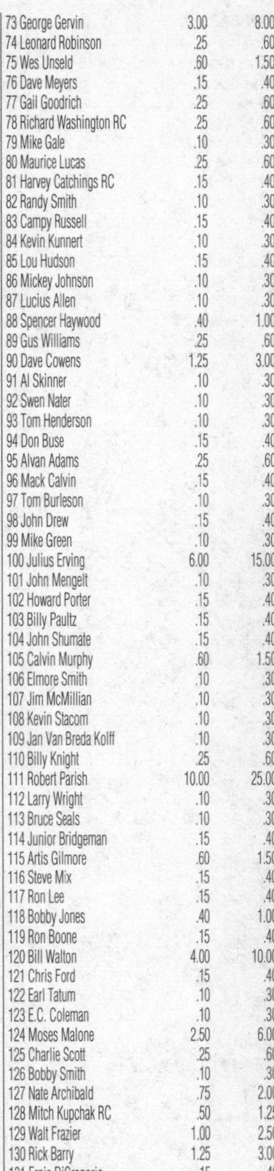

1978-79 Topps

The 1978-79 Topps basketball card set contains 132 standard-size cards. Cards were issued in 10-card packs with 36 packs per box. Card fronts feature the player and team name down the left border and a small head shot inserted at bottom right. Card backs are printed in orange and brown on gray card stock. The key Rookie Cards in this set inlcude Quinn Buckner, Walter Davis, James "Buddha" Edwards, Dennis Johnson, Marques Johnson, Bernard King, Norm Nixon and Jack Sikma.

Card	Low	High
COMPLETE SET (132)	25.00	60.00
1 Bill Walton !	4.00	10.00
2 Doug Collins	.60	1.50
3 Jamaal Wilkes	.30	.75
4 Wilbur Holland	.10	.30
5 Bob McAdoo	.50	1.25
6 Lucius Allen	.10	.30
7 Wes Unseld	.50	1.25
8 Dave Meyers	.20	.50
9 Austin Carr	.20	.50
10 Walter Davis RC	3.00	8.00
11 John Williamson	.10	.30
12 E.C. Coleman	.10	.30
13 Calvin Murphy	.50	1.25

14 Bobby Jones .30 .75
15 Chris Ford .20 .50
16 Kermit Washington .20 .50
17 Butch Beard .20 .50
18 Steve Mix .30 .75
19 Marvin Webster .20 .50
20 George Gervin 2.50 6.00
21 Steve Hawes .10 .30
22 Johnny Davis RC .20 .50
23 Swen Nater .10 .30
24 Lou Hudson .20 .50
25 Elvin Hayes .60 1.50
26 Nate Archibald .60 1.50
27 James Edwards RC 1.25 3.00
28 Howard Porter .20 .50
29 Quinn Buckner RC .50 1.25
30 Leonard Robinson .20 .50
31 Jim Cleamons .10 .30
32 Campy Russell .20 .50
33 Phil Smith .10 .30
34 Darryl Dawkins .75 2.00
35 Don Buse .20 .50
36 Mickey Johnson .10 .30
37 Mike Gale .10 .30
38 Moses Malone 1.50 4.00
39 Gus Williams .30 .75
40 Dave Cowens .75 2.00
41 Bobby Wilkerson RC .20 .50
42 Wilbert Jones .10 .30
43 Charlie Scott .20 .50
44 John Drew .20 .50
45 Earl Monroe .50 1.25
46 John Shumate .20 .50
47 Earl Tatum .10 .30
48 Mitch Kupchak .20 .50
49 Ron Boone .20 .50
50 Maurice Lucas .40 1.00
51 Louie Dampier .20 .50
52 Aaron James .10 .30
53 John Mengelt .10 .30
54 Garfield Heard .20 .50
55 George Johnson .10 .30
56 Junior Bridgeman .10 .30
57 Elmore Smith .10 .30
58 Rudy Tomjanovich .60 1.50
59 Fred Brown .20 .50
60 Rick Barry UER .75 2.00
61 Dave Bing .50 1.25
62 Anthony Roberts .20 .50
63 Norm Nixon RC .75 2.00
64 Leon Douglas RC .20 .50
65 Henry Bibby .20 .50
66 Lonnie Shelton .20 .50
67 Checklist 1-132 .75 2.00
68 Tom Henderson .10 .30
69 Dan Roundfield .20 .50
70 Armond Hill RC .20 .50
71 Larry Kenon .20 .50
72 Billy Knight .20 .50
73 Artis Gilmore .60 1.50
74 Lionel Hollins .20 .50
75 Bernard King RC 3.00 8.00
76 Brian Winters .30 .75
77 Alvan Adams .30 .75
78 Dennis Johnson RC 3.00 8.00
79 Scott Wedman .10 .30
80 Pete Maravich 4.00 10.00
81 Dan Issel .60 1.50
82 M.L. Carr .30 .75
83 Walt Frazier .60 1.50
84 Dwight Jones .10 .30
85 Jo Jo White .30 .75
86 Robert Parish 2.00 5.00
87 Charlie Criss RC .20 .50
88 Jim McMillian .10 .30
89 Chuck Williams .10 .30
90 George McGinnis .30 .75
91 Billy Paultz .20 .50
92 Bob Dandridge .20 .50
93 Ricky Sobers .10 .30
94 Paul Silas .20 .50
95 Gail Goodrich .30 .75
96 Tim Bassett .10 .30
97 Ron Lee .10 .30
98 Bob Gross .20 .50
99 Sam Lacey .20 .50
100 David Thompson 1.50 4.00
101 John Gianelli .10 .30
102 Norm Van Lier .20 .50
103 Caldwell Jones .20 .50
104 Eric Money .10 .30
105 Jim Chones .20 .50
106 John Lucas .40 1.00
107 Spencer Haywood .30 .75
108 Eddie Johnson RC .10 .30
109 Sidney Wicks .30 .75
110 Kareem Abdul-Jabbar 4.00 10.00
111 Sonny Parker RC .20 .50
112 Randy Smith .10 .30
113 Kevin Grevey .20 .50
114 Rich Kelley .10 .30
115 Scott May .20 .50
116 Lloyd Free .30 .75
117 Jack Sikma RC .75 2.00
118 Kevin Porter .20 .50
119 Darnell Hillman .20 .50
120 Paul Westphal .40 1.00
121 Richard Washington .10 .30
122 Dave Twardzik .20 .50
123 Mike Bantom .10 .30
124 Mike Newlin .10 .30
125 Bob Lanier .60 1.50
126 Marques Johnson RC 1.50 4.00
127 Foots Walker RC .20 .50
128 Cedric Maxwell RC .60 1.50
129 Ray Williams RC .20 .50
130 Julius Erving 5.00 12.00
131 Clifford Ray .10 .30
132 Adrian Dantley ! 1.25 3.00

1979-80 Topps

The 1979-80 Topps basketball set contains 132 standard-size cards. Cards were issued in 12-card packs along with a stick of bubble gum. The player's name, team and position are at the bottom. The team name is wrapped around a basketball. Card backs are printed in red and black on gray card stock. All-Star selections are designated as AS1 for first team selections and AS2 for second team selections and are denoted on the front of the player's regular card. Notable Rookie Cards in this set include Alex English, Reggie Theus, and Mychal Thompson.

COMPLETE SET (132) 40.00 80.00
1 George Gervin ! 2.50 6.00
2 Mitch Kupchak .15 .40
3 Henry Bibby .15 .40
4 Bob Gross .25 .60
5 Dave Cowens .75 2.00
6 Dennis Johnson .60 1.50
7 Scott Wedman .15 .40
8 Earl Monroe .50 1.25
9 Mike Bantom .10 .30
10 Kareem Abdul-Jabbar AS 3.00 8.00
11 Jo Jo White .30 .75
12 Spencer Haywood .25 .60
13 Kevin Porter .15 .40
14 Bernard King .60 1.50
15 Mike Newlin .10 .30
16 Sidney Wicks .25 .60
17 Dan Issel .50 1.25
18 Tom Henderson .10 .30
19 Jim Chones .15 .40
20 Julius Erving 5.00 12.00
21 Brian Winters .25 .60
22 Billy Paultz .15 .40
23 Cedric Maxwell .15 .40
24 Eddie Johnson .10 .30
25 Artis Gilmore .30 .75
26 Maurice Lucas .25 .60
27 Gus Williams .25 .60
28 Sam Lacey .15 .40
29 Toby Knight .10 .30
30 Paul Westphal AS1 .25 .60
31 Alex English RC 5.00 12.00
32 Gail Goodrich .25 .60
33 Caldwell Jones .15 .40
34 Kevin Grevey .15 .40
35 Jamaal Wilkes .25 .60
36 Sonny Parker .10 .30
37 John Gianelli .10 .30
38 John Long RC .15 .40
39 George Johnson .10 .30
40 Lloyd Free AS2 .25 .60
41 Rudy Tomjanovich .50 1.25
42 Foots Walker .15 .40
43 Dan Roundfield .15 .40
44 Reggie Theus RC 1.25 3.00
45 Bill Walton 1.25 3.00
46 Fred Brown .15 .40
47 Darnell Hillman .15 .40
48 Ray Williams .10 .30
49 Larry Kenon .15 .40
50 David Thompson .75 2.00
51 Billy Knight .25 .60
52 Alvan Adams .25 .60
53 Phil Smith .10 .30
54 Adrian Dantley .50 1.25
55 John Williamson .10 .30
56 Campy Russell .15 .40
57 Armond Hill .15 .40
58 Bob Lanier .50 1.25
59 Mickey Johnson .10 .30
60 Pete Maravich 4.00 10.00
61 Nick Weatherspoon .10 .30
62 Robert Reid RC .25 .60
63 Mychal Thompson RC .60 1.50
64 Doug Collins .40 1.00
65 Wes Unseld .50 1.25
66 Jack Sikma .25 .60
67 Bobby Wilkerson .10 .30
68 Bill Robinzine .10 .30
69 Joe Meriweather .10 .30
70 Marques Johnson AS1 .15 .40
71 Ricky Sobers .10 .30
72 Clifford Ray .10 .30
73 Tim Bassett .15 .40
74 James Silas .15 .40
75 Bob McAdoo .30 .75
76 Austin Carr .15 .40
77 Don Ford .10 .30
78 Steve Hawes .10 .30
79 Ron Brewer RC .10 .30
80 Walter Davis .40 1.00
81 Calvin Murphy .40 1.00
82 Tom Boswell .10 .30
83 Lonnie Shelton .10 .30
84 Terry Tyler RC .15 .40
85 Randy Smith .10 .30
86 Rich Kelley .10 .30
87 Otis Birdsong RC .25 .60
88 Marvin Webster .10 .30
89 Eric Money .10 .30
90 Elvin Hayes AS1 .60 1.50
91 Junior Bridgeman .10 .30
92 Johnny Davis .10 .30
93 Robert Parish 1.50 4.00
94 Eddie Jordan .15 .40
95 Leonard Robinson .15 .40
96 Rick Robey RC .15 .40
97 Norm Nixon .25 .60
98 Mark Olberding .10 .30
99 Wilbur Holland .10 .30
100 Moses Malone AS1 1.25 3.00
101 Checklist 1-132 .75 2.00
102 Tom Owens .10 .30
103 Phil Chenier .15 .40
104 John Johnson .10 .30
105 Darryl Dawkins .40 1.00
106 Charlie Scott .15 .40
107 M.L. Carr .25 .60
108 Phil Ford RC 1.00 2.50
109 Swen Nater .10 .30
110 Nate Archibald .60 1.50
111 Aaron James .10 .30
112 Jim Cleamons .10 .30
113 James Edwards .25 .60
114 Don Buse .15 .40
115 Steve Mix .15 .40
116 Charles Johnson .10 .30
117 Elmore Smith .10 .30
118 John Drew .10 .30
119 Lou Hudson .15 .40
120 Rick Barry .75 2.00
121 Kent Benson RC .25 .60
122 Mike Gale .10 .30
123 Jan Van Breda Kolff .10 .30
124 Chris Ford .15 .40
125 George McGinnis .25 .60
126 Leon Douglas .10 .30
127 John Lucas .25 .60
128 Kermit Washington .15 .40
129 Lionel Hollins .15 .40
130 Bob Dandridge AS2 .15 .40
131 James McElroy .10 .30
132 Bobby Jones ! .60 1.50

1980-81 Topps

The 1980-81 Topps basketball card set contains 264 different individual players (1 1/6" by 2 1/2") on 176 different panels of three (2 1/2" by 3 1/2"). This set was issued in packs of eight cards costing 25 cents per pack which came 36 packs per box. The cards come with three individual players per standard card. A perforation line segments each card into three players. In all, there are 176 different complete cards, however, the same player will be on more than one card. The variations stem from the fact that the cards in this set were printed on two separate sheets. In the checklist below, the first 88 cards comprise a complete set of all 264 players. The second 88 cards (89-176) provide a slight rearrangement of players within the card, but still contain the same 264 players. The cards are numbered within each series of 88 by any ordering of the left-hand player's number when the card is viewed from the back. In the checklist below, SD refers to a "Slam Dunk" star card. The letters AS in the checklist refer to an All-Star selection pictured on the front of the checklist card. There are a number of Team Leader (TL) cards which depict the team's leader in assists, scoring or rebounds. Prices given below are for complete panels, as that is the typical way these cards are collected. Cards which have been separated into the three parts are relatively valueless. The key card in this set features Larry Bird, Julius Erving and Magic Johnson. It is the Rookie Card for Bird and Magic. In addition to Bird and Magic, other noteworthy players making their first card appearance in this set include Bill Cartwright, Maurice Cheeks, Michael Cooper, Sidney Moncrief and Tree Rollins. Other lesser-known players making their first card appearance include James Bailey, Greg Ballard, Dudley Bradley, Mike Bratz, Joe Bryant, Kenny Carr, Wayne Cooper, David Greenwood, Phil Hubbard, Geoff Huston, Abdul Jeelani, Greg Kelser, Reggie King, Tom LaGarde, Mark Landsberger, Allen Leavell, Calvin

COMPLETE SET (176) 250.00 450.00
1 3/Erving/258 Brewer 2.00 5.00
2 7 Malone AS/185/Parish TL .60 1.50
3 12 Gus Williams AS .25 .60
4 24/32/248 Elvin Hayes .40 1.00
5 29 Dan Roundfield .40 1.00
6 34 Bird RC/Erving/Magic RC 150.00 400.00
7 36 Cowens/186/Wilkes .60 1.50
8 38 Maravich/264/194 DJ 2.50 6.00
9 40 Rick Robey .25 .60
10 47 Scott May .25 .60
11 55 Don Ford .10 .30
12 58 Campy Russell .10 .30
13 60 Foots Walker .10 .30
14 61/Jabbar AS/200 Natt 1.25 3.00
15 63 Jim Cleamons .25 .60
16 69 Tom LaGarde .10 .30
17 71 Jerome Whitehead .25 .60
18 74 John Roche TL .10 .30
19 75 English/2/68 .50 1.25
20 82 Terry Tyler TL .10 .30
21 84 Kent Benson .25 .60
22 86/Parish TL/126 .60 1.50
23 88/Erving AS/Sobers 1.25 3.00
24 90 Eric Money .10 .30
25 95 Wayne Cooper .10 .30
26 97 Parish/187/46 .75 2.00
27 98 Sonny Parker .10 .30
28 105 Barry/122/48 .40 1.00
29 106 Allen Leavell .10 .30
30 108/176 Cheeks TL/87 .25 .60
31 110 Robert Reid .25 .60
32 111 Rudy Tomjanovich .25 .60
33 112/28 Tree Rollins/15 .10 .30
34 115 Mike Bantom .25 .60
35 116 Dudley Bradley .10 .30
36 118 James Edwards .10 .30
37 119 Mickey Johnson .10 .30
38 120 Billy Knight .25 .60
39 121 George McGinnis .25 .60
40 124 Phil Ford TL .10 .30
41 127 Phil Ford .25 .60
42 131 Scott Wedman .25 .60
43 132 Jabbar TL/Mitch/81 1.25 3.00
44 135 Jabbar/79/216 2.00 5.00
45 137 Coop/Malone TL/148 .60 1.50
46 140/Lanier AS/Walton .60 1.50
47 141 Norm Nixon .25 .60
48 143/30 Bird TL/Sikma 10.00 25.00
49 146/31 Bird TL/Brewer 8.00 20.00
50 147/133 Jabbar TL/207 1.25 3.00
51 149/262 Erving SD/62 1.25 3.00
52 151 Moncrief/260/220 1.25 3.00
53 156 George Johnson .25 .60
54 158 Maurice Lucas .25 .60
55 159 Mike Newlin .10 .30
56 160 Roger Phegley .10 .30
57 161 Cliff Robinson .10 .30
58 162 Jan V.Breda Kolff .25 .60
59 165/214/Gilmore .10 .30
60 166 Cartwright/244/25 .60 1.50
61 168/14/Dantley .10 .30
62 169 Joe Meriweather .25 .60
63 170 Monroe/27/85 .25 .60
64 172 Marvin Webster .25 .60
65 173 Ray Williams .10 .30
66 178 Cheeks/Magic AS/237 6.00 15.00
67 183 Bobby Jones .40 1.00
68 189/163/Issel .40 1.00
69 190 Don Buse .25 .60
70 191 Davis/Gervin AS/136 .40 1.00
71 192/Malone TL/64 .40 1.00
72 201 Tom Owens .10 .30
73 208 Gervin/Issel TL/249 .60 1.50
74 217/263/107 Malone .60 1.50
75 219 Swen Nater .25 .60
76 221 Brian Taylor .10 .30
77 228 Fred Brown .10 .30
78 230/W.Davis AS/Archibald .40 1.00
79 231 Lonnie Shelton .25 .60
80 233 Gus Williams .10 .30
81 236 Allan Bristow TL .10 .30
82 238/109/Lanier .40 1.00
83 241 Ben Poquette .40 1.00
84 245 Greg Ballard .10 .30
85 246 Bob Dandridge .25 .60
86 250 Kevin Porter .10 .30
87 251 Unseld/195/78 .25 .60
88 257 Hayes SD/144/McAdoo .25 .60
89 3 Dan Roundfield .25 .60
90 7 Malone AS/247/52 .40 1.00
91 12 Gus Williams .10 .30
92 24 Steve Hawes .10 .30
93 29 Dan Roundfield .10 .30
94 34 Bird/Cartwright/23 15.00 40.00
95 36 Cowens/16/59 .40 1.00
96 38 Maravich/187/46 3.00 8.00
97 40 Rick Robey .25 .60
98 47/30 Bird TL/Sikma 8.00 20.00
99 55 Don Ford .40 1.00
100 58 Campy Russell .25 .60
101 60 Foots Walker .10 .30
102 61 Austin Carr .10 .30
103 63 Jim Cleamons .10 .30
104 69/109/Bob Lanier .40 1.00
105 71 Jerome Whitehead .25 .60
106 74/28 Tree Rollins/15 .10 .30
107 75 English/Malone TL/64 .60 1.50
108 82 Terry Tyler TL .10 .30
109 84 Kent Benson .25 .60
110 86 Phil Hubbard .10 .30
111 88/18 Magic AS/237 6.00 15.00
112 90 Eric Money .10 .30
113 95 Wayne Cooper .10 .30
114 97 Parish/Malone TL/148 .75 2.00
115 98 Sonny Parker .25 .60
116 105 Barry/123/54 .40 1.00
117 106 Allen Leavell .10 .30
118 108 Calvin Murphy .25 .60
119 110 Robert Reid .25 .60
120 111 Rudy Tomjanovich .40 1.00
121 112/264/D.Johnson .40 1.00
122 115 Mike Bantom .25 .60
123 116 Dudley Bradley .40 1.00
124 118/Archibald TL/Hayes .50 1.25
125 119 Mickey Johnson .40 1.00
126 120 Billy Knight .10 .30
127 121/Lanier AS/Walton .60 1.50
128 124 Phil Ford TL .25 .60
129 127 Phil Ford .25 .60
130 131 Scott Wedman .10 .30
131 132 Jabbar TL/Par.TL/126 1.50 4.00
132 135 Jabbar/253/167 2.00 5.00
133 137 M.Cooper/212/229 .50 1.25
134 140/214/Gilmore .25 .60
135 141 Norm Nixon .25 .60
136 143 Marq.Johnson TL .10 .30
137 146/Erving AS/Sobers 1.25 3.00
138 147 Quinn Buckner .25 .60
139 149 Marques Johnson .10 .30
140 151 Moncrief/Jabb.TL/207 1.50 4.00
141 156 George Johnson .10 .30
142 158/262 Erving SD/62 1.25 3.00
143 159 Mike Newlin .25 .60
144 160 Roger Phegley .10 .30
145 161 Cliff Robinson .10 .30
146 162/Erving SD/139 Magic 15.00 40.00
147 165/185/Parish TL .40 1.00
148 166 Cartwright/13/179 .40 1.00
149 168 Toby Knight .25 .60
150 169 Joe Meriweather .10 .30
151 170 Monroe/206/91 .10 .30
152 172 Marvin Webster .25 .60
153 173 Ray Williams .10 .30
154 178 Cheeks/Gervin AS/136 1.50 4.00
155 183 Bobby Jones .25 .60
156 189/14/Dantley .25 .60

157 190 Don Buse	.25	.60
158 191 Walter Davis	.25	.60
159 192/263/107 Malone	.60	1.50
160 201 Tom Owens	.25	.60
161 208 Gervin/53/223	.60	1.50
162 217/8 Jabbar AS/Natt	1.25	3.00
163 219 Swen Nater	.10	.30
164 221 Brian Taylor	.10	.30
165 228/31 Bird TL/Brewer	8.00	20.00
166 230/163/Issel	.40	1.00
167 231 Lonnie Shelton	.10	.30
168 233 Gus Williams	.25	.60
169 236 Allan Bristow TL	.10	.30
170 238 Tom Boswell	.10	.30
171 241/Cheeks TL/87	.40	1.00
172 245/W.Davis AS/Archibald	.40	1.00
173 246 Bob Dandridge	.10	.30
174 250 Kevin Porter	.10	.30
175 251 Unseld/67/5	.40	1.00
176 257 Hayes SD/Erving/258	2.00	5.00

1980-81 Topps Team Posters

This set of 16 numbered team mini-posters was issued as a folded insert (one per pack) in regular wax packs of 1980-81 Topps basketball cards. The small posters feature a full-color posed team picture, with the team name in the frame line. These posters are on thin, white paper stock and measure approximately 4 7/8" by 6 7/8" when unfolded. Since the copies were originally folded by Topps prior to insertion into the packs, they are still considered Mint with fold lines.

COMPLETE SET (16)	12.00	30.00
1 Atlanta Hawks	.40	1.00
2 Boston Celtics	3.00	8.00
3 Chicago Bulls	.40	1.00
4 Cleveland Cavaliers	.40	1.00
5 Detroit Pistons	.40	1.00
6 Houston Rockets	.40	1.00
7 Indiana Pacers	.40	1.00
8 Los Angeles Lakers	2.50	6.00
9 Milwaukee Bucks	.40	1.00
10 New Jersey Nets	.40	1.00
11 New York Knicks	.40	1.00
12 Philadelphia 76ers	.75	2.00
13 Phoenix Suns	.40	1.00
14 Portland Blazers	.40	1.00
15 Seattle Sonics	.40	1.00
16 Washington Bullets	.40	1.00

1948 Topps Magic Photos

The 1948 Topps Magic Photos set contains 252 small (approximately 7/8" by 1 7/16") individual cards featuring sport and non-sport subjects. They were issued in 19 lettered series with cards numbered within each series. The fronts were developed, much like a photograph, from a "blank" appearance by using moisture and sunlight. Due to varying degrees of photographic sensitivity, the clarity of these cards ranges from fully developed to poorly developed. This set contains Topps' first baseball cards. A premium album holding 126-cards was also issued. The set is sometimes confused with Topps' 1956 Hocus-Focus set, although the cards in this set are slightly smaller than those in the Hocus-Focus set. The checklist below is presented by series. Poorly developed cards are considered in lesser condition and hence have lesser value. The catalog designation for this set is R714-27. Each type of card subject has a letter prefix as follows: Boxing Champions (A), All-American Basketball (B), All-American Football (C), Wrestling Champions (D), Track and Field Champions (E), Stars of Stage and Screen (F), American Dogs (G), General Sports (H), Movie Stars (J), Baseball Hall of Fame (K), Aviation Pioneers (L), Famous Landmarks (M), American Inventors (N), American Military Leaders (O), American Explorers (P), Basketball Thrills (Q), Football Thrills (R), Figures of the Wild West (S), and General Sports (T).

COMPLETE SET (252)	3,000.00	5,000.00
B1 Ralph Beard	25.00	50.00
B2 Murray Weir	15.00	30.00
B3 Ed Macauley	40.00	80.00
B4 Kevin O'Shea	12.50	25.00
B5 Jim McIntyre	15.00	30.00
B6 Manhattan Beats	12.50	25.00

1975-76 Trail Blazers Iron Ons

Sponsored by PayLess Drug Store, this is a set of seven iron ons. Printed on very thin paper and measuring 5" by 7 7/8", they feature black-and-white player portraits. The players' jerseys are outlined in red. A facsimile autograph, also in red, is printed on the bottom. The iron ons are unnumbered and checklisted below in alphabetical order.

COMPLETE SET (7)	20.00	40.00
1 Dan Anderson	1.25	3.00
2 Barry Clemens	1.25	3.00
3 Bob Gross	1.50	4.00
4 LaRue Martin	1.25	3.00
5 Larry Steele	1.50	4.00
6 Bill Walton	12.50	25.00
7 Sidney Wicks	3.00	8.00

1977-78 Trail Blazers Police

This set contains 14 cards measuring approximately 2 5/8" by 4 1/8" featuring the Portland Trail Blazers. The cards are unnumbered except for uniform number. Backs contain safety tips ("Tips from the Blazers") and are written in black ink with red accent. The set was sponsored by the Kiwanis and the Police Department. According to informed sources, 26, 000 sets were produced.

COMPLETE SET (14)	25.00	50.00
10 Corky Calhoun	1.25	3.00
13 Dave Twardzik	2.00	5.00
14 Lionel Hollins	2.00	5.00
15 Larry Steele	2.00	5.00
16 Johnny Davis	1.50	4.00
20 Maurice Lucas	3.00	8.00
23 T.R. Dunn	1.50	4.00
25 Tom Owens	1.25	3.00
30 Bob Gross	1.50	4.00
32 Bill Walton	10.00	20.00
36 Lloyd Neal	1.25	3.00
NNO Jack Ramsay CO	2.50	6.00
NNO Jack McKinney ACO	2.00	5.00
NNO Ron Culp TR	1.25	3.00

1979-80 Trail Blazers Police

This set contains 16 cards measuring 2 5/8" by 4 1/8" featuring the Portland Trail Blazers. Backs contain safety tips and are available with either light red or maroon printing on the backs. The year of issue and a facsimile autograph are printed on the front of the cards. The set was sponsored by 7-Up, Safeway, Kiwanis, KEX-1190AM, and the Police Departments. The cards are ordered below according to uniform number. The set features an early professional card of Mychal Thompson.

COMPLETE SET (16)	4.00	10.00
4 Jim Paxson	.75	2.00
9 Lionel Hollins	.60	1.50
10 Ron Brewer	.30	.75
11 Abdul Jeelani	.30	.75
13 Dave Twardzik	.60	1.50
15 Larry Steele	.50	1.25
20 Maurice Lucas	.75	2.00
23 T.R. Dunn	.40	1.00
25 Tom Owens	.30	.75
30 Bob Gross	.40	1.00
42 Kermit Washington	.50	1.25
43 Mychal Thompson	.75	2.00
44 Kevin Kunnert	.30	.75
xx Jack Ramsay CO	.60	1.50
xx Bucky Buckwalter ACO	.30	.75
xx Bill Schonely ANN	.30	.75

1978-79 Trail Blazers Portfolio

These collector prints of Portland Trail Blazers were sponsored by The Benj. Franklin Federal Savings and Loan Association in Portland as a special gift to Blazer-Savers. They were produced by artist Michael Lundy and measure approximately 11" by 14". The Lucas print is in color, while the rest of the prints are in black and white. Two Trail Blazers are depicted together on two of the prints. The backs are blank. The prints are unnumbered and checklisted below in alphabetical order.

COMPLETE SET (10)	20.00	40.00
1 Kim Anderson and Clemon Johnson	1.25	3.00
2 T.R. Dunn	1.50	4.00
3 Bob Gross	1.50	4.00
4 Lionel Hollins	2.50	6.00
5 Maurice Lucas	3.00	8.00
6 Lloyd Neal	1.25	3.00
7 Tom Owens	1.25	3.00
8 Willie Smith and Ron Brewer	1.25	3.00
9 Larry Steele	2.50	6.00
10 Dave Twardzik	2.50	6.00

1977-78 Trail Blazers RC Glasses

These approximately 6 3/8" tall glasses were produced to celebrate the Portland Trailblazers 1976-77 NBA Championship. The glasses have a head shot with the players name, height and position, a facsimile signature, and other personal data below the player. The back of the glass has the "Me and my RC" slogan, and the glass is ringed with "RC Salutes the Champs-Portland Players" in black type over the blue ring. The checklist below may be incomplete, and any additions would be welcomed.

COMPLETE SET (8)	50.00	100.00
1 Johnny Davis	5.00	10.00
2 Bob Gross	5.00	10.00
3 Lionel Hollins	5.00	10.00
4 Maurice Lucas	7.50	15.00
5 Lloyd Neal	5.00	10.00
6 Larry Steele	5.00	10.00
7 Dave Twardzik	5.00	10.00
8 Bill Walton	20.00	40.00

1972-73 Trail Blazers Team Issue

Measuring 8" x 10", this 25-photo set features members from the 1972-73 Portland Trail Blazers. Each photo features either a close-up posed shot and an in action shot of each player in black and white. The player's name, height and college are listed on the front, as well as the team logo. The backs are blank. The photos are not numbered and listed below alphabetically.

COMPLETE SET (25)	65.00	125.00
1 Rick Adelman	3.00	8.00
2 Rick Adelman IA	2.50	6.00
3 Bob Davis	2.00	5.00
4 Bob Davis IA	2.00	5.00
5 Bobby Fields	2.00	5.00
6 Bobby Fields IA	2.00	5.00
7 Stu Inman VP	2.00	5.00
8 Neil Johnston ACO	3.00	8.00
9 Ollie Johnson	2.00	5.00
10 Ollie Johnson IA	2.00	5.00
11 LaRue Martin	2.00	5.00
12 LaRue Martin IA	2.00	5.00
13 Leo Marty TR	2.00	5.00
14 Jack McCloskey CO	2.00	5.00
15 Stan McKenzie	2.00	5.00
16 Stan McKenzie IA	2.00	5.00
17 Lloyd Neal	2.00	5.00
18 Lloyd Neal IA	2.00	5.00
19 Geoffrey Petrie	5.00	10.00
20 Geoffrey Petrie IA	3.00	8.00
21 Dale Schlueter	2.00	5.00
22 Dale Schlueter IA	2.00	5.00
23 Larry Steele	3.00	8.00
24 Larry Steele IA	2.50	6.00
25 Sidney Wicks IA	7.50	15.00

1976-77 Trail Blazers Team Issue

This 8" x10" set was produced for the Portland Trailblazers during the 1976-77 season. The set features 15 black and white cards of the team's players and coaches.

COMPLETE SET (15)	20.00	40.00
1 Dan Anderson	1.25	3.00
2 Barry Clemens	1.25	3.00
3 Bob Gross	1.25	3.00
4 Steve Hawes	1.25	3.00
5 Lionel Hollins	1.50	4.00
6 Maurice Lucas	2.50	6.00
7 Lloyd Neal	1.25	3.00
8 Larry Steele	1.25	3.00
9 Dave Twardzik	1.25	3.00
10 Wally Walker	1.25	3.00
11 Stu Inman VP	1.25	3.00
12 Ron Culp TR	1.25	3.00
13 Jack McKinney CO	1.25	3.00
14 Harry Glickman EVP	1.25	3.00
15 Larry Weinberg PRES	1.25	3.00

1977-78 Trail Blazers Team Issue

These color photos, which measure 5 7/8" by 9" and are blank-backed, feature members of the Portland Trail Blazers who were the defending NBA champs. Since these photos are unnumbered, we have sequenced them in alphabetical order.

COMPLETE SET (13)	17.50	35.00
1 Corky Calhoun	.75	2.00
2 Johnny Davis	.75	2.00
3 T.R. Dunn	.75	2.00
4 Bob Gross	.75	2.00
5 Lionel Hollins	.75	2.00
6 Maurice Lucas	1.50	4.00
7 Lloyd Neal	.75	2.00
8 Tom Owens	.75	2.00
9 Jack Ramsey CO	1.50	4.00
10 Larry Steele	.75	2.00
11 Dave Twardzik	.75	2.00
12 Bill Walton	3.00	8.00
13 Portland Trail Blazers Team Composite	1.50	4.00

1971-72 Trail Blazers Texaco

This 12-card set was sponsored by Texaco. The cards measure approximately 8" by 9 5/8" and feature full-bleed, posed player photos. The player's name is printed in white script lettering in the upper right corner. The card backs have biographical information and career statistics. The Texaco logo is printed at the bottom of the card. The cards are unnumbered and checklisted below in alphabetical order.

COMPLETE SET (12)	30.00	60.00
1 Rick Adelman	5.00	12.00
2 Gary Gregor	3.00	8.00
3 Ron Knight	3.00	8.00
4 Jim Marsh	3.00	8.00
5 Willie McCarter	3.00	8.00
6 Stan McKenzie	3.00	8.00
7 Geoff Petrie	5.00	12.00
8 Dale Schlueter	3.00	8.00
9 Bill Smith	3.00	8.00
10 Larry Steele	3.00	8.00
11 Sidney Wicks	6.00	15.00
12 Charles Yelverton	3.00	8.00

1957-59 Union Oil Booklets

These booklets were distributed by Union Oil. The front cover of each booklet features a drawing of the subject player. The booklets are numbered and were issued over several years beginning in 1957. These are 12-page pamphlets and are approximately 4" by 5 1/2". The set is subtitled "Family Sports Fun." This was apparently primarily a Southern California promotion.

COMPLETE SET (44)	200.00	400.00
5 Bill Russell BK 57	20.00	40.00
6 Forrest Twogood BK57	6.00	12.00
8 Phil Woolpert BK 58	6.00	12.00
9 Bill Sharman BK 58	10.00	20.00
31 George Yardley BK 58	7.50	15.00
32 John Wooden BK 58	20.00	40.00
34 Bob Cousy BK 59	17.50	35.00
36 Slats Gill BK 59	7.50	15.00

1961 Union Oil Chiefs

The 1961 Union Oil basketball card set contains 10 oversized (3" by 3 15/16"), attractive, brown-tinted cards. The cards feature players from the Hawaii Chiefs of the American Basketball League. The backs, printed in dark blue ink, feature a short biography of the player, an ad for KGU radio and the Union Oil circle 76 logo. The catalog number for this set is UO-17. These unnumbered cards are ordered alphabetically by player in the checklist below. Rick Herrscher would go on to have a short career with the 1962 New York Mets baseball team.

COMPLETE SET (10)	125.00	250.00
1 Frank Burgess	12.50	25.00
2 Jeff Cohen	12.50	25.00
3 Lee Harman	12.50	25.00
4 Rick Herrscher	15.00	40.00
5 Lowery Kirk	12.50	25.00
6 Dave Mills	12.50	25.00
7 Max Perry	12.50	25.00
8 George Price	12.50	25.00
9 Fred Sawyer	12.50	25.00
10 Dale Wise	12.50	25.00

1971-72 Warriors Team Issue

This 1971-72 Golden State Warriors set consists of 13 team-issued photos, each measuring approximately 10" by 8 1/8". The fronts feature one black-and-white posed action player photograph on the right side, and a smaller black-and-white player portrait in the top left corner. The player's name appears under the photo, with the team logo in the lower left. The backs are blank. The photos are unnumbered and checklisted below in alphabetical order. The set's date is based on the fact that Odis Allison and Vic Bartolome only played in 1971-72.

COMPLETE SET (13)	40.00	80.00
1 Odis Allison	1.50	4.00
2 Al Attles	5.00	10.00
3 Jim Barnett	2.00	5.00
4 Vic Bartolome	1.50	4.00
5 Joe Ellis	2.00	5.00
6 Nick Jones	1.50	4.00
7 Clyde Lee	2.00	5.00
8 Jeff Mullins	5.00	10.00
9 Bob Portman	1.50	4.00
10 Cazzie Russell	6.00	12.00
11 Nate Thurmond	10.00	20.00
12 Bill Turner	1.50	4.00
13 Ron(Fritz) Williams	2.00	5.00

1924 Willard's Chocolates Sports Champions V122

42 Edmonton Grads
Women's Basketball

1951 Wheaties

The cards in this six-card set measure approximately 2 1/2" by 3 1/4". Cards of the 1951 Wheaties set are actually the backs of small individual boxes of Wheaties. The cards are waxed and depict three baseball players, one football player, one basketball player, and one golfer. They are occasionally found as complete boxes, which are worth 50 percent more than the prices listed below. The catalog designation for this set is F272-3. The cards are blank-backed and unnumbered; they are numbered below in alphabetical order for convenience.

COMPLETE SET (6)	300.00	600.00
3 George Mikan	100.00	200.00

1952 Wheaties

The cards in this 60-card set measure 2" by 2 3/4". The 1952 Wheaties set of orange, blue and white, unnumbered cards was issued in panels of eight or ten cards on the backs of Wheaties cereal boxes. Each player appears in an action pose, designated in the checklist with an "A", and as a portrait, listed in the checklist with a "B". The catalog designation is F272-4. The cards are blank-backed and unnumbered, but have been assigned numbers below using a sport prefix (BB- baseball, BK- basketball, FB- football, G- Golf, OT- other).

COMPLETE SET (60)	600.00	1,000.00
BK1A Bob Davies Action	12.50	20.00
BK1B Bob Davies Portrait	12.50	20.00
BK2A George Mikan Action	75.00	125.00
BK2B George Mikan Portrait	75.00	125.00
BK3A Jim Pollard Action	10.00	25.00
BK3B Jim Pollard Portrait	10.00	25.00

College/Draft Picks

1980-81 Arizona

This 19-card standard-size set was co-sponsored by Golden Eagle Distributors and the Tucson Police Department. The cards feature on the fronts color posed close-up photos, with the players in uniform and holding a basketball in their hands. The pictures are full-bleed on three sides, with the player's name and number in the bottom white border. The backs have biographical information, a discussion or definition of an aspect of basketball, and a safety message. The cards are unnumbered and checklisted below in alphabetical order. The two SP cards (Cook and Mosebar) are very difficult to find as they were pulled from the set before the set went into general distribution.

COMPLETE SET (19)	75.00	150.00
1 John Belobraydic	1.25	3.00
2 Russell Brown	1.25	3.00
3 Jeff Collins	1.25	3.00
4 Greg Cook SP	40.00	80.00
5 Ron Davis	1.25	3.00
6 Robbie Dosty	1.25	3.00
7 Mike Frink ACO	1.25	3.00
8 Len Gordy ACO	1.50	4.00
9 Mike Green ACO	1.25	3.00
10 Jack Magno	1.25	3.00
11 Donald Mellon	1.25	3.00
12 Charles Miller	1.25	3.00
13 David Mosebar SP	25.00	50.00
14 Frank Smith	1.25	3.00
15 John Smith	1.25	3.00
16 Fred Snowden CO	1.50	4.00
17 Harvey Thompson	1.25	3.00
18 Ernie Valenzuela	1.25	3.00
19 Ricky Walker	1.50	4.00

1972-73 Bradley Schedules

These five schedule cards measure approximately 2 1/2" by 3 3/4" and are printed on heavy cardboard stock. Each card shows a black and white photo of a player on the front with a Bradley schedule for the 1972-73 basketball season on the back. The cards have rounded corners; on the front, the player's name appears on a white stripe beneath the posed black-and-white player photo.

COMPLETE SET (5)	40.00	80.00
1 Sam Allen	10.00	20.00
2 Mark Dohner	10.00	20.00
3 Dave Klobucher	10.00	20.00
4 Seymour Reed	12.50	25.00
5 Doug Shank	10.00	20.00

1910 College Athlete Felts B-33

Issued as a cigarette redemption premium, most prominently by Egyptiene Cigarettes, but other companies also probably offered these as premiums. Many of the backs have a listing on the reverse side listing a factory and district number. Although 10 different sports are included in this series, we are only listing the colleges in which basketball figures are known to exist. Although these are not numbered, we are putting these in alphabetical order for convenience.

COMPLETE SET	2,000.00	3,300.00
1 Amherst	50.00	100.00
2 Army	75.00	150.00
3 Brown	75.00	150.00
4 Bucknell	50.00	100.00
5 California	50.00	100.00
6 Chicago	50.00	100.00
7 Colgate	50.00	100.00
8 Colorado	50.00	100.00
9 Columbia	75.00	150.00
10 Cornell	75.00	150.00
11 Dartmouth	75.00	150.00
12 Harvard	100.00	200.00
13 Johns Hopkins	60.00	120.00
14 Knox	50.00	100.00
15 Michigan	75.00	150.00
16 Navy	50.00	100.00
17 Oregon	50.00	100.00
18 Pennsylvania	75.00	150.00
19 Princeton	100.00	200.00
20 Rutgers	50.00	100.00
21 St Louis	50.00	100.00
22 Stanford	100.00	200.00
23 Syracuse	50.00	100.00
24 Trinity	50.00	100.00
25 Tufts	50.00	100.00
26 Utah	50.00	100.00
27 Vermont	50.00	100.00
28 Williams	60.00	120.00
29 Wisconsin	50.00	100.00
30 Yale	100.00	200.00

1974-75 Duke Schedules

1 Tate Armstrong	2.00	5.00
2 Kevin Billerman	2.00	5.00
3 Bob Fleischer	2.00	5.00
4 Willie Hodge	2.00	5.00
5 Pete Kramer	2.00	5.00
6 George Moses	2.00	5.00
7 Kenneth Young	2.00	5.00
8 Coaching Staff	2.00	5.00

1975-76 Duke Schedules

1 Tate Armstrong	2.00	5.00
2 Bruce Bell	2.00	5.00
3 Terry Chili	2.00	5.00
4 Rick Gomez	2.00	5.00
5 Scott Goetsch	2.00	5.00
6 Steve Gray	2.00	5.00
7 Cameron Hall	2.00	5.00
8 George Moses	2.00	5.00

1976-77 Duke Schedules

1 Tate Armstrong	2.00	5.00

1978-79 Duke Schedules

1 Gene Banks	2.00	5.00
2 Kenny Dennard	2.00	5.00
3 Mike Gminski	3.00	8.00
4 John Harrell	2.00	5.00
5 Jim Spanarkel	2.00	5.00

1979-80 Duke Schedules

1 Gene Banks	2.00	5.00
2 Kenny Dennard	2.00	5.00

1980-81 Duke Schedules

1 Gene Banks	.40	1.00

1921 Holy Cross

This set was issued around 1922 and features cards of coaches and team captains for various Holy Cross University sports. The six cards measrue roughly 2 1/2" by 3 3/4" and were issued inside a "wrap-around" style folder that included a photo of the football team. Each card is blankbacked and was printed on thick cream colored stock.

COMPLETE SET (7)	100.00	200.00
4 McLaughlin BK	10.00	20.00

1980-81 Illinois

This 15-card standard-size set was sponsored by Arby's Restaurants and features players of the 1980-81 Fighting Illini squad. The player's signature and an Arby's advertisement appear below a color posed photo of the player. The horizontally oriented back provides biographical and statistical information. The cards are numbered for convenience alphabetically in the checklist below. Key cards in the set include the first cards of NBA veterans Derek Harper and Eddie Johnson.

COMPLETE SET (15)	15.00	30.00
1 Kevin Bontemps	.40	1.00
2 James Griffin	.40	1.00
3 Derek Harper	7.50	15.00
4 Lou Henson CO	1.50	4.00
5 Derek Holcomb	.75	2.00
6 Eddie Johnson	6.00	12.00
7 Bryan Leonard	.40	1.00
8 Dick Nagy ACO	.40	1.00
9 Perry Range	.40	1.00
10 Quinn Richardson	.40	1.00
11 Mark Smith	.40	1.00
12 Neale Stoner	.40	1.00
13 Craig Tucker	.40	1.00
14 Tony Yates ACO	.75	2.00
15 Team Photo	1.50	4.00

1976-77 Kentucky Schedules

This 12-card set features schedule cards each measuring approximately 2 1/4" by 3 3/4". The fronts display borderless dark blue-tinted player photos. Player information is given in the white stripe below the picture. On white backgrounds in dark blue lettering, the backs carry the 1976-77 basketball schedule. The cards are unnumbered and checklisted below in alphabetical order. These schedule cards were passed out individually at games by booster clubs.

COMPLETE SET (12)	15.00	30.00
1 Dwane Casey	2.00	5.00
2 Truman Claytor	1.25	3.00
3 Jack Givens	2.50	6.00
4 Merion Haskins	.75	2.00
5 Larry Johnson	1.25	3.00
6 James Lee	1.25	3.00
7 Kyle Macy	3.00	8.00
8 Mike Phillips	1.25	3.00
9 Rick Robey	2.50	6.00
10 Jay Shidler	1.25	3.00
11 Tim Stephens	1.25	3.00
12 LaVon Williams	1.25	3.00

1977-78 Kentucky

This 22-card set measures 2 1/2" by 3 3/4" and was produced by Wildcat News. The front features a black and white action photo with a royal blue border on white card stock. The player cards have the Wildcat logo, year, and the card number (in a basketball) across the top of the card face. The player's name and position appear below the picture. The back has a black and white head shot of the player in the upper right corner, with biographical and statistical information filling in the remainder of the space. This set features early cards of Kyle Macy and Rick Robey, who later played with different NBA teams. This set features the team that won the 1977-78 NCAA Championship.

COMPLETE SET (22)	22.50	45.00
1 The Fabulous Five	2.50	6.00
2 Joe Hall's First UK Team (Team Photo)	.75	2.00
3 1975 NCAA Runners-Up (Team photo in plaid blazers)	.75	2.00
4 1977-78 Wildcats	.75	2.00
5 Leonard Hamilton CO	1.25	3.00
6 Joe Dean CO	.75	2.00
7 Joe B. Hall CO	1.25	3.00
8 Dick Parsons CO	.75	2.00
9 Scott Courts	.40	1.00
10 Chuck Aleksinas	.75	2.00
11 LaVon Williams	.75	2.00
12 Chris Gettelfinger	.40	1.00
13 Dwane Casey	1.25	3.00
14 Fred Cowan	.75	2.00
15 Kyle Macy	3.00	8.00
16 Tim Stephens	.40	1.00
17 James Lee	1.25	3.00
18 Jay Shidler	1.25	3.00
19 Rick Robey	2.00	5.00
20 Truman Claytor	.75	2.00
21 Jack Givens	2.50	6.00
22 Mike Phillips	.75	2.00

1977-78 Kentucky Schedules

This 19-card set features schedule cards each measuring approximately 2 1/4" by 3 3/4". These schedule cards were passed out individually at games by booster clubs. The fronts display borderless dark blue-tinted player photos. Player information is given in the white stripe below the picture. On white backgrounds in dark blue lettering, the backs carry the 1977-78 basketball schedule. Included in this set is a second card of head coach Joe B. Hall featuring a full-bleed color photo. The cards are unnumbered and checklisted below in alphabetical order.

COMPLETE SET (19)	20.00	40.00
1 Chuck Aleksinas	1.25	3.00
2 Dwane Casey	1.50	4.00
3 Truman Claytor	1.25	3.00
4 Scott Courts	.75	2.00
5 Fred Cowan	1.25	3.00
6 Joe Dean ACO	.75	2.00
7 Joe B. Hall CO	1.25	3.00
8 Joe B. Hall CO	1.25	3.00
9 Leonard Hamilton ACO	1.25	3.00
10 Chris Gettelfinger	.75	2.00
11 Jack Givens	2.00	5.00
12 James Lee	1.50	4.00
13 Kyle Macy	2.50	6.00
14 Dick Parsons ACO	.75	2.00
15 Mike Phillips	1.25	3.00
16 Rick Robey	2.00	5.00
17 Jay Shidler	1.25	3.00
18 Tim Stephens	.75	2.00
19 LaVon Williams	.75	2.00

1978-79 Kentucky

This 22-card set was produced by Wildcat News and sponsored by Food Town. The cards were originally given out one per week at the participating grocery stores. The cards measure approximately 2 1/2" by 3 3/4". The front features a black and white action photo, with the Wildcat logo, year, and the card number (in a basketball) to the left of the picture. The player's name and position appear below the picture, and a royal blue border outlines the card face. The back has a black and white head shot of the player in the upper right corner, with biographical and statistical information filling in the remainder of the space. This set features an early card of Kyle Macy, who later played in the NBA.

COMPLETE SET (22)	7.50	15.00
1 Homeward Bound (Joe B. Hall and wife)	.60	1.50
2 Jack Givens Mike Phillips Rick Robey James Lee	.60	1.50
3 Moment of Glory (Jack Givens)	.75	2.00
4 Cliff Hagan's Hall of Fame Induction	.75	2.00
5 1978-79 Wildcats Team Photo	.60	1.50
6 1978 NCAA Champions Team Photo	.60	1.50
7 Dwight Anderson	.75	2.00
8 Clarence Tillman	.30	.75
9 Chuck Verderber	.60	1.50
10 Dwane Casey	.75	2.00
11 Truman Claytor	.60	1.50
12 Tim Stephens	.30	.75
13 Kyle Macy	1.50	4.00
14 LaVon Williams	.60	1.50
15 Jay Shidler	.60	1.50
16 Freddie Cowan	.60	1.50
17 Chuck Aleksinas	.60	1.50
18 Chris Gettelfinger	.30	.75
19 Joe B. Hall CO	.75	2.00
20 Dick Parsons ACO	.60	1.50
21 Leonard Hamilton ACO	.60	1.50
22 Joe Dean ACO	.30	.75

1978-79 Kentucky Schedules

This 16-card set features schedule cards each measuring approximately 2 1/4" by 3 3/4". These schedule cards were passed out individually at games by booster clubs. The fronts feature borderless dark blue-tinted player photos. Player information is given in the white stripe below the picture. In dark blue lettering on a white background, the backs have the 1978-79 basketball schedule. The cards are unnumbered and checklisted below in alphabetical order.

COMPLETE SET (16)	15.00	30.00
1 Chuck Aleksinas	.75	2.00
2 Dwight Anderson	1.25	3.00
3 Dwane Casey	1.25	3.00
4 Truman Claytor	1.25	3.00
5 Fred Cowan	.75	2.00
6 Joe Dean ACO	.75	2.00
7 Chris Gettelfinger	.75	2.00
8 Joe B. Hall CO	1.25	3.00
9 Leonard Hamilton ACO	1.25	3.00
10 Kyle Macy	1.50	4.00
11 Dick Parsons ACO	.75	2.00
12 Jay Shidler	1.25	3.00
13 Tim Stephens	.75	2.00
14 Clarence Tillman	.75	2.00
15 Chuck Verderber	1.25	3.00
16 LaVon Williams	.75	2.00

1979-80 Kentucky

This 22-card set was sponsored by Food Town. The cards measures approximately 2 1/2" by 3 3/4". The front features a black and white action photo, with the player's name printed vertically to the right of the picture. The card number (in a basketball), the year, and the Wildcat logo appear at the bottom of the card face. A royal blue border outlines the card face. The back has a black and white head shot of the player in the upper right corner, with biographical information filling in the remainder of the space. This set features cards of Kyle Macy, Sam Bowie, and Dirk Minniefield, who later played with different NBA teams.

COMPLETE SET (22)	10.00	20.00
1 1979-1980 Wildcats Team Photo	.40	1.00
2 Kyle Macy	1.25	3.00
3 Jay Shidler	.40	1.00
4 LaVon Williams	.40	1.00
5 Chris Gettelfinger	.30	.75
6 Fred Cowan	.40	1.00
7 Dwight Anderson	.60	1.50
8 Bo Lanter	.30	.75
9 Chuck Verderber	.30	.75
10 Dirk Minniefield	1.00	2.50
11 Sam Bowie	2.50	6.00
12 Charles Hurt	.75	2.00
13 Derrick Hord	.60	1.50
14 Tom Heitz	.30	.75
15 Joe Dean CO	.30	.75
16 Leonard Hamilton CO	.60	1.50
17 Dick Parsons CO	.40	1.00
18 Joe B. Hall CO	.60	1.50
19 Rupp Arena	.30	.75
20 Kyle Macy Pan Am Gold Medalist (Schedule on back)	.75	2.00
21 Sam Bowie Tom Heitz Derrick Hord Charles Hurt Dirk Minniefield	.75	2.00
22 Kyle Macy LaVon Williams Jay Shidler	.75	2.00

1979-80 Kentucky Schedules

This 17-card set features schedule cards each measuring approximately 2 1/4" by 3 3/4". These schedule cards were passed out individually at games by booster clubs. The fronts feature borderless dark blue-tinted player photos. Player information is given in the white stripe below the picture. In dark blue lettering, the backs have the 1979-80 basketball schedule. The cards are unnumbered and checklisted below in alphabetical order.

COMPLETE SET (17)	10.00	20.00
1 Dwight Anderson	.75	2.00
2 Sam Bowie	2.00	5.00
3 Fred Cowan	.40	1.00
4 Joe Dean ACO	.40	1.00
5 Chris Gettelfinger	.40	1.00
6 Joe B. Hall CO	.60	1.50
7 Leonard Hamilton ACO	.60	1.50
8 Tom Heitz	.40	1.00
9 Derrick Hord	.75	2.00
10 Charles Hurt	.75	2.00
11 Bo Lanter	.40	1.00
12 Kyle Macy	1.25	3.00
13 Dirk Minniefield	1.25	3.00
14 Dick Parsons ACO	.40	1.00
15 Jay Shidler	.60	1.50
16 Chuck Verderber	.40	1.00
17 LaVon Williams	.40	1.00

1980-81 Kentucky Schedules

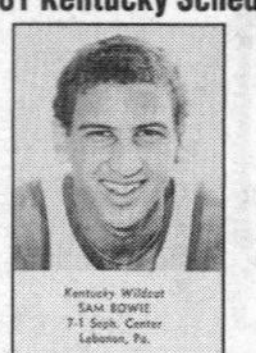

This 16-card set features schedule cards each measuring approximately 2 1/4" by 3 3/4". These schedule cards were passed out individually at games by booster clubs. The fronts feature borderless dark blue-tinted player photos. Player information is given in the white stripe below the picture. In dark blue lettering, the backs have the 1980-81 basketball schedule. The only color photo in this set is of head coach Joe B. Hall. The cards are unnumbered and checklisted below in alphabetical order.

COMPLETE SET (16)	10.00	20.00
1 Dicky Beal	.40	1.00

2 Bret Bearup .40 1.00
3 Sam Bowie 1.50 4.00
4 Fred Cowan .40 1.00
5 Joe Dean ACO .40 1.00
6 Chris Gettelfinger .40 1.00
7 Joe B. Hall CO .60 1.50
8 Leonard Hamilton ACO .60 1.50
9 Tom Heitz .40 1.00
10 Derrick Hord .60 1.50
11 Charles Hurt .60 1.50
12 Bo Lanter .40 1.00
13 Jim Master .75 2.00
14 Dirk Minniefield .75 2.00
15 Melvin Turpin 1.25 3.00
16 Chuck Verderber .40 1.00

1970-71 North Carolina Schedules

1 Dean Smith 10.00 20.00

1972-73 North Carolina Schedules

1 Donn Johnston 2.00 5.00
2 George Karl 4.00 10.00

1973-74 North Carolina Playing Cards

This 54-card standard-size set features North Carolina players. The set is designed like a playing card set and has rounded corners. On a white background, the fronts feature black-and-white player photos, with the player's name printed below. The backs are blue on white and carry the team name and logo. The cards are checklisted in playing card order by suits and numbers are assigned to Aces (1), Jacks (11), Queens (12), and Kings (13).

COMP. FACT SET (54) 75.00 150.00
1C 1956-57 National Champs 1.00 2.50
1D Bobby Jones 4.00 10.00
1H Homer Rice DIR 1.00 2.50
1S Dean Smith CO 20.00 35.00
2C Bob Lewis 1.00 2.50
2D Dave Hanners 1.00 2.50
2H Jerry Vayda 1.25 3.00
2S James Smith 1.00 2.50
3C Dennis Wuycik 1.00 2.50
3D Billy Chambers 1.00 2.50
3H Steve Previs 1.00 2.50
3S Bruce Buckley 1.00 2.50
4C Billy Cunningham 5.00 10.00
4D Mickey Bell 1.00 2.50
4H Dick Grubar 1.00 2.50
4S Tommy LaGarde 1.25 3.00
5C Lee Shaffer 1.00 2.50
5D Charles Waddell 1.00 2.50
5H Rusty Clark 1.00 2.50
5S John Kuester 1.00 2.50
6C Hook Dillon 1.00 2.50
6D Brad Hoffman 1.00 2.50
6H Joe Quigg 1.00 2.50
6S Tony Shaver 1.00 2.50
7C York Larese 1.50 4.00
7D Ray Hite 1.00 2.50
7H Tommy Kearns 1.25 3.00
7S Eddie Fogler 2.00 5.00
8C Jim Jorden 1.00 2.50
8D Walter Davis 5.00 12.00
8H Bill Bunting 1.00 2.50
8S Bill Guthridge 5.00 12.00
9C Doug Moe 3.00 8.00
9D Ed Stahl 1.00 2.50
9H Larry Brown 5.00 12.00
9S 1971-72 Third Nationally 1.00 2.50
10C Pete Brennan 1.50 4.00
10D Mitch Kupchak 3.00 8.00
10H Bill Chamberlain 1.00 2.50
10S 1970-71 NIT Champs 1.00 2.50
11C Charlie Scott 3.00 8.00
11D John O'Donnell 1.00 2.50
11H Robert McAdoo 6.00 15.00
11S 1968-69 ACC Champs 1.00 2.50
12C Larry Miller 2.50 6.00
12D Ray Harrison 1.00 2.50
12H Lailee McNair 1.00 2.50
12S 1967-68 Second Nationally 1.25 3.00
13C Lennie Rosenbluth 2.50 6.00
13D Darrell Elston 1.00 2.50
13H George Karl 4.00 10.00
13S 1966-67 ACC Champs 1.25 3.00
JK Bell Tower 1.00 2.50
JK Old Well 1.00 2.50

1973-74 North Carolina Schedules

1 Bobby Jones 3.00 8.00

1974-75 North Carolina Schedules

This three-card set was issued by the University of North Carolina. Each card measures approximately 2 3/8" by 3 1/2". The fronts feature full-bleed close-up color player photos, with the player's name and jersey number at the bottom of the card. The backs list the 1974-75 varsity basketball schedule. The cards are unnumbered and checklisted below in alphabetical order.

COMPLETE SET (3) 7.50 15.00
1 Mickey Bell 2.00 5.00
2 Brad Hoffman 2.00 5.00
3 Ed Stahl 2.00 5.00

1975-76 North Carolina Schedules

This three-card set was issued by the University of North Carolina. Each card measures approximately 2 3/8" by 3 1/2". The fronts feature full-bleed close-up color player photos, with the player's name and jersey number at the bottom of the card. The backs list the 1975-76 varsity basketball schedule. The cards are unnumbered and checklisted below in alphabetical order.

COMPLETE SET (3) 7.50 15.00
1 Bill Chambers 1.50 4.00
2 Dave Hanners 1.50 4.00
3 Mitch Kupchak 5.00 10.00

1976-77 North Carolina Schedules

This five-card set was issued by the University of North Carolina. Each card measures approximately 2 3/8" by 3 1/2". The fronts feature full-bleed close-up color player photos, with the player's name and jersey number at the bottom of the card. The backs list the 1976-77 varsity basketball schedule. The cards are unnumbered and checklisted below in alphabetical order.

COMPLETE SET (5) 12.50 25.00
1 Bruce Buckley 1.25 3.00
2 Woody Coley 1.25 3.00
3 Walter Davis 5.00 10.00
4 John Kuester 1.50 4.00
5 Tommy LaGarde 2.50 6.00

1977-78 North Carolina Schedules

This three-card set was issued by the University of North Carolina. Each card measures approximately 2 3/8" by 3 1/2". The fronts feature full-bleed close-up color player photos, with the player's name and jersey number at the bottom of the card. The backs list the 1977-78 varsity basketball schedule. The cards are unnumbered and checklisted below in alphabetical order.

COMPLETE SET (3) 5.00 10.00
1 Geoff Crompton 1.25 3.00
2 Phil Ford 2.50 6.00
3 Tom Zaliagiris 1.25 3.00

1978-79 North Carolina Schedules

This three-card set was issued by the University of North Carolina. Each card measures approximately 2 3/8" by 3 1/2". The fronts feature full-bleed close-up color player photos, with the player's name and jersey number at the bottom of the card. The backs list the 1978-79 varsity basketball schedule. The cards are unnumbered and checklisted below in alphabetical order.

COMPLETE SET (3) 4.00 8.00
1 Dudley Bradley 1.50 4.00
2 Ged Doughton 1.25 3.00
3 Randy Wiel 1.25 3.00

1979-80 North Carolina Schedules

This five-card set was issued by the University of North Carolina. Each card measures approximately 2 3/8" by 3 1/2". The fronts feature full-bleed close-up color player photos, with the player's name and jersey number at the bottom of the card. The backs list the 1979-80 varsity basketball schedule. The cards are unnumbered and checklisted below in alphabetical order.

COMPLETE SET (5) 6.00 12.00
1 Dave Colescott .75 2.00
2 Mike O'Koren 1.50 4.00
3 John Virgil .75 2.00
4 Jeff Wolf 1.25 3.00
5 Rich Yonakor 1.25 3.00

1980-81 North Carolina Schedules

These four cards were apparently issued by the Athletic Department of the University of North Carolina. Each card measures approximately 2 3/8" by 3 3/8". The fronts feature full-bleed close-up color photos, with the player's name and jersey number at the bottom of the card face. The backs list the 1980-81 varsity basketball schedule. The cards are unnumbered and checklisted below in alphabetical order.

COMPLETE SET (4) 3.00 6.00
1 Pete Budko .60 1.50
2 Eric Kenny .60 1.50
3 Mike Pepper .60 1.50
4 Al Wood 1.25 3.00

1972-73 North Carolina State Schedules

1 Tom Burleson 2.00 5.00

1973-74 North Carolina State Playing Cards

This 54-card standard size set features former North Carolina State University All-America players and team photos of ACC champions. The set is designed like a playing card set and has rounded corners and black-and-white photos on white backgrounds. The backs are red on white and display the N.C. State mascot and have the words "Pack Power" printed above the mascot and "Wolfpack Country" printed below in red outlined block letters. Since the set is similar to a playing card deck, it is checklisted below as if it were a playing card set. In the checklist C means Clubs, D means Diamonds, H means Hearts, S means Spades, and JK means Joker. The cards are checklisted in playing card order by suits and numbers are assigned to Aces (1), Jacks (11), Queens (12), and Kings (13). The jokers are unnumbered and listed at the end.

COMPLETE SET (54) 50.00 120.00
C1 Willis Casey AD .40 1.00
C2 Ken Gehring .40 1.00
C3 Steve Smith .75 2.00
C4 Dwight Johnson .40 1.00
C5 Jerry Hunt .40 1.00
C6 Tommy Burleson 2.00 5.00
C7 John Richter .40 1.00
C8 Lou Pucillo .40 1.00
C9 Vic Molodet .40 1.00
C10 Ronnie Shavlik .40 1.00
C11 Bob Speight .40 1.00
C12 Sammy Ranzino .40 1.00
C13 Dick Dickey .40 1.00
D1 Everett Case CO 1.25 3.00
D2 1965 ACC Champs .75 2.00
D3 1959 ACC Champs .75 2.00
D4 1956 ACC Champs .75 2.00
D5 1955 ACC Champs .75 2.00
D6 1954 ACC Champs .75 2.00
D7 1953 Dixie Classic .75 2.00
D8 1952 S.C. Champs .75 2.00
D9 1951 S.C. Champs .75 2.00
D10 1950 S.C. Champs .75 2.00
D11 1949 S.C. Champs .75 2.00
D12 1948 S.C. Champs .75 2.00
D13 1947 S.C. Champs .75 2.00
H1 Tommy Burleson 2.00 5.00
H2 Bruce Dayhuff .40 1.00
H3 Bill Lake .40 1.00
H4 Mike Buurma .40 1.00
H5 Greg Hawkins .40 1.00
H6 Craig Kuszmaul .40 1.00
H7 Mark Moeller .40 1.00
H8 Phil Spence .40 1.00
H9 Steve Nuce .75 2.00
H10 Moe Rivers .75 2.00
H11 Tim Stoddard .75 2.00
H12 Monte Towe 1.50 4.00
H13 David Thompson 12.00 30.00
S1 Norm Sloan CO 4.00 10.00
S2 Vann Williford .75 2.00
S3 Jo Ann Sloan .40 1.00
S4 Everett Case CO 1.25 3.00
S5 Tommy Burleson 2.00 5.00
S6 Three All-Americans 5.00 12.00
S7 David Thompson 10.00 25.00
S8 David Thompson 10.00 25.00
S9 1970 ACC Champs .75 2.00
S10 1973 ACC Champs 1.25 3.00
S11 Sam Esposito ACO .75 2.00
S12 Art Musselman ACO .40 1.00
S13 Eddie Bierderbach ACO .40 1.00
JK Pack Power .75 2.00
JK Reynolds Coliseum .75 2.00

1973-74 North Carolina State Schedules

1 David Thompson 5.00 12.00

1974-75 North Carolina State Schedules

1 David Thompson 3.00 8.00

1975-76 North Carolina State Schedules

1 Kenny Carr 2.00 5.00

1977-78 North Carolina State Schedules

1 Hawkeye Whitney 2.00 5.00

1978-79 North Carolina State Schedules

1 Clyde Austin 2.00 5.00

1979-80 North Carolina State Schedules

1 Hawkeye Whitney 2.00 5.00

1980-81 North Carolina State Schedules

1 Sidney Lowe 1.00 2.50

1910 Richmond College Silks S23

These colorful silks were issued around 1910 by Richmond Straight Cut Cigarettes. Each measures roughly 4" by 5 1/2" and are often called "College Flag, Seal, Song, and Yell" due to the content found on each one. More importantly to most sports collectors is the image found in the lower right hand bottom corner. A few feature a mainstream sports' subject such as a generic player or piece of equipment, while most include a realistic image of the school's mascot or image of the founder or the school's namesake.

28 Oberlin BK Player 75.00 150.00
32 Rochester Basketball 60.00 120.00

1979-80 St. Bonaventure

This 18-card set measures the standard size, 2 1/2" by 3 1/2". The front features a sepia-toned photo with the player's name above and jersey number in a basketball logo at upper right hand corner; the team name "Bonnies" appears below the photo. The photo is also enframed by a thin brown border on white card stock. The back is filled with biographical and statistical information. The set is ordered below alphabetically for convenience. At time of issue, a collector could order this set from St Bonaventure for $1.

COMPLETE SET (18) 20.00 40.00
1 Earl Belcher 25 1.50 4.00
2 Dan Burns 41 1.25 3.00
3 Bruno DeGiglio 24 1.25 3.00
4 Jim Elenz 10 1.25 3.00
5 Lacey Fulmer 20 1.25 3.00
6 Delmar Harrod 52 1.25 3.00
7 Alfonza Jones 12 1.25 3.00
8 Mark Jones 11 1.50 4.00
9 Bill Kalbaugh CO 1.25 3.00
10 Lloyd Praedel 44 1.25 3.00
11 Pat Rodgers 35 1.25 3.00
12 Bob Sassone CO 1.25 3.00
13 Jim Satalin CO 1.25 3.00
14 Mark Spencer 15 1.25 3.00
15 Eric Stover 40 1.25 3.00
16 Shawn Waterman 33 1.25 3.00
17 Brian West 30 1.25 3.00
18 Title Card 2.00 5.00

1977-78 West Virginia Schedules

This set of four schedule cards measures the standard size, 2 1/2" by 3 1/2". Printed on cardboard stock, the fronts show black-and-white action shots or portraits enframed by thick white borders. In team color-coded print, the school name, logo, and "Basketball 1977-78" appear above the pictures, while player information is presented below the pictures. On a white background, the back lists the 1978-78 basketball schedule, again in team color-coded print. The schedule cards are unnumbered and checklisted below in alphabetical order.

COMPLETE SET (4) 4.00 8.00
1 Sid Bostick .75 2.00
2 Dennis Hosey .75 2.00
3 Tommy Roberts .75 2.00
4 Maurice Robinson 1.50 4.00

1978-79 West Virginia Schedules

This set of 15 schedule cards measures approximately 2 5/16" by 3 1/2". Printed on cardboard stock, the fronts show black-and-white closeup player photos enframed by thick white borders. In blue print, the school name and "Basketball '79" appear above the pictures, while player information is presented below the pictures. On a white background, the back lists the 1978-78 basketball schedule, again in blue print. The schedule cards are unnumbered and checklisted below in alphabetical order.

COMPLETE SET (15) 7.50 15.00
1 Gale Catlett CO .75 2.00
2 John Goots .40 1.00
3 Vic Herbert .40 1.00
4 Dennis Hosey .40 1.00
5 Junius Lewis .40 1.00
6 Steve McCune .40 1.00
7 Lowes Moore .75 2.00
8 Noah Moore .40 1.00
9 Greg Nance .40 1.00
10 Dana Perno .40 1.00
11 Mike Richardson .40 1.00
12 Jeff Szczepanski .40 1.00
13 Lanny Van Eman ACO .75 2.00
14 Coaching Staff .40 1.00
15 Eastern Eight Logo .40 1.00

1980-81 Wichita State

This 15-card standard size (2 1/2" by 3 1/2") set was sponsored by Service Auto Glass and the Wichita Police Department. The cards were given away at the Wichita State athletic banquet and also by police officers. The fronts feature a close-up of the player enclosed by a border. The slogan "Love 'Ya Shockers" appears in the upper right corner, while player information is printed beneath the picture. Each card back carries a different safety message and a reminder to call 911. The cards are unnumbered and checklisted below in alphabetical order. Key cards in the set include the first cards of Antoine Carr and Cliff Levingston.

COMPLETE SET (15) 50.00 100.00
1 Antoine Carr 20.00 40.00
2 Mike Denny 1.50 4.00
3 Zarko Djuricic 1.50 4.00
4 James Gibbs 1.50 4.00
5 Jay Jackson 1.50 4.00
6 Mike Jones 1.50 4.00
7 Ozell Jones 4.00 10.00
8 Eric Kuhn 1.50 4.00
9 Cliff Levingston 15.00 30.00
10 Tony Martin 1.50 4.00
11 Karl Papke 1.50 4.00
12 Zoran Rdovic 1.50 4.00
13 Gene Smithson CO 1.50 4.00
14 Randy Smithson 1.50 4.00
15 Team Photo 2.50 6.00

Football Card Price Guide

1972 All Pro Graphics

These 8 1/2" by 10 1/2" color photos were produced by All Pro Graphics Inc. of Miami Florida. Each card carries an attractive color photo of the player with a facsimile signature on the front and the player's name above the photo. The cardbacks include biographical player information and carry the company name "Dimensional Sales Corporation, All Pro Graphics" all in lower case letters. Any additions to the checklist below are appreciated.

1 Buck Buchanan	7.50	15.00
2 Nick Buoniconti	7.50	15.00
3 Mike Curtis	6.00	12.00
4 Len Dawson	12.50	25.00
5 Mel Farr	5.00	10.00
6 Ted Hendricks	6.00	12.00
7 Leroy Kelly	7.50	15.00
8 Jim Kiick	6.00	12.00
9 Willie Lanier	6.00	12.00
10 Archie Manning	10.00	20.00
11 Earl Morrall	6.00	12.00
12 Steve Owens	6.00	12.00
13 Altie Taylor	5.00	10.00
14 Otis Taylor	6.00	12.00
15 Garo Yepremian	6.00	12.00

1973 All Pro Graphics

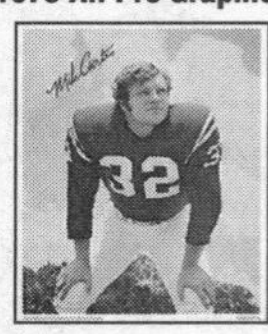

These 8" by 10" color photos were produced by All Pro Graphics Inc. of Miami Florida around 1973. Each blankbacked photo carries an attractive color photo of the player with a facsimile signature. Below the photo are the manufacturer's name on the left and the player's name on the right side. This list is thought to be incomplete as All Pro Graphics issued many photos in varying styles over a number of years. Any additions are appreciated.

1 John Brockington	6.00	12.00
2 Wally Chambers	5.00	10.00
3 Mike Curtis	6.00	12.00
4 Roman Gabriel	7.50	15.00
5 Joe Greene	12.00	20.00
6 John Hadl	7.50	15.00
7 Ron Johnson	5.00	10.00
8 Steve Owens	7.50	15.00
9 Alan Page	7.50	15.00
10 Jim Plunkett	7.50	15.00
11 Jan Stenerud	6.00	12.00

1966 American Oil All-Pro

The 1966 American Oil All-Pro set featured 20 stamps, each measuring approximately 15/16" by 1 1/8". To participate in the contest, the consumer needed to acquire an 8 1/2" by 11" collection sheet from a participating American Oil dealer. This sheet is horizontally oriented and presents rules governing the contest as well as 20 slots in which to paste the stamps. The 20 slots are arranged in five rows in the shape of an inverted triangle (6, 5, 4, 3, and 2 stamps per row as one moves from top to bottom) with the prizes listed to the left of each row. The consumer also received envelopes from participating dealers that contained small sheets of three perforated player stamps each. Each 3-stamp sheet was numbered with a letter as noted below making some of the stamps known double prints. Each stamp features a color head shot with the player wearing his helmet. After separating the stamps, the consumer was instructed to paste them on the matching squares of the collection sheet. If all the stamps in a particular prize group row were collected, the consumer won that particular prize. Top prize for all six stamps in the top group was a 1967 Ford Mustang. The other prizes were $250, $25, $5, and $1 for five-, four-, three-, and two-stamp prize groups respectively. Prizes were to be redeemed within 15 days after the closing of the promotion, but no later than March 1, 1967 in any event. Complete three stamp panels carry a 50 percent premium. The stamps are blank backed and unnumbered, and have been checklisted below alphabetically. Wayne Walker and Tommy Nobis were required to win $1; Herb Adderley and Dave Parks and Lenny Moore were required to win $5; John Unitas and Dave Jones, Mick Tingelhoff, and Alex Karras were required to win $25; Dick Butkus and Charley Johnson, Gary Ballman, Frank Ryan, and Willie Davis were required to win $250; and Gary Collins and Tucker Frederickson, Pete Retzlaff, Sam Huff, Gale Sayers, and Bob Lilly were required to win the 1967 Mustang. The winner cards indicated below are not priced (and not considered necessary for a complete set) since each is thought to have been largely redeemed and very few sales have been reported on existing copies. A 3-stamp advertising strip (roughly 3 1/4" by 6 3/4") was also produced and listed below.

COMPLETE SET (15)	100.00	200.00
WRAPPER	3.00	8.00
1 Herb Adderley		
2 Gary Ballman	5.00	12.00
3 Dick Butkus		
4 Gary Collins		
5 Willie Davis	6.00	15.00
6 Tucker Frederickson	5.00	12.00
7 Sam Huff	10.00	20.00
8 Charley Johnson C/L	6.00	15.00
9 Deacon Jones	8.00	20.00
10 Alex Karras	8.00	20.00
11 Bob Lilly	12.50	25.00
12 Lenny Moore	12.50	25.00
13 Tommy Nobis	6.00	15.00
14 Dave Parks	5.00	12.00
15 Pete Retzlaff	5.00	12.00
16 Frank Ryan	5.00	12.00
17 Gale Sayers	20.00	35.00
18 Mick Tingelhoff	6.00	15.00
19 Johnny Unitas		
20 Wayne Walker	100.00	200.00
NNO Ad Strip	75.00	150.00
NNO Saver Sheet	50.00	100.00

1967 American Oil All-Pro

The 1967 American Oil All-Pro set featured 21-stamps with each measuring approximately 7/8" by 1 1/8". The contestant needed to acquire an 8 1/2" by 11" collection sheet from a participating American Oil dealer on which he would place the stamps. The sheet was arranged in five rows with the prize level listed above each row. Each 3-stamp sheet was numbered with a letter as noted below. The consumer received envelopes from participating dealers that contained sheets of two perforated player stamps and one Mustang car stamp. Note that the Jim Taylor sheet contained a "Service Award" stamp instead of a second player. If all stamps in a particular prize group were collected, the consumer won that particular prize: the grand prize of a 1968 Ford Mustang, $100, $25, $5, or $1 cash. The $1 prize could be won by acquiring the stamps of Johnny Morris, Tommy Nobis, and Jim Taylor. The $5 prize required the stamps of Timmy Brown, Jimmy Orr, Fran Tarkenton, and Brady Keys. The $25 prize required stamps of John Unitas, Bob Hayes, Bill Brown, and Junior Coffey. The $100 prize required Gary Collins, Sonny Jurgensen, Charley Johnson, Gale Sayers, and Merlin Olsen. To win the 1968 Mustang required stamps of Bart Starr, Wayne Walker, Charley Taylor, Larry Wilson, and Ken Willard. The "winning" player for each prize group is fairly scarce, (and not necessary for a complete set) since each is thought to have been largely redeemed. Each stamp front features a color action player photo. The stamps are blank-backed and unnumbered and have been checklisted below alphabetically.

COMPLETE SET (19)	350.00	600.00
1 Bill Brown F	15.00	30.00
2 Timmy Brown J	15.00	30.00
3 Junior Coffey H	15.00	30.00
4 Gary Collins E	15.00	30.00
5 Bob Hayes D	25.00	40.00
6 Charley Johnson J	15.00	30.00
7 Sonny Jurgensen B	30.00	50.00
8 Brady Keys B	15.00	30.00
9 Johnny Morris A/M/P	15.00	30.00
10 Tommy Nobis ($1 winner)	60.00	100.00
11 Merlin Olsen M/P	25.00	35.00
12 Jimmy Orr H	15.00	30.00
13 Gale Sayers ($100 winner)	60.00	100.00
14 Bart Starr A	60.00	100.00
15 Fran Tarkenton ($5 winner)	30.00	50.00
16 Charley Taylor E	20.00	35.00
17 Jim Taylor N	40.00	75.00
18 John Unitas ($25 winner)		
19 Wayne Walker (Winner 1968 Mustang)		
20 Ken Willard F	15.00	30.00
21 Larry Wilson A/D	18.00	30.00
NNO Saver Sheet	50.00	100.00

1968 American Oil Mr. and Mrs.

This 32-card set was produced by Glendinning Companies and distributed by the American Oil Company. The cards measure approximately 2 1/8" by 3 7/16". The set is made up of 16 player cards and 16 wife/family cards that were originally connected by perforation in pairs. The cards were distributed as pieces of the "Mr. and Mrs. NFL" game. If a matched pair (i.e. a player card and his wife/family card) were obtained, the holder was an instant winner of either a 1969 Ford (choice of Mustang Mach I or Country Squire), $500, $100, $10, $5, $1, or 50-cents. The cards are most frequently found as detached halves. The horizontally oriented fronts feature action color player photos or color family photos featuring the wife. On the player card, the player's name is printed above the picture. On the wife card, the woman's married name (i.e. Mrs. Bobby Mitchell) and a caption defining the activity shown are above the picture. Each card is bordered in a different color and the prize corresponding to that card is printed in the border. The backs of the cards vary. In each pair that were originally connected, the wife card back features contest rules in a blue box on a red background with darker red car silhouettes. The player card back carries the game title (Mr. and Mrs. NFL), the American Oil Company logo, and the words "Win 1969 Fords and Cash" on the same background. In addition, attached to each pair at either end and forming a 12" strip, two more cardlike pieces contained further information and a game piece for predicting the 1969 Super Bowl scores. The smaller of the two (approximately 1 7/8" by 2 1/8") is printed with the NFL players and the corresponding prizes. The larger of the two (2 1/8" by 3 1/4") is the game piece for the second part of the contest with blanks for recording a score prediction for one NFL and one AFL team. This piece was mailed in to Super Bowl Scoreboard in New York. Each correct entry would share equally in the $100,000 Super Bowl Scoreboard cash prize. The cards are checklisted below alphabetically. The prize corresponding to each married couple is listed under the tougher of the pair. Prices listed are for single cards. Complete two-card panels are valued at approximately double the value of the individual cards. There are 16 tougher pieces that were the cards needed to win prizes. These 16 are not considered necessary for a complete set.

COMPLETE SET (16)	100.00	200.00
1 Kermit Alexander	250.00	400.00
2 Mrs. Kermit Alexander	6.00	12.00
3 Jim Bakken	6.00	12.00
4 Mrs. Jim Bakken	50.00	80.00
5 Gary Collins		
6A Mrs. Gary Collins	6.00	12.00
6B Mrs. Gary Collins Enjoying the Outdoors, pink frame	6.00	12.00
7 Jim Grabowski		
8 Mrs. Jim Grabowski	6.00	12.00
9 Earl Gros	50.00	80.00
10 Mrs. Earl Gros	6.00	12.00
11 Deacon Jones	12.00	20.00
12 Mrs. Deacon Jones		
13 Billy Lothridge		
14 Mrs. Billy Lothridge	6.00	12.00
15 Tom Matte	10.00	15.00
16 Mrs. Tom Matte		
17 Bobby Mitchell	90.00	150.00
18 Mrs. Bobby Mitchell	6.00	12.00
19 Joe Morrison	6.00	12.00
20 Mrs. Joe Morrison		
21A Dave Osborn	6.00	12.00
21B Dave Osborn silver frame		
22 Mrs. Dave Osborn		
23 Dan Reeves	40.00	80.00
24 Mrs. Dan Reeves	6.00	12.00
25 Gale Sayers	25.00	40.00
26 Mrs. Gale Sayers		
27 Norm Snead	60.00	100.00
28 Mrs. Norm Snead	6.00	12.00
29 Steve Stonebreaker	6.00	12.00
30 Mrs. Steve Stonebreaker	6.00	12.00
31 Wayne Walker	50.00	80.00
32 Mrs. Wayne Walker	6.00	12.00

1968 American Oil Winners Circle

This set of 12 perforated game cards measures approximately 2 5/8" by 2 1/8". There are "left side" and "right side" game cards which had to be matched to win a car or a cash prize. The "right side" game cards have a color drawing of a sports personality in a circle on the left, surrounded by laurel leaf twigs, and a short career summary on the right. There is a color bar on the bottom of the game piece carrying a dollar amount and the words "right side". The "left side" game cards carry a rectangular drawing of a sports personality or a photo of a Camaro or a Corvette. A different color bar with a dollar amount and the words "left side" are under the picture. On a dark blue background, the "right side" backs carry the rules of the game, and the "left side" cards show a "Winners Circle". The cards are unnumbered and checklisted below in alphabetical order.

COMPLETE SET (12)	75.00	150.00
11 Gale Sayers Left side	7.50	15.00
12 Bart Starr Right side	10.00	20.00

1961 American Tract Society

These cards are quite attractive and feature the "pure card" concept that is always popular with collectors (no card borders simply pure photo on front). The cards are numbered on the back and are skip-numbered below due to the fact that these singles are part of a much larger (sport and non-sport) set. The issue features Christian ballplayers giving first-person testimonies on the cardbacks describing how Jesus has changed their lives. These cards are often referred to as "Tracards." Each measures approximately 2 3/4" X 3 1/2". Many of the baseball subjects contain variations. No known variations exist for the football cards.

21 Donn Moomaw	10.00	20.00
50 Joe Romig	10.00	20.00

1978 Atlanta Convention

This 24-card standard-size set features circular black-and-white player photos framed in light green and bordered in white. The player's name is printed in black across the top with his position, team name, and logo at the bottom. The white backs carry the player's name and career information. The cards are unnumbered and checklisted below in alphabetical order. Almost all of the players in this set played for the Braves at one time.

COMPLETE SET (24)	7.50	15.00
19 Tommy Nobis	.75	1.50

1945 Autographs Playing Cards

Cards from this set are part of a playing card game released in 1945 by Leister Game Co. of Toledo Ohio. The cards feature a photo of a famous person, such as an actor or writer, or athlete on the top half of the card with his signature across the middle. A photo appears in the upper left hand corner along with some biographical information about him printed in orange in the center. The bottom half of the cardfront features a drawing along with information about a second personality in the same field or vocation. Those two characters are featured on another card with the positions reversed top and bottom. Note that a card number was also used in the upper left corner with each pair being featured on two of the same card number. We've listed the player who's photo appears on the card first, followed by the personality featured at the bottom of the card.

COMPLETE SET (55)	200.00	400.00
7A Bernie Bierman CO Knute Rockne CO	10.00	20.00
7A Knute Rockne CO Bernie Bierman	10.00	20.00
10 Red Grange Tom Harmon	12.50	25.00
10 Tom Harmon Red Grange	12.50	25.00

1959 Bazooka

The 1959 Bazooka football cards made up the back of the Bazooka Bubble Gum boxes of that year. The cards are blank backed and measure approximately 2 13/16" by 4 15/16". Comparable to the Bazooka baseball cards of that year, they are relatively difficult to obtain and fairly attractive considering they form part of the box. The full boxes contained 20 pieces of chewing gum. The cards are unnumbered but have been numbered alphabetically in the checklist below for your convenience. The cards marked with

SP in the checklist below were apparently printed in shorter supply and are more difficult to find. The catalog number for this set is R414-15A. The value of complete intact boxes would be 50 percent greater than the prices listed below.

COMPLETE SET (18)	6,000.00	9,500.00
1 Alan Ameche	175.00	300.00
2 Jon Arnett	150.00	250.00
3 Jim Brown	400.00	700.00
4 Rick Casares	200.00	350.00
5A Charley Conerly SP	350.00	500.00
5B Charley Conerly SP	350.00	500.00
6 Howard Ferguson	175.00	300.00
7 Frank Gifford	200.00	350.00
8 Lou Groza SP	1,250.00	1,800.00
9 Bobby Layne	200.00	350.00
10 Eddie LeBaron	175.00	300.00
11 Woodley Lewis	150.00	250.00
12 Ollie Matson	175.00	300.00
13 Joe Perry	175.00	300.00
14 Pete Retzlaff	150.00	250.00
15 Tobin Rote	150.00	250.00
16 Y.A. Tittle	250.00	400.00
17 Tom Tracy SP	1,500.00	2,500.00
18 Johnny Unitas	350.00	650.00

1971 Bazooka

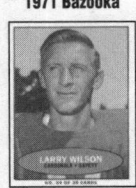

The 1971 Bazooka football cards were issued as twelve panels of three on the backs of Bazooka Bubble Gum boxes. Consequently, cards are seen in panels of three or as individual cards which have been cut from panels of three. The individual cards measure approxiamtely 1 15/16" by 2 5/8" and the panels of three measure 2 5/8" by 5 7/8". The 36 individual blank-backed cards are numbered on the card front. The checklist below presents prices for the individual cards. Complete panels are worth 25 percent more than the sum of the individual players making up the panel; complete boxes are worth approximately 50 percent more (i.e., an additional 25 percent premium) than the sum of the three players on the box. With regard to cut single cards, the mid-panel cards (2, 5, 8, ...) seem to be somewhat easier to find in nice shape.

COMPLETE SET (36)	300.00	450.00
1 Joe Namath	25.00	50.00
2 Larry Brown	6.00	12.00
3 Bobby Bell	6.00	12.00
4 Dick Butkus	18.00	30.00
5 Charlie Sanders	6.00	12.00
6 Chuck Howley	6.00	12.00
7 Gale Gillingham	5.00	10.00
8 Leroy Kelly	6.00	12.00
9 Floyd Little	6.00	12.00
10 Dan Abramowicz	5.00	10.00
11 Sonny Jurgensen	10.00	20.00
12 Andy Russell	5.00	10.00
13 Tommy Nobis	6.00	12.00
14 O.J. Simpson	10.00	20.00
15 Tom Woodeshick	5.00	10.00
16 Roman Gabriel	6.00	12.00
17 Claude Humphrey	5.00	10.00
18 Merlin Olsen	7.50	15.00
19 Daryle Lamonica	6.00	12.00
20 Fred Cox	5.00	10.00
21 Bart Starr	30.00	50.00
22 John Brodie	7.50	15.00
23 Jim Nance	5.00	10.00
24 Gary Garrison	5.00	10.00
25 Fran Tarkenton	12.50	25.00
26 Johnny Robinson	5.00	10.00
27 Gale Sayers	18.00	30.00
28 Johnny Unitas	30.00	50.00
29 Jerry LeVias	5.00	10.00
30 Virgil Carter	5.00	10.00
31 Bill Nelsen	5.00	10.00
32 Dave Osborn	5.00	10.00
33 Matt Snell	5.00	10.00
34 Larry Wilson	6.00	12.00
35 Bob Griese	15.00	25.00
36 Lance Alworth	10.00	20.00

1972 Bazooka Official Signals

This 12-card set was issued on the bottom of Bazooka Bubble Gum boxes. The box bottom measures approximately 6 1/4" by 2 7/8". The bottoms are numbered in the upper left corner and the text appears between cartoon characters on the sides of the bottom. The material is entitled "A children's guide to TV football," having been extracted from the book Football Lingo. Cards 1-8 provide definitions of numerous terms associated with football. Card number 9 lists the six different officials and describes their responsibilities. Cards 10-12 picture the officials' signals and explain their meanings. The value of complete intact boxes would be 50 percent greater than the prices listed below.

COMPLETE SET (12)	62.50	125.00
1 Football Lingo	6.00	12.00
2 Football Lingo	6.00	12.00
3 Football Lingo	6.00	12.00
4 Football Lingo	6.00	12.00
5 Football Lingo	6.00	12.00
6 Football Lingo	6.00	12.00
7 Football Lingo	6.00	12.00
8 Football Lingo	6.00	12.00
9 Officials' Duties	6.00	12.00
10 Officials' Duties	6.00	12.00
11 Officials' Signals	6.00	12.00
12 Officials' Signals	6.00	12.00

1964 Bears McCarthy Postcards

This 11-card set of the Chicago Bears features posed and action player photos taken by J.D. McCarthy and printed on postcard-size cards. Each is unnumbered and checklisted below in alphabetical order.

COMPLETE SET (11)	45.00	90.00
1 Charlie Bivins	2.50	5.00
2 Ronnie Bull	4.00	8.00
3 Mike Ditka	15.00	25.00
4 John Farrington	2.50	5.00
5 Sid Luckman CO	7.50	15.00
6 Joe Marconi	4.00	8.00
7 Billy Martin HB	2.50	5.00
8 Billy Martin E	2.50	5.00
9 Johnny Morris	4.00	8.00
10 Mike Rabold	2.50	5.00
11 Gene Schroeder CO	2.50	5.00

1967 Bears Pro's Pizza

These cards are actually discs that measure roughly 4 3/4" in diameter. They were printed on Pro's Pizza packages sold in the Chicago area and at stadiums. The player's image, with the athlete dressed in street clothes, appears on the front and the backs are blank.

COMPLETE SET (12)	3,000.00	4,500.00
1 Doug Atkins	175.00	300.00
2 Ronnie Bull	150.00	250.00
3 Dick Butkus	500.00	800.00
4 Mike Ditka	500.00	800.00
5 Dick Evey	150.00	250.00
6 Johnny Morris	150.00	250.00
7 Richie Petitbon	150.00	250.00
8 Jim Purnell	150.00	250.00
9 Mike Pyle	150.00	250.00
10 Gale Sayers	500.00	800.00
11 Roosevelt Taylor	150.00	250.00
12 Bob Wetoska	150.00	250.00

1967 Bears Team Issue

These black and white player photos were released by the Chicago Bears around 1967. Each measures approximately 5" by 7" and includes the player's name, his position (spelled out in full) and team name below the photo. They are blankbacked and unnumbered. Any additions to this list are appreciated.

COMPLETE SET (10)	75.00	125.00
1 Ronnie Bull	6.00	12.00
2 Rudy Bukich	5.00	10.00
3 Jack Concannon	5.00	10.00
4 Joe Fortunato	5.00	10.00
5 Richie Petitbon	6.00	12.00
6 Jim Purnell	5.00	10.00
7 Mike Pyle	5.00	10.00
8 Mike Rabold	5.00	10.00
9 Gale Sayers	15.00	30.00
10 Roosevelt Taylor	6.00	12.00

1968-69 Bears Team Issue

The Chicago Bears issued these black and white glossy photos for fans primarily for autograph purposes and mail requests. Each measures roughly 8" by 10" and includes the player's name and team name below the photo. Many also include the player's position or abbreviated position initials below the photo. As is common with many team issued photos, they were issued during more than one season and many contain different printed type styles and sizes. Any additions to this checklist are appreciated.

COMPLETE SET (43)	200.00	400.00
1 Doug Buffone	5.00	10.00
2 Ronnie Bull	6.00	12.00
3 Dick Butkus	15.00	30.00
4 Jim Cadile	5.00	10.00
5 Virgil Carter	5.00	10.00
6 Jack Concannon	5.00	10.00
7 Frank Cornish	5.00	10.00
8 Frank Cornish	5.00	10.00
9 Austin Denney	5.00	10.00
10 Dick Evey	5.00	10.00
11 Dick Evey	5.00	10.00
12 Bobby Joe Green	5.00	10.00
13 Willie Holman	5.00	10.00
14 Mike Hull	5.00	10.00
15 Randy Jackson	5.00	10.00
16 John Johnson DT	5.00	10.00
17 Jimmy Jones TE	5.00	10.00
18 Doug Kriewald	5.00	10.00
19 Rudy Kuechenberg	5.00	10.00
20 Ralph Kurek	5.00	10.00
21 Andy Livingston	5.00	10.00
22 Garry Lyle	5.00	10.00
23 Wayne Mass	5.00	10.00
24 Bennie McRae	5.00	10.00
25 Ed O'Bradovich	5.00	10.00
26 Richie Petitbon	6.00	12.00
27 Loyd Phillips	5.00	10.00
28 Loyd Phillips	5.00	10.00
29 Brian Piccolo	15.00	30.00
30 Brian Piccolo	15.00	30.00
31 Bob Pickens	5.00	10.00
32 Jim Purnell	5.00	10.00
33 Mike Pyle	5.00	10.00
34 Larry Rakestraw	5.00	10.00
35 Mike Reilly	5.00	10.00
36 Gale Sayers	18.00	30.00
37 Gale Sayers	18.00	30.00
38 Gale Sayers	18.00	30.00
39 Joe Taylor	5.00	10.00
40 Roosevelt Taylor	6.00	12.00
41 Cecil Turner	5.00	10.00
42 Bob Wallace	5.00	10.00
43 Bob Wetoska	5.00	10.00

1968 Bears Tasco Prints

1 Dick Butkus	20.00	40.00
2 Gale Sayers	20.00	40.00

1969 Bears Kroger

Similar to the Chiefs set issued the same year, this eight-card release was sponsored by Kroger Stores and measures approximately 8" by 9 3/4." The fronts feature a color painting of the player by artist John Wheeldon with the player's name inscribed across the bottom of the picture. The back has player biographical and statistical information and a brief note about the artist.

COMPLETE SET (8)	150.00	300.00
1 Dick Butkus	40.00	80.00
2 Virgil Carter	8.00	12.00
3 Jack Concannon	10.00	15.00
4 Dick Gordon	8.00	12.00
5 Bennie McRae	8.00	12.00
6 Brian Piccolo	60.00	100.00
7 Gale Sayers	35.00	60.00
8 Roosevelt Taylor	10.00	15.00

1971 Bears Team Issue

These twelve black and white photos were released as a set by the Chicago Bears in 1971. Each measures approximately 4 1/2" by 7" and includes the player's name and team name below the photo. They are blankbacked and unnumbered.

COMPLETE SET (12)	75.00	125.00
1 Doug Buffone	5.00	10.00
2 Dick Butkus	12.50	25.00
3 Rich Coady	5.00	10.00
4 Jack Concannon	5.00	10.00
5 Bobby Douglass	6.00	12.00
6 Dick Gordon	5.00	10.00
7 Jim Grabowski	5.00	10.00
8 Willie Holman	5.00	10.00
9 Randy Jackson	5.00	10.00
10 Gale Sayers	12.50	25.00
11 George Seals	5.00	10.00
12 Aaron Thomas	5.00	10.00

1973 Bears Team Issue Color

The NFLPA worked with many teams in 1973 to issued photo packs to be sold at stadium concession stands. Each measures approximately 7" by 8-5/8" and features a color player photo with a blank back. A small sheet with a player checklist was included in each 12-photo pack. These twelve color photos are thought to have also been released by Jewel Foods in Chicago.

COMPLETE SET (12)	40.00	80.00
1 Doug Buffone	5.00	8.00
2 Dick Butkus	10.00	20.00
3 Bobby Douglass	5.00	10.00
4 George Farmer	5.00	8.00
5 Carl Garrett	5.00	8.00
6 Jimmy Gunn	5.00	8.00
7 Jim Harrison	5.00	8.00
8 Willie Holman	5.00	8.00
9 Mac Percival	5.00	8.00
10 Jim Seymour	5.00	8.00
11 Don Shy	5.00	8.00
12 Cecil Turner	5.00	8.00

1973 Bears Team Sheets

This set of photos of the Chicago Bears was distributed on glossy paper stock each measuring approximately 8" by 10". The fronts feature black-and-white player and/or coach portraits with eight pictures to a sheet along with the Bears helmet and team name. The backs are blank and the sheets are not numbered.

COMPLETE SET (7)	35.00	60.00
1 Lionel Antoine Bob Asher Rich Coady Craig Cotto	5.00	8.00
2 Buffone Butkus Chambers Gunn Holman McGee Os	6.00	12.00
3 Clark Ellis Graham Lawson Rives Sanderson Pe	5.00	8.00
4 Clemons Hale Horton Hrivnak Janet Jeter Lyle	5.00	8.00
5 Douglass Farmer Huff Garrett Harrison Kozins#	6.00	10.00
6 Abe Gibron Zeke Bratkowski Chuck Cherundolo Whi	5.00	8.00
7 Coaches Players	10.00	20.00

1974 Bears Team Sheets

This set of photos of the Chicago Bears was distributed on six glossy sheets with each measuring approximately 8" by 10". The fronts feature black-and-white player or coach portraits with eight pictures to a sheet along with the year of issue. The backs are blank and the sheets are numbered on the fronts 1-5.

COMPLETE SET (5)	25.00	40.00
1 Sheet 1	6.00	10.00
2 Sheet 2	10.00	15.00
3 Sheet 3	5.00	8.00
4 Sheet 4	5.00	8.00
5 Sheet 5	5.00	8.00

1976 Bears Coke Discs

The cards in this 22-player disc set are unnumbered so they are listed below alphabetically. All players in the set are members of the Chicago Bears suggesting that these cards were issued as part of a local Chicago Coca-Cola promotion. The discs measure approximately 3 3/8" in diameter but with the hang tab intact the whole card is 5 1/4" long. There are two versions of the Doug Plank disc (green and yellow) and two versions of Clemons (yellow and orange); both of these variations were printed in the same quantities as all the other cards in the set and hence are not that difficult to find. The discs were produced by Mike Schechter Associates (MSA). These cards are frequently found with their hang tabs intact and hence they are priced that way in the list below. The back of each disc contains the phrase, "Coke adds life to ... halftime fun." The set price below includes all the variation cards. The set is also noteworthy in that it contains another card (albeit round) of Walter Payton in 1976, the same year as his Topps Rookie Card.

COMPLETE SET (24)	50.00	100.00
1 Lionel Antoine	1.00	2.50
2 Bob Avellini	1.25	3.00
3 Waymond Bryant	1.00	2.50
4 Doug Buffone	1.25	3.00
5 Wally Chambers	1.25	3.00

6A Craig Clemons	1.00	2.50
6B Craig Clemons	1.00	2.50
7 Allan Ellis	1.00	2.50
8 Roland Harper	1.00	2.50
9 Mike Hartenstine	1.00	2.50
10 Noah Jackson	1.00	2.50
11 Virgil Livers	1.00	2.50
12 Jim Osborne	1.00	2.50
13 Bob Parsons	1.25	3.00
14 Walter Payton	40.00	75.00
15 Dan Peiffer	1.00	2.50
16A Doug Plank	1.25	3.00
16B Doug Plank	1.25	3.00
17 Bo Rather	1.00	2.50
18 Don Rives	1.00	2.50
19 Jeff Sevy	1.00	2.50
20 Ron Shanklin	1.00	2.50
21 Revie Sorey	1.00	2.50
22 Roger Stillwell	1.00	2.50

1980 Bears Team Sheets

This set of photos was released by the Bears. Each measures roughly 8" by 10" and features 8-players or coaches on each sheet. The sheets are blankbacked and numbered on the fronts of 7.

COMPLETE SET (7)	20.00	40.00
1 Neill Armstrong	2.00	5.00
Jerry Frei		
Dale Haupt		
Hank Kuhl		
2 Ted Albrecht	3.00	8.00
Bob Avellini		
Brian Baschnagel		
Gary		
3 Gary Fencik	3.00	8.00
Robert Fisher		
Wentford Gaines		
Kris		
4 Bruce Herron	2.00	5.00
Tom Hicks		
Noah Jackson		
Dan Jiggett		
5 Willie McClendon	6.00	15.00
Rocco Moore		
Jerry Muckensturm		
6 Mike Phipps	3.00	8.00
Doug Plank		
Ron Rydalch		
Terry Schmid		
7 Matt Suhey	2.00	5.00
Paul Tabor		
Bob Thomas		
Mike Ulmer		
Le		

1968 Bengals Royal Crown Photos

These black and white blankbacked photos measure roughly 4" by 5 5/8" and feature members of the Bengals. Printed below the player photo are "Compliments of Royal Crown Cola" along with the player's name. A facsimile autograph is also included across each photo.

1 Frank Buncom	10.00	20.00
2 Sherrill Headrick	10.00	20.00
3 Dewey Warren	10.00	20.00
4 Ernie Wright	10.00	20.00

1968 Bengals Team Issue

The Cincinnati Bengals issued and distributed these player photos. Each measures approximately 8 1/2" by 11" and features a black and white photo. The player's name and position appear in the bottom border below the photo.

COMPLETE SET (15)	100.00	200.00
1 Al Beauchamp	7.50	15.00
2 Paul Brown CO	15.00	25.00
3 Frank Buncom	7.50	15.00
4 Greg Cook	7.50	15.00
5 Sherrill Headrick	7.50	15.00
6 Bob Johnson	7.50	15.00
7 Warren McVea	7.50	15.00
8 Jess Phillips	7.50	15.00
10 Fletcher Smith	7.50	15.00
11 Bill Staley	7.50	15.00
12 John Stofa	7.50	15.00
13 Bob Trumpy	7.50	15.00
14 Dewey Warren	7.50	15.00
15 Ernie Wright	7.50	15.00
16 Sam Wyche	10.00	20.00

1969 Bengals Team Issue

COMPLETE SET (6)	40.00	80.00
1 Paul Brown	10.00	20.00
2 Greg Cook	6.00	12.00
3 Bill Bergey	7.50	15.00
4 Bob Johnson	6.00	12.00
5 Horst Muhlmann	6.00	12.00
6 Paul Robinson	6.00	12.00

1969 Bengals Tresler Comet

The 1969 Tresler Comet set contains 20 cards featuring Cincinnati Bengals only. The cards measure 2 1/2" by 3 1/2". The set is quite attractive in its sepia and orange color front with a facsimile autograph of the player portrayed. The cards are unnumbered but have been listed below in alphabetical order for convenience. The card of Bob Johnson is much scarcer than the other cards, although some collectors and dealers consider Howard Fest, Harry Gunner, and Warren McVea to be somewhat more difficult to find as well. The backs contain biographical and statistical data of the player and the Tresler Comet logo. An offer to obtain a free set of these cards at a Tresler Comet (gasoline) dealer is stated at the bottom on the back.

COMPLETE SET (20)	300.00	450.00
1 Al Beauchamp	5.00	10.00
2 Bill Bergey	6.00	12.00
3 Royce Berry	5.00	10.00
4 Paul Brown CO	25.00	40.00
5 Frank Buncom	5.00	10.00
6 Greg Cook	5.00	10.00
7 Howard Fest SP	30.00	50.00
8 Harry Gunner SP	30.00	50.00
9 Bobby Hunt	5.00	10.00
10 Bob Johnson SP	75.00	125.00
11 Charley King	5.00	10.00
12 Dale Livingston	5.00	10.00
13 Warren McVea SP	30.00	50.00
14 Bill Peterson	5.00	10.00
15 Jess Phillips	5.00	10.00
16 Andy Rice	5.00	10.00
17 Bill Staley	5.00	10.00
18 Bob Trumpy	6.00	12.00
19 Ernie Wright	5.00	10.00
20 Sam Wyche	7.50	15.00

1971 Bengals Team Issue

The Bengals issued this photo pack set in 1971. Each borderless photo measures roughly 4 3/4" by 6 3/4" and features a facsimile autograph of the player over the photo. The cardbacks are blank and unnumbered. The set was typically released in an envelope labeled "Travel With the Champs" with the checklist on the outside of the envelope.

COMPLETE SET (6)	30.00	60.00
1 Virgil Carter	6.00	12.00
2 Greg Cook	6.00	12.00
3 Bob Johnson	6.00	12.00
4 Horst Muhlman	6.00	12.00
5 Lamar Parrish	6.00	12.00
6 Mike Reid	7.50	15.00

1972-74 Bengals Team Issue

The Bengals issued this set of player photos in the mid-1970s. Each measures roughly 8" by 10" and was printed on glossy black and white stock. The photos are blankbacked and unnumbered and checklisted below in alphabetical order. Each photo typically includes the player's name, position (spelled out) and team name below the photo seperated by dashes. The type sizes and styles vary with many of the photos in this list suggesting that they were issued in different years. Any additions to the list below are appreciated.

1 Doug Adams	5.00	10.00
2 Ken Anderson	7.50	15.00
3 Ken Avery	5.00	10.00
4 Al Beauchamp	5.00	10.00
5A Royce Berry wht jsy	5.00	10.00
5B Royce Berry brwn jsy	5.00	10.00
6 Lyle Blackwood	5.00	10.00
7 Paul Brown CO	7.50	15.00
8 Ron Carpenter	5.00	10.00
9 Virgil Carter wht jsy	5.00	10.00
10 Tommy Casanova	5.00	10.00
11 Al Chandler	5.00	10.00
12 Steve Chomyszak	5.00	10.00
13 Boobie Clark	6.00	12.00
14 Charles Clark	5.00	10.00
15 Wayne Clark	5.00	10.00
16 Bruce Coslet	5.00	10.00
17 Neal Craig	5.00	10.00
18 Isaac Curtis	5.00	10.00
19 Charles Davis	5.00	10.00
20 Doug Dressler	5.00	10.00
21 Lenvil Elliott	5.00	10.00
22 Mike Ernst	5.00	10.00
23 Howard Fest	5.00	10.00
24 Dave Green	5.00	10.00
25 Vern Holland	5.00	10.00
26 Bernard Jackson	5.00	10.00
27 Bob Johnson wht jsy	6.00	12.00
28 Ken Johnson DT	5.00	10.00
29 Charlie Joiner	7.50	15.00
30 Evan Jolitz wht jsy	5.00	10.00
31 Bob Jones S	5.00	10.00
32 Tim Kearney	5.00	10.00
33 Bill Kollar	5.00	10.00
34 Dave Lapham	5.00	10.00
35 Steve Lawson	5.00	10.00
36 Jim LeClair	5.00	10.00
37 Dave Lewis wht jsy	5.00	10.00
38 Pat Matson	5.00	10.00
39 Rufus Mayes	5.00	10.00
40 John McDaniel	5.00	10.00
41 Horst Muhlmann	5.00	10.00
42 Chip Myers	5.00	10.00
43 Lemar Parrish	6.00	12.00
44 Ron Pritchard	5.00	10.00
45 Mike Reid	6.00	12.00
46 Ken Riley	6.00	12.00
47 Paul Robinson wht jsy	5.00	10.00
48 Ken Sawyer wht jsy	5.00	10.00
49 John Shinners	5.00	10.00
50 Fletcher Smith	5.00	10.00
51 Bob Trumpy	6.00	12.00
52 Stan Walters	5.00	10.00
53 Sherman White	5.00	10.00
54 Fred Willis wht jsy	5.00	10.00

1976 Bengals MSA Cups

This set of plastic cups was issued for the Cincinnati Bengals in 1976 and licensed through MSA. Each features an artist's rendering of a Bengals' player. Some players also appeared in the nationally issued 1976 MSA Cups set with only slight differences in each. The unnumbered cups are listed below alphabetically. Confirmed additions to this checklist are appreciated.

1 Ken Anderson	5.00	10.00
2 Archie Griffin	4.00	8.00
3 Essex Johnson	3.00	6.00

1975-77 Bengals Team Issue

The Bengals issued this set of player photos between 1975 and 1977. Each measures roughly 5" by 8" with a black and white photo. The photos are blankbacked and unnumbered and checklisted below in alphabetical order. Each card includes the player's name, position initials and team name below the photo in large all capital letters. They look very similar to the 1978-79 photos but feature a larger type size. The white border below the player image is generally smaller as well but some players were also issued with a larger border and larger type size which would indicate a multiple year issue.

1 Al Beauchamp	4.00	8.00
2 Lyle Blackwood	4.00	8.00
3 Billy Brooks	4.00	8.00
4A Bob Brown	4.00	8.00
4B Bob Brown	4.00	8.00
5 Glenn Bujnoch	4.00	8.00
6 Gary Burley	4.00	8.00
7 Glenn Cameron	4.00	8.00
8 Ron Carpenter	4.00	8.00
9 Tommy Casanova	4.00	8.00
10 Boobie Clark	4.00	8.00
11 Marvin Cobb	4.00	8.00
12 Bruce Coslet	4.00	8.00
13 Brad Cousino	4.00	8.00
14 Isaac Curtis	5.00	10.00
15 Tony Davis	4.00	8.00
16 Lenvil Elliott	4.00	8.00
17 Greg Fairchild	4.00	8.00
18 Howard Fest	4.00	8.00
19 Stan Fritts	4.00	8.00
20A Vern Holland	4.00	8.00
20B Vern Holland	4.00	8.00
21 Ron Hunt	4.00	8.00
22 Bob Johnson	4.00	8.00
23 Essex Johnson	4.00	8.00
24 Ken Johnson	4.00	8.00
25 Charlie Joiner	6.00	12.00
26 Bill Kollar	4.00	8.00
27 Al Krevis	4.00	8.00
28A Dave Lapham	4.00	8.00
28B Dave Lapham	4.00	8.00
29 Jim LeClair	4.00	8.00
30 Rufus Mayes	4.00	8.00
31A John McDaniel	4.00	8.00
31B John McDaniel	4.00	8.00
32 Pat McInally	4.00	8.00
33 Maulty Moore	4.00	8.00
34 Melvin Morgan	4.00	8.00
35 Jack Novak	4.00	8.00
36 Lemar Parrish	5.00	10.00
37 Scott Perry	4.00	8.00
38A Ron Pritchard	4.00	8.00
38B Ron Pritchard	4.00	8.00
39 John Reaves	4.00	8.00
40 Ken Riley	5.00	10.00
41 Willie Shelby	4.00	8.00
42A John Shinners	4.00	8.00
42B John Shinners	4.00	8.00
43 Rick Walker	4.00	8.00
44 Sherman White	4.00	8.00
45 Ed Williams	4.00	8.00
46A Reggie Williams	5.00	10.00
46B Reggie Williams	5.00	10.00

1978-79 Bengals Team Issue

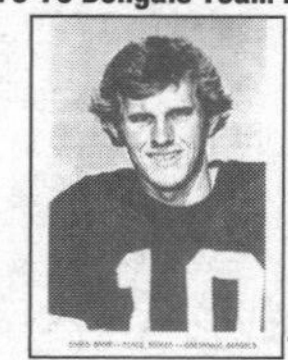

The Bengals issued this set of player photos in 1978. The 5 x 8 black and white photos are blankbacked and unnumbered and checklisted below in alphabetical order. Each card includes the player's name, position (spelled out) and team name below the photo. They look very similar to the 1975-77 photos but feature a smaller type size and a larger white border below the player image.

COMPLETE SET (30)	100.00	200.00
1 Ken Anderson	6.00	12.00
2 Chris Bahr	4.00	8.00
3 Don Bass	4.00	8.00
4 Louis Breeden	4.00	8.00
5 Ross Browner	4.00	8.00
6 Glenn Bujnoch	4.00	8.00
7 Gary Burley	4.00	8.00
8 Blair Bush	4.00	8.00
9 Glenn Cameron	4.00	8.00
10 Marvin Cobb	4.00	8.00
11 Jim Corbett	4.00	8.00
12 Tom DePaso	4.00	8.00
13 Tom Dinkel	4.00	8.00
14 Mark Donahue	4.00	8.00
15 Eddie Edwards	4.00	8.00
16 Lenvil Elliott	4.00	8.00
17 Archie Griffin	6.00	12.00
18 Ray Griffin	4.00	8.00
19 Bo Harris	4.00	8.00
20 Ron Hunt	4.00	8.00
21 Pete Johnson	5.00	10.00
22 Dave Lapham	4.00	8.00
23 Dennis Law	4.00	8.00
24 Jim LeClair	4.00	8.00
25 Pat McInally	4.00	8.00
26 Ken Riley	5.00	10.00
27 Ron Shumon	4.00	8.00
28 Dave Turner	4.00	8.00
29 Ted Vincent	4.00	8.00
30 Wilson Whitley	4.00	8.00

1951 Berk Ross

The 1951 Berk Ross set consists of 72 cards (each measuring approximately 2 1/16" by 2 1/2") with tinted photographs, divided evenly into four series (designated in the checklist as 1, 2, 3 and 4). The cards were marketed in boxes containing two card panels, without gum, and the set includes stars of other sports as well as baseball players. The set is sometimes still found in the original packaging. Intact panels command a premium over the listed prices. The catalog designation for this set is W532-1. In every series the first ten cards are baseball players; the set has a heavy emphasis on Yankees and Phillies players as they were in the World Series the year before. The set includes the first card of Bob Cousy as well as a card of Whitey Ford in his Rookie Card year.

COMPLETE SET (72)	900.00	1,500.00
14-Jan Leon Hart Football	7.50	15.00
15-Jan James Martin Football	6.00	12.00
14-Feb Doak Walker Football	10.00	20.00
15-Feb Emil Sitko Football	6.00	12.00
14-Mar Wade Walker Football	7.50	15.00
15-Mar Rodney Franz Football	6.00	12.00
14-Apr Arnold Galiffa Football	6.00	12.00
15-Apr Charlie Justice Football	7.50	15.00

1960 Bills Team Issue

Issued by the team, this set of 40 black-and-white photos each measures roughly 4 7/8" by 6 3/4" and was given to 1960 Bills season ticketholders in complete set form. The photos are unnumbered and checklisted below in alphabetical order. The photos are frequently found personally autographed.

COMPLETE SET (40)	250.00	400.00
1 Bill Atkins	7.50	15.00
2 Bob Barrett	7.50	15.00
3 Phil Blazer	7.50	15.00
4 Bob Brodhead	7.50	15.00
5 Dick Brubaker	7.50	15.00

6 Bernie Buzyniski	7.50	15.00
7 Wray Carlton	7.50	15.00
8 Don Chelf	7.50	15.00
9 Monte Crockett	7.50	15.00
10 Bob Dove CO	7.50	15.00
11 Elbert Dubenion	10.00	20.00
12 Fred Ford	7.50	15.00
13 Dick Gallagher GM	7.50	15.00
14 Darrell Harper	7.50	15.00
15 Harvey Johnson CO	7.50	15.00
16 Jack Johnson	7.50	15.00
17 Billy Kinard DB	7.50	15.00
18 Joe Kulbacki	7.50	15.00
19 John Laraway	7.50	15.00
20 Richie Lucas	7.50	15.00
21 Archie Matsos	7.50	15.00
22 Rich McCabe	7.50	15.00
23 Dan McGrew	7.50	15.00
24 Chuck McMurtry	7.50	15.00
25 Ed Meyer	7.50	15.00
26 Ed Muelhaupt	7.50	15.00
27 Tom O'Connell	7.50	15.00
28 Harold Olson	7.50	15.00
29 Buster Ramsey CO	7.50	15.00
30 Floyd Reid CO	7.50	15.00
31 Tom Rychlec	7.50	15.00
32 Joe Schaffer	7.50	15.00
33 John Scott	7.50	15.00
34 Bob Sedlock	7.50	15.00
35 Carl Smith	7.50	15.00
36 Jim Sorey	7.50	15.00
37 Laverne Torczon	7.50	15.00
38 Jim Wagstaff	7.50	15.00
39 Ralph Wilson OWN	15.00	30.00
40 Mack Yoho	7.50	15.00

1963 Bills Jones-Rich Dairy

This set of 40-crude drawings features members of the Buffalo Bills and were produced in a variety of versions and variations, but not all players have been verified for all versions. These "cards" are actually either blankbacked cardboard cut-outs from the sides of milk cartons or actual cap liners originally inserted into milk bottles. The bottle cap liners were produced with or without a small pull-out tab on the fronts and include the Jones-Rich logo on the backs. The flat (non-tab) version of the bottle caps liners were also produced in two versions with one being printed with a slightly larger player name printed on the front and larger company logo printed on the back. It is not yet known which players appeared in the large versus small print or the flat versus tab cap version. The milk carton version was produced in both a red and black ink variety with a further slight difference being found in the red ink variety (some can be found with a red ink circle around the player image along with the yellow ink dotted line). Most, if not all, of the players appear to be available in both varieties as well as both milk cap versions. The black ink carton variety seems to be very difficult to find. These circular cards measure approximately 1" in diameter and are frequently found miscut, i.e., off-centered. A display sheet that featured Bill's owner, Ralph Wilson, and Head Coach, Lou Saban, was also produced to house some of the caps and liners. Collectors at the time were challenged to complete a line-up of the 1963 Bills team, attach the caps and liners to the sheet and mail it in for a chance to win tickets to a Bill's game. The ACC catalog designation for this set is F118-1.

*CAP LINERS: .5X TO 1.2X CARTON CUT-OUTS

1 Ray Abruzzese	150.00	300.00
2 Art Baker	150.00	300.00
3 Stew Barber	200.00	350.00
4 Glenn Bass	150.00	300.00
5 Dave Behrman	150.00	300.00
6 Al Bemiller	150.00	300.00
7 Wray Carlton	150.00	300.00
8 Carl Charon	150.00	300.00
9 Monte Crockett	150.00	300.00
10 Wayne Crow	150.00	300.00
11 Tom Day	150.00	300.00
12 Elbert Dubenion	200.00	350.00
13 Jim Dunaway	200.00	350.00
14 Booker Edgerson	150.00	300.00
15 Cookie Gilchrist	250.00	400.00
16 Dick Hudson	150.00	300.00
17 Frank Jackunas	150.00	300.00
18 Harry Jacobs	150.00	300.00
19 Jack Kemp	500.00	800.00
20 Roger Kochman	150.00	300.00
21 Daryle Lamonica	250.00	400.00
22 Charley Leo	150.00	300.00
23 Marv Matuszak	150.00	300.00
24 Bill Miller	150.00	300.00
25 Leroy Moore	150.00	300.00
26 Harold Olson	150.00	300.00
27 Herb Paterra	150.00	300.00
28 Ken Rice	150.00	300.00
29 Henry Rivera	150.00	300.00
30 Ed Rutkowski	150.00	300.00
31 George Saimes	150.00	300.00
32 Tom Sestak	150.00	300.00
33 Billy Shaw	250.00	400.00
34 Mike Stratton	150.00	300.00
35 Gene Sykes	150.00	300.00
36 John Tracey	150.00	300.00
37 Ernie Warlick	150.00	300.00
38 Willie West	150.00	300.00
39 Mack Yoho	150.00	300.00
40 Sid Youngelman	150.00	300.00
NNO Display Sheet	500.00	750.00

1965 Bills Matchbooks

This 1965 Buffalo Bills release contains at least 3-different matchbooks. Each features a Bills player printed in blue on white paper stock along with the team's 1965 season schedule. Any additions to the checklist below would be greatly appreciated.

COMPLETE SET (3)	40.00	75.00
1 Elbert Dubenion	18.00	30.00
2 Billy Shaw	20.00	35.00
3 Tom Sestak	15.00	25.00

1965 Bills Super Duper Markets

Super Duper Food Markets offered these black-and-white (approximately 8 1/2" by 11") Buffalo Bills photos to shoppers during the fall of 1965. The photos were a weekly giveaway during the football season by Super Duper markets in western New York. The photos are unnumbered and checklisted below in alphabetical order.

COMPLETE SET (10)	150.00	250.00
1 Glenn Bass	7.50	15.00
2 Elbert Dubenion	10.00	20.00
3 Billy Joe	7.50	15.00
4 Jack Kemp	40.00	80.00
5 Daryle Lamonica	25.00	40.00
6 Tom Sestak	7.50	15.00
7 Billy Shaw	10.00	20.00
8 Mike Stratton	7.50	15.00
9 Ernie Warlick	7.50	15.00
10 Team Photo	15.00	30.00

1965 Bills Team Issue

Issued by the team, this set of black-and-white photos each measures roughly 8" by 10" and was issued to fulfill fan requests and for player appearances in the mid 1960s. Unless noted below, the text within the bottom border includes the player's name in all caps, his position in lower case letters, and the team name in all caps. The photos are unnumbered, blankbacked, and checklisted below in alphabetical order.

1 Cookie Gilchrist	7.50	15.00
2 Daryle Lamonica	10.00	20.00
3 Tom Janik	6.00	12.00

1965 Bills Volpe Tumblers

These Bills artist's renderings were part of a plastic cup tumbler produced in 1965 and distributed through Sunoco gasoline stations. The noted sports artist Volpe created the artwork which includes an action scene and a player portrait. These paper inserts are unnumbered, each measures approximately 5" by 8 1/2" and is curved in the shape required to fit inside a plastic cup.

COMPLETE SET (12)	300.00	500.00
1 Glenn Bass	25.00	40.00
2 Butch Byrd	30.00	50.00
3 Wray Carlton	25.00	40.00
4 Tom Day	25.00	40.00
5 Billy Joe	30.00	50.00
6 Jack Kemp	60.00	100.00
7 Daryle Lamonica	40.00	75.00
8 Lou Saban CO	30.00	50.00
9 George Saimes	25.00	40.00
10 Tom Sestak	25.00	40.00
11 Billy Shaw	35.00	60.00
12 Mike Stratton	30.00	50.00

1966 Bills Matchbooks

The 1966 Bills Matchbook set features the team's 1966 season schedule along with a blue player photo and sponsor logos. Any additions to the checklist below would be greatly appreciated.

COMPLETE SET (4)	100.00	175.00
1 Butch Byrd	7.50	15.00
2 Elbert Dubenion	18.00	30.00
3 Jack Kemp	75.00	125.00
4 Mike Stratton	15.00	25.00

1967 Bills Jones-Rich Dairy

Through a special mail-in offer, Jones-Rich Milk Co. offered this set of six Buffalo Bills' highlight action photos from the 1965 and 1966 seasons. These black-and-white photos measure approximately 8 1/2" by 11".

COMPLETE SET (6)	75.00	125.00
1 George Butch Byrd	12.50	25.00
2 Wray Carlton	12.50	25.00
3 Hagood Clarke	10.00	20.00
4 Paul Costa	10.00	20.00
5 Jim Dunaway	10.00	20.00
6 Jack Spikes	12.50	25.00

1967 Bills Matchbooks

The 1967 Buffalo Bills matchbook set contains 4-different matchbooks. Each includes the team's 1967 season schedule along with a player photo printed in blue ink. Any additions to the checklist below would be greatly appreciated.

COMPLETE SET (4)	50.00	80.00
1 Bobby Burnett	15.00	25.00
2 Butch Byrd	18.00	30.00
3 Roland McDole	15.00	25.00
4 Ed Rutkowski	15.00	25.00

1967 Bills Team Issue

Issued by the team, this set of black-and-white photos each measures roughly 8" by 10" and was issued to fulfill fan requests and for player appearances in the mid 1960s. Unless noted below, the text within the bottom border includes on the far left the photographer's ID, then (in all caps) the player's position, his name, and the team name, followed by the team logo on the far right. The photos are unnumbered, blankbacked, and checklisted below in alphabetical order.

1 Joe Collier CO	6.00	12.00
2 Jack Kemp	20.00	35.00

1968 Bills Matchbooks

This Buffalo Bills matchbook set contains only one known matchbook. It includes the team's 1968 season schedule along with a player photo printed in black ink. Any additions to the checklist below would be greatly appreciated.

1 Keith Lincoln	25.00	40.00
2 Billy Shaw	25.00	40.00

1972 Bills Buffalo News Posters

These posters were created by the Buffalo News and issued as "pages" in the daily newspapers during the 1972 season. Each large poster includes a color artist's rendition of a Bills player on the front with a typical newspaper page back. We've included the date when the photo appeared when known.

COMPLETE SET (10)	50.00	100.00
1 Paul Costa	4.00	10.00
2 Al Cowlings	4.00	10.00
3 Paul Guidry	4.00	10.00
4 J.D. Hill	4.00	10.00
5 Spike Jones	4.00	10.00
6 Reggie McKenzie	6.00	15.00
7 Wayne Patrick	4.00	10.00
8 Walt Patulski	4.00	10.00
9 Dennis Shaw	5.00	12.00
10 O.J. Simpson	12.50	25.00

1973 Bills Buffalo News Posters

These posters were created by the Buffalo News and issued as "pages" in the daily newspapers during the 1973 season. Each large poster includes a color artist's rendition of a Bills player on the front with a typical newspaper page back. We've included the date when the photo appeared when known. Any additions to this list are appreciated.

COMPLETE SET (16)	75.00	150.00
1 Jim Braxton	4.00	10.00
2 Bob Chandler	5.00	12.00
3 Jim Cheyunski	4.00	10.00
4 Earl Edwards	4.00	10.00
5 Joe Ferguson	6.00	15.00
6 Tony Greene	4.00	10.00
7 Bob James	4.00	10.00
8 Bruce Jarvis	4.00	10.00
9 Reggie McKenzie	6.00	15.00
10 Ahmad Rashad	6.00	15.00
11 Lou Saban CO	4.00	10.00
12 Paul Seymour	4.00	10.00
13 Dennis Shaw	5.00	12.00
14 O.J. Simpson	15.00	30.00
15 John Skorupan	4.00	10.00
16 Larry Watkins	4.00	10.00

1973 Bills Team Issue Color

The NFLPA worked with many teams in 1973 to issued photo packs to be sold at stadium concession stands. Each measures approximately 7" by 8-5/8" and features a color player photo with a blank back. A small sheet with a player checklist was included in each 6-photo pack.

COMPLETE SET (12)	40.00	80.00
1 Jim Braxton	4.00	8.00
2 Bob Chandler	4.00	8.00
3 Jim Cheyunski	4.00	8.00
4 Earl Edwards	4.00	8.00
5 Joe Ferguson	5.00	10.00
6 Dave Foley	4.00	8.00
7 Robert James	4.00	8.00
8 Reggie McKenzie	4.00	8.00
9 Jerry Patton	4.00	8.00
10 Walt Patulski	4.00	8.00
11 John Skorupan	4.00	8.00
12 O.J. Simpson	10.00	20.00

1974 Bills Buffalo News Posters

These posters were created by the Buffalo News and issued as "pages" in the daily newspapers during the 1974 season. Each large poster includes a color artist's rendition of a Bills player on the front with a typical newspaper page back. We've included the date when the photo appeared when known. Any additions to this list are appreciated.

COMPLETE SET (12)	60.00	120.00
1 Doug Allen	4.00	10.00
2 Jim Braxton	4.00	10.00
3 Joe DeLamielleure	6.00	15.00
4 Reuben Gant	4.00	10.00
5 Dwight Harrison	4.00	10.00
6 Mike Kadish	4.00	10.00
7 John Leypoldt	4.00	10.00
8 Reggie McKenzie	6.00	15.00
9 Mike Montler	4.00	10.00
10 Walt Patulski	4.00	10.00
11 Ahmad Rashad	6.00	15.00
12 O.J. Simpson	12.50	25.00

1975 Bills Buffalo News Posters

These posters were created by the Buffalo News and issued as "pages" in the daily newspapers during the 1975 season. Each large poster includes a color artist's rendition of a Bills player on the front with a typical newspaper page back. We've included the date when the photo appeared when known. Any additions to this list are appreciated.

COMPLETE SET (13)	50.00	100.00
1 Marv Bateman	3.00	8.00
2 Bo Cornell	3.00	8.00
3 Don Croft	3.00	8.00
4 Dave Foley	3.00	8.00
5 Gary Hayman	3.00	8.00
6 John Holland	3.00	8.00
7 Merv Krakau	3.00	8.00
8 Gary Marangi	3.00	8.00
9 Willie Parker	3.00	8.00
10 Tom Ruud	3.00	8.00
11 Pat Toomay	3.00	8.00
12 Vic Washington	3.00	8.00
13 Jeff Winans	3.00	8.00

1976 Bills Buffalo News Posters

These posters were created by the Buffalo News and issued as "pages" in the daily newspapers during the 1976 season. Each large poster includes a color artist's rendition of a Bills player on the front with a typical newspaper page back. We've included the date when the photo appeared when known. Any additions to this list are appreciated.

COMPLETE SET (11)	40.00	80.00
1 Bill Adams	3.00	8.00
2 Mario Clark	3.00	8.00
3 Joe Ferguson	5.00	12.00
4 Steve Freeman	3.00	8.00
5 Dan Jilek	3.00	8.00
6 Doug Jones	3.00	8.00
7 Ken Jones	3.00	8.00
8 Merv Krakau	3.00	8.00
9 Gary Marangi	3.00	8.00
10 Eddie Ray	3.00	8.00
11 Sherman White	3.00	8.00

1976 Bills McDonald's

This set of three photos was sponsored by McDonald's in conjunction with WBEN-TV. These "Player of the Week" photos were given away free with the purchase of a Quarter Pounder at participating McDonald's restaurants of Western New York. The offer was valid while supplies lasted but ended Nov. 28, 1976. Each photo measures approximately 8" by 10" and features a posed color close-up photo bordered in white. The player's name and team name are printed in black in the bottom white border, and his facsimile autograph is inscribed across the photo toward the lower right corner. The top portion of the back has biographical information, career summary, and career statistics (except the McKenzie back omits statistics). Inside a rectangle, the bottom portion describes the promotion and presents the 1976-77 football schedule on WBEN-TV. The photos are unnumbered and are checklisted below alphabetically.

COMPLETE SET (3)	12.50	25.00
1 Bob Chandler	4.00	8.00
2 Joe Ferguson	6.00	12.00
3 Reggie McKenzie	4.00	8.00

1977 Bills Buffalo News Posters

These posters were created by the Buffalo News and issued as "pages" in the daily newspapers during the 1977 season. Each large poster includes a color artist's rendition of a Bills player on the front with a typical newspaper page back. We've included the date when the photo appeared when known. Any additions to this list are appreciated.

COMPLETE SET (8)	30.00	60.00
1 Joe Devlin	3.00	8.00
2 Phil Dokes	3.00	8.00
3 Bill Dunstan	3.00	8.00
4 Roland Hooks	3.00	8.00
5 Ken Johnson	3.00	8.00
6 Keith Moody	3.00	8.00
7 Shane Nelson	3.00	8.00
8 Ben Williams	3.00	8.00

1978 Bills Buffalo News Posters

These posters were created by the Buffalo News and issued as "pages" in the daily newspapers during the 1978 season. Each large poster includes a color artist's rendition of a Bills player on the front with a typical newspaper page back. We've included the date when the photo appeared when known. Any additions to this list are appreciated.

1 Dee Hardison 6.00 8.00
2 Scott Hutchinson 6.00 8.00
3 Frank Lewis 4.00 10.00
4 Terry Miller 6.00 8.00
5 Charles Romes 6.00 8.00
6 Lucius Sanford 6.00 8.00

1978 Bills Postcards

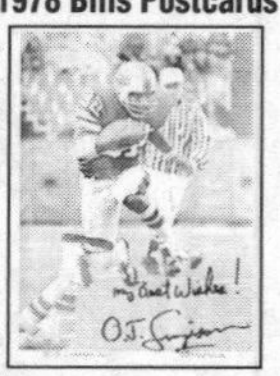

These Bills Team Issue photos were sent out to fans requesting autographs. The cardbacks include a message from the player to fans along with an area for the fan's name and address similar to a postcard. We've included prices below for unsigned copies of the cards. Two different Simpson photos were released that contain the same cardback.

COMPLETE SET (5) 20.00 40.00
1 Jim Braxton 2.00 4.00
2 Bob Chandler 3.00 6.00
3 Joe Ferguson 3.00 6.00
4 O.J. Simpson 7.50 15.00
5 O.J. Simpson 7.50 15.00

1978 Bills Team Issue

This set of 8" by 10" black and white photos was issued by the Bills around 1978. Each photo was produced in one of two styles: with player name, position, and team name below the photo, or with jersey number, player name, position, and team name below. All photos also include the photographer's notation (Photo by Robert L. Smith) below the photo. Each is blankbacked and listed alphabetically below.

COMPLETE SET (22) 35.00 60.00
1 Mario Celotto 2.00 4.00
2 Mike Collier 2.00 4.00
3 Elbert Drungo 2.00 4.00
4 Mike Franckowiak 2.00 4.00
5 Tom Graham 2.00 4.00
6 Will Grant 2.00 4.00
7 Tony Greene 2.00 4.00
8 Dee Hardison 2.00 4.00
9 Scott Hutchinson 2.00 4.00
10 Dennis Johnson 2.00 4.00
11 Ken Johnson 2.00 4.00
12 Mike Kadish 2.00 4.00
13 Frank Lewis 2.50 5.00
14 John Little 2.00 4.00
15 Carson Long 2.00 4.00
16 David Mays 2.00 4.00
17 Terry Miller 2.00 4.00
18 Keith Moody 2.00 4.00
19 Bill Munson 2.50 5.00
20 Shane Nelson 2.00 4.00
21 Lucius Sanford 2.00 4.00
22 Connie Zelencik 2.00 4.00

1979 Bills Bell's Market

The 1979 Bell's Market Buffalo Bills set contains 11 photos which were issued one per week, with purchase, at Bell's Markets during the football season. The cards measure approximately 7 5/8" by 10" and were printed on thin stock. The Bills' logo as well as the Bell's Markets logo appears on the back along with information and statistics about the players. The cards show the player portrayed in action in full color. The photos are unnumbered and are listed below in alphabetical order by name.

COMPLETE SET (11) 20.00 40.00
1 Curtis Brown 1.50 3.00
2 Bob Chandler 3.00 6.00
3 Joe DeLamielleure 2.00 4.00
4 Joe Ferguson 4.00 8.00
5 Reuben Gant 2.00 4.00
6 Dee Hardison 1.50 3.00
7 Frank Lewis 2.00 4.00
8 Reggie McKenzie 2.00 4.00
9 Terry Miller 2.00 4.00
10 Shane Nelson 1.50 3.00
11 Lucius Sanford 1.50 3.00

1979 Bills Buffalo News Posters

These posters were created by the Buffalo News and issued as "pages" in the daily newspapers during the 1979 season. Each large poster includes a color artist's rendition of a Bills player on the front with a typical newspaper page back. We've included the date when the photo appeared when known. Any additions to this list are appreciated.

1 Curtis Brown 3.00 8.00
2 Jerry Butler 4.00 10.00
3 Jim Haslett 3.00 8.00
4 Isiah Robertson 4.00 10.00
5 Fred Smerlas 3.00 8.00

1980 Bills Bell's Market

The 1980 Bell's Market Buffalo Bills cards were available in ten strips of two (connected together by a perforation) or singly as 20 individual cards. The individual cards measure approximately 2 1/2" by 3 1/2". The cards are in full color and contain a red frame line on the front. The back features blue printing listing player biographies, statistics and the Bell's Markets logo. The prices below are for the individual cards. The value of a connected pair is approximately the sum of the two individual cards listed below. The pairings were as follows: 1-2, 3-4, 5-6, 7-8, 9-10, 11-12, 13-14, 15-16, 17-18, and 19-20.

COMPLETE SET (20) 5.00 10.00
1 Curtis Brown .20 .50
2 Shane Nelson .20 .50
3 Jerry Butler .30 .75
4 Joe Ferguson .60 1.50
5 Joe Cribbs .40 1.00
6 Reggie McKenzie .30 .75
7 Joe Devlin .30 .75
8 Ken Jones .20 .50
9 Steve Freeman .20 .50
10 Mike Kadish .20 .50
11 Jim Haslett .75 2.00
12 Isiah Robertson .30 .75
13 Frank Lewis .30 .75
14 Jeff Nixon .20 .50
15 Nick Mike-Mayer .20 .50
16 Jim Ritcher .30 .75
17 Charles Romes .20 .50
18 Fred Smerlas .40 1.00
19 Ben Williams .20 .50
20 Roland Hooks .20 .50

1980 Bills Buffalo News Posters

These posters were created by the Buffalo News and issued as "pages" in the daily newspapers during the 1979 season. Each large poster includes a color artist's rendition of a Bills player on the front with a typical newspaper page back. We've included the date when the photo appeared when known. Any additions to this list are appreciated.

COMPLETE SET (9) 30.00 60.00
1 Joe Cribbs 4.00 10.00
2 Conrad Dobler 4.00 10.00
3 Joe Ferguson 4.00 10.00
4 Roosevelt Leaks 3.00 8.00
5 Reggie McKenzie 5.00 12.00
6 Nick Mike-Mayer 3.00 8.00
7 Jeff Nixon 3.00 8.00
8 Lou Piccone 3.00 8.00
9 Team Picture 4.00 10.00

1974 Birmingham Americans WFL Cups

These plastic drinking cups were sponsored by Jack's Hamburgers and WBRC-TV Channel 6 in Birmingham and feature members of the WFL Birmingham Americans. Each week of the WFL season a different player was featured on a cup. Any additions to the list below are appreciated.

1 John Andrews 7.50 15.00
2 George Mira 7.50 15.00
3 Paul Robinson 7.50 15.00

1975 Birmingham Vulcans WFL Team Issue 8X10

These photos measure roughly 8" x 10" and include a large black and white player image on the front with only the player's name below photo. The backs are blank.

1 Matthew Reed 7.50 15.00

1975 Birmingham Vulcans WFL Team Issue Dual Photo 8X10

These photos measure roughly 8" x 10" and include black and white images with a smaller head-and-shoulders photo to the left with the player's name and team logo beneath it and a larger action shot to the right. The backs are blank.

1 William Bryant 7.50 15.00
2 Denny Duron 7.50 15.00
3 Larry Estes 7.50 15.00
4 Mike Hayes 7.50 15.00
5 Dennis Homan 7.50 15.00
6 Pat Kelley 7.50 15.00
7 Steve Manstedt 7.50 15.00
8 Johnny Musso 7.50 15.00
9 Ted Powell 7.50 15.00
10 Joe Profit 7.50 15.00
11 Matthew Reed 7.50 15.00
12 Ron Slovensky 7.50 15.00
13 Bob Tatarek 7.50 15.00
14 Larry Willingham 7.50 15.00
15 Wimpy Winther 7.50 15.00
16 Jesse Wolf 7.50 15.00

1948 Bowman

The 1948 Bowman set is considered the first football set of the modern era. The set consists of 108 cards measuring 2 1/16" by 2 1/2". Cards were issued in one-card penny packs. The entire front is comprised of a black and white photo. The backs contain a write-up and an offer for a football. The cards were printed in three sheets; the third sheet (containing all the card numbers divisible by three, i.e., 3, 6, 9, 12, 15, etc.) being printed in much lesser quantities. Hence, cards with numbers divisible by three are substantially more valuable than the other cards in the set. The second sheet (numbers 2, 5, 8, 11, 14, etc.) is also regarded as slightly tougher to obtain than the first sheet (numbers 1, 4, 7, 10, 13, etc.) which contains the most plentiful cards. An album with which to house the set was produced. Key Rookie Cards in this set are Sammy Baugh, Charley Conerly, Sid Luckman, Johnny Lujack, Pete Pihos, Bulldog Turner, Steve Van Buren, and Bob Waterfield.

COMPLETE SET (108) 4,500.00 7,000.00
WRAPPER (1-CENT) 150.00 250.00
1 Joe Tereshinski RC 80.00 150.00
2 Larry Olsonoski RC 15.00 25.00
3 Johnny Lujack SP RC 250.00 350.00
4 Ray Poole RC 12.00 20.00
5 Bill DeCorrevont RC 15.00 25.00
6 Paul Briggs SP RC 65.00 100.00
7 Steve Van Buren RC 125.00 200.00
8 Kenny Washington RC 40.00 60.00
9 Nolan Luhn SP RC 65.00 100.00
10 Chris Iversen RC 12.00 20.00
11 Jack Wiley RC 15.00 25.00
12 Charley Conerly SP RC 250.00 350.00
13 Hugh Taylor RC 15.00 25.00
14 Frank Seno RC 15.00 25.00
15 Gil Bouley SP RC 65.00 100.00
16 Tommy Thompson RC 20.00 35.00
17 Charley Trippi RC 60.00 100.00
18 Vince Banonis SP RC 65.00 100.00
19 Art Faircloth RC 12.00 20.00
20 Clyde Goodnight RC 15.00 25.00
21 Bill Chipley SP RC 65.00 100.00
22 Sammy Baugh RC 350.00 500.00
23 Don Kindt RC 15.00 25.00
24 John Koniszewski SP RC 65.00 100.00
25 Pat McHugh RC 12.00 20.00
26 Bob Waterfield RC 125.00 200.00
27 Tony Compagno SP RC 65.00 100.00
28 Paul Governali RC 15.00 25.00
29 Pat Harder RC 40.00 60.00
30 Vic Lindskog SP RC 65.00 100.00
31 Salvatore Rosato RC 12.00 20.00
32 John Mastrangelo RC 15.00 25.00
33 Fred Gehrke SP RC 65.00 100.00
34 Bosh Pritchard RC 12.00 20.00
35 Mike Micka RC 15.00 25.00
36 Bulldog Turner SP RC 150.00 250.00
37 Len Younce RC 12.00 20.00
38 Pat West RC 15.00 25.00
39 Russ Thomas SP RC 65.00 100.00
40 James Peebles RC 12.00 20.00
41 Bob Skoglund RC 15.00 25.00
42 Walt Stickle SP RC 65.00 100.00
43 Whitey Wistert RC 15.00 25.00
44 Paul Christman RC 40.00 60.00
45 Jay Rhodemyre SP RC 65.00 100.00
46 Tony Minisi RC 12.00 20.00
47 Bob Mann RC 15.00 25.00
48 Mal Kutner SP RC 75.00 125.00
49 Dick Poillon RC 12.00 20.00
50 Charles Cherundolo RC 15.00 25.00
51 Gerald Cowhig SP RC 65.00 100.00
52 Neill Armstrong RC UER 15.00 25.00
53 Frank Maznicki RC 15.00 25.00
54 John Sanchez SP RC 65.00 100.00
55 Frank Reagan RC 12.00 20.00
56 Jim Hardy RC 15.00 25.00
57 John Badaczewski SP 65.00 100.00
58 Robert Nussbaumer RC 12.00 20.00
59 Mervin Pregulman RC 15.00 25.00
60 Elbie Nickel SP RC 75.00 125.00
61 Alex Wojciechowicz RC 90.00 150.00
62 Walt Schlinkman RC 15.00 25.00
63 Pete Pihos SP RC 150.00 225.00
64 Joseph Sulaitis RC 12.00 20.00
65 Mike Holovak RC 30.00 50.00
66 Cy Souders SP RC 65.00 100.00
67 Paul McKee RC 12.00 20.00
68 Bill Moore RC 15.00 25.00
69 Frank Minini SP RC 65.00 100.00
70 Jack Ferrante RC 12.00 20.00
71 Les Horvath RC 35.00 50.00
72 Ted Fritsch Sr. SP RC 75.00 125.00
73 Tex Coulter RC 15.00 25.00
74 Boley Dancewicz RC 15.00 25.00
75 Dante Mangani SP RC 65.00 100.00
76 James Hefti RC 12.00 20.00
77 Paul Sarringhaus RC 15.00 25.00
78 Joe Scott SP RC 65.00 100.00
79 Bucko Kilroy RC 15.00 25.00
80 Bill Dudley RC 75.00 125.00
81 Mar.Goldberg SP RC 75.00 125.00
82 John Cannady RC 12.00 20.00
83 Perry Moss RC 15.00 25.00
84 Harold Crisler SP RC 75.00 125.00
85 Bill Gray RC 12.00 20.00
86 John Clement RC 15.00 25.00
87 Dan Sandifer SP RC 65.00 100.00
88 Ben Kish RC 12.00 20.00
89 Herbert Banta RC 15.00 25.00
90 Bill Garnaas SP RC 65.00 100.00
91 Jim White RC 18.00 30.00
92 Frank Barzilauskas RC 15.00 25.00
93 Vic Sears SP RC 65.00 100.00
94 John Adams RC 12.00 20.00
95 George McAfee RC 90.00 150.00
96 Ralph Heywood SP RC 65.00 100.00
97 Joe Muha RC 12.00 20.00
98 Fred Enke RC 15.00 25.00
99 Harry Gilmer SP RC 100.00 175.00
100 Bill Miklich RC 12.00 20.00
101 Joe Gottlieb RC 15.00 25.00
102 Bud Angsman SP RC 75.00 125.00
103 Tom Farmer RC 12.00 20.00
104 Bruce Smith RC 40.00 75.00
105 Bob Cifers SP RC 65.00 100.00
106 Ernie Steele RC 12.00 20.00
107 Sid Luckman RC 175.00 300.00
108 Buford Ray SP RC 250.00 400.00
NNO c 200.00 350.00

1950 Bowman

After a one year hiatus, Bowman issued its first color football set for 1950. The set comprises 144 cards measuring 2 1/16" by 2 1/2". Cards were issued in six-card nickel packs with two pieces of gum. The fronts contain a black and white photo that was colored in. The card backs, which contain a write-up, feature black printing except for the player's name and the logo for the "5-Star Bowman Picture Card Collectors Club" which are both in red. The set features the Rookie Cards of Tony Canadeo, Glenn Davis, Tom Fears, Otto Graham, Lou Groza, Elroy Hirsch, Dante Lavelli, Marion Motley, Joe Perry, and Y.A. Tittle. With a few exceptions the set numbering is arranged so that trios of players from the same team are numbered together in sequence.

COMPLETE SET (144) 3,000.00 4,500.00
WRAPPER (5-CENT) 100.00 175.00
1 Doak Walker 150.00 250.00
2 John Greene RC 18.00 25.00
3 Bob Nowasky RC 18.00 25.00
4 Jonathan Jenkins RC 18.00 25.00
5 Y.A.Tittle RC 175.00 250.00
6 Lou Groza RC 100.00 175.00
7 Alex Agase RC 20.00 30.00
8 Mac Speedie RC 30.00 50.00
9 Tony Canadeo RC 50.00 90.00
10 Larry Craig RC 20.00 30.00
11 Ted Fritsch Sr. 20.00 30.00
12 Joe Golding RC 18.00 25.00
13 Martin Ruby RC 18.00 25.00
14 George Taliaferro 20.00 30.00
15 Tank Younger RC 30.00 50.00
16 Glenn Davis RC 75.00 125.00
17 Bob Waterfield 75.00 125.00
18 Val Jansante RC 18.00 25.00
19 Joe Geri RC 18.00 25.00
20 Jerry Nuzum RC 18.00 25.00
21 Elmer Bud Angsman 18.00 25.00
22 Billy Dewell 18.00 25.00
23 Steve Van Buren 50.00 90.00
24 Cliff Patton RC 18.00 25.00
25 Bosh Pritchard 18.00 25.00
26 Johnny Lujack 50.00 80.00
27 Sid Luckman 75.00 125.00
28 Bulldog Turner 35.00 60.00
29 Bill Dudley 35.00 60.00
30 Hugh Taylor 20.00 30.00
31 George Thomas RC 18.00 25.00
32 Ray Poole 18.00 25.00
33 Travis Tidwell RC 18.00 25.00
34 Gail Bruce RC 18.00 25.00
35 Joe Perry RC 125.00 200.00
36 Frankie Albert RC 30.00 50.00
37 Bobby Layne 125.00 200.00
38 Leon Hart 25.00 40.00
39 B.Hoernschemeyer RC 20.00 30.00
40 Dick Barwegan RC 18.00 25.00
41 Adrian Burk RC 20.00 30.00
42 Barry French RC 18.00 25.00
43 Marion Motley RC 150.00 250.00
44 Jim Martin 20.00 30.00
45 Otto Graham RC 300.00 450.00
46 Al Baldwin RC 18.00 25.00
47 Larry Coutre RC 20.00 30.00
48 John Rauch 18.00 25.00
49 Sam Tamburo RC 18.00 25.00
50 Mike Swistowicz RC 18.00 25.00
51 Tom Fears RC 90.00 150.00
52 Elroy Hirsch RC 125.00 225.00
53 Dick Huffman RC 18.00 25.00
54 Bob Gage RC 18.00 25.00
55 Buddy Tinsley RC 18.00 25.00
56 Bill Blackburn RC 18.00 25.00
57 John Cochran RC 18.00 25.00
58 Bill Fischer 18.00 25.00
59 Whitey Wistert 20.00 30.00
60 Clyde Scott RC 18.00 25.00
61 Walter Barnes RC 18.00 25.00
62 Bob Perina RC 18.00 25.00
63 Bill Wightkin RC 18.00 25.00
64 Bob Goode RC 18.00 25.00
65 Al Demao RC 18.00 25.00
66 Harry Gilmer 20.00 30.00
67 Bill Austin RC 18.00 25.00
68 Joe Scott 18.00 25.00
69 Tex Coulter 20.00 30.00
70 Paul Salata RC 18.00 25.00
71 Emil Sitko 20.00 30.00
72 Bill Johnson C RC 18.00 25.00
73 Don Doll RC 18.00 25.00
74 Dan Sandifer RC 18.00 25.00
75 John Panelli RC 18.00 25.00
76 Bill Leonard RC 18.00 25.00
77 Bob Kelly RC 18.00 25.00
78 Dante Lavelli RC 100.00 175.00
79 Tony Adamle RC 20.00 30.00

Card	Low	High
80 Dick Wildung RC	18.00	25.00
81 Tobin Rote RC	30.00	50.00
82 Paul Burris RC	18.00	25.00
83 Lowell Tew RC	18.00	25.00
84 Barney Poole RC	18.00	25.00
85 Fred Naumetz RC	18.00	25.00
86 Dick Hoerner RC	18.00	25.00
87 Bob Reinhard RC	18.00	25.00
88 Howard Hartley RC	18.00	25.00
89 Darrell Hogan RC	18.00	25.00
90 Jerry Shipkey RC	18.00	25.00
91 Frank Tripucka	20.00	30.00
92 Buster Ramsey RC	18.00	25.00
93 Pat Harder	20.00	30.00
94 Vic Sears RC	18.00	25.00
95 Tommy Thompson QB	20.00	30.00
96 Bucko Kilroy	20.00	30.00
97 George Connor	30.00	50.00
98 Fred Morrison RC	18.00	25.00
99 Jim Keane RC	18.00	25.00
100 Sammy Baugh	150.00	250.00
101 Harry Ulinski	18.00	25.00
102 Frank Spaniel RC	18.00	25.00
103 Charley Conerly	50.00	90.00
104 Dick Hensley RC	18.00	25.00
105 Eddie Price RC	18.00	25.00
106 Ed Carr RC	18.00	25.00
107 Leo Nomellini	45.00	75.00
108 Verl Lillywhite RC	18.00	25.00
109 Wallace Triplett RC	18.00	25.00
110 Joe Watson RC	18.00	25.00
111 Cloyce Box RC	20.00	30.00
112 Billy Stone RC	18.00	25.00
113 Earl Murray RC	18.00	25.00
114 Chet Mutryn RC	20.00	30.00
115 Ken Carpenter RC	20.00	30.00
116 Lou Rymkus RC	20.00	30.00
117 Dub Jones RC	25.00	40.00
118 Clayton Tonnemaker	18.00	25.00
119 Walt Schlinkman RC	18.00	25.00
120 Billy Grimes RC	18.00	25.00
121 George Ratterman RC	20.00	30.00
122 Bob Mann	18.00	25.00
123 Buddy Young RC	30.00	50.00
124 Jack Zilly RC	18.00	25.00
125 Tom Kalmanir RC	18.00	25.00
126 Frank Sinkovitz RC	18.00	25.00
127 Elbert Nickel	20.00	30.00
128 Jim Finks RC	40.00	75.00
129 Charley Trippi	35.00	60.00
130 Tom Wham RC	18.00	25.00
131 Ventan Yablonski RC	18.00	25.00
132 Chuck Bednarik	75.00	125.00
133 Joe Muha	18.00	25.00
134 Pete Pihos	45.00	80.00
135 Washington Serini RC	18.00	25.00
136 George Gulyanics RC	18.00	25.00
137 Ken Kavanaugh	20.00	30.00
138 Howie Livingston RC	18.00	25.00
139 Joe Tereshinski	18.00	25.00
140 Jim White	25.00	40.00
141 Gene Roberts RC	18.00	25.00
142 Bill Swiacki	20.00	30.00
143 Norm Standlee RC	18.00	25.00
144 Knox Ramsey RC	50.00	100.00

1951 Bowman

The 1951 Bowman set of 144 numbered cards witnessed an increase in card size from previous Bowman football sets. Cards were issued in six-card nickel packs and one-card penny packs. The cards were enlarged from the previous year to 2 1/16" by 3 1/8". The set is very similar in format to the baseball card set of that year. The fronts feature black and white photos that were colored in. The player's name is in a bar toward the bottom that runs from the right border toward the middle of the photo. A team logo or mascot is on top of the bar. The card backs are printed in maroon and blue on gray card stock and contain a write-up. The set features the Rookie Cards of Tom Landry, Emlen Tunnell, and Norm Van Brocklin. The Bill Walsh in this set went to Notre Dame and is not the Bill Walsh who coached the San Francisco 49ers in the 1980s. The set numbering is arranged so that two, three, or four players from the same team are together. Three blank backed proof cards have recently been uncovered and added to the listings below. The proofs are very similar to the corresponding base card. However, the artwork varies somewhat versus the base card.

Card	Low	High
COMPLETE SET (144)	2,500.00	3,500.00
WRAPPER (1-CENT)	150.00	250.00
WRAPPER (5-CENT)	175.00	300.00
1 Weldon Humble RC	50.00	80.00
2 Otto Graham	150.00	250.00
3 Mac Speedie	20.00	35.00
4 Norm Van Brocklin RC	200.00	300.00
5 Woodley Lewis RC	15.00	25.00
6 Tom Fears	30.00	50.00
7 George Musacco RC	12.00	20.00
8 George Taliaferro	15.00	25.00
9 Barney Poole	12.00	20.00
10 Steve Van Buren	35.00	60.00
11 Whitey Wistert	15.00	25.00
12 Chuck Bednarik	50.00	80.00
13 Bulldog Turner	30.00	50.00
14 Bob Williams RC	12.00	20.00
15 Johnny Lujack	35.00	60.00
16 Roy Rebel Steiner	12.00	20.00
17 Jug Girard	15.00	25.00
18 Bill Neal RC	12.00	20.00
19 Travis Tidwell	12.00	20.00
20 Tom Landry RC	350.00	500.00
21 Arnie Weinmeister RC	35.00	60.00
22 Joe Geri	12.00	20.00
23 Bill Walsh C RC	15.00	30.00
24 Fran Rogel	12.00	20.00
25 Doak Walker	35.00	60.00
26 Leon Hart	20.00	35.00
27 Thurman McGraw RC	12.00	20.00
28 Buster Ramsey	12.00	20.00
29 Frank Tripucka	20.00	35.00
30 Don Paul DB RC	12.00	20.00
31 Alex Loyd RC	12.00	20.00
32 Y.A.Tittle	75.00	135.00
33 Verl Lillywhite	12.00	20.00
34 Sammy Baugh	110.00	175.00
35 Chuck Drazenovich RC	12.00	20.00
36 Bob Goode	12.00	20.00
37 Horace Gillom RC	15.00	25.00
38 Lou Rymkus	15.00	25.00
39 Ken Carpenter	12.00	20.00
40 Bob Waterfield	45.00	75.00
41 Vitamin Smith RC	15.00	25.00
42 Glenn Davis	35.00	60.00
43 Dan Edwards RC	12.00	20.00
44 John Rauch	12.00	20.00
45 Zollie Toth RC	12.00	20.00
46 Pete Pihos	35.00	60.00
47 Russ Craft RC	12.00	20.00
48 Walter Barnes	12.00	20.00
49 Fred Morrison	12.00	20.00
50 Ray Bray RC	12.00	20.00
51 Ed Sprinkle RC	15.00	25.00
52 Floyd Reid RC	12.00	20.00
53 Billy Grimes	12.00	20.00
54 Ted Fritsch Sr.	15.00	25.00
55 Al DeRogatis RC	15.00	25.00
56 Charley Conerly	45.00	75.00
57 Jon Baker RC	12.00	20.00
58 Tom McWilliams	12.00	20.00
59 Jerry Shipkey	12.00	20.00
60 Lynn Chandnois RC	15.00	25.00
61 Don Doll	12.00	20.00
62 Lou Creekmur	30.00	50.00
63 Bob Hoernschemeyer	15.00	25.00
64 Tom Wham	12.00	20.00
65 Bill Fischer	12.00	20.00
66 Robert Nussbaumer	12.00	20.00
67 Gordy Soltau RC	12.00	20.00
68 Visco Grgich RC	12.00	20.00
69 John Strzykalski RC	12.00	20.00
70 Pete Stout RC	12.00	20.00
71 Paul Lipscomb RC	12.00	20.00
72 Harry Gilmer	20.00	35.00
73 Dante Lavelli	30.00	50.00
74 Dub Jones	15.00	25.00
75 Lou Groza	45.00	75.00
76 Elroy Hirsch	45.00	75.00
77 Tom Kalmanir	12.00	20.00
78 Jack Zilly	12.00	20.00
79 Bruce Alford RC	12.00	20.00
80 Art Weiner	12.00	20.00
81 Brad Ecklund RC	12.00	20.00
82 Bosh Pritchard	12.00	20.00
83 John Green RC	12.00	20.00
84 Ebert Van Buren RC	12.00	20.00
85 Julie Rykovich RC	12.00	20.00
86 Fred Davis	12.00	20.00
87 John Hoffman RC	12.00	20.00
88 Tobin Rote	15.00	25.00
89 Paul Burris	12.00	20.00
90 Tony Canadeo	30.00	50.00
91 Emlen Tunnell RC	60.00	100.00
92 Otto Schnellbacher RC	12.00	20.00
93 Ray Poole	12.00	20.00
94 Darrell Hogan	12.00	20.00
95 Frank Sinkovitz	12.00	20.00
96 Ernie Stautner	60.00	100.00
97 Elmer Bud Angsman	12.00	20.00
98 Jack Jennings RC	12.00	20.00
99 Jerry Groom RC	12.00	20.00
100 John Prchlik RC	12.00	20.00
101 J. Robert Smith RC	12.00	20.00
102 Bobby Layne	75.00	135.00
103 Frankie Albert	20.00	35.00
104 Gail Bruce	12.00	20.00
105 Joe Perry	45.00	75.00
106 Leon Heath RC	12.00	20.00
107 Ed Quirk RC	12.00	20.00
108 Hugh Taylor	15.00	25.00
109 Marion Motley	60.00	100.00
110 Tony Adamle	12.00	20.00
111 Alex Agase	15.00	25.00
112 Tank Younger	20.00	35.00
113 Bob Boyd RC	12.00	20.00
114 Jerry Williams RC	12.00	20.00
115 Joe Golding	12.00	20.00
116 Sherman Howard RC	12.00	20.00
117 John Wozniak RC	12.00	20.00
118 Frank Reagan	12.00	20.00
119 Vic Sears	12.00	20.00
120 Clyde Scott	12.00	20.00
121 George Gulyanics	12.00	20.00
122 Bill Wightkin	12.00	20.00
123 Chuck Hunsinger RC	12.00	20.00
124 Jack Cloud	12.00	20.00
125 Abner Wimberly RC	12.00	20.00
126 Dick Wildung	12.00	20.00
127 Eddie Price	12.00	20.00
128 Joe Scott	12.00	20.00
129 Jerry Nuzum	12.00	20.00
130 Jim Finks	20.00	35.00
131 Bob Gage	12.00	20.00
132 Bill Swiacki	15.00	25.00
133 Joe Watson	12.00	20.00
134 Ollie Cline RC	12.00	20.00
135 Jack Lininger RC	12.00	20.00
136 Fran Polsfoot RC	12.00	20.00
137 Charley Trippi	30.00	50.00
138 Ventan Yablonski	12.00	20.00
139 Emil Sitko	12.00	20.00
140 Leo Nomellini	30.00	60.00
141 Norm Standlee	12.00	20.00
142 Eddie Saenz RC	12.00	20.00
143 Al Demao	12.00	20.00
144 Bill Dudley	75.00	150.00
NNO Johnny Lujack Proof	175.00	300.00
NNO Bob Gage Proof	75.00	125.00
NNO Darrell Hogan Proof	75.00	125.00

1952 Bowman Large

One of two different sized sets produced by Bowman in 1952, the large version measures 2 1/2" by 3 3/4". Cards were issued in five-card, five-cent packs. The 144-card issue is identical to the smaller version in every respect except size. Either horizontal or vertical fronts contain a player portrait, a white banner with the player's name and a bar containing the team name and logo. Horizontal backs have a small write-up, previous year's stats and biographical information. Certain numbers were systematically printed in lesser quantities due to the fact that Bowman apparently could not fit each 72-card series on their respective sheets. The affected cards are those which are divisible by nine (i.e. 9, 18, 27 etc.) and those which are numbered one more than those divisible by nine (i.e. 10, 19, 28 etc.). These short-print cards are marked in the checklist below by SP. The set features NFL veterans and college players that entered the pro ranks in '52. The set features the Rookie Cards of Paul Brown, Jack Christiansen, Art Donovan, Frank Gifford, George Halas, Yale Lary, Gino Marchetti, Ollie Matson, Hugh McElhenny, and Andy Robustelli. The last card in the set, No. 144 Jim Lansford, is among the toughest football cards to acquire. It is generally accepted among hobbyists that the card was located at the bottom right corner of the production sheet and was subject to much abuse including numerous poor cuts. The problem was such that many copies never made it out of the factory as they were discarded. This card is also indicated below by SP.

Card	Low	High
COMPLETE SET (144)	9,500.00	12,500.00
WRAPPER (5-CENT)	30.00	60.00
1 Norm Van Brocklin SP	350.00	500.00
2 Otto Graham	200.00	300.00
3 Doak Walker	60.00	100.00
4 Steve Owen CO RC	50.00	80.00
5 Frankie Albert	30.00	50.00
6 Laurie Niemi RC	20.00	35.00
7 Chuck Hunsinger	20.00	35.00
8 Ed Modzelewski	30.00	50.00
9 Joe Spencer SP RC	40.00	75.00
10 Chuck Bednarik SP	200.00	350.00
11 Barney Poole	20.00	35.00
12 Charley Trippi	40.00	75.00
13 Tom Fears	40.00	75.00
14 Paul Brown CO RC	150.00	250.00
15 Leon Hart	30.00	50.00
16 Frank Gifford RC	350.00	500.00
17 Y.A.Tittle	200.00	300.00
18 Charlie Justice SP	100.00	175.00
19 George Connor SP	100.00	175.00
20 Lynn Chandnois	20.00	35.00
21 Billy Howton RC	30.00	50.00
22 Kenneth Snyder RC	20.00	35.00
23 Gino Marchetti RC	150.00	250.00
24 John Karras	20.00	35.00
25 Tank Younger	30.00	50.00
26 Tommy Thompson LB RC	20.00	35.00
27 Bob Miller SP RC	200.00	300.00
28 Kyle Rote SP RC	100.00	175.00
29 Hugh McElhenny RC	150.00	250.00
30 Sammy Baugh	225.00	350.00
31 Jim Dooley RC	25.00	45.00
32 Ray Mathews	20.00	35.00
33 Fred Cone RC	20.00	35.00
34 Al Pollard RC	20.00	35.00
35 Brad Ecklund	20.00	35.00
36 John Hancock SP RC	250.00	350.00
37 Elroy Hirsch SP	125.00	200.00
38 Keever Jankovich RC	20.00	35.00
39 Emlen Tunnell	75.00	125.00
40 Steve Dowden RC	20.00	35.00
41 Claude Hipps RC	20.00	35.00
42 Norm Standlee	20.00	35.00
43 Dick Todd CO RC	20.00	35.00
44 Babe Parilli	30.00	50.00
45 Steve Van Buren SP	200.00	300.00
46 Art Donovan SP RC	250.00	350.00
47 Bill Fischer	20.00	35.00
48 George Halas CO RC	160.00	275.00
49 Jerrell Price	20.00	35.00
50 John Sandusky RC	25.00	40.00
51 Ray Beck	20.00	35.00
52 Jim Martin	25.00	45.00
53 Joe Bach CO RC	20.00	35.00
54 Glen Christian SP RC	40.00	75.00
55 Andy Davis SP RC	40.00	75.00
56 Tobin Rote	25.00	50.00
57 Wayne Millner CO RC	50.00	90.00
58 Zollie Toth	20.00	35.00
59 Jack Jennings	20.00	35.00
60 Bill McColl RC	20.00	35.00
61 Les Richter RC	35.00	60.00
62 Walt Michaels RC	25.00	45.00
63 Charley Conerly SP	500.00	750.00
64 Howard Hartley SP	40.00	75.00
65 Jerome Smith RC	20.00	35.00
66 James Clark RC	20.00	35.00
67 Dick Logan RC	20.00	35.00
68 Wayne Robinson RC	20.00	35.00
69 James Hammond RC	20.00	35.00
70 Gene Schroeder RC	20.00	35.00
71 Tex Coulter	25.00	45.00
72 John Schweder SP RC	400.00	600.00
73 Vitamin Smith SP	75.00	125.00
74 Joe Campanella RC	25.00	40.00
75 Joe Kuharich CO RC	30.00	50.00
76 Herman Clark RC	25.00	40.00
77 Dan Edwards	25.00	40.00
78 Bobby Layne	175.00	300.00
79 Bob Hoernschemeyer	30.00	50.00
80 John Carr Blount RC	25.00	40.00
81 John Kastan SP RC	90.00	150.00
82 Harry Minarik SP RC	90.00	150.00
83 Joe Perry	75.00	125.00
84 Buddy Parker CO RC	30.00	50.00
85 Andy Robustelli RC	125.00	200.00
86 Dub Jones	30.00	50.00
87 Mal Cook RC	25.00	40.00
88 Billy Stone	25.00	40.00
89 George Taliaferro	30.00	50.00
90 Thomas Johnson SP RC	90.00	150.00
91 Leon Heath SP	60.00	100.00
92 Pete Pihos	60.00	100.00
93 Fred Benners RC	25.00	40.00
94 George Tarasovic RC	25.00	40.00
95 Buck Shaw CO RC	25.00	40.00
96 Bill Wightkin	25.00	40.00
97 John Wozniak	25.00	40.00
98 Bobby Dillon RC	30.00	50.00
99 Joe Stydahar SP RC	450.00	650.00
100 Dick Alban SP RC	90.00	150.00
101 Arnie Weinmeister	35.00	60.00
102 Bobby Cross RC	25.00	40.00
103 Don Paul DB	25.00	40.00
104 Buddy Young	35.00	60.00
105 Lou Groza	75.00	125.00
106 Ray Pelfrey RC	25.00	40.00
107 Maurice Nipp RC	25.00	40.00
108 Hubert Johnston SP RC	450.00	650.00
109 Vol.Quinlan SP RC	60.00	100.00
110 Jack Simmons RC	25.00	40.00
111 George Ratterman	30.00	50.00
112 John Badaczewski RC	25.00	40.00
113 Bill Reichardt	25.00	40.00
114 Art Weiner	25.00	40.00
115 Keith Flowers RC	25.00	40.00
116 Russ Craft	25.00	40.00
117 Jim O'Donahue SP RC	90.00	150.00
118 Darrell Hogan SP	60.00	100.00
119 Frank Ziegler RC	25.00	40.00
120 Dan Towler	35.00	60.00
121 Fred Williams RC	25.00	40.00
122 Jimmy Phelan CO RC	25.00	40.00
123 Eddie Price	25.00	40.00
124 Chet Ostrowski RC	25.00	40.00
125 Leo Nomellini	60.00	100.00
126 Steve Romanik SP RC	200.00	300.00
127 Ollie Matson SP RC	200.00	300.00
128 Dante Lavelli	50.00	90.00
129 Jack Christiansen RC	100.00	175.00
130 Dom Moselle RC	25.00	40.00
131 John Rapacz RC	25.00	40.00
132 Chuck Ortmann UER RC	25.00	40.00
133 Bob Williams	25.00	40.00
134 Chuck Ulrich RC	25.00	40.00
135 Gene Ronzani CO SP RC	450.00	700.00
136 Bert Rechichar SP	60.00	100.00
137 Bob Waterfield	75.00	125.00
138 Bobby Walston RC	30.00	50.00
139 Jerry Shipkey	25.00	40.00
140 Yale Lary RC	125.00	200.00
141 Gordy Soltau	25.00	40.00
142 Tom Landry	450.00	600.00
143 John Papit RC	25.00	40.00
144 Jim Lansford SP RC	1,800.00	3,000.00

1952 Bowman Small

One of two different sized sets issued by Bowman in 1952, this 144-card set is identical in every respect to the large version except for the smaller size of 2 1/16" by 3 1/8". Cards were issued in one-card penny packs. The fronts are either horizontal or vertical and feature a player protrait, a white banner with the player's name and a bar containing the team name and logo. All backs are horizontal and contain a brief write-up, previous year's stats and a bio. The set features NFL veterans and college players that entered the pro ranks in '52. The set features the Rookie Cards of Paul Brown, Jack Christiansen, Art Donovan, Frank Gifford, George Halas, Yale Lary, Gino Marchetti, Ollie Matson, Hugh McElhenny, and Andy Robustelli.

COMPLETE SET (144) 3,500.00 5,000.00
WRAPPER (1-CENT) 40.00 60.00
1 Norm Van Brocklin 200.00 350.00
2 Otto Graham 125.00 200.00
3 Doak Walker 35.00 60.00
4 Steve Owen CO RC 35.00 60.00
5 Frankie Albert 20.00 35.00
6 Laurie Niemi RC 15.00 25.00
7 Chuck Hunsinger 15.00 25.00
8 Ed Modzelewski 20.00 35.00
9 Joe Spencer RC 15.00 25.00
10 Chuck Bednarik 45.00 75.00
11 Barney Poole 15.00 25.00
12 Charley Trippi 35.00 60.00
13 Tom Fears 35.00 60.00
14 Paul Brown CO RC 90.00 150.00
15 Leon Hart 20.00 35.00
16 Frank Gifford 200.00 400.00
17 Y.A.Tittle 75.00 125.00
18 Charlie Justice 30.00 50.00
19 George Connor 20.00 35.00
20 Lynn Chandnois 15.00 25.00
21 Billy Howton RC 25.00 40.00
22 Kenneth Snyder RC 15.00 25.00
23 Gino Marchetti RC 75.00 125.00
24 John Karras 15.00 25.00
25 Tank Younger 20.00 35.00
26 Tommy Thompson LB RC 15.00 25.00
27 Bob Miller RC 15.00 25.00
28 Kyle Rote RC 30.00 50.00
29 Hugh McElhenny RC 100.00 175.00
30 Sammy Baugh 150.00 250.00
31 Jim Dooley RC 18.00 30.00
32 Ray Mathews 15.00 25.00
33 Fred Cone RC 15.00 25.00
34 Al Pollard RC 15.00 25.00
35 Brad Ecklund 15.00 25.00
36 John Lee Hancock RC 15.00 25.00
37 Elroy Hirsch 35.00 60.00
38 Keever Jankovich 15.00 25.00
39 Emlen Tunnell 30.00 50.00
40 Steve Dowden RC 15.00 25.00
41 Claude Hipps 15.00 25.00
42 Norm Standlee 15.00 25.00
43 Dick Todd CO RC 15.00 25.00
44 Babe Parilli 20.00 35.00
45 Steve Van Buren 40.00 75.00
46 Art Donovan RC 125.00 200.00
47 Bill Fischer 15.00 25.00
48 George Halas CO RC 150.00 250.00
49 Jerrell Price 15.00 25.00
50 John Sandusky RC 15.00 25.00
51 Ray Beck 15.00 25.00
52 Jim Martin 18.00 30.00
53 Joe Bach CO RC 15.00 25.00
54 Glen Christian RC 15.00 25.00
55 Andy Davis RC 15.00 25.00
56 Tobin Rote 18.00 30.00
57 Wayne Millner RC CO 30.00 50.00
58 Zollie Toth 15.00 25.00
59 Jack Jennings 15.00 25.00
60 Bill McColl RC 15.00 25.00
61 Les Richter RC 35.00 60.00
62 Walt Michaels RC 18.00 30.00
63 Charley Conerly 40.00 75.00
64 Howard Hartley 15.00 25.00
65 Jerome Smith RC 15.00 25.00
66 James Clark 15.00 25.00
67 Dick Logan 15.00 25.00
68 Wayne Robinson RC 15.00 25.00
69 James Hammond 15.00 25.00
70 Gene Schroeder RC 15.00 25.00
71 Tex Coulter 18.00 30.00
72 John Schweder 15.00 25.00
73 Vitamin Smith 20.00 35.00
74 Joe Campanella RC 18.00 30.00
75 Joe Kuharich CO RC 20.00 35.00
76 Herman Clark 18.00 30.00
77 Dan Edwards 18.00 30.00
78 Bobby Layne 90.00 150.00
79 Bob Hoernschemeyer 20.00 35.00
80 John Carr Blount RC 18.00 30.00
81 John Kastan RC 18.00 30.00
82 Harry Minarik 18.00 30.00
83 Joe Perry 40.00 75.00
84 Buddy Parker CO RC 20.00 35.00
85 Andy Robustelli RC 75.00 125.00
86 Dub Jones 20.00 35.00
87 Mal Cook 18.00 30.00
88 Billy Stone 18.00 30.00
89 George Taliaferro 20.00 35.00
90 Thomas Johnson RC 18.00 30.00
91 Leon Heath 18.00 30.00
92 Pete Pihos 35.00 50.00
93 Fred Benners 18.00 30.00
94 George Tarasovic RC 18.00 30.00
95 Buck Shaw CO RC 18.00 30.00
96 Bill Wightkin 18.00 30.00
97 John Wozniak 18.00 30.00
98 Bobby Dillon RC 20.00 35.00
99 Joe Stydahar RC CO 50.00 80.00
100 Dick Alban RC 18.00 30.00
101 Arnie Weinmeister 25.00 40.00
102 Bobby Cross RC 18.00 30.00
103 Don Paul DB 18.00 30.00
104 Buddy Young 25.00 40.00
105 Lou Groza 45.00 75.00
106 Ray Pelfrey 18.00 30.00
107 Maurice Nipp RC 18.00 30.00
108 Hubert Johnston RC 18.00 30.00
109 Volney Quinlan RC 18.00 30.00
110 Jack Simmons RC 18.00 30.00
111 George Ratterman 20.00 35.00
112 John Badaczewski 18.00 30.00
113 Bill Reichardt 18.00 30.00
114 Art Weiner 18.00 30.00
115 Keith Flowers RC 18.00 30.00
116 Russ Craft 18.00 30.00
117 Jim O'Donahue RC 18.00 30.00
118 Darrell Hogan 18.00 30.00
119 Frank Ziegler RC 18.00 30.00
120 Dan Towler 25.00 40.00
121 Fred Williams RC 18.00 30.00
122 Jimmy Phelan CO RC 18.00 30.00
123 Eddie Price 18.00 30.00
124 Chet Ostrowski RC 18.00 30.00
125 Leo Nomellini 40.00 75.00
126 Steve Romanik RC 18.00 30.00
127 Ollie Matson RC 75.00 125.00
128 Dante Lavelli 35.00 60.00
129 Jack Christiansen RC 50.00 80.00
130 Dom Moselle RC 18.00 30.00
131 John Rapacz RC 18.00 30.00
132 Chuck Ortmann UER RC 18.00 30.00
133 Bob Williams 18.00 30.00
134 Chuck Ulrich RC 18.00 30.00
135 Gene Ronzani CO RC 18.00 30.00
136 Bert Rechichar 20.00 35.00
137 Bob Waterfield 45.00 75.00
138 Bobby Walston RC 20.00 35.00
139 Jerry Shipkey 18.00 30.00
140 Yale Lary RC 50.00 80.00
141 Gordy Soltau 18.00 30.00
142 Tom Landry 250.00 400.00
143 John Papit RC 18.00 30.00
144 Jim Lansford RC 100.00 175.00

1953 Bowman

The 1953 Bowman set of 96 cards measures approximately 2 1/2" by 3 3/4". Cards were issued in five-card, five-cent packs. The set is somewhat smaller in number than would be thought since Bowman was the only major producer of football cards during this year. The fronts feature a player portrait with a football that contains player and team names. Horizontal backs contain a brief write-up, previous year's stats, a bio and a quiz. There are 24 cards marked SP in the checklist below which are considered in shorter supply than the other cards in the set. The Bill Walsh in this set went to Notre Dame and is not the Bill Walsh who coached the San Francisco 49ers in the 1980s. The most notable Rookie Card in this set is Eddie LeBaron.

COMPLETE SET (96) 2,500.00 3,500.00
WRAPPER (5-CENT) 90.00 150.00
1 Eddie LeBaron RC 75.00 125.00
2 John Dottley 18.00 30.00
3 Babe Parilli 20.00 35.00
4 Bucko Kilroy 20.00 35.00
5 Joe Tereshinski 18.00 30.00
6 Doak Walker 45.00 75.00
7 Fran Polsfoot 18.00 30.00
8 Sisto Averno RC 18.00 30.00
9 Marion Motley 45.00 100.00
10 Pat Brady RC 18.00 30.00
11 Norm Van Brocklin 75.00 125.00
12 Bill McColl 18.00 30.00
13 Jerry Groom 18.00 30.00
14 Al Pollard 18.00 30.00
15 Dante Lavelli 30.00 50.00
16 Eddie Price 18.00 30.00
17 Charley Trippi 30.00 50.00
18 Elbert Nickel 20.00 35.00
19 George Taliaferro 20.00 35.00
20 Charley Conerly 50.00 80.00
21 Bobby Layne 75.00 125.00
22 Elroy Hirsch 60.00 100.00
23 Jim Finks 25.00 40.00
24 Chuck Bednarik 45.00 75.00
25 Kyle Rote 25.00 40.00
26 Otto Graham 100.00 200.00
27 Harry Gilmer 20.00 35.00
28 Tobin Rote 20.00 35.00
29 Billy Stone 18.00 30.00
30 Buddy Young 25.00 40.00
31 Leon Hart 25.00 40.00
32 Hugh McElhenny 45.00 75.00
33 Dale Samuels 18.00 30.00
34 Lou Creekmur 30.00 50.00
35 Tom Catlin RC 18.00 30.00
36 Tom Fears 35.00 60.00
37 George Connor 25.00 40.00
38 Bill Walsh C 18.00 30.00
39 Leo Sanford SP RC 30.00 50.00
40 Horace Gillom 20.00 35.00
41 John Schweder SP 30.00 50.00
42 Tom O'Connell RC 18.00 30.00
43 Frank Gifford SP 175.00 300.00
44 Frank Continetti SP RC 30.00 50.00
45 John Olszewski SP RC 30.00 50.00
46 Dub Jones 20.00 35.00
47 Don Paul LB SP RC 30.00 50.00
48 Gerald Weatherly RC 18.00 30.00
49 Fred Bruney SP RC 30.00 50.00
50 Jack Scarbath RC 18.00 30.00
51 John Karras 18.00 30.00
52 Al Conway RC 18.00 30.00
53 Emlen Tunnell SP 75.00 125.00
54 Gern Nagler SP RC 30.00 50.00
55 Kenneth Snyder SP 30.00 50.00
56 Y.A.Tittle 90.00 150.00
57 John Rapacz SP 30.00 50.00
58 Harley Sewell SP RC 30.00 50.00
59 Don Bingham RC 18.00 30.00
60 Darrell Hogan 18.00 30.00
61 Tony Curcillo RC 18.00 30.00
62 Ray Renfro SP RC 35.00 60.00
63 Leon Heath 18.00 30.00
64 Tex Coulter SP 30.00 50.00
65 Dewayne Douglas RC 18.00 30.00
66 J. Robert Smith SP 30.00 50.00
67 Bob McChesney SP RC 30.00 50.00
68 Dick Alban SP 30.00 50.00
69 Andy Kozar RC 18.00 30.00
70 Merwin Hodel SP RC 30.00 50.00
71 Thurman McGraw 18.00 30.00
72 Cliff Anderson RC 18.00 30.00
73 Pete Pihos 35.00 60.00
74 Julie Rykovich 18.00 30.00
75 John Kreamcheck SP RC 30.00 50.00
76 Lynn Chandnois 18.00 30.00
77 Cloyce Box SP 30.00 50.00
78 Ray Mathews 18.00 30.00
79 Bobby Walston 20.00 35.00
80 Jim Dooley 18.00 30.00
81 Pat Harder SP 30.00 50.00
82 Jerry Shipkey 18.00 30.00
83 Bobby Thomason RC 18.00 30.00
84 Hugh Taylor 20.00 35.00
85 George Ratterman 20.00 35.00
86 Don Stonesifer RC 18.00 30.00
87 John Williams SP RC 30.00 50.00
88 Leo Nomellini 30.00 50.00
89 Frank Ziegler 18.00 30.00
90 Don Paul DB UER 18.00 30.00
91 Tom Dublinski 18.00 30.00
92 Ken Carpenter 18.00 30.00
93 Ted Marchibroda RC 30.00 50.00
94 Chuck Drazenovich 18.00 30.00
95 Lou Groza SP 75.00 125.00
96 William Cross SP RC 50.00 100.00

1954 Bowman

Measuring 2 1/2" by 3 3/4", the 1954 set consists of 128 cards. Cards were issued in seven-card five-cent packs and one-card penny packs. Toward the bottom of the photo is a white banner that contains the player's name, team name and mascot. The card backs feature the player's name in black print inside a red outline of a football. The player's statistical information from the previous season and a quiz are also on back. The "Whizzer" White in the set (125) is not Byron White, the Supreme Court Justice, but Wilford White. Wilford is the father of former Dallas Cowboys quarterback Danny White. The Bill Walsh in this set went to Notre Dame and is not the Bill Walsh who coached the San Francisco 49ers in the 1980s. The mid-series, cards 65-96, is very tough to find in relationship to other series. Rookie Cards in this set include Doug Atkins and George Blanda.

COMPLETE SET (128) 1,200.00 1,800.00
WRAPPER (1-CENT) 10.00 15.00
WRAPPER (5-CENT) 25.00 30.00
1 Ray Mathews 15.00 30.00
2 John Huzvar RC 3.00 5.00
3 Jack Scarbath 3.00 5.00
4 Doug Atkins RC 30.00 50.00
5 Bill Stits RC 3.00 5.00
6 Joe Perry 18.00 30.00
7 Kyle Rote 7.50 15.00
8 Norm Van Brocklin 25.00 50.00
9 Pete Pihos 12.00 20.00
10 Babe Parilli 4.00 8.00
11 Zeke Bratkowski RC 15.00 25.00
12 Ollie Matson 15.00 25.00
13 Pat Brady 3.00 5.00
14 Fred Enke 3.00 5.00
15 Harry Ulinski 3.00 5.00
16 Bob Garrett RC 3.00 5.00
17 Bill Bowman RC 3.00 5.00
18 Leo Rucka RC 3.00 5.00
19 John Cannady 3.00 5.00
20 Tom Fears 15.00 25.00
21 Norm Willey RC 3.00 5.00
22 Floyd Reid 3.00 5.00
23 George Blanda RC 100.00 175.00
24 Don Doheney RC 3.00 5.00
25 John Schweder 3.00 5.00
26 Bert Rechichar 3.00 5.00
27 Harry Dowda RC 3.00 5.00
28 John Sandusky 3.00 5.00
29 Les Bingaman RC 7.50 15.00
30 Joe Arenas RC 3.00 5.00
31 Ray Wietecha RC 3.00 5.00
32 Elroy Hirsch 18.00 30.00
33 Harold Giancanelli RC 3.00 5.00
34 Billy Howton 4.00 8.00
35 Fred Morrison 3.00 5.00
36 Bobby Cavazos RC 3.00 5.00
37 Darrell Hogan 3.00 5.00
38 Buddy Young 4.00 8.00
39 Charlie Justice 12.00 20.00
40 Otto Graham 50.00 80.00
41 Doak Walker 20.00 35.00
42 Y.A.Tittle 35.00 60.00
43 Buford Long RC 3.00 5.00
44 Volney Quinlan 3.00 5.00
45 Bobby Thomason 3.00 5.00
46 Fred Cone 3.00 5.00
47 Gerald Weatherly 3.00 5.00
48 Don Stonesifer 3.00 5.00
49A Lynn Chandnois ERR 3.00 5.00
49B Lynn Chandnois COR 3.00 5.00
50 George Taliaferro 3.00 5.00
51 Dick Alban 3.00 5.00
52 Lou Groza 20.00 35.00
53 Bobby Layne 35.00 60.00
54 Hugh McElhenny 20.00 40.00
55 Frank Gifford 60.00 100.00
56 Leon McLaughlin RC 3.00 5.00
57 Chuck Bednarik 20.00 40.00
58 Art Hunter RC 3.00 5.00
59 Bill McColl 3.00 5.00
60 Charley Trippi 15.00 25.00
61 Jim Finks 7.50 15.00
62 Bill Lange G RC 3.00 5.00
63 Laurie Niemi 3.00 5.00
64 Ray Renfro 4.00 8.00
65 Dick Chapman SP RC 15.00 25.00
66 Bob Hantla SP RC 15.00 25.00
67 Ralph Starkey SP RC 15.00 25.00
68 Don Paul LB SP 15.00 25.00
69 Kenneth Snyder SP 15.00 25.00
70 Tobin Rote SP 18.00 30.00
71 Art DeCarlo SP RC 15.00 25.00
72 Tom Keane SP RC 15.00 25.00
73 Hugh Taylor SP 18.00 30.00
74 Warren Lahr SP RC 15.00 25.00
75 Jim Neal SP RC 15.00 25.00
76 Leo Nomellini SP 35.00 60.00
77 Dick Yelvington SP RC 15.00 25.00
78 Les Richter SP 18.00 30.00
79 Bucko Kilroy SP 18.00 30.00
80 John Martinkovic SP RC 15.00 25.00
81 Dale Dodrill SP RC 15.00 25.00
82 Ken Jackson SP RC 15.00 25.00
83 Paul Lipscomb SP 15.00 25.00
84 John Bauer SP RC 15.00 25.00
85 Lou Creekmur SP 30.00 50.00
86 Eddie Price SP 15.00 25.00
87 Kenneth Farragut SP RC 15.00 25.00
88 Dave Hanner SP RC 18.00 30.00
89 Don Boll SP RC 15.00 25.00
90 Chet Hanulak SP RC 15.00 25.00
91 Thurman McGraw SP 15.00 25.00
92 Don Heinrich SP RC 18.00 30.00
93 Dan McKown SP RC 15.00 25.00
94 Bob Fleck SP RC 15.00 25.00
95 Jerry Hilgenberg SP RC 15.00 25.00
96 Bill Walsh C SP 15.00 25.00
97A Tom Finnin ERR 35.00 60.00
97B Tom Finnan COR RC 4.00 8.00
98 Paul Barry RC 3.00 5.00
99 Chick Jagade 3.00 5.00
100 Jack Christiansen 12.00 25.00
101 Gordy Soltau 3.00 5.00
102A Emlen Tunnell ERR 15.00 25.00
102B Emlen Tunnell COR 12.00 20.00
102C Emlen Tunnell COR 12.00 20.00
103 Stan West RC 3.00 5.00
104 Jerry Williams 3.00 5.00
105 Veryl Switzer RC 3.00 5.00
106 Billy Stone 3.00 5.00
107 Jerry Watford RC 3.00 5.00
108 Elbert Nickel 4.00 8.00
109 Ed Sharkey RC 3.00 5.00
110 Steve Meilinger RC 3.00 5.00
111 Dante Lavelli 12.00 20.00
112 Leon Hart 7.50 15.00
113 Charley Conerly 18.00 30.00
114 Richard Lemmon RC 3.00 5.00
115 Al Carmichael RC 3.00 5.00
116 George Connor 12.00 20.00
117 John Olszewski 3.00 5.00
118 Ernie Stautner 15.00 25.00
119 Ray Smith RC 3.00 5.00
120 Neil Worden RC 3.00 5.00
121 Jim Dooley 3.00 5.00
122 Arnold Galiffa 3.00 5.00
123 Kline Gilbert RC 3.00 5.00
124 Bob Hoernschemeyer 4.00 8.00
125 Wilford White RC 7.50 15.00
126 Art Spinney RC 3.00 5.00
127 Joe Koch RC 3.00 5.00
128 John Lattner RC 40.00 80.00

1955 Bowman

The 1955 Bowman set of 160 cards was Bowman's last sports issue before the company was purchased by Topps in January of 1956. The cards were issued in seven-card, five-cent packs and one-card penny packs and measure approximately 2 1/2" by 3 3/4". The fronts contain player photos with the player name and team logo at the bottom and the team name at the top. The card backs are printed in red and blue on gray card stock and a short player bio is included. On the bottom of most of the card backs is a play diagram. Cards 65-160 are slightly more difficult to obtain. The notable Rookie Cards in this set are Alan Ameche, Len Ford, Frank Gatski, John Henry Johnson, Mike McCormack, Jim Ringo, Bob St. Clair, and Pat Summerall.

COMPLETE SET (160)	1,000.00	1,600.00
WRAPPER (1-CENT)	150.00	225.00
WRAPPER (5-CENT)	60.00	120.00
1 Doak Walker	40.00	75.00
2 Mike McCormack RC	18.00	30.00
3 John Olszewski	3.00	5.00
4 Dorne Dibble RC	3.00	5.00
5 Lindon Crow RC	3.00	5.00
6 Hugh Taylor UER	4.00	8.00
7 Frank Gifford	35.00	60.00
8 Alan Ameche RC	25.00	40.00
9 Don Stonesifer	3.00	5.00
10 Pete Pihos	7.50	15.00
11 Bill Austin	3.00	5.00
12 Dick Alban	3.00	5.00
13 Bobby Walston	4.00	8.00
14 Len Ford RC	25.00	40.00
15 Jug Girard	3.00	5.00
16 Charley Conerly	15.00	25.00
17 Volney Peters RC	3.00	5.00
18 Max Boydston RC	3.00	5.00
19 Leon Hart	6.00	12.00
20 Bert Rechichar	3.00	5.00
21 Lee Riley RC	3.00	5.00
22 Johnny Carson RC	3.00	5.00
23 Harry Thompson	3.00	5.00
24 Ray Wietecha	3.00	5.00
25 Ollie Matson	15.00	25.00
26 Eddie LeBaron	7.50	15.00
27 Jack Simmons	3.00	5.00
28 Jack Christiansen	7.50	15.00
29 Bucko Kilroy	4.00	8.00
30 Tom Keane	3.00	5.00
31 Dave Leggett RC	3.00	5.00
32 Norm Van Brocklin	25.00	40.00
33 Harlon Hill RC	6.00	12.00
34 Robert Haner RC	3.00	5.00
35 Veryl Switzer	3.00	5.00
36 Dick Stanfel RC	6.00	12.00
37 Lou Groza	15.00	25.00
38 Tank Younger	6.00	12.00
39 Dick Flanagan RC	3.00	5.00
40 Jim Dooley	3.00	5.00
41 Ray Collins RC	3.00	5.00
42 John Henry Johnson RC	25.00	50.00
43 Tom Fears	7.50	15.00
44 Joe Perry	18.00	30.00
45 Gene Brito RC	3.00	5.00
46 Bill Johnson C	3.00	5.00
47 Dan Towler	6.00	12.00
48 Dick Moegle RC	4.00	8.00
49 Kline Gilbert	3.00	5.00
50 Les Gobel RC	3.00	5.00
51 Ray Krouse RC	3.00	5.00
52 Pat Summerall RC	35.00	70.00
53 Ed Brown RC	7.50	15.00
54 Lynn Chandnois	3.00	5.00
55 Joe Heap RC	3.00	5.00
56 John Hoffman	3.00	5.00
57 Howard Ferguson RC	3.00	5.00
58 Bobby Watkins RC	3.00	5.00
59 Charlie Ane RC	3.00	5.00
60 Ken MacAfee E RC	4.00	8.00
61 Ralph Guglielmi RC	4.00	8.00
62 George Blanda	35.00	60.00
63 Kenneth Snyder	3.00	5.00
64 Chet Ostrowski	3.00	5.00
65 Buddy Young	7.50	15.00
66 Gordy Soltau	5.00	8.00
67 Eddie Bell RC	5.00	8.00
68 Ben Agajanian RC	6.00	12.00
69 Tom Dahms RC	5.00	8.00
70 Jim Ringo RC	30.00	50.00
71 Bobby Layne	45.00	75.00
72 Y.A.Tittle	45.00	75.00
73 Bob Gaona RC	5.00	8.00
74 Tobin Rote	6.00	12.00
75 Hugh McElhenny	18.00	30.00
76 John Kreamcheck	5.00	8.00
77 Al Dorow RC	6.00	12.00
78 Bill Wade	7.50	15.00
79 Dale Dodrill	5.00	8.00
80 Chuck Drazenovich	5.00	8.00
81 Billy Wilson RC	6.00	12.00
82 Les Richter	6.00	12.00
83 Pat Brady	5.00	8.00
84 Bob Hoernschemeyer	6.00	12.00
85 Joe Arenas	5.00	8.00
86 Len Szafaryn UER RC	5.00	8.00
87 Rick Casares RC	12.00	20.00
88 Leon McLaughlin	5.00	8.00
89 Charley Toogood RC	5.00	8.00
90 Tom Bettis RC	5.00	8.00
91 John Sandusky	5.00	8.00
92 Bill Wightkin	5.00	8.00
93 Darrel Brewster RC	5.00	8.00
94 Marion Campbell	7.50	15.00
95 Floyd Reid	5.00	8.00
96 Chick Jagade	5.00	8.00
97 George Taliaferro	5.00	8.00
98 Carlton Massey RC	5.00	8.00
99 Fran Rogel	5.00	8.00
100 Alex Sandusky RC	5.00	8.00
101 Bob St.Clair RC	30.00	60.00
102 Al Carmichael	5.00	8.00
103 Carl Taseff RC	5.00	8.00
104 Leo Nomellini	15.00	25.00
105 Tom Scott	5.00	8.00
106 Ted Marchibroda	7.50	15.00
107 Art Spinney	5.00	8.00
108 Wayne Robinson	5.00	8.00
109 Jim Ricca RC	5.00	8.00
110 Lou Ferry RC	5.00	8.00
111 Roger Zatkoff RC	5.00	8.00
112 Lou Creekmur	7.50	15.00
113 Kenny Konz RC	5.00	8.00
114 Doug Eggers RC	5.00	8.00
115 Bobby Thomason	5.00	8.00
116 Bill McPeak RC	5.00	8.00
117 William Brown RC	5.00	8.00
118 Royce Womble RC	5.00	8.00
119 Frank Gatski RC	20.00	40.00
120 Jim Finks	7.50	15.00
121 Andy Robustelli	15.00	25.00
122 Bobby Dillon	5.00	8.00
123 Leo Sanford	5.00	8.00
124 Elbert Nickel	6.00	12.00
125 Wayne Hansen RC	5.00	8.00
126 Buck Lansford RC	5.00	8.00
127 Gern Nagler	5.00	8.00
128 Jim Salsbury RC	5.00	8.00
129 Dale Atkeson RC	5.00	8.00
130 John Schweder	5.00	8.00
131 Dave Hanner	6.00	12.00
132 Eddie Price	5.00	8.00
133 Vic Janowicz	15.00	30.00
134 Ernie Stautner	15.00	25.00
135 James Parmer RC	5.00	8.00
136 Emlen Tunnell UER	12.00	20.00
137 Kyle Rote	7.50	15.00
138 Norm Willey	5.00	8.00
139 Charley Trippi	12.00	20.00
140 Billy Howton	6.00	12.00
141 Bobby Clatterbuck RC	5.00	8.00
142 Bob Boyd	5.00	8.00
143 Bob Toneff RC	6.00	12.00
144 Jerry Helluin RC	5.00	8.00
145 Adrian Burk	5.00	8.00
146 Walt Michaels	6.00	12.00
147 Zollie Toth	5.00	8.00
148 Frank Varrichione RC	5.00	8.00
149 Dick Bielski RC	5.00	8.00
150 George Ratterman	6.00	12.00
151 Mike Jarmoluk RC	5.00	8.00
152 Tom Landry	125.00	200.00
153 Ray Renfro	6.00	12.00
154 Zeke Bratkowski	6.00	12.00
155 Jerry Norton RC	5.00	8.00
156 Maurice Bassett RC	5.00	8.00
157 Volney Quinlan	5.00	8.00
158 Chuck Bednarik	18.00	30.00
159 Don Colo RC	5.00	8.00
160 L.G. Dupre RC	20.00	40.00

1977 Bowmar Reading Kit

The 50-card series consisting of the Bowmar NFL Reading Kit was originally issued to promote reading within school classrooms. The cards would be used to reward school children who correctly answered the questions relating to the biography on the cards. It was distributed in complete set form along with study materials, card dividers, and a colorful storage box. Each card measures roughly 8 3/8" by 13" and includes a color photo on front with a text intensive cardback.

COMPLETE SET (50)	100.00	200.00
1 Terry Metcalf	2.00	4.00
2 O.J. Simpson	2.00	4.00
3 Paul Brown	4.00	8.00
4 George Izo	2.00	4.00
5 Ernie Davis	4.00	8.00
6 Fred Gehrke Bob Waterfield	2.00	4.00
7 Bronko Nagurski	2.00	4.00
8 Don Hutson	2.00	4.00
9 Growth of Pro Football Helmets	.75	2.00
10 The Men in the Striped Shirts Referees	.75	2.00
11 Bert Jones	2.00	4.00
12 Jack Lambert	4.00	8.00
13 Charley Taylor	2.00	4.00
14 Frank Gifford	4.00	8.00
15 Roger Staubach	7.50	15.00
16 Joe Namath	10.00	20.00
17 Teddy Roosevelt	2.00	4.00
18 Sammy Baugh	4.00	8.00
19 George Halas	4.00	8.00
20 Y. A. Tittle	4.00	8.00
21 Dan Abramowicz	2.00	4.00
22 Fran Tarkenton	4.00	8.00
23 Johnny Unitas	10.00	20.00
24 Vince Lombardi	6.00	12.00
25 Csonka Clarence Davis	2.00	4.00
26 Ken Houston	2.00	4.00
27 Don Shula	5.00	10.00
28 LeBaron T.McDonald Cl.Davis G.Pruitt	2.00	4.00
29 Jim Brown	7.50	15.00
30 Franco Harris	2.00	4.00
31 Lydell Mitchell Franco Harris	2.00	4.00
32 Players No One Watches	2.00	4.00
33 Gale Sayers	4.00	8.00
34 Tom Dempsey	2.00	4.00
35 Sonny Jurgensen	2.00	4.00
36 George Blanda	2.00	4.00
37 Bart Starr	10.00	20.00
38 Chuck Noll Terry Bradshaw	6.00	12.00
39 Longest Football Game	2.00	4.00
40 Rocky Bleier	2.00	4.00
41 Walter Payton	15.00	25.00
42 Ken Anderson	2.00	4.00
43 Stadiums: From the Coliseum to the Superdome	.75	2.00
44 Coldest Championship Game Bart Starr	5.00	10.00
45 Jim Bakken	2.00	4.00
46 PP and K: A Super Bowl for Young Players	.75	2.00
47 Game that Made Pro Football	2.00	4.00
48 Purple People Eaters	2.00	4.00
49 Super Game R.Staubach J.Lambert P.Pearson	4.00	8.00
50 Pro Bowl: A Dream that Came True	2.00	4.00

1950 Bread for Health

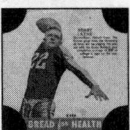

The 1950 Bread for Health football card (actually bread end labels) set contains 32 bread-end labels of players in the National Football League. The cards (actually paper thin labels) measure approximately 2 3/4" by 2 3/4". These labels are not usually found in top condition due to the difficulty in removing them from the bread package. While all the bakeries who issued this set are not presently known, Fisher's Bread in the New Jersey, New York and Pennsylvania area and NBC Bread in the Michigan area are two of the bakeries that have been confirmed to date. As with many of the bread label sets of the early 1950's, an album to house the set was probably issued. Each label contains the B.E.B. copyright found on so many of the labels of this period. Labels which contain "Bread for Energy" at the bottom are not a part of the set but part of a series of movie, western and sport stars issued during the same approximate time period. The catalog designation for this set is D290-15. The cards are unnumbered but are arranged alphabetically below for convenience.

COMPLETE SET (32)	8,000.00	12,000.00
1 Frankie Albert	150.00	300.00
2 Elmer Bud Angsman	125.00	250.00
3 Dick Barwegan	125.00	250.00
4 Sammy Baugh	500.00	800.00
5 Charley Conerly	200.00	400.00
6 Glenn Davis	150.00	300.00
7 Don Doll	150.00	300.00
8 Tom Fears	200.00	350.00
9 Harry Gilmer	150.00	300.00
10 Otto Graham	500.00	800.00
11 Pat Harder	150.00	300.00
12 Bobby Layne	400.00	700.00
13 Sid Luckman	400.00	700.00
14 Johnny Lujack	250.00	500.00
15 John Panelli	150.00	300.00
16 Barney Poole	150.00	300.00
17 George Ratterman	150.00	300.00
18 Tobin Rote	150.00	300.00
19 Jack Russell	200.00	400.00
20 Lou Rymkus	150.00	300.00
21 Joe Signiago	150.00	300.00
22 Mac Speedie	200.00	400.00
23 Bill Swiacki	150.00	300.00
24 Tommy Thompson QB	150.00	300.00
25 Y.A. Tittle	300.00	600.00
26 Clayton Tonnemaker	150.00	300.00
27 Charley Trippi	150.00	300.00
28 Bulldog Turner	200.00	400.00
29 Steve Van Buren	200.00	400.00
30 Bill Walsh C	150.00	300.00
31 Bob Waterfield	250.00	500.00
32 Jim White	150.00	300.00

1951 Bread For Energy

The 1951 Bread for Energy bread end labels set contains 11 known labels of players in the National Football League, professional basketball, pro boxing, and famous actors. Each measures approximately 2 3/4" by 2 3/4" with the corners cut out in typical bread label style. These labels are not usually found in top condition due to the difficulty in removing them from the bread package. While all the bakeries who issued this set are not presently known, Junge's Brand Bread in the New England area is one bakery that has been confirmed. As with many of the bread label sets of the early 1950's, an album to house the set was probably issued. Each label was printed with a red, yellow, and blue background. The cards are unnumbered but are arranged alphabetically within subject below.

37 Otto Graham FB	800.00	1,200.00
38 Johnny Lujack FB	200.00	400.00
39 Johnny Rauch FB	150.00	300.00
40 Buddy Young FB	150.00	300.00

1962 Broncos Team Issue

The Broncos issued several series of player photos in the early 1960s with some invariably being released in multiple years. Each of the photos in this group are black-and-white and measure approximately 8" by 10" and are blankbacked. The line of text below the image contains the following from left to right: player name and team name in all caps.

1 George Herring/(dropping back to pass)	7.50	15.00
2 George Herring/(running pose)	7.50	15.00
3 George Herring/(punting pose)	7.50	15.00
4 Tom Higginbotham	7.50	15.00

1963 Broncos Team Issue

The Broncos issued several series of player photos in the early 1960s with some invariably being released in multiple years. Each of the photos in this group are black-and-white and measure approximately 8" by 10" and are blankbacked. The line of text below the image contains the following from left to right: player name, position spelled out, height, weight and team name in all caps.

1 George Herring/(portrait)	7.50	15.00
2 George Herring/(handing off the ball)	7.50	15.00
3 Jack Hill	7.50	15.00
4 Jerry Hopkins	7.50	15.00

1967-68 Broncos Team Issue

The Broncos issued several series of player photos in the late 1960s through early 1970s with many invariably being released in multiple years. The format is the same for most of the sets with only subtle differences in the type (size and style) and information contained below the photo. Each of the photos in this group are black-and-white measuring approximately 5" by 7" and are blankbacked and unnumbered. The line of text contains the following from left to right: player name, position (completely spelled out), height, weight, and team name. We've included what is thought to be the year of issue. The 1967 photos were printed with both upper and lower case lettering, while the 1968 issue was done in all caps. We've listed the only known photos in the set.

COMPLETE SET (4)	25.00	50.00
1 Carl Cunningham 67	7.50	15.00
2 Al Denson 67	7.50	15.00
3 Wallace Dickey 68	7.50	15.00
4 Charlie Greer 68	7.50	15.00

1969 Broncos Team Issue

The Broncos issued several series of player photos in the 1960s and 1970s with many invariably being released in multiple years. The format is the same for most of the sets with only subtle differences in the type (size and style) and information contained below the photo. Each of these black-and-white photos measures approximately 5" by 7" and is blankbacked and unnumbered. The line of text for the 1969 issue contains the following from left to right: player name (in all caps), position (spelled out in all caps), height, weight, and team name (in all caps). We've listed the only known photos in the set.

COMPLETE SET (16)	100.00	200.00
1 Tom Beer	7.50	15.00
2 Phil Brady	7.50	15.00
3 Sam Brunelli	7.50	15.00
4 George Burrell	7.50	15.00
5 Grady Cavness	7.50	15.00
6 Ken Criter	7.50	15.00
7 Al Denson	7.50	15.00
8 John Embree	7.50	15.00
9 Walter Highsmith	7.50	15.00
10 Gus Hollomon	7.50	15.00
11 Pete Liske	7.50	15.00
12 Rex Mirich	7.50	15.00
13 Tom Oberg	7.50	15.00
14 Frank Richter	7.50	15.00
15 Paul Smith	7.50	15.00
16 Bob Young	7.50	15.00

1970 Broncos Carlson-Frink Dairy Coaches

These large (roughly 6" by 11 7/8") cards were issued by Carlson-Frink Dairy in the Denver area about 1970. Each is blankbacked and features a black and white photo of a then current Denver Broncos coach. A written "Football Tip" is also included below the coach's photo. The set includes just one unique photo for each coach but it is included on five different card numbers that begin with the first initial of the coach's last name. The "Football Tip" is unique to each of the five cards per coach. Lou Saban has also been found only in an unnumbered card version. Any confirmed additions to this list are appreciated.

COMPLETE SET (36)	2,500.00	4,000.00
COMP.SHORT SET (8)	500.00	800.00
C1 Joe Collier	60.00	100.00
C2 Joe Collier	60.00	100.00
C3 Joe Collier	60.00	100.00
C4 Joe Collier	60.00	100.00
C5 Joe Collier	60.00	100.00
D1 Whitey Dovell	60.00	100.00
D2 Whitey Dovell	60.00	100.00
D3 Whitey Dovell	60.00	100.00
D4 Whitey Dovell	60.00	100.00
D5 Whitey Dovell	60.00	100.00
E1 Hunter Enis	60.00	100.00
E2 Hunter Enis	60.00	100.00
E3 Hunter Enis	60.00	100.00
E4 Hunter Enis	60.00	100.00
E5 Hunter Enis	60.00	100.00
G1 Fred Gehrke	60.00	100.00
G2 Fred Gehrke	60.00	100.00
G3 Fred Gehrke	60.00	100.00
G4 Fred Gehrke	60.00	100.00
G5 Fred Gehrke	60.00	100.00
J1 Stan Jones	75.00	125.00
J2 Stan Jones	75.00	125.00
J3 Stan Jones	75.00	125.00
J4 Stan Jones	75.00	125.00
J5 Stan Jones	75.00	125.00
M1 Dick MacPherson	60.00	100.00
M2 Dick MacPherson	60.00	100.00
M3 Dick MacPherson	60.00	100.00
M4 Dick MacPherson	60.00	100.00
M5 Dick MacPherson	60.00	100.00
R1 Sam Rutigliano	75.00	125.00
R2 Sam Rutigliano	75.00	125.00
R3 Sam Rutigliano	75.00	125.00
R4 Sam Rutigliano	75.00	125.00
R5 Sam Rutigliano	75.00	125.00
S1 Lou Saban	75.00	125.00
S2 Lou Saban	75.00	125.00
S3 Lou Saban	75.00	125.00
S4 Lou Saban	75.00	125.00
S5 Lou Saban	75.00	125.00
NNO Lou Saban	75.00	125.00

1970 Broncos Team Issue

The Broncos issued several series of player photos in the 1960s and 1970s with many invariably being released in multiple years. The format is the same for most of the sets with only subtle differences in the type (size and style) and information contained below the photo. Each of these black-and-white photos measures approximately 5" by 7" and is blankbacked and unnumbered. The line of text for the 1970 issue contains the following from left to right: player name (in upper and lower case), position (initials), and team name (in upper and lower case). We've listed the only known photos in the set.

COMPLETE SET (11)	50.00	100.00
1 Bob Anderson	6.00	12.00
2 Dave Costa	6.00	12.00
3 Ken Criter	6.00	12.00
4 Mike Current	6.00	12.00
5 Fred Forsberg	6.00	12.00
6 Charles Greer	6.00	12.00
7 Larry Kaminski	6.00	12.00
8 Fran Lynch	6.00	12.00
9 Mike Schnitker	6.00	12.00
10 Paul Smith	6.00	12.00
11 Dave Washington	6.00	12.00

1970 Broncos Texaco

The Broncos and Texaco released this set in 1970. Each card is actually an artist's rendering in an 8" by 10" format. The backs are unnumbered and contain extensive player information as well information about the artist, Von Schroeder.

COMPLETE SET (10)	100.00	175.00
1 Bob Anderson RB	7.50	15.00
2 Dave Costa	7.50	15.00
3 Pete Duranko	7.50	15.00
4 George Goeddeke SP	15.00	30.00
5 Mike Haffner	7.50	15.00
6 Rich Jackson	7.50	15.00
7 Larry Kaminski	7.50	15.00
8 Floyd Little	10.00	20.00
9 Pete Liske SP	15.00	30.00
10 Bill Van Heusen	7.50	15.00

1971 Broncos Team Issue 5x7

The Broncos issued several series of player photos in the 1960s and 1970s with many invariably being released in multiple years. The format is the same for most of the sets with only subtle differences in the type (size and style) and information contained below the photo. Each of these black-and-white photos measures approximately 5" by 7" and is blankbacked and unnumbered. The line of text for the 1971 issue contains the following from left to right: player name (in upper and lower case), height, weight, position (initials), and team name (in upper and lower case). We've listed the only known photos in the set.

COMPLETE SET (6)	25.00	40.00
1 Jack Gehrke	4.00	8.00
2 Dwight Harrison	4.00	8.00
3 Randy Montgomery	4.00	8.00
4 Steve Ramsey	4.00	8.00
5 Roger Shoals	4.00	8.00
6 Olen Underwood	4.00	8.00

1971-72 Broncos Team Issue 8x10

The Broncos issued several series of player photos in the 1960s and 1970s with many invariably being released in multiple years. The format is roughly the same for most of the sets with only subtle differences in the type (size and style) and information contained below the photo. Each of these black-and-white photos measures approximately 8" by 10" and is blankbacked and unnumbered.

COMPLETE SET (10)	50.00	100.00
1 Lyle Alzado	7.50	15.00
2 Mike Current	5.00	10.00
3 Fred Forsberg	5.00	10.00
4 Charles Greer	5.00	10.00
5 Don Horn	5.00	10.00
6 Bill McKoy	5.00	10.00
7 George Saimes	5.00	10.00
8 Paul Smith	5.00	10.00
9 Bill Thompson	5.00	10.00
10 Jim Turner	5.00	10.00
Don Horn		

1972 Broncos Team Issue

The Broncos issued several series of player photos in the 1960s and 1970s with many invariably being released in multiple years. The format is the same for most of the sets with only subtle differences in the type (size and style) and information contained below the photo. Each of these black-and-white photos measures approximately 5" by 7" and is blankbacked and unnumbered. The line of text for the 1972 issue contains the following from left to right: player name (in all caps), position (initials in all caps), and team city and team name (in all caps). We've listed only the known photos in the set, additions to this list are welcomed.

COMPLETE SET (6)	25.00	50.00
1 Carter Campbell	5.00	10.00
2 Cornell Gordon	5.00	10.00
3 Larron Jackson	5.00	10.00
4 Tommy Lyons	5.00	10.00
5 Bobby Maples	5.00	10.00
6 Jerry Simmons	5.00	10.00

1973 Broncos Team Issue

The Broncos issued several series of player photos in the 1960s and 1970s with many invariably being released in multiple years. The format is the same for most of the sets with only subtle differences in the type (size and style) and information contained below the photo. Each of these black-and-white photos measures approximately 5" by 7" and is blankbacked and unnumbered. The line of text for the 1973 issue contains the following from left to right: player name (in all caps), position (initials in all caps) followed by a comma, and team city and team name (in all caps). We've listed only the known photos in the set, additions to this list are welcomed.

COMPLETE SET (16)	75.00	150.00
1 Lyle Alzado	6.00	12.00
2 Otis Armstrong	6.00	12.00
3 Barney Chavous	5.00	10.00
4 Mike Current	5.00	10.00
5 Joe Dawkins	5.00	10.00
6 John Grant	5.00	10.00
7 Larron Jackson 73	5.00	10.00
8 Calvin Jones	5.00	10.00
9 Larry Kaminski	5.00	10.00
10 Bill Laskey	5.00	10.00
11 Tom Lyons	5.00	10.00
12 Randy Montgomery	5.00	10.00
13 Riley Odoms	5.00	10.00
14 Oliver Ross	5.00	10.00
15 Ed Smith	5.00	10.00
16 Bill Van Heusen	5.00	10.00

1975 Broncos Team Issue

The Broncos issued several series of player photos in the 1960s and 1970s with many invariably being released in multiple years. The format is very similar for most of the sets with only subtle differences in the type (size and style) and information contained below the photo. Each of these black-and-white photos measures approximately 5" by 7" and is blankbacked and unnumbered. The line of text for the 1975 issue contains the following from left to right: player name (in all caps), position (initials in all caps), and team city (in all caps). We've listed only the known photos in the set, additions to this list are welcomed.

COMPLETE SET (15)	60.00	120.00
1 Stan Rogers	5.00	10.00
2 John Rowser	5.00	10.00
3 Bob Swenson	5.00	10.00
4 Paul Smith	5.00	10.00
5 Jeff Severson	5.00	10.00
6 Boyd Brown	5.00	10.00
7 Rubin Carter	5.00	10.00
8 Jack Dolbin	5.00	10.00
9 Mike Franckowiak	5.00	10.00
10 Randy Gradishar	6.00	12.00
11 Paul Howard	5.00	10.00
12 Claudie Minor	5.00	10.00
13 Phil Olsen	5.00	10.00
14 Steve Ramsey	5.00	10.00
15 Joe Rizzo	5.00	10.00

1976 Broncos Team Issue

The Broncos issued several series of player photos in the 1960s and 1970s with many invariably being released in multiple years. The format is very similar for most of the sets with only subtle differences in the type (size and style) and information contained below the photo. Each of these black-and-white photos measures approximately 5" by 7" and is blankbacked and unnumbered. The line of text for the 1975 issue contains the following from left to right: player name (in upper and lower case letters), position (initials or spelled out fully in upper and lower case), and team city (in upper and lower case). We've listed only the known photos in the set, additions to this list are welcomed.

1 Randy Poltl	5.00	10.00
2 Earlie Thomas	5.00	10.00

1977 Broncos Burger King Glasses

Burger King restaurants released this set of 6-drinking glasses during the 1977 NFL season in Denver area stores. Each features a black and white photo of a Broncos player with his name and team name below the picture.

COMPLETE SET (6)	45.00	90.00
1 Lyle Alzado	12.50	25.00
2 Randy Gradishar	10.00	20.00
3 Tom Jackson	10.00	20.00
4 Craig Morton	12.50	25.00
5 Haven Moses	7.50	15.00
6 Riley Odoms	7.50	15.00

1977 Broncos Orange Crush Cans

This can set features player images of the Denver Broncos printed on Orange Crush Soda cans. The set is unnumbered and checklisted below in alphabetical order. Reportedly, there were 64-different cans made. Any additions to the below list are appreciated.

COMPLETE SET (64)	200.00	350.00
1 Henry Allison	2.50	5.00
2 Lyle Alzado	5.00	10.00
3 Steve Antonopulos TR	2.50	5.00
4 Otis Armstrong	4.00	8.00
5 Rick Baska	2.50	5.00
6 Ronnie Bill EQ MGR	2.50	5.00
7 Marv Braden CO	2.50	5.00
8 Rubin Carter	2.50	5.00
9 Barney Chavous	3.00	6.00
10 Joe Collier CO	2.50	5.00
11 Bucky Dilts	2.50	5.00
12 Jack Dolbin	3.00	6.00
13 Larry Elliot EQ MGR	2.50	5.00
14 Larry Evans	2.50	5.00
15 Dave Frei DIR	2.50	5.00
16 Steve Foley	3.00	6.00
17 Ron Egloff	2.50	5.00
18 Bob Gambold CO	2.50	5.00
19 Fred Gehrke GM	2.50	5.00
20 Tom Glassic	2.50	5.00
21 Randy Gradishar	5.00	10.00
22 John Grant	2.50	5.00
23 Ken Gray CO	2.50	5.00
24 Paul Howard	2.50	5.00
25 Allen Hurst TR	2.50	5.00
26 Glenn Hyde	2.50	5.00
27 Bernard Jackson	2.50	5.00
28 Tom Jackson	5.00	10.00
29 Jim Jensen	2.50	5.00
30 Stan Jones CO	4.00	8.00
31 Rob Lytle	3.00	6.00
32 Jon Keyworth	3.00	6.00
33 Brison Manor	2.50	5.00
34 Bobby Maples	2.50	5.00
35 Andy Maurer	2.50	5.00
36 Red Miller CO	4.00	8.00
37 Claudie Minor	2.50	5.00
38 Mike Montler	2.50	5.00
39 Myrel Moore CO	2.50	5.00
40 Craig Morton	5.00	10.00
41 Haven Moses	4.00	8.00
42 Rob Nairne	2.50	5.00
43 Riley Odoms	3.00	6.00
44 Babe Parilli CO	3.00	6.00
45 Bob Peck	2.50	5.00
46 Craig Penrose	2.50	5.00
47 Lonnie Perrin	2.50	5.00
48 Fran Polsfoot CO	2.50	5.00
49 Randy Poltl	2.50	5.00
50 Randy Rich	2.50	5.00
51 Larry Riley	2.50	5.00
52 Joe Rizzo	2.50	5.00
53 Paul Roach CO	2.50	5.00
54 Steve Schindler	2.50	5.00
55 John Schultz	2.50	5.00
56 Paul Smith	3.00	6.00
57 Gail Stuckey	2.50	5.00
58 Bob Swenson	2.50	5.00
59 Bill Thompson	3.00	6.00
60 Godwin Turk	2.50	5.00
61 Jim Turner	3.00	6.00
62 Rick Upchurch	4.00	8.00
63 Norris Weese	2.50	5.00
64 Louis Wright	3.00	6.00

1980 Broncos Stamps Police

The 1980 Denver Broncos set are not cards but stamps each measuring approximately 3" by 3". Each stamp actually contains three smaller stamps, two player stamps and the Denver Broncos logo stamp. The set is co-sponsored by Albertson's, the Kiwanis Club, and the local law enforcement agency. A different stamp pair was given away each week for nine weeks by Albertson's food stores in the Denver Metro area. The set is unnumbered, although player uniform numbers appear on each small stamp. The set has been listed below in alphabetical order based on the player stamp on the left side. The back of each pair states "Support your local Law Enforcement Agency" and gives instructions on how to reach the police by phone. The backs of the stamps contain 1980 NFL and NFL Player's Association copyright dates. There was also a poster (to hold the stamps) issued which originally was priced at 99 cents. It was a color action picture of four Broncos tackling a Chargers running back measuring approximately 21" by 29"; the poster is much more difficult to find now than the set of stamps.

COMPLETE SET (9)	7.50	15.00
1 Barney Chavous	.60	1.50
2 Bernard Jackson	.60	1.50
3 Tom Jackson	1.25	3.00
4 Brison Manor	.60	1.50
5 Claudie Minor	.60	1.50
6 Craig Morton	1.25	3.00
7 Jim Turner	.75	2.00
8 Rick Upchurch	1.00	2.50
9 Louis Wright	.75	2.00

1946 Browns Sears

These eight cards measure approximately 2 1/2" by 4". They were issued by Sears and Roebuck and feature players from the debut season of the Cleveland Browns. The cards were printed on heavy white paper stock and include a black and white photo of the featured player on the front with a team schedule on back. Cardfronts also included a message to follow the Browns and shop at Sears Stores. Several very early cards of Hall of Famers are included in this set. We have checklisted this set in alphabetical order.

COMPLETE SET (8)	1,000.00	1,800.00
1 Ernie Blandin	90.00	150.00
2 Jim Daniell	90.00	150.00
3 Fred Evans	90.00	150.00
4 Frank Gatski	150.00	250.00
5 Otto Graham	350.00	600.00
6 Dante Lavelli	175.00	300.00
7 Mel Maceau	90.00	150.00
8 George Young	125.00	200.00

1948 Browns Sohio

These large (measure either 8" by 9 7/8" or 7 3/4" by 9 7/8") black and white photos are issued by Cleveland area Sohio stores in 1948. They are very simiar to the 1949 release and were printed on heavy card stock and each includes a black and white photo along with brief biographical information on the cardfronts and "Compliments of Sohio" printed within the bottom border. Since the photos are unnumbered, we have sequenced them in alphabetical order.

COMPLETE SET (3)	150.00	300.00
1 Horace Gillom	25.00	50.00
2 Marion Motley	100.00	175.00
3 Bill Willis	40.00	80.00

1949 Browns Sohio

These large black and white photos were issued by Cleveland area Sohio stores in 1949 as a complete set in an envelope. The exact size of each photo varies slightly by as much as 1/16" but roughly each measures 8" by 9 3/4". They were printed on heavy card stock and each includes a black and white photo along with brief biographical information on the cardfronts. Since the photos are unnumbered, we have sequenced them in alphabetical order. Note that most of the photos in this release have been reproduced with slight differences in paper stock and size.

COMPLETE SET (11)	500.00	800.00
1 Bob Gaudio	25.00	40.00
2 Otto Graham	175.00	300.00
3 Lou Groza	90.00	150.00
4 Lin Houston	25.00	40.00
5 Weldon Humble	25.00	40.00
6 Tommy James	25.00	40.00
7 Edgar Jones	30.00	50.00
8 Dante Lavelli	60.00	100.00
9 Marion Motley	100.00	175.00
10 Lou Saban	30.00	50.00
11 Mac Speedie	50.00	80.00

1950 Browns Team Issue 6x9

This set of team-issued photos measures approximately 6 1/4" by 9" and was printed on thin paper stock and issued as a set. The fronts feature black-and-white posed action shots framed by white borders with a facsimile autogrpah near the bottoom of the photo. The cardbacks are blank and unnumbered and the photos are checklisted below in alphabetical order.

COMPLETE SET (25)	600.00	1,000.00
1 Tony Adamle	18.00	30.00
2 Paul Brown	50.00	80.00
3 Rex Bumgardner	18.00	30.00
4 Frank Gatski	30.00	50.00
5 Abe Gibron	18.00	30.00
6 Otto Graham	125.00	200.00
7 Forrest Grigg	18.00	30.00
8 Lou Groza	60.00	100.00
9 Hal Herring	18.00	30.00
10 Lin Houston	18.00	30.00
11 Tommy James	18.00	30.00
12 Dub Jones	20.00	35.00
13 Warren Lahr	18.00	30.00
14 Dante Lavelli	40.00	75.00
15 Cliff Lewis	18.00	30.00
16 Dom Moselle	18.00	30.00
17 Marion Motley	60.00	100.00
18 Derrell F. Palmer	18.00	30.00
19 Don Phelps	18.00	30.00
20 John Russell	18.00	30.00
21 Lou Rymkus	20.00	35.00
22 Mac Speedie	30.00	50.00
23 Thomas Thompson	18.00	30.00
24 Bill Willis	35.00	60.00
25 George Young	25.00	40.00

1950 Browns Team Issue 8x10

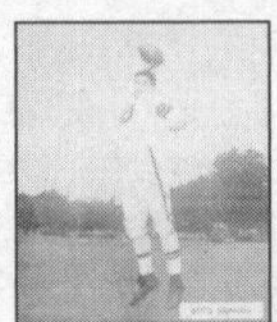

This set of Cleveland Browns photos measures approximately 8" by 10" and features black and white posed action shots framed by white borders. The year is an estimate based upon when the players appeared on the same Browns' team. The player's name appears in a small white box close to the bottom of the photo and the cardbacks are blank. Each is unnumbered and checklisted below in alphabetical order. It is thought that the set could have been released by Sohio. These photos are identical to the 1954 set and some players may have been issued both years. Any additions to either checklist is appreciated.

COMPLETE SET (11)	400.00	750.00
1 Tony Adamle	25.00	40.00
2 Otto Graham	125.00	200.00
3 Horace Gillom	25.00	40.00
4 Chubby Grigg	25.00	40.00
5 Lou Groza	75.00	125.00
6 Lin Houston	25.00	40.00
7 Dub Jones	30.00	50.00
8 Dante Lavelli	40.00	75.00
9 Marion Motley	75.00	125.00
10 Mac Speedie	35.00	60.00
11 Bill Willis	35.00	60.00

1951 Browns Team Issue 6x9

This set of team-issued photos measures approximately 6 1/2" by 9" and features black and white posed action shots framed by white borders. The set was distributed in an attractive off-white envelope with orange and brown trim titled "Cleveland Browns Photographs". The set is similar to the 1950 issue, but the player's name appears in script close to the photo. The backs are blank. The cards are unnumbered and checklisted below in alphabetical order.

COMPLETE SET (25)	600.00	1,000.00
1 Tony Adamle	18.00	30.00
2 Alex Agase	18.00	30.00
3 Rex Bumgardner	18.00	30.00
4 Emerson Cole	18.00	30.00
5 Len Ford	35.00	60.00
6 Frank Gatski	30.00	50.00
7 Horace Gillom	18.00	30.00
8 Ken Gorgal	18.00	30.00
9 Otto Graham	125.00	200.00
10 Forrest Grigg	18.00	30.00
11 Lou Groza	60.00	100.00
12 Hal Herring	18.00	30.00
13 Lin Houston	18.00	30.00
14 Weldon Humble	18.00	30.00
15 Tommy James	18.00	30.00
16 Dub Jones	20.00	35.00
17 Warren Lahr	18.00	30.00
18 Dante Lavelli	40.00	75.00
19 Cliff Lewis	18.00	30.00
20 Marion Motley	60.00	100.00
21 Lou Rymkus	20.00	35.00
22 Mac Speedie	30.00	50.00
23 Tommy Thompson LB	18.00	30.00
24 Bill Willis	35.00	60.00
25 George Young	25.00	40.00

1952 Browns Team Issue

This set of team-issued photos measures approximately 8" by 10" and features black and white posed action shots framed by white borders. Each photo was issued with the player's name, position, and team name stamped on the back making it quite different than other Browns photos of the era. The photos are unnumbered and checklisted below in alphabetical order.

1 Doug Atkins	25.00	40.00
2 Darrel Brewster	15.00	30.00
3 Ken Carpenter	15.00	30.00
4 Tom Catlin	15.00	30.00
5 Don Colo	15.00	30.00
6 Gene Donaldson	15.00	30.00
7 Abe Gibron	15.00	30.00
8 Horace Gillom	15.00	30.00
9 Jerry Helluin	15.00	30.00
10 Sherm Howard	15.00	30.00
11 Dub Jones	20.00	35.00
12 Warren Lahr	15.00	30.00
13 Chuck Noll	30.00	50.00
14 Derrell Palmer	15.00	30.00
15 George Ratterman	15.00	30.00
16 Ray Renfro	20.00	35.00
17 John Sandusky	15.00	30.00
18 Tommy Thompson	15.00	30.00

1953 Browns Carling Beer

This set of ten black and white posed action shots was sponsored by Carling Black Label Beer and features members of the Cleveland Browns. The pictures measure approximately 8" by 12 1/4" and have white borders. The sponsor's name and the team name appear below the picture in black lettering. The photos are very similar to the 1954 issue but with several different players and four players with different images. Each is unnumbered and the backs are blank. The serial number in the lower right corner on the fronts reads "DBL 54" plus a unique letter for each player. The photos were shot against a background of an open field with trees.

COMPLETE SET (10)	250.00	400.00
54F Dante Lavelli	25.00	40.00
54G Otto Graham	75.00	125.00
54H Lou Groza	40.00	75.00
54J Dub Jones	20.00	35.00
54K Gorgal	18.00	30.00
54L Len Ford	25.00	40.00
54M Bill Willis	25.00	40.00
54N Thompson	18.00	30.00
54O Frank Gatski	20.00	35.00
54P Jagade	18.00	30.00

1953 Browns Team Issue

The Cleveland Browns issued and distributed this 12-photo set. Each measures approximately 8 1/2" by 10 1/4" and features a black and white photo. The player's name and position appear in a small white box near the photo.

COMPLETE SET (12)	300.00	450.00
1 Len Ford	20.00	35.00
2 Frank Gatski	20.00	35.00
3 Abe Gibron	15.00	25.00
4 Ken Gorgal	12.00	20.00
5 Otto Graham	75.00	135.00
6 Lou Groza	35.00	60.00
7 Harry Jagade	12.00	20.00
8 Dub Jones	15.00	25.00
9 Dante Lavelli	30.00	50.00
10 Ray Renfro	15.00	25.00
11 Tommy Thompson	15.00	25.00
12 Bill Willis	20.00	35.00

1954 Browns Fisher Foods

This 10-card set features 8 1/2" by 10 1/2" black-and-white photos of the 1954 Cleveland Browns sponsored by Fisher Foods. The photos are very similar to many of the Browns Team Issue sets of the era but can be differentiated by the "Fisher Foods" type within the bottom border. Some or all of the photos an also be found missing the Fisher Foods name. The backs are blank. The cards are unnumbered and checklisted below in alphabetical order.

COMPLETE SET (10)	250.00	400.00
1 Darrel Brewster	12.00	20.00
2 Tom Catlin	12.00	20.00
3 Len Ford	20.00	35.00
4 Otto Graham	60.00	100.00
5 Lou Groza	30.00	50.00
6 Kenny Konz	15.00	25.00
7 Dante Lavelli	25.00	40.00
8 Mike McCormack	20.00	35.00
9 Fred Morrison	12.00	20.00
10 Chuck Noll	60.00	100.00

1954 Browns Team Issue

This photo set features 8 1/2" by 10 1/2" black-and-white photos of the 1954 Cleveland Browns. The photos are very similar to many of the Browns Team Issue sets of the era and are identical to the Fisher Foods set except for the omission of the company name in the bottom border. The player's name and position appear inside a box found near the player's image. The backs are blank. The cards are unnumbered and checklisted below in alphabetical order.

COMPLETE SET (10)	250.00	400.00
1 Tom Catlin	12.00	20.00
2 Len Ford	20.00	35.00
3 Abe Gibron	12.00	20.00
4 Otto Graham	60.00	100.00
5 Lou Groza	30.00	50.00
6 Dante Lavelli	25.00	40.00
7 Mike McCormack	20.00	35.00
8 Fred Morrison	12.00	20.00
9 Chuck Noll	60.00	100.00
10 Tommy Thompson	12.00	20.00

1954 Browns Team Issue 8x10

The Cleveland Browns released this set of photos with each measuring approximately 8" by 10" - slightly smaller than the Fisher Foods photos. The photos feature black and white posed action shots framed by white borders with just the player's name on the front. The year is an estimate based upon when the players appeared on the same Browns' team. Each is blankbacked and unnumbered and checklisted below in alphabetical order. It is thought that the set could have been released by Sohio. These photos are identical in style to the 1947 set and some players may have been issued both years. Any additions to either checklist is appreciated.

COMPLETE SET (8)	90.00	150.00
1 Darrell Brewster	12.00	20.00
2 Len Ford	15.00	25.00
3 Kenny Konz	12.00	20.00
4 Warren Lahr	12.00	20.00
5 Mike McCormack	15.00	25.00
6 Fred Morrison	12.00	20.00
7 Don Phelps	12.00	20.00
8 Tommy Thompson	12.00	20.00

1955-56 Browns Team Issue

This set consists of 8 1/2" by 10" posed player photos, with white borders and blank backs. Most of the photos are poses shot from the waist up; a few (Colo, Ford, and Lahr) picture the player in an action pose. The player's name and position are printed in the bottom white border in large letters. The photos are unnumbered and checklisted below in alphabetical order.

COMPLETE SET (23)	250.00	400.00
1 Maurice Bassett	7.50	15.00
2 Harold Bradley	7.50	15.00
3 Darrell(Pete) Brewster	7.50	15.00
4 Don Colo	7.50	15.00
5 Len Ford	15.00	25.00
6 Bobby Freeman	7.50	15.00
7 Bob Gain	7.50	15.00
8 Frank Gatski	15.00	25.00
9 Abe Gibron	7.50	15.00
10 Lou Groza	25.00	40.00
11 Tommy James	7.50	15.00
12 Dub Jones	10.00	20.00
13 Kenny Konz	7.50	15.00
14 Warren Lahr	7.50	15.00
15 Dante Lavelli	18.00	30.00
16 Carlton Massey	7.50	15.00
17 Mike McCormack	15.00	25.00
18 Walt Michaels	10.00	20.00
19 Chuck Noll	40.00	75.00
20 Babe Parilli	10.00	20.00
21 Don Paul DB	7.50	15.00
22 Ray Renfro	10.00	20.00
23 George Ratterman	10.00	20.00

1954 Browns Carling Beer

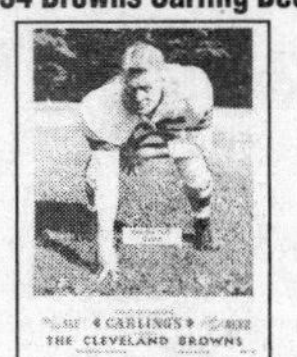

This set of black and white posed action shots was sponsored by Carling Black Label Beer and features members of the Cleveland Browns. The pictures measure approximately 8" by 12 1/4" and have white borders. The sponsor's name and the team name appear below the picture in black lettering. The photos are very similar to the 1953 issue with several new players and updated pictures on four players. Each of the backs are blank and the photo numbering in the lower right corner reads "DBL 54" followed by a unique letter for each player. We've included those numbers/letters below when known. The photos were shot against a background of an open field with trees.

COMPLETE SET (10)	300.00	500.00
1 Darrel Brewster	18.00	30.00
2 Tom Catlin	18.00	30.00
3 Len Ford	25.00	40.00
4 Otto Graham	75.00	125.00
5 Lou Groza	40.00	75.00
6 Kenny Konz	18.00	30.00
7 Dante Lavelli	25.00	40.00
8 Mike McCormack	20.00	35.00
9 Fred Morrison	18.00	30.00
10 Chuck Noll	50.00	100.00

1955 Browns Color Postcards

Measuring approximately 6" by 9", these color postcards feature Cleveland Browns players. The cards have rounded corners are are thought to have been distributed directly by the Browns.

COMPLETE SET (6)	125.00	225.00
1 Maurice Bassett	12.50	25.00
2 Don Colo	12.50	25.00
3 Frank Gatski	25.00	40.00
4 Lou Groza	40.00	75.00
5 Dante Lavelli	35.00	60.00
6 George Ratterman	12.50	25.00

1956 Browns Team Issue

This set was issued by the Cleveland Browns. Each photo is very similar to the 1954-55 set except for the size which is 6 3/4" by 8 1/2." All are black and white player photos with white borders and blankbacks. The player's name and position are printed in the bottom white border. The photos are unnumbered and checklisted below in alphabetical order.

COMPLETE SET (7)	125.00	200.00
1 Otto Graham	35.00	60.00
2 Dante Lavelli	15.00	25.00
3 Carlton Massey	7.50	15.00
4 Chuck Noll	25.00	50.00
5 Babe Parilli	10.00	20.00
6 George Ratterman	10.00	20.00
7 Ray Renfro	10.00	20.00

1958 Browns Carling Beer

This set of black-and-white posed action shots was sponsored by Carling Black Label Beer and features members of the Cleveland Browns. The pictures measure approximately 8 1/2" by 11 1/2" and have white borders. The sponsor's name and the team name appear below the picture in black lettering. The backs are blank and the pictures are numbered on the fronts with a "DBL" prefix on the card numbers.

COMPLETE SET (10)	350.00	600.00
227A Ray Renfro	20.00	40.00
227B Jim Brown	150.00	250.00
227C Art Hunter	20.00	40.00
227D Lowe Wren	20.00	40.00
227E Vince Costello	20.00	40.00
227F Chuck Noll	60.00	120.00
227G Paul Wiggin	20.00	40.00
227H Lou Groza	30.00	60.00
227I Bob Gain	20.00	40.00
227J Milt Plum	25.00	50.00

1958-59 Browns Team Issue

These cards are an unnumbered, blank-backed, team issue set of black and white photographs of the Cleveland Browns measuring approximately 8 1/2" by 10 1/2". The set features posed action shots of players whose name and position appear in a white reverse-out block burned into the bottom of each picture. The photos are very similar to the 1961 Browns

Team Issue therefore differences are included below for player in both sets. The unnumbered cards are listed below alphabetically.

COMPLETE SET (28)	175.00	300.00
1 Leroy Bolden	6.00	12.00
2 Lew Carpenter	6.00	12.00
3 Tom Catlin	6.00	12.00
4 Don Colo	6.00	12.00
5 Vince Costello	6.00	12.00
6 Galen Fiss	6.00	12.00
7 Bob Gain	6.00	12.00
8 Gene Hickerson	10.00	20.00
9 Art Hunter	6.00	12.00
10 Hank Jordan	10.00	20.00
11 Ken Konz	6.00	12.00
12 Warren Lahr	6.00	12.00
13 Willie McClung	6.00	12.00
14 Mike McCormack	7.50	15.00
15 Walt Michaels	7.50	15.00
16 Bobby Mitchell	10.00	20.00
17 Ed Modzelewski	6.00	12.00
18 Jim Ninowski	6.00	12.00
19 Chuck Noll	12.50	25.00
20 Fran O'Brien	6.00	12.00
21 Bernie Parrish	6.00	12.00
22 Don Paul	6.00	12.00
23 Milt Plum	7.50	15.00
24 Bill Quinlan	6.00	12.00
25 Ray Renfro	7.50	15.00
26 Jim Shofner	7.50	15.00
27 Paul Wiggin	6.00	12.00
28 Lowe Wren	6.00	12.00

1959 Browns Carling Beer

This set of black and white posed action shots was sponsored by Carling Black Label Beer and features members of the Cleveland Browns. The pictures measure approximately 8 1/2" by 11 1/2" and have white borders. The sponsor's name and the team name appear below the picture in black lettering. The backs are typically blank and were printed on glossy paper stock. The pictures are numbered in the lower right corner on the fronts. The photos were shot against a background of an open field with trees. The set is dated by the fact that Billy Howton's last year with Cleveland was 1959. This set was reprinted in the late 1980's; the reprints are on slightly thicker cardboard stock and typically show the Henry M. Barr stamp on the back.

COMPLETE SET (10)	350.00	600.00
302A Leroy Bolden	25.00	40.00
302B Vince Costello	25.00	40.00
302C Galen Fiss	25.00	40.00
302D Jim Brown	100.00	200.00
302E Lou Groza	40.00	75.00
302F Walt Michaels	30.00	50.00
302G Bobby Mitchell	35.00	60.00
302J Bob Gain	25.00	40.00
302K Bill Howton	30.00	50.00
302H Milt Plum	30.00	50.00

1959 Browns Shell Posters

This set of posters was distributed by Shell Oil in 1959. The pictures are black and white drawings with a light sepia color and measure approximately 11 3/4" by 13 3/4". The unnumbered posters are arranged alphabetically by the player's last name and feature members of the Cleveland Browns. Any additions to this list are appreciated.

COMPLETE SET (4)	75.00	125.00
1 Preston Carpenter	15.00	25.00
2 Lou Groza	30.00	50.00
3 Milt Plum	18.00	30.00
4 Jim Ray Smith	15.00	25.00

1960 Browns Team Issue

These large photos are an unnumbered, blank-backed, team issue set of black and white photographs of the Cleveland Browns. Each measures approximately 6" by 9 1/8" and was printed on thin glossy paper stock. The set features posed action shots of players with a facsimile autograph across the image. The cardbacks are blank and they are listed below alphabetically.

COMPLETE SET (32)	300.00	500.00
1 Sam Baker	6.00	12.00
2 Jim Brown	50.00	80.00
3 Paul Brown CO	15.00	30.00
4 Vince Costello	6.00	12.00
5 Len Dawson	30.00	50.00
6 Bob Denton	6.00	12.00
7 Ross Fichtner	6.00	12.00
8 Galen Fiss	6.00	12.00
9 Don Fleming	6.00	12.00
10 Bobby Franklin	6.00	12.00
11 Bob Gain	6.00	12.00
12 Prentice Gautt	6.00	12.00
13 Gene Hickerson	10.00	20.00
14 Jim Houston	6.00	12.00
15 Rich Kreitling	6.00	12.00
16 Dave Lloyd	6.00	12.00
17 Mike McCormack	10.00	20.00
18 Walt Michaels	7.50	15.00
19 Bobby Mitchell	12.50	25.00
20 John Morrow	6.00	12.00
21 Rich Mostardo	6.00	12.00
22 Fred Murphy	6.00	12.00
23 Gern Nagler	6.00	12.00
24 Bernie Parrish	6.00	12.00
25 Floyd Peters	6.00	12.00
26 Milt Plum	7.50	15.00
27 Jim Prestel	6.00	12.00
28 Dick Schafrath	7.50	15.00
29 Jim Shofner	7.50	15.00
30 Jim Ray Smith	6.00	12.00
31 Paul Wiggin	6.00	12.00
32 John Wooten	6.00	12.00

1961 Browns Carling Beer

This set of ten black and white posed action shots was sponsored by Carling Black Label Beer and features members of the Cleveland Browns. The pictures measure approximately 8 1/2" by 11 1/2" and have white borders. The sponsor's name and the team name appear below the picture in black lettering. The banks are blank. The pictures are numbered in the lower right corner on the fronts. The set is dated by the fact that Jim Houston's first year was 1960 and Bobby Mitchell and Milt Plum's last year with the Browns was 1961.

COMPLETE SET (10)	350.00	600.00
439A Milt Plum	30.00	50.00
439B Mike McCormack	30.00	50.00
439C Bob Gain	25.00	40.00
439D John Morrow	25.00	40.00
439E Jim Brown	100.00	200.00
439F Bobby Mitchell	35.00	60.00
439G Bobby Franklin	25.00	40.00
439H Jim Ray Smith	25.00	40.00
439K Jim Houston	25.00	40.00
439L Ray Renfro	30.00	50.00

1961 Browns National City Bank

The 1961 National City Bank Cleveland Browns football card set contains 36 brown and white cards each measuring approximately 2 1/2" by 3 9/16". The cards were issued in sheets of six cards, with each sheet of six given a set number and each individual card within the sheet given a player number. In the checklist below the cards have been numbered consecutively from one to 36. On the actual card, set/sheet number one will appear on cards 1 through 6, set number two on cards 7 through 12, etc. The front of the card states that the card is a "Quarterback Club Brownie Card". The backs of the cards contain the card number, a short biography and an ad for the National City Bank. Cards still in uncut (sheet of six) form are valued at one to two times the sum of the single card prices listed below. Len Dawson's card predates his 1963 Fleer Rookie Card by two years. It has been reported that cards #25-30 are in shorter supply than the rest.

COMPLETE SET (36)	1,200.00	2,000.00
1 Mike McCormack	30.00	60.00
2 Jim Brown	300.00	500.00
3 Leon Clarke	20.00	35.00
4 Walt Michaels	25.00	40.00
5 Jim Ray Smith	20.00	35.00
6 Quarterback Club	40.00	80.00
7 Len Dawson	250.00	400.00
8 John Morrow	20.00	35.00
9 Bernie Parrish	25.00	40.00
10 Floyd Peters	25.00	40.00
11 Paul Wiggin	25.00	40.00
12 John Wooten	25.00	40.00
13 Ray Renfro	25.00	40.00
14 Galen Fiss	20.00	35.00
15 Dave Lloyd	20.00	35.00
16 Dick Schafrath	30.00	50.00
17 Ross Fichtner	20.00	35.00
18 Gern Nagler	20.00	35.00
19 Rich Kreitling	20.00	35.00
20 Duane Putnam	20.00	35.00
21 Vince Costello	20.00	35.00
22 Jim Shofner	25.00	40.00
23 Sam Baker	25.00	40.00
24 Bob Gain	25.00	40.00
25 Lou Groza	100.00	175.00
26 Don Fleming	35.00	60.00
27 Tom Watkins	30.00	50.00
28 Jim Houston	35.00	60.00
29 Larry Stephens	30.00	50.00
30 Bobby Mitchell	90.00	150.00
31 Bobby Franklin	20.00	35.00
32 Charley Ferguson	20.00	35.00
33 Johnny Brewer	20.00	35.00
34 Bob Crespino	20.00	35.00
35 Milt Plum	35.00	60.00
36 Preston Powell	20.00	35.00

1961 Browns Team Issue Large

These large photo cards are an unnumbered, blank-backed, team issue set of black and white photographs of the Cleveland Browns measuring approximately 8 1/2" by 10 1/2". The set features posed action shots of players whose name and position appear in a white reverse-out block burned into the bottom of each picture. The cards are listed below alphabetically.

COMPLETE SET (20)	175.00	300.00
1 Jim Brown	50.00	75.00
2 Galen Fiss	6.00	12.00
3 Don Fleming	6.00	12.00
4 Bobby Franklin	6.00	12.00
5 Bob Gain	6.00	12.00
6 Jim Houston	6.00	12.00
7 Rich Kreitling	6.00	12.00
8 Dave Lloyd	6.00	12.00
9 Mike McCormack	12.00	20.00
10 Bobby Mitchell	15.00	25.00
11 John Morrow	6.00	12.00
12 Bernie Parrish	6.00	12.00
13 Milt Plum	7.50	15.00
14 Ray Renfro	7.50	15.00
15 Dick Schafrath	7.50	15.00
16 Jim Shofner	7.50	15.00
17 Jim Ray Smith	6.00	12.00
18 Tom Watkins	6.00	12.00
19 Paul Wiggin	6.00	12.00
20 John Wooten	6.00	12.00

1961 Browns Team Issue Small

These photos are an unnumbered, blank-backed, team issue set of black and white images of the Cleveland Browns. The photos are virtually identical to the 1960 Team Issue set except for the slightly different size. Each measures approximately 6 1/8" by 9" and was printed on thin glossy paper stock. The set features posed action shots of players with a facsimile autograph across the image. Many of the same photos were used for the 1961 Browns National City card set. The cardbacks are blank and the photos are listed below alphabetically.

COMPLETE SET (30)	200.00	350.00
1 Sam Baker	5.00	10.00
2 Jim Brown	50.00	75.00
3 Paul Brown CO	15.00	25.00
4 Vince Costello	5.00	10.00
5 Len Dawson	25.00	40.00
6 Charley Ferguson	5.00	10.00
7 Ross Fichtner	5.00	10.00
8 Galen Fiss	5.00	10.00
9 Don Fleming	5.00	10.00
10 Bobby Franklin	5.00	10.00
11 Bob Gain	5.00	10.00
12 Prentice Gautt	5.00	10.00
13 Lou Groza	15.00	25.00
14 Jim Houston	5.00	10.00
15 Dave Lloyd	5.00	10.00
16 Mike McCormack	7.50	15.00
17 Walt Michaels	6.00	12.00
18 Bobby Mitchell	10.00	20.00
19 John Morrow	5.00	10.00
20 Bernie Parrish	5.00	10.00
21 Floyd Peters	5.00	10.00
22 Milt Plum	6.00	12.00
23 Preston Powell	5.00	10.00
24 Duane Putnam	5.00	10.00
25 Ray Renfro	6.00	12.00
26 Jim Shofner	6.00	12.00
27 Jim Ray Smith	5.00	10.00
28 Tom Watkins	5.00	10.00
29 Paul Wiggin	5.00	10.00
30 John Wooten	5.00	10.00

1963 Browns Team Issue

These large photos measure approximately 7 1/2" by 9 1/2" and feature a black-and-white player photo on blankbacked glossy paper stock. Each includes the player's name, position (initials) and team name in the bottom border. They are very similar in design to the 1964-66 set, but can be differentiated by the 1/4" space between the player's name, position, and team name. The photos are unnumbered and checklisted below in alphabetical order.

COMPLETE SET (28)	150.00	250.00
1 Johnny Brewer	5.00	10.00
2 Monte Clark	5.00	10.00
3 Blanton Collier CO	5.00	10.00
4 Gary Collins	6.00	12.00
5 Vince Costello	5.00	10.00
6 Bob Crespino	5.00	10.00
7 Ross Fichtner	5.00	10.00
8 Galen Fiss	5.00	10.00
9 Bob Gain	5.00	10.00
10 Bill Glass	5.00	10.00
11 Ernie Green	6.00	12.00
12 Lou Groza	10.00	20.00
13 Gene Hickerson	7.50	15.00
14 Jim Houston	5.00	10.00
15A Tom Hutchinson	5.00	10.00
15B Tom Hutchinson	5.00	10.00
16 Rich Kreitling	5.00	10.00
17 Mike Lucci	6.00	12.00
18 John Morrow	5.00	10.00
19 Jim Ninowski	6.00	12.00
20 Frank Parker	5.00	10.00
21 Bernie Parrish	5.00	10.00
22 Ray Renfro	6.00	12.00
23 Dick Schafrath	5.00	10.00
24 Jim Shofner	6.00	12.00
25 Ken Webb	5.00	10.00
26 Paul Wiggin	5.00	10.00
27 John Wooten	5.00	10.00

1964-66 Browns Team Issue Large

These large photos measure approximately 7 3/8" by 9 3/8" and feature a black-and-white player photo on blankbacked glossy paper stock. Each includes the player's name, position (initials) and team name in the bottom border. They are very similar in design to the 1963 set, but can be differentiated by the 1" space between the player's name, position, and team name. The Blanton Collier and John Wooten photos are the only exception to this design. Some players were issued over several years with no differences in the photos or only very slight differences in the photo cropping or text as noted below. Each photo is unnumbered and checklisted below in alphabetical order.

COMPLETE SET (42)	250.00	400.00
1 Walter Beach	5.00	10.00
2 Larry Benz	5.00	10.00
3 John Brewer	5.00	10.00
4 John Brown T	5.00	10.00
5 Jim Brown	35.00	60.00
6 Monte Clark	5.00	10.00
7 Blanton Collier CO	5.00	10.00
8 Gary Collins	6.00	12.00
9 Gary Collins	6.00	12.00
10 Vince Costello	5.00	10.00
11 Vince Costello	5.00	10.00
12 Galen Fiss	5.00	10.00
13 Galen Fiss	5.00	10.00
14 Bill Glass DE	5.00	10.00
15 Bill Glass DE	5.00	10.00
16 Ernie Green	5.00	10.00
17 Lou Groza	12.00	20.00
18 Gene Hickerson	7.50	15.00
19 Gene Hickerson	7.50	15.00
20 Jim Houston LB	5.00	10.00
21 Jim Houston LB	5.00	10.00
22 Jim Kanicki	5.00	10.00
23 Jim Kanicki	5.00	10.00
24 Leroy Kelly	12.00	20.00
25 Dick Modzelewski	5.00	10.00
26 Milt Morin	5.00	10.00
27 John Morrow	5.00	10.00
28 John Morrow	5.00	10.00
29 Jim Ninowski	6.00	12.00
30 Frank Parker	5.00	10.00
31 Bernie Parrish	5.00	10.00
32 Walter Roberts	5.00	10.00
33 Frank Ryan	6.00	12.00
34 Frank Ryan	6.00	12.00
35 Dick Schafrath	5.00	10.00
36 Dick Schafrath	5.00	10.00
37 Paul Warfield	15.00	25.00
38 Paul Warfield	15.00	25.00
39 Paul Wiggin	5.00	10.00
40 Paul Wiggin	5.00	10.00
41 John Wooten	5.00	10.00
42 John Wooten	5.00	10.00

1964-66 Browns Team Issue Small

1 Vince Costello	5.00	10.00
2 Ross Fichtner	5.00	10.00
3 Ernie Green	5.00	10.00
4 Gene Hickerson	7.50	15.00
5 Jim Kanicki	5.00	10.00
6 Rich Kreitling	5.00	10.00
7 Dick Scharafth	5.00	10.00

1965 Browns Volpe Tumblers

These Browns artist's renderings were part of a plastic cup tumbler product produced in 1965, which celebrated the 1964 Browns World Championship. These cups were promoted by Fisher's, Fazio's and Costa's Supermarkets in Cleveland The noted sports artist Volpe created the artwork which includes an action scene and a player portrait. The "cards" are unnumbered, each measures approximately 5" by 8 1/2" and is curved in the shape required to fit inside a plastic cup.

COMPLETE SET (12)	350.00	600.00
1 Jim Brown	75.00	125.00
2 Blanton Collier CO	20.00	35.00
3 Gary Collins	25.00	40.00
4 Vince Costello	20.00	35.00
5 Bill Glass	20.00	35.00
6 Lou Groza	40.00	75.00
7 Jim Houston	25.00	40.00
8 Jim Kanicki	20.00	35.00
9 Dick Modzelewski	25.00	40.00
10 Frank Ryan	25.00	40.00
11 Dick Schafrath	25.00	40.00
12 Paul Warfield	40.00	75.00

1966 Browns Team Sheets

Each of these team issued sheets features four black and white player photos and measures roughly 8" x10". The player's name, position and team name appear below each photo and the cardbacks are blank. Any additions to list below are appreciated.

COMPLETE SET (8)	25.00	50.00
1 E.Barnes	2.50	5.00
B.Matheson		
J.Gregory		
L.Conjar		
2 J.Brewer	2.50	5.00
J.Houston		
J.Kanicki		
P.Wiggin		
3 G.Collins	3.00	6.00
F.Ryan		
F.Hoaglin		
J.Wooten		
4 B.Davis	2.50	5.00
R.Smith		
D.Schafrath		
M.Morin		
5 R.Fichtner	6.00	12.00
M.Howell		
M.Clark		
P.Warfield		
6 G.Hickerson	5.00	10.00
B.Collier		
E.Green		
L.Kelly		
7 W.Johnson	6.00	12.00
B.Glass		
E.Kellerman		
L.Groza		
8 G.Lane	2.50	5.00
D.Lindsey		
V.Costello		
F.Parker		

1968 Browns Team Issue 7x8

The Cleveland Browns issued and distributed this set of player photos around 1968. Each measures approximately 6 7/8" by 8 1/2" and features a black and white photo on the front and a blank back. The player's name, position (spelled out), and team name appear in the bottom border below the photo. There is also a facsimile autograph of the featured player printed on each photo. Any additions to this list are appreciated.

COMPLETE SET (7)	50.00	100.00
1 Gary Collins	6.00	12.00
2 Ernie Green	5.00	10.00
3 Leroy Kelly	10.00	20.00
4 Bill Nelsen	6.00	12.00
5 Frank Ryan	6.00	12.00
6 Dick Schafrath	6.00	12.00
7 Paul Warfield	12.50	25.00

1968 Browns Team Issue 8x10

The Cleveland Browns issued and distributed this set of player photos. Each measures approximately 8" by 10" and features a black and white photo. The player's name and position appear in the bottom border below the photo. Any additions to this list are appreciated.

COMPLETE SET (12)	75.00	135.00
1 Don Cockroft	5.00	10.00
2 Gary Collins	6.00	12.00
3 Ernie Green	5.00	10.00
4 Jack Gregory	5.00	10.00
5 Gene Hickerson	7.50	15.00
6 Ernie Kellerman	5.00	10.00
7 Leroy Kelly	10.00	20.00
8 Milt Morin	5.00	10.00
9 Frank Ryan	6.00	12.00
10 Marvin Upshaw	5.00	10.00
11 Paul Warfield	12.50	25.00
12 Coaching Staff	6.00	12.00

1968 Browns Team Sheets

These 8" by 10" sheets were issued primarily to the media for use as player images for print. Each features 7 or 8-players and coaches with the player's name beneath his picture. The sheets are blankbacked and unnumbered. Any additions to this list are appreciated.

1 Collier	6.00	15.00
Houston		
Keller.		
Hick.		
Kelly		
Warfield		
Schaf		
2 Howell	5.00	12.00
Kanicki		
Greg.		
Collins		
Lindsey		
Math.		
Mitch		
N		

1969 Browns Team Issue

The Cleveland Browns issued and distributed this set of player photos in the late 1960s. They closely resemble other photos issued by the team throughout the decade. Each measures approximately 7 1/2" by 9 1/2" and features a black and white photo. The player's name, position (spelled out completely), and team name appear in the bottom border below the photo with roughly a 1/2" to 1" white space between the words.

COMPLETE SET (27)	150.00	225.00
1 Bill Andrews	5.00	10.00
2 Erich Barnes	5.00	10.00
3 Monte Clark	5.00	10.00
4 Don Cockroft	5.00	10.00
5 Gary Collins	6.00	12.00
6 Ben Davis	5.00	10.00
7 John DeMarie	5.00	10.00
8 Jack Gregory	5.00	10.00
9 Gene Hickerson	7.50	15.00
10 Fred Hoaglin	5.00	10.00
11 Jim Houston	5.00	10.00
12 Mike Howell	5.00	10.00
13 Ron Johnson	6.00	12.00
14 Jim Kanicki	5.00	10.00
15 Walter Johnson	5.00	10.00
16 Ernie Kellerman	5.00	10.00
17 Leroy Kelly	12.00	20.00
18 Dale Lindsey	5.00	10.00
19 Bob Matheson	5.00	10.00
20 Reece Morrison	5.00	10.00
21 Milt Morin	5.00	10.00
22 Bill Nelsen	6.00	12.00
23 Dick Schafrath	5.00	10.00
24 Ron Snidow	5.00	10.00
25 Walt Sumner	5.00	10.00
26 Marvin Upshaw	5.00	10.00
27 Paul Warfield	12.50	25.00

1971 Browns Boy Scouts

These standard sized cards were issued for the Boy Scouts as rewards for the 1971 "Roundup" membership drive in the Cleveland area. Each was printed on thin stock and features a black and white photo of a Browns player on the front and Boy Scouts membership information on the backs. The cards are often found with the player's autograph on the back as well as the member's hand written name.

1 Jim Houston	20.00	50.00
2 Leroy Kelly	40.00	75.00
3 Bill Nelsen	35.00	60.00
4 Bo Scott	20.00	50.00

1978 Browns Wendy's

This set of oversized (roughly 5" by 7") black and white photos was sponsored by Wendy's. Each includes a Browns player photo with the player's name below the photo and to the left and the Wendy's logo to the right. The backs are blank and unnumbered. Any additions to the list below are appreciated.

COMPLETE SET (19)	100.00	200.00
1 Dick Ambrose	6.00	12.00
2 Ron Bolton	6.00	12.00
3 Larry Colliins	6.00	12.00
4 Oliver Davis	6.00	12.00
5 Johnny Evans	6.00	12.00
6 Ricky Feacher	6.00	12.00
7 Dave Graf	6.00	12.00
8 Charlie Hall	6.00	12.00
9 Calvin Hill	7.50	15.00
10 Gerald Irons	6.00	12.00
11 Robert L. Jackson	6.00	12.00
12 Ricky Jones	6.00	12.00
13 Clay Mathews	10.00	20.00
14 Cleo Miller	6.00	12.00
15 Mark Miller	6.00	12.00
16 Sam Rutigliano CO	6.00	12.00
17 Henry Sheppard	6.00	12.00
18 Mickey Sims	6.00	12.00
19 Gerry Sullivan	6.00	12.00

1979 Browns Team Sheets

The 1979 Browns Team Issue Sheets were issued to fans and total six known sheets. Each measures roughly 8" by 10" and includes seven or eight small black and white player photos.

COMPLETE SET (6)	12.50	25.00
1 Clinton Burrell	1.50	3.00
Clarence Scott		
Willis Adams		
Law		
2 Oliver Davis	2.50	5.00
Ricky Feacher		
Charlie Hall		
Don Coc		
3 Jack Gregory	1.50	3.00
Dave Graf		
Cleo Miller		
Ricky Jones#		
4 Art Modell	2.50	5.00
Sam Rutigliano		
Jerry Sherk		
Greg Prui		
5 Henry Sheppard	3.00	6.00
Mike Pruitt		
Gerry Sullivan		
Curti		
6 Mickey Sims	2.50	5.00
Mark Miller		
Clay Matthews		
Robert E.		

1978 Buccaneers Team Issue

These 8" by 10" black and white Photos were issued by the Buccaneers for player signing sessions and to fill fan requests. Each includes the player's name, his position initials and the team name below the player photo in all capital letters. It is believed that there were more photos issued in the series, thus any additional submissions would be welcomed.

1 Ricky Bell	3.00	6.00
2 Dave Pear	2.50	5.00
3 Lee Roy Selmon	6.00	12.00

1978 Buccaneers Team Sheets

This set consists of 8" by 10" glossy photo sheets that display eight black-and-white player/coach photos. Each individual photo on the sheet measures approximately 2 1/8" by 3 1/4". Two Buccaneers logos appear in the upper left and right corners of the sheet. The backs are blank. The sheets are unnumbered and checklisted below alphabetically according to the player featured in the upper left corner.

COMPLETE SET (4)	20.00	40.00
1 Sheet 1	7.50	15.00
2 Sheet 2	4.00	8.00
3 Sheet 3	4.00	8.00
4 Sheet 4	6.00	12.00

1979 Buccaneers Team Issue

These 8 1/2" by 11" black and white blank backed photos were given out for publicity purposes by the Buccaneers. Each includes the player's name, his position (spelled out) and the team name below the player photo. It is believed that there were more photos issued in the series, thus any additional submissions would be welcomed.

1 Jimmy DuBose	2.50	5.00
2 Doug Williams	4.00	8.00

1980 Buccaneers Police

This set is complete at 56 cards measuring approximately 2 5/8" by 4 1/8". Since there are no numbers on the cards, the set has been listed in alphabetical order by player. In addition to player cards, an assortment of coaches, mascots, and Swash-Buc-Lers (cheerleaders) are included. The set was sponsored by the Greater Tampa Chamber of Commerce Law Enforcement Council, the local law enforcement agencies, and Coca-Cola. Tips from the Buccaneers are written on the backs. The fronts contain the Tampa Bay helmet logo. Cards are also available with a tougher Paradyne (Corporation) cardback sponsorship.

COMPLETE SET (56)	75.00	150.00
*PARADYNE BACKS: 1.5X TO 2.5X		
1 Ricky Bell	3.00	8.00
2 Rick Berns	1.50	4.00
3 Tom Blanchard	1.25	3.00
4 Scot Brantley	1.25	3.00
5 Aaron Brown LB	1.25	3.00
6 Cedric Brown	1.25	3.00
7 Mark Cotney	1.25	3.00
8 Randy Crowder	1.25	3.00
9 Gary Davis	1.25	3.00
10 Johnny Davis	1.50	4.00
11 Tony Davis	1.25	3.00
12 Jerry Eckwood	2.00	5.00
13 Chuck Fusina	1.50	4.00
14 Jimmie Giles	2.00	5.00
15 Isaac Hagins	1.25	3.00
16 Charley Hannah	1.25	3.00
17 Andy Hawkins	1.25	3.00
18 Kevin House	2.00	5.00
19 Cecil Johnson	1.25	3.00
20 Gordon Jones	1.50	4.00
21 Curtis Jordan	1.25	3.00
22 Bill Kollar	1.25	3.00
23 Jim Leonard	1.25	3.00
24 David Lewis	1.50	4.00
25 Reggie Lewis	1.25	3.00
26 David Logan	1.50	4.00
27 Larry Mucker	1.25	3.00
28 Jim O'Bradovich	1.50	4.00
29 Mike Rae	1.25	3.00
30 Dave Reavis	1.25	3.00
31 Danny Reece	1.25	3.00
32 Greg Roberts	1.25	3.00
33 Gene Sanders	1.25	3.00
34 Dewey Selmon	2.00	5.00
35 Lee Roy Selmon	8.00	20.00
36 Ray Snell	1.25	3.00
37 Dave Stalls	1.25	3.00
38 Norris Thomas	1.25	3.00
39 Mike Washington	1.25	3.00
40 Doug Williams	4.00	10.00
41 Steve Wilson	1.25	3.00
42 Richard Wood	1.50	4.00
43 George Yarno	1.25	3.00
44 Garo Yepremian	2.00	5.00
45 Logo Card	1.25	3.00
46 Team Photo	2.00	5.00
47 Hugh Culverhouse OWN	1.50	4.00
48 John McKay CO	1.50	4.00
49 Mascot Capt. Crush	1.25	3.00
50 Cheerleaders:	1.50	4.00
51 Swash-Buc-Lers	1.50	4.00
52 Swash-Buc-Lers	1.50	4.00
53 Swash-Buc-Lers	1.50	4.00
54 Swash-Buc-Lers	1.50	4.00
55 Swash-Buc-Lers (Pass	1.50	4.00
56 Swash-Buc-Lers	1.50	4.00

1980 Buccaneers Team Issue

These paper thin 5" by 7" black and white blank backed photos were given out for publicity purposes. Each includes the player's name (all caps), a facsimile signature, and the team name (all caps) below the player photo. It is believed that there were more photos issued in the series, thus any additional submissions would be welcomed.

COMPLETE SET (5)	12.50	25.00
1 Jerry Eckwood	2.00	5.00
2 Lee Roy Selmon	3.00	8.00
3 1980 Team Photo	2.00	5.00
4 Doug Williams	3.00	8.00
5 Garo Yepremian	2.00	5.00

1976 Buckmans Discs

The 1976 Buckmans football disc set of 20 is unnumbered and features star players from the National Football League. The circular cards measure approximately 3 3/8" in diameter. The players' pictures are in black and white with a colored arc serving as the disc border. Four stars complete the border at the top. The backs of the most common version contain the address of the Buckmans Ice Cream outlet in Rochester, New York. A much scarcer blankbacked version of the set was also prodcued and though to have been issued in packages of Safelon lunch bags. Another version that reads "Customized Sports Discs" on the back exists and is thought to have been issued as promotional pieces or samples. The MSA marking, signifying Michael Schechter Associates, is featured on the backs as well. Since the set is unnumbered, the cards are listed below alphabetically by player's name.

COMPLETE SET (20) 40.00 80.00
*BLANKBACK: 4X TO 10X
*CUSTOMIZED: 8X TO 20X
1 Otis Armstrong 1.00 2.50
2 Steve Bartkowski 1.00 2.50
3 Terry Bradshaw 15.00 25.00
4 Doug Buffone .75 2.00
5 Wally Chambers .75 2.00
6 Chuck Foreman 1.00 2.50
7 Roman Gabriel 1.25 3.00
8 Mel Gray 1.00 2.50
9 Franco Harris 5.00 10.00
10 James Harris 1.00 2.50
11 Jim Hart 1.00 2.50
12 Gary Huff .75 2.00
13 Billy Kilmer 1.00 2.50
14 Terry Metcalf 1.00 2.50
15 Jim Otis .75 2.00
16 Jim Plunkett 1.25 3.00
17 Greg Pruitt 1.00 2.50
18 Roger Staubach 15.00 25.00
19 Jan Stenerud 1.00 2.50
20 Roger Wehrli 1.00 2.50

1972 Burger King Ice Milk Cups

These white cups with brown detail were issued in 1972 by Burger King to promote their Ice Milk dessert. These cups are approximately 4" high and feature a detailed portrait on the front of the cup with a biography on the back and a Burger King logo at the bottom. The cups are listed below in alphabetical order. These thin cups are condition sensitive since they are highly susceptible to cracking.

1 Dan Abramowicz 6.00 12.00
2 Julius Adams 6.00 12.00
3 Bob Anderson 6.00 12.00
4 Dick Anderson 6.00 12.00
5 George Andrie 6.00 12.00
6 Jim Bakken 6.00 12.00
7 Pete Banaszak 6.00 12.00
8 Pete Beathard 6.00 12.00
9 Bill Bergey 7.50 15.00
10 Forrest Blue 6.00 12.00
11 Terry Bradshaw 20.00 40.00
12 John Brockington 6.00 12.00
13 Buck Buchanan 7.50 15.00
14 Norm Bulaich 6.00 12.00
15 Nick Buoniconti 7.50 15.00
16 Virgil Carter 6.00 12.00
17 Richard Caster 6.00 12.00
18 Jack Concannon 6.00 12.00
19 Dave Costa 6.00 12.00
20 Larry Csonka 10.00 20.00
21 Mike Curtis 6.00 12.00
22 Len Dawson 12.50 25.00
23 Bobby Douglass 6.00 12.00
24 Bobby Duhon 6.00 12.00
25 Carl Eller 7.50 15.00
26 Mel Farr 6.00 12.00
27 Manny Fernandez 6.00 12.00
28 John Fuqua 7.50 15.00
29 Walt Garrison 6.00 12.00
30 John Gilliam 6.00 12.00
31 Dick Gordon 6.00 12.00
32 Joe Greene 10.00 20.00
33 Bob Griese 12.50 25.00
34 John Hadl 7.50 15.00
35 Don Hansen 6.00 12.00
36 Cliff Harris 7.50 15.00
37 Dave Herman 6.00 12.00
38 J.D. Hill 6.00 12.00
39 Jim Houston 6.00 12.00
40 Delles Howell 6.00 12.00
41 Rich Jackson 6.00 12.00
42 Ron Johnson 6.00 12.00
43 Walter Johnson 6.00 12.00
44 Clint Jones 6.00 12.00
45 Deacon Jones 10.00 20.00
46 Lee Roy Jordan 10.00 20.00
47 Leroy Kelly 10.00 20.00
48 Leroy Keyes 6.00 12.00
49 Jim Kiick 7.50 15.00
50 George Kunz 6.00 12.00
51 Jake Kupp 6.00 12.00
52 Greg Landry 7.50 15.00
53 Willie Lanier 7.50 15.00
54 Pete Liske 6.00 12.00
55 Floyd Little 7.50 15.00
56 Mike Lucci 6.00 12.00
57 Jim Lynch 6.00 12.00
58 Milt Morin 6.00 12.00
59 Earl Morrall 7.50 15.00
60 Mercury Morris 7.50 15.00
61 Haven Moses 6.00 12.00
62 John Niland 6.00 12.00
63 Frank Nunley 6.00 12.00
64 Merlin Olsen 10.00 20.00
65 Steve Owens 7.50 15.00
66 Lemar Parrish 6.00 12.00
67 Dan Pastorini 6.00 12.00
68 Jim Plunkett 10.00 20.00
69 Ed Podolak 6.00 12.00
70 Ron Pritchard 6.00 12.00
71 Isiah Robertson 6.00 12.00
72 Dave Robinson 6.00 12.00
73 Tim Rossovich 6.00 12.00
74 Andy Russell 7.50 15.00
75 Charlie Sanders 7.50 15.00
76 Jake Scott 7.50 15.00
77 George Seals 6.00 12.00
78 Dennis Shaw 6.00 12.00
79 Jackie Smith 7.50 15.00
80 Jerry Smith 6.00 12.00
81 Royce Smith 6.00 12.00
82 Jack Snow 6.00 12.00
83 Walt Sweeney 6.00 12.00
84 Steve Tannen 6.00 12.00
85 Fran Tarkenton 12.50 25.00
86 Altie Taylor 6.00 12.00
87 Otis Taylor 7.50 15.00
88 Billy Truax 6.00 12.00
89 Bob Tucker 6.00 12.00
90 Randy Vataha 6.00 12.00
91 Paul Warfield 10.00 20.00
92 Gene Washington 7.50 15.00
93 George Webster 6.00 12.00
94 Dave Wilcox 7.50 15.00
95 Ken Willard 6.00 12.00
96 Larry Wilson 10.00 20.00
97 Garo Yepremian 6.00 12.00

1932 Briggs Chocolate

This set was issued by C.A. Briggs Chocolate company in 1932. The cards feature 31-different sports with each card including an artist's rendering of a sporting event. Although players are not named, it is thought that most were modeled after famous athletes of the time. The cardbacks include a written portion about the sport and an offer from Briggs for free baseball equipment for building a compete set of cards.

11 Football 800.00 1,200.00

1976 Canada Dry Cans

Canada Dry released soda cans in 1976 featuring the logos of NFL teams along with a brief history of the featured team. The pricing below is for opened cans.

COMPLETE SET (28) 100.00 200.00
1 Atlanta Falcons 4.00 8.00
2 Baltimore Colts 4.00 8.00
3 Buffalo Bills 5.00 10.00
4 Chicago Bears 4.00 8.00
5 Cincinnati Bengals 4.00 8.00
6 Cleveland Browns 5.00 10.00
7 Dallas Cowboys 7.50 15.00
8 Denver Broncos 4.00 8.00
9 Detroit Lions 4.00 8.00
10 Green Bay Packers 7.50 15.00
11 Houston Oilers 4.00 8.00
12 Kansas City Chiefs 4.00 8.00
13 Los Angeles Rams 4.00 8.00
14 Miami Dolphins 7.50 15.00
15 Minnesota Vikings 5.00 10.00
16 New England Patriots 4.00 8.00
17 New Orleans Saints 4.00 8.00
18 New York Giants 5.00 10.00
19 New York Jets 5.00 10.00
20 Oakland Raiders 7.50 15.00
21 Philadelphia Eagles 4.00 8.00
22 Pittsburgh Steelers 5.00 10.00
23 St. Louis Cardinals 4.00 8.00
24 San Diego Chargers 4.00 8.00
25 San Francisco 49ers 5.00 10.00
26 Seattle Seahawks 4.00 8.00
27 Tampa Bay Buccaneers 4.00 8.00
28 Washington Redskins 7.50 15.00

1964 Caprolan Nylon All-Star Buttons

These buttons were issued in the mid-1960s and feature a black and white image of an AFL or NFL player. The fronts also feature the words " A Caprolan Nylon All-Star Performer" along with the player's name printed in blue ink above the photo. Any additions to this list are appreciated.

COMPLETE SET (5) 100.00 200.00
1 Maxie Baughan 25.00 40.00
2 Gino Cappelletti 25.00 40.00
3 Matt Hazeltine UER 25.00 40.00
4 Merlin Olsen 30.00 50.00
5 Andy Robustelli 30.00 50.00

1967 Caprolan Nylon Photos

These 8" x 10" glossy black-and-white photos were issued to promote the Caprolan company. Each includes the player's name, team name, and "A Caprolan All-Star" below the image.

1 Gary Ballman 12.50 25.00
2 Gino Cappelletti 12.50 25.00
3 Mike Ditka 20.00 40.00
4 Matt Hazeltine 12.50 25.00
5 Pete Retzlaff 12.50 25.00
6 Andy Robustelli 15.00 30.00
7 Frank Ryan 12.50 25.00

1953 Cardinals Team Issue

Photos in this set of the Chicago Cardinals measure approximately 8" by 10" and feature a black-and-white player image on the front printed on high gloss stock. The player's name and position can sometimes be found written on the backs but no player identification is otherwise given. The photos are unnumbered and checklisted below in alphabetical order.

COMPLETE SET (31) 350.00 600.00
1 Cliff Anderson 10.00 20.00
2 Roy Barni 10.00 20.00
3 Tom Bienemann 10.00 20.00
4 Al Campana 10.00 20.00
5 Nick Chickillo 10.00 20.00
6 Billy Cross 10.00 20.00
7 Tony Curcillo 10.00 20.00
8 Jerry Groom 10.00 20.00
9 Ed Husmann 10.00 20.00
10 Don Joyce 10.00 20.00
11 Ed Listopad 10.00 20.00
12 Ollie Matson 15.00 30.00
13 Gern Nagler 10.00 20.00
14 Johnny Olszewski 10.00 20.00
15 John Panelli 10.00 20.00
16 Volney Peters 10.00 20.00
17 Gordon Polofsky 10.00 20.00
18 Jim Psaltis 10.00 20.00
19 Ray Ramsey 10.00 20.00
20 Jack Simmons 10.00 20.00
21 Emil Sitko 10.00 20.00
22 Don Stonesifer 10.00 20.00
23 Joe Stydahar CO 12.50 25.00
24 Leo Sugar 10.00 20.00
25 Dave Suminski 10.00 20.00
26 Pat Summerall 15.00 30.00
27 Bill Svoboda 10.00 20.00
28 Charley Trippi 12.50 25.00
29 Fred Wallner 10.00 20.00
30 Jerry Watford 10.00 20.00
31 Team Photo 12.50 25.00

1960 Cardinals Mayrose Franks

The Mayrose Franks set of 11 cards features players on the St. Louis (Football) Cardinals and first hit store shelves in Septmber 1960. The cards are plastic coated (they were intended as inserts in hot dog and bacon packages) with slightly rounded corners and are numbered. The cards measure approximately 2 1/2" by 3 1/2". The fronts, with a black and white photograph of the player and a red background, contain the card number, player statistics and the Cardinal's logo. The backs contain a description of the Big Mayrose Football Contest.

COMPLETE SET (11) 80.00 125.00
1 Don Gillis 6.00 12.00
2 Frank Fuller 6.00 12.00
3 George Izo 6.00 12.00
4 Woodley Lewis 6.00 12.00
5 King Hill 6.00 12.00
6 John David Crow 7.50 15.00
7 Bill Stacy 6.00 12.00
8 Ted Bates 6.00 12.00
9 Mike McGee 6.00 12.00
10 Bobby Joe Conrad 6.00 12.00
11 Ken Panfil 6.00 12.00

1961 Cardinals Jay Publishing

This 12-card set features (approximately) 5" by 7" black-and-white player photos. The pictures show players in traditional poses with the quarterback preparing to throw, the runner heading downfield, and the defensive player ready for the tackle. These cards were packaged 12 to a packet and originally sold for 25 cents. The backs are blank. The cards are unnumbered and checklisted below in alphabetical order.

COMPLETE SET (12) 40.00 80.00
1 Joe Childress 4.00 8.00
2 Sam Etcheverry 4.00 8.00
3 Ed Henke 4.00 8.00
4 Jimmy Hill 4.00 8.00
5 Bill Koman 4.00 8.00
6 Roland McDole 4.00 8.00
7 Mike McGee 4.00 8.00
8 Dale Meinert 4.00 8.00
9 Jerry Norton 4.00 8.00
10 Sonny Randle 4.00 8.00
11 Joe Robb 4.00 8.00
12 Billy Stacy 4.00 8.00

1963-64 Cardinals Team Issue

The Cardinals likely issued these photos over a period of years during the mid-1960s. Each measures approximately 5" by 7" and features a black and white player photo along with player information below the photo. Some photos contain only the player's name, positon and team name in all caps, while others also include the player's height and weight with the team name in upper and lower case letters. They are unnumbered and blankbacked and listed below alphabetically.

COMPLETE SET (15) 100.00 175.00
1 Taz Anderson 6.00 12.00
2 Garland Boyette 6.00 12.00
3 Don Brumm 6.00 12.00
4A Jim Burson 6.00 12.00
4B Jim Burson 6.00 12.00
5 Irv Goode 6.00 12.00
6 John Houser 6.00 12.00
7 Bill Koman 6.00 12.00
8 Ernie McMillan 6.00 12.00
9A Luke Owens 6.00 12.00
9B Luke Owens 6.00 12.00
10 Bob Paremore 6.00 12.00
11A Bob Reynolds 6.00 12.00
11B Bob Reynolds 6.00 12.00
12 Joe Robb 6.00 12.00
13 Sam Silas 6.00 12.00
14 Jerry Stovall 6.00 12.00
15A Bill Triplett 6.00 12.00
15B Bill Triplett 6.00 12.00

1965 Cardinals Big Red Biographies

This set was featured during the 1965 football season as the side panels of half-gallon milk cartons from Adams Dairy in St. Louis. When cut, the cards measure approximately 3 1/16" by 5 9/16". The printing on the cards is in purple and orange. All cards feature members of the St. Louis Cardinals. The catalog designation for this set is F112. Two different Cardinals logos in the upper right hand corner we used on the cards, but no variations of the same card are known. We've identified known logo versions below with: 1) cards featuring the white jersey Cardinal beneath the Arch, and 2) cards featuring the red jersey Cardinal and no Arch. Complete milk cartons would be valued at double the prices listed below.

COMPLETE SET (27) 3,000.00 5,000.00
1 Monk Bailey 150.00 250.00
2 Jim Bakken 1 175.00 300.00
3 Don Brumm 2 150.00 250.00
4 Jim Burson 150.00 250.00
5 Joe Childress 2 150.00 250.00
6 Willis Crenshaw 1 150.00 250.00
7 Bob DeMarco 1 150.00 250.00
8 Pat Fischer 1 150.00 250.00
9 Billy Gambrell 150.00 250.00
10 Irv Goode 1 150.00 250.00
11 Ken Gray 1 150.00 250.00
12 Charley Johnson 2 175.00 300.00
13 Bill Koman 1 150.00 250.00
14 Dave Meggysey 1 150.00 250.00
15 Dale Meinert 2 150.00 250.00
16 Mike Melinkovich 1 150.00 250.00
17 Sonny Randle 150.00 250.00
18 Bob Reynolds 1 150.00 250.00
19 Joe Robb 150.00 250.00
20 Marion Rushing 150.00 250.00
21 Sam Silas 150.00 250.00
22 Carl Silvestri 1 150.00 250.00
23 Dave Simmons 1 150.00 250.00
24 Jackie Smith 1 200.00 350.00
25 Bill(Thunder) Thornton 1 150.00 250.00
26 Bill Triplett 2 150.00 250.00
27 Herschel Turner 1 150.00 250.00

1965 Cardinals McCarthy Postcards

This two-card set features posed player photos of the Cardinals team printed on postcard-size cards. The cards are unnumbered and checklisted below in alphabetical order.

1 Dick Lane 2.50 5.00
2 Ollie Matson 2.50 5.00

1965 Cardinals Team Issue

This 10-card set of the St. Louis Cardinals measures approximately 7 3/8" by 9 3/8" and features black-and-white player photos in a white border. The player's name, position and team are printed in the wide bottom margin. The backs are blank. The cards are unnumbered and checklisted below in alphabetical order.

COMPLETE SET (10) 60.00 120.00
1 Don Brumm 6.00 12.00
2 Bobby Joe Conrad 6.00 12.00

3 Bob DeMarco 6.00 12.00
4 Charley Johnson 7.50 15.00
5 Ernie McMillan 6.00 12.00
6 Dale Meinert 6.00 12.00
7 Luke Owens 6.00 12.00
8 Sonny Randle 6.00 12.00
9 Joe Robb 6.00 12.00
10 Jerry Stovall 6.00 12.00

1967 Cardinals Team Issue

These photos are very similar in design to several other Cardinals Team Issue releases. Like the other sets, this set was likely released over a period of years. Each photo measures approximately 5" by 7" and features a black and white player photo along with player information below the photo. The player's name and positon are in all caps with the team name in upper and lower case letters. They are unnumbered and blankbacked and listed below alphabetically.

COMPLETE SET (16) 90.00 150.00
1 Don Brumm 6.00 12.00
2 Charlie Bryant 6.00 12.00
3 Jim Burson 6.00 12.00
4 Irv Goode 6.00 12.00
5 Mal Hammack 6.00 12.00
6 Bill Koman 6.00 12.00
7 Chuck Logan 6.00 12.00
8 Dave Long 6.00 12.00
9 John McDowell 6.00 12.00
10 Ernie McMillan 6.00 12.00
11 Dave O'Brien OL 6.00 12.00
12 Bob Reynolds 6.00 12.00
13 Joe Robb 6.00 12.00
14 Roy Shivers 6.00 12.00
15 Chuck Walker 6.00 12.00
16 Bobby Williams DB 6.00 12.00

1969 Cardinals Team Issue

These photos are very similar in design to several other Cardinals Team Issue releases. Like the other sets, this set was likely released over a period of years. Each photo measures approximately 5" by 7" and features a black and white player photo along with player information below the photo. The player's name and positon are in all caps with the team name in upper and lower case letters. The type size and style differs slightly from one photo to the next, but all include a slightly wider or round letter "C" in the word Cardinals than the 1971 set. They are unnumbered and blankbacked and listed below alphabetically.

COMPLETE SET (31) 150.00 250.00
1 Robert Atkins 5.00 10.00
2 Jim Bakken 6.00 12.00
3 Bob Brown 5.00 10.00
4 Terry Brown 5.00 10.00
5 Willis Crenshaw 5.00 10.00
6 Jerry Daanen 5.00 10.00
7 Irv Goode 5.00 10.00
8 Chip Healy 5.00 10.00
9 Fred Heron 5.00 10.00
10 King Hill 5.00 10.00
11 Fred Hyatt 5.00 10.00
12 Rolf Krueger 5.00 10.00
13 MacArthur Lane 6.00 12.00
14 Ernie McMillan 5.00 10.00
15 Wayne Mulligan 5.00 10.00
16 Dave Olerich 5.00 10.00
17 Bob Reynolds 5.00 10.00
18 Jamie Rivers 5.00 10.00
19 Johnny Roland 5.00 10.00
20 Rocky Rosema 5.00 10.00
21 Bob Rowe 5.00 10.00
22 Lonnie Sanders 5.00 10.00
23 Joe Schmiesing 5.00 10.00
24 Roy Shivers 5.00 10.00
25 Cal Snowden 5.00 10.00
26 Rick Sortun 5.00 10.00
27 Chuck Walker 5.00 10.00
28 Clyde Williams 5.00 10.00
29 Dave Williams 5.00 10.00
30 Charley Winner CO 5.00 10.00
31 Nate Wright 5.00 10.00

1971 Cardinals Team Issue

These photos are very similar in design to many other Cardinals Team Issue set listings. Like the others, these photos were likely released over a period of years. Each photo measures approximately 5" by 7" and features a black and white player photo along with player information below the photo. The player's name and positon are in all caps with the team name in upper and lower case letters. The type size and style differs slightly from one photo to the next, but all include a slightly more narrow letter "C" in the word Cardinals than the 1969 set. They are unnumbered and blankbacked and listed below alphabetically.

COMPLETE SET (22) 100.00 175.00
1 Tom Banks 5.00 10.00
2 Dale Hackbart 5.00 10.00
3 Jim Hargrove 5.00 10.00
4 Fred Heron 5.00 10.00
5 Bob Hollway CO 5.00 10.00
6 Mike McGill 5.00 10.00
7 Dave Meggysey 5.00 10.00
8 Terry Miller LB 5.00 10.00
9 Don Parish 5.00 10.00
10 Charlie Pittman 5.00 10.00
11 Rocky Rosema 5.00 10.00
12 Lonnie Sanders 5.00 10.00
13 Joe Schmiesing 5.00 10.00
14 Mike Siwek 5.00 10.00
15 Larry Stegent 5.00 10.00
16 Norm Thompson 5.00 10.00
17 Tim Van Galder 5.00 10.00
18 Chuck Walker 5.00 10.00
19 Dave Williams 5.00 10.00
20 Larry Willingham 5.00 10.00
21 Nate Wright 5.00 10.00
22 Ron Yankowski 5.00 10.00

1972 Cardinals Team Issue

The Cardinals issued these photos likely over a period of years. Each measures approximately 5" by 7" and features a black and white player photo along with the player's name, positon, height, weight, and team name below the photo. The type size and style used is virtually the same for all of the photos and the team name reads "St. Louis Cardinals." The player's name is printed in upper and lower case letters. They are unnumbered and blankbacked and listed below alphabetically.

COMPLETE SET (37) 125.00 225.00
1 Jeff Allen 4.00 8.00
2 Tom Banks 4.00 8.00
3 Craig Baynham 4.00 8.00
4 Pete Beathard 4.00 8.00
5 Tom Beckman 4.00 8.00
6 Terry Brown 4.00 8.00
7 Gary Cuozzo 5.00 10.00
8 Paul Dickson 4.00 8.00
9 Miller Farr 4.00 8.00
10 Walker Gillette 4.00 8.00
11 John Gilliam 5.00 10.00
12 Dale Hackbart 4.00 8.00
13 Jim Hargrove 4.00 8.00
14 Jim Hart 6.00 12.00
15 Fred Heron 4.00 8.00
16 George Hoey 4.00 8.00
17 Bob Hollway CO 4.00 8.00
18 Chuck Hutchison 4.00 8.00
19 Fred Hyatt 4.00 8.00
20 Martin Imhof 4.00 8.00
21 Jeff Lyman 4.00 8.00
22 Mike McGill 4.00 8.00
23 Ernie McMillan 4.00 8.00
24 Terry Miller LB 4.00 8.00
25 Bobby Moore 10.00 20.00
(Ahmad Rashad)
26 Wayne Mulligan 4.00 8.00
27 Bob Reynolds 4.00 8.00
28 Jamie Rivers 4.00 8.00
29 Johnny Roland 5.00 10.00
30 Bob Rowe 4.00 8.00
31 Roy Shivers 4.00 8.00
32 Tim Van Galder 4.00 8.00
33 Chuck Walker 4.00 8.00
34 Eric Washington 4.00 8.00
35 Clyde Williams 4.00 8.00
36 Larry Willingham 4.00 8.00
37 Ron Yankowski 4.00 8.00

1973 Cardinals Team Issue

The Cardinals issued these photos likely over a period of years as this set looks very similar to the 1972 issue. Each measures approximately 5" by 7" and features a black and white player photo along with the player's name, positon, height, weight, and team name below the photo. The type size and style used is different than the 1972 set and varies slightly from photo to photo. The team name reads "St. Louis Football Cardinals" on all these photos unless noted below. They are unnumbered and blankbacked and listed below alphabetically.

COMPLETE SET (43) 150.00 250.00
1 Donny Anderson 5.00 10.00
2 Tom Banks 4.00 8.00
3 Chuck Beatty 4.00 8.00
4 Tom Beckman 4.00 8.00
5 Willie Belton 4.00 8.00
6 Leon Burns 4.00 8.00
7 Dave Butz 4.00 8.00
8 Steve Conley 4.00 8.00
9 Dwayne Crump 4.00 8.00
10 Ron Davis 4.00 8.00
11 Rod Dowhower CO 4.00 8.00
12 Miller Farr 4.00 8.00
13 Ken Garrett 4.00 8.00
14 Joe Gibbs CO 15.00 30.00
15 Walker Gillette 4.00 8.00
16 Jim Hanifan CO 4.00 8.00
17 Sid Hall CO 4.00 8.00
18 Chuck Hutchison 4.00 8.00
19 Fred Hyatt 4.00 8.00
20 Martin Imhoff 4.00 8.00
21 Gary Keithley 4.00 8.00
22 Don Maynard 6.00 12.00
23 Ernie McMillan 4.00 8.00
25 Terry Miller LB 4.00 8.00
26 Wayne Mulligan 4.00 8.00
27 Jim Otis 5.00 10.00
28 Marv Owens 4.00 8.00
29 Ara Person 4.00 8.00
30 Ahmad Rashad 7.50 15.00
31 John Richardson 4.00 8.00
32 Jamie Rivers 4.00 8.00
33 Johnny Roland 4.00 8.00
34 Don Shy 4.00 8.00
35 Jackie Simpson CO 4.00 8.00
36 Maurice Spencer 4.00 8.00
37 Jeff Staggs 4.00 8.00
38 Norm Thompson 4.00 8.00
39 Jim Tolbert 4.00 8.00
40 Eric Washington 4.00 8.00
41 Bob Wicks 4.00 8.00
42 Ray Willsey CO 4.00 8.00
43 Bob Young 4.00 8.00
24A Terry Metcalf 5.00 10.00
24B Terry Metcalf 5.00 10.00

1974 Cardinals Team Issue

The Cardinals issued these photos likely over a period of years as this set looks very similar to the 1972 and 1973 issues. Each measures approximately 5" by 7" and features a black and white player photo along with the player's name, positon, height, weight, and team name below the photo. The type size and style used is different than the 1972 and 1973 sets with the 1974 printing being slightly larger. The team name reads "St. Louis Football Cardinals" on all these photos with most, but not all, being in all capitals letters. They are unnumbered and blankbacked and listed below alphabetically.

COMPLETE SET (17) 50.00 100.00
1 Tom Banks 4.00 8.00
2 Jim Champion CO 4.00 8.00
3 Gene Hamlin 4.00 8.00
4 Reggie Harrison 4.00 8.00
5 Eddie Moss 4.00 8.00
6 Steve Neils 4.00 8.00
7 Jim Otis 5.00 10.00
8 Ken Reaves 4.00 8.00
9 Hal Roberts 4.00 8.00
10 Hurles Scales 4.00 8.00
11 Wayne Sevier CO 4.00 8.00
12 Dennis Shaw 4.00 8.00
13 Maurice Spencer 4.00 8.00
14 Larry Stallings 4.00 8.00
15 Scott Stringer 4.00 8.00
16 Earl Thomas 4.00 8.00
17 Cal Withrow 4.00 8.00

1976 Cardinals Team Issue

The St. Louis Cardinals issued this series of player photos quite possibly over a number of years. Each photo is very similar in design and is only differentiated by the size and type style of the print. The unnumbered black and white photos measure approximately 5 1/8" by 7" and all, except John Zook, include the player's name, position, height and weight below the photo along with "St. Louis Football Cardinals." The team name printed on the cards varies in size and print type from photo to photo. Although they likely were issued over a period of years, we've included them all as a 1976 release since all players performed for that year's team.

COMPLETE SET (51) 150.00 300.00
1 Mark Arneson 4.00 8.00
2 Jim Bakken 5.00 10.00
3 Rodrigo Barnes 4.00 8.00
4 Al Beauchamp 4.00 8.00
5 Bob Bell 4.00 8.00
6 Tom Brahaney 4.00 8.00
7 Leo Brooks 4.00 8.00
8 J.V. Cain 4.00 8.00
9 Don Coryell CO 5.00 10.00
10 Dwayne Crump 4.00 8.00
11 Charlie Davis 4.00 8.00
12 Mike Dawson 4.00 8.00
13 Dan Dierdorf 6.00 12.00
14 Conrad Dobler 5.00 10.00
15 Bill Donckers 4.00 8.00
16 Clarence Duren 4.00 8.00
17 Roger Finnie 4.00 8.00
18 Carl Gersbach 4.00 8.00
19 Harry Gilmer CO 5.00 10.00
20 Mel Gray 5.00 10.00
21 Tim Gray 4.00 8.00
22 Gary Hammond 4.00 8.00
23 Ike Harris 4.00 8.00
24 Jim Hart 5.00 10.00
25 Steve Jones 4.00 8.00
26 Terry Joyce 4.00 8.00
27 Tim Kearney 4.00 8.00
28 Jerry Latin 4.00 8.00
29 Mike McGraw 4.00 8.00
30 Terry Metcalf 5.00 10.00
31 Wayne Morris 4.00 8.00
32 Steve Neils 4.00 8.00
33 Brad Oates 4.00 8.00
34 Steve Okoniewski 4.00 8.00
35 Walt Patulski 4.00 8.00
36 Ken Reaves 4.00 8.00
37 Mike Sensibaugh 4.00 8.00
38 Jeff Severson 4.00 8.00
39 Jackie Smith 6.00 12.00
40 Larry Stallings 4.00 8.00
41 Norm Thompson 4.00 8.00
42 Pat Tilley 5.00 10.00
43 Jim Tolbert 4.00 8.00
44 Marvin Upshaw 4.00 8.00
45 Roger Wehrli 5.00 10.00
46 Jeff West 4.00 8.00
47 Ray White 4.00 8.00
48 Sam Wyche 5.00 10.00
49 Ron Yankowski 4.00 8.00
50 Bob Young 4.00 8.00
51 John Zook 4.00 8.00

1977-78 Cardinals Team Issue

The St. Louis Cardinals issued this series of player photos quite possibly over a number of years. Each photo is nearly identical in design. The unnumbered black and white photos measure approximately 5 1/8" by 7" and all include the player's name, position, height and weight below the photo along with "ST. LOUIS FOOTBALL CARDINALS" in all capital letters. We've cataloged them all as a 1977-78 release since all of the players performed during those years and the type style matches on each photo.

COMPLETE SET (28) 100.00 200.00
1 Kurt Allerman 4.00 8.00
2 Dan Audick 4.00 8.00
3 John Barefield 4.00 8.00
4 Tim Black 4.00 8.00
5 Dan Brooks CO 4.00 8.00
6 Duane Carrell 4.00 8.00
7 Al Chandler 4.00 8.00
8 Jim Childs 4.00 8.00
9 George Collins 4.00 8.00
10 Dan Dierdorf 5.00 10.00
11 Bob Giblin 4.00 8.00
12 Randy Gill 4.00 8.00
13 Doug Greene 4.00 8.00
14 Ken Greene 4.00 8.00
15 Willard Harrell 4.00 8.00
16 Jim Hart 5.00 10.00
17 Steve Little 4.00 8.00
18 Steve Pisarkiewicz 4.00 8.00
19 Bob Pollard 4.00 8.00
20 Eason Ramson 4.00 8.00
21 Keith Simons 4.00 8.00
22 Perry Smith 4.00 8.00
23 Dave Stief 4.00 8.00
24 Terry Stieve 4.00 8.00
25 Ken Stone 4.00 8.00
26 Pat Tilley 5.00 10.00
27 Eric Williams 4.00 8.00
28 Keith Wortman 4.00 8.00

1980 Cardinals Police

The 15-card 1980 St. Louis Cardinals set was sponsored by the local law enforcement agency, the St. Louis Cardinals, KMOX Radio (which broadcasts the Cardinals' games), and Community Federal Savings and Loan: the last three of which have their logos on the backs of the cards. The cards measure approximately 2 5/8" by 4 1/8". The set is unnumbered but has been listed by player uniform number in the checklist below. The backs present "Cardinal Tips" and information on how to contact a police officer by telephone. Card backs feature black print with red trim on white card stock. Ottis Anderson appears in his Rookie Card year.

COMPLETE SET (15)	7.50	15.00
17 Jim Hart	.75	2.00
22 Roger Wehrli	.60	1.50
24 Wayne Morris	.30	.75
32 Ottis Anderson	1.00	2.50
33 Theotis Brown	.30	.75
37 Ken Greene	.30	.75
55 Eric Williams LB	.30	.75
56 Tim Kearney	.30	.75
59 Calvin Favron	.30	.75
68 Terry Stieve	.30	.75
72 Dan Dierdorf	1.25	3.00
73 Mike Dawson	.30	.75
82 Bob Pollard	.30	.75
83 Pat Tilley	.50	1.25
85 Mel Gray	.60	1.50

1980 Cardinals Team Issue

The St. Louis Cardinals issued this series of player photos around 1980. Each photo is very similar in design to the 1976 issue and is only differentiated by slight differences in type size and style. The unnumbered black and white photos measure approximately 5 1/8" by 7" and all include the player's name, position, height and weight below the photo along with "St. Louis Football Cardinals."

COMPLETE SET (12)	30.00	60.00
1 Mark Arneson	2.50	6.00
2 Tom Banks	2.50	6.00
3 Joe Bostic	3.00	8.00
4 Dan Dierdorf	4.00	10.00
4 Barney Cotton	2.50	6.00
5 Calvin Favron	2.50	6.00
6 Harry Gilmer CO	3.00	8.00
7 Tim Kearney	2.50	6.00
7 Jim Hart	3.00	8.00
8 Dave Stief	2.50	6.00
9 Ken Stone	2.50	6.00
10 Ron Yankowski	2.50	6.00

1968 Champion Corn Flakes

These cards were thought to have been issued on Champion Corn Flakes boxes around 1968, but the year has yet to have been confirmed. Each card measures approximately 2 1/16" by 3 3/16, is blankbacked, and features perforations on the edges. The cardfronts feature a color action player photo surrounded by a thin black border on three sides with the player's name and number at the bottom within a thick black border. The cards are apparently reprints of Sports Illustrated posters that were made available in the late 1960s. The card number consists of a numerical team code and AFL or NFL league letter assigned to each team (Examples: 7N for Packers and NFL, 6A for Chiefs and AFL) followed by the player's jersey number. Any additional confirmed information or additions to this list are appreciated. The recently discovered Floyd Little and Lance Rentzel cards were apparently issued without a player image on the cardfronts and have not yet been priced due to perceived scarcity.

1A35 Jim Nance	35.00	60.00
1N34 Junior Coffey	35.00	60.00
1N60 Tommy Nobis	50.00	80.00
2A15 Jack Kemp	125.00	200.00
2N41 Tom Matte	50.00	80.00
2N88 John Mackey	50.00	80.00
3A42 Warren McVea UER	35.00	60.00
3N40 Gale Sayers	175.00	300.00
3N51 Dick Butkus	175.00	300.00
4A44 Floyd Little ERR No Photo		
4N13 Frank Ryan	50.00	80.00
4N44 Leroy Kelly	60.00	100.00
5A90 George Webster	50.00	80.00
5N19 Lance Rentzel ERR No Photo		
5N30 Dan Reeves	60.00	100.00
5N74 Bob Lilly	125.00	200.00
6A16 Len Dawson	125.00	200.00
6A21 Mike Garrett	35.00	60.00
6N20 Lem Barney	50.00	80.00
6N24 Mel Farr	35.00	60.00
7A12 Bob Griese	150.00	250.00
7A39 Larry Csonka	150.00	250.00
7N15 Bart Starr	300.00	500.00
7N33 Jim Grabowski	50.00	80.00
7N66 Ray Nitschke	125.00	200.00
8A12 Joe Namath	300.00	500.00
8A13 Don Maynard	90.00	150.00
8A83 George Sauer	50.00	80.00
8N18 Roman Gabriel	60.00	100.00
8N75 Deacon Jones	60.00	100.00
9A13 Daryle Lamonica	60.00	100.00
9A40 Pete Banaszak	35.00	60.00
9N30 Bill Brown RB	35.00	60.00
9N84 Gene Washington Vik	35.00	60.00
10A19 Lance Alworth	125.00	200.00
10A21 John Hadl	60.00	100.00
10N17 Billy Kilmer	50.00	80.00
10N31 Jim Taylor	125.00	200.00
11N45 Homer Jones	35.00	60.00
12N16 Norm Snead	50.00	80.00
12N18 Ben Hawkins	35.00	60.00
13N10 Kent Nix	35.00	60.00
13N24 Andy Russell	50.00	80.00
13N47 Marv Woodson	35.00	60.00
14N12 Charley Johnson	50.00	80.00
14N25 Jim Bakken	35.00	60.00
15N12 John Brodie	75.00	125.00
16N9 Sonny Jurgensen	90.00	150.00
16N42 Charley Taylor	50.00	80.00

1960 Chargers Team Issue 5x7

The Chargers released these photos in 1960 - their only year in Los Angeles. Each measures approximately 5" by 7" and includes a black and white photo on the cardfront with a blankback. The player's name appears below the photo to the left with the team name oriented to the right.

1 Charlie Flowers	7.50	15.00
2 Jim Sears	7.50	15.00

1960 Chargers Team Issue 8x10

The Chargers released these photos in 1960 - their only year in Los Angeles. Each measures approximately 5" by 7" and includes a black and white photo on the cardfront with a blankback. The player's name appears below the photo to the left with the team name oriented to the right.

1 Howie Ferguson	10.00	20.00
2 Jack Kemp	20.00	40.00

1961 Chargers Golden Tulip

The 1961 Golden Tulip Chips football card set contains 22 black and white cards featuring San Diego (Los Angeles in 1960) Chargers AFL players. The cards measure approximately 2" by 3" and are commonly found with roughly cut or irregularly shaped edges. The fronts contain the player's name, a short biography, and vital statistics. The backs, which are the same for all cards, contain an ad for XETV television, a premium offer for (approximately) 8" by 10" photos and an ad for a free ticket contest. The cards are unnumbered but have been numbered in alphabetical order in the checklist below for your convenience. The catalog designation for this set is F395.

COMPLETE SET (22)	1,200.00	1,800.00
1 Ron Botchan	40.00	75.00
2 Howard Clark	40.00	75.00
3 Fred Cole	40.00	75.00
4 Sam DeLuca	40.00	75.00
5 Orlando Ferrante	40.00	75.00
6 Charlie Flowers	40.00	75.00
7 Dick Harris	40.00	75.00
8 Emil Karas	40.00	75.00
9 Jack Kemp	300.00	500.00
10 Dave Kocourek	40.00	75.00
11 Bob Laraba	40.00	75.00
12 Paul Lowe	50.00	100.00
13 Paul Maguire	50.00	100.00
14 Charlie McNeil	40.00	75.00
15 Ron Mix	75.00	150.00
16 Ron Nery	40.00	75.00
17 Don Norton	40.00	75.00
18 Volney Peters	40.00	75.00
19 Don Rogers	40.00	75.00
20 Maury Schleicher	50.00	100.00
21 Ernie Wright	50.00	100.00
22 Bob Zeman	40.00	75.00

1961 Chargers Golden Tulip Premiums

These oversized (roughly 8" by 10") photos were issued as premiums for collectors in 1961. Each was mailed in exchange for 5-Golden Tulip cards of the featured player. The photos are black and white and include a facsimile player autograph on the front along with a small Golden Tulip Potato Chips logo.

1 Charlie Flowers	125.00	200.00
2 Dick Harris	125.00	200.00
3 Jack Kemp	350.00	600.00
4 Dave Kocourek	125.00	200.00
5 Paul Maguire	150.00	250.00
6 Charlie McNeil	125.00	200.00
7 Ron Mix	175.00	300.00
8 Don Norton	125.00	200.00
9 Volney Peters	125.00	200.00
10 Don Rogers	125.00	200.00
11 Ernie Wright	150.00	250.00
12 Bob Zeman	125.00	200.00

1961-64 Chargers Team Issue 8x10

The Chargers released these photos over a number of seasons. Each measures approximately 8" by 10" and includes a black and white photo on the cardfront with a blankback. The player's name appears below the photo and to the left with the team name oriented to the right. As is common with many team issued photos, the text style and size varies slightly from photo to photo. We've noted known photo variations below and added a number in parenthesis for other players with reported variations.

1 Chuck Allen	7.50	15.00
2 Lance Alworth (2)	15.00	30.00
3 Alworth Kocourek Carolan	12.50	25.00
4 Alworth D.Norton Kocourek Carolan	12.50	25.00
5 Ernie Barnes	7.50	15.00
6 George Blair	7.50	15.00
7 Frank Buncom	7.50	15.00
8 Reg Carolan	7.50	15.00
9 Ron Carpenter	7.50	15.00
10 Bert Coan	7.50	15.00
11 Sam DeLuca (2)	7.50	15.00
12 Hunter Enis	7.50	15.00
13 Earl Faison	7.50	15.00
14 Claude Gibson	7.50	15.00
15 Sid Gillman	10.00	20.00
16 Ken Graham	7.50	15.00
17 George Gross	7.50	15.00
18 Sam Gruneisen	7.50	15.00
19 John Hadl	12.50	25.00
20 John Hadl Willie Frazier	12.50	25.00
21 Dick Harris	7.50	15.00
22 Bill Hudson Richard Hudson	7.50	15.00
23 Richard Hudson	7.50	15.00
24 Bob Jackson	7.50	15.00
25 Emil Karas	7.50	15.00
26A Jack Kemp	15.00	30.00
26B Jack Kemp	15.00	30.00
26C Jack Kemp	15.00	30.00
27 Keith Kinderman	7.50	15.00
28 Gary Kirner	7.50	15.00
29 Dave Kocourek (2)	7.50	15.00
30 Ernie Ladd (3)	10.00	20.00
31 Bob Lane (2)	7.50	15.00
32 Keith Lincoln (3)	10.00	20.00
33 Paul Lowe (2)	10.00	20.00
34A Jacque MacKinnon	7.50	15.00
34B Jacque MacKinnon	7.50	15.00
34C Jacque MacKinnon	7.50	15.00
34D Jacque MacKinnon	7.50	15.00
35 Joe Madro	7.50	15.00
36A Paul Maguire	10.00	20.00
36B Paul Maguire	10.00	20.00
37 Charlie McNeil (2)	7.50	15.00
38 Tommy Minter	7.50	15.00
39 Bob Mitinger	7.50	15.00
40 Ron Mix	12.50	25.00
41 Ron Nery	7.50	15.00
42 Don Norton	7.50	15.00
43 Ernie Park	7.50	15.00
44 Bob Petrich (2)	7.50	15.00
45 Bo Roberson	7.50	15.00
46 Jerry Robinson	7.50	15.00
47 Don Rogers	7.50	15.00
48 Tobin Rote (2)	10.00	20.00
49 Tobin Rote Keith Linclon	10.00	20.00
50 Alvin Roy Keith Linclon	10.00	20.00
51 Henry Schmidt	7.50	15.00
52 Pat Shea	7.50	15.00
53 Walt Sweeney (2)	7.50	15.00
54 Jim Warren	7.50	15.00
55 Dick Westmoreland (2)	7.50	15.00
56 Bud Whitehead	7.50	15.00
57 Ernie Wright (2)	7.50	15.00
58 1964 Coaching Staff	7.50	15.00
59 1961 Team Photo	10.00	20.00
60 1962 Team Photo	10.00	20.00
61 1963 Team Photo	10.00	20.00
62 1964 Team Photo	10.00	20.00

1962 Chargers Golden Arrow Dairy Bottle Caps

This set of milk caps was issued in 1962, and possibly 1963, by the Golden Arrow Dairy in the San Diego area. Each blankbacked paper milk bottle cap features a black and white drawing of a player or other AFL or team subject along with the team name printed above and his position printed bleow the image. These milk caps are exceedingly scarce and were cataloged for the first time in 2008. The saver sheet is a white paper poster with a football field printed on it along with spaces to align the milk caps into a football play formation. The saver sheet reports that 35 different player caps were produced, therefore it is thought that our list below is not fully complete.

1 Chuck Allen	75.00	150.00
2 Lance Alworth	175.00	300.00
3 Ernie Barnes	75.00	150.00
4 Jim Bates	75.00	150.00
5 Frank Buncom	75.00	150.00
6 Bert Coan	75.00	150.00
7 Earl Faison	75.00	150.00
8 Joe Foss Comm.	75.00	150.00
9 Claude Gibson	75.00	150.00
10 Sid Gillman CO	100.00	200.00
11 George Gross	75.00	150.00
12 John Hadl	150.00	250.00
13 Dick Harris	75.00	150.00
14 Barron Hilton Pres.	75.00	150.00
15 Bill Hudson	75.00	150.00
16 Dick Hudson	75.00	150.00
17 Bob Jackson	75.00	150.00
18 Emil Karas	75.00	150.00
19 Jack Kemp	200.00	400.00
20 Ernie Ladd	100.00	200.00
21 Keith Lincoln	100.00	200.00
22 Paul Lowe	100.00	200.00
23 Jacque MacKinnon	75.00	150.00
24 Paul Maguire	100.00	200.00
25 Bob Mitinger	75.00	150.00
26 Ron Mix	150.00	250.00
27 Ron Nery	75.00	150.00
28 Don Norton	75.00	150.00
29 Sherman Plunkett	75.00	150.00
30 Don Rogers	75.00	150.00
31 Tobin Rote	100.00	200.00
32 Maury Schleicher	75.00	150.00
33 Mark Schmidt	75.00	150.00
34 Bud Whitehead	75.00	150.00
35 Ernie Wright	75.00	150.00
36 Saver Sheet	75.00	150.00

1962 Chargers Union Oil

The set was sponsored by Union 76. All players featured in the set are members of the San Diego Chargers. They are derived from sketches by the artist, Patrick. The cards are black and white, approximately 6" by 8" with player biography and Union Oil logo on backs. The catalog designation for the set is UO35-2. The cards were reportedly issued with an album with 24 spaces for the photos. The key cards in this set are quarterback Jack Kemp, who would later gain fame as a politician, as well as cards issued during the rookie season of future Hall of Famer Lance Alworth and star quarterback John Hadl.

COMPLETE SET (16)	350.00	600.00
1 Chuck Allen	10.00	20.00
2 Lance Alworth	75.00	125.00
3 Earl Faison	10.00	20.00
4 John Hadl	25.00	40.00
5 Dick Harris	10.00	20.00
6 Bill Hudson	10.00	20.00
7 Jack Kemp	125.00	250.00
8 Dave Kocourek	10.00	20.00
9 Ernie Ladd	20.00	35.00
10 Keith Lincoln	12.50	25.00
11 Paul Lowe	12.50	25.00
12 Charlie McNeil	10.00	20.00
13 Ron Mix	20.00	35.00
14 Ron Nery	10.00	20.00
15 Don Norton	10.00	20.00
16 Team Photo	15.00	30.00

1962-63 Chargers Team Issue 5x7

The Chargers released these photos over a number of seasons. Each measures approximately 5" by 7" and includes a black and white photo on the cardfront with a blankback. The player's name appears below the photo to the left, while the team name appears on the right. The type styles and sizes vary slightly from photo to photo and many players were issued with photo variations as noted below.

1964 Chargers Team Issue

Photos from this set, measuring approximately 5 1/2" by 8 1/2", were issued over a number of years. Each features black and white close-up player photos on off-white linen weave paper (same as 1965-67 Chargers Team Issue). The player's facsimile autograph is centered beneath each picture above the team name. The 1964 issue has biographical and statistical information on the backs that helps to identify the year of issue. Because the set is unnumbered, players and coaches are listed alphabetically.

COMPLETE SET (36)	150.00	300.00
1 Chuck Allen	6.00	12.00
2 Lance Alworth	12.50	25.00
3 George Blair	6.00	12.00
4 Frank Buncom	6.00	12.00
5 Earl Faison	6.00	12.00
6 Sid Gillman CO	7.50	15.00
7 George Gross	6.00	12.00
8 Sam Gruneisen	6.00	12.00
9 Walt Hackett CO	6.00	12.00
10 John Hadl	10.00	20.00
11 Dick Harris	6.00	12.00
12 Bob Jackson	6.00	12.00
13 Emil Karas	6.00	12.00
14 Dave Kocourek	6.00	12.00
15 Ernie Ladd	7.50	15.00
16 Keith Lincoln	7.50	15.00
17 Paul Lowe	7.50	15.00
18 Jacque MacKinnon	6.00	12.00
19 Joe Madro CO	6.00	12.00
20 Gerry McDougall	6.00	12.00
21 Charlie McNeil	6.00	12.00
22 Bob Mitinger	6.00	12.00
23 Ron Mix	10.00	20.00
24 Chuck Noll CO	10.00	20.00
25 Don Norton	6.00	12.00
26 Bob Petrich	6.00	12.00
27 Jerry Robinson	6.00	12.00
28 Don Rogers	6.00	12.00

29 Tobin Rote 7.50 15.00
30 Hank Schmidt 6.00 12.00
31 Pat Shea 6.00 12.00
32 Walt Sweeney 7.50 15.00
33 Dick Westmoreland 6.00 12.00
34 Bud Whitehead 6.00 12.00
35 Ernie Wright 6.00 12.00
36 1963 Team Photo 7.50 15.00

1965-67 Chargers Team Issue

This team issue set, with photos measuring approximately 5 1/2" by 8 1/2", was issued over at least a couple of years, with a few personnel changes reflected each year. This series features black and white close-up player photos on off-white linen weave paper. The player's facsimile autograph is centered beneath each picture above the team name. Some photos were issued with biographical information on the back (primarily in 1964 and 1966), while others have blank backs (issued primarily in 1967). We've included known variations below, but the checklist is thought to be incomplete. Because the set is unnumbered, players and coaches are listed alphabetically. This set is interesting in that it features an early issue of Bum Phillips.

1A Chuck Allen 6.00 12.00
blank backed
1B Chuck Allen 6.00 12.00
1966 bio on back
2A Jim Allison 6.00 12.00
blank backed
2B Jim Allison 6.00 12.00
1966 bio on back
3A Lance Alworth 25.00 40.00
blank backed
3B Lance Alworth 25.00 40.00
1966 bio on back
4A Tom Bass CO 6.00 12.00
blank backed
4B Tom Bass CO 6.00 12.00
1966 bio on back
5A Joe Beauchamp 6.00 12.00
blank backed
6A Frank Buncom 6.00 12.00
blank backed
6B Frank Buncom 6.00 12.00
1966 bio on back
7A Ron Carpenter 6.00 12.00
blank backed
7B Ron Carpenter 6.00 12.00
1966 bio on back
8A Richard Degen 6.00 12.00
blank backed
9A Steve DeLong 6.00 12.00
blank backed
9B Steve DeLong 6.00 12.00
1966 bio on back
10A Speedy Duncan 6.00 12.00
blank backed
10B Speedy Duncan 6.00 12.00
1966 bio on back
11A Earl Faison 6.00 12.00
(1966 bio on back
12A John Farris 6.00 12.00
(blank backed
12B John Farris 6.00 12.00
(1966 bio on back
13A Gene Foster 6.00 12.00
blank backed
13B Gene Foster 6.00 12.00
1966 bio on back
14A Willie Frazier 6.00 12.00
blank backed
15A Gary Garrison 6.00 12.00
blank backed
15B Gary Garrison 6.00 12.00
1966 bio on back
16A Sid Gillman CO 7.50 15.00
blank backed
16B Sid Gillman CO 7.50 15.00
coaching record on back
through 1965)
17A Kenny Graham 6.00 12.00
blank backed)
17B Kenny Graham 6.00 12.00
1966 bio on back)
18A Jim Griffin 6.00 12.00
(blank backed)
18B Jim Griffin 6.00 12.00
(1966 bio on back)
19A George Gross 6.00 12.00
blank backed)
19B George Gross 6.00 12.00
1967 bio on back)
20A Sam Gruneisen 6.00 12.00
blank backed)
20B Sam Gruneisen 6.00 12.00
1966 bio on back)
21A Walt Hackett CO 6.00 12.00
(blank backed)
22A John Hadl 15.00 25.00
(blank backed)
22B John Hadl 15.00 25.00
(1966 bio on back)
23A Dick Harris 6.00 12.00
blank backed)
23B Dick Harris 6.00 12.00
1966 bio on back)
24A Dan Henning 6.00 12.00
blank backed)
25A Bob Horton 6.00 12.00
26A Harry Johnston CO 6.00 12.00
blank backed)
27A Howard Kindig 6.00 12.00
blank backed)
28A Gary Kirner 6.00 12.00
(blank backed)
28B Gary Kirner 6.00 12.00
(1966 bio on back)
29A Dave Kocourek 6.00 12.00
(1966 bio on back)
30A Ernie Ladd 7.50 15.00
(1966 bio on back)
31A Mike London 6.00 12.00
(1966 bio on back)
32A Jacque MacKinnon 6.00 12.00
blank backed)
32B Jacque MacKinnon 6.00 12.00
1966 bio on back)
33A Joe Madro CO 6.00 12.00
blank backed)
33B Joe Madro CO 6.00 12.00
1966 bio on back)
34A Lloyd McCoy 6.00 12.00
(blank backed)
35A Ed Mitchell 6.00 12.00
blank backed)
35B Ron Mix 10.00 20.00
(blank backed)
36A Fred Moore 6.00 12.00
blank backed)
36B Fred Moore 6.00 12.00
1966 bio on back)
37A Chuck Noll CO 10.00 20.00
(blank backed)
38A Don Norton 6.00 12.00
blank backed)
38B Don Norton 6.00 12.00
1966 bio on back)
39A Terry Owens 6.00 12.00
(blank backed)
39B Terry Owens 6.00 12.00
(1966 bio on back)
40A Bob Petrich 6.00 12.00
(blank backed)
40B Bob Petrich 6.00 12.00
(1966 bio on back)
41A Bum Phillips CO 7.50 15.00
blank backed)
42A Dave Plump 6.00 12.00
blank backed)
43A Rick Redman 6.00 12.00
blank backed)
43B Rick Redman 6.00 12.00
1966 bio on back)
44A Houston Ridge 6.00 12.00
blank backed)
45A Hank Schmidt 6.00 12.00
(blank backed)
46A Pat Shea 6.00 12.00
blank backed)
46B Pat Shea 6.00 12.00
(1966 bio on back)
47A Jackie Simpson CO 6.00 12.00
blank backed)
48A Walt Sweeney 7.50 15.00
blank backed)
48B Walt Sweeney 7.50 15.00
1966 bio on back)
49A Sammy Taylor 6.00 12.00
49B Steve Tensi 6.00 12.00
blank backed)
50A Herb Travenio 6.00 12.00
51A John Travis 6.00 12.00
blank backed)
52A Dick Van Raaphorst 6.00 12.00
blank backed)
53A Charlie Waller CO 6.00 12.00
blank backed)
53B Charlie Waller CO 6.00 12.00
1966 bio on back)
54A Bud Whitehead 6.00 12.00
blank backed)
54B Bud Whitehead 6.00 12.00
1966 bio on back)
55A Nat Whitmyer 6.00 12.00
blank backed)
55B Nat Whitmyer 6.00 12.00
1966 bio on back)
56A Ernie Wright 7.50 15.00
blank backed)
56B Ernie Wright 7.50 15.00
1966 bio on back)
57A Bob Zeman 6.00 12.00
(1966 bio on back)
58A 1965 Team Photo 10.00 20.00
58B 1966 Team Photo 10.00 20.00

1965-69 Chargers Team Issue 8x10

The Chargers released these photos over a number of seasons. Each measures approximately 8" by 10" and includes a black and white photo on the cardfront with a blankback. The player's name appears below the photo to the left, with the player's position spelled out in the middle and the team name to the right. Each also includes the newer Chargers' team logo with the goalpost style H. The text style and size varies slightly from photo to photo and the checklist is thought to be incomplete. Any additions to this list are appreciated.

1966-68 Chargers Team Issue 5X7

The Chargers released these photos over a number of seasons. Each measures approximately 5" by 7" and includes a black and white photo on the cardfront with a blankback. The player's name appears below the photo to the left with his position centered. The Chargers' team name appears on the right and is in the style with the goalpost shaped H. The type styles and sizes can vary slightly from photo to photo.

COMPLETE SET (15) 60.00 120.00
1 Harold Akin 5.00 10.00
2 Scott Appleton 5.00 10.00
3 Tom Denman CO 5.00 10.00
4 Ken Dyer 5.00 10.00
5 Willie Frazier 5.00 10.00
6 Barron Hilton OWN 5.00 10.00
7 Brad Hubbert 5.00 10.00
8 Harry Johnston CO 5.00 10.00
9 Irv Kaze OFF 5.00 10.00
10 Paul Lowe 6.00 12.00
11 Don Norton 5.00 10.00
12 Dick Van Raaphorst 5.00 10.00
13 Charlie Waller CO 5.00 10.00
14 Bob Wells 5.00 10.00
15 Bob Zeman 5.00 10.00

1968 Chargers Team Issue 7x9

The Chargers released these photos over a number of seasons. Each measures approximately 7" by 9" and includes a black and white photo on the cardfront with a blankback. The player's name appears below the photo to the left with his position centered. The Chargers' team name appears on the right and is in the style with the goalpost shaped H. The type styles and sizes can vary slightly from photo to photo.

COMPLETE SET (23) 100.00 200.00
1 Chuck Allen 5.00 10.00
2A Lance Alworth 12.50 25.00
2B Lance Alworth 12.50 25.00
3 Scott Appleton 5.00 10.00
4 Jon Brittenum 5.00 10.00
5 Steve DeLong 5.00 10.00
6 Les Duncan 6.00 12.00
7 Dick Farley 5.00 10.00
8 Gene Foster 5.00 10.00
9 Willie Frazier 5.00 10.00
10 Gary Garrison 5.00 10.00
11 Ken Graham 5.00 10.00
12 Sam Gruneisen 5.00 10.00
13 John Hadl 7.50 15.00
14 Bob Howard 5.00 10.00
15 Gary Kirner 5.00 10.00
16 Larry Little 10.00 20.00
17 Ron Mix 10.00 20.00
18 Terry Owens 5.00 10.00
19 Dick Post 5.00 10.00
20 Rick Redman 5.00 10.00
21 Houston Ridge 5.00 10.00
22 Jeff Staggs 5.00 10.00
23 Walt Sweeney 5.00 10.00

1968 Chargers Team Issue 8x11

This set featuring members of the 1968 San Diego Chargers features sepia toned player photos measuring approximately 8 1/2" by 11". The backs are blank. The cards are unnumbered and checklisted below in alphabetical order. The 1968 photos are nearly identical to the 1969 issue but can be differentiated by the slightly larger type size. Also, most of the photos were produced with the facsimile autograph appearing over the image of the player.

COMPLETE SET (8) 50.00 100.00
1 Lance Alworth 12.50 25.00
2 John Hadl 7.50 15.00
3 Bob Howard 6.00 12.00
4 Brad Hubbert 6.00 12.00
5 Ron Mix 7.50 15.00
6 Dick Post 6.00 12.00
7 Jeff Staggs 6.00 12.00
8 Walt Sweeney 6.00 12.00

1968 Chargers Volpe Tumblers

These Chargers artist's renderings were part of a plastic cup tumbler product produced in 1968 and distributed by White Front Stores. The noted sports artist Volpe created the artwork which includes an action scene and a player portrait. Each is unnumbered, measures approximately 5" by 8 1/2" when flat, and is curved in the shape required to fit inside a plastic cup. The manufacturer notation PGC (Programs General Corp) is printed on each piece as well. There are thought to be 6-cups included in this set. Any additions to this list are appreciated.

1 Chuck Allen 20.00 40.00
2 Kenny Graham 20.00 40.00
3 John Hadl 25.00 50.00
4 Dick Post 20.00 40.00

1969 Chargers Team Issue 8x11

This set of the 1969 San Diego Chargers was issued by the team. Each features a black-and-white player photo measuring approximately 8 1/2" by 11". The backs are blank. The cards are unnumbered and checklisted below in alphabetical order. The 1969 photos are nearly identical to the 1968 issue but can be differentiated by the smaller type size. Also all of the photos were produced with the facsimile autograph appearing away from the player image.

COMPLETE SET (11) 60.00 120.00
1 Lance Alworth 10.00 20.00
2 Les Duncan 5.00 10.00
3 Gary Garrison 5.00 10.00
4 Kenny Graham 5.00 10.00
5 John Hadl 7.50 15.00
6 Ron Mix 7.50 15.00
7 Dick Post 5.00 10.00
8 Jeff Staggs 5.00 10.00
9 Walt Sweeney 6.00 12.00
10 Russ Washington 5.00 10.00
11 Team Photo 6.00 12.00

1970 Chargers Team Issue 8X10

This set of photos featuring the 1970 San Diego Chargers was issued by the team. Each features a black-and-white player photo measuring approximately 8" by 10" with blank backs. The player's name is included below the image oriented to the left with his position in the center and the Chargers' team name to the right. Each player is pictured in a posed kneeling photo with his hand on his helmet which includes the player's jersey number. The photos are unnumbered and checklisted below in alphabetical order.

COMPLETE SET (20) 75.00 150.00
1 Lance Alworth 10.00 20.00
2 Bob Babich 5.00 10.00
3 Pete Barnes 5.00 10.00
4 Joe Beauchamp 5.00 10.00
5 Ron Billingsley 5.00 10.00
6 Gene Ferguson 5.00 10.00
7 Gene Foster 5.00 10.00
8 Mike Garrett 6.00 12.00
9 Gary Garrison 5.00 10.00
10 Ira Gordon 5.00 10.00
11 Sam Gruneisen 5.00 10.00
12 Jim Hill 5.00 10.00
13 Bob Howard 5.00 10.00
14 Joe Owens 5.00 10.00
15 Dennis Partee 5.00 10.00
16 Dick Post 5.00 10.00
17 Jeff Staggs 5.00 10.00
18 Walt Sweeney 6.00 12.00
19 Jim Tolbert 5.00 10.00
20 Russ Washington 5.00 10.00

1974 Chargers Team Issue

Photos in this set were issued by the team to fulfill fan requests. Each features a black-and-white player photo measuring approximately 8 1/2" by 11" with blank backs. The team name "Chargers" is printed to the far left below the image and the player's name and position (spelled out) are oriented to the far right side. The photos are unnumbered and checklisted below in alphabetical order.

1 Harrison Davis 5.00 10.00
2 Jesse Freitas 5.00 10.00
3 John Teerlink 5.00 10.00

1976 Chargers Dean's Photo

This 10-card set was sponsored by Dean's Photo Service and features nine San Diego Chargers' players. The cards were released on an uncut perforated sheet with each card measuring approximately 5" by 8." The player photos are black and white, but the team helmet is printed in color. The cards are blank backed and unnumbered.

COMPLETE SET (10) 30.00 60.00
1 Pat Curran 2.50 5.00
2 Chris Fletcher 2.50 5.00
3 Dan Fouts 10.00 20.00
4 Gary Garrison 3.00 6.00
5 Louie Kelcher 3.00 6.00
6 Joe Washington 3.00 6.00
7 Russ Washington 2.50 5.00
8 Doug Wilkerson 2.50 5.00
9 Don Woods 2.50 5.00
10 Schedule Card 2.50 5.00

1976 Chargers Team Sheets

The San Diego Chargers issued these sheets of black-and-white player photos around 1976. Each measures roughly 8"

by 10 1/4" and was printed on glossy stock with white borders. Each sheet includes photos of 3-players and/or coaches. Below each player's image is his jersey number, his name, position and the team name. The photos are blankbacked.

COMPLETE SET (16)	75.00	125.00
1 Charles Anthony	5.00	10.00
Doug Wilkerson		
Louie Kelcher		
2 Ken Bernich	4.00	8.00
Mark Markovich		
Floyd Rice		
3 Bob Brown	4.00	8.00
Coy Bacon		
Dwight McDonald		
4 Booker Brown	4.00	8.00
Billy Shields		
Ira Gordon		
5 Earnel Durden CO	4.00	8.00
Bobb McKittrick CO		
Howard Mudd CO		
6 Rudy Feldman CO	4.00	8.00
Dick Coury CO		
George Dickson CO		
7 Jesse Freitas	4.00	8.00
Mike Williams		
Glen Bonner		
8 Mike Fuller	4.00	8.00
Chris Fletcher		
Sam Williams		
9 Gary Garrison	5.00	10.00
Dennis Partee		
Don Woods		
10 Don Goode	4.00	8.00
Ed Flanagan		
Carl Gersbach		
11 Neal Jeffrey	10.00	20.00
Dan Fouts		
Ray Wersching		
12 Dave Lowe/Terry Owens/John Teerlinck	4.00	8.00
13 Tommy Prothro CO	5.00	10.00
John David Crow CO		
Jackie Simpson CO		
14 Bob Thomas	4.00	8.00
Joe Beauchamp		
Bo Matthews		
15 Charles Wadnelk	4.00	8.00
Harrison Davis		
Wayne Stewart		
16 Russ Washington	5.00	10.00
Fred Dean		
Gary Johnson		

1970 Chase and Sanborn Stickers

This 26-card set features colored stickers of team logos on silver backgrounds. The backs carry a Chase and Sanborn Coffee send-in ad for a complete set of the 26 NFL team emblems. The cards are unnumbered and checklisted below in alphabetical order according to team nickname.

COMPLETE SET (26)	150.00	300.00
1 Chicago Bears	7.50	15.00
2 Cincinnati Bengals	7.50	15.00
3 Buffalo Bills	7.50	15.00
4 Denver Broncos	7.50	15.00
5 Cleveland Browns	7.50	15.00
6 St.Louis Cardinals	7.50	15.00
7 San Diego Chargers	7.50	15.00
8 Kansas City Chiefs	7.50	15.00
9 Baltimore Colts	7.50	15.00
10 Dallas Cowboys	10.00	20.00
11 Miami Dolphins	7.50	15.00
12 Philadelphia Eagles	7.50	15.00
13 Atlanta Falcons	7.50	15.00
14 San Francisco 49ers	7.50	15.00
15 New York Giants	7.50	15.00
16 New York Jets	7.50	15.00
17 Detroit Lions	7.50	15.00
18 Houston Oilers	7.50	15.00
19 Green Bay Packers	10.00	20.00
20 New England Patriots	7.50	15.00
21 Oakland Raiders	10.00	20.00
22 Los Angeles Rams	7.50	15.00
23 Washington Redskins	10.00	20.00
24 New Orleans Saints	7.50	15.00
25 Pittsburgh Steelers	7.50	15.00
26 Minnesota Vikings	7.50	15.00

1969 Chemtoy AFL Superballs

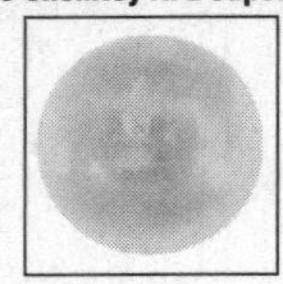

These little high bouncing 1" balls were produced by Chemtoy and featured AFL players. The player's picture is on the front with their name and team affiliation on the back of the paper piece inside the ball. Since these are not numbered, we have sequenced them in alphabetical order.

COMPLETE SET (26)	600.00	1,000.00
1 Lance Alworth	60.00	100.00
2 Pete Beathard	18.00	30.00
3 Bobby Bell	30.00	50.00
4 Emerson Boozer	18.00	30.00
5 Nick Buoniconti	35.00	60.00
6 Billy Cannon	25.00	40.00
7 Gino Cappelletti	25.00	40.00
8 Jack Clancy	18.00	30.00
9 Larry Csonka	60.00	100.00
10 Ben Davidson	25.00	40.00
11 Len Dawson	60.00	100.00
12 Mike Garrett	18.00	30.00
13 Bob Griese	80.00	120.00
14 John Hadl	30.00	50.00
15 Jack Kemp	90.00	150.00
16 Don Maynard	50.00	80.00
17 Ron McDole	18.00	30.00
18 Ron Mix	30.00	50.00
20 Dick Post	18.00	30.00
20 Jim Otto	30.00	50.00
21 George Saimes	18.00	30.00
22 George Sauer	18.00	30.00
23 Jan Stenerud	30.00	50.00
24 Matt Snell	25.00	40.00
25 Jim Turner	18.00	30.00
26 George Webster	18.00	30.00

1963-65 Chiefs Fairmont Dairy

These cards were featured as the side panels of half-gallon milk cartons in the Kansas City area by Fairmont Dairy. Similar cards were apparently issued during more than one season as there are several styles with different sizes and colors. Any one individual card can be identified using either the age of the player or "years pro" that is printed on the card. The cards below were likely issued between 1963 and 1965 based upon this information or have not been confirmed as to year of issue. When cut, each card measures approximately 2 1/4" by 3 1/4" to the outside dotted line. The printing on the cards is in red and may also have been printed in black as well. The fronts feature close-up player photos with the player's biographical information appearing to the right. The cards have blank backs as is the case with most milk carton issues. Complete milk cartons would be valued at double the prices listed below. Additions to the list below are welcomed.

1 Bobby Bell	300.00	500.00
2 Mel Branch	200.00	350.00
(Age: 27; 1964 issue		
3 Len Dawson	350.00	600.00
4 Dave Grayson	200.00	350.00
5 Abner Haynes	250.00	400.00
6 Sherrill Headrick	200.00	350.00
7 Dave Hill	200.00	350.00
8 Bobby Hunt	200.00	350.00
9 Frank Jackson	200.00	350.00
10 Curtis McClinton	250.00	400.00
11 Bobby Ply	200.00	350.00
12 Al Reynolds	200.00	350.00
13 Smokey Stover	200.00	350.00

1965 Chiefs Team Issue 8 x 10

This set of photos was released around 1965. Each features a Chiefs player on glossy photographic stock measuring roughly 8" by 10." The player's position (initials), name and team name is spelled out below the player's photo. The photo backs are blank and can often be found with a photographer's imprint and year of issue. These photos look very similar to the 1967 set, but the team name is roughly 1 3/4" to 1 7/8" long. Any additions to this list are appreciated.

COMPLETE SET (17)	100.00	200.00
1 Pete Beathard	7.50	15.00
2 Buck Buchanan	12.50	25.00
3 Ed Budde	7.50	15.00
4 Chris Burford	7.50	15.00
5 Len Dawson	20.00	35.00
6 Sherrill Headrick	7.50	15.00
7 Mack Lee Hill	7.50	15.00
8 E.J. Holub	7.50	15.00
9 Bobby Hunt	7.50	15.00
10 Frank Jackson	7.50	15.00
11 Ed Lothamer	7.50	15.00
12 Jerry Mays	7.50	15.00
13 Curtis McClinton	10.00	20.00
14 Johnny Robinson	10.00	20.00
15 Jim Tyrer	10.00	20.00
16 Fred Williamson	10.00	20.00
17 Jerrel Wilson	7.50	15.00

1966 Chiefs Team Issue

The Kansas City Chiefs issued these player photos around 1966. Some likely were released over a period years. The type style and size varies slightly from photo to photo. Each measures roughly 7 1/4" by 9 1/2" and features a black and white photo. They are unnumbered and checklisted below in alphabetical order. Any additions to the list are appreciated.

COMPLETE SET (15)	125.00	250.00
1 Pete Beathard	7.50	15.00
2 Bobby Bell	10.00	20.00
3 Tommy Brooker	7.50	15.00
4 Ed Budde	7.50	15.00
5 Bert Coan	7.50	15.00
6 Len Dawson	15.00	30.00
7 Mike Garrett	7.50	15.00
8 Sherrill Headrick	7.50	15.00
9 Jerry Mays	7.50	15.00
10 Curtis McClinton	7.50	15.00
11 Bobby Ply	7.50	15.00
12 Johnny Robinson	7.50	15.00
13 Hank Stram CO	12.50	25.00
14 Otis Taylor	10.00	20.00
15 Fred Williamson	10.00	20.00

1967 Chiefs Fairmont Dairy

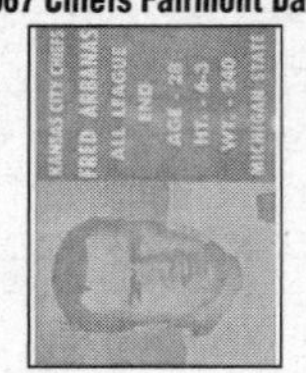

These cards were featured as the side panels of half-gallon milk cartons in the Kansas City area by Fairmont Dairy. Similar cards were apparently issued during more than one season as there are several styles with different sizes and colors. Any one individual card can be identified using the age of the player that is printed on the card. The cards below were issued in 1967 based upon this information and we've noted that below when known. When cut, each card measures approximately 2 3/8" by 3 3/8" to the outside dotted line. The printing on all confirmed cards is in red but may also have been printed in black as well. The fronts feature a close-up player photo with the player's team, his name, position, height, weight, age, and college information appearing to the right. The cards have blank backs as is the case with most milk carton issues. Complete milk cartons would be valued at double the prices listed below. Additions to the list below are welcomed.

COMPLETE SET (23)	1,500.00	2,500.00
1 Fred Arbanas	175.00	300.00
2 Pete Beathard	175.00	300.00
3 Bobby Bell	250.00	400.00
4 Aaron Brown	150.00	250.00
5 Buck Buchanan	250.00	400.00
6 Ed Budde	150.00	250.00
7 Chris Burford	175.00	300.00
8 Bert Coan	150.00	250.00
9 Len Dawson	350.00	600.00
10 Mike Garrett	175.00	300.00
11 Jon Gilliam	150.00	250.00
12 E.J. Holub	175.00	300.00
13 Bobby Hunt	150.00	250.00
14 Chuck Hurston	150.00	250.00
15 Ed Lothamer	150.00	250.00
16 Curtis McClinton	175.00	300.00
17 Curt Merz	150.00	250.00
18 Willie Mitchell	150.00	250.00
19 Johnny Robinson	175.00	300.00
20 Otis Taylor	200.00	350.00
21 Jim Tyrer	175.00	300.00
22 Fred Williamson	200.00	350.00
23 Jerrel Wilson	150.00	250.00

1967 Chiefs Team Issue

This set of photos was released around 1967. Each features a Chiefs player on glossy stock measuring roughly 8" by 10." The player's name and team name is spelled out below the player's photo with some photos also including the player's position listed before his name. These photos look very similar to the 1965 set, but the team name is roughly 1 1/2" long. Any additions to this list are appreciated.

COMPLETE SET (11)	100.00	175.00
1 Bobby Bell	10.00	20.00
2 Aaron Brown	7.50	15.00
3 Ed Budde	7.50	15.00
4 Chris Burford	7.50	15.00
5 Bert Coan	7.50	15.00
6 Len Dawson	15.00	30.00
7 Willie Lanier	10.00	20.00
8 Curt Merz	7.50	15.00
9 Jan Stenerud	10.00	20.00
10 Otis Taylor	10.00	20.00
11 Jim Tyrer	10.00	20.00

1968 Chiefs Fairmont Dairy

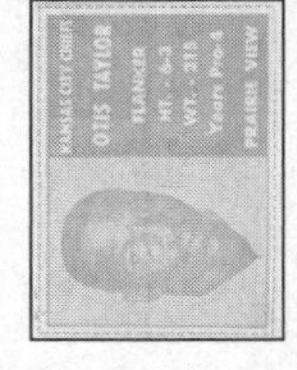

These cards were featured as the side panels of half-gallon milk cartons in the Kansas City area by Fairmont Dairy. Similar cards were apparently issued during more than one season as there are several styles with different sizes and colors. Any one individual card can be identified using the "years pro" of the player that is printed on the card. The cards below were issued in 1968 based upon this information and we've noted that below when known. When cut, each card measures approximately 2 3/8" by 3 3/8" to the outside dotted lines. The printing on the confirmed cards is in red but may also have been printed in black as well. The fronts feature close-up player photos with the player's team, his name, position, biographical information, and years pro appearing to the right. Most were printed with a very thin (roughly 1/16") white border, while a few featured a thicker (roughly 1/4") white border. The cards have blank backs as is the case with most milk carton issues. Complete milk cartons would be valued at double the prices listed below. Additions to the list below are welcomed.

COMPLETE SET (23)	1,500.00	2,500.00
1 Bud Abell	150.00	250.00
2 Fred Arbanas	175.00	300.00
3 Aaron Brown	150.00	250.00
4 Buck Buchanan	250.00	400.00
5 Ed Budde	150.00	250.00
6 Wendell Hayes	175.00	300.00
7 Dave Hill	150.00	250.00
8 E.J. Holub	175.00	300.00
9 Jim Kearney	150.00	250.00
10 Ernie Ladd	200.00	350.00
11 Willie Lanier	250.00	400.00
12 Jacky Lee	175.00	300.00
13 Ed Lothamer	150.00	250.00
14 Jim Lynch	150.00	250.00
15 Jerry Mays	150.00	250.00
16 Curtis McClinton	175.00	300.00
17 Willie Mitchell	150.00	250.00
18 Johnny Robinson	175.00	300.00
19 Noland Smith	150.00	250.00
20 Jan Stenerud	200.00	350.00
21 Otis Taylor	200.00	350.00
22 Jim Tyrer	175.00	300.00
23 Jerrel Wilson	150.00	250.00

1968 Chiefs Team Issue

The Chiefs issued these player photos in the late 1960s. Each photo measures roughly 8 1/2" by 10 5/16" and features a black and white photo along with a white facsimile autograph. The Len Dawson can be found with either a white or black signature. The player's position initials, name, and team name appear below the photo. They are unnumbered and checklisted below in alphabetical order.

COMPLETE SET (22)	150.00	300.00
1 Bobby Bell	10.00	20.00
2 Buck Buchanan	10.00	20.00
3 Reg Carolan	7.50	15.00
4 Len Dawson WHT	15.00	30.00
5 Len Dawson BLK	15.00	30.00
6 Mike Garrett	7.50	15.00
7 E.J. Holub	7.50	15.00
8 Jim Kearney	7.50	15.00
9 Ernie Ladd	7.50	15.00
10 Willie Lanier	10.00	20.00
11 Jacky Lee	7.50	15.00
12 Ed Lothamer	7.50	15.00
13 Curtis McClinton	7.50	15.00
14 Willie Mitchell	7.50	15.00
15 Frank Pitts	7.50	15.00
16 Johnny Robinson	7.50	15.00
17 Goldie Sellers	7.50	15.00
18 Noland Smith	7.50	15.00
19 Hank Stram CO	12.50	25.00
20 Otis Taylor	10.00	20.00
21 Fred Williamson	10.00	20.00
22 Jerrel Wilson	7.50	15.00

1969 Chiefs Fairmont Dairy

These cards were featured as the side panels of half-gallon milk cartons in the Kansas City area by Fairmont Dairy. Similar cards were apparently issued during more than one season as there are several styles with different sizes and colors. Any one individual card can be identified using either the age of the player or "years pro" that is printed on the card. The cards below were issued in 1969 based upon this information and we've noted that below when known. When cut, each card measures approximately 1 5/8" by 3 1/2" to the outside dotted line. The printing on the confirmed cards is in black ink but some may also have been printed in red ink as well. The fronts feature close-up player photos with the player's team, his jersey number, his name, position, biographical information, and years pro appearing to the right. The cards have blank backs as is the case with most milk carton issues. Complete milk cartons would be valued at double the prices listed below. Additions to the list below are welcomed.

COMPLETE SET (25)	1,800.00	3,000.00
1 Fred Arbanas	60.00	100.00
2 Bobby Bell	125.00	200.00
(Years Pro 7)		
3 Aaron Brown	60.00	100.00
4 Buck Buchanan	100.00	200.00
5 Ed Budde	60.00	100.00
6 Curley Culp	100.00	175.00
(Years Pro 2)		
7 George Daney	60.00	100.00
8 Len Dawson	200.00	350.00
9 Wendell Hayes	75.00	125.00

10 E.J. Holub 75.00 125.00
11 Ernie Ladd 90.00 150.00
12 Mike Livingston 75.00 125.00
13 Ed Lothamer 60.00 100.00
14 Jim Marsalis 60.00 100.00
(First Year Pro)
15 Jerry Mays 60.00 100.00
16 Curtis McClinton 75.00 125.00
17 Willie Mitchell 60.00 100.00
18 Mo Moorman 60.00 100.00
19 Frank Pitts 60.00 100.00
(Years Pro 5)
20 Gloster Richardson 60.00 100.00
21 Johnny Robinson 75.00 125.00
22 Otis Taylor 90.00 150.00
23 Emmitt Thomas 75.00 125.00
24 Jim Tyrer 60.00 100.00
25 Jerrel Wilson 60.00 100.00

1969 Chiefs Kroger

This eight-card, unnumbered set was sponsored by Kroger and measures approximately 8" by 9 3/4". The front features a color painting of the player by artist John Wheeldon, with the player's name inscribed across the bottom of the picture. The back has biographical and statistical information about the player and a brief note about the artist.

COMPLETE SET (8) 75.00 150.00
1 Buck Buchanan 10.00 20.00
2 Len Dawson 25.00 40.00
3 Mike Garrett 7.50 15.00
4 Willie Lanier 10.00 20.00
5 Jerry Mays 7.50 15.00
6 Johnny Robinson 7.50 15.00
7 Jan Stenerud 10.00 20.00
8 Jim Tyrer 7.50 15.00

1969 Chiefs Team Issue

These photos of the Kansas City Chiefs measures approximately 8 1/2" by 10 3/8" and feature black-and-white player images with a white border. The player's name and team name are included below each photo. The backs are blank and unnumbered so the photos are checklisted below in alpabetical order.

COMPLETE SET (5) 25.00 50.00
1 Caesar Belser 6.00 12.00
2 Curley Culp 6.00 12.00
3 George Daney 6.00 12.00
4 Mo Moorman 6.00 12.00
5 Frank Pitts 6.00 12.00

1970 Chiefs Team Issue

This 17-card set of the Kansas City Chiefs measures approximately 8" by 10 3/8" and features black-and-white player photos with a white border. The player's facsimile autograph appears across the photo with his name and team name below each photo. The backs are blank and unnumbered so the photos are checklisted below in alpabetical order.

COMPLETE SET (17) 75.00 150.00
1 Fred Arbanas 5.00 10.00
2 Bobby Bell 7.50 15.00
3 Aaron Brown 5.00 10.00
4 Billy Cannon 6.00 12.00
5 Robert Holmes 5.00 10.00
6 Mike Livingston 5.00 10.00
7 Jim Lynch 5.00 10.00
8 Jim Marsalis 5.00 10.00
9 Warren McVea 5.00 10.00
10 Willie Mitchell 5.00 10.00
11 Mo Moorman 5.00 10.00
12 Ed Podolak 5.00 10.00
13 Bob Stein 5.00 10.00
14 Jan Stenerud 7.50 15.00
15 Morris Stroud 5.00 10.00
16 Otis Taylor 6.00 12.00
17 Jerrel Wilson 5.00 10.00

1971 Chiefs Team Issue

This set of photos is a team-issued set. Each photo measures approximately 7 1/4" by 10" and features a black-and-white head shot bordered in white. The player's name and team name are printed in the lower white border, while the player's facsimile autograph is inscribed across the picture. The backs carry biography and career summary; some of the backs also have statistics. The photos are unnumbered and checklisted below in alphabetical order.

COMPLETE SET (13) 60.00 120.00
1 Bobby Bell 7.50 15.00
2 Wendell Hayes 5.00 10.00
3 Ed Lothamer 5.00 10.00
4 Jim Lynch 5.00 10.00
5 Mike Oriard 5.00 10.00
6 Jack Rudnay 5.00 10.00
7 Sid Smith 5.00 10.00
8 Bob Stein 5.00 10.00
9 Jan Stenerud 7.50 15.00
10 Hank Stram CO 7.50 15.00
11 Otis Taylor 6.00 12.00
12 Jim Tyrer 6.00 12.00
13 Marvin Upshaw 5.00 10.00

1972 Chiefs Team Issue

This set of photos was released by the Chiefs. Each photo measures approximately 7 1/4" by 10" and features a black-and-white head shot bordered in white. The player's name and team name are printed in the lower white border, while the player's facsimile autograph is inscribed across the picture. The backs on most carry biography and career summaries and other statistics while some were issued blankbacked as well. The photos are unnumbered and checklisted below in alphabetical order. Any additions to this list are appreciated.

COMPLETE SET (34) 150.00 300.00
1 Mike Adamle 5.00 10.00
2 Nate Allen 5.00 10.00
3 Buck Buchanan 7.50 15.00
4 Ed Budde 5.00 10.00
5 Curley Culp 5.00 10.00
6 George Daney 5.00 10.00
7 Willie Frazier 5.00 10.00
8 Wendell Hayes 5.00 10.00
9 Dave Hill 5.00 10.00
10 Dennis Homan 5.00 10.00
11 Bruce Jankowski 5.00 10.00
12 Jim Kearney 5.00 10.00
13 Jeff Kinney 5.00 10.00
14A Willie Lanier 7.50 15.00
14B Willie Lanier 7.50 15.00
15 Mike Livingston 5.00 10.00
16 Ed Lothamer 5.00 10.00
17 Jim Lynch 5.00 10.00
18 Jim Marsalis 5.00 10.00
19 Larry Marshall 5.00 10.00
20 Mo Moorman 5.00 10.00
21 Mike Oriard 5.00 10.00
22 Jim Otis 5.00 10.00
23 Ed Podolak 5.00 10.00
24 Kerry Reardon 5.00 10.00
25 Jack Rudnay 5.00 10.00
26A Mike Sensibaugh 5.00 10.00
26B Mike Sensibaugh 5.00 10.00
27 Sid Smith 5.00 10.00
28 Jan Stenerud 7.50 15.00
29 Otis Taylor 6.00 12.00
30 Jim Tyrer 5.00 10.00
31 Clyde Werner 5.00 10.00
32 Jerrel Wilson 5.00 10.00
33 Elmo Wright 5.00 10.00
34 Wilbur Young 5.00 10.00

1973 Chiefs Team Issue Color

The NFLPA worked with many teams in 1973 to issued photo packs to be sold at stadium concession stands. Each measures approximately 7" by 8-5/8" and features a color player photo with a blank back. A small sheet with a player checklist was included in each 6-photo pack.

COMPLETE SET (6) 30.00 60.00
1 Len Dawson 7.50 15.00
2 Bobby Bell 5.00 10.00
3 Willie Lanier 5.00 10.00
4 Jan Stenerud 5.00 10.00
5 Otis Taylor 4.00 8.00
6 Aaron Brown 4.00 8.00

1973-74 Chiefs Team Issue 5x7

This 18-card set of the Kansas City Chiefs measures approximately 5" by 7" and features black-and-white player photos with a white border. The backs are blank. The cards are unnumbered and checklisted below in alpabetical order.

COMPLETE SET (18) 60.00 120.00
1 Bob Briggs 4.00 8.00
2 Larry Brunson 4.00 8.00
3 Gary Butler 4.00 8.00
4 Dean Carlson 4.00 8.00
5 Tom Condon 4.00 8.00
6 George Daney 4.00 8.00
7 Andy Hamilton 4.00 8.00
8 Dave Hill 4.00 8.00
9 Jim Kearney 4.00 8.00
10 Mike Livingston 4.00 8.00
11 Jim Marsalis 4.00 8.00
12 Barry Pearson 4.00 8.00
13 Francis Peay 4.00 8.00
14 Kerry Reardon 4.00 8.00
15 Mike Sensibaugh 4.00 8.00
16 Bill Thomas 4.00 8.00
17 Marvin Upshaw 4.00 8.00
18 Clyde Werner 4.00 8.00

1973 Chiefs Team Issue 7x10

This set of the Kansas City Chiefs measures approximately 7 1/4" by 10 1/2" and features black-and-white player photos with a white border. The player's facsimile autograph appears across the photo with his name, position (initials), and team name below each photo. The backs are blank. The cards are unnumbered and checklisted below in alpabetical order.

COMPLETE SET (12) 50.00 100.00
1 Pete Beathard 5.00 10.00
2 Gary Butler 5.00 10.00
3 Dean Carlson 5.00 10.00
4 Willie Ellison 5.00 10.00
5 Andy Hamilton 5.00 10.00
6 Pat Holmes 5.00 10.00
7 Leroy Keyes 5.00 10.00
8 John Lohmeyer 5.00 10.00
9 Al Palewicz 5.00 10.00
10 Francis Peay 5.00 10.00
11 George Seals 5.00 10.00
12 Wayne Walton 5.00 10.00

1974 Chiefs Team Issue 7x10

Photos in this set of the Kansas City Chiefs measure approximately 7 1/4" by 10 1/4" and feature a black-and-white player image with a white border. The player's facsimile autograph appears across the photo with his name, position initials (unless noted below) and team name below each photo in small (1/8") letters. The backs are blank. The cards are unnumbered and checklisted below in alpabetical order.

COMPLETE SET (14) 50.00 100.00
1 Bobby Bell 5.00 10.00
2 Larry Brunson 4.00 8.00
3 Tom Condon 4.00 8.00
4 Len Dawson 7.50 15.00
5 Charlie Getty 4.00 8.00
6 Woody Green 4.00 8.00
7 Dave Jaynes 4.00 8.00
8 Doug Jones 4.00 8.00
9 Tom Keating 4.00 8.00
10 Cleo Miller 4.00 8.00
11 Jim Nicholson 4.00 8.00
12 Bill Thomas 4.00 8.00
13 Bob Thornbladh 4.00 8.00
14 Marvin Upshaw 4.00 8.00

1975 Chiefs Team Issue

Each of these photos measures approximately 7 1/4" by 10" and features a black-and-white head shot bordered in white. The player's name, his position (initials), and team name are printed in the lower white border, while the player's facsimile autograph is inscribed across the picture. The player name and position is printed in a different font (resembles typewriter print) than the 1976 issue. The backs carry a player biography and career summary; some of the backs also have statistics. The photos are unnumbered and checklisted below in alphabetical order. Any additions to this list are appreciated.

COMPLETE SET (19) 75.00 150.00
1 Tony Adams 4.00 8.00
2 Charlie Ane III 4.00 8.00
3 Ken Avery 4.00 8.00
4 Charlie Getty 4.00 8.00
5 Woody Green 4.00 8.00
6 Tim Kearney 4.00 8.00
7 Morris LaGrand 4.00 8.00
8 MacArthur Lane 4.00 10.00
9 Willie Lanier 5.00 10.00
10 Jim Lynch 4.00 8.00
11 Bob Maddox 4.00 8.00
12 Don Martin 4.00 8.00
13 Billy Masters 4.00 8.00
14 John Matuszak 5.00 10.00
15 Bill Peterson 4.00 8.00
16 Jan Stenerud 6.00 12.00
17 Charlie Thomas 4.00 8.00
18 Walter White 4.00 8.00
19 Paul Wiggin CO 4.00 8.00

1976 Chiefs Team Issue

This set of photos was released by the Chiefs with each measuring approximately 7 1/4" by 10." The photos include a black-and-white head shot bordered in white. The player's name appears at the left with his position (initials) in the middle and team name printed in script to the right all within the lower white border. The player's facsimile autograph is inscribed across the picture. The backs carry biography and career summary; some of the backs also have statistics. The photos are unnumbered and checklisted below in alphabetical order. Any additions to this list are appreciated.

COMPLETE SET (31) 100.00 200.00
1 Tony Adams 4.00 8.00
2 Billy Andrews 4.00 8.00
3 Charlie Ane III 4.00 8.00
4 Gary Barbaro 4.00 8.00
5 Larry Brunson 4.00 8.00
6 Tim Collier 4.00 8.00
7 Tom Condon 4.00 8.00
8 Jimbo Elrod 4.00 8.00
9 Lawrence Estes 4.00 8.00
10 Tim Gray 4.00 8.00
11 Matt Herkenhoff 4.00 8.00
12 MacArthur Lane 5.00 10.00
13 Willie Lee 4.00 8.00
14 John Lohmeyer 4.00 8.00
15 Henry Marshall 5.00 10.00
16 Billy Masters 4.00 8.00
17 Pat McNeil 4.00 8.00
18 Mike Nott 4.00 8.00
19 Orrin Olsen 4.00 8.00
20 Whitney Paul 4.00 8.00
21 Jack Rudnay 4.00 8.00
22 Keith Simons 4.00 8.00
23 Jan Stenerud 5.00 10.00
24 Steve Taylor 4.00 8.00
25 Emmitt Thomas 5.00 10.00
26 Rod Walters 4.00 8.00
27 Walter White 4.00 8.00
28 Larry Williams 4.00 8.00
29 Jerrel Wilson 4.00 8.00
30 Jim Wolf 4.00 8.00
31 Wilbur Young 4.00 8.00

1977 Chiefs Team Issue

This set of photos was released by the Chiefs with each measuring approximately 7 1/4" by 10." The photos include a black-and-white head shot bordered in white. The player's name appears at the left with his position in the middle and team name printed in script to the right all below the photo. The player's facsimile autograph is inscribed across the picture. The backs carry biographical information and/or a career summary and statistics. The photos are unnumbered and checklisted below in alphabetical order. Any additions to this list are appreciated.

COMPLETE SET (10) 40.00 80.00
1 Mark Bailey 4.00 8.00
2 Tom Bettis CO 4.00 8.00
3 John Brockington 5.00 10.00
4 Ricky Davis 4.00 8.00
5 Cliff Frazier 4.00 8.00
6 Darius Helton 4.00 8.00
7 Thomas Howard 4.00 8.00
8 Dave Rozumek 4.00 8.00
9 Bob Simmons 4.00 8.00
10 Ricky Wesson 4.00 8.00

1979 Chiefs Frito Lay

These black and white photos include the player's name, position (initials) and team name below the picture on the front. The cardbacks contain an extensive player bio and career statistics.

COMPLETE SET (8) 30.00 60.00
1 Brad Budde 4.00 8.00
2 Steve Gaunty 4.00 8.00
3 Dave Lindstrom 4.00 8.00
4 Arnold Morgado 4.00 8.00
5 Tony Samuels 4.00 8.00
6 Bob Simmons 4.00 8.00
7 Jan Stenerud 5.00 10.00
8 Art Still 4.00 8.00

1979 Chiefs Police

The 1979 Kansas City Chiefs Police set consists of ten cards co-sponsored by Hardee's Restaurants and the Kansas City (Missouri) Police Department, in addition to the Chiefs' football club. The cards measure approximately 2 5/8" by 4 1/8". The card backs discuss a football term and related legal/safety issue in a section entitled "Chief's Tips". The set is unnumbered but the player's uniform number appears on the front of the cards; the cards are numbered and ordered below by uniform number. The Chiefs' helmet logo is found on both the fronts and backs of the cards.

COMPLETE SET (10) 7.50 15.00
1 Bob Grupp .75 1.50
4 Steve Fuller 1.00 2.00
22 Ted McKnight .75 1.50

24 Gary Green	.75	1.50
26 Gary Barbaro	.75	1.50
32 Tony Reed	1.00	2.00
58 Jack Rudnay	.75	1.50
67 Art Still	1.00	2.00
73 Bob Simmons	.75	1.50
NNO Marv Levy CO	2.00	4.00

1979 Chiefs Team Issue

This set of Kansas City Chiefs players measures approximately 5" by 7" and features black-and-white player photos with a white border. The fronts include the player's name, position initials, and team name below the photo. The backs contain a player profile and stats but no sponsor logos. The cards are unnumbered and checklisted below in alpabetical order.

COMPLETE SET (20)	75.00	150.00
1 Mike Bell	4.00	8.00
2 Jerry Blanton	4.00	8.00
3 M.L. Carter	4.00	8.00
4 Earl Gant	4.00	8.00
5 Steve Gaunty	4.00	8.00
6 Bob Grupp	4.00	8.00
7 Charles Jackson	4.00	8.00
8 Gerald Jackson	4.00	8.00
9 Ken Kremer	4.00	8.00
10 Dave Lindstrom	4.00	8.00
11 Frank Manumaleuga	4.00	8.00
12 Arnold Morgado	4.00	8.00
13 Horace Perkins	4.00	8.00
14 Cal Peterson	4.00	8.00
15 Jerry Reese	4.00	8.00
16 Tony Samuels	4.00	8.00
17 Bob Simmons	4.00	8.00
18 J.T. Smith	5.00	10.00
19 Art Still	4.00	8.00
20 Mike Williams	4.00	8.00

1980 Chiefs Frito Lay

These black and white photos include the player's name, position initials and team name below the picture on the front. The cardbacks contain an extensive player bio and career statistics along with the Frito Lay logo.

COMPLETE SET (35)	125.00	250.00
1 Gary Barbaro	3.00	8.00
2 Ed Beckman	3.00	8.00
3 Mike Bell	3.00	8.00
4 Horace Belton	3.00	8.00
5 Jerry Blanton	3.00	8.00
6 Brad Budde	3.00	8.00
7 Carlos Carson	3.00	8.00
8 M.L. Carter	3.00	8.00
9 Herb Christopher	3.00	8.00
10 Tom Clements	4.00	10.00
11 Paul Dombrowski	3.00	8.00
12 Steve Fuller	3.00	8.00
13 Charlie Getty	3.00	8.00
14 Gary Green	3.00	8.00
15 Bob Grupp	3.00	8.00
16 James Hadnot	3.00	8.00
17 Eric Harris	3.00	8.00
18 Matt Herkenhoff	3.00	8.00
19 Thomas Howard	3.00	8.00
20 Charles Jackson	3.00	8.00
21 Dave Lindstrom	3.00	8.00
22 Mike Livingston	3.00	8.00
23 Nick Lowery	3.00	8.00
24 Dino Mangiero	3.00	8.00
25 Frank Manumaleuga	3.00	8.00
26 Henry Marshall	3.00	8.00
27 Ted McKnight	3.00	8.00
28 Don Parrish	3.00	8.00
29 Whitney Paul	3.00	8.00
30 Cal Peterson	3.00	8.00
31 Jim Rourke	3.00	8.00
32 J.T. Smith	4.00	10.00
33 Gary Spani	3.00	8.00
34 Art Still	3.00	8.00
35 Mike Williams	3.00	8.00

1980 Chiefs Police

The unnumbered, ten-card, 1980 Kansas City Chiefs Police set has been listed by the player's uniform number in the checklist below. The cards measure approximately 2 5/8" by 4 1/8". The Stenerud card was supposedly distributed on a limited basis and is thus more difficult to obtain. In addition to the Chiefs and the local law enforcement agencies, the set is sponsored by the Kiwanis Club and Frito-Lay, whose logos appear on the backs of the cards. The 1980 date can be found on the back of the cards as can "Chiefs Tips".

COMPLETE SET (10)	5.00	10.00
1 Bob Grupp	.40	1.00
3 Jan Stenerud SP	1.50	4.00
32 Tony Reed	.50	1.25
53 Whitney Paul	.40	1.00
59 Gary Spani	.40	1.00
67 Art Still	.60	1.50
86 J.T. Smith	.60	1.50
99 Mike Bell	.40	1.00
NNO Defensive Team	.50	1.25
NNO Offensive Team	.50	1.25

1980 Chiefs Team Issue

The Kansas City Chiefs issued this set of unnumbered photos that measure approximately 5" by 7" and contain black and white player photos. Each is similar to the Frito Lay photos except that there are no sponsor logos and the backs are blank. Any additions to this checklist would be appreciated.

COMPLETE SET (34)	125.00	250.00
1 Earl Gant	3.00	8.00
2 Bob Grupp	3.00	8.00
3 James Hadnot	3.00	8.00
4 Larry Heater	3.00	8.00
5 Matt Herkenhoff	3.00	8.00
6 Sylvester Hicks	3.00	8.00
7 Thomas Howard	3.00	8.00
8 Charles Jackson	3.00	8.00
9 Gerald Jackson	3.00	8.00
10 Bill Kellar	3.00	8.00
11 Bill Kenney	3.00	8.00
12 Bruce Kirchner	3.00	8.00
13 Ken Kremer	3.00	8.00
14 Frank Manumaleuga	3.00	8.00
15 Dale Markham	3.00	8.00
16 Henry Marshall	3.00	8.00
17 Ted McKnight	3.00	8.00
18 Arnold Morgado	3.00	8.00
19 Don Parrish	3.00	8.00
20 Cal Peterson	3.00	8.00
21 Tony Reed	3.00	8.00
22 Jerry Reese	3.00	8.00
23 Stan Rome	3.00	8.00
24 Donovan Rose	3.00	8.00
25 Jim Rourke	3.00	8.00
26 Jack Rudnay	3.00	8.00
27 Tony Samuels	3.00	8.00
28 Bob Simmons	3.00	8.00
29 Franky Smith	3.00	8.00
30 Kelvin Smith	3.00	8.00
31 Sam Stepney	3.00	8.00
32 Rod Walters	3.00	8.00
33 Mike Williams	3.00	8.00
34 Cecil Youngblood	3.00	8.00

1970 Chiquita Team Logo Stickers

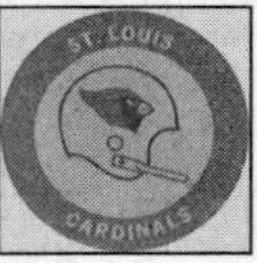

In 1970, Chiquita produced team logo stickers for the 26 pro football teams. We have sequenced these unnumbered stickers alphabetically below. Both Boston and New England Patriots versions of that team's sticker were issued allowing that these stickers may have first appeared in the late 1960s.

COMPLETE SET (26)	175.00	350.00
1 Atlanta Falcons	6.00	12.00
2 Baltimore Colts	7.50	15.00
3 Boston Patriots	20.00	40.00
4 Buffalo Bills	7.50	15.00
5 Chicago Bears	7.50	15.00
6 Cincinnati Bengals	6.00	12.00
7 Cleveland Browns	7.50	15.00
8 Dallas Cowboys	10.00	20.00
9 Denver Broncos	7.50	15.00
10 Detroit Lions	6.00	12.00
11 Green Bay Packers	10.00	20.00
12 Houston Oilers	6.00	12.00
13 Kansas City Chiefs	6.00	12.00
14 Los Angeles Rams	6.00	12.00
15 Miami Dolphins	7.50	15.00
16 Minnesota Vikings	7.50	15.00
17 New England Patriots	6.00	12.00
18 New Orleans Saints	6.00	12.00
19 New York Giants	7.50	15.00
20 New York Jets	7.50	15.00
21 Oakland Raiders	10.00	20.00
22 Philadelphia Eagles	6.00	12.00
23 Pittsburgh Steelers	10.00	20.00
24 San Diego Chargers	6.00	12.00
25 San Francisco 49ers	7.50	15.00
26 St. Louis Cardinals	6.00	12.00
27 Washington Redskins	7.50	15.00

1972 Chiquita NFL Slides

This set consists of 13-slides and a plastic viewer for viewing the slides. Each slide measures approximately 3 9/16" by 1 3/4" and features two players (one on each side); each of the 26 NFL teams is represented by one player. Each side has a player summary on its middle portion, with two small color action slides at each end stacked one above the other. When the slide is placed in the viewer, the two bottom slides, which are identical, reveal the first player. Flipping the slide over reveals the other player biography and enables one to view the other two slides, which show the second player. The text on each slide can be found printed in either black or blue ink. Each side of the slides is numbered as listed below. The set is considered complete without the viewer. In 1972, collectors could receive a viewer and a complete set of 13-slides by sending in 35-cents, 5-NFL Logo Stickers from Chiquita bananas, and a cash register receipt showing $15 worth of produce purchases made at the store.

COMPLETE SET (13)	40.00	100.00
*BLUE: .5X TO 1.2X BLACK		
1 Joe Greene B.Lilly	12.50	30.00
3 Bill Bergey G.Collins	5.00	12.00
5 Walt Sweeney Bub.Smith	4.00	10.00
7 Larry Wilson Fred Carr	5.00	12.00
9 Mac Percival John Brodie	5.00	12.00
11 Lem Barney Ron Yary	5.00	12.00
13 Curt Knight A.Haymond	4.00	10.00
15 Floyd Little G.Philbin	5.00	12.00
17 Jim Mitchell Paul Costa	4.00	10.00
19 Jake Kupp Ben Hawkins	4.00	10.00
21 Johnny Robinson G.Webster	4.00	10.00
23 Mercury Morris Willie Brown	6.00	15.00
25 Ron Johnson Jon Morris	4.00	10.00
NNO Yellow Viewer	6.00	15.00
NNO Red Viewer	6.00	15.00
NNO Blue Viewer	6.00	15.00

1970 Clark Volpe

This 66-card set is actually a collection of team sets. Each team subset contains between six and nine cards. These unnumbered cards are listed below alphabetically by player within team as follows: Chicago Bears (1-8), Cincinnati Bengals (9-14), Cleveland Browns (15-21), Detroit Lions (22-30), Green Bay Packers (31-39), Kansas City Chiefs (40-48), Minnesota Vikings (49-57), St. Louis Cardinals (58-66). The cards measure approximately 7 1/2" by 9 15/16" (or 7 1/2" by 14" with mail-in tab intact). The back of the (top) drawing portion describes the mail-in offers for tumblers, posters, etc. The bottom tab is a business-reply mail-in card addressed to Clark Oil and Refining Corporation to the attention of Alex Karras. The artist for these drawings was Nicholas Volpe. The cards are typically found with tabs intact and hence they are priced that way below.

COMPLETE SET (66)	200.00	400.00
1 Ronnie Bull	4.00	8.00
2 Dick Butkus	15.00	30.00
3 Lee Roy Caffey	4.00	8.00
4 Bobby Douglass	4.00	8.00
5 Dick Gordon	4.00	8.00
6 Bennie McRae	4.00	8.00
7 Ed O'Bradovich	4.00	8.00
8 George Seals	4.00	8.00
9 Bill Bergey	5.00	10.00
10 Jess Phillips	4.00	8.00
11 Mike Reid	5.00	10.00
12 Paul Robinson	4.00	8.00
13 Bob Trumpy	5.00	10.00
14 Sam Wyche	5.00	10.00
15 Erich Barnes	4.00	8.00
16 Gary Collins	4.00	8.00
17 Gene Hickerson	5.00	10.00
18 Jim Houston	4.00	8.00
19 Leroy Kelly	6.00	12.00
20 Ernie Kellerman	4.00	8.00
21 Bill Nelsen	4.00	8.00
22 Lem Barney	6.00	12.00
23 Mel Farr	4.00	8.00
24 Larry Hand	4.00	8.00
25 Alex Karras	7.50	15.00
26 Mike Lucci	4.00	8.00
27 Bill Munson	4.00	8.00
28 Charlie Sanders	5.00	10.00
29 Tom Vaughn	4.00	8.00
30 Wayne Walker	4.00	8.00
31 Lionel Aldridge	4.00	8.00
32 Donny Anderson	5.00	10.00
33 Ken Bowman	4.00	8.00
34 Carroll Dale	4.00	8.00
35 Jim Grabowski	4.00	8.00
36 Ray Nitschke	7.50	15.00
37 Dave Robinson	5.00	10.00
38 Travis Williams	4.00	8.00
39 Willie Wood	6.00	12.00
40 Fred Arbanas	4.00	8.00
41 Bobby Bell	6.00	12.00
42 Aaron Brown	4.00	8.00
43 Buck Buchanan	6.00	12.00
44 Len Dawson	12.50	25.00
45 Jim Marsalis	4.00	8.00
46 Jerry Mays	4.00	8.00
47 Johnny Robinson	4.00	8.00
48 Jim Tyrer	4.00	8.00
49 Bill Brown	5.00	10.00
50 Fred Cox	4.00	8.00
51 Gary Cuozzo	4.00	8.00
52 Carl Eller	6.00	12.00
53 Jim Marshall	6.00	12.00
54 Dave Osborn	4.00	8.00
55 Alan Page	7.50	15.00
56 Mick Tingelhoff	5.00	10.00
57 Gene Washington Vik	4.00	8.00
58 Pete Beathard	4.00	8.00
59 John Gilliam	4.00	8.00
60 Jim Hart	5.00	10.00
61 Johnny Roland	4.00	8.00
62 Jackie Smith	6.00	12.00
63 Larry Stallings	4.00	8.00
64 Roger Wehrli	5.00	10.00
65 Dave Williams	4.00	8.00
66 Larry Wilson	6.00	12.00

1962 Cleveland Bulldogs UFL Picture Pack

Big League Books produced and distributed this set of 5" by 7" photos for the Cleveland Bulldogs of the United Football League. This semi-pro league was centered in the Midwest and consisted of 7-teams. It's likely that each of the teams had a similar set produced, and any additional information on those would be appreciated.

COMPLETE SET (10)	75.00	150.00
1 Dave Adams Gordon Helms	7.50	15.00
2 Bob Alford Leo Bland	7.50	15.00
3 Bob Brodhead	10.00	20.00
4 John Drew Bill Eyesdom Ed Nemetz	7.50	15.00
5 Clay Hill Gary Hostetler	7.50	15.00
6 Clark Kellogg Bill Slacas	7.50	15.00
7 Dick Louis Frank Mancini	7.50	15.00
8 Dick Newsome Paul Pirrone	7.50	15.00
9 Coaching Staff	7.50	15.00
10 Officers	7.50	15.00

1963 Coke Caps Chargers

Little is actually known about these recently discovered Coke Caps but they are thought to be a scarce test issue to the more common Coke Cap series released nationally from 1964-1966. Each is similar in format to the 1964 release but coaches were included in this test issue and the player caps include the player's jersey number and position initials below the image. The set includes the earliest known Al Davis football collectible.

1 Lance Alworth	25.00	50.00
2 Frank Buncom	10.00	20.00
3 Reg Carolan	10.00	20.00
4 Al Davis CO	60.00	100.00
5 Wayne Frazier	10.00	20.00
6 Sid Gillman CO	15.00	30.00
7 George Gross	10.00	20.00
8 Sam Gruneisen	10.00	20.00
9 Rufus Guthrie	10.00	20.00
10 John Hadl	15.00	30.00
11 Bob Jackson	10.00	20.00
12 Emil Karas	10.00	20.00
13 Keith Kinderman	10.00	20.00
14 Ernie Ladd	12.50	25.00
15 Keith Lincoln	12.50	25.00
16 Gerry McDougall	10.00	20.00
17 Charlie McNeil	10.00	20.00
18 Ron Mix	15.00	30.00
19 Chuck Noll CO	25.00	50.00
20 Tobin Rote	12.50	25.00
21 Pat Shea	10.00	20.00

1964 Coke Caps All-Stars AFL

These AFL All-Star caps were issued in AFL cities (and a few other cities as well) along with the local team caps as part of the Go with the Pros promotion. The AFL team Cap Saver sheets had separate sections in which to affix the local team's player caps, the AFL team logos, and the All-Stars' caps. The caps measure approximately 1 1/8" in diameter and have the drink logo and a football on the outside, while the inside has the player's face printed in black, with text surrounding the face. The consumer could turn in his completed saver sheet to receive various prizes. The caps are unnumbered, but have been alphabetically listed below. These caps were also produced for 1964 on Sprite and King Size Coke bottles. Sprite caps typically carry a slight premium over the value of the Coke version.

COMPLETE SET (44)	100.00	200.00
1 Tommy Addison	1.75	3.50
2 Dalva Allen	1.75	3.50
3 Lance Alworth	7.50	15.00
4 Houston Antwine	1.75	3.50
5 Fred Arbanas	1.75	3.50
6 Tony Banfield	1.75	3.50
7 Stew Barber	1.75	3.50
8 George Blair	1.75	3.50
9 Mel Branch	1.75	3.50
10 Nick Buoniconti	3.75	7.50
11 Doug Cline	1.75	3.50
12 Eldon Danenhauer	1.75	3.50
13 Clem Daniels	2.00	4.00
14 Larry Eisenhauer	1.75	3.50
15 Earl Faison	1.75	3.50
16 Cookie Gilchrist	2.00	5.00
17 Freddy Glick	1.75	3.50
18 Larry Grantham	2.00	4.00
19 Ron Hall	1.75	3.50
20 Charlie Hennigan	2.00	4.00
21 E.J. Holub	2.00	4.00
22 Ed Husmann	1.75	3.50
23 Jack Kemp	12.50	25.00
24 Dave Kocourek	1.75	3.50
25 Keith Lincoln	2.00	4.00
26 Charles Long	1.75	3.50
27 Paul Lowe	2.00	4.00
28 Archie Matsos	1.75	3.50
29 Jerry Mays	2.00	4.00
30 Ron Mix	3.00	6.00
31 Tom Morrow	1.75	3.50
32 Billy Neighbors	2.00	4.00
33 Jim Otto	3.75	7.50
34 Art Powell	2.00	4.00
35 Johnny Robinson	2.00	4.00
36 Tobin Rote	2.00	4.00
37 Bob Schmidt	1.75	3.50
38 Tom Sestak	1.75	3.50
39 Billy Shaw	2.00	4.00
40 Bob Talamini	1.75	3.50
41 Lionel Taylor	2.00	4.00
42 Jim Tyrer	2.00	4.00
43 Dick Westmoreland	1.75	3.50
44 Fred Williamson	2.00	5.00

1964 Coke Caps All-Stars NFL

These NFL All-Star caps were issued in NFL cities (and a few other cities as well) along with the local team caps as part of the Go with the Pros promotion. The NFL team Cap Saver sheets had separate sections in which to affix the local team's player caps, the NFL team logos, and the All-Stars' caps. The caps measure approximately 1 1/8" in diameter and have the drink logo and a football on the outside, while the inside has the player's face printed in black, with text surrounding the face. The consumer could turn in his completed saver sheet to receive various prizes. The caps are unnumbered, but have been alphabetically listed below. These caps were also produced for 1964 on Sprite and King Size Coke bottles. Sprite caps typically carry a slight premium over the value of the Coke version.

COMPLETE SET (44)	100.00	200.00
1 Doug Atkins	3.00	6.00
2 Terry Barr	1.25	2.50
3 Jim Brown	12.50	25.00
4 Roger Brown	2.00	4.00
5 Roosevelt Brown	2.50	5.00
6 Timmy Brown	2.00	4.00
7 Bobby Joe Conrad	2.00	4.00
8 Willie Davis	3.00	6.00
9 Bob DeMarco	1.25	2.50
10 Darrell Dess	1.25	2.50
11 Mike Ditka	7.50	15.00
12 Bill Forester	1.25	2.50
13 Joe Fortunato	1.25	2.50
14 Bill George	3.00	6.00
15 Ken Gray	1.25	2.50
16 Forrest Gregg	3.00	6.00
17 Roosevelt Grier	2.50	5.00
18 Hank Jordan	3.00	6.00
19 Jim Katcavage	2.00	4.00
20 Jerry Kramer	2.50	5.00
21 Ron Kramer	1.25	2.50
22 Dick Lane	3.00	6.00
23 Dick Lynch	1.25	2.50
24 Gino Marchetti	3.00	6.00
25 Tommy Mason	2.00	4.00
26 Ed Meador	1.25	2.50
27 Bobby Mitchell	3.00	6.00
28 Larry Morris	1.25	2.50
29 Merlin Olsen	4.00	8.00
30 Jim Parker	2.50	5.00
31 Jim Patton	2.00	4.00
32 Myron Pottios	1.25	2.50
33 Jim Ringo	2.50	5.00
34 Dick Schafrath	1.25	2.50
35 Joe Schmidt	3.00	6.00
36 Del Shofner	2.00	4.00
37 Bob St. Clair	2.50	5.00
38 Jim Taylor	4.00	8.00
39 Roosevelt Taylor	2.00	4.00
40 Y.A. Tittle	5.00	10.00
41 Johnny Unitas	7.50	15.00
42 Larry Wilson	3.00	6.00
43 Willie Wood	3.00	6.00
44 Abe Woodson	2.00	4.00

1964 Coke Caps Bears

Coke caps were issued in each NFL city (except for the St.Louis Cardinals) featuring 35-members of that team along with the NFL All-Stars caps as part of the 1964 Go with the Pros promotion. The NFL team Cap Saver sheets had separate sections in which to affix both the local team's caps, the NFL team logos, and the All-Stars' caps. The caps measure approximately 1 1/8" in diameter and have the drink logo and a football on the outside, while the inside has the player's face printed in black with the team name above the photo, the player's name below, his jersey number to the left and his position to the right. Most caps were issued with either a plastic or cork liner on the inside. The consumer could turn in his completed saver sheet (before the expiration date of Nov. 21, 1964) to receive various prizes. The 1964 caps look very similar to those issued in 1965 and 1966 but were numbered only according to the player's jersey number. We've arranged them alphabetically by team for ease in cataloging. Football caps were produced for Coca-Cola, Sprite and King Size Coke bottles. Sprite caps typically carry a slight premium over the value of the Coke version.

COMPLETE SET (35)	75.00	150.00
1 Doug Atkins	4.00	8.00
2 Steve Barnett	1.50	3.00
3 Charlie Bivins	1.50	3.00
4 Rudy Bukich	2.50	4.00
5 Ronnie Bull	2.50	4.00
6 Jim Cadile	1.50	3.00
7 J.C. Caroline	1.50	3.00
8 Rick Casares	2.50	4.00
9 Roger Davis	1.50	3.00
10 Mike Ditka	6.00	12.00
11 John Farrington	1.50	3.00
12 Joe Fortunato	1.50	3.00
13 Willie Galimore	2.50	4.00
14 Bill George	3.50	6.00
15 Larry Glueck	1.50	3.00
16 Bobby Joe Green	1.50	3.00
17 Bob Jencks	1.50	3.00
18 John Johnson	1.50	3.00
19 Stan Jones	3.50	6.00
20 Ted Karras	1.50	3.00
21 Bob Kilcullen	1.50	3.00
22 Roger LeClerc	1.50	3.00
23 Herman Lee	1.50	3.00
24 Earl Leggett	1.50	3.00
25 Joe Marconi	1.50	3.00
26 Bennie McRae	1.50	3.00
27 Johnny Morris	1.50	3.00
28 Larry Morris	1.50	3.00
29 Ed O'Bradovich	1.50	3.00
30 Richie Petitbon	2.50	4.00
31 Mike Pyle	1.50	3.00
32 Roosevelt Taylor	2.50	4.00
33 Bill Wade	2.50	4.00
34 Bob Wetoska	1.50	3.00
35 Dave Whitsell	1.50	3.00
NNO Bears Saver Sheet	15.00	30.00

1964 Coke Caps Browns

Please see the 1964 Coke Caps Bears listing for information on this set.

COMPLETE SET (35)	75.00	150.00
1 Walter Beach	1.50	3.00
2 Larry Benz	1.50	3.00
3 Johnny Brewer	1.50	3.00
4 Jim Brown	15.00	30.00
5 John Brown	1.50	3.00
6 Monte Clark	1.50	3.00
7 Gary Collins	2.50	5.00
8 Vince Costello	1.50	3.00
9 Ross Fichtner	1.50	3.00
10 Galen Fiss	1.50	3.00
11 Bobby Franklin	1.50	3.00
12 Bob Gain	2.00	4.00
13 Bill Glass	2.00	4.00
14 Ernie Green	1.50	3.00
15 Lou Groza	5.00	10.00
16 Gene Hickerson	2.00	4.00
17 Jim Houston	1.50	3.00
18 Tom Hutchinson	1.50	3.00
19 Jim Kanicki	1.50	3.00
20 Mike Lucci	2.00	4.00
21 Dick Modzelewski	2.00	4.00
22 John Morrow	1.50	3.00
23 Jim Ninowski	2.00	4.00
24 Frank Parker	1.50	3.00
25 Bernie Parrish	2.00	4.00
26 Frank Ryan	2.50	5.00
27 Charlie Scales	1.50	3.00
28 Dick Schafrath	2.00	4.00
29 Roger Shoals	1.50	3.00
30 Jim Shorter	1.50	3.00
31 Billy Truax	2.00	4.00
32 Paul Warfield	7.50	15.00
33 Ken Webb	1.50	3.00
34 Paul Wiggin	1.50	3.00
35 John Wooten	2.00	4.00
NNO Browns Saver Sheet	15.00	30.00

1964 Coke Caps Chargers

Coke caps were issued in each AFL city, except Buffalo, featuring 35-members of that team along with the AFL All-Stars caps as part of the 1964 Go with the Pros promotion. The AFL team Cap Saver sheets had separate sections in which to affix both the local team's caps, all of the AFL team logos, and the AFL All-Star caps. The caps measure approximately 1 1/8" in diameter and have the drink logo and a football on the outside, while the inside has the player's face printed in black with the team name above the photo, the player's name below, his jersey number to the left and his position to the right. Most caps were issued with either a plastic or cork liner on the inside. The consumer could turn in his completed saver sheet (before the expiration date of Nov. 21, 1964) to receive various prizes. The 1964 caps look very similar to those issued in 1965 and 1966 but were numbered only according to the player's jersey number. We've arranged them alphabetically by team for ease in cataloging. Football caps were produced for Coca-Cola, Sprite and King Size Coke bottles. Sprite caps typically carry a slight premium over the value of the Coke version.

COMPLETE SET (35)	100.00	175.00
1 Chuck Allen	2.50	5.00
2 Lance Alworth	10.00	20.00
3 George Blair	2.00	4.00
4 Frank Buncom	2.00	4.00
5 Earl Faison	2.50	5.00
6 Kenny Graham	2.00	4.00
7 George Gross	2.00	4.00
8 Sam Gruneisen	2.00	4.00
9 John Hadl	5.00	10.00
10 Dick Harris	2.50	5.00
11 Bob Jackson FB	2.00	4.00
12 Emil Karas	2.00	4.00
13 Dave Kocourek	2.00	4.00
14 Ernie Ladd	5.00	10.00
15 Bob Lane	2.00	4.00
16 Keith Lincoln	3.00	6.00
17 Paul Lowe	3.00	6.00
18 Jacque MacKinnon	2.00	4.00
19 Gerry McDougall	2.00	4.00
20 Charlie McNeil	2.50	5.00
21 Bob Mitinger	2.00	4.00
22 Ron Mix	5.00	10.00
23 Don Norton	2.00	4.00
24 Ernie Park	2.00	4.00
25 Bob Petrich	2.00	4.00
26 Jerry Robinson	2.00	4.00
27 Don Rogers	2.00	4.00
28 Tobin Rote	2.50	5.00
29 Henry Schmidt	2.00	4.00
30 Pat Shea	2.00	4.00
31 Walt Sweeney	2.50	5.00
32 Jim Warren	2.00	4.00
33 Dick Westmoreland	2.50	5.00
34 Bud Whitehead	2.00	4.00
35 Ernie Wright	2.50	5.00
NNO Chargers Saver Sheet	15.00	30.00

1964 Coke Caps Eagles

Please see the 1964 Coke Caps Bears listing for information on this set.

COMPLETE SET (35)	75.00	150.00
1 Mickey Babb	2.00	3.00
2 Sam Baker	2.00	3.00
3 Maxie Baughan	2.00	3.00
4 Ed Blaine	2.00	3.00
5 Bob Brown	2.50	4.00
6 Timmy Brown	2.50	4.00
7 Don Burroughs	2.00	3.00
8 Pete Case	2.00	3.00
9 Jack Concannon	2.50	4.00
10 Claude Crabb	2.00	3.00
11 Glenn Glass	2.00	3.00
12 Ron Goodwin	2.00	3.00
13 Dave Graham	2.00	3.00
14 Earl Gros	2.00	3.00
15 Riley Gunnels	2.00	3.00
16 King Hill	2.50	4.00
17 Lynn Hoyem	2.00	3.00
18 Don Hultz	2.00	3.00
19 Terry Kosens	2.00	3.00
20 Chuck Lamson	2.00	3.00
21 Dave Lloyd	2.00	3.00
22 Red Mack	2.00	3.00
23 Ollie Matson	6.00	10.00
24 John Mellekas	2.00	3.00
25 John Meyers	2.00	3.00
26 Floyd Peters	2.50	4.00
27 Ray Poage	2.00	3.00
28 Nate Ramsey	2.00	3.00
29 Pete Retzlaff	2.50	4.00
30 Jim Ringo	5.00	8.00
31 Jim Skaggs	2.00	3.00
32 Ralph Smith	2.00	3.00
33 Norm Snead	3.00	5.00
34 George Tarasovic	2.00	3.00
35 Tom Woodeshick	2.50	4.00
NNO Eagles Saver Sheet	15.00	30.00

1964 Coke Caps 49ers

Please see the 1964 Coke Caps Bears listing for information on this set.

COMPLETE SET (35)	75.00	150.00
1 Kermit Alexander	2.00	3.00
2 Bruce Bosley	2.00	3.00
3 John Brodie	4.00	8.00
4 Vern Burke	2.00	3.00
5 Bernie Casey	2.50	4.00
6 Dan Colchico	2.00	3.00
7 Clyde Conner	2.00	3.00
8 Bill Cooper	2.00	3.00
9 Tommy Davis	2.50	4.00
10 Leon Donohue	2.00	3.00
11 Mike Dowdle	2.00	3.00
12 Matt Hazeltine	2.00	3.00
13 Jim Johnson	3.00	5.00
14 Billy Kilmer	3.60	6.00
15 Elbert Kimbrough	2.00	3.00
16 Charlie Krueger	2.00	3.00
17 Roland Lakes	2.00	3.00
18 Don Lisbon	2.00	3.00
19 Mike Magac	2.00	3.00
20 Jerry Mertens	2.00	3.00
21 Dave Messer	2.00	3.00
22 Clark Miller	2.00	3.00
23 George Mira	2.50	4.00
24 Dave Parks	2.50	4.00
25 Ed Pine	2.00	3.00
26 Walter Rock	2.00	3.00
27 Len Rohde	2.00	3.00
28 Karl Rubke	2.00	3.00
29 Bob St. Clair	3.00	5.00
30 Charlie Sieminski	2.00	3.00
31 J.D. Smith	2.50	4.00
32 Monty Stickles	2.00	3.00
33 John Thomas	2.00	3.00
34 Jim Vollenweider	2.00	3.00
35 Abe Woodson	2.50	4.00
NNO 49ers Saver Sheet	15.00	30.00

1964 Coke Caps Giants

Please see the 1964 Coke Caps Bears listing for information on this set.

COMPLETE SET (38)	75.00	150.00
1 Roger Anderson	1.50	4.00
2 Erich Barnes	1.50	4.00
3 Bookie Bolin UER	1.50	4.00
4 Ken Byers	1.50	4.00
5 Roosevelt Brown	2.50	6.00
6 Don Chandler	2.00	5.00
7 Bob Crespino	1.50	4.00
8 Darrell Dess	1.50	4.00
9 Ed Dove	1.50	4.00
10 Frank Gifford	5.00	4.00
11 Glynn Griffing	1.50	4.00
12 Jerry Hillebrand	1.50	4.00
13 Lane Howell	1.50	4.00
14 Dick James	1.50	4.00
15 Jim Katcavage	2.00	5.00
16 Charlie Killett	1.50	4.00
17 Phil King	1.50	4.00
18 Lou Kirouac	1.50	4.00
19 Greg Larson	1.50	4.00
20 Joe Don Looney	2.00	5.00
21 John LoVetere	1.50	4.00
22 Dick Lynch	1.50	4.00
23 Jim Moran	1.50	4.00
24 Joe Morrison	2.00	5.00
25 Jimmy Patton	1.50	4.00
26 Dick Pesonen	1.50	4.00
27 Tom Scott	1.50	4.00
28 Del Shofner	2.00	5.00
29 Jack Stroud	1.50	4.00
30 Andy Stynchula	1.50	4.00
31 Aaron Thomas	1.50	4.00
32 Bob Timberlake	1.50	4.00
33 Y.A. Tittle	6.00	12.00
34 Mickey Walker	1.50	4.00
35 Joe Walton	1.50	4.00
36 Allan Webb	1.50	4.00
37 Alex Webster	2.00	5.00
38 Bill Winter	1.50	4.00

1964 Coke Caps Lions

Please see the 1964 Coke Caps Bears listing for information on this set.

COMPLETE SET (35)	75.00	150.00
1 Terry Barr	1.50	3.00
2 Carl Brettschneider	1.50	3.00
3 Roger Brown	2.00	4.00
4 Mike Bundra	1.50	3.00
5 Ernie Clark	1.50	3.00
6 Gail Cogdill	2.00	4.00
7 Larry Ferguson	1.50	3.00
8 Dennis Gaubatz	1.50	3.00
9 Jim Gibbons	2.00	4.00
10 John Gonzaga	1.50	3.00
11 John Gordy	1.50	3.00
12 Tom Hall	1.50	3.00
13 Alex Karras	5.00	10.00
14 Dick Lane	4.00	8.00
15 Dan LaRose	1.50	3.00
16 Yale Lary	4.00	8.00
17 Dick LeBeau	2.00	4.00
18 Dan Lewis	1.50	3.00
19 Gary Lowe	1.50	3.00
20 Bruce Maher	1.50	3.00
21 Darris McCord	1.50	3.00
22 Max Messner	1.50	3.00
23 Earl Morrall	3.00	6.00
24 Nick Pietrosante	2.00	4.00
25 Milt Plum	2.50	5.00
26 Daryl Sanders	1.50	3.00
27 Joe Schmidt	5.00	10.00
28 Bob Scholtz	1.50	3.00

29 J.D. Smith T	2.00	4.00
30 Pat Studstill	2.00	4.00
31 Larry Vargo	1.50	3.00
32 Wayne Walker	2.00	4.00
33 Tom Watkins	1.50	3.00
34 Bob Whitlow	1.50	3.00
35 Sam Williams	1.50	3.00
NNO Lions Saver Sheet	15.00	30.00

1964 Coke Caps National NFL

This set of 68 Coke caps was issued on bottled soft drinks primarily in cities without an NFL team. The caps were issued along with their own Saver Sheet. Each measures approximately 1 1/8" in diameter and has the drink logo and a football on the outside, while the inside has the player's face printed with text surrounding the face. An "NFL ALL STARS" title appears above the player's photo, therefore some players below appear in both this set and the NFL All-Stars set listing. The consumer could turn in his completed saver sheet to receive various prizes. The caps are unnumbered and checklisted below in alphabetical order. Football caps were also produced for Sprite and King Size Coke bottles. Sprite caps typically carry a slight premium over the value of the Coke version.

COMPLETE SET (68)	125.00	250.00
1 Herb Adderley	2.50	5.00
2 Grady Alderman	1.50	3.00
3 Doug Atkins	3.00	6.00
4 Sam Baker	1.50	3.00
5 Erich Barnes	1.50	3.00
6 Terry Barr	1.50	3.00
7 Dick Bass	1.50	3.00
8 Maxie Baughan	1.50	3.00
9 Raymond Berry	3.00	6.00
10 Charley Bradshaw	1.50	3.00
11 Jim Brown	12.50	25.00
12 Roger Brown	1.50	3.00
13 Timmy Brown	1.50	3.00
14 Gail Cogdill	1.50	3.00
15 Tommy Davis	1.50	3.00
16 Willie Davis	1.50	3.00
17 Bob DeMarco	1.50	3.00
18 Darrell Dess	1.50	3.00
19 Buddy Dial	2.00	4.00
20 Mike Ditka	7.50	15.00
21 Galen Fiss	1.50	3.00
22 Lee Folkins	1.50	3.00
23 Joe Fortunato	1.50	3.00
24 Bill Glass	1.50	3.00
25 John Gordy	1.50	3.00
26 Ken Gray	1.50	3.00
27 Forrest Gregg	3.00	6.00
28 Rip Hawkins	1.50	3.00
29 Charley Johnson	2.00	4.00
30 John Henry Johnson	2.50	5.00
31 Hank Jordan	2.50	5.00
32 Jim Katcavage	1.50	3.00
33 Jerry Kramer	2.50	5.00
34 Joe Krupa	1.50	3.00
35 John Lovetere	1.50	3.00
36 Dick Lynch	1.50	3.00
37 John Mackey	3.00	6.00
38 Gino Marchetti	2.50	5.00
39 Joe Marconi	1.50	3.00
40 Tommy Mason	1.50	3.00
41 Dale Meinert	1.50	3.00
42 Lou Michaels	2.00	4.00
43 Bobby Mitchell	3.00	6.00
44 John Morrow	1.50	3.00
45 Merlin Olsen	4.00	8.00
46 Jack Pardee	2.00	4.00
47 Jim Parker	1.50	3.00
48 Bernie Parrish	1.50	3.00
49 Don Perkins	2.00	4.00
50 Richie Petitbon	1.50	3.00
51 Myron Pottios	1.50	3.00
52 Vince Promuto	1.50	3.00
53 Mike Pyle	1.50	3.00
54 Pete Retzlaff	2.00	4.00
55 Jim Ringo	2.50	5.00
56 Joe Rutgens	1.50	3.00
57 Dick Schafrath	1.50	3.00
58 Del Shofner	1.50	3.00
59 Jim Taylor	3.75	7.50
60 Roosevelt Taylor	1.50	3.00
61 Clendon Thomas	1.50	3.00
62 Y.A. Tittle	5.00	10.00
63 John Unitas	7.50	15.00
64 Bill Wade	1.50	3.00
65 Wayne Walker	1.50	3.00
66 Jesse Whittenton	2.00	4.00
67 Larry Wilson	2.50	5.00
68 Abe Woodson	2.00	4.00
NNO NFL All-Star Saver Sheet	15.00	30.00

1964 Coke Caps Oilers

Please see the 1964 Coke Caps Chargers listing for information on this set.

COMPLETE SET (35)	90.00	150.00
1 Scott Appleton	2.00	4.00
2 Johnny Baker	2.00	4.00
3 Tony Banfield	2.00	4.00
4 George Blanda	10.00	20.00
5 Danny Brabham	2.00	4.00
6 Ode Burrell	2.00	4.00
7 Billy Cannon	3.00	6.00
8 Doug Cline	2.00	4.00
9 Bobby Crenshaw	2.00	4.00
10 Gary Cutsinger	2.00	4.00
11 Willard Dewveall	2.00	4.00
12 Mike Dukes	2.00	4.00
13 Staley Faulkner	2.00	4.00
14 Don Floyd	2.00	4.00
15 Freddy Glick	2.00	4.00
16 Tom Goode	2.00	4.00
17 Charlie Hennigan	2.50	5.00
18 Ed Husmann	2.00	4.00
19 Bobby Jancik	2.00	4.00
20 Mark Johnston	2.00	4.00
21 Jacky Lee	2.50	5.00
22 Bob McLeod	2.00	4.00
23 Dudley Meredith	2.00	4.00
24 Rich Michael	2.00	4.00
25 Benny Nelson	2.00	4.00
26 Jim Norton	2.50	5.00
27 Larry Onesti	2.00	4.00
28 Bob Schmidt	2.00	4.00
29 Dave Smith	2.00	4.00
30 Walt Suggs	2.00	4.00
31 Bob Talamini	2.00	4.00
32 Charley Tolar	2.00	4.00
33 Don Trull	2.50	5.00
34 John Varnell	2.00	4.00
35 Hogan Wharton	2.00	4.00

1964 Coke Caps Packers

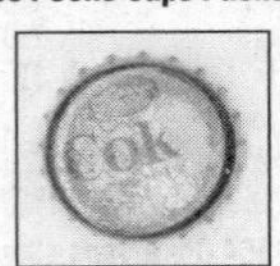

Please see the 1964 Coke Caps Bears listing for information on this set.

COMPLETE SET (35)	125.00	225.00
1 Herb Adderley	4.00	8.00
2 Lionel Aldridge	3.00	5.00
3 Zeke Bratkowski	3.00	5.00
4 Lee Roy Caffey	2.50	4.00
5 Dennis Claridge	2.50	4.00
6 Dan Currie	2.50	4.00
7 Willie Davis	4.00	8.00
8 Boyd Dowler	3.00	5.00
9 Marv Fleming	3.00	5.00
10 Forrest Gregg	4.00	8.00
11 Hank Gremminger	2.50	4.00
12 Dan Grimm	2.50	4.00
13 Dave Hanner	3.00	5.00
14 Urban Henry	2.50	4.00
15 Paul Hornung	10.00	20.00
16 Bob Jeter	3.00	5.00
17 Hank Jordan	4.00	8.00
18 Ron Kostelnik	2.50	4.00
19 Jerry Kramer	3.00	6.00
20 Ron Kramer	2.50	4.00
21 Norm Masters	2.50	4.00
22 Max McGee	3.00	5.00
23 Frank Mestnik	2.50	4.00
24 Tom Moore	3.00	5.00
25 Ray Nitschke	6.00	12.00
26 Jerry Norton	2.50	4.00
27 Elijah Pitts	3.00	5.00
28 Dave Robinson	3.50	6.00
29 Bob Skoronski	2.50	4.00
30 Bart Starr	12.50	25.00
31 Jim Taylor	6.00	12.00
32 Fuzzy Thurston	4.00	8.00
33 Lloyd Voss	2.50	4.00
34 Jesse Whittenton	2.50	4.00
35 Willie Wood	4.00	8.00
NNO Packers Saver Sheet	20.00	40.00

1964 Coke Caps Patriots

Please see the 1964 Coke Caps Chargers listing for information on this set.

COMPLETE SET (35)	75.00	150.00
1 Tom Addison	2.50	4.00
2 Houston Antwine	2.50	4.00
3 Nick Buoniconti	6.00	10.00
4 Ron Burton	3.00	5.00
5 Gino Cappelletti	3.50	6.00
6 Jim Colclough	2.50	4.00
7 Harry Crump	2.50	4.00
8 Bob Dee	2.50	4.00
9 Bob Dentel	2.50	4.00
10 Larry Eisenhauer	2.50	4.00
11 Dick Felt	2.50	4.00
12 Larry Garron	2.50	4.00
13 Art Graham	3.00	5.00
14 Ron Hall	2.50	4.00
15 Jim Hunt	2.50	4.00
16 Charles Long	2.50	4.00
17 Don McKinnon	2.50	4.00
18 Jon Morris	2.50	4.00
19 Billy Neighbors	2.50	4.00
20 Tom Neumann	2.50	4.00
21 Don Oakes	2.50	4.00
22 Ross O'Hanley	2.50	4.00
23 Babe Parilli	3.00	5.00
24 Jesse Richardson	2.50	4.00
25 Tony Romeo	2.50	4.00
26 Jack Rudolph	2.50	4.00
27 Chuck Shonta	2.50	4.00
28 Al Snyder	2.50	4.00
29 Nick Spinelli	2.50	4.00
30 Bob Suci	2.50	4.00
31 Dave Watson	2.50	4.00
32 Don Webb	2.50	4.00
33 Bob Yates	2.50	4.00
34 Tom Yewcic	2.50	4.00
35 Mack Yoho	2.50	4.00

1964 Coke Caps Raiders

Please see the 1964 Coke Caps Chargers listing for information on this set.

1 Jan Barrett	3.00	6.00
2 Dan Birdwell	3.00	6.00
3 Sonny Bishop	3.00	6.00
4 Bill Budness	3.00	6.00
5 Dave Costa	3.00	6.00
6 Dobie Craig	3.00	6.00
7 Clem Daniels	4.00	8.00
8 Claude Gibson	3.00	6.00
9 Wayne Hawkins	4.00	8.00
10 Ken Herock	3.00	6.00
11 Dick Klein	3.00	6.00
12 Jim McMillin	3.00	6.00
13 Chuck McMurtry	3.00	6.00
14 Mike Mercer	3.00	6.00
15 Al Miller	3.00	6.00
16 Rex Mirich	3.00	6.00
17 Bob Mischak	3.00	6.00
18 Jim Norris	3.00	6.00
19 Jim Otto	7.50	15.00
20 Art Powell	4.00	8.00
21 Warren Powers	3.00	6.00
22 Ken Rice	3.00	6.00
23 Bo Roberson	3.00	6.00
24 Jack Simpson	3.00	6.00
25 Fred Williamson	5.00	10.00
26 Frank Youso	3.00	6.00

1964 Coke Caps Rams

Please see the 1964 Coke Caps Bears listing for information on this set.

COMPLETE SET (35)	75.00	150.00
1 Jon Arnett	2.50	4.00
2 Pervis Atkins	1.50	3.00
3 Terry Baker RB	3.00	5.00
4 Dick Bass	2.50	4.00
5 Charley Britt	1.50	3.00
6 Willie Brown WR	2.50	4.00
7 Joe Carollo	1.50	3.00
8 Don Chuy	1.50	3.00
9 Charlie Cowan	1.50	3.00
10 Lindon Crow	1.50	3.00
11 Carroll Dale	2.50	4.00
12 Roman Gabriel	4.00	8.00
13 Roosevelt Grier	3.00	6.00
14 Mike Henry	1.50	3.00
15 Art Hunter	1.50	3.00
16 Ken Iman	1.50	3.00
17 Deacon Jones	5.00	10.00
18 Cliff Livingston	1.50	3.00
19 Lamar Lundy	2.50	4.00
20 Marlin McKeever	1.50	3.00
21 Ed Meador	1.50	3.00
22 Bill Munson	2.50	4.00
23 Merlin Olsen	6.00	12.00
24 Jack Pardee	2.50	4.00
25 Art Perkins	1.50	3.00
26 Jim Phillips	2.50	4.00
27 Roger Pillath	1.50	3.00
28 Mel Profit	1.50	3.00
29 Joe Scibelli	1.50	3.00
30 Carver Shannon	1.50	3.00
31 Bobby Smith	1.50	3.00
32 Bill Swain	1.50	3.00
33 Frank Varrichione	1.50	3.00
34 Danny Villanueva	1.50	3.00
35 Nat Whitmyer	1.50	3.00
NNO Rams Saver Sheet	15.00	30.00

1964 Coke Caps Redskins

Please see the 1964 Coke Caps Bears listing for information on this set.

COMPLETE SET (35)	90.00	150.00
1 Bill Barnes	2.50	4.00
2 Don Bosseler	2.50	4.00
3 Rod Breedlove	2.50	4.00
4 Frank Budd	2.50	4.00
5 Henry Butsko	2.50	4.00
6 Jimmy Carr	2.50	4.00
7 Bill Clay	2.50	4.00
8 Angelo Coia	2.50	4.00
9 Fred Dugan	2.50	4.00
10 Fred Hageman	2.50	4.00
11 Sam Huff	5.00	10.00
12 George Izo	3.00	5.00
13 Sonny Jurgensen	5.00	10.00
14 Carl Kammerer	2.50	4.00
15 Gordon Kelley	2.50	4.00
16 Bob Khayat	2.50	4.00
17 Paul Krause	3.50	6.00
18 J.W. Lockett	2.50	4.00
19 Riley Mattson	2.50	4.00
20 Bobby Mitchell	4.00	8.00
21 John Nisby	2.50	4.00
22 Fran O'Brien	2.50	4.00
23 John Paluck	2.50	4.00
24 Jack Pardee	3.50	6.00
25 Bob Pellegrini	2.50	4.00
26 Vince Promuto	2.50	4.00
27 Pat Richter	3.00	5.00
28 Johnny Sample	3.00	5.00
29 Lonnie Sanders	2.50	4.00
30 Dick Shiner	2.50	4.00
31 Ron Snidow	2.50	4.00
32 Jim Steffen	2.50	4.00
33 Charley Taylor	5.00	10.00
34 Tom Tracy	3.00	5.00
35 Fred Williams	2.50	4.00
NNO Redskins Saver Sheet	15.00	30.00

1964 Coke Caps Steelers

Please see the 1964 Coke Caps Bears listing for information on this set.

COMPLETE SET (35)	75.00	150.00
1 Art Anderson	2.50	4.00
2 Frank Atkinson	2.50	4.00
3 Gary Ballman	2.50	4.00
4 John Baker	2.50	4.00
5 Charley Bradshaw	2.50	4.00
6 Jim Bradshaw	2.50	4.00
7 Ed Brown	3.00	5.00
8 John Burrell	2.50	4.00
9 Preston Carpenter	3.00	5.00
10 Lou Cordileone	2.50	4.00
11 Willie Daniel	2.50	4.00
12 Dick Haley	2.50	4.00
13 Bob Harrison	2.50	4.00
14 Dick Hoak	3.00	5.00
15 Dan James	2.50	4.00
16 Tom Jenkins	2.50	4.00
17 John Henry Johnson	5.00	10.00
18 Jim Kelly TE	2.50	4.00
19 Brady Keys	2.50	4.00
20 Joe Krupa	2.50	4.00
21 Ray Lemek	2.50	4.00
22 Paul Martha	2.50	4.00
23 Lou Michaels	3.00	5.00
24 Bill Nelsen	3.00	6.00
25 Terry Nofsinger	2.50	4.00
26 Buzz Nutter	2.50	4.00
27 Clarence Peaks	2.50	4.00
28 Myron Pottios	2.50	4.00
29 John Reger	2.50	4.00
30 Mike Sandusky	2.50	4.00
31 Theron Sapp	2.50	4.00
32 Bob Schmitz	2.50	4.00
33 Ron Stehouwer	2.50	4.00
34 Clendon Thomas	2.50	4.00
35 Joe Womack	2.50	4.00

1964 Coke Caps Team Emblems AFL

Each 1964 Coke Caps saver sheet had a section for collecting caps featuring the team emblem for all eight AFL teams. The caps are unnumbered and checklisted below in alphabetical order. These "Coke" caps were also available on Sprite bottles. Sprite caps typically carry a 1.5X-2X premium over the Coke version.

COMPLETE SET (8)	20.00	40.00
1 Boston Patriots	2.50	5.00
2 Buffalo Bills	2.50	5.00
3 Denver Broncos	3.00	6.00
4 Houston Oilers	2.50	5.00
5 Kansas City Chiefs	2.50	5.00
6 New York Jets	2.50	5.00
7 Oakland Raiders	3.00	6.00
8 San Diego Chargers	2.50	5.00

1964 Coke Caps Team Emblems NFL

Each 1964 Coke Caps saver sheet had a section for collecting caps featuring the team emblem for all fourteen NFL teams. The caps are unnumbered and checklisted below in alphabetical order. These "Coke" caps were also available on Sprite bottles. Sprite caps typically carry a 1.5X-2X premium over the Coke version.

COMPLETE SET (14)	30.00	60.00
1 Baltimore Colts	2.50	5.00
2 Chicago Bears	2.50	5.00

3 Cleveland Browns	2.50	5.00
4 Dallas Cowboys	3.00	6.00
5 Detroit Lions	2.50	5.00
6 Green Bay Packers	3.00	6.00
7 Los Angeles Rams	2.50	5.00
8 Minnesota Vikings	2.50	5.00
9 New York Giants	2.50	5.00
10 Philadelphia Eagles	2.50	5.00
11 Pittsburgh Steelers	2.50	5.00
12 San Francisco 49ers	2.50	5.00
13 St. Louis Cardinals	2.50	5.00
14 Washington Redskins	3.00	6.00

1964 Coke Caps Vikings

Please see the 1964 Coke Caps Bears listing for information on this set.

COMPLETE SET (35)	75.00	150.00
1 Grady Alderman	2.50	5.00
2 Hal Bedsole	2.00	4.00
3 Larry Bowie	2.00	4.00
4 Jim Boylan	2.00	4.00
5 Bill Brown	2.50	5.00
6 Bill Butler	2.00	4.00
7 Lee Calland	2.00	4.00
8 John Campbell	2.00	4.00
9 Fred Cox	2.50	5.00
10 Ted Dean	2.00	4.00
11 Bob Denton	2.00	4.00
12 Paul Dickson	2.00	4.00
13 Carl Eller	6.00	10.00
14 Paul Flatley	2.00	4.00
15 Tom Franckhauser	2.00	4.00
16 Rip Hawkins	2.00	4.00
17 Bill Jobko	2.00	4.00
18 Karl Kassulke	2.00	4.00
19 John Kirby	2.00	4.00
20 Bob Lacey	2.00	4.00
21 Errol Linden	2.00	4.00
22 Jim Marshall	6.00	10.00
23 Tommy Mason	2.50	5.00
24 Dave O'Brien	2.00	4.00
25 Palmer Pike	2.00	4.00
26 Jim Prestel	2.00	4.00
27 Jerry Reichow	2.00	4.00
28 George Rose	2.00	4.00
29 Ed Sharockman	2.00	4.00
30 Gordon Smith	2.00	4.00
31 Fran Tarkenton	15.00	25.00
32 Mick Tingelhoff	2.50	5.00
33 Ron Vanderkelen	2.00	4.00
34 Tom Wilson	2.00	4.00
35 Roy Winston	2.50	5.00

1965 Coke Caps All-Stars AFL

These AFL All-Star caps were issued in AFL cities (and a few other cities as well) along with the local team caps as part of the Go with the Pros promotion. The AFL team Cap Saver sheets had separate sections in which to affix both the local team's caps and the All-Stars' caps. The caps measure approximately 1 1/8" in diameter and have the drink logo and a football on the outside, while the inside has the player's face printed in black or red, with text surrounding the face. The consumer could turn in his completed saver sheet to receive various prizes. The caps are numbered with a "C" prefix. The 1965 caps are very similar to the 1966 issue and many of the players are the same in both years. However, the 1965 caps do not have the words "Caramel Colored" on the outside of the cap as do the 1966 caps. These caps were also produced for 1965 on other Coca-Cola products: TAB, Fanta and Sprite. The other drink caps typically carry a slight premium (1.5-2 times) over the value of the Coke version.

COMPLETE SET (34)	87.50	175.00
C37 Jerry Mays	1.50	3.00
C38 Cookie Gilchrist	2.00	4.00
C39 Lionel Taylor	2.00	4.00
C40 Goose Gonsoulin	2.00	4.00
C41 Gino Cappelletti	2.00	4.00
C42 Nick Buoniconti	2.50	5.00
C43 Larry Eisenhauer	1.50	3.00
C44 Babe Parilli	2.00	4.00
C45 Jack Kemp	12.50	25.00
C46 Billy Shaw	2.00	4.00
C47 Scott Appleton	1.50	3.00
C48 Matt Snell	2.00	4.00
C49 Charlie Hennigan	2.00	4.00
C50 Tom Flores	2.50	5.00
C51 Clem Daniels	2.00	4.00
C52 George Blanda	7.50	15.00
C53 Art Powell	2.00	4.00
C54 Jim Otto	5.00	10.00
C55 Larry Grantham	1.50	3.00
C56 Don Maynard	6.00	12.00
C57 Gerry Philbin	1.50	3.00
C58 E.J. Holub	1.50	3.00
C59 Chris Burford	1.50	3.00
C60 Ron Mix	3.75	7.50
C61 Ernie Ladd	3.75	7.50
C62 Fred Arbanas	1.50	3.00
C63 Tom Sestak	1.50	3.00
C64 Elbert Dubenion	2.00	4.00
C65 Mike Stratton	1.50	3.00
C66 Willie Brown	5.00	10.00
C67 Sid Blanks	1.50	3.00
C68 Len Dawson	6.00	12.00
C69 Lance Alworth	6.00	12.00
C70 Keith Lincoln	2.00	4.00

1965 Coke Caps All-Stars NFL

These NFL All-Star caps were issued in NFL cities (and a few other cities as well) along with the local team caps as part of the Go with the Pros promotion. The NFL team Cap Saver sheets had separate sections in which to affix both the local team's caps and the All-Stars' caps. The caps measure approximately 1 1/8" in diameter and have the drink logo and a football on the outside, while the inside has the player's face printed in black or red with text surrounding the face. The 1965 caps are very similar to the 1966 issue and many of the players are the same in both years. However, the 1965 caps do not have the words "Caramel Colored" on the outside of the cap as do the 1966 caps. The consumer could turn in his completed saver sheet to receive various prizes. The caps are numbered with a "C" prefix. These caps were also produced for 1965 on other Coca-Cola products: TAB, Fanta and Sprite. The other drink caps typically carry a slight premium (1.5-2 times) over the value of the Coke version.

COMPLETE SET (34)	50.00	100.00
C37 Sonny Jurgensen	2.50	6.00
C38 Fran Tarkenton	3.00	8.00
C39 Frank Ryan	1.25	3.00
C40 Johnny Unitas	5.00	12.00
C41 Tommy Mason	1.25	3.00
C42 Mel Renfro	1.50	4.00
C43 Ed Meador	1.00	2.50
C44 Paul Krause	1.50	4.00
C45 Irv Cross	1.25	3.00
C46 Bill Brown	1.25	3.00
C47 Joe Fortunato	1.00	2.50
C48 Jim Taylor	2.50	6.00
C49 John Henry Johnson	1.50	4.00
C50 Pat Fischer	1.00	2.50
C51 Bob Boyd DB	1.00	2.50
C52 Terry Barr	1.00	2.50
C53 Charley Taylor	1.50	4.00
C54 Paul Warfield	2.50	6.00
C55 Pete Retzlaff	1.25	3.00
C56 Maxie Baughan	1.00	2.50
C57 Matt Hazeltine	1.00	2.50
C58 Ken Gray	1.00	2.50
C59 Ray Nitschke	2.50	6.00
C60 Myron Pottios	1.00	2.50
C61 Charlie Krueger	1.00	2.50
C62 Deacon Jones	2.00	5.00
C63 Bob Lilly	2.50	6.00
C64 Merlin Olsen	2.00	5.00
C65 Jim Parker	1.50	4.00
C66 Roosevelt Brown	1.50	4.00
C67 Jim Gibbons	1.00	2.50
C68 Mike Ditka	3.00	8.00
C69 Willie Davis	1.50	4.00
C70 Aaron Thomas	1.00	2.50

1965 Coke Caps Bears

Coke caps were again issued for each NFL team in 1965 primarily in that team's local area along with the NFL All-Stars caps as part of the Go with the Pros promotion. The NFL team Cap Saver sheets had separate sections in which to affix both the local team's caps and the All-Stars' caps. The caps measure approximately 1 1/8" in diameter and have the drink logo and a football on the outside, while the inside has the player's face printed in red or black, with the team name above the photo, the player's name below, his position to the right and the cap number to the left. Some teams are also known to exist in a version that features a slightly smaller player photo. Cap numbers included a "C" prefix on all NFL teams except the Giants which had two sets using either a "C" or "G" prefix. The consumer could turn in his completed saver sheet to receive various prizes. The 1965 caps are very similar to the 1966 issue and many of the players are the same in both years. However, the 1965 caps do not have the words "Caramel Colored" on the outside of the cap as do the 1966 caps. Football caps were also produced for 1965 on other Coca-Cola products: Coke lift top, TAB (Low-Calorie Beverage), TAB lift top, Fanta Grape, Fanta Grapefruit, Fanta Orange, King Size Coke and Sprite. The other drink caps typically carry a slight premium over the value of the basic Coke version.

C1 Bennie McRae	1.50	3.00
C2 Johnny Morris	1.50	3.00
C3 Roosevelt Taylor	2.50	4.00
C4 Larry Morris	1.50	3.00
C5 Ed O'Bradovich	1.50	3.00
C6 Richie Petitbon	2.50	4.00
C7 Mike Pyle	1.50	3.00
C8 Dave Whitsell	1.50	3.00
C9 Billy Martin	1.50	3.00
C10 John Johnson	1.50	3.00
C11 Stan Jones	3.50	6.00
C12 Ted Karras	1.50	3.00
C13 Bob Kilcullen	1.50	3.00
C14 Roger LeClerc	1.50	3.00
C15 Herman Lee	1.50	3.00
C16 Earl Leggett	1.50	3.00
C17 Joe Marconi	1.50	3.00
C18 Rudy Bukich	2.50	4.00
C19 Mike Reilly	1.50	3.00
C20 Mike Ditka	6.00	12.00
C21 Dick Evey	1.50	3.00
C22 Joe Fortunato	1.50	3.00
C23 Bill Wade	2.50	4.00
C24 Bill George	3.50	6.00
C25 Larry Glueck	1.50	3.00
C26 Bobby Joe Green	1.50	3.00
C27 Bob Wetoska	1.50	3.00
C28 Doug Atkins	4.00	8.00
C29 Jon Arnett	2.50	4.00
C30 Dick Butkus	18.00	30.00
C31 Charlie Bivins	1.50	3.00
C32 Ronnie Bull	2.50	4.00
C33 Jim Cadile	1.50	3.00
C34 J.C. Caroline	1.50	3.00
C35 Gale Sayers	18.00	30.00
C36 Team Logo	1.50	3.00
NNO Saver Sheet	15.00	30.00

1965 Coke Caps Bills B

Coke caps were again issued for each AFL team in 1965 primarily in that team's local area along with the AFL All-Stars caps as part of the Go with the Pros promotion. The AFL team Cap Saver sheets had separate sections in which to affix both the local team's caps and the All-Stars' caps. The caps measure approximately 1 1/8" in diameter and have the drink logo and a football on the outside, while the inside has the player's face printed in red or black, with the team name above the photo, the player's name below, his position to the right and the cap number to the left. Some teams are also known to exist in a version that features a slightly smaller player photo. Cap numbers included a "C" prefix on all AFL teams except the Jets (J prefix) and Bills (B prefix). The consumer could turn in his completed saver sheet to receive various prizes. The 1965 caps are very similar to the 1966 issue and many of the players are the same in both years. However, the 1965 caps do not have the words "Caramel Colored" on the outside of the cap as do the 1966 caps. Football caps were also produced for 1965 on other Coca-Cola products: TAB, Fanta, King Size Coke and Sprite. The other drink caps typically carry a slight premium over the value of the basic Coke version.

COMPLETE SET (35)	75.00	150.00
*C CAPS: .4X TO 1X B CAPS		
B1 Ray Abruzzese	1.50	3.00
B2 Joe Auer	1.50	3.00
B3 Stew Barber	2.00	4.00
B4 Glenn Bass	1.50	3.00
B5 Dave Behrman	1.50	3.00
B6 Al Bemiller	1.50	3.00
B7 George Butch Byrd	2.00	4.00
B8 Wray Carlton	2.00	4.00
B9 Hagood Clarke	1.50	3.00
B10 Jack Kemp	15.00	30.00
B11 Oliver Dobbins	1.50	3.00
B12 Elbert Dubenion	2.00	4.00
B13 Jim Dunaway	2.00	4.00
B14 Booker Edgerson	1.50	3.00
B15 George Flint	1.50	3.00
B16 Pete Gogolak	2.00	4.00
B17 Dick Hudson	2.00	4.00
B18 Harry Jacobs	2.00	4.00
B19 Tom Keating	1.50	3.00
B20 Tom Day	1.50	3.00
B21 Daryle Lamonica	6.00	12.00
B22 Paul Maguire	3.00	6.00
B23 Roland McDole	2.00	4.00
B24 Dudley Meredith	1.50	3.00
B25 Joe O'Donnell	1.50	3.00
B26 Willie Ross	1.50	3.00
B27 Ed Rutkowski	1.50	3.00
B28 George Saimes	2.00	4.00
B29 Tom Sestak	2.00	4.00
B30 Billy Shaw	2.00	4.00
B31 Bob Lee Smith	1.50	3.00
B32 Mike Stratton	2.00	4.00
B33 Gene Sykes	1.50	3.00
B34 John Tracey	1.50	3.00
B35 Ernie Warlick	1.50	3.00
NNO Bills Saver Sheet	15.00	30.00

1965 Coke Caps Bills C

Please see the 1965 Coke Caps Bills B listing for information on this set.

1965 Coke Caps Broncos

Please see the 1965 Coke Caps Bills listing for information on this set.

COMPLETE SET (36)	125.00	225.00
C1 Odell Barry	3.00	6.00
C2 Willie Brown	6.00	12.00
C3 Bob Scarpitto	3.00	6.00
C4 Ed Cooke	3.00	6.00
C5 Al Denson	3.00	6.00
C6 Tom Erlandson	3.00	6.00
C7 Hewritt Dixon	3.00	6.00
C8 Mickey Slaughter	3.00	6.00
C9 Lionel Taylor	4.00	8.00
C10 Jerry Sturm	3.00	6.00
C11 Jerry Hopkins	3.00	6.00
C12 Charlie Mitchell	3.00	6.00
C13 Ray Jacobs	3.00	6.00
C14 Larry Jordan	3.00	6.00
C15 Charlie Janerette	3.00	6.00
C16 Ray Kubala	3.00	6.00
C17 Leroy Moore	3.00	6.00
C18 Bob Breitenstein	3.00	6.00
C19 Eldon Danenhauer	3.00	6.00
C20 Miller Farr	3.00	6.00
C21 Max Leetzow	3.00	6.00
C22 Gene Jeter	3.00	6.00
C23 Tom Janik	3.00	6.00
C24 Gerry Bussell	3.00	6.00
C25 Bob McCullough	3.00	6.00
C26 Jim McMillin	3.00	6.00
C27 Abner Haynes	4.00	8.00
C28 John McGeever	3.00	6.00
C29 Cookie Gilchrist	4.00	8.00
C30 John McCormick	3.00	6.00
C31 Don Shackelford	3.00	6.00
C32 Goose Gonsoulin	3.00	6.00
C33 Jim Perkins	3.00	6.00
C34 Marv Matuszak	3.00	6.00
C35 Jacky Lee	3.00	6.00
C36 Team Logo	3.00	6.00

1965 Coke Caps Browns

Please see the 1965 Coke Caps Bears listing for information on this set.

COMPLETE SET (36)	75.00	125.00
C1 Jim Ninowski	2.50	4.00
C2 Leroy Kelly	5.00	10.00
C3 Lou Groza	4.00	8.00
C4 Gary Collins	2.50	4.00
C5 Bill Glass	2.50	4.00
C6 Bobby Franklin	1.50	3.00
C7 Galen Fiss	1.50	3.00
C8 Ross Fichtner	1.50	3.00
C9 John Wooten	2.50	4.00
C10 Clifton McNeil	1.50	3.00
C11 Paul Wiggin	2.50	4.00
C12 Gene Hickerson	2.50	4.00
C13 Ernie Green	1.50	3.00
C14 Dale Memmelaar	1.50	3.00
C15 Dick Schafrath	1.50	3.00
C16 Sidney Williams	1.50	3.00
C17 Frank Ryan	2.50	4.00
C18 Bernie Parrish	1.50	3.00
C19 Vince Costello	1.50	3.00
C20 John Brown	1.50	3.00
C21 Monte Clark	1.50	3.00
C22 Walter Roberts	1.50	3.00
C23 Johnny Brewer	1.50	3.00
C24 Walter Beach	1.50	3.00
C25 Dick Modzelewski	1.50	3.00
C26 Larry Benz	1.50	3.00
C27 Jim Houston	1.50	3.00
C28 Mike Lucci	1.50	3.00
C29 Mel Anthony	1.50	3.00
C30 Tom Hutchinson	1.50	3.00
C31 John Morrow	1.50	3.00
C32 Jim Kanicki	1.50	3.00
C33 Paul Warfield	5.00	10.00
C34 Jim Garcia	1.50	3.00
C35 Walter Johnson	1.50	3.00
C36 Team Logo	1.50	3.00

1965 Coke Caps Cardinals

Please see the 1965 Coke Caps Bears listing for information on this set.

C1 Pat Fischer	4.00	8.00
C2 Sonny Randle	3.00	6.00
C3 Joe Childress	3.00	6.00
C4 Dave Meggysey	4.00	8.00
C5 Joe Robb	3.00	6.00
C6 Jerry Stovall	3.00	6.00
C7 Ernie McMillan	3.00	6.00
C8 Dale Meinert	3.00	6.00
C9 Irv Goode	3.00	6.00
C10 Bob DeMarco	3.00	6.00
C11 Mal Hammack	3.00	6.00
C12 Jim Bakken	3.00	6.00
C13 Bill Thornton	3.00	6.00
C14 Buddy Humphrey	3.00	6.00
C15 Bill Koman	3.00	6.00
C16 Larry Wilson	5.00	10.00
C17 Ed Cook	3.00	6.00
C18 Prentice Gautt	3.00	6.00
C19 Charlie Johnson	4.00	8.00
C20 Ken Gray	3.00	6.00
C21 Taz Anderson	3.00	6.00
C22 Sam Silas	3.00	6.00
C23 Larry Stallings	3.00	6.00
C24 Don Brumm	3.00	6.00
C25 Bobby Joe Conrad	3.00	6.00
C26 Bill Triplett	3.00	6.00
C27 Luke Owens	3.00	6.00
C28 Jackie Smith	5.00	10.00
C29 Bob Reynolds	3.00	6.00
C30 Abe Woodson	3.00	6.00
C31 Jim Burson	3.00	6.00
C32 Willis Crenshaw	3.00	6.00
C33 Billy Gambrell	3.00	6.00
C34 Tom Redmond	3.00	6.00
C35 Herschel Turner	3.00	6.00
C36 Team Logo	3.00	6.00

1965 Coke Caps Chiefs

Please see the 1965 Coke Caps Bills listing for information on this set.

COMPLETE SET (36)		
C1 E.J. Holub	4.00	8.00
C2 Al Reynolds	3.00	6.00

C3 Buck Buchanan	5.00	10.00
C4 Curt Merz	3.00	6.00
C5 Dave Hill	3.00	6.00
C6 Bobby Hunt	3.00	6.00
C7 Jerry Mays	3.00	6.00
C8 Jon Gilliam	3.00	6.00
C9 Walt Corey	3.00	6.00
C10 Curt Farrier	3.00	6.00
C11 Jerry Cornelison	3.00	6.00
C12 Bert Coan	3.00	6.00
C13 Ed Budde	3.00	6.00
C14 Tommy Brooker	3.00	6.00
C15 Bobby Bell	5.00	10.00
C16 Smokey Stover	3.00	6.00
C17 Curtis McClinton	4.00	8.00
C18 Jerrel Wilson	3.00	6.00
C19 Jim Fraser	3.00	6.00
C20 Mack Lee Hill	3.00	6.00
C21 Jim Tyrer	3.00	6.00
C22 Johnny Robinson	4.00	8.00
C23 Bobby Ply	3.00	6.00
C24 Frank Jackson	3.00	6.00
C25 Ed Lothamer	3.00	6.00
C26 Sherrill Headrick	3.00	6.00
C27 Fred Williamson	4.00	8.00
C28 Chris Burford	3.00	6.00
C29 Willie Mitchell	3.00	6.00
C30 Mel Branch	3.00	6.00
C31 Fred Arbanas	3.00	6.00
C32 Hatch Rosdahl	3.00	6.00
C33 Reggie Carolan	3.00	6.00
C34 Len Dawson	6.00	12.00
C35 Pete Beathard	3.00	6.00
C36 Team Logo	2.50	5.00

1965 Coke Caps Colts

Please see the 1965 Coke Caps Bears listing for information on this set.

COMPLETE SET (36)	75.00	150.00
C1 Ted Davis	1.50	3.00
C2 Bob Boyd DB	1.50	3.00
C3 Lenny Moore	6.00	12.00
C4 Lou Kirouac	1.50	3.00
C5 Jimmy Orr	2.00	4.00
C6 Wendell Harris	1.50	3.00
C7 Mike Curtis	4.00	8.00
C8 Jerry Logan	1.50	3.00
C9 Steve Stonebreaker	1.50	3.00
C10 John Mackey	5.00	10.00
C11 Dennis Gaubatz	1.50	3.00
C12 Don Shinnick	1.50	3.00
C13 Dick Szymanski	1.50	3.00
C14 Ordell Braase	1.50	3.00
C15 Lenny Lyles	1.50	3.00
C16 John Campbell	1.50	3.00
C17 Dan Sullivan	1.50	3.00
C18 Lou Michaels	2.00	4.00
C19 Gary Cuozzo	2.00	4.00
C20 Butch Wilson	1.50	3.00
C21 Alex Sandusky	1.50	3.00
C22 Jim Welch	1.50	3.00
C23 Tony Lorick	1.50	3.00
C24 Billy Ray Smith	2.00	4.00
C25 Fred Miller	1.50	3.00
C26 Tom Matte	3.00	6.00
C27 Johnny Unitas	10.00	20.00
C28 Glenn Ressler	1.50	3.00
C29 Alex Hawkins	2.00	4.00
C30 Jim Parker	4.00	8.00
C31 Guy Reese	1.50	3.00
C32 Bob Vogel	1.50	3.00
C33 Jerry Hill	1.50	3.00
C34 Raymond Berry	6.00	12.00
C35 George Preas	1.50	3.00
C36 Team Logo	1.50	3.00
NNO Colts Saver Sheet	15.00	30.00

1965 Coke Caps Cowboys

Please see the 1965 Coke Caps Bears listing for information on this set.

COMPLETE SET (36)	100.00	175.00
C1 Mike Connelly	2.50	5.00
C2 Tony Liscio	2.50	5.00
C3 Maury Youmans	2.50	5.00
C4 Larry Stephens	2.50	5.00
C5 Jim Colvin	2.50	5.00
C6 Malcolm Walker	2.50	5.00
C7 Danny Villanueva	2.50	5.00
C8 Frank Clarke	3.00	6.00
C9 Don Meredith	10.00	20.00
C10 George Andrie	2.50	5.00
C11 Mel Renfro	5.00	10.00
C12 Pettis Norman	2.50	5.00
C13 Buddy Dial	3.00	6.00
C14 Lee Folkins	2.50	5.00
C15 Jerry Rhome	2.50	5.00
C16 Bob Hayes	7.50	15.00
C17 Mike Gaechter	2.50	5.00
C18 Joe Bob Isbell	2.50	5.00
C19 Harold Hays	2.50	5.00
C20 Craig Morton	4.00	8.00
C21 Jake Kupp	2.50	5.00
C22 Cornell Green	2.50	5.00
C23 Perry Lee Dunn	2.50	5.00
C24 Don Talbert	2.50	5.00
C25 Dave Manders	2.50	5.00
C26 Warren Livingston	2.50	5.00
C27 Bob Lilly	7.50	15.00
C28 Chuck Howley	4.00	8.00
C29 Don Bishop	2.50	5.00
C30 Don Perkins	3.00	6.00
C31 Jim Boeke	2.50	5.00
C32 Dave Edwards	2.50	5.00
C33 Lee Roy Jordan	3.00	6.00
C34 Jerry Tubbs	2.50	5.00
C35 Amos Marsh	2.50	5.00
C36 Team Logo	2.00	4.00

1965 Coke Caps Eagles

Please see the 1965 Coke Caps Bears listing for information on this set.

COMPLETE SET (36)	80.00	120.00
C1 Norm Snead	2.50	5.00
C2 Al Nelson	1.50	3.00
C3 Jim Skaggs	1.50	3.00
C4 Glenn Glass	1.50	3.00
C5 Pete Retzlaff	2.00	4.00
C6 Bill Mack	1.50	3.00
C7 Ray Rissmiller	1.50	3.00
C8 Lynn Hoyem	1.50	3.00
C9 King Hill	2.00	4.00
C10 Timmy Brown	2.50	5.00
C11 Ollie Matson	5.00	10.00
C12 Dave Lloyd	2.00	4.00
C13 Jim Ringo	3.50	7.00
C14 Floyd Peters	2.00	4.00
C15 Riley Gunnels	1.50	3.00
C16 Claude Crabb	1.50	3.00
C17 Earl Gros	2.00	4.00
C18 Fred Hill	1.50	3.00
C19 Don Hultz	1.50	3.00
C20 Ray Poage	1.50	3.00
C21 Irv Cross	2.50	5.00
C22 Mike Morgan	1.50	3.00
C23 Maxie Baughan	2.00	4.00
C24 Ed Blaine	1.50	3.00
C25 Jack Concannon	2.00	4.00
C26 Sam Baker	1.50	3.00
C27 Tom Woodeshick	2.00	4.00
C28 Joe Scarpati	1.50	3.00
C29 John Meyers	1.50	3.00
C30 Nate Ramsey	1.50	3.00
C31 George Tarasovic	1.50	3.00
C32 Bob Brown T	2.50	5.00
C33 Ralph Smith	1.50	3.00
C34 Ron Goodwin	1.50	3.00
C35 Dave Graham	1.50	3.00
C36 Team Logo	1.50	3.00
NNO Eagles Saver Sheet	15.00	30.00

1965 Coke Caps Giants C

Please see the 1965 Coke Caps Bears listing for information on this set.

COMPLETE SET (36)	75.00	125.00
C1 Ernie Koy	2.50	4.00
C2 Chuck Mercein	2.50	4.00
C3 Bob Timberlake	1.75	3.00
C4 Jim Katcavage	2.50	4.00
C5 Mickey Walker	1.75	3.00
C6 Roger Anderson	1.75	3.00
C7 Jerry Hillebrand	1.75	3.00
C8 Tucker Frederickson	2.50	4.00
C9 Jim Moran	1.75	3.00
C10 Bill Winter	1.75	3.00
C11 Aaron Thomas	2.50	4.00
C12 Clarence Childs	1.75	3.00
C13 Jim Patton	2.50	4.00
C14 Joe Morrison	2.50	4.00
C15 Homer Jones	2.50	4.00
C16 Dick Lynch	2.50	4.00
C17 John Lovetere	1.75	3.00
C18 Greg Larson	2.50	4.00
C19 Lou Slaby	1.75	3.00
C20 Tom Costello	1.75	3.00
C21 Darrell Dess	1.75	3.00
C22 Frank Lasky	1.75	3.00
C23 Dick Pesonen	1.75	3.00
C24 Tom Scott	1.75	3.00
C25 Erich Barnes	2.50	4.00
C26 Roosevelt Brown	3.50	6.00
C27 Del Shofner	2.50	4.00
C28 Dick James	1.75	3.00
C29 Andy Stynchula	1.75	3.00
C30 Tony Dimidio	1.75	3.00
C31 Steve Thurlow	1.75	3.00
C32 Ernie Wheelwright	1.75	3.00
C33 Bookie Bolin	1.75	3.00
C34 Gary Wood	2.50	4.00
C35 John Contoulis	1.75	3.00
C36 Team Logo	1.75	3.00

1965 Coke Caps Giants G

Please see the 1965 Coke Caps Bears listing for information on this set.

COMPLETE SET (35)	75.00	150.00
G1 Joe Morrison	2.00	4.00
G2 Dick Lynch	2.00	4.00
G3 Andy Stynchula	1.50	3.00
G4 Clarence Childs	1.50	3.00
G5 Aaron Thomas	2.00	4.00
G6 Mickey Walker	1.50	3.00
G7 Bill Winter	1.50	3.00
G8 Bookie Bolin	1.50	3.00
G9 Tom Scott	1.50	3.00
G10 John Lovetere	1.50	3.00
G11 Jim Patton	2.00	4.00
G12 Darrell Dess	1.50	3.00
G13 Dick James	1.50	3.00
G14 Jerry Hillebrand	1.50	3.00
G15 Dick Pesonen	1.50	3.00
G16 Del Shofner	2.00	4.00
G17 Erich Barnes	2.00	4.00
G18 Roosevelt Brown	3.00	6.00
G19 Greg Larson	2.00	4.00
G20 Jim Katcavage	2.00	4.00
G21 Frank Lasky	1.50	3.00
G22 Lou Slaby	1.50	3.00
G23 Jim Moran	1.50	3.00
G24 Roger Anderson	1.50	3.00
G25 Steve Thurlow	1.50	3.00
G26 Ernie Wheelwright	1.50	3.00
G27 Gary Wood	2.00	4.00
G28 Tony Dimidio	1.50	3.00
G29 John Contoulis	1.50	3.00
G30 Tucker Frederickson	2.00	4.00
G31 Bob Timberlake	1.50	3.00
G32 Chuck Mercein	2.00	4.00
G33 Ernie Koy	2.00	4.00
G34 Tom Costello	1.50	3.00
G35 Homer Jones	2.00	4.00
NNO Giants Saver Sheet	15.00	30.00

1965 Coke Caps Jets

Please see the 1965 Coke Caps Bills listing for information on this set.

COMPLETE SET (35)	125.00	200.00
J1 Don Maynard	6.00	12.00
J2 George Sauer Jr.	3.00	6.00
J3 Cosmo Iacavazzi	2.00	4.00
J4 Jim O'Mahoney	2.00	4.00
J5 Matt Snell	3.00	6.00
J6 Clyde Washington	2.00	4.00
J7 Jim Turner	2.50	5.00
J8 Mike Taliaferro	2.00	4.00
J9 Marshall Starks	2.00	4.00
J10 Mark Smolinski	2.00	4.00
J11 Bob Schweickert	2.00	4.00
J12 Paul Rochester	2.00	4.00
J13 Sherman Plunkett	2.50	5.00
J14 Gerry Philbin	2.50	5.00
J15 Pete Perreault	2.00	4.00
J16 Dainard Paulson	2.00	4.00
J17 Joe Namath	30.00	50.00
J18 Winston Hill	2.50	5.00
J19 Dee Mackey	2.00	4.00
J20 Curley Johnson	2.00	4.00
J21 Mike Hudock	2.00	4.00
J22 John Huarte	3.00	6.00
J23 Gordy Holz	2.00	4.00
J24 Gene Heeter	2.50	5.00
J25 Larry Grantham	2.50	5.00
J26 Dan Ficca	2.00	4.00
J27 Sam DeLuca	2.50	5.00
J28 Bill Baird	2.00	4.00
J29 Ralph Baker	2.00	4.00
J30 Wahoo McDaniel	6.00	12.00
J31 Jim Evans	2.00	4.00
J32 Dave Herman	2.50	5.00
J33 John Schmitt	2.00	4.00
J34 Jim Harris	2.00	4.00
J35 Bake Turner	2.50	5.00
NNO Jets Saver Sheet	15.00	30.00

1965 Coke Caps Lions

Please see the 1965 Coke Caps Bears listing for information on this set.

COMPLETE SET (36)	75.00	150.00
C1 Pat Studstill	2.00	4.00
C2 Bob Whitlow	1.50	3.00
C3 Wayne Walker	2.00	4.00
C4 Tom Watkins	1.50	3.00
C5 Jim Simon	1.50	3.00
C6 Sam Williams	1.50	3.00
C7 Terry Barr	1.50	3.00
C8 Jerry Rush	1.50	3.00
C9 Roger Brown	2.00	4.00
C10 Tom Nowatzke	2.00	4.00
C11 Dick Lane	4.00	8.00
C12 Dick Compton	1.50	3.00
C13 Yale Lary	4.00	8.00
C14 Dick Lebeau	2.00	4.00
C15 Dan Lewis	2.00	4.00
C16 Wally Hilgenberg	2.00	4.00
C17 Bruce Maher	1.50	3.00
C18 Darris McCord	1.50	3.00
C19 Hugh McInnis	1.50	3.00
C20 Ernie Clark	1.50	3.00
C21 Gail Cogdill	2.00	4.00
C22 Wayne Rasmussen	1.50	3.00
C23 Joe Don Looney	5.00	10.00
C24 Jim Gibbons	2.00	4.00
C25 John Gonzaga	1.50	3.00
C26 John Gordy	1.50	3.00
C27 Bobby Thompson DB	1.50	3.00
C28 J.D. Smith T	2.00	4.00
C29 Earl Morrall	2.50	5.00
C30 Alex Karras	5.00	10.00
C31 Nick Pietrosante	2.00	4.00
C32 Milt Plum	2.00	4.00
C33 Daryl Sanders	1.50	3.00
C34 Joe Schmidt	5.00	10.00
C35 Bob Scholtz	1.50	3.00
C36 Team Logo	1.50	3.00
NNO Lions Saver Sheet	15.00	30.00

1965 Coke Caps National NFL

This set of 70 Coke caps was issued on bottled soft drinks primarily in cities without an NFL team. The caps were issued along with their own Saver Sheet. Each measures approximately 1 1/8" in diameter and has the drink logo and a football on the outside, while the inside has the player's face printed in black or red, with NFL ALL STARS above the player image. The 1965 caps are very similar to the 1966 issue and many of the players are the same in both years. However, the 1965 caps do not have the words "Caramel Colored" on the outside of the cap as do the 1966 caps. An "NFL ALL STARS" title appears above the player's photo so some caps were issued with this set and the NFL All-Stars set. The consumer could turn in his completed saver sheet to receive various prizes. These caps were also produced for 1965 on other Coca-Cola products: TAB, Fanta and Sprite. The other drink caps typically carry a slight premium (1.5-2 times) over the value of the Coke version.

COMPLETE SET (70)	112.50	225.00
C1 Herb Adderley	2.50	5.00
C2 Yale Lary	2.50	5.00
C3 Dick LeBeau	1.50	3.00
C4 Bill Brown	2.00	4.00
C5 Jim Taylor	3.75	7.50
C6 Joe Fortunato	1.50	3.00
C7 Bob Boyd DB	1.50	3.00
C8 Terry Barr	1.50	3.00
C9 Dick Szymanski	1.50	3.00
C10 Mick Tingelhoff	2.00	4.00
C11 Wayne Walker	1.50	3.00
C12 Matt Hazeltine	1.50	3.00
C13 Ray Nitschke	3.75	7.50
C14 Grady Alderman	1.50	3.00
C15 Charlie Krueger	1.50	3.00
C16 Tommy Mason	1.50	3.00
C17 Willie Wood	2.50	5.00
C18 John Unitas	6.00	12.00
C19 Lenny Moore	3.00	6.00
C20 Fran Tarkenton	5.00	10.00
C21 Deacon Jones	3.00	6.00
C22 Bob Vogel	1.50	3.00
C23 John Gordy	1.50	3.00
C24 Jim Parker	2.50	5.00
C25 Jim Gibbons	1.50	3.00
C26 Merlin Olsen	3.00	6.00
C27 Forrest Gregg	2.50	5.00
C28 Roger Brown	1.50	3.00
C29 Dave Parks	1.50	3.00
C30 Raymond Berry	3.00	6.00
C31 Mike Ditka	6.00	12.00
C32 Gino Marchetti	3.00	6.00
C33 Willie Davis	3.00	6.00
C34 Ed Meador	1.50	3.00
C35 Browns Logo	1.50	3.00
C36 Colts Logo	1.50	3.00
C37 Sam Baker	1.50	3.00
C38 Irv Cross	2.00	4.00
C39 Maxie Baughan	1.50	3.00
C40 Vince Promuto	1.50	3.00
C41 Paul Krause	1.50	3.00
C42 Charley Taylor	3.00	6.00
C43 John Paluck	1.50	3.00
C44 Paul Warfield	5.00	10.00
C45 Dick Modzelewski	1.50	3.00
C46 Myron Pottios	1.50	3.00
C47 Erich Barnes	1.50	3.00
C48 Bill Koman	1.50	3.00
C49 John Thomas	1.50	3.00
C50 Gary Ballman	1.50	3.00
C51 Sam Huff	3.00	6.00
C52 Ken Gray	1.50	3.00
C53 Roosevelt Brown	2.50	5.00
C54 Bobby Joe Conrad	1.50	3.00
C55 Pat Fischer	1.50	3.00
C56 Irv Goode	1.50	3.00
C57 Floyd Peters	1.50	3.00

C58 Charley Johnson 2.00 4.00
C59 John Henry Johnson 3.00 6.00
C60 Charles Bradshaw 1.50 3.00
C61 Jim Ringo 2.50 5.00
C62 Pete Retzlaff 2.00 4.00
C63 Sonny Jurgensen 3.50 7.00
C64 Don Meredith 6.00 12.00
C65 Bob Lilly 5.00 10.00
C66 Bill Glass 1.50 3.00
C67 Dick Schafrath 1.50 3.00
C68 Mel Renfro 3.00 6.00
C69 Jim Houston 1.50 3.00
C70 Frank Ryan 2.00 4.00
NNO NFL Saver Sheet 15.00 30.00

1965 Coke Caps Packers

Please see the 1965 Coke Caps Bears listing for information on this set.

COMPLETE SET (36) 125.00 200.00
C1 Herb Adderley 4.00 8.00
C2 Lionel Aldridge 3.00 5.00
C3 Hank Gremminger 2.50 4.00
C4 Willie Davis 4.00 8.00
C5 Boyd Dowler 3.00 5.00
C6 Marv Fleming 3.00 5.00
C7 Ken Bowman 3.00 5.00
C8 Tom Brown 2.50 4.00
C9 Doug Hart 2.50 4.00
C10 Dan Grimm 2.50 4.00
C11 Dennis Claridge 2.50 4.00
C12 Dave Hanner 3.00 5.00
C13 Tommy Crutcher 2.50 4.00
C14 Fred Thurston 4.00 8.00
C15 Elijah Pitts 3.00 5.00
C16 Lloyd Voss 2.50 4.00
C17 Lee Roy Caffey 2.50 4.00
C18 Dave Robinson 3.50 6.00
C19 Bart Starr 10.00 20.00
C20 Ray Nitschke 6.00 12.00
C21 Max McGee 3.00 5.00
C22 Don Chandler 3.00 5.00
C23 Norman Masters 2.50 4.00
C24 Ron Kostelnik 2.50 4.00
C25 Carroll Dale 3.00 5.00
C26 Hank Jordan 4.00 8.00
C27 Bob Jeter 3.00 5.00
C28 Bob Skoronski 2.50 4.00
C29 Jerry Kramer 3.50 6.00
C30 Willie Wood 4.00 8.00
C31 Paul Hornung 7.50 15.00
C32 Forrest Gregg 4.00 8.00
C33 Zeke Bratkowski 3.00 5.00
C34 Tom Moore 3.00 5.00
C35 Jim Taylor 6.00 12.00
C36 Team Logo 2.50 4.00
NNO Packers Saver Sheet 15.00 30.00

1965 Coke Caps Patriots

Please see the 1965 Coke Caps Bills listing for information on this set.

COMPLETE SET (36) 75.00 135.00
C1 Jon Morris 2.50 4.00
C2 Don Webb 2.50 4.00
C3 Charles Long 2.50 4.00
C4 Tony Romeo 2.50 4.00
C5 Bob Dee 2.50 4.00
C6 Tommy Addison 3.00 5.00
C7 Bob Yates 2.50 4.00
C8 Ron Hall 2.50 4.00
C9 Billy Neighbors 2.50 4.00
C10 Jack Rudolph 2.50 4.00
C11 Don Oakes 2.50 4.00
C12 Tom Yewcic 2.50 4.00
C13 Ron Burton 3.00 5.00
C14 Jim Colclough 2.50 4.00
C15 Larry Garron 2.50 4.00
C16 Dave Watson 2.50 4.00
C17 Art Graham 3.00 5.00
C18 Babe Parilli 3.00 6.00
C19 Jim Hunt 2.50 4.00
C20 Don McKinnon 2.50 4.00
C21 Houston Antwine 2.50 4.00
C22 Nick Buoniconti 5.00 10.00
C23 Ross O'Hanley 2.50 4.00
C24 Gino Cappelletti 3.00 6.00
C25 Chuck Shonta 2.50 4.00
C26 Dick Felt 2.50 4.00
C27 Mike Dukes 2.50 4.00
C28 Larry Eisenhauer 2.50 4.00
C29 Bob Schmidt 2.50 4.00
C30 Len St. Jean 2.50 4.00
C31 J.D. Garrett 2.50 4.00
C32 Jim Whalen 2.50 4.00
C33 Jim Nance 3.00 6.00
C34 Eddie Wilson 2.50 4.00
C35 Lonnie Farmer 2.50 4.00
C36 Boston Patriots Logo 2.50 4.00
NNO Patriots Saver Sheet 15.00 30.00

1965 Coke Caps Raiders

Please see the 1965 Coke Caps Bills listing for information on this set.

COMPLETE SET (36) 100.00 175.00
C1 Fred Biletnikoff 6.00 12.00
C2 Gus Otto 2.50 5.00
C3 Harry Schuh 2.50 5.00
C4 Ken Herock 2.50 5.00
C5 Claude Gibson 2.50 5.00
C6 Cotton Davidson 2.50 5.00
C7 Rich Zecher 2.50 5.00
C8 Ben Davidson 3.00 6.00
C9 Frank Youso 2.50 5.00
C10 Bob Svihus 2.50 5.00
C11 John R. Williamson 2.50 5.00
C12 Dave Grayson 2.50 5.00
C13 Archie Matsos 2.50 5.00
C14 Dave Costa 2.50 5.00
C15 Bo Roberson 2.50 5.00
C16 Alan Miller 2.50 5.00
C17 Billy Cannon 4.00 8.00
C18 Wayne Hawkins 3.00 6.00
C19 Warren Powers 2.50 5.00
C20 Clancy Osborne 2.50 5.00
C21 Dan Conners 2.50 5.00
C22 Jim Otto 5.00 10.00
C23 Clem Daniels 3.00 6.00
C24 Tom Flores 4.00 8.00
C25 Art Powell 3.00 6.00
C26 Rex Mirich 2.50 5.00
C27 Dick Klein 2.50 5.00
C28 Dan Birdwell 2.50 5.00
C29 Dalva Allen 2.50 5.00
C30 Mike Mercer 2.50 5.00
C31 Ken Rice 2.50 5.00
C32 Bill Budness 2.50 5.00
C33 Tommy Morrow 2.50 5.00
C34 Joe Krakoski 2.50 5.00
C35 Bob Mischak 2.50 5.00
C36 Team Logo 2.50 5.00

1965 Coke Caps Rams

Please see the 1965 Coke Caps Bears listing for information on this set.

COMPLETE SET (36) 75.00 125.00
C1 Jerry Richardson 2.50 4.00
C2 Bobby Smith 1.50 3.00
C3 Bill Munson 2.50 4.00
C4 Frank Varrichione 1.50 3.00
C5 Joe Carollo 1.50 3.00
C6 Dick Bass 2.50 4.00
C7 Ken Iman 1.50 3.00
C8 Charlie Cowan 1.50 3.00
C9 Terry Baker 3.00 5.00
C10 Don Chuy 1.50 3.00
C11 Cliff Livingston 1.50 3.00
C12 Lamar Lundy 2.50 4.00
C13 Duane Allen 1.50 3.00
C14 Roman Gabriel 3.00 6.00
C15 Roosevelt Grier 3.00 6.00
C16 Mike Henry 1.50 3.00
C17 Merlin Olsen 5.00 10.00
C18 Deacon Jones 5.00 10.00
C19 Joe Scibelli 1.50 3.00
C20 Marlin McKeever 1.50 3.00
C21 Fred Brown 1.50 3.00
C22 Frank Budka 1.50 3.00
C23 Dan Currie 1.50 3.00
C24 Roger Davis 1.50 3.00
C25 Bruce Gossett 2.50 4.00
C26 Les Josephson 2.50 4.00
C27 Ed Meador 1.50 3.00
C28 Joe Krupa 1.50 3.00
C29 Aaron Martin 1.50 3.00
C30 Tommy McDonald 3.00 5.00
C31 Bucky Pope 1.50 3.00
C32 Jack Snow 2.50 4.00
C33 Joe Wendryhoski 1.50 3.00
C34 Clancy Williams 1.50 3.00
C35 Ben Wilson 1.50 3.00
C36 Team Logo 1.50 3.00

1965 Coke Caps Redskins

Please see the 1965 Coke Caps Bears listing for information on this set.

COMPLETE SET (36) 62.50 125.00
C1 Jimmy Carr 1.50 3.00
C2 Fred Mazurek 1.50 3.00
C3 Lonnie Sanders 1.50 3.00
C4 Jim Steffen 1.50 3.00
C5 John Nisby 1.50 3.00
C6 George Izo 2.50 4.00
C7 Vince Promuto 1.50 3.00
C8 Johnny Sample 2.50 4.00
C9 Pat Richter 2.50 4.00
C10 Preston Carpenter 1.50 3.00
C11 Sam Huff 5.00 10.00
C12 Pervis Atkins 1.50 3.00
C13 Steve Barnett 1.50 3.00
C14 Len Hauss 2.50 4.00
C15 Bill Anderson 1.50 3.00
C16 John Reger 1.50 3.00
C17 George Seals 1.50 3.00
C18 J.W. Lockett 1.50 3.00
C19 Tom Walters 1.50 3.00
C20 Joe Rutgens 1.50 3.00
C21 John Paluck 1.50 3.00
C22 Fran O'Brien 1.50 3.00
C23 Willie Adams 1.50 3.00
C24 Rod Breedlove 1.50 3.00
C25 Bob Pellegrini 1.50 3.00
C26 Bob Jencks 1.50 3.00
C27 Joe Hernandez 1.50 3.00
C28 Sonny Jurgensen 5.00 10.00
C29 Bob Toneff 1.50 3.00
C30 Charley Taylor 5.00 10.00
C31 Dick Shiner 1.50 3.00
C32 Bobby Williams 1.50 3.00
C33 Angelo Coia 1.50 3.00
C34 Ron Snidow 1.50 3.00
C35 Paul Krause 3.00 6.00
C36 Team Logo 1.50 3.00
NNO Redskins Saver Sheet 15.00 30.00

1965 Coke Caps Southern Pros

This set of Coke caps was created for and, apparently, only issued in the south as part of the Go with the Pros promotion. The player selection focused on athletes playing in the south or those who had college careers in the south. Most of the players appear in the various team sets as well but carry a different cap number in this set. The caps measure approximately 1 1/8" in diameter and have the drink logo and a football on the outside, while the inside has the player's face printed in black, with his team name above the photo, the player's name below, his position to the right and the cap number to the left including a "C" prefix. The 1965 caps are very similar to the 1966 issue but the 1965 caps do not have the words "Caramel Colored" on the outside of the cap. Football caps were also produced for 1965 on other Coca-Cola products: TAB (Low-Calorie Beverage), Fanta, King Size Coke and Sprite. The other drink caps typically carry a slight premium over the value of the basic Coke version.

C1 Bart Starr 12.50 25.00
C2 Roman Gabriel 4.00 8.00
C3 Tommy Mason 3.00 6.00
C4 Jim Patton 2.50 5.00
C5 Maxie Baughan 2.50 5.00
C6 Johnny Unitas 12.50 25.00
C7 Richie Petitbon 3.00 6.00
C8 Johnny Brewer 2.50 5.00
C9 Lee Roy Jordan 3.00 6.00
C10 John Gordy 2.50 5.00
C11 Theron Sapp 2.50 5.00
C12 Joe Childress 2.50 5.00
C13 Tommy Davis 2.50 5.00
C14 Sam Huff 4.00 8.00
C15 Clendon Thomas 2.50 5.00
C16 Jerry Stovall 2.50 5.00
C17 George Mira 2.50 5.00
C18 Sonny Jurgensen 6.00 12.00
C19 Jim Taylor 7.50 15.00
C20 Deacon Jones 4.00 8.00
C21 Fran Tarkenton 6.00 12.00
C22 Bookie Bolin 2.50 5.00
C23 Earl Gros 2.50 5.00
C24 Raymond Berry 6.00 12.00
C25 Bill Wade 3.00 6.00
C26 Ernie Green 2.50 5.00
C27 Bob Lilly 6.00 12.00
C28 Yale Lary 4.00 8.00
C29 Jimmy Orr 3.00 6.00
C30 Larry Morris 2.50 5.00
C31 Gene Hickerson 4.00 8.00
C32 Don Meredith 10.00 20.00
C33 Darris McCord 2.50 5.00
C34 Willie Davis 5.00 10.00
C35 Ed Meador 2.50 5.00
C36 Rip Hawkins 2.50 5.00
C37 Clarence Childs 2.50 5.00
C38 Norm Snead 4.00 8.00
C39 Charley Bradshaw 2.50 5.00
C40 Bill Koman 2.50 5.00
C41 J.D. Smith 3.00 6.00
C42 Preston Carpenter 2.50 5.00
C43 Buzz Nutter 2.50 5.00
C44 Sonny Randle 2.50 5.00
C45 John David Crow 3.00 6.00
C46 Tom Tracy 3.00 6.00
C47 Lou Michaels 3.00 6.00
C48 Joe Fortunato 2.50 5.00
C49 Bernie Parrish 2.50 5.00
C50 Harold Hays 2.50 5.00
C51 Pat Studstill 3.00 6.00
C52 Tom Moore 3.00 6.00
C53 Bucky Pope 2.50 5.00
C54 Jim Phillips 2.50 5.00
C55 Darrell Dess 2.50 5.00
C56 Riley Gunnels 2.50 5.00
C57 Don Chandler 2.50 5.00
C58 Tommy McDonald 4.00 8.00
C59 Bobby Walden 2.50 5.00
C60 Frank Lasky 2.50 5.00
C61 Tom Woodeshick 2.50 5.00
C62 Fred Miller 2.50 5.00
C63 Bobby Joe Green 2.50 5.00
C64 Frank Ryan 3.00 6.00
C65 Bob Hayes 7.50 15.00
C66 Hugh McInnis 2.50 5.00
C67 Ben McGee 2.50 5.00
C68 Bobby Joe Conrad 2.50 5.00
C69 Charlie Krueger 2.50 5.00
C70 Rick Casares 3.00 6.00

1965 Coke Caps Steelers

Please see the 1965 Coke Caps Bears listing for information on this set.

COMPLETE SET (36) 75.00 150.00
C1 John Baker 2.00 5.00
C2 Ed Brown 2.00 5.00
C3 Jim Kelly 2.00 5.00
C4 Willie Daniel 2.00 5.00
C5 Bob Harrison 2.00 5.00
C6 Dick Haley 2.00 5.00
C7 Dan James 2.00 5.00
C8 Gary Ballman 2.00 5.00
C9 Brady Keys 2.00 5.00
C10 Charlie Bradshaw 2.00 5.00
C11 Jim Bradshaw 2.00 5.00
C12 Bill Saul 2.00 5.00
C13 Paul Martha 2.00 5.00
C14 Mike Clark 2.00 5.00
C15 Ray Lemek 2.00 5.00
C16 Clarence Peaks 2.00 5.00
C17 Theron Sapp 2.00 5.00
C18 Ray Mansfield 2.00 5.00
C19 Chuck Hinton 2.00 5.00
C20 Bill Nelsen 2.50 6.00
C21 Dan LaRose 2.00 5.00
C22 Buzz Nutter 2.00 5.00
C23 Ben McGee 2.00 5.00
C24 Myron Pottios 2.00 5.00
C25 Max Messner 2.00 5.00
C26 Andy Russell 2.50 6.00
C27 Mike Sandusky 2.00 5.00
C28 Bob Schmitz 2.00 5.00
C29 Ron Stehouwer 2.00 5.00
C30 Clendon Thomas 2.00 5.00
C31 Tommy Wade 2.00 5.00
C32 Dick Hoak 2.00 5.00
C33 Marv Woodson 2.00 5.00
C34 John Burrell 2.00 5.00
C35 John Henry Johnson 4.00 8.00
C36 Team Logo 2.00 5.00

1965 Coke Caps Vikings

Please see the 1965 Coke Caps Bears listing for information on this set.

COMPLETE SET (36) 90.00 150.00
C1 Jerry Reichow 1.25 3.00
C2 Jim Prestel 1.25 3.00
C3 Jim Marshall 3.00 6.00
C4 Errol Linden 1.25 3.00
C5 Bob Lacey 1.25 3.00
C6 Rip Hawkins 1.25 3.00
C7 John Kirby 1.25 3.00
C8 Roy Winston 1.50 4.00
C9 Ron Vanderkelen 1.25 3.00
C10 Gordon Smith 1.25 3.00
C11 Larry Bowie 1.25 3.00
C12 Paul Flatley 1.50 4.00
C13 Grady Alderman 1.50 4.00
C14 Mick Tingelhoff 2.00 5.00
C15 Lee Calland 1.25 3.00
C16 Fred Cox 1.50 4.00
C17 Bill Brown 1.50 4.00
C18 Ed Sharockman 1.25 3.00
C19 George Rose 1.25 3.00
C20 Paul Dickson 1.25 3.00
C21 Tommy Mason 1.50 4.00
C22 Carl Eller 2.00 5.00
C23 Bill Jobko 1.25 3.00
C24 Hal Bedsole 1.25 3.00
C25 Karl Kassulke 1.25 3.00
C26 Fran Tarkenton 7.50 15.00
C27 Tom Hall 1.25 3.00
C28 Archie Sutton 1.25 3.00
C29 Jim Phillips 1.25 3.00
C30 Bill Swain 1.25 3.00
C31 Larry Vargo 1.25 3.00
C32 Bobby Walden 1.25 3.00
C33 Bob Berry 1.50 4.00
C34 Jeff Jordan 1.25 3.00
C35 Lance Rentzel 1.50 4.00
C36 Vikings Logo 1.25 3.00
NNO Vikings Saver Sheet 15.00 30.00

1966 Coke Caps All-Stars AFL

The AFL All-Star caps were issued in AFL cities (and a few other cities as well) along with the local team caps as part of the Score with the Pros promotion. The local team cap saver sheets had separate sections in which to affix both the local team's caps and the All-Stars' caps. The caps measure approximately 1 1/8" in diameter and have the drink logo and a football on the outside, while the inside has the player's face printed in black, with the words "AFL ALL STAR" above the player photo and his name below. The consumer could turn in his completed saver sheet to receive various prizes. The caps are numbered with a "C" prefix. These caps were also produced for 1966 on other Coca-Cola products: Tab,

Fanta, Fresca and Sprite. The other drink caps typically carry a slight premium over the value of the basic Coke version.

COMPLETE SET (34)	90.00	150.00
C37 Babe Parilli	1.50	3.00
C38 Mike Stratton	1.00	2.00
C39 Jack Kemp	12.50	25.00
C40 Len Dawson	3.75	7.50
C41 Fred Arbanas	1.00	2.00
C42 Bobby Bell	2.50	5.00
C43 Willie Brown	2.50	5.00
C44 Buck Buchanan	2.50	5.00
C45 Frank Buncom	1.00	2.00
C46 Nick Buoniconti	2.00	4.00
C47 Gino Cappelletti	1.50	3.00
C48 Eldon Danenhauer	1.00	2.00
C49 Clem Daniels	1.50	3.00
C50 Les Speedy Duncan	1.50	3.00
C51 Willie Frazier	1.00	2.00
C52 Cookie Gilchrist	1.50	3.00
C53 Dave Grayson	1.00	2.00
C54 John Hadl	2.00	4.00
C55 Wayne Hawkins	1.00	2.00
C56 Sherrill Headrick	1.00	2.00
C57 Charlie Hennigan	1.50	3.00
C58 E.J. Holub	1.00	2.00
C59 Curley Johnson	1.00	2.00
C60 Keith Lincoln	1.50	3.00
C61 Paul Lowe	1.50	3.00
C62 Don Maynard	3.00	6.00
C63 Jon Morris	1.00	2.00
C64 Joe Namath	15.00	30.00
C65 Jim Otto	2.50	5.00
C66 Dainard Paulson	1.00	2.00
C67 Art Powell	1.50	3.00
C68 Walt Sweeney	1.50	3.00
C69 Bob Talamini	1.00	2.00
C70 Lance Alworth UER	3.75	7.50

1966 Coke Caps All-Stars NFL

These NFL All-Star caps were issued in NFL cities (and a few other cities as well) along with the local team caps as part of the Score with the Pros promotion. The local team cap saver sheets had separate sections in which to affix both the local team's caps and the All-Stars' caps. The caps measure approximately 1 1/8" in diameter and have the drink logo and a football on the outside, while the inside has the player's face printed in black, with the words "NFL ALL STAR" above the player photo and his name below. The consumer could turn in his completed saver sheet to receive various prizes. The caps are numbered with a "C" prefix. These caps were also produced for 1966 on other Coca-Cola products: Tab, Fanta, Fresca and Sprite. The other drink caps typically carry a slight premium over the value of the basic Coke version.

COMPLETE SET (34)	50.00	100.00
C37 Frank Ryan	1.00	2.50
C38 Timmy Brown	1.00	2.50
C39 Tucker Frederickson	.75	2.00
C40 Cornell Green	1.00	2.50
C41 Bob Hayes	1.50	4.00
C42 Charley Taylor	1.25	3.00
C43 Pete Retzlaff	1.00	2.50
C44 Jim Ringo	1.25	3.00
C45 John Wooten	.75	2.00
C46 Dale Meinert	.75	2.00
C47 Bob Lilly	2.00	5.00
C48 Sam Silas	.75	2.00
C49 Roosevelt Brown	1.25	3.00
C50 Gary Ballman	.75	2.00
C51 Gary Collins	.75	2.00
C52 Sonny Randle	.75	2.00
C53 Charlie Johnson UER	1.00	2.50
C54 Herb Adderley	1.25	3.00
C55 Doug Atkins	1.25	3.00
C56 Roger Brown	.75	2.00
C57 Dick Butkus	4.00	10.00
C58 Willie Davis	1.25	3.00
C59 Tommy McDonald	1.00	2.50
C60 Alex Karras	1.50	4.00
C61 John Mackey	1.25	3.00
C62 Ed Meador	.75	2.00
C63 Merlin Olsen	1.50	4.00
C64 Dave Parks	.75	2.00
C65 Gale Sayers	4.00	10.00
C66 Fran Tarkenton	2.50	6.00
C67 Mick Tingelhoff	.75	2.00
C68 Ken Willard	.75	2.00
C69 Willie Wood	1.25	3.00
C70 Bill Brown	1.00	2.50

1966 Coke Caps Bears

Coca-Cola issued its final run of football caps in 1966. Each NFL team had a set released in their area along with the NFL All-Stars caps as part of the "Score with the Pros" promotion. Each team's Saver Sheets had separate sections in which to affix both the local team's caps and the All-Stars' caps. The caps measure approximately 1 1/8" in diameter and have the drink logo and a football on the outside, while the inside has the player's face printed in black with the team name above the photo, the player's name below, his position to the right and the cap number to the left. Some teams are also known to exist in a version that features a slightly smaller player photo. Cap numbers included a "C" prefix on all NFL teams except the Giants which had two versions with either "C" or "G" prefixes. The consumer could turn in his completed saver sheet to receive various prizes. The 1966 caps are very similar to the 1965 issue and many of the players are the same in both years. However, the 1966 caps have the words "Caramel Colored" on the outside of the cap while the 1965 caps do not. Most caps were also produced for 1966 on other Coca-Cola products: Tab (Dietary Beverage), Fanta, Fresca, King Size Coke and Sprite. These other drink caps typically carry a slight premium over the value of the Coke version.

COMPLETE SET (36)	75.00	135.00
C1 Bennie McRae	1.25	2.50
C2 Johnny Morris	1.25	2.50
C3 Roosevelt Taylor	2.00	4.00
C4 Doug Buffone	1.25	2.50
C5 Ed O'Bradovich	1.25	2.50
C6 Richie Petitbon	2.00	4.00
C7 Mike Pyle	1.25	2.50
C8 Dave Whitsell	1.25	2.50
C9 Dick Gordon	1.25	2.50
C10 John Johnson DT	1.25	2.50
C11 Jim Jones	1.25	2.50
C12 Andy Livingston	1.25	2.50
C13 Bob Kilcullen	1.25	2.50
C14 Roger LeClerc	1.25	2.50
C15 Herman Lee	1.25	2.50
C16 Earl Leggett	1.25	2.50
C17 Joe Marconi	1.25	2.50
C18 Rudy Bukich	2.00	4.00
C19 Mike Reilly	1.25	2.50
C20 Mike Ditka	5.00	10.00
C21 Dick Evey	1.25	2.50
C22 Joe Fortunato	1.25	2.50
C23 Bill Wade	3.00	5.00
C24 Jim Purnell	1.25	2.50
C25 Larry Glueck	1.25	2.50
C26 Mike Rabold	1.25	2.50
C27 Bob Wetoska	1.25	2.50
C28 Mike Rabold	1.25	2.50
C29 Jon Arnett	2.00	4.00
C30 Dick Butkus	15.00	25.00
C31 Charlie Bivins	1.25	2.50
C32 Ronnie Bull	2.00	4.00
C33 Jim Cadile	1.25	2.50
C34 George Seals	1.25	2.50
C35 Gale Sayers	15.00	25.00
C36 Bears Logo	1.25	2.50

1966 Coke Caps Bills

Coca-Cola issued its final run of football caps in 1966. Each AFL team had a set released in their area along with the AFL All-Stars caps as part of the "Score with the Pros" promotion. Each team's Saver Sheets had separate sections in which to affix both the local team's caps and the All-Stars' caps. The caps measure approximately 1 1/8" in diameter and have the drink logo and a football on the outside, while the inside has the player's face printed in black with the team name above the photo, the player's name below, his position to the right and the cap number to the left. Some teams are also known to exist in a version that features a slightly smaller player photo. Cap numbers included a "C" prefix on all AFL teams except the Jets (J prefix) and Bills (B prefix). The consumer could turn in his completed saver sheet to receive various prizes. The 1966 caps are very similar to the 1965 issue and many of the players are the same in both years. However, the 1966 caps have the words "Caramel Colored" on the outside of the cap while the 1965 caps do not. Most caps were also produced for 1966 on other Coca-Cola products: Tab, Fanta, Fresca, King Size Coke and Sprite. These other drink caps typically carry a slight premium over the value of the Coke version.

COMPLETE SET (35)	90.00	150.00
B1 Bill Laskey	1.25	2.50
B2 Marty Schottenheimer	6.00	12.00
B3 Stew Barber	2.50	4.00
B4 Glenn Bass	1.25	2.50
B5 Remi Prudhomme	1.25	2.50
B6 Al Bemiller	1.25	2.50
B7 George Butch Byrd	2.50	4.00
B8 Wray Carlton	2.50	4.00
B9 Hagood Clarke	1.25	2.50
B10 Jack Kemp	15.00	30.00
B11 Charley Warner	1.25	2.50
B12 Elbert Dubenion	2.50	4.00
B13 Jim Dunaway	2.50	4.00
B14 Booker Edgerson	2.50	4.00
B15 Paul Costa	1.25	2.50
B16 Henry Schmidt	1.25	2.50
B17 Dick Hudson	1.25	2.50
B18 Harry Jacobs	2.50	4.00
B19 Tom Janik	1.25	2.50
B20 Tom Day	2.50	4.00
B21 Daryle Lamonica	4.00	8.00
B22 Paul Maguire	3.00	6.00
B23 Roland McDole	2.50	4.00
B24 Dudley Meredith	1.25	2.50
B25 Joe O'Donnell	1.25	2.50
B26 Charley Ferguson	1.25	2.50
B27 Ed Rutkowski	1.25	2.50
B28 George Saimes	2.50	4.00
B29 Tom Sestak	2.50	4.00
B30 Billy Shaw	2.50	4.00
B31 Bob Lee Smith	1.25	2.50
B32 Mike Stratton	2.50	4.00
B33 Gene Sykes	1.25	2.50
B34 John Tracey	1.25	2.50
B35 Ernie Warlick	1.25	2.50
NNO Bills Saver Sheet	15.00	30.00

1966 Coke Caps Broncos

Please see the 1966 Coke Caps Bills listing for information on this set.

COMPLETE SET (36)	70.00	120.00
C1 Fred Forsberg	1.50	3.00
C2 Willie Brown DB	5.00	10.00
C3 Bob Scarpitto	2.50	4.00
C4 Butch Davis	1.50	3.00
C5 Al Denson	2.50	4.00
C6 Ron Sbranti	1.50	3.00
C7 John Bramlett	1.50	3.00
C8 Mickey Slaughter	1.50	3.00
C9 Lionel Taylor	3.00	5.00
C10 Jerry Sturm	1.50	3.00
C11 Jerry Hopkins	1.50	3.00
C12 Charlie Mitchell	1.50	3.00
C13 Ray Jacobs	1.50	3.00
C14 Lonnie Wright	1.50	3.00
C15 Goldie Sellers	1.50	3.00
C16 Ray Kubala	1.50	3.00
C17 John Griffin	1.50	3.00
C18 Bob Breitenstein	1.50	3.00
C19 Eldon Danenhauer	1.50	3.00
C20 Wendell Haynes	2.50	4.00
C21 Max Leetzow	1.50	3.00
C22 Nemiah Wilson	2.50	4.00
C23 Jim Thibert	1.50	3.00
C24 Gerry Bussell	1.50	3.00
C25 Bob McCullough	1.50	3.00
C26 Jim McMillin	1.50	3.00
C27 Abner Haynes	3.00	5.00
C28 Darrell Lester	1.50	3.00
C29 Cookie Gilchrist	3.00	5.00
C30 John McCormick	2.50	4.00
C31 Lee Bernet	1.50	3.00
C32 Goose Gonsoulin	2.50	4.00
C33 Scotty Glacken	1.50	3.00
C34 Bob Hadrick	1.50	3.00
C35 Archie Matsos	2.50	4.00
C36 Broncos Logo	1.50	3.00

1966 Coke Caps Browns

Please see the 1966 Coke Caps Bears listing for information on this set.

COMPLETE SET (36)	75.00	125.00
C1 Jim Ninowski	2.00	3.50
C2 Leroy Kelly	4.00	8.00
C3 Lou Groza	4.00	8.00
C4 Gary Collins	2.00	3.50
C5 Bill Glass	2.00	3.50
C6 Dale Lindsey	1.25	2.50
C7 Galen Fiss	1.25	2.50
C8 Ross Fichtner	1.25	2.50
C9 John Wooten	2.00	3.50
C10 Clifton McNeil	1.25	2.50
C11 Paul Wiggin	2.00	3.50
C12 Gene Hickerson	2.00	3.50
C13 Ernie Green	1.25	2.50
C14 Mike Howell	1.25	2.50
C15 Dick Schafrath	1.25	2.50
C16 Sidney Williams	1.25	2.50
C17 Frank Ryan	2.00	3.50
C18 Bernie Parrish	1.25	2.50
C19 Vince Costello	1.25	2.50
C20 John Brown OT	1.25	2.50
C21 Monte Clark	1.25	2.50
C22 Walter Roberts	1.25	2.50
C23 Johnny Brewer	1.25	2.50
C24 Walter Beach	1.25	2.50
C25 Dick Modzelewski	1.25	2.50
C26 Gary Lane	1.25	2.50
C27 Jim Houston	1.25	2.50
C28 Milt Morin	1.25	2.50
C29 Erich Barnes	1.25	2.50
C30 Tom Hutchinson	1.25	2.50
C31 John Morrow	1.25	2.50
C32 Jim Kanicki	1.25	2.50
C33 Paul Warfield	4.00	8.00
C34 Jim Garcia	1.25	2.50
C35 Walter Johnson	1.25	2.50
C36 Browns Logo	1.25	2.50
NNO Browns Saver Sheet	15.00	30.00

1966 Coke Caps Cardinals

Please see the 1966 Coke Caps Bears listing for information on this set.

COMPLETE SET (36)	50.00	100.00
C1 Pat Fischer	1.75	3.50
C2 Sonny Randle	1.75	3.50
C3 Joe Childress	1.25	2.50
C4 Dave Meggysey UER	2.50	5.00
C5 Joe Robb	1.25	2.50
C6 Jerry Stovall	1.25	2.50
C7 Ernie McMillan	1.75	3.50
C8 Dale Meinert	1.25	2.50
C9 Irv Goode	1.25	2.50
C10 Bob DeMarco	1.25	2.50
C11 Mal Hammack	1.25	2.50
C12 Jim Bakken	1.75	3.50
C13 Bill Thornton	1.25	2.50
C14 Buddy Humphrey	1.25	2.50
C15 Bill Koman	1.25	2.50
C16 Larry Wilson	3.00	6.00
C17 Charles Walker	1.25	2.50
C18 Prentice Gautt	1.25	2.50
C19 Charlie Johnson UER	2.00	4.00
C20 Ken Gray	1.25	2.50
C21 Dave Simmons	1.25	2.50
C22 Sam Silas	1.25	2.50
C23 Larry Stallings	1.25	2.50
C24 Don Brumm	1.25	2.50
C25 Bobby Joe Conrad	1.75	3.50
C26 Bill Triplett	1.25	2.50
C27 Luke Owens	1.25	2.50
C28 Jackie Smith	3.00	6.00
C29 Bob Reynolds	1.25	2.50
C30 Abe Woodson	1.75	3.50
C31 Jim Burson	1.25	2.50
C32 Willis Crenshaw	1.25	2.50
C33 Billy Gambrell	1.25	2.50
C34 Ray Ogden	1.25	2.50
C35 Herschel Turner	1.25	2.50
C36 Cardinals Logo	1.25	2.50
NNO Cardinals Saver Sheet	15.00	30.00

1966 Coke Caps Chargers

Please see the 1966 Coke Caps Bills listing for information on this set.

COMPLETE SET (36)	70.00	120.00
C1 John Hadl	4.00	8.00
C2 George Gross	1.50	3.00
C3 Frank Buncom	1.50	3.00
C4 Lance Alworth	4.00	8.00
C5 Paul Lowe	3.00	5.00
C6 Herb Travenio	1.50	3.00
C7 Dick Degen	1.50	3.00
C8 Jacque MacKinnon	1.50	3.00
C9 Les Duncan	2.50	4.00
C10 John Farris	1.50	3.00
C11 Willie Frazier	2.50	4.00
C12 Howard Kindig	1.50	3.00
C13 Pat Shea	1.50	3.00
C14 Fred Moore	1.50	3.00
C15 Bob Petrich	1.50	3.00
C16 Ron Mix	3.00	6.00
C17 Miller Farr	1.50	3.00
C18 Keith Lincoln	3.00	5.00
C19 Sam Gruneisen	1.50	3.00
C20 Jim Allison	1.50	3.00
C21 Chuck Allen	1.50	3.00
C22 Gene Foster	1.50	3.00
C23 Rick Redman	1.50	3.00
C24 Steve DeLong	1.50	3.00
C25 Gary Kirner	1.50	3.00
C26 Steve Tensi	1.50	3.00
C27 Kenny Graham	1.50	3.00
C28 Bud Whitehead	1.50	3.00
C29 Walt Sweeney	1.50	3.00
C30 Bob Zeman	1.50	3.00
C31 Gary Garrison	2.50	4.00
C32 Don Norton	1.50	3.00
C33 Ernie Wright	2.50	4.00
C34 Ron Carpenter	1.50	3.00
C35 Pete Jacques	1.50	3.00
C36 Team Logo	1.50	3.00

1966 Coke Caps Chiefs

Please see the 1966 Coke Caps Bills listing for information on this set.

COMPLETE SET (36)	75.00	150.00
C1 E.J. Holub	2.00	4.00
C2 Al Reynolds	1.50	3.00
C3 Buck Buchanan	4.00	8.00
C4 Curt Merz SP	4.00	8.00
C5 Dave Hill	1.50	3.00
C6 Bobby Hunt	1.50	3.00
C7 Jerry Mays	2.00	4.00
C8 Jon Gilliam	1.50	3.00
C9 Walt Corey	2.00	4.00
C10 Solomon Brannan	1.50	3.00
C11 Aaron Brown	1.50	3.00
C12 Bert Coan	1.50	3.00
C13 Ed Budde	2.00	4.00
C14 Tommy Brooker	1.50	3.00
C15 Bobby Bell	4.00	8.00
C16 Smokey Stover	1.50	3.00
C17 Curtis McClinton	2.00	4.00
C18 Jerrel Wilson	2.00	4.00
C19 Ron Burton	2.00	4.00
C20 Mike Garrett	2.50	5.00
C21 Jim Tyrer	2.00	4.00
C22 Johnny Robinson	2.00	4.00
C23 Bobby Ply	1.50	3.00
C24 Frank Pitts	1.50	3.00
C25 Ed Lothamer	1.50	3.00
C26 Sherrill Headrick	2.00	4.00
C27 Fred Williamson	3.00	6.00
C28 Chris Burford	2.00	4.00
C29 Willie Mitchell	1.50	3.00
C30 Otis Taylor	3.00	6.00
C31 Fred Arbanas	2.00	4.00

C32 Hatch Rosdahl 1.50 3.00
C33 Reg Carolan 1.50 3.00
C34 Len Dawson 6.00 12.00
C35 Pete Beathard 2.00 4.00
C36 Chiefs Logo 1.50 3.00
NNO Chiefs Saver Sheet 15.00 30.00

1966 Coke Caps Colts

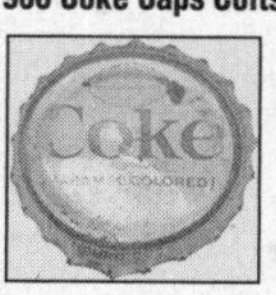

Please see the 1966 Coke Caps Bears listing for information on this set.

COMPLETE SET (36) 75.00 135.00
C1 Ted Davis 1.25 2.50
C2 Bob Boyd DB 1.25 2.50
C3 Lenny Moore 5.00 10.00
C4 Jackie Burkett 1.25 2.50
C5 Jimmy Orr 1.50 3.50
C6 Andy Stynchula 1.25 2.50
C7 Mike Curtis 3.00 6.00
C8 Jerry Logan 1.25 2.50
C9 Steve Stonebreaker 1.25 2.50
C10 John Mackey 4.00 8.00
C11 Dennis Gaubatz 1.25 2.50
C12 Don Shinnick 1.25 2.50
C13 Dick Szymanski 1.25 2.50
C14 Ordell Braase 1.25 2.50
C15 Lenny Lyles 1.25 2.50
C16 Rick Kestner 1.25 2.50
C17 Dan Sullivan 1.25 2.50
C18 Lou Michaels 1.50 3.50
C19 Gary Cuozzo 1.50 3.50
C20 Butch Wilson 1.25 2.50
C21 Willie Richardson 1.50 3.50
C22 Jim Welch 1.25 2.50
C23 Tony Lorick 1.25 2.50
C24 Billy Ray Smith 1.50 3.50
C25 Fred Miller 1.25 2.50
C26 Tom Matte 2.50 5.00
C27 Johnny Unitas 7.50 15.00
C28 Glenn Ressler 1.25 2.50
C29 Alvin Haymond 1.50 3.50
C30 Jim Parker 3.00 6.00
C31 Butch Allison 1.25 2.50
C32 Bob Vogel 1.25 2.50
C33 Jerry Hill 1.25 2.50
C34 Raymond Berry 5.00 10.00
C35 Sam Ball 1.25 2.50
C36 Colts Team Logo 1.25 2.50
NNO Colts Saver Sheet 15.00 30.00

1966 Coke Caps Cowboys

Please see the 1966 Coke Caps Bears listing for information on this set.

COMPLETE SET (36) 100.00 175.00
C1 Mike Connelly 2.00 4.00
C2 Tony Liscio 1.50 3.00
C3 Jethro Pugh 2.00 4.00
C4 Larry Stephens 1.50 3.00
C5 Jim Colvin 1.50 3.00
C6 Malcolm Walker 1.50 3.00
C7 Danny Villanueva 1.50 3.00
C8 Frank Clarke 2.00 4.00
C9 Don Meredith 7.50 15.00
C10 George Andrie 2.00 4.00
C11 Mel Renfro 5.00 10.00
C12 Pettis Norman 2.00 4.00
C13 Buddy Dial 2.00 4.00
C14 Pete Gent 2.00 4.00
C15 Jerry Rhome 2.00 4.00
C16 Bob Hayes 7.50 15.00
C17 Mike Gaechter 1.50 3.00
C18 Joe Bob Isbell 1.50 3.00
C19 Harold Hays 1.50 3.00
C20 Craig Morton 4.00 8.00
C21 Jake Kupp 1.50 3.00
C22 Cornell Green 2.00 4.00
C23 Dan Reeves 5.00 10.00
C24 Leon Donohue 1.50 3.00
C25 Dave Manders 1.50 3.00
C26 Warren Livingston 1.50 3.00
C27 Bob Lilly 6.00 12.00
C28 Chuck Howley 3.00 6.00
C29 Don Bishop 2.00 4.00
C30 Don Perkins 2.00 4.00
C31 Jim Boeke 1.50 3.00
C32 Dave Edwards 2.00 4.00
C33 Lee Roy Jordan 3.00 6.00
C34 Obert Logan 1.50 3.00
C35 Ralph Neely 2.00 4.00
C36 Cowboys Logo 1.50 3.00
NNO Cowboys Saver Sheet 15.00 30.00

1966 Coke Caps Eagles

Please see the 1966 Coke Caps Bears listing for information on this set.

COMPLETE SET (36) 75.00 135.00
C1 Norm Snead 2.00 4.00
C2 Al Nelson 1.25 2.50
C3 Jim Skaggs 1.25 2.50
C4 Glenn Glass 1.25 2.50
C5 Pete Retzlaff 1.75 3.50
C6 John Osmond 1.25 2.50
C7 Ray Rissmiller 1.25 2.50
C8 Lynn Hoyem 1.25 2.50
C9 King Hill 1.75 3.50
C10 Timmy Brown 1.75 3.50
C11 Ollie Matson 3.75 7.50
C12 Dave Lloyd 1.75 3.50
C13 Jim Ringo 3.00 6.00
C14 Floyd Peters 1.75 3.50
C15 Gary Pettigrew 1.25 2.50
C16 Frank Molden 1.25 2.50
C17 Earl Gros 1.75 3.50
C18 Fred Hill 1.25 2.50
C19 Don Hultz 1.25 2.50
C20 Ray Poage 1.25 2.50
C21 Aaron Martin 1.25 2.50
C22 Mike Morgan 1.25 2.50
C23 Lane Howell 1.25 2.50
C24 Ed Blaine 1.25 2.50
C25 Jack Concannon 1.75 3.50
C26 Sam Baker 1.25 2.50
C27 Tom Woodeshick 1.75 3.50
C28 Joe Scarpati 1.25 2.50
C29 John Meyers 1.25 2.50
C30 Nate Ramsey 1.75 3.50
C31 Ben Hawkins 1.25 2.50
C32 Bob Brown T 1.75 3.50
C33 Willie Brown WR 1.25 2.50
C34 Ron Goodwin 1.25 2.50
C35 Randy Beisler 1.25 2.50
C36 Team Logo 1.25 2.50
NNO Eagles Saver Sheet 15.00 30.00

1966 Coke Caps Falcons

Please see the 1966 Coke Caps Bears listing for information on this set.

COMPLETE SET (36) 50.00 100.00
C1 Tommy Nobis 4.00 8.00
C2 Ernie Wheelwright 1.75 3.50
C3 Lee Calland 1.25 2.50
C4 Chuck Sieminski 1.25 2.50
C5 Dennis Claridge 1.75 3.50
C6 Ralph Heck 1.25 2.50
C7 Alex Hawkins 1.75 3.50
C8 Dan Grimm 1.75 3.50
C9 Marion Rushing 1.25 2.50
C10 Bobbie Johnson 1.25 2.50
C11 Bobby Franklin 1.25 2.50
C12 Bill McWatters 1.25 2.50
C13 Billy Lothridge 1.75 3.50
C14 Billy Martin E 1.75 3.50
C15 Tom Wilson 1.25 2.50
C16 Dennis Murphy 1.25 2.50
C17 Randy Johnson 1.75 3.50
C18 Guy Reese 1.25 2.50
C19 Frank Marchlewski 1.25 2.50
C20 Don Talbert 1.25 2.50
C21 Errol Linden 1.25 2.50
C22 Dan Lewis 1.25 2.50
C23 Ed Cook 1.25 2.50
C24 Hugh McInnis 1.25 2.50
C25 Frank Lasky 1.25 2.50
C26 Bob Jencks 1.25 2.50
C27 Bill Jobko 1.25 2.50
C28 Nick Rassas 1.25 2.50
C29 Bob Riggle 1.25 2.50
C30 Ken Reaves 1.75 3.50
C31 Bob Sanders 1.25 2.50
C32 Steve Sloan 1.75 3.50
C33 Ron Smith 1.75 3.50
C34 Bob Whitlow 1.25 2.50
C35 Roger Anderson 1.25 2.50
C36 Falcons Logo 1.25 2.50
NNO Falcons Saver Sheet 15.00 30.00

1966 Coke Caps 49ers

Please see the 1966 Coke Caps Bears listing for information on this set.

COMPLETE SET (36) 75.00 135.00
C1 Bernie Casey 1.75 3.50
C2 Bruce Bosley 1.75 3.50
C3 Kermit Alexander 1.75 3.50
C4 John Brodie 3.75 7.50
C5 Dave Parks 1.75 3.50
C6 Len Rohde 1.75 3.50
C7 Walter Rock 1.75 3.50
C8 George Mira 2.50 5.00
C9 Karl Rubke 1.25 2.50
C10 Ken Willard 1.75 3.50
C11 John David Crow UER 2.00 4.00
C12 George Donnelly 1.25 2.50
C13 Dave Wilcox 2.00 4.00
C14 Vern Burke 1.25 2.50
C15 Wayne Swinford 1.25 2.50
C16 Elbert Kimbrough 1.25 2.50
C17 Clark Miller 1.25 2.50
C18 Dave Kopay 1.75 3.50
C19 Joe Cerne 1.25 2.50
C20 Roland Lakes 1.25 2.50
C21 Charlie Krueger 1.75 3.50
C22 Billy Kilmer 2.50 5.00
C23 Jim Johnson 3.00 6.00
C24 Matt Hazeltine 1.75 3.50
C25 Mike Dowdle 1.25 2.50
C26 Jim Wilson 1.25 2.50
C27 Tommy Davis 1.75 3.50
C28 Jim Norton 1.25 2.50
C29 Jack Chapple 1.25 2.50
C30 Ed Beard 1.25 2.50
C31 John Thomas 1.25 2.50
C32 Monty Stickles 1.25 2.50
C33 Kay McFarland 1.25 2.50
C34 Gary Lewis 1.25 2.50
C35 Howard Mudd 1.25 2.50
C36 49ers Logo 1.25 2.50
NNO 49ers Saver Sheet 15.00 30.00

1966 Coke Caps Giants C

Please see the 1966 Coke Caps Bears listing for information on this set.

COMPLETE SET (36) 60.00 100.00
C1 Joe Morrison 2.00 3.50
C2 Dick Lynch 2.00 3.50
C3 Pete Case 2.00 3.50
C4 Clarence Childs 1.50 2.50
C5 Aaron Thomas 2.00 3.50
C6 Jim Carroll 1.50 2.50
C7 Henry Carr 2.00 3.50
C8 Bookie Bolin 1.50 2.50
C9 Roosevelt Davis 1.50 2.50
C10 John Lovetere 1.50 2.50
C11 Jim Patton 2.00 3.50
C12 Wendell Harris 1.50 2.50
C13 Roger LaLonde 1.50 2.50
C14 Jerry Hillebrand 1.50 2.50
C15 Spider Lockhart 2.00 3.50
C16 Del Shofner 2.00 3.50
C17 Earl Morrall 3.00 5.00
C18 Roosevelt Brown 3.00 5.00
C19 Greg Larson 2.00 3.50
C20 Jim Katcavage 2.00 3.50
C21 Smith Reed 1.50 2.50
C22 Lou Slaby 1.50 2.50
C23 Jim Moran 1.50 2.50
C24 Bill Swain 1.50 2.50
C25 Steve Thurlow 1.50 2.50
C26 Olen Underwood 1.50 2.50
C27 Gary Wood 2.00 3.50
C28 Larry Vargo 1.50 2.50
C29 Jim Prestel 1.50 2.50
C30 Tucker Frederickson 2.00 3.50
C31 Bob Timberlake 1.50 2.50
C32 Chuck Mercein 2.50 4.00
C33 Ernie Koy 2.00 3.50
C34 Tom Costello 1.50 2.50
C35 Homer Jones 2.00 3.50
C36 Team Logo 1.50 2.50

1966 Coke Caps Giants G

Please see the 1966 Coke Caps Bears listing for information on this set.

COMPLETE SET (35) 60.00 100.00
G1 Joe Morrison 2.00 3.50
G2 Dick Lynch 2.00 3.50
G3 Pete Case 2.00 3.50
G4 Clarence Childs 1.50 2.50
G5 Aaron Thomas 2.00 3.50
G6 Jim Carroll 1.50 2.50
G7 Henry Carr 2.00 3.50
G8 Bookie Bolin 1.50 2.50
G9 Roosevelt Davis 1.50 2.50
G10 John Lovetere 1.50 2.50
G11 Jim Patton 2.00 3.50
G12 Wendell Harris 1.50 2.50
G13 Roger LaLonde 1.50 2.50
G14 Jerry Hillebrand 1.50 2.50
G15 Spider Lockhart 2.00 3.50
G16 Del Shofner 2.00 3.50
G17 Earl Morrall 2.50 5.00
G18 Roosevelt Brown 2.50 5.00
G19 Greg Larson 2.00 3.50
G20 Jim Katcavage 2.00 3.50
G21 Smith Reed 1.50 2.50
G22 Lou Slaby 1.50 2.50
G23 Jim Moran 1.50 2.50
G24 Bill Swain 1.50 2.50
G25 Steve Thurlow 1.50 2.50
G26 Olen Underwood 1.50 2.50
G27 Gary Wood 2.00 3.50
G28 Larry Vargo 1.50 2.50
G29 Jim Prestel 1.50 2.50
G30 Tucker Frederickson 2.00 3.50
G31 Bob Timberlake 1.50 2.50
G32 Chuck Mercein 2.50 4.00
G33 Ernie Koy 2.00 3.50
G34 Tom Costello 1.50 2.50
G35 Homer Jones 2.00 3.50
NNO Giants Saver Sheet 15.00 30.00

1966 Coke Caps Jets

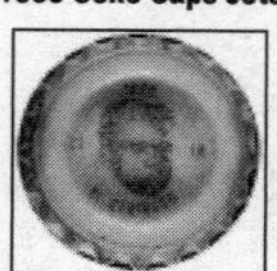

Please see the 1966 Coke Caps Bills listing for information on this set.

COMPLETE SET (35) 75.00 150.00
J1 Don Maynard 5.00 10.00
J2 George Sauer Jr. 2.50 5.00
J3 Paul Crane 1.25 2.50
J4 Jim Colclough 1.25 2.50
J5 Matt Snell 3.00 6.00
J6 Sherman Lewis 3.00 6.00
J7 Jim Turner 1.75 3.50
J8 Mike Taliaferro 1.25 2.50
J9 Cornell Gordon 1.75 3.50
J10 Mark Smolinski 1.25 2.50
J11 Al Atkinson 1.75 3.50
J12 Paul Rochester 1.25 2.50
J13 Sherman Plunkett 1.25 2.50
J14 Gerry Philbin 1.75 3.50
J15 Pete Lammons 1.75 3.50
J16 Dainard Paulson 1.25 2.50
J17 Joe Namath 25.00 50.00
J18 Winston Hill 1.75 3.50
J19 Dee Mackey 1.25 2.50
J20 Curley Johnson 1.25 2.50
J21 Verlon Biggs 1.75 3.50
J22 Bill Mathis 1.75 3.50
J23 Carl McAdams 1.25 2.50
J24 Bert Wilder 1.25 2.50
J25 Larry Grantham 1.75 3.50
J26 Bill Yearby 1.25 2.50
J27 Sam DeLuca 1.25 2.50
J28 Bill Baird 1.25 2.50
J29 Ralph Baker 1.75 3.50
J30 Ray Abruzzese 1.25 2.50
J31 Jim Hudson 1.25 2.50
J32 Dave Herman 1.75 3.50
J33 John Schmitt 1.25 2.50
J34 Jim Harris 1.25 2.50
J35 Bake Turner 1.75 3.50
NNO Jets Saver Sheet 15.00 30.00

1966 Coke Caps Lions

Please see the 1966 Coke Caps Bears listing for information on this set.

COMPLETE SET (36) 50.00 100.00
C1 Pat Studstill 1.75 3.50
C2 Ed Flanagan 1.75 3.50
C3 Wayne Walker 1.75 3.50
C4 Tom Watkins 1.25 2.50
C5 Tommy Vaughn 1.25 2.50
C6 Jim Kearney 1.25 2.50
C7 Larry Hand 1.75 3.50
C8 Jerry Rush 1.25 2.50
C9 Roger Brown 1.75 3.50
C10 Tom Nowatzke 1.75 3.50
C11 John Henderson 1.25 2.50
C12 Tom Myers QB 1.25 2.50
C13 Ron Kramer 1.75 3.50
C14 Dick LeBeau 1.75 3.50
C15 Amos Marsh 1.75 3.50
C16 Wally Hilgenberg 1.75 3.50
C17 Bruce Maher 1.25 2.50
C18 Darris McCord 1.75 3.50
C19 Ted Karras 1.25 2.50
C20 Ernie Clark 1.25 2.50
C21 Gail Cogdill 1.75 3.50
C22 Wayne Rasmussen 1.25 2.50
C23 Joe Don Looney 4.00 8.00
C24 Jim Gibbons 1.75 3.50
C25 John Gonzaga 1.25 2.50
C26 John Gordy 1.25 2.50
C27 Bobby Thompson 1.25 2.50
C28 J.D. Smith 1.25 2.50
C29 Roger Shoals 1.25 2.50
C30 Alex Karras 3.50 7.00
C31 Nick Pietrosante 1.75 3.50
C32 Milt Plum 2.00 4.00
C33 Daryl Sanders 1.25 2.50
C34 Mike Lucci 1.75 3.50
C35 George Izo 1.75 3.50
C36 Lions Logo 1.25 2.50

1966 Coke Caps National NFL

As part of an advertising promotion, Coca-Cola issued 21 sets of bottle caps, covering the 14 NFL cities, the six AFL cities, and a separate National set for cities not reached by the leagues. This National issue was released primarily in non-NFL cities as part of the Score with the Pros promotion. There was a separate Saver Sheet for the National set. The caps measure approximately 1 1/8" in diameter and have the drink logo and a football on the outside, while the inside has the player's face printed in black, with text surrounding the face. The consumer could turn in his completed saver sheet to receive various prizes. The caps are numbered with a "C" prefix. These caps were also produced for 1966 on other Coca-Cola products: Tab, Fanta, Fresca and Sprite. The other drink caps typically carry a slight premium of 1.5X to 2X the value of the Coke version.

COMPLETE SET (70) 112.50 225.00
C1 Larry Wilson 2.50 5.00
C2 Frank Ryan 1.75 3.50
C3 Norm Snead 1.75 3.50
C4 Mel Renfro 2.50 5.00
C5 Timmy Brown 1.75 3.50
C6 Tucker Frederickson 1.25 2.50

C7 Jim Bakken 1.25 2.50
C8 Paul Krause 2.00 4.00
C9 Irv Cross 1.25 2.50
C10 Cornell Green 1.75 3.50
C11 Pat Fischer 1.25 2.50
C12 Bob Hayes 3.00 6.00
C13 Charley Taylor 2.50 5.00
C14 Pete Retzlaff 1.75 3.50
C15 Jim Ringo 2.50 5.00
C16 Maxie Baughan 1.25 2.50
C17 Chuck Howley 1.50 3.00
C18 John Wooten 1.25 2.50
C19 Bob DeMarco 1.25 2.50
C20 Dale Meinert 1.25 2.50
C21 Gene Hickerson 1.25 2.50
C22 George Andrie 1.25 2.50
C23 Joe Rutgens 1.25 2.50
C24 Bob Lilly 5.00 10.00
C25 Sam Silas 1.25 2.50
C26 Bob Brown OT 1.75 3.50
C27 Dick Schafrath 1.25 2.50
C28 Roosevelt Brown 2.50 5.00
C29 Jim Houston 1.25 2.50
C30 Paul Wiggin 1.25 2.50
C31 Gary Ballman 1.25 2.50
C32 Gary Collins 1.75 3.50
C33 Sonny Randle 1.25 2.50
C34 Charley Johnson 1.75 3.50
C35 Browns Logo 1.25 2.50
C36 Packers Logo 1.25 2.50
C37 Herb Adderley 2.50 5.00
C38 Grady Alderman 1.25 2.50
C39 Doug Atkins 2.50 5.00
C40 Bruce Bosley UER 1.25 2.50
C41 John Brodie UER 2.50 5.00
C42 Roger Brown 1.25 2.50
C43 Bill Brown 1.25 2.50
C44 Dick Butkus 7.50 15.00
C45 Lee Roy Caffey 1.25 2.50
C46 John David Crow UER 1.75 3.50
C47 Willie Davis 2.50 5.00
C48 Mike Ditka 6.00 12.00
C49 Joe Fortunato 1.25 2.50
C50 John Gordy 1.25 2.50
C51 Deacon Jones 2.50 5.00
C52 Alex Karras 3.75 7.50
C53 Dick LeBeau 1.25 2.50
C54 Jerry Logan 1.25 2.50
C55 John Mackey 2.50 5.00
C56 Ed Meador 1.25 2.50
C57 Tommy McDonald 1.75 3.50
C58 Merlin Olsen 3.75 7.50
C59 Jimmy Orr 1.75 3.50
C60 Jim Parker 2.50 5.00
C61 Dave Parks 1.25 2.50
C62 Walter Rock 1.25 2.50
C63 Gale Sayers 7.50 15.00
C64 Pat Studstill 1.25 2.50
C65 Fran Tarkenton 6.00 12.00
C66 Mick Tingelhoff 1.75 3.50
C67 Bob Vogel 1.25 2.50
C68 Wayne Walker 1.25 2.50
C69 Ken Willard 1.25 2.50
C70 Willie Wood 2.50 5.00
NNO National Saver Sheet 7.50 15.00

1966 Coke Caps Oilers

Please see the 1966 Coke Caps Bills listing for information on this set.

COMPLETE SET (36) 62.50 125.00
C1 Scott Appleton 1.50 3.00
C2 George Allen 2.50 4.00
C3 Don Floyd 1.50 3.00
C4 Ronnie Caveness 1.50 3.00
C5 Jim Norton 1.50 3.00
C6 Jacky Lee 2.50 4.00
C7 George Blanda 7.50 15.00
C8 Tony Banfield 2.50 4.00
C9 George Rice 1.50 3.00
C10 Charley Tolar 2.50 4.00
C11 Bobby Jancik 1.50 3.00
C12 Freddy Glick 1.50 3.00
C13 Ode Burrell 2.50 4.00
C14 Walt Suggs 2.50 4.00
C15 Bob McLeod 1.50 3.00
C16 Johnny Baker 1.50 3.00
C17 Danny Brabham 1.50 3.00
C18 Gary Cutsinger 2.50 4.00
C19 Doug Cline 1.50 3.00
C20 Hoyle Granger 2.50 4.00
C21 Bob Talamini 2.50 4.00
C22 Don Trull 2.50 4.00
C23 Charlie Hennigan 2.50 4.00
C24 Sid Blanks 2.50 4.00
C25 Pat Holmes 1.50 3.00
C26 John Frongillo 1.50 3.00
C27 John Wittenborn 1.50 3.00
C28 George Kinney 1.50 3.00
C29 Charles Frazier 1.50 3.00
C30 Ernie Ladd 4.00 8.00
C31 W.K. Hicks 1.50 3.00
C32 Sonny Bishop 2.50 4.00
C33 Larry Elkins 2.50 4.00
C34 Glen Ray Hines 2.50 4.00
C35 Bobby Maples 2.50 4.00
C36 Oilers Logo 1.50 3.00
NNO Oilers Saver Sheet 15.00 30.00

1966 Coke Caps Packers

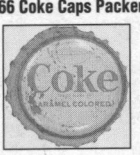

Please see the 1966 Coke Caps Bears listing for information on this set.

COMPLETE SET (31) 100.00 175.00
C1 Herb Adderley 4.00 8.00
C2 Lionel Aldridge 2.50 4.00
C3 Bob Long 1.50 3.00
C4 Willie Davis 4.00 8.00
C5 Boyd Dowler 2.50 4.00
C6 Marv Fleming 2.50 4.00
C7 Ken Bowman 2.50 4.00
C8 Tom Brown 1.50 3.00
C9 Doug Hart 1.50 3.00
C10 Steve Wright 1.50 3.00
C11 Bill Anderson 1.50 3.00
C12 Bill Curry 2.50 4.00
C13 Tommy Crutcher 1.50 3.00
C14 Fred Thurston 4.00 8.00
C15 Elijah Pitts 2.50 4.00
C16 Lloyd Voss 1.50 3.00
C17 Lee Roy Caffey 1.50 3.00
C18 Dave Robinson 3.00 5.00
C19 Bart Starr 7.50 15.00
C20 Ray Nitschke 5.00 10.00
C21 Max McGee 2.50 4.00
C22 Don Chandler 2.50 4.00
C23 Rich Marshall 1.50 3.00
C24 Ron Kostelnik 1.50 3.00
C25 Carroll Dale 2.50 4.00
C26 Hank Jordan 4.00 8.00
C27 Bob Jeter 2.50 4.00
C28 Bob Skoronski 1.50 3.00
C29 Jerry Kramer 3.00 6.00
C30 Willie Wood 4.00 8.00
C31 Paul Hornung 7.50 15.00
C32 Forrest Gregg 4.00 8.00
C33 Zeke Bratkowski 2.50 4.00
C34 Tom Moore 2.50 4.00
C35 Jim Taylor 5.00 10.00
C36 Packers Team Emblem 1.50 3.00
NNO Packers Saver Sheet 15.00 30.00

1966 Coke Caps Patriots

Please see the 1966 Coke Caps Bills listing for information on this set.

COMPLETE SET (36) 75.00 125.00
C1 Jon Morris 2.50 4.00
C2 Don Webb 1.50 3.00
C3 Charles Long 1.50 3.00
C4 Tony Romeo 1.50 3.00
C5 Bob Dee 2.50 4.00
C6 Tommy Addison 2.50 4.00
C7 Tom Neville 2.50 4.00
C8 Ron Hall 1.50 3.00
C9 White Graves 1.50 3.00
C10 Ellis Johnson 1.50 3.00
C11 Don Oakes 1.50 3.00
C12 Tom Yewcic 1.50 3.00
C13 Tom Hennessey 1.50 3.00
C14 Jay Cunningham 1.50 3.00
C15 Larry Garron 2.50 4.00
C16 Justin Canale 1.50 3.00
C17 Art Graham 2.50 4.00
C18 Babe Parilli 2.50 4.00
C19 Jim Hunt 2.50 4.00
C20 Karl Singer 1.50 3.00
C21 Houston Antwine 2.50 4.00
C22 Nick Buoniconti 3.00 6.00
C23 John Huarte 2.50 5.00
C24 Gino Cappelletti 2.50 4.00
C25 Chuck Shonta 1.50 3.00
C26 Dick Felt 2.50 4.00
C27 Mike Dukes 1.50 3.00
C28 Larry Eisenhauer 2.50 4.00
C29 Jim Fraser 1.50 3.00
C30 Len St. Jean 2.50 4.00
C31 J.D. Garrett 1.50 3.00
C32 Jim Whalen 1.50 3.00
C33 Jim Nance 2.50 5.00
C34 Dick Arrington 1.50 3.00
C35 Lonnie Farmer 1.50 3.00
C36 Patriots Logo 1.50 3.00
NNO Patriots Saver Sheet 15.00 30.00

1966 Coke Caps Raiders

Please see the 1966 Coke Caps Bills listing for information on this set.

COMPLETE SET (36) 70.00 120.00
C1 Fred Biletnikoff 4.00 8.00
C2 Gus Otto 1.50 3.00
C3 Harry Schuh 1.50 3.00
C4 Ken Herock 1.50 3.00
C5 Claude Gibson 1.50 3.00
C6 Cotton Davidson 2.50 4.00
C7 Cliff Kenney 1.50 3.00
C8 Ben Davidson 3.00 5.00
C9 Roger Hagberg 1.50 3.00
C10 Bob Svihus 1.50 3.00
C11 John R. Williamson 1.50 3.00
C12 Dave Grayson 1.50 3.00
C13 Hewritt Dixon 2.50 4.00
C14 Dave Costa 1.50 3.00
C15 Tom Keating 1.50 3.00
C16 Alan Miller 1.50 3.00
C17 Billy Cannon 3.00 5.00
C18 Wayne Hawkins 2.50 4.00
C19 Warren Powers 1.50 3.00
C20 Joe Labruzzo 1.50 3.00
C21 Dan Conners 1.50 3.00
C22 Jim Otto 3.00 6.00
C23 Clem Daniels 2.50 4.00
C24 Tom Flores 3.00 5.00
C25 Art Powell 2.50 4.00
C26 Larry Todd 1.50 3.00
C27 James Harvey 1.50 3.00
C28 Dan Birdwell 1.50 3.00
C29 Carleton Oats 1.50 3.00
C30 Mike Mercer 1.50 3.00
C31 Pete Banaszak 1.50 3.00
C32 Bill Budness 1.50 3.00
C33 Kent McCloughan 1.50 3.00
C34 Howie Williams 1.50 3.00
C35 Rodger Bird 1.50 3.00
C36 Team Logo 1.50 3.00

1966 Coke Caps Rams

Please see the 1966 Coke Caps Bears listing for information on this set.

COMPLETE SET (36) 62.50 125.00
C1 Tom Mack 4.00 8.00
C2 Tom Moore 1.25 2.50
C3 Bill Munson 2.00 3.50
C4 Bill George 3.00 6.00
C5 Joe Carollo 1.25 2.50
C6 Dick Bass 2.00 3.50
C7 Ken Iman 1.25 2.50
C8 Charlie Cowan 2.00 3.50
C9 Terry Baker RB 3.00 5.00
C10 Don Chuy 1.25 2.50
C11 Jack Pardee 2.00 3.50
C12 Lamar Lundy 2.00 3.50
C13 Bill Anderson 1.25 2.50
C14 Roman Gabriel 3.00 6.00
C15 Roosevelt Grier 3.00 6.00
C16 Billy Truax 2.00 3.50
C17 Merlin Olsen 4.00 8.00
C18 Deacon Jones 4.00 8.00
C19 Joe Scibelli 1.25 2.50
C20 Marlin McKeever 1.25 2.50
C21 Doug Woodlief 1.25 2.50
C22 Chuck Lamson 1.25 2.50
C23 Dan Currie 1.25 2.50
C24 Maxie Baughan 2.00 3.50
C25 Bruce Gossett 2.00 3.50
C26 Les Josephson 2.00 3.50
C27 Ed Meador 1.25 2.50
C28 Anthony Guillory 1.25 2.50
C29 Irv Cross 2.00 3.50
C30 Tommy McDonald 3.00 5.00
C31 Bucky Pope 1.25 2.50
C32 Jack Snow 2.00 3.50
C33 Joe Wendryhoski 1.25 2.50
C34 Clancy Williams 1.25 2.50
C35 Ben Wilson 1.25 2.50
C36 Rams Logo 1.25 2.50
NNO Rams Saver Sheet 15.00 30.00

1966 Coke Caps Redskins

Please see the 1966 Coke Caps Bears listing for information on this set.

COMPLETE SET (36) 75.00 125.00
C1 Don Croftcheck 1.50 3.00
C2 Fred Mazurek 1.50 3.00
C3 Lonnie Sanders 1.50 3.00
C4 Jim Steffen 1.50 3.00
C5 Jim Shofner 2.00 4.00
C6 Bill Hunter 1.50 3.00
C7 Vince Promuto 1.50 3.00
C8 Jerry Smith 1.50 3.00
C9 Pat Richter 1.50 3.00
C10 Preston Carpenter 1.50 3.00
C11 Sam Huff 4.00 8.00
C12 Darrell Dess 1.50 3.00
C13 Jim Snowden 1.50 3.00
C14 Len Hauss 1.50 3.00
C15 Chris Hanburger 2.00 4.00
C16 John Reger 1.50 3.00
C17 George Hughley 1.50 3.00
C18 Rickie Harris 1.50 3.00
C19 Tom Walters 1.50 3.00
C20 Joe Rutgens 1.50 3.00
C21 Carl Kammerer 1.50 3.00
C22 Fran O'Brien 1.50 3.00
C23 Willie Adams 1.50 3.00
C24 Bill Clay 1.50 3.00
C25 Charlie Gogolak 1.50 3.00
C26 Dick Lemay 1.50 3.00
C27 Walter Barnes 1.50 3.00
C28 Sonny Jurgensen 4.00 8.00
C29 John Strohmeyer 1.50 3.00
C30 Charley Taylor 4.00 8.00
C31 Dick Shiner 1.50 3.00
C32 Fred Williams 1.50 3.00
C33 Angelo Coia 1.50 3.00
C34 Ron Snidow 1.50 3.00
C35 Paul Krause 2.50 5.00
C36 Team Logo 1.50 3.00

1966 Coke Caps Steelers

Please see the 1966 Coke Caps Bears listing for information on this set.

COMPLETE SET (36) 70.00 120.00
C1 John Baker 1.50 3.00
C2 Mike Lind 2.50 4.00
C3 Ken Kortas 1.50 3.00
C4 Willie Daniel 1.50 3.00
C5 Roy Jefferson 2.50 4.00
C6 Bob Hohn 1.50 3.00
C7 Dan James 1.50 3.00
C8 Gary Ballman 2.50 4.00
C9 Brady Keys 1.50 3.00
C10 Charley Bradshaw 2.50 4.00
C11 Jim Bradshaw 1.50 3.00
C12 Jim Butler 2.50 4.00
C13 Paul Martha 2.50 4.00
C14 Mike Clark 1.50 3.00
C15 Ray Lemek 1.50 3.00
C16 Clarence Peaks 2.50 4.00
C17 Theron Sapp 1.50 3.00
C18 Ray Mansfield 2.50 4.00
C19 Chuck Hinton 1.50 3.00
C20 Bill Nelsen 2.50 4.00
C21 Rod Breedlove 1.50 3.00
C22 Frank Lambert 1.50 3.00
C23 Ben McGee 1.50 3.00
C24 Myron Pottios 2.50 4.00
C25 John Campbell 1.50 3.00
C26 Andy Russell 2.50 5.00
C27 Mike Sandusky 1.50 3.00
C28 Bob Schmitz 1.50 3.00
C29 Riley Gunnels 1.50 3.00
C30 Clendon Thomas 2.50 4.00
C31 Tommy Wade 1.50 3.00
C32 Dick Hoak 2.50 4.00
C33 Marv Woodson 1.50 3.00
C34 Bob Nichols 1.50 3.00
C35 John Henry Johnson 3.00 6.00
C36 Steelers Logo 1.50 3.00
NNO Steelers Saver Sheet 15.00 30.00

1966 Coke Caps Vikings

Please see the 1966 Coke Caps Bears listing for information on this set.

COMPLETE SET (36) 50.00 100.00
C1 Milt Sunde 1.75 3.50
C2 Don Hansen 1.25 2.50
C3 Jim Marshall 3.00 6.00
C4 Jerry Shay 1.25 2.50
C5 Ken Byers 1.25 2.50
C6 Rip Hawkins 1.25 2.50
C7 John Kirby 1.25 2.50
C8 Roy Winston 1.75 3.50
C9 Ron VanderKelen 1.75 3.50
C10 Jim Lindsey 1.25 2.50
C11 Paul Flatley 1.75 3.50
C12 Larry Bowie 1.25 2.50
C13 Grady Alderman 1.75 3.50
C14 Mick Tingelhoff 2.50 5.00
C15 Lonnie Warwick 1.75 3.50
C16 Fred Cox 1.75 3.50
C17 Bill Brown 1.75 3.50
C18 Ed Sharockman 1.75 3.50
C19 George Rose 1.25 2.50
C20 Paul Dickson 1.25 2.50
C21 Tommy Mason 1.75 3.50
C22 Carl Eller 3.00 6.00
C23 Jim Young 1.25 2.50
C24 Hal Bedsole 1.25 2.50
C25 Karl Kassulke 1.75 3.50
C26 Fran Tarkenton 6.00 12.00
C27 Tom Hall 1.25 2.50
C28 Archie Sutton 1.25 2.50
C29 Jim Phillips 1.25 2.50
C30 Gary Larsen 1.75 3.50
C31 Phil King 1.25 2.50
C32 Bobby Walden 1.25 2.50
C33 Bob Berry 1.75 3.50
C34 Jeff Jordan 1.25 2.50
C35 Lance Rentzel 1.75 3.50
C36 Team Logo 1.25 2.50
NNO Vikings Saver Sheet 15.00 30.00

1971 Coke Caps Packers

This is a 22-player set of Coca-Cola bottle caps featuring members of the Green Bay Packers. They have the Coke logo and a football on the outside, while the inside has the player's face printed in black, with the player's name below the picture. The caps measure approximately 1 1/8" in diameter. A cap-saver sheet was also issued to aid in collecting the bottle caps, and the consumer could turn in his completed sheet to receive various prizes. The caps are unnumbered and therefore listed below alphabetically. The caps were also produced in a twist-off version with red printing.

COMPLETE SET (22) 25.00 50.00
*TWIST-OFF CAPS: .6X TO 1.5X
1 Ken Bowman 1.00 2.00
2 John Brockington 1.50 3.00
3 Bob Brown DT .75 1.50
4 Fred Carr 1.00 2.00

5 Jim Carter	.75	1.50
6 Carroll Dale	1.00	2.00
7 Ken Ellis	1.00	2.00
8 Gale Gillingham	1.00	2.00
9 Dave Hampton	.75	1.50
10 Doug Hart	.75	1.50
11 Jim Hill	.75	1.50
12 Dick Himes	.75	1.50
13 Scott Hunter	1.00	2.00
14 MacArthur Lane	1.50	3.00
15 Bill Lueck	.75	1.50
16 Al Matthews	.75	1.50
17 Rich McGeorge	1.00	1.50
18 Ray Nitschke	3.00	8.00
19 Francis Peay	.75	1.50
20 Dave Robinson	1.50	3.00
21 Alden Roche	.75	1.50
22 Bart Starr	7.50	15.00
NNO Saver Sheet	12.50	25.00

1971 Coke Fun Kit Photos

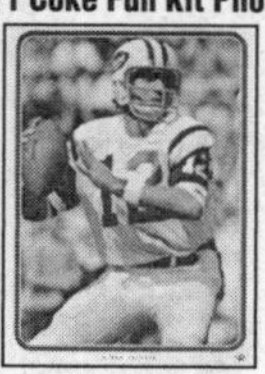

These color photos were released around 1971 with packages of Coca-Cola drinks in packages of four. Each is blankbacked, measures roughly 7" by 10" and includes a color photo of the featured player with his name and team name below the photo. The photos were printed on thin white paper stock. No Coca-Cola logos appear on the photos only that of the NFL Player's Association. Any additions to this list are appreciated.

COMPLETE SET (106)	500.00	800.00
1 Donny Anderson	4.00	8.00
2 Tony Baker	3.00	6.00
3 Pete Barnes	3.00	6.00
4 Lem Barney	4.00	8.00
5 Bill Bergey	4.00	8.00
6 Fred Biletnikoff	10.00	18.00
7 George Blanda	12.00	20.00
8 Lee Bouggess	3.00	6.00
9 Marlin Briscoe	3.00	6.00
10 John Brodie	6.00	12.00
11 Larry Brown	4.00	8.00
12 Willie Brown	4.00	8.00
13 Nick Buoniconti	6.00	12.00
14 Dick Butkus	18.00	30.00
15 Butch Byrd	3.00	6.00
16 Fred Carr	3.00	6.00
17 Virgil Carter	3.00	6.00
18 Gary Collins	3.00	6.00
19 Jack Concannon	3.00	6.00
20 Greg Cook	3.00	6.00
21 Dave Costa	3.00	6.00
22 Paul Costa	3.00	6.00
23 Larry Csonka	15.00	25.00
24 Carroll Dale	3.00	6.00
25 Len Dawson	12.00	20.00
26 Tom Dempsey	3.00	6.00
27 Al Dodd	3.00	6.00
28 Fred Dryer	4.00	8.00
29 Carl Eller	4.00	8.00
30 Mel Farr	3.00	6.00
31 Jim Files	3.00	6.00
32 John Fuqua	3.00	6.00
33 Roman Gabriel	6.00	12.00
34 Gary Garrison	3.00	6.00
35 Walt Garrison	4.00	8.00
36 Joe Greene	12.00	20.00
37 Bob Griese	15.00	25.00
38 John Hadl	6.00	12.00
39 Terry Hanratty	3.00	6.00
40 Jim Hart	6.00	12.00
41 Ben Hawkins	3.00	6.00
42 Alvin Haymond	3.00	6.00
43 Eddie Hinton	3.00	6.00
44 Claude Humphrey	3.00	6.00
45 Rich Jackson	3.00	6.00
46 Charley Johnson	3.00	6.00
47 Ron Johnson	4.00	8.00
48 Walter Johnson	3.00	6.00
49 Deacon Jones	10.00	15.00
50 Lee Roy Jordan	6.00	12.00
51 Joe Kapp	4.00	8.00
52 Leroy Kelly	6.00	12.00
53 Curt Knight	3.00	6.00
54 Charlie Krueger	3.00	6.00
55 Jake Kupp	3.00	6.00
56 MacArthur Lane	3.00	6.00
57 Willie Lanier	6.00	12.00
58 Jerry Levias	3.00	6.00
59 Bob Lilly	10.00	18.00
60 Floyd Little	4.00	8.00
61 Mike Lucci	4.00	8.00
62 Jim Marshall	6.00	12.00
62 Dave Manders	3.00	6.00
63 Tom Matte	4.00	8.00
64 Don Maynard	10.00	18.00
65 Mike McCoy	3.00	6.00
66 Jim Mitchell	3.00	6.00
67 Jon Morris	3.00	6.00
68 Joe Namath	25.00	40.00
69 Jim Nance	4.00	8.00
70 Bill Nelsen	4.00	8.00
72 Tommy Nobis	4.00	8.00
73 Merlin Olsen	10.00	15.00
74 Dave Osborn	3.00	6.00
76 Alan Page	6.00	12.00
77 Preston Pearson	4.00	8.00
78 Mac Percival	3.00	6.00
79 Gerry Philbin	3.00	6.00
80 Jess Phillips	3.00	6.00
81 Tom Regner	3.00	6.00
82 Mel Renfro	6.00	12.00
83 Johnny Robinson	3.00	6.00
84 Tim Rossovich	3.00	6.00
85 Charlie Sanders	3.00	6.00
86 Gale Sayers	18.00	30.00
87 Ron Sellers	3.00	6.00
88 Dennis Shaw	3.00	6.00
89 Bubba Smith	6.00	12.00
90 Charlie Smith	3.00	6.00
91 Jerry Smith	3.00	6.00
92 Matt Snell	4.00	8.00
93 Larry Stallings	3.00	6.00
94 Walt Sweeney	3.00	6.00
95 Fran Tarkenton	12.00	20.00
96 Bruce Taylor	3.00	6.00
97 Charley Taylor	6.00	12.00
98 Otis Taylor	4.00	8.00
99 Bill Thompson	3.00	6.00
100 Johnny Unitas	18.00	30.00
101 Harmon Wages	3.00	6.00
102 Paul Warfield	10.00	18.00
103 Gene Washington 49er	4.00	8.00
104 George Webster	3.00	6.00
104 Gene Washington Vik	3.00	6.00
105 Larry Wilson	6.00	12.00
106 Tom Woodeshick	3.00	6.00

1973 Coke Cap Team Logos

This set of caps were issued in bottles of Coca-Cola in the Milwaukee area in 1973. Each clear plastic liner inside the cap features a black and white NFL team logo. The inside liners were to be attached to a saver sheet that could be partially or completely filled in order to be exchanged for various prizes from Coke.

COMPLETE SET (26)	30.00	60.00
1 Atlanta Falcons	1.00	2.50
2 Baltimore Colts	1.25	3.00
3 Buffalo Bills	1.00	2.50
4 Chicago Bears	1.25	3.00
5 Cincinnati Bengals	1.00	2.50
6 Cleveland Browns	1.25	3.00
7 Dallas Cowboys	2.00	4.00
8 Denver Broncos	1.25	3.00
9 Detroit Lions	1.00	2.50
10 Green Bay Packers	2.00	4.00
11 Houston Oilers	1.00	2.50
12 Kansas City Chiefs	1.00	2.50
13 Los Angeles Rams	1.00	2.50
14 Miami Dolphins	2.00	4.00
15 Minnesota Vikings	1.25	3.00
16 New England Patriots	1.00	2.50
17 New Orleans Saints	1.00	2.50
18 New York Giants	1.00	2.50
19 New York Jets	1.00	2.50
20 Oakland Raiders	2.00	4.00
21 Philadelphia Eagles	1.00	2.50
22 Pittsburgh Steelers	2.00	4.00
23 San Diego Chargers	1.00	2.50
24 San Francisco 49ers	2.00	4.00
25 St. Louis Cardinals	1.00	2.50
26 Washington Redskins	2.00	4.00

1973 Coke Prints

These prints were released around 1973 through retailers as an inducement to their customers to purchase Coke flavored Icee or Frozen Coca-Cola drinks. Each measures roughly 8 1/2" x 11" and features a black and white artist's rendering of the player along with two characatures of football players and a facsimile autograph in blue ink. The backs feature a brief write-up on the player printed in blue ink along with either a large Frozen Coke or Icee ad. Some players were issued with both back versions as noted below. Any additions to this checklist are appreciated.

COMPLETE SET (49)	500.00	800.00
1 Danny Abramowicz	10.00	20.00
2 Julius Adams	10.00	20.00
3 Bobby Anderson	10.00	20.00
4 Dick Anderson	12.50	25.00
5 Terry Bradshaw	40.00	75.00
6 Larry Brown	12.50	25.00
7A Nick Buoniconti	15.00	30.00
7B Nick Buoniconti	15.00	30.00
8 Ken Burrow	12.50	25.00
9 Richard Caster	12.50	25.00
10 Larry Csonka	30.00	50.00
11A Mike Curtis	12.50	25.00
11B Mike Curtis	12.50	25.00
12 John Elliott	10.00	20.00
13 Manny Fernandez	10.00	20.00
14A John Fuqua	12.50	25.00
14B John Fuqua	12.50	25.00
15 Walt Garrison	10.00	20.00
16 Joe Greene	25.00	40.00
17A Bob Griese	30.00	50.00
17B Bob Griese	30.00	50.00
18 Paul Guidry	10.00	20.00
19 Don Hansen	10.00	20.00
20A Ted Hendricks	15.00	30.00
20B Ted Hendricks	15.00	30.00
21 Dave Herman	10.00	20.00
22 J.D. Hill	10.00	20.00
23 Fred Hoaglin	10.00	20.00
24 Jim Houston	10.00	20.00
25A Rich Jackson	10.00	20.00
25B Rich Jackson	10.00	20.00
26 Walter Johnson	10.00	20.00
27A Leroy Kelly	15.00	30.00
27B Leroy Kelly	15.00	30.00
28A Jim Kiick	12.50	25.00
28B Jim Kiick	12.50	25.00
29 George Kunz	10.00	20.00
30 Floyd Little	12.50	25.00
31 Archie Manning	15.00	30.00
32 Milt Morin	10.00	20.00
33A Earl Morrall	12.50	25.00
33B Earl Morrall	12.50	25.00
34 Mercury Morris	15.00	30.00
35 Haven Moses	12.50	25.00
36A John Niland	10.00	20.00
36B John Niland	10.00	20.00
37A Walt Patulski	10.00	20.00
37B Walt Patulski	10.00	20.00
38A Jim Plunkett	15.00	30.00
38B Jim Plunkett	15.00	30.00
39 Andy Russell	12.50	25.00
40 Jake Scott	12.50	25.00
41 Jerry Smith	12.50	25.00
42A Royce Smith	10.00	20.00
42B Royce Smith	10.00	20.00
43 Steve Tannen	10.00	20.00
44 Charley Taylor	15.00	30.00
45 Billy Truax	10.00	20.00
46 Randy Vataha	10.00	20.00
47A Rick Volk	10.00	20.00
47B Rick Volk	10.00	20.00
48 Paul Warfield	15.00	30.00
49 Garo Yepremian	10.00	20.00

1948 Colts Matchbooks

These standard sized (1 1/2" by 4 1/2") matchbooks were thought to have been released during the 1948 season. Each was printed in blue ink with a player head shot on gray card stock. Complete covers with matches intact are valued at approximately 1 1/2 times the prices listed below.

COMPLETE SET (10)	800.00	1,200.00
1 Dick Barwegan	90.00	150.00
2 Lamar Davis	75.00	125.00
3 Spiro Dellerba	75.00	125.00
4 Lou Gambino	75.00	125.00
5 Rex Grossman	75.00	125.00
6 Jake Leicht	75.00	125.00
7 Charlie O'Rourke	75.00	125.00
8 Y.A. Tittle	250.00	500.00
9 Sam Vacanti	75.00	125.00
10 Herman Wedemeyer	90.00	150.00

1949 Colts Silber's Bakery

This rare set of cards was issued by Silber's Bakery only in the Baltimore area in 1949 and featured members of the AAFC Baltimore Colts including future Hall of Famer Y.A. Tittle. Each card measures roughly 2 1/4" by 3 1/4" and features a black and white photo on the front with basic vital statistics for the player below the image. "Silber's Trading Cards" appears above the photo. The cardbacks include brief rules to a contest using a letter printed on the cards to spell SILBER'S in exchange for various prizes. The team's home game schedule is also included on the backs. Any additions to this list are appreciated.

1 Dick Barwegan	800.00	1,200.00
2 Hub Bechtol	600.00	1,000.00
3 Ernie Blandin	600.00	1,000.00
4 Lamar Davis	600.00	1,000.00
5 Barry French	600.00	1,000.00
6 Lou Gambino	600.00	1,000.00
7 Dub Garrett	600.00	1,000.00
8 Rex Grossman	600.00	1,000.00
9 Johnny Mellus	600.00	1,000.00
10 Bus Mertes	600.00	1,000.00
11 John North	600.00	1,000.00
12 Charlie O'Rouke	600.00	1,000.00
13 Paul Page	600.00	1,000.00
14 Bob Pfohl	600.00	1,000.00
15 Billy Stone	600.00	1,000.00
16 Y.A. Tittle	2,000.00	3,500.00
17 Sam Vacanti	600.00	1,000.00
18 Win Williams	600.00	1,000.00

1957 Colts Team Issue

These photos were issued around 1957 by the Baltimore Colts. Each features a black and white player photo with the player's name and team name in a white box near the picture. They measure approximately 8" by 10 1/4" and are blankbacked and unnumbered. Any additions to this list are welcomed.

COMPLETE SET (7)	50.00	100.00
1 Alan Ameche	10.00	20.00
2 L.G. Dupre	7.50	15.00
3 Bill Pellington	7.50	15.00
4 Bert Rechichar	7.50	15.00
5 George Shaw	7.50	15.00
6 Art Spinney	7.50	15.00
7 Carl Taseff	7.50	15.00

1958-60 Colts Team Issue

This set of photos was likely issued over a number of years by the Baltimore Colts. Each card features a black and white player photo with just the player's name and team name below the picture. They measure approximately 8" by 10 1/4" and are blankbacked and unnumbered. There are two known Johnny Unitas photo variations. Any additions to this list are welcomed.

COMPLETE SET (41)	400.00	700.00
1 Alan Ameche	10.00	20.00
2 Raymond Berry	18.00	30.00
3 Ordell Braase	7.50	15.00
4 Ray Brown	7.50	15.00
5 Milt Davis	7.50	15.00
6 Art DeCarlo	7.50	15.00
7 Art Donovan	15.00	25.00
8 L.G. Dupre	7.50	15.00
9 Weeb Ewbank CO	10.00	20.00
10 Alex Hawkins	7.50	15.00
11 Don Joyce	7.50	15.00
12 Ray Krouse	7.50	15.00
13 Harold Lewis	7.50	15.00
14 Gene Lipscomb	10.00	20.00
15 Gino Marchetti	15.00	25.00
16 Marv Matuszak	7.50	15.00
17 Lenny Moore	18.00	30.00
18 Jim Mutscheller	7.50	15.00
19 Steve Myhra	7.50	15.00
20 Andy Nelson	7.50	15.00
21 Buzz Nutter	7.50	15.00
22 Jim Parker	15.00	25.00
23 Bill Pellington	7.50	15.00
24 Sherman Plunkett	7.50	15.00
25 George Preas	7.50	15.00
26 Billy Pricer	7.50	15.00
27 Palmer Pyle	7.50	15.00
28 Bert Rechichar	7.50	15.00
29 Jerry Richardson	7.50	15.00
30 Johnny Sample	7.50	15.00
31 Alex Sandusky	7.50	15.00
32 Dave Sherer	7.50	15.00
33 Don Shinnick	7.50	15.00
34 Jackie Simpson	7.50	15.00
35 Art Spinney	7.50	15.00
36 Dick Szymanski	7.50	15.00
37 Carl Taseff	7.50	15.00
38A Johnny Unitas	40.00	75.00
38B Johnny Unitas	40.00	75.00
39 Jim Welch	7.50	15.00
40 1958 Team Picture	30.00	50.00

1960 Colts Jay Publishing

This 12-card photo set features 5" by 7" black-and-white photos of Baltimore Colts players. The photos show players in traditional posed action shots and were originally packaged 12 to a set. Sets sold primarily through Jay Publishing's Pro Football Yearbook in 1960 and originally sold for 25-cents. The backs are blank. The cards are unnumbered and checklisted below in alphabetical order.

COMPLETE SET (12)	75.00	135.00
1 Alan Ameche	6.00	12.00
2 Raymond Berry	7.50	15.00
3 Art Donovan	6.00	12.00
4 Don Joyce	5.00	10.00
5 Gene Lipscomb	6.00	12.00
6 Gino Marchetti	6.00	12.00
7 Lenny Moore	7.50	15.00
8 Jim Mutscheller	5.00	10.00
9 Steve Myhra	5.00	10.00
10 Jim Parker	6.00	12.00
11 Bill Pellington	5.00	10.00
12 Johnny Unitas	15.00	30.00

1961 Colts Jay Publishing

This 12-card set features (approximately) 5" by 7" black-and-white player photos. The photos show players in traditional poses with the quarterback preparing to throw, the runner heading downfield, and the defenseman ready for the tackle. These cards were packaged 12 to a packet and originally sold for 25 cents. The backs are blank. The cards are unnumbered and checklisted below in alphabetical order.

COMPLETE SET (12)	75.00	135.00
1 Raymond Berry	7.50	15.00
2 Art Donovan	6.00	12.00
3 Weeb Ewbank CO	6.00	12.00
4 Alex Hawkins	5.00	10.00
5 Gino Marchetti	6.00	12.00
6 Lenny Moore	7.50	15.00
7 Jim Mutscheller	5.00	10.00
8 Steve Myhra	5.00	10.00
9 Jimmy Orr	5.00	10.00
10 Jim Parker	6.00	12.00
11 Joe Perry	7.50	15.00
12 Johnny Unitas	15.00	30.00

1963-64 Colts Team Issue

These large photo cards were produced and distributed by the Baltimore Colts. Each photo measures approximately 7 7/8" by 10 1/4" and is black-and-white, blank backed, and printed on glossy heavy paper stock. The player's name appears in bold lettering below the photo with the team name and player's position, height, weight, and college below that. Except for size, these cards are virtually identical to the 1967 and 1968 sets with differences in the photos or text noted below on like players. The cards are unnumbered and checklisted below in alphabetical order. Any additions to this list are appreciated.

COMPLETE SET (34)	250.00	450.00
1 Raymond Berry	12.50	25.00
2 Jackie Burkett	7.50	15.00
3 Jim Colvin	7.50	15.00
4 Gary Cuozzo	10.00	20.00
5 Wiley Feagin	7.50	15.00
6 Tom Gilburg	7.50	15.00
7 Wendell Harris	7.50	15.00
8 Alex Hawkins	7.50	15.00
9 Jerry Hill	7.50	15.00
10 J.W. Lockett	7.50	15.00
11 Tony Lorick	7.50	15.00
12 Lenny Lyles	7.50	15.00
13 Dee Mackey	7.50	15.00
14 John Mackey	10.00	20.00
15 Butch Maples	7.50	15.00
16 Lou Michaels	7.50	15.00
17 Fred Miller	7.50	15.00
18 Lenny Moore	12.50	25.00
19 Andy Nelson	7.50	15.00
20 Jimmy Orr	7.50	15.00
21 Bill Pellington	7.50	15.00
22 Palmer Pyle	7.50	15.00
23 Alex Sandusky	7.50	15.00
24 Don Shinnick	7.50	15.00
25 Don Shula CO	18.00	30.00
26 Billy Ray Smith	7.50	15.00
27 Steve Stonebreaker	7.50	15.00
28 Dick Szymanski	7.50	15.00
29 Don Thompson	7.50	15.00
30 Johnny Unitas	25.00	40.00
31 Bob Vogel	7.50	15.00
32 Jim Welch	7.50	15.00
33 Butch Wilson	7.50	15.00
34 1963 Coaching Staff	10.00	20.00
35 1964 Coaching Staff	10.00	20.00

1965 Colts Team Issue

These large photos were produced and distributed by the Baltimore Colts. Each photo measures approximately 7 7/8" by 10" and is black-and-white, blank backed, and printed on heavy glossy stock. The player's name appears in bold lettering below the photo with the team name and player's position, height, weight, and college below that. Except for the slightly smaller size, these photos are virtually identical to the 1963-64 set and exactly the same format as the 1967 and 1968 sets. However, there are noticable differences from one year to the next in terms of the photos or text featured below each photo. We've made note of key changes below on like players from 1965-1968. The cards are unnumbered and checklisted below in alphabetical order.

COMPLETE SET (18)	125.00	250.00
1 Raymond Berry	10.00	20.00
2 Bob Boyd	6.00	12.00
3 Gary Cuozzo	7.50	15.00
4 Dennis Gaubatz	6.00	12.00
5 Jerry Hill	6.00	12.00
7 Tony Lorick	6.00	12.00
8 John Mackey	7.50	15.00
9 Fred Miller	6.00	12.00
10 Lenny Moore	10.00	20.00
11 Jimmy Orr	6.00	12.00
12 Jim Parker	7.50	15.00
14 Willie Richardson	6.00	12.00
15 Don Shinnick	6.00	12.00
16 Steve Stonebreaker	6.00	12.00
17 Johnny Unitas	25.00	40.00
18 Bob Vogel	6.00	12.00

1967 Colts Johnny Pro

These 41 die-cut punchouts were issued (six or seven per page) in an album which itself measured approximately 11" by 14". Each punchout is approximately 4 1/8" tall and 2 7/8" wide at its base. A stand came with each punchout, and by inserting the punchout in it, the player stood upright. Each punchout consisted of a color player photo against a green grass background. The player's jersey number, name, and position are printed in a white box toward the bottom. The punchouts are unnumbered and checklisted below in alphabetical order.

COMPLETE SET (41)	500.00	850.00
1 Sam Ball	7.50	15.00
2 Raymond Berry	25.00	50.00
3 Bob Boyd DB	7.50	15.00
4 Ordell Braase	7.50	15.00
5 Barry Brown	7.50	15.00
6 Bill Curry	12.50	25.00
7 Mike Curtis	12.50	25.00
8 Norman Davis	7.50	15.00
9 Jim Detwiler	7.50	15.00
10 Dennis Gaubatz	7.50	15.00
11 Alvin Haymond	7.50	15.00
12 Jerry Hill	7.50	15.00
13 Roy Hilton	10.00	20.00
14 David Lee	7.50	15.00
15 Jerry Logan	10.00	20.00
16 Tony Lorick	10.00	20.00
17 Lenny Lyles	10.00	20.00
18 John Mackey	17.50	35.00
19 Tom Matte	12.50	25.00
20 Lou Michaels	10.00	20.00
21 Fred Miller	7.50	15.00
22 Lenny Moore	25.00	50.00
23 Jimmy Orr	10.00	20.00
24 Jim Parker	17.50	35.00
25 Ray Perkins	10.00	20.00
26 Glenn Ressler	7.50	15.00
27 Willie Richardson	10.00	20.00
28 Don Shinnick	7.50	15.00
29 Billy Ray Smith	10.00	20.00
30 Bubba Smith	20.00	40.00
31 Charlie Stukes	7.50	15.00
32 Andy Stynchula	7.50	15.00
33 Dan Sullivan	7.50	15.00
34 Dick Szymanski	7.50	15.00
35 Johnny Unitas	50.00	100.00
36 Bob Vogel	10.00	20.00
37 Rick Volk	10.00	20.00
38 Bob Wade	7.50	15.00
39 Jim Ward	7.50	15.00
40 Jim Welch	7.50	15.00
41 Butch Wilson	7.50	15.00

1967 Colts Team Issue

These large photos were produced and distributed by the Baltimore Colts in 1967. Each photo measures approximately 7 7/8" by 10" (with a few measuring a slightly larger 10 1/4") and is black-and-white, blank backed, and printed on heavy glossy stock. The player's name appears in bold lettering below the photo with the team name and player's position, height, weight, and college below that. Except for the slightly smaller size on most, these photos are virtually identical to the 1963-64 set and exactly the same format as the 1965 and 1968 sets. However, there are noticable differences from one year to the next in terms of the photos or text featured below each photo. We've made note of key changes below on like players from 1965-1968. The cards are unnumbered and checklisted below in alphabetical order.

COMPLETE SET (44)	200.00	400.00
1 Bob Baldwin	6.00	12.00
2 Sam Ball	6.00	12.00
3 Raymond Berry	10.00	20.00
4 Bob Boyd	6.00	12.00
5 Jackie Burkett	6.00	12.00
6 Gary Cuozzo	6.00	12.00
7 Bill Curry	6.00	12.00
8 Mike Curtis	7.50	15.00
9 Norman Davis	6.00	12.00
10 Jim Detwiler	6.00	12.00
11 Dennis Gaubatz	6.00	12.00
12 Alvin Haymond	6.00	12.00
13 Jerry Hill	6.00	12.00
14 Roy Hilton	6.00	12.00
15 David Lee	6.00	12.00
16 Jerry Logan	6.00	12.00
17 Tony Lorick	6.00	12.00
18 Lenny Lyles	6.00	12.00
19 John Mackey	7.50	15.00
20 Tom Matte	7.50	15.00
21 Dale Memmelaar	6.00	12.00
22 Lou Michaels	6.00	12.00
23 Fred Miller	6.00	12.00
24 Lenny Moore	10.00	20.00
25 Jimmy Orr	6.00	12.00
26 Jim Parker	7.50	15.00
27 Ray Perkins	6.00	12.00
28 Glenn Ressler	6.00	12.00
29 Alex Sandusky	6.00	12.00
30 Willie Richardson	6.00	12.00
31 Don Shinnick	6.00	12.00
32 Don Shula CO	15.00	25.00
33 Billy Ray Smith	6.00	12.00
34 Bubba Smith	7.50	15.00
35 Andy Stynchula	6.00	12.00
36 Dan Sullivan	6.00	12.00
37 Dick Szymanski	6.00	12.00
38 Johnny Unitas	18.00	30.00
39 Bob Vogel	6.00	12.00
40 Rick Volk	6.00	12.00
41 Jim Ward	6.00	12.00
42 Jim Welch	6.00	12.00
43 Butch Wilson	6.00	12.00
44 1967 Coaches Arns Shula Noll Biel Sand Rutl McCa	7.50	15.00

1968 Colts Team Issue

These large photos were produced and distributed by the Baltimore Colts in 1968. Each photo measures approximately 8" by 10" and is black-and-white, blank backed, and printed on heavy glossy stock. The player's name appears in bold lettering below the photo with the team name and player's position, height, weight, and college below that. Except for the smaller size, these cards are virtually identical to the 1963-64 set and almost exactly the same format as the 1965 and 1967 sets. However, there are noticable differences from one year to the next in terms of the photos or text featured below each photo. We've made note of key changes below on like players from 1965-1968. The cards are unnumbered and checklisted below in alphabetical order.

COMPLETE SET (30)	200.00	350.00
1 Don Alley	6.00	12.00
2 Ordell Braase	6.00	12.00
3 Timmy Brown	6.00	12.00
4 Terry Cole	6.00	12.00
5 Mike Curtis	7.50	15.00
6 Bill Curry	6.00	12.00
7 Dennis Gaubatz	6.00	12.00
8 Alex Hawkins	6.00	12.00
9 Jerry Hill	6.00	12.00
10 Cornelius Johnson	6.00	12.00
11 Lenny Lyles	6.00	12.00
12 John Mackey	7.50	15.00
13 Tom Matte	7.50	15.00
14 Lou Michaels	6.00	12.00
15 Fred Miller	6.00	12.00
16 Earl Morrall	7.50	15.00
17 Preston Pearson	7.50	15.00
18 Ron Porter	6.00	12.00
19 Willie Richardson	6.00	12.00
20 Don Shinnick	6.00	12.00
21 Billy Ray Smith	6.00	12.00
22 Bubba Smith	7.50	15.00
23 Charlie Stukes	6.00	12.00
24 Dick Szymanski	6.00	12.00
25 Bob Vogel	6.00	12.00
26 Rick Volk	6.00	12.00
27 Jim Ward	6.00	12.00
28 John Williams T	6.00	12.00
29 Coaching Staff	7.50	15.00
30 Team Photo	10.00	20.00

1969-70 Colts Team Issue

This set of photos issued by the Colts measure roughly 8" by 10" and feature black and white player images with vital statistics below the photo. Each is blankbacked and features much of the same information as the 1967 and 1968 sets, but presented in much larger text. The player's name can be found with two different sized letters. Unless noted below, all these photos feature a player name with letters that are 3/16" tall. The small names feature letters only 1/8" tall. Any additions to this list are appreciated.

COMPLETE SET (29)	200.00	350.00
1 Ocie Austin	6.00	12.00
2 Sam Ball	6.00	12.00
3 Terry Cole	6.00	12.00
4 Tom Curtis	6.00	12.00
5 Jim Duncan	6.00	12.00
6 Speedy Duncan	6.00	12.00
7 Perry Lee Dunn	6.00	12.00
8 Bob Grant	6.00	12.00
9 Sam Havrilak	6.00	12.00
10 Ted Hendricks	7.50	15.00
11 Jerry Hill	6.00	12.00
12 Ron Kostelnik	6.00	12.00
13 Lenny Lyles	6.00	12.00
14 Tom Matte	7.50	15.00
15 Tom Maxwell	6.00	12.00
16 Lou Michaels	6.00	12.00
17 Fred Miller	6.00	12.00
18 Tom Mitchell	6.00	12.00
19 Earl Morrall	7.50	15.00
20 Jimmy Orr	6.00	12.00
21 Ray Perkins	6.00	12.00
22 Billy Ray Smith	6.00	12.00
23 Bubba Smith	7.50	15.00
24 Charlie Stukes	6.00	12.00
25 Dan Sullivan	6.00	12.00
26A Johnny Unitas Action	15.00	30.00
26B Johnny Unitas Portrait	15.00	30.00
27 Bob Vogel	6.00	12.00
28 Rick Volk	6.00	12.00
29 John Williams	6.00	12.00

1971 Colts Baltimore Sunday Sun Posters

These oversized (roughly 14 1/4" by 21 1/2") posters were to be cut from weekly issues of the Baltimore Sunday Sun newspaper in 1971. Each was printed in color and features typical newsprint pages on the backs. Any additions to this list are appreciated.

COMPLETE SET (17)	100.00	200.00
1 Norm Bulaich	5.00	10.00
2 Mike Curtis	6.00	12.00
3 Jim Duncan	5.00	10.00
4 Ted Hendricks	10.00	20.00
5 Roy Hilton	5.00	10.00
6 Eddie Hinton	5.00	10.00
7 Jerry Logan	5.00	10.00
8 John Mackey	7.50	15.00
9 Tom Matte	6.00	12.00
10 Tom Mitchell	5.00	10.00
11 Earl Morrall	7.50	15.00
12 Jim O'Brien	5.00	10.00
13 Bubba Smith	7.50	15.00
14 Charlie Stukes	5.00	10.00
15 Dan Sullivan	5.00	10.00
16 Bob Vogel	5.00	10.00
17 Rick Volk	5.00	10.00

1971 Colts Jewel Foods

These six color photos are thought to have been released by Jewel Foods in Baltimore. Each measures approximately 7" by 8 3/4" and includes the player's name and team name below the photo. They are blankbacked and unnumbered.

COMPLETE SET (6)	30.00	60.00
1 Norm Bulaich	2.50	5.00
2 Mike Curtis	5.00	10.00
3 Ted Hendricks	6.00	12.00
4 Tom Matte	5.00	10.00
5 Bubba Smith	6.00	12.00
6 Johnny Unitas	12.50	25.00

1971 Colts Team Issue

This set of photos was issued by the Baltimore Colts in 1971. Each photo measures 8" by 10" and includes a black and white player photo on the front with the player's name (printed in large or small letters) and team name below the photo. The photos are blank backed, unnumbered and checklisted below in alphabetical order. Photos in this set are very similar to the 1973 Colts photos except for the smaller font size (measures roughly 1 3/8") used in the team name. They are identical in design to the 1974 set except this year features all players in action photos unless noted below.

COMPLETE SET (10)	50.00	100.00
1 Karl Douglas	5.00	10.00
2 Ted Hendricks	7.50	15.00
3 Lonnie Hepburn	5.00	10.00
4 Dennis Nelson	5.00	10.00
5 Billy Newsome	5.00	10.00
6 Don Nottingham	5.00	10.00
7 Charlie Pittman	5.00	10.00
8A Bubba Smith	7.50	15.00
8B Bubba Smith	7.50	15.00
9 Rick Volk	5.00	10.00

1972 Colts Team Issue

This set of photos was issued by the Baltimore Colts around 1972. Many of these Colts team issue photos were issued over a period of years as players were added to the roster or left the team, therefore the year of issue is an estimate. Each photo in this group is of one of two distinctly different designs or formats. The first style measures 8" by 10" and includes a black and white player photo on the front. Below the photo are: the player's jersey number to the far right, followed by his name and team name printed in large letters. The second style features only the player's name and team name below the photo in small letters resembling that of typewriter type. All of the photos are blank backed, unnumbered and checklisted below in alphabetical order.

COMPLETE SET (20)	100.00	175.00
1 Dick Amman	5.00	10.00
2 Jim Bailey	5.00	10.00
3 Mike Curtis	6.00	12.00
4 Marty Domres	5.00	10.00
5 Glenn Doughty	5.00	10.00
6 Tom Drougas	5.00	10.00
7 Randy Edmunds	5.00	10.00
8 Chuck Hinton	5.00	10.00
9 Cornelius Johnson	5.00	10.00
10 Bruce Laird	5.00	10.00
11 Don McCauley	5.00	10.00

12 Ken Mendenhall 5.00 10.00
13 Jack Mildren 5.00 10.00
14 Lydell Mitchell 6.00 12.00
15 Nelson Munsey 5.00 10.00
16 Dennis Nelson 5.00 10.00
17 Billy Newsome 5.00 10.00
18 Cotton Speyrer 5.00 10.00
19 Dan Sullivan 5.00 10.00
20 Rick Volk 6.00 12.00

1973 Colts McDonald's

These 11" by 14" color posters were sponsored by and distributed through McDonald's stores. Each includes an artist's rendering of one or two Colts players along with the year and the "McDonald's Superstars Collector's Series" notation below the picture.

COMPLETE SET (4) 50.00 80.00
1 Raymond Chester 10.00 15.00
2 Mike Curtis 12.00 20.00
3 Ted Hendricks 15.00 25.00
Rick Volk
4 Bert Jones 15.00 25.00

1973 Colts Team Issue B&W

This set of photos was issued by the Baltimore Colts in 1973. Each photo measures 8" by 10" and includes a black and white player photo on the front with the player's name and team below the photo. The photos are blank backed, unnumbered and checklisted below in alphabetical order. Photos in this set are very similar to the 1974 Colts photos except for the larger font size (measures roughly 2') used in the team name.

COMPLETE SET (28) 100.00 175.00
1 Dick Amman 4.00 8.00
2 Mike Barnes 4.00 8.00
3 Stan Cherry 4.00 8.00
4 Raymond Chester 5.00 10.00
5 Larry Christoff 4.00 8.00
6 Elmer Collett 4.00 8.00
7 Glenn Doughty 4.00 8.00
8 Tom Drougas 4.00 8.00
9 Joe Ehrmann 4.00 8.00
10 Hubert Ginn 4.00 8.00
11 Brian Herosian 4.00 8.00
12 Fred Hoaglin 4.00 8.00
13 George Hunt 4.00 8.00
14 Bert Jones 6.00 12.00
15 Mike Kaczmarek 4.00 8.00
16 Ed Mooney 4.00 8.00
17 Nelson Munsey 4.00 8.00
18 Dan Neal 4.00 8.00
19 Ray Oldham 4.00 8.00
20 Bill Olds 4.00 8.00
21 Gery Palmer 4.00 8.00
22 Tom Pierantozzi 4.00 8.00
23 Joe Schmiesing 4.00 8.00
24 Howard Schnellenberger CO 5.00 10.00
25 Ollie Smith 4.00 8.00
26 David Taylor T 4.00 8.00
27 Stan White LB 4.00 8.00
28 Bill Windauer 4.00 8.00

1973 Colts Team Issue Color

The NFLPA worked with many teams in 1973 to issued photo packs to be sold at stadium concession stands. Each measures approximately 7" by 8-5/8" and features a color player photo with a blank back. A small sheet with a player checklist was included in each 6-photo pack. Any additions to this list are appreciated.

1 Norm Bulaich 2.50 5.00
2 Mike Curtis 3.00 6.00
3 Ted Hendricks 4.00 8.00
4 Tom Matte 3.00 6.00
5 Bubba Smith 4.00 8.00

1974 Colts Team Issue

This set of photos was issued by the Baltimore Colts in 1974. Each photo measures 8" by 10" and includes a black and white player photo on the front with the player's name (printed in large letters) and team name below the photo. The players name is oriented to the far left unless noted below. The photos are blank backed, unnumbered and checklisted below in alphabetical order. Photos in this set are very similar to the 1973 Colts photos except for the smaller font size (measures roughly 1 3/8') used in the team name. The photos with the name to the far left are also identical in design to the 1971 set except this year features all players in portrait photos -- no action shots.

COMPLETE SET (34) 125.00 250.00
1 John Andrews 4.00 8.00
2 Jim Bailey 4.00 8.00
3 Mike Barnes 4.00 8.00
4 Tim Berra 4.00 8.00
5 Tony Bertuca 4.00 8.00
6 Roger Carr 5.00 10.00
7 Fred Cook 4.00 8.00
8 Mike Curtis 5.00 10.00
9 Dan Dickel 4.00 8.00
10 Glenn Doughty 4.00 8.00
11 John Dutton 5.00 10.00
12 Joe Ehrmann 4.00 8.00
13 Randy Hall 4.00 8.00
14 Ted Hendricks 6.00 12.00
15 Bert Jones 6.00 12.00
16 Rex Kern 4.00 8.00
17 Bruce Laird 4.00 8.00
18 Toni Linhart 4.00 8.00
19 Tom MacLeod 4.00 8.00
20 Ted Marchibroda CO 5.00 10.00
21 Jack Mildren 4.00 8.00
22 Nelson Munsey 4.00 8.00
23 Doug Nettles 4.00 8.00
24 Ray Oldham 4.00 8.00
25 Bill Olds 4.00 8.00
26 Joe Orduna 4.00 8.00
27 Robert Pratt 4.00 8.00
28 Danny Rhodes 4.00 8.00
29 Tim Rudnick 4.00 8.00
30 Freddie Scott 5.00 10.00
31 Dave Simonson 4.00 8.00
32 Bob Van Duyne 4.00 8.00
33 Steve Williams 4.00 8.00
34 Bill Windauer 4.00 8.00

1976 Colts Team Issue 5x7

This set of photos was issued by the Baltimore Colts in 1976. Each photo measures approximately 5" by 7". The fronts feature a black and white photo with player's name (on the left in large capital letters) and team name (on the right in slightly smaller letters) below the photo. The photos are blank backed, unnumbered and checklisted below in alphabetical order.

COMPLETE SET (12) 15.00 30.00
1 Roger Carr 2.00 4.00
2 Raymond Chester 2.00 4.00
3 Jim Cheyunski 1.50 3.00
4 Elmer Collett 1.50 3.00
5 Fred Cook 1.50 3.00
6 John Dutton 2.00 4.00
7 Joe Ehrmann 1.50 3.00
8 Bert Jones 2.50 5.00
9 Bruce Laird 1.50 3.00
10 Roosevelt Leaks 2.00 4.00
11 Lydell Mitchell 2.00 4.00
12 Lloyd Mumphord 1.50 3.00

1976 Colts Team Issue 8x10

This set of photos was issued by the Baltimore Colts in 1976. Each photo measures 8" by 10" and includes a black and white player photo on the front with the player's name (printed in bold letters) and team name below the photo. The players name is oriented to the far left and the team name to the far right. The photos are blank backed, unnumbered and checklisted below in alphabetical order. The photo style used in this set is nearly identical to the 1974 Colts photos except for the slightly different font style and size used in the player and team name. All of the photos are close-up portrait shots.

COMPLETE SET (44) 150.00 300.00
1 Mike Barnes 4.00 8.00
2 Tim Baylor 4.00 8.00
3 Forrest Blue 4.00 8.00
4 Roger Carr 5.00 10.00
5 Raymond Chester 5.00 10.00
6 Jim Cheyunski 4.00 8.00
7 Elmer Collett 4.00 8.00
8 Fred Cook 4.00 8.00
9 Dan Dickel 4.00 8.00
10 Glenn Doughty 4.00 8.00
11 John Dutton 5.00 10.00
12 Joe Ehrmann 4.00 8.00
13 Ron Fernandes 4.00 8.00
14 Randy Hall 4.00 8.00
15 Ken Huff 4.00 8.00
16 Bert Jones 6.00 12.00
17 Jimmie Kennedy 4.00 8.00
18 Mike Kirkland 4.00 8.00
19 Bruce Laird 4.00 8.00
20 Roosevelt Leaks 5.00 10.00
21 David Lee 4.00 8.00
22 Ron Lee 4.00 8.00
23 Toni Linhart 4.00 8.00
24 Derrel Luce 4.00 8.00
25 Ted Marchibroda CO 5.00 10.00
26 Don McCauley 4.00 8.00
27 Ken Mendenhall 4.00 8.00
28 Lydell Mitchell 5.00 10.00
29 Lloyd Mumphord 4.00 8.00
30 Nelson Munsey 4.00 8.00
31 Doug Nettles 4.00 8.00
32 Ken Novak 4.00 8.00
33 Ray Oldham 4.00 8.00
34 Robert Pratt 4.00 8.00
35 Freddie Scott 5.00 10.00
36 Sanders Shiver 4.00 8.00
37 Ed Simonini 4.00 8.00
38 Howard Stevens 4.00 8.00
39 David Taylor 4.00 8.00
40 Ricky Thompson 4.00 8.00
41 Bill Troup 4.00 8.00
42 Bob Van Duyne 4.00 8.00
43 Jackie Wallace 4.00 8.00
44 Stan White 4.00 8.00

1977 Colts Book Covers

These book covers were sponsored by Amoco and feature a member of the Baltimore Colts on the front in a black and white photo. The Colts team photo and schedule is printed on the back side once the cover is folded. Each measures roughly 13" by 20".

COMPLETE SET (5) 25.00 50.00
1 Glenn Doughty 4.00 10.00
2 Joe Ehrmann 4.00 10.00
3 Bert Jones 6.00 15.00
4 Ted Marchibroda CO 4.00 10.00
5 Lydell Mitchell 5.00 12.00

1977 Colts Team Issue

This set of photos was issued by the Baltimore Colts in 1977. Each photo measures approximately 5" by 7". The fronts feature a black and white photo with player's name (on the left) and team name (on the right) below the photo in small letters. The date "8/77" is also include just below the team name. The photos are blank backed, unnumbered and checklisted below in alphabetical order.

COMPLETE SET (12) 30.00 60.00
1 Mack Alston 3.00 6.00
2 Mike Barnes 3.00 6.00
3 Lyle Blackwood 3.00 6.00
4 Bert Jones 5.00 10.00
5 Ed Khayat CO 3.00 6.00
6 George Kunz 3.00 6.00
7 Darrell Luce 3.00 6.00
8 Ted Marchibroda CO 4.00 8.00
9 Robert Pratt 3.00 6.00
10 Norm Thompson 3.00 6.00
11 Bob Van Duyne 3.00 6.00
12 Stan White 3.00 6.00

1978-81 Colts Team Issue

This set of photos was issued by the Baltimore Colts. Each photo measures approximately 5" by 7". The fronts display player portrait photos with player name, postion, and team below the photo. The photos are blank backed, unnumbered and checklisted below in alphabetical order. This set listings is likely comprised of photos issued over a number of years. Any additions or confirmed variations on player photos or text styles are appreciated.

1 Mack Alston 2.00 5.00
2 Kim Anderson 2.00 5.00
3 Ron Baker 2.00 5.00
4 Mike Barnes 2.00 5.00
5 Tim Baylor 2.00 5.00
6 Lyle Blackwood 2.00 5.00
7 Mike Bragg 2.00 5.00
8 Larry Braziel 2.00 5.00
9 Randy Burke 2.00 5.00
10 Raymond Butler 2.50 6.00
11 Roger Carr 2.50 6.00
12 Fred Cook 2.00 5.00
13 Brian DeRoo 2.00 5.00
14 Curtis Dickey 2.50 6.00
15 Zachary Dixon 2.00 5.00
16 Ray Donaldson 2.00 5.00
17 Glenn Doughty 2.00 5.00
18 Joe Ehrmann 2.00 5.00
19 Greg Fields 2.00 5.00
20 Ron Fernandes 2.00 5.00
21 Chris Foote 2.00 5.00
22 Cleveland Franklin 2.00 5.00
23 Mike Garrett 2.50 6.00
24 Nesby Glasgow 2.00 5.00
25 Bubba Green 2.00 5.00
26 Wade Griffin 2.00 5.00
27 Lee Gross 2.00 5.00
28 Don Hardeman 2.00 5.00
29 Dwight Harrison 2.00 5.00
30 Jeff Hart 2.00 5.00
31 Derrick Hatchett 2.00 5.00
32 Dallas Hickman 2.00 5.00
33 Ken Huff 2.00 5.00
34 Marshall Johnson 2.00 5.00
35 Bert Jones 3.00 8.00
36 Ricky Jones 2.00 5.00
37 Barry Krauss 2.00 5.00
38 George Kunz 2.00 5.00
39 Bruce Laird 2.00 5.00
40 Greg Landry 3.00 8.00
41 Roosevelt Leaks 2.50 6.00
42 David Lee 2.00 5.00
43 Ron Lee FB 2.00 5.00
44 Toni Linhart 2.00 5.00
45 Derrel Luce 2.00 5.00
46 Reese McCall 2.00 5.00
47 Don McCauley 2.00 5.00
48 Randy McMillan 2.00 5.00
49 Ken Mendenhall 2.00 5.00
50 Steve Mike-Mayer 2.00 5.00
51 Jim Moore 2.00 5.00
52 Don Morrison 2.00 5.00
53 Lloyd Mumphord 2.00 5.00
54 Doug Nettles 2.00 5.00
55 Calvin O'Neal 2.00 5.00
56 Herb Orvis 2.00 5.00
57 Mike Ozdowski 2.00 5.00
58 Reggie Pinkney 2.00 5.00
59 Robert Pratt 2.00 5.00
60 Dave Rowe 2.00 5.00
61 Tim Sherwin 2.00 5.00
62A Sanders Shiver ERR 2.00 5.00
62B Sanders Shiver COR 2.00 5.00
63 David Shula 2.50 6.00
64 Mike Siani 2.00 5.00
65 Ed Simonini 2.00 5.00
66 Marvin Sims 2.00 5.00
67 Ed Smith 2.00 5.00
68 Hosea Taylor 2.00 5.00
69 Donnell Thompson 2.00 5.00
70 Norm Thompson 2.00 5.00
71 Bill Troup 2.00 5.00
72 Randy Van Diver 2.00 5.00
73 Bob Van Duyne 2.00 5.00
74 Joe Washington 2.50 6.00
75 Stan White 2.00 5.00
76 Mike Wood 2.00 5.00
77 Mike Woods 2.00 5.00
78 Steve Zabel 2.00 5.00

1959 Comet Sweets Olympic Achievements

Celebrating various Olympic events, ceremonies, and their history, this 25-card set was issued by Comet Sweets. The cards are printed on thin cardboard stock and measure 1 7/16" by 2 9/16". Inside white borders, the fronts display water color paintings of various Olympic events. Some cards are horizontally oriented; others are vertically oriented. The set title "Olympic Achievements" appears at the top on the backs, with a discussion of the event below. This set is the first series; the cards are numbered "X to 25."

COMPLETE SET (25) 30.00 60.00
18 Football 1.50 3.00

1960 Cowboys Team Sheets

This set of press photo sheets was released to publicize players signed early to the first Cowboys' team. Each sheet includes four black and white photos, measures roughly 8 1/2" X 11" and is blankbacked. Some of these player images were also issued as separate 8 x 10 photos as well.

COMPLETE SET (10) 150.00 250.00
1 T.Braatz 15.00 25.00
L.G.Dupre
J.Patera
B.Butler DB
2 G.Babb 15.00 25.00
D.Putnam
N.Borden
D.Heinrich
3 F.Clarke 15.00 25.00
D.Sherer
D.McIlhenny
B.Bradfute
4 M.Falls 15.00 25.00
D.Bishop
P.Dickson
B.Bercich
5 Bob Fry/Jim Doran/Fred Dugan/Fred Cone/Don Heinrich
15.00 25.00
6 W.Hansen 15.00 25.00
W.Kowalczyk
D.Klein
J.Houser
7 D.Healy 15.00 25.00
D.Bielski
B.Herchman
J.Tubbs
8 Meredith 35.00 60.00
Gonzaga
Guy
Frankhouser
9 Hussman 20.00 35.00
Mathews
LeBaron
Cronin
10 Lewis 18.00 30.00
Howton
Connelly
Mooty

1960-62 Cowboys Team Issue 5x7

These team issued photos feature black-and-white player images taken of just head-and-shoulders. Each measures approximately 5" by 7" and was printed on glossy photographic paper stock. Most feature four white borders around the player image but some were created with just one white border at the bottom: noted below. Each photo is a portrait with the player wearing a blue early 1960s era stars-on-the-shoulder Cowboys jersey. The white border at the bottom contains just the player's name and team name printed in all capital letters. These cards are blankbacked and unnumbered. Any additions to the below list are appreciated.

COMPLETE SET (22)	125.00	250.00
1 Dick Bielski	6.00	12.00
2 Frank Clarke	7.50	15.00
3 Donnie Davis	6.00	12.00
4 Jim Doran	6.00	12.00
5 Ken Frost	6.00	12.00
6 Bob Fry	6.00	12.00
7 Mike Gaechter	6.00	12.00
8 John Gonzaga	6.00	12.00
9 Don Healy	6.00	12.00
10 Bill Herchman	6.00	12.00
11 Billy Howton	7.50	15.00
12 Lynn Hoyem	6.00	12.00
13 Walt Kowalczyk	6.00	12.00
14 Eddie LeBaron	7.50	15.00
15 Bob Lilly	12.50	25.00
16 Don McIlhenny	6.00	12.00
17 Don Meredith	18.00	30.00
18 Don Perkins	7.50	15.00
19 Duane Putnam	6.00	12.00
20 Guy Reese	6.00	12.00
21 Lorenzo Stanford	6.00	12.00
22 Don Talbert	6.00	12.00

1960-63 Cowboys Team Issue 8x10

The Dallas Cowboys issued these black-and-white photos and all feature the player wearing the original stars-on-the-sleeves blue jersey. Each measures 8" by 10" and was printed on glossy stock with white borders. Each photo features a posed action shot with the border below the photo containing just the player's name and team name. The type style and size may vary slightly on some photos, and some players have more than one photo, so this may indicate that they were released over a period of years. The photos are blankbacked and unnumbered. Any additions to the below list are appreciated.

1 Gene Babb	7.50	15.00
2 Bob Bercich	7.50	15.00
3A Dick Bielski	7.50	15.00
3B Dick Bielski	7.50	15.00
4 Don Bishop	7.50	15.00
5 Nate Borden	7.50	15.00
6 Amos Bullocks	7.50	15.00
7A Frank Clarke	10.00	20.00
7B Frank Clarke	10.00	20.00
8 Mike Connelly	7.50	15.00
9 Andy Cvercko	7.50	15.00
10 Gerry DeLucca	7.50	15.00
11 Jim Doran	7.50	15.00
12 L.G. Dupre	7.50	15.00
13 Ken Frost	7.50	15.00
14 Don Healy	7.50	15.00
15 Don Heinrich	7.50	15.00
16 Bill Herchman	7.50	15.00
17 John Houser	7.50	15.00
18A Billy Howton	10.00	20.00
18B Billy Howton	10.00	20.00
18C Billy Howton	10.00	20.00
19 Lee Roy Jordan	12.50	25.00
20A Eddie LeBaron	10.00	20.00
20B Eddie LeBaron	10.00	20.00
20C Eddie LeBaron	10.00	20.00
20D Eddie LeBaron	10.00	20.00
20E Eddie LeBaron portrait	10.00	20.00
21 Bob Lilly portrait	15.00	30.00
22 Warren Livingston	7.50	15.00
23 J.W. Lockett	7.50	15.00
24 Amos Marsh	7.50	15.00
25A Don Meredith	25.00	40.00
25B Don Meredith	25.00	40.00
25C Don Meredith	25.00	40.00
25D Don Meredith	25.00	40.00
26 Dick Nolan	7.50	15.00
27 Don Perkins	10.00	20.00
28 Larry Stephens	7.50	15.00
29A Jerry Tubbs	7.50	15.00
29B Jerry Tubbs	7.50	15.00
29C Jerry Tubbs	7.50	15.00

1961 Cowboys Team Issue 7x9

These team issued photos feature black-and-white player images taken of just head-and-shoulders. They were most likely issued as set in "photo pack" style but that has yet to be confirmed. Each measures approximately 7 1/2" by 9 1/2" and was printed on thin matte finish paper stock. They have four wide white borders and the bottom contains just the player's name and team name, unless noted below. These photos are blankbacked and unnumbered. They look very similar to the 1962 7x9 set but feature a much wider white border around the photos as well as unique images.

COMPLETE SET (8)	75.00	125.00
1 Dick Bielski	6.00	12.00
2 Frank Clarke	7.50	15.00
3 Billy Howton	7.50	15.00
4 Eddie LeBaron	7.50	15.00
5 Bob Lilly	10.00	20.00
6 Amos Marsh	6.00	12.00
7 Don Meredith	20.00	35.00
8 Jerry Tubbs	6.00	12.00

1961-62 Cowboys Team Issue 5x6

These team issued photos feature black-and-white player portraits taken of just head-and-shoulders. Each measures approximately 5" by 6 1/2" and was printed on thin matte-finish paper stock with four white borders. The bottom border contains just the player's name and team name with both oriented near the outside edges of the player images. This style, very similar to the Jay Publishing issues of the period, would be used by the Cowboys well into the 1980s. The photos are blankbacked and unnumbered.

COMPLETE SET (6)	40.00	80.00
1 L.G. Dupre	6.00	12.00
2 Don Healy	6.00	12.00
3 Eddie LeBaron	7.50	15.00
4 Don McIlhenny	6.00	12.00
5 Don Meredith	18.00	30.00
6 Jerry Tubbs	6.00	12.00

1962 Cowboys Team Issue 7x9 Photo Pack

These team issued photos feature black-and-white player images taken of just head-and-shoulders. They were issued as set in "photo pack" style. Each measures approximately 7 1/2" by 9 1/2" and was printed on thin matte finish paper stock. They have four white borders and the bottom contains just the player's name and team name, unless noted below. These cards are blankbacked and unnumbered. They look very similar to the 1961 7x9 set but feature a much thinner white border around the photos.

COMPLETE SET (10)	75.00	150.00
1 Don Bishop	6.00	12.00
2 Frank Clarke	7.50	15.00
3 Mike Gaechter	6.00	12.00
4 Sonny Gibbs	6.00	12.00
5 Billy Howton	7.50	15.00
6 Eddie LeBaron	7.50	15.00
7 Amos Marsh	6.00	12.00
8 Don Meredith	20.00	35.00
9 Don Perkins	7.50	15.00
10 Jerry Tubbs	6.00	12.00

1962-63 Cowboys Team Issue Sepia

These photos were issued by the Cowboys most likely over the course of the 1962 and 1963 seasons. Each features a sepia-toned posed action photo, measures approximately 4 7/8" by 6 1/2" and was printed on thin paper stock. A wide border at the bottom contains the player's name, position spelled out, and team name. The photos are blankbacked and unnumbered. Any additions to the below list are appreciated.

COMPLETE SET (17)	125.00	250.00
1 Bob Bercich	7.50	15.00
2 Mike Connelly	7.50	15.00
3 L.G. Dupre	7.50	15.00
4 Sonny Gibbs	7.50	15.00
5 Don Healy	7.50	15.00
6 Bill Herchman	7.50	15.00
7 Eddie LeBaron	10.00	20.00
8 Bob Lilly	15.00	30.00
9 Don Meredith	25.00	40.00
10 Bobby Plummer	7.50	15.00
11 Guy Reese Action	7.50	15.00
12 Guy Reese Port	7.50	15.00
13 Ray Schoenke	7.50	15.00
14 Jim Ray Smith	7.50	15.00
15 Don Talbert (college photo)	7.50	15.00
16 Jerry Tubbs	7.50	15.00
17 Team Photo	12.50	25.00

1963-64 Cowboys Team Issue 7x9

These team issued photos feature black-and-white player images taken of just head-and-shoulders. They may have been issued as a set in "photo pack" style but that has not been confirmed. Each measures approximately 7 1/2" by 9 1/2" and was printed on glossy stock. They have four white borders and the bottom contains the player's name, position initals, and team name. These cards are blankbacked and unnumbered. They look very similar to the 1962 7x9 set with the thinner white border but these also include the player's position on every photo. The Clarke and Tubbs photos are virtually identical to the 1962 issue except for this position addition.

1 Frank Clarke	7.50	15.00
2 Buddy Dial	6.00	12.00
3 Cornell Green	6.00	12.00
4 Lee Roy Jordan	7.50	15.00
5 Tommy McDonald	7.50	15.00
6 Don Perkins	7.50	15.00
7 Jerry Tubbs	6.00	12.00

1964-66 Cowboys Team Issue 5x7

These team issued photos feature black-and-white images with roughly the player's chest up to his head in view. The player's are wearing the new solid white or solid blue 1964 era Cowboys jersey unless noted below. Each photo measures approximately 5" by 7" and was printed on glossy photographic paper stock with four white borders unless noted below. The bottom border contains just the player's name and team name. These cards are blankbacked and unnumbered. Any additions to the below list are appreciated.

COMPLETE SET (31)	200.00	350.00
1 George Andrie	6.00	12.00
2 Don Bishop	6.00	12.00
3 Jim Boeke	6.00	12.00
4 Frank Clarke	7.50	15.00
5 Jim Colvin	6.00	12.00
6 Dick Daniels	6.00	12.00
7 Austin Denney (wearing t-shirt)	6.00	12.00
8A Buddy Dial	7.50	15.00
8B Buddy Dial	7.50	15.00
8C Buddy Dial	7.50	15.00
9 Leon Donohue	6.00	12.00
10 Lee Folkins	6.00	12.00
11 Cornell Green	7.50	15.00
12 Bob Hayes	15.00	25.00
13 Harold Hays	6.00	12.00
14 Chuck Howley	7.50	15.00
15 Jake Kupp	6.00	12.00
16 Tom Landry CO	15.00	25.00
17 Obert Logan	6.00	12.00
18 Billy Lothridge	6.00	12.00
19 Don Meredith	20.00	35.00
20 Ralph Neely	6.00	12.00
21 Don Perkins	7.50	15.00
22 Dan Reeves	10.00	20.00
23 Mel Renfro	10.00	20.00
24 Jerry Rhome	6.00	12.00
25 Ray Schoenke	6.00	12.00
26 Jim Ray Smith	6.00	12.00
27 Willie Townes	6.00	12.00
28 Danny Villanueva	6.00	12.00
29 Malcolm Walker	6.00	12.00

1965 Cowboys Team Issue 5x6

This team-issued set features black-and-white head-to-foot posed action player photos with white borders. Each photo measures approximately 5 1/2" by 6 1/2" but the exact width is known to vary due to inconsistent cutting. The player's name and team name appear below the image. Most players appear in their white jersey, but a few have been found with the road blue as noted below. The photos were printed on thick card stock with a dull matte finish and have unnumbered blankbacks.

COMPLETE SET (43)	300.00	500.00
1 George Andrie	6.00	12.00
2 Don Bishop	6.00	12.00
3 Jim Boeke	6.00	12.00
4A Frank Clarke Blue	7.50	15.00
4B Frank Clarke Wht	7.50	15.00
5 Jim Colvin	6.00	12.00
6 Mike Connelly	6.00	12.00
7 Buddy Dial	7.50	15.00
8 Leon Donohue Blue	6.00	12.00
9 Perry Lee Dunn	6.00	12.00
10A Dave Edwards Blue	6.00	12.00
10B Dave Edwards Wht	6.00	12.00
11 Mike Gaechter	6.00	12.00
12 Pete Gent	6.00	12.00
13 Cornell Green	6.00	12.00
14 Bob Hayes	12.50	25.00
15 Harold Hays	6.00	12.00
16 Chuck Howley	10.00	20.00
17 Joe Bob Isbell	6.00	12.00
18 Mitch Johnson Blue	6.00	12.00
19 Lee Roy Jordan	10.00	20.00
20 Jake Kupp	6.00	12.00
21 Bob Lilly	12.50	25.00
22 Tony Liscio	6.00	12.00
23 Warren Livingston	6.00	12.00
24 Obert Logan Blue	6.00	12.00
25 Dave Manders	6.00	12.00
26A Don Meredith Blue	18.00	30.00
26B Don Meredith Wht	18.00	30.00
27 Craig Morton Blue	10.00	20.00
28 Ralph Neely Blue	6.00	12.00
29 Pettis Norman	6.00	12.00
30 Don Perkins	7.50	15.00
31 Jethro Pugh Blue	6.00	12.00
32 Dan Reeves Blue	10.00	20.00
33 Mel Renfro	10.00	20.00
34 Jerry Rhome Blue	6.00	12.00
35 Colin Ridgway Blue	6.00	12.00
36 J.D. Smith Blue	6.00	12.00
37 Larry Stephens	6.00	12.00
38 Jim Stiger	6.00	12.00
39 Don Talbert Blue	6.00	12.00
40 Jerry Tubbs	6.00	12.00
41 Danny Villanueva Blue	6.00	12.00
42 Russell Wayt Blue	6.00	12.00
43 Maury Youmans	6.00	12.00

1965-66 Cowboys Team Issue 5-1/4x7 Position

These team issued photos feature black-and-white images with roughly the player's chest up to his head in view. The player's are pictured wearing the solid white Cowboys jersey unless noted below. Each photo measures approximately 5 1/4" by 7" and was printed on matte-finish paper stock with four white borders. The bottom border contains the player's name, position intials, and team name in all caps. These photos are blankbacked and unnumbered. Any additions to the below list are appreciated.

1 Frank Clarke	7.50	15.00
2 Buddy Dial	6.00	12.00
3 Lee Roy Jordan	7.50	15.00
4 Bob Lilly	10.00	20.00
5 Ralph Neely	6.00	12.00
6 Pettis Norman	6.00	12.00
7 Don Perkins	7.50	15.00
8 Jerry Tubbs	6.00	12.00

1966-67 Cowboys Team Issue 5x7

These team issued photos feature black-and-white images, measure approximately 5" by 7" and were printed on matte-finish thin paper stock with four white borders. The bottom border contains the player's name, position spelled out, and team name in uppre and lower case letters - making these unique to most Cowboys issues of the era. These photos are blankbacked and unnumbered. Any additions to the below list are appreciated.

1 George Andrie	6.00	12.00
2 Frank Clarke	7.50	15.00
3 Pete Gent	6.00	12.00
4 Bob Hayes	10.00	20.00
5 Lee Roy Jordan	7.50	15.00
6 Bob Lilly	10.00	20.00
7 Dave Manders	6.00	12.00
8 Don Meredith	18.00	30.00
9 Mel Renfro	7.50	15.00

1966-67 Cowboys Team Issue 8x10

The Dallas Cowboys issued these black-and-white player photos printed on glossy photographic paper. Each measures 8" by 10" and was printed on glossy stock with white borders. Each player photo is a posed action shot head-to-foot and features the player in the blue jersey unless noted below. The border below the photo contains just the player's name and team name in all caps. The type style and size varies slightly on some photos so this may indicate that they were released over a period of years. The photos are blankbacked and unnumbered but can often be found with a photographer's imprint on the backs along with a date. Any additions to the below list are appreciated.

COMPLETE SET (33)	300.00	500.00
1 George Andrie Wht	7.50	15.00
2 Don Bishop	7.50	15.00
3 Phil Clark Wht	7.50	15.00
4 Frank Clarke Wht	10.00	20.00
5 Buddy Dial	7.50	15.00
6 Ron East Wht	7.50	15.00
7 Walt Garrison	7.50	15.00
8 Bob Hayes	15.00	30.00
9 Harold Hays	7.50	15.00
10 Chuck Howley	10.00	20.00
11 Mitch Johnson	7.50	15.00
12 Lee Roy Jordan	10.00	20.00
13 Jake Kupp	7.50	15.00
14 Bob Lilly	15.00	25.00
15 Don Meredith	25.00	40.00
16 Craig Morton Wht	10.00	20.00
17 Ralph Neely	7.50	15.00
18 John Niland	7.50	15.00
19 Pettis Norman	7.50	15.00
20 Brig Owens	7.50	15.00
21 Don Perkins	10.00	20.00
22 Jethro Pugh Wht	7.50	15.00
23 Dan Reeves	10.00	20.00
24 Mel Renfro	10.00	20.00
25A Jerry Rhome Blue	7.50	15.00
25B Jerry Rhome Wht	7.50	15.00
26 Ernie Stautner ACO	10.00	20.00
27 Don Talbert	7.50	15.00
28 Willie Townes	7.50	15.00
29 Malcolm Walker	7.50	15.00
30 A.D. Whitfield	7.50	15.00
31 John Wilbur	7.50	15.00
32 Rayfield Wright Wht	10.00	20.00
33 Maury Youmans	7.50	15.00

1968 Cowboys Team Issue 8x10

The Dallas Cowboys issued these black-and-white player photos printed on glossy photographic paper stock. Each measures 8" by 10" and was printed with four white borders with the player's image as a posed action shot. The border below the photo contains the player's name, his position initials, and team name. The type style and size varies slightly on some photos so this may indicate that they were released over a period of years. The photos are blankbacked and unnumbered. Any additions to the below list are appreciated.

1 Raymond Berry ACO	10.00	20.00
2 Larry Cole	7.50	15.00
3 Dennis Homan	7.50	15.00
4 Tom Landry CO	15.00	25.00
5 Obert Logan	7.50	15.00
6 David McDaniels	7.50	15.00
7 Blaine Nye	7.50	15.00
8 Ron Widby	7.50	15.00

1969 Cowboys Tasco Prints

Tasco Associates produced this set of small Dallas Cowboys posters. The fronts feature a color artist's rendering of the player along with the player's name and position. The backs are blank. The prints measure approximately 11 1/2" by 16."

1 Chuck Howley	12.50	25.00
2 Bob Lilly	15.00	30.00
3 Ralph Neely	10.00	20.00
5 Dan Reeves	12.50	25.00
6 Mel Renfro	12.50	25.00

1969 Cowboys Team Issue 5x6

These team-issued photos feature black-and-white posed action player photos with white borders. Each measures approximately 5" by 6 1/2" and are virtually identical in style to the 1970 and 1971 listings. We've noted specific differences below (identified by the poses) for players that appear in more than one of the sets. Many of these photos were issued for more than one year but we've cataloged them just one time within the set listing that seems to fit best in terms of the pose style and the years the players were on the roster. A wide white border at the bottom contains only the player's name and team name. These cards are printed on thin card stock, have blankbacks and are unnumbered.

COMPLETE SET (25) 150.00 300.00
1 George Andrie 6.00 12.00
2 Craig Baynham 6.00 12.00
3 Ron East 6.00 12.00
4 Walt Garrison 6.00 12.00
5 Pete Gent 6.00 12.00
6 Bob Hayes 12.50 25.00
7 Chuck Howley 7.50 15.00
8 Lee Roy Jordan 7.50 15.00
9 Bob Lilly 12.50 25.00
10 Tony Liscio 6.00 12.00
11 Dave Manders 6.00 12.00
12 Don Meredith 20.00 35.00
13 Craig Morton 7.50 15.00
14 Ralph Neely 6.00 12.00
15 John Niland 6.00 12.00
16 Pettis Norman 6.00 12.00
17 Don Perkins 7.50 15.00
18A Dan Reeves 10.00 20.00
18B Dan Reeves 10.00 20.00
19 Mel Renfro 7.50 15.00
20 Lance Rentzel 6.00 12.00
21A Roger Staubach 25.00 40.00
21B Roger Staubach 25.00 40.00
22 Malcolm Walker 6.00 12.00
23 Ron Widby 6.00 12.00
24 John Wilbur 6.00 12.00
25 Rayfield Wright 7.50 15.00
(wearing jersey #85)

1969-72 Cowboys Team Issue 5x7

These team-issued photos feature black-and-white player images with white borders on four sides, unless otherwise noted below. Each photo measures approximately 5" by 7" and was printed on glossy photographic paper stock. Each photo is a portrait showing the player wearing a white jersey with just half of his jersey number showing. A thick white border at the bottom contains only the player's name and team name except for a few that also include initials for the player's position. They were issued over a period of years and feature a variety of type styles and type sizes for the lettering within the bottom border. We've noted differences in the player The photos are blankbacked and unnumbered.

1 Margene Adkins 6.00 12.00
2 George Andrie 6.00 12.00
3 Bob Asher 6.00 12.00
4 Mike Clark 6.00 12.00
5 Phil Clark 6.00 12.00
6 Ralph Coleman 6.00 12.00
7 Mike Ditka 10.00 20.00
8 Ron East 6.00 12.00
9 John Fitzgerald 6.00 12.00
10 Richmond Flowers 6.00 12.00
11 Walt Garrison 7.50 15.00
12 Cornell Green 6.00 15.00
13 Halvor Hagen 6.00 12.00
14A Bob Hayes 10.00 20.00
14B Bob Hayes 10.00 20.00
15A Calvin Hill 7.50 15.00
15B Calvin Hill 7.50 15.00
16 Dennis Homan 6.00 12.00
17 Mike Johnson 6.00 12.00
18A Lee Roy Jordan 7.50 15.00
18B Lee Roy Jordan 7.50 15.00
19 Tom Landry CO 12.50 25.00
20 D.D. Lewis 6.00 12.00
21 Bob Lilly 12.50 25.00
22 Dave Manders 6.00 12.00
23A Craig Morton 7.50 15.00
23B Craig Morton 7.50 15.00
24A Ralph Neely 6.00 12.00
24B Ralph Neely 6.00 12.00
25A John Niland 6.00 12.00
25B John Niland 6.00 12.00
26 Pettis Norman 6.00 12.00
27 Blaine Nye 6.00 12.00
28 Billy Parks 6.00 12.00
29 Dan Reeves 7.50 15.00
30A Mel Renfro 7.50 15.00
30B Mel Renfro 7.50 15.00
31 Lance Rentzel 6.00 12.00
32 Reggie Rucker 6.00 12.00
33 Les Shy 6.00 12.00
34 Tody Smith 6.00 12.00
35A Roger Staubach 20.00 35.00
35B Roger Staubach 20.00 35.00
35C Roger Staubach 20.00 35.00
35D Roger Staubach 20.00 35.00
36 Ernie Stautner ACO 6.00 12.00
37 Tom Stincic 6.00 12.00
38 Bill Thomas 6.00 12.00
39 Duane Thomas 6.00 12.00
40 Isaac Thomas 6.00 12.00
41 Willie Townes 6.00 12.00
42 Mark Washington 6.00 12.00
43 Claxton Welch 6.00 12.00
44 Fred Whittingham 6.00 12.00
45 Ron Widby 6.00 12.00
46A Rayfield Wright 7.50 15.00
46B Rayfield Wright 7.50 15.00

1970 Cowboys Team Issue 5x6

These team-issued photos feature black-and-white posed action player photos with white borders. Each measures approximately 5" by 6 1/2" and are virtually identical in style to the 1969 and 1971 listings. We've noted specific differences below (identified by the poses) for players that appear in more than one of the sets. Many of these photos were issued for more than one year but we've cataloged them just one time within the set listing that seems to fit best in terms of the pose style and the years the players were on the roster. A wide white border at the bottom contains only the player's name and team name. These cards are printed on thin card stock, have blankbacks and are unnumbered.

COMPLETE SET (30) 200.00 350.00
1 Herb Adderley 7.50 15.00
2 Margene Adkins 6.00 12.00
3 George Andrie 6.00 12.00
4 Bob Asher 6.00 12.00
5 Mike Clark 6.00 12.00
6 Mike Ditka 6.00 12.00
7 Dave Edwards 6.00 12.00
8 Walt Garrison 6.00 12.00
9 Cornell Green 6.00 12.00
10 Cliff Harris 7.50 15.00
11 Bob Hayes 10.00 20.00
12 Calvin Hill 7.50 15.00
13 Chuck Howley 7.50 15.00
14 Lee Roy Jordan 7.50 15.00
15 D.D. Lewis 6.00 12.00
16 Bob Lilly 10.00 20.00
17 Craig Morton 7.50 15.00
18 Ralph Neely 6.00 12.00
19 John Niland 6.00 12.00
20 Blaine Nye 6.00 12.00
21 Jethro Pugh 6.00 12.00
22 Dan Reeves 7.50 15.00
23 Mel Renfro 10.00 20.00
24 Roger Staubach 25.00 40.00
25 Duane Thomas 6.00 12.00
26 Pat Toomay 6.00 12.00
27 Mark Washington 6.00 12.00
28 Claxton Welch 6.00 12.00
29 Ron Widby 6.00 12.00
30 Rayfield Wright 7.50 15.00
(wearing jersey #70)

1970 Cowboys Team Issue 8x10

The Dallas Cowboys issued these black-and-white player photos, measuring 8" by 10," and printed on glossy stock with white borders. Each player photo is a posed action shot. The border below the photo contains just the player's name and team name. The type style and size varies slightly on some photos so this may indicate that they were released over a period of years. The photos are blankbacked and unnumbered. Any additions to the below list are appreciated.

1 Ron East 7.50 15.00
2 Halvor Hagen 7.50 15.00
3 Calvin Hill 10.00 20.00
4 Bob Lilly 12.50 25.00
(left foot off of the ground)
5 Blaine Nye 7.50 15.00
6 Tom Stincic 7.50 15.00

1971 Cowboys Team Issue 5x6

These team-issued photos feature black-and-white posed action player photos with white borders. Each measures approximately 5" by 6 1/2" and are virtually identical in style to the 1969 and 1970 listings. We've noted specific differences below (identified by the poses) for players that appear in more than one of the sets. Many of these photos were issued for more than one year but we've cataloged them just one time within the set listing that seems to fit best in terms of the pose style and the years the players were on the roster. A wide white border at the bottom contains only the player's name and team name. These cards are printed on thin card stock, have blankbacks and are unnumbered.

COMPLETE SET (23) 150.00 300.00
1 Lance Alworth 7.50 15.00
2 George Andrie 6.00 12.00
(cutting right, right foot raised)
3 Larry Cole 6.00 12.00
4 Mike Ditka 10.00 20.00
(with mustache)
5 John Fitzgerald 6.00 12.00
6 Toni Fritsch 6.00 12.00
7 Forrest Gregg 7.50 15.00
8 Bill Gregory 6.00 12.00
9 Bob Hayes 7.50 15.00
(white jersey; football in hands)
10 Chuck Howley 7.50 15.00
(white jersey; right foot raised)
11 Lee Roy Jordan 7.50 15.00
(white jersey; no clouds in background)
12 Tom Landry CO 12.50 25.00
13 D.D. Lewis 6.00 12.00
(with mustache)
14 Dave Manders 6.00 12.00
(both feet on ground)
15 John Niland 6.00 12.00
(white jersey; running to his left)
16 Gloster Richardson 6.00 12.00
17 Tody Smith 6.00 12.00
18 Don Talbert 6.00 12.00
19 Isaac Thomas 6.00 12.00
20 Pat Toomay 6.00 12.00
(right foot raised)
21 Billy Truax 6.00 12.00
22 Rodney Wallace 6.00 12.00
23 Charlie Waters 6.00 12.00

1972 Cowboys Team Issue 4x5-1/2

These team issued photos feature black-and-white posed action player photos with white borders. Many of the photos are identical to the larger sized pictures from 1971, but this series measures approximately 4 1/4" by 5 1/2" and was likely issued over a period of years. Each features the player's facsimile autograph on the front with a white border at the bottom containing the player's name and team name. These cards are printed on thin card stock and have unnumbered blank backs. They closely resemble the 1975-76 Team Issue set so we've noted differences below on players common to both sets.

COMPLETE SET (43) 200.00 400.00
1 Herb Adderley 6.00 12.00
2 Lance Alworth 7.50 15.00
3 George Andrie 5.00 10.00
4 John Babinecz 5.00 10.00
5 Benny Barnes 5.00 10.00
6 Marv Bateman 5.00 10.00
7 Larry Cole 5.00 10.00
(cutting to his right)
8 Jack Concannon 5.00 10.00
9 Mike Ditka 7.50 15.00
10 Dave Edwards 5.00 10.00
11 John Fitzgerald 5.00 10.00
12 Toni Fritsch 5.00 10.00
13 Jean Fugett 5.00 10.00
14 Walt Garrison 5.00 10.00
15 Cornell Green 6.00 12.00
16 Bill Gregory 5.00 10.00
17 Cliff Harris 6.00 12.00
(no mustache)
18 Bob Hayes 7.50 15.00
19 Calvin Hill 6.00 12.00
20 Chuck Howley 6.00 12.00
21 Lee Roy Jordan 6.00 12.00
(left foot raised)
22 Mike Keller 5.00 10.00
23 Tom Landry CO 10.00 20.00
24 D.D. Lewis 5.00 10.00
(with mustache)
25 Bob Lilly 10.00 20.00
26 Dave Manders 5.00 10.00
27 Mike Montgomery 5.00 10.00
28 Craig Morton 6.00 12.00
29 Ralph Neely 5.00 10.00
30 Robert Newhouse 5.00 10.00
31 John Niland 5.00 10.00
32 Blaine Nye 5.00 10.00
33 Billy Parks 5.00 10.00
34 Jethro Pugh 5.00 10.00
(left foot raised)
35 Dan Reeves 6.00 12.00
36 Mel Renfro 6.00 12.00
(left foot raised)
37 Roger Staubach 15.00 30.00
(jersey #12 on shoulder)
38 Pat Toomay 5.00 10.00
39 Billy Truax 5.00 10.00
40 Rodney Wallace 5.00 10.00
41 Mark Washington 5.00 10.00
42 Charlie Waters 6.00 12.00
(left foot raised)
43 Rayfield Wright 6.00 12.00
(charging forward)

1973 Cowboys McDonald's

This set of photos was sponsored by McDonald's. Each photo measures approximately 8" by 10" and features a posed color close-up photo bordered in white. The player's name and team name are printed in black in the bottom white border. The top portion of the back has biographical information, career summary, and career statistics. The bottom portion carries the Cowboys 1973 game schedule. The photos are unnumbered and are checklisted below alphabetically.

COMPLETE SET (4) 45.00 90.00
1 Walt Garrison 5.00 10.00
2 Calvin Hill 7.50 15.00
3 Bob Lilly 12.50 25.00
4 Roger Staubach 25.00 50.00

1973 Cowboys Team Issue 4x5-1/2

These team issued photos feature black-and-white posed player photos with white borders. Each photo measures approximately 4 1/4" by 5 1/2" and features the player's name and team name below the player image. Every player is shown in his white jersey and the images were cropped to show no more than half of the jersey number. Some images were also used to create the 5x7-1/2 version. Each photo was printed on thin paper stock, has a blankback and was not numbered. We've listed all known subjects; any additions to this list are appreciated.

COMPLETE SET (15) 60.00 120.00
1 Jim Arneson 4.00 8.00
2 Rodrigo Barnes 4.00 8.00
3 Marv Bateman 4.00 8.00
4 Jack Concannon 4.00 8.00
5 Billy Joe Dupree 5.00 10.00
6 Harvey Martin 5.00 10.00
7 Robert Newhouse 4.00 8.00
8 Billy Parks 4.00 8.00
9 Drew Pearson 7.50 15.00
10 Cyril Pinder 4.00 8.00
11 Golden Richards 4.00 8.00
12 Larry Robinson 4.00 8.00
13 Otto Stowe 4.00 8.00
14 Les Strayhorn 4.00 8.00
15 Bruce Walton 4.00 8.00

1973 Cowboys Team Issue 5x7-1/2

These team-issued photos feature black-and-white player pictures with a blank back. Each measures approximately 5 1/8" by 7 1/2" and was printed on glossy stock. A thick (3/8") white border surrounds the photo with the player's name and team name below. They are nearly identical to our list for 1974-76 except for the slightly larger overall size and different player photos. The 1973 photos typically show the player waist up with his full jersey number in view while the 1974-76 photos were taken more close-up. Any additions to the below list are appreciated.

COMPLETE SET (24) 75.00 150.00
1 Jim Arneson 4.00 8.00
2 John Babinecz 4.00 8.00
3 Gil Brandt PD 4.00 8.00
4 Larry Cole 4.00 8.00
5 Billy Joe DuPree 5.00 10.00
6 Walt Garrison 4.00 8.00
7 Bob Hayes 6.00 12.00
8 Calvin Hill 5.00 10.00
9 Ed Hughes ACO 4.00 8.00
10 Lee Roy Jordan 5.00 10.00
11 Tom Landry CO 7.50 15.00
12 Dave Manders 4.00 8.00
13 Harvey Martin 5.00 10.00
14 Robert Newhouse 4.00 8.00
15 John Niland 4.00 8.00
16 Blaine Nye 4.00 8.00
17 Jethro Pugh 4.00 8.00
18 Mel Renfro 6.00 12.00
19 John Smith 4.00 8.00
20 Otto Stowe 4.00 8.00
21 Pat Toomay 4.00 8.00
22 Bruce Walton 4.00 8.00
23 Charlie Waters 5.00 10.00
24 Rayfield Wright 5.00 10.00

1974-76 Cowboys Team Issue 5x7

These team-issued photos feature black-and-white player pictures with a blank back. Each measures approximately 5" by 7" and was printed on glossy photo paper stock. A thick (3/8") white border surrounds the photo with the player's name and team name below. They closely resemble the 1973 set but are generally cropped more closely with only a partial jersey number showing versus the 1973 photos. These were likely issued over a number of years as many variations can be found in the photos, but the text size is very close to the same on all of the photos. Any additions to the below list are appreciated.

1 Jim Arneson 4.00 8.00
2A Benny Barnes 4.00 8.00
(slight smile)
2B Benny Barnes 4.00 8.00
(no smile)
3 Bob Breunig 4.00 8.00
4 Warren Capone 4.00 8.00
5A Larry Cole 4.00 8.00
(jersey number barely shows)
5B Larry Cole 4.00 8.00
(half of jersey number shows)
6 Kyle Davis 4.00 8.00
7A Doug Dennison 4.00 8.00
(Jersey # to the right)
7B Doug Dennison 4.00 8.00
(Jersey # to the left)
8 Mike Ditka ACO 6.00 12.00
9 Pat Donovan 4.00 8.00
10A Billy Joe DuPree 5.00 10.00
(slight smile)
10B Billy Joe DuPree 5.00 10.00
(no smile)

11A Dave Edwards	4.00	8.00
(jersey # barely shows)		
11B Dave Edwards	4.00	8.00
(half of jersey # shows)		
12A John Fitzgerald	4.00	8.00
(jersey # barely shows)		
12B John Fitzgerald	4.00	8.00
(half of jersey # shows)		
13 Toni Fritsch	4.00	8.00
14A Jean Fugett	4.00	8.00
(smiling)		
14B Jean Fugett	4.00	8.00
(not smiling)		
15A Walt Garrison	4.00	8.00
(facing straight)		
15B Walt Garrison	4.00	8.00
(looking slightly to his left)		
16A Cornell Green	4.00	8.00
(4 on shoulder visible)		
16B Cornell Green	4.00	8.00
(4 on shoulder not visible)		
17A Bill Gregory	4.00	8.00
(1/2 of jersey number shows)		
17B Bill Gregory	4.00	8.00
(1/3 of jersey number shows)		
18A Cliff Harris	5.00	10.00
18B Cliff Harris	5.00	10.00
19 Bob Hayes	6.00	12.00
20 Thomas Henderson	5.00	10.00
21 Efren Herrera	4.00	8.00
22 Calvin Hill	5.00	10.00
23 Mitch Hoopes	4.00	8.00
24 Bill Houston	4.00	8.00
25 Percy Howard	4.00	8.00
26A Ron Howard	4.00	8.00
(smiling)		
26B Ron Howard	4.00	8.00
(not smiling)		
27 Randy Hughes	4.00	8.00
28 Ken Hutcherson	4.00	8.00
29 Ed Too Tall Jones	5.00	10.00
30A Lee Roy Jordan	5.00	10.00
(half of jersey # shows)		
30B Lee Roy Jordan	5.00	10.00
(3/4 of jersey # shows)		
31 Gene Killian	4.00	8.00
32 Burton Lawless	4.00	8.00
33A D.D. Lewis	4.00	8.00
(no mustache)		
33B D.D. Lewis	4.00	8.00
(with mustache)		
34 Bob Lilly	7.50	15.00
35 Clint Longley	4.00	8.00
36 Dave Manders	4.00	8.00
37A Harvey Martin	5.00	10.00
37B Harvey Martin	5.00	10.00
38 Dennis Morgan	4.00	8.00
39A Ralph Neely	4.00	8.00
(facing slightly to his right)		
39B Ralph Neely	4.00	8.00
(facing slightly to his left)		
40A Robert Newhouse	5.00	10.00
(half of jersey # shows)		
40B Robert Newhouse	5.00	10.00
(jersey # not visible)		
41A Blaine Nye/(smiling)	4.00	8.00
41B Blaine Nye/(slight smile)	4.00	8.00
42 Drew Pearson	6.00	12.00
43A Cal Peterson	4.00	8.00
(name listed Calvin)		
43B Cal Peterson	4.00	8.00
(name listed Cal)		
44A Jethro Pugh	4.00	8.00
44B Jethro Pugh	4.00	8.00
45 Dan Reeves ACO	5.00	10.00
46A Mel Renfro	5.00	10.00
46B Mel Renfro	5.00	10.00
47A Golden Richards	4.00	8.00
(looking to his right)		
47B Golden Richards	4.00	8.00
(facing straight)		
48 Herb Scott	4.00	8.00
49 Ron Sellers	4.00	8.00
50A Roger Staubach	12.50	25.00
50B Roger Staubach	12.50	25.00
51 Les Strayhorn	4.00	8.00
52 Pat Toomay	4.00	8.00
53 Louie Walker	4.00	8.00
54A Bruce Walton	4.00	8.00
(half jersey # visible)		
54B Bruce Walton	4.00	8.00
(full jersey # visible)		
55A Mark Washington	4.00	8.00
(not smiling)		
55B Mark Washington	4.00	8.00
(smiling)		
56A Charlie Waters	5.00	10.00
(no shoulder #'s visible)		
56B Charlie Waters	5.00	10.00
(1 on shoulder visible)		
57 Randy White	7.50	15.00
58 Rollie Woolsey	4.00	8.00
59 Rayfield Wright	5.00	10.00
60A Charlie Young	4.00	8.00
(half jersey # shows)		
60B Charlie Young	4.00	8.00
(jersey # shows slightly)		

1975-76 Cowboys Team Issue 4x5-1/2

This team issued photo set features black-and-white posed action player photos with white borders. Each photo measures approximately 4 1/2" by 5 1/2" and features a facsimile autograph on the front unless noted below. A wider (1/2") white border at the bottom contains the player's name and team. These cards are printed on thin card stock and have unnumbered blank backs. They closely resemble the 1972 Team Issue set so we've noted differences below on players common to both sets.

COMPLETE SET (28)	100.00	200.00
1 Benny Barnes	4.00	8.00
(no facsimile)		
2 Bob Breunig	4.00	8.00
3 Larry Cole	4.00	8.00
(charging forward)		
4 Kyle Davis	4.00	8.00
5 Pat Donovan	4.00	8.00
6 Cliff Harris	5.00	10.00
(with mustache; no facsimile)		
7 Thomas Henderson	5.00	10.00
8 Efren Herrera	4.00	8.00
9 Mitch Hoopes	4.00	8.00
10 Ed Too Tall Jones	5.00	10.00
11 Lee Roy Jordan	5.00	10.00
(right foot raised)		
12 Scott Laidlaw	4.00	8.00
13 Burton Lawless	4.00	8.00
14 D.D. Lewis	4.00	8.00
(no mustache)		
15 Clint Longley	4.00	8.00
16 Harvey Martin	5.00	10.00
(no facsimile)		
17 Robert Newhouse	4.00	8.00
(no facsimile)		
18 Drew Pearson	5.00	10.00
(no facsimile)		
19 Preston Pearson	5.00	10.00
20 Jethro Pugh	4.00	8.00
(right foot raised)		
21 Mel Renfro	6.00	12.00
(right foot raised)		
22 Golden Richards	4.00	8.00
23 Herb Scott	4.00	8.00
24 Roger Staubach	10.00	20.00
(no jersey number on shoulder)		
25 Charlie Waters	4.00	8.00
(right foot raised)		
26 Randy White	7.50	15.00
27 Rayfield Wright	5.00	10.00
(cutting to his left)		
28 Charles Young	4.00	8.00

1976-78 Cowboys Team Issue 8x10

These photos were released by the Cowboys for player appearances and fan mail requests from roughly 1976-78. Each measures approximately 8" by 10" and fetures a black and white player photo. The player's name and team name appear immediately below the photo with slightly different font size and style used on the text for some of the photos. Many players were issued in more than one pose with some featuring only slight differences. Each is unnumbered and checklisted below alphabetically.

1A Bob Breunig	5.00	10.00
1B Bob Breunig	5.00	10.00
1C Bob Breunig	5.00	10.00
1D Bob Breunig	5.00	10.00
2 Glenn Carano	5.00	10.00
3 Larry Cole	5.00	10.00
(left foot off of the ground)		
4 Jim Cooper	5.00	10.00
5A Doug Dennison	5.00	10.00
5B Doug Dennison	5.00	10.00
6 Pat Donovan	5.00	10.00
7 Tony Dorsett	10.00	20.00
8 Billy Joe DuPree	5.00	10.00
9 Jim Eidson	5.00	10.00
10 John Fitzgerald	5.00	10.00
11A Bill Gregory	5.00	10.00
11B Bill Gregory	5.00	10.00
12A Cliff Harris	6.00	12.00
12B Cliff Harris	6.00	12.00
12C Cliff Harris	6.00	12.00
13 Mike Hegman	5.00	10.00
14A Thomas Henderson	6.00	12.00
14B Thomas Henderson	6.00	12.00
14C Thomas Henderson	6.00	12.00
15A Efren Herrera	5.00	10.00
15B Efren Herrera	5.00	10.00
16A Tony Hill	6.00	12.00
16B Tony Hill	6.00	12.00
17 Randy Hughes	5.00	10.00
18A Bruce Huther	5.00	10.00
18B Bruce Huther	5.00	10.00
19 Jim Jensen	5.00	10.00
20A Butch Johnson	5.00	10.00
20B Butch Johnson	5.00	10.00
21A Ed Too Tall Jones	6.00	12.00
21B Ed Too Tall Jones	6.00	12.00
21C Ed Too Tall Jones	6.00	12.00
21D Ed Too Tall Jones	6.00	12.00
22 Lee Roy Jordan	6.00	12.00
23A Aaron Kyle	5.00	10.00
23B Aaron Kyle	5.00	10.00
24 Scott Laidlaw	5.00	10.00
25 Burton Lawless	5.00	10.00
26A D.D. Lewis	5.00	10.00
26B D.D. Lewis	5.00	10.00
27A Harvey Martin	6.00	12.00
27B Harvey Martin	5.00	10.00
28A Ralph Neely	5.00	10.00
28B Ralph Neely	5.00	10.00
29A Robert Newhouse	5.00	10.00
29B Robert Newhouse	5.00	10.00
30 Blaine Nye	5.00	10.00
31A Drew Pearson	6.00	12.00
31B Drew Pearson	6.00	12.00
31C Drew Pearson	6.00	12.00
32A Preston Pearson	6.00	12.00
32B Preston Pearson	6.00	12.00
33A Jethro Pugh	5.00	10.00
33B Jethro Pugh	5.00	10.00
33C Jethro Pugh	5.00	10.00
34 Tom Rafferty	5.00	10.00
35 Tom Randall	5.00	10.00
36A Mel Renfro	7.50	15.00
36B Mel Renfro	7.50	15.00
37A Golden Richards	5.00	10.00
37B Golden Richards	5.00	10.00
38 Jay Saldi	5.00	10.00
39 Rafael Septien	5.00	10.00
40A Roger Staubach	10.00	20.00
40B Roger Staubach	10.00	20.00
41A Mark Washington	5.00	10.00
41B Mark Washington	5.00	10.00
42A Charlie Waters	6.00	12.00
42B Charlie Waters	6.00	12.00
43A Randy White	10.00	20.00
43B Randy White	10.00	20.00
44 Rayfield Wright	6.00	12.00
45 Charlie Young	5.00	10.00

1977 Cowboys Burger King Glasses

Burger King restaurants in conjunction with Dr. Pepper released this set of 6-drinking glasses during the 1977 NFL season in Dallas area stores. Each features a black and white photo of a Cowboys player with his name and team name below the picture. This set can be differentiated from the 1978 Burger King due to the row of stars that encircle the glass, as well as the different player selection.

COMPLETE SET (6)	25.00	50.00
1 Billy Joe DuPree	5.00	10.00
2 Efren Herrera	3.75	7.50
3 Harvey Martin	6.00	12.00
4 Drew Pearson	6.00	12.00
5 Charlie Waters	5.00	10.00
6 Randy White	7.50	15.00

1978 Cowboys Burger King Glasses

Burger King restaurants in conjunction with Dr. Pepper released this set of 6-drinking glasses during the 1978 NFL season in Dallas area stores. Each features a black and white photo of a Cowboys player with his name and team name below the picture.

COMPLETE SET (6)	20.00	40.00
1 Bob Breunig	3.00	6.00
2 Pat Donovan	3.00	6.00
3 Cliff Harris	4.00	8.00
4 D.D. Lewis	4.00	8.00
5 Robert Newhouse	4.00	8.00
6 Golden Richards	3.00	6.00

1978 Cowboys Team Sheets

These 8" by 10" sheets were issued primarily to media outlets in need of player photos. Each sheet includes small photos for 8-players (except for the final sheet) with the player's name and position below each image. The "Dallas Cowboys" name is at the top of each sheet. The backs are blank

COMPLETE SET (6)	40.00	80.00
1 Sheet 1	5.00	10.00
2 Sheet 2	10.00	20.00
3 Sheet 3	6.00	12.00
4 Sheet 4	6.00	12.00
5 Sheet 5	12.50	25.00
6 Sheet 6	7.50	15.00

1979 Cowboys Police

The 1979 Dallas Cowboy Police set consists of 15 cards sponsored by the Kiwanis Clubs, the Dallas Cowboys Weekly (the official fan newspaper), and the local law enforcement agency. The cards measure approximately 2 5/8" by 4 1/8". The cards are unnumbered but have been numbered in the checklist below by the player's uniform number which appears on the fronts of the cards. The backs contain "Cowboys Tips" which draw analogies between action on the football field and law abiding action in real life. D.D. Lewis replaced Thomas (Hollywood) Henderson midway through the season; hence, both of these cards are available in lesser quantities than the other cards in this set.

COMPLETE SET (15)	10.00	20.00
12 Roger Staubach	4.00	8.00
33 Tony Dorsett	2.50	5.00
41 Charlie Waters	.50	1.00
43 Cliff Harris	.50	1.00
44 Robert Newhouse	.25	.50
50 D.D. Lewis SP	1.50	3.00
53 Bob Breunig	.25	.50
54 Randy White	1.25	2.50
56 Thomas Henderson SP	1.50	3.00
67 Pat Donovan	.25	.50
79 Harvey Martin	.50	1.00
80 Tony Hill	.50	1.00
88 Drew Pearson	.60	1.50
89 Billy Joe DuPree	.50	1.00
NNO Tom Landry CO	2.00	4.00

1979 Cowboys Team Issue Bios

These photos were released by the Cowboys for player appearances and fan mail requests. This style and format was used for a number of years (from roughly 1979-1985) so we've included descriptions below to differentiate players released in more than one year. Each measures approximately 4" by 5 1/2" and was printed on thick paper stock. The white-bordered fronts display black-and-white player photos. The player's name and jersey number appear immediately below the photo with his position, height, weight, and college below that. The Cowboys helmet logo on included on the left. The backs are blank are unnumbered.

COMPLETE SET (53)	250.00	400.00
1 Benny Barnes	4.00	8.00
2 Larry Bethea	4.00	8.00
3 Alois Blackwell	4.00	8.00
4 Bob Breunig	4.00	8.00
(running to his left)		
6 Guy Brown	4.00	8.00
7 Glenn Carano	4.00	8.00
(right foot raised)		
8 Larry Cole	4.00	8.00
8 Jim Cooper	4.00	8.00
(no mustache; offensive tackle)		
10 Doug Cosbie	4.00	8.00
(football in hands)		
11 Anthony Dickerson	4.00	8.00
(left leg straight)		
12 Pat Donovan	4.00	8.00
(jersey #7 obscured)		
13 Tony Dorsett	7.50	15.00
(football in right hand)		
14 Billy Joe Dupree	5.00	10.00
15 John Dutton	4.00	8.00
(cutting to his left slightly)		
16 John Fitzgerald	4.00	8.00
(snapping the ball)		
17 Andy Frederick	4.00	8.00
18 Richard Grimmett	4.00	8.00
19 Cliff Harris	5.00	10.00
20 Mike Hegman	4.00	8.00
(left hand at left shoulder)		
21 Thomas Henderson	5.00	10.00
22 Tony Hill	5.00	10.00
(football up by shoulder)		
23 Randy Hughes	4.00	8.00
24 Bruce Huther	4.00	8.00
25 Butch Johnson	4.00	8.00
(football up near head)		
26 Ed Too Tall Jones	5.00	10.00
(cutting to his right)		
29 Tom Landry CO	6.00	12.00
(star next to helmet logo)		
31 D.D. Lewis	4.00	8.00
33 Harvey Martin	5.00	10.00
(jersey #7 partially obscured)		
34 Aaron Mitchell	4.00	8.00
35 Robert Newhouse	5.00	10.00
(football in left arm)		
36 Drew Pearson	6.00	12.00
(jersey #8 obscured; weight:183)		
37 Preston Pearson	5.00	10.00
38 Tom Rafferty	4.00	8.00
39 Jay Saldi	4.00	8.00
40 Tex Schramm GM	5.00	10.00
41 Herb Scott	4.00	8.00
42 Rafael Septien	4.00	8.00
(right foot at left knee)		
43 Robert Shaw	4.00	8.00
44 Ron Springs	4.00	8.00
(right foot at left knee)		
45 Dave Stalls	4.00	8.00
46 Roger Staubach	15.00	25.00
47 Bruce Thornton	4.00	8.00
48 Dennis Thurman	4.00	8.00
(left leg raised)		
49 Charlie Waters	5.00	10.00
50 Danny White	6.00	12.00
(feet planted)		

51 Randy White (running to his right)	7.50	15.00
52 Steve Wilson (wearing jersey #81)	4.00	8.00

1979 Cowboys Team Sheets

These 8" by 10" sheets were issued primarily to media outlets in need of player photos. Each sheet includes small photos for 8-players with the player's jersey number, name and position below each image. The "Dallas Cowboys" name is at the top of each sheet. The backs are blank

COMPLETE SET (6)	40.00	80.00
1 Larry Bethea	5.00	10.00
Benny Barnes		
Alois Blackwell		
Bob Breunig		
Larry Brinson		
Guy Brown		
Glenn Carano		
Larry Cole		
2 Jim Cooper	7.50	15.00
Doug Cosbie		
Pat Donovan		
Tony Dorsett		
Billy Joe Dupree		
John Fitzgerald		
Andy Frederick		
Richard Grimmett		
3 Cliff Harris	5.00	10.00
Mike Hegman		
Thomas Henderson		
Tony Hill		
Randy Hughes		
Bruce Huther		
Butch Johnson		
Aaron Kyle		
4 Scott Laidlaw	6.00	12.00
Burton Lawless		
D.D. Lewis		
Wade Manning		
Harvey Martin		
Aaron Mitchell		
Robert Newhouse		
Drew Pearson		
5 Preston Pearson	5.00	10.00
Tom Rafferty		
Jay Saldi		
Herb Scott		
Rafael Septien		
Robert Shaw		
Ron Springs		
Dave Stalls		
6 Roger Staubach	12.50	25.00
Bruce Thornton		
Dennis Thurman		
Charlie Waters		
Danny White		
Randy White		
Steve Wilson		
Rayfield Wright		

1979-80 Cowboys Team Issue 4x5-1/2

These team issued photos feature black-and-white posed action player photos with white borders. Each photo measures approximately 4 1/4" by 5 1/2" and features the player's name and team name below the player image. Every player is shown in his white jersey and each photo was printed on thin paper matte-finish stock, has a blankback and was not numbered. We've listed all known subjects; any additions to this list are appreciated.

1 Tony Dorsett	6.00	12.00
2 Billy Joe DuPree	4.00	8.00
3 James Jones	4.00	8.00
4 D.D. Lewis	4.00	8.00
5 Drew Pearson	5.00	10.00
6 Roger Staubach	10.00	20.00
7 Danny White	6.00	12.00
8 Randy White	6.00	12.00

1980 Cowboys McDonald's

These cards were issued two per box on three different Happy Meal type boxes numbered "Super Box I" through "Super Box III." The individual cards, meant to be cut from the boxes, are unnumbered and blankbacked. We've listed prices for single cards, neatly cut from the box, below alphabetically according to the box on which the player appears. Complete Happy Meal Boxes carry a premium of 1.5X to 2X the prices listed below.

COMPLETE SET (6)	125.00	200.00
1 Chuck Howley	10.00	25.00
2 Don Perkins	10.00	25.00
3 Bob Lilly	12.00	30.00
4 Don Meredith	15.00	40.00
5 Walt Garrison	8.00	20.00
6 Roger Staubach	50.00	100.00

1980 Cowboys Police

Quite similar to the 1979 set, the 1980 Dallas Cowboys police set is unnumbered other than the player's uniform number (as is listed in the checklist below). The cards in this 14-card set measure approximately 2 5/8" by 4 1/8". The sponsors are the same as those of the 1979 issue and the section entitled "Cowboys Tips" is contained on the back. The Kiwanis and Cowboys helmet logos appear on the fronts of the cards.

COMPLETE SET (14)	6.00	12.00
1 Rafael Septien	.40	1.00
11 Danny White	1.00	2.50
25 Aaron Kyle	.25	.60
26 Preston Pearson	.60	1.50
31 Benny Barnes	.40	1.00
35 Scott Laidlaw	.25	.60
42 Randy Hughes	.25	.60
62 John Fitzgerald	.40	1.00
63 Larry Cole	.40	1.00
64 Tom Rafferty	.40	1.00
68 Herb Scott	.25	.60
70 Rayfield Wright	.40	1.00
78 John Dutton	.40	1.00
87 Jay Saldi	.40	1.00

1980 Cowboys Team Issue

These photos were released by the Cowboys for player appearances and fan mail requests. This style and format was used for a number of years (from roughly 1979-1985) so we've included descriptions below to differentiate players released in more than one year. Each measures approximately 4" by 5 1/2" and was printed on thick paper stock. The white-bordered fronts display black-and-white player photos. The player's name and jersey number appear immediately below the photo with his position, height, weight, and college below that. The Cowboys helmet logo on included on the left. The backs are blank are unnumbered.

COMPLETE SET (27)	100.00	200.00
1 Bob Breunig	3.00	8.00
2 Glenn Carano	3.00	8.00
3 Dextor Clinkscale	3.00	8.00
4 Jim Cooper	3.00	8.00
5 Doug Cosbie	3.00	8.00
6 Anthony Dickerson	3.00	8.00
7 Pat Donovan	3.00	8.00
8 Tony Dorsett	6.00	15.00
9 John Dutton	3.00	8.00
12 Tony Hill	4.00	10.00
10 John Fitzgerald (charging forward)	3.00	8.00
13 Gary Hogeboom	3.00	8.00
11 Mike Hegman (left hand on jersey #5)	3.00	8.00
14 Butch Johnson	3.00	8.00
16 James Jones	3.00	8.00
15 Ed Too Tall Jones	4.00	10.00
17 Tom Landry CO	5.00	12.00
18 Harvey Martin	4.00	10.00
19 Robert Newhouse	3.00	8.00
20 Timmy Newsome	3.00	8.00
21 Drew Pearson	4.00	10.00
22 Kurt Petersen	3.00	8.00
23 Bill Roe	3.00	8.00
24 Rafael Septien	3.00	8.00
25 Roland Solomon	3.00	8.00
26 Ron Springs	3.00	8.00
27 Dennis Thurman	3.00	8.00
28 Norm Wells	3.00	8.00
29 Danny White	5.00	12.00
30 Randy White	6.00	15.00
31 Steve Wilson (wearing jersey #45)	3.00	8.00

1980 Cowboys Team Sheets

These 8" by 10" sheets were issued primarily to media outlets in need of player photos. Each sheet includes small photos for 8-players with the player's jersey number, name and position below each image. "The Dallas Cowboys Football Club" is printed at the top of each sheet and the backs are blank

COMPLETE SET (7)	40.00	80.00
1 Benny Barnes	4.00	10.00
Larry Bethea		
Bob Breunig		
Guy Brown		
Glenn Carano		
Dextor Clinkscale		
Larry Cole		
Jim Cooper		
2 Doug Cosbie	6.00	15.00
Anthony Dickerson		
Pat Donovan		
Tony Dorsett		
Billy Joe Dupree		
John Dutton		
John Fitzgerald		
Andy Frederick		
3 Mike Hegman	5.00	12.00
Tony Hill		
Gary Hogeboom		
Randy Hughes		
Eric Hurt		
Bruce Huther		
Butch Johnson		
Ed Jones		
4 James Jones	5.00	12.00
Aaron Kyle		
D.D. Lewis		
Harvey Martin		
Aaron Mitchell		
Robert Newhouse		
Timmy Newsome		
Drew Pearson		
5 Preston Pearson	4.00	10.00
Kurt Petersen		
Tom Rafferty		
Bill Roe		
Jay Saldi		
Herb Scott		
Rafael Septien		
Robert Shaw		
6 Roland Soloman	6.00	15.00
Ron Springs		
Bruce Thornton		
Dennis Thurman		
Charlie Waters		
Norm Wells		
Danny White		
Randy White		
Steve Wilson		
7 Coaching Staff	6.00	15.00
Tom Landry		
Ermal Allen		
Mike Ditka		
Al Lavan		
Jim Myers		
Dan Reeves		
Gene Stallings		
Ernie Stautner		
Jerry Tubbs		
Bob Ward		

1974 Cowboys Team Issue 8x10

The Dallas Cowboys issued these black-and-white player photos, measuring 8" by 10," and printed on glossy stock with white borders. Each player photo is a posed action shot. The border below the photo contains just the player's name and team name. The type style and size varies slightly on some photos so this may indicate that they were released over a period of years. The photos are blankbacked and unnumbered. Any additions to the below list are appreciated.

1 Larry Cole (right foot off of the ground)	6.00	12.00
2 Bob Hayes	7.50	15.00
3 Ron Howard	6.00	12.00
4 Cornell Green	6.00	12.00
5 Bob Lilly	10.00	20.00
6 Ralph Neely	6.00	12.00
7 Mel Renfro	7.50	15.00

1976 Crane Discs

The 1976 Crane football disc set of 30 cards contains a black and white photo of the player surrounded by a colored border. These circular cards measure 3 3/8" in diameter. The word Crane completes the circle of the border. The backs contain a Crane (Potato Chips) advertisement and the letters MSA, signifying Michael Schechter Associates. A recently discovered version of the discs was apparently inserted into potato chip packages as several players have been found printed without the "National Football League Players" notation around the small football logo on the fronts. Known discs from this version also feature food product stains as would be expected. Franco Harris can only be found in this "product inserted" version of the discs. None of the second version of the discs are considered part of the complete set price below due to their scarcity. Any additions to the checklist of this version of the discs is appreciated. These discs were also available as a complete set via a mail-in offer on the potato chip wrappers; consequently they are commonly found in nice condition. Of these, there are 12 discs that were produced in shorter supply than the other 18 and are noted by SP in the checklist below. These extras found their way into the hobby when Crane sold their leftovers to a major midwestern dealer. Since the cards are unnumbered, they are ordered below alphabetically. The discs can also be found with the sponsor Saga Philadelphia School District on the cardback. The Saga discs are much more difficult to find and are listed as a separate release.

COMPLETE SET (30)	12.50	25.00
1 Ken Anderson	.30	.60
2 Otis Armstrong	.20	.40
3 Steve Bartkowski	.20	.40
4 Terry Bradshaw	1.50	3.00
5 John Brockington SP	.18	.35
6 Doug Buffone	.13	.25
7 Wally Chambers	.13	.25
8 Isaac Curtis SP	.25	.50
9 Chuck Foreman	.20	.40
10 Roman Gabriel SP	.25	.50
11 Mel Gray	.20	.40
12 Joe Greene	.50	1.00
13 Franco Harris SP	7.50	15.00
14 James Harris SP	.18	.35
15 Jim Hart	.20	.40
16 Billy Kilmer	.20	.40
17 Greg Landry SP	.25	.50
18 Ed Marinaro SP	.25	.50
19 Lawrence McCutcheon SP	.25	.50
20 Terry Metcalf	.20	.40
21 Lydell Mitchell SP	.25	.50
22 Jim Otis	.13	.25
23 Alan Page	.30	.60
24 Walter Payton SP	7.50	15.00
25A Greg Pruitt SP	.25	.50
25B Greg Pruitt SP	2.50	5.00
26 Charlie Sanders SP	.30	.75
27 Ron Shanklin SP	.18	.35
28 Roger Staubach	2.00	4.00
29 Jan Stenerud	.20	.40
30 Charley Taylor	.30	.60
31 Roger Wehrli	.20	.50

1970 Dayton Daily News

Each of these "bubble gum-less cards" are actually a cut-out photo from The Dayton Daily News newspaper. Each card measures approximately 3 1/2" by 4" when properly cut. The checklist below is incomplete, any additions to it would be appreciated.

1 Herb Adderley	5.00	10.00
2 Virgil Carter	2.50	5.00
4 Gary Cuozzo	3.00	6.00
6 Ken Dyer	2.50	5.00
7 Walt Garrison	3.00	6.00
8 Bob Hayes	4.00	8.00
9 Bob Lilly	6.00	12.00
13 Joe Morrison	3.00	6.00
14 Craig Morton	4.00	8.00
16 Bart Starr	15.00	30.00
17 Fran Tarkenton	10.00	20.00
161 Bill Bergey	3.00	6.00
172 Don Cockroft UER	2.50	5.00
174 John DeMarie	2.50	5.00
176A Dale Lindsey ERR	2.50	5.00
176B Dale Lindsey COR	2.50	5.00
182 Fred Hoaglin	2.50	5.00
190 Mike Howell	2.50	5.00
191 Al Jenkins	2.50	5.00
194 Milt Morin	2.50	5.00
200 Donny Anderson	3.00	6.00
201 Fred Carr	2.50	5.00
209 Pete Case	2.50	5.00
214 Tucker Frederickson	3.00	6.00
217 Mike Wilson G	2.50	5.00
220 Bill Munson	3.00	6.00
221 Bennie McRae	2.50	5.00
224 Bubba Smith	4.00	8.00
226 John Brodie	4.00	8.00
229 Ken Willard	3.00	6.00
234 John Mackey	5.00	10.00
236 Mike Curtis	3.00	6.00
241 Earl Morrall	3.00	6.00
242 Jim O'Brien	2.50	5.00

1971-72 Dell Photos

Measuring approximately 8 1/4" by 10 3/4", the 1971-72 Dell Pro Football Guide features a center insert that unfolds to display 48 color player photos that are framed by black and yellow border stripes. Each picture measures approximately 1 3/4" by 3" and is not perforated. The player's name and team name are printed beneath the picture. The backs have various color action shots that are framed by a black-and-white film type pattern. Biographies on the NFL stars featured on the insert are found throughout the guide. The uncut set still in the book brings up to a 25 percent premium over the complete set price. The pictures are unnumbered and checklisted below in alphabetical order.

COMPLETE SET (48)	40.00	80.00
1 Dan Abramowicz	.40	1.00
2 Herb Adderley	1.00	2.00
3 Lem Barney	.60	1.50
4 Bobby Bell	.60	1.50
5 George Blanda	2.00	4.00
6 Terry Bradshaw	5.00	10.00
7 John Brodie	1.00	2.00
8 Larry Brown	.50	1.25
9 Dick Butkus	4.00	8.00
10 Fred Carr	.40	1.00
11 Virgil Carter	.40	1.00
12 Mike Curtis	.50	1.25
13 Len Dawson	1.25	3.00
14 Carl Eller	.60	1.50
15 Mel Farr	.40	1.00
16 Roman Gabriel	.60	1.50
17 Gary Garrison	.40	1.00
18 Dick Gordon	.40	1.00
19 Bob Griese	3.00	6.00
20 Bob Hayes	1.00	2.00
21 Rich Jackson	.40	1.00
22 Charley Johnson	.50	1.25
23 Ron Johnson	.40	1.00
24 Deacon Jones	.60	1.50
25 Sonny Jurgensen	1.00	2.00
26 Leroy Kelly	1.00	2.00
27 Daryle Lamonica	.60	1.50
28 MacArthur Lane	.40	1.00
29 Willie Lanier	.60	1.50
30 Bob Lilly	1.00	2.50
31 Floyd Little	.50	1.25
32 Mike Lucci	.40	1.00
33 Don Maynard	1.00	2.50
34 Joe Namath	5.00	10.00
35 Tommy Nobis	.60	1.50
36 Merlin Olsen	1.00	2.00
37 Alan Page	1.00	2.00

38 Gerry Philbin	.40	1.00
39 Jim Plunkett	.60	1.50
40 Tim Rossovich	.40	1.00
41 Gale Sayers	4.00	8.00
42 Dennis Shaw	.40	1.00
43 O.J. Simpson	3.00	8.00
44 Fran Tarkenton	2.00	5.00
45 Johnny Unitas	5.00	12.00
46 Paul Warfield	1.25	3.00
47 Gene Washington 49er	.50	1.25
48 Larry Wilson	.60	1.50

1933 Diamond Matchbooks Silver

Diamond Match Co. produced their first football matchbook set in 1933. Many covers appear with both a green and pink background on the text area surrounded by a silver border, although a few cards appear in only one color. This set is clearly the most difficult to complete of all the football Diamond Matchbooks. Each cover measures approximately 1 1/2" by 4 1/2" (when completely folded out) and is priced below as unfolded with the matches removed. Complete covers with matches intact sometimes sell for as much as 1-1/2 ttimes the prices listed below. Although the covers are not numbered, we've assigned numbers alphabetically with the white bordered All-American Seal leading off and the color variations listed with a G (green) and P (pink) suffix. Several covers are thought to be much more difficult to find; we've labeled those as SP below.

1 All-American Board Seal	30.00	60.00
2G Gene Alford	40.00	75.00
2P Gene Alford	40.00	75.00
3G Marger Apsit	40.00	75.00
3P Marger Apsit	40.00	75.00
4G Red Badgro	75.00	125.00
4P Red Badgro	75.00	125.00
5G Cliff Battles	100.00	175.00
5P Cliff Battles	100.00	175.00
6P Maury Bodenger	40.00	75.00
7P Jim Bowdoin	40.00	75.00
8G John Boylan	40.00	75.00
8P John Boylan	40.00	75.00
9G Hank Bruder	60.00	100.00
9P Hank Bruder	60.00	100.00
10G Carl Brumbaugh	40.00	75.00
10P Carl Brumbaugh	40.00	75.00
11P Bill Buckler	40.00	75.00
12G Jerome Buckley	40.00	75.00
12P Jerome Buckley	40.00	75.00
13G Dale Burnett	40.00	75.00
13P Dale Burnett	40.00	75.00
14P Ernie Caddel	60.00	100.00
15G1 Chris Cagle OFB	60.00	100.00
15G2 Chris Cagle WFB	75.00	150.00
15P Chris Cagle	60.00	100.00
16G Glen Campbell	40.00	75.00
16P Glen Campbell	40.00	75.00
17G John Cannella	40.00	75.00
18P Zuck Carlson	40.00	75.00
19P George Christensen	75.00	125.00
20G Stu Clancy	40.00	75.00
21G Paul(Rip) Collins	40.00	75.00
21P Paul(Rip) Collins	40.00	75.00
22P Jack Connell	40.00	75.00
23P George Corbett	40.00	75.00
24G Orien Crow	40.00	75.00
24P Orien Crow	40.00	75.00
25G Ed Danowski	40.00	75.00
25P Ed Danowski	40.00	75.00
26G Sylvester(Red) Davis	40.00	75.00
26P Sylvester(Red) Davis	40.00	75.00
27G Johnny Dell Isola	60.00	100.00
27P Johnny Dell Isola	60.00	100.00
28P John Doehring	40.00	75.00
29G Turk Edwards	175.00	300.00
29P Turk Edwards	175.00	300.00
30G Earl Elser	40.00	75.00
30P Earl Elser	40.00	75.00
31G Ox Emerson	60.00	100.00
31P Ox Emerson	60.00	100.00
32G Tiny Feather SP	75.00	125.00
33G Ray Flaherty	75.00	125.00
33P Ray Flaherty	75.00	125.00
34G Ike Frankian	40.00	75.00
34P Ike Frankian	40.00	75.00
35G Red Grange	300.00	500.00
35P Red Grange	300.00	500.00
36G Len Grant	40.00	75.00
37G Ace Gutowsky	75.00	125.00
37P Ace Gutowsky	75.00	125.00
38G Mel Hein	300.00	500.00
39P Arnie Herber	600.00	1,000.00
40G Bill Hewitt	350.00	600.00
40P Bill Hewitt	350.00	600.00
41G Herman Hickman	60.00	100.00
41P Herman Hickman	60.00	100.00
42G Clarke Hinkle	350.00	600.00
42P Clarke Hinkle	350.00	600.00
43G Cal Hubbard	600.00	1,000.00
43P Cal Hubbard	600.00	1,000.00
44G George Hurley	40.00	75.00
44P George Hurley	40.00	75.00
45P Herman Hussey SP	75.00	125.00
46G Cecil (Tex) Irvin	40.00	75.00
47G Luke Johnsos	75.00	125.00
47P Luke Johnsos	75.00	125.00
48G Bruce Jones	40.00	75.00
48P Bruce Jones	40.00	75.00
49G Potsy Jones	40.00	75.00
50P Thacker Kaye SP	75.00	125.00
51G Shipwreck Kelly	60.00	100.00
51P Shipwreck Kelly	60.00	100.00
52P Joe Doc Kopcha	60.00	100.00
53G Joe Kurth	90.00	150.00
53P Joe Kurth	90.00	150.00
54G Milo Lubratevich	40.00	75.00
54P Milo Lubratevich	40.00	75.00
55G Father Lumpkin	60.00	100.00
55P Father Lumpkin	60.00	100.00
56G Jim MacMurdo	40.00	75.00
56P Jim MacMurdo	40.00	75.00
57P Joe Maniaci	40.00	75.00
58G Jack McBride	40.00	75.00
59G Ookie Miller	40.00	75.00
59P Ookie Miller	40.00	75.00
60P Buster Mitchell	40.00	75.00
61P Keith Molesworth	40.00	75.00
62P Bob Monnett	90.00	150.00
63G Hap Moran	40.00	75.00
63P Hap Moran	40.00	75.00
64G Bill Morgan	40.00	75.00
65P Maynard Morrison SP	75.00	125.00
66P Mathew Murray	40.00	75.00
67G Jim Musick	40.00	75.00
67P Jim Musick	40.00	75.00
68P Bronko Nagurski SP	600.00	1,000.00
69P Dick Nesbitt	40.00	75.00
70G Harry Newman	60.00	100.00
71G1 Bill Owen ERR	75.00	125.00
71G2 Bill Owen COR	40.00	75.00
72G Steve Owen SP	150.00	250.00
73P Andy Pavlicovic	60.00	100.00
74P Bert Pearson	40.00	75.00
75G William Pendergast	40.00	75.00
75P William Pendergast	40.00	75.00
76P Jerry Pepper	40.00	75.00
77P Stan Piawlock	40.00	75.00
78G Erny Pinckert	60.00	100.00
78P Erny Pinckert	60.00	100.00
79G Glenn Presnell	40.00	75.00
79P Glenn Presnell	40.00	75.00
80P Jess Quatse	90.00	150.00
81G Hank Reese	40.00	75.00
82G Dick Richards	40.00	75.00
82P Dick Richards	40.00	75.00
83P Tony Sarausky	40.00	75.00
84G Elmer Schaake	40.00	75.00
84P Elmer Schaake	40.00	75.00
85G John Schneller	40.00	75.00
85P John Schneller	40.00	75.00
86P Johnny Sisk	40.00	75.00
87G Mike Steponovich	40.00	75.00
87P Mike Steponovich	40.00	75.00
88G Ken Strong	250.00	400.00
89P Charles Tackwell	60.00	100.00
90G Harry Thayer	40.00	75.00
90P Harry Thayer	40.00	75.00
91P Walt Uzdavinis	40.00	75.00
92P John Welch	40.00	75.00
93P William Whalen	40.00	75.00
94G Mule Wilson	60.00	100.00
94P Mule Wilson	60.00	100.00
95G Frank Babe Wright	40.00	75.00
95P Frank Babe Wright	40.00	75.00

1934 Diamond Matchbooks

The 1934 Diamond Matchbook set is the first of many issues from the company printed with colorful borders. Four border colors were used for this set: blue, green, red, and tan. Many players appear with three border color variations, while some only appear with one, two or four different border colors. We've noted below known border colors for each matchbook. It is thought that a complete checklist with all color variations is still unknown. A Tan colored Bronko Nagurski matchbook was recently discovered as was a Green Clarke Hinkle. There is no player position included nor picture frame border shown on the player photo. The text printing is in black ink and each cover measures approximately 1 1/2" by 4 1/2" when completely unfolded. The set is very similar in appearance to the 1935 issues, but can be distinguished by the single lined manufacturer's identification "The Diamond Match Co., N.Y.C." Complete covers with matches intact sometimes sell for as much as 1-1/2 ttimes the prices listed below. Although the covers are not numbered, we've assigned numbers alphabetically. Several covers are thought to be much more difficult to find; we've labeled those as SP below.

1 Arvo Antilla G/R/T	18.00	30.00
2 Red Badgro B/G/R/T	35.00	60.00
3 Norbert Bartell R SP	150.00	300.00
4 Cliff Battles G/R/T	50.00	80.00
5 Chuck Bennis B/G/R/T	18.00	30.00
6 Jack Beynon G/R/T	18.00	30.00
7 Maury Bodenger G/R/T (misspelled Morry)	18.00	30.00
8 John Bond G/R/T	18.00	30.00
9 John Brown G/R/T	18.00	30.00
10 Carl Brumbaugh R/T SP	150.00	300.00
11 Dale Burnett B/G/R/T	18.00	30.00
12 Ernie Caddel R SP	50.00	100.00
13 Chris Red Cagle G SP	50.00	100.00
14 Glen Campbell G/R/T	18.00	30.00
15 John Cannella G/R/T	18.00	30.00
16 Joe Carter T SP	150.00	300.00
17 Les Caywood B SP	50.00	100.00
18 George Buck Chapman G/R/T	18.00	30.00
19 Frank Christensen G	18.00	30.00
20 Stu Clancy G/R/T	18.00	30.00
21 Myers Algy Clark B/G/R/T	18.00	30.00
22 Paul Rip Collins G/R/T	18.00	30.00
23 Jack Connell G/R/T SP	50.00	100.00
24 Orien Crow G/R/T	18.00	30.00
25 Lone Star Dietz CO G/R/T SP	50.00	100.00
26 John Doehring T SP	150.00	300.00
27 Jimmie Downey T SP	150.00	300.00
28 Turk Edwards B/G/R/T	50.00	80.00
29 Ox Emerson R	20.00	35.00
30 Tiny Feather B/G/R/T	18.00	30.00
31 Ray Flaherty G/R/T	35.00	60.00
32 Frank Froschauer G/R/T	18.00	30.00
33 Chuck Galbreath G/R/T	18.00	30.00
34 Red Gragg G/R/T	18.00	30.00
35 Red Grange G/R/T SP	800.00	1,200.00
36 Cy Grant G/R/T	18.00	30.00
37 Leonard Grant B/G/R/T	18.00	30.00
38 Ross Grant B	18.00	30.00
39 Jack Griffith B/G/R	18.00	30.00
40 Ed Gryboski G/R/T	18.00	30.00
41 Ace Gutowsky G/R/T	25.00	40.00
42 Swede Hanson G/R/T	18.00	30.00
43 Mel Hein G/R/T	35.00	60.00
44 Warren Heller G/R/T	18.00	30.00
45 Bill Hewitt R SP	500.00	800.00
46 Clarke Hinkle G SP	500.00	800.00
47 Cecil Tex Irvin G/R/T	18.00	30.00
48 Frank Johnson G/R/T	18.00	30.00
49 Jack Johnson G	18.00	30.00
50 Robert Jones G SP	150.00	300.00
51 Potsy Jones B/G/R/T	18.00	30.00
52 Carl Jorgensen G/R SP	150.00	300.00
53 John Karcis G/R/T	18.00	30.00
54 Eddie Kawal G/R SP	50.00	100.00
55 Shipwreck Kelly G SP	150.00	300.00
56 George Kenneally T SP	150.00	300.00
57 Walt Kiesling G/R SP	1,000.00	1,500.00
58 Jack Knapper T SP	150.00	300.00
59 Frank Knox R SP	50.00	100.00
60 Joe Doc Kopcha G/R SP	150.00	300.00
61 Joe Kresky T SP	150.00	300.00
62 Joe Laws G/R SP	150.00	300.00
63 Russ Lay G/R/T	18.00	30.00
64 Hilary Biff Lee B/G/R/T	18.00	30.00
65 Gil LeFebvre B/G/R/T	18.00	30.00
66 Jim Leonard G/R/T	18.00	30.00
67 Les Lindberg B/G/R/T	18.00	30.00
68 John Lipski T	18.00	30.00
69 Milo Lubratevich G/T	18.00	30.00
70 Father Lumpkin G/R SP	50.00	100.00
71 Link Lyman T SP	500.00	800.00
72 Jim MacMurdo T	18.00	30.00
73 Ed Matesic R SP	150.00	300.00
74 Dave McCollough B/G/R/T	18.00	30.00
75 John McKnight G/R/T	18.00	30.00
76 Johnny Blood McNally G/R/T	250.00	400.00
77 Al Minot G/R/T	18.00	30.00
78 Keith Molesworth SP	35.00	60.00
79 Jim Mooney B/G/R/T	18.00	30.00
80 Leroy Moorehead G/R/T	18.00	30.00
81 Bill Morgan G/R/T	18.00	30.00
82 Bob Moser R/T SP	50.00	100.00
83 Lee Mulleneaux B	18.00	30.00
84 George Munday G/R/T	18.00	30.00
85 George Musso R/T SP	1,000.00	1,500.00
86 Bronko Nagurski T SP	500.00	800.00
87 Harry Newman G	20.00	35.00
88 Al Norgard G SP	150.00	300.00
89 John Oehler G/R/T	18.00	30.00
90 Charlie Opper G/R/T	18.00	30.00
91 Bill Owen G/R/T	18.00	30.00
92 Steve Owen G/R/T	35.00	60.00
93 Bert Pearson T SP	150.00	300.00
94 Tom Perkinson B/G/R/T	18.00	30.00
95 Mace Pike R SP	35.00	60.00
96 Joe Pilconis R SP	150.00	300.00
97 Lew Pope B	18.00	30.00
98 Crain Portman G/R/T	18.00	30.00
99 Glenn Presnell B/G/R/T	18.00	30.00
100 Jess Quatse G/R/T SP	50.00	100.00
101 Clare Randolph G/T SP	50.00	100.00
102 Hank Reese G/R/T	18.00	30.00
103 Paul Riblett B/R/T SP	150.00	300.00
104 Dick Richards G SP	150.00	300.00
105 Jack Roberts G/R/T	18.00	30.00
106 John Lee Rogers B/G/R/T	18.00	30.00
107 Gene Ronzani G/R SP	150.00	300.00
108 Bob Rowe R SP	35.00	60.00
109 John Schneller T SP	35.00	60.00
110 Adolph Schwammel G SP	150.00	300.00
111 Earl Red Seick T SP	150.00	300.00
112 Allen Shi G/R/T	18.00	30.00
113 Ben Smith G/R/T	18.00	30.00
114 Ken Strong G/R/T	60.00	100.00
115 Elmer Taber R T SP	50.00	100.00
116 Charles Tackwell B	18.00	30.00
117 Ray Tesser G/R/T	18.00	30.00
118 John Thomason G/R/T	18.00	30.00
119 Charlie Turbyville G/R/T (misspelled Turbeyville)	18.00	30.00
120 Claude Urevig R SP	50.00	100.00
121 John Harp Vaughan G/R/T	18.00	30.00
122 Henry Wagnon G/R/T	18.00	30.00
123 John West G/R/T	18.00	30.00
124 Lee Woodruff G/R/T	18.00	30.00
125 Jim Zyntell G/R/T	18.00	30.00

1934 Diamond Matchbooks College Rivals

Diamond Match Co. produced this set issued in 1934. Each cover features a top college rivalry with a short write-up about the latest games between the two teams. The covers contain a single line manufacturer's identification "The Diamond Match Co. N.Y.C." This set is very similar to the 1935 issue, but can be distinguished by the last line of type in the text as indicated below. Each of the twelve unnumbered covers was produced with either a black or tan colored border. Some collectors attempt to assemble a complete 24-card set with all variations. Complete covers with matches intact sometimes sell for as much as 1-1/2 times the prices listed below.

COMPLETE SET (12)	175.00	300.00
1 Alabama vs. Fordham SP	75.00	125.00
2 Army vs. Navy	12.50	25.00
3 Fordham vs. St. Mary's	10.00	20.00
4 Georgia vs. Georgia Tech	10.00	20.00
5 Holy Cross vs. Boston College	10.00	20.00
6 Lafayette vs. Lehigh	10.00	20.00
7 Michigan vs. Ohio State	12.50	25.00
8 Notre Dame vs. Army	12.50	25.00
9 Penn vs. Cornell	10.00	20.00
10 USC vs. Notre Dame	12.50	25.00
11 Yale vs. Harvard	10.00	20.00
12 Yale vs. Princeton	10.00	20.00

1935 Diamond Matchbooks

The 1935 Diamond Matchbook set is very similar in design to the 1934 set, but can be distinguished by the double lined manufacturer's identification "Made in U.S.A./The Diamond Match Co., N.Y.C." Only three border colors were used for this set: green, red, and tan and each player appears with only one border color. There is no player position included nor picture frame border shown on the player photo. The text printing is in black ink and each cover measures approximately 1 1/2" by 4 1/2" when completely unfolded. Complete covers with matches intact sometimes sell for as much as 1-1/2 ttimes the prices listed below. Although the covers are not numbered, we've assigned numbers alphabetically.

1 Alf Anderson	15.00	25.00
2 Alec Ashford	15.00	25.00
3 Gene Augusterfer SP	30.00	60.00
4 Red Badgro	20.00	35.00
5 Cliff Battles	35.00	60.00
6 Harry Benson	15.00	25.00
7 Tony Blazine	15.00	25.00
8 John Bond	15.00	25.00
9 Maurice (Mule) Bray	15.00	25.00
10 Dale Burnett	15.00	25.00
11 Charles(Cocky) Bush	15.00	25.00
12 Ernie Caddel	18.00	30.00
13 Zuck Carlson	15.00	25.00
14 Joe Carter	15.00	25.00
15 Cy Casper	15.00	25.00
16 Paul Causey	15.00	25.00
17 Frank Christensen	15.00	25.00
18 Stu Clancy	15.00	25.00
19 Dutch Clark	90.00	150.00
20 Paul(Rip) Collins	15.00	25.00
21 Dave Cook	15.00	25.00
22 Fred Crawford	15.00	25.00
23 Paul Cuba	15.00	25.00
24 Harry Ebding	15.00	25.00
25 Turk Edwards	35.00	60.00
26 Marvin(Swede) Ellstrom	15.00	25.00
27 Beattie Feathers	25.00	40.00
28 Ray Flaherty	20.00	35.00
29 John Gildea	15.00	25.00
30 Tom Graham	15.00	25.00
31 Len Grant	15.00	25.00
32 Maurice Green	15.00	25.00
33 Norman Greeney	15.00	25.00
34 Ace Gutowsky	18.00	30.00
35 Julius Hall	15.00	25.00
36 Swede Hanson	15.00	25.00
37 Charles Harold	15.00	25.00
38 Tom Haywood	15.00	25.00
39 Mel Hein	75.00	125.00
40 Bill Hewitt	90.00	150.00
41 Cecil(Tex) Irvin	15.00	25.00
42 Frank Johnson	15.00	25.00
43 Jack Johnson	15.00	25.00
44 Luke Johnsos	18.00	30.00
45 Potsy Jones	15.00	25.00
46 Carl Jorgensen	25.00	40.00

47 George Kenneally	15.00	25.00
48 Roger(Reds) Kirkman	15.00	25.00
49 Frank Knox	15.00	25.00
50 Joe Doc Kopcha	18.00	30.00
51 Rick Lackman	15.00	25.00
52 Jim Leonard	15.00	25.00
53 Joe(Hunk) Malkovich	15.00	25.00
54 Ed Manske	15.00	25.00
55 Bernie Masterson	18.00	30.00
56 James McMillen	15.00	25.00
57 Mike Mikulak	15.00	25.00
58 Ookie Miller	15.00	25.00
59 Milford(Dub) Miller	15.00	25.00
60 Al Minot	15.00	25.00
61 Buster Mitchell	15.00	25.00
62 Bill Morgan	15.00	25.00
63 George Musso	35.00	60.00
64 Harry Newman	18.00	30.00
65 Al Nichelini	15.00	25.00
66 Bill(Red) Owen	15.00	25.00
67 Steve Owen	20.00	35.00
68 Max Padlow	15.00	25.00
69 Hal Pangle	15.00	25.00
70 Melvin(Swede) Pittman	15.00	25.00
71 William(Red) Pollock	15.00	25.00
72 Glenn Presnell	15.00	25.00
73 George(Mousie) Rado	15.00	25.00
74 Clare Randolph	15.00	25.00
75 Hank Reese	15.00	25.00
76 Ray Richards	15.00	25.00
77 Doug Russell	15.00	25.00
78 Sandy Sandberg	15.00	25.00
79 Phil Sarboe	15.00	25.00
80 Big John Schneller	15.00	25.00
81 Michael Sebastian	15.00	25.00
82 Allen Shi	15.00	25.00
83 Johnny Sisk	15.00	25.00
84 James(Red) Stacy	15.00	25.00
85 Ed Storm	15.00	25.00
86 Ken Strong	35.00	60.00
87 Art Strutt	15.00	25.00
88 Frank Sullivan	15.00	25.00
89 Charles Treadaway	15.00	25.00
90 John Turley	15.00	25.00
91 Claude Urevig	15.00	25.00
92 Charles(Pug) Vaughan	15.00	25.00
93 Izzy Weinstock	15.00	25.00
94 Henry Wiesenbaugh	15.00	25.00
95 Joe Zeller	15.00	25.00
96 Vince Zizak	15.00	25.00

1935 Diamond Matchbooks College Rivals

Diamond Match Co. produced this set issued in 1935. Each cover features a top college rivalry with a short write-up about the latest games between the two teams. The covers contain either a single line or a double line manufacturer's identification "Made in U.S.A./The Diamond Match Co. N.Y.C." This set is very similar to the 1934 issue but can be distinguished by the last line of type in the text as indicated below. Each of the unnumbered covers was produced with three versions. The manufacturer's name can be found as a single line with either a black or a tan colored border and the covers can be found in tan with a double lined manufacturer's name. Some collectors attempt to assemble a complete 36-book set with all variations. Complete covers with matches intact sometimes sell for as much as 1-1/2 times the prices listed below.

COMPLETE SET (11)	125.00	200.00
1 Alabama vs. Fordham	20.00	40.00
2 Army vs. Navy	12.50	25.00
3 Fordham vs. St. Mary's	10.00	20.00
4 Georgia vs. Georgia Tech	10.00	20.00
5 Holy Cross vs. Boston College	10.00	20.00
6 Lafayette vs. Lehigh	10.00	20.00
7 Michigan vs. Ohio State	12.50	25.00
8 Notre Dame vs. Army	12.50	25.00
9 Penn vs. Cornell	10.00	20.00
10 USC vs. Notre Dame	12.50	25.00
11 Yale vs. Harvard	10.00	20.00
12 Yale vs. Princeton	10.00	20.00

1936 Diamond Matchbooks

The Diamond Match Co. produced these matchbook covers featuring players of the Chicago Bears and Philadelphia Eagles. They measure approximately 1 1/2" by 4 1/2" (when completely folded out). We've listed below the players alphabetically by team with the Bears first. Each of the covers was produced with either black or brown ink on the text. Three border colors (green, red and tan) were used on the covers, but each player appears with only one border color in black ink and one border color in brown ink. The only exception is Ray Nolting who appears with two border colors with both black and brown ink versions. A picture frame design is included on the left and right sides of the player photo. Don Jackson's and all of the Bears' players' positions are included before the bio. Some collectors consider these two or more separate issues due to the variations and assemble "sets" with either the brown or black printing. Since no price differences are seen between variations and the text and photos are identical for each version, we've listed them together. With all variations, a total of 96-covers were produced. A few of the players are included in the 1937 set as well with only slight differences between the two issues. For those players, we've included the first or last lines of text to help identify the year. Complete covers with matches intact sometimes sell for as much as 1-1/2 ttimes the prices listed below.

COMPLETE SET (47)	500.00	800.00
1 Carl Brumbaugh	10.00	20.00
2 Zuck Carlson	10.00	20.00
3 George Corbett	10.00	20.00
4 John Doehring	10.00	20.00
5 Beattie Feathers	12.50	25.00
6 Dan Fortmann	12.50	25.00
7 George Grosvenor	10.00	20.00
8 Bill Hewitt	18.00	30.00
9 Luke Johnsos	10.00	20.00
10 William Karr	10.00	20.00
11 Eddie Kawal	10.00	20.00
12 Jack Manders	10.00	20.00
13 Bernie Masterson	10.00	20.00
14 Eddie Michaels	10.00	20.00
15 Ookie Miller	10.00	20.00
16 Keith Molesworth	10.00	20.00
17 George Musso	12.50	25.00
18 Bronko Nagurski	150.00	250.00
19 Ray Nolting	10.00	20.00
20 Vernon Oech	10.00	20.00
21 William(Red) Pollock	10.00	20.00
22 Gene Ronzani	10.00	20.00
23 Ted Rosequist	10.00	20.00
24 Johnny Sisk	10.00	20.00
25 Joe Stydahar	12.50	25.00
26 Frank Sullivan	10.00	20.00
27 Russell Thompson	10.00	20.00
28 Milt Trost	10.00	20.00
29 Joe Zeller	10.00	20.00
30 Bill Brian	7.50	15.00
31 Art Buss	7.50	15.00
32 Joe Carter	7.50	15.00
33 Swede Hanson	7.50	15.00
34 Don Jackson	7.50	15.00
35 John Kusko	7.50	15.00
36 Jim Leonard	7.50	15.00
37 Jim MacMurdo	7.50	15.00
38 Ed Manske	7.50	15.00
39 Forrest McPherson	7.50	15.00
40 George Mulligan	7.50	15.00
41 Joe Pilconis	7.50	15.00
42 Hank Reese	7.50	15.00
43 Jim Russell	7.50	15.00
44 Dave Smukler	7.50	15.00
45 Pete Stevens	7.50	15.00
46 John Thomason	7.50	15.00
47 Vince Zizak	7.50	15.00

1937 Diamond Matchbooks

The Diamond Match Co. produced these matchbook covers featuring players of the Chicago Bears. They measure approximately 1 1/2" by 4 1/2" (when completely folded out). The covers look very similar to the 1936 set, but use a slightly smaller print type. Each of the 24-covers was produced with either black or brown ink on the text. Three border colors (green, red and tan) were used on the covers, with all three used for each of the brown ink varieties. Only one border color was used for each cover printed in black ink. Similar to the 1936 issue, a picture frame design is included on the left and right sides of the player photo. Some collectors consider these two separate issues due to the variations and assemble "sets" with either the brown or black printing. Since no price differences are seen between variations and the text and photos are identical for each version, we've listed them together. With all variations, a total of 96-covers were produced. Several of the players are included in the 1936 set as well with only slight differences between the two issues. For those players, we've included the first or last lines of text to help identify the year. Complete covers with matches intact sometimes sell for as much as 1-1/2 times the prices listed below. Although the covers are not numbered, we've assigned numbers alphabetically.

COMPLETE SET (24)	200.00	350.00
1 Frank Bausch	7.50	15.00
2 Delbert Bjork	7.50	15.00
3 William(Red) Conkright	7.50	15.00
4 George Corbett	7.50	15.00
5 John Doehring	7.50	15.00
6 Beattie Feathers	10.00	20.00
7 Dan Fortmann	10.00	20.00
8 Sam Francis	7.50	15.00
9 Henry Hammond	7.50	15.00
10 William Karr	7.50	15.00
11 Jack Manders	7.50	15.00
12 Ed Manske	7.50	15.00
13 Bernie Masterson	7.50	15.00
14 Keith Molesworth	7.50	15.00
15 George Musso	10.00	20.00
16 Ray Nolting	7.50	15.00
17 Richard Plasman	7.50	15.00
18 Gene Ronzani	7.50	15.00
19 Joe Stydahar	10.00	20.00
20 Frank Sullivan	7.50	15.00
21 Russell Thompson	7.50	15.00
22 Milt Trost	7.50	15.00
23 George Wilson	7.50	15.00
24 Joe Zeller	7.50	15.00

1938 Diamond Matchbooks

Diamond Match Co. again produced a matchcover set for 1938 featuring players from the Bears and Lions. They measure approximately 1 1/2" by 4 1/2" (when completely folded out). The overall border color is silver with the bio background color being red for the Bears (1-12) and blue for the Lions (13-24). The Lions players seem to be much tougher to find than the Bears. We've assigned card numbers below alphabetically by the two teams included. There are no known variations. Complete covers with matches intact sometimes sell for as much as 1-1/2 ttimes the prices listed below.

COMPLETE SET (24)	600.00	1,000.00
1 Delbert Bjork	15.00	25.00
2 Raymond Buivid	15.00	25.00
3 Gary Famiglietti	15.00	25.00
4 Dan Fortmann	20.00	35.00
5 Bert Johnson	15.00	25.00
6 Jack Manders	15.00	25.00
7 Joe Maniaci	15.00	25.00
8 Lester McDonald	15.00	25.00
9 Frank Sullivan	15.00	25.00
10 Robert Swisher	15.00	25.00
11 Russell Thompson	15.00	25.00
12 Gust Zarnas	15.00	25.00
13 Ernie Caddel	35.00	60.00
14 Lloyd Cardwell	30.00	50.00
15 Dutch Clark	175.00	300.00
16 Jack Johnson	30.00	50.00
17 Ed Klewicki	30.00	50.00
18 James McDonald	30.00	50.00
19 James(Monk) Moscrip	30.00	50.00
20 Maurice (Babe) Patt	30.00	50.00
21 Bob Reynolds	30.00	50.00
22 Kent Ryan	30.00	50.00
23 Fred Vanzo	30.00	50.00
24 Alex Wojciechowicz	125.00	200.00

1938 Dixie Lids Small

This unnumbered set of lids is actually a combined sport and non-sport set with 24 different lids. The lids are found in more than one size, approximately 2 11/16" in diameter as well as 2 5/16" in diameter. The catalog designation is F7-1. The 1938 lids are distinguished from the 1937 Dixie Lids by the fact that the 1938 lids are printed in blue ink whereas the 1938 lids are printed in black or wine-colored ink. In the checklist below only the sports subjects are checklisted; non-sport subjects (celebrities) included in this 24 card set are Don Ameche, Annabella, Gene Autry, Warner Baxter, William Boyd, Bobby Breen, Gary Cooper, Alice Fay, Sonja Henie, Tommy Kelly, June Lang, Colonel Tim McCoy, Tyrone Power, Tex Ritter, Simone Simon, Bob Steele, The Three Musquiteers and Jane Withers.

COMPLETE SPORT SET (6)	250.00	500.00
*LARGE: .6X TO 1.5X SMALL		
1 Sam Baugh	75.00	125.00
6 Bronko Nagurski	90.00	150.00

1938 Dixie Premiums

This is a parallel issue to the lids -- an attractive "premium" large picture of each of the subjects in the Dixie Lids set. The premiums are printed on thick stock and feature a large color drawing on the front; each unnumbered premium measures approximately 8" X 10". The 1938 premiums are distinguished from the 1937 Dixie Lid premiums by the fact that the 1938 premiums contain a light green border whereas the 1937 premiums have a darker green border completely around the photo. Also, on the reverse, the 1938 premiums have a single gray sline line at the top leading to the player's name in script. Again, we have only checklisted the sports personalities.

COMPLETE SET (6)	375.00	750.00
1 Sam Baugh	150.00	250.00
6 Bronko Nagurski	150.00	250.00

1967 Dolphins Royal Castle

This 27-card set was issued by Royal Castle, a south Florida hamburger stand, at a rate of two new cards every week during the season. These unnumbered cards measure approximately 3" by 4 3/8". The front features a black and white (almost sepia-toned) posed photo of the player enframed by an orange border, with the player's signature below the photo. Biographical information is given on the back (including player's nickname where appropriate), along with the logos for the Miami Dolphins and Royal Castle. This set features a card of Bob Griese during his rookie season. There may be a 28th card of George Wilson Jr., but it has never been substantiated. There are 17-cards that are easier than the others; rather than calling these double prints, the other ten cards are marked as SP's in the checklist below.

COMPLETE SET (27)	4,500.00	7,000.00
1 Joe Auer SP	175.00	300.00
2 Tom Beier	75.00	125.00
3 Mel Branch	75.00	125.00
4 Jon Brittenum	75.00	125.00
5 George Chesser	75.00	125.00
6 Edward Cooke	75.00	125.00
7 Frank Emanuel SP	175.00	300.00
8 Tom Erlandson SP	175.00	300.00
9 Norm Evans SP	200.00	350.00
10 Bob Griese SP	1,800.00	3,000.00
11 Abner Haynes SP	250.00	400.00
12 Jerry Hopkins SP	175.00	300.00
13 Frank Jackson	75.00	125.00
14 Billy Joe	75.00	125.00
15 Wahoo McDaniel	150.00	250.00
16 Robert Neff	75.00	125.00
17 Billy Neighbors	75.00	125.00
18 Rick Norton	75.00	125.00
19 Bob Petrich	75.00	125.00
20 Jim Riley	75.00	125.00
21 John Stofa SP	175.00	300.00
22 Laverne Torczon	75.00	125.00
23 Howard Twilley	75.00	125.00
24 Jim Warren SP	175.00	300.00
25 Dick Westmoreland	75.00	125.00
26 Maxie Williams	75.00	125.00
27 George Wilson Sr. SP	200.00	350.00

1970 Dolphins Team Issue

The Miami Dolphins likely issued this series of player photos over a two or three year period around 1970. The format is the same for each photo with only subtle differences in the type (size and style) and player position (some spelled out and others initials only). Each of these black-and-white photos measures approximately 5" by 7" and is blankbacked and unnumbered.

COMPLETE SET (12)	60.00	120.00
1 Dean Brown	6.00	12.00
2 Frank Cornish DT	6.00	12.00
3 Ted Davis	6.00	12.00
4 Norm Evans	6.00	12.00
5 Hubert Ginn	6.00	12.00
6 Mike Kolen	6.00	12.00
7 Bob Kuechenberg	7.50	15.00
8 Stan Mitchell	6.00	12.00
9 Lloyd Mumphord	6.00	12.00
10 Dick Palmer	6.00	12.00
11 Barry Pryor	6.00	12.00
12 Bill Stanfill	6.00	12.00

1970-71 Dolphins Team Issue

The Miami Dolphins likely issued this series of player photos over a two or three year period around 1970. The format is the same for each photo with only subtle differences in the type (size and style) and player position (some are included while others are not). Each of these black-and-white photos measures approximately 8" by 10" and is blankbacked and unnumbered.

COMPLETE SET (22)	125.00	250.00
1 Dick Anderson	6.00	12.00
2 Dick Anderson	6.00	12.00
3 Nick Buoniconti	7.50	15.00
4 Larry Csonka	10.00	18.00
5 Manny Fernandez	6.00	12.00
6 Tom Goode	6.00	12.00
7 Bob Griese	12.00	20.00
8 Jimmy Hines	6.00	12.00
9 Jim Kiick	7.50	15.00
10 Mike Kolen	6.00	12.00
11 Larry Little	7.50	15.00
12 Bob Matheson	6.00	12.00
13 Mercury Morris	7.50	15.00
14 Bob Petrella	6.00	12.00
15 Larry Seiple	6.00	12.00
16 Don Shula CO	12.00	20.00
18 Otto Stowe	6.00	12.00
19 Howard Twilley	6.00	12.00
20 Paul Warfield	7.50	15.00
21 Paul Warfield	7.50	15.00
22 Garo Yepremian	6.00	12.00

1972 Dolphins Glasses

This set of player glasses was thought to have been issued in 1972. Each features a color artist's rendition of a Dolphins player against a background of white. The reverse includes a short bio of the player. The glasses stand roughly 5 1/2" tall with a diameter of 2 3/4."

COMPLETE SET (8)	50.00	100.00
1 Larry Csonka	15.00	25.00
1 Larry Little	6.00	12.00
2 Jim Kiick	6.00	12.00
2 Nick Buoniconti	7.50	15.00
3 Bob Griese	15.00	25.00
4 Mercury Morris	6.00	12.00

5 Paul Warfield	10.00	20.00
6 Manny Fernandez	6.00	12.00

1972 Dolphins Koole Frozen Cups

This set of plastic cups was sponsored by Koole Frozen Foods and Coca-Cola. Each looks very similar to the 1972 7-11 cups with a color artist's rendering of the featured player along with a cup number of 20 in the set. Each cup measures roughly 5 1/4" tall with a diameter at the top of 3 1/4."

COMPLETE SET (20)	100.00	200.00
1 Dick Anderson	6.00	12.00
2 Nick Buoniconti	7.50	15.00
3 Bob Griese	15.00	25.00
4 Bob Kuechenberg	6.00	12.00
5 Bill Stanfill	4.00	8.00
6 Jake Scott	6.00	12.00
7 Manny Fernandez	6.00	12.00
8 Earl Morrall	7.50	15.00
9 Larry Csonka	15.00	25.00
10 Jim Kiick	7.50	15.00
11 Bob Heinz	4.00	8.00
12 Jim Langer	7.50	15.00
13 Bob Matheson	4.00	8.00
14 Vern Den Herder	4.00	8.00
15 Larry Little	7.50	15.00
16 Curtis Johnson	4.00	8.00
17 Mercury Morris	6.00	12.00
18 Paul Warfield	12.00	20.00
19 Marv Fleming	6.00	12.00
20 Lloyd Mumphord	4.00	8.00

1972 Dolphins Team Issue

These large (approximately 8 1/2" by 11") black and white photos were issued by the Dolphins around 1972. Each features the player's name, position initals and team name below the photo with a facsimile autograph on the image.

COMPLETE SET (12)	60.00	120.00
1 Dick Anderson	5.00	10.00
2 Marlin Briscoe	5.00	10.00
3 Nick Buoniconti	6.00	12.00
4 Larry Csonka	7.50	15.00
5 Manny Fernandez	5.00	10.00
6 Bob Griese	10.00	20.00
7 Jim Kiick	6.00	12.00
8 Larry Little	6.00	12.00
9 Earl Morrall	5.00	10.00
10 Mercury Morris	6.00	12.00
11 Don Shula CO	10.00	20.00
12 Garo Yepremian	5.00	10.00

1972 Dolphins Team Issue Color

These color photos, issued in 1972, measure roughly 8 3/8" by 10 1/2" and feature a player photo surrounded by a white border with the player's name and position in the upper border. The photo backs include a detailed player bio and statistics as well as the name "Dolphins Graphics, Miami Florida" at the bottom.

COMPLETE SET (6)	40.00	80.00
1 Nick Buoniconti	7.50	15.00
2 Larry Csonka	10.00	20.00
3 Manny Fernandez	5.00	10.00
4 Bob Griese	12.50	25.00
5 Jim Kiick	6.00	12.00
6 Paul Warfield	10.00	20.00

1974 Dolphins All-Pro Graphics

Each of these ten photos measures approximately 8 1/4" by 10 3/4". The fronts feature color action photos bordered in white. The player's name, position, and team name appear in the top border, while the copyright year (1974) and the manufacturer "All Pro Graphics, Inc." are printed in the bottom white border at the left. It is reported that several of these photos do not have the tagline in the lower left corner. The backs are blank. The photos are unnumbered and checklisted below in alphabetical order.

COMPLETE SET (10)	62.50	125.00
1 Dick Anderson	6.00	12.00
2 Nick Buoniconti	7.50	15.00
3 Larry Csonka	10.00	20.00
4 Manny Fernandez	4.00	8.00
5 Bob Griese	12.50	25.00
6 Jim Kiick	6.00	12.00
7 Earl Morrall	7.50	15.00
8 Mercury Morris	6.00	12.00
9 Jake Scott	5.00	10.00
10 Garo Yepremian	4.00	8.00

1974 Dolphins Team Issue

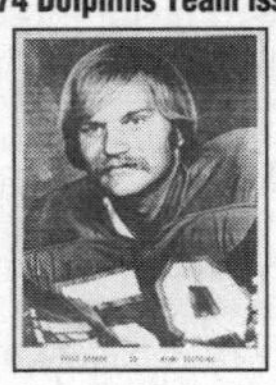

The Miami Dolphins likely issued this series of player photos over a two or three year period around 1974. The format is the same for each photo with only subtle differences in the type size and style. The photos are similar to the 1970 release but feature a distinctly different type style. Each of these black-and-white photos measures approximately 5" by 7" and is blankbacked and unnumbered.

COMPLETE SET (21)	75.00	150.00
1 Charlie Babb	4.00	8.00
2 Mel Baker	4.00	8.00
3 Bruce Bannon	4.00	8.00
4 Randy Crowder	4.00	8.00
5 Norm Evans	4.00	8.00
6 Hubert Ginn	4.00	8.00
7 Irv Goode	4.00	8.00
8 Bob Heinz	4.00	8.00
9 Curtis Johnson	4.00	8.00
10 Bob Kuechenberg	5.00	10.00
11 Nat Moore	5.00	10.00
12 Wayne Moore	4.00	8.00
13 Lloyd Mumphord	4.00	8.00
14 Ed Newman	4.00	8.00
15 Don Reese	4.00	8.00
16 Larry Seiple	4.00	8.00
17 Bill Stanfill	5.00	10.00
18 Henry Stuckey	4.00	8.00
19 Doug Swift	4.00	8.00
20 Jeris White	4.00	8.00
21 Tom Wickert	4.00	8.00

1976 Dolphins McDonald's

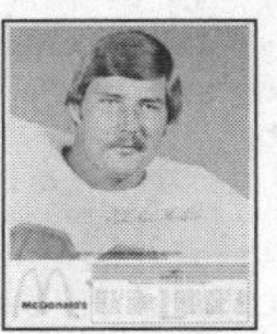

This set of photos was sponsored by McDonald's. Each photo measures approximately 8" by 10" and features a posed color close-up photo bordered in white. The player's name and team name are printed in black below the player's photo with the Dolphin's 1976 regular season schedule below it. The top portion of the back has a black and white photo and biographical information on the player. The bottom portion carries an ad for McDonald's. The photos are unnumbered and are checklisted below alphabetically.

COMPLETE SET (4)	15.00	30.00
1 Dick Anderson	5.00	10.00
2 Vern Den Herder	4.00	8.00
3 Nat Moore	5.00	10.00
4 Don Nottingham	4.00	8.00

1980 Dolphins Police

The 1980 Miami Dolphins set contains 16 unnumbered cards, which have been listed by player uniform number in the checklist below. The cards measure approximately 2 5/8" by 4 1/8". The set was sponsored by the Kiwanis Club, the local law enforcement agency, and the Miami Dolphins. The backs contain "Dolphins Tips" and the Miami Dolphins logo. The backs are printed in black with blue accent on white card stock. The fronts contain the Kiwanis logo, but not the Dolphins logo as in the following year. The card of Larry Little is reportedly more difficult to obtain than other cards in this set.

COMPLETE SET (16)	50.00	100.00
5 Uwe Von Schamann	1.25	3.00
10 Don Strock	2.50	6.00
12 Bob Griese	6.00	15.00
22 Tony Nathan	2.50	6.00
24 Delvin Williams	2.50	6.00
25 Tim Foley	1.50	4.00
50 Larry Gordon	1.25	3.00
58 Kim Bokamper	1.25	3.00
64 Ed Newman	1.25	3.00
66 Larry Little SP	8.00	20.00
67 Bob Kuechenberg	2.50	6.00
73 Bob Baumhower	1.50	4.00
77 A.J. Duhe	2.50	6.00
82 Duriel Harris	1.50	4.00
89 Nat Moore	2.50	6.00
NNO Don Shula CO	6.00	15.00

1949 Eagles Team Issue

This set of black and white photos was issued in 1949 by the Eagles in celebration of their 1948 NFL Championship team. Each photo measures roughly 8 3/4" by 10 1/2" and includes a facsimile autograph, the player's position, weight, height, and college below the photo. The photos are blankbacked and unnumbered.

COMPLETE SET (20)	250.00	400.00
1 Neill Armstrong	12.00	20.00
2 Russ Craft	12.00	20.00
3 Jack Ferrante	12.00	20.00
4 Noble Doss	12.00	20.00
4 Bucko Kilroy	15.00	25.00
5 Mario Giannelli	12.00	20.00
5 Vic Lindskog	12.00	20.00
6 Pat McHugh	12.00	20.00
7 Joe Muha	12.00	20.00
8 Jack Myers	12.00	20.00
9 Pete Pihos	25.00	40.00
10 Bosh Pritchard	15.00	25.00
11 George Savitsky	12.00	20.00
12 Vic Sears	12.00	20.00
13 Ernie Steele	12.00	20.00
14 Tommy Thompson	18.00	30.00
15 Steve Van Buren	35.00	60.00
16 Al Wistert	15.00	25.00
17 Alex Wojciechowicz	18.00	30.00
18 Team Photo	18.00	30.00

1950 Eagles Bulletin Pin-ups

These black and white premium photos measure roughly 8" x 10" and were issued by The Bulletin newspaper in the Philadelphia area. The photos are blankbacked and feature the newspaper's logo in the upper left corner, the team name in the lower left corner and the player's facsimile autograph in the lower right corner.

1 Greasy Neale	10.00	20.00
2 Bosh Pritchard	10.00	20.00
3 Steve Van Buren	15.00	30.00

1950 Eagles Team Issue

This set of black and white photos was issued around 1950 by the Eagles. Each photo is very similar to the 1949 issue with the differences being found in the text included below the player image. Some players were featured with the same photo in both years with only the difference in text. Each photo measures roughly 8 3/4" by 11" and includes a printed player name on a top row, followed by the player's position, height, weight, and college on a bottom row of type below the photo. The photos are blankbacked and unnumbered.

COMPLETE SET (10)		
1 Neill Armstrong	12.00	20.00
2 Russ Craft	12.00	20.00
3 Bucko Kilroy	15.00	25.00
4 Pat McHugh	12.00	20.00
5 Joe Muha	12.00	20.00
6 Pete Pihos	25.00	40.00
7 Bosh Pritchard	15.00	25.00
8 Vic Sears	12.00	20.00
9 Steve Van Buren	35.00	60.00
10 Whitey Wistert	15.00	25.00

1956 Eagles Team Issue

The Philadelphia Eagles issued and distributed this set of player photos. Each measures approximately 8" by 10" and features a black and white photo on the cardfront with a blank cardback. The player's name, position (abbreviated), height, weight, and college affiliation appear below the photo with the team name above the picture. The checklist is thought to be incomplete. Any additions to this list are greatly appreciated.

1 Bibbles Bawel	10.00	20.00
2 Eddie Bell	10.00	20.00
3 Ken Keller	10.00	20.00
4 Bob Kelley	10.00	20.00
5 Bob Pellegrini	10.00	20.00
6 Rocky Ryan	10.00	20.00
7 Bill Stribling	10.00	20.00
8 Neil Worden	10.00	20.00

1959 Eagles Jay Publishing

This set features (approximately) 5" by 7" black-and-white player photos with the players in traditional football poses. The photos were packaged 12-per set and originally sold for 25-cents. The fronts include the player's name and team name (Philadelphia Eagles) below the player image. The backs are blank, unnumbered, and checklisted below in alphabetical order.

COMPLETE SET (11)	50.00	100.00
1 Bill Barnes	4.00	8.00
2 Chuck Bednarik	10.00	20.00
3 Tom Brookshier	5.00	10.00
4 Marion Campbell	4.00	8.00
5 Tommy McDonald	6.00	12.00
6 Clarence Peaks	4.00	8.00
7 Pete Retzlaff	5.00	10.00
8 Jesse Richardson	4.00	8.00
9 Norm Van Brocklin	10.00	20.00
10 Bobby Walston	4.00	8.00
11 Chuck Weber	4.00	8.00

1959 Eagles San Giorgio Flipbooks

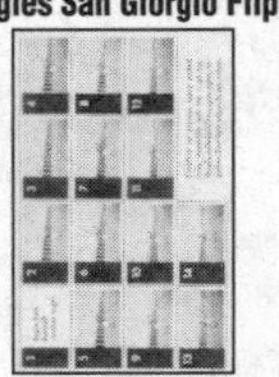

This set features members of the Philadelphia Eagles printed on velum type paper stock created in a multi-image action sequence. The set is commonly referenced as the San Giorgio Macaroni Football Flipbooks. Members of the Philadelphia Eagles, Pittsburgh Steelers, and Washington Redskins were produced regionally with 15-players, reportedly, issued per team. Some players were produced in more than one sequence of poses with different captions and/or slightly different photos used. When the flipbooks are still in uncut form (which is most desirable), they measure approximately 5 3/4" by 3 9/16". The sheets are blank backed, in black and white, and provide 14-small numbered pages when cut apart. Collectors were encouraged to cut out each photo and stack them in such a way as to create a moving image of the player when flipped with the fingers. Any additions to this list are appreciated.

1A Bill Barnes	90.00	150.00
1B Bill Barnes	90.00	150.00
2 Chuck Bednarik	250.00	400.00
3 Proverb Jacobs	90.00	150.00
4 Tommy McDonald	175.00	300.00
5A Ed Meadows	90.00	150.00
5B Ed Meadows	90.00	150.00
6A Clarence Peaks	90.00	150.00
6B Clarence Peaks	90.00	150.00
7 Bob Pellegrini	90.00	150.00
8A Pete Retzlaff	100.00	175.00
8B Pete Retzlaff	100.00	175.00
8C Pete Retzlaff	100.00	175.00
9 Bobby Walston	90.00	150.00
10 Chuck Weber	90.00	150.00

1960 Eagles Team Issue

This 11-card team issued set measures approximately 5" by 7" and is printed on thin, slick card stock. The fronts feature black-and-white posed action player photos with white borders. The player's name is printed in black below the picture along with the team name "Eagles." The backs are blank. The cards are unnumbered and checklisted below in alphabetical order. Any additions to this list are appreciated.

COMPLETE SET (11)	60.00	120.00
1 Maxie Baughan	6.00	12.00
2 Chuck Bednarik	12.50	25.00
3 Don Burroughs	5.00	10.00
4 Jimmy Carr	6.00	12.00
5 Howard Keys	5.00	10.00
6 Ed Khayat	5.00	10.00
7 Jim McCusker	5.00	10.00
8 John Nocera	5.00	10.00
9 Nick Skorich CO	5.00	10.00
10 J.D. Smith	6.00	12.00
11 John Wittenborn	5.00	10.00

1961 Eagles Jay Publishing

This 12-card set features (approximately) 5" by 7" black-and-white player photos. The photos show players in traditional poses with the quarterback preparing to throw, the runner heading downfield, and the defenseman ready for the tackle. These cards were packaged 12 to a packet and originally sold for 25 cents. The backs are blank. The cards are unnumbered and checklisted below in alphabetical order.

COMPLETE SET (12)	40.00	80.00
1 Maxie Baughan	4.00	8.00
2 Jim McCusker	4.00	8.00
3 Tommy McDonald	6.00	12.00
4 Bob Pellegrini	4.00	8.00
5 Pete Retzlaff	5.00	10.00
6 Jesse Richardson	4.00	8.00
7 Joe Robb	4.00	8.00
8 Theron Sapp	4.00	8.00
9 J.D. Smith T	4.00	8.00
10 Bobby Walston	4.00	8.00
11 Jerry Williams ACO	4.00	8.00
12 John Wittenborn	4.00	8.00

1960-62 Eagles Team Issue

The Eagles issued this set of black and white player photos. Each measures approximately 8" by 10" and features the team name above the player photo with his name, vital statistics and college below. The backs are blank and unnumbered. The checklist below includes the known photos at this time. It's likely there were more produced. Any additions to this list would be appreciated.

COMPLETE SET (25)	150.00	300.00
1 Timmy Brown	7.50	15.00
2 Don Burroughs	7.50	15.00
3 Jimmy Carr	7.50	15.00
4 Irv Cross	7.50	15.00
5 Gene Gossage	7.50	15.00
6 Riley Gunnels	7.50	15.00
7 Bob Harrison	7.50	15.00
8 King Hill	7.50	15.00
9 Sonny Jurgensen	15.00	30.00
10 Jim McCusker	7.50	15.00
11 Alan Miller	7.50	15.00
12 John Nocera	7.50	15.00
13 Don Oakes	7.50	15.00
14 Clarence Peaks	7.50	15.00
15 Will Renfro	7.50	15.00
16 Theron Sapp	7.50	15.00
17 Buck Shaw CO	7.50	15.00
18 Nick Skorich CO	7.50	15.00
19 J.D. Smith T	7.50	15.00
20 Leo Sugar	7.50	15.00
21 Carl Taseff	7.50	15.00
22 John Tracey	7.50	15.00
23 Bobby Walston	7.50	15.00
24 Chuck Weber	7.50	15.00
25 John Wittenborn	7.50	15.00

1961 Eagles Team Issue 5x7

This team issued set measures approximately 5" by 7" and is printed on thin, slick card stock. The fronts feature black-and-white posed action player photos with white borders. The player's name is printed in black below the picture along with the team name "Philadelphia Eagles." The backs are blank. The cards are unnumbered and checklisted below in alphabetical order. Any additions to this list are appreciated.

COMPLETE SET (12)	75.00	150.00
1 Bill Barnes	6.00	12.00
2 Chuck Bednarik	10.00	20.00
3 Tom Brookshier	7.50	15.00
4 Timmy Brown	7.50	15.00
5 Marion Campbell	7.50	15.00
6 Stan Campbell	6.00	12.00
7 Jimmy Carr	6.00	12.00
8 Irv Cross	7.50	15.00
9 Sonny Jurgensen	15.00	25.00
10 Clarence Peaks	6.00	12.00
11 Jesse Richardson	6.00	12.00
12 Nick Skorich CO	6.00	12.00

1963 Eagles Phillies' Cigars

This attractive color football photo was part of a premium promotion for Phillies Cigars. It measures 6 1/2" by 9" and features a facsimile autograph on the cardfront. The cardback is blank.

1 Tommy McDonald	15.00	25.00

1964-66 Eagles Program Inserts

These photos were actually bound into Philadelphia Eagles game programs from 1964-66. Each one when cleanly cut from the program measures roughly 8 3/8" by 11" and features a black and white photo of an Eagles player (except for the photo of Giants Y.A. Tittle) on one side and a bio on the back along with two small photos. A facsimile autograph is included on the photo and the first 43-pictures in the series are numbered within the left side border while the remaining were issued without numbers. Early photos include a white border around all sides of the photo while later issues are borderless on three sides.

COMPLETE SET (53)	150.00	300.00
1 Timmy Brown	4.00	8.00
2 Ron Goodwin	3.00	6.00
3 Pete Retzlaff	4.00	8.00
4 Maxie Baughan	4.00	8.00
5 Y.A. Tittle	10.00	20.00
6 Don Burroughs	3.00	6.00
7 Norm Snead	6.00	12.00
8 Jim Ringo	6.00	12.00
9 Riley Gunnels	3.00	6.00
10 George Tarasovic	3.00	6.00
11 Earl Gros	3.00	6.00
12 Bob Brown	4.00	8.00
13 Irv Cross	4.00	8.00
14 Sam Baker	3.00	6.00
15 Ed Blaine	3.00	6.00
16 Nate Ramsey	3.00	6.00
17 Dave Lloyd	3.00	6.00
18 Ollie Matson	7.50	15.00
19 Pete Case	3.00	6.00
20 Mike Morgan	3.00	6.00
21 Bob Richards	3.00	6.00
22 Ray Poage	3.00	6.00
23 Don Hultz	3.00	6.00
24 Dave Graham	3.00	6.00
25 Floyd Peters	3.00	6.00
26 King Hill	4.00	8.00
27 John Meyers	3.00	6.00
28 Lynn Hoyem	3.00	6.00
29 Joe Scarpati	3.00	6.00
30 Jack Concannon	4.00	8.00
31 Jim Skaggs	3.00	6.00
32 Glenn Glass	3.00	6.00
33 Ralph Heck	3.00	6.00
34 Claude Crabb	3.00	6.00
35 Israel Lang	3.00	6.00
36 Tom Woodeshick	4.00	8.00
37 Ed Khayat	3.00	6.00
38 Roger Gill	3.00	6.00
39 Harold Wells	3.00	6.00
40 Lane Howell	3.00	6.00
41 Dave Recher	3.00	6.00
42 Fred Hill	3.00	6.00
43 Al Nelson	3.00	6.00
NNO Randy Beisler	3.00	6.00
NNO Dave Cahill	3.00	6.00
NNO Ben Hawkins	3.00	6.00
NNO Ike Kelley	3.00	6.00
NNO Aaron Martin	3.00	6.00
NNO Ron Medved	3.00	6.00
NNO Jim Nettles	3.00	6.00
NNO Gary Pettigrew	3.00	6.00
NNO Arunas Vasys	3.00	6.00
NNO Fred Whittingham	3.00	6.00

1965-66 Eagles Team Issue

The Eagles issued these black and white glossy player photos likely over a period of years. Each measures approximately 8" by 10" and features the player's name, position (spelled out in full) and team name below the photo. The backs are blank and unnumbered. The checklist below includes the known photos at this time. Any additions to this list would be appreciated.

COMPLETE SET (16)	125.00	250.00
1 Sam Baker	5.00	10.00
2 Sam Baker	5.00	10.00
3 Ed Blaine	5.00	10.00
4 Bob Brown T	6.00	12.00
5 Bob Brown T	6.00	12.00
6 Timmy Brown	6.00	12.00
7 Jack Concannon	5.00	10.00
8 Dave Graham	5.00	10.00
9 Earl Gros	5.00	10.00
10 Fred Hill	5.00	10.00
11 Lynn Hoyem	5.00	10.00
12 Dwight Kelley	5.00	10.00
13 Ed Khayat	5.00	10.00
14 Israel Lang	5.00	10.00
15 Dave Lloyd	5.00	10.00
16 Aaron Martin	5.00	10.00
17 Mike Morgan LB	5.00	10.00
18 Al Nelson	5.00	10.00
19 Jim Nettles	5.00	10.00
20 Floyd Peters	5.00	10.00
21 Ray Poage	5.00	10.00
22 Pete Retzlaff	6.00	12.00
23 Jim Ringo	6.00	12.00
24 Jim Skaggs	5.00	10.00
25 Norm Snead	6.00	12.00
26 Norm Snead	6.00	12.00
27 Norm Snead	6.00	12.00

1967 Eagles Program Inserts

These photos were actually bound into Philadelphia Eagles game programs from 1967 and are entitled "Eagles Portraits." Each one when cleanly cut from the program measures roughly 8 3/8" by 11" and features a black and white photo of an Eagles player on one side and a bio on the back along with two small photos. A facsimile autograph is included on the photo and each photo is numbered within the left side border. Each photo is borderless on three sides.

COMPLETE SET (14)	40.00	80.00
1 Timmy Brown	4.00	8.00
2 Dave Lloyd	3.00	6.00
3 Joe Scarpati	3.00	6.00
4 Bob Brown	4.00	8.00
5 Jim Ringo	6.00	12.00
6 Nate Ramsey	3.00	6.00
7 Israel Lang	3.00	6.00
8 Jim Skaggs	3.00	6.00
9 Norm Snead	6.00	12.00
10 Sam Baker	3.00	6.00
11 Tom Woodeshick	3.00	6.00
12 Tom Woodeshick	4.00	8.00
13 Don Hultz	3.00	6.00
14 Harold Wells	3.00	6.00

1968 Eagles Postcards

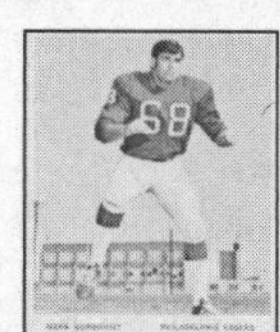

These photos measure approximately 4 1/4" by 5 1/2" and feature posed action black-and-white player photos with white borders. Each photo was taken outside unless noted below. The player's name and team name (measuring either 1 9/16" or 1 3/8") are printed in the bottom border. The Eagles issued Postcards over a number of years and this set is differentiated by the lack of a facsimile autograph on the cardfronts. Since the set is nearly identical to the 1969 issue, we've noted differences of like players below. Unless noted below, the backs include a postcard style format. The cards are unnumbered and checklisted below in alphabetical order.

COMPLETE SET (40)	150.00	300.00
1 Sam Baker	4.00	8.00
2 Gary Ballman	4.00	8.00
3 Randy Beisler	4.00	8.00
4 Bob Brown	6.00	12.00
5 Fred Brown	4.00	8.00
6 Gene Ceppetelli	4.00	8.00
7 Wayne Colman	4.00	8.00
8 Mike Ditka	10.00	20.00
9 Rick Duncan	4.00	8.00
10 Ron Goodwin	4.00	8.00
11 Ben Hawkins	4.00	8.00
12 Alvin Haymond	4.00	8.00
13 King Hill	4.00	8.00
14 John Huarte	4.00	8.00
15 Don Hultz	4.00	8.00
16 Ike Kelley	4.00	8.00
17 Jim Kelly	4.00	8.00
18 Izzy Lang	4.00	8.00
19 Dave Lloyd	4.00	8.00
20 John Mallory	4.00	8.00
21 Ron Medved	4.00	8.00
22 Frank Molden	4.00	8.00
23 Al Nelson	4.00	8.00
24 Jim Nettles	4.00	8.00
25 Mark Nordquist	4.00	8.00
26 Floyd Peters	4.00	8.00
27 Gary Pettigrew	4.00	8.00
28 Cyril Pinder	4.00	8.00
29 Nate Ramsey	4.00	8.00
30 Dave Recher	4.00	8.00
31 Tim Rossovich	4.00	8.00
32 Joe Scarpati	4.00	8.00
33 Norm Snead	5.00	10.00
34 Mel Tom	4.00	8.00
35 Arunas Vasys	4.00	8.00
36 Harold Wells	4.00	8.00
37 Harry Wilson	4.00	8.00
38 Tom Woodeshick	4.00	8.00
39 Adrian Young	4.00	8.00
40 Coaching Staff	4.00	8.00

1969 Eagles Postcards

These photos measure approximately 4 1/4" by 5 1/2" and feature posed action black-and-white player photos with white borders. Each photo was taken outside unless noted below. The player's name and team name (measuring either 1 9/16" or 1 3/8") are printed in the bottom border. The Eagles issued Postcards over a number of years and this set is differentiated by the lack of a facsimile autograph on the cardfronts. Since the set is nearly identical to the 1968 issue, we've noted differences of like players below. Unless noted below, the backs include a postcard style format. The cards are unnumbered and checklisted below in alphabetical order.

COMPLETE SET (41)	150.00	300.00
1 Sam Baker	4.00	8.00
2 Gary Ballman	4.00	8.00
3 Ronnie Blye	4.00	8.00
4 Bill Bradley	5.00	10.00
5 Ernest Calloway	4.00	8.00
6 Joe Carollo	4.00	8.00
7 Irv Cross	4.00	8.00
8 Mike Dirks	4.00	8.00
9 Mike Evans	4.00	8.00
10 Dave Graham	4.00	8.00
11 Tony Guillory	4.00	8.00
12 Dick Hart	4.00	8.00
13 Fred Hill	4.00	8.00
14 William Hobbs	4.00	8.00
15 Lane Howell	4.00	8.00
16 Chuck Hughes	4.00	8.00
17 Don Hultz	4.00	8.00
18 Harold Jackson	6.00	12.00
19 Harry Jones	4.00	8.00
20 Ike Kelley	4.00	8.00
21 Wade Key	4.00	8.00
22 Leroy Keyes	4.00	8.00
23 Kent Lawrence	4.00	8.00
24 Dave Lloyd	4.00	8.00
25 Ron Medved	4.00	8.00
26 George Mira	4.00	8.00
27 Al Nelson	4.00	8.00
28 Mark Nordquist	4.00	8.00
29 Floyd Peters	4.00	8.00
30 Gary Pettigrew	4.00	8.00
31 Cyril Pinder	4.00	8.00
32 Ron Porter	4.00	8.00
33 Nate Ramsey	4.00	8.00
34 Jimmy Raye	4.00	8.00
35 Tim Rossovich	4.00	8.00
36 Joe Scarpati	4.00	8.00
37 Jim Skaggs	4.00	8.00
38 Norm Snead	5.00	10.00
39 Mel Tom	4.00	8.00
40 Tom Woodeshick	4.00	8.00
41 Adrian Young	4.00	8.00

1970-71 Eagles Postcards

These postcards measure approximately 4 1/4" by 5 1/2" and feature posed action black-and-white player photos with white borders. Each photo was taken outside unless noted below. The player's name and team name (measuring either 1 9/16" or 1 3/8") are printed in the bottom border. The Eagles issued Postcards over a number of years and this set is differentiated by the facsimile autograph on the cardfronts. It is likely that our listing combines postcards that were released in 1970 and 1971. Several have been found with a Boy Scouts "BSA" logo near the photo. Unless noted below, the backs include a postcard style format. The cards are unnumbered and checklisted below in alphabetical order.

COMPLETE SET (53)	125.00	250.00
1 Henry Allison	3.00	6.00
2 Rick Arrington	3.00	6.00
3 Tom Bailey	3.00	6.00
4 Gary Ballman	3.00	6.00
5 Lee Bouggess	3.00	6.00
6 Lee Bouggess BSA	3.00	6.00
7 Bill Bradley	4.00	8.00
8 Ernie Calloway	3.00	6.00
9 Harold Carmichael	8.00	12.00
10 Joe Carollo	3.00	6.00
11 Bob Creech	3.00	6.00
12 Norm Davis	3.00	6.00
13 Tom Dempsey	3.00	6.00
14 Tom Dempsey BSA	3.00	6.00
15 Mike Dirks	3.00	6.00
16 Mike Evans	3.00	6.00
17 Happy Feller	3.00	6.00
18 Carl Gersbach	3.00	6.00
19 Dave Graham	3.00	6.00
20 Richard Harris	3.00	6.00
21 Dick Hart	3.00	6.00
22 Ben Hawkins	3.00	6.00
23 Fred Hill	3.00	6.00
24 Bill Hobbs	3.00	6.00
25 Don Hultz	3.00	6.00
26 Harold Jackson	4.00	8.00
27 Jay Johnson	3.00	6.00
28 Harry Jones	3.00	6.00
29 Ray Jones	3.00	6.00
30 Ike Kelley	3.00	6.00
31 Wade Key	3.00	6.00
32 Leroy Keyes	3.00	6.00
33 Pete Liske	3.00	6.00
34 Pete Liske BSA	3.00	6.00
35 Dave Lloyd	3.00	6.00
36 Ron Medved	3.00	6.00
37 Tom McNeill BSA	3.00	6.00
38 Mark Moseley	4.00	8.00
39 Al Nelson	3.00	6.00
40 Mark Nordquist	3.00	6.00
41 Gary Pettigrew	3.00	6.00
42 Steve Preece	3.00	6.00
43 Ron Porter	3.00	6.00
44 Nate Ramsey	3.00	6.00
45 Tim Rossovich	3.00	6.00
46 Jim Skaggs	3.00	6.00
47 Steve Smith T	3.00	6.00
48 Richard Stevens	3.00	6.00
49 Bill Walik	3.00	6.00
50 Jim Ward	3.00	6.00
51 Larry Watkins	3.00	6.00
52 Adrian Young	3.00	6.00
53 Coaching Staff	8.00	12.00

Cross
Levy

1972 Eagles Postcards

These photos measure approximately 4 1/4" by 5 1/2" and feature posed action black-and-white player photos with white borders. Each photo was taken outside unless noted below. The player's name and team name (measuring about 1 9/16") are printed in the bottom border. The Eagles issued Postcards over a number of years and this set is differentiated from the 1970-71 list by the lack of a facsimile autograph on the cardfronts. Unless noted below, the backs include a postcard style format. The cards are unnumbered and checklisted below in alphabetical order.

COMPLETE SET (6)	20.00	35.00
1 Henry Allison	3.00	6.00
2 Houston Antwine	3.00	6.00
3 Tony Baker	3.00	6.00
4 Larry Crowe	3.00	6.00
5 Harold Jackson	4.00	8.00
6 Jim Thrower	3.00	6.00

1972-73 Eagles Team Issue

These Philadelphia Eagles team issued photos measure approximately 8" by 10" and feature a black and white player photo on a glossy blankbacked card stock. The photos were likely issued over a number of years with many players issued in both a portrait and posed action format. Just the player's name and team name appear below the photo. The checklist is likely incomplete; any additions to this list would be appreciated.

COMPLETE SET (29)	75.00	150.00
1 Tom Bailey Portrait	3.00	6.00
2 Herman Ball	3.00	6.00
3 Bill Bradley Posed Action	4.00	8.00
4 Ron Bull	3.00	6.00
5 John Bunting	3.00	6.00
6 John Bunting	3.00	6.00
7 Bill Cody Portrait	3.00	6.00
8 Larry Crowe	3.00	6.00
9 Larry Crowe	3.00	6.00
10 Albert Davis	3.00	6.00
11 Albert Davis	3.00	6.00
12 Stanley Davis	3.00	6.00
13 Stanley Davis	3.00	6.00
14 Mike Dunstan	3.00	6.00
15 Mike Dunstan	3.00	6.00
16 Lawrence Estes Portrait	3.00	6.00
17 Mike Evans	3.00	6.00
18 Pat Gibbs Posed Action	3.00	6.00
19 Harold Jackson Posed Action	4.00	8.00
20 Wade Key Posed Action	3.00	6.00
21 Kent Kramer Portrait	3.00	6.00
22 Randy Logan Posed Action	3.00	6.00
23 Tom Luken Posed Action	3.00	6.00
24 Tom McNeill	3.00	6.00
25 Tom McNeill	3.00	6.00
26 Gary Pettigrew Posed Action	3.00	6.00
27 Bob Picard Posed Action	3.00	6.00
28 Ron Porter Posed Action	3.00	6.00
29 Jerry Wampfler CO	3.00	6.00
30 Vern Winfield Posed Action	3.00	6.00
31 Steve Zabel Posed Action	3.00	6.00

1974 Eagles Postcards

These photos measure approximately 4 1/4" by 5 1/2" and feature posed action or portrait style black-and-white player photos with white borders. The player's name and team name (measuring about 1 9/16") are printed in the bottom border. The Eagles issued Postcards over a number of years and this set is very similar to the 1972 issue. The backs include a postcard style format. The photos are unnumbered and checklisted below in alphabetical order.

COMPLETE SET (45)	125.00	250.00
1 Tom Bailey	3.00	6.00
2 Bill Bergey	4.00	8.00
3 Mike Boryla	3.00	6.00
4 Bill Bradley	3.00	6.00
5 Norm Bulaich	3.00	6.00
6 John Bunting	3.00	6.00
7 Jim Cagle	3.00	6.00
8 Harold Carmichael	6.00	12.00
9 Wes Chesson	3.00	6.00
10 Tom Dempsey	3.00	6.00
11 Bill Dunstan	3.00	6.00
12 Charlie Ford	3.00	6.00
13 Roman Gabriel	5.00	10.00
14 Dean Halverson	3.00	6.00
15 Randy Jackson	3.00	6.00
16 Po James	3.00	6.00
17 Joe Jones	3.00	6.00
18 Roy Kirksey	3.00	6.00
19 Merritt Kersey	3.00	6.00
20 Wade Key	3.00	6.00
21 Kent Kramer	3.00	6.00
22 Joe Lavender	3.00	6.00
23 Frank LeMaster	3.00	6.00
24 Tom Luken	3.00	6.00
25 Larry Marshall	3.00	6.00
26 Guy Morriss	3.00	6.00
27 Mark Nordquist	3.00	6.00
28 Greg Oliver	3.00	6.00
29 John Outlaw	3.00	6.00
30 Artimus Parker	3.00	6.00
31 Jerry Patton	3.00	6.00
32 Bob Picard	3.00	6.00
33 John Reaves	3.00	6.00
34 Marion Reeves	3.00	6.00
35 Kevin Reilly	3.00	6.00
36 Charles Smith	3.00	6.00
37 Steve Smith	3.00	6.00
38 Jerry Sisemore	3.00	6.00
39 Richard Stevens	3.00	6.00
40 Mitch Sutton	3.00	6.00
41 Tom Sullivan	3.00	6.00
42 Will Wynn	3.00	6.00
43 Charlie Young	3.00	6.00
44 Steve Zabel	3.00	6.00
45 Don Zimmerman	3.00	6.00

1975 Eagles Postcards

Cards from this set measure approximately 4 1/4" by 5 1/2" and feature game action black-and-white player photos with white borders. The player's name, position (initials), Eagles logo and team name are printed in the bottom white margin. The backs include a postcard style format. The cards are unnumbered and checklisted below in alphabetical order. Any additions to the list below are appreciated.

COMPLETE SET (26)	75.00	135.00
1 George Amundson	3.00	6.00
2 Mike Boryla	3.00	6.00
3 Bill Bradley	3.00	6.00
4 Cliff Brooks	3.00	6.00
5 John Bunting	3.00	6.00
6 Tom Ehler	3.00	6.00
7 Roman Gabriel	6.00	10.00
8 Spike Jones	3.00	6.00
9 Keith Krepfle	3.00	6.00
10 Joe Lavender	3.00	6.00
11 Ron Lou	3.00	6.00
12 Art Malone	3.00	6.00
13 Rosie Manning	3.00	6.00
14 James McAlister	3.00	6.00
15 Guy Morriss	3.00	6.00
16 Horst Muhlmann	3.00	6.00
17 John Niland	3.00	6.00
18 John Outlaw	3.00	6.00
19 Artimus Parker	3.00	6.00
20 Don Ratliff	3.00	6.00
21 Jerry Sisemore	3.00	6.00
22 Charles Smith	3.00	6.00
23 Tom Sullivan	3.00	6.00
24 Stan Walters	3.00	6.00
25 Will Wynn	3.00	6.00
26 Don Zimmerman	3.00	6.00

1976 Eagles Team Issue

The Eagles issued these black and white glossy player photos in 1976. Each measures approximately 5" by 7" and features the player's name and position (initials) below the photo. The team name and year appear above the photo. The backs are blank and unnumbered. The checklist below includes the known photos at this time. Any additions to this list would be appreciated.

COMPLETE SET (7)	20.00	40.00
1 John Bunting	3.00	6.00
2 Harold Carmichael	4.00	8.00
3 Pete Lazetich	3.00	6.00
4 Guy Morriss	3.00	6.00
5 Jerry Sisemore	3.00	6.00
6 Charles Smith	3.00	6.00
7 Dick Vermeil CO	6.00	12.00

1977 Eagles Frito Lay

Cards from this set measure approximately 4 1/4" by 5 1/2" and feature portrait player photos on the fronts. The photo type differentiates this set from the 1978 set which otherwise follows the same type style and printing. It's likely that some of these player photos were released during both years. The team name and logo appear in the top border while the player's name, position, and Frito Lay (FL) logo appear in the bottom border. Most feature postcard style cardbacks. This release can be identified by the shorter "FL" Frito Lay logo in the lower right corner and the 1/8" left and right borders. Because this set is unnumbered, the cards are listed alphabetically.

COMPLETE SET (34)	100.00	200.00
1 Bill Bergey	4.00	8.00
2 John Bunting	3.00	6.00
3 Lem Burnham	3.00	6.00
4 Harold Carmichael	5.00	10.00
5 Mike Cordova	3.00	6.00
6 Herman Edwards	4.00	8.00
7 Tom Ehler	3.00	6.00
8 Cleveland Franklin	3.00	6.00
9 Dennis Franks	3.00	6.00
10 Roman Gabriel	5.00	10.00
11 Carl Hairston	3.00	6.00
12 Mike Hogan	3.00	6.00
13 Charlie Johnson	3.00	6.00
14 Eric Johnson	3.00	6.00
15 Wade Key	3.00	6.00
16 Pete Lazetich	3.00	6.00
17 Randy Logan	3.00	6.00
18 Herb Lusk	3.00	6.00
19 Larry Marshall	3.00	6.00
20 Wilbert Montgomery	4.00	8.00
21 Rocco Moore	3.00	6.00
22 Guy Morriss	3.00	6.00
23 Horst Muhlmann	3.00	6.00
24 John Outlaw	3.00	6.00
25 Vince Papale	7.50	15.00
26 James Reed	3.00	6.00
27 Kevin Russell	3.00	6.00
28 Jerry Sisemore	3.00	6.00
29 Manny Sistrunk	3.00	6.00
30 Charles Smith	3.00	6.00
31 Terry Tautolo	3.00	6.00
32 Art Thoms	3.00	6.00
33 Stan Walters	4.00	8.00
34 John Walton	3.00	6.00

1978 Eagles Frito Lay

Cards from this set measure approximately 4 1/4" by 5 1/2" and feature an action player photo on the fronts. The photo type differentiates this set from the 1977 set which otherwise follows the same type style and printing. It's likely that some of these player photos were released during both years. The team name and logo appear in the top border while the player's name, position, and Frito Lay (FL) logo appear in the bottom border. Most feature postcard style cardbacks. This release can be identified by the shorter "FL" Frito Lay logo in the lower right corner and the 1/8" left and right borders. Because this set is unnumbered, the cards are listed alphabetically.

COMPLETE SET (11)	30.00	60.00
1 Bill Bergey	4.00	8.00
2 Ken Clarke	3.00	6.00
3 Bob Howard	3.00	6.00
4 Keith Krepfle	3.00	6.00
5 Frank LeMaster	3.00	6.00
6 Mike Michel	3.00	6.00
7 Oren Middlebrook	3.00	6.00
8 Wilbert Montgomery	4.00	8.00
9 Mike Osborn	3.00	6.00
10 Reggie Wilkes	3.00	6.00
11 Charles Williams	3.00	6.00

1978 Eagles Team Issue

The Eagles issued these black and white glossy player photos in 1976. Each measures approximately 5" by 7" and features the player's name and position (initials) below the photo. The team name and year appear above the photo. The backs are blank and unnumbered. The checklist below includes the known photos at this time. Any additions to this list would be appreciated.

COMPLETE SET (15)	40.00	80.00
1 Rick Engles	3.00	6.00
2 Cleveland Franklin	3.00	6.00
3 Dennis Franks	3.00	6.00
4 Ed George	3.00	6.00
5 Eric Johnson	3.00	6.00
6 Oren Middlebrook	3.00	6.00
7 Mike Osborn	3.00	6.00
8 Richard Osborne	3.00	6.00
9 John Outlaw	3.00	6.00
10 Ken Payne	3.00	6.00
11 John Sanders	3.00	6.00
12 Manny Sistrunk	3.00	6.00
13 Terry Tautolo	3.00	6.00
14 John Walton	3.00	6.00
15 Charles Williams	3.00	6.00

1979 Eagles Frito Lay

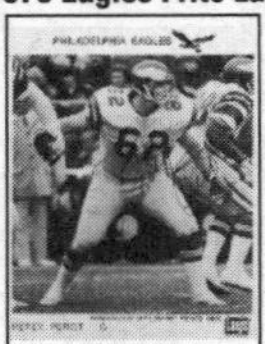

The 1979 Frito Lay Eagles cards measure approximately 4 1/4" by 5 1/2" and feature an action player shot enclosed within a white border. The team name and mascot appear in the top border while the player's name, position, and "Lay's Brand Potato Chips" logo appear in the bottom border. Most feature postcard style cardbacks. Frito Lay sponsored several Eagles sets throughout the 1970s and '80s and it is likely that photos from this set were released over a period of years. This release can be specifically identified by the unique "Lay's Potato Chips" logo in the lower right corner. Because this set is unnumbered, the cards are listed alphabetically.

COMPLETE SET (30)	90.00	150.00
1 Larry Barnes	3.00	6.00
2 John Bunting	3.00	6.00
3 Lem Burnham	3.00	6.00
4 Billy Campfield	3.00	6.00
5 Harold Carmichael	5.00	10.00
6 Ken Clarke	3.00	6.00
7 Scott Fritzkee	3.00	6.00
8 Louie Giammona	3.00	6.00
9 Leroy Harris	3.00	6.00
10 Wally Henry	3.00	6.00
11 Bobby Lee Howard	3.00	6.00
12 Claude Humphrey	4.00	8.00
13 Charlie Johnson	3.00	6.00
14 Wade Key	3.00	6.00
15 Keith Krepfle	4.00	8.00
16 Frank LeMaster	3.00	6.00
17 Randy Logan	3.00	6.00
18 Rufus Mayes	3.00	6.00
19 Jerrold McRae	3.00	6.00
20 Wilbert Montgomery	4.00	8.00
21 Woody Peoples	3.00	6.00
22 Petey Perot	3.00	6.00
23 John Sanders	3.00	6.00
24 John Sciarra	3.00	6.00
25 Manny Sistrunk	3.00	6.00
26 Mark Slater	3.00	6.00
27 John Spagnola	3.00	6.00
28 Stan Walters	3.00	6.00
29 Reggie Wilkes	3.00	6.00
30 Brenard Wilson	3.00	6.00

1979 Eagles Team Sheets

This set consists of six 8" by 10" sheets that display five or eight glossy black-and-white player/coaches photos each. Each individual photo on the sheets measures approximately 2 1/4" by 3 1/4". An Eagles logo, team name and year appear above the photos at the top of each sheet and the backs are blank. The sheets are unnumbered and checklisted below alphabetically according to the player featured in the upper left corner.

COMPLETE SET (6)	20.00	40.00
1 Sheet 1	3.00	6.00
2 Sheet 2	4.00	8.00
3 Sheet 3	4.00	8.00
4 Sheet 4	3.00	6.00
5 Sheet 5	3.00	6.00
6 Sheet 6	5.00	10.00

1980 Eagles Frito Lay

COMPLETE SET (48)	125.00	250.00
1 Bill Bergey	3.00	8.00
2 Richard Blackmore	2.50	6.00
3 Thomas Brown	2.50	6.00
4 John Bunting	2.50	6.00
5 Lem Burnham	2.50	6.00
6 Billy Campfield	2.50	6.00
7 Harold Carmichael	4.00	10.00
8 Al Chesley	2.50	6.00
9 Ken Clarke	2.50	6.00
10 Ken Dunek	2.50	6.00
11 Herman Edwards	2.50	6.00
12 Scott Fitzkee	2.50	6.00
13 Tony Franklin	3.00	8.00
14 Louie Giammona	2.50	6.00
15 Carl Hairston	3.00	8.00
16 Perry Harrington	2.50	6.00
17 Leroy Harris	2.50	6.00
18 Dennis Harrison	2.50	6.00
19 Zac Henderson	2.50	6.00
20 Wally Henry	2.50	6.00
21 Rob Hertel	2.50	6.00
22 Claude Humphrey	3.00	8.00
23 Ron Jaworski	5.00	12.00
24 Charlie Johnson	2.50	6.00
25 Steve Kenney	2.50	6.00
26 Keith Krepfle	3.00	8.00
27 Frank LeMaster	2.50	6.00
28 Randy Logan	2.50	6.00
29 Wilbert Montgomery	3.00	8.00
30 Guy Morriss	2.50	6.00
31 Rodney Parker	2.50	6.00
32 Woody Peoples	2.50	6.00
33 Pete Perot	2.50	6.00
34 Ray Phillips	2.50	6.00
35 Joe Pisarcik	3.00	8.00
36 Jerry Robinson	2.50	6.00
37 Max Runager	2.50	6.00
38 John Sciarra	2.50	6.00
39 Jerry Sisemore	2.50	6.00
40 Mark Slater	2.50	6.00
41 Charles Smith	2.50	6.00
42 John Spagnola	2.50	6.00
43 Dick Vermeil	6.00	15.00
44 Steve Wagner	2.50	6.00
45 Stan Walters	2.50	6.00
46 Reggie Wilkes	2.50	6.00
47 Brenard Wilson	2.50	6.00
48 Roynell Young	2.50	6.00

1980 Eagles McDonald's Glasses

These standard-sized glasses were distributed by McDonald's in the Philadelphia area in 1980. Each glass contains 2 player drawings, with each player represented by a crude action drawing and a head shot superimposed over a football, with their name in script underneath the football. The glasses are unnumbered, and are catalogued below in alphabetical order by the first player name.

COMPLETE SET (5)	12.50	25.00
1 Bill Bergey John Bunting	2.50	6.00
2 Billy Campfield Wilbert Montgomery	2.50	6.00
3 Harold Carmichael Randy Logan	2.00	5.00
4 Tony Franklin Stan Walters	2.00	5.00
5 Ron Jaworski Keith Krepfle	3.00	8.00

1967-73 Equitable Sports Hall of Fame

This set consists of copies of art work found over a number of years in many national magazines, especially "Sports Illustrated," honoring sports heroes that Equitable Life Assurance Society selected to be in its very own Sports Hall of Fame. The cards consists of charcoal-type drawings on white backgrounds by artists, George Loh and Robert Riger, and measure approximately 11" by 7 3/4". The unnumbered cards have been assigned numbers below using a sport prefix (BB- baseball, BK- basketball, FB- football, HK- hockey, OT-other).

COMPLETE SET (95)	250.00	500.00
FB1 Jim Brown	4.00	8.00
FB2 Charley Conerly	2.00	4.00
FB3 Bill Dudley	1.25	2.50
FB4 Roman Gabriel	1.25	2.50
FB5 Red Grange	4.00	8.00
FB6 Elroy Hirsch	2.00	4.00
FB7 Jerry Kramer	2.00	4.00
FB8 Vince Lombardi	4.00	8.00
FB9 Earl Morrall	1.25	2.50
FB10 Bronko Nagurski	3.00	6.00
FB11 Gale Sayers	4.00	8.00
FB12 Jim Thorpe	4.00	8.00
FB13 Johnny Unitas	4.00	8.00
FB14 Alex Webster	2.00	4.00

1969 Eskimo Pie

The 1969 Eskimo Pie football card set contains 15 panel pairs of American Football League players. Each pair of individual player cards is most commonly collected together and, thus, cataloged as pairs below. Each could be cut off of Eskimo Pie Ice Cream boxes at the time and most, if not all, can also be found in a thinner sticker version originally attached to a green colored backing paper - two cards per panel for a total of four players. We've cataloged the card/box version below with a "C" suffix after the card number and an "S" suffix for the known sticker versions. This thin sticker version appears to be more difficult to find than the card/box version. The panels measure approximately 2 1/2" by 3" when neatly cut. The unnumbered pairs are checklisted below alphabetically according to the last name of the player on the left. The names are mistakenly reversed on the card containing Jim Otto and Len Dawson (card number 14). Finally, a 16th sticker was uncovered in 2012 which included an offer for four different NFL team logo jewelry premiums: tie clasp, tie tac, pendant, and charm bracelet with the Jets team logo featured. This premium offer sticker was issued along with the Lamonica/Frazier sticker pair and it measures the same size as a standard sticker pair. The catalog designation for this set is F73.

1C L.Alworth/J.Charles	100.00	200.00
1S L.Alworth/J.Charles	175.00	300.00
2C Al Atkinson/G.Goeddeke	100.00	200.00
2S Al Atkinson/G.Goeddeke	175.00	300.00
3S M.Briscoe/B.Shaw SP	350.00	600.00
4C G.Cappelletti/D.Livingston SP	250.00	400.00
4S G.Cappelletti/D.Livingston SP	350.00	600.00
5C E.Crabtree/J.Dunaway	100.00	200.00
5S E.Crabtree/J.Dunaway	175.00	300.00
6C B.Davidson/B.Griese	250.00	400.00
6S B.Davidson/B.Griese	400.00	600.00
7C H.Dixon/P.Beathard	100.00	175.00
7S H.Dixon/P.Beathard	150.00	250.00
8S M.Garrett/B.Hunt SP	250.00	400.00
9C D.Lamonica/W.Frazier	150.00	300.00
10C J.Lynch.J.Hadl	100.00	200.00
11C K.McCloughan/T.Regner	100.00	200.00
12C J.Nance/B.Neighbors SP	250.00	400.00
12S J.Nance/B.Neighbors SP	350.00	600.00
13C R.Norton/P.Costa	100.00	200.00
13S R.Norton/P.Costa	175.00	300.00
14C J.Otto/L.Dawson	250.00	400.00
15C M.Snell/D.Post	100.00	175.00
15S M.Snell/D.Post	150.00	250.00
16S Premium Offer Sticker	500.00	750.00

1948-52 Exhibit W468 Black and White

Produced by the Exhibit Supply Company of Chicago, the 1948-52 Football Exhibit cards are unnumbered, blank-backed, and produced on thick card stock. Although we list the more common black and white cards below, some of the cards were issued in other colors as well including sepia, tan, green, red, pink, blue, and yellow. The primary method of distribution for the cards was through mechanical vending machines. Advertising panels on the front of these machines displayed from one to nine cards as well as the price for a card which was originally one-cent but later raised to two-cents. Each card measures approximately 3 1/4" by 5 3/8" and features a pro or college player. Several cards in the checklist below (Sammy Baugh, Glenn Dobbs, Otto Graham, Pat Harder, Jack Jacobs, Sid Luckman, Johnny Lujack, Marion Motley, Emil Sitko, Steve Van Buren, Bob Waterfield, and Tank Younger) have the same photo as in the Exhibit Sports Champions set of 1948; however, cards in this series do not have the single agate line of type describing the player at the bottom of the card. The cards were issued in three groups of 32 primarily during 1948, 1950, and 1951. We've included what is thought to be the year/years of issue for each card. The 16-cards in the 1951/1952 group are the most plentiful as they were reissued intact in sepia tone in 1952 (and perhaps 1953 as well). Some veteran collectors believe the second group may have been issued in 1949 rather than 1950. Cards issued during and after 1951 are marked as DP's as they are quite common compared to the other cards in the set. Several players, such as Creekmur, Houck, and Martin, are rumored to exist, but they have not been verified and are assumed not to exist in the checklist below. The American Card Catalog designation is W468. A football exhibit checklist card has also been found but was apparently produced in very limited quantity in 1950 only. This checklist card is known to exist in green and black-and-white and is identical to the Bednarik card but has the 32 players from the 1950 set listed on its front. The Bednarik checklist is usually found on the 9-card advertising display piece

COMPLETE SET (59)	2,500.00	5,000.00
1 Frankie Albert DP	3.00	8.00
2 Dick Barwegan DP	2.50	6.00
3 Sammy Baugh DP	12.50	25.00
4 Chuck Bednarik SP50	90.00	150.00
5 Tony Canadeo DP	6.00	15.00
6 Paul Christman	25.00	40.00
7 Bob Cifers SP48	175.00	300.00
8 Irv Comp SP48	175.00	300.00
9A Charley Conerly DP	6.00	15.00
9B Charley Conerly DP	6.00	15.00
10 George Connor DP	4.00	10.00
11 Tex Coulter SP48	175.00	300.00
12 Glenn Davis SP50	175.00	300.00
13 Glenn Dobbs	25.00	40.00
14 John Dottley DP	2.50	6.00
15 Bill Dudley	35.00	60.00
16 Tom Fears DP	5.00	12.00
17 Joe Geri DP	2.50	6.00
18 Otto Graham DP	15.00	30.00
19 Pat Harder	25.00	40.00
20 Elroy Hirsch DP	6.00	15.00
21 Dick Hoerner SP50	60.00	100.00
22 Bob Hoernschemeyer DP	2.50	6.00
23 Les Horvath SP48	175.00	300.00
24 Jack Jacobs SP48	175.00	300.00
25 Nate Johnson SP48	175.00	300.00
26 Charlie Justice SP50	90.00	150.00
27 Bobby Layne DP	10.00	25.00
28 Clyde LeForce SP48	175.00	300.00
29 Sid Luckman	45.00	80.00
30 Johnny Lujack	35.00	60.00
31 John Mastrangelo SP48	175.00	300.00
32 Ollie Matson DP	6.00	15.00
33 Bill McColl DP	2.50	6.00
34 Fred Morrison DP	2.50	6.00
35 Marion Motley DP	10.00	20.00
36 Chuck Ortmann DP	2.50	6.00
37 Joe Perry SP50	75.00	135.00
38 Pete Pihos	30.00	50.00
39 Steve Pritko SP48	175.00	300.00
40 George Ratterman DP	2.50	6.00
41 Jay Rhodemyre DP	2.50	6.00
42 Martin Ruby SP50	75.00	125.00
43 Julie Rykovich DP	2.50	6.00
44 Walt Schlinkman SP48	175.00	300.00
45 Emil Sitko DP	2.50	6.00
46 Vitamin Smith DP	2.50	6.00
47 Norm Standlee	25.00	40.00
48 George Taliaferro DP	2.50	6.00
49 Y.A. Tittle HOR	60.00	100.00
50 Charley Trippi DP	4.00	10.00
51 Frank Tripucka DP	3.00	8.00
52 Emlen Tunnell DP	5.00	12.00
53 Bulldog Turner DP	5.00	12.00
54 Steve Van Buren	35.00	60.00
55 Bob Waterfield DP	7.50	20.00
56 Herm Wedemeyer SP48	500.00	800.00
57 Bob Williams DP	2.50	6.00
58 Buddy Young DP	3.00	8.00
59 Tank Younger DP	3.00	8.00
NNO Checklist Card SP50	500.00	800.00

1948-52 Exhibit W468 Variations

1A Frankie Albert B&W PC	12.50	25.00
1B Frankie Albert Sepia	7.50	15.00
2B Dick Barwegan Sepia	6.00	12.00
3A Sammy Baugh B&W PC	25.00	50.00
3B Sammy Baugh Yellow	75.00	125.00
5B Tony Canadeo Sepia	15.00	30.00
6A Paul Christman Lt.Blue	60.00	100.00
7A Bob Cifers Dark Green	200.00	350.00
7B Bob Cifers Yellow	200.00	350.00
8A Irv Comp Yellow	200.00	350.00
9A Charley Conerly B&W PC	20.00	40.00
10B George Connor Sepia	10.00	20.00
11A Tex Coulter Green	200.00	350.00
11B Tex Coulter Pink	200.00	350.00
14B John Dottley Sepia	6.00	12.00
15A Bill Dudley Red	60.00	100.00
16A Tom Fears B&W PC	12.50	25.00
16B Tom Fears Sepia	12.50	25.00
17A Joe Geri Sepia	6.00	12.00
18A Otto Graham B&W PC	30.00	60.00
18B Otto Graham Sepia	30.00	60.00
19A Pat Harder Blue	50.00	80.00
20A Elroy Hirsch B&W PC	20.00	40.00
20B Elroy Hirsch Sepia	15.00	30.00
22B Bob Hoernschemeyer Sepia	6.00	12.00
23A Les Horvath Dark Red	200.00	350.00
23B Les Horvath Yellow	200.00	350.00
24A Jack Jacobs Dark Green	200.00	350.00
25A Nate Johnson Green	200.00	350.00
25B Nate Johnson Dark Red	200.00	350.00
27A Bobby Layne B&W PC	25.00	50.00
27B Bobby Layne Sepia	25.00	50.00
28A Clyde LeForce Green	200.00	350.00
29A Sid Luckman Lt.Green	90.00	150.00
30A Johnny Lujack Yellow	75.00	125.00
30B Johnny Lujack Pink	75.00	125.00
31A John Mastrangelo Lt.Blue	175.00	300.00
32A Ollie Matson B&W PC	20.00	40.00
32B Ollie Matson Sepia	15.00	30.00
33B Bill McColl Sepia	6.00	15.00
34A Fred Morrison B&W PC	25.00	50.00
34B Fred Morrison Sepia	6.00	12.00
34C Fred Morrison Tan	7.50	15.00
35A Marion Motley B&W PC	25.00	50.00
35B Marion Motley Sepia	20.00	40.00
36B Chuck Ortmann Sepia	6.00	12.00
38A Pete Pihos Yellow	60.00	100.00
39A Steve Pritko Yellow	200.00	350.00
40A George Ratterman B&W PC	12.50	25.00
40B George Ratterman Sepia	6.00	12.00
41B Jay Rhodemyre Sepia	6.00	12.00
41C Jay Rhodemyre Tan	7.50	15.00
43A Julie Rykovich B&W PC	12.50	25.00
43B Julie Rykovich Sepia	6.00	12.00
44A Walt Schlinkman Pink	200.00	350.00
45B Emil Sitko Sepia	6.00	12.00
48B George Taliaferro Sepia	6.00	12.00
48C George Taliaferro Tan	7.50	15.00
49A Y.A. Tittle Green	90.00	150.00
49B Y.A. Tittle Yellow	90.00	150.00
50A Charley Trippi B&W PC	15.00	30.00
50B Charley Trippi Sepia	10.00	20.00
51B Frank Tripucka Sepia	7.50	15.00
52B Emlen Tunnell Sepia	12.50	25.00
53A Bulldog Turner B&W PC	25.00	50.00
53B Bulldog Turner Green	60.00	100.00
53C Bulldog Turner Sepia	12.50	25.00
54A Steve Van Buren Lt.Blue	75.00	125.00
55A Bob Waterfield B&W PC	25.00	50.00
55B Bob Waterfield Sepia	15.00	40.00
56A Herm Wedemeyer Lt.Green	600.00	1,000.00
57A Bob Williams B&W PC	25.00	50.00
57B Bob Williams Sepia	6.00	12.00
58A Buddy Young B&W PC	12.50	25.00
58B Buddy Young Sepia	7.50	15.00
58C Buddy Young Yellow	60.00	100.00
59B Tank Younger Sepia	6.00	12.00
NNO Chuck Bednarik CL Green	500.00	800.00

1926 Exhibit Red Grange One Minute to Play

These Exhibit cards were issued for the movie "One Minute to play" starring Red Grange. Each was produced in the standard oversized Exhibit style with a single color cardfront picturing Grange in a scene from the movie. The backs are blank.

1 Red Grange Green

2 Red Grange in sweater

1971 Facsimile Photos

1 Danny Abramowicz	6.00	15.00
2 Lem Barney	8.00	20.00
3 Emerson Boozer	6.00	15.00
4 Terry Bradshaw	15.00	40.00
5 Larry Brown	6.00	15.00
6 Nick Buoniconti	8.00	20.00
7 Paul Costa	5.00	12.00
8 Bobby Douglass	6.00	15.00
9 Carl Eller	6.00	15.00
10 Jim Hart	6.00	15.00
11 Charley Johnson	6.00	15.00
12 Daryle Lamonica	6.00	15.00
13 Floyd Little	6.00	15.00
14 Spider Lockhart	5.00	12.00
15 Bill Nelsen	6.00	15.00
16 Ray Nitschke	10.00	25.00
17 Tommy Nobis	6.00	15.00
18 Johnny Robinson	6.00	15.00
19 Paul Robinson	5.00	12.00
20 Ron Sellers	5.00	12.00
21 Bubba Smith	8.00	20.00
22 Gene Washington	6.00	15.00
23 Tom Woodeshick	6.00	15.00

1968-69 Falcons Team Issue

Printed on glossy thick paper stock, each of these black-and-white photos measure approximately 7 1/2" by 9 1/2" and have white borders. With the exception of the Berry photo (a portrait), all the photos are posed action shots. The cardbacks are blank. The photos are unnumbered and checklisted below in alphabetical order. Each includes the player's name and team name below the photo in the card border. This series can be differentiated from the 1970 and 1971 issues by the much larger type used in printing the player name and team name below the photo.

COMPLETE SET (23)	100.00	200.00
1 Bob Berry	5.00	10.00
2 Greg Brezina	5.00	10.00
3 Junior Coffey	5.00	10.00
4 Carlton Dabney	5.00	10.00
5 Bob Etter	5.00	10.00
6 Paul Gipson	5.00	10.00
7 Don Hansen	5.00	10.00
8 Bill Harris	5.00	10.00
9 Ralph Heck	5.00	10.00
10 Claude Humphrey	6.00	12.00
11 Randy Johnson	5.00	10.00
12 George Kunz	5.00	10.00
13 Errol Linden	5.00	10.00
14 Billy Lothridge	5.00	10.00
15 Tommy McDonald	7.50	15.00
16 Jim Mitchell	5.00	10.00
17 Tommy Nobis	7.50	15.00
18 Ken Reaves	5.00	10.00
19 Jerry Shay	5.00	10.00
20 John Small	5.00	10.00
21 Norm Van Brocklin CO	7.50	15.00
22 Harmon Wages	5.00	10.00
23 John Zook	5.00	10.00

1970 Falcons Stadium Issue

This 10-card set of the Atlanta Falcons features black and white player portraits in a white border and measures approximately 5 1/2" by 7 1/2". The backs are blank. The cards are unnumbered and checklisted below in alphabetical order.

COMPLETE SET (10)	40.00	80.00
1 Mike Brunson	5.00	10.00
2 Charlie Bryant	5.00	10.00
3 Sonny Campbell	5.00	10.00
4 Dean Halverson	5.00	10.00
5 Greg Lens	5.00	10.00
6 Randy Marshall	5.00	10.00
7 John Matlock	5.00	10.00
8 Gary Roberts	5.00	10.00
9 Jim Sullivan	5.00	10.00
10 Kenny Vinyard	5.00	10.00

1970 Falcons Team Issue

This set of the Atlanta Falcons features 8" by 10" black-and-white player photos with white borders. The photos are very similar to the 1971 set except that most players are wearing their black Falcons jersey and the pictures were taken inside the stadium. Unless noted below, all players also include their position (initials) below the photo along with their name and team name. The backs are blank. The cards are unnumbered and checklisted below in alphabetical order.

COMPLETE SET (41)	150.00	300.00
1 Ron Acks	5.00	10.00
2 Grady Allen	5.00	10.00
3A Bob Berry ERR	5.00	10.00
3B Bob Berry COR	5.00	10.00
4 Bob Breitenstein	5.00	10.00
5 Greg Brezina	5.00	10.00
6 Jim Butler	5.00	10.00
7 Gail Cogdill	5.00	10.00
8 Glen Condren	5.00	10.00
9 Ted Cottrell	5.00	10.00
10 Carlton Dabney	5.00	10.00
11 Mike Donohoe	5.00	10.00
12 Dick Enderle	5.00	10.00
13 Paul Flatley	5.00	10.00
14 Mike Freeman	5.00	10.00
15 Paul Gipson	5.00	10.00

16 Don Hansen	5.00	10.00
17 Tom Hayes	5.00	10.00
18 Dave Hettema	5.00	10.00
19 Claude Humphrey	6.00	12.00
20 Randy Johnson	6.00	12.00
21 George Kunz	5.00	10.00
22 Al Lavan	5.00	10.00
23 Bruce Lemmerman	5.00	10.00
24 Billy Lothridge	5.00	10.00
25 John Mallory	5.00	10.00
26 Art Malone	5.00	10.00
27 Andy Maurer	5.00	10.00
28 Tom McCauley	5.00	10.00
29 Jim Mitchell	5.00	10.00
30A Tommy Nobis	6.00	12.00
30B Tommy Nobis	6.00	12.00
31 Rudy Redmond	5.00	10.00
32 Bill Sandeman	5.00	10.00
33 Dick Shiner	5.00	10.00
34 John Small	5.00	10.00
35 Malcolm Snider	5.00	10.00
36 Todd Snyder	5.00	10.00
37 Norm Van Brocklin CO	6.00	12.00
38 Jeff Van Note	5.00	10.00
39 Harmon Wages	5.00	10.00
40 John Zook	5.00	10.00
41 Team Photo	5.00	10.00

1971 Falcons Team Issue

The 1971 Falcons Team Issue set consists of black-and-white photos measuring 8" by 10" with a white border on all four sides. The photos are similar to the 1970 set, but each player is wearing his red Falcons jersey and the pictures were taken outdoors. Only the player's name and team name appear below the photo. They are unnumbered and checklisted in alphabetical order.

COMPLETE SET (15)	75.00	150.00
1 Bob Berry	5.00	10.00
2 Mike Brunson	5.00	10.00
3 Ken Burrow	5.00	10.00
4 Sonny Campbell	5.00	10.00
5 Don Hansen	5.00	10.00
6 Leo Hart	5.00	10.00
7 Claude Humphrey	5.00	10.00
8 Ray Jarvis	5.00	10.00
9 Greg Lens	5.00	10.00
10 John Matlock	5.00	10.00
11 Tommy Nobis	6.00	12.00
12 Malcolm Snider	5.00	10.00
13 Pat Sullivan	6.00	12.00
14 Norm Van Brocklin CO	6.00	12.00
15 Harmon Wages	5.00	10.00

1973 Falcons Team Issue

The 1973 Falcons Team Issue features black-and-white photos measuring 8" by 10" with a white border. The photos are similar to the 1970 and 1972 sets, but the player's name and position initials (on the left) and the team name (on the right) are oriented very close to the outside borders. They are blankbacked, unnumbered and checklisted below in alphabetical order.

COMPLETE SET (11)	40.00	80.00
1 Greg Brezina	4.00	8.00
2 Ray Brown	4.00	8.00
3 Ken Burrow	4.00	8.00
4 Dave Hampton	4.00	8.00
5 Don Hansen	4.00	8.00
6A Claude Humphrey (vertical)	5.00	10.00
6B Claude Humphrey (horizontal)	5.00	10.00
7 Art Malone	4.00	8.00
8 Tommy Nobis	5.00	10.00
9 Ken Reaves	4.00	8.00
10 Bill Sandeman	4.00	8.00
11 Pat Sullivan	5.00	10.00

1975 Falcons Team Sheets

This three-card set was printed on sheets each measuring approximately 8 1/2" by 11" and features black-and-white player portraits. They were produced to be used by media and as public relations photos. Sheet 3 contains 15-players and the set title, while sheets 1 and 2 contain 16 players. The backs are blank.

COMPLETE SET (3)	10.00	20.00
1 Greg Brezina Ray Brown Ken Burrow Rick Byas La	2.50	5.00
2 Marion Campbell/	5.00	10.00
3 Title Card/	2.50	5.00

1978 Falcons Kinnett Dairies

These six blank-backed white panels measure approximately 4 1/4" by 6" and feature four black-and-white player headshots per panel, all framed by a thin red line. A narrow strip running across the center of the panel contains the sponsor name, the words "Atlanta Player Cards," and the NFLPA logo. The cards are unnumbered and checklisted below in the alphabetical order of the players shown in the upper left corners.

COMPLETE SET (6)	20.00	40.00
1 William Andrews	3.75	7.50
2 Warren Bryant	5.00	10.00
3 Wallace Francis Mitchell TE Van Note East.	3.75	7.50
4 Dewey McClain	2.50	5.00
5 Robert Pennywell	2.50	5.00
6 Haskel Stanback	3.75	7.50

1980 Falcons Police

The 1980 Atlanta Falcons set contains 30 unnumbered cards each measuring approximately 2 5/8" by 4 1/8". Although uniform numbers can be found on the front of the cards, the cards have been listed alphabetically on the checklist below for convenience. Logos of the three sponsors, the Atlanta Police Athletic League, the Northside Atlanta Jaycees, and Coca-Cola, can be found on the back of the cards with short "Tips from the Falcons". Card backs have black printing with red accent. The Falcon helmet and stylized logo appear on the front of the cards with the player's name, uniform number, position, height, weight and college.

COMPLETE SET (30)	25.00	50.00
1 William Andrews	2.00	5.00
2 Steve Bartkowski	3.00	8.00
3 Bubba Bean	.75	2.00
4 Warren Bryant	.60	1.50
5 Rick Byas	.60	1.50
6 Lynn Cain	1.25	3.00
7 Buddy Curry	.60	1.50
8 Edgar Fields	.60	1.50
9 Wallace Francis	1.50	4.00
10 Alfred Jackson	1.25	3.00
11 John James	.60	1.50
12 Alfred Jenkins	1.50	4.00
13 Kenny Johnson	.60	1.50
14 Mike Kenn	1.25	3.00
15 Fulton Kuykendall	.75	2.00
16 Rolland Lawrence	.75	2.00
17 Tim Mazzetti	.60	1.50
18 Dewey McLean	.60	1.50
19 Jeff Merrow	.75	2.00
20 Junior Miller	.75	2.00
21 Tom Pridemore	.60	1.50
22 Frank Reed	.60	1.50
23 Al Richardson	.60	1.50
24 Dave Scott	.60	1.50
25 Don Smith	.60	1.50
26 Reggie Smith	.60	1.50
27 R.C. Thielemann	.75	2.00
28 Jeff Van Note	1.25	3.00
29 Joel Williams	.60	1.50
30 Jeff Yeates	.60	1.50

1960 Fleer

The 1960 Fleer set of 132 standard-size cards was Fleer's first venture into football card production. This set features players of the American Football League's debut season. Several well-known coaches are featured in the set; the set is the last regular issue set to feature coaches (on their own specific card) until the 1989 Pro Set release. The card backs are printed in red and black. The key card in the set is Jack Kemp's Rookie Card. Other Rookie Cards include Sid Gillman, Ron Mix and Hank Stram. The cards are frequently found off-centered as Fleer's first effort into the football card market left much to be desired in the area of quality control. A large quantity of color separations and "proofs" are widely available.

COMPLETE SET (132)	500.00	750.00
WRAPPER (5-CENT)	20.00	25.00
1 Harvey White RC	12.00	20.00
2 Tom Corky Tharp RC	2.00	4.00
3 Dan McGrew RC	2.00	4.00
4 Bob White RC	2.00	4.00
5 Dick Jamieson RC	2.00	4.00
6 Sam Salerno RC	2.00	4.00
7 Sid Gillman CO RC	12.00	20.00
8 Ben Preston RC	2.00	4.00
9 George Blanch RC	2.00	4.00
10 Bob Stransky RC	2.00	4.00
11 Fran Curci RC	2.00	4.00
12 George Shirkey RC	2.00	4.00
13 Paul Larson	2.00	4.00
14 John Stolte RC	2.00	4.00
15 Serafino Fazio RC	2.50	5.00
16 Tom Dimitroff RC	2.00	4.00
17 Elbert Dubenion RC	6.00	12.00
18 Hogan Wharton RC	2.00	4.00
19 Tom O'Connell	2.00	4.00
20 Sammy Baugh CO	25.00	40.00
21 Tony Sardisco RC	2.00	4.00
22 Alan Cann RC	2.00	4.00
23 Mike Hudock RC	2.00	4.00
24 Bill Atkins RC	2.00	4.00
25 Charlie Jackson RC	2.00	4.00
26 Frank Tripucka	3.00	6.00
27 Tony Teresa RC	2.00	4.00
28 Joe Amstutz RC	2.00	4.00
29 Bob Fee RC	2.00	4.00
30 Jim Baldwin RC	2.00	4.00
31 Jim Yates RC	2.00	4.00
32 Don Flynn RC	2.00	4.00
33 Ken Adamson RC	2.00	4.00
34 Ron Drzewiecki	2.00	4.00
35 J.W. Slack RC	2.00	4.00
36 Bob Yates RC	2.00	4.00
37 Gary Cobb RC	2.00	4.00
38 Jacky Lee RC	2.50	5.00
39 Jack Spikes RC	2.50	5.00
40 Jim Padgett RC	2.00	4.00
41 Jack Larscheid UER RC	2.00	4.00
42 Bob Reifsnyder RC	2.00	4.00
43 Fran Rogel	2.00	4.00
44 Ray Moss RC	2.00	4.00
45 Tony Banfield RC	2.50	5.00
46 George Herring RC	2.00	4.00
47 Willie Smith RC	2.00	4.00
48 Buddy Allen RC	2.00	4.00
49 Bill Brown LB RC	2.00	4.00
50 Ken Ford RC	2.00	4.00
51 Billy Kinard RC	2.00	4.00
52 Buddy Mayfield RC	2.00	4.00
53 Bill Krisher RC	2.00	4.00
54 Frank Bernardi RC	2.00	4.00
55 Lou Saban CO RC	2.50	5.00
56 Gene Cockrell RC	2.00	4.00
57 Sam Sanders RC	2.00	4.00
58 George Blanda	30.00	50.00
59 Sherrill Headrick RC	2.50	5.00
60 Carl Larpenter RC	2.00	4.00
61 Gene Prebola RC	2.00	4.00
62 Dick Chorovich RC	2.00	4.00
63 Bob McNamara RC	2.00	4.00
64 Tom Saidock RC	2.00	4.00
65 Willie Evans RC	2.00	4.00
66 Billy Cannon RC UER	10.00	20.00
67 Sam McCord RC	2.00	4.00
68 Mike Simmons RC	2.00	4.00
69 Jim Swink RC	2.50	5.00
70 Don Hitt RC	2.00	4.00
71 Gerhard Schwedes RC	2.00	4.00
72 Thurlow Cooper RC	2.00	4.00
73 Abner Haynes RC	10.00	20.00
74 Billy Shoemake RC	2.00	4.00
75 Marv Lasater RC	2.00	4.00
76 Paul Lowe RC	7.50	15.00
77 Bruce Hartman RC	2.00	4.00
78 Blanche Martin RC	2.00	4.00
79 Gene Grabosky RC	2.00	4.00
80 Lou Rymkus CO	2.50	5.00
81 Chris Burford RC	4.00	8.00
82 Don Allen RC	2.00	4.00
83 Bob Nelson C RC	2.00	4.00
84 Jim Woodard RC	2.00	4.00
85 Tom Rychlec RC	2.00	4.00
86 Bob Cox RC	2.00	4.00
87 Jerry Cornelison RC	2.00	4.00
88 Jack Work	2.00	4.00
89 Sam DeLuca RC	2.00	4.00
90 Rommie Loudd RC	2.00	4.00
91 Teddy Edmondson RC	2.00	4.00
92 Buster Ramsey CO	2.00	4.00
93 Doug Asad RC	2.00	4.00
94 Jimmy Harris	2.00	4.00
95 Larry Cundiff RC	2.00	4.00
96 Richie Lucas RC	3.00	6.00
97 Don Norwood RC	2.00	4.00
98 Larry Grantham RC	2.50	5.00
99 Bill Mathis RC	3.00	6.00
100 Mel Branch RC	2.50	5.00
101 Marvin Terrell RC	2.00	4.00
102 Charlie Flowers RC	2.00	4.00
103 John McMullan RC	2.00	4.00
104 Charlie Kaaihue RC	2.00	4.00
105 Joe Schaffer RC	2.00	4.00
106 Al Day RC	2.00	4.00
107 Johnny Carson	2.00	4.00
108 Alan Goldstein RC	2.00	4.00
109 Doug Cline RC	2.00	4.00
110 Al Carmichael	2.00	4.00
111 Bob Dee RC	2.00	4.00
112 John Bredice RC	2.00	4.00
113 Don Floyd RC	2.00	4.00
114 Ronnie Cain RC	2.00	4.00
115 Stan Flowers RC	2.00	4.00
116 Hank Stram CO RC	25.00	40.00
117 Bob Dougherty RC	2.00	4.00
118 Ron Mix RC	25.00	40.00
119 Roger Ellis RC	2.00	4.00
120 Elvin Caldwell RC	2.00	4.00
121 Bill Kimber RC	2.00	4.00
122 Jim Matheny RC	2.00	4.00
123 Curley Johnson RC	2.00	4.00
124 Jack Kemp RC	60.00	120.00
125 Ed Denk RC	2.00	4.00
126 Jerry McFarland RC	2.00	4.00
127 Dan Lanphear RC	2.00	4.00
128 Paul Maguire RC	10.00	18.00
129 Ray Collins	2.00	4.00
130 Ron Burton RC	3.00	6.00
131 Eddie Erdelatz CO RC	2.00	4.00
132 Ron Beagle RC !	7.50	15.00

1960 Fleer AFL Team Decals

This set of nine logo decals was inserted with the 1960 Fleer regular issue inaugural AFL football set. These inserts measure approximately 2 1/4" by 3" and one decal was to be inserted in each wax pack. The decals are unnumbered and are ordered below alphabetically by team name for convenience. There is one decal for each of the eight AFL teams as well as a decal with the league logo. The backs of the decal backing contained instructions on the proper application of the decal.

COMPLETE SET (9)	100.00	200.00
1 AFL Logo	12.50	25.00
2 Boston Patriots	10.00	20.00
3 Buffalo Bills	12.50	25.00
4 Dallas Texans	15.00	30.00
5 Denver Broncos	12.50	25.00
6 Houston Oilers	12.50	25.00
7 Los Angeles Chargers	12.50	25.00
8 New York Titans	10.00	20.00
9 Oakland Raiders	15.00	30.00

1960 Fleer College Pennant Decals

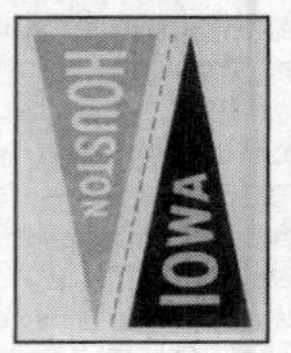

This set of 19 pennant decal pairs was distributed as an insert with the 1960 Fleer regular issue inaugural AFL football set along with and at the same time as the AFL Team Decals described immediately above. Some dealers feel that these college decals are tougher to find than the AFL team decals. These inserts were approximately 2 1/4" by 3" and one decal was to be inserted in each wax pack. The decals are unnumbered and are ordered below alphabetically according to the lower alphabetically of each college pair. The backs of the decal backing contained instructions on the proper application of the decal printed in very light blue.

COMPLETE SET (19)	87.50	175.00
1 Alabama Yale	6.00	12.00
2 Army Mississippi	3.75	7.50
3 California Indiana	3.75	7.50
4 Duke Notre Dame	10.00	20.00
5 Florida St. Kentucky	6.00	12.00
6 Georgia Oklahoma	6.00	12.00
7 Houston Iowa	3.75	7.50
8 Idaho St. Penn.	3.75	7.50
9 Iowa St. Penn State	6.00	12.00
10 Kansas UCLA	5.00	10.00
11 Marquette New Mexico	3.75	7.50
12 Maryland Missouri	3.75	7.50
13 Miss.South. N.Carolina	3.75	7.50
14 Navy Stanford	5.00	10.00
15 Nebraska Purdue	6.00	12.00
16 Pittsburgh Utah	3.75	7.50
17 SMU West Virginia	3.75	7.50
18 So.Carolina USC	5.00	10.00
19 Wake Forest Wisconsin	3.75	7.50

1961 Fleer

The 1961 Fleer football set contains 220 standard-size cards. The set contains NFL (1-132) and AFL (133-220) players. The cards are grouped alphabetically by team nicknames within league. The backs are printed in black and lime green on a white card stock. The AFL cards are often found in uncut sheet form. The key Rookie Cards in this set are John Brodie, Tom Flores, Don Maynard, Don Meredith, and Jim Otto.

COMPLETE SET (220)	1,000.00	1,600.00
WRAPPER (5-CENT, SER.1)	20.00	25.00
WRAPPER (5-CENT, SER.2)	25.00	30.00
1 Ed Brown	7.50	15.00
2 Rick Casares	3.00	6.00
3 Willie Galimore	3.00	6.00
4 Jim Dooley	2.50	4.00
5 Harlon Hill	2.50	4.00
6 Stan Jones	4.00	8.00
7 J.C. Caroline	2.50	4.00
8 Joe Fortunato	2.50	4.00
9 Doug Atkins	4.00	8.00
10 Milt Plum	3.00	6.00
11 Jim Brown	90.00	150.00
12 Bobby Mitchell	5.00	10.00
13 Ray Renfro	3.00	6.00
14 Gern Nagler	2.50	4.00
15 Jim Shofner	2.50	4.00
16 Vince Costello	2.50	4.00
17 Galen Fiss RC	2.50	4.00
18 Walt Michaels	3.00	6.00
19 Bob Gain	2.50	4.00
20 Mal Hammack	2.50	4.00
21 Frank Mestnik RC	2.50	4.00
22 Bobby Joe Conrad	3.00	6.00
23 John David Crow	3.00	6.00
24 Sonny Randle RC	3.00	6.00
25 Don Gillis	2.50	4.00
26 Jerry Norton	2.50	4.00
27 Bill Stacy RC	2.50	4.00
28 Leo Sugar	2.50	4.00
29 Frank Fuller	2.50	4.00
30 Johnny Unitas	35.00	60.00
31 Alan Ameche	4.00	8.00
32 Lenny Moore	7.50	15.00
33 Raymond Berry	7.50	15.00
34 Jim Mutscheller	2.50	4.00
35 Jim Parker	4.00	8.00
36 Bill Pellington	2.50	4.00
37 Gino Marchetti	5.00	10.00
38 Gene Lipscomb	4.00	8.00
39 Art Donovan	7.50	15.00
40 Eddie LeBaron	3.00	6.00
41 Don Meredith RC	90.00	150.00
42 Don McIlhenny	2.50	4.00
43 L.G. Dupre	2.50	4.00
44 Fred Dugan RC	2.50	4.00
45 Billy Howton	3.00	6.00
46 Duane Putnam	2.50	4.00
47 Gene Cronin	2.50	4.00
48 Jerry Tubbs	2.50	4.00
49 Clarence Peaks	2.50	4.00
50 Ted Dean RC	2.50	4.00
51 Tommy McDonald	4.00	8.00
52 Bill Barnes	2.50	4.00
53 Pete Retzlaff	3.00	6.00
54 Bobby Walston	2.50	4.00
55 Chuck Bednarik	6.00	12.00
56 Maxie Baughan RC	3.00	6.00
57 Bob Pellegrini	2.50	4.00
58 Jesse Richardson	2.50	4.00
59 John Brodie RC	30.00	50.00
60 J.D. Smith RB	3.00	6.00
61 Ray Norton RC	2.50	4.00
62 Monty Stickles RC	2.50	4.00
63 Bob St.Clair	4.00	8.00
64 Dave Baker RC	2.50	4.00
65 Abe Woodson	2.50	4.00
66 Matt Hazeltine	2.50	4.00
67 Leo Nomellini	5.00	10.00
68 Charley Conerly	5.00	10.00
69 Kyle Rote	4.00	8.00
70 Jack Stroud RC	2.50	4.00
71 Roosevelt Brown	4.00	8.00
72 Jim Patton	2.50	4.00
73 Erich Barnes	2.50	4.00
74 Sam Huff	7.50	15.00
75 Andy Robustelli	5.00	10.00
76 Dick Modzelewski RC	2.50	4.00
77 Roosevelt Grier	4.00	8.00
78 Earl Morrall	4.00	8.00
79 Jim Ninowski	2.50	4.00
80 Nick Pietrosante RC	3.00	6.00
81 Howard Cassady	3.00	6.00
82 Jim Gibbons	2.50	4.00
83 Gail Cogdill RC	3.00	6.00
84 Dick Lane	4.00	8.00
85 Yale Lary	4.00	8.00
86 Joe Schmidt	4.00	8.00
87 Darris McCord	2.50	4.00
88 Bart Starr	35.00	60.00
89 Jim Taylor	30.00	50.00
90 Paul Hornung	30.00	55.00
91 Tom Moore RC	4.00	8.00
92 Boyd Dowler RC	7.50	15.00
93 Max McGee	4.00	8.00
94 Forrest Gregg	5.00	10.00
95 Jerry Kramer	5.00	10.00
96 Jim Ringo	4.00	8.00
97 Bill Forester	3.00	6.00
98 Frank Ryan	3.00	6.00
99 Ollie Matson	6.00	12.00
100 Jon Arnett	3.00	6.00
101 Dick Bass RC	3.00	6.00
102 Jim Phillips	2.50	4.00
103 Del Shofner	3.00	6.00
104 Art Hunter	2.50	4.00
105 Lindon Crow	2.50	4.00
106 Les Richter	3.00	6.00
107 Lou Michaels	2.50	4.00
108 Ralph Guglielmi	2.50	4.00
109 Don Bosseler	2.50	4.00
110 John Olszewski	2.50	4.00
111 Bill Anderson	2.50	4.00
112 Joe Walton	2.50	4.00
113 Jim Schrader	2.50	4.00
114 Gary Glick	2.50	4.00
115 Ralph Felton	2.50	4.00
116 Bob Toneff	2.50	4.00
117 Bobby Layne	25.00	40.00
118 John Henry Johnson	4.00	8.00
119 Tom Tracy	3.00	6.00
120 Jimmy Orr RC	4.00	8.00
121 John Nisby	2.50	4.00
122 Dean Derby	2.50	4.00
123 John Reger	2.50	4.00
124 George Tarasovic	2.50	4.00
125 Ernie Stautner	5.00	10.00
126 George Shaw	2.50	4.00
127 Hugh McElhenny	6.00	12.00
128 Dick Haley RC	2.50	4.00
129 Dave Middleton	2.50	4.00
130 Perry Richards RC	2.50	4.00
131 Gene Johnson DB RC	2.50	4.00
132 Don Joyce RC	2.50	4.00
133 Johnny Green RC	4.00	8.00
134 Wray Carlton RC	4.00	8.00
135 Richie Lucas	4.00	8.00
136 Elbert Dubenion	4.00	8.00
137 Tom Rychlec	3.50	6.00
138 Mack Yoho RC	3.50	6.00
139 Phil Blazer RC	3.50	6.00
140 Dan McGrew	3.50	6.00
141 Bill Atkins	3.50	6.00
142 Archie Matsos RC	3.50	6.00
143 Gene Grabosky	3.50	6.00
144 Frank Tripucka	5.00	10.00
145 Al Carmichael	3.50	6.00
146 Bob McNamara	3.50	6.00
147 Lionel Taylor RC	7.50	15.00
148 Eldon Danenhauer RC	3.50	6.00
149 Willie Smith	3.50	6.00
150 Carl Larpenter	3.50	6.00
151 Ken Adamson	3.50	6.00
152 Goose Gonsoulin UER RC	5.00	10.00
153 Joe Young RC	3.50	6.00
154 Gordy Holz RC	3.50	6.00
155 Jack Kemp	35.00	60.00
156 Charlie Flowers	3.50	6.00
157 Paul Lowe	5.00	10.00
158 Don Norton RC	3.50	6.00
159 Howard Clark RC	3.50	6.00
160 Paul Maguire	7.50	15.00
161 Ernie Wright RC	4.00	8.00
162 Ron Mix	7.50	15.00
163 Fred Cole RC	3.50	6.00
164 Jim Sears RC	3.50	6.00
165 Volney Peters	3.50	6.00
166 George Blanda	25.00	40.00
167 Jacky Lee	4.00	8.00
168 Bob White	3.50	6.00
169 Doug Cline	3.50	6.00
170 Dave Smith RB RC	3.50	6.00
171 Billy Cannon	7.50	15.00
172 Bill Groman RC	3.50	6.00
173 Al Jamison RC	3.50	6.00
174 Jim Norton RC	3.50	6.00
175 Dennit Morris RC	3.50	6.00
176 Don Floyd	3.50	6.00
177 Butch Songin	3.50	6.00
178 Billy Lott RC	3.50	6.00
179 Ron Burton	5.00	10.00
180 Jim Colclough RC	3.50	6.00
181 Charley Leo RC	3.50	6.00
182 Walt Cudzik RC	3.50	6.00
183 Fred Bruney	3.50	6.00
184 Ross O'Hanley RC	3.50	6.00
185 Tony Sardisco	3.50	6.00
186 Harry Jacobs RC	3.50	6.00
187 Bob Dee	3.50	6.00
188 Tom Flores RC	15.00	30.00
189 Jack Larscheid	3.50	6.00
190 Dick Christy RC	3.50	6.00
191 Alan Miller RC	3.50	6.00
192 James Smith	3.50	6.00
193 Gerald Burch RC	3.50	6.00
194 Gene Prebola	3.50	6.00
195 Alan Goldstein	3.50	6.00
196 Don Manoukian RC	3.50	6.00
197 Jim Otto RC	40.00	75.00
198 Wayne Crow	3.50	6.00
199 Cotton Davidson RC	4.00	8.00
200 Randy Duncan RC	4.00	8.00
201 Jack Spikes	4.00	8.00
202 Johnny Robinson RC	7.50	15.00
203 Abner Haynes	7.50	15.00
204 Chris Burford	4.00	8.00
205 Bill Krisher	3.50	6.00
206 Marvin Terrell	3.50	6.00
207 Jimmy Harris	3.50	6.00
208 Mel Branch	4.00	8.00
209 Paul Miller	3.50	6.00
210 Al Dorow	3.50	6.00
211 Dick Jamieson	3.50	6.00
212 Pete Hart RC	3.50	6.00
213 Bill Shockley RC	3.50	6.00
214 Dewey Bohling RC	3.50	6.00
215 Don Maynard RC	40.00	80.00
216 Bob Mischak RC	3.50	6.00
217 Mike Hudock	3.50	6.00
218 Bob Reifsnyder	3.50	6.00
219 Tom Saidock	3.50	6.00
220 Sid Youngelman	12.00	20.00

1961 Fleer Magic Message Blue Inserts

This unattractive set contains 40 cards that were inserted in 1961 Fleer football wax packs. The cards are light blue in color and measure approximately 3" by 2 1/8". The fronts feature a question and a crude line drawing. For the answer, the collector is instructed to "Turn card and wet; when dry, wet again." A tag line at the bottom of the front indicates that the cards were printed by Business Service of Long Island, New York. The backs are blank, and the cards are numbered on the front in the lower right corner.

COMPLETE SET (40)	75.00	150.00
1 When was the first	2.00	4.00
2 Which school was	2.00	4.00
3 What famous coach was	2.00	4.00
4 Which college coach	2.00	4.00
5 What is meant by two	2.00	4.00
6 When was the only	2.00	4.00
7 What is a Sudden	2.00	4.00
8 What is the longest	2.00	4.00
9 What famous Colorado	2.00	4.00
10 What Michigan All-	3.00	6.00
11 The North-South game	2.00	4.00
12 The Army-Navy game has	2.00	4.00
13 What slugging major	2.00	4.00
14 What All-Americans were	2.00	4.00
15 Which team was called	2.00	4.00
16 When was the first	2.00	4.00
17 What is the record	2.00	4.00
18 What is the longest	2.00	4.00
19 Who was the first	2.00	4.00
20 Which team was the	2.00	4.00
21 Who was the first	2.00	4.00
22 When was the first	2.00	4.00
23 What is the longest	2.00	4.00
24 What is the origin of	2.00	4.00
25 What player was	3.00	6.00
26 What is the record	2.00	4.00
27 What player ran the	2.00	4.00
28 When was the first	2.00	4.00
29 When and by whom was	2.00	4.00
30 When was the forward	2.00	4.00
31 What was the first	2.00	4.00
32 When was the first	2.00	4.00
33 Where is the Football	2.00	4.00
34 Who were the Four	2.00	4.00
35 When was the first	2.00	4.00
36 Who holds the record	2.00	4.00
37 Who was known as the	3.00	6.00
38 Has the Rose Bowl	2.00	4.00
39 Which team featured	2.00	4.00
40 Where and when was the	3.00	6.00

1961 Fleer Wallet Pictures

These "cards" were issued as part of the 1961-62 issue of Complete Sports Pro-Football Illustrated magazine. The magazine section was entitled "Wallet Picture Album, photos courtesy of Frank H. Fleer Corp." The AFL and NFL sections were issued seperately and each photo inside the magazine was printed in black and white on newsprint stock. The pictures were to be cut from the pages and, once neatly cut, the photos measure roughly 2 1/2" by 3 3/8" with the backs including only the player's name and team name. The interior pages included 52-NFL players and 90-AFL players. Twelve additional photos were included as the back cover to the magazine and they measure roughly 2 3/8" by 2 3/8" when neatly cut out. Those twleve were printed on white stock with a light single color tone. Most of the photos were the same as used for the 1961 Fleer card set. We've arranged the unnumbered photos below alphabetically by team and then by player starting with the AFL (1-90) then the NFL (91-145).

COMPLETE SET (145)	125.00	300.00
1 Tommy Addison	.75	2.00
2 Jim Colclough	.75	2.00
3 Walt Cudzik	.75	2.00
4 Bob Dee	.75	2.00
5 Harry Jacobs	.75	2.00
6 Charley Leo	.75	2.00
7 Billy Lott	.75	2.00
8 Ross O'Hanley	.75	2.00
9 Tony Sardisco UER	.75	2.00
10 Butch Songin	.75	2.00
11 Bill Atkins	.75	2.00
12 Phil Blazer	.75	2.00
13 Wray Carlton	.75	2.00
14 Monte Crockett	.75	2.00
15 Elbert Dubenion	1.00	2.00
16 Willmer Fowler	.75	2.00
17 Gene Grabosky	.75	2.00
18 Richie Lucas	1.00	2.50
19 Archie Matsos	.75	2.00
20 Richard McCabe	.75	2.00
21 Dan McGrew UER	.75	2.00
22 Tom Rychlec	.75	2.00
23 Laverne Torczon	.75	2.00
24 Mack Yoho	.75	2.00
25 Mel Branch	.75	2.00
26 Chris Burford	.75	2.00
27 Cotton Davidson	.75	2.00
28 Randy Duncan	.75	2.00
29 Jimmy Harris	.75	2.00
30 E.J. Holub	.75	2.00
31 Bill Krisher	.75	2.00
32 Paul Miller	.75	2.00
33 Johnny Robinson	1.00	2.50
34 Jack Spikes	.75	2.00
35 Marvin Terrell	.75	2.00
36 Ken Adamson	.75	2.00
37 Al Carmichael	.75	2.00
38 Eldon Danenhauer	.75	2.00
39 Goose Gonsoulin	.75	2.00
40 Gordy Holz	.75	2.00
41 Carl Larpenter	.75	2.00
42 Bud McFadin	.75	2.00
43 Bob McNamara	.75	2.00
44 Dave Rolle	.75	2.00
45 Willie Smith	.75	2.00
46 Lionel Taylor	1.50	4.00
47 Frank Tripucka UER	1.50	4.00
48 Joe Young	.75	2.00
49 George Blanda	4.00	10.00
50 Doug Cline	.75	2.00
51 Don Floyd	.75	2.00
52 Bobby Gordon	.75	2.00
53 Bill Groman	.75	2.00
54 Al Jamison	.75	2.00
55 Jacky Lee	.75	2.00
56 Richard Michael	.75	2.00
57 Dennit Morris	.75	2.00
58 Jim Norton	.75	2.00
59 Dave Smith	.75	2.00
60 Bob White	.75	2.00
61 Dewey Bohling	.75	2.00
62 Pete Hart	.75	2.00
63 Mike Hudock	.75	2.00
64 Bob Mischak	.75	2.00
65 Sid Youngelman	.75	2.00
66 Gerald Burch	.75	2.00
67 Dick Christy	.75	2.00
68 Bob Coolbaugh	.75	2.00
69 Wayne Crow	.75	2.00
70 Don Deskins	.75	2.00
71 Tom Flores	1.50	4.00
72 Alan Goldstein	.75	2.00
73 Jack Larscheid	.75	2.00
74 Dan Manoukian	.75	2.00
75 Alan Miller UER	.75	2.00
76 Jim Otto	3.00	8.00
77 Charley Powell	.75	2.00
78 Gene Prebola	.75	2.00
79 Jim Smith RB	.75	2.00
80 Howard Clark	.75	2.00
81 Fred Cole	.75	2.00
82 Charlie Flowers	.75	2.00
83 Dick Harris	.75	2.00
84 Jack Kemp	6.00	15.00
85 Paul Lowe	1.00	2.50
86 Ron Mix	1.50	4.00
87 Don Norton	.75	2.00
88 Volney Peters	.75	2.00
89 Jim Sears	.75	2.00
90 Ernie Wright	1.00	2.50
91 Alan Ameche	1.00	2.50
92 Raymond Berry	3.00	8.00
93 Lenny Moore	2.50	6.00
94 Jim Mutscheller	.75	2.00
95 Ed Brown	1.00	2.50
96 Rick Casares	1.00	2.50
97 J.C. Caroline	.75	2.00
98 Willie Galimore	.75	2.00
99 Harlon Hill UER	.75	2.00
100 Bobby Mitchell	2.00	5.00
101 Gern Nagler	.75	2.00
102 Milt Plum	1.00	2.50
103 Ray Renfro	1.00	2.50
104 Billy Howton UER	1.00	2.50
105 Don Meredith	6.00	15.00
106 Howard Cassady	1.00	2.50
107 Gail Cogdill	.75	2.00
108 Dick Lane	1.50	4.00
109 Nick Pietrosante	.75	2.00
110 Paul Hornung	6.00	15.00
111 Tom Moore	1.00	2.50
112 Bart Starr	10.00	25.00
113 Jim Taylor	5.00	12.00
114 Les Richter	.75	2.00
115 Frank Ryan	1.00	2.50
116 Del Shofner	.75	2.00
117 Dick Haley UER	.75	2.00
118 Perry Richards	.75	2.00
119 Charley Conerly UER	2.00	5.00
120 Kyle Rote	1.00	2.50
121 Bill Barnes	.75	2.00
122 Chuck Bednarik	2.00	5.00
123 Clarence Peaks	.75	2.00
124 Pete Retzlaff	1.00	2.50
125 Bobby Walston	.75	2.00
126 Dean Derby	.75	2.00
127 John Henry Johnson	1.50	4.00
128 Bobby Layne	4.00	10.00
129 Jimmy Orr	1.00	2.50
130 Tom Tracy	1.00	2.50
131 Bobby Joe Conrad	.75	2.00
132 John David Crow	1.00	2.50

133 Mal Hammack .75 2.00
134 Sonny Randle .75 2.00
135 Bill Stacy UER .75 2.00
136 Dave Baker .75 2.00
137 John Brodie 3.00 8.00
138 Matt Hazeltine .75 2.00
139 Ray Norton .75 2.00
140 J.D.Smith RB .75 2.00
141 Bill Anderson .75 2.00
142 Don Bosseler .75 2.00
143 Ralph Guglielmi .75 2.00
144 John Olszewski .75 2.00
145 Joe Walton .75 2.00

1962 Fleer

The 1962 Fleer football set contains 88 standard-size cards featuring AFL players only. The set was issued in six-card nickel packs which came 24 packs to a box with a slab of bubble gum. Card numbering is alphabetical by team city. The card backs are printed in black and blue on a white card stock. Key Rookie Cards in this set are Gino Cappelletti, Charlie Hennigan, Ernie Ladd and Fred Williamson.

COMPLETE SET (88) 500.00 900.00
WRAPPER (5-CENT) 100.00 200.00
1 Billy Lott 8.00 16.00
2 Ron Burton 5.00 10.00
3 Gino Cappelletti RC 10.00 20.00
4 Babe Parilli 5.00 10.00
5 Jim Colclough 3.50 7.00
6 Tony Sardisco 3.50 7.00
7 Walt Cudzik 3.50 7.00
8 Bob Dee 3.50 7.00
9 Tommy Addison RC 4.00 8.00
10 Harry Jacobs 3.50 7.00
11 Ross O'Hanley 3.50 7.00
12 Art Baker 3.50 7.00
13 Johnny Green 3.50 7.00
14 Elbert Dubenion 5.00 10.00
15 Tom Rychlec 3.50 7.00
16 Billy Shaw RC 20.00 40.00
17 Ken Rice 3.50 7.00
18 Bill Atkins 3.50 7.00
19 Richie Lucas 4.00 8.00
20 Archie Matsos 3.50 7.00
21 Laverne Torczon 3.50 7.00
22 Warren Rabb RC UER 3.50 7.00
23 Jack Spikes 4.00 8.00
24 Cotton Davidson 4.00 8.00
25 Abner Haynes 7.50 15.00
26 Jimmy Saxton RC 3.50 7.00
27 Chris Burford 4.00 8.00
28 Bill Miller RC 3.50 7.00
29 Sherrill Headrick 4.00 8.00
30 E.J.Holub RC 4.00 8.00
31 Jerry Mays RC 5.00 10.00
32 Mel Branch 4.00 8.00
33 Paul Rochester RC 3.50 7.00
34 Frank Tripucka 5.00 10.00
35 Gene Mingo 3.50 7.00
36 Lionel Taylor 6.00 12.00
37 Ken Adamson 3.50 7.00
38 Eldon Danenhauer 3.50 7.00
39 Goose Gonsoulin 5.00 10.00
40 Gordy Holz 3.50 7.00
41 Bud McFadin 4.00 8.00
42 Jim Stinnette RC 3.50 7.00
43 Bob Hudson RC 3.50 7.00
44 George Herring 3.50 7.00
45 Charley Tolar RC 3.50 7.00
46 George Blanda 30.00 50.00
47 Billy Cannon 7.50 15.00
48 Charlie Hennigan RC 7.50 15.00
49 Bill Groman 3.50 7.00
50 Al Jamison 3.50 7.00
51 Tony Banfield 3.50 7.00
52 Jim Norton 3.50 7.00
53 Dennit Morris 3.50 7.00
54 Don Floyd 3.50 7.00
55 Ed Husmann UER RC 3.50 7.00
56 Robert Brooks RC 3.50 7.00
57 Al Dorow 3.50 7.00
58 Dick Christy 3.50 7.00
59 Don Maynard 30.00 50.00
60 Art Powell 5.00 10.00
61 Mike Hudock 3.50 7.00
62 Bill Mathis 4.00 8.00
63 Butch Songin 3.50 7.00
64 Larry Grantham 3.50 7.00
65 Nick Mumley RC 3.50 7.00
66 Tom Saidock 3.50 7.00
67 Alan Miller 3.50 7.00
68 Tom Flores 7.50 15.00
69 Bob Coolbaugh 3.50 7.00
70 George Fleming RC 3.50 7.00
71 Wayne Hawkins RC 4.00 8.00
72 Jim Otto 25.00 40.00
73 Wayne Crow 3.50 7.00
74 Fred Williamson RC 18.00 30.00
75 Tom Louderback RC 3.50 7.00
76 Volney Peters 3.50 7.00
77 Charley Powell RC 3.50 7.00
78 Don Norton 3.50 7.00
79 Jack Kemp 50.00 100.00
80 Paul Lowe 5.00 10.00
81 Dave Kocourek 3.50 7.00
82 Ron Mix 7.50 15.00
83 Ernie Wright 5.00 10.00
84 Dick Harris RC 3.50 7.00
85 Bill Hudson RC 3.50 7.00
86 Ernie Ladd RC 15.00 25.00
87 Earl Faison RC 4.00 8.00
88 Ron Nery 9.00 18.00

1963 Fleer

The 1963 Fleer football set of 88 standard-size cards features AFL players only. Card numbers is in team order. Card numbers 6 and 64 are more difficult to obtain than the other cards in the set; their shortage is believed to be attributable to their possible replacement on the printing sheet by the unnumbered checklist. The card backs are printed in red and black on a white card stock. The set price below does not include the checklist card. Cards with numbers divisible by four can be found with or without a red stripe on the bottom of the card back; it is thought that those without the red stripe are in lesser supply. Currently, there is no difference in value. The key Rookie Cards in this set are Lance Alworth, Nick Buoniconti, and Len Dawson.

COMPLETE SET (88) 1,200.00 1,800.00
WRAPPER (5-CENT) 60.00 120.00
1 Larry Garron RC 10.00 20.00
2 Babe Parilli 5.00 10.00
3 Ron Burton 6.00 12.00
4 Jim Colclough 4.00 8.00
4B Jim Colclough NS 4.00 8.00
5 Gino Cappelletti 6.00 12.00
6 Charles Long SP RC 45.00 80.00
7 Billy Neighbors RC 4.00 8.00
8 Dick Felt RC 4.00 8.00
8B Dick Felt NS RC 4.00 8.00
9 Tommy Addison 4.00 8.00
10 Nick Buoniconti RC 45.00 80.00
11 Larry Eisenhauer RC 4.00 8.00
12 Bill Mathis 4.00 8.00
12B Bill Mathis NS 4.00 8.00
13 Lee Grosscup RC 5.00 10.00
14 Dick Christy 4.00 8.00
15 Don Maynard 30.00 50.00
16 Alex Kroll RC 4.00 8.00
16B Alex Kroll NS RC 4.00 8.00
17 Bob Mischak 4.00 8.00
18 Dainard Paulson RC 4.00 8.00
19 Lee Riley 4.00 8.00
20 Larry Grantham 5.00 10.00
20B Larry Grantham NS 5.00 10.00
21 Hubert Bobo RC 4.00 8.00
22 Nick Mumley 4.00 8.00
23 Cookie Gilchrist RC 30.00 50.00
24 Jack Kemp 75.00 150.00
24B Jack Kemp NS 75.00 150.00
25 Wray Carlton 4.00 8.00
26 Elbert Dubenion 5.00 10.00
27 Ernie Warlick RC 5.00 10.00
28 Billy Shaw 7.50 15.00
28B Billy Shaw NS 7.50 15.00
29 Ken Rice 4.00 8.00
30 Booker Edgerson RC 4.00 8.00
31 Ray Abruzzese RC UER 4.00 8.00
(name misspelled Abbruzzese)
32 Mike Stratton RC 7.50 15.00
32B Mike Stratton NS RC 7.50 15.00
33 Tom Sestak RC 6.00 12.00
34 Charley Tolar 4.00 8.00
35 Dave Smith RB 4.00 8.00
36 George Blanda 30.00 50.00
36B George Blanda NS 30.00 50.00
37 Billy Cannon 7.50 15.00
38 Charlie Hennigan 5.00 10.00
39 Bob Talamini RC 4.00 8.00
40 Jim Norton 4.00 8.00
40B Jim Norton NS 4.00 8.00
41 Tony Banfield 4.00 8.00
42 Doug Cline 4.00 8.00
43 Don Floyd 4.00 8.00
44 Ed Husmann 4.00 8.00
44B Ed Husmann NS 4.00 8.00
45 Curtis McClinton RC 7.50 15.00
46 Jack Spikes 5.00 10.00
47 Len Dawson RC 150.00 250.00
48 Abner Haynes 7.50 15.00
48B Abner Haynes NS 7.50 15.00
49 Chris Burford 5.00 10.00
50 Fred Arbanas RC 6.00 12.00
51 Johnny Robinson 5.00 10.00
52 E.J. Holub 5.00 10.00
52B E.J. Holub NS 5.00 10.00
53 Sherrill Headrick 5.00 10.00
54 Mel Branch 5.00 10.00
55 Jerry Mays 5.00 10.00
56 Cotton Davidson 5.00 10.00
56B Cotton Davidson NS 5.00 10.00
57 Clem Daniels RC 10.00 20.00
58 Bo Roberson RC 5.00 10.00
59 Art Powell 6.00 12.00
60 Bob Coolbaugh 4.00 8.00
60B Bob Coolbaugh NS 4.00 8.00
61 Wayne Hawkins 4.00 8.00
62 Jim Otto 18.00 30.00
63 Fred Williamson 10.00 20.00
64 Bob Dougherty SP 60.00 120.00
64B Bob Dougherty SP NS 60.00 120.00
65 Dalva Allen RC 4.00 8.00
66 Chuck McMurtry RC 4.00 8.00
67 Gerry McDougall RC 4.00 8.00
68 Tobin Rote 5.00 10.00
68B Tobin Rote NS 5.00 10.00
69 Paul Lowe 6.00 12.00
70 Keith Lincoln RC 25.00 40.00
71 Dave Kocourek 4.00 8.00
72 Lance Alworth RC 125.00 250.00
72B Lance Alworth NS RC 125.00 250.00
73 Ron Mix 15.00 25.00
74 Charlie McNeil RC 4.00 8.00
75 Emil Karas RC 4.00 8.00
76 Ernie Ladd 10.00 20.00
76B Ernie Ladd NS 10.00 20.00
77 Earl Faison 4.00 8.00
78 Jim Stinnette 4.00 8.00
79 Frank Tripucka 6.00 12.00
80 Don Stone RC 4.00 8.00
80B Don Stone NS RC 4.00 8.00
81 Bob Scarpitto RC 4.00 8.00
82 Lionel Taylor 6.00 12.00
83 Jerry Tarr RC 4.00 8.00
84 Eldon Danenhauer 4.00 8.00
84B Eldon Danenhauer NS 4.00 8.00
85 Goose Gonsoulin 5.00 10.00
86 Jim Fraser RC 4.00 8.00
87 Chuck Gavin RC 4.00 8.00
88 Bud McFadin ! 10.00 20.00
88B Bud McFadin NS 10.00 20.00
NNO Checklist SP ! 250.00 350.00

1968 Fleer Big Signs

This set of 26 "Big Signs" was produced by Fleer. They are blank backed and measure approximately 7 3/4" by 11 1/2" with rounded corners. They are unnumbered so they are listed below alphabetically by team city name. They are credited at the bottom as 1968 in roman numerals, but in fact were probably issued several years later, perhaps as late as 1974. As another point of reference in dating the set, the New England Patriots changed their name from Boston in 1970. There were two distinct versions of this set, with each version including all 26 teams. The 1970 version was issued in a green box, while the 1974 version was issued in a brown box. Both boxes carry a 1968 copyright date; however, 1974 is generally considered to be the issue date of the second series. Though they are considerably different in design, the size of the collectibles is similar. The generic drawings (of a faceless player from each team) are in color with a white border. The set was licensed by NFL Properties so there are no players shown.

COMPLETE SET (26) 150.00 250.00
1 Atlanta Falcons 5.00 10.00
2 Baltimore Colts 5.00 10.00
3 Buffalo Bills 5.00 10.00
4 Chicago Bears 6.00 12.00
5 Cincinnati Bengals 5.00 10.00
6 Cleveland Browns 5.00 10.00
7 Dallas Cowboys 10.00 20.00
8 Denver Broncos 5.00 10.00
9 Detroit Lions 5.00 10.00
10 Green Bay Packers 10.00 20.00
11 Houston Oilers 5.00 10.00
12 Kansas City Chiefs 5.00 10.00
13 Los Angeles Rams 5.00 10.00
14 Miami Dolphins 7.50 15.00
15 Minnesota Vikings 5.00 10.00
16 New England Patriots 5.00 10.00
17 New Orleans Saints 5.00 10.00
18 New York Giants 5.00 10.00
19 New York Jets 5.00 10.00
20 Oakland Raiders 10.00 20.00
21 Philadelphia Eagles 5.00 10.00
22 Pittsburgh Steelers 7.50 15.00
23 St. Louis Cardinals 5.00 10.00
24 San Diego Chargers 5.00 10.00
25 San Francisco 49ers 7.50 15.00
26 Washington Redskins 7.50 15.00

1972 Fleer Quiz

The 28 cards in this set measure approximately 2 1/2" by 4" and feature three questions and (upside down) answers about football players and events. The cards were issued one per pack with Fleer cloth team patches. The words "Official Football Quiz" are printed at the top and are accented by the NFL logo. The backs are blank. The cards are numbered in the lower right hand corner.

COMPLETE SET (28) 25.00 50.00
COMMON CARD (1-28) 1.00 2.00

1972-73 Fleer Cloth Patches

These cloth stickers were issued 3-per pack as a stand alone product, inserted one per pack in 1972 Fleer Quiz, and two per pack in 1973 Fleer Pro Scouting Report. Each blankbacked sticker includes one small team name sticker at the top and a larger team helmet or team logo at the bottom. We've catalogued and priced the stickers as pairs according to the smaller team name sticker first and the larger sticker second. Many of the stickers were identical for both years (and all contain a 1972 copyright date) except for the conference champions stickers as noted below. Variations on some sticker combinations do exist and we have cataloged all known versions below. The 1972-73 helmet stickers can be differentiated from the 1974-75 listings (those also feature a 1972 copyright year) by a single-bar face mask design instead of dual-bar. The glue used for these stickers tends to break down over time and will cause spots to bleed through to the fronts and separation of the sticker from the backing is quite common, therefore they are extremely condition sensitive.

COMPLETE SET (64) 125.00 250.00
1 Bears Name 4.00 8.00
Cowboys Small Helmet
2 Bears Name 3.00 6.00
Jets helmet
3 Bengals Name 2.50 5.00
Cardinals Helmet
4 Bengals Name 3.00 6.00
Giants Logo Blue
5A Bills Name 4.00 10.00
Chiefs Logo ERR
5B Bills Name 2.50 5.00
Chiefs Logo Gold
6 Bills Name 4.00 8.00
Cowboys Large Helmet
7 Broncos Name 2.50 5.00
Colts Helmet
8 Broncos Name 2.50 5.00
Patriots Logo
9 Broncos Name 4.00 8.00
Redskins Helmet
10 Browns Name 2.50 5.00
Chargers Helmet
11 Browns Name 2.50 5.00
Saints Helmet
12 Cardinals Name Gold 2.50 5.00
Bengals Logo
13 Cardinals Name 4.00 8.00
Raiders Helmet
14A Chargers Name Lt Blue 3.00 6.00
Bears Helmet White C
14B Chargers Name Lt Blue 3.00 6.00
Bears Helmet Orange C
15 Chiefs Name 2.50 5.00
Browns Helmet
16 Chiefs Name 2.50 5.00
NFL Logo
17 Chiefs Name 2.50 5.00
Rams Helmet
18 Colts Name 2.50 5.00
Saints Logo
19 Colts Name 4.00 8.00
Steelers Logo
20 Cowboys Name 4.00 8.00
Broncos Helmet
21A Cowboys Name 4.00 8.00
Dolphins Helmet Print
21B Cowboys Name 4.00 8.00
Dolphins Helmet Script
22 Dolphins Name 3.00 6.00
Vikings Helmet
23 Eagles Name 2.50 5.00
Chiefs Helmet
24 Eagles Name 4.00 8.00
Steelers Helmet
25 Falcons Name 3.00 6.00
Browns Logo
26 Falcons Name 3.00 6.00
Giants Logo Red
27 Falcons Name 2.50 5.00
Oilers Helmet
28 49ers Name 3.00 6.00
Colts Logo
29 49ers Name 4.00 8.00
Packers Logo
30 Giants Name Red 3.00 6.00
Bills Logo
31 Giants Name Blue 2.50 5.00
Lions Logo
32 Jets Name 4.00 8.00
Broncos Logo
33 Jets Name 2.50 5.00
Falcons Logo
34 Lions Name 2.50 5.00
Oilers Logo
35 Lions Name 2.50 5.00
Rams Logo Y
36 Lions Name 2.50 5.00
Rams Logo W
37 Oilers Name 2.50 5.00
Cardinals Logo
38 Oilers Name 2.50 5.00
Eagles Helmet
39 Packers Name 3.00 6.00
Chargers Logo Lt Blue
40 Packers Name 3.00 6.00
Eagles Logo
41 Patriots Name 2.50 5.00
Falcons Helmet
42 Patriots Name 3.00 6.00
Jets Logo
43 Raiders Name 4.00 8.00
Redskins Logo Gold
44 Raiders Name 3.00 6.00
Giants Helmet
45A Rams Name 4.00 8.00
Dolphins Logo Print

45B Rams Name Dolphins Logo Script	4.00	8.00
46 Rams Name/49ers Logo	4.00	8.00
47 Redskins Name Bengals Helmet	2.50	5.00
48 Redskins Name/49ers Helmet	4.00	8.00
49 Saints Name Lions Helmet	2.50	5.00
50 Saints Name Raiders Logo	4.00	8.00
51 Steelers Name Packers Helmet	4.00	8.00
52 Steelers Name Rams Helmet	3.00	6.00
53 Steelers Name Vikings Logo	3.00	6.00
54 Vikings Name Bears Logo	3.00	6.00
55 Vikings Name Bills Helmet	3.00	6.00
56 Vikings Name Patriots Helmet	2.50	5.00
57 AFC Champ Dolphins NFL Logo	4.00	8.00
58 AFC Conference NFL Logo	4.00	8.00
59 NFC Champ Redskins NFL Logo	4.00	8.00
60 NFC Conference NFL Logo	4.00	8.00

1973 Fleer Pro Bowl Scouting Report

The 14 cards in this set measure approximately 2 1/2" by 4" and feature an explanation of the ideal size, responsibilities, and assignments of each player on the team. Each card shows a different position. Color artwork illustrates examples of how a player might appear. A diagram shows the position on the field. The words "AFC-NFC Pro Bowl Scouting Cards" are printed at the top and are accented by the NFL logo and underscored by a blue stripe. The backs are blank. The cards are unnumbered and checklisted below in alphabetical order. The cards came one per pack with two cloth football logo patches that are dated 1972. It appears that the same cloth patches were sold each year from 1972 to 1975. In the first year, they were sold alone in packs, while in the following years, they were sold again through packs with the Scouting Report and Hall of Fame issues, respectively.

COMPLETE SET (14)	20.00	40.00
1 Center	1.50	3.00
2 Cornerback	1.50	3.00
3 Defensive End	1.50	3.00
4 Defensive Tackle	1.50	3.00
5 Guard	1.50	3.00
6 Kicker	1.50	3.00
7 Linebacker	1.50	3.00
8 Offensive Tackle	1.50	3.00
9 Punter	1.50	3.00
10 Quarterback	1.50	3.00
11 Running Back	1.50	3.00
12 Safety	1.50	3.00
13 Tight End	1.50	3.00
14 Wide Receiver	1.50	3.00

1974 Fleer Big Signs

This set of 26 "Big Signs" was produced by Fleer in 1974. They are blank backed and measure approximately 7 3/4" by 11 1/2" with rounded corners. They are unnumbered so they are listed below alphabetically by team city name. They are credited at the bottom as 1968 in roman numerals, but in fact were probably issued several years later, perhaps as late as 1974. As another point of reference in dating the set, the New England Patriots changed their name from Boston in 1970. There were two distinct versions of this set, with each version including all 26 teams. The 1968 version was issued in a green box, while the 1974 version was issued in a brown box. Both boxes carry a 1968 copyright date; however, 1974 is generally considered to be the issue date of this second series. Though they are considerably different in design, the size of the collectibles is similar. The generic drawings (of a faceless player from each team) are in color with a white border. The set was licensed by NFL Properties so there are no players identifiably shown.

COMPLETE SET (26)	60.00	100.00
1 Atlanta Falcons	2.00	4.00
2 Baltimore Colts	2.00	4.00
3 Buffalo Bills	2.00	4.00
4 Chicago Bears	2.00	4.00
5 Cincinnati Bengals	2.00	4.00
6 Cleveland Browns	2.00	4.00
7 Dallas Cowboys	4.00	8.00
8 Denver Broncos	2.00	4.00
9 Detroit Lions	2.00	4.00
10 Green Bay Packers	4.00	8.00
11 Houston Oilers	2.00	4.00
12 Kansas City Chiefs	2.00	4.00
13 Los Angeles Rams	2.00	4.00
14 Miami Dolphins	3.00	6.00
15 Minnesota Vikings	2.00	4.00
16 New England Patriots	2.00	4.00
17 New Orleans Saints	2.00	4.00
18 New York Giants	2.00	4.00
19 New York Jets	2.00	4.00
20 Oakland Raiders	4.00	8.00
21 Philadelphia Eagles	2.00	4.00
22 Pittsburgh Steelers	3.00	6.00
23 St. Louis Cardinals	2.00	4.00
24 San Diego Chargers	2.00	4.00
25 San Francisco 49ers	3.00	6.00
26 Washington Redskins	3.00	6.00

1974 Fleer Hall of Fame

The 1974 Fleer Hall of Fame football card set contains 50 players inducted into the Pro Football Hall of Fame in Canton, Ohio. The cards measure approximately 2 1/2" by 4". The fronts feature black and white photos, white borders, and a cartoon head of a football player flanked by the words "The Immortal Roll." The backs contain biographical data and a stylized Pro Football Hall of Fame logo. The cards are unnumbered and can be distinguished from cards of the 1975 Fleer Hall of Fame set by this lack of numbering as well as the white border on the fronts. The cards are arranged and numbered below alphabetically by player's name for convenience. The cards were originally issued in wax packs with one Hall of Fame card and two cloth team logo stickers.

COMPLETE SET (50)	35.00	70.00
1 Cliff Battles	.50	1.25
2 Sammy Baugh	1.50	3.00
3 Chuck Bednarik	.75	1.50
4 Bert Bell COMM OWN	.40	1.00
5 Paul Brown CO OWN FOUND	1.00	2.00
6 Joe Carr PRES	.40	1.00
7 Guy Chamberlin	.40	1.00
8 Dutch Clark	.50	1.25
9 Jimmy Conzelman	.40	1.00
10 Art Donovan	.75	1.50
11 Paddy Driscoll	.40	1.00
12 Bill Dudley	.50	1.25
13 Dan Fortmann	.40	1.00
14 Otto Graham	1.50	3.00
15 Red Grange	2.00	4.00
16 George Halas CO OWN	1.00	2.00
17 Mel Hein	.40	1.00
18 Fats Henry	.40	1.00
19 Bill Hewitt	.40	1.00
20 Clarke Hinkle	.40	1.00
21 Elroy Hirsch	.75	1.50
22 Robert(Cal) Hubbard	.40	1.00
23 Lamar Hunt OWN FOUNDER	.40	1.00
24 Don Hutson	.50	1.25
25 Earl Lambeau CO	.40	1.00
26 Bobby Layne	1.25	2.50
27 Vince Lombardi CO	2.00	4.00
28 Sid Luckman	1.00	2.00
29 Gino Marchetti	.50	1.25
30 Ollie Matson	.75	1.50
31 George McAfee	.50	1.25
32 Hugh McElhenny	.75	1.50
33 Johnny Blood McNally	.40	1.00
34 Marion Motley	.75	1.50
35 Bronko Nagurski	1.25	2.50
36 Ernie Nevers	.50	1.25
37 Leo Nomellini	.50	1.25
38 Steve Owen CO	.40	1.00
39 Joe Perry	.75	1.50
40 Pete Pihos	.50	1.25
41 Andy Robustelli	.75	1.50
42 Ken Strong	.50	1.25
43 Jim Thorpe	2.00	4.00
44 Y.A. Tittle	1.25	2.50
45 Charley Trippi	.50	1.25
46 Emlen Tunnell	.50	1.25
47 Bulldog Turner	.75	1.50
48 Norm Van Brocklin	1.00	2.00
49 Steve Van Buren	.75	1.50
50 Bob Waterfield	1.00	2.00

1974-75 Fleer Cloth Patches

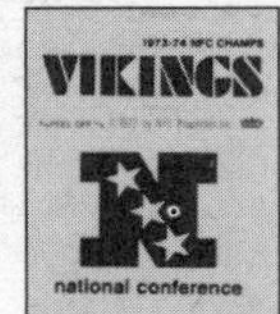

These cloth stickers were inserted one per pack in 1974 and 1975 Fleer Hall of Fame packs although each includes a 1972 copyright year on the fronts. The blankbacked stickers include one small team name sticker at the top and a larger team helmet or team logo at the bottom. We've catalogued and priced the stickers as pairs according to the smaller team name sticker first and the larger sticker second. Most of the stickers were nearly identical for both years except that the 1974 issue features no trademark (TM) notation on the fronts while the 1975 stickers include two trademark (TM) symbols. They are also very similar to the 1972-73 stickers and are often confused with them due to the 1972 copyright year printed on the fronts. However, the helmet stickers can be differentiated from the 1972-73 listings by the double-bar face mask design instead of single-bar. Most of the 1974 team logo stickers cannot be differentiated from the 1972-73 logo stickers and therefore are not listed below. However, the 1975 team logo stickers are priced below (marked with an *) since they do feature the trademark (TM) symbol distinction on the logo sticker portion. The glue used for these stickers tends to break down over time and will cause spots to bleed through to the fronts and separation of the sticker from the backing is quite common, therefore they are extremely condition sensitive.

COMPLETE SET (62)	125.00	250.00
1 Bears Name Cowboys Small Helmet	4.00	8.00
2 Bears Name Jets helmet	3.00	6.00
3 Bengals Name Cardinals Helmet	2.50	5.00
4 Bengals Name Giants Logo TM *	3.00	6.00
5A Bills Name Chiefs Logo Yellow No TM	2.50	5.00
5B Bills Name Chiefs Logo Yellow TM	2.50	5.00
6 Bills Name Cowboys Large Helmet	4.00	8.00
7 Broncos Name Colts Helmet	2.50	5.00
8 Broncos Name Patriots Logo *	2.50	5.00
9 Broncos Name Redskins Helmet	4.00	8.00
10 Browns Name Chargers Helmet	2.50	5.00
11 Browns Name Saints Helmet	2.50	5.00
12A Cardinals Name Yell No TM Bengals Logo	2.50	5.00
12B Cardinals Name Yellow TM Bengals Logo	2.50	5.00
13 Cardinals Name Raiders Helmet	4.00	8.00
14 Chargers Name Dark Blue Bears Helmet Orange C	3.00	6.00
15 Chiefs Name Browns Helmet	2.50	5.00
16 Chiefs Name NFL Logo *	2.50	5.00
17 Colts Name Saints Logo *	2.50	5.00
18 Colts Name Steelers Logo *	4.00	8.00
19 Cowboys Name Broncos Helmet	4.00	8.00
20 Cowboys Name Dolphins Helmet	4.00	8.00
21 Dolphins Name Vikings Helmet	3.00	6.00
22 Eagles Name Chiefs Helmet	2.50	5.00
23 Eagles Name Steelers Helmet	4.00	8.00
24 Falcons Name Browns Logo *	3.00	6.00
25 Falcons Name Giants Logo *	3.00	6.00
26 Falcons Name Oilers Helmet	2.50	5.00
27 49ers Name Colts Logo *	3.00	6.00
28 49ers Name Packers Logo *	4.00	8.00
29 Giants Name Bills Logo *	3.00	6.00
30 Giants Name Lions Logo *	2.50	5.00
31 Jets Name Broncos Logo *	4.00	8.00
32 Jets Name Falcons Logo *	2.50	5.00
33 Lions Name Oilers Logo *	2.50	5.00
34 Lions Name Rams Logo Y	2.50	5.00
35 Oilers Name Cardinals Logo *	2.50	5.00
36 Oilers Name Eagles Helmet	2.50	5.00
37A Packers Name Chargers Logo dark blue No TM	3.00	6.00
37B Packers Name/Chargers Logo *	3.00	6.00
38 Packers Name Eagles Logo *	3.00	6.00
39 Patriots Name Falcons Helmet	2.50	5.00
40 Patriots Name Jets Logo *	3.00	6.00
41A Raiders Name Redskins Logo Yellow TM	4.00	8.00
41B Raiders Name/Redskins Logo *	4.00	8.00
42 Raiders Name Giants Helmet	3.00	6.00
43 Rams Name Dolphins Logo *	4.00	8.00
44 Rams Name/49ers Logo *	4.00	8.00
45 Redskins Name Bengals Helmet	2.50	5.00
46 Redskins Name/49ers Helmet	4.00	8.00
47 Saints Name Lions Helmet	2.50	5.00
48 Saints Name Raiders Logo *	4.00	8.00
49 Steelers Name Packers Helmet	4.00	8.00
50 Steelers Name Rams Helmet	3.00	6.00
51 Steelers Name Vikings Logo *	3.00	6.00
52 Vikings Name Bears Logo *	3.00	6.00
53 Vikings Name Bills Helmet	3.00	6.00
54 Vikings Name Patriots Helmet	2.50	5.00
55 AFC Conference AFC Logo	4.00	8.00
56 AFC Conference AFC Logo	4.00	8.00
57 NFC Conference/NFC Logo	4.00	8.00
58 NFC Conference NFC Logo	4.00	8.00

1975 Fleer Hall of Fame

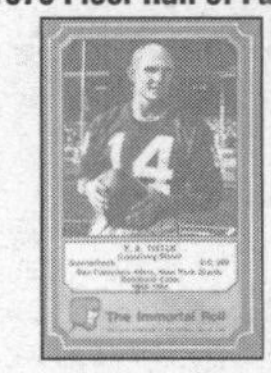

The 1975 Fleer Hall of Fame football card set contains 84 cards. The cards measure 2 1/2" by 4". Except for the change in border color from white to brown and the different set numbering contained on the backs of the cards, fifty of the cards in this set are very similar to the cards in the 1974 Fleer set. Thirty-four additional cards have been added to this set in comparison to the 1974 set. These cards are numbered and were issued in wax packs with cloth team logo stickers.

COMPLETE SET (84)	40.00	80.00
1 Jim Thorpe	1.50	3.00
2 Cliff Battles	.40	1.00
3 Bronko Nagurski	1.00	2.00
4 Red Grange	1.50	3.00
5 Guy Chamberlin	.30	.75
6 Joe Carr PRES	.30	.75
7 George Halas CO/OWN//FOUNDER	.75	1.50
8 Jimmy Conzelman	.30	.75
9 George McAfee	.40	1.00
10 Clarke Hinkle	.30	.75
11 Paddy Driscoll	.30	.75
12 Mel Hein	.30	.75
13 Johnny Blood McNally	.30	.75
14 Dutch Clark	.40	1.00
15 Steve Owen CO	.30	.75
16 Bill Hewitt	.30	.75
17 Cal Hubbard	.30	.75
18 Don Hutson	.63	1.25
19 Ernie Nevers	.40	1.00
20 Dan Fortmann	.30	.75
21 Ken Strong	.40	1.00
22 Chuck Bednarik	.63	1.25
23 Bert Bell COMM/OWN	.30	.75
24 Paul Brown CO/OWN/FOUND	.75	1.50
25 Art Donovan	.63	1.25
26 Bill Dudley	.40	1.00
27 Otto Graham	1.00	2.00
28 Fats Henry	.40	1.00
29 Elroy Hirsch	.63	1.25
30 Lamar Hunt OWN/FOUND	.30	.75
31 Curly Lambeau CO/OWN/FOUNDER	.30	.75
32 Vince Lombardi CO	1.50	3.00
33 Sid Luckman	.75	1.50
34 Gino Marchetti	.40	1.00
35 Ollie Matson	.63	1.25
36 Hugh McElhenny	.63	1.25
37 Marion Motley	.40	1.00
38 Leo Nomellini	.40	1.00
39 Joe Perry	.63	1.25
40 Andy Robustelli	.40	1.00
41 Pete Pihos	.40	1.00
42 Y.A. Tittle	1.00	2.00
43 Charley Trippi	.40	1.00
44 Emlen Tunnell	.40	1.00
45 Bulldog Turner	.63	1.25
46 Norm Van Brocklin	.75	1.50
47 Steve Van Buren	.63	1.25
48 Bob Waterfield	.75	1.50
49 Bobby Layne	1.00	2.00
50 Sammy Baugh	1.25	2.50
51 Joe Guyon	.30	.75
52 Roy(Link) Lyman	.30	.75
53 George Trafton	.30	.75
54 Turk Edwards	.30	.75
55 Ed Healey	.30	.75
56 Mike Michalske	.30	.75
57 Alex Wojciechowicz	.30	.75
58 Dante Lavelli	.63	1.25
59 George Connor	.40	1.00
60 Wayne Millner	.30	.75
61 Jack Christiansen	.30	.75
62 Roosevelt Brown	.30	.75
63 Joe Stydahar	.30	.75
64 Ernie Stautner	.40	1.00

Card	Low	High
65 Jim Parker	.40	1.00
66 Raymond Berry	.63	1.25
67 George Preston Marshall OWN/FOUND	.30	.75
68 Clarence(Ace) Parker	.30	.75
69 Greasy Neale CO	.30	.75
70 Tim Mara OWN/FOUND	.30	.75
71 Hugh (Shorty) Ray OFF	.30	.75
72 Tom Fears	.40	1.00
73 Arnie Herber	.30	.75
74 Walt Kiesling	.30	.75
75 Frank (Bruiser) Kinard	.30	.75
76 Tony Canadeo	.30	.75
77 Bill George	.30	.75
78 Art Rooney FOUND/OWN/ADMIN	.30	.75
79 Joe Schmidt	.40	1.00
80 Dan Reeves OWN	.30	.75
81 Lou Groza	.63	1.25
82 Charles W. Bidwill OWN	.30	.75
83 Lenny Moore	.63	1.25
84 Dick (Night Train) Lane	.40	1.00

1976 Fleer Cloth Patches

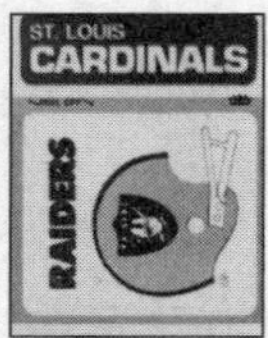

These cloth stickers were sold as a stand alone product and do not feature any copyright year on them. The blankbacked stickers include one small team name sticker at the top and a larger team helmet or team logo at the bottom. We've catalogued and priced the stickers as pairs according to the smaller team name sticker first and the larger sticker second. Many of the stickers can be confused with the 1972-73 and 1974-75 sets, but this year has no date designation. The glue used for these stickers tends to break down over time and will cause spots to bleed through to the fronts and separation of the sticker from the backing is quite common, therefore they are extremely condition sensitive.

Card	Low	High
1 Bears Name Cowboys Small Helmet	3.00	6.00
2 Bears Name Jets helmet	2.50	5.00
3 Bengals Name Cardinals Helmet	2.00	4.00
4 Bengals Name Giants Logo	2.50	5.00
5 Bills Name Chiefs Logo	2.00	4.00
6 Bills Name Cowboys Large Helmet	3.00	6.00
7 Broncos Name Colts Helmet	2.00	4.00
8 Broncos Name Patriots Logo	2.00	4.00
9 Broncos Name Redskins Helmet	3.00	6.00
10 Browns Name Chargers Helmet	2.00	4.00
11 Browns Name Saints Helmet	2.00	4.00
12 Buccaneers Name Seahawks Helmet	2.00	4.00
13 Buccaneers Name Seahawks Logo	2.00	4.00
14 Cardinals Name Bengals Logo	2.00	4.00
15 Cardinals Name Raiders Helmet	3.00	6.00
16 Chargers Name Bears Helmet	2.50	5.00
17 Chiefs Name Browns Helmet	2.50	5.00
18 Colts Name Saints Logo	2.00	4.00
19 Colts Name Steelers Logo	3.00	6.00
20 Cowboys Name Broncos Helmet	3.00	6.00
21 Cowboys Name Dolphins Helmet	3.00	6.00
22 Dolphins Name Vikings Logo	2.50	5.00
23 Eagles Name Chiefs Helmet	2.00	4.00
24 Eagles Name Steelers Helmet	3.00	6.00
25 Falcons Name Browns Logo	2.50	5.00
26 Falcons Name Oilers Helmet	2.00	4.00
27 49ers Name Colts Logo	2.50	5.00
28 49ers Name Packers Logo	3.00	6.00
29 Giants Name Bills Logo	2.50	5.00
30 Giants Name Lions Logo	2.00	4.00
31 Jets Name Broncos Logo	3.00	6.00
32 Jets Name Falcons Logo	2.00	4.00
33 Lions Name Oilers Helmet	2.00	4.00
34 Lions Name Rams Logo	2.00	4.00
35 Oilers Name Cardinals Logo	2.00	4.00
36 Oilers Name Eagles Helmet	2.00	4.00
37 Packers Name Chargers Logo	2.50	5.00
38 Packers Name Eagles Logo	2.50	5.00
39 Patriots Name Falcons Helmet	2.00	4.00
40 Patriots Name Jets Logo	2.50	5.00
41 Raiders Name Redskins Logo	3.00	6.00
42 Raiders Name Giants Helmet	2.50	5.00
43 Rams Name Dolphins Logo	3.00	6.00
44 Rams Name/49ers Logo	3.00	6.00
45 Redskins Name Bengals Helmet	2.00	4.00
46 Redskins Name/49ers Helmet	3.00	6.00
47 Saints Name Lions Helmet	2.00	4.00
48 Seahawks Name Buccaneers Helmet	2.00	4.00
49 Saints Name Raiders Logo	3.00	6.00
50 Seahawks Name Buccaneers Logo	2.00	4.00
51 Steelers Name Packers Helmet	3.00	6.00
52 Steelers Name Rams Helmet	2.50	5.00
53 Steelers Name Vikings Logo	2.50	5.00
54 Vikings Name Bears Logo	2.50	5.00
55 Vikings Name Bills Helmet	2.50	5.00
56 Vikings Name Patriots Helmet	2.00	4.00

1976 Fleer Hi Gloss Patches

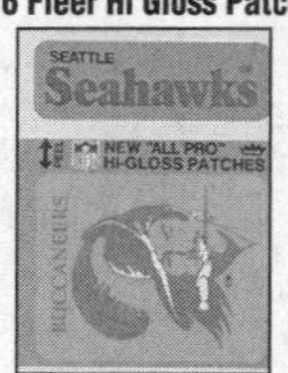

Fleer issued these helmet and logo stickers in 1976 as a separate product packaged in its own wrapper with two Hi Gloss paper stickers and one Cloth Patch in each pack. Each card is blankbacked and features a small team name sticker at the top and a larger logo or helmet sticker at the bottom. We've cataloged the set in order by the team name on top. Note that no year of issue was printed on the stickers.

Card	Low	High
COMPLETE SET (56)	125.00	225.00
*CLOTH VERSION: .5X TO 1.2X		
1 Bears Name Cowboys Small Helmet	3.00	6.00
2 Bears Name Jets helmet	2.50	5.00
3 Bengals Name Cardinals Helmet	2.00	4.00
4 Bengals Name Giants Logo	2.50	5.00
5 Bills Name Chiefs Logo	2.00	4.00
6 Bills Name Cowboys Large Helmet	3.00	6.00
7 Broncos Name Colts Helmet	2.00	4.00
8 Broncos Name Patriots Logo	2.00	4.00
9 Broncos Name Redskins Helmet	3.00	6.00
10 Browns Name Chargers Helmet	2.00	4.00
11 Browns Name Saints Helmet	2.00	4.00
12 Buccaneers Name Seahawks Helmet	2.00	4.00
13 Buccaneers Name Seahawks Logo	2.00	4.00
14 Cardinals Name Bengals Logo	2.00	4.00
15 Cardinals Name Raiders Helmet	3.00	6.00
16 Chargers Name Bears Helmet	2.50	5.00
17 Chiefs Name Browns Helmet	2.50	5.00
18 Colts Name Saints Logo	2.00	4.00
19 Colts Name Steelers Logo	3.00	6.00
20 Cowboys Name Broncos Helmet	3.00	6.00
21 Cowboys Name Dolphins Helmet	3.00	6.00
22 Dolphins Name Vikings Logo	2.50	5.00
23 Eagles Name Chiefs Helmet	2.00	4.00
24 Eagles Name Steelers Helmet	3.00	6.00
25 Falcons Name Browns Logo	2.50	5.00
26 Falcons Name Oilers Helmet	2.00	4.00
27 49ers Name Colts Logo	2.50	5.00
28 49ers Name Packers Logo	3.00	6.00
29 Giants Name Bills Logo	2.50	5.00
30 Giants Name Lions Logo	2.00	4.00
31 Jets Name Broncos Logo	3.00	6.00
32 Jets Name Falcons Logo	2.00	4.00
33 Lions Name Oilers Helmet	2.00	4.00
34 Lions Name Rams Logo	2.00	4.00
35 Oilers Name Cardinals Logo	2.00	4.00
36 Oilers Name Eagles Helmet	2.00	4.00
37 Packers Name Chargers Logo	2.50	5.00
38 Packers Name Eagles Logo	2.50	5.00
39 Patriots Name Falcons Helmet	2.00	4.00
40 Patriots Name Jets Logo	2.50	5.00
41 Raiders Name Giants Helmet	2.50	5.00
42 Raiders Name Redskins Logo	3.00	6.00
43 Rams Name Dolphins Logo	3.00	6.00
44 Rams Name/49ers Logo	3.00	6.00
45 Redskins Name Bengals Helmet	2.00	4.00
46 Redskins Name/49ers Helmet	3.00	6.00
47 Saints Name Lions Helmet	2.00	4.00
48 Saints Name Raiders Logo	3.00	6.00
49 Seahawks Name Buccaneers Helmet	2.00	4.00
50 Seahawks Name Buccaneers Logo	2.00	4.00
51 Steelers Name Packers Helmet	3.00	6.00
52 Steelers Name Rams Helmet	2.50	5.00
53 Steelers Name Vikings Logo	2.50	5.00
54 Vikings Name Bears Logo	2.50	5.00
55 Vikings Name Bills Helmet	2.50	5.00
56 Vikings Name Patriots Helmet	2.00	4.00

1976 Fleer Team Action

This 66-card standard-size set contains cards picturing action scenes with two cards for every NFL team and then a card for each previous Super Bowl. The first card in each team pair, i.e., the odd-numbered card, is an offensive card; the even-numbered cards are defensive scenes. Cards have a white border with a red outline on the front; the backs are printed with black ink on white cardboard stock with a light blue NFL emblem superimposed in the middle of the write-up on the back of the card. These cards are actually stickers as they may be peeled and stuck. The instructions on the back of the sticker say, "For use as sticker, bend corner and peel." The cards were issued in four-card packs with no inserts, unlike earlier Fleer football issues.

Card	Low	High
COMPLETE SET (66)	300.00	600.00
1 Baltimore Colts	4.50	9.00
2 Baltimore Colts	4.00	8.00
3 Buffalo Bills	4.00	8.00
4 Buffalo Bills	4.00	8.00
5 Cincinnati Bengals	4.00	8.00
6 Cincinnati Bengals	6.00	12.00
7 Cleveland Browns	4.00	8.00
8 Cleveland Browns	4.00	8.00
9 Denver Broncos	4.00	8.00
10 Denver Broncos	4.00	8.00
11 Houston Oilers	5.00	10.00
12 Houston Oilers	6.00	12.00
13 Kansas City Chiefs	4.00	8.00
14 Kansas City Chiefs	4.00	8.00
15 Miami Dolphins	6.00	12.00
16 Miami Dolphins	5.00	10.00
17 New England Patriots	4.00	8.00
18 New England Patriots	4.00	8.00
19 New York Jets	7.50	15.00
20 New York Jets	6.00	12.00
21 Oakland Raiders	5.00	10.00
22 Oakland Raiders	5.00	10.00
23 Pittsburgh Steelers	7.50	15.00
24 Pittsburgh Steelers	6.00	12.00
25 San Diego Chargers	4.00	8.00
26 San Diego Chargers	4.00	8.00
27 Tampa Bay Buccaneers	4.00	8.00
28 Tampa Bay Buccaneers	4.00	8.00
29 Atlanta Falcons	4.00	8.00
30 Atlanta Falcons	4.00	8.00
31 Chicago Bears	4.00	8.00
32 Chicago Bears	4.00	8.00
33 Dallas Cowboys	5.00	10.00
34 Dallas Cowboys	5.00	10.00
35 Detroit Lions	4.00	8.00
36 Detroit Lions	4.00	8.00
37 Green Bay Packers	4.00	8.00
38 Green Bay Packers	4.00	8.00
39 Los Angeles Rams	4.00	8.00
40 Los Angeles Rams	4.00	8.00
41 Minnesota Vikings	6.00	12.00
42 Minnesota Vikings	4.00	8.00
43 New York Giants	4.00	8.00
44 New York Giants	4.00	8.00
45 New Orleans Saints	5.00	10.00
46 New Orleans Saints	4.00	8.00
47 Philadelphia Eagles	4.00	8.00
48 Philadelphia Eagles	4.00	8.00
49 San Francisco 49ers	4.00	8.00
50 San Francisco 49ers	4.00	8.00
51 St. Louis Cardinals	5.00	10.00
52 St. Louis Cardinals	4.00	8.00
53 Seattle Seahawks	4.00	8.00
54 Seattle Seahawks	4.00	8.00
55 Washington Redskins	5.00	10.00
56 Washington Redskins	4.00	8.00
57 Super Bowl I	6.00	12.00
58 Super Bowl II	6.00	12.00
59 Super Bowl III	6.00	12.00
60 Super Bowl IV	6.00	12.00
61 Super Bowl V	6.00	12.00
62 Super Bowl VI	10.00	20.00
63 Super Bowl VII	7.50	15.00
64 Super Bowl VIII	7.50	15.00
65 Super Bowl IX	6.00	12.00
66 Super Bowl X	25.00	40.00

1977 Fleer Team Action

The 1977 Fleer Teams in Action football set contains 67 standard-size cards depicting action scenes. There are two cards for each NFL team and one card for each Super Bowl. The first card in each team pair, i.e., the odd-numbered card, is an offensive card; the even-numbered cards are defensive scenes. The cards have white borders and the backs are printed in dark blue ink on gray stock. The cards are numbered and contain a 1977 copyright date. The cards were issued in four-card wax packs along with four team logo stickers.

Card	Low	High
COMPLETE SET (67)	40.00	80.00
1 Baltimore Colts	1.25	2.50
2 Baltimore Colts	.63	1.25
3 Buffalo Bills	.63	1.25
4 Buffalo Bills	.63	1.25
5 Cincinnati Bengals	1.00	2.00
6 Cincinnati Bengals	.63	1.25
7 Cleveland Browns	.75	1.50
8 Cleveland Browns	.63	1.25
9 Denver Broncos	.63	1.25
10 Denver Broncos	.63	1.25
11 Houston Oilers	.63	1.25
12 Houston Oilers	.63	1.25
13 Kansas City Chiefs	.63	1.25
14 Kansas City Chiefs	.63	1.25
15 Miami Dolphins	.75	1.50
16 Miami Dolphins	.75	1.50
17 New England Patriots	.63	1.25
18 New England Patriots	.63	1.25
19 New York Jets	4.00	8.00
20 New York Jets	.63	1.25
21 Oakland Raiders	.75	1.50
22 Oakland Raiders	.75	1.50
23 Pittsburgh Steelers	1.00	2.00
24 Pittsburgh Steelers	.75	1.50
25 San Diego Chargers	2.00	4.00
26 San Diego Chargers	.63	1.25
27 Seattle Seahawks	1.00	2.00
28 Seattle Seahawks	.75	1.50
29 Atlanta Falcons	.63	1.25
30 Atlanta Falcons	.63	1.25
31 Chicago Bears	3.00	6.00
32 Chicago Bears	.63	1.25
33 Dallas Cowboys	.75	1.50
34 Dallas Cowboys	1.25	2.50
35 Detroit Lions	.63	1.25
36 Detroit Lions	.63	1.25
37 Green Bay Packers	.63	1.25
38 Green Bay Packers	3.00	6.00
39 Los Angeles Rams	.63	1.25
40 Los Angeles Rams	.63	1.25
41 Minnesota Vikings	.63	1.25
42 Minnesota Vikings	.63	1.25
43 New Orleans Saints	.63	1.25
44 New Orleans Saints	.63	1.25
45 New York Giants	.63	1.25
46 New York Giants	.63	1.25
47 Philadelphia Eagles	.63	1.25
48 Philadelphia Eagles	.63	1.25
49 St. Louis Cardinals	.75	1.50
50 St. Louis Cardinals	.63	1.25
51 San Francisco 49ers	.75	1.50

52 San Francisco 49ers .75 1.50
53 Tampa Bay Buccaneers .63 1.25
54 Tampa Bay Buccaneers .63 1.25
55 Washington Redskins 1.25 2.50
56 Washington Redskins .75 1.50
57 Super Bowl I .75 1.50
58 Super Bowl II .75 1.50
59 Super Bowl III .75 1.50
60 Super Bowl IV .75 1.50
61 Super Bowl V .75 1.50
62 Super Bowl VI 2.00 4.00
63 Super Bowl VII 1.25 2.50
64 Super Bowl VIII 1.25 2.50
65 Super Bowl IX .75 1.50
66 Super Bowl X 2.00 4.00
67 Super Bowl XI 2.00 4.00

1977 Fleer Team Action Stickers

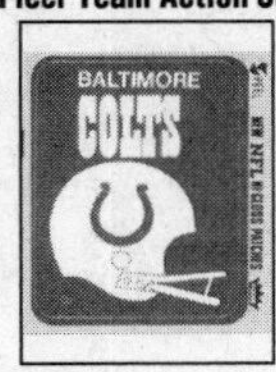

This set of stickers was issued one per pack in the 1977 Fleer Team Action card release. Each NFL team is represented with two stickers, with all but the Cowboys and Seahawks having both a helmet sticker and logo/insignia sticker. Several were produced with slight color variations in the border as noted below. Although these and other similar stickers were released over a number of years, the exact year of issue can be identified by the unique sticker back -- an artist's drawing of fingers peeling away a Jets helmet sticker. Two separate posters were also released to house the stickers; one for each conference. Each sticker measures roughly 2 3/8" by 2 3/4."

COMPLETE SET (65) 100.00 200.00
1A Atlanta Falcons Helmet 1.25 3.00
1B Atlanta Falcons Helmet 1.25 3.00
2 Atlanta Falcons 1.25 3.00
Logo
3A Baltimore Colts Helmet 1.25 3.00
3B Baltimore Colts Helmet 1.25 3.00
4 Baltimore Colts 1.25 3.00
Logo
5 Buffalo Bills 1.50 4.00
Helmet
6 Buffalo Bills 1.50 4.00
Logo
7A Chicago Bears Helmet 1.50 4.00
7B Chicago Bears 1.50 4.00
Helmet
(red border)
8 Chicago Bears 1.50 4.00
Logo
9 Cincinnati Bengals 1.25 3.00
Helmet
10 Cincinnati Bengals 1.25 3.00
Logo
11 Cleveland Browns 1.50 4.00
Helmet
12 Cleveland Browns 1.50 4.00
Logo
13 Dallas Cowboys Helmet 2.00 5.00
14 Dallas Cowboys Helmet 2.00 5.00
15 Denver Broncos 2.00 5.00
Helmet
16 Denver Broncos 2.00 5.00
Logo
17 Detroit Lions 1.25 3.00
Helmet
18 Detroit Lions 1.25 3.00
Logo
19 Green Bay Packers 2.00 5.00
Helmet
20 Green Bay Packers 2.00 5.00
Logo
21 Houston Oilers 1.25 3.00
Helmet
22 Houston Oilers 1.25 3.00
Logo
23 Kansas City Chiefs 1.25 3.00
Helmet
24 Kansas City Chiefs 1.25 3.00
Logo
25 Los Angeles Rams 1.25 3.00
Helmet
26A Los Angeles Rams Logo 1.25 3.00
26B Los Angeles Rams Logo 1.25 3.00
27 Miami Dolphins 2.00 5.00
Helmet
28 Miami Dolphins 2.00 5.00
Logo
29 Minnesota Vikings 1.50 4.00
Helmet
30 Minnesota Vikings 1.50 4.00
Logo
31A New England Patriots Helmet 1.25 3.00
31B New England Patriots Helmet 1.25 3.00
32 New England Patriots 1.25 3.00
Logo
33 New Orleans Saints 1.25 3.00
Helmet
34 New Orleans Saints 1.25 3.00
Logo
35 New York Giants 1.50 4.00
Helmet
36 New York Giants 1.50 4.00
Logo
37 New York Jets 1.50 4.00
Helmet
38A New York Jets Logo 1.50 4.00
38B New York Jets 1.50 4.00
Logo
(green border)
39 Oakland Raiders 2.00 5.00
Helmet
40A Oakland Raiders Logo 2.00 5.00
40B Oakland Raiders Logo 2.00 5.00
41A Philadelphia Eagles Helmet 1.25 3.00
41B Philadelphia Eagles 1.25 3.00
Helmet
(green border)
42 Philadelphia Eagles 1.25 3.00
Logo
43 Pittsburgh Steelers 2.00 5.00
Helmet
44A Pittsburgh Steelers Logo 2.00 5.00
44B Pittsburgh Steelers 2.00 5.00
Logo
(yellow border)
45 St. Louis Cardinals 1.25 3.00
Helmet
46 St. Louis Cardinals 1.25 3.00
Logo
47 San Diego Chargers 1.25 3.00
Helmet
48 San Diego Chargers 1.25 3.00
Logo
49 San Francisco 49ers 2.00 5.00
Helmet
50 San Francisco 49ers 2.00 5.00
Logo
51 Seattle Seahawks Helmet 1.25 3.00
52 Seattle Seahawks Helmet 1.25 3.00
53 Tampa Bay Bucs 1.25 3.00
Helmet
54 Tampa Bay Bucs 1.25 3.00
Logo
55 Washington Redskins 2.00 5.00
Helmet
56 Washington Redskins 2.00 5.00
Logo
NNO AFC Poster 5.00 10.00
NNO NFC Poster 5.00 10.00

1978 Fleer Team Action

The 1978 Fleer Teams in Action football set contains 68 action scenes. The cards measure the standard size. As in the previous year, each team is depicted on two cards and each Super Bowl is depicted on one card. The additional card in comparison to last year's set comes from the additional Super Bowl which was played during the year. The fronts have yellow borders. The card backs are printed with black ink on gray stock. The cards are numbered and feature a 1978 copyright date. Cards were issued in wax packs of seven team cards plus four team logo stickers.

COMPLETE SET (68) 20.00 40.00
1 Atlanta Falcons .63 1.25
2 Atlanta Falcons .25 .50
3 Baltimore Colts .25 .50
4 Baltimore Colts .25 .50
5 Buffalo Bills .25 .50
6 Buffalo Bills .25 .50
7 Chicago Bears 3.00 6.00
8 Chicago Bears .25 .50
9 Cincinnati Bengals .75 1.50
10 Cincinnati Bengals .25 .50
11 Cleveland Browns .38 .75
12 Cleveland Browns .50 1.00
13 Dallas Cowboys 3.00 6.00
14 Dallas Cowboys .50 1.00
15 Denver Broncos .25 .50
16 Denver Broncos 2.00 4.00
17 Detroit Lions .25 .50
18 Detroit Lions .25 .50
19 Green Bay Packers .25 .50
20 Green Bay Packers .25 .50
21 Houston Oilers .25 .50
22 Houston Oilers .25 .50
23 Kansas City Chiefs .25 .50
24 Kansas City Chiefs .25 .50
25 Los Angeles Rams .25 .50
26 Los Angeles Rams .25 .50
27 Miami Dolphins 1.50 3.00
28 Miami Dolphins .38 .75
29 Minnesota Vikings .50 1.00
30 Minnesota Vikings .25 .50
31 New England Patriots .25 .50
32 New England Patriots .25 .50
33 New Orleans Saints .25 .50
34 New Orleans Saints .25 .50
35 New York Giants .25 .50
36 New York Giants .25 .50
37 New York Jets .25 .50
38 New York Jets .25 .50
39 Oakland Raiders .50 1.00
40 Oakland Raiders .50 1.00
41 Philadelphia Eagles .40 1.00
42 Philadelphia Eagles .25 .50
43 Pittsburgh Steelers .38 .75
44 Pittsburgh Steelers .75 1.50
45 St. Louis Cardinals .25 .50
46 St. Louis Cardinals .25 .50
47 San Diego Chargers .25 .50
48 San Diego Chargers .25 .50
49 San Francisco 49ers .50 1.00
50 San Francisco 49ers .50 1.00
51 Seattle Seahawks .25 .50
52 Seattle Seahawks .25 .50
53 Tampa Bay Buccaneers .25 .50
54 Tampa Bay Buccaneers .25 .50
55 Washington Redskins .38 .75
56 Washington Redskins .38 .75
57 Super Bowl I 1.00 2.00
58 Super Bowl II .38 .75
59 Super Bowl III .38 .75
60 Super Bowl IV .38 .75
61 Super Bowl V .38 .75
62 Super Bowl VI .38 .75
63 Super Bowl VII .38 .75
64 Super Bowl VIII 1.00 2.00
65 Super Bowl IX 1.50 3.00
66 Super Bowl X .38 .75
67 Super Bowl XI .75 1.50
68 Super Bowl XII 2.00 4.00

1978 Fleer Team Action Stickers

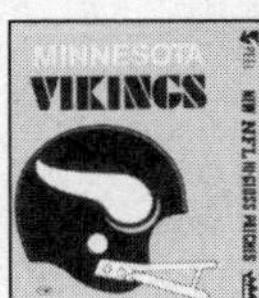

This set of stickers was issued one per pack in the 1978 Fleer Team Action card release and is virtually identical to the 1979 set. Each NFL team is represented with two stickers, with all but the Cowboys and Seahawks having both a helmet sticker and logo/insignia sticker. Several were produced with slight color variations in the border as noted below. Although these and other similar stickers were released over a number of years, the exact year of issue can be identified by the unique sticker back -- a puzzle piece that forms a photo from Super Bowl XII when fully assembled. Note that there are a number of puzzle back variations for each team. Very few collectors attempt to assemble a full set with all back variations. Reportedly, there are 170-total different sticker combinations of fronts and backs. We've noted the number of known back variations for each sticker below. Each sticker measures roughly 2 3/8" by 2 3/4."

COMPLETE SET (65) 70.00 120.00
1A Atlanta Falcons Helmet 1 .75 1.50
1B Atlanta Falcons Helmet 3 .75 1.50
2 Atlanta Falcons .75 1.50
Logo 3
3A Baltimore Colts Helmet 1 1.25 2.50
3B Baltimore Colts 1.25 2.50
Helmet 2
(yellow border)
4 Baltimore Colts 1.25 2.50
Logo 3
5 Buffalo Bills 1.25 2.50
Helmet 3
6 Buffalo Bills 1.25 2.50
Logo 3
7A Chicago Bears Helmet 1 1.25 2.50
7B Chicago Bears .75 1.50
Helmet 2
(red border)
8 Chicago Bears 1.25 2.50
Logo 3
9 Cincinnati Bengals .75 1.50
Helmet 3
10 Cincinnati Bengals .75 1.50
Logo 3
11 Cleveland Browns 1.25 2.50
Helmet 3
12 Cleveland Browns 1.25 2.50
Logo 3
13 Dallas Cowboys 2.00 4.00
Helmet 3
14 Dallas Cowboys 2.00 4.00
Helmet 3
15 Denver Broncos 2.00 4.00
Helmet 2
16 Denver Broncos .75 1.50
Logo 3
17 Detroit Lions .75 1.50
Helmet 2
18 Detroit Lions .75 1.50
Logo 3
19 Green Bay Packers 2.00 4.00
Helmet 3
20 Green Bay Packers 2.00 4.00
Logo 3
21 Houston Oilers .75 1.50
Helmet 4
22 Houston Oilers .75 1.50
Logo 3
23 Kansas City Chiefs .75 1.50
Helmet 3
24 Kansas City Chiefs .75 1.50
Logo 3
25 Los Angeles Rams .75 1.50
Helmet 3
26A Los Angeles Rams blue .75 1.50
26B Los Angeles Rams Red .75 1.50
27 Miami Dolphins 2.00 4.00
Helmet 3
28 Miami Dolphins 1.50 3.00
Logo 3
29 Minnesota Vikings 1.25 2.50
Helmet 3
30 Minnesota Vikings 1.25 2.50
Logo 3
31A New England Pats .75 1.50
Helmet 1
(blue border)
31B New England Pats Helmet 2 .75 1.50
32 New England Pats .75 1.50
Logo 3
33 New Orleans Saints .75 1.50
Helmet 3
34 New Orleans Saints .75 1.50
Logo 3
35 New York Giants 1.25 2.50
Helmet 3
36 New York Giants 1.25 2.50
Logo 3
37 New York Jets 1.25 2.50
Helmet 3
38A New York Jets .75 1.50
Logo 1
(blue border)
38B New York Jets Logo 3 1.25 2.50
39 Oakland Raiders 2.00 4.00
Helmet 3
40A Oakland Raiders .75 1.50
Logo 1
(blue border)
40B Oakland Raiders Logo 3 2.00 4.00
41A Philadelphia Eagles Helmet 1 .75 1.50
41B Philadelphia Eagles Helmet 2 .75 1.50
42 Philadelphia Eagles .75 1.50
Logo 3
43 Pittsburgh Steelers 2.00 4.00
Helmet 3
44A Pittsburgh Steelers Logo 1 .75 1.50
44B Pittsburgh Steelers Logo 3 2.00 4.00
45 St. Louis Cardinals .75 1.50
Helmet 3
46 St. Louis Cardinals .75 1.50
Logo 3
47 San Diego Chargers .75 1.50
Helmet 2
48 San Diego Chargers .75 1.50
Logo 3
49 San Francisco 49ers 2.00 4.00
Helmet 3
50 San Francisco 49ers 2.00 4.00
Logo 3
51 Seattle Seahawks Helmet 3 .75 1.50
52 Seattle Seahawks Helmet 3 .75 1.50
53 Tampa Bay Bucs .75 1.50
Helmet 3
54 Tampa Bay Bucs .75 1.50
Logo 3
55 Washington Redskins 2.00 4.00
Helmet 3
56 Washington Redskins 2.00 4.00
Logo 3

1979 Fleer Team Action

The 1979 Fleer Teams in Action football set mirrors the previous two sets in design (colorful action scenes with specific players not identified) and contains an additional card for the most recent Super Bowl making a total of 69 standard-size cards in the set. The fronts have white borders, and the backs are printed in black ink on gray stock. The backs have a 1979 copyright date. The card numbering follows team name alphabetical order followed by Super Bowl cards in chronological order. Cards were issued in wax packs of seven team cards plus three team logo stickers.

COMPLETE SET (69) 15.00 30.00
1 Atlanta Falcons .50 1.00
2 Atlanta Falcons .20 .40
3 Baltimore Colts .20 .40
4 Baltimore Colts .20 .40
5 Buffalo Bills .20 .40
6 Buffalo Bills .20 .40
7 Chicago Bears .20 .40
8 Chicago Bears .20 .40
9 Cincinnati Bengals .20 .40
10 Cincinnati Bengals .20 .40
11 Cleveland Browns .20 .40
12 Cleveland Browns .20 .40
13 Dallas Cowboys 1.50 3.00
14 Dallas Cowboys .30 .60
15 Denver Broncos .20 .40
16 Denver Broncos .20 .40
17 Detroit Lions .20 .40
18 Detroit Lions .20 .40
19 Green Bay Packers .20 .40
20 Green Bay Packers .20 .40
21 Houston Oilers 3.00 6.00
22 Houston Oilers .20 .40
23 Kansas City Chiefs .20 .40
24 Kansas City Chiefs .20 .40
25 Los Angeles Rams .20 .40
26 Los Angeles Rams .20 .40
27 Miami Dolphins .30 .60
28 Miami Dolphins .30 .60
29 Minnesota Vikings .20 .40
30 Minnesota Vikings .20 .40
31 New England Patriots .20 .40

Card	Low	High
32 New England Patriots	.20	.40
33 New Orleans Saints	.50	1.00
34 New Orleans Saints	.20	.40
35 New York Giants	.20	.40
36 New York Giants	.20	.40
37 New York Jets	.20	.40
38 New York Jets	.20	.40
39 Oakland Raiders	1.00	2.00
40 Oakland Raiders	.30	.60
41 Philadelphia Eagles	.20	.40
42 Philadelphia Eagles	.20	.40
43 Pittsburgh Steelers	.30	.60
44 Pittsburgh Steelers	.50	1.00
45 St. Louis Cardinals	.30	.60
46 St. Louis Cardinals	.20	.40
47 San Diego Chargers	.20	.40
48 San Diego Chargers	.20	.40
49 San Francisco 49ers	.30	.60
50 San Francisco 49ers	.30	.60
51 Seattle Seahawks	.20	.40
52 Seattle Seahawks	.20	.40
53 Tampa Bay Buccaneers	.20	.40
54 Tampa Bay Buccaneers	.20	.40
55 Washington Redskins	.30	.60
56 Washington Redskins	.30	.60
57 Super Bowl I	.50	1.00
58 Super Bowl II	.75	1.50
59 Super Bowl III	.30	.60
60 Super Bowl IV	.30	.60
61 Super Bowl V	.30	.60
62 Super Bowl VI	1.00	2.00
63 Super Bowl VII	.30	.60
64 Super Bowl VIII	1.00	2.00
65 Super Bowl IX	1.50	3.00
66 Super Bowl X	.30	.60
67 Super Bowl XI	.30	.60
68 Super Bowl XII	.30	.60
69 Super Bowl XIII	.75	1.50

1979 Fleer Team Action Stickers

This set of stickers was issued one per pack in the 1979 Fleer Team Action card release and is virtually identical to the 1978 set. Each NFL team is represented with two stickers, with all but the Cowboys and Seahawks having both a helmet sticker and logo/insignia sticker. Several were produced with slight color variations in the border as noted below. Although these and other similar stickers were released over a number of years, the exact year of issue can be identified by the unique sticker back -- a puzzle piece that forms a photo from Super Bowl XIII when fully assembled. Note that there are a number of puzzle back variations for each team. Very few collectors attempt to assemble a full set with all back variations. Reportedly, there are 170-total different sticker combinations of fronts and backs. We've noted the number of known back variations for each sticker below. Each sticker measures roughly 2 3/8" by 2 3/4."

Card	Low	High
COMPLETE SET (65)	30.00	60.00
1A Atlanta Falcons Helmet 1	.50	1.00
1B Atlanta Falcons Helmet 3	.50	1.00
2 Atlanta Falcons Logo 3	.50	1.00
3A Baltimore Colts Helmet 1	.75	1.50
3B Baltimore Colts Helmet 2 (yellow border)	.75	1.50
4 Baltimore Colts Logo 3	.75	1.50
5 Buffalo Bills Helmet 3	.75	1.50
6 Buffalo Bills Logo 3	.75	1.50
7A Chicago Bears Helmet 1	.75	1.50
7B Chicago Bears Helmet 2 (red border)	.75	1.50
8 Chicago Bears Logo 3	.75	1.50
9 Cincinnati Bengals Helmet 3	.50	1.00
10 Cincinnati Bengals Logo 3	.50	1.00
11 Cleveland Browns Helmet 3	.75	1.50
12 Cleveland Browns Logo 3	.75	1.50
13 Dallas Cowboys Helmet 3	1.25	2.50
14 Dallas Cowboys Helmet 3	1.25	2.50
15 Denver Broncos Helmet 2	.75	1.50
16 Denver Broncos Logo 3	.75	1.50
17 Detroit Lions Helmet 2	.50	1.00
18 Detroit Lions Logo 3	.50	1.00
19 Green Bay Packers Helmet 3	1.25	2.50
20 Green Bay Packers Logo 3-	1.25	2.50
21 Houston Oilers Helmet 4	.50	1.00
22 Houston Oilers Logo 3	.50	1.00
23 Kansas City Chiefs Helmet 3	.50	1.00
24 Kansas City Chiefs Logo 3	.50	1.00
25 Los Angeles Rams Helmet 3	.50	1.00
26A Los Angeles Rams Logo 1#(blue border)	.50	1.00
26B Los Angeles Rams Logo 3	.50	1.00
27 Miami Dolphins Helmet 3	1.25	2.50
28 Miami Dolphins Logo 3	1.25	2.50
29 Minnesota Vikings Helmet 3	.75	1.50
30 Minnesota Vikings Logo 3	.75	1.50
31A New England Pats Helmet 1 (blue border)	.50	1.00
31B New England Pats Helmet 2	.50	1.00
32 New England Pats Logo 3	.50	1.00
33 New Orleans Saints Helmet 3	.50	1.00
34 New Orleans Saints Logo 3	.50	1.00
35 New York Giants Helmet 3	.75	1.50
36 New York Giants Logo 3	.75	1.50
37 New York Jets Helmet 3	.75	1.50
38A New York Jets Logo 1 (blue border)	.75	1.50
38B New York Jets Logo 3	.75	1.50
39 Oakland Raiders Helmet 3	1.25	2.50
40A Oakland Raiders Logo 1 (blue border)	1.25	2.50
40B Oakland Raiders Logo 3	1.25	2.50
41A Philadelphia Eagles Helmet 1	.50	1.00
41B Philadelphia Eagles Helmet 2	.50	1.00
42 Philadelphia Eagles Logo 3	.50	1.00
43 Pittsburgh Steelers Helmet 3	1.25	2.50
44A Pittsburgh Steelers Logo 1	1.25	2.50
44B Pittsburgh Steelers Logo 3	1.25	2.50
45 St. Louis Cardinals Helmet 3	.50	1.00
46 St. Louis Cardinals Logo 3	.50	1.00
47 San Diego Chargers Helmet 2	.50	1.00
48 San Diego Chargers Logo 3	.50	1.00
49 San Francisco 49ers Helmet 3	1.25	2.50
50 San Francisco 49ers Logo 3	1.25	2.50
51 Seattle Seahawks Helmet 3	.50	1.00
52 Seattle Seahawks Helmet 3	.50	1.00
53 Tampa Bay Bucs Helmet 3	.50	1.00
54 Tampa Bay Bucs Logo 3	.50	1.00
55 Washington Redskins Helmet 3	.75	1.50
56 Washington Redskins Logo 3	.75	1.50

1980 Fleer Team Action

The 1980 Fleer Teams in Action football set continues the tradition of earlier sets but has one additional card for the most recent Super Bowl, i.e., now 70 full color standard-size cards in the set. The fronts have white borders and the backs are printed in black on gray stock. The cards are numbered on back and feature a 1980 copyright date. The card numbering follows team name alphabetical order followed by Super Bowl cards in chronological order. Cards were issued in seven-card wax packs along with three team logo stickers.

Card	Low	High
COMPLETE SET (70)	10.00	20.00
1 Atlanta Falcons	.30	.75
2 Atlanta Falcons	.12	.30
3 Baltimore Colts	.12	.30
4 Baltimore Colts	.12	.30
5 Buffalo Bills	.12	.30
6 Buffalo Bills	.12	.30
7 Chicago Bears	1.50	4.00
8 Chicago Bears	.12	.30
9 Cincinnati Bengals	.12	.30
10 Cincinnati Bengals	.12	.30
11 Cleveland Browns	.40	1.00
12 Cleveland Browns	.12	.30
13 Dallas Cowboys	.75	2.00
14 Dallas Cowboys	.25	.60
15 Denver Broncos	.12	.30
16 Denver Broncos	.12	.30
17 Detroit Lions	.12	.30
18 Detroit Lions	.12	.30
19 Green Bay Packers	.12	.30
20 Green Bay Packers	.12	.30
21 Houston Oilers	.12	.30
22 Houston Oilers	.12	.30
23 Kansas City Chiefs	.12	.30
24 Kansas City Chiefs	.12	.30
25 Los Angeles Rams	.12	.30
26 Los Angeles Rams	.12	.30
27 Miami Dolphins	.12	.30
28 Miami Dolphins	.12	.30
29 Minnesota Vikings	.12	.30
30 Minnesota Vikings	.12	.30
31 New England Patriots	.12	.30
32 New England Patriots	.12	.30
33 New Orleans Saints	.12	.30
34 New Orleans Saints	.40	1.00
35 New York Giants	1.00	2.50
36 New York Giants	.12	.30
37 New York Jets	.12	.30
38 New York Jets	.12	.30
39 Oakland Raiders	.12	.30
40 Oakland Raiders	.12	.30
41 Philadelphia Eagles	.12	.30
42 Philadelphia Eagles	.12	.30
43 Pittsburgh Steelers	.75	2.00
44 Pittsburgh Steelers	.12	.30
45 St. Louis Cardinals	.40	1.00
46 St. Louis Cardinals	.12	.30
47 San Diego Chargers	.12	.30
48 San Diego Chargers	.12	.30
49 San Francisco 49ers	.12	.30
50 San Francisco 49ers	.12	.30
51 Seattle Seahawks	.12	.30
52 Seattle Seahawks	.12	.30
53 Tampa Bay Buccaneers	.12	.30
54 Tampa Bay Buccaneers	1.25	3.00
55 Washington Redskins	.12	.30
56 Washington Redskins	.12	.30
57 Super Bowl I	.20	.50
58 Super Bowl II	.40	1.00
59 Super Bowl III	1.00	2.50
60 Super Bowl IV	.20	.50
61 Super Bowl V	.20	.50
62 Super Bowl VI	1.00	2.50
63 Super Bowl VII	.20	.50
64 Super Bowl VIII	.20	.50
65 Super Bowl IX	.60	1.50
66 Super Bowl X	.40	1.00
67 Super Bowl XI	.20	.50
68 Super Bowl XII	.20	.50
69 Super Bowl XIII	.75	2.00
70 Super Bowl XIV	.60	1.50

1980 Fleer Team Action Stickers

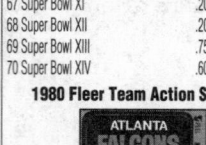

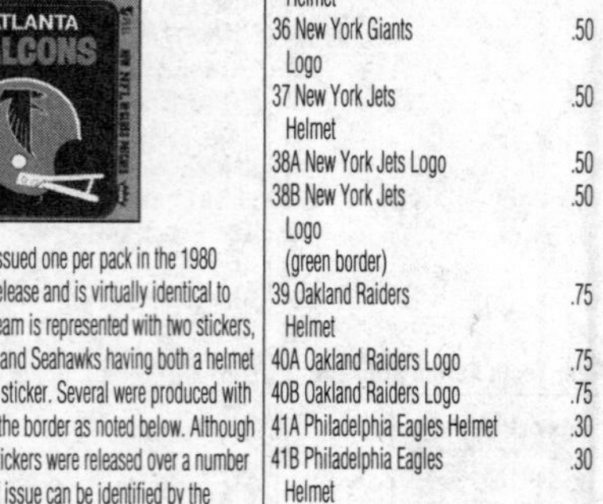

This set of stickers was issued one per pack in the 1980 Fleer Team Action card release and is virtually identical to the 1977 set. Each NFL team is represented with two stickers, with all but the Cowboys and Seahawks having both a helmet sticker and logo/insignia sticker. Several were produced with slight color variations in the border as noted below. Although these and other similar stickers were released over a number of years, the exact year of issue can be identified by the unique blank white sticker back. Each sticker measures roughly 2 3/8" by 2 3/4."

Card	Low	High
COMPLETE SET (65)	25.00	50.00
1A Atlanta Falcons Helmet	.30	.75
1B Atlanta Falcons Helmet	.30	.75
2 Atlanta Falcons Logo	.30	.75
3A Baltimore Colts Helmet	.50	1.25
3B Baltimore Colts Helmet	.50	1.25
4 Baltimore Colts Logo	.50	1.25
5 Buffalo Bills Helmet	.50	1.25
6 Buffalo Bills Logo	.50	1.25
7A Chicago Bears Helmet	.50	1.25
7B Chicago Bears Helmet (red border)	.50	1.25
8 Chicago Bears Logo	.50	1.25
9 Cincinnati Bengals Helmet	.30	.75
10 Cincinnati Bengals Logo	.30	.75
11 Cleveland Browns Helmet	.50	1.25
12 Cleveland Browns Logo	.50	1.25
13 Dallas Cowboys Helmet	.75	2.00
14 Dallas Cowboys Helmet	.75	2.00
15 Denver Broncos Helmet	.50	1.25
16 Denver Broncos Logo	.50	1.25
17 Detroit Lions Helmet	.30	.75
18 Detroit Lions Logo	.30	.75
19 Green Bay Packers Helmet	.75	2.00
20 Green Bay Packers Logo	.75	2.00
21 Houston Oilers Helmet	.30	.75
22 Houston Oilers Logo	.30	.75
23 Kansas City Chiefs Helmet	.30	.75
24 Kansas City Chiefs Logo	.30	.75
25 Los Angeles Rams Helmet	.30	.75
26A Los Angeles Rams Logo	.30	.75
26B Los Angeles Rams Logo	.30	.75
27 Miami Dolphins Helmet	.75	2.00
28 Miami Dolphins Logo	.75	2.00
29 Minnesota Vikings Helmet	.50	1.25
30 Minnesota Vikings Logo	.50	1.25
31A New England Patriots Helmet	.30	.75
31B New England Patriots Helmet	.30	.75
32 New England Patriots Logo	.30	.75
33 New Orleans Saints Helmet	.30	.75
34 New Orleans Saints Logo	.30	.75
35 New York Giants Helmet	.50	1.25
36 New York Giants Logo	.50	1.25
37 New York Jets Helmet	.50	1.25
38A New York Jets Logo	.50	1.25
38B New York Jets Logo (green border)	.50	1.25
39 Oakland Raiders Helmet	.75	2.00
40A Oakland Raiders Logo	.75	2.00
40B Oakland Raiders Logo	.75	2.00
41A Philadelphia Eagles Helmet	.30	.75
41B Philadelphia Eagles Helmet (green border)	.30	.75
42 Philadelphia Eagles Logo	.30	.75
43 Pittsburgh Steelers Helmet	.75	2.00
44A Pittsburgh Steelers Logo	.75	2.00
44B Pittsburgh Steelers Logo (yellow border)	.75	2.00
45 St. Louis Cardinals Helmet	.30	.75
46 St. Louis Cardinals Logo	.30	.75
47 San Diego Chargers Helmet	.30	.75
48 San Diego Chargers Logo	.30	.75
49 San Francisco 49ers Helmet	.75	2.00
50 San Francisco 49ers Logo	.75	2.00
51 Seattle Seahawks Helmet	.30	.75
52 Seattle Seahawks Helmet	.30	.75
53 Tampa Bay Bucs Helmet	.30	.75
54 Tampa Bay Bucs Logo	.30	.75
55 Washington Redskins Helmet	.50	1.25
56 Washington Redskins Logo	.50	1.25

1974 Florida Blazers WFL Team Issue

These photos were issued by the team for promotional purposes and fan mail requests. Each includes a black and white image printed above the subject's name and team logo. Each measures 5 1/2" by 7."

Card	Low	High
COMPLETE SET (10)	25.00	60.00
1 Chuck Beatty	3.00	8.00
2 Bob Davis	3.00	8.00
3 Billy Hobbs	3.00	8.00
4 Billie Hayes	3.00	8.00
5 Rommie Loudd Mgr.	3.00	8.00
6 Jack Pardee CO	4.00	10.00
7 Tommy Reamon	3.00	8.00
8 John Ricca	3.00	8.00
9 Lou Ross	3.00	8.00
10 Paul Vellano	3.00	8.00

1966 Fortune Shoes

Fortune Shoe Company sponsored this set of 9" by 12" black-and-white pencil sketches. The unnumbered cards are blankbacked and were printed on thick paper stock. Any additions to this list would be appreciated.

Card	Low	High
COMPLETE SET (9)	125.00	250.00
1 Roman Gabriel	12.50	25.00
2 Charley Johnson	10.00	20.00
3 John Henry Johnson	15.00	25.00
4 Don Meredith	15.00	30.00
5 Lenny Moore	15.00	25.00
6 Frank Ryan	10.00	20.00

7 Gale Sayers	25.00	50.00
8 Jim Taylor	15.00	30.00
9 John Unitas	25.00	50.00

1953-55 49ers Burgermeister Beer Team Photos

These oversized (roughly 6 1/4" by 9") color team photos were sponsored by Burgermeister Beer and distributed in the San Francisco area. Each were printed on thin card stock and featured a Burgermeister ad on the back along with the 49ers logo.

1953 San Francisco 49ers	25.00	50.00
1954 San Francisco 49ers	25.00	50.00
1955 San Francisco 49ers	25.00	50.00

1955 49ers Christopher Dairy

These cards were part of milk cartons released around 1955 by Christopher Dairy Farms. Two players were apparently included on each carton and printed in blue and white with the player's name and position next to the image. Three unfolded cartons were uncovered in 2001, but it is not yet known if these 6 constitute a full set. Any additions to this list are appreciated.

COMPLETE SET (6)	500.00	800.00
1 John Henry Johnson	125.00	200.00
2 Clay Matthews Sr.	75.00	125.00
3 Dick Moegle	75.00	125.00
4 Joe Perry	150.00	250.00
5 Bob St.Clair	90.00	150.00
6 Bob Toneff	75.00	125.00

1955 49ers Team Issue

This 38-card set measures approximately 4 1/4" by 6 1/4". The front features a black and white posed action photo enclosed by a white border, with the player's signature across the bottom portion of the picture. The back of the card lists the player's name, position, height, weight, and college, along with basic biographical information. Many of the cards in this and the other similar team issue sets are only distinguishable as to year by comparing text on the card back; the first few words of text are provided for many of the cards parenthetically below. The set was available direct from the team as part of a package for their fans. The cards are unnumbered and hence are listed alphabetically for convenience.

COMPLETE SET (38)	250.00	400.00
1 Frankie Albert CO	5.00	10.00
2 Joe Arenas	4.00	8.00
3 Harry Babcock	4.00	8.00
4 Ed Beatty	4.00	8.00
5 Phil Bengtson CO	4.00	8.00
6 Rex Berry	4.00	8.00
7 Hardy Brown	4.00	10.00
8 Marion Campbell	4.00	10.00
9 Al Carapella	4.00	8.00
10 Paul Carr	4.00	8.00
11 Maury Duncan	4.00	8.00
12 Bob Hantla	4.00	8.00
13 Carroll Hardy	4.00	8.00
14 Matt Hazeltine	4.00	8.00
15 Howard(Red) Hickey CO	4.00	8.00
16 Doug Hogland	4.00	8.00
17 Bill Johnson C	4.00	8.00
18 John Henry Johnson	15.00	30.00
19 Eldred Kraemer	4.00	8.00
20 Bud Laughlin	4.00	8.00
21 Bobby Luna	4.00	8.00
22 George Maderos	4.00	8.00
23 Clay Matthews Sr.	4.00	10.00
24 Hugh McElhenny	15.00	30.00
25 Dick Moegle	5.00	10.00
26 Leo Nomellini	12.50	25.00
27 Lou Palatella	4.00	8.00
28 Joe Perry	15.00	30.00
29 Charley Powell	4.00	8.00
30 Gordy Soltau	4.00	8.00
31 Bob St. Clair	12.50	25.00
32 Tom Stolhandske	4.00	8.00
33 R.Storey	4.00	8.00
B.Fouts		
Strader		
34 Red Strader CO	4.00	8.00
35 Y.A. Tittle	20.00	40.00
36 Bob Toneff	4.00	8.00
37 Billy Wilson	4.00	10.00
38 Sid Youngelman	4.00	8.00

1956 49ers Team Issue

This set measures approximately 4 1/8" by 6 1/4". The front features a black and white posed action photo enclosed by a white border, with the player's signature across the bottom portion of the picture. The back of the card lists the player's name, position, height, weight, and college, along with basic biographical information. Many of the cards in this and the other similar team issue sets are only distinguishable as to year by comparing text on the card back; the first few words of text are provided for many of the cards parenthetically below. The set was available direct from the team as part of a package for their fans. The cards are unnumbered and hence are listed alphabetically for convenience. It is likely that this set contains more than the number of cards listed below. Any additions to this list are appreciated.

COMPLETE SET (35)	200.00	350.00
1 Frankie Albert CO	5.00	10.00
2 Joe Arenas	4.00	8.00
3 Ed Beatty	4.00	8.00
4 Phil Bengtson CO	4.00	8.00
5 Rex Berry	4.00	8.00
6 Bruce Bosley	4.00	8.00
7 Fred Bruney	4.00	8.00
8 Paul Carr	4.00	8.00
9 Clyde Conner	4.00	8.00
10 Paul Goad	4.00	8.00
11 Matt Hazeltine	4.00	8.00
12 Ed Henke	4.00	8.00
13 Bill Herchman	4.00	8.00
14 Howard(Red) Hickey CO	4.00	8.00
15 Bill Jessup	4.00	8.00
16 Bill Johnson C	4.00	8.00
17 John Henry Johnson	18.00	30.00
18 George Maderos	4.00	8.00
19 Hugh McElhenny	15.00	30.00
20 Dick Moegle	5.00	10.00
21 Earl Morrall	12.00	20.00
22 George Morris	4.00	8.00
23 Leo Nomellini	12.50	25.00
24 Lou Palatella	4.00	8.00
25 Joe Perry	15.00	30.00
26 Charley Powell	4.00	8.00
27 Leo Rucka	4.00	8.00
28 Ed Sharkey	4.00	8.00
29 Charles Smith	4.00	8.00
30 Gordy Soltau	4.00	8.00
31 R.Storey	4.00	8.00
B.Fouts		
32 Bob St. Clair	10.00	20.00
33 Y.A. Tittle	25.00	40.00
34 Bob Toneff	4.00	8.00
35 Billy Wilson	4.00	8.00

1956-61 49ers Falstaff Beer Team Photos

These oversized (roughly 6 1/4" by 9") color team photos were sponsored by Falstaff Beer and distributed in the San Francisco area. Each was printed on card stock and features advertising and/or photos of the coaching staff on the back. Note that blankbacked reprints of the photos have circulated for a number of years.

1956 San Francisco 49ers	20.00	40.00
1957 San Francisco 49ers	20.00	40.00
1958 San Francisco 49ers	20.00	40.00
1959 San Francisco 49ers	20.00	40.00
1960 San Francisco 49ers	20.00	40.00
1961 San Francisco 49ers	20.00	40.00

1957 49ers Team Issue

This 43-card set measures approximately 4 1/8" by 6 1/4". The front features a black and white posed action photo enclosed by a white border, with the player's signature across the bottom portion of the picture. For those players who were included in the 1956 set, the same photos were used in the 1957 set, with the exception of Bill Johnson, who appears as a coach in the 1957 set. The back lists the player's name, position, height, weight, and college, along with basic biographical information. Many of the cards in this and the other similar team issue sets are only distinguishable as to year by comparing text on the card back; the first few words of text are provided for many of the cards parenthetically below. The set was available direct from the team as part of a package for their fans. The John Brodie card in this set predates his Topps and Fleer Rookie Cards by four years. The cards are unnumbered and hence are listed alphabetically for convenience.

COMPLETE SET (43)	250.00	400.00
1 Frankie Albert CO	5.00	10.00
2 Joe Arenas	4.00	8.00
3 Gene Babb	4.00	8.00
4 Larry Barnes	4.00	8.00
5 Phil Bengtson CO	4.00	8.00
6 Bruce Bosley	4.00	8.00
7 John Brodie	20.00	40.00
8 Paul Carr	4.00	8.00
9 Clyde Conner	4.00	8.00
10 Ted Connolly	4.00	8.00
11 Bobby Cross	4.00	8.00
12 Mark Duncan CO	4.00	8.00
13 B.Fouts	4.00	8.00
L.Simmons		
Albert		
14 John Gonzaga	4.00	8.00
15 Tom Harmon ANN	5.00	10.00
16 Matt Hazeltine	4.00	8.00
17 Ed Henke	4.00	8.00
18 Bill Herchman	4.00	8.00
19 Howard(Red) Hickey CO	4.00	8.00
20 Bob Holladay	4.00	8.00
21 Bill Jessup	4.00	8.00
22 Bill Johnson CO	4.00	8.00
23 Marv Matuszak	4.00	8.00
24 Hugh McElhenny	12.50	25.00
25 Dick Moegle	5.00	10.00
26 Frank Morze	4.00	8.00
27 Leo Nomellini	10.00	20.00
28 R.C. Owens	5.00	10.00
29 Lou Palatella	4.00	8.00
30 Joe Perry	12.50	25.00
31 Charley Powell	4.00	8.00
32 Jim Ridlon	4.00	8.00
33 Karl Rubke	4.00	8.00
34 J.D. Smith	5.00	10.00
35 Gordy Soltau	4.00	8.00
36 Bob St. Clair	7.50	15.00
37 Bill Stits	4.00	8.00
38 Y.A. Tittle	20.00	40.00
39 Bob Toneff	4.00	8.00
40A Lynn Waldorf Dir.	4.00	8.00
40B Lynn Waldorf Dir.	4.00	8.00
41 Val Joe Walker	4.00	8.00
42 Billy Wilson	4.00	8.00
43 49ers Coaches	5.00	10.00

1958 49ers Team Issue

This 44-card set measures approximately 4 1/8" by 6 1/4". The front features a black and white posed action photo enclosed by a white border, with the player's signature across the bottom portion of the picture. The back lists the player's name, position, height, weight, and college, along with basic biographical information. Many of the cards in this and the other similar team issue sets are only distinguishable as to year by comparing text on the card back; the first few words of text are provided for many of the cards parenthetically below. The set was available direct from the team as part of a package for their fans. The John Brodie card in this set holds particular interest to some collectors in that it precedes Brodie's Topps and Fleer Rookie Cards by three years. The cards are unnumbered and hence are listed alphabetically for convenience.

COMPLETE SET (44)	250.00	400.00
1 Frankie Albert CO	5.00	10.00
2 Bill Atkins	4.00	8.00
3 Gene Babb	4.00	8.00
4 Phil Bengtson CO	4.00	8.00
5 Bruce Bosley	4.00	8.00
6 John Brodie	15.00	30.00
7 Clyde Conner	4.00	8.00
8 Ted Connolly	4.00	8.00
9 Fred Dugan	4.00	8.00
10 Mark Duncan CO	4.00	8.00
11 Bob Fouts	4.00	8.00
Simmons		
Albert		
12 John Gonzaga	4.00	8.00
13 Tom Harmon ANN	5.00	10.00
14 Matt Hazeltine	4.00	8.00
15 Ed Henke	4.00	8.00
16 Bill Herchman	4.00	8.00
17 Howard(Red) Hickey CO	4.00	8.00
18 Bill Jessup	4.00	8.00
19 Bill Johnson CO	4.00	8.00
20 Marv Matuszak	4.00	8.00
21 Hugh McElhenny	12.50	25.00
22 Jerry Mertens	4.00	8.00
23 Dick Moegle	5.00	10.00
24 Dennit Morris	4.00	8.00
25 Frank Morze	4.00	8.00
26 Leo Nomellini	10.00	20.00
27 R.C. Owens	5.00	10.00
28 Jim Pace	4.00	8.00
29 Lou Palatella	4.00	8.00
30 Joe Perry	12.50	25.00
31 Jim Ridlon	4.00	8.00
32 Karl Rubke	4.00	8.00
33 J.D. Smith	5.00	10.00
34 Gordy Soltau	4.00	8.00
35 Bob St. Clair	7.50	15.00
36 Bill Stits	4.00	8.00
37 John Thomas	4.00	8.00
38 Y.A. Tittle	17.50	35.00
39 Bob Toneff	4.00	8.00
40 Lynn Waldorf Dir.	4.00	8.00
41 Billy Wilson	4.00	8.00
42 John Wittenborn	4.00	8.00
43 Abe Woodson	5.00	10.00
44 49ers Coaches	5.00	10.00

1959 49ers Team Issue

This 45-card set measures approximately 4 1/8" by 6 1/4". The front features a black and white posed action photo enclosed by a white border, with the player's signature across the bottom portion of the picture. The back lists the player's name, position, height, weight, and college, along with basic biographical information. Many of the cards in this and the other similar team issue sets are only distinguishable as to year by comparing text on the card back; the first few words of text are provided for many of the cards parenthetically below. The set was available direct from the team as part of a package for their fans. The cards are unnumbered and hence are listed alphabetically for convenience.

COMPLETE SET (45)	250.00	400.00
1 Bill Atkins	4.00	8.00
2 Dave Baker	4.00	8.00
3 Bruce Bosley	4.00	8.00
4 John Brodie	12.50	25.00
5 Jack Christiansen CO	7.50	15.00
6 Monte Clark	4.00	8.00
7 Clyde Conner	4.00	8.00
8 Ted Connolly	4.00	8.00
9 Tommy Davis	4.00	8.00
10 Eddie Dove	4.00	8.00
11 Fred Dugan	4.00	8.00
12 Mark Duncan CO	4.00	8.00
13 Bob Fouts ANN	4.00	8.00
14 John Gonzaga	4.00	8.00
15 Bob Harrison	4.00	8.00
16 Matt Hazeltine	4.00	8.00
17 Ed Henke	4.00	8.00
18 Bill Herchman	4.00	8.00
19 Howard(Red) Hickey CO	4.00	8.00
20 Russ Hodges ANN	4.00	8.00
21 Bill Johnson CO	4.00	8.00
22 Charlie Krueger	4.00	8.00
23 Lenny Lyles	4.00	8.00
24 Hugh McElhenny	12.50	25.00
25 Jerry Mertens	4.00	8.00
26 Dick Moegle	5.00	10.00
27 Frank Morze	4.00	8.00
28 Leo Nomellini	10.00	20.00
29 Clancy Osborne	4.00	8.00
30 R.C. Owens	5.00	10.00
31 Joe Perry	12.50	25.00
32 Jim Ridlon	4.00	8.00
33 Karl Rubke	4.00	8.00
34 Bob St.Clair	7.50	15.00
35 Henry Schmidt	4.00	8.00
36 Bob Shaw CO	4.00	8.00
37 Lon Simmons ANN	4.00	8.00
38 J.D. Smith	5.00	10.00
39 John Thomas	4.00	8.00
40 Y.A. Tittle	15.00	30.00
41 Jerry Tubbs	4.00	8.00
42 Lynn Waldorf Dir.	4.00	8.00
43 Billy Wilson	4.00	8.00
44 John Wittenborn	4.00	8.00
45 Abe Woodson	5.00	10.00

1960 49ers Team Issue

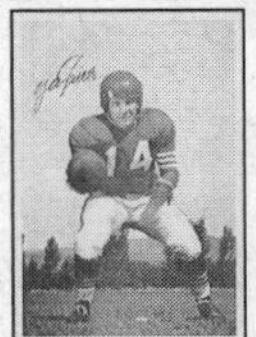

This 44-card set measures approximately 4 1/8" by 6 1/4". The front features a black-and-white posed action photo with white borders. The player's facsimile autograph is inscribed across the picture. The back lists the player's name, position, height, weight, age, college, along with career summary and biographical notes. The set was available direct from the team as part of a package for their fans. The photos are unnumbered and checklisted below in alphabetical order.

COMPLETE SET (44)	200.00	350.00
1 Dave Baker	4.00	8.00
2 Bruce Bosley	4.00	8.00
3 John Brodie	12.50	25.00
4 Jack Christiansen ACO	6.00	12.00
5 Monte Clark	4.00	8.00
6 Dan Colchico	4.00	8.00
7 Clyde Conner	4.00	8.00
8 Ted Connolly	4.00	8.00
9 Tommy Davis	4.00	8.00
10 Eddie Dove	4.00	8.00
11 Mark Duncan ACO	4.00	8.00
12 Bob Fouts ANN	4.00	8.00
13 Bob Harrison	4.00	8.00
14 Matt Hazeltine	4.00	8.00
15 Ed Henke	4.00	8.00
16 Howard(Red) Hickey CO	4.00	8.00
17 Russ Hodges ANN	4.00	8.00
18 Bill Johnson CO	4.00	8.00
19 Gordon Kelley	4.00	8.00
20 Charlie Krueger	4.00	8.00
21 Lenny Lyles	4.00	8.00
22 Hugh McElhenny	12.50	25.00
23 Mike Magac	4.00	8.00
24 Jerry Mertens	4.00	8.00
25 Frank Morze	4.00	8.00
26 Leo Nomellini	10.00	20.00
27 Clancy Osborne	4.00	8.00
28 R.C. Owens	5.00	10.00
29 Jim Ridlon	4.00	8.00
30 C.R. Roberts	4.00	8.00
31 Len Rohde	4.00	8.00
32 Karl Rubke	4.00	8.00
33 Bob St.Clair	6.00	12.00

34 Henry Schmidt 4.00 8.00
35 Lon Simmons ANN 4.00 8.00
36 J.D. Smith 4.00 8.00
37 Gordy Soltau ANN 4.00 8.00
38 Monty Stickles 4.00 8.00
39 John Thomas 4.00 8.00
40 Y.A. Tittle 15.00 30.00
41 Lynn Waldorf Dir. 4.00 8.00
42 Bobby Waters 4.00 8.00
43 Billy Wilson 4.00 8.00
44 Abe Woodson 5.00 10.00

1961 49ers Team Issue

The 49ers issued this set of large (approximately 8" by 10") black and white player photos in 1961. The team logo (old style) and basic player information is contained beneath the player image. The photos are unnumbered and listed below alphabetically. Note that these photos are similar to other 49ers photos, but can be identified by the size (8" by 10") and by the text (position is in lower and upper case letters) and format used to identify the player's weight (example of style: 6-1).

COMPLETE SET (31) 125.00 250.00
1 Bruce Bosley 4.00 8.00
2 John Brodie 10.00 20.00
3 Bernie Casey 4.00 8.00
4 Monte Clark 4.00 8.00
5 Clyde Conner 4.00 8.00
6 Bill Cooper 4.00 8.00
7 Lou Cordileone 4.00 8.00
8 Tommy Davis 5.00 10.00
9 Bob Harrison 4.00 8.00
10 Matt Hazeltine 4.00 8.00
11 Ed Henke 4.00 8.00
12 Howard Red Hickey CO 4.00 8.00
13 Jim Johnson 5.00 10.00
14 Carl Kammerer 4.00 8.00
15 Billy Kilmer 7.50 15.00
16 Roland Lakes 4.00 8.00
17 Bill Lopasky 4.00 8.00
18 Hugh McElhenny 7.50 15.00
19 Dale Messer 4.00 8.00
20 Leo Nomellini 6.00 12.00
21 Ray Norton 4.00 8.00
22 R.C. Owens 5.00 10.00
23 Jim Ridlon 4.00 8.00
24 Karl Rubke 4.00 8.00
25 Bob St. Clair 5.00 10.00
26 Monty Stickles 4.00 8.00
27 Aaron Thomas 4.00 8.00
28 John Thomas 4.00 8.00
29 Y.A. Tittle 12.50 25.00
30 Abe Woodson 5.00 10.00
31 Bill Johnson 7.50 15.00
Jack Christiansen
Billy Wilson

1963 49ers Team Issue

The 49ers issued this set of large (approximately 8" by 10 7/8") black and white player photos around 1963. The team logo (old style) and basic player information is contained beneath the player image. The photos are unnumbered and listed below alphabetically. Note that these photos are similar to other 49ers photos, but can be identified by the larger size (8" by 10 7/8") and by the larger text used on the player's name (4/32" high) as well as the format used to identify the player's weight (example of style: 6' 1"). Note that the player's position was also printed in upper and lower case letters which helps to differentiate this year from later years.

COMPLETE SET (7) 25.00 50.00
1 Eddie Dove 4.00 8.00
2 Mike Magac 4.00 8.00
3 Ed Pine 4.00 8.00
4 Len Rohde 4.00 8.00
5 Monty Stickles 4.00 8.00
6 John Thomas 4.00 8.00
7 Bob Waters 4.00 8.00

1964 49ers Team Issue

The 49ers issued this set of large (approximately 8" by 10 7/8") black and white player photos around 1964. The team logo (old style) and basic player information is contained beneath the player image. The photos are unnumbered and listed below alphabetically. Note that these photos are similar to other 49ers photos, but can be identified by the larger size (8" by 10 7/8") and by the smaller text used on the player's name (3/32" high) and the format used to identify the player's height (example of style: 6' 1"). Note that the player's position was also printed in upper and lower case letters which helps to differentiate this year from later years.

COMPLETE SET (16) 60.00 120.00
1 Kermit Alexander 4.00 8.00
2 John Brodie 7.50 15.00
3 Bernie Casey 5.00 10.00
4 Jack Christiansen CO 6.00 12.00
5 Dan Colchico 4.00 8.00
6 Tommy Davis 5.00 10.00
7 Leon Donohue 4.00 8.00
8 Charlie Krueger 4.00 8.00
9 Roland Lakes 4.00 8.00
10 Don Lisbon 4.00 8.00
11 Clark Miller 4.00 8.00
12 Walter Rock 4.00 8.00
13 Karl Rubke 4.00 8.00
14 Chuck Sieminski 4.00 8.00
15 J.D. Smith 5.00 10.00
16 Abe Woodson 4.00 8.00

1965 49ers Team Issue

The 49ers issued this set of large (approximately 8" by 10 7/8") black and white player photos around 1965. The team logo (old style) and basic player information is contained beneath the player image. The photos are unnumbered and listed below alphabetically. Note that these are virtually identical to the 1964 photos and likely were issued over a period of years. However, we've cataloged below photos which include distinct variations over the 1964 issue.

1 Kermit Alexander 4.00 8.00
2 John Brodie 7.50 15.00
3 Bernie Casey 4.00 8.00
4 Dave Wilcox 5.00 10.00

1966 49ers Team Issue

The 49ers issued this set of large (approximately 8" by 10 7/8") black and white player photos around 1966. The team logo (old style) and basic player information is contained beneath the player image. The photos are unnumbered and listed below alphabetically. Note that these photos are similar to other 49ers photos, but can be identified by the larger size (8" by 10 7/8") and by the text style used on the player's position which was printed in all capital letters.

COMPLETE SET (8) 40.00 80.00
1 Kermit Alexander 4.00 8.00
2 Tommy Davis 5.00 10.00
3 Billy Kilmer 7.50 15.00
4 Elbert Kimbrough 4.00 8.00
5 Dave Kopay 4.00 8.00
6 Charlie Krueger 4.00 8.00
7 Gary Lewis 4.00 8.00
8 George Mira 4.00 8.00
9 Ken Willard 5.00 10.00

1967 49ers Team Issue

This team issue set measures approximately 8" by 11" and features black and white posed action photos of the San Francisco 49ers on thin card stock. The backs are blank. The player's name, position, height, and weight are printed in the white lower border in all caps. The set is very similar to the 1968 and 1971-72 releases, but the size is slightly smaller. The team logo that appears in the white border below the player photo is also slightly different than the 1968 photos. Because this set is unnumbered, the photos are listed alphabetically.

COMPLETE SET 60.00 120.00
1 John David Crow 5.00 10.00
2 Tommy Davis 5.00 10.00
3 George Donnelly 4.00 8.00
4 Charlie Johnson DT 4.00 8.00
5 John Brodie 7.50 15.00
6 George Mira 4.00 8.00
7 Howard Mudd 4.00 8.00
8 Sonny Randle 4.00 8.00
9 Dave Wilcox 5.00 10.00
10 Dick Witcher 4.00 8.00
11 Ken Willard 5.00 10.00
12 Bob Windsor 4.00 8.00
13 Steve Spurrier 20.00 40.00

1968 49ers Team Issue

This team issue set measures approximately 8 1/2" by 11" and features black and white posed action photos of the San Francisco 49ers on thin card stock. The backs are blank. The player's name, position, height, and weight are printed in the white lower border in all caps. The set is very similar to the 1971-72 release, but the team logo is printed in black and silver. It also appears in the white border below the player information. Because this set is unnumbered, the players and coaches are listed alphabetically. Steve Spurrier's card predates his Rookie Card by four years.

COMPLETE SET (38) 125.00 250.00
1 Kermit Alexander 5.00 10.00
2 Cas Banaszek 4.00 8.00
3 Ed Beard 4.00 8.00
4 Forrest Blue 4.00 8.00
5 Bruce Bosley 4.00 8.00
6 John Brodie 7.50 15.00
7 Elmer Collett 4.00 8.00
8 Doug Cunningham 4.00 8.00
9 Tommy Davis 5.00 10.00
10 Earl Edwards 4.00 8.00
11 Kevin Hardy 4.00 8.00
12 Matt Hazeltine 4.00 8.00
13 Stan Hindman 4.00 8.00
14 Tom Holzer 4.00 8.00
15 Jim Johnson 6.00 12.00
16 Charlie Krueger 4.00 8.00
17 Roland Lakes 4.00 8.00
18 Gary Lewis 4.00 8.00
19 Kay McFarland 4.00 8.00
20 Clifton McNeil 4.00 8.00
21 George Mira 5.00 10.00
22 Eugene Moore 4.00 8.00
23 Howard Mudd 4.00 8.00
24 Dick Nolan CO 4.00 8.00
25 Frank Nunley 4.00 8.00
26 Don Parker 4.00 8.00
27 Mel Phillips 4.00 8.00
28 Al Randolph 4.00 8.00
29 Len Rohde 4.00 8.00
30 Steve Spurrier 20.00 40.00
31 John Thomas 4.00 8.00
32 Bill Tucker 4.00 8.00
33 Gene Washington 5.00 10.00
34 Dave Wilcox 5.00 10.00
35 Ken Willard 5.00 10.00
36 Bob Windsor 4.00 8.00
37 Dick Witcher 4.00 8.00
38 Team Photo 7.50 15.00

1968 49ers Volpe Tumblers

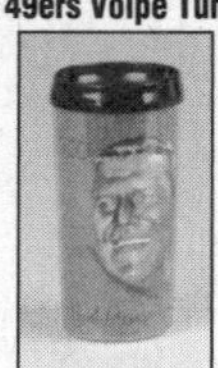

These 49ers artist's renderings were part of a plastic cup tumbler product produced in 1968. The noted sports artist Volpe created the artwork which includes an action scene and a player portrait. The "cards" are unnumbered, each measures approximately 5" by 8 1/2" and is curved in the shape required to fit inside a plastic cup. There are likely 12 cups included in this set. Any additions to this list are appreciated.

COMPLETE SET (3) 62.50 125.00
1 John Brodie 30.00 60.00
2 John David Crow 20.00 40.00
3 Charlie Krueger 15.00 30.00

1969 49ers Team Issue 4X5

These small (roughly 4" by 5") black and white photos look very similar to the 1971 release. Each includes a player photo along with his team name, player name, and position. The cardbacks are blank. We've noted text or photo differences below on players that were included in both sets.

COMPLETE SET (20) 40.00 80.00
1 Elmer Collett 2.50 5.00
2 Tommy Davis 3.00 6.00
3 Earl Edwards 2.50 5.00
4 Johnny Fuller 2.50 5.00
5 Harold Hays 2.50 5.00
6 Stan Hindman 2.50 5.00
7 Roland Lakes 2.50 5.00
8 Gary Lewis 2.50 5.00
9 Frank Nunley 2.50 5.00
10 Clifton McNeil 2.50 5.00
11 Mel Phillips 2.50 5.00
12 Al Randolph 2.50 5.00
13 Len Rohde 2.50 5.00
14 Jim Sniadecki 2.50 5.00
15 Sam Silas 2.50 5.00
16 Jimmy Thomas 2.50 5.00
17 Bill Tucker 2.50 5.00
18 Bob Windsor 2.50 5.00
19 Dick Witcher 3.00 6.00
20 John Woitt 2.50 5.00

1971 49ers Team Issue 4X5

These small (roughly 4" by 5") black and white photos look very similar to the 1969 release. Each includes a player photo along with his team name, player name, and position. The cardbacks are blank. We've noted text or photo differences below on players that were included in both sets.

COMPLETE SET (20) 40.00 80.00
1 Elmer Collett 2.50 4.00
2 Earl Edwards 2.50 4.00
3 Johnny Fuller 2.50 4.00
4 Tony Harris 2.50 4.00
5 Tommy Hart 3.00 6.00
6 Stan Hindman 2.50 4.00
7 Bob Hoskins 2.50 4.00
8 John Isenbarger 2.50 4.00
9 Jim McCann 2.50 4.00
10 Frank Nunley 2.50 4.00
11 Mel Phillips 2.50 4.00
12 Preston Riley 2.50 4.00
13 Len Rohde 2.50 5.00
14 Larry Schreiber 2.50 4.00
15 Mike Simpson 2.50 4.00
16 Jim Sniadecki 2.50 4.00
17 Jimmy Thomas 2.50 4.00
18 Vic Washington 2.50 5.00
19 Bob Windsor 2.50 5.00
20 Dick Witcher 2.50 5.00

1971 49ers Postcards

The San Francisco 49ers distributed this set of oversized postcards in 1971. Each measures approximately 5 3/4" by 8 7/8" and features a borderless black and white player photo on front with a postcard style back. The player's name, position, helmet logo, and some vital statistics are featured within a white border area below the photo. The unnumbered cardbacks also contain extensive player career information and stats.

COMPLETE SET (47) 200.00 400.00
1 Cas Banaszak 6.25 12.50
2 Ed Beard 5.00 10.00
3 Randy Beisler 5.00 10.00
4 Bill Belk 6.25 12.50
5 Forrest Blue 6.25 12.50
6 John Brodie 10.00 20.00
7 Elmer Collett 5.00 10.00
8 Doug Cunningham 5.00 10.00
9 Earl Edwards 5.00 10.00
10 Johnny Fuller 5.00 10.00
11 Bruce Gossett 6.25 12.50
12 Cedrick Hardman 6.25 12.50
13 Tony Harris 5.00 10.00
14 Tommy Hart 6.25 12.50
15 Stan Hindman 5.00 10.00
16 Bob Hoskins 5.00 10.00
17 Marty Huff 5.00 10.00
18 John Isenbarger 5.00 10.00
19 Ernie Janet 5.00 10.00
20 Jimmy Johnson 7.50 15.00
21 Charlie Krueger 6.25 12.50
22 Ted Kwalick 6.25 12.50
23 Jim McCann 5.00 10.00
24 Dick Nolan CO 6.25 12.50
25 Frank Nunley 5.00 10.00
26 Joe Orduna 5.00 10.00
27 Willie Parker 5.00 10.00
28 Woody Peoples 5.00 10.00
29 Mel Phillips 6.25 12.50
30 Joe Reed 6.25 12.50
31 Preston Riley 5.00 10.00
32 Len Rohde 6.25 12.50
33 Larry Schreiber 5.00 10.00
34 Sam Silas 5.00 10.00
35 Mike Simpson 5.00 10.00
36 Jim Sniadecki 5.00 10.00
37 Steve Spurrier 20.00 40.00
38 Bruce Taylor 6.25 12.50
39 Jimmy Thomas 5.00 10.00
40 Skip Vanderbundt 6.25 12.50
41 Gene Washington 6.25 12.50
42 Vic Washington 6.25 12.50
43 John Watson 5.00 10.00
44 Dave Wilcox 6.25 12.50
45 Ken Willard 6.25 12.50
46 Bob Windsor 5.00 10.00
47 Dick Witcher 5.00 10.00
48 Coaching Staff 6.25 12.50

1971-72 49ers Team Issue

This team issue set measures approximately 8 1/2" by 11" and features black and white posed action photos of the San Francisco 49ers on thin card stock. The backs are blank. The player's name, position, height, and weight are printed in the white lower border in all caps. The set is very similar to the 1967 and 1968 releases, but the team logo is printed in all black and appears in the white border below the player information. Because this set is unnumbered, the players are listed alphabetically.

COMPLETE SET (5) 15.00 30.00
1 Ed Beard 4.00 8.00
2 Bill Belk 4.00 8.00
3 John Brodie 7.50 15.00
4 Bruce Gossett 4.00 8.00
5 Ted Kwalick 4.00 8.00

1972 49ers Redwood City Tribune

This set of six (approximately) 3" by 5 1/2" facsimile autograph cards features black-and-white head shots with white borders. The player's name is printed beneath the picture and in a large space immediately beneath, the card carries the player's signature. The bottom of the front reads "49er autograph card courtesy of Redwood City Tribune." The cards are unnumbered and checklisted below in alphabetical order. The set's date is bracketed by the fact that Frank Edwards last year with the San Francisco 49ers was 1972 and Larry Schreiber's first year with the 49ers was 1971.

COMPLETE SET (6) 37.50 75.00
1 Earl Edwards 3.75 7.50
2 Frank Nunley 3.75 7.50
3 Len Rohde 3.75 7.50

4 Larry Schreiber	3.75	7.50
5 Steve Spurrier	20.00	40.00
6 Gene Washington	6.25	12.50

1972-75 49ers Team Issue

The 49ers released similar player photos over a period of years in the 1970s. For ease in cataloging, we've included them together below. There are likely many missing from the checklist, any additions to the list would be appreciated. Each photo measures approximately 7" by 11" and was printed on very thin glossy stock. The fronts feature black-and-white action player photos on a white background. The player's picture measures roughly 6 1/4" by 7 1/2" and the cardbacks are blanks. The player's name, biographical information, career highlights, and a personal profile are printed in the white margin at the bottom. Most also include a 49ers helmet logo below the image. The player's statistics and years pro notation help in identifying the year of issue. The cards are unnumbered and checklisted below in alphabetical order.

1 Cas Banaszek	4.00	8.00
2 Forrest Blue	4.00	8.00
3 Bruce Gossett	4.00	8.00
4 Windlan Hall 1974	4.00	8.00
5 Cedrick Hardman	4.00	8.00
6 Mike Holmes	4.00	8.00
7 Tom Hull 1974	4.00	8.00
8 Wilbur Jackson 1974	5.00	10.00
9 Jim Johnson 1974	6.00	12.00
10 Manfred Moore 1974	4.00	8.00
11 Mel Phillips 1972	4.00	8.00
12 Steve Spurrier 1974	12.50	25.00
13 Bruce Taylor	4.00	8.00
14 Skip Vanderbundt	4.00	8.00
15 Gene Washington 1973	5.00	10.00
16 Gene Washington 1975	5.00	10.00
17 John Watson 1974	4.00	8.00

1977 49ers Team Issue

These team issued photos of the San Francisco 49ers measure approximately 5" by 8" and feature black-and-white player photos within a white border. The player's name is pirnted in all caps below the picture with his jersey number, position, height, weight, and college printed below that. The backs are blank so the cards are unnumbered and checklisted below in alphabetical order. It is thought that these photos may have been issued over a period of years since they closely resemble the 1980-82 release.

1 Cleveland Elam	2.00	5.00
2 Jim Plunkett	3.00	8.00
3 Dave Washington	2.00	5.00

1980-82 49ers Team Issue

This team issue set of the San Francisco 49ers measures approximately 5" by 8" and features a black-and-white player photo in a white border. The players name, jersey number, height, weight, and college are printed in the wide bottom margin. The backs are blank. The cards are unnumbered and checklisted below in alphabetical order. It is thought that these photos may have been issued over a period of years since some feature the player's name in all caps while others use both upper and lower case letters. The set features an early Joe Montana card that is thought to have been issued in 1982.

COMPLETE SET (55)	125.00	250.00
1 Dan Audick	1.25	3.00
2 John Ayers	1.25	3.00
3 Jean Barrett	1.25	3.00
4 Guy Benjamin	1.25	3.00
5 Dwaine Board	1.25	3.00
6 Bob Bruer	1.25	3.00
7 Ken Bungarda	1.25	3.00
8 Dan Bunz	1.25	3.00
9 John Choma	1.25	3.00
10 Ricky Churchman	1.25	3.00
11 Dwight Clark	3.00	8.00
12 Earl Cooper	1.25	3.00
13 Randy Cross	1.50	4.00
14 Johnny Davis	1.25	3.00
15 Fred Dean	1.50	4.00
16 Walt Downing	1.25	3.00
17 Walt Easley	1.25	3.00
18 Lenvil Elliott	1.25	3.00
19 Keith Fahnhorst	1.25	3.00
20 Bob Ferrell	1.25	3.00
21 Phil Francis	1.25	3.00
22 Rick Gervais	1.25	3.00
23 Willie Harper	1.25	3.00
24 John Harty	1.25	3.00
25 Dwight Hicks	1.50	4.00
26 Scott Hilton	1.25	3.00
27 Paul Hofer	1.25	3.00
28 Pete Kugler	1.25	3.00
29 Amos Lawrence	1.25	3.00
30 Bobby Leopold	1.25	3.00
31 Ronnie Lott	6.00	15.00
32 Saladin Martin	1.25	3.00
33 Milt McColl	1.25	3.00
34 Jim Miller P	1.25	3.00
35 Joe Montana	90.00	150.00
36 Ricky Patton	1.25	3.00
37 Lawrence Pillers	1.25	3.00
38 Craig Puki	1.25	3.00
39 Fred Quillan	1.25	3.00
40 Eason Ramson	1.25	3.00
41 Archie Reese	1.25	3.00
42 Jack Reynolds	1.50	4.00
43 Bill Ring	1.25	3.00
44 Mike Shumann	1.25	3.00
45 Freddie Solomon	2.00	5.00
46 Scott Stauch	1.25	3.00
47 Jim Stuckey	1.25	3.00
48 Lynn Thomas	1.25	3.00
49 Keena Turner	1.25	3.00
50 Jimmy Webb	1.25	3.00
51 Ray Wersching	1.25	3.00
52 Carlton Williamson	1.25	3.00
53 Mike Wilson	1.25	3.00
54 Eric Wright	1.50	4.00
55 Charlie Young	1.50	4.00

1972-74 Franklin Mint HOF Coins Bronze

Issued by the Pro Football Hall of Fame in Canton, Ohio and the Franklin Mint, this collection of 50-coins honors inducted players and coaches chosen by the Hall's Selection Committee. The larger coins were released by subscription over the course of three years. The year of issue can be found on the serrated edge of the coin in very fine print. Reported mintage figures were 1,946 silver coins and 1,802 bronze coins with each coin containing 1-ounce of metal. The fronts feature a double image: a large portrait and an action scene. The unnumbered backs carry the Hall of Fame Logo, the player's name, position and a summary of his accomplishments. Each set came with a colorful album with a black-and-white action pencil drawing and a biography for each player. Another cardboard "mount" album was issued for use in housing the larger coin set. In 1976, the set was re-released in miniature form (roughly 1/2" diameter) as a complete set. These "minis" were issued sealed on a backer board and came with a jewelry style case to house the coins.

COMPLETE SET (50)	250.00	500.00
*SILVER MINI COINS: .3X TO .8X BRONZE		
1 Cliff Battles	4.00	10.00
2 Sammy Baugh	10.00	25.00
3 Chuck Bednarik	6.00	15.00
4 Bert Bell	4.00	10.00
5 Paul Brown 74	6.00	15.00
6 Joe Carr	4.00	10.00
7 Guy Chamberlin	4.00	10.00
8 Dutch Clark	5.00	12.00
9 Jimmy Conzelman	4.00	10.00
10 Art Donovan	6.00	15.00
11 Paddy Driscoll	4.00	10.00
12 Bill Dudley	5.00	12.00
13 Dan Fortmann	4.00	10.00
14 Otto Graham 73	10.00	25.00
15 Red Grange 72	12.00	30.00
16 George Halas 74	8.00	20.00
17 Mel Hein	4.00	10.00
18 Fats Henry	5.00	12.00
19 Bill Hewitt	4.00	10.00
20 Clarke Hinkle	4.00	10.00
21 Elroy Hirsch 73	6.00	15.00
22 Cal Hubbard	4.00	10.00
23 Lamar Hunt 74	4.00	10.00
24 Don Hutson	6.00	15.00
25 Curly Lambeau	5.00	12.00
26 Bobby Layne 73	8.00	20.00
27 Vince Lombardi 74	15.00	40.00
28 Sid Luckman	8.00	20.00
29 Gino Marchetti	5.00	12.00
30 Ollie Matson	6.00	15.00
31 George McAfee	5.00	12.00
32 Hugh McElhenny 73	6.00	15.00
33 Johnny Blood McNally	4.00	10.00
34 Marion Motley 73	6.00	15.00
35 Bronko Nagurski	12.00	30.00
36 Ernie Nevers 72	5.00	12.00
37 Leo Nomellini 74	5.00	12.00
38 Steve Owen	4.00	10.00
39 Joe Perry 73	5.00	12.00
40 Pete Pihos 73	5.00	12.00
41 Andy Robustelli	5.00	12.00
42 Ken Strong	5.00	12.00
43 Jim Thorpe	12.00	30.00
44 Y.A. Tittle 74	8.00	20.00
45 Charley Trippi 73	5.00	12.00
46 Emlen Tunnell 74	5.00	12.00
47 Bulldog Turner	5.00	12.00
48 Norm Van Brocklin 74	6.00	15.00
49 Steve Van Buren 73	6.00	15.00
50 Bob Waterfield 73	6.00	15.00

1972-74 Franklin Mint HOF Coins Silver

1 Cliff Battles	30.00	40.00
2 Sammy Baugh	30.00	40.00
3 Chuck Bednarik	30.00	40.00
4 Bert Bell	30.00	40.00
5 Paul Brown 74	30.00	40.00
6 Joe Carr	30.00	40.00
7 Guy Chamberlin	30.00	40.00
8 Dutch Clark	30.00	40.00
9 Jimmy Conzelman	30.00	40.00
10 Art Donovan	30.00	40.00
11 Paddy Driscoll	30.00	40.00
12 Bill Dudley	30.00	40.00
13 Dan Fortmann	30.00	40.00
14 Otto Graham 73	30.00	40.00
15 Red Grange 72	30.00	50.00
16 George Halas 74	30.00	40.00
17 Mel Hein	30.00	40.00
18 Fats Henry	30.00	40.00
19 Bill Hewitt	30.00	40.00
20 Clarke Hinkle	30.00	40.00
21 Elroy Hirsch 73	30.00	40.00
22 Cal Hubbard	30.00	40.00
23 Lamar Hunt 74	30.00	40.00
24 Don Hutson	30.00	40.00
25 Curly Lambeau	30.00	40.00
26 Bobby Layne 73	30.00	40.00
27 Vince Lombardi 74	30.00	60.00
28 Sid Luckman	30.00	40.00
29 Gino Marchetti	30.00	40.00
30 Ollie Matson	30.00	40.00
31 George McAfee	30.00	40.00
32 Hugh McElhenny 73	30.00	40.00
33 Johnny Blood McNally	30.00	40.00
34 Marion Motley 73	30.00	40.00
35 Bronko Nagurski	30.00	50.00
36 Ernie Nevers 72	30.00	40.00
37 Leo Nomellini 74	30.00	40.00
38 Steve Owen	30.00	40.00
39 Joe Perry 73	30.00	40.00
40 Pete Pihos 73	30.00	40.00
41 Andy Robustelli	30.00	40.00
42 Ken Strong	30.00	40.00
43 Jim Thorpe	30.00	50.00
44 Y.A. Tittle 74	30.00	40.00
45 Charley Trippi 73	30.00	40.00
46 Emlen Tunnell 74	30.00	40.00
47 Bulldog Turner	30.00	40.00
48 Norm Van Brocklin 74	30.00	40.00
49 Steve Van Buren 73	30.00	40.00
50 Bob Waterfield 73	30.00	40.00

1963 Gad Fun Cards

This set of 1963 Fun Cards were issued by a sports illustrator by the name of Gad from Minneapolis, Minnesota. The cards are printed on cardboard stock paper. The borderless fronts have black and white line drawings. A fun sport's fact or player career statistic is depicted in the drawing. The backs of the first six cards display numbers used to play the game explained on card number 6. The other backs carry a cartoon with a joke or riddle. Copyright information is listed on the lower portion of the card.

COMPLETE SET (84)	37.50	75.00
74 Minnesota Football Team/1949	.25	.50
81 Highest Football Game Score	.25	.50

1971 Gatorade Team Lids

These lids were actually the tops off bottles of Gatorade sold during the 1971 and 1972 NFL seasons. Each white colored lid had a dark outline of an NFL helmet with the team name printed underneath.

COMPLETE SET (26)	75.00	150.00
1 Atlanta Falcons	2.50	5.00
2 Baltimore Colts	3.00	6.00
3 Buffalo Bills	2.50	5.00
4 Chicago Bears	3.00	6.00
5 Cincinnati Bengals	2.50	5.00
6 Cleveland Browns	3.00	6.00
7 Dallas Cowboys	4.00	8.00
8 Denver Broncos	3.00	6.00
9 Detroit Lions	2.50	5.00
10 Green Bay Packers	4.00	8.00
11A Houston Oilers	4.00	10.00
11B Houston Oilers	2.50	5.00
12 Kansas City Chiefs	2.50	5.00
13A Los Angeles Rams	4.00	10.00
13B Los Angeles Rams	2.50	5.00
14 Miami Dolphins	4.00	8.00
15 Minnesota Vikings	3.00	6.00
16 New England Patriots	2.50	5.00
17 New Orleans Saints	2.50	5.00
18 New York Giants	2.50	5.00
19 New York Jets	2.50	5.00
20 Oakland Raiders	4.00	8.00
21 Philadelphia Eagles	2.50	5.00
22 Pittsburgh Steelers	4.00	8.00
23 San Diego Chargers	2.50	5.00
24 San Francisco 49ers	4.00	8.00
25 St. Louis Cardinals	2.50	5.00
26A Washington Redskins	4.00	8.00
26B Washington Redskins	4.00	8.00

1956 Giants Team Issue

The 1956 Giants Team Issue set contains 36 cards measuring approximately 4 7/8" by 6 7/8". The fronts have black and white posed player photos with white borders. A facsimile autograph appears below the picture. The backs have brief biographical information and career highlights. The cards are unnumbered and checklisted below in alphabetical order. Many of the cards in this set are similar to the 1957 release and are only distinguishable by the differences noted below in parenthesis. We've included the first line of text on the cardback of some to help differentiate the two sets.

COMPLETE SET (36)	125.00	250.00
1 Bill Austin	4.00	8.00
2 Ray Beck	4.00	8.00
3 Roosevelt Brown	6.00	12.00
4 Hank Burnine	4.00	8.00
5 Don Chandler	4.00	8.00
6 Bobby Clatterbuck	4.00	8.00
7 Charley Conerly	10.00	20.00
8 Frank Gifford	20.00	40.00
9 Roosevelt Grier	6.00	12.00
10 Don Heinrich	4.00	8.00
11 John Hermann	4.00	8.00
12 Jim Lee Howell CO	4.00	8.00
13 Sam Huff	10.00	20.00
14 Ed Hughes	4.00	8.00
15 Gerald Huth	4.00	8.00
16 Jim Katcavage	4.00	8.00
17 Gene Kirby ANN	4.00	8.00
18 Ken MacAfee E	4.00	8.00
19 Dick Modzelewski	4.00	8.00
20 Henry Moore	4.00	8.00
21 Dick Nolan	4.00	8.00
22 Jim Patton	4.00	8.00
23 Andy Robustelli	7.50	15.00
24 Kyle Rote	5.00	10.00
25 Chris Schenkel ANN	4.00	8.00
26 Bob Schnelker	4.00	8.00
27 Jack Stroud	4.00	8.00
28 Harland Svare	4.00	8.00
29 Bill Svoboda	4.00	8.00
30 Bob Topp	4.00	8.00
31 Mel Triplett	4.00	8.00
32 Emlen Tunnell	6.00	12.00
33 Alex Webster	5.00	10.00
34 Ray Wietecha	4.00	8.00
35 Dick Yelvington	4.00	8.00
36 Walt Yowarsky	4.00	8.00

1957 Giants Team Issue

This 36-card set measures approximately 4 7/8" by 6 7/8". The cardfronts have a black and white player photo printed on thin card stock with a white border. The cardbacks give biographical and statistical information. This set features one of the earliest Vince Lombardi cards. The cards are unnumbered and checklisted below in alphabetical order. Many of the cards in this set are similar to the 1956 release and are only distinguishable by the differences noted below in parenthesis. We've included the first line of text on the cardback of some to help differentiate the two sets.

COMPLETE SET (36)	150.00	300.00
1 Ben Agajanian	4.00	8.00
2 Bill Austin	4.00	8.00
3 Ray Beck	4.00	8.00
4 John Bookman	4.00	8.00
5 Roosevelt Brown	6.00	12.00
6 Don Chandler	4.00	8.00
7 Bobby Clatterbuck	4.00	8.00
8 Charley Conerly	10.00	20.00
9 Gene Filipski	4.00	8.00
10 Frank Gifford	15.00	30.00
11 Don Heinrich	4.00	8.00
12 Sam Huff	6.00	12.00
13 Ed Hughes	4.00	8.00
14 Gerald Huth	4.00	8.00
15 Jim Katcavage	4.00	8.00
16 Les Keiter ANN	4.00	8.00
17 Cliff Livingston	4.00	8.00
18 Ken MacAfee E	4.00	8.00
19 Dennis Mendyk	4.00	8.00
20 Dick Modzelewski	4.00	8.00
21 Dick Nolan	4.00	8.00
22 Jim Patton	4.00	8.00
23 Andy Robustelli	6.00	12.00
24 Kyle Rote	5.00	10.00
25 Chris Schenkel ANN	4.00	8.00
26 Jack Spinks	4.00	8.00
27 Jack Stroud	4.00	8.00
28 Harland Svare	4.00	8.00
29 Bill Svoboda	4.00	8.00
30 Mel Triplett	4.00	8.00
31 Emlen Tunnell	6.00	12.00
32 Alex Webster	5.00	10.00
33 Ray Wietecha	4.00	8.00
34 Dick Yelvington	4.00	8.00
35 Walt Yowarsky	4.00	8.00
36 Giants Coaches	30.00	60.00

1959 Giants Shell Glasses

These four drinking glasses were issued by Shell Gasoline Stations around 1959. Each features the same artwork and captions found on the 1959 Giants Shell Posters with the image etched on the glass with a frosted background.

COMPLETE SET (4)	100.00	200.00
1 Frank Gifford	40.00	80.00
2 Sam Huff	30.00	60.00
3 Dick Modzelewski	20.00	40.00
4 Kyle Rote	25.00	50.00

1959 Giants Shell Posters

This set of ten posters was distributed by Shell Oil in 1959. The pictures are black and white drawings by Robert Riger, and measure approximately 11 3/4" by 13 3/4". The unnumbered posters are arranged alphabetically by the player's last name and feature members of the New York Giants.

COMPLETE SET (10)	75.00	150.00
1 Charley Conerly	7.50	15.00
2 Frank Gifford	18.00	30.00
3 Sam Huff	12.00	20.00
4 Dick Modzelewski	6.00	12.00
5 Jim Patton	6.00	12.00
6 Andy Robustelli	7.50	15.00
7 Kyle Rote	7.50	15.00
8 Bob Schnelker	6.00	12.00
9 Pat Summerall	7.50	15.00
10 Alex Webster	7.50	15.00
R.Brown		

1960 Giants Jay Publishing

This 12-card set features (approximately) 5" by 7" black-and-white player photos. The photos show players in traditional poses with the quarterback preparing to throw, the runner heading downfield, and the defenseman ready for the tackle. These cards were packaged 12 to a packet and originally sold for 25 cents. The backs are blank. The cards are unnumbered and checklisted in alphabetical order.

COMPLETE SET (12)	75.00	135.00
1 Roosevelt Brown	6.00	12.00
2 Don Chandler	3.00	6.00
3 Charley Conerly	10.00	20.00
4 Frank Gifford	17.50	35.00
5 Roosevelt Grier	5.00	10.00
6 Sam Huff	10.00	20.00
7 Phil King	3.00	6.00
8 Andy Robustelli	7.50	15.00
9 Kyle Rote	4.00	8.00
10 Bob Schnelker	3.00	6.00
11 Pat Summerall	7.50	15.00
12 Alex Webster	4.00	8.00

1961 Giants Jay Publishing

This 12-card set features (approximately) 5" by 7" black-and-white player photos. The photos show players in traditional poses with the quarterback preparing to throw, the runner heading downfield, and the defenseman ready for the tackle. These cards were packaged 12 to a packet and originally sold for 25 cents. The backs are blank. The cards are unnumbered and checklisted below in alphabetical order.

COMPLETE SET (12)	50.00	100.00
1 Roosevelt Brown	4.00	8.00
2 Don Chandler	3.00	6.00
3 Charley Conerly	7.50	15.00
4 Roosevelt Grier	4.00	8.00
5 Sam Huff	6.00	12.00
6 Dick Modzelewski	3.00	6.00
7 Jimmy Patton	3.00	6.00
8 Jim Podoley	3.00	6.00
9 Andy Robustelli	5.00	10.00
10 Allie Sherman CO	3.00	6.00
11 Del Shofner	4.00	8.00
12 Y.A. Tittle	12.50	25.00

1962 Giants Team Issue

The New York Giants issued this set of player photos in 1962. The photos were distributed in set form complete with a paper checklist of the 10-players. Each measures approximately 8" by 10" and features a black and white photo with only the player's name directly below the picture within the border. The cards are blankbacked and unnumbered.

COMPLETE SET (10)	75.00	150.00
1 Roosevelt Brown	7.50	15.00
2 Don Chandler	6.00	12.00
3 Frank Gifford	17.50	35.00
4 Sam Huff	10.00	20.00
5 Dick Lynch	6.00	12.00
6 Jim Patton	6.00	12.00
7 Andy Robustelli	10.00	20.00
8 Del Shofner	7.50	15.00
9 Y.A. Tittle	12.50	25.00
10 Alex Webster	6.00	12.00

1965 Giants Team Issue Color

This set was originally released as a poster-sized sheet of color photos with facsimile player signatures. When cut, the photos measure roughly 5" by 7". The set is unnumbered and listed below alphabetically with prices for cut cards..

COMPLETE SET (15)	75.00	150.00
1 Roosevelt Brown	7.50	15.00
2 Tucker Frederickson	5.00	10.00
3 Jerry Hillebrand	5.00	10.00
4 Jim Katcavage	5.00	10.00
5 Spider Lockhart	6.00	12.00
6 Dick Lynch	5.00	10.00
7 Chuck Mercein	5.00	10.00
8 Earl Morrall	6.00	12.00
9 Joe Morrison	6.00	12.00
10 Del Shofner	6.00	12.00
11 Lou Slaby	5.00	10.00
12 Aaron Thomas	5.00	10.00
13 Steve Thurlow	5.00	10.00
14 Ernie Wheelwright	5.00	10.00
15 Giants Team Photo	6.00	12.00

1965-68 Giants Team Issue

The Giants issued a large number of roughly 8" x 10" black and white photos in the mid 1960s. Each photo includes only the player's name and position below the image in all capital letters and the backs are blank. Many player's were issued in various different poses as well as with variations in the text below the photo. We've included this detail below when known. Additions to this list are appreciated.

1A Erich Barnes	5.00	10.00
(Def. Halfback)		
1B Erich Barnes	5.00	10.00
(Def. Halfback)		
1C Erich Barnes	5.00	10.00
(Defensive Back)		
2 Roosevelt Brown	7.50	15.00
3 Henry Carr	5.00	10.00
4A Clarence Childs	5.00	10.00
Defensive Back, name		
and position 1 1/4-in apart)		
4B Clarence Childs	5.00	10.00
Defensive Back, name		
and position 1 1/4-in apart)		
5 Darrell Dess	5.00	10.00
6 Scott Eaton	5.00	10.00
7 Tucker Frederickson	6.00	12.00
8A Jerry Hillebrand	5.00	10.00
(Linebacker, name and		
position 1 3/8-in apart)		
8B Jerry Hillebrand	5.00	10.00
(Linebacker, name and		
position 3/4-in apart)		
9A Jim Katcavage	5.00	10.00
(Defensive End)		
9B Jim Katcavage	5.00	10.00
(Def. End, name and		
position 2 3/8-in apart)		
9C Jim Katcavage	5.00	10.00
(Def. End, name and		
position 1 1/4-in apart)		
10A Ernie Koy	6.00	12.00
(Offensive Back)		
10B Ernie Koy	6.00	12.00
(Running Back)		
11 Greg Larson	5.00	10.00
12 Dick Lynch	5.00	10.00
13 Earl Morrall	6.00	12.00
14 Joe Morrison	6.00	12.00
15 Allie Sherman CO	6.00	12.00
(At chalkboard)		
16 Del Shofner	6.00	12.00
17 Andy Stynchula	5.00	10.00
18 Fran Tarkenton	12.50	25.00
19 Aaron Thomas	5.00	10.00

1966 Giants Team Issue Color

This set was originally released as a poster-sized sheet of color photos with facsimile player signatures. When cut, the photos measure roughly 5" by 7". The set is unnumbered and listed below alphabetically with prices for cut photos.

1 Henry Carr	5.00	10.00
2 Tucker Frederickson	5.00	10.00
3 Pete Gogolak	5.00	10.00
4 Jerry Hillebrand	5.00	10.00
5 Homer Jones	5.00	10.00
6 Jim Katcavage	5.00	10.00
7 Ernie Koy	5.00	10.00
8 Spider Lockhart	6.00	12.00
9 Chuck Mercein	5.00	10.00
10 Earl Morrall	7.50	15.00
11 Joe Morrison	6.00	12.00
12 Jim Prestel	5.00	10.00
13 Aaron Thomas	5.00	10.00
14 Go-Go Giants '66 Title	5.00	10.00
15 Earl Morrall Action 7x10	6.00	12.00

1972 Giants Team Issue

These photos were issued by the Giants in 1972. Each measures roughly 4" by 5" with a white border on all 4-sides of the player image. The player's name and position is included below the photo and the cardbacks are blank and unnumbered.

COMPLETE SET (18)	50.00	100.00
1 Pete Athas	4.00	8.00
2 Bobby Duhon	4.00	8.00
3 Charlie Evans	4.00	8.00
4 Jim Files	4.00	8.00
5 Pete Gogolak	4.00	8.00
6 Jack Gregory	4.00	8.00
7 Bob Grim	4.00	8.00
8 Don Herrmann	4.00	8.00
9 Rich Houston	4.00	8.00
10 Pat Hughes	4.00	8.00
11 Randy Johnson	5.00	10.00
12 Ron Johnson	4.00	8.00
13 Carl Lockhart	4.00	8.00
14 Eldridge Small	4.00	8.00
15 Joe Taffoni	4.00	8.00
16 Rocky Thompson	4.00	8.00
17 Dave Tipton	4.00	8.00
18 Willie Williams	4.00	8.00

1973 Giants Color Litho

Each of these color lithos measures approximately 8 1/2" by 11" and is blank backed. There is no card border and a facsimile autograph appears within a white triangle below the player photo.

COMPLETE SET (8)	25.00	50.00
1 Jim Files	3.00	6.00
2 Jack Gregory	3.00	6.00
3 Ron Johnson	4.00	8.00
4 Greg Larson	3.00	6.00
5 Spider Lockhart	4.00	8.00
6 Norm Snead	5.00	10.00
7 Bob Tucker	4.00	8.00
8 Brad Van Pelt	4.00	8.00

1974 Giants Color Litho

Each of these color photos measures approximately 8 1/2" by 11" and is blankbacked. The photos are borderless and the player's name appears in white in the lower left or right of the player image.

COMPLETE SET (8)	25.00	50.00
1 Pete Athas	3.00	6.00
2 Pete Gogolak	3.00	6.00
3 Bob Grim	4.00	8.00
4 Don Herrmann	3.00	6.00
5 Pat Hughes	3.00	6.00
6 Bob Hyland	3.00	6.00
7 Ron Johnson	4.00	8.00
8 John Mendenhall	3.00	6.00

1974 Giants Team Issue

This photo pack set was issued by the Giants in 1974. Each photo measures roughly 8 1/2" by 10" with a white border on all 4-sides of the player image. The player's name and position is included below the photo and the cardbacks are blank and unnumbered.

COMPLETE SET (8)	25.00	50.00
1 Chuck Crist	3.00	6.00
2 Pete Gogolak	3.00	6.00
3 Bob Grim	3.00	6.00
4 Brian Kelley	3.00	6.00
5 Spider Lockhart	4.00	8.00
6 Norm Snead	5.00	10.00
7 Doug Van Horn	3.00	6.00
8 Willie Young	3.00	6.00

1975 Giants Team Issue

This photos were issued by the Giants around 1975. Each measures roughly 8" by 10" with a white border on all 4-sides of the player image. Just the player's name and position are included below the photo and the backs are blank and unnumbered.

1 Bobby Brooks	5.00	10.00
2 Pete Gogolak	5.00	10.00
3 Ron Johnson	6.00	12.00
4 Norm Snead	6.00	12.00
5 Willie Young	5.00	10.00

1979 Giants Team Sheets

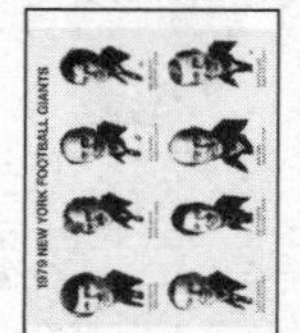

This set consists of eight 8" by 10" sheets that display 5-8 black-and-white player/coach photos on each. Each individual photo measures approximately 2 1/4" by 3 1/4" and includes the player's name, jersey number, position, and brief vital stats below the photo. "1979 New York Football Giants" appears across the top of each sheet and the backs are blank. The sheets are unnumbered and checklisted below alphabetically according to the player featured in the upper left corner.

COMPLETE SET (8)	25.00	50.00
1 Sheet 1	4.00	8.00
2 Sheet 2	3.00	6.00
3 Sheet 3	5.00	10.00
4 Sheet 4	3.00	6.00
5 Sheet 5	3.00	6.00
6 Sheet 6	5.00	10.00
7 Sheet 7	3.00	6.00
8 Sheet 8	3.00	6.00

1969 Glendale Stamps

This set contains 312 stamps featuring NFL players each measuring approximately 1 13/16" by 2 15/16". The stamps were meant to be pasted in an accompanying album, which itself measures approximately 9" by 12". The stamps and the album positions are unnumbered so the stamps are ordered and numbered below according to the team order that they appear in the book. The team order is alphabetical as well, according to the city name. The stamp of O.J. Simpson predates his 1970 Topps Rookie Card by one year and the stamp of Gene Upshaw predates his Rookie Card by three years.

COMPLETE SET (312)	200.00	350.00
1 Bob Berry	.30	.75
2 Clark Miller	.30	.75
3 Jim Butler	.30	.75
4 Junior Coffey	.30	.75
5 Paul Flatley	.30	.75
6 Randy Johnson	.30	.75
7 Charlie Bryant	.30	.75
8 Billy Lothridge	.30	.75
9 Tommy Nobis	.75	1.50
10 Claude Humphrey	.30	.75
11 Ken Reaves	.30	.75
12 Jerry Simmons	.30	.75
13 Mike Curtis	.40	1.00
14 Dennis Gaubatz	.30	.75
15 Jerry Logan	.30	.75
16 Lenny Lyles	.30	.75
17 John Mackey	1.00	2.00
18 Tom Matte	.30	.75
19 Lou Michaels	.30	.75
20 Jimmy Orr	.30	.75
21 Willie Richardson	.30	.75
22 Don Shinnick	.30	.75
23 Dan Sullivan	.30	.75
24 Johnny Unitas	10.00	20.00
25 Houston Antwine	.30	.75
26 John Bramlett	.30	.75
27 Aaron Marsh	.30	.75
28 R.C. Gamble	.30	.75
29 Gino Cappelletti	.40	1.00
30 John Charles	.30	.75
31 Larry Eisenhauer	.30	.75
32 Jon Morris	.30	.75
33 Jim Nance	.30	.75
34 Len St. Jean	.30	.75
35 Mike Taliaferro	.30	.75
36 Jim Whalen	.30	.75
37 Stew Barber	.30	.75
38 Al Bemiller	.30	.75
39 George(Butch) Byrd	.30	.75
40 Booker Edgerson	.30	.75
41 Harry Jacobs	.30	.75
42 Jack Kemp	10.00	20.00
43 Ron McDole	.30	.75
44 Joe O'Donnell	.30	.75
45 John Pitts	.30	.75
46 George Saimes	.30	.75
47 Mike Stratton	.30	.75
48 O.J. Simpson	7.50	15.00
49 Ronnie Bull	.30	.75
50 Dick Butkus	7.50	15.00
51 Jim Cadile	.30	.75
52 Jack Concannon	.30	.75
53 Dick Evey	.30	.75
54 Bennie McRae	.30	.75
55 Ed O'Bradovich	.30	.75
56 Brian Piccolo	12.50	25.00
57 Mike Pyle	.30	.75
58 Gale Sayers	7.50	15.00
59 Dick Gordon	.30	.75
60 Roosevelt Taylor	.30	.75
61 Al Beauchamp	.30	.75
62 Dave Middendorf	.30	.75
63 Harry Gunner	.30	.75
64 Bobby Hunt	.30	.75
65 Bob Johnson	.30	.75
66 Charley King	.30	.75
67 Andy Rice	.30	.75
68 Paul Robinson	.30	.75
69 Bill Staley	.30	.75
70 Pat Matson	.30	.75
71 Bob Trumpy	.50	1.25
72 Sam Wyche	2.00	4.00
73 Erich Barnes	.30	.75
74 Gary Collins	.30	.75
75 Ben Davis	.30	.75
76 John Demarie	.30	.75
77 Gene Hickerson	.40	1.00
78 Jim Houston	.30	.75
79 Ernie Kellerman	.30	.75
80 Leroy Kelly	1.25	2.50
81 Dale Lindsey	.30	.75
82 Bill Nelsen	.30	.75
83 Jim Kanicki	.30	.75
84 Dick Schafrath	.30	.75
85 George Andrie	.30	.75
86 Mike Clark	.30	.75
87 Cornell Green	.30	.75

88 Bob Hayes	1.00	2.00
89 Chuck Howley	.40	1.00
90 Lee Roy Jordan	.75	1.50
91 Bob Lilly	2.50	5.00
92 Craig Morton	.40	1.00
93 John Niland	.30	.75
94 Dan Reeves	2.50	5.00
95 Mel Renfro	1.00	2.00
96 Lance Rentzel	.30	.75
97 Tom Beer	.30	.75
98 Billy Van Heusen	.30	.75
99 Mike Current	.30	.75
100 Al Denson	.30	.75
101 Pete Duranko	.30	.75
102 George Goeddeke	.30	.75
103 John Huard	.30	.75
104 Rich Jackson	.30	.75
105 Pete Jacques	.30	.75
106 Fran Lynch	.30	.75
107 Floyd Little	.75	1.50
108 Steve Tensi	.30	.75
109 Lem Barney	1.25	2.50
110 Nick Eddy	.30	.75
111 Mel Farr	.30	.75
112 Ed Flanagan	.30	.75
113 Larry Hand	.30	.75
114 Alex Karras	1.25	2.50
115 Dick LeBeau	.30	.75
116 Mike Lucci	.30	.75
117 Earl McCullouch	.30	.75
118 Bill Munson	.30	.75
119 Jerry Rush	.30	.75
120 Wayne Walker	.30	.75
121 Herb Adderley	1.00	2.00
122 Donny Anderson	.40	1.00
123 Lee Roy Caffey	.30	.75
124 Carroll Dale	.30	.75
125 Willie Davis	1.00	2.00
126 Boyd Dowler	.30	.75
127 Marv Fleming	.30	.75
128 Bob Jeter	.30	.75
129 Hank Jordan	1.00	2.00
130 Dave Robinson	.40	1.00
131 Bart Starr	10.00	20.00
132 Willie Wood	1.00	2.00
133 Pete Beathard	.30	.75
134 Jim Beirne	.30	.75
135 Garland Boyette	.30	.75
136 Woody Campbell	.30	.75
137 Miller Farr	.30	.75
138 Hoyle Granger	.30	.75
139 Mac Haik	.30	.75
140 Ken Houston	1.25	2.50
141 Bobby Maples	.30	.75
142 Alvin Reed	.30	.75
143 Don Trull	.30	.75
144 George Webster	.30	.75
145 Bobby Bell	1.00	2.00
146 Aaron Brown	.30	.75
147 Buck Buchanan	1.00	2.00
148 Len Dawson	4.00	8.00
149 Mike Garrett	.40	1.00
150 Robert Holmes	.30	.75
151 Willie Lanier	1.25	2.50
152 Frank Pitts	.30	.75
153 Johnny Robinson	.40	1.00
154 Jan Stenerud	1.25	2.50
155 Otis Taylor	.40	1.00
156 Jim Tyrer	.30	.75
157 Dick Bass	.30	.75
158 Maxie Baughan	.30	.75
159 Richie Petitbon	.30	.75
160 Roger Brown	.30	.75
161 Roman Gabriel	.50	1.25
162 Bruce Gossett	.30	.75
163 Deacon Jones	1.00	2.00
164 Tom Mack	.50	1.25
165 Tommy Mason	.30	.75
166 Ed Meador	.30	.75
167 Merlin Olsen	1.25	2.50
168 Pat Studstill	.30	.75
169 Jack Clancy	.30	.75
170 Maxie Williams	.30	.75
171 Larry Csonka	7.50	15.00
172 Jim Warren	.30	.75
173 Norm Evans	.30	.75
174 Rick Norton	.30	.75
175 Bob Griese	6.00	12.00
176 Howard Twilley	.30	.75
177 Billy Neighbors	.30	.75
178 Nick Buoniconti	.75	1.50
179 Tom Goode	.30	.75
180 Dick Westmoreland	.30	.75
181 Grady Alderman	.30	.75
182 Bill Brown	.30	.75
183 Fred Cox	.30	.75
184 Clint Jones	.30	.75
185 Joe Kapp	.40	1.00
186 Paul Krause	.40	1.00
187 Gary Larsen	.30	.75
188 Jim Marshall	1.00	2.00
189 Dave Osborn	.30	.75
190 Alan Page	2.50	5.00
191 Mick Tingelhoff	.40	1.00
192 Roy Winston	.30	.75
193 Dan Abramowicz	.30	.75
194 Doug Atkins	1.00	2.00
195 Bo Burris	.30	.75
196 John Douglas	.30	.75
197 Don Shy	.30	.75
198 Billy Kilmer	.40	1.00
199 Tony Lorick	.30	.75
200 Dave Parks	.30	.75
201 Dave Rowe	.30	.75
202 Monty Stickles	.30	.75
203 Steve Stonebreaker	.30	.75
204 Del Williams	.30	.75
205 Pete Case	.30	.75
206 Tommy Crutcher	.30	.75
207 Scott Eaton	.30	.75
208 Tucker Frederickson	.30	.75
209 Pete Gogolak	.30	.75
210 Homer Jones	.30	.75
211 Ernie Koy	.30	.75
212 Spider Lockhart	.30	.75
213 Bruce Maher	.30	.75
214 Aaron Thomas	.30	.75
215 Fran Tarkenton	6.00	12.00
216 Jim Katcavage	.30	.75
217 Al Atkinson	.30	.75
218 Emerson Boozer	.30	.75
219 John Elliott	.30	.75
220 Dave Herman	.30	.75
221 Winston Hill	.30	.75
222 Jim Hudson	.30	.75
223 Pete Lammons	.30	.75
224 Gerry Philbin	.30	.75
225 George Sauer Jr.	.30	.75
226 Joe Namath	12.50	25.00
227 Matt Snell	.40	1.00
228 Jim Turner	.30	.75
229 Fred Biletnikoff	2.00	4.00
230 Willie Brown	1.00	2.00
231 Billy Cannon	.40	1.00
232 Dan Conners	.30	.75
233 Ben Davidson	.40	1.00
234 Hewritt Dixon	.30	.75
235 Daryle Lamonica	.50	1.25
236 Ike Lassiter	.30	.75
237 Kent McCloughan	.30	.75
238 Jim Otto	1.00	2.00
239 Harry Schuh	.30	.75
240 Gene Upshaw	1.25	2.50
241 Gary Ballman	.30	.75
242 Joe Carollo	.30	.75
243 Dave Lloyd	.30	.75
244 Fred Hill	.30	.75
245 Al Nelson	.30	.75
246 Joe Scarpati	.30	.75
247 Sam Baker	.30	.75
248 Fred Brown	.30	.75
249 Floyd Peters	.30	.75
250 Nate Ramsey	.30	.75
251 Norm Snead	.40	1.00
252 Tom Woodeshick	.30	.75
253 John Hilton	.30	.75
254 Kent Nix	.30	.75
255 Paul Martha	.30	.75
256 Ben McGee	.30	.75
257 Andy Russell	.40	1.00
258 Dick Shiner	.30	.75
259 J.R. Wilburn	.30	.75
260 Marv Woodson	.30	.75
261 Earl Gros	.30	.75
262 Dick Hoak	.30	.75
263 Roy Jefferson	.30	.75
264 Larry Gagner	.30	.75
265 Johnny Roland	.30	.75
266 Jackie Smith	1.00	2.00
267 Jim Bakken	.30	.75
268 Don Brumm	.30	.75
269 Bob DeMarco	.30	.75
270 Irv Goode	.30	.75
271 Ken Gray	.30	.75
272 Charley Johnson	.40	1.00
273 Ernie McMillan	.30	.75
274 Larry Stallings	.30	.75
275 Jerry Stovall	.30	.75
276 Larry Wilson	.75	1.50
277 Chuck Allen	.30	.75
278 Lance Alworth	2.50	5.00
279 Kenny Graham	.30	.75
280 Steve DeLong	.30	.75
281 Willie Frazier	.30	.75
282 Gary Garrison	.30	.75
283 Sam Gruneisen	.30	.75
284 John Hadl	.50	1.25
285 Brad Hubbert	.30	.75
286 Ron Mix	.75	1.50
287 Dick Post	.30	.75
288 Walt Sweeney	.30	.75
289 Kermit Alexander	.30	.75
290 Ed Beard	.30	.75
291 Bruce Bosley	.30	.75
292 John Brodie	1.25	2.50
293 Stan Hindman	.30	.75
294 Jim Johnson	1.00	2.00
295 Charlie Krueger	.30	.75
296 Clifton McNeil	.30	.75
297 Gary Lewis	.30	.75
298 Howard Mudd	.30	.75
299 Dave Wilcox	.40	1.00
300 Ken Willard	.30	.75
301 Charlie Gogolak	.30	.75
302 Len Hauss	.30	.75
303 Sonny Jurgensen	2.50	5.00
304 Carl Kammerer	.30	.75
305 Walter Rock	.30	.75
306 Ray Schoenke	.30	.75
307 Chris Hanburger	.40	1.00
308 Tom Brown	.30	.75
309 Sam Huff	1.25	2.50
310 Bob Long	.30	.75
311 Vince Promuto	.30	.75
312 Pat Richter	.30	.75
NNO Stamp Album	10.00	20.00

1888 Goodwin Champions N162

This 50-card set issued by Goodwin was one of the major competitors to the N28 and N29 sets marketed by Allen and Ginter. It contains individuals representing 18 sports, with eight baseball players pictured. Each color card is backlisted and bears advertising for "Old Judge" and "Gypsy Queen" cigarettes on the front. The set was released to the public in 1888 and an album (catalog: A36) is associated with it as a premium issue.

12 Harry Beecher (Football)	3,000.00	4,500.00

1939 Gridiron Greats Blotters

This set of 12 ink blotters was produced by the Louis F. Dow Company in honor of great college football players. These blotters were issued in two different sizes: legal sized blotter at approximately 9" by 3 7/8" and a smaller version at 3 3/8" by 6 1/4." They were issued in a brown paper sleeve as a complete set. The left portion of the blotter front has a head and shoulders sepia-toned drawing, with the player wearing either a red or a blue jersey. The right portion of the blotter has a brief player profile and one or more or even none of the following: a sponsor advertisement and/or monthly calendar (a different month on each of the 12 blotters). The backs are blank with just the felt-like blotter material and each is numbered in small print on the front. Many of these player blotters were issued over a period of years as some have been found with different calendar years, no calendar at all, and/or various advertisors such as Syracuse Letter Co., Famous Energy, or Pyott Foundry. Louis Dow also produced larger wall type calendars for some, or all, of these player works of art as well as bound notebooks using the player images on the covers.

COMPLETE SET (12)	7,000.00	10,000.00
B3941 Jim Thorpe	900.00	1,500.00
B3942 Walter Eckersall	300.00	500.00
B3943 Edward Mahan	300.00	500.00
B3944 Sammy Baugh	750.00	1,250.00
B3945 Thomas Shevlin	300.00	500.00
B3946 Red Grange	900.00	1,500.00
B3947 Ernie Nevers	400.00	750.00
B3948 George Gipp	600.00	1,000.00
B3949 Pudge Heffelfinger	300.00	500.00
B3950 Bronko Nagurski	900.00	1,500.00
B3951 Willie Heston	300.00	500.00
B3952 Jay Berwanger	300.00	500.00

1939 Gridiron Greats Notebooks

These notebook covers were produced by the Louis F. Dow Company in honor of great college football players. Each measures slightly smaller than 8" by 10" and was blank backed. They can be found bound with pages or with the pages carefully removed.

1 Jay Berwanger	300.00	500.00
2 George Gipp	600.00	1,000.00
3 Willie Heston	300.00	500.00
4 Bronko Nagurski	900.00	1,500.00

1941 Gridiron Greats Blotters

These oversized blotters are virtually identical to the 1939 Gridiron Greats Blotters and were produced by Louis F. Dow Company. The artwork featured for each player is the same but the calendar is for the year 1941. It is believed that there are likely a number of different advertising sponsors used on the calendars as well as the full complement of players.

1 Red Grange	900.00	1,500.00

1943 Gridiron Greats Calendars

These oversized calendars are very similar to the 1939 Gridiron Greats Blotters and were produced by Louis F. Dow Company. The artwork featured for each player is the same but these calendars are vertically oriented. The fronts contain a small attached calendar for the year 1943 along with sponsor advertising. It is believed that there are likely a number of different advertising sponsors used on the calendars as well as the full complement of players.

M3902 Walter Eckersall	250.00	400.00
M3910 Bronko Nagurski	600.00	1,000.00
M3952 Jay Berwanger	250.00	400.00

1963 Hall of Fame Postcards

1 Sammy Baugh	10.00	20.00
2 Dutch Clark	7.50	15.00
3 Fats Henry	7.50	15.00
4 Johnny Blood McNally	7.50	15.00
5 Ernie Nevers	7.50	15.00
6 Jim Thorpe	12.50	25.00

1974 Hawaii Hawaiians WFL Team Issue

These photos were issued by the team for promotional purposes and fan mail requests. Each includes a black and white image printed above the subject's name and team logo. Each measures 5 1/2" by 7."

COMPLETE SET (9)	25.00	60.00
1 Gary Baccus	3.00	8.00
2 Damone Bame CO	3.00	8.00
3 Lem Burnham	3.00	8.00
4 Ron East	3.00	8.00
5 John Kelsey	3.00	8.00
6 Al Oliver	3.00	8.00
7 Greg Slough	3.00	8.00
8 Levi Stanley	3.00	8.00
9 Norris Weese	3.00	8.00

1970 Hi-C Mini-Posters

This set of ten posters were the insides of the Hi-C drink can labels. They are numbered very subtly below the player's picture but they are listed below in alphabetical order. The players selected for the set were leaders at their positions during the 1969 season. The mini-posters measure approximately 6 5/8" by 13 3/4".

COMPLETE SET (10)	300.00	600.00
1 Greg Cook	30.00	60.00
2 Fred Cox	30.00	60.00
3 Sonny Jurgensen	50.00	100.00
4 David Lee	25.00	50.00
5 Dennis Partee	25.00	50.00
6 Dick Post	25.00	50.00
7 Mel Renfro	50.00	100.00
8 Gale Sayers	75.00	150.00
9 Emmitt Thomas	30.00	60.00
10 Jim Turner	25.00	50.00

1974 Houston Texans WFL Team Issue 8X10

The photos measure roughly 8" x 10" and include black and white images with the player's name in the lower left below the photo, his position centered, and the team name on the right side below the photo. The backs are blank.

1 Garland Boyette	7.50	15.00
2 Joe Robb	7.50	15.00

1938 Huskies Cereal

These cards are actually entire backs of Huskies cereal boxes from the late 1930s. Each box back features an artist's rendering of the University of Washington Huskies coach Jimmy Phelan and one NFL player (or just a single player) at the top along with brief bios on each. A series of smaller drawings appears below the two that were intended to be cut out and used to form a moving picture simulating football action when flipped by the collector.

1 J.Phelan S.Baugh	350.00	600.00
2 Dutch Clark	300.00	500.00
3 J.Phelan D.Hutson	350.00	600.00

1974 Jacksonville Sharks WFL Team Issue

These black and white photos were issued by the team and measure roughly 3 1/2" x 4 3/4." The backs are blank but the fronts include a large amount of information within the space below the player image: jersey number, player's name, team logo, position initials, height, and weight.

1 Tommy Durrance	6.00	12.00
2 Dennis Hughes	6.00	12.00
3 Grant Guthrie	6.00	12.00
4 Kay Stephenson	6.00	12.00

1975 Jacksonville Express Team Issue

The Jacksonville Express of the World Football League distributed this set of player photos. Each photo measures approximately 4 1/2" by 5" and features a black and white player picture with a blank cardback. The photos contain no player names nor any other identifying text. We've listed the photos below according to the player's jersey number.

COMPLETE SET (38)	450.00	900.00
2 Johnny Osborne	12.50	25.00
3 Lee McGriff	12.50	25.00
6 Dan Callahan	12.50	25.00

7 Steve Barrios	12.50	25.00
8 Steve Foley	15.00	30.00
10 George Mira	15.00	30.00
12 David Fowler	12.50	25.00
16 Ron Coppenbarger	12.50	25.00
18 Abb Ansley	12.50	25.00
20 Jimmy Poulos	12.50	25.00
21 Tommy Reamon	12.50	25.00
23 Alfred Haywood	12.50	25.00
30 Jeff Davis RB	12.50	25.00
31 Fletcher Smith	12.50	25.00
32 Brian Duncan	12.50	25.00
42 Canary Simmons	12.50	25.00
44 Skip Johns	12.50	25.00
46 Willie Jackson DB	15.00	30.00
50 Rick Thomann	12.50	25.00
Ted Jarnov		
51 Jay Casey	12.50	25.00
52 Glen Gaspard	12.50	25.00
54 Howard Kindig	12.50	25.00
55 Fred Abbott	12.50	25.00
57 Ted Jarnov	12.50	25.00
58 Chip Myrtle	15.00	30.00
59 Sherman Miller	12.50	25.00
63 Tom Walker	12.50	25.00
68 Carleton Oats	12.50	25.00
70 Buck Baker	12.50	25.00
76 Carl Taibi	12.50	25.00
77 Joe Jackson	12.50	25.00
78 Kenny Moore	12.50	25.00
79 Larry Gagner	12.50	25.00
80 Dennis Hughes	12.50	25.00
81 Charles Hall	12.50	25.00
82 Don Brumm	15.00	30.00
87 Mike Creaney	12.50	25.00
88 Witt Beckman	12.50	25.00

1963 Jets Team Issue

These 4" by 5" Black and White cards were issued by the New York Jets in their first season as the Jets. They had been the Titans for the previous three seasons. There are small facsimile autographs on the bottom of the cardfronts. As these cards are not numbered we have sequenced them in alphabetical order.

COMPLETE SET (8)	60.00	120.00
1 Weeb Ewbank CO	10.00	20.00
2 Larry Grantham	7.50	15.00
3 Gene Heeter	7.50	15.00
4 Bill Mathis	7.50	15.00
5 Don Maynard	12.50	25.00
6 Mark Smolinski	7.50	15.00
7 Bake Turner	7.50	15.00
8 Dick Wood	7.50	15.00

1963 Jets Team Issue 5x7

This set of the New York Jets measures approximately 5" by 7" and look very similar to the Jay Publishing issues of the early 1960s and the 1965-66 Jets set listings. The fronts feature black-and-white player photos with just the player's name and team name below the photo. It is very likely that the Jets issued these photos in groups over a number of years as they can be found in 6 or 8-card envelopes. The backs are blank. The cards are unnumbered and checklisted below in alphabetical order.

1 Bill Atkins	6.00	12.00
2 Dick Christy	6.00	12.00
3 Larry Grantham	6.00	12.00
4 Dick Guesman	6.00	12.00
5 Mike Hudock	6.00	12.00
6 Charlie Janerette	6.00	12.00
7 Don Maynard	10.00	20.00
8 Bill Mathis	6.00	12.00
9 LaVerne Torczon	6.00	12.00

1965 Jets Team Issue 8x10

This set of the New York Jets photos measures approximately 8 1/2" by 10 1/4" and are very similar in design to other Jets photos issued in the 1960s and 1970s. The fronts feature black and white player photos with just the player's name and position (spelled out on most) below the photo along with the team's logo. This year can be identified by the slightly slanted position of the Jets' logo below the player image. The blankbacked photos are unnumbered and checklisted below in alphabetical order.

COMPLETE SET (10)	125.00	200.00
1 Emerson Boozer	7.50	15.00
2 Larry Grantham	6.00	12.00
3 John Huarte	6.00	12.00
4 Bill Mathis	6.00	12.00
5 Don Maynard	12.50	25.00
6 Wahoo McDaniel	7.50	15.00
7 Joe Namath	50.00	100.00
8 George Sauer	6.00	12.00
9 Matt Snell	7.50	15.00
10 Bake Turner	6.00	12.00

1965-66 Jets Team Issue 5x7

This set of the New York Jets measures approximately 5" by 7" and look very similar to the Jay Publishing issues of the early 1960s. The fronts feature black-and-white player photos with just the player's name and team name below the photo. It is very likely that the Jets issued these photos in groups over a number of years as they can be found in 6 or 8-card envelopes. The backs are blank. The cards are unnumbered and checklisted below in alphabetical order.

COMPLETE SET (10)	100.00	175.00
1 Ralph Baker	6.00	12.00
2 Dan Ficca	6.00	12.00
3 Wahoo McDaniel	7.50	15.00
4 Joe Namath	45.00	80.00
5 Dainard Paulson	6.00	12.00
6 Gerry Philbin	6.00	12.00
7 Mark Smolinski	6.00	12.00
8 Matt Snell	7.50	15.00
9 Bake Turner	6.00	12.00
10 Dick Wood	6.00	12.00

1969 Jets Tasco Prints

Tasco Associates produced this set of New York Jets prints. The fronts feature a large color artist's rendering of the player along with the player's name and position. The backs are blank. The prints measure approximately 11" by 16."

COMPLETE SET (6)	75.00	125.00
1 Winston Hill	7.50	15.00
2 Joe Namath	35.00	60.00
3 Gerry Philbin	7.50	15.00
4 Johnny Sample	7.50	15.00
5 Matt Snell	10.00	20.00
6 Jim Turner	7.50	15.00

1969 Jets Team Issue 8x10

This set of the New York Jets photos measures approximately 8" by 10" and are very similar in design to the 1965 issue except for the logo. The fronts feature black and white player photos with just the player's name and position (spelled out on most in all caps) below the photo along with the team's logo. This year can be identified by the horizontal position of the Jets' logo below the player image. The blankbacked photos are unnumbered and checklisted below in alphabetical order.

1 Al Atkinson	6.00	12.00
2 Verlon Biggs	6.00	12.00
3 Emerson Boozer	7.50	15.00
4 Earl Christy	6.00	12.00
5 Mike D'Amato	6.00	12.00
6 John Dockery	7.50	15.00
7 John Elliott	6.00	12.00
8 Roger Finnie	6.00	12.00
9 Dave Foley	6.00	12.00
10 Karl Henke	6.00	12.00
11 Billy Joe	7.50	15.00
12 Cecil Leonard	6.00	12.00
13 Bill Mathis	6.00	12.00
14 Carl McAdams	6.00	12.00
15 George Nock	6.00	12.00
16 Bill Rademacher	6.00	12.00
17 Randy Rasmussen	6.00	12.00
18 Jeff Richardson	6.00	12.00
19 Paul Rochester	6.00	12.00
20 Johnny Sample	7.50	15.00
21 George Sauer	6.00	12.00
22 John Schmitt	6.00	12.00
23 Mark Smolinski	6.00	12.00
24 Wayne Stewart	6.00	12.00
25 Mike Stromberg	6.00	12.00
26 Bob Talamini	6.00	12.00
27 Bake Turner	7.50	15.00
28 Sam Walton	6.00	12.00
29 Lee White	6.00	12.00
30 Al Woodall	7.50	15.00

1973-76 Jets Team Issue

The Jets issued these 8" by 10" photos over the course of several years in the mid-1970s. Each includes a black and white photo of a Jets player with the older style (JETS within an oval) team logo, his name, and his position listed below the image. The type style and size varies slightly from photo to photo and several players were likely issued in differing styles. The backs are blank. Any additions to this list are appreciated.

1 Mike Adamle	5.00	10.00
4 Ralph Baker	5.00	10.00
6 Carl Barzilauskas	5.00	10.00
7 Mike Battle	5.00	10.00
9 Roger Bernhardt	5.00	10.00
10 Hank Bjorklund	5.00	10.00
11 Emerson Boozer	6.00	12.00
12 Willie Brister	5.00	10.00
13 Gordon Brown	5.00	10.00
14 Bob Burns	5.00	10.00
15 Greg Buttle	5.00	10.00
16 Duane Carrell	5.00	10.00
18 Bill Demory	5.00	10.00
19 John Dockery	5.00	10.00
21 Bill Ferguson	5.00	10.00
23 Richmond Flowers	5.00	10.00
25 Ed Galigher	5.00	10.00
26 Greg Gantt	5.00	10.00
27 Bruce Harper	5.00	10.00
28 Dave Herman	5.00	10.00
29 Winston Hill	5.00	10.00
2A Al Atkinson (jersey number fully visible)	5.00	10.00
2B Al Atkinson (half of jersey number visible)	5.00	10.00
30 Lou Holtz CO (press conference holding ball)	7.50	15.00
31 Delles Howell	5.00	10.00
32 Bobby Howfield	5.00	10.00
33 Clarence Jackson	5.00	10.00
34 J.J. Jones	5.00	10.00
35 Larry Keller	5.00	10.00
36 David Knight	5.00	10.00
37 Warren Koegel	5.00	10.00
38 Pete Lammons	5.00	10.00
39 Pat Leahy	5.00	10.00
3A Darrell Austin (with neck pad)	5.00	10.00
3B Darrell Austin (without neck pad)	5.00	10.00
40 John Little	5.00	10.00
41 Mark Lomas	5.00	10.00
42 Bob Martin	5.00	10.00
43 Don Maynard	10.00	20.00
44 Wayne Mulligan	5.00	10.00
45 Joe Namath Action	20.00	35.00
46 Jim Nance	6.00	12.00
47 Richard Neal	5.00	10.00
48 Burgess Owens	5.00	10.00
49 Gerry Philbin (all-pro defensive end)	5.00	10.00
50 Lou Piccone	5.00	10.00
51 Lawrence Pillers	5.00	10.00
52 Garry Puetz	5.00	10.00
53 Randy Rasmussen	5.00	10.00
54 Steve Reese	5.00	10.00
56 Jamie Rivers	5.00	10.00
57 Travis Roach	5.00	10.00
58 Joe Schmiesing	5.00	10.00
59 John Schmitt	5.00	10.00
5A Jerome Barkum (photo from waist up)	5.00	10.00
5B Jerome Barkum (close-up of face)	5.00	10.00
60 Richard Sowells	5.00	10.00
61 Shafer Suggs	5.00	10.00
62 Bob Svihus	5.00	10.00
63 Steve Tannen	5.00	10.00
64 Ed Taylor	5.00	10.00
65 Earlie Thomas	5.00	10.00
67 Godwin Turk	5.00	10.00
68 Phil Wise	5.00	10.00
70 Larry Woods	5.00	10.00
71 Robert Woods	5.00	10.00
72 Roscoe Word	5.00	10.00
8A Ed Bell (facing straight forward)	5.00	10.00
8B Ed Bell (turned to his side)	5.00	10.00
17A Richard Caster (listed as Richard)	6.00	12.00
17B Richard Caster (listed as Rich)	6.00	12.00
20A John Ebersole Port	5.00	10.00
20B John Ebersole Port	5.00	10.00
20C John Ebersole On field	5.00	10.00
22A Joe Fields mustache	5.00	10.00
22B Joe Fields smiling	5.00	10.00
24A Clark Gaines Action	5.00	10.00
24B Clark Gaines Jacket	5.00	10.00
55A John Riggins (close up portrait)	10.00	20.00
55B John Riggins Action	10.00	20.00
66A Richard Todd (action photo)	7.50	15.00
66B Richard Todd (portrait)	7.50	15.00
69A Al Woodall (green jersey)	5.00	10.00
69B Al Woodall (white jersey)	5.00	10.00

1963 Jewish Sports Champions

The 16 cards in this set, measuring roughly 2 2/3" x 3", are cut out of an "Activity Funbook" entitled Jewish Sports Champions. The set pays tribute to famous Jewish athletes from baseball, football, bull fighting to chess. The cards have a green border with a yellow background and a player close-up illustration. Cards that are still attached carry a premium over those that have been cut-out. The cards are unnumbered and listed below in alphabetical order with an assigned sport prefix (BB-baseball, BK- basketball, BX- boxing, FB-football, OT- other).

COMPLETE SET (16)	100.00	200.00
FB1 Benny Friedman FB	6.00	12.00
FB2 Sid Luckman FB	10.00	20.00

1959 Kahn's

The 1959 Kahn's football set of 31 black and white cards features players from the Cleveland Browns and the Pittsburgh Steelers. The cards measure approximately 3 1/4" by 3 15/16". The backs contain height, weight and short football career data. The statistics on the back are single spaced. The cards are unnumbered and hence are listed below alphabetically for convenience.

COMPLETE SET (31)	3,000.00	5,000.00
1 Dick Alban	75.00	125.00
2 Jim Brown	800.00	1,200.00
3 Jack Butler	75.00	125.00
4 Lew Carpenter	75.00	125.00
5 Preston Carpenter	75.00	125.00
6 Vince Costello	75.00	125.00
7 Dale Dodrill	75.00	125.00
8 Bob Gain	75.00	125.00
9 Gary Glick	75.00	125.00
10 Lou Groza	125.00	200.00
11 Gene Hickerson	150.00	250.00
12 Bill Howton	90.00	150.00
13 Art Hunter	75.00	125.00
14 Joe Krupa	75.00	125.00
15 Bobby Layne	175.00	300.00
16 Joe Lewis	75.00	125.00
17 Jack McClairen	75.00	125.00
18 Mike McCormack	100.00	175.00
19 Walt Michaels	90.00	150.00
20 Bobby Mitchell	150.00	250.00
21 Jim Ninowski	75.00	125.00
22 Chuck Noll	500.00	800.00
23 Jimmy Orr	75.00	125.00
24 Milt Plum	90.00	150.00
25 Ray Renfro	90.00	150.00
26 Mike Sandusky	75.00	125.00
27 Billy Ray Smith	75.00	125.00
28 Jim Ray Smith	75.00	125.00
29 Ernie Stautner	150.00	250.00
30 Tom Tracy	90.00	150.00
31 Frank Varrichione	75.00	125.00

1960 Kahn's

The 1960 Kahn's football set of 38 cards features Cleveland Browns and Pittsburgh Steelers. The cards measure approximately 3 1/4" by 3 15/16". In addition to data similar to the backs of the 1959 Kahn's cards, the backs of the 1960 Kahn's cards contain an ad for a free professional album and instruction booklet, which could be obtained by sending two labels to Kahn's. The cards are unnumbered and hence are listed below alphabetically for convenience. Willie Davis' card predates his 1964 Philadelphia Rookie Card by four years.

COMPLETE SET (38)	3,500.00	6,000.00
1 Sam Baker	50.00	80.00
2 Jim Brown SP	900.00	1,500.00
3 Ray Campbell	50.00	80.00
4 Preston Carpenter	50.00	80.00
5 Vince Costello	50.00	80.00
6 Willie Davis	75.00	125.00
7 Galen Fiss	50.00	80.00
8 Bob Gain	50.00	80.00
9 Lou Groza	90.00	150.00
10 Gene Hickerson	100.00	175.00
11 John Henry Johnson	75.00	125.00
12 Rich Kreitling	50.00	80.00
13 Joe Krupa	50.00	80.00
14 Bobby Layne	150.00	250.00
15 Jack McClairen	50.00	80.00
16 Mike McCormack	75.00	125.00
17 Walt Michaels	50.00	100.00
18 Bobby Mitchell	90.00	150.00
19 Dick Moegle	50.00	100.00
20 John Morrow	50.00	80.00
21 Gern Nagler	50.00	80.00
22 John Nisby	50.00	80.00
23 Jimmy Orr	50.00	100.00
24 Bernie Parrish	50.00	80.00
25 Milt Plum	50.00	100.00
26 John Reger	50.00	80.00
27 Ray Renfro	50.00	100.00
28 Will Renfro	50.00	80.00
29 Mike Sandusky	50.00	80.00
30 Dick Schafrath	50.00	80.00
31 Jim Ray Smith	50.00	80.00
32 Billy Ray Smith	50.00	100.00
33 Ernie Stautner	90.00	150.00
34 George Tarasovic	50.00	80.00
35 Tom Tracy	50.00	100.00
36 Frank Varrichione	50.00	80.00
37 John Wooten	50.00	80.00
38 Lowe Wren	50.00	80.00

1961 Kahn's

The 1961 Kahn's football set of 36 cards features Cleveland and Pittsburgh players. The cards measure approximately 3 1/4" by 4 1/16". The backs are the same as the 1960 Kahn's cards; however, the free booklet ad requires but one label to be sent in rather than the two labels required for the 1960 offer. Pictures of Larry Krutko and Tom Tracy are reversed. The cards are unnumbered and hence are listed below alphabetically for convenience.

COMPLETE SET (36)	1,200.00	2,000.00
1 Sam Baker	25.00	40.00
2 Jim Brown	250.00	400.00
3 Preston Carpenter	25.00	40.00
4 Vince Costello	25.00	40.00
5 Dean Derby	25.00	40.00
6 Buddy Dial	25.00	40.00
7 Don Fleming	25.00	40.00
8 Bob Gain	25.00	40.00
9 Bobby Joe Green	25.00	40.00
10 Gene Hickerson	60.00	100.00
11 Jim Houston	25.00	40.00
12 Dan James	25.00	40.00
13 John Henry Johnson	60.00	100.00
14 Rich Kreitling	25.00	40.00
15 Joe Krupa	25.00	40.00
16 Larry Krutko UER	25.00	40.00
17 Bobby Layne	100.00	175.00
18 Joe Lewis	25.00	40.00
19 Gene Lipscomb	40.00	80.00
20 Mike McCormack	60.00	100.00
21 Bobby Mitchell	75.00	125.00
22 John Morrow	25.00	40.00
23 John Nisby	25.00	40.00
24 Jimmy Orr	25.00	40.00
25 Milt Plum	30.00	50.00
26 John Reger	25.00	40.00
27 Ray Renfro	30.00	50.00
28 Will Renfro	25.00	40.00
29 Mike Sandusky	25.00	40.00
30 Dick Schafrath	25.00	40.00
31 Jim Ray Smith	25.00	40.00
32 Ernie Stautner	60.00	100.00
33 George Tarasovic	25.00	40.00
34 Tom Tracy UER	30.00	50.00
35 Frank Varrichione	25.00	40.00
36 John Wooten	25.00	40.00

1962 Kahn's

The 1962 Kahn's football card set contains 38 players from eight different teams. New teams added in this year's set are the Chicago Bears, Detroit Lions, and Minnesota Vikings. The cards measure approximately 3 1/4" by 4 3/16". The backs contain information comparable to the backs of previous years; however, the statistics are double spaced, and the player's name on the back is in bold-faced type. The cards are unnumbered and hence are listed below alphabetically for convenience. An album was also issued to house the set.

COMPLETE SET (38)	1,200.00	2,000.00
1 Maxie Baughan	25.00	40.00
2 Charley Britt	25.00	40.00
3 Jim Brown	200.00	350.00
4 Preston Carpenter	25.00	40.00
5 Pete Case	25.00	40.00
6 Howard Cassady	25.00	50.00
7 Vince Costello	25.00	40.00
8 Buddy Dial	25.00	50.00
9 Gene Hickerson	40.00	80.00
10 Jim Houston	25.00	40.00
11 Dan James	25.00	40.00
12 Rich Kreitling	25.00	40.00
13 Joe Krupa	25.00	40.00
14 Bobby Layne	90.00	150.00
15 Ray Lemek	25.00	40.00
16 Gene Lipscomb	30.00	60.00
17 Dave Lloyd	25.00	40.00
18 Lou Michaels	25.00	40.00
19 Larry Morris	25.00	40.00
20 John Morrow	25.00	40.00
21 Jim Ninowski	25.00	40.00
22 Buzz Nutter	25.00	40.00
23 Jimmy Orr	25.00	40.00
24 Bernie Parrish	25.00	40.00
25 Milt Plum	25.00	50.00
26 Myron Pottios	25.00	40.00
27 John Reger	25.00	40.00
28 Ray Renfro	25.00	50.00
29 Frank Ryan	25.00	50.00
30 Johnny Sample	25.00	40.00
31 Mike Sandusky	25.00	40.00
32 Dick Schafrath	25.00	40.00
33 Jim Shofner	25.00	50.00
34 Jim Ray Smith	25.00	40.00
35 Ernie Stautner	40.00	80.00
36 Fran Tarkenton	150.00	250.00
37 Paul Wiggin	25.00	40.00
38 John Wooten	25.00	40.00

1963 Kahn's

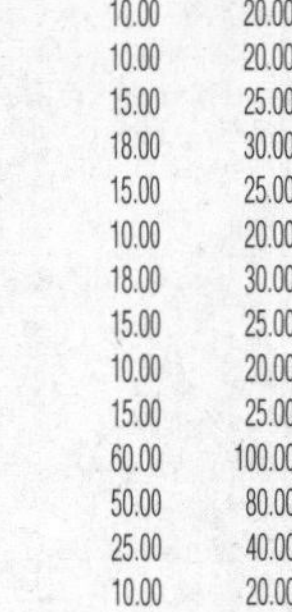

The 1963 Kahn's football card set includes players from six new teams not appearing in previous Kahn sets. All 14 NFL teams are represented in this set. The new teams are Dallas Cowboys, Green Bay Packers, New York Giants, St. Louis Cardinals, San Francisco 49ers and Washington Redskins. The cards measure approximately 3 1/4" by 4 3/16". The backs contain player statistics comparable to previous years; however, this set may be distinguished from Kahn's sets of other years because it is the only Kahn's football card set that has a distinct white border surrounding the picture on the obverse. With a total of 92 different cards, this is the largest Kahn's football issue. The cards are unnumbered and hence are listed below alphabetically for convenience.

COMPLETE SET (92)	1,800.00	3,000.00
1 Bill Barnes	15.00	25.00
2 Erich Barnes	15.00	25.00
3 Dick Bass	18.00	30.00
4 Don Bosseler	15.00	25.00
5 Jim Brown	175.00	300.00
6 Roger Brown	15.00	25.00
7 Roosevelt Brown	25.00	40.00
8 Ronnie Bull	18.00	30.00
9 Preston Carpenter	15.00	25.00
10 Frank Clarke	25.00	40.00
11 Gail Cogdill	15.00	25.00
12 Bobby Joe Conrad	15.00	25.00
13 John David Crow	18.00	30.00
14 Dan Currie	18.00	30.00
15 Buddy Dial	18.00	30.00
16 Mike Ditka	90.00	150.00
17 Fred Dugan	15.00	25.00
18 Galen Fiss	15.00	25.00
19 Bill Forester	18.00	30.00
20 Bob Gain	15.00	25.00
21 Willie Galimore	18.00	30.00
22 Bill George	25.00	40.00
23 Frank Gifford	60.00	100.00
24 Bill Glass	18.00	30.00
25 Forrest Gregg	25.00	40.00
26 Fred Hageman	15.00	25.00
27 Jimmy Hill	15.00	25.00
28 Sam Huff	35.00	60.00
29 Dan James	15.00	25.00
30 John Henry Johnson	25.00	40.00
31 Sonny Jurgensen	35.00	60.00
32 Jim Katcavage	18.00	30.00
33 Ron Kostelnik	15.00	25.00
34 Jerry Kramer	25.00	40.00
35 Ron Kramer	18.00	30.00
36 Dick Lane	25.00	40.00
37 Yale Lary	25.00	40.00
38 Eddie LeBaron	25.00	40.00
39 Dick Lynch	15.00	25.00
40 Tommy Mason	18.00	30.00
41 Tommy McDonald	25.00	40.00
42 Lou Michaels	18.00	30.00
43 Bobby Mitchell	30.00	50.00
44 Dick Modzelewski	15.00	25.00
45 Lenny Moore	35.00	60.00
46 John Morrow	15.00	25.00
47 John Nisby	15.00	25.00
48 Ray Nitschke	50.00	80.00
49 Leo Nomellini	25.00	40.00
50 Jimmy Orr	15.00	25.00
51 John Paluck	15.00	25.00
52 Jim Parker	25.00	40.00
53 Bernie Parrish	15.00	25.00
54 Jim Patton	15.00	25.00
55 Don Perkins	25.00	40.00
56 Richie Petitbon	18.00	30.00
57 Jim Phillips	15.00	25.00
58 Nick Pietrosante	15.00	25.00
59 Milt Plum	18.00	30.00
60 Myron Pottios	15.00	25.00
61 Sonny Randle	18.00	30.00
62 John Reger	15.00	25.00
63 Ray Renfro	18.00	30.00
64 Pete Retzlaff	18.00	30.00
65 Pat Richter	15.00	25.00
66 Jim Ringo	25.00	40.00
67 Andy Robustelli	30.00	50.00
68 Joe Rutgens	15.00	25.00
69 Bob St. Clair	25.00	40.00
70 Johnny Sample	18.00	30.00
71 Lonnie Sanders	15.00	25.00
72 Dick Schafrath	15.00	25.00
73 Joe Schmidt	30.00	50.00
74 Del Shofner	18.00	30.00
75 J.D. Smith	15.00	25.00
76 Norm Snead	25.00	40.00
77 Bill Stacy	15.00	25.00
78 Bart Starr	125.00	225.00
79 Ernie Stautner	30.00	50.00
80 Jim Steffen	15.00	25.00
81 Andy Stynchula	15.00	25.00
82 Fran Tarkenton	60.00	100.00
83 Jim Taylor	50.00	80.00
84 Clendon Thomas	15.00	25.00
85 Fuzzy Thurston	25.00	40.00
86 Y.A. Tittle	60.00	100.00
87 Bob Toneff	15.00	25.00
88 Jerry Tubbs	25.00	40.00
89 Johnny Unitas	150.00	250.00
90 Bill Wade	18.00	30.00
91 Willie Wood	25.00	40.00
92 Abe Woodson	18.00	30.00

1964 Kahn's

The 1964 Kahn's football card set of 53 is the only Kahn's football card set in full color. It is also the only set which does not contain the statement "Compliments of Kahn's, the Wiener the World Awaited" on the cardfront. This slogan is contained on the back of the card which also contains player data similar to cards of other years. The cards measure approximately 3" by 3 5/8". The cards are unnumbered and hence are listed below alphabetically for convenience. Paul Warfield's card holds special interest in that it was issued very early in his career.

COMPLETE SET (53)	900.00	1,500.00
1 Doug Atkins	18.00	30.00
2 Terry Barr	10.00	20.00
3 Dick Bass	15.00	25.00
4 Ordell Braase	10.00	20.00
5 Ed Brown	15.00	25.00
6 Jimmy Brown	90.00	150.00
7 Gary Collins	15.00	25.00
8 Bobby Joe Conrad	10.00	20.00
9 Mike Ditka	60.00	100.00
10 Galen Fiss	10.00	20.00
11 Paul Flatley	15.00	25.00
12 Joe Fortunato	10.00	20.00
13 Bill George	18.00	30.00
14 Bill Glass	15.00	25.00
15 Ernie Green	15.00	25.00
16 Dick Hoak	10.00	20.00
17 Paul Hornung	30.00	50.00
18 Sam Huff	20.00	35.00
19 Charley Johnson	15.00	25.00
20 John Henry Johnson	18.00	30.00
21 Alex Karras	18.00	30.00
22 Jim Katcavage	15.00	25.00
23 Joe Krupa	10.00	20.00
24 Dick Lane	18.00	30.00
25 Tommy Mason	15.00	25.00
26 Don Meredith	50.00	80.00
27 Bobby Mitchell	20.00	35.00
28 Larry Morris	10.00	20.00
29 Jimmy Orr	15.00	25.00
30 Jim Parker	18.00	30.00
31 Bernie Parrish	10.00	20.00
32 Don Perkins	15.00	25.00
33 Jim Phillips	10.00	20.00
34 Sonny Randle	10.00	20.00
35 Pete Retzlaff	15.00	25.00
36 Jim Ringo	18.00	30.00
37 Frank Ryan	15.00	25.00
38 Dick Schafrath	10.00	20.00
39 Joe Schmidt	18.00	30.00
40 Del Shofner	15.00	25.00
41 J.D. Smith	10.00	20.00
42 Norm Snead	15.00	25.00
43 Bart Starr	60.00	100.00
44 Fran Tarkenton	50.00	80.00
45 Jim Taylor	25.00	40.00
46 Clendon Thomas	10.00	20.00
47 Y.A. Tittle	30.00	50.00
48 Jerry Tubbs	15.00	25.00
49 Johnny Unitas	60.00	100.00
50 Bill Wade	15.00	25.00
51 Paul Warfield	35.00	60.00
52 Alex Webster	15.00	25.00
53 Abe Woodson	10.00	20.00

1971 Keds KedKards

This set is composed of crude artistic renditions of popular subjects from various sports from 1971 who were apparently celebrity endorsers of Keds shoes. The cards actually form a complete panel on the Keds tennis shoes box. The three different panels are actually different sizes; the Bing panel contains smaller cards. The smaller Bubba Smith shows him without beard and standing straight; the large Bubba shows him leaning over, with beard, and jersey number partially visible. The individual player card portions of the card panels measure approximately 2 15/16" by 2 3/4" and 2 5/16" by 2 3/16" respectively, although it should noted that there are slight size differences among the individual cards even on the same panel. The panel background is colored in black and yellow. On the Bench/Reed card (number 3 below) each player measures approximately 5 1/4" by 3 1/2". A facsimile autograph appears in the upper left corner of each player's drawing. The Bench/Reed was issued with the Keds Champion boys basketball shoe box, printed on the box top with a black broken line around the card to follow when cutting the card out.

COMPLETE SET (3)	112.50	225.00
1FB Bubba Smith with beard	30.00	60.00
2FB Bubba Smith no beard	30.00	60.00

1937 Kellogg's Pep Stamps

Kellogg's distributed these multi-sport stamps inside specially marked Pep brand cereal boxes in 1937. They were originally issued in four-stamp blocks along with an instructional type tab at the top. The tab contained the sheet number. We've noted the sheet number after each athlete's name below. Note that six athletes appear on two sheets, thereby making those six double prints. There were 24-different sheets produced. We've catalogued the unnumbered stamps below in single loose form according to sport (AR- auto racing, AV- aviation, BB- baseball, BX- boxing, FB- football, GO- golf, HO- horses, SW- swimming, TN- tennis). Stamps can often be found intact in blocks of four along with the tab. Complete blocks of stamps are valued at roughly 50 percent more than the total value of the four individual stamps as priced below. An album was also produced to house the set.

COMPLETE SET (90)	1,000.00	2,000.00
FB1 Bill Alexander 2	12.00	20.00
FB2 Matty Bell 3	12.00	20.00
FB3 Fritz Crisler 14	25.00	40.00
FB4 Bill Cunningham 23	12.00	20.00
FB5 Red Grange 16/22	125.00	200.00
FB6 Howard Jones 18	15.00	25.00
FB7 Andy Kerr 4	15.00	25.00
FB8 Harry Kipke 19	12.00	20.00
FB9 Lou Little 8	25.00	40.00
FB10 Ed Madigan 12	12.00	20.00
FB11 Bronko Nagurski 15	125.00	200.00
FB12 Ernie Nevers 21	35.00	60.00
FB13 Jimmy Phelan 20	12.00	20.00
FB14 Bill Shakespeare 10	15.00	25.00
FB15 Frank Thomas 5	15.00	25.00
FB16 Tiny Thornhill 9	12.00	20.00
FB17 Jim Thorpe 17	125.00	200.00
FB18 Wallace Wade 11	12.00	20.00

1948 Kellogg's All Wheat Sport Tips Series 1

21 Football: Punting	3.00	8.00
22 Football: Passing	3.00	8.00
23 Football: Placement Kick	3.00	8.00
24 Football: Ball Carrying	3.00	8.00

1948 Kellogg's All Wheat Sport Tips Series 2

12 Football: Shoulder Block	3.00	8.00
26 Football: Cross Body Block	3.00	8.00
27 Football: Holding the Ball	3.00	8.00
28 Football: Punt	3.00	8.00

1948 Kellogg's Pep

These small cards measure approximately 1 7/16" by 1 5/8". The card front presents a black and white head-and-shoulders shot of the player, with a white border. The back has the player's name and a brief description of his accomplishments. The cards are unnumbered, but have been assigned numbers below using a sport (BB- baseball, FB- football, BK- basketball, OT- other) prefix. Other Movie Star Kellogg's Pep cards exist, but they are not listed below. The catalog designation for this set is F273-19. An album was also produced to house the set.

COMPLETE SET (20)	700.00	1,400.00
FB1 Lou Groza	80.00	120.00
FB2 George McAfee	25.00	40.00
FB3 Norm Standlee	18.00	30.00
FB4A Charley Trippi	50.00	80.00
FB4B Charley Trippi	50.00	80.00
FB5 Bob Waterfield	80.00	120.00

1970 Kellogg's

The 1970 Kellogg's football set of 60 cards was Kellogg's first football issue. The cards have a 3D effect and are approximately 2 1/4" by 3 1/2". The cards could be obtained from boxes of cereal or as a set from a box top offer. The 1970 Kellogg's set can easily be distinguished from the 1971 Kellogg's set by recognizing the color of the helmet logo on the front of each card. In the 1970 set this helmet logo is blue, whereas with the 1971 set the helmet logo is red. The 1971 set also is distinguished by its thick blue (with white spots) border on each card front as well as by the small inset photo in the upper left corner of each reverse. The key card in the set is O.J. Simpson as 1970 was O.J.'s rookie year for cards.

COMPLETE SET (60)	50.00	100.00
1 Carl Eller	.60	1.50
2 Jim Otto	.60	1.50
3 Tom Matte	.40	1.00
4 Bill Nelsen	.30	.75
5 Travis Williams	.30	.75
6 Len Dawson	2.00	4.00
7 Gene Washington Vik	.30	.75
8 Jim Nance	.30	.75
9 Norm Snead	.40	1.00
10 Dick Butkus	4.00	8.00
11 George Sauer Jr.	.40	1.00
12 Billy Kilmer	.50	1.25
13 Alex Karras	1.25	2.50
14 Larry Wilson	.60	1.50
15 Dave Robinson	.40	1.00
16 Bill Brown	.30	.75
17 Bob Griese	3.00	6.00
18 Al Denson	.30	.75
19 Dick Post	.30	.75
20 Jan Stenerud	.60	1.50
21 Paul Warfield	2.00	4.00
22 Mel Farr	.30	.75
23 Mel Renfro	.60	1.50
24 Roy Jefferson	.30	.75
25 Mike Garrett	.30	.75
26 Harry Jacobs	.30	.75

27 Carl Garrett .30 .75
28 Dave Wilcox .50 1.25
29 Matt Snell .40 1.00
30 Tom Woodeshick .30 .75
31 Leroy Kelly .75 2.00
32 Floyd Little .40 1.00
33 Ken Willard .30 .75
34 John Mackey .75 2.00
35 Merlin Olsen 1.50 3.00
36 Dave Grayson .30 .75
37 Lem Barney 1.25 2.50
38 Deacon Jones 1.25 2.50
39 Bob Hayes 1.25 2.50
40 Lance Alworth 2.00 4.00
41 Larry Csonka 3.00 6.00
42 Bobby Bell .75 2.00
43 George Webster .30 .75
44 Johnny Roland .30 .75
45 Dick Shiner .30 .75
46 Bubba Smith 1.25 2.50
47 Daryle Lamonica .50 1.25
48 O.J. Simpson 5.00 10.00
49 Calvin Hill .50 1.25
50 Fred Biletnikoff 2.00 4.00
51 Gale Sayers 4.00 8.00
52 Homer Jones .30 .75
53 Sonny Jurgensen 2.00 4.00
54 Bob Lilly 1.50 3.00
55 Johnny Unitas 6.00 12.00
56 Tommy Nobis .50 1.25
57 Ed Meador .30 .75
58 Spider Lockhart .30 .75
59 Don Maynard 2.00 4.00
60 Greg Cook .30 .75

1971 Kellogg's

The 1971 Kellogg's set of 60 cards could be obtained only from boxes of cereal. One card was inserted in each specially marked box of Kellogg's Corn Flakes and Kellogg's Raisin Bran cereals. The cards measure approximately 2 1/4" by 3 1/2". This set is much more difficult to obtain than the previous Kellogg's set since no box top offer was available. The 1971 Kellogg's set can easily be distinguished from the 1970 Kellogg's set by recognizing the color of the helmet logo on the front of each card. In the 1970 set this helmet logo is blue, whereas with the 1971 set the helmet logo is red. The 1971 set also is distinguished by its thick blue (with white spots) border on each card front as well as by the small inset photo in the uppper left corner of each reverse. Among the key cards in the set is Joe Greene as 1971 was "Mean" Joe's rookie year for cards.

COMPLETE SET (60) 200.00 400.00
1 Tom Barrington 2.50 5.00
2 Chris Hanburger 3.00 6.00
3 Frank Nunley 2.50 5.00
4 Houston Antwine 2.50 5.00
5 Ron Johnson 3.00 6.00
6 Craig Morton 4.00 8.00
7 Jack Snow 3.00 6.00
8 Mel Renfro 5.00 10.00
9 Les Josephson 2.50 5.00
10 Gary Garrison 2.50 5.00
11 Dave Herman 2.50 5.00
12 Fred Dryer 4.00 8.00
13 Larry Brown 3.00 6.00
14 Gene Washington 49er 3.00 6.00
15 Joe Greene 10.00 20.00
16 Marlin Briscoe 2.50 5.00
17 Bob Grant 2.50 5.00
18 Dan Conners 2.50 5.00
19 Mike Curtis 3.00 6.00
20 Harry Schuh 2.50 5.00
21 Rich Jackson 2.50 5.00
22 Clint Jones 2.50 5.00
23 Hewritt Dixon 2.50 5.00
24 Jess Phillips 2.50 5.00
25 Gary Cuozzo 2.50 5.00
26 Bo Scott 2.50 5.00
27 Glen Ray Hines 2.50 5.00
28 Johnny Unitas 17.50 35.00
29 John Gilliam 2.50 5.00
30 Harmon Wages 2.50 5.00
31 Walt Sweeney 2.50 5.00
32 Bruce Taylor 2.50 5.00
33 George Blanda 10.00 20.00
34 Ken Bowman 2.50 5.00
35 Johnny Robinson 3.00 6.00
36 Ed Podolak 2.50 5.00
37 Curley Culp 2.50 5.00
38 Jim Hart 3.00 6.00
39 Dick Butkus 12.50 25.00
40 Floyd Little 3.00 6.00
41 Nick Buoniconti 4.00 8.00
42 Larry Smith RB 2.50 5.00
43 Wayne Walker 3.00 6.00
44 MacArthur Lane 2.50 5.00
45 John Brodie 6.00 12.00
46 Dick LeBeau 2.50 5.00
47 Claude Humphrey 2.50 5.00
48 Jerry LeVias 2.50 5.00
49 Erich Barnes 2.50 5.00
50 Andy Russell 3.00 6.00
51 Donny Anderson 3.00 6.00
52 Mike Reid 4.00 8.00
53 Al Atkinson 2.50 5.00
54 Tom Dempsey 2.50 5.00
55 Bob Griese 10.00 20.00
56 Dick Gordon 2.50 5.00
57 Charlie Sanders 3.00 6.00
58 Doug Cunningham 2.50 5.00
59 Cyril Pinder 2.50 5.00
60 Dave Osborn 2.50 5.00

1978 Kellogg's Stickers

These stickers measure approximately 2 1/2" by 2 5/8". The fronts feature color team helmets with the team's name below. The backs carry a short team history and a quiz about referee's signals. The stickers are numbered on the back "X of 28."

COMPLETE SET (28) 60.00 100.00
1 Atlanta Falcons 3.00 6.00
2 Baltimore Colts 3.00 6.00
3 Buffalo Bills 3.00 6.00
4 Chicago Bears 4.00 8.00
5 Cincinnati Bengals 3.00 6.00
6 Cleveland Browns 4.00 8.00
7 Dallas Cowboys 4.00 8.00
8 Denver Broncos 3.00 6.00
9 Detroit Lions 3.00 6.00
10 Green Bay Packers 4.00 8.00
11 Houston Oilers 3.00 6.00
12 Kansas City Chiefs 3.00 6.00
13 Los Angeles Rams 3.00 6.00
14 Miami Dolphins 4.00 8.00
15 Minnesota Vikings 3.00 6.00
16 New England Patriots 3.00 6.00
17 New Orleans Saints 3.00 6.00
18 New York Giants 3.00 6.00
19 New York Jets 3.00 6.00
20 Oakland Raiders 4.00 8.00
21 Philadelphia Eagles 3.00 6.00
22 Pittsburgh Steelers 4.00 8.00
23 St. Louis Cardinals 3.00 6.00
24 San Diego Chargers 3.00 6.00
25 San Francisco 49ers 3.00 6.00
26 Seattle Seahawks 3.00 6.00
27 Tampa Bay Buccaneers 3.00 6.00
28 Washington Redskins 4.00 8.00

1969 Kelly's Chips Zip Stickers

This set of small stickers was inserted one per package in Kelly's Brand Chips in 1969. Each includes a black and white head photo of the player against a red/orange (cards #1-6), green (#7-12), or blue (#13-20) colored background along with the word "ZIP" on the fronts. The backs contain the sticker number and instructions on obtaining a full color action signed photo of a player. Each sticker measures roughly 2" by 3" and often are found in slightly varying sizes and miscuts.

1 Dave Williams UER 50.00 80.00
2 Johnny Roland 50.00 80.00
3 Willis Crenshaw 50.00 80.00
4 Jim Bakken 50.00 80.00
5 Chuck Walker 50.00 80.00
6 Larry Wilson 60.00 100.00
7 Bart Starr 300.00 500.00
8 John Mackey 60.00 100.00
9 Joe Namath 300.00 500.00
10 Ray Nitschke UER 100.00 175.00
11 Jim Grabowski 60.00 100.00
12 Bob Hayes 90.00 150.00
13 Gale Sayers 175.00 300.00
14 Dick Butkus 175.00 300.00
15 Ed O'Bradovich 50.00 80.00
16 Brian Piccolo 175.00 300.00
17 Mike Pyle 50.00 80.00
19 Roman Gabriel 60.00 100.00
20 Bill Brown 60.00 100.00

1971 Lake County Rifles Milk Cartons

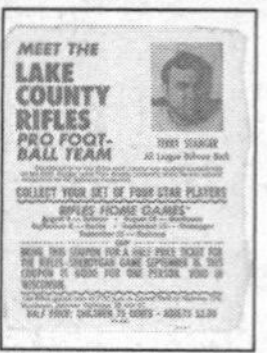

These cards were cut from milk cartons and feature a small single color player image from the Lake County (Illinois) semi-pro football team. Each card also include a very short bio of the player as well as the team's season schedule. A coupon good for a discounted game ticket was also included at the bottom, but presumably would be removed from most cards. The cardbacks are blank.

1 Clifford Boyd 5.00 10.00
2 Bruce Hart 5.00 10.00
3 Terry Stanger 5.00 10.00

1976 Sports Deck Landsman Playing Cards

These decks of playing cards were released in the mid-1970s and feature a Landsman black and white artwork image of one player per deck of cards. We've listed only one player name below although each player can be found in all 54-card versions of a standard deck of playing cards. Any additions to this list are appreciated.

COMP.FOREMAN DECK (54) 15.00 30.00
COMP.NAMATH DECK (54) 20.00 50.00
COMP.SAYERS DECK (54) 15.00 40.00
COMP.STABLER DECK (54) 15.00 40.00
COMP.STARR DECK (54) 20.00 50.00
COMP.TARKENTON (54) 15.00 40.00
1 Chuck Foreman .40 1.00
2 Joe Namath 1.00 2.50
3 Gale Sayers .60 1.50
4 Ken Stabler .75 2.00
5 Bart Starr .75 2.00
6 Fran Tarkenton .60 1.50

1976 Landsman Portraits

These 8 1/2" by 11" black-and-white portraits were issued around 1976 and feature art by Landsman. The checklist below is thought to be incomplete, however any additional information would be appreciated.

COMPLETE SET (3) 25.00 50.00
1 Chuck Foreman 5.00 10.00
2 Ken Stabler 12.50 25.00
3 Fran Tarkenton 7.50 15.00

1975 Laughlin Flaky Football

This 26-card set measures approximately 2 1/2" by 3 3/8". The title card indicates that the set was copyrighted in 1975 by noted artist, R.G. Laughlin. The typical orientation of the cards is that the city name is printed on the top of the card, with the mock team name running from top to bottom down the left side. The cartoon pictures are oriented horizontally inside the right angle formed by these two lines of text. The cards are numbered in the lower right hand corner (usually) and the backs of the cards are blank.

COMPLETE SET (27) 125.00 225.00
1 Pittsburgh Stealers 8.00 12.00
2 Minnesota Spikings 8.00 12.00
3 Cincinnati Bungles 6.00 10.00
4 Chicago Bares 8.00 12.00
5 Miami Dullfins 8.00 12.00
6 Philadelphia Eggles 6.00 10.00
7 Cleveland Brawns 8.00 12.00
8 New York Gianuts 8.00 12.00
9 Buffalo Bulls 6.00 10.00
10 Dallas Plowboys 8.00 12.00
11 New England Pastry Nuts 6.00 10.00
12 Green Bay Porkers 8.00 12.00
13 Denver Bongos 6.00 10.00
14 St. Louis Cigardinals 6.00 10.00
15 New York Jests 8.00 12.00
16 Washington Redshins 8.00 12.00
17 Oakland Waders 8.00 12.00
18 Los Angeles Yams 6.00 10.00
19 Baltimore Kilts 6.00 10.00
20 New Orleans Scents 6.00 10.00
21 San Diego Charges 6.00 10.00
22 Detroit Loins 6.00 10.00
23 Kansas City Chefs 6.00 10.00
24 Atlanta Fakin's 6.00 10.00
25 Houston Owlers 6.00 10.00
26 San Francisco 40 Miners 8.00 12.00
NNO Title Card 8.00 12.00

1948 Leaf

The 1948 Leaf set of 98-cards features black and white player portraits against a solid colored background. The player's uniforms were also colored and quite a number of variations have been reported in the player's uniform and background colors. We've included the most collected/recognized variations in the listing below but any additions to the variations list are appreciated. The cards measure approximately 2 3/8" by 2 7/8" and can be found on gray or cream colored card stock or a lighter, nearly white, stock. These differences in paper stock may account for the large number of color variations discovered. The second series (50-98) cards are much more difficult to obtain than the first series (1-49). This set features the Rookie Cards of many football stars since it was, along with the 1948 Bowman set, the first major post-war set. The set included then current NFL players as well as current college players.

COMPLETE SET (98) 4,500.00 6,000.00
WRAPPER (5-CENT) 110.00 160.00
1A Sid Luckman YB RC 250.00 400.00
1B Sid Luckman WB RC
2 Steve Suhey RC 20.00 30.00
3A Bull.Turner RB BYP RC 75.00 135.00
3B Bull.Turner RB DYP RC 75.00 135.00
3C Bull.Turner WB RC 100.00 175.00
4A Doak Walker BYB RC 125.00 200.00
4B Doak Walker WB RC
5A Levi Jackson BJ RC 25.00 40.00
5B Levi Jackson WJ RC 30.00 50.00
6A Bobby Layne YP RC 250.00 400.00
6B Bobby Layne RP RC 300.00 500.00
7A Bill Fischer RB BYP RC 20.00 30.00
7B Bill Fischer RB DYP RC 20.00 30.00
7C Bill Fischer WB RC 25.00 40.00
8A Vince Banonis BL RC 20.00 30.00
8B Vince Banonis WL RC 30.00 50.00
8C Vince Banonis WB RC
9A Tommy Thompson YJN RC 25.00 40.00
9B Tommy Thompson BJN RC 40.00 80.00
9C Tommy Thompson GJN RC 40.00 80.00
10A Perry Moss BFB RC 20.00 30.00
10B Perry Moss TFB RC 20.00 30.00
11A Terry Brennan BYP RC 25.00 40.00
11B Terry Brennan DYP RC 25.00 40.00
12A Bill Swiacki BL RC 20.00 30.00
12B Bill Swiacki WL RC 30.00 50.00
13A Johnny Lujack RC 125.00 200.00
13B Johnny Lujack ERR RC 175.00 300.00
14A Mal Kutner BL RC 20.00 30.00
14B Mal Kutner WL RC 30.00 50.00
15 Charlie Justice RC 50.00 90.00
16A Pete Pihos YJN RC 90.00 150.00
16B Pete Pihos BJN RC 125.00 200.00
17A Kenny Washington BL RC 35.00 60.00
17B Kenny Washington WL RC 50.00 80.00
18A Harry Gilmer MJ RC 30.00 50.00
18B Harry Gilmer PJ RC 30.00 50.00
18C Harry Gilmer RJ RC 30.00 50.00
19A George McAfee RC 90.00 150.00
19B George McAfee ERR RC 125.00 200.00
20A George Taliaferro YB RC 25.00 40.00
20B George Taliaferro WB RC 30.00 50.00
21 Paul Christman RC 30.00 50.00
22A Steve Van Buren GJ RC 150.00 250.00
22B Steve Van Buren YJ RC 175.00 300.00
22C Steve Van Buren GJ BS RC 200.00 350.00
22D Steve Van Buren BJ GS RC 200.00 350.00
22E Steve Van Buren GJ GS RC
23A Ken Kavanaugh YS RC 25.00 40.00
23B Ken Kavanaugh RS RC
24A Jim Martin RB BYP RC 25.00 40.00
24B Jim Martin RB DYP RC 25.00 40.00
24C Jim Martin WB RC 30.00 50.00
25A Bud Angsman BL RC 25.00 40.00
25B Bud Angsman WL RC 35.00 60.00
25C Bud Angsman WB RC
26A Bob Waterfield BL RC 150.00 250.00
26B Bob Waterfield WL RC 300.00 450.00
27A Fred Davis YB RC 20.00 30.00
27B Fred Davis WB RC 30.00 50.00
28A Whitey Wistert YJ RC 25.00 40.00
28B Whitey Wistert GJ RC 30.00 50.00
29 Charley Trippi RC 65.00 110.00
30A Paul Governali BRH RC 25.00 40.00
30B Paul Governali TH RC 25.00 40.00
30C Paul Governali BH RC 30.00 50.00
31A Tom McWilliams MJ RC 20.00 30.00
31B Tom McWilliams RJ RC 25.00 40.00
32A Leroy Zimmerman GNN RC 20.00 30.00
32B Leroy Zimmerman YN RC 20.00 30.00
32C Leroy Zimmerman GYN RC 20.00 30.00
33 Pat Harder UER RC 30.00 50.00
34A Sammy Baugh MJ RC 400.00 600.00
34B Sammy Baugh RJ RC 400.00 600.00
35A Ted Fritsch Sr. DJN RC 25.00 40.00
35B Ted Fritsch Sr. FJN RC 25.00 40.00
36 Bill Dudley RC 75.00 125.00
37A George Connor BYP RC 50.00 100.00
37B George Connor DYP RC 50.00 100.00
38A Frank Dancewicz GNN RC 20.00 30.00
38B Frank Dancewicz BN RC 20.00 40.00
38C Frank Dancewicz GYN RC 20.00 40.00
39 Billy Dewell RC 20.00 30.00
40A John Nolan GN RC 20.00 30.00
40B John Nolan BN RC 20.00 40.00
40C John Nolan YN RC 20.00 40.00
41A Harry Szulborski OP RC 20.00 30.00
41B Harry Szulborski YP RC 30.00 50.00
41C Harry Szulborski YP RC
Orange Pants, bright yellow jersey)
42 Tex Coulter RC 25.00 40.00
43A Robert Nussbaumer MJ RC 20.00 30.00
43B Robert Nussbaumer RJ RC 30.00 50.00
43C Robert Nussbaumer WB RC
44 Bob Mann RC 20.00 30.00
45A Jim White BB RC 25.00 40.00
45B Jim White WB RC
46A Jack Jacobs JN RC 20.00 30.00
46B Jack Jacobs NJN RC 30.00 50.00
47A John Clement BFB BYJ RC 20.00 30.00
47B John Clement BFB DYJ RC 20.00 30.00
47C John Clement YFB RC 60.00 100.00
48 Frank Reagan RC 20.00 30.00
49 Frank Tripucka RC 25.00 40.00
50 John Rauch RC 100.00 175.00
51A Mike DiMitro BYP RC 100.00 175.00

51B Mike DiMitro DYP RC	100.00	175.00
52A Leo Nomellini BBMJ RC	300.00	450.00
52B Leo Nomellini BBRJ RC	350.00	500.00
52C Leo Nomellini WB RC	350.00	500.00
53 Charley Conerly BB RC	300.00	450.00
53B Charley Conerly WB RC		
54A Chuck Bednarik YB RC	350.00	500.00
54B Chuck Bednarik WB RC	350.00	500.00
55 Chick Jagade RC	100.00	175.00
56A Bob Folsom BB RC	125.00	200.00
56B Bob Folsom WB RC		
57 Gene Rossides RC	125.00	200.00
58 Art Weiner RC	100.00	175.00
59 Alex Sarkistian RC	100.00	175.00
60 Dick Harris RC	100.00	175.00
61 Len Younce RC	100.00	175.00
62 Gene Derricotte RC	100.00	175.00
63A Roy Rebel Steiner RJ RC	100.00	175.00
63B Roy Rebel Steiner WJ RC	125.00	200.00
64A Frank Seno YN RC	100.00	175.00
64B Frank Seno GN RC	100.00	175.00
65A Bob Hendren BYP RC	100.00	175.00
65B Bob Hendren DYP RC	100.00	175.00
66A Jack Cloud BB YJ RC	100.00	175.00
66B Jack Cloud BB GJ RC	100.00	175.00
66C Jack Cloud WB RC	125.00	200.00
67 Harrell Collins RC	100.00	175.00
68A Clyde LeForce RB RC	100.00	175.00
68B Clyde LeForce WB RC	125.00	200.00
69 Larry Joe RC	100.00	175.00
70 Phil O'Reilly RC	100.00	175.00
71 Paul Campbell RC	100.00	175.00
72A Ray Evans RC	100.00	175.00
72B Ray Evans RC	100.00	175.00
73A Jackie Jensen RB RC	250.00	400.00
73B Jackie Jensen WB RC	300.00	450.00
74 Russ Steger RC	100.00	175.00
75 Tony Minisi RC	100.00	175.00
76A Clayton Tonnemaker BYP RC	100.00	175.00
76B Clayton Tonnemaker DYP RC	100.00	175.00
77A George Savitsky GS BYP RC	100.00	175.00
77B George Savitsky GS DYP RC	100.00	175.00
77C George Savitsky NGS RC	125.00	200.00
78 Clarence Self RC	100.00	175.00
79 Rod Franz RC	100.00	175.00
80A Jim Youle RB BYP RC	100.00	175.00
80B Jim Youle RB DYP RC	100.00	175.00
80C Jim Youle WB RC	125.00	200.00
81A Billy Bye YPMJ RC	100.00	175.00
81B Billy Bye YPRJ RC	125.00	200.00
81C Billy Bye WPMJ RC	125.00	200.00
82 Fred Enke RC	100.00	175.00
83A Fred Folger GJ RC	100.00	175.00
83B Fred Folger WJ RC	125.00	200.00
84 Jug Girard RC	125.00	200.00
85 Joe Scott RC	100.00	175.00
86A Bob DeMoss BYP RC	100.00	175.00
86B Bob DeMoss DYP RC	100.00	175.00
87 Dave Templeton RC	100.00	175.00
88A Herb Siegert BYP RC	100.00	175.00
88B Herb Siegert DYP RC	100.00	175.00
89A Bucky O'Conner BJ RC	100.00	175.00
89B Bucky O'Conner WJ RC	150.00	250.00
90 Joe Whisler RC	100.00	175.00
91 Leon Hart RC	150.00	250.00
92 Earl Banks RC	100.00	175.00
93A Frank Aschenbrenner PJ RC	100.00	175.00
93B Frank Aschenbrenner BJ RC	100.00	175.00
94 John Goldsberry RC	100.00	175.00
95 Porter Payne RC	100.00	175.00
96A Pete Perini BB RC	100.00	175.00
96B Pete Perini WB RC		
97A Jay Rhodemyre BYJ RC	100.00	175.00
97B Jay Rhodemyre DYJ RC	100.00	175.00
98A Al DiMarco BYP RC	125.00	250.00
98B Al DiMarco DYP RC	125.00	250.00

1949 Leaf

Measuring approximately 2 3/8" by 2 7/8", the 1949 Leaf set contains 49 cards that are skip-numbered from 1 to 150. Designed much like the 1948 issue (use of many of the same portraits), the fronts feature player portraits againts a solid background. The player's name is at the bottom. The backs carry career highlights and a bio. The cards can be found on either gray or cream colored card stock. The card backs detail an offer to send in five wrappers and a dime for a 12" by 6" felt pennant of one of the teams listed on the different card backs including college and pro teams. Unlike the 1948 set, all the players portrayed were in the NFL. There are no key Rookie Cards in this set as virtually all of the players in the 1949 set were also in the 1948 Leaf set.

COMPLETE SET (49)	1,500.00	2,200.00
WRAPPER (5-CENT)	250.00	300.00
1 Bob Hendren	40.00	80.00
2 Joe Scott	18.00	30.00
3 Frank Reagan	18.00	30.00
4 John Rauch	18.00	30.00
7 Bill Fischer	18.00	30.00
9 Elmer Bud Angsman	20.00	35.00
10 Billy Dewell	18.00	30.00
13 Tommy Thompson QB	25.00	35.00
15 Sid Luckman	75.00	125.00
16 Charley Trippi	35.00	60.00
17 Bob Mann	18.00	30.00
19 Paul Christman	25.00	35.00
22 Bill Dudley	35.00	60.00
23 Clyde LeForce	18.00	30.00
26 Sammy Baugh	200.00	350.00
28 Pete Pihos	50.00	70.00
31 Tex Coulter	25.00	35.00
32 Mal Kutner	25.00	35.00
35 Whitey Wistert	25.00	35.00
37 Ted Fritsch Sr.	25.00	35.00
38 Vince Banonis	18.00	30.00
39 Jim White	18.00	30.00
40 George Connor	35.00	60.00
41 George McAfee	35.00	60.00
43 Frank Tripucka	30.00	50.00
47 Fred Enke	18.00	30.00
49 Charley Conerly	60.00	100.00
51 Ken Kavanaugh	25.00	35.00
52 Bob Demoss	18.00	30.00
56 Johnny Lujack	60.00	100.00
57 Jim Youle	18.00	30.00
62 Harry Gilmer	25.00	35.00
65 Robert Nussbaumer	18.00	30.00
67 Bobby Layne	125.00	200.00
70 Herb Siegert	18.00	30.00
74 Tony Minisi	18.00	30.00
79 Steve Van Buren	90.00	150.00
81 Perry Moss	18.00	30.00
89 Bob Waterfield	75.00	125.00
90 Jack Jacobs	18.00	30.00
95 Kenny Washington	30.00	50.00
101 Pat Harder UER	25.00	35.00
110 Bill Swiacki	25.00	35.00
118 Fred Davis	18.00	30.00
126 Jay Rhodemyre	18.00	30.00
127 Frank Seno	18.00	30.00
134 Chuck Bednarik	110.00	175.00
144 George Savitsky	18.00	30.00
150 Bulldog Turner	90.00	150.00

1950 Lions Matchbooks

Universal Match Corp. produced these Detroit Lions matchcovers. Each measures approximately 1 1/2" by 4 1/2" (when completely folded out) and features a blue bordered front with the player's photo in black and white along with an advertisement for either Mello Crisp Potato Chips or Ray Whyte Chevy. Backs contain the 1950 Lions' seasaon schedule. The prices given are for full covers (with strikers) missing the actual matches. This is the form in which the matchbooks are most commonly found. Complete books with matches typically carry a 50% premium. Books missing the striker are considered VG at best.

1 Leon Hart	12.50	25.00
2 Doak Walker	15.00	30.00

1953-59 Lions McCarthy Postcards

Photographer J.D. McCarthy released a number of postcards throughout the 1950s to the early 1980s with many issued over a number of years. This group was most likely released during the 1950s as most feature older photographs and follow the same format of featuring a facsimile autograph on the cardfronts. Several players are featured on more than one card type with the differences noted below. Most also include a typical postcard style cardback, but some were printed blankbacked and many do contain back variations. There are two slightly different sizes that were used as well: larger 3 5/8" by 5 1/2" and smaller 3 1/4" by 5 1/2". It is thought that many of the postcards were reprinted from time to time, thus the reasoning behind what may seem like undervalued prices.

COMPLETE SET (108)	500.00	1,000.00
1A Charlie Ane	6.00	12.00
1B Charlie Ane (standing)	6.00	12.00
2A Vince Banonis	4.00	8.00
2B Vince Banonis	4.00	8.00
2C Vince Banonis	4.00	8.00
2D Vince Banonis	4.00	8.00
3 Terry Barr	6.00	12.00
4A Les Bingaman	6.00	12.00
4B Les Bingaman	6.00	12.00
4C Les Bingaman	6.00	12.00
5 Bill Bowman	4.00	8.00
6 Cloyce Box	7.50	15.00
7 Jim Cain DE	4.00	8.00
8 Stan Campbell	4.00	8.00
9 Lew Carpenter	4.00	8.00
10A Howard Cassady (With ball)	7.50	15.00
10B Howard Cassady (Standing)	7.50	15.00
11A Jack Christiansen	10.00	20.00
11B Jack Christiansen	10.00	20.00
11C Jack Christiansen	10.00	20.00
12A Ollie Cline	4.00	8.00
12B Ollie Cline	4.00	8.00
13A Lou Creekmur	10.00	20.00
13B Lou Creekmur	10.00	20.00
14 Gene Cronin	4.00	8.00
15A Jim David	6.00	12.00
15B Jim David	6.00	12.00
16A Dorne Dibble	4.00	8.00
16B Dorne Dibble	4.00	8.00
17A Don Doll	6.00	12.00
17B Don Doll	4.00	8.00
18A Jim Doran	6.00	12.00
18B Jim Doran	6.00	12.00
18C Jim Doran	6.00	12.00
19 Bob Dove	4.00	8.00
20 Tom Dublinski	4.00	8.00
21 Sonny Gandee	4.00	8.00
22 Gene Gedman	4.00	8.00
23A Jim Gibbons	4.00	8.00
23B Jim Gibbons	4.00	8.00
23C Jim Gibbons (catching pass)	4.00	8.00
24 Jug Girard	6.00	12.00
25 Bill Glass	4.00	8.00
26 Pat Harder	7.50	15.00
27 Leon Hart	12.50	25.00
28 Bob Hoernschemeyer	6.00	12.00
29 Doug Hogland	4.00	8.00
30A John Henry Johnson	12.50	25.00
30B John Henry Johnson	12.50	25.00
31 Steve Junker	4.00	8.00
32 Carl Karilivacz	4.00	8.00
33 Alex Karras	12.50	25.00
34 Ray Krouse	4.00	8.00
35A Dick Lane	10.00	20.00
35B Dick Lane	10.00	20.00
36A Yale Lary	10.00	20.00
36B Yale Lary	10.00	20.00
36C Yale Lary	10.00	20.00
37A Bobby Layne	20.00	40.00
37B Bobby Layne	20.00	40.00
38 Dan Lewis	4.00	8.00
39 Gary Lowe	4.00	8.00
40A Gil Mains	4.00	8.00
40B Gil Mains	4.00	8.00
41A Jim Martin (punting pose)	6.00	12.00
41B Jim Martin	6.00	12.00
41C Jim Martin	6.00	12.00
42 Darris McCord	4.00	8.00
43A Thurman McGraw	4.00	8.00
43B Thurman McGraw	6.00	12.00
43C Thurman McGraw	6.00	12.00
44 Don McIlhenny	6.00	12.00
45 Andy Miketa	4.00	8.00
46A Dave Middleton	4.00	8.00
46B Dave Middleton	4.00	8.00
47 Bob Miller	4.00	8.00
48A Earl Morrall	7.50	15.00
48B Earl Morrall	7.50	15.00
49 Buddy Parker CO	6.00	12.00
50 Gerry Perry	4.00	8.00
51 Nick Pietrosante	6.00	12.00
52A John Prchlik	4.00	8.00
53B John Prchlik	4.00	8.00
54 Jerry Reichow	4.00	8.00
55 Perry Richards	4.00	8.00
56 Lee Riley	4.00	8.00
57 Ken Russell	4.00	8.00
58 Tobin Rote	7.50	15.00
59 Tom Rychlec	4.00	8.00
60 Jim Salsbury	4.00	8.00
61A Joe Schmidt (hands on knees)	12.50	25.00
61B Joe Schmidt (kneeling pose)	12.50	25.00
62 Harley Sewell	6.00	12.00
63 Bob Smith RB	6.00	12.00
64 Oliver Spencer	4.00	8.00
65 Dick Stanfel	4.00	8.00
66 Bill Stits	4.00	8.00
67 Lavern Torgeson	4.00	8.00
68A Tom Tracy	4.00	8.00
68B Tom Tracy	4.00	8.00
69A Doak Walker (larger card)	17.50	35.00
69B Doak Walker (smaller card)	17.50	35.00
70A Wayne Walker (running pose)	6.00	12.00
70B Wayne Walker (portrait)	6.00	12.00
71 Ken Webb	4.00	8.00
72 Dave Whitsell	4.00	8.00
73A George Wilson CO	6.00	12.00
73B George Wilson CO	6.00	12.00
74 Roger Zatkoff	4.00	8.00

1960-85 Lions McCarthy Postcards

Photographer J.D. McCarthy released a number of postcards throughout the 1950s to the mid-1980s with many issued over a number of years. This group was most likely released gradually between 1960-1980 as most feature newer photographs and follow the similar format of including the player's name within a name plate below the photo. Several players are featured on more than one card type with the differences noted below. Most also include a typical postcard style cardback, but some were printed blankbacked and many do contain back variations. It is thought that many of the postcards were reprinted from time to time, thus the reasoning behind what may seem like undervalued prices.

COMPLETE SET (92)	200.00	400.00
1 Jimmy Allen	2.00	4.00
2 Al Baker	4.00	8.00
3 Larry Ball	2.00	4.00
4A Lem Barney ((portrait)	7.50	15.00
4B Lem Barney (kneeling pose)	7.50	15.00
5A Lynn Boden (standing)	2.00	4.00
5B Lynn Boden (kneeling)	2.00	4.00
6 Craig Cotton	2.00	4.00
7 Leon Crosswhite	2.00	4.00
8A Gary Danielson	3.00	6.00
8B Gary Danielson	3.00	6.00
8C Gary Danielson	2.00	4.00
8D Gary Danielson	3.00	6.00
9 Nick Eddy	2.00	4.00
10A Doug English (action photos)	3.00	6.00
10B Doug English (kneeling pose)	3.00	6.00
11A Mel Farr (standing)	3.00	6.00
11B Mel Farr (kneeling)	3.00	6.00
12 Bobby Felts	2.00	4.00
13 Ed Flanagan	2.00	4.00
14 Rockne Freitas	2.00	4.00
15 Frank Gallagher	2.00	4.00
16 Billy Gambrell	2.00	4.00
17A Jim Gibbons	2.00	4.00
17B Jim Gibbons (White background, Palmer Moving ad o	3.00	6.00
18 Bob Grottkau	2.00	4.00
19 Larry Hand	3.00	6.00
20 R.W. Hicks	2.00	4.00
21 Billy Howard	2.00	4.00
22 James Hunter	2.00	4.00
23 Ray Jarvis	2.00	4.00
24 Dick Jauron	4.00	8.00
25A Ron Jessie	3.00	6.00
25B Ron Jessie	3.00	6.00
26 Levi Johnson	2.00	4.00
27 Horace King	2.00	4.00
28A Bob Kowalkowski	2.00	4.00
28B Bob Kowalkowski	2.00	4.00
28C Bob Kowalkowski	2.00	4.00
29A Greg Landry	4.00	8.00
29B Greg Landry	4.00	8.00
29C Greg Landry	4.00	8.00
30 Dick Lane (kneeling pose)	5.00	10.00
31A Dick Lebeau	3.00	6.00
31B Dick Lebeau	3.00	6.00
32A Mike Lucci	3.00	6.00
32B Mike Lucci	3.00	6.00
32C Mike Lucci	3.00	6.00
32D Mike Lucci	3.00	6.00
32E Mike Lucci	3.00	6.00
33 Bruce Maher	2.00	4.00
34A Errol Mann (hands on hips)	2.00	4.00
34B Errol Mann (standing holding helmet)	2.00	4.00
35 Amos Marsh	2.00	4.00
36 Earl McCullouch	2.00	4.00
37 Jim Mitchell	2.00	4.00
38 Bill Munson	3.00	6.00
39 Eddie Murray	3.00	6.00
40 Paul Naumoff	2.00	4.00
41 Orlando Nelson	2.00	4.00
42 Herb Orvis	2.00	4.00
43A Steve Owens (right hand on helmet)	5.00	10.00
43B Steve Owens	5.00	10.00
43C Steve Owens	5.00	10.00
43D Steve Owens	5.00	10.00
43E Steve Owens	5.00	10.00
43F Steve Owens	2.00	4.00
44 Ernie Price	2.00	4.00
45 Wayne Rasmussen	2.00	4.00
46 Rudy Redmond	2.00	4.00
47A Charlie Sanders	4.00	8.00
47B Charlie Sanders	4.00	8.00
47C Charlie Sanders (squatting pose)	4.00	8.00
47D Charlie Sanders	4.00	8.00
47E Charlie Sanders ch	4.00	8.00
47F Charlie Sanders	4.00	8.00
47G Charlie Sanders	4.00	8.00
48 Freddie Scott	3.00	6.00
49 Bobby Thompson	2.00	4.00
50 Leonard Thompson	3.00	6.00
51A Bill Triplett	2.00	4.00
51B Bill Triplett	2.00	4.00
52A Wayne Walker	3.00	6.00
52B Wayne Walker	3.00	6.00
53 Jim Weatherall	2.00	4.00
54 Charlie Weaver	2.00	4.00
55 Herman Weaver	2.00	4.00
56A Mike Weger	2.00	4.00
56B Mike Weger	2.00	4.00
57 Bobby Williams	2.00	4.00
58 Jim Yarbrough	2.00	4.00
59 Garo Yepremian	4.00	8.00

1961 Lions Jay Publishing

This 12-card set features (approximately) 5" by 7" black-and-white player photos. The photos show players in traditional poses with the quarterback preparing to throw, the runner heading downfield, and the defenseman ready for the tackle. These cards were packaged 12 to a packet and originally sold for 25 cents. The backs are blank. The cards are unnumbered and checklisted below in alphabetical order.

COMPLETE SET (12)	50.00	100.00
1 Carl Brettschneider	4.00	8.00
2 Howard Cassady	5.00	10.00
3 Gail Cogdill	4.00	8.00
4 Jim Gibbons	4.00	8.00
5 Alex Karras	6.00	12.00
6 Yale Lary	6.00	12.00
7 Jim Martin	4.00	8.00
8 Earl Morrall	5.00	10.00
9 Jim Ninowski	5.00	10.00
10 Nick Pietrosante	4.00	8.00
11 Joe Schmidt	6.00	12.00
12 George Wilson CO	4.00	8.00

1961 Lions Team Issue

The Lions issued these photos around 1961. Each features a black and white player image, measures roughly 7 3/4" by 9 1/2" and is surrounded by a thin white border. The player's name and position is printed in a small box within the photo. The backs are blank and we've listed the photos alphabetically below.

COMPLETE SET (12)	75.00	125.00
1 Terry Barr	5.00	10.00
2 Howard Cassady	6.00	12.00
3 Gail Cogdill	5.00	10.00
4 Jim Gibbons	6.00	12.00
5 Dick Lane	7.50	15.00
6 Yale Lary	7.50	15.00
7 Dan Lewis	5.00	10.00
8 Jim Martin	5.00	10.00
9 Earl Morrall	7.50	15.00
10 Jim Ninowski	6.00	12.00
11 Nick Pietrosante	5.00	10.00
12 Joe Schmidt	10.00	20.00

1961-62 Lions Falstaff Beer Team Photos

These oversized (roughly 6 1/4" by 9") color team photos were sponsored by Falstaff Beer and distributed in the Detroit area. Each was printed on card stock and included advertising messages and the Lions season schedule on the back.

1961 Lions Team	18.00	30.00
1962 Lions Team	18.00	30.00

1963-67 Lions Team Issue 8x10

The Detroit Lions issued these photos printed on glossy photographic stock. Each measures approximately 8" by 10" and features a black and white photo. The player's name, position, and team name appear below the photo on most of the pictures. However, a few photos catalogued below do not include the player's position. Therefore it is likely that the photos were released over a period of years. A photographer's imprint can often be found on the backs.

COMPLETE SET (23)	100.00	200.00
1 Lem Barney	7.50	15.00
2 Charley Bradshaw	5.00	10.00
3 Roger Brown DT	5.00	10.00
4 Ernie Clark	5.00	10.00
5 Gail Cogdill	5.00	10.00
6 John Gordy	5.00	10.00
7 Wally Hilgenberg	6.00	12.00
8 Alex Karras	7.50	15.00
9 Alex Karras	7.50	15.00
10 Bob Kowalkowski	5.00	10.00
11 Dick LeBeau	5.00	10.00
12 Joe Don Looney	6.00	12.00
13 Mike Lucci	6.00	12.00
14 Bruce Maher	5.00	10.00
15 Paul Naumoff	5.00	10.00
16 Tom Nowatzke	5.00	10.00
17 Milt Plum	6.00	12.00
18 Pat Studstill	5.00	10.00
19 Pat Studstill	5.00	10.00
20 Pat Studstill	5.00	10.00
21 Karl Sweetan	5.00	10.00
22 Bobby Thompson	5.00	10.00
23 Wayne Walker	5.00	10.00

1964-65 Lions Team Issue

The Lions issued single photos and photo packs to fans throughout the mid 1960s. Each photo in this set is a black and white 7 3/8" by 9 3/8" posed action shot surrounded by a white border. The player's name, position, and team name are printed on a single line below the photo. The print type, style, and size are identical on each photo. However, some of the players were issued in one or more years as some of the cards can be found with a date (either Oct. 1, 1964 or Sep. 24, 1965) stamped in blue ink on the cardback while others have no stamp. Of those known to be stamped, we've included the year(s) below. The cards also look identical to the 1966 issue. Players found in both sets have the specific differences noted below.

COMPLETE SET (40)	150.00	300.00
1 Terry Barr 65	5.00	10.00
2 Roger Brown DT 65	5.00	10.00
3 Gail Cogdill 64	5.00	10.00
4 Dick Compton 64/65	5.00	10.00
5 Larry Ferguson 65	5.00	10.00
6 Dennis Gaubatz 64/65	5.00	10.00
7 Jim Gibbons 64/65	6.00	12.00
8 John Gonzaga 64/65	5.00	10.00
9 John Gordy 64/65	5.00	10.00
10 Tom Hall 65	5.00	10.00
11 Ron Kramer	5.00	10.00
12 Roger LaLonde 65	5.00	10.00
13 Dick Lane 64	7.50	15.00
14 Dan LaRose 65	5.00	10.00
15 Yale Lary 64/65	7.50	15.00
16 Dick LeBeau 65	5.00	10.00
17 Monte Lee 65	5.00	10.00
18 Dan Lewis 64/65	5.00	10.00
19 Gary Lowe 65	5.00	10.00
20 Bruce Maher 64	5.00	10.00
21 Darris McCord 64/65	5.00	10.00
22 Hugh McInnis 65	5.00	10.00
23 Max Messner 65	5.00	10.00
24 Floyd Peters 65	5.00	10.00
25 Nick Pietrosante 65	5.00	10.00
26 Milt Plum 65	6.00	12.00
27 Bill Quinlan 65	5.00	10.00
28 Nick Ryder 65	5.00	10.00
29 Daryl Sanders 65	5.00	10.00
30 Joe Schmidt 64/65	7.50	15.00
31 Bob Scholtz 65	5.00	10.00
32 James Simon 64	5.00	10.00
33 J.D. Smith T 65	5.00	10.00
34 Pat Studstill 65	5.00	10.00
35 Larry Vargo 65	5.00	10.00
36 Wayne Walker 64/65	5.00	10.00
37 Tom Watkins 64/65	5.00	10.00
38 Warren Wells 65	5.00	10.00
39 Bob Whitlow 65	5.00	10.00
40 Sam Williams 64	5.00	10.00

1966 Lions Marathon Oil

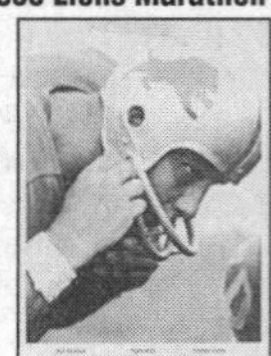

This set consists of seven photos measuring approximately 5" by 7" thought to have been released by Marathon Oil. The fronts feature black-and-white photos with white borders. The player's name, position, and team name are printed in the bottom border. The backs are blank. The cards are unnumbered and checklisted below in alphabetical order.

COMPLETE SET (7)	30.00	60.00
1 Gail Cogdill	5.00	10.00
2 John Gordy	5.00	10.00
3 Alex Karras	7.50	15.00
4 Ron Kramer	5.00	10.00
5 Milt Plum	6.00	12.00
6 Wayne Rasmussen	5.00	10.00
7 Daryl Sanders	5.00	10.00

1966 Lions Team Issue

The Detroit Lions issued this set of large photos to Lions' fans who requested player pictures in 1966. Each measures approximately 7 1/2" by 9 1/2" and features a black and white photo. The player's name, position, and team name appear below the photo. The cards look identical to the 1964-65 issue. Players found in both sets have the specific differences noted below.

COMPLETE SET (41)	150.00	300.00
1 Mike Alford	5.00	10.00
2 Roger Brown	5.00	10.00
3 Ernie Clark	5.00	10.00
4 Bill Cody	5.00	10.00
5 Gail Cogdill	5.00	10.00
6 Ed Flanagan	5.00	10.00
7 Jim Gibbons	5.00	10.00
8 John Gordy	5.00	10.00
9 Larry Hand	5.00	10.00
10 John Henderson	5.00	10.00
11 Wally Hilgenberg	6.00	12.00
12 Alex Karras	7.50	15.00
13 Bob Kowalkowski	5.00	10.00
14 Ron Kramer	5.00	10.00
15 Dick LeBeau	5.00	10.00
16 Joe Don Looney	6.00	12.00
17 Mike Lucci	6.00	12.00
18 Bruce Maher	5.00	10.00
19 Bill Malinchak	5.00	10.00
20 Amos Marsh	5.00	10.00
21 Jerry Mazzanti	5.00	10.00
22 Darris McCord	5.00	10.00
23 Bruce McLenna	5.00	10.00
24 Tom Nowatzke	5.00	10.00
25 Milt Plum	6.00	12.00
26 Wayne Rasmussen	5.00	10.00
27 Johnnie Robinson DB	5.00	10.00
28 Jerry Rush	5.00	10.00
29 Daryl Sanders	5.00	10.00
30 Bobby Smith	5.00	10.00
31 J.D. Smith	5.00	10.00
32 Pat Studstill	5.00	10.00
33 Karl Sweetan	5.00	10.00
34 Bobby Thompson	5.00	10.00
35 Jim Todd	5.00	10.00
36 Doug Van Horn	5.00	10.00
37 Tom Vaughn	5.00	10.00
38 Wayne Walker	5.00	10.00
39 Willie Walker	5.00	10.00
40 Tom Watkins	5.00	10.00
41 Coaching Staff	10.00	20.00

1968 Lions Tasco Prints

Tasco Associates produced this set of Detroit Lions prints. The fronts feature a large color artist's rendering of the player along with the player's name and position. The backs are blank. The prints measure approximately 11 1/2" by 16."

COMPLETE SET (7)	50.00	100.00
1 Lem Barney	7.50	15.00
2 Mel Farr	5.00	10.00
3 Alex Karras	15.00	25.00
4 Dick LeBeau	5.00	10.00
5 Mike Lucci	6.00	12.00
6 Earl McCullouch	5.00	10.00
7 Bill Munson	6.00	12.00
8 Wayne Rasmussen	5.00	10.00
9 Jerry Rush	5.00	10.00

1968 MacGregor Advisory Staff

MacGregor released a number of player photos during the 1960s. Each measures roughly 8" by 10 1/2" and carries a black and white photo of the player. Included below the photo is a note that the player is a member of MacGregor's advisory staff. The photos are blankbacked and unnumbered and checklisted below in alphabetical order. Any additions to the list below are appreciated.

1 Mike Ditka	15.00	30.00
2 Joe Namath	30.00	60.00
3 Bart Starr	15.00	30.00
4 Johnny Unitas	20.00	40.00

1973-87 Mardi Gras Parade Doubloons

These Mardi Gras Parade Doubloons or coins were thrown into the crowds by passing floats during the celebration each year in New Orleans. Although many different subject matters appear on these types of coins, we've only listed the football players below. Each includes a sculpted portrait of the player on one side and the parade logo on the other on a gold or bronze colored coin; all are from the Gladiators Parade unless noted below. We've listed the coins by their year of issue. Any additions to the list below are appreciated.

COMPLETE SET (16)	15.00	30.00
1973 Danny Abramowicz	1.00	2.00
1974 George Blanda	1.50	3.00
1975 Ken Stabler	2.50	5.00
1977 Bert Jones	1.00	2.00
1978 Joe Ferguson	1.00	2.00
1979 Ray Guy	1.00	2.00
1980 Norris Weese	1.00	2.00
1981 Billy Kilmer	1.00	2.00
1982 Sonny Jurgensen	1.50	3.00
1983 Danny Abramowicz	1.00	2.00
1984 Archie Manning	1.50	3.00
1985 Richard Todd	1.00	2.00
1986 Brian Hansen	1.00	2.00
1987 Morten Andersen	1.00	2.00
1995 Jim Finks Green	1.00	2.00
1995 Jim Finks Silver	1.00	2.00

1977 Marketcom Test

The 1977 Marketcom Test checklist below includes known mini-posters with each measuring approximately 5 1/2" by 8 1/2". They were printed on paper-thin stock and are virtually always found with fold creases. Marketcom is credited at the bottom of most of them along with the year 1977. Some are blankbacked while others include an advertisement for obtaining a large version of the poster. These posters are unnumbered and listed below in alphabetical order.

1 Otis Armstrong	20.00	40.00
2 Ken Burrough	20.00	40.00
3 Greg Pruitt	20.00	40.00
4 Jack Youngblood	20.00	40.00

1978-79 Marketcom Test

The 1978-79 Marketcom set includes mini-posters measuring approximately 5 1/2" by 8 1/2". They were printed on paper-thin stock and are virtually always found with fold creases. Marketcom is credited at the bottom of each poster front and some include a year designation while others do not. Most poster backs are blank but others have been found with an advertisement on the back for full sized posters. Finally, another version of many of the posters was also printed on thin cardboard stock without any folds. These cardboard versions are blankbacked and thicker than the paper version but slightly thinner than the 1980 posters. The posters are unnumbered and listed below in alphabetical order.

COMPLETE SET (34)	250.00	450.00
1 Otis Armstrong SP	5.00	10.00
2 Steve Bartkowski SP	6.00	12.00
3 Terry Bradshaw SP	20.00	40.00
4 Ken Burrough	3.00	6.00
5 Earl Campbell	15.00	30.00
6 Dave Casper	4.00	8.00
7 Gary Danielson	3.00	6.00
8 Dan Dierdorf SP	6.00	12.00
9 Tony Dorsett SP	20.00	40.00
10 Dan Fouts SP	12.50	25.00
11 Wallace Francis	4.00	8.00
12 Tony Galbreath	3.00	6.00
13 Randy Gradishar SP	5.00	10.00
14 Bob Griese SP	12.50	25.00
15 Steve Grogan	4.00	8.00
16 Ray Guy	4.00	8.00
17 Pat Haden SP	6.00	12.00
18 Jack Ham	6.00	12.00
19 Cliff Harris SP	5.00	10.00
20 Franco Harris	7.50	15.00
21 Jim Hart	4.00	8.00
22 Ron Jaworski	4.00	8.00
23 John Jefferson	5.00	10.00
24 Bert Jones SP	6.00	12.00
25 Jack Lambert SP	10.00	20.00
26 Archie Manning	6.00	12.00
27 Harvey Martin SP	5.00	10.00
28 Reggie McKenzie	3.00	6.00
29 Karl Mecklenburg SP	5.00	10.00
30 Craig Morton	4.00	8.00
31 Dan Pastorini	3.00	6.00
32 Walter Payton SP	20.00	40.00
33 Lee Roy Selmon	5.00	10.00
34 Roger Staubach SP	20.00	40.00
35 Joe Theismann UER	6.00	12.00
36 Wesley Walker SP	5.00	10.00
37 Randy White	6.00	12.00
38 Jack Youngblood SP	5.00	10.00
39 Jim Zorn	4.00	8.00

1980 Marketcom

In 1980, Marketcom issued a set of 50 Football Mini-Posters. These 5 1/2" by 8 1/2" cards are very attractive, featuring a large full color (action scene) picture of each player with a white border. The cards have the player's name on front at top and have a facsimile autograph on the picture as well; cards are numbered on the back at the bottom as "x of 50". A very tough to find Rocky Bleier card (numbered 51) was produced as well, but is not listed below due to lack of market information.

COMPLETE SET (50)	30.00	60.00
1 Ottis Anderson	.75	2.00
2 Brian Sipe	.40	1.00
3 Lawrence McCutcheon	.40	1.00
4 Ken Anderson	.75	2.00
5 Roland Harper	.40	1.00
6 Chuck Foreman	.40	1.00
7 Gary Danielson	.40	1.00
8 Wallace Francis	.40	1.00
9 John Jefferson	.50	1.25
10 Charlie Waters	.50	1.25
11 Jack Ham	.75	2.00
12 Jack Lambert	.75	2.00
13 Walter Payton	5.00	12.00
14 Bert Jones	.50	1.25
15 Harvey Martin	.50	1.25
16 Jim Hart	.40	1.00
17 Craig Morton	.50	1.25

Card	Low	High
18 Reggie McKenzie	.40	1.00
19 Keith Wortman	.40	1.00
20 Otis Armstrong	.40	1.00
21 Steve Grogan	.50	1.25
22 Jim Zorn	.40	1.00
23 Bob Griese	1.25	3.00
24 Tony Dorsett	2.00	5.00
25 Wesley Walker	.40	1.00
26 Dan Fouts	1.00	2.50
27 Dan Dierdorf	.75	2.00
28 Steve Bartkowski	.50	1.25
29 Archie Manning	.50	1.25
30 Randy Gradishar	.50	1.25
31 Randy White	.75	2.00
32 Joe Theismann	.75	2.00
33 Tony Galbreath	.40	1.00
34 Cliff Harris	.50	1.25
35 Ray Guy	.50	1.25
36 Dave Casper	.50	1.25
37 Ron Jaworski	.50	1.25
38 Greg Pruitt	.40	1.00
39 Ken Burrough	.40	1.00
40 Robert Brazile	.40	1.00
41 Pat Haden	.50	1.25
42 Dan Pastorini	.40	1.00
43 Lee Roy Selmon	.75	2.00
44 Franco Harris	1.25	3.00
45 Jack Youngblood	.50	1.25
46 Terry Bradshaw	3.00	8.00
47 Roger Staubach	3.00	8.00
48 Earl Campbell	2.00	5.00
49 Phil Simms	1.25	3.00
50 Delvin Williams	.40	1.00

1971 Mattel Mini-Records

This set was designed to be played on a special Mattel mini-record player, which is not included in the complete set price. Each black plastic disc, approximately 2 1/2" in diameter, features a recording on one side and a color drawing of the player on the other. The picture appears on a paper disk that is glued onto the smooth unrecorded side of the mini-record. On the recorded side, the player's name and the set's subtitle appear in arcs stamped in the central portion of the mini-record. The hand-engraved player's name appears again along with a production number, copyright symbol, and the Mattel name and year of production in the ring between the central portion of the record and the grooves. The ivory discs are the ones which are double sided and are considered to be tougher than the black discs. They were also known as "Mattel Show 'N Tell". The discs are unnumbered and checklisted below in alphabetical order according to sport

Card	Low	High
COMPLETE SET (18)	200.00	400.00
FB1 Donny Anderson	1.25	3.00
FB2 Lem Barney	1.50	4.00
FB3 John Brodie DP	1.50	4.00
FB4 Dick Butkus DP	3.00	8.00
FB5 Bob Hayes DP	1.50	4.00
FB6 Sonny Jurgensen	2.50	6.00
FB7 Alex Karras	2.50	6.00
FB8 Leroy Kelly	2.00	5.00
FB9 Daryle Lamonica DP	1.25	3.00
FB10 John Mackey DP	1.50	4.00
FB11 Earl Morrall	1.25	3.00
FB12 Joe Namath	15.00	30.00
FB13 Merlin Olsen DP	1.50	4.00
FB14 Alan Page	2.00	5.00
FB15 Gale Sayers DP	3.00	8.00
FB16 O.J. Simpson DP	3.00	8.00
FB17 Bart Starr	12.50	25.00

1937 Mayfair Candies Touchdown 100 Yards

Mayfair Candies produced this perforated card set in 1937. Each unnumbered card features an unidentified football action photo on the front and a football play description on the back. The set involved a contest whereby the collector tried to accumulate "100 Yards" based on football plays described on the cardbacks. The offer expired on February 15, 1938 and winners could exchange the cards for an official sized football. The ACC designation is R343 and each card measures approximately 1 3/4" by 2 3/4" and was unnumbered. Since there are no card numbers and no identification of players, we have cataloged the cards below using the first several words found at the top of the cardbacks. We have also included the cardfront photo's background color and number of players featured in the image for each card to help catalog the cardfronts. Note that four cardfronts exist with two different cardbacks each. Red Grange is the only player of note that has been positively identified.

Card	Low	High
COMPLETE SET (24)	5,000.00	8,000.00
1 2 Yards to go!...	200.00	350.00
2 3 Yards to go...	200.00	350.00
3 Again the off tackle...	200.00	350.00
4 Being in perfect position...	200.00	350.00
5 Changing quickly from...	200.00	350.00
6 Charging hard...	200.00	350.00
7 Coming from in front...	200.00	350.00
8 Coming out of a....	200.00	350.00
9 Digging in their heels...	200.00	350.00
10 Early in the third...	200.00	350.00
11 Flipping a underhand....	200.00	350.00
12 Giving every ounce...	200.00	350.00
13 In a play that fizzled...	200.00	350.00
14 Indecision on the part...	200.00	350.00
15 Late in the same...	200.00	350.00
16 Left Tackle is called....	200.00	350.00
17 Line holds beautifully... (Red Grange pictured)	900.00	1,500.00
18 Only intense rivalry...	200.00	350.00
19 Outmaneuvered....	200.00	350.00
20 Quarterback runs...	200.00	350.00
21 Revealing for the first...	200.00	350.00
22 Same old story...	200.00	350.00
23 Smashing close behind...	200.00	350.00
24 Snapping out of their...	200.00	350.00
25 The fullback driving...	200.00	350.00
26 Three unsuccessful...	200.00	350.00
27 Trying the old...	200.00	350.00
28 What have we here?...	200.00	350.00

1894 Mayo

The 1894 Mayo college football series contains 35-cards of top Ivy League players. The cards feature sepia photos of the player surrounded by a black border, in which the player's name, his college, and a Mayo Cut Plug ad appears. The cards have solid black backs and measure approximately 1 5/8" by 2 7/8". Each card is unnumbered, but we've assigned card numbers alphabetically in the checklist below for your convenience. One of the cards has no specific identification of the player (John Dunlop of Harvard) and is listed below as being anonymous. It's one of the most highly sought after of all football cards and seldom seen. We've not included it in the complete set price due to its scarcity. Those players who were All-American selections are listed below with the year(s) of selection. The Poe (likely Neilson Poe) in the set is a direct descendant of the famous writer Edgar Allan Poe.

Card	Low	High
COMPLETE SET (34)	15,000.00	25,000.00
1 Robert Acton (Harvard)	500.00	800.00
2 George Adee (Yale)	500.00	800.00
3 Richard Armstrong (Yale)	500.00	800.00
4 H.W.Barnett (Princeton)	500.00	800.00
5 Art Beale (Harvard)	500.00	800.00
6 Anson Beard (Yale)	500.00	800.00
7 Charles Brewer (Harvard)	500.00	800.00
8 H.D.Brown (Princeton)	500.00	800.00
9 C.D. Burt (Princeton)	500.00	800.00
10 Frank Butterworth (Yale)	550.00	850.00
11 Eddie Crowdis (Princeton)	500.00	800.00
12 Robert Emmons (Harvard)	500.00	800.00
13 Madison Gonterman UER (Har)	500.00	800.00
14 George Gray (Harvard)	500.00	800.00
15 John Greenway (Yale)	550.00	850.00
16 William Hickok (Yale)	550.00	850.00
17 Frank Hinkey (Yale)	800.00	1,200.00
18 Augustus Holly (Princeton)	500.00	800.00
19 Langdon Lea (Princeton)	550.00	850.00
20 William Mackie (Harvard)	500.00	800.00
21 Tom Manahan (Harvard)	500.00	800.00
22 Jim McCrea (Yale)	500.00	800.00
23 Frank Morse (Princeton)	500.00	800.00
24 Fred Murphy (Yale)	550.00	850.00
25 Neilson Poe (Princeton)	800.00	1,200.00
26 Dudley Riggs (Princeton)	550.00	850.00
27 Phillip Stillman (Yale)	500.00	800.00
28 Knox Taylor (Princeton)	500.00	800.00
29 Brinck Thorne (Yale)	500.00	800.00
30 T.Trenchard (Princeton)	550.00	850.00
31 William Ward (Princeton)	500.00	800.00
32 Bert Waters (Harvard)	550.00	850.00
33 A. Wheeler (Princeton)	550.00	850.00
34 Edgar Wrightington (Har)	500.00	800.00
35 Anonymous (J.Dunlop)	12,000.00	18,000.00

1975 McDonald's Quarterbacks

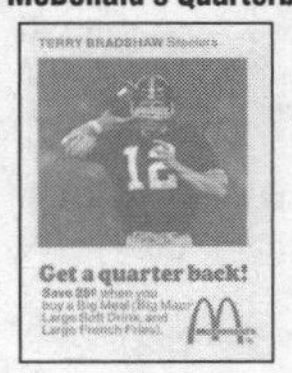

The 1975 McDonald's Quarterbacks set contains four cards, each of which was used as a promotion for McDonald's hamburger restaurants. The cards measure 2 1/2" by 3 7/16". One might get a quarter back if the coupon at the bottom of the card were presented at one of McDonald's retail establishments. Each coupon was valid for only one week, that particular week clearly marked on the coupon. The cards themselves are in color with yellow borders on the front and statistics on the back. The back of each card is a different color. Statistics are given for each of the quarterback's previous seasons record passing and rushing. The prices below are for the cards with coupons intact as that is the way they are usually found.

Card	Low	High
COMPLETE SET (4)	12.50	25.00
1 Terry Bradshaw	7.50	15.00
2 Joe Ferguson	2.00	5.00
3 Ken Stabler	4.00	10.00
4 Al Woodall	1.50	4.00

1976 MSA Cups

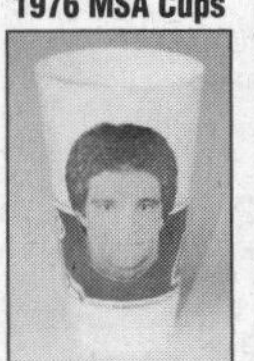

This set of cups was produced by MSA and distributed at various outlets and stores in 1976. Each features a photo of the player without the use of team logos. It is thought that two different 20-cup sets were released throughout the country. Any additions to this list are appreciated.

Card	Low	High
1 Ken Anderson	4.00	8.00
2 Lem Barney	4.00	8.00
3 Steve Bartkowski	3.00	6.00
4 Fred Biletnikoff	5.00	10.00
5 Terry Bradshaw	12.00	25.00
6 Gary Danielson	2.50	5.00
7 Joe Ferguson	3.00	6.00
8 Chuck Foreman	3.00	6.00
9 Dan Fouts	6.00	12.00
10 Randy Gradishar	3.00	6.00
11 Bob Griese	6.00	12.00
12 Archie Griffin	3.00	6.00
13 Steve Grogan	3.00	6.00
14 Pat Haden	3.00	6.00
15 Jim Hart	2.50	5.00
16 Gary Huff	2.50	5.00
17 Ron Jaworski	3.00	6.00
18 Billy Johnson	2.50	5.00
19 Essex Johnson	2.50	5.00
20 Bert Jones	3.00	6.00
21 Billy Kilmer	3.00	6.00
22 Mike Livingston	2.50	5.00
23 Archie Manning	2.50	5.00
24 Ed Marinaro	4.00	8.00
25 Lawrence McCutchen	2.50	5.00
26 Craig Morton	3.00	6.00
27 Dan Pastorini	3.00	6.00
28 Walter Payton	25.00	40.00
29 Jim Plunkett	5.00	10.00
30 Greg Pruitt	2.50	5.00
31 John Riggins	6.00	12.00
32 Brian Sipe	3.00	6.00
33 Steve Spurrier	10.00	20.00
34 Roger Staubach	12.50	25.00
35 Mark Van Eeghen	3.00	6.00
36 Brad Van Pelt	2.50	5.00
37 David Whitehurst	2.50	5.00

1974 Nabisco Sugar Daddy

This set of 25 tiny (approximately 1 1/16" by 2 3/4") cards features athletes from a variety of popular pro sports. One card was included in specially marked Sugar Daddy and Sugar Mama candy bars. The cards were designed to be placed on a 18" by 24" poster, which could only be obtained through a mail-in offer direct from Nabisco. The set is referred to as "Pro Faces" as the cards show an enlarged head photo with a small caricature body. Cards 1-10 are football players, cards 11-16 and 22 are hockey players, and cards 17-21 and 23-25 are basketball players. Each card was produced in two printings. The first printing has a copyright date of 1973 printed on the backs (although the cards are thought to have been released in early 1974) and the second printing is missing a copyright date altogether.

Card	Low	High
COMPLETE SET (25)	75.00	150.00
1 Roger Staubach	15.00	30.00
2 Floyd Little	2.50	6.00
3 Steve Owens	2.50	6.00
4 Roman Gabriel	2.50	6.00
5 Bobby Douglass	2.00	5.00
6 John Gilliam	2.00	5.00
7 Bob Lilly	5.00	10.00
8 John Brockington	2.00	5.00
9 Jim Plunkett	2.50	6.00
10 Greg Landry	2.00	5.00

1975 Nabisco Sugar Daddy

This set of 25 tiny (approximately 1 1/16" by 2 3/4") cards features athletes from a variety of popular pro sports. One card was included in specially marked Sugar Daddy and Sugar Mama candy bars. The cards were designed to be placed on a 18" by 24" poster, which could only be obtained through a mail-in offer direct from Nabisco. The set is referred to as "Sugar Daddy All-Stars". As with the set of the previous year, the cards show an enlarged head photo with a small caricature body with a flag background of stars and stripes. This set is referred on the back as Series No. 2 and has a red, white, and blue background behind the picture on the front of the card. Cards 1-10 are pro football players and the remainder are pro basketball (17-21, 23-25) and hockey (11-16, 22) players.

Card	Low	High
COMPLETE SET (25)	75.00	150.00
1 Roger Staubach	12.00	30.00
2 Floyd Little	2.50	6.00
3 Alan Page	2.50	6.00
4 Merlin Olsen	4.00	8.00
5 Wally Chambers	2.00	5.00
6 John Gilliam	2.00	5.00
7 Bob Lilly	4.00	10.00
8 John Brockington	2.00	5.00
9 Jim Plunkett	2.50	6.00
10 Willie Lanier	2.50	6.00

1976 Nabisco Sugar Daddy 1

This set of 25 tiny (approximately 1 1/16" by 2 3/4") cards features action scenes from a variety of popular sports from around the world. One card was included in specially marked Sugar Daddy and Sugar Mama candy bars. The set is referred to as "Sugar Daddy Sports World - Series 1" on the backs of the cards. The cards are in color with a relatively wide white border around the front of the cards.

Card	Low	High
COMPLETE SET (25)	40.00	80.00
6 Football Charley Johnson	5.00	12.00

1976 Nabisco Sugar Daddy 2

This set of 25 tiny (approximately 1 1/16" by 2 3/4") cards features action scenes from a variety of popular sports from around the world. One card was included in specially marked Sugar Daddy and Sugar Mama candy bars. The set is referred to as "Sugar Daddy Sports World - Series 2" on the backs of the cards. The cards are in color with a relatively wide white border around the front of the cards.

Card	Low	High
COMPLETE SET (25)	40.00	80.00
4 Football (Sonny Jurgensen)	7.50	15.00

1935 National Chicle

The 1935 National Chicle set was the first nationally distributed bubble gum set dedicated exclusively to football players. The cards measure 2 3/8" by 2 7/8". Card numbers 25 to 36 are more difficult to obtain than other cards in this set. The Knute Rockne and Bronko Nagurski cards are two of the most valuable football cards in existence. The set features NFL players except for the Rockne card. There are variations on the backs of each of the first series (1-24) cards with respect to the size of Eddie Casey's facsimile signature. The variation of Casey's name printed in larger letters appears to be in shorter supply and that larger name is the only version appearing on the backs of the high series (25-36) cards. This leads us to believe that the first series large name variations were inserted into high series packs. Please note that many different reprints of these cards exist (particularly Rockne and Nagurski) so caution should be taken before paying a large sum for a card. The original cards were printed with blue ink on the back not green. Some reprints feature the word "reprint" on the front or back while others do not. A close look at the dot pattern on the front of the card is a tell tale sign of a reprint card. The originals do not show a dot pattern under magnification.

Card	Low	High
COMPLETE SET (36)	10,000.00	15,000.00
COMMON CARD (1-24)	100.00	175.00
COMMON CARD (25-36)	400.00	600.00
WRAPPER (1-CENT)	200.00	400.00
1A Dutch Clark SN RC	300.00	600.00
1B Dutch Clark LN	500.00	900.00
2A Bo Molenda SN RC	100.00	175.00
2B Bo Molenda LN	150.00	250.00
3A George Kenneally SN RC	100.00	175.00
3B George Kenneally LN	150.00	250.00
4A Ed Matesic SN RC	100.00	175.00
4B Ed Matesic LN	150.00	250.00
4C Ed Matesic LN ERR		
5A Glenn Presnell SN RC	100.00	175.00
5B Glenn Presnell LN	150.00	250.00
6A Pug Rentner SN RC	100.00	175.00
6B Pug Rentner LN	150.00	250.00
7A Ken Strong SN RC	250.00	400.00
7B Ken Strong LN	350.00	600.00
8A Jim Zyntell SN RC	100.00	175.00
8B Jim Zyntell LN	150.00	250.00
9A Knute Rockne CO SN	1,000.00	1,600.00
9B Knute Rockne CO LN	1,200.00	2,200.00
10A Cliff Battles SN RC	250.00	400.00
10B Cliff Battles LN	350.00	600.00
11A Turk Edwards SN RC	250.00	400.00
11B Turk Edwards LN	350.00	600.00
12A Tom Hupke SN RC	100.00	175.00
12B Tom Hupke LN	150.00	250.00
13A Homer Griffiths SN RC	100.00	175.00
13B Homer Griffiths LN	150.00	250.00
14A Phil Sarboe SN RC UER	100.00	175.00
14B Phil Sarboe LN UER	150.00	250.00
15A Ben Ciccone SN RC UER	100.00	175.00
15B Ben Ciccone LN	150.00	250.00
16A Ben Smith SN RC UER	100.00	175.00
16B Ben Smith LN	150.00	250.00
17A Tom Jones SN RC	100.00	175.00
17B Tom Jones LN	150.00	250.00
18A Mike Mikulak SN RC	100.00	175.00
18B Mike Mikulak LN	150.00	250.00
19 Ralph Kercheval SN RC UER	100.00	175.00
19B Ralph Kercheval LN COR	150.00	250.00
20A Warren Heller SN RC UER	100.00	175.00
20B Warren Heller LN	150.00	250.00
21A Cliff Montgomery SN RC	100.00	175.00
21B Cliff Montgomery LN	150.00	250.00
22A Shipwreck Kelly SN RC UER	100.00	175.00
22B Shipwreck Kelly LN UER	150.00	250.00
23A Beattie Feathers SN RC UER	175.00	300.00
23B Beattie Feathers LN	250.00	450.00
24A Clarke Hinkle SN RC UER	400.00	600.00
24B Clarke Hinkle LN	500.00	900.00
25 Dale Burnett RC	400.00	600.00
26 John Dell Isola RC	400.00	600.00
27 Bull Tosi RC	600.00	1,000.00
28 Stan Kostka RC	400.00	600.00
29 Jim MacMurdo RC	400.00	600.00
30 Ernie Caddel RC	400.00	600.00
31 Nic Niccola RC	400.00	600.00
32 Swede Johnston RC	400.00	600.00
33 Ernie Smith RC	400.00	600.00
34 Bronko Nagurski RC	3,500.00	5,000.00
35 Luke Johnsos RC	400.00	600.00
36 Bernie Masterson RC	350.00	800.00

1974 New York News This Day in Sports

These cards are newspaper clippings of drawings by Hollreiser and are accompanied by textual description highlighting a player's unique sports feat. Cards are approximately 2" X 4 1/4". These are multisport cards and aranged in chronological order.

COMPLETE SET	50.00	120.00
25 Doc Blanchard Glenn Davis Sept. 30, 1944	1.50	3.00
27 Archie Manning Oct. 4, 1969	1.50	3.00
31 Harold Jackson Oct. 14, 1973	1.00	2.00
32 O.J. Simpson Oct. 21, 1967	1.50	3.00
33 Doc Blanchard Nov. 11, 1944	1.00	2.00
35 Bronko Nagurski Nov. 23, 1929	1.50	3.00
37 New York Giants Dec. 9, 1934	1.00	2.00
38 John Brodie Dec. 20, 1970	1.00	2.00
39 Roger Staubach Dec. 23, 1972	2.00	4.00
40 Paul Brown Otto Graham Dec. 26, 1954	1.50	3.00

1974 New York Stars WFL Team Issue 8X10

The photos measure roughly 8" x 10" and include black and white images with the player's name centered below the photo, the team logo to the left and the player's position to the right. The backs are blank.

1 Howard Baldwin Pres.	5.00	10.00
2 Robert Keating VP	5.00	10.00
3 Babe Parilli CO	7.50	15.00

1972 NFL Properties Cloth Patches

This set of team logos and team helmet stickers was produced by NFL Properties in 1972. Each measures roughly 1 1/2" by 1 3/4" and was printed on cloth sticker stock with a blank back. The stickers closely resemble the early cloth patches used in many of the Fleer releases from that era. It is thought by many hobbyists that this set was actually released in Schwebel Bread products in 1975.

COMPLETE SET (52)	150.00	300.00
1 Chicago Bears	3.00	6.00
2 Chicago Bears	3.00	6.00
3 Cincinnati Bengals (logo)	3.00	6.00
4 Cincinnati Bengals (helmet)	3.00	6.00
5 Buffalo Bills (logo)	3.00	6.00
6 Buffalo Bills (helmet)	3.00	6.00
7 Denver Broncos (logo)	3.00	6.00
8 Denver Broncos (helmet)	3.00	6.00
9 Cleveland Browns (logo)	5.00	10.00
10 Cleveland Browns (helmet)	4.00	8.00
11 St.Louis Cardinals (logo)	3.00	6.00
12 St.Louis Cardinals (helmet)	3.00	6.00
13 San Diego Chargers (logo)	3.00	6.00
14 San Diego Chargers (helmet)	3.00	6.00
15 Kansas City Chiefs (logo)	3.00	6.00
16 Kansas City Chiefs (helmet)	3.00	6.00
17 Baltimore Colts (logo)	3.00	6.00
18 Baltimore Colts (helmet)	3.00	6.00
19 Dallas Cowboys (logo)	5.00	10.00
20 Dallas Cowboys (helmet)	5.00	10.00
21 Miami Dolphins (logo)	5.00	10.00
22 Miami Dolphins (helmet)	5.00	10.00
23 Philadelphia Eagles (logo)	3.00	6.00
24 Philadelphia Eagles (helmet)	3.00	6.00
25 Atlanta Falcons (logo)	3.00	6.00
26 Atlanta Falcons (helmet)	3.00	6.00
27 San Francisco 49ers (logo)	4.00	8.00
28 San Francisco 49ers (helmet)	4.00	8.00
29 New York Giants (logo)	4.00	8.00
30 New York Giants (helmet)	4.00	8.00
31 New York Jets (logo)	3.00	6.00
32 New York Jets (helmet)	3.00	6.00
33 Detroit Lions (logo)	3.00	6.00
34 Detroit Lions (helmet)	3.00	6.00
35 Houston Oilers (logo)	3.00	6.00
36 Houston Oilers (helmet)	3.00	6.00
37 Green Bay Packers (logo)	4.00	8.00
38 Green Bay Packers (helmet)	4.00	8.00
39 New England Patriots (logo)	3.00	6.00
40 New England Patriots (helmet)	3.00	6.00
41 Oakland Raiders (logo)	5.00	10.00
42 Oakland Raiders {(helmet)	5.00	10.00
43 Los Angeles Rams (logo)	3.00	6.00
44 Los Angeles Rams (helmet)	3.00	6.00
45 Washington Redskins (logo)	5.00	10.00
46 Washington Redskins (helmet)	5.00	10.00
47 New Orleans Saints (logo)	3.00	6.00
48 New Orleans Saints (helmet)	3.00	6.00
49 Pittsburgh Steelers (logo)	4.00	8.00
50 Pittsburgh Steelers (helmet)	4.00	8.00
51 Minnesota Vikings (logo)	4.00	8.00
52 Minnesota Vikings (helmet)	4.00	8.00

1971 NFLPA Wonderful World Stamps

This set of 390 stamps was issued in both 1971 and 1972 under the auspices of the NFL Players Association in conjunction with an album entitled "The Wonderful World of Pro Football USA." The album features a photo of Earl Morrall and Mark Washington from Super Bowl V. The stamps are numbered and measure approximately 1 15/16" by 2 7/8". The team order of the album is arranged alphabetically according to the city name and then alphabetically by player name within each team The picture stamp album contains 30 pages measuring approximately 9 1/2" by 13 1/4". The text narrates the story of pro football in the United States. The album includes spaces for 390 color player stamps. The checklist and stamp numbering below is according to the album. There are some numbering and very slight text variations between the 1971 and 1972 issues on some stamps, as noted below.

COMPLETE SET (390)	350.00	600.00
1 Bob Berry	.40	1.00
2 Greg Brezina	.40	1.00
3 Ken Burrow	.40	1.00
4 Jim Butler	.40	1.00
5 Paul Gipson	.40	1.00
6 Claude Humphrey	.50	1.25
7 George Kunz	.40	1.00
8 Tom McCauley	.40	1.00
9 Jim Mitchell	.40	1.00
10 Tommy Nobis	.75	1.50
11 Ken Reaves	.40	1.00
12 Rudy Redmond	.40	1.00
13 John Small	.40	1.00
14 Harmon Wages	.40	1.00
15 John Zook	.40	1.00
16 Norm Bulaich	.40	1.00
17 Mike Curtis	.50	1.25
18 Jim Duncan	.40	1.00
19 Ted Hendricks	1.00	2.00
20 Roy Hilton	.40	1.00
21 Eddie Hinton	.40	1.00
22 David Lee	.40	1.00
23 Jerry Logan	.40	1.00
24 John Mackey	1.00	2.00
25 Tom Matte	.50	1.25
26 Jim O'Brien	.40	1.00
27 Glenn Ressler	.40	1.00
28 Johnny Unitas	6.00	12.00
29 Bob Vogel	.40	1.00
30 Rick Volk	.40	1.00
31 Butch Byrd	.40	1.00
32 Edgar Chandler	.40	1.00
33 Paul Costa	.40	1.00
34 Jim Dunaway	.40	1.00
35 Paul Guidry	.40	1.00
36 Jim Harris	.40	1.00
37 Robert James	.40	1.00
38 Mike McBath	.40	1.00
39 Haven Moses	.40	1.00
40 John Pitts	.40	1.00
41 Jim Reilly	.40	1.00
42 Dennis Shaw	.40	1.00
43 O.J. Simpson	5.00	10.00
44 Mike Stratton	.40	1.00
45 Bob Tatarek	.40	1.00
46 Craig Baynham	.40	1.00
47 Dick Butkus	5.00	10.00
48 Jim Cadile	.40	1.00
49 Lee Roy Caffey	.40	1.00
50 Jack Concannon	.50	1.25
51 Bobby Douglass	.50	1.25
52 Dick Gordon	.40	1.00
53 Bobby Joe Green	.40	1.00
54 Bob Hyland	.40	1.00
55 Ed O'Bradovich	.40	1.00
56 Mac Percival	.40	1.00
57 Gale Sayers	5.00	10.00
58 George Seals	.40	1.00
59 Bill Staley	.40	1.00
60 Cecil Turner	.40	1.00
61 Al Beauchamp	.40	1.00
62 Virgil Carter	.40	1.00
63 Vernon Holland	.40	1.00
64 Bob Johnson TE	.40	1.00
65 Ron Lamb	.40	1.00
66 Dave Lewis	.40	1.00
67 Rufus Mayes	.40	1.00
68 Horst Muhlmann	.40	1.00
69 Lemar Parrish	.50	1.25
70 Jess Phillips	.40	1.00
71 Mike Reid	.75	1.50
72 Ken Riley	.50	1.25
73 Paul Robinson	.40	1.00
74 Bob Trumpy	.50	1.25
75 Ernie Wright	.40	1.00
76 Don Cockroft	.40	1.00
77 Gary Collins	.50	1.25
78 Gene Hickerson	.40	1.00
79 Jim Houston	.40	1.00
80 Walter Johnson	.40	1.00
81 Joe Jones DE	.40	1.00
82 Leroy Kelly	1.00	2.00
83 Bob Matheson	.40	1.00
84 Milt Morin	.40	1.00
85 Bill Nelsen	.50	1.25
86 Mike Phipps	.50	1.25
87 Dick Schafrath	.50	1.25
88 Bo Scott	.50	1.25
89 Jerry Sherk	.40	1.00
90 Ron Snidow	.40	1.00
91 Herb Adderley	1.00	2.00
92 George Andrie	.40	1.00
93 Mike Clark	.40	1.00
94 Dave Edwards	.40	1.00
95 Walt Garrison	.50	1.25
96 Cornell Green	.50	1.25
97 Bob Hayes	1.00	2.00
98 Calvin Hill	.75	1.50
99 Chuck Howley	.50	1.25
100 Lee Roy Jordan	.75	1.50
101 Dave Manders	.40	1.00
102 Craig Morton	.75	1.50
103 Ralph Neely	.40	1.00
104 Mel Renfro	1.00	2.00
105 Roger Staubach	10.00	20.00
106 Bob Anderson	.40	1.00
107 Sam Brunelli	.40	1.00
108 Dave Costa	.40	1.00
109 Mike Current	.40	1.00
110 Pete Duranko	.40	1.00
111 Cornell Gordon	.40	1.00
112 Mike Haffner	.40	1.00
113 Don Horn	.40	1.00
114 Rich Jackson	.40	1.00
115 Floyd Little	.75	1.50
116 Dick Post	.50	1.25
117 Paul Smith	.40	1.00
118 Billy Thompson	.50	1.25
119 Dave Washington	.40	1.00
120 Jim Whalen	.40	1.00
121 Lem Barney	1.00	2.00
122 Nick Eddy	.40	1.00
123 Mel Farr	.40	1.00
124 Ed Flanagan	.40	1.00
125 Larry Hand	.40	1.00
126 Alex Karras	1.50	3.00
127 Greg Landry	.50	1.25
128 Dick LeBeau	.40	1.00
129 Mike Lucci	.50	1.25
130 Earl McCullouch	.40	1.00
131 Bill Munson	.50	1.25
132 Joe Robb	.40	1.00
133 Jerry Rush	.40	1.00
134 Altie Taylor	.40	1.00
135 Wayne Walker	.50	1.25
136 Lionel Aldridge	.40	1.00
137 Ken Bowman	.40	1.00
138 Fred Carr	.40	1.00
139 Carroll Dale	.50	1.25
140 Ken Ellis	.40	1.00
141 Gale Gillingham	.40	1.00
142 Dave Hampton	.40	1.00
143 Doug Hart	.40	1.00
144 John Hilton	.40	1.00
145 Mike McCoy	.40	1.00
146 Ray Nitschke	1.00	2.00
147 Frank Patrick	.40	1.00
148 Francis Peay	.40	1.00
149 Dave Robinson	.50	1.25
150 Bart Starr	6.00	12.00
151 Elvin Bethea	.75	1.50
152 Garland Boyette	.40	1.00
153 Ken Burrough	.50	1.25
154 Woody Campbell	.40	1.00
155 Joe Dawkins	.40	1.00
156 Lynn Dickey	.50	1.25
157 Elbert Drungo	.40	1.00
158 Gene Ferguson	.40	1.00
159 Willie Frazier	.40	1.00
160 Charley Johnson	.50	1.25
161 Charlie Joiner	1.25	2.50
162 Dan Pastorini	.75	1.50
163 Dave Rowe	.40	1.00
164 Walt Suggs	.40	1.00
165 Mike Tilleman	.40	1.00
166 Bobby Bell	1.00	2.00
167 Aaron Brown	.40	1.00
168 Buck Buchanan	1.00	2.00
169 Ed Budde	.40	1.00
170 Curley Culp	.50	1.25
171 Len Dawson	2.50	5.00
172 Robert Holmes	.40	1.00
173 Jim Lynch	.40	1.00
174 Jim Marsalis	.40	1.00
175 Mo Moorman	.40	1.00
176 Ed Podolak	.50	1.25
177 Johnny Robinson	.50	1.25
178 Jan Stenerud	.75	1.50
179 Otis Taylor	.75	1.50
180 Jim Tyrer	.40	1.00
181 Kermit Alexander	.40	1.00
182 Coy Bacon	.40	1.00
183 Roman Gabriel	.75	1.50
184 Ken Iman	.40	1.00
185 Deacon Jones	1.25	2.50
186 Les Josephson	.40	1.00
187 Marlin McKeever	.40	1.00
188 Merlin Olsen	2.00	4.00
189 Phil Olsen	.40	1.00
190 Richie Petitbon	.50	1.25
191 David Ray	.40	1.00
192 Lance Rentzel	.50	1.25
193 Isiah Robertson	.50	1.25
194 Larry Smith	.40	1.00
195 Jack Snow	.50	1.25
196 Nick Buoniconti	.75	1.50
197 Doug Crusan	.40	1.00
198 Larry Csonka	5.00	10.00
199 Bob DeMarco	.40	1.00
200 Marv Fleming	.50	1.25
201 Bob Griese	4.00	8.00
202 Jim Kiick	.75	1.50
203 Mercury Morris	.75	1.50
204 John Richardson	.40	1.00
205 Jim Riley	.40	1.00
206 Jake Scott	.75	1.50
207 Howard Twilley	.50	1.25
208 Paul Warfield	2.00	4.00
209 Ed Weisacosky	.40	1.00
210 Garo Yepremian	.50	1.25
211 Grady Alderman	.50	1.25
212 John Beasley	.40	1.00
213 Gary Cuozzo	.50	1.25
214 John Henderson	.40	1.00
215 Wally Hilgenberg	.40	1.00
216 Clinton Jones	.40	1.00
217 Karl Kassulke	.40	1.00
218 Paul Krause	.75	1.50
219 Dave Osborn	.50	1.25
220 Alan Page	1.00	2.00
221 Ed Sharockman	.40	1.00
222 Norm Snead	.50	1.25
223 Mick Tingelhoff	.50	1.25
224 Lon Warwick	.40	1.00
225 Gene Washington Vik.	.50	1.25
226 Hank Barton	.40	1.00
227 Larry Carwell	.40	1.00
228 Tom Funchess	.40	1.00
229 Carl Garrett	.50	1.25
230 Jim Hunt	.40	1.00
231 Daryle Johnson	.40	1.00
232 Joe Kapp	.50	1.25
233 Tim Kelly	.40	1.00
234 Jon Morris	.40	1.00
235 Jim Nance	.50	1.25
236 Jim Plunkett	1.50	3.00
237 Dan Schneiss	.40	1.00
238 Ron Sellers	.40	1.00
239 Ed Toner	.40	1.00
240 Gerald Warren	.40	1.00
241 Dan Abramowicz	.50	1.25
242 Tony Baker FB	.50	1.25
243 Leo Carroll	.40	1.00
244 Dick Davis	.40	1.00
245 Tom Dempsey	.50	1.25
246 Al Dodd	.40	1.00
247 Jim Flanigan LB	.40	1.00
248 Hoyle Granger	.40	1.00
249 Edd Hargett	.40	1.00
250 Gene Howard	.40	1.00
251 Jake Kupp	.40	1.00
252 Dave Long	.40	1.00
253 Dick Lyons	.40	1.00
254 Mike Morgan	.40	1.00
255 Del Williams	.40	1.00
256 Fred Dryer	.75	1.50
257 Bobby Duhon	.40	1.00
258 Jim Files	.40	1.00
259 Tucker Frederickson	.50	1.25
260 Pete Gogolak	.40	1.00
261 Don Herrmann	.40	1.00
262 Ron Johnson	.40	1.00
263 Jim Kanicki	.40	1.00
264 Ernie Koy	.40	1.00

265 Spider Lockhart .40 1.00
266 Clifton McNeil .40 1.00
267 Joe Morrison .40 1.00
268 Fran Tarkenton 4.00 8.00
269 Willie Williams .40 1.00
270 Willie Young .40 1.00
271 Al Atkinson .40 1.00
272 Ralph Baker .40 1.00
273 Emerson Boozer .50 1.25
274 Mike Battle .40 1.00
275 John Elliott .40 1.00
276 Dave Herman .40 1.00
277 Winston Hill .40 1.00
278 Gus Hollomon .40 1.00
279 Bobby Howfield .40 1.00
280 Pete Lammons .40 1.00
281 Joe Namath 10.00 20.00
282 Gerry Philbin UER .40 1.00
283 Matt Snell .50 1.25
284 Steve Tannen .40 1.00
285 Al Woodall .40 1.00
286 Fred Biletnikoff 2.00 4.00
287 George Blanda 3.00 6.00
288 Willie Brown 1.00 2.00
289 Raymond Chester .50 1.25
290 Tony Cline .40 1.00
291 Dan Conners .40 1.00
292 Ben Davidson .50 1.25
293 Hewritt Dixon .40 1.00
294 Bill Enyart .40 1.00
295 Daryle Lamonica .75 1.50
296 Gus Otto .40 1.00
297 Jim Otto 1.00 2.00
298 Charlie Smith .40 1.00
299 Gene Upshaw 1.00 2.00
300 Warren Wells .40 1.00
301 Rick Arrington .40 1.00
302 Gary Ballman .40 1.00
303 Lee Bouggess .40 1.00
304 Bill Bradley .50 1.25
305 Richard Harris .40 1.00
306 Ben Hawkins .40 1.00
307 Harold Jackson .75 1.50
308 Pete Liske .40 1.00
309 Al Nelson .40 1.00
310 Gary Pettigrew .40 1.00
311 Cyril Pinder .40 1.00
312 Tim Rossovich .50 1.25
313 Tom Woodeshick .50 1.25
314 Adrian Young .40 1.00
315 Steve Zabel .40 1.00
316 Chuck Allen .40 1.00
317 Warren Bankston .40 1.00
318 Chuck Beatty .40 1.00
319 Terry Bradshaw 10.00 20.00
320 John Fuqua .40 1.00
321 Terry Hanratty .50 1.25
322 Chuck Hinton DT .40 1.00
323 Ray Mansfield .40 1.00
324 Ben McGee .40 1.00
325 Andy Russell .50 1.25
326 Ron Shanklin .40 1.00
327 Bruce Van Dyke .40 1.00
328 Lloyd Voss .40 1.00
329 Bobby Walden .40 1.00
330 Allen Watson .40 1.00
331 Jim Bakken .50 1.25
332 Pete Beathard .40 1.00
333 Miller Farr .40 1.00
334 Mel Gray .75 1.50
335 Jim Hart .75 1.50
336 MacArthur Lane .50 1.25
337 Chuck Latourette .40 1.00
338 Ernie McMillan .40 1.00
339 Bob Reynolds .40 1.00
340 Jackie Smith 1.00 2.00
341 Larry Stallings .40 1.00
342 Jerry Stovall .40 1.00
343 Chuck Walker .40 1.00
344 Roger Wehrli .50 1.25
345 Larry Wilson 1.00 2.00
346 Bob Babich .40 1.00
347 Pete Barnes .40 1.00
348 Marty Domres .40 1.00
349 Steve DeLong .40 1.00
350 Gary Garrison .50 1.25
351 Walker Gillette .40 1.00
352 Dave Grayson .40 1.00
353 John Hadl .75 1.50
354 Jim Hill .40 1.00
355 Bob Howard DB .40 1.00
356 Tony Liscio .40 1.00
357 Dennis Partee .40 1.00
358 Andy Rice .40 1.00
359 Russ Washington .40 1.00
360 Doug Wilkerson .40 1.00
361 John Brodie 1.25 2.50
362 Doug Cunningham .40 1.00
363 Bruce Gossett .40 1.00
364 Stan Hindman .40 1.00
365 John Isenbarger .40 1.00
366 Charlie Krueger .40 1.00
367 Frank Nunley .40 1.00
368 Woody Peoples .40 1.00
369 Len Rohde .40 1.00
370 Steve Spurrier 6.00 12.00
371 Gene Washington 49er .50 1.25
372 Dave Wilcox .50 1.25
373 Ken Willard .40 1.00
374 Bob Windsor .40 1.00
375 Dick Witcher .40 1.00
376 Maxie Baughan .40 1.00
377 Larry Brown RB .75 1.50
378 Boyd Dowler .50 1.25
379 Chris Hanburger .50 1.25
380 Charlie Harraway .40 1.00
381 Rickie Harris .40 1.00
382 Sonny Jurgensen 2.00 4.00
383 Billy Kilmer .75 1.50
384 Tommy Mason .50 1.25
385 Brig Owens .40 1.00
386 Jack Pardee .50 1.25
387 Myron Pottios .40 1.00
388 Jerry Smith .40 1.00
389 Diron Talbert .40 1.00
390 Charley Taylor 1.50 3.00
NNO Wonderful World Album 50.00 100.00

1972 NFLPA Wonderful World Stamps

This set of 390 stamps was issued in both 1971 and 1972 under the auspices of the NFL Players Association in conjunction with an album entitled "The Wonderful World of Pro Football USA." The album pictures Walt Garrison being tackled during Super Bowl VI. The stamps are numbered and are approximately 1 15/16" by 2 7/8". The team order of the album is arranged alphabetically according to the city name and then alphabetically by player name within each team The picture stamp album contains 30 pages measuring approximately 9 1/2" by 13 1/4". The text narrates the story of pro football in the United States. The album includes spaces for 390 color player stamps. The checklist and stamp numbering below is according to the album. There are some numbering and very slight text variations between the 1971 and 1972 issues on some stamps, as noted below.

COMPLETE SET (390) 250.00 400.00
1 Bob Berry .50 1.25
2 Greg Brezina .40 1.00
3 Ken Burrow .40 1.00
4 Jim Butler .40 1.00
5 Wes Chesson .40 1.00
6 Claude Humphrey .40 1.00
7 George Kunz .40 1.00
8 Tom McCauley .40 1.00
9 Jim Mitchell TE .40 1.00
10 Tommy Nobis .75 1.50
11 Ken Reaves .40 1.00
12 Bill Sandeman .40 1.00
13 John Small .40 1.00
14 Harmon Wages .40 1.00
15 John Zook .40 1.00
16 Norm Bulaich .50 1.25
17 Bill Curry .50 1.25
18 Mike Curtis .50 1.25
19 Ted Hendricks 1.00 2.00
20 Roy Hilton .40 1.00
21 Eddie Hinton .40 1.00
22 David Lee .40 1.00
23 Jerry Logan .40 1.00
24 John Mackey 1.00 2.00
25 Tom Matte .50 1.25
26 Jim O'Brien .50 1.25
27 Glenn Ressler .40 1.00
28 Johnny Unitas 6.00 12.00
29 Bob Vogel .40 1.00
30 Rick Volk .40 1.00
31 Paul Costa .40 1.00
32 Jim Dunaway .40 1.00
33 Paul Guidry .40 1.00
34 Jim Harris .40 1.00
35 Robert James .40 1.00
36 Mike McBath .40 1.00
37 Haven Moses .50 1.25
38 Wayne Patrick .40 1.00
39 John Pitts .40 1.00
40 Jim Reilly T .40 1.00
41 Pete Richardson .40 1.00
42 Dennis Shaw .50 1.25
43 O.J. Simpson 4.00 8.00
44 Mike Stratton .40 1.00
45 Bob Tatarek .40 1.00
46 Dick Butkus 5.00 10.00
47 Jim Cadile .40 1.00
48 Jack Concannon .50 1.25
49 Bobby Douglass .50 1.25
50 George Farmer .40 1.00
51 Dick Gordon .40 1.00
52 Bobby Joe Green .40 1.00
53 Ed O'Bradovich .40 1.00
54 Mac Percival .40 1.00
55 Gale Sayers 5.00 10.00
56 George Seals .40 1.00
57 Jim Seymour .40 1.00
58 Ron Smith .40 1.00
59 Bill Staley .40 1.00
60 Cecil Turner .40 1.00
61 Al Beauchamp .40 1.00
62 Virgil Carter .40 1.00
63 Vern Holland .40 1.00
64 Bob Johnson .50 1.25
65 Ron Lamb .40 1.00
66 Dave Lewis .40 1.00
67 Rufus Mayes .40 1.00
68 Horst Muhlmann .40 1.00
69 Lemar Parrish .50 1.25
70 Jess Phillips .40 1.00
71 Mike Reid 1.00 2.00
72 Ken Riley .50 1.25
73 Paul Robinson .40 1.00
74 Bob Trumpy .50 1.25
75 Fred Willis .50 1.25
76 Don Cockroft .40 1.00
77 Gary Collins .40 1.00
78 Gene Hickerson .40 1.00
79 Fair Hooker .40 1.00
80 Jim Houston .40 1.00
81 Walter Johnson .40 1.00
82 Joe Jones DE .40 1.00
83 Leroy Kelly 1.00 2.00
84 Milt Morin .40 1.00
85 Reece Morrison .40 1.00
86 Bill Nelsen .50 1.25
87 Mike Phipps .50 1.25
88 Bo Scott .40 1.00
89 Jerry Sherk .40 1.00
90 Ron Snidow .40 1.00
91 Herb Adderley 1.00 2.00
92 George Andrie .40 1.00
93 Mike Clark .40 1.00
94 Dave Edwards .40 1.00
95 Walt Garrison .50 1.25
96 Cornell Green .50 1.25
97 Bob Hayes 1.00 2.00
98 Calvin Hill .75 1.50
99 Chuck Howley .50 1.25
100 Lee Roy Jordan 1.00 2.00
101 Dave Manders .40 1.00
102 Craig Morton .75 1.50
103 Ralph Neely .40 1.00
104 Mel Renfro 1.00 2.00
105 Roger Staubach 10.00 20.00
106 Bob Anderson .40 1.00
107 Sam Brunelli .40 1.00
108 Dave Costa .40 1.00
109 Mike Current .40 1.00
110 Pete Duranko .40 1.00
111 George Goeddeke .40 1.00
112 Cornell Gordon .40 1.00
113 Don Horn .40 1.00
114 Rich Jackson .40 1.00
115 Larry Kaminski .40 1.00
116 Floyd Little .75 1.50
117 Marv Montgomery .40 1.00
118 Steve Ramsey .40 1.00
119 Paul Smith .40 1.00
120 Bill Thompson .40 1.00
121 Lem Barney 1.00 2.00
122 Nick Eddy .40 1.00
123 Mel Farr .40 1.00
124 Ed Flanagan .40 1.00
125 Larry Hand .40 1.00
126 Greg Landry .50 1.25
127 Dick LeBeau .50 1.25
128 Mike Lucci .50 1.25
129 Earl McCullouch .40 1.00
130 Bill Munson .50 1.25
131 Wayne Rasmussen .40 1.00
132 Joe Robb .40 1.00
133 Jerry Rush .40 1.00
134 Altie Taylor .40 1.00
135 Wayne Walker .50 1.25
136 Ken Bowman .40 1.00
137 John Brockington .50 1.25
138 Fred Carr .40 1.00
139 Carroll Dale .50 1.25
140 Ken Ellis .40 1.00
141 Gale Gillingham .40 1.00
142 Dave Hampton .40 1.00
143 Doug Hart .40 1.00
144 MacArthur Lane .50 1.25
145 Mike McCoy DT .40 1.00
146 Ray Nitschke 1.00 2.00
147 Frank Patrick .40 1.00
148 Francis Peay .40 1.00
149 Dave Robinson .50 1.25
150 Bart Starr 6.00 12.00
151 Bob Atkins .40 1.00
152 Elvin Bethea .75 1.50
153 Garland Boyette .40 1.00
154 Ken Burrough .50 1.25
155 Woody Campbell .40 1.00
156 John Charles .40 1.00
157 Lynn Dickey .50 1.25
158 Elbert Drungo .40 1.00
159 Gene Ferguson .40 1.00
160 Charley Johnson .50 1.25
161 Charlie Joiner 1.25 2.50
162 Dan Pastorini .75 1.50
163 Ron Pritchard .40 1.00
164 Walt Suggs .40 1.00
165 Mike Tilleman .40 1.00
166 Bobby Bell 1.00 2.00
167 Aaron Brown .40 1.00
168 Buck Buchanan 1.00 2.00
169 Ed Budde .40 1.00
170 Curley Culp .40 1.00
171 Len Dawson 2.50 5.00
172 Willie Lanier 1.25 2.50
173 Jim Lynch .40 1.00
174 Jim Marsalis .40 1.00
175 Mo Moorman .40 1.00
176 Ed Podolak .50 1.25
177 Johnny Robinson .50 1.25
178 Jan Stenerud .75 1.50
179 Otis Taylor .75 1.50
180 Jim Tyrer .40 1.00
181 Kermit Alexander .40 1.00
182 Coy Bacon .40 1.00
183 Dick Buzin .40 1.00
184 Roman Gabriel .75 1.50
185 Gene Howard .40 1.00
186 Ken Iman .40 1.00
187 Les Josephson .40 1.00
188 Marlin McKeever .40 1.00
189 Merlin Olsen 2.00 4.00
190 Phil Olsen .40 1.00
191 David Ray .40 1.00
192 Lance Rentzel .50 1.25
193 Isiah Robertson .50 1.25
194 Larry Smith RB .40 1.00
195 Jack Snow .50 1.25
196 Nick Buoniconti .75 1.50
197 Doug Crusan .40 1.00
198 Larry Csonka 5.00 10.00
199 Bob DeMarco .40 1.00
200 Marv Fleming .50 1.25
201 Bob Griese 4.00 8.00
202 Jim Kiick .75 1.50
203 Bob Kuechenberg .50 1.25
204 Mercury Morris .75 1.50
205 John Richardson .40 1.00
206 Jim Riley .40 1.00
207 Jake Scott .50 1.25
208 Howard Twilley .50 1.25
209 Paul Warfield 2.00 4.00
210 Garo Yepremian .50 1.25
211 Grady Alderman .40 1.00
212 John Beasley .40 1.00
213 John Henderson .40 1.00
214 Wally Hilgenberg .40 1.00
215 Clint Jones .40 1.00
216 Karl Kassulke .40 1.00
217 Paul Krause .75 1.50
218 Dave Osborn .40 1.00
219 Alan Page 1.00 2.00
220 Ed Sharockman .40 1.00
221 Fran Tarkenton 4.00 8.00
222 Mick Tingelhoff .50 1.25
223 Charlie West .40 1.00
224 Lonnie Warwick .40 1.00
225 Gene Washington Vik .50 1.25
226 Hank Barton .40 1.00
227 Ron Berger .40 1.00
228 Larry Carwell .40 1.00
229 Jim Cheyunski .40 1.00
230 Carl Garrett .40 1.00
231 Rickie Harris .40 1.00
232 Daryle Johnson .40 1.00
233 Steve Kiner .40 1.00
234 Jon Morris .40 1.00
235 Jim Nance .50 1.25
236 Tom Neville .40 1.00
237 Jim Plunkett 1.25 2.50
238 Ron Sellers .40 1.00
239 Len St. Jean .40 1.00
240 Don Webb .40 1.00
241 Dan Abramowicz .50 1.25
242 Dick Absher .40 1.00
243 Leo Carroll .40 1.00
244 Jim Duncan .40 1.00
245 Al Dodd .40 1.00
246 Jim Flanigan LB .40 1.00
247 Hoyle Granger .40 1.00
248 Edd Hargett .40 1.00
249 Glen Ray Hines .40 1.00
250 Hugo Hollas .40 1.00
251 Jake Kupp .40 1.00
252 Dave Long .40 1.00
253 Mike Morgan LB .40 1.00
254 Tom Roussel .40 1.00
255 Del Williams .40 1.00
256 Otto Brown .40 1.00
257 Bobby Duhon .40 1.00
258 Scott Eaton .40 1.00
259 Jim Files .40 1.00
260 Tucker Frederickson .50 1.25
261 Pete Gogolak .40 1.00
262 Bob Grim .40 1.00
263 Don Herrmann .40 1.00
264 Ron Johnson .50 1.25
265 Jim Kanicki .40 1.00
266 Spider Lockhart .50 1.25
267 Joe Morrison .50 1.25
268 Bob Tucker .50 1.25
269 Willie Williams .40 1.00
270 Willie Young .40 1.00
271 Al Atkinson .40 1.00
272 Ralph Baker .40 1.00
273 Emerson Boozer .50 1.25
274 John Elliott .40 1.00
275 Dave Herman .40 1.00
276 Winston Hill .40 1.00
277 Gus Hollomon .40 1.00
278 Bobby Howfield .40 1.00
279 Pete Lammons .40 1.00
280 Joe Namath 10.00 20.00
281 Gerry Philbin .40 1.00
282 Matt Snell .50 1.25
283 Steve Tannen .40 1.00
284 Earlie Thomas .40 1.00
285 Al Woodall .40 1.00
286 Fred Biletnikoff 2.00 4.00
287 George Blanda 3.00 6.00
288 Willie Brown 1.00 2.00
289 Raymond Chester .50 1.25
290 Tony Cline .40 1.00
291 Dan Conners .40 1.00
292 Ben Davidson .50 1.25

Card	Low	High
293 Hewritt Dixon	.40	1.00
294 Tom Keating	.40	1.00
295 Daryle Lamonica	.75	1.50
296 Gus Otto	.40	1.00
297 Jim Otto	1.00	2.00
298 Rod Sherman	.40	1.00
299 Charlie Smith RB	.40	1.00
300 Gene Upshaw	1.00	2.00
301 Rick Arrington	.40	1.00
302 Gary Ballman	.40	1.00
303 Lee Bouggess	.40	1.00
304 Bill Bradley	.50	1.25
305 Happy Feller	.40	1.00
306 Richard Harris	.40	1.00
307 Ben Hawkins	.40	1.00
308 Harold Jackson	.50	1.25
309 Pete Liske	.40	1.00
310 Al Nelson	.40	1.00
311 Gary Pettigrew	.40	1.00
312 Tim Rossovich	.40	1.00
313 Tom Woodeshick	.40	1.00
314 Adrian Young	.40	1.00
315 Steve Zabel	.40	1.00
316 Chuck Allen	.50	1.25
317 Warren Bankston	.40	1.00
318 Chuck Beatty	.40	1.00
319 Terry Bradshaw	10.00	20.00
320 John Fuqua	.40	1.00
321 Terry Hanratty	.50	1.25
322 Ray Mansfield	.40	1.00
323 Ben McGee	.40	1.00
324 John Rowser	.40	1.00
325 Andy Russell	.50	1.25
326 Ron Shanklin	.40	1.00
327 Dave Smith WR	.40	1.00
328 Bruce Van Dyke	.40	1.00
329 Lloyd Voss	.40	1.00
330 Bobby Walden	.40	1.00
331 Donny Anderson	.50	1.25
332 Jim Bakken	.50	1.25
333 Pete Beathard	.40	1.00
334 Miller Farr	.40	1.00
335 Mel Gray	.50	1.25
336 Jim Hart	.75	1.50
337 Rolf Krueger	.40	1.00
338 Chuck Latourette	.40	1.00
339 Ernie McMillan	.40	1.00
340 Bob Reynolds	.40	1.00
341 Jackie Smith	1.00	2.00
342 Larry Stallings	.40	1.00
343 Chuck Walker	.40	1.00
344 Roger Wehrli	.50	1.25
345 Larry Wilson	1.00	2.00
346 Bob Babich	.40	1.00
347 Pete Barnes	.40	1.00
348 Steve DeLong	.40	1.00
349 Marty Domres	.40	1.00
350 Gary Garrison	.50	1.25
351 John Hadl	.75	1.50
352 Kevin Hardy	.40	1.00
353 Bob Howard	.40	1.00
354 Deacon Jones	1.25	2.50
355 Terry Owens	.40	1.00
356 Dennis Partee	.40	1.00
357 Jeff Queen	.40	1.00
358 Jim Tolbert	.40	1.00
359 Russ Washington	.40	1.00
360 Doug Wilkerson	.40	1.00
361 John Brodie	1.25	2.50
362 Doug Cunningham	.40	1.00
363 Bruce Gossett	.40	1.00
364 Stan Hindman	.40	1.00
365 John Isenbarger	.40	1.00
366 Charlie Krueger	.40	1.00
367 Frank Nunley	.40	1.00
368 Woody Peoples	.40	1.00
369 Len Rohde	.40	1.00
370 Steve Spurrier	6.00	12.00
371 Gene Washington 49er	.50	1.25
372 Dave Wilcox	.50	1.25
373 Ken Willard	.50	1.25
374 Bob Windsor	.40	1.00
375 Dick Witcher	.40	1.00
376 Verlon Biggs	.40	1.00
377 Larry Brown	.75	1.50
378 Speedy Duncan	.50	1.25
379 Chris Hanburger	.50	1.25
380 Charlie Harraway	.40	1.00
381 Sonny Jurgensen	2.00	4.00
382 Billy Kilmer	.75	1.50
383 Tommy Mason	.50	1.25
384 Ron McDole	.40	1.00
385 Brig Owens	.40	1.00
386 Jack Pardee	.50	1.25
387 Myron Pottios	.40	1.00
388 Jerry Smith	.40	1.00
389 Diron Talbert	.40	1.00
390 Charley Taylor	1.50	3.00
NNO Wonderful World Album	10.00	20.00

1972 NFLPA Fabric Cards

The 1972 NFLPA Fabric Cards set includes 35 cards printed on cloth. These thin fabric cards measure approximately 2 1/4" by 3 1/2" and are blank backed. The cards are sometimes referred to as "Iron Ons" as they were intended to be semi-permanently ironed on to clothes. The full color portrait of the player is surrounded by a black border. Below the player's name at the bottom of the card is indicated copyright by the NFL Players Association in 1972. The cards may have been illegally reprinted. There is some additional interest in the Staubach card due to the fact that his 1972 Topps card (that same year) is considered his Rookie Card. Since they are unnumbered, they are listed below in alphabetical order according to the player's name. These fabric cards were originally available in vending machines at retail stores and other outlets.

Card	Low	High
COMPLETE SET (35)	75.00	150.00
1 Donny Anderson	1.00	2.50
2 George Blanda	3.00	6.00
3 Terry Bradshaw	7.50	15.00
4 John Brockington	1.00	2.50
5 John Brodie	2.00	4.00
6 Dick Butkus	5.00	10.00
7 Larry Csonka	3.00	6.00
8 Mike Curtis	1.00	2.50
9 Len Dawson	2.50	5.00
10 Carl Eller	1.25	3.00
11 Mike Garrett	1.00	2.50
12 Joe Greene	4.00	8.00
13 Bob Griese	3.00	6.00
14 Dick Gordon	1.00	2.50
15 John Hadl	1.25	3.00
16 Bob Hayes	1.50	4.00
17 Ron Johnson	1.00	2.50
18 Deacon Jones	1.50	4.00
19 Sonny Jurgensen	2.50	5.00
20 Leroy Kelly	1.50	4.00
21 Jim Kiick	1.25	3.00
22 Greg Landry	1.00	2.50
23 Floyd Little	1.25	3.00
24 Mike Lucci	1.00	2.50
25 Archie Manning	2.00	4.00
26 Joe Namath	10.00	20.00
27 Tommy Nobis	1.25	3.00
28 Alan Page	1.50	4.00
29 Jim Plunkett	2.00	4.00
30 Gale Sayers	5.00	10.00
31 O.J. Simpson	5.00	10.00
32 Roger Staubach	10.00	20.00
33 Duane Thomas	1.25	3.00
34 Johnny Unitas	10.00	20.00
35 Paul Warfield	3.00	6.00

1972 NFLPA Vinyl Stickers

The 1972 NFLPA Vinyl Stickers set contains 20 stand-up type stickers depicting the players in a caricature-like style with big heads. These irregularly shaped stickers are approximately 2 3/4" by 4 3/4". Below the player's name at the bottom of the card is indicated copyright by the NFL Players Association in 1972. The set is sometimes offered as a short set excluding the shorter-printed cards, i.e., those listed by SP in the checklist below. Since they are unnumbered, they are listed below in alphabetical order according to the player's name. The Roger Staubach card holds special interest in that 1972 represents Roger's rookie year for cards. These stickers were originally available in vending machines at retail stores and other outlets. The Dick Butkus and Joe Namath stickers exist as reverse negatives. The set is considered complete with either Butkus or Namath variation.

Card	Low	High
COMPLETE SET (20)	100.00	175.00
1 Donny Anderson	1.50	4.00
2 George Blanda	3.00	6.00
3 Terry Bradshaw	7.50	15.00
4 John Brockington	1.50	4.00
5 John Brodie	2.50	6.00
6A Dick Butkus	5.00	10.00
6B Dick Butkus	5.00	10.00
7 Dick Gordon	1.50	4.00
8 Joe Greene	2.50	6.00
9 John Hadl	2.00	5.00
10 Bob Hayes	2.50	6.00
11 Ron Johnson SP	4.00	8.00
12 Floyd Little	1.50	4.00
13A Joe Namath	10.00	20.00
13B Joe Namath	10.00	20.00
14 Tommy Nobis	2.00	5.00
15 Alan Page SP	6.00	12.00
16 Jim Plunkett	2.50	5.00
17 Gale Sayers	5.00	10.00
18 Roger Staubach	10.00	20.00
19 Johnny Unitas	10.00	20.00
20 Paul Warfield	2.50	6.00

1972 NFLPA Woodburning Kit

This Woodburning set was sold as an arts and crafts kit with 16-individual player wooden plaques measuring roughly 4" by 4 1/4", 2-generic football player plaques measuring 2 3/8" by 4 1/2" and two larger (roughly 8" by 10") plaques featuring 5-players on each. Each plaque is unnumbered and blankbacked with bright red or maroon printing on the front featuring a drawing of an NFL player. It is thought that each can be found with either the bright red printing or the darker maroon printing. The player image was supposed to be burning out with a tool and then painted by the collector.

Card	Low	High
1 Lance Alworth	10.00	25.00
2 Terry Bradshaw	15.00	40.00
3 Nick Buoniconti	8.00	20.00
4 Dick Butkus	12.00	30.00
5 Roy Jefferson	6.00	15.00
6 Ron Johnson	6.00	15.00
7 Sonny Jurgensen	10.00	25.00
8 Daryle Lamonica	8.00	20.00
9 Alan Page	8.00	20.00
10 O.J. Simpson	10.00	25.00
11 Matt Snell	8.00	20.00
12 Gene Washington Minn.	6.00	15.00
17 Generic Player	4.00	10.00
18 Quarterbacks	8.00	20.00
19 Running Backs	8.00	20.00

1979 NFLPA Pennant Stickers

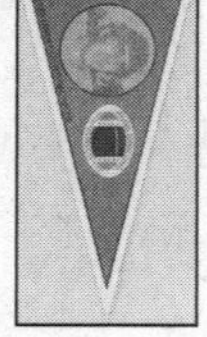

The 1979 NFL Player's Association Pennant Stickers set contains stickers measuring approximately 2 1/2" by 5". The pennant-shaped stickers show a circular (black and white) photo of the player next to the NFL Players Association football logo. The set was apparently not approved by the NFL as the team logos are not shown on the cards. The player's name, position, and team are given at the bottom of the card. The backs are blank as it is a peel-off backing only. Some of the stickers can be found with more than one color background and have been listed accordingly below. The complete set price includes just one sticker for each player.

Card	Low	High
COMPLETE SET (55)	300.00	600.00
1 Lyle Alzado	3.00	6.00
2 Ken Anderson	4.00	8.00
3 Steve Bartkowski SP	12.50	25.00
4 Ricky Bell	3.00	6.00
5 Elvin Bethea	3.00	6.00
6A Tom Blanchard	2.50	5.00
6B Tom Blanchard (Red)	2.50	5.00
6C Tom Blanchard (Yellow)	2.50	5.00
7A Terry Bradshaw	25.00	50.00
7B Terry Bradshaw (Yellow)	25.00	50.00
8A Bob Breunig	2.50	5.00
8B Bob Breunig (Yellow)	2.50	5.00
9A Greg Brezina	2.50	5.00
9B Greg Brezina (Red)	2.50	5.00
9C Greg Brezina (Yellow)	2.50	5.00
10 Doug Buffone SP	12.50	25.00
11 Earl Campbell	15.00	30.00
12 John Cappelletti	4.00	8.00
13 Harold Carmichael	3.00	6.00
14 Chuck Crist SP	12.50	25.00
15 Sam Cunningham	2.50	5.00
16 Isaac Curtis SP (Blue)	12.50	25.00
17 Joe DeLamielleure	4.00	8.00
18A Tom Dempsey	2.50	5.00
18B Tom Dempsey (Red)	2.50	5.00
18C Tom Dempsey (Yellow)	2.50	5.00
19 Tony Dorsett	10.00	20.00
20 Dan Fouts SP	15.00	30.00
21A Roy Gerela	2.50	5.00
21B Roy Gerela (Yellow)	2.50	5.00
22 Bob Griese UER	10.00	20.00
23A Franco Harris Red	10.00	20.00
23B Franco Harris Yellow	10.00	20.00
23C Franco Harris SP Green	25.00	50.00
24 Jim Hart SP	12.50	25.00
25 Charlie Joiner	4.00	8.00
26 Doug Kotar SP	25.00	50.00
27 Paul Krause	4.00	8.00
28 Bob Kuechenberg	2.50	5.00
29 Greg Landry	3.00	6.00
30 Archie Manning	3.00	6.00
31 Chester Marcol	2.50	5.00
32A Harvey Martin	3.00	6.00
32B Harvey Martin Yellow	3.00	6.00
33 Lawrence McCutcheon SP	12.50	25.00
34 Craig Morton	3.00	6.00
35 Haven Moses	2.50	5.00
36 Steve Odom	2.50	5.00
37 Morris Owens	2.50	5.00
38 Dan Pastorini SP	12.50	25.00
39 Walter Payton	25.00	50.00
40 Greg Pruitt SP	12.50	25.00
41 John Riggins	6.00	12.00
42 Jake Scott	2.50	5.00
43 Jerry Sherk SP	12.50	25.00
44 Ken Stabler SP	30.00	60.00
45 Mike Siani SP	12.50	25.00
46 Roger Staubach	25.00	50.00
47 Jan Stenerud	3.00	6.00
48 Art Still SP	12.50	25.00
49 Mick Tingelhoff	2.50	5.00
50 Richard Todd	2.50	5.00
51 Brad Van Pelt SP	30.00	50.00
52 Phil Villapiano SP	12.50	25.00
53A Wesley Walker	3.00	6.00
53B Wesley Walker (Yellow)	3.00	6.00
54 Roger Wehrli SP	12.50	25.00
55 Jim Zorn SP	12.50	25.00

1960 Oilers Matchbooks

The 1960 Oilers Matchbook set was produced by Universal Match Corp. and features the team's logo and mascot on one side when flattened. The other side includes a small black and white player photo along with the Universal Match Corporation logo.

Card	Low	High
COMPLETE SET (10)	100.00	175.00
1 George Blanda	20.00	40.00
2 Johnny Carson	10.00	20.00
3 Doug Cline	10.00	20.00
4 Don Hitt	10.00	20.00
5 Mark Johnston	10.00	20.00
6 Dan Lanphear	10.00	20.00
7 Jacky Lee	10.00	20.00
8 Bill Mathis	10.00	20.00
9 Hogan Wharton	10.00	20.00
10 Bob White	10.00	20.00

1961 Oilers Jay Publishing

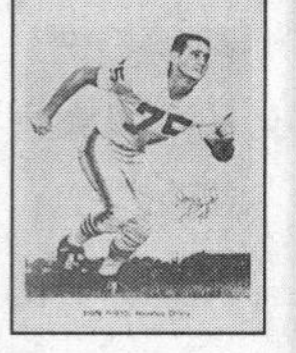

This 24-card set features (approximately) 5" by 7" black-and-white player photos. The photos show players in traditional poses with the quarterback preparing to throw, the runner heading downfield, and the defenseman ready for the tackle. These cards were packaged 12 to a packet and originally sold for 25 cents. The backs are blank. The cards are unnumbered and checklisted below in alphabetical order.

Card	Low	High
COMPLETE SET (24)	100.00	175.00
1 Dalva Allen	4.00	8.00
2 Tony Banfield	4.00	8.00
3 George Blanda	15.00	30.00
4 Billy Cannon	6.00	12.00
5 Doug Cline	4.00	8.00
6 Willard Dewveall	4.00	8.00
7 Mike Dukes	4.00	8.00
8 Don Floyd	4.00	8.00
9 Freddy Glick	4.00	8.00
10 Bill Groman	4.00	8.00
11 Charlie Hennigan	5.00	10.00
12 Ed Husmann	4.00	8.00
13 Al Jamison	4.00	8.00
14 Mark Johnston	4.00	8.00
15 Jacky Lee	4.00	8.00
16 Bob McLeod	4.00	8.00
17 Rich Michael	4.00	8.00
18 Dennit Morris	4.00	8.00
19 Jim Norton	4.00	8.00
20 Bob Schmidt	4.00	8.00
21 Dave Smith RB	4.00	8.00
22 Bob Talamini	4.00	8.00
23 Charley Tolar	4.00	8.00
24 Hogan Wharton	4.00	8.00

1965 Oilers Team Issue 8X10

These photos measure 8" by 10" and feature black-and-white player images with white borders. Most of the photos feature posed action shots. The player's position (spelled out completely), name, and team name are printed in the bottom white border in all caps. The backs are blank and the photos are unnumbered and checklisted below in alphabetical order.

Card	Low	High
COMPLETE SET (38)	200.00	350.00
1 Scott Appleton	6.00	12.00
2 Johnny Baker	6.00	12.00
3 Johnny Baker	6.00	12.00
4 Tony Banfield	6.00	12.00

5 Sonny Bishop	6.00	12.00
6A Sid Blanks	6.00	12.00
6B Sid Blanks (position: Halfback)	6.00	12.00
7 Danny Brabham	6.00	12.00
8 Ode Burrell	6.00	12.00
9 Doug Cline	6.00	12.00
10 Gary Cutsinger	6.00	12.00
11 Norm Evans	6.00	12.00
12 Don Floyd	6.00	12.00
13 Wayne Frazier	6.00	12.00
14 Willie Frazier	6.00	12.00
15 John Frongillo	6.00	12.00
16 Freddy Glick	6.00	12.00
17 Tom Goode	6.00	12.00
18 Jim Hayes	6.00	12.00
19 Charlie Hennigan	6.00	12.00
20 W.K. Hicks	6.00	12.00
21 W.K. Hicks	6.00	12.00
22 Ed Husmann	6.00	12.00
23 Bobby Jancik	6.00	12.00
24 Pete Jacques	6.00	12.00
25 Bobby Maples	6.00	12.00
26 Bud McFadin	6.00	12.00
27 Bob McLeod	6.00	12.00
28 Bob McLeod	6.00	12.00
29 Jim Norton	6.00	12.00
30 Larry Onesti	6.00	12.00
31 Jack Spikes	6.00	12.00
32 Walt Suggs	6.00	12.00
33 Bob Talamini	6.00	12.00
34 Charley Tolar	6.00	12.00
35 Don Trull	6.00	12.00
36 Don Trull	6.00	12.00
37 Maxie Williams	6.00	12.00
38 John Wittenborn	6.00	12.00

1965 Oilers Team Issue Color

This team-issued set of 16 player photos measures approximately 7 3/4" by 9 3/4" and features color posed shots of players in uniform. Eight photos were grouped together as a set and packaged in plastic bags; set 1 and 2 each originally sold for 50 cents. The photos were printed on thin paper stock and white borders frame each picture. A facsimile autograph is inscribed across the pictures in black ink. The backs are blank. The photos are unnumbered and checklisted below in alphabetical order.

COMPLETE SET (16)	75.00	150.00
1 Scott Appleton	5.00	10.00
2 Tony Banfield	5.00	10.00
3 Sonny Bishop	5.00	10.00
4 George Blanda	15.00	30.00
5 Sid Blanks	5.00	10.00
6 Danny Brabham	5.00	10.00
7 Ode Burrell	5.00	10.00
8 Doug Cline	5.00	10.00
9 Don Floyd	5.00	10.00
10 Freddy Glick	5.00	10.00
11 Charlie Hennigan	5.00	10.00
12 Ed Husmann	5.00	10.00
13 Walt Suggs	5.00	10.00
14 Bob Talamini	5.00	10.00
15 Charley Tolar	5.00	10.00
16 Don Trull	5.00	10.00

1966 Oilers Team Issue 8X10

These photos measure 8" by 10" and feature black-and-white player images with white borders. Most of the photos feature posed action shots. The player's position (initials), name, and team name are printed in the bottom white border in all caps. The backs are blank and the photos are unnumbered and checklisted below in alphabetical order.

COMPLETE SET (5)	25.00	50.00
1 Scott Appleton	6.00	12.00
2 Ode Burrell	6.00	12.00
3 Jacky Lee	6.00	12.00
4 Walt Suggs	6.00	12.00
5 Charley Tolar	6.00	12.00

1967 Oilers Team Issue 5X7

This 14-card set of the Houston Oilers measures approximately 5 1/8" by 7" and features black-and-white player photos. The backs are blank. The cards are unnumbered and checklisted below in alphabetical order.

COMPLETE SET (14)	50.00	100.00
1 Pete Barnes	4.00	8.00
2 Sonny Bishop	4.00	8.00
3 Ode Burrell	4.00	8.00
4 Ronnie Caveness	4.00	8.00
5 Joe Childress CO	4.00	8.00
6 Glen Ray Hines	4.00	8.00
7 Pat Holmes	4.00	8.00
8 Bobby Jancik	4.00	8.00
9 Pete Johns	4.00	8.00
10 Jim Norton	4.00	8.00
11 Willie Parker	4.00	8.00
12 Bob Poole	4.00	8.00
13 Alvin Reed	4.00	8.00
14 Olen Underwood	4.00	8.00

1968 Oilers Team Issue 5X7

These 5" by 7" black-and-white photos have a 3/8" white border and include a facsimile signature of the featured player. The player's name, position (initials), and team name are printed in the bottom white border. The backs are blank and the photos are unnumbered, thus checklisted below in alphabetical order.

COMPLETE SET (12)	40.00	80.00
1 Pete Beathard	5.00	10.00
2 Garland Boyette	4.00	8.00
3 Ode Burrell	4.00	8.00
4 Miller Farr	4.00	8.00
5 Hoyle Granger	4.00	8.00
6 Pat Holmes	4.00	8.00
7 Bobby Maples	4.00	8.00
8 Jim Norton	4.00	8.00
9 George Rice	4.00	8.00
10 Walt Suggs	4.00	8.00
11 Bob Talamini	4.00	8.00
12 George Webster	5.00	10.00

1968-69 Oilers Team Issue 8X10

These approximately 8" by 10" black-and-white photos have white borders. Most of the photos feature posed action shots. The player's name, position (initials), and team name are printed in the bottom white border in all caps. The coaches photos feature a slightly different text style. The backs are blank and the photos are unnumbered and checklisted below in alphabetical order.

COMPLETE SET (40)	150.00	300.00
1A Jim Beirne (position WR)	6.00	12.00
1B Jim Beirne position SE		
2 Elvin Bethea	7.50	15.00
3 Sonny Bishop	6.00	12.00
4 Garland Boyette	6.00	12.00
5 Ode Burrell	6.00	12.00
6 Ed Carrington	6.00	12.00
7 Joe Childress CO	6.00	12.00
8 Bob Davis QB	6.00	12.00
9 Hugh Devore CO	6.00	12.00
10 Tom Domres	6.00	12.00
11 F.A. Dry CO	6.00	12.00
12 Miller Farr	6.00	12.00
13 Charles Frazier	6.00	12.00
14 Hoyle Granger	6.00	12.00
15 Mac Haik	6.00	12.00
16 W.K. Hicks	6.00	12.00
17 Glen Ray Hines	6.00	12.00
18A Pat Holmes (position: DE)	6.00	12.00
18B Pat Holmes (position: DT)	6.00	12.00
19 Roy Hopkins	6.00	12.00
20 Wally Lemm CO	6.00	12.00
21 Jim LeMoine	6.00	12.00
22 Bobby Maples	6.00	12.00
23 Richard Marshall	6.00	12.00
24 Bud McFadin CO	6.00	12.00
25 Zeke Moore	6.00	12.00
26 Willie Parker DT	6.00	12.00
27 Johnny Peacock	6.00	12.00
28 Fran Polsfoot CO	6.00	12.00
29 Ron Pritchard (Preparing to fend off blocker)	6.00	12.00
30 Alvin Reed	6.00	12.00
31 Tom Regner	6.00	12.00
32 George Rice	6.00	12.00
33 Bob Robertson	6.00	12.00
34 Walt Suggs	6.00	12.00
35 Don Trull	6.00	12.00
36 Olen Underwood	6.00	12.00
37 Loyd Wainscott	6.00	12.00
38 Wayne Walker	7.50	15.00
39 George Webster	7.50	15.00
40 Glenn Woods	6.00	12.00

1969 Oilers Postcards

These postcards were issued in the late 1960s or possibly early 1970s. Each features a black and white photo of an Oilers player on the front along with his name printed below the photo and to the left. The backs feature a postcard format with most also including a list of Oiler's souvenir items that could be ordered from the team. The postcards measure roughly 3 1/4" by 5 1/2." Any additions to this list are appreciated.

COMPLETE SET (6)	20.00	40.00
1 Jim Beirne	4.00	8.00
2 Woody Campbell	4.00	8.00
3 Alvin Reed	4.00	8.00
4 Tom Regner	4.00	8.00
5 Walt Suggs	4.00	8.00
6 George Webster	5.00	10.00

1971 Oilers Team Issue 4X5

This 23-card set measures approximately 4" by 5 1/2" and features black-and-white, close-up, player photos, bordered in white and printed on a textured paper stock. The team name appears at the top between an Oilers helmet and the NFL logo, while the player's name and position are printed in the bottom border. The cards are unnumbered and checklisted below in alphabetical order. The set's date is defined by the fact that Willie Alexander, Ron Billingsley, Ken Burrough, Lynn Dickey, Robert Holmes, Dan Pastorini, Floyd Rice, Mike Tilleman's first year with the Houston Oilers was 1971, and Charlie Johnson's last year with the Oilers was 1971.

COMPLETE SET (23)	75.00	150.00
1 Willie Alexander	4.00	8.00
2 Jim Beirne	4.00	8.00
3 Elvin Bethea	6.00	12.00
4 Ron Billingsley	4.00	8.00
5 Garland Boyette	4.00	8.00
6 Leo Brooks	4.00	8.00
7 Ken Burrough	5.00	10.00
8 Woody Campbell	4.00	8.00
9 Lynn Dickey	5.00	10.00
10 Elbert Drungo	4.00	8.00
11 Pat Holmes	4.00	8.00
12 Robert Holmes	4.00	8.00
13 Ken Houston	6.00	12.00
14 Charley Johnson	5.00	10.00
15 Charlie Joiner	10.00	20.00
16 Zeke Moore	4.00	8.00
17 Mark Moseley	5.00	10.00
18 Dan Pastorini	5.00	10.00
19 Alvin Reed	4.00	8.00
20 Tom Regner	4.00	8.00
21 Floyd Rice	4.00	8.00
22 Mike Tilleman	4.00	8.00
23 George Webster	5.00	10.00

1971 Oilers Team Issue 5X7

This set of the Houston Oilers measures approximately 5" by 7" and features borderless black-and-white player photos. The photos are very similar to the 1972 release but can be differentiated by the slight difference in the positioning of the player's name and team name below the photo. The 1972 photos feature both names much closer to the photos edge than the 1971 set. The cards are unnumbered and checklisted below in alphabetical order.

COMPLETE SET (15)	50.00	100.00
1 Allen Aldridge	4.00	8.00
2 Jim Beirne	4.00	8.00
3 Elvin Bethea	5.00	10.00
4 Ron Billingsley	4.00	8.00
5 Ken Burrough	5.00	10.00
6 John Charles	4.00	8.00
7 Joe Dawkins	4.00	8.00
8 Calvin Fox	4.00	8.00
9 Johnny Gonzalez Eq.Mgr.	4.00	8.00
10 Cleo Johnson	4.00	8.00
11 Spike Jones	4.00	8.00
12 Alvin Reed	4.00	8.00
13 Floyd Rice	4.00	8.00
14 Mike Tilleman	4.00	8.00
15 George Webster	5.00	10.00

1972 Oilers Team Issue 5X7

This set of the Houston Oilers measures approximately 5" by 7" and features borderless black-and-white player photos. The backs are blank. The cards are unnumbered and checklisted below in alphabetical order. The photos are very similar to the 1971 release but can be differentiated by the slight difference in the positioning of player's name and team name below the photo. The 1972 photos feature both names much closer to the photos edge than the 1971 set

COMPLETE SET (12)	40.00	80.00
1 Ron Billingsley	4.00	8.00
2 Garland Boyette	4.00	8.00
3 Levert Carr	4.00	8.00
4 Walter Highsmith	4.00	8.00
5 Al Johnson	4.00	8.00
6 Benny Johnson	4.00	8.00
7 Guy Murdock	4.00	8.00
8 Willie Rodgers	4.00	8.00
9 Ron Saul	4.00	8.00
10 Mike Tilleman	4.00	8.00
11 Ward Walsh	4.00	8.00
12 George Webster	5.00	10.00

1973 Oilers McDonald's

This set of photos was sponsored by McDonald's. Each photo measures approximately 8" by 10" and features a posed color close-up photo bordered in white. The player's name and team name are printed in black in the bottom white border. The top portion of the back has biographical information, career summary, and career statistics. The bottom portion carries the Oilers 1973 game schedule. The photos are unnumbered and are checklisted below alphabetically.

COMPLETE SET (4)	25.00	50.00
1 Bill Curry	5.00	10.00
2 John Matuszak	7.50	15.00
3 Zeke Moore	5.00	10.00
4 Dan Pastorini	7.50	15.00

1973 Oilers Team Issue

This 17-card set of the Houston Oilers measures approximately 5" by 8" and features black-and-white player photos with a white border. The backs are blank. The cards are unnumbered and checklisted below in alphabetical order.

COMPLETE SET (17)	50.00	100.00
1 Mack Alston	4.00	8.00
2 Bob Atkins	4.00	8.00
3 Skip Butler	4.00	8.00
4 Al Cowlings	4.00	8.00
5 Lynn Dickey	5.00	10.00
6 Mike Fanucci	4.00	8.00
7 Edd Hargett	4.00	8.00
8 Lewis Jolley	4.00	8.00
9 Clifton McNeil	4.00	8.00
10 Ralph Miller	4.00	8.00
11 Zeke Moore	4.00	8.00
12 Dave Parks	4.00	8.00
13 Willie Rodgers	4.00	8.00
14 Greg Sampson	4.00	8.00
15 Finn Seemann	4.00	8.00
16 Jeff Severson	4.00	8.00
17 Fred Willis	4.00	8.00

1974 Oilers Team Issue

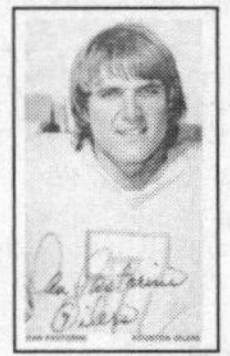

These photos measure approximately 5" by 7" and contain black and white player shots on heavy paper stock. Each carries a facsimile signature and was produced around 1974. These cardbacks are blank. The Bethea, Bingham, Gresham, and Smith card are smaller in size than the rest of the series (approximately 5" by 6 1/2") and could possibly have been issued in another year.

COMPLETE SET (15)	50.00	100.00
1 Mack Alston	4.00	8.00
2 George Amundson	4.00	8.00
3 Elvin Bethea	6.00	12.00
4 Gregg Bingham UER	4.00	8.00
5 Ken Burrough	5.00	10.00
6 Skip Butler	4.00	8.00
7 Al Cowlings	4.00	8.00
8 Lynn Dickey	5.00	10.00
9 Bob Gresham	4.00	8.00
10 Zeke Moore	4.00	8.00
11 Billy Parks	4.00	8.00
12 Dan Pastorini	5.00	10.00
13 Greg Sampson	4.00	8.00
14 Jeff Severson	4.00	8.00
15 Tody Smith	4.00	8.00

1975 Oilers Team Issue

These photos measure approximately 5" by 7" and contain black and white player shots printed on heavy paper stock. Unlike the 1974 issue, these photos do not carry a facsimile signature. The cardbacks are blank and some of the photos are cropped smaller than others.

COMPLETE SET (12)	50.00	100.00
1 Willie Alexander	4.00	8.00
2 Elvin Bethea	6.00	12.00
3 Ken Burrough	5.00	10.00
4 Lynn Dickey	5.00	10.00
5 Fred Hoaglin	4.00	8.00
6 Billy Johnson	6.00	12.00
7 Steve Kiner	4.00	8.00
8 Zeke Moore	4.00	8.00
9 Guy Roberts	4.00	8.00
10 Willie Rodgers	4.00	8.00
11 Ted Washington	4.00	8.00
12 Fred Willis	4.00	8.00

1975 Oilers Team Sheets

This set consists of three 8" by 10" sheets that display a group of black-and-white player photos on each. The player's name is printed below each photo and the backs are blank. The sheets are unnumbered and checklisted below alphabetically according to the player featured in the upper left corner.

COMPLETE SET (3)	10.00	20.00
1 Sheet 1	4.00	8.00
2 Sheet 3	4.00	8.00
3 Sheet 2	3.00	6.00

1980 Oilers Police

The 14-card set of the 1980 Houston Oilers is unnumbered and checklist below in alphabetical order. The cards measure approximately 2 5/8" by 4 1/8". The Kiwanis Club, the local law enforcement agency, and the Houston Oilers sponsored this set. The backs feature "Oilers Tips" and a Kiwanis logo. The fronts feature logos of the Kiwanis and the City of Houston.

COMPLETE SET (14)	10.00	20.00
1 Gregg Bingham	.40	1.00
2 Robert Brazile	.50	1.25
3 Ken Burrough	.60	1.50
4 Rob Carpenter	.50	1.25
5 Ronnie Coleman	.40	1.00
6 Curley Culp	.50	1.25
7 Carter Hartwig	.40	1.00
8 Billy Johnson	.60	1.50
9 Carl Mauck	.40	1.00
10 Gifford Nielsen	.40	1.00
11 Cliff Parsley	.40	1.00
12 Bum Phillips CO	.75	2.00
13 Mike Renfro	.40	1.00
14 Ken Stabler	3.00	8.00

1979 Open Pantry

This set is an unnumbered, 12-card issue featuring players from Milwaukee area professional sports teams with five Brewers baseball (1-5), five Bucks basketball (6-10), and two Packers football (11-12). Cards are black and white with red trim and measure approximately 5" by 6". Cards were sponsored by Open Pantry, Lake to Lake, and MACC (Milwaukee Athletes against Childhood Cancer). The cards are unnumbered and hence are listed and numbered below alphabetically within sport.

COMPLETE SET (12)	12.50	25.00
11 Rich McGeorge	1.00	2.00
12 Steve Wagner	1.00	2.00

1938-42 Overland All American Roll Candy Wrappers

These unnumbered candy wrappers measure roughly 5" by 5 1/4" and were issued over a period of time in the late 1930's and early 1940's. A drawing of the player is at the top of the wrapper with his name, team name, and a short biography below. All players known thus far are post college athletes with some playing in the NFL and some on the military teams which were so popular during World War II. The product name and price "All American Football Roll 1-cent" appears at the bottom with the Overland Candy Corporation mentioned below that. The backs are blank and the wrappers are nearly always found with multiple creases. Any additions to this list are appreciated.

1 Sammy Baugh	800.00	1,200.00
2 Bill DeCorrevont	350.00	600.00
3 Rudy Mucha	350.00	600.00
4 Bruce Smith	500.00	800.00

1932 Packers Walker's Cleaners

This set of photos was issued in early 1932 by Walker's Cleaners in the Green Bay area to commemorate the 1929-1931 3-time World Champions. Each large photo was printed in sepia tone and included a facsimile autograph of the featured player as well as the photographer's notation. Each photo also includes a strip on the left side with two holes punched in order to fit into an album that was made available to anyone who built a complete set.. The photos are often found with the two-hole section trimmed off. Lastly a small cover sheet was included with each photo that featured a photo number, sponsorship mentions, a bio of the player and information about obtaining the album. Photos with the cover sheet still attached are valued at roughly double photos without. We've listed the blank backed photos below according to the photo number on the small cover sheets.

COMPLETE SET (27)	6,000.00	10,000.00
1 Curly Lambeau	800.00	1,200.00
2 Frank Baker	150.00	300.00
3 Russ Saunders	150.00	300.00
4 Wuert Engelmann	150.00	300.00
5 Hank Bruder	200.00	400.00
6 Waldo Don Carlos	150.00	300.00
7 Roger Grove	150.00	300.00
8 Mike Michalske	250.00	500.00
9 Milt Gantenbein	150.00	300.00
10 Lavie Dilweg	200.00	400.00
11 Verne Lewellen	200.00	400.00
12 Red Dunn	150.00	300.00
13 Johnny Blood McNally	300.00	600.00
14 Jug Earp	200.00	400.00
15 Arnie Herber	300.00	600.00
16 Dick Stahlman	150.00	300.00
17 Red Sleight	150.00	300.00
18 Rudy Comstock	150.00	300.00
19 Jim Bowdoin	150.00	300.00
20 Hurdis McCrary	150.00	300.00
21 Bo Molenda	150.00	300.00
22 Cal Hubbard	500.00	800.00
23 Paul Fitzgibbon	150.00	300.00
24 Tom Nash	150.00	300.00
25 Mule Wilson	200.00	400.00
26 Howard Woodin	150.00	300.00
27 Nate Barragar	150.00	300.00
NNO Album	200.00	400.00

1955 Packers Miller Brewing Postcards

1 Tobin Rote	20.00	40.00

1955 Packers Team Issue

This set of large (roughly 8 1/2" by 10 1/2") black and white photos was issued by the Packers around 1955. Each photo was printed on thick stock and includes the player's name and team name within a white box on the front. The photos are blankbacked. Any additions to the list below are appreciated.

1 Charlie Brackens	75.00	150.00
3 Al Carmichael	35.00	60.00
4 Howard Ferguson	35.00	60.00
5 Billy Howton	50.00	80.00
6 Gary Knafelc	35.00	60.00
10 Veryl Switzer	35.00	60.00

1959 Packers Team Issue

The Packers released this set of photos to fans in 1959. They were commonly released in a Green Bay Packers envelope with each measuring roughly 5" by 7" featuring a black and white player photo. The team name appears above the photo and the player's name, position, college, height, and weight is included below the photo. Some photos vary slightly in size and style of print type used while others have sponsor logos on the fronts as noted below. All photos, except Nitschke, feature action shots and a facsimile autograph. The photos were also printed on thin paper stock, are blankbacked, and listed below alphabetically.

COMPLETE SET (30)	400.00	700.00
1 Tom Bettis	7.50	15.00
2 Nate Borden	7.50	15.00
3 Lew Carpenter	7.50	15.00
4 Dan Currie	7.50	15.00
5 Bill Forester	7.50	15.00
6 Bob Freeman	7.50	15.00
7 Forrest Gregg	20.00	35.00
8 Hank Gremminger	7.50	15.00
9 Dave Hanner	7.50	15.00
10 Jerry Helluin	7.50	15.00
11 Paul Hornung	35.00	60.00
12 Gary Knafelc	7.50	15.00
13 Jerry Kramer	20.00	35.00
14 Vince Lombardi CO	125.00	200.00
15 Norm Masters	7.50	15.00
16 Lamar McHan	7.50	15.00
17 Max McGee	10.00	20.00
18 Don McIlhenny	7.50	15.00
19 Steve Meilinger	7.50	15.00
20 Ray Nitschke	30.00	50.00
21 Babe Parilli	10.00	20.00
22 Bill Quinlan	7.50	15.00
23 Jim Ringo	20.00	35.00
24 Al Romine	7.50	15.00
25 Bob Skoronski	10.00	20.00
26 Bart Starr	40.00	75.00
27 John Symank	7.50	15.00
28 Jim Taylor	30.00	50.00
29 Jim Temp	7.50	15.00
30 Emlen Tunnell	20.00	35.00

1961 Packers Lake to Lake

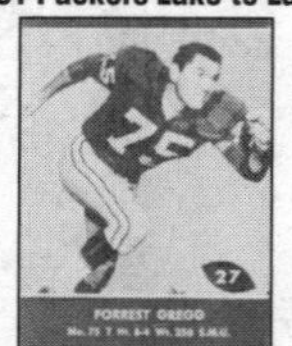

The 1961 Lake to Lake Green Bay Packers set consists of 36 unnumbered, green and white cards each measuring approximately 2 1/2" by 3 1/4". The fronts contain the card number, the player's uniform number, his position, and his height, weight, and college. The backs contain advertisements for the Packer fans to obtain Lake to Lake premiums. Card numbers 1-8 and 17-24 are the most difficult cards to obtain and cards #33-36 are also in shorter supply than #9-16 and #25-32 which are the easiest cards in the set. Lineman Ken Iman's card was issued ten years before his Rookie Card; Defensive back Herb Adderley's card was issued three years before his Rookie Card.

COMPLETE SET (36)	1,800.00	3,000.00
1 Jerry Kramer SP	100.00	175.00
2 Norm Masters SP	75.00	125.00
3 Willie Davis SP	100.00	175.00
4 Bill Quinlan SP	75.00	125.00
5 Jim Temp SP	75.00	125.00
6 Emlen Tunnell SP	90.00	150.00
7 Gary Knafelc SP	75.00	125.00
8 Hank Jordan SP	125.00	200.00
9 Bill Forester	4.00	8.00
10 Paul Hornung	15.00	25.00
11 Jesse Whittenton	4.00	8.00
12 Andy Cvercko	4.00	8.00
13 Jim Taylor	10.00	20.00
14 Hank Gremminger	4.00	8.00
15 Tom Moore	4.00	8.00
16 John Symank	4.00	8.00
17 Max McGee SP	90.00	150.00
18 Bart Starr SP	250.00	400.00
19 Ray Nitschke SP	150.00	250.00
20 Dave Hanner SP	75.00	125.00
21 Tom Bettis SP	75.00	125.00
22 Fuzzy Thurston SP	90.00	150.00
23 Lew Carpenter SP	75.00	125.00
24 Boyd Dowler SP	90.00	150.00
25 Ken Iman	4.00	8.00
26 Bob Skoronski	4.00	8.00
27 Forrest Gregg	6.00	12.00
28 Jim Ringo	6.00	12.00
29 Ron Kramer	4.00	8.00
30 Herb Adderley	7.50	15.00
31 Dan Currie	4.00	8.00
32 John Roach	4.00	8.00
33 Dale Hackbart SP	75.00	125.00
34 Larry Hickman SP	75.00	125.00
35 Nelson Toburen SP	75.00	125.00
36 Willie Wood SP	100.00	175.00

1965 Packers Team Issue

This set of small (5" by 7") black and white photos was issued by the Packers around 1965. Each photo was printed on thick stock, includes the player name, position, and team name below the photo and are blankbacked. Any additions to the list below are appreciated.

1 Herb Adderley	7.50	15.00
2 Lionel Aldridge	6.00	12.00
3 Jim Taylor	15.00	25.00
4 Fuzzy Thurston	7.50	15.00

1966 Packers Mobil Posters

This eight-poster set of the Green Bay Packers measures approximately 11" by 14" and features art prints suitable for framing of various game action pictures. The fronts carry a color action art piece and the backs are blank. The posters were distributed in envelopes that included the title of the artwork and the poster number. Although players are not specifically identified, we've made attempts to identify some key players. The prints are listed below according to the number and title on the envelope.

COMPLETE SET (8)	125.00	250.00
1 The Pass	30.00	60.00
2 The Block	15.00	30.00
3 The Punt	12.50	25.00
4 The Sweep	18.00	30.00
5 The Catch	15.00	30.00
6 The Tackle	12.50	25.00
7 The Touchdown	12.50	25.00
8 The Extra Point	20.00	40.00

1966 Packers Team Issue

The Green Bay Packers issued player photos over a number of years in the late 1960s. Most of the 8" by 10" photos may have even been issued across a number of years. This set was most likely released in 1966 and can be differentiated by the text included below the black and white player photo. Included (reading left to right) are the player's position (initials), his name in all caps, and full team name in all caps. Any additions to this list are appreciated.

1 Donny Anderson	7.50	15.00
2 Gale Gillingham	6.00	12.00
3 Jim Grabowski	6.00	12.00

1967 Packers Socka-Tumee Prints

These large (roughly 9' x 10 1/2") art prints feature a Packers player in contact with another NFL player in an exagerated action scene that includes a portion of the picture's frame being broken away. While the player is not specifically identified, the artwork is detailed enough to identify a specific player as noted below.

1 Jim Grabowski	25.00	50.00
2 Ray Nitschke	60.00	100.00
3 Don Chandler	25.00	50.00

1967 Packers Team Issue 5x7

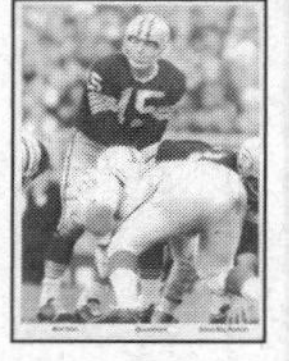

These black and white player photos were released by the Green Bay Packers around 1967. Each measures approximately 5" by 7" and includes the player's name, his position (spelled out in full) and team name below the photo. They are blankbacked and unnumbered. Any additions to this list are appreciated.

COMPLETE SET (13)	100.00	175.00
1 Donny Anderson	6.00	12.00
2 Zeke Bratkowski	6.00	12.00
3 Willie Davis	7.50	15.00
4 Gale Gillingham	5.00	10.00
5 Bob Jeter	5.00	10.00
6 Hank Jordan	7.50	15.00
7 Ron Kostelnik	5.00	10.00
8 Jerry Kramer	7.50	15.00
9 Ray Nitschke	10.00	20.00
10 Dave Robinson	7.50	15.00
11 Bob Skoronski	5.00	10.00
12 Bart Starr	20.00	40.00
13 Travis Williams	5.00	10.00

1967 Packers Team Issue 8x10

The Green Bay Packers issued roughly 8" by 10" player photos over a number of years in the late 1960s. Most of the photos were issued across a number of years. This set was most likely released in 1967 and can be differentiated by the text included below the black and white player photo. Included (reading left to right) are the player's name in all caps, position spelled out in caps, and the city "GREEN BAY" in all caps. Any additions to this list are appreciated.

1 Boyd Dowler	7.50	15.00
2 Bart Starr	20.00	40.00
3 Bart Starr	20.00	40.00
4 Bart Starr	20.00	40.00

1968-69 Packers Team Issu

This team-issued set consists of black-and-white player photos with each measuring approximately 8" by 10". They were printed on thin glossy paper and likely released over a number of years. The player's name, position, and team name are printed in black in the bottom white border. Although they are very similar to the 1971-72 release, the printing used for the text is generally larger. The team name is approximately 1 3/4" to 2" long. The cardbacks are blank. The photos are unnumbered and checklisted below in alphabetical order.

COMPLETE SET (51)	250.00	500.00
1 Herb Adderley	7.50	15.00
2 Herb Adderley	7.50	15.00
3 Larry Agajanian	6.00	12.00
4 Lionel Aldridge	6.00	12.00
5 Phil Bengston CO	6.00	12.00
6 Ken Bowman	6.00	12.00
7 Dave Bradley	6.00	12.00
8 Zeke Bratkowski	7.50	15.00
9 Bob Brown	6.00	12.00

Card	Low	High
10 Lee Roy Caffey	6.00	12.00
11 Fred Carr	6.00	12.00
12 Fred Carr	6.00	12.00
13 Don Chandler	6.00	12.00
14 Carroll Dale	7.50	15.00
15 Willie Davis	7.50	15.00
16 Willie Davis	7.50	15.00
17 Boyd Dowler	7.50	15.00
18 Jim Flanigan	6.00	12.00
19 Marv Fleming	7.50	15.00
20 Forrest Gregg	7.50	15.00
21 Dave Hampton	6.00	12.00
22 Leon Harden	6.00	12.00
23 Doug Hart	6.00	12.00
24 Bill Hayhoe	6.00	12.00
25 Dick Himes	6.00	12.00
26 Don Horn	6.00	12.00
27 Bob Hyland	6.00	12.00
28 Claudis James	6.00	12.00
29 Bob Jeter	6.00	12.00
30 Ron Jones	6.00	12.00
31 Jerry Kramer	7.50	15.00
32 Vince Lombardi CO	15.00	30.00
33 Bill Lueck	6.00	12.00
34 Max McGee	7.50	15.00
35 Mike Mercer	6.00	12.00
36 Rich Moore	6.00	12.00
37 Ray Nitschke	10.00	20.00
38 Francis Peay	6.00	12.00
39 Elijah Pitts	6.00	12.00
40 Dave Robinson LB	7.50	15.00
41 John Rowser	6.00	12.00
42 Gordon Rule	6.00	12.00
43 John Spilis	6.00	12.00
44 Bart Starr	15.00	30.00
45 Bill Stevens	6.00	12.00
46 Phil Vandersea	6.00	12.00
47 Jim Weatherwax	6.00	12.00
48 Perry Williams	6.00	12.00
49 Travis Williams	6.00	12.00
50 Francis Winkler	6.00	12.00
51 Willie Wood	7.50	15.00

1969 Packers Drenks Potato Chip Pins

The 1969 Packers Drenks Potato Chip set contains 20 pins, each measuring approximately 1 1/8" in diameter. The fronts have a green and white background, with a black and white headshot in the center of the white football-shaped area. The team name at the top and player information at the bottom follow the curve of the pin. The pins are unnumbered and checklisted below in alphabetical order.

Card	Low	High
COMPLETE SET (20)	75.00	150.00
1 Herb Adderley	5.00	10.00
2 Lionel Aldridge	3.00	6.00
3 Donny Anderson	4.00	8.00
4 Ken Bowman	3.00	6.00
5 Carroll Dale	3.00	6.00
6 Willie Davis	5.00	10.00
7 Boyd Dowler	4.00	8.00
8 Marv Fleming	4.00	8.00
9 Gale Gillingham	3.00	6.00
10 Jim Grabowski	3.00	6.00
11 Forrest Gregg	5.00	10.00
12 Don Horn	3.00	6.00
13 Bob Jeter	3.00	6.00
14 Hank Jordan	5.00	10.00
15 Ray Nitschke	7.50	15.00
16 Elijah Pitts	3.00	6.00
17 Dave Robinson	4.00	8.00
18 Bart Starr	12.50	25.00
19 Travis Williams	3.00	6.00
20 Willie Wood	5.00	10.00

1969 Packers Tasco Prints

Tasco Associates produced this set of Green Bay Packers prints. The fronts feature a large color artist's rendering of the player along with the player's name and position. The backs are blank and unnumbered. The prints measure approximately 11" by 16."

Card	Low	High
COMPLETE SET (8)	175.00	300.00
1 Donny Anderson	20.00	35.00
2 Willie Davis	25.00	40.00
3 Boyd Dowler	20.00	35.00
4 Jim Grabowski	18.00	30.00
5 Hank Jordan	25.00	40.00
6 Ray Nitschke	30.00	50.00
7 Bart Starr	50.00	80.00
8 Willie Wood	25.00	40.00

1970 Packers Volpe Tumblers

Card	Low	High
1 Ray Nitschke	20.00	40.00
2 Dave Robinson	10.00	20.00
3 Carroll Dale	10.00	20.00
4 Donny Anderson	10.00	20.00
5 Willie Wood	12.50	25.00

1971-72 Packers Team Issue

This team-issued set consists of black-and-white player photos with each measuring approximately 8" by 10". They were printed on thin glossy paper. The player's name, position, and team name are printed in black in the bottom white border. Although they are very similar to the 1968-69 release, the printing used for the text is generally smaller. The team name is approximately 1 1/2" long. The cardbacks are blank. Several players have two photos in the set. Furthermore, Napper never played in the NFL, and Pittman never played for the Packers, suggesting that these photos may have been taken during training camp or preseason. The photos are unnumbered and checklisted below in alphabetical order.

Card	Low	High
COMPLETE SET (44)	150.00	300.00
1 John Brockington	6.00	12.00
2 Bob Brown DT	5.00	10.00
3 Willie Buchanon	6.00	12.00
4 Jim Carter	5.00	10.00
5 Carroll Dale	6.00	12.00
6 Dan Devine CO GM	6.00	12.00
7 Ken Ellis	5.00	10.00
8 Len Garrett	5.00	10.00
9 Gale Gillingham	5.00	10.00
10 Leland Glass	5.00	10.00
11 Charlie Hall DB	5.00	10.00
12 Jim Hill	5.00	10.00
13 Dick Himes	5.00	10.00
14 Bob Hudson	5.00	10.00
15 Bob Hudson	5.00	10.00
16 Kevin Hunt	5.00	10.00
17 Scott Hunter Passing action posed	6.00	12.00
18 Scott Hunter Arm raised to pass Thin paper stock	6.00	12.00
19 Dave Kopay	5.00	10.00
20 Bob Kroll	5.00	10.00
21 Pete Lammons	5.00	10.00
22 MacArthur Lane	6.00	12.00
23 Bill Lueck	5.00	10.00
24 Al Matthews	5.00	10.00
25 Mike McCoy DT	5.00	10.00
26 Rich McGeorge	5.00	10.00
27 Lou Michaels	6.00	12.00
28 Charlie Napper	5.00	10.00
29 Ray Nitschke	7.50	15.00
30 Charlie Pittman	5.00	10.00
31 Alden Roche	5.00	10.00
32 Malcolm Snider	5.00	10.00
33 Malcolm Snider	5.00	10.00
34 Jon Staggers	5.00	10.00
35 Jerry Tagge	5.00	10.00
36 Isaac Thomas	5.00	10.00
37 Isaac Thomas	5.00	10.00
38 Vern Vanoy	5.00	10.00
39 Ron Widby	5.00	10.00
40 Ron Widby	5.00	10.00
41 Clarence Williams	5.00	10.00
42 Perry Williams RB	5.00	10.00
43 Keith Wortman	5.00	10.00
44 Coaching Staff	7.50	15.00

1972 Packers Coke Cap Liners

This set of cap liners were issued inside the caps of bottles of Coca-Cola in the Green Bay area in 1972. Each clear plastic liner features a black and white photo of the featured player. They were to be attached to a saver sheet that could be partially or completely filled in order to be exchanged for various prizes from Coke.

Card	Low	High
COMPLETE SET (22)	50.00	100.00
1 Ken Bowman	2.50	5.00
2 John Brockington	3.00	6.00
3 Bob Brown	2.50	5.00
4 Fred Carr	2.50	5.00
5 Jim Carter	2.50	5.00
6 Carroll Dale	3.00	6.00
7 Ken Ellis	2.50	5.00
8 Gale Gillingham	2.50	5.00
9 Dave Hampton	2.50	5.00
10 Doug Hart	2.50	5.00
11 Jim Hill	2.50	5.00
12 Dick Himes	2.50	5.00
13 Scott Hunter	2.50	5.00
14 MacArthur Lane	3.00	6.00
15 Bill Lueck	2.50	5.00
16 Al Matthews	2.50	5.00
17 Rich McGeorge	2.50	5.00
18 Ray Nitschke	6.00	12.00
19 Francis Peay	2.50	5.00
20 Dave Robinson	4.00	8.00
21 Alden Roche	2.50	5.00
22 Bart Starr	10.00	20.00

1975 Packers Pizza Hut Glasses

This set of glasses was issued by Pizza Hut in the mid-1970s to honor past Green Bay Packers greats. Each glass includes Packer green and gold colored highlights with a black and white picture of the featured player.

Card	Low	High
COMPLETE SET (6)	50.00	100.00
1 Wille Davis	5.00	10.00
2 Paul Hornung	10.00	20.00
3 Jerry Kramer	5.00	10.00
4 Vince Lombardi	20.00	40.00
5 Ray Nitschke	7.50	15.00
6 Bart Starr	12.50	25.00

1975 Packers Team Issue

The Green Bay Packers issued this set of 15-photos along with a saver album sponsored by Roundy's Food Store. Each measures approximately 6" by 9". The fronts feature posed color photos of the players kneeling with their right hand resting on their helmets. Facsimile autographs are inscribed across the pictures. The backs are blank. The cards are unnumbered and checklisted below in alphabetical order.

Card	Low	High
COMPLETE SET (15)	50.00	100.00
1 John Brockington	5.00	10.00
2 Willie Buchanon	5.00	10.00
3 Fred Carr	4.00	8.00
4 Jim Carter	4.00	8.00
5 Jack Concannon	4.00	8.00
6 Bill Curry	5.00	10.00
7 John Hadl	6.00	12.00
8 Bill Lueck	4.00	8.00
9 Chester Marcol	4.00	8.00
10 Al Matthews	4.00	8.00
11 Rich McGeorge	4.00	8.00
12 Alden Roche	4.00	8.00
13 Barry Smith	4.00	8.00
14 Barty Smith	4.00	8.00
15 Clarence Williams	4.00	8.00
NNO Saver Album	10.00	20.00

1976-77 Packers Team Issue 5x7

These photos were issued by the Packers, feature black-and-white player images, and measure approximately 5" by 7". They were printed on thin glossy paper with the player's name and position initials on the top line and the team name on the bottom line of type printed below the player's image. The photos are blankbacked, unnumbered and checklisted below in alphabetical order.

Card	Low	High
COMPLETE SET (28)	75.00	125.00
1 Bert Askson	3.00	6.00
2 John Brockington	4.00	8.00
3 Willie Buchanon	4.00	8.00
4 Mike Butler	3.00	6.00
5 Fred Carr	3.00	6.00
6 Jim Carter	3.00	6.00
7 Charlie Hall	3.00	6.00
8 Willard Harrell 1	3.00	6.00
9 Willard Harrell 2	3.00	6.00
10 Bob Hyland	3.00	6.00
11 Melvin Jackson	3.00	6.00
12 Ezra Johnson	3.00	6.00
13 Mark Koncar	3.00	6.00
14 Steve Luke	3.00	6.00
15 Chester Marcol	3.00	6.00
16 Mike McCoy DB	3.00	6.00
17 Mike Mccoy DT	3.00	6.00
18 Rich Mcgeorge	3.00	6.00
19 Steve Odom	3.00	6.00
20 Ken Payne	3.00	6.00
21 Tom Perko	3.00	6.00
22 Dave Pureifory	3.00	6.00
23 Alden Roche	3.00	6.00
24 Barty Smith 1	3.00	6.00
25 Barty Smith 2	3.00	6.00
26 Perry Smith	3.00	6.00
27 Cliff Taylor	3.00	6.00
28 Tom Toner	3.00	6.00

1976-77 Packers Team Issue 8x10

These team-issued photos feature black-and-white player images with each measuring approximately 8" by 10". They were printed on thin glossy paper with the player's name, position (initials), and team name printed in black in the bottom white border. Most feature the player in a kneeling pose with his hand on his helmet. The photos are blankbacked, unnumbered and checklisted below in alphabetical order.

Card	Low	High
COMPLETE SET (33)	125.00	250.00
1 Dave Beverly	4.00	8.00
2 Mike Butler	4.00	8.00
3 Jim Culbreath	4.00	8.00
4 Lynn Dickey	5.00	10.00
5 Derrel Gofourth	4.00	8.00
6 Johnnie Gray	4.00	8.00
7 Will Harrell	4.00	8.00
8 Dennis Havig	4.00	8.00
9 Melvin Jackson	4.00	8.00
10 Greg Koch	4.00	8.00
11 Mark Koncar	4.00	8.00
12 Larry McCarren	4.00	8.00
13 Mike McCoy DB	4.00	8.00
14 Mike McCoy DT	4.00	8.00
15 Terdell Middleton	4.00	8.00
16 Tim Moresco	4.00	8.00
17 Steve Okoniewski	4.00	8.00
18 Tom Perko	4.00	8.00
19 Terry Randolph	4.00	8.00
20 Alden Roche	4.00	8.00
21 Dave Roller	4.00	8.00
22 Barty Smith	4.00	8.00
23 Ollie Smith	4.00	8.00
24 Clifton Taylor	4.00	8.00
25 Aundra Thompson	4.00	8.00
26 Tom Toner	4.00	8.00
27 Eric Torkelson	4.00	8.00
28 Bruce Van Dyke	4.00	8.00
29 Randy Vataha	4.00	8.00
30 Steve Wagner	4.00	8.00
31 David Whitehurst	5.00	10.00
32 Clarence Williams	4.00	8.00
33 Keith Wortman	4.00	8.00

1968-70 Partridge Meats

These black and white (with some red trim and text) photo-like cards feature players from all three Cincinnati major league sports teams of that time: Cincinnati Reds baseball (BB1-BB20), Cincinnati Bengals football (FB1-FB5), and Cincinnati Royals basketball (BK1-BK2). The cards measure approximately 4" by 5" or 3-3/4" by 5-1/2" and were issued over a period of years. The cards are blank backed and a "Mr. Whopper" card was also issued in honor of the 7'-3" company spokesperson. The Tom Rhoads football card was only recently discovered, in 2012, adding to the prevailing thought that these cards were issued over a period of years since its format matches some of the baseball cards and not the other four more well-known football cards in the set. Joe Morgan was also recently added to the checklist indicating that more cards could turn up in the future. This card follows the same format as Gullett, May, Perez, and Tolan (all measuring 3-3/4" by 5-1/2") missing the team's logo on the cap, missing the team's nickname in the text, and missing the company's slogan below the image. Some collectors believe this style to be consistent with a 1972 release.

Card	Low	High
COMPLETE SET (14)	400.00	800.00
FB1 Bob Johnson (measures 4" x 5")	6.00	15.00
FB2 Paul Robinson SP	25.00	50.00
FB3 John Stofa SP (measures 4" x 5")	25.00	50.00
FB4 Bob Trumpy (measures 4" x 5")	6.00	15.00
FB5 Tom Rhoads SP (measures 4" x 5")	75.00	150.00

1961 Patriots Team Issue

The Patriots issued these photos around 1961. Each measures roughly 8" by 10" and includes a black and white player image with the player's name and team name (Boston Patriots) to the left and the team logo and address to the right below the image. The backs are blank.

Card	Low	High
COMPLETE SET	50.00	100.00
1 Ron Burton	7.50	15.00
2 Gerry Delucca	6.00	12.00
3 Mike Holovak	7.50	15.00
4 Jim Hunt	6.00	12.00
5 Harry Jacobs	6.00	12.00
6 Dick Klein	6.00	12.00
7 Tommy Stephens	6.00	12.00
8 Clyde Washington	6.00	12.00

1965 Patriots Team Issue

Card	Low	High
1 Tom Addison All-League Linebacker	7.50	15.00
2 Houston Antwine DT	6.00	12.00
3 Jim Boudreaux Tackle	6.00	12.00
4 John Charles Defensive Back	6.00	12.00
5 Jim Colclough Offensive End	6.00	12.00
6 Jay Cunningham DB	6.00	12.00
7 Tom Fussell Defensive End	6.00	12.00
8 J.D. Garrett Halfback	6.00	12.00
9 Art Graham Split End	7.50	15.00
10 White Graves DB	6.00	12.00
11 Tom Hennessey DB	6.00	12.00
12 John Huarte Quarterback	7.50	15.00
13 Ray Ilg Linebacker	6.00	12.00
14 LeRoy Mitchell Defensive Back	6.00	12.00
15 Don Oakes T.	6.00	12.00
16 Babe Parilli Q.B. (team name under player name)	7.50	15.00
17 Vic Purvis DB	6.00	12.00
18 Chuck Shonta Defensive Back	6.00	12.00
19 Terry Swanson Punter	6.00	12.00
20 Don Webb DB	6.00	12.00
21 Jim Whalen E	6.00	12.00

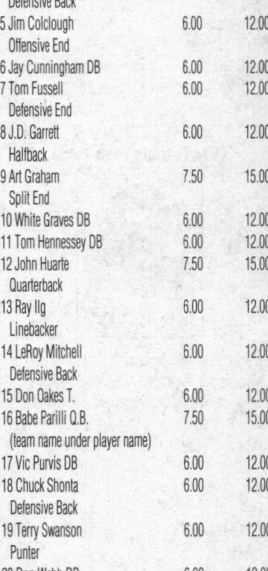

1967 Patriots Team Issue

The Patriots issued this set of photos and distributed them to fans through mail requests. Each measures roughly 8" by 10 1/8" and includes a black and white player photo. The cards are unnumbered and checklisted below in alphabetical order.

Card	Low	High
COMPLETE SET (8)	50.00	100.00
1 Houston Antwine	6.00	12.00
2 Gino Cappelletti	7.50	15.00
3 John Charles	6.00	12.00
4 Jim Hunt	6.00	12.00
5 Leroy Mitchell	6.00	12.00
6 Babe Parilli	7.50	15.00
7 Don Trull	6.00	12.00
8 Jim Whalen	6.00	12.00

1971 Patriots Team Sheets

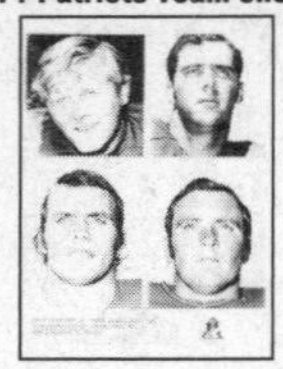

The New England Patriots issued these sheets of black-and-white player photos around 1971. Each measures roughly 8" by 10 1/8" and was printed on glossy stock with white borders. Each sheet includes photos of 4-players with the player's names, positions, team name and logo grouped below the photos. The coaches photo is a simple group shot with their names and positions listed below. The photo sheets are blankbacked.

COMPLETE SET (10)	50.00	100.00
1 Houston Antwine	5.00	10.00
2 Randall Edmunds	5.00	10.00
3 Halvor Hagen	5.00	10.00
4 Jon Morris	5.00	10.00
5 Jim Nance	6.00	12.00
6 John Outlaw	5.00	10.00
7 Jim Plunkett	7.50	15.00
8 Perry Pruett	5.00	10.00
9 Sam Rutigliano CO	5.00	10.00
10 Ron Sellers	5.00	10.00

1974 Patriots Linnett

Noted sports Artist Charles Linnett drew these charcoal portraits of New England Patriots players. The 8 1/2" by 11" portraits were sold three per pack. Each is blankbacked and includes the player's name below the artwork.

COMPLETE SET (9)	35.00	60.00
1 Jim Plunkett	6.00	12.00
2 Jon Morris	3.00	6.00
3 Julius Adams	3.00	6.00
4 Randy Vataha	3.00	6.00
5 Sam Cunningham	4.00	8.00
6 Reggie Rucker	4.00	8.00
7 Tom Neville	3.00	6.00
8 Mack Herron	3.00	6.00
9 John Smith	3.00	6.00

1974 Patriots Team Issue

The Patriots issued this set of player photos for the purpose of media use only. The 4 7/8" by 7 1/8" black and white photos are blankbanked and unnumbered and checklisted below in alphabetical order.

COMPLETE SET (29)	75.00	150.00
1 Bob Adams	3.00	6.00
2 Julius Adams	3.00	6.00
3 Sam Adams	4.00	8.00
4 Josh Ashton	3.00	6.00
5 Bruce Barnes	3.00	6.00
6 Sam Cunningham	5.00	10.00
7 Sandy Durko	3.00	6.00
8 Allen Gallaher	3.00	6.00
9 Neil Graff	3.00	6.00
10 Leon Gray	4.00	8.00
11 John Hannah	7.50	15.00
12 Craig Hanneman	3.00	6.00
13 Andy Johnson	3.00	6.00
14 Steve King	3.00	6.00
15 Bill Lenkaitis	3.00	6.00
16 Prentice McCray	3.00	6.00
17 Jack Mildren	3.00	6.00
18 Arthur Moore	3.00	6.00
19 Jon Morris	3.00	6.00
20 Reggie Rucker	4.00	8.00
21 John Sanders	3.00	6.00
22 Steve Schubert	3.00	6.00
23 John Smith	3.00	6.00
24 John Tanner	3.00	6.00
25 John Tarver	3.00	6.00
26 Randy Vataha	3.00	6.00
27 George Webster	4.00	8.00
28 Joe Wilson	3.00	6.00
29 Bob Windsor	3.00	6.00

1976 Patriots Frito Lay

The New England Patriots issued this set sponsored by Frito Lay. The cards are blankbacked, measure approximately 5" by 7", and feature black and white player photos. The cards can be distinguished from other Patriots Frito Lay issues by the notation "Compliments of Frito Lay" contained at the bottom of the cardfront along with the "FL" logo. The left and right hand borders are much wider than the 1977-78 release. The player's are not identified on the photos and each appears in a kneeling (one hand on helmet) pose. Any additions to the list below are appreciated.

COMPLETE SET (44)		
1 Julius Adams	3.00	8.00
2 Sam Adams	4.00	10.00
3 Pete Barnes	3.00	8.00
4 Doug Beaudoin	3.00	8.00
5 Richard Bishop	3.00	8.00
6 Marlin Briscoe	3.00	8.00
7 Peter Brock	3.00	8.00
8 Steve Burks	3.00	8.00
9 Don Calhoun	3.00	8.00
10 Al Chandler	3.00	8.00
11 Dick Conn	3.00	8.00
12 Sam Cunningham	4.00	10.00
13 Ike Forte	3.00	8.00
14 Tim Fox	4.00	10.00
15 Russ Francis	5.00	12.00
16 Willie Germany	3.00	8.00
17 Leon Gray	3.00	8.00
18 Steve Grogan	6.00	15.00
19 Ray Hamilton	3.00	8.00
20 John Hannah	8.00	20.00
21 Mike Haynes	5.00	12.00
22 Bob Howard	3.00	8.00
23 Sam Hunt	3.00	8.00
24 Andy Johnson	3.00	8.00
25 Steve King	3.00	8.00
26 Bill Lenkaitis	3.00	8.00
27 Prentice McCray	3.00	8.00
28 Tony McGee	4.00	10.00
29 Bob McKay	3.00	8.00
30 Arthur Moore	3.00	8.00
31 Steve Nelson	3.00	8.00
32 Tom Neville	3.00	8.00
33 Tom Owen	3.00	8.00
34 Mike Patrick	3.00	8.00
35 Jess Phillips	3.00	8.00
36 Jim Romaniszyn	3.00	8.00
37 John Smith	3.00	8.00
38 Darryl Stingley	4.00	10.00
39 Fred Sturt	3.00	8.00
40 Randy Vataha	3.00	8.00
41 George Webster	3.00	8.00
42 Steve Zabel	3.00	8.00
43 R.Miller Erhardt Perkins Dotsch	3.00	8.00
44 Team Photo	3.00	8.00

1977-78 Patriots Frito Lay

The New England Patriots issued this set sponsored by Frito Lay. The cards are blankbacked, measure approximately 5" by 7", and feature black and white player photos. The cards can be distinguished from other Patriots Frito Lay issues by the simple notation "Compliments of Frito Lay" contained at the bottom of the cardfront along with the "FL" logo. The left and right hand borders around the image are much thinner than the 1976 release, but otherwise the photos look the same. The player's are not identified on the photos and each appears in a kneeling (one hand on helmet) pose unless noted. Any additions to the list below are appreciated.

1 Richard Bishop	3.00	8.00
2 Sam Cunningham	4.00	10.00
3 Tim Fox	3.00	8.00
4 Leon Gray	3.00	8.00
5A Steve Grogan kneeling	6.00	15.00
5B Steve Grogan snap	6.00	15.00
5C Steve Grogan pass	6.00	15.00
6A Don Hasselbeck kneeling	3.00	8.00
6B Don Hasselbeck action	3.00	8.00
7A Stanley Morgan kneeling	5.00	12.00
7B Stanley Morgan action	5.00	12.00
8 Steve Nelson	3.00	8.00
9 Mike Patrick	3.00	8.00

1979 Patriots Frito Lay

The New England Patriots issued this set sponsored by Frito Lay. The cards are blankbacked, measure approximately 3 7/8" by 5 3/4", and contain black and white player photos. The cards can be distinguished from other Patriots Frito Lay issues by the notation "A WINNING TEAM" in all caps contained at the bottom of the cardfront. Each player's name is also printed below the photo with full first and last names. Any additions to the list below are appreciated.

COMPLETE SET (27)	100.00	200.00
1 Julius Adams	4.00	8.00
2 Sam Adams	4.00	8.00
3 Doug Beaudoin	4.00	8.00
4 Richard Bishop	4.00	8.00
5 Mark Buben	4.00	8.00
6 Matt Cavanaugh	5.00	10.00
7 Allan Clark	4.00	8.00
8 Ray Costict	4.00	8.00
9 Sam Cunningham	5.00	10.00
10 Russ Francis	5.00	10.00
11 Bob Golic	5.00	10.00
12 Ray Hamilton	4.00	8.00
13 John Hannah	6.00	12.00
14 Eddie Hare	4.00	8.00
15 Mike Hawkins	4.00	8.00
16 Horace Ivory	4.00	8.00
17 Harold Jackson	6.00	12.00
18 Andy Johnson	4.00	8.00
19 Shelby Jordan	4.00	8.00
20 Bill Lenkaitis	4.00	8.00
21 Bill Matthews	4.00	8.00
22 Stanley Morgan	4.00	8.00
23 Steve Nelson	4.00	8.00
24 Tom Owen	4.00	8.00
25 Carlos Pennywell	4.00	8.00
26 John Smith	4.00	8.00
27 Mosi Tatupu	4.00	8.00

1976 Pepsi Discs

The 1976 Pepsi Discs set contains 40 numbered discs, each measuring approximately 3 1/2" in diameter. Each disc has a player photo, biographical information, and 1975 statistics. Disc numbers 1-20 are from many different teams and are known as "All-Stars." Numbers 21-40 feature Cincinnati Bengals, since this set was a regional issue produced in the Cincinnati area. Numbers 1, 5, 7, 8, and 14 are much scarcer than the other 35 and are marked SP in the checklist below. Ed Marinaro also exists as a New York Jet, which is very difficult to find. It has been reported that Ed Marinaro may be a sixth SP. The checklist for the set is printed on the tab; the checklist below values the discs with the tabs intact as that is the way they are most commonly found.

COMPLETE SET (40)	75.00	150.00
1 Steve Bartkowski SP	10.00	20.00
2 Lydell Mitchell	1.25	3.00
3 Wally Chambers	1.00	2.50
4 Doug Buffone	1.00	2.50
5 Jerry Sherk SP	7.50	15.00
6 Drew Pearson	1.50	4.00
7 Otis Armstrong SP	7.50	15.00
8 Charlie Sanders SP	7.50	15.00
9 John Brockington	1.25	3.00
10 Curley Culp	1.25	3.00
11 Jan Stenerud	1.25	3.00
12 Lawrence McCutchen	1.25	3.00
13 Chuck Foreman	1.25	3.00
14 Bob Pollard SP	7.50	15.00
15 Ed Marinaro	2.00	5.00
16 Jack Lambert	4.00	8.00
17 Terry Metcalf	1.25	3.00
18 Mel Gray	1.25	3.00
19 Russ Washington	1.00	2.50
20 Charley Taylor	1.50	4.00
21 Ken Anderson	2.00	5.00
22 Bob Brown DT	1.00	2.50
23 Ron Carpenter	1.00	2.50
24 Tommy Casanova	1.00	2.50
25 Boobie Clark	1.00	2.50
26 Isaac Curtis	1.25	3.00
27 Lenvil Elliott	1.00	2.50
28 Stan Fritts	1.00	2.50
29 Vern Holland	1.00	2.50
30 Bob Johnson	1.25	3.00
31 Ken Johnson DT	1.00	2.50
32 Bill Kollar	1.00	2.50
33 Jim LeClair	1.00	2.50
34 Chip Myers	1.00	2.50
35 Lemar Parrish	1.25	3.00
36 Ron Pritchard	1.00	2.50
37 Bob Trumpy	1.25	3.00
38 Sherman White	1.00	2.50
39 Archie Griffin	1.50	4.00
40 John Shinners	1.00	2.50

1964 Philadelphia

The 1964 Philadelphia Gum set of 198 standard-size cards, featuring National Football League players, is the first of four annual issues released by the company. The cards were issued in one-card penny packs, five-card nickel packs, as well as cello packs. Each card has a question about that player in a cartoon at the bottom of the reverse; the answer is given upside down in blue ink. Each team has a team picture card as well as a card diagramming one of the team's plays; this "play card" shows a small black and white picture of the team's coach on the front of the card. The card backs are printed in blue and black on a gray card stock. Within each team group the players are arranged alphabetically by last name. The two checklist cards erroneously say "Official 1963 Checklist" at the top. The key Rookie Cards in this set are Herb Adderley, Willie Davis, Jim Johnson, John Mackey and Merlin Olsen. Tatoo Transfers sheets were included as inserts in packs.

COMPLETE SET (198)	600.00	900.00
WRAPPER (1-CENT)	35.00	60.00
WRAPPER (5-CENT)	10.00	20.00
1 Raymond Berry	10.00	20.00
2 Tom Gilburg	1.25	2.50
3 John Mackey RC	20.00	40.00
4 Gino Marchetti	2.50	5.00
5 Jim Martin	1.25	2.50
6 Tom Matte RC	3.00	6.00
7 Jimmy Orr	1.50	3.00
8 Jim Parker	2.00	4.00
9 Bill Pellington	1.25	2.50
10 Alex Sandusky	1.25	2.50
11 Dick Szymanski	1.25	2.50
12 Johnny Unitas	25.00	50.00
13 Baltimore Colts	1.50	3.00
14 Colts Play Don Shula	20.00	35.00
15 Doug Atkins	2.50	5.00
16 Ronnie Bull	1.25	2.50
17 Mike Ditka	25.00	40.00
18 Joe Fortunato	1.25	2.50
19 Willie Galimore	1.50	3.00
20 Joe Marconi	1.25	2.50
21 Bennie McRae RC	1.25	2.50
22 Johnny Morris	1.25	2.50
23 Richie Petitbon	1.25	2.50
24 Mike Pyle RC	1.25	2.50
25 Roosevelt Taylor RC	2.00	4.00
26 Bill Wade	1.50	3.00
27 Chicago Bears	1.50	3.00
28 Bears Play George Halas	6.00	12.00
29 Johnny Brewer RC	1.25	2.50
30 Jim Brown	50.00	90.00
31 Gary Collins RC	4.00	8.00
32 Vince Costello	1.25	2.50
33 Galen Fiss	1.25	2.50
34 Bill Glass	1.25	2.50
35 Ernie Green RC	1.50	3.00
36 Rich Kreitling	1.25	2.50
37 John Morrow	1.25	2.50
38 Frank Ryan	1.50	3.00
39 Charlie Scales RC	1.25	2.50
40 Dick Schafrath RC	1.25	2.50
41 Cleveland Browns	1.50	3.00
42 Cleveland Browns Play	1.25	2.50
43 Don Bishop	1.25	2.50
44 Frank Clarke RC	1.50	3.00
45 Mike Connelly	1.25	2.50
46 Lee Folkins RC	1.25	2.50
47 Cornell Green RC	4.00	8.00
48 Bob Lilly	25.00	40.00
49 Amos Marsh	1.25	2.50
50 Tommy McDonald	2.50	5.00
51 Don Meredith	20.00	35.00
52 Pettis Norman RC	1.50	3.00
53 Don Perkins	2.00	4.00
54 Guy Reese RC	1.25	2.50
55 Dallas Cowboys	2.00	4.00
56 Cowboys Play T.Landry	12.00	20.00
57 Terry Barr	1.25	2.50
58 Roger Brown	1.50	3.00
59 Gail Cogdill	1.25	2.50
60 John Gordy RC	1.25	2.50
61 Dick Lane	2.00	4.00
62 Yale Lary	2.00	4.00
63 Dan Lewis	1.25	2.50
64 Darris McCord	1.25	2.50
65 Earl Morrall	1.50	3.00
66 Joe Schmidt	2.50	5.00
67 Pat Studstill RC	1.50	3.00
68 Wayne Walker RC	1.50	3.00
69 Detroit Lions	1.50	3.00
70 Detroit Lions	1.25	2.50
71 Herb Adderley RC	20.00	35.00
72 Willie Davis RC	18.00	30.00
73 Forrest Gregg	2.50	5.00
74 Paul Hornung	20.00	35.00
75 Hank Jordan	2.50	5.00
76 Jerry Kramer	3.00	6.00
77 Tom Moore	1.50	3.00
78 Jim Ringo	2.50	5.00
79 Bart Starr	35.00	60.00
80 Jim Taylor	15.00	25.00
81 Jesse Whittenton RC	1.50	3.00
82 Willie Wood	4.00	8.00
83 Green Bay Packers	3.00	6.00
84 Packers Play Lombardi	20.00	35.00
85 Jon Arnett	1.25	2.50
86 Pervis Atkins RC	1.25	2.50
87 Dick Bass	1.50	3.00
88 Carroll Dale	2.00	4.00
89 Roman Gabriel	3.00	6.00
90 Ed Meador	1.25	2.50
91 Merlin Olsen RC	30.00	50.00
92 Jack Pardee RC	2.00	4.00
93 Jim Phillips	1.25	2.50
94 Carver Shannon RC	1.25	2.50
95 Frank Varrichione	1.25	2.50
96 Danny Villanueva	1.25	2.50
97 Los Angeles Rams	1.50	3.00
98 Los Angeles Rams Play	1.25	2.50
99 Grady Alderman RC	1.50	3.00
100 Larry Bowie RC	1.25	2.50
101 Bill Brown RC	3.00	6.00
102 Paul Flatley RC	1.25	2.50
103 Rip Hawkins	1.25	2.50
104 Jim Marshall	4.00	8.00
105 Tommy Mason	1.50	3.00
106 Jim Prestel	1.25	2.50
107 Jerry Reichow	1.25	2.50
108 Ed Sharockman	1.25	2.50
109 Fran Tarkenton	20.00	35.00
110 Mick Tingelhoff RC	3.00	6.00
111 Minnesota Vikings	1.50	3.00
112 Vikings Play Van Brock.	2.00	4.00
113 Erich Barnes	1.25	2.50
114 Roosevelt Brown	2.00	4.00
115 Don Chandler	1.25	2.50
116 Darrell Dess	1.25	2.50
117 Frank Gifford	20.00	35.00
118 Dick James	1.25	2.50

119 Jim Katcavage 1.25 2.50
120 John Lovetere RC 1.25 2.50
121 Dick Lynch RC 1.50 3.00
122 Jim Patton 1.25 2.50
123 Del Shofner 1.25 2.50
124 Y.A.Tittle 10.00 20.00
125 New York Giants 1.50 3.00
126 New York Giants Play 1.25 2.50
127 Sam Baker 1.25 2.50
128 Maxie Baughan 1.25 2.50
129 Timmy Brown 1.50 3.00
130 Mike Clark RC 1.25 2.50
131 Irv Cross RC 2.00 4.00
132 Ted Dean 1.25 2.50
133 Ron Goodwin RC 1.25 2.50
134 King Hill 1.25 2.50
135 Clarence Peaks 1.25 2.50
136 Pete Retzlaff 1.50 3.00
137 Jim Schrader 1.25 2.50
138 Norm Snead 1.50 3.00
139 Philadelphia Eagles 1.50 3.00
140 Philadelphia Eagles Play 1.25 2.50
141 Gary Ballman RC 1.25 2.50
142 Charley Bradshaw RC 1.25 2.50
143 Ed Brown 1.50 3.00
144 John Henry Johnson 2.00 4.00
145 Joe Krupa 1.25 2.50
146 Bill Mack 1.25 2.50
147 Lou Michaels 1.25 2.50
148 Buzz Nutter 1.25 2.50
149 Myron Pottios 1.25 2.50
150 John Reger 1.25 2.50
151 Mike Sandusky 1.25 2.50
152 Clendon Thomas 1.25 2.50
153 Pittsburgh Steelers 1.50 3.00
154 Pittsburgh Steelers Play 1.25 2.50
155 Kermit Alexander RC 1.50 3.00
156 Bernie Casey 1.50 3.00
157 Dan Colchico 1.25 2.50
158 Clyde Conner 1.25 2.50
159 Tommy Davis 1.25 2.50
160 Matt Hazeltine 1.25 2.50
161 Jim Johnson RC 15.00 25.00
162 Don Lisbon RC 1.25 2.50
163 Lamar McHan 1.25 2.50
164 Bob St.Clair 2.00 4.00
165 J.D. Smith 1.25 2.50
166 Abe Woodson 1.25 2.50
167 San Francisco 49ers 1.50 3.00
168 San Francisco 49ers Play 1.25 2.50
169 Garland Boyette UER RC 1.25 2.50
170 Bobby Joe Conrad 1.50 3.00
171 Bob DeMarco RC 1.25 2.50
172 Ken Gray RC 1.25 2.50
173 Jimmy Hill 1.25 2.50
174 Charley Johnson 1.50 3.00
175 Ernie McMillan 1.25 2.50
176 Dale Meinert RC 1.25 2.50
177 Luke Owens RC 1.25 2.50
178 Sonny Randle 1.25 2.50
179 Joe Robb RC 1.25 2.50
180 Bill Stacy 1.25 2.50
181 St. Louis Cardinals 1.50 3.00
182 St. Louis Cardinals Play 1.25 2.50
183 Bill Barnes 1.25 2.50
184 Don Bosseler 1.25 2.50
185 Sam Huff 3.00 6.00
186 Sonny Jurgensen 10.00 20.00
187 Bob Khayat RC 1.25 2.50
188 Riley Mattson 1.25 2.50
189 Bobby Mitchell 3.00 6.00
190 John Nisby 1.25 2.50
191 Vince Promuto 1.25 2.50
192 Joe Rutgens RC 1.25 2.50
193 Lonnie Sanders RC 1.25 2.50
194 Jim Steffen RC 1.25 2.50
195 Washington Redskins 1.50 3.00
196 Washington Redskins Play 1.25 2.50
197 Checklist 1 UER 18.00 30.00
198 Checklist 2 UER 30.00 55.00

1965 Philadelphia

The 1965 Philadelphia Gum set of NFL players consists of 198 standard-size cards. The cards were issued in five-card nickel packs and cello packs. The card fronts have the player's name, team name and position in a black box beneath the photo. The NFL logo is at bottom right. The card backs feature statistics and a question and answer section that requires a coin to rub and reveal the answer. The card backs are printed in maroon on a gray card stock. Each team has a team picture card as well as a card featuring a diagram of one of the team's plays; this play card shows a small coach's picture in black and white on the front of the card. The card backs are printed in maroon on a gray card stock. The cards are numbered within team with the players arranged alphabetically by last name. The key Rookie Cards in this set are Carl Eller, Paul Krause, Mel Renfro, Charley Taylor, and Paul Warfield. Comic Transfers sheets were included as inserts into packs.

COMPLETE SET (198) 500.00 800.00
WRAPPER (5-CENT) 10.00 20.00
1 Colts Team 7.50 15.00
2 Raymond Berry 5.00 10.00
3 Bob Boyd DB 1.00 2.00
4 Wendell Harris 1.00 2.00
5 Jerry Logan RC 1.00 2.00
6 Tony Lorick RC 1.00 2.00
7 Lou Michaels 1.00 2.00
8 Lenny Moore 4.00 8.00
9 Jimmy Orr 1.50 3.00
10 Jim Parker 2.00 4.00
11 Dick Szymanski 1.00 2.00
12 Johnny Unitas 25.00 40.00
13 Bob Vogel RC 1.00 2.00
14 Colts Play 12.00 20.00
Don Shula
15 Chicago Bears 1.50 3.00
16 Jon Arnett 1.00 2.00
17 Doug Atkins 2.50 5.00
18 Rudy Bukich RC 1.50 3.00
19 Mike Ditka 25.00 40.00
20 Dick Evey RC 1.00 2.00
21 Joe Fortunato 1.00 2.00
22 Bobby Joe Green RC 1.00 2.00
23 Johnny Morris 1.00 2.00
24 Mike Pyle 1.00 2.00
25 Roosevelt Taylor 1.50 3.00
26 Bill Wade 1.50 3.00
27 Bob Wetoska RC 1.00 2.00
28 Bears Play 4.00 8.00
George Halas
29 Cleveland Browns 1.50 3.00
30 Walter Beach RC 1.00 2.00
31 Jim Brown 50.00 80.00
32 Gary Collins 1.50 3.00
33 Bill Glass 1.00 2.00
34 Ernie Green 1.00 2.00
35 Jim Houston RC 1.00 2.00
36 Dick Modzelewski 1.00 2.00
37 Bernie Parrish 1.00 2.00
38 Walter Roberts RC 1.00 2.00
39 Frank Ryan 1.50 3.00
40 Dick Schafrath 1.00 2.00
41 Paul Warfield RC 50.00 90.00
42 Cleveland Browns 1.00 2.00
43 Dallas Cowboys 1.50 3.00
44 Frank Clarke 1.50 3.00
45 Mike Connelly 1.00 2.00
46 Buddy Dial 1.00 2.00
47 Bob Lilly 20.00 35.00
48 Tony Liscio RC 1.00 2.00
49 Tommy McDonald 2.50 5.00
50 Don Meredith 15.00 25.00
51 Pettis Norman 1.00 2.00
52 Don Perkins 2.00 4.00
53 Mel Renfro RC 35.00 50.00
54 Jim Ridlon 1.00 2.00
55 Jerry Tubbs 1.00 2.00
56 Cowboys Play 7.50 15.00
T.Landry
57 Detroit Lions 1.50 3.00
58 Terry Barr 1.00 2.00
59 Roger Brown 1.00 2.00
60 Gail Cogdill 1.00 2.00
61 Jim Gibbons 1.00 2.00
62 John Gordy 1.00 2.00
63 Yale Lary 2.00 4.00
64 Dick LeBeau RC 25.00 40.00
65 Earl Morrall 1.50 3.00
66 Nick Pietrosante 1.00 2.00
67 Pat Studstill 1.00 2.00
68 Wayne Walker 1.50 3.00
69 Tom Watkins RC 1.00 2.00
70 Detroit Lions 1.50 3.00
71 Green Bay Packers 4.00 8.00
72 Herb Adderley 4.00 8.00
73 Willie Davis DE 4.00 8.00
74 Boyd Dowler 2.00 4.00
75 Forrest Gregg 2.50 5.00
76 Paul Hornung 20.00 35.00
77 Hank Jordan 2.50 5.00
78 Tom Moore 1.50 3.00
79 Ray Nitschke 12.00 20.00
80 Elijah Pitts RC 4.00 8.00
81 Bart Starr 30.00 50.00
82 Jim Taylor 12.00 20.00
83 Willie Wood 3.00 6.00
84 Packers Play 12.00 20.00
Lombardi
85 Los Angeles Rams 1.50 3.00
86 Dick Bass 1.50 3.00
87 Roman Gabriel 2.50 5.00
88 Roosevelt Grier 2.00 4.00
89 Deacon Jones 5.00 10.00
90 Lamar Lundy RC 2.00 4.00
91 Marlin McKeever 1.00 2.00
92 Ed Meador 1.00 2.00
93 Bill Munson RC 2.00 4.00
94 Merlin Olsen 7.50 15.00
95 Bobby Smith RC 1.00 2.00
96 Frank Varrichione 1.00 2.00
97 Ben Wilson RC 1.00 2.00
98 Los Angeles Rams 1.00 2.00
99 Minnesota Vikings 1.50 3.00
100 Grady Alderman 1.00 2.00
101 Hal Bedsole RC 1.00 2.00
102 Bill Brown 1.50 3.00
103 Bill Butler RC 1.00 2.00
104 Fred Cox RC 1.50 3.00
105 Carl Eller RC 18.00 30.00
106 Paul Flatley 1.00 2.00
107 Jim Marshall 3.00 6.00
108 Tommy Mason 1.00 2.00
109 George Rose RC 1.00 2.00
110 Fran Tarkenton 15.00 25.00
111 Mick Tingelhoff 1.50 3.00
112 Vikings Play 2.00 4.00
Van Brock.
113 New York Giants 1.50 3.00
114 Erich Barnes 1.00 2.00
115 Roosevelt Brown 2.00 4.00
116 Clarence Childs RC 1.00 2.00
117 Jerry Hillebrand 1.00 2.00
118 Greg Larson RC 1.00 2.00
119 Dick Lynch 1.00 2.00
120 Joe Morrison RC 2.00 4.00
121 Lou Slaby RC 1.00 2.00
122 Aaron Thomas RC 1.00 2.00
123 Steve Thurlow RC 1.00 2.00
124 Ernie Wheelwright RC 1.00 2.00
125 Gary Wood RC 1.50 3.00
126 New York Giants 1.00 2.00
127 Philadelphia Eagles 1.50 3.00
128 Sam Baker 1.00 2.00
129 Maxie Baughan 1.00 2.00
130 Timmy Brown 1.50 3.00
131 Jack Concannon RC 1.00 2.00
132 Irv Cross 1.50 3.00
133 Earl Gros 1.00 2.00
134 Dave Lloyd RC 1.00 2.00
135 Floyd Peters RC 1.00 2.00
136 Nate Ramsey RC 1.00 2.00
137 Pete Retzlaff 1.50 3.00
138 Jim Ringo 2.00 4.00
139 Norm Snead 2.00 4.00
140 Philadelphia Eagles 1.00 2.00
141 Pittsburgh Steelers 1.50 3.00
142 John Baker 1.00 2.00
143 Gary Ballman 1.00 2.00
144 Charley Bradshaw 1.00 2.00
145 Ed Brown 1.00 2.00
146 Dick Haley 1.00 2.00
147 John Henry Johnson 2.00 4.00
148 Brady Keys RC 1.00 2.00
149 Ray Lemek 1.00 2.00
150 Ben McGee RC 1.00 2.00
151 Clarence Peaks UER 1.00 2.00
152 Myron Pottios 1.00 2.00
153 Clendon Thomas 1.00 2.00
154 Pittsburgh Steelers 1.00 2.00
155 St. Louis Cardinals 1.50 3.00
156 Jim Bakken RC 1.50 3.00
157 Joe Childress 1.00 2.00
158 Bobby Joe Conrad 1.50 3.00
159 Bob DeMarco 1.00 2.00
160 Pat Fischer RC 2.00 4.00
161 Irv Goode RC 1.00 2.00
162 Ken Gray 1.00 2.00
163 Charley Johnson 1.50 3.00
164 Bill Koman 1.00 2.00
165 Dale Meinert 1.00 2.00
166 Jerry Stovall RC 1.50 3.00
167 Abe Woodson 1.00 2.00
168 St. Louis Cardinals 1.00 2.00
169 San Francisco 49ers 1.50 3.00
170 Kermit Alexander 1.00 2.00
171 John Brodie 5.00 10.00
172 Bernie Casey 1.50 3.00
173 John David Crow 1.50 3.00
174 Tommy Davis 1.00 2.00
175 Matt Hazeltine 1.00 2.00
176 Jim Johnson 2.00 4.00
177 Charlie Krueger RC 1.00 2.00
178 Roland Lakes RC 1.00 2.00
179 George Mira RC 1.50 3.00
180 Dave Parks RC 1.50 3.00
181 John Thomas RC 1.00 2.00
182 49ers Play 1.00 2.00
Christiansen
183 Washington Redskins 1.50 3.00
184 Pervis Atkins 1.00 2.00
185 Preston Carpenter 1.00 2.00
186 Angelo Coia 1.00 2.00
187 Sam Huff 3.00 6.00
188 Sonny Jurgensen 7.50 15.00
189 Paul Krause RC 20.00 40.00
190 Jim Martin 1.00 2.00
191 Bobby Mitchell 2.50 5.00
192 John Nisby 1.00 2.00
193 John Paluck 1.00 2.00
194 Vince Promuto 1.00 2.00
195 Charley Taylor RC 30.00 50.00
196 Washington Redskins 1.00 2.00
197 Checklist 1 15.00 30.00
198 Checklist 2 UER 25.00 50.00

1966 Philadelphia

The 1966 Philadelphia Gum football card set contains 198 standard-size cards featuring NFL players. The cards were issued in five-card nickel packs which came 24 packs to a box and cello packs. The card fronts feature the player's name, team name and position in a color bar above the photo. The NFL logo is at upper left. The card backs are printed in green and black on a white card stock. The backs contain the player's name, a card number, a short biography, and a "Guess Who" quiz. The quiz answer is found on another card. The last two cards in the set are checklist cards. Each team's "play card" shows a color photo of actual game action, described on the back. The cards are numbered within team with the players arranged alphabetically by last name. The set features the debut of Hall of Fame Chicago Bears' greats Dick Butkus and Gale Sayers. Other Rookie Cards include Cowboys Bob Hayes and Chuck Howley. Comic Transfers sheets were included as inserts into packs.

COMPLETE SET (198) 600.00 900.00
WRAPPER (5-CENT) 10.00 20.00
1 Atlanta Falcons Logo 6.00 12.00
2 Larry Benz RC 1.00 2.00
3 Dennis Claridge RC 1.00 2.00
4 Perry Lee Dunn RC 1.00 2.00
5 Dan Grimm RC 1.00 2.00
6 Alex Hawkins 1.00 2.00
7 Ralph Heck RC 1.00 2.00
8 Frank Lasky RC 1.00 2.00
9 Guy Reese 1.00 2.00
10 Bob Richards RC 1.00 2.00
11 Ron Smith RC 1.00 2.00
12 Ernie Wheelwright 1.00 2.00
13 Atlanta Falcons Roster 1.50 3.00
14 Baltimore Colts Team 1.50 3.00
15 Raymond Berry 4.00 8.00
16 Bob Boyd DB 1.00 2.00
17 Jerry Logan 1.00 2.00
18 John Mackey 3.00 6.00
19 Tom Matte 2.00 4.00
20 Lou Michaels 1.00 2.00
21 Lenny Moore 4.00 8.00
22 Jimmy Orr 1.50 3.00
23 Jim Parker 2.00 4.00
24 Johnny Unitas 30.00 50.00
25 Bob Vogel 1.00 2.00
26 Colts Play 2.00 4.00
Lenny Moore
Jim Parker
27 Chicago Bears Team 1.50 3.00
28 Doug Atkins 2.00 4.00
29 Rudy Bukich 1.00 2.00
30 Ronnie Bull 1.00 2.00
31 Dick Butkus RC 150.00 250.00
32 Mike Ditka 20.00 35.00
33 Joe Fortunato 1.00 2.00
34 Bobby Joe Green 1.00 2.00
35 Roger LeClerc 1.00 2.00
36 Johnny Morris 1.00 2.00
37 Mike Pyle 1.00 2.00
38 Gale Sayers RC 125.00 225.00
39 Bears Play 20.00 35.00
Gale Sayers
40 Cleveland Browns Team 1.50 3.00
41 Jim Brown 50.00 80.00
42 Gary Collins 1.50 3.00
43 Ross Fichtner RC 1.00 2.00
44 Ernie Green 1.00 2.00
45 Gene Hickerson RC 15.00 25.00
46 Jim Houston 1.00 2.00
47 John Morrow 1.00 2.00
48 Walter Roberts 1.00 2.00
49 Frank Ryan 1.50 3.00
50 Dick Schafrath 1.00 2.00
51 Paul Wiggin RC 1.00 2.00
52 Cleveland Browns Play 1.00 2.00
53 Dallas Cowboys Team 1.50 3.00
54 George Andrie UER RC 2.00 4.00
55 Frank Clarke 1.50 3.00
56 Mike Connelly 1.00 2.00
57 Cornell Green 2.00 4.00
58 Bob Hayes RC 45.00 75.00
59 Chuck Howley RC 15.00 30.00
60 Bob Lilly 12.00 20.00
61 Don Meredith 15.00 30.00
62 Don Perkins 1.50 3.00
63 Mel Renfro 7.50 15.00
64 Danny Villanueva 1.00 2.00
65 Dallas Cowboys Play 1.00 2.00
66 Detroit Lions Team 1.50 3.00
67 Roger Brown 1.00 2.00
68 John Gordy 1.00 2.00
69 Alex Karras 5.00 10.00
70 Dick LeBeau 3.00 6.00
71 Amos Marsh 1.00 2.00
72 Milt Plum 1.50 3.00
73 Bobby Smith 1.00 2.00
74 Wayne Rasmussen RC 1.00 2.00
75 Pat Studstill 1.00 2.00
76 Wayne Walker 1.00 2.00
77 Tom Watkins 1.00 2.00
78 Detroit Lions Play 1.00 2.00
79 Green Bay Packers Team 3.00 6.00
80 Herb Adderley 3.00 6.00
81 Lee Roy Caffey RC 2.00 4.00
82 Don Chandler 1.50 3.00
83 Willie Davis DE 3.00 6.00
84 Boyd Dowler 2.00 4.00
85 Forrest Gregg 2.00 4.00
86 Tom Moore 1.50 3.00
87 Ray Nitschke 7.50 15.00
88 Bart Starr 30.00 50.00
89 Jim Taylor 12.00 20.00
90 Willie Wood 3.00 6.00
91 Green Bay Packers Play 1.00 2.00

92 Los Angeles Rams Team 1.50 3.00
93 Willie Brown RC 1.00 2.00
94 Roman Gabriel 2.00 4.00
Dick Bass
95 Bruce Gossett RC 1.50 3.00
96 Deacon Jones 3.00 6.00
97 Tommy McDonald 2.50 5.00
98 Marlin McKeever 1.00 2.00
99 Aaron Martin RC 1.00 2.00
100 Ed Meador 1.00 2.00
101 Bill Munson 1.50 3.00
102 Merlin Olsen 4.00 8.00
103 Jim Stiger RC 1.00 2.00
104 Rams Play 1.50 3.00
Willie Brown
105 Minnesota Vikings Team 1.50 3.00
106 Grady Alderman 1.00 2.00
107 Bill Brown 1.50 3.00
108 Fred Cox 1.00 2.00
109 Paul Flatley 1.00 2.00
110 Rip Hawkins 1.00 2.00
111 Tommy Mason 1.00 2.00
112 Ed Sharockman 1.00 2.00
113 Gordon Smith RC 1.00 2.00
114 Fran Tarkenton 15.00 30.00
115 Mick Tingelhoff 1.50 3.00
116 Bobby Walden RC 1.00 2.00
117 Minnesota Vikings Play 1.00 2.00
118 New York Giants Team 1.50 3.00
119 Roosevelt Brown 2.00 4.00
120 Henry Carr RC 1.50 3.00
121 Clarence Childs 1.00 2.00
122 Tucker Frederickson RC 1.50 3.00
123 Jerry Hillebrand 1.00 2.00
124 Greg Larson 1.00 2.00
125 Spider Lockhart RC 1.50 3.00
126 Dick Lynch 1.00 2.00
127 Earl Morrall 1.50 3.00
Bob Scholtz
128 Joe Morrison 1.00 2.00
129 Steve Thurlow 1.00 2.00
130 New York Giants Play 1.00 2.00
131 Philadelphia Eagles Team 1.50 3.00
132 Sam Baker 1.00 2.00
133 Maxie Baughan 1.00 2.00
134 Bob Brown OT RC 7.50 15.00
135 Timmy Brown 1.50 3.00
136 Irv Cross 1.50 3.00
137 Earl Gros 1.00 2.00
138 Ray Poage RC 1.00 2.00
139 Nate Ramsey 1.00 2.00
140 Pete Retzlaff 1.50 3.00
141 Jim Ringo 2.00 4.00
142 Norm Snead 2.00 4.00
143 Philadelphia Eagles Play 1.00 2.00
144 Pittsburgh Steelers Team 1.50 3.00
145 Gary Ballman 1.00 2.00
146 Jim Bradshaw 1.00 2.00
147 Jim Butler RC 1.00 2.00
148 Mike Clark 1.00 2.00
149 Dick Hoak RC 1.00 2.00
150 Roy Jefferson RC 1.50 3.00
151 Frank Lambert RC 1.00 2.00
152 Mike Lind RC 1.00 2.00
153 Bill Nelsen RC 2.00 4.00
154 Clarence Peaks 1.00 2.00
155 Clendon Thomas 1.00 2.00
156 Pittsburgh Steelers Play 1.00 2.00
157 St. Louis Cardinals Team 1.50 3.00
158 Jim Bakken 1.00 2.00
159 Bobby Joe Conrad 1.50 3.00
160 Willis Crenshaw RC 1.00 2.00
161 Bob DeMarco 1.00 2.00
162 Pat Fischer 1.50 3.00
163 Charley Johnson 1.50 3.00
164 Dale Meinert 1.00 2.00
165 Sonny Randle 1.00 2.00
166 Sam Silas RC 1.00 2.00
167 Bill Triplett RC 1.00 2.00
168 Larry Wilson 2.00 4.00
169 St. Louis Cardinals Play 1.00 2.00
170 San Francisco 49ers Team 1.50 3.00
171 Kermit Alexander 1.00 2.00
172 Bruce Bosley 1.00 2.00
173 John Brodie 3.00 6.00
174 Bernie Casey 1.50 3.00
175 John David Crow 2.00 4.00
176 Tommy Davis 1.00 2.00
177 Jim Johnson 2.00 4.00
178 Gary Lewis RC 1.00 2.00
179 Dave Parks 1.00 2.00
180 Walter Rock RC 1.50 3.00
181 Ken Willard RC 2.00 4.00
182 San Francisco 49ers Play 1.00 2.00
183 Washington Redskins Team 1.50 3.00
184 Rickie Harris RC 1.00 2.00
185 Sonny Jurgensen 4.00 8.00
186 Paul Krause 3.00 6.00
187 Bobby Mitchell 3.00 6.00
188 Vince Promuto 1.00 2.00
189 Pat Richter RC 1.00 2.00
190 Joe Rutgens 1.00 2.00
191 Johnny Sample 1.00 2.00
192 Lonnie Sanders 1.00 2.00
193 Jim Steffen 1.00 2.00
194 Charley Taylor 7.50 15.00
195 Washington Redskins Play 1.00 2.00
196 Referee Signals 1.50 3.00
197 Checklist 1 12.50 25.00
198 Checklist 2 UER 25.00 50.00

1967 Philadelphia

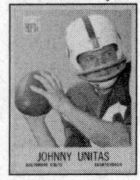

The 1967 Philadelphia Gum set of NFL players consists of 198 standard-size cards. It was the company's last issue. Cards were issued in five-card nickel packs and cello packs. This set is easily distinguished from the other Philadelphia football sets by its yellow border on the fronts of the cards. The player's name, team name and position are at the bottom in a color bar. The NFL logo is at the top right or left. Horizontally designed backs are printed in brown on a white card stock. The left side of the back contains a trivia question that requires a coin to scratch to reveal the answer. The right side has a brief write-up. The cards are numbered within team with players arranged alphabetically by last name. The key Rookie Cards in this set are Lee Roy Jordan, Leroy Kelly, Tommy Nobis, Dan Reeves and Jackie Smith.

COMPLETE SET (198) 400.00 650.00
WRAPPER (5-CENT) 10.00 20.00
1 Falcons Team 5.00 10.00
2 Junior Coffey RC 1.50 3.00
3 Alex Hawkins 1.00 2.00
4 Randy Johnson RC 1.50 3.00
5 Lou Kirouac RC 1.00 2.00
6 Billy Martin RC 1.00 2.00
7 Tommy Nobis RC 10.00 20.00
8 Jerry Richardson RC 2.00 4.00
9 Marion Rushing RC 1.00 2.00
10 Ron Smith 1.00 2.00
11 Ernie Wheelwright UER 1.00 2.00
12 Atlanta Falcons 1.00 2.00
13 Baltimore Colts 1.50 3.00
14 Raymond Berry UER 3.50 7.00
15 Bob Boyd DB 1.00 2.00
16 Ordell Braase RC 1.00 2.00
17 Alvin Haymond RC 1.00 2.00
18 Tony Lorick 1.00 2.00
19 Lenny Lyles RC 1.00 2.00
20 John Mackey 2.50 5.00
21 Tom Matte 1.50 3.00
22 Lou Michaels 1.00 2.00
23 Johnny Unitas 25.00 40.00
24 Baltimore Colts 1.00 2.00
25 Chicago Bears 1.50 3.00
26 Rudy Bukich UER 1.00 2.00
27 Ronnie Bull 1.00 2.00
28 Dick Butkus 45.00 75.00
29 Mike Ditka 18.00 30.00
30 Dick Gordon RC 1.50 3.00
31 Roger LeClerc 1.00 2.00
32 Bennie McRae 1.00 2.00
33 Richie Petitbon 1.00 2.00
34 Mike Pyle 1.00 2.00
35 Gale Sayers 45.00 75.00
36 Chicago Bears 1.00 2.00
37 Cleveland Browns 1.50 3.00
38 Johnny Brewer 1.00 2.00
39 Gary Collins 1.50 3.00
40 Ross Fichtner 1.00 2.00
41 Ernie Green 1.00 2.00
42 Gene Hickerson 2.50 5.00
43 Leroy Kelly RC 25.00 50.00
44 Frank Ryan 1.50 3.00
45 Dick Schafrath 1.00 2.00
46 Paul Warfield 10.00 18.00
47 John Wooten RC 1.00 2.00
48 Cleveland Browns 1.00 2.00
49 Dallas Cowboys 1.50 3.00
50 George Andrie 1.00 2.00
51 Cornell Green 1.50 3.00
52 Bob Hayes 10.00 20.00
53 Chuck Howley 2.00 4.00
54 Lee Roy Jordan RC 12.00 20.00
55 Bob Lilly 7.50 15.00
56 Dave Manders RC 1.00 2.00
57 Don Meredith 15.00 25.00
58 Dan Reeves RC 18.00 30.00
59 Mel Renfro 3.00 6.00
60 Dallas Cowboys 1.50 3.00
61 Detroit Lions 1.50 3.00
62 Roger Brown 1.50 3.00
63 Gail Cogdill 1.00 2.00
64 John Gordy 1.00 2.00
65 Ron Kramer 1.00 2.00
66 Dick LeBeau 2.00 4.00
67 Mike Lucci RC 2.00 4.00
68 Amos Marsh 1.00 2.00
69 Tom Nowatzke RC 1.00 2.00
70 Pat Studstill 1.00 2.00
71 Karl Sweetan RC 1.00 2.00
72 Detroit Lions 1.00 2.00
73 Green Bay Packers 2.50 5.00
74 Herb Adderley UER 3.00 6.00
75 Lee Roy Caffey 1.50 3.00
76 Willie Davis DE 2.50 5.00
77 Forrest Gregg 2.00 4.00
78 Hank Jordan 2.00 4.00
79 Ray Nitschke 6.00 12.00
80 Dave Robinson RC 18.00 30.00
81 Bob Skoronski RC 1.50 3.00
82 Bart Starr 30.00 50.00
83 Willie Wood 2.50 5.00
84 Green Bay Packers 1.50 3.00
85 Los Angeles Rams 1.50 3.00
86 Dick Bass 1.50 3.00
87 Maxie Baughan 1.00 2.00
88 Roman Gabriel 2.00 4.00
89 Bruce Gossett 1.00 2.00
90 Deacon Jones 2.50 5.00
91 Tommy McDonald 2.50 5.00
92 Marlin McKeever 1.00 2.00
93 Tom Moore 1.00 2.00
94 Merlin Olsen 3.00 6.00
95 Clancy Williams RC 1.00 2.00
96 Los Angeles Rams 1.00 2.00
97 Minnesota Vikings 1.50 3.00
98 Grady Alderman 1.00 2.00
99 Bill Brown 1.50 3.00
100 Fred Cox 1.00 2.00
101 Paul Flatley 1.00 2.00
102 Dale Hackbart RC 1.00 2.00
103 Jim Marshall 2.00 4.00
104 Tommy Mason 1.00 2.00
105 Milt Sunde RC 1.00 2.00
106 Fran Tarkenton 10.00 20.00
107 Mick Tingelhoff 1.50 3.00
108 Minnesota Vikings 1.00 2.00
109 New York Giants 1.50 3.00
110 Henry Carr 1.00 2.00
111 Clarence Childs 1.00 2.00
112 Allen Jacobs RC 1.00 2.00
113 Homer Jones RC 1.50 3.00
114 Tom Kennedy RC 1.00 2.00
115 Spider Lockhart 1.00 2.00
116 Joe Morrison 1.00 2.00
117 Francis Peay RC 1.00 2.00
118 Jeff Smith LB RC 1.00 2.00
119 Aaron Thomas 1.00 2.00
120 New York Giants 1.00 2.00
121 Saints Insignia 1.50 3.00
122 Charley Bradshaw 1.00 2.00
123 Paul Hornung 12.50 25.00
124 Elbert Kimbrough RC 1.00 2.00
125 Earl Leggett RC 1.00 2.00
126 Obert Logan RC 1.00 2.00
127 Riley Mattson 1.00 2.00
128 John Morrow 1.00 2.00
129 Bob Scholtz RC 1.00 2.00
130 Dave Whitsell RC 1.00 2.00
131 Gary Wood 1.00 2.00
132 Saints Roster UER 121 1.50 3.00
133 Philadelphia Eagles 1.50 3.00
134 Sam Baker 1.00 2.00
135 Bob Brown OT 2.00 5.00
136 Timmy Brown 1.50 3.00
137 Earl Gros 1.00 2.00
138 Dave Lloyd 1.00 2.00
139 Floyd Peters 1.00 2.00
140 Pete Retzlaff 1.50 3.00
141 Joe Scarpati RC 1.00 2.00
142 Norm Snead 1.50 3.00
143 Jim Skaggs RC 1.00 2.00
144 Philadelphia Eagles 1.00 2.00
145 Pittsburgh Steelers 1.50 3.00
146 Bill Asbury RC 1.00 2.00
147 John Baker 1.00 2.00
148 Gary Ballman 1.00 2.00
149 Mike Clark 1.00 2.00
150 Riley Gunnels 1.00 2.00
151 John Hilton RC 1.00 2.00
152 Roy Jefferson 1.50 3.00
153 Brady Keys 1.00 2.00
154 Ben McGee 1.00 2.00
155 Bill Nelsen 1.50 3.00
156 Pittsburgh Steelers 1.00 2.00
157 St. Louis Cardinals 1.50 3.00
158 Jim Bakken 1.00 2.00
159 Bobby Joe Conrad 1.50 3.00
160 Ken Gray 1.00 2.00
161 Charley Johnson 1.50 3.00
162 Joe Robb 1.00 2.00
163 Johnny Roland RC 1.50 3.00
164 Roy Shivers RC 1.00 2.00
165 Jackie Smith RC 10.00 20.00
166 Jerry Stovall 1.00 2.00
167 Larry Wilson 2.00 4.00
168 St. Louis Cardinals 1.00 2.00
169 San Francisco 49ers 1.50 3.00
170 Kermit Alexander 1.00 2.00
171 Bruce Bosley 1.00 2.00
172 John Brodie 3.00 6.00
173 Bernie Casey 1.50 3.00
174 Tommy Davis 1.00 2.00
175 Howard Mudd RC 2.00 4.00
176 Dave Parks 1.00 2.00
177 John Thomas 1.00 2.00
178 Dave Wilcox RC 12.50 25.00
179 Ken Willard 1.50 3.00
180 San Francisco 49ers 1.00 2.00
181 Washington Redskins 1.50 3.00
182 Charlie Gogolak RC 1.00 2.00
183 Chris Hanburger RC 7.50 15.00
184 Len Hauss RC 1.50 3.00
185 Sonny Jurgensen 3.50 7.00
186 Bobby Mitchell 2.50 5.00
187 Brig Owens RC 1.00 2.00
188 Jim Shorter RC 1.00 2.00
189 Jerry Smith RC 1.50 3.00
190 Charley Taylor 4.00 8.00
191 A.D. Whitfield RC 1.00 2.00
192 Washington Redskins 1.00 2.00
193 Browns Play 3.00 6.00
Leroy Kelly
194 New York Giants PC 1.00 2.00
195 Atlanta Falcons PC 1.00 2.00
196 Referee Signals 1.50 3.00
197 Checklist 1 12.00 20.00
198 Checklist 2 UER 20.00 40.00

1974 Philadelphia Bell WFL Team Issue

These photos were issued by the team for promotional purposes and fan mail requests. Each includes a black and white image printed above the subject's name and team logo. Each measures 5 1/2" by 7."

COMPLETE SET (8) 50.00 100.00
1 John Bosacco Pres. 6.00 12.00
2 Jim Corcoran 6.00 12.00
3 Richard Iannarella GM 6.00 12.00
4 J.J. Jennings 6.00 12.00
5 Ted Kwalick 6.00 12.00
6 Tim Rossovich 6.00 12.00
7 Claude Watts 6.00 12.00
8 Willie Wood 7.50 15.00

1972 Phoenix Blazers Shamrock Dairy

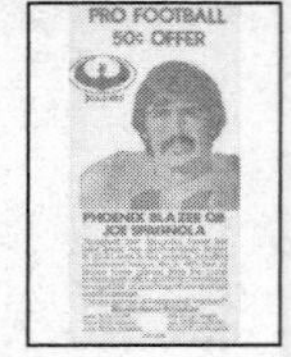

The Shamrock Dairy issued these cards on the sides of milk cartons in 1972. Each features a member of the Phoenix Blazers minor league football team and was printed in green ink. The blankbacked cards when cut cleanly to the edges of the carton measure roughly 3 3/4" by 7 1/2" and include a brief player bio and Blazers home schedule. Any additions to this list are appreicated.

1 Darby Jones 10.00 20.00
2 Joe Spagnola 10.00 20.00

1976 Popsicle Teams

This set of 28 teams is printed on plastic material similar to that found on thin credit cards. There is a variation on the New York Giants card; one version shows the helmet logo as Giants and the other shows it as New York. The title card appears to be short-printed and reads, "Pro Quarterback, Pro Football's Leading Magazine". The cards measure approximately 3 3/8" by 2 1/8", have rounded corners, and are slightly thinner than a credit card. Below the NFL logo and the team, the front features a color helmet shot and a color action photo. We've noted below prominent players that can be identified in the photos. The backs contais a brief team history. Some consider the new expansion teams, Tampa Bay and Seattle, to be somewhat tougher to find. The cards are unnumbered and are ordered below alphabetically by team location name. The set is considered complete with just the 28 team cards.

COMPLETE SET (28) 40.00 80.00
1 Atlanta Falcons 1.50 3.00
2 Baltimore Colts 1.50 3.00
3 Buffalo Bills 1.50 3.00
4 Chicago Bears 1.50 3.00
5 Cincinnati Bengals 1.50 3.00
6 Cleveland Browns 1.50 3.00
7 Dallas Cowboys 2.00 4.00
8 Denver Broncos 1.50 3.00
9 Detroit Lions 1.50 3.00
10 Green Bay Packers 1.50 3.00
11 Houston Oilers 1.50 3.00
12 Kansas City Chiefs 1.50 3.00
13 Los Angeles Rams 1.50 3.00
14 Miami Dolphins 2.00 4.00
15 Minnesota Vikings 1.50 3.00
16 New England Patriots 1.50 3.00
17 New Orleans Saints 1.50 3.00
18A New York Giants 1.50 3.00
18B New York Giants 1.50 3.00
19 New York Jets 1.50 3.00
20 Oakland Raiders 2.00 4.00
21 Philadelphia Eagles 1.50 3.00
22 Pittsburgh Steelers 2.00 4.00
23 St. Louis Cardinals 1.50 3.00
24 San Diego Chargers 1.50 3.00
25 San Francisco 49ers 2.00 4.00
26 Seattle Seahawks 1.50 3.00
27 Tampa Bay Buccaneers 1.50 3.00
28 Washington Redskins 2.00 4.00
NNO Title Card SP 15.00 30.00

1974 Portland Storm WFL Team Issue 5X7

The photos measure roughly 5" x 7 1/2" and feature black and white images with the player's name in the lower left below the photo, his position (initials) centered, and the team name on the right side below the photo. The backs are blank.

1 Dick Coury CO 6.00 12.00
2 Marv Kendricks 6.00 12.00
3 Mike Taylor 6.00 12.00
4 Tony Terry 6.00 12.00

1960 Post Cereal

These large cards measure approximately 7" by 8 3/4". The 1960 Post Cereal Sports Stars set contains nine cards depicting current baseball, football and basketball players. Each card comprised the entire back of a Grape Nuts Flakes Box and is blank backed. The color player photos are set on a colored background surrounded by a wooden frame design, and they are unnumbered (assigned numbers below for reference according to sport). The catalog designation is F278-26.

COMPLETE SET (9) 3,000.00 5,000.00
FB1 Frank Gifford 200.00 400.00
FB2 John Unitas 350.00 600.00

1962 Post Cereal

The 1962 Post Cereal set of 200 cards is Post's only American football issue. The cards were distributed on the back panels of various flavors of Post Cereals. As is typical of the Post package-back issues, the cards are blank-backed and are typically found poorly cut from the cereal box. The cards (when properly trimmed) measure 2 1/2" by 3 1/2". The cards are grouped in order of the team's 1961 season finish. The players within each team are also grouped in alphabetical order with the exception of 135 Frank Clarke of the Cowboys. Certain cards printed only on unpopular types of cereal are relatively difficult to obtain. Thirty-one such cards are known and are indicated by an SP (short printed) in the checklist. Some players who had been traded had asterisks after their positions. Jim Ninowski (57) and Sam Baker (74) can be found with either a red or black (traded) asterisk. The set price below does not include both variations. The cards of Jim Johnson, Bob Lilly, and Larry Wilson predate their Rookie Cards. Also noteworthy is the card of Fran Tarkenton, whose rookie year for cards is 1962.

COMPLETE SET (200) 2,700.00 4,500.00
1 Dan Currie 3.50 7.00
2 Boyd Dowler 3.50 7.00
3 Bill Forester 2.50 5.00
4 Forrest Gregg 4.00 8.00
5 Dave Hanner 2.50 5.00
6 Paul Hornung 10.00 20.00
7 Hank Jordan 4.00 8.00
8 Jerry Kramer SP 25.00 40.00
9 Max McGee SP 15.00 25.00
10 Tom Moore SP 125.00 200.00
11 Jim Ringo 4.00 8.00
12 Bart Starr 15.00 25.00
13 Jim Taylor 7.50 15.00
14 Fuzzy Thurston 3.50 7.00
15 Jesse Whittenton 2.00 4.00
16 Erich Barnes 2.50 5.00
17 Roosevelt Brown 3.50 7.00
18 Bob Gaiters 2.00 4.00
19 Roosevelt Grier 3.50 7.00
20 Sam Huff 5.00 10.00
21 Jim Katcavage 2.50 5.00
22 Cliff Livingston 2.00 4.00
23 Dick Lynch 2.00 4.00
24 Joe Morrison SP 35.00 60.00
25 Dick Nolan SP 30.00 50.00
26 Andy Robustelli 4.00 8.00
27 Kyle Rote 3.50 7.00
28 Del Shofner SP 60.00 100.00
29 Y.A. Tittle SP 75.00 125.00
30 Alex Webster 2.50 5.00
31 Bill Barnes 2.00 4.00
32 Maxie Baughan 2.50 5.00
33 Chuck Bednarik 5.00 10.00
34 Tom Brookshier 3.50 7.00
35 Jimmy Carr 2.00 4.00
36 Ted Dean SP 30.00 50.00
37 Sonny Jurgensen 7.50 15.00
38 Tommy McDonald 3.50 7.00
39 Clarence Peaks 2.00 4.00
40 Pete Retzlaff 2.50 5.00
41 Jesse Richardson SP 50.00 100.00
42 Leo Sugar 2.00 4.00
43 Bobby Walston SP 35.00 70.00
44 Chuck Weber 5.00 10.00
45 Ed Khayat 2.00 4.00
46 Howard Cassady 2.50 5.00
47 Gail Cogdill 2.00 4.00
48 Jim Gibbons SP 25.00 50.00
49 Bill Glass 2.00 4.00
50 Alex Karras 5.00 10.00
51 Dick Lane 3.50 7.00
52 Yale Lary 3.50 7.00
53 Dan Lewis 2.00 4.00
54 Darris McCord SP 40.00 80.00
55 Jim Martin 2.00 4.00
56 Earl Morrall 2.50 5.00
57A Jim Ninowski (red*) 2.50 5.00
57B Jim Ninowski (blk*) 2.50 5.00
58 Nick Pietrosante 2.50 5.00
59 Joe Schmidt SP 60.00 100.00
60 Harley Sewell 2.00 4.00
61 Jim Brown 40.00 75.00
62 Galen Fiss SP 35.00 60.00
63 Bob Gain 2.00 4.00
64 Jim Houston 2.00 4.00
65 Mike McCormack 3.50 7.00
66 Gene Hickerson 5.00 10.00
67 Bobby Mitchell 4.00 8.00
68 John Morrow 2.00 4.00
69 Bernie Parrish 2.00 4.00
70 Milt Plum 2.50 5.00
71 Ray Renfro 2.50 5.00
72 Dick Schafrath 2.50 5.00
73 Jim Ray Smith 2.00 4.00
74A Sam Baker SP red* 200.00 350.00
74B Sam Baker SP blk* 175.00 300.00
75 Paul Wiggin SP 15.00 30.00
76 Raymond Berry 5.00 10.00
77 Bob Boyd DB 2.00 4.00
78 Ordell Braase 2.00 4.00
79 Art Donovan 5.00 10.00
80 Dee Mackey 2.00 4.00
81 Gino Marchetti 4.00 8.00
82 Lenny Moore 5.00 10.00
83 Jim Mutscheller 2.00 4.00
84 Steve Myhra 2.00 4.00
85 Jimmy Orr 2.50 5.00
86 Jim Parker 4.00 8.00
87 Bill Pellington 2.00 4.00
88 Alex Sandusky 2.00 4.00
89 Dick Szymanski 2.00 4.00
90 Johnny Unitas 15.00 30.00
91 Bruce Bosley 2.00 4.00
92 John Brodie 6.00 12.00
93 Dave Baker SP 250.00 450.00
94 Tommy Davis 2.00 4.00
95 Bob Harrison 2.00 4.00
96 Matt Hazeltine 2.00 4.00
97 Jim Johnson SP 35.00 70.00
98 Billy Kilmer 3.50 7.00
99 Jerry Mertens 2.00 4.00
100 Frank Morze 2.00 4.00
101 R.C. Owens 2.50 5.00
102 J.D. Smith 2.00 4.00
103 Bob St. Clair SP 45.00 80.00
104 Monty Stickles 2.00 4.00
105 Abe Woodson 2.00 4.00
106 Doug Atkins 4.00 8.00
107 Ed Brown 2.50 5.00
108 J.C. Caroline 2.00 4.00
109 Rick Casares 2.50 5.00
110 Angelo Coia SP 150.00 250.00
111 Mike Ditka SP 75.00 125.00
112 Joe Fortunato 2.00 4.00
113 Willie Galimore 2.50 5.00
114 Bill George 3.50 7.00
115 Stan Jones 3.50 7.00
116 Johnny Morris 2.50 5.00
117 Larry Morris SP 35.00 60.00
118 Richie Petitbon 2.50 5.00
119 Bill Wade 2.50 5.00
120 Maury Youmans 2.00 4.00
121 Preston Carpenter 2.00 4.00
122 Buddy Dial 2.50 5.00
123 Bobby Joe Green 2.00 4.00
124 Mike Henry 2.00 4.00
125 John Henry Johnson 4.00 8.00
126 Bobby Layne 10.00 20.00
127 Gene Lipscomb 3.50 7.00
128 Lou Michaels 2.50 5.00
129 John Nisby 2.00 4.00
130 John Reger 2.00 4.00
131 Mike Sandusky 2.00 4.00
132 George Tarasovic 2.00 4.00
133 Tom Tracy SP 70.00 110.00
134 Glynn Gregory 2.00 4.00
135 Frank Clarke SP 45.00 80.00
136 Mike Connelly SP 35.00 70.00
137 L.G. Dupre 2.00 4.00
138 Bob Fry 2.00 4.00
139 Allen Green SP 75.00 125.00
140 Billy Howton 2.50 5.00
141 Bob Lilly 25.00 40.00
142 Don Meredith 20.00 35.00
143 Dick Moegle 2.00 4.00
144 Don Perkins 3.50 7.00
145 Jerry Tubbs SP 75.00 125.00
146 J.W. Lockett 2.00 4.00
147 Ed Cook 2.00 4.00
148 John David Crow 2.50 5.00
149 Sam Etcheverry 2.00 4.00
150 Frank Fuller 2.00 4.00
151 Prentice Gautt 2.00 4.00
152 Jimmy Hill 2.00 4.00
153 Bill Koman SP 30.00 50.00
154 Larry Wilson 7.50 15.00
155 Dale Meinert 2.00 4.00
156 Ed Henke 2.00 4.00
157 Sonny Randle 2.00 4.00
158 Ralph Guglielmi SP 30.00 50.00
159 Joe Childress 2.00 4.00
160 Jon Arnett 2.50 5.00
161 Dick Bass 2.00 4.00
162 Zeke Bratkowski 2.50 5.00
163 Carroll Dale SP 25.00 40.00
164 Art Hunter 2.00 4.00
165 John Lovetere 2.00 4.00
166 Lamar Lundy 2.50 5.00
167 Ollie Matson 5.00 10.00
168 Ed Meador 2.00 4.00
169 Jack Pardee SP 45.00 80.00
170 Jim Phillips 2.00 4.00
171 Les Richter 2.50 5.00
172 Frank Ryan 2.50 5.00
173 Frank Varrichione 2.00 4.00
174 Grady Alderman 2.50 5.00
175 Rip Hawkins 2.00 4.00
176 Don Joyce SP 75.00 125.00
177 Bill Lapham 2.00 4.00
178 Tommy Mason 2.50 5.00
179 Hugh McElhenny 5.00 10.00
180 Dave Middleton 2.00 4.00
181 Dick Pesonen SP 20.00 35.00
182 Karl Rubke 2.00 4.00
183 George Shaw 2.00 4.00
184 Fran Tarkenton 30.00 50.00
185 Mel Triplett 2.00 4.00
186 Frank Youso SP 60.00 100.00
187 Bill Bishop 2.50 5.00
188 Bill Anderson SP 40.00 75.00
189 Don Bosseler 2.00 4.00
190 Fred Hageman 2.00 4.00
191 Sam Horner 2.00 4.00
192 Jim Kerr 2.00 4.00
193 Joe Krakoski SP 150.00 250.00
194 Fred Dugan 2.00 4.00
195 John Paluck 2.00 4.00
196 Vince Promuto 2.00 4.00
197 Joe Rutgens 2.00 4.00
198 Norm Snead 3.50 7.00
199 Andy Stynchula 2.00 4.00
200 Bob Toneff 2.00 4.00

1962 Post Booklets

Each of these booklets measures approximately 5" by 3" and contained fifteen pages. The front cover carries the title of each booklet and a color cartoon headshot of the player inside a circle. While the first page presents biography and career summary, the remainder of each booklet consists of various tips, diagrams of basic formations and plays, officials' signals, football lingo, statistics, or team standings. The booklets are illustrated throughout by crude color drawings. These booklets are numbered on the front page in the upper right corner.

COMPLETE SET (4) 75.00 150.00
1 Jon Arnett 15.00 30.00
2 Paul Hornung 25.00 50.00
3 Sonny Jurgensen 20.00 40.00
4 Sam Huff 20.00 40.00

1926 Pottsville Maroons Postcards

1 Heinie Benkert 600.00 1,000.00
2 Charlie Berry 1,250.00 2,000.00
3 Jesse Brown 600.00 1,000.00
4 Frank Bucher 600.00 1,000.00
5 Jack Ernst 800.00 1,200.00
6 Hoot Flanagan 800.00 1,200.00
7 Russ Hathaway 600.00 1,000.00
8 Heinie Jawish 600.00 1,000.00
9 George Kenneally 600.00 1,000.00
10 Tony Latone 900.00 1,500.00
11 Bob Millman 600.00 1,000.00
12 Duke Osborn 800.00 1,200.00
13 Frank Racis 600.00 1,000.00
14 Herb Stein 800.00 1,200.00
15 Jim Welsh 600.00 1,000.00
16 Barney Wentz 800.00 1,200.00
17 Zeke Wissinger 600.00 1,000.00
18 Frank Youngfleish 600.00 1,000.00

1977 Pottsville Maroons 1925

Reportedly issued in 1977, this standard-size 17-card set features helmetless player photos of the disputed 1925 NFL champion Pottsville Maroons on the card fronts. The pictures are white-bordered and red-screened, with the player's name, card number, and team name in red beneath each photo. The player's name, team, and card number appear again at the top of the card back, along with the name of the college (if any) attended previous to playing for the Maroons and brief biographical information, all in red. The set producer's name, Joseph C. Zacko Sr., appears at the bottom, along with the copyright date, 1977.

COMPLETE SET (17) 10.00 20.00
1 Team History .75 2.00
2 The Symbolic Shoe .75 1.50
3 Jack Ernst .75 2.00
4 Tony Latone .75 1.50
5 Duke Osborn .75 1.50
6 Frank Bucher .75 1.50
7 Frankie Racis .75 1.50
8 Russ Hathaway .75 1.50
9 W.H.(Hoot) Flanagan .75 1.50
10 Charlie Berry 1.00 2.00
11 Russ Stein .75 1.50
12 Howard Lebengood .75 1.50
13 Denny Hughes .75 1.50
14 Barney Wentz .75 1.50
15 Eddie Doyle UER .75 1.50
16 Walter French .75 1.50
17 Dick Rauch .75 2.00

1950 Prest-o-Lite Postcards

These postcards were issued to promote the "Prest-O-Lite" batteries. The front contains an action photo of the star while the back has a promotion for those batteries. There might be more photos so any additions are appreiciated.

1 Leon Hart 12.50 25.00

1954 Quaker Sports Oddities

This 27-card set features strange moments in sports and was issued as an insert inside Quaker Puffed Rice cereal boxes. Fronts of the cards are drawings depicting the person or the event. In a stripe at the top of the card face appear the words "Sports Oddities." Two colorful drawings fill the remaining space: the left half is a portrait, while the right half is action-oriented. A variety of sports are included. The cards measure approximately 2 1/4" by 3 1/2" and have rounded corners. The last line on the back of each card declares, "It's Odd but True." A person could also buy the complete set for fifteen cents and two box tops from Quaker Puffed Wheat or Quaker Rice. If a collector did send in their material to Quaker Oats the set came back in a specially marked box with the cards in cellophane wrapping. Sets in original wrapping are valued at 1.25x to 1.5X the high column listings in our checklist.

COMPLETE SET (27) 125.00 250.00
1 Johnny Miller 3.00 6.00
6 Wake Forest College 3.00 6.00
7 Amos Alonzo Stagg 12.50 25.00
19 George Halas 15.00 30.00
25 Texas University Northwestern 3.00 6.00
26 Bronko Nagurski 30.00 60.00

1935 R311-2 National Chicle Premiums

The R311-2 (as referenced in the American Card Catalog) Football Stars and Scenes set consists of 17 glossy, unnumbered, 6" by 8" photos. Both professional and collegiate players are pictured on these photos. These blank-back photos have been numbered in the checklist below alphabetically by the player's name or title. These premium photos were available from National Chicle with one premium given for every 20 wrappers turned in to the retailer.

COMPLETE SET (17) 3,000.00 4,500.00
1 Joe Bach SP 350.00 500.00
2 Eddie Casey 150.00 250.00
3 George Christensen SP 350.00 500.00
4 Red Grange 400.00 750.00
5 Stan Kostka 125.00 200.00
6 Joe Maniaci SP 200.00 350.00
7 Harry Newman 125.00 200.00
8 Walter Switzer 125.00 200.00
9 Chicago Bears Team 250.00 400.00
10 New York Giants Team 200.00 350.00
11 Bill Shakespeare punting 175.00 300.00
12 Pittsburgh U. in Rough 125.00 200.00
13 Pittsburgh Pirates 175.00 300.00
14 S.L. Morton 125.00 200.00
15 Dixie Howell 150.00 250.00
16 Cotton Warburton 150.00 250.00
17 A.Gutowsky/S.Hokuf 150.00 250.00

1962 Raiders Team Issue

The Raiders likely released these photos over a number of seasons. Each measures approximately 8" by 10" and includes a black and white photo on the cardfront with a blank cardback. The team name, player's name, and position (abbreviated) appear below the photo from left to right. The checklist is thought to be incomplete. Any additions to this list are appreciated.

COMPLETE SET (4) 35.00 60.00
1 Clem Daniels 10.00 20.00
2 Wayne Hawkins 10.00 20.00
3 Jon Jelacic 7.50 15.00
4 Chuck McMurtry 7.50 15.00
5 Pete Nicklas 7.50 15.00

1964 Raiders Team Issue

The Raiders likely released these photos over a number of seasons. Each measures approximately 8" by 10" and includes a black and white photo on the front with a blank back. The player's name, position (spelled out in full) and team name appear below the photo. The text style and size varies slightly from photo to photo and the checklist is thought to be incomplete. Any additions to this list are appreciated.

COMPLETE SET (19) 150.00 250.00
1 Bill Budness 7.50 15.00
2 Billy Cannon 12.50 25.00
3 Clem Daniels 10.00 20.00
4 Ben Davidson 12.50 25.00
5 Cotton Davidson 10.00 20.00
6 Claude Gibson 7.50 15.00
7 Wayne Hawkins 10.00 20.00
8 Ken Herock 7.50 15.00
9 Jon Jelacic 7.50 15.00
10 Dick Klein 7.50 15.00
11 Joe Krakoski 7.50 15.00

12 Mike Mercer	7.50	15.00
13 Tommy Morrow	7.50	15.00
14 Clancy Osborne	7.50	15.00
15 Jim Otto	20.00	35.00
16 Art Powell	10.00	20.00
17 Ken Rice	7.50	15.00
18 Bo Roberson	7.50	15.00
19 Howie Williams	7.50	15.00

1968 Raiders Team Issue

The Raiders likely released these photos over a number of seasons. Each measures approximately 8" by 10 1/4" to 8 1/2" by 10 1/2" in size and includes a black and white photo on the cardfront with a blank cardback. All of the photos were taken outdoors with a rolling hillside in the far background. The player's name, position initials and team name appear below the photo. The text style and size varies slightly from photo to photo. The 1969 issue looks very similar to this set, but it was printed on slightly thicker, larger, and slightly less glossy paper stock than this 1968 release. Any additions to this list are appreciated.

COMPLETE SET (34)	200.00	400.00
1 Fred Biletnikoff	12.50	25.00
2 Dan Birdwell	6.00	12.00
3 Bill Budness	6.00	12.00
4 Billy Cannon	7.50	15.00
5 Dan Conners	6.00	12.00
6 Ben Davidson (portrait holding helmet)	7.50	15.00
7 Cotton Davidson	6.00	12.00
8 Eldridge Dickey	6.00	12.00
9A Hewritt Dixon	6.00	12.00
9B Hewritt Dixon (position omitted)	6.00	12.00
10 John Eason	6.00	12.00
11 Mike Eischeid	6.00	12.00
12 Dave Grayson	6.00	12.00
13 Roger Hagberg	6.00	12.00
14 James Harvey	6.00	12.00
15 Wayne Hawkins	6.00	12.00
16 Tom Keating	6.00	12.00
17 Bob Kruse	6.00	12.00
18A Daryle Lamonica	10.00	20.00
18B Daryle Lamonica (passing pose)	10.00	20.00
19 Ike Lassiter	6.00	12.00
20 Marv Marinovich (portrait)	6.00	12.00
21 Kent McCloughan	6.00	12.00
22 Bill Miller	6.00	12.00
23 Carleton Oats	6.00	12.00
24 Gus Otto	6.00	12.00
25 Jim Otto	10.00	20.00
26 Warren Powers	6.00	12.00
27 John Rauch CO	6.00	12.00
28A Harry Schuh (position is OT)	6.00	12.00
28B Harry Schuh (position omitted)	6.00	12.00
29 Art Shell	15.00	30.00
30 Charlie Smith	6.00	12.00
31 Bob Svihus	6.00	12.00
32 Larry Todd	6.00	12.00
33 Warren Wells	6.00	12.00
34 Howie Williams	6.00	12.00

1969 Raiders Team Issue

The Raiders issued these photos shrink wrapped in a package of 8 defensive or offensive players along with a small paper checklist. Each measures approximately 8 1/2" by 10 3/8" and includes a black and white photo on the cardfront with a blank cardback. The player's name, position initials (except Dave Grayson) and team name appear below the photo. The text style and size and some of the photos are nearly identical to the 1968 listing. This issue was printed on thicker, slightly less glossy, paper stock than the 1968 photos along with difference in size.

COMPLETE SET (8)	100.00	200.00
1 George Atkinson	6.00	12.00
2 Fred Biletnikoff	12.50	25.00
3 Willie Brown	10.00	20.00
4 Dan Conners	6.00	12.00
5 Ben Davidson	7.50	15.00
6 Hewritt Dixon	7.50	15.00
7 Dave Grayson	6.00	12.00
8 Tom Keating	6.00	12.00
9 Daryle Lamonica	10.00	20.00
10 Carleton Oats	6.00	12.00
11 Gus Otto	6.00	12.00
12 Jim Otto	10.00	20.00
13 Harry Schuh	6.00	12.00
14 Charlie Smith	6.00	12.00
15 Gene Upshaw	10.00	20.00
16 Warren Wells	6.00	12.00

1950 Rams Admiral

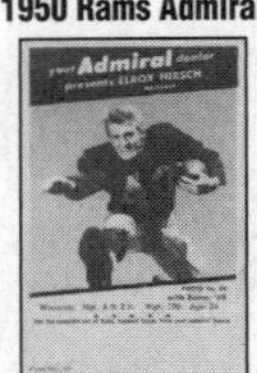

This 35-card set was sponsored by Admiral Televisions and features cards measuring approximately 3 1/2" by 5 1/2" (#1-25) and 3 1/8" by 5 3/8" (#26-35). The front design has a black and white action pose of the player, without borders on the sides of the picture. The words "Your Admiral dealer presents" followed by the player's name and position appear in the black stripe at the top of each card. A black border separates the bottom of the picture from the biographical information below. In a horizontal format, the backs are blank on the right half, and have a season schedule as well as Admiral advertisements on the left half (#1-25) or are blankbacked (#26-35). The cards are numbered on the front underneath the photos. Norm Van Brocklin appears in his Rookie Card year.

COMPLETE SET (35)	4,000.00	7,000.00
1 Joe Stydahar CO	125.00	200.00
2 Hampton Pool CO	100.00	175.00
3 Fred Naumetz	100.00	175.00
4 Jack Finlay	100.00	175.00
5 Gil Bouley	100.00	175.00
6 Bob Reinhard	100.00	175.00
7 Bob Boyd	100.00	175.00
8 Bob Waterfield	300.00	500.00
9 Mel Hein CO	125.00	200.00
10 Howard(Red) Hickey CO	100.00	175.00
11 Ralph Pasquariello	100.00	175.00
12 Jack Zilly	100.00	175.00
13 Tom Kalmanir	100.00	175.00
14 Norm Van Brocklin	400.00	750.00
15 Woodley Lewis	100.00	175.00
16 Glenn Davis	150.00	250.00
17 Dick Hoerner	100.00	175.00
18 Bob Kelley ANN	100.00	175.00
19 Paul (Tank) Younger	125.00	200.00
20 George Sims	100.00	175.00
21 Dick Huffman	100.00	175.00
22 Tom Fears	175.00	300.00
23 Vitamin T. Smith	100.00	175.00
24 Elroy Hirsch	350.00	600.00
25 Don Paul	100.00	175.00
26 Bill Lange	100.00	175.00
27 Paul Barry	100.00	175.00
28 Deacon Dan Towler	125.00	200.00
29 Vic Vasicek	100.00	175.00
30 Bill Smyth	100.00	175.00
31 Larry Brink	100.00	175.00
32 Jerry Williams	100.00	175.00
33 Stan West	100.00	175.00
34 Art Statuto	100.00	175.00
35 Ed Champagne	100.00	175.00

1950 Rams Matchbooks

These matchbook covers were produced by Universal Match Corporation around 1950 and feature members of the Los Angeles Rams. Each cover features a blue border and yellow-tinted player photo along with the Rams team logo. The inside or "back" of the covers is blank. Any additions to the list below are appreciated.

1 Bob Waterfield	20.00	40.00

1953 Rams Team Issue

This 36-card unnumbered set measures approximately 4 1/4" by 6 3/8" and was issued by the Los Angeles Rams for their fans. This set has black borders on the front framing posed action shots with the player's signature across the bottom portion of the picture. Biographical information on the back relating to the player pictured listing the player's name, height, weight, age, and college is also included. Among the interesting cards in this set are early cards of Dick "Night-Train" Lane and Andy Robustelli. The cards were available directly from the team as a complete set. We have checklisted this set in alphabetical order. Many cards from the 1953-1955 and 1957 Rams Team Issue Black Border sets are identical except for text differences on the card backs. Player stat lines are also helpful in identifying year of issue; the year of issue is typically the next year after the last year on the stats. The first few words of the first line of text is listed for players without stat lines.

COMPLETE SET (36)	250.00	400.00
1 Ben Agajanian	5.00	8.00
2 Bob Boyd	5.00	8.00
3 Larry Brink	5.00	8.00
4 Rudy Bukich	5.00	8.00
5 Tom Dahms	5.00	8.00
6 Dick Daugherty	5.00	8.00
7 Jack Dwyer	5.00	8.00
8 Tom Fears	15.00	30.00
9 Bob Fry	5.00	8.00
10 Frank Fuller	5.00	8.00
11 Norbert Hecker	5.00	8.00
12 Elroy Hirsch	25.00	40.00
13 John Hock	5.00	8.00
14 Bob Kelley ANN	5.00	8.00
15 Dick Lane	15.00	30.00
16 Woodley Lewis	5.00	8.00
17 Tom McCormick	5.00	8.00
18 Lewis(Bud) McFadin	5.00	8.00
19 Leon McLaughlin	5.00	8.00
20 Brad Myers	5.00	8.00
21 Don Paul LB	5.00	8.00
22 Hampton Pool CO	5.00	8.00
23 Duane Putnam	5.00	8.00
24 Volney Quinlan	5.00	8.00
25 Herb Rich	5.00	8.00
26 Andy Robustelli	20.00	35.00
27 Vitamin T. Smith	5.00	8.00
28 Harland Svare	5.00	8.00
29 Len Teeuws	5.00	8.00
30 Harry Thompson	5.00	8.00
31 Charley Toogood	5.00	8.00
32 Deacon Dan Towler	6.00	10.00
33 Norm Van Brocklin	35.00	60.00
34 Stan West	5.00	8.00
35 Paul(Tank) Younger	6.00	10.00
36 Coaches: John Sauer&	5.00	8.00

1953-54 Rams Burgermeister Beer Team Photos

These oversized (roughly 6 1/4" by 9") color team photos were sponsored by Burgermeister Beer and distributed in the Los Angeles area. Each were printed on card stock and included advertising messages on the back.

1953 Los Angeles Rams	35.00	60.00
1954 Los Angeles Rams	35.00	60.00

1954 Rams Team Issue

This 36-card set measures approximately 4 1/4" by 6 3/8". The front features a black and white posed action photo enclosed by a black border, with the player's signature across the bottom portion of the picture. The back lists the player's name, height, weight, age, and college, along with basic biographical information. The set was available direct from the team as part of a package for their fans. The cards are listed alphabetically below since they are unnumbered. Many cards from the 1953-1955 and 1957 Rams Team Issue Black Border sets are identical except for text differences on the card backs. Player stat lines are also helpful in identifying year of issue; the year of issue is typically the next year after the last year on the stats. The first few words of the first line of text is listed for players without stat lines. The set features the first card appearance of Gene "Big Daddy" Lipscomb.

COMPLETE SET (36)	200.00	400.00
1 Bob Boyd	4.00	8.00
2 Bob Carey	4.00	8.00
3 Bobby Cross	4.00	8.00
4 Tom Dahms	4.00	8.00
5 Don Doll	4.00	8.00
6 Jack Dwyer	4.00	8.00
7 Tom Fears	12.50	25.00
8 Bob Griffin	4.00	8.00
9 Art Hauser	4.00	8.00
10 Hall Haynes	4.00	8.00
11 Elroy Hirsch	20.00	35.00
12 Ed Hughes	4.00	8.00
13 Bob Kelley ANN	4.00	8.00
14 Woodley Lewis	4.00	8.00
15 Gene Lipscomb	10.00	20.00
16 Tom McCormick	4.00	8.00
17 Bud McFadin	4.00	8.00
18 Leon McLaughlin	4.00	8.00
19 Paul Miller	4.00	8.00
20 Don Paul LB	4.00	8.00
21 Hampton Pool CO	4.00	8.00
22 Duane Putnam	4.00	8.00
23 Volney Quinlan	4.00	8.00
24 Les Richter	4.00	8.00
25 Andy Robustelli	12.50	25.00
26 Willard Sherman	4.00	8.00
27 Harland Svare	4.00	8.00
28 Harry Thompson	4.00	8.00
29 Charley Toogood	4.00	8.00
30 Deacon Dan Towler	5.00	10.00
31 Norm Van Brocklin	25.00	50.00
32 Bill Wade	7.50	15.00
33 Duane Wardlow	4.00	8.00
34 Stan West	4.00	8.00
35 Paul(Tank) Younger	5.00	10.00
36 Coaches Card	4.00	8.00

1955 Rams Team Issue

This 37-card set measures approximately 4 1/4" by 6 3/8". The front features a black and white posed action photo enclosed by a black border, with the player's signature across the bottom portion of the picture. The back lists the player's name, height, weight, age, and college, along with basic biographical information. The set was available direct from the team as part of a package for their fans. The cards are listed alphabetically below since they are unnumbered. Many cards from the 1953-1955 and 1957 Rams Team Issue Black Border sets are identical except for text differences on the card backs. Player stat lines are also helpful in identifying year of issue; the year of issue is typically the next year after the last year on the stats. The first few words of the first line of text is listed for players without stat lines.

COMPLETE SET (37)	200.00	325.00
1 Jack Bighead	4.00	8.00
2 Bob Boyd	4.00	8.00
3 Don Burroughs	4.00	8.00
4 Jim Cason	4.00	8.00
5 Bobby Cross	4.00	8.00
6 Jack Ellena	4.00	8.00
7 Tom Fears	7.50	15.00
8 Sid Fournet	4.00	8.00
9 Frank Fuller	4.00	8.00
10 Sid Gillman and staff	6.00	12.00
11 Bob Griffin	4.00	8.00
12 Art Hauser	4.00	8.00
13 Hall Haynes	4.00	8.00
14 Elroy Hirsch	15.00	30.00
15 John Hock	4.00	8.00
16 Glenn Holtzman	4.00	8.00
17 Ed Hughes	4.00	8.00
18 Woodley Lewis	4.00	8.00
19 Gene Lipscomb	7.50	15.00
20 Tom McCormick	4.00	8.00
21 Bud McFadin	4.00	8.00
22 Leon McLaughlin	4.00	8.00
23 Paul Miller	4.00	8.00
24 Larry Morris	4.00	8.00
25 Don Paul LB	4.00	8.00
26 Duane Putnam	4.00	8.00
27 Volney Quinlan	4.00	8.00
28 Les Richter	4.00	8.00
29 Andy Robustelli	7.50	15.00
30 Willard Sherman	4.00	8.00
31 Corky Taylor	4.00	8.00
32 Charley Toogood	4.00	8.00
33 Deacon Dan Towler	5.00	10.00
34 Norm Van Brocklin	20.00	40.00
35 Bill Wade	6.00	12.00
36 Ron Waller	4.00	8.00
37 Paul(Tank) Younger	5.00	10.00

1956 Rams Team Issue

This 37-card team-issued set measures approximately 4 1/4" by 6 3/8" and features members of the Los Angeles Rams. The set has posed action shots on the front framed by a white border with the player's signature across the picture, while the back has biographical information about the player listing the player's name, height, weight, age, number of years in NFL, and college. We have checklisted this (unnumbered) set in alphabetical order. The set was initially available for fans direct from the team for $1.

COMPLETE SET (37)	150.00	300.00
1 Bob Boyd	4.00	8.00
2 Rudy Bukich	4.00	8.00
3 Don Burroughs	4.00	8.00
4 Jim Cason	4.00	8.00
5 Leon Clarke	4.00	8.00
6 Dick Daugherty	4.00	8.00
7 Jack Ellena	4.00	8.00
8 Tom Fears	7.50	15.00
9 Sid Fournet	4.00	8.00
10 Bob Fry	4.00	8.00
11 Coaches	6.00	12.00
12 Bob Griffin	4.00	8.00
13 Art Hauser	4.00	8.00
14 Elroy Hirsch	12.50	25.00
15 John Hock	4.00	8.00
16 Bob Holladay	4.00	8.00
17 Glenn Holtzman	4.00	8.00
18 Bob Kelley ANN	4.00	8.00
19 Joe Marconi	4.00	8.00
20 Bud McFadin	4.00	8.00
21 Paul Miller	4.00	8.00
22 Ron Miller DE	4.00	8.00
23 Larry Morris	4.00	8.00
24 John Morrow	4.00	8.00
25 Brad Myers	4.00	8.00
26 Hugh Pitts	4.00	8.00
27 Duane Putnam	4.00	8.00
28 Les Richter	4.00	8.00
29 Willard Sherman	4.00	8.00
30 Charley Toogood	4.00	8.00
31 Norm Van Brocklin	17.50	35.00
32 Bill Wade	6.00	12.00
33 Ron Waller	4.00	8.00
34 Duane Wardlow	4.00	8.00
35 Jesse Whittenton	4.00	8.00
36 Tom Wilson	4.00	8.00
37 Paul(Tank) Younger	5.00	10.00

1957-61 Rams Falstaff Beer Team Photos

These oversized (roughly 6 1/4" by 9") color team photos were sponsored by Falstaff Beer and distributed in the Los Angeles area. Each was printed on card stock and included advertising and/or photos of the team's coaching staff on the back.

1957 Rams Team	30.00	50.00
1958 Rams Team	30.00	50.00
1959 Rams Team	30.00	50.00
1960 Rams Team	25.00	40.00
1961 Rams Team	25.00	40.00

1957 Rams Team Issue

This 38-card team-issued set measures approximately 4 1/4" by 6 3/8" and features posed action shots on the front surrounded by black borders with the player's signature across the picture. The card backs contain biographical information about the player listing the player's name, height, weight, age, number of years in NFL, and college. We have checklisted this (unnumbered) set in alphabetical order. The set was available direct from the team as part of a package for their fans. Many cards from the 1953-1955 and 1957 Rams Team Issue Black Border sets are identical except for text differences on the card backs. Player stat lines are also helpful in identifying year of issue; the year of issue is typically the next year after the last year on the stats. The first few words of the first line of text is listed for players without stat lines. The set features the first card appearance of Jack Pardee.

COMPLETE SET (38)	150.00	300.00
1 Jon Arnett	5.00	10.00
2 Bob Boyd	4.00	8.00
3 Alex Bravo	4.00	8.00
4 Bill Brundige ANN	4.00	8.00
5 Don Burroughs	4.00	8.00
6 Jerry Castete	4.00	8.00
7 Leon Clarke	4.00	8.00
8 Paige Cothren	4.00	8.00
9 Dick Daugherty	4.00	8.00
10 Bob Dougherty	4.00	8.00
11 Bob Fry	4.00	8.00
12 Frank Fuller	4.00	8.00
13 Coaches: Sid Gillman	12.50	25.00
14 Bob Griffin	4.00	8.00
15 Art Hauser	4.00	8.00
16 Elroy Hirsch	12.50	25.00
17 John Hock	4.00	8.00
18 Glenn Holtzman	4.00	8.00
19 John Houser	4.00	8.00
20 Bob Kelley ANN	4.00	8.00
21 Lamar Lundy	5.00	10.00
22 Joe Marconi	4.00	8.00
23 Paul Miller	4.00	8.00
24 Larry Morris	4.00	8.00
25 Ken Panfil	4.00	8.00
26 Jack Pardee	6.00	12.00
27 Duane Putnam	4.00	8.00
28 Les Richter	4.00	8.00
29 Willard Sherman	4.00	8.00
30 Del Shofner	5.00	10.00
31 Billy Ray Smith	4.00	8.00
32 George Strugar	4.00	8.00
33 Norm Van Brocklin	15.00	30.00
34 Bill Wade	6.00	12.00
35 Ron Waller	4.00	8.00
36 Jesse Whittenton	4.00	8.00
37 Tom Wilson	4.00	8.00
38 Paul(Tank) Younger	5.00	10.00

1959 Rams Bell Brand

The 1959 Bell Brand Los Angeles Rams set contains 40-regular issue standard-size cards. The catalog designation for this set is F387-1. The obverses contain white-bordered color photos of the player with a facsimile autograph. The backs contain the card number, a short biography and vital statistics of the player, a Bell Brand ad, and advertisements for Los Angeles Rams' merchandise. These cards were issued as inserts in potato chip and corn chip bags in the Los Angeles area and are frequently found with oil stains from the chips. Cards #41 Bill Jobko and #43 Tom Franckhauer were recently discovered. Much like the 1960 Gene Selawski card #2, it is thought that the Jobko and Franckhauser cards were withdrawn early in production and available only upon request from the company. It is not considered part of the complete set price below.

COMPLETE SET (40)	1,200.00	2,000.00
1 Bill Wade	40.00	75.00
2 Buddy Humphrey	30.00	50.00
3 Frank Ryan	35.00	60.00
4 Ed Meador	30.00	50.00
5 Tom Wilson	30.00	50.00
6 Don Burroughs	30.00	50.00
7 Jon Arnett	35.00	60.00
8 Del Shofner	35.00	60.00
9 Jack Pardee	35.00	60.00
10 Ollie Matson	60.00	100.00
11 Joe Marconi	30.00	50.00
12 Jim Jones	30.00	50.00
13 Jack Morris	30.00	50.00
14 Willard Sherman	30.00	50.00
15 Clendon Thomas	30.00	50.00
16 Les Richter	35.00	60.00
17 John Morrow	30.00	50.00
18 Lou Michaels	35.00	60.00
19 Bob Reifsnyder	30.00	50.00
20 John Guzik	30.00	50.00
21 Duane Putnam	30.00	50.00
22 John Houser	30.00	50.00
23 Buck Lansford	30.00	50.00
24 Gene Selawski	30.00	50.00
25 John Baker	30.00	50.00
26 Bob Fry	30.00	50.00
27 John Lovetere	30.00	50.00
28 George Strugar	30.00	50.00
29 Roy Wilkins	30.00	50.00
30 Charley Bradshaw	30.00	50.00
31 Gene Brito	30.00	50.00
32 Jim Phillips	35.00	60.00
33 Leon Clarke	30.00	50.00
34 Lamar Lundy	40.00	75.00
35 Sam Williams	30.00	50.00
36 Sid Gillman CO	50.00	80.00
37 Jack Faulkner CO	30.00	50.00
38 Joe Madro CO	30.00	50.00
39 Don Paul LB CO	30.00	50.00
40 Lou Rymkus CO	35.00	60.00
41 Bill Jobko SP	1,200.00	2,000.00
43 Tom Franckhauser SP	1,200.00	2,000.00

1960 Rams Bell Brand

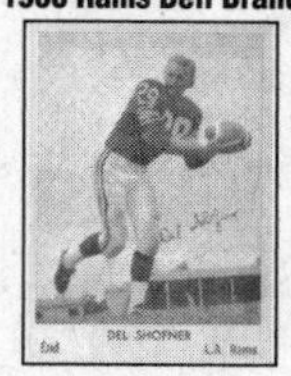

The 1960 Bell Brand Los Angeles Rams Football set contains 39 standard-size cards in a format similar to the 1959 Bell Brand set. The fronts of the cards have distinctive yellow borders. The catalog designation for this set is F387-2. Card numbers 1-18, except number 2, are repeated photos from the 1959 set and were available throughout the season. Numbers 19-39 were available later in the 1960 season. These cards were issued as inserts in potato chip and corn chip bags in the Los Angeles area and are frequently found with oil stains from the chips. Card number 2 Selawski was withdrawn early in the year (after he was cut from the team) and was reportedly available only upon request from the company. It is not considered part of the complete set price below.

COMPLETE SET (38)	1,500.00	2,500.00
COMMON CARD (1-18)	30.00	50.00
COMMON CARD (19-39)	50.00	80.00
1 Joe Marconi	30.00	50.00
2 Gene Selawski SP	1,200.00	2,000.00
3 Frank Ryan	30.00	50.00
4 Ed Meador	35.00	60.00
5 Tom Wilson	30.00	50.00
6 Gene Brito	35.00	60.00
7 Jon Arnett	30.00	50.00
8 Buck Lansford	30.00	50.00
9 Jack Pardee	30.00	50.00
10 Ollie Matson	50.00	80.00
11 John Lovetere	30.00	50.00
12 Bill Jolko	30.00	50.00
13 Jim Phillips	35.00	60.00
14 Lamar Lundy	30.00	50.00
15 Del Shofner	30.00	50.00
16 Les Richter	35.00	60.00
17 Bill Wade	30.00	50.00
18 Lou Michaels	35.00	60.00
19 Dick Bass	60.00	100.00
20 Charley Britt	50.00	80.00
21 Willard Sherman	50.00	80.00
22 George Strugar	50.00	80.00
23 Bob Long LB	50.00	80.00
24 Danny Villanueva	50.00	80.00
25 Jim Boeke	50.00	80.00
26 Clendon Thomas	50.00	80.00
27 Art Hunter	50.00	80.00
28 Carl Karilivacz	50.00	80.00
29 John Baker	50.00	80.00
30 Charley Bradshaw	50.00	80.00
31 John Guzik	50.00	80.00
32 Buddy Humphrey	50.00	80.00
33 Carroll Dale	50.00	80.00
34 Don Ellersick	50.00	80.00
35 Roy Hord	50.00	80.00
36 Charlie Janerette	50.00	80.00
37 John Kennerson	50.00	80.00
38 Jerry Stalcup	50.00	80.00
39 Bob Waterfield CO	125.00	200.00

1967 Rams Team Issue

The Los Angeles Rams issued these black and white player photos around 1967. Each includes the player's name and team name below the photo, measures roughly 5 1/4" by 7" and is blankbacked.

COMPLETE SET (27)	125.00	250.00
1 Maxie Baughan	6.00	12.00
2 Joe Carollo	6.00	12.00
3 Bernie Casey	6.00	12.00
4 Don Chuy	6.00	12.00
5 Charlie Cowan	6.00	12.00
6 Irv Cross	6.00	12.00
7 Dan Currie	6.00	12.00
8 Willie Daniel	6.00	12.00
9 Willie Ellison	6.00	12.00
10 Roman Gabriel	7.50	15.00
11 Bruce Gossett	6.00	12.00
12 Roosevelt Grier	7.50	15.00
13 Anthony Guillory	6.00	12.00
14 Ken Iman	6.00	12.00
15 Deacon Jones	7.50	15.00
16 Les Josephson	6.00	12.00
17 Chuck Lamson	6.00	12.00
18 Tom Mack	7.50	15.00
19 Tommy Mason	6.00	12.00
20 Marlin McKeever	6.00	12.00
21 Bill Munson	6.00	12.00
22 Jack Pardee	6.00	12.00
23 Myron Pottios	6.00	12.00
24 Joe Scibelli	6.00	12.00
25 Jack Snow	6.00	12.00
26 Clancy Williams	6.00	12.00
27 Doug Woodlief	6.00	12.00

1968 Rams Team Issue

The Los Angeles Rams issued these black and white player photos. Each measures roughly 8" by 10" and is blank backed. The checklist below is thought to be incomplete.

COMPLETE SET (9)	50.00	100.00
1 George Allen CO	10.00	20.00
2 Dick Bass	5.00	10.00
3 Bernie Casey	5.00	10.00
4 Lamar Lundy	6.00	12.00
5 Deacon Jones	7.50	15.00
6 Les Josephson	5.00	10.00
7 Merlin Olsen	7.50	15.00
8 Jack Snow	5.00	10.00
9 Team Photo	5.00	10.00

1968 Rams Volpe Tumblers

These Rams artist's renderings were part of a plastic cup tumbler product produced in 1968 and distributed by White Front Stroes. The noted sports artist Volpe created the artwork which includes an action scene and a player portrait. The "cards" are unnumbered, each measures approximately 5" by 8 1/2" and is curved in the shape required to fit inside a plastic cup. The manufacturer notation PGC (programs General Corp) is printed on each piece as well. There are thought to be 6-cups included in this set. Any additions to this list are appreciated.

COMPLETE SET (6)	100.00	200.00
1 Dick Bass	15.00	30.00
2 Roger Brown	15.00	30.00
3 Roman Gabriel	25.00	50.00
4 Deacon Jones	25.00	50.00
5 Lamar Lundy	15.00	30.00
6 Merlin Olsen	30.00	60.00

1973 Rams Team Issue Color

The NFLPA worked with many teams in 1973 to issued photo packs to be sold at stadium concession stands. Each measures approximately 7" by 8-5/8" and features a color player photo with a blank back. A small sheet with a player checklist was included in each 6-photo pack.

COMPLETE SET (6)	25.00	50.00
1 Jim Bertelsen	4.00	8.00
2 John Hadl	6.00	12.00
3 Harold Jackson	5.00	10.00
4 Merlin Olsen	6.00	12.00
5 Isiah Robertson	4.00	8.00
6 Jack Snow	4.00	8.00

1974 Rams Team Issue

The Rams issued this group of photos around 1974. Each measures roughly 5" by 7 1/4" and features a black and white player photo on blankbacked paper stock. There is a thin white border on three sides with roughly a 1" border below the photo. The team's helmet logo, player's name and position (initials) are included in the border below the photo. The Rams' helmet logo has a single bar facemask, is oriented to the left on all the photos unless noted below, and measures roughly 5/8" high. The photos are identical in format to the 1978 team issue. Any additions to the list below are appreciated.

COMPLETE SET (30)	100.00	200.00
1 Larry Brooks	4.00	8.00
2 Mike Burke	4.00	8.00
3 Bud Carson CO	5.00	10.00
4 Al Clark	4.00	8.00
5 Bill Curry	4.00	8.00
6 Dave Elmendorf	4.00	8.00
7 Clyde Evans ASST	4.00	8.00
8 Jack Faulkner ASST	4.00	8.00
9 Chuck Knox CO	5.00	10.00
10 Paul Lanham CO	4.00	8.00
11 Frank Lauterbur CO	4.00	8.00
12 Tom Mack	6.00	12.00
13 Lawrence McCutcheon	5.00	10.00
14 Willie McGee	4.00	8.00
15 Eddie McMillan	4.00	8.00
16 Phil Olsen	4.00	8.00
17 Jim Peterson	4.00	8.00
18 Tony Plummer	4.00	8.00
19 Steve Preece	4.00	8.00
20 David Ray	4.00	8.00
21 Jack Reynolds	5.00	10.00
22 Isiah Robertson	5.00	10.00
23 Rich Saul	4.00	8.00
24 Rob Scribner	4.00	8.00
25 Bob Stein	4.00	8.00
26 Tim Stokes	4.00	8.00
27 Charlie Stukes	4.00	8.00
28 Lionel Taylor CO	5.00	10.00
29 LaVern Torgeson CO	4.00	8.00
30 John Williams G	4.00	8.00

1978 Rams Team Issue

The Rams issued this group of photos around 1978. Each measures roughly 5" by 7 1/4" and features a black and white player photo on blankbacked paper stock. There is a thin white border on three sides with roughly a 1" border below the photo. The team's helmet logo, player's name and position (initials) are included in the border below the photo. The Rams' helmet logo has a single bar facemask, is oriented to the left on all the photos unless noted below, and measures roughly 5/8" high. The photos are identical in format to the 1974 team issue. Any additions to the list below are appreciated.

COMPLETE SET (37)	100.00	200.00
1 Bob Brudzinski	3.00	6.00
2 Frank Corral	3.00	6.00
3 Nolan Cromwell	3.00	6.00
4 Reggie Doss	3.00	6.00
5 Fred Dryer	4.00	8.00
6 Carl Ekern	3.00	6.00
7 Mike Fanning	3.00	6.00
8 Vince Ferragamo	4.00	8.00
9 Doug France	3.00	6.00
10 Ed Fulton	3.00	6.00
11 Pat Haden	4.00	8.00
12 Dennis Harrah	3.00	6.00
13 Greg Horton	3.00	6.00
14 Ron Jaworski	5.00	10.00
15 Ron Jessie	3.00	6.00
16 Jim Jodat	3.00	6.00
17 Cody Jones	3.00	6.00
18 Lawrence McCutcheon	3.00	6.00
19 Kevin McLain	3.00	6.00
20 Willie Miller	3.00	6.00
21 Joe Namath	12.50	25.00
22 Terry Nelson	3.00	6.00
23 Rod Perry	3.00	6.00
24 Rod Phillips	3.00	6.00
25 Jack Reynolds	4.00	8.00
26 Dan Ryczek	3.00	6.00
27 Bill Simpson	3.00	6.00
28 Jackie Slater	6.00	12.00
29 Doug Smith C	3.00	6.00
30 Ron Smith WR	3.00	6.00
31 Pat Thomas	3.00	6.00
32 Wendell Tyler	3.00	6.00
33 Billy Waddy	3.00	6.00
34 Glen Walker	3.00	6.00
35 Charle Young	3.00	6.00
36 Jack Youngblood	5.00	10.00
37 Jim Youngblood	3.00	6.00

1979 Rams Team Issue

The Rams issued this group of photos around 1979. Each measures roughly 5" by 7 1/4" and features a black and white player photo on blankbacked paper stock. There is a thin white border on three sides with roughly a 1" border below the photo. The team's helmet logo, player's name and position (initials) are included in the border below the photo. The Rams' helmet logo has a double bar facemask that is oriented to the left on all of the photos and measures roughly 5/8" high. The photos are identical in format to the 1978 team issue except for the double bar facemask instead of single. Any additions to the list below are appreciated.

COMPLETE SET (34)	75.00	150.00
1 George Andrews	3.00	6.00
2 Larry Brooks	3.00	6.00
3 Dave Elmendorf	3.00	6.00
4 Doug France	3.00	6.00
5 Dennis Harrah	3.00	6.00
6 Drew Hill	5.00	10.00
7 Eddie Hill	3.00	6.00
8 Bill Hickman ASST	3.00	6.00
9 Kent Hill	3.00	6.00
10 Ron Jessie	4.00	8.00
11 Jim Jodat	3.00	6.00
12 Cody Jones	3.00	6.00
13 Sid Justin	3.00	6.00
14 Lawrence McCutcheon	4.00	8.00
15 Kevin McLain	3.00	6.00
16 Terry Nelson	3.00	6.00
17 Dwayne O'Steen	3.00	6.00

18 Elvis Peacock 3.00 6.00
19 Rod Perry 3.00 6.00
20 Dan Radakovich CO 3.00 6.00
21 Jack Reynolds 4.00 8.00
22 Jeff Rutledge 3.00 6.00
23 Dan Ryczek 3.00 6.00
24 Rich Saul 3.00 6.00
25 Jackie Slater 6.00 12.00
26 Doug Smith 3.00 6.00
27 Ron Smith WR 3.00 6.00
28 Pat Thomas 3.00 6.00
29 Wendell Tyler 4.00 8.00
30 Billy Waddy 4.00 8.00
31 Jerry Wilkinson 3.00 6.00
32 Charle Young 4.00 8.00
33 Jack Youngblood 6.00 12.00
34 Jim Youngblood 3.00 6.00

1980 Rams Police

This unnumbered, 14-card set has been listed in the checklist below by uniform number, which appears on the fronts of the cards. The cards measure approximately 2 5/8" by 4 1/8". The Kiwanis Club, who sponsored this set along with the local law enforcement agency and the Rams, has their logo on the fronts of the cards. These cards, which contain "Rams Tips" on the backs, were distributed by police officers, one per week over a 14-week period.

COMPLETE SET (14) 10.00 20.00
11 Pat Haden 1.50 4.00
15 Vince Ferragamo 1.00 2.50
21 Nolan Cromwell 1.00 2.50
26 Wendell Tyler .75 2.00
32 Cullen Bryant .50 1.25
53 Jim Youngblood .50 1.25
59 Bob Brudzinski .40 1.00
61 Rich Saul .40 1.00
77 Doug France .40 1.00
82 Willie Miller .40 1.00
85 Jack Youngblood 2.00 5.00
88 Preston Dennard .40 1.00
90 Larry Brooks .40 1.00
NNO Ray Malavasi CO .40 1.00

1980 Rams Team Issue

The Rams issued this group of photos around 1980. Each measures roughly 5" by 7" or 5" by 7 1/4" and features a black and white player photo on blankbacked paper stock. There is a thin white border on three sides with roughly a 1" border below the photo. The team's helmet logo, player's name and position (spelled out) are included in the border below the photo. The Rams' helmet logo has a double bar facemask that is oriented to the left on all of the photos and measures roughly 1" high. The photos are identical in format to the 1979 team issue except for the larger (1") helmet logo. Any additions to the list below are appreciated.

COMPLETE SET (52) 100.00 200.00
1 George Andrews 2.00 5.00
2 Walt Arnold 2.00 5.00
3 Bill Bain 2.00 5.00
4 Larry Brooks 2.00 5.00
5 Bob Brudzinski 2.00 5.00
6 Cullen Bryant 2.00 5.00
7 Howard Carson 2.00 5.00
8 Frank Corral 2.00 5.00
9 Nolan Cromwell 2.00 5.00
10 Nolan Cromwell 2.00 5.00
11 Jeff Delaney 2.00 5.00
12 Preston Dennard 2.00 5.00
13 Reggie Doss 2.00 5.00
14 Fred Dryer 2.50 6.00
15 Carl Ekern 2.00 5.00
16 Mike Fanning 2.00 5.00
17 Doug France 2.00 5.00
18 Mike Guman 2.00 5.00
19 Pat Haden 2.50 6.00
20 Dennis Harrah 2.00 5.00
21 Joe Harris 2.00 5.00
22 Victor Hicks 2.00 5.00
23 Drew Hill 3.00 8.00
24 Eddie Hill 2.00 5.00
25 Kent Hill 2.00 5.00
26 LeRoy Irvin 2.00 5.00
27 Johnnie Johnson 2.00 5.00
28 Cody Jones 2.00 5.00
29 Jeff Kemp 2.00 5.00
30 Bob Lee 2.00 5.00
31 Ray Malavasi CO 2.00 5.00
32 Willie Miller 2.00 5.00
33 Jeff Moore 2.00 5.00
34 Phil Murphy 2.00 5.00
35 Terry Nelson 2.00 5.00
36 Irv Pankey 2.00 5.00
37 Herb Paterra CO 2.00 5.00
38 Elvis Peacock 2.00 5.00
39 Rod Perry 2.00 5.00
40 Jack Reynolds 2.50 6.00
41 Jeff Rutledge 2.00 5.00
42 Rich Saul 2.00 5.00
43 Jackie Slater 3.00 8.00
44 Doug Smith C 2.00 5.00
45 Lucious Smith 2.00 5.00
46 Ivory Sully 2.00 5.00
47 Jewerl Thomas 2.00 5.00
48 Pat Thomas 2.00 5.00
49 Wendell Tyler 2.50 6.00
50 Billy Waddy 2.50 6.00
51 Jack Youngblood 3.00 8.00
52 Jim Youngblood 2.00 5.00

1961 Random House Football Portfolio

These color photos were issued as a set in the early 1960s by Random House. They were distributed in a colorful folder that featured the title "Football Portfolio" at the top and the Random House identification at the bottom. The body of the folder included the image of the Giants and Packers with Y.A. Tittle in the foreground. Each photo features a color image of a player or game action with only the photographer's notation on the front to use as identification. The backs are blank and the photos are borderless and measure roughly 7 7/8" by 11".

COMPLETE SET (6) 75.00 150.00
1 Bart Starr 15.00 40.00
2 Jim Taylor 12.50 30.00
3 Bart Starr 12.50 30.00
Jerry Kramer
4 Jim Taylor being tackled 10.00 25.00
5 Giants vs. Packers game action 12.50 30.00
6 Don Chandler 7.50 20.00
Phil King

1962-66 Rawlings Advisory Staff Photos

These photos were likely issued over a period of years in the early to mid-1960s. Each is unnumbered and checklisted below in alphabetical order. The cards measure roughly 8 1/8" by 10 1/8" and include a white box containing the player's facsimile autograph and Rawlings Advisory Staff identification lines. Any additions to the list below are appreciated.

COMMON CARD (1-13) 7.50 15.00
1 Jim Bakken 7.50 15.00
2 Billy Cannon 10.00 20.00
3 Roman Gabriel 15.00 25.00
4 John Hadl 15.00 25.00
5 Jim Hart 15.00 25.00
6 Harlon Hill 7.50 15.00
7 Bobby Layne 20.00 40.00
8 Don Meredith 20.00 40.00
9 Sonny Randle 7.50 15.00
10 Kyle Rote 10.00 20.00
11 Tobin Rote 7.50 15.00
12 John Stofa 7.50 15.00
13 Alex Webster 7.50 15.00

1976 RC Cola Colts Cans

This set of RC Cola cans was release in the Baltimore area and featured members of the Colts. The cans are blue and feature a black and white player photo. They are similar in design to the nationally issued 1977 set but include a red banner below the player's photo as well as different statistics for each player versus the 1977 release. Prices below reflect that of opened empty cans.

COMPLETE SET (43) 50.00 100.00
1 Mike Barnes 1.50 3.00
2 Tim Baylor 1.50 3.00
3 Forrest Blue 2.00 4.00
4 Roger Carr 1.50 3.00
5 Raymond Chester 2.00 4.00
6 Jim Cheyunski 1.50 3.00
7 Elmer Collett 1.50 3.00
8 Fred Cook 1.50 3.00
9 Dan Dickel 1.50 3.00
10 John Dutton 1.50 3.00
11 Joe Ehrmann 2.00 4.00
12 Ron Fernandes 1.50 3.00
13 Glenn Doughty 1.50 3.00
14 Randy Hall 1.50 3.00
15 Ken Huff 1.50 3.00
16 Bert Jones 3.00 6.00
17 Jimmie Kennedy 1.50 3.00
18 Mike Kirkland 1.50 3.00
19 George Kunz 1.50 3.00
20 Bruce Laird 1.50 3.00
21 Roosevelt Leaks 2.00 4.00
22 David Lee 2.00 4.00
23 Ron Lee 1.50 3.00
24 Toni Linhart 1.50 3.00
25 Derrel Luce 1.50 3.00
26 Don McCauley 2.00 4.00
27 Ken Mendenhall 1.50 3.00
28 Lydell Mitchell 3.00 6.00
29 Lloyd Mumphord 2.00 4.00
30 Nelson Munsey 1.50 3.00
31 Ken Novak 1.50 3.00
32 Ray Oldham 1.50 3.00
33 Robert Pratt 1.50 3.00
34 Sanders Shiver 1.50 3.00
35 Freddie Scott 1.50 3.00
36 Ed Simonini 1.50 3.00
37 Howard Stevens 1.50 3.00
38 David Taylor 1.50 3.00
39 Ricky Thompson 1.50 3.00
40 Bill Troup 1.50 3.00
41 Jackie Wallace 1.50 3.00
42 Bob Van Duyne 1.50 3.00
43 Stan White 2.00 4.00

1977 RC Cola Cans

RC Cola distributed this set of cans regionally in NFL team areas. Each can features a black and white NFL player photo along with a brief player summary and a football trivia question. Quite a few variations exist with regards to the trivia question presented on the can and we've included the first few words of the trivia question for those known variations. Ten players were issued for each NFL team, except for the Washington Redskins which featured over 40. We've catalogued the set below according to team (alphabetized). Prices below reflect opened empty cans.

COMPLETE SET (298) 500.00 1,000.00
1 Steve Bartkowski 3.00 6.00
2 Bubba Bean 2.00 4.00
3 Ray Brown 2.00 4.00
4A John Gilliam 2.00 4.00
(Jake Scott holds...)
4B John Gilliam 2.00 4.00
(Ken Anderson completed...)
5 Claude Humphrey 3.00 6.00
6A Alfred Jenkins 2.00 4.00
(Jackie Smith holds...)
6B Alfred Jenkins 2.00 4.00
(Don Cockroft is...)
7A Nick Mike-Mayer 2.00 4.00
(Bert Jones holds...)
7B Nick Mike-Mayer 2.00 4.00
(Walter Payton had...)
8 Jim Mitchell 2.00 4.00
9 Ralph Ortega 2.00 4.00
10A Jeff Van Note 2.00 4.00
(Bert Jones holds...)
10B Jeff Van Note 2.00 4.00
(Don Woods set...)
11 Forrest Blue 2.00 4.00
12 Raymond Chester 2.00 4.00
13 Joe Ehrmann 2.00 4.00
14 Bert Jones 3.00 6.00
15 Roosevelt Leaks 2.00 4.00
16 David Lee 2.00 4.00
17 Don McCauley 2.00 4.00
18 Lydell Mitchell 2.00 4.00
19 Lloyd Mumphord 2.00 4.00
20 Stan White 2.00 4.00
21 Marv Bateman 2.00 4.00
22 Bob Chandler 3.00 6.00
23 Joe DeLamielleure 3.00 6.00
24 Joe Ferguson 3.00 6.00
25 Dave Foley 2.00 4.00
26 Steve Freeman 2.00 4.00
27 Mike Kadish 2.00 4.00
28 Jeff Lloyd 2.00 4.00
29 Reggie McKenzie 3.00 6.00
30 Bob Nelson 2.00 4.00
31 Lionel Antoine 2.00 4.00
32 Bob Avellini 2.00 4.00
33 Brian Baschnagel 2.00 4.00
34 Waymond Bryant 2.00 4.00
35 Doug Buffone 2.00 4.00
36A Wally Chambers 2.00 4.00
(Jackie Smith holds...)
36B Wally Chambers 2.00 4.00
(Don Cockroft is...)
37A Virgil Livers 2.00 4.00
(Walter Payton had...)
37B Virgil Livers 2.00 4.00
(Jake Scott holds...)
38 Johnny Musso 2.00 4.00
39 Walter Payton 20.00 40.00
40 Bo Rather 2.00 4.00
41 Ken Anderson 3.00 6.00
42 Coy Bacon 2.00 4.00
43A Tommy Casanova 2.00 4.00
(Lydell Mitchell had...)
43B Tommy Casanova 2.00 4.00
(Fred Dryer holds...)
44A Boobie Clark 2.00 4.00
(Lydell Mitchell had...)
44B Boobie Clark 2.00 4.00
(MacArthur Lane caught...)
45A Archie Griffin 3.00 6.00
(Dan Pastorini holds...)
45B Archie Griffin 3.00 6.00
(Rocky Bleier rushed...)
46A Jim LeClair 2.00 4.00
Ken Houston holds...)
46B Jim LeClair 2.00 4.00
Steve Grogan ran...)
47A Rufus Mayes 2.00 4.00
(John Hicks offensive...)
47B Rufus Mayes 2.00 4.00
(Fred Dryer holds...)
48A Chip Myers 2.00 4.00
(Jackie Smith holds...)
48B Chip Myers 2.00 4.00
(Lydell Mitchell had...)
49A Ken Riley 2.00 4.00
(MacArthur Lane caught...)
49B Ken Riley 2.00 4.00
(Don Woods set...)
50A Bob Trumpy 2.00 4.00
(Dan Pastorini holds...)
50B Bob Trumpy 2.00 4.00
(Ken Houston holds...)
51 Don Cockroft 2.00 4.00
52A Thom Darden 2.00 4.00
(Dan Pastorini holds...)
52B Thom Darden 2.00 4.00
(Dick Anderson tied...)
53A Tom DeLeone 2.00 4.00
(Jim Turner holds...)
53B Tom DeLeone 2.00 4.00
(Roger Wehrli attended...)
54A John Garlington 2.00 4.00
(Jack Youngblood a...)
54B John Garlington 2.00 4.00
(Dick Anderson tied...)
55A Walter Johnson 2.00 4.00
(Bert Jones holds...)
55B Walter Johnson 2.00 4.00
(Ed To Tall Jones...)
56A Joe Jones 2.00 4.00
(Jim Turner holds...)
56B Joe Jones 2.00 4.00
(Ken Anderson completed...)
57 Cleo Miller 2.00 4.00
58 Greg Pruitt 3.00 6.00
59A Reggie Rucker 2.00 4.00
(Jack Youngblood a...)
59B Reggie Rucker 2.00 4.00
(MacArthur Lane...)
60 Paul Warfield 5.00 10.00
61A Cliff Harris 3.00 6.00
(Ken Houston holds...)
61B Cliff Harris 3.00 6.00
(Dan Pastorini holds...)
62 Ed Too Tall Jones 5.00 10.00
63A Ralph Neely 2.00 4.00
(Lydell Mitchell had...)
63B Ralph Neely 2.00 4.00
(Fred Dryer holds...)
64 Robert Newhouse 2.00 4.00
65 Drew Pearson 4.00 8.00
66A Jethro Pugh 2.00 4.00
(Fred Dryer holds...)
66B Jethro Pugh 2.00 4.00
(John Hicks offensive...)
67 Mel Renfro 4.00 8.00
68A Golden Richards 2.00 4.00
(MacArthur Lane...)
68B Golden Richards 2.00 4.00
(Don Woods set...)
69 Charlie Waters 3.00 6.00
70 Randy White 6.00 12.00
71A Otis Armstrong 2.00 4.00
(Jake Scott holds...)
71B Otis Armstrong 2.00 4.00
(Jackie Smith holds...)
72 Jon Keyworth 2.00 4.00
73 Jim Kiick 3.00 6.00
74 Craig Morton 3.00 6.00
75A Haven Moses 2.00 4.00
(Don Woods set...)
75B Haven Moses 2.00 4.00
(Levi Johnson had...)
76 Riley Odoms 2.00 4.00
77 Bill Thompson 2.00 4.00
78 Jim Turner 2.00 4.00
79 Rick Upchurch 3.00 6.00
80 Louis Wright 3.00 6.00
81 Lem Barney 2.00 4.00
82A Larry Hand 2.00 4.00
(Fred Cox holds...)
82B Larry Hand 2.00 4.00
(Cliff Harris attended...)
83A J.D. Hill 2.00 4.00
(Pat Haden is...)
83B J.D. Hill 2.00 4.00
(Ed Too Tall Jones...)
84A Levi Johnson 2.00 4.00
(Fred Cox holds...)
84B Levi Johnson 2.00 4.00
(Terry Metcalf set...)
85A Greg Landry 2.00 4.00
(Fred Cox holds...)
85B Greg Landry 2.00 4.00
(Fred Dryer holds...)
86 Jon Morris 2.00 4.00
87 Paul Naumoff 2.00 4.00
88 Charlie Sanders 2.00 4.00
89 Charlie West 2.00 4.00
90 Jim Yarbrough 2.00 4.00
91 John Brockington 2.00 4.00
92 Willie Buchanon 2.00 4.00
93 Fred Carr 2.00 4.00
94 Lynn Dickey 2.00 4.00
95A Bob Hyland 2.00 4.00
(Mike Curtis linebacker...)
95B Bob Hyland 2.00 4.00
(Dan Pastorini holds...)
96A Chester Marcol 2.00 4.00
(Roman Gabriel recovered...)
96B Chester Marcol 2.00 4.00
(Jim Turner holds...)
97 Mike McCoy 2.00 4.00
98 Rich McGeorge 2.00 4.00
99A Steve Odom 2.00 4.00

(Cliff Harris attended...)
99B Steve Odom 2.00 4.00
(Ken Stabler threw...)
100A Clarence Williams 2.00 4.00
(Pat Haden is...)
100B Clarence Williams 2.00 4.00
(Mike Curtis linebacker...)
101A Willie Alexander 2.00 4.00
(Ken Anderson completed...)
101B Willie Alexander 2.00 4.00
(Jim Turner holds...)
102A Duane Benson 2.00 4.00
(Dick Anderson tied...)
102B Duane Benson 2.00 4.00
(Jake Scott holds...)
103A Elvin Bethea 3.00 6.00
(Roger Wehrli attended...)
103B Elvin Bethea 3.00 6.00
(Don Woods set...)
104A Ken Burrough 2.50 5.00
(MacArthur Lane...)
104B Ken Burrough 2.50 5.00
(Jack Youngblood a...)
105A Skip Butler 2.00 4.00
(Dan Pastorini holds...)
105B Skip Butler 2.00 4.00
(Ed Too Tall Jones...)
106A Curley Culp 3.00 6.00
(Jim Turner holds...)
106B Curley Culp 3.00 6.00
(MacArthur lane caught...)
107A Elbert Drungo 2.00 4.00
(Dick Anderson tied...)
107B Elbert Drungo 2.00 4.00
(Dan Pastorini holds...)
108A Billy Johnson 2.50 5.00
(Dick Anderson tied...)
108B Billy Johnson 2.50 5.00
(Roger Wehrli attended...)
109A Carl Mauck 2.00 4.00
(Jack Youngblood a...)
109B Carl Mauck 2.00 4.00
(Dick Anderson tied...)
110A Dan Pastorini 2.50 5.00
(Ed Too Tall Jones...)
110B Dan Pastorini 2.50 5.00
(Jim Turner holds...)
111 Tom Condon 2.00 4.00
112 MacArthur Lane 2.00 4.00
113 Willie Lee 2.00 4.00
114 Mike Livingston 2.00 4.00
115 Jim Nicholson 2.00 4.00
116A Jim Lynch 2.00 4.00
(Dan Pastorini holds...)
116B Jim Lynch 2.00 4.00
(Rocky Bleier rushed...)
117 Barry Pearson 2.00 4.00
118 Ed Podolak 2.00 4.00
119A Jan Stenerud 3.00 6.00
(MacArthur Lane caught...)
119B Jan Stenerud 3.00 6.00
(Don Woods set...)
120 Walter White 2.00 4.00
121 Jim Bertelsen 2.00 4.00
122 John Cappelletti 3.00 6.00
123 Fred Dryer 3.00 6.00
124 Pat Haden 3.00 6.00
125 Harold Jackson 3.00 6.00
126 Ron Jessie 2.00 4.00
127 Lawrence McCutcheon 2.00 4.00
128 Isiah Robertson 2.00 4.00
129 Bucky Scribner 2.00 4.00
130 Jack Youngblood 3.00 6.00
131 Dick Anderson 6.00 12.00
132 Norm Bulaich 5.00 10.00
133 Dave Foley 5.00 10.00
134 Vern Den Herder 5.00 10.00
135A Bob Kuechenberg 5.00 10.00
(Alfred Jenkins caught...)
135B Bob Kuechenberg 5.00 10.00
(Ken Houston holds...)
136A Larry Little 6.00 12.00
(Fred Cox holds...)
136B Larry Little 6.00 12.00
(Fred Dryer holds...)
137A Jim Mandich 5.00 10.00
(Cliff Harris attended...)
137B Jim Mandich 5.00 10.00
(Lydell Mitchell had...)
138 Don Nottingham 5.00 10.00
139 Larry Seiple 5.00 10.00
140 Howard Twilley 5.00 10.00
141 Bobby Bryant 2.00 4.00
142 Fred Cox 2.00 4.00
143 Carl Eller 3.00 6.00
144 Chuck Foreman 2.00 4.00
145 Paul Krause 3.00 6.00
146 Jeff Siemon 2.00 4.00
147 Mick Tingelhoff 2.00 4.00
148 Ed White 2.00 4.00
149 Nate Wright 2.00 4.00
150 Ron Yary 3.00 6.00
151 Marlin Briscoe 2.00 4.00
152 Sam Cunningham 2.00 4.00
153 Steve Grogan 3.00 6.00
154 John Hannah 4.00 8.00
155 Andy Johnson 2.00 4.00
156 Tony McGee DE 2.00 4.00
157 John Sanders 2.00 4.00
158 Randy Vataha 2.00 4.00
159 George Webster 2.00 4.00
160 Steve Zabel 2.00 4.00
161 Larry Burton 2.00 4.00
162 Tony Galbreath 2.00 4.00
163 Don Herrmann 2.00 4.00
164 Archie Manning 5.00 10.00
165 Alvin Maxson 2.00 4.00
166 Jim Merlo 2.00 4.00
167 Derland Moore 2.00 4.00
168 Chuck Muncie 3.00 6.00
169 Tom Myers 2.00 4.00
170 Bob Pollard 2.00 4.00
171 Rich Dvorak 2.00 4.00
172 Walker Gillette 2.00 4.00
173 Jack Gregory 2.00 4.00
174 John Hicks 2.00 4.00
175 Brian Kelley 2.00 4.00
176 John Mendenhall 2.00 4.00
177 Clyde Powers 2.00 4.00
178 Bob Tucker 3.00 6.00
179 Doug Van Horn 2.00 4.00
180 Brad Van Pelt 3.00 6.00
181 Jerome Barkum 2.00 4.00
182 Richard Caster 2.00 4.00
183 Clark Gaines 2.00 4.00
184 Pat Leahy 2.00 4.00
185 Ed Marinaro 3.00 6.00
186 Richard Neal 2.00 4.00
187 Lou Piccone 2.00 4.00
188 Walt Suggs 2.00 4.00
189 Richard Todd 3.00 6.00
190 Phil Wise 2.00 4.00
191 Fred Biletnikoff 6.00 12.00
192A Dave Casper 3.00 6.00
(Pat Haden is...)
192B Dave Casper 3.00 6.00
(Ed Too Tall Jones...)
193 Ted Hendricks 4.00 8.00
194 Marv Hubbard 2.00 4.00
195 Ted Kwalick 2.00 4.00
196 Otis Sistrunk 3.00 6.00
197 Ken Stabler 10.00 20.00
198 Gene Upshaw 4.00 8.00
199 Mark Van Eeghen 3.00 6.00
200 Phil Villapiano 3.00 6.00
201 Bill Bergey 3.00 6.00
202 Harold Carmichael 3.00 6.00
203 Roman Gabriel 3.00 6.00
204 Art Malone 2.00 4.00
205 James McAlister 2.00 4.00
206 John Outlaw 2.00 4.00
207 Jerry Sisemore 2.00 4.00
208 Manny Sistrunk 2.00 4.00
209 Tom Sullivan 2.00 4.00
210 Will Wynn 2.00 4.00
211 Rocky Bleier 3.00 6.00
212 Mel Blount 4.00 8.00
213 Terry Bradshaw 12.50 25.00
214 Roy Gerela 2.00 4.00
215 Joe Greene 5.00 10.00
216 Jack Ham 4.00 8.00
217 Ernie Holmes 2.00 4.00
218 Jack Lambert 6.00 12.00
219 Ray Mansfield 2.00 4.00
220 Dwight White 2.00 4.00
221A Tom Banks 2.00 4.00
(In 1970 Bruce Taylor...)
221B Tom Banks 2.00 4.00
(Roman Gabriel recovered...)
222A Dan Dierdorf 4.00 8.00
(Clark Gaines led...)
222B Dan Dierdorf 4.00 8.00
(Ken Stone intercepted...)
223A Conrad Dobler 2.00 4.00
(Archie Manning QB...)
223B Conrad Dobler 2.00 4.00
(Marv Bateman punter...)
224 Mel Gray 3.00 6.00
225A Terry Metcalf 3.00 6.00
(Ken Stabler threw...)
225B Terry Metcalf 3.00 6.00
(Don Cockroft is...)
226A Jackie Smith 4.00 8.00
(Levi Johnson had...)
226B Jackie Smith 4.00 8.00
(1970 Bruce Taylor...)
227 Roger Wehrli 3.00 6.00
228 Ron Yankowski 2.00 4.00
229 Bob Young 2.00 4.00
230A John Zook 2.00 4.00
(Don Cockroft is...)
230B John Zook 2.00 4.00
(Clark Gaines led...)
231 Pat Curran 2.00 4.00
232 Fred Dean 2.00 4.00
233A Ed Flanagan 2.00 4.00
(Marv Bateman punter...)
233B Ed Flanagan 2.00 4.00
(Terry Metcalf set...)
234A Mike Fuller 2.00 4.00
(Ken Stabler threw...)
234B Mike Fuller 2.00 4.00
(Alfred Jenkins caught...)
235 Don Goode 2.00 4.00
236 Charlie Joiner 5.00 10.00
237 Louie Kelcher 3.00 6.00
238 Bo Matthews 2.00 4.00
239 Hal Stringert 2.00 4.00
240 Don Woods 2.00 4.00
241A Cas Banaszek 2.00 4.00
(In 1970 Bruce Taylor...)
241B Cas Banaszek 2.00 4.00
(Roman Gabriel recovered...)
242 Cedrick Hardman 2.00 4.00
243 Tommy Hart 2.00 4.00
244 Wilbur Jackson 2.00 4.00
245 Mel Phillips 2.00 4.00
246 Jim Plunkett 4.00 8.00
247A Bruce Taylor 2.00 4.00
(Walter Payton had...)
247B Bruce Taylor 2.00 4.00
(Archie Manning QB...)
248 Gene Washington 49er 3.00 6.00
249 Delvin Williams 2.00 4.00
250 Skip Vanderbundt 2.00 4.00
251 Mike Curtis 3.00 6.00
252 Norm Evans 2.00 4.00
253 Don Hansen 2.00 4.00
254 Fred Hoaglin 2.00 4.00
255 Ron Howard 2.00 4.00
256 Al Matthews 2.00 4.00
257 Sam McCullum 2.00 4.00
258 Eddie McMillan 2.00 4.00
259 Steve Niehaus 2.00 4.00
260 Jim Zorn 3.00 6.00
261A Mike Boryla 2.00 4.00
(Chester Marcol...)
261B Mike Boryla 2.00 4.00
(In 1970 Bruce Taylor...)
262A Anthony Davis 3.00 6.00
(Archie Manning QB...)
262B Anthony Davis 3.00 6.00
(Walter Payton had...)
263A Jimmy DuBose 2.00 4.00
(John Hicks offensive...)
263B Jimmy DuBose 2.00 4.00
(in 1970 Bruce Taylor...)
264 Jimmy Gunn 2.00 4.00
265A Essex Johnson 2.00 4.00
(Steve Grogan ran...)
265B Essex Johnson 2.00 4.00
(Ken Stone intercepted...)
266A Bob Moore TE 2.00 4.00
(John Hicks offensive...)
266B Bob Moore TE 2.00 4.00
(Chester Marcol in...)
267 Jim Peterson 2.00 4.00
268 Dan Ryczek 2.00 4.00
269A Barry Smith 2.00 4.00
(Rocky Bleier rushed...)
269B Barry Smith 2.00 4.00
(John Hicks offensive...)
270A Ken Stone 2.00 4.00
(Mike Curtis linebacker...)
270B Ken Stone 2.00 4.00
(Steve Grogan ran...)
271 Mike Bragg 2.00 4.00
272 Eddie Brown 2.00 4.00
273 Bill Brundige 2.00 4.00
274 Dave Butz 2.00 4.00
275 Brad Dusek 2.00 4.00
276 Pat Fischer 3.00 6.00
277 Jean Fugett 2.00 4.00
278 Frank Grant 2.00 4.00
279 Chris Hanburger 3.00 6.00
280 Len Hauss 2.00 4.00
281 Terry Hermeling 2.00 4.00
282 Calvin Hill 2.00 4.00
283 Ken Houston 3.00 6.00
284 Bob Kuziel 2.00 4.00
285 Joe Lavender 2.00 4.00
286 Mark Moseley 2.00 4.00
287 Dan Nugent 2.00 4.00
288 Brig Owens 2.00 4.00
289 John Riggins 6.00 12.00
290 Ron Saul 2.00 4.00
291 Jake Scott 3.00 6.00
292 George Starke 2.00 4.00
293 Tim Stokes 2.00 4.00
294 Diron Talbert 2.00 4.00
295 Charley Taylor 3.00 6.00
296 Joe Theismann 6.00 12.00
297 Mike Thomas 2.00 4.00
298 Pete Wysocki 2.00 4.00

1939 Redskins Matchbooks

Sponsored by Ross Jewelers, these 20 matchbooks measure approximately 1 1/2" by 4 1/2" (when completely folded out) and feature black-and-white photos of the 1939 Washington Redskins, with simulated autographs on the inside panel. The player's position and college, along with his height and weight, appear below the photo. The bottom half of the inside panel reads "This is one of 20 autographed pictures of the Washington Redskins compliments of the Ross Jewelry Co." In maroon lettering upon a gold background, the top half of the outside of the matchbook carries on its front the Ross Company name and address within a drawing of a football. the Redskins 1939 home game schedule is shown on the bottom half. This is the only distinguishing characteristic between the 1939 and 1940 issues. The covers of Jim Barber and Steve Slivinski are considered scarce. The matchbooks are unnumbered and checklisted below in alphabetical order. The prices given are for full covers (with strikers) missing the actual matches. This is the form in which the matchbooks are most commonly found. Complete books with matches typically carry a 50% premium. Books missing the striker are considered VG at best.

COMPLETE SET (20) 1,000.00 1,500.00
1 Jim Barber SP 250.00 400.00
2 Sammy Baugh 90.00 150.00
3 Hal Bradley 20.00 35.00
4 Vic Carroll 20.00 35.00
5 Bud Erickson 20.00 35.00
6 Andy Farkas 20.00 35.00
7 Frank Filchock 20.00 35.00
8 Ray Flaherty CO 25.00 40.00
9 Don Irwin 20.00 35.00
10 Ed Justice 20.00 35.00
11 Jim Karcher 20.00 35.00
12 Max Krause 20.00 35.00
13 Charley Malone 20.00 35.00
14 Bob Masterson 20.00 35.00
15 Wayne Millner 25.00 40.00
16 Mickey Parks 20.00 35.00
17 Erny Pinckert 20.00 35.00
18 Steve Slivinski SP 250.00 400.00
19 Clem Stralka 20.00 35.00
20 Jay Turner 20.00 35.00

1939 Redskins Postcards

This series of postcards was produced for and issued by the team in 1939. Each card measures roughly 3 1/2" by 5 1/2" and features a typically postcard style back with a black and white player photo on the front. The player's name, position, and team name is included within the player photo.

COMPLETE SET (15) 1,200.00 1,800.00
1 Jim Barber 75.00 125.00
2 Sammy Baugh 300.00 500.00
3 Andy Farkas 75.00 125.00
4 Jimmy German 75.00 125.00
5 Don Irwin 75.00 125.00
6 Jimmy Johnston 75.00 125.00
7 Ed Justice 75.00 125.00
8 Jim Karcher 75.00 125.00
9 Charley Malone 75.00 125.00
10 Bob McChesney 75.00 125.00
11 Jim Meade 75.00 125.00
12 Boyd Morgan 75.00 125.00
13 Bo Russell 75.00 125.00
14 Clyde Shugart 75.00 125.00
15 Bill Young 75.00 125.00

1940 Redskins Matchbooks

Made for Ross Jewelers by the Universal Match Corp. of Philadelphia, these 20 matchbooks measure approximately 1 1/2" by 4 1/2" (when completely folded out) and feature black-and-white photos of the 1940 Washington Redskins, with simulated autographs, on the inside panel. The player's position and college, along with his height and weight, appear below the photo. The bottom half of the inside panel reads "This is one of 20 autographed pictures of the Washington Redskins compliments of Ross Jewelry Co." In maroon lettering upon a gold background, the top half of the outside of the matchbook carries on its front the Ross Company name and address within a drawing of a football. On the bottom half is shown the Redskins 1940 home game schedule. This is the only distinguishing characteristic between the 1939 and 1940 issues. The matchbooks are unnumbered and checklisted below in alphabetical order. The prices given are for full covers (with strikers) missing the actual matches. This is the form in which the matchbooks are most commonly found. Complete books with matches typically carry a 50% premium. Books missing the striker are considered VG at best.

COMPLETE SET (20) 200.00 350.00
1 Jim Barber 10.00 18.00
2 Sammy Baugh 50.00 80.00
3 Vic Carroll 10.00 18.00
4 Turk Edwards 18.00 30.00
5 Andy Farkas 10.00 18.00
6 Dick Farman 10.00 18.00
7 Bob Hoffman 10.00 18.00
8 Don Irwin 10.00 18.00
9 Charley Malone 10.00 18.00
10 Bob Masterson 10.00 18.00
11 Wayne Millner 12.00 20.00
12 Mickey Parks 10.00 18.00
13 Erny Pinckert 10.00 18.00
14 Bo Russell 10.00 18.00
15 Clyde Shugart 10.00 18.00
16 Steve Slivinski 10.00 18.00
17 Clem Stralka 10.00 18.00
18 Dick Todd 10.00 18.00
19 Bill Young 10.00 18.00
20 Roy Zimmerman 10.00 18.00

1941 Redskins Matchbooks

Made for Home Laundry by the Maryland Match Co. of Baltimore, these 20 matchbooks measure approximately 1 1/2" by 4 1/2" (when completely folded out) and feature black-and-white photos of the 1941 Washington Redskins, with simulated autographs on the inside panel. The player's position and college, along with his height and weight, appear below the photo. The bottom half of the inside panel reads "This is one of 20 autographed pictures of the Washington Redskins compliments of Home Laundry," followed by the business's 1941 six-digit phone number, ATlantic 2400. In gold lettering upon a maroon background, the outside of the matchbook carries on its front the Home Laundry name and telephone number within a drawing of a football. On the back is shown the Redskins 1941 home game schedule, which ended with a game against Philadelphia, on Sunday, Dec. 7, 1941. The matchbooks are unnumbered and checklisted below in alphabetical order. The prices given are for full covers (with strikers) missing the actual matches. This is the form in which the matchbooks are most commonly found. Complete books with matches typically carry a 50% premium. Books missing the striker are considered VG at best.

COMPLETE SET (20)	150.00	250.00
1 Ki Aldrich	7.00	12.00
2 Jim Barber	7.00	12.00
3 Sammy Baugh	35.00	60.00
4 Vic Carroll	7.00	12.00
5 Fred Davis	7.00	12.00
6 Andy Farkas	7.00	12.00
7 Dick Farman	7.00	12.00
8 Frank Filchock	7.00	12.00
9 Ray Flaherty CO	9.00	15.00
10 Bob Masterson	7.00	12.00
11 Bob McChesney	7.00	12.00
12 Wayne Millner	9.00	15.00
13 Wilbur Moore	7.00	12.00
14 Bob Seymour	7.00	12.00
15 Clyde Shugart	7.00	12.00
16 Clem Stralka	7.00	12.00
17 Robert Titchenal	7.00	12.00
18 Dick Todd	7.00	12.00
19 Bill Young	7.00	12.00
20 Roy Zimmerman	7.00	12.00

1942 Redskins Matchbooks

Made for Home Laundry by the Maryland Match Co. of Baltimore, these 20 matchbooks measure approximately 1 1/2" by 4 1/2" (when completely folded out) and feature black-and-white photos of the 1942 Washington Redskins, with simulated autographs, on the inside panel. The player's position and college, along with his height and weight, appear below the photo. The bottom half of the inside panel reads "This is one of 20 autographed pictures of the Washington Redskins compliments of Home Laundry," followed by the business's 1942 six-digit phone number, ATlantic 2400. In maroon lettering upon a yellow-orange background, the outside of the matchbook carries on its front the Home Laundry name and telephone number within a drawing of a football. On the back is shown the Redskins 1942 home game schedule. The matchbooks are unnumbered and checklisted below in alphabetical order. The prices given are for full covers (with strikers) missing the actual matches. This is the form in which the matchbooks are most commonly found. Complete books with matches typically carry a 50% premium. Books missing the striker are considered VG at best.

COMPLETE SET (20)	150.00	250.00
1 Ki Aldrich	7.00	12.00
2 Sammy Baugh	35.00	60.00
3 Joe Beinor	7.00	12.00
4 Vic Carroll	7.00	12.00
5 Ed Cifers	7.00	12.00
6 Fred Davis	7.00	12.00
7 Turk Edwards	12.00	20.00
8 Andy Farkas	7.00	12.00
9 Dick Farman	7.00	12.00
10 Ray Flaherty CO	9.00	15.00
11 Al Krueger	7.00	12.00
12 Bob Masterson	7.00	12.00
13 Bob McChesney	7.00	12.00
14 Wilbur Moore	7.00	12.00
15 Bob Seymour	7.00	12.00
16 Clyde Shugart	7.00	12.00
17 Clem Stralka	7.00	12.00
18 Dick Todd	7.00	12.00
19 Willie Wilkin	7.00	12.00
20 Bill Young	7.00	12.00

1951-52 Redskins Matchbooks

Sponsored by Arcade Pontiac and produced by the Universal Match Corp.,Washington D.C., these matchbooks measure approximately 1 1/2" by 4 1/2" (when completely folded out) and feature small black-and-white photos of Washington Redskins with simulated autographs on the inside panel. The player's position and college, along with his height and weight, appear below the photo. The bottom half of the inside panel reads "This is one of 20 autographed pictures of the Washington Redskins compliments of Jack Blank, President Arcade Pontiac Co.," followed by the business' 1950s six-digit phone number, ADams 8500. The outside of the matchbook carries on its top half the Arcade Pontiac name along with a logo on a black and gold background. On the bottom half is shown the Redskins logo on a gold background. The matchbooks are unnumbered and checklisted below in alphabetical order. Although the covers read "20" to the set, it is thought that only 17-matchbooks were released in 1951 and 19 in 1952. Many of the matchbooks were released in both 1951 and 1952 with a few containing only very minor differences in the photo cropping. Otherwise, the two sets are indistinguishable. Thus, we've listed the two sets together for ease in cataloging. Major variations between the two years (only the Herman Ball cover) and covers reportedly issued only one year are listed below as such. The prices given are for full covers (with strikers) missing the actual matches. This is the form in which the matchbooks are most commonly found. Complete books with matches typically carry a 50% premium. Books missing the striker are considered VG at best.

COMPLETE SET (25)	250.00	400.00
1 John Badaczewski	5.00	10.00
2A Herman Ball CO	6.00	12.00
2B Herman Ball CO	6.00	12.00
3 Sammy Baugh	25.00	50.00
4 Ed Berrang 1951	6.00	12.00
5 Dan Brown 1951	6.00	12.00
6 Al DeMao	5.00	10.00
7 Harry Dowda 1952	10.00	20.00
8 Chuck Drazenovich	5.00	10.00
9 Bill Dudley 1951	10.00	20.00
10 Harry Gilmer	7.50	15.00
11 Bob Goode 1951	6.00	12.00
12 Leon Heath 1952	10.00	20.00
13 Charlie Justice 1952	12.50	25.00
14 Lou Karras	5.00	10.00
15 Eddie LeBaron 1952	15.00	30.00
16 Paul Lipscomb	5.00	10.00
17 Laurie Niemi	5.00	10.00
18 Johnny Papit 1952	10.00	20.00
19 James Peebles 1951	6.00	12.00
20 Ed Quirk	5.00	10.00
21 Jim Ricca 1952	10.00	20.00
22 James Staton 1951	6.00	12.00
23 Hugh Taylor	6.00	12.00
24 Joe Tereshinski	5.00	10.00
25 Dick Todd CO 1952	10.00	20.00

1952 Redskins Postcards

1 Dick Alban	30.00	50.00
2 Don Boll	30.00	50.00
3 Gene Brito	30.00	50.00
4 Jack Cloud	30.00	50.00
5 Al Demao	30.00	50.00
6 Chuck Drazenovich	30.00	50.00
7 Harry Gilmer	35.00	60.00
8 Jerry Hennessy	30.00	50.00
9 Paul Lipscomb	30.00	50.00
10 Laurie Niemi	30.00	50.00
11 Knox Ramsey	30.00	50.00
12 Julie Rykovich	30.00	50.00
13 Jack Scarbath	30.00	50.00
14 Joe Tereshinski	30.00	50.00
15 Johnny Williams	30.00	50.00

1957 Redskins Team Issue 5x7

This set of 5x7 photos was issued by the team to fulfill fan requests and for player appearances. Each includes a black and white photo of a Redskins player with just his name below the image. The backs are blank and unnumbered.

COMPLETE SET (12)	75.00	150.00
1 Sam Baker	7.50	15.00
2 Don Bosseler	7.50	15.00
3 Gene Brito	7.50	15.00
4 John Carson	7.50	15.00
5 Chuck Drazenovich	7.50	15.00
6 Ralph Guglielmi	7.50	15.00
7 Dick James	7.50	15.00
8 Eddie LeBaron	12.50	25.00
9 Jim Podoley	7.50	15.00
10 Jim Schrader	7.50	15.00
11 Ed Sutton	7.50	15.00
12 Albert Zagers	7.50	15.00

1957 Redskins Team Issue 8x10

This set of black and white photos was issued by the team for fan requests and public appearances. Each measures roughly 8" by 10 1/4" with a 1/4" white border around all four sides. The team name and player name appear below the photo and the backs are blank and unnumbered.

COMPLETE SET (14)	125.00	250.00
1 Sam Baker	10.00	20.00
2 Gene Brito	10.00	20.00
3 John Carson	10.00	20.00
4 Bob Dee	10.00	20.00
5 Chuck Drazenovich	10.00	20.00
6 Ralph Felton	10.00	20.00
7 Norb Hecker	10.00	20.00
8 Dick James	10.00	20.00
9 Eddie LeBaron	15.00	30.00
10 Ray Lemek	10.00	20.00
11 Volney Peters	10.00	20.00
12 Joe Scudero	10.00	20.00
13 Dick Stanfel	12.50	25.00
14 Lavern Torgeson	10.00	20.00

1958-59 Redskins Matchbooks

Sponsored by First Federal Savings and produced by Universal Match Corp., Washington D.C., these 20 matchcovers measure approximately 1 1/2" by 4 1/2" (when completely folded out). Each front cover features a small black-and-white photo of a popular Washington Redskins player with the Redskins logo and the title "Famous Redskins" on the bottom half and a First Federal Savings advertisement on the top half. A player profile is given at the top of the matchcover back along with the words "This is one of twenty famous Redskins presented for you by your 1st Federal Savings and Loan Association of Washington& Bethesda Branch," followed by the address. The matchbooks are unnumbered and checklisted below in alphabetical order. It is most commonly thought that the set was issued in two ten-cover series over a two-year period. We've included the presumed year of issue after each cover. The matchbooks are very similar to the 1960-61 issue, but can be distinguished by their light gray colored paper stock instead of off-white. The prices given are for full covers (with strikers) missing the actual matches. This is the form in which the matchbooks are most commonly found. Complete books with matches typically carry a 50% premium. Books missing the striker are considered VG at best.

COMPLETE SET (20)	125.00	250.00
1 Steve Bagarus 58	5.00	10.00
2 Cliff Battles 58	10.00	20.00
3 Sammy Baugh 58	20.00	40.00
4 Gene Brito 58	5.00	10.00
5 Jim Castiglia 58	5.00	10.00
6 Al DeMao 58	5.00	10.00
7 Chuck Drazenovich 59	5.00	10.00
8 Bill Dudley 59	10.00	20.00
9 Al Fiorentino 59	5.00	10.00
10 Don Irwin 59	5.00	10.00
11 Eddie LeBaron 58	7.50	15.00
12 Wayne Millner 58	7.50	15.00
13 Wilbur Moore 58	5.00	10.00
14 Jim Schrader 59	5.00	10.00
15 Riley Smith 59	5.00	10.00
16 Mike Sommer 59	5.00	10.00
17 Joe Tereshinski 58	5.00	10.00
18 Dick Todd 59	6.00	12.00
19 Willie Wilkin 59	5.00	10.00
20 Casimir Witucki 59	5.00	10.00

1959 Redskins San Giorgio Flipbooks

This set features members of the Washington Redskins printed on velum type paper stock created in a multi-image action sequence. The set is commonly referenced as the San Giorgio Macaroni Football Flipbooks. Members of the Philadelphia Eagles, Pittsburgh Steelers, and Washington Redskins were produced regionally with 15-players, reportedly, issued per team. Some players were produced in more than one sequence of poses with different captions and/or slightly different photos used. When the flipbooks are still in uncut form (which is most desirable), they measure approximately 5 3/4" by 3 9/16". The sheets are blank backed, in black and white, and provide 14-small numbered pages when cut apart. Collectors were encouraged to cut out each photo and stack them in such a way as to create a moving image of the player when flipped with the fingers. Any additions to this list are appreciated.

1 Sam Baker	100.00	175.00
2 Don Bosseler	90.00	150.00
3 Eddei LeBaron	150.00	250.00
4 Mike Sommer	90.00	150.00

1960-61 Redskins Matchbooks

Sponsored by First Federal Savings and produced by Universal Match Corp., Washington D.C., these 20 matchcovers measure approximately 1 1/2" by 4 1/2" (when completely folded out). Each front cover features a small black-and-white photo of a popular Washington Redskins player with the Redskins logo and the title "Famous Redskins" on the bottom half and a First Federal Savings advertisement on the top half. A player profile is given at the top of the matchcover back along with the words "This is one of twenty famous Redskins presented for you by your 1st Federal Savings and Loan Association of Washington, Bethesda Branch," followed by the address and a Universal Match Corporation company logo. The matchbooks are unnumbered and checklisted below in alphabetical order. It is most commonly thought that the set was issued in two ten-cover series over a two-year period. We've included the presumed year of issue after each cover. The matchbooks are very similar to the 1958-59 issue& but can be distinguished by their off-white colored paper stock instead of light gray. The prices given are for full covers (with strikers) missing the actual matches. This is the form in which the matchbooks are most commonly found. Complete books with matches typically carry a 50% premium. Books missing the striker are considered VG at best.

COMPLETE SET (20)	100.00	200.00
1 Bill Anderson 61	6.00	12.00
2 Don Bosseler 60	6.00	12.00
3 Turk Edwards 60	12.50	25.00
4 Ralph Guglielmi 61	6.00	12.00
5 Bill Hartman 60	5.00	10.00
6 Norb Hecker 61	5.00	10.00
7 Dick James 61	6.00	12.00
8 Charlie Justice 60	10.00	20.00
9 Ray Krouse 61	5.00	10.00
10 Ray Lemek 61	5.00	10.00
11 Tommy Mont 60	5.00	10.00
12 John Olszewski 61	6.00	12.00
13 John Paluck 61	5.00	10.00
14 Jim Peebles 60	5.00	10.00
15 Bo Russell 60	5.00	10.00
16 Jim Schrader 61	5.00	10.00
17 Louis Stephens 61	5.00	10.00
18 Ed Sutton 60	5.00	10.00
19 Bob Toneff 60	6.00	12.00
20 Lavern Torgeson 60	6.00	12.00

1960 Redskins Jay Publishing

This 12-card set features (approximately) 5" by 7" black-and-white player photos. The photos show players in traditional poses with the quarterback preparing to throw, the runner heading downfield, and the defenseman ready for the tackle. These cards were packaged 12 to a packet and originally sold for 25 cents. The backs are blank. The cards are unnumbered and checklisted below in alphabetical order.

COMPLETE SET (12)	40.00	80.00
1 Sam Baker	4.00	8.00
2 Don Bosseler	4.00	8.00
3 Gene Brito	4.00	8.00
4 Johnny Carson	4.00	8.00
5 Chuck Drazenovich	4.00	8.00
6 Ralph Guglielmi	4.00	8.00
7 Dick James	4.00	8.00
8 Eddie LeBaron	6.00	12.00
9 Jim Podoley	4.00	8.00
10 Jim Schrader	4.00	8.00
11 Ed Sutton	4.00	8.00
12 Albert Zagers	4.00	8.00

1961 Redskins Jay Publishing

This 12-card set features 5" by 7" black-and-white player photos. The photos show players in traditional poses with the quarterback preparing to throw, the runner heading downfield, and the defenseman ready for the tackle. These cards were packaged 12 to a packet and originally sold for 25 cents through Jay Publishing's annual football magazine. The backs are blank. The cards are unnumbered and checklisted below in alphabetical order.

COMPLETE SET (12)	50.00	100.00
1 Don Bosseler	5.00	10.00
2 Eagle Day	4.00	8.00
3 Fred Dugan	4.00	8.00
4 Gary Glick	4.00	8.00
5 Sam Horner	4.00	8.00
6 Dick James	5.00	10.00
7 Bob Khayat	4.00	8.00
8 Bill McPeak CO	4.00	8.00
9 Jim Schrader	4.00	8.00
10 Norm Snead	7.50	15.00
11 Bob Toneff	4.00	8.00
12 Ed Vereb	4.00	8.00

1965 Redskins Team Issue

These black and white photos were issued by the Redskins in the mid-1960s. Each was printed on high gloss stock with a blankback and no identifying marks on the fronts. The Redskins often stamped the name of the player on the photo backs.

COMPLETE SET (10)	50.00	100.00
1 Willie Adams	6.00	12.00
2 Len Hauss	6.00	12.00
3 Bob Jencks	6.00	12.00
4 Bob Pellegrini	6.00	12.00
5 Jim Steffen	6.00	12.00
6 Pat Richter	6.00	12.00
7 Fred Williams	6.00	12.00
8 Unidentified Player #24	6.00	12.00
9 Unidentified Player #27	6.00	12.00
10 Unidentified Player #71	6.00	12.00

1965 Redskins Volpe Tumblers

These Redskins artist's renderings were inserted into a plastic cup tumbler produced in 1965. The noted sports artist Volpe created the artwork which includes an action scene and a player portrait. The paper inserts are unnumbered, each measures approximately 5" by 8 1/2" and are curved in the shape required to fit inside the plastic cup. This set is believed to contain up to 12-cups. Any additions to this list are welcomed.

1 Sam Huff	50.00	80.00
2 Sonny Jurgensen	60.00	100.00
3 Paul Krause	30.00	50.00
4 Bobby Mitchell	35.00	60.00
5 John Paluck	25.00	40.00
6 Joe Rutgens	25.00	40.00
7 Charley Taylor	35.00	60.00

1966 Redskins Team Issue

This set of photos was issued in the mid-1960s and features a black and white photo of a Redskins player on each. The photos measure roughly 5" by 7" and include the player's name, his position (spelled out), and the team name below the each player image. The backs are blank. A complete set is thought to include 12-photos, therefore any additions to this list are appreciated.

COMPLETE SET (6)	40.00	80.00
1 Chris Hanburger	7.50	15.00
2 Sonny Jurgensen	12.50	25.00
3 Bobby Mitchell	10.00	20.00
4 Brig Owens	6.00	12.00
5 Joe Rutgens	6.00	12.00
6 Ron Snidow	6.00	12.00

1969 Redskins High's Dairy

This eight-card set was sponsored by High's Dairy Stores and measures approximately 8" by 10". The front has white borders and a full color painting of the player by Alex Fournier, with the player's signature near the bottom of the portrait. The plain white back gives biographical and statistical information on the player on its left side, and information about Fournier on the right. Reportedly 70,000 of each photo was produced. Collectors could receive a free card for each two half gallons of milk they purchased or could buy them from High's Dairy Stores for ten cents each. The cards are unnumbered and checklisted below in alphabetical order. Reportedly, Bobby Mitchell was drawn for this set but never printed as he retired before the 1969 season began.

COMPLETE SET (8)	75.00	125.00
1 Chris Hanburger	7.50	15.00
2 Len Hauss	6.00	12.00
3 Sam Huff	10.00	20.00
4 Sonny Jurgensen	20.00	35.00
5 Carl Kammerer	6.00	12.00
6 Brig Owens	6.00	12.00
7 Pat Richter	6.00	12.00
8 Charley Taylor	10.00	20.00

1971 Redskins Team Issue

This set of black and white player photos was released around 1971. Each measures roughly 8" by 10 1/8" and features the player in the yellow Redskins helmet. No player names are identified on the fronts but either a stamped or written name was often included on the, otherwise blank, cardbacks. They look very similar to the 1973 set but can be identified by the yellow player helmets.

COMPLETE SET (20)	100.00	200.00
1 Verlon Biggs	5.00	10.00
2 Larry Brown	6.00	12.00
3 George Burman	5.00	10.00
4 Boyd Dowler	6.00	12.00
5 Pat Fischer	5.00	10.00
6 Chris Hanburger	6.00	12.00
7 Charlie Harraway	5.00	10.00
8 Jon Jaqua	5.00	10.00
9 Sonny Jurgensen	10.00	20.00
10 Billy Kilmer	7.50	15.00
11 Curt Knight	5.00	10.00
12 Tommy Mason	5.00	10.00
13 Clifton McNeil	5.00	10.00
14 Brig Owens	5.00	10.00
15 Jack Pardee	6.00	12.00
16 Jerry Smith	5.00	10.00
17 Diron Talbert	5.00	10.00
18 Charley Taylor	7.50	15.00
19 Ted Vactor	5.00	10.00
20 John Wilbur	5.00	10.00

1972 Redskins Characatures

This set was produced by Dick Shuman and Compu-Set, Inc. in 1972 and features players of the Washington Redskins. Each card measures approximatley 8" by 10" and features a characature drawing of the player with his name printed below. The cards are unnumbered and blankbacked.

COMPLETE SET (31)	200.00	350.00
1 Mack Alston	6.00	12.00
2 Mike Bass	7.50	15.00
3 Verlon Biggs	6.00	12.00
4 Mike Bragg	6.00	12.00
5 Larry Brown	10.00	20.00
6 Speedy Duncan	7.50	15.00
7 Pat Fischer	7.50	15.00
8 Chris Hanburger	7.50	15.00
9 Charlie Harraway	6.00	12.00
10 Len Hauss	6.00	12.00
11 Roy Jefferson	7.50	15.00
12 Sonny Jurgensen	12.50	25.00
13 Billy Kilmer	10.00	20.00
14 Curt Knight	6.00	12.00
15 Ron McDole	6.00	12.00
16 Clifton McNeil	6.00	12.00
17 George Nock	6.00	12.00
18 Brig Owens	6.00	12.00
19 Jack Pardee	7.50	15.00
20 Richie Petitbon	7.50	15.00
21 Myron Pottios	6.00	12.00
22 Walter Rock	6.00	12.00
23 Ray Schoenke	6.00	12.00
24 Manny Sistrunk	6.00	12.00
25 Jerry Smith	6.00	12.00
26 Jim Snowden	6.00	12.00
27 Diron Talbert	6.00	12.00
28 Charley Taylor	10.00	20.00
29 Ted Vactor	6.00	12.00
30 John Wilbur	6.00	12.00
31 Cover Card Pardee M.Bass M.Sistrunk Hanburger	7.50	15.00

1972 Redskins Picture Pack

This set of 8 1/2" by 11" photos was distributed in two separate "picture packs" with 14-defensive players in one and 16-offensive players in the other envelope. The fronts feature a player photo with his jersey number and name below the photo and the team name below that. The backs are blank and unnumbered.

COMPLETE SET (30)	75.00	150.00
1 Mack Alston	2.50	5.00
2 Mike Bass	2.50	5.00
3 Verlon Biggs	2.50	5.00
4 Larry Brown	4.00	8.00
5 Bill Brundige	2.50	5.00
6 Bob Brunet	2.50	5.00
7 Pat Fischer	2.50	5.00
8 Chris Hanburger	3.00	6.00
9 Charlie Harraway	2.50	5.00
10 Len Hauss	2.50	5.00
11 Terry Hermeling	2.50	5.00
12 Jon Jaqua	2.50	5.00
13 Roy Jefferson	3.00	6.00
14 Sonny Jurgensen	6.00	12.00
15 Billy Kilmer	5.00	10.00
16 Paul Laaveg	2.50	5.00
17 Harold McLinton	2.50	5.00
18 Ron McDole	2.50	5.00
19 Clifton McNeil	2.50	5.00
20 Brig Owens	2.50	5.00
21 Jack Pardee	3.00	6.00
22 Myron Pottios	2.50	5.00
23 Walter Rock	2.50	5.00
24 Manny Sistrunk	2.50	5.00
25 Jerry Smith	2.50	5.00
26 Diron Talbert	2.50	5.00
27 Charley Taylor	5.00	10.00
28 Roosevelt Taylor	3.00	6.00
29 Ted Vactor	2.50	5.00
30 John Wilbur	2.50	5.00

1973 Redskins McDonald's

These 11" by 14" color posters were sponsored by and distributed through McDonald's stores. Each includes an artist's rendering of one Redskins player along with the year and the "McDonald's Superstars Collector's Series" notation below the picture. Reprints can often be found of these prints but can be identified by the new white flat finish paper stock. The originals were printed on glossy cream colored stock.

COMPLETE SET (4)	60.00	100.00
1 Chris Hanburger	12.00	20.00
2 Sonny Jurgensen	25.00	40.00
3 Billy Kilmer	15.00	25.00
4 Charley Taylor	15.00	25.00

1973 Redskins Newspaper Posters

These oversized (roughly 14 1/4" by 21 1/2") posters were inserted into issues of The Sunday Star and The Washington Daily News throughout the 1973 season. Each poster features an artist's rendering of a player with just his name printed inside the image. Within the border below the image are the names of the two newspapers. The backs feature newsprint from another page of the paper. There were thought to have been 26-different posters produced. Any additions to this list are appreciated.

COMPLETE SET (24)	175.00	300.00
1 George Allen CO	12.50	25.00
2 Mike Bass	6.00	12.00
3 Verlon Biggs	6.00	12.00
4 Mike Bragg	6.00	12.00
5 Larry Brown	10.00	20.00
6 Speedy Duncan	7.50	15.00
7 Pat Fischer	7.50	15.00
8 Chris Hanburger	7.50	15.00
9 Charlie Harraway	6.00	12.00
10 Len Hauss	6.00	12.00
11 Roy Jefferson	6.00	12.00
12 Sonny Jurgensen	12.50	25.00
13 Billy Kilmer	10.00	20.00
14 Curt Knight	6.00	12.00
15 Paul Laaveg	6.00	12.00
16 Ron McDole	6.00	12.00
17 Brig Owens	6.00	12.00
18 Walter Rock	6.00	12.00
19 Ray Schoenke	6.00	12.00
20 Manny Sistrunk	6.00	12.00
21 Jerry Smith	6.00	12.00
22 Diron Talbert	6.00	12.00
23 Charley Taylor	10.00	20.00
24 Roosevelt Taylor	7.50	15.00

1973 Redskins Team Issue

This set of black and white player photos was released around 1973. Each measures roughly 8" by 10 1/8" and features the player in the red Redskins helmet in a kneeling pose. No player names are identified on the fronts but either a stamped or written name was often included on the, otherwise blank, cardbacks. They look very similar to the 1971 set but can be identified by the red player helmets.

COMPLETE SET (43)	175.00	300.00
1 George Allen CO	10.00	20.00
2 Mike Bass	5.00	10.00
3 Verlon Biggs	5.00	10.00
4 Mike Bragg	5.00	10.00
5 Larry Brown	6.00	12.00
6 Bill Brundige	5.00	10.00
7 Bob Brunet	5.00	10.00
8 Speedy Duncan	5.00	10.00
9 Brad Dusek	5.00	10.00
10 Pat Fischer	5.00	10.00
11 Frank Grant	5.00	10.00
12 Charlie Harraway	5.00	10.00
13 Chris Hanburger	6.00	12.00
14 Mike Hancock	5.00	10.00
15 Len Hauss	5.00	10.00
16 Terry Hermeling	5.00	10.00
17 Mike Hull	5.00	10.00
18 Dennis Johnson	5.00	10.00
19 Jimmie Jones	5.00	10.00
20 Sonny Jurgensen	10.00	20.00
21 Billy Kilmer	7.50	15.00
22 Curt Knight	5.00	10.00
23 Paul Laaveg	5.00	10.00
24 Bill Malinchak	5.00	10.00
25 Ron McDole	5.00	10.00
26 Harold McLinton	5.00	10.00
27 Herb Mul-Key	5.00	10.00
28 Brig Owens	5.00	10.00
29 Richie Petitbon	5.00	10.00
30 Myron Pottios	5.00	10.00
31 Walter Rock	5.00	10.00
32 Dan Ryczek	5.00	10.00
33 Ray Schoenke	5.00	10.00
34 Manny Sistrunk	5.00	10.00
35 Jerry Smith	5.00	10.00
36 Diron Talbert	5.00	10.00
37 Charley Taylor	7.50	15.00
38 Roosevelt Taylor	6.00	12.00
39 Duane Thomas	5.00	10.00
40 Russell Tillman	5.00	10.00
41 Ted Vactor	5.00	10.00
42 John Wilbur	5.00	10.00
43 Sam Wyche	6.00	12.00

1973 Redskins Team Issue Color

The NFLPA worked with many teams in 1973 to issued photo packs to be sold at stadium concession stands. Each measures approximately 7" by 8-5/8" and features a color player photo with a blank back. A small sheet with a player checklist was included in each 6-photo pack.

COMPLETE SET (6)	25.00	40.00
1 Larry Brown	4.00	8.00
2 Chris Hanburger	4.00	8.00
3 Sonny Jurgensen	6.00	12.00
4 Billy Kilmer	5.00	10.00
5 Charley Taylor	5.00	10.00
6 Duane Thomas	4.00	8.00

1974 Redskins McDonald's

For the second year, these 11" by 14" color posters were sponsored by and distributed through McDonald's stores. Each includes an artist's rendering of a Redskins player along with the year and the "McDonald's Superstars Collector's Series" notation below the picture. Reprints can often be found of these prints but can be identified by the new white flat finish paper stock. The originals were printed on glossy cream colored stock.

COMPLETE SET (4)	35.00	60.00
1 Larry Brown	12.00	20.00
2 Roy Jefferson	12.00	20.00
3 Herb Mul-Key	10.00	15.00
4 Diron Talbert	10.00	15.00

1977 Redskins Team Issue

This set of photos was released by the Washington Redskins. Each measures roughly 5" by 7" and includes a player photo on the front with a 1/2" white border on the top and bottom and a 3/8" border on the left and right. There is no player identification except for the facsimile autograph that appears on some of the photos. The backs are blank and unnumbered. The photos are similar in appearance to the 1979 issue. Any additions to this list are appreciated.

COMPLETE SET (7)	30.00	60.00
1 Eddie Brown	4.00	8.00
2 Chris Hanburger	5.00	10.00
3 Terry Hermeling	4.00	8.00
4 Billy Kilmer	6.00	12.00
5 Joe Theismann	10.00	20.00
6 Jersey #50	4.00	8.00
7 Jersey #57	4.00	8.00

1979 Redskins Team Issue

This set of photos was released by the Washington Redskins. Each measures roughly 5" by 7" and includes a player photo on the front with a 1/4" white border on all four sides. There is no player identification except for the facsimile autograph that appears on the photo. The backs are blank and unnumbered. The photos are similar in appearance to the 1977 issue.

COMPLETE SET (14)	50.00	100.00
1 Coy Bacon	4.00	8.00
2 Mike Curtis	5.00	10.00
3 Fred Dean	5.00	10.00
4 Greg Dubinetz	4.00	8.00
5 Phil DuBois	4.00	8.00
6 Ted Fritsch	4.00	8.00
7 Don Harris	4.00	8.00
8 Don Hover	4.00	8.00
9 Benny Malone	4.00	8.00
10 Kim McQuilken	4.00	8.00
11 Jack Pardee CO	5.00	10.00
12 Paul Smith	4.00	8.00
13 Diron Talbert	4.00	8.00
14 Joe Theismann	10.00	20.00

1930 Rogers Peet

The Rogers Peet Department Store in New York released this set in early 1930. The cards were given out four at time to employees at the store for enrolling boys in Ropeco (the store's magazine club). Employees who completed the set, and pasted them in the album designed to house the cards, were eligible to win prizes. The blankbacked cards measure roughly 1 3/4" by 2 1/2" and feature a black and white photo of the famous athlete with his name and card number below the picture. Additions to this list are appreciated.

31 Red Grange Football	800.00	1,200.00
33 Ken Strong Football	250.00	400.00
37 Ed Wittmer Football	100.00	175.00
41 Chris Cagle Football	125.00	200.00

1979 Sacramento Buffaloes Schedules

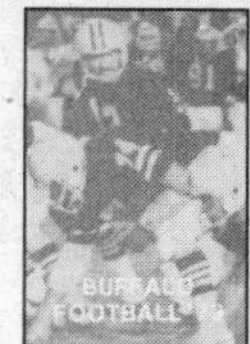

This set of black and white cards features members of the California Football League Sacramento Buffaloes. Each features a game action photo on the front and the team's schedule on the back with the player identified at the bottom.

COMPLETE SET (6)	12.50	25.00
1 Wayne Dalkse Bill Shiflett	2.50	5.00
2 Jim Gabriel Rod Lung	2.50	5.00
3 Earl Green	2.50	5.00
4 Ron Killion	2.50	5.00
5 Rod Lung	2.50	5.00
6 Bob Morris	2.50	5.00

1948-1950 Safe-T-Card

Cards from this set were issued in the Washington D.C. area in the late 1940s and early 1950s. Each card was printed in either black or red and features an artist's rendering of a famous area athlete or personality from a variety of sports. The card backs feature an ad for Jim Gibbons Cartoon-A-Quiz television show along with an ad from a local business. The player's facsimile autograph and team or sport affiliation is included on the fronts.

1 John Adams FB	15.00	30.00
5 Herman Ball FB	15.00	30.00
6 Sammy Baugh FB	50.00	100.00
7 Sammy Baugh QB FB	50.00	100.00
8 Bryan Bell FB	15.00	30.00
14 Billy Conn FB	15.00	30.00
16 Andy Davis FB	15.00	30.00
17 Doug DeGroot CO FB	15.00	30.00
18 Al Demao FB	15.00	30.00
20 Mush Dubofsky CO FB	15.00	30.00
22 Turk Edwards FB	30.00	60.00

24 Tom Farmer FB	15.00	30.00
26 Lou Gambino FB	15.00	30.00
27 Harry Gilmer Hel FB	20.00	40.00
28 Harry Gilmer No Hel FB	20.00	40.00
31 Art Guepe CO FB	15.00	30.00
39 Jan Jankowski CO FB	15.00	30.00
42 Bob Margarita CO FB	15.00	30.00
43 Corrine Griffith Marshall actress	15.00	30.00
44 Dick McCann GM FB	15.00	30.00
47 Wilbur Moore FB	20.00	40.00
51 Dick Poillon FB	15.00	30.00
53 Bo Rowland CO FB	15.00	30.00
54 Dan Sandifer FB	15.00	30.00
55 George Sauer CO FB	15.00	30.00
58 Jim Tatum CO FB	15.00	30.00
59 Joe Tereshinski FB	20.00	40.00
60 Dick Todd FB	15.00	30.00
61 Vic Turyn FB	15.00	30.00
63 Bob Waterfield FB	40.00	80.00
64 John Welchel CO FB	15.00	30.00

1976 Saga Discs

These cards parallel the 1976 Crane Discs set. Instead of the Crane sponsor logo on back, each features the "Saga" logo. The Saga versions are much more difficult to find than their Crane counterparts.

COMPLETE SET (30)	300.00	500.00
1 Ken Anderson	5.00	12.00
2 Otis Armstrong	3.00	8.00
3 Steve Bartkowski	4.00	10.00
4 Terry Bradshaw	25.00	60.00
5 John Brockington	2.50	6.00
6 Doug Buffone	2.50	6.00
7 Wally Chambers	2.50	6.00
8 Isaac Curtis	2.50	6.00
9 Chuck Foreman	3.00	8.00
10 Roman Gabriel	4.00	10.00
11 Mel Gray	3.00	8.00
12 Joe Greene	12.00	30.00
13 James Harris	2.50	6.00
14 Jim Hart	3.00	8.00
15 Billy Kilmer	4.00	10.00
16 Greg Landry	3.00	8.00
17 Ed Marinaro	2.50	6.00
18 Lawrence McCutcheon	3.00	8.00
19 Terry Metcalf	3.00	8.00
20 Lydell Mitchell	2.50	6.00
21 Jim Otis	2.50	6.00
22 Alan Page	4.00	10.00
23 Walter Payton	125.00	250.00
24 Greg Pruitt	3.00	8.00
25 Charlie Sanders	4.00	10.00
26 Ron Shanklin	2.50	6.00
27 Roger Staubach	25.00	60.00
28 Jan Stenerud	4.00	10.00
29 Charley Taylor	5.00	12.00
30 Roger Wehrli	3.00	8.00

1967 Saints Team Doubloons

For a number of years, the New Orleans Saints included one Doubloon (coin) per game day program. The 1967 coins featured on the fronts a player wearing the team helmet for each home game match-up for the Saints season including one pre-season game. The coin backs included an advertisement for Jax Beer. The year of issue is also featured on the coin front and each was produced using a silver colored aluminum metal. We've numbered the set in the order of release.

COMPLETE SET (8)	15.00	30.00
1 Saints vs. Falcons	2.00	4.00
2 Saints vs. Rams	2.00	4.00
3 Saints vs. Redskins	2.50	5.00
4 Saints vs. Browns	2.50	5.00
5 Saints vs. Steelers	2.50	5.00
6 Saints vs. Eagles	2.00	4.00
7 Saints vs. Cowboys	2.50	5.00
8 Saints vs. Falcons	2.00	4.00

1967 Saints Team Issue 5X7 Bordered

The Saints issued several different sets of 5" by 7" photos, presumably over a period of years. Many of the photographs of the same players in either the bordered or borderless sets are identical. The text size and style of each photo in this release are exactly the same. The players full name is to the left, with his position initials in the center, and the full team name printed in all caps to the right. All are head and chest shots instead of action. Each is unnumbered and blankbacked.

COMPLETE SET (20)	75.00	150.00
1 Danny Abramowicz	5.00	10.00
2 Doug Atkins	6.00	12.00
3 Tom Barrington	4.00	8.00
4 Lou Cordileone	4.00	8.00
5 Bruce Cortez	4.00	8.00
6 Gary Cuozzo	5.00	10.00
7 Ted Davis	4.00	8.00
8 Jim Hester	4.00	8.00
9 Les Kelley	4.00	8.00
10 Kent Kramer	4.00	8.00
11 Jake Kupp	4.00	8.00
12 Obert Logan	4.00	8.00
13 Don McCall	4.00	8.00
14 Thomas McNeill	4.00	8.00
15 Ray Ogden	4.00	8.00
16 Ray Rissmiller	4.00	8.00
17 Walter Roberts	4.00	8.00
18 George Rose	4.00	8.00
19 Bill Sandeman	4.00	8.00
20 Phil Vandersea	4.00	8.00
21 Joe Wendryhoski	4.00	8.00
22 Dave Whitsell	4.00	8.00
23 Gary Wood	4.00	8.00

1967-68 Saints Team Issue 5X7 Borderless

The Saints issued two different sets of 5" by 7" photos, presumably over a period of years. The photographs of the same players in both sets are identical except for the white border or lack of a border. The text size and style varies from photo to photo as does the player information below the picture. All are head and chest shots instead of action. The two groups were likely issued together but have been separated for ease in cataloging. Each is unnumbered and blankbacked.

COMPLETE SET (28)	100.00	200.00
1 Charlie Brown RB	4.00	8.00
2 Vern Burke	4.00	8.00
3 Jackie Burkett	4.00	8.00
4 Bill Carr	4.00	8.00
5 Bill Cody	4.00	8.00
6 Ted Davis	4.00	8.00
7 Jim Garcia	4.00	8.00
8 Tom Hall	4.00	8.00
9 Jimmy Heidel	4.00	8.00
10 Les Kelley	4.00	8.00
11 Jake Kupp	4.00	8.00
12 Herman Lee	4.00	8.00
13 John Morrow	4.00	8.00
14 Ray Ogden	4.00	8.00
15 Ray Rissmiller	4.00	8.00
16 Bert Rose GM	4.00	8.00
17 Bill Sandeman	4.00	8.00
18 Roy Schmidt	4.00	8.00
19 Brian Schweda	4.00	8.00
20 Dave Simmons	4.00	8.00
21 Jerry Simmons	4.00	8.00
22 Mike Tilleman	4.00	8.00
23 Joe Wendryhoski	4.00	8.00
24 Ernie Wheelwright UER	4.00	8.00
25 Fred Whittingham	4.00	8.00
26 Del Williams	4.00	8.00
27 Bo Wood	4.00	8.00
28 Gary Wood	4.00	8.00

1967-68 Saints Team Issue 8X10

The Saints released these posed action photos primarily for fans and to fulfill autograph reguests. Each measures roughly 8" by 10" and features a black and white player photo with information in the border below the picture. They were likely released over a period of years as the type style and size used varies from photo to photo. There appear to be several distinct types issued with text as follows reading left to right: (1) player's name in all caps, position initials only, and team name in all caps, (2) player's name, position spelled out completely and team in all capital letters, (3) player's name in caps, position spelled out in upper and lower case letters, and team in upper and lower case letters, (4) player's name in all caps (no position) and team name in all caps, (5) player's name in all caps, position spelled out in caps, and team name in all caps, (6) player's name in all caps, no position, team name in upper and lower case letters. Some also appear to have been released through Maison Blanche department stores in New Orleans along with the store's logo stamped on front. These Maison Blanche variations typically sell for a premium as listed below. Any additions to this list and confirmation of Maison Blanche checklist is appreciated.

*MAISON BLANCHE: .75X TO 1.5X

1 Dan Abramowicz 1	6.00	12.00
2 Doug Atkins 1	7.50	15.00
3 Tony Baker 1	5.00	10.00
4A Tom Barrington 1	5.00	10.00
4B Tom Barrington 1	5.00	10.00
5 Jim Boeke 2	5.00	10.00
6 Johnny Brewer 2	5.00	10.00
7 Jackie Burkett 1	5.00	10.00
8 Bo Burris 4	5.00	10.00
9 Bill Cody 4	5.00	10.00
10 Gary Cuozzo 1	6.00	12.00
11 Ted Davis 1	5.00	10.00
12 Tom Dempsey 2	6.00	12.00
13 Al Dodd 1	5.00	10.00
14 John Douglas 1	5.00	10.00
15 Julian Fagan	5.00	10.00
16 Jim Garcia 1	5.00	10.00
17 John Gilliam 4	5.00	10.00
18A Tom Hall 1	5.00	10.00
18B Tom Hall 6	5.00	10.00
19 Kevin Hardy 2	5.00	10.00
20 Edd Hargett	5.00	10.00
21 George Harvey 1	5.00	10.00
22 Jimmy Heidel 1	5.00	10.00
23 Jim Hester 1	5.00	10.00
24 Paul Hornung 6	10.00	20.00
25 Gene Howard 3	5.00	10.00
26 Harry Jacobs	5.00	10.00
27A Les Kelley 1	5.00	10.00
27B Les Kelley 3	5.00	10.00
28 Billy Kilmer	7.50	15.00
29 Elbert Kimbrough	5.00	10.00
30 Kent Kramer 1	5.00	10.00
31 Jake Kupp 1	5.00	10.00
32 Earl Leggett 1	5.00	10.00
33 Andy Livingston 1	5.00	10.00
34 Obert Logan 1	5.00	10.00
35 Tony Lorick 1	5.00	10.00
36 Ray Ogden 1	5.00	10.00
37 Don McCall 1	5.00	10.00
38A Tom McNeill 1	5.00	10.00
38B Tom McNeill 3	5.00	10.00
39 Mike Morgan	5.00	10.00
40 John Morrow 1	5.00	10.00
41 Elijah Nevett 5	5.00	10.00
42 Bob Newland	5.00	10.00
43 Ray Poage 4	5.00	10.00
44 Ray Rissmiller 1	5.00	10.00
45 Walter Roberts 1	5.00	10.00
46 George Rose 1	5.00	10.00
47 David Rowe 4	5.00	10.00
48 Roy Schmidt 4	5.00	10.00
49 Bob Scholtz 6	5.00	10.00
50 Randy Schultz 4	5.00	10.00
51 Brian Schweda 1	5.00	10.00
52 Dave Simmons 1	5.00	10.00
53 Larry Stephens 6	5.00	10.00
54 Monty Stickles 3	5.00	10.00
55 Steve Stonebreaker 1	5.00	10.00
56 Jim Taylor 1	7.50	15.00
57 Mike Tilleman 1	5.00	10.00
58 Willie Townes	5.00	10.00
59 Phil Vandersea 1	5.00	10.00
60 Joe Wendryhoski 1	5.00	10.00
61 Ernie Wheelwright	5.00	10.00
62 Dave Whitsell 1	5.00	10.00
63 Fred Whittingham 1	5.00	10.00
64 Del Williams 1	5.00	10.00
65 Gary Wood 1	5.00	10.00
66 Doug Wyatt	5.00	10.00
67 Team Photo	6.00	12.00

1968 Saints Team Doubloons

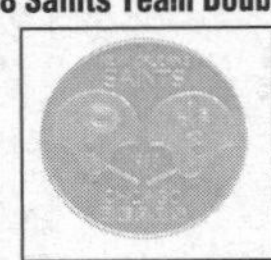

For a number of years, the New Orleans Saints included one Doubloon (coin) per game day program. The 1968 coins featured on the fronts the team helmets for each home game match-up for the Saints season including two pre-season games. The coin backs included an advertisement for Jax Beer. The year of issue is also featured on the coin front and each was produced using both a silver colored aluminum and a gold colored metal. We've numbered the set in the order of release.

COMPLETE SET (9)	20.00	40.00
*GOLD COINS: 1X TO 2X SILVERS		
1 Saints vs. Patriots	2.00	4.00
2 Saints vs. Browns	2.50	5.00
3 Saints vs. Browns	2.50	5.00
4 Saints vs. Redskins	2.50	5.00
5 Saints vs. Cardinals	2.00	4.00
6 Saints vs. Vikings	2.50	5.00
7 Saints vs. Cowboys	2.50	5.00
8 Saints vs. Bears	2.50	5.00
9 Saints vs. Steelers	2.50	5.00

1968 Saints Team Issue 5X7 Bordered

The Saints issued several different sets of 5" by 7" photos, presumably over a period of years. Many of the photographs of the same players in either the bordered or borderless sets are identical. The text size and style of each photo in this release are different than the 1967 set and differ from each other as noted below. Some photos in this group do not have the player identified at all, as noted below. These photos presumably were issued in haste by the team as several players didn't make the Saints rosters. All are head and chest shots instead of action. This group was not likely issued together but has been combined for ease in cataloging and identification. Each is unnumbered and blankbacked.

COMPLETE SET (17)	60.00	120.00
1 Tom Barrington	4.00	8.00
2 Charlie Brown RB	4.00	8.00
3 Bo Burris	4.00	8.00
4 Bill Cody	4.00	8.00
5 Willie Crittendon	4.00	8.00
6A Charles Durkee	4.00	8.00
6B Charles Durkee	4.00	8.00
7 Jim Hester	4.00	8.00
8 Jerry Jones T	4.00	8.00
9 Elijah Nevett	4.00	8.00
10 Mike Rengel	4.00	8.00
11A Randy Schultz	4.00	8.00
11B Randy Schultz	4.00	8.00
12 Brian Schweda	4.00	8.00
13 Jerry Sturm	4.00	8.00
14 Ernie Wheelwright	4.00	8.00
15 Del Williams G	4.00	8.00

1969 Saints Pro Players Doubloons

These coins were produced by Pro Players Doubloons, Inc. and distributed by the New Orleans Saints at games during the 1969 season. Each coin is unnumbered and measures approximately 1 1/2" in diameter. There were at least three different colored coins (silver, brass, and light gold) with each featuring a player bust on front with a short player bio and copyright information on back.

COMPLETE SET (24)	62.50	125.00
1 Dan Abramowicz	3.00	6.00
2 Doug Atkins	6.00	12.00
3 Tom Barrington	2.50	5.00
4 Johnny Brewer	2.50	5.00
5 Bo Burris	2.50	5.00
6 Ted Davis	2.50	5.00
7 John Douglas	2.50	5.00
8 Charlie Durkee	2.50	5.00
9 Gene Howard	2.50	5.00
10 Billy Kilmer	5.00	10.00
11 Jake Kupp	2.50	5.00
12 Errol Linden	2.50	5.00
13 Tony Lorick	2.50	5.00
14 Don McCall	2.50	5.00
15 Dave Parks	3.00	6.00
16 Dave Rowe	2.50	5.00
17 Brian Schweda	2.50	5.00
18 Monte Stickles	2.50	5.00
19 Jerry Sturm	2.50	5.00
20 Mike Tilleman	2.50	5.00
21 Joe Wendryhoski	2.50	5.00
22 Dave Whitsell	3.00	6.00
23 Fred Whittingham	2.50	5.00
24 Del Williams	2.50	5.00

1969 Saints Team Doubloons

For a number of years, the New Orleans Saints included one Doubloon (coin) per game day program. The 1969 coins featured on the fronts two footballs printed with the team names for each home game match-up for the Saints, as well as the team logos. Seven regular season games and two pre-season games were included. The coin backs included an advertisement for Volkswagon. The year of issue is also featured on the coin front and each was produced using both a silver colored aluminum and a gold colored metal. We've numbered the set in the order of release.

COMPLETE SET (9)	17.50	35.00
1 Saints vs. Falcons	2.00	4.00
2 Saints vs. Oilers	2.00	4.00
3 Saints vs. Redskins	2.50	5.00
4 Saints vs. Cowboys	2.50	5.00
5 Saints vs. Browns	2.50	5.00
6 Saints vs. Colts	2.00	4.00
7 Saints vs. 49ers	2.50	5.00
8 Saints vs. Eagles	2.00	4.00
9 Saints vs. Steelers	2.50	5.00

1970 Saints Team Doubloons

For a number of years, the New Orleans Saints included one Doubloon (coin) per game day program. The 1970 coins featured on the fronts a generic figure of a quarterback with the team names for each home game match-up for the Saints, as well as the team logos. Seven regular season games and two pre-season games were included. The coin backs included the crest of the NFL and the names of both conferences. The year of issue is also featured on the coin front and each was produced using both a silver colored aluminum and a gold colored metal. We've numbered the set in the order of release.

COMPLETE SET (9)	17.50	35.00
1 Saints vs. Lions	2.00	4.00

2 Saints vs. Chargers	2.00	4.00
3 Saints vs. Falcons	2.00	4.00
4 Saints vs. Giants	2.00	4.00
5 Saints vs. Rams	2.00	4.00
6 Saints vs. Lions	2.00	4.00
7 Saints vs. Broncos	2.00	4.00
8 Saints vs. 49ers	2.50	5.00
9 Saints vs. Bears	2.50	5.00

1971-76 Saints Circle Inset

Each of these photos measures approximately 8" by 10." The fronts feature black-and-white action player photos with white borders. Near one of the corners a black-and-white headshot photo appears within a circle. The player's name, position, and team name are typically printed in the lower border in a variety of different type sizes and styles. Some photos are horizontally oriented while others are vertical. The backs are blank. The photos are unnumbered and checklisted below in alphabetical order with some players having more than one type. The year of issue for this set is an estimate with the likelihood of the photos being released over a period of years.

1 Steve Baumgartner	4.00	8.00
2 John Beasley	4.00	8.00
3 Tom Blanchard	4.00	8.00
4 Larry Burton	4.00	8.00
5 Warren Capone	4.00	8.00
6 Rusty Chambers	4.00	8.00
7 Henry Childs	4.00	8.00
8 Larry Cipa	4.00	8.00
9 Don Coleman	4.00	8.00
10 Wayne Colman	4.00	8.00
11 Chuck Crist	4.00	8.00
12 Jack DeGrenier	4.00	8.00
13 Jim Deratt	4.00	8.00
14 John Didion	4.00	8.00
15 Andy Dorris	4.00	8.00
16 Bobby Douglass	5.00	10.00
17 Joe Federspiel	4.00	8.00
18 Jim Flanigan LB	4.00	8.00
19 Johnny Fuller	4.00	8.00
20 Elois Grooms	4.00	8.00
21 Andy Hamilton	4.00	8.00
22 Don Herrmann	4.00	8.00
23 Hugo Hollas	4.00	8.00
24 Ernie Jackson	4.00	8.00
25 Andrew Jones	4.00	8.00
26 Rick Kingrea	4.00	8.00
27 Jake Kupp	4.00	8.00
28 Phil LaPorta	4.00	8.00
29 Odell Lawson	4.00	8.00
30 Archie Manning	12.50	25.00
31 Andy Maurer	4.00	8.00
32 Alvin Maxson	4.00	8.00
33 Bill McClard	4.00	8.00
34 Rod McNeill	4.00	8.00
35 Leon McQuay	4.00	8.00
37 Rick Middleton	4.00	8.00
38 Mark Montgomery	4.00	8.00
39 Derland Moore	4.00	8.00
40 Jerry Moore	4.00	8.00
41 Chuck Muncie	6.00	12.00
43 Joe Owens	4.00	8.00
44 Tinker Owens	4.00	8.00
46 Jess Phillips	4.00	8.00
48 Elex Price	4.00	8.00
49 Ken Reaves	4.00	8.00
50 Steve Rogers	4.00	8.00
51 Terry Schmidt	4.00	8.00
52 Kurt Schumacher	4.00	8.00
53 Bobby Scott	4.00	8.00
54 Paul Seal	4.00	8.00
55 Royce Smith	4.00	8.00
56 Maurice Spencer	4.00	8.00
57 Mike Strachan	4.00	8.00
58 Hank Stram CO	6.00	12.00
59 Rich Szaro	4.00	8.00
60 Jim Thaxton	4.00	8.00
61 Dave Thompson	4.00	8.00
36A Jim Merlo	4.00	8.00
36B Jim Merlo	4.00	8.00

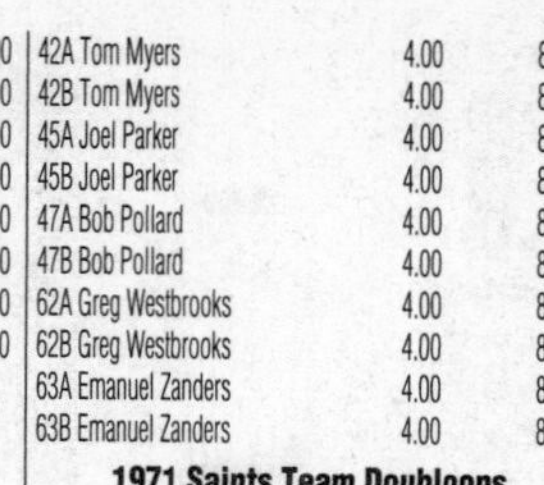

42A Tom Myers	4.00	8.00
42B Tom Myers	4.00	8.00
45A Joel Parker	4.00	8.00
45B Joel Parker	4.00	8.00
47A Bob Pollard	4.00	8.00
47B Bob Pollard	4.00	8.00
62A Greg Westbrooks	4.00	8.00
62B Greg Westbrooks	4.00	8.00
63A Emanuel Zanders	4.00	8.00
63B Emanuel Zanders	4.00	8.00

1971 Saints Team Doubloons

For a number of years, the New Orleans Saints included one Doubloon (coin) per game day program. The 1971 coins featured on the fronts a generic player profile with the team names for each home game match-up for the Saints. Seven regular season games and two pre-season games were included. The coin backs included an advertisement for New Orleans Magazine. The year of issue is also featured on the coin front and each was produced using a silver colored aluminum only. We've numbered the set in the order of release.

COMPLETE SET (9)	17.50	35.00
1 Saints vs. Eagles	2.00	4.00
2 Saints vs. Oilers	2.00	4.00
3 Saints vs. Rams	2.00	4.00
4 Saints vs. 49ers	2.50	5.00
5 Saints vs. Cowboys	2.50	5.00
6 Saints vs. Raiders	2.50	5.00
7 Saints vs. Vikings	2.50	5.00
8 Saints vs. Browns	2.50	5.00
9 Saints vs. Falcons	2.00	4.00

1971-72 Saints Team Issue 4X5

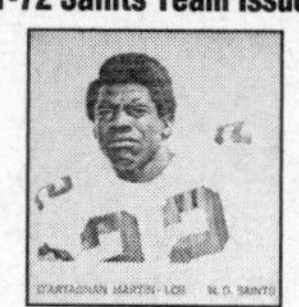

The Saints issued several very similar photo series in the early 1970s. This set was likely issued between 1971 and 1972. Each black and white portrait (no action) photo measures approximately 4" by 5" and carries the player's name and team in the border below the picture. Most include the player's name in large capital letters with the team name abbreviated "N.O. Saints." We've also included a few photos that feature the player's name and team in bold block letters. Any additions to this list are appreciated.

COMPLETE SET (14)	50.00	100.00
1 Carl Cunningham	4.00	8.00
2 Al Dodd	4.00	8.00
3 Julian Fagan	4.00	8.00
4 Edd Hargett	4.00	8.00
5 Glen Ray Hines	4.00	8.00
6 Jake Kupp	4.00	8.00
7 Bivian Lee	4.00	8.00
8 D'Artagnan Martin	4.00	8.00
9 Reynaud Moore	4.00	8.00
10 Don Morrison	4.00	8.00
11 Joe Owens	4.00	8.00
12 Dave Parks	4.00	8.00
13 John Shinners	4.00	8.00
14 Doug Wyatt UER	4.00	8.00

1972 Saints Square Inset

Each of these photos measures approximately 8" by 10." The fronts feature black-and-white action player photos with white borders. Near one of the corners, a black-and-white headshot appears within a square. The player's name, position initials, and team name are printed within one border. The backs are blank and the unnumbered photos are checklisted below in alphabetical order. The list below is thought to be incomplete. Any checklist additions would be appreciated.

COMPLETE SET (9)	30.00	60.00
1 Don Burchfield	4.00	8.00
2 John Didion	4.00	8.00
3 James Ford	4.00	8.00
4 Bob Gresham	4.00	8.00
5 Richard Neal	4.00	8.00
6 Bob Newland	4.00	8.00
7 Dave Parks	4.00	8.00
8 Virgil Robinson	4.00	8.00
9 Jim Strong	4.00	8.00

1972 Saints Team Doubloons

For a number of years, the New Orleans Saints included one Doubloon (coin) per game day program. The 1972 coins featured on the fronts a generic player profile with the team names for each home game match-up for the Saints. Seven regular season games and two pre-season games were included. The coin backs included an advertisement for Burger King. The year of issue is also featured on the coin front and each was produced using a silver colored aluminum only. We've numbered the set in the order of release.

COMPLETE SET (9)	17.50	35.00
1 Saints vs. Cowboys	2.50	5.00
2 Saints vs. Chargers	2.00	4.00
3 Saints vs. Chiefs	2.00	4.00
4 Saints vs. 49ers	2.50	5.00
5 Saints vs. Falcons	2.00	4.00
6 Saints vs. Eagles	2.00	4.00
7 Saints vs. Rams	2.00	4.00
8 Saints vs. Patriots	2.00	4.00
9 Saints vs. Packers	2.50	5.00

1972 Saints Team Issue

The Saints issued several very similar photo series in the early 1970s. This set was most likely released in 1972. Each black and white portrait (no action) photo measures approximately 4" by 5" and carries no pre-printed player identification nor team on the picture at all. Apparently, player names were sometimes written on the photo fronts by a New Orleans Saints employee prior to being shipped out to fans as many are found with this type of written ID.

COMPLETE SET (17)	60.00	120.00
1 Bill Butler	4.00	8.00
2 Al Dodd	4.00	8.00
3 Lawrence Estes	4.00	8.00
4 James Ford	4.00	8.00
5 Edd Hargett	4.00	8.00
6 Glen Ray Hines	4.00	8.00
7 Dave Kopay	4.00	8.00
8 Jake Kupp	4.00	8.00
9 Toni Linhart	4.00	8.00
10 Dave Long	4.00	8.00
11 Don Morrison	4.00	8.00
12 Richard Neal	4.00	8.00
13A Bob Newland	4.00	8.00
13B Bob Newland	4.00	8.00
14 Joe Owens	4.00	8.00
15 Virgil Robinson	4.00	8.00
16 Royce Smith	4.00	8.00

1973 Saints McDonald's

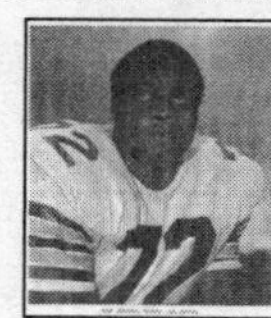

This set of four photos was sponsored by McDonald's. Each photo measures approximately 8" by 10" and features a posed color close-up photo bordered in white. The player's name and team name are printed in black in the bottom white border, and his facsimile autograph is inscribed across the photo. The top portion of the back has biographical information, career summary, and career statistics. The bottom portion includes a list of local McDonald's store addresses and presents the 1973 football schedule for the Saints, Tulane University and LSU. The photos are unnumbered and are checklisted below alphabetically.

COMPLETE SET (4)	17.50	35.00
1 Joe Federspiel	5.00	10.00
2 Jake Kupp	5.00	10.00
3 Joe Owens	5.00	10.00
4 Del Williams	5.00	10.00

1973 Saints Team Doubloons

For a number of years, the New Orleans Saints included one Doubloon (coin) per game day program. The 1973 coins featured on the fronts a generic player profile with the team names for each home game match-up for the Saints. Seven regular season games and two pre-season games were included. The coin backs included an advertisement for Burger King. The year of issue is also featured on the coin front and each was produced using a silver colored aluminum only. We've numbered the set in the order of release.

COMPLETE SET (9)	17.50	35.00
1 Saints vs. Patriots	2.00	4.00
2 Saints vs. Oilers	2.00	4.00
3 Saints vs. Falcons	2.00	4.00
4 Saints vs. Bears	2.50	5.00
5 Saints vs. Lions	2.00	4.00
6 Saints vs. Redskins	2.50	5.00
7 Saints vs. Bills	2.00	4.00
8 Saints vs. Rams	2.00	4.00
9 Saints vs. 49ers	2.50	5.00

1973 Saints Team Issue

The Saints issued several very similar photo series in the early 1970s. This set was most likely issued in 1973. Each black and white portrait (no action) photo measures approximately 4" by 5" and carries the player's name, postion (initials) and team in the border below the picture. The type style used was small (all caps) block lettering with the team name spelled out completely.

COMPLETE SET (17)	60.00	120.00
1 Bill Butler	4.00	8.00
2 Drew Buie	4.00	8.00
3 Bob Davis	4.00	8.00
4 Ernie Jackson	4.00	8.00
5 Ernie Jackson	4.00	8.00
6 Mike Kelly	4.00	8.00
7 Jake Kupp	4.00	8.00
8 Jim Merlo	4.00	8.00
9 Don Morrison	4.00	8.00
10 Bob Newland	4.00	8.00
11 Joe Owens	4.00	8.00
12 Dick Palmer	4.00	8.00
13 Elex Price	4.00	8.00
14 Preston Riley	4.00	8.00
15 Bobby Scott	4.00	8.00
16 Royce Smith	4.00	8.00
17 Howard Stevens	4.00	8.00

1974 Saints Team Doubloons

For a number of years, the New Orleans Saints included one Doubloon (coin) per game day program. The 1974 coins featured on the fronts a generic player profile with the team names for each home game match-up for the Saints. Seven regular season games and two pre-season games were included. The coin backs included an advertisement for Burger King. The year of issue is also featured on the coin front and each was produced using a silver colored aluminum only. We've numbered the set in the order of release.

COMPLETE SET (9)	17.50	35.00
1 Saints vs. Cowboys	2.50	5.00
2 Saints vs. Steelers	2.50	5.00
3 Saints vs. 49ers	2.50	5.00
4 Saints vs. Falcons	2.00	4.00
5 Saints vs. Eagles	2.00	4.00
6 Saints vs. Dolphins	2.50	5.00
7 Saints vs. Rams	2.00	4.00
8 Saints vs. Steelers	2.50	5.00
9 Saints vs. Cardinals	2.00	4.00

1974 Saints Team Issue

The Saints issued several very similar photo series in the early 1970s. This set was most likely issued in 1974. Each black and white portrait (no action) photo measures approximately 4" by 5" and carries the player's name, postion (initials) and team in the border below the picture. The type style used was small italicized block lettering with the team name spelled out completely.

COMPLETE SET (13)	40.00	80.00
1 Andy Dorris	4.00	8.00
2 Paul Fersen	4.00	8.00
3 Len Garrett	4.00	8.00
4 Rick Kingrea	4.00	8.00
5 Odell Lawson	4.00	8.00
6 Jim Merlo	4.00	8.00
7 Jerry Moore	4.00	8.00
8 Don Morrison	4.00	8.00
9 Bob Newland	4.00	8.00
10 Joe Owens	4.00	8.00
11 Elex Price	4.00	8.00
12 Bobby Scott	4.00	8.00
13 Howard Stevens	4.00	8.00

1977 Saints Team Issue

This set of blankbacked photos issued by the Saints was most likely released in 1977. Each black and white action photo measures approximately 8" by 10" and includes the player's name, postion (initials) and team name printed in all upper case letters. The player's facsimile autograph is also printed across the photo.

1 Tony Galbreath	4.00	8.00
2 Archie Manning	7.50	15.00
3 Pollard Fultz	4.00	8.00
4 Bobby Scott	4.00	8.00
5 K.Schumacher C.Muncie	5.00	10.00

1979 Saints Coke

The 1979 Coca-Cola New Orleans Saints set contains 45 black and white standard-size cards with red borders. The Coca-Cola logo appears in the upper right hand corner while a New Orleans Saints helmet appears in the lower left. The backs of this gray stock card contain minimal biographical data, the card number and the Coke logo. The cards were produced in conjunction with Topps. There were also unnumbered ad cards for Mr. Pibb and Sprite, one of which was included in each pack of cards.

COMPLETE SET (45)	40.00	80.00
1 Archie Manning	5.00	10.00
2 Ed Burns	1.00	2.00
3 Bobby Scott	1.00	2.00
4 Russell Erxleben	1.00	2.00
5 Eric Felton	1.00	2.00
6 David Gray	1.00	2.00
7 Ricky Ray	1.00	2.00
8 Clarence Chapman	1.00	2.00
9 Kim Jones	1.00	2.00
10 Mike Strachan	1.00	2.00

11 Tony Galbreath	1.25	2.50
12 Tom Myers	1.00	2.00
13 Chuck Muncie	2.50	5.00
14 Jack Holmes	1.00	2.00
15 Don Schwartz	1.00	2.00
16 Ralph McGill	1.00	2.00
17 Ken Bordelon	1.00	2.00
18 Jim Kovach	1.00	2.00
19 Pat Hughes	1.00	2.00
20 Reggie Mathis	1.00	2.00
21 Jim Merlo	1.00	2.00
22 Joe Federspiel	1.00	2.00
23 Don Reese	1.00	2.00
24 Roger Finnie	1.00	2.00
25 John Hill	1.00	2.00
26 Barry Bennett	1.00	2.00
27 Dave Lafary	1.00	2.00
28 Robert Woods	1.00	2.00
29 Conrad Dobler	1.50	3.00
30 John Watson	1.00	2.00
31 Fred Sturt	1.00	2.00
32 J.T. Taylor	1.00	2.00
33 Mike Fultz	1.00	2.00
34 Joe Campbell DT	1.00	2.00
35 Derland Moore	1.00	2.00
36 Elex Price	1.00	2.00
37 Elois Grooms	1.00	2.00
38 Emanuel Zanders	1.00	2.00
39 Ike Harris	1.00	2.00
40 Tinker Owens	1.00	2.00
41 Rich Mauti	1.00	2.00
42 Henry Childs	1.50	3.00
43 Larry Hardy	1.00	2.00
44 Brooks Williams	1.00	2.00
45 Wes Chandler	2.50	5.00
AD1 Mr.Pibb Ad Card	.20	.50
AD2 Sprite Ad Card	.20	.50

1980 Saints Team Issue

These photos were released by the Saints for fans and for player signing appearances. Each measures roughly 8" by 10" and includes a black and white photo of the player with the player's name (in all caps), his position (intials), and team name (New Orleans Saints stacked) below the picture. The backs are blank and unnumbered.

COMPLETE SET (7)	15.00	30.00
1 Russell Erxleben	2.00	5.00
2 Elois Grooms	2.00	5.00
3 Jack Holmes	2.00	5.00
4 Dave LaFary	2.00	5.00
5 Derland Moore	2.00	5.00
6 Benny Ricardo	2.00	5.00
7 Emanuel Zanders	2.00	5.00

1962-63 Salada Coins

This 154-coin set features popular NFL and AFL players from selected teams. Each team had a specific rim color. The numbering of the coins is essentially by teams, i.e., Colts (1-11 blue), Packers (12-22 green), 49ers (23-33 salmon), Bears (34-44 black), Rams (45-55 yellow), Browns (56-66 black), Steelers (67-77 yellow), Lions (78-88 blue), Redskins (89-99 yellow), Eagles (100-110 green), Giants (111-121 blue), Patriots (122-132 salmon), Titans (133-143 blue), and Bills (144-154 salmon). All players are pictured without their helmets. The coins measure approximately 1 1/2" in diameter. The coin backs give the player's name, position, pro team, college, height, and weight. The coins were originally produced on sheets measuring 31 1/2" by 25"; the 255 coins on the sheet included the complete set as well as duplicates and triplicates. Double prints (DP) and triple prints (TP) are listed below. The double-printed coins are generally from certain teams, i.e., Packers, Bears, Browns, Lions, Eagles, Giants, Patriots, Titans, and Bills. Those coins below not listed explicitly as to the frequency of printing are in fact single printed (SP) and hence more difficult to find. The set is sometimes found intact as a presentation set in its own custom box; such a set would be valued 25 percent higher than the complete set price below.

COMPLETE SET (154)	1,250.00	2,500.00
1 Johnny Unitas	75.00	150.00
2 Lenny Moore	40.00	80.00
3 Jim Parker	25.00	50.00
4 Gino Marchetti	25.00	50.00
5 Dick Szymanski	15.00	30.00
6 Alex Sandusky	15.00	30.00
7 Raymond Berry	40.00	80.00
8 Jimmy Orr	15.00	30.00
9 Ordell Braase	15.00	30.00
10 Bill Pellington	15.00	30.00
11 Bob Boyd DB	15.00	30.00
12 Paul Hornung DP	20.00	40.00
13 Jim Taylor DP	15.00	30.00
14 Hank Jordan DP	5.00	10.00
15 Dan Currie DP	4.00	8.00
16 Bill Forester DP	4.00	8.00
17 Dave Hanner DP	4.00	8.00
18 Bart Starr DP	25.00	50.00
19 Max McGee DP	5.00	10.00
20 Jerry Kramer DP	6.00	12.00
21 Forrest Gregg DP	6.00	12.00
22 Jim Ringo DP	6.00	12.00
23 Billy Kilmer	25.00	50.00
24 Charlie Krueger	15.00	30.00
25 Bob St. Clair	25.00	50.00
26 Abe Woodson	15.00	30.00
27 Jim Johnson	25.00	50.00
28 Matt Hazeltine	15.00	30.00
29 Bruce Bosley	15.00	30.00
30 Clyde Conner	15.00	30.00
31 John Brodie	30.00	60.00
32 J.D. Smith	15.00	30.00
33 Monty Stickles	15.00	30.00
34 Johnny Morris DP	3.00	6.00
35 Stan Jones DP	5.00	10.00
36 J.C. Caroline DP	2.50	5.00
37 Richie Petitbon DP	3.00	6.00
38 Joe Fortunato DP	3.00	6.00
39 Larry Morris DP	2.50	5.00
40 Doug Atkins DP	6.00	12.00
41 Bill Wade DP	3.00	6.00
42 Rick Casares DP	3.00	6.00
43 Willie Galimore DP	3.00	6.00
44 Angelo Coia DP	2.50	5.00
45 Ollie Matson	30.00	60.00
46 Carroll Dale	15.00	30.00
47 Ed Meador	15.00	30.00
48 Jon Arnett	15.00	30.00
49 Joe Marconi	15.00	30.00
50 John LoVetere	15.00	30.00
51 Red Phillips	15.00	30.00
52 Zeke Bratkowski	20.00	40.00
53 Dick Bass	15.00	30.00
54 Les Richter	15.00	30.00
55 Art Hunter	15.00	30.00
56 Jim Brown TP	25.00	50.00
57 Mike McCormack DP	5.00	10.00
58 Bob Gain DP	2.50	5.00
59 Paul Wiggin DP	2.50	5.00
60 Jim Houston DP	2.50	5.00
61 Ray Renfro DP	3.00	6.00
62 Galen Fiss DP	2.50	5.00
63 J.R. Smith DP	2.50	5.00
64 John Morrow DP	2.50	5.00
65 Gene Hickerson DP	3.00	6.00
66 Jim Ninowski DP	2.50	5.00
67 Tom Tracy	15.00	30.00
68 Buddy Dial	15.00	30.00
69 Mike Sandusky	15.00	30.00
70 Lou Michaels	15.00	30.00
71 Preston Carpenter	15.00	30.00
72 John Reger	15.00	30.00
73 John Henry Johnson	30.00	60.00
74 Gene Lipscomb	20.00	35.00
75 Mike Henry	15.00	30.00
76 George Tarasovic	15.00	30.00
77 Bobby Layne	50.00	100.00
78 Harley Sewell DP	2.50	5.00
79 Darris McCord DP	2.50	5.00
80 Yale Lary DP	5.00	10.00
81 Jim Gibbons DP	3.00	6.00
82 Gail Cogdill DP	2.50	5.00
83 Nick Pietrosante DP	2.50	5.00
84 Alex Karras DP	7.50	15.00
85 Dick Lane DP	5.00	10.00
86 Joe Schmidt DP	6.00	12.00
87 John Gordy DP	2.50	5.00
88 Milt Plum DP	3.00	6.00
89 Andy Stynchula	15.00	30.00
90 Bob Toneff	15.00	30.00
91 Bill Anderson	15.00	30.00
92 Sam Horner	15.00	30.00
93 Norm Snead	20.00	40.00
94 Bobby Mitchell	30.00	60.00
95 Bill Barnes	15.00	30.00
96 Rod Breedlove	15.00	30.00
97 Fred Hageman	15.00	30.00
98 Vince Promuto	15.00	30.00
99 Joe Rutgens	15.00	30.00
100 Maxie Baughan DP	2.50	5.00
101 Pete Retzlaff DP	3.00	6.00
102 Tom Brookshier DP	3.00	6.00
103 Sonny Jurgensen DP	9.00	18.00
104 Ed Khayat DP	2.50	5.00
105 Chuck Bednarik DP	7.50	15.00
106 Tommy McDonald DP	4.00	8.00
107 Bobby Walston DP	2.50	5.00
108 Ted Dean DP	2.50	5.00
109 Clarence Peaks DP	3.00	6.00
110 Jimmy Carr DP	2.50	5.00
111 Sam Huff DP	7.50	15.00
112 Erich Barnes DP	2.50	5.00
113 Del Shofner DP	3.00	6.00
114 Bob Gaiters DP	2.50	5.00
115 Alex Webster DP	3.00	6.00
116 Dick Modzelewski DP	2.50	5.00
117 Jim Katcavage DP	3.00	6.00
118 Roosevelt Brown DP	5.00	10.00
119 Y.A. Tittle DP	12.50	25.00
120 Andy Robustelli DP	6.00	12.00
121 Dick Lynch DP	2.50	5.00
122 Don Webb DP	2.50	5.00
123 Larry Eisenhauer DP	2.50	5.00
124 Babe Parilli DP	3.00	6.00
125 Charles Long DP	2.50	5.00
126 Billy Lott DP	2.50	5.00
127 Harry Jacobs DP	2.50	5.00
128 Bob Dee DP	2.50	5.00
129 Ron Burton DP	3.00	6.00
130 Jim Colclough TP	1.50	3.00
131 Gino Cappelletti DP	3.00	6.00
132 Tommy Addison DP	2.50	5.00
133 Larry Grantham DP	2.50	5.00
134 Dick Christy DP	2.50	5.00
135 Bill Mathis DP	3.00	6.00
136 Butch Songin DP	2.50	5.00
137 Dainard Paulson DP	2.50	5.00
138 Roger Ellis DP	2.50	5.00
139 Mike Hudock DP	2.50	5.00
140 Don Maynard DP	10.00	20.00
141 Al Dorow DP	2.50	5.00
142 Jack Klotz DP	2.50	5.00
143 Lee Riley DP	2.50	5.00
144 Bill Atkins DP	2.50	5.00
145 Art Baker DP	2.50	5.00
146 Stew Barber DP	2.50	5.00
147 Glenn Bass DP	2.50	5.00
148 Al Bemiller DP	2.50	5.00
149 Richie Lucas DP	2.50	5.00
150 Archie Matsos DP	2.50	5.00
151 Warren Rabb DP	2.50	5.00
152 Ken Rice DP	2.50	5.00
153 Billy Shaw DP	3.00	6.00
154 Laverne Torczon DP	2.50	5.00

1975 San Antonio Wings WFL Team Issue

This set of black and white photos was issued by the San Antonio Wings to fulfill fan requests and for player appearances. Each measures roughly 5" by 7" and includes the player's name, position, and team name below the photo in varying type styles and sizes. The photo backs are blank.

COMPLETE SET (5)	25.00	50.00
1 Rick Cash	5.00	10.00
2 Luther Palmer	5.00	10.00
3 Dick Pesonen CO	5.00	10.00
4 Lonnie Warwick	5.00	10.00
5 Craig Wiseman	5.00	10.00

1976 Seahawks Post-Intelligencer

This 57-card set was issued at the start of training camp for the Seattle Seahawks first season. The cards measure approximately 6 1/2" by 3" and were printed in the sports section of the local newspaper. The fronts feature headshot drawings of the player and his background and have a black dotted line to help cut them out of the newspaper.

COMPLETE SET (57)	125.00	250.00
1 Jack Patera	3.00	6.00
2 Dave Williams WR	3.00	6.00
3 Bill Olds	3.00	6.00
4 Mike Curtis	4.00	8.00
5 Norm Evans	3.00	6.00
6 Ron Howard	3.00	6.00
7 John Demarie	3.00	6.00
8 Ken Geddes	3.00	6.00
9 Don Hansen	3.00	6.00
10 Rollie Woolsey	3.00	6.00
11 Sam McCullum	3.00	6.00
12 Eddie McMillan	3.00	6.00
13 Gordon Jolley	3.00	6.00
14 John McMakin	3.00	6.00
15 Nick Bebout	3.00	6.00
16 Carl Barisich	3.00	6.00
17 Gary Hayman	3.00	6.00
18 Al Matthews	3.00	6.00
19 Fred Hoaglin	3.00	6.00
20 Ahmad Rashad	6.00	12.00
21 Wayne Baker	3.00	6.00
22 Dave Brown	3.00	6.00
23 Larry Woods	3.00	6.00
24 Dave Tipton DE	3.00	6.00
25 Ed Bradley	3.00	6.00
26 Bob Penchion	3.00	6.00
27 Steve Niehaus	3.00	6.00
28 Gary Keithley	3.00	6.00
29 Bob Picard	3.00	6.00
30 Joe Owens	3.00	6.00
31 Steve Myer	3.00	6.00
32 Lyle Blackwood	3.00	6.00
33 Sherman Smith	3.00	6.00
34 Don Bitterlich	3.00	6.00
35 Neil Graff	3.00	6.00
36 Steve Taylor DB	3.00	6.00
37 Kerry Marbury	3.00	6.00
38 Charles Waddell	3.00	6.00
39 Art Kuehn	3.00	6.00
40 Jerry Davis	3.00	6.00
41 Sammy Green	3.00	6.00
42 Rocky Rasley	3.00	6.00
43 Ken Hutcherson	3.00	6.00
44 Dwayne Crump	3.00	6.00
45 Steve Raible	3.00	6.00
45 Larry Bates	3.00	6.00
46 Rondy Colbert	3.00	6.00
47 Randy Johnson	3.00	6.00
48 Andy Bolton	3.00	6.00
49 Jeff Lloyd	3.00	6.00
50 Don Dufek Jr.	3.00	6.00
51 Rick Engles	3.00	6.00
52 Alvis Darby	3.00	6.00
53 Ernie Jones DB	3.00	6.00
55 Jim Zorn	5.00	10.00
56 Don Clune	3.00	6.00
57 Bill Munson	4.00	8.00

1976 Seahawks Team Issue 8.5x11

These blank-backed photos measure approximately 8 1/2" by 11" and feature black-and-white full-bleed head shots of Seattle Seahawks players. The player's name, team name, facsimile autograph, and Seahawks logo appear near the bottom. The photos are unnumbered and checklisted below in alphabetical order. We've included all known photos. Any addtions to this list are appreciated.

COMPLETE SET (12)	60.00	120.00
1 Ed Bradley	5.00	10.00
2 Mike Curtis	6.00	12.00
3 Norm Evans	5.00	10.00
4 Ken Geddes	5.00	10.00
5 Sammy Green	5.00	10.00
6 Fred Hoaglin	5.00	10.00
7 Ron Howard	5.00	10.00
8 Eddie McMillan	5.00	10.00
9 Steve Niehaus	5.00	10.00
10 Jack Patera	5.00	10.00
11 Bob Penchion	5.00	10.00
12 Jim Zorn	7.50	15.00

1976-77 Seahawks Team Issue 5x7

These blank-backed photos measure approximately 5" by 7" and feature black-and-white full-bleed head shots of Seattle Seahawks players. The player's name, team, facsimile autograph, and Seahawks logo appear near the bottom. Some of the photos have the text and helmet printed in black ink while others use white ink. The photos are unnumbered and checklisted below in alphabetical order. We've included all known photos. Any addtions to this list are appreciated.

COMPLETE SET (37)	150.00	300.00
1 Sam Adkins	4.00	8.00
2 Steve August	4.00	8.00
3 Carl Barisich	4.00	8.00
4 Nick Bebout	4.00	8.00
5 Dennis Boyd	4.00	8.00
6 Dave Brown	4.00	8.00
7 Ron Coder	4.00	8.00
8 Mike Curtis	5.00	10.00
9 John DeMarie	4.00	8.00
10 Dan Doornink	4.00	8.00
11 Norm Evans	4.00	8.00
12 Efren Herrera	4.00	8.00
13 Fred Hoaglin	4.00	8.00
14 Ron Howard	4.00	8.00
15 Steve Largent	15.00	25.00
16 Steve Largent	15.00	25.00
17 John Leypoldt	4.00	8.00
18 Bob Lurtsema	4.00	8.00
19 Al Matthews	4.00	8.00
20 Sam McCullum	4.00	8.00
21 John McMakin	4.00	8.00
22 Bill Munson	5.00	10.00
23 Steve Myer	4.00	8.00
24 Steve Niehaus	4.00	8.00
25 Jack Patera CO	4.00	8.00
26 Steve Raible	4.00	8.00
27 John Sawyer	4.00	8.00
28 Sherman Smith	4.00	8.00
29 Don Testerman	4.00	8.00
30 Dave Tipton	4.00	8.00
31 Manu Tuiasosopo	4.00	8.00
32 Herman Weaver	4.00	8.00
33 Cornell Webster	4.00	8.00
34 Rollie Woolsey	4.00	8.00
35 Jim Zorn	7.50	15.00
36 Jim Zorn	7.50	15.00
37 Seahawk Mascot	4.00	8.00

1977 Seahawks Fred Meyer

Sponsored by Fred Meyer Department Stores and subtitled "Savings Selections Quality Service," this set consists of 14 photos (approximately 6" by 7 1/4") printed on thin glossy paper stock. The cards were reportedly given out one per week. The fronts feature either posed or action color player photos with black borders. The player's name, uniform number, and brief player information appear in one of the bottom corners. Most photos have a small color closeup in one of the lower corners; several others do not (photo numbers 3, 5, 12, 13A). Only Jim Zorn is represented twice in the set, by an action photo with a small color closeup and a portrait without an inset closeup. The backs are blank. The cards are unnumbered and checklisted below in alphabetical order. The set features a card of Steve Largent in his Rookie Card year.

COMPLETE SET (14)	75.00	150.00
1 Steve August	5.00	10.00
2 Autry Beamon	5.00	10.00
3 Terry Beeson	5.00	10.00
4 Dennis Boyd	5.00	10.00
5 Norm Evans	5.00	10.00
6 Sammy Green	5.00	10.00
7 Ron Howard	5.00	10.00

8 Steve Largent	20.00	40.00
9 Steve Myer	5.00	10.00
10 Steve Niehaus	5.00	10.00
11 Sherman Smith	5.00	10.00
12 Don Testerman	5.00	10.00
13A Jim Zorn	7.50	15.00
13B Jim Zorn	7.50	15.00

1978 Seahawks Nalley's

The 1978 Nalley's Chips Seattle Seahawks cards are actually the back panels of large (nine ounce) Nalley's boxes of Dippers, Barbecue Chips, and Potato Chips. The cards themselves measure approximately 9" by 10 3/4" and include a facsimile autograph. The back of the potato chip box features a color posed photo of the player with his facsimile autograph. One side of the box has the Seahawks game schedule, while the other side provides biographical and statistical information on the player. The front of the box includes the player's name and card number. The prices listed below refer to complete boxes.

COMPLETE SET (8)	350.00	500.00
1 Steve Largent	200.00	350.00
2 Autry Beamon	15.00	25.00
3 Jim Zorn	35.00	60.00
4 Sherman Smith	18.00	30.00
5 Ron Coder	15.00	25.00
6 Terry Beeson	15.00	25.00
7 Steve Niehaus	15.00	25.00
8 Ron Howard	15.00	25.00

1979 Seahawks Nalley's

The 1979 Nalley's Chips Seattle Seahawks cards are actually the back panels of large (nine ounce) Nalley's boxes of Dippers, Barbecue Chips, and Potato Chips. The cards themselves measure approximately 9" by 10 3/4" and include a facsimile autograph. The back of the potato chip box features a color photo of the player with his facsimile autograph. One side of the box has the Seahawks game schedule, while the other side provides biographical and statistical information on the player. The front of the box features the player's name and a card number that is a continuation of previous year's cards. The prices listed below refer to complete boxes.

COMPLETE SET (8)	75.00	135.00
9 Steve Myer	12.00	20.00
10 Tom Lynch	12.00	20.00
11 David Sims	12.00	20.00
12 John Yarno	12.00	20.00
13 Bill Gregory	12.00	20.00
14 Steve Raible	12.00	20.00
15 Dennis Boyd	12.00	20.00
16 Steve August	12.00	20.00

1979 Seahawks Police

The 1979 Seattle Seahawks Police set consists of 16 cards each measuring approximately 2 5/8" by 4 1/8". In addition to the local law enforcement agency, the set was sponsored by the Washington State Crime Prevention Association, the Kiwanis Club, and Coca-Cola, the logos of which all appear on the back of the cards. In addition to the 13 player cards, cards for the mascot, coach, and Sea Gal were issued. The set is unnumbered but has been listed below in alphabetical order by subject. The backs contain "Tips from the Seahawks". A 1979 copyright date can be found on the back of the cards.

COMPLETE SET (16)	12.50	25.00
1 Steve August	.50	1.00
2 Autry Beamon	.50	1.00
3 Terry Beeson	.50	1.00
4 Dennis Boyd	.50	1.00
5 Dave Brown	.63	1.25
6 Efren Herrera	.50	1.00
7 Steve Largent	6.00	12.00
8 Tom Lynch	.50	1.00
9 Bob Newton	.50	1.00
10 Jack Patera CO	.63	1.25
11 Sea Gal (Keri Truscan)	.50	1.00
12 Seahawk (Mascot)	.50	1.00
13 David Sims	.50	1.00
14 Sherman Smith	.63	1.25
15 John Yarno	.50	1.00
16 Jim Zorn	1.50	3.00

1980 Seahawks Nalley's

The 1980 Nalley's Chips Seattle Seahawks cards are actually the back panels of large (nine ounce) Nalley's boxes of Dippers, Barbecue Chips, and Potato Chips. The cards themselves measure approximately 9" by 10 3/4" and include a facsimile autograph. The back of the potato chip box features a color photo of the player with his facsimile autograph. One side of the box has the Seahawks game schedule, while the other side provides biographical and statistical information on the player. The front of the box features the player's name and a card number that is a continuation of previous year's cards. The prices listed below refer to complete boxes.

COMPLETE SET (8)	75.00	135.00
17 Keith Simpson	8.00	20.00
18 Michael Jackson	8.00	20.00
19 Manu Tuiasosopo	8.00	20.00
20 Sam McCullum	8.00	20.00
21 Keith Butler	8.00	20.00
22 Sam Adkins	8.00	20.00
23 Dan Doornink	8.00	20.00
24 Dave Brown	8.00	20.00

1980 Seahawks Police

The 1980 Seattle Seahawks set of 16 cards is numbered and contains the 1980 date on the back. The cards measure approximately 2 5/8" by 4 1/8". In addition to the local law enforcement agency, the set is sponsored by the Washington State Crime Prevention Association, the Kiwanis Club, Coca-Cola, and the Ernst Home Centers, each of which has their logo appearing on the back. Also appearing on the backs of the cards are "Tips from the Seahawks". The card backs have blue printing with red accent on white card stock. A stylized Seahawks helmet logo appears on the front.

COMPLETE SET (16)	7.50	15.00
1 Sam McCullum	.30	.75
2 Dan Doornink	.25	.60
3 Sherman Smith	.40	1.00
4 Efren Herrera	.25	.60
5 Bill Gregory	.25	.60
6 Keith Simpson	.25	.60
7 Manu Tuiasosopo	.30	.75
8 Michael Jackson	.25	.60
9 Steve Raible	.25	.60
10 Steve Largent	2.50	6.00
11 Jim Zorn	.75	2.00
12 Nick Bebout	.25	.60
13 The Seahawk (mascot)	.25	.60
14 Jack Patera CO	.30	.75
15 Robert Hardy	.25	.60
16 Keith Butler	.25	.60

1980 Seahawks 7-Up

This "7-Up/Seahawks Collectors Series" (as noted on the cardbacks) measures approximately 2 3/8" by 3 1/4" and is printed on thin card stock. Each card was issued on a slightly larger panel (roughly 3 7/8" by 3 1/4") with both the left and right side of the panel being intended to be removed leaving a perforation on both sides of the final separated card. The cardfronts carry a color player photo enclosed in a white border with the Seahawks' helmet, player's name, and 7-Up logo in the bottom border. The card backs feature brief player vital statistics and sponsor logos. The cards are unnumbered and checklisted below alphabetically. Steve Largent and Jim Zorn were not included in the set due to their sponsorship of Darigold Dairy Products.

COMPLETE SET (10)	75.00	150.00
1 Steve August	6.00	15.00
2 Terry Beeson	6.00	15.00
3 Dan Doornink	6.00	15.00
4 Michael Jackson	6.00	15.00
5 Tom Lynch	6.00	15.00
6 Steve Myer	6.00	15.00
7 Steve Raible	6.00	15.00
8 Sherman Smith	8.00	20.00
9 Manu Tuiasosopo	6.00	15.00
10 John Yarno	6.00	15.00

1972 7-Eleven Slurpee Cups

Seven-Eleven stores released two series of football player cups in the early 1970s. Each white plastic cup measures roughly 5-1/4" tall, 3-1/4" in diameter at the mouth and 2" at the base. The fronts feature a color portrait of a player along with his name and team name. In many cases, a facsimile autograph appears between the bottom of the portrait and the player's name. All of the players pictured are helmetless. The backs include basic biographical information along with the 7-Eleven logo at the top and the player's team helmet at the bottom. The unnumbered cups are arranged below alphabetically. Both years are very similar in design. The 1972 release is distinguished by the smaller type face used on the player's name (1/16" tall) and the lack of the "Made in USA" tag that runs down the sides of the 1973 cups.

COMPLETE SET (60)	75.00	150.00
1 Donny Anderson	1.00	2.50
2 Elvin Bethea	1.00	2.50
3 Fred Biletnikoff	2.00	5.00
4 Bill Bradley	.75	2.00
5 Terry Bradshaw	5.00	12.00
6 Larry Brown	1.00	2.50
7 Willie Brown	1.25	3.00
8 Norm Bulaich	.75	2.00
9 Dick Butkus	3.00	8.00
10 Ray Chester	.75	2.00
11 Bill Curry	.75	2.00
12 Len Dawson	1.50	4.00
13 Willie Ellison	.75	2.00
14 Ed Flanagan	.75	2.00
15 Gary Garrison	.75	2.00
16 Gale Gillingham	.75	2.00
17 Joe Greene	1.50	4.00
18 Cedrick Hardman	.75	2.00
19 Jim Hart	1.25	3.00
20 Ted Hendricks	1.25	3.00
21 Winston Hill	.75	2.00
22 Ken Houston	1.25	3.00
23 Chuck Howley	1.00	2.50
24 Claude Humphrey	.75	2.00
25 Roy Jefferson	.75	2.00
26 Sonny Jurgensen	1.50	4.00
27 Leroy Kelly	1.25	3.00
28 Paul Krause	1.00	2.50
29 George Kunz	.75	2.00
30 Jake Kupp	.75	2.00
31 Ted Kwalick	.75	2.00
32 Willie Lanier	1.25	3.00
33 Bob Lilly	1.50	4.00
34 Floyd Little	1.00	2.50
35 Larry Little	1.25	3.00
36 Tom Mack	1.00	2.50
37 Milt Morin	.75	2.00
38 Mercury Morris	1.25	3.00
39 John Niland	.75	2.00
40 Jim Otto	1.25	3.00
41 Steve Owens	1.00	2.50
42 Alan Page	1.25	3.00
43 Jim Plunkett	1.25	3.00
44 Mike Reid	1.25	3.00
45 Mel Renfro	1.25	3.00
46 Isiah Robertson	.75	2.00
47 Andy Russell	1.00	2.50
48 Charlie Sanders	1.00	2.50
49 O.J. Simpson	2.50	6.00
50 Bubba Smith	1.25	3.00
51 Bill Stanfill	1.00	2.50
52 Jan Stenerud	1.25	3.00
53 Walt Sweeney	.75	2.00
54 Bob Tucker	.75	2.00
55 Jim Tyrer	.75	2.00
56 Rick Volk	.75	2.00
57 Gene Washington 49er	1.00	2.50
58 Dave Wilcox	1.00	2.50
59 Del Williams	.75	2.00
60 Ron Yary	1.25	3.00
NNO Picture Checklist	6.00	15.00

1973 7-Eleven Slurpee Cups

Seven-Eleven stores released two series of football player cups in the early 1970s. Each white plastic cup measures roughly 5-1/4" tall, 3-1/4" in diameter at the mouth and 2" at the base. The fronts feature a color portrait of a player along with his name and team name. In many cases, a facsimile autograph appears between the bottom of the portrait and the player's name. All of the players pictured are helmetless. The backs include basic biographical information along with the 7-Eleven logo at the top and the player's team helmet at the bottom. The unnumbered cups are arranged below alphabetically. Both years are very similar in design. The 1973 issue is distinguished by the larger type face used on the player's name (1/8" tall) and the words "Made in USA" that run down the sides of the cups.

COMPLETE SET (1-80)	125.00	250.00
1 Dan Abramowicz	1.25	3.00
2 Ken Anderson	2.00	5.00
3 Jim Beirne	1.00	2.50
4 Ed Bell	1.00	2.50
5 Bob Berry	1.00	2.50
6 Jim Bertelsen	1.00	2.50
7 Marlin Briscoe	1.00	2.50
8 John Brockington	1.00	2.50
9 Larry Brown	1.25	3.00
10 Buck Buchanan	1.50	4.00
11 Dick Butkus	5.00	12.00
12 Larry Carwell	1.00	2.50
13 Rich Caster	1.00	2.50
14 Bobby Douglass	1.00	2.50
15 Pete Duranko	1.00	2.50
16 Cid Edwards	1.00	2.50
17 Mel Farr	1.00	2.50
18 Pat Fischer	1.00	2.50
19 Mike Garrett	1.25	3.00
20 Walt Garrison	1.25	3.00
21 George Goeddeke	1.00	2.50
22 Bob Gresham	1.00	2.50
23 Jack Ham	2.50	6.00
24 Chris Hanburger	1.25	3.00
25 Franco Harris	5.00	12.00
26 Calvin Hill	1.25	3.00
27 J.D. Hill	1.00	2.50
28 Marv Hubbard	1.00	2.50
29 Scott Hunter	1.00	2.50
30 Harold Jackson	1.25	3.00
31 Randy Jackson	1.00	2.50
32 Bob Johnson	1.00	2.50
33 Jim Johnson	1.50	4.00
34 Ron Johnson	1.00	2.50
35 Leroy Keyes	1.00	2.50
36 Greg Landry	1.25	3.00
37 Gary Larsen	1.00	2.50
38 Frank Lewis	1.00	2.50
39 Bob Lilly	2.00	5.00
40 Dale Lindsey	1.00	2.50
41 Larry Little	1.50	4.00
42 Spider Lockhart	1.00	2.50
43 Mike Lucci	1.00	2.50
44 Jim Lynch	1.00	2.50
45 Art Malone	1.00	2.50
46 Ed Marinaro	1.25	3.00
47 Jim Marshall	1.50	4.00
48 Ray May	1.00	2.50
49 Don Maynard	2.00	5.00
50 Don McCauley	1.00	2.50
51 Mike McCoy	1.00	2.50
52 Tom Mitchell	1.00	2.50
53 Tommy Nobis	1.25	3.00
54 Dan Pastorini	1.25	3.00
55 Mac Percival	1.00	2.50
56 Mike Phipps	1.25	3.00
57 Ed Podolak	1.00	2.50
58 John Reaves	1.00	2.50
59 Tim Rossovich	1.00	2.50
60 Bo Scott	1.00	2.50
61 Ron Sellers	1.00	2.50
62 Dennis Shaw	1.00	2.50
63 Mike Siani	1.00	2.50
64 O.J. Simpson	3.00	8.00
65 Bubba Smith	1.50	4.00
66 Larry Smith	1.00	2.50
67 Jackie Smith	1.50	4.00
68 Norm Snead	1.25	3.00
69 Jack Snow	1.25	3.00
70 Steve Spurrier	2.50	6.00
71 Doug Swift	1.00	2.50
72 Jack Tatum	1.50	4.00
73 Bruce Taylor	1.00	2.50
74 Otis Taylor	1.25	3.00
75 Bob Trumpy	1.25	3.00
76 Jim Turner	1.00	2.50
77 Phil Villapiano	1.25	3.00
78 Roger Wehrli	1.25	3.00
79 Ken Willard	1.00	2.50
80 Jack Youngblood	1.50	4.00
NNO Picture Checklist	10.00	25.00

1926 Shotwell Red Grange Ad Back

Shotwell Candy issued two different sets featuring Red Grange. Each card in the "ad back" version measures roughly 2" by 3 1/8" (slightly larger than the blankbacks) and was printed on very thin newspaper type paper stock. Each features Red Grange in a black and white photo from the motion picture "One Minute to Play." The cards were issued as inserts into Shotwell Candies so many are found with creases and other damage from the original packaging. Many of the same photos were used in this version as the first 12-cards of the blankbacked set. However, the captions are worded differently. Each also includes an advertisement on the cardback for Shotwell Candies, a Grange album, and Grange photos. A second, presumably much more scarce, version of card #9 was confirmed in 2011 featuring a photo of Grange wearing his famous jersey #77. It has been speculated that this card may have been pulled early in production or issued very late in the promotion or even issued as a seperate sample card.

COMPLETE SET (12)	2,500.00	4,000.00
1 Red Grange (Getting Under Way)	250.00	400.00
2 Red Grange (A Forward Pass)	200.00	350.00
3 Red Grange (The start of one of those famous 50-yard runs)	200.00	350.00
4 Red Grange (Passing it Along)	250.00	400.00
5 Red Grange (Picking a High One)	200.00	350.00
6 Red Grange (Raccoon coat photo)	250.00	400.00
7 Red Grange (America's Most Famous Ice Man)	200.00	350.00
8 Red Grange (The Famous Smile)	200.00	350.00
9A Red Grange (Illinois Famous Half Back)	250.00	400.00
9B Red Grange SP (Red calls this his lucky number)		
10 Red Grange (The Kick That Put it Over)	250.00	400.00
11 Red Grange (On the Run)	250.00	400.00
12 Red Grange (Himself)	250.00	400.00

1926 Shotwell Red Grange Blankbacked

Shotwell Candy issued two different sets featuring Red Grange. Each card in the blankbacked version measures roughly 1-15/16" by 3" and features a black and white photo from the motion picture "One Minute to Play." The cards were issued as inserts into Shotwell Candies. Photos that feature Grange in football attire generally fetch a slight premium over the movie photo cards.

COMPLETE SET (24)	5,000.00	8,000.00
WRAPPER	1,000.00	1,500.00
1 Red Grange	250.00	400.00
2 Red Grange	200.00	350.00
3 Red Grange	200.00	350.00
4 Red Grange	200.00	350.00
5 Red Grange	200.00	350.00
6 Red Grange	200.00	350.00
7 Red Grange	250.00	400.00
8 Red Grange	200.00	350.00
9 Red Grange	200.00	350.00
10 Red Grange	200.00	350.00
11 Red Grange	200.00	350.00
12 Red Grange	200.00	350.00
13 Red Grange	250.00	400.00
14 Red Grange	250.00	400.00
15 Red Grange	250.00	400.00
16 Red Grange	200.00	350.00
17 Red Grange	200.00	350.00
18 Red Grange	200.00	350.00
19 Red Grange	200.00	350.00
20 Red Grange	250.00	400.00
21 Red Grange	200.00	350.00
22 Red Grange	200.00	350.00
23 Red Grange	200.00	350.00
24 Red Grange	250.00	400.00

1978 Slim Jim

The 1978 Slim Jim football discs were issued on the backs of Slim Jim packages with each package back containing two discs. There were six package colors (flavors): blue (mild), green (pizza), dark green (pepperoni), maroon (salami), orange (bacon), and red (spicy). The large display boxes originally contained 12 small packages and each large box featured one Slim Jim player disc. It is thought that all 70 discs appeared on at least one large box. The complete set consists of 35 connected pairs or 70 individual discs. The individual discs measure approximately 2 3/8" in diameter whereas the complete panel is 3" by 5 3/4". The discs themselves are either yellow, red or brown with black lettering. The same two players are always paired on a particular package. The discs are numbered for convenience in alphabetical order below and prices are for single punched or neatly cut out discs.

COMPLETE SET (70)	200.00	400.00
*UNCUT BOXES: .6X TO 1.5X PAIRS		
*LARGE OUTER BOXES: 2X TO 4X		
1 Lyle Alzado	3.00	8.00
2 Otis Armstrong	2.50	6.00
3 Jerome Barkum	1.50	4.00
4 Bill Bergey	2.00	5.00
5 Elvin Bethea	3.00	8.00
6 Fred Biletnikoff	6.00	15.00
7 Rocky Bleier	5.00	12.00
8 Willie Buchanon	1.50	4.00
9 Doug Buffone	1.50	4.00
10 Dexter Bussey	1.50	4.00
11 John Cappelletti	3.00	8.00
12 Fred Carr	1.50	4.00
13 Tommy Casanova	1.50	4.00
14 Richard Caster	1.50	4.00
15 Bob Chandler	1.50	4.00
16 Larry Csonka	10.00	20.00
17 Isaac Curtis	2.00	5.00
18 Joe DeLamielleure	3.00	8.00
19 Dan Dierdorf	3.00	8.00
20 Glenn Doughty	1.50	4.00
21 Billy Joe DuPree	2.00	5.00
22 John Dutton	1.50	4.00
23 Glen Edwards	1.50	4.00
24 Leon Gray	1.50	4.00
25 Mel Gray	2.00	5.00
26 Joe Greene	6.00	15.00
27 Jack Gregory	1.50	4.00
28 Steve Grogan	3.00	8.00
29 John Hannah	4.00	10.00
30 Jim Hart	2.50	6.00
31 Tommy Hart	1.50	4.00
32 Ron Howard	1.50	4.00
33 Claude Humphrey	2.00	5.00
34 Wilbur Jackson	1.50	4.00
35 Ron Jaworski	3.00	8.00
36 Ron Jessie	1.50	4.00
37 Billy Johnson	2.00	5.00
38 Charlie Joiner	3.00	8.00
39 Paul Krause	3.00	8.00
40 Larry Little	4.00	10.00
41 Archie Manning	5.00	12.00
42 Ron McDole	1.50	4.00
43 Lydell Mitchell	2.00	5.00
44 Nat Moore	2.00	5.00
45 Robert Newhouse	2.50	6.00
46 Riley Odoms	1.50	4.00
47 Alan Page	4.00	10.00
48 Lemar Parrish	2.00	5.00
49 Walter Payton	30.00	60.00
50 Greg Pruitt	2.00	5.00
51 Ahmad Rashad	4.00	10.00
52 Golden Richards	2.00	5.00
53 John Riggins	6.00	15.00
54 Isiah Robertson	1.50	4.00
55 Charlie Sanders	2.50	6.00
56 Clarence Scott	1.50	4.00
57 Lee Roy Selmon	6.00	15.00
58 Otis Sistrunk	2.50	6.00
59 Darryl Stingley	2.50	6.00
60 Bruce Taylor	1.50	4.00
61 Emmitt Thomas	2.00	5.00
62 Mike Thomas	1.50	4.00
63 Gene Upshaw	3.00	8.00
64 Jeff Van Note	1.50	4.00
65 Brad Van Pelt	1.50	4.00
66 Gene Washington 49ers	2.00	5.00
67 Ted Washington	1.50	4.00
68 Roger Wehrli	2.00	5.00
69 Clarence Williams	1.50	4.00
70 Don Woods	1.50	4.00

1974 Southern California Sun WFL Team Issue 8X10

These photos measure roughly 8" x 10" and include black and white images with the player's name in the lower right below the photo and the team name in the upper left corner above the photo. The backs are blank.

1 Anthony Davis	10.00	20.00
2 Dave Roller	7.50	15.00

1974 Southern California Sun WFL Team Sheets

These team issued sheets feature player photos, measuring roughly 8" x 10" overall, with black and white images of either three or four players. The format varies from eight small photos of four players to a sheet to three larger photos on one sheet. The team name and year are included near the bottom and each player's name is printed below his image.

COMPLETE SET (11)	75.00	125.00
1 Booker Brown/Joe Carollo Jack Conners/Dennis Crane	7.50	15.00
2 Alonzo Emery/Wayne Estabrook Kevin Fletcher/Kevin Grady	7.50	15.00
3 Steve Gunther/Tim Guy/Ike Harris John Hoffman DE	7.50	15.00
4 Gene Howard/Clay Jefferies Eric Johnson DB/Kermit Johnson	7.50	15.00
5 Jimmie Jones RB/Durwood Keeton Younger Klippert/Ed Kezirian	7.50	15.00
6 Ken Lee/Terry Lindsey Jacque MacKinnon/Greg Mason	7.50	15.00
7 Ralph Nelson/Jim Bowman Charles DeJurnett	7.50	15.00
8 Eric Patton/Ed Philpott/Dan Pride/Bill Reid	7.50	15.00
9 Dave Roller/Mike Ryan Steve Schroder/Ted Seifert	7.50	15.00
10 Neal Skarin/Dave Szymakowski Ron Thomas WR/ Gary Valbuena	7.50	15.00
11 Cleveland Vann/Jim Williams DB Dave Williams WR	7.50	15.00

1975 Southern California Sun WFL Team Issue 5X7

These photos were released by the team to fulfill fan requests. Each measures roughly 5" x 7" and includes a black and white image with no player names or writing on the fronts. The backs are blank.

1 Kevin Fletcher	6.00	12.00
2 Jim Jones	6.00	12.00
3 Jim Norton	6.00	12.00
4 Scott Palmer	6.00	12.00
5 Don Parish	6.00	12.00
6 Ron Thomas	6.00	12.00

1975 Southern California Sun WFL Team Issue 8X10

These team issued photos measure roughly 8" x 10" and feature black and white player images with no names or identification on the fronts, The photo backs sometimes contain hand written player identification.

1 Kermit Johnson	7.50	15.00
2 Jimmie Lee Jones	7.50	15.00
3 Younger Klippert	7.50	15.00
4 Daryle Lamonica	10.00	20.00
5 James McAlister	7.50	15.00
6 Bill Reid	7.50	15.00
7 Paul Seiler	7.50	15.00
8 Dave Williams	7.50	15.00

1963-66 Spalding Advisory Staff Photos

Spalding released a number of player photos during the 1960s. Each measures roughly 8" by 10" and carries a black and white photo of the player surrounding by a white border. Included below the photo is a note that the player is a member of Spalding's advisory staff. Some include the Spalding logo while other do not. The photos are blankbacked and unnumbered and checklisted below in alphabetical order. Since many of the photos differ in type style and design, it is thought that they were released over a number of years. Any additions to the list below are appreciated.

1 Jon Arnett	7.50	15.00
2 Ronnie Bull	7.50	15.00
3 Gail Cogdill	7.50	15.00
4 John David Crow	7.50	15.00
5 Len Dawson	12.50	25.00
6 Sonny Gibbs	7.50	15.00
7 Pete Retzlaff	7.50	15.00
8 Fran Tarkenton	15.00	30.00
9 Norm Van Brocklin	15.00	30.00
10 Bill Wade	7.50	15.00

1966 Spalding Brown Frame Photos

These photos are similar to other Spalding photos of the era except for the brown wood grain frame border that surrounds the picture. Spalding released a number of player photos during the 1960s. Each measures roughly 8" by 10" and carries a black and white photo of the player. The photos are blankbacked and unnumbered and checklisted below in alphabetical order. Any additions to the list below are appreciated.

1 Roman Gabriel	10.00	20.00
2 Johnny Unitas	30.00	50.00

1967 Spalding Red Border Photos

This group of photos is similar to other Spalding photos of the era except for the red border that surrounds the picture. Spalding released a number of player photos during the 1960s. Each measures roughly 8" by 10" and carries a black and white photo of the player. The photos are blankbacked and unnumbered and checklisted below in alphabetical order. Any additions to the list below are appreciated.

1 Norm Snead	10.00	15.00
2 Johnny Unitas	30.00	50.00

1968 Spalding Green Frame Photos

This group of photos is similar to other Spalding photos of the era except for the green frame border that surrounds the picture. Spalding released a number of player photos during the 1960s. Each measures roughly 8" by 10" and carries a black and white photo of the player. The photos are blankbacked and unnumbered and checklisted below in alphabetical order. Any additions to the list below are appreciated.

COMPLETE SET (5)	60.00	120.00
1 Len Dawson	10.00	20.00
2 Bobby Mitchell	10.00	20.00
3 Fran Tarkenton	15.00	30.00
4 Charley Taylor	10.00	20.00
5 Johnny Unitas	20.00	40.00

1926 Sport Company of America

This 151-card set encompasses athletes from a multitude of different sports. There are 49-cards representing baseball and 14-cards for football. Each includes a black-and-white player photo within a fancy frame border. The player's name and sport are printed at the bottom. The backs carry a short player biography and statistics. The cards originally came in a small glassine envelope along with a coupon that could be redeemed for sporting equipment and are often still found in this form. The cards are unnumbered and have been checklisted below in alphabetical order within sport. We've assigned prefixes to the card numbers which serves to group the cards by sport (BB- baseball, FB- football).

FB1 Peggy Flournoy	100.00	200.00
FB1B Peggy Flournoy AD	125.00	250.00
FB2 Benny Friedman	175.00	300.00
FB3 Ed Garbisch	100.00	200.00
FB4 Red Grango Promo	1,500.00	2,500.00
FB5 Homer Hazel	100.00	200.00
FB6 Walter Koppisch	125.00	250.00
FB6B Walter Koppisch AD	150.00	300.00
FB7 Edward McGinley	100.00	200.00
FB8 Edward McMillan	125.00	250.00
FB8B Edward McMillan AD	150.00	300.00
FB9 Harry Stuhldreher	250.00	500.00
FB9B Harry Stuhldreher AD	300.00	600.00
FB10 Brick Muller	100.00	200.00
FB11 Ernie Nevers	1,000.00	1,500.00
FB12 Swede Oberlander	100.00	200.00
FB12B Swede Oberlander AD	125.00	250.00
FB13 Edward Tryon	125.00	250.00
FB14 Ed Weir	100.00	200.00
FB15 George Wilson	125.00	250.00
FB15B George Wilson AD	150.00	300.00

1933 Sport Kings

The cards in this 48-card set measure 2 3/8" by 2 7/8". The 1933 Sport Kings set, issued by the Goudey Gum Company, contains cards for the most famous athletic heroes of the times. No less than 18 different sports are represented in the set. The baseball cards of Cobb, Hubbell, and Ruth, and the football cards of Rockne, Grange and Thorpe command premium prices. The cards were issued in one-card penny packs which came 100 packs to a box along with a piece of gum. The catalog designation for this set is R338.

COMPLETE SET	10,000.00	16,000.00
4 Red Grange RC FB	500.00	800.00
6 Jim Thorpe RC FB	600.00	1,000.00
35 Knute Rockne RC FB	350.00	600.00

1934 Sport Kings Varsity Game

Goudey Gum Co. produced this 24-card set in wax packs under the Sport Kings Gum label. The year of issue is thought to be 1934, one year after the first set of Sport Kings. Each 2 3/8" by 2 7/8" card features the same front, but a slightly different back. The backs contain a card number followed by play results under the headings of kick off, rush, forward pass, punt, place kick, and goal after touchdown. The play results were designed to be used in a football card game played with the set. The first few words, when available, of the top line of text are included below to help identify each card.

1 Game Card	12.50	25.00
2 Game Card	12.50	25.00
3 Game Card	12.50	25.00
4 Game Card	12.50	25.00
5 Game Card	12.50	25.00
6 Game Card	12.50	25.00
7 Game Card	12.50	25.00
8 Game Card	12.50	25.00
9 Game Card	12.50	25.00
10 Game Card	12.50	25.00
11 Game Card	12.50	25.00
12 Game Card	12.50	25.00
13 Game Card SP	125.00	200.00
14 Game Card	12.50	25.00
15 Game Card	12.50	25.00
16 Game Card	12.50	25.00
17 Game Card	12.50	25.00
18 Game Card	12.50	25.00
19 Game Card SP	75.00	150.00
20 Game Card	12.50	25.00
21 Game Card SP	75.00	150.00
22 Game Card	12.50	25.00
23 Game Card	12.50	25.00
24 Game Card SP	75.00	150.00

1953 Sport Magazine Premiums

This 10-card set features 5 1/2" by 7" color portraits and was issued as a subscription premium by Sport Magazine. These photos were taken by noted sports photographer Ozzie Sweet. Each features a top player from a number of different sports. The photo backs are blank and unnumbered. We've checklisted the set below in alphabetical order.

COMPLETE SET (10)	30.00	60.00
3 Elroy Hirsch FB	7.50	15.00
7 John Olszewski FB	4.00	8.00

1968-73 Sport Pix

These 8" by 10" blank-backed photos feature black and white photos with the players name and the words "Sport Pix" on the bottom. The address for Sport Pix is also on the bottom. Since the cards are not numbered, we have sequenced them in alphabetical order.

COMPLETE SET (22)	150.00	300.00
1 Sammy Baugh	7.50	15.00
2 Jim Brown	10.00	20.00
3 Billy Cannon	5.00	10.00
4 Red Grange	7.50	15.00
6 Paul Hornung	7.50	15.00
7 Sam Huff	6.00	12.00
13 Bobby Mitchell	5.00	10.00
15 Bronko Nagurski Not in football uniform	6.00	12.00
17 Jim Taylor	6.00	12.00
18 Jim Thorpe	7.50	15.00
19 Y.A. Tittle	6.00	12.00
20 Johnny Unitas	10.00	20.00

1977-79 Sportscaster Series 1

COMPLETE SET (24)	17.50	35.00
115 Johnny Unitas	2.00	4.00
120 Jets vs. Colts	.75	1.50

1977-79 Sportscaster Series 2

COMPLETE SET (24)	30.00	60.00
204 George Blanda	1.00	2.00

1977-79 Sportscaster Series 3

COMPLETE SET (24)	15.00	30.00
307 O.J. Simpson	1.50	4.00
320 Joe Namath	2.50	6.00

1977-79 Sportscaster Series 5

COMPLETE SET (24)	12.50	25.00
523 Gale Sayers	2.00	4.00

1977-79 Sportscaster Series 6

COMPLETE SET (24)	12.50	25.00
613 Red Grange	2.00	4.00
618 Jimmy Brown	2.50	5.00

1977-79 Sportscaster Series 7

COMPLETE SET (24)	15.00	30.00
715 1967 Green Bay Packers	.75	2.00

1977-79 Sportscaster Series 8

COMPLETE SET (24)	12.50	25.00
806 Fran Tarkenton	1.25	2.50

1977-79 Sportscaster Series 9

COMPLETE SET (24)	15.00	30.00
922 The Rose Bowl	.75	1.50

1977-79 Sportscaster Series 10

COMPLETE SET (24)	17.50	35.00
1024 Tony Dorsett	2.00	4.00

1977-79 Sportscaster Series 11

COMPLETE SET (25)	20.00	40.00
1113 Larry Csonka and Jim Kiick	1.50	3.00

1977-79 Sportscaster Series 12

COMPLETE SET (24)	12.50	25.00
1206 A Very Warlike Game	.75	1.50
1209 Joe Greene	2.00	4.00

1977-79 Sportscaster Series 13

COMPLETE SET (24)	12.50	25.00
1306 Archie Griffin	1.00	2.50
1321 Miami Dolphins vs. Kansas City	1.00	2.00

1977-79 Sportscaster Series 16

COMPLETE SET (24)	15.00	30.00
1612 Paul Hornung	1.50	3.00

1977-79 Sportscaster Series 17

COMPLETE SET (24)	10.00	20.00
1701 Jim Taylor	1.25	2.50
1715 Ken Stabler	2.00	4.00

1977-79 Sportscaster Series 20

COMPLETE SET (24)	7.50	15.00
2020 Ken Anderson	1.25	2.50

1977-79 Sportscaster Series 21

COMPLETE SET (24)	15.00	30.00
2118 College AS Game	1.00	2.00

1977-79 Sportscaster Series 22

COMPLETE SET (24)	15.00	30.00
2216 Lingo	1.50	4.00

1977-79 Sportscaster Series 23

COMPLETE SET (24)	20.00	40.00
2311 Super Bowl	.75	1.50

1977-79 Sportscaster Series 24

COMPLETE SET (24)	10.00	20.00
2405 Bert Jones	.75	1.50

1977-79 Sportscaster Series 25

COMPLETE SET (24)	10.00	20.00
2523 Charley Taylor	.75	1.50

1977-79 Sportscaster Series 26

COMPLETE SET (24)	15.00	30.00
2611 Presidents in Sport Gerald Ford	5.00	10.00
2614 Walter Payton	4.00	8.00

1977-79 Sportscaster Series 27

COMPLETE SET (24)	12.50	25.00
2706 Packers vs. Bears	.50	1.00

1977-79 Sportscaster Series 29

COMPLETE SET (24)	17.50	35.00
2907 Defensive Formations	3.00	6.00
2916 NFL History	.75	1.50

1977-79 Sportscaster Series 31

COMPLETE SET (24)	12.50	25.00
3102 Trick Plays	.75	1.50

1977-79 Sportscaster Series 32

COMPLETE SET (24)	17.50	35.00
3203 Offensive Alignments	.75	1.50

1977-79 Sportscaster Series 33

COMPLETE SET (24)	10.00	20.00
3301 Holding	.75	1.50
3314 Chuck Foreman	.75	1.50
3322 Gene Upshaw	1.00	2.00

1977-79 Sportscaster Series 34

COMPLETE SET (24)	15.00	30.00
3418 Preston Pearson	.75	2.00

1977-79 Sportscaster Series 35

COMPLETE SET (24)	15.00	30.00
3518 Jim Bakken	.50	1.00

1977-79 Sportscaster Series 36

COMPLETE SET (24)	15.00	30.00
3617 Goal Line Defense	.75	1.50
3620 Two-Minute Offense	1.50	3.00

1977-79 Sportscaster Series 37

Please note that cards number 4 and 17 are not listed. Any information on the two missing cards is very appreciated.

COMPLETE SET (24)	12.50	25.00
3715 Legal and Illegal	.25	.50
3717 Lynn Swann	2.00	5.00

1977-79 Sportscaster Series 38

COMPLETE SET (24)	20.00	40.00
3822 Jack Youngblood	1.00	2.00

1977-79 Sportscaster Series 39

COMPLETE SET (24)	7.50	15.00
3917 Ball Control	.75	1.50
3921 Grabbing the Face Mask	.75	1.50
3922 Harvey Martin	1.00	2.00

1977-79 Sportscaster Series 40

COMPLETE SET (24)	10.00	20.00
4004 Pass Interference	.75	1.50
4010 Rick Upchurch	.50	1.00

1977-79 Sportscaster Series 42

COMPLETE SET (24)	15.00	30.00
4213 Curley Culp	.50	1.00
4224 Cheerleading	.75	1.50

1977-79 Sportscaster Series 43

COMPLETE SET (24)	12.50	25.00
4312 Holding the Ball	.75	1.50

1977-79 Sportscaster Series 44

COMPLETE SET (24)	12.50	25.00
4422 Punting	1.25	2.50
4424 Special Team Defense	.50	1.00

1977-79 Sportscaster Series 45

Card number 11 is not in our checklist. Any information on this missing card is greatly appreciated.

COMPLETE SET (24)	20.00	40.00
4504 Throwing the Ball	1.50	3.00
4509 Punt Returns	1.00	2.00

1977-79 Sportscaster Series 46

COMPLETE SET (24)	12.50	25.00
4601 NFL Draft	1.25	2.50
4613 Kickoff Returns	2.00	4.00

1977-79 Sportscaster Series 47

COMPLETE SET (24)	17.50	35.00
4721 Tom Jackson	2.00	4.00

1977-79 Sportscaster Series 50

COMPLETE SET (24)	15.00	30.00
5001 Equipment	.75	1.50
5020 Ernie Nevers	1.00	2.00

1977-79 Sportscaster Series 53

COMPLETE SET (24)	15.00	30.00
5310 The Sidelines	.75	1.50
5317 Joe Namath GM	1.50	4.00

1977-79 Sportscaster Series 54

COMPLETE SET (24)	15.00	30.00
5414 Joe Kapp	1.00	2.00
5420 Jim Thorpe	4.00	8.00

1977-79 Sportscaster Series 55

COMPLETE SET (24)	12.50	25.00
5501 Dave Casper	1.00	2.00

1977-79 Sportscaster Series 56

COMPLETE SET (24)	37.50	75.00
5615 Ray Guy	2.50	5.00
5618 Great Moments	7.50	15.00

1977-79 Sportscaster Series 57

COMPLETE SET (24)	40.00	80.00
5701 Willie Lanier	2.50	5.00

1977-79 Sportscaster Series 59

COMPLETE SET (24)	50.00	100.00
5902 Roger Staubach	5.00	10.00

1977-79 Sportscaster Series 60

COMPLETE SET (24)	37.50	75.00
6004 Whizzer White	4.00	8.00

1977-79 Sportscaster Series 61

COMPLETE SET (24)	50.00	100.00
6120 Heisman Trophy	5.00	10.00

1977-79 Sportscaster Series 62

COMPLETE SET (24)	40.00	80.00
6214 Eddie Lee Ivery	2.00	4.00

1977-79 Sportscaster Series 63

COMPLETE SET (24)	30.00	60.00
6302 17-0 Dolphins	5.00	10.00
6316 Outland Award	1.00	2.00

1977-79 Sportscaster Series 64

COMPLETE SET (24)	25.00	50.00
6411 Harvard Stadium	2.00	4.00
6419 Floyd Little	2.50	5.00

1977-79 Sportscaster Series 65

COMPLETE SET (24)	40.00	80.00
6524 Franco Harris	3.00	8.00

1977-79 Sportscaster Series 66

COMPLETE SET (24)	37.50	75.00
6607 The Four Horsemen	7.50	15.00

1977-79 Sportscaster Series 67

COMPLETE SET (24)	40.00	80.00
6705 The Bahr Family	2.50	5.00

1977-79 Sportscaster Series 68

COMPLETE SET (24)	40.00	80.00
6806 Incredible Playoff	2.00	4.00
6820 John Cappelletti	2.50	5.00

1977-79 Sportscaster Series 69

COMPLETE SET (24)	40.00	80.00
6902 Terry Bradshaw	5.00	10.00
6912 First Televised	1.00	2.00
6915 Indian HOF	4.00	8.00

1977-79 Sportscaster Series 70

COMPLETE SET (24)	30.00	60.00
7010 Pro Bowl	2.50	5.00

1977-79 Sportscaster Series 71

COMPLETE SET (24)	40.00	80.00
7101 Dave Jennings	2.00	4.00
7123 Chuck Noll	6.00	12.00

1977-79 Sportscaster Series 72

COMPLETE SET (24)	50.00	100.00
7217 Joe Paterno Jeff Hostetler	10.00	20.00
7221 Greg Pruitt	2.50	5.00

1977-79 Sportscaster Series 73

COMPLETE SET (24)	40.00	80.00
7306 Bear Bryant	10.00	20.00

1977-79 Sportscaster Series 75

COMPLETE SET (24)	30.00	60.00
7502 Nick Buoniconti	2.50	5.00

1977-79 Sportscaster Series 76

COMPLETE SET (24)	30.00	60.00
7605 NFL Hall of Fame	2.00	4.00
7624 Walter Camp All-	2.00	4.00

1977-79 Sportscaster Series 78

COMPLETE SET (24)	150.00	300.00
7809 Tom Landry	7.50	15.00
7820 Rating Passers	5.00	10.00

1977-79 Sportscaster Series 79

COMPLETE SET (24)	60.00	120.00
7922 College Football	10.00	20.00

1977-79 Sportscaster Series 80

COMPLETE SET (24)	62.50	125.00
8019 Jim Marshall	4.00	8.00

1977-79 Sportscaster Series 81

COMPLETE SET (24)	62.50	125.00
8118 Dan Pastorini	3.00	6.00
8122 Billy Sims	4.00	8.00

1977-79 Sportscaster Series 82

COMPLETE SET (24)	50.00	100.00
8203 Jerome Holland	2.00	4.00
8221 Tom Cousineau	2.50	5.00

1977-79 Sportscaster Series 83

COMPLETE SET (24)	62.50	125.00
8310 Ed Too Tall Jones	4.00	8.00

1977-79 Sportscaster Series 85

COMPLETE SET (24)	62.50	125.00
8502 Barefoot Athletes	3.00	6.00
8510 Protecting the	3.00	6.00
8520 Lou Holtz FB	10.00	20.00

1977-79 Sportscaster Series 86

COMPLETE SET (24)	50.00	100.00
8601 Grambling	3.00	6.00

1977-79 Sportscaster Series 88

COMPLETE SET (24)	50.00	100.00
8811 Ernie Davis	7.50	15.00

1977-79 Sportscaster Series 101

COMPLETE SET (24)	62.50	125.00
10117 Pat Haden	2.00	5.00

1977-79 Sportscaster Series 102

COMPLETE SET (24)	75.00	150.00
10220 NCAA Records Steve Owens	4.00	8.00

1977-79 Sportscaster Series 103

COMPLETE SET (24)	87.50	175.00
10301 Jim Turner	4.00	8.00
10316 Longest Runs	4.00	8.00

1977 Sports Illustrated Ad Cards

This set is a multi-sport set and features cards with action player photos from various sports as they appeared on different covers of Sports Illustrated Magazine. The cards measure approximately 3 1/2" by 4 3/4" with the backs displaying the player's name and team name and information on how to subscribe to the magazine at a special rate. It was issued by Mrs. Carter Breads.

COMPLETE SET	12.50	25.00
4 Oakland Raiders	2.50	5.00
5 Michigan Wolverines FB	2.50	5.00

1976 Sportstix

These ten blank-backed irregularly shaped stickers measure approximately 3 1/2" in diameter and feature borderless color player action photos. Team markings were crudely obliterated from the players' helmets. The numbering is a continuation from other non-football Sportstix. The stickers came in packs of five, with stickers 31-35 in packs marked "Series 3B" and stickers 36-40 in packs marked "Series 4B." The player's name, along with the sticker's number& appears in black lettering (except the Drew Pearson and Gary Huff stickers have white lettering). The stickers are numbered on the front.

COMPLETE SET (11)	100.00	175.00
31 Carl Eller Minnesota Vikings	6.00	15.00
32 Fred Biletnikoff UER Oakland Raiders (Misspelled	10.00	25.00
33 Terry Metcalf St. Louis Cardinals	5.00	12.00
34 Gary Huff Chicago Bears	4.00	10.00
35 Steve Bartkowski Atlanta Falcons	6.00	15.00
36 Dan Pastorini Houston Oilers	5.00	12.00
37 Drew Pearson UER Dallas Cowboys (Photo is of Gl	7.50	20.00
38 Bert Jones Baltimore Colts	5.00	12.00
39 Otis Armstrong Denver Broncos	5.00	12.00
40 Don Woods San Diego Chargers	4.00	10.00
C Dick Butkus Chicago Bears	15.00	40.00

1963 Stancraft Playing Cards

This 54-card set, subtitled "Official NFL All-Time Greats," commemorates outstanding NFL players and was issued in conjunction with the opening of the Pro Football Hall of Fame in Canton, Ohio. It should be noted that several of the players in the set are not in the Pro Football Hall of Fame. The back of the cards was produced two different ways. One style has a checkerboard pattern, with the NFL logo in the middle and logos for the 14 NFL teams surrounding it against a red background; the other style has the 14 NFL team helmets floating on a green background. The set was issued in a plastic box which fit into a cardboard outer slip-case box. Apart from the aces and two jokers (featuring the NFL logo), the fronts of the other cards have a skillfully drawn picture (in brown ink) of the player, with his name, position, year(s), and team below the drawing. The set was also reportedly made in a pinochle format. We have checklisted this set in playing card order by suits and assigned numbers to Aces (1), Jacks (11), Queens (12), and Kings (13). Each card measures approximately 2 1/4" by 3 1/2" with rounded corners.

COMPLETE SET (54)	125.00	250.00
*GREEN BACKS: SAME PRICE		
1C NFL Logo	1.50	3.00
1D NFL Logo	1.50	3.00
1H NFL Logo	1.50	3.00
1S NFL Logo	1.50	3.00
2C Johnny Blood McNally	2.00	4.00
2D Frankie Albert	1.50	3.00
2H Paul Hornung	5.00	10.00
2S Eddie LeBaron	2.00	4.00
3C Bobby Mitchell	3.00	6.00
3D Del Shofner	1.50	3.00
3H Johnny Unitas	7.50	15.00
3S Don Hutson	3.00	6.00
4C Billy Howton	1.50	3.00
4D Ollie Matson	3.00	6.00
4H Doak Walker	3.00	6.00
4S Clarke Hinkle	2.00	4.00
5C Fats Henry	2.00	4.00
5D Mike Ditka	6.00	12.00
5H Tom Fears	3.00	6.00
5S Charley Conerly	3.00	6.00
6C Tony Canadeo	2.50	5.00
6D Otto Graham	5.00	10.00
6H Jim Thorpe	7.50	15.00
6S Earl(Curly) Lambeau	1.50	3.00
7C Bulldog Turner	3.00	6.00
7D Chuck Bednarik	4.00	8.00
7H Gino Marchetti	3.00	6.00
7S Sid Luckman	4.00	8.00
8C Charley Trippi	3.00	6.00
8D Jim Taylor	4.00	8.00
8H Claude(Buddy) Young	1.50	3.00
8S Pete Pihos	2.50	5.00
9C Tommy Mason	1.50	3.00
9D Mel Hein	2.00	4.00
9H Jim Benton	1.50	3.00
9S Dante Lavelli	3.00	6.00
10C Dutch Clark	2.50	5.00
10D Eddie Price	1.50	3.00
10H Jim Brown	10.00	20.00
10S Norm Van Brocklin	4.00	8.00
11C Y.A. Tittle	4.00	8.00
11D Sonny Randle	1.50	3.00
11H George Halas	5.00	10.00
11S Cloyce Box	1.50	3.00
12C Lou Groza	3.00	6.00
12D Joe Perry	3.00	6.00
12H Sammy Baugh	5.00	10.00
12S Joe Schmidt	3.00	6.00
13C Bobby Layne	4.00	8.00
13D Bob Waterfield	4.00	8.00
13H Bill Dudley	2.50	5.00
13S Elroy Hirsch	3.00	6.00
NNO Joker (NFL Logo)	1.50	3.00
NNO Joker (NFL Logo)	1.50	3.00

1928 Star Player Candy

This recently discovered set of cards is thought to have been issued by Dockman and Son's candy company since it closely resembles the 1928 Star Player Candy baseball card set. Based upon the players in the set, the year of issue is thought to be 1928 so it is possible that both the football and baseball players were packaged together. Red Grange is listed as Illinois instead of Professional so the true year of issue often comes under question. Each card is blankbacked and features a sepia colored photo of the player on the cardfront along with his name and either name of his university or the word "professional" (noted below) for those few players in the pros at the time. Each card measures roughly 2" by 3."

1 Russell Avery	150.00	300.00
2 Bullet Baker	150.00	300.00
3 Richard Black	150.00	300.00
4 E.J. Burke	150.00	300.00
5 Jack Chevigney	200.00	400.00
6 Fred Collins	200.00	400.00
7 A.C. Cornsweet	150.00	300.00
8 Jus Dart	150.00	300.00
9 Paddy Driscoll	1,200.00	2,000.00
10A Bruce Dumont	150.00	300.00
10B Bruce Dumont ERR	150.00	300.00
11 Fred Ellis	150.00	300.00
12 Benny Friedman	1,200.00	2,000.00
13 Gene Fritz	150.00	300.00
14 Walter Gebert	150.00	300.00
15 Louis Gilbert	150.00	300.00
16 Red Grange	1,500.00	2,500.00
17 Glen Harmeson	150.00	300.00
18 John Hazen	150.00	300.00
19 Gibson Holliday	150.00	300.00
20 Walt Holmer	150.00	300.00
21 John Karcis	150.00	300.00
22 Harry Lindblom	150.00	300.00
23 Jim McMillen UER	150.00	300.00
24 Hugh Mendenhall	150.00	300.00
25 Fred Miller	150.00	300.00
26 John Murrell	150.00	300.00
27 John Niemiec	150.00	300.00
28 A.J. Nowak	150.00	300.00
29 Irvine Phillips	150.00	300.00
30 E.H. Rose	150.00	300.00
31 Stanley Rosen	150.00	300.00
32 Paul Scull	150.00	300.00
33 J.W. Slagle	150.00	300.00
34 John Smith Ford.	150.00	300.00
35 John Smith Penn.	150.00	300.00
36 Euil Snitz Snider	150.00	300.00
37 M.E. Bud Sprague	150.00	300.00
38 Joe Sternaman	600.00	1,000.00
39 Eddie Tryon	350.00	600.00
40 Rube Wagner	150.00	300.00
41 Saul Weislow	150.00	300.00
42 Ralph Welch	150.00	300.00
43 George Wilson	250.00	500.00

1959 Steelers San Giorgio Flipbooks

This set features members of the Pittsburgh Steelers printed on velum type paper stock created in a multi-image action sequence. The set is commonly referenced as the San Giorgio Macaroni Football Flipbooks. Members of the

Philadelphia Eagles, Pittsburgh Steelers, and Washington Redskins were produced regionally with 15-players, reportedly, issued per team. Some players were produced in more than one sequence of poses with different captions and/or slightly different photos used. When the flipbooks are still in uncut form (which is most desirable), they measure approximately 5 3/4" by 3 9/16". The sheets are blank backed, in black and white, and provide 14-small numbered pages when cut apart. Collectors were encouraged to cut out each photo and stack them in such a way as to create a moving image of the player when flipped with the fingers. Any additions to this list are appreciated.

1 Darrel Brewster 90.00 150.00
2 Jack Butler 90.00 150.00
3 Gern Nagler 90.00 150.00
4 Tom Tracy 100.00 175.00

1961 Steelers Jay Publishing

This 12-card set features (approximately) 5" by 7" black-and-white player photos. The photos show players in traditional poses with the quarterback preparing to throw, the runner heading downfield, and the defenseman ready for the tackle. These cards were packaged 12 to a packet and originally sold for 25 cents. The backs are blank. The cards are unnumbered and checklisted below in alphabetical order.

COMPLETE SET (12) 75.00 150.00
1 Preston Carpenter 5.00 10.00
2 Dean Derby 5.00 10.00
3 Buddy Dial 5.00 10.00
4 John Henry Johnson 10.00 20.00
5 Bobby Layne 15.00 30.00
6 Gene Lipscomb 6.00 12.00
7 Bill Mack 5.00 10.00
8 Fred Mautino 5.00 10.00
9 Lou Michaels 5.00 10.00
10 Buddy Parker CO 5.00 10.00
11 Myron Pottios 5.00 10.00
12 Tom Tracy 5.00 10.00

1963 Steelers IDL

This unnumbered black and white card set (featuring the Pittsburgh Steelers) is complete at 26 cards. The cards feature an identifying logo of IDL Drug Store on the front left corner of the card. The cards measure approximately 4" by 5". Cards are blank backed and unnumbered and hence are ordered alphabetically in the checklist below.

COMPLETE SET (26) 125.00 250.00
1 Frank Atkinson 6.00 12.00
2 Jim Bradshaw 6.00 12.00
3 Ed Brown 6.00 12.00
4 John Burrell 6.00 12.00
5 Preston Carpenter 6.00 12.00
6 Lou Cordileone 6.00 12.00
7 Buddy Dial 6.00 12.00
8 Bob Ferguson 6.00 12.00
9 Glenn Glass 6.00 12.00
10 Dick Haley 6.00 12.00
11 Dick Hoak 7.50 15.00
12 John Henry Johnson 10.00 25.00
13 Brady Keys 6.00 12.00
14 Joe Krupa 6.00 12.00
15 Ray Lemek 6.00 12.00
16 Bill(Red) Mack 6.00 12.00
17 Lou Michaels 6.00 12.00
18 Bill Nelsen 6.00 12.00
19 Buzz Nutter 6.00 12.00
20 Myron Pottios 6.00 12.00
21 John Reger 6.00 12.00
22 Mike Sandusky 6.00 12.00
23 Ernie Stautner 10.00 25.00
24 George Tarasovic 6.00 12.00
25 Clendon Thomas 6.00 12.00
26 Tom Tracy 7.50 15.00

1963 Steelers McCarthy Postcards

This set of the Pittsburgh Steelers features posed player photos printed on postcard-size cards. Each was produced from photos taken by photographer J.D. McCarthy and likely distributed over a number of years. The cards are unnumbered and checklisted below in alphabetical order. Any additions to the checklist below are appreciated.

COMPLETE SET (3) 15.00 30.00
1 John Henry Johnson 7.50 15.00
2 Brady Keys 4.00 8.00
3 Buzz Nutter 4.00 8.00

1964 Steelers Emenee Electric Football

These sepia toned photos were sponsored by Emenee Electric Pro Football Game and KDKA TV and radio. Each includes a large photo of a Steelers player with an advertisement for the Emenee Football Game below the photo, as well as a mail in contest offer for fans to guess Steelers game yardage totals. The backs are blank and the photos have been arranged alphabetically below.

COMPLETE SET (9) 800.00 1,400.00
1 Frank Atkinson 75.00 125.00
2 Gary Ballman 75.00 125.00
3 Ed Brown 90.00 150.00
4 Dick Hoak 75.00 125.00
5 Dan James 75.00 125.00
6 John Henry Johnson 100.00 175.00
7 Jim Kelly 75.00 125.00
8 Ray Lemek 75.00 125.00
9 Paul Martha 75.00 125.00
10 Buzz Nutter 75.00 125.00
11 Mike Sandusky 75.00 125.00

1965 Steelers Program Inserts

The Steelers issued these black and white player photos bound into game programs during the 1965-68 seasons. The 1965 version includes a large player photo along with bio information below the image on the front and another page of the program on the back.

1 Gary Ballman 3.00 8.00
2 Jim Bradshaw 3.00 8.00
3 Dan James 3.00 8.00
4 Ray Lemek 3.00 8.00

1966 Steelers Program Inserts

The Steelers issued these black and white player photos bound into home game programs during the 1965-68 seasons. The 1966 set was issued in two different styles. Version 1 follows the 1965 fomat and includes a large player photo along with bio information below the image on the front. Version two features a large player photo and bio as well as three circles intended to direct the collector to punch them out and insert the photos into a binder. Both versions have another page of the program on the back.

COMPLETE SET (12) 40.00 100.00
1 Gary Ballman 2 3.00 8.00
2 Charlie Bradshaw 1 3.00 8.00
3 John Campbell 1 3.00 8.00
4 Riley Gunnels 1 3.00 8.00
5 Chuck Hinton 1 3.00 8.00
6 Dick Hoak 2 3.00 8.00
7 Brady Keys 2 3.00 8.00
8 Ken Kortas 2 3.00 8.00
9 Ben McGee 1 3.00 8.00
10 Andy Russell 2 4.00 10.00
11 Bill Saul 1 3.00 8.00
12 Marv Woodson 2 3.00 8.00

1966 Steelers Team Issue

These photos were issued in the mid-1960s by the Pittsburgh Steelers. Each measures roughly 8" by 10", contains a black and white photo and was printed on glossy stock. The photos look nearly identical to the 1969 Team Issue set. The photo backs are blank and unnumbered.

COMPLETE SET (24) 100.00 200.00
1 Mike Clark 5.00 10.00
2 Dick Compton 5.00 10.00
3 Sam Davis G 5.00 10.00
4 Mike Haggerty 5.00 10.00
5 John Hilton 5.00 10.00
6 Chuck Hinton 5.00 10.00
7 Dick Hoak 5.00 10.00
8 Bob Hohn 5.00 10.00
9 Roy Jefferson 6.00 12.00
10 Ken Kortas 5.00 10.00
11 Ray Mansfield 5.00 10.00
12 Paul Martha 5.00 10.00
13 Ray May 5.00 10.00
14 Ben McGee 5.00 10.00
15 Bill Nelsen 6.00 12.00
16 Andy Russell 6.00 12.00
17 Bill Saul 5.00 10.00
18 Don Shy 5.00 10.00
19 Clendon Thomas 5.00 10.00
20 Bruce Van Dyke 5.00 10.00
21 Lloyd Voss 5.00 10.00
22 J.R. Wilburn 5.00 10.00
23 Marv Woodson 5.00 10.00
24 Coaching Staff 5.00 10.00

1967 Steelers Program Inserts

The Steelers issued these black and white player photos bound into home game programs during the 1965-68 seasons. The 1967 set was issued one, two or three per program and includes a large player photo along with bio information below the image on the front as well as three circles intended to direct the collector to punch them out and insert the photos into a binder. Each has another page of the program on the back.

COMPLETE SET (10) 40.00 80.00
1 John Baker 3.00 8.00
2 Jim Butler 3.00 8.00
3 Dick Compton 3.00 8.00
4 Larry Gagner 3.00 8.00
5 John Hilton 3.00 8.00
6 Ray Mansfield 3.00 8.00
7 Bill Saul 3.00 8.00
8 Clendon Thomas 3.00 8.00
9 J.R. Wilburn 3.00 8.00
10 Marv Woodson 3.00 8.00

1968 Steelers KDKA

The 1968 KDKA Pittsburgh Steelers card set contains 15 cards with horizontal poses of several players per card. The cards measure approximately 2 3/8" by 4 1/8". Each card depicts players of a particular position (defensive backs, tight ends, linebackers). The backs are essentially advertisements for radio station KDKA, the sponsor of the card set. The cards are unnumbered and hence are listed below alphabetically by position name for convenience.

COMPLETE SET (15) 75.00 150.00
1 Centers: 5.00 10.00
2 Coaches: 6.00 12.00
3 Defensive Backs: 5.00 10.00
4 Defensive Backs: 5.00 10.00
5 Defensive Linemen: 5.00 10.00
6 Flankers: 5.00 10.00
7 Fullbacks: 5.00 10.00
8 Guards: 5.00 10.00
9 Linebackers: 6.00 12.00
10 Quarterbacks: 5.00 10.00
11 Rookies: 5.00 10.00
12 Running Backs: 5.00 10.00
13 Split Ends: 5.00 10.00
14 Tackles: 5.00 10.00
15 Tight Ends: 5.00 10.00

1968 Steelers Program Inserts

The Steelers issued these black and white player photos bound into home game programs during the 1965-68 seasons. The 1968 set was issued one per program and includes a large player photo along with bio information below the image on the front as well as three circles intended to direct the collector to punch them out and insert the photos into a binder. Each has another page of the program on the back.

1 Roy Jefferson 3.00 8.00
2 Ben McGee 3.00 8.00

1968 Steelers Team Issue

These photos were issued around 1968 by the Pittsburgh Steelers. Each measures roughly 5" by 7" and contains a black and white photo printed on paper stock. The photo backs are blank and unnumbered.

COMPLETE SET (5) 25.00 50.00
1 Earl Gros 5.00 10.00
2 Paul Martha 5.00 10.00
3 Kent Nix 5.00 10.00
4 Andy Russell 6.00 12.00
5 Marv Woodson 5.00 10.00

1969 Steelers Team Issue

These photos were issued around 1969 by the Pittsburgh Steelers. Each measures roughly 8" by 10", contains a black and white photo and was printed on glossy stock. The photos look nearly identical to the 1966 Team Issue set. The photo backs are blank and unnumbered.

COMPLETE SET (6) 25.00 50.00
1 Earl Gros 5.00 10.00
2 Jerry Hillebrand 5.00 10.00
3 Gene Mingo 5.00 10.00
4 Dick Shiner 5.00 10.00
5 Bobby Walden 5.00 10.00
6 Erwin Williams 5.00 10.00

1972 Steelers Team Sheets

This set consists of eight 8" by 10" sheets that display eight glossy black-and-white player photos each. Each individual photo measures approximately 2" by 3". The player's name, number, and position are printed below the photo. A Steelers helmet icon appears in the lower left corner of the sheet. The backs are blank. The sheets are unnumbered and checklisted below alphabetically according to the player featured in the upper left corner.

COMPLETE SET (8) 75.00 150.00
1 Ralph Anderson 6.00 15.00
2 Jim Brumfield 7.50 20.00
3 Bud Carson CO 7.50 20.00
4 Jack Ham 7.50 20.00
5 Joe Greene 10.00 25.00
6 Chuck Noll CO 15.00 30.00
7 Dick Post 10.00 25.00
8 Mike Wagner 6.00 15.00

1973 Steelers Team Issue

The NFLPA worked with many teams in 1973 to issued photo packs to be sold at stadium concession stands. Each measures approximately 7" by 8-5/8" and features a color player photo with a blank back. A small sheet with a player checklist was included in each 6-photo pack which was also assigned a series number as follows: A (cards #1-6), B (cards #7-12), and C (cards #13-18).

COMPLETE SET (18) 60.00 120.00
1 Jim Clack 4.00 8.00
2 Henry Davis 4.00 8.00
3 Franco Harris 7.50 15.00
4 Ron Shanklin 4.00 8.00
5 Bruce Van Dyke 4.00 8.00
6 Dwight White 5.00 10.00
7 Terry Bradshaw 12.50 25.00
8 Larry Brown 4.00 8.00
9 Roy Gerela 4.00 8.00
10 L.C. Greenwood 6.00 12.00
11 Frank Lewis 4.00 8.00
12 Andy Russell 5.00 10.00
13 John Fuqua 5.00 10.00
14 Joe Greene 6.00 12.00
15 Jack Ham 6.00 12.00
16 Terry Hanratty 4.00 8.00
17 Ray Mansfield 4.00 8.00
18 Preston Pearson 5.00 10.00

1973 Steelers Team Issue Color

The NFLPA worked with many teams in 1973 to issued photo packs to be sold at stadium concession stands. Each measures approximately 7" by 8-5/8" and features a color player photo with a blank back. A small sheet with a player checklist was included in each 6-photo pack.

COMPLETE SET (6) 25.00 50.00
1 Jim Clack 4.00 8.00
2 Henry Davis 4.00 8.00
3 Franco Harris 7.50 15.00
4 Ron Shanklin 4.00 8.00
5 Bruce Van Dyke 4.00 8.00
6 Dwight White 5.00 10.00

1973 Steelers Team Sheets

This set consists of eight 8" by 10" sheets that display eight glossy black-and-white player photos each. Each individual photo on the sheets measures approximately 2" by 3". A Steelers helmet icon appears in the lower left corner of the sheet. The backs are blank. The sheets are unnumbered and checklisted below alphabetically according to the player featured in the upper left corner.

COMPLETE SET (8) 50.00 100.00
1 Ander./Clack/Davis/Kolb
Mansfield/Davis/Ham/Bernhardt 6.00 12.00
2 Edwards/Vincent/Dockery/Young
Harris/Fuqua/Russell/Davis 7.50 15.00
3 Hanratty/Gerela/Bradshaw/Gilliam
Bleier/Wagner/Shanklin/Pearson 12.50 25.00
4 Mullins/Greene/Holmes/White/Pear.
Brown/McMakin/Webster 6.00 12.00
5 Noll/Carson/Fry/Hoak/Parilli/Perles
Riecke/Taylor/Uram/Widen. 6.00 12.00
6 Phares/Brad./Walden/Meyer/Lewis
Bankston/Blount/Rowser 6.00 12.00
7 Glenn Scolnik 5.00 10.00
James Thomas
Loren Toews
Gail Clark
Lee Nystrom
Nate Dorsey
Bracey Bonham
Tom Keating
8 Sten./Holmes/Furn./Van
Dyke/Henne./Greenwood/Curl/Gravelle 6.00 12.00

1974 Steelers Tribune-Review Posters

These posters (measuring roughly 14" by 21 1/2") were issued one per Greensburg Tribune-Review newspaper in 1974. Each includes a black and white photo of a Steelers' player on one side and another page from the newspaper on the back. We've listed them below in alphabetical order.

1 Mel Blount 7.50 15.00
2 Roy Gerela 5.00 10.00
3 Joe Greene 7.50 15.00
4 Jack Ham 7.50 15.00
5 Andy Russell 5.00 10.00
6 Ron Shanklin 5.00 10.00
7 Dwight White 6.00 12.00

1974 Steelers WTAE

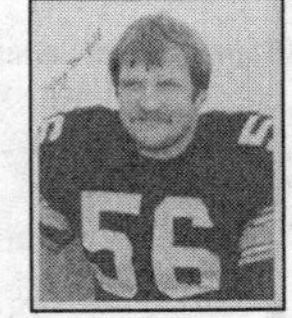

These color 8" X 10" photos feature players of the Pittsburgh Steelers. The cards were sponsored by radio station WTAE and the cardbacks include player bio information. The cards may have been distributed by Arby's Restaurants as well. The set is thought to contain 14-different photos. Any additions to this checklist are appreciated.

1 Terry Bradshaw 75.00 125.00
2 Sam Davis 15.00 30.00
3 Glen Edwards 15.00 30.00
4 John Fuqua 25.00 40.00
5 Roy Gerela 15.00 30.00
6 Joe Gilliam 15.00 30.00
7 Joe Greene 35.00 60.00
8 Jack Ham 35.00 60.00
9 Terry Hanratty 25.00 40.00
10 Franco Harris 40.00 75.00
11 Ray Mansfield 15.00 30.00
12 Ron Shanklin 15.00 30.00
13 Mike Wagner 15.00 30.00

1976 Steelers Glasses

This set of glasses was issued for the Pittsburgh Steelers in 1976, licensed through MSA and sponsored by WTAE. Each features a black and white photo of a Steelers' player along with a gold and black stripe running above and below the photo. Any additions to the list below are appreciated. These glasses were available at the Isaly or Sweet William restaurants.

COMPLETE SET (7)	50.00	100.00
1 Rocky Bleier	6.00	12.00
2 Terry Bradshaw	15.00	30.00
3 Mel Blount	6.00	12.00
4 Joe Greene	7.50	15.00
5 Jack Ham	6.00	12.00
6 Jack Lambert	7.50	15.00
7 Andy Russell	5.00	10.00

1976 Steelers MSA Cups

This set of plastic cups was issued for the Pittsburgh Steelers in 1976 and licensed through MSA. Each features an artist's rendering of a Steelers' player wearing a black jersey. Some players also appeared in the nationally issued 1976 MSA Cups set with only slight differences in each. The unnumbered cups are listed below alphabetically.

COMPLETE SET (23)	100.00	200.00
1 Rocky Bleier	5.00	10.00
2 Mel Blount	5.00	10.00
3 Terry Bradshaw	10.00	20.00
4 Jim Clack	4.00	8.00
5 Sam Davis	4.00	8.00
6 Roy Gerela	4.00	8.00
7 Gordon Gravelle	4.00	8.00
8 Joe Greene	6.00	12.00
9 L.C. Greenwood	5.00	10.00
10 Randy Grossman	4.00	8.00
11 Jack Ham	5.00	10.00
12 Franco Harris	7.50	15.00
13 Marv Kellum	4.00	8.00
14 Jon Kolb	4.00	8.00
15 Jack Lambert	7.50	15.00
16 Ray Mansfield	4.00	8.00
17 Andy Russell	4.00	8.00
18 John Stallworth	6.00	12.00
19 Lynn Swann	7.50	15.00
20 J.T. Thomas	4.00	8.00
21 Loren Toews	4.00	8.00
22 Mike Wagner	4.00	8.00
23 Bobby Walden	4.00	8.00

1978 Steelers Team Issue

This set consists of 5" by 7" glossy black-and-white player photos. The player's jersey number, name, position (initials), and team name are printed in all caps below the photo. Each is blankbacked, unnumbered and checklisted below alphabetically.

1 Rocky Bleier	6.00	12.00
2 Mel Blount	6.00	12.00
3 Terry Bradshaw	12.50	25.00
4 Joe Greene	7.50	15.00
5 L.C. Greenwood	6.00	12.00
6 Jack Ham	7.50	15.00

1978 Steelers Team Sheets

This set consists of eight 10" by 8" sheets that display eight glossy black-and-white player photos each. Each photo measures approximately 2" by 3". The player's name, number, and position are printed below the photo. The sheets are blankbacked, unnumbered and checklisted below alphabetically according to the player featured in the upper left corner.

COMPLETE SET (8)	40.00	80.00
1 B Carr	6.00	12.00
Harr		
Blou		
Becker		
Brz		
Toew		
Webs		
Winst		
2 Delo	5.00	10.00
Gains		
Thorn		
Moser		
Reut		
Terr		
Lew		
BWag		
3 Fry	6.00	12.00
Furn		
Beas		
Pet		
Dunn		
Gree		
FAnd		
LRey		
4 LaC	6.00	12.00
Kolb		
Cole		
SDav		
Lamb		
Ham		
Cous		
Hicks		
5 Mull	6.00	12.00
Pure		
Pinn		
Green		
Bana		
Cour		
DWhit		
LBrow		
6 Noll	10.00	20.00
Colq		
Ger		
Brad		
Kruc		
Stou		
Blei		
Dungy		
7 Stall	7.50	15.00
Bell		
Gross		
Keys		
JSmith		
McC		
Swa		
Cunn		
8 Wagner	6.00	12.00
R Scott		
G Edward		
AMaxson		
RJohnson DB		
LAnder		

1979 Steelers McDonald's Glasses

McDonald's stores issued this set of glasses in the Pittsburgh area in 1979 following Super Bowl XIII. Each features a black and white photo of three different Steelers players with the McDonald's logo circling the bottom of the glass.

COMPLETE SET (4)	30.00	60.00
1 J.Banaszak	7.50	15.00
Sam Davis		
Lambert		
2 Bleier	7.50	15.00
Ham		
Shell		
3 Bradshaw	12.50	25.00
Greenwood		
Webster		
4 Greene	7.50	15.00
Stallworth		
Wagner		

1979 Steelers Notebook Pittsburgh Press

These small posters measure roughly 5 1/2" by 8" when properly cut. Each was issued in Pittsburgh Press newspapers in 1979 and includes a black and white photo of a Steelers' player or coach with extensive bio information on the front. The backs feature another page from the newspaper. We've listed them below in alphabetical order.

COMPLETE SET (56)	125.00	250.00
1 Anthony Anderson	3.00	6.00
2 Larry Anderson	3.00	6.00
3 Matt Bahr	3.00	6.00
4 John Banaszak	3.00	6.00
5 Tom Beasley	3.00	6.00
6 Theo Bell	3.00	6.00
7 Rocky Bleier	4.00	8.00
8 Mel Blount	5.00	10.00
9 Terry Bradshaw	10.00	20.00
10 Larry Brown	3.00	6.00
11 Robin Cole	3.00	6.00
12 Craig Colquitt	3.00	6.00
13 Steve Courson	3.00	6.00
14 Bennie Cunningham	3.00	6.00
15 Sam Davis	3.00	6.00
16 Tom Dornbrook	3.00	6.00
17 Rollie Dotsch CO	3.00	6.00
18 Gary Dunn	3.00	6.00
19 Steve Furness	3.00	6.00
20 Roy Gerela	3.00	6.00
21 Joe Greene	6.00	12.00
22 L.C. Greenwood	5.00	10.00
23 Randy Grossman	4.00	8.00
24 Jack Ham	5.00	10.00
25 Franco Harris	6.00	12.00
26 Greg Hawthorne	3.00	6.00
27 Dick Hoak CO	3.00	6.00
28 Ron Johnson	3.00	6.00
29 Jon Kolb	3.00	6.00
30 Mike Kruczek	3.00	6.00
31 Jack Lambert	6.00	12.00
32 Tom Moore CO	3.00	6.00
33 Rick Moser	3.00	6.00
34 Gerry Mullins	3.00	6.00
35 Chuck Noll CO	7.50	15.00
36 George Perles CO	3.00	6.00
37 Ted Peterson	3.00	6.00
38 Ray Pinney	3.00	6.00
39 Lou Riecke CO	3.00	6.00
40 Donnie Shell	4.00	8.00
41 Jim Smith	4.00	8.00
42 John Stallworth	6.00	12.00
43 Cliff Stoudt	4.00	8.00
44 Lynn Swann	7.50	15.00
45 Loren Toews	3.00	6.00
46 J.T. Thomas	3.00	6.00
47 Sidney Thornton	3.00	6.00
48 Paul Uram CO	3.00	6.00
49 Zack Valentine CO	3.00	6.00
50 Mike Wagner	3.00	6.00
51 Dick Walker CO	3.00	6.00
52 Mike Webster	5.00	10.00
53 Dwight White	4.00	8.00
54 Woody Widenhofer CO	3.00	6.00
55 Dennis Winston	3.00	6.00
56 Dwayne Woodruff	3.00	6.00

1979-80 Steelers Postcards

The Steelers released these postcards presumably in the late 1970s. The Bradshaw and Greene cards were printed by Coastal Printing and include a typical postcard format on the back with a color player photo on the front. The Swann card was printed by Ellie's and is slightly different in back design. Each measures roughly 6" by 9." The checklist below is thought to be incomplete.

COMPLETE SET (3)	20.00	40.00
1 Terry Bradshaw	10.00	20.00
2 Joe Greene	5.00	10.00
3 Lynn Swann	6.00	12.00

1980 Steelers McDonald's Glasses

McDonald's stores issued this set of glasses in the Pittsburgh area in 1980 following Super Bowl XIV. Each features a black and white photo of three different Steelers players with the McDonald's logo circling the bottom of the glass. The logos for the NFL Player's Association and MSA also appear.

COMPLETE SET (4)	17.50	35.00
1 Rocky Bleier	3.00	8.00
John Stallworth		
Roy Winston		
2 Mel Blount	3.00	8.00
Jon Kolb		
Jack Lambert		
3 Terry Bradshaw	6.00	15.00
Sam Davis		
Jack Ham		
4 Matt Bahr	3.00	8.00
Joe Greene		
Sidney Thornton		

1980 Steelers Pittsburgh Press Posters

These small posters (measuring roughly 13 1/2" by 21") were issued one per Pittsburgh Press newspaper in 1980. Each includes a color artist's rendering of a Steelers' player with a facsimile autograph below the image along with a copyright line and date. The backs feature a comics page from the newspaper. We've listed them below in alphabetical order.

COMPLETE SET (12)	50.00	100.00
1 Chris Bahr	2.50	6.00
2 Mel Blount	4.00	10.00
3 Terry Bradshaw	8.00	20.00
4 Sam Davis	2.50	6.00
5 Jack Ham	4.00	10.00
6 Franco Harris	5.00	12.00
7 Jon Kolb	2.50	6.00
8 Chuck Noll CO	4.00	10.00
9 Donnie Shell	3.00	8.00
10 John Stallworth	4.00	10.00
11 Lynn Swann	5.00	12.00
12 Mike Webster	3.00	8.00

1980-82 Steelers Boy Scouts

These standard sized cards were issued for the Boy Scouts and used as membership cards. Each was printed on thin stock and features a Steelers player on the front and Boy Scouts membership information on the back.

1 Rocky Bleier	20.00	40.00
2 Terry Bradshaw 1982	40.00	75.00
3 Franco Harris	25.00	50.00
4 John Stallworth 1981	20.00	40.00
5 Cliff Stoudt 1981	15.00	30.00
6 Lynn Swann	25.00	50.00
7 Mike Webster 1981	20.00	40.00

1979 Stop'N'Go

The 1979 Stop 'N' Go Markets set contains 18 3-D cards. The cards measure approximately 2 1/8" by 3 1/4". They are numbered and contain both a 1979 National Football League Players Association copyright date and a Xograph (predecessor of Sportflics and Score) trademark registration on the back. The set shows a heavy emphasis on players from the two Texas teams, the Dallas Cowboys and Houston Oilers, as they were issued primarily in the south.

COMPLETE SET (18)	40.00	75.00
1 Gregg Bingham	.60	1.50
2 Ken Burrough	.75	2.00
3 Preston Pearson	.75	2.00
4 Sam Cunningham	.75	2.00
5 Robert Newhouse	.75	2.00
6 Walter Payton	15.00	30.00
7 Robert Brazile	.60	1.50
8 Rocky Bleier	2.00	4.00
9 Toni Fritsch	.60	1.50
10 Jack Ham	2.00	4.00
11 Jay Saldi	.60	1.50
12 Roger Staubach	12.00	20.00
13 Franco Harris	4.00	8.00
14 Otis Armstrong	1.50	3.00
15 Lyle Alzado	1.50	3.00
16 Billy Johnson	.75	2.00
17 Elvin Bethea	1.50	3.00
18 Joe Greene	3.00	6.00

1980 Stop'N'Go

The 1980 Stop 'N' Go Markets football card set contains 48 3-D cards. The cards measure approximately 2 1/8" by 3 1/4". Although similar to the 1979 issue, the cards can easily be distinguished by the two stars surrounding the name plaque on the front of the 1980 set and the obvious copyright date on the respective backs. One card was given out with each soda fountain drink purchased through September at participating Stop'N'Go and Doty stores. While players from National Football League teams, other than those in Texas, are indeed contained in the set, the emphasis remains on the Cowboys and Oilers. Cards with a "Doty" logo on back are more difficult to find than the base Stop'N'Go.

COMPLETE SET (48)	25.00	40.00
*DOTY BACKS: 2.5X TO 6X		
1 John Jefferson	.40	1.00
2 Herb Scott	.25	.60
3 Pat Donovan	.25	.60
4 William Andrews	.40	1.00
5 Frank Corral	.25	.60
6 Fred Dryer	.40	1.00
7 Franco Harris	2.50	6.00
8 Leon Gray	.25	.60
9 Gregg Bingham	.25	.60
10 Louie Kelcher	.25	.60
11 Robert Newhouse	.30	.75
12 Preston Pearson	.40	1.00
13 Wallace Francis	.30	.75
14 Pat Haden	.40	1.00
15 Jim Youngblood	.25	.60
16 Rocky Bleier	.75	2.00
17 Gifford Nielsen	.25	.60
18 Elvin Bethea	.40	1.00
19 Charlie Joiner	.75	2.00
20 Tony Hill	.40	1.00
21 Drew Pearson	.75	2.00
22 Alfred Jenkins	.30	.75
23 Dave Elmendorf	.25	.60
24 Jack Reynolds	.30	.75
25 Joe Greene	1.50	4.00
26 Robert Brazile	.25	.60
27 Mike Reinfeldt	.25	.60
28 Bob Griese	2.50	6.00
29 Harold Carmichael	.60	1.50
30 Ottis Anderson	1.25	3.00
31 Ahmad Rashad	.75	2.00
32 Archie Manning	.60	1.50
33 Ricky Bell	.40	1.00
34 Jay Saldi	.25	.60
35 Ken Burrough	.30	.75
36 Don Woods	.25	.60
37 Henry Childs	.25	.60
38 Wilbur Jackson	.25	.60
39 Steve DeBerg	.40	1.00
40 Ron Jessie	.30	.75
41 Mel Blount	.75	2.00
42 Cliff Branch	.75	2.00
43 Chuck Muncie	.30	.75
44 Ken MacAfee	.25	.60
45 Charlie Young	.30	.75
46 Cody Jones	.25	.60
47 Jack Ham	1.00	2.50
48 Ray Guy	.40	1.00

1976 Sunbeam NFL Die Cuts

This 28-card set features standard size cards. The cards are die-cut so that they can stand up when the perforation is popped. The team's helmet, team nickname, and a generic player drawing are pictured on each card front. The card back features a narrative about the team and the Sunbeam logo. The cards were printed on white or gray card stock. The cards are unnumbered and may be found with or without the Sunbeam logo on the white stock version. A header card was produced announcing the 1976 season. There was also a card saver book issued. All the prices below are for unpunched cards.

COMPLETE SET (29)	137.50	275.00
1 Atlanta Falcons	6.00	12.00
2 Baltimore Colts	6.00	12.00
3 Buffalo Bills	6.00	12.00
4 Chicago Bears	7.50	15.00
5 Cincinnati Bengals	6.00	12.00
6 Cleveland Browns	6.00	12.00
7 Dallas Cowboys	7.50	15.00
8 Denver Broncos	6.00	12.00
9 Detroit Lions	6.00	12.00
10 Green Bay Packers	7.50	15.00
11 Houston Oilers	6.00	12.00
12 Kansas City Chiefs	6.00	12.00
13 Los Angeles Rams	6.00	12.00
14 Miami Dolphins	7.50	15.00

15 Minnesota Vikings	7.50	15.00
16 New England Patriots	6.00	12.00
17 New Orleans Saints	6.00	12.00
18 New York Giants	6.00	12.00
19 New York Jets	6.00	12.00
20 Oakland Raiders	7.50	15.00
21 Philadelphia Eagles	6.00	12.00
22 Pittsburgh Steelers	7.50	15.00
23 St. Louis Cardinals	6.00	12.00
24 San Diego Chargers	6.00	12.00
25 San Francisco 49ers	7.50	15.00
26 Seattle Seahawks	6.00	12.00
27 Tampa Bay Buccaneers	6.00	12.00
28 Washington Redskins	7.50	15.00
NNO NFL Logo	7.50	15.00
NNO Saver Book	12.50	25.00

1976 Sunbeam NFL Pennant Stickers

This set of stickers was issued along with the logo cards and was intended to be pasted into the saver album. Each measures roughly 1 3/4" by 2 7/8" and includes the team's logo and name within a pennant shaped design. The backs feature the team's all-time record along with a Sunbeam ad.

COMPLETE SET (28)	137.50	275.00
1 Atlanta Falcons	6.00	12.00
2 Baltimore Colts	6.00	12.00
3 Buffalo Bills	6.00	12.00
4 Chicago Bears	7.50	15.00
5 Cincinnati Bengals	6.00	12.00
6 Cleveland Browns	7.50	15.00
7 Dallas Cowboys	7.50	15.00
8 Denver Broncos	6.00	12.00
9 Detroit Lions	6.00	12.00
10 Green Bay Packers	7.50	15.00
11 Houston Oilers	6.00	12.00
12 Kansas City Chiefs	6.00	12.00
13 Los Angeles Rams	6.00	12.00
14 Miami Dolphins	7.50	15.00
15 Minnesota Vikings	7.50	15.00
16 New England Patriots	6.00	12.00
17 New Orleans Saints	6.00	12.00
18 New York Giants	7.50	15.00
19 New York Jets	6.00	12.00
20 Oakland Raiders	7.50	15.00
21 Philadelphia Eagles	6.00	12.00
22 Pittsburgh Steelers	7.50	15.00
23 St. Louis Cardinals	6.00	12.00
24 San Diego Chargers	6.00	12.00
25 San Francisco 49ers	7.50	15.00
26 Seattle Seahawks	6.00	12.00
27 Tampa Bay Buccaneers	6.00	12.00
28 Washington Redskins	7.50	15.00

1972 Sunoco Stamps

In 1972, the Sun Oil Company issued a stamp set and two types of albums. Each stamp measures approximately 1 5/8" by 2 3/8" whereas the albums are approximately 10 3/8" by 10 15/16". The logo on the cover of the 56-page stamp album indicates "NFL Action '72". The other "deluxe" album contains 128 pages. Each team was represented with 12 offensive and 12 defensive player stamps. There are a total of 624 unnumbered stamps in the set, which made this stamp set the largest football set to date at that time. The albums indicate where each stamp is to be placed. The square for each player's stamp was marked by the player's number, name, position, height, weight, age, and college attended. When the album was issued, the back of the book included perforated sheets of stamps comprising more than one fourth of the set. The album also had sheets of tabs which were to be used for putting the stamps in the book, rather than licking the entire stamp. Each week of the promotion a purchase of gasoline yielded an additional nine-player perforated stamp sheet. The stamps and the album positions are unnumbered so the stamps are ordered and numbered below according to the team order in which they appear in the book. The team order is alphabetical. Since the same 144 stamps were included as an insert with each album; these 144 stamps are easier to find and are marked as DP's in the checklist below. The stamp set is considered in very good condition at best when glued in the album. There are a number of players appearing in this set in (or before) their Rookie Card year: Lyle Alzado, Mel Blount, Harold Carmichael, Dan Dierdorf, L.C. Greenwood, Jack Ham, Cliff Harris, Ted Hendricks, Charlie Joiner, Bob Kuechenberg, Larry Little, Archie Manning, Ray Perkins, Jim Plunkett, John Riggins, Art Shell, Steve Spurrier, Roger Staubach, Gene Upshaw, Jeff Van Note, and Jack Youngblood.

COMPLETE SET (624)	75.00	150.00
1 Ken Burrow	.10	.20
2 Bill Sandeman	.10	.20
3 Andy Maurer DP	.08	.15
4 Jeff Van Note DP	.13	.25
5 Malcolm Snider	.10	.20
6 George Kunz	.10	.20
7 Jim Mitchell TE	.10	.20
8 Wes Chesson	.10	.20
9 Bob Berry	.10	.20
10 Dick Shiner	.10	.20
11 Jim Butler	.10	.20
12 Art Malone	.10	.20
13 Claude Humphrey DP	.13	.25
14 John Small DP	.08	.15
15 Glen Condren	.10	.20
16 John Zook	.10	.20
17 Don Hansen	.10	.20
18 Tommy Nobis	.30	.60
19 Greg Brezina	.10	.20
20 Ken Reaves	.10	.20
21 Tom Hayes	.10	.20
22 Tom McCauley DP	.08	.15
23 Bill Bell K DP	.08	.15
24 Billy Lothridge	.10	.20
25 Eddie Hinton	.10	.20
26 Bob Vogel DP	.08	.15
27 Glenn Ressler	.10	.20
28 Bill Curry DP	.08	.15
29 John Williams G	.10	.20
30 Dan Sullivan	.10	.20
31 Tom Mitchell	.10	.20
32 John Mackey	.50	1.00
33 Ray Perkins	.25	.50
34 Johnny Unitas	2.50	5.00
35 Tom Matte	.15	.30
36 Norm Bulaich	.10	.20
37 Bubba Smith DP	.38	.75
38 Billy Newsome	.10	.20
39 Fred Miller DP	.08	.15
40 Roy Hilton	.10	.20
41 Ray May DP	.08	.15
42 Ted Hendricks	.50	1.00
43 Charlie Stukes	.10	.20
44 Rex Kern	.10	.20
45 Jerry Logan	.10	.20
46 Rick Volk	.10	.20
47 David Lee	.10	.20
48 Jim O'Brien	.15	.30
49 J.D. Hill	.15	.30
50 Willie Young Alcorn	.10	.20
51 Jim Reilly T	.10	.20
52 Bruce Jarvis DP	.08	.15
53 Levert Carr	.10	.20
54 Donnie Green DP	.08	.15
55 Jan White DP	.08	.15
56 Marlin Briscoe	.10	.20
57 Dennis Shaw	.15	.30
58 O.J. Simpson	2.00	4.00
59 Wayne Patrick	.10	.20
60 John Leypoldt	.10	.20
61 Al Cowlings	.15	.30
62 Jim Dunaway DP	.08	.15
63 Bob Tatarek	.10	.20
64 Cal Snowden	.10	.20
65 Paul Guidry	.10	.20
66 Edgar Chandler	.10	.20
67 Al Andrews DP	.08	.15
68 Robert James	.10	.20
69 Alvin Wyatt	.10	.20
70 John Pitts DP	.08	.15
71 Pete Richardson	.10	.20
72 Spike Jones	.10	.20
73 Dick Gordon	.10	.20
74 Randy Jackson DP	.08	.15
75 Glen Holloway	.10	.20
76 Rich Coady DP	.08	.15
77 Jim Cadile DP	.08	.15
78 Steve Wright	.10	.20
79 Bob Wallace	.10	.20
80 George Farmer	.10	.20
81 Bobby Douglass	.15	.30
82 Don Shy	.10	.20
83 Cyril Pinder	.10	.20
84 Mac Percival	.10	.20
85 Willie Holman	.10	.20
86 George Seals DP	.08	.15
87 Bill Staley	.10	.20
88 Ed O'Bradovich DP	.08	.15
89 Doug Buffone DP	.08	.15
90 Dick Butkus	2.00	4.00
91 Ross Brupbacher	.10	.20
92 Charlie Ford	.10	.20
93 Joe Taylor	.10	.20
94 Ron Smith	.15	.30
95 Jerry Moore	.10	.20
96 Bobby Joe Green	.10	.20
97 Chip Myers	.10	.20
98 Rufus Mayes DP	.08	.15
99 Howard Fest	.10	.20
100 Bob Johnson	.15	.30
101 Pat Matson DP	.08	.15
102 Vern Holland	.10	.20
103 Bruce Coslet	.15	.30
104 Bob Trumpy	.20	.40
105 Virgil Carter	.10	.20
106 Fred Willis	.10	.20
107 Jess Phillips	.10	.20
108 Horst Muhlmann	.10	.20
109 Royce Berry	.10	.20
110 Mike Reid DP	.25	.50
111 Steve Chomyszak DP	.08	.15
112 Ron Carpenter	.10	.20
113 Al Beauchamp DP	.08	.15
114 Bill Bergey	.15	.30
115 Ken Avery	.10	.20
116 Lemar Parrish	.15	.30
117 Ken Riley	.15	.30
118 Sandy Durko DP	.08	.15
119 Dave Lewis	.10	.20
120 Paul Robinson	.10	.20
121 Fair Hooker	.10	.20
122 Doug Dieken DP	.08	.15
123 John Demarie	.10	.20
124 Jim Copeland	.10	.20
125 Gene Hickerson DP	.10	.25
126 Bob McKay	.10	.20
127 Milt Morin	.10	.20
128 Frank Pitts	.10	.20
129 Mike Phipps	.15	.30
130 Leroy Kelly	.50	1.00
131 Bo Scott	.15	.30
132 Don Cockroft	.10	.20
133 Ron Snidow	.10	.20
134 Walter Johnson DP	.08	.15
135 Jerry Sherk	.15	.30
136 Jack Gregory	.10	.20
137 Jim Houston DP	.08	.15
138 Dale Lindsey	.10	.20
139 Bill Andrews	.10	.20
140 Clarence Scott	.10	.20
141 Ernie Kellerman	.10	.20
142 Walt Sumner	.10	.20
143 Mike Howell DP	.08	.15
144 Reece Morrison	.10	.20
145 Bob Hayes	.50	1.00
146 Ralph Neely	.10	.20
147 John Niland DP	.08	.15
148 Dave Manders	.10	.20
149 Blaine Nye	.10	.20
150 Rayfield Wright	.10	.20
151 Billy Truax	.10	.20
152 Lance Alworth	1.00	2.00
153 Roger Staubach	4.00	8.00
154 Duane Thomas	.25	.50
155 Walt Garrison	.15	.30
156 Mike Clark	.10	.20
157 Larry Cole DP	.08	.15
158 Jethro Pugh	.10	.20
159 Bob Lilly	.75	1.50
160 George Andrie	.10	.20
161 Dave Edwards DP	.08	.15
162 Lee Roy Jordan	.38	.75
163 Chuck Howley	.15	.30
164 Herb Adderley DP	.38	.75
165 Mel Renfro	.50	1.00
166 Cornell Green	.15	.30
167 Cliff Harris DP	.20	.40
168 Ron Widby	.10	.20
169 Jerry Simmons	.10	.20
170 Roger Shoals	.10	.20
171 Larron Jackson	.10	.20
172 George Goeddeke DP	.08	.15
173 Mike Schnitker	.10	.20
174 Mike Current	.10	.20
175 Billy Masters	.10	.20
176 Jack Gehrke	.10	.20
177 Don Horn	.10	.20
178 Floyd Little	.30	.60
179 Bob Anderson	.10	.20
180 Jim Turner DP	.13	.25
181 Rich Jackson	.10	.20
182 Paul Smith DP	.08	.15
183 Dave Costa	.10	.20
184 Lyle Alzado DP	.38	.75
185 Olen Underwood	.10	.20
186 Fred Forsberg DP	.08	.15
187 Chip Myrtle	.10	.20
188 Leroy Mitchell	.10	.20
189 Bill Thompson DP	.08	.15
190 Charlie Greer	.10	.20
191 George Saimes	.10	.20
192 Billy Van Heusen	.10	.20
193 Earl McCullouch	.15	.30
194 Jim Yarbrough	.10	.20
195 Chuck Walton	.10	.20
196 Ed Flanagan	.10	.20
197 Frank Gallagher	.10	.20
198 Rockne Freitas	.10	.20
199 Charlie Sanders DP	.13	.25
200 Larry Walton	.10	.20
201 Greg Landry	.20	.40
202 Altie Taylor	.10	.20
203 Steve Owens	.20	.40
204 Errol Mann DP	.08	.15
205 Joe Robb	.10	.20
206 Dick Evey	.10	.20
207 Jerry Rush	.10	.20
208 Larry Hand DP	.08	.15
209 Paul Naumoff	.10	.20
210 Mike Lucci	.15	.30
211 Wayne Walker DP	.13	.25
212 Lem Barney DP	.38	.75
213 Dick LeBeau DP	.08	.15
214 Mike Weger	.10	.20
215 Wayne Rasmussen	.10	.20
216 Herman Weaver	.10	.20
217 John Spilis	.10	.20
218 Francis Peay DP	.08	.15
219 Bill Lueck	.10	.20
220 Ken Bowman DP	.08	.15
221 Gale Gillingham DP	.08	.15
222 Dick Himes DP	.08	.15
223 Rich McGeorge	.10	.20
224 Carroll Dale	.15	.30
225 Bart Starr	2.00	4.00
226 Scott Hunter	.15	.30
227 John Brockington	.15	.30
228 Dave Hampton	.10	.20
229 Clarence Williams	.10	.20
230 Mike McCoy DT	.10	.20
231 Bob Brown DT	.10	.20
232 Alden Roche	.10	.20
233 Dave Robinson DP	.13	.25
234 Jim Carter	.10	.20
235 Fred Carr	.10	.20
236 Ken Ellis	.10	.20
237 Doug Hart	.10	.20
238 Al Randolph	.10	.20
239 Al Matthews	.10	.20
240 Tim Webster	.10	.20
241 Jim Beirne DP	.08	.15
242 Bob Young	.10	.20
243 Elbert Drungo	.10	.20
244 Sam Walton	.10	.20
245 Alvin Reed	.10	.20
246 Charlie Joiner	.75	1.50
247 Dan Pastorini	.20	.40
248 Charley Johnson	.15	.30
249 Lynn Dickey	.15	.30
250 Woody Campbell	.10	.20
251 Robert Holmes	.10	.20
252 Mark Moseley	.15	.30
253 Pat Holmes	.10	.20
254 Mike Tilleman DP	.08	.15
255 Leo Brooks	.10	.20
256 Elvin Bethea	.15	.30
257 George Webster	.15	.30
258 Garland Boyette	.10	.20
259 Ron Pritchard	.10	.20
260 Zeke Moore DP	.13	.25
261 Willie Alexander	.10	.20
262 Ken Houston	.50	1.00
263 John Charles DP	.08	.15
264 Linzy Cole DP	.08	.15
265 Elmo Wright	.10	.20
266 Jim Tyrer DP	.13	.25
267 Ed Budde	.10	.20
268 Jack Rudnay DP	.08	.15
269 Mo Moorman	.10	.20
270 Dave Hill	.10	.20
271 Morris Stroud	.10	.20
272 Otis Taylor	.20	.40
273 Len Dawson	1.00	2.00
274 Ed Podolak	.15	.30
275 Wendell Hayes	.15	.30
276 Jan Stenerud	.38	.75
277 Marvin Upshaw DP	.08	.15
278 Curley Culp	.15	.30
279 Buck Buchanan	.50	1.00
280 Aaron Brown	.10	.20
281 Bobby Bell	.50	1.00
282 Willie Lanier	.50	1.00
283 Jim Lynch	.10	.20
284 Jim Marsalis DP	.08	.15
285 Emmitt Thomas	.30	.75
286 Jim Kearney DP	.08	.15
287 Johnny Robinson	.15	.30
288 Jerrel Wilson DP	.08	.15
289 Jack Snow	.15	.30
290 Charlie Cowan	.10	.20
291 Tom Mack DP	.13	.25
292 Ken Iman	.10	.20
293 Joe Scibelli	.10	.20
294 Harry Schuh DP	.08	.15
295 Bob Klein	.10	.20
296 Lance Rentzel	.15	.30
297 Roman Gabriel	.25	.50
298 Les Josephson	.15	.30
299 Willie Ellison	.10	.20
300 David Ray	.10	.20
301 Jack Youngblood	.50	1.00
302 Merlin Olsen	.50	1.00
303 Phil Olsen	.15	.30
304 Coy Bacon	.15	.30
305 Jim Purnell DP	.08	.15
306 Marlin McKeever	.10	.20
307 Isiah Robertson	.15	.30
308 Jim Nettles DP	.08	.15
309 Gene Howard DP	.08	.15
310 Kermit Alexander	.15	.30
311 Dave Elmendorf DP	.08	.15
312 Pat Studstill	.10	.20
313 Paul Warfield	1.00	2.00
314 Doug Crusan	.10	.20
315 Bob Kuechenberg	.15	.30
316 Bob DeMarco DP	.08	.15
317 Larry Little	.50	1.00
318 Norm Evans DP	.13	.25
319 Marv Fleming DP	.13	.25
320 Howard Twilley	.15	.30
321 Bob Griese	1.25	2.50
322 Jim Kiick	.20	.40
323 Larry Csonka	1.00	2.00
324 Garo Yepremian	.15	.30
325 Jim Riley DP	.08	.15
326 Manny Fernandez	.15	.30
327 Bob Heinz DP	.08	.15
328 Bill Stanfill	.15	.30
329 Doug Swift	.10	.20
330 Nick Buoniconti	.38	.75
331 Mike Kolen	.10	.20
332 Tim Foley	.15	.30
333 Curtis Johnson	.10	.20
334 Dick Anderson	.15	.30
335 Jake Scott	.20	.40
336 Larry Seiple	.10	.20
337 Gene Washington Vik	.15	.30
338 Grady Alderman	.10	.20
339 Ed White DP	.13	.25
340 Mick Tingelhoff DP	.13	.25
341 Milt Sunde DP	.08	.15

Card	Low	High
342 Ron Yary	.15	.30
343 John Beasley	.10	.20
344 John Henderson	.10	.20
345 Fran Tarkenton	1.25	2.50
346 Clint Jones	.10	.20
347 Dave Osborn	.15	.30
348 Fred Cox	.15	.30
349 Carl Eller DP	.25	.50
350 Gary Larsen DP	.08	.15
351 Alan Page	.50	1.00
352 Jim Marshall	.38	.75
353 Roy Winston	.10	.20
354 Lonnie Warwick	.10	.20
355 Wally Hilgenberg	.10	.20
356 Bobby Bryant	.10	.20
357 Ed Sharockman	.10	.20
358 Charlie West	.10	.20
359 Paul Krause	.25	.50
360 Bob Lee	.10	.20
361 Randy Vataha	.10	.20
362 Mike Montler DP	.08	.15
363 Halvor Hagen	.10	.20
364 Jon Morris DP	.08	.15
365 Len St. Jean	.10	.20
366 Tom Neville	.10	.20
367 Tom Beer	.10	.20
368 Ron Sellers	.10	.20
369 Jim Plunkett	.63	1.25
370 Carl Garrett	.15	.30
371 Jim Nance	.15	.30
372 Charlie Gogolak	.10	.20
373 Ike Lassiter DP	.08	.15
374 Dave Rowe	.10	.20
375 Julius Adams	.10	.20
376 Dennis Wirgowski	.10	.20
377 Ed Weisacosky	.10	.20
378 Jim Cheyunski DP	.08	.15
379 Steve Kiner	.10	.20
380 Larry Carwell DP	.08	.15
381 John Outlaw	.10	.20
382 Rickie Harris	.10	.20
383 Don Webb DP	.08	.15
384 Tom Janik	.10	.20
385 Al Dodd DP	.08	.15
386 Don Morrison	.10	.20
387 Jake Kupp	.10	.20
388 John Didion	.10	.20
389 Del Williams	.10	.20
390 Glen Ray Hines	.10	.20
391 Dave Parks DP	.08	.15
392 Dan Abramowicz	.15	.30
393 Archie Manning	.63	1.25
394 Bob Gresham	.10	.20
395 Virgil Robinson	.10	.20
396 Charlie Durkee	.10	.20
397 Richard Neal	.10	.20
398 Bob Pollard DP	.08	.15
399 Dave Long DP	.08	.15
400 Joe Owens	.10	.20
401 Carl Cunningham	.10	.20
402 Jim Flanigan LB	.10	.20
403 Wayne Colman	.10	.20
404 D'Artagnan Martin DP	.08	.15
405 Delles Howell	.10	.20
406 Hugo Hollas	.10	.20
407 Doug Wyatt DP	.08	.15
408 Julian Fagan	.10	.20
409 Don Herrmann	.10	.20
410 Willie Young	.10	.20
411 Bob Hyland	.10	.20
412 Greg Larson DP	.08	.15
413 Doug Van Horn	.10	.20
414 Charlie Harper DP	.08	.15
415 Bob Tucker	.15	.30
416 Joe Morrison	.15	.30
417 Randy Johnson	.15	.30
418 Tucker Frederickson	.15	.30
419 Ron Johnson	.15	.30
420 Pete Gogolak	.15	.30
421 Henry Reed	.10	.20
422 Jim Kanicki DP	.08	.15
423 Roland Lakes	.10	.20
424 John Douglas DP	.08	.15
425 Ron Hornsby DP	.08	.15
426 Jim Files	.10	.20
427 Willie Williams DP	.08	.15
428 Otto Brown	.10	.20
429 Scott Eaton	.10	.20
430 Spider Lockhart	.15	.30
431 Tom Blanchard	.10	.20
432 Rocky Thompson	.10	.20
433 Richard Caster	.15	.30
434 Randy Rasmussen	.10	.20
435 John Schmitt	.10	.20
436 Dave Herman DP	.08	.15
437 Winston Hill DP	.08	.15
438 Pete Lammons	.10	.20
439 Don Maynard	1.00	2.00
440 Joe Namath	4.00	8.00
441 Emerson Boozer	.15	.30
442 John Riggins	1.25	2.50
443 George Nock	.10	.20
444 Bobby Howfield	.10	.20
445 Gerry Philbin	.10	.20
446 John Little DT DP	.08	.15
447 Chuck Hinton	.10	.20
448 Mark Lomas	.10	.20
449 Ralph Baker	.10	.20
450 Al Atkinson DP	.08	.15
451 Larry Grantham DP	.08	.15
452 John Dockery	.10	.20
453 Earlie Thomas DP	.08	.15
454 Phil Wise	.10	.20
455 W.K. Hicks	.10	.20
456 Steve O'Neal	.10	.20
457 Drew Buie	.10	.20
458 Art Shell	.50	1.00
459 Gene Upshaw	.38	.75
460 Jim Otto DP	.38	.75
461 George Buehler	.10	.20
462 Bob Brown OT	.15	.30
463 Raymond Chester	.15	.30
464 Fred Biletnikoff	1.00	2.00
465 Daryle Lamonica	.30	.60
466 Marv Hubbard	.15	.30
467 Clarence Davis	.10	.20
468 George Blanda	1.00	2.00
469 Tony Cline	.10	.20
470 Art Thoms	.10	.20
471 Tom Keating DP	.08	.15
472 Ben Davidson	.25	.50
473 Phil Villapiano	.15	.30
474 Dan Conners DP	.08	.15
475 Duane Benson DP	.08	.15
476 Nemiah Wilson DP	.08	.15
477 Willie Brown DP	.38	.75
478 George Atkinson	.10	.20
479 Jack Tatum	.20	.40
480 Jerry DePoyster	.10	.20
481 Harold Jackson	.20	.40
482 Wade Key DP	.08	.15
483 Henry Allison DP	.08	.15
484 Mike Evans DP C	.08	.15
485 Steve Smith T	.10	.20
486 Harold Carmichael	.50	1.00
487 Ben Hawkins	.10	.20
488 Pete Liske	.15	.30
489 Rick Arrington	.10	.20
490 Lee Bouggess	.10	.20
491 Tom Woodeshick	.10	.20
492 Tom Dempsey	.15	.30
493 Richard Harris	.10	.20
494 Don Hultz	.10	.20
495 Ernie Calloway	.10	.20
496 Mel Tom DP	.08	.15
497 Steve Zabel	.10	.20
498 Tim Rossovich DP	.08	.15
499 Ron Porter	.10	.20
500 Al Nelson	.10	.20
501 Nate Ramsey	.10	.20
502 Leroy Keyes	.15	.30
503 Bill Bradley	.15	.30
504 Tom McNeill	.10	.20
505 Dave Smith WR	.10	.20
506 Jon Kolb	.08	.15
507 Gerry Mullins	.10	.20
508 Ray Mansfield DP	.08	.15
509 Bruce Van Dyke DP	.08	.15
510 John Brown DP	.08	.15
511 Ron Shanklin	.10	.20
512 Terry Bradshaw	3.00	6.00
513 Terry Hanratty	.15	.30
514 Preston Pearson	.20	.40
515 John Fuqua	.15	.30
516 Roy Gerela	.10	.20
517 L.C. Greenwood	.38	.75
518 Joe Greene	1.00	2.00
519 Lloyd Voss DP	.08	.15
520 Dwight White DP	.13	.25
521 Jack Ham	1.25	2.50
522 Chuck Allen	.10	.20
523 Brian Stenger	.10	.20
524 Andy Russell	.15	.30
525 John Rowser	.10	.20
526 Mel Blount	1.00	2.00
527 Mike Wagner	.15	.30
528 Bobby Walden	.10	.20
529 Mel Gray	.20	.40
530 Bob Reynolds	.10	.20
531 Dan Dierdorf DP	.38	.75
532 Wayne Mulligan	.10	.20
533 Clyde Williams	.10	.20
534 Ernie McMillan	.10	.20
535 Jackie Smith	.38	.75
536 John Gilliam DP	.13	.25
537 Jim Hart	.25	.50
538 Pete Beathard	.15	.30
539 Johnny Roland	.15	.30
540 Jim Bakken	.15	.30
541 Ron Yankowski DP	.08	.15
542 Fred Heron	.10	.20
543 Bob Rowe	.10	.20
544 Chuck Walker	.10	.20
545 Larry Stallings	.10	.20
546 Jamie Rivers DP	.08	.15
547 Mike McGill	.10	.20
548 Miller Farr	.10	.20
549 Roger Wehrli	.15	.30
550 Larry Willingham DP	.08	.15
551 Larry Wilson	.50	1.00
552 Chuck Latourette	.10	.20
553 Billy Parks	.10	.20
554 Terry Owens	.15	.30
555 Doug Wilkerson	.10	.20
556 Carl Mauck DP	.08	.15
557 Walt Sweeney	.10	.20
558 Russ Washington DP	.08	.15
559 Pettis Norman	.10	.20
560 Gary Garrison	.15	.30
561 John Hadl	.25	.50
562 Mike Montgomery	.10	.20
563 Mike Garrett	.15	.30
564 Dennis Partee DP	.08	.15
565 Deacon Jones	.50	1.00
566 Ron East DP	.08	.15
567 Kevin Hardy	.10	.20
568 Steve DeLong	.10	.20
569 Rick Redman DP	.08	.15
570 Bob Babich	.10	.20
571 Pete Barnes	.10	.20
572 Bob Howard	.10	.20
573 Joe Beauchamp	.10	.20
574 Bryant Salter	.10	.20
575 Chris Fletcher	.10	.20
576 Jerry LeVias	.15	.30
577 Dick Witcher	.10	.20
578 Len Rohde	.10	.20
579 Randy Beisler	.10	.20
580 Forrest Blue	.10	.20
581 Woody Peoples	.10	.20
582 Cas Banaszek	.10	.20
583 Ted Kwalick	.15	.30
584 Gene Washington 49er	.15	.30
585 John Brodie	.50	1.00
586 Ken Willard	.15	.30
587 Vic Washington	.10	.20
588 Bruce Gossett DP	.08	.15
589 Tommy Hart	.10	.20
590 Charlie Krueger	.10	.20
591 Earl Edwards	.10	.20
592 Cedrick Hardman DP	.08	.15
593 Dave Wilcox DP	.13	.25
594 Frank Nunley	.10	.20
595 Skip Vanderbundt DP	.08	.15
596 Jim Johnson DP	.38	.75
597 Bruce Taylor	.10	.20
598 Mel Phillips	.10	.20
599 Roosevelt Taylor	.15	.30
600 Steve Spurrier	2.00	4.00
601 Charley Taylor	.50	1.00
602 Jim Snowden DP	.08	.15
603 Ray Schoenke	.10	.20
604 Len Hauss DP	.08	.15
605 John Wilbur	.10	.20
606 Walter Rock DP	.08	.15
607 Jerry Smith	.15	.30
608 Roy Jefferson	.15	.30
609 Billy Kilmer	.30	.60
610 Larry Brown	.38	.75
611 Charlie Harraway	.10	.20
612 Curt Knight	.10	.20
613 Ron McDole	.10	.20
614 Manny Sistrunk DP	.13	.25
615 Diron Talbert	.10	.20
616 Verlon Biggs DP	.08	.15
617 Jack Pardee	.20	.40
618 Myron Pottios	.10	.20
619 Chris Hanburger	.15	.30
620 Pat Fischer	.15	.30
621 Mike Bass	.10	.20
622 Richie Petitbon DP	.13	.25
623 Brig Owens	.10	.20
624 Mike Bragg	.10	.20
NNO Album (64 pages)	5.00	10.00
NNO Deluxe Album	7.50	15.00

1972 Sunoco Stamps Update

The players listed below are those who are not explicitly listed in the 1972 Sunoco stamp album. They are otherwise indistinguishable from the 1972 Sunoco stamps listed immediately above. These unnumbered stamps are ordered below in team order and alphabetically within team. The stamps measure approximately 1 5/8" by 2 3/8" and were issued later in the year as part of complete team sheets. Uncut team sheets typically sell for $15-50 per team, except for the Bears and Raiders sheets which are the toughest to find. There are a number of players appearing in this set before their Rookie Card year: Cliff Branch, Jim Langer, and Bobby Moore (later known as Ahmad Rashad).

Card	Low	High
COMPLETE SET (82)	125.00	200.00
1 Clarence Ellis	1.50	4.00
2 Dave Hampton	1.50	4.00
3 Dennis Havig	1.25	3.00
4 John James	1.25	3.00
5 Joe Profit	1.25	3.00
6 Lonnie Hepburn	1.25	3.00
7 Dennis Nelson	1.25	3.00
8 Mike McBath	1.25	3.00
9 Walt Patulski	1.25	3.00
10 Bob Asher	10.00	20.00
11 Steve DeLong	10.00	20.00
12 Tony McGee	10.00	20.00
13 Jim Osborne	10.00	20.00
14 Jim Seymour	10.00	20.00
15 Tommy Casanova	1.50	4.00
16 Neal Craig	1.25	3.00
17 Essex Johnson	1.25	3.00
18 Sherman White	1.25	3.00
19 Bob Briggs	1.25	3.00
20 Thom Darden	1.25	3.00
21 Marv Bateman	1.25	3.00
22 Toni Fritsch	1.25	3.00
23 Calvin Hill	2.00	5.00
24 Pat Toomay	1.25	3.00
25 Pete Duranko	1.25	3.00
26 Marv Montgomery	1.25	3.00
27 Rod Sherman	1.25	3.00
28 Bob Kowalkowski	1.25	3.00
29 Jim Mitchell DT	1.25	3.00
30 Larry Woods	1.25	3.00
31 Willie Buchanon	1.50	4.00
32 Leland Glass	1.25	3.00
33 MacArthur Lane	1.50	4.00
34 Chester Marcol	1.25	3.00
35 Ron Widby	1.25	3.00
36 Ken Burrough	1.50	4.00
37 Calvin Hunt	1.25	3.00
38 Ron Saul	1.25	3.00
39 Greg Simpson	1.25	3.00
40 Mike Sensibaugh	1.50	4.00
41 Dave Chapple	1.25	3.00
42 Jim Langer	2.50	6.00
43 Mike Eischeid	1.25	3.00
44 John Gilliam	1.50	4.00
45 Ron Acks	1.25	3.00
46 Bob Gladieux	1.25	3.00
47 Honor Jackson	1.25	3.00
48 Reggie Rucker	1.50	4.00
49 Pat Studstill	1.25	3.00
50 Bob Windsor	1.25	3.00
51 Joe Federspiel	1.25	3.00
52 Bob Newland	1.25	3.00
53 Pete Athas	1.25	3.00
54 Charlie Evans	1.25	3.00
55 Jack Gregory	1.25	3.00
56 John Mendenhall	1.25	3.00
57 Ed Bell	1.25	3.00
58 John Elliott	1.25	3.00
59 Chris Farasopoulos	1.25	3.00
60 Bob Svihus	1.25	3.00
61 Steve Tannen	1.25	3.00
62 Cliff Branch	12.50	25.00
63 Gus Otto	10.00	20.00
64 Otis Sistrunk	10.00	20.00
65 Charlie Smith RB	10.00	20.00
66 John Reaves	1.25	3.00
67 Larry Watkins	1.25	3.00
68 Henry Davis	1.25	3.00
69 Ben McGee	1.25	3.00
70 Donny Anderson	2.00	5.00
71 Walker Gillette	1.25	3.00
72 Martin Imhoff	1.25	3.00
73 Bobby Moore	5.00	10.00
74 Norm Thompson	1.25	3.00
75 Lionel Aldridge	1.50	4.00
76 Dave Costa	1.25	3.00
77 Cid Edwards	1.25	3.00
78 Tim Rossovich	1.25	3.00
79 Dave Williams	1.25	3.00
80 Johnny Fuller	1.25	3.00
81 Terry Hermeling	1.25	3.00
82 Paul Laaveg	1.25	3.00

1962 Tang Team Photos

Each team in the NFL is represented in this set of 10" by 8" white-bordered color team photos. The team logo is superimposed over the picture at the lower right, and all the players and team personnel are identified by rows in wider white border. The backs are completely blank and the paper stock is thin. While Tang is not specifically identified as the sponsor on the photos, advertising pieces exist to verify this fact. Originally, complete sets were available via mail for 50-cents each with one innerseal from a Tang drink mix jar. The team photos are listed below in alphabetical order. Beware reprints.

Card	Low	High
COMPLETE SET (14)	150.00	250.00
1 Baltimore Colts	12.00	20.00
2 Chicago Bears	15.00	25.00
3 Cleveland Browns	20.00	35.00
4 Dallas Cowboys	20.00	35.00
5 Detroit Lions	12.00	20.00
6 Green Bay Packers	25.00	40.00
7 Los Angeles Rams	12.00	20.00
8 Minnesota Vikings	15.00	25.00
9 New York Giants	12.00	20.00
10 Philadelphia Eagles	12.00	20.00
11 Pittsburgh Steelers	12.00	20.00
12 St. Louis Cardinals	12.00	20.00
13 San Francisco 49ers	15.00	25.00
14 Washington Redskins	20.00	35.00

1960 Texans 7-Eleven

This set was issued by 7-11 convenience stores in the Dallas area in 1960. Each card measures the standard size 2 1/2" by 3 1/2" and was unnumbered. The fronts include a posed sepia toned photo of the player with no border. The player's name, position, and school are listed below the picture in small print. The font size used on three of the cards is about 50% larger: Boydston, Burford, and Haynes. On all cards but two, the team name is printed from bottom to top along the right or left hand sides. The exceptions are Ray Collins, which is missing the team altogether, and Cotton Davidson which was printed with the team name along the top. The backs include biographical information running the length of the card in typewriter style print. A Paul Miller card is rumored to exist and was once cataloged. We've removed the card from the checklist after years of research trying to verify its existence. Since the cards are unnumbered, they are listed below alphabetically.

COMPLETE SET (11)	2,000.00	3,000.00
1 Max Boydston	175.00	300.00
2 Mel Branch	175.00	300.00
3 Chris Burford	175.00	300.00
4 Ray Collins UER	175.00	300.00
5 Cotton Davidson	175.00	300.00
6 Abner Haynes	200.00	350.00
7 Sherrill Headrick	175.00	300.00
8 Bill Krisher	175.00	300.00
9 Johnny Robinson	175.00	300.00
10 Jack Spikes	175.00	300.00

1960 Texans Team Issue

These photos were issued around 1960 by the Dallas Texans. Each features a black and white player photo with the player's position, name and team name printed below the picture. They measure approximately 8" by 10 1/4" and include a brief player bio on the unnumbered cardbacks. Any additions to this list are welcomed.

COMPLETE SET (12)	75.00	150.00
1 Max Boydston	6.00	12.00
2 Mel Branch	6.00	12.00
3 Chris Burford	6.00	12.00
4 Cotton Davidson	6.00	12.00
5 Abner Haynes	10.00	20.00
6 Charlie Jackson	6.00	12.00
7 Curley Johnson	6.00	12.00
8 Paul Miller	6.00	12.00
9 Johnny Robinson	7.50	15.00
10 Jack Spikes	6.00	12.00
11 Hank Stram CO	12.50	25.00
12 Jim Swink	6.00	12.00

1962 Texans Team Issue

These photos were issued in 1962 by the Dallas Texans. Each features a black and white player photo with the player's facsimile autograph printed within the picture. They measure approximately 5" by 7" and were printed on thick blankbacked paper stock.

1 Chris Burford	6.00	12.00
2 Walt Corey	6.00	12.00
3 Bobby Hunt	6.00	12.00
4 Curtis McClinton	7.50	15.00
5 Curt Merz	6.00	12.00
6 Al Reynolds	6.00	12.00
8 Jim Tyrer	6.00	12.00
7 Smokey Stover	6.00	12.00

1937 Thrilling Moments

Doughnut Company of America produced these cards and distributed them on the outside of doughnut boxes twelve per box. The cards were to be cut from the boxes and affixed to an album that housed the set. The set's full name is Thrilling Moments in the Lives of Famous Americans. Only seven athletes were included among 65-other famous non-sport American figures. Each blankbacked card measures roughly 1 7/8" by 2 7/8" when neatly trimmed. The set was produced in four different colored backgrounds: blue, green, orange, and yellow with each subject being printed in only one background color.

28 Red Grange FB	800.00	1,200.00
55 Knute Rockne FB	800.00	1,200.00

1961 Titans Jay Publishing

This 12-card set features (approximately) 5" by 7" black-and-white player photos of the New York Titans, one of the original AFL teams who later became the New York Jets. The photos show players in traditional poses with the quarterback preparing to throw, the runner heading downfield, and the defenseman ready for the tackle. The player's name and the team name appear in the wider bottom border. These cards were packaged 12 to a packet and originally sold for 25 cents through various Jay Publishing products. The backs are blank. The cards are unnumbered and checklisted below in alphabetical order.

COMPLETE SET (12)	60.00	120.00
1 Al Dorow	5.00	10.00
2 Larry Grantham	5.00	10.00
3 Mike Hagler	5.00	10.00
4 Mike Hudock	5.00	10.00
5 Bob Jewett	5.00	10.00
6 Jack Klotz	5.00	10.00
7 Don Maynard	15.00	30.00
8 John McMullan	5.00	10.00
9 Bob Mischak	5.00	10.00
10 Art Powell	6.00	12.00
11 Bob Reifsnyder	5.00	10.00
12 Sid Youngelman	5.00	10.00

1949 Topps Felt Backs

The 1949 Topps Felt Backs set contains 100-cards with each measuring approximately 7/8" by 1 7/16". The cards are unnumbered and arranged in alphabetical order below. The cardbacks are made of felt and depict a college pennant. Twenty-five of the cards were produced with either a brown or yellow background on the cardfront. For years the yellow version was thought to be slightly more difficult to find, but in recent years it has become apparent that the brown background version is actually the most difficult to find. Sheets of 25 cards with the same color background are often found. For more than 30 years, the set had been cataloged as a 1950 release, but evidence began to build that suggested the actual year of release was 1949. The wrapper actually has the year 1949 printed on it, the player selection matches the 1949 college football season much better than 1950, and a recent advertising piece from the period mentions a mail-in offer that expired in December, 1949. Perhaps the cards were released in both 1949 and 1950, but certainly 1949 was the initial release year.

COMPLETE SET (100)	6,000.00	8,000.00
WRAPPER (1-CENT)	60.00	120.00
1 Lou Allen RC	35.00	60.00
2 Morris Bailey RC	35.00	60.00
3 George Bell RC	35.00	60.00
4 Lindy Berry HOR RC	35.00	60.00
5A Mike Boldin Brn RC	50.00	80.00
5B Mike Boldin Yel RC	35.00	60.00
6A Bernie Botula Brn RC	50.00	80.00
6B Bernie Botula Yel RC	35.00	60.00
7 Bob Bowlby RC	35.00	60.00
8 Bob Bucher RC	35.00	60.00
9A Al Burnett Brn RC	50.00	80.00
9B Al Burnett Yel RC	35.00	60.00
10 Don Burson RC	35.00	60.00
11 Paul Campbell	35.00	60.00
12 Herb Carey RC	35.00	60.00
13A Bimbo Cecconi Brn RC	50.00	80.00
13B Bimbo Cecconi Yel RC	35.00	60.00
14 Bill Chauncey RC	35.00	60.00
15 Dick Clark RC	35.00	60.00
16 Tom Coleman RC	35.00	60.00
17 Billy Conn RC	35.00	60.00
18 John Cox RC	35.00	60.00
19 Lou Creekmur RC	90.00	150.00
20 Richard Glen Davis RC	40.00	75.00
21 Warren Davis RC	35.00	60.00
22 Bob Deuber RC	35.00	60.00
23 Ray Dooney RC	35.00	60.00
24 Tom Dublinski RC	40.00	75.00
25 Jeff Fleischman RC	35.00	60.00
26 Jack Friedland RC	35.00	60.00
27 Bob Fuchs RC	35.00	60.00
28 Arnold Galiffa RC	40.00	75.00
29 Dick Gilman RC	35.00	60.00
30A Frank Gitschier Brn RC	50.00	80.00
30B Frank Gitschier Yel RC	35.00	60.00
31 Gene Glick	35.00	60.00
32 Bill Gregus RC	35.00	60.00
33 Harold Hagan RC	35.00	60.00
34 Charles Hall RC	35.00	60.00
35A Leon Hart Brn	100.00	175.00
35B Leon Hart Yel	90.00	150.00
36A Bob Hester Brn RC	50.00	80.00
36B Bob Hester Yel RC	35.00	60.00
37 George Hughes RC	35.00	60.00
38 Levi Jackson	40.00	75.00
39A Jack Jensen Brn	125.00	200.00
39B Jack Jensen Yel	100.00	175.00
40 Charlie Justice	90.00	150.00
41 Gary Kerkorian RC	35.00	60.00
42 Bernie Krueger RC	35.00	60.00
43 Bill Kuhn RC	35.00	60.00
44 Dean Laun RC	35.00	60.00
45 Chet Leach RC	35.00	60.00
46A Bobby Lee Brn RC	50.00	80.00
46B Bobby Lee Yel RC	35.00	60.00
47 Roger Lehew RC	35.00	60.00
48 Glenn Lippman RC	35.00	60.00
49 Melvin Lyle RC	35.00	60.00
50 Len Makowski RC	35.00	60.00
51A Al Malekoff Brn RC	50.00	80.00
51B Al Malekoff Yel RC	35.00	60.00
52A Jim Martin Brn	60.00	100.00
52B Jim Martin Yel	50.00	80.00
53 Frank Mataya RC	35.00	60.00
54A Ray Mathews Brn RC	60.00	100.00
54B Ray Mathews Yel RC	50.00	80.00
55A Dick McKissack Brn RC	50.00	80.00
55B Dick McKissack Yel RC	35.00	60.00
56 Frank Miller RC	35.00	60.00
57A John Miller Brn RC	50.00	80.00
57B John Miller Yel RC	35.00	60.00
58 Ed Modzelewski RC	40.00	75.00
59 Don Mouser RC	35.00	60.00
60 James Murphy RC	35.00	60.00
61A Ray Nagle Brn RC	50.00	80.00
61B Ray Nagle Yel RC	35.00	60.00
62 Leo Nomellini	200.00	350.00
63 James O'Day RC	35.00	60.00
64 Joe Paterno RC	1,200.00	2,000.00
65 Andy Pavich RC	35.00	60.00
66A Pete Perini Brn	50.00	80.00
66B Pete Perini Yel	35.00	60.00
67 Jim Powers RC	35.00	60.00
68 Dave Rakestraw RC	35.00	60.00
69 Herb Rich RC	35.00	60.00
70 Fran Rogel RC	35.00	60.00
71A Darrell Royal Brn RC	300.00	500.00
71B Darrell Royal Yel RC	250.00	400.00
72 Steve Sawle RC	35.00	60.00
73 Nick Sebek RC	35.00	60.00
74 Herb Seidell RC	35.00	60.00
75A Charles Shaw Brn RC	50.00	80.00
75B Charles Shaw Yel RC	35.00	60.00
76A Emil Sitko Brn RC	50.00	80.00
76B Emil Sitko Yel RC	35.00	60.00
77 Butch Songin RC	40.00	75.00
78A Mariano Stalloni Brn RC	50.00	80.00
78B Mariano Stalloni Yel RC	35.00	60.00
79 Ernie Stautner RC	175.00	300.00
80 Don Stehley RC	35.00	60.00
81 Gil Stevenson RC	35.00	60.00
82 Bishop Strickland RC	35.00	60.00
83 Harry Szulborski	35.00	60.00
84A Wally Teninga Brn RC	50.00	80.00
84B Wally Teninga Yel RC	35.00	60.00
85 Clayton Tonnemaker	35.00	60.00
86A Dan Towler Brn RC	125.00	200.00
86B Dan Towler Yel RC	100.00	175.00
87A Bert Turek Brn RC	50.00	80.00
87B Bert Turek Yel RC	35.00	60.00
88 Harry Ulinski RC	35.00	60.00
89 Leon Van Billingham RC	35.00	60.00
90 Langdon Viracola RC	35.00	60.00
91 Leo Wagner RC	35.00	60.00
92A Doak Walker Brn	350.00	500.00
92B Doak Walker Yel	250.00	400.00
93 Jim Ward RC	35.00	60.00
94 Art Weiner	35.00	60.00
95 Dick Weiss RC	35.00	60.00
96 Froggie Williams RC	35.00	60.00
97 Robert Wilson RC	35.00	60.00
98 Roger Red Wilson RC	35.00	60.00
99 Carl Wren RC	35.00	60.00
100A Pete Zinaich Brn RC	50.00	80.00
100B Pete Zinaich Yel RC	35.00	60.00

1951 Topps Magic

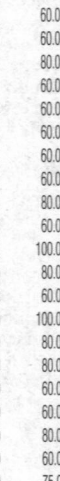

The 1951 Topps Magic football set was Topps' second major college football issue and featured 75 different players. The cards measure approximately 2 1/16" by 2 15/16" and were produced with a perforated edge along the bottom. Two different distinct perforation configurations have been found - one with a very tight pattern of dimples and the other with the dimples roughly 3/16" apart. The tight pattern version are usually found slightly diamond cut. Despite the perforation, the cards were issued as single cards and not as pairs in 1951. The fronts contain color portraits with the player's name, position and team nickname in a black box at the bottom. The backs contain a brief write-up, a black and white photo of the player's college or university within a 'scratch-off' section (unscratched cards still show the silver substance) which gives the answer to a football quiz. Cards with the scratch-off back intact are valued at 50 percent more than the prices listed below. Rookie Cards in this set include Marion Campbell, Vic Janowicz, Babe Parilli, Bert Rechichar, Bill Wade and George Young.

COMPLETE SET (75)	800.00	1,200.00
*BACK UNSCRATCHED: 1.5X TO 2.5X		
WRAPPER (1-CENT)	150.00	200.00
WRAPPER (5-CENT)	250.00	300.00
1 Jimmy Monahan RC	15.00	30.00
2 Bill Wade RC	30.00	50.00
3 Bill Reichardt RC	10.00	18.00
4 Babe Parilli RC	30.00	50.00
5 Billie Burkhalter RC	10.00	18.00
6 Ed Weber RC	10.00	18.00
7 Tom Scott RC	15.00	25.00
8 Frank Guthridge RC	10.00	18.00
9 John Karras	10.00	18.00
10 Vic Janowicz RC	100.00	175.00
11 Lloyd Hill RC	10.00	18.00
12 Jim Weatherall RC	15.00	25.00
13 Howard Hansen RC	10.00	18.00
14 Lou D'Achille RC	10.00	18.00
15 Johnny Turco RC	10.00	18.00
16 Jerrell Price RC	10.00	18.00
17 John Coatta RC	10.00	18.00
18 Bruce Patton RC	10.00	18.00
19 Marion Campbell RC	20.00	35.00
20 Blaine Earon RC	10.00	18.00
21 Dewey McConnell RC	10.00	18.00
22 Ray Beck RC	10.00	18.00
23 Jim Prewett RC	10.00	18.00
24 Bob Steele RC	10.00	18.00
25 Art Betts RC	10.00	18.00
26 Walt Trillhaase RC	10.00	18.00
27 Gil Bartosh RC	10.00	18.00
28 Bob Bestwick RC	10.00	18.00
29 Tom Rushing RC	10.00	18.00
30 Bert Rechichar RC	20.00	35.00
31 Bill Owens RC	10.00	18.00
32 Mike Goggins RC	10.00	18.00
33 John Petitbon RC	10.00	18.00
34 Byron Townsend RC	10.00	18.00
35 Ed Rotticci RC	10.00	18.00
36 Steve Wadiak RC	10.00	18.00
37 Bobby Marlow RC	15.00	25.00
38 Bill Fuchs RC	10.00	18.00
39 Ralph Staub RC	10.00	18.00
40 Bill Vesprini RC	10.00	18.00
41 Zack Jordan RC	10.00	18.00
42 Bob Smith RC	15.00	25.00
43 Charles Hanson RC	10.00	18.00
44 Glenn Smith RC	10.00	18.00
45 Armand Kitto RC	10.00	18.00
46 Vinnie Drake RC	10.00	18.00
47 Bill Putich RC	10.00	18.00
48 George Young RC	30.00	50.00
49 Don McRae RC	10.00	18.00
50 Frank Smith RC	10.00	18.00
51 Dick Hightower RC	10.00	18.00
52 Clyde Pickard RC	10.00	18.00
53 Bob Reynolds RC	15.00	25.00
54 Dick Gregory RC	10.00	18.00
55 Dale Samuels RC	10.00	18.00
56 Gale Galloway RC	10.00	18.00
57 Vic Pujo RC	10.00	18.00
58 Dave Waters RC	10.00	18.00
59 Joe Ernest RC	10.00	18.00
60 Elmer Costa RC	10.00	18.00
61 Nick Liotta RC	10.00	18.00
62 John Dottley RC	10.00	18.00
63 Hi Faubion RC	10.00	18.00
64 David Harr RC	10.00	18.00
65 Bill Matthews RC	10.00	18.00
66 Carroll McDonald RC	10.00	18.00
67 Dick Dewing RC	10.00	18.00
68 Joe Johnson RB RC	10.00	18.00
69 Arnold Burwitz RC	10.00	18.00
70 Ed Dobrowolski RC	10.00	18.00
71 Joe Dudeck RC	10.00	18.00
72 Johnny Bright RC	15.00	25.00
73 Harold Loehlein RC	10.00	18.00
74 Lawrence Hairston RC	10.00	18.00
75 Bob Carey RC	15.00	25.00

1955 Topps All American

Issued in one-card penny packs, nine-card nickel packs as well as 22-card cello packs, the 1955 Topps All-American set features 100-cards of college football greats from years past. The cards measure approximately 2 5/8" by 3 5/8". Card fronts contain a color player photo superimposed over a black and white action photo. The player's college logo is in one upper corner and an All-American logo is at the bottom with the player's name and position. The backs contain collegiate highlights and a cartoon. There are many numbers which were printed in lesser supply. These short-printed cards are denoted in the checklist below by SP. The key Rookie Cards in this set are Doc Blanchard, Tommy Harmon, Don Hutson, Ernie Nevers and Amos Alonzo Stagg. The Four Horsemen (Notre Dame backfield in 1924), Knute Rockne, Jim Thorpe, Red Grange and former Supreme Court Justice Whizzer White are also key cards. Wrongbacks can be found on some cards with the Amos A. Stagg card seemingly the most common of those wrongbacks. They are not cataloged below as error cards.

COMPLETE SET (100)	2,800.00	3,800.00
WRAPPER (1-CENT)	250.00	400.00
WRAPPER (5-CENT)	200.00	350.00
1 Herman Hickman RC	65.00	125.00
2 John Kimbrough RC	10.00	18.00
3 Ed Weir RC	10.00	18.00
4 Erny Pinckert RC	10.00	18.00
5 Bobby Grayson RC	10.00	18.00
6 Nile Kinnick UER RC	75.00	135.00
7 Andy Bershak RC	10.00	18.00
8 George Cafego RC	10.00	18.00
9 Tom Hamilton SP RC	20.00	30.00
10 Bill Dudley	25.00	40.00
11 Bobby Dodd SP RC	20.00	30.00
12 Otto Graham	100.00	200.00
13 Aaron Rosenberg	10.00	18.00
14A Gaynell Tinsley ERR RC	50.00	100.00
14B Gaynell Tinsley COR RC	15.00	25.00
15 Ed Kaw SP	20.00	30.00
16 Knute Rockne	175.00	275.00
17 Bob Reynolds	10.00	18.00
18 Pudge Heffelfinger SP RC	25.00	40.00
19 Bruce Smith	25.00	40.00
20 Sammy Baugh	125.00	200.00
21A W.White RC SP ERR	150.00	250.00
21B W.White RC SP COR	60.00	100.00
22 Brick Muller RC	10.00	18.00
23 Dick Kazmaier RC	15.00	25.00
24 Ken Strong	30.00	50.00
25 Casimir Myslinski SP RC	20.00	30.00
26 Larry Kelley SP RC	25.00	40.00
27 Red Grange UER	200.00	300.00
28 Mel Hein SP RC	60.00	100.00
29 Leo Nomellini SP	50.00	80.00
30 Wes Fesler RC	10.00	18.00
31 George Sauer Sr. RC	15.00	25.00
32 Hank Foldberg RC	10.00	18.00
33 Bob Higgins RC	10.00	18.00
34 Davey O'Brien RC	30.00	50.00
35 Tom Harmon SP RC	60.00	100.00
36 Turk Edwards SP	35.00	60.00

37 Jim Thorpe 275.00 400.00
38 Amos A. Stagg RC 40.00 75.00
39 Jerome Holland RC 15.00 25.00
40 Donn Moomaw RC 10.00 18.00
41 Joseph Alexander SP RC 20.00 30.00
42 Eddie Tryon SP RC 25.00 40.00
43 George Savitsky 10.00 18.00
44 Ed Garbisch RC 10.00 18.00
45 Elmer Oliphant RC 10.00 18.00
46 Arnold Lassman RC 10.00 18.00
47 Bo McMillin RC 15.00 25.00
48 Ed Widseth RC 10.00 18.00
49 Don Gordon Zimmerman RC 10.00 18.00
50 Ken Kavanaugh 15.00 25.00
51 Duane Purvis SP RC 20.00 30.00
52 Johnny Lujack 50.00 90.00
53 John F. Green RC 10.00 18.00
54 Edwin Dooley SP RC 20.00 30.00
55 Frank Merritt SP RC 20.00 30.00
56 Ernie Nevers RC 75.00 125.00
57 Vic Hanson SP RC 20.00 30.00
58 Ed Franco RC 10.00 18.00
59 Doc Blanchard RC 30.00 50.00
60 Dan Hill RC 10.00 18.00
61 Charles Brickley SP RC 20.00 30.00
62 Harry Newman RC 15.00 30.00
63 Charlie Justice 20.00 35.00
64 Benny Friedman RC 20.00 35.00
65 Joe Donchess SP RC 20.00 30.00
66 Bruiser Kinard RC 20.00 35.00
67 Frankie Albert 15.00 25.00
68 Four Horsemen SP RC 325.00 500.00
69 Frank Sinkwich RC 15.00 25.00
70 Bill Daddio RC 10.00 18.00
71 Bobby Wilson 10.00 18.00
72 Chub Peabody RC 10.00 18.00
73 Paul Governali RC 15.00 25.00
74 Gene McEver RC 10.00 18.00
75 Hugh Gallarneau RC 10.00 18.00
76 Angelo Bertelli RC 15.00 25.00
77 Bowden Wyatt SP RC 20.00 30.00
78 Jay Berwanger RC 20.00 35.00
79 Pug Lund RC 10.00 18.00
80 Bennie Oosterbaan RC 10.00 18.00
81 Cotton Warburton RC 10.00 18.00
82 Alex Wojciechowicz 20.00 35.00
83 Ted Coy SP RC 20.00 30.00
84 Ace Parker SP RC 30.00 60.00
85 Sid Luckman 60.00 120.00
86 Albie Booth SP RC 20.00 30.00
87 Adolph Schultz SP 20.00 30.00
88 Ralph Kercheval 10.00 18.00
89 Marshall Goldberg 18.00 30.00
90 Charlie O'Rourke RC 10.00 18.00
91 Bob Odell UER RC 10.00 18.00
92 Biggie Munn RC 10.00 18.00
93 Willie Heston SP RC 25.00 40.00
94 Joe Bernard SP RC 25.00 40.00
95 Chris Cagle SP RC 25.00 40.00
96 Bill Hollenback SP 25.00 40.00
97 Don Hutson SP RC 150.00 225.00
98 Beattie Feathers SP 60.00 100.00
99 Don Whitmire SP RC 25.00 40.00
100 Fats Henry SP RC 100.00 200.00

1956 Topps

The 1956 set of 120 player cards marks Topps' first standard NFL football card set since acquiring Bowman. The cards measure 2 5/8" by 3 5/8" and were issued in one-card penny packs, nickel packs and 15-card cello packs. The card fronts have a player photo superimposed over a solid color background. The team logo is an upper corner with the player's name, team name and position grouped in a box toward the bottom of the photo. The card backs were printed in red and black on gray card stock. Statistical information from the immediate past season and career totals are given at the bottom. Players from the Washington Redskins and the Chicago Cardinals were apparently produced in lesser quantities, as they are more difficult to find compared to the other teams. Some veteran collectors believe that cards of members of the Baltimore Colts, Chicago Bears, and Cleveland Browns may also be slightly more difficult to find as well. An unnumbered checklist card and six contest cards were also issued along with this set, although in much lesser quantities. The contest cards have advertisements on both sides for Bazooka Bubble Gum. Both sides have orange-red and blue type on an off-white background. The fronts of the contest cards feature an offer to win one of three prizes (basketball, football, or autographed baseball glove) in the Bazooka Bubble Gum football contest, and the rules governing the contest are listed on the back. Any eligible contestant (not over 15 years old) who mailed in (before November 19th) the correct scores to the two NFL football games listed on the front of that particular card and includes five one-cent Bazooka Bubble Gum wrappers or one nickel Bazooka wrapper with the entry received a choice of one of the three above-mentioned prizes. The cards are either numbered (1-3) or lettered (A-C). Some dealers have doubted the existence of Contest Card C. Any proof of this card would be greatly appreciated. There also exists a three-card advertising panel consis

COMPLETE SET (120) 1,200.00 1,800.00
WRAPPER (1-CENT) 200.00 250.00
WRAPPER (5-CENT) 60.00 100.00
1 Johnny Carson SP 40.00 80.00
2 Gordy Soltau 3.50 6.00
3 Frank Varrichione 3.50 6.00
4 Eddie Bell 3.50 6.00
5 Alex Webster RC 7.50 15.00
6 Norm Van Brocklin 18.00 30.00
7 Green Bay Packers 15.00 25.00
8 Lou Creekmur 7.50 15.00
9 Lou Groza 15.00 25.00
10 Tom Bienemann SP RC 15.00 25.00
11 George Blanda 30.00 50.00
12 Alan Ameche 6.00 12.00
13 Vic Janowicz SP 25.00 45.00
14 Dick Moegle 4.00 8.00
15 Fran Rogel 3.50 6.00
16 Harold Giancanelli 3.50 6.00
17 Emlen Tunnell 7.50 15.00
18 Tank Younger 6.00 12.00
19 Billy Howton 4.00 8.00
20 Jack Christiansen 7.50 15.00
21 Darrel Brewster 3.50 6.00
22 Chicago Cardinals SP 60.00 100.00
23 Ed Brown 4.00 8.00
24 Joe Campanella 3.50 6.00
25 Leon Heath SP 15.00 25.00
26 San Francisco 49ers 10.00 18.00
27 Dick Flanagan RC 3.50 6.00
28 Chuck Bednarik 15.00 25.00
29 Kyle Rote 6.00 12.00
30 Les Richter 4.00 8.00
31 Howard Ferguson 3.50 6.00
32 Dorne Dibble 3.50 6.00
33 Kenny Konz 3.50 6.00
34 Dave Mann SP RC 15.00 25.00
35 Rick Casares 6.00 12.00
36 Art Donovan 18.00 30.00
37 Chuck Drazenovich SP 15.00 25.00
38 Joe Arenas 3.50 6.00
39 Lynn Chandnois 3.50 6.00
40 Philadelphia Eagles 10.00 18.00
41 Roosevelt Brown RC 25.00 40.00
42 Tom Fears 15.00 25.00
43 Gary Knafelc RC 3.50 6.00
44 Joe Schmidt RC 35.00 60.00
45 Cleveland Browns 10.00 18.00
46 Len Teeuws SP RC 15.00 25.00
47 Bill George RC 25.00 40.00
48 Baltimore Colts 10.00 18.00
49 Eddie LeBaron SP 25.00 50.00
50 Hugh McElhenny 18.00 30.00
51 Ted Marchibroda 6.00 12.00
52 Adrian Burk 3.50 6.00
53 Frank Gifford 35.00 60.00
54 Charley Toogood 3.50 6.00
55 Tobin Rote 4.00 8.00
56 Bill Stits 3.50 6.00
57 Don Colo 3.50 6.00
58 Ollie Matson SP 35.00 60.00
59 Harlon Hill 4.00 8.00
60 Lenny Moore RC 75.00 125.00
61 Wash.Redskins SP 50.00 90.00
62 Billy Wilson 3.50 6.00
63 Pittsburgh Steelers 10.00 18.00
64 Bob Pellegrini RC 3.50 6.00
65 Ken MacAfee E 3.50 6.00
66 Willard Sherman RC 3.50 6.00
67 Roger Zatkoff 3.50 6.00
68 Dave Middleton RC 3.50 6.00
69 Ray Renfro 4.00 8.00
70 Don Stonesifer SP 15.00 25.00
71 Stan Jones RC 25.00 40.00
72 Jim Mutscheller RC 3.50 6.00
73 Volney Peters SP 15.00 25.00
74 Leo Nomellini 12.00 20.00
75 Ray Mathews 3.50 6.00
76 Dick Bielski 3.50 6.00
77 Charley Conerly 15.00 25.00
78 Elroy Hirsch 18.00 30.00
79 Bill Forester RC 4.00 8.00
80 Jim Doran RC 3.50 6.00
81 Fred Morrison 3.50 6.00
82 Jack Simmons SP 15.00 25.00
83 Bill McColl 3.50 6.00
84 Bert Rechichar 3.50 6.00
85 Joe Scudero SP RC 15.00 25.00
86 Y.A.Tittle 30.00 50.00
87 Ernie Stautner 12.00 20.00
88 Norm Willey 3.50 6.00
89 Bob Schnelker RC 3.50 6.00
90 Dan Towler 6.00 12.00
91 John Martinkovic 3.50 6.00
92 Detroit Lions 10.00 18.00
93 George Ratterman 4.00 8.00
94 Chuck Ulrich SP 15.00 25.00
95 Bobby Watkins 3.50 6.00
96 Buddy Young 6.00 12.00
97 Billy Wells SP RC 15.00 25.00
98 Bob Toneff 3.50 6.00
99 Bill McPeak 3.50 6.00
100 Bobby Thomason 3.50 6.00
101 Roosevelt Grier RC 30.00 50.00
102 Ron Waller RC 3.50 6.00
103 Bobby Dillon 3.50 6.00
104 Leon Hart 6.00 12.00
105 Mike McCormack 7.50 15.00
106 John Olszewski SP 15.00 25.00
107 Bill Wightkin 3.50 6.00
108 George Shaw RC 4.00 8.00
109 Dale Atkeson SP 15.00 25.00
110 Joe Perry 15.00 25.00
111 Dale Dodrill 3.50 6.00
112 Tom Scott 3.50 6.00
113 New York Giants 10.00 18.00
114 Los Angeles Rams 10.00 18.00
115 Al Carmichael 3.50 6.00
116 Bobby Layne 30.00 50.00
117 Ed Modzelewski 3.50 6.00
118 Lamar McHan RC SP 15.00 25.00
119 Chicago Bears 10.00 18.00
120 Billy Vessels RC 20.00 40.00
AD1 Advertising Panel 500.00 800.00
Lou Groza
Don Colo
Darrel Brewster
NNO Checklist SP NNO! 250.00 400.00
C1 Contest Card 1 ! 45.00 80.00
C2 Contest Card 2 ! 45.00 80.00
C3 Contest Card 3 ! 45.00 80.00
CA Contest Card A ! 50.00 90.00
CB Contest Card B ! 70.00 110.00

1957 Topps

The 1957 Topps football set contains 154 standard-size cards of NFL players. Cards were issued in penny, nickel and cello packs. Horizontally designed fronts have a close-up photo (with player name) on the left and an in-action pose (with position and team name) to the right. Both have solid color backgrounds. The card backs were printed in red and black on gray card stock. Backs are also divided in two with statistical information on one side and a cartoon on the other. The Rookie Cards of Johnny Unitas, Bart Starr, and Paul Hornung are included in this set. Other notable Rookie Cards in this set are Raymond Berry, Dick "Night Train" Lane, Tommy McDonald and Earl Morrall. The second series (89-154) is generally more difficult to obtain than the first series. A number of cards (22) from the second series are much easier to find than the other 44, making those double prints (DP). It's thought that the John Unitas Rookie card is among the 22-DPs. An unnumbered checklist card was also issued with this set. The checklist card was printed in red, yellow, and blue or in red, white, and blue; neither variety currently is recognized as having any additional premium value above the price listed below. There also were produced several three-card advertising panels consisting of the card fronts of three players with ad copy on the reverse of the top two cards and a player's cardback at the bottom. The complete set price below refers to the 154 numbered cards minus the unnumbered checklist card.

COMPLETE SET (154) 1,600.00 2,200.00
WRAPPER (1-CENT) 30.00 50.00
WRAPPER (5-CENT) 50.00 75.00
1 Eddie LeBaron 30.00 50.00
2 Pete Retzlaff RC 7.50 15.00
3 Mike McCormack 6.00 12.00
4 Lou Baldacci RC 2.50 4.00
5 Gino Marchetti 10.00 20.00
6 Leo Nomellini 10.00 20.00
7 Bobby Watkins 2.50 4.00
8 Dave Middleton 2.50 4.00
9 Bobby Dillon 2.50 4.00
10 Les Richter 3.50 6.00
11 Roosevelt Brown 10.00 20.00
12 Lavern Torgeson RC 2.50 4.00
13 Dick Bielski 2.50 4.00
14 Pat Summerall 10.00 20.00
15 Jack Butler RC 15.00 25.00
16 John Henry Johnson 7.50 15.00
17 Art Spinney 2.50 4.00
18 Bob St. Clair 6.00 12.00
19 Perry Jeter RC 2.50 4.00
20 Lou Creekmur 6.00 12.00
21 Dave Hanner 3.50 6.00
22 Norm Van Brocklin 18.00 30.00
23 Don Chandler RC 5.00 10.00
24 Al Dorow 2.50 4.00
25 Tom Scott 2.50 4.00
26 Ollie Matson 12.00 20.00
27 Fran Rogel 2.50 4.00
28 Lou Groza 15.00 25.00
29 Billy Vessels 3.50 6.00
30 Y.A.Tittle 25.00 40.00
31 George Blanda 25.00 40.00
32 Bobby Layne 25.00 40.00
33 Billy Howton 3.50 6.00
34 Bill Wade 5.00 10.00
35 Emlen Tunnell 7.50 15.00
36 Leo Elter RC 2.50 4.00
37 Clarence Peaks RC 3.50 6.00
38 Don Stonesifer 2.50 4.00
39 George Tarasovic 2.50 4.00
40 Darrel Brewster 2.50 4.00
41 Bert Rechichar 2.50 4.00
42 Billy Wilson 2.50 4.00
43 Ed Brown 3.50 6.00
44 Gene Gedman RC 2.50 4.00
45 Gary Knafelc 2.50 4.00
46 Elroy Hirsch 18.00 30.00
47 Don Heinrich 3.50 6.00
48 Gene Brito 2.50 4.00
49 Chuck Bednarik 15.00 25.00
50 Dave Mann 2.50 4.00
51 Bill McPeak 2.50 4.00
52 Kenny Konz 2.50 4.00
53 Alan Ameche 5.00 10.00
54 Gordy Soltau 2.50 4.00
55 Rick Casares 3.50 6.00
56 Charlie Ane 2.50 4.00
57 Al Carmichael 2.50 4.00
58A W.Sherman ERR no pos/team 175.00 300.00
58B Willard Sherman COR 2.50 4.00
58C W.Sherman ERR no team 125.00 200.00
59 Kyle Rote 5.00 10.00
60 Chuck Drazenovich 2.50 4.00
61 Bobby Walston 2.50 4.00
62 John Olszewski 2.50 4.00
63 Ray Mathews 2.50 4.00
64 Maurice Bassett 2.50 4.00
65 Art Donovan 15.00 25.00
66 Joe Arenas 2.50 4.00
67 Harlon Hill 3.50 6.00
68 Yale Lary 6.00 12.00
69 Bill Forester 3.50 6.00
70 Bob Boyd 2.50 4.00
71 Andy Robustelli 12.00 20.00
72 Sam Baker RC 3.50 6.00
73 Bob Pellegrini 2.50 4.00
74 Leo Sanford 2.50 4.00
75 Sid Watson RC 2.50 4.00
76 Ray Renfro 3.50 6.00
77 Carl Taseff UER 2.50 4.00
78 Clyde Conner RC 2.50 4.00
79 J.C. Caroline RC 2.50 4.00
80 Howard Cassady RC 7.50 15.00
81 Tobin Rote 3.50 6.00
82 Ron Waller 2.50 4.00
83 Jim Patton RC 3.50 6.00
84 Volney Peters 2.50 4.00
85 Dick Lane RC 35.00 60.00
86 Royce Womble 2.50 4.00
87 Duane Putnam RC 3.50 6.00
88 Frank Gifford 30.00 60.00
89 Steve Meilinger 5.00 10.00
90 Buck Lansford 5.00 10.00
91 Lindon Crow DP 4.00 8.00
92 Ernie Stautner DP 12.50 25.00
93 Preston Carpenter DP RC 4.00 8.00
94 Raymond Berry RC 75.00 150.00
95 Hugh McElhenny 18.00 30.00
96 Stan Jones 15.00 25.00
97 Dorne Dibble 5.00 10.00
98 Joe Scudero DP 4.00 8.00
99 Eddie Bell 5.00 10.00
100 Joe Childress DP RC 4.00 8.00
101 Elbert Nickel 6.00 12.00
102 Walt Michaels 6.00 12.00
103 Jim Mutscheller DP 4.00 8.00
104 Earl Morrall RC 35.00 60.00
105 Larry Strickland RC 5.00 10.00
106 Jack Christiansen 7.50 15.00
107 Fred Cone DP 4.00 8.00
108 Bud McFadin RC 6.00 12.00
109 Charley Conerly 18.00 30.00
110 Tom Runnels DP RC 4.00 8.00
111 Ken Keller DP RC 4.00 8.00
112 James Root RC 5.00 10.00
113 Ted Marchibroda DP 5.00 10.00
114 Don Paul DB 5.00 10.00
115 George Shaw 6.00 12.00
116 Dick Moegle 6.00 12.00
117 Don Bingham 5.00 10.00
118 Leon Hart 7.50 15.00
119 Bart Starr RC 400.00 750.00
120 Paul Miller DP RC 4.00 8.00
121 Alex Webster 6.00 12.00
122 Ray Wietecha DP 4.00 8.00
123 Johnny Carson 5.00 10.00
124 Tom. McDonald DP RC 25.00 40.00
125 Jerry Tubbs RC 6.00 12.00
126 Jack Scarbath 5.00 10.00
127 Ed Modzelewski DP 4.00 8.00
128 Lenny Moore 30.00 50.00
129 Joe Perry DP 15.00 25.00
130 Bill Wightkin 5.00 10.00
131 Jim Doran 5.00 10.00
132 Howard Ferguson UER 5.00 10.00
133 Tom Wilson RC 5.00 10.00
134 Dick James RC 5.00 10.00
135 Jimmy Harris RC 5.00 10.00
136 Chuck Ulrich 5.00 10.00
137 Lynn Chandnois 5.00 10.00
138 Johnny Unitas DP RC 300.00 450.00
139 Jim Ridlon DP RC 4.00 8.00
140 Zeke Bratkowski DP 5.00 10.00
141 Ray Krouse 5.00 10.00
142 John Martinkovic 5.00 10.00
143 Jim Cason DP RC 4.00 8.00
144 Ken MacAfee E 5.00 10.00
145 Sid Youngelman RC 6.00 12.00
146 Paul Larson RC 5.00 10.00
147 Len Ford 18.00 30.00
148 Bob Toneff DP 4.00 8.00
149 Ronnie Knox DP RC 4.00 8.00
150 Jim David RC 6.00 12.00
151 Paul Hornung RC 250.00 400.00
152 Tank Younger 7.50 15.00
153 Bill Svoboda DP RC 4.00 8.00
154 Fred Morrison 35.00 70.00
AD1 Al Dorow 400.00 700.00
Harlon Hill
Bert Rechich
AD2 B.Watkins 400.00 700.00
G.Marchetti
C.Peaks

AD3 M.McCormack 400.00 700.00
L.Elter
J.Caroline
CL1 Checklist Bazooka SP 500.00 750.00
CL2 Checklist Blony SP 500.00 750.00

1958 Topps

The 1958 Topps set of 132 standard-size cards contains NFL players. After a one-year interruption, team cards returned to the Topps lineup. The cards were issued in penny, nickel and cello packs. Card fronts have an oval player photo surrounded by a solid color that varies according to team. The player's name, position and team are at the bottom. The backs are easily distinguished from other years, as they are printed in bright red ink on white stock. The right-hand side has a trivia question with which the answer could be obtained by rubbing with a coin over the blank space. The left side has stats and highlights. The key Rookie Cards in this set are Jim Brown and Sonny Jurgensen. Topps also randomly inserted in packs a card with the words "Free Felt Initial" across the top. The horizontally oriented front pictures a boy in a red shirt and a girl in a blue shirt, with a large yellow "L" and "A" respectively on each of their shirts. The card back indicates an initial could be obtained by sending in three Bazooka or Blony wrappers and a self-addressed stamped envelope with the initial of choice printed on the front and back of the envelope. According to a note in the December 15th, 1958 issue of Sports Illustrated, 110 million cards were produced for this issue.

COMPLETE SET (132) 850.00 1,250.00
WRAPPER (1-CENT) 35.00 60.00
WRAPPER (5-CENT) 75.00 125.00
1 Gene Filipski RC 7.50 15.00
2 Bobby Layne 20.00 35.00
3 Joe Schmidt 6.00 12.00
4 Bill Barnes RC 2.00 4.00
5 Milt Plum RC 5.00 10.00
6 Billy Howton UER 2.50 5.00
7 Howard Cassady 2.50 5.00
8 Jim Dooley 2.00 4.00
9 Cleveland Browns 3.00 6.00
10 Lenny Moore 15.00 30.00
11 Darrel Brewster 2.00 4.00
12 Alan Ameche 4.00 8.00
13 Jim David 2.00 4.00
14 Jim Mutscheller 2.00 4.00
15 Andy Robustelli 5.00 10.00
16 Gino Marchetti 6.00 12.00
17 Ray Renfro 2.50 5.00
18 Yale Lary 4.00 8.00
19 Gary Glick RC 2.00 4.00
20 Jon Arnett RC 4.00 8.00
21 Bob Boyd 2.00 4.00
22 Johnny Unitas UER 90.00 150.00
23 Zeke Bratkowski 2.50 5.00
24 Sid Youngelman UER 2.00 4.00
25 Leo Elter 2.00 4.00
26 Kenny Konz 2.00 4.00
27 Washington Redskins 3.00 6.00
28 Carl Brettschneider RC 2.00 4.00
29 Chicago Bears 3.00 6.00
30 Alex Webster 2.50 5.00
31 Al Carmichael 2.00 4.00
32 Bobby Dillon 2.00 4.00
33 Steve Meilinger 2.00 4.00
34 Sam Baker 2.00 4.00
35 Chuck Bednarik 7.50 15.00
36 Bert Vic Zucco RC 2.00 4.00
37 George Tarasovic 2.00 4.00
38 Bill Wade 4.00 8.00
39 Dick Stanfel 2.50 5.00
40 Jerry Norton 2.00 4.00
41 San Francisco 49ers 3.00 6.00
42 Emlen Tunnell 5.00 10.00
43 Jim Doran 2.00 4.00
44 Ted Marchibroda 4.00 8.00
45 Chet Hanulak 2.00 4.00
46 Dale Dodrill 2.00 4.00
47 Johnny Carson 2.00 4.00
48 Dick Deschaine RC 2.00 4.00
49 Billy Wells UER 2.00 4.00
50 Larry Morris RC 2.00 4.00
51 Jack McClairen RC 2.00 4.00
52 Lou Groza 7.50 15.00
53 Rick Casares 2.50 5.00
54 Don Chandler 2.50 5.00
55 Duane Putnam 2.00 4.00
56 Gary Knafelc 2.00 4.00
57 Earl Morrall 5.00 10.00
58 Ron Kramer RC 2.50 5.00
59 Mike McCormack 4.00 8.00
60 Gern Nagler 2.00 4.00
61 New York Giants 3.00 6.00
62 Jim Brown RC 350.00 500.00
63 Joe Marconi RC 2.00 4.00
64 R.C. Owens UER RC 2.50 5.00
65 Jimmy Carr RC 2.50 5.00
66 Bart Starr UER 90.00 150.00
67 Tom Wilson 2.00 4.00
68 Lamar McHan 2.00 4.00
69 Chicago Cardinals 3.00 6.00
70 Jack Christiansen 4.00 8.00
71 Don McIlhenny RC 2.00 4.00
72 Ron Waller 2.00 4.00
73 Frank Gifford 25.00 50.00
74 Bert Rechichar 2.00 4.00
75 John Henry Johnson 5.00 10.00
76 Jack Butler 4.00 8.00
77 Frank Varrichione 2.00 4.00
78 Ray Mathews 2.00 4.00
79 Marv Matuszak UER RC 2.00 4.00
80 Harlon Hill UER 2.00 4.00
81 Lou Creekmur 4.00 8.00
82 Woodley Lewis UER 2.00 4.00
83 Don Heinrich 2.00 4.00
84 Charley Conerly 7.50 15.00
85 Los Angeles Rams 3.00 6.00
86 Y.A.Tittle 18.00 30.00
87 Bobby Walston 2.00 4.00
88 Earl Putman RC 2.00 4.00
89 Leo Nomellini 7.50 15.00
90 Sonny Jurgensen RC 60.00 100.00
91 Don Paul DB 2.00 4.00
92 Paige Cothren RC 2.00 4.00
93 Joe Perry 7.50 15.00
94 Tobin Rote 2.50 5.00
95 Billy Wilson 2.00 4.00
96 Green Bay Packers 7.50 15.00
97 Lavern Torgeson 2.00 4.00
98 Milt Davis RC 2.00 4.00
99 Larry Strickland 2.00 4.00
100 Matt Hazeltine RC 2.50 5.00
101 Walt Yowarsky RC 2.00 4.00
102 Roosevelt Brown 4.00 8.00
103 Jim Ringo 5.00 10.00
104 Joe Krupa RC 2.00 4.00
105 Les Richter 2.50 5.00
106 Art Donovan 12.00 20.00
107 John Olszewski 2.00 4.00
108 Ken Keller 2.00 4.00
109 Philadelphia Eagles 3.00 6.00
110 Baltimore Colts 3.00 6.00
111 Dick Bielski 2.00 4.00
112 Eddie LeBaron 4.00 8.00
113 Gene Brito 2.00 4.00
114 Willie Galimore RC 5.00 10.00
115 Detroit Lions 3.00 6.00
116 Pittsburgh Steelers 3.00 6.00
117 L.G. Dupre 2.50 5.00
118 Babe Parilli 2.50 5.00
119 Bill George 5.00 10.00
120 Raymond Berry 25.00 40.00
121 Jim Podoley UER RC 2.00 4.00
122 Hugh McElhenny 7.50 15.00
123 Ed Brown 2.50 5.00
124 Dick Moegle 2.50 5.00
125 Tom Scott 2.00 4.00
126 Tommy McDonald 6.00 12.00
127 Ollie Matson 10.00 20.00
128 Preston Carpenter 2.00 4.00
129 George Blanda 18.00 30.00
130 Gordy Soltau 2.00 4.00
131 Dick Nolan RC 2.50 5.00
132 Don Bosseler RC 10.00 20.00
AD1 Ad Panel 450.00 700.00
Leo Nomellini
Chet Hanulak
Cardinals Team
Gordy Soltau back
NNO Free Felt Initial Card 15.00 25.00

1959 Topps

The 1959 Topps football set contains 176 standard-size cards which were issued in two series of 88. The cards were issued in penny, nickel and cello packs. The cello packs contained 12 cards at a cost of 10 cents per and were packed 36 to a box. Card fronts contain a player photo over a solid background. Beneath the photo, is the player's name in red and blue letters. Beneath the name are the player's position and team. The card backs were printed in gray on white card stock. Statistical information from the immediate past season and career totals are given on the reverse. Card backs include a scratch-off quiz. Team cards (with checklist backs) as well as team pennant cards are included in the set. The key Rookie Cards in this set are Sam Huff, Alex Karras, Jerry Kramer, Bobby Mitchell, Jim Parker and Jim Taylor. The Taylor card was supposed to portray the great Packers running back. Instead, the card depicts the Cardinals linebacker.

COMPLETE SET (176) 600.00 900.00
WRAPPER (1-CENT) 50.00 90.00
WRAPPER (1-CENT, REP) 50.00 80.00
WRAPPER (5-CENT) 75.00 125.00
1 Johnny Unitas 60.00 120.00
2 Gene Brito 1.50 3.00
3 Detroit Lions CL 3.00 6.00
4 Max McGee RC 15.00 30.00
5 Hugh McElhenny 7.50 15.00
6 Joe Schmidt 4.00 8.00
7 Kyle Rote 3.00 6.00
8 Clarence Peaks 1.50 3.00
9 Steelers Pennant 1.75 3.50
10 Jim Brown 90.00 150.00
11 Ray Mathews 1.50 3.00
12 Bobby Dillon 1.50 3.00
13 Joe Childress 1.50 3.00
14 Terry Barr RC 1.50 3.00
15 Del Shofner RC 2.00 4.00
16 Bob Pellegrini UER 1.50 3.00
17 Baltimore Colts CL 3.00 6.00
18 Preston Carpenter 1.50 3.00
19 Leo Nomellini 5.00 10.00
20 Frank Gifford 25.00 40.00
21 Charlie Ane 1.50 3.00
22 Jack Butler 2.50 6.00
23 Bart Starr 35.00 60.00
24 Cardinals Pennant 1.75 3.50
25 Bill Barnes 1.50 3.00
26 Walt Michaels 2.00 4.00
27 Clyde Conner UER 1.50 3.00
28 Paige Cothren 1.50 3.00
29 Roosevelt Grier 3.00 6.00
30 Alan Ameche 3.00 6.00
31 Philadelphia Eagles CL 3.00 6.00
32 Dick Nolan 2.00 4.00
33 R.C. Owens 2.00 4.00
34 Dale Dodrill 1.50 3.00
35 Gene Gedman 1.50 3.00
36 Gene Lipscomb RC 5.00 10.00
37 Ray Renfro 2.00 4.00
38 Browns Pennant 1.75 3.50
39 Bill Forester 2.00 4.00
40 Bobby Layne 15.00 25.00
41 Pat Summerall 5.00 10.00
42 Jerry Mertens RC 1.50 3.00
43 Steve Myhra RC 1.50 3.00
44 John Henry Johnson 4.00 8.00
45 Woodley Lewis UER 1.50 3.00
46 Green Bay Packers CL 5.00 10.00
47 Don Owens UER RC 1.50 3.00
48 Ed Beatty RC 1.50 3.00
49 Don Chandler 1.50 3.00
50 Ollie Matson 6.00 12.00
51 Sam Huff RC 30.00 50.00
52 Tom Miner RC 1.50 3.00
53 Giants Pennant 1.75 3.50
54 Kenny Konz 1.50 3.00
55 Raymond Berry 10.00 20.00
56 Howard Ferguson UER 1.50 3.00
57 Chuck Ulrich 1.50 3.00
58 Bob St.Clair 3.00 6.00
59 Don Burroughs RC 1.50 3.00
60 Lou Groza 7.50 15.00
61 San Francisco 49ers CL 3.00 6.00
62 Andy Nelson RC 1.50 3.00
63 Harold Bradley RC 1.50 3.00
64 Dave Hanner 2.00 4.00
65 Charley Conerly 6.00 12.00
66 Gene Cronin RC 1.50 3.00
67 Duane Putnam 1.50 3.00
68 Colts Pennant 1.75 3.50
69 Ernie Stautner 4.00 8.00
70 Jon Arnett 2.00 4.00
71 Ken Panfil RC 1.50 3.00
72 Matt Hazeltine 1.50 3.00
73 Harley Sewell 1.50 3.00
74 Mike McCormack 3.00 6.00
75 Jim Ringo 4.00 8.00
76 Los Angeles Rams CL 3.00 6.00
77 Bob Gain RC 1.50 3.00
78 Buzz Nutter RC 1.50 3.00
79 Jerry Norton 1.50 3.00
80 Joe Perry 6.00 12.00
81 Carl Brettschneider 1.50 3.00
82 Paul Hornung 30.00 60.00
83 Eagles Pennant 1.75 3.50
84 Les Richter 2.00 4.00
85 Howard Cassady 2.00 4.00
86 Art Donovan 7.50 15.00
87 Jim Patton 2.00 4.00
88 Pete Retzlaff 2.00 4.00
89 Jim Mutscheller 1.00 2.00
90 Zeke Bratkowski 1.50 3.00
91 Washington Redskins CL 2.00 4.00
92 Art Hunter 1.00 2.00
93 Gern Nagler 1.00 2.00
94 Chuck Weber RC 1.00 2.00
95 Lew Carpenter RC 1.50 3.00
96 Stan Jones 2.50 5.00
97 Ralph Guglielmi UER 1.50 3.00
98 Packers Pennant 2.00 4.00
99 Ray Wietecha 1.00 2.00
100 Lenny Moore 6.00 12.00
101 Jim Ray Smith UER RC 1.50 3.00
102 Abe Woodson RC 1.50 3.00
103 Alex Karras RC 25.00 40.00
104 Chicago Bears CL 2.00 4.00
105 John David Crow RC 6.00 12.00
106 Joe Fortunato RC 1.00 2.00
107 Babe Parilli 1.50 3.00
108 Proverb Jacobs RC 1.00 2.00
109 Gino Marchetti 4.00 8.00
110 Bill Wade 1.50 3.00
111 49ers Pennant 1.50 3.00
112 Karl Rubke RC 1.00 2.00
113 Dave Middleton UER 1.00 2.00
114 Roosevelt Brown 2.50 5.00
115 John Olszewski 1.00 2.00
116 Jerry Kramer RC 18.00 30.00
117 King Hill RC 1.50 3.00
118 Chicago Cardinals CL 2.00 4.00
119 Frank Varrichione 1.00 2.00
120 Rick Casares 1.50 3.00
121 George Strugar RC 1.00 2.00
122 Bill Glass RC 1.50 3.00
123 Don Bosseler 1.00 2.00
124 John Reger RC 1.00 2.00
125 Jim Ninowski RC 1.00 2.00
126 Rams Pennant 1.50 3.00
127 Willard Sherman 1.00 2.00
128 Bob Schnelker 1.00 2.00
129 Ollie Spencer RC 1.00 2.00
130 Y.A.Tittle 15.00 25.00
131 Yale Lary 2.50 5.00
132 Jim Parker RC 15.00 30.00
133 New York Giants CL 2.00 4.00
134 Jim Schrader RC 1.00 2.00
135 M.C. Reynolds RC 1.00 2.00
136 Mike Sandusky RC 1.00 2.00
137 Ed Brown 1.50 3.00
138 Al Barry RC 1.00 2.00
139 Lions Pennant 1.50 3.00
140 Bobby Mitchell RC 20.00 35.00
141 Larry Morris 1.00 2.00
142 Jim Phillips RC 1.50 3.00
143 Jim David 1.00 2.00
144 Joe Krupa 1.00 2.00
145 Willie Galimore 1.50 3.00
146 Pittsburgh Steelers CL 2.00 4.00
147 Andy Robustelli 4.00 8.00
148 Billy Wilson 1.00 2.00
149 Leo Sanford 1.00 2.00
150 Eddie LeBaron 2.50 5.00
151 Bill McColl 1.00 2.00
152 Buck Lansford UER 1.00 2.00
153 Bears Pennant 1.50 3.00
154 Leo Sugar RC 1.00 2.00
155 Jim Taylor UER RC 20.00 35.00
156 Lindon Crow 1.00 2.00
157 Jack McClairen 1.00 2.00
158 Vince Costello RC UER 1.00 2.00
159 Stan Wallace RC 1.00 2.00
160 Mel Triplett RC 1.00 2.00
161 Cleveland Browns CL 2.00 4.00
162 Dan Currie RC 2.00 4.00
163 L.G. Dupre UER 1.50 3.00
164 John Morrow UER RC 1.00 2.00
165 Jim Podoley 1.00 2.00
166 Bruce Bosley RC 1.00 2.00
167 Harlon Hill 1.00 2.00
168 Redskins Pennant 1.50 3.00
169 Junior Wren RC 1.00 2.00
170 Tobin Rote 1.50 3.00
171 Art Spinney 1.00 2.00
172 Chuck Drazenovich UER 1.00 2.00
173 Bobby Joe Conrad RC 1.50 3.00
174 Jesse Richardson RC 1.00 2.00
175 Sam Baker 1.00 2.00
176 Tom Tracy RC 4.00 8.00
AD1 Ad Panel 350.00 500.00
Bill Forrester
Bobby Dillon
Ernie Stautner
Gene Cronin back

1960 Topps

The 1960 Topps football set contains 132 standard-size cards. Card fronts have a "pure card" effect in that the player photo dominates the card. The only design on front is the player's name, team name and position within a football-shaped icon toward the bottom of the file. The card backs are printed in green on white card stock. Statistical information from the immediate past season and career totals are given on the reverse. The set marks the debut of the Dallas Cowboys into the NFL. The backs feature a "Football Funnies" scratch-off quiz; answer was revealed by rubbing with an edge of a coin. The team cards feature numerical checklist backs. The team cards that have the 67-132 checklist backs (card Nos. 60, 102, 112, 122, 132) all misspell 124 Don Bosseler as Bossler along with a number of other like errors. Several 3-card panel advertisement sheets were released to promote the set. Each features the cardfronts of three base cards with the sheet back including a Gene Cronin mock cardback and several Topps ads.

COMPLETE SET (132) 400.00 600.00
WRAPPER (1-CENT) 60.00 100.00
WRAPPER (1-CENT, REP) 250.00 400.00
WRAPPER (5-CENT) 50.00 80.00
1 Johnny Unitas 40.00 80.00
2 Alan Ameche 2.00 4.00
3 Lenny Moore 5.00 10.00
4 Raymond Berry 6.00 12.00
5 Jim Parker 4.00 8.00
6 George Preas RC 1.25 2.50
7 Art Spinney 1.25 2.50
8 Bill Pellington RC 1.50 3.00
9 Johnny Sample RC 1.50 3.00
10 Gene Lipscomb 1.50 3.00
11 Baltimore Colts 1.50 3.00
12 Ed Brown 1.50 3.00
13 Rick Casares 1.50 3.00
14 Willie Galimore 1.50 3.00
15 Jim Dooley 1.25 2.50
16 Harlon Hill UER 1.25 2.50
17 Stan Jones 2.00 4.00
18 Bill George 2.00 4.00
19 Erich Barnes RC 1.50 3.00
20 Doug Atkins 3.00 6.00
21 Chicago Bears 1.50 3.00
22 Milt Plum 1.50 3.00
23 Jim Brown 60.00 100.00

Card	Low	High
24 Sam Baker	1.25	2.50
25 Bobby Mitchell	5.00	10.00
26 Ray Renfro	1.50	3.00
27 Billy Howton	1.50	3.00
28 Jim Ray Smith	1.25	2.50
29 Jim Shofner RC	1.50	3.00
30 Bob Gain	1.25	2.50
31 Cleveland Browns	1.50	3.00
32 Don Heinrich	1.25	2.50
33 Ed Modzelewski UER	1.25	2.50
34 Fred Cone	1.25	2.50
35 L.G. Dupre	1.50	3.00
36 Dick Bielski	1.25	2.50
37 Charlie Ane UER	1.25	2.50
38 Jerry Tubbs	1.50	3.00
39 Doyle Nix RC	1.25	2.50
40 Ray Krouse	1.25	2.50
41 Earl Morrall	2.00	4.00
42 Howard Cassady	1.50	3.00
43 Dave Middleton	1.25	2.50
44 Jim Gibbons RC	1.50	3.00
45 Darris McCord RC	1.25	2.50
46 Joe Schmidt	3.00	6.00
47 Terry Barr	1.25	2.50
48 Yale Lary	2.00	4.00
49 Gil Mains RC	1.25	2.50
50 Detroit Lions	1.50	3.00
51 Bart Starr	30.00	50.00
52 Jim Taylor UER	4.00	8.00
53 Lew Carpenter	1.50	3.00
54 Paul Hornung	30.00	45.00
55 Max McGee	2.00	4.00
56 Forrest Gregg RC UER	25.00	40.00
57 Jim Ringo	2.50	5.00
58 Bill Forester	1.50	3.00
59 Dave Hanner	1.50	3.00
60 Green Bay Packers	4.00	8.00
61 Bill Wade	1.50	3.00
62 Frank Ryan RC	2.50	5.00
63 Ollie Matson	5.00	10.00
64 Jon Arnett	1.50	3.00
65 Del Shofner	1.50	3.00
66 Jim Phillips	1.25	2.50
67 Art Hunter	1.25	2.50
68 Les Richter	1.50	3.00
69 Lou Michaels RC	1.50	3.00
70 John Baker RC	1.25	2.50
71 Los Angeles Rams	1.50	3.00
72 Charley Conerly	4.00	8.00
73 Mel Triplett	1.25	2.50
74 Frank Gifford	20.00	35.00
75 Alex Webster	1.50	3.00
76 Bob Schnelker	1.25	2.50
77 Pat Summerall	4.00	8.00
78 Roosevelt Brown	2.00	4.00
79 Jim Patton	1.25	2.50
80 Sam Huff	10.00	20.00
81 Andy Robustelli	3.00	6.00
82 New York Giants	1.50	3.00
83 Clarence Peaks	1.25	2.50
84 Bill Barnes	1.25	2.50
85 Pete Retzlaff	1.50	3.00
86 Bobby Walston	1.25	2.50
87 Chuck Bednarik UER	4.00	8.00
88 Bob Pellegrini	1.25	2.50
89 Tom Brookshier RC	1.50	3.00
90 Marion Campbell	1.50	3.00
91 Jesse Richardson	1.25	2.50
92 Philadelphia Eagles	1.50	3.00
93 Bobby Layne	18.00	30.00
94 John Henry Johnson	3.00	6.00
95 Tom Tracy UER	1.50	3.00
96 Preston Carpenter	1.25	2.50
97 Frank Varrichione UER	1.25	2.50
98 John Nisby RC	1.25	2.50
99 Dean Derby RC	1.25	2.50
100 George Tarasovic	1.25	2.50
101 Ernie Stautner	2.50	5.00
102 Pittsburgh Steelers	1.50	3.00
103 King Hill	1.25	2.50
104 Mal Hammack RC	1.25	2.50
105 John David Crow	1.50	3.00
106 Bobby Joe Conrad	1.50	3.00
107 Woodley Lewis	1.25	2.50
108 Don Gillis RC	1.25	2.50
109 Carl Brettschneider	1.25	2.50
110 Leo Sugar	1.25	2.50
111 Frank Fuller RC	1.25	2.50
112 St. Louis Cardinals	1.50	3.00
113 Y.A.Tittle	18.00	30.00
114 Joe Perry	4.00	8.00
115 J.D.Smith RC	1.50	3.00
116 Hugh McElhenny	4.00	8.00
117 Billy Wilson	1.25	2.50
118 Bob St.Clair	2.00	4.00
119 Matt Hazeltine	1.25	2.50
120 Abe Woodson	1.25	2.50
121 Leo Nomellini	2.50	5.00
122 San Francisco 49ers	1.50	3.00
123 Ralph Guglielmi UER	1.25	2.50
124 Don Bosseler	1.25	2.50
125 John Olszewski	1.25	2.50
126 Bill Anderson UER RC	1.25	2.50
127 Joe Walton RC	1.50	3.00
128 Jim Schrader	1.25	2.50
129 Ralph Felton RC	1.25	2.50
130 Gary Glick	1.25	2.50
131 Bob Toneff	1.25	2.50
132 Redskins Team	18.00	30.00
AD1 Alan Ameche	200.00	350.00
Paul Hornung		
Tom Tracy		
AD2 Del Shofner	125.00	200.00
Milt Plum		
Jim Patton		
AD3 Bob St.Clair	125.00	200.00
Jim Shofner		
Gil Mains		
AD4 Tom Brookshier	125.00	200.00
Packers Team		
George Preas		
AD5 Jimmy Patton	500.00	800.00
Bobby Joe Conrad		
Sam Huff		

1960 Topps Metallic Stickers Inserts

This set of 33 metallic team emblem stickers was inserted with the 1960 Topps regular issue football set. The stickers are unnumbered and are ordered below alphabetically within type. NFL teams are listed first (1-13) followed by college teams (14-33). The stickers measure approximately 2 1/8" by 3 1/16". The sticker fronts are either silver, gold, or blue with a black border.

Card	Low	High
COMPLETE SET (33)	200.00	400.00
1 Baltimore Colts	7.50	15.00
2 Chicago Bears	12.50	25.00
3 Cleveland Browns	12.50	25.00
4 Dallas Cowboys	12.50	25.00
5 Detroit Lions	7.50	15.00
6 Green Bay Packers	15.00	30.00
7 Los Angeles Rams	7.50	15.00
8 New York Giants	7.50	15.00
9 Philadelphia Eagles	7.50	15.00
10 Pittsburgh Steelers	7.50	15.00
11 St. Louis Cardinals	7.50	15.00
12 San Francisco 49ers	12.50	25.00
13 Washington Redskins	12.50	25.00
14 Air Force Falcons	5.00	10.00
15 Army Cadets	5.00	10.00
16 California Golden Bears	5.00	10.00
17 Dartmouth Indians	5.00	10.00
18 Duke Blue Devils	5.00	10.00
19 LSU Tigers	7.50	15.00
20 Michigan Wolverines	10.00	20.00
21 Minnesota Golden Gophers	5.00	10.00
22 Mississippi Rebels	5.00	10.00
23 Navy Midshipmen	5.00	10.00
24 Notre Dame Fight.Irish	12.50	25.00
25 SMU Mustangs	5.00	10.00
26 USC Trojans	7.50	15.00
27 Syracuse Orangemen	5.00	10.00
28 Tennessee Volunteers	7.50	15.00
29 Texas Longhorns	7.50	15.00
30 UCLA Bruins	7.50	15.00
31 Washington Huskies	5.00	10.00
32 Wisconsin Badgers	5.00	10.00
33 Yale Bulldogs	5.00	10.00

1960 Topps Tattoos

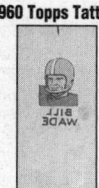

This set was thought to have been distributed in 1960 like the corresponding baseball issue. It appears they were issued as a separate set by both Topps and O-Pee-Chee in Canada. Each is actually the inside surface of the outer wrapper (measuring roughly 1 9/16" by 3 1/2") in which the collector would apply the tatoo by moistening the skin and then pressing the tattoo to the moistened spot. The tattoos are unnumbered and where produced in color. Any additions to the list below are appreciated.

Card	Low	High
1 Bill Anderson	125.00	250.00
2 Jim Brown	350.00	600.00
3 Rick Casares	125.00	250.00
4 Howard Cassady	125.00	250.00
5 Frank Gifford	200.00	350.00
6 Paul Hornung	250.00	400.00
7 Bobby Layne	200.00	350.00
8 Y.A. Tittle	200.00	350.00
9 Johnny Unitas	350.00	600.00
10 Bill Wade	125.00	250.00
11 Chicago Bears	50.00	100.00
12 Cleveland Browns	40.00	80.00
13 Dallas Cowboys	125.00	200.00
14 Detroit Lions	40.00	80.00
15 Green Bay Packers	125.00	200.00
16 New York Giants	40.00	80.00
17 Pittsburgh Steelers	60.00	120.00
18 St.Louis Cardinals	40.00	80.00
19 San Francisco 49ers	40.00	80.00
20 Washington Redskins	90.00	150.00
21 Air Force	30.00	60.00
22 Army	30.00	60.00
23 Baylor	30.00	60.00
24 Boston College	30.00	60.00
25 California	30.00	60.00
26 Duke	30.00	60.00
27 Illinois	30.00	60.00
28 Indiana	30.00	60.00
29 Iowa	30.00	60.00
30 Kentucky	40.00	80.00
31 Michigan	50.00	100.00
32 Michigan State	30.00	60.00
33 Minnesota	30.00	60.00
34 Mississippi	30.00	60.00
35 Navy	30.00	60.00
36 Nebraska	40.00	80.00
37 Northwestern	30.00	60.00
38 Notre Dame	75.00	150.00
39 Oklahoma	40.00	80.00
40 Oregon	30.00	60.00
41 Oregon State	30.00	60.00
42 Penn State	50.00	100.00
43 Pennsylvania	30.00	60.00
44 Pittsburgh	30.00	60.00
45 Princeton	30.00	60.00
46 Rice	30.00	60.00
47 Rutgers	30.00	60.00
48 SMU	30.00	60.00
49 South Carolina	30.00	60.00
50 Stanford	30.00	60.00
51 TCU	30.00	60.00
52 Tennessee	40.00	80.00
53 Texas	40.00	80.00
54 UCLA	40.00	80.00
55 USC	40.00	80.00
56 Washington State	30.00	60.00
57 Wisconsin	30.00	60.00
58 Wyoming	30.00	50.00
59 Generic	15.00	30.00
Actual Kicking of Football		
60 Generic	15.00	30.00
Catching a Pass		
61 Generic	15.00	30.00
Chasing a fumble		
62 Generic	15.00	30.00
Defender is grabbing shirt		
63 Generic	15.00	30.00
Defender trying to block kick		
64 Generic	15.00	30.00
Kicking Follow Through		
65 Generic	15.00	30.00
Lateral		
66 Generic	15.00	30.00
Passer ready to throw		
67 Generic	15.00	30.00
Player #8 is charging		
68 Generic	15.00	30.00
Player yelling at Referee		
69 Generic	15.00	30.00
Profile view of Passer		
70 Generic	15.00	30.00
Receiver and Defender		
71 Generic	15.00	30.00
Runner being tackled		
72 Generic	15.00	30.00
Runner is falling down		
73 Generic	15.00	30.00
Runner is Fumbling		
74 Generic	15.00	30.00
Runner using stiff arm		
75 Generic	15.00	30.00
Runner with football		
76 Generic	15.00	30.00
Taking a snap on one knee		

1961 Topps

The 1961 Topps football set of 198 standard-size cards contains NFL players (1-132) and AFL players (133-197). The fronts are very similar to the Topps 1961 baseball issue with the player's name, team and position at beneath posed player photos. The card backs are printed in light blue on white card stock. Statistical information from the immediate past season and career totals are given on the reverse. A "coin-rub" picture was featured on the right of the reverse. Cards are essentially numbered in team order by league. There are three checklist cards in the set, numbers 67, 122, and 198. The key Rookie Cards in this set are John Brodie, Tom Flores, Henry Jordan, Don Maynard, and Jim Otto. A 3-card advertising panel was issued as well.

Card	Low	High
COMPLETE SET (198)	650.00	1,000.00
WRAPPER (1-CENT)	250.00	400.00
WRAPPER (1-CENT, REP)	125.00	200.00
WRAPPER (5-CENT)	60.00	100.00
1 Johnny Unitas	50.00	100.00
2 Lenny Moore	6.00	12.00
3 Alan Ameche	2.00	4.00
4 Raymond Berry	6.00	12.00
5 Jim Mutscheller	1.25	2.50
6 Jim Parker	2.50	5.00
7 Gino Marchetti	3.00	6.00
8 Gene Lipscomb	2.00	4.00
9 Baltimore Colts	1.50	3.00
10 Bill Wade	1.50	3.00
11 Johnny Morris RC	3.00	6.00
12 Rick Casares	1.50	3.00
13 Harlon Hill	1.25	2.50
14 Stan Jones	2.00	4.00
15 Doug Atkins	2.50	5.00
16 Bill George	2.00	4.00
17 J.C. Caroline	1.25	2.50
18 Chicago Bears	1.50	3.00
19 Eddie LeBaron IA	1.50	3.00
20 Eddie LeBaron	1.50	3.00
21 Don McIlhenny	1.25	2.50
22 L.G. Dupre	1.50	3.00
23 Jim Doran	1.25	2.50
24 Billy Howton	1.50	3.00
25 Buzz Guy RC	1.25	2.50
26 Jack Patera RC	1.25	2.50
27 Tom Franckhauser RC	1.25	2.50
28 Cowboys Team	7.50	15.00
29 Jim Ninowski	1.25	2.50
30 Dan Lewis RC	1.25	2.50
31 Nick Pietrosante RC	1.50	3.00
32 Gail Cogdill RC	1.50	3.00
33 Jim Gibbons	1.25	2.50
34 Jim Martin	1.25	2.50
35 Alex Karras	7.50	15.00
36 Joe Schmidt	2.50	5.00
37 Detroit Lions	1.50	3.00
38 Paul Hornung IA	9.00	18.00
39 Bart Starr	25.00	40.00
40 Paul Hornung	25.00	40.00
41 Jim Taylor	20.00	35.00
42 Max McGee	2.00	4.00
43 Boyd Dowler RC	5.00	10.00
44 Jim Ringo	2.50	5.00
45 Hank Jordan RC	20.00	40.00
46 Bill Forester	1.50	3.00
47 Green Bay Packers	7.50	15.00
48 Frank Ryan	1.50	3.00
49 Jon Arnett	1.50	3.00
50 Ollie Matson	4.00	8.00
51 Jim Phillips	1.25	2.50
52 Del Shofner	1.50	3.00
53 Art Hunter	1.25	2.50
54 Gene Brito	1.25	2.50
55 Lindon Crow	1.25	2.50
56 Los Angeles Rams	1.50	3.00
57 Johnny Unitas IA	15.00	25.00
58 Y.A.Tittle	18.00	30.00
59 John Brodie RC	25.00	40.00
60 J.D. Smith	1.25	2.50
61 R.C. Owens	1.50	3.00
62 Clyde Conner	1.25	2.50
63 Bob St.Clair	2.00	4.00
64 Leo Nomellini	3.00	6.00
65 Abe Woodson	1.25	2.50
66 San Francisco 49ers	1.50	3.00
67 Checklist Card	25.00	40.00
68 Milt Plum	1.50	3.00
69 Ray Renfro	1.50	3.00
70 Bobby Mitchell	4.00	8.00
71 Jim Brown	75.00	125.00
72 Mike McCormack	2.00	4.00
73 Jim Ray Smith	1.25	2.50
74 Sam Baker	1.25	2.50
75 Walt Michaels	1.50	3.00
76 Cleveland Browns	1.50	3.00
77 Jim Brown IA	25.00	40.00
78 George Shaw	1.25	2.50
79 Hugh McElhenny	4.00	8.00
80 Clancy Osborne RC	1.25	2.50
81 Dave Middleton	1.25	2.50
82 Frank Youso RC	1.25	2.50
83 Don Joyce RC	1.25	2.50
84 Ed Culpepper RC	1.25	2.50
85 Charley Conerly	4.00	8.00
86 Mel Triplett	1.25	2.50
87 Kyle Rote	1.50	3.00
88 Roosevelt Brown	2.00	4.00
89 Ray Wietecha	1.25	2.50
90 Andy Robustelli	2.50	5.00
91 Sam Huff	4.00	8.00
92 Jim Patton	1.25	2.50
93 New York Giants	1.50	3.00
94 Charley Conerly IA	3.00	6.00
95 Sonny Jurgensen	15.00	25.00
96 Tommy McDonald	2.50	5.00
97 Bill Barnes	1.25	2.50
98 Bobby Walston	1.25	2.50
99 Pete Retzlaff	1.50	3.00
100 Jim McCusker RC	1.25	2.50
101 Chuck Bednarik	4.00	8.00
102 Tom Brookshier	1.50	3.00
103 Philadelphia Eagles	1.50	3.00
104 Bobby Layne	18.00	30.00
105 John Henry Johnson	2.00	4.00
106 Tom Tracy	1.50	3.00
107 Buddy Dial RC	1.25	2.50
108 Jimmy Orr RC	3.00	6.00
109 Mike Sandusky	1.25	2.50
110 John Reger	1.25	2.50
111 Junior Wren	1.25	2.50
112 Pittsburgh Steelers	1.50	3.00
113 Bobby Layne IA	5.00	10.00
114 John Roach RC	1.25	2.50
115 Sam Etcheverry RC	1.50	3.00
116 John David Crow	1.50	3.00
117 Mal Hammack	1.25	2.50
118 Sonny Randle RC	1.50	3.00
119 Leo Sugar	1.25	2.50
120 Jerry Norton	1.25	2.50
121 St. Louis Cardinals	1.50	3.00
122 Checklist Card	30.00	50.00
123 Ralph Guglielmi	1.25	2.50
124 Dick James	1.25	2.50
125 Don Bosseler	1.25	2.50
126 Joe Walton	1.25	2.50
127 Bill Anderson	1.25	2.50

128 Vince Promuto RC	1.25	2.50
129 Bob Toneff	1.25	2.50
130 John Paluck RC	1.25	2.50
131 Washington Redskins	1.50	3.00
132 Milt Plum IA !	1.25	2.50
133 Abner Haynes !	4.00	8.00
134 Mel Branch UER	2.00	4.00
135 Jerry Cornelison UER	1.50	3.00
136 Bill Krisher	1.50	3.00
137 Paul Miller	1.50	3.00
138 Jack Spikes	2.00	4.00
139 Johnny Robinson RC	4.00	8.00
140 Cotton Davidson RC	2.00	4.00
141 Dave Smith RB	1.50	3.00
142 Bill Groman	1.50	3.00
143 Rich Michael RC	1.50	3.00
144 Mike Dukes RC	1.50	3.00
145 George Blanda	15.00	25.00
146 Billy Cannon	3.00	6.00
147 Dennit Morris RC	1.50	3.00
148 Jacky Lee UER	2.00	4.00
149 Al Dorow	1.50	3.00
150 Don Maynard RC	25.00	50.00
151 Art Powell RC	4.00	8.00
152 Sid Youngelman	1.50	3.00
153 Bob Mischak RC	1.50	3.00
154 Larry Grantham	1.50	3.00
155 Tom Saidock	1.50	3.00
156 Roger Donnahoo RC	1.50	3.00
157 Laverne Torczon RC	1.50	3.00
158 Archie Matsos RC	2.00	4.00
159 Elbert Dubenion	2.00	4.00
160 Wray Carlton RC	2.00	4.00
161 Rich McCabe RC	1.50	3.00
162 Ken Rice RC	1.50	3.00
163 Art Baker RC	1.50	3.00
164 Tom Rychlec	1.50	3.00
165 Mack Yoho	1.50	3.00
166 Jack Kemp	35.00	60.00
167 Paul Lowe	3.00	6.00
168 Ron Mix	5.00	10.00
169 Paul Maguire UER	3.00	6.00
170 Volney Peters	1.50	3.00
171 Ernie Wright RC	2.00	4.00
172 Ron Nery RC	1.50	3.00
173 Dave Kocourek RC	2.00	4.00
174 Jim Colclough RC	1.50	3.00
175 Babe Parilli	2.00	4.00
176 Billy Lott	1.50	3.00
177 Fred Bruney	1.50	3.00
178 Ross O'Hanley RC	1.50	3.00
179 Walt Cudzik RC	1.50	3.00
180 Charley Leo	1.50	3.00
181 Bob Dee	1.50	3.00
182 Jim Otto RC	25.00	40.00
183 Eddie Macon RC	1.50	3.00
184 Dick Christy RC	1.50	3.00
185 Alan Miller RC	1.50	3.00
186 Tom Flores RC	10.00	20.00
187 Joe Cannavino RC	1.50	3.00
188 Don Manoukian	1.50	3.00
189 Bob Coolbaugh RC	1.50	3.00
190 Lionel Taylor RC	4.00	8.00
191 Bud McFadin	1.50	3.00
192 Goose Gonsoulin RC	3.00	6.00
193 Frank Tripucka	2.00	4.00
194 Gene Mingo RC	2.00	4.00
195 Eldon Danenhauer RC	1.50	3.00
196 Bob McNamara	1.50	3.00
197 Dave Rolle UER RC	1.50	3.00
198 Checklist UER	40.00	80.00
AD1 Advertising Panel	150.00	250.00
Jim Martin		
George Shaw		
Jim Ray Smith		
AD2 Advertising Panel	175.00	300.00
Alex Karras		
Charley Conerly IA		
Jon Arnett		

1961 Topps Flocked Stickers Inserts

This set of 48 flocked stickers was inserted with the 1961 Topps regular issue football set. The stickers are unnumbered and are ordered below alphabetically within type. NFL teams are listed first (1-15), followed by AFL teams (16-24), and college teams (25-48). The capital letters in the listing below signify the letter on the detachable tab. The stickers measure approximately 2" by 2 3/4" without the letter tab and 2" by 3 3/8" with the letter tab. The prices below are for the stickers with tabs intact; stickers without tabs would be considered VG-E at best. There are letter tab variations on 12 of the stickers as noted by the double letters below. The complete set price below considers the set complete with the 48 different distinct teams, i.e., not including all 60 different tab combinations.

COMPLETE SET (48)	500.00	800.00
1 NFL Emblem N	10.00	20.00
2 Baltimore Colts U	10.00	20.00
3 Chicago Bears H	10.00	20.00
4 Cleveland Browns I	10.00	20.00
5 Dallas Cowboys K	25.00	40.00
6 Detroit Lions E	10.00	20.00
7 Green Bay Packers A	25.00	40.00
8 Los Angeles Rams M	10.00	20.00
9 Minnesota Vikings R	10.00	20.00
10 New York Giants D	10.00	20.00
11 Philadelphia Eagles O	10.00	20.00
12 Pittsburgh Steelers S	12.50	25.00
13 San Francisco 49ers P	10.00	20.00
14 St. Louis Cardinals L	10.00	20.00
15 Washington Redskins J	12.50	25.00
16 AFL Emblem A/G	10.00	20.00
17 Boston Patriots F/T	10.00	20.00
18 Buffalo Bills I/M	10.00	20.00
19 Dallas Texans P/R	12.50	25.00
20 Denver Broncos G/I	12.50	25.00
21 Houston Oilers A/H	10.00	20.00
22 Oakland Raiders B/O	18.00	30.00
23 San Diego Chargers E/K	10.00	20.00
24 New York Titans D/E	10.00	20.00
25 Air Force Falcons V	7.50	15.00
26 Alabama Crimson Tide L	10.00	20.00
27 Arkansas Razorbacks A	7.50	15.00
28 Army Cadets G	7.50	15.00
29 Baylor Bears E	7.50	15.00
30 California Golden Bears T	7.50	15.00
31 Georgia Tech F	7.50	15.00
32 Illinois Fighting Illini C	7.50	15.00
33 Kansas Jayhawks J	7.50	15.00
34 Kentucky Wildcats R	7.50	15.00
35 Miami Hurricanes H	7.50	15.00
36 Michigan Wolverines W	15.00	25.00
37 Missouri Tigers B	7.50	15.00
38 Navy Midshipmen J/S	7.50	15.00
39 Oregon Ducks C/N	7.50	15.00
40 Penn State Nittany Lions Z	10.00	20.00
41 Pittsburgh Panthers G	7.50	15.00
42 Purdue Boilermakers B	7.50	15.00
43 USC Trojans Y	7.50	15.00
44 Stanford Indians L/O	7.50	15.00
45 TCU Horned Frogs C	7.50	15.00
46 Virginia Cavaliers S	7.50	15.00
47 Washington Huskies D	7.50	15.00
48 Washington St.Cougers M UER	7.50	15.00

1962 Topps

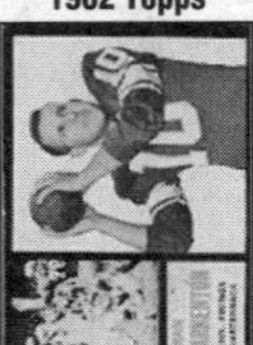

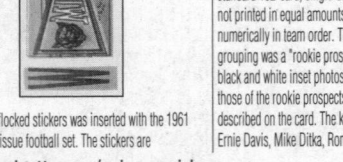

The 1962 Topps football set contains 176 black-bordered standard-size cards. In designing the 1962 set, Topps chose a horizontally oriented card front for the first time since 1957. Two photos include a small action photo to the left that is joined by the player's name, team name and position. An up-close photo to the right covers majority of the card. Black borders, which are prone to chipping, make it quite difficult to put together a set in top grades. The short-printed (SP) cards are indicated in the checklist below. The shortage is probably attributable to the fact that the set size is not the standard 132-card, single-sheet size; hence all cards were not printed in equal amounts. Cards are again organized numerically in team order. The last card within each team grouping was a "rookie prospect" for that team. Many of the black and white inset photos on the card fronts (especially those of the rookie prospects) are not the player pictured and described on the card. The key Rookie Cards in this set are Ernie Davis, Mike Ditka, Roman Gabriel, Bill Kilmer, Norm Snead and Fran Tarkenton.

COMPLETE SET (176)	1,200.00	2,000.00
WRAPPER (1-CENT)	175.00	250.00
WRAPPER (5-CENT,STARS)	25.00	50.00
WRAPPER (5-CENT,BUCKS)	25.00	40.00
1 Johnny Unitas	125.00	200.00
2 Lenny Moore	6.00	12.00
3 Alex Hawkins SP RC	5.00	10.00
4 Joe Perry	4.00	8.00
5 Raymond Berry SP	25.00	40.00
6 Steve Myhra	2.00	4.00
7 Tom Gilburg SP RC	4.00	8.00
8 Gino Marchetti	4.00	8.00
9 Bill Pellington	2.00	4.00
10 Andy Nelson	2.00	4.00
11 Wendell Harris SP RC	4.00	8.00
12 Baltimore Colts Team	3.00	6.00
13 Bill Wade SP	5.00	10.00
14 Willie Galimore	2.50	5.00
15 Johnny Morris SP	4.00	8.00
16 Rick Casares	2.50	5.00
17 Mike Ditka RC	175.00	300.00
18 Stan Jones	3.00	6.00
19 Roger LeClerc RC	2.00	4.00
20 Angelo Coia RC	2.00	4.00
21 Doug Atkins	4.00	8.00
22 Bill George	3.00	6.00
23 Richie Petitbon RC	2.50	5.00
24 Ronnie Bull SP RC	4.00	8.00
25 Chicago Bears Team	3.00	6.00
26 Howard Cassady	2.50	5.00
27 Ray Renfro SP	5.00	10.00
28 Jim Brown	100.00	175.00
29 Rich Kreitling RC	2.00	4.00
30 Jim Ray Smith	2.00	4.00
31 John Morrow	2.00	4.00
32 Lou Groza	7.50	15.00
33 Bob Gain	2.00	4.00
34 Bernie Parrish RC	2.00	4.00
35 Jim Shofner	2.00	4.00
36 Ernie Davis SP RC	90.00	150.00
37 Cleveland Browns Team	3.00	6.00
38 Eddie LeBaron	2.50	5.00
39 Don Meredith SP	60.00	100.00
40 J.W. Lockett SP RC	4.00	8.00
41 Don Perkins RC	7.50	15.00
42 Billy Howton	2.50	5.00
43 Dick Bielski	2.00	4.00
44 Mike Connelly RC	2.00	4.00
45 Jerry Tubbs SP	4.00	8.00
46 Don Bishop SP RC	4.00	8.00
47 Dick Moegle	2.00	4.00
48 Bobby Plummer SP RC	4.00	8.00
49 Dallas Cowboys Team	12.00	20.00
50 Milt Plum	2.50	5.00
51 Dan Lewis	2.00	4.00
52 Nick Pietrosante SP	4.00	8.00
53 Gail Cogdill	2.00	4.00
54 Jim Gibbons	2.00	4.00
55 Jim Martin	2.00	4.00
56 Yale Lary	3.00	6.00
57 Darris McCord	2.00	4.00
58 Alex Karras	15.00	25.00
59 Joe Schmidt	4.00	8.00
60 Dick Lane	3.00	6.00
61 John Lomakoski SP RC	4.00	8.00
62 Detroit Lions Team SP	10.00	18.00
63 Bart Starr SP	75.00	125.00
64 Paul Hornung SP	60.00	100.00
65 Tom Moore SP	6.00	12.00
66 Jim Taylor SP	30.00	50.00
67 Max McGee SP	6.00	15.00
68 Jim Ringo SP	7.50	15.00
69 Fuzzy Thurston SP RC	18.00	30.00
70 Forrest Gregg	4.00	8.00
71 Boyd Dowler	3.00	6.00
72 Hank Jordan SP	7.50	15.00
73 Bill Forester SP	5.00	10.00
74 Earl Gros SP RC	4.00	8.00
75 Green Bay Packers Team SP	25.00	40.00
76 Checklist SP	50.00	80.00
77 Zeke Bratkowski SP	5.00	10.00
78 Jon Arnett SP	5.00	10.00
79 Ollie Matson SP	20.00	35.00
80 Dick Bass SP	5.00	10.00
81 Jim Phillips	2.00	4.00
82 Carroll Dale RC	2.50	5.00
83 Frank Varrichione	2.00	4.00
84 Art Hunter	2.00	4.00
85 Danny Villanueva RC	2.00	4.00
86 Les Richter SP	4.00	8.00
87 Lindon Crow	2.00	4.00
88 Roman Gabriel SP RC	35.00	60.00
89 Los Angeles Rams Team SP	10.00	18.00
90 Fran Tarkenton SP RC	125.00	225.00
91 Jerry Reichow SP RC	4.00	8.00
92 Hugh McElhenny SP	18.00	30.00
93 Mel Triplett SP	4.00	8.00
94 Tommy Mason SP RC	6.00	12.00
95 Dave Middleton SP	4.00	8.00
96 Frank Youso SP	4.00	8.00
97 Mike Mercer SP RC	4.00	8.00
98 Rip Hawkins SP	4.00	8.00
99 Cliff Livingston SP RC	4.00	8.00
100 Roy Winston SP RC	4.00	8.00
101 Minnesota Vikings Team SP	15.00	25.00
102 Y.A.Tittle	25.00	40.00
103 Joe Walton	2.00	4.00
104 Frank Gifford	30.00	50.00
105 Alex Webster	2.50	5.00
106 Del Shofner	2.50	5.00
107 Don Chandler	2.00	4.00
108 Andy Robustelli	4.00	8.00
109 Jim Katcavage RC	2.50	5.00
110 Sam Huff SP	25.00	40.00
111 Erich Barnes	2.00	4.00
112 Jim Patton	2.00	4.00
113 Jerry Hillebrand SP RC	4.00	8.00
114 New York Giants Team	3.00	6.00
115 Sonny Jurgensen	25.00	40.00
116 Tommy McDonald	4.00	8.00
117 Ted Dean SP	4.00	8.00
118 Clarence Peaks	2.00	4.00
119 Bobby Walston	2.00	4.00
120 Pete Retzlaff SP	5.00	10.00
121 Jim Schrader SP	4.00	8.00
122 J.D. Smith T RC	2.00	4.00
123 King Hill	2.00	4.00
124 Maxie Baughan	2.50	5.00
125 Pete Case SP RC	4.00	8.00
126 Philadelphia Eagles Team	3.00	6.00
127 Bobby Layne UER	25.00	40.00
128 Tom Tracy	2.50	5.00
129 John Henry Johnson	3.00	6.00
130 Buddy Dial SP	5.00	10.00
131 Preston Carpenter	2.00	4.00
132 Lou Michaels SP	4.00	8.00
133 Gene Lipscomb SP	5.00	10.00
134 Ernie Stautner SP	12.00	20.00
135 John Reger SP	4.00	8.00
136 Myron Pottios RC	2.00	4.00
137 Bob Ferguson SP RC	4.00	8.00
138 Pittsburgh Steelers Team SP	10.00	18.00
139 Sam Etcheverry	2.50	5.00
140 John David Crow SP	5.00	10.00
141 Bobby Joe Conrad SP	5.00	10.00
142 Prentice Gautt SP RC	4.00	8.00
143 Frank Mestnik	2.00	4.00
144 Sonny Randle	2.50	5.00
145 Gerry Perry UER RC	2.00	4.00
146 Jerry Norton	2.00	4.00
147 Jimmy Hill RC	2.00	4.00
148 Bill Stacy	2.00	4.00
149 Fate Echols SP RC	4.00	8.00
150 St. Louis Cardinals Team	3.00	6.00
151 Billy Kilmer RC	25.00	40.00
152 John Brodie	10.00	18.00
153 J.D. Smith RB	2.50	5.00
154 C.R. Roberts SP RC	4.00	8.00
155 Monty Stickles	2.00	4.00
156 Clyde Conner UER	2.00	4.00
157 Bob St.Clair	3.00	6.00
158 Tommy Davis RC	2.00	4.00
159 Leo Nomellini	4.00	8.00
160 Matt Hazeltine	2.00	4.00
161 Abe Woodson	2.00	4.00
162 Dave Baker	2.00	4.00
163 San Francisco 49ers Team	3.00	6.00
164 Norm Snead SP RC	18.00	30.00
165 Dick James	2.50	5.00
166 Bobby Mitchell	4.00	8.00
167 Sam Horner RC	2.00	4.00
168 Bill Barnes	2.00	4.00
169 Bill Anderson	2.00	4.00
170 Fred Dugan	2.00	4.00
171 John Aveni SP RC	4.00	8.00
172 Bob Toneff	2.00	4.00
173 Jim Kerr RC	2.00	4.00
174 Leroy Jackson SP RC	4.00	8.00
175 Washington Redskins Team	5.00	10.00
176 Checklist	60.00	100.00

1962 Topps Bucks Inserts

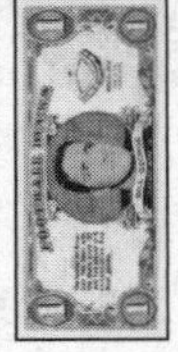

The 1962 Topps Football Bucks set contains 48 cards and was issued as an insert into wax packs of the 1962 Topps regular issue of football cards. Printing was done with black and green ink on off-white (very thin) paper stock. Bucks are typically found with a fold crease in the middle as they were inserted in packs in that manner. These "football bucks" measure approximately 1 1/4" by 4 1/4". Mike Ditka and Fran Tarkenton appear in their Rookie Card year.

COMPLETE SET (48)	350.00	450.00
1 J.D. Smith	2.00	4.00
2 Bart Starr	15.00	30.00
3 Dick James	2.00	4.00
4 Alex Webster	2.50	5.00
5 Paul Hornung	10.00	20.00
6 John David Crow	2.50	5.00
7 Jim Brown	30.00	50.00
8 Don Perkins	2.50	5.00
9 Bobby Walston	2.00	4.00
10 Jim Phillips	2.00	4.00
11 Y.A. Tittle	7.50	15.00
12 Sonny Randle	2.00	4.00
13 Jerry Reichow	2.00	4.00
14 Yale Lary	3.00	6.00
15 Buddy Dial	2.50	5.00
16 Ray Renfro	2.50	5.00
17 Norm Snead	3.00	6.00
18 Leo Nomellini	3.00	6.00
19 Hugh McElhenny	5.00	10.00
20 Eddie LeBaron	2.50	5.00
21 Billy Howton	2.50	5.00
22 Bobby Mitchell	4.00	8.00
23 Nick Pietrosante	2.00	4.00
24 Johnny Unitas	20.00	40.00
25 Raymond Berry	5.00	10.00
26 Billy Kilmer	4.00	8.00
27 Lenny Moore	5.00	10.00
28 Tommy McDonald	3.00	6.00
29 Del Shofner	2.50	5.00
30 Jim Taylor	7.50	15.00
31 Joe Schmidt	4.00	8.00
32 Bill George	3.00	6.00
33 Fran Tarkenton	30.00	50.00
34 Willie Galimore	2.50	5.00
35 Bobby Layne	7.50	15.00
36 Max McGee	2.50	5.00
37 Jon Arnett	2.50	5.00
38 Lou Groza	6.00	12.00
39 Frank Varrichione	2.00	4.00
40 Milt Plum	2.50	5.00
41 Prentice Gautt	2.00	4.00
42 Bill Wade	2.50	5.00
43 Gino Marchetti	4.00	8.00
44 John Brodie	5.00	10.00
45 Sonny Jurgensen UER	7.50	15.00
46 Clarence Peaks	2.50	5.00
47 Mike Ditka	15.00	30.00
48 John Henry Johnson	4.00	8.00

1963 Topps

The 1963 Topps set contains 170 standard-size cards of NFL players grouped together by teams. The card backs are printed in light orange ink on white card stock. Statistical information from the immediate past season and career totals are given on the reverse. The illustrated trivia question on the reverse (of each card) could be answered by placing red cellophane paper (which was inserted into wax packs) over the card. The 76 cards indicated by SP below are in shorter supply than the others because the set size is not the standard 132-card, single-sheet size; hence, all cards were not printed in equal amounts. There also exists a three-card advertising panel consisting of card fronts of Charlie Johnson, John David Crow and Bobby Joe Conrad. The back of the latter two players contains ad copy and a Y.A. Tittle card back on Johnson. Interestingly, Y.A. Tittle was also used as the player featured on the full box of packs. Finally, many of the cards in the set were printed with color variations in the background of the player photo, thus resulting in one version of the photo that appears to have a purple tinted background while the other is a color corrected blue background. This is most evident on cards with a large portion of sky in the background of the photo. Most collectors feel that the "purple" sky version was generally printed in shorter supply, but the market has not yet clearly indicated any price differences thus far.

COMPLETE SET (170)	850.00	1,350.00
WRAPPER (1-CENT)	1,000.00	1,500.00
WRAPPER (5-CENT)	50.00	80.00
1 Johnny Unitas	75.00	135.00
2 Lenny Moore	4.00	8.00
3 Jimmy Orr	1.50	3.00
4 Raymond Berry	4.00	8.00
5 Jim Parker	2.50	5.00
6 Alex Sandusky	1.25	2.50
7 Dick Szymanski RC	1.25	2.50
8 Gino Marchetti	3.00	6.00
9 Billy Ray Smith RC	1.50	3.00
10 Bill Pellington	1.25	2.50
11 Bob Boyd DB RC	1.25	2.50
12 Baltimore Colts SP	5.00	10.00
13 Frank Ryan SP	4.00	8.00
14 Jim Brown SP	100.00	200.00
15 Ray Renfro SP	4.00	8.00
16 Rich Kreitling SP	3.50	6.00
17 Mike McCormack SP	5.00	10.00
18 Jim Ray Smith SP	3.50	6.00
19 Lou Groza SP	15.00	25.00
20 Bill Glass SP	3.50	6.00
21 Galen Fiss SP	3.50	6.00
22 Don Fleming SP RC	4.00	8.00
23 Bob Gain SP	3.50	6.00
24 Cleveland Browns SP	5.00	10.00
25 Milt Plum	1.50	3.00
26 Dan Lewis	1.25	2.50
27 Nick Pietrosante	1.25	2.50
28 Gail Cogdill	1.25	2.50
29 Harley Sewell	1.25	2.50
30 Jim Gibbons	1.25	2.50
31 Carl Brettschneider	1.25	2.50
32 Dick Lane	2.50	5.00
33 Yale Lary	2.50	5.00
34 Roger Brown RC	1.50	3.00
35 Joe Schmidt	3.00	6.00
36 Detroit Lions SP	5.00	10.00
37 Roman Gabriel	4.00	8.00
38 Zeke Bratkowski	1.50	3.00
39 Dick Bass	1.50	3.00
40 Jon Arnett	1.50	3.00
41 Jim Phillips	1.25	2.50
42 Frank Varrichione	1.25	2.50
43 Danny Villanueva	1.25	2.50
44 Deacon Jones RC	35.00	60.00
45 Lindon Crow	1.25	2.50
46 Marlin McKeever RC	1.25	2.50
47 Ed Meador RC	1.25	2.50
48 Los Angeles Rams	2.00	4.00
49 Y.A.Tittle SP	30.00	50.00
50 Del Shofner SP	3.50	6.00
51 Alex Webster SP	4.00	8.00
52 Phil King SP RC	3.50	6.00
53 Jack Stroud SP	3.50	6.00
54 Darrell Dess SP	3.50	6.00
55 Jim Katcavage SP	3.50	6.00
56 Roosevelt Grier SP	5.00	10.00
57 Erich Barnes SP	3.50	6.00
58 Jim Patton SP	3.50	6.00
59 Sam Huff SP	12.00	20.00
60 New York Giants	2.00	4.00
61 Bill Wade	1.50	3.00
62 Mike Ditka	35.00	60.00
63 Johnny Morris	1.25	2.50
64 Roger LeClerc	1.25	2.50
65 Roger Davis RC	1.25	2.50
66 Joe Marconi	1.25	2.50
67 Herman Lee RC	1.25	2.50
68 Doug Atkins	3.00	6.00
69 Joe Fortunato	1.25	2.50
70 Bill George	2.50	5.00
71 Richie Petitbon	1.50	3.00
72 Bears Team SP	5.00	10.00
73 Eddie LeBaron SP	5.00	10.00
74 Don Meredith SP	35.00	60.00
75 Don Perkins SP	5.00	10.00
76 Amos Marsh SP RC	3.50	6.00
77 Billy Howton SP	4.00	8.00
78 Andy Cvercko SP RC	3.50	6.00
79 Sam Baker SP	3.50	6.00
80 Jerry Tubbs SP	3.50	6.00
81 Don Bishop SP	3.50	6.00
82 Bob Lilly SP RC	100.00	175.00
83 Jerry Norton SP	3.50	6.00
84 Cowboys Team SP	12.00	20.00
85 Checklist 1	15.00	25.00
86 Bart Starr	40.00	75.00
87 Jim Taylor	18.00	30.00
88 Boyd Dowler	2.50	5.00
89 Forrest Gregg	3.00	6.00
90 Fuzzy Thurston	3.00	6.00
91 Jim Ringo	3.00	6.00
92 Ron Kramer	1.50	3.00
93 Hank Jordan	3.00	6.00
94 Bill Forester	1.50	3.00
95 Willie Wood RC	25.00	40.00
96 Ray Nitschke RC	90.00	150.00
97 Green Bay Packers	7.50	15.00
98 Fran Tarkenton	35.00	60.00
99 Tommy Mason	1.50	3.00
100 Mel Triplett	1.25	2.50
101 Jerry Reichow	1.25	2.50
102 Frank Youso	1.25	2.50
103 Hugh McElhenny	4.00	8.00
104 Gerald Huth RC	1.25	2.50
105 Ed Sharockman RC	1.25	2.50
106 Rip Hawkins	1.25	2.50
107 Jim Marshall RC	20.00	40.00
108 Jim Prestel RC	1.25	2.50
109 Minnesota Vikings	2.00	4.00
110 Sonny Jurgensen SP	15.00	25.00
111 Timmy Brown SP RC	5.00	10.00
112 Tommy McDonald SP	7.50	15.00
113 Clarence Peaks SP	3.50	6.00
114 Pete Retzlaff SP	4.00	8.00
115 Jim Schrader SP	3.50	6.00
116 Jim McCusker SP	3.50	6.00
117 Don Burroughs SP	3.50	6.00
118 Maxie Baughan SP	3.50	6.00
119 Riley Gunnels SP RC	3.50	6.00
120 Jimmy Carr SP	3.50	6.00
121 Philadelphia Eagles SP	5.00	10.00
122 Ed Brown SP	4.00	8.00
123 John H.Johnson SP	7.50	15.00
124 Buddy Dial SP	3.50	6.00
125 Bill Red Mack SP RC	3.50	6.00
126 Preston Carpenter SP	3.50	6.00
127 Ray Lemek SP RC	3.50	6.00
128 Buzz Nutter SP	3.50	6.00
129 Ernie Stautner SP	7.50	15.00
130 Lou Michaels SP	3.50	6.00
131 Clendon Thomas SP RC	3.50	6.00
132 Tom Bettis SP	3.50	6.00
133 Pittsburgh Steelers SP	5.00	10.00
134 John Brodie	4.00	8.00
135 J.D. Smith	1.25	2.50
136 Billy Kilmer	2.50	5.00
137 Bernie Casey RC	1.50	3.00
138 Tommy Davis	1.25	2.50
139 Ted Connolly RC	1.25	2.50
140 Bob St.Clair	2.50	5.00
141 Abe Woodson	1.25	2.50
142 Matt Hazeltine	1.25	2.50
143 Leo Nomellini	3.00	6.00
144 Dan Colchico RC	1.25	2.50
145 San Francisco 49ers SP	5.00	10.00
146 Charley Johnson RC	4.00	8.00
147 John David Crow	3.50	6.00
148 Bobby Joe Conrad	1.50	3.00
149 Sonny Randle	1.25	2.50
150 Prentice Gautt	1.25	2.50
151 Taz Anderson RC	1.25	2.50
152 Ernie McMillan RC	1.50	3.00
153 Jimmy Hill	1.25	2.50
154 Bill Koman RC	1.25	2.50
155 Larry Wilson RC	12.00	20.00
156 Don Owens	1.25	2.50
157 St. Louis Cardinals SP	5.00	10.00
158 Norm Snead SP	5.00	10.00
159 Bobby Mitchell SP	7.50	15.00
160 Bill Barnes SP	3.50	6.00
161 Fred Dugan SP	3.50	6.00
162 Don Bosseler SP	3.50	6.00
163 John Nisby SP	3.50	6.00
164 Riley Mattson SP RC	3.50	6.00
165 Bob Toneff SP	3.50	6.00
166 Rod Breedlove SP RC	3.50	6.00
167 Dick James SP	3.50	6.00
168 Claude Crabb SP RC	3.50	6.00
169 Washington Redskins SP	5.00	10.00
170 Checklist 2 UER	30.00	50.00
AD1 C.Johnson/Crow/Conrad AD	600.00	1,000.00

1964 Topps

The 1964 Topps football set begins a run of four straight years that Topps issued cards of American Football League (AFL) player cards. The cards in this 176-card set measure the standard size and are grouped by teams. Because the cards were not printed on a standard 132-card sheet, some cards are printed in lesser quantities than others. These cards are marked in the checklist with SP for short print. Cards fronts feature white boders with tiny red stars outlining the photo. The player's name, team and position are in a black box beneath the photo. The backs of the cards contain the card number, vital statistics, a short biography, the player's record for the past year and his career, and a cartoon-illustrated question and answer section. The cards are organized alphabetically within teams. The key Rookie Cards in this set are Bobby Bell, Buck Buchanan, John Hadl, and Daryle Lamonica.

COMPLETE SET (176)	1,000.00	1,500.00
WRAPPER (1-CENT)	60.00	100.00
WRAPPER (5-CENT, PENN)	75.00	125.00
WRAP. (5-CENT, 8-CARD)	90.00	150.00
1 Tommy Addison SP	15.00	40.00
2 Houston Antwine RC	2.00	4.00
3 Nick Buoniconti	15.00	25.00
4 Ron Burton SP	5.00	10.00
5 Gino Cappelletti	2.50	5.00
6 Jim Colclough SP	3.00	6.00
7 Bob Dee SP	3.00	6.00
8 Larry Eisenhauer	2.00	4.00
9 Dick Felt SP	3.00	6.00
10 Larry Garron	2.00	4.00
11 Art Graham RC	2.00	4.00
12 Ron Hall DB RC	2.00	4.00
13 Charles Long	2.00	4.00
14 Don McKinnon RC	2.00	4.00
15 Don Oakes SP RC	3.00	6.00
16 Ross O'Hanley SP	3.00	6.00
17 Babe Parilli SP	5.00	10.00
18 Jesse Richardson SP	3.00	6.00
19 Jack Rudolph SP RC	3.00	6.00
20 Don Webb RC	2.00	4.00
21 Boston Patriots	3.00	6.00
22 Ray Abruzzese UER	2.00	4.00
23 Stew Barber RC	2.00	4.00
24 Dave Behrman RC	2.00	4.00
25 Al Bemiller RC	2.00	4.00
26 Elbert Dubenion SP	5.00	10.00
27 Jim Dunaway SP RC	3.00	6.00
28 Booker Edgerson SP	3.00	6.00
29 Cookie Gilchrist SP	15.00	25.00
30 Jack Kemp SP	50.00	100.00
31 Daryle Lamonica RC	35.00	60.00
32 Bill Miller	2.00	4.00
33 Herb Paterra RC	2.00	4.00
34 Ken Rice SP	3.00	6.00
35 Ed Rutkowski UER RC	2.00	4.00
36 George Saimes RC	2.00	4.00
37 Tom Sestak	2.00	4.00
38 Billy Shaw SP	7.50	15.00
39 Mike Stratton	2.50	5.00
40 Gene Sykes RC	2.00	4.00
41 John Tracey SP RC	3.00	6.00
42 Sid Youngelman SP	3.00	6.00
43 Buffalo Bills	3.00	6.00
44 Eldon Danenhauer SP	3.00	6.00
45 Jim Fraser SP	3.00	6.00
46 Chuck Gavin SP	3.00	6.00
47 Goose Gonsoulin SP	5.00	10.00
48 Ernie Barnes SP RC	2.00	4.00
49 Tom Janik RC	2.00	4.00
50 Billy Joe RC	2.50	5.00
51 Ike Lassiter RC	2.00	4.00
52 John McCormick SP RC	3.00	6.00
53 Bud McFadin SP	3.00	6.00
54 Gene Mingo SP	3.00	6.00
55 Charlie Mitchell RC	2.00	4.00
56 John Nocera SP RC	3.00	6.00
57 Tom Nomina RC	2.00	4.00
58 Harold Olson SP RC	3.00	6.00
59 Bob Scarpitto	2.00	4.00
60 John Sklopan RC	2.00	4.00
61 Mickey Slaughter RC	2.00	4.00
62 Don Stone	2.00	4.00
63 Jerry Sturm RC	2.00	4.00
64 Lionel Taylor SP	6.00	12.00
65 Broncos Team SP	10.00	20.00
66 Scott Appleton RC	2.00	4.00
67 Tony Banfield SP	3.00	6.00
68 George Blanda SP	40.00	80.00
69 Billy Cannon	3.00	6.00
70 Doug Cline SP	3.00	6.00
71 Gary Cutsinger SP RC	3.00	6.00
72 Willard Dewveall SP RC	3.00	6.00
73 Don Floyd SP	3.00	6.00
74 Freddy Glick SP RC	3.00	6.00
75 Charlie Hennigan SP	5.00	10.00
76 Ed Husmann SP	3.00	6.00
77 Bobby Jancik SP RC	3.00	6.00
78 Jacky Lee SP	5.00	10.00
79 Bob McLeod SP RC	3.00	6.00
80 Rich Michael SP	3.00	6.00
81 Larry Onesti RC	2.00	4.00
82 Checklist Card UER	30.00	60.00
83 Bob Schmidt SP RC	3.00	6.00
84 Walt Suggs SP RC	3.00	6.00
85 Bob Talamini SP	3.00	6.00
86 Charley Tolar SP	3.00	6.00
87 Don Trull RC	2.00	4.00
88 Houston Oilers	3.00	6.00
89 Fred Arbanas	2.00	4.00
90 Bobby Bell RC	25.00	40.00
91 Mel Branch SP	5.00	10.00
92 Buck Buchanan RC	25.00	40.00
93 Ed Budde RC	2.00	4.00
94 Chris Burford SP	5.00	10.00
95 Walt Corey RC	2.50	5.00
96 Len Dawson SP	40.00	75.00
97 Dave Grayson RC	2.00	4.00
98 Abner Haynes	3.00	6.00
99 Sherrill Headrick SP	5.00	10.00
100 E.J. Holub	2.00	4.00
101 Bobby Hunt RC	2.00	4.00
102 Frank Jackson SP	3.00	6.00
103 Curtis McClinton	2.50	5.00
104 Jerry Mays SP	5.00	10.00
105 Johnny Robinson SP	6.00	12.00
106 Jack Spikes SP	3.00	6.00
107 Smokey Stover SP RC	3.00	6.00
108 Jim Tyrer RC	5.00	10.00
109 Duane Wood SP RC	3.00	6.00
110 Kansas City Chiefs	3.00	6.00
111 Dick Christy SP	3.00	6.00
112 Dan Ficca SP RC	3.00	6.00
113 Larry Grantham	2.00	4.00
114 Curley Johnson SP	3.00	6.00
115 Gene Heeter RC	2.00	4.00
116 Jack Klotz RC	2.00	4.00
117 Pete Liske RC	2.50	5.00
118 Bob McAdam RC	2.00	4.00
119 Dee Mackey SP RC	3.00	6.00
120 Bill Mathis SP	5.00	10.00
121 Don Maynard	20.00	35.00
122 Dainard Paulson SP	3.00	6.00
123 Gerry Philbin RC	2.50	5.00
124 Mark Smolinski SP RC	3.00	6.00
125 Matt Snell RC	10.00	20.00
126 Mike Taliaferro RC	2.00	4.00
127 Bake Turner SP RC	5.00	10.00
128 Jeff Ware RC	2.00	4.00
129 Clyde Washington RC	2.00	4.00
130 Dick Wood RC	2.00	4.00
131 New York Jets	3.00	6.00
132 Dalva Allen SP	3.00	6.00
133 Dan Birdwell RC	2.00	4.00
134 Dave Costa RC	2.00	4.00
135 Dobie Craig RC	2.00	4.00
136 Clem Daniels	2.50	5.00
137 Cotton Davidson SP	5.00	10.00
138 Claude Gibson RC	2.00	4.00
139 Tom Flores SP	7.50	15.00
140 Wayne Hawkins SP	3.00	6.00
141 Ken Herock RC	2.00	4.00
142 Jon Jelacic SP RC	3.00	6.00
143 Joe Krakoski RC	2.00	4.00
144 Archie Matsos SP	3.00	6.00
145 Mike Mercer	2.00	4.00
146 Alan Miller SP	3.00	6.00
147 Bob Mischak SP	3.00	6.00
148 Jim Otto SP	18.00	30.00
149 Clancy Osborne SP	3.00	6.00
150 Art Powell SP	6.00	12.00
151 Bo Roberson	2.00	4.00
152 Fred Williamson SP	18.00	30.00
153 Oakland Raiders	3.00	6.00
154 Chuck Allen SP RC	5.00	10.00
155 Lance Alworth	30.00	50.00
156 George Blair RC	2.00	4.00
157 Earl Faison	2.00	4.00
158 Sam Gruneisen RC	2.00	4.00
159 John Hadl RC	25.00	40.00
160 Dick Harris SP	3.00	6.00
161 Emil Karas SP RC	3.00	6.00
162 Dave Kocourek SP	3.00	6.00
163 Ernie Ladd	4.00	8.00
164 Keith Lincoln	3.00	6.00
165 Paul Lowe SP	6.00	12.00
166 Charlie McNeil	2.00	4.00
167 Jacque MacKinnon SP RC	3.00	6.00
168 Ron Mix SP	10.00	20.00
169 Don Norton SP	3.00	6.00
170 Don Rogers SP RC	3.00	6.00
171 Tobin Rote SP	5.00	10.00
172 Henry Schmidt SP RC	3.00	6.00
173 Bud Whitehead RC	2.00	4.00
174 Ernie Wright SP	5.00	10.00
175 San Diego Chargers	3.00	6.00
176 Checklist SP UER	80.00	160.00
AD1 Advertising Panel	250.00	400.00
Larry Eisenhauer		
Bo Roberson		
K.C. Chiefs Team		

1964 Topps Pennant Stickers Inserts

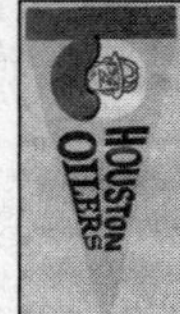

This set of 24 pennant stickers was inserted into the 1964 Topps regular issue AFL set. These inserts are actually 2 1/8" by 4 1/2" glassine type peel-offs on gray backing. The pennants are unnumbered and are ordered below alphabetically within type. The stickers were folded in order to fit into the 1964 Topps wax packs, so they are virtually always found with a crease or fold.

COMPLETE SET (24)	750.00	1,500.00
1 Boston Patriots	50.00	100.00
2 Buffalo Bills	50.00	100.00
3 Denver Broncos	60.00	120.00
4 Houston Oilers	50.00	100.00
5 Kansas City Chiefs	50.00	100.00
6 New York Jets	50.00	100.00
7 Oakland Raiders	60.00	120.00
8 San Diego Chargers	50.00	100.00
9 Air Force Falcons	30.00	60.00
10 Army Cadets	30.00	60.00
11 Dartmouth Indians	30.00	60.00
12 Duke Blue Devils	30.00	60.00
13 Michigan Wolverines	37.50	75.00
14 Minnesota Golden Gophers	30.00	60.00
15 Mississippi Rebels	30.00	60.00
16 Navy Midshipmen	30.00	60.00
17 Notre Dame Fight.Irish	75.00	150.00
18 SMU Mustangs	30.00	60.00
19 USC Trojans	30.00	60.00
20 Syracuse Orangemen	30.00	60.00
21 Texas Longhorns	30.00	60.00
22 Washington Huskies	30.00	60.00
23 Wisconsin Badgers	30.00	60.00
24 Yale Bulldogs	30.00	60.00

1965 Topps

The 1965 Topps football card set contains 176 oversized (2 1/2" by 4 11/16") cards of American Football League players.

Colorful card fronts have a player photo over a solid color background. The team name is at the top with the player's name and position at the bottom. Horizontal backs contain highlights and statistics to the left with a cartoon pertaining to the player to the right. The cards are grouped together and numbered in basic alphabetical order by teams. Since this set was not printed in the standard fashion, many of the cards were printed in lesser quantities than others. These cards are marked in the checklist with SP for short print. This set is somewhat significant in that it contains the Rookie Card of Joe Namath. Other notable Rookie Cards in this set of Oakland Raiders stars Fred Biletnikoff, Willie Brown and Ben Davidson.

COMPLETE SET (176)	2,500.00	4,000.00
WRAPPER (5-CENT)	90.00	150.00
1 Tommy Addison SP	20.00	35.00
2 Houston Antwine SP	7.00	12.00
3 Nick Buoniconti SP	18.00	30.00
4 Ron Burton SP	10.00	20.00
5 Gino Cappelletti SP	10.00	20.00
6 Jim Colclough	3.50	7.00
7 Bob Dee SP	7.00	12.00
8 Larry Eisenhauer	3.50	7.00
9 J.D. Garrett RC	3.50	7.00
10 Larry Garron	3.50	7.00
11 Art Graham SP	7.00	12.00
12 Ron Hall DB	3.50	7.00
13 Charles Long	3.50	7.00
14 Jon Morris RC	5.00	10.00
15 Billy Neighbors SP	7.00	12.00
16 Ross O'Hanley	3.50	7.00
17 Babe Parilli SP	10.00	20.00
18 Tony Romeo SP RC	7.00	12.00
19 Jack Rudolph SP	7.00	12.00
20 Bob Schmidt	3.50	7.00
21 Don Webb SP	7.00	12.00
22 Jim Whalen SP RC	7.00	12.00
23 Stew Barber	3.50	7.00
24 Glenn Bass SP RC	7.00	12.00
25 Al Bemiller SP	7.00	12.00
26 Wray Carlton SP	7.00	12.00
27 Tom Day RC	3.50	7.00
28 Elbert Dubenion SP	7.50	15.00
29 Jim Dunaway	3.50	7.00
30 Pete Gogolak SP RC	10.00	20.00
31 Dick Hudson SP	7.00	12.00
32 Harry Jacobs SP	7.00	12.00
33 Billy Joe SP	7.50	15.00
34 Tom Keating SP RC	7.00	12.00
35 Jack Kemp SP	75.00	150.00
36 Daryle Lamonica SP	30.00	50.00
37 Paul Maguire SP	10.00	20.00
38 Ron McDole SP RC	7.00	12.00
39 George Saimes SP	7.00	12.00
40 Tom Sestak SP	7.00	12.00
41 Billy Shaw SP	10.00	20.00
42 Mike Stratton SP	7.00	12.00
43 John Tracey SP	7.00	12.00
44 Ernie Warlick	3.50	7.00
45 Odell Barry RC	3.50	7.00
46 Willie Brown SP RC	75.00	135.00
47 Gerry Bussell SP RC	7.00	12.00
48 Eldon Danenhauer SP	7.00	12.00
49 Al Denson SP RC	7.00	12.00
50 Hewritt Dixon SP RC	7.50	15.00
51 Cookie Gilchrist SP	18.00	30.00
52 Goose Gonsoulin SP	7.50	15.00
53 Abner Haynes SP	10.00	20.00
54 Jerry Hopkins RC	3.50	7.00
55 Ray Jacobs SP	7.00	12.00
56 Jacky Lee SP	7.50	15.00
57 John McCormick QB	3.50	7.00
58 Bob McCullough SP	7.00	12.00
59 John McGeever RC	3.50	7.00
60 Charlie Mitchell SP	7.00	12.00
61 Jim Perkins SP RC	7.00	12.00
62 Bob Scarpitto SP	7.00	12.00
63 Mickey Slaughter SP	7.00	12.00
64 Jerry Sturm SP	7.00	12.00
65 Lionel Taylor SP	10.00	20.00
66 Scott Appleton SP	7.00	12.00
67 Johnny Baker SP RC	7.00	12.00
68 Sonny Bishop SP RC	7.00	12.00
69 George Blanda SP	75.00	125.00
70 Sid Blanks SP RC	7.00	12.00
71 Ode Burrell SP RC	7.00	12.00
72 Doug Cline SP	7.00	12.00
73 Willard Dewveall	3.50	7.00
74 Larry Elkins RC	3.50	7.00
75 Don Floyd SP	7.00	12.00
76 Freddy Glick	3.50	7.00
77 Tom Goode SP RC	7.00	12.00
78 Charlie Hennigan SP	10.00	20.00
79 Ed Husmann	3.50	7.00
80 Bobby Jancik SP	7.00	12.00
81 Bud McFadin SP	7.00	12.00
82 Bob McLeod SP	7.00	12.00
83 Jim Norton SP	7.00	12.00
84 Walt Suggs	3.50	7.00
85 Bob Talamini	3.50	7.00
86 Charley Tolar SP	7.00	12.00
87 Checklist SP	100.00	175.00
88 Don Trull SP	7.00	12.00
89 Fred Arbanas SP	7.00	12.00
90 Pete Beathard SP RC	7.00	12.00
91 Bobby Bell SP	25.00	40.00
92 Mel Branch SP	7.00	12.00
93 Tommy Brooker SP RC	7.00	12.00
94 Buck Buchanan SP	20.00	35.00
95 Ed Budde SP	7.00	12.00
96 Chris Burford SP	7.00	12.00
97 Walt Corey	3.50	7.00
98 Jerry Cornelison	3.50	7.00
99 Len Dawson SP	60.00	100.00
100 Jon Gilliam SP RC	7.00	12.00
101 Sherrill Headrick SP UER	7.00	12.00
102 Dave Hill SP RC	7.00	12.00
103 E.J. Holub SP	7.00	12.00
104 Bobby Hunt SP	7.00	12.00
105 Frank Jackson SP	7.00	12.00
106 Jerry Mays	5.00	10.00
107 Curtis McClinton SP	7.50	15.00
108 Bobby Ply SP RC	7.00	12.00
109 Johnny Robinson SP	7.50	15.00
110 Jim Tyrer SP	7.00	12.00
111 Bill Baird SP RC	7.00	12.00
112 Ralph Baker SP RC	7.00	12.00
113 Sam DeLuca SP	7.00	12.00
114 Larry Grantham SP	7.50	15.00
115 Gene Heeter SP	7.00	12.00
116 Winston Hill SP RC	10.00	20.00
117 John Huarte SP RC	18.00	30.00
118 Cosmo Iacavazzi SP RC	7.00	12.00
119 Curley Johnson SP	7.00	12.00
120 Dee Mackey UER	3.50	7.00
121 Don Maynard	30.00	50.00
122 Joe Namath SP RC	1,200.00	1,800.00
123 Dainard Paulson	3.50	7.00
124 Gerry Philbin SP	7.00	12.00
125 Sherman Plunkett SP RC	7.50	15.00
126 Mark Smolinski	3.50	7.00
127 Matt Snell SP	18.00	30.00
128 Mike Taliaferro SP	7.00	12.00
129 Bake Turner SP	7.00	12.00
130 Clyde Washington SP	7.00	12.00
131 Verlon Biggs SP RC	7.00	12.00
132 Dalva Allen	3.50	7.00
133 Fred Biletnikoff SP RC	150.00	250.00
134 Billy Cannon SP	10.00	20.00
135 Dave Costa SP	7.00	12.00
136 Clem Daniels SP	7.50	15.00
137 Ben Davidson SP RC	35.00	60.00
138 Cotton Davidson SP	7.50	15.00
139 Tom Flores SP	10.00	20.00
140 Claude Gibson	3.50	7.00
141 Wayne Hawkins	3.50	7.00
142 Archie Matsos SP	7.00	12.00
143 Mike Mercer SP	7.00	12.00
144 Bob Mischak SP	7.00	12.00
145 Jim Otto	18.00	30.00
146 Art Powell UER	5.00	10.00
147 Warren Powers SP RC	7.00	12.00
148 Ken Rice SP	7.00	12.00
149 Bo Roberson SP	7.00	12.00
150 Harry Schuh RC	3.50	7.00
151 Larry Todd SP RC	7.00	12.00
152 Fred Williamson SP	15.00	30.00
153 J.R. Williamson RC	3.50	7.00
154 Chuck Allen	5.00	10.00
155 Lance Alworth	50.00	75.00
156 Frank Buncom RC	3.50	7.00
157 Steve DeLong SP RC	7.00	12.00
158 Earl Faison SP	7.50	15.00
159 Kenny Graham SP RC	7.00	12.00
160 George Gross SP RC	7.00	12.00
161 John Hadl SP	20.00	35.00
162 Emil Karas SP	7.00	12.00
163 Dave Kocourek SP	7.00	12.00
164 Ernie Ladd SP	10.00	20.00
165 Keith Lincoln SP	12.00	25.00
166 Paul Lowe SP	10.00	20.00
167 Jacque MacKinnon	3.50	7.00
168 Ron Mix	12.00	20.00
169 Don Norton SP	7.00	12.00
170 Bob Petrich RC	3.50	7.00
171 Rick Redman SP RC	7.00	12.00
172 Pat Shea RC	3.50	7.00
173 Walt Sweeney SP RC	7.50	15.00
174 Dick Westmoreland RC	3.50	7.00
175 Ernie Wright SP	10.00	20.00
176 Checklist SP	125.00	225.00

1965 Topps Magic Rub-Off Inserts

This set of 36 rub-off team emblems was inserted into packs of the 1965 Topps AFL regular football issue. They are very similar to the 1961 Topps Baseball Magic Rub-Offs. Each rub-off measures 2" by 3"; eight AFL teams and 28 college teams are featured. The rub-offs are unnumbered and, hence, are numbered below alphabetically within type, i.e., AFL teams 1-8 and college teams 9-36.

COMPLETE SET (36)	400.00	800.00
1 Boston Patriots	15.00	30.00
2 Buffalo Bills	15.00	30.00
3 Denver Broncos	20.00	40.00
4 Houston Oilers	15.00	30.00
5 Kansas City Chiefs	15.00	30.00
6 New York Jets	15.00	30.00
7 Oakland Raiders	20.00	40.00
8 San Diego Chargers	15.00	30.00
9 Alabama Crimson Tide	12.50	25.00
10 Air Force Falcons	10.00	20.00
11 Arkansas Razorbacks	10.00	20.00
12 Army Cadets	10.00	20.00
13 Boston College Eagles	10.00	20.00
14 Duke Blue Devils	10.00	20.00
15 Illinois Fighting Illini	10.00	20.00
16 Kansas Jayhawks	10.00	20.00
17 Kentucky Wildcats	10.00	20.00
18 Maryland Terrapins	10.00	20.00
19 Miami Hurricanes	10.00	20.00
20 Minnesota Golden Gophers	10.00	20.00
21 Mississippi Rebels	10.00	20.00
22 Navy Midshipmen	10.00	20.00
23 Nebraska Cornhuskers	10.00	20.00
24 Notre Dame Fight.Irish	20.00	40.00
25 Penn State Nittany Lions	12.50	25.00
26 Purdue Boilermakers	10.00	20.00
27 SMU Mustangs	10.00	20.00
28 USC Trojans	10.00	20.00
29 Stanford Indians	10.00	20.00
30 Syracuse Orangemen	10.00	20.00
31 TCU Horned Frogs	10.00	20.00
32 Texas Longhorns	10.00	20.00
33 Virginia Cavaliers	10.00	20.00
34 Washington Huskies	10.00	20.00
35 Wisconsin Badgers	10.00	20.00
36 Yale Bulldogs	10.00	20.00

1966 Topps

The 1966 Topps set of 132 standard-size cards contains AFL players grouped together and numbered alphabetically within teams. The set marks the debut into the AFL of the Miami Dolphins. Card fronts are horizontal with woodgrain borders. Such a border offers a challenge to locate cards in top grades. The player's name, team and position are within the border below the photo. The card backs are printed in black and pink on white card stock. In actuality, card number 15 is not a football card at all but a "Funny Ring" checklist card; nevertheless, it is considered part of the set and is now regarded as the toughest card in the set to find in mint condition. Funny Ring cards were inserted one per pack but measure only 2 1/2" by 3 3/8". Notable Rookie Cards in this set include Wendell Hayes, George Sauer Jr., Otis Taylor, and Jim Turner.

COMPLETE SET (132)	950.00	1,500.00
WRAPPER (5-CENT)	30.00	60.00
1 Tommy Addison	10.00	20.00
2 Houston Antwine	3.00	5.00
3 Nick Buoniconti	5.00	10.00
4 Gino Cappelletti	4.00	8.00
5 Bob Dee	3.00	5.00
6 Larry Garron	3.00	5.00
7 Art Graham	3.00	5.00
8 Ron Hall DB	3.00	5.00
9 Charles Long	3.00	5.00
10 Jon Morris	3.00	5.00
11 Don Oakes	3.00	5.00
12 Babe Parilli	4.00	8.00
13 Don Webb	3.00	5.00
14 Jim Whalen	3.00	5.00
15 Funny Ring Checklist !	200.00	300.00
16 Stew Barber	3.00	5.00
17 Glenn Bass	3.00	5.00
18 Dave Behrman	3.00	5.00
19 Al Bemiller	3.00	5.00
20 Butch Byrd RC	4.00	8.00
21 Wray Carlton	3.00	5.00
22 Tom Day	3.00	5.00
23 Elbert Dubenion	4.00	8.00
24 Jim Dunaway	3.00	5.00
25 Dick Hudson	3.00	5.00
26 Jack Kemp	60.00	120.00
27 Daryle Lamonica	12.00	20.00
28 Tom Sestak	3.00	5.00
29 Billy Shaw	5.00	10.00
30 Mike Stratton	3.00	5.00
31 Eldon Danenhauer	3.00	5.00
32 Cookie Gilchrist	5.00	10.00
33 Goose Gonsoulin	4.00	8.00
34 Wendell Hayes RC	5.00	10.00
35 Abner Haynes	5.00	10.00
36 Jerry Hopkins	3.00	5.00
37 Ray Jacobs	3.00	5.00
38 Charlie Janerette RC	3.00	5.00
39 Ray Kubala RC	3.00	5.00
40 John McCormick QB	3.00	5.00
41 Leroy Moore RC	3.00	5.00
42 Bob Scarpitto	3.00	5.00
43 Mickey Slaughter	3.00	5.00
44 Jerry Sturm	3.00	5.00
45 Lionel Taylor	5.00	10.00
46 Scott Appleton	3.00	5.00
47 Johnny Baker	3.00	5.00
48 George Blanda	20.00	35.00
49 Sid Blanks	3.00	5.00
50 Danny Brabham RC	3.00	5.00
51 Ode Burrell	3.00	5.00
52 Gary Cutsinger	3.00	5.00
53 Larry Elkins	3.00	5.00
54 Don Floyd	3.00	5.00
55 Willie Frazier RC	4.00	8.00
56 Freddy Glick	3.00	5.00
57 Charlie Hennigan	4.00	8.00
58 Bobby Jancik	3.00	5.00
59 Rich Michael	3.00	5.00
60 Don Trull	3.00	5.00
61 Checklist	30.00	55.00
62 Fred Arbanas	3.00	5.00
63 Pete Beathard	3.00	5.00
64 Bobby Bell	5.00	10.00
65 Ed Budde	3.00	5.00
66 Chris Burford	3.00	5.00
67 Len Dawson	25.00	40.00
68 Jon Gilliam	3.00	5.00
69 Sherrill Headrick	3.00	5.00
70 E.J. Holub UER	3.00	5.00
71 Bobby Hunt	3.00	5.00
72 Curtis McClinton	4.00	8.00
73 Jerry Mays	3.00	5.00
74 Johnny Robinson	4.00	8.00
75 Otis Taylor RC	15.00	25.00
76 Tom Erlandson RC	4.00	8.00
77 Norm Evans RC	5.00	10.00
78 Tom Goode	4.00	8.00
79 Mike Hudock	4.00	8.00
80 Frank Jackson	4.00	8.00
81 Billy Joe	4.00	8.00
82 Dave Kocourek	4.00	8.00
83 Bo Roberson	4.00	8.00
84 Jack Spikes	4.00	8.00
85 Jim Warren RC	4.00	8.00
86 Willie West RC	4.00	8.00
87 Dick Westmoreland	4.00	8.00
88 Eddie Wilson RC	4.00	8.00
89 Dick Wood	4.00	8.00
90 Verlon Biggs	4.00	8.00
91 Sam DeLuca	3.00	5.00
92 Winston Hill	3.00	5.00
93 Dee Mackey	3.00	5.00
94 Bill Mathis	3.00	5.00
95 Don Maynard	18.00	30.00
96 Joe Namath	150.00	250.00
97 Dainard Paulson	3.00	5.00
98 Gerry Philbin	4.00	8.00
99 Sherman Plunkett	3.00	5.00
100 Paul Rochester	3.00	5.00
101 George Sauer Jr. RC	7.50	15.00
102 Matt Snell	5.00	10.00
103 Jim Turner RC	4.00	8.00
104 Fred Biletnikoff UER	30.00	50.00
105 Bill Budness RC	3.00	5.00
106 Billy Cannon	5.00	10.00
107 Clem Daniels	4.00	8.00
108 Ben Davidson	7.50	15.00
109 Cotton Davidson	4.00	8.00
110 Claude Gibson	3.00	5.00
111 Wayne Hawkins	3.00	5.00
112 Ken Herock	3.00	5.00
113 Bob Mischak	3.00	5.00
114 Gus Otto RC	3.00	5.00
115 Jim Otto	12.00	20.00
116 Art Powell	5.00	10.00
117 Harry Schuh	3.00	5.00
118 Chuck Allen	3.00	5.00
119 Lance Alworth	25.00	40.00
120 Frank Buncom	3.00	5.00
121 Steve DeLong	3.00	5.00
122 John Farris RC	3.00	5.00
123 Kenny Graham	3.00	5.00
124 Sam Gruneisen	3.00	5.00
125 John Hadl	5.00	10.00
126 Walt Sweeney	3.00	5.00
127 Keith Lincoln	5.00	10.00
128 Ron Mix	5.00	10.00
129 Don Norton	3.00	5.00
130 Pat Shea	3.00	5.00
131 Ernie Wright	5.00	10.00
132 Checklist	50.00	100.00

1967 Topps

The 1967 Topps set of 132 standard-size cards contains AFL players only, with players grouped together and numbered by teams. The cardfronts include an oval design player photo surrounded by a team color. The cardbacks are printed in black text with a dark yellow or gold colored background on white card stock. A question (with upside-down answer) is given on the bottom of the cardbacks. Additionally, some cards were also issued along with the "Win-A-Card" board game from Milton Bradley that included cards from the 1965 Topps Hot Rods and 1968 Topps baseball card sets. This version of the cards is somewhat difficult to distinguish, but are often found with a slight touch of the 1968 baseball set border on the front top or bottom edge as well as a brighter yellow card back instead of the darker yellow or gold color. Known cards issued in this version include: #2, 12, 13, 18, 22, 28, 30, 31, 32, 48, 49, 51, 58, 60, 67, 68, 71, 84, 86, 87, 88, 92, 95, 98, 103, 106, 110, 116, 117, 121, 124, 125, and 130.

COMPLETE SET (132)	400.00	700.00
WRAPPER (5-CENT)	30.00	60.00
1 John Huarte	10.00	18.00
2 Babe Parilli	2.00	4.00
3 Gino Cappelletti	2.00	4.00
4 Larry Garron	1.50	3.00
5 Tommy Addison	1.50	3.00
6 Jon Morris	1.50	3.00
7 Houston Antwine	1.50	3.00
8 Don Oakes	1.50	3.00
9 Larry Eisenhauer	1.50	3.00
10 Jim Hunt RC	1.50	3.00
11 Jim Whalen	1.50	3.00

12 Art Graham 1.50 3.00
13 Nick Buoniconti 3.00 6.00
14 Bob Dee 1.50 3.00
15 Keith Lincoln 3.00 6.00
16 Tom Flores 2.00 4.00
17 Art Powell 2.00 4.00
18 Stew Barber 1.50 3.00
19 Wray Carlton 1.50 3.00
20 Elbert Dubenion 2.00 4.00
21 Jim Dunaway 1.50 3.00
22 Dick Hudson 1.50 3.00
23 Harry Jacobs 1.50 3.00
24 Jack Kemp 40.00 80.00
25 Ron McDole 1.50 3.00
26 George Saimes 1.50 3.00
27 Tom Sestak 1.50 3.00
28 Billy Shaw 3.00 6.00
29 Mike Stratton 1.50 3.00
30 Nemiah Wilson RC 1.50 3.00
31 John McCormick QB 1.50 3.00
32 Rex Mirich RC 1.50 3.00
33 Dave Costa 1.50 3.00
34 Goose Gonsoulin 2.00 4.00
35 Abner Haynes 3.00 6.00
36 Wendell Hayes 2.00 4.00
37 Archie Matsos 1.50 3.00
38 John Bramlett RC 1.50 3.00
39 Jerry Sturm 1.50 3.00
40 Max Leetzow RC 1.50 3.00
41 Bob Scarpitto 1.50 3.00
42 Lionel Taylor 3.00 6.00
43 Al Denson 1.50 3.00
44 Miller Farr RC 1.50 3.00
45 Don Trull 1.50 3.00
46 Jacky Lee 2.00 4.00
47 Bobby Jancik 1.50 3.00
48 Ode Burrell 1.50 3.00
49 Larry Elkins 1.50 3.00
50 W.K. Hicks RC 1.50 3.00
51 Sid Blanks 1.50 3.00
52 Jim Norton 1.50 3.00
53 Bobby Maples RC 1.50 3.00
54 Bob Talamini 1.50 3.00
55 Walt Suggs 1.50 3.00
56 Gary Cutsinger 1.50 3.00
57 Danny Brabham 1.50 3.00
58 Ernie Ladd 3.00 6.00
59 Checklist 25.00 50.00
60 Pete Beathard 1.50 3.00
61 Len Dawson 18.00 30.00
62 Bobby Hunt 1.50 3.00
63 Bert Coan RC 1.50 3.00
64 Curtis McClinton 2.00 4.00
65 Johnny Robinson 2.00 4.00
66 E.J. Holub 1.50 3.00
67 Jerry Mays 1.50 3.00
68 Jim Tyrer 2.00 4.00
69 Bobby Bell 3.00 6.00
70 Fred Arbanas 1.50 3.00
71 Buck Buchanan 3.00 6.00
72 Chris Burford 1.50 3.00
73 Otis Taylor 3.00 6.00
74 Cookie Gilchrist 4.00 8.00
75 Earl Faison 1.50 3.00
76 George Wilson Jr. RC 2.00 4.00
77 Rick Norton RC 1.50 3.00
78 Frank Jackson 2.00 4.00
79 Joe Auer RC 1.50 3.00
80 Willie West 1.50 3.00
81 Jim Warren 1.50 3.00
82 Wahoo McDaniel RC 30.00 50.00
83 Ernie Park RC 1.50 3.00
84 Billy Neighbors 1.50 3.00
85 Norm Evans 2.00 4.00
86 Tom Nomina 1.50 3.00
87 Rich Zecher RC 1.50 3.00
88 Dave Kocourek 1.50 3.00
89 Bill Baird 1.50 3.00
90 Ralph Baker 1.50 3.00
91 Verlon Biggs 1.50 3.00
92 Sam DeLuca 1.50 3.00
93 Larry Grantham 2.00 4.00
94 Jim Harris RC 1.50 3.00
95 Winston Hill 1.50 3.00
96 Bill Mathis 1.50 3.00
97 Don Maynard 12.00 20.00
98 Joe Namath 75.00 150.00
99 Gerry Philbin 2.00 4.00
100 Paul Rochester 1.50 3.00
101 George Sauer Jr. 2.00 4.00
102 Matt Snell 3.00 6.00
103 Daryle Lamonica 5.00 10.00
104 Glenn Bass 1.50 3.00
105 Jim Otto 3.00 6.00
106 Fred Biletnikoff 18.00 30.00
107 Cotton Davidson 2.00 4.00
108 Larry Todd 1.50 3.00
109 Billy Cannon 3.00 6.00
110 Clem Daniels 2.00 4.00
111 Dave Grayson 1.50 3.00
112 Kent McCloughan UER RC 1.50 3.00
113 Bob Svihus RC 1.50 3.00
114 Ike Lassiter 1.50 3.00
115 Harry Schuh 1.50 3.00
116 Ben Davidson 4.00 8.00
117 Tom Day 1.50 3.00
118 Scott Appleton 1.50 3.00
119 Steve Tensi RC 1.50 3.00
120 John Hadl 3.00 6.00
121 Paul Lowe 2.00 4.00
122 Jim Allison RC 1.50 3.00
123 Lance Alworth 20.00 35.00
124 Jacque MacKinnon 1.50 3.00
125 Ron Mix 3.00 6.00
126 Bob Petrich 1.50 3.00
127 Howard Kindig RC 1.50 3.00
128 Steve DeLong 1.50 3.00
129 Chuck Allen 1.50 3.00
130 Frank Buncom 1.50 3.00
131 Speedy Duncan RC 2.50 5.00
132 Checklist 35.00 70.00

1967 Topps Comic Pennants

This set was issued as an insert with the 1967 Topps regular issue football cards as well as being issued separately. The stickers are standard size, and the backs are blank. The set can also be found in adhesive form with the pennant merely printed on card stock. They are numbered in the upper right corner, although reportedly they can also occasionally be found without numbers. Many of the cards feature sayings or depictions that are in poor taste, i.e., sick humor. Perhaps they were discontinued or recalled before the end of the season, which would explain their relative scarcity.

COMPLETE SET (31) 300.00 600.00
1 Navel Academy 10.00 25.00
2 City College 10.00 25.00
3 Notre Dame 20.00 40.00
4 Psychedelic State 10.00 25.00
5 Minneapolis Mini-skirts 10.00 25.00
6 School of Art 10.00 25.00
7 Washington 10.00 25.00
8 School of Hard Knocks 10.00 25.00
9 Alaska 10.00 25.00
10 Confused State 10.00 25.00
11 Yale Locks 10.00 25.00
12 University of 10.00 25.00
13 Down With Teachers 10.00 25.00
14 Cornell 10.00 25.00
15 Houston Oilers 10.00 25.00
16 Harvard 10.00 25.00
17 Diskotech 10.00 25.00
18 Dropout U. 10.00 25.00
19 Air Force 10.00 25.00
20 Nutstu U. 10.00 25.00
21 Michigan State Pen 10.00 25.00
22 Denver Broncos 15.00 30.00
23 Buffalo Bills 12.50 30.00
24 Army of Dropouts 10.00 25.00
25 Miami Dolphins 15.00 30.00
26 Kansas City (Has Too 10.00 25.00
27 Boston Patriots 10.00 25.00
28 (Fat People In) Oakland 15.00 30.00
29 (I'd Go) West (If You'd 10.00 25.00
30 New York Jets 12.50 30.00
31 San Diego Chargers 10.00 25.00

1968 Topps

The 1968 set marks the beginning of a 21-year run of Topps being the only major producer of football cards. The two-series set of 219 standard-size cards is Topps' first set in seven years (since 1961) to contain players from both leagues. The set marks the AFL debut of the Cincinnati Bengals. Card fronts feature the player photo over a solid background. A team logo is in an upper corner. The player's name, team name and position are in a colored cicular box at the bottom. Cards for players from the previous year's Super Bowl teams, the Green Bay Packers and the Oakland Raiders, are the only cards to contain horizontally designed fronts. In addition, these cards also have color boders at top and bottom and the player photo is superimposed over yellow tinted game action artwork. The backs have statistics and highlights as well as a rub-off cartoon at the bottom. The cards in the second series have blue printing on the back whereas the cards in the first series had green printing on the back. Card backs of some of the cards in the second series can be used to form a ten-card puzzle of Bart Starr (141, 148, 153, 155, 168, 172, 186, 197, 201, and 213) or Len Dawson (145, 146, 151, 152, 163, 166, 170, 195, 199, and 200). The set features the Rookie Cards of quarterbacks Bob Griese, Jim Hart, and Craig Morton, and (ex-Syracuse) running backs Floyd Little and Jim Nance. The second series (132-219) is slightly more difficult to obtain than the first series. This set was issued in five card wax packs which cost five cents and came 24 packs to a box.

COMPLETE SET (219) 350.00 550.00
WRAPPER (5-CENT, SER.1) 10.00 20.00
WRAPPER (5-CENT, SER.2) 20.00 30.00
1 Bart Starr 25.00 40.00
2 Dick Bass 1.00 2.00
3 Grady Alderman .75 1.50
4 Obert Logan .75 1.50
5 Ernie Koy RC 1.00 2.00
6 Don Hultz RC .75 1.50
7 Earl Gros .75 1.50
8 Jim Bakken .75 1.50
9 George Mira 1.00 2.00
10 Carl Kammerer RC .75 1.50
11 Willie Frazier .75 1.50
12 Kent McCloughan UER .75 1.50
13 George Sauer Jr. 1.00 2.00
14 Jack Clancy RC .75 1.50
15 Jim Tyrer 1.00 2.00
16 Bobby Maples .75 1.50
17 Bo Hickey RC .75 1.50
18 Frank Buncom .75 1.50
19 Keith Lincoln 1.00 2.00
20 Jim Whalen .75 1.50
21 Junior Coffey .75 1.50
22 Billy Ray Smith .75 1.50
23 Johnny Morris .75 1.50
24 Ernie Green .75 1.50
25 Don Meredith 15.00 25.00
26 Wayne Walker .75 1.50
27 Carroll Dale 1.00 2.00
28 Bernie Casey 1.00 2.00
29 Dave Osborn RC 1.00 2.00
30 Ray Poage .75 1.50
31 Homer Jones .75 1.50
32 Sam Baker .75 1.50
33 Bill Saul RC .75 1.50
34 Ken Willard 1.00 2.00
35 Bobby Mitchell 2.00 4.00
36 Gary Garrison RC 1.00 2.00
37 Billy Cannon 1.00 2.00
38 Ralph Baker .75 1.50
39 Howard Twilley RC 2.00 4.00
40 Wendell Hayes 1.00 2.00
41 Jim Norton .75 1.50
42 Tom Beer RC .75 1.50
43 Chris Burford .75 1.50
44 Stew Barber .75 1.50
45 Leroy Mitchell UER RC .75 1.50
46 Dan Grimm .75 1.50
47 Jerry Logan .75 1.50
48 Andy Livingston RC .75 1.50
49 Paul Warfield 7.50 15.00
50 Don Perkins 1.50 3.00
51 Ron Kramer .75 1.50
52 Bob Jeter RC 1.00 2.00
53 Les Josephson RC 1.00 2.00
54 Bobby Walden .75 1.50
55 Checklist 7.50 15.00
56 Walter Roberts .75 1.50
57 Henry Carr .75 1.50
58 Gary Ballman .75 1.50
59 J.R. Wilburn RC .75 1.50
60 Jim Hart RC 5.00 10.00
61 Jim Johnson 1.50 3.00
62 Chris Hanburger 1.00 2.00
63 John Hadl 1.50 3.00
64 Hewritt Dixon 1.00 2.00
65 Joe Namath 50.00 80.00
66 Jim Warren .75 1.50
67 Curtis McClinton 1.00 2.00
68 Bob Talamini .75 1.50
69 Steve Tensi .75 1.50
70 Dick Van Raaphorst UER RC .75 1.50
71 Art Powell 1.00 2.00
72 Jim Nance RC 2.00 4.00
73 Bob Riggle RC .75 1.50
74 John Mackey 2.50 5.00
75 Gale Sayers 25.00 40.00
76 Gene Hickerson 1.25 2.50
77 Dan Reeves 5.00 10.00
78 Tom Nowatzke .75 1.50
79 Elijah Pitts 1.50 3.00
80 Lamar Lundy 1.00 2.00
81 Paul Flatley .75 1.50
82 Dave Whitsell .75 1.50
83 Spider Lockhart 1.00 2.00
84 Dave Lloyd .75 1.50
85 Roy Jefferson 1.00 2.00
86 Jackie Smith 3.00 6.00
87 John David Crow 1.00 2.00
88 Sonny Jurgensen 3.00 6.00
89 Ron Mix 1.50 3.00
90 Clem Daniels 1.00 2.00
91 Cornell Gordon RC .75 1.50
92 Tom Goode .75 1.50
93 Bobby Bell 1.50 3.00
94 Walt Suggs .75 1.50
95 Eric Crabtree RC .75 1.50
96 Sherrill Headrick .75 1.50
97 Wray Carlton .75 1.50
98 Gino Cappelletti 1.00 2.00
99 Tommy McDonald 2.00 4.00
100 Johnny Unitas 25.00 40.00
101 Richie Petitbon .75 1.50
102 Erich Barnes .75 1.50
103 Bob Hayes 5.00 10.00
104 Milt Plum 1.00 2.00
105 Boyd Dowler 1.00 2.00
106 Ed Meador .75 1.50
107 Fred Cox .75 1.50
108 Steve Stonebreaker RC .75 1.50
109 Aaron Thomas .75 1.50
110 Norm Snead 1.00 2.00
111 Paul Martha RC .75 1.50
112 Jerry Stovall .75 1.50
113 Kay McFarland RC .75 1.50
114 Pat Richter .75 1.50
115 Rick Redman .75 1.50
116 Tom Keating .75 1.50
117 Matt Snell 1.00 2.00
118 Dick Westmoreland .75 1.50
119 Jerry Mays .75 1.50
120 Sid Blanks .75 1.50
121 Al Denson .75 1.50
122 Bobby Hunt .75 1.50
123 Mike Mercer .75 1.50
124 Nick Buoniconti 1.50 3.00
125 Ron Vanderkelen RC .75 1.50
126 Ordell Braase .75 1.50
127 Dick Butkus 30.00 50.00
128 Gary Collins 1.00 2.00
129 Mel Renfro 3.00 6.00
130 Alex Karras 2.50 5.00
131 Herb Adderley 2.50 5.00
132 Roman Gabriel 2.00 4.00
133 Bill Brown 1.25 2.50
134 Kent Kramer RC 1.00 2.00
135 Tucker Frederickson 1.25 2.50
136 Nate Ramsey 1.00 2.00
137 Marv Woodson RC 1.00 2.00
138 Ken Gray 1.00 2.00
139 John Brodie 2.50 5.00
140 Jerry Smith 1.00 2.00
141 Brad Hubbert RC 1.00 2.00
142 George Blanda 10.00 20.00
143 Pete Lammons RC 1.00 2.00
144 Doug Moreau RC 1.00 2.00
145 E.J. Holub 1.00 2.00
146 Ode Burrell 1.00 2.00
147 Bob Scarpitto 1.00 2.00
148 Andre White RC 1.00 2.00
149 Jack Kemp 30.00 50.00
150 Art Graham 1.00 2.00
151 Tommy Nobis 3.00 6.00
152 Willie Richardson RC 1.25 2.50
153 Jack Concannon 1.00 2.00
154 Bill Glass 1.00 2.00
155 Craig Morton RC 5.00 10.00
156 Pat Studstill 1.00 2.00
157 Ray Nitschke 5.00 10.00
158 Roger Brown 1.00 2.00
159 Joe Kapp RC 2.50 5.00
160 Jim Taylor 7.50 15.00
161 Fran Tarkenton 10.00 20.00
162 Mike Ditka 18.00 30.00
163 Andy Russell RC 4.00 8.00
164 Larry Wilson 2.00 4.00
165 Tommy Davis 1.00 2.00
166 Paul Krause 2.00 4.00
167 Speedy Duncan 1.00 2.00
168 Fred Biletnikoff 7.50 15.00
169 Don Maynard 5.00 10.00
170 Frank Emanuel RC 1.00 2.00
171 Len Dawson 7.50 15.00
172 Miller Farr 1.00 2.00
173 Floyd Little RC 12.50 25.00
174 Lonnie Wright RC 1.00 2.00
175 Paul Costa RC 1.00 2.00
176 Don Trull 1.00 2.00
177 Jerry Simmons RC 1.00 2.00
178 Tom Matte 1.25 2.50
179 Bennie McRae 1.00 2.00
180 Jim Kanicki RC 1.00 2.00
181 Bob Lilly 7.50 15.00
182 Tom Watkins 1.00 2.00
183 Jim Grabowski RC 3.00 6.00
184 Jack Snow RC 2.00 4.00
185 Gary Cuozzo RC 1.25 2.50
186 Billy Kilmer 2.00 4.00
187 Jim Katcavage 1.00 2.00
188 Floyd Peters 1.00 2.00
189 Bill Nelsen 1.25 2.50
190 Bobby Joe Conrad 1.25 2.50
191 Kermit Alexander 1.00 2.00
192 Charley Taylor UER 3.00 6.00
193 Lance Alworth 10.00 20.00
194 Daryle Lamonica 2.50 5.00
195 Al Atkinson RC 1.00 2.00
196 Bob Griese RC 60.00 100.00
197 Buck Buchanan 2.00 4.00
198 Pete Beathard 1.00 2.00
199 Nemiah Wilson 1.00 2.00
200 Ernie Wright 1.00 2.00
201 George Saimes 1.00 2.00
202 John Charles RC 1.00 2.00
203 Randy Johnson 1.00 2.00
204 Tony Lorick 1.00 2.00
205 Dick Evey 1.00 2.00
206 Leroy Kelly 5.00 10.00
207 Lee Roy Jordan 3.00 6.00
208 Jim Gibbons 1.00 2.00
209 Donny Anderson RC 2.00 4.00
210 Maxie Baughan 1.00 2.00
211 Joe Morrison 1.00 2.00
212 Jim Snowden RC 1.00 2.00
213 Lenny Lyles 1.00 2.00
214 Bobby Joe Green 1.00 2.00
215 Frank Ryan 1.25 2.50
216 Cornell Green 1.25 2.50
217 Karl Sweetan 1.00 2.00
218 Dave Williams RC 1.00 2.00
219A Checklist Green 10.00 18.00
219B Checklist Blue 12.00 20.00

1968 Topps Posters Inserts

The 1968 Topps Football Posters set contains 16 NFL and AFL players on paper stock; the cards (posters) measure approximately 5" by 7". The posters, folded twice for insertion into first series wax packs, are numbered on the obverse at the lower left hand corner. The backs of these posters are blank. Fold marks are normal and do not detract from the poster's condition. These posters are the same style as the 1967 Topps baseball

COMPLETE SET (16)	40.00	80.00
1 Johnny Unitas	10.00	20.00
2 Leroy Kelly	2.50	5.00
3 Bob Hayes	3.00	6.00
4 Bart Starr	7.50	15.00
5 Charley Taylor	2.50	5.00
6 Fran Tarkenton	5.00	10.00
7 Jim Bakken	1.50	3.00
8 Gale Sayers	6.00	12.00
9 Gary Cuozzo	1.50	3.00
10 Les Josephson	1.50	3.00
11 Jim Nance	1.50	3.00
12 Brad Hubbert	1.50	3.00
13 Keith Lincoln	1.50	3.00
14 Don Maynard	3.00	6.00
15 Len Dawson	4.00	8.00
16 Jack Clancy	1.50	3.00

1968 Topps Stand-Ups Inserts

The 22-card 1968 Topps Football Stand-Ups standard-size set is unnumbered but has been numbered alphabetically in the checklist below for your convenience. Values listed below are for complete cards; the value is greatly reduced if the backs are detached, and such a card can be considered fair to good at best. The cards were issued as an insert in second series packs of 1968 Topps football cards, one per pack.

COMPLETE SET (22)	150.00	250.00
1 Sid Blanks	3.00	6.00
2 John Brodie	6.00	12.00
3 Jack Concannon	3.00	6.00
4 Roman Gabriel	4.00	8.00
5 Art Graham	3.00	6.00
6 Jim Grabowski	3.00	6.00
7 John Hadl	4.00	8.00
8 Jim Hart	4.00	8.00
9 Homer Jones	3.00	6.00
10 Sonny Jurgensen	6.00	12.00
11 Alex Karras	5.00	10.00
12 Billy Kilmer	4.00	8.00
13 Daryle Lamonica	4.00	8.00
14 Floyd Little	4.00	8.00
15 Curtis McClinton	3.00	6.00
16 Don Meredith	20.00	40.00
17 Joe Namath	40.00	80.00
18 Bill Nelsen	3.50	7.00
19 Dave Osborn	3.00	6.00
20 Willie Richardson	3.00	6.00
21 Frank Ryan	3.50	7.00
22 Norm Snead	3.50	7.00

1968 Topps Test Teams

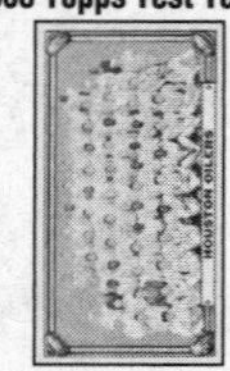

The 25-card set of team cards was issued as a stand alone wax pack (10-cents per pack) product with cloth patch/sticker inserts. The fronts provide a black and white picture of the team while the backs give the names of the players in the picture in red print on vanilla card stock. Due to their positioning within the pack, these test team cards are typically found with gum stains on the card backs. The cards measure approximately 2 1/2" by 4 11/16" and are numbered on the back.

COMPLETE SET (25)	1,800.00	3,000.00
WRAPPER (10-cent)	250.00	350.00
1 Green Bay Packers	100.00	175.00
2 New Orleans Saints	50.00	100.00
3 New York Jets	75.00	150.00
4 Miami Dolphins	100.00	175.00
5 Pittsburgh Steelers	75.00	125.00
6 Detroit Lions	50.00	100.00
7 Los Angeles Rams	50.00	100.00
8 Atlanta Falcons	50.00	100.00
9 New York Giants	75.00	125.00
10 Denver Broncos	175.00	300.00
11 Dallas Cowboys	250.00	400.00
12 Buffalo Bills	75.00	125.00
13 Cleveland Browns	75.00	125.00
14 San Francisco 49ers	75.00	125.00
15 Baltimore Colts	50.00	100.00
16 San Diego Chargers	50.00	100.00
17 Oakland Raiders	100.00	200.00
18 Houston Oilers	50.00	100.00
19 Minnesota Vikings	75.00	125.00
20 Washington Redskins	100.00	175.00
21 St. Louis Cardinals	50.00	100.00
22 Kansas City Chiefs	50.00	100.00
23 Boston Patriots	50.00	100.00
24 Chicago Bears	75.00	135.00
25 Philadelphia Eagles	50.00	100.00

1968 Topps Test Team Patches

These team emblem cloth patches/stickers were distributed as an insert with the 1968 Topps Test Teams: one sticker per 10 cent pack along with one test team. In fact according to the wrapper, these stickers were the featured item; however the hobby has deemed the team cards to be more collectible and hence more valuable than these rather bland, but scarce, logo stickers. The complete set of 44 patches consisted of team emblems, the letters A through Z, and the numbers 0 through 9. The letters and number patches contained two letters or numbers on each patch. The number patches are printed in black on a blue background, the letter patches are white on a red background, and the team emblems were done in the team colors. The stickers measure 2 1/2" by 3 1/2". The backs are blank.

COMPLETE SET (44)	1,000.00	2,000.00
1 1 and 2	6.00	12.00
2 3 and 4	6.00	12.00
3 5 and 6	6.00	12.00
4 7 and 8	6.00	12.00
5 9 and 0	6.00	12.00
6 A and B	6.00	12.00
7 C and D	6.00	12.00
8 E and F	6.00	12.00
9 G and H	6.00	12.00
10 I and W	6.00	12.00
11 J and X	6.00	12.00
12 Atlanta Falcons	30.00	60.00
13 Baltimore Colts	30.00	60.00
14 Chicago Bears	45.00	90.00
15 Cleveland Browns	30.00	60.00
16 Dallas Cowboys	100.00	175.00
17 Detroit Lions	30.00	60.00
18 Green Bay Packers	75.00	125.00
19 Los Angeles Rams	30.00	60.00
20 Minnesota Vikings	45.00	90.00
21 New Orleans Saints	30.00	60.00
22 New York Giants	45.00	90.00
23 K and L	6.00	12.00
24 M and O	6.00	12.00
25 N and P	6.00	12.00
26 Q and R	6.00	12.00
27 S and T	6.00	12.00
28 U and V	6.00	12.00
29 Y and Z	6.00	12.00
30 Philadelphia Eagles	30.00	60.00
31 Pittsburgh Steelers	45.00	90.00
32 St. Louis Cardinals	30.00	60.00
33 San Francisco 49ers	30.00	60.00
34 Washington Redskins	100.00	200.00
35 Boston Patriots	30.00	60.00
36 Buffalo Bills	30.00	60.00
37 Denver Broncos	67.50	135.00
38 Houston Oilers	30.00	60.00
39 Kansas City Chiefs	30.00	60.00
40 Miami Dolphins	75.00	150.00
41 New York Jets	30.00	60.00
42 Oakland Raiders	75.00	150.00
43 San Diego Chargers	30.00	60.00
44 Cincinnati Bengals	30.00	60.00

1969 Topps

The 1969 Topps set of 263 standard-size cards was issued in two series. First series cards (1-132) are borderless whereas the second series (133-263) cards have white borders. The lack of borders makes the first series especially difficult to find in mint condition. The checklist card (132) was obviously printed with each series as it is found in both styles (with and without borders). The set was issued in 12-card 10-cent packs. Though the borders differ, the fronts have otherwise consistent designs. A player photo is superimposed over a solid color background with the team logo, player's name, team name and position at the bottom. The backs of the cards are predominantly black, but with a green and white accent. Card backs of some of the cards in the second series can be used to form a ten-card puzzle of Fran Tarkenton (137, 145, 168, 174, 177, 194, 211, 219, 224, and 256). This set is distinctive in that it contains the late Brian Piccolo's only regular issue card. Another notable Rookie Card in this set is Larry Csonka.

COMPLETE SET (263)	350.00	550.00
WRAPPER (5-CENT)	15.00	30.00
1 Leroy Kelly	10.00	20.00
2 Paul Flatley	.75	1.50
3 Jim Cadile RC	.75	1.50
4 Erich Barnes	.75	1.50
5 Willie Richardson	.75	1.50
6 Bob Hayes	4.00	8.00
7 Bob Jeter	.75	1.50
8 Jim Colclough	.75	1.50
9 Sherrill Headrick	.75	1.50
10 Jim Dunaway	.75	1.50
11 Bill Munson	1.00	2.00
12 Jack Pardee	1.00	2.00
13 Jim Lindsey RC	.75	1.50
14 Dave Whitsell	.75	1.50
15 Tucker Frederickson	.75	1.50
16 Alvin Haymond	1.00	2.00
17 Andy Russell	1.00	2.00
18 Tom Beer	.75	1.50
19 Bobby Maples	.75	1.50
20 Len Dawson	4.00	8.00
21 Willis Crenshaw	.75	1.50
22 Tommy Davis	.75	1.50
23 Rickie Harris	.75	1.50
24 Jerry Simmons	.75	1.50
25 Johnny Unitas	25.00	50.00
26 Brian Piccolo UER RC	50.00	80.00
27 Bob Matheson RC	.75	1.50
28 Howard Twilley	1.00	2.00
29 Jim Turner	1.00	2.00
30 Pete Banaszak RC	1.00	2.00
31 Lance Rentzel RC	1.00	2.00
32 Bill Triplett	.75	1.50
33 Boyd Dowler	1.00	2.00
34 Merlin Olsen	2.50	5.00
35 Joe Kapp	1.50	3.00
36 Dan Abramowicz RC	2.00	4.00
37 Spider Lockhart	1.00	2.00
38 Tom Day	.75	1.50
39 Art Graham	.75	1.50
40 Bob Cappadona RC	.75	1.50
41 Gary Ballman	.75	1.50
42 Clendon Thomas	.75	1.50
43 Jackie Smith	2.00	4.00
44 Dave Wilcox	1.50	3.00
45 Jerry Smith	.75	1.50
46 Dan Grimm	.75	1.50
47 Tom Matte	1.00	2.00
48 John Stofa RC	.75	1.50
49 Rex Mirich	.75	1.50
50 Miller Farr	.75	1.50
51 Gale Sayers	25.00	40.00
52 Bill Nelsen	1.00	2.00
53 Bob Lilly	3.00	6.00
54 Wayne Walker	.75	1.50
55 Ray Nitschke	2.50	5.00
56 Ed Meador	.75	1.50
57 Lonnie Warwick RC	.75	1.50
58 Wendell Hayes	.75	1.50
59 Dick Anderson RC	2.50	5.00
60 Don Maynard	3.00	6.00
61 Tony Lorick	.75	1.50
62 Pete Gogolak	.75	1.50
63 Nate Ramsey	.75	1.50
64 Dick Shiner RC	.75	1.50
65 Larry Wilson UER	1.50	3.00
66 Ken Willard	1.00	2.00
67 Charley Taylor	2.50	5.00
68 Billy Cannon	1.00	2.00
69 Lance Alworth	4.00	8.00
70 Jim Nance	1.00	2.00
71 Nick Rassas RC	.75	1.50
72 Lenny Lyles	.75	1.50
73 Bennie McRae	.75	1.50
74 Bill Glass	.75	1.50
75 Don Meredith	15.00	25.00
76 Dick LeBeau	1.00	2.50
77 Carroll Dale	1.00	2.00
78 Ron McDole	.75	1.50
79 Charley King RC	.75	1.50
80 Checklist UER	7.50	15.00
81 Dick Bass	1.00	2.00
82 Roy Winston	.75	1.50
83 Don McCall RC	.75	1.50
84 Jim Katcavage	1.00	2.00
85 Norm Snead	1.00	2.00
86 Earl Gros	.75	1.50
87 Don Brumm RC	.75	1.50
88 Sonny Bishop	.75	1.50
89 Fred Arbanas	.75	1.50
90 Karl Noonan RC	.75	1.50
91 Dick Witcher RC	.75	1.50
92 Vince Promuto	.75	1.50
93 Tommy Nobis	2.00	4.00
94 Jerry Hill RC	.75	1.50
95 Ed O'Bradovich RC	.75	1.50
96 Ernie Kellerman RC	.75	1.50
97 Chuck Howley	1.00	2.00
98 Hewritt Dixon	.75	1.50
99 Ron Mix	1.50	3.00
100 Joe Namath	40.00	75.00
101 Billy Gambrell RC	.75	1.50
102 Elijah Pitts	1.00	2.00
103 Billy Truax RC	1.00	2.00
104 Ed Sharockman	.75	1.50
105 Doug Atkins	1.50	3.00
106 Greg Larson	.75	1.50
107 Israel Lang RC	.75	1.50
108 Houston Antwine	.75	1.50
109 Paul Guidry RC	.75	1.50
110 Al Denson	.75	1.50
111 Roy Jefferson	1.00	2.00
112 Chuck Latourette RC	.75	1.50
113 Jim Johnson	1.50	3.00
114 Bobby Mitchell	2.00	4.00
115 Randy Johnson	.75	1.50
116 Lou Michaels	.75	1.50
117 Rudy Kuechenberg RC	.75	1.50
118 Walt Suggs	.75	1.50
119 Goldie Sellers RC	.75	1.50
120 Larry Csonka RC	40.00	75.00
121 Jim Houston	.75	1.50
122 Craig Baynham RC	.75	1.50
123 Alex Karras	2.50	5.00
124 Jim Grabowski	1.00	2.00
125 Roman Gabriel	1.50	3.00
126 Larry Bowie	.75	1.50
127 Dave Parks	1.00	2.00
128 Ben Davidson	1.50	3.00
129 Steve DeLong	.75	1.50
130 Fred Hill RC	.75	1.50
131 Ernie Koy	1.00	2.00
132A Checklist no border	7.50	15.00
132B Checklist bordered	10.00	20.00
133 Dick Hoak	1.00	2.00
134 Larry Stallings RC	1.00	2.00
135 Clifton McNeil RC	1.00	2.00
136 Walter Rock	1.00	2.00
137 Billy Lothridge RC	1.00	2.00
138 Bob Vogel	1.00	2.00
139 Dick Butkus	25.00	40.00
140 Frank Ryan	1.25	2.50
141 Larry Garron	1.00	2.00
142 George Saimes	1.00	2.00
143 Frank Buncom	1.00	2.00
144 Don Perkins	1.25	2.50
145 Johnnie Robinson UER RC	1.00	2.00
146 Lee Roy Caffey	1.25	2.50
147 Bernie Casey	1.25	2.50
148 Billy Martin E	1.00	2.00
149 Gene Howard RC	1.00	2.00
150 Fran Tarkenton	10.00	20.00
151 Eric Crabtree	1.00	2.00
152 W.K. Hicks	1.00	2.00
153 Bobby Bell	2.00	4.00
154 Sam Baker	1.00	2.00
155 Marv Woodson	1.00	2.00
156 Dave Williams	1.00	2.00
157 Bruce Bosley UER	1.00	2.00
158 Carl Kammerer	1.00	2.00
159 Jim Burson RC	1.00	2.00
160 Roy Hilton RC	1.00	2.00
161 Bob Griese	15.00	25.00
162 Bob Talamini	1.00	2.00
163 Jim Otto	2.00	4.00
164 Ronnie Bull	1.00	2.00
165 Walter Johnson RC	1.00	2.00
166 Lee Roy Jordan	2.00	4.00
167 Mike Lucci	1.25	2.50
168 Willie Wood	2.00	4.00
169 Maxie Baughan	1.00	2.00
170 Bill Brown	1.25	2.50
171 John Hadl	2.00	4.00
172 Gino Cappelletti	1.25	2.50
173 George Butch Byrd	1.25	2.50
174 Steve Stonebreaker	1.00	2.00
175 Joe Morrison	1.00	2.00
176 Joe Scarpati	1.00	2.00
177 Bobby Walden	1.00	2.00
178 Roy Shivers	1.00	2.00
179 Kermit Alexander	1.00	2.00
180 Pat Richter	1.00	2.00
181 Pete Perreault RC	1.00	2.00
182 Pete Duranko RC	1.00	2.00
183 Leroy Mitchell	1.00	2.00
184 Jim Simon RC	1.00	2.00
185 Billy Ray Smith	1.00	2.00
186 Jack Concannon	1.00	2.00
187 Ben Davis RC	1.00	2.00
188 Mike Clark	1.00	2.00
189 Jim Gibbons	1.00	2.00
190 Dave Robinson	3.00	6.00
191 Otis Taylor	1.25	2.50
192 Nick Buoniconti	2.00	4.00
193 Matt Snell	1.25	2.50
194 Bruce Gossett	1.00	2.00
195 Mick Tingelhoff	1.25	2.50
196 Earl Leggett	1.00	2.00
197 Pete Case	1.00	2.00
198 Tom Woodeshick RC	1.00	2.00
199 Ken Kortas RC	1.00	2.00
200 Jim Hart	2.00	4.00
201 Fred Biletnikoff	5.00	10.00
202 Jacque MacKinnon	1.00	2.00
203 Jim Whalen	1.00	2.00
204 Matt Hazeltine	1.00	2.00
205 Charlie Gogolak	1.00	2.00
206 Ray Ogden RC	1.00	2.00
207 John Mackey	2.00	4.00
208 Roosevelt Taylor	1.00	2.00
209 Gene Hickerson	1.25	2.50
210 Dave Edwards RC	1.25	2.50
211 Tom Sestak	1.00	2.00
212 Ernie Wright	1.00	2.00
213 Dave Costa	1.00	2.00
214 Tom Vaughn RC	1.00	2.00
215 Bart Starr	25.00	40.00
216 Les Josephson	1.00	2.00
217 Fred Cox	1.00	2.00
218 Mike Tilleman RC	1.00	2.00
219 Darrell Dess	1.00	2.00
220 Dave Lloyd	1.00	2.00
221 Pete Beathard	1.00	2.00
222 Buck Buchanan	2.00	4.00
223 Frank Emanuel	1.00	2.00
224 Paul Martha	1.00	2.00
225 Johnny Roland	1.00	2.00
226 Gary Lewis	1.00	2.00
227 Sonny Jurgensen UER	3.00	6.00
228 Jim Butler	1.00	2.00
229 Mike Curtis RC	4.00	8.00
230 Richie Petitbon	1.00	2.00
231 George Sauer Jr.	1.25	2.50
232 George Blanda	10.00	20.00
233 Gary Garrison	1.00	2.00

234 Gary Collins 1.25 2.50
235 Craig Morton 2.00 4.00
236 Tom Nowatzke 1.00 2.00
237 Donny Anderson 1.25 2.50
238 Deacon Jones 2.00 4.00
239 Grady Alderman 1.00 2.00
240 Billy Kilmer 2.00 4.00
241 Mike Taliaferro 1.00 2.00
242 Stew Barber 1.00 2.00
243 Bobby Hunt 1.00 2.00
244 Homer Jones 1.00 2.00
245 Bob Brown OT 2.00 4.00
246 Bill Asbury 1.00 2.00
247 Charley Johnson 1.25 2.50
248 Chris Hanburger 1.25 2.50
249 John Brodie 3.00 6.00
250 Earl Morrall 1.25 2.50
251 Floyd Little 2.50 5.00
252 Jerrel Wilson RC 1.00 2.00
253 Jim Keyes RC 1.00 2.00
254 Mel Renfro 2.00 4.00
255 Herb Adderley 2.00 4.00
256 Jack Snow 1.25 2.50
257 Charlie Durkee RC 1.00 2.00
258 Charlie Harper RC 1.00 2.00
259 J.R. Wilburn 1.00 2.00
260 Charlie Krueger 1.00 2.00
261 Pete Jacques RC 1.00 2.00
262 Gerry Philbin 1.00 2.00
263 Daryle Lamonica 5.00 10.00

1969 Topps Four-in-One Inserts

The 1969 Topps Four-in-One set contains 66 cards (each measuring the standard size) with each card having four small (1" by 1 1/2") cardboard stamps on the front. Cards 27 and 28 are the same except for colors. The cards were issued as inserts to the 1969 Topps regular football card set. The cards are unnumbered, but have been numbered in the checklist below for convenience in alphabetical order by the player in the northwest quadrant of the card. Prices below are for complete cards; individual stamps are not priced. An album exists to house the stamps on these cards (see 1969 Topps Mini Albums). It is interesting to note that not all the players appearing in this set also appear in the 1969 Topps regular issue set especially since there are almost the same number of players in each set. Jack Kemp is included in this set but not in the regular 1969 Topps set. Bryan Piccolo also appears in his only Topps appearance other than the 1969 Topps regular issue set. There are 19 players in this set who do not appear in the regular issue 1969 Topps set; they are marked by asterisks in the list below.

COMPLETE SET (66) 150.00 300.00
1 Gale Sayers 6.00 12.00
2 Jim Allison * 1.75 3.50
3 Lance Alworth/Maynard 3.00 6.00
4 Fred Biletnikoff 3.00 6.00
5 Ralph Baker 2.50 5.00
6 Gary Ballman 1.75 3.50
7 Tom Beer 1.75 3.50
8 Sonny Bishop 1.75 3.50
9 Bruce Bosley 1.75 3.50
10 Larry Bowie 1.75 3.50
11 Nick Buoniconti 2.50 5.00
12 Jim Burson 1.75 3.50
13 Reg Carolan * 1.75 3.50
14 Bert Coan * 2.50 5.00
15 Joe Namath 15.00 30.00
16 Fran Tarkenton 5.00 10.00
17 Pete Gogolak 1.75 3.50
18 Bob Griese 5.00 10.00
19 Jim Hart 1.75 3.50
20 Alvin Haymond 1.75 3.50
21 Dick Butkus 6.00 12.00
22 Fred Hill 2.50 5.00
23 Dick Hoak 2.50 5.00
24 Jim Houston 1.75 3.50
25 Gene Howard 1.75 3.50
26 Brian Piccolo 12.50 25.00
27 C.Johnson R 1.75 3.50
Katcav
G.Lewis
Triplett W
28 C.Johnson W 1.75 3.50
Katcav
G.Lewis
Triplett R
29 Walter Johnson 1.75 3.50
30 Sonny Jurgensen 4.00 8.00
31 Bart Starr 7.50 15.00
32 Charley King 1.75 3.50
33 Daryle Lamonica 2.50 5.00
34 Bob Lilly/Brodie 3.00 6.00
35 Jim Lindsey 2.50 5.00
36 Billy Lothridge 2.50 5.00
37 Bobby Maples 1.75 3.50
38 Don Meredith 6.00 12.00
39 Rex Mirich 1.75 3.50
40 Leroy Mitchell 1.75 3.50
41 Larry Csonka 6.00 12.00
42 Bill Nelsen 1.75 3.50
43 Jim Otto 2.50 5.00
44 Jack Pardee 1.75 3.50
45 Richie Petitbon 1.75 3.50
46 Nick Rassas 2.50 5.00
47 Pat Richter 1.75 3.50
48 Johnny Roland 1.75 3.50
49 Alex Karras 3.00 6.00
50 Joe Scarpati 1.75 3.50
51 Tom Sestak 1.75 3.50
52 Bob Hayes 2.50 5.00
53 Jackie Smith/C.Taylor 3.00 6.00
54 Larry Stallings 2.50 5.00
55 Mike Stratton * 1.75 3.50
56 Len Dawson 3.00 6.00
57 Jack Kemp/Blanda 12.50 25.00
58 Clendon Thomas 1.75 3.50
59 Don Trull * 2.50 5.00
60 Johnny Unitas 7.50 15.00
61 Merlin Olsen 2.50 5.00
62 Willie West * 1.75 3.50
63 Jerrel Wilson 1.75 3.50
64 Larry Wilson 2.50 5.00
65 Willie Wood 2.50 5.00
66 Tom Woodeshick 2.50 5.00

1969 Topps Mini-Albums Inserts

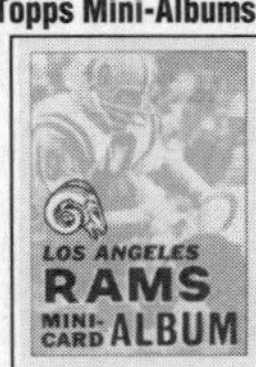

The 1969 Topps Mini-Card Team Albums is a set of 26 small (2 1/2" by 3 1/2") booklets which were issued in conjunction with the 1969 Four-in-One inserts. Each of these booklets has eight pages and a game action photo on the front. Many of the cover photos were from games from the early 1960s. We've included the player's names when known. A picture of each player is contained in the album, over which the stamps from the Four-in-One inserts were to be pasted. In order to be mint, the album must have no stamps pasted in it. The booklets are printed in blue and black ink on thick white paper and are numbered on the last page of the album. The card numbering cooresponds to an alphabetical listing by team name within each league.

COMPLETE SET (26) 37.50 75.00
1 Atlanta Falcons 1.50 3.00
2 Baltimore Colts 3.00 6.00
3 Chicago Bears 1.50 3.00
4 Cleveland Browns 2.00 4.00
5 Dallas Cowboys 2.50 5.00
6 Detroit Lions 1.50 3.00
7 Green Bay Packers 3.00 6.00
8 Los Angeles Rams 1.50 3.00
9 Minnesota Vikings 1.50 3.00
10 New Orleans Saints 1.50 3.00
11 New York Giants 1.50 3.00
12 Philadelphia Eagles 2.00 4.00
13 Pittsburgh Steelers 2.00 4.00
14 St. Louis Cardinals 1.50 3.00
15 San Francisco 49ers 1.50 3.00
16 Washington Redskins 1.50 3.00
17 Boston Patriots 1.50 3.00
18 Buffalo Bills 2.00 4.00
19 Cincinnati Bengals 2.00 4.00
20 Denver Broncos 1.50 3.00
21 Houston Oilers 1.50 3.00
22 Kansas City Chiefs 3.00 6.00
23 Miami Dolphins 2.00 4.00
24 New York Jets 2.00 4.00
25 Oakland Raiders 2.50 5.00
26 San Diego Chargers 1.50 3.00

1970 Topps

The 1970 Topps football set contains 263 standard-size cards that were issued in two series. The second series (133-263) was printed in slightly lesser quantities than the first series. This set was issued in 10 count, 10 cent packs which came 24 packs to a box. Card fronts have an oval photo surrounded by tan borders. At the bottom of photo is a color banner that contains the player's name and team. A football at bottom right contain the player's position. The card backs are done in orange, purple, and white and are horizontally designed. Statistics, highlights and a player cartoon adorn the backs. In the second series, card backs of offensive and defensive linemen have a coin rub-off cartoon rather than a printed cartoon as seen on all the other cards in the set. O.J. Simpson's Rookie Card appears in this set. Other notable Rookie Cards in this set are Lem Barney, Bill Bergey, Larry Brown, Fred Dryer, Mike Garrett, Calvin Hill, Harold Jackson, Tom Mack, Alan Page, Bubba Smith, Jan Stenerud, Bob Trumpy, and both Gene Washingtons.

COMPLETE SET (263) 300.00 475.00
WRAPPER (10-CENT) 8.00 12.00
1 Len Dawson UER 12.00 20.00
2 Doug Hart RC .40 1.00
3 Verlon Biggs .40 1.00
4 Ralph Neely RC .60 1.50
5 Harmon Wages RC .40 1.00
6 Dan Conners RC .40 1.00
7 Gino Cappelletti .60 1.50
8 Erich Barnes .40 1.00
9 Checklist 5.00 10.00
10 Bob Griese 7.50 15.00
11 Ed Flanagan RC .40 1.00
12 George Seals RC .40 1.00
13 Harry Jacobs .40 1.00
14 Mike Haffner RC .40 1.00
15 Bob Vogel .40 1.00
16 Bill Peterson RC .40 1.00
17 Spider Lockhart .40 1.00
18 Billy Truax .40 1.00
19 Jim Beirne RC .40 1.00
20 Leroy Kelly 3.00 6.00
21 Dave Lloyd .40 1.00
22 Mike Tilleman .40 1.00
23 Gary Garrison .40 1.00
24 Larry Brown RC 4.00 12.00
25 Jan Stenerud RC 6.00 12.00
26 Rolf Krueger RC .40 1.00
27 Roland Lakes .40 1.00
28 Dick Hoak .40 1.00
29 Gene Washington Vik RC 1.25 2.50
30 Bart Starr 12.50 25.00
31 Dave Grayson .40 1.00
32 Jerry Rush RC .40 1.00
33 Len St. Jean RC .40 1.00
34 Randy Edmunds RC .40 1.00
35 Matt Snell .60 1.50
36 Paul Costa .40 1.00
37 Mike Pyle .40 1.00
38 Roy Hilton .40 1.00
39 Steve Tensi .40 1.00
40 Tommy Nobis 1.25 2.50
41 Pete Case .40 1.00
42 Andy Rice RC .40 1.00
43 Elvin Bethea RC 4.00 8.00
44 Jack Snow .60 1.50
45 Mel Renfro 1.25 2.50
46 Andy Livingston .40 1.00
47 Gary Ballman .40 1.00
48 Bob DeMarco .40 1.00
49 Steve DeLong .40 1.00
50 Daryle Lamonica 2.00 4.00
51 Jim Lynch RC .40 1.00
52 Mel Farr RC .40 1.00
53 Bob Long RC .40 1.00
54 John Elliott RC .40 1.00
55 Ray Nitschke 2.50 5.00
56 Jim Shorter .40 1.00
57 Dave Wilcox 1.25 2.50
58 Eric Crabtree .40 1.00
59 Alan Page RC 15.00 30.00
60 Jim Nance .60 1.50
61 Glen Ray Hines RC .40 1.00
62 John Mackey 1.25 2.50
63 Ron McDole .40 1.00
64 Tom Beier RC .40 1.00
65 Bill Nelsen .60 1.50
66 Paul Flatley .40 1.00
67 Sam Brunelli RC .40 1.00
68 Jack Pardee .60 1.50
69 Brig Owens .40 1.00
70 Gale Sayers 12.50 25.00
71 Lee Roy Jordan 1.25 2.50
72 Harold Jackson RC 2.50 5.00
73 John Hadl 1.25 2.50
74 Dave Parks .40 1.00
75 Lem Barney RC 7.50 15.00
76 Johnny Roland .40 1.00
77 Ed Budde .40 1.00
78 Ben McGee .40 1.00
79 Ken Bowman RC .40 1.00
80 Fran Tarkenton 7.50 15.00
81 Gene Washington 49er RC 2.50 5.00
82 Larry Grantham .40 1.00
83 Bill Brown .60 1.50
84 John Charles .40 1.00
85 Fred Biletnikoff 3.50 7.00
86 Royce Berry RC .40 1.00
87 Bob Lilly 2.50 5.00
88 Earl Morrall .60 1.50
89 Jerry LeVias RC .60 1.50
90 O.J. Simpson 40.00 80.00
91 Mike Howell RC .40 1.00
92 Ken Gray .40 1.00
93 Chris Hanburger .40 1.00
94 Larry Seiple RC .40 1.00
95 Rich Jackson RC .40 1.00
96 Rockne Freitas RC .40 1.00
97 Dick Post RC .60 1.50
98 Ben Hawkins RC .40 1.00
99 Ken Reaves RC .40 1.00
100 Roman Gabriel 1.25 2.50
101 Dave Rowe RC .40 1.00
102 Dave Robinson .75 2.00
103 Otis Taylor .60 1.50
104 Jim Turner .40 1.00
105 Joe Morrison .40 1.00
106 Dick Evey .40 1.00
107 Ray Mansfield RC .40 1.00
108 Grady Alderman .40 1.00
109 Bruce Gossett .40 1.00
110 Bob Trumpy RC 2.00 4.00
111 Jim Hunt .40 1.00
112 Larry Stallings .40 1.00
113A Lance Rentzel Red .60 1.50
113B Lance Rentzel Black .60 1.50
114 Bubba Smith RC 12.50 25.00
115 Norm Snead .60 1.50
116 Jim Otto 1.25 2.50
117 Bo Scott RC .40 1.00
118 Rick Redman .40 1.00
119 George Butch Byrd .40 1.00
120 George Webster RC .60 1.50
121 Chuck Walton RC .40 1.00
122 Dave Costa .40 1.00
123 Al Dodd RC .40 1.00
124 Len Hauss .40 1.00
125 Deacon Jones 1.25 2.50
126 Randy Johnson .40 1.00
127 Ralph Heck .40 1.00
128 Emerson Boozer RC .60 1.50
129 Johnny Robinson .60 1.50
130 John Brodie 2.50 5.00
131 Gale Gillingham RC .40 1.00
132 Checklist DP 3.00 6.00
133 Chuck Walker RC .50 1.25
134 Bennie McRae .50 1.25
135 Paul Warfield 3.50 7.00
136 Dan Darragh RC .50 1.25
137 Paul Robinson RC .50 1.25
138 Ed Philpott RC .50 1.25
139 Craig Morton 1.50 3.00
140 Tom Dempsey RC .75 2.00
141 Al Nelson RC .50 1.25
142 Tom Matte .75 2.00
143 Dick Schafrath .50 1.25
144 Willie Brown 2.00 4.00
145 Charley Taylor UER 2.50 5.00
146 John Huard RC .50 1.25
147 Dave Osborn .50 1.25
148 Gene Mingo .50 1.25
149 Larry Hand RC .50 1.25
150 Joe Namath 25.00 50.00
151 Tom Mack RC 5.00 10.00
152 Kenny Graham .50 1.25
153 Don Herrmann RC .50 1.25
154 Bobby Bell 1.50 3.00
155 Hoyle Granger RC .50 1.25
156 Claude Humphrey RC 12.00 20.00
157 Clifton McNeil .50 1.25
158 Mick Tingelhoff .75 2.00
159 Don Horn RC .50 1.25
160 Larry Wilson 1.50 3.00
161 Tom Neville RC .50 1.25
162 Larry Csonka 10.00 20.00
163 Doug Buffone RC .50 1.25
164 Cornell Green .75 2.00
165 Haven Moses RC .75 2.00
166 Billy Kilmer 1.50 3.00
167 Tim Rossovich RC .50 1.25
168 Bill Bergey RC 2.00 4.00
169 Gary Collins .75 2.00
170 Floyd Little 1.50 3.00
171 Tom Keating .50 1.25
172 Pat Fischer .50 1.25
173 Walt Sweeney .50 1.25
174 Greg Larson .50 1.25
175 Carl Eller 1.50 3.00
176 George Sauer Jr. .75 2.00
177 Jim Hart 1.50 3.00
178 Bob Brown OT 1.50 3.00
179 Mike Garrett RC .75 2.00
180 Johnny Unitas 15.00 25.00
181 Tom Regner RC .50 1.25
182 Bob Jeter .50 1.25
183 Gail Cogdill .50 1.25
184 Earl Gros .50 1.25
185 Dennis Partee RC .50 1.25
186 Charlie Krueger .50 1.25
187 Martin Baccaglio RC .50 1.25
188 Charles Long .50 1.25
189 Bob Hayes 3.00 6.00
190 Dick Butkus 12.50 25.00
191 Al Bemiller .50 1.25
192 Dick Westmoreland .50 1.25
193 Joe Scarpati .50 1.25
194 Ron Snidow RC .50 1.25
195 Earl McCullouch RC .50 1.25
196 Jake Kupp RC .50 1.25
197 Bob Lurtsema RC .50 1.25
198 Mike Current RC .50 1.25
199 Charlie Smith RB RC .50 1.25
200 Sonny Jurgensen 3.00 6.00
201 Mike Curtis .75 2.00
202 Aaron Brown RC .50 1.25
203 Richie Petitbon .50 1.25
204 Walt Suggs .50 1.25
205 Roy Jefferson .50 1.25
206 Russ Washington RC .50 1.25
207 Woody Peoples RC .50 1.25
208 Dave Williams .50 1.25
209 John Zook RC .50 1.25
210 Tom Woodeshick .50 1.25
211 Howard Fest RC .50 1.25
212 Jack Concannon .50 1.25
213 Jim Marshall 1.50 3.00
214 Jon Morris .50 1.25
215 Dan Abramowicz .75 2.00
216 Paul Martha .50 1.25
217 Ken Willard .50 1.25
218 Walter Rock .50 1.25
219 Garland Boyette .50 1.25
220 Buck Buchanan 1.50 3.00
221 Bill Munson .75 2.00
222 David Lee RC .50 1.25
223 Karl Noonan .50 1.25
224 Harry Schuh .50 1.25
225 Jackie Smith 1.50 3.00
226 Gerry Philbin .50 1.25
227 Ernie Koy .50 1.25
228 Chuck Howley .75 2.00
229 Billy Shaw 1.50 3.00
230 Jerry Hillebrand .50 1.25
231 Bill Thompson RC .75 2.00
232 Carroll Dale .75 2.00

233 Gene Hickerson	1.50	3.00
234 Jim Butler	.50	1.25
235 Greg Cook RC	.50	1.25
236 Lee Roy Caffey	.50	1.25
237 Merlin Olsen	2.00	4.00
238 Fred Cox	.50	1.25
239 Nate Ramsey	.50	1.25
240 Lance Alworth	3.50	7.00
241 Chuck Hinton RC	.50	1.25
242 Jerry Smith	.50	1.25
243 Tony Baker FB RC	.50	1.25
244 Nick Buoniconti	1.50	3.00
245 Jim Johnson	1.50	3.00
246 Willie Richardson	.50	1.25
247 Fred Dryer RC	5.00	10.00
248 Bobby Maples	.50	1.25
249 Alex Karras	2.00	4.00
250 Joe Kapp	.75	2.00
251 Ben Davidson	1.50	3.00
252 Mike Stratton	.50	1.25
253 Les Josephson	.50	1.25
254 Don Maynard	3.00	6.00
255 Houston Antwine	.50	1.25
256 Mac Percival RC	.50	1.25
257 George Goeddeke RC	.50	1.25
258 Homer Jones	.50	1.25
259 Bob Berry RC	.50	1.25
260A Calvin Hill Red RC	7.50	15.00
260B Calvin Hill Black RC	10.00	20.00
261 Willie Wood	1.50	3.00
262 Ed Weisacosky RC	.50	1.25
263 Jim Tyrer	1.50	3.00

1970 Topps Glossy Inserts

The 1970 Topps Super Glossy football set features 33 full-color, thick-stock, glossy cards each measuring 2 1/4" by 3 1/4". The corners are rounded and the backs contain only the player's name, his position, his team and the card number. The set numbering follows the player's team location within league (NFC 1-20 and AFC 21-33). The cards are quite attractive and a favorite with collectors. The cards were inserted in 1970 Topps first series football wax packs. The key cards in the set are Joe Namath and O.J. Simpson, appearing in his Rookie Card year.

COMPLETE SET (33)	150.00	250.00
1 Tommy Nobis	3.00	6.00
2 Johnny Unitas	20.00	40.00
3 Tom Matte	2.50	5.00
4 Mac Percival	2.00	4.00
5 Leroy Kelly	3.00	6.00
6 Mel Renfro	3.00	6.00
7 Bob Hayes	3.00	6.00
8 Earl McCullouch	2.00	4.00
9 Bart Starr	15.00	30.00
10 Willie Wood	3.00	6.00
11 Jack Snow	2.00	4.00
12 Joe Kapp	2.50	5.00
13 Dave Osborn	2.00	4.00
14 Dan Abramowicz	2.00	4.00
15 Fran Tarkenton	10.00	20.00
16 Tom Woodeshick	2.00	4.00
17 Roy Jefferson	2.00	4.00
18 Jackie Smith	2.50	5.00
19 Jim Johnson	2.50	5.00
20 Sonny Jurgensen	5.00	10.00
21 Houston Antwine	2.00	4.00
22 O.J. Simpson	10.00	20.00
23 Greg Cook	2.00	4.00
24 Floyd Little	2.50	5.00
25 Rich Jackson	2.00	4.00
26 George Webster	2.00	4.00
27 Len Dawson	5.00	10.00
28 Bob Griese	7.50	15.00
29 Joe Namath	20.00	40.00
30 Matt Snell	2.50	5.00
31 Daryle Lamonica	3.00	6.00
32 Fred Biletnikoff	5.00	10.00
33 Dick Post	2.00	4.00

1970 Topps Posters Inserts

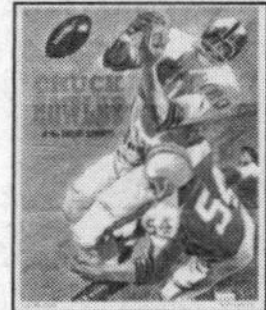

This insert set of 24 folded thin paper posters was issued with the 1970 Topps regular football card issue. The posters are approximately 8" by 10" and were inserted in wax packs along with the 1970 Topps regular issue (second series) football cards. The posters are blank backed.

COMPLETE SET (24)	60.00	100.00
1 Gale Sayers	7.50	15.00
2 Bobby Bell	2.00	4.00
3 Roman Gabriel	1.50	3.00
4 Jim Tyrer	1.25	2.50
5 Willie Brown	2.00	4.00
6 Carl Eller	1.50	3.00
7 Tom Mack	1.50	3.00
8 Deacon Jones	2.00	4.00
9 Johnny Robinson	1.25	2.50
10 Jan Stenerud	1.50	3.00
11 Dick Butkus	7.50	15.00
12 Lem Barney	2.00	4.00
13 David Lee	1.25	2.50
14 Larry Wilson	1.50	3.00
15 Gene Hickerson	1.25	3.00
16 Lance Alworth	4.00	8.00
17 Merlin Olsen	2.50	5.00
18 Bob Trumpy	1.50	3.00
19 Bob Lilly	3.00	6.00
20 Mick Tingelhoff SP	3.00	6.00
21 Calvin Hill	1.50	3.00
22 Paul Warfield	4.00	8.00
23 Chuck Howley	1.50	3.00
24 Bob Brown OT	1.50	3.00

1970 Topps Super

The 1970 Topps Super set contains 35 cards. The cards measure approximately 3 1/8" by 5 1/4". The backs of the cards are identical in format to the regular football issue of 1970. The cards were sold in packs of three with a stick of gum for a dime and are on very thick card stock. The last seven cards in the set were printed in smaller quantities, i.e., short printed; these seven are designated SP in the checklist below. The cards were printed in sheets of seven rows and nine columns or 63 cards; thus 28 cards were double printed and seven cards were single printed. In more recent years wrongbacks and uncut sheets of the cards have been uncovered as well as some featuring square corners instead of rounded.

COMPLETE SET (35)	125.00	250.00
WRAPPER (10-CENT)	10.00	20.00
1 Fran Tarkenton	6.00	12.00
2 Floyd Little	1.50	4.00
3 Bart Starr	12.50	25.00
4 Len Dawson	4.00	8.00
5 Dick Post	1.25	3.00
6 Sonny Jurgensen	4.00	8.00
7 Deacon Jones	2.00	5.00
8 Leroy Kelly	2.00	5.00
9 Larry Wilson	1.50	4.00
10 Greg Cook	1.25	3.00
11 Carl Eller	1.50	4.00
12 Lem Barney	2.00	5.00
13 Lance Alworth	5.00	10.00
14 Dick Butkus	7.50	15.00
15 Johnny Unitas	15.00	30.00
16 Roy Jefferson	1.25	3.00
17 Bobby Bell	2.00	5.00
18 John Brodie	3.00	6.00
19 Dan Abramowicz	1.25	3.00
20 Matt Snell	1.50	4.00
21 Tom Matte	1.25	3.00
22 Gale Sayers	7.50	15.00
23 Tom Woodeshick	1.25	3.00
24 O.J. Simpson	7.50	15.00
25 Roman Gabriel	1.50	4.00
26 Jim Nance	1.25	3.00
27 Joe Morrison	1.25	3.00
28 Calvin Hill	1.50	4.00
29 Tommy Nobis SP	3.00	6.00
30 Bob Hayes SP	4.00	8.00
31 Joe Kapp SP	2.00	4.00
32 Daryle Lamonica SP	3.00	6.00
33 Joe Namath SP	25.00	50.00
34 George Webster SP	2.00	4.00
35 Bob Griese SP	10.00	20.00

1971 Topps

The 1971 Topps set contains 263 standard-size cards issued in two series. The second series (133-263) was printed in slightly lesser quantities than the first series. Card have a player photo surrounded by either a red (AFC), blue (NFC) or blue and red (All-Pros) border. The player's name, team name, position and conference are within the bottom border. An animated cartoon-like player icon appears by the position listing at the bottom. The card backs are printed in black ink with a gold accent on gray card stock. The content includes highlights and, a first for Topps football cards, yearly statistics. A player cartoon is at the top. The first cards of two Steeler greats, Terry Bradshaw and Mean Joe Greene, appear in this set. Other notable Rookie Cards in this set are Hall of Famers Ken Houston and Willie Lanier.

COMPLETE SET (263)	300.00	500.00
WRAPPER (10-CENT)	10.00	20.00
1 Johnny Unitas	15.00	30.00
2 Jim Butler	.40	1.00
3 Marty Schottenheimer RC	6.00	12.00
4 Joe O'Donnell RC	.40	1.00
5 Tom Dempsey	.50	1.25
6 Chuck Allen	.40	1.00
7 Ernie Kellerman	.40	1.00
8 Walt Garrison RC	.75	2.00
9 Bill Van Heusen RC	.40	1.00
10 Lance Alworth	4.00	8.00
11 Greg Landry RC	.75	2.00
12 Larry Krause RC	.40	1.00
13 Buck Buchanan	.75	2.00
14 Roy Gerela RC	.50	1.25
15 Clifton McNeil	.40	1.00
16 Bob Brown OT	.75	2.00
17 Lloyd Mumphord RC	.40	1.00
18 Gary Cuozzo	.40	1.00
19 Don Maynard	2.50	5.00
20 Larry Wilson	.75	2.00
21 Charlie Smith RB	.40	1.00
22 Ken Avery RC	.40	1.00
23 Billy Walik RC	.40	1.00
24 Jim Johnson	.75	2.00
25 Dick Butkus	12.50	25.00
26 Charley Taylor UER	2.00	4.00
27 Checklist UER	4.00	12.00
28 Lionel Aldridge RC	.40	1.00
29 Billy Lothridge	.40	1.00
30 Terry Hanratty RC	.50	1.25
31 Lee Roy Jordan	.75	2.00
32 Rick Volk RC	.40	1.00
33 Howard Kindig	.40	1.00
34 Carl Garrett RC	.40	1.00
35 Bobby Bell	.75	2.00
36 Gene Hickerson	.75	2.00
37 Dave Parks	.40	1.00
38 Paul Martha	.40	1.00
39 George Blanda	7.50	15.00
40 Tom Woodeshick	.40	1.00
41 Alex Karras	1.50	3.00
42 Rick Redman	.40	1.00
43 Zeke Moore RC	.40	1.00
44 Jack Snow	.50	1.25
45 Larry Csonka	7.50	15.00
46 Karl Kassulke RC	.40	1.00
47 Jim Hart	.75	2.00
48 Al Atkinson	.40	1.00
49 Horst Muhlmann RC	.40	1.00
50 Sonny Jurgensen	2.50	5.00
51 Ron Johnson RC	.50	1.25
52 Cas Banaszek RC	.40	1.00
53 Bubba Smith	4.00	8.00
54 Bobby Douglass RC	.50	1.25
55 Willie Wood	.75	2.00
56 Bake Turner	.40	1.00
57 Mike Morgan LB RC	.40	1.00
58 George Butch Byrd	.50	1.25
59 Don Horn	.40	1.00
60 Tommy Nobis	.75	2.00
61 Jan Stenerud	2.00	4.00
62 Altie Taylor RC	.40	1.00
63 Gary Pettigrew RC	.40	1.00
64 Spike Jones RC	.40	1.00
65 Duane Thomas RC	.75	2.00
66 Marty Domres RC	.40	1.00
67 Dick Anderson	.50	1.25
68 Ken Iman RC	.40	1.00
69 Miller Farr	.40	1.00
70 Daryle Lamonica	1.50	3.00
71 Alan Page	6.00	12.00
72 Pat Matson RC	.40	1.00
73 Emerson Boozer	.40	1.00
74 Pat Fischer	.40	1.00
75 Gary Collins	.50	1.25
76 John Fuqua RC	.50	1.25
77 Bruce Gossett	.40	1.00
78 Ed O'Bradovich	.40	1.00
79 Bob Tucker RC	.50	1.25
80 Mike Curtis	.50	1.25
81 Rich Jackson	.40	1.00
82 Tom Janik	.40	1.00
83 Gale Gillingham	.40	1.00
84 Jim Mitchell TE RC	.40	1.00
85 Charley Johnson	.50	1.25
86 Edgar Chandler RC	.40	1.00
87 Cyril Pinder RC	.40	1.00
88 Johnny Robinson	.50	1.25
89 Ralph Neely	.40	1.00
90 Dan Abramowicz	.40	1.00
91 Mercury Morris RC	5.00	10.00
92 Steve DeLong	.40	1.00
93 Larry Stallings	.40	1.00
94 Tom Mack	.75	2.00
95 Hewritt Dixon	.40	1.00
96 Fred Cox	.40	1.00
97 Chris Hanburger	.40	1.00
98 Gerry Philbin	.40	1.00
99 Ernie Wright	.40	1.00
100 John Brodie	2.00	4.00
101 Tucker Frederickson	.40	1.00
102 Bobby Walden	.40	1.00
103 Dick Gordon	.40	1.00
104 Walter Johnson	.40	1.00
105 Mike Lucci	.50	1.25
106 Checklist DP	3.00	6.00
107 Ron Berger RC	.40	1.00
108 Dan Sullivan RC	.40	1.00
109 George Kunz RC	.40	1.00
110 Floyd Little	.75	2.00
111 Zeke Bratkowski	.50	1.25
112 Haven Moses	.50	1.25
113 Ken Houston RC	7.50	15.00
114 Willie Lanier RC	7.50	15.00
115 Larry Brown	.75	2.00
116 Tim Rossovich	.40	1.00
117 Errol Linden RC	.40	1.00
118 Mel Renfro	.75	2.00
119 Mike Garrett	.40	1.00
120 Fran Tarkenton	7.50	15.00
121 Garo Yepremian RC	.75	2.00
122 Glen Condren RC	.40	1.00
123 Johnny Roland	.40	1.00
124 Dave Herman	.40	1.00
125 Merlin Olsen	1.50	3.00
126 Doug Buffone	.40	1.00
127 Earl McCullouch	.40	1.00
128 Spider Lockhart	.40	1.00
129 Ken Willard	.40	1.00
130 Gene Washington Vik	.40	1.00
131 Mike Phipps RC	.50	1.25
132 Andy Russell	.50	1.25
133 Ray Nitschke	2.00	6.00
134 Jerry Logan	.50	1.25
135 MacArthur Lane RC	.60	1.50
136 Jim Turner	.50	1.25
137 Kent McCloughan	.50	1.25
138 Paul Guidry	.50	1.25
139 Otis Taylor	.60	1.50
140 Virgil Carter RC	.50	1.25
141 Joe Dawkins RC	.50	1.25
142 Steve Preece RC	.50	1.25
143 Mike Bragg RC	.50	1.25
144 Bob Lilly	2.50	5.00
145 Joe Kapp	.60	1.50
146 Al Dodd	.50	1.25
147 Nick Buoniconti	1.25	2.50
148 Speedy Duncan	.50	1.25
149 Cedrick Hardman RC	.50	1.25
150 Gale Sayers	15.00	30.00
151 Jim Otto	1.25	2.50
152 Billy Truax	.50	1.25
153 John Elliott	.50	1.25
154 Dick LeBeau	1.25	2.50
155 Bill Bergey	.60	1.50
156 Terry Bradshaw RC !	125.00	200.00
157 Leroy Kelly	3.00	6.00
158 Paul Krause	1.25	2.50
159 Ted Vactor RC	.50	1.25
160 Bob Griese	7.50	15.00
161 Ernie McMillan	.50	1.25
162 Donny Anderson	.60	1.50
163 John Pitts RC	.50	1.25
164 Dave Costa	.50	1.25
165 Gene Washington 49er	.60	1.50
166 John Zook	.50	1.25
167 Pete Gogolak	.50	1.25
168 Erich Barnes	.50	1.25
169 Alvin Reed RC	.50	1.25
170 Jim Nance	.60	1.50
171 Craig Morton	1.25	2.50
172 Gary Garrison	.50	1.25
173 Joe Scarpati	.50	1.25
174 Adrian Young UER RC	.50	1.25
175 John Mackey	1.25	2.50
176 Mac Percival	.50	1.25
177 Preston Pearson RC	2.00	4.00
178 Fred Biletnikoff	4.00	8.00
179 Mike Battle RC	.50	1.25
180 Len Dawson	4.00	8.00
181 Les Josephson	.50	1.25
182 Royce Berry	.50	1.25
183 Herman Weaver RC	.50	1.25
184 Norm Snead	.60	1.50
185 Sam Brunelli	.50	1.25
186 Jim Kiick RC	2.50	5.00
187 Austin Denney RC	.50	1.25
188 Roger Wehrli RC	7.50	15.00
189 Dave Wilcox	1.25	2.50
190 Bob Hayes	2.00	4.00
191 Joe Morrison	.50	1.25
192 Manny Sistrunk RC	.50	1.25
193 Don Cockroft RC	.50	1.25
194 Lee Bouggess RC	.50	1.25
195 Bob Berry	.50	1.25
196 Ron Sellers RC	.50	1.25
197 George Webster	.50	1.25
198 Hoyle Granger	.50	1.25
199 Bob Vogel	.50	1.25
200 Bart Starr	10.00	25.00
201 Mike Mercer	.50	1.25
202 Dave Smith WR	.50	1.25
203 Lee Roy Caffey	.50	1.25
204 Mick Tingelhoff	.60	1.50
205 Matt Snell	.60	1.50
206 Jim Tyrer	.50	1.25
207 Willie Brown	1.25	2.50
208 Bob Johnson RC	.50	1.25
209 Deacon Jones	1.25	2.50
210 Charlie Sanders RC	6.00	12.00
211 Jake Scott RC	3.00	6.00
212 Bob Anderson RC	.50	1.25
213 Charlie Krueger	.50	1.25
214 Jim Bakken	.50	1.25
215 Harold Jackson	.60	1.50
216 Bill Brundige RC	.50	1.25
217 Calvin Hill	2.50	5.00
218 Claude Humphrey	.60	1.50
219 Glen Ray Hines	.50	1.25
220 Bill Nelsen	.60	1.50
221 Roy Hilton	.50	1.25
222 Don Herrmann	.50	1.25
223 John Bramlett	.50	1.25
224 Ken Ellis RC	.50	1.25
225 Dave Osborn	.60	1.50
226 Edd Hargett RC	.50	1.25
227 Gene Mingo	.50	1.25
228 Larry Grantham	.50	1.25
229 Dick Post	.50	1.25
230 Roman Gabriel	1.25	2.50

231 Mike Eischeid RC	.50	1.25
232 Jim Lynch	.50	1.25
233 Lemar Parrish RC	.60	1.50
234 Cecil Turner RC	.50	1.25
235 Dennis Shaw RC	.50	1.25
236 Mel Farr	.50	1.25
237 Curt Knight RC	.50	1.25
238 Chuck Howley	.60	1.50
239 Bruce Taylor RC	.50	1.25
240 Jerry LeVias	.50	1.25
241 Bob Lurtsema	.50	1.25
242 Earl Morrall	.60	1.50
243 Kermit Alexander	.50	1.25
244 Jackie Smith	1.25	2.50
245 Joe Greene RC	35.00	60.00
246 Harmon Wages	.50	1.25
247 Errol Mann	.50	1.25
248 Mike McCoy DT RC	.50	1.25
249 Milt Morin RC	.50	1.25
250 Joe Namath	35.00	60.00
251 Jackie Burkett	.50	1.25
252 Steve Chomyszak RC	.50	1.25
253 Ed Sharockman	.50	1.25
254 Robert Holmes RC	.50	1.25
255 John Hadl	1.25	2.50
256 Cornell Gordon	.50	1.25
257 Mark Moseley RC	.60	1.50
258 Gus Otto	.50	1.25
259 Mike Taliaferro	.50	1.25
260 O.J.Simpson	12.50	25.00
261 Paul Warfield	4.00	8.00
262 Jack Concannon	.50	1.25
263 Tom Matte	1.25	2.50

1971 Topps Game Inserts

The 1971 Topps Game cards were issued as inserts with the 1971 regular issue football cards. The cards measure 2 1/4" by 3 1/4" with rounded corners. The cards can be used for a table game of football. The 52 player cards in the set are numbered and have light blue backs. The 53rd card (actually unnumbered) is a field position/first down marker which is used in the table game. Six of the cards in the set were double printed and are marked as DP in the checklist below. The key card in the set is Terry Bradshaw, appearing in his Rookie Card year.

COMPLETE SET (53)	75.00	125.00
1 Dick Butkus DP	3.00	6.00
2 Bob Berry DP	.30	.60
3 Joe Namath DP	6.00	12.00
4 Mike Curtis	.30	.60
5 Jim Nance	.30	.60
6 Ron Berger	.30	.60
7 O.J. Simpson	7.50	15.00
8 Haven Moses	.50	1.00
9 Tommy Nobis	.50	1.00
10 Gale Sayers	6.00	12.00
11 Virgil Carter	.30	.60
12 Andy Russell DP	.30	.60
13 Bill Nelsen	.30	.60
14 Gary Collins	.30	.60
15 Duane Thomas	.50	1.00
16 Bob Hayes	1.00	2.00
17 Floyd Little	.50	1.00
18 Sam Brunelli	.30	.60
19 Charlie Sanders	.40	1.00
20 Mike Lucci	.30	.60
21 Gene Washington 49er	.50	1.00
22 Willie Wood	1.00	2.00
23 Jerry LeVias	.30	.60
24 Charley Johnson	.50	1.00
25 Len Dawson	2.00	4.00
26 Bobby Bell	1.00	2.00
27 Merlin Olsen	1.50	3.00
28 Roman Gabriel	1.00	2.00
29 Bob Griese	3.00	6.00
30 Larry Csonka	3.00	6.00
31 Dave Osborn	.30	.60
32 Gene Washington Vik	.30	.60
33 Dan Abramowicz	.30	.60
34 Tom Dempsey	.30	.60
35 Fran Tarkenton	4.00	8.00
36 Clifton McNeil	.30	.60
37 Johnny Unitas	7.50	15.00
38 Matt Snell	.50	1.00
39 Daryle Lamonica	1.00	2.00
40 Hewritt Dixon	.30	.60
41 Tom Woodeshick DP	.30	.60
42 Harold Jackson	.50	1.00
43 Terry Bradshaw	12.50	25.00
44 Ken Avery	.30	.60
45 MacArthur Lane	.30	.60
46 Larry Wilson	.50	1.00
47 John Hadl	.50	1.00
48 Lance Alworth	2.00	4.00
49 John Brodie	1.50	3.00
50 Bart Starr DP	4.00	8.00
51 Sonny Jurgensen	2.50	5.00
52 Larry Brown	.50	1.00
NNO Field Marker	.30	.60

1971 Topps Posters Inserts

The 1971 Topps Football pin-up posters are a set of 32 paper inserts each folded twice for insertion into gum packs. The cards (small posters) measure 4 7/8" by 6 7/8". The lower left hand corner of the obverse contains the pin-up number while the back features a green simulated football field upon which a football card game could be played as well as the instructions to accompany the card insert game. Inexplicably the second half of the set seems to be somewhat more difficult to find.

COMPLETE SET (32)	50.00	100.00
1 Gene Washington 49er	.75	1.50
2 Andy Russell	.75	1.50
3 Harold Jackson	.75	1.50
4 Joe Namath	7.50	15.00
5 Fran Tarkenton	2.00	4.00
6 Dave Osborn	.50	1.00
7 Bob Griese	2.50	5.00
8 Roman Gabriel	1.00	2.00
9 Jerry LeVias	.50	1.00
10 Bart Starr	6.00	12.00
11 Bob Hayes	1.50	3.00
12 Gale Sayers	4.00	8.00
13 O.J. Simpson	4.00	8.00
14 Sam Brunelli	.50	1.00
15 Jim Nance	.75	1.50
16 Bill Nelsen	.50	1.00
17 Sonny Jurgensen	2.00	4.00
18 John Brodie	2.00	4.00
19 Lance Alworth	2.50	5.00
20 Larry Wilson	1.50	3.00
21 Daryle Lamonica	1.50	3.00
22 Dan Abramowicz	1.00	2.00
23 Gene Washington Vik	1.00	2.00
24 Bobby Bell	2.00	4.00
25 Merlin Olsen	2.00	4.00
26 Charlie Sanders	1.25	2.50
27 Virgil Carter	1.00	2.00
28 Dick Butkus	4.00	8.00
29 Johnny Unitas	7.50	15.00
30 Tommy Nobis	1.50	3.00
31 Floyd Little	1.50	3.00
32 Larry Brown	1.00	2.00

1972 Topps

The 1972 Topps set contains 351 standard size cards that were issued in three series. The third series (264-351) is considerably more difficult to obtain than cards in the first two series. Card fronts are either horizontal and vertical and contain player photos that are bordered by a color that, for the most part, is part of the player's team color scheme. Vertical photos have team names at the top and horizontal photos have team names to the left. In either case, the player's name and position are at the bottom of the photo. The card backs are printed in blue and green on gray card stock. The backs have yearly statistics and a cartoon. Subsets include league leaders (1-8), In-Action cards (119-132, 250-263, 338-351), 1971 Playoffs (133-139) and All-Pro (264-287). The key Rookie Cards in this set are Lyle Alzado, L.C. Greenwood, Ted Hendricks, Charlie Joiner, Larry Little, Archie Manning, Jim Plunkett, John Riggins, Steve Spurrier, Roger Staubach, and Gene Upshaw. The cards were isssued in 10 cents wax packs.

COMPLETE SET (351)	1,500.00	2,500.00
WRAPPER (10-CENT)	6.00	10.00
WRAPPER SER.3 (10-CENT)	15.00	20.00
1 L.Csonka/Litt/Hubb LL	2.00	4.00
2 NFC Rushing Leaders	.25	.60
3 B.Griese/Dawson/Cart LL	.75	2.00
4 R.Staubach/Lan/Kil LL	2.50	5.00
5 AFC Receiving Leaders	.50	1.25
6 NFC Receiving Leaders	.25	.60
7 Yepre/Stener/O'Brien LL	.25	.60
8 NFC Scoring Leaders	.25	.60
9 Jim Kiick	.75	2.00
10 Otis Taylor	.50	1.25
11 Bobby Joe Green	.25	.60
12 Ken Ellis	.25	.60
13 John Riggins RC	10.00	20.00
14 Dave Parks	.25	.60
15 John Hadl	.75	2.00
16 Ron Hornsby RC	.25	.60
17 Chip Myers RC	.25	.60
18 Billy Kilmer	.75	2.00
19 Fred Hoaglin RC	.25	.60
20 Carl Eller	.75	2.00
21 Steve Zabel RC	.25	.60
22 Vic Washington RC	.25	.60
23 Len St. Jean	.25	.60
24 Bill Thompson	.25	.60
25 Steve Owens RC	1.25	3.00
26 Ken Burrough RC	.50	1.25
27 Mike Clark	.25	.60
28 Willie Brown	.75	2.00
29 Checklist 1-132	3.00	6.00
30 Marlin Briscoe RC	.25	.60
31 Jerry Logan	.25	.60
32 Donny Anderson	.50	1.25
33 Rich McGeorge RC	.25	.60
34 Charlie Durkee	.25	.60
35 Willie Lanier	2.00	4.00
36 Chris Farasopoulos RC	.25	.60
37 Ron Shanklin RC	.25	.60
38 Forrest Blue RC	.25	.60
39 Ken Reaves	.25	.60
40 Roman Gabriel	.75	2.00
41 Mac Percival	.25	.60
42 Lem Barney	1.50	3.00
43 Nick Buoniconti	.75	2.00
44 Charlie Gogolak	.25	.60
45 Bill Bradley RC	.50	1.25
46 Joe Jones DE RC	.25	.60
47 Dave Williams	.25	.60
48 Pete Athas RC	.25	.60
49 Virgil Carter	.25	.60
50 Floyd Little	.75	2.00
51 Curt Knight	.25	.60
52 Bobby Maples	.25	.60
53 Charlie West RC	.25	.60
54 Marv Hubbard RC	.50	1.25
55 Archie Manning RC	10.00	25.00
56 Jim O'Brien RC	.50	1.25
57 Wayne Patrick RC	.25	.60
58 Ken Bowman	.25	.60
59 Roger Wehrli	.50	1.25
60 Charlie Sanders	.50	1.25
61 Jan Stenerud	.75	2.00
62 Willie Ellison RC	.25	.60
63 Walt Sweeney	.25	.60
64 Ron Smith	.25	.60
65 Jim Plunkett RC	10.00	20.00
66 Herb Adderley UER	.75	2.00
67 Mike Reid RC	.75	2.00
68 Richard Caster RC	.50	1.25
69 Dave Wilcox	.75	2.00
70 Leroy Kelly	1.50	3.00
71 Bob Lee RC	.25	.60
72 Verlon Biggs	.25	.60
73 Henry Allison RC	.25	.60
74 Steve Ramsey RC	.25	.60
75 Claude Humphrey	.60	1.50
76 Bob Grim RC	.25	.60
77 John Fuqua	.50	1.25
78 Ken Houston	2.00	4.00
79 Checklist 133-263 DP	2.50	5.00
80 Bob Griese	4.00	8.00
81 Lance Rentzel	.50	1.25
82 Ed Podolak RC	.50	1.25
83 Ike Hill RC	.25	.60
84 George Farmer RC	.25	.60
85 John Brockington RC	.75	2.00
86 Jim Otto	.75	2.00
87 Richard Neal RC	.25	.60
88 Jim Hart	.75	2.00
89 Bob Babich RC	.25	.60
90 Gene Washington 49er	.50	1.25
91 John Zook	.25	.60
92 Bobby Duhon RC	.25	.60
93 Ted Hendricks RC	7.50	15.00
94 Rockne Freitas	.25	.60
95 Larry Brown	.75	2.00
96 Mike Phipps	.50	1.25
97 Julius Adams RC	.25	.60
98 Dick Anderson	.50	1.25
99 Fred Willis RC	.25	.60
100 Joe Namath	20.00	35.00
101 L.C. Greenwood RC	7.50	15.00
102 Mark Nordquist RC	.25	.60
103 Robert Holmes	.25	.60
104 Ron Yary RC	2.00	5.00
105 Bob Hayes	1.00	2.50
106 Lyle Alzado RC	7.50	15.00
107 Bob Berry	.25	.60
108 Phil Villapiano RC	.50	1.25
109 Dave Elmendorf RC	.25	.60
110 Gale Sayers	10.00	20.00
111 Jim Tyrer	.25	.60
112 Mel Gray RC	.75	2.00
113 Gerry Philbin	.25	.60
114 Bob James RC	.25	.60
115 Garo Yepremian	.50	1.25
116 Dave Robinson	.50	1.25
117 Jeff Queen RC	.25	.60
118 Norm Snead	.50	1.25
119 Jim Nance IA	.50	1.25
120 Terry Bradshaw IA	7.50	15.00
121 Jim Kiick IA	.50	1.25
122 Roger Staubach IA	12.00	20.00
123 Bo Scott IA	.25	.60
124 John Brodie IA	.75	2.00
125 Rick Volk IA	.25	.60
126 John Riggins IA	3.00	6.00
127 Bubba Smith IA	.75	2.00
128 Roman Gabriel IA	.50	1.25
129 Calvin Hill IA	.50	1.25
130 Bill Nelsen IA	.25	.60
131 Tom Matte IA	.50	1.25
132 Bob Griese IA	2.00	4.00
133 AFC Semi-Final	.50	1.25
134 NFC Semi-Final	.50	1.25
135 AFC Semi-Final	.50	1.25
136 NFC Semi-Final	.50	1.25
137 AFC Title Game/Unitas	1.50	3.00
138 NFC Title Game/Bob Lilly	.75	2.00
139 Super Bowl VI/Staubach	2.50	5.00
140 Larry Csonka	4.00	8.00
141 Rick Volk	.30	.75
142 Roy Jefferson	.50	1.25
143 Raymond Chester RC	.50	1.25
144 Bobby Douglass	.30	.75
145 Bob Lilly	2.50	5.00
146 Harold Jackson	.50	1.25
147 Pete Gogolak	.30	.75
148 Art Malone RC	.30	.75
149 Ed Flanagan	.30	.75
150 Terry Bradshaw	25.00	40.00
151 MacArthur Lane	.50	1.25
152 Jack Snow	.50	1.25
153 Al Beauchamp RC	.30	.75
154 Bob Anderson	.30	.75
155 Ted Kwalick RC	.30	.75
156 Dan Pastorini RC	1.00	2.50
157 Emmitt Thomas RC	10.00	20.00
158 Randy Vataha RC	.30	.75
159 Al Atkinson	.30	.75
160 O.J. Simpson	7.50	15.00
161 Jackie Smith	.75	2.00
162 Ernie Kellerman	.30	.75
163 Dennis Partee	.30	.75
164 Jake Kupp	.30	.75
165 John Unitas	12.50	25.00
166 Clint Jones RC	.30	.75
167 Paul Warfield	3.00	6.00
168 Roland McDole RC	.30	.75
169 Daryle Lamonica	.75	2.00
170 Dick Butkus	7.50	15.00
171 Jim Butler	.30	.75
172 Mike McCoy	.30	.75
173 Dave Smith WR	.30	.75
174 Greg Landry	.50	1.25
175 Tom Dempsey	.50	1.25
176 John Charles	.30	.75
177 Bobby Bell	.75	2.00
178 Don Horn	.30	.75
179 Bob Trumpy	.75	2.00
180 Duane Thomas	.50	1.25
181 Merlin Olsen	1.50	3.00
182 Dave Herman	.30	.75
183 Jim Nance	.50	1.25
184 Pete Beathard	.30	.75
185 Bob Tucker	.30	.75
186 Gene Upshaw RC	7.50	15.00
187 Bo Scott	.30	.75
188 J.D. Hill RC	.30	.75
189 Bruce Gossett	.30	.75
190 Bubba Smith	2.00	4.00
191 Edd Hargett	.30	.75
192 Gary Garrison	.30	.75
193 Jake Scott	.50	1.25
194 Fred Cox	.30	.75
195 Sonny Jurgensen	2.00	4.00
196 Greg Brezina RC	.30	.75
197 Ed O'Bradovich	.30	.75
198 John Rowser RC	.30	.75
199 Altie Taylor UER	.30	.75
200 Roger Staubach RC	100.00	175.00
201 Leroy Keyes RC	.30	.75
202 Garland Boyette	.30	.75
203 Tom Beer	.30	.75
204 Buck Buchanan	.75	2.00
205 Larry Wilson	.75	2.00
206 Scott Hunter RC	.30	.75
207 Ron Johnson	.30	.75
208 Sam Brunelli	.30	.75
209 Deacon Jones	.75	2.00
210 Fred Biletnikoff	3.00	6.00
211 Bill Nelsen	.50	1.25
212 George Nock RC	.30	.75
213 Dan Abramowicz	.50	1.25
214 Irv Goode	.30	.75
215 Isiah Robertson RC	.50	1.25
216 Tom Matte	.50	1.25
217 Pat Fischer	.30	.75
218 Gene Washington Vik	.30	.75
219 Paul Robinson	.30	.75
220 John Brodie	2.00	4.00
221 Manny Fernandez RC	.50	1.25
222 Errol Mann	.30	.75
223 Dick Gordon	.30	.75
224 Calvin Hill	.75	2.00
225 Fran Tarkenton	6.00	12.00
226 Jim Turner	.30	.75
227 Jim Mitchell	.30	.75
228 Pete Liske	.30	.75
229 Carl Garrett	.30	.75
230 Joe Greene	10.00	20.00
231 Gale Gillingham	.30	.75
232 Norm Bulaich RC	.50	1.25
233 Spider Lockhart	.30	.75
234 Ken Willard	.30	.75
235 George Blanda	6.00	12.00
236 Wayne Mulligan RC	.30	.75
237 Dave Lewis RC	.30	.75
238 Dennis Shaw	.30	.75
239 Fair Hooker RC	.30	.75
240 Larry Little RC	7.50	15.00
241 Mike Garrett	.30	.75
242 Glen Ray Hines	.30	.75
243 Myron Pottios	.30	.75
244 Charlie Joiner RC	10.00	20.00
245 Len Dawson	3.00	6.00
246 W.K. Hicks	.30	.75
247 Les Josephson	.30	.75
248 Lance Alworth UER	3.00	6.00
249 Frank Nunley RC	.30	.75
250 Mel Farr IA	.30	.75
251 Johnny Unitas IA	4.00	8.00
252 George Farmer IA	.30	.75
253 Duane Thomas IA	.50	1.25
254 John Hadl IA	.75	2.00
255 Vic Washington IA	.30	.75

256 Don Horn IA	.30	.75
257 L.C. Greenwood IA	.75	2.00
258 Bob Lee IA	.30	.75
259 Larry Csonka IA	2.00	4.00
260 Mike McCoy IA	.30	.75
261 Greg Landry IA	.50	1.25
262 Ray May IA	.30	.75
263 Bobby Douglass IA	.30	.75
264 Charlie Sanders AP	15.00	30.00
265 Ron Yary AP	15.00	30.00
266 Rayfield Wright AP	20.00	40.00
267 Larry Little AP	20.00	35.00
268 John Niland AP	15.00	30.00
269 Forrest Blue AP	15.00	30.00
270 Otis Taylor AP	15.00	30.00
271 Paul Warfield AP	30.00	50.00
272 Bob Griese AP	40.00	70.00
273 John Brockington AP	15.00	30.00
274 Floyd Little AP	15.00	30.00
275 Garo Yepremian AP	15.00	30.00
276 Jerrel Wilson AP	10.00	18.00
277 Carl Eller AP	15.00	30.00
278 Bubba Smith AP	25.00	40.00
279 Alan Page AP	25.00	40.00
280 Bob Lilly AP	30.00	60.00
281 Ted Hendricks AP	30.00	50.00
282 Dave Wilcox AP	15.00	30.00
283 Willie Lanier AP	20.00	35.00
284 Jim Johnson AP	15.00	30.00
285 Willie Brown AP	20.00	35.00
286 Bill Bradley AP	15.00	30.00
287 Ken Houston AP	20.00	35.00
288 Mel Farr	10.00	18.00
289 Kermit Alexander	10.00	18.00
290 John Gilliam RC	15.00	30.00
291 Steve Spurrier RC	50.00	100.00
292 Walter Johnson	10.00	18.00
293 Jack Pardee	12.50	25.00
294 Checklist UER	50.00	80.00
295 Winston Hill	10.00	18.00
296 Hugo Hollas RC	10.00	18.00
297 Ray May RC	10.00	18.00
298 Jim Bakken	10.00	18.00
299 Larry Carwell RC	10.00	18.00
300 Alan Page	30.00	50.00
301 Walt Garrison	12.50	25.00
302 Mike Lucci	12.50	25.00
303 Nemiah Wilson	10.00	18.00
304 Carroll Dale	12.50	25.00
305 Jim Kanicki	10.00	18.00
306 Preston Pearson	15.00	30.00
307 Lemar Parrish	12.50	25.00
308 Earl Morrall	12.50	25.00
309 Tommy Nobis	12.50	25.00
310 Rich Jackson	10.00	18.00
311 Doug Cunningham RC	10.00	18.00
312 Jim Marsalis RC	10.00	18.00
313 Jim Beirne	10.00	18.00
314 Tom McNeill RC	10.00	18.00
315 Milt Morin	10.00	18.00
316 Rayfield Wright RC	30.00	50.00
317 Jerry LeVias	12.50	25.00
318 Travis Williams RC	12.50	25.00
319 Edgar Chandler	10.00	18.00
320 Bob Wallace RC	10.00	18.00
321 Delles Howell RC	10.00	18.00
322 Emerson Boozer	12.50	25.00
323 George Atkinson RC	12.50	25.00
324 Mike Montler RC	10.00	18.00
325 Randy Johnson	10.00	18.00
326 Mike Curtis UER	12.50	25.00
327 Miller Farr	10.00	18.00
328 Horst Muhlmann	10.00	18.00
329 John Niland RC	15.00	30.00
330 Andy Russell	15.00	30.00
331 Mercury Morris	25.00	40.00
332 Jim Johnson	15.00	30.00
333 Jerrel Wilson	10.00	18.00
334 Charley Taylor	25.00	40.00
335 Dick LeBeau	10.00	18.00
336 Jim Marshall	15.00	30.00
337 Tom Mack	15.00	30.00
338 Steve Spurrier IA	30.00	60.00
339 Floyd Little IA	12.50	25.00
340 Len Dawson IA	25.00	40.00
341 Dick Butkus IA	40.00	70.00
342 Larry Brown IA	12.50	25.00
343 Joe Namath IA	75.00	150.00
344 Jim Turner IA	10.00	18.00
345 Doug Cunningham IA	10.00	18.00
346 Edd Hargett IA	10.00	18.00
347 Steve Owens IA	10.00	18.00
348 George Blanda IA	30.00	50.00
349 Ed Podolak IA	10.00	18.00
350 Rich Jackson IA	10.00	18.00
351 Ken Willard IA	25.00	40.00

1973 Topps

The 1973 set marks the first of ten years in a row that Topps produced a 528-card football standard-size set issued in a single series. The fronts have the players name at the top and position and team name at the bottom. The player's first name and team name are in a color that corresponds to one of the colors in a small banner-like design that emanates from the photo. The card backs are printed in blue ink with a red background on gray card stock. Highlights and statistics are accompanied by a cartoon and trivia question and answer. The first six cards in the set are statistical league leader cards. Cards 133-139 show the results of the previous season's playoff games. Cards 265-267 are Kid Pictures (KP) showing the player in a boyhood photo. Rookie Cards include this set are Ken Anderson, Al Cowlings, Dan Dierdorf, Jack Ham, Franco Harris, Jim Langer, Art Shell, Ken Stabler, and Jack Youngblood. An uncut sheet of team checklist cards was also available via a mail-in offer on wax pack wrappers.

COMPLETE SET (528)	200.00	400.00
1 Simpson/L.Brown LL	3.00	8.00
2 Passing Leaders	.40	1.00
3 Jackson/Biletnikoff LL	.60	1.50
4 Scoring Leaders	.25	.60
5 Interception Leaders	.25	.60
6 Punting Leaders	.25	.60
7 Bob Trumpy	.60	1.50
8 Mel Tom RC	.25	.60
9 Clarence Ellis RC	.25	.60
10 John Niland	.25	.60
11 Randy Jackson RC	.25	.60
12 Greg Landry	.60	1.50
13 Cid Edwards RC	.25	.60
14 Phil Olsen RC	.25	.60
15 Terry Bradshaw	15.00	25.00
16 Al Cowlings RC	.60	1.50
17 Walker Gillette RC	.25	.60
18 Bob Atkins RC	.25	.60
19 Diron Talbert RC	.25	.60
20 Jim Johnson	.60	1.50
21 Howard Twilley	.40	1.00
22 Dick Enderle RC	.25	.60
23 Wayne Colman RC	.25	.60
24 John Schmitt RC	.25	.60
25 George Blanda	5.00	10.00
26 Milt Morin	.25	.60
27 Mike Current	.25	.60
28 Rex Kern RC	.25	.60
29 MacArthur Lane	.40	1.00
30 Alan Page	1.50	3.00
31 Randy Vataha	.25	.60
32 Jim Kearney RC	.25	.60
33 Steve Smith T RC	.25	.60
34 Ken Anderson RC	7.50	15.00
35 Calvin Hill	.60	1.50
36 Andy Maurer RC	.25	.60
37 Joe Taylor RC	.25	.60
38 Deacon Jones	.60	1.50
39 Mike Weger RC	.25	.60
40 Roy Gerela	.40	1.00
41 Les Josephson	.25	.60
42 Dave Washington RC	.25	.60
43 Bill Curry RC	.40	1.00
44 Fred Heron RC	.25	.60
45 John Brodie	1.50	3.00
46 Roy Winston	.25	.60
47 Mike Bragg	.25	.60
48 Mercury Morris	.60	1.50
49 Jim Files RC	.25	.60
50 Gene Upshaw	1.50	3.00
51 Hugo Hollas	.25	.60
52 Rod Sherman RC	.25	.60
53 Ron Snidow	.25	.60
54 Steve Tannen RC	.25	.60
55 Jim Carter RC	.25	.60
56 Lydell Mitchell RC	.60	1.50
57 Jack Rudnay RC	.25	.60
58 Halvor Hagen RC	.25	.60
59 Tom Dempsey	.40	1.00
60 Fran Tarkenton	5.00	10.00
61 Lance Alworth	2.50	5.00
62 Vern Holland RC	.25	.60
63 Steve DeLong	.25	.60
64 Art Malone	.25	.60
65 Isiah Robertson	.40	1.00
66 Jerry Rush	.25	.60
67 Bryant Salter RC	.25	.60
68 Checklist 1-132	2.50	5.00
69 J.D. Hill	.25	.60
70 Forrest Blue	.25	.60
71 Myron Pottios	.25	.60
72 Norm Thompson RC	.25	.60
73 Paul Robinson	.25	.60
74 Larry Grantham	.25	.60
75 Manny Fernandez	.40	1.00
76 Kent Nix RC	.25	.60
77 Art Shell RC	7.50	15.00
78 George Saimes	.25	.60
79 Don Cockroft	.25	.60
80 Bob Tucker	.40	1.00
81 Don McCauley RC	.25	.60
82 Bob Brown DT RC	.25	.60
83 Larry Carwell	.25	.60
84 Mo Moorman RC	.25	.60
85 John Gilliam	.40	1.00
86 Wade Key RC	.25	.60
87 Ross Brupbacher RC	.25	.60
88 Dave Lewis	.25	.60
89 Franco Harris RC	25.00	50.00
90 Tom Mack	.60	1.50
91 Mike Tilleman	.25	.60
92 Carl Mauck RC	.25	.60
93 Larry Hand	.25	.60
94 Dave Foley RC	.25	.60
95 Frank Nunley	.25	.60
96 John Charles	.25	.60
97 Jim Bakken	.25	.60
98 Pat Fischer	.40	1.00
99 Randy Rasmussen RC	.25	.60
100 Larry Csonka	3.00	6.00
101 Mike Siani RC	.25	.60
102 Tom Roussel RC	.25	.60
103 Clarence Scott RC	.40	1.00
104 Charley Johnson	.40	1.00
105 Rick Volk	.25	.60
106 Willie Young RC	.25	.60
107 Emmitt Thomas	.60	1.50
108 Jon Morris	.25	.60
109 Clarence Williams RC	.25	.60
110 Rayfield Wright	.40	1.00
111 Norm Bulaich	.25	.60
112 Mike Eischeid	.25	.60
113 Speedy Thomas RC	.25	.60
114 Glen Holloway RC	.25	.60
115 Jack Ham RC	15.00	30.00
116 Jim Nettles RC	.25	.60
117 Errol Mann	.25	.60
118 John Mackey	.60	1.50
119 George Kunz	.25	.60
120 Bob James	.25	.60
121 Garland Boyette	.25	.60
122 Mel Phillips RC	.25	.60
123 Johnny Roland	.25	.60
124 Doug Swift RC	.25	.60
125 Archie Manning	2.00	4.00
126 Dave Herman	.25	.60
127 Carleton Oats RC	.25	.60
128 Bill Van Heusen	.25	.60
129 Rich Jackson	.25	.60
130 Len Hauss	.40	1.00
131 Billy Parks RC	.25	.60
132 Ray May	.25	.60
133 NFC Semi/R.Staubach	2.00	5.00
134 AFC Semi/Immac.Rec.	1.00	2.50
135 NFC Semi-Final	.40	1.00
136 AFC Semi/L.Csonka	.75	2.00
137 NFC Title Game/Kilmer	.60	1.50
138 AFC Title Game	.40	1.00
139 Super Bowl VII	.60	1.50
140 Dwight White RC	2.00	5.00
141 Jim Marsalis	.25	.60
142 Doug Van Horn RC	.25	.60
143 Al Matthews RC	.25	.60
144 Bob Windsor RC	.25	.60
145 Dave Hampton RC	.25	.60
146 Horst Muhlmann	.25	.60
147 Wally Hilgenberg RC	.25	.60
148 Ron Smith	.25	.60
149 Coy Bacon RC	.40	1.00
150 Winston Hill	.25	.60
151 Ron Jessie RC	.40	1.00
152 Ken Iman	.25	.60
153 Ron Saul RC	.25	.60
154 Jim Braxton RC	.40	1.00
155 Bubba Smith	1.25	2.50
156 Gary Cuozzo	.40	1.00
157 Charlie Krueger	.40	1.00
158 Tim Foley RC	.40	1.00
159 Lee Roy Jordan	.60	1.50
160 Bob Brown OT	.60	1.50
161 Margene Adkins RC	.25	.60
162 Ron Widby RC	.25	.60
163 Jim Houston	.25	.60
164 Joe Dawkins	.25	.60
165 L.C. Greenwood	2.00	4.00
166 Richmond Flowers RC	.25	.60
167 Curley Culp RC	6.00	20.00
168 Len St. Jean	.25	.60
169 Walter Rock	.25	.60
170 Bill Bradley	.40	1.00
171 Ken Riley RC	.60	1.50
172 Rich Coady RC	.25	.60
173 Don Hansen RC	.25	.60
174 Lionel Aldridge	.25	.60
175 Don Maynard	2.00	4.00
176 Dave Osborn	.40	1.00
177 Jim Bailey	.25	.60
178 John Pitts	.25	.60
179 Dave Parks	.25	.60
180 Chester Marcol RC	.25	.60
181 Len Rohde RC	.25	.60
182 Jeff Staggs RC	.25	.60
183 Gene Hickerson	.60	1.25
184 Charlie Evans RC	.25	.60
185 Mel Renfro	.60	1.50
186 Marvin Upshaw RC	.25	.60
187 George Atkinson	.40	1.00
188 Norm Evans	.40	1.00
189 Steve Ramsey	.25	.60
190 Dave Chapple RC	.25	.60
191 Gerry Mullins RC	.25	.60
192 John Didion RC	.25	.60
193 Bob Gladieux RC	.25	.60
194 Don Hultz	.25	.60
195 Mike Lucci	.25	.60
196 John Wilbur RC	.25	.60
197 George Farmer	.25	.60
198 Tommy Casanova RC	.40	1.00
199 Russ Washington	.25	.60
200 Claude Humphrey	.60	1.50
201 Pat Hughes RC	.25	.60
202 Zeke Moore	.25	.60
203 Chip Glass RC	.25	.60
204 Glenn Ressler RC	.25	.60
205 Willie Ellison	.40	1.00
206 John Leypoldt RC	.25	.60
207 Johnny Fuller RC	.25	.60
208 Bill Hayhoe RC	.25	.60
209 Ed Bell RC	.25	.60
210 Willie Brown	.60	1.50
211 Carl Eller	.60	1.50
212 Mark Nordquist	.25	.60
213 Larry Willingham RC	.25	.60
214 Nick Buoniconti	.60	1.50
215 John Hadl	.60	1.50
216 Jethro Pugh RC	.60	1.50
217 Leroy Mitchell	.25	.60
218 Billy Newsome RC	.25	.60
219 John McMakin RC	.25	.60
220 Larry Brown	.60	1.50
221 Clarence Scott RC	.25	.60
222 Paul Naumoff RC	.25	.60
223 Ted Fritsch Jr. RC	.25	.60
224 Checklist 133-264	2.50	5.00
225 Dan Pastorini	.60	1.50
226 Joe Beauchamp UER RC	.25	.60
227 Pat Matson	.25	.60
228 Tony McGee DT RC	.25	.60
229 Mike Phipps	.40	1.00
230 Harold Jackson	.60	1.50
231 Willie Williams RC	.25	.60
232 Spike Jones	.25	.60
233 Jim Tyrer	.25	.60
234 Roy Hilton	.25	.60
235 Phil Villapiano	.40	1.00
236 Charley Taylor UER	1.50	3.00
237 Malcolm Snider RC	.25	.60
238 Vic Washington	.25	.60
239 Grady Alderman	.25	.60
240 Dick Anderson	.40	1.00
241 Ron Yankowski RC	.25	.60
242 Billy Masters RC	.25	.60
243 Herb Adderley	.60	1.50
244 David Ray RC	.25	.60
245 John Riggins	4.00	8.00
246 Mike Wagner RC	1.25	3.00
247 Don Morrison RC	.25	.60
248 Earl McCullouch	.25	.60
249 Dennis Wirgowski RC	.25	.60
250 Chris Hanburger	.40	1.00
251 Pat Sullivan RC	.60	1.50
252 Walt Sweeney	.25	.60
253 Willie Alexander RC	.25	.60
254 Doug Dressler RC	.25	.60
255 Walter Johnson	.25	.60
256 Ron Hornsby	.25	.60
257 Ben Hawkins	.25	.60
258 Donnie Green RC	.25	.60
259 Fred Hoaglin	.25	.60
260 Jerrel Wilson	.25	.60
261 Horace Jones	.25	.60
262 Woody Peoples	.25	.60
263 Jim Hill RC	.25	.60
264 John Fuqua	.25	.60
265 Donny Anderson KP	.40	1.00
266 Roman Gabriel KP	.60	1.50
267 Mike Garrett KP	.40	1.00
268 Rufus Mayes RC	.25	.60
269 Chip Myrtle RC	.25	.60
270 Bill Stanfill RC	.40	1.00
271 Clint Jones	.25	.60
272 Miller Farr	.25	.60
273 Harry Schuh	.25	.60
274 Bob Hayes	.75	2.00
275 Bobby Douglass	.40	1.00
276 Gus Hollomon RC	.25	.60
277 Del Williams RC	.25	.60
278 Julius Adams	.25	.60
279 Herman Weaver	.25	.60
280 Joe Greene	4.00	8.00
281 Wes Chesson RC	.25	.60
282 Charlie Harraway RC	.25	.60
283 Paul Guidry	.25	.60
284 Terry Owens RC	.25	.60
285 Jan Stenerud	.60	1.50
286 Pete Athas	.25	.60
287 Dale Lindsey RC	.25	.60
288 Jack Tatum RC	6.00	20.00
289 Floyd Little	.60	1.50
290 Bob Johnson	.25	.60
291 Tommy Hart RC	.25	.60
292 Tom Mitchell RC	.25	.60
293 Walt Patulski RC	.25	.60
294 Jim Skaggs	.25	.60
295 Bob Griese	3.00	6.00
296 Mike McCoy	.25	.60
297 Mel Gray	.40	1.00
298 Bobby Bryant RC	.25	.60
299 Blaine Nye RC	.25	.60
300 Dick Butkus	6.00	12.00
301 Charlie Cowan RC	.25	.60
302 Mark Lomas RC	.25	.60
303 Josh Ashton RC	.25	.60
304 Happy Feller RC	.25	.60
305 Ron Shanklin	.25	.60
306 Wayne Rasmussen	.25	.60
307 Jerry Smith	.25	.60
308 Ken Reaves	.25	.60
309 Ron East RC	.25	.60
310 Otis Taylor	.60	1.50
311 John Garlington RC	.25	.60
312 Lyle Alzado	2.00	4.00
313 Remi Prudhomme RC	.25	.60
314 Cornelius Johnson RC	.25	.60
315 Lemar Parrish	.40	1.00
316 Jim Kiick	.60	1.50
317 Steve Zabel	.25	.60
318 Alden Roche RC	.25	.60
319 Tom Blanchard RC	.25	.60
320 Fred Biletnikoff	2.00	4.00
321 Ralph Neely	.40	1.00
322 Dan Dierdorf RC	7.50	20.00
323 Richard Caster	.40	1.00
324 Gene Howard	.25	.60
325 Elvin Bethea	.60	1.50
326 Carl Garrett	.40	1.00
327 Ron Billingsley RC	.25	.60
328 Charlie West	.25	.60
329 Tom Neville	.25	.60

330 Ted Kwalick .40 1.00
331 Rudy Redmond RC .25 .60
332 Henry Davis RC .25 .60
333 John Zook .25 .60
334 Jim Turner .25 .60
335 Len Dawson 2.50 5.00
336 Bob Chandler RC .40 1.00
337 Al Beauchamp .25 .60
338 Tom Matte .40 1.00
339 Paul Laaveg RC .25 .60
340 Ken Ellis .25 .60
341 Jim Langer RC 6.00 12.00
342 Ron Porter .25 .60
343 Jack Youngblood RC 7.50 15.00
344 Cornell Green .60 1.50
345 Marv Hubbard .40 1.00
346 Bruce Taylor .25 .60
347 Sam Havrilak RC .25 .60
348 Walt Sumner RC .25 .60
349 Steve O'Neal RC .25 .60
350 Ron Johnson .40 1.00
351 Rockne Freitas .25 .60
352 Larry Stallings .25 .60
353 Jim Cadile .25 .60
354 Ken Burrough .40 1.00
355 Jim Plunkett 2.00 4.00
356 Dave Long RC .25 .60
357 Ralph Anderson RC .25 .60
358 Checklist 265-396 2.50 5.00
359 Gene Washington Vik .40 1.00
360 Dave Wilcox .60 1.50
361 Paul Smith RC .25 .60
362 Alvin Wyatt RC .25 .60
363 Charlie Smith RB .25 .60
364 Royce Berry .25 .60
365 Dave Elmendorf .25 .60
366 Scott Hunter .40 1.00
367 Bob Kuechenberg RC 1.25 3.00
368 Pete Gogolak .25 .60
369 Dave Edwards .25 .60
370 Lem Barney 1.25 2.50
371 Verlon Biggs .25 .60
372 John Reaves RC .25 .60
373 Ed Podolak .40 1.00
374 Chris Farasopoulos .25 .60
375 Gary Garrison .25 .60
376 Tom Funchess RC .25 .60
377 Bobby Joe Green .25 .60
378 Don Brumm .25 .60
379 Jim O'Brien .25 .60
380 Paul Krause .60 1.50
381 Leroy Kelly 1.25 2.50
382 Ray Mansfield .25 .60
383 Dan Abramowicz .40 1.00
384 John Outlaw RC .25 .60
385 Tommy Nobis .60 1.50
386 Tom Domres RC .25 .60
387 Ken Willard .25 .60
388 Mike Stratton .25 .60
389 Fred Dryer 1.25 2.50
390 Jake Scott .60 1.50
391 Rich Houston RC .25 .60
392 Virgil Carter .25 .60
393 Tody Smith RC .25 .60
394 Ernie Calloway RC .25 .60
395 Charlie Sanders .60 1.50
396 Fred Willis .25 .60
397 Curt Knight .25 .60
398 Nemiah Wilson .25 .60
399 Carroll Dale .40 1.00
400 Joe Namath 18.00 35.00
401 Wayne Mulligan .25 .60
402 Jim Harrison RC .25 .60
403 Tim Rossovich .25 .60
404 David Lee .25 .60
405 Frank Pitts RC .25 .60
406 Jim Marshall .60 1.50
407 Bob Brown TE .25 .60
408 John Rowser .25 .60
409 Mike Montler .25 .60
410 Willie Lanier .60 1.50
411 Bill Bell K RC .25 .60
412 Cedrick Hardman .25 .60
413 Bob Anderson .25 .60
414 Earl Morrall .60 1.50
415 Ken Houston .60 1.50
416 Jack Snow .40 1.00
417 Dick Cunningham RC .25 .60
418 Greg Larson .25 .60
419 Mike Bass RC .40 1.00
420 Mike Reid .60 1.50
421 Walt Garrison .60 1.50
422 Pete Liske .25 .60
423 Jim Yarbrough RC .25 .60
424 Rich McGeorge .25 .60
425 Bobby Howfield RC .25 .60
426 Pete Banaszak .25 .60
427 Willie Holman RC .25 .60
428 Dale Hackbart .25 .60
429 Fair Hooker .25 .60
430 Ted Hendricks 2.50 5.00
431 Mike Garrett .40 1.00
432 Glen Ray Hines .25 .60
433 Fred Cox .25 .60
434 Bobby Walden .25 .60
435 Bobby Bell .60 1.50
436 Dave Rowe .25 .60
437 Bob Berry .25 .60
438 Bill Thompson .25 .60
439 Jim Beirne .25 .60
440 Larry Little 1.50 3.00
441 Rocky Thompson RC .25 .60
442 Brig Owens .25 .60
443 Richard Neal .25 .60
444 Al Nelson .25 .60
445 Chip Myers .25 .60
446 Ken Bowman .25 .60
447 Jim Purnell RC .25 .60
448 Altie Taylor .25 .60
449 Linzy Cole .25 .60
450 Bob Lilly 2.50 5.00
451 Charlie Ford RC .25 .60
452 Milt Sunde .25 .60
453 Doug Wyatt RC .25 .60
454 Don Nottingham RC .40 1.00
455 John Unitas 7.50 15.00
456 Frank Lewis RC .40 1.00
457 Roger Wehrli .40 1.00
458 Jim Cheyunski RC .25 .60
459 Jerry Sherk RC .40 1.00
460 Gene Washington 49er .40 1.00
461 Jim Otto .60 1.50
462 Ed Budde .25 .60
463 Jim Mitchell .40 1.00
464 Emerson Boozer .40 1.00
465 Garo Yepremian .60 1.50
466 Pete Duranko .25 .60
467 Charlie Joiner 4.00 8.00
468 Spider Lockhart .40 1.00
469 Marty Domres .25 .60
470 John Brockington .60 1.50
471 Ed Flanagan .25 .60
472 Roy Jefferson .40 1.00
473 Julian Fagan RC .25 .60
474 Bill Brown .40 1.00
475 Roger Staubach 15.00 30.00
476 Jan White RC .25 .60
477 Pat Holmes RC .25 .60
478 Bob DeMarco .25 .60
479 Merlin Olsen 1.25 2.50
480 Andy Russell .60 1.50
481 Steve Spurrier 10.00 20.00
482 Nate Ramsey .25 .60
483 Dennis Partee .25 .60
484 Jerry Simmons .25 .60
485 Donny Anderson .60 1.50
486 Ralph Baker .25 .60
487 Ken Stabler RC 35.00 60.00
488 Ernie McMillan .25 .60
489 Ken Burrow RC .25 .60
490 Jack Gregory RC .25 .60
491 Larry Seiple .40 1.00
492 Mick Tingelhoff .40 1.00
493 Craig Morton .60 1.50
494 Cecil Turner .25 .60
495 Steve Owens .60 1.50
496 Rickie Harris .25 .60
497 Buck Buchanan .60 1.50
498 Checklist 397-528 2.50 5.00
499 Billy Kilmer .60 1.50
500 O.J. Simpson 7.50 15.00
501 Bruce Gossett .25 .60
502 Art Thoms RC .25 .60
503 Larry Kaminski RC .25 .60
504 Larry Smith RB RC .25 .60
505 Bruce Van Dyke RC .25 .60
506 Alvin Reed .25 .60
507 Delles Howell .25 .60
508 Leroy Keyes .25 .60
509 Bo Scott .40 1.00
510 Ron Yary .60 1.50
511 Paul Warfield 2.50 5.00
512 Mac Percival .25 .60
513 Essex Johnson RC .25 .60
514 Jackie Smith .60 1.50
515 Norm Snead .60 1.50
516 Charlie Stukes RC .25 .60
517 Reggie Rucker RC .40 1.00
518 Bill Sandeman UER RC .25 .60
519 Mel Farr .40 1.00
520 Raymond Chester .40 1.00
521 Fred Carr RC .40 1.00
522 Jerry LeVias .40 1.00
523 Jim Strong RC .25 .60
524 Roland McDole .25 .60
525 Dennis Shaw .25 .60
526 Dave Manders .25 .60
527 Skip Vanderbundt RC .25 .60
528 Mike Sensibaugh RC .60 1.50

1973 Topps Team Checklists

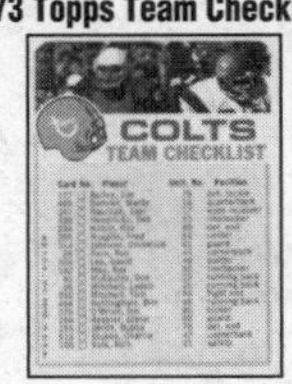

The 1973 Topps Team Checklist set contains 26 checklist cards, one for each of the 26 NFL teams. The cards measure 2 1/2" by 3 1/2" and were inserted into regular issue 1973 Topps football wax packs. The fronts show action scenes at the top of the card and a Topps helmet with the team name at its immediate right. The bottom portion of the card contains the checklist, complete with boxes in which to place check marks. Uniform numbers and positions are also given with the player's name. The backs of the cards form puzzles of Joe Namath and Larry Brown. These unnumbered cards are numbered below for convenience in alphabetical order by team name. The cards can all be found with one or two asterisks on the front and in a blank backed version.

COMPLETE SET (26) 50.00 100.00
1 Atlanta Falcons 2.00 4.00
2 Baltimore Colts 2.00 4.00
3 Buffalo Bills 2.00 4.00
4 Chicago Bears 2.50 5.00
5 Cincinnati Bengals 2.00 4.00
6 Cleveland Browns 2.50 5.00
7 Dallas Cowboys 3.00 6.00
8 Denver Broncos 2.00 4.00
9 Detroit Lions 2.00 4.00
10 Green Bay Packers 2.50 5.00
11 Houston Oilers 2.00 4.00
12 Kansas City Chiefs 2.00 4.00
13 Los Angeles Rams 2.00 4.00
14 Miami Dolphins 2.50 5.00
15 Minnesota Vikings 2.50 5.00
16 New England Patriots 2.00 4.00
17 New Orleans Saints 2.00 4.00
18 New York Giants 2.00 4.00
19 New York Jets 2.00 4.00
20 Oakland Raiders 3.00 6.00
21 Philadelphia Eagles 2.00 4.00
22 Pittsburgh Steelers 2.50 5.00
23 St. Louis Cardinals 2.00 4.00
24 San Diego Chargers 2.00 4.00
25 San Francisco 49ers 2.50 5.00
26 Washington Redskins 2.50 5.00

1974 Topps

The 1974 Topps set contains 528 standard-size cards. Card fronts have photos that are bordered on either side by uprights of a goal post. The goal post has a different color depending upon the player's team. The team name is in a color bar at the bottom. The player's name and position are beneath the crossbar. The card backs are printed in blue and yellow on gray card stock and include statistics and highlights. The bottom of the back provides part of a simulated football game which could be played by drawing cards. Subsets inlcude All-Pro (121-144), league leaders (328-333) and post-season action (460-463). This set contains the Rookie Cards of Harold Carmichael, Chuck Foreman, Ray Guy, John Hannah, Bert Jones, Ed Marinaro, John Matuszak and Ahmad Rashad. An uncut sheet of team checklist cards was also available via a mail-in offer on wax pack wrappers. There are a number of cards with copyright variations. On cards 26, 129, 130, 156, 162, 219, 265-364, 367-422, and 424-528, there are two asterisks with the copyright line. The rest of the cards have one asterisk. Topps also printed a very similar (and very confusing) 50-card set for Parker Brothers in early 1974 as part of its Pro Draft football board game. The only players in this set (game) were offensive players (with an emphasis on the skill positions) that were among the first 132 cards in the 1974 Topps set. There are several notable differences between these Parker Brothers Pro Draft cards and the basic issue. Those cards ending with 1972 statistics on the back (unlike the basic issue which go through 1973) are Parker Brothers cards. Parker Brothers game cards can also be distinguished by the presence of two asterisks rather than one on the copyright line. However, as noted above, there are cards in the regular 1974 Topps set that do have two asterisks but are not Parker Brothers Pro Draft cards. In fact, variations 23A, 49A, 116A, 124A, 126A, and 127A listed in the checklist below were issued with a later

COMPLETE SET (528) 175.00 300.00
1 O.J.Simpson RB UER 10.00 20.00
2 Blaine Nye .25 .60
3 Don Hansen .25 .60
4 Ken Bowman .25 .60
5 Carl Eller .60 1.50
6 Jerry Smith .25 .60
7 Ed Podolak .25 .60
8 Mel Gray .60 1.50
9 Pat Matson .25 .60
10 Floyd Little .60 1.50
11 Frank Pitts .25 .60
12 Vern Den Herder RC .40 1.00
13 John Fuqua .40 1.00
14 Jack Tatum .75 2.00
15 Winston Hill .25 .60
16 John Beasley RC .25 .60
17 David Lee .25 .60
18 Rich Coady .25 .60
19 Ken Willard .25 .60
20 Coy Bacon .40 1.00
21 Ben Hawkins .25 .60
22 Paul Guidry .25 .60
23 Norm Snead HOR .40 1.00
24 Jim Yarbrough .25 .60
25 Jack Reynolds RC 1.25 3.00
26 Josh Ashton .25 .60
27 Donnie Green .25 .60
28 Bob Hayes .75 2.00
29 John Zook .25 .60
30 Bobby Bryant .25 .60
31 Scott Hunter .40 1.00
32 Dan Dierdorf 3.00 6.00
33 Curt Knight .25 .60
34 Elmo Wright RC .25 .60
35 Essex Johnson .25 .60
36 Walt Sumner .25 .60
37 Marv Montgomery RC .25 .60
38 Tim Foley .40 1.00
39 Mike Siani .25 .60
40 Joe Greene 3.00 6.00
41 Bobby Howfield .25 .60
42 Del Williams .25 .60
43 Don McCauley .25 .60
44 Randy Jackson .25 .60
45 Ron Smith .25 .60
46 Gene Washington 49er .40 1.00
47 Po James RC .25 .60
48 Solomon Freelon RC .25 .60
49 Bob Windsor HOR .25 .60
50 John Hadl .60 1.50
51 Greg Larson .25 .60
52 Steve Owens .40 1.00
53 Jim Cheyunski .25 .60
54 Rayfield Wright .40 1.00
55 Dave Hampton .25 .60
56 Ron Widby .25 .60
57 Milt Sunde .25 .60
58 Billy Kilmer .60 1.50
59 Bobby Bell .60 1.50
60 Jim Bakken .25 .60
61 Rufus Mayes .25 .60
62 Vic Washington .25 .60
63 Gene Washington Vik .40 1.00
64 Clarence Scott .25 .60
65 Gene Upshaw .75 2.00
66 Larry Seiple .40 1.00
67 John McMakin .25 .60
68 Ralph Baker .25 .60
69 Lydell Mitchell .40 1.00
70 Archie Manning 1.25 2.50
71 George Farmer .25 .60
72 Ron East .25 .60
73 Al Nelson .25 .60
74 Pat Hughes .25 .60
75 Fred Willis .25 .60
76 Larry Walton RC .25 .60
77 Tom Neville .25 .60
78 Ted Kwalick .25 .60
79 Walt Patulski .25 .60
80 John Niland .25 .60
81 Ted Fritsch Jr. .25 .60
82 Paul Krause .60 1.50
83 Jack Snow .40 1.00
84 Mike Bass .25 .60
85 Jim Tyrer .25 .60
86 Ron Yankowski .25 .60
87 Mike Phipps .40 1.00
88 Al Beauchamp .25 .60
89 Riley Odoms RC .60 1.50
90 MacArthur Lane .25 .60
91 Art Thoms .25 .60
92 Marlin Briscoe .25 .60
93 Bruce Van Dyke .25 .60
94 Tom Myers RC .25 .60
95 Calvin Hill .60 1.50
96 Bruce Laird RC .25 .60
97 Tony McGee DT .25 .60
98 Len Rohde .25 .60
99 Tom McNeill .25 .60
100 Delles Howell .25 .60
101 Gary Garrison .25 .60
102 Dan Goich RC .25 .60
103 Len St. Jean .25 .60
104 Zeke Moore .25 .60
105 Ahmad Rashad RC 10.00 20.00
106 Mel Renfro .60 1.50
107 Jim Mitchell .25 .60
108 Ed Budde .25 .60
109 Harry Schuh .25 .60
110 Greg Pruitt RC 2.00 4.00
111 Ed Flanagan .25 .60
112 Larry Stallings .25 .60
113 Chuck Foreman RC 4.00 8.00
114 Royce Berry .25 .60
115 Gale Gillingham .25 .60
116 Charlie Johnson HOR .60 1.50
117 Checklist 1-132 UER 2.00 4.00
118 Bill Butler RC .25 .60
119 Roy Jefferson .40 1.00
120 Bobby Douglass .40 1.00
121 Harold Carmichael RC 6.00 12.00
122 George Kunz AP .25 .60
123 Larry Little AP .75 2.00
124 Forrest Blue AP .25 .60
125 Ron Yary AP .60 1.50
126 Tom Mack AP .60 1.50
127 Bob Tucker AP .40 1.00
128 Paul Warfield AP 2.00 4.00
129 Fran Tarkenton AP 5.00 10.00
130 O.J. Simpson AP 6.00 12.00
131 Larry Csonka AP 3.00 6.00
132 Bruce Gossett AP .25 .60
133 Bill Stanfill AP .40 1.00
134 Alan Page AP 1.25 2.50
135 Paul Smith AP .25 .60
136 Claude Humphrey AP .50 1.25
137 Jack Ham AP 5.00 10.00
138 Lee Roy Jordan AP .60 1.50
139 Phil Villapiano AP .40 1.00
140 Ken Ellis AP .25 .60
141 Willie Brown AP .60 1.50
142 Dick Anderson AP .40 1.00
143 Bill Bradley AP .40 1.00
144 Jerrel Wilson AP .25 .60
145 Reggie Rucker .40 1.00
146 Marty Domres .25 .60
147 Bob Kowalkowski RC .25 .60
148 John Matuszak RC 2.50 6.00
149 Mike Adamle RC .40 1.00
150 Johnny Unitas 7.50 15.00

151 Charlie Ford .25 .60
152 Bob Klein RC .25 .60
153 Jim Merlo RC .25 .60
154 Willie Young .25 .60
155 Donny Anderson .40 1.00
156 Brig Owens .25 .60
157 Bruce Jarvis RC .25 .60
158 Ron Carpenter RC .25 .60
159 Don Cockroft .25 .60
160 Tommy Nobis .60 1.50
161 Craig Morton .60 1.50
162 Jon Staggers RC .25 .60
163 Mike Eischeid .25 .60
164 Jerry Sisemore RC .25 .60
165 Cedrick Hardman .25 .60
166 Bill Thompson .40 1.00
167 Jim Lynch .40 1.00
168 Bob Moore RC .25 .60
169 Glen Edwards RC .25 .60
170 Mercury Morris .60 1.50
171 Julius Adams .25 .60
172 Cotton Speyrer RC .25 .60
173 Bill Munson .40 1.00
174 Benny Johnson .25 .60
175 Burgess Owens RC .25 .60
176 Cid Edwards .25 .60
177 Doug Buffone .25 .60
178 Charlie Cowan .25 .60
179 Bob Newland RC .25 .60
180 Ron Johnson .40 1.00
181 Bob Rowe RC .25 .60
182 Len Hauss .25 .60
183 Joe DeLamielleure RC 6.00 12.00
184 Sherman White RC .25 .60
185 Fair Hooker .25 .60
186 Nick Mike-Mayer RC .25 .60
187 Ralph Neely .25 .60
188 Rich McGeorge .25 .60
189 Ed Marinaro RC 1.50 4.00
190 Dave Wilcox .60 1.50
191 Joe Owens RC .25 .60
192 Bill Van Heusen .25 .60
193 Jim Kearney .25 .60
194 Otis Sistrunk RC .60 1.50
195 Ron Shanklin .25 .60
196 Bill Lenkaitis RC .25 .60
197 Tom Drougas RC .25 .60
198 Larry Hand .25 .60
199 Mack Alston RC .25 .60
200 Bob Griese 3.00 6.00
201 Earlie Thomas RC .25 .60
202 Carl Gersbach RC .25 .60
203 Jim Harrison .25 .60
204 Jake Kupp .25 .60
205 Merlin Olsen .75 2.00
206 Spider Lockhart .40 1.00
207 Walker Gillette .25 .60
208 Verlon Biggs .25 .60
209 Bob James .25 .60
210 Bob Trumpy .60 1.50
211 Jerry Sherk .25 .60
212 Andy Maurer .25 .60
213 Fred Carr .25 .60
214 Mick Tingelhoff .40 1.00
215 Steve Spurrier 7.50 15.00
216 Richard Harris RC .25 .60
217 Charlie Greer RC .25 .60
218 Buck Buchanan .60 1.50
219 Ray Guy RC 10.00 20.00
220 Franco Harris 6.00 12.00
221 Darryl Stingley RC .60 1.50
222 Rex Kern .25 .60
223 Toni Fritsch RC .40 1.00
224 Levi Johnson RC .25 .60
225 Bob Kuechenberg .40 1.00
226 Elvin Bethea .60 1.50
227 Al Woodall RC .40 1.00
228 Terry Owens .25 .60
229 Bivian Lee RC .25 .60
230 Dick Butkus 5.00 10.00
231 Jim Bertelsen RC .40 1.00
232 John Mendenhall RC .25 .60
233 Conrad Dobler RC .60 1.50
234 J.D. Hill .40 1.00
235 Ken Houston .60 1.50
236 Dave Lewis .25 .60
237 John Garlington .25 .60
238 Bill Sandeman .25 .60
239 Alden Roche .25 .60
240 John Gilliam .40 1.00
241 Bruce Taylor .25 .60
242 Vern Winfield RC .25 .60
243 Bobby Maples .25 .60
244 Wendell Hayes .25 .60
245 George Blanda 4.00 8.00
246 Dwight White .40 1.00
247 Sandy Durko RC .25 .60
248 Tom Mitchell .25 .60
249 Chuck Walton .25 .60
250 Bob Lilly 2.00 4.00
251 Doug Swift .25 .60
252 Lynn Dickey RC .60 1.50
253 Jerome Barkum RC .25 .60
254 Clint Jones .25 .60
255 Billy Newsome .25 .60
256 Bob Asher RC .25 .60
257 Joe Scibelli RC .25 .60
258 Tom Blanchard .25 .60
259 Norm Thompson .25 .60
260 Larry Brown .60 1.50
261 Paul Seymour RC .25 .60
262 Checklist 133-264 2.00 4.00
263 Doug Dieken RC .25 .60
264 Lemar Parrish .40 1.00
265 Bob Lee UER .25 .60
266 Bob Brown DT .25 .60
267 Roy Winston .25 .60
268 Randy Beisler RC .25 .60
269 Joe Dawkins .25 .60
270 Tom Dempsey .40 1.00
271 Jack Rudnay .25 .60
272 Art Shell 2.50 5.00
273 Mike Wagner .40 1.00
274 Rick Cash RC .25 .60
275 Greg Landry .60 1.50
276 Glenn Ressler .25 .60
277 Billy Joe DuPree RC 1.25 3.00
278 Norm Evans .25 .60
279 Billy Parks .25 .60
280 John Riggins 3.00 6.00
281 Lionel Aldridge .25 .60
282 Steve O'Neal .25 .60
283 Craig Clemons RC .25 .60
284 Willie Williams .25 .60
285 Isiah Robertson .40 1.00
286 Dennis Shaw .25 .60
287 Bill Brundige .25 .60
288 John Leypoldt .25 .60
289 John DeMarie RC .25 .60
290 Mike Reid .60 1.50
291 Greg Brezina .25 .60
292 Willie Buchanon RC .25 .60
293 Dave Osborn .40 1.00
294 Mel Phillips .25 .60
295 Haven Moses .40 1.00
296 Wade Key .25 .60
297 Marvin Upshaw .25 .60
298 Ray Mansfield .25 .60
299 Edgar Chandler .25 .60
300 Marv Hubbard .40 1.00
301 Herman Weaver .25 .60
302 Jim Bailey .25 .60
303 D.D. Lewis RC .60 1.50
304 Ken Burrough .40 1.00
305 Jake Scott .60 1.50
306 Randy Rasmussen .25 .60
307 Pettis Norman .25 .60
308 Carl Johnson RC .25 .60
309 Joe Taylor .25 .60
310 Pete Gogolak .25 .60
311 Tony Baker FB .25 .60
312 John Richardson RC .25 .60
313 Dave Robinson .40 1.00
314 Reggie McKenzie RC .60 1.50
315 Isaac Curtis RC .60 1.50
316 Thom Darden RC .25 .60
317 Ken Reaves .25 .60
318 Malcolm Snider .25 .60
319 Jeff Siemon RC .40 1.00
320 Dan Abramowicz .40 1.00
321 Lyle Alzado .75 2.00
322 John Reaves .25 .60
323 Morris Stroud RC .25 .60
324 Bobby Walden .25 .60
325 Randy Vataha .25 .60
326 Nemiah Wilson .25 .60
327 Paul Naumoff .25 .60
328 O.J.Simpson/Brock. LL 1.50 3.00
329 R.Staubach/Stabler LL 2.50 5.00
330 Harold Carmichael/Wil LL .60 1.50
331 Scoring Leaders .40 1.00
332 Interception Leaders .40 1.00
333 Punting Leaders .40 1.00
334 Dennis Nelson RC .25 .60
335 Walt Garrison .40 1.00
336 Tody Smith .25 .60
337 Ed Bell .25 .60
338 Bryant Salter .25 .60
339 Wayne Colman .25 .60
340 Garo Yepremian .40 1.00
341 Bob Newton RC .25 .60
342 Vince Clements RC .25 .60
343 Ken Iman .25 .60
344 Jim Tolbert RC .25 .60
345 Chris Hanburger .40 1.00
346 Dave Foley .25 .60
347 Tommy Casanova .40 1.00
348 John James RC .25 .60
349 Clarence Williams .25 .60
350 Leroy Kelly .60 1.50
351 Stu Voigt RC .40 1.00
352 Skip Vanderbundt .25 .60
353 Pete Duranko .25 .60
354 John Outlaw .25 .60
355 Jan Stenerud .60 1.50
356 Barry Pearson RC .25 .60
357 Brian Dowling RC .25 .60
358 Dan Conners .25 .60
359 Bob Bell RC .25 .60
360 Rick Volk .25 .60
361 Pat Toomay RC .40 1.00
362 Bob Gresham RC .25 .60
363 John Schmitt .25 .60
364 Mel Rogers RC .25 .60
365 Manny Fernandez .40 1.00
366 Ernie Jackson RC .25 .60
367 Gary Huff RC .40 1.00
368 Bob Grim .25 .60
369 Ernie McMillan .25 .60
370 Dave Elmendorf .25 .60
371 Mike Bragg .25 .60
372 John Skorupan RC .25 .60
373 Howard Fest .25 .60
374 Jerry Tagge RC .40 1.00
375 Art Malone .25 .60
376 Bob Babich .25 .60
377 Jim Marshall .60 1.50
378 Bob Hoskins RC .25 .60
379 Don Zimmerman RC .25 .60
380 Ray May .25 .60
381 Emmitt Thomas .40 1.00
382 Terry Hanratty .40 1.00
383 John Hannah RC 10.00 20.00
384 George Atkinson .25 .60
385 Ted Hendricks 1.50 3.00
386 Jim O'Brien .25 .60
387 Jethro Pugh .40 1.00
388 Elbert Drungo RC .25 .60
389 Richard Caster .40 1.00
390 Deacon Jones .60 1.50
391 Checklist 265-396 2.00 4.00
392 Jess Phillips RC .25 .60
393 Garry Lyle UER RC .25 .60
394 Jim Files .25 .60
395 Jim Hart .60 1.50
396 Dave Chapple .25 .60
397 Jim Langer .75 2.00
398 John Wilbur .25 .60
399 Dwight Harrison RC .25 .60
400 John Brockington .40 1.00
401 Ken Anderson 3.00 6.00
402 Mike Tilleman .25 .60
403 Charlie Hall RC .25 .60
404 Tommy Hart .25 .60
405 Norm Bulaich .40 1.00
406 Jim Turner .25 .60
407 Mo Moorman .25 .60
408 Ralph Anderson .25 .60
409 Jim Otto .60 1.50
410 Andy Russell .60 1.50
411 Glenn Doughty RC .25 .60
412 Altie Taylor .25 .60
413 Marv Bateman RC .25 .60
414 Willie Alexander .25 .60
415 Bill Zapalac RC .25 .60
416 Russ Washington .25 .60
417 Joe Federspiel RC .25 .60
418 Craig Cotton RC .25 .60
419 Randy Johnson .25 .60
420 Harold Jackson .60 1.50
421 Roger Wehrli .40 1.00
422 Charlie Harraway .25 .60
423 Spike Jones .25 .60
424 Bob Johnson .25 .60
425 Mike McCoy DT .25 .60
426 Dennis Havig RC .25 .60
427 Bob McKay RC .25 .60
428 Steve Zabel .25 .60
429 Horace Jones .25 .60
430 Jim Johnson .60 1.50
431 Roy Gerela .40 1.00
432 Tom Graham RC .25 .60
433 Curley Culp 1.00 2.50
434 Ken Mendenhall RC .25 .60
435 Jim Plunkett 1.25 2.50
436 Julian Fagan .25 .60
437 Mike Garrett .40 1.00
438 Bobby Joe Green .25 .60
439 Jack Gregory .25 .60
440 Charlie Sanders .40 1.00
441 Bill Curry .40 1.00
442 Bob Pollard RC .25 .60
443 David Ray .25 .60
444 Terry Metcalf RC 1.50 3.00
445 Pat Fischer .40 1.00
446 Bob Chandler .40 1.00
447 Bill Bergey .40 1.00
448 Walter Johnson .25 .60
449 Charle Young RC .60 1.50
450 Chester Marcol .25 .60
451 Ken Stabler 10.00 20.00
452 Preston Pearson .60 1.50
453 Mike Current .25 .60
454 Ron Bolton RC .25 .60
455 Mark Lomas .25 .60
456 Raymond Chester .40 1.00
457 Jerry LeVias .40 1.00
458 Skip Butler RC .25 .60
459 Mike Livingston RC .25 .60
460 AFC Semi-Final .40 1.00
461 NFC Semi/R.Staubach 2.00 4.00
462 Playoff Champs/Stabler 1.50 3.00
463 Super Bowl/Dolphins 24/Vikings 7/(Larry Csonka pictured) .75 2.00
464 Wayne Mulligan .25 .60
465 Horst Muhlmann .25 .60
466 Milt Morin .25 .60
467 Don Parish RC .25 .60
468 Richard Neal .25 .60
469 Ron Jessie .40 1.00
470 Terry Bradshaw 12.50 25.00
471 Fred Dryer .60 1.50
472 Jim Carter .25 .60
473 Ken Burrow .25 .60
474 Wally Chambers RC .40 1.00
475 Dan Pastorini .60 1.50
476 Don Morrison .25 .60
477 Carl Mauck .25 .60
478 Larry Cole RC .40 1.00
479 Jim Kiick .60 1.50
480 Willie Lanier .60 1.50
481 Don Herrmann .40 1.00
482 George Hunt RC .25 .60
483 Bob Howard RC .25 .60
484 Myron Pottios .25 .60
485 Jackie Smith .60 1.50
486 Vern Holland .25 .60
487 Jim Braxton .25 .60
488 Joe Reed RC .25 .60
489 Wally Hilgenberg .25 .60
490 Fred Biletnikoff 2.00 4.00
491 Bob DeMarco .25 .60
492 Mark Nordquist .25 .60
493 Larry Brooks RC .25 .60
494 Pete Athas .25 .60
495 Emerson Boozer .40 1.00
496 L.C. Greenwood .75 2.00
497 Rockne Freitas .25 .60
498 Checklist 397-528 UER 2.00 4.00
499 Joe Schmiesing RC .25 .60
500 Roger Staubach 12.50 25.00
501 Al Cowlings UER .40 1.00
502 Sam Cunningham RC .60 1.50
503 Dennis Partee .25 .60
504 John Didion .25 .60
505 Nick Buoniconti .60 1.50
506 Carl Garrett .40 1.00
507 Doug Van Horn .25 .60
508 Jamie Rivers RC .25 .60
509 Jack Youngblood 2.00 4.00
510 Charley Taylor UER 1.25 2.50
511 Ken Riley .60 1.50
512 Joe Ferguson RC 1.25 3.00
513 Bill Lueck RC .25 .60
514 Ray Brown DB RC .25 .60
515 Fred Cox .25 .60
516 Joe Jones .25 .60
517 Larry Schreiber RC .25 .60
518 Dennis Wirgowski .25 .60
519 Leroy Mitchell .25 .60
520 Otis Taylor .60 1.50
521 Henry Davis .25 .60
522 Bruce Barnes RC .25 .60
523 Charlie Smith RB .25 .60
524 Bert Jones RC 3.00 6.00
525 Lem Barney .75 2.00
526 John Fitzgerald RC .25 .60
527 Tom Funchess .25 .60
528 Steve Tannen .60 1.50

1974 Topps Parker Brothers Pro Draft

This 50-card standard-size set was printed by Topps for distribution by Parker Brothers in early 1974 as part of a football board game. The only players in this set (game) are offensive players (with an emphasis on the skill positions) and all come from the first 132 cards in the 1974 Topps football card set. The cards are very similar and often confused with the 1974 Topps regular issue football cards. There are several notable differences between these cards and the 1974 Topps regular issue: cards with 1972 statistics on the back (unlike the 1974 Topps regular issue) are indicated in the checklist below with an asterisk and cards with pose variations (different from the 1974 Topps) are noted as well parenthetically; these six pose variations are numbers 23, 49, 116, 124, 126, and 127. Parker Brothers game cards can also be distinguished by the presence of two asterisks rather than one on the copyright line. However, there are cards in the regular 1974 Topps set that do have two asterisks but are not Parker Brothers Pro Draft cards. Cards in the 1974 Topps regular set with two asterisks include 26, 129, 130, 156, 162, 219, 265-364, 367-422, and 424-528; the rest have only one asterisk. The Parker Brothers cards are skip-numbered with the number on the back corresponding to that player's number in the Topps regular issue.

COMPLETE SET (50) 62.50 125.00
4 Ken Bowman .50 1.00
6 Jerry Smith * 1.00 2.00
7 Ed Podolak * 1.00 2.00
9 Pat Matson .50 1.00
11 Frank Pitts * 1.00 2.00
15 Winston Hill .50 1.00
18 Rich Coady * 1.00 2.00
19 Ken Willard * 1.25 2.50
21 Ben Hawkins * 1.00 2.00
23A Norm Snead * 2.00 5.00
23B Norm Snead * 2.00 5.00
24 Jim Yarbrough * 1.00 2.00
28 Bob Hayes * 2.50 5.00
32 Dan Dierdorf * 3.00 6.00
35 Essex Johnson * 1.00 2.00
39 Mike Siani .50 1.00
42 Del Williams .50 1.00
43 Don McCauley * 1.00 2.00
44 Randy Jackson * 1.00 2.00
46 Gene Washington 49er * 1.50 3.00
49A Bob Windsor * 1.50 3.00
49B Bob Windsor * 1.50 3.00
50 John Hadl * 2.00 4.00
52 Steve Owens * 2.00 4.00
54 Rayfield Wright * 1.00 2.00
57 Milt Sunde * 1.00 2.00
58 Billy Kilmer * 2.00 4.00
61 Rufus Mayes * 1.00 2.00
63 Gene Washington Vik * 1.25 2.50
65 Gene Upshaw 2.50 5.00
75 Fred Willis * 1.00 2.00

Card	Low	High
77 Tom Neville	.50	1.00
78 Ted Kwalick *	1.25	2.50
80 John Niland *	1.00	2.00
81 Ted Fritsch Jr.	.50	1.00
83 Jack Snow *	1.50	3.00
87 Mike Phipps *	1.50	3.00
90 MacArthur Lane *	1.50	3.00
95 Calvin Hill *	1.00	2.00
98 Len Rohde	.50	1.00
101 Gary Garrison *	1.00	2.00
103 Len St. Jean	.50	1.00
107 Jim Mitchell *	1.00	2.00
109 Harry Schuh	.50	1.00
110 Greg Pruitt *	2.00	4.00
111 Ed Flanagan	.50	1.00
113 Chuck Foreman *	2.00	4.00
116A Charlie Johnson *	2.00	5.00
116B Charlie Johnson *	2.00	5.00
119 Roy Jefferson *	1.25	2.50
124A Forrest Blue *	1.50	3.00
124B Forrest Blue *	1.50	3.00
126A Tom Mack *	4.00	8.00
126B Tom Mack *	4.00	8.00
127B Bob Tucker *	1.50	3.00
127A Bob Tucker *	1.50	3.00

1974 Topps Team Checklists

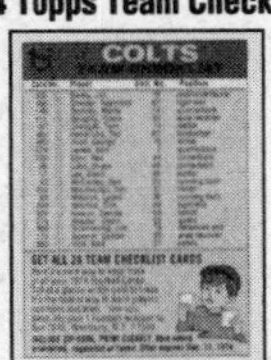

The 1974 Topps Team Checklist set contains 26 standard-size cards. The cards were inserted into regular issue 1974 Topps football wax packs. The Topps logo and team name appear at the top of the card, while the mid-portion of the card contains the actual checklist giving each player's card number, check-off box, name, uniform number, and position. The lower portion of the card contains an ad to obtain all 26 team checklists. A picture of a boy collector is shown in the lower right corner. The back of the card contains rules for a football game to be played with the 1974 Topps football cards. These unnumbered cards are numbered below for convenience in alphabetical order by team name. Twenty of the 26 checklist cards show players out of alphabetical order on the card front. The cards can all be found with one or two asterisks on the front. The set was also available directly from Topps as a mail-away offer as a pair of unperforated uncut sheets, which had blank backs. Measuring approximately 13 1/2" by 10 1/2", each sheet featured thirteen team checklist cards and an offer for a football action poster.

Card	Low	High
COMPLETE SET (26)	37.50	75.00
*BLANKBACKS: 2X TO 4X BASIC CARDS		
1 Atlanta Falcons	1.50	3.00
2 Baltimore Colts	1.50	3.00
3 Buffalo Bills	1.50	3.00
4 Chicago Bears	2.00	4.00
5 Cincinnati Bengals	1.50	3.00
6 Cleveland Browns UER	1.50	3.00
7 Dallas Cowboys	2.50	5.00
8 Denver Broncos	1.50	3.00
9 Detroit Lions	1.50	3.00
10 Green Bay Packers	2.00	4.00
11 Houston Oilers	1.50	3.00
12 Kansas City Chiefs	1.50	3.00
13 Los Angeles Rams	1.50	3.00
14 Miami Dolphins	2.00	4.00
15 Minnesota Vikings	2.00	4.00
16 New England Patriots	1.50	3.00
17 New Orleans Saints	1.50	3.00
18 New York Giants	2.00	4.00
19 New York Jets	1.50	3.00
20 Oakland Raiders	2.50	5.00
21 Philadelphia Eagles	1.50	3.00
22 Pittsburgh Steelers	2.00	4.00
23 St. Louis Cardinals	1.50	3.00
24 San Diego Chargers	1.50	3.00
25 San Francisco 49ers	2.00	4.00
26 Washington Redskins UER	2.00	4.00

1975 Topps

The 1975 Topps football set contains 528 standard-size cards. Beneath a color photo, card fronts contain a banner with the team name. Both were done in a team color. To the right of the banner is a football helmet the includes the player's position. The player's name is at the bottom. Subsets include leaders (1-6), All-Pro (201-225), Record Breakers (351-356), Highlights (452-460) and playoffs (526-528). The card backs are printed in black ink with a green background on gray card stock and contain statistics and highlights. The key Rookie Cards in this set are Otis Armstrong, Rocky Bleier, Mel Blount, Cliff Branch, Dan Fouts, Cliff Harris, Drew Pearson, Lynn Swann and Charlie Waters. The set also includes Joe Theismann's first NFL card after having performed in the Canadian Football League. An uncut sheet of team checklist cards was also available via a mail-in offer wax pack wrappers.

Card	Low	High
COMPLETE SET (528)	175.00	300.00
1 McCutcheon Armstrong LL	.60	1.50
2 Jurgensen K.Anderson LL	.60	1.50
3 Receiving Leaders	.60	1.50
4 Scoring Leaders	.30	.75
5 Interception Leaders	.30	.75
6 Punting Leaders	.60	1.50
7 George Blanda HL	2.50	5.00
8 George Blanda	2.50	5.00
9 Ralph Baker	.20	.50
10 Don Woods RC	.20	.50
11 Bob Asher	.20	.50
12 Mel Blount RC	10.00	20.00
13 Sam Cunningham	.30	.75
14 Jackie Smith	.60	1.50
15 Greg Landry	.30	.75
16 Buck Buchanan	.60	1.50
17 Haven Moses	.30	.75
18 Clarence Ellis	.20	.50
19 Jim Carter	.20	.50
20 Charley Taylor UER	.75	2.00
21 Jess Phillips	.20	.50
22 Larry Seiple	.20	.50
23 Doug Dieken	.20	.50
24 Ron Saul	.20	.50
25 Isaac Curtis	.60	1.50
26 Gary Larsen RC	.20	.50
27 Bruce Jarvis	.20	.50
28 Steve Zabel	.20	.50
29 John Mendenhall	.20	.50
30 Rick Volk	.20	.50
31 Checklist 1-132	2.00	4.00
32 Dan Abramowicz	.30	.75
33 Bubba Smith	.60	1.50
34 David Ray	.20	.50
35 Dan Dierdorf	2.00	4.00
36 Randy Rasmussen	.20	.50
37 Bob Howard	.20	.50
38 Gary Huff	.30	.75
39 Rocky Bleier RC	10.00	20.00
40 Mel Gray	.30	.75
41 Tony McGee DT	.20	.50
42 Larry Hand	.20	.50
43 Wendell Hayes	.20	.50
44 Doug Wilkerson RC	.20	.50
45 Paul Smith	.20	.50
46 Dave Robinson	.40	1.00
47 Bivian Lee	.20	.50
48 Jim Mandich RC	.30	.75
49 Greg Pruitt	.60	1.50
50 Dan Pastorini	.60	1.50
51 Ron Pritchard RC	.20	.50
52 Dan Conners	.20	.50
53 Fred Cox	.20	.50
54 Tony Greene RC	.20	.50
55 Craig Morton	.60	1.50
56 Jerry Sisemore	.20	.50
57 Glenn Doughty	.20	.50
58 Larry Schreiber	.20	.50
59 Charlie Waters RC	2.00	4.00
60 Jack Youngblood	.60	1.50
61 Bill Lenkaitis	.20	.50
62 Greg Brezina	.20	.50
63 Bob Pollard	.20	.50
64 Mack Alston	.20	.50
65 Drew Pearson RC	10.00	20.00
66 Charlie Stukes	.20	.50
67 Emerson Boozer	.30	.75
68 Dennis Partee	.20	.50
69 Bob Newton	.20	.50
70 Jack Tatum	.60	1.50
71 Frank Lewis	.20	.50
72 Bob Young RC	.20	.50
73 Julius Adams	.20	.50
74 Paul Naumoff	.20	.50
75 Otis Taylor	.60	1.50
76 Dave Hampton	.20	.50
77 Mike Current	.20	.50
78 Brig Owens	.20	.50
79 Bobby Scott RC	.20	.50
80 Harold Carmichael	1.50	3.00
81 Bill Stanfill	.20	.50
82 Bob Babich	.20	.50
83 Vic Washington	.20	.50
84 Mick Tingelhoff	.30	.75
85 Bob Trumpy	.60	1.50
86 Earl Edwards RC	.20	.50
87 Ron Hornsby	.20	.50
88 Don McCauley	.20	.50
89 Jim Johnson	.60	1.50
90 Andy Russell	.30	.75
91 Cornell Green	.60	1.50
92 Charlie Cowan	.20	.50
93 Jon Staggers	.20	.50
94 Billy Newsome	.20	.50
95 Willie Brown	.60	1.50
96 Carl Mauck	.20	.50
97 Doug Buffone	.20	.50
98 Preston Pearson	.30	.75
99 Jim Bakken	.20	.50
100 Bob Griese	2.50	5.00
101 Bob Windsor	.20	.50
102 Rockne Freitas	.20	.50
103 Jim Marsalis	.20	.50
104 Bill Thompson	.30	.75
105 Ken Burrow	.20	.50
106 Diron Talbert	.20	.50
107 Joe Federspiel	.20	.50
108 Norm Bulaich	.30	.75
109 Bob DeMarco	.20	.50
110 Tom Wittum RC	.20	.50
111 Larry Hefner RC	.20	.50
112 Tody Smith	.20	.50
113 Stu Voigt	.20	.50
114 Horst Muhlmann	.20	.50
115 Ahmad Rashad	3.00	6.00
116 Joe Dawkins	.20	.50
117 George Kunz	.20	.50
118 D.D. Lewis	.30	.75
119 Levi Johnson	.20	.50
120 Len Dawson	2.00	4.00
121 Jim Bertelsen	.20	.50
122 Ed Bell	.20	.50
123 Art Thoms	.20	.50
124 Joe Beauchamp	.20	.50
125 Jack Ham	3.00	6.00
126 Carl Garrett	.20	.50
127 Roger Finnie RC	.20	.50
128 Howard Twilley	.30	.75
129 Bruce Barnes	.20	.50
130 Nate Wright RC	.20	.50
131 Jerry Tagge	.20	.50
132 Floyd Little	.60	1.50
133 John Zook	.20	.50
134 Len Hauss	.20	.50
135 Archie Manning	.60	1.50
136 Po James	.20	.50
137 Walt Sumner	.20	.50
138 Randy Beisler	.20	.50
139 Willie Alexander	.20	.50
140 Garo Yepremian	.30	.75
141 Chip Myers	.20	.50
142 Jim Braxton	.20	.50
143 Doug Van Horn	.20	.50
144 Stan White RC	.20	.50
145 Roger Staubach	10.00	20.00
146 Herman Weaver	.20	.50
147 Marvin Upshaw	.20	.50
148 Bob Klein	.20	.50
149 Earlie Thomas	.20	.50
150 John Brockington	.30	.75
151 Mike Siani	.20	.50
152 Sam Davis RC	.20	.50
153 Mike Wagner	.30	.75
154 Larry Stallings	.20	.50
155 Wally Chambers	.20	.50
156 Randy Vataha	.20	.50
157 Jim Marshall	.60	1.50
158 Jim Turner	.20	.50
159 Walt Sweeney	.20	.50
160 Ken Anderson	2.00	4.00
161 Ray Brown	.20	.50
162 John Didion	.20	.50
163 Tom Dempsey	.20	.50
164 Clarence Scott	.20	.50
165 Gene Washington 49er	.30	.75
166 Willie Rodgers RC	.20	.50
167 Doug Swift	.20	.50
168 Rufus Mayes	.20	.50
169 Marv Bateman	.20	.50
170 Lydell Mitchell	.30	.75
171 Ron Smith	.20	.50
172 Bill Munson	.30	.75
173 Bob Grim	.20	.50
174 Ed Budde	.20	.50
175 Bob Lilly UER	2.00	4.00
176 Jim Youngblood RC	.60	1.50
177 Steve Tannen	.20	.50
178 Rich McGeorge	.20	.50
179 Jim Tyrer	.20	.50
180 Forrest Blue	.20	.50
181 Jerry LeVias	.30	.75
182 Joe Gilliam RC	.60	1.50
183 Jim Otis RC	.30	.75
184 Mel Tom	.20	.50
185 Paul Seymour	.20	.50
186 George Webster	.20	.50
187 Pete Duranko	.20	.50
188 Essex Johnson	.20	.50
189 Bob Lee	.30	.75
190 Gene Upshaw	.60	1.50
191 Tom Myers	.20	.50
192 Don Zimmerman	.20	.50
193 John Garlington	.20	.50
194 Skip Butler	.20	.50
195 Tom Mitchell	.20	.50
196 Jim Langer	.60	1.50
197 Ron Carpenter	.20	.50
198 Dave Foley	.20	.50
199 Bert Jones	.60	1.50
200 Larry Brown	.30	.75
201 Biletnikoff C.Taylor AP	.75	2.00
202 All Pro Tackles	.20	.50
203 L.Little T.Mack AP	.60	1.50
204 All Pro Centers	.20	.50
205 Hannah Gillingham AP	.60	1.50
206 Dan Dierdorf W.Hill AP	.60	1.50
207 All Pro Tight Ends	.30	.75
208 F.Tarkenton Stabler AP	2.00	4.00
209 Simpson McCutch. AP	1.50	3.00
210 All Pro Backs	.30	.75
211 All Pro Receivers	.30	.75
212 All Pro Kickers	.20	.50
213 Youngblood Bethea AP	.60	1.50
214 All Pro Tackles	.30	.75
215 M.Olsen M.Reid AP	.60	1.50
216 Carl Eller L.Alzado AP	.60	1.50
217 Hendricks Villapiano AP	.60	1.50
218 Willie Lanier Jordan AP	.60	1.50
219 All Pro Linebackers	.30	.75
220 All Pro Cornerbacks	.20	.50
221 All Pro Cornerbacks	.20	.50
222 K.Houston D.Anderson AP	.30	.75
223 Cliff Harris J.Tatum AP	.60	1.50
224 All Pro Punters	.30	.75
225 All Pro Returners	.30	.75
226 Ted Kwalick	.20	.50
227 Spider Lockhart	.30	.75
228 Mike Livingston	.20	.50
229 Larry Cole	.20	.50
230 Gary Garrison	.20	.50
231 Larry Brooks	.20	.50
232 Bobby Howfield	.20	.50
233 Fred Carr	.20	.50
234 Norm Evans	.20	.50
235 Dwight White	.30	.75
236 Conrad Dobler	.30	.75
237 Garry Lyle	.20	.50
238 Darryl Stingley	.60	1.50
239 Tom Graham	.20	.50
240 Chuck Foreman	.60	1.50
241 Ken Riley	.30	.75
242 Don Morrison	.20	.50
243 Lynn Dickey	.30	.75
244 Don Cockroft	.20	.50
245 Claude Humphrey	.40	1.00
246 John Skorupan	.20	.50
247 Raymond Chester	.30	.75
248 Cas Banaszek	.20	.50
249 Art Malone	.20	.50
250 Ed Flanagan	.20	.50
251 Checklist 133-264	2.00	4.00
252 Nemiah Wilson	.20	.50
253 Ron Jessie	.20	.50
254 Jim Lynch	.20	.50
255 Bob Tucker	.30	.75
256 Terry Owens	.20	.50
257 John Fitzgerald	.20	.50
258 Jack Snow	.30	.75
259 Garry Puetz RC	.20	.50
260 Mike Phipps	.30	.75
261 Al Matthews	.20	.50
262 Bob Kuechenberg	.20	.50
263 Ron Yankowski	.20	.50
264 Ron Shanklin	.20	.50
265 Bobby Douglass	.30	.75
266 Josh Ashton	.20	.50
267 Bill Van Heusen	.20	.50
268 Jeff Siemon	.20	.50
269 Bob Newland	.20	.50
270 Gale Gillingham	.20	.50
271 Zeke Moore	.20	.50
272 Mike Tilleman	.20	.50
273 John Leypoldt	.20	.50
274 Ken Mendenhall	.20	.50
275 Norm Snead	.30	.75
276 Bill Bradley	.30	.75
277 Jerry Smith	.20	.50
278 Clarence Davis RC	.20	.50
279 Jim Yarbrough	.20	.50
280 Lemar Parrish	.20	.50
281 Bobby Bell	.60	1.50
282 Lynn Swann UER RC	30.00	60.00
283 John Hicks RC	.20	.50
284 Coy Bacon	.30	.75
285 Lee Roy Jordan	.60	1.50
286 Willie Buchanon	.20	.50
287 Al Woodall	.20	.50
288 Reggie Rucker	.30	.75
289 John Schmitt	.20	.50
290 Carl Eller	.60	1.50
291 Jake Scott	.30	.75
292 Donny Anderson	.30	.75
293 Charley Wade RC	.20	.50
294 John Tanner RC	.20	.50
295 Charley Johnson	.30	.75
296 Tom Blanchard	.20	.50
297 Curley Culp	.75	2.00
298 Jeff Van Note RC	.30	.75
299 Bob James	.20	.50
300 Franco Harris	4.00	8.00
301 Tim Berra RC	.30	.75
302 Bruce Gossett	.20	.50
303 Verlon Biggs	.20	.50
304 Bob Kowalkowski	.20	.50
305 Marv Hubbard	.20	.50
306 Ken Avery	.20	.50
307 Mike Adamle	.20	.50
308 Don Herrmann	.20	.50
309 Chris Fletcherv RC	.20	.50
310 Roman Gabriel	.60	1.50
311 Billy Joe DuPree	.60	1.50
312 Fred Dryer	.60	1.50
313 John Riggins	2.50	5.00
314 Bob McKay	.20	.50

Card	Low	High
315 Ted Hendricks	.60	1.50
316 Bobby Bryant	.20	.50
317 Don Nottingham	.20	.50
318 John Hannah	2.00	4.00
319 Rich Coady	.20	.50
320 Phil Villapiano	.30	.75
321 Jim Plunkett	.60	1.50
322 Lyle Alzado	.60	1.50
323 Ernie Jackson	.20	.50
324 Billy Parks	.20	.50
325 Willie Lanier	.60	1.50
326 John James	.20	.50
327 Joe Ferguson	.30	.75
328 Ernie Holmes RC	3.00	6.00
329 Bruce Laird	.20	.50
330 Chester Marcol	.20	.50
331 Dave Wilcox	.60	1.50
332 Pat Fischer	.30	.75
333 Steve Owens	.30	.75
334 Royce Berry	.20	.50
335 Russ Washington	.20	.50
336 Walker Gillette	.20	.50
337 Mark Nordquist	.20	.50
338 James Harris RC	1.00	2.50
339 Warren Koegel RC	.20	.50
340 Emmitt Thomas	.30	.75
341 Walt Garrison	.30	.75
342 Thom Darden	.20	.50
343 Mike Eischeid	.20	.50
344 Ernie McMillan	.20	.50
345 Nick Buoniconti	.60	1.50
346 George Farmer	.20	.50
347 Sam Adams	.20	.50
348 Larry Cipa RC	.20	.50
349 Bob Moore	.20	.50
350 Otis Armstrong RC	.60	1.50
351 George Blanda RB	1.50	3.00
352 Fred Cox RB	.30	.75
353 Tom Dempsey RB	.30	.75
354 Ken Houston RB	.60	1.50
355 O.J.Simpson RB	2.50	5.00
356 Ron Smith RB	.30	.75
357 Bob Atkins	.20	.50
358 Pat Sullivan	.30	.75
359 Joe DeLamielleure	1.00	2.50
360 Lawrence McCutcheon RC	.60	1.50
361 David Lee	.20	.50
362 Mike McCoy DT	.20	.50
363 Skip Vanderbundt	.20	.50
364 Mark Moseley	.30	.75
365 Lem Barney	.60	1.50
366 Doug Dressler	.20	.50
367 Dan Fouts RC	20.00	40.00
368 Bob Hyland RC	.20	.50
369 John Outlaw	.20	.50
370 Roy Gerela	.20	.50
371 Isiah Robertson	.30	.75
372 Jerome Barkum	.20	.50
373 Ed Podolak	.20	.50
374 Milt Morin	.20	.50
375 John Niland	.20	.50
376 Checklist 265-396 UER	2.00	4.00
377 Ken Iman	.20	.50
378 Manny Fernandez	.30	.75
379 Dave Gallagher RC	.20	.50
380 Ken Stabler	7.50	15.00
381 Mack Herron RC	.20	.50
382 Bill McClard RC	.20	.50
383 Ray May	.20	.50
384 Don Hansen	.20	.50
385 Elvin Bethea	.60	1.50
386 Joe Scibelli	.20	.50
387 Neal Craig RC	.20	.50
388 Marty Domres	.20	.50
389 Ken Ellis	.20	.50
390 Charle Young	.30	.75
391 Tommy Hart	.20	.50
392 Moses Denson RC	.20	.50
393 Larry Walton	.20	.50
394 Dave Green RC	.20	.50
395 Ron Johnson	.30	.75
396 Ed Bradley RC	.20	.50
397 J.T. Thomas RC	.20	.50
398 Jim Bailey	.20	.50
399 Barry Pearson	.20	.50
400 Fran Tarkenton	4.00	8.00
401 Jack Rudnay	.20	.50
402 Rayfield Wright	.30	.75
403 Roger Wehrli	.40	1.00
404 Vern Den Herder	.20	.50
405 Fred Biletnikoff	1.50	3.00
406 Ken Grandberry RC	.20	.50
407 Bob Adams RC	.20	.50
408 Jim Merlo	.20	.50
409 John Pitts	.20	.50
410 Dave Osborn	.30	.75
411 Dennis Havig	.20	.50
412 Bob Johnson	.20	.50
413 Ken Burrough UER	.30	.75
414 Jim Cheyunski	.20	.50
415 MacArthur Lane	.20	.50
416 Joe Theismann RC	12.50	25.00
417 Mike Boryla RC	.20	.50
418 Bruce Taylor	.20	.50
419 Chris Hanburger	.30	.75
420 Tom Mack	.60	1.50
421 Errol Mann	.20	.50
422 Jack Gregory	.20	.50
423 Harrison Davis RC	.20	.50
424 Burgess Owens	.20	.50
425 Joe Greene	2.50	5.00
426 Morris Stroud	.20	.50
427 John DeMarie	.20	.50
428 Mel Renfro	.60	1.50
429 Cid Edwards	.20	.50
430 Mike Reid	.60	1.50
431 Jack Mildren RC	.20	.50
432 Jerry Simmons	.20	.50
433 Ron Yary	.60	1.50
434 Howard Stevens RC	.20	.50
435 Ray Guy	.75	2.00
436 Tommy Nobis	.60	1.50
437 Solomon Freelon	.20	.50
438 J.D. Hill	.30	.75
439 Toni Linhart RC	.20	.50
440 Dick Anderson	.30	.75
441 Guy Morriss RC	.20	.50
442 Bob Hoskins	.20	.50
443 John Hadl	.60	1.50
444 Roy Jefferson	.20	.50
445 Charlie Sanders	.40	1.00
446 Pat Curran RC	.20	.50
447 David Knight RC	.20	.50
448 Bob Brown DT	.20	.50
449 Pete Gogolak	.20	.50
450 Terry Metcalf	.60	1.50
451 Bill Bergey	.60	1.50
452 Dan Abramowicz HL	.30	.75
453 Otis Armstrong HL	.30	.75
454 Cliff Branch HL	.60	1.50
455 John James HL	.20	.50
456 Lydell Mitchell HL	.30	.75
457 Lemar Parrish HL	.30	.75
458 Ken Stabler HL	2.50	5.00
459 Lynn Swann HL	4.00	8.00
460 Emmitt Thomas HL	.20	.50
461 Terry Bradshaw	10.00	20.00
462 Jerrel Wilson	.20	.50
463 Walter Johnson	.20	.50
464 Golden Richards RC	.30	.75
465 Tommy Casanova	.30	.75
466 Randy Jackson	.20	.50
467 Ron Bolton	.20	.50
468 Joe Owens	.20	.50
469 Wally Hilgenberg	.20	.50
470 Riley Odoms	.30	.75
471 Otis Sistrunk	.30	.75
472 Eddie Ray RC	.20	.50
473 Reggie McKenzie	.30	.75
474 Elbert Drungo	.20	.50
475 Mercury Morris	.60	1.50
476 Dan Dickel RC	.20	.50
477 Merritt Kersey RC	.20	.50
478 Mike Holmes RC	.20	.50
479 Clarence Williams	.20	.50
480 Billy Kilmer	.60	1.50
481 Altie Taylor	.20	.50
482 Dave Elmendorf	.20	.50
483 Bob Rowe	.20	.50
484 Pete Athas	.20	.50
485 Winston Hill	.20	.50
486 Bo Matthews RC	.20	.50
487 Earl Thomas RC	.20	.50
488 Jan Stenerud	.60	1.50
489 Steve Holden RC	.20	.50
490 Cliff Harris RC	3.00	6.00
491 Boobie Clark RC	.30	.75
492 Joe Taylor	.20	.50
493 Tom Neville	.20	.50
494 Wayne Colman	.20	.50
495 Jim Mitchell	.20	.50
496 Paul Krause	.60	1.50
497 Jim Otto	.60	1.50
498 John Rowser	.20	.50
499 Larry Little	.60	1.50
500 O.J. Simpson	5.00	10.00
501 John Dutton RC	.60	1.50
502 Pat Hughes	.20	.50
503 Malcolm Snider	.20	.50
504 Fred Willis	.20	.50
505 Harold Jackson	.60	1.50
506 Mike Bragg	.20	.50
507 Jerry Sherk	.30	.75
508 Mirro Roder RC	.20	.50
509 Tom Sullivan RC	.20	.50
510 Jim Hart	.60	1.50
511 Cedrick Hardman	.20	.50
512 Blaine Nye	.20	.50
513 Elmo Wright	.20	.50
514 Herb Orvis RC	.20	.50
515 Richard Caster	.30	.75
516 Doug Kotar RC	.20	.50
517 Checklist 397-528	2.00	4.00
518 Jesse Freitas RC	.20	.50
519 Ken Houston	.60	1.50
520 Alan Page	.60	1.50
521 Tim Foley	.30	.75
522 Bill Olds RC	.20	.50
523 Bobby Maples	.20	.50
524 Cliff Branch RC	7.50	15.00
525 Merlin Olsen	.60	1.50
526 AFC Champs Brad. Harris	2.00	4.00
527 NFC Champs Foreman	.60	1.50
528 Super Bowl IX Bradshaw	2.50	5.00

1975 Topps Team Checklists

The 1975 Topps Team Checklist set contains 26 standard-size cards, one for each of the 26 NFL teams. The front of the card has the 1975 schedule, while the back of the card contains the checklist, complete with boxes in which to place check marks. The player's position is also listed with his name. The set was only available directly from Topps as a send-off offer as an uncut sheet; the prices below apply equally to uncut sheets as they are frequently found in their original uncut condition. As for individual cards, thin card stock mkaes it a challenge to find these cards in top grades. These unnumbered cards are numbered below for convenience in alphabetical order by team name.

Card	Low	High
COMPLETE SET (26)	125.00	250.00
1 Atlanta Falcons	5.00	10.00
2 Baltimore Colts	5.00	10.00
3 Buffalo Bills	5.00	10.00
4 Chicago Bears	7.50	15.00
5 Cincinnati Bengals	5.00	10.00
6 Cleveland Browns	7.50	15.00
7 Dallas Cowboys	10.00	20.00
8 Denver Broncos	5.00	10.00
9 Detroit Lions	5.00	10.00
10 Green Bay Packers	7.50	15.00
11 Houston Oilers	5.00	10.00
12 Kansas City Chiefs	5.00	10.00
13 Los Angeles Rams	5.00	10.00
14 Miami Dolphins	7.50	15.00
15 Minnesota Vikings	7.50	15.00
16 New England Patriots	5.00	10.00
17 New York Giants	7.50	15.00
18 New York Jets	5.00	10.00
19 New Orleans Saints	5.00	10.00
20 Oakland Raiders	10.00	20.00
21 Philadelphia Eagles	5.00	10.00
22 Pittsburgh Steelers	7.50	15.00
23 St. Louis Cardinals	5.00	10.00
24 San Diego Chargers	5.00	10.00
25 San Francisco 49ers	7.50	15.00
26 Washington Redskins	7.50	15.00

1976 Topps

The 1976 Topps football set contains 528 standard-size cards including the first year cards of Seattle Seahawks and Tampa Bay Buccaneers. Underneath photos that are bordered by a team color, card fronts contain a team colored football at bottom left with the team name within. The player's name and position are also at the bottom. The card backs are printed in orange and blue on gray card stock and are horizontally designed. The content includes statistics, highlights and a trivia question with answer. Subsets include Record Breakers (1-8), league leaders (201-206), playoffs (331-333) and team checklist (451-478) cards. The key Rookie Card belongs to all-time rushing leader Walter Payton. Other Rookie Cards include Randy Gradishar, Ed Too Tall Jones, Jack Lambert, Harvey Martin, and Randy White. An uncut sheet of team checklist cards was also available via a mail-in offer on wax packs.

Card	Low	High
COMPLETE SET (528)	200.00	350.00
1 George Blanda RB	2.50	5.00
2 Neal Colzie RB	.30	.75
3 Chuck Foreman RB	.30	.75
4 Jim Marshall RB	.30	.75
5 Terry Metcalf RB	.30	.75
6 O.J.Simpson RB	1.50	3.00
7 Fran Tarkenton RB	1.50	3.00
8 Charley Taylor RB	.60	1.50
9 Ernie Holmes	.30	.75
10 Ken Anderson AP	.60	1.50
11 Bobby Bryant	.20	.50
12 Jerry Smith	.30	.75
13 David Lee	.20	.50
14 Robert Newhouse RC	.60	1.50
15 Vern Den Herder	.20	.50
16 John Hannah	.60	1.50
17 J.D. Hill	.30	.75
18 James Harris	.30	.75
19 Willie Buchanon	.20	.50
20 Charle Young	.30	.75
21 Jim Yarbrough	.20	.50
22 Ronnie Coleman RC	.20	.50
23 Don Cockroft	.20	.50
24 Willie Lanier	.60	1.50
25 Fred Biletnikoff	1.50	3.00
26 Ron Yankowski	.20	.50
27 Spider Lockhart	.20	.50
28 Bob Johnson	.20	.50
29 J.T. Thomas	.20	.50
30 Ron Yary	.60	1.50
31 Brad Dusek RC	.20	.50
32 Raymond Chester	.30	.75
33 Larry Little	.60	1.50
34 Pat Leahy RC	.60	1.50
35 Steve Bartkowski RC	2.00	4.00
36 Tom Myers	.20	.50
37 Bill Van Heusen	.20	.50
38 Russ Washington	.20	.50
39 Tom Sullivan	.20	.50
40 Curley Culp	.75	2.00
41 Johnnie Gray RC	.20	.50
42 Bob Klein	.20	.50
43 Lem Barney	.60	1.50
44 Harvey Martin RC	3.00	6.00
45 Reggie Rucker	.30	.75
46 Neil Clabo RC	.20	.50
47 Ray Hamilton RC	.20	.50
48 Joe Ferguson	.30	.75
49 Ed Podolak	.20	.50
50 Ray Guy AP	.60	1.50
51 Glen Edwards	.20	.50
52 Jim LeClair RC	.20	.50
53 Mike Barnes RC	.20	.50
54 Nat Moore RC	.60	1.50
55 Billy Kilmer	.60	1.50
56 Larry Stallings	.20	.50
57 Jack Gregory	.20	.50
58 Steve Mike-Mayer RC	.20	.50
59 Virgil Livers RC	.20	.50
60 Jerry Sherk	.30	.75
61 Guy Morriss	.20	.50
62 Barty Smith	.20	.50
63 Jerome Barkum	.20	.50
64 Ira Gordon RC	.20	.50
65 Paul Krause	.60	1.50
66 John McMakin	.20	.50
67 Checklist 1-132	1.50	3.00
68 Charlie Johnson UER	.30	.75
69 Tommy Nobis	.60	1.50
70 Lydell Mitchell	.30	.75
71 Vern Holland	.20	.50
72 Tim Foley	.30	.75
73 Golden Richards	.30	.75
74 Bryant Salter	.20	.50
75 Terry Bradshaw	10.00	20.00
76 Ted Hendricks	.60	1.50
77 Rich Saul RC	.20	.50
78 John Smith RC	.20	.50
79 Altie Taylor	.20	.50
80 Cedrick Hardman	.20	.50
81 Ken Payne RC	.20	.50
82 Zeke Moore	.20	.50
83 Alvin Maxson RC	.20	.50
84 Wally Hilgenberg	.20	.50
85 John Niland	.20	.50
86 Mike Sensibaugh	.20	.50
87 Ron Johnson	.30	.75
88 Winston Hill	.20	.50
89 Charlie Joiner	2.00	4.00
90 Roger Wehrli	.30	.75
91 Mike Bragg	.20	.50
92 Dan Dickel	.20	.50
93 Earl Morrall	.30	.75
94 Pat Toomay	.20	.50
95 Gary Garrison	.20	.50
96 Ken Geddes RC	.20	.50
97 Mike Current	.20	.50
98 Bob Avellini RC	.30	.75
99 Dave Pureifory RC	.20	.50
100 Franco Harris AP	4.00	8.00
101 Randy Logan RC	.20	.50
102 John Fitzgerald	.20	.50
103 Gregg Bingham RC	.30	.75
104 Jim Plunkett	.60	1.50
105 Carl Eller	.60	1.50
106 Larry Walton	.20	.50
107 Clarence Scott	.20	.50
108 Skip Vanderbundt	.20	.50
109 Boobie Clark	.30	.75
110 Tom Mack	.60	1.50
111 Bruce Laird	.20	.50
112 Dave Dalby RC	.20	.50
113 John Leypoldt	.20	.50
114 Barry Pearson	.20	.50
115 Larry Brown	.30	.75
116 Jackie Smith	.60	1.50
117 Pat Hughes	.20	.50
118 Al Woodall	.20	.50
119 John Zook	.20	.50
120 Jake Scott	.30	.75
121 Rich Glover RC	.20	.50
122 Ernie Jackson	.20	.50
123 Otis Armstrong	.60	1.50
124 Bob Grim	.20	.50
125 Jeff Siemon	.30	.75
126 Harold Hart RC	.20	.50
127 John DeMarie	.20	.50
128 Dan Fouts	6.00	12.00
129 Jim Kearney	.20	.50
130 John Dutton AP	.30	.75
131 Calvin Hill	.60	1.50
132 Toni Fritsch	.20	.50
133 Ron Jessie	.20	.50
134 Don Nottingham	.20	.50
135 Lemar Parrish	.20	.50
136 Russ Francis RC	.60	1.50
137 Joe Reed	.20	.50
138 C.L. Whittington RC	.20	.50
139 Otis Sistrunk	.30	.75
140 Lynn Swann AP	10.00	20.00
141 Jim Carter	.20	.50
142 Mike Montler	.20	.50
143 Walter Johnson	.20	.50
144 Doug Kotar	.20	.50
145 Roman Gabriel	.60	1.50
146 Billy Newsome	.20	.50
147 Ed Bradley	.20	.50
148 Walter Payton RC	125.00	250.00
149 Johnny Fuller	.20	.50
150 Alan Page AP	.60	1.50
151 Frank Grant RC	.20	.50

152 Dave Green .20 .50
153 Nelson Munsey RC .20 .50
154 Jim Mandich .20 .50
155 Lawrence McCutcheon .60 1.50
156 Steve Ramsey .20 .50
157 Ed Flanagan .20 .50
158 Randy White RC 10.00 20.00
159 Gerry Mullins .20 .50
160 Jan Stenerud AP .60 1.50
161 Steve Odom RC .20 .50
162 Roger Finnie .20 .50
163 Norm Snead .30 .75
164 Jeff Van Note .30 .75
165 Bill Bergey .60 1.50
166 Allen Carter RC .20 .50
167 Steve Holden .20 .50
168 Sherman White .20 .50
169 Bob Berry .20 .50
170 Ken Houston AP .60 1.50
171 Bill Olds .20 .50
172 Larry Seiple .20 .50
173 Cliff Branch 2.00 4.00
174 Reggie McKenzie .30 .75
175 Dan Pastorini .60 1.50
176 Paul Naumoff .20 .50
177 Checklist 133-264 1.50 3.00
178 Durwood Keeton RC .20 .50
179 Earl Thomas .20 .50
180 L.C. Greenwood AP .60 1.50
181 John Outlaw .20 .50
182 Frank Nunley .20 .50
183 Dave Jennings RC .30 .75
184 MacArthur Lane .20 .50
185 Chester Marcol .20 .50
186 J.J. Jones RC .20 .50
187 Tom DeLeone RC .20 .50
188 Steve Zabel .20 .50
189 Ken Johnson DT RC .20 .50
190 Rayfield Wright .30 .75
191 Brent McClanahan RC .20 .50
192 Pat Fischer .30 .75
193 Roger Carr RC .30 .75
194 Manny Fernandez .30 .75
195 Roy Gerela .20 .50
196 Dave Elmendorf .20 .50
197 Bob Kowalkowski .20 .50
198 Phil Villapiano .30 .75
199 Will Wynn RC .20 .50
200 Terry Metcalf .60 1.50
201 Tarkenton Anderson LL .75 2.00
202 Receiving Leaders .30 .75
203 O.J.Simpson J.Otis LL 1.25 2.50
204 Simpson Foreman LL 1.25 2.50
205 M.Blount P.Krause LL .60 1.50
206 Punting Leaders .30 .75
207 Ken Ellis .20 .50
208 Ron Saul .20 .50
209 Toni Linhart .20 .50
210 Jim Langer AP .60 1.50
211 Jeff Wright S RC .20 .50
212 Moses Denson .20 .50
213 Earl Edwards .20 .50
214 Walker Gillette .20 .50
215 Bob Trumpy .30 .75
216 Emmitt Thomas .30 .75
217 Lyle Alzado .60 1.50
218 Carl Garrett .30 .75
219 Van Green RC .20 .50
220 Jack Lambert AP RC 20.00 35.00
221 Spike Jones .20 .50
222 John Hadl .60 1.50
223 Billy Johnson RC .60 1.50
224 Tony McGee DT .20 .50
225 Preston Pearson .30 .75
226 Isiah Robertson .30 .75
227 Errol Mann .20 .50
228 Paul Seal RC .20 .50
229 Roland Harper RC .20 .50
230 Ed White RC .30 .75
231 Joe Theismann 3.00 6.00
232 Jim Cheyunski .20 .50
233 Bill Stanfill .30 .75
234 Marv Hubbard .20 .50
235 Tommy Casanova .30 .75
236 Bob Hyland .20 .50
237 Jesse Freitas .20 .50
238 Norm Thompson .20 .50
239 Charlie Smith WR .20 .50
240 John James .20 .50
241 Alden Roche .20 .50
242 Gordon Jolley RC .20 .50
243 Larry Ely RC .20 .50
244 Richard Caster .20 .50
245 Joe Greene 2.00 5.00
246 Larry Schreiber .20 .50
247 Terry Schmidt RC .20 .50
248 Jerrel Wilson .20 .50
249 Marty Domres .20 .50
250 Isaac Curtis .30 .75
251 Harold McLinton RC .20 .50
252 Fred Dryer .60 1.50
253 Bill Lenkaitis .20 .50
254 Don Hardeman RC .20 .50
255 Bob Griese 2.00 4.00
256 Oscar Roan RC .20 .50
257 Randy Gradishar RC 2.00 5.00
258 Bob Thomas RC .20 .50
259 Joe Owens .20 .50
260 Cliff Harris AP .60 1.50
261 Frank Lewis .20 .50
262 Mike McCoy .20 .50
263 Rickey Young RC .20 .50
264 Brian Kelley RC .20 .50
265 Charlie Sanders .30 .75
266 Jim Hart .60 1.50
267 Greg Gantt RC .20 .50
268 John Ward RC .20 .50
269 Al Beauchamp .20 .50
270 Jack Tatum .60 1.50
271 Jim Lash RC .20 .50
272 Diron Talbert .20 .50
273 Checklist 265-396 1.50 3.00
274 Steve Spurrier 3.00 8.00
275 Greg Pruitt .60 1.50
276 Jim Mitchell .20 .50
277 Jack Rudnay .20 .50
278 Freddie Solomon RC .30 .75
279 Frank LeMaster RC .20 .50
280 Wally Chambers .20 .50
281 Mike Collier RC .20 .50
282 Clarence Williams .20 .50
283 Mitch Hoopes RC .20 .50
284 Ron Bolton .20 .50
285 Harold Jackson .60 1.50
286 Greg Landry .30 .75
287 Tony Greene .20 .50
288 Howard Stevens .20 .50
289 Roy Jefferson .20 .50
290 Jim Bakken .20 .50
291 Doug Sutherland RC .20 .50
292 Marvin Cobb RC .20 .50
293 Mack Alston .20 .50
294 Rod McNeill RC .20 .50
295 Gene Upshaw .60 1.50
296 Dave Gallagher .20 .50
297 Larry Ball RC .20 .50
298 Ron Howard RC .20 .50
299 Don Strock RC .60 1.50
300 O.J. Simpson AP 4.00 8.00
301 Ray Mansfield .20 .50
302 Larry Marshall RC .20 .50
303 Dick Himes RC .20 .50
304 Ray Wersching RC .20 .50
305 John Riggins 2.00 4.00
306 Bob Parsons RC .20 .50
307 Ray Brown .20 .50
308 Len Dawson 1.50 3.00
309 Andy Maurer .20 .50
310 Jack Youngblood AP .60 1.50
311 Essex Johnson .20 .50
312 Stan White .20 .50
313 Drew Pearson 2.00 5.00
314 Rockne Freitas .20 .50
315 Mercury Morris .60 1.50
316 Willie Alexander .20 .50
317 Paul Warfield 1.50 3.00
318 Bob Chandler .30 .75
319 Bobby Walden .20 .50
320 Riley Odoms .30 .75
321 Mike Boryla .20 .50
322 Bruce Van Dyke .20 .50
323 Pete Banaszak .20 .50
324 Darryl Stingley .60 1.50
325 John Mendenhall .20 .50
326 Dan Dierdorf .75 2.00
327 Bruce Taylor .20 .50
328 Don McCauley .20 .50
329 John Reaves UER .20 .50
330 Chris Hanburger .30 .75
331 NFC Champs Staubach 1.50 3.00
332 AFC Champs F.Harris .75 2.00
333 Super Bowl X Bradshaw 1.25 2.50
334 Godwin Turk RC .20 .50
335 Dick Anderson .30 .75
336 Woody Green RC .20 .50
337 Pat Curran .20 .50
338 Council Rudolph RC .20 .50
339 Joe Lavender RC .20 .50
340 John Gilliam .30 .75
341 Steve Furness RC .30 .75
342 D.D. Lewis .30 .75
343 Duane Carrell RC .20 .50
344 Jon Morris .20 .50
345 John Brockington .30 .75
346 Mike Phipps .30 .75
347 Lyle Blackwood RC .20 .50
348 Julius Adams .20 .50
349 Terry Hermeling RC .20 .50
350 Rolland Lawrence AP RC .20 .50
351 Glenn Doughty .20 .50
352 Doug Swift .20 .50
353 Mike Strachan RC .20 .50
354 Craig Morton .60 1.50
355 George Blanda 2.50 5.00
356 Garry Puetz .20 .50
357 Carl Mauck .20 .50
358 Walt Patulski .20 .50
359 Stu Voigt .20 .50
360 Fred Carr .20 .50
361 Po James .20 .50
362 Otis Taylor .60 1.50
363 Jeff West RC .20 .50
364 Gary Huff .30 .75
365 Dwight White .30 .75
366 Dan Ryczek RC .20 .50
367 Jon Keyworth RC .20 .50
368 Mel Renfro .60 1.50
369 Bruce Coslet RC .60 1.50
370 Len Hauss .20 .50
371 Rick Volk .20 .50
372 Howard Twilley .30 .75
373 Cullen Bryant RC .30 .75
374 Bob Babich .20 .50
375 Herman Weaver .20 .50
376 Steve Grogan RC 1.25 3.00
377 Bubba Smith .60 1.50
378 Burgess Owens .20 .50
379 Al Matthews .20 .50
380 Art Shell .60 1.50
381 Larry Brown .20 .50
382 Horst Muhlmann .20 .50
383 Ahmad Rashad 1.25 2.50
384 Bobby Maples .20 .50
385 Jim Marshall .60 1.50
386 Joe Dawkins .20 .50
387 Dennis Partee .20 .50
388 Eddie McMillan RC .20 .50
389 Randy Johnson .20 .50
390 Bob Kuechenberg .20 .50
391 Rufus Mayes .20 .50
392 Lloyd Mumphord .20 .50
393 Ike Harris RC .20 .50
394 Dave Hampton .20 .50
395 Roger Staubach 10.00 20.00
396 Doug Buffone .20 .50
397 Howard Fest .20 .50
398 Wayne Mulligan .20 .50
399 Bill Bradley .30 .75
400 Chuck Foreman AP .60 1.50
401 Jack Snow .30 .75
402 Bob Howard .20 .50
403 John Matuszak .60 1.50
404 Bill Munson .30 .75
405 Andy Russell .30 .75
406 Skip Butler .20 .50
407 Hugh McKinnis RC .20 .50
408 Bob Penchion RC .20 .50
409 Mike Bass .20 .50
410 George Kunz .20 .50
411 Ron Pritchard .20 .50
412 Barry Smith RC .20 .50
413 Norm Bulaich .20 .50
414 Marv Bateman .20 .50
415 Ken Stabler 6.00 12.00
416 Conrad Dobler .30 .75
417 Bob Tucker .30 .75
418 Gene Washington 49er .30 .75
419 Ed Marinaro .60 1.50
420 Jack Ham AP 2.00 4.00
421 Jim Turner .20 .50
422 Chris Fletcher .20 .50
423 Carl Barzilauskas RC .20 .50
424 Robert Brazile RC 2.00 5.00
425 Harold Carmichael .75 2.00
426 Ron Jaworski RC 3.00 6.00
427 Ed Too Tall Jones RC 10.00 20.00
428 Larry McCarren RC .20 .50
429 Mike Thomas RC .20 .50
430 Joe DeLamielleure .60 1.50
431 Tom Blanchard .20 .50
432 Ron Carpenter .20 .50
433 Levi Johnson .20 .50
434 Sam Cunningham .30 .75
435 Garo Yepremian .30 .75
436 Mike Livingston .20 .50
437 Larry Csonka 2.00 4.00
438 Doug Dieken .30 .75
439 Bill Lueck .20 .50
440 Tom MacLeod RC .20 .50
441 Mick Tingelhoff .30 .75
442 Terry Hanratty .30 .75
443 Mike Siani .20 .50
444 Dwight Harrison .20 .50
445 Jim Otis .30 .75
446 Jack Reynolds .30 .75
447 Jean Fugett RC .30 .75
448 Dave Beverly RC .20 .50
449 Bernard Jackson RC .20 .50
450 Charley Taylor .75 2.00
451 Atlanta Falcons CL .75 2.00
452 Baltimore Colts CL .75 2.00
453 Buffalo Bills CL .75 2.00
454 Chicago Bears CL .75 2.00
455 Cincinnati Bengals CL .75 2.00
456 Cleveland Browns CL .75 2.00
457 Dallas Cowboys CL .75 2.00
458 Denver Broncos CL UER .75 2.00
459 Detroit Lions CL .75 2.00
460 Green Bay Packers CL .75 2.00
461 Houston Oilers CL .75 2.00
462 Kansas City Chiefs CL .75 2.00
463 Los Angeles Rams CL .75 2.00
464 Miami Dolphins CL .75 2.00
465 Minnesota Vikings CL .75 2.00
466 New England Patriots CL .75 2.00
467 New Orleans Saints CL .75 2.00
468 New York Giants CL .75 2.00
469 New York Jets CL .75 2.00
470 Oakland Raiders CL .75 2.00
471 Philadelphia Eagles CL .75 2.00
472 Pittsburgh Steelers CL .75 2.00
473 St. Louis Cardinals CL .75 2.00
474 San Diego Chargers CL .75 2.00
475 San Francisco 49ers CL .75 2.00
476 Seattle Seahawks CL .75 2.00
477 Tampa Bay Buccaneers CL .75 2.00
478 Washington Redskins CL .75 2.00
479 Fred Cox .20 .50
480 Mel Blount AP 3.00 6.00
481 John Bunting RC .30 .75
482 Ken Mendenhall .20 .50
483 Will Harrell RC .20 .50
484 Marlin Briscoe .20 .50
485 Archie Manning .60 1.50
486 Tody Smith .20 .50
487 George Hunt .20 .50
488 Roscoe Word RC .20 .50
489 Paul Seymour .20 .50
490 Lee Roy Jordan AP .60 1.50
491 Chip Myers .20 .50
492 Norm Evans .20 .50
493 Jim Bertelsen .20 .50
494 Mark Moseley .30 .75
495 George Buehler RC .20 .50
496 Charlie Hall .20 .50
497 Marvin Upshaw .20 .50
498 Tom Banks RC .20 .50
499 Randy Vataha .20 .50
500 Fran Tarkenton AP 3.00 6.00
501 Mike Wagner .30 .75
502 Art Malone .20 .50
503 Fred Cook RC .20 .50
504 Rich McGeorge .20 .50
505 Ken Burrough .30 .75
506 Nick Mike-Mayer .20 .50
507 Checklist 397-528 1.50 3.00
508 Steve Owens .30 .75
509 Brad Van Pelt RC .20 .50
510 Ken Riley .30 .75
511 Art Thoms .20 .50
512 Ed Bell .20 .50
513 Tom Wittum .20 .50
514 Jim Braxton .20 .50
515 Nick Buoniconti .60 1.50
516 Brian Sipe RC 2.50 6.00
517 Jim Lynch .20 .50
518 Prentice McCray RC .20 .50
519 Tom Dempsey .20 .50
520 Mel Gray .30 .75
521 Nate Wright .20 .50
522 Rocky Bleier 3.00 6.00
523 Dennis Johnson RC .20 .50
524 Jerry Sisemore .20 .50
525 Bert Jones .20 .50
526 Perry Smith RC .20 .50
527 Blaine Nye .20 .50
528 Bob Moore .60 1.50

1976 Topps Team Checklists

The 1976 Topps Team Checklist set contains 30 standard-size cards, one for each of the 28 NFL teams plus two checklist cards. The front of the card has the 1976 Topps checklist for that particular team, complete with boxes in which to place check marks. The set was only available directly from Topps as a send-off offer as an uncut sheet; the prices below apply equally to uncut sheets as they are frequently found in their original uncut condition. As for individual cards, thin card stock makes it a challenge to obtain singles in top grades. These unnumbered cards are numbered below for convenience in alphabetical order by team name.

COMPLETE SET (30) 62.50 125.00
1 Atlanta Falcons 2.50 5.00
2 Baltimore Colts 2.50 5.00
3 Buffalo Bills 2.50 5.00
4 Chicago Bears 2.50 5.00
5 Cincinnati Bengals 2.50 5.00
6 Cleveland Browns 2.50 5.00
7 Dallas Cowboys 5.00 10.00
8 Denver Broncos 2.50 5.00
9 Detroit Lions 2.50 5.00
10 Green Bay Packers 3.75 7.50
11 Houston Oilers 2.50 5.00
12 Kansas City Chiefs 2.50 5.00
13 Los Angeles Rams 2.50 5.00
14 Miami Dolphins 3.75 7.50
15 Minnesota Vikings 2.50 5.00
16 New England Patriots 2.50 5.00
17 New York Giants 2.50 5.00
18 New York Jets 2.50 5.00
19 New Orleans Saints 2.50 5.00
20 Oakland Raiders 5.00 10.00
21 Philadelphia Eagles 2.50 5.00
22 Pittsburgh Steelers 3.75 7.50
23 St. Louis Cardinals 2.50 5.00
24 San Diego Chargers 2.50 5.00
25 San Francisco 49ers 3.75 7.50
26 Seattle Seahawks 2.50 5.00
27 Tampa Bay Buccaneers 2.50 5.00
28 Washington Redskins 3.75 7.50
29 Checklist 1-132 2.50 5.00
30 Checklist 133-264 2.50 5.00

1977 Topps

The 1977 Topps football set contains 528 standard-size cards. Card fronts have a banner (with team name), the player's name and position at the top. Backs that rushed for 1,000 yards have a "1,000 Yarder" football logo on front. The card backs are printed in purple and black on gray card stock. The backs contain yearly statistics, highlights and a note on the player's college career. Subsets include league leaders (1-6), team checklist cards (201-208), Record Breakers (451-455) and playoffs (526-528). The key Rookie Card is Steve Largent. Other Rookie Cards include Harry Carson, Dave Casper, Archie Griffin, Mike Haynes, Ray Rhodes, Lee Roy Selmon, Mike Webster, Danny White and Jim Zorn. An uncut sheet of team checklist cards was also available via a mail-in offer on wax pack wrappers. A Mexican version of this set was produced. All text is in Spanish (front and back) and is quite a bit tougher to find than the basic issue.

COMPLETE SET (528) 125.00 250.00
1 K.Stabler/J.Harris LL 1.25 2.50
2 Drew Pearson/M.Lane LL .40 1.00
3 W.Payton/Simpson LL 5.00 10.00
4 Scoring Leaders .25 .60
5 Interception Leaders .25 .60
6 Punting Leaders .15 .40
7 Mike Phipps .25 .60
8 Rick Volk .15 .40
9 Steve Furness .25 .60
10 Isaac Curtis .25 .60
11 Nate Wright .25 .60
12 Jean Fugett .15 .40
13 Ken Mendenhall .15 .40
14 Sam Adams .15 .40
15 Charlie Waters .40 1.00
16 Bill Stanfill .15 .40
17 John Holland RC .15 .40
18 Pat Haden RC .75 2.00
19 Bob Young .15 .40
20 Wally Chambers .15 .40
21 Lawrence Gaines RC .15 .40
22 Larry McCarren .15 .40
23 Horst Muhlmann .15 .40
24 Phil Villapiano .25 .60
25 Greg Pruitt .25 .60
26 Ron Howard .15 .40
27 Craig Morton .40 1.00
28 Rufus Mayes .15 .40
29 Lee Roy Selmon UER RC 7.50 15.00
30 Ed White .25 .60
31 Harold McLinton .15 .40
32 Glenn Doughty .15 .40
33 Bob Kuechenberg .40 1.00
34 Duane Carrell .15 .40
35 Riley Odoms .15 .40
36 Bobby Scott .15 .40
37 Nick Mike-Mayer .15 .40
38 Bill Lenkaitis .15 .40
39 Roland Harper .25 .60
40 Tommy Hart .15 .40
41 Mike Sensibaugh .15 .40
42 Rusty Jackson RC .15 .40
43 Levi Johnson .15 .40
44 Mike McCoy .15 .40
45 Roger Staubach 10.00 20.00
46 Fred Cox .15 .40
47 Bob Babich .15 .40
48 Reggie McKenzie .25 .60
49 Dave Jennings .15 .40
50 Mike Haynes RC 4.00 10.00
51 Larry Brown .25 .60
52 Marvin Cobb .15 .40
53 Fred Cook .15 .40
54 Freddie Solomon .25 .60
55 John Riggins 1.25 2.50
56 John Bunting .25 .60
57 Ray Wersching .25 .60
58 Mike Livingston .15 .40
59 Billy Johnson .25 .60
60 Mike Wagner .15 .40
61 Waymond Bryant RC .15 .40
62 Jim Otis .25 .60
63 Ed Galigher RC .15 .40
64 Randy Vataha .15 .40
65 Jim Zorn RC 2.00 5.00
66 Jon Keyworth .15 .40
67 Checklist 1-132 .75 2.00
68 Henry Childs RC .15 .40
69 Thom Darden .15 .40
70 George Kunz .15 .40
71 Lenvil Elliott RC .15 .40
72 Curtis Johnson RC .15 .40
73 Doug Van Horn .15 .40
74 Joe Theismann 2.00 4.00
75 Dwight White .25 .60
76 Scott Laidlaw RC .15 .40
77 Monte Johnson RC .15 .40
78 Dave Beverly .15 .40
79 Jim Mitchell .15 .40
80 Jack Youngblood AP .40 1.00
81 Mel Gray .25 .60
82 Dwight Harrison .15 .40
83 John Hadl .25 .60
84 Matt Blair RC .40 1.00
85 Charlie Sanders .25 .60
86 Noah Jackson RC .15 .40
87 Ed Marinaro .25 .60
88 Bob Howard .15 .40
89 John McDaniel RC .15 .40
90 Dan Dierdorf AP .60 1.50
91 Mark Moseley .25 .60
92 Cleo Miller RC .15 .40
93 Andre Tillman RC .15 .40
94 Bruce Taylor .15 .40
95 Bert Jones .40 1.00
96 Anthony Davis RC .40 1.00
97 Don Goode RC .15 .40
98 Ray Rhodes RC 2.00 6.00
99 Mike Webster RC 6.00 12.00
100 O.J. Simpson AP 3.00 6.00
101 Doug Plank RC .15 .40
102 Efren Herrera RC .25 .60
103 Charlie Smith .15 .40
104 Carlos Brown RC .40 1.00
105 Jim Marshall .40 1.00
106 Paul Naumoff .15 .40
107 Walter White RC .15 .40
108 John Cappelletti RC 1.25 3.00
109 Chip Myers .15 .40
110 Ken Stabler AP 5.00 10.00
111 Joe Ehrmann RC .15 .40
112 Rick Engles RC .15 .40
113 Jack Dolbin RC .15 .40
114 Ron Bolton .15 .40
115 Mike Thomas .15 .40
116 Mike Fuller RC .15 .40
117 John Hill RC .15 .40
118 Richard Todd RC .40 1.00
119 Duriel Harris RC .40 1.00
120 John James .15 .40
121 Lionel Antoine RC .15 .40
122 John Skorupan .15 .40
123 Skip Butler .15 .40
124 Bob Tucker .15 .40
125 Paul Krause .40 1.00
126 Dave Hampton .15 .40
127 Tom Wittum .15 .40
128 Gary Huff .25 .60
129 Emmitt Thomas .25 .60
130 Drew Pearson AP .75 2.00
131 Ron Saul .15 .40
132 Steve Niehaus RC .15 .40
133 Fred Carr .40 1.00
134 Norm Bulaich .15 .40
135 Bob Trumpy .25 .60
136 Greg Landry .25 .60
137 George Buehler .15 .40
138 Reggie Rucker .25 .60
139 Julius Adams .15 .40
140 Jack Ham AP 1.25 2.50
141 Wayne Morris RC .15 .40
142 Marv Bateman .15 .40
143 Bobby Maples .15 .40
144 Harold Carmichael .40 1.00
145 Bob Avellini .25 .60
146 Harry Carson RC 2.50 5.00
147 Lawrence Pillers RC .15 .40
148 Ed Williams RC .15 .40
149 Dan Pastorini .25 .60
150 Ron Yary .40 1.00
151 Joe Lavender .15 .40
152 Pat McInally RC .25 .60
153 Lloyd Mumphord .15 .40
154 Cullen Bryant .25 .60
155 Willie Lanier .40 1.00
156 Gene Washington 49er .25 .60
157 Scott Hunter .15 .40
158 Jim Merlo .15 .40
159 Randy Grossman RC .25 .60
160 Blaine Nye .15 .40
161 Ike Harris .15 .40
162 Doug Dieken .15 .40
163 Guy Morriss .15 .40
164 Bob Parsons .15 .40
165 Steve Grogan .40 1.00
166 John Brockington .25 .60
167 Charlie Joiner 1.25 2.50
168 Ron Carpenter .15 .40
169 Jeff Wright .15 .40
170 Chris Hanburger .15 .40
171 Roosevelt Leaks RC .25 .60
172 Larry Little .40 1.00
173 John Matuszak .25 .60
174 Joe Ferguson .25 .60
175 Brad Van Pelt .25 .60
176 Dexter Bussey RC .25 .60
177 Steve Largent RC 20.00 40.00
178 Dewey Selmon RC .25 .60
179 Randy Gradishar .40 1.00
180 Mel Blount AP 1.50 3.00
181 Dan Neal RC .15 .40
182 Rich Szaro RC .15 .40
183 Mike Boryla .15 .40
184 Steve Jones RC .15 .40
185 Paul Warfield 1.25 2.50
186 Greg Buttle RC .15 .40
187 Rich McGeorge .15 .40
188 Leon Gray RC .25 .60
189 John Shinners RC .15 .40
190 Toni Linhart .15 .40
191 Robert Miller RC .15 .40
192 Jake Scott .15 .40
193 Jon Morris .15 .40
194 Randy Crowder RC .15 .40
195 Lynn Swann UER 10.00 18.00
196 Marsh White RC .15 .40
197 Rod Perry RC .40 1.00
198 Willie Hall RC .15 .40
199 Mike Hartenstine RC .15 .40
200 Jim Bakken .15 .40
201 Atlanta Falcons CL UER .50 1.25
202 Baltimore Colts CL .50 1.25
203 Buffalo Bills CL .50 1.25
204 Chicago Bears CL .50 1.25
205 Cincinnati Bengals CL .50 1.25
206 Cleveland Browns CL .50 1.25
207 Dallas Cowboys CL .50 1.25
208 Denver Broncos CL .50 1.25
209 Detroit Lions CL .50 1.25
210 Green Bay Packers CL .50 1.25
211 Houston Oilers CL .50 1.25
212 Kansas City Chiefs CL .50 1.25
213 Los Angeles Rams CL .50 1.25
214 Miami Dolphins CL .50 1.25
215 Minnesota Vikings CL .50 1.25
216 New England Patriots CL .50 1.25
217 New Orleans Saints CL .50 1.25
218 New York Giants CL .50 1.25
219 New York Jets CL .50 1.25
220 Oakland Raiders CL .50 1.25
221 Philadelphia Eagles CL .50 1.25
222 Pittsburgh Steelers CL .50 1.25
223 St. Louis Cardinals CL .50 1.25
224 San Diego Chargers CL .50 1.25
225 San Francisco 49ers CL .50 1.25
226 Seattle Seahawks CL .50 1.25
227 Tampa Bay Buccaneers CL .50 1.25
228 Washington Redskins CL .50 1.25
229 Sam Cunningham .25 .60
230 Alan Page AP .40 1.00
231 Eddie Brown S RC .15 .40
232 Stan White .15 .40
233 Vern Den Herder .15 .40
234 Clarence Davis .15 .40
235 Ken Anderson .40 1.00
236 Karl Chandler RC .15 .40
237 Will Harrell .15 .40
238 Clarence Scott .15 .40
239 Bo Rather RC .15 .40
240 Robert Brazile AP .25 .60
241 Bob Bell .15 .40
242 Rolland Lawrence .15 .40
243 Tom Sullivan .15 .40
244 Larry Brunson RC .15 .40
245 Terry Bradshaw 10.00 20.00
246 Rich Saul .15 .40
247 Cleveland Elam RC .15 .40
248 Don Woods .15 .40
249 Bruce Laird .15 .40
250 Coy Bacon .25 .60
251 Russ Francis .40 1.00
252 Jim Braxton .15 .40
253 Perry Smith .15 .40
254 Jerome Barkum .15 .40
255 Garo Yepremian .25 .60
256 Checklist 133-264 .75 2.00
257 Tony Galbreath RC .25 .60
258 Troy Archer RC .15 .40
259 Brian Sipe .40 1.00
260 Billy Joe DuPree AP .25 .60
261 Bobby Walden .15 .40
262 Larry Marshall .15 .40
263 Ted Fritsch Jr. .15 .40
264 Larry Hand .15 .40
265 Tom Mack .40 1.00
266 Ed Bradley .15 .40
267 Pat Leahy .25 .60
268 Louis Carter RC .15 .40
269 Archie Griffin RC 3.00 6.00
270 Art Shell AP .40 1.00
271 Stu Voigt .15 .40
272 Prentice McCray .15 .40
273 MacArthur Lane .15 .40
274 Dan Fouts 3.00 6.00
275 Charle Young .25 .60
276 Wilbur Jackson RC .15 .40
277 John Hicks .25 .60
278 Nat Moore .40 1.00
279 Virgil Livers .15 .40
280 Curley Culp .40 1.00
281 Rocky Bleier 1.25 2.50
282 John Zook .15 .40
283 Tom DeLeone .15 .40
284 Danny White RC 6.00 12.00
285 Otis Armstrong .25 .60
286 Larry Walton .15 .40
287 Jim Carter .15 .40
288 Don McCauley .15 .40
289 Frank Grant .15 .40
290 Roger Wehrli .25 .60
291 Mick Tingelhoff .25 .60
292 Bernard Jackson .15 .40
293 Tom Owen RC .15 .40
294 Mike Esposito RC .15 .40
295 Fred Biletnikoff 1.25 2.50
296 Revie Sorey RC .15 .40
297 John McMakin .15 .40
298 Dan Ryczek .15 .40
299 Wayne Moore RC .15 .40
300 Franco Harris AP 2.00 4.00
301 Rick Upchurch RC .40 1.00
302 Jim Stienke RC .15 .40
303 Charlie Davis RC .15 .40
304 Don Cockroft .15 .40
305 Ken Burrough .25 .60
306 Clark Gaines RC .15 .40
307 Bobby Douglass .15 .40
308 Ralph Perretta RC .15 .40
309 Wally Hilgenberg .15 .40
310 Monte Jackson AP RC .25 .60
311 Chris Bahr RC .25 .60
312 Jim Cheyunski .15 .40
313 Mike Patrick RC .15 .40
314 Ed Too Tall Jones 2.50 5.00
315 Bill Bradley .15 .40
316 Benny Malone RC .15 .40
317 Paul Seymour .15 .40
318 Jim Laslavic RC .15 .40
319 Frank Lewis .25 .60
320 Ray Guy AP .40 1.00
321 Allan Ellis RC .15 .40
322 Conrad Dobler .25 .60
323 Chester Marcol .15 .40
324 Doug Kotar .15 .40
325 Lemar Parrish .25 .60
326 Steve Holden .15 .40
327 Jeff Van Note .25 .60
328 Howard Stevens .15 .40
329 Brad Dusek .25 .60
330 Joe DeLamielleure .40 1.00
331 Jim Plunkett .40 1.00
332 Checklist 265-396 .75 2.00
333 Lou Piccone RC .15 .40
334 Ray Hamilton .15 .40
335 Jan Stenerud .40 1.00
336 Jeris White RC .15 .40
337 Sherman Smith RC .15 .40
338 Dave Green .15 .40
339 Terry Schmidt .15 .40
340 Sammie White RC .50 1.25
341 Jon Kolb RC .15 .40
342 Randy White 4.00 8.00
343 Bob Klein .15 .40
344 Bob Kowalkowski .15 .40
345 Terry Metcalf .25 .60
346 Joe Danelo RC .15 .40
347 Ken Payne .15 .40
348 Neal Craig .15 .40
349 Dennis Johnson .15 .40
350 Bill Bergey AP .25 .60
351 Raymond Chester .15 .40
352 Bob Matheson .15 .40
353 Mike Kadish RC .15 .40
354 Mark Van Eeghen RC .60 1.50
355 L.C. Greenwood .40 1.00
356 Sam Hunt RC .15 .40
357 Darrell Austin RC .15 .40
358 Jim Turner .15 .40
359 Ahmad Rashad .75 2.00
360 Walter Payton AP 15.00 40.00
361 Mark Arneson RC .15 .40
362 Jerrel Wilson .15 .40
363 Steve Bartkowski .40 1.00
364 John Watson RC .15 .40
365 Ken Riley .25 .60
366 Gregg Bingham .15 .40
367 Golden Richards .25 .60
368 Clyde Powers RC .15 .40
369 Diron Talbert .15 .40
370 Lydell Mitchell .25 .60
371 Bob Jackson RC .15 .40
372 Jim Mandich .15 .40
373 Frank LeMaster .15 .40
374 Benny Ricardo RC .15 .40
375 Lawrence McCutcheon .25 .60
376 Lynn Dickey .25 .60
377 Phil Wise RC .15 .40
378 Tony McGee .15 .40
379 Norm Thompson .15 .40
380 Dave Casper RC 2.00 5.00
381 Glen Edwards .15 .40
382 Bob Thomas .15 .40
383 Bob Chandler .25 .60
384 Rickey Young .25 .60
385 Carl Eller .40 1.00
386 Lyle Alzado .40 1.00
387 John Leypoldt .15 .40
388 Gordon Bell RC .15 .40
389 Mike Bragg .15 .40
390 Jim Langer AP .40 1.00
391 Vern Holland .15 .40
392 Nelson Munsey .15 .40
393 Mack Mitchell RC .15 .40
394 Tony Adams RC .15 .40
395 Preston Pearson .25 .60
396 Emanuel Zanders RC .15 .40
397 Vince Papale RC 8.00 20.00
398 Joe Fields RC .25 .60
399 Craig Clemons .15 .40
400 Fran Tarkenton AP 2.50 5.00
401 Andy Johnson RC .15 .40
402 Willie Buchanon .15 .40
403 Pat Curran .15 .40
404 Ray Jarvis RC .15 .40
405 Joe Greene 1.25 2.50
406 Bill Simpson RC .15 .40
407 Ronnie Coleman .15 .40
408 J.K. McKay RC .25 .60
409 Pat Fischer .25 .60
410 John Dutton .25 .60
411 Boobie Clark .15 .40
412 Pat Tilley RC .40 1.00
413 Don Strock .25 .60
414 Brian Kelley .15 .40
415 Gene Upshaw .40 1.00
416 Mike Montler .15 .40
417 Checklist 397-528 .75 2.00

418 John Gilliam	.15	.40
419 Brent McClanahan	.15	.40
420 Jerry Sherk	.15	.40
421 Roy Gerela	.15	.40
422 Tim Fox RC	.25	.60
423 John Ebersole RC	.15	.40
424 James Scott RC	.15	.40
425 Delvin Williams RC	.25	.60
426 Spike Jones	.15	.40
427 Harvey Martin	.40	1.00
428 Don Herrmann	.15	.40
429 Calvin Hill	.25	.60
430 Isiah Robertson	.15	.40
431 Tony Greene	.15	.40
432 Bob Johnson	.15	.40
433 Lem Barney	.40	1.00
434 Eric Torkelson RC	.15	.40
435 John Mendenhall	.15	.40
436 Larry Seiple	.25	.60
437 Art Kuehn RC	.15	.40
438 John Vella RC	.15	.40
439 Greg Latta RC	.15	.40
440 Roger Carr	.25	.60
441 Doug Sutherland	.15	.40
442 Mike Kruczek RC	.15	.40
443 Steve Zabel	.15	.40
444 Mike Pruitt RC	.40	1.00
445 Harold Jackson	.25	.60
446 George Jakowenko RC	.15	.40
447 John Fitzgerald	.15	.40
448 Carey Joyce RC	.15	.40
449 Jim LeClair	.15	.40
450 Ken Houston AP	.40	1.00
451 Steve Grogan RB	.25	.60
452 Jim Marshall RB	.25	.60
453 O.J.Simpson RB	1.25	2.50
454 Fran Tarkenton RB	1.50	3.00
455 Jim Zorn RB	.40	1.00
456 Robert Pratt RC	.15	.40
457 Walker Gillette	.15	.40
458 Charlie Hall	.15	.40
459 Robert Newhouse	.25	.60
460 John Hannah AP	.40	1.00
461 Ken Reaves	.15	.40
462 Herman Weaver	.15	.40
463 James Harris	.25	.60
464 Howard Twilley	.25	.60
465 Jeff Siemon	.25	.60
466 John Outlaw	.15	.40
467 Chuck Muncie RC	.40	1.00
468 Bob Moore	.15	.40
469 Robert Woods RC	.15	.40
470 Cliff Branch AP	.75	2.00
471 Johnnie Gray	.15	.40
472 Don Hardeman	.15	.40
473 Steve Ramsey	.15	.40
474 Steve Mike-Mayer	.15	.40
475 Gary Garrison	.15	.40
476 Walter Johnson	.15	.40
477 Neil Clabo	.15	.40
478 Len Hauss	.15	.40
479 Darryl Stingley	.25	.60
480 Jack Lambert AP	4.00	8.00
481 Mike Adamle	.25	.60
482 David Lee	.15	.40
483 Tom Mullen RC	.15	.40
484 Claude Humphrey	.15	.40
485 Jim Hart	.40	1.00
486 Bobby Thompson RC	.15	.40
487 Jack Rudnay	.15	.40
488 Rich Sowells RC	.15	.40
489 Reuben Gant RC	.15	.40
490 Cliff Harris AP	.40	1.00
491 Bob Brown DT	.15	.40
492 Don Nottingham	.15	.40
493 Ron Jessie	.15	.40
494 Otis Sistrunk	.25	.60
495 Billy Kilmer	.25	.60
496 Oscar Roan	.15	.40
497 Bill Van Heusen	.15	.40
498 Randy Logan	.15	.40
499 John Smith	.15	.40
500 Chuck Foreman AP	.25	.60
501 J.T. Thomas	.15	.40
502 Steve Schubert RC	.15	.40
503 Mike Barnes	.15	.40
504 J.V. Cain RC	.15	.40
505 Larry Csonka	1.50	3.00
506 Elvin Bethea	.40	1.00
507 Ray Easterling RC	.15	.40
508 Joe Reed	.15	.40
509 Steve Odom	.15	.40
510 Tommy Casanova	.15	.40
511 Dave Dalby	.15	.40
512 Richard Caster	.15	.40
513 Fred Dryer	.40	1.00
514 Jeff Kinney RC	.15	.40
515 Bob Griese	1.50	3.00
516 Butch Johnson RC	.40	1.00
517 Gerald Irons RC	.15	.40
518 Don Calhoun RC	.15	.40
519 Jack Gregory	.15	.40
520 Tom Banks	.15	.40
521 Bobby Bryant	.15	.40
522 Reggie Harrison RC	.15	.40
523 Terry Hermeling	.15	.40
524 David Taylor RC	.15	.40
525 Brian Baschnagel RC	.25	.60
526 AFC Champ/Stabler	.40	1.00
527 NFC Championship	.25	.60
528 Super Bowl XI	.60	1.50

1977 Topps Holsum Packers/Vikings

In 1977 Topps produced a set of 11 Green Bay Packers (1-11) and 11 Minnesota Vikings (12-22) for Holsum Bread for distribution in the general area of those teams. One card was packed inside each loaf of bread. Unfortunately, nowhere on the card is Holsum mentioned leading to frequent misclassification of this set. The cards are in color and are standard size. An uncut production sheet was offered in the 1989 Topps Archives auction. The personal data on the card back is printed in brown and orange.

COMPLETE SET (22)	25.00	50.00
1 Lynn Dickey	1.25	3.00
2 John Brockington	1.00	2.50
3 Will Harrell	.75	2.00
4 Ken Payne	.75	2.00
5 Rich McGeorge	.75	2.00
6 Steve Odom	.75	2.00
7 Jim Carter	.75	2.00
8 Fred Carr	.75	2.00
9 Willie Buchanon	1.00	2.50
10 Mike McCoy DT	.75	2.00
11 Chester Marcol	.75	2.00
12 Chuck Foreman	2.00	4.00
13 Ahmad Rashad	3.00	6.00
14 Sammie White	1.25	3.00
15 Stu Voigt	.75	2.00
16 Fred Cox	.75	2.00
17 Carl Eller	2.00	4.00
18 Alan Page	3.00	6.00
19 Jeff Siemon	.75	2.00
20 Bobby Bryant	.75	2.00
21 Paul Krause	1.25	3.00
22 Ron Yary	1.25	3.00

1977 Topps Mexican

The Mexican version of the 1977 Topps football series contains the same 528 players as the American issue. The cards were issued in 2-card packs with a stick of gum, or in scarcer four-card packs without gum. All text is in Spanish (front and back). Several cases of cards made their way into the organized hobby in the early 1990s. Since then, all cards have been discovered. However, some cards are considered to be tougher to obtain and are priced below at higher levels than otherwise might be expected. Some collectors also pursue the wrappers, which feature various NFL stars on them.

COMPLETE SET (528)	5,000.00	10,000.00
1 Passing Leaders SP	75.00	125.00
2 Drew Pearson M.Lane LL SP	200.00	400.00
3 Rushing Leaders SP	300.00	600.00
4 Scoring Leaders SP	200.00	400.00
5 Interception Leaders SP	200.00	400.00
6 Punting Leaders	125.00	250.00
7 Mike Phipps	4.00	8.00
8 Rick Volk SP	150.00	300.00
9 Steve Furness	4.00	8.00
10 Isaac Curtis	4.00	8.00
11 Nate Wright	4.00	8.00
12 Jean Fugett	6.00	12.00
13 Ken Mendenhall	3.00	6.00
14 Sam Adams OL	3.00	6.00
15 Charlie Waters	5.00	10.00
16 Bill Stanfill SP	50.00	100.00
17 John Holland	3.00	6.00
18 Pat Haden	20.00	40.00
19 Bob Young	3.00	6.00
20 Wally Chambers SP	100.00	200.00
21 Lawrence Gaines SP	125.00	250.00
22 Larry McCarren	3.00	6.00
23 Horst Muhlmann	3.00	6.00
24 Phil Villapiano	4.00	8.00
25 Greg Pruitt	40.00	80.00
26 Ron Howard	6.00	12.00
27 Craig Morton	5.00	10.00
28 Rufus Mayes	3.00	6.00
29 Lee Roy Selmon UER	100.00	200.00
30 Ed White SP	75.00	150.00
31 Harold McLinton SP	50.00	100.00
32 Glenn Doughty	3.00	6.00
33 Bob Kuechenberg	3.00	6.00
34 Duane Carrell	3.00	6.00
35 Riley Odoms	3.00	6.00
36 Bobby Scott	3.00	6.00
37 Nick Mike-Mayer	3.00	6.00
38 Bill Lenkaitis	3.00	6.00
39 Roland Harper	3.00	6.00
40 Tommy Hart SP	100.00	200.00
41 Mike Sensibaugh	3.00	6.00
42 Rusty Jackson	3.00	6.00
43 Levi Johnson	3.00	6.00
44 Mike McCoy DT	6.00	12.00
45 Roger Staubach	75.00	150.00
46 Fred Cox	3.00	6.00
47 Bob Babich	3.00	6.00
48 Reggie McKenzie	3.00	6.00
49 Dave Jennings SP	50.00	100.00
50 Mike Haynes	12.50	25.00
51 Larry Brown	4.00	8.00
52 Marvin Cobb	3.00	6.00
53 Fred Cook	3.00	6.00
54 Freddie Solomon	6.00	12.00
55 John Riggins	25.00	50.00
56 John Bunting	3.00	6.00
57 Ray Wersching	3.00	6.00
58 Mike Livingston	3.00	6.00
59 Billy Johnson	40.00	80.00
60 Mike Wagner AP	6.00	12.00
61 Waymond Bryant	3.00	6.00
62 Jim Otis	3.00	6.00
63 Ed Galigher SP	50.00	100.00
64 Randy Vataha	3.00	6.00
65 Jim Zorn	15.00	30.00
66 Jon Keyworth SP	50.00	100.00
67 Checklist 1-132	4.00	8.00
68 Henry Childs	3.00	6.00
69 Thom Darden	3.00	6.00
70 George Kunz AP	3.00	6.00
71 Lenvil Elliott	3.00	6.00
72 Curtis Johnson	3.00	6.00
73 Doug Van Horn	3.00	6.00
74 Joe Theismann	20.00	40.00
75 Dwight White	4.00	8.00
76 Scott Laidlaw	3.00	6.00
77 Monte Johnson	3.00	6.00
78 Dave Beverly	3.00	6.00
79 Jim Mitchell TE	40.00	80.00
80 Jack Youngblood	7.50	15.00
81 Mel Gray	3.00	6.00
82 Dwight Harrison	3.00	6.00
83 John Hadl	4.00	8.00
84 Matt Blair	4.00	8.00
85 Charlie Sanders	4.00	8.00
86 Noah Jackson	3.00	6.00
87 Ed Marinaro	5.00	10.00
88 Bob Howard	3.00	6.00
89 John McDaniel SP	150.00	300.00
90 Dan Dierdorf	6.00	12.00
91 Mark Moseley	3.00	6.00
92 Cleo Miller	3.00	6.00
93 Andre Tillman	3.00	6.00
94 Bruce Taylor	3.00	6.00
95 Bert Jones	5.00	10.00
96 Anthony Davis	50.00	100.00
97 Don Goode	3.00	6.00
98 Ray Rhodes SP	150.00	300.00
99 Mike Webster SP	60.00	120.00
100 O.J. Simpson AP	50.00	100.00
101 Doug Plank	3.00	6.00
102 Efren Herrera	3.00	6.00
103 Charlie Smith WR SP	75.00	150.00
104 Carlos Brown	40.00	80.00
105 Jim Marshall	5.00	10.00
106 Paul Naumoff	6.00	12.00
107 Walter White	6.00	12.00
108 John Cappelletti	7.50	15.00
109 Chip Myers	3.00	6.00
110 Ken Stabler AP	100.00	200.00
111 Joe Ehrmann	3.00	6.00
112 Rick Engles	3.00	6.00
113 Jack Dolbin	3.00	6.00
114 Ron Bolton	3.00	6.00
115 Mike Thomas	3.00	6.00
116 Mike Fuller	3.00	6.00
117 John Hill	3.00	6.00
118 Richard Todd SP	60.00	120.00
119 Duriel Harris	3.00	6.00
120 John James AP	3.00	6.00
121 Lionel Antoine	3.00	6.00
122 John Skorupan	3.00	6.00
123 Skip Butler	3.00	6.00
124 Bob Tucker	3.00	6.00
125 Paul Krause	3.00	6.00
126 Dave Hampton SP	75.00	150.00
127 Tom Wittum	3.00	6.00
128 Gary Huff	3.00	6.00
129 Emmitt Thomas	3.00	6.00
130 Drew Pearson	12.50	25.00
131 Ron Saul	6.00	12.00
132 Steve Niehaus	3.00	6.00
133 Fred Carr	3.00	6.00
134 Norm Bulaich	3.00	6.00
135 Bob Trumpy	5.00	10.00
136 Greg Landry	4.00	8.00
137 George Buehler	3.00	6.00
138 Reggie Rucker	3.00	6.00
139 Julius Adams	3.00	6.00
140 Jack Ham	15.00	30.00
141 Wayne Morris	3.00	6.00
142 Marv Bateman	6.00	12.00
143 Bobby Maples	3.00	6.00
144 Harold Carmichael	5.00	10.00
145 Bob Avellini	3.00	6.00
146 Harry Carson	20.00	40.00
147 Lawrence Pillers SP	75.00	150.00
148 Ed Williams	3.00	6.00
149 Dan Pastorini	3.00	6.00
150 Ron Yary AP	5.00	10.00
151 Joe Lavender	3.00	6.00
152 Pat McInally	3.00	6.00
153 Lloyd Mumphord	3.00	6.00
154 Cullen Bryant	3.00	6.00
155 Willie Lanier	30.00	60.00
156 Gene Washington 49er	4.00	8.00
157 Scott Hunter	3.00	6.00
158 Jim Merlo	3.00	6.00
159 Randy Grossman	3.00	6.00
160 Blaine Nye AP	3.00	6.00
161 Ike Harris	3.00	6.00
162 Doug Dieken	3.00	6.00
163 Guy Morriss SP	50.00	100.00
164 Bob Parsons SP	50.00	100.00
165 Steve Grogan	40.00	80.00
166 John Brockington	3.00	6.00
167 Charlie Joiner	7.50	15.00
168 Ron Carpenter	40.00	80.00
169 Jeff Wright S	40.00	80.00
170 Chris Hanburger AP	4.00	8.00
171 Roosevelt Leaks	3.00	6.00
172 Larry Little	4.00	8.00
173 John Matuszak	7.50	15.00
174 Joe Ferguson	3.00	6.00
175 Brad Van Pelt	40.00	80.00
176 Dexter Bussey SP	150.00	300.00
177 Steve Largent	300.00	500.00
178 Dewey Selmon	4.00	8.00
179 Randy Gradishar	5.00	10.00
180 Mel Blount	20.00	35.00
181 Dan Neal	40.00	80.00
182 Rich Szaro SP	75.00	150.00
183 Mike Boryla	6.00	12.00
184 Steve Jones	3.00	6.00
185 Paul Warfield	20.00	35.00
186 Greg Buttle SP	75.00	150.00
187 Rich McGeorge	3.00	6.00
188 Leon Gray SP	75.00	150.00
189 John Shinners	3.00	6.00
190 Toni Linhart AP	3.00	6.00
191 Robert Miller	3.00	6.00
192 Jake Scott	3.00	6.00
193 Jon Morris	40.00	80.00
194 Randy Crowder	3.00	6.00
195 Lynn Swann	60.00	120.00
196 Marsh White	3.00	6.00
197 Rod Perry	3.00	6.00
198 Willie Hall	3.00	6.00
199 Mike Hartenstine	3.00	6.00
200 Jim Bakken AP	3.00	6.00
201 Atlanta Falcons UER	50.00	100.00
202 Baltimore Colts	4.00	8.00
203 Buffalo Bills	10.00	20.00
204 Chicago Bears	4.00	8.00
205 Cincinnati Bengals	4.00	8.00
206 Cleveland Browns	4.00	8.00
207 Dallas Cowboys SP	75.00	150.00
208 Denver Broncos	4.00	8.00
209 Detroit Lions	4.00	8.00
210 Green Bay Packers	4.00	8.00
211 Houston Oilers	4.00	8.00
212 Kansas City Chiefs	4.00	8.00
213 Los Angeles Rams SP	50.00	100.00
214 Miami Dolphins	4.00	8.00
215 Minnesota Vikings	4.00	8.00
216 New England Patriots	4.00	8.00
217 New Orleans Saints	10.00	20.00
218 New York Giants	4.00	8.00
219 New York Jets	4.00	8.00
220 Oakland Raiders	4.00	8.00
221 Philadelphia Eagles	4.00	8.00
222 Pittsburgh Steelers	4.00	8.00
223 St. Louis Cardinals	4.00	8.00
224 San Diego Chargers	4.00	8.00
225 San Francisco 49ers	4.00	8.00
226 Seattle Seahawks SP	50.00	100.00
227 Tampa Bay Buccaneers	4.00	8.00
228 Washington Redskins SP	75.00	150.00
229 Sam Cunningham	4.00	8.00
230 Alan Page	7.50	15.00
231 Eddie Brown S SP	125.00	250.00
232 Stan White	3.00	6.00
233 Vern Den Herder	3.00	6.00
234 Clarence Davis	3.00	6.00
235 Ken Anderson	10.00	20.00
236 Karl Chandler	6.00	12.00
237 Will Harrell SP	100.00	200.00
238 Clarence Scott	3.00	6.00
239 Bo Rather	3.00	6.00
240 Robert Brazile	3.00	6.00
241 Bob Bell	3.00	6.00
242 Rolland Lawrence	3.00	6.00
243 Tom Sullivan SP	50.00	100.00
244 Larry Brunson	3.00	6.00
245 Terry Bradshaw	65.00	125.00
246 Rich Saul	3.00	6.00
247 Cleveland Elam	3.00	6.00
248 Don Woods	3.00	6.00
249 Bruce Laird	3.00	6.00
250 Coy Bacon AP	3.00	6.00
251 Russ Francis	5.00	10.00
252 Jim Braxton	3.00	6.00
253 Perry Smith	30.00	60.00
254 Jerome Barkum	3.00	6.00
255 Garo Yepremian	3.00	6.00
256 Checklist 133-264	4.00	8.00
257 Tony Galbreath	3.00	6.00
258 Troy Archer	3.00	6.00
259 Brian Sipe	5.00	10.00
260 Billy Joe DuPree	10.00	20.00
261 Bobby Walden	3.00	6.00
262 Larry Marshall	3.00	6.00
263 Ted Fritsch Jr.	3.00	6.00
264 Larry Hand	3.00	6.00
265 Tom Mack SP	50.00	100.00
266 Ed Bradley	3.00	6.00
267 Pat Leahy	3.00	6.00
268 Louis Carter SP	50.00	100.00
269 Archie Griffin SP	150.00	300.00

270 Art Shell 6.00 12.00
271 Stu Voigt 3.00 6.00
272 Prentice McCray 3.00 6.00
273 MacArthur Lane 7.50 15.00
274 Dan Fouts 25.00 50.00
275 Charle Young 3.00 6.00
276 Wilbur Jackson 125.00 250.00
277 John Hicks 3.00 6.00
278 Nat Moore 3.00 6.00
279 Virgil Livers 3.00 6.00
280 Curley Culp AP 4.00 10.00
281 Rocky Bleier 15.00 30.00
282 John Zook 7.50 15.00
283 Tom DeLeone 3.00 6.00
284 Danny White SP 150.00 300.00
285 Otis Armstrong 4.00 8.00
286 Larry Walton 3.00 6.00
287 Jim Carter 3.00 6.00
288 Don McCauley 3.00 6.00
289 Frank Grant 7.50 15.00
290 Roger Wehrli AP 4.00 8.00
291 Mick Tingelhoff 10.00 20.00
292 Bernard Jackson 7.50 15.00
293 Tom Owen 6.00 12.00
294 Mike Esposito 3.00 6.00
295 Fred Biletnikoff SP 200.00 400.00
296 Revie Sorey 3.00 6.00
297 John McMakin 3.00 6.00
298 Dan Ryczek 3.00 6.00
299 Wayne Moore 7.50 15.00
300 Franco Harris AP 60.00 120.00
301 Rick Upchurch 4.00 8.00
302 Jim Stienke 3.00 6.00
303 Charlie Davis 3.00 6.00
304 Don Cockroft 3.00 6.00
305 Ken Burrough 3.00 6.00
306 Clark Gaines SP 75.00 150.00
307 Bobby Douglass 4.00 8.00
308 Ralph Perretta 3.00 6.00
309 Wally Hilgenberg 3.00 6.00
310 Monte Jackson 3.00 6.00
311 Chris Bahr 3.00 6.00
312 Jim Cheyunski 3.00 6.00
313 Mike Patrick 3.00 6.00
314 Ed Too Tall Jones 75.00 150.00
315 Bill Bradley 3.00 6.00
316 Benny Malone 3.00 6.00
317 Paul Seymour 3.00 6.00
318 Jim Laslavic 3.00 6.00
319 Frank Lewis 3.00 6.00
320 Ray Guy 40.00 80.00
321 Allan Ellis 3.00 6.00
322 Conrad Dobler 3.00 6.00
323 Chester Marcol 3.00 6.00
324 Doug Kotar 3.00 6.00
325 Lemar Parrish 3.00 6.00
326 Steve Holden 3.00 6.00
327 Jeff Van Note 4.00 8.00
328 Howard Stevens 3.00 6.00
329 Brad Dusek 3.00 6.00
330 Joe DeLamielleure AP 5.00 10.00
331 Jim Plunkett SP 100.00 200.00
332 Checklist 265-396 SP 100.00 200.00
333 Lou Piccone 3.00 6.00
334 Ray Hamilton 3.00 6.00
335 Jan Stenerud 5.00 10.00
336 Jeris White 3.00 6.00
337 Sherman Smith 4.00 8.00
338 Dave Green 3.00 6.00
339 Terry Schmidt 3.00 6.00
340 Sammie White 4.00 8.00
341 Jon Kolb 7.50 15.00
342 Randy White 25.00 50.00
343 Bob Klein 3.00 6.00
344 Bob Kowalkowski 6.00 12.00
345 Terry Metcalf 4.00 8.00
346 Joe Danelo 3.00 6.00
347 Ken Payne 3.00 6.00
348 Neal Craig 3.00 6.00
349 Dennis Johnson 3.00 6.00
350 Bill Bergey 7.50 15.00
351 Raymond Chester SP 75.00 150.00
352 Bob Matheson 4.00 8.00
353 Mike Kadish 3.00 6.00
354 Mark Van Eeghen 5.00 10.00
355 L.C.Greenwood 6.00 12.00
356 Sam Hunt 3.00 6.00
357 Darrell Austin 3.00 6.00
358 Jim Turner 3.00 6.00
359 Ahmad Rashad 10.00 20.00
360 Walter Payton AP 250.00 400.00
361 Mark Arneson 3.00 6.00
362 Jerrel Wilson 3.00 6.00
363 Steve Bartkowski 5.00 10.00
364 John Watson 3.00 6.00
365 Ken Riley 3.00 6.00
366 Gregg Bingham 30.00 60.00
367 Golden Richards 4.00 8.00
368 Clyde Powers 3.00 6.00
369 Diron Talbert 7.50 15.00
370 Lydell Mitchell 20.00 40.00
371 Bob Jackson 3.00 6.00
372 Jim Mandich SP 75.00 150.00
373 Frank LeMaster 30.00 60.00
374 Benny Ricardo SP 125.00 250.00
375 Lawrence McCutcheon 3.00 6.00
376 Lynn Dickey 4.00 8.00
377 Phil Wise 3.00 6.00
378 Tony McGee DT 3.00 6.00
379 Norm Thompson 3.00 6.00
380 Dave Casper 20.00 40.00
381 Glen Edwards 3.00 6.00
382 Bob Thomas 3.00 6.00
383 Bob Chandler 3.00 6.00
384 Rickey Young 3.00 6.00
385 Carl Eller 5.00 10.00
386 Lyle Alzado 5.00 10.00
387 John Leypoldt 3.00 6.00
388 Gordon Bell SP 125.00 250.00
389 Mike Bragg 3.00 6.00
390 Jim Langer 4.00 8.00
391 Vern Holland 3.00 6.00
392 Nelson Munsey 3.00 6.00
393 Mack Mitchell 3.00 6.00
394 Tony Adams 3.00 6.00
395 Preston Pearson 4.00 8.00
396 Emanuel Zanders 3.00 6.00
397 Vince Papale 12.50 25.00
398 Joe Fields 3.00 6.00
399 Craig Clemons 3.00 6.00
400 Fran Tarkenton AP 30.00 60.00
401 Andy Johnson 3.00 6.00
402 Willie Buchanon 7.50 15.00
403 Pat Curran 3.00 6.00
404 Ray Jarvis SP 125.00 250.00
405 Joe Greene 20.00 35.00
406 Bill Simpson 3.00 6.00
407 Ronnie Coleman 3.00 6.00
408 J.K. McKay 3.00 6.00
409 Pat Fischer 10.00 20.00
410 John Dutton AP 3.00 6.00
411 Boobie Clark 3.00 6.00
412 Pat Tilley 6.00 12.00
413 Don Strock SP 75.00 150.00
414 Brian Kelley 3.00 6.00
415 Gene Upshaw 7.50 15.00
416 Mike Montler 3.00 6.00
417 Checklist 397-528 SP 100.00 200.00
418 John Gilliam 3.00 6.00
419 Brent McClanahan 3.00 6.00
420 Jerry Sherk AP 3.00 6.00
421 Roy Gerela 3.00 6.00
422 Tim Fox 3.00 6.00
423 John Ebersole SP 75.00 150.00
424 James Scott SP 75.00 150.00
425 Delvin Williams 30.00 60.00
426 Spike Jones 30.00 60.00
427 Harvey Martin SP 50.00 100.00
428 Don Herrmann 3.00 6.00
429 Calvin Hill 5.00 10.00
430 Isiah Robertson AP 30.00 60.00
431 Tony Greene 3.00 6.00
432 Bob Johnson 3.00 6.00
433 Lem Barney SP 100.00 200.00
434 Eric Torkelson SP 125.00 250.00
435 John Mendenhall 3.00 6.00
436 Larry Seiple 3.00 6.00
437 Art Kuehn 3.00 6.00
438 John Vella 3.00 6.00
439 Greg Latta 3.00 6.00
440 Roger Carr AP 3.00 6.00
441 Doug Sutherland 3.00 6.00
442 Mike Kruczek 6.00 12.00
443 Steve Zabel 3.00 6.00
444 Mike Pruitt SP 125.00 250.00
445 Harold Jackson SP 75.00 150.00
446 George Jakowenko 3.00 6.00
447 John Fitzgerald 3.00 6.00
448 Carey Joyce 3.00 6.00
449 Jim LeClair 4.00 8.00
450 Ken Houston 5.00 10.00
451 Steve Grogan RB 5.00 10.00
452 Jim Marshall RB 5.00 10.00
453 O.J. Simpson RB 75.00 150.00
454 Fran Tarkenton RB 20.00 40.00
455 Jim Zorn RB 25.00 50.00
456 Robert Pratt 3.00 6.00
457 Walker Gillette 6.00 12.00
458 Charlie Hall 3.00 6.00
459 Robert Newhouse 4.00 8.00
460 John Hannah 5.00 10.00
461 Ken Reaves 3.00 6.00
462 Herman Weaver 3.00 6.00
463 James Harris 3.00 6.00
464 Howard Twilley 3.00 6.00
465 Jeff Siemon SP 75.00 150.00
466 John Outlaw 3.00 6.00
467 Chuck Muncie 5.00 10.00
468 Bob Moore 3.00 6.00
469 Robert Woods 3.00 6.00
470 Cliff Branch SP 125.00 250.00
471 Johnnie Gray 3.00 6.00
472 Don Hardeman 3.00 6.00
473 Steve Ramsey 3.00 6.00
474 Steve Mike-Mayer SP 75.00 150.00
475 Gary Garrison 4.00 8.00
476 Walter Johnson 3.00 6.00
477 Neil Clabo 6.00 12.00
478 Len Hauss 3.00 6.00
479 Darryl Stingley 4.00 8.00
480 Jack Lambert AP 40.00 80.00
481 Mike Adamle 4.00 8.00
482 David Lee 3.00 6.00
483 Tom Mullen 3.00 6.00
484 Claude Humphrey 3.00 6.00
485 Jim Hart 3.00 6.00
486 Bobby Thompson SP 100.00 200.00
487 Jack Rudnay 3.00 6.00
488 Rich Sowells SP 125.00 250.00
489 Reuben Gant SP 100.00 200.00
490 Cliff Harris 5.00 10.00
491 Bob Brown DT 3.00 6.00
492 Don Nottingham 6.00 12.00
493 Ron Jessie SP 75.00 150.00
494 Otis Sistrunk 12.50 25.00
495 Billy Kilmer 4.00 8.00
496 Oscar Roan 3.00 6.00
497 Bill Van Heusen 3.00 6.00
498 Randy Logan 30.00 60.00
499 John Smith 3.00 6.00
500 Chuck Foreman SP 60.00 120.00
501 J.T. Thomas 3.00 6.00
502 Steve Schubert 3.00 6.00
503 Mike Barnes 3.00 6.00
504 J.V. Cain 3.00 6.00
505 Larry Csonka 30.00 60.00
506 Elvin Bethea 5.00 10.00
507 Ray Easterling 3.00 6.00
508 Joe Reed 6.00 12.00
509 Steve Odom 3.00 6.00
510 Tommy Casanova AP 4.00 8.00
511 Dave Dalby 3.00 6.00
512 Richard Caster 3.00 6.00
513 Fred Dryer SP 100.00 200.00
514 Jeff Kinney 6.00 12.00
515 Bob Griese 25.00 50.00
516 Butch Johnson 3.00 6.00
517 Gerald Irons 3.00 6.00
518 Don Calhoun 3.00 6.00
519 Jack Gregory 3.00 6.00
520 Tom Banks AP 3.00 6.00
521 Bobby Bryant 3.00 6.00
522 Reggie Harrison 3.00 6.00
523 Terry Hermeling 3.00 6.00
524 David Taylor 3.00 6.00
525 Brian Baschnagel 3.00 6.00
526 AFC Championship 30.00 60.00
527 NFC Championship 30.00 60.00
528 Super Bowl XI SP 500.00 800.00

1977 Topps Team Checklists

The 1977 Topps Team Checklist set contains 30 standard-size cards. The 28 NFL teams as well as 2 regular checklists were printed in this set. The front of the card has the 1977 Topps checklist for that particular team, complete with boxes in which to place check marks. The set was only available directly from Topps as a send-off offer as an uncut sheet; the prices below apply equally to uncut sheets as they are frequently found in their original uncut condition. As for individual cards, thin white card (almost paper-thin) stock makes it a challenge to find singles in top grades. These unnumbered cards are numbered below for convenience in alphabetical order by team name.

COMPLETE SET (30) 55.00 110.00
1 Atlanta Falcons 2.50 5.00
2 Baltimore Colts 2.50 5.00
3 Buffalo Bills 2.50 5.00
4 Chicago Bears 3.75 7.50
5 Cincinnati Bengals 2.50 5.00
6 Cleveland Browns 2.50 5.00
7 Dallas Cowboys 5.00 10.00
8 Denver Broncos 2.50 5.00
9 Detroit Lions 2.50 5.00
10 Green Bay Packers 5.00 10.00
11 Houston Oilers 2.50 5.00
12 Kansas City Chiefs 2.50 5.00
13 Los Angeles Rams 2.50 5.00
14 Miami Dolphins 3.75 7.50
15 Minnesota Vikings 2.50 5.00
16 New England Patriots 2.50 5.00
17 New York Giants 2.50 5.00
18 New York Jets 2.50 5.00
19 New Orleans Saints 2.50 5.00
20 Oakland Raiders 3.75 7.50
21 Philadelphia Eagles 2.50 5.00
22 Pittsburgh Steelers 3.75 7.50
23 St. Louis Cardinals 2.50 5.00
24 San Diego Chargers 2.50 5.00
25 San Francisco 49ers 3.75 7.50
26 Seattle Seahawks 2.50 5.00
27 Tampa Bay Buccaneers 2.50 5.00
28 Washington Redskins 3.75 7.50
NNO1 Checklist 1-132 2.50 5.00
NNO2 Checklist 133-264 2.50 5.00

1978 Topps

The 1978 Topps football set contains 528 standard-size cards. Card fronts have a color border that runs up the left side and contains the team name. The player's name is at the top and his position is within a football at the bottom right of the photo. The card backs are printed in black and green on gray card stock and are horizontally designed. Statistics, highlights and a player fact carttton are inlcuded. Subsets include Highlights (1-6), playoffs (166-168), league leaders (331-336) and team leaders (501-528). Rookie Cards include Tony Dorsett, Randy Cross, Tom Jackson, Joe Klecko, Stanley Morgan, John Stallworth, Wesley Walker and Reggie Williams.

COMPLETE SET (528) 80.00 150.00
1 Gary Huff HL .40 1.00
2 Craig Morton HL .40 1.00
3 Walter Payton HL 3.00 8.00
4 O.J.Simpson HL .75 2.00
5 Fran Tarkenton HL .75 2.00
6 Bob Thomas HL .10 .30
7 Joe Pisarcik RC .20 .50
8 Skip Thomas RC .10 .30
9 Roosevelt Leaks .10 .30
10 Ken Houston AP .40 1.00
11 Tom Blanchard .10 .30
12 Jim Turner .10 .30
13 Tom DeLeone .10 .30
14 Jim LeClair .10 .30
15 Bob Avellini .20 .50
16 Tony McGee DT .10 .30
17 James Harris .20 .50
18 Terry Nelson RC .10 .30
19 Rocky Bleier .75 2.00
20 Joe DeLamielleure .40 1.00
21 Richard Caster .10 .30
22 A.J. Duhe RC .40 1.00
23 John Outlaw .10 .30
24 Danny White .50 1.25
25 Larry Csonka 1.00 2.50
26 David Hill RC .20 .50
27 Mark Arneson .10 .30
28 Jack Tatum .20 .50
29 Norm Thompson .10 .30
30 Sammie White .20 .50
31 Dennis Johnson .10 .30
32 Robin Earl RC .10 .30
33 Don Cockroft .10 .30
34 Bob Johnson .10 .30
35 John Hannah .40 1.00
36 Scott Hunter .10 .30
37 Ken Burrough .20 .50
38 Wilbur Jackson .20 .50
39 Rich McGeorge .10 .30
40 Lyle Alzado AP .40 1.00
41 John Ebersole .10 .30
42 Gary Green RC .10 .30
43 Art Kuehn .10 .30
44 Glen Edwards .20 .50
45 Lawrence McCutcheon .20 .50
46 Duriel Harris .10 .30
47 Rich Szaro .10 .30
48 Mike Washington RC .10 .30
49 Stan White .10 .30
50 Dave Casper AP .40 1.00
51 Len Hauss .10 .30
52 James Scott .10 .30
53 Brian Sipe .40 1.00
54 Gary Shirk RC .10 .30
55 Archie Griffin .40 1.00
56 Mike Patrick .10 .30
57 Mario Clark RC .10 .30
58 Jeff Siemon .10 .30
59 Steve Mike-Mayer .10 .30
60 Randy White AP 2.00 4.00
61 Darrell Austin .10 .30
62 Tom Sullivan .10 .30
63 Johnny Rodgers RC .40 1.00
64 Ken Reaves .10 .30
65 Terry Bradshaw 6.00 12.00
66 Fred Steinfort RC .10 .30
67 Curley Culp .40 1.00
68 Ted Hendricks .40 1.00
69 Raymond Chester .10 .30
70 Jim Langer AP .40 1.00
71 Calvin Hill .20 .50
72 Mike Hartenstine .10 .30
73 Gerald Irons .10 .30
74 Billy Brooks RC .20 .50
75 John Mendenhall .10 .30
76 Andy Johnson .10 .30
77 Tom Wittum .10 .30
78 Lynn Dickey .20 .50
79 Carl Eller .40 1.00
80 Tom Mack .40 1.00
81 Clark Gaines .10 .30
82 Lem Barney .40 1.00
83 Mike Montler .10 .30
84 Jon Kolb .10 .30
85 Bob Chandler .20 .50
86 Robert Newhouse .20 .50
87 Frank LeMaster .10 .30
88 Jeff West .10 .30
89 Lyle Blackwood .20 .50
90 Gene Upshaw AP .40 1.00
91 Frank Grant .10 .30
92 Tom Hicks RC .10 .30
93 Mike Pruitt .20 .50
94 Chris Bahr .10 .30
95 Russ Francis .20 .50
96 Norris Thomas RC .10 .30
97 Gary Barbaro RC .20 .50
98 Jim Merlo .10 .30
99 Karl Chandler .10 .30
100 Fran Tarkenton 1.50 4.00
101 Abdul Salaam RC .10 .30
102 Marv Kellum RC .10 .30

1977 Topps Team Checklists

103 Herman Weaver	.10	.30
104 Roy Gerela	.10	.30
105 Harold Jackson	.20	.50
106 Dewey Selmon	.20	.50
107 Checklist 1-132	.40	1.00
108 Clarence Davis	.10	.30
109 Robert Pratt	.10	.30
110 Harvey Martin AP	.40	1.00
111 Brad Dusek	.10	.30
112 Greg Latta	.10	.30
113 Tony Peters RC	.10	.30
114 Jim Braxton	.10	.30
115 Ken Riley	.20	.50
116 Steve Nelson RC	.10	.30
117 Rick Upchurch	.20	.50
118 Spike Jones	.10	.30
119 Doug Kotar	.10	.30
120 Bob Griese AP	1.00	2.50
121 Burgess Owens	.10	.30
122 Rolf Benirschke RC	.20	.50
123 Haskel Stanback RC	.10	.30
124 J.T. Thomas	.10	.30
125 Ahmad Rashad	.60	1.50
126 Rick Kane RC	.10	.30
127 Elvin Bethea	.40	1.00
128 Dave Dalby	.10	.30
129 Mike Barnes	.10	.30
130 Isiah Robertson	.10	.30
131 Jim Plunkett	.40	1.00
132 Allan Ellis	.10	.30
133 Mike Bragg	.10	.30
134 Bob Jackson	.10	.30
135 Coy Bacon	.10	.30
136 John Smith	.10	.30
137 Chuck Muncie	.20	.50
138 Johnnie Gray	.10	.30
139 Jimmy Robinson RC	.10	.30
140 Tom Banks	.10	.30
141 Marvin Powell RC	.10	.30
142 Jerrel Wilson	.10	.30
143 Ron Howard	.10	.30
144 Rob Lytle RC	.20	.50
145 L.C. Greenwood	.40	1.00
146 Morris Owens RC	.10	.30
147 Joe Reed	.10	.30
148 Mike Kadish	.10	.30
149 Phil Villapiano	.20	.50
150 Lydell Mitchell	.20	.50
151 Randy Logan	.10	.30
152 Mike Williams RC	.10	.30
153 Jeff Van Note	.20	.50
154 Steve Schubert	.10	.30
155 Billy Kilmer	.20	.50
156 Boobie Clark	.10	.30
157 Charlie Hall	.10	.30
158 Raymond Clayborn RC	.40	1.00
159 Jack Gregory	.10	.30
160 Cliff Harris AP	.40	1.00
161 Joe Fields	.10	.30
162 Don Nottingham	.10	.30
163 Ed White	.20	.50
164 Toni Fritsch	.10	.30
165 Jack Lambert	2.00	4.00
166 NFC Champs/Staubach	.60	1.50
167 AFC Champs/Lytle	.20	.50
168 Super Bowl XII/Dorsett	1.50	3.00
169 Neal Colzie RC	.10	.30
170 Cleveland Elam	.10	.30
171 David Lee	.10	.30
172 Jim Otis	.10	.30
173 Archie Manning	.40	1.00
174 Jim Carter	.10	.30
175 Jean Fugett	.10	.30
176 Willie Parker RC	.10	.30
177 Haven Moses	.20	.50
178 Horace King RC	.10	.30
179 Bob Thomas	.10	.30
180 Monte Jackson	.10	.30
181 Steve Zabel	.10	.30
182 John Fitzgerald	.10	.30
183 Mike Livingston	.10	.30
184 Larry Poole RC	.10	.30
185 Isaac Curtis	.20	.50
186 Chuck Ramsey RC	.10	.30
187 Bob Klein	.10	.30
188 Ray Rhodes	.40	1.00
189 Otis Sistrunk	.20	.50
190 Bill Bergey	.20	.50
191 Sherman Smith	.20	.50
192 Dave Green	.10	.30
193 Carl Mauck	.10	.30
194 Reggie Harrison	.10	.30
195 Roger Carr	.20	.50
196 Steve Bartkowski	.40	1.00
197 Ray Wersching	.10	.30
198 Willie Buchanon	.10	.30
199 Neil Clabo	.10	.30
200 Walter Payton UER	12.50	25.00
201 Sam Adams	.10	.30
202 Larry Gordon RC	.10	.30
203 Pat Tilley	.20	.50
204 Mack Mitchell	.10	.30
205 Ken Anderson	.40	1.00
206 Scott Dierking RC	.10	.30
207 Jack Rudnay	.10	.30
208 Jim Stienke	.10	.30
209 Bill Simpson	.10	.30
210 Errol Mann	.10	.30
211 Bucky Dilts RC	.10	.30
212 Reuben Gant	.10	.30
213 Thomas Henderson RC	.60	1.50
214 Steve Furness	.20	.50
215 John Riggins	.75	2.00
216 Keith Krepfle RC	.10	.30
217 Fred Dean RC	6.00	12.00
218 Emanuel Zanders	.10	.30
219 Don Testerman RC	.10	.30
220 George Kunz	.10	.30
221 Darryl Stingley	.20	.50
222 Ken Sanders RC	.10	.30
223 Gary Huff	.10	.30
224 Gregg Bingham	.10	.30
225 Jerry Sherk	.10	.30
226 Doug Plank	.10	.30
227 Ed Taylor RC	.10	.30
228 Emery Moorehead RC	.10	.30
229 Reggie Williams RC	.40	1.00
230 Claude Humphrey	.10	.30
231 Randy Cross RC	1.25	3.00
232 Jim Hart	.40	1.00
233 Bobby Bryant	.10	.30
234 Larry Brown	.10	.30
235 Mark Van Eeghen	.20	.50
236 Terry Hermeling	.10	.30
237 Steve Odom	.10	.30
238 Jan Stenerud	.40	1.00
239 Andre Tillman	.10	.30
240 Tom Jackson RC	2.00	5.00
241 Ken Mendenhall	.10	.30
242 Tim Fox	.10	.30
243 Don Herrmann	.10	.30
244 Eddie McMillan	.10	.30
245 Greg Pruitt	.20	.50
246 J.K. McKay	.10	.30
247 Larry Keller RC	.10	.30
248 Dave Jennings	.20	.50
249 Bo Harris RC	.10	.30
250 Revie Sorey	.10	.30
251 Tony Greene	.10	.30
252 Butch Johnson	.20	.50
253 Paul Naumoff	.10	.30
254 Rickey Young	.20	.50
255 Dwight White	.20	.50
256 Joe Lavender	.10	.30
257 Checklist 133-264	.40	1.00
258 Ronnie Coleman	.10	.30
259 Charlie Smith WR	.10	.30
260 Ray Guy AP	.40	1.00
261 David Taylor	.10	.30
262 Bill Lenkaitis	.10	.30
263 Jim Mitchell	.10	.30
264 Delvin Williams	.10	.30
265 Jack Youngblood	.40	1.00
266 Chuck Crist RC	.10	.30
267 Richard Todd	.20	.50
268 Dave Logan RC	.40	1.00
269 Rufus Mayes	.10	.30
270 Brad Van Pelt	.10	.30
271 Chester Marcol	.10	.30
272 J.V. Cain	.10	.30
273 Larry Seiple	.10	.30
274 Brent McClanahan	.10	.30
275 Mike Wagner	.10	.30
276 Diron Talbert	.10	.30
277 Brian Baschnagel	.10	.30
278 Ed Podolak	.10	.30
279 Don Goode	.10	.30
280 John Dutton	.20	.50
281 Don Calhoun	.10	.30
282 Monte Johnson	.10	.30
283 Ron Jessie	.10	.30
284 Jon Morris	.10	.30
285 Riley Odoms	.10	.30
286 Marv Bateman	.10	.30
287 Joe Klecko RC	.40	1.00
288 Oliver Davis RC	.10	.30
289 John McDaniel	.10	.30
290 Roger Staubach	6.00	12.00
291 Brian Kelley	.10	.30
292 Mike Hogan RC	.10	.30
293 John Leypoldt	.10	.30
294 Jack Novak RC	.10	.30
295 Joe Greene	.75	2.00
296 John Hill	.10	.30
297 Danny Buggs RC	.10	.30
298 Ted Albrecht RC	.10	.30
299 Nelson Munsey	.10	.30
300 Chuck Foreman	.20	.50
301 Dan Pastorini	.20	.50
302 Tommy Hart	.10	.30
303 Dave Beverly	.10	.30
304 Tony Reed RC	.20	.50
305 Cliff Branch	.60	1.50
306 Clarence Duren RC	.10	.30
307 Randy Rasmussen	.10	.30
308 Oscar Roan	.10	.30
309 Lenvil Elliott	.10	.30
310 Dan Dierdorf AP	.40	1.00
311 Johnny Perkins RC	.10	.30
312 Rafael Septien RC	.20	.50
313 Terry Beeson RC	.10	.30
314 Lee Roy Selmon	.75	2.00
315 Tony Dorsett RC	25.00	40.00
316 Greg Landry	.20	.50
317 Jake Scott	.10	.30
318 Dan Peiffer RC	.10	.30
319 John Bunting	.20	.50
320 John Stallworth RC	10.00	20.00
321 Bob Howard	.10	.30
322 Larry Little	.40	1.00
323 Reggie McKenzie	.20	.50
324 Duane Carrell	.10	.30
325 Ed Simonini RC	.10	.30
326 John Vella	.10	.30
327 Wesley Walker RC	1.50	3.00
328 Jon Keyworth	.10	.30
329 Ron Bolton	.10	.30
330 Tommy Casanova	.10	.30
331 R.Staubach/B.Griese LL	2.00	4.00
332 A.Rashad/Mitchell LL	.40	1.00
333 W.Payton VanEeghenLL	1.25	3.00
334 W.Payton E.Mann LL	1.25	3.00
335 Interception Leaders	.10	.30
336 Punting Leaders	.20	.50
337 Robert Brazile	.20	.50
338 Charlie Joiner	.60	1.50
339 Joe Ferguson	.20	.50
340 Bill Thompson	.10	.30
341 Sam Cunningham	.20	.50
342 Curtis Johnson	.10	.30
343 Jim Marshall	.40	1.00
344 Charlie Sanders	.20	.50
345 Willie Hall	.10	.30
346 Pat Haden	.40	1.00
347 Jim Bakken	.10	.30
348 Bruce Taylor	.10	.30
349 Barty Smith	.10	.30
350 Drew Pearson AP	.60	1.50
351 Mike Webster	1.00	2.50
352 Bobby Hammond RC	.10	.30
353 Dave Mays RC	.10	.30
354 Pat McInally	.10	.30
355 Toni Linhart	.10	.30
356 Larry Hand	.10	.30
357 Ted Fritsch Jr.	.10	.30
358 Larry Marshall	.10	.30
359 Waymond Bryant	.10	.30
360 Louie Kelcher RC	.20	.50
361 Stanley Morgan RC	.75	2.00
362 Bruce Harper RC	.20	.50
363 Bernard Jackson	.10	.30
364 Walter White	.10	.30
365 Ken Stabler	4.00	8.00
366 Fred Dryer	.40	1.00
367 Ike Harris	.10	.30
368 Norm Bulaich	.10	.30
369 Merv Krakau RC	.10	.30
370 John James	.10	.30
371 Bennie Cunningham RC	.10	.30
372 Doug Van Horn	.10	.30
373 Thom Darden	.10	.30
374 Eddie Edwards RC	.10	.30
375 Mike Thomas	.10	.30
376 Fred Cook	.10	.30
377 Mike Phipps	.20	.50
378 Paul Krause	.40	1.00
379 Harold Carmichael	.40	1.00
380 Mike Haynes AP	.40	1.00
381 Wayne Morris	.10	.30
382 Greg Buttle	.10	.30
383 Jim Zorn	.40	1.00
384 Jack Dolbin	.10	.30
385 Charlie Waters	.20	.50
386 Dan Ryczek	.10	.30
387 Joe Washington RC	.40	1.00
388 Checklist 265-396	.40	1.00
389 James Hunter RC	.10	.30
390 Billy Johnson	.20	.50
391 Jim Allen RC	.10	.30
392 George Buehler	.10	.30
393 Harry Carson	.40	1.00
394 Cleo Miller	.10	.30
395 Gary Burley RC	.10	.30
396 Mark Moseley	.20	.50
397 Virgil Livers	.10	.30
398 Joe Ehrmann	.10	.30
399 Freddie Solomon	.10	.30
400 O.J. Simpson	2.00	4.00
401 Julius Adams	.10	.30
402 Artimus Parker RC	.10	.30
403 Gene Washington 49er	.20	.50
404 Herman Edwards RC	.20	.50
405 Craig Morton	.40	1.00
406 Alan Page	.40	1.00
407 Larry McCarren	.10	.30
408 Tony Galbreath	.20	.50
409 Roman Gabriel	.40	1.00
410 Efren Herrera	.10	.30
411 Jim Smith RC	.40	1.00
412 Bill Bryant RC	.10	.30
413 Doug Dieken	.10	.30
414 Marvin Cobb	.10	.30
415 Fred Biletnikoff	.75	2.00
416 Joe Theismann	1.00	2.50
417 Roland Harper	.10	.30
418 Derrel Luce RC	.10	.30
419 Ralph Perretta	.10	.30
420 Louis Wright RC	.40	1.00
421 Prentice McCray	.10	.30
422 Garry Puetz	.10	.30
423 Alfred Jenkins RC	.40	1.00
424 Paul Seymour	.10	.30
425 Garo Yepremian	.20	.50
426 Emmitt Thomas	.20	.50
427 Dexter Bussey	.10	.30
428 John Sanders RC	.10	.30
429 Ed Too Tall Jones	.75	2.00
430 Ron Yary	.40	1.00
431 Frank Lewis	.20	.50
432 Jerry Golsteyn RC	.10	.30
433 Clarence Scott	.10	.30
434 Pete Johnson RC	.40	1.00
435 Charle Young	.20	.50
436 Harold McLinton	.10	.30
437 Noah Jackson	.10	.30
438 Bruce Laird	.10	.30
439 John Matuszak	.20	.50
440 Nat Moore AP	.20	.50
441 Leon Gray	.10	.30
442 Jerome Barkum	.10	.30
443 Steve Largent	6.00	12.00
444 John Zook	.10	.30
445 Preston Pearson	.20	.50
446 Conrad Dobler	.20	.50
447 Wilbur Summers RC	.10	.30
448 Lou Piccone	.10	.30
449 Ron Jaworski	.40	1.00
450 Jack Ham AP	.60	1.50
451 Mick Tingelhoff	.20	.50
452 Clyde Powers	.10	.30
453 John Cappelletti	.40	1.00
454 Dick Ambrose RC	.10	.30
455 Lemar Parrish	.10	.30
456 Ron Saul	.10	.30
457 Bob Parsons	.10	.30
458 Glenn Doughty	.10	.30
459 Don Woods	.10	.30
460 Art Shell AP	.40	1.00
461 Sam Hunt	.10	.30
462 Lawrence Pillers	.10	.30
463 Henry Childs	.10	.30
464 Roger Wehrli	.20	.50
465 Otis Armstrong	.20	.50
466 Bob Baumhower RC	.75	2.00
467 Ray Jarvis	.10	.30
468 Guy Morriss	.10	.30
469 Matt Blair	.20	.50
470 Billy Joe DuPree	.20	.50
471 Roland Hooks RC	.10	.30
472 Joe Danelo	.10	.30
473 Reggie Rucker	.20	.50
474 Vern Holland	.10	.30
475 Mel Blount	.60	1.50
476 Eddie Brown	.10	.30
477 Bo Rather	.10	.30
478 Don McCauley	.10	.30
479 Glen Walker RC	.10	.30
480 Randy Gradishar AP	.40	1.00
481 Dave Rowe	.10	.30
482 Pat Leahy	.20	.50
483 Mike Fuller	.10	.30
484 David Lewis RC	.10	.30
485 Steve Grogan	.40	1.00
486 Mel Gray	.20	.50
487 Eddie Payton RC	.20	.50
488 Checklist 397-528	.40	1.00
489 Stu Voigt	.10	.30
490 Rolland Lawrence	.10	.30
491 Nick Mike-Mayer	.10	.30
492 Troy Archer	.10	.30
493 Benny Malone	.10	.30
494 Golden Richards	.20	.50
495 Chris Hanburger	.10	.30
496 Dwight Harrison	.10	.30
497 Gary Fencik RC	.40	1.00
498 Rich Saul	.10	.30
499 Dan Fouts	2.00	4.00
500 Franco Harris AP	2.00	4.00
501 Atlanta Falcons TL	.30	.75
502 Baltimore Colts TL	.30	.75
503 Bills TL/O.J.Simpson	.60	1.50
504 Bears TL/W.Payton	.75	2.00
505 Bengals TL/Reg.Williams	.30	.75
506 Cleveland Browns TL	.30	.75
507 Cowboys TL/T.Dorsett	1.00	2.50
508 Denver Broncos TL	.40	1.00
509 Detroit Lions TL	.30	.75
510 Green Bay Packers TL	.40	1.00
511 Houston Oilers TL	.30	.75
512 Kansas City Chiefs TL	.30	.75
513 Los Angeles Rams TL	.30	.75
514 Miami Dolphins TL	.40	1.00
515 Minnesota Vikings TL	.30	.75
516 New England Patriots TL	.30	.75
517 New Orleans Saints TL	.30	.75
518 New York Giants TL	.30	.75
519 Jets TL/Wesley Walker	.30	.75
520 Oakland Raiders TL	.40	1.00
521 Philadelphia Eagles TL	.30	.75
522 Steelers TL/Harris/Blount	.40	1.00
523 St.Louis Cardinals TL	.30	.75
524 San Diego Chargers TL	.40	1.00
525 San Francisco 49ers TL	.30	.75
526 Seahawks TL/S.Largent	.60	1.50
527 Tampa Bay Bucs TL	.30	.75
528 Redskins TL/Ken Houston	.40	1.00

1978 Topps Holsum

In 1978, Topps produced a set of 33 NFL full-color standard-size cards for Holsum Bread. One card was packed inside each loaf of bread. Unfortunately, nowhere on the card is Holsum mentioned, leading to frequent misclassification of this set. An uncut production sheet was offered in the 1989 Topps Archives auction. The personal data on the card back is printed in yellow and green. Each card can be found with either one or two asterisks on the copyright line.

COMPLETE SET (33)	150.00	300.00
1 Rolland Lawrence	2.00	4.00
2 Walter Payton	60.00	120.00
3 Lydell Mitchell	2.50	5.00
4 Joe DeLamielleure	3.50	6.00
5 Ken Anderson	5.00	10.00
6 Greg Pruitt	2.50	5.00
7 Harvey Martin	3.00	6.00
8 Tom Jackson	3.00	6.00
9 Chester Marcol	2.00	4.00
10 Jim Carter	2.00	4.00
11 Will Harrell	2.00	4.00
12 Greg Landry	2.50	5.00
13 Billy Johnson	2.50	5.00
14 Jan Stenerud	3.00	6.00
15 Lawrence McCutcheon	2.50	5.00
16 Bob Griese	12.50	25.00
17 Chuck Foreman	2.50	5.00
18 Sammie White	2.50	5.00
19 Jeff Siemon	2.00	4.00
20 Mike Haynes	4.00	8.00
21 Archie Manning	7.50	15.00
22 Brad Van Pelt	2.00	4.00
23 Richard Todd	2.50	5.00
24 Dave Casper	4.00	8.00
25 Bill Bergey	2.50	5.00
26 Franco Harris	12.50	25.00
27 Mel Gray	2.50	5.00
28 Louie Kelcher	2.00	4.00
29 O.J. Simpson	15.00	30.00
30 Jim Zorn	2.50	5.00
31 Lee Roy Selmon	4.00	8.00
32 Ken Houston	3.00	6.00
33 Checklist Card	10.00	20.00

1978 Topps Team Checklists

These cards are essentially a parallel to the base 1978 Topps team checklist subset cards. The set was only available directly from Topps as a send-off offer in uncut sheet form. The prices below apply equally to uncut sheets as they are frequently found in their original uncut condition. As for individual cards, thin white card (almost paper-thin) stock makes it a challenge to find singles in top grades.

COMPLETE SET (28)	62.50	125.00
501 Atlanta Falcons TL	2.00	4.00
502 Baltimore Colts TL	2.00	4.00
503 Bills TL O.J.Simpson	4.00	8.00
504 Bears TL Walter Payton	7.50	15.00
505 Bengals TL Reg.Williams	2.00	4.00
506 Cleveland Browns TL	2.00	4.00
507 Cowboys TL T.Dorsett	5.00	10.00
508 Denver Broncos TL	3.00	6.00
509 Detroit Lions TL	2.00	4.00
510 Green Bay Packers TL	3.00	6.00
511 Houston Oilers TL	2.00	4.00
512 Kansas City Chiefs TL	2.00	4.00
513 Los Angeles Rams TL	2.00	4.00
514 Miami Dolphins TL	3.00	6.00
515 Minnesota Vikings TL	3.00	6.00
516 New England Patriots TL	2.00	4.00
517 New Orleans Saints TL	2.00	4.00
518 New York Giants TL	2.00	4.00
519 Jets TL Wesley Walker	2.00	4.00
520 Oakland Raiders TL	3.00	6.00
521 Philadelphia Eagles TL	3.00	6.00
522 Steelers TL Harris Blount	4.00	8.00
523 St.Louis Cardinals TL	2.00	4.00
524 San Diego Chargers TL	3.00	6.00
525 San Francisco 49ers TL	3.00	6.00
526 Seahawks TL S.Largent	4.00	8.00
527 Tampa Bay Bucs TL	3.00	6.00
528 Redskins TL Ken Houston	3.00	6.00

1979 Topps

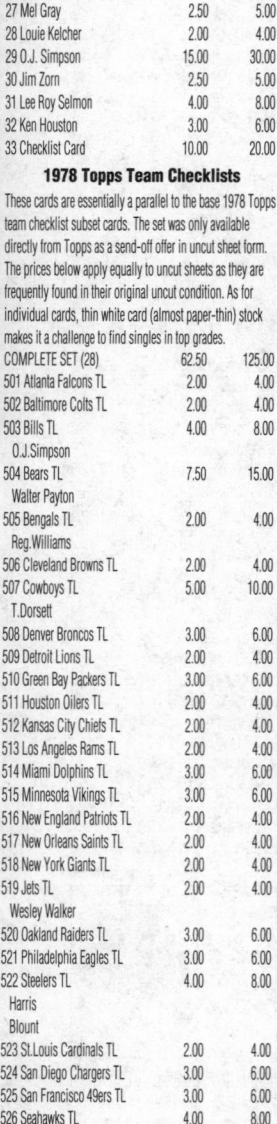

The 1979 Topps football set contains 528 standard-size cards. The cardfronts have the player's name, team name and position at the top and the position is within a football that is part of a banner-like design. The backs contain yearly statistics, highlights and a player cartoon. Subsets include League Leaders (1-6), Playoffs (166-168) and Record Breakers (331-336). Team Leaders (TL) depict team leaders in various categories on front and a team checklist on back. An uncut sheet of the 28-Team Leaders cards along with two checklists was available via a wrapper mail order offer. The set features the first and only major issue cards of Earl Campbell. Other Rookie Cards include Steve DeBerg, James Lofton, Ozzie Newsome and Doug Williams. Finally, every card was printed on the standard dark colored gray card stock as well as a thinner cream colored card stock that is slightly more difficult to find.

COMPLETE SET (528)	75.00	150.00
*CREAM BACK: .4X TO 1X GRAY BACK		
1 Staubach/Bradshaw LL	4.00	8.00
2 S.Largent/R.Young LL	.40	1.00
3 E.Campbell/W.Payton LL	4.00	8.00
4 Scoring Leaders	.10	.30
5 Interception Leaders	.10	.30
6 Punting Leaders	.10	.30
7 Johnny Perkins	.10	.30
8 Charles Phillips RC	.10	.30
9 Derrel Luce	.10	.30
10 John Riggins	.50	1.25
11 Chester Marcol	.10	.30
12 Bernard Jackson	.10	.30
13 Dave Logan	.10	.30
14 Bo Harris	.10	.30
15 Alan Page	.40	1.00
16 John Smith	.10	.30
17 Dwight McDonald RC	.10	.30
18 John Cappelletti	.20	.50
19 Steelers TL/Harris/Dungy	5.00	12.00
20A Bill Bergey AP (Eagles printed in pink on front)	.20	.50
20B Bill Bergey AP Red	1.25	3.00
21 Jerome Barkum	.10	.30
22 Larry Csonka	1.00	2.50
23 Joe Ferguson	.20	.50
24 Ed Too Tall Jones	.50	1.25
25 Dave Jennings	.20	.50
26 Horace King	.10	.30
27 Steve Little RC	.20	.50
28 Morris Bradshaw RC	.10	.30
29 Joe Ehrmann	.10	.30
30 Ahmad Rashad AP	.40	1.00
31 Joe Lavender	.10	.30
32 Dan Neal	.10	.30
33 Johnny Evans RC	.10	.30
34 Pete Johnson	.20	.50
35 Mike Haynes AP	.40	1.00
36 Tim Mazzetti RC	.10	.30
37 Mike Barber RC	.10	.30
38 49ers TL/O.J.Simpson	.60	1.50
39 Bill Gregory RC	.10	.30
40 Randy Gradishar AP	.40	1.00
41 Richard Todd	.20	.50
42 Henry Marshall	.10	.30
43 John Hill	.10	.30
44 Sidney Thornton RC	.10	.30
45 Ron Jessie	.10	.30
46 Bob Baumhower	.20	.50
47 Johnnie Gray	.10	.30
48 Doug Williams RC	3.00	6.00
49 Don McCauley	.10	.30
50 Ray Guy AP	.20	.50
51 Bob Klein	.10	.30
52 Golden Richards	.10	.30
53 Mark Miller QB RC	.10	.30
54 John Sanders	.10	.30
55 Gary Burley	.10	.30
56 Steve Nelson	.10	.30
57 Buffalo Bills TL	.30	.75
58 Bobby Bryant	.10	.30
59 Rick Kane	.10	.30
60 Larry Little	.40	1.00
61 Ted Fritsch Jr.	.10	.30
62 Larry Mallory RC	.10	.30
63 Marvin Powell	.10	.30
64 Jim Hart	.40	1.00
65 Joe Greene AP	.60	1.50
66 Walter White	.10	.30
67 Gregg Bingham	.10	.30
68 Errol Mann	.10	.30
69 Bruce Laird	.10	.30
70 Drew Pearson	.40	1.00
71 Steve Bartkowski	.40	1.00
72 Ted Albrecht	.10	.30
73 Charlie Hall	.10	.30
74 Pat McInally	.10	.30
75 Bubba Baker RC	.40	1.00
76 New England Pats TL	.30	.75
77 Steve DeBerg RC	.75	2.00
78 John Yarno RC	.10	.30
79 Stu Voigt	.10	.30
80 Frank Corral AP RC	.10	.30
81 Troy Archer	.10	.30
82 Bruce Harper	.10	.30
83 Tom Jackson	.60	1.50
84 Larry Brown	.20	.50
85A Wilbert Montgomery AP RC	.40	1.00
85B Wilbert Montgomery AP Red	1.50	4.00
86 Butch Johnson	.20	.50
87 Mike Kadish	.10	.30
88 Ralph Perretta	.10	.30
89 David Lee	.10	.30
90 Mark Van Eeghen	.20	.50
91 John McDaniel	.10	.30
92 Gary Fencik	.20	.50
93 Mack Mitchell	.10	.30
94 Cincinnati Bengals TL/Jauron	.40	1.00
95 Steve Grogan	.40	1.00
96 Garo Yepremian	.20	.50
97 Barty Smith	.10	.30
98 Frank Reed RC	.10	.30
99 Jim Clack RC	.10	.30
100 Chuck Foreman	.20	.50
101 Joe Klecko	.40	1.00
102 Pat Tilley	.20	.50
103 Conrad Dobler	.20	.50
104 Craig Colquitt RC	.10	.30
105 Dan Pastorini	.20	.50
106 Rod Perry AP	.10	.30
107 Nick Mike-Mayer	.10	.30
108 John Matuszak	.20	.50
109 David Taylor	.10	.30
110 Billy Joe DuPree AP	.20	.50
111 Harold McLinton	.10	.30
112 Virgil Livers	.10	.30
113 Cleveland Browns TL	.30	.75
114 Checklist 1-132	.40	1.00
115 Ken Anderson	.40	1.00
116 Bill Lenkaitis	.10	.30
117 Bucky Dilts	.10	.30
118 Tony Greene	.10	.30
119 Bobby Hammond	.10	.30
120 Nat Moore	.20	.50
121 Pat Leahy AP	.20	.50
122 James Harris	.20	.50
123 Lee Roy Selmon	.50	1.25
124 Bennie Cunningham	.20	.50
125 Matt Blair AP	.20	.50
126 Jim Allen	.10	.30
127 Alfred Jenkins	.20	.50
128 Arthur Whittington RC	.10	.30
129 Norm Thompson	.10	.30
130 Pat Haden	.40	1.00
131 Freddie Solomon	.10	.30
132 Bears TL/W.Payton	.75	2.00
133 Mark Moseley	.10	.30
134 Cleo Miller	.10	.30
135 Ross Browner RC	.20	.50
136 Don Calhoun	.10	.30
137 David Whitehurst RC	.10	.30
138 Terry Beeson	.10	.30
139 Ken Stone RC	.10	.30
140 Brad Van Pelt AP	.10	.30
141 Wesley Walker AP	.40	1.00
142 Jan Stenerud	.40	1.00
143 Henry Childs	.10	.30
144 Otis Armstrong	.40	1.00
145 Dwight White	.20	.50
146 Steve Wilson RC	.10	.30
147 Tom Skladany RC	.10	.30
148 Lou Piccone	.10	.30
149 Monte Johnson	.10	.30
150 Joe Washington	.20	.50
151 Eagles TL/W.Montgomery	.30	.75
152 Fred Dean	.40	1.00
153 Rolland Lawrence	.10	.30
154 Brian Baschnagel	.10	.30
155 Joe Theismann	.75	2.00
156 Marvin Cobb	.10	.30
157 Dick Ambrose	.10	.30
158 Mike Patrick	.10	.30
159 Gary Shirk	.10	.30
160 Tony Dorsett	6.00	12.00
161 Greg Buttle	.10	.30
162 A.J. Duhe	.20	.50
163 Mick Tingelhoff	.20	.50
164 Ken Burrough	.20	.50
165 Mike Wagner	.10	.30
166 AFC Champs/F.Harris	.40	1.00
167 NFC Championship	.20	.50
168 Super Bowl XIII/Harris	.50	1.25
169 Raiders TL/Ted Hendricks	.40	1.00
170 O.J. Simpson	1.50	4.00
171 Doug Nettles RC	.10	.30
172 Dan Dierdorf AP	.40	1.00
173 Dave Beverly	.10	.30
174 Jim Zorn	.40	1.00
175 Mike Thomas	.10	.30
176 John Outlaw	.10	.30
177 Jim Turner	.10	.30
178 Freddie Scott RC	.10	.30
179 Mike Phipps	.20	.50
180 Jack Youngblood AP	.40	1.00
181 Sam Hunt	.10	.30
182 Tony Hill RC	.40	1.00
183 Gary Barbaro	.10	.30
184 Archie Griffin	.20	.50
185 Jerry Sherk	.10	.30
186 Bobby Jackson RC	.10	.30
187 Don Woods	.10	.30
188 New York Giants TL	.30	.75
189 Raymond Chester	.10	.30
190 Joe DeLamielleure AP	.40	1.00
191 Tony Galbreath	.20	.50
192 Robert Brazile AP	.20	.50
193 Neil O'Donoghue RC	.10	.30
194 Mike Webster AP	.40	1.00
195 Ed Simonini	.10	.30
196 Benny Malone	.10	.30
197 Tom Wittum	.10	.30
198 Steve Largent AP	4.00	8.00
199 Tommy Hart	.10	.30
200 Fran Tarkenton	1.50	3.00
201 Leon Gray AP	.10	.30
202 Leroy Harris RC	.10	.30
203 Eric Williams LB RC	.10	.30
204 Thom Darden AP	.10	.30
205 Ken Riley	.20	.50
206 Clark Gaines	.10	.30
207 Kansas City Chiefs TL	.30	.75
208 Joe Danelo	.10	.30
209 Glen Walker	.10	.30
210 Art Shell	.40	1.00
211 Jon Keyworth	.10	.30
212 Herman Edwards	.10	.30
213 John Fitzgerald	.10	.30
214 Jim Smith	.20	.50
215 Coy Bacon	.20	.50
216 Dennis Johnson RBK RC	.10	.30
217 John Jefferson RC	1.50	3.00
218 Gary Weaver RC	.10	.30
219 Tom Blanchard	.10	.30
220 Bert Jones	.40	1.00
221 Stanley Morgan	.40	1.00
222 James Hunter	.10	.30
223 Jim O'Bradovich RC	.10	.30
224 Carl Mauck	.10	.30
225 Chris Bahr	.10	.30
226 Jets TL/Wesley Walker	.30	.75
227 Roland Harper	.10	.30
228 Randy Dean RC	.10	.30
229 Bob Jackson	.10	.30
230 Sammie White	.20	.50
231 Mike Dawson RC	.10	.30
232 Checklist 133-264	.40	1.00
233 Ken MacAfee RC	.10	.30
234 Jon Kolb AP	.10	.30
235 Willie Hall	.10	.30
236 Ron Saul AP	.10	.30
237 Haskel Stanback	.10	.30
238 Zenon Andrusyshyn RC	.10	.30
239 Norris Thomas	.10	.30
240 Rick Upchurch	.20	.50
241 Robert Pratt	.10	.30
242 Julius Adams	.10	.30
243 Rich McGeorge	.10	.30
244 Seahawks TL/S.Largent	.50	1.25
245 Blair Bush RC	.10	.30
246 Billy Johnson	.20	.50
247 Randy Rasmussen	.10	.30
248 Brian Kelley	.10	.30
249 Mike Pruitt	.20	.50
250 Harold Carmichael AP	.40	1.00
251 Mike Hartenstine	.10	.30
252 Robert Newhouse	.20	.50
253 Gary Danielson RC	.40	1.00
254 Mike Fuller	.10	.30
255 L.C. Greenwood AP	.40	1.00
256 Lemar Parrish	.10	.30
257 Ike Harris	.10	.30
258 Ricky Bell RC	.40	1.00
259 Willie Parker C	.10	.30
260 Gene Upshaw	.40	1.00
261 Glenn Doughty	.10	.30
262 Steve Zabel	.10	.30
263 Atlanta Falcons TL	.30	.75
264 Ray Wersching	.10	.30
265 Lawrence McCutcheon	.20	.50
266 Willie Buchanon AP	.10	.30
267 Matt Robinson RC	.10	.30
268 Reggie Rucker	.20	.50
269 Doug Van Horn	.10	.30
270 Lydell Mitchell	.20	.50
271 Vern Holland	.10	.30
272 Eason Ramson RC	.10	.30
273 Steve Towle RC	.10	.30
274 Jim Marshall	.40	1.00
275 Mel Blount	.50	1.25
276 Bob Kuziel RC	.10	.30
277 James Scott	.10	.30
278 Tony Reed	.10	.30
279 Dave Green	.10	.30
280 Toni Linhart	.10	.30
281 Andy Johnson	.10	.30
282 Los Angeles Rams TL	.30	.75
283 Phil Villapiano	.20	.50
284 Dexter Bussey	.10	.30
285 Craig Morton	.40	1.00
286 Guy Morriss	.10	.30
287 Lawrence Pillers	.10	.30
288 Gerald Irons	.10	.30
289 Scott Perry RC	.10	.30
290 Randy White AP	.75	2.00
291 Jack Gregory	.10	.30
292 Bob Chandler	.10	.30
293 Rich Szaro	.10	.30
294 Sherman Smith	.10	.30
295 Tom Banks AP	.10	.30
296 Revie Sorey AP	.10	.30
297 Ricky Thompson RC	.10	.30
298 Ron Yary	.40	1.00
299 Lyle Blackwood	.10	.30
300 Franco Harris	1.25	2.50
301 Oilers TL/E.Campbell	1.50	3.00
302 Scott Bull RC	.10	.30
303 Dewey Selmon	.20	.50
304 Jack Rudnay	.10	.30
305 Fred Biletnikoff	.75	2.00
306 Jeff West	.10	.30
307 Shafer Suggs RC	.10	.30
308 Ozzie Newsome RC	6.00	12.00
309 Boobie Clark	.10	.30
310 James Lofton RC	6.00	15.00
311 Joe Pisarcik	.10	.30
312 Bill Simpson AP	.10	.30
313 Haven Moses	.20	.50
314 Jim Merlo	.10	.30
315 Preston Pearson	.20	.50
316 Larry Tearry RC	.10	.30
317 Tom Dempsey	.10	.30
318 Greg Latta	.10	.30
319 Redskins TL/John Riggins	.60	1.50
320 Jack Ham AP	.50	1.25
321 Harold Jackson	.20	.50
322 George Roberts RC	.10	.30
323 Ron Jaworski	.40	1.00
324 Jim Otis	.10	.30
325 Roger Carr	.20	.50

326 Jack Tatum .20 .50
327 Derrick Gaffney RC .10 .30
328 Reggie Williams .40 1.00
329 Doug Dieken .10 .30
330 Efren Herrera .10 .30
331 Earl Campbell RB 3.00 6.00
332 Tony Galbreath RB .10 .30
333 Bruce Harper RB .10 .30
334 John James RB .10 .30
335 Walter Payton RB 1.50 4.00
336 Rickey Young RB .10 .30
337 Jeff Van Note .20 .50
338 Chargers TL/J.Jefferson .40 1.00
339 Stan Walters RC .10 .30
340 Louis Wright AP .20 .50
341 Horace Ivory RC .10 .30
342 Andre Tillman .10 .30
343 Greg Coleman RC .10 .30
344 Doug English AP RC .40 1.00
345 Ted Hendricks .40 1.00
346 Rich Saul .10 .30
347 Mel Gray .20 .50
348 Toni Fritsch .10 .30
349 Cornell Webster RC .10 .30
350 Ken Houston .40 1.00
351 Ron Johnson DB RC .20 .50
352 Doug Kotar .10 .30
353 Brian Sipe .40 1.00
354 Billy Brooks .10 .30
355 John Dutton .20 .50
356 Don Goode .10 .30
357 Detroit Lions TL .30 .75
358 Reuben Gant .10 .30
359 Bob Parsons .10 .30
360 Cliff Harris AP .40 1.00
361 Raymond Clayborn .20 .50
362 Scott Dierking .10 .30
363 Bill Bryan RC .10 .30
364 Mike Livingston .10 .30
365 Otis Sistrunk .20 .50
366 Charle Young .20 .50
367 Keith Wortman RC .10 .30
368 Checklist 265-396 .40 1.00
369 Mike Michel RC .10 .30
370 Delvin Williams AP .10 .30
371 Steve Furness .20 .50
372 Emery Moorehead .10 .30
373 Clarence Scott .10 .30
374 Rufus Mayes .10 .30
375 Chris Hanburger .10 .30
376 Baltimore Colts TL .30 .75
377 Bob Avellini .20 .50
378 Jeff Siemon .10 .30
379 Roland Hooks .10 .30
380 Russ Francis .20 .50
381 Roger Wehrli .20 .50
382 Joe Fields .10 .30
383 Archie Manning .40 1.00
384 Rob Lytle .10 .30
385 Thomas Henderson .20 .50
386 Morris Owens .10 .30
387 Dan Fouts 1.50 3.00
388 Chuck Crist .10 .30
389 Ed O'Neil RC .10 .30
390 Earl Campbell RC 15.00 30.00
391 Randy Grossman .10 .30
392 Monte Jackson .10 .30
393 John Mendenhall .10 .30
394 Miami Dolphins TL .40 1.00
395 Isaac Curtis .20 .50
396 Mike Bragg .10 .30
397 Doug Plank .10 .30
398 Mike Barnes .10 .30
399 Calvin Hill .20 .50
400 Roger Staubach AP 5.00 10.00
401 Doug Beaudoin RC .10 .30
402 Chuck Ramsey .10 .30
403 Mike Hogan .10 .30
404 Mario Clark .10 .30
405 Riley Odoms .10 .30
406 Carl Eller .40 1.00
407 Packers TL/J.Lofton .60 1.50
408 Mark Arneson .10 .30
409 Vince Ferragamo RC .40 1.00
410 Cleveland Elam .10 .30
411 Donnie Shell RC 1.50 4.00
412 Ray Rhodes .40 1.00
413 Don Cockroft .10 .30
414 Don Bass RC .20 .50
415 Cliff Branch .40 1.00
416 Diron Talbert .10 .30
417 Tom Hicks .10 .30
418 Roosevelt Leaks .10 .30
419 Charlie Joiner .40 1.00
420 Lyle Alzado AP .40 1.00
421 Sam Cunningham .20 .50
422 Larry Keller .10 .30
423 Jim Mitchell .10 .30
424 Randy Logan .10 .30
425 Jim Langer .40 1.00
426 Gary Green .10 .30
427 Luther Blue RC .10 .30
428 Dennis Johnson .10 .30
429 Danny White .40 1.00
430 Roy Gerela .10 .30
431 Jimmy Robinson .10 .30
432 Minnesota Vikings TL .30 .75
433 Oliver Davis .10 .30
434 Lenvil Elliott .10 .30
435 Willie Miller RC .10 .30
436 Brad Dusek .10 .30
437 Bob Thomas .10 .30
438 Ken Mendenhall .10 .30
439 Clarence Davis .10 .30
440 Bob Griese 1.00 2.50
441 Tony McGee .10 .30
442 Ed Taylor .10 .30
443 Ron Howard .10 .30
444 Wayne Morris .10 .30
445 Charlie Waters .20 .50
446 Rick Danmeier RC .10 .30
447 Paul Naumoff .10 .30
448 Keith Krepfle .10 .30
449 Rusty Jackson .10 .30
450 John Stallworth 2.00 4.00
451 New Orleans Saints TL .30 .75
452 Ron Mikolajczyk RC .10 .30
453 Fred Dryer .40 1.00
454 Jim LeClair .10 .30
455 Greg Pruitt .20 .50
456 Jake Scott .10 .30
457 Steve Schubert .10 .30
458 George Kunz .10 .30
459 Mike Williams .10 .30
460 Dave Casper AP .40 1.00
461 Sam Adams .10 .30
462 Abdul Salaam .10 .30
463 Terdell Middleton RC .20 .50
464 Mike Wood RC .10 .30
465 Bill Thompson AP .10 .30
466 Larry Gordon .10 .30
467 Benny Ricardo .10 .30
468 Reggie McKenzie .20 .50
469 Cowboys TL/T.Dorsett .60 1.50
470 Rickey Young .20 .50
471 Charlie Smith .10 .30
472 Al Dixon RC .10 .30
473 Tom DeLeone .10 .30
474 Louis Breeden RC .20 .50
475 Jack Lambert .75 2.00
476 Terry Hermeling .10 .30
477 J.K. McKay .10 .30
478 Stan White .10 .30
479 Terry Nelson .10 .30
480 Walter Payton AP 10.00 20.00
481 Dave Dalby .10 .30
482 Burgess Owens .10 .30
483 Rolf Benirschke .10 .30
484 Jack Dolbin .10 .30
485 John Hannah AP .40 1.00
486 Checklist 397-528 .40 1.00
487 Greg Landry .20 .50
488 St. Louis Cardinals TL .30 .75
489 Paul Krause .40 1.00
490 John James .10 .30
491 Merv Krakau .10 .30
492 Dan Doornink RC .10 .30
493 Curtis Johnson .10 .30
494 Rafael Septien .10 .30
495 Jean Fugett .10 .30
496 Frank LeMaster .10 .30
497 Allan Ellis .10 .30
498 Billy Waddy RC .20 .50
499 Hank Bauer RC .10 .30
500 Terry Bradshaw UER 5.00 10.00
501 Larry McCarren .10 .30
502 Fred Cook .10 .30
503 Chuck Muncie .20 .50
504 Herman Weaver .10 .30
505 Eddie Edwards .10 .30
506 Tony Peters .10 .30
507 Denver Broncos TL .30 .75
508 Jimbo Elrod RC .10 .30
509 David Hill .10 .30
510 Harvey Martin .20 .50
511 Terry Miller RC .20 .50
512 June Jones RC .20 .50
513 Randy Cross .40 1.00
514 Duriel Harris .10 .30
515 Harry Carson .40 1.00
516 Tim Fox .10 .30
517 John Zook .10 .30
518 Bob Tucker .10 .30
519 Kevin Long RC .10 .30
520 Ken Stabler 3.00 6.00
521 John Bunting .20 .50
522 Rocky Bleier .50 1.25
523 Noah Jackson .10 .30
524 Cliff Parsley RC .10 .30
525 Louie Kelcher AP .20 .50
526 Bucs TL/Ricky Bell .30 .75
527 Bob Brudzinski RC .10 .30
528 Danny Buggs .10 .30

1979 Topps Team Checklists

These cards are essentially a parallel to the base 1979 Topps team checklist subset cards. The set was only available directly from Topps as a send-off offer in uncut sheet form. The prices below apply equally to uncut sheets as they are frequently found in their original uncut condition. As for individual cards, thin white card (almost paper-thin) stock makes it a challenge to find singles in top grades.

COMPLETE SET (28) 62.50 125.00
19 Steelers TL 5.00 10.00
F.Harris
Dungy
38 49ers TL 4.00 8.00
O.J.Simpson
57 Buffalo Bills TL 2.00 4.00
76 New England Pats TL 2.00 4.00
94 Cincinnati Bengals TL 4.00 8.00
Jauron
113 Cleveland Browns TL 2.00 4.00
132 Bears TL 6.00 12.00
Walter Payton
151 Eagles TL 3.00 6.00
W.Montgomery
169 Raiders TL 4.00 8.00
Ted Hendricks
188 New York Giants TL 2.00 4.00
207 Kansas City Chiefs TL 2.00 4.00
226 Jets TL 2.00 4.00
Wesley Walker
244 Seahawks TL 4.00 8.00
S.Largent
263 Atlanta Falcons TL 2.00 4.00
282 Los Angeles Rams TL 2.00 4.00
301 Oilers TL 6.00 12.00
Earl Campbell
319 Redskins TL 4.00 8.00
John Riggins
338 Chargers TL 3.00 6.00
J.Jefferson
357 Detroit Lions TL 2.00 4.00
376 Baltimore Colts TL 2.00 4.00
394 Miami Dolphins TL 2.00 4.00
407 Packers TL 5.00 10.00
James Lofton
432 Minnesota Vikings TL 3.00 6.00
451 New Orleans Saints TL 2.00 4.00
469 Cowboys TL 5.00 10.00
Tony Dorsett
488 St. Louis Cardinals TL 2.00 4.00
507 Denver Broncos TL 3.00 6.00
526 Bucs TL 3.00 6.00
Ricky Bell

1980 Topps

The 1980 Topps football card set contains 528 standard-size cards of NFL players. The set was issued in 12-card packs along with a bubble gum slab. The fronts feature a football at the bottom of the photo. Within the football is the player's team and position. A bar with the player's name runs through the center of the football. The backs of the cards contain year-by-year and career statistics and a cartoon-illustrated fact section. Subsets include Record-Breakers (1-6), league leaders (331-336) and playoffs (492-494). Team Leader (TL) cards depict team statistical leaders on the front and a team checklist on the back. The key Rookie Cards in this set are Ottis Anderson, Clay Matthews, and Phil Simms.

COMPLETE SET (528) 40.00 75.00
1 Ottis Anderson RB .40 1.00
2 Harold Carmichael RB .40 1.00
3 Dan Fouts RB .40 1.00
4 Paul Krause RB .20 .50
5 Rick Upchurch RB .20 .50
6 Garo Yepremian RB .10 .25
7 Harold Jackson .20 .50
8 Mike Williams .10 .25
9 Calvin Hill .20 .50
10 Jack Ham AP .40 1.00
11 Dan Melville .10 .25
12 Matt Robinson .10 .25
13 Billy Campfield RC .10 .25
14 Phil Tabor RC .10 .25
15 Randy Hughes UER RC .10 .25
16 Andre Tillman .10 .25
17 Isaac Curtis .20 .50
18 Charley Hannah .10 .25
19 Redskins TL/J.Riggins .40 1.00
20 Jim Zorn .20 .50
21 Brian Baschnagel .10 .25
22 Jon Keyworth .10 .25
23 Phil Villapiano .10 .25
24 Richard Osborne .10 .25
25 Rich Saul AP .10 .25
26 Doug Beaudoin .10 .25
27 Cleveland Elam .10 .25
28 Charlie Joiner .40 1.00
29 Dick Ambrose .10 .25
30 Mike Reinfeldt RC .10 .25
31 Matt Bahr RC .40 1.00
32 Keith Krepfle .10 .25
33 Herb Scott .10 .25
34 Doug Kotar .10 .25
35 Bob Griese .60 1.50
36 Jerry Butler RC .40 1.00
37 Rolland Lawrence .10 .25
38 Gary Weaver .10 .25
39 Chiefs TL/J.T.Smith .20 .50
40 Chuck Muncie .20 .50
41 Mike Hartenstine .10 .25
42 Sammie White .20 .50
43 Ken Clark .10 .25
44 Clarence Harmon .10 .25
45 Bert Jones .40 1.00
46 Mike Washington .10 .25
47 Joe Fields .10 .25
48 Mike Wood .10 .25
49 Oliver Davis .10 .25
50 Stan Walters AP .10 .25
51 Riley Odoms .10 .25
52 Steve Pisarkiewicz .10 .25
53 Tony Hill .40 1.00
54 Scott Perry .10 .25
55 George Martin RC .10 .25
56 George Roberts .10 .25
57 Seahawks TL/S. Largent .40 1.00
58 Billy Johnson .20 .50
59 Reuben Gant .10 .25
60 Dennis Harrah RC .10 .25
61 Rocky Bleier .40 1.00
62 Sam Hunt .10 .25
63 Allan Ellis .10 .25
64 Ricky Thompson .10 .25
65 Ken Stabler 1.50 4.00
66 Dexter Bussey .10 .25
67 Ken Mendenhall .10 .25
68 Woodrow Lowe .10 .25
69 Thom Darden .10 .25
70 Randy White AP .60 1.50
71 Ken MacAfee .10 .25
72 Ron Jaworski .40 1.00
73 William Andrews RC .40 1.00
74 Jimmy Robinson .10 .25
75 Roger Wehrli AP .20 .50
76 Dolphins TL/L.Csonka .40 1.00
77 Jack Rudnay .10 .25
78 James Lofton .75 2.00
79 Robert Brazile .20 .50
80 Russ Francis .20 .50
81 Ricky Bell .40 1.00
82 Bob Avellini .20 .50
83 Bobby Jackson .10 .25
84 Mike Bragg .10 .25
85 Cliff Branch .40 1.00
86 Blair Bush .10 .25
87 Sherman Smith .10 .25
88 Glen Edwards .10 .25
89 Don Cockroft .10 .25
90 Louis Wright AP .20 .50
91 Randy Grossman .10 .25
92 Carl Hairston RC .40 1.00
93 Archie Manning .40 1.00
94 New York Giants TL .20 .50
95 Preston Pearson .20 .50
96 Rusty Chambers .10 .25
97 Greg Coleman .10 .25
98 Charle Young .10 .25
99 Matt Cavanaugh RC .20 .50
100 Jesse Baker .10 .25
101 Doug Plank .10 .25
102 Checklist 1-132 .30 .75
103 Luther Bradley RC .10 .25
104 Bob Kuziel .10 .25
105 Craig Morton .20 .50
106 Sherman White .10 .25
107 Jim Breech RC .20 .50
108 Hank Bauer .10 .25
109 Tom Blanchard .10 .25
110 Ozzie Newsome AP .75 2.00
111 Steve Furness .10 .25
112 Frank LeMaster .10 .25
113 Cowboys TL/T.Dorsett .40 1.00
114 Doug Van Horn .10 .25
115 Delvin Williams .10 .25
116 Lyle Blackwood .10 .25
117 Derrick Gaffney .10 .25
118 Cornell Webster .10 .25
119 Sam Cunningham .20 .50
120 Jim Youngblood AP .20 .50
121 Bob Thomas .10 .25
122 Jack Thompson RC .20 .50
123 Randy Cross .40 1.00
124 Karl Lorch RC .10 .25
125 Mel Gray .10 .25
126 John James .10 .25
127 Terdell Middleton .10 .25
128 Leroy Jones .10 .25
129 Tom DeLeone .10 .25
130 John Stallworth AP .60 1.50
131 Jimmie Giles RC .20 .50
132 Philadelphia Eagles TL .40 1.00
133 Gary Green .10 .25
134 John Dutton .20 .50
135 Harry Carson AP .40 1.00
136 Bob Kuechenberg .20 .50
137 Ike Harris .10 .25
138 Tommy Kramer RC .40 1.00
139 Sam Adams OL .10 .25
140 Doug English AP .20 .50
141 Steve Schubert .10 .25
142 Rusty Jackson .10 .25
143 Reese McCall .10 .25
144 Scott Dierking .10 .25
145 Ken Houston AP .40 1.00
146 Bob Martin .10 .25
147 Sam McCullum .10 .25
148 Tom Banks .10 .25
149 Willie Buchanon .10 .25
150 Greg Pruitt .20 .50
151 Denver Broncos TL .40 1.00
152 Don Smith RC .10 .25
153 Pete Johnson .20 .50
154 Charlie Smith WR .10 .25
155 Mel Blount .40 1.00
156 John Mendenhall .10 .25
157 Danny White .40 1.00
158 Jimmy Cefalo RC .20 .50
159 Richard Bishop AP .10 .25
160 Walter Payton AP 5.00 12.00
161 Dave Dalby .10 .25
162 Preston Dennard .10 .25
163 Johnnie Gray .10 .25
164 Russell Erxleben .10 .25
165 Toni Fritsch AP .10 .25
166 Terry Hermeling .10 .25
167 Roland Hooks .10 .25

168 Roger Carr .10 .25
169 San Diego Chargers TL .40 1.00
170 Ottis Anderson RC 1.50 4.00
171 Brian Sipe .40 1.00
172 Leonard Thompson .10 .25
173 Tony Reed .10 .25
174 Bob Tucker .10 .25
175 Joe Greene .40 1.00
176 Jack Dolbin .10 .25
177 Chuck Ramsey .10 .25
178 Paul Hofer .10 .25
179 Randy Logan .10 .25
180 David Lewis AP .10 .25
181 Duriel Harris .10 .25
182 June Jones .20 .50
183 Larry McCarren .10 .25
184 Ken Johnson RB .10 .25
185 Charlie Waters .20 .50
186 Noah Jackson .10 .25
187 Reggie Williams .20 .50
188 New England Patriots TL .20 .50
189 Carl Eller .40 1.00
190 Ed White AP .10 .25
191 Mario Clark .10 .25
192 Roosevelt Leaks .10 .25
193 Ted McKnight .10 .25
194 Danny Buggs .10 .25
195 Lester Hayes RC 1.50 4.00
196 Clarence Scott .10 .25
197 Saints TL/Wes Chandler .20 .50
198 Richard Caster .10 .25
199 Louie Giammona RC .10 .25
200 Terry Bradshaw 3.00 8.00
201 Ed Newman .10 .25
202 Fred Dryer .40 1.00
203 Dennis Franks .10 .25
204 Bob Breunig RC .20 .50
205 Alan Page .40 1.00
206 Earnest Gray RC .10 .25
207 Vikings TL/A.Rashad .40 1.00
208 Horace Ivory .10 .25
209 Isaac Hagins .10 .25
210 Gary Johnson AP .10 .25
211 Kevin Long .10 .25
212 Bill Thompson .10 .25
213 Don Bass .10 .25
214 George Starke RC .10 .25
215 Efren Herrera .10 .25
216 Theo Bell .10 .25
217 Monte Jackson .10 .25
218 Reggie McKenzie .10 .25
219 Bucky Dilts .10 .25
220 Lyle Alzado .40 1.00
221 Tim Foley .10 .25
222 Mark Arneson .10 .25
223 Fred Quillan .10 .25
224 Benny Ricardo .10 .25
225 Phil Simms RC 4.00 10.00
226 Bears TL/Walter Payton .50 1.25
227 Max Runager .10 .25
228 Barty Smith .10 .25
229 Jay Saldi .20 .50
230 John Hannah AP .40 1.00
231 Tim Wilson .10 .25
232 Jeff Van Note .10 .25
233 Henry Marshall .10 .25
234 Diron Talbert .10 .25
235 Garo Yepremian .20 .50
236 Larry Brown .10 .25
237 Clarence Williams RB RC .10 .25
238 Burgess Owens .10 .25
239 Vince Ferragamo .20 .50
240 Rickey Young .10 .25
241 Dave Logan .10 .25
242 Larry Gordon .10 .25
243 Terry Miller .10 .25
244 Baltimore Colts TL .40 1.00
245 Steve DeBerg .40 1.00
246 Checklist 133-264 .30 .75
247 Greg Latta .10 .25
248 Raymond Clayborn .20 .50
249 Jim Clack .10 .25
250 Drew Pearson .40 1.00
251 John Bunting .20 .50
252 Rob Lytle .10 .25
253 Jim Hart .40 1.00
254 John McDaniel .10 .25
255 Dave Pear AP .10 .25
256 Donnie Shell .40 1.00
257 Dan Doornink .10 .25
258 Wallace Francis RC .40 1.00
259 Dave Beverly .10 .25
260 Lee Roy Selmon AP .40 1.00
261 Doug Dieken .10 .25
262 Gary Davis RC .10 .25
263 Bob Rush .10 .25
264 Buffalo Bills TL .20 .50
265 Greg Landry .20 .50
266 Jan Stenerud .40 1.00
267 Tom Hicks .10 .25
268 Pat McInally .10 .25
269 Tim Fox .10 .25
270 Harvey Martin .20 .50
271 Dan Lloyd RC .10 .25
272 Mike Barber .10 .25
273 Wendell Tyler RC .40 1.00
274 Jeff Komlo RC .10 .25
275 Wes Chandler RC .40 1.00
276 Brad Dusek .10 .25
277 Charlie Johnson NT .10 .25
278 Dennis Swilley .10 .25
279 Johnny Evans .10 .25
280 Jack Lambert AP .60 1.50
281 Vern Den Herder .10 .25
282 Tampa Bay Bucs TL .40 1.00
283 Bob Klein .10 .25
284 Jim Turner .10 .25
285 Marvin Powell AP .20 .50
286 Aaron Kyle .10 .25
287 Dan Neal .10 .25
288 Wayne Morris .10 .25
289 Steve Bartkowski .20 .50
290 Dave Jennings AP .20 .50
291 John Smith .10 .25
292 Bill Gregory .10 .25
293 Frank Lewis .10 .25
294 Fred Cook .10 .25
295 David Hill AP .10 .25
296 Wade Key .10 .25
297 Sidney Thornton .10 .25
298 Charlie Hall .10 .25
299 Joe Lavender .10 .25
300 Tom Rafferty RC .10 .25
301 Mike Renfro RC .20 .50
302 Wilbur Jackson .20 .50
303 Packers TL/J.Lofton .40 1.00
304 Henry Childs .10 .25
305 Russ Washington AP .10 .25
306 Jim LeClair .10 .25
307 Tommy Hart .10 .25
308 Gary Barbaro .10 .25
309 Billy Taylor .10 .25
310 Ray Guy .20 .50
311 Don Hasselbeck RC .20 .50
312 Doug Williams .40 1.00
313 Nick Mike-Mayer .10 .25
314 Don McCauley .10 .25
315 Wesley Walker .40 1.00
316 Dan Dierdorf .40 1.00
317 Dave Brown DB RC .20 .50
318 Leroy Harris .10 .25
319 Steelers TL/Harris/Lambrt .40 1.00
320 Mark Moseley AP UER .10 .25
321 Mark Dennard .10 .25
322 Terry Nelson .10 .25
323 Tom Jackson .40 1.00
324 Rick Kane .10 .25
325 Jerry Sherk .10 .25
326 Ray Preston .10 .25
327 Golden Richards .10 .25
328 Randy Dean .10 .25
329 Rick Danmeier .10 .25
330 Tony Dorsett 2.50 6.00
331 R.Staubach/Fouts LL 1.25 3.00
332 Receiving Leaders .20 .50
333 Sacks Leaders .40 1.00
334 Scoring Leaders .40 1.00
335 Interception Leaders .40 1.00
336 Punting Leaders .40 1.00
337 Freddie Solomon .10 .25
338 Cincinnati Bengals TL/Jauron .40 1.00
339 Ken Stone .10 .25
340 Greg Buttle AP .10 .25
341 Bob Baumhower .20 .50
342 Billy Waddy .10 .25
343 Cliff Parsley .10 .25
344 Walter White .10 .25
345 Mike Thomas .10 .25
346 Neil O'Donoghue .10 .25
347 Freddie Scott .10 .25
348 Joe Ferguson .20 .50
349 Doug Nettles .10 .25
350 Mike Webster AP .40 1.00
351 Ron Saul .10 .25
352 Julius Adams .10 .25
353 Rafael Septien .10 .25
354 Cleo Miller .10 .25
355 Keith Simpson AP .10 .25
356 Johnny Perkins .10 .25
357 Jerry Sisemore .10 .25
358 Arthur Whittington .10 .25
359 Cardinals TL/Anderson .40 1.00
360 Rick Upchurch .20 .50
361 Kim Bokamper RC .10 .25
362 Roland Harper .10 .25
363 Pat Leahy .10 .25
364 Louis Breeden .10 .25
365 John Jefferson .40 1.00
366 Jerry Eckwood .10 .25
367 David Whitehurst .10 .25
368 Willie Parker C .10 .25
369 Ed Simonini .10 .25
370 Jack Youngblood AP .40 1.00
371 Don Warren RC .40 1.00
372 Andy Johnson .10 .25
373 D.D. Lewis .20 .50
374A Beasley Reece ERR RC .40 1.00
374B Beasley Reece COR RC .20 .50
375 L.C. Greenwood .40 1.00
376 Cleveland Browns TL .20 .50
377 Herman Edwards .10 .25
378 Rob Carpenter RC .10 .25
379 Herman Weaver .10 .25
380 Gary Fencik .10 .25
381 Don Strock .20 .50
382 Art Shell .40 1.00
383 Tim Mazzetti .10 .25
384 Bruce Harper .10 .25
385 Al (Bubba) Baker .20 .50
386 Conrad Dobler .10 .25
387 Stu Voigt .10 .25
388 Ken Anderson .40 1.00
389 Pat Tilley .10 .25
390 John Riggins .40 1.00
391 Checklist 265-396 .30 .75
392 Fred Dean .20 .50
393 Benny Barnes RC .10 .25
394 Los Angeles Rams TL .20 .50
395 Brad Van Pelt .10 .25
396 Eddie Hare .10 .25
397 John Sciarra RC .10 .25
398 Bob Jackson .10 .25
399 John Yarno .10 .25
400 Franco Harris AP .75 2.00
401 Ray Wersching .10 .25
402 Virgil Livers .10 .25
403 Raymond Chester .10 .25
404 Leon Gray .10 .25
405 Richard Todd .20 .50
406 Larry Little .40 1.00
407 Ted Fritsch Jr. .10 .25
408 Larry Mucker .10 .25
409 Jim Allen .10 .25
410 Randy Gradishar .40 1.00
411 Atlanta Falcons TL .40 1.00
412 Louie Kelcher .20 .50
413 Robert Newhouse .20 .50
414 Gary Shirk .10 .25
415 Mike Haynes AP .40 1.00
416 Craig Colquitt .10 .25
417 Lou Piccone .10 .25
418 Clay Matthews RC 1.50 4.00
419 Marvin Cobb .10 .25
420 Harold Carmichael AP .40 1.00
421 Uwe Von Schamann RC .20 .50
422 Mike Phipps .20 .50
423 Nolan Cromwell RC .40 1.00
424 Glenn Doughty .10 .25
425 Bob Young AP .10 .25
426 Tony Galbreath .10 .25
427 Luke Prestridge RC .10 .25
428 Terry Beeson .10 .25
429 Jack Tatum .20 .50
430 Lemar Parrish AP .10 .25
431 Chester Marcol .10 .25
432 Houston Oilers TL .40 1.00
433 John Fitzgerald .10 .25
434 Gary Jeter RC .20 .50
435 Steve Grogan .40 1.00
436 Jon Kolb UER .10 .25
437 Jim O'Bradovich UER .10 .25
438 Gerald Irons .10 .25
439 Jeff West .10 .25
440 Wilbert Montgomery .20 .50
441 Norris Thomas .10 .25
442 James Scott .10 .25
443 Curtis Brown .10 .25
444 Ken Fantetti .10 .25
445 Pat Haden .40 1.00
446 Carl Mauck .10 .25
447 Bruce Laird .10 .25
448 Otis Armstrong .10 .25
449 Gene Upshaw .40 1.00
450 Steve Largent AP 2.50 6.00
451 Benny Malone .10 .25
452 Steve Nelson .10 .25
453 Mark Cotney RC .10 .25
454 Joe Danelo .10 .25
455 Billy Joe DuPree .20 .50
456 Ron Johnson DB .10 .25
457 Archie Griffin .20 .50
458 Reggie Rucker .10 .25
459 Claude Humphrey .10 .25
460 Lydell Mitchell .20 .50
461 Steve Towle .10 .25
462 Revie Sorey .10 .25
463 Tom Skladany .10 .25
464 Clark Gaines .10 .25
465 Frank Corral .10 .25
466 Steve Fuller RC .20 .50
467 Ahmad Rashad AP .40 1.00
468 Oakland Raiders TL .40 1.00
469 Brian Peets .10 .25
470 Pat Donovan RC .20 .50
471 Ken Burrough .10 .25
472 Don Calhoun .10 .25
473 Bill Bryan .10 .25
474 Terry Jackson .10 .25
475 Joe Theismann .50 1.25
476 Jim Smith .20 .50
477 Joe DeLamielleure .40 1.00
478 Mike Pruitt AP .20 .50
479 Steve Mike-Mayer .10 .25
480 Bill Bergey .20 .50
481 Mike Fuller .10 .25
482 Bob Parsons .10 .25
483 Billy Brooks .10 .25
484 Jerome Barkum .10 .25
485 Larry Csonka .60 1.50
486 John Hill .10 .25
487 Mike Dawson .10 .25
488 Detroit Lions TL .20 .50
489 Ted Hendricks .40 1.00
490 Dan Pastorini .20 .50
491 Stanley Morgan .40 1.00
492 AFC Champs/Bleier .40 1.00
493 NFC Champs/Ferragamo .20 .50
494 Super Bowl XIV .40 1.00
495 Dwight White .20 .50
496 Haven Moses .10 .25
497 Guy Morriss .10 .25
498 Dewey Selmon .20 .50
499 Dave Butz RC .40 1.00
500 Chuck Foreman .20 .50
501 Chris Bahr .10 .25
502 Mark Miller QB .10 .25
503 Tony Greene .10 .25
504 Brian Kelley .10 .25
505 Joe Washington .20 .50
506 Butch Johnson .20 .50
507 New York Jets TL .20 .50
508 Steve Little .10 .25
509 Checklist 397-528 .30 .75
510 Mark Van Eeghen .10 .25
511 Gary Danielson .20 .50
512 Manu Tuiasosopo RC .10 .25
513 Paul Coffman RC .20 .50
514 Cullen Bryant .20 .50
515 Nat Moore .20 .50
516 Bill Lenkaitis .10 .25
517 Lynn Cain RC .10 .25
518 Gregg Bingham .10 .25
519 Ted Albrecht .10 .25
520 Dan Fouts AP .75 2.00
521 Bernard Jackson .10 .25
522 Coy Bacon .10 .25
523 Tony Franklin RC .20 .50
524 Bo Harris .10 .25
525 Bob Grupp AP .10 .25
526 San Francisco 49ers TL .40 1.00
527 Steve Wilson .10 .25
528 Bennie Cunningham .20 .50

1980 Topps Super

The 1980 Topps Superstar Photo Football set features 30 large (approximately 4 7/8" by 6 7/8") and very colorful cards. This set, a football counterpart to Topps' Superstar Photo Baseball set of the same year, is numbered and is printed on white stock. The cards in this set, sold over the counter without gum at retail establishments, could be individually chosen by the buyer.

COMPLETE SET (30) 7.50 15.00
1 Franco Harris .75 2.00
2 Bob Griese .75 2.00
3 Archie Manning .20 .50
4 Harold Carmichael .20 .50
5 Wesley Walker .20 .50
6 Richard Todd .15 .40
7 Dan Fouts .60 1.50
8 Ken Stabler 1.25 3.00
9 Jack Youngblood .20 .50
10 Jim Zorn .20 .50
11 Tony Dorsett 1.25 3.00
12 Lee Roy Selmon .30 .75
13 Russ Francis .15 .40
14 John Stallworth .30 .75
15 Terry Bradshaw 1.50 4.00
16 Joe Theismann .50 1.25
17 Ottis Anderson .30 .75
18 John Jefferson .30 .75
19 Jack Ham .30 .75
20 Joe Greene .40 1.00
21 Chuck Muncie .15 .40
22 Ron Jaworski .20 .50
23 John Hannah .20 .50
24 Randy Gradishar .15 .40
25 Jack Lambert .40 1.00
26 Ricky Bell .15 .40
27 Drew Pearson .30 .75
28 Rick Upchurch .15 .40
29 Brad Van Pelt .15 .40
30 Walter Payton 2.50 6.00

1980 Topps Team Checklists

These cards are essentially a parallel to the base 1980 Topps team checklist subset cards. The set was only available directly from Topps as a send-off offer in uncut sheet form. The prices below apply equally to uncut sheets as they are frequently found in their original uncut condition. As for individual cards, thin white card (almost paper-thin) stock makes it a challenge to find singles in top grades. We've cataloged the cards below for convenience in alphabetical order by team name.

COMPLETE SET (28) 50.00 100.00
19 Redskins TL 2.50 6.00
John Riggins
39 Chiefs TL 1.25 3.00
J.T.Smith
57 Seahawks TL 2.50 6.00
Steve Largent
76 Dolphins TL 2.50 6.00
Larry Csonka
94 New York Giants TL 1.25 3.00
113 Cowboys TL 3.00 8.00
Tony Dorsett
132 Philadelphia Eagles TL 1.50 4.00
151 Denver Broncos TL 1.50 4.00
169 San Diego Chargers TL 1.50 4.00
188 New England Patriots TL 1.25 3.00
197 Saints TL 1.25 3.00
Wes Chandler
207 Vikings TL 1.50 4.00
Ahmad Rashad
226 Bears TL 4.00 10.00
Walter Payton
244 Baltimore Colts TL 1.25 3.00
264 Buffalo Bills TL 1.25 3.00
282 Tampa Bay Bucs TL 1.50 4.00

303 Packers TL	1.50	4.00
James Lofton		
319 Steelers TL	2.50	6.00
Harris		
Lambrt		
338 Cincinnati Bengals TL	2.50	6.00
Jauron		
359 Cardinals TL	2.50	6.00
O.Anderson		
376 Cleveland Browns TL	1.25	3.00
394 Los Angeles Rams TL	1.50	4.00
411 Atlanta Falcons TL	1.50	4.00
432 Houston Oilers TL	1.50	4.00
468 Oakland Raiders TL	1.50	4.00
488 Detroit Lions TL	1.25	3.00
507 New York Jets TL	1.25	3.00
526 San Francisco 49ers TL	1.50	4.00

1956 Topps Hocus Focus

The 1956 Topps Hocus Focus set is very similar in size and design to the 1948 Topps Magic Photos set. It contains at least 96 small (approximately 7/8" by 1 5/8") individual cards featuring a variety of sports and non-sport subjects. They were printed with both a series card number (by subject matter) on the back as well as a card number reflecting the entire set. The fronts were developed, much like a photograph, from a blank appearance by using moisture and sunlight. Due to varying degrees of photographic sensitivity, the clarity of these cards ranges from fully developed to poorly developed. A premium album holding 126-cards was also issued leading to the theory that there are actually 126 different cards. A few High Series (#97-126) cards have been discovered and cataloged below although a full 126-card checklist is yet unknown. The cards do reference the set name "Hocus Focus" on the backs unlike the 1948 Magic Photos. Finally, a slightly smaller version (roughly 7/8" by 1 7/16") of some of the cards has also been found, but a full checklist is not known.

10 Southern Cal Football	12.50	25.00

1948 Topps Magic Photos

The 1948 Topps Magic Photos set contains 252 small (approximately 7/8" by 1 7/16") individual cards featuring sport and non-sport subjects. They were issued in 19 lettered series with cards numbered within each series. The fronts were developed, much like a photograph, from a "blank" appearance by using moisture and sunlight. Due to varying degrees of photographic sensitivity, the clarity of these cards ranges from fully developed to poorly developed. This set contains Topps' first baseball cards. A premium album holding 126-cards was also issued. The set is sometimes confused with Topps' 1956 Hocus-Focus set, although the cards in this set are slightly smaller than those in the Hocus-Focus set. The checklist below is presented by series. Poorly developed cards are considered in lesser condition and hence have lesser value. The catalog designation for this set is R714-27. Each type of card subject has a letter prefix as follows: Boxing Champions (A), All-American Basketball (B), All-American Football (C), Wrestling Champions (D), Track and Field Champions (E), Stars of Stage and Screen (F), American Dogs (G), General Sports (H), Movie Stars (J), Baseball Hall of Fame (K), Aviation Pioneers (L), Famous Landmarks (M), American Inventors (N), American Military Leaders (O), American Explorers (P), Basketball Thrills (Q), Football Thrills (R), Figures of the Wild West (S), and General Sports (T).

COMPLETE SET (252)	3,000.00	5,000.00
C1 Barney Poole	12.50	25.00
C2 Pete Elliott	7.50	15.00
C3 Doak Walker	25.00	50.00
C4 Bill Swiacki	10.00	20.00
C5 Bill Fischer	7.50	15.00
C6 Johnny Lujack	25.00	50.00
C7 Chuck Bednarik	25.00	50.00
C8 Joe Steffy	7.50	15.00
C9 George Connor	15.00	30.00
C10 Steve Suhey	10.00	20.00
C11 Bob Chappuis	10.00	20.00
C12 Bill Swiacki	7.50	15.00
Columbia 23		
Navy 14		
C13 Army-Notre Dame	12.50	25.00
R1 Wally Triplett	5.00	10.00
R2 Gil Stevenson	5.00	10.00
R3 Northwestern	5.00	10.00
R4 Yale vs. Columbia	5.00	10.00
R5 Cornell	5.00	10.00
NNO Sid Luckman Ad Poster	175.00	300.00

1977 Touchdown Club

This 50-card set was initially targeted toward football autograph collectors as the set featured only living (at the time) ex-football players many of whom were or are now in the Pro Football Hall of Fame in Canton, Ohio. The set was originally sold for $5.95 along with a printed address list for the players in the set. The cards are black and white (typically showing the player in his prime) and are numbered on the back. The cards measure approximately 2 1/4" by 3 1/4". Card backs list career honors the player received.

COMPLETE SET (50)	60.00	120.00
1 Red Grange	4.00	8.00
2 George Halas	4.00	8.00
3 Benny Friedman UER	1.00	2.50
4 Cliff Battles	1.25	3.00
5 Mike Michalske	1.25	3.00
6 George McAfee	1.50	3.00
7 Beattie Feathers	1.25	3.00
8 Ernie Caddel	1.00	2.50
9 George Musso	1.25	3.00
10 Sid Luckman	2.50	5.00
11 Cecil Isbell	1.25	3.00
12 Bronko Nagurski	4.00	8.00
13 Hunk Anderson	1.00	2.50
14 Dick Farman	1.00	2.50
15 Aldo Forte	1.00	2.50
16 Ki Aldrich	1.00	2.50
17 Jim Lee Howell	1.00	2.50
18 Ray Flaherty	1.25	3.00
19 Hampton Pool	1.00	2.50
20 Alex Wojciechowicz	1.25	3.00
21 Bill Osmanski	1.00	2.50
22 Hank Soar	1.00	2.50
23 Dutch Clark	1.50	3.00
24 Joe Muha	1.00	2.50
25 Don Hutson	2.00	4.00
26 Jim Poole	1.00	2.50
27 Charley Malone	1.00	2.50
28 Charley Trippi	1.50	3.00
29 Andy Farkas	1.00	2.50
30 Clarke Hinkle	1.25	3.00
31 Gary Famiglietti	1.00	2.50
32 Bulldog Turner	1.50	3.00
33 Sammy Baugh	4.00	8.00
34 Pat Harder	1.00	2.50
35 Tuffy Leemans	1.00	2.50
36 Ken Strong	1.50	3.00
37 Barney Poole	1.00	2.50
38 Frank(Bruiser) Kinard	1.25	3.00
39 Buford Ray	1.00	2.50
40 Clarence(Ace) Parker	1.25	3.00
41 Buddy Parker	1.00	2.50
42 Mel Hein	1.25	3.00
43 Ed Danowski	1.00	2.50
44 Bill Dudley	1.50	3.00
45 Paul Stenn	1.00	2.50
46 George Connor	1.25	3.00
47 George Sauer Sr.	1.00	2.50
48 Armand Niccolai	1.00	2.50
49 Tony Canadeo	1.25	3.00
50 Bill Willis	1.50	4.00

1957-59 Union Oil Booklets

These booklets were distributed by Union Oil. The front cover of each booklet features a drawing of the subject player. The booklets are numbered and were issued over several years beginning in 1957. These are 12-page pamphlets and are approximately 4" by 5 1/2". The set is subtitled "Family Sports Fun." This was apparently primarily a Southern California promotion.

COMPLETE SET (44)	200.00	400.00
1 Elroy Hirsch FB 57	10.00	20.00
2 Les Richter FB 57	2.00	4.00
3 Frankie Albert FB 57	7.50	15.00
4 Y.A. Tittle FB 57	10.00	20.00
27 Bob Waterfield FB 58	10.00	20.00
28 Pete Elliott FB 58	5.00	10.00
29 Elroy Hirsch FB 58	7.50	15.00
30 Frank Gifford FB 58	10.00	20.00

1966 Van Heusen Photos

1 Len Dawson	20.00	40.00

1961 Vikings Team Issue

These large photos measure approximately 5" by 7" and feature black-and-white player photos. The set was issued in "Picture Pak" form in its own envelope by the team. Each has a large white border below the player photo with his position (initials), name, and team (Minnesota) printed in the border. The player photos carry a brief bio on the backs with stats when applicable; the coaches photos are blankbacked. The cards are unnumbered and checklisted below in alphabetical order.

COMPLETE SET (48)	300.00	500.00
1 Grady Alderman	6.00	12.00
2 Bill Bishop	6.00	12.00
3 Darrel Brewster CO	6.00	12.00
4 Jamie Caleb	6.00	12.00
5 Ed Culpepper	6.00	12.00
6 Bob Denton	6.00	12.00
7 Paul Dickson	6.00	12.00
8 Billy Gault	6.00	12.00
9 Harry Gilmer CO	7.50	15.00
10 Dick Grecni	6.00	12.00
11 Dick Haley	6.00	12.00
12 Rip Hawkins	6.00	12.00
13 Raymond Hayes	6.00	12.00
14 Gerry Huth	6.00	12.00
15 Gene Johnson	6.00	12.00
16 Don Joyce	6.00	12.00
17 Bill Lapham	6.00	12.00
18 Jim Leo	6.00	12.00
19 Jim Marshall	10.00	20.00
20 Tommy Mason	7.50	15.00
21 Doug Mayberry	6.00	12.00
22 Hugh McElhenny	10.00	20.00
23 Mike Mercer	6.00	12.00
24 Dave Middleton	6.00	12.00
25 Jack Morris	6.00	12.00
26 Rich Mostardo	6.00	12.00
27 Fred Murphy	6.00	12.00
28 Clancy Osborne	6.00	12.00
29 Dick Pesonen	6.00	12.00
30 Ken Petersen	6.00	12.00
31 Jim Prestel	6.00	12.00
32 Mike Rabold	6.00	12.00
33 Jerry Reichow	6.00	12.00
34 Karl Rubke	6.00	12.00
35 Bob Schnelker	6.00	12.00
36 Ed Sharockman	6.00	12.00
37 George Shaw	7.50	15.00
38 Willard Sherman	6.00	12.00
39 Lebron Shields	6.00	12.00
40 Gordon Smith	6.00	12.00
41 Charlie Sumner	6.00	12.00
42 Fran Tarkenton	20.00	40.00
43 Mel Triplett	6.00	12.00
44 Norm Van Brocklin CO	7.50	15.00
45 Stan West CO	6.00	12.00
46 A.D. Wiliams	6.00	12.00
47 Frank Youso	6.00	12.00
48 Walt Yowarsky CO	6.00	12.00

1963-64 Vikings Team Issue

This 20-card set of the Minnesota Vikings measures approximately 5" by 7" and features black-and-white borderless player portraits with the players position, name and team in a bar at the card bottom. The photos were likely issued over a number of years. Either a Vikings or Minnesota name can be found on the cardfronts.The backs are blank. The cards are unnumbered and checklisted below in alphabetical order.

COMPLETE SET (20)	100.00	200.00
1 Jim Battle	6.00	12.00
2 Larry Bowie	6.00	12.00
3 Bill Butler	6.00	12.00
4 Lee Calland	6.00	12.00
5 John Campbell	6.00	12.00
6 Leon Clarke	6.00	12.00
7 Paul Dickson	6.00	12.00
8 Terry Dillon	6.00	12.00
9 Paul Flatley	6.00	12.00
10 Tom Franckhauser	6.00	12.00
11 Rip Hawkins	6.00	12.00
12 Don Hultz	6.00	12.00
13 Errol Linden	6.00	12.00
14 Mike Mercer	6.00	12.00
15 Ray Poage	6.00	12.00
16 Jim Prestel	6.00	12.00
17 Jerry Reichow	6.00	12.00
18 Ed Sharockman	6.00	12.00
19 Gordon Smith	6.00	12.00
20 Tom Wilson	6.00	12.00

1965 Vikings Team Issue

This set of photos from the Minnesota Vikings measures approximately 4 1/4" by 5 1/2" and features black-and-white player portraits with the players position (appreviated), name and team "Vikings" in a bar at the card bottom. Most of the players in the set are shown wearing their white jersey and most include a facsimile autograph. Some photos were issued with variations on the placement of the facsimilie signature on the front. The photos were likely issued over a number of years and vary slightly in text style and size. The cardbacks are blank; each is unnumbered and checklisted below in alphabetical order.

COMPLETE SET (27)	150.00	300.00
1 Larry Bowie	6.00	12.00
2 Bill Brown	7.50	15.00
3 Fred Cox	10.00	20.00
(with Fran Tarkenton holding)		
4 Doug Davis	6.00	12.00
(facsimile sig in upper right)		
5 Paul Dickson	6.00	12.00
(facsimile sig in upper right)		
6 Carl Eller	7.50	15.00
8 Dale Hackbart	6.00	12.00
8 Paul Flatley	6.00	12.00
(facsimile sig in upper right)		
9 Rip Hawkins	6.00	12.00
10 Jeff Jordan	6.00	12.00
(facsimile sig in upper left)		
11 Karl Kassulke	6.00	12.00
(no facsimilie sig)		
12 Phil King	6.00	12.00
(facsimile sig in upper left)		
13 John Kirby	6.00	12.00
(facsimile sig in upper right)		
14 Gary Larsen	6.00	12.00
(facsimile sig in upper left)		
15 Jim Lindsey	6.00	12.00
(facsimile sig in upper right)		
16 Jim Marshall	7.50	15.00
(facsimile sig in upper right)		
17 Tommy Mason	6.00	12.00
18A Jim Phillips	6.00	12.00
(facsimile sig in upper right)		
18B Jim Phillips	6.00	12.00
(facsimile sig in upper left)		
19 Ed Sharockman	6.00	12.00
20 Milt Sunde	6.00	12.00
(facsimile sig in upper right)		
21 Fran Tarkenton	12.50	25.00
22 Mick Tingelhoff	7.50	15.00
no facsimile, small type size)		
23 Norm Van Brocklin CO	7.50	15.00
24 Ron Vanderkelen	6.00	12.00
25 Bobby Walden	6.00	12.00
(facsimile sig in upper left)		
26 Lonnie Warwick	6.00	12.00
27 Roy Winston	6.00	12.00

1966 Vikings Team Issue

These large photo cards are approximately 8" by 10" and feature black-and-white player photos. Each has a white border and was printed on thick glossy stock. The cards are unnumbered and checklisted below in alphabetical order. They are very similar to the 1967 and 1968 issues, but can be differentiated by the player's position, name, and then team name spread out across the border below the photo. Any additions to the checklist below are appreciated.

COMPLETE SET (3)	15.00	30.00
1 Larry Bowie	6.00	12.00
2 Dave Tobey	6.00	12.00
3 Ron Vanderkelen	6.00	12.00

1967 Vikings Team Issue

These large photo cards are approximately 8" by 10" and feature black-and-white player photos. Each has a white border and was printed on thick glossy stock. The cards are unnumbered and checklisted below in alphabetical order. They are very similar to the 1966 and 1968 issues, but can be differentiated by the player's name, postion, and team name tightly arranged in the border below the photo.

COMPLETE SET (23)	100.00	200.00
1 Grady Alderman	7.50	15.00
2 John Beasley	6.00	12.00
3 Bob Berry	6.00	12.00
4 Doug Davis	6.00	12.00
5 Paul Dickson	6.00	12.00
6 Paul Flatley	6.00	12.00
7 Bob Grim	6.00	12.00
8 Dale Hackbart	6.00	12.00
9 Don Hansen	6.00	12.00
10 Jim Hargrove	6.00	12.00
11 Clint Jones	6.00	12.00
12 Jeff Jordan	6.00	12.00
13 Joe Kapp	7.50	15.00
14 John Kirby	6.00	12.00
15 Gary Larsen	6.00	12.00
16 Earsell Mackbee	6.00	12.00
17 Marlin McKeever	6.00	12.00
18 Milt Sunde	6.00	12.00
19 Jim Vellone	6.00	12.00
20 Bobby Walden	6.00	12.00
21 Lonnie Warwick	6.00	12.00
22 Gene Washington	6.00	12.00
23 Roy Winston	6.00	12.00

1968 Vikings Team Issue

These large photo cards are approximately 8" by 10" and feature black-and-white player photos. Each has a white border and was printed on thick glossy stock. The cards are unnumbered and checklisted below in alphabetical order. They are very similar to the 1966 and 1967 issues, but can be differentiated by the player's name, postion (initial), and team name loosely arranged in the border below the photo.

COMPLETE SET (3)	15.00	30.00
1 Grady Alderman	6.00	12.00
2 Gary Cuozzo	6.00	12.00
3 Gene Washington	6.00	12.00

1969 Vikings Team Issue

This 27-card set of the Minnesota Vikings measures approximately 5" by 6 7/8" and features black-and-white borderless player portraits with the players name, position and team in a wide bar at the bottom. The backs are blank. Although similar to earlier Vikings' team issues, these photos can be differentiated by the order in which the player details are listed at the bottom of the card. The cards are unnumbered and checklisted below in alphabetical order.

COMPLETE SET (27)	100.00	200.00

1 Bookie Bolin	5.00	10.00
2 Bobby Bryant	5.00	10.00
3 John Beasley	5.00	10.00
4 Gary Cuozzo	6.00	12.00
5 Doug Davis	5.00	10.00
6 Paul Dickson	5.00	10.00
7 Bob Grim	5.00	10.00
8 Dale Hackbart	5.00	10.00
9 Jim Hargrove	5.00	10.00
10 John Henderson	5.00	10.00
11 Wally Hilgenberg	5.00	10.00
12 Clinton Jones	5.00	10.00
13 Karl Kassulke	5.00	10.00
14 Kent Kramer	5.00	10.00
15 Gary Larsen	5.00	10.00
16 Bob Lee	5.00	10.00
17 Jim Lindsey	5.00	10.00
18 Earsell Mackbee	5.00	10.00
19 Mike McGill	5.00	10.00
20 Oscar Reed	5.00	10.00
21 Ed Sharockman	5.00	10.00
22 Steve Smith	5.00	10.00
23 Milt Sunde	5.00	10.00
24 Jim Vellone	5.00	10.00
25 Lonnie Warwick	5.00	10.00
26 Gene Washington	5.00	10.00
27 Charlie West	5.00	10.00

1970-71 Vikings Team Issue

This 17-card set of the Minnesota Vikings measures approximately 5" by 7" and features black-and-white borderless player portraits with the players name and team name only in a wide bar at the bottom. The backs are blank. The photos were likely issued over a number of years due to the different type styles used on the photo's text. The cards are unnumbered and checklisted below in alphabetical order. Any additions to this checklist would be greatly appreciated.

COMPLETE SET (17)	60.00	120.00
1 John Beasley	5.00	10.00
2 Doug Davis	5.00	10.00
3 Paul Dickson	5.00	10.00
4 Bob Grim	5.00	10.00
5 Jim Hargrove	5.00	10.00
6 John Henderson	5.00	10.00
7 Clint Jones	5.00	10.00
8 Bob Lee	5.00	10.00
9 Jim Lindsey	5.00	10.00
10 Oscar Reed	5.00	10.00
11 Ed Sharockman	5.00	10.00
12 Steve Smith	5.00	10.00
13 Milt Sunde	5.00	10.00
14 Dave Tobey	5.00	10.00
15 Jim Vellone	5.00	10.00
16 John Ward	5.00	10.00
17 Charlie West	5.00	10.00

1971 Vikings Color Photos

Issued in the late summer of 1971 (preseason), this team-issued set consists of 49 four-color close-up photos printed on thin paper stock. Each photo measures approximately 5" by 7 7/16". The player's name, position, and team name appear in a white bottom border. The backs are blank. The cards are unnumbered and checklisted below in alphabetical order.

COMPLETE SET (52)	175.00	300.00
1 Grady Alderman	4.00	8.00
2 Neill Armstrong CO	3.00	6.00
3 John Beasley	3.00	6.00
4 Bill Brown	4.00	8.00
5 Bob Brown	3.00	6.00
6 Bobby Bryant	4.00	8.00
7 Jerry Burns CO	3.00	6.00
8 Fred Cox	4.00	8.00
9 Gary Cuozzo	4.00	8.00
10 Doug Davis	3.00	6.00
11 Al Denson	3.00	6.00
12 Paul Dickson	3.00	6.00
13 Carl Eller	5.00	10.00
14 Bud Grant CO	7.50	15.00
15 Bob Grim	3.00	6.00
16 Leo Hayden	3.00	6.00
17 John Henderson	3.00	6.00
18 Wally Hilgenberg	4.00	8.00
19 Noel Jenke	3.00	6.00
20 Clint Jones	3.00	6.00
21 Karl Kassulke	3.00	6.00
22 Paul Krause	5.00	10.00
23 Gary Larsen	4.00	8.00
24 Bob Lee	3.00	6.00
25 Jim Lindsey	3.00	6.00
26 Jim Marshall	5.00	10.00
27 Bus Mertes CO	3.00	6.00
28 John Michels CO	3.00	6.00
29 Jocko Nelson CO	3.00	6.00
30 Dave Osborn	4.00	8.00
31 Alan Page	7.50	15.00
32 Jack Patera CO	3.00	6.00
33 Jerry Patton	3.00	6.00
34 Pete Perreault	3.00	6.00
35 Oscar Reed	3.00	6.00
36 Ed Sharockman	3.00	6.00
37 Norm Snead	4.00	8.00
38 Milt Sunde	3.00	6.00
39 Doug Sutherland	3.00	6.00
40 Mick Tingelhoff	4.00	8.00
41 Stu Voigt	3.00	6.00
42 John Ward	3.00	6.00
43 Lonnie Warwick	3.00	6.00
44 Gene Washington	4.00	8.00
45 Charlie West	3.00	6.00
46 Ed White	4.00	8.00
47 Carl Winfrey	3.00	6.00
48 Roy Winston	4.00	8.00
49 Jeff Wright S	3.00	6.00
50 Nate Wright	4.00	8.00
51 Ron Yary	4.00	8.00
52 Godfrey Zaunbrecher	3.00	6.00

1971 Vikings Color Postcards

This 19-card set measures roughly 5" by 7 1/2" and features posed color close-up photos on the fronts. These cards were issued after the season had begun and may have been sold at the stadium. The player's name, position, and team name appear in a white bottom border. As with a postcard, the horizontal backs are divided into two sections by a thin black stripe. Brief biographical information is given at the upper left corner, while a box for the stamp is printed at the upper right corner. The cards are unnumbered and checklisted below in alphabetical order.

COMPLETE SET (19)	75.00	125.00
1 Grady Alderman	4.00	8.00
2 Neill Armstrong CO	3.00	6.00
3 John Beasley	3.00	6.00
4 Paul Dickson	3.00	6.00
5 Bud Grant CO	7.50	15.00
6 Wally Hilgenberg	4.00	8.00
7 Noel Jenke	3.00	6.00
8 Paul Krause	5.00	10.00
9 Gary Larsen	4.00	8.00
10 Dave Osborn	4.00	8.00
11 Alan Page	7.50	15.00
12 Jerry Patton	3.00	6.00
13 Doug Sutherland	4.00	8.00
14 Mick Tingelhoff	5.00	10.00
15 Lonnie Warwick	3.00	6.00
16 Charlie West	3.00	6.00
17 Jeff Wright S	3.00	6.00
18 Nate Wright	4.00	8.00
19 Godfrey Zaunbrecher	3.00	6.00

1972 Vikings Color Postcards

Cards in this set measure roughly 4" by 5 7/8" and feature color close-up player photos. These cards were issued after the season had begun and likely were sold at the stadium. The player's name, position, and team name appear in a white bottom border. The backs included a typical postcard format although some have been found without the postcard format. The cards are unnumbered and checklisted below in alphabetical order.

COMPLETE SET ()		
1 John Beasley	3.00	6.00
2 Fran Tarkenton	7.50	15.00
3 Godfrey Zaunbrecher (blank backed)	3.00	6.00

1973 Vikings Team Issue

This 17-card set of the Minnesota Vikings measures roughly 5" by 7". The fronts feature white bordered black-and-white player portraits with the player's name and team in the bottom wide margin. The backs are blank. The photos can be differentiated from previous Vikings Team Issues by the distinctive white borders and scripted team name on the card fronts. The cards are unnumbered and checklisted below in alphabetical order.

COMPLETE SET (17)	50.00	100.00
1 John Beasley	4.00	8.00
2 Bob Berry	4.00	8.00
3 Terry Brown	4.00	8.00
4 Bobby Bryant	4.00	8.00
5 Larry Dibbles	4.00	8.00
6 Mike Eischeid	4.00	8.00
7 Charles Goodrum	4.00	8.00
8 Neil Graff	4.00	8.00
9 Wally Hilgenberg	4.00	8.00
10 Amos Martin	4.00	8.00
11 Brent McClanahan	4.00	8.00
12 John Michels	4.00	8.00
13 Oscar Reed	4.00	8.00
14 John Ward	4.00	8.00
15 Charlie West	4.00	8.00
16 Jeff Wright	4.00	8.00
17 Nate Wright	4.00	8.00

1974 Vikings Team Issue

These all-color blankbacked photos were released by the Vikings around 1974 presumably to fans via mail. Each includes the player's name and team name below the photo.

COMPLETE SET (11)	50.00	100.00
1 Bobby Bryant	4.00	8.00
2 Carl Eller	5.00	10.00
3 Chuck Foreman	5.00	10.00
4 John Gilliam	4.00	8.00
5 Paul Krause	5.00	10.00
6 Jim Marshall	5.00	10.00
7 Alan Page	6.00	12.00
8 Fran Tarkenton	7.50	15.00
9 Mick Tingelhoff	4.00	8.00
10 Ed White	4.00	8.00
11 Ron Yary	5.00	10.00

1975 Vikings Team Sheets

The Vikings issued these black and white player photo sheets for use in publicity opportunities. Each sheet features a number of small player images along with vital information about the player. Each sheet measures roughly 8" by 10" and is blankbacked.

COMPLETE SET (4)	20.00	40.00
1 Players A-H	5.00	10.00
2 Players H-R	5.00	10.00
3 Players K-M	5.00	10.00
4 Players O-Y	7.50	15.00

1976 Vikings Team Sheets

The Vikings issued these black and white player photo sheets for use in publicity opportunities and to fill media requests. Each sheet features a group of small player/coach images along with vital information about the player below the image. Each sheet measures roughly 8" by 10" and is blankbacked.

COMPLETE SET (3)	20.00	35.00
1 Sheet 1	5.00	10.00
2 Sheet 2	5.00	10.00
3 Sheet 3	7.50	15.00

1978 Vikings Country Kitchen

This seven-card set was sponsored by Country Kitchen Restaurants and measures approximately 5" by 7". The front features a black and white head shot of the player. The card backs have biographical and statistical information. The cards are unnumbered and hence are listed alphabetically below.

COMPLETE SET (7)	25.00	50.00
1 Bobby Bryant	3.00	6.00
2 Tommy Kramer	5.00	10.00
3 Paul Krause	5.00	10.00
4 Ahmad Rashad	7.50	15.00
5 Jeff Siemon	3.00	6.00
6 Mick Tingelhoff	4.00	8.00
7 Sammie White	4.00	8.00

1979 Vikings SuperAmerica

The 1979 SuperAmerica Vikings set was distributed through the SuperAmerica convenience stores with a fill-up of gasoline. These 10" by 12" unnumbered sepia posters display watercolor art of the player in action, with a write-up about his career in the top third of the poster. The bottom third of the poster shows a watercolor close-up of the particular player along with a descriptive cutline for the poster. The posters are cataloged in alphabetical order below. There are seven known posters.

COMPLETE SET (7)	40.00	80.00
1 Bill Brown	5.00	10.00
2 Karl Kassulke	4.00	8.00
3 Jim Marshall	7.50	15.00
4 Hugh McElhenny	10.00	20.00
5 Dave Osborn	4.00	8.00
6 Fran Tarkenton	15.00	30.00
7 Gene Washington	5.00	10.00

1925-31 W590 Athletes

Issued over a period of years, this set (which measure approximately 1 3/8" by 2 1/2") features some of the leading athletes from the 1920's. The fronts have a B&W photo with the players name, position and team on the bottom for the baseball players and sport and additional short bio info on the other athletes. The backs are blank and as these cards are unnumbered we have sequenced them in alphabetical order within sport. They were initally issued in strips and panels and can often be found intact. A number of the baseball players were re-issued from year-to-year with updated team information.

60 Red Grange FB	350.00	600.00
61 Walter Koppisch FB	60.00	100.00

1935 Wheaties All-Americans of 1934

This set of cards is very similar to the 1934 Fancy Frames issue and is often referred to as "Wheaties FB2." They are differentiated by the printed "All American...1934" title line. Each features a blue and white photo of the player surrounded by a blue frame border design which is often referred to as "fancy frames." The cardbacks are blank and each measures roughly 6" by 6 1/4" when cut around the frame border. The George Barclay and William Shepherd cards are thought to be the toughest to find.

COMPLETE SET (12)	1,500.00	2,500.00
1 George Barclay	100.00	175.00
2 Charles Hartwig	100.00	175.00
3 Dixie Howell	175.00	300.00
4 Don Hutson	350.00	600.00
5 Stan Kostka	100.00	175.00
6 Frank Larson	100.00	175.00
7 Bill Lee	100.00	175.00
8 George Maddox	100.00	175.00
9 Regis Monahan	100.00	175.00
10 John J. Robinson	100.00	175.00
11 William Shepherd	100.00	175.00
12 Cotton Warburton	100.00	175.00

1935 Wheaties Fancy Frames

Cards from this set could be cut from boxes of Wheaties cereals in the 1930s and are commonly found mis-cut. Each features a blue and white photo of a famous player or coach surrounded by a blue frame border design. The cards are often called "Wheaties FB1" as well as "Fancy Frames." In appearance they are very similar to the 1935 All-Americans issue, except for the player's name written in script on the cardfront. The cardbacks are blank and each measures roughly 6" by 6 1/4" when cut around the frame border. The Benny Friedman and Pop Warner cards are thought to be slightly tougher to find.

COMPLETE SET (8)	1,500.00	2,200.00
1 Jack Armstrong	75.00	150.00
2 Chris Cagle	100.00	175.00
3 Benny Friedman	175.00	300.00
4 Red Grange	500.00	800.00
5 Howard Jones CO	100.00	175.00
6 Harry Kipke	100.00	175.00
7 Ernie Nevers	250.00	400.00
8 Pop Warner CO	175.00	300.00

1936 Wheaties All-Americans of 1935

This set is often referred to as "Wheaties FB3" or the "All American of 1935" set due to that title line appearing on the cardfronts. As was the case with most Wheaties cards, the fronts were printed in blue and white on an orange background. Bernie Bierman is thought to be tougher to find than the rest.

COMPLETE SET (12)	1,800.00	2,800.00
1 Sheldon Beise	150.00	250.00
2 Bernie Bierman SP	175.00	300.00
3 Darrell Lester TX	150.00	250.00
4 Eddie Michaels	150.00	250.00
5 Wayne Millner	250.00	400.00
6 Monk Moscrip	150.00	250.00
7 Andy Pilney	150.00	250.00
8 Dick Smith	150.00	250.00
9 Riley Smith	150.00	250.00
10 Truman Spain	150.00	250.00
11 Charles Wasicek	150.00	250.00
12 Bobby Wilson	150.00	250.00

1936 Wheaties Coaches

These cards are actually advertising panels cut from the backs of Wheaties cereal boxes. Unlike many of the other Wheaties cards from the era, they do not offer instructions on how or where to cut the cards from the boxes. Each includes a famous coach's picture along with a short quote and measures roughly 6" by 8 1/4" when cut cleanly. The Harry Stuhldreher is thought to be the toughest panel to find.

COMPLETE SET (7)	600.00	1,200.00
1 Bernie Bierman	100.00	175.00
2 Jim Crowley	125.00	200.00
3 Red Dawson	100.00	175.00
4 Andy Kerr	100.00	175.00
5 Bo McMillin	100.00	175.00

6 Harry Stuhldreher	150.00	250.00
7 Lynn Waldorf	100.00	175.00

1936 Wheaties Six-Man

Famous coaches are featured on this set of Wheaties box panels discussing the unique rules and strategy involved with 6-man football. Each measures roughly 6" by 8 1/4" when cut from the box and was printed with the familiar blue and orange color scheme. The Red Dawson and Ossie Solem cards are thought to be the toughest to find.

COMPLETE SET (6)	800.00	1,200.00
1 Bernie Bierman	150.00	250.00
2 Red Dawson	125.00	200.00
3 Tiny Hollingsberry	125.00	200.00
4 Andy Kerr	125.00	200.00
5 Ossie Solem	125.00	200.00
6 Tiny Thornhill	150.00	250.00

1937 Wheaties Big Ten Football

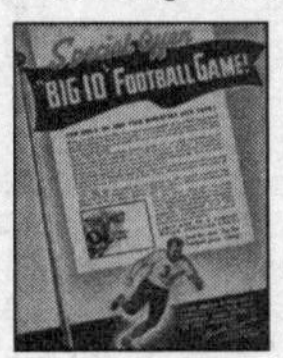

These Wheaties cards are actually advertisements cut from the backs of Wheaties cereal boxes. Each features a popular pro football player touting the "Big Ten Football Game" offered for sale on the box back. There was also a football field game board as part of the set that could be used to play a form of game with a football radio broadcast. The cards were printed in blue, white, and orange and each measures roughly 6" by 8 1/4" when cut cleanly from the box.

COMPLETE SET (5)	1,200.00	1,800.00
1 Ed Danowski	125.00	200.00
2 Arnie Herber	175.00	300.00
3 Ralph Kercheval	125.00	200.00
4 Ed Manske	125.00	200.00
5 Bronko Nagurski	600.00	1,000.00
6 Football Game Board	175.00	300.00

1940 Wheaties M4

This set is referred to as the "Champs in the USA" The cards measure about 6" 8 1'4" and are numbered. The drawing portion (inside the dotted lines) measures approximately 6" X 6". There is a Baseball player on each card and they are joined by football players, football coaches, race car drivers, airline pilots, a circus clown, ice skater, hockey star and golfers. Each athlete appears in what looks like a stamp with a serrated edge. The stamps appear one above the other with a brief block of copy describing his or her achievements. There appears to have been three printings, resulting in some variation panels. The full panels tell the cereal buyer to look for either 27, 39, or 63 champ stamps. The first nine panels apparently were printed more than once, since all the unknown variations occur with those numbers.

COMPLETE SET (20)	400.00	800.00
3 J. Foxx/B. Dickey	35.00	60.00
4 M. Arnovich/D. Clark	15.00	25.00
5 Joe Medwick Matty Bell Ab Jenkins	15.00	25.00
6A J. Mize/D. O'Brien Ralph Guldahl/(27 stamp	15.00	25.00
6C G. Hartnett/D. O'Brien Ralph Guldahl/(unk	15.00	25.00
7A J. Cronin/Byron Nelson/(27 stamp	15.00	25.00
7C P. Derringer/Byron Nelson/(unkno	15.00	25.00
8A J. Manders/E. Lombardi George I. Myers/(27	15.00	25.00
10 A. Inge/B. Herman	15.00	25.00
11 Dolph Camilli Antoinette Concello Wallace Wade	15.00	25.00

1941 Wheaties M5

This set is also referred to as "Champs of the U.S.A." These numbered cards made up the back of the Wheaties box; the whole panel measures 6" X 8 1/4" but the drawing portion (inside the dotted lines) is apparently 6" X 6". Each athlete appears in what looks like a stamp with a serrated edge. The stamps appear one above the other with a brief block of copy describing his or her achievements. The format is the same as the previous M4 set -- even the numbering system continues where the M4 set stops.

COMPLETE SET (8)	175.00	350.00
15 B. Bierman/B. Feller/Jessie McLeod	20.00	40.00
16 Hank Greenberg Lowell Red Dawson J.W. Stoker	20.00	40.00

1951 Wheaties

The cards in this six-card set measure approximately 2 1/2" by 3 1/4". Cards of the 1951 Wheaties set are actually the backs of small individual boxes of Wheaties. The cards are waxed and depict three baseball players, one football player, one basketball player, and one golfer. They are occasionally found as complete boxes, which are worth 50 percent more than the prices listed below. The catalog designation for this set is F272-3. The cards are blank-backed and unnumbered; they are numbered below in alphabetical order for convenience.

COMPLETE SET (6)	300.00	600.00
2 Johnny Lujack	40.00	80.00

1952 Wheaties

The cards in this 60-card set measure 2" by 2 3/4". The 1952 Wheaties set of orange, blue and white, unnumbered cards was issued in panels of eight or ten cards on the backs of Wheaties cereal boxes. Each player appears in an action pose, designated in the checklist with an "A", and as a portrait, listed in the checklist with a "B". The catalog designation is F272-4. The cards are blank-backed and unnumbered, but have been assigned numbers below using a sport prefix (BB- baseball, BK- basketball, FB- football, G- Golf, OT- other).

COMPLETE SET (60)	600.00	1,000.00
FB1A Glenn Davis Action	4.00	8.00
FB1B Glenn Davis Portrait	4.00	8.00
FB2A Tom Fears Action	4.00	8.00
FB2B Tom Fears Portrait	4.00	8.00
FB3A Otto Graham Action	10.00	20.00
FB3B Otto Graham Portrait	10.00	20.00
FB4A Johnny Lujack Action	4.00	8.00
FB4B Johnny Lujack Portrait	4.00	8.00
FB5A Doak Walker Action	7.50	15.00
FB5B Doak Walker Portrait	7.50	15.00
FB6A Bob Waterfield Action	12.50	25.00
FB6B Bob Waterfield Portrait	12.50	25.00

1964 Wheaties Stamps

This set of 74 stamps was issued perforated within a 48-page album. There were 70 players and four team logo stamps bound into the album as six pages of 12 stamps each plus two stamps attached to the inside front cover. In fact, they are typically found this way, still bound into the album. The stamps measure approximately 2 1/2" by 2 3/4" and are unnumbered. The album itself measures approximately 8 1/8" by 11" and is entitled "Pro Bowl Football Player Stamp Album". The stamp list below has been alphabetized for convenience. Each player stamp has a facsimile autograph on the front. Note that there are no spaces in the album for Joe Schmidt, Y.A.Tittle, or the four team emblem stamps.

COMPLETE SET (74)	175.00	300.00
1 Herb Adderley	5.00	10.00
2 Grady Alderman	1.50	3.00
3 Doug Atkins	4.00	8.00
4 Sam Baker	1.50	3.00
5 Erich Barnes	1.50	3.00
6 Terry Barr	1.50	3.00
7 Dick Bass	2.00	4.00
8 Maxie Baughan	1.50	3.00
9 Raymond Berry	5.00	10.00
10 Charley Bradshaw	1.50	3.00
11 Jim Brown	20.00	40.00
12 Roger Brown	1.50	3.00
13 Timmy Brown	2.00	4.00
14 Gail Cogdill	1.50	3.00
15 Tommy Davis	1.50	3.00
16 Willie Davis	5.00	10.00
17 Bob DeMarco	1.50	3.00
18 Darrell Dess	1.50	3.00
19 Buddy Dial	1.50	3.00
20 Mike Ditka	10.00	20.00
21 Galen Fiss	1.50	3.00
22 Lee Folkins	1.50	3.00
23 Joe Fortunato	1.50	3.00
24 Bill Glass	1.50	3.00
25 John Gordy	1.50	3.00
26 Ken Gray	1.50	3.00
27 Forrest Gregg	4.00	8.00
28 Rip Hawkins	1.50	3.00
29 Charley Johnson	2.00	4.00
30 John Henry Johnson	4.00	8.00
31 Hank Jordan	4.00	8.00
32 Jim Katcavage	1.50	3.00
33 Jerry Kramer	4.00	8.00
34 Joe Krupa	1.50	3.00
35 John LoVetere	1.50	3.00
36 Dick Lynch	1.50	3.00
37 Gino Marchetti	4.00	8.00
38 Joe Marconi	1.50	3.00
39 Tommy Mason	2.00	4.00
40 Dale Meinert	1.50	3.00
41 Lou Michaels	2.00	4.00
42 Minnesota Vikings	1.50	3.00
43 Bobby Mitchell	4.00	8.00
44 John Morrow	1.50	3.00
45 New York Giants	1.50	3.00
46 Merlin Olsen	6.00	12.00
47 Jack Pardee	2.00	4.00
48 Jim Parker	3.00	6.00
49 Bernie Parrish	1.50	3.00
50 Don Perkins	3.00	6.00
51 Richie Petitbon	1.50	3.00
52 Vince Promuto	1.50	3.00
53 Myron Pottios	1.50	3.00
54 Mike Pyle	1.50	3.00
55 Pete Retzlaff	2.00	4.00
56 Jim Ringo	4.00	8.00
57 Joe Rutgens	1.50	3.00
58 St. Louis Cardinals	1.50	3.00
59 San Francisco 49ers	1.50	3.00
60 Dick Schafrath	1.50	3.00
61 Joe Schmidt	4.00	8.00
62 Del Shofner	2.00	4.00
63 Norm Snead	2.00	4.00
64 Bart Starr	18.00	30.00
65 Jim Taylor	10.00	20.00
66 Roosevelt Taylor	2.00	4.00
67 Clendon Thomas	1.50	3.00
68 Y.A. Tittle	7.50	15.00
69 Johnny Unitas	20.00	35.00
70 Bill Wade	2.00	4.00
71 Wayne Walker	1.50	3.00
72 Jesse Whittenton	1.50	3.00
73 Larry Wilson	3.00	6.00
74 Abe Woodson	1.50	3.00
NNO Stamp Album	10.00	20.00

1966 Williams Portraits Packers

This set consists of charcoal portraits of Green Bay Packers players with each portrait measuring approximately 8" by 10" This set preceded the complete NFL Williams Portraits released in 1967. The prints look very similar to the 1967 set, with each including the player's name and position beneath the charcoal portrait with blankbacks. The 1966 set is distinguished primarily by the lack of a year on the copyright line. The portraits are unnumbered and have been checklisted below alphabetically. An album was also produced to house the complete set.

COMPLETE SET (34)	175.00	300.00
1 Herb Adderley	10.00	15.00
2 Lionel Aldridge	5.00	8.00
3 Donny Anderson	6.00	10.00
4 Ken Bowman	5.00	8.00
5 Zeke Bratkowski	6.00	10.00
6 Bob Brown SP	6.00	10.00
7 Tom Brown	5.00	8.00
8 Lee Roy Caffey	5.00	8.00
9 Don Chandler	5.00	8.00
10 Tommy Crutcher	5.00	8.00
11 Bill Curry SP		
12 Carroll Dale	6.00	10.00
13 Willie Davis	8.00	12.00
14 Boyd Dowler	6.00	10.00
15 Marv Fleming	6.00	10.00
16 Gale Gillingham SP	5.00	8.00
17 Jim Grabowski	5.00	8.00
18 Forrest Gregg	8.00	12.00
19 Doug Hart SP	5.00	8.00
20 Paul Hornung	15.00	25.00
21 Bob Jeter	5.00	8.00
22 Hank Jordan	8.00	12.00
23 Ron Kostelnik	5.00	8.00
24 Jerry Kramer	8.00	12.00
25 Bob Long	5.00	8.00
26 Max McGee	6.00	10.00
27 Ray Nitschke	15.00	25.00
28 Elijah Pitts	5.00	8.00
29 Dave Robinson	7.50	15.00
30 Bob Skoronski	5.00	8.00
31 Bart Starr	25.00	40.00
32 Jim Taylor	12.00	20.00
33 Fuzzy Thurston	8.00	12.00
34 Steve Wright SP	5.00	8.00
35 Willie Wood	8.00	12.00

1967 Williams Portraits

This set consists of charcoal art portraits of NFL players. Each portrait measures approximately 8" by 10", and they were sold in sets of eight for $1 along with the end flap from Velveeta, or a front label from Kraft Deluxe Slices or Singles, Cracker Barrel Cheddar or Kraft Sliced Natural Cheese. There were four eight-portrait groups for each of the 16 NFL teams. Moreover, an official NFL portrait album which would hold 32 portraits was offered for $2. The player's name and position were printed beneath the charcoal portrait. The backs are blank. The portraits are unnumbered and have been checklisted below alphabetically according to team. A checklist sheet (8" by 10") was produced, but is not considered a card. The Redskins and Packers sets appear to be the easiest to find. Popular players issued in their Rookie Card year include Leroy Kelly, Tommy Nobis, Dan Reeves and Jackie Smith. Players issued before their Rookie Card year include Lem Barney, Brian Piccolo, Bubba Smith and Steve Spurrier. It is believed that six players on this checklist did not have portraits produced while several other player listed are incorrect. Several players apparently were switched out for new players in their respective sets: Chuck Walton replaced Mike Alford and Bob Pickens replaced Bob Jones as examples. Lastly, a Vince Lombardi Williams Portrait was issued for a Downtown Businessman's function for the Green Bay Chamber of Commerce on August 7, 1968. We price this photo below as well although it is not considered part of the complete set.

COMPLETE SET (512)	5,000.00	8,000.00
1 Taz Anderson	10.00	20.00
2 Gary Barnes	10.00	20.00
3 Lee Calland	10.00	20.00
4 Junior Coffey	10.00	20.00
5 Ed Cook	10.00	20.00
6 Perry Lee Dunn	10.00	20.00
7 Dan Grimm	10.00	20.00
8 Alex Hawkins	12.50	25.00
9 Randy Johnson	10.00	20.00
10 Lou Kirouac	10.00	20.00
11 Errol Linden	10.00	20.00
12 Billy Lothridge	10.00	20.00
13 Frank Marchlewski	10.00	20.00
14 Rich Marshall	10.00	20.00
15 Billy Martin E	10.00	20.00
16 Tom Moore	12.50	25.00
17 Tommy Nobis	15.00	30.00
18 Jim Norton	10.00	20.00
19 Nick Rassas	10.00	20.00
20 Ken Reaves	10.00	20.00
21 Bobby Richards	10.00	20.00
22 Jerry Richardson	10.00	20.00
23 Bob Riggle	10.00	20.00
24 Karl Rubke	10.00	20.00
25 Marion Rushing	10.00	20.00
26 Chuck Sieminski	10.00	20.00
27 Steve Sloan	10.00	20.00
28 Ron Smith	10.00	20.00
29 Don Talbert	10.00	20.00
30 Ernie Wheelwright	10.00	20.00
31 Sam Williams	10.00	20.00
32 Jim Wilson	10.00	20.00
33 Sam Ball	10.00	20.00
34 Raymond Berry	20.00	40.00
35 Bob Boyd DB	10.00	20.00
36 Ordell Braase	10.00	20.00
37 Barry Brown	10.00	20.00
38 Bill Curry	10.00	20.00
39 Mike Curtis	12.50	25.00
40 Alvin Haymond	10.00	20.00
41 Jerry Hill	10.00	20.00
42 David Lee	10.00	20.00
43 Jerry Logan	10.00	20.00
44 Tony Lorick	10.00	20.00
45 Lenny Lyles	10.00	20.00
46 John Mackey	15.00	30.00
47 Tom Matte	12.50	25.00
48 Lou Michaels	12.50	25.00
49 Fred Miller	10.00	20.00
50 Lenny Moore	20.00	40.00
51 Jimmy Orr	10.00	20.00
52 Jim Parker	15.00	30.00
53 Glenn Ressler	10.00	20.00
54 Willie Richardson	10.00	20.00
55 Don Shinnick	10.00	20.00
56 Billy Ray Smith	10.00	20.00
57 Bubba Smith	15.00	30.00
58 Dan Sullivan	10.00	20.00
59 Dick Szymanski	10.00	20.00
60 Johnny Unitas	60.00	100.00
61 Bob Vogel	10.00	20.00
62 Rick Volk	10.00	20.00
63 Jim Welch	10.00	20.00
64 Butch Wilson	10.00	20.00
65 Charlie Bivins	12.50	25.00
66 Charlie Brown DB	12.50	25.00
67 Doug Buffone	12.50	25.00
68 Rudy Bukich	12.50	25.00
69 Ronnie Bull	12.50	25.00
70 Dick Butkus	40.00	75.00
71 Jim Cadile	12.50	25.00
72 Jack Concannon	12.50	25.00
73 Frank Cornish DT	12.50	25.00
74 Don Croftcheck	12.50	25.00
75 Dick Evey	12.50	25.00
76 Joe Fortunato	12.50	25.00
77 Curtis Gentry	12.50	25.00
78 Bobby Joe Green	12.50	25.00
79 John Johnson DT	12.50	25.00
80 Jimmy Jones	12.50	25.00
81 Ralph Kurek	12.50	25.00
82 Roger LeClerc	12.50	25.00
83 Andy Livingston	12.50	25.00
84 Bennie McRae	12.50	25.00
85 Johnny Morris	12.50	25.00
86 Richie Petitbon	12.50	25.00
87 Loyd Phillips	12.50	25.00
88 Brian Piccolo	40.00	75.00
89 Bob Pickens	12.50	25.00
90 Jim Purnell	12.50	25.00
91 Mike Pyle	12.50	25.00
92 Mike Reilly	12.50	25.00
93 Gale Sayers	40.00	75.00
94 George Seals	12.50	25.00
95 Roosevelt Taylor	15.00	30.00
96 Bob Wetoska	12.50	25.00
97 Erich Barnes	10.00	20.00
98 Johnny Brewer	10.00	20.00
99 Monte Clark	10.00	20.00
100 Gary Collins	12.50	25.00
101 Larry Conjar	10.00	20.00
102 Vince Costello	10.00	20.00
103 Ross Fichtner	10.00	20.00
104 Bill Glass	10.00	20.00
105 Ernie Green	10.00	20.00

106 Jack Gregory 10.00 20.00
107 Charlie Harraway 10.00 20.00
108 Gene Hickerson 10.00 20.00
109 Fred Hoaglin 10.00 20.00
110 Jim Houston 10.00 20.00
111 Mike Howell 10.00 20.00
112 Joe Bob Isbell 10.00 20.00
113 Walter Johnson 10.00 20.00
114 Jim Kanicki 10.00 20.00
115 Ernie Kellerman 10.00 20.00
116 Leroy Kelly 15.00 30.00
117 Dale Lindsey 10.00 20.00
118 Clifton McNeil 10.00 20.00
119 Milt Morin 10.00 20.00
120 Nick Pietrosante 10.00 20.00
121 Frank Ryan 12.50 25.00
122 Dick Schafrath 10.00 20.00
123 Randy Schultz 10.00 20.00
124 Ralph Smith 10.00 20.00
125 Carl Ward 10.00 20.00
126 Paul Warfield 15.00 30.00
127 Paul Wiggin 10.00 20.00
128 John Wooten 10.00 20.00
129 George Andrie 12.50 25.00
130 Jim Boeke 12.50 25.00
131 Frank Clarke 15.00 30.00
132 Mike Connelly 12.50 25.00
133 Buddy Dial 12.50 25.00
134 Leon Donohue 12.50 25.00
135 Dave Edwards 12.50 25.00
136 Mike Gaechter 12.50 25.00
137 Walt Garrison 15.00 30.00
138 Pete Gent 12.50 25.00
139 Cornell Green 15.00 30.00
140 Bob Hayes 20.00 40.00
141 Chuck Howley 20.00 40.00
142 Lee Roy Jordan 20.00 40.00
143 Bob Lilly 35.00 60.00
144 Tony Liscio 12.50 25.00
145 Warren Livingston 12.50 25.00
146 Dave Manders 12.50 25.00
147 Don Meredith 40.00 75.00
148 Ralph Neely 12.50 25.00
149 John Niland 12.50 25.00
150 Pettis Norman 12.50 25.00
151 Don Perkins 15.00 30.00
152 Jethro Pugh 12.50 25.00
153 Dan Reeves 25.00 50.00
154 Mel Renfro 20.00 40.00
155 Jerry Rhome 12.50 25.00
156 Les Shy 12.50 25.00
157 J.D. Smith 12.50 25.00
158 Willie Townes 12.50 25.00
159 Danny Villanueva 12.50 25.00
160 John Wilbur 12.50 25.00
161 Lem Barney 15.00 30.00
162 Charley Bradshaw 10.00 20.00
163 Roger Brown 12.50 25.00
164 Ernie Clark 10.00 20.00
165 Gail Cogdill 10.00 20.00
166 Nick Eddy 10.00 20.00
167 Mel Farr 10.00 20.00
168 Bobby Felts 10.00 20.00
169 Ed Flanagan 10.00 20.00
170 Jim Gibbons 12.50 25.00
171 John Gordy 10.00 20.00
172 Larry Hand 10.00 20.00
173 Wally Hilgenberg 10.00 20.00
174 Alex Karras 20.00 40.00
175 Bob Kowalkowski 10.00 20.00
176 Ron Kramer 10.00 20.00
177 Mike Lucci 10.00 20.00
178 Bruce Maher 10.00 20.00
179 Amos Marsh 10.00 20.00
180 Darris McCord 10.00 20.00
181 Tom Nowatzke 10.00 20.00
182 Milt Plum 12.50 25.00
183 Wayne Rasmussen 10.00 20.00
184 Roger Shoals 10.00 20.00
185 Pat Studstill 10.00 20.00
186 Karl Sweetan 10.00 20.00
187 Bobby Thompson DB 10.00 20.00
188 Doug Van Horn 10.00 20.00
189 Wayne Walker 10.00 20.00
190 Tommy Watkins 10.00 20.00
191 Chuck Walton 10.00 20.00
192 Garo Yepremian 12.50 25.00
193 Herb Adderley 10.00 20.00
194 Lionel Aldridge 5.00 10.00
195 Donny Anderson 6.00 12.00
196 Ken Bowman 5.00 10.00
197 Zeke Bratkowski 6.00 12.00
198 Bob Brown DT 5.00 10.00
199 Tom Brown 5.00 10.00
200 Lee Roy Caffey 5.00 10.00
201 Don Chandler 6.00 12.00
202 Tommy Crutcher 5.00 10.00
203 Carroll Dale 6.00 12.00
204 Willie Davis 7.50 15.00
205 Boyd Dowler 6.00 12.00
206 Marv Fleming 6.00 12.00
207 Gale Gillingham 5.00 10.00
208 Jim Grabowski 5.00 10.00
209 Forrest Gregg 10.00 20.00
210 Doug Hart 5.00 10.00
211 Bob Jeter 5.00 10.00
212 Hank Jordan 7.50 15.00
213 Ron Kostelnik 5.00 10.00
214 Jerry Kramer 7.50 15.00
215 Bob Long 5.00 10.00
216 Max McGee 6.00 12.00
217 Ray Nitschke 12.50 25.00
218 Elijah Pitts 6.00 12.00
219 Dave Robinson 6.00 12.00
220 Bob Skoronski 5.00 10.00
221 Bart Starr 25.00 50.00
222 Fred Thurston 7.50 15.00
223 Willie Wood 10.00 20.00
224 Steve Wright 5.00 10.00
225 Dick Bass 12.50 25.00
226 Maxie Baughan 10.00 20.00
227 Joe Carollo 10.00 20.00
228 Bernie Casey 10.00 20.00
229 Don Chuy 10.00 20.00
230 Charlie Cowan 10.00 20.00
231 Irv Cross 10.00 20.00
232 Willie Ellison 10.00 20.00
233 Roman Gabriel 15.00 30.00
234 Bruce Gossett 10.00 20.00
235 Roosevelt Grier 12.50 25.00
236 Tony Guillory 10.00 20.00
237 Ken Iman 10.00 20.00
238 Deacon Jones 20.00 40.00
239 Les Josephson 10.00 20.00
240 Jon Kilgore 10.00 20.00
241 Chuck Lamson 10.00 20.00
242 Lamar Lundy 12.50 25.00
243 Tom Mack 15.00 30.00
244 Tommy Mason 12.50 25.00
245 Tommy McDonald 12.50 25.00
246 Ed Meador 10.00 20.00
247 Bill Munson 10.00 20.00
248 Bob Nichols 10.00 20.00
249 Merlin Olsen 20.00 40.00
250 Jack Pardee 12.50 25.00
251 Bucky Pope 10.00 20.00
252 Joe Scibelli 10.00 20.00
253 Jack Snow 12.50 25.00
254 Billy Truax 10.00 20.00
255 Clancy Williams 10.00 20.00
256 Doug Woodlief 10.00 20.00
257 Grady Alderman 12.50 25.00
258 John Beasley 10.00 20.00
259 Bob Berry 10.00 20.00
260 Larry Bowie 10.00 20.00
261 Bill Brown 12.50 25.00
262 Fred Cox 12.50 25.00
263 Doug Davis 10.00 20.00
264 Paul Dickson 10.00 20.00
265 Carl Eller 15.00 30.00
266 Paul Flatley 10.00 20.00
267 Dale Hackbart 10.00 20.00
268 Don Hansen 10.00 20.00
269 Clint Jones 10.00 20.00
270 Jeff Jordan 10.00 20.00
271 Karl Kassulke 10.00 20.00
272 John Kirby 10.00 20.00
273 Gary Larsen 10.00 20.00
274 Jim Lindsey 10.00 20.00
275 Earsell Mackbee 10.00 20.00
276 Jim Marshall 15.00 30.00
277 Marlin McKeever 10.00 20.00
278 Dave Osborn 10.00 20.00
279 Jim Phillips 10.00 20.00
280 Ed Sharockman 10.00 20.00
281 Jerry Shay 10.00 20.00
282 Milt Sunde 10.00 20.00
283 Archie Sutton 10.00 20.00
284 Mick Tingelhoff 12.50 25.00
285 Ron VanderKelen 10.00 20.00
286 Jim Vellone 10.00 20.00
287 Lonnie Warwick 10.00 20.00
288 Roy Winston 10.00 20.00
289 Doug Atkins 15.00 30.00
290 Vern Burke 10.00 20.00
291 Bruce Cortez 10.00 20.00
292 Gary Cuozzo 12.50 25.00
293 Ted Davis 10.00 20.00
294 John Douglas 10.00 20.00
295 Jim Garcia 10.00 20.00
296 Tom Hall 10.00 20.00
297 Jim Heidel 10.00 20.00
298 Leslie Kelley 10.00 20.00
299 Billy Kilmer 12.50 25.00
300 Kent Kramer 10.00 20.00
301 Jake Kupp 10.00 20.00
302 Earl Leggett 10.00 20.00
303 Obert Logan 10.00 20.00
304 Tom McNeill 10.00 20.00
305 John Morrow 10.00 20.00
306 Ray Ogden 10.00 20.00
307 Ray Rissmiller 10.00 20.00
308 George Rose 10.00 20.00
309 Dave Rowe 10.00 20.00
310 Brian Schweda 10.00 20.00
311 Dave Simmons 10.00 20.00
312 Jerry Simmons 10.00 20.00
313 Steve Stonebreaker 10.00 20.00
314 Jim Taylor 20.00 40.00
315 Mike Tilleman 10.00 20.00
316 Phil Vandersea 10.00 20.00
317 Joe Wendryhoski 10.00 20.00
318 Dave Whitsell 10.00 20.00
319 Fred Whittingham 10.00 20.00
320 Gary Wood 10.00 20.00
321 Ken Avery 10.00 20.00
322 Bookie Bolin 10.00 20.00
323 Henry Carr 12.50 25.00
324 Pete Case 10.00 20.00
325 Clarence Childs 10.00 20.00
326 Mike Ciccolella 10.00 20.00
327 Glen Condren 10.00 20.00
328 Bob Crespino 10.00 20.00
329 Don Davis 10.00 20.00
330 Tucker Frederickson 12.50 25.00
331 Charlie Harper 10.00 20.00
332 Phil Harris 10.00 20.00
333 Allen Jacobs 10.00 20.00
334 Homer Jones 10.00 20.00
335 Jim Katcavage 10.00 20.00
336 Tom Kennedy 10.00 20.00
337 Ernie Koy 10.00 20.00
338 Greg Larson 10.00 20.00
339 Spider Lockhart 10.00 20.00
340 Chuck Mercein 10.00 20.00
341 Jim Moran 10.00 20.00
342 Earl Morrall 12.50 25.00
343 Joe Morrison 10.00 20.00
344 Francis Peay 10.00 20.00
345 Del Shofner 12.50 25.00
346 Jeff Smith LB 10.00 20.00
347 Fran Tarkenton 30.00 60.00
348 Aaron Thomas 10.00 20.00
349 Larry Vargo 10.00 20.00
350 Freeman White 10.00 20.00
351 Sidney Williams 10.00 20.00
352 Willie Young 10.00 20.00
353 Sam Baker 10.00 20.00
354 Gary Ballman 10.00 20.00
355 Randy Beisler 10.00 20.00
356 Bob Brown OT 12.50 25.00
357 Timmy Brown 12.50 25.00
358 Mike Ditka 40.00 75.00
359 Dave Graham 10.00 20.00
360 Ben Hawkins 10.00 20.00
361 Fred Hill 10.00 20.00
362 King Hill 10.00 20.00
363 Lynn Hoyem 10.00 20.00
364 Don Hultz 10.00 20.00
365 Dwight Kelley 10.00 20.00
366 Israel Lang 10.00 20.00
367 Dave Lloyd 10.00 20.00
368 Aaron Martin 10.00 20.00
369 Ron Medved 10.00 20.00
370 John Meyers 10.00 20.00
371 Mike Morgan LB 10.00 20.00
372 Al Nelson 10.00 20.00
373 Jim Nettles 10.00 20.00
374 Floyd Peters 10.00 20.00
375 Gary Pettigrew 10.00 20.00
376 Ray Poage 10.00 20.00
377 Nate Ramsey 10.00 20.00
378 Dave Recher 10.00 20.00
379 Jim Ringo 10.00 20.00
380 Joe Scarpati 10.00 20.00
381 Jim Skaggs 10.00 20.00
382 Norm Snead 12.50 25.00
383 Harold Wells 10.00 20.00
384 Tom Woodeshick 10.00 20.00
385 Bill Asbury 12.50 25.00
386 John Baker 12.50 25.00
387 Jim Bradshaw 12.50 25.00
388 Rod Breedlove 12.50 25.00
389 John Brown 12.50 25.00
390 Amos Bullocks 12.50 25.00
391 Jim Butler 12.50 25.00
392 John Campbell 12.50 25.00
393 Mike Clark 12.50 25.00
394 Larry Gagner 12.50 25.00
395 Earl Gros 12.50 25.00
396 John Hilton 12.50 25.00
397 Dick Hoak 12.50 25.00
398 Roy Jefferson 12.50 25.00
399 Tony Jeter 12.50 25.00
400 Brady Keys 12.50 25.00
401 Ken Kortas 12.50 25.00
402 Ray Mansfield 12.50 25.00
403 Paul Martha 12.50 25.00
404 Ben McGee 12.50 25.00
405 Bill Nelsen 15.00 30.00
406 Kent Nix 12.50 25.00
407 Fran O'Brien 12.50 25.00
408 Andy Russell 15.00 30.00
409 Bill Saul 12.50 25.00
410 Don Shy 12.50 25.00
411 Clendon Thomas 12.50 25.00
412 Bruce Van Dyke 12.50 25.00
413 Lloyd Voss 12.50 25.00
414 Ralph Wenzel 12.50 25.00
415 J.R. Wilburn 12.50 25.00
416 Marv Woodson 12.50 25.00
417 Jim Bakken 10.00 20.00
418 Don Brumm 10.00 20.00
419 Vidal Carlin 10.00 20.00
420 Bobby Joe Conrad 10.00 20.00
421 Willis Crenshaw 10.00 20.00
422 Bob DeMarco 10.00 20.00
423 Pat Fischer 12.50 25.00
424 Billy Gambrell 10.00 20.00
425 Prentice Gautt 10.00 20.00
426 Ken Gray 10.00 20.00
427 Jerry Hillebrand 10.00 20.00
428 Charley Johnson 12.50 25.00
429 Bill Koman 10.00 20.00
430 Dave Long 10.00 20.00
431 Ernie McMillan 10.00 20.00
432 Dave Meggysey 10.00 20.00
433 Dale Meinert 10.00 20.00
434 Mike Melinkovich 10.00 20.00
435 Dave O'Brien 10.00 20.00
436 Sonny Randle 10.00 20.00
437 Bob Reynolds 10.00 20.00
438 Joe Robb 10.00 20.00
439 Johnny Roland 10.00 20.00
440 Roy Shivers 10.00 20.00
441 Sam Silas 10.00 20.00
442 Jackie Smith 15.00 30.00
443 Rick Sortun 10.00 20.00
444 Jerry Stovall 10.00 20.00
445 Chuck Walker 10.00 20.00
446 Bobby Williams 10.00 20.00
447 Dave Williams 10.00 20.00
448 Larry Wilson 15.00 30.00
449 Kermit Alexander 10.00 20.00
450 Cas Banaszek 10.00 20.00
451 Bruce Bosley 10.00 20.00
452 John Brodie 20.00 40.00
453 Joe Cerne 10.00 20.00
454 John David Crow 12.50 25.00
455 Tommy Davis 10.00 20.00
456 Bob Harrison 10.00 20.00
457 Matt Hazeltine 10.00 20.00
458 Stan Hindman 10.00 20.00
459 Charlie Johnson DT 10.00 20.00
460 Jim Johnson 12.50 25.00
461 Dave Kopay 10.00 20.00
462 Charlie Krueger 10.00 20.00
463 Roland Lakes 10.00 20.00
464 Gary Lewis 10.00 20.00
465 Dave McCormick 10.00 20.00
466 Kay McFarland 10.00 20.00
467 Clark Miller 10.00 20.00
468 George Mira 10.00 20.00
469 Howard Mudd 10.00 20.00
470 Frank Nunley 10.00 20.00
471 Dave Parks 10.00 20.00
472 Walter Rock 10.00 20.00
473 Len Rohde 10.00 20.00
474 Steve Spurrier 30.00 60.00
475 Monty Stickles 10.00 20.00
476 John Thomas 10.00 20.00
477 Bill Tucker 10.00 20.00
478 Dave Wilcox 12.50 25.00
479 Ken Willard 10.00 20.00
480 Dick Witcher 10.00 20.00
481 Willie Adams 6.00 12.00
482 Walt Barnes DL 6.00 12.00
483 Jim Carroll 6.00 12.00
484 Dave Crossan 6.00 12.00
485 Charlie Gogolak 6.00 12.00
486 Tom Goosby 6.00 12.00
487 Chris Hanburger 7.50 15.00
488 Rickie Harris 6.00 12.00
489 Len Hauss 6.00 12.00
490 Sam Huff 12.50 25.00
491 Steve Jackson LB 6.00 12.00
492 Mitch Johnson 6.00 12.00
493 Sonny Jurgensen 12.50 25.00
494 Carl Kammerer 6.00 12.00
495 Paul Krause 10.00 20.00
496 Joe Don Looney 7.50 15.00
497 Ray McDonald 6.00 12.00
498 Bobby Mitchell 10.00 20.00
499 Jim Ninowski 6.00 12.00
500 Brig Owens 6.00 12.00
501 Vince Promuto 6.00 12.00
502 Pat Richter 6.00 12.00
503 Joe Rutgens 6.00 12.00
504 Lonnie Sanders 6.00 12.00
505 Ray Schoenke 6.00 12.00
506 Jim Shorter 6.00 12.00
507 Jerry Smith 6.00 12.00
508 Ron Snidow 6.00 12.00
509 Jim Snowden 6.00 12.00
510 Charley Taylor 10.00 20.00
511 Steve Thurlow 6.00 12.00
512 A.D. Whitfield 6.00 12.00
513 Vince Lombardi CO 60.00 100.00
514 Portrait Album 30.00 50.00

1948 Wilson Advisory Staff

These glossy black and white photos measure roughly 8 1/8" by 10" and were likely issued over a number of years. Each features a top player or coach photo with the Wilson advisory staff line of text below the picture. They also include facsimile autographs.

COMPLETE SET (5) 100.00 200.00
1 Paul Christman 20.00 40.00
2 Johnny Lujack 37.50 75.00
3 Clark Shaughnessy 15.00 30.00
4 Charley Trippi 25.00 50.00
5 Lynn Waldorf 15.00 30.00

1962-66 Wilson Advisory Staff

These 8X10 glossy photos were likely issued over a number of years in the 1960s. Each features a top player or coach photo printed in black and white with the Wilson advisory staff line of text below the picture. Some also include facsimile autographs.

COMPLETE SET (4) 45.00 90.00
1 Bernie Bierman 7.50 15.00
2 Boyd Dowler 10.00 20.00
3 Hugh McElhenny 12.50 25.00
4 Gale Sayers 20.00 40.00

1974 Wonder Bread

The 1974 Wonder Bread Football set features 30 standard-size cards with colored borders and color photographs of the players on the front. Season by season records are given on the back of the cards as well as a particular football technique. A "Topps Chewing Gum, Inc." copyright appears on the reverse. A parallel version of the cards was also distributed by Town Talk Bread.

COMPLETE SET (30)	25.00	50.00
1 Jim Bakken	.60	1.50
2 Forrest Blue	.60	1.50
3 Bill Bradley	.60	1.50
4 Willie Brown	1.00	2.50
5 Larry Csonka	3.00	6.00
6 Ken Ellis	.60	1.50
7 Bruce Gossett	.60	1.50
8 Bob Griese	3.00	6.00
9 Chris Hanburger	.60	1.50
10 Winston Hill	.60	1.50
11 Jim Johnson	.75	2.00
12 Paul Krause	.75	2.00
13 Ted Kwalick	.60	1.50
14 Willie Lanier	1.00	2.50
15 Tom Mack	.75	2.00
16 Jim Otto	1.00	2.50
17 Alan Page	1.00	2.50
18 Frank Pitts	.60	1.50
19 Jim Plunkett	1.00	2.50
20 Mike Reid	.75	2.00
21 Paul Smith	.60	1.50
22 Bob Tucker	.60	1.50
23 Jim Tyrer	.60	1.50
24 Gene Upshaw	1.00	2.50
25 Phil Villapiano	.60	1.50
26 Paul Warfield	1.50	4.00
27 Dwight White	.75	2.00
28 Steve Owens	.75	2.00
29 Jerrel Wilson	.60	1.50
30 Ron Yary	.75	2.00

1974 Wonder Bread/Town Talk

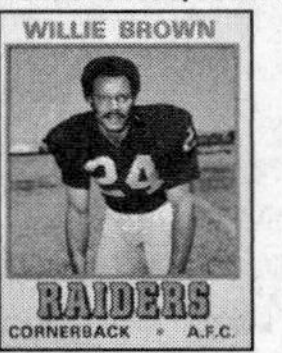

The 1974 Town Talk Bread set features 30 standard-size cards with colored borders and color photographs of the players on the front. The cards are essentially a parallel version of the 1974 Wonder Bread release, but were distributed through Town Talk Bread products. A "Topps Chewing Gum, Inc." copyright appears on the reverse. These Town Talk cards are more difficult to find and are priced using the multiplier line given below. They are distinguished from the Wonder Bread issue by the absence of a credit line at the top of the cardback.

COMPLETE SET (30) 125.00 250.00
*TOWN TALK: 3X TO 6X BASIC CARDS

1975 Wonder Bread

The 1975 Wonder Bread Football card set contains 24 standard-size cards with either blue (7-18) or red (1-6 and 19-24) borders. The backs feature several questions (about the player and the game of football) whose answers could be determined by turning the card upside down and reading the answers to the corresponding questions. The words "Topps Chewing Gum, Inc." appears at the bottom of the reverse of the card. Wonder Bread also produced a saver sheet and album for this set. A parallel version of the cards was also produced by Town Talk Bread.

COMPLETE SET (24)	20.00	40.00
1 Alan Page	.75	2.00
2 Emmitt Thomas	.60	1.50
3 John Mendenhall	.50	1.25
4 Ken Houston	.60	1.50
5 Jack Ham	1.50	4.00
6 L.C. Greenwood	.75	2.00
7 Tom Mack	.60	1.50
8 Winston Hill	.50	1.25
9 Isaac Curtis	.50	1.25
10 Terry Owens	.50	1.25
11 Drew Pearson	1.25	3.00
12 Don Cockroft	.50	1.25
13 Bob Griese	2.00	5.00
14 Riley Odoms	.50	1.25
15 Chuck Foreman	.60	1.50
16 Forrest Blue	.50	1.25
17 Franco Harris	2.50	6.00
18 Larry Little	.60	1.50
19 Bill Bergey	.50	1.25
20 Ray Guy	.60	1.50
21 Ted Hendricks	.75	2.00
22 Levi Johnson	.50	1.25
23 Jack Mildren	.50	1.25
24 Mel Tom	.50	1.25

1975 Wonder Bread/Town Talk

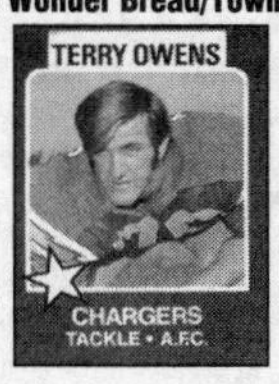

The 1975 Town Talk Bread card set contains 24 standard-size cards with either blue (7-18) or red (1-6 and 19-24) borders. The cards are essentially a parallel to the Wonder Bread issue. The words "Topps Chewing Gum, Inc." appears at the bottom of the cardback. These Town Talk cards are more difficult to find and are priced using the multiplier line given below. They are distinguished by the different "Town Talk" credit line at the top of the cardback.

COMPLETE SET (24) 125.00 250.00
*TOWN TALK: 4X TO 8X BASIC CARDS

1976 Wonder Bread

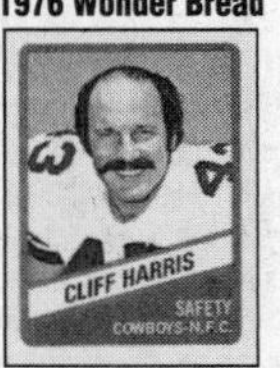

The 1976 Wonder Bread Football Card set features 24 colored standard-size cards with red or blue frame lines and white borders. The first 12 cards (1-12) in the set feature offensive players with a blue frame and the last 12 cards (13-24) feature defensive players with a red frame. The backs feature one of coach Hank Stram's favorite plays, with a football diagram and a text listing each offensive player's assignments of the particular play. The "Topps Chewing Gum, Inc." copyright appears at the bottom on the cardback. A parallel version of the cards was also produced by Town Talk Bread.

COMPLETE SET (24)	2.50	5.00
1 Craig Morton	.25	.50
2 Chuck Foreman	.15	.40
3 Franco Harris	.50	1.25
4 Mel Gray	.15	.40
5 Charley Taylor	.30	.75
6 Richard Caster	.10	.30
7 George Kunz	.10	.30
8 Rayfield Wright	.10	.30
9 Gene Upshaw	.25	.50
10 Tom Mack	.15	.40
11 Len Hauss	.10	.30
12 Garo Yepremian	.10	.30
13 Cedrick Hardman	.10	.30
14 Jack Youngblood	.25	.50
15 Wally Chambers	.10	.30
16 Jerry Sherk	.10	.30
17 Bill Bergey	.10	.30
18 Jack Ham	.30	.75
19 Fred Carr	.10	.30
20 Jack Tatum	.15	.40
21 Cliff Harris	.25	.50
22 Emmitt Thomas	.10	.30
23 Ken Riley	.10	.30
24 Ray Guy	.25	.50

1976 Wonder Bread/Town Talk

The 1976 Town Talk Bread football card set features 24 colored standard-size cards with red or blue frame lines and white borders. The cards are essentially a parallel version to the Wonder Bread release. The "Topps Chewing Gum, Inc." copyright appears at the bottom on the cardback. These Town Talk cards are more difficult to find than the Wonder Bread issue and are priced using the multiplier line given below. They are distinguished by the different credit line at the top of the cardback.

COMPLETE SET (24) 50.00 100.00
*TOWN TALK: 6X TO 12X BASIC CARDS

1964 Yuban Coffee Canvas Premiums

These large portraits were issued by Yuban Coffee around 1964. Each features a current NFL star in a painting format printed on canvas. The backs are blank. Any additions to this list are appreciated.

COMPLETE SET (17)	2,500.00	4,000.00
1 Gary Ballman	100.00	200.00
2 Jim Brown	500.00	800.00
3 Gail Cogdill	100.00	200.00
4 Bill George	125.00	250.00
5 Frank Gifford	125.00	250.00
6 Matt Hazeltine	100.00	200.00
7 Paul Hornung	200.00	400.00
8 Charley Johnson	100.00	200.00
9 Don Meredith	200.00	350.00
10 Bobby Mitchell	125.00	250.00
11 Earl Morrall	125.00	250.00
12 Jack Pardee	100.00	200.00
13 Nick Pietrosante	100.00	200.00
14 Pete Retzlaff	125.00	250.00
15 Fran Tarkenton	250.00	500.00
16 Y.A. Tittle	200.00	400.00
17 Johnny Unitas	400.00	800.00

1967 Air Force Team Issue

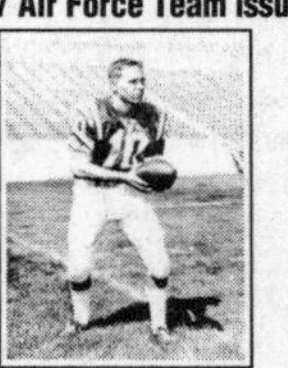

These 5" by 7" black and white photos were issued by the Air Force Academy. Each features a member of the football team without any player identfiication on the front. The backs were produced blank, however the player's identification is usually hand written on the backs.

COMPLETE SET (7)	25.00	50.00
1 Gerry Cormany	3.00	8.00
2 George Gibson	3.00	8.00
3 Don Heckert	3.00	8.00
4 Mike Mueller	3.00	8.00
5 Neal Starkey	3.00	8.00
6 Paul Stein	3.00	8.00
7 Rich Wolfe	3.00	8.00

1971 Alabama Team Sheets

These six sheets measure approximately 8" by 9". The fronts feature twelve black-and-white player portraits arranged in three rows of four portraits per row. The player's name is printed under the photo. The backs are blank. The sheets are unnumbered and checklisted below in alphabetical order beginning with the player in the upper left hand corner.

COMPLETE SET (6)	40.00	80.00
1 Sheet 1	6.00	12.00
2 Sheet 2	6.00	12.00
3 Sheet 3	7.50	15.00
4 Sheet 4	6.00	12.00
5 Sheet 5	7.50	15.00
6 Sheet 6	7.50	15.00

1972 Alabama Playing Cards

This 54-card standard-size set was issued in a box as a playing card deck through the Alabama University bookstore. The cards have rounded corners and the typical playing card finish. The fronts feature black-and-white posed action photos of helmetless players in their uniforms. A white border surrounds each picture and contains the card number and suit designation in the upper left corner and again, but inverted, in the lower right. The player's name and hometown appear just beneath the photo. The white-bordered crimson backs all have the Alabama "A" logo in white and the year of issue, 1972. The name Alabama Crimson Tide also appears on the backs. Since the set is similar to a playing card set, the set is arranged just like a card deck and checklisted below accordingly. In the checklist below S means Spades, D means Diamonds, C means Clubs, H means Hearts, and JK means Joker. The cards are checklisted below in playing card order by suits and numbers are assigned to Aces (1), Jacks (11), Queens (12), and Kings (13). The jokers are unnumbered and listed at the end. Key cards in the set are early cards of coaching legend Paul "Bear" Bryant and lineman John Hannah. This set was available directly from Alabama for $2.50

COMPLETE SET (54)	90.00	150.00
1C Skip Kubelius	1.00	2.50
1D Terry Davis	1.25	3.00
1H Robert Fraley	1.00	2.50
1S Paul(Bear) Bryant CO	20.00	35.00
2C David Watkins	1.00	2.50
2D Bobby McKinney	1.00	2.50
2H Dexter Wood	1.00	2.50
2S Chuck Strickland	1.00	2.50
3C John Hannah	12.00	20.00
3D Tom Lusk	1.00	2.50
3H Jim Krapf	1.00	2.50
3S Warren Dyar	1.00	2.50
4C Greg Gantt	1.25	3.00
4D Johnny Sharpless	1.00	2.50
4H Steve Wade	1.00	2.50
4S John Rogers	1.00	2.50
5C Doug Faust	1.00	2.50
5D Jeff Rouzie	1.00	2.50
5H Buddy Brown	1.00	2.50
5S Randy Moore	1.00	2.50
6C David Knapp	1.25	3.00
6D Lanny Norris	1.00	2.50
6H Paul Spivey	1.00	2.50
6S Pat Raines	1.00	2.50
7C Pete Pappas	1.00	2.50
7D Ed Hines	1.00	2.50
7H Mike Washington	1.00	2.50
7S David McMakin	1.25	3.00
8C Steve Dean	1.00	2.50
8D Joe LaBue	1.00	2.50
8H John Croyle	1.00	2.50
8S Noah Miller	1.00	2.50
9C Bobby Stanford	1.00	2.50
9D Sylvester Croom	1.50	4.00
9H Wilbur Jackson	4.00	8.00
9S Ellis Beck	1.00	2.50
10C Steve Bisceglia	1.00	2.50
10D Andy Cross	1.00	2.50
10H John Mitchell	1.25	3.00
10S Bill Davis	1.00	2.50
11C Gary Rutledge	1.25	3.00
11D Randy Billingsley	1.00	2.50
11H Randy Hall	1.00	2.50
11S Ralph Stokes	1.00	2.50
12C Jeff Blitz	1.00	2.50
12D Robby Rowan	1.00	2.50
12H Mike Raines	1.00	2.50
12S Wayne Wheeler	1.00	2.50
13C Steve Sprayberry	1.00	2.50
13D Wayne Hall	1.25	3.00
13H Morris Hunt	1.00	2.50
13S Butch Norman	1.00	2.50
JOK1 Denny Stadium	1.00	2.50
JOK2 Memorial Coliseum	1.00	2.50

1973 Alabama Playing Cards

These 54 standard-size playing cards have rounded corners and the typical playing card finish The cards were sold through the Alabama University bookstore. The fronts feature black-and-white posed action photos of helmetless players in their uniforms. A white border surrounds each picture and contains the card number and suit designation in the upper left corner and again, but inverted, in the lower right. The player's name and hometown appear just beneath the photo. The white-bordered crimson backs all have the Alabama "A" logo in white and the year of issue, 1973. The name Alabama Crimson Tide also appears on the backs. Since this is a set of playing cards, the set is checklisted below accordingly. In the checklist below S means Spades, D means Diamonds, C means Clubs, H means Hearts, and JK means Joker. The cards are in playing card order by suits and numbers are assigned to Aces (1), Jacks (11), Queens (12), and Kings (13). The jokers are unnumbered and listed at the end. If a player was in the 1972 set, they have the same pose in this set. This set was originally available from Alabama for $3.50.

COMPLETE SET (54)	90.00	150.00
1C Skip Kubelius	1.00	2.50
1D Mark Prudhomme	1.00	2.50
1H Robert Fraley	1.00	2.50
1S Paul(Bear) Bryant CO	15.00	30.00
2C David Watkins	1.00	2.50
2D Richard Todd	6.00	12.00
2H Buddy Pope	1.00	2.50
2S Chuck Strickland	1.00	2.50
3C Bob Bryan	1.00	2.50
3D Gary Hanrahan	1.00	2.50
3H Greg Montgomery LB	1.00	2.50
3S Warren Dyar	1.00	2.50
4C Greg Gantt	1.25	3.00
4D Johnny Sharpless	1.00	2.50
4H Rick Watson	1.00	2.50
4S John Rogers	1.00	2.50
5C George Pugh	1.25	3.00
5D Jeff Rouzie	1.00	2.50
5H Buddy Brown	1.00	2.50
5S Randy Moore	1.00	2.50
6C Ray Maxwell	1.00	2.50
6D Alan Pizzitola	1.00	2.50
6H Paul Spivey	1.00	2.50
6S Ron Robertson	1.00	2.50
7C Pete Pappas	1.00	2.50
7D Steve Kulback	1.00	2.50
7H Mike Washington	1.00	2.50
7S David McMakin	1.25	3.00
8C Steve Dean	1.00	2.50
8D Jerry Brown	1.00	2.50
8H John Croyle	1.00	2.50
8S Noah Miller	1.00	2.50
9C Leroy Cook	1.00	2.50
9D Sylvester Croom	1.50	4.00
9H Wilbur Jackson	3.00	6.00
9S Ellis Beck	1.00	2.50
10C Tyrone King	1.00	2.50
10D Mike Stock	1.00	2.50
10H Mike DuBose	1.00	2.50
10S Bill Davis	1.00	2.50
11C Gary Rutledge	1.25	3.00
11D Randy Billingsley	1.00	2.50
11H Randy Hall	1.00	2.50
11S Ralph Stokes	1.00	2.50
12C Woodrow Lowe	3.00	6.00
12D Marvin Barron	1.00	2.50
12H Mike Raines	1.00	2.50
12S Wayne Wheeler	1.00	2.50
13C Steve Sprayberry	1.00	2.50
13D Wayne Hall	1.25	3.00
13H Morris Hunt	1.00	2.50
13S Butch Norman	1.00	2.50
JOK1 Denny Stadium	1.00	2.50
JOK2 Memorial Coliseum	1.00	2.50

1929 Albert Richard Co. All American Photos

This set of blankbacked photos was issued by the Albert Richard Company to honor the clothing firm's selection of 1929 college All Americans. Each photo measures roughly 8" by 10" and features a sepia toned photo of the player wearing an Albert Richard coat. A thick white border surrounds the image and the player's name and a brief bio is included in the bottom border. Each photo also includes a facsimile autograph. Finally, an additional cover or header sheet accompanied the set.

COMPLETE SET (12)	500.00	800.00
1 George Ackerman	30.00	60.00
2 Chris Cagle	30.00	60.00
3 John Cannon	30.00	60.00
4 Frank Carideo	30.00	60.00
5 Joe Donchess	30.00	60.00
6 Bill Glassgow	30.00	60.00
7 Ray Montgomery	30.00	60.00
8 Bronko Nagurski	250.00	400.00
9 Elmer Sleight	30.00	60.00
10 Francis Tap Tappaan	30.00	60.00

11 Ralph Welch	30.00	60.00
12 Header Sheet	6.00	15.00

1980 Arizona Police

The 1980 University of Arizona Police set contains 24 cards measuring approximately 2 7/16" by 3 3/4". The fronts have borderless color player photos, with the player's name and jersey number in a white stripe beneath the picture. The backs have brief biographical information and safety tips. The cards are unnumbered and checklisted below in alphabetical order. Reportedly the Reggie Ware card is very difficult to find.

COMPLETE SET (24)	50.00	100.00
1 Brian Clifford	1.25	3.00
2 Mark Fulcher	1.25	3.00
3 Bob Gareeb	1.25	3.00
4 Marcellus Green	1.50	4.00
5 Drew Hardville	1.25	3.00
6 Neal Harris	1.25	3.00
7 Richard Hersey	1.25	3.00
8 Alfondia Hill	1.25	3.00
9 Tim Holmes	1.25	3.00
10 Jack Housley	1.25	3.00
11 Glenn Hutchinson	1.25	3.00
12 Bill Jensen	1.25	3.00
13 Frank Kalil	1.25	3.00
14 Dave Liggins	1.25	3.00
15 Tom Manno	1.25	3.00
16 Bill Nettling	1.25	3.00
17 Hubie Oliver	2.50	6.00
18 Glenn Perkins	1.25	3.00
19 John Ramseyer	1.25	3.00
20 Mike Robinson	1.25	3.00
21 Chris Schultz	1.50	4.00
22 Larry Smith CO	2.00	5.00
23 Reggie Ware SP	15.00	40.00
24 Bill Zivic	1.25	3.00

1972 Auburn Playing Cards

This 54-card standard-size set was issued in a playing card deck box. The cards have rounded corners and the typical playing card finish. The fronts feature black-and-white posed photos of helmetless players in their uniforms. A white border surrounds each picture and contains the card number and suit designation in the upper left corner and again, but inverted, in the lower right. The player's name and hometown appear just beneath the photo. The white-bordered orange backs all have the Auburn "AU" logo in navy blue and orange and white outlines. The the year of issue, 1972, and the name "Auburn Tigers" also appears on the backs. Since the set is similar to a playing card set, it is arranged just like a card deck and checklisted below accordingly. In the checklist below C means Clubs, D means Diamonds, H means Hearts, S means Spades and JOK means Joker. Numbers are assigned to Aces (1), Jacks (11), Queens (12), and Kings (13). The jokers are unnumbered and listed at the end.

COMPLETE SET (54)	50.00	100.00
1C Ken Calleja	.75	2.00
1D James Owens FB	.75	2.00
1H Mac Lorendo	.75	2.00
1S Ralph(Shug) Jordan CO	3.00	6.00
2C Rick Neel	.75	2.00
2D Ted Smith QB	.75	2.00
2H Eddie Welch	.75	2.00
2S Mike Neel	.75	2.00
3C Larry Taylor	.75	2.00
3D Rett Davis	.75	2.00
3H Rusty Fuller	.75	2.00
3S Lee Gross	.75	2.00
4C Bruce Evans	.75	2.00
4D Rusty Deen	.75	2.00
4H Johnny Simmons	.75	2.00
4S Bill Newton	.75	2.00
5C Dave Beverly	1.25	3.00
5D Dave Lyon	.75	2.00
5H Mike Fuller	2.00	5.00
5S Bill Luka	.75	2.00
6C Ken Bernich	.75	2.00
6D Andy Steele	.75	2.00
6H Wade Whatley	.75	2.00
6S Bob Newton	1.25	3.00
7C Benny Sivley	1.00	2.50
7D Gardner Jett	1.00	2.50
7H Rob Spivey	1.00	2.50
7S Jay Casey	.75	2.00
8C David Langner	.75	2.00
8D Terry Henley	.75	2.00
8H Thomas Gossom	.75	2.00
8S Joe Tanory	.75	2.00
9C Chris Linderman	.75	2.00
9D Harry Unger	.75	2.00
9H Kenny Burks	.75	2.00
9S Sandy Cannon	.75	2.00
10C Roger Mitchell	.75	2.00
10D Jim McKinney	.75	2.00
10H Gaines Lanier	.75	2.00
10S Dave Beck	.75	2.00
11C Bob Farrior	.75	2.00
11D Miles Jones	.75	2.00
11H Tres Rogers	.75	2.00
11S David Hughes DE	.75	2.00
12C Sherman Moon	.75	2.00
12D Danny Sanspree	.75	2.00
12H Steve Taylor	.75	2.00
12S Randy Walls	.75	2.00
13C Steve Wilson LB	.75	2.00
13D Bobby Davis	.75	2.00
13H Hamlin Caldwell	.75	2.00
13S Dan Nugent	.75	2.00
JOK1 Joker	.75	2.00
JOK2 Joker	.75	2.00

1973 Auburn Playing Cards

This 54-card standard-size set was issued in a playing card deck box. The cards have rounded corners and the typical playing card finish. The fronts feature black-and-white posed photos of helmetless players in their uniforms. A white border surrounds each picture and contains the card number and suit designation in the upper left corner and again, but inverted, in the lower right. The player's name and hometown appear just beneath the photo. The white-bordered navy blue backs all have the Auburn "AU" logo in navy blue and orange and white outlines. The the year of issue, 1973, and the name "Auburn Tigers" also appears on the backs. Since the set is similar to a playing card set, it is arranged just like a card deck and checklisted below accordingly. In the checklist below C means Clubs, D means Diamonds, H means Hearts, S means Spades and JOK means Joker. Numbers are assigned to Aces (1), Jacks (11), Queens (12), and Kings (13). The jokers are unnumbered and listed at the end.

COMPLETE SET (54)	50.00	100.00
1C Ken Calleja	.75	2.00
1D Chris Wilson K	.75	2.00
1H Lee Hayley	.75	2.00
1S Ralph(Shug) Jordan CO	2.50	5.00
2C Rick Neel	.75	2.00
2D Johnny Sumner	.75	2.00
2H Mitzi Jackson	.75	2.00
2S Jim Pitts	.75	2.00
3C Steve Stanaland	.75	2.00
3D Rett Davis	.75	2.00
3H Rusty Fuller	.75	2.00
3S Lee Gross	.75	2.00
4C Bruce Evans	.75	2.00
4D Rusty Deen	.75	2.00
4H Liston Eddins	.75	2.00
4S Bill Newton	.75	2.00
5C Jimmy Sirmans	.75	2.00
5D Harry Ward	.75	2.00
5H Mike Fuller	1.25	3.00
5S Bill Luka	.75	2.00
6C Ken Bernich	.75	2.00
6D Andy Steele	.75	2.00
6H Wade Whatley	.75	2.00
6S Bob Newton	1.00	2.50
7C Benny Sivley	1.00	2.50
7D Rick Telhiard	1.00	2.50
7H Rob Spivey	1.00	2.50
7S David Williams OL	.75	2.00
8C David Langner	.75	2.00
8D Chuck Fletcher	.75	2.00
8H Thomas Gossom	.75	2.00
8S Holley Caldwell	.75	2.00
9C Chris Linderman	.75	2.00
9D Ed Butler	.75	2.00
9H Kenny Burks	.75	2.00
9S Mike Flynn	.75	2.00
10C Roger Mitchell	.75	2.00
10D Jim McKinney	.75	2.00
10H Gaines Lanier	.75	2.00
10S Carl Hubbard	.75	2.00
11C Bob Farrior	.75	2.00
11D Ronnie Jones	.75	2.00
11H Billy Woods	.75	2.00
11S David Hughes DE	.75	2.00
12C Sherman Moon	.75	2.00
12D Mike Gates	.75	2.00
12H Steve Taylor	.75	2.00
12S Randy Walls	.75	2.00
13C Roger Pruett	.75	2.00
13D Bobby Davis	.75	2.00
13H Hamlin Caldwell	.75	2.00
13S Dan Nugent	.75	2.00
JOK1 Joker	.75	2.00
JOK2 Joker	.75	2.00

1905 Bergman College Postcards

The 1905 J. Bergman postcard series includes various collegiate football teams printed by the Illustrated Post Card Company. Each card features a color art rendering of a generic college co-ed waving the school's pennant against a solid colored background. A copyright date is also included on the cardfront and the cardback is typical postcard style. We've listed the known postcards. Any additions to this list are appreciated.

1 Columbia	25.00	40.00
2 Cornell	25.00	40.00
3 Harvard	25.00	40.00
4 Pennsylvania	25.00	40.00
5 Princeton	25.00	40.00
6 Yale	25.00	40.00

1970 BYU Team Issue

These glossy black and white photos measure roughly 8" by 10" and feature members of the BYU football team. Each includes the school name spelled out "Brigham Young University, Provo Utah" below the photo along with a facsimile player signature on the image itself. The backs are blank. Any additions to this list are appreciated.

COMPLETE SET (4)	12.00	20.00
1 Golden Richards	5.00	8.00
2 Pete Van Valkenberg	3.00	5.00
3 Gordon Gravelle	3.00	5.00
4 Joe Lilginquist	3.00	5.00

1907 Christy College Series 7 Postcards

This postcard series features various schools. Each card, measuring roughly 3 1/2" by 5 3/8," includes an embossed artist's rendering of a woman fan with a football player seated at a table with the school's banner underneath. The copyright line reads "COPYRIGHT 1907 F. EARL CHRISTY" and the back features a standard postcard design. The title "College Series No. 7" is included on the cardback as well.

COMPLETE SET (8)	90.00	175.00
1 Chicago	15.00	25.00
2 Columbia	15.00	25.00
3 Cornell	15.00	25.00
4 Harvard	15.00	25.00
5 Michigan	18.00	30.00
6 Penn	15.00	25.00
7 Princeton	15.00	25.00
8 Yale	15.00	25.00

1907 Christy College Series 95 Postcards

Much like the Series 7 set, these postcards feature Ivy League schools. Each card, measuring roughly 3 1/2" by 5 3/8," includes an embossed artist's rendering of a woman fan with a football player sitting on top of a large image of a football with the school's banner being held by the woman fan. The copyright line on the front reads 'COPYRIGHT 1907 Julius Bien and Company' and a card number is printed on the front as well. The backs feature a standard postcard design along with the set name College Series 95.

COMPLETE SET (6)	75.00	125.00
950 Yale	15.00	25.00
951 Harvard	15.00	25.00
952 Columbia	15.00	25.00
953 Penn	15.00	25.00
954 Princeton	15.00	25.00
955 Cornell	15.00	25.00

1958 Cincinnati

These blankbacked cards were issued around 1958 and measure roughly 8 1/2" by 10 5/8." Each features one black and white photo of a University of Cincinnati football player surrounded by a thick red border with the player's name and position below the photo. The backs are blank and the cards were printed on thick white or gray card stock. It is likely that these were issued in more than one year. Any additions to this list are appreciated.

COMPLETE SET (4)	20.00	40.00
1 Ron Couch	5.00	12.00
2 Ed Denk	5.00	12.00
3 Gene Johnson	5.00	12.00
4 Dick Seomin	5.00	12.00

1966 Cincinnati

These oversized (roughly 8 1/2" by 10 1/2") cards were issued around 1966 and feature one black and white photo of a University of Cincinnati football player surrounded by a thick red border with just his name below the photo. The backs are blank and the cards were printed on glossy thick card stock. It is likely that they were issued over a period of years. Any additions to this list are appreciated.

COMPLETE SET (10)	50.00	100.00
1 Bob Amburgey	6.00	12.00
1 Jay Bachman	6.00	12.00
2 Tony Jackson	6.00	12.00
2 Milt Balkum	6.00	12.00
3 Ken Jordan	6.00	12.00
3 Bob Miller	6.00	12.00
4 Tom Macejko	6.00	12.00
4 Lloyd Pate	6.00	12.00
5 Ron Nelson	6.00	12.00
6 Ed Nemann	6.00	12.00

1969 Cincinnati

1 Joe Bardaro	6.00	12.00
2 Bob Bell Mike Miller	6.00	12.00
3 Dutch Foreman	6.00	12.00
4 Bob Merkich	6.00	12.00
5 Jim O'Brien	7.50	15.00
6 Jim Ousley	6.00	12.00
7 Benny Rhoads	6.00	12.00
8 Earl Willson	6.00	12.00

1970 Clemson Team Issue

These photos were issued by the school to promote the football program. Each measures roughly 8" by 10" and features a black and white image of a player. The player's name, position (initials) and school are printed below each photo and the backs are blank.

COMPLETE SET (23)	75.00	150.00
1 Ben Anderson	4.00	8.00
2 Tony Anderson P/DB	4.00	8.00
3 Tony Anderson E	4.00	8.00
4 John Bolubasz	4.00	8.00
5 Mike Buckner	4.00	8.00
6 Ralph Daniel	4.00	8.00
7 Heide Davis	4.00	8.00
8 Luke Deanhardt	4.00	8.00
9 Pete Galuska	4.00	8.00
10 Don Kelley	4.00	8.00
11 Tommy Kemdrick	4.00	8.00
12 Larry Lawson	4.00	8.00
13 Steve Lewter	4.00	8.00
14 John McMakin	4.00	8.00
15 Ken Pengitore	4.00	8.00
16 John Price	4.00	8.00
17 Marion Reeves	4.00	8.00
18 Tommy Richardson	4.00	8.00
19 Eddie Seigler	4.00	8.00
20 Jack Sokohl	4.00	8.00
21 Jim Sursavage	4.00	8.00
22 Dave Thompson	4.00	8.00
23 Ray Yauger	4.00	8.00

1904 College Captains and Teams Postcards

This set of postcards was issued in 1904. Each card features small black and white photos of two team captains that competed in a college football game that year. The two team's pennants (in school colors) are also included on the cardfronts. Any additions to the below list are appreciated.

1 Bush/Heston	50.00	100.00
2 Speik/Heston	50.00	100.00
3 Schwinn/Knibbs	35.00	60.00

1905 College Captains and Teams Postcards

This set of postcards was issued in 1905. Each card features small black and white photos of two team captains that competed in a college football game that year. The two team's pennants (in one school color) are also included on the cardfronts along with a blank box score to be filled out upon completion of the game. Any additions to the below list are appreciated.

1 Russ/Main	30.00	50.00
2 Vanderbloom/Mark Catlin	30.00	50.00
3 Vanderbloom/F.Norcross	30.00	50.00
4 M.Catlin/F.Norcross	30.00	50.00

1906 College Captains and Teams Postcards

This set of postcards was issued in 1906. Each card features small black and white photos of two team captains that competed in a college game that year. The two team's pennants are also included on the cardfronts along with a blank box score to be filled out upon completion of the game. Any additions to the below list are appreciated.

1 Schwartz/Glaze 40.00 80.00
2 Lincoln/Bradford 60.00 100.00
3 Ohio St. vs. Ohio Medical 60.00 100.00
James Lincoln (OSU)
William Cann (OMU)

1907 College Captains and Teams Postcards

This set of postcards was issued in 1907 and features small black and white photos of two team captains that competed in a college football game that year. The player's images and date of the game are included on the fronts. The Michigan-Wabash card features the player images within a black and white ink drawing outline of a football while the others includes color pennants for both teams. The cardbacks feature a typical postcard design.

1 P.Magoffin/Gipe 40.00 80.00
2 Berkheiser/Callicrate 40.00 80.00
3 DeTray/Lyles 40.00 80.00

1908 College Captains and Teams Postcards

This set of postcards was issued in 1908. Each card features small black and white photos of two team captains that competed in a college game that year. The two team's pennants are also included on the cardfronts with some also including a blank box score to be filled out upon completion of the game. Any additions to the below list are appreciated.

1 Purdue vs. DePauw 35.00 60.00
(October 31, 1908)
A.E. Holloway (Purdue)
Jackson (DePauw)
2 Purdue vs. Indiana 35.00 60.00
(November 21, 1908)
A.E. Holloway (Purdue)
Scott Paddock (Indiana)
3 Oregon vs. Oregon State 35.00 60.00
(Nov. 21, 1908)
Fred Moullen (Oregon)
Carl Wolff (Oregon State)

1910 College Captains and Teams Postcards

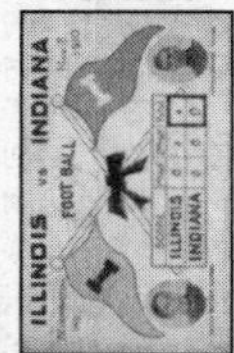

These postcards were issued in 1910 and feature small black and white photos of two team captains that competed in a college game that year. The two team's pennants are also included on the cardfronts with some also including a blank box score to be filled out upon completion of the game. Any additions to the below list are appreciated.

1 Illinois vs. Indiana/(November 5, 1910)/Butzer (Illinois)/Berndt (Indian 30.00 50.00

1911 College Captains and Teams Postcards

These postcards were issued in 1911 and feature small black and white photos of two team captains that competed in a college game that year. The two team's pennants are also included on the cardfronts with some also including a blank box score to be filled out upon completion of the game. Any additions to the below list are appreciated.

1 Purdue vs. Indiana 30.00 50.00
(November 25, 1911)
Tavey (Purdue)
Gill (Indiana)

1912 College Captains and Teams Postcards

These postcards were issued in 1912 and feature small black and white photos of two team captains that competed in a college game that year. The two team's pennants are also included on the cardfronts with some also including a blank box score to be filled out upon completion of the game. Any additions to the below list are appreciated.

1 Purdue vs. Illinois 30.00 50.00
(November 9, 1912)
Hutchison (Purdue)
Woolston (Illinois)

1933 College Captains

These postcard sized cards feature a black and white photo on the fronts with a blank cardback. They were thought to have been released in 1933 as arcade trading cards. Below the photo is a short write-up on the featured college football captain with the college name printed above the photo. The unnumbered cards are listed below alphabetically.

COMPLETE SET (10) 150.00 250.00
1 Gil Berry 15.00 30.00
2 Raymond Brown 20.00 35.00
3 Walter Haas 20.00 35.00
4 Lew Hinchman 15.00 30.00
5 Paul Host 15.00 30.00
6 Gregory Kabat 15.00 30.00
7 John Oehler 15.00 30.00
8 Pug Rentner 20.00 35.00
9 Stanley Sokolis 15.00 30.00
10 Ivan Williamson 15.00 30.00

1950 C.O.P. Betsy Ross

Subtitled C.O.P.'s Player of the Week, this seven-card set features outstanding players from College of the Pacific. The date of the set is fixed by the Eddie LeBaron card, which listed him as a senior. The oversized cards measure approximately 5" by 7" and are printed on thin paper stock. The fronts feature black-and-white posed action shots that are tilted slightly to the left and have rounded corners. The top stripe carries brief biographical information and career highlights. The bottom stripe notes that these cards were distributed "as a public service by your neighborhood Grocer and Betsy Ross Bread." The bread company's logo is located at the lower right corner. Although LeBaron is the most well known player in the set, he appears to be more plentiful than the others. Additional cards may belong to this set. The backs are blank and the unnumbered cards are listed below in alphabetical order.

COMPLETE SET (7) 400.00 800.00
1 Don Campora 50.00 100.00
2 Don Hardey 50.00 100.00
3 Robert Klein 25.00 60.00
4 Eddie LeBaron 40.00 75.00
5 Eddie Macon 50.00 100.00
6 Walter Polenske SP 175.00 300.00
7 John Rohde 50.00 100.00

1974 Colorado Playing Cards

This 54-card set of playing cards measures 2 1/4" by 3 1/2". The cardbacks feature the Colorado Buffaloes logo against a black background. The cardfronts feature a black and white player photo with the player's name below. The cards are checklisted below in playing card order by suit (C for Clubs, D for Diamonds, H for Hearts, S for Spades, and JOK for the Jokers) and numbers are assigned to Aces (1), Jacks (11), Queens (12), and Kings (13).

COMPELTE SET (54) 90.00 150.00
1C Doug Payton 1.25 3.00
1D Buck Arnold 1.25 3.00
1H Larry Williams 1.25 3.00
1S Bill Mallory CO 1.25 3.00
2C Whitney Paul 1.25 3.00
2D Pete Brock 1.25 3.00
2H Dave Williams 1.25 3.00
2S Eddie Crowder AD 1.25 3.00
3C Vic Odegard 1.25 3.00
3D Gary Campbell 1.25 3.00
3H Leon White 1.50 4.00
3S Tom Batta Asst.CO 1.25 3.00
4C Emery Moorehead 1.50 4.00
4D Dennis Cimmino 1.25 3.00
4H Billy Waddy 2.00 5.00
4S George Belu COORD 1.25 3.00
5C Mike Metoyer 1.25 3.00
5D Clyde Crutchmer 1.25 3.00
5H Jeff Turcotte 1.25 3.00
5S Ron Corradini Asst.CO 1.25 3.00
6C Jerry Martinez 1.25 3.00
6D Bill Donnell 1.25 3.00
6H Tom Tesone 1.25 3.00
6S Gary Durchik Asst.CO 1.25 3.00
7C David Logan 1.25 3.00
7D Rick Ellwood 1.25 3.00
7H Rick Stearns 1.25 3.00
7S Floyd Keith Asst.CO 1.25 3.00
8C Tom Likovich 1.25 3.00
8D Jeff Geiser 1.25 3.00
8H Mike Spivey 1.25 3.00
8S Bob Reublin COORD 1.25 3.00
9C Terry Kunz 1.25 3.00
9D Harvey Goodman 1.25 3.00
9H Bob Simpson 1.25 3.00
9S Dan Stavely Asst.DIR 1.25 3.00
10C Jeff Kensinger 1.25 3.00
10D Steve Haggerty 1.25 3.00
10H Ed Shoen 1.25 3.00
10S Les Steckel Asst.CO 2.00 5.00
11C Jim Kelleher 1.25 3.00
11D Steve Hakes 1.25 3.00
11H Tom Perry 1.25 3.00
11S Milan Vooletich Asst.CO 1.25 3.00
12C Melvin Johnson 1.25 3.00
12D Brad Harris 1.25 3.00
12H Rod Perry 1.50 4.00
12S Dwight Wallace Asst.CO 1.25 3.00
13C Bobby Hunt 1.25 3.00
13D Don Hasselbeck 1.50 4.00
13H Horace Perkins 1.25 3.00
13S Blake Arnold 1.25 3.00
JOK1 Team Logo Black 1.25 3.00
JOK2 Team Logo Red 1.25 3.00

1973 Colorado State Schedules

The 1973 Colorado State football set consists of eight cards, measuring approximately 2 1/2" by 3 3/4". The set was sponsored by Poudre Valley Dairy Foods. The fronts display green-tinted posed action shots with rounded corners and green borders. The words "1973 CSU Football" appear in the top border while the player's name and position are printed in the bottom border. The horizontal backs present the 1973 football schedule. Reportedly, the Stuebbe and Simpson cards are more difficult to obtain because they were given out to the public before hobbyists began to collect the set. Best known among the players is Willie Miller, who played for the Los Angeles Rams. The cards are unnumbered and checklisted below in alphabetical order.

COMPLETE SET (8) 45.00 90.00
1 Wes Cerveny 5.00 10.00
2 Mark Driscoll 5.00 10.00
3 Jimmie Kennedy 5.00 10.00
4 Greg Kuhn 5.00 10.00
5 Willie Miller 10.00 20.00
6 Al Simpson SP 7.50 15.00
7 Jan Stuebbe SP 7.50 15.00
8 Tom Wallace 5.00 10.00

1974 Colorado State Schedules

The 1974 Colorado State football set reportedly consists of just one card measuring roughly 2 1/2" by 3 3/4". Like the 1973 issue, the card was sponsored by Poudre Valley Dairy Foods. The words "1974 CSU Football" appear in the top border while the coach's name printed in the bottom border. The horizontal cardback presents the 1974 football schedule.

1 Sark Arslanian CO 2.50 5.00

1916 Cornell Postcards

These black and white Cornell Postcards were issued around 1916 by the University. The cards feature a standard postcard style back with the player's last name printed near his photo on the front. Any additions or information on the checklist below would be appreciated.

1 Charles Barrett 30.00 50.00
2 Fritz Shiverick 30.00 50.00

1972 Davidson College Team Issue

These photos were issued by the school to promote the football program. Each measures roughly 8" by 10" and features two players with a black and white image for each player. The school name appears at the top and the player's name is included below. The backs are blank.

COMPLETE SET (10) 30.00 60.00
1 John Barbee 4.00 8.00
Greg Sikes
2 Jim Ellison 4.00 8.00
Randy Parker
3 Bill Garrett 4.00 8.00
Mike Sikes
4 Bill Nicklas 4.00 8.00
Larry Spears
5 Robert Norris 4.00 8.00
Rick Kemmerlin
6 Johnny Ribet 4.00 8.00
Carl Rizzo
7 Scotty Shipp 4.00 8.00
Gary Coulter
8 Scotty Shipp 4.00 8.00
Robert Elliott
9 Walt Walker 4.00 8.00
John Webel
10 Terry Woodlief 4.00 8.00
Joe Poteat

1905 Dominoe Postcards

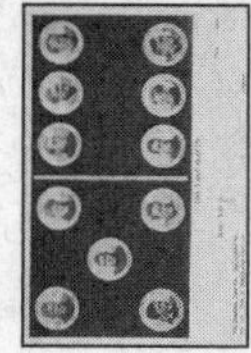

These postcards were issued in 1905 and include small photos of the starting eleven of the featured school. Each was produced by Boston Postcard Company in a typical postcard style on the backs and a dominoe layout on the fronts. Most of the postcards include a space below the images for writing in the score of a game and the date of the game while some include a schedule below the player photos. The Ivy League schools are the easiest to find with the lower level schools generally the most difficult to locate. We've listed the known cards below - any additions to this list are appreciated.

1 Brown 20.00 35.00
2 Carlisle 40.00 80.00
3 Dartmouth 20.00 35.00
4 Dean Academy 15.00 30.00
5 Harvard 20.00 35.00
6 Penn Captain/Harvard Captain 20.00 35.00
7 Rindge Training School 15.00 30.00
8 Somerville High School 25.00 50.00
9 Yale 20.00 35.00

1976 Duke Team Issue

These photos were issued by the school to promote the football program. Each measures roughly 5" by 8" and features a black and white image of a player with the player's name, position, and school name below each photo. The backs are blank. It is likely that these photos were originally issued as two player panels.

COMPLETE SET (16) 40.00 80.00
1 Mike Barney 3.00 6.00
2 Billy Bryan 3.00 6.00
3 Ernie Clark 3.00 6.00
4 Bob Corbett 3.00 6.00
5 Dave Dusek 3.00 6.00
6 Vince Fusco 3.00 6.00
7 Art Gore 3.00 6.00
8 Jeff Green 3.00 6.00
9 Larry Martinez 3.00 6.00
10 Dave Meier 3.00 6.00
11 Gary Pellom 3.00 6.00
12 Bob Pruitt 3.00 6.00
13 Troy Slade 3.00 6.00
14 Hal Spears 3.00 6.00
15 Larry Upshaw 3.00 6.00
16 Chuck Williamson 3.00 6.00

1973 Florida Playing Cards

This set was issued in a playing card deck box. The cards have rounded corners and the typical playing card format. The fronts feature black-and-white posed photos of helmetless players in their uniforms. A white border surrounds each picture and contains the card number and suit designation in the upper left corner and again, but inverted, in the lower right. The player's name and position initials appear just beneath the photo. The orange backs all feature the "Fighting Gators" logo. The cards were also produced with a blue cardback variation. The year of issue, 1973, is included on the schedule card. Since the set is similar to a playing card set, it is arranged just like a card deck and checklisted below accordingly. In the checklist below C means Clubs, D means Diamonds, H means Hearts, S means Spades and JK means Joker. Numbers are assigned to Aces (1), Jacks (11), Queens (12), and Kings (13). The jokers are unnumbered and listed at the end.

COMPLETE SET (54)	75.00	135.00
1C Kris Anderson	1.00	2.50
1D David Bowden	1.00	2.50
1H Nat Moore	5.00	10.00
1S Doug Dickey CO	1.50	3.00
2C Gary Padgett	1.00	2.50
2D Tom Dolfi	1.00	2.50
2H Sammy Green	1.00	2.50
2S Scott Nugent	1.00	2.50
3C Joel Parker	1.00	2.50
3D Don Gaffney	1.00	2.50
3H Andy Summers	1.00	2.50
3S Joe Wunderly	1.00	2.50
4C George Nicholas	1.00	2.50
4D Hank Foldberg	2.50	5.00
4H Jimmy DuBose	1.00	2.50
4S David Starkey	1.00	2.50
5C Buster Morrison	1.00	2.50
5D Mike Williams	1.00	2.50
5H David Hitchcock	1.00	2.50
5S Glenn Cameron	1.00	2.50
6C Mike Moore DE	1.00	2.50
6D Chan Gailey	3.00	6.00
6H John Williams	1.00	2.50
6S Eddie Sirmons	1.00	2.50
7C Roy Mallory	1.00	2.50
7D Mike Smith DE	1.00	2.50
7H Glenn Sever	1.00	2.50
7S Ward Eastman	1.00	2.50
8C Lee McGriff	1.00	2.50
8D Carey Geiger	1.00	2.50
8H Andy Wade	1.00	2.50
8S Robbie Davis	1.00	2.50
9C Chris McCoun	1.00	2.50
9D Preston Kendrick	1.00	2.50
9H Jim Revels	1.00	2.50
9S Robby Ball	1.00	2.50
10C Burton Lawless	2.50	5.00
10D Clint Griffith	1.00	2.50
10H Alvin Butler	2.50	5.00
10S Thom Clifford	1.00	2.50
11C Jimbo Kynes	1.00	2.50
11D Al Darby	1.00	2.50
11H Hollis Boardman	1.00	2.50
11S Ricky Browne	1.00	2.50
12C Randy Talbot	1.00	2.50
12D Mike Stanfield	1.00	2.50
12H Paul Parker	1.00	2.50
12S John Lacer	1.00	2.50
13C Tyson Sever	1.00	2.50
13D Wayne Fields	1.00	2.50
13H Vince Kendrick	1.00	2.50
13S Ralph Ortega	1.00	2.50
J1 Schedule Card	1.00	2.50
J2 Joker	1.00	2.50

1973 Harvard Team Sheets

These photos were issued by the school to promote the football program. Each measures roughly 8" by 10" and features ten black and white images of players with the school name and year appearing at the top. The player's name, position, and brief vital stats is printed below each photo. The backs are blank.

1 Joe Restic (HC)	4.00	8.00
Dave Pierre		
Jim Stoeckel		
Milt Holt		
Jeff Bone		
Mitch Berger		
S		

1921 Holy Cross

This set was issued around 1922 and features cards of coaches and team captains for various Holy Cross University sports. The six cards measrue roughly 2 1/2" by 3 3/4" and were issued inside a "wrap-around" style folder that included a photo of the football team. Each card is blankbacked and was printed on thick cream colored stock.

COMPLETE SET (7)	100.00	200.00
2 Gildea FB	12.50	25.00
6 Cleo O'Donnell CO FB	10.00	20.00
7 Football Team Folder	7.50	15.00

1909-21 Illinois Postcards

A large number of postcards were issued over a period of years between 1910-1921 by Illinois University. Most of them feature campus buildings or scenes, while others feature football players or game action photography. We've cataloged just the postcards below that feature individual football players, team photos, coaches, and game action scenes that are identifiable. The cards feature a standard postcard style back with "U of I Student Life Series, by Strauch Photo Craft House" printed on the backs of some, but not all of the cards. The fronts are printed in sepia or black-and-white with the player's last name typically printed near the photo. Some also include extra data such as the year or "captain." The photographer's name "Lloyde, Aristo, or Strauch" is sometimes printed on the fronts as well. Any additions or information on the checklist below would be appreciated.

1 L.S. Bernstein	30.00	50.00
2 Glenn Butzer	30.00	50.00
3 Arthur Hall CO	30.00	50.00
4 Ralph Jones CO	40.00	75.00
5 Reynold Kraft	30.00	50.00
6 Justa Lindgren CO	30.00	50.00
7 Bart Macomber	75.00	125.00
8 Bart Macomber Capt. Bart	50.00	80.00
9 J.R. Merriman	30.00	50.00
10 Albert Mohr	30.00	50.00
11 James Richards	30.00	50.00
12 Chester Roberts	30.00	50.00
13 Enos Rowe	30.00	50.00
14 Elmer Rundquist ERR	30.00	50.00
15 Otto Seiler	30.00	50.00
16 Dutch Sternaman	125.00	200.00
17 J.O. Tupper	30.00	50.00
18 Forest Van Hook Pom Sinnock	30.00	50.00
19 John Weiss	30.00	50.00
20 Bob Zuppke CO	75.00	125.00
21 1909 Team Photo	35.00	60.00
22 1910 Team Photo	35.00	60.00
23 1911 Team Photo	35.00	60.00
24 1912 Team Photo (1912 Varsity, U of I)	35.00	60.00
25 1912 Team Photo ('12 Class team)	30.00	50.00
26 1916 Team Photo	60.00	100.00
27 Illinois 6 vs. Indiana 5 (1909)	25.00	40.00
28 Chicago 14 vs. Illinois 8 (1909)	25.00	40.00
29 Illinois 23 vs. Millikin 0 (1909)	25.00	40.00
30 Illinois 3 vs. Chicago 0, '10	25.00	40.00
31 Illinois 3 vs. Chicago 0 (1910)	25.00	40.00
32 Illinois 3 vs. Chicago 0, Oct.15, 1910	25.00	40.00
33 Chicago 0 vs. Illinois 3, Oct.15, 1910	25.00	40.00
34 Illinois 3 vs. Chicago 0, Oct.15, 1910	25.00	40.00
35 Illinois 29 vs. Drake 0, Oct.8, 1910	25.00	40.00
36 Illinois 3 vs. Indiana 0, Nov.5, 1910	25.00	40.00
37 Illinois 9 vs. St. Louis 0, Oct. 14, 1911	25.00	40.00
38 Illinois 12 vs. Purdue 3, Nov. 4, 1911	25.00	40.00
39 Illinois 12 vs. Purdue 3, Nov. 4, 1911	25.00	40.00
40 Illinois 9 vs. Purdue 9, Nov. 9, 1912	25.00	40.00
41 Kentucky 0 vs. Illinois 21, 1913	25.00	40.00
42 Missouri 7 vs. Illinois 25, 1913	25.00	40.00
43 Illinois 7 vs. Chicago 28, 1913	25.00	40.00
44 Illinois 37 vs. Ohio St. 0 Oct. 17, 1914 (passing play)	25.00	40.00
45 Illinois 37 vs. CBC 0 (1914), Touchdown (runner scoring at goal line)	25.00	40.00
46 Illinois 33 vs. Northwestern 0 Oct. 24, 1914 (close-up action at line)	25.00	40.00
47 Illinois 21 vs. Chicago 7, Homecoming Nov.14 (1914)	25.00	40.00
48 Illinois 17 vs. Wisconsin 9, Nov. 21, 1914	25.00	40.00
49 Illinois 6 vs. Minnesota 6, Homecoming (1915)	25.00	40.00
50 Illinois 0 vs. Purdue 0, Nov. 15, 1915	25.00	40.00
51 Illinois 17 vs. Wisconsin 3, 1915	25.00	40.00
52 Illinois 17 vs. Wisconsin 3, 1915	25.00	40.00
53 Illinois 17 vs. Wisconsin 3 (1915)	25.00	40.00
54 Illinois vs. Purdue, '16	25.00	40.00
55 Illinois 0 vs. Wisconsin 20 (1921)	25.00	40.00

1974 Illinois Team Sheets

These photos were issued by the school to promote the football program. Each measures roughly 8 by 10 and features eight black and white images of players with the school name appearing at the top. The backs are blank.

1 Bob Blackman CO	4.00	8.00
Lonnie Perrin		
Jim Kopatz		
Tracy Campbell		
Tom Hicks		
Mike McCr		
2 Mark Petersen	4.00	8.00
Bruce Beaman		
Steve Greene		
Ty McMillin		
Jim Phillips		
Revie Sore		

1974 Indiana Team Sheets

These photos were issued by the school to promote the football program. Each measures roughly 8" by 10" and features eight black and white images of players with the school name appearing at the top. The backs are blank.

1 Larry Atkinson	4.00	10.00
Rod Lawson		
Mark Deming		
Jim Shuck		
Willie Jones		
Bob Kramer		
Tom		
2 Lee Corso CO	4.00	10.00
Trent Smock		
Mike Flanagan		
Dennis Cremeens		
Courtney Snyder		
Larr		

1971 Iowa Team Photos

This 32-player University of Iowa photo set was issued as four sheets measuring approximately 8" by 10" featuring eight black and white player portraits. The backs are blank. We have arranged the photos in order alphabetically by the player in the upper left hand corner.

COMPLETE SET (4)	15.00	30.00
1 Sheet 1	5.00	10.00
2 Sheet 2	3.50	7.00
3 Sheet 3	3.50	7.00
4 Sheet 4	3.50	7.00

1974 Iowa Team Shee

These photos were issued by the school to promote the football program. Each measures roughly 8" by 10" and features eight black and white images of players with the school name appearing at the top. The backs are blank.

1 Bob Commings CO	4.00	8.00
Rodney Wellington		
Andre Jackson		
Rick Penney		
Butch Caldwell		
2 Lester Washington	4.00	8.00
Tyrone Dye		
Jim Jensen		
David Bryant		
Mark Fetter		
Lynn Heil		

1907 Gordon Ivy League Postcards

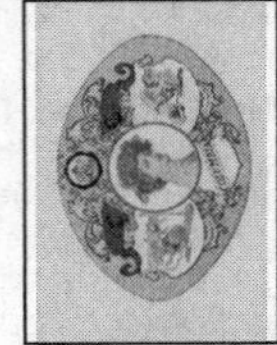

This postcard series features schools of the Ivy League. Each card (3 5/8" by 5 1/2") includes an artist's rendering of a woman's face surrounded by two football action scenes within the outline of a football. The copyright line reads "1907 P.Gordon" and the back features a standard postcard design. The title "No. 5100 Football Series 8 Subjects" is included on the cardback as well.

COMPLETE SET (8)	125.00	200.00
1 Brown	15.00	25.00
2 Columbia	15.00	25.00
3 Cornell	15.00	25.00
4 Dartmouth	15.00	25.00
5 Harvard	18.00	30.00
6 Pennsylvania	15.00	25.00
7 Princeton	18.00	30.00
8 Yale	18.00	30.00

1912 Lafayette Post Cards

1 Ross Boas	35.00	60.00
2 Edgar Furry	35.00	60.00
3 Bill Gross	35.00	60.00
4 Arthur Hammond	35.00	60.00
5 Ernest Roth	35.00	60.00

1924 Lafayette

This blankbacked set of cards was issued by the team and printed on thin cardboard stock with sepia toned player images. The cards measure roughly 2 1/2" by 4 1/4" and include only the player's last name below the photo. They were released as a complete set in a yellow envelope presumably at souvenir stands at home games. The year and team "1924 Lafayette" is printed on the envelope. Several players in the set went on to play in the NFL including Charlie Berry and Jack Ernst who both were major contributors to the Pottsville Maroons disputed NFL championship of 1925.

COMPLETE SET (20)	2,500.00	4,000.00
1 Charlie Berry	250.00	400.00
2 Don Booz	100.00	200.00
3 William Brown	100.00	200.00
4 John Budd	100.00	200.00
5 Frank Chicknoski	100.00	200.00
6 Doug Crate	100.00	200.00
7 Robert Duffy	100.00	200.00
8 Jack Ernst	125.00	250.00
9 Adrian Ford	100.00	200.00
10 Louis Gebhard UER	100.00	200.00
11 Cullen Gourley Asst.CO	100.00	200.00
12 Charles Grantier	100.00	200.00
13 William Highberger	100.00	200.00
14 Frank Kirkleski	100.00	200.00
15 Daniel Lyons	100.00	200.00
16 Herb McCracken CO	100.00	200.00
17 Jim McGarvey	100.00	200.00
18 Bob Millman	100.00	200.00
19 Sheldon Pollock	100.00	200.00
20 Weldon Asst.CO	100.00	200.00

1969 Maryland Team Sheets

These six sheets measure approximately 8" by 10". The fronts feature two rows of four black-and-white player portraits each. The player's name is printed under the photo. The backs are blank. The sheets are unnumbered and checklisted below in alphabetical order according to the first player (or coach) listed.

COMPLETE SET (6)	25.00	50.00
1 Bill Backus	4.00	10.00
2 Bill Bell CO	4.00	10.00
3 Pat Burke	4.00	10.00
4 Steve Ciambor	4.00	10.00
5 Bob Colbert	4.00	10.00
6 Paul Fitzpatrick	4.00	10.00

1905 Michigan Postcards

This postcard set features members of the University of Michigan football team. Each features a black and white player photo (head and shoulders pose) on the front along with just the player's last name. The fronts feature a white border below the image in which to write a note. The cardbacks are printed in a generic postcard style with no manufacturer's identification.

1 John Curtis	40.00	80.00
2 Tom Hammond	40.00	80.00
4 Fred Norcross	40.00	80.00
5 Germany Schultz	100.00	175.00
6 Fielding Yost CO	125.00	200.00

1907 Michigan Dietsche Postcards

This set features members of the University of Michigan football team on postcard back cards. The ACC catalog designation for this set is PC765-3. Each card features a black and white player photo on front and a postcard back complete with a short player write-up. The A.C. Dietsche copyright line also appears on the back.

COMPLETE SET (15)	1,200.00	1,800.00
1 Dave Allerdice	75.00	125.00
2 William Casey	75.00	125.00
3 William Embs	75.00	125.00
4 Keene Fitzpatrick TR	75.00	125.00
5 Red Flanagan	75.00	125.00
6 Walter Graham	75.00	125.00
7 Harry Hammond	75.00	125.00
8 John Loell	75.00	125.00
9 Paul Magoffin	75.00	125.00
10 James Joy Miller	75.00	125.00
11 Walter Rheinschild	75.00	125.00
12 Mason Rumney	75.00	125.00
13 Adolph (Germany) Schultz	150.00	250.00
14 William Wasmund	75.00	125.00
15 Fielding Yost CO	175.00	300.00

1908 Michigan White Postcards

This postcard set features members of the University of Michigan football team. Most feature a black and white studio photo on the front along with just the player's last name while others feature an action photo with a short caption. The cardbacks are printed in a generic postcard style along with the manufacturer's identification: White Post Card Co., Ann Arbor, Mich.

1 William Casey	40.00	75.00
2 Prentiss Douglas	40.00	75.00
3 John Loell	40.00	75.00
4 Paul Magoffin	40.00	75.00
5 Adolph (Germany) Schultz	100.00	175.00
6 William Wasmund	40.00	75.00
7 William Wasmund ACT	35.00	60.00

1910 Michigan Longman Postcards

1 William Edmunds	40.00	75.00
2 George Lawton	40.00	75.00
3 Joe Magidsohn	125.00	200.00
4 Neil McMillan	40.00	75.00
5 Curtis Redden	40.00	75.00
6 Stan Wells	40.00	75.00

1913 Michigan Hoppe Postcards

This postcard set features members of the University of Michigan football team. Each features a black and white photo of the player on the field with just the player's last name and photographer's name on the front. The cardbacks are printed in a generic postcard style along with the manufacturer's identification: O.P. Hoppe, 619 E. Liberty St., Ann Arbor, Mich.

1 Capt. Conklin	30.00	60.00
2 Pontius	30.00	60.00
3 Craig	30.00	60.00
4 Harrington	30.00	60.00

1951 Michigan Team Issue

This set of photos was issued in its own envelope and presumaby mailed out to fans. Each photo is blankbacked, black and white and measures roughly 6 1/2" by 9." The player's name is printed in script on the fronts and each has a thin white border on all four sides.

COMPLETE SET (17)	200.00	350.00
1 Harry Allis	12.00	20.00
2 Art Dunne	12.00	20.00
3 John Hess	12.00	20.00
4 David Hill	12.00	20.00
5 Gene Hinton	12.00	20.00
6 Frank Howell	12.00	20.00
7 Tom Johnson	15.00	25.00
8 Tom Kelsey	12.00	20.00
9 Leo Koceski	12.00	20.00
10 Wayne Melchiori	12.00	20.00
11 Terry Nuff	12.00	20.00
12 Bill Ohlenroth	12.00	20.00
13 Bill Putich	15.00	25.00
14 Clyde Reeme	12.00	20.00
15 Robert Timm	12.00	20.00
16 Ted Topor	15.00	25.00
17 James Wolter	12.00	20.00

1977 Michigan Postcards

Produced by Stommen Enterprises, this 21-card postcard size (approximately 3 1/2" by 5 1/2") set features the 1977 Michigan Wolverines. Bordered in blue, the fronts divide into three registers. The top register is pale yellow and carries "Michigan" in block lettering. The middle register displays a color posed photo of the player in uniform holding his helmet. The bottom register is pale yellow and has the player's name, position, and a drawing of the mascot, all in blue. The horizontal backs are divided down the middle by two thin bluish-purple stripes, and Michigan's 1977 schedule appears in the same color ink on the upper left. Three cards, those of Giesler, Stephenson, and Szara, have an additional feature on their backs, an order blank printed on the right side. The order blank speaks of the "entire set of 18" and goes on to state "also available at the gates before and after the games." It appears that these three cards may have been produced or distributed later than the other eighteen.

COMPLETE SET (21)	15.00	30.00
1 John Anderson	.60	1.50
2 Russell Davis	.60	1.50
3 Mark Donahue	.50	1.25
4 Walt Downing	.50	1.25
5 Bill Dufek	.60	1.50
6 Jon Giesler SP	1.25	2.50
7 Steve Graves	.50	1.25
8 Curtis Greer	.75	2.00
9 Dwight Hicks	1.25	3.00
10 Derek Howard	.50	1.25
11 Harlan Huckleby	1.00	2.50
12 Gene Johnson TE	.50	1.25
13 Dale Keitz	.50	1.25
14 Mike Kenn	1.00	2.50
15 Rick Leach	1.50	4.00
16 Mark Schmerge	.50	1.25
17 Ron Simpkins	.60	1.50
18 Curt Stephenson SP	1.25	2.50
19 Gerry Szara SP	1.25	2.50
20 Rick White	.50	1.25
21 Gregg Willner	.50	1.25

1977 Michigan Schedules

These team schedules measure roughly 3 3/8" by 5 3/8" and include a color image of the featured player. Each unnumbered card includes a 1977 Michigan schedule on the back.

COMPLETE SET (4)	10.00	20.00
1 John Anderson	2.50	5.00
2 Walt Downing	2.50	5.00
3 Harlan Huckleby	2.50	5.00
4 Dwight Hicks	4.00	8.00

1974 Michigan State Team Sheets

These photos were issued by the school to promote the football program. Each measures roughly 8" by 10" and features eight black and white images of players with the school name appearing at the top. The backs are blank.

1 Mike Hurd	4.00	8.00
Tyrone Willingham		
Tom Hannon		
Tyrone Wilson		
Rich Baes		
Mike Duda		
Ch		
2 Denny Stolz CO	4.00	8.00
Jim Taubert		
Terry McClowry		
Charles Baggett		
Clarence Bullock		

1973 Minnesota Team Issue

These photos were issued by the school to promote the football program. Each measures roughly 8" by 10" and features a black and white image of a player. The backs are blank or sometimes can be found with a typed player identification. Otherwise no player identification is included.

COMPLETE SET (23)	75.00	125.00
1 George Adzick	3.00	6.00
2 Tim Alderson	3.00	6.00
3 Ollie Bakken	3.00	6.00
4 Doug Beaudoin	3.00	6.00
5 Keith Fahnkorst	3.00	6.00
6 Dale Hagland	3.00	6.00
7 Matt Herkenhoff	3.00	6.00
8 Michael Hunt	3.00	6.00
9 Mike Jones	3.00	6.00
10 Doug Kingsriter	3.00	6.00
11 Tom Macleod	3.00	6.00
12 Art Meadowcroft	3.00	6.00
13 Jeff Morrow	3.00	6.00
14 Steve Neils	3.00	6.00
15 J. Dexter Pride	3.00	6.00
16 Jim Ronan	3.00	6.00
17 Keith Simons	3.00	6.00
18 Dave Simonson	3.00	6.00
19 Mark Slater	3.00	6.00
20 Steve Stewart	3.00	6.00
21 Stan Sytsma	3.00	6.00
22 Rick Upchurch	6.00	12.00
23 Mike White	3.00	6.00

1974 Minnesota Team Sheets

These photos were issued by the school to promote the football program. Each measures roughly 8" by 10" and features eight black and white images of players with the school name appearing at the top. The backs are blank.

1 Dan Christensen	5.00	10.00
Orville Gilmore		
Ollie Bakken		
John Jones		
Steve Goldberg		
Greg		
2 Cal Stoll CO	5.00	10.00
Paul Giel AD		
Rick Upchurch		
Doug Beaudoin		
Keith Simons		
Tony Dun		

1907 Missouri Postcards

These black and white photo Missouri Postcards were issued in 1907 by the University Co-Operative Store. The cards feature a postcard style back with a brief write-up on the player and closely resemble the 1907 Michigan Dietsche Postcard issue. Just the player's last name or nickname is included on the cardfronts.

1 Aubrey Alexander	30.00	50.00
2 William Carothers	30.00	50.00
3 William Deatherage	30.00	50.00
4 William Driver	30.00	50.00
5 Dorcet Tubby Graves	30.00	50.00
6 William Jackson	30.00	50.00
7 Edwin Miller	30.00	50.00
8 Bill Monilaw CO	30.00	50.00
9 James Patrick Nixon	30.00	50.00
10 Carl Ristine	30.00	50.00
11 Prewett Roberts	30.00	50.00
12 H.K. Rutherford	30.00	50.00
13 Melverne Sigler	30.00	50.00
14 F.L. Williams	30.00	50.00
16 Team Photo	30.00	50.00

1909 Missouri Postcards

These black and white Missouri Postcards were issued in 1909. The cards feature a postcard style back with the player's name and weight printed on the front along with his photo. Any additions or information on the checklist below would be appreciated.

1 Aubrey Alexander	25.00	40.00
2 James Bluck	25.00	40.00
3 John Clare	25.00	40.00
4 Henry Crain	25.00	40.00
5 William Deatherage	25.00	40.00
6 H.S. Gove	25.00	40.00
7 Theodore D. Hackney	25.00	40.00
8 Eugene Hall	25.00	40.00
9 Arthur Idler	25.00	40.00
10 Warren Roberts	25.00	40.00
11 William Roper CO	25.00	40.00
12 L.E. Thatcher	25.00	40.00
13 Allen Wilder	25.00	40.00

1913 Missouri Postcards

These black and white Missouri football photo postcards were issued in 1913 by the University. The cards feature a postcard style back and often include a mention of the photographer: Volney McFadden, Student Photographer, Columbia, Mo. on the back or Aristo on the front. The player's last name is printed below his photo on the front or a score and/or caption included for action photos. Any additions or information on the checklist below would be appreciated.

2 Missouri 3, Kansas 0	25.00	40.00
4 Missouri 20, Oklahoma 17	25.00	40.00

1914 Missouri Postcards

These black and white photo Missouri Postcards were issued around 1914 by the University. The cards feature a postcard style back with a mention of the photographer: A.M. Finley, Student Photographer, Columbia, Mo. The player's last name is printed below his photo on the front. Any additions or information on the checklist below would be appreciated.

1 Harry Lansing (standing pose)	30.00	50.00
2 Missouri 46, W.J. 0 (William Jewel; action scene)	20.00	40.00

1915 Missouri Postcards

These black and white photo Missouri Postcards were issued around 1915 by the University. The cards feature a postcard style back with a mention of the photographer: A.M. Finley, Volney McFadden, or E.L. Ocker, Student Photographer, Columbia, Mo. The player's last name is printed below his photo on the front. Any additions or information on the checklist below would be appreciated.

1 Frank Herndon	30.00	50.00
2 Capt. Harry Lansing	30.00	50.00
3 Henry Schulte CO	30.00	50.00
4 Jacob Speelman	30.00	50.00
5 Van Dyne	30.00	50.00

1910 Murad College Silks S21

Each of these silks was issued by Murad Cigarettes around 1910 with a college emblem and an artist's rendering of a generic athlete on the front. The backs are blank. Each of the S21 silks measures roughly 5" by 7" and there was a smaller version created (roughly 3 1/2" by 5 1/2") of each and cataloged as S22.

*SMALLER S22: .3X TO .8X LARGER S21

1FB Army (West Point) football	30.00	60.00
2FB Brown football	30.00	60.00
3FB California football	30.00	60.00
4FB Chicago football	30.00	60.00
5FB Colorado football	30.00	60.00
6FB Columbia football	30.00	60.00
7FB Cornell football	30.00	60.00
8FB Dartmouth football	30.00	60.00
9FB Georgetown football	30.00	60.00
10FB Harvard football	30.00	60.00
11FB Illinois football	30.00	60.00
12FB Michigan football	30.00	60.00
13FB Minnesota football	30.00	60.00
14FB Missouri football	30.00	60.00
15FB Navy (Annapolis) football	30.00	60.00
16FB Ohio State football	30.00	60.00
17FB Pennsylvania football	30.00	60.00
18FB Purdue football	30.00	60.00
19FB Stanford football	30.00	60.00
20FB Stanford football	30.00	60.00
21FB Syracuse football	30.00	60.00
22FB Texas football	30.00	60.00
23FB Wisconsin football	30.00	60.00
24FB Yale football	30.00	60.00

1911 Murad College Series T51

These colorful cigarette cards featured several colleges and a variety of sports and recreations of the day and were issued in packs of Murad Cigarettes. The cards measure approximately 2" by 3". Two variations of each of the first 50 cards were produced; one variation says "College Series" on back, the other, "2nd Series". The drawings on cards of the 2nd Series are slightly different from those of the College Series. There are 6 different series of 25 in the College Series and they are listed here in the order that they appear on the checklist on the cardbacks. There is also a larger version (5" x 8") that was available for the first 25 cards as a premium (catalog designation T6) offer that could be obtained in exchange for 15 Murad cigarette coupons; the offers expired June 30, 1911.

*2ND SERIES: .4X TO 1X COLLEGE SERIES

10 Harvard Football	25.00	50.00
13 Michigan Football	25.00	50.00
39 S.U.N.D.(Univ. of N.Dakota) Football	25.00	50.00
43 Tufts College Football	25.00	50.00
54 C (Coalgate) Football	25.00	50.00
102 Buchtel Football	25.00	50.00

1911 Murad College Series Premiums T6

10 Harvard Football	250.00	400.00
13 Michigan#(Football	250.00	400.00

1939 Nebraska Don Leon Coffee

These cards were thought to have been produced in the late 1930s and early 1940s and released as a premium for purchasing Don Leon Coffee. Each card measures roughly 1-7/8" by 2-3/4" and features a black and white photo of the player on the cardfront along with just his name, position, and hometown. No height and weight information is included on the 1939 cards. The unnumbered cardbacks containing rules for a card set building contest along with an ad for Don Leon Coffee. Listed below are the known cards, any additions to this list are appreciated.

1 Elmer Dohrmann	125.00	200.00
2 Lowell English	125.00	200.00
3 Perry Franks	125.00	200.00
4 John Richardson	125.00	200.00
5 Fred Shirey	125.00	200.00
6 Kenneth Shindo	125.00	200.00

1940 Nebraska Don Leon Coffee

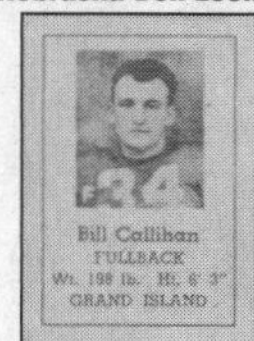

These cards were thought to have been produced in the late 1930s and early 1940s and released as a premium for purchasing Don Leon Coffee. Each card measures roughly 1-7/8" by 2-3/4" and features a black and white photo of the player on the cardfront along with his name, position, weight and height information and hometown. The unnumbered cardbacks containing rules for a card set building contest along with an ad for Don Leon Coffee. Listed below are the known cards, any additions to this list are appreciated.

COMPLETE SET (19)	2,500.00	3,500.00
1 Forrest Behm	175.00	300.00
2 Charles Brock	200.00	350.00
3 Bill Callihan	150.00	250.00
4 Elmer Dohrmann	125.00	200.00
5 Jack Dodd	150.00	250.00
6 Lloyd Grimm	125.00	200.00
7 Lowell English	125.00	200.00
8 Perry Franks	125.00	200.00
9 Harry Hopp	150.00	250.00
10 Robert Kahler	125.00	200.00
11 Royal Kahler	125.00	200.00
12 Vernon Neprud	125.00	200.00
13 E. Nuernberger	125.00	200.00
14 William Pfeiff	125.00	200.00
15 George Porter	150.00	250.00
16 John Richardson	125.00	200.00
17 Fred Preston	125.00	200.00
18 Glen Schluckebier	125.00	200.00
19 Fred Shirey	125.00	200.00
20 Kenneth Shindo	125.00	200.00

1966 Nebraska Team Issue

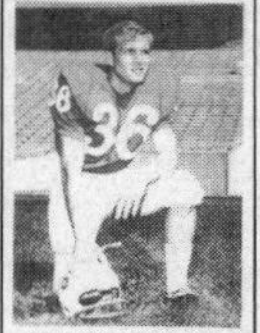

These 5" by 7" black and white photos were issued by Nebraska. Each features a member of the football team without any player identifiication on the front. The backs were produced blank, however the player's identification is usually hand written or even stamped on the backs.

COMPLETE SET (9)	25.00	50.00
1 LaVerne Allers	3.00	6.00
2 Bob Churchich	4.00	8.00
3 Dick Fitzgerald	3.00	6.00
4 Wayne Meylan	3.00	6.00
5 Bob Pickens	3.00	6.00
6 Lynn Senkbeil	3.00	6.00
7 Pete Tatman	3.00	6.00
8 Larry Wacholtz	3.00	6.00
9 Harry Wilson	4.00	8.00

1973 Nebraska Playing Cards

This 54-card set of playing cards measures 2 1/4" by 3 1/2". The cardbacks feature the words "Go Big Red" and "Nebraska" in the shape of a football helmet against either a red or white background color -- there were two versions of the set in either white or red colored backs. The cardfronts feature a black and white player photo with the player's name below. The cards are checklisted below in playing card order by suit (C for Clubs, D for Diamonds, H for Hearts, S for Spades, and JOK for the Jokers) and numbers are assigned to Aces (1), Jacks (11), Queens (12), and Kings (13). This set was released in 1973 and very closely resembles the 1974 set with a few of the differences as noted below. It also includes the first card of legendary head coach Tom Osborne.

COMPLETE SET (54)	90.00	150.00
1C Terry Rogers	.75	2.00
1D Richard Duda	1.25	2.50
1H Zaven Yaralian	.75	2.00
1S Tom Osborne CO	35.00	50.00
2C Bob Revelle	.75	2.00
2D John Dutton	3.00	5.00
2H Bob Wolfe	.75	2.00
2S Tom Alward	.75	2.00
3C Tom Pate	.75	2.00
3D Pat Fischer	2.50	4.00
3H Steve Wieser	.75	2.00
3S Dan Anderson	.75	2.00
4C Mike O'Holleran	.75	2.00
4D Marvin Crenshaw	1.25	2.50
4H Daryl White	.75	2.00
4S Frosty Anderson	.75	2.00
5C Ron Pruitt	.75	2.00
5D Dean Gissler	.75	2.00
5H Bob Thornton	.75	2.00
5S Al Austin	.75	2.00
6C Bob Nelson	1.25	2.50
6D Dave Goeller	.75	2.00
6H John Starkebaum	.75	2.00
6S Ritch Bahe	.75	2.00
7C Larry Mushinskie	.75	2.00
7D Percy Eichelberger	.75	2.00
7H Dave Shamblin	.75	2.00
7S John Bell	.75	2.00
8C Jeff Moran	.75	2.00
8D Stan Hegener	.75	2.00
8H Don Westbrook	1.25	2.50
8S Rik Bonness	1.25	2.50
9C Bob Martin	.75	2.00
9D Dave Humm	3.00	5.00
9H Bob Schmit	1.25	2.50
9S Randy Borg	.75	2.00
10C Ralph Powell	.75	2.00
10D Ardell Johnson	.75	2.00
10H Rich Sanger	.75	2.00
10S Rich Costanzo	.75	2.00
11C Steve Manstedt	.75	2.00
11D Doug Johnson	.75	2.00
11H Willie Thornton	1.25	2.50
11S Maury Damkroger	1.25	2.50
12C Brent Longwell	.75	2.00
12D Chuck Jones	.75	2.00
12H Tom Ruud	1.25	2.50
12S Tony Davis	1.25	2.50
13C George Kyros	.75	2.00
13D Wonder Monds	1.25	2.50
13H Steve Runty	.75	2.00
13S Mark Doak	.75	2.00
JOK1 Memorial Stadium Black	.75	2.00
JOK2 Memorial Stadium Red	.75	2.00

1974 Nebraska Playing Cards

This 54-card set of playing cards measures 2 1/4" by 3 1/2". The cardbacks feature the words "Go Big Red" and "Nebraska" in the shape of a football helmet against either a red or white background color -- there were two versions of the set in either white or red colored backs. The cardfronts feature a black and white player photo with the player's name below. The cards are checklisted below in playing card order by suit (C for Clubs, D for Diamonds, H for Hearts, S for Spades, and JOK for the Jokers) and numbers are assigned to Aces (1), Jacks (11), Queens (12), and Kings (13). This set was released in 1974 and very closely resembles the 1973 set with a few of the differences as noted below. It also includes the first card of legendary head coach Tom Osborne.

COMPLETE SET (54)	75.00	135.00
1C Rik Bonness	1.25	2.50
1D Don Westbrook	.75	2.00
1H Ron Pruitt	.75	2.00
1S Tom Osborne CO	25.00	40.00
2C Mark Doak	.75	2.00
2D Mike Offner	.75	2.00
2H Tony Davis	1.25	2.50
2S Terry Rogers	.75	2.00
3C John Lee DE	.75	2.00
3D Stan Waldemore	.75	2.00
3H Mike Fultz	.75	2.00
3S Tom Ruud	1.25	2.50
4C Mike Coyle	.75	2.00
4D Stan Hegener	.75	2.00
4H Chad Leonardi	.75	2.00
4S Jeff Schneider	.75	2.00
5C George Kyros	.75	2.00
5D Bobby Thomas	.75	2.00
5H John Starkebaum	.75	2.00
5S Mark Heydorff	.75	2.00
6C Gary Higgs	.75	2.00
6D Bob Martin	.75	2.00
6H Marvin Crenshaw	1.25	2.50
6S Dean Gissler	.75	2.00
7C Dennis Pavelka	.75	2.00
7D Ritch Bahe	.75	2.00
7H Larry Mushinskie	.75	2.00
7S Jim Burrow	.75	2.00
8C Jeff Moran	.75	2.00
8D Tom Heiser	.75	2.00
8H Tom Pate	.75	2.00
8S Al Eveland	.75	2.00
9C John O'Leary DL	.75	2.00
9D Steve Wieser	.75	2.00
9H Dave Humm	3.00	5.00
9S Chuck Jones	.75	2.00
10C Percy Eichelberger	.75	2.00
10D Ardell Johnson	.75	2.00
10H Willie Thornton	1.25	2.50
10S Brad Jenkins	.75	2.00
11C Greg Jorgensen	.75	2.00
11D Chuck Malito	.75	2.00
11H Dave Redding	.75	2.00
11S Dave Butterfield	.75	2.00
12C George Mills	.75	2.00
12D Bob Lingenfelter	.75	2.00
12H Dave Shamblin	.75	2.00
12S Rich Duda	1.25	2.50
13C Terry Luck	.75	2.00
13D Wonder Monds	1.25	2.50
13H Earl Everett	.75	2.00
13S Steve Hoins	.75	2.00
JOK1 Bob Nelson	1.25	2.50
JOK2 Memorial Stadium	1.25	2.50

1969 North Carolina State Team Issue

These photos were issued by the school to promote the football program. Each measures roughly 8" by 10" and features a pair of black and white images of players with the player's name, position, and school name below each photo. The backs are blank.

COMPLETE SET (11)	50.00	100.00
1 Bill Clark Don Bradley	5.00	10.00
2 Ed Hoffman Dick Curran	5.00	10.00
3 Don Jordan Dave Rodgers	5.00	10.00
4 Pat Korsnick Pat Kenney	5.00	10.00
5 Mike Mallan Gary Moser	5.00	10.00
6 Robert McLean Gary Yount	5.00	10.00
7 Paul Sharp Jack Whitley	5.00	10.00
8 George Smith Pat Korsnick	5.00	10.00
9 Pete Sowirka Bill Miller	5.00	10.00
10 Van Walker Clyde Chesney	5.00	10.00
11 Bryan Wall Bill Miller	5.00	10.00

1979 North Carolina Schedules

This four-card set was apparently issued by the Department of Athletics at North Carolina (Chapel Hill) and partially sponsored by Hardee's. The cards measure approximately 2 3/8" by 3 3/8". The card front features a full-bleed head shot of the player, with the player's name and jersey number burned into the bottom portion of the picture. The backs carry the 1979 varsity football schedule. The cards are unnumbered and checklisted below in alphabetical order.

COMPLETE SET (4)	6.00	12.00
1 Ricky Barden	1.50	3.00
2 Steve Junkman	1.50	3.00
3 Matt Kupec	2.00	4.00
4 Doug Paschal	1.50	3.00

1931 Northwestern Postcards

1 Carl Hall	25.00	50.00
2 Will Lewis	25.00	50.00
3 Al Moore UER	25.00	50.00
4 Reb Russell	30.00	60.00

1974 Northwestern Team Sheets

These photos were issued by the school to promote the football program. Each measures roughly 8" by 10" and features eight black and white images of players with the school name appearing at the top. The backs are blank.

1 Rich Boothe Wayne Frederickson Rob Mason Carl Patrnchak Joe Patrnchak Mark	4.00	8.00
2 John Pont CO Mitch Anderson Greg Boykin Billy Stevens Larry Lilja Paul Hiem	4.00	8.00

1923 Notre Dame Postcards

Each of the postcards in this set covers a specific 1923 Notre Dame football game with the date, opponent, and final score included on the cardfront printed in blue along with a gold colored border near the card's edges. The cardbacks feature a typical postcard design with "Souvenir Post Card" printed at the top. The cards are unnumbered and listed below alphabetically. Any additions to this list are appreciated.

1 Elmer Layden	150.00	250.00
2 Bill Maher (Oct. 6, 1923)	100.00	175.00
3 Don Miller	150.00	250.00
4 Gene Oberst	100.00	175.00
5 Harry Stuhldreher	150.00	250.00

1924 Notre Dame Postcards

Each of the postcards in this set was issued in 1924. The cardfronts were printed in blue along with a thin gold colored border near the card's edges on most. The cardbacks feature a typical postcard design with "Souvenir Post Card" printed at the top and "Published by Jay R. Masenich U.N.D." printed in blue at the bottom. The cards are unnumbered and listed below alphabetically. Any additions to this list are appreciated.

1 Football Player Artwork	30.00	60.00
2 The Four Horseman	150.00	300.00
3 Student Trip to Wisconsin	30.00	60.00
4 Capt. Adam Walsh	50.00	100.00

1925 Notre Dame Postcards

Each of the postcards in this set was issued in 1925. The cardfronts were printed in black and white or blue and white along with a thin gold colored border near the card's edges on most. The cardbacks feature a typical postcard design with "Souvenir Post Card" printed at the top. The cards are unnumbered and listed below alphabetically. Any additions to this list are appreciated.

1 Dick Hanousek	100.00	200.00
2 Minneapolis Bound Art	75.00	150.00

1926 Notre Dame Postcards

Notre Dame issued postcard sets over a number of years to fans as a momento of each game of the season. They can often be found signed by the player(s) featured. Each of these postcards covers a specific 1926 Notre Dame game with the date and opponent and final score printed on the cardfront. The printing is a single color blue or dark sepia tone. The cards are unnumbered and listed below alphabetically. Any additions to this list are appreciated.

1 Benda O'Boyle Wallace	50.00	100.00
2 Boeringer R.Smith Voedisch A.Walsh	50.00	100.00
3 J.Boland F.Collins Horsemen	175.00	300.00
4 Christie Flanagan	50.00	100.00
5 Hearden Rockne Edwards	350.00	600.00
6 John Niemiec	50.00	100.00
7 C.Riley V.McNally Parisien Maxwell Walsh	50.00	100.00

1927 Notre Dame Postcards

Notre Dame issued postcard sets over a number of years to fans as a momento of each game of the season. They can often be found signed by the player featured. Each of these postcards covers a specific 1927 Notre Dame game with the date and opponent included on the cardfront. The printing on the fronts is a single color blue or dark sepia tone. The cards are unnumbered and listed below alphabetically. Any additions to this list are appreciated.

1 Christie Flanagan	50.00	100.00
2 B.Dahman J.Chevigney	60.00	120.00
3 Knute Rockne	350.00	500.00
4 K.Rockne Smith	250.00	400.00
5 John Niemiec	50.00	100.00
6 C.Riley F.Collins	50.00	100.00
7 Frederick Voedisch Walsh	50.00	100.00

1929 Notre Dame Postcards

Each of the postcards in this set covers a specific 1929 Notre Dame football game with the date and opponent included on the cardfront. They are often found with the game's score written on the front and sometimes autographed by the player. The cardbacks are a typical postcards design. The cards are unnumbered and listed below alphabetically. Any additions to this list are appreciated.

1 Jack Cannon	50.00	100.00
2 Eddie Collins	50.00	100.00
3 Jack Elder	50.00	100.00
4 Tim Moynihan	60.00	120.00
5 Larry Moon Mullins	60.00	120.00

1930 Notre Dame Postcards

Notre Dame issued this postcard set with the intention of fans to have each card autographed and game score recorded as a momento of the game featured. Each of the postcards covers a specific 1930 Notre Dame game with the date and opponent included on the cardfront. The cards are unnumbered and listed below alphabetically.

COMPLETE SET (25)	1,000.00	1,800.00
1 Marty Brill	40.00	80.00
2 Frank Carideo	60.00	120.00
3 Tom Conley	40.00	80.00
4 Al Culver	40.00	80.00
5 Dick Donaghue	40.00	80.00
6 Nordy Hoffman	40.00	80.00
7 Al Howard	40.00	80.00
8 Chuck Jaskwich	40.00	80.00
9 Clarence Kaplan	40.00	80.00
10 Tom Kassis	40.00	80.00
11 Ed Kosky	40.00	80.00
12 Joe Kurth	50.00	100.00
13 Bernie Leahy	50.00	100.00
14 Frank Leahy	150.00	250.00
15 Dick Mahoney	40.00	80.00
16 Art McManmon	40.00	80.00
17 Bert Metzger	40.00	80.00
18 Larry Moon Mullins	50.00	100.00
19 John O'Brien	40.00	80.00
20 Bucky O'Connor	40.00	80.00
21 Joe Savoldi	60.00	120.00
22 Marchmont Schwartz	50.00	100.00
23 Robert Terlaak	40.00	80.00
24 George Vlk	40.00	80.00
25 Tommy Yarr	40.00	80.00

1931 Notre Dame Postcards

Similar to the 1930 release, Notre Dame issued this postcard set with the intention of fans having each card autographed and the game score recorded as a momento of the game featured. Each of the postcards covers a specific 1931 Notre Dame game with the date and opponent included on the cardfront. The cards are unnumbered and listed below alphabetically. The set is thought to contain well over 20-different postcards. Any additions to this list are appreciated.

1 Hunk Anderson CO	75.00	150.00
2 Jack Chevigney CO	50.00	100.00
3 Tom Gorman	50.00	100.00
4 Knute Rockne	300.00	500.00
5 Tommy Yarr	50.00	100.00

1932 Notre Dame Postcards

Similar to previous releases, Notre Dame issued this postcard set with the intention of fans having each card autographed and the game score recorded as a souvenir. Unlike other years, the 1932 issue does not include a specific game on the front, but does have a player photo printed in blue along with a yellow-gold border. The words "Notre Dame Varsity 1932" appear above the player image. The cardbacks feature a typical postcard format. The cards are unnumbered and listed below alphabetically. Any additions to this list are appreciated.

1 Ben Alexander	40.00	80.00
2 Steve Banas	40.00	80.00
3 Ray Brancheau	40.00	80.00
4 Sturla Canale	40.00	80.00
5 Hugh DeVore	40.00	80.00
6 Tom Gorman	40.00	80.00
7 Norman Greeney	40.00	80.00
8 Jim Harris	40.00	80.00
9 Paul Host	50.00	100.00
10 Chuck Jaskwich	40.00	80.00
11 Mike Koken	40.00	80.00
12 Ed Kosky	40.00	80.00
13 Ed Krause	40.00	80.00
14 Joe Kurth	50.00	100.00
15 Mike Leding	40.00	80.00
16 James Leonard	50.00	100.00
17 Nick Lukats	40.00	80.00
18 George Melinkovitch	40.00	80.00
19 Emmett Murphy	40.00	80.00
20 Bill Pierce	50.00	100.00
21 Tom Roach	40.00	80.00
22 Joe Sheeketski	40.00	80.00
23 Laurie Vejar	40.00	80.00
24 Harry Wunsch	40.00	80.00
25 Season Schedule	40.00	80.00

1966 Notre Dame Team Issue

These photos were issued by the school to promote the football program. Each measures roughly 8" by 10" and features a black and white image of a player. The backs are blank or sometimes can be found with a typed player identification. Otherwise no player identification is included.

COMPLETE SET (7)	30.00	60.00
1 John Atamiam	5.00	10.00
2 Alex Bonvechio	5.00	10.00
3 Ken Ivan	5.00	10.00
4 Joseph Kantor	5.00	10.00
5 Marty Olosky	5.00	10.00
6 Tom Talaga	5.00	10.00
7 Bill Wolski	5.00	10.00

1967 Notre Dame Team Issue

Notre Dame issued these black-and-white player photos around 1967. Each measures 8" by 10" and was printed on glossy stock with white borders. The border below the photo contains the player's position, his name and school name. These photos are blankbacked and unnumbered. Any additions to the below list are appreciated. Some of the players who would later have professional cards include: Rocky Bleier, Pete Duranko, George Goeddeke, Terry Hanratty, Jim Lynch, Tom Regner and Jim Seymour.

COMPLETE SET (15)	75.00	150.00
1 Rocky Bleier	10.00	20.00
2 Larry Conjar	5.00	10.00
3 Pete Duranko	6.00	12.00
4 Don Gmitter	5.00	10.00
5 George Goeddeke	5.00	10.00
6 Terry Hanratty	6.00	12.00
7 Kevin Hardy	5.00	10.00
8 Curt Heneghan	5.00	10.00
9 Jim Lynch	6.00	12.00
10 Dave Martin	5.00	10.00
11 Mike McGill	5.00	10.00
12 Coley O'Brien	5.00	10.00
13 Tom Regner	5.00	10.00
14 Tom Schoen	5.00	10.00
15 Jim Seymour	5.00	10.00

1961 Nu-Card

The 1961 Nu-Card set of 80 standard-size cards features college players. One odd feature of the set is that the card numbers start with the number 101. The set features the first nationally distributed cards of Ernie Davis, Roman Gabriel, and John Hadl.

COMPLETE SET (80)	100.00	200.00
WRAPPER (5-cent)	5.00	10.00
101 Bob Ferguson	2.50	5.00
102 Ron Snidow	1.50	3.00
103 Steve Barnett	1.25	2.50
104 Greg Mather	1.25	2.50
105 Vern Von Sydow	1.25	2.50
106 John Hewitt	1.25	2.50
107 Eddie Johns	1.25	2.50
108 Walt Rappold	1.25	2.50
109 Roy Winston	1.50	3.00
110 Bob Boyda	1.25	2.50
111 Billy Neighbors	1.50	3.00
112 Don Purcell	1.25	2.50
113 Ken Byers	1.25	2.50
114 Ed Pine	1.25	2.50
115 Fred Oblak	1.25	2.50
116 Bobby Iles	1.25	2.50
117 John Hadl	10.00	20.00
118 Charlie Mitchell	1.25	2.50
119 Bill Swinford	1.25	2.50
120 Bill King	1.25	2.50
121 Mike Lucci	3.00	6.00
122 Dave Sarette	1.25	2.50
123 Alex Kroll	1.50	3.00
124 Steve Bauwens	1.25	2.50
125 Jimmy Saxton	1.50	3.00
126 Steve Simms	1.25	2.50
127 Andy Timura	1.25	2.50
128 Gary Collins	6.00	12.00
129 Ron Taylor	1.25	2.50
130 Bobby Dodd Flor.	2.50	5.00
131 Curtis McClinton	4.00	8.00
132 Ray Poage	1.50	3.00
133 Gus Gonzales	1.25	2.50
134 Dick Locke	1.25	2.50
135 Larry Libertore	1.25	2.50
136 Stan Sczurek	1.25	2.50
137 Pete Case	1.50	3.00
138 Jesse Bradford	1.25	2.50
139 Coolidge Hunt	1.25	2.50
140 Walter Doleschal	1.25	2.50
141 Bill Williamson	1.25	2.50
142 Pat Trammell	2.50	5.00
143 Ernie Davis	30.00	60.00
144 Chuck Lamson	1.25	2.50
145 Bobby Plummer	1.50	3.00
146 Sonny Gibbs	1.50	3.00
147 Joe Eilers	1.25	2.50
148 Roger Kochman	1.25	2.50
149 Norman Beal	1.25	2.50
150 Sherwyn Torson	1.25	2.50
151 Russ Hepner	1.25	2.50
152 Joe Romig	1.25	2.50
153 Larry Thompson T	1.25	2.50
154 Tom Perdue	1.25	2.50
155 Ken Bolin	1.25	2.50
156 Art Perkins	1.25	2.50
157 Jim Sanderson	1.25	2.50
158 Bob Asack	1.25	2.50
159 Dan Celoni G	1.25	2.50
160 Bill McGuirt	1.25	2.50
161 Dave Hoppmann	1.25	2.50
162 Gary Barnes	1.25	2.50
163 Don Lisbon	1.50	3.00
164 Jerry Gross	1.25	2.50
165 George Pierovich	1.25	2.50
166 Roman Gabriel	10.00	20.00
167 Billy White	1.25	2.50
168 Gale Weidner	1.25	2.50
169 Charles Rieves	1.25	2.50
170 Jim Furlong	1.25	2.50
171 Tom Hutchinson	1.50	3.00
172 Galen Hall	5.00	10.00
173 Wilburn Hollis	1.25	2.50
174 Don Kasso	1.25	2.50
175 Bill Miller	1.50	3.00
176 Ron Miller QB	1.25	2.50
177 Joe Williams	1.25	2.50
178 Mel Melin UER((misspelled Mellin)	1.25	2.50
179 Tom Vassell	1.25	2.50
180 Mike Cotten	1.50	3.00

1961 Nu-Card Pennant Inserts

This set of pennant sticker pairs was inserted with the 1961 Nu-Card regular issue college football set. These inserts are actually 1 1/2" by 3 7/16" and one pair was to be inserted in each wax pack. The pennant pairs were printed with several different ink colors (orange, light blue, navy blue, purple, green, black, and red) on several different paper stock colors (white, red, gray, orange, and yellow). The pennant pairs are unnumbered and are ordered below alphabetically according to the lowest alphabetical member of the pair. Many of the teams are available paired with several different other colleges. Any additions to this list below would be welcome.

COMPLETE SET (270)	400.00	750.00
1 Air Force/Georgetown	1.50	4.00
2 Air Force/Queens	1.50	4.00
3 Air Force/Upsala	1.50	4.00
4 Alabama/Boston U.	2.50	5.00
5 Alabama/Cornell	2.50	5.00
6 Alabama/Detroit	2.50	5.00
7 Alabama/Harvard	2.50	5.00
8 Alabama/Miami	2.50	5.00
9 Alabama/North Carolina State	2.50	5.00
10 Alabama/Wisconsin	2.50	5.00
11 Allegheny/Colorado St.	1.50	4.00
12 Allegheny/Oregon	1.50	4.00
13 Allegheny/Piedmont	1.50	4.00
14 Allegheny/Wm.and Mary	1.50	4.00
15 Arizona/Kansas	1.50	4.00
16 Arizona/Mississippi	1.50	4.00
17 Arizona/Pennsylvania	1.50	4.00
18 Arizona/S.M.U.	1.50	4.00
19 Army/Ga.Tech	1.50	4.00
20 Army/Iowa	1.50	4.00
21 Army/Johns Hopkins	1.50	4.00
22 Army/Maryland	1.50	4.00
23 Army/Missouri	1.50	4.00
24 Army/Pratt	1.50	4.00
25 Army/Purdue	1.50	4.00
26 Auburn/Florida	2.00	5.00
27 Auburn/Gettysburg	1.50	4.00
28 Auburn/Illinois	2.00	5.00
29 Auburn/Syracuse	2.00	5.00
30 Auburn/Virginia	2.00	5.00
31 Barnard/Columbia	1.50	4.00
32 Barnard/Maine	1.50	4.00
33 Barnard/N.Carolina	1.50	4.00
34 Baylor/Colorado St.	1.50	4.00
35 Baylor/Drew	1.50	4.00
36 Baylor/Oregon	1.50	4.00
37 Baylor/Piedmont	1.50	4.00
38 Boston Coll./Minnesota	1.50	4.00
39 Boston Coll./Norwich	1.50	4.00
40 Boston Coll./Winthrop	1.50	4.00
41 Boston U./Cornell	1.50	4.00
42 Boston U. Rensselaer	1.50	4.00
43 Boston U./Stanford	1.50	4.00
44 Boston U./Temple	1.50	4.00
45 Boston U./Utah State	1.50	4.00
46 Bridgeport/Holy Cross	1.50	4.00
47 Bridgeport/N.Y.U.	1.50	4.00
48 Bridgeport/Northwestrn	1.50	4.00
49 Bucknell/Illinois	1.50	4.00
50 Bucknell/Syracuse	1.50	4.00
51 Bucknell/Virginia	1.50	4.00
52 C.O.P./Oklahoma St.	1.50	4.00
53 C.O.P./Oregon St.	1.50	4.00
54 C.O.P./Princeton	1.50	4.00
55 California/Delaware	1.50	4.00
56 California/Hofstra	1.50	4.00
57 California/Kentucky	1.50	4.00
58 California/Marquette	1.50	4.00
59 California/Michigan	2.50	5.00
60 California/Notre Dame	4.00	8.00
61 California/Wingate	1.50	4.00
62 Charleston/Dickinson	1.50	4.00
63 Charleston/Lafayette	1.50	4.00
64 Charleston/U.of Mass.	1.50	4.00
65 Cincinnati/Maine	1.50	4.00
66 Cincinnati/Ohio Wesl.	1.50	4.00
67 Citadel/Columbia	1.50	4.00
68 Citadel/Maine	1.50	4.00
69 Citadel/N.Carolina	1.50	4.00
70 Coast Guard/Drake	1.50	4.00
71 Coast Guard/Penn St.	1.50	4.00
72 Coast Guard/Yale	1.50	4.00
73 Coker/UCLA	1.50	4.00
74 Coker/Wingate	1.50	4.00
75 Colby/Kings Point	1.50	4.00
76 Colby/Queens	1.50	4.00
77 Colby/Rice	1.50	4.00
78 Colby/Upsala	1.50	4.00
79 Colgate/Dickinson	1.50	4.00
80 Colgate/Lafayette	1.50	4.00
81 Colgate/Springfield	1.50	4.00
82 Colgate/Texas AM	1.50	4.00
83 Colgate/U.of Mass.	1.50	4.00
84 Colo.St./Drew	1.50	4.00
85 Colo.St./Oregon	1.50	4.00
86 Colo.St./Piedmont	1.50	4.00
87 Colo.St./Wm.and Mary	1.50	4.00
88 Columbia/Dominican	1.50	4.00
89 Columbia/Maine	1.50	4.00
90 Columbia/N.Carolina	1.50	4.00
91 Cornell/Harvard	1.50	4.00
92 Cornell/Rensselaer	1.50	4.00
93 Cornell/Stanford	1.50	4.00
94 Cornell/Wisconsin	1.50	4.00
95 Dartmouth/Mich.St.	1.50	4.00
96 Dartmouth/Ohio U.	1.50	4.00
97 Dartmouth/Wagner	1.50	4.00
98 Davidson/Ohio Wesl.	1.50	4.00
99 Davidson/S.Carolina	1.50	4.00
100 Davidson/Texas Tech	1.50	4.00
101 Delaware/Marquette	1.50	4.00
102 Delaware/Michigan	1.50	4.00
103 Delaware/Notre Dame	4.00	8.00
104 Delaware/UCLA	1.50	4.00
105 Denver/Florida State	2.00	5.00
106 Denver/Indiana	1.50	4.00
107 Denver/Iowa State	1.50	4.00
108 Denver/USC	1.50	4.00
109 Denver/VMI	1.50	4.00
110 Detroit/Harvard	1.50	4.00
111 Detroit/Rensselaer	1.50	4.00
112 Detroit/Stanford	1.50	4.00
113 Detroit/Utah State	1.50	4.00
114 Dickinson/Regis	1.50	4.00
115 Dickinson/Springfield	1.50	4.00
116 Dickinson/Texas AM	1.50	4.00
117 Dickinson/U.of Mass.	1.50	4.00
118 Dominican/North Car.	1.50	4.00
119 Drake/Duke	1.50	4.00
120 Drake/Kentucky	1.50	4.00
121 Drake/Middlebury	1.50	4.00
122 Drake/Penn St.	1.50	4.00
123 Drake/St. Peters	1.50	4.00
124 Drake/Yale	1.50	4.00
125 Drew/Middlebury	1.50	4.00
126 Drew/Oregon	1.50	4.00
127 Drew/Piedmont	1.50	4.00
128 Drew/Wm. and Mary	1.50	4.00
129 Duke/Middlebury	1.50	4.00
130 Duke/Rhode Island	1.50	4.00
131 Duke/Seton Hall	1.50	4.00
133 Duke/Yale	1.50	4.00
134 Finch/Long Island AT	1.50	4.00
135 Finch/Michigan St.	1.50	4.00
136 Finch/Ohio U.	1.50	4.00
137 Finch/Wagner	1.50	4.00
138 Florida St./Indiana	2.00	5.00
139 Florida St./Iowa St.	2.00	5.00
140 Florida St./So.Cal.	2.00	5.00
141 Florida St./VMI	2.00	5.00
142 Florida/Gettysburg	1.50	4.00
143 Florida/Illinois	2.00	5.00
144 Florida/Syracuse	2.00	5.00
145 Florida/Virginia	2.00	5.00
146 Ga.Tech/Johns Hopkins	1.50	4.00
147 Ga.Tech/Maryland	1.50	4.00
148 Ga.Tech/Missouri	1.50	4.00
149 Georgetown/Kings Point	1.50	4.00
150 Georgetown/Rice	1.50	4.00
151 Georgia/Missouri	2.00	5.00
152 Georgia/Ohio Wesleyan	1.50	4.00
153 Georgia/Rutgers	1.50	4.00
154 Georgia/So.Carolina	2.00	5.00
155 Gettysburg/Syracuse	1.50	4.00
156 Harvard/Miami	2.00	5.00
157 Harvard/NC State	1.50	4.00
158 Harvard/Stanford	1.50	4.00
159 Harvard/Utah State	1.50	4.00
160 Harvard/Wisconsin	1.50	4.00
161 Hofstra/Marquette	1.50	4.00
162 Hofstra/Michigan	2.50	5.00
163 Hofstra/Navy	1.50	4.00
164 Hofstra/Notre Dame	4.00	8.00
165 Hofstra/UCLA	1.50	4.00
166 Holy Cross/Navy	1.50	4.00
167 Holy Cross/New York	1.50	4.00
168 Holy Cross/N'western	1.50	4.00
169 Holy Cross/Nyack	1.50	4.00
170 Howard/Kentucky	1.50	4.00
171 Howard/Villanova	1.50	4.00
172 Illinois/Syracuse	1.50	4.00
173 Indiana/Iowa State	1.50	4.00
174 Indiana/V.M.I.	1.50	4.00
175 Iowa State/So.Cal.	2.00	5.00
176 Iowa/Maryland	1.50	4.00
177 Iowa/Missouri	1.50	4.00
178 Iowa/Pratt	1.50	4.00
179 Johns Hopkins/Pratt	1.50	4.00
180 Johns Hopkins/Purdue	1.50	4.00
181 Kansas State/N.Y.U.	1.50	4.00
182 Kansas State/T.C.U.	1.50	4.00
183 Kansas/S.M.U.	1.50	4.00
184 Kansas/St.Francis	1.50	4.00
185 Kentucky/Maryland	1.50	4.00
186 Kentucky/Middlebury	1.50	4.00
187 Kentucky/New Hampsh.	1.50	4.00
188 Kentucky/Penn State	2.50	5.00
189 Kentucky/Rhode Island	1.50	4.00
190 Kentucky/Seton Hall	1.50	4.00
191 Kentucky/St.Peter's	1.50	4.00
192 Kentucky/Villanova	1.50	4.00
194 Kings Point/Queens	1.50	4.00
195 Kings Point/Rice	1.50	4.00
196 Kings Point/Upsala	1.50	4.00
197 Lafayette/Regis	1.50	4.00
198 Lafayette/U.of Mass.	1.50	4.00
199 Long Isl. AT/Mich.St.	1.50	4.00
200 Long Isl. AT/Ohio U.	1.50	4.00
201 Long Isl. AT/Wagner	1.50	4.00
202 Loyola/Minnesota	1.50	4.00
203 Loyola/Norwich	1.50	4.00
204 Loyola/Winthrop	1.50	4.00
205 Marquette/Michigan	2.50	5.00
206 Marquette/Navy	1.50	4.00
207 Marquette/New Platz	1.50	4.00
208 Marquette/Notre Dame	4.00	8.00
209 Marquette/UCLA	1.50	4.00
210 Maryland/Missouri	1.50	4.00
211 Mass./Regis	1.50	4.00
212 Mass./Springfield	1.50	4.00
213 Mass./Texas AM	1.50	4.00
214 Michigan St./Ohio U.	1.50	4.00
215 Michigan St./Wagner	1.50	4.00
216 Michigan/Navy	2.50	5.00
217 Michigan/New Platz	1.50	4.00
218 Michigan/UCLA	2.50	5.00
219 Middlebury/Penn St.	1.50	4.00
220 Middlebury/Yale	1.50	4.00
221 Minnesota/Norwich	1.50	4.00
222 Minnesota/Winthrop	1.50	4.00

223 Mississippi/Penn	1.50	4.00
224 Mississippi/St.Francis	1.50	4.00
225 Missouri/Purdue	1.50	4.00
226 N.Y.U./Northwestern	1.50	4.00
227 Navy/Notre Dame	4.00	8.00
228 Navy/UCLA	2.00	5.00
229 Navy/Wingate	1.50	4.00
230 NC State/Temple	1.50	4.00
231 NCE/Temple	1.50	4.00
232 NCE/Wisconsin	1.50	4.00
233 New Hamp./Villanova	1.50	4.00
234 Northwestern/TCU	1.50	4.00
235 Norwich/Winthrop	1.50	4.00
236 Notre Dame/UCLA	4.00	8.00
237 Notre Dame/Wingate	2.50	5.00
238 Ohio U./Wagner	1.50	4.00
239 Ohio Wesl./Roberts	1.50	4.00
240 Ohio Wesl./S.Carolina	1.50	4.00
241 Okla. St./Pacific	1.50	4.00
242 Okla.St./Oregon St.	1.50	4.00
243 Okla.St./Princeton	1.50	4.00
244 Oregon St./Princeton	1.50	4.00
245 Oregon/Piedmont	1.50	4.00
246 Oregon/Wm.and Mary	1.50	4.00
247 Penn State/Seton Hall	1.50	4.00
248 Penn State/St.Peter's	1.50	4.00
249 Penn State/Yale	1.50	4.00
250 Penn/S.M.U.	1.50	4.00
251 Penn/St.Francis	1.50	4.00
252 Queens/Rice	1.50	4.00
253 Queens/Upsala	1.50	4.00
254 Rensselaer/Stanford	1.50	4.00
255 Rensselaer/Temple	1.50	4.00
256 Rensselaer/Utah State	1.50	4.00
257 Rhode Island/Yale	1.50	4.00
258 Rice/Upsala	1.50	4.00
259 Roberts/So.Carolina	1.50	4.00
260 Roberts/Texas Tech	1.50	4.00
261 Rutgers/So.Carolina	1.50	4.00
262 So.California/VMI	2.00	5.00
263 So.Carolina/Texas Tech	1.50	4.00
264 St.Francis/S.M.U.	1.50	4.00
265 St.Peter's/Villanova	1.50	4.00
266 St.Peter's/Yale	1.50	4.00
267 Syracuse/Virginia	1.50	4.00
268 Temple/Wisconsin	1.50	4.00
269 UCLA/Wingate	2.00	5.00
270 Kentucky/Yale	1.50	4.00
270 Utah State/Wisconsin	1.50	4.00
271 Villanova/Yale	1.50	4.00

1955 Ohio University

This set of black and white player photos was released by the University of Ohio. Each was printed on high gloss paper stock and measures roughly 8" by 10." The players are not specifically identified but are often found with a hand typed ID on the backs. The set is unnumbered and checklisted below in alphabetical order.

COMPLETE SET (10)	45.00	90.00
1 Bob Kappes	5.00	10.00
Cliff Heffelfinger		
Joe Dean		
Bill Hes		
2 Bob Beach	5.00	10.00
3 James Brown	5.00	10.00
4 Cleve Bryant	5.00	10.00
5 Dick Conley	5.00	10.00
6 Bob Houmard	5.00	10.00
7 Dave LeVeck	5.00	10.00
8 Dave Mueller	5.00	10.00
9 John Smith	5.00	10.00
10 Frank Spolrich	5.00	10.00

1945 Ohio State

This black and white team issue photo set was released by the school in a white envelope that pictured a game action photo from a Minnesota versus OSU contest. Each photo measures roughly 2 3/4" by 3 1/4" and is bankbacked.

COMPLETE SET (18)	200.00	400.00
1 Warren Amling	12.50	25.00
2 Paul Bixler CO	12.50	25.00
3 Matt Brown	12.50	25.00
4 Ollie Cline	12.50	25.00
5 Thornton Dixon	12.50	25.00
6 Bob Dove	12.50	25.00
7 Ernest Godfrey CO	12.50	25.00
8 Bill Hackett	12.50	25.00
9 Dick Jackson	12.50	25.00
10 Jerry Krall	12.50	25.00
11 Jim Lininger	12.50	25.00
12 Ernie Santora	12.50	25.00
13 Paul Sarringhaus	15.00	30.00
14 Russ Thomas	12.50	25.00
15 Alex Verdova	12.50	25.00
16 Carroll Widdoes CO	12.50	25.00
17 Sam Winter	12.50	25.00
18 Ward Wright	12.50	25.00

1974 Ohio State Team Sheets

These photos were issued by the school to promote the football program. Each measures roughly 8" by 10" and features eight black and white images of players with the school name appearing at the top. The backs are blank.

1 Brian Baschnagel	4.00	8.00
Jim Cope		
Dave Purdy		
Tim Fox		
Dick Mack		
Arnie Jones		
Harold H		
2 Woody Hayes CO	7.50	15.00
Archie Griffin		
Cornelius Green		
Neal Colzie		
Pete Cusick		
Steve		

1979 Ohio State Greats 1916-1965

This set features Ohio State football players and coaches who obtained All-American or College Football Hall of Fame status from 1916 through 1965. The cards were issued in playing card format and each card measures approximately 2 1/2" by 3 1/4". The fronts feature a close-up photograph of the player in an octagon frame. The backs feature a collage of Ohio State players within an octagon border with "All-Americans, National Football Hall of Famers" at the bottom. Because this set is similar to a playing card set, the set is arranged just like a card deck and checklisted below as follows: C means Clubs, D means Diamonds, H means Hearts, S means Spades, and JK means Joker. The cards are checklisted below in playing card order by suits and numbers are assigned to Aces (1), Jacks (11), Queens (12), and Kings (13). The joker is listed at the end.

COMPLETE SET (52)	50.00	100.00
1C Howard Cassady 1955	1.25	3.00
1D Wes Fesler 1928	.75	2.00
1H Doug Van Horn	.75	2.00
1S Chic Harley 1916	.75	2.00
2C Dean Dugger	.75	2.00
2D Wes Fesler 1929	.75	2.00
2H Ike Kelley 1965	.75	2.00
2S Robert Karch	.75	2.00
3C Howard Cassady 1954	1.25	3.00
3D Wes Fesler 1930	.75	2.00
3H Jim Davidson	.75	2.00
3S Charles Bolen	.75	2.00
4C Mike Takacs	.75	2.00
4D Joseph Gailus	.75	2.00
4H Ike Kelley 1964	.75	2.00
4S Chic Harley 1917	.75	2.00
5C Robert Momsen	.75	2.00
5D Regis Monahan	.75	2.00
5H Arnold Chonko	.75	2.00
5S Chic Harley 1919	.75	2.00
6C Robert McCullough	.75	2.00
6D Gomer Jones	.75	2.00
6H Bob Ferguson 1961	.75	2.00
6S Iolas Huffman 1920	.75	2.00
7C Vic Janowicz	1.00	2.50
7D Inwood Smith	.75	2.00
7H Bob Ferguson 1960	.75	2.00
7S Gaylord Stinchcomb	.75	2.00
8C Warren Amling 1946	.75	2.00
8D Gust Zarnas	.75	2.00
8H Jim Houston 1959	.75	2.00
8S Iolas Huffman 1921	.75	2.00
9C Warren Amling 1945	.75	2.00
9D Esco Sarkkinen	.75	2.00
9H Jim Marshall	1.25	3.00
9S Harold Cuningham	.75	2.00
10C Bill Willis	1.50	4.00
10D Don Scott	.75	2.00
10H Jim Houston 1958	.75	2.00
10S Edwin Hess 1925	.75	2.00
11C Les Horvath	1.00	2.50
11D Charles Csuri	.75	2.00
11H Aurelius Thomas	.75	2.00
11S Edwin Hess 1926	.75	2.00
12C Bill Hackett	.75	2.00
12D Lindell Houston	.75	2.00
12H Jim Parker 1956	2.00	5.00
12S Martin Karow	.75	2.00
13C Jack Dugger	.75	2.00
13D Bob Shaw	1.00	2.50
13H Jim Parker 1955	2.00	5.00
13S Leo Raskowski	.75	2.00

1979 Ohio State Greats 1966-1978

This 53-card set contains all the Ohio State football players and coaches who obtained All-American or National Football (college) Hall of Fame status from 1966 through 1978. The cards were issued in the playing card format, and each card measures approximately 2 1/2" by 3 1/4". The fronts feature a close-up photograph of the player in an octagon frame. Those cards with two stars in the octagon frame indicate those players voted into the National Football Hall of Fame. The red colored backs feature a collage of Ohio State players within an octagon border with "All-Americans, National Football Hall of Famers" at the bottom. Because this set is similar to a playing card set, the set is arranged just like a card deck and checklisted below as follows: C means Clubs, D means Diamonds, H means Hearts, S means Spades, and JK means Joker. The cards are checklisted below in playing card order by suits and numbers are assigned to Aces (1), Jacks (11), Queens (12), and Kings (13). The joker is listed at the end.

COMPLETE SET (53)	75.00	150.00
1C Chris Ward	.75	2.00
1D Jan White	1.25	2.50
1H Ernest R. Godfrey ACO	.75	2.00
1S Ray Pryor	.75	2.00
2C Ray Griffin	1.25	2.50
2D Tom Deleone	1.25	2.50
2H Francis A. Schmidt CO	1.25	2.50
2S Dave Foley	1.25	2.50
3C Tom Cousineau	2.00	4.00
3D Randy Gradishar	2.50	5.00
3H Jim Parker	3.00	6.00
3S Rufus Mayes	1.25	2.50
4C Aaron Brown LB	1.25	2.50
4D John Hicks	2.00	4.00
4H Vic Janowicz	2.50	5.00
4S Rex Kern	2.00	4.00
5C Chris Ward	.75	2.00
5D Van Decree	.75	2.00
5H Les Horvath	2.00	5.00
5S Jim Otis	2.00	5.00
6C Tom Skladany	1.25	2.50
6D Randy Gradishar	2.50	5.00
6H Bill Willis	2.00	5.00
6S Ted Provost	.75	2.00
7C Bob Brudzinski	1.25	2.50
7D Archie Griffin	3.00	6.00
7H James Daniell	.75	2.00
7S Jim Stillwagon	1.25	2.50
8C Ted Smith	.75	2.00
8D John Hicks	2.00	4.00
8H Gust Zarnas	.75	2.00
8S Jack Tatum	2.00	5.00
9C Tom Skladany	1.25	2.50
9D Neal Colzie	1.25	2.50
9H Gomer Jones	.75	2.00
9S Tim Anderson DB	.75	2.00
10C Archie Griffin	3.00	6.00
10D Pete Cusick	.75	2.00
10H Wes Fesler	1.25	2.50
10S John Brockington	2.00	5.00
11C Tim Fox	1.25	2.50
11D Van Decree	.75	2.00
11H Pete Stinchcomb	.75	2.00
11S Mike Sensibaugh	1.25	2.50
12C Tom Skladany	1.25	2.50
12D Archie Griffin	3.00	6.00
12H Chic Harley	.75	2.00
12S Jim Stillwagon	1.25	2.50
13C Kurt Schumacher	1.25	2.50
13D Steve Meyers	1.25	2.50
13H Tom Cousineau	2.00	4.00
13S Jack Tatum	2.00	5.00
JK Howard Jones CO	1.25	2.50

1962 Oklahoma Team Issue

This set of black and white photos was issued by Oklahoma and released in 1962. Each features a player or coach on a photo measuring roughly 4" by 5" printed on photographic quality paper stock. Each photo is blankbacked and unnumbered.

COMPLETE SET (31)	100.00	200.00
1 Virgil Boll	4.00	8.00
2 Allen Bumgardner	4.00	8.00
3 Newt Burton	4.00	8.00
4 Duane Cook	4.00	8.00
5 Glen Condren	4.00	8.00
6 Jackie Cowan	4.00	8.00
7 Leon Cross	4.00	8.00
8 Monte Deere	4.00	8.00
9 Bud Dempsey	4.00	8.00
10 John Flynn	4.00	8.00
12 Paul Lea	4.00	8.00
13 Alvin Lear	4.00	8.00
14 Wayne Lee	4.00	8.00
15 Joe Don Looney	5.00	10.00
16 Charles Mayhue	4.00	8.00
17 Rick McCurdy	4.00	8.00
18 Ed McQuarters	4.00	8.00
19 Butch Metcalf	4.00	8.00
20 Ralph Neely	7.50	15.00
21 Bobby Page	4.00	8.00
22 John Porterfield	4.00	8.00
23 Mel Sandersfeld	4.00	8.00
24 Wes Skidgel	4.00	8.00
25 Norman Smith	4.00	8.00
26 George Stokes	4.00	8.00
27 Larry Vermillion	4.00	8.00
28 David Voiles	4.00	8.00
29 Dennis Ward	4.00	8.00
30 Bud Wilkinson CO	10.00	20.00
31 Gary Wylie	4.00	8.00

1976 Oklahoma Team Issue

These photos were issued by the school to promote the football program. Each measures roughly 8" by 10" and features a black and white image of a player with the player's name and school name below each photo. The backs are blank.

COMPLETE SET (22)	75.00	150.00
1 Jerry Anderson	4.00	8.00
2 Dean Blevins	4.00	8.00
3 Sidney Brown	4.00	8.00
4 Victor Brown	4.00	8.00
5 Kevin Craig	4.00	8.00
6 Jim Culbreath	4.00	8.00
7 Bill Dalke	4.00	8.00
8 Zac Henderson	4.00	8.00
9 Victor Hicks	4.00	8.00
10 Horace Ivory	5.00	10.00
11 Kenny King	5.00	10.00
12 Reggie Kinlaw	4.00	8.00
13 Thomas Lott	5.00	10.00
14 Jaime Melendez	4.00	8.00
15 Richard Murray	4.00	8.00
16 Elvis Peacock	5.00	10.00
17 Terry Peters	4.00	8.00
18 Mike Phillips	4.00	8.00
19 Jerry Reese	4.00	8.00
20 Greg Roberts	4.00	8.00
21 Myron Shoate	4.00	8.00
22 Uwe Von Schamann	5.00	10.00

1953 Oregon

This 20-card set measures roughly 2 1/4" x 3 1/2". The fronts feature a posed action photo, with player information appearing in handwritten script in a white box toward the bottom of the picture. Below the motto "Football is Fun," the backs have a list of locations where adult tickets can be purchased and a Knothole Gang membership offer. The cards are unnumbered and checklisted below in alphabetical order.

COMPLETE SET (20)	600.00	1,000.00
1 Farrell Albright	30.00	50.00
2 Ted Anderson	30.00	50.00
3 Len Berrie	30.00	50.00
4 Tom Elliott	30.00	50.00
5 Tim Flaherty	30.00	50.00
6 Cecil Hodges	30.00	50.00
7 Barney Holland	30.00	50.00
8 Dick James	35.00	60.00
9 Harry Johnson	30.00	50.00
10 Dave Lowe	30.00	50.00
11 Jack Patera	35.00	60.00
12 Ron Pheister	30.00	50.00
13 John Reed	30.00	50.00
14 Hal Reeve	30.00	50.00
15 Larry Rose	30.00	50.00
16 George Shaw	50.00	80.00
17 Lon Stiner Jr.	30.00	50.00
18 Ken Sweitzer	30.00	50.00
19 Keith Tucker	30.00	50.00
20 Dean Van Leuven	30.00	50.00

1956 Oregon

This 19-card set measures the standard size (2 1/2" x 3 1/2"). The fronts feature a posed action photo, with player information appearing in a white box toward the bottom of the picture. Below the motto "Follow the Ducks," the backs have schedule information and a list of locations where adult tickets can be purchased. The cards are unnumbered and checklisted below in alphabetical order.

COMPLETE SET (19)	500.00	800.00
1 Bruce Brenn	30.00	50.00
2 Jack Brown	30.00	50.00
3 Reanous Cochran	30.00	50.00
4 Jack Crabtree	35.00	60.00
5 Tom Crabtree	30.00	50.00

6 Tom Hale	30.00	50.00
7 Spike Hillstrom	30.00	50.00
8 Jim Linden	30.00	50.00
9 Hank Loumena	30.00	50.00
10 Nick Markulis	30.00	50.00
11 Phil McHugh	30.00	50.00
12 Fred Miklancic	30.00	50.00
13 Harry Mondale	30.00	50.00
14 Leroy Phelps	30.00	50.00
15 Jack Pocock	30.00	50.00
16 John Raventos	30.00	50.00
17 Jim Shanley	30.00	50.00
18 Ron Stover	30.00	50.00
19 J.C. Wheeler	30.00	50.00

1958 Oregon

This 20-card set measures approximately 2 1/4" by 3 1/2". The fronts feature a posed action player photo with player information in the white border beneath the picture. The cards are unnumbered and checklisted below in alphabetical order.

COMPLETE SET (20)	500.00	800.00
1 Greg Altenhofen	30.00	50.00
2 Darrel Aschbacher	30.00	50.00
3 Dave Fish	30.00	50.00
4 Sandy Fraser	30.00	50.00
5 Dave Grosz	30.00	50.00
6 Bob Grottkau	30.00	50.00
7 Marlan Holland	30.00	50.00
8 Tom Keele	30.00	50.00
9 Alden Kimbrough	30.00	50.00
10 Don Laudenslager	30.00	50.00
11 Riley Mattson	35.00	60.00
12 Bob Peterson	30.00	50.00
13 Dave Powell	30.00	50.00
14 Len Read	30.00	50.00
15 Will Reeve	30.00	50.00
16 Joe Schaffeld	30.00	50.00
17 Charlie Tourville	30.00	50.00
18 Dave Urell	30.00	50.00
19 Pete Welch	30.00	50.00
20 Willie West	35.00	60.00

1963 Oregon

1 Ron Berg	25.00	40.00
2 Len Casanova CO	25.00	40.00
3 Lowell Dean		
4 Larry Hill	25.00	40.00
5 Milt Kanehe	25.00	40.00
6 Dennis Keller		
7 Mel Renfro		
8 Ron Stratten	25.00	40.00

1972 Oregon Schedules

COMPLETE SET (16)	125.00	250.00
1 Maurice Anderson	7.50	15.00
2 Steve Bailey	7.50	15.00
3 Chuck Bradley	7.50	15.00
4 Pete Carlson	7.50	15.00
5 Ken Carter	7.50	15.00
6 Charley Cobb	7.50	15.00
7 Steve Herr	7.50	15.00
8 Rick Lessel	7.50	15.00
9 Fred Manuel	7.50	15.00
10 Joe Muse	7.50	15.00
11 Tony Rapolla	7.50	15.00
12 Don Reynolds	7.50	15.00
13 Tim Slapnicka	7.50	15.00
14 Greg Specht	7.50	15.00
15 Marc Traut	7.50	15.00
16 Norv Turner	15.00	30.00

1909 Penn State Postcards

These black and white postcards were issued around 1909. The player's name and position are usually included at the bottom of the card front and the backs feature a typical postcard style format. The photographer's ID is also typically included on the fronts and was McNary and Swope.

1 Larry Vorhis	35.00	60.00
2 State Varsity 1909	60.00	100.00
3 Team in Offensive Formation	50.00	80.00

1910 Penn State Postcards

This set of black and white postcards was issued around 1910 and is entitled "State Star Series" as printed on the cardfronts. The player's last name and position are included at the bottom of the card and a card number is included near the set name. The backs feature a typical postcard style format.

1 Bull McCleary	30.00	50.00
4 A.B. Gray	30.00	50.00
11 H.A.Weaver	30.00	50.00

1911 Penn State Postcards

This set of black and white postcards was issued around 1911. The player's name and position are included at the bottom of the card along with "Penn State Varsity." The backs feature a typical postcard style format with a mention of the photographer: Swope and Zerby, College Photographers, State College, PA.

1 Shorty Miller	30.00	50.00

1950 Pennsylvania Bulletin Pin-ups

These black and white premium photos measure roughly 8" x 10" and were issued by The Bulletin newspaper in the Philadelphia area. The photos are blankbacked and feature the newspaper's logo in the upper left corner, the school's pennant in the lower left corner and the player's facsimile autograph in the lower right corner.

1 Francis Bagnell	10.00	20.00
2 Bill Deuber	10.00	20.00
3 Bernie Lemonick	10.00	20.00

1974 Purdue Team Sheets

These photos were issued by the school to promote the football program. Each measures roughly 8" by 10" and features eight black and white images of players with the school name appearing at the top. The backs are blank.

1 Alex Agase CO	4.00	8.00
Larry Burton		
Ken Novak		
Mike Worthington		
Scott Dierking		
Ralph		
2 Stan Parker	4.00	8.00
Mark Vitali		
Steve Schmidt		
Fred Cooper		
Randy Clark		
Pete Gross		
Ma		

1910 Richmond College Silks S23

These colorful silks were issued around 1910 by Richmond Straight Cut Cigarettes. Each measures roughly 4" by 5 1/2" and are often called "College Flag, Seal, Song, and Yell" due to the content found on each one. More importantly to most sports collectors is the image found in the lower right hand-bottom corner. A few feature a mainstream sports' subject such as a generic player or piece of equipment, while most include a realistic image of the school's mascot or image of the founder or the school's namesake.

7 Chicago FB Player	75.00	150.00
29 Pennsylvania Football	60.00	120.00

1908 Rotograph Celebrity Series Postcards

The Rotograph Co. of New York issued a Celebrity Series set of postcards in 1908 that included one football subject. The set has an ACC designation of PC438.

1 Fielding Yost	75.00	150.00

1936 Seal Craft Discs

This series of discs was issued by Seal Craft Gum around 1936. The entire set consists of 240-discs featuring various non-sport subjects from animals and american indians to sports oriented college pennants. Each disc featuring a sports theme includes a college pennant in the center with artwork of the team's mascot and a generic representative sport above and below the pennant. The backs feature a brief history of the school and a football icon at the top and artwork of a tennis player at the bottom along with a card number.

91 Stanford	20.00	40.00
92 Kentucky	15.00	30.00
93 Pitt	15.00	30.00
94 Vermont	15.00	30.00
95 Princeton	15.00	30.00
96 Fordham	15.00	30.00
97 UCLA	20.00	40.00
98 NYU	15.00	30.00
99 Notre Dame	40.00	80.00
100 Southern California	20.00	40.00
101 Florida	20.00	40.00
102 Army	15.00	30.00
103 California	15.00	30.00
104 Columbia	15.00	30.00
105 Cornell	15.00	30.00
106 Yale	15.00	30.00
107 Dartmouth	15.00	30.00

1969 South Carolina Team Sheets

These six sheets measure approximately 8" by 10". The fronts feature two rows of five black-and-white player portraits each. The player's name, position and home town are printed under the photo. The backs are blank. The sheets are unnumbered and checklisted below in alphabetical order according to the first player listed.

COMPLETE SET (6)	25.00	50.00
1 Tim Bice	4.00	8.00
2 Allen Brown	4.00	8.00
3 Andy Chavous	4.00	8.00
4 Paul Dietzel CO	10.00	20.00
5 Ben Garnto	4.00	8.00
6 Jimmy Killen	4.00	8.00

1974 Southern Cal Discs

This 30-disc set was issued inside a miniature plastic football display holder, sitting on a red stand that reads "Trojans 1974". The discs measure approximately 2 5/16" in diameter and feature borderless color glossy player photos, shot from the waist up. The backs have biographical information, including the high school attended in the player's hometown. The discs are unnumbered and are listed alphabetically below. The set was reportedly produced and sold by Photo Sports for $2.50 (under the name Foto Ball) during Southern Cal's homecoming week the Fall of 1974. The miniature football card holder is priced below but is not considered part of the set.

COMPLETE SET (30)	50.00	100.00
1 Bill Bain	1.50	3.00
2 Otha Bradley	1.50	3.00
3 Kevin Bruce	1.00	2.00
4 Mario Celotto	1.00	2.00
5 Marvin Cobb	2.00	4.00
6 Anthony Davis	4.00	8.00
7 Joe Davis G	1.00	2.00
8 Shelton Diggs	1.50	3.00
9 Dave Farmer	1.50	3.00
10 Pat Haden	7.50	15.00
11 Donnie Hickman	1.00	2.00
12 Doug Hogan	1.00	2.00
13 Mike Howell TE	1.00	2.00
14 Gary Jeter	2.00	4.00
15 Steve Knutson	1.00	2.00
16 Chris Limahelu	1.50	3.00
17 Bob McCaffrey	1.00	2.00
18 J.K. McKay	2.00	4.00
19 John McKay CO	4.00	8.00
20 Jim O'Bradovich	2.00	4.00
21 Charles Phillips	1.50	3.00
22 Ed Powell	1.00	2.00
23 Marvin Powell	2.00	4.00
24 Danny Reece	1.50	3.00
25 Art Riley	1.00	2.00
26 Traveller II and	1.50	3.00
27 Tommy Trojan	1.50	3.00
28 USC Song Girls	1.00	2.00
29 USC Song Girls	1.00	2.00
30 Richard Wood	2.00	4.00
NNO Football Card Holder	10.00	20.00

1979 Stanford Playing Cards

This set was issued as a playing card deck. Each card has rounded corners and a typical playing card format. The fronts feature black-and-white photos with the card number and suit designation in the upper left corner and again, but inverted, in the lower right. The player's name and position initials appear just beneath the photo. The red cardbacks feature the title "The Stanford Cards." A few cards do not feature a player image but simply text about a Stanford football event or record. Since the set is similar to a playing card set, it is arranged just like a card deck and checklisted below accordingly. In the checklist below C means Clubs, D means Diamonds, H means Hearts, S means Spades and JOK means Joker. Numbers are assigned to Aces (1), Jacks (11), Queens (12), and Kings (13).

COMPLETE SET (54)	20.00	40.00
1C 1979 Football Schedule	.30	.75
1D Heisman Winners	.30	.75
1H Rod Dowhower CO	.30	.75
1S Stanford Stadium	.30	.75
2C 1980 Football Schedule	.30	.75
2D Players in Pro FB	.30	.75
2H Russel Charles Asst.CO	.30	.75
2S All-Time Leaders	.30	.75
3C 1978 Football Results	.30	.75
3D All-Time Leaders	.30	.75
3H Bill Dutton Asst.CO	.30	.75
3S All-Time Leaders	.30	.75
4C 1978 Team Leaders	.30	.75
4D All-Time Leaders	.30	.75
4H Jim Fassel Asst.CO	.40	1.00
4S All-Time Leaders	.30	.75
5C 1978 UPI Football Poll	.30	.75
5D All-Time Leaders	.30	.75
5H John Gooden Asst.CO	.30	.75
5S All-Time Leaders	.30	.75
6C 1978 AP Football Poll	.30	.75
6D All-Time Leaders	.30	.75
6H Ray Handley Asst.CO	.30	.75
6S All-Time Leaders	.30	.75
7C Football Bowl Record	.30	.75
7D All-Time Leaders	.30	.75
7H Al Lavan Asst.CO	.30	.75
7S All-Time Leaders	.30	.75
8C 1924-1935 All-Americans	.30	.75
8D All-Time Leaders	.30	.75
8H Tom Lovat Asst.CO	.30	.75
8S All-Time Leaders	.30	.75
9C 1940-1959 All-Americans	.30	.75
9D Gordon Banks	.30	.75
9H George Seifert Asst.CO	2.00	5.00
9S All-Time Leaders	.30	.75
10C 1960-1979 All-Americans	.30	.75
10D Rick Parker	.30	.75
10H 1979 Seniors	.30	.75
10S All-Time Leaders	.30	.75
11C Andre Tyler	.30	.75
11D Brian Holloway	.40	1.00
11H Turk Schonert	.30	.75
11S All-Time Leaders	.30	.75
12C John MacAulay	.30	.75
12D Milt McColl	.30	.75
12H Ken Margerum	.40	1.00
12S All-Time Leaders	.30	.75
13C Pat Bowe	.30	.75
13D Chuck Evans	.30	.75
13H Darrin Nelson	.50	1.25
13S All-Time Leaders	.30	.75
JOK1 Andy Geiger AD	.30	.75
JOK2 Garry Cavalli Assoc.AD	.30	.75

1970-86 Sugar Bowl Doubloons

COMPLETE SET (9)	6.00	12.00
1970 Arkansas vs Mississippi	.75	1.50
1972 Auburn vs. Oklahoma	.75	1.50
1973 Oklahoma vs. Penn State Blue	.75	1.50
1973 Oklahoma vs. Penn State Gold	.75	1.50
1974 Alabama vs. Notre Dame	.75	1.50
1975 Florida vs. Nebraska	.75	1.50
1979 Alabama vs. Penn State	.75	1.50
1980 Alabama vs. Arkansas	.75	1.50
1986 Miami vs. Tennessee	.75	1.50

1976 Sunbeam SEC Die Cuts

Produced by Arnold Harris Associates Inc. (Cherry Hill, New Jersey), each one of these twenty standard-size cards was inserted in specially-marked loaves of Sunbeam bread. Sunbeam also issued a 4" by 9" "Stand-up Trading Card Saver Book" to hold the cards. This book features pictures of all the fronts with instructions to put the corners of the cards in the slots indicated by the arrows. The team profile cards display the team helmet, an ink drawing of a football action scene, and the team name. The white backs profile the coach and team. The schedule cards show the mascot, another ink drawing of a football action scene, and the team name. The gray backs carry the 1976 football schedule. Both cards are perforated in an arc. The cards are unnumbered; they are checklisted below alphabetically as presented in the saver book.

COMPLETE SET (20)	100.00	200.00
1 Alabama Crimson Tide	6.00	15.00
2 Alabama Crimson Tide	6.00	15.00
3 Auburn War Eagle	4.00	10.00
4 Auburn War Eagle	4.00	10.00
5 Florida Gators	6.00	15.00
6 Florida Gators	6.00	15.00
7 Georgia Bulldogs	4.00	10.00
8 Georgia Bulldogs	4.00	10.00
9 Kentucky Wildcats	4.00	10.00
10 Kentucky Wildcats	4.00	10.00
11 Louisiana St. Tigers	4.00	10.00
12 Louisiana St. Tigers	4.00	10.00
13 Miss. St. Bulldogs	4.00	10.00
14 Miss. St. Bulldogs	4.00	10.00
15 Ole Miss Rebels	4.00	10.00
16 Ole Miss Rebels	4.00	10.00
17 Tennessee Volunteers	5.00	12.00
18 Tennessee Volunteers	5.00	12.00
19 Vanderbilt Commodores	4.00	10.00
20 Vanderbilt Commodores	4.00	10.00

1977 Syracuse Team Sheets

These photos were issued by the school to promote the football program. Each measures roughly 8" by 10" and features ten black and white images of players with the school name appearing at the top. The player's name, position, and brief vital stats is printed below each photo. The backs are blank.

1 Dan Breznay 4.00 8.00
John Cameron
Jim Collins
Ron Farneski
Warren Harvey
Willie McCu
2 Bill Hurley 4.00 8.00
Pete Prather
Larry Archis
Rich Rosen
Mike Jones
Bill Zanovitch

1965 Tennessee Team Sheets

The University of Tennessee issued these sheets of black-and-white player photos in 1865. Each measures roughly 7 7/8" by 10" and was printed on glossy stock with white borders. Each sheet includes photos of 10-players with his position and name printed below the image. The top of the sheets reads "University of Tennessee 1965 Football." The photos are blankbacked.

1 Sheet 1 7.50 15.00
2 Sheet 2 10.00 20.00
3 Sheet 3 10.00 20.00

1975 Tennessee Team Sheets

These photos were issued by the school to promote the football program. Each measures roughly 8" by 10" and features ten black and white images of players with the school name and year appearing at the top. The backs are blank.

1 Charles Anderson 4.00 8.00
Keith Autry
Dave Brady
Mike Caldwell
Phil Clabo
Bill Cole

2 Joe Gallagher 4.00 8.00
Mike Gayles
Jim Gaylor
Mike Huskisson
Paul Johnson
Ron McCart
3 John Murphy 4.00 8.00
David Page
David Parsons
Steve Poole
Gary Roach
Thomas Rowsey
P
4 Al Szawara 4.00 8.00
Randy Verner
Randy Wallace
Ernie Ward
Brent Watson
Tommy West
St

1980 Tennessee Police

The 1980 Tennessee Police Set features 19 cards measuring approximately 2 5/8" by 4 3/16". The fronts have color photos bordered in white; the vertically oriented backs feature football terminology and safety tips. The cards are unnumbered, so they are listed alphabetically by subject's name. The key player in this set is longtime Cowboy special team star Bill Bates.

COMPLETE SET (19) 25.00 50.00
1 Bill Bates 6.00 15.00
2 James Berry .75 2.00
3 Chris Bolton .75 2.00
4 Mike L. Cofer 2.50 6.00
5 Glenn Ford .75 2.00
6 Anthony Hancock 1.25 3.00
7 Brian Ingram .75 2.00
8 Tim Irwin 2.00 5.00
9 Kenny Jones .75 2.00
10 Wilbert Jones .75 2.00
11 Johnny Majors CO 3.00 8.00
12 Bill Marren .75 2.00
13 Danny Martin .75 2.00
14 Jim Noonan .75 2.00
15 Lee North .75 2.00
16 Hubert Simpson 1.25 3.00
17 Danny Spradlin 1.25 3.00
18 John Warren 1.25 3.00
19 Brad White .75 2.00

1908 Tuck's College Postcards

This set of postcards was issued by Tuck's and features a college co-ed portrait inside the image of a vintage football. The featured school's pennant is prominantly displayed as well on the cardfront. The cardbacks feature a typical postcard design.

COMPLETE SET (6) 60.00 120.00
1 Columbia 10.00 20.00
2 Cornell 10.00 20.00
3 Harvard 10.00 20.00
4 Missouri 10.00 20.00
5 Pennsylvania 10.00 20.00
6 Princeton 10.00 20.00
7 Yale 10.00 20.00

1978 Tulane Team Issue

These photos were issued by the school to promote the football program. Each measures roughly 8" by 10" and features between six and eight black and white images of players with the school name and year appearing at the top. The player's name is printed below each photo. The backs are blank.

COMPLETE SET (9) 30.00 60.00
1 John Ammerman 4.00 8.00
Marcus Anderson
Steve Athas
Tommie Barlow
Bob Becnel
James Be
2 Larry Bizzotto 4.00 8.00
Owen Brennan
Gary Brown
Willard Browner
Larry Burke
Jeff Car
3 Kevin Cole 4.00 8.00
Terry Daffin
Darryl Dawkins
Tony Delaughter
Arnie Diaz
Chris Doy
4 Carl Duvigneaud 4.00 8.00
Chip Forte
Jeff Forte
Nolan Franz
Nolan Gallo
Donald Garret
5 Darrell Griffin 4.00 8.00
Nickie Hall
Terry Harris
Fred Hicks
Tommy Hightower
Dwain H
6 Rob Indicott 4.00 8.00
Ken Johnston
Al Jones
Clayton Jones
Clifton Jones
Jeff Jones
J
7 Donald Louviere 4.00 8.00
Dee Methvin
Percy Millett
Mark Montini
Scott Morrell
Paul M
8 Jim Price 4.00 8.00
Nick Ray
Donnie Rice
Andre Robert
Frank Robinson
Gerry Sheridan
J
9 Mike Sims 4.00 8.00
Ricky Smith
Rory Stone
Phil Townsend
Mike Wasilieleski
Frank Wills

1905 Ullman Postcards

The 1905 Ullman Mfg. Co. postcard series includes various collegiate football teams. Each postcard features a color art rendering of a generic football player along with the team's mascot or emblem. A copyright date is also included on the cardfront and the cardback is typical postcard style. We've listed the known postcards. Any additions to this list are appreciated.

COMPLETE SET (7) 75.00 125.00
1 Chicago 12.00 20.00
2 Columbia 12.00 20.00
3 Cornell 12.00 20.00
4 Penn 12.00 20.00
5 Princeton 12.00 20.00
6 Stanford 12.00 20.00
7 Yale 12.00 20.00

1905 University Ivy League Postcards

These cards were issued by the University Post Card Company in 1905. Each card includes a black and white player photo to the left and a smaller football action photo in the upper right corner. The player's name is included in a banner at the top along with a caption for the action photo. The backs feature a very basic postcard style. The notation "Published by University Post Card Company" appears on the card front on the left side. Any additions to this list are appreciated.

1 Robert Folwell 35.00 60.00
2 Harold Gaston 35.00 60.00
3 Daniel Hurley 35.00 60.00
4 Robert Torrey 35.00 60.00

1906 University Ivy League Postcards

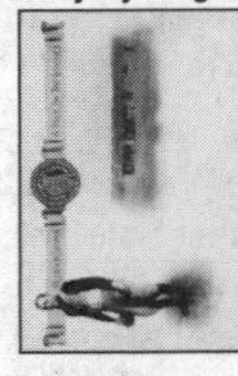

These cards were issued by the University Post Card Company in 1906. Each card includes a black and white player photo to the left and a smaller football action photo in the upper right corner. The player's name is included in a banner at the top along with a caption for the action photo. The backs feature a decorative Post Card style design along with the copyright " The University Post Card Company, Andover, Massachusetts" printed on the left side. Any additions to this list are appreciated.

1 Bebee 35.00 60.00
(Yale)
2 Edward Bennis 35.00 60.00
(Penn; A Play Through Tackle)
3 W.Z. Carr 35.00 60.00
(Harvard)
4 Dexter Draper 35.00 60.00
(Penn, A Talk by the Coaches)
5 Harold Gaston 35.00 60.00
(Penn, Tackling the Dummy)
6 MacDonald ERR 35.00 60.00
(Harvard, misspelled McDonald)
7 James Robinson 35.00 60.00
(Penn, Franklin Field)
8 William Rooke 35.00 60.00
(Pennsylvania)
9 Howard Roome 35.00 60.00
(Yale)
10 J Howard Sheble 60.00 100.00
(Penn; A Good Punt)
11 Vincent Stevenson 75.00 150.00
(Penn; A Good Start)
12 Roswell Tripp 35.00 60.00
(Yale)
13 Paul Veeder 35.00 60.00
(Yale)
14 John Wendell 35.00 60.00
(Harvard)
15 Gus Zeigler 35.00 60.00
(Pennsylvania)

1971 Virginia Team Sheets

The University of Virginia issued these sheets of black-and-white player photos. Each measures roughly 8" by 10 1/4" and was printed on glossy stock with white borders. Each sheet includes photos of 10-players and/or coaches. Below each player's image is his name and position. The photos are blankbacked.

COMPLETE SET (7) 25.00 50.00
STATED ODDS
1 Athletic Staff 4.00 8.00
2 Defensive Soph Performers 4.00 8.00
3 Defensive Sophomore Performers 4.00 8.00
4 Defensive Veterans 4.00 8.00
5 U. of Virginia Cavaliers 4.00 8.00
6 Veteran Offensive Backs-Ends 4.00 8.00
7 Veteran Offensive Linemen 4.00 8.00

1972 Virginia Team Sheets

The University of Virginia issued these sheets of black-and-white player photos. Each measures roughly 8" by 10 1/8" and was printed on glossy stock with white borders. Each sheet includes photos of 2-players. Below each player's image is his name, position, and school. The photos are blankbacked.

COMPLETE SET (8) 30.00 60.00
1 Bill Davis 4.00 8.00
Joe Smith
2 Harrison Davis 4.00 8.00
Dave Sullivan
3 Tom Kennedy 4.00 8.00
Bill Maxwell
4 Jimmy Lacey 4.00 8.00
Gary Helman
5 Steve Shawley 4.00 8.00
Greg Godfrey
6 Leroy Still 4.00 8.00
Gerald Mullins
7 Dennis Scott 4.00 8.00
Billy Williams
8 Kent Merritt 4.00 8.00
Stanley Land

1927 W560 Black

Cards in this set feature athletes from baseball and college football, along with an assortment of other sports and non-sports. The cards were issued in strips and full sheets and follow a standard playing card design. Quite a few Joker cards were produced. We've numbered the cards below according to the suit and playing card number (face cards were assigned numbers as well). It is thought there were at least three different printings and that the baseball and football players were added in the second printing replacing other subjects. All are baseball players below unless otherwise noted. Many cards were printed in a single color red, single color black, and a black/red dual color printing, thereby creating up to three versions. The full set, with just one of each different subject, contains 88-different cards. It is thought that the two-color cards are slightly tougher to find than the single color version.

COMPLETE SET (63) 900.00 1,500.00
*RED: .4X TO 1X BLACK
*BLACK/RED: .5X TO 1.2X BLACK
D1 Dutch Loud 4.00 8.00
(football)
D2 Chris Cagle 7.50 15.00
(football)
D10 D.A. Lowry 4.00 8.00
(misspelled Lowery
(football)
H6 Bruce T. Dumont (football) 4.00 8.00
H9 Al Lassman (football) 4.00 8.00
H12 M.E. Sprague (football) 4.00 8.00
JOK Ken Strong 10.00 20.00

1967 Wake Forest Team Issue

These photos were issued by the school to promote the football program. Each measures roughly 8" by 10" and features a pair of black and white images of players with the school name and year appearing at the top and the player's name and position below each photo. The backs are blank.

COMPLETE SET (9) 40.00 80.00
1 Fred Angerman 5.00 10.00
Rick Decker
2 Eddie Arrington 5.00 10.00
Don Hensley
3 Phil Cheatwood 5.00 10.00
Larry Hambrick
4 Ken Erickson 5.00 10.00
Roman Wszelaki
5 Chick George 5.00 10.00
Bob Flynn
6 Robert Grant 5.00 10.00
Caryle Pate
7 Lloyd Halvorson 5.00 10.00
Tom Deacon
8 Ron Jurewicz 5.00 10.00
Jimmy Clack
9 Bill Overton 5.00 10.00
Joe Theriault

1967 Wake Forest Team Sheets

These photos were issued by the school to promote the football program. Each measures roughly 8" by 10" and features ten black and white images of players with the school name and year appearing at the top. The backs are blank.

COMPLETE SET (3) 20.00 35.00
1 Jack Dolbin 6.00 12.00
Rick White
Fred Angerman
Phil Cheatwood
Fred Barden
Tom Deacon

2 Ron Jurewicz 6.00 12.00
Eddie Arrington
Buz Leavitt
Ken Erickson
Butch Henry
Rick Deck
3 Howard Stanback 6.00 12.00
Ed Atkinson
Digit Laughridge
Carlton Baker
Jimmy Clack
Cary

1968 Wake Forest Team Sheets

These photos were issued by the school to promote the football program. Each measures roughly 8" by 10" and features ten black and white images of players with the school name and year appearing at the top. The backs are blank.

COMPLETE SET (3) 20.00 35.00
1 Jack Dolbin 6.00 12.00
Rick White
Fred Augerman
Jon Schubert
Dick Bozoian
Tom Deacom
J
2 Ron Jurewicz 6.00 12.00
Eddie Arrington
Buz Leavitt
Dave Connors
Larry Russell
Joe Dob
3 Howard Stanback 6.00 12.00
Tom Gavin
Digit Laughridge
Ed George
Jimmy Clack
Caryle Pat

1973 Washington KFC

Sponsored by Kentucky Fried Chicken and KIRO (Radio Northwest 710), these 30 cards measure approximately 3" by 4" and are printed on thick card stock. The fronts feature posed black-and-white head shots with white borders. The Kentucky Fried Chicken logo is in the top border, while player information is printed in the bottom border. The backs are blank. The cards are unnumbered and checklisted below in alphabetical order. The cards were given out by KFC with purchase of their product. Also distributed to purchasers of 5.00 or more was a color team photo or coaches picture measuring approximately 8" by 10".

COMPLETE SET (30) 225.00 450.00
1 Jim Anderson 7.50 15.00
2 Jim Andrilenas 7.50 15.00
3 Glen Bonner 7.50 15.00
4 Bob Boustead 7.50 15.00
5 Skip Boyd 7.50 15.00
6 Gordie Bronson 7.50 15.00
7 Reggie Brown 7.50 15.00
8 Dan Celoni CO 7.50 15.00
9 Brian Daheny 7.50 15.00
10 Fred Dean FL 7.50 15.00
11 Pete Elswick 7.50 15.00
12 Dennis Fitzpatrick 7.50 15.00
13 Bob Graves 7.50 15.00
14 Pedro Hawkins 7.50 15.00
15 Rick Hayes 7.50 15.00
16 Barry Houlihan 7.50 15.00
17 Roberto Jourdan 7.50 15.00
18 Washington Keenan 7.50 15.00
19 Eddie King 7.50 15.00
20 Jim Kristoff 7.50 15.00
21 Murphy McFarland 7.50 15.00
22 Walter Oldes 7.50 15.00
23 Louis Quinn 7.50 15.00
24 Frank Reed 7.50 15.00
25 Dain Rodwell 7.50 15.00
26 Ron Stanley 7.50 15.00
27 Joe Tabor 7.50 15.00
28 Pete Taggares 7.50 15.00
29 John Whitacre 7.50 15.00
30 Hans Woldseth 7.50 15.00
NNO Color Team Photo 10.00 20.00
NNO Coaches Photo 12.50 25.00

1967 Western Michigan Team Issue

These photos were issued by the school to promote the football program. Each measures roughly 5" by 7" and features a black and white image of a player. The backs are blank or sometimes can be found with a typed player identification. Otherwise no player identification is included.

COMPLETE SET (20) 75.00 150.00
1 Sam Antonazzo 4.00 8.00
2 Marty Barski 4.00 8.00
3 Dennis Bridges 4.00 8.00
4 Larry Butler 4.00 8.00
5 Glenn Cherup 4.00 8.00
6 Bill Devine 4.00 8.00
7 Clarence Harville 4.00 8.00
8 John Messenger 4.00 8.00
9 Pete Mitchell 4.00 8.00
10 Steve Mitchell 4.00 8.00
11 Gary Parent 4.00 8.00
12 Terry Pierce 4.00 8.00
13 Gary Rowe 4.00 8.00
14 Tom Randolph 4.00 8.00
15 Tom Saewert 4.00 8.00
16 Orv Schneider 4.00 8.00
17 Ron Seifert 4.00 8.00
18 Michael Sobol 4.00 8.00
19 Rolf Strout 4.00 8.00
20 Rick Trudeau 4.00 8.00

1974 West Virginia Playing Cards

This 54-card set was sponsored by the Student Foundation, a non-profit campus development group. The cards were issued in the playing card format, and each card measures approximately 2 1/8" by 3 1/8". The fronts feature either close-ups or posed action shots of the players. Card backs feature a line drawing of a West Virginia Mountaineer, with the four corners cut off to create triangles. There are two different card backs, same design, but either blue or gold. The set is arranged just like a card deck and checklisted below as follows: C means Clubs, D means Diamonds, H means Hearts, S means Spades, and JOK means Joker. The cards are checklisted below in playing card order by suits and numbers are assigned to Aces (1), Jacks (11), Queens (12), and Kings (13). The jokers are listed at the end. The key card in the set is coach Bobby Bowden.

COMPLETE SET (54) 60.00 120.00
1C Stu Wolpert .60 1.50
1D Mountaineer Coaches 2.50 5.00
1H Leland Byrd AD .60 1.50
1S Bobby Bowden CO 20.00 40.00
2C Jay Sheehan .60 1.50
2D Tom Brandner .60 1.50
2H Tommy Bowden 6.00 12.00
2S Chuck Smith T .60 1.50
3C Ray Marshall .60 1.50
3D Randy Swinson .60 1.50
3H Tom Loadman .60 1.50
3S Bob Kaminski .75 2.00
4C Ron Lee FB 1.50 3.00
4D Kirk Lewis .60 1.50
4H Greg Dorn .60 1.50
4S Emil Ros .60 1.50
5C Mark Burke .60 1.50
5D Rory Fields .60 1.50
5H Gary Lombard .60 1.50
5S Brian Gates .60 1.50
6C John Schell .60 1.50
6D Paul Jordan .60 1.50
6H Mike Hubbard .60 1.50
6S Chuck Kelly .60 1.50
7C Rick Pennypacker .75 2.00
7D Heywood Smith .60 1.50
7H Jack Eastwood .60 1.50
7S Andy Peters .60 1.50
8C Steve Dunlap .60 1.50
8D Dave Wilcher .75 2.00
8H Greg Anderson .60 1.50
8S Ken Culbertson .60 1.50
9C David Van Halanger .60 1.50
9D Rick Shaffer .60 1.50
9H Rich Lukowski .60 1.50
9S Al Gluchoski .60 1.50
10C Dwayne Woods .60 1.50
10D Ben Williams .75 2.00
10H John Adams .60 1.50
10S Tom Florence .60 1.50
11C Marcus Mauney .60 1.50
11D John Spraggins .60 1.50
11H Bruce Huffman .60 1.50
11S Bernie Kirchner .60 1.50
12C Artie Owens .75 2.00
12D Charlie Miller .60 1.50
12H 1974 Cheerleaders .60 1.50
12S Eddie Russell .60 1.50
13C Danny Buggs 2.50 5.00
13D Marshall Mills .60 1.50
13H John Everly .60 1.50
13S Jeff Merrow 2.00 4.00
JOK1 Student Foundation Logo .60 1.50
JOK2 Student Foundation Info .60 1.50

1933 Wheaties College Photo Premiums

This series of team photos was apparently issued as a premium from Wheaties in 1933. Each includes a college football team photo printed on parchment style paper stock. The backs are blank.

NNO Loyola U. 50.00 80.00
NNO San Francisco U. 50.00 80.00
NNO Stanford 50.00 80.00

1908-09 Wisconsin Postcards

These black and white postcards was issued from roughly 1908-1909. The player's last name is included below the photo and the backs feature a typical postcard style format. Any additions to the list below are appreciated.

1 F.E. Boyle 30.00 50.00
2 Moll 30.00 50.00
3 Osthoff 30.00 50.00
4 Jumbo Stiehm 35.00 60.00
5 Wilce 30.00 50.00

1915-20 Wisconsin Postcards

These black and white postcards was issued from roughly 1915-1920 primarily by the Photoart House in Madison, Wisconsin. The player's name is typically included in small letters across his chest with the company name appearing at his belt. A number of different game action shots were also produced and we've cataloged those that include players on them along with the card's printed description. The backs feature a typical postcard style format with the manufacturer's name and address. Any additions to the list below are appreciated.

1 Cub Buck 200.00 350.00
2 George Bunge 30.00 50.00
3 Dow Beyers UER 30.00 50.00
(Photoart, spelled Byers)
4 Dow Beyers UER 30.00 50.00
(McKillop Photo, spelled Byers)
5 Rowdy Elliott 30.00 50.00
6 William Juneau CO 30.00 50.00
7 Louis Kreuz 30.00 50.00
8 Arlie Mucks 30.00 50.00
9 Lynwood Smith 30.00 50.00
10 Glenn Taylor 30.00 50.00
11 Action; Smith - Wis. with ball 30.00 50.00
(action shot of Lynwood Smith)
12 Action; Wisc 3 - Minn 20 25.00 50.00

1951-53 Wisconsin Hall of Fame Postcards

These 12 postcards were issued by the Wisconsin Hall of Fame and feature some of the leading athletes out of Milwaukee. The sepia illustrations have a relief of the player as well as some information about them. Since these cards are unnumbered, we have sequenced them in alphabetical order.

COMPLETE SET (12) 175.00 350.00
6 Ernie Nevers FB 40.00 80.00
8 Pat O'Dea FB 15.00 30.00
9 Dave Schreiner FB 7.50 15.00
12 Bob Zuppke CO FB 20.00 40.00

1972 Wisconsin Team Sheets

The University of Wisconsin issued these sheets of black-and-white player photos. Each measures roughly 8" by 10" and was printed on glossy stock with white borders. Each sheet includes photos of 10-players and/or coaches. Below each player's image is his jersey number, name, school class, position, height, and weight. The photos are blankbacked.

COMPLETE SET (2) 15.00 30.00
1 Rick Jakious 10.00 20.00
2 Rufus Ferguson 5.00 10.00

1974 Wisconsin Team Sheets

These photos were issued by the school to promote the football program. Each measures roughly 8" by 10" and features eight black and white images of players with the school name appearing at the top. The backs are blank.

1 John Jardine CO 4.00 8.00
Dennis Lick
Bill Marek
Gregg Bohlig
Art Sanger
Jeff Mack
Ja
2 Rodney Rhodes 4.00 8.00
Ken Starch
Larry Canada
Mark Zakula
Rick Jarious
Terry Stieve

1909 Yale Postcards

These postcards were issued in 1909 and feature members of the Yale football team. The fronts include a large black and white image of the player with his name, position, and school identified below the photo. The backs featue a standard "private mailing card" style design with the publisher's name: B. B. Steiber.

COMPLETE SET (14) 300.00 500.00
1 Ham Andrus 30.00 50.00
2 Biddle 30.00 50.00
3 Bob Burch 30.00 50.00
4 Art Brides 30.00 50.00
5 Carrol Cooney 30.00 50.00
6 Ted Coy 30.00 50.00
7 Bill Goebel 30.00 50.00
8 Haines 30.00 50.00
9 Henry Hobbs 30.00 50.00
10 Tad Jones CO 30.00 50.00
11 Reed Kilpatrick 30.00 50.00
12 W.S. Logan 30.00 50.00
13 Steve Philbin 30.00 50.00
14 Wheaton 30.00 50.00

1955 B.C. Lions Team Issue

These 8" by 10" photos feature members of the B.C. Lions and were issued by the team. Each includes the player's name and position along with the team name and photographer (Artray Ltd.) notation. The photo backs are generally blank except for those that can often by found with the photographer's (Artray Ltd.) stamp.

COMPLETE SET (8) 50.00 100.00
1 By Bailey 12.50 25.00
2 Ron Baker 5.00 10.00
3 Ken Higgs 5.00 10.00
4 Laurie Niemi 5.00 10.00
5 Al Pollard 5.00 10.00
6 Mac Speedie 10.00 20.00
7 Primo Villanueva 5.00 10.00
8 Arnie Weinmeister 12.50 25.00

1956 B.C. Lions Team Issue

These 8" by 10" sepia toned photos feature members of the B.C. Lions and were issued by the team. Each includes the player's name, height, weight, position, team name and year in the border below the image. The photo backs are generally blank except for those that can often by found with the photographer's (Graphic Industries Ltd.) stamp.

COMPLETE SET (38) 175.00 300.00
1 Ken Arkell 5.00 10.00
2 By Bailey 12.50 25.00
3 Ron Baker 5.00 10.00
4 Bob Brady 5.00 10.00
5 Paul Cameron 5.00 10.00

6 Vic Chapman 5.00 10.00
7 Glen Christian 5.00 10.00
8 Ron Clinkscale 5.00 10.00
9 Chuck Dubuque 5.00 10.00
10 Dan Edwards 5.00 10.00
11 Norm Fieldgate 10.00 20.00
12 Arnie Galiffa 6.00 12.00
13 Jerry Gustafson 5.00 10.00
14 Bob Hantla 5.00 10.00
15 Ken Higgs 5.00 10.00
16 Bill Hortie 5.00 10.00
17 John Jankins 5.00 10.00
18 Roy Jenson 5.00 10.00
19 Ivan Livingstone 6.00 12.00
20 Don Lord 5.00 10.00
21 Rommie Loudd 5.00 10.00
22 Norm Masters 6.00 12.00
23 Carl Mayes 5.00 10.00
24 Jim Mitchener 5.00 10.00
25 Brian Mulhern 5.00 10.00
26 Steve Palmer 5.00 10.00
27 Doug Peters 5.00 10.00
28 Al Pollard 5.00 10.00
29 Chuck Quilter 5.00 10.00
30 Fred Robinson 5.00 10.00
31 Don Ross 5.00 10.00
32 Rae Ross 5.00 10.00
33 Frank Smith 5.00 10.00
34 Ken Stallwell 5.00 10.00
35 Bill Stuart 5.00 10.00
36 Tony Teresa 5.00 10.00
37 Primo Villanueva 5.00 10.00
38 Ron Watton 5.00 10.00

1957 B.C. Lions Team Issue 5x8

These 5" by 8" photos feature members of the B.C. Lions and were issued by the team. Each includes the player's name, position, team name and year in the border below the image. The photo backs are blank. A larger size photo was also issued for each player.

COMPLETE SET (64) 250.00 400.00
1 Tom Allman 4.00 10.00
2 Ken Arkell 4.00 10.00
3 By Bailey 10.00 20.00
4 Emery Barnes 4.00 10.00
5 Bob Brady 4.00 10.00
6 Rudy Brooks 4.00 10.00
7 Mike Cacic 4.00 10.00
8 Paul Cameron 4.00 10.00
9 Bill Carrington 4.00 10.00
10 Vic Chapman 4.00 10.00
11 Glen Christian 4.00 10.00
12 Bob Dickie 4.00 10.00
13 Chuck Dubuque 4.00 10.00
14 Jerry Duncan 5.00 12.00
15 Maury Duncan 4.00 10.00
16 Dan Edwards 4.00 10.00
17 Norm Fieldgate 7.50 15.00
18 Dick Foster 4.00 10.00
19 Chuck Frank 4.00 10.00
20 Mel Gillett 4.00 10.00
21 Vern Hallback 4.00 10.00
22 Bob Hantla 4.00 10.00
23 Sherman Hood 4.00 10.00
24 Ted Hunt 4.00 10.00
25 Jerry Janes 4.00 10.00
26 John Jankins 4.00 10.00
27 Roy Jenson 4.00 10.00
28 Rick Kaser 4.00 10.00
29 Al Kopare 4.00 10.00
30 Cas Krol 4.00 10.00
31 Ray Lackner 4.00 10.00
32 Paul Larson 4.00 10.00
33 Henry Laughlin 4.00 10.00
34 Wally Lencz 4.00 10.00
35 Vic Lindskog 4.00 10.00
36 Vern Lofstrom 4.00 10.00
37 Don Lord 4.00 10.00
38 Rommie Loudd 4.00 10.00
39 Walt Mazur 4.00 10.00
40 Harrison McDonald 4.00 10.00
41 Jim Mitchener 4.00 10.00
42 Steve Palmer 4.00 10.00
43 Matt Phillips 4.00 10.00
44 Joe Poirier 5.00 12.00
45 Chuck Quilter 4.00 10.00
46 Lorne Reid 4.00 10.00
47 Don Ross 4.00 10.00
48 Rae Ross 4.00 10.00
49 Leo Rucka 4.00 10.00
50 Art Shannon 4.00 10.00
51 Ed Sharkey 4.00 10.00
52 Frank Smith 4.00 10.00
53 Hal Sparrow 4.00 10.00
54 Ian Stewart 4.00 10.00
55 Tony Teresa 4.00 10.00
56 Toppy Vann 4.00 10.00
57 Don Vicic 4.00 10.00
58 Primo Villanueva 4.00 10.00
59 Ron Watton 4.00 10.00
60 Dave West 4.00 10.00
61 Ken Whitten 4.00 10.00
62 Phil Wright 4.00 10.00
63 Joe Yamauchi 4.00 10.00
64 Team Photo 5.00 10.00

1957 B.C. Lions Team Issue 8x10

These 8" by 10" sepia toned photos feature members of the B.C. Lions and were issued by the team. Each includes the player's name, position, team name and year in the border below the image. The photo backs are generally blank except for those that can often by found with the photographer's (Graphic Industries Ltd.) stamp. A smaller size photo was also issued for each player.

COMPLETE SET (64) 300.00 500.00
1 Tom Allman 5.00 10.00
2 Ken Arkell 5.00 10.00
3 By Bailey 12.50 25.00
4 Emery Barnes 5.00 10.00
5 Bob Brady 5.00 10.00
6 Rudy Brooks 5.00 10.00
7 Mike Cacic 5.00 10.00
8 Paul Cameron 5.00 10.00
9 Bill Carrington 5.00 10.00
10 Vic Chapman 5.00 10.00
11 Glen Christian 5.00 10.00
12 Bob Dickie 5.00 10.00
13 Chuck Dubuque 5.00 10.00
14 Jerry Duncan 6.00 12.00
15 Maury Duncan 5.00 10.00
16 Dan Edwards 5.00 10.00
17 Norm Fieldgate 10.00 20.00
18 Dick Foster 5.00 10.00
19 Chuck Frank 5.00 10.00
20 Mel Gillett 5.00 10.00
21 Vern Hallback 5.00 10.00
22 Bob Hantla 5.00 10.00
23 Sherman Hood 5.00 10.00
24 Ted Hunt 5.00 10.00
25 Jerry Janes 5.00 10.00
26 John Jankins 5.00 10.00
27 Roy Jenson 5.00 10.00
28 Rick Kaser 5.00 10.00
29 Al Kopare 5.00 10.00
30 Cas Krol 5.00 10.00
31 Ray Lackner 5.00 10.00
32 Paul Larson 5.00 10.00
33 Henry Laughlin 5.00 10.00
34 Wally Lencz 5.00 10.00
35 Vic Lindskog 5.00 10.00
36 Vern Lofstrom 5.00 10.00
37 Don Lord 5.00 10.00
38 Rommie Loudd 5.00 10.00
39 Walt Mazur 5.00 10.00
40 Harrison McDonald 5.00 10.00
41 Jim Mitchener 5.00 10.00
42 Steve Palmer 5.00 10.00
43 Matt Phillips 5.00 10.00
44 Joe Poirier 6.00 12.00
45 Chuck Quilter 5.00 10.00
46 Lorne Reid 5.00 10.00
47 Don Ross 5.00 10.00
48 Rae Ross 5.00 10.00
49 Leo Rucka 5.00 10.00
50 Art Shannon 5.00 10.00
51 Ed Sharkey 5.00 10.00
52 Frank Smith 5.00 10.00
53 Hal Sparrow 5.00 10.00
54 Ian Stewart 5.00 10.00
55 Tony Teresa 5.00 10.00
56 Toppy Vann 5.00 10.00
57 Don Vicic 5.00 10.00
58 Primo Villanueva 5.00 10.00
59 Ron Watton 5.00 10.00
60 Dave West 5.00 10.00
61 Ken Whitten 5.00 10.00
62 Phil Wright 5.00 10.00
63 Joe Yamauchi 5.00 10.00
64 Team Photo 6.00 12.00

1958 B.C. Lions Clearbrook Farms

Measuring 3 3/4" by 5", these cards were sponsored by Clearbrook Farm Milk and House of Shannon. The fronts feature black-and-white photos with the player's name, position, team name, and year below the photo. The cards are unnumbered and checklisted below in alphabetical order.

1 By Bailey 15.00 30.00
2 John Bayuk 10.00 20.00
3 Don Bingham 10.00 20.00
4 Bob Brady 10.00 20.00
5 Bill Britton 10.00 20.00
6 Pete Brown 10.00 20.00
7 Mike Cacic 10.00 20.00
8 Paul Cameron 81 10.00 20.00
9 Paul Cameron 90 10.00 20.00
10 Vic Chapman 10.00 20.00
11 Gord Chiarot 10.00 20.00
12 Dick Chrobak 10.00 20.00
13 Mike Davies 10.00 20.00
14 Bob Dickie 10.00 20.00
15 Hugh Drake 10.00 20.00
16 Chuck Dubuque 10.00 20.00
17 Jerry Duncan 10.00 20.00
18 Dan Edwards 10.00 20.00
19 Alvie Elliott 10.00 20.00
20 Maurice Elias 10.00 20.00
21 Ed Enos 10.00 20.00
22 Norm Fieldgate 12.50 25.00
23 Chuck Frank 10.00 20.00
24 Mel Gillett 10.00 20.00
25 Larry Goble 10.00 20.00
26 John Groom 10.00 20.00
27 Jerry Gustafson 10.00 20.00
28 Urban Henry 10.00 20.00
29 George Herring 10.00 20.00
30 Tom Hinton 10.00 20.00
31 Laurie Hodgson 10.00 20.00
32 Sonny Homer 10.00 20.00
33 Ted Hunt 10.00 20.00
34 Curt Iaukea 10.00 20.00
35 Jerry Janes 10.00 20.00
36 Jerry Johnson 10.00 20.00
37 Steve Kapasky 10.00 20.00
38 Rick Kaser 10.00 20.00
39 Earl Keeley 10.00 20.00
40 Ray Lackner 10.00 20.00
41 Vern Lofstrom 10.00 20.00
42 Don Lord 10.00 20.00
43 Marty Martinello 10.00 20.00
44 Norm Masters 10.00 20.00
45 Gordie Mitchell 10.00 20.00
46 Gordie MacDonald 10.00 20.00
47 Baz Nagle 10.00 20.00
48 Pete Neft 10.00 20.00
49 Rod Pantages 10.00 20.00
50 Matt Phillips 10.00 20.00
51 Joe Poirier 10.00 20.00
52 Roger Power 10.00 20.00
53 Chuck Quilter 10.00 20.00
54 Howard Schnellenberger 12.50 25.00
55 Art Shannon 10.00 20.00
56 Ed Sharkey 10.00 20.00
57 Billy Clyde Smith 10.00 20.00
58 Harold Sparrow 10.00 20.00
59 Ed Vereb 10.00 20.00
60 Don Vicic 10.00 20.00
61 Primo Villanueva 10.00 20.00
62 Bob Ward 10.00 20.00
63 Duke Washington 10.00 20.00
64 Ron Watton 10.00 20.00
65 Hall Whitley 10.00 20.00
66 Bob Winters 10.00 20.00
67 Joe Yamauchi 10.00 20.00

1958 B.C. Lions Puritan Meats

Measuring 2 1/4 by 3 3/8", these cards were distributed with Puritan canned meat products in late 1958. The fronts feature black-and-white posed action photos inside white borders. In bold black lettering, the player's name, position, height, and weight are given. Immediately after in italic print is a player profile. In addition to a team logo, the back carries an offer for a 1958 B.C. Lions album for three Puritan product wrappers and 20 cents. The cards are unnumbered and checklisted below in alphabetical order. Although the album contains spaces for just 33-cards, more than that have been confirmed.

COMPLETE SET (46) 600.00 1,000.00
1 By Bailey 30.00 50.00
2 Bob Brady 15.00 25.00
3 Bill Britton 15.00 25.00
3 Curt Iaukea 15.00 25.00
4 Pete Brown 15.00 25.00
5 Mike Cacic 15.00 25.00
6 Paul Cameron 15.00 25.00
7 Vic Chapman 15.00 25.00
8 Gord Chiarot 15.00 25.00
9 Mike Davies 15.00 25.00
10 Chuck Dubuque 15.00 25.00
11 Dan Edwards 15.00 25.00
12 Ed Enos 15.00 25.00
13 Norm Fieldgate 20.00 35.00
14 Chuck Frank 15.00 25.00
15 Mel Gillett 15.00 25.00
16 Larry Goble 15.00 25.00
17 Urban Henry 15.00 25.00
18 George Herring 15.00 25.00
19 Tom Hinton 15.00 25.00
20 Laurie Hodgson 15.00 25.00
21 Sonny Homer 15.00 25.00
22 Ted Hunt 15.00 25.00
24 Gerry James 25.00 40.00
25 Steve Kapasky 15.00 25.00
26 Rick Kaser 15.00 25.00
27 Earl Keeley 15.00 25.00
28 Ray Lackner 15.00 25.00
29 Don Lord 15.00 25.00
30 Gordie MacDonald 15.00 25.00
31 Marty Martinello 15.00 25.00
32 Gordie Mitchell 15.00 25.00
33 Baz Nagle 15.00 25.00
34 Pete Neft 15.00 25.00
35 Matt Phillips 15.00 25.00
36 Joe Poirier 15.00 25.00
37 Roger Power 15.00 25.00
38 Chuck Quilter 15.00 25.00
39 Howard Schnellenberger 25.00 40.00
40 Ed Sharkey 15.00 25.00
41 Billy Clyde Smith 15.00 25.00
42 Ed Vereb 15.00 25.00
43 Don Vicic 15.00 25.00
44 Primo Villanueva 15.00 25.00
45 Bob Ward 15.00 25.00
46 Duke Washington 15.00 25.00
47 Ron Watton 15.00 25.00
48 Hall Whitley 15.00 25.00
49 Bob Winters 15.00 25.00
50 Joe Yamauchi 15.00 25.00

1959 B.C. Lions Program Inserts

Cards from this set were inserted in 1959 Lions programs - one per program. Each measures roughly 4" by 5" and features a black and white player image with his name, position, and year printed below the photo. The blankbacked photos do not feature any sponsorship logos.

COMPLETE SET (42) 250.00 400.00
1 By Bailey 10.00 20.00
2 Bob Brady 5.00 10.00
3 Bill Britton 5.00 10.00
4 Bruce Claridge 5.00 10.00
5 Chuck Diamond 5.00 10.00
6 Al Dorow 10.00 20.00
7 Chuck Dubuque 5.00 10.00
8 Randy Duncan 10.00 20.00
9 Norm Fieldgate 10.00 20.00
10 Willie Fleming 12.50 25.00
11 Jim Furey 5.00 10.00
12 Chuck Gavin 5.00 10.00
13 Mel Gillett 5.00 10.00
14 Urban Henry 6.00 12.00
15 Tom Hinton 6.00 12.00
16 Sonny Homer 6.00 12.00
17 Curt Iaukea 5.00 10.00
18 Gerry James 12.50 25.00
19 Bill Jessup 5.00 10.00
20 Roy Jokanovich 5.00 10.00
21 Earl Keeley 6.00 12.00
22 Vic Kristopaitis 5.00 10.00
23 Lavern Lofstrom 5.00 10.00
24 Don Lord 5.00 10.00
25 Marty Martinello 5.00 10.00
26 Gordie Mitchell 5.00 10.00
27 Baz Nagle 5.00 10.00
28 Chuck Quilter 5.00 10.00
29 Ted Roman 5.00 10.00
30 Vince Scorsone 5.00 10.00
31 Hal Sparrow 5.00 10.00
32 Ed Sullivan 5.00 10.00
33 Ted Tully 5.00 10.00
34 Don Vassos 5.00 10.00
35 Ed Vereb 5.00 10.00
36 Don Vicic 5.00 10.00
37 Ron Watton 5.00 10.00
38 Hank Whitley 5.00 10.00
39 Jim Wood 5.00 10.00
40 Joe Yamauchi 5.00 10.00
41 Coaches 5.00 10.00
42 Team Photo 6.00 12.00

1959 B.C. Lions Woodward's

These 4" by 5" photos are virtually identical to the 1959 B.C. Lions Team Issue photos with the addition of the "Woodward's" logo in the lower right hand corner. Each photo features a facsimile autograph printed in blue ink across the player image.

COMPLETE SET (4) 25.00 50.00
1 By Bailey 12.50 25.00
2 Don Vassos 5.00 10.00
3 Baz Nagle 5.00 10.00
4 Hank Whitley 5.00 10.00

1960 B.C. Lions CKWX Program Inserts

Cards from this set were inserted in 1960 Lions programs one card per program. Each measures roughly 4" by 5" and features a black and white player image with his name, position, and year printed below the photo. The photos were sponsored by CKWX radio and feature a facsimilie player autograph. At the time, a complete set of 40-photos could be ordered for $2 via a program offer.

COMPLETE SET (40) 175.00 300.00
1 By Bailey 10.00 20.00
2 Dave Barrus 4.00 8.00
3 Nub Beamer 4.00 8.00
4 Neil Beaumont 5.00 10.00
5 Bill Britton 4.00 8.00
6 Mike Cacic 4.00 8.00
7 Roy Cameron 4.00 8.00
8 Jim Carphin 4.00 8.00

9 Joe Carruthers 4.00 8.00
10 Bruce Claridge 4.00 8.00
11 Steve Cotter 4.00 8.00
12 Lonnie Dennis 4.00 8.00
13 Randy Duncan 7.50 15.00
14 Norm Fieldgate 7.50 15.00
15 Willie Fleming 10.00 20.00
16 Jim Furey 4.00 8.00
17 Frank Gilliam 4.00 8.00
18 George Grant 4.00 8.00
19 Urban Henry 5.00 10.00
20 Bill Herron 4.00 8.00
21 Tom Hinton 5.00 10.00
22 Sonny Homer 5.00 10.00
23 Bob Jeter 7.50 15.00
24 Jim Jones 4.00 8.00
25 Earl Keeley 5.00 10.00
26 Vic Kristopaitis 4.00 8.00
27 John Land 4.00 8.00
28 Vern Lofstrom 4.00 8.00
29 Doug Mitchell 4.00 8.00
30 Gordie Mitchell 4.00 8.00
31 Baz Nagle 4.00 8.00
32 Ted Roman 4.00 8.00
33 Harold Sparrow 4.00 8.00
34 Ed Sullivan 5.00 10.00
35 Don Vassos 4.00 8.00
36 Don Vicic 4.00 8.00
37 Jim Walden 4.00 8.00
38 Ron Watton 4.00 8.00
39 Joe Yamauchi 4.00 8.00
40 Coaches Photo 4.00 8.00

1961 B.C. Lions CKNW Program Inserts

Each of these photos measure approximately 3 7/8" by 5 1/2". Inside white borders, the fronts feature black-and-white posed action photos. The player's facsimile autograph is written across the picture in either black or orange colored ink. Immediately below the picture in small print are player information and "Graphic Industries Limited Photo." The wider white bottom border also carries sponsor information and a five- or six-digit serial number. Apparently the photos were primarily sponsored by CKNW (a radio station), which appears on every photo, and various other co-sponsors that may vary from card to card. The photos show signs of perforation as they were originally issued in game programs. The backs display various advertisements. The photos are unnumbered and checklisted below in alphabetical order. The co-sponsors (listed on the card front) are also listed below. The set can be distinguished from the set of the following year by the presence of the set's date in the lower left corner of the cardfront.

COMPLETE SET (30) 125.00 200.00
1 By Bailey 7.50 15.00
2 Nub Beamer 3.00 6.00
3 Bob Belak 3.00 6.00
4 Neil Beaumont 4.00 8.00
5 Bill Britton 3.00 6.00
6 Tom Brown 4.00 8.00
7 Mike Cacic 3.00 6.00
8 Jim Carphin 3.00 6.00
9 Bruce Claridge 3.00 6.00
10 Pat Claridge 3.00 6.00
11 Steve Cotter 3.00 6.00
12 Lonnie Dennis 3.00 6.00
13 Norm Fieldgate 5.00 8.00
14 Willie Fleming 10.00 20.00
15 George Grant 3.00 6.00
16 Tom Hinton 4.00 8.00
17 Sonny Homer 4.00 8.00
18 Bob Jeter 5.00 10.00
19 Dick Johnson 3.00 6.00
20 Joe Kapp 10.00 20.00
21 Earl Keeley 4.00 8.00
22 Vic Kristopaitis 3.00 6.00
23 Vern Lofstrom 3.00 6.00
24 Gordie Mitchell 3.00 6.00
25 Rae Ross 3.00 6.00
26 Bob Schloredt 4.00 8.00
27 Mel Semenko 3.00 6.00
28 Ed Sullivan 4.00 8.00
29 Barney Therrien 3.00 6.00
30 Ed Vereb 3.00 6.00
31 Don Vicic 3.00 6.00
32 Ron Watton 3.00 6.00

1961 B.C. Lions Team Issue

These 8" by 10" black and white photos feature members of the B.C. Lions and were issued by the team. Each photo includes the player's name, position, team name and year in the border below the image. The photo backs are blank.

COMPLETE SET (32) 150.00 300.00
1 By Bailey 10.00 20.00
2 Nub Beamer 5.00 10.00
3 Neil Beaumont 6.00 12.00
4 Bob Belak 5.00 10.00
5 Bill Britton 5.00 10.00
6 Tom Brown 6.00 12.00
7 Mike Cacic 5.00 10.00
8 Jim Carphin 5.00 10.00
9 Bruce Claridge 5.00 10.00
10 Pat Claridge 5.00 10.00
11 Lonnie Dennis 5.00 10.00
12 Norm Fieldgate 7.50 15.00
13 Willie Fleming 10.00 20.00
14 George Grant 5.00 10.00
15 Tom Hinton 6.00 12.00
16 Sonny Homer 6.00 12.00
17 Bob Jeter 7.50 15.00
18 Dick Johnson 5.00 10.00
19 Jim Jones 5.00 10.00
20 Earl Keeley 6.00 12.00
21 Vic Kristopaitis 5.00 10.00
22 Vern Lofstrom 5.00 10.00
23 Gordie Mitchell 5.00 10.00
24 Ed O'Bradovich 6.00 12.00
25 Bob Schloredt 6.00 12.00
26 Mel Semenko 5.00 10.00
27 Barney Therrien 5.00 10.00
28 Don Vicic 5.00 10.00
29 Jim Walden 5.00 10.00
30 Ron Watton 5.00 10.00
31 Joe Wendryhoski 5.00 10.00
32 Coaches 5.00 10.00

1962 B.C. Lions CKNW Program Inserts

Each of these photos measure approximately 3 7/8" by 5 1/2". Inside white borders, the fronts feature black-and-white posed action photos. The player's facsimile autograph is written across the picture; on most of the cards it is in red ink. Immediately below the picture in small print are player information and "Graphic Industries Limited Photo." The wider white bottom border also carries sponsor information and a five- or six-digit serial number. Apparently the photos were primarily sponsored by CKNW (a radio station), which appears on every photo, and various other co-sponsors that may vary from card to card. The photos show signs of perforation as they were originally issued in game programs. The backs display various advertisements. The photos are unnumbered and checklisted below in alphabetical order. The co-sponsors are also listed below. The set can be distinguished from the set of the previous year by the presence of the set's date in the lower left corner of the cardfront.

COMPLETE SET (32) 125.00 200.00
1 By Bailey 7.50 15.00
2 Nub Beamer 3.50 6.00
3 Neil Beaumont 5.00 8.00
4 Bob Belak 3.50 6.00
5 Walt Bilicki 3.50 6.00
6 Tom Brown 5.00 8.00
7 Mack Burton 5.00 8.00
8 Mike Cacic 3.50 6.00
9 Jim Carphin 3.50 6.00
10 Pat Claridge 3.50 6.00
11 Steve Cotter 3.50 6.00
12 Lonnie Dennis 3.50 6.00
13 Norm Fieldgate 3.50 6.00
14 Willie Fleming 10.00 20.00
15 Dick Fouts 5.00 8.00
16 George Grant 3.50 6.00
17 Ian Hagemoen 3.50 6.00
18 Tommy Hinton 5.00 8.00
19 Sonny Homer 5.00 8.00
20 Joe Kapp 10.00 20.00
21 Earl Keeley 5.00 8.00
22 Vic Kristopaitis 3.50 6.00
23 Tom Larscheid 3.50 6.00
24 Mike Martin 3.50 6.00
25 Gordie Mitchell 3.50 6.00
26 Baz Nagle 3.50 6.00
27 Bob Schloredt 5.00 8.00
28 Gary Schwertfeger 3.50 6.00
29 Willie Taylor 5.00 8.00
30 Barney Therrien 3.50 6.00
31 Don Vicic 3.50 6.00
32 Tom Walker 3.50 6.00

1962 B.C. Lions Team Issue

These 4 1/2" by 6" black and white photos feature members of the B.C. Lions and were issued by the team. Each includes the player's name, position, team name and year in the border below the image. The photo backs are blank.

COMPLETE SET (12) 75.00 125.00
1 By Bailey 7.50 15.00
2 Neil Beaumont 5.00 10.00
3 Walt Bilicki 4.00 8.00
4 Tom Brown 5.00 10.00
5 Pat Claridge 4.00 8.00
6 Norm Fieldgate 7.50 15.00
7 Willie Fleming 10.00 20.00
8 Dick Fouts 5.00 10.00
9 Joe Kapp 10.00 20.00
10 Vic Kristopaitis 4.00 8.00
11 Gordie Mitchell 4.00 8.00
12 Don Vicic 4.00 8.00

1963 B.C. Lions Photo Gallery Program Inserts

These photo gallery sheets were actually page inserts into 1963 Lions game programs. Each features four Lions players on the front under the title "B.C. Lions Photo Gallery -- 1963." The backs feature another page from the program with advertising or other game related text. We've listed them below as uncut sheets in order by game program date.

COMPLETE SET (10) 60.00 100.00
1 1-Aug 10.00 20.00
2 12-Aug 7.50 15.00
3 19-Aug 6.00 12.00
4 7-Sep 4.00 8.00
5 16-Sep 4.00 8.00
6 30-Sep 5.00 10.00
7 12-Oct 6.00 12.00
8 19-Oct 4.00 8.00
9 3-Nov 4.00 8.00
10 November 20,23 10.00 20.00

1963 B.C. Lions Team Issue

These 4 1/2" by 5 1/2" black and white photos feature members of the B.C. Lions and were issued by the team. Each includes the player's name and year in the border below the image. The photo backs are blank.

COMPLETE SET (10) 50.00 100.00
1 By Bailey 7.50 15.00
2 Neil Beaumont 5.00 10.00
3 Walt Bilicki 4.00 8.00
4 Tom Brown 5.00 10.00
5 Pat Claridge 4.00 8.00
6 Steve Cotter 4.00 8.00
7 Norm Fieldgate 6.00 12.00
8 Willie Fleming 7.50 15.00
9 Dick Fouts 5.00 10.00
10 Joe Kapp 10.00 20.00

1964 B.C. Lions CKWX Program Inserts

Each of these photos was sponsored by CKWX radio and measure roughly 3 7/8" by 5 1/4". The fronts feature black-and-white photos of B.C. Lions players. The player's facsimile autograph is written across the picture in red ink. Immediately below the picture in small print is the player's name, position, jersey number, team and year of issue. The wider bottom border carries the sponsor information and a five- or six-digit serial number. The photos were primarily sponsored by CKWX and other co-sponsors on the card fronts that may vary from card to card. The photos show signs of perforation as they were originally issued 4-per page in Lions game programs. The backs display various advertisements. The photos are unnumbered and checklisted below in alphabetical order. Any additions to this list are appreciated.

COMPLETE SET (35) 125.00 200.00
1 By Bailey 7.50 15.00
2 Emery Barnes 3.00 6.00
3 Neil Beaumont 4.00 8.00
4 Walt Bilicki 3.00 6.00
5 Tom Brown 4.00 8.00
6 Mack Burton 4.00 8.00
7 Mike Cacic 3.00 6.00
8 Jim Carphin 3.00 6.00
9 Pat Claridge 3.00 6.00
10 Steve Cotter 3.00 6.00
11 Lonnie Dennis 3.00 6.00
12 Norm Fieldgate 5.00 10.00
13 Greg Findlay 3.00 6.00
14 Willie Fleming 7.50 15.00
15 Dick Fouts 4.00 8.00
16 Bill Frank 3.00 6.00
17 Tom Hinton 4.00 8.00
18 Lou Holland 3.00 6.00
19 Sonny Homer 4.00 8.00
20 Joe Kapp 7.50 15.00
21 Gus Kasapis 3.00 6.00
22 Peter Kempf 3.00 6.00
23 Bill Lasseter 3.00 6.00
24 Mike Martin 3.00 6.00
25 Mel Melin 3.00 6.00
26 Ron Morris 3.00 6.00
27 Bill Munsey 4.00 8.00
28 Pete Ohler 3.00 6.00
29 Gary Schwertfeger 3.00 6.00
30 Paul Seale 3.00 6.00
31 Steve Shafer 3.00 6.00
32 Ken Sugarman 3.00 6.00
33 Bob Swift 3.00 6.00
34 Don Vicic 3.00 6.00
35 Jesse Williams 3.00 6.00

1964 B.C. Lions Team Issue

These 8" by 10" photos feature members of the B.C. Lions and were issued by the team. Each includes two photos of the featured player along with an extensive bio on the front. The photo backs are blank.

COMPLETE SET (35) 125.00 250.00
1 By Bailey 7.50 15.00
2 Emery Barnes 4.00 8.00
3 Neil Beaumont 5.00 10.00
4 Walt Bilicki 4.00 8.00
5 Tom Brown 5.00 10.00
6 Mack Burton 5.00 10.00
7 Mike Cacic 4.00 8.00
8 Jim Carphin 4.00 8.00
9 Pat Claridge 4.00 8.00
10 Steve Cotter 4.00 8.00
11 Lonnie Dennis 4.00 8.00
12 Norm Fieldgate 6.00 12.00
13 Greg Findlay 4.00 8.00
14 Willie Fleming 7.50 15.00
15 Dick Fouts 5.00 10.00
16 Bill Frank 4.00 8.00
17 Tom Hinton 5.00 10.00
18 Louie Holland 4.00 8.00
19 Sonny Homer 5.00 10.00
20 Joe Kapp 10.00 20.00
21 Gus Kasapis 4.00 8.00
22 Peter Kempf 4.00 8.00
23 Bill Lasseter 4.00 8.00
24 Mike Martin 4.00 8.00
25 Mel Melin 4.00 8.00
26 Ron Morris 4.00 8.00
27 Bill Munsey 5.00 10.00
28 Pete Ohler 4.00 8.00
29 Gary Schwertfeger 4.00 8.00
30 Paul Seale 4.00 8.00
31 Steve Shafer 4.00 8.00
32 Ken Sugarman 4.00 8.00
33 Bob Swift 4.00 8.00
34 Don Vicic 4.00 8.00
35 Jesse Williams 4.00 8.00

1965 B.C. Lions Program Inserts

Each of these photos did not include a sponsor like previous years and measure roughly 3 7/8" by 5 1/4". The fronts feature black-and-white photos of B.C. Lions players. The player's facsimile autograph is written below the player photo along with the player's name, position, jersey number, team and year of issue. The photos show signs of perforation as they were originally issued 4-per page in Lions game programs. The backs display various advertisements. The photos are unnumbered and checklisted below in alphabetical order. Any additions to this list are appreciated.

COMPLETE SET (30) 125.00 200.00
1 Ernie Allen 3.00 6.00
2 Neil Beaumont 4.00 8.00
3 Walt Bilicki 3.00 6.00
4 Tom Brown 4.00 8.00
5 Mack Burton 4.00 8.00
6 Mike Cacic 3.00 6.00
7 Jim Carphin 3.00 6.00
8 Pat Claridge 3.00 6.00
9 Steve Cotter 3.00 6.00
10 Lonnie Dennis 3.00 6.00
11 Norm Fieldgate 6.00 12.00
12 Greg Findlay 3.00 6.00
13 Willie Fleming 7.50 15.00
14 Dick Fouts 4.00 8.00
15 Tom Hinton 4.00 8.00
16 Sonny Homer 4.00 8.00
17 Joe Kapp 7.50 15.00
18 Gus Kasapis 3.00 6.00
19 Peter Kempf 3.00 6.00
20 Bill Lasseter 3.00 6.00
21 Mike Martin 3.00 6.00
22 Ron Morris 3.00 6.00
23 Bill Munsey 4.00 8.00
24 Gary Schwertfeger 3.00 6.00
25 Paul Seale 3.00 6.00
26 Steve Shafer 3.00 6.00
27 Roy Shatzko 3.00 6.00
28 Ken Sugarman 3.00 6.00
29 Bob Swift 3.00 6.00
30 Jesse Williams 3.00 6.00

1966 B.C. Lions Program Inserts

The B.C. Lions continued their tradition of inserting player photos into game programs in 1966. However, this was the first year for color player images. Each also measured a much larger 7 3/4" by 10 1/2" and the set featured only 8-players. Each included a sponsor notation below the image as well as a page number as any other page from the program.

COMPLETE SET (8) 35.00 60.00
1 Neil Beaumont 4.00 8.00
2 Tom Brown 4.00 8.00
3 Mike Cacic 3.50 6.00
4 Norm Fieldgate 6.00 12.00
5 Willie Fleming 7.50 15.00

6 Dick Fouts	4.00	8.00
7 Tom Hinton	4.00	8.00
8 Joe Kapp	7.50	15.00

1967 B.C. Lions Team Issue

These 8" by 10" photos feature members of the B.C. Lions and were issued by the team. Each includes two photos of the featured player along with an extensive bio on the front. The photo backs are blank.

COMPLETE SET (26)	100.00	175.00
1 Ernie Allen	4.00	8.00
2 Neil Beaumont	5.00	10.00
3 Tom Brown	5.00	10.00
4 Mike Cacic	4.00	8.00
5 Dwayne Czupka	4.00	8.00
6 Lonnie Dennis	4.00	8.00
7 Larry Eilmes	5.00	10.00
8 Bernie Faldney	4.00	8.00
9 Norm Fieldgate	6.00	12.00
10 Greg Findlay	4.00	8.00
11 Wayne Foster	4.00	8.00
12 Ted Gerela	5.00	10.00
13 Sonny Homer	5.00	10.00
14 Bill Lasseter	4.00	8.00
15 Mike Martin	4.00	8.00
16 Bill Mitchell	4.00	8.00
17 Dave Moton	4.00	8.00
18 Bill Munsey	5.00	10.00
19 Craig Murray	4.00	8.00
20 Rudy Resche	4.00	8.00
21 Henry Schichtle	4.00	8.00
22 Steve Shafer	4.00	8.00
23 Leroy Sledge	4.00	8.00
24 Ken Sugarman	4.00	8.00
25 Jerry West	4.00	8.00
26 Jim Young	10.00	20.00

1968 B.C. Lions Team Issue

These photos feature members of the B.C. Lions and were issued by the team. Each measures 8" by 10" and includes two photos of the featured player along with an extensive bio on the front. The photo backs are blank.

COMPLETE SET (14)	50.00	10.00
1 Paul Brothers	4.00	8.00
2 Bill Bufton	4.00	8.00
3 Jim Carphin	4.00	8.00
4 Skip Diaz	4.00	8.00
5 Jim Evenson	4.00	8.00
6 Ted Gerela	5.00	10.00
7 John Griffin	4.00	8.00
8 Lynn Hendrickson	4.00	8.00
9 Lach Heron	4.00	8.00
10 Sonny Homer	5.00	10.00
11 Bill Lasseter	4.00	8.00
12 Mike Martin	4.00	8.00
13 Jim Sioie	4.00	8.00
14 Leroy Sledge	4.00	8.00

1971 B.C. Lions Chevron

This card set of the British Columbia Lions measures approximately 3" by 4 1/2" and was distributed by Standard Oil Company. The unnumbered cards were originally attached in complete sheet form. The fronts feature color player portraits and player information on a white background. The backs carry information about the Canadian Football League. A plastic folded "wallet" was produced to house the set with the words "Chevron Touchdown Cards" on the cover. Cards 3,7,11,22, 27,28,33,44 and 46 were bonus cards added later and therefore considered tougher to find.

COMPLETE SET (50)	175.00	300.00
1 George Anderson	3.00	6.00
2 Josh Ashton	4.00	8.00
3 Ross Boice SP	10.00	20.00
4 Paul Brothers	3.00	6.00
5 Tom Cassese	3.00	6.00
6 Roy Cavallin	3.00	6.00
7 Rusty Clark SP	10.00	20.00
8 Owen Dejanovich CO	3.00	6.00
9 Dave Denny	3.00	6.00
10 Brian Donnelly	3.00	6.00
11 Steve Duich SP	10.00	20.00
12 Jim Duke	3.00	6.00
13 Dave Easley	3.00	6.00
14 Trevor Ekdahl	4.00	8.00
15 Jim Evenson	4.00	8.00
16 Greg Findlay	3.00	6.00
17 Ted Gerela	3.00	6.00
18 Dave Golinsky	3.00	6.00
19 Lefty Hendrickson	3.00	6.00
20 Lach Heron	4.00	8.00
21 Gerry Herron	3.00	6.00
22 Larry Highbaugh SP	10.00	20.00
23 Wayne Holm	3.00	6.00
24 Bob Howes	3.00	6.00
25 Max Huber	3.00	6.00
26 Garrett Hunsperger	3.00	6.00
27 Lawrence James SP	10.00	20.00
28 Brian Kelsey SP	10.00	20.00
29 Eagle Keys CO	4.00	8.00
30 Mike Leveille	3.00	6.00
31 John Love	3.00	6.00
32 Ray Lychak	3.00	6.00
33 Dick Lyons SP	10.00	20.00
34 Wayne Matherne	3.00	6.00
35 Ken McCullough CO	3.00	6.00
36 Don Moorhead	3.00	6.00
37 Pete Palmer	3.00	6.00
38 Jackie Parker GM	6.00	12.00
39 Ken Phillips	3.00	6.00
40 Cliff Powell	3.00	6.00
41 Gary Robinson	3.00	6.00
42 Ken Sugarman	4.00	8.00
43 Bruce Taupier	3.00	6.00
44 Jim Tomlin SP	10.00	20.00
45 Bud Tynes CO	3.00	6.00
46 Carl Weathers SP	10.00	20.00
47 Jim White	3.00	6.00
48 Mike Wilson	3.00	6.00
49 Jim Young	5.00	10.00
50 Contest Card	3.00	6.00

1971 B.C. Lions Royal Bank

This 16-photo set of the CFL's British Columbia Lions was sponsored by Royal Bank. Each black-and-white, blank-backed picture measures approximately 5" by 7" and features a white-bordered posed action photo and a facsimile autograph inscribed across it. The sponsor logo appears in black in each corner of the bottom margin. The photos are unnumbered and checklisted below in alphabetical order.

COMPLETE SET (16)	50.00	100.00
1 George Anderson	3.00	6.00
2 Paul Brothers	3.00	6.00
3 Brian Donnelly	3.00	6.00
4 Dave Easley	3.00	6.00
5 Trevor Ekdahl	4.00	8.00
6 Jim Evenson	4.00	8.00
7 Greg Findlay	3.00	6.00
8 Lefty Hendrickson	3.00	6.00
9 Bob Howes	3.00	6.00
10 Garrett Hunsperger	3.00	6.00
11 Wayne Matherne	3.00	6.00
12 Don Moorhead	3.00	6.00
13 Ken Phillips	3.00	6.00
14 Ken Sugarman	4.00	8.00
15 Tom Wilkinson	5.00	10.00
16 Jim Young	5.00	10.00

1972 B.C. Lions Royal Bank

This set of 16 photos was sponsored by Royal Bank. They measure approximately 5" by 7" and are printed on thin glossy paper. The color posed player photos are bordered in white. A facsimile autograph is inscribed across the picture. At the bottom of the front, the words "Royal Bank Leo's Leaders, B.C. Lions Player of the Week" are printed between the sponsor's logo and the Lions' logo. The backs are blank. The photos are unnumbered and checklisted below in alphabetical order. One noteworthy card in the set is Carl Weathers, who went on to acting fame as Apollo Creed in Sylvester Stallone's popular "Rocky" movies.

COMPLETE SET (16)	60.00	120.00
1 George Anderson	3.00	6.00
2 Brian Donnelly	3.00	6.00
3 Dave Easley	3.00	6.00
4 Trevor Ekdahl	4.00	8.00
5 Ron Estay	3.00	6.00
6 Jim Evenson	4.00	8.00
7 Dave Golinsky	3.00	6.00
8 Larry Highbaugh	4.00	8.00
9 Garrett Hunsperger	3.00	6.00
10 Don Moorhead	3.00	6.00
11 Johnny Musso	6.00	12.00
12 Ray Nettles	3.00	6.00
13 Willie Postler	3.00	6.00
14 Carl Weathers	7.50	15.00
15 Jim Young	5.00	10.00
16 Coaching Staff	4.00	8.00

1973 B.C. Lions Royal Bank

This set of 18-photos (including all variations) was sponsored by Royal Bank. They measure approximately 5" by 7" and were printed on thin glossy paper. The color posed action shots are bordered in white. A facsimile autograph is inscribed across the picture. At the bottom of the front, the words "Royal Leaders, B.C. Lions Player of the Week" are printed between the sponsor's logo and the Lions' logo. The set includes three Don Moorhead cards, and two of these have borders around the picture. The third Moorhead photo and one of the Matherne photos has a black stripe at the bottom to cover up a wrong signature. The backs are blank, unnumbered and checklisted below in alphabetical order.

COMPLETE SET (18)	60.00	120.00
1 Barry Ardern	3.00	6.00
2 Monroe Eley	4.00	8.00
3 Bob Friend	3.00	6.00
4 Eric Guthrie	3.00	6.00
5 Garrett Hunsperger	3.00	6.00
6 Wayne Matherne	3.00	6.00
7 Wayne Matherne	3.00	6.00
8 Don Moorhead	3.00	6.00
9 Don Moorhead	3.00	6.00
10 Don Moorhead	3.00	6.00
11 Johnny Musso	6.00	12.00
12 Ray Nettles	3.00	6.00
13 Pete Palmer	3.00	6.00
14 Gary Robinson SP	12.00	20.00
15 Al Wilson	3.00	6.00
16 Mike Wilson	3.00	6.00
17 Jim Young	5.00	10.00
18 Coaches	4.00	8.00

1974 B.C. Lions Royal Bank

This blank-backed 14-photo color set was sponsored by Royal Bank. Each posed and bordered CFL Lions player's photo measures approximately 5" by 7" and carries a facsimile autograph across it. The sponsor logo appears in the lower left corner while the team logo is in the lower right corner. The photos are unnumbered and checklisted below in alphabetical order.

COMPLETE SET (14)	40.00	80.00
1 Bill Baker	4.00	8.00
2 Karl Douglas	2.50	5.00
3 Layne McDowell	2.50	5.00
4 Ivan MacMillan	2.50	5.00
5 Bud Magrum	2.50	5.00
6 Don Moorhead	2.50	5.00
7 Johnny Musso	5.00	10.00
8 Ray Nettles	2.50	5.00
9 Brian Sopatyk	2.50	5.00
10 Curtis Wester	3.00	6.00
11 Slade Willis	2.50	5.00
12 Al Wilson	2.50	5.00
13 Jim Young	4.00	8.00
14 Coaching Staff	3.00	6.00

1974 B.C. Lions Team Issue

These black and white photos were issued by the B.C. Lions around 1974. Each includes the player's name and team name below the photo on the front and the backs are blank. The photos measure roughly 5" by 8".

COMPLETE SET (25)	50.00	100.00
1 Barry Ardern	2.00	5.00
2 Brock Ansley	2.00	5.00
3 Terry Bailey	2.00	5.00
4 Bill Baker	3.00	6.00
5 Elton Baker	2.00	5.00
6 Grady Cavness	3.00	6.00
7 Brian Donnelly	2.00	5.00
8 Karl Douglas	2.00	5.00
9 Joe Fourqurean	2.00	5.00
10 Lou Harris	3.00	6.00
11 Garrett Hunsperger	2.00	5.00
12 Mike Lahood	2.00	5.00
13 Ivan MacMillan	2.00	5.00
14 Bud Magrum	2.00	5.00
15 Wayne Matherne	2.00	5.00
16 Don Moorhead	2.00	5.00
17 Johnny Musso	4.00	8.00
18 Ray Nettles	2.00	5.00
19 Peter Palmer	2.00	5.00
20 Brian Sopatyk	2.00	5.00
21 Slade Willis	2.00	5.00
22 Carl Winfrey	2.00	5.00
23 Al Wilson	2.00	5.00
24 Mike Wilson	2.00	5.00
25 Jim Young	4.00	8.00

1975 B.C. Lions Royal Bank

Royal Bank sponsored this 14-photo set. Each photo measures approximately 5 1/4" by 6". The photos are unnumbered and checklisted below in alphabetical order.

COMPLETE SET (14)	30.00	60.00
1 Brock Ansley	2.50	5.00
2 Terry Bailey	2.50	5.00
3 Bill Baker	4.00	8.00
4 Elton Brown	2.50	5.00
5 Grady Cavness	3.00	6.00
6 Ross Clarkson	2.50	5.00
7 Joe Fourqurean	2.50	5.00
8 Lou Harris	3.00	6.00
9 Layne McDowell	2.50	5.00
10 Don Moorhead	2.50	5.00
11 Tony Moro	2.50	5.00
12 Ray Nettles	2.50	5.00
13 Curtis Wester	3.00	6.00
14 Jim Young	4.00	8.00

1975 B.C. Lions Team Issued Buttons

These buttons were issued by the B.C. Lions and feature members of the team. Each measures roughly 2 1/4" in diameter and includes a black and white player photo against an orange background. A "nickname" for the player is included along with his jersey number, but no other identification is given.

COMPLETE SET (36)	125.00	200.00
1 Barry Ardern	3.00	5.00
2 Brock Ansley	3.00	5.00
3 Bill Baker	8.00	12.00
4 Larry Cameron	5.00	8.00
5 Elton Brown	3.00	5.00
6 Doug Carlson	3.00	5.00
7 Grady Cavness	5.00	8.00
8 Ross Clarkson	3.00	5.00
9 Jerry Ellison	3.00	5.00
10 Allen Gallagher	3.00	5.00
11 Paul Giroday	3.00	5.00
12 Eric Guthrie	3.00	5.00
13 Lou Harris	5.00	8.00
14 Bob Hornes	3.00	5.00
15 Barry Houlihan	3.00	5.00
16 Andy Jonassen	3.00	5.00
17 Pete Liske	8.00	12.00
18 Rocky Long	3.00	5.00
19 Ivan MacMillan	3.00	5.00
20 Dan McDonough	3.00	5.00
21 Layne McDowell	3.00	5.00
22 Don Moorhead	3.00	5.00
23 Tony Moro	3.00	5.00
24 Wayne Moseley	3.00	5.00
25 Ray Nettles	3.00	5.00
26 Pete Palmer	5.00	8.00
27 Gary Robinson	3.00	5.00
28 Wally Saunders	3.00	5.00
29 Jim Schneitz	3.00	5.00
30 Brian Sopatyk	3.00	5.00
31 Michael Strickland	3.00	5.00
32 Lorne Watters	3.00	5.00
33 Curtis Wester	5.00	8.00
34 Slade Willis	3.00	5.00
35 Don Wunderley	3.00	5.00
36 Jim Young	10.00	15.00

1975 B.C. Lions Team Sheets

This group of 32-players and coaches of the B.C. Lions was produced on four glossy sheets each measuring approximately 8" by 10". The fronts feature black-and-white player portraits with eight pictures to a sheet. The year and the "CP" (printer) logo appears at the top of each sheet. The backs are blank. The cards are unnumbered and checklisted below in alphabetical order, with the player pictured in the upper left hand corner of the sheet listed first.

COMPLETE SET (4)	12.50	25.00
1 Aynsley Moro Watters Cavness Willis Fourqurean Wester Moorhead	2.50	5.00
2 Howard Sopatyk Clarkson MacMillan Dever Ardern Robinson Liske	3.00	6.00
3 Keys McDonough Harris	5.00	10.00

Bailey		
Wilson		
Brown		
La Hood		
Young		
4 Wunderly	3.00	6.00
Guthrie		
Hornes		
Baker		
Nettles		
Johnson		
Palmer		
McDowell		

1976 B.C. Lions Royal Bank

This set of 15 photos was sponsored by Royal Bank. They measure approximately 5 1/4" by 6" and are printed on thin glossy paper. The color posed player shots (from the waist up) are bordered in white. A facsimile autograph is inscribed across the picture. At the bottom of the front, the words "1976 Royal Leaders, B.C. Lions Player of the Week" are printed between the sponsor's logo and the Lions' logo. The backs are blank. The photos are unnumbered and checklisted below in alphabetical order.

COMPLETE SET (15)	40.00	80.00
1 Terry Bailey	2.50	5.00
2 Bill Baker	4.00	8.00
3 Ted Dushinski	2.50	5.00
4 Eric Guthrie	2.50	5.00
5 Lou Harris	3.00	6.00
6 Glen Jackson	2.50	5.00
7 Rocky Long	2.50	5.00
8 Layne McDowell	2.50	5.00
9 Ray Nettles	2.50	5.00
10 Gary Robinson	2.50	5.00
11 John Sciarra	4.00	8.00
12 Wayne Smith	2.50	5.00
13 Michael Strickland	2.50	5.00
14 Al Wilson	2.50	5.00
15 Jim Young	4.00	8.00

1977 B.C. Lions Royal Bank

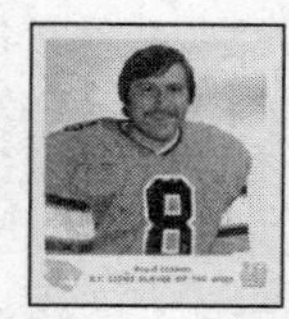

This set of 12 photos was sponsored by Royal Bank. They measure approximately 4 3/4" by 5 3/8" and are printed on thin glossy paper. The color head and shoulders shots are bordered in white. A facsimile autograph is inscribed across the picture. At the bottom of the front, the words "Royal Leaders, B.C. Lions Player of the Week" are printed between the Lions' logo and the sponsor's logo. The backs are blank. The photos are unnumbered and checklisted below in alphabetical order.

COMPLETE SET (12)	30.00	60.00
1 Doug Carlson	2.50	5.00
2 Sam Cvijanovich	2.50	5.00
3 Ted Dushinski	2.50	5.00
4 Paul Giroday	2.50	5.00
5 Glen Jackson	2.50	5.00
6 Frank Landy	2.50	5.00
7 Lui Passaglia	4.00	8.00
8 John Sciarra	3.00	6.00
9 Michael Strickland	2.50	5.00
10 Jerry Tagge	4.00	8.00
11 Al Wilson	2.50	5.00
12 Jim Young	4.00	8.00

1977-78 B.C. Lions Team Sheets

This group of 32-players and coaches of the B.C. Lions was produced on four glossy sheets each measuring approximately 8" by 10". The fronts feature black-and-white player portraits with eight pictures to a sheet. The year, the Lions logo, and the CFL logo appear at the top of each sheet. The backs are blank. The cards are unnumbered and checklisted below in alphabetical order, with the player pictured in the upper left hand corner of the sheet listed first.

COMPLETE SET (4)	12.50	25.00
1 B.Ackles	3.00	6.00
J.Farley		
V.Tobin		
V.Rapp		
M.McCartney		
B.Quinter		
D.Wunderly		
R.Appleby		
2 G.Inglish	2.50	5.00
G.Jackson		
G.Keithley		
T.Kudaea		
F.Landy		
G.Leach		
R.Long		
L.McDowell		
3 R.McLaren	4.00	8.00
J.O'Neal		
L.Passaglia		
G.Robinson		
J.Schnietz		
J.Sciarra		
D.Seymour		
H.Sovio		
4 J.Tagge	4.00	8.00
M.Strickland		
T.Uperesa		
L.Watkins		
A.Wilson		
D.Ratliff		
T.Bailey		
J.Harrison		

1978 B.C. Lions Royal Bank

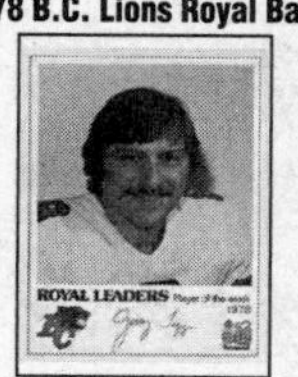

Royal Bank sponsored this 12-photo set again featuring the player's of the week as chosen by Royal Bank. Each photo measures approximately 4 1/4" by 5 1/2". The photos are unnumbered and checklisted below in alphabetical order.

COMPLETE SET (12)	30.00	60.00
1 Terry Bailey	2.00	4.00
2 Leon Bright	3.00	6.00
3 Doug Carlson	2.00	4.00
4 Grady Cavness	2.50	5.00
5 Al Charuk	2.00	4.00
6 Paul Giroday	2.00	4.00
7 Larry Key	2.00	4.00
8 Frank Landy	2.00	4.00
9 Lui Passaglia	4.00	8.00
10 Jerry Tagge	4.00	8.00
11 Al Wilson	2.00	4.00
12 Jim Young	4.00	8.00

1979 B.C. Lions Team Sheets

This group of 32-players and coaches of the B.C. Lions was produced on four glossy sheets each measuring approximately 8" by 10". The fronts feature black-and-white player portraits with eight pictures to a sheet. The year, the Lions logo, and the CFL logo appear at the top of each sheet. The backs are blank. The cards are unnumbered and checklisted below in alphabetical order, with the player pictured in the upper left hand corner of the sheet listed first.

COMPLETE SET (4)	10.00	25.00
1 A.Anderson	3.00	6.00
T.Bailey		
J.Beaton		
J.Blain		
J.Blake		
L.Bright		
S.Britts		
D.Carlson		
2 A.Charuk	3.00	6.00
J.Fourqurean		
D.Ford		
P.Giroday		
R.Goltz		
N.Hebeler		
K.Hinton		
H.Holt		
3 M.Houghton	2.50	5.00
G.Jackson		
L.Key		
T.Kudaba		
F.Landy		
G.Leonhard		
J.Lohmann		
R.Morehouse		
4 J.White	4.00	8.00
A.Wilson		
J.Young		
B.Ackles		
B.Quinter		
J.Farley		
V.Rapp		

1954 Blue Ribbon Tea

The 1954 Blue Ribbon Tea set contains 80 color cards of CFL players. The cards measure 2 1/4" by 4" and the pictures on the front are posed rather than action shots. The backs of the cards contain biographical data in both English and French. An album for this set was prodcued to house the cards. The set was printed in Canada by a firm called Colorgraphic.

COMPLETE SET (80)	5,000.00	9,000.00
1 Jack Jacobs	100.00	200.00
2 Neill Armstrong	60.00	100.00
3 Lorne Benson	50.00	80.00
4 Tom Casey	60.00	100.00
5 Vinnie Drake	50.00	80.00
6 Tommy Ford	50.00	80.00
7 Bud Grant	350.00	600.00
8 Dick Huffman	60.00	100.00
9 Gerry James	75.00	150.00
10 Bud Korchak	50.00	80.00
11 Thomas Lumsden	50.00	80.00
12 Steve Patrick	50.00	80.00
13 Keith Pearce	50.00	80.00
14 Jesse Thomas	50.00	80.00
15 Buddy Tinsley	60.00	100.00
16 Alan Scott Wiley	50.00	80.00
17 Winty Young	50.00	80.00
18 Joseph Zaleski	50.00	80.00
19 Ron Vaccher	50.00	80.00
20 John Gramling	50.00	80.00
21 Bob Simpson	75.00	150.00
22 Bruno Bitkowski	60.00	100.00
23 Kaye Vaughan	60.00	100.00
24 Don Carter	50.00	80.00
25 Gene Roberts	50.00	80.00
26 Howie Turner	50.00	80.00
27 Avatus Stone	50.00	80.00
28 Tom McHugh	50.00	80.00
29 Clyde Bennett	50.00	80.00
30 Bill Berezowski	50.00	80.00
31 Eddie Bevan	50.00	80.00
32 Dick Brown	50.00	80.00
33 Bernie Custis	60.00	100.00
34 Merle Hapes	60.00	100.00
35 Tip Logan	50.00	80.00
36 Vince Mazza	60.00	100.00
37 Pete Neumann	60.00	100.00
38 Vince Scott	60.00	100.00
39 Ralph Toohy	50.00	80.00
40 Frank Anderson	50.00	80.00
41 Bob Dean	50.00	80.00
42 Leon Manley	50.00	80.00
43 Bill Zock	60.00	100.00
44 Frank Morris	75.00	150.00
45 Jim Quondamatteo	50.00	80.00
46 Eagle Keys	75.00	150.00
47 Bernie Faloney	200.00	400.00
48 Jackie Parker	300.00	500.00
49 Ray Willsey	50.00	80.00
50 Mike King	50.00	80.00
51 Johnny Bright	200.00	350.00
52 Gene Brito	60.00	100.00
53 Stan Heath	60.00	100.00
54 Roy Jenson	50.00	80.00
55 Don Loney	50.00	80.00
56 Eddie Macon	50.00	80.00
57 Peter Maxwell-Muir	50.00	80.00
58 Tom Miner	50.00	80.00
59 Jim Prewett	50.00	80.00
60 Lowell Wagner	50.00	80.00
61 Red O'Quinn	60.00	100.00
62 Ray Poole	60.00	100.00
63 Jim Staton	50.00	80.00
64 Alex Webster	100.00	200.00
65 Al Dekdebruin	50.00	80.00
66 Ed Bradley	50.00	80.00
67 Tex Coulter	75.00	150.00
68 Sam Etcheverry	300.00	500.00
69 Larry Grigg	50.00	80.00
70 Tom Hugo	50.00	80.00
71 Chuck Hunsinger	50.00	80.00
72 Herb Trawick	75.00	150.00
73 Virgil Wagner	60.00	100.00
74 Phil Adrian	50.00	80.00
75 Bruce Coulter	50.00	80.00
76 Jim Miller	50.00	80.00
77 Jim Mitchener	50.00	80.00
78 Tom Moran	50.00	80.00
79 Doug McNichol	50.00	80.00
80 Joey Pal	50.00	80.00
NNO Card Album	175.00	350.00

1969 Calgary Stampeders Team Issue

The Stampeders issued this set of player photos around 1969. Each includes two black-and-white player photos with one being a posed action shot along with a smaller portrait image. The roughly 8" by 10 1/8" photos include the player's name, a short bio and team logo on the cardfronts. The backs are blank and unnumbered.

COMPLETE SET (28)	100.00	200.00
1 Frank Andruski	4.00	8.00
2 Lanny Boleski	4.00	8.00
3 Ron Capham	4.00	8.00
4 Terry Evanshen	7.50	15.00
5 Joe Forzani	5.00	10.00
6 Jim Furlong	4.00	8.00
7 Wayne Harris	7.50	15.00
8 Herman Harrison	6.00	12.00
9 John Helton	6.00	12.00
10 Fred James	4.00	8.00
11 Jerry Keeling	6.00	12.00
12 Roger Kramer	5.00	10.00
13 Granville Liggins	5.00	10.00
14 Rudy Linterman	5.00	10.00
15 Bob Lueck	4.00	8.00
16 Don Luzzi	4.00	8.00
17 Bob McCarthy	4.00	8.00
18 Ron Payne	4.00	8.00
19 Larry Robinson	5.00	10.00
20 Billy Roy	4.00	8.00
21 Herb Schumn	4.00	8.00
22 Gerry Shaw	4.00	8.00
23 Rick Shaw	4.00	8.00
24 Jim Sillye	4.00	8.00
25 Ward Smith	4.00	8.00
26 Howard Starks	4.00	8.00
27 Terry Wilson	4.00	8.00
28 Ted Woods	4.00	8.00

1971 Calgary Stampeders Team Issue

The Stampeders issued this set of player photos around 1971. Each includes two black-and-white player photos with one being a posed action shot along with a smaller portrait image. The roughly 8" by 10 1/8" photos include the player's name and team logo on the cardfronts. The backs are blank and unnumbered.

COMPLETE SET (22)	75.00	150.00
1 Frank Andruski	4.00	8.00
2 Basil Bark	4.00	8.00
3 Lanny Boleski	4.00	8.00
4 Jim Bond	4.00	8.00
5 Joe Forzani	5.00	10.00
6 John Forzani	4.00	8.00
7 Jim Furlong	4.00	8.00
8 Wayne Harris	6.00	12.00
9 Herman Harrison	6.00	12.00
10 John Helton	5.00	10.00
11 Fred James	4.00	8.00
12 Jerry Keeling	6.00	12.00
13 Craig Koinzan	4.00	8.00
14 Granville Liggins	5.00	10.00
15 Jim Lindsey	4.00	8.00
16 Rudy Linterman	5.00	10.00
17 Brian Marcil	4.00	8.00
18 Hugh McInnis	4.00	8.00
19 Herb Schumn	4.00	8.00
20 John Senst	4.00	8.00
21 Gerry Shaw	4.00	8.00
22 Howard Starks	4.00	8.00

1973 Calgary Stampeders Team Issue

The Stampeders issued this set of player photos around 1973. Each includes two black-and-white player photos with one being a posed action shot along with a smaller portrait image. The roughly 8" by 10 1/8" photos include the player's name and team logo on the cardfronts. The backs are blank and unnumbered.

COMPLETE SET (18)	60.00	120.00
1 Frank Andruski	4.00	8.00
2 Lanny Boleski	4.00	8.00
3 John Forzani	4.00	8.00
4 Jim Furlong	4.00	8.00
5 John Helton	5.00	10.00
6 Dave Herbert	4.00	8.00
7 Fred James	4.00	8.00
8 Blain Lamoreaux	4.00	8.00
9 Marion Latimore	4.00	8.00
10 Jim Lindsey	4.00	8.00
11 Pete Liske	10.00	20.00
12 John Senst	4.00	8.00
13 Larry Robinson	5.00	10.00
14 Fritz Seyferth	4.00	8.00
15 Gerry Shaw	4.00	8.00
16 Jim Sillye	4.00	8.00
17 Howard Starks	4.00	8.00
18 Bob Wyatt	4.00	8.00

1975 Calgary Stampeders Team Sheets

This group of 32-players and coaches of the Stampeders was produced on four glossy sheets each measuring approximately 8" by 10". The fronts feature black-and-white player portraits with eight pictures to a sheet with the year printed at the top. The backs are blank. The cards are unnumbered and checklisted below in alphabetical order, with the player pictured in the upper left hand corner of the sheet listed first.

COMPLETE SET (4) 15.00 30.00
1 J.Forzani/M.Jackson/K.Douglas/F.James/T.Bachman
B.Line/G.Murdock/R.Galbos 4.00 8.00
2 J.Helton/W.Burden/P.McKay/B.Lamoureux/G.Stewart
J.Forzani/R.Bark/T.Forzani 4.00 8.00
3 C.McFall/J.Pisarcik/R.Goree/O.Collier/L.Sherbina
J.Silye/R.Linterman/J.Wood 5.00 10.00
4 D.Wesolowski/H.Sovio/O.Morgan/D.Moulton
J.Bond/H.Starks/L.Cates/H.Holton 4.00 8.00

1977-78 Calgary Stampeders Team Sheets

This group of 40-players and coaches of the Stampeders was produced on five glossy sheets each measuring approximately 8" by 10". The fronts feature black-and-white player portraits with eight pictures to a sheet with the year printed at the top. The backs are blank. The cards are unnumbered and checklisted below in alphabetical order, with the player pictured in the upper left hand corner of the sheet listed first.

COMPLETE SET (5) 12.50 25.00
1 A.Burleson 3.00 6.00
B.Gervais
W.Armsteadd
B.Lamoureux
D.Falconer
O.Bakken
J.Palazeti
L.Leathem
2 A.Evans 2.50 5.00
A.Wiegandt
J.Spavital
J.Gotta
E.Zwahlen
L.Fairbanks
R.Galbos
B.Bark
3 B.Martin 3.00 6.00
J.Jones
J.Medord
R.Woodward
T.Forzani
C.McFall
D.Meyer
W.Thomas
4 R.Odums 2.50 5.00
J.Harris
H.Holton
J.Baker
R.Linterman
B.Viccars
G.Murdock
J.Helton
5 L.Tittley 3.00 6.00
L.Sherbina
B.Palmer
A.Jonasen
W.Burden
B.McLaughlin
M.Wilson
J.Hufnagel

1978 Calgary Stampeders Team Sheets

This group of 40-players and coaches of the Stampeders was produced on five glossy sheets each measuring approximately 8" by 10". The fronts feature black-and-white player portraits with eight pictures to a sheet with the year printed at the top. The backs are blank. The cards are unnumbered and checklisted below in alphabetical order, with the player pictured in the upper left hand corner of the sheet listed first.

COMPLETE SET (5) 15.00 30.00
1 O.Bakken/M.Reed/R.Lewis/J.Baker
L.Fairbanks/E.McAleney/L.Tittley/A.Morris 4.00 8.00
2 J.Helton/W.Burden/A.Burleson/T.Irvin
B.Lamoureux/R.Odums
H.Holton/W.Armstead 4.00 8.00
3 D.Kirzinger/A.Jonassen/A.Dickerson
D.Falconer/J.Palazeti/T.Reimer
T.Forzani/J.Hufnagel 4.00 8.00
4 R.Koswin/A.Evans/J.Gotta/J.Tiller
W.Thomas/M.Gorrell/A.Johnson
B.Lubig 3.00 6.00
5 J.Malinosky/C.McFall/A.MacLean/K.Kirk/R.Harber
R.Kochel/G.Sykes/B.Viccars 4.00 8.00

1980 Calgary Stampeders Team Sheets

This group of 40-players and coaches of the Stampeders was produced on five glossy sheets each measuring approximately 8" by 10". The fronts feature black-and-white player portraits with eight pictures to a sheet with the year printed at the top. The backs are blank. The cards are unnumbered and checklisted below in alphabetical order, with the player pictured in the upper left hand corner of the sheet listed first.

COMPLETE SET (5) 12.50 25.00
1 W.Armstead/D.Battershill/W.Burden/J.Palazeti
K.Dombrowski/L.Fairbanks
R.Forbes/T.Gillespie 2.50 6.00
2 M.Gorrell/J.Gotta CO/J.Hay/T.Hicks/M.Horton/J.Inglis
T.Irvin/K.Johnson 2.50 6.00
3 S.Kearns/K.Kirk/D.Kirzinger/T.Krebs
L.Lewis/R.Lewis/R.Lubig/D.Moir 2.50 6.00
4 E.McAleney/M.McTague/M.Nelson/R.Odums/R.Paggett
R.Sparks/J.Sykes/B.Threadgill 2.00 5.00
5 B.Viccars/M.Walker/L.Woznesensky/A.Wiegandt/R.Kochel
S.Schwartz CO/D.Meyer CO/M.Bass CO 2.00 5.00

1971 Chiquita CFL All-Stars

This set of CFL All-Stars actually consists of 13 slides which were intended to be viewed by a special yellow Chiquita viewer. Each slide measures approximately 1 3/4" by 3 5/8" and contains four small color slides showing two views of two players. Each side has a player summary on its middle portion, with two small color action slides at each end stacked one above the other. When the slide is placed in the viewer, the two bottom slides, which are identical, reveal the first player. Flipping the slide over reveals the other player biography and enables one to view the other two slides, which show the second player. Each side of the slides is numbered as listed below. The set is considered complete without the yellow viewer.

COMPLETE SET (13) 100.00 200.00
1 Bill Baker 6.00 15.00
3 Wayne Giardino 6.00 15.00
5 Leon McQuay 7.50 20.00
7 George Reed 6.00 15.00
9 Tommy Joe Coffey 7.50 20.00
11 Jim Young 6.00 15.00
13 Ron Forwick 5.00 12.00
15 Don Jonas 6.00 15.00
17 Joe Theismann 15.00 40.00
19 Ed George 5.00 12.00
21 Ted Dushinski 5.00 12.00
23 John Lagrone 5.00 12.00
25 Garney Henley 6.00 15.00
NNO Yellow Viewer 6.00 15.00

1965 Coke Caps CFL

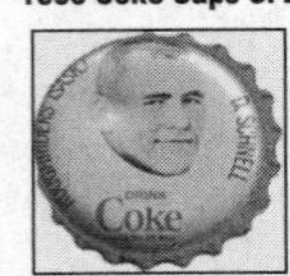

This set of 230 Coke caps was issued on bottled soft drinks and featured CFL players. The caps measure approximately one inch in diameter. The outside of the cap exhibits a black-and-white photo of the player's face, with a Coke (or Sprite) advertisement below the picture. Sprite caps are harder to find and are valued using the multiplier line below. The player's team name is written vertically on the left side, following the curve of the bottle cap, and likewise for the player's name on the right side. The players are listed in alphabetical order within their teams, and the teams are arranged alphabetically. Three players appear twice with two different teams, Don Fuell, Hal Ledyard, and L. Tomlinson. A plastic holder measuring approximately 14" by 16" was also available. The caps were available in French and English, the difference being "Drink Coke" or "Bovez Coke" under the player photo.

COMPLETE SET (230) 600.00 1,000.00
*SPRITE CAPS: 1.5X TO 2.5X
*FRENCH CAPS: 1.25X TO 2X
1 Neil Beaumont 3.00 6.00
2 Tom Brown 4.00 8.00
3 Mack Burton 2.50 5.00
4 Mike Cacic 2.50 5.00
5 Pat Claridge 2.50 5.00
6 Steve Cotter 2.50 5.00
7 Norm Fieldgate 4.00 8.00
8 Greg Findlay 2.50 5.00
9 Willie Fleming 8.00 12.00
10 Dick Fouts 2.50 5.00
11 Tom Hinton 4.00 8.00
12 Sonny Homer 3.00 6.00
13 Joe Kapp 15.00 25.00
14 Gus Kasapis 2.50 5.00
15 Peter Kempf 2.50 5.00
16 Bill Lasseter 2.50 5.00
17 Mike Martin 2.50 5.00
18 Ron Morris 2.50 5.00
19 Bill Munsey 2.50 5.00
20 Paul Seale 2.50 5.00
21 Steve Shafer 2.50 5.00
22 Ken Sugarman 3.00 6.00
23 Bob Swift 2.50 5.00
24 Jesse Williams 2.50 5.00
25 Ron Albright UER 2.50 5.00
26 Lu Bain 2.50 5.00
27 Frank Budd 2.50 5.00
28 Lovell Coleman 3.00 6.00
29 Eagle Day 5.00 10.00
30 Paul Dudley 2.50 5.00
31 Jim Furlong 2.50 5.00
32 George Hansen 2.50 5.00
33 Wayne Harris 8.00 12.00
34 Herman Harrison 4.00 8.00
35 Pat Holmes 2.50 5.00
36 Art Johnson 2.50 5.00
37 Jerry Keeling 4.00 8.00
38 Roger Kramer 3.00 6.00
39 Hal Krebs 2.50 5.00
40 Don Luzzi 4.00 8.00
41 Pete Manning 2.50 5.00
42 Dale Parsons 2.50 5.00
43 Ron Payne 2.50 5.00
44 Larry Robinson 3.00 6.00
45 Gerry Shaw 2.50 5.00
46 Don Stephenson 2.50 5.00
47 Bob Taylor 3.00 6.00
48 Ted Woods 2.50 5.00
49 Jon Anabo 2.50 5.00
50 Ray Ash 2.50 5.00
51 Jim Battle 2.50 5.00
52 Charlie Brown 2.50 5.00
53 Tommy Joe Coffey 10.00 15.00
54 Marcel Deleeuw 2.50 5.00
55 Al Ecuyer 2.50 5.00
56 Ron Forwick 2.50 5.00
57 Jim Higgins 2.50 5.00
58 Henry Huth 2.50 5.00
59 Randy Kerbow 2.50 5.00
60 Oscar Kruger 2.50 5.00
61 Tom Machan 2.50 5.00
62 Grant McKee 2.50 5.00
63 Bill Mitchell 2.50 5.00
64 Barry Mitchelson 2.50 5.00
65 Roger Nelson 4.00 8.00
66 Bill Redell 2.50 5.00
67 Morley Rohliser 2.50 5.00
68 Howie Schumm 2.50 5.00
69 E.A. Sims 2.50 5.00
70 John Sklopan 2.50 5.00
71 Jim Stinnette 2.50 5.00
72 Barney Therrien 2.50 5.00
73 Jim Thomas 2.50 5.00
74 Neil Thomas 2.50 5.00
75 Bill Tobin 3.00 6.00
76 Terry Wilson 2.50 5.00
77 Art Baker 4.00 8.00
78 John Barrow 4.00 8.00
79 Gene Ceppetelli 2.50 5.00
80 John Cimba 2.50 5.00
81 Dick Cohee 2.50 5.00
82 Frank Cosentino 3.00 6.00
83 Johnny Counts 2.50 5.00
84 Stan Crisson 2.50 5.00
85 Tommy Grant 4.00 8.00
86 Garney Henley 4.00 8.00
87 Ed Hoerster 2.50 5.00
88 Zeno Karcz 3.00 6.00
89 Ellison Kelly 4.00 8.00
90 Bob Krouse 2.50 5.00
91 Billy Ray Locklin 2.50 5.00
92 Chet Miksza 2.50 5.00
93 Angelo Mosca 12.00 20.00
94 Bronko Nagurski Jr. 4.00 8.00
95 Ted Page 2.50 5.00
96 Don Sutherin 5.00 10.00
97 Dave Viti 2.50 5.00
98 Dick Walton 2.50 5.00
99 Billy Wayte 2.50 5.00
100 Joe Zuger 2.50 5.00
101 Jim Andreotti 3.00 6.00
102 John Baker 3.00 6.00
103 Gino Beretta 2.50 5.00
104 Bill Bewley 3.00 6.00
105 Garland Boyette 3.00 6.00
106 Doug Daigneault 2.50 5.00
107 George Dixon 4.00 8.00
108 D. Dolatri 2.50 5.00
109 Ted Elsby 2.50 5.00
110 Don Estes 2.50 5.00
111 Terry Evenshen 8.00 12.00
112 Clare Exelby 2.50 5.00
113 Larry Fairholm 3.00 6.00
114 Bernie Faloney 12.00 20.00
115 Don Fuell 2.50 5.00
116 Mike Gibbons 2.50 5.00
117 Ralph Goldston 3.00 6.00
118 Al Irwin 2.50 5.00
119 John Kennerson 2.50 5.00
120 Ed Learn 2.50 5.00
121 Moe Levesque 2.50 5.00
122 Bob Minihane 2.50 5.00
123 Jim Reynolds 2.50 5.00
124 Billy Roy 2.50 5.00
125 Larry Tomlinson 2.50 5.00
126 Ernie White 2.50 5.00
127 Rick Black 2.50 5.00
128 Mike Blum 2.50 5.00
129 Billy Joe Booth 2.50 5.00
130 Jim Cain 2.50 5.00
131 Bill Cline 2.50 5.00
132 Merv Collins 2.50 5.00
133 Jim Conroy 3.00 6.00
134 Larry DeGraw 2.50 5.00
135 Jim Dillard 2.50 5.00
136 Gene Gaines 4.00 8.00
137 Don Gilbert 2.50 5.00
138 Russ Jackson 12.00 20.00
139 Ken Lehmann 3.00 6.00
140 Bob O'Billovich 2.50 5.00
141 John Pentecost 2.50 5.00
142 Joe Poirier 3.00 6.00
143 Moe Racine 2.50 5.00
144 Sam Scoccia 2.50 5.00
145 Bo Scott 5.00 10.00
146 Jerry Selinger 2.50 5.00
147 Marshall Shirk 2.50 5.00
148 Bill Siekierski 2.50 5.00
149 Ron Stewart 5.00 10.00
150 Whit Tucker 4.00 8.00
151 Ron Atchison 5.00 10.00
152 Al Benecick 2.50 5.00
153 Clyde Brock 2.50 5.00
154 Ed Buchanan 2.50 5.00
155 Roy Cameron 2.50 5.00
156 Hugh Campbell 4.00 8.00
157 Henry Dorsch 2.50 5.00
158 Larry Dumelie 2.50 5.00
159 Garner Ekstran 3.00 6.00
160 Martin Fabi 2.50 5.00
161 Bob Good 2.50 5.00
162 Bob Kosid 2.50 5.00
163 Ron Lancaster 12.00 20.00
164 Hal Ledyard 2.50 5.00
165 Len Legault 2.50 5.00
166 Ron Meadmore 2.50 5.00
167 Bob Ptacek 3.00 6.00
168 George Reed 8.00 12.00
169 Dick Schnell 2.50 5.00
170 Wayne Shaw 2.50 5.00
171 Ted Urness 4.00 8.00
172 Dale West 3.00 6.00
173 Reg Whitehouse 2.50 5.00
174 Gene Wlasiuk 2.50 5.00
175 Jim Worden 2.50 5.00
176 Dick Aldridge 2.50 5.00
177 Walt Balasiuk 2.50 5.00
178 Ron Brewer 2.50 5.00
179 W. Dickey 2.50 5.00
180 Bob Dugan 3.00 6.00
181 Larry Ferguson 3.00 6.00
182 Don Fuell 2.50 5.00
183 Ed Harrington 3.00 6.00
184 Ron Howell 2.50 5.00
185 Francis LaRoue 2.50 5.00
186 Sherman Lewis 3.00 6.00
187 Marv Luster 4.00 8.00
188 Dave Mann 3.00 6.00
189 Pete Martin 2.50 5.00
190 Marty Martinello 2.50 5.00
191 Lamar McHan 4.00 8.00
192 Danny Nykoluk 2.50 5.00
193 Jackie Parker 15.00 25.00
194 Dave Pivec 2.50 5.00
195 Jim Rountree 2.50 5.00
196 Dick Shatto 4.00 8.00
197 Billy Shipp 2.50 5.00
198 Len Sparks 2.50 5.00
199 Dave Still 2.50 5.00
200 Norm Stoneburgh 2.50 5.00
201 Dave Thelen 5.00 10.00
202 John Vilanus 2.50 5.00
203 Jim Walter 2.50 5.00
204 Pat Watson 2.50 5.00
205 John Wydareny 3.00 6.00
206 Billy Cooper 2.50 5.00
207 Wayne Dennis 2.50 5.00
208 Paul Desjardins 3.00 6.00
209 Noel Dunford 2.50 5.00
210 Farrell Funston 3.00 6.00
211 Herb Gray 4.00 8.00
212 Roger Hamelin 2.50 5.00
213 Barrie Hansen 2.50 5.00
214 Henry Janzen 3.00 6.00
215 Hal Ledyard 2.50 5.00
216 Leo Lewis 5.00 10.00
217 Brian Palmer 2.50 5.00
218 Art Perkins 2.50 5.00
219 Cornel Piper 2.50 5.00
220 Ernie Pitts 2.50 5.00
221 Kenny Ploen 5.00 10.00
222 Dave Raimey 3.00 6.00
223 Norm Rauhaus 3.00 6.00
224 Frank Rigney 4.00 8.00
225 Roger Savoie 2.50 5.00
226 Jackie Simpson 4.00 8.00
227 Dick Thornton 3.00 6.00
228 Sherwyn Thorson 2.50 5.00
229 Ed Ulmer 2.50 5.00
230 Bill Whisler 2.50 5.00

1952 Crown Brand Photos

This set of 48 pictures was distributed by Crown Brand Corn Syrup. The collection of the complete set of pictures involved a mail-in offer: one label or cone top from a tin of Crown Brand Corn Syrup and 10 cents for two pictures; or two labels and 25 cents for seven pictures. The photos measure approximately 7" by 8 1/4" and feature a posed photo of the player, with player information below. The back has a checklist of all 48 players included in the set. Hall of Famers included in this set are Tom Casey, Dick Huffman, Jack Jacobs, Martin Ruby, Buddy Tinsley, and Frank Morris. The photos are listed below in alphabetical order according to their teams.

COMPLETE SET (48) 1,000.00 2,000.00
1 John Brown 25.00 50.00
2 Tom Casey 37.50 75.00
3 Tommy Ford 25.00 50.00
4 Ian Gibb 25.00 50.00
5 Dick Huffman 37.50 75.00
6 Jack Jacobs 50.00 100.00
7 Thomas Lumsden 25.00 50.00
8 George McPhail 25.00 50.00
9 Jim McPherson 25.00 50.00
10 Buddy Tinsley 37.50 75.00
11 Ron Vaccher 25.00 50.00
12 Al Wiley 25.00 50.00
13 Ken Charlton 37.50 75.00
14 Glenn Dobbs 37.50 75.00
15 Sully Glasser 25.00 50.00
16 Nelson Greene 25.00 50.00
17 Bert Iannone 25.00 50.00
18 Art McEwan 25.00 50.00
19 Jimmy McFaul 25.00 50.00
20 Bob Pelling 25.00 50.00
21 Chuck Radley 25.00 50.00
22 Martin Ruby 37.50 75.00
23 Jack Russell 25.00 50.00
24 Roy Wright 25.00 50.00
25 Paul Alford 25.00 50.00
26 Sugarfoot Anderson 25.00 50.00
27 Dick Bradley 25.00 50.00
28 Bob Bryant 25.00 50.00
29 Cliff Cyr 25.00 50.00
30 Cal Green 25.00 50.00
31 Stan Heath 37.50 75.00

32 Stan Kaluznick	25.00	50.00
33 Guss Knickerhm	25.00	50.00
34 Paul Salata	25.00	50.00
35 Murry Sullivan	25.00	50.00
36 Dave West	25.00	50.00
37 Joe Aguirre	25.00	50.00
38 Claude Arnold	25.00	50.00
39 Bill Briggs	25.00	50.00
40 Mario DeMarco	25.00	50.00
41 Mike King	25.00	50.00
42 Donald Lord	25.00	50.00
43 Frank Morris	37.50	75.00
44 Gayle Pace	25.00	50.00
45 Rod Pantages	25.00	50.00
46 Rollin Prather	25.00	50.00
47 Chuck Quilter	25.00	50.00
48 Jim Quondamatteo	25.00	50.00

1972-83 Dimanche/Derniere Heure

The blank-backed photo sheets in this multi-sport set measure approximately 8 1/2" by 11" and feature white-bordered color sports star photos from Dimanche Derniere Heure, a Montreal newspaper. The player's name, position and biographical information appear within the lower white margin. All text is in French. A white vinyl album was available for storing the photo sheets. Printed on the album's spine are the words, "Mes Vedettes du Sport" (My Stars of Sport).The photos are unnumbered and are checklisted below in alphabetical order according to sport or team as follows: Montreal Expos baseball players (1-117; National League baseball players (118-130); Montreal Canadiens hockey players (131-177); wrestlers (178-202); prize fighters (203-204); auto racing drivers (205-208); women's golf (209); Patof the circus clown (210); and CFL (211-278).

214 Peter Dalla Riva 10/23/77	2.00	5.00
215 Don Sweet 10/30/77	2.00	5.00
216 Mark Jackson 11/6/77	2.00	5.00
217 Tony Proudfoot 11/13/77	2.00	5.00
218 Dan Yochum 11/20/77	2.00	5.00
219 1977 Team Photo 11/27/77	2.00	5.00
220 Wayne Conrad 12/77	2.00	5.00
221 Vernon Perry 12/11/77	2.50	6.00
222 Carl Crennel 12/17/77	2.00	5.00
223 Sonny Wade	5.00	10.00
Marv Levy 12/25/77		
224 John O'Leary 8/6/78	2.00	5.00
225 Dickie Harris 8/13/78	2.50	6.00
226 Glen Weir 8/20/78	2.00	5.00
227 Gabriel Gregoire 8/27/78	2.00	5.00
228 Larry Smith 9/3/78	2.00	5.00
229 Gerry Dattilio 9/10/78	2.00	5.00
230 Ken Starch 9/17/78	2.00	5.00
231 Larry Uteck 9/24/78	2.00	5.00
232 Jim Burrow 10/1/78	2.50	6.00
233 Randy Rhino 10/8/78	2.00	5.00
234 Chuck McMann 10/15/78	2.00	5.00
235 Gordon Judges 10/22/78	2.00	5.00
236 Doug Payton 10/29/78	2.00	5.00
237 Ty Morris 11/5/78	2.00	5.00
238 Wally Buono 11/12/78	2.00	5.00
239 1978 Team Photo 11/19/78	2.50	6.00
240 Ray Watrin 11/26/78	2.00	5.00
241 Junior Ah You 12/3/78	3.00	8.00
242 David Green 10/7/79	2.50	6.00
243 Ron Calgagni 10/14/79	2.00	5.00
244 Bobby Husea 10/21/79	2.00	5.00
245 Nick Arakgi 10/28/79	2.00	5.00
246 Joe Barnes 11/4/79	3.00	8.00
247 Keith Baker 11/11/79	2.00	5.00
248 Tony Petruccio 11/18/79	2.00	5.00
249 Tom Cousineau 11/25/79	3.00	8.00
250 Doug Scott 10/5/80	2.00	5.00
251 Dickie Harris 10/12/80	2.50	6.00
252 Gabriel Gregoire 10/19/80	2.00	5.00
253 Fred Biletnikoff 10/26/80	10.00	20.00
254 Tom Cousineau 11/2/80	3.00	8.00
255 Chuck McMann 11/9/80	2.00	5.00
256 Junior Ah You 11/16/80	3.00	8.00
257 Gerry Dattilio 11/23/80	2.00	5.00
258 Vince Ferragamo 7/19/81	3.00	8.00
259 Joe Scannella 7/26/81	2.00	5.00
260 Billy Johnson 8/2/81	3.00	8.00
261 Joe Hawco 8/9/81	2.00	5.00
262 Gerry McGrath 8/16/81	2.00	5.00
263 Joe Taylor 8/23/81	2.00	5.00
264 Doug Scott 8/30/81	2.00	5.00
265 Tom Cousineau 9/6/81	3.00	8.00
266 Nick Arakgi 9/13/81	2.00	5.00
267 Mike Hameluck 8/20/81	2.00	5.00
268 Doug Payton 9/27/81	2.00	5.00
269 James Scott 10/4/81	2.50	6.00
270 Keith Gary 10/11/81	2.00	5.00
271 David Overstreet 10/18/81	3.00	8.00
272 Peter Dalla Riva 10/25/81	2.00	5.00
273 Marc Lacelle 11/1/81	2.00	5.00
274 Luc Tousignant 9/19/82	2.00	5.00
275 Denny Ferdinand 9/26/82	2.00	5.00
276 Joe Galat 10/3/82	2.00	5.00
277 Lester Brown 10/10/82	2.00	5.00
278 Dom Vetro 10/17/82	2.00	5.00
279 Preston Young 10/24/82	2.00	5.00
280 Eugene Beliveau 10/31/82	2.00	5.00
281 Ken Miller 11/7/82	2.00	5.00

1925 Dominion Chocolates V31

2 Roy Chantler FB	125.00	200.00
8 Carl Voss FB	125.00	200.00
15 Gibb McKelvie FB	125.00	200.00
21 Johnny Evans FB	125.00	200.00
22 Morris Hughes FB	125.00	200.00
77 Alex Pontin FB	125.00	200.00
91 Johnny Laing	125.00	200.00
Lacrosse, Football		

1962 Edmonton Eskimos Program Inserts

Each of these photos measures approximately 3 7/8" by 5 3/8". Inside white borders, the fronts feature black-and-white posed action photos. The player's facsimile autograph is written across the photo in red ink. Immediately below the picture is the player's name and position. The wider white bottom border also carries some sponsor information and a red ink printed serial number. The photos were primarily sponsored by CFRN radio and/or A&W Drive-in. The photos were initially issued in perforated sheets of four per Eskimos game programs. The backs display various advertisements. The photos are unnumbered and checklisted below in alphabetical order.

COMPLETE SET (32)	125.00	225.00
1 Ray Baillie	3.00	6.00
2 Johnny Bright	6.00	12.00
3 Tommy Joe Coffey	6.00	12.00
4 Toby Deese	3.00	6.00
5 Don Duncalfe	3.00	6.00
6 Nat Dye	3.00	6.00
7 Pat Dye	12.00	20.00
8 Al Ecuyer	3.00	6.00
9 Larry Fleisher	3.00	6.00
10 Gino Fracas	4.00	8.00
11 Ted Frechette	3.00	6.00
12 Don Getty	6.00	12.00
13 Ed Gray	3.00	6.00
14 Dunc Harvey	4.00	8.00
15 Tony Kehrer	3.00	6.00
16 Mike Kmeche	3.00	6.00
17 Oscar Kruger	4.00	8.00
18 Jack Lamb	3.00	6.00
19 Mike Lashuk	3.00	6.00
20 Jim Letcavits	3.00	6.00
21 Bill McKenny	3.00	6.00
22 Roger Nelson	6.00	12.00
23 Jackie Parker	12.00	20.00
24 Howie Schumm	3.00	6.00
25 E.A. Sims	3.00	6.00
26 Bill Smith	3.00	6.00
27 Don Stephenson	3.00	6.00
28 Roy Stevenson	3.00	6.00
29 Ted Tully	3.00	6.00
30 Len Vella	3.00	6.00
31 Mike Volcan	3.00	6.00
32 Bobby Walden	4.00	8.00

1962 Edmonton Eskimos Team Issue 4x5

This set of photos was issued by the Eskimos to fill fan requests. Each photo measures roughly 4" by 5" and includes a black and white photo of the player in street clothes instead of in uniform. There is no identification on the fronts, but the player's name is usually included on the backs of the photos. The unnumbered photos are listed alphabetically below.

COMPLETE SET (20)	75.00	150.00
1 Don Barry	4.00	8.00
2 Steve Bendiak	4.00	8.00
3 Johnny Bright	6.00	12.00
4 Gino Fracas	4.00	8.00
5 Don Getty	5.00	10.00
6 Ed Gray	4.00	8.00
7 Mike Kmeche	4.00	8.00
8 Oscar Kruger	4.00	8.00
9 Mike Lashuk	4.00	8.00
10 Jim Letcavits	4.00	8.00
11 Rollie Miles	4.00	8.00
12 Jackie Parker	7.50	15.00
13 Roger Nelson	5.00	10.00
14 Jim Shipka	4.00	8.00
15 Bill Smith	4.00	8.00
16 Joe-Bob Smith	4.00	8.00
17 Roy Stevenson	4.00	8.00
18 Don Stephenson	4.00	8.00
19 Mike Volcan	4.00	8.00
20 Art Walker	4.00	8.00

1962 Edmonton Eskimos Team Issue 8x10

This set of Eskimos player photos was issued by the team to fill fan requests. Each photo measures roughly 8" by 10" and includes the player's name, position (spelled out), height, and weight to the far left below the photo. The Eskimo logo appears in the lower right hand corner. The unnumbered backs are blank.

COMPLETE SET (6)	30.00	60.00
1 Ray Baillie	5.00	10.00
2 Gino Fracas	6.00	12.00
3 Ted Frechette	5.00	10.00
4 Tony Kehrer	5.00	10.00
5 E.A. Sims	5.00	10.00
6 Mike Volcan	5.00	10.00

1963 Edmonton Eskimos Team Issue

This set of Eskimos player photos was issued by the team to fill fan requests and looks nearly identical to the 1962 photos. Each photo measures roughly 8" by 10" and includes the player's name, position (spelled out), height, and weight below the photo but about 1 1/2" from the left edge. The Eskimo logo appears in the lower right hand corner. The unnumbered backs are blank.

COMPLETE SET (7)	25.00	50.00
1 Charlie Brown	4.00	8.00
2 Marcel Deleeuw	4.00	8.00
3 Ted Frechette	4.00	8.00
4 Sammie Harris	4.00	8.00
5 Dunc Harvey	5.00	10.00
6 Ken Reed	4.00	8.00
7 James Earl Wright	4.00	8.00

1964 Edmonton Eskimos Team Issue

This set of Eskimos player photos was issued by the team to fill fan requests. Each photo measures roughly 8" by 10" and includes the player's name, position (initials), height, and weight to the left below the photo. The Eskimo logo appears in the lower right hand corner. The unnumbered backs are blank.

COMPLETE SET (5)	20.00	40.00
1 Clair Branch	4.00	8.00
2 Junior Hawthorne	4.00	8.00
3 Ken Sigaty	4.00	8.00
4 Jim Stinnette	4.00	8.00
5 Jim Thibert	4.00	8.00

1965 Edmonton Eskimos Team Issue

This set of Eskimos player photos was issued by the team to fill fan requests. Each photo measures roughly 8" by 10" and includes the player's name, position (initials), height, and weight centered below the photo. The Eskimo logo appears in the lower right hand corner. The unnumbered backs are blank.

COMPLETE SET (9)	30.00	60.00
1 Charlie Brown	4.00	8.00
2 Ron Forwick	4.00	8.00
3 Bill Mitchell	4.00	8.00
4 Barry Mitchelson	4.00	8.00
5 John Sklopan	5.00	10.00
6 Jim Stinnette	4.00	8.00
7 Barney Therrien	4.00	8.00
8 Norman Thomas	4.00	8.00
9 Terry Wilson	4.00	8.00

1966 Edmonton Eskimos Program Inserts

Each of these photos measures approximately 3 7/8" by 5 1/8". Inside white borders, the fronts feature black-and-white posed action photos with the player's name and position below the image. The wider white bottom border carries the sponsor -- Canada Dry. The photos were initially issued in perforated sheets of four in each Eskimos game program for the season. The unnumbered backs include various advertisements.

COMPLETE SET (32)	75.00	125.00
1 Neill Armstrong CO	2.50	5.00
2 Mickey Bitsko	2.00	4.00
3 Ron Brewer	2.50	5.00
4 Ron Capham	2.00	4.00
5 Tommy Joe Coffey	4.00	8.00
6 Merv Collins	2.00	4.00
7 Steve Cotter	2.00	4.00
8 Ron Forwick	2.00	4.00
9 Ed Husmann	2.00	4.00
10 Art Johnson	2.00	4.00
11 Randy Kerbow	2.00	4.00
12 Garry Lefebvre	2.00	4.00
13 Ian MacLeod	2.00	4.00
14 Rusty Martin	2.00	4.00
15 Barry Mitchelson	2.00	4.00
16 Roger Nelson	4.00	8.00
17 Ken Perkins	2.00	4.00
18 Edgar Poles	2.00	4.00
19 Bill Redell	2.00	4.00
20 Billy Roy	2.00	4.00
21 Howie Schumm	2.00	4.00
22 Ken Sigaty	2.00	4.00
23 E.A. Sims	2.00	4.00
24 Bob Spanach	2.00	4.00
25 Marshall Starks	2.00	4.00
26 Jim Stinnette	2.00	4.00
27 Barney Therrien	2.00	4.00
28 Jim Thomas	2.00	4.00
29 Ed Turek	2.00	4.00
30 Trent Walters	2.00	4.00
31 Terry Wilson	2.00	4.00
32 John Wydareny	2.50	5.00

1966 Edmonton Eskimos Team Issue

This set of Eskimos player photos was issued by the team to fill fan requests and is very similar to the 1964 and 1965 issues. Each photo measures roughly 8" by 10" and includes the player's name, position (initials), height, and weight to the far left below the photo. The Eskimo logo appears in the lower right hand corner. The unnumbered backs are blank.

COMPLETE SET (11)	40.00	80.00
1 Mickey Bitsko	4.00	8.00
2 Ron Capham	4.00	8.00
3 Merv Collins	4.00	8.00
4 Steve Cotter	4.00	8.00
5 Norm Kimball GM	4.00	8.00
6 Rusty Martin	4.00	8.00
7 Willie Shine	4.00	8.00
8 Bob Spanach	4.00	8.00
9 Jon Sterling	4.00	8.00
10 Trent Walters	4.00	8.00
11 Terry Wilson	4.00	8.00

1967 Edmonton Eskimos Team Issue

The Eskimos issued this set of player photos around 1967. Each includes two black-and-white player photos with one being an action shot along with a smaller portrait image. The roughly 8" by 10 1/8" photos include the player's name, position underneath the name, college, vital stats, years pro, and team logo on the cardfronts. The coaches and GM photos measure a smaller 5" by 10 1/4" and include only his position, name, and team logo below the photo. The backs are blank and unnumbered.

COMPLETE SET (24)	75.00	150.00
1 Neill Armstrong CO	5.00	10.00
2 Brent Berry	4.00	8.00
3 David Campbell	4.00	8.00
4 Frank Cosentino	4.00	8.00
5 Steve Cotter	4.00	8.00
6 Doug Dersch	4.00	8.00
7 Earl Edwards	5.00	10.00
8 Charles Fulton	4.00	8.00
9 Jerry Griffin	4.00	8.00
10 Joe Hernandez	4.00	8.00
11 Ray Jauch CO	4.00	8.00
12 Peter Kempf	4.00	8.00
13 Randy Kerbow	4.00	8.00
14 Norm Kimball GM	4.00	8.00
15 Garry Lefebvre	4.00	8.00
16 Don Lisbon	4.00	8.00
17 Gordon Lund	4.00	8.00
18 Art Perkins	4.00	8.00
19 Edgar Poles	4.00	8.00
20 E.A. Sims	4.00	8.00
21 Bob Spanach	4.00	8.00
22 Phil Tucker	4.00	8.00
23 Trent Walters	4.00	8.00
24 John Wilson	4.00	8.00

1971 Edmonton Eskimos Team Issue

The Eskimos issued this set of player photos around 1971. Each includes two black-and-white player photos with one being an action shot along with a smaller portrait image. The roughly 8" by 10 1/8" photos include the player's name, position, vital stats, and team logo on the cardfronts. The backs are blank and unnumbered.

COMPLETE SET (13)	35.00	60.00
1 Rusty Clark	3.00	6.00
2 Fred Dunn	3.00	6.00
3 Mike Eben	3.00	6.00
4 Dave Fahrner	3.00	6.00
5 Ken Ferguson	3.00	6.00
6 James Henshal	3.00	6.00
7 Chip Kell	3.00	6.00
8 Henry King	3.00	6.00
9 Larry Kerychuk	3.00	6.00

10 Lance Olssen	3.00	6.00
11 Peter Travis	3.00	6.00
12 Don Trull	4.00	8.00
13 Willie Young	3.00	6.00

1972 Edmonton Eskimos Team Issue

The Eskimos issued this set of player photos. Each includes a black-and-white player photo on thin card stock. The photos measure roughly 7" by 9" and include the player's name, vital stats, college, and team logo on the cardfronts. The cardbacks are blank.

COMPLETE SET (10)	30.00	60.00
1 Ron Forwick	3.00	6.00
2 Gene Foster	3.00	6.00
3 Jim Henshall	3.00	6.00
4 Garry Lefebvre	3.00	6.00
5 Ed Molstad	3.00	6.00
6 Bayne Norrie	3.00	6.00
7 Dave Syme	3.00	6.00
8 Peter Travis	3.00	6.00
9 Charlie Turner	3.00	6.00
10 Tom Wilkinson	5.00	10.00

1960-61 Hamilton Tiger-Cats Team Issue

These 5" by 7" black and white photos were issued by the team to fill fan requests for souvenirs. Each photo was printed on glossy stock and includes the player's name, position, height, weight, and team name below the photo. The backs are blank and unnumbered.

COMPLETE SET (8)	30.00	60.00
1 Geno DeNobile	4.00	8.00
2 Jamie Colet	4.00	8.00
3 Grant McKee	4.00	8.00
4 Bob Minihane	4.00	8.00
5 Tom Moulton	4.00	8.00
6 Ron Ray	4.00	8.00
7 Butch Rogers	4.00	8.00
8 Willie Taylor	5.00	10.00

1962 Hamilton Tiger-Cats Team Issue

These 5" by 8" black and white photos were issued by the team to fill fan requests for souvenirs. Each photo was printed on glossy stock and includes the player's name, position, height, weight, and team name below the photo. In addition to the difference in length, the print size used for the 1962 photos is much larger than that used for 1960-61. Otherwise, the photos appear to be very similar. The backs are blank and unnumbered.

COMPLETE SET (12)	40.00	80.00
1 Art Baker	5.00	10.00
2 Don Caraway	4.00	8.00
3 Dick Cohee	5.00	10.00
4 Dick Easterly	4.00	8.00
5 Sam Fernandez	4.00	8.00
6 Larry Hickman	4.00	8.00
7 Willie McClung	4.00	8.00
8 Tom Moran	4.00	8.00
9 Jim Pace	4.00	8.00
10 Tim Reid	4.00	8.00
11 Milam Wall	4.00	8.00
12 Dave Viti	4.00	8.00

1964 Hamilton Tiger-Cats Team Issue

These 5" by 7" black and white photos were issued by the team to fill fan requests for souvenirs. Each photo was printed on glossy stock and includes the player's name, position, height, weight, and team name below the photo. Note there is no "--" between the player's name and position like exists on the 1960-61 photos. The backs are blank and unnumbered.

COMPLETE SET (6)	20.00	40.00
1 Joe Cannavino UER	4.00	8.00
2 Gene Ceppetelli	4.00	8.00
3 John Cimba	4.00	8.00
4 Stan Crisson	4.00	8.00
5 Bob Gaiters	5.00	10.00
6 Steve Hmiel	4.00	8.00

1965 Hamilton Tiger-Cats Team Issue

These 5" by 8" black and white photos were issued by the team to fill fan requests for souvenirs. Each photo was printed on glossy stock and includes the player's name, height and weight in a single line below the photo followed by the team name in the lower right corner. The backs are blank and unnumbered.

1 Dick Cohee	5.00	10.00
2 Billy Ray Locklin	4.00	8.00
3 Ted Page	4.00	8.00
4 Jim Reynolds	4.00	8.00
5 Dave Viti	4.00	8.00
6 Billy Wayte	4.00	8.00

1966 Hamilton Tiger-Cats Team Issue

These 5" by 8" black and white photos were issued by the team to fill fan requests for souvenirs. Each photo was printed on glossy stock and includes the player's name, position, height and weight in two lines of type below the photo followed by the team name in the lower right corner. The backs are blank and unnumbered.

COMPLETE SET (3)	10.00	20.00
1 Gene Ceppetelli	4.00	8.00
2 Billy Ray Locklin	4.00	8.00
3 Bob Steiner	4.00	8.00

1967 Hamilton Tiger-Cats Team Issue

These 5" by 8" black and white photos were issued by the team to fill fan requests for souvenirs. Each photo was printed on glossy stock and includes the player's name, height and weight in a single line below the photo followed by the team name in the lower right corner. The backs are blank and unnumbered.

COMPLETE SET (5)	20.00	40.00
1 Gordan Christian	4.00	8.00
2 Barrie Hansen	4.00	8.00
3 Doug Mitchell	4.00	8.00
4 Bob Storey	5.00	10.00
5 Ted Watkins	4.00	8.00

1977-78 Hamilton Tiger-Cats Team Sheets

This group of 32-players and coaches of the Tiger-Cats was produced on four glossy sheets each measuring approximately 8" by 10". The fronts feature black-and-white player portraits with eight pictures to a sheet with the year printed at the top. The backs are blank. The cards are unnumbered and checklisted below in alphabetical order, with the player pictured in the upper left hand corner of the sheet listed first.

COMPLETE SET (4)	10.00	20.00
1 B.Evans	2.50	5.00
S.Britts		
J.Jones		
N.Jambrosic		
L.Butler		
D.Shaw		
M.Harris		
P.Sheridan		
2 F.Gibson	3.00	6.00
B.Shaw		
R.Sazio		
W.Bauer		
M.Wilson		
L.Porter		
M.Perrelli		
P.Donley		
3 C.Jensen	2.50	5.00
G.Shaw		
K.Strayhorn		
J.Martini		
L.Skolrood		
J.Kinch		
J.Worobec		
T.Berryman		
4 A.Moffat	2.50	5.00
K.Carter		
L.Brune		
B.Finlay		
S.Gelley		
M.Samples		
H.Waszczuk		
K.Clark		

1980 Hamilton Tiger-Cats Team Sheets

This group of 40-players and coaches of the Tiger-Cats was produced on five glossy sheets each measuring approximately 8" by 10". The fronts feature black-and-white player portraits with eight pictures to a sheet with the year printed at the top. The backs are blank. The cards are unnumbered and checklisted below in alphabetical order, with the player pictured in the upper left hand corner of the sheet listed first.

COMPLETE SET (5)	12.50	25.00
1 J.Anderson	2.50	6.00
B.Aynsley		
J.Blair		
W.Carter		
P.Colwell		
R.Crawford		
C.Crennel		
C.Curran		
2 L.Davidson	2.00	5.00
B.Dutton CO		
R.DiPietro		
A.Dosant		
R.Gaddis		
E.George		
R.Graham		
J.Haering CO		
3 J.Holland	2.00	5.00
C.Labbett		
B.Lemmerman		
D.Marler		
W.Martin		
J.Muller		
F.Moffatt		
B.Macauley		
4 B.McBride	2.00	5.00
E.Nielsen		
G.Paterson		
L.Paul		
L.Pettersen		
R.Rowland		
B.Rozier		
B.Ruoff		
5 D.Shaw	2.50	6.00
G.Thiessen		
G.Wall		
H.Waszczuk		
H.Woods		
B.Zambiasi		
R.Honey		
M.Cyncar		

1971 Mac's Milk CFL Cloth Stickers

These, roughly 3" in diameter, cloth sticker discs feature a color image of a CFL player or team helmet. The backs are blank and the discs are thought to have been issued by Mac's Milk.

COMPLETE SET (20)	75.00	150.00
1 Greg Barton	3.00	8.00
2 Tommy Joe Coffey	5.00	12.00
3 Garney Henley	3.00	8.00
4 Marv Luster	3.00	8.00
5 Leon McQuay	3.00	8.00
6 Angelo Mosca	5.00	12.00
7 Mel Profit	3.00	8.00
8 Dave Raimey	3.00	8.00
9 Joe Theismann	7.50	15.00
10 John Williams	3.00	8.00
11 Alouettes Helmet	3.00	8.00
12 Argonauts Helmet	3.00	8.00
13 B.C. Lions Helmet	3.00	8.00
14 Blue Bombers Helmet	3.00	8.00
15 CFL Helmet	3.00	8.00
16 Eskimos Helmet	3.00	8.00
17 Rough Riders Helmet	3.00	8.00
18 Roughriders Helmet	3.00	8.00
19 Stampeders Helmet	3.00	8.00
20 Tiger-Cats Helmet	3.00	8.00

1963 Montreal Alouettes Bank of Montreal

Each of these photos measure approximately 3 7/8" by 5 3/8". Inside white borders, the fronts feature black-and-white posed action photos. Immediately below the picture in small print is the player's name. The wider white bottom border carries the sponsor (Bank of Montreal) information. The photos were perforated as they were originally issued in game programs as pairs. The backs display various advertisements. The photos are unnumbered and checklisted below in alphabetical order.

COMPLETE SET (14)	50.00	100.00
1 Dick Aboud	4.00	10.00
2 Jim Andreotti	4.00	10.00
3 Ross Buckle	4.00	10.00
4 Don Clark	4.00	10.00
5 Tom Cloutier	4.00	10.00
6 Ted Elsby	4.00	10.00
7 Jack Espenship	4.00	10.00
8 Bob Geary	4.00	10.00
9 Robert LeBlanc	4.00	10.00
10 Billy Ray Locklin	4.00	10.00
11 Ron Maddocks	5.00	12.00
12 Don Paquette	4.00	10.00
13 Dick Schnell	4.00	10.00
14 Billy Wayte	4.00	10.00

1970-72 Montreal Alouettes Matin Sports Weekend Posters

These posters were actually newspaper page cut-outs. Each is oversized and features a color photo of the featured player surrounded by cardlike graphics. The posters were printed on newsprint type stock or a period of years. The backs are simply another page from the newspaper. Any additions to the below checklist are appreciated.

1 Bruce Van Ness	7.50	15.00
2 Terry Evanshen 1970	15.00	30.00
3 Terry Evanshen 1971	15.00	30.00
4 Gene Gaines	15.00	30.00
5 Gino Cappelletti	15.00	30.00
6 Pierre Desjardins	7.50	15.00
7 Dennis Duncan	7.50	15.00
8 Russ Jackson	15.00	30.00
9 Joe Theismann	25.00	50.00
10 S.Etcheverry	15.00	30.00
S.Wade		
Passander		
11 Moses Denson	10.00	20.00
12 Jim Chasey	7.50	15.00

1974-76 Montreal Alouettes Team Issue

These oversized (roughly 3 1/2" by 5 1/2") photos feature black and white player photos and were issued by the Alouettes for player appearances and fan mail. Each is blankbacked and features the team name and logo below the photo with only a facsimile player signature to help identify the athlete. The photos were likely issued over a number of years. Any additions to this list are appreciated.

COMPLETE SET (38)	125.00	200.00
1 Junior Ah-You	6.00	10.00
2 Brock Ansley	3.00	5.00
3 Joe Barnes	6.00	10.00
4 Pat Bonnet	3.00	5.00
5 Dave Braggins	3.00	5.00
6 Wally Buono	3.00	5.00
7 Gary Chown	3.00	5.00
8 Wayne Conrad	3.00	5.00
9 Carl Crennell	3.00	5.00
10 Peter Dalla Riva	3.50	6.00
11 Gerry Dattilio	3.00	5.00
12 Marvin Davis	3.00	5.00
13 Rudy Florio	3.00	5.00
14 Gene Gaines	6.00	10.00
15 Pierre Gelesiar	3.00	5.00
16 Gabriel Gregoire	3.00	5.00
17 Dickie Harris	3.00	5.00
18 Andy Hopkins	3.00	5.00
19 Gordon Judges	3.00	5.00
20 Glen Leach	3.00	5.00
21 Chuck McMann	3.00	5.00
22 Ian Mofford	3.00	5.00
23 Joe Petty	3.00	5.00
24 Frank Pomarico	3.00	5.00
25 Phil Price	3.00	5.00
26 Barry Randall	3.00	5.00
27 Randy Rhino	3.00	5.00
28 Johnny Rodgers	6.00	10.00
29 Johnny Rodgers	6.00	10.00
30 Doug Smith	3.00	5.00
31 Larry Smith	3.00	5.00
32 Don Sweet	3.00	5.00
33 John Tanner	3.00	5.00
34 Sonny Wade	3.00	5.00
35 Glen Weir	3.00	5.00
36 Mike Widger	3.00	5.00
37 Dan Yochum	3.00	5.00
38 Chuck Zapiec	3.00	5.00

1978 Montreal Alouettes Redpath Sugar

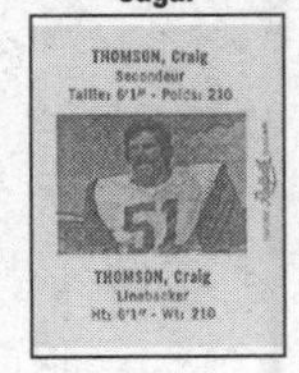

Redpath Sugar produced small (roughly 1 5/8" by 2 1/2") sugar packets featuring Alouette players for distribution in the Montreal area. Each is unnumbered and includes a small color photo of the player on the front along with his name, position, and vital information in both French and English. The back of the sugar packet includes an Alouettes logo and a short player bio. Any additions to this checklist are appreciated.

COMPLETE SET (11)	25.00	50.00
1 Jim Burrow	3.75	7.50
2 Gary Chown	2.50	5.00
3 Dan Diebert TR	2.50	5.00
4 Gabriel Gregoire	2.50	5.00
5 Dickie Harris	3.75	7.50
6 Max Huber	2.50	5.00
7 Mark Jackson	3.75	7.50
8 Larry Pasquale	2.50	5.00
9 Craig Thomson	2.50	5.00
10 Sonny Wade	2.50	5.00
11 Alouettes Mascot	2.50	5.00

1978 Montreal Alouettes Team Sheets

This group of 32-players of the Montreal Alouettes was produced on four glossy sheets each measuring approximately 8" by 10". The fronts feature black-and-white player portraits with eight pictures to a sheet. The backs are blank. The cards are unnumbered and checklisted below in alphabetical order, with the player pictured in the upper left hand corner of the sheet listed first.

COMPLETE SET (4)	10.00	20.00
1 G.Dattilio	3.00	6.00
P.Dalla Riva		
W.Conrad		
J.Burrow		
W.Buono		
P.Bonnett		
J.Barnes		
C.Zapiec		
2 J.Friesen	3.00	6.00
J.Olenchalk		
C.Alapa		
C.Crennel		
J.Ah You		
E.Fiatoa		
B.Watson		
G.Weir		
3 B.Gaddis	2.50	5.00
V.Perry		
G.Gregoire		
D.Harris		
C.Labbett		
C.McMann		
T.Morris		
J.O'Leary		
4 R.Watrin	2.50	5.00
S.Wade		
L.Uteck		
J.Taylor		
K.Starch		
L.Smith		
D.Sweet		
D.Payton		

1963 Nalley's Coins

This 160-coin set is difficult to complete due to the fact that within every team grouping, the last ten coins are much tougher to find. The back of the coin is hard plastic, but also see-through. The coins can be found with sponsors Nalley's Potato Chips, Hunter's Potato Chips, Krun-Chee Potato Chips, and Humpty Dumpty Potato Chips. Humpty Dumpty coins were printed in French and English, instead of just English. The coins can also be found without sponsor names. There are no price differences between the variations. Eight of the nine CFL teams are represented. The coins measure approximately 1 3/8" in diameter. Shields to hold the coins were also issued; these shields are also very collectible and are listed at the end of the list below, with the prefix S. The shields are not included in the complete set price.

COMPLETE SET (160)	1,500.00	3,000.00
1 Jackie Parker	10.00	20.00
2 Dick Shatto	4.00	8.00
3 Dave Mann	3.00	6.00
4 Danny Nykoluk	2.50	5.00
5 Billy Shipp	2.50	5.00
6 Doug McNichol	2.50	5.00
7 Jim Rountree	2.50	5.00
8 Art Johnson	2.50	5.00
9 Walt Radzick	2.50	5.00
10 Jim Andreotti	3.00	6.00
11 Gerry Philip	10.00	20.00
12 Lynn Bottoms	10.00	20.00
13 Ron Morris SP	40.00	80.00
14 Nobby Wirkowski CO	10.00	20.00
15 John Wydareny	10.00	20.00
16 Gerry Wilson	10.00	20.00
17 Gerry Patrick SP	25.00	50.00
18 Aubrey Linne	10.00	20.00
19 Norm Stoneburgh	10.00	20.00
20 Ken Beck	10.00	20.00
21 Russ Jackson	7.50	15.00
22 Kaye Vaughan	4.00	8.00
23 Dave Thelen	4.00	8.00
24 Ron Stewart	4.00	8.00
25 Moe Racine	2.50	5.00
26 Jim Conroy	3.00	6.00
27 Joe Poirier	3.00	6.00
28 Mel Seminko	2.50	5.00
29 Whit Tucker	4.00	8.00
30 Ernie White	2.50	5.00
31 Frank Clair CO	10.00	20.00
32 Merv Bevan	10.00	20.00
33 Jerry Selinger	10.00	20.00
34 Jim Cain	10.00	20.00
35 Mike Snodgrass	10.00	20.00
36 Ted Smale	10.00	20.00
37 Billy Joe Booth	10.00	20.00
38 Len Chandler	10.00	20.00
39 Rick Black	10.00	20.00
40 Allen Schau	10.00	20.00
41 Bernie Faloney	7.50	15.00
42 Bobby Kuntz	3.00	6.00
43 Joe Zuger	3.00	6.00
44 Hal Patterson	6.00	12.00
45 Bronko Nagurski Jr.	5.00	10.00
46 Zeno Karcz	3.00	6.00
47 Hardiman Cureton	2.50	5.00
48 John Barrow	4.00	8.00
49 Tommy Grant	4.00	8.00
50 Garney Henley	4.00	8.00
51 Dick Easterly	10.00	20.00
52 Frank Cosentino	10.00	20.00
53 Geno DeNobile	10.00	20.00
54 Ralph Goldston	10.00	20.00
55 Chet Miksza	10.00	20.00
56 Bob Minihane	10.00	20.00
57 Don Sutherin	20.00	40.00
58 Ralph Sazio CO	10.00	20.00
59 Dave Viti SP	17.50	35.00
60 Angelo Mosca SP	62.50	125.00
61 Sandy Stephens	4.00	8.00
62 George Dixon	4.00	8.00
63 Don Clark	3.00	6.00
64 Don Paquette	2.50	5.00
65 Billy Wayte	2.50	5.00
66 Ed Nickla	2.50	5.00
67 Marv Luster	4.00	8.00
68 Joe Stracini	2.50	5.00
69 Bobby Jack Oliver	3.00	6.00
70 Ted Elsby	2.50	5.00
71 Jim Trimble CO	5.00	10.00
72 Bob Leblanc	5.00	10.00
73 Dick Schnell	5.00	10.00
74 Milt Crain	5.00	10.00
75 Dick Dalatri	5.00	10.00
76 Billy Roy	5.00	10.00
77 Dave Hoppmann	5.00	10.00
78 Billy Ray Locklin	5.00	10.00
79 Ed Learn SP	75.00	150.00
80 Meco Poliziani SP	20.00	40.00
81 Leo Lewis	4.00	8.00
82 Kenny Ploen	4.00	8.00
83 Steve Patrick	2.50	5.00
84 Farrell Funston	3.00	6.00
85 Charlie Shepard	3.00	6.00
86 Ronnie Latourelle	2.50	5.00
87 Gord Rowland	3.00	6.00
88 Frank Rigney	3.00	6.00
89 Cornel Piper	2.50	5.00
90 Ernie Pitts	2.50	5.00
91 Roger Hagberg	7.50	15.00
92 Herb Gray	15.00	30.00
93 Jack Delveaux	5.00	10.00
94 Roger Savoie	5.00	10.00
95 Nick Miller	5.00	10.00
96 Norm Rauhaus	5.00	10.00
97 Cec Luining	5.00	10.00
98 Hal Ledyard	5.00	10.00
99 Neil Thomas	5.00	10.00
100 Bud Grant CO	40.00	80.00
101 Eagle Keys CO	4.00	8.00
102 Mike Wicklum	2.50	5.00
103 Bill Mitchell	2.50	5.00
104 Mike Lashuk	2.50	5.00
105 Tommy Joe Coffey	4.00	8.00
106 Zeke Smith	2.50	5.00
107 Joe Hernandez	2.50	5.00
108 Johnny Bright	4.00	8.00
109 Don Getty	4.00	8.00
110 Nat Dye	2.50	5.00
111 James Earl Wright	5.00	10.00
112 Mike Volcan SP	17.50	35.00
113 Jon Rechner	5.00	10.00
114 Len Vella	5.00	10.00
115 Ted Frechette	5.00	10.00
116 Larry Fleisher	5.00	10.00
117 Oscar Kruger	5.00	10.00
118 Ken Petersen	5.00	10.00
119 Bobby Walden	5.00	10.00
120 Mickey Ording	5.00	10.00
121 Pete Manning	2.50	5.00
122 Harvey Wylie	3.00	6.00
123 Tony Pajaczkowski	4.00	8.00
124 Wayne Harris	5.00	10.00
125 Earl Lunsford	4.00	8.00
126 Don Luzzi	3.00	6.00
127 Ed Buckanan	2.50	5.00
128 Lovell Coleman	3.00	6.00
129 Hal Krebs	2.50	5.00
130 Eagle Day	4.00	8.00
131 Bobby Dobbs CO	5.00	10.00
132 George Hansen	5.00	10.00
133 Roy Jokanovich SP	40.00	80.00
134 Jerry Keeling	15.00	30.00
135 Larry Anderson	5.00	10.00
136 Bill Crawford	5.00	10.00
137 Ron Albright	5.00	10.00
138 Bill Britton	5.00	10.00
139 Jim Dillard	5.00	10.00
140 Jim Furlong	5.00	10.00
141 Dave Skrien CO	2.50	5.00
142 Willie Fleming	5.00	10.00
143 Nub Beamer	2.50	5.00
144 Norm Fieldgate	4.00	8.00
145 Joe Kapp	17.50	35.00
146 Tom Hinton	4.00	8.00
147 Pat Claridge	2.50	5.00
148 Bill Munsey	2.50	5.00
149 Mike Martin	2.50	5.00
150 Tom Brown	4.00	8.00
151 Ian Hagemoen	5.00	10.00
152 Jim Carphin	5.00	10.00
153 By Bailey	15.00	30.00
154 Steve Cotter	5.00	10.00
155 Mike Cacic	5.00	10.00
156 Neil Beaumont	5.00	10.00
157 Lonnie Dennis	5.00	10.00
158 Barney Therrien	5.00	10.00
159 Sonny Homer	5.00	10.00
160 Walt Bilicki	5.00	10.00
S1 Toronto Shield	25.00	50.00
S2 Ottawa Shield	25.00	50.00
S3 Hamilton Shield	25.00	50.00
S4 Montreal Shield	25.00	50.00
S5 Winnipeg Shield	25.00	50.00
S6 Edmonton Shield	25.00	50.00
S7 Calgary Shield	25.00	50.00
S8 British Columbia	25.00	50.00

1964 Nalley's Coins

This 100-coin set is very similar to the set from the previous year except that there are no real distribution scarcities. The backs of the coins are plastic, but not see-through. No specific information about the player, as in the previous year, is included. The coins were sponsored by Nalley's Potato Chips and packaged one per box of chips. The set numbering is in team order. The coins measure approximately 1 3/8" in diameter. Shields to hold the coins were also issued; these shields are also very collectible and are listed at the end of the list below with the prefix "S". The shields are not included in the complete set price. Only teams from the Western Conference of the CFL were included.

COMPLETE SET (100)	375.00	750.00
1 Joe Kapp	15.00	30.00
2 Willie Fleming	5.00	10.00
3 Norm Fieldgate	4.00	8.00
4 Bill Murray	2.50	5.00
5 Tom Brown	5.00	10.00
6 Neil Beaumont	3.00	6.00
7 Sonny Homer	3.00	6.00
8 Lonnie Dennis	2.50	5.00
9 Dave Skrien	2.50	5.00
10 Dick Fouts CO	2.50	5.00
11 Paul Seale	2.50	5.00
12 Peter Kempf	2.50	5.00
13 Steve Shafer	2.50	5.00
14 Tom Hinton	4.00	8.00
15 Pat Claridge	2.50	5.00
16 By Bailey	4.00	8.00
17 Nub Beamer	3.00	6.00
18 Steve Cotter	2.50	5.00
19 Mike Cacic	2.50	5.00
20 Mike Martin	2.50	5.00
21 Eagle Day	7.50	15.00
22 Jim Dillard	2.50	5.00
23 Pete Murray	2.50	5.00
24 Tony Pajaczkowski	4.00	8.00
25 Don Luzzi	3.00	6.00
26 Wayne Harris	5.00	10.00
27 Harvey Wylie	3.00	6.00
28 Bill Crawford	2.50	5.00
29 Jim Furlong	2.50	5.00
30 Lovell Coleman	3.00	6.00
31 Pat Haines	2.50	5.00
32 Bob Taylor	3.00	6.00
33 Ernie Danjean	2.50	5.00
34 Jerry Keeling	4.00	8.00
35 Larry Robinson	3.00	6.00
36 George Hansen	2.50	5.00
37 Ron Albright	2.50	5.00
38 Larry Anderson	2.50	5.00
39 Bill Miller	2.50	5.00
40 Bill Britton	2.50	5.00
41 Lynn Amadee	4.00	8.00
42 Mike Lashuk	2.50	5.00
43 Tommy Joe Coffey	4.00	8.00
44 Junior Hawthorne	2.50	5.00
45 Nat Dye	2.50	5.00
46 Al Ecuyer	2.50	5.00
47 Howie Schumm	2.50	5.00
48 Zeke Smith	2.50	5.00
49 Mike Wicklum	2.50	5.00
50 Mike Volcan	2.50	5.00
51 E.A. Sims	2.50	5.00
52 Bill Mitchell	2.50	5.00
53 Ken Reed	2.50	5.00
54 Len Vella	2.50	5.00
55 Johnny Bright	4.00	8.00
56 Don Getty	4.00	8.00
57 Oscar Kruger	2.50	5.00
58 Ted Frechette	2.50	5.00
59 James Earl Wright	2.50	5.00
60 Roger Nelson	2.50	5.00
61 Ron Lancaster	6.00	12.00
62 Bill Clarke	2.50	5.00
63 Bob Shaw	2.50	5.00
64 Ray Purdin	2.50	5.00
65 Ron Atchison	4.00	8.00
66 Ted Urness	4.00	8.00
67 Bob Ptacek	2.50	5.00
68 Neil Habig	2.50	5.00
69 Garner Ekstran	3.00	6.00
70 Gene Wlasiuk	2.50	5.00
71 Jack Gotta	3.00	6.00
72 Dick Cohee	2.50	5.00
73 Ron Meadmore	2.50	5.00
74 Martin Fabi	2.50	5.00
75 Bob Good	2.50	5.00
76 Len Legault	2.50	5.00
77 Al Benecick	2.50	5.00
78 Dale West	3.00	6.00
79 Reg Whitehouse	2.50	5.00
80 George Reed	5.00	10.00
81 Kenny Ploen	4.00	8.00
82 Leo Lewis	6.00	12.00
83 Dick Thornton	3.00	6.00
84 Steve Patrick	2.50	5.00
85 Frank Rigney	3.00	6.00
86 Cornel Piper	2.50	5.00
87 Sherwyn Thorson	2.50	5.00
88 Ernie Pitts	2.50	5.00
89 Roger Hagberg	3.00	6.00
90 Bud Grant CO	25.00	50.00
91 Jack Delveaux	2.50	5.00
92 Farrell Funston	3.00	6.00
93 Ronnie Latourelle	2.50	5.00
94 Roger Hamelin	2.50	5.00
95 Gord Rowland	3.00	6.00
96 Herb Gray	5.00	10.00
97 Nick Miller	2.50	5.00
98 Norm Rauhaus	3.00	6.00
99 Bill Whisler	2.50	5.00
100 Hal Ledyard	2.50	5.00
S1 British Columbia	22.50	45.00
S2 Calgary Shield	22.50	45.00
S3 Edmonton Shield	22.50	45.00
S4 Saskatchewan Shield	22.50	45.00
S5 Winnipeg Shield	22.50	45.00

1976 Nalley's Chips

This 31-card set was distributed in Western Canada in boxes of Nalley's Plain or Salt 'n Vinegar potato chips. The cards measure approximately 3 3/8" by 5 1/2" and feature posed color photos of the player, with the Nalley company name and player's signature below the picture. These blank-backed, unnumbered cards are listed below in alphabetical order.

COMPLETE SET (31)	250.00	400.00
1 Bill Baker	12.50	25.00
2 Willie Burden	20.00	35.00
3 Larry Cates	5.00	10.00
4 Dave Cutler	10.00	20.00
5 Lloyd Fairbanks	7.50	15.00
6 Joe Forzani	6.00	12.00
7 Tom Forzani	5.00	10.00
8 Rick Galbos	5.00	10.00
9 Eric Guthrie	5.00	10.00
10 Lou Harris	6.00	12.00
11 John Helton	10.00	20.00
12 Larry Highbaugh	7.50	15.00
13 Harold Holton	5.00	10.00
14 John Konihowski	5.00	10.00
15 Bruce Lemmerman	6.00	12.00
16 Rudy Linterman	7.50	15.00
17 Layne McDowell	5.00	10.00
18 George McGowan	7.50	15.00
19 Ray Nettles	5.00	10.00
20 Lui Passaglia	15.00	30.00
21 Joe Pisarcik	10.00	20.00
22 Dale Potter	5.00	10.00
23 John Sciarra	10.00	20.00
24 Wayne Smith	5.00	10.00
25 Michael Strickland	5.00	10.00
26 Charlie Turner	5.00	10.00
27 Tyrone Walls	6.00	12.00
28 Don Warrington	5.00	10.00
29 Tom Wilkinson	15.00	30.00
30 Jim Young	15.00	30.00
31 Cover Card	5.00	10.00

1953 Northern Photo Services Giant Postcards

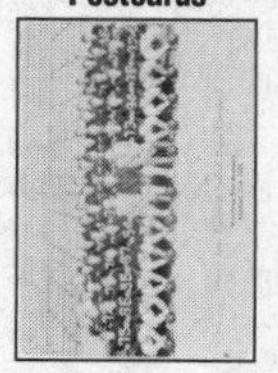

These large (roughly) postcards were produced by Northern Photo Services and feature the four teams of the Western Interprovincial Football Union of the CFL. Each was produced in Ektachrome color, features rounded corners, and includes a postcard style cardback.

NNO Winnipeg Blue Bombers	90.00	150.00
NNO Edmonton Eskimos	90.00	150.00
NNO Saskatchewan Roughriders	90.00	150.00
NNO Calgary Stampeders	90.00	150.00

1968 O-Pee-Chee CFL

The 1968 O-Pee-Chee CFL set of 132 standard-size cards received limited distribution and is considered by some to be a test set. The card backs are written in English and French in green ink on yellowish card stock. The cards are ordered by teams. A complete checklist is given on card number 132. The card front design is similar to the design of the 1968 Topps NFL set.

COMPLETE SET (132)	900.00	1,500.00
1 Roger Murphy	6.00	12.00
2 Charlie Parker	5.00	10.00
3 Mike Webster	5.00	10.00
4 Carroll Williams	5.00	10.00
5 Phil Brady	5.00	10.00
6 Dave Lewis	5.00	10.00
7 John Baker	5.00	10.00
8 Basil Bark	5.00	10.00
9 Donnie Davis	5.00	10.00
10 Pierre Desjardins	5.00	10.00
11 Larry Fairholm	5.00	10.00
12 Peter Paquette	5.00	10.00
13 Ray Lychak	5.00	10.00
14 Ted Collins	5.00	10.00
15 Margene Adkins	6.00	12.00
16 Ron Stewart	10.00	20.00
17 Russ Jackson	20.00	35.00
18 Bo Scott	7.50	15.00
19 Joe Poirier	5.00	10.00
20 Wayne Giardino	5.00	10.00
21 Gene Gaines	7.50	15.00
22 Billy Joe Booth	5.00	10.00
23 Whit Tucker	7.50	15.00
24 Rick Black	5.00	10.00
25 Ken Lehmann	6.00	12.00
26 Bob Brown	5.00	10.00
27 Moe Racine	5.00	10.00
28 Dick Thornton	5.00	10.00
29 Bob Taylor	5.00	10.00
30 Mel Profit	6.00	12.00
31 Dave Mann	6.00	12.00
32 Marv Luster	6.00	12.00
33 Ed Buchanan	5.00	10.00
34 Ed Harrington	5.00	10.00
35 Jim Dillard	5.00	10.00
36 Bob Taylor	5.00	10.00
37 Ron Arends	5.00	10.00
38 Mike Wadsworth	5.00	10.00
39 Wally Gabler	6.00	12.00
40 Pete Martin	5.00	10.00
41 Danny Nykoluk	5.00	10.00
42 Bill Frank	5.00	10.00
43 Gordon Christian	5.00	10.00
44 Tommy Joe Coffey	10.00	20.00
45 Ellison Kelly	10.00	20.00
46 Angelo Mosca	15.00	30.00
47 John Barrow	10.00	20.00
48 Bill Danychuk	6.00	12.00
49 Jon Hohman	5.00	10.00
50 Bill Redell	5.00	10.00
51 Joe Zuger	5.00	10.00

52 Willie Bethea 6.00 12.00
53 Dick Cohee 5.00 10.00
54 Tommy Grant 7.50 15.00
55 Garney Henley 10.00 20.00
56 Ted Page 5.00 10.00
57 Bob Krouse 5.00 10.00
58 Phil Minnick 5.00 10.00
59 Butch Pressley 5.00 10.00
60 Dave Raimey 5.00 10.00
61 Sherwyn Thorson 5.00 10.00
62 Bill Whisler 5.00 10.00
63 Roger Hamelin 5.00 10.00
64 Chuck Harrison 5.00 10.00
65 Ken Nielsen 6.00 12.00
66 Ernie Pitts 5.00 10.00
67 Mitch Zainasky 5.00 10.00
68 John Schneider 5.00 10.00
69 Ron Kirkland 5.00 10.00
70 Paul Desjardins 5.00 10.00
71 Luther Selbo 5.00 10.00
72 Don Gilbert 5.00 10.00
73 Bob Lueck 5.00 10.00
74 Gerry Shaw 5.00 10.00
75 Chuck Zickefoose 5.00 10.00
76 Frank Andruski 5.00 10.00
77 Lanny Boleski 5.00 10.00
78 Terry Evanshen 10.00 20.00
79 Jim Furlong 5.00 10.00
80 Wayne Harris 10.00 20.00
81 Jerry Keeling 6.00 12.00
82 Roger Kramer 5.00 10.00
83 Pete Liske 10.00 20.00
84 Dick Suderman 6.00 12.00
85 Granville Liggins 10.00 20.00
86 George Reed 12.50 25.00
87 Ron Lancaster 15.00 30.00
88 Alan Ford 5.00 10.00
89 Gordon Barwell 5.00 10.00
90 Wayne Shaw 5.00 10.00
91 Bruce Bennett 7.50 15.00
92 Henry Dorsch 5.00 10.00
93 Ken Reed 5.00 10.00
94 Ron Atchison 7.50 15.00
95 Clyde Brock 5.00 10.00
96 Al Benecick 5.00 10.00
97 Ted Urness 6.00 12.00
98 Wally Dempsey 5.00 10.00
99 Don Gerhardt 5.00 10.00
100 Ted Dushinski 5.00 10.00
101 Ed McQuarters 6.00 12.00
102 Bob Kosid 5.00 10.00
103 Gary Brandt 5.00 10.00
104 John Wydareny 5.00 10.00
105 Jim Thomas 5.00 10.00
106 Art Perkins 5.00 10.00
107 Frank Cosentino 6.00 12.00
108 Earl Edwards 5.00 10.00
109 Garry Lefebvre 5.00 10.00
110 Greg Pipes 5.00 10.00
111 Ian MacLeod 5.00 10.00
112 Dick Dupuis 5.00 10.00
113 Ron Forwick 5.00 10.00
114 Jerry Griffin 5.00 10.00
115 John LaGrone 6.00 12.00
116 E.A. Sims 5.00 10.00
117 Greenard Poles 5.00 10.00
118 Leroy Sledge 5.00 10.00
119 Ken Sugarman 5.00 10.00
120 Jim Young 12.50 25.00
121 Garner Ekstran 5.00 10.00
122 Jim Evenson 6.00 12.00
123 Greg Findlay 5.00 10.00
124 Ted Gerela 5.00 10.00
125 Lach Heron 5.00 10.00
126 Mike Martin 5.00 10.00
127 Craig Murray 5.00 10.00
128 Pete Ohler 5.00 10.00
129 Sonny Homer 5.00 10.00
130 Bill Lasseter 5.00 10.00
131 John McDowell 5.00 10.00
132 Checklist Card 60.00 120.00

1968 O-Pee-Chee CFL Poster Inserts

This 16-card set of color posters featuring all-stars of the Canadian Football League was inserted in wax packs along with the regular issue of 1968 O-Pee-Chee CFL cards. These (approximately) 5" by 7" posters were folded twice in order to fit in the wax packs. They are unnumbered and are blank on the back. They were printed on very thin paper. These posters are similar in appearance to the 1967 Topps baseball and 1968 Topps football poster inserts.

COMPLETE SET (16) 150.00 300.00
1 Margene Adkins 9.00 18.00
2 Tommy Joe Coffey 12.50 25.00
3 Frank Cosentino 9.00 18.00
4 Terry Evanshen 12.50 25.00
5 Larry Fairholm 7.50 15.00
6 Wally Gabler 7.50 15.00
7 Russ Jackson 17.50 35.00
8 Ron Lancaster 17.50 35.00
9 Pete Liske 12.50 25.00
10 Dave Mann 9.00 18.00
11 Ken Nielsen 9.00 18.00
12 Dave Raimey 9.00 18.00
13 George Reed 15.00 30.00
14 Carroll Williams 7.50 15.00
15 Jim Young 15.00 30.00
16 Joe Zuger 7.50 15.00

1970 O-Pee-Chee CFL

The 1970 O-Pee-Chee CFL set features 115 standard-size cards ordered by teams. The design of these cards is very similar to the 1969 Topps NFL football issue. The card backs are written in French and English; the card back is predominantly black with white lettering and green accent. Six miscellaneous special feature cards comprise cards numbered 110-115.

COMPLETE SET (115) 175.00 350.00
1 Ed Harrington 2.00 4.00
2 Danny Nykoluk 1.25 2.50
3 Marv Luster 2.50 5.00
4 Dave Raimey 2.00 4.00
5 Bill Symons 2.50 5.00
6 Tom Wilkinson 10.00 20.00
7 Mike Wadsworth 1.25 2.50
8 Dick Thornton 2.00 4.00
9 Jim Tomlin 1.25 2.50
10 Mel Profit 2.00 4.00
11 Bob Taylor 2.50 5.00
12 Dave Mann 2.00 4.00
13 Tommy Joe Coffey 3.00 6.00
14 Angelo Mosca 9.00 18.00
15 Joe Zuger 2.00 4.00
16 Garney Henley 5.00 10.00
17 Mike Strofolino 1.25 2.50
18 Billy Ray Locklin 1.25 2.50
19 Ted Page 1.25 2.50
20 Bill Danychuk 2.00 4.00
21 Bob Krouse 1.25 2.50
22 John Reid 1.25 2.50
23 Dick Wesolowski 1.25 2.50
24 Willie Bethea 2.00 4.00
25 Ken Sugarman 2.00 4.00
26 Rich Robinson 1.25 2.50
27 Dave Tobey 1.25 2.50
28 Paul Brothers 1.25 2.50
29 Charlie Brown RB 1.25 2.50
30 Jerry Bradley 1.25 2.50
31 Ted Gerela 2.00 4.00
32 Jim Young 4.00 8.00
33 Gary Robinson 1.25 2.50
34 Bob Howes 1.25 2.50
35 Greg Findlay 1.25 2.50
36 Trevor Ekdahl 2.00 4.00
37 Ron Stewart 3.00 6.00
38 Joe Poirier 2.00 4.00
39 Wayne Giardino 1.25 2.50
40 Tom Schuette 1.25 2.50
41 Roger Perdrix 1.25 2.50
42 Jim Mankins 1.25 2.50
43 Jay Roberts 1.25 2.50
44 Ken Lehmann 2.00 4.00
45 Jerry Campbell 2.00 4.00
46 Billy Joe Booth 2.00 4.00
47 Whit Tucker 3.00 6.00
48 Moe Racine 1.25 2.50
49 Corey Colehour 2.00 4.00
50 Dave Gasser 1.25 2.50
51 Jerry Griffin 1.25 2.50
52 Greg Pipes 2.00 4.00
53 Roy Shatzko 1.25 2.50
54 Ron Forwick 1.25 2.50
55 Ed Molstad 1.25 2.50
56 Ken Ferguson 1.25 2.50
57 Terry Swarn 3.00 6.00
58 Tom Nettles 1.25 2.50
59 John Wydareny 2.00 4.00
60 Bayne Norrie 1.25 2.50
61 Wally Gabler 2.00 4.00
62 Paul Desjardins 1.25 2.50
63 Peter Francis 1.25 2.50
64 Bill Frank 1.25 2.50
65 Chuck Harrison 1.25 2.50
66 Gene Lakusiak 1.25 2.50
67 Phil Minnick 1.25 2.50
68 Doug Strong 1.25 2.50
69 Glen Schapansky 1.25 2.50
70 Ed Ulmer 1.25 2.50
71 Bill Whisler 1.25 2.50
72 Ted Collins 1.25 2.50
73 Larry DeGraw 1.25 2.50
74 Henry Dorsch 1.25 2.50
75 Alan Ford 1.25 2.50
76 Ron Lancaster 10.00 20.00
77 Bob Kosid 1.25 2.50
78 Bobby Thompson 1.25 2.50
79 Ted Dushinski 1.25 2.50
80 Bruce Bennett 2.50 5.00
81 George Reed 7.50 15.00
82 Wayne Shaw 1.25 2.50
83 Cliff Shaw 1.25 2.50
84 Jack Abendschan 2.00 4.00
85 Ed McQuarters 3.00 6.00
86 Jerry Keeling 3.00 6.00
87 Gerry Shaw 1.25 2.50
88 Basil Bark UER 1.25 2.50
89 Wayne Harris 4.00 8.00
90 Jim Furlong 1.25 2.50
91 Larry Robinson 2.50 5.00
92 John Helton 5.00 10.00
93 Dave Cranmer 1.25 2.50
94 Lanny Boleski UER 1.25 2.50
95 Herman Harrison 3.00 6.00
96 Granville Liggins 2.50 5.00
97 Joe Forzani 2.00 4.00
98 Terry Evanshen 4.00 8.00
99 Sonny Wade 3.00 6.00
100 Dennis Duncan 1.25 2.50
101 Al Phaneuf 2.00 4.00
102 Larry Fairholm 1.25 2.50
103 Moses Denson 2.50 5.00
104 Gino Baretta 1.25 2.50
105 Gene Ceppetelli 1.25 2.50
106 Dick Smith 1.25 2.50
107 Gordon Judges 1.25 2.50
108 Harry Olszewski 1.25 2.50
109 Mike Webster 1.25 2.50
110 Checklist 1-115 15.00 30.00
111 Outstanding Player 4.00 8.00
112 Player of the Year 4.00 8.00
113 Lineman of the Year 3.00 6.00
114 CFL Coaches 3.00 6.00
115 Identifying Player 7.50 15.00

1970 O-Pee-Chee CFL Push-Out Inserts

This attractive set of 16 push-out inserts features players in the Canadian Football League. The cards are standard size, but are actually stickers, if the backs are moistened. The cards are numbered at the bottom and the backs are blank. Instructions on the front (upper left corner) are written in both English and French. Each player's team is identified on his card under his name. The player is shown superimposed over a football; the push-out area is essentially the football.

COMPLETE SET (16) 150.00 300.00
1 Ed Harrington 7.50 15.00
2 Danny Nykoluk 7.50 15.00
3 Tommy Joe Coffey 12.50 25.00
4 Angelo Mosca 20.00 35.00
5 Ken Sugarman 10.00 20.00
6 Jay Roberts 7.50 15.00
7 Joe Poirier 10.00 20.00
8 Corey Colehour 7.50 15.00
9 Dave Gasser 7.50 15.00
10 Wally Gabler 10.00 20.00
11 Paul Desjardins 7.50 15.00
12 Larry DeGraw 7.50 15.00
13 Jerry Keeling 12.50 25.00
14 Gerry Shaw 7.50 15.00
15 Terry Evanshen 12.50 25.00
16 Sonny Wade 10.00 20.00

1971 O-Pee-Chee CFL

The 1971 O-Pee-Chee CFL set features 132 standard-size cards ordered by teams. The card fronts feature a bright red border. The card backs are written in French and English. A complete checklist is given on card number 132. The key card in the set is Joe Theismann, which is his first professional card and predates his entry into the NFL.

COMPLETE SET (132) 200.00 400.00
1 Bill Symons 1.25 3.00
2 Mel Profit 1.25 3.00
3 Jim Tomlin 1.00 2.50
4 Ed Harrington 1.25 3.00
5 Jim Corrigall 1.50 4.00
6 Chip Barrett 1.00 2.50
7 Marv Luster 1.25 3.00
8 Ellison Kelly 1.50 4.00
9 Charlie Bray 1.00 2.50
10 Pete Martin 1.00 2.50
11 Tony Moro 1.00 2.50
12 Dave Raimey 1.25 3.00
13 Joe Theismann 30.00 60.00
14 Greg Barton 3.00 6.00
15 Leon McQuay 3.00 6.00
16 Don Jonas 3.00 6.00
17 Doug Strong 1.00 2.50
18 Paul Brule 1.00 2.50
19 Bill Frank 1.00 2.50
20 Joe Critchlow 1.00 2.50
21 Chuck Liebrock 1.00 2.50
22 Rob McLaren 1.00 2.50
23 Bob Swift 1.00 2.50
24 Rick Shaw 1.00 2.50
25 Ross Richardson 1.00 2.50
26 Benji Dial 1.00 2.50
27 Jim Heighton 1.00 2.50
28 Ed Ulmer 1.00 2.50
29 Glen Schapansky 1.00 2.50
30 Larry Slagle 1.00 2.50
31 Tom Cassese 1.00 2.50
32 Ted Gerela 1.00 2.50
33 Bob Howes 1.00 2.50
34 Ken Sugarman 1.25 3.00
35 A.D. Whitfield 1.25 3.00
36 Jim Young 3.00 6.00
37 Tom Wilkinson 4.00 8.00
38 Lefty Hendrickson 1.00 2.50
39 Dave Golinsky 1.00 2.50
40 Gerry Herron 1.00 2.50
41 Jim Evenson 1.25 3.00
42 Greg Findlay 1.00 2.50
43 Garrett Hunsperger 1.00 2.50
44 Jerry Bradley 1.00 2.50
45 Trevor Ekdahl 1.25 3.00
46 Bayne Norrie 1.00 2.50
47 Henry King 1.00 2.50
48 Terry Swarn 1.25 3.00
49 Jim Thomas 1.25 3.00
50 Bob Houmard 1.00 2.50
51 Don Trull 1.25 3.00
52 Dave Cutler 4.00 8.00
53 Mike Law 1.00 2.50
54 Dick Dupuis 1.25 3.00
55 Dave Gasser 1.00 2.50
56 Ron Forwick 1.00 2.50
57 John LaGrone 1.25 3.00
58 Greg Pipes 1.25 3.00
59 Ted Page 1.00 2.50
60 John Wydareny 1.25 3.00
61 Joe Zuger 1.25 3.00
62 Tommy Joe Coffey 3.00 6.00
63 Rensi Perdoni 1.00 2.50
64 Bob Taylor 1.25 3.00
65 Garney Henley 3.00 6.00
66 Dick Wesolowski 1.00 2.50
67 Dave Fleming 1.00 2.50
68 Bill Danychuk 1.25 3.00
69 Angelo Mosca 7.50 15.00
70 Bob Krouse 1.00 2.50
71 Tony Gabriel 7.50 15.00
72 Wally Gabler 1.25 3.00
73 Bob Steiner 1.00 2.50
74 John Reid 1.00 2.50
75 Jon Hohman 1.00 2.50
76 Barry Ardern 1.00 2.50
77 Jerry Campbell 1.25 3.00
78 Billy Cooper 1.00 2.50
79 Dave Braggins 1.00 2.50
80 Tom Schuette 1.00 2.50
81 Dennis Duncan 1.00 2.50
82 Moe Racine 1.00 2.50
83 Rod Woodward 1.00 2.50
84 Al Marcelin 1.25 3.00
85 Gary Wood 2.50 5.00
86 Wayne Giardino 1.00 2.50
87 Roger Perdrix 1.00 2.50
88 Hugh Oldham 1.00 2.50
89 Rick Cassatta 1.25 3.00
90 Jack Abendschan 1.25 3.00
91 Don Bahnuik 1.00 2.50
92 Bill Baker 4.00 8.00
93 Gordon Barwell 1.00 2.50
94 Gary Brandt 1.00 2.50
95 Henry Dorsch 1.00 2.50
96 Ted Dushinski 1.00 2.50
97 Alan Ford 1.00 2.50
98 Ken Frith 1.00 2.50
99 Ralph Galloway 1.00 2.50
100 Bob Kosid 1.00 2.50
101 Ron Lancaster 6.00 12.00
102 Silas McKinnie 1.00 2.50
103 George Reed 4.00 8.00
104 Gene Ceppetelli 1.00 2.50
105 Merl Code 1.00 2.50
106 Peter Dalla Riva 4.00 8.00
107 Moses Denson 1.25 3.00
108 Pierre Desjardins 1.00 2.50
109 Terry Evanshen 3.00 6.00
110 Larry Fairholm 1.25 3.00
111 Gene Gaines 2.50 5.00
112 Ed George 1.25 3.00
113 Gordon Judges 1.00 2.50
114 Garry Lefebvre 1.00 2.50
115 Al Phaneuf 1.25 3.00
116 Steve Smear 2.50 5.00
117 Sonny Wade 1.50 4.00
118 Frank Andruski 1.00 2.50
119 Basil Bark 1.00 2.50
120 Lanny Boleski 1.00 2.50
121 Joe Forzani 1.25 3.00
122 Jim Furlong 1.00 2.50
123 Wayne Harris 3.00 6.00
124 Herman Harrison 2.50 5.00
125 John Helton 1.50 4.00
126 Wayne Holm 1.00 2.50
127 Fred James 1.00 2.50
128 Jerry Keeling 2.50 5.00
129 Rudy Linterman 1.25 3.00
130 Larry Robinson 1.50 4.00
131 Gerry Shaw 1.00 2.50
132 Checklist Card 15.00 30.00

1971 O-Pee-Chee CFL Poster Inserts

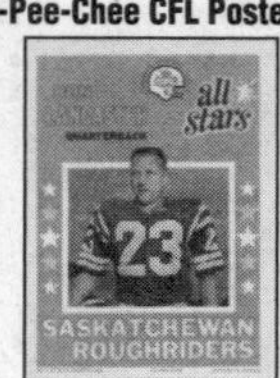

This 16-card set of posters featuring all-stars of the Canadian Football League was inserted in wax packs along with the regular issue of O-Pee-Chee cards. These 5" by 7" posters were folded twice in order to fit in the wax packs. They are numbered at the bottom and are blank on the back. These posters are somewhat similar in appearance to the Topps football poster inserts of 1971.

COMPLETE SET (16)	75.00	150.00
1 Tommy Joe Coffey	6.00	12.00
2 Herman Harrison	6.00	12.00
3 Bill Frank	4.00	8.00
4 Ellison Kelly	5.00	10.00
5 Charlie Bray	4.00	8.00
6 Bill Danychuk	5.00	10.00
7 Ron Lancaster	7.50	15.00
8 Bill Symons	5.00	10.00
9 Steve Smear	5.00	10.00
10 Angelo Mosca	7.50	15.00
11 Wayne Harris	6.00	12.00
12 Greg Findlay	4.00	8.00
13 John Wydareny	5.00	10.00
14 Garney Henley	6.00	12.00
15 Al Phaneuf	5.00	10.00
16 Ed Harrington	5.00	10.00

1972 O-Pee-Chee CFL

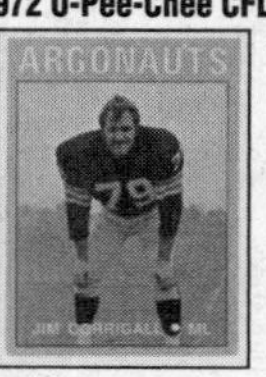

The 1972 O-Pee-Chee CFL set of 132 standard-size cards is the last O-Pee-Chee CFL issue to date. Cards are ordered by teams. The card backs are written in French and English; card back is blue and green print on white card stock. Fourteen Pro-Action cards (118-131) and a checklist card (132) complete the set. The key card in the set is Joe Theismann. The cards were originally sold in ten-cent wax packs with eight cards and a piece of bubble gum.

COMPLETE SET (132)	125.00	250.00
1 Bob Krouse	1.50	3.00
2 John Williams	.50	1.25
3 Garney Henley	3.00	6.00
4 Dick Wesolowski	.50	1.25
5 Paul McKay	.50	1.25
6 Bill Danychuk	.75	2.00
7 Angelo Mosca	5.00	10.00
8 Tommy Joe Coffey	2.50	5.00
9 Tony Gabriel	4.00	8.00
10 Mike Blum	.50	1.25
11 Doug Mitchell	.50	1.25
12 Emery Hicks	.50	1.25
13 Max Anderson	.50	1.25
14 Ed George	.75	2.00
15 Mark Kosmos	.75	2.00
16 Ted Collins	.50	1.25
17 Peter Dalla Riva	2.50	5.00
18 Pierre Desjardins	.50	1.25
19 Terry Evanshen	3.00	6.00
20 Larry Fairholm	.75	2.00
21 Jim Foley	.75	2.00
22 Gordon Judges	.50	1.25
23 Barry Randall	.50	1.25
24 Brad Upshaw	.50	1.25
25 Jorma Kuisma	.50	1.25
26 Mike Widger	.50	1.25
27 Joe Theismann	15.00	30.00
28 Greg Barton	2.00	4.00
29 Bill Symons	1.50	3.00
30 Leon McQuay	2.00	4.00
31 Jim Corrigall	2.00	4.00
32 Jim Stillwagon	2.50	5.00
33 Dick Thornton	.75	2.00
34 Marv Luster	2.00	4.00
35 Paul Desjardins	.50	1.25
36 Mike Eben	.50	1.25
37 Eric Allen	2.50	5.00
38 Chip Barrett	.50	1.25
39 Noah Jackson	1.50	3.00
40 Jim Young	3.00	6.00
41 Trevor Ekdahl	.75	2.00
42 Garrett Hunsperger	.50	1.25
43 Willie Postler	.50	1.25
44 George Anderson	.50	1.25
45 Ron Estay	.50	1.25
46 Johnny Musso	6.00	12.00
47 Eric Guthrie	.50	1.25
48 Monroe Eley	.50	1.25
49 Don Bunce	2.50	5.00
50 Jim Evenson	.75	2.00
51 Ken Sugarman	.75	2.00
52 Dave Golinsky	.50	1.25
53 Wayne Harris	2.50	5.00
54 Jerry Keeling	2.00	4.00
55 Herman Harrison	2.00	4.00
56 Larry Robinson	1.50	3.00
57 John Helton	2.00	4.00
58 Gerry Shaw	.50	1.25
59 Frank Andruski	.50	1.25
60 Basil Bark	.50	1.25
61 Joe Forzani	.75	2.00
62 Jim Furlong	.50	1.25
63 Rudy Linterman	.75	2.00
64 Granville Liggins	1.50	3.00
65 Lanny Boleski	.50	1.25
66 Hugh Oldham	.50	1.25
67 Dave Braggins	.50	1.25
68 Jerry Campbell	.75	2.00
69 Al Marcelin	.75	2.00
70 Tom Pullen	.50	1.25
71 Rudy Sims	.50	1.25
72 Marshall Shirk	.50	1.25
73 Tom Laputka	.50	1.25
74 Barry Ardern	.50	1.25
75 Billy Cooper	.50	1.25
76 Dan Deever	.50	1.25
77 Wayne Giardino	.50	1.25
78 Terry Wellesley	.50	1.25
79 Ron Lancaster	5.00	10.00
80 George Reed	4.00	8.00
81 Bobby Thompson	.50	1.25
82 Jack Abendschan	.75	2.00
83 Ed McQuarters	1.50	3.00
84 Bruce Bennett	1.50	3.00
85 Bill Baker	2.50	5.00
86 Don Bahnuik	.50	1.25
87 Gary Brandt	.50	1.25
88 Henry Dorsch	.50	1.25
89 Ted Dushinski	.50	1.25
90 Alan Ford	.50	1.25
91 Bob Kosid	.50	1.25
92 Greg Pipes	.75	2.00
93 John LaGrone	.75	2.00
94 Dave Gasser	.50	1.25
95 Bob Taylor	.75	2.00
96 Dave Cutler	3.00	6.00
97 Dick Dupuis	.50	1.25
98 Ron Forwick	.50	1.25
99 Bayne Norrie	.50	1.25
100 Jim Henshall	.50	1.25
101 Charlie Turner	.50	1.25
102 Fred Dunn	.50	1.25
103 Sam Scarber	.50	1.25
104 Bruce Lemmerman	3.00	6.00
105 Don Jonas	2.50	5.00
106 Doug Strong	.50	1.25
107 Ed Williams	.50	1.25
108 Paul Markle	.50	1.25
109 Gene Lakusiak	.50	1.25
110 Bob LaRose	.50	1.25
111 Rob McLaren	.50	1.25
112 Pete Ribbins	.50	1.25
113 Bill Frank	.50	1.25
114 Bob Swift	.50	1.25
115 Chuck Liebrock	.50	1.25
116 Joe Critchlow	.50	1.25
117 Paul Williams	.50	1.25
118 Pro Action M.Anderson	.50	1.25
119 Pro Action	.50	1.25
120 Pro Action	.50	1.25
121 Pro Action	.50	1.25
122 Pro Action	.50	1.25
123 Pro Action	.50	1.25
124 Pro Action	.50	1.25
125 Pro Action	.50	1.25
126 Pro Action	.50	1.25
127 Pro Action	.75	2.00
128 Pro Action	.75	2.00
129 Pro Action	.50	1.25
130 Pro Action	6.00	12.00
131 Pro Action	.50	1.25
132 Checklist Card	15.00	30.00

1972 O-Pee-Chee CFL Trio Sticker Inserts

Issued with the 1972 CFL regular cards was this 24-card set of trio peel-off sticker inserts. These blank-backed panels of three small stickers are 2 1/2" by 3 1/2" and have a distinctive black border around an inner white border. Each individual player is numbered in the upper corner of his card; the player's name and team are given below the player's picture in the black border. The copyright notation (O.P.C. Printed in Canada) is overprinted in the picture area of the card.

COMPLETE SET (24)	125.00	225.00
1 Johnny Musso/2 Ron Lancaster/3 Don Jonas	15.00	30.00
4 Jerry Campbell/5 Bill Symons/6 Ted Collins	4.00	8.00
7 Dave Cutler/8 Paul McKay/9 Rudy Sims	5.00	10.00
10 Wayne Harris/11 Greg Pipes/12 Chuck Ealey	10.00	20.00
13 Ron Estay/14 Jack Abendschan/15 Paul Markle	4.00	8.00
16 Jim Stillwagon/17 Terry Evanshen/18 Willie Postler	7.50	15.00
19 Hugh Oldham/20 Joe Theismann/21 Ed George	17.50	35.00
22 Larry Robinson/23 Bruce Lemmerman/24 Garney Henley	5.00	10.00
25 Bill Baker/26 Bob LaRose/27 Frank Andruski	5.00	10.00
28 Don Bunce/29 George Reed/30 Doug Strong	6.00	12.00
31 Al Marcelin/32 Leon McQuay/33 Peter Dalla Riva	5.00	10.00
34 Dick Dupuis/35 Bill Danychuk/36 Marshall Shirk	4.00	8.00
37 Jerry Keeling/38 John LaGrone/39 Bob Krouse	5.00	10.00
40 Jim Young/41 Ed McQuarters/42 Gene Lakusiak	5.00	10.00
43 Dick Thornton/44 Larry Fairholm/45 Garrett Hunsperger	4.00	8.00
46 Dave Braggins/47 Greg Barton/48 Mark Kosmos	5.00	10.00
49 John Helton/50 Bobby Taylor/51 Dick Wesolowski	5.00	10.00
52 Don Bahnuik/53 Rob McLaren/54 Granville Liggins	4.00	8.00
55 Monroe Eley/56 Bob Thompson/57 Ed Williams	4.00	8.00
58 Tom Pullen/59 Jim Corrigall/60 Pierre Desjardins	4.00	8.00
61 Ron Forwick/62 Angelo Mosca/63 Tom Laputka	10.00	20.00
64 Herman Harrison/65 Dave Gasser/66 John Williams	4.00	8.00
67 Trevor Ekdahl/68 Bruce Bennett/69 Gerry Shaw	4.00	8.00
70 Jim Foley/71 Pete Ribbins/72 Marv Luster	4.00	8.00

1951 Ottawa Rough Riders Team Issue

This set of Rough Riders player photos was issued by the team to fill fan requests. Each photo measures roughly 8 1/2" by 11" and includes the player's name and position (spelled out) below the photo. The unnumbered backs are blank.

COMPLETE SET (12)	100.00	200.00
1 Alton Baldwin	12.50	25.00
2 Bruce Cummings	12.50	25.00
3 Jake Dunlop	12.50	25.00
4 Bob Gain	12.50	25.00
5 Steve Hatfield	12.50	25.00
6 Bill Larochelle	12.50	25.00
7 Benny MacDonnell	12.50	25.00
8 Tom O'Malley	12.50	25.00
9 Bob Simpson	12.50	25.00
10 Bill Stanton	12.50	25.00
11 Howie Turner	12.50	25.00
12 John Wagoner	12.50	25.00

1960 Ottawa Rough Riders Team Issue

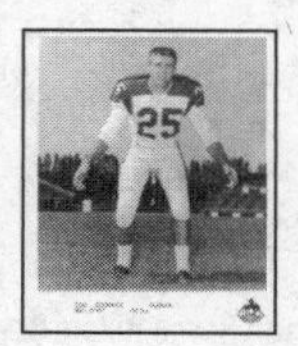

This set of Rough Riders player photos was issued by the team to fill fan requests. Each photo measures roughly 8" by 10" and includes the player's name, position (spelled out), height, and weight slightly to the left below the photo. The Rough Riders logo appears in the lower right hand corner. The unnumbered backs are blank.

COMPLETE SET (4)	25.00	50.00
1 Jim Conroy	7.50	15.00
2 Joe Poirier	7.50	15.00
3 Gary Schreider	6.00	12.00
4 George Terlep GM	6.00	12.00

1961 Ottawa Rough Riders Team Issue

This set of Rough Riders player photos was issued by the team to fill fan requests. Each photo measures roughly 8" by 10" and includes the player's name, position (spelled out), height, and weight to the far left below the photo. The Rough Riders logo appears in the lower right hand corner. The unnumbered backs are blank.

COMPLETE SET (40)	200.00	400.00
1 Gilles Archambeault	6.00	12.00
2 Merv Bevan	7.50	15.00
3 Bruno Bitkowski	6.00	12.00
4 Billy Joe Booth	6.00	12.00
5 George Brancato	6.00	12.00
6 Jim Cain	6.00	12.00
7 Len Chandler	6.00	12.00
8 Edward Chlebek	6.00	12.00
9 Merv Collins	6.00	12.00
10 Jim Conroy	6.00	12.00
11 Doug Daigneault	6.00	12.00
12 Paul D'Arras	6.00	12.00
13 Dick Desmarais	6.00	12.00
14 Millard Flemming	6.00	12.00
15 David Herne	6.00	12.00
16 Ron Koes	6.00	12.00
17 Russ Jackson	15.00	25.00
18 Tom Jones	6.00	12.00
19 Ron Lancaster	18.00	30.00
20 Donald Scott Maentz	6.00	12.00
21 Joe Poirier	6.00	12.00
22 Moe Racine	6.00	12.00
23 Jim Reynolds	6.00	12.00
24 Tom Rodgers	6.00	12.00
25 Norb Roy	6.00	12.00
26 Sam Scoccia	6.00	12.00
27 Jerry Selinger	6.00	12.00
28 Bob Simpson	12.00	20.00
29 Ted Smale	6.00	12.00
30 Mike Snodgras	6.00	12.00
31 Ron Stewart	15.00	25.00
32 Chuck Stanley	6.00	12.00
33 Dave Thelen	12.00	20.00
34 Whit Tucker	7.50	15.00
35 Kaye Vaughan	7.50	15.00
36 Ernie White	6.00	12.00
37 Chuck Wood	6.00	12.00
38 Branby / Clair / Smyth CO	6.00	12.00
39 Frank Clair CO	6.00	12.00
40 Bill Smyth CO	6.00	12.00

1962 Ottawa Rough Riders Team Issue

This set of Rough Riders player photos was issued by the team to fill fan requests. Each photo measures roughly 8" by 10 1/4" and includes the player's name, position, height, and weight in large letters below the photo. The Rough Riders logo appears in the lower right hand corner. The unnumbered backs are blank.

COMPLETE SET (30)	150.00	300.00
1 Merv Bevan	7.50	15.00
2 Rick Black	6.00	12.00
3 Don Branby ASST. CO	6.00	12.00
4 Billy Joe Booth	6.00	12.00
5 Jim Cain	6.00	12.00
6 Frank Clair Head CO	6.00	12.00
7 Merv Collins	6.00	12.00
8 Larry DeGraw	6.00	12.00
9 Gene Gaines	7.50	15.00
10 Russ Jackson	15.00	25.00
11 Bill Johnson	6.00	12.00
12 Roger Kramer	6.00	12.00
13 Tommy Lee	6.00	12.00
14 Bob O'Billovich	6.00	12.00
15 Joe Poirier	6.00	12.00
16 Peter Quinn	6.00	12.00
17 Bill Quinter	6.00	12.00
18 Moe Racine	6.00	12.00
19 Sam Scoccia	6.00	12.00
20 Jerry Selinger	6.00	12.00
21 Mel Semenko	6.00	12.00
22 Bill Siekierski	6.00	12.00
23 Billy Smyth ASST. CO	6.00	12.00
24 Ron Stewart	15.00	25.00
25 Dave Thelen	12.00	20.00
26 Oscar Thorsland	6.00	12.00
27 Whit Tucker	7.50	15.00
28 Kaye Vaughan	7.50	15.00
29 Ted Watkins	6.00	12.00
30 Ernie White	6.00	12.00

1967 Ottawa Rough Riders Rideau Trust

These photos measure roughly 4" by 6" and feature three members of the 1967 Ottawa Rough Riders. The Rideau Trust Company logo appears below each player's black and white photo. A facsimile autograph also appears below the photo for each player as well. The unnumbered backs feature a bio for each of the three players. We've cataloged the photos with the player on the far left listed first on each card.

COMPLETE SET (12)	175.00	300.00
1 Mike Blum / Russ Jackson / Chuck Harrison	20.00	35.00
2 Billy Joe Booth / Russ Jackson / Jay Roberts	25.00	40.00
3 Coaches / Al Bruno / Kelley Mote / Frank Clair	10.00	20.00
4 Jim Cain / Bo Scott / Larry DeGraw	20.00	35.00
5 Bill Cline / Whit Tucker / Ted Collins	12.50	25.00
6 Wayne Giardino / Margene Adkins / Moe Levesque	10.00	20.00
7 Roger Pardin / Ken Lehmann / Doug Specht	10.00	20.00
8 Joe Poirier / Rick Black	12.50	25.00

Bob Brown		
9 Tom Schuette	10.00	20.00
Moe Racine		
Jerry Selinger		
10 Don Sutherlin	20.00	35.00
Ron Stewart		
Jim Conroy		
11 Peter Thompson	10.00	20.00
Bob O'Billovich		
Don Gilbert		
12 Mike Walderzak	12.50	25.00
Gene Gaines		
Marshall Shirk		

1967 Ottawa Rough Riders Team Issue

The Rough Riders issued this set of player photos around 1967. Each includes two black-and-white player photos with one being a posed action shot along with a smaller portrait image. The roughly 8" by 10 1/8" photos include the player's name, position, college, age, birthplace, a short bio, and team logo on the cardfronts. The backs are blank and unnumbered.

COMPLETE SET (14)	60.00	120.00
1 Rick Black	5.00	10.00
2 Terry Black	5.00	10.00
3 Mike Blum	5.00	10.00
4 Jim Cain	5.00	10.00
5 Bill Cline	5.00	10.00
6 Ted Collins	5.00	10.00
7 Gene Gaines	6.00	12.00
8 Don Gilbert	5.00	10.00
9 Chuck Harrison	5.00	10.00
10 Ed Joyner	5.00	10.00
11 Moe Levesque	5.00	10.00
12 Bob O'Billovich	5.00	10.00
13 Jerry Selinger	5.00	10.00
14 Mike Walderzak	5.00	10.00

1970 Ottawa Rough Riders Team Issue

The Rough Riders issued this set of player photos around 1970. Each includes two black-and-white player photos with one being a larger posed action shot and the other a smaller portrait image. The roughly 8" by 10 1/8" photos include only the player's name and team logo on the cardfronts below the smaller image. The backs are blank and unnumbered.

COMPLETE SET (32)	100.00	200.00
1 Dick Adams	4.00	8.00
2 Barry Ardern	4.00	8.00
3 Allan Barclay	4.00	8.00
4 Charles Brandon	4.00	8.00
5A Paul Brothers (black jersey)	4.00	8.00
5B Paul Brothers (white jersey)	4.00	8.00
6 Jerry Campbell	4.00	8.00
7 Arthur Cantrelle	4.00	8.00
8 Rick Cassatta	4.00	8.00
9 Marcel Deleeuw	4.00	8.00
10 Dennis Duncan	4.00	8.00
11A Skip Eaman (black jersey)	4.00	8.00
11B Skip Eaman (white jersey)	4.00	8.00
12 James Elder	4.00	8.00
13 Bob Houmard	4.00	8.00
14 John Kennedy	4.00	8.00
15 John Kruspe	4.00	8.00
16 Tom Laputka	4.00	8.00
17 Art Laster	4.00	8.00
18 Richard Lolotai	4.00	8.00
19 Bob McKeown	4.00	8.00
20 Rhome Nixon	4.00	8.00
21 Gerry Organ	5.00	10.00
22 Jim Piaskoski	4.00	8.00
23 Dave Pivec	4.00	8.00
24 Gus Revenberg	4.00	8.00
25 Rudy Sims	4.00	8.00
26 Tom Schultz	4.00	8.00
27 Wayne Tosh	4.00	8.00
28 Bill Van Burkleo	4.00	8.00
29 Gary Wood	5.00	10.00
30 Rod Woodward	4.00	8.00
31 Ulysses Young	4.00	8.00
32 K.Mote	4.00	8.00
F.Clair		
J.Gotta		

1971 Ottawa Rough Riders Royal Bank

These photos were issued by Royal Bank and feature members of the Rough Riders. Each photo measures roughly 5" by 7" and includes a black and white photo of the player with his jersey number and name above the picture. The Royal Bank logo and set title "Royal Bank Leo's Leaders Rough Riders Player of the Week" appear below the photo in French and English. The photo backs are blank.

COMPLETE SET (7)	18.00	30.00
1 Billy Cooper	2.50	5.00
2 Wayne Giardino	2.50	5.00
3 Al Marcelin	2.50	5.00
4 Bob McKeown	2.50	5.00
5 Rhome Nixon	2.50	5.00
6 Hugh Oldham	2.50	5.00
7 Moe Racine	2.50	5.00

1971 Ottawa Rough Riders Team Issue

The Rough Riders issued this set of player photos around 1971. Each includes two black-and-white player photos with one being a posed action shot along with a smaller portrait image. The roughly 8" by 10 1/8" photos include the player's name, position, college, vital stats, a lengthy bio, and team logo on the cardfronts. The backs are blank and unnumbered.

COMPLETE SET (18)	40.00	80.00
1 Irby Augustine	4.00	8.00
2 Bob Brown	4.00	8.00
3 Lovell Coleman	5.00	10.00
4 Tom Deacon	4.00	8.00
5 Ivan MacMillan	4.00	8.00
6 Jim Mankins	4.00	8.00
7 Allen Marcelin	4.00	8.00
8 Hugh Oldham	4.00	8.00
9 LeVerle Pratt	4.00	8.00
10 Tom Pullen	4.00	8.00
11 Frank Reid	4.00	8.00
12 Gus Revenberg	4.00	8.00
13 Ken Shaw	4.00	8.00
14 Greg Thompson	4.00	8.00
15 Bill Van Burkleo	4.00	8.00
16 Joe Vijuk	4.00	8.00
17 Terry Wellesley	4.00	8.00
18 Gary Wood	5.00	10.00

1952 Parkhurst

The 1952 Parkhurst CFL set of 100 cards is the earliest known CFL issue. Features include the four Eastern teams: Toronto Argonauts (20-40), Montreal Alouettes (41-61), Ottawa Rough Riders (63-78, 100), and Hamilton Tiger-Cats (79-99), as well as 19 instructional artwork cards (1-19). These small cards measure approximately 1 7/8" by 2 3/4". There are two different number 58's and card number 62 does not exist.

COMPLETE SET (100)	1,800.00	3,000.00
1 Watch the games	30.00	50.00
2 Teamwork	12.50	25.00
3 Football Equipment	12.50	25.00
4 Hang onto the ball	12.50	25.00
5 The head on tackle	12.50	25.00
6 The football field	12.50	25.00
7 The Lineman's Stance	12.50	25.00
8 Centre's spiral pass	12.50	25.00
9 The lineman	12.50	25.00
10 The place kick	12.50	25.00
11 The cross-body block	12.50	25.00
12 T formation	12.50	25.00
13 Falling on the ball	12.50	25.00
14 The throw	12.50	25.00
15 Breaking from tackle	12.50	25.00
16 How to catch a pass	12.50	25.00
17 The punt	12.50	25.00
18 Shifting the ball	12.50	25.00
19 Penalty signals	12.50	25.00
20 Leslie Ascott	18.00	30.00
21 Robert Marshall	18.00	30.00
22 Tom Harpley	18.00	30.00
23 Robert McClelland	18.00	30.00
24 Rod Smylie	18.00	30.00
25 Bill Bass	18.00	30.00
26 Fred Black	18.00	30.00
27 Jack Carpenter	18.00	30.00
28 Bob Hack	18.00	30.00
29 Ulysses Curtis	18.00	30.00
30 Nobby Wirkowski	30.00	50.00
31 George Arnett	18.00	30.00
32 Lorne Parkin	18.00	30.00
33 Alex Toogood	18.00	30.00
34 Marshall Haymes	18.00	30.00
35 Shanty McKenzie	18.00	30.00
36 Byron Karrys	18.00	30.00
37 George Rooks	18.00	30.00
38 Red Ettinger	18.00	30.00
39 Al Bruno	25.00	40.00
40 Stephen Karrys	18.00	30.00
41 Herb Trawick	30.00	50.00
42 Sam Etcheverry	200.00	350.00
43 Marv Melrowitz	18.00	30.00
44 John Red O'Quinn	30.00	50.00
45 Jim Ostendarp	18.00	30.00
46 Tom Tofaute	18.00	30.00
47 Joey Pal	18.00	30.00
48 Ray Cicia	18.00	30.00
49 Bruce Coulter	25.00	40.00
50 Jim Mitchener	18.00	30.00
51 Lally Lalonde	18.00	30.00
52 Jim Staton	18.00	30.00
53 Glenn Douglas	18.00	30.00
54 Dave Tomlinson	18.00	30.00
55 Ed Salem	18.00	30.00
56 Virgil Wagner	30.00	50.00
57 Dawson Tilley	18.00	30.00
58A Cec Findlay	25.00	40.00
58B Tommy Manastersky	25.00	40.00
59 Frank Nable	18.00	30.00
60 Chuck Anderson	18.00	30.00
61 Charlie Hubbard	18.00	30.00
63 Benny MacDonnell	18.00	30.00
64 Peter Karpuk	18.00	30.00
65 Tom O'Malley	18.00	30.00
66 Bill Stanton	18.00	30.00
67 Matt Anthony	18.00	30.00
68 John Morneau	18.00	30.00
69 Howie Turner	18.00	30.00
70 Alton Baldwin	18.00	30.00
71 John Bovey	18.00	30.00
72 Bruno Bitkowski	25.00	40.00
73 Gene Roberts	18.00	30.00
74 John Wagoner	18.00	30.00
75 Ted MacLarty	18.00	30.00
76 Jerry Lefebvre	18.00	30.00
77 Buck Rogers	18.00	30.00
78 Bruce Cummings	18.00	30.00
79 Hal Wagner	25.00	40.00
80 Joe Shinn	18.00	30.00
81 Eddie Bevan	18.00	30.00
82 Ralph Sazio	30.00	50.00
83 Bob McDonald	18.00	30.00
84 Vince Scott	25.00	40.00
85 Jack Stewart	18.00	30.00
86 Ralph Bartolini	18.00	30.00
87 Blake Taylor	18.00	30.00
88 Richard Brown	18.00	30.00
89 Douglas Gray	18.00	30.00
90 Alex Muzyka	18.00	30.00
91 Pete Neumann	30.00	50.00
92 Jack Rogers	18.00	30.00
93 Bernie Custis	25.00	40.00
94 Cam Fraser	18.00	30.00
95 Vince Mazza	25.00	40.00
96 Peter Wooley	18.00	30.00
97 Earl Valiquette	18.00	30.00
98 Floyd Cooper	18.00	30.00
99 Louis DiFrancisco	18.00	30.00
100 Robert Simpson	90.00	150.00

1956 Parkhurst

The 1956 Parkhurst CFL set of 50 cards features ten players from each of five teams: Edmonton Eskimos (1-10), Saskatchewan Roughriders (11-20), Calgary Stampeders (21-30), Winnipeg Blue Bombers (31-40), and Montreal Alouettes (41-50). Cards are numbered on the front. The cards measure approximately 1 3/4" by 1 7/8". The cards were sold in wax boxes of 48 five-cent wax packs each containing cards and gum. The set features an early card of Bud Grant, who later coached the Minnesota Vikings.

COMPLETE SET (50)	2,000.00	3,500.00
1 Art Walker	50.00	80.00
2 Frank Anderson	25.00	40.00
3 Normie Kwong	90.00	150.00
4 Johnny Bright	90.00	150.00
5 Jackie Parker	250.00	400.00
6 Bob Dean	25.00	40.00
7 Don Getty	75.00	125.00
8 Rollie Miles	60.00	100.00
9 Ted Tully	25.00	40.00
10 Frank Morris	60.00	100.00
11 Martin Ruby	35.00	60.00
12 Mel Becket	50.00	80.00
13 Bill Clarke	25.00	40.00
14 John Wozniak	25.00	40.00
15 Larry Isbell	25.00	40.00
16 Ken Carpenter	50.00	80.00
17 Sully Glasser	25.00	40.00
18 Bobby Marlow	60.00	100.00
19 Paul Anderson	35.00	60.00
20 Gord Sturtridge	50.00	80.00
21 Alex Macklin	25.00	40.00
22 Duke Cook	25.00	40.00
23 Bill Stevenson	25.00	40.00
24 Lynn Bottoms	50.00	80.00
25 Aramis Dandoy	25.00	40.00
26 Peter Muir	35.00	60.00
27 Harvey Wylie	50.00	80.00
28 Joe Yamauchi	25.00	40.00
29 John Alderton	25.00	40.00
30 Bill McKenna	25.00	40.00
31 Edward Kotowich	25.00	40.00
32 Herb Gray	60.00	100.00
33 Calvin Jones	90.00	150.00
34 Herman Day	25.00	40.00
35 Buddy Leake	25.00	40.00
36 Robert McNamara	25.00	40.00
37 Bud Grant	300.00	500.00
38 Gord Rowland	35.00	60.00
39 Glen McWhinney	25.00	40.00
40 Lorne Benson	25.00	40.00
41 Sam Etcheverry	175.00	300.00
42 Joey Pal	25.00	40.00
43 Tom Hugo	25.00	40.00
44 Tex Coulter	35.00	60.00
45 Doug McNichol	25.00	40.00
46 Tom Moran	25.00	40.00
47 Red O'Quinn	50.00	80.00
48 Hal Patterson	125.00	200.00
49 Jacques Belec	25.00	40.00
50 Pat Abrzi	60.00	100.00

1962 Post Cereal CFL

The 1962 Post Cereal CFL set is the first of two Post Cereal Canadian Football issues. The cards measure the standard size. The cards were issued on the backs of boxes of Post Cereals distributed in Canada. Cards were not available directly from the company via a send-in offer as with other Post Cereal issues. Cards which are marked as SP are considered somewhat shorter printed and more limited in supply. Many of these short-printed cards have backs that are not the typical brown color but rather white. The cards are arranged according to teams.

COMPLETE SET (137)	750.00	1,500.00
1A Don Clark	12.00	20.00
1B Don Clark SP	30.00	60.00
2 Ed Meadows	4.00	8.00
3 Meco Poliziani	4.00	8.00
4 George Dixon	12.00	20.00
5 Bobby Jack Oliver	5.00	10.00
6 Ross Buckle	4.00	8.00
7 Jack Espenship	4.00	8.00
8 Howard Cissell	4.00	8.00
9 Ed Nickla	4.00	8.00
10 Ed Learn	4.00	8.00
11 Billy Ray Locklin	4.00	8.00
12 Don Paquette	4.00	8.00
13 Milt Crain	5.00	10.00
14 Dick Schnell	4.00	8.00
15 Dick Cohee	5.00	10.00
16 Joe Francis	5.00	10.00
17 Gilles Archambeault	4.00	8.00
18 Angelo Mosca	18.00	30.00
19 Ernie White	4.00	8.00
20 George Brancato	5.00	10.00
21 Ron Lancaster	18.00	30.00
22 Jim Cain	4.00	8.00
23 Gerry Nesbitt	4.00	8.00
24 Russ Jackson	18.00	30.00
25 Bob Simpson	10.00	20.00
26 Sam Scoccia	4.00	8.00
27 Tom Jones	4.00	8.00
28 Kaye Vaughan	7.50	15.00
29 Chuck Stanley	4.00	8.00
30 Dave Thelen	7.50	15.00
31 Gary Schreider	4.00	8.00
32 Jim Reynolds	4.00	8.00
33 Doug Daigneault	4.00	8.00
34 Joe Poirier	4.00	8.00
35 Clare Exelby	4.00	8.00
36 Art Johnson	4.00	8.00
37 Menan Schriewer	4.00	8.00
38 Art Darch	4.00	8.00
39 Cookie Gilchrist	18.00	30.00
40 Brian Aston	4.00	8.00
41 Bobby Kuntz SP	25.00	50.00
42 Gerry Patrick	4.00	8.00
43 Norm Stoneburgh	4.00	8.00
44 Billy Shipp	5.00	10.00
45 Jim Andreotti	7.50	15.00
46 Tobin Rote	12.00	20.00
47 Dick Shatto	7.50	15.00
48 Dave Mann	5.00	10.00
49 Ron Morris	4.00	8.00
50 Lynn Bottoms	5.00	10.00
51 Jim Rountree	5.00	10.00
52 Bill Mitchell	4.00	8.00
53 Wes Gideon SP	25.00	50.00
54 Boyd Carter	4.00	8.00
55 Ron Howell	5.00	10.00
56 John Barrow	7.50	15.00
57 Bernie Faloney	18.00	30.00
58 Ron Ray	4.00	8.00
59 Don Sutherin	7.50	15.00
60 Frank Cosentino	5.00	10.00
61 Hardiman Cureton	4.00	8.00
62 Hal Patterson	10.00	20.00
63 Ralph Goldston	5.00	10.00
64 Tommy Grant	7.50	15.00
65 Larry Hickman	5.00	10.00
66 Zeno Karcz	5.00	10.00
67 Garney Henley	10.00	20.00

68 Gerry McDougall 5.00 10.00
69 Vince Scott 6.00 12.00
70 Gerry James 7.50 15.00
71 Roger Hagberg 5.00 10.00
72 Gord Rowland 5.00 10.00
73 Ernie Pitts 4.00 8.00
74 Frank Rigney 6.00 12.00
75 Norm Rauhaus 6.00 12.00
76 Leo Lewis 10.00 20.00
77 Mike Wright 4.00 8.00
78 Jack Delveaux 5.00 10.00
79 Steve Patrick 4.00 8.00
80 Dave Burkholder 4.00 8.00
81 Charlie Shepard 5.00 10.00
82 Kenny Ploen 10.00 20.00
83 Ronnie Latourelle 4.00 8.00
84 Herb Gray 7.50 15.00
85 Hal Ledyard 4.00 8.00
86 Cornel Piper SP 25.00 50.00
87 Farrell Funston 5.00 10.00
88 Ray Smith 4.00 8.00
89 Clair Branch 4.00 8.00
90 Fred Burket 4.00 8.00
91 Dave Grosz 4.00 8.00
92 Bob Golic 5.00 10.00
93 Billy Gray 4.00 8.00
94 Neil Habig 4.00 8.00
95 Reg Whitehouse 4.00 8.00
96 Jack Gotta 5.00 10.00
97 Bob Ptacek 6.00 12.00
98 Jerry Keeling 7.50 15.00
99 Ernie Danjean 4.00 8.00
100 Don Luzzi 6.00 12.00
101 Wayne Harris 12.00 20.00
102 Tony Pajaczkowski 7.50 15.00
103 Earl Lunsford 7.50 15.00
104 Ernie Warlick 6.00 12.00
105 Gene Filipski 6.00 12.00
106 Eagle Day 10.00 20.00
107 Bill Crawford 4.00 8.00
108 Oscar Kruger 4.00 8.00
109 Gino Fracas 5.00 10.00
110 Don Stephenson 4.00 8.00
111 Jim Letcavits 4.00 8.00
112 Howie Schumm 4.00 8.00
113 Jackie Parker 20.00 40.00
114 Rollie Miles 7.50 15.00
115 Johnny Bright 15.00 25.00
116 Don Getty 7.50 15.00
117 Bobby Walden 5.00 10.00
118 Roger Nelson 7.50 15.00
119 Al Ecuyer 4.00 8.00
120 Ed Gray 4.00 8.00
121 Vic Chapman SP 25.00 50.00
122 Earl Keeley 4.00 8.00
123 Sonny Homer 4.00 8.00
124 Bob Jeter 10.00 20.00
125 Jim Carphin 4.00 8.00
126 By Bailey 10.00 20.00
127 Norm Fieldgate 7.50 15.00
128 Vic Kristopaitis 4.00 8.00
129 Willie Fleming 10.00 20.00
130 Don Vicic 4.00 8.00
131 Tom Brown SP 25.00 50.00
132 Tom Hinton SP 25.00 50.00
133 Pat Claridge 4.00 8.00
134 Bill Britton 4.00 8.00
135 Neil Beaumont 6.00 12.00
136 Nub Beamer SP 25.00 50.00
137 Joe Kapp 30.00 60.00

1963 Post Cereal CFL

The 1963 Post Cereal CFL set was issued on backs of boxes of Post Cereals in Canada. The cards measure 2 1/2" by 3 1/2". Cards could also be obtained from an order-by-number offer during 1963 from Post's Canadian affiliate. Cards are numbered and ordered within the set according to team. An album for the cards was also produced for this set and is relatively hard to find.

COMPLETE SET (160) 400.00 800.00
1 Larry Hickman 4.00 8.00
2 Dick Schnell 2.50 5.00
3 Don Clark 4.00 8.00
4 Ted Page 2.50 5.00
5 Milt Crain 4.00 8.00
6 George Dixon 7.50 15.00
7 Ed Nickla 2.50 5.00
8 Barrie Hansen 2.50 5.00
9 Ed Learn 2.50 5.00
10 Billy Ray Locklin 2.50 5.00
11 Bobby Jack Oliver 4.00 8.00
12 Don Paquette 2.50 5.00
13 Sandy Stephens 6.00 12.00
14 Billy Wayte 2.50 5.00
15 Jim Reynolds 2.50 5.00
16 Ross Buckle 2.50 5.00
17 Bob Geary 2.50 5.00
18 Bobby Lee Thompson 2.50 5.00
19 Mike Snodgrass 2.50 5.00
20 Billy Joe Booth 4.00 8.00
21 Jim Cain 2.50 5.00
22 Kaye Vaughan 5.00 10.00
23 Doug Daigneault 2.50 5.00
24 Millard Flemming 4.00 8.00
25 Russ Jackson 12.50 25.00
26 Joe Poirier 4.00 8.00
27 Moe Racine 2.50 5.00
28 Norb Roy 2.50 5.00
29 Ted Smale 2.50 5.00
30 Ernie White 2.50 5.00
31 Whit Tucker 5.00 10.00
32 Dave Thelen 5.00 10.00
33 Len Chandler 2.50 5.00
34 Jim Conroy 4.00 8.00
35 Jerry Selinger 2.50 5.00
36 Ron Stewart 6.00 12.00
37 Jim Andreotti 4.00 8.00
38 Jackie Parker 12.50 25.00
39 Lynn Bottoms 4.00 8.00
40 Gerry Patrick 2.50 5.00
41 Gerry Philip 2.50 5.00
42 Art Johnson 2.50 5.00
43 Aubrey Linne 2.50 5.00
44 Dave Mann 4.00 8.00
45 Marty Martinello 2.50 5.00
46 Doug McNichol 2.50 5.00
47 Ron Morris 2.50 5.00
48 Walt Radzick 2.50 5.00
49 Jim Rountree 4.00 8.00
50 Dick Shatto 5.00 10.00
51 Billy Shipp 4.00 8.00
52 Norm Stoneburgh 2.50 5.00
53 Gerry Wilson 2.50 5.00
54 Danny Nykoluk 2.50 5.00
55 John Barrow 5.00 10.00
56 Frank Cosentino 4.00 8.00
57 Hardiman Cureton 2.50 5.00
58 Bobby Kuntz 4.00 8.00
59 Bernie Faloney 10.00 20.00
60 Garney Henley 6.00 12.00
61 Zeno Karcz 4.00 8.00
62 Dick Easterly 2.50 5.00
63 Bronko Nagurski Jr. 6.00 12.00
64 Hal Patterson 7.50 15.00
65 Ron Ray 2.50 5.00
66 Don Sutherin 4.00 8.00
67 Dave Viti 2.50 5.00
68 Joe Zuger 4.00 8.00
69 Angelo Mosca 10.00 20.00
70 Ralph Goldston 4.00 8.00
71 Tommy Grant 5.00 10.00
72 Geno DeNobile 2.50 5.00
73 Dave Burkholder 2.50 5.00
74 Jack Delveaux 4.00 8.00
75 Farrell Funston 4.00 8.00
76 Herb Gray 5.00 10.00
77 Roger Hagberg 4.00 8.00
78 Henry Janzen 4.00 8.00
79 Ronnie Latourelle 2.50 5.00
80 Leo Lewis 5.00 10.00
81 Cornel Piper 2.50 5.00
82 Ernie Pitts 2.50 5.00
83 Kenny Ploen 5.00 10.00
84 Norm Rauhaus 4.00 8.00
85 Charlie Shepard 4.00 8.00
86 Gar Warren 2.50 5.00
87 Dick Thornton 4.00 8.00
88 Hal Ledyard 2.50 5.00
89 Frank Rigney 4.00 8.00
90 Gord Rowland 4.00 8.00
91 Don Walsh 2.50 5.00
92 Bill Burrell 2.50 5.00
93 Ron Atchison 5.00 10.00
94 Billy Gray 2.50 5.00
95 Neil Habig 2.50 5.00
96 Bob Ptacek 4.00 8.00
97 Ray Purdin 2.50 5.00
98 Ted Urness 4.00 8.00
99 Dale West 4.00 8.00
100 Reg Whitehouse 2.50 5.00
101 Clair Branch 2.50 5.00
102 Bill Clarke 2.50 5.00
103 Garner Ekstran 4.00 8.00
104 Jack Gotta 4.00 8.00
105 Len Legault 2.50 5.00
106 Larry Dumelie 2.50 5.00
107 Bill Britton 2.50 5.00
108 Ed Buchanan 2.50 5.00
109 Lovell Coleman 4.00 8.00
110 Bill Crawford 2.50 5.00
111 Ernie Danjean 2.50 5.00
112 Eagle Day 5.00 10.00
113 Jim Furlong 2.50 5.00
114 Wayne Harris 7.50 15.00
115 Roy Jakanovich 2.50 5.00
116 Phil Lohmann 2.50 5.00
117 Earl Lunsford 4.00 8.00
118 Don Luzzi 4.00 8.00
119 Tony Pajaczkowski 4.00 8.00
120 Pete Manning 4.00 8.00
121 Harvey Wylie 4.00 8.00
122 George Hansen 2.50 5.00
123 Pat Holmes 4.00 8.00
124 Larry Robinson 4.00 8.00
125 Johnny Bright 7.50 15.00
126 Jon Rechner 2.50 5.00
127 Al Ecuyer 2.50 5.00
128 Don Getty 6.00 12.00
129 Ed Gray 2.50 5.00
130 Oscar Kruger 2.50 5.00
131 Jim Letcavits 2.50 5.00
132 Mike Lashuk 2.50 5.00
133 Don Duncalfe 2.50 5.00
134 Bobby Walden 4.00 8.00
135 Tommy Joe Coffey 6.00 12.00
136 Nat Dye 4.00 8.00
137 Roy Stevenson 2.50 5.00
138 Howie Schumm 2.50 5.00
139 Roger Nelson 4.00 8.00
140 Larry Fleisher 4.00 8.00
141 Dunc Harvey 2.50 5.00
142 James Earl Wright 4.00 8.00
143 By Bailey 6.00 12.00
144 Nub Beamer 2.50 5.00
145 Neil Beaumont 4.00 8.00
146 Tom Brown 4.00 8.00
147 Pat Claridge 4.00 8.00
148 Lonnie Dennis 4.00 8.00
149 Norm Fieldgate 4.00 8.00
150 Willie Fleming 6.00 12.00
151 Dick Fouts 4.00 8.00
152 Tom Hinton 4.00 8.00
153 Sonny Homer 4.00 8.00
154 Joe Kapp 12.50 25.00
155 Tom Larscheid 2.50 5.00
156 Mike Martin 2.50 5.00
157 Mel Melin 2.50 5.00
158 Mike Cacic 2.50 5.00
159 Walt Bilicki 2.50 5.00
160 Earl Keeley 2.50 5.00
NNO Post Album English 20.00 40.00
NNO Post Album French 20.00 40.00
NNO Checklist 60.00 100.00

1971 Sargent Promotions Stamps

This photo album, measuring approximately 10 3/4" by 13", features 225 players from nine Canadian Football League teams. The set was sponsored by Eddie Sargent Promotions and is completely bi-lingual. The collector completed the set by purchasing a different picture packet from a participating food store each week. There were 16 different picture packets, with 14 color stickers per packet. After a general introduction, the album is divided into team sections, with two pages devoted to each team. A brief history of each team is presented, followed by 25 numbered sticker slots. Each sticker measures approximately 2" by 2 1/2" and has a posed color player photo with white borders. The player's name and team affiliation are indicated in the bottom white border. Biographical information and career summary appear below each sticker slot on the page itself. The stickers are numbered on the front and checklisted below alphabetically according to teams.

COMPLETE SET (225) 300.00 600.00
1 Jim Young 7.50 15.00
2 Trevor Ekdahl 1.50 3.00
3 Ted Gerela 1.50 3.00
4 Jim Evenson 1.50 3.00
5 Ray Lychak 1.00 2.00
6 Dave Golinsky 1.00 2.00
7 Ted Warkentin 1.00 2.00
8 A.D. Whitfield 1.50 3.00
9 Lach Heron 1.50 3.00
10 Ken Phillips 1.00 2.00
11 Lefty Hendrickson 1.00 2.00
12 Paul Brothers 1.00 2.00
13 Eagle Keys CO 2.00 4.00
14 Garrett Hunsperger 1.00 2.00
15 Greg Findlay 1.00 2.00
16 Dave Easley 1.00 2.00
17 Barrie Hansen 1.00 2.00
18 Wayne Dennis 1.00 2.00
19 Jerry Bradley 1.00 2.00
20 Gerry Herron 1.00 2.00
21 Gary Robinson 1.00 2.00
22 Bill Whisler 1.00 2.00
23 Bob Howes 1.00 2.00
24 Tom Wilkinson 6.00 12.00
25 Tom Cassese 1.00 2.00
26 Dick Suderman 1.50 3.00
27 Jerry Keeling 3.00 6.00
28 John Helton 3.00 6.00
29 Jim Furlong 1.00 2.00
30 Fred James 1.00 2.00
31 Howard Starks 1.00 2.00
32 Craig Koinzan 1.00 2.00
33 Frank Andruski 1.00 2.00
34 Joe Forzani 1.50 3.00
35 Herb Schumn 1.00 2.00
36 Gerry Shaw 1.00 2.00
37 Lanny Boleski 1.00 2.00
38 Jim Duncan CO 1.00 2.00
39 Hugh McKinnis 1.00 2.00
40 Basil Bark 1.00 2.00
41 Herman Harrison 3.00 6.00
42 Larry Robinson 1.50 3.00
43 Larry Lawrence 1.00 2.00
44 Granville Liggins 2.00 4.00
45 Wayne Harris 3.00 6.00
46 John Atamian 1.00 2.00
47 Wayne Holm 1.00 2.00
48 Rudy Linterman 1.50 3.00
49 Jim Sillye 1.00 2.00
50 Terry Wilson 1.00 2.00
51 Don Trull 2.00 4.00
52 Rusty Clark 1.00 2.00
53 Ted Page 1.00 2.00
54 Ken Ferguson 1.00 2.00
55 Alan Pitcaithley 1.00 2.00
56 Bayne Norrie 1.00 2.00
57 Dave Gasser 1.00 2.00
58 Jim Thomas 1.00 2.00
59 Terry Swarn 1.50 3.00
60 Ron Forwick 1.00 2.00
61 Henry King 1.00 2.00
62 John Wydareny 1.50 3.00
63 Ray Jauch CO 1.50 3.00
64 Jim Henshall 1.00 2.00
65 Dave Cutler 3.00 6.00
66 Fred Dunn 1.00 2.00
67 Dick Dupuis 1.50 3.00
68 Fritz Greenlee 1.00 2.00
69 Jerry Griffin 1.50 3.00
70 Allen Ische 1.00 2.00
71 John LaGrone 1.50 3.00
72 Mike Law 1.00 2.00
73 Ed Molstad 1.00 2.00
74 Greg Pipes 1.50 3.00
75 Roy Shatzko 1.00 2.00
76 Joe Zuger 1.50 3.00
77 Wally Gabler 1.50 3.00
78 Tony Gabriel 6.00 12.00
79 John Reid 1.00 2.00
80 Dave Fleming 1.00 2.00
81 Jon Hohman 1.00 2.00
82 Tommy Joe Coffey 4.00 8.00
83 Dick Wesolowski 1.00 2.00
84 Gordon Christian 1.00 2.00
85 Steve Worster 5.00 10.00
86 Bob Taylor 1.50 3.00
87 Doug Mitchell 1.00 2.00
88 Al Dorow CO 1.50 3.00
89 Angelo Mosca 10.00 20.00
90 Bill Danychuk 1.50 3.00
91 Mike Blum 1.00 2.00
92 Garney Henley 5.00 10.00
93 Bob Steiner 1.00 2.00
94 John Manel 1.00 2.00
95 Bob Krouse 1.00 2.00
96 John Williams 1.00 2.00
97 Scott Henderson 1.00 2.00
98 Ed Chalupka 1.00 2.00
99 Paul McKay 1.00 2.00
100 Rensi Perdoni 1.00 2.00
101 Ed George 1.50 3.00
102 Al Phaneuf 1.50 3.00
103 Sonny Wade 2.00 4.00
104 Moses Denson 2.00 4.00
105 Terry Evanshen 5.00 10.00
106 Pierre Desjardins 1.00 2.00
107 Larry Fairholm 1.00 2.00
108 Gene Gaines 3.00 6.00
109 Bobby Lee Thompson 1.00 2.00
110 Mike Widger 1.00 2.00
111 Gene Ceppetelli 1.00 2.00
112 Barry Randall 1.00 2.00
113 Sam Etcheverry CO 2.00 4.00
114 Mark Kosmos 1.50 3.00
115 Peter Dalla Riva 2.00 4.00
116 Ted Collins 1.00 2.00
117 John Couture 1.00 2.00
118 Tony Passander 1.00 2.00
119 Garry Lefebvre 1.00 2.00
120 George Springate 1.00 2.00
121 Gordon Judges 1.00 2.00
122 Steve Smear 2.00 4.00
123 Tom Pullen 1.00 2.00
124 Merl Code 1.00 2.00
125 Steve Bocras 1.00 2.00
126 Hugh Oldham 1.00 2.00
127 Moe Racine 1.00 2.00
128 John Kruspe 1.00 2.00
129 Ken Lehmann 1.50 3.00
130 Billy Cooper 1.00 2.00
131 Marshall Shirk 1.00 2.00
132 Tom Schuette 1.00 2.00
133 Doug Specht 1.00 2.00
134 Dennis Duncan 1.00 2.00
135 Jerry Campbell 1.50 3.00
136 Wayne Giardino 1.00 2.00
137 Roger Perdrix 1.00 2.00
138 Jack Gotta CO 1.50 3.00
139 Terry Wellesley 1.00 2.00
140 Dave Braggins 1.00 2.00
141 Dave Pivec 1.00 2.00
142 Rod Woodward 1.00 2.00
143 Gary Wood 2.00 4.00
144 Al Marcelin 1.50 3.00
145 Dan Dever 1.00 2.00
146 Ivan MacMillan 1.00 2.00
147 Wayne Smith 1.00 2.00
148 Barry Ardern 1.00 2.00
149 Rick Cassatta 1.50 3.00
150 Bill Van Burkleo 1.00 2.00
151 Ron Lancaster 6.00 12.00
152 Wayne Shaw 1.00 2.00
153 Bob Kosid 1.00 2.00
154 George Reed 7.50 15.00
155 Don Bahnuik 1.00 2.00
156 Gordon Barwell 1.00 2.00
157 Clyde Brock 1.00 2.00
158 Alan Ford 1.00 2.00
159 Jack Abendschan 1.50 3.00
160 Steve Molnar 1.00 2.00
161 Al Rankin 1.00 2.00
162 Bobby Thompson 1.00 2.00
163 Dave Skrien CO 1.00 2.00
164 Nolan Bailey 1.00 2.00
165 Bill Baker 4.00 8.00
166 Bruce Bennett 2.00 4.00
167 Gary Brandt 1.00 2.00
168 Charlie Collins 1.00 2.00
169 Henry Dorsch 1.00 2.00
170 Ted Dushinski 1.00 2.00
171 Bruce Gainer 1.00 2.00
172 Ralph Galloway 1.00 2.00
173 Ken Frith 1.00 2.00
174 Cliff Shaw 1.00 2.00
175 Silas McKinnie 1.00 2.00

176 Mike Eben	1.00	2.00
177 Greg Barton	2.00	4.00
178 Joe Theismann	25.00	50.00
179 Charlie Bray	1.00	2.00
180 Roger Scales	1.00	2.00
181 Bob Hudspeth	1.00	2.00
182 Bill Symons	1.50	3.00
183 Dave Raimey	1.50	3.00
184 Dave Cranmer	1.50	3.00
185 Mel Profit	1.50	3.00
186 Paul Desjardins	1.00	2.00
187 Tony Moro	1.00	2.00
188 Leo Cahill CO	1.00	2.00
189 Chip Barrett	1.00	2.00
190 Pete Martin	1.00	2.00
191 Walt Balasiuk	1.00	2.00
192 Jim Corrigall	1.50	3.00
193 Ellison Kelly	4.00	8.00
194 Jim Tomlin	1.00	2.00
195 Marv Luster	2.00	4.00
196 Jim Thorpe	2.00	4.00
197 Jim Stillwagon	3.00	6.00
198 Ed Harrington	1.00	2.00
199 Jim Dye	1.00	2.00
200 Leon McQuay	2.00	4.00
201 Rob McLaren	1.00	2.00
202 Benji Dial	1.00	2.00
203 Chuck Liebrock	1.00	2.00
204 Glen Schapansky	1.00	2.00
205 Ed Ulmer	1.00	2.00
206 Ross Richardson	1.00	2.00
207 Lou Andrus	1.00	2.00
208 Paul Robson	1.00	2.00
209 Paul Brule	1.00	2.00
210 Doug Strong	1.00	2.00
211 Dick Smith	1.00	2.00
212 Bill Frank	1.00	2.00
213 Jim Spavital CO	1.00	2.00
214 Rick Shaw	1.00	2.00
215 Joe Critchlow	1.00	2.00
216 Don Jonas	2.00	4.00
217 Bob Swift	1.00	2.00
218 Larry Kerychuk	1.00	2.00
219 Bob McCarthy	1.00	2.00
220 Gene Lakusiak	1.00	2.00
221 Jim Heighton	1.00	2.00
222 Chuck Harrison	1.00	2.00
223 Lance Fletcher	1.00	2.00
224 Larry Slagle	1.00	2.00
225 Wayne Giesbrecht	1.00	2.00

1970-71 Saskatchewan Roughriders Gulf

Gulf Canada gasoline stations issued this set of player photos during both the 1970 and 1971 seasons. Each measures roughly 8" by 10" and features a black and white player photo to the right. Both the Roughriders and Gulf Canada logos are included on the cardfronts to the left. The cardbacks are blank. Three players were issued only for the 1971 and were thought to be printed in shorter supply. We've marked those three as short prints (SP).

COMPLETE SET (37)	75.00	150.00
1 Jack Abendschan	2.50	5.00
2 Barry Aldag	2.50	5.00
3 Don Bahnuik	2.00	4.00
4 Nolan Bailey	2.00	4.00
5 Bill Baker	6.00	12.00
6 Gord Barwell	2.00	4.00
7 Bruce Bennett	3.00	6.00
8 Gary Brandt	2.00	4.00
9 Clyde Brock	2.00	4.00
10 Larry DeGraw	2.00	4.00
11 Dave Denny	2.00	4.00
12 Henry Dorsch	2.00	4.00
13 Ted Dushinski	2.00	4.00
14 Alan Ford	2.00	4.00
15 Ken Frith	2.00	4.00
16 Bruce Gainer	2.00	4.00
17 Ralph Galloway	2.00	4.00
18 Eagle Keys CO	3.00	6.00
19 Bob Kosid	2.00	4.00
20 Chuck Kyle	2.00	4.00
21 Ron Lancaster	7.50	15.00
22 Gary Lane SP	7.50	15.00
23 Ken McCullough CO	2.00	4.00
24 Silas McKinnie	2.00	4.00
25 Ed McQuarters	2.00	4.00
26 Steve Molnar	2.00	4.00
27 Bob Pearce SP	7.50	15.00
28 Al Rankin	2.00	4.00
29 George Reed	10.00	20.00
30 Ken Reed	2.00	4.00
31 Don Seaman	2.00	4.00
32 Cliff Shaw	2.00	4.00
33 Wayne Shaw	2.00	4.00
34 Dave Skrien CO	2.00	4.00
35 Bobby Thompson	2.00	4.00
36 Ted Urness	3.00	6.00
37 Jim Walter SP	7.50	15.00

1975 Saskatchewan Roughriders Team Sheets

This group of 32-players and coaches of the Roughriders was produced on four glossy sheets each measuring approximately 8" by 10". The fronts feature black-and-white player portraits with eight pictures to a sheet with the year printed at the top. The backs are blank. The cards are unnumbered and checklisted below in alphabetical order, with the player pictured in the upper left hand corner of the sheet listed first.

COMPLETE SET (4)	10.00	20.00
1 L.Benard	2.50	5.00
C.Collins		
B.Manchuk		
R.Mattingly		
C.Brock		
T.Bulych		
F.Landy		
P.Watson		
2 M.Dirks	2.50	5.00
T.Campana		
T.Dushinski		
R.Dawson		
S.Mazurak		
S.Molnar		
R.Galloway		
S.Smear		
3 L.Peterson	4.00	8.00
A.Ford		
G.Reed		
L.Richardson		
B.Berg		
T.Roth		
J.Hopson		
R.Lancaster		
4 G.Wells	3.00	6.00
K.McEachern		
B.Pearce		
L.Bird		
T.Provost		
J.Elder		
B.Richardson		
G.Brandt		

1976 Saskatchewan Roughriders Team Sheets

This group of 40-players and coaches of the Roughriders was produced on five glossy sheets each measuring approximately 8" by 10". The fronts feature black-and-white player portraits with eight pictures to a sheet with the year printed at the top. The backs are blank. The cards are unnumbered and checklisted below in alphabetical order, with the player pictured in the upper left hand corner of the sheet listed first.

COMPLETE SET (5)	12.50	25.00
1 L.Bird	4.00	8.00
K.McEachern		
B.Richardson		
G.Brandt		
S.Mazurak		
R.Galloway		
T.Campana		
R.Lancaster		
2 S.Mazurak	2.50	5.00
J.Washington		
B.Bertefeuille		
G.Wells		
J.Hopson		
R.Graham		
P.Valkenburg		
C.Vann		
3 L.Richardson	2.50	5.00
B.Macoritti		
T.McEachern		
R.Cherkas		
R.Dawson		
A.Ford		
B.O'Hara		
L.Pettersen		
4 D.Smarsh	2.50	5.00
T.Roth		
S.Molnar		
J.Marshall		
R.Goree		
B.Manchuk		
R.Odums		
S.Holden		
5 D.Syme	3.00	6.00
T.Provost		
M.Dirks		
J.O'Neal		
P.Williams		
J.Payne		
K.Preston		
B.Cowie		

1977-78 Saskatchewan Roughriders Team Sheets

This group of 40-players and coaches of the Roughriders was produced on five glossy sheets each measuring approximately 8" by 10". The fronts feature black-and-white player portraits with eight pictures to a sheet with the year printed at the top. The backs are blank. The cards are unnumbered and checklisted below in alphabetical order, with the player pictured in the upper left hand corner of the sheet listed first.

COMPLETE SET (5)	12.50	25.00
1 B.Ardern	4.00	8.00
B.Richardson		
G.Brandt		
T.Campana		
R.Lancaster		
E.Guthrie		
P.Price		
L.Cook		
2 L.Clare	2.50	5.00
K.McEachern		
T.Provost		
R.Cherkas		
S.McGee		
R.Graham		
J.Miller		
S.Mazurak		
3 S.Dennis	3.00	6.00
R.Galloway		
C.Roaches		
M.Dirks		
L.Pettersen		
C.Vann		
D.Hadden		
R.Goree		
4 B.Macoritti	3.00	6.00
P.Williams		
B.Baker		
R.Aldag		
S.Holden		
B.O'Hara		
E.Nielsen		
B.Manchuk		
5 K.Preston	2.50	5.00
B.Clarke		
B.Cowie		
J.Eddy		
L.Bird		
T.Roth		
S.Molnar		
G.Wells		

1978 Saskatchewan Roughriders Team Sheets

This group of 40-players and coaches of the Roughriders was produced on five glossy sheets each measuring approximately 8" by 10". The fronts feature black-and-white player portraits with eight pictures to a sheet with the year printed at the top. The backs are blank. The cards are unnumbered and checklisted below in alphabetical order, with the player pictured in the upper left hand corner of the sheet listed first.

COMPLETE SET (5)	12.50	25.00
1 B.Clarke	4.00	8.00
B.Cowie		
J.Eddy		
H.Dorsch		
P.Young		
R.Wellington		
J.Walters		
R.Lancaster		
2 S.Dennis	2.50	5.00
J.Wolf		
C.Vann		
R.Goree		
B.O'Hara		
L.Dick		
C.Thomson		
J.Worobec		
3 S.Molnar	2.50	5.00
G.Wells		
L.Clare		
J.Miller		
R.Cherkas		
M.Strickland		
S.Holden		
K.McEachern		
4 B.Richardson	3.00	6.00
E.Nielsen		
B.Manchuk		
R.Aldag		
B.Baker		
P.Williams		
B.Macoritti		
L.Bird		
5 H.Woods	2.50	5.00
R.Galloway		
S.Mazurak		
M.Dirks		
B.Bruer		
S.McGee		
E.Jones		
S.Gelley		

1980 Saskatchewan Roughriders Team Sheets

This group of 40-players and coaches of the Roughriders was produced on five glossy sheets each measuring approximately 8" by 10". The fronts feature black-and-white player portraits with eight pictures to a sheet with the year printed at the top. The backs are blank. The cards are unnumbered and checklisted below in alphabetical order, with the player pictured in the upper left hand corner of the sheet listed first.

COMPLETE SET (5)	12.50	25.00
1 R.Aldag	2.00	5.00
V.Anderson		
C.Carteri		
A.Chorney		
F.Dark		
S.Dennis		
G.Fellner		
S.Fraser		
2 R.Gill	2.50	6.00
R.Goree		
G.Harris		
K.Helms		
C.Henderson		
T.Hook		
G.Hornett		
J.Hufnagel		
3 B.Illerbrun	2.00	5.00
A.Johns		
Z.Jones		
J.Kinch		
B.Lamoureux		
B.Macoritti		
B.Manchuk		
S.Mazurak		
4 J.Miller	2.00	5.00
R.Milo		
K.McEachern		
D.McIver		
D.Petzke		
B.Poley		
N.Quilter		
T.Roberts		
5 D.Robey	2.00	5.00
T.Rozantz		
M.Samples		
D.Sanders		
K.Smith		
J.Spavital CO		
Cleveland Vann		
A.Walker		

1956 Shredded Wheat

The 1956 Shredded Wheat CFL football card set contains 105 cards portraying CFL players. The cards measure 2 1/2" by 3 1/2". The fronts of the cards contain a black and white portrait photo of the player on a one-color striped background. The lower 1/2" of the front contains the card number and the player's name below a dashed line. This lower portion of the card was presumably connected with a premium offer, as the back indicates such an offer, in both English and French, on the bottom. The backs contain brief biographical data in both English and French. Each letter prefix corresponds to a team, e.g., A: Calgary Stampeders, B: Edmonton Eskimos, C: Winnipeg Blue Bombers, D: Hamilton Tiger-Cats, E: Toronto Argonauts, F: Saskatchewan Roughriders, and G: Ottawa Rough Riders.

COMPLETE SET (105)	5,000.00	9,000.00
A1 Peter Muir	60.00	100.00
A2 Harry Langford	50.00	80.00
A3 Tony Pajaczkowski	90.00	150.00
A4 Bob Morgan	50.00	80.00
A5 Baz Nagle	50.00	80.00
A6 Alex Macklin	50.00	80.00
A7 Bob Geary	50.00	80.00
A8 Don Klosterman	75.00	125.00
A9 Bill McKenna	50.00	80.00
A10 Bill Stevenson	50.00	80.00
A11 Ray Baillie	50.00	80.00
A12 Berdett Hess	50.00	80.00
A13 Lynn Bottoms	60.00	100.00
A14 Doug Brown	50.00	80.00
A15 Jack Hennemier	50.00	80.00
B1 Frank Anderson	50.00	80.00
B2 Don Barry	50.00	80.00
B3 Johnny Bright	125.00	200.00
B4 Kurt Burris	50.00	80.00
B5 Bob Dean	50.00	80.00
B6 Don Getty	90.00	150.00
B7 Normie Kwong	125.00	200.00
B8 Earl Lindley	50.00	80.00
B9 Art Walker	60.00	100.00
B10 Rollie Miles	75.00	125.00
B11 Frank Morris	75.00	125.00
B12 Jackie Parker	175.00	300.00
B13 Ted Tully	50.00	80.00
B14 Frank Ivy	60.00	100.00
B15 Bill Rowekamp	50.00	80.00
C1 Allie Sherman	60.00	100.00
C2 Larry Cabrelli	50.00	80.00
C3 Ron Kelly	50.00	80.00
C4 Edward Kotowich	50.00	80.00
C5 Buddy Leake	60.00	100.00
C6 Thomas Lumsden	50.00	80.00
C7 Bill Smitiuk	50.00	80.00
C8 Buddy Tinsley	75.00	125.00
C9 Ron Vaccher	50.00	80.00
C10 Eagle Day	90.00	150.00
C11 Buddy Allison	50.00	80.00
C12 Bob Haas	60.00	100.00
C13 Steve Patrick	50.00	80.00
C14 Keith Pearce UER	50.00	80.00
C15 Lorne Benson	50.00	80.00
D1 George Arnett	50.00	80.00
D2 Eddie Bevan	50.00	80.00
D3 Art Darch	50.00	80.00
D4 John Fedosoff	50.00	80.00
D5 Cam Fraser	50.00	80.00
D6 Ron Howell	60.00	100.00
D7 Alex Muzyka	60.00	100.00
D8 Chet Miksza	50.00	80.00
D9 Walt Nikorak	50.00	80.00
D10 Pete Neumann	75.00	125.00
D11 Steve Oneschuk	50.00	80.00
D12 Vince Scott	75.00	125.00
D13 Ralph Toohy	50.00	80.00
D14 Ray Truant	50.00	80.00
D15 Nobby Wirkowski	60.00	100.00
E1 Pete Bennett	50.00	80.00
E2 Fred Black	50.00	80.00
E3 Jim Copeland	50.00	80.00
E4 Al Pfeifer	60.00	100.00
E5 Ron Albright	50.00	80.00
E6 Tom Dublinski	60.00	100.00
E7 Billy Shipp	60.00	100.00
E8 Baz Mackie	50.00	80.00
E9 Bill McFarlane	50.00	80.00
E10 John Sopinka	60.00	100.00
E11 Dick Brown	50.00	80.00
E12 Gerry Doucette	50.00	80.00
E13 Dan Shaw	50.00	80.00
E14 Dick Shatto	100.00	175.00

E15 Bill Swiacki	60.00	100.00
F1 Ray Syrnyk	50.00	80.00
F2 Martin Ruby	90.00	150.00
F3 Bobby Marlow	75.00	125.00
F4 Doug Kiloh	50.00	80.00
F5 Gord Sturtridge	60.00	100.00
F6 Stan Williams	50.00	80.00
F7 Larry Isbell	50.00	80.00
F8 Ken Casner	50.00	80.00
F9 Mel Becket	60.00	100.00
F10 Reg Whitehouse	50.00	80.00
F11 Harry Lampman	50.00	80.00
F12 Mario DeMarco	60.00	100.00
F13 Ken Carpenter	60.00	100.00
F14 Frank Filchock	60.00	100.00
F15 Frank Tripucka	90.00	150.00
G1 Tom Tracy	90.00	150.00
G2 Pete Ladygo	50.00	80.00
G3 Sam Scoccia	50.00	80.00
G4 Joe Upton	50.00	80.00
G5 Bob Simpson	90.00	150.00
G6 Bruno Bitkowski	60.00	100.00
G7 Joe Stracini UER	50.00	80.00
G8 Hal Ledyard	50.00	80.00
G9 Milt Graham	50.00	80.00
G10 Bill Sowalski	50.00	80.00
G11 Avatus Stone	50.00	80.00
G12 John Boich	60.00	100.00
G13 Don Pinhey UER	50.00	80.00
G14 Peter Karpuk	50.00	80.00
G15 Frank Clair	75.00	125.00

1952 Star Weekly Posters

These posters were actually pages from a newspaper weekly magazine. Each measures roughly 11" by 14" and features a color photo of a top CFL player. The posters were printed on newsprint type stock and unnumbered. The backs are simply another page from the magazine. We've arranged them below in order of their publication date which can be found along the top or bottom edge. Additions to this list are appreciated.

1 Herb Trawick	25.00	50.00
2 Ed Salem	15.00	30.00
3 Lally Lalonde	15.00	30.00

1958 Star Weekly Posters

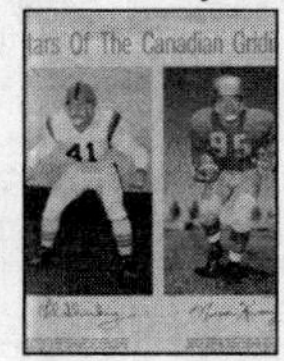

These posters were actually pages from a newspaper weekly magazine. Each measures roughly 11" by 14" and features two color photos of top CFL players at the bottom and a "Stars of the Canadian Gridiron" title at the top. The posters were printed on newsprint type stock and each was not numbered. The backs are simply another page from the magazine.

1 P.Abbruzzi H.Gray	15.00	30.00
2 J.Bright D.Renfro	20.00	40.00
3 J.Doucette S.Oneschuk	15.00	30.00
4 S.Etcheverry G.James	25.00	50.00
5 C.Gilchrist F.Rogel	20.00	40.00
6 T.Hunt M.Graham	15.00	30.00
7 L.Isbell D.Shatto	15.00	30.00
8 G.McDougall B.Tinsley	25.00	50.00
9 R.Nelson J.Gotta	15.00	30.00
10 J.Parker C.Zickefoose	20.00	50.00
11 H.Patterson K.Ploen	15.00	30.00
12 E.Sharkey N.Kwong	25.00	50.00

1959 Star Weekly Posters

These posters were actually magazine page cut-outs designed to form a football player photo album. Each uncut page measures roughly 11" by 14" and features two color photos of top CFL players at the bottom and a "Great Moments in Canadian Football" note at the top. The posters were printed on newsprint type stock and each was not numbered. The backs are simply another page from the magazine.

COMPLETE SET (7)	125.00	200.00
1 Bernie Faloney Randy Duncan	25.00	50.00
2 Jack Hill Russ Jackson	15.00	30.00
3 Gerry James Frank Tripucka	20.00	40.00
4 Ronnie Knox Jim Van Pelt	12.50	25.00
5 Bobby Kuntz Bruce Claridge	15.00	30.00
6 Tony Pajaczkowski Ron Howell	12.50	25.00
7 Billy Shipp Don Getty	12.50	25.00

1963 Star Weekly Posters

These small posters were actually newspaper color magazine page cut-outs measuring roughly 11" by 14." The posters feature a color photo of a top CFL player to the right and a detailed player bio to the left. The posters were printed on newsprint type stock and not numbered. The backs are simply another page from the magazine.

1 George Dixon	12.50	25.00
2 Willie Fleming	20.00	40.00
3 Leo Lewis	12.50	25.00
4 Ray Purdin	10.00	20.00
5 Jim Rountree	10.00	20.00
6 Whit Tucker	15.00	30.00
7 James Earl Wright	10.00	20.00
8 Harvey Wylie	10.00	20.00

1958 Topps CFL

The 1958 Topps CFL set features eight of the nine Canadian Football League teams, excluding Montreal. The cards measure the standard size. This first Topps Canadian issue is very similar in format to the 1958 Topps NFL issue. The cards were sold in wax boxes containing 36 five-cent wax packs. The card backs feature a "Rub-a-coin" quiz along with the typical biographical and statistical information. The set features the first card of Cookie Gilchrist, who later led the AFL in rushing twice.

COMPLETE SET (88)	500.00	900.00
1 Paul Anderson	5.00	10.00
2 Leigh McMillan	4.00	8.00
3 Vic Chapman	4.00	8.00
4 Bobby Marlow	7.50	15.00
5 Mike Cacic	4.00	8.00
6 Ron Pawlowski	4.00	8.00
7 Frank Morris	5.00	10.00
8 Earl Keeley	4.00	8.00
9 Don Walsh	4.00	8.00
10 Bryan Engram	4.00	8.00
11 Bobby Kuntz	4.00	8.00
12 Jerry Janes	4.00	8.00
13 Don Bingham	4.00	8.00
14 Paul Fedor	4.00	8.00
15 Tommy Grant	6.00	12.00
16 Don Getty	7.50	15.00
17 George Brancato	4.00	8.00
18 Jackie Parker	20.00	40.00
19 Alan Valdes	4.00	8.00
20 Paul Dekker	4.00	8.00
21 Frank Tripucka	6.00	12.00
22 Gerry McDougall	5.00	10.00
23 Willard Dewveall	5.00	10.00
24 Ted Smale	4.00	8.00
25 Tony Pajaczkowski	6.00	12.00
26 Don Pinhey	4.00	8.00
27 Buddy Tinsley	6.00	12.00
28 Cookie Gilchrist	20.00	40.00
29 Larry Isbell	4.00	8.00
30 Bob Kelley	4.00	8.00
31 Thomas(Corky) Tharp	5.00	10.00
32 Steve Patrick	4.00	8.00
33 Hardiman Cureton	4.00	8.00
34 Joe Mobra	4.00	8.00
35 Harry Lunn	4.00	8.00
36 Gord Rowland	4.00	8.00
37 Herb Gray	7.50	15.00
38 Bob Simpson	7.50	15.00
39 Cam Fraser	4.00	8.00
40 Kenny Ploen	10.00	20.00
41 Lynn Bottoms	4.00	8.00
42 Bill Stevenson	4.00	8.00
43 Jerry Selinger	4.00	8.00
44 Oscar Kruger	5.00	10.00
45 Gerry James	7.50	15.00
46 Dave Mann	6.00	12.00
47 Tom Dimitroff	5.00	10.00
48 Vince Scott	6.00	12.00
49 Fran Rogel	5.00	10.00
50 Henry Hair	4.00	8.00
51 Bob Brady	4.00	8.00
52 Gerry Doucette	4.00	8.00
53 Ken Carpenter	5.00	10.00
54 Bernie Faloney	12.50	25.00
55 John Barrow	10.00	20.00
56 George Druxman	4.00	8.00
57 Rollie Miles	6.00	12.00
58 Jerry Cornelison	4.00	8.00
59 Harry Langford	4.00	8.00
60 Johnny Bright	10.00	20.00
61 Ron Clinkscale	4.00	8.00
62 Jack Hill	4.00	8.00
63 Ron Quillian	4.00	8.00
64 Ted Tully	4.00	8.00
65 Pete Neft	5.00	10.00
66 Arvyd Buntins	4.00	8.00
67 Normie Kwong	10.00	20.00
68 Matt Phillips	4.00	8.00
69 Pete Bennett	4.00	8.00
70 Vern Lofstrom	4.00	8.00
71 Norm Stoneburgh	4.00	8.00
72 Danny Nykoluk	4.00	8.00
73 Chuck Dubuque	4.00	8.00
74 John Varone	4.00	8.00
75 Bob Kimoff	4.00	8.00
76 John Pyeatt	4.00	8.00
77 Pete Neumann	6.00	12.00
78 Ernie Pitts	5.00	10.00
79 Steve Oneschuk	4.00	8.00
80 Kaye Vaughan	6.00	12.00
81 Joe Yamauchi	4.00	8.00
82 Harvey Wylie	5.00	10.00
83 Berdett Hess	4.00	8.00
84 Dick Shatto	10.00	20.00
85 Floyd Harrawood	4.00	8.00
86 Ron Atchison	6.00	12.00
87 Bobby Judd	4.00	8.00
88 Keith Pearce	5.00	10.00
NNO Free Felt Initial Card	7.50	15.00

1959 Topps CFL

The 1959 Topps CFL set features cards grouped by teams. The cards measure the standard size. Checklists are given on the backs of card number 15 (1-44) and card number 44 (45-88). The issue is very similar to the Topps 1959 NFL issue. The cards were originally sold in five-cent wax packs with gum.

COMPLETE SET (88)	400.00	750.00
1 Norm Rauhaus	5.00	10.00
2 Cornel Piper UER	3.00	6.00
3 Leo Lewis	10.00	20.00
4 Roger Savoie	3.00	6.00
5 Jim Van Pelt	5.00	10.00
6 Herb Gray	5.00	10.00
7 Gerry James	5.00	10.00
8 By Bailey	6.00	15.00
9 Tom Hinton	4.00	8.00
10 Chuck Quilter	3.00	6.00
11 Mel Gillett	3.00	6.00
12 Ted Hunt	3.00	6.00
13 Sonny Homer	3.00	6.00
14 Bill Jessup	3.00	6.00
15 Al Dorow CL	12.00	20.00
16 Norm Fieldgate	6.00	12.00
17 Urban Henry	3.00	6.00
18 Paul Cameron	3.00	6.00
19 Bruce Claridge	3.00	6.00
20 Jim Bakhtiar	3.00	6.00
21 Earl Lunsford	6.00	12.00
22 Walt Radzick	3.00	6.00
23 Ron Albright	4.00	8.00
24 Art Scullion	3.00	6.00
25 Ernie Warlick	5.00	10.00
26 Nobby Wirkowski	3.00	6.00
27 Harvey Wylie	4.00	8.00
28 Gordon Brown	3.00	6.00
29 Don Luzzi	5.00	10.00
30 Hal Patterson	10.00	20.00
31 Jackie Simpson	7.50	15.00
32 Doug McNichol	3.00	6.00
33 Bob MacLellan	3.00	6.00
34 Ted Elsby	3.00	6.00
35 Mike Kovac	3.00	6.00
36 Bob Leary	3.00	6.00
37 Hal Krebs	3.00	6.00
38 Steve Jennings	3.00	6.00
39 Don Getty	6.00	12.00
40 Normie Kwong	7.50	15.00
41 Johnny Bright	7.50	15.00
42 Art Walker	4.00	8.00
43 Jackie Parker UER	17.50	35.00
44 Don Barry CL	10.00	20.00
45 Tommy Joe Coffey	12.50	25.00
46 Mike Volcan	3.00	6.00
47 Stan Renning	3.00	6.00
48 Gino Fracas	4.00	8.00
49 Ted Smale	3.00	6.00
50 Mack Yoho	4.00	8.00
51 Bobby Gravens	3.00	6.00
52 Milt Graham	3.00	6.00
53 Lou Bruce	3.00	6.00
54 Bob Simpson	6.00	15.00
55 Bill Sowalski	3.00	6.00
56 Russ Jackson	20.00	40.00
57 Don Clark	4.00	8.00
58 Dave Thelen	5.00	10.00
59 Larry Cowart	3.00	6.00
60 Dave Mann	3.00	6.00
61 Norm Stoneburgh UER	3.00	6.00
62 Ronnie Knox	4.00	8.00
63 Dick Shatto	6.00	12.00
64 Bobby Kuntz	3.00	6.00
65 Phil Muntz	3.00	6.00
66 Gerry Doucette	3.00	6.00
67 Sam DeLuca	4.00	8.00
68 Boyd Carter	3.00	6.00
69 Vic Kristopaitis	4.00	8.00
70 Gerry McDougall UER	4.00	8.00
71 Vince Scott	5.00	10.00
72 Angelo Mosca	17.50	35.00
73 Chet Miksza	3.00	6.00
74 Eddie Macon	3.00	6.00
75 Harry Lampman	3.00	6.00
76 Bill Graham	3.00	6.00
77 Ralph Goldston	3.00	6.00
78 Cam Fraser	3.00	6.00
79 Ron Dundas	3.00	6.00
80 Bill Clarke	3.00	6.00
81 Len Legault	3.00	6.00
82 Reg Whitehouse	3.00	6.00
83 Dale Parsons	3.00	6.00
84 Doug Kiloh	3.00	6.00
85 Tom Whitehouse	3.00	6.00
86 Mike Hagler	3.00	6.00
87 Paul Anderson	3.00	6.00
88 Danny Banda	3.00	6.00

1960 Topps CFL

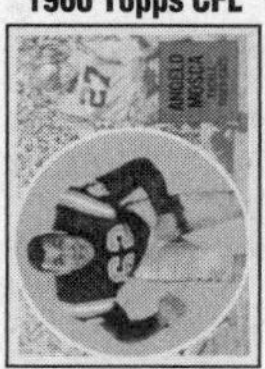

The 1960 Topps CFL set features cards grouped by teams. The cards measure the standard size. Checklists are given on the backs of card number 14 (1-44) and card number 45 (45-88). The issue is very similar in format to the Topps NFL issue of 1960. The set features a card of Gerry James, who also played in the National Hockey League.

COMPLETE SET (88)	400.00	750.00
1 By Bailey	7.50	15.00
2 Paul Cameron	2.50	5.00
3 Bruce Claridge	2.50	5.00
4 Chuck Dubuque	2.50	5.00
5 Randy Duncan	6.00	12.00
6 Norm Fieldgate	5.00	10.00
7 Urban Henry	3.00	6.00
8 Ted Hunt	2.50	5.00
9 Bill Jessup	2.50	5.00
10 Ted Tully	2.50	5.00
11 Vic Chapman	2.50	5.00
12 Gino Fracas	3.00	6.00
13 Don Getty	5.00	10.00
14 Ed Gray	2.50	5.00
15 Oscar Kruger	10.00	20.00
16 Rollie Miles	5.00	10.00
17 Jackie Parker	15.00	30.00
18 Joe-Bob Smith UER	2.50	5.00
19 Mike Volcan	2.50	5.00
20 Art Walker	4.00	8.00
21 Ron Albright	3.00	6.00
22 Jim Bakhtiar	2.50	5.00
23 Lynn Bottoms	3.00	6.00
24 Jack Gotta	4.00	8.00
25 Joe Kapp	25.00	50.00
26 Earl Lunsford	4.00	8.00
27 Don Luzzi	4.00	8.00
28 Art Scullion	2.50	5.00
29 Hugh Simpson	2.50	5.00
30 Ernie Warlick	5.00	10.00
31 John Barrow	6.00	12.00
32 Paul Dekker	2.50	5.00
33 Bernie Faloney	12.50	25.00
34 Cam Fraser	2.50	5.00
35 Ralph Goldston	3.00	6.00
36 Ron Howell	5.00	10.00
37 Gerry McDougall UER	3.00	6.00
38 Angelo Mosca	10.00	20.00
39 Pete Neumann	4.00	8.00
40 Vince Scott	4.00	8.00
41 Ted Elsby	2.50	5.00
42 Sam Etcheverry	15.00	30.00
43 Mike Kovac	2.50	5.00
44 Ed Learn	2.50	5.00
45 Ivan Livingstone CL	10.00	20.00
46 Hal Patterson	10.00	20.00
47 Jackie Simpson	6.00	12.00
48 Veryl Switzer	2.50	5.00
49 Bill Bewley	4.00	8.00
50 Joel Wells	2.50	5.00
51 Ron Atchison	4.00	8.00
52 Ken Carpenter	3.00	6.00
53 Bill Clarke	2.50	5.00
54 Ron Dundas	2.50	5.00
55 Mike Hagler	2.50	5.00
56 Jack Hill	2.50	5.00
57 Doug Kiloh	2.50	5.00
58 Bobby Marlow	6.00	12.00
59 Bob Mulgado	2.50	5.00
60 George Brancato	3.00	6.00
61 Lou Bruce	2.50	5.00
62 Hardiman Cureton	2.50	5.00
63 Russ Jackson	15.00	30.00
64 Gerry Nesbitt	2.50	5.00
65 Bob Simpson	5.00	12.00
66 Ted Smale	2.50	5.00
67 Dave Thelen	5.00	10.00
68 Kaye Vaughan	4.00	8.00
69 Pete Bennett	2.50	5.00
70 Boyd Carter	2.50	5.00
71 Gerry Doucette	2.50	5.00
72 Bobby Kuntz	3.00	6.00

73 Alex Panton 2.50 5.00
74 Tobin Rote 12.50 25.00
75 Jim Rountree 3.00 6.00
76 Dick Shatto 5.00 10.00
77 Norm Stoneburgh 2.50 5.00
78 Thomas(Corky) Tharp 4.00 8.00
79 George Druxman 2.50 5.00
80 Herb Gray 5.00 10.00
81 Gerry James 5.00 10.00
82 Leo Lewis 5.00 10.00
83 Ernie Pitts 3.00 6.00
84 Kenny Ploen 7.50 15.00
85 Norm Rauhaus 3.00 6.00
86 Gord Rowland 3.00 6.00
87 Charlie Shepard 3.00 6.00
88 Don Clark 4.00 8.00

1961 Topps CFL

The 1961 Topps CFL set features cards grouped by teams with the team picture last in the sequence. The cards measure the standard size. Card number 102 gives the full set checklist. Although the T.C.G. trademark appears on these cards, they were printed in Canada by O-Pee-Chee.

COMPLETE SET (132) 700.00 1,200.00
1 By Bailey 7.50 15.00
2 Bruce Claridge 3.00 6.00
3 Norm Fieldgate 6.00 12.00
4 Willie Fleming 10.00 20.00
5 Urban Henry 4.00 8.00
6 Bill Herron 3.00 6.00
7 Tom Hinton 5.00 10.00
8 Sonny Homer 4.00 8.00
9 Bob Jeter 7.50 15.00
10 Vic Kristopaitis 3.00 6.00
11 Baz Nagle 3.00 6.00
12 Ron Watton 3.00 6.00
13 Joe Yamauchi 3.00 6.00
14 Bob Schloredt 7.50 15.00
15 B.C. Lions Team 6.00 12.00
16 Ron Albright 4.00 8.00
17 Gordon Brown 3.00 6.00
18 Gerry Doucette 3.00 6.00
19 Gene Filipski 6.00 12.00
20 Joe Kapp 15.00 30.00
21 Earl Lunsford 6.00 12.00
22 Don Luzzi 6.00 12.00
23 Bill McKenna 3.00 6.00
24 Ron Morris 3.00 6.00
25 Tony Pajaczkowski 6.00 12.00
26 Lorne Reid 3.00 6.00
27 Art Scullion 3.00 6.00
28 Ernie Warlick 6.00 12.00
29 Stampeders Team 6.00 12.00
30 Johnny Bright 7.50 15.00
31 Vic Chapman 3.00 6.00
32 Gino Fracas 4.00 8.00
33 Tommy Joe Coffey 9.00 18.00
34 Don Getty 7.50 15.00
35 Ed Gray 3.00 6.00
36 Oscar Kruger 4.00 8.00
37 Rollie Miles 6.00 12.00
38 Roger Nelson 6.00 12.00
39 Jackie Parker 20.00 35.00
40 Howie Schumm 3.00 6.00
41 Joe-Bob Smith UER 3.00 6.00
42 Art Walker 5.00 10.00
43 Eskimos Team 6.00 12.00
44 John Barrow 7.50 15.00
45 Paul Dekker 3.00 6.00
46 Tom Dublinski 4.00 8.00
47 Bernie Faloney 12.50 25.00
48 Cam Fraser 3.00 6.00
49 Ralph Goldston 4.00 8.00
50 Ron Howell 5.00 10.00
51 Gerry McDougall 4.00 8.00
52 Pete Neumann 6.00 12.00
53 Bronko Nagurski Jr. 7.50 15.00
54 Vince Scott 5.00 10.00
55 Steve Oneschuk 4.00 8.00
56 Hal Patterson 10.00 20.00
57 Jim Taylor LB 4.00 8.00
58 Tiger-Cats Team 6.00 12.00
59 Ted Elsby 3.00 6.00
60 Don Clark 5.00 10.00
61 Dick Cohee 5.00 10.00
62 George Dixon 10.00 20.00
63 Wes Gideon 3.00 6.00
64 Harry Lampman 3.00 6.00
65 Meco Poliziani 3.00 6.00
66 Ray Baillie 3.00 6.00
67 Howard Cissell 3.00 6.00
68 Ed Learn 3.00 6.00
69 Tom Moran 3.00 6.00
70 Jackie Simpson 6.00 12.00
71 Bill Bewley 4.00 8.00
72 Tom Hugo 3.00 6.00
73 Alouettes Team 7.50 15.00
74 Gilles Archambeault 3.00 6.00
75 Lou Bruce 3.00 6.00
76 Russ Jackson 15.00 30.00
77 Tom Jones 3.00 6.00
78 Gerry Nesbitt 3.00 6.00
79 Ron Lancaster 20.00 40.00
80 Joe Kelley 3.00 6.00
81 Joe Poirier 4.00 8.00
82 Doug Daigneault 3.00 6.00
83 Kaye Vaughan 5.00 10.00
84 Dave Thelen 7.50 15.00
85 Ron Stewart 12.50 25.00
86 Ted Smale 3.00 6.00
87 Bob Simpson 7.50 15.00
88 Ottawa Rough Riders 6.00 12.00
89 Don Allard 3.00 6.00
90 Ron Atchison 6.00 12.00
91 Bill Clarke 3.00 6.00
92 Ron Dundas 3.00 6.00
93 Jack Gotta 5.00 10.00
94 Bob Golic 4.00 8.00
95 Jack Hill 3.00 6.00
96 Doug Kiloh 3.00 6.00
97 Len Legault 3.00 6.00
98 Doug McKenzie 3.00 6.00
99 Bob Ptacek 4.00 8.00
100 Roy Smith 3.00 6.00
101 Saskatchewan Roughriders UER 6.00 12.00
102 Checklist 1-132 50.00 100.00
103 Jim Andreotti 4.00 8.00
104 Boyd Carter 3.00 6.00
105 Dick Fouts 4.00 8.00
106 Cookie Gilchrist 12.50 25.00
107 Bobby Kuntz 4.00 8.00
108 Jim Rountree 4.00 8.00
109 Dick Shatto 7.50 15.00
110 Norm Stoneburgh 3.00 6.00
111 Dave Mann 4.00 8.00
112 Ed Ochiena 3.00 6.00
113 Bill Stribling 3.00 6.00
114 Tobin Rote 10.00 20.00
115 Stan Wallace 3.00 6.00
116 Billy Shipp 4.00 8.00
117 Argonauts Team 7.50 15.00
118 Dave Burkholder 3.00 6.00
119 Jack Delveaux 4.00 8.00
120 George Druxman 3.00 6.00
121 Farrell Funston 4.00 8.00
122 Herb Gray 6.00 12.00
123 Gerry James 6.00 12.00
124 Ronnie Latourelle 3.00 6.00
125 Leo Lewis 7.50 15.00
126 Steve Patrick 4.00 8.00
127 Ernie Pitts 4.00 8.00
128 Kenny Ploen 7.50 15.00
129 Norm Rauhaus 4.00 8.00
130 Gord Rowland 4.00 8.00
131 Charlie Shepard 4.00 8.00
132 Winnipeg Blue Bombers 10.00 20.00

1961 Topps CFL Transfers

There were 27 transfers inserted in Topps CFL wax packs issued in 1961. The transfers measure approximately 2" by 3" and feature players, logos, and pennants of the CFL teams. After placing the transfer against any surface, the collector could apply the transfer by rubbing the top side with a coin. The top side carried instructions for applying the transfers. The pictures on the transfers are done in five basic colors: reddish orange, yellow, blue, black, and green. The transfers are unnumbered and are checklisted below alphabetically according to players (1-15) and teams (19-27). The set price below is only for the 24 players and team cards that we currently list. Three Transfers (#16-18) are yet to be identified. Any additional information on the other players that were contained in this set would be appreciated.

COMPLETE SET (24) 375.00 750.00
1 Don Clark 17.50 35.00
2 Gene Filipski 17.50 35.00
3 Willie Fleming 20.00 40.00
4 Cookie Gilchrist 25.00 50.00
5 Jack Hill 15.00 30.00
6 Bob Jeter 17.50 35.00
7 Joe Kapp 30.00 60.00
8 Leo Lewis 20.00 40.00
9 Gerry McDougall 17.50 35.00
10 Jackie Parker 30.00 60.00
11 Hal Patterson 20.00 40.00
12 Kenny Ploen 20.00 40.00
13 Bob Ptacek 17.50 35.00
14 Ron Stewart 20.00 40.00
15 Dave Thelen 20.00 40.00
19 British Columbia Lions 10.00 20.00
20 Calgary Stampeders 10.00 20.00
21 Edmonton Eskimos 10.00 20.00
22 Hamilton Tiger-Cats 10.00 20.00
23 Montreal Alouettes 10.00 20.00
24 Ottawa Rough Riders 10.00 20.00
25 Saskatchewan Roughriders 10.00 20.00
26 Toronto Argonauts 10.00 20.00
27 Winnipeg Blue Bombers 10.00 20.00

1962 Topps CFL

This 1962 Topps CFL set features 169-different numbered cards originally issued in perforated pairs. We've priced the cards below as separate cards; pairs are worth up to a slight premium over the value of both cards. Note that there are many variations on which two cards were paired together. Each card measures 1 1/4" by 2 1/2" individually and 2 1/2" by 3 1/2" as a pair. The team cards contain a team checklist on the reverse side and the players preceding the team cards belong to the respective teams. Although the T.C.G. trademark appears on the cards, they were printed in Canada by O-Pee-Chee.

COMPLETE SET (169) 400.00 700.00
1 By Bailey 4.00 8.00
2 Nub Beamer 1.00 2.50
3 Tom Brown 4.00 8.00
4 Mack Burton 1.00 2.50
5 Mike Cacic 1.00 2.50
6 Pat Claridge 1.00 2.50
7 Steve Cotter 1.00 2.50
8 Lonnie Dennis 1.00 2.50
9 Norm Fieldgate 2.50 5.00
10 Willie Fleming 5.00 10.00
11 Tom Hinton 2.00 4.00
12 Sonny Homer 1.50 3.00
13 Joe Kapp 7.50 15.00
14 Tom Larscheid 1.00 2.50
15 Gordie Mitchell 1.00 2.50
16 Baz Nagle 1.00 2.50
17 Norris Stevenson 1.00 2.50
18 Barney Therrien UER 1.00 2.50
19 Don Vicic 2.00 4.00
20 B.C. Lions Team 4.00 8.00
21 Ed Buchanan 1.00 2.50
22 Joe Carruthers 1.00 2.50
23 Lovell Coleman 1.50 3.00
24 Barrie Cyr 1.00 2.50
25 Ernie Danjean 1.00 2.50
26 Gene Filipski 2.00 4.00
27 George Hansen 1.00 2.50
28 Earl Lunsford 2.50 5.00
29 Don Luzzi 1.50 3.00
30 Bill McKenna 1.00 2.50
31 Tony Pajaczkowski 2.00 4.00
32 Chuck Quilter 1.00 2.50
33 Lorne Reid 1.00 2.50
34 Art Scullion 1.00 2.50
35 Jim Walden 1.00 2.50
36 Harvey Wylie 2.00 4.00
37 Calgary Stampeders 4.00 8.00
38 Johnny Bright 5.00 10.00
39 Vic Chapman 1.00 2.50
40 Marion Drew Deese 1.00 2.50
41 Al Ecuyer 1.00 2.50
42 Gino Fracas 1.50 3.00
43 Don Getty 3.00 6.00
44 Ed Gray 1.00 2.50
45 Urban Henry 1.50 3.00
46 Bill Hill 1.00 2.50
47 Mike Kmeche 1.00 2.50
48 Oscar Kruger 1.50 3.00
49 Mike Lashuk 1.00 2.50
50 Jim Letcavits 1.00 2.50
51 Roger Nelson 2.00 4.00
52 Jackie Parker 7.50 15.00
53 Howie Schumm 1.00 2.50
54 Jim Shipka 1.00 2.50
55 Bill Smith 1.00 2.50
56 Joe-Bob Smith 1.00 2.50
57 Art Walker 2.00 4.00
58 Edmonton Eskimos 4.00 8.00
59 John Barrow 4.00 8.00
60 Hardiman Cureton 1.00 2.50
61 Geno DeNobile 1.00 2.50
62 Tom Dublinski 1.50 3.00
63 Bernie Faloney 6.00 12.00
64 Cam Fraser 1.00 2.50
65 Ralph Goldston 1.50 3.00
66 Tommy Grant 3.50 7.00
67 Garney Henley 7.50 15.00
68 Ron Howell 2.00 5.00
69 Zeno Karcz 1.50 3.00
70 Gerry McDougall UER 1.50 3.00
71 Chet Miksza 1.00 2.50
72 Bronko Nagurski Jr. 3.00 6.00
73 Hal Patterson 5.00 10.00
74 George Scott 1.00 2.50
75 Vince Scott 2.00 4.00
76 Hamilton Tiger-Cats 4.00 8.00
77 Ron Brewer 1.50 3.00
78 Ron Brooks 1.00 2.50
79 Howard Cissell 1.00 2.50
80 Don Clark 2.00 4.00
81 Dick Cohee 1.50 3.00
82 John Conroy 1.00 2.50
83 Milt Crain 1.50 3.00
84 Ted Elsby 1.00 2.50
85 Joe Francis 1.50 3.00
86 Gene Gaines 4.00 8.00
87 Barrie Hansen 1.00 2.50
88 Mike Kovac 1.00 2.50
89 Ed Learn 1.00 2.50
90 Billy Ray Locklin 1.00 2.50
91 Marv Luster 3.00 6.00
92 Bobby Jack Oliver 1.50 3.00
93 Sandy Stephens 4.00 8.00
94 Montreal Alouettes 5.00 10.00
95 Gilles Archambeault 1.00 2.50
96 Bruno Bitkowski 1.50 3.00
97 Jim Conroy 1.50 3.00
98 Doug Daigneault 1.00 2.50
99 Dick Desmarais 1.00 2.50
100 Russ Jackson 7.50 15.00
101 Tom Jones 1.00 2.50
102 Ron Lancaster 10.00 20.00
103 Angelo Mosca 7.50 15.00
104 Gerry Nesbitt 1.00 2.50
105 Joe Poirier 1.50 3.00
106 Moe Racine 1.00 2.50
107 Gary Schreider 1.00 2.50
108 Bob Simpson 3.00 6.00
109 Ted Smale 1.00 2.50
110 Ron Stewart 3.50 7.00
111 Dave Thelen 3.00 6.00
112 Kaye Vaughan 2.00 4.00
113 Ottawa Rough Riders 4.00 8.00
114 Ron Atchison UER 2.00 4.00
115 Danny Banda 1.00 2.50
116 Al Benecick 1.00 2.50
117 Clair Branch 1.00 2.50
118 Fred Burket 1.00 2.50
119 Bill Clarke 1.00 2.50
120 Jim Copeland 1.00 2.50
121 Ron Dundas 1.00 2.50
122 Bob Golic 1.50 3.00
123 Jack Gotta 2.00 4.00
124 Dave Grosz 1.00 2.50
125 Neil Habig 1.50 3.00
126 Jack Hill 1.00 2.50
127 Len Legault 1.00 2.50
128 Bob Ptacek 1.00 2.50
129 Roy Smith 1.00 2.50
130 Saskatchewan Rough- 4.00 8.00
131 Lynn Bottoms 1.50 3.00
132 Dick Fouts 1.50 3.00
133 Wes Gideon 1.00 2.50
134 Cookie Gilchrist 7.50 15.00
135 Art Johnson 1.00 2.50
136 Bobby Kuntz 1.50 3.00
137 Dave Mann 1.50 3.00
138 Marty Martinello 1.00 2.50
139 Doug McNichol 1.00 2.50
140 Bill Mitchell 1.00 2.50
141 Danny Nykoluk 1.00 2.50
142 Walt Radzick 1.00 2.50
143 Tobin Rote 5.00 10.00
144 Jim Rountree 1.50 3.00
145 Dick Shatto 4.00 8.00
146 Billy Shipp 1.50 3.00
147 Norm Stoneburgh 1.00 2.50
148 Toronto Argonauts 5.00 10.00
149 Dave Burkholder 1.00 2.50
150 Jack Delveaux 1.50 3.00
151 George Druxman 1.00 2.50
152 Farrell Funston 1.50 3.00
153 Herb Gray 2.50 5.00
154 Roger Hagberg 1.50 3.00
155 Gerry James 3.00 6.00
156 Henry Janzen 1.50 3.00
157 Ronnie Latourelle 1.00 2.50
158 Hal Ledyard 1.00 2.50
159 Leo Lewis 3.00 6.00
160 Steve Patrick 1.50 3.00
161 Cornel Piper 1.00 2.50
162 Ernie Pitts 1.50 3.00
163 Kenny Ploen 4.00 8.00
164 Norm Rauhaus 1.50 3.00
165 Frank Rigney 3.00 6.00
166 Gord Rowland 1.50 3.00
167 Roger Savoie 1.00 2.50
168 Charlie Shepard 1.50 3.00
169 Winnipeg Blue Bombers 10.00 20.00

1963 Topps CFL

The 1963 Topps CFL set features cards ordered by teams (which are in alphabetical order) with players preceding their respective team cards. Although the T.C.G. trademark appears on the cards, they were printed in Canada by O-Pee-Chee.

COMPLETE SET (88) 300.00 500.00
1 Willie Fleming 6.00 12.00
2 Dick Fouts 2.00 4.00
3 Joe Kapp 7.50 15.00
4 Nub Beamer 1.25 2.50
5 By Bailey 3.00 6.00
6 Tom Walker 1.25 2.50
7 Sonny Homer 2.00 4.00
8 Tom Hinton 2.50 5.00
9 Lonnie Dennis 1.25 2.50
10 British Columbia Lions 4.00 8.00
11 Ed Buchanan 1.25 2.50
12 Ernie Danjean 1.25 2.50
13 Eagle Day 3.00 6.00
14 Earl Lunsford 2.50 5.00
15 Don Luzzi 2.50 5.00
16 Tony Pajaczkowski 2.50 5.00
17 Jerry Keeling 7.50 15.00
18 Pat Holmes 2.00 4.00
19 Wayne Harris 7.50 15.00
20 Calgary Stampeders 4.00 8.00
21 Tommy Joe Coffey 4.00 8.00
22 Mike Lashuk 1.25 2.50
23 Bobby Walden 2.00 4.00
24 Don Getty 4.00 8.00
25 Len Vella 1.25 2.50

26 Ted Frechette 1.25 2.50
27 E.A. Sims 1.25 2.50
28 Nat Dye 1.25 2.50
29 Edmonton Eskimos 4.00 8.00
30 Bernie Faloney 5.00 10.00
31 Hal Patterson 4.00 8.00
32 John Barrow 3.00 6.00
33 Sam Fernandez 1.25 2.50
34 Garney Henley 6.00 12.00
35 Joe Zuger 2.00 4.00
36 Hardiman Cureton 1.25 2.50
37 Zeno Karcz 2.00 4.00
38 Bobby Kuntz 2.00 4.00
39 Hamilton Tiger-Cats 4.00 8.00
40 George Dixon 3.00 6.00
41 Don Clark 2.50 5.00
42 Marv Luster 3.00 6.00
43 Bobby Jack Oliver 2.00 4.00
44 Billy Ray Locklin 1.25 2.50
45 Sandy Stephens 3.00 6.00
46 Milt Crain 2.00 4.00
47 Meco Poliziani 1.25 2.50
48 Ted Elsby 1.25 2.50
49 Montreal Alouettes 4.00 8.00
50 Russ Jackson 7.50 15.00
51 Ron Stewart 4.00 8.00
52 Dave Thelen 3.00 6.00
53 Kaye Vaughan 2.50 5.00
54 Joe Poirier 2.00 4.00
55 Moe Racine 1.25 2.50
56 Whit Tucker 5.00 10.00
57 Ernie White 1.25 2.50
58 Ottawa Rough Riders 4.00 8.00
59 Bob Ptacek 1.25 2.50
60 Ray Purdin 1.25 2.50
61 Dale West 2.00 4.00
62 Neil Habig 1.25 2.50
63 Jack Gotta 2.00 4.00
64 Billy Gray 1.25 2.50
65 Don Walsh 1.25 2.50
66 Bill Clarke 1.25 2.50
67 Saskatchewan Rough- 4.00 8.00
68 Jackie Parker 7.50 15.00
69 Dave Mann 2.00 4.00
70 Dick Shatto 3.00 6.00
71 Norm Stoneburgh UER 1.25 2.50
72 Clare Exelby 1.25 2.50
73 Art Johnson 1.25 2.50
74 Doug McNichol 1.25 2.50
75 Danny Nykoluk 1.25 2.50
76 Walt Radzick 1.25 2.50
77 Toronto Argonauts 4.00 8.00
78 Leo Lewis 3.00 6.00
79 Kenny Ploen 4.00 8.00
80 Henry Janzen 2.00 4.00
81 Charlie Shepard 2.00 4.00
82 Roger Hagberg 2.00 4.00
83 Herb Gray 3.00 6.00
84 Frank Rigney 2.50 5.00
85 Jack Delveaux 2.00 4.00
86 Ronnie Latourelle 1.25 2.50
87 Winnipeg Blue Bombers 4.00 8.00
88 Checklist Card 30.00 60.00

1964 Topps CFL

The 1964 Topps CFL set features cards ordered by teams (which are in alphabetical order) with players preceding their respective team cards. Although the T.C.G. trademark appears on the cards, they were printed in Canada by O-Pee-Chee.

COMPLETE SET (88) 300.00 500.00
1 Willie Fleming 6.00 12.00
2 Dick Fouts 2.00 4.00
3 Joe Kapp 7.50 15.00
4 Nub Beamer 1.25 2.50
5 Tom Brown 2.50 5.00
6 Tom Walker 1.25 2.50
7 Sonny Homer 2.00 4.00
8 Tom Hinton 2.50 5.00
9 Lonnie Dennis 1.25 2.50
10 B.C. Lions Team 4.00 8.00
11 Lovell Coleman 2.00 4.00
12 Ernie Danjean 1.25 2.50
13 Eagle Day 2.50 5.00
14 Jim Furlong 1.25 2.50
15 Don Luzzi 2.50 5.00
16 Tony Pajaczkowski 2.50 5.00
17 Jerry Keeling 3.00 6.00
18 Pat Holmes 2.00 4.00
19 Wayne Harris 4.00 8.00
20 Calgary Stampeders 4.00 8.00
21 Tommy Joe Coffey 4.00 8.00
22 Al Ecuyer 1.25 2.50
23 Checklist Card 20.00 40.00
24 Don Getty 3.00 6.00
25 Len Vella 1.25 2.50
26 Ted Frechette 1.25 2.50
27 E.A. Sims 1.25 2.50
28 Nat Dye 1.25 2.50
29 Edmonton Eskimos 4.00 8.00
30 Bernie Faloney 7.50 15.00
31 Hal Patterson 4.00 8.00
32 John Barrow 3.00 6.00
33 Tommy Grant 3.00 6.00
34 Garney Henley 4.00 8.00
35 Joe Zuger 2.00 4.00
36 Hardiman Cureton 1.25 2.50
37 Zeno Karcz 2.00 4.00
38 Bobby Kuntz 2.00 4.00
39 Hamilton Tiger-Cats 4.00 8.00
40 George Dixon 4.00 8.00
41 Dave Hoppmann 1.25 2.50
42 Dick Walton 1.25 2.50
43 Jim Andreotti 2.00 4.00
44 Billy Ray Locklin 1.25 2.50
45 Fred Burket 1.25 2.50
46 Milt Crain 2.00 4.00
47 Meco Poliziani 1.25 2.50
48 Ted Elsby 1.25 2.50
49 Montreal Alouettes 5.00 10.00
50 Russ Jackson 7.50 15.00
51 Ron Stewart 4.00 8.00
52 Dave Thelen 2.50 5.00
53 Kaye Vaughan 2.50 5.00
54 Joe Poirier 2.00 4.00
55 Moe Racine 1.25 2.50
56 Whit Tucker 3.00 6.00
57 Ernie White 1.25 2.50
58 Ottawa Rough Riders 4.00 8.00
59 Bob Ptacek 1.25 2.50
60 Ray Purdin 1.25 2.50
61 Dale West 2.00 4.00
62 Neil Habig 1.25 2.50
63 Jack Gotta 2.00 4.00
64 Billy Gray 1.25 2.50
65 Don Walsh 1.25 2.50
66 Bill Clarke 1.25 2.50
67 Saskatchewan Rough- 4.00 8.00
68 Jackie Parker 7.50 15.00
69 Dave Mann 2.00 4.00
70 Dick Shatto 3.00 6.00
71 Norm Stoneburgh 1.25 2.50
72 Clare Exelby 1.25 2.50
73 Jim Christopherson 1.25 2.50
74 Sherman Lewis 3.00 6.00
75 Danny Nykoluk 1.25 2.50
76 Walt Radzick 1.25 2.50
77 Toronto Argonauts 5.00 10.00
78 Leo Lewis 3.00 6.00
79 Kenny Ploen 3.00 6.00
80 Henry Janzen 2.00 4.00
81 Charlie Shepard 2.00 4.00
82 Roger Hagberg 2.00 4.00
83 Herb Gray 3.00 6.00
84 Frank Rigney 2.50 5.00
85 Jack Delveaux 2.00 4.00
86 Ronnie Latourelle 1.25 2.50
87 Winnipeg Blue 4.00 8.00
88 Checklist Card 25.00 50.00

1965 Topps CFL

The 1965 Topps CFL set features 132 cards ordered by teams (which are in alphabetical order) with players also in alphabetical order. Card numbers 60 (1-60) and 132 (61-132) are checklist cards. Don Sutherlin, number 57, has number 51 on the back. Although the T.C.G. trademark appears on the cards, they were printed in Canada by O-Pee-Chee.

COMPLETE SET (132) 350.00 600.00
1 Neil Beaumont 3.00 6.00
2 Tom Brown 3.00 6.00
3 Mike Cacic 1.25 2.50
4 Pat Claridge 1.25 2.50
5 Steve Cotter 1.25 2.50
6 Lonnie Dennis 1.25 2.50
7 Norm Fieldgate 2.50 5.00
8 Willie Fleming 6.00 12.00
9 Dick Fouts 2.00 4.00
10 Tom Hinton 2.50 5.00
11 Sonny Homer 2.00 4.00
12 Joe Kapp 7.50 15.00
13 Paul Seale 1.25 2.50
14 Steve Shafer 1.25 2.50
15 Bob Swift 1.25 2.50
16 Larry Anderson 1.25 2.50
17 Lu Bain 1.25 2.50
18 Lovell Coleman 2.00 4.00
19 Eagle Day 2.50 5.00
20 Jim Furlong 1.25 2.50
21 Wayne Harris 3.50 7.00
22 Herman Harrison 6.00 12.00
23 Jerry Keeling 3.00 6.00
24 Hal Krebs 1.25 2.50
25 Don Luzzi 2.50 5.00
26 Tony Pajaczkowski 2.50 5.00
27 Larry Robinson 2.50 5.00
28 Bob Taylor 2.00 4.00
29 Ted Woods 1.25 2.50
30 Jon Anabo 1.25 2.50
31 Jim Battle 1.25 2.50
32 Charlie Brown 1.25 2.50
33 Tommy Joe Coffey 5.00 10.00
34 Marcel Deleeuw 1.25 2.50
35 Al Ecuyer 1.25 2.50
36 Jim Higgins 1.25 2.50
37 Oscar Kruger 2.00 4.00
38 Barry Mitchelson 1.25 2.50
39 Roger Nelson 2.50 5.00
40 Bill Redell 1.25 2.50
41 E.A. Sims 1.25 2.50
42 Jim Stinnette 1.25 2.50
43 Jim Thomas 1.25 2.50
44 Terry Wilson 1.25 2.50
45 Art Baker 2.00 4.00
46 John Barrow 3.00 6.00
47 Dick Cohee 2.00 4.00
48 Frank Cosentino 2.50 5.00
49 Johnny Counts 1.25 2.50
50 Tommy Grant 2.50 5.00
51 Garney Henley 4.00 8.00
52 Zeno Karcz 2.00 4.00
53 Ellison Kelly 6.00 12.00
54 Bobby Kuntz 2.00 4.00
55 Angelo Mosca 7.50 15.00
56 Bronko Nagurski Jr. 3.50 7.00
57 Don Sutherin UER 6.00 12.00
58 Dave Viti 1.25 2.50
59 Joe Zuger 2.00 4.00
60 Checklist 1-60 17.50 35.00
61 Jim Andreotti 2.00 4.00
62 Harold Cooley 1.25 2.50
63 Nat Craddock 1.25 2.50
64 George Dixon 3.00 6.00
65 Ted Elsby 1.25 2.50
66 Clare Exelby 1.25 2.50
67 Bernie Faloney 7.50 15.00
68 Al Irwin 1.25 2.50
69 Ed Learn 1.25 2.50
70 Moe Levesque 1.25 2.50
71 Bob Minihane 1.25 2.50
72 Jim Reynolds 1.25 2.50
73 Billy Roy 1.25 2.50
74 Billy Joe Booth 2.00 4.00
75 Jim Cain 1.25 2.50
76 Larry DeGraw 1.25 2.50
77 Don Estes 1.25 2.50
78 Gene Gaines 2.50 5.00
79 John Kennerson 1.25 2.50
80 Roger Kramer 2.00 4.00
81 Ken Lehmann 2.00 4.00
82 Bob O'Billovich 1.25 2.50
83 Joe Poirier 2.00 4.00
84 Bill Quinter 1.25 2.50
85 Jerry Selinger 1.25 2.50
86 Bill Siekierski 1.25 2.50
87 Len Sparks 1.25 2.50
88 Whit Tucker 2.50 5.00
89 Ron Atchison 2.50 5.00
90 Ed Buchanan 1.25 2.50
91 Hugh Campbell 5.00 10.00
92 Henry Dorsch 1.25 2.50
93 Garner Ekstran 2.00 4.00
94 Martin Fabi 1.25 2.50
95 Bob Good 1.25 2.50
96 Ron Lancaster 7.50 15.00
97 Bob Ptacek 1.25 2.50
98 George Reed 12.50 25.00
99 Wayne Shaw 1.25 2.50
100 Dale West 2.00 4.00
101 Reg Whitehouse 1.25 2.50
102 Jim Worden 1.25 2.50
103 Ron Brewer 2.00 4.00
104 Don Fuell 1.25 2.50
105 Ed Harrington 2.00 4.00
106 George Hughley 1.25 2.50
107 Dave Mann 2.00 4.00
108 Marty Martinello 1.25 2.50
109 Danny Nykoluk 1.25 2.50
110 Jackie Parker 10.00 20.00
111 Dave Pivec 1.25 2.50
112 Walt Radzick 1.25 2.50
113 Lee Sampson 1.25 2.50
114 Dick Shatto 2.50 5.00
115 Norm Stoneburgh 1.25 2.50
116 Jim Vollenweider 1.25 2.50
117 John Wydareny 2.00 4.00
118 Billy Cooper 1.25 2.50
119 Farrell Funston 2.00 4.00
120 Herb Gray 2.50 5.00
121 Henry Janzen 2.00 4.00
122 Leo Lewis 3.50 7.00
123 Brian Palmer 1.25 2.50
124 Cornel Piper 1.25 2.50
125 Ernie Pitts 1.25 2.50
126 Kenny Ploen 3.50 7.00
127 Norm Rauhaus 2.00 4.00
128 Frank Rigney 2.50 5.00
129 Roger Savoie 1.25 2.50
130 Dick Thornton 2.50 5.00
131 Bill Whisler 1.25 2.50
132 Checklist 61-132 25.00 50.00

1965 Topps CFL Transfers

These four-color transfers were inserts in 1965 Topps CFL packs, measure approximately 2" by 3," and closely resemble the 1961 set. The 1965 inserts are distinguished from the 1961 release by the addition of the notation "Printed in U.S.A.".

COMPLETE SET (27) 250.00 500.00
1 British Columbia Lions Crest 10.00 20.00
2 British Columbia Lions Pennant 10.00 20.00
3 Calgary Stampeders Crest 10.00 20.00
4 Calgary Stampeders Pennant 10.00 20.00
5 Edmonton Eskimos Crest 10.00 20.00
6 Edmonton Eskimos Pennant 10.00 20.00
7 Hamilton Tiger-Cats Crest 10.00 20.00
8 Hamilton Tiger-Cats Pennant 10.00 20.00
9 Montreal Alouettes Crest 10.00 20.00
10 Montreal Alouettes Pennant 10.00 20.00
11 Ottawa Rough Riders Crest 10.00 20.00
12 Ottawa Rough Riders Pennant 10.00 20.00
13 Saskatchewan Roughriders Crest 10.00 20.00
14 Saskatchewan Roughriders Pennant 10.00 20.00
15 Toronto Argonauts Crest 10.00 20.00
16 Toronto Argonauts Pennant 10.00 20.00
17 Winnipeg Blue Bombers Crest 10.00 20.00
18 Winnipeg Blue Bombers Pennant 10.00 20.00
19 Quebec Provincial Crest 10.00 20.00
20 Ontario Provincial Crest 10.00 20.00
21 Manitoba Provincial Crest 10.00 20.00
22 Saskatchewan Provincial Crest 10.00 20.00
23 Alberta Provincial Crest 10.00 20.00
24 British Columbia Provincial Crest 10.00 20.00
25 Northwest Territories Territorial Crest 10.00 20.00
26 Yukon Territory Territorial Crest 10.00 20.00
27 Canada 12.50 25.00

1967 Toronto Argonauts Team Issue

1 Richard Aboud 4.00 8.00
2 Gordon Ackerman CO 4.00 8.00
3 Dick Aldridge 4.00 8.00
4 Ron Arends 4.00 8.00
5 Walt Balasiuk 4.00 8.00
6 Jerry Bradley 4.00 8.00
7 Frank Johnston CO 4.00 8.00
8 Donald Kopplin 4.00 8.00
9 Ed Learn 4.00 8.00
10 Ian MacDonald 4.00 8.00
11 Mario Mariani 4.00 8.00
12 Peter Martin 4.00 8.00
13 Mel Profit 4.00 8.00
14 Merl Prophet CO 4.00 8.00
15 John Reykdal 4.00 8.00
16 Norm Stoneburgh 4.00 8.00
17 Steve Sucic CO 4.00 8.00
18 Mike Wicklum 4.00 8.00

1968 Toronto Argonauts Team Issue

1 Allen Aldridge 4.00 8.00
2 Dick Aldridge 4.00 8.00
3 Ron Arends 4.00 8.00
4 Walt Balasiuk 4.00 8.00
5 Jimmy Dye 4.00 8.00
6 Mike Eben 4.00 8.00
7 Dave Knechtel 4.00 8.00
8 Ed Learn 4.00 8.00
9 Charles Liebrock 4.00 8.00
10 Marv Luster 4.00 8.00
11 Paul Markle 4.00 8.00
12 Peter Martin 4.00 8.00
13 Danny Nykoluk 4.00 8.00
14 Bob Peterson 4.00 8.00
15 Gil Petmanis 4.00 8.00
16 Neil Smith 4.00 8.00
17 Bobby Taylor 4.00 8.00
18 Coaches 4.00 8.00
Frank Johnston
Gordon Ackerman

1969 Toronto Argonauts Team Issue

1 Allen Aldridge 4.00 8.00
2 Dick Aldridge 4.00 8.00
3 Walt Balasiuk 4.00 8.00
4 Mike Blum 4.00 8.00
5 Charlie Bray 4.00 8.00
6 Mike Eben 4.00 8.00
7 Jim Henderson 4.00 8.00
8 Dave Knechtel 4.00 8.00
9 Ed Learn 4.00 8.00
10 Charles Liebrock 4.00 8.00
11 Paul Markle 4.00 8.00
12 Peter Martin 4.00 8.00
13 Bob Morgan 4.00 8.00
14 James Moore 4.00 8.00
15 Gil Petmanis 4.00 8.00
16 Mel Profit 4.00 8.00
17 Roger Scales 4.00 8.00
18 Gerry Sternberg 4.00 8.00
19 Coaches 4.00 8.00
Frank Johnston
Gordon Ackerman

1970 Toronto Argonauts Team Issue

1 Dick Aldridge 4.00 8.00
2 Ron Arends 4.00 8.00
3 Walt Balasiuk 4.00 8.00
4 Chip Barrett 4.00 8.00
5 Tom Bland 4.00 8.00
6 Mike Blum 4.00 8.00
7 Charlie Bray 4.00 8.00
8 Ron Capham 4.00 8.00
9 Ed Harrington 4.00 8.00
10 Bob Hudspeth 4.00 8.00
11 Dave Knechtel 4.00 8.00
12 Marv Luster 4.00 8.00
13 Dave Mann 5.00 10.00
14 Paul Markle 4.00 8.00
15 Peter Martin 4.00 8.00
16 Danny Nykoluk 4.00 8.00
17 Gerry Sternberg 4.00 8.00
18 Bill Symons 5.00 10.00
19 Bobby Taylor 4.00 8.00

20 Larry Watkins 4.00 8.00
21 Coaches 4.00 8.00
Frank Johnston
Gordon Ackerman

1971 Toronto Argonauts Team Issue

1 Harry Abofs 4.00 8.00
2 Dick Aldridge 4.00 8.00
3 Chip Barrett 4.00 8.00
4 Charlie Bray 4.00 8.00
5 Paul Desjardins 4.00 8.00
6 Mike Eben 4.00 8.00
7 Bob Hamilton 4.00 8.00
8 Ed Harrington 4.00 8.00
9 Jim Henderson 4.00 8.00
10 Dave Knechtel 4.00 8.00
11 Marv Luster 4.00 8.00
12 Gene Mack 4.00 8.00
13 Peter Martin 4.00 8.00
14 Peter Paquette 4.00 8.00
15 Roger Scales 4.00 8.00
16 Gerry Sternberg 4.00 8.00
17 Bill Symons 5.00 10.00
18 John Trainor 4.00 8.00

1972 Toronto Argonauts Team Issue

The Argonauts issued player photos over a number of years in the 1960s and 1970s with similar designs and styles. We've attempted to group them according to year by assembling like styles together. Each photo in this set includes two black-and-white player images, with one being a posed action shot along with a smaller portrait image. The roughly 8" by 10" photos also include the player's name and team logo on the cardfronts but no year. The backs are blank and unnumbered.

COMPLETE SET (15) 60.00 120.00
1 Harry Abofs 4.00 8.00
2 Dick Aldridge 4.00 8.00
3 Chip Barrett 4.00 8.00
4 Charlie Bray 4.00 8.00
5 Paul Desjardins 4.00 8.00
6 Jim Henderson 4.00 8.00
7 Noah Jackson 5.00 10.00
8 Dave Knechtel 4.00 8.00
9 Gene Mack 4.00 8.00
10 Peter Martin 4.00 8.00
11 Peter Paquette 4.00 8.00
12 Roger Scales 4.00 8.00
13 Bill Symons 5.00 10.00
14 Joe Theismann 15.00 25.00
15 John Trainor 4.00 8.00

1976 Toronto Argonauts Team Sheets

This group of 40-players and coaches of the Argonauts was produced on five glossy sheets each measuring approximately 8" by 10". The fronts feature black-and-white player portraits with eight pictures to a sheet with the year printed at the top. The backs are blank. The cards are unnumbered and checklisted below in alphabetical order, with the player pictured in the upper left hand corner of the sheet listed first.

COMPLETE SET (5) 15.00 30.00
1 Sheet 1 3.00 6.00
2 Sheet 2 4.00 8.00
3 Sheet 3 3.00 6.00
4 Sheet 4 4.00 8.00
5 Sheet 5 3.00 6.00

1977-78 Toronto Argonauts Team Sheets

This group of 40-players and coaches of the Argonauts was produced on five glossy sheets each measuring approximately 8" by 10". The fronts feature black-and-white player portraits with eight pictures to a sheet with the year printed at the top. The backs are blank. The cards are unnumbered and checklisted below in alphabetical order, with the player pictured in the upper left hand corner of the sheet listed first.

COMPLETE SET (5) 15.00 30.00
1 Sheet 1 3.00 6.00
2 Sheet 2 3.00 6.00
3 Sheet 3 3.00 6.00
4 Sheet 4 3.00 6.00
5 Sheet 5 4.00 8.00

1957 Weekend Magazine Posters

These posters were actually magazine page cut-outs. Each measures roughly 11" by 15" and features a color photo of the featured player on the left and a bio of the player on the right. The posters were printed on newsprint type stock and each was numbered in the lower right hand corner. The backs are simply another page from the magazine. Any additions to the below checklist are appreciated.

COMPLETE SET (11) 125.00 200.00
35 Normie Kwong 20.00 35.00
36 Hal Patterson 12.00 20.00
37 Dick Huffman 12.00 20.00
38 Bob Simpson 12.00 20.00
39 By Bailey 20.00 35.00
40 Vince Scott 12.00 20.00
41 Ken Carpenter 15.00 25.00
42 Sam Etcheverry 15.00 25.00
43 Bob McNamara 12.00 20.00
44 Jackie Parker 20.00 35.00
45 Kaye Vaughan 12.00 20.00

1958 Weekend Magazine Posters

These posters were actually magazine page cut-outs. Each measures roughly 11" by 15" and features a color photo of the featured player. The numbered posters were printed on newsprint stock. The poster backs are simply another page from the magazine.

37 Tony Curcillo 10.00 20.00
38 Gerry James 15.00 30.00
39 Johnny Bright 20.00 40.00
40 Pat Abruzzi 12.50 25.00
41 Ted Hunt 10.00 20.00
42 Bobby Judd 10.00 20.00
43 Reg Whitehouse 10.00 20.00
44 Ernie Warlick 12.50 25.00
45 Dave Mann 12.50 25.00
46 Ken Carpenter 12.50 25.00

1959 Weekend Magazine Posters

These posters were actually magazine page cut-outs. Each measures roughly 11" by 15" and features a color art portrait, by former player Tex Coulter, of the featured player on the left and a bio of the player on the right. The posters were printed on newsprint type stock and each was numbered on the right hand side. The backs are simply another page from the magazine.

33 Jim Van Pelt 12.50 25.00
34 Ron Howell 10.00 20.00
35 Jackie Parker 25.00 40.00
36 Dick Shatto 12.50 25.00
37 Don Luzzi 12.50 25.00
38 Sam Etcheverry 15.00 30.00
39 Bob Simpson 10.00 20.00
40 By Bailey 20.00 35.00
41 Jack Hill 10.00 20.00

1959 Wheaties CFL

The 1959 Wheaties CFL set contains 48 cards, each measuring 2 1/2" by 3 1/2". The fronts contain a black and white photo on a one-colored striped field, with the player's name and team in black within a white rectangle at the lower portion. The back contains the player's name and team, his position, and brief biographical data in both English and French. The cards are quite similar in appearance to the 1956 Shredded Wheat set. These unnumbered cards are ordered below in alphabetical order. Every 1959 CFL game program contained a full-page ad for the Wheaties Grey Cup Game Contest. The ad detailed the card program which indicated that each specially marked package of Wheaties contained four cards.

COMPLETE SET (48) 3,000.00 4,500.00
1 Ron Adam 35.00 60.00
2 Bill Bewley 45.00 80.00
3 Lynn Bottoms 45.00 80.00
4 Johnny Bright 90.00 150.00
5 Ken Carpenter 45.00 80.00
6 Tony Curcillo 45.00 80.00
7 Sam Etcheverry 150.00 250.00
8 Bernie Faloney 125.00 200.00
9 Cam Fraser 45.00 80.00
10 Don Getty 75.00 125.00
11 Jack Gotta 45.00 80.00
12 Milt Graham 35.00 60.00
13 Jack Hill 35.00 60.00
14 Ron Howell 45.00 80.00
15 Russ Jackson 125.00 200.00
16 Gerry James 75.00 125.00
17 Doug Kiloh 35.00 60.00
18 Ronnie Knox 45.00 80.00
19 Vic Kristopaitis 35.00 60.00
20 Oscar Kruger 35.00 60.00
21 Bobby Kuntz 45.00 80.00
22 Normie Kwong 100.00 175.00
23 Leo Lewis 90.00 150.00
24 Harry Lunn 35.00 60.00
25 Don Luzzi 60.00 100.00
26 Dave Mann 45.00 80.00
27 Bobby Marlow 60.00 100.00
28 Gerry McDougall 45.00 80.00
29 Doug McNichol 35.00 60.00
30 Rollie Miles 60.00 100.00
31 Red O'Quinn 60.00 100.00
32 Jackie Parker 175.00 300.00
33 Hal Patterson 90.00 150.00
34 Don Pinhey 35.00 60.00
35 Kenny Ploen 75.00 125.00
36 Gord Rowland 45.00 80.00
37 Vince Scott 60.00 100.00
38 Art Scullion 35.00 60.00
39 Dick Shatto 75.00 125.00
40 Bob Simpson 75.00 125.00
41 Jackie Simpson UER 60.00 100.00
42 Bill Sowalski 35.00 60.00
43 Norm Stoneburgh 35.00 60.00
44 Buddy Tinsley 60.00 100.00
45 Frank Tripucka 75.00 125.00
46 Jim Van Pelt 45.00 80.00
47 Ernie Warlick 60.00 100.00
48 Nobby Wirkowski 60.00 100.00

1962 Wheaties Great Moments in Canadian Sports

This 25 card set, which measure approximately 3 1/2" by 2 1/2" was issued in Canada one per cereal box. The fronts have a color drawing of an important event in Canadian sport history while the backs have a description in both English and French as to what the significance of the event was.

COMPLETE SET (25)
4 McGill Player 2.00 5.00
Introduction of Football to America
6 Jackie Parker/1954 Grey Cup 3.00 8.00
13 Red Storey/1938 Grey Cup 2.00 5.00
18 Ron Stewart/1960 Grey Cup 2.50 6.00

1924 Willard's Chocolates Sports Champions V122

6 A.H. Cap Fear Football

1976 Winnipeg Blue Bombers Team Sheets

This group of 40-players and coaches of the Blue Bombers was produced on five glossy sheets each measuring approximately 8" by 10". The fronts feature black-and-white player portraits with eight pictures to a sheet with the year printed at the top. The backs are blank. The cards are unnumbered and checklisted below in alphabetical order, with the player pictured in the upper left hand corner of the sheet listed first.

COMPLETE SET (5) 12.50 25.00
1 L.Benard 2.50 5.00
B.Swift
M.Reeves
S.Williams
M.Hoban
B.Toogood
R.Brock
B.LaRose
2 D.Craig 3.00 6.00
C.Liebrock
B.Herosian
J.Jackson
G.Anderson
S.Beaird
D.Bowman
M.McDonald
3 R.Halsall 2.50 5.00
J.Heighton
B.Brown
G.Paterson
C.Wills
R.Crump
H.Knight
B.Ruoff
4 R.Southwick 2.50 5.00
O.Bakken
R.Koswin
H.Walters
J.Bonk
B.Norman
E.Lunsford
B.Riley
5 J.Washington 3.00 6.00
B.Frank
T.Scott
B.Jack
T.Walker
M.Walker
D.Knechtel
P.Ribbins

1977-78 Winnipeg Blue Bombers Team Sheets

This group of 32-players and coaches of the Blue Bombers was produced on four glossy sheets each measuring approximately 8" by 10". The fronts feature black-and-white player portraits with eight pictures to a sheet with the year printed at the top. The backs are blank. The cards are unnumbered and checklisted below in alphabetical order, with the player pictured in the upper left hand corner of the sheet listed first.

COMPLETE SET (4) 10.00 20.00
1 J.Bonk 3.00 6.00
J.Babinecz
D.Hubbard
R.Crump
J.Heighton
S.Scully
R.Honey
C.Wills
2 M.McDonald 2.50 5.00
B.Herosian
C.Liebrock
H.Walters
R.Southwick
B.Norman
R.Brock
T.Walker
3 M.Walker 3.00 6.00
E.Brown
J.Washington
B.Swift
R.Koswin
G.Rosolowich
T.Scott
L.Benard
4 S.Willis 2.50 5.00
H.Knight
L.Woznesensky
V.Phason
B.Ruoff
G.Krahn
J.Walters
G.Paterson

1978 Winnipeg Blue Bombers Team Sheets

This group of 40-players and coaches of the Blue Bombers was produced on five glossy sheets each measuring approximately 8" by 10". The fronts feature black-and-white player portraits with eight pictures to a sheet with the year printed at the top. The backs are blank. The cards are unnumbered and checklisted below in alphabetical order, with the player pictured in the upper left hand corner of the sheet listed first.

COMPLETE SET (5) 12.50 25.00
1 E.Brown 2.50 5.00
B.Hardeman
R.Halsall
J.McCorquindale
W.Allison
M.McDonald
D.Knechtel
R.Pierson
2 B.Herosian 2.50 5.00
H.Walters
B.Brown
B.Morrison
E.Hiebert
E.Lunsford
R.Jauch
M.Holmes
3 H.Knight 3.00 6.00
B.Norman
B.Howard
G.Paterson
J.Washington
R.Brock
M.Walker
J.Heighton
4 I.Watley 3.00 6.00
B.Ruoff
L.Woznesensky
V.Phason
R.Crump
S.Okoniewski
R.Clark
B.Toogood
5 C.Wills 2.50 5.00
G.Rosolowich
D.MacKinlay
R.Southwick
J.Hart
T.Walker
J.Bonk
L.Ezerins

1980 Winnipeg Blue Bombers Team Sheets

This group of 32-players and coaches of the Blue Bombers was produced on four glossy sheets each measuring approximately 8" by 10". The fronts feature black-and-white player portraits with eight pictures to a sheet with the year printed at the top. The backs are blank. The cards are unnumbered and checklisted below in alphabetical order, with the player pictured in the upper left hand corner of the sheet listed first.

COMPLETE SET (4) 10.00 20.00
1 M.Allemang 2.50 6.00
N.Bastaja
J.Bonk
M.Bragagnolo
R.Brock
E.Burley
L.Butler
B.Cameron
2 B.Gervais 2.00 5.00
C.Williams
J.Helton
B.Holland
M.Holmes
R.House
J.Krohn
H.Kruger
3 J.Martini 2.50 6.00
B.Norman
W.Passaglia
V.Phason
T.Kennerd
R.Pierson
J.Poplawski
M.Rieker
4 G.Rosolowich 2.50 6.00
T.Schulz
C.Cobb
G.Seidel
W.Thomas
B.Toogood
J.Washington
R.Wesson

1946-49 AAFC Championship Press Pins

1 1946 Browns vs Yankees
2 1947 Browns vs Yankees 300.00 500.00
3 1948 Browns vs Bills 300.00 500.00
4 1949 Browns vs 49ers 250.00 400.00

1946-49 AAFC Championship Programs

The All-America Football Conference began play in 1946 and folded after the 1949 season. The AAFC was the brainchild of Chicago Sportswriter and sports promoter, Arch Ward. The AAFC was comprised of eight teams representing the cities of: Cleveland (Browns), San Francisco (49ers), Los Angeles (Dons), Chicago (Rockets, Hornets), New York (Yankees), Brooklyn (Dodgers), Buffalo (Bills) and Miami. The Miami Seahawks folded after the 1946 season and were replaced by the Baltimore Colts. The Cleveland Browns, with a combined record of 47-4-3, won the AAFC title game in each of the league's four seasons. Three AAFC franchises, the San Francisco 49ers, Baltimore Colts and Cleveland Browns merged with the NFL for the 1950 season.

1 1946 Browns vs Yankees	350.00	600.00
2 1947 Browns vs Yankees	350.00	600.00
3 1948 Browns vs Bills	350.00	600.00
4 1949 Browns vs 49ers	350.00	600.00

1946-49 AAFC Championship Ticket Stubs

Complete AAFC Championship tickets are nearly impossible to obtain and would command a premium above and beyond the values below.

1 1946 Browns vs Yankees	200.00	350.00
2 1947 Browns vs Yankees	200.00	325.00
3 1948 Browns vs Bills	200.00	325.00
4 1949 Browns vs 49ers	200.00	325.00

1947-49 AAFC Record Manuals

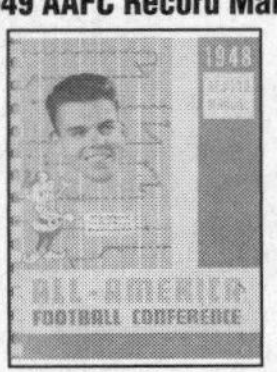

These guides or manuals were issued by the league and include AAFC records, lists of league leaders, championship teams, etc. Most years also include a basic league rules section. We've noted the subject matter on each front cover when known.

1947 Record Manual	40.00	80.00
1948 Record Manual	50.00	100.00
1949 Record Manual	40.00	80.00

1960-69 AFL Championship Programs

1 1960 Chargers vs Oilers	400.00	800.00
2 1961 Oilers vs Chargers	250.00	500.00
3 1962 Texans vs Oilers	250.00	500.00
4 1963 Patriots vs Chargers	250.00	500.00
5 1964 Chargers vs Bills	250.00	500.00
6 1965 Bills vs Chargers	200.00	350.00
7 1966 Chiefs vs Bills	200.00	350.00
8 1967 Oilers vs Raiders	200.00	350.00
9 1968 Raiders vs Jets	200.00	350.00
10 1969 Chiefs vs Raiders	150.00	300.00

1960-69 AFL Championship Ticket Stubs

1 1960 Chargers vs Oilers	300.00	600.00
2 1961 Oilers vs Chargers	250.00	500.00
3 1962 Texans vs Oilers	250.00	500.00
4 1963 Patriots vs Chargers	250.00	500.00
5 1964 Chargers vs Bills	150.00	300.00
6 1965 Bills vs Chargers	150.00	300.00
7 1966 Chiefs vs Bills	150.00	300.00
8 1967 Oilers vs Raiders	125.00	250.00
9 1968 Raiders vs Jets	125.00	250.00
10 1969 Chiefs vs Raiders	125.00	250.00

1933-69 NFL Championship Programs

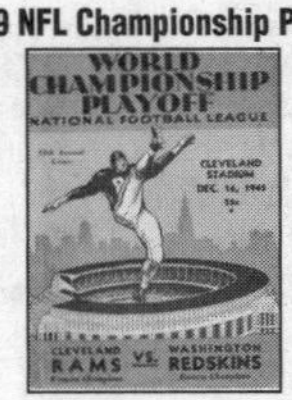

Pre-War programs are difficult to obtain in top condition and are graded Vg-Ex below. Post-War programs are priced in Ex-Mt condition.

1 1933 Giants vs Bears	3,000.00	4,500.00
2 1934 Bears vs Giants	2,000.00	3,000.00
3 1935 Giants vs Lions	2,000.00	3,000.00
4 1936 Packers vs Redskins	2,500.00	3,500.00
5 1937 Redskins vs Bears	1,800.00	3,000.00
6 1938 Giants vs Packers	1,800.00	3,000.00
7 1939 Packers vs Giants	1,500.00	2,500.00
8 1940 Bears vs Redskins	1,200.00	2,000.00
9 1941 Bears vs Giants	1,000.00	1,800.00
10 1942 Redskins vs Bears	1,000.00	1,600.00
11 1943 Bears vs Redskins	800.00	1,200.00
12 1944 Packers vs Giants	800.00	1,200.00
13 1945 Rams vs Redskins	500.00	800.00
14 1946 Bears vs Giants	350.00	600.00
15 1947 Cardinals vs Eagles	300.00	500.00
16 1948 Eagles vs Cardinals	300.00	500.00
17 1949 Eagles vs Rams	250.00	400.00
18 1950 Browns vs Rams	250.00	400.00
19 1951 Rams vs Browns	175.00	300.00
20 1952 Lions vs Browns	175.00	300.00
21 1953 Browns vs Lions	175.00	300.00
22 1954 Lions vs Browns	175.00	300.00
23 1955 Browns vs Rams	150.00	250.00
24 1956 Bears vs Giants	150.00	250.00
25 1957 Browns vs Lions	150.00	250.00
26 1958 Colts vs Giants	175.00	300.00
27 1959 Giants vs Colts	125.00	200.00
28 1960 Packers vs Eagles	175.00	300.00
29 1961 Giants vs Packers	150.00	250.00
30 1962 Giants vs Packers	150.00	250.00
31 1963 Giants vs Bears	100.00	175.00
32 1964 Colts vs Browns	100.00	175.00
33 1965 Browns vs Packers	150.00	250.00
34 1966 Packers vs Cowboys	150.00	250.00
35 1967 Cowboys vs Packers	175.00	300.00
36 1968 Colts vs Browns	75.00	125.00
37 1969 Browns vs Vikings	60.00	100.00

1933-69 NFL Championship Ticket Stubs

Pre-war ticket stubs are difficult to obtain in top condition and are graded Vg-Ex and Ex-Mt below. Complete tickets are valued 3 to 5 times that of a stub.

1 1933 Giants vs Bears	250.00	500.00
2 1934 Bears vs Giants	225.00	450.00
3 1935 Giants vs Lions	225.00	450.00
4 1936 Packers vs Redskins	175.00	350.00
5 1937 Redskins vs Bears	150.00	300.00
6 1938 Giants vs Packers	125.00	250.00
7 1939 Packers vs Giants	125.00	250.00
8 1940 Bears vs Redskins	175.00	350.00
9 1941 Bears vs Giants	125.00	250.00
10 1942 Redskins vs Bears	125.00	250.00
11 1943 Bears vs Redskins	125.00	250.00
12 1944 Packers vs Giants	125.00	250.00
13 1945 Rams vs Redskins	112.50	225.00
14 1946 Bears vs Giants	100.00	200.00
15 1947 Cardinals vs Eagles	87.50	175.00
16 1948 Eagles vs Cardinals	75.00	150.00
17 1949 Eagles vs Rams	75.00	150.00
18 1950 Browns vs Rams	75.00	150.00
19 1951 Rams vs Browns	75.00	150.00
20 1952 Lions vs Browns	75.00	150.00
21 1953 Browns vs Lions	75.00	150.00
22 1954 Lions vs Browns	62.50	125.00
23 1955 Browns vs Rams	62.50	125.00
24 1956 Bears vs Giants	62.50	125.00
25 1957 Browns vs Lions	62.50	125.00
26 1958 Colts vs Giants	125.00	200.00
27 1959 Giants vs Colts	50.00	100.00
28 1960 Packers vs Eagles	62.50	125.00
29 1961 Giants vs Packers	62.50	125.00
30 1962 Giants vs Packers	75.00	125.00
31 1963 Giants vs Bears	50.00	100.00
32 1964 Colts vs Browns	62.50	125.00
33 1965 Browns vs Packers	50.00	100.00
34 1966 Packers vs Cowboys	75.00	150.00
35 1967 Cowboys vs Packers	75.00	125.00
36 1968 Colts vs Browns	30.00	60.00
37 1969 Browns vs Vikings	30.00	60.00

1941-63 NFL Record Manuals

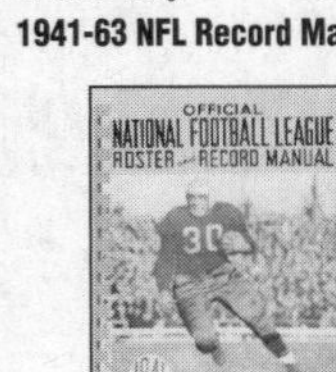

These guides or manuals were issued by the league and include historical NFL records, lists of past league leaders, championship teams, etc. Most years also include a basic league rules section. We've noted the subject matter on each front cover when known.

1941 Roster and Record Manual	60.00	100.00
1942 Roster and Record Manual	60.00	100.00
1943 Roster and Record Manual	60.00	100.00
1944 Record and Rules Manual	60.00	100.00
1945 Record and Rules Manual	60.00	100.00
1946 Record and Rules Manual	50.00	80.00
1947 Record and Rules Manual	50.00	80.00
1948 Record and Rules Manual	35.00	60.00
1949 Record and Rules Manual	35.00	60.00
1950 Record and Rules Manual	35.00	60.00
1951 Record and Rules Manual	35.00	60.00
1952 Record and Rules Manual	35.00	60.00
1953 Record and Rules Manual	30.00	50.00
1954 Record and Rules Manual	30.00	50.00
1955 Record and Rules Manual	35.00	60.00
1956 Record and Rules Manual	35.00	60.00
1957 Record and Rules Manual	30.00	50.00
1958 Record and Rules Manual	25.00	50.00
1959 Record and Rules Manual	25.00	50.00
1960 Record and Rules Manual	25.00	50.00
1961 Record and Rules Manual	25.00	50.00
1962 Record Manual	100.00	175.00
1963 Record Manual	40.00	80.00
1964 Record Manual	25.00	50.00
1965 Record Manual	20.00	40.00
1966 Record Manual	20.00	40.00
1967 Record Manual	25.00	50.00
1968 Record Manual	25.00	50.00
1969 Record Manual	20.00	40.00

1935-40 Spalding NFL Guides

These guides were issued by Spalding and include historical NFL records, lists of past league leaders, championship teams, please photos and bios of then current NFL teams. Most years also include a basic league rules section and a cover photo from the previous year's championship game. We've noted the subject matter on each front cover when known.

1935 Guide and Pro Football Rules	45.00	80.00
1936 Guide and Pro Football Rules	45.00	80.00
1937 Guide and Pro Football Rules	45.00	80.00
1938 Guide and Pro Football Rules	45.00	80.00
1939 Guide and Pro Football Rules	35.00	60.00
1940 Guide and Pro Football Rules	35.00	60.00

1946-50 Spink NFL Guides

These guides and manuals were published by the Charles Spink and Son Company and include historical NFL records, lists of past league leaders, championship teams, etc. Most years also include a feature on one significant football player or contributor. We've noted the subject matter on each front cover when known.

1946 Official Pro Rules	20.00	40.00
1947 Official Pro Rules	20.00	40.00
1948 NFL Record and Rule Book	20.00	40.00
1949 NFL Record and Rule Book	20.00	40.00
1950 NFL Record and Rule Book	20.00	40.00

1962-70 Sporting News AFL Football Guide

1 1962 Game Action	37.50	75.00
2 1963 Game Action	30.00	60.00
3 1964 Game Action	25.00	50.00
4 1965 Tobin Rote	20.00	40.00
5 1966 Sherrill Headrick	17.50	35.00
6 1967 Bobby Burnett	17.50	35.00
7 1968 Multi-Players	17.50	35.00
8 1969 Game Action	15.00	30.00
9 1970 Lance Alworth	15.00	30.00

1970-03 Sporting News NFL Football Guide

1 1970 Hank Stram	25.00	50.00
2 1971 Jim Bakken	20.00	40.00
3 1972 Roger Staubach	15.00	30.00
4 1973 Mercury Morris	12.50	25.00
5 1974 Larry Csonka	12.50	25.00
6 1975 Franco Harris	12.50	25.00
7 1976 Lynn Swann	10.00	20.00
8 1977 Kenny Stabler	10.00	20.00
9 1978 Roger Staubach	10.00	20.00
10 1979 Terry Bradshaw	10.00	20.00
11 1980 Swann Stallworth	10.00	20.00
12 1981 Billy Simms	7.50	15.00
13 1982 Kenny Anderson	7.50	15.00
14 1983 Mark Moesley	7.50	15.00
15 1984 Eric Dickerson	7.50	15.00
16 1985 Dan Marino	10.00	20.00
17 1986-PRESENT	5.00	10.00

1966-03 Sporting News NFL Football Register

1 1966 St. Louis Cardinals	25.00	50.00
2 1967 Mike Garrett	20.00	40.00
3 1968 Unidentified	20.00	40.00
4 1969 Dick Butkus	20.00	40.00
5 1970 Roman Gabriel	15.00	30.00
6 1971 Sonny Jurgensen	15.00	30.00
7 1972 Larry Wilson	15.00	30.00
8 1973 Terry Bradshaw	15.00	30.00
9 1974 O.J. Simpson	12.50	25.00
10 1975 Kenny Stabler	10.00	20.00
11 1976 Fran Tarkenton	10.00	20.00
12 1977 Bert Jones	10.00	20.00
13 1978 Walter Payton	12.50	25.00
14 1979 Earl Campbell	12.50	25.00
15 1980 Dan Fouts	10.00	20.00
16 1981 Brian Sipe	7.50	15.00
17 1982 Geroge Rogers	7.50	15.00
18 1983 Marcus Allen	7.50	15.00
19 1984 Dan Marino	10.00	20.00
20 1985 Walter Payton	10.00	20.00
21 1986 -PRESENT	5.00	10.00

1963-03 Street and Smith's Pro Football Yearbook

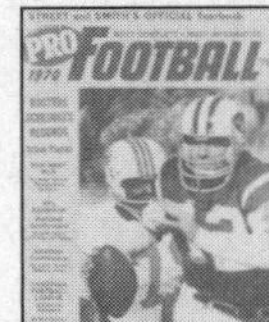

Street and Smith's was one of the first sports magazines to feature regional covers.

1 1963 Milt Plum	30.00	60.00
2 1963 Roman Gabriel	30.00	60.00
3 1963 Y.A. Tittle	37.50	75.00
4 1964 Terry Baker	25.00	50.00
5 1964 Jim Katcavage	25.00	50.00
6 1964 Bart Starr	30.00	60.00
7 1965 Johnny Unitas	25.00	50.00
8 1965 Frank Ryan	20.00	40.00
9 1965 Dick Bass	20.00	40.00
10 1966 Charley Johnson	17.50	35.00
11 1966 Ken Willard	17.50	35.00
12 1966 LaLonde Hillebrand	17.50	35.00
13 1967 Vogel Lorick	15.00	30.00
14 1967 Dick Bass	15.00	30.00
15 1967 Gale Sayers	20.00	40.00
16 1968 Norm Snead	15.00	30.00
17 1968 Raiders (action)	15.00	30.00
18 1968 Don Meredith	17.50	35.00
19 1969 John Brodie	15.00	30.00
20 1969 Joe Namath	22.50	45.00
21 1969 Jack Concannon	12.50	25.00
22 1970 Joe Namath	20.00	40.00
23 1970 Roman Gabriel	12.50	25.00
24 1970 Joe Kapp	12.50	25.00
25 1971 Earl Morrall	12.50	25.00
26 1971 Thomas Neely	12.50	25.00
27 1971 Brodie Willard	12.50	25.00
28 1972 Roger Staubach	15.00	30.00
29 1972 John Hadl	10.00	20.00
30 1972 Bob Griese	12.50	25.00
31 1973 Larry Csonka	12.50	25.00
32 1973 Chester Marcol	10.00	20.00
33 1973 Steve Spurrier	12.50	25.00
34 1974 Roger Staubach	12.50	25.00
35 1974 O.J. Simpson	12.50	25.00
36 1974 Jim Bertelsen	10.00	20.00
37 1975 Jim Hart	10.00	20.00
38 1975 Franco Harris	12.50	25.00
39 1975 Lawrence McCutchen	10.00	20.00
40 1976 Roger Staubach	10.00	20.00
41 1976 Terry Bradshaw	10.00	20.00
42 1976 Ken Stabler	10.00	20.00
43 1977 Walter Payton	10.00	20.00
44 1977 Bert Jones	7.50	15.00
45 1977 John Cappelletti	7.50	15.00
46 1978 Bob Griese	10.00	20.00
47 1978 Mark Van Eeghen	7.50	15.00
48 1978 Tony Dorsett	10.00	20.00
49 1979 Jim Zorn	7.50	15.00
50 1979 Terry Bradshaw	10.00	20.00
51 1979 Roger Staubach	10.00	20.00
52 1980 Terry Bradshaw	10.00	20.00
53 1980 Walter Payton	10.00	20.00
54 1980 Dan Fouts	7.50	15.00
55 1981 Campbell Bartkowski	10.00	20.00
56 1981 Plunkett Zorn	7.50	15.00
57 1981 Sipe Kramer	7.50	15.00
58 1982 Joe Montana	12.50	25.00
59 1982 Ken Anderson	7.50	15.00
60 1982 Lawrence Taylor	7.50	15.00
61 1982 Tony Dorsett	7.50	15.00
62 1983 Marcus Allen	7.50	15.00
63 1983 Ken Anderson	6.00	12.00
64 1983 Joe Theismann	7.50	15.00
65 1983 A.J. Duhe	6.00	12.00
66 1984 Walter Payton	7.50	15.00
67 1984 Dan Marino	10.00	20.00
68 1984 Marcus Allen	7.50	15.00
69 1984 John Riggins	7.50	15.00
70 1985 Walter Payton	7.50	15.00
71 1985 Phil Simms	6.00	12.00
72 1985 Dan Marino	10.00	20.00
73 1985 Joe Montana	7.50	15.00
74 1986-PRESENT	5.00	10.00

1967-04 Super Bowl Media Guides

1 1967 (I) Packers vs Chiefs 150.00 450.00
2 1968 (II) Packers vs Raiders 350.00 600.00
3 1969 (III) Jets vs Colts 350.00 600.00
4 1970 (IV) Chiefs vs Vikings 150.00 300.00
5 1971 (V) Colts vs Cowboys 150.00 300.00
6 1972 (VI) Cowboys vs Dolphins 125.00 250.00
7 1973 (VII) Dolphins vs Redskins 125.00 250.00
8 1974 (VIII) Dolphins vs Vikings 125.00 250.00
9 1975 (IX) Steelers vs Vikings 75.00 150.00
10 1976 (X) Steelers vs Cowboys 75.00 150.00
11 1977 (XI) Raiders vs Vikings 50.00 100.00
12 1978 (XII) Broncos vs Cowboys 50.00 100.00
13 1979 (XIII) Steelers vs Cowboys 37.50 75.00
14 1980 (XIV) Steelers vs Rams 37.50 75.00
15 1981 (XV) Eagles vs Raiders 25.00 50.00
16 1982 (XVI) 49ers vs Bengals 25.00 50.00
17 1983 (XVII) Redskins vs Dolphins 25.00 50.00
18 1984 (XVIII) Raiders vs Redskins 25.00 50.00
19 1985 (XIX) 49ers vs Dolphins 25.00 50.00
20 1986 (XX) Bears vs Patriots 25.00 50.00
21 1987 (XXI) Giants vs Broncos 20.00 40.00
22 1988 (XXII) Redskins vs Broncos 20.00 40.00
23 1989 (XXIII) 49ers vs Bengals 20.00 40.00
24 1990 (XXIV) 49ers vs Broncos 20.00 40.00
25 1991 (XXV) Giants vs Bills 12.50 25.00
26 1992 (XXVI) Redskins vs Bills 12.50 25.00
27 1993 (XXVII) Bills vs Cowboys 12.50 25.00
28 1994 (XXVIII) Bills vs Cowboys 12.50 25.00
29 1995 (XXIX) 49ers vs Chargers 12.50 25.00
30 1996 (XXX) Steelers vs Cowboys 12.50 25.00
31 1997 (XXXI) Packers vs Patriots 12.50 25.00
32 1998 (XXXII) Broncos vs Packers 12.50 25.00
33 1999 (XXXIII) Broncos vs Falcons 12.50 25.00
34 2000 (XXXIV) 12.50 25.00
St Louis Rams
Tennessee Titans
35 2001 (XXXV) 25.00 40.00
Baltimore Ravens
New York Giants
36 2002 (XXXVI) 15.00 30.00
New England Patriots
St.Louis Rams
37 2003 (XXXVII) 15.00 30.00
Tampa Bay Buccaneers
Oakland Raiders
38 2004 (XXXVIII) 15.00 30.00
Carolina Panthers
New England Pat
39 2005 (XXXIX) 15.00 30.00
New England Patriots
Philadelphia Eagles
40 2006 (XL) 15.00 30.00
Pittsburgh Steelers
Seattle Seahawks

1967-04 Super Bowl Patches

Super Bowl patches were intended to be sold at each Super Bowl venue as a souvenir. In recent years most patches have been reprinted. It's difficult to differentiate original Super Bowl patches from reprints. However, original patches prior to Super Bow XIV do not have the plastic coating applied to the backside like the current patches do.

1 1967 (I) 40.00 80.00
{Packers vs Chiefs
2 1968 (II) 40.00 80.00
{Packers vs Raiders
3 1969 (III) 30.00 60.00
{Jets vs Colts
4 1970 (IV) 25.00 50.00
{Chiefs vs Vikings
5 1971 (V) 25.00 50.00
{Colts vs Cowboys
6 1972 (VI) 25.00 50.00
{Cowboys vs Dolphins
7 1973 (VII) 20.00 40.00
{Dolphins vs Redskins
8 1974 (VIII) 10.00 25.00
{Dolphins vs Vikings
9 1975 (IX) 10.00 25.00
{Steelers vs Vikings
10 1976 (X) Steelers vs Cowboys 10.00 25.00
11 1977 (XI) Raiders vs Vikings 10.00 25.00
12 1978 (XII) Broncos vs Cowboys 10.00 25.00
13 1979 (XIII) Steelers vs Cowboys 10.00 25.00
14 1980 (XIV) Steelers vs Rams 10.00 25.00
15 1981 (XV) Eagles vs Raiders 10.00 25.00
16 1982 (XVI) 49ers vs Bengals 10.00 25.00
17 1983 (XVII) Redskins vs Dolphins 10.00 25.00
18 1984 (XVIII) Raiders vs Redskins 10.00 25.00
19 1985 (XIX) 49ers vs Dolphins 10.00 25.00
20 1986 (XX) Bears vs Patriots 10.00 25.00
21 1987 (XXI) Giants vs Broncos 7.50 20.00
22 1988 (XXII) Redskins vs Broncos 7.50 20.00
23 1989 (XXIII) 49ers vs Bengals 7.50 20.00
24 1990 (XXIV) 49ers vs Broncos 7.50 20.00
25 1991 (XXV) Giants vs Bills 7.50 20.00
26 1992 (XXVI) Redskins vs Bills 7.50 20.00
27 1993 (XXVII) Bills vs Cowboys 7.50 20.00
28 1994 (XXVIII) Bills vs Cowboys 7.50 20.00
29 1995 (XXIX) 49ers vs Chargers 7.50 20.00
30 1996 (XXX) Steelers vs Cowboys 6.00 15.00
31 1997 (XXXI) Packers vs Patriots 6.00 15.00
32 1998 (XXXII) Broncos vs Packers 6.00 15.00
33 1999 (XXXIII) Broncos vs Falcons 6.00 15.00
34 2000 (XXXIV) 6.00 15.00
{Tennessee Titans
St Louis Rams
35 2001 (XXXV) 6.00 15.00
Baltimore Ravens
New York Giants
36 2002 (XXXVI) 7.50 15.00
New England Patriots
St.Louis Rams
37A 2003 (XXXVII) 20.00 40.00
Tampa Bay Buccaneers
Oakland Raiders
37B 2003 (XXXVII) 7.50 20.00
Tampa Bay Buccaneers
Oakland Raide
38 2004 (XXXVIII) 7.50 20.00
Carolina Panthers
New England Pat
39 2005 (XXXIX) 10.00 20.00
New England Patriots
Philadelphia Eagles
40 2006 (XL) 10.00 20.00
Pittsburgh Steelers
Seattle Seahawks

1967-04 Super Bowl Press Pins

Press pins are given to members of the media attending the Super Bowl. The value for Super Bowl I pin includes the tie-bar and cuff links. The value of the Super Bowl I pin by itself would be $900. There was no pin issued for Super Bowl II. The media received a charm. Also, the media attending Super Bowl III were given a tie-clasp rather than the traditional press pin. There were no press pins issued for either Super Bowl IV or V.

1 1967 (I) (Tie Clasp) 1,200.00 2,000.00
Green Bay Packers
Kansas City Chiefs
2 1968 (II) 1,500.00 2,500.00
Green Bay Packers
Oakland Raiders
3 1969 (III) (Tie Clasp) 750.00 1,500.00
New York Jets
Baltimore Colts
4 1970 (IV) 500.00 800.00
{Kansas City Chiefs
Minnesota Vikings
5 1971 (V) 500.00 800.00
{Baltimore Colts
Dallas Cowboys
6 1972 (VI) 250.00 400.00
{Dallas Cowboys
Miami Dolphins
7 1973 (VII) 200.00 350.00
{Miami Dolphins
Washington Redskins
8 1974 (VIII) 200.00 350.00
{Miami Dolphins
Minnesota Vikings
9 1975 (IX) 175.00 300.00
Pittsburgh Steelers
Minnesota Vikings
10 1976 (X) 175.00 300.00
Pittsburgh Steelers
Dallas Cowboys
11 1977 (XI) 150.00 250.00
{Oakland Raiders
Minnesota Vikings
12 1978 (XII) 150.00 250.00
{Denver Broncos
Dallas Cowboys
13 1979 (XIII) 125.00 225.00
Pittsburgh Steelers
Dallas Cowboys
14 1980 (XIV) 125.00 225.00
Pittsburgh Steelers
Los Angeles Rams
15 1981 (XV) 125.00 200.00
Philadelphia Eagles
Oakland Raiders
16 1982 (XVI) 175.00 300.00
{San Francisco 49ers
Cincinnati Bengals
17 1983 (XVII) 125.00 250.00
Washington Redskins
Miami Dolphins
18 1984 (XVIII) 75.00 150.00
{Los Angeles Raiders
Washington Redskins
19 1985 (XIX) 62.50 125.00
San Francisco 49ers
Miami Dolphins
20 1986 (XX) 62.50 125.00
{Chicago Bears
New England Patriots
21 1987 (XXI) 62.50 125.00
{New York Giants
Denver Broncos
22 1988 (XXII) 50.00 100.00
Washington Redskins
Denver Broncos
23 1989 (XXIII) 50.00 100.00
{San Francisco 49ers
Cincinnati Bengals
24 1990 (XXIV) 50.00 100.00
San Francisco 49ers
Denver Broncos
25 1991 (XXV) 50.00 100.00
New York Giants
Buffalo Bills
26 1992 (XXVI) 62.50 125.00
{Washington Redskins
Buffalo Bills
27 1993 (XXVII) 62.50 125.00
{Buffalo Bills
Dallas Cowboys
28 1994 (XXVIII) 62.50 125.00
{Buffalo Bills
Dallas Cowboys
29 1995 (XXIX) 62.50 125.00
{San Francisco 49ers
San Diego Chargers
30 1996 (XXX) 75.00 150.00
Pittsburgh Steelers
Dallas Cowboys
31 1997 (XXXI) 62.50 125.00
Green Bay Packers
New England Patriots
32 1998 (XXXII) 62.50 125.00
Denver Broncos
Green Bay Packers
33 1999 (XXXIII) 62.50 125.00
Denver Broncos
Atlanta Falcons
34 2000 (XXXIV) 62.50 125.00
St. Louis Rams
Tennessee Titans
35 2001 (XXXV) 62.50 125.00
Baltimore Ravens
New York Giants
36 2002 (XXXVI) 50.00 100.00
New England Patriots
St.Louis Rams
37 2003 (XXXVII)/5225 25.00 50.00
Tampa Bay Buccaneers
Oakland Raiders
38 2004 (XXXVIII)/5000 50.00 100.00
Carolina Panthers
New England Patriots

1967-13 Super Bowl Programs

The program for Super Bowl V is sold at a premium due to a limited number being available on game day. Reportedly, a semi-truck carrying a quantity of programs crashed and overturned in route to the stadium. These programs were later destroyed. Beginning with Super Bowl X, game programs were available through the mail, thus the drop-off in values.

1 1967 (I) 300.00 500.00
{Green Bay Packers
Kansas City Chiefs
2 1968 (II) 300.00 500.00
{Green Bay Packers
Oakland Raiders
3 1969 (III) 250.00 400.00
{New York Jets
Baltimore Colts
4 1970 (IV) 150.00 250.00
{Kansas City Chiefs
Minnesota Vikings (game)
4A 1970 (IV) 50.00 100.00
Kansas City Chiefs
Minnesota Vikings (newsstand)
5 1971 (V) 200.00 350.00
{Baltimore Colts
Dallas Cowboys
6 1972 (VI) 125.00 200.00
{Dallas Cowboys
Miami Dolphins
7 1973 (VII) 100.00 175.00
{Miami Dolphins
Washington Redskins
8 1974 (VIII) 100.00 175.00
{Miami Dolphins
Minnesota Vikings
9 1975 (IX) 75.00 125.00
Pittsburgh Steelers
Minnesota Vikings
10 1976 (X) 75.00 125.00
Pittsburgh Steelers
Dallas Cowboys
11 1977 (XI) 40.00 75.00
Oakland Raiders
Minnesota Vikings
12 1978 (XII) 40.00 75.00
Denver Broncos
Dallas Cowboys
13 1979 (XIII) 35.00 60.00
Pittsburgh Steelers
Dallas Cowboys
14 1980 (XIV) 30.00 50.00
Pittsburgh Steelers
Los Angeles Rams
15 1981 (XV) 17.50 35.00
Philadelphia Eagles
Oakland Raiders
16 1982 (XVI) 17.50 35.00
San Francisco 49ers
Cincinnati Bengals
17 1983 (XVII) 15.00 30.00
Washington Redskins
Miami Dolphins
18 1984 (XVIII) 15.00 30.00
Oakland Raiders
Washington Redskins
19 1985 (XIX) 15.00 30.00
San Francisco 49ers
Miami Dolphins
20 1986 (XX) 15.00 30.00
Chicago Bears
New England Patriots
21 1987 (XXI) 12.50 25.00
New York Giants
Denver Broncos
22 1988 (XXII) 12.50 25.00
Washington Redskins
Denver Broncos
23 1989 (XXIII) 12.50 25.00
San Francisco 49ers
Denver Bengals
24 1990 (XXIV) 10.00 20.00
San Francisco 49ers
Denver Broncos
25 1991 (XXV) 10.00 20.00
New York Giants
Buffalo Bills
26 1992 (XXVI) 10.00 20.00
Washington Redskins
Buffalo Bills
27 1993 (XXVII) 10.00 20.00
Buffalo Bills
Dallas Cowboys
28 1994 (XXVIII) 10.00 20.00
Buffalo Bills
Dallas Cowboys
29 1995 (XXIX) 10.00 20.00
San Francisco 49ers
San Diego Chargers
30 1996 (XXX) 10.00 20.00
Pittsburgh Steelers
Dallas Cowboys
31 1997 (XXXI) 10.00 20.00
Green Bay Packers
New England Patriots
32 1998 (XXXII) 10.00 20.00
Denver Broncos
Green Bay Packers
33 1999 (XXXIII) 10.00 20.00
Denver Broncos
Atlanta Falcons
34 2000 (XXXIV) 10.00 20.00
St Louis Rams
Tennessee Titans
35 2001 (XXXV) 10.00 20.00
Baltimore Ravens
New York Giants
36 2002 (XXXVI) 10.00 20.00
New England Patriots
St.Louis Rams
37 2003 (XXXVII) 10.00 20.00
Tampa Bay Buccaneers
Oakland Raiders
38A 2004 (XXXVIII) 10.00 20.00
Carolina Panthers
New England Patriots
(Holographic Cover Stadium Version)
38B 2004 (XXXVIII) 6.00 15.00
Carolina Panthers
New England Patriots
(Mass Market Version)
39 2005 (XXXIX) 10.00 20.00
New England Patriots
Philadelphia Eagles
40 2006 (XL) 10.00 20.00
Pittsburgh Steelers
Seattle Seahawks
41 2007 (XLI) 10.00 20.00
Indianapolis Colts
Chicago Bears
42 2008 (XLII) 10.00 20.00
New York Giants
New England Patriots
43 2009 (XLIII) 10.00 20.00
Pittsburgh Steelers
Arizona Cardinals
44 2010 (XLIV) 10.00 20.00
New Orleans Saints
Indianapolis Colts
45 2011 (XLV) 10.00 20.00
Green Bay Packers
Pittsburgh Steelers
46 2012 (XLVI) 10.00 20.00
New York Giants
New England Patriots
47 2013 (XLVII) 10.00 20.00
Baltimore Ravens
San Francisco 49ers

1967-13 Super Bowl Full Tickets

Cataloged below are all known color variations for full Super Bowl tickets. The variations in color generally represent the different sections of the stadium in which the game was played and usually can be found on the "stub" portion of the ticket or in the background color of the ticket. Many of these variations are quite scarce with just a few known high quality examples in existence. Those are not priced below due to their scarcity but some can command prices well over $1000, with a few of the scarcest known high grade examples reported to have sold for more than $10,000. Note that full tickets for some recent Super Bowls are much easier to obtain since the NFL began scanning full tickets at some games instead of tearing them. Consequently, full tickets for the early games are quite scarce since nearly all were torn at the stadium. Be aware that souvenir tickets, often called Z-Tickets (because of the section #Z printed on many of them), were issued for some games and, while still collectible in their own right, are not priced below. Prices below are for full game tickets, not stubs, and represent the market for tickets in Excellent (EX) condition for vintage (generally 1960s and 1970s games) and Near-Mint for modern era (1980s-present) games.

1A 1967 (I) Blue
Green Bay Packers
Kansas City Chiefs
1B 1967 (I) Gold
Green Bay Packers
Kansas City Chiefs
1C 1967 (I) White
Green Bay Packers
Kansas City Chiefs
2A 1968 (II) Blue
Green Bay Packers
Oakland Raiders
2B 1968 (II) White
Green Bay Packers
Oakland Raiders
2C 1968 (II) Yellow
Green Bay Packers
Oakland Raiders
3A 1969 (III) Blue
New York Jets
Baltimore Colts
3B 1969 (III) White
New York Jets
Baltimore Colts
3C 1969 (III) Yellow
New York Jets
Baltimore Colts
4A 1970 (IV) Black
Kansas City Chiefs
Minnesota Vikings
4B 1970 (IV) Blue
Kansas City Chiefs
Minnesota Vikings
4C 1970 (IV) Red
Kansas City Chiefs
Minnesota Vikings
4D 1970 (IV) White
Kansas City Chiefs
Minnesota Vikings
5A 1971 (V) Blue
Baltimore Colts
Dallas Cowboys
5B 1971 (V) Orange
Baltimore Colts
Dallas Cowboys
5C 1971 (V) Red
Baltimore Colts
Dallas Cowboys
5D 1971 (V) White
Baltimore Colts
Dallas Cowboys
6A 1972 (VI) Black
Dallas Cowboys
Miami Dolphins
6B 1972 (VI) Blue
Dallas Cowboys
Miami Dolphins
6C 1972 (VI) Red
Dallas Cowboys
Miami Dolphins
6D 1972 (VI) White
Dallas Cowboys
Miami Dolphins
7A 1973 (VII) White
Miami Dolphins
Washington Redskins
8A 1974 (VIII) White 150.00 225.00
Miami Dolphins
Minnesota Vikings
9A 1975 (IX) Blue
Pittsburgh Steelers
Minnesota Vikings
9B 1975 (IX) Gray
Pittsburgh Steelers
Minnesota Vikings
9C 1975 (IX) Red
Pittsburgh Steelers
Minnesota Vikings
9D 1975 (IX) White 250.00 400.00
Pittsburgh Steelers
Minnesota Vikings
10A 1976 (X) White 350.00 600.00
Pittsburgh Steelers
Dallas Cowboys
11A 1977 (XI) White 300.00 500.00
Oakland Raiders
Minnesota Vikings
12A 1978 (XII) White
Denver Broncos
Dallas Cowboys
12B 1978 (XII) Yellow
Denver Broncos
Dallas Cowboys
13A 1979 (XIII) Silver 250.00 450.00
Pittsburgh Steelers
Dallas Cowboys
14A 1980 (XIV) Green 200.00 350.00
Pittsburgh Steelers
Los Angeles Rams
15A 1981 (XV) Gold 200.00 350.00
Philadelphia Eagles
Oakland Raiders
15B 1981 (XV) White
Philadelphia Eagles
Oakland Raiders
16A 1982 (XVI) Silver 600.00 1,000.00
San Francisco 49ers
Cincinnati Bengals
17A 1983 (XVII) Blue 250.00 400.00
Washington Redskins
Miami Dolphins
18A 1984 (XVIII) Yellow 250.00 400.00
Oakland Raiders
Washington Redskins
19A 1985 (XIX) Silver 350.00 600.00
San Francisco 49ers
Miami Dolphins
20A 1986 (XX) Silver 500.00 800.00
Chicago Bears
New England Patriots
20B 1986 (XX) White
Chicago Bears
New England Patriots
21A 1987 (XXI) Blue 250.00 500.00
New York Giants
Denver Broncos
22A 1988 (XXII) Purple 150.00 300.00
Washington Redskins
Denver Broncos
23A 1989 (XXIII) Coral 150.00 300.00
San Francisco 49ers
Denver Bengals
24A 1990 (XXIV) Purple 150.00 250.00
San Francisco 49ers
Denver Broncos
24B 1990 (XXIV) Teal 500.00 800.00
San Francisco 49ers
Denver Broncos
25A 1991 (XXV) Blue 125.00 200.00
New York Giants
Buffalo Bills
26A 1992 (XXVI) Light Purple 125.00 250.00
Washington Redskins
Buffalo Bills
27A 1993 (XXVII) Blue 125.00 200.00
Buffalo Bills
Dallas Cowboys
27B 1993 (XXVII) Gold 125.00 200.00
Buffalo Bills
Dallas Cowboys
28A 1994 (XXVIII) Orange 125.00 250.00
Buffalo Bills
Dallas Cowboys
28B 1994 (XXVIII) Purple 150.00 300.00
Buffalo Bills
Dallas Cowboys
29A 1995 (XXIX) Blue 125.00 250.00
San Francisco 49ers
San Diego Chargers
29B 1995 (XXIX) Tan 125.00 250.00
San Francisco 49ers
San Diego Chargers
30A 1996 (XXX) Green 125.00 225.00
Pittsburgh Steelers
Dallas Cowboys
30B 1996 (XXX) Purple 125.00 225.00
Pittsburgh Steelers
Dallas Cowboys
30C 1996 (XXX) Tan 125.00 225.00
Pittsburgh Steelers
Dallas Cowboys
31A 1997 (XXXI) Blue
Green Bay Packers
New England Patriots
31B 1997 (XXXI) Gold 125.00 250.00
Green Bay Packers
New England Patriots
31C 1997 (XXXI) Green 125.00 250.00
Green Bay Packers
New England Patriots
31D 1997 (XXXI) Purple 125.00 250.00
Green Bay Packers
New England Patriots
32A 1998 (XXXII) Blue 125.00 225.00
Denver Broncos
Green Bay Packers
32B 1998 (XXXII) Copper 125.00 250.00
Denver Broncos
Green Bay Packers
32C 1998 (XXXII) Gold 100.00 200.00
Denver Broncos
Green Bay Packers
32D 1998 (XXXII) Green 100.00 200.00
Denver Broncos
Green Bay Packers
32E 1998 (XXXII) Purple 100.00 200.00
Denver Broncos
Green Bay Packers
32F 1998 (XXXII) Silver 125.00 250.00
Denver Broncos
Green Bay Packers
33A 1999 (XXXIII) Blue 125.00 250.00
Denver Broncos
Atlanta Falcons
33B 1999 (XXXIII) Gold 100.00 200.00
Denver Broncos
Atlanta Falcons
33C 1999 (XXXIII) Green 100.00 200.00
Denver Broncos
Atlanta Falcons
34A 2000 (XXXIV) Blue
St Louis Rams
Tennessee Titans
34B 2000 (XXXIV) Gold 100.00 200.00
St Louis Rams
Tennessee Titans
34C 2000 (XXXIV) Purple 100.00 200.00
St Louis Rams
Tennessee Titans
34D 2000 (XXXIV) Silver 125.00 250.00
St Louis Rams
Tennessee Titans
34E 2000 (XXXIV) Tan
St Louis Rams
Tennessee Titans
35A 2001 (XXXV) Blue 150.00 300.00
Baltimore Ravens
New York Giants
35B 2001 (XXXV) Gold 100.00 200.00
Baltimore Ravens
New York Giants
35C 2001 (XXXV) Green 125.00 250.00
Baltimore Ravens
New York Giants
35D 2001 (XXXV) Orange 100.00 200.00
Baltimore Ravens
New York Giants
35E 2001 (XXXV) Purple 100.00 200.00
Baltimore Ravens
New York Giants
35F 2001 (XXXV) Yellow 100.00 200.00
Baltimore Ravens
New York Giants
36A 2002 (XXXVI) Blue 75.00 125.00
New England Patriots
St.Louis Rams
36B 2002 (XXXVI) Gold 75.00 125.00
New England Patriots
St.Louis Rams
36C 2002 (XXXVI) Green 75.00 125.00
New England Patriots
St.Louis Rams
36D 2002 (XXXVI) Light Tan 75.00 125.00
New England Patriots
St.Louis Rams
36E 2002 (XXXVI) Silver 75.00 125.00
New England Patriots
St.Louis Rams
37A 2003 (XXXVII) Blue 75.00 150.00
Tampa Bay Buccaneers
Oakland Raiders
37B 2003 (XXXVII) Green 75.00 150.00
Tampa Bay Buccaneers
Oakland Raiders
37C 2003 (XXXVII) Light Purple 75.00 150.00
Tampa Bay Buccaneers
Oakland Raiders
37D 2003 (XXXVII) Yellow 75.00 150.00
Tampa Bay Buccaneers
Oakland Raiders
38A 2004 (XXXVIII) Blue 75.00 150.00
Carolina Panthers
New England Patriots
38B 2004 (XXXVIII) Gold 75.00 150.00
Carolina Panthers
New England Patriots
38C 2004 (XXXVIII) Green 75.00 150.00
Carolina Panthers
New England Patriots
38D 2004 (XXXVIII) Purple 75.00 150.00
Carolina Panthers
New England Patriots
38E 2004 (XXXVIII) Yellow
Carolina Panthers
New England Patriots
39A 2005 (XXXIX) Blue
New England Patriots
Philadelphia Eagles
39B 2005 (XXXIX) Brown 100.00 200.00
New England Patriots
Philadelphia Eagles
39C 2005 (XXXIX) Green 100.00 200.00
New England Patriots
Philadelphia Eagles
39D 2005 (XXXIX) Orange 75.00 150.00
New England Patriots
Philadelphia Eagles
39E 2005 (XXXIX) Purple 100.00 200.00
New England Patriots
Philadelphia Eagles
39F 2005 (XXXIX) Yellow 75.00 150.00
New England Patriots
Philadelphia Eagles
40A 2006 (XL) Blue 75.00 150.00
Pittsburgh Steelers
Seattle Seahawks
40B 2006 (XL) Green 75.00 150.00
Pittsburgh Steelers
Seattle Seahawks
40C 2006 (XL) Orange 75.00 150.00
Pittsburgh Steelers
Seattle Seahawks
40D 2006 (XL) Red 75.00 150.00
Pittsburgh Steelers
Seattle Seahawks
40E 2006 (XL) Silver 75.00 150.00
Pittsburgh Steelers
Seattle Seahawks
41A 2007 (XLI) Blue 125.00 250.00
Indianapolis Colts
Chicago Bears
41B 2007 (XLI) Orange 75.00 125.00
Indianapolis Colts
Chicago Bears
41C 2007 (XLI) Silver 75.00 125.00
Indianapolis Colts
Chicago Bears
41D 2007 (XLI) Teal 200.00 400.00
Indianapolis Colts
Chicago Bears
42A 2008 (XLII) Blue 100.00 200.00
New York Giants
New England Patriots
42B 2008 (XLII) Gold 100.00 200.00
New York Giants
New England Patriots
42C 2008 (XLII) Green
New York Giants
New England Patriots
42D 2008 (XLII) Red
New York Giants
New England Patriots
42E 2008 (XLII) Silver 100.00 200.00
New York Giants
New England Patriots
42F 2008 (XLII) Teal 100.00 200.00
New York Giants
New England Patriots
43A 2009 (XLIII) Blue 75.00 150.00
Pittsburgh Steelers
Arizona Cardinals
43B 2009 (XLIII) Gold 75.00 150.00
Pittsburgh Steelers
Arizona Cardinals
43C 2009 (XLIII) Green 75.00 150.00
Pittsburgh Steelers
Arizona Cardinals
43D 2009 (XLIII) Red 75.00 150.00
Pittsburgh Steelers
Arizona Cardinals
43E 2009 (XLIII) Silver 100.00 200.00
Pittsburgh Steelers
Arizona Cardinals
44A 2010 (XLIV) Blue 75.00 150.00
New Orleans Saints
Indianapolis Colts
44B 2010 (XLIV) Gold 75.00 150.00
New Orleans Saints
Indianapolis Colts
44C 2010 (XLIV) Green 250.00 500.00
New Orleans Saints
Indianapolis Colts
44D 2010 (XLIV) Orange 75.00 150.00
New Orleans Saints
Indianapolis Colts
44E 2010 (XLIV) Red 75.00 150.00
New Orleans Saints
Indianapolis Colts
45A 2011 (XLV) Blue 75.00 125.00
Green Bay Packers
Pittsburgh Steelers
45B 2011 (XLV) Gold 75.00 125.00
Green Bay Packers
Pittsburgh Steelers
45C 2011 (XLV) Green 75.00 125.00
Green Bay Packers
Pittsburgh Steelers
45D 2011 (XLV) Red 75.00 125.00
Green Bay Packers
Pittsburgh Steelers
46A 2012 (XLVI) Blue 75.00 150.00
New York Giants
New England Patriots
46B 2012 (XLVI) Gold 250.00 500.00
New York Giants
New England Patriots
46C 2012 (XLVI) Red 75.00 125.00
New York Giants
New England Patriots
47A 2013 (XLVII) Purple 75.00 150.00
Baltimore Ravens
San Francisco 49ers
47B 2013 (XLVII) Teal 60.00 120.00
Baltimore Ravens
San Francisco 49ers

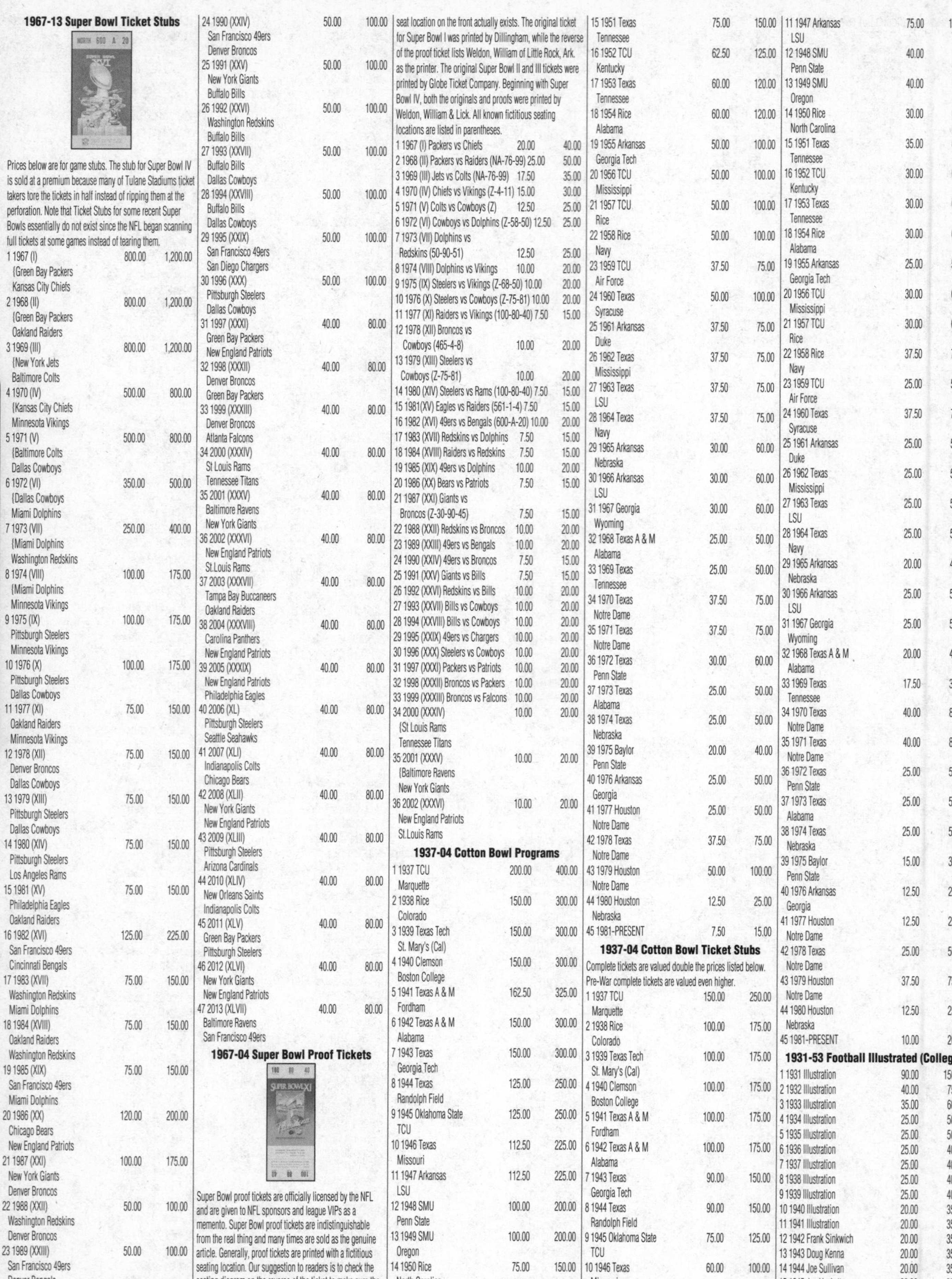

1967-13 Super Bowl Ticket Stubs

Prices below are for game stubs. The stub for Super Bowl IV is sold at a premium because many of Tulane Stadiums ticket takers tore the tickets in half instead of ripping them at the perforation. Note that Ticket Stubs for some recent Super Bowls essentially do not exist since the NFL began scanning full tickets at some games instead of tearing them.

Item	Low	High
1 1967 (I) {Green Bay Packers Kansas City Chiefs	800.00	1,200.00
2 1968 (II) {Green Bay Packers Oakland Raiders	800.00	1,200.00
3 1969 (III) {New York Jets Baltimore Colts	800.00	1,200.00
4 1970 (IV) {Kansas City Chiefs Minnesota Vikings	500.00	800.00
5 1971 (V) {Baltimore Colts Dallas Cowboys	500.00	800.00
6 1972 (VI) {Dallas Cowboys Miami Dolphins	350.00	500.00
7 1973 (VII) {Miami Dolphins Washington Redskins	250.00	400.00
8 1974 (VIII) {Miami Dolphins Minnesota Vikings	100.00	175.00
9 1975 (IX) Pittsburgh Steelers Minnesota Vikings	100.00	175.00
10 1976 (X) Pittsburgh Steelers Dallas Cowboys	100.00	175.00
11 1977 (XI) Oakland Raiders Minnesota Vikings	75.00	150.00
12 1978 (XII) Denver Broncos Dallas Cowboys	75.00	150.00
13 1979 (XIII) Pittsburgh Steelers Dallas Cowboys	75.00	150.00
14 1980 (XIV) Pittsburgh Steelers Los Angeles Rams	75.00	150.00
15 1981 (XV) Philadelphia Eagles Oakland Raiders	75.00	150.00
16 1982 (XVI) San Francisco 49ers Cincinnati Bengals	125.00	225.00
17 1983 (XVII) Washington Redskins Miami Dolphins	75.00	150.00
18 1984 (XVIII) Oakland Raiders Washington Redskins	75.00	150.00
19 1985 (XIX) San Francisco 49ers Miami Dolphins	75.00	150.00
20 1986 (XX) Chicago Bears New England Patriots	120.00	200.00
21 1987 (XXI) New York Giants Denver Broncos	100.00	175.00
22 1988 (XXII) Washington Redskins Denver Broncos	50.00	100.00
23 1989 (XXIII) San Francisco 49ers Denver Bengals	50.00	100.00
24 1990 (XXIV) San Francisco 49ers Denver Broncos	50.00	100.00
25 1991 (XXV) New York Giants Buffalo Bills	50.00	100.00
26 1992 (XXVI) Washington Redskins Buffalo Bills	50.00	100.00
27 1993 (XXVII) Buffalo Bills Dallas Cowboys	50.00	100.00
28 1994 (XXVIII) Buffalo Bills Dallas Cowboys	50.00	100.00
29 1995 (XXIX) San Francisco 49ers San Diego Chargers	50.00	100.00
30 1996 (XXX) Pittsburgh Steelers Dallas Cowboys	50.00	100.00
31 1997 (XXXI) Green Bay Packers New England Patriots	40.00	80.00
32 1998 (XXXII) Denver Broncos Green Bay Packers	40.00	80.00
33 1999 (XXXIII) Denver Broncos Atlanta Falcons	40.00	80.00
34 2000 (XXXIV) St Louis Rams Tennessee Titans	40.00	80.00
35 2001 (XXXV) Baltimore Ravens New York Giants	40.00	80.00
36 2002 (XXXVI) New England Patriots St.Louis Rams	40.00	80.00
37 2003 (XXXVII) Tampa Bay Buccaneers Oakland Raiders	40.00	80.00
38 2004 (XXXVIII) Carolina Panthers New England Patriots	40.00	80.00
39 2005 (XXXIX) New England Patriots Philadelphia Eagles	40.00	80.00
40 2006 (XL) Pittsburgh Steelers Seattle Seahawks	40.00	80.00
41 2007 (XLI) Indianapolis Colts Chicago Bears	40.00	80.00
42 2008 (XLII) New York Giants New England Patriots	40.00	80.00
43 2009 (XLIII) Pittsburgh Steelers Arizona Cardinals	40.00	80.00
44 2010 (XLIV) New Orleans Saints Indianapolis Colts	40.00	80.00
45 2011 (XLV) Green Bay Packers Pittsburgh Steelers	40.00	80.00
46 2012 (XLVI) New York Giants New England Patriots	40.00	80.00
47 2013 (XLVII) Baltimore Ravens San Francisco 49ers	40.00	80.00

1967-04 Super Bowl Proof Tickets

Super Bowl proof tickets are officially licensed by the NFL and are given to NFL sponsors and league VIPs as a memento. Super Bowl proof tickets are indistinguishable from the real thing and many times are sold as the genuine article. Generally, proof tickets are printed with a fictitious seating location. Our suggestion to readers is to check the seating diagram on the reverse of the ticket to make sure the seat location on the front actually exists. The original ticket for Super Bowl I was printed by Dillingham, while the reverse of the proof ticket lists Weldon, William of Little Rock, Ark. as the printer. The original Super Bowl II and III tickets were printed by Globe Ticket Company. Beginning with Super Bowl IV, both the originals and proofs were printed by Weldon, William & Lick. All known fictitious seating locations are listed in parentheses.

Item	Low	High
1 1967 (I) Packers vs Chiefs	20.00	40.00
2 1968 (II) Packers vs Raiders (NA-76-99)	25.00	50.00
3 1969 (III) Jets vs Colts (NA-76-99)	17.50	35.00
4 1970 (IV) Chiefs vs Vikings (Z-4-11)	15.00	30.00
5 1971 (V) Colts vs Cowboys (Z)	12.50	25.00
6 1972 (VI) Cowboys vs Dolphins (Z-58-50)	12.50	25.00
7 1973 (VII) Dolphins vs Redskins (50-90-51)	12.50	25.00
8 1974 (VIII) Dolphins vs Vikings	10.00	20.00
9 1975 (IX) Steelers vs Vikings (Z-68-50)	10.00	20.00
10 1976 (X) Steelers vs Cowboys (Z-75-81)	10.00	20.00
11 1977 (XI) Raiders vs Vikings (100-80-40)	7.50	15.00
12 1978 (XII) Broncos vs Cowboys (465-4-8)	10.00	20.00
13 1979 (XIII) Steelers vs Cowboys (Z-75-81)	10.00	20.00
14 1980 (XIV) Steelers vs Rams (100-80-40)	7.50	15.00
15 1981(XV) Eagles vs Raiders (561-1-4)	7.50	15.00
16 1982 (XVI) 49ers vs Bengals (600-A-20)	10.00	20.00
17 1983 (XVII) Redskins vs Dolphins	7.50	15.00
18 1984 (XVIII) Raiders vs Redskins	7.50	15.00
19 1985 (XIX) 49ers vs Dolphins	10.00	20.00
20 1986 (XX) Bears vs Patriots	7.50	15.00
21 1987 (XXI) Giants vs Broncos (Z-30-90-45)	7.50	15.00
22 1988 (XXII) Redskins vs Broncos	10.00	20.00
23 1989 (XXIII) 49ers vs Bengals	10.00	20.00
24 1990 (XXIV) 49ers vs Broncos	7.50	15.00
25 1991 (XXV) Giants vs Bills	7.50	15.00
26 1992 (XXVI) Redskins vs Bills	10.00	20.00
27 1993 (XXVII) Bills vs Cowboys	10.00	20.00
28 1994 (XXVIII) Bills vs Cowboys	10.00	20.00
29 1995 (XXIX) 49ers vs Chargers	10.00	20.00
30 1996 (XXX) Steelers vs Cowboys	10.00	20.00
31 1997 (XXXI) Packers vs Patriots	10.00	20.00
32 1998 (XXXII) Broncos vs Packers	10.00	20.00
33 1999 (XXXIII) Broncos vs Falcons	10.00	20.00
34 2000 (XXXIV) {St Louis Rams Tennessee Titans	10.00	20.00
35 2001 (XXXV) {Baltimore Ravens New York Giants	10.00	20.00
36 2002 (XXXVI) New England Patriots St.Louis Rams	10.00	20.00

1937-04 Cotton Bowl Programs

Item	Low	High
1 1937 TCU Marquette	200.00	400.00
2 1938 Rice Colorado	150.00	300.00
3 1939 Texas Tech St. Mary's (Cal)	150.00	300.00
4 1940 Clemson Boston College	150.00	300.00
5 1941 Texas A & M Fordham	162.50	325.00
6 1942 Texas A & M Alabama	150.00	300.00
7 1943 Texas Georgia Tech	150.00	300.00
8 1944 Texas Randolph Field	125.00	250.00
9 1945 Oklahoma State TCU	125.00	250.00
10 1946 Texas Missouri	112.50	225.00
11 1947 Arkansas LSU	112.50	225.00
12 1948 SMU Penn State	100.00	200.00
13 1949 SMU Oregon	100.00	200.00
14 1950 Rice North Carolina	75.00	150.00
15 1951 Texas Tennessee	75.00	150.00
16 1952 TCU Kentucky	62.50	125.00
17 1953 Texas Tennessee	60.00	120.00
18 1954 Rice Alabama	60.00	120.00
19 1955 Arkansas Georgia Tech	50.00	100.00
20 1956 TCU Mississippi	50.00	100.00
21 1957 TCU Rice	50.00	100.00
22 1958 Rice Navy	50.00	100.00
23 1959 TCU Air Force	37.50	75.00
24 1960 Texas Syracuse	50.00	100.00
25 1961 Arkansas Duke	37.50	75.00
26 1962 Texas Mississippi	37.50	75.00
27 1963 Texas LSU	37.50	75.00
28 1964 Texas Navy	37.50	75.00
29 1965 Arkansas Nebraska	30.00	60.00
30 1966 Arkansas LSU	30.00	60.00
31 1967 Georgia Wyoming	30.00	60.00
32 1968 Texas A & M Alabama	25.00	50.00
33 1969 Texas Tennessee	25.00	50.00
34 1970 Texas Notre Dame	37.50	75.00
35 1971 Texas Notre Dame	37.50	75.00
36 1972 Texas Penn State	30.00	60.00
37 1973 Texas Alabama	25.00	50.00
38 1974 Texas Nebraska	25.00	50.00
39 1975 Baylor Penn State	20.00	40.00
40 1976 Arkansas Georgia	25.00	50.00
41 1977 Houston Notre Dame	25.00	50.00
42 1978 Texas Notre Dame	37.50	75.00
43 1979 Houston Notre Dame	50.00	100.00
44 1980 Houston Nebraska	12.50	25.00
45 1981-PRESENT	7.50	15.00

1937-04 Cotton Bowl Ticket Stubs

Complete tickets are valued double the prices listed below. Pre-War complete tickets are valued even higher.

Item	Low	High
1 1937 TCU Marquette	150.00	250.00
2 1938 Rice Colorado	100.00	175.00
3 1939 Texas Tech St. Mary's (Cal)	100.00	175.00
4 1940 Clemson Boston College	100.00	175.00
5 1941 Texas A & M Fordham	100.00	175.00
6 1942 Texas A & M Alabama	100.00	175.00
7 1943 Texas Georgia Tech	90.00	150.00
8 1944 Texas Randolph Field	90.00	150.00
9 1945 Oklahoma State TCU	75.00	125.00
10 1946 Texas Missouri	60.00	100.00
11 1947 Arkansas LSU	75.00	125.00
12 1948 SMU Penn State	40.00	75.00
13 1949 SMU Oregon	40.00	75.00
14 1950 Rice North Carolina	30.00	60.00
15 1951 Texas Tennessee	35.00	60.00
16 1952 TCU Kentucky	30.00	60.00
17 1953 Texas Tennessee	30.00	60.00
18 1954 Rice Alabama	30.00	60.00
19 1955 Arkansas Georgia Tech	25.00	50.00
20 1956 TCU Mississippi	30.00	60.00
21 1957 TCU Rice	30.00	60.00
22 1958 Rice Navy	37.50	75.00
23 1959 TCU Air Force	25.00	50.00
24 1960 Texas Syracuse	37.50	75.00
25 1961 Arkansas Duke	25.00	50.00
26 1962 Texas Mississippi	25.00	50.00
27 1963 Texas LSU	25.00	50.00
28 1964 Texas Navy	25.00	50.00
29 1965 Arkansas Nebraska	20.00	40.00
30 1966 Arkansas LSU	25.00	50.00
31 1967 Georgia Wyoming	25.00	50.00
32 1968 Texas A & M Alabama	20.00	40.00
33 1969 Texas Tennessee	17.50	35.00
34 1970 Texas Notre Dame	40.00	80.00
35 1971 Texas Notre Dame	40.00	80.00
36 1972 Texas Penn State	25.00	50.00
37 1973 Texas Alabama	25.00	50.00
38 1974 Texas Nebraska	25.00	50.00
39 1975 Baylor Penn State	15.00	30.00
40 1976 Arkansas Georgia	12.50	25.00
41 1977 Houston Notre Dame	12.50	25.00
42 1978 Texas Notre Dame	25.00	50.00
43 1979 Houston Notre Dame	37.50	75.00
44 1980 Houston Nebraska	12.50	25.00
45 1981-PRESENT	10.00	20.00

1931-53 Football Illustrated (College)

Item	Low	High
1 1931 Illustration	90.00	150.00
2 1932 Illustration	40.00	75.00
3 1933 Illustration	35.00	60.00
4 1934 Illustration	25.00	50.00
5 1935 Illustration	25.00	50.00
6 1936 Illustration	25.00	40.00
7 1937 Illustration	25.00	40.00
8 1938 Illustration	25.00	40.00
9 1939 Illustration	25.00	40.00
10 1940 Illustration	20.00	35.00
11 1941 Illustration	20.00	35.00
12 1942 Frank Sinkwich	20.00	35.00
13 1943 Doug Kenna	20.00	35.00
14 1944 Joe Sullivan	20.00	35.00
15 1945 Joe Hackett	20.00	35.00

16 1946 Herman Wedemeyer 20.00 35.00
17 1947 Bobby Layne 30.00 50.00
18 1948 Chuck Bednarik 30.00 50.00
19 1949 Jim Owens 20.00 40.00
20 1950 Billy Cox 20.00 35.00
21 1951 Les Richter 20.00 35.00
22 1952 Bob Kennedy 20.00 35.00
23 1953 Illustration 18.00 30.00

1935-04 Orange Bowl Programs

1 1935 Bucknell 250.00 500.00
Miami
2 1936 Mississippi 150.00 300.00
Catholic U.
3 1937 Mississippi State 137.50 275.00
Duquesne
4 1938 Auburn 125.00 250.00
Michigan State
5 1939 Tennessee 150.00 300.00
Oklahoma
6 1940 Georgia Tech 137.50 275.00
Missouri
7 1941 Mississippi St. 125.00 250.00
Georgetwon
8 1942 Georgia 125.00 250.00
TCU
9 1943 Alabama 125.00 250.00
Boston College
10 1944 LSU 112.50 225.00
Texas A & M
11 1945 Georgia Tech 100.00 200.00
Tulsa
12 1946 Miami 100.00 200.00
Holy Cross
13 1947 Tennessee 75.00 150.00
Rice
14 1948 Georgia Tech 62.50 125.00
Kansas
15 1949 Georgia 50.00 100.00
Texas
16 1950 Kentucky 50.00 100.00
Santa Clara
17 1951 Miami 62.50 125.00
Clemson
18 1952 Georgia Tech 50.00 100.00
Baylor
19 1953 Alabama 50.00 100.00
Syracuse
20 1954 Maryland 50.00 100.00
Oklahoma
21 1955 Duke 75.00 150.00
Nebraska
22 1956 Maryland 50.00 100.00
Oklahoma
23 1957 Clemson 50.00 100.00
Colorado
24 1958 Duke 50.00 100.00
Oklahoma
25 1959 Syracuse 50.00 100.00
Oklahoma
26 1960 Gerogia 37.50 75.00
Missouri
27 1961 Navy 37.50 75.00
Missouri
28 1962 LSU 37.50 75.00
Colorado
29 1963 Alabama 30.00 60.00
Oklahoma
30 1964 Auburn 30.00 60.00
Nebraska
31 1965 Alabama 50.00 100.00
Texas
32 1966 Alabama 30.00 60.00
Nebraska
33 1967 Florida 25.00 50.00
Georgia Tech
34 1968 Tennessee 25.00 50.00
Oklahoma
35 1969 Penn State 25.00 50.00
Kansas
36 1970 Penn State 20.00 40.00
Missouri
37 1971 LSU 17.50 35.00
Nebraska
38 1972 Alabama 17.50 35.00
Nebraska
39 1973 Notre Dame 17.50 35.00
Nebraska
40 1974 LSU 17.50 35.00
Penn State
41 1975 Alabama 17.50 35.00
Notre Dame
42 1976 Oklahoma 15.00 30.00
Michigan
43 1977 Ohio State 15.00 30.00
Colorado
44 1978 Arkansas 12.50 25.00
Oklahoma
45 1979 Oklahoma 10.00 20.00
Nebraska
46 1980 Oklahoma 10.00 20.00
Florida State
47 1981-PRESENT 7.50 15.00

1935-04 Orange Bowl Ticket Stubs

1 1935 Bucknell 150.00 300.00
Miami
2 1936 Mississippi 75.00 150.00
Catholic U.
3 1937 Mississippi State 75.00 150.00
Duquesne
4 1938 Auburn 75.00 150.00
Michigan State
5 1939 Tennessee 87.50 175.00
Oklahoma
6 1940 Georgia Tech 62.50 125.00
Missouri
7 1941 Mississippi St. 50.00 100.00
Georgetwon
8 1942 Georgia 62.50 125.00
TCU
9 1943 Alabama 62.50 125.00
Boston College
10 1944 LSU 50.00 100.00
Texas A & M
11 1945 Georgia Tech 37.50 75.00
Tulsa
12 1946 Miami 37.50 75.00
Holy Cross
13 1947 Tennessee 37.50 75.00
Rice
14 1948 Georgia Tech 37.50 75.00
Kansas
15 1949 Georgia 30.00 60.00
Texas
16 1950 Kentucky 30.00 60.00
Santa Clara
17 1951 Miami 30.00 60.00
Clemson
18 1952 Georgia Tech 30.00 60.00
Baylor
19 1953 Alabama 30.00 60.00
Syracuse
20 1954 Maryland 30.00 60.00
Oklahoma
21 1955 Duke 37.50 75.00
Nebraska
22 1956 Maryland 30.00 60.00
Oklahoma
23 1957 Clemson 30.00 60.00
Colorado
24 1958 Duke 30.00 60.00
Oklahoma
25 1959 Syracuse 37.50 75.00
Oklahoma
26 1960 Gerogia 25.00 50.00
Missouri
27 1961 Navy 25.00 50.00
Missouri
28 1962 LSU 25.00 50.00
Colorado
29 1963 Alabama 25.00 50.00
Oklahoma
30 1964 Auburn 20.00 40.00
Nebraska
31 1965 Alabama 37.50 75.00
Texas
32 1966 Alabama 30.00 60.00
Nebraska
33 1967 Florida 20.00 40.00
Georgia Tech
34 1968 Tennessee 20.00 40.00
Oklahoma
35 1969 Penn State 20.00 40.00
Kansas
36 1970 Penn State 15.00 30.00
Missouri
37 1971 LSU 15.00 30.00
Nebraska
38 1972 Alabama 15.00 30.00
Nebraska
39 1973 Notre Dame 20.00 40.00
Nebraska
40 1974 LSU 17.50 35.00
Penn State
41 1975 Alabama 20.00 40.00
Notre Dame
42 1976 Oklahoma 12.50 25.00
Michigan
43 1977 Ohio State 12.50 25.00
Colorado
44 1978 Arkansas 12.50 25.00
Oklahoma
45 1979 Oklahoma 12.50 25.00
Nebraska
46 1980 Oklahoma 12.50 25.00
Florida State
47 1981-PRESENT 10.00 20.00

1902-07 Rose Bowl Programs

Pre-war bowl programs and ticket stubs are rarely found in Nr-Mt condition. These programs and ticket stubs are graded at Ex-Mt and Ex condition.

1 1902 Stanford 1,000.00 15,000.00
Michigan
2 1916 Wash. State 1,250.00 2,500.00
Brown
3 1917 Oregon 750.00 1,500.00
Penn.
4 1918 Mare Isle. 600.00 1,200.00
Camp Lewis
5 1919 Mare Isle 600.00 1,200.00
Great Lakes
6 1920 Oregon 500.00 1,000.00
Harvard
7 1921 California 600.00 1,200.00
Ohio State
8 1922 Cal. 500.00 1,000.00
Wash. & Jeff.
9 1923 USC 750.00 1,500.00
Penn State
10 1924 Washington 500.00 1,000.00
Navy
11 1925 Stan. 900.00 1,800.00
Notre Dame
12 1926 Washington 600.00 1,200.00
Alabama
13 1927 Stanford 600.00 1,000.00
Alabama
14 1928 Stanford 350.00 700.00
Pittsburgh
15 1929 Cal. 500.00 1,000.00
Georgia Tech
16 1930 USC 400.00 750.00
Pittsburgh
17 1931 Wash. St 900.00 1,400.00
Alabama
18 1932 USC 250.00 500.00
Tulane
19 1933 USC 250.00 500.00
Pittsburgh
20 1934 Stanford 300.00 600.00
Columbia
21 1935 Stanford 250.00 500.00
Alabama
22 1936 Stanford 175.00 350.00
LSU
23 1937 Wash 150.00 300.00
Pittsburgh
24 1938 California 150.00 300.00
Alabama
25 1939 USC 125.00 250.00
Duke
26 1940 USC 125.00 250.00
Tennessee
27 1941 Stanford 125.00 250.00
Nebraska
28 1942 Oregon State 400.00 800.00
Duke
29 1943 UCLA 150.00 300.00
Georgia
30 1944 USC 100.00 200.00
Washington
31 1945 USC 87.50 175.00
Tennessee
32 1946 USC 75.00 150.00
Alabama
33 1947 UCLA 75.00 150.00
Illinois
34 1948 USC 75.00 150.00
Michigan
35 1949 Cal. 62.50 125.00
Northwestern
36 1950 California 62.50 125.00
Ohio State
37 1951 California 62.50 125.00
Michigan
38 1952 Stanford 50.00 100.00
Illinois
39 1953 UCLA 50.00 100.00
Wisconsin
40 1954 UCLA 50.00 100.00
Michigan State
41 1955 USC 50.00 100.00
Ohio State
42 1956 UCLA 37.50 75.00
Michigan State
43 1957 Oregon State 30.00 60.00
Iowa
44 1958 Oregon 37.50 75.00
Ohio State
45 1959 California 30.00 60.00
Iowa
46 1960 Washington 30.00 60.00
Wisconsin
47 1961 Washington 25.00 50.00
Minnesota
48 1962 UCLA 25.00 50.00
Minnesota
49 1963 USC 37.50 75.00
Wisconsin
50 1964 Washigotn 25.00 50.00
Illinois
51 1965 Oregon State 25.00 50.00
Michigan
52 1966 UCLA 30.00 60.00
Michigan State
53 1967 USC 25.00 50.00
Purdue
54 1968 USC 37.50 75.00
Indiana
55 1969 USC 25.00 50.00
Ohio State
56 1970 USC 17.50 35.00
Michigan
57 1971 Stanford 17.50 35.00
Ohio State
58 1972 Stanford 17.50 35.00
Michigan
59 1973 USC 17.50 35.00
Ohio State
60 1974 USC 17.50 35.00
Ohio State
61 1975 USC 17.50 35.00
Ohio State
62 1976 UCLA 12.50 25.00
Ohio State
63 1977 USC 12.50 25.00
Michigan
64 1978 Washington 12.50 25.00
Michigan
65 1979 USC 10.00 20.00
Michigan
66 1980 USC 10.00 20.00
Ohio State
67 1981-PRESENT 7.50 15.00

1902-04 Rose Bowl Ticket Stubs

1 1902 Stanford 1,500.00 3,000.00
Michigan
2 1916 Wash. State 600.00 1,200.00
Brown
3 1917 Oregon 375.00 750.00
Penn.
4 1918 Mare Isle. 300.00 600.00
Camp Lewis
5 1919 Mare Isle 300.00 600.00
Great Lakes
6 1920 Oregon 250.00 500.00
Harvard
7 1921 California 300.00 600.00
Ohio State
8 1922 Cal. 250.00 500.00
Wash.&Jeff.
9 1923 USC 375.00 750.00
Penn State
10 1924 Washington 250.00 500.00
Navy
11 1925 Stan. 450.00 900.00
Notre Dame
12 1926 Washington 250.00 500.00
Alabama
13 1927 Stanford 175.00 350.00
Alabama
14 1928 Stanford 150.00 300.00
Pittsburgh
15 1929 Cal. 150.00 300.00
Georgia Tech
16 1930 USC 150.00 300.00
Pittsburgh
17 1931 Wash. St 250.00 500.00
alabama
18 1932 USC 125.00 250.00
Tulane
19 1933 USC 125.00 250.00
Pittsburgh
20 1934 Stanford 125.00 250.00
Columbia
21 1935 Stanford 100.00 200.00
Alabama
22 1936 Stanford 75.00 150.00
LSU
23 1937 Wash 50.00 100.00
Pittsburgh
24 1938 California 62.50 125.00
Alabama
25 1939 USC 62.50 125.00
Duke

26 1940 USC Tennessee	50.00	100.00
27 1941 Stanford Nebraska	200.00	400.00
28 1942 Oregon State Duke	100.00	200.00
29 1943 UCLA Georgia	37.50	75.00
30 1944 USC Washington	37.50	75.00
31 1945 USC Tennessee	37.50	75.00
32 1946 USC Alabama	37.50	75.00
33 1947 UCLA Illinois	37.50	75.00
34 1948 USC Michigan	30.00	60.00
35 1949 Cal. Northwestern	30.00	60.00
36 1950 California Ohio State	37.50	75.00
37 1951 California Michigan	37.50	75.00
38 1952 Stanford Illinois	30.00	60.00
39 1953 UCLA Wisconsin	30.00	60.00
40 1954 UCLA Michigan State	30.00	60.00
41 1955 USC Ohio State	30.00	60.00
42 1956 UCLA Michigan State	25.00	50.00
43 1957 Oregon State Iowa	20.00	40.00
44 1958 Oregon Ohio State	25.00	50.00
45 1959 California Iowa	25.00	50.00
46 1960 Washington Wisconsin	25.00	50.00
47 1961 Washington Minnesota	20.00	40.00
48 1962 UCLA Minnesota	20.00	40.00
49 1963 USC Wisconsin	25.00	50.00
50 1964 Washingtn Illinois	20.00	40.00
51 1965 Oregon State Michigan	20.00	40.00
52 1966 UCLA Michigan State	20.00	40.00
53 1967 USC Purdue	15.00	30.00
54 1968 USC Indiana	25.00	50.00
55 1969 USC Ohio State	25.00	50.00
56 1970 USC Michigan	15.00	30.00
57 1971 Stanford Ohio State	15.00	30.00
58 1972 Stanford Michigan	15.00	30.00
59 1973 USC Ohio State	15.00	30.00
60 1974 USC Ohio State	12.50	25.00
61 1975 USC Ohio State	12.50	25.00
62 1976 UCLA Ohio State	12.50	25.00
63 1977 USC Michigan	12.50	25.00
64 1978 Washington Michigan	12.50	25.00
65 1979 USC Michigan	12.50	25.00
66 1980 USC Ohio State	12.50	25.00
67 1981-PRESENT	10.00	20.00

1940-04 Street and Smith's College Football Yearbook

1 1940 Illustration	125.00	250.00
2 1941 Frankie Albert	62.50	125.00
3 1942 Allen Cameron	50.00	100.00
4 1943 Steve Juzwik	37.50	75.00
5 1944 Bob Kelly	37.50	75.00
6 1945 Bob Jenkins	37.50	75.00
7 1946 John Ferraro	30.00	60.00
8 1947 George Connor	37.50	75.00
9 1948 Jack Cloud	30.00	60.00
10 1949 Charley Justice	37.50	75.00
11 1950 Leon Heath	25.00	50.00
12 1951 Bob Smith	25.00	50.00
13 1952 Johnny Olszewski	25.00	50.00
14 1953 Ike Eisenhower	25.00	50.00
15 1954 Ralph Guglielmi	25.00	50.00
16 1955 Howard Cassidy	25.00	50.00
17 1956 Jim Swink	20.00	40.00
18 1957 Clendon Thomas	20.00	40.00
19 1958 Bob White	20.00	40.00
20 1959 Notre Dame	25.00	50.00
21 1960 Rich Mayo	20.00	40.00
22 1961 Ronnie Bull	20.00	40.00
23 1962 Jay Wilkerson	17.50	35.00
24 1963 Pete Beathard	17.50	35.00
25 1963 Paul Martha	17.50	35.00
26 1963 Tom Myers	15.00	30.00
27 1964 Dick Butkus	20.00	40.00
28 1964 Craig Morton	15.00	30.00
29 1964 Roger Staubach	20.00	40.00
30 1965 Roger Bird	12.50	25.00
31 1965 Ray Handley	12.50	25.00
32 1965 Phil Sheridan	12.50	25.00
33 1966 Bob Griese	15.00	30.00
34 1967 Ron Drake	12.50	25.00
35 1967 Terry Hanratty	12.50	25.00
36 1967 Ted Hendricks	15.00	30.00
37 1968 Chris Gilbert	12.50	25.00
38 1968 Larry Smith	12.50	25.00
39 1969 Rex Kern	12.50	25.00
40 1969 Steve Kiner	12.50	25.00
41 1970 Archie Manning	15.00	30.00
42 1970 Jim Plunkett	15.00	30.00
43 1970 Steve Worcester	10.00	20.00
44 1971 Joe Ferguson	10.00	20.00
45 1971 Sonny Sixkiller	10.00	20.00
46 1971 Pat Sullivan	10.00	20.00
47 1972 Pete Adams	10.00	20.00
48 1972 John Hufnagel	10.00	20.00
49 1972 Brad Van Pelt	10.00	20.00
50 1973 Champ Henson	7.50	15.00
51 1973 Kermit Johnson	7.50	15.00
52 1973 Wayne Wheeler	7.50	15.00
53 1974 Tom Clements	7.50	15.00
54 1974 Brad Davis	7.50	15.00
55 1974 Pat Haden	9.00	18.00
56 1975 Archie Griffin	10.00	20.00
57 1975 Richard Todd	7.50	15.00
58 1975 John Sciarra	7.50	15.00
59 1976 Ricky Bell	7.50	15.00
60 1976 Tony Dorsett	10.00	20.00
61 1976 Rob Lytle	7.50	15.00
62 1977 Guy Benjamin	7.50	15.00
63 1977 Ken McAfee	7.50	15.00
64 1977 Ben Zambiasi	7.50	15.00
65 1978 Rick Leach	7.50	15.00
66 1978 Jeff Rutledge	7.50	15.00
67 1978 Jack Thompson	7.50	15.00
68 1979 Mark Hermann	7.50	15.00
69 1979 Jeff Pyburn	6.00	12.00
70 1979 Charles White	7.50	15.00
71 1980 Rick Campbell	6.00	12.00
72 1980 Art Schlichter	6.00	12.00
73 1980 Scott Woerner	6.00	12.00
74 1981 A. Carter B. Crable	7.50	15.00
75 1981 John Elway	12.50	25.00
76 1981 D. Marino J. Morris	12.50	25.00
77 1981 H. Walker B. Bryant	10.00	20.00
78 1982 T. Eason M. Marek	7.50	15.00
79 1982 John Elway	12.50	25.00
80 1982 D. Marino C. Warner	10.00	20.00
81 1982 Herschel Walker	7.50	15.00
82 1983 Marcus Dupree	6.00	12.00
83 1983 Ken Jackson	6.00	12.00
84 1983 Johnny Robinson	6.00	12.00
85 1983 Mike Rozier	6.00	12.00
86 1984 Jack Del Rio	6.00	12.00
87 1984 Doug Flutie	7.50	15.00
88 1984 Bo Jackson	7.50	15.00
89 1984 Jack Trudeau	6.00	12.00
90 1985 Robie Bosco	5.00	10.00
91 1985 Keith Byers	5.00	10.00
92 1985 D.J. Dozier	5.00	10.00
93 1985 Jeff Wickersham	5.00	10.00
94 1986-PRESENT	5.00	10.00

1935-04 Sugar Bowl Programs

1 1935 Tulane Temple	450.00	900.00
2 1936 LSU TCU	300.00	600.00
3 1937 LSU Santa Clara	300.00	600.00
4 1938 LSU Santa Clara	250.00	500.00
5 1939 TCU Carnegie Tech.	175.00	350.00
6 1940 Texas A & M Tulane	150.00	300.00
7 1941 Tennessee Boston College	125.00	250.00
8 1942 Missouri Fordham	87.50	175.00
9 1943 Tennessee Tulsa	87.50	175.00
10 1944 Georgia Tech Tulsa	87.50	175.00
11 1945 Alabama Duke	75.00	150.00
12 1946 Okla. A & M St. Mary's	75.00	150.00
13 1947 Georgia North Carolina	75.00	150.00
14 1948 Alabama Texas	87.50	175.00
15 1949 Oklahoma North Carolina	75.00	150.00
16 1950 Oklahoma LSU	62.50	125.00
17 1951 Oklahoma Kentucky	62.50	125.00
18 1952 Tennessee Maryland	50.00	100.00
19 1953 Mississippi Georgia Tech	50.00	100.00
20 1954 Georgia Tech W. Virginia	50.00	100.00
21 1955 Mississippi Navy	37.50	100.00
22 1956 Georgia Tech Pittsburgh	37.50	100.00
23 1957 Tennessee Baylor	37.50	100.00
24 1958 Mississippi LSU	60.00	100.00
25 1959 LSU Clemson	37.50	100.00
26 1960 Mississippi LSU	60.00	100.00
27 1961 Mississippi Rice	30.00	75.00
28 1962 Alabama Arkansas	30.00	75.00
29 1963 Mississippi Arkansas	25.00	60.00
30 1964 Mississippi Alabama	30.00	60.00
31 1965 LSU Syracuse	25.00	50.00
32 1966 Florida Missouri	25.00	60.00
33 1967 Alabama Nebraska	30.00	60.00
34 1968 LSU Wyoming	20.00	40.00
35 1969 Georgia Arkansas	20.00	40.00
36 1970 Mississippi Arkansas	20.00	40.00
37 1971 Tennessee Air Force	17.50	35.00
38 1972 Auburn Oklahoma	17.50	35.00
39 1973 Oklahoma Penn State	17.50	35.00
40 1974 Alabama Nortre Dame	20.00	40.00
41 1975 Florida Nebraska	15.00	30.00
42 1976 Alabama Penn State	15.00	30.00
43 1977 Georgia Pittsburgh	15.00	30.00
44 1978 Alabama Ohio State	10.00	20.00
45 1979 Alabama Penn State	15.00	30.00
46 1980 Alabama Arkansas	10.00	20.00
47 1981-PRESENT	7.50	15.00

1935-04 Sugar Bowl Ticket Stubs

1 1935 Tulane Temple	250.00	500.00
2 1936 LSU TCU	150.00	300.00
3 1937 LSU Santa Clara	125.00	250.00
4 1938 LSU Santa Clara	75.00	150.00
5 1939 TCU Carnegie Tech.	75.00	150.00
6 1940 Texas A & M Tulane	62.50	125.00
7 1941 Tennessee Boston College	50.00	100.00
8 1942 Missouri Fordham	62.50	125.00
9 1943 Tennessee Tulsa	50.00	100.00
10 1944 Georgia Tech Tulsa	37.50	75.00
11 1945 Alabama Duke	37.50	75.00
12 1946 Okla. A & M St. Mary's	37.50	75.00
13 1947 Georgia North Carolina	37.50	75.00
14 1948 Alabama Texas	50.00	100.00
15 1949 Oklahoma North Carolina	37.50	75.00
16 1950 Oklahoma LSU	37.50	75.00
17 1951 Oklahoma Kentucky	30.00	60.00
18 1952 Tennessee Maryland	30.00	60.00
19 1953 Mississippi Georgia Tech	30.00	60.00
20 1954 Georgia Tech W. Virginia	30.00	60.00
21 1955 Mississippi Navy	25.00	50.00
22 1956 Georgia Tech Pittsburgh	30.00	60.00
23 1957 Tennessee Baylor	25.00	50.00
24 1958 Mississippi LSU	30.00	60.00
25 1959 LSU Clemson	37.50	75.00
26 1960 Mississippi LSU	25.00	50.00
27 1961 Mississippi Rice	20.00	40.00
28 1962 Alabama Arkansas	25.00	50.00
29 1963 Mississippi Arkansas	25.00	50.00
30 1964 Mississippi Alabama	25.00	50.00
31 1965 LSU Syracuse	25.00	50.00
32 1966 Florida Missouri	25.00	50.00
33 1967 Alabama Nebraska	25.00	50.00
34 1968 LSU Wyoming	20.00	40.00
35 1969 Georgia Arkansas	20.00	40.00
36 1970 Mississippi Arkansas	20.00	40.00
37 1971 Tennessee Air Force	15.00	30.00
38 1972 Auburn Oklahoma	15.00	30.00
39 1973 Oklahoma Penn State	20.00	40.00
40 1974 Alabama Notre Dame	20.00	40.00
41 1975 Florida Nebraska	15.00	30.00
42 1976 Alabama Penn State	15.00	30.00
43 1977 Georgia Pittsburgh	15.00	30.00
44 1978 Alabama Ohio State	12.50	25.00
45 1979 Alabama Penn State	12.50	25.00
46 1980 Alabama Arkansas	12.50	25.00
47 1981-PRESENT	10.00	20.00

1965 Aurora Sports Model Kits

This set of six plastic models was released in 1965 and 1966. Each model, when fully assembled, measures approx. 6" high. Prices below are for complete, unbuilt models accompanied by the box. Model kits still in factory wrapped boxes are considered to be Nr-Mt-Mt . Built-up models minus the box are valued at 20 to 50 percent of the Nr-Mt prices below.

1 Jim Brown	150.00	350.00
2 Jack Dempsey	50.00	100.00
5 Johnny Unitas	150.00	250.00

1961-62 Bobbin Heads Football AFL Toes Up

This set is identified by the distinctive "toes up" pose of the players. The Dolls are standing on a ceramic round base painted in the color of the jersey. A city name and team name decal is usually applied with one on the jersey and the other on the base. However, they can often be found with only one or no decal(s) at all. Dolls still in original boxes are worth approximately 1.5 times the value of loose pieces.

1 Boston Patriots	350.00	600.00
2 Buffalo Bills	350.00	600.00
3 Dallas Texans	1,000.00	1,800.00
4 Denver Broncos	350.00	600.00
5 Houston Oilers	350.00	600.00
6 New York Titans	1,000.00	1,800.00
7 Oakland Raiders	500.00	800.00
8 San Diego Chargers	350.00	600.00

1961-62 Bobbin Heads Football NFL Square Base Ceramic

The statues in this series feature boy-like faces and have a ceramic molded base painted in varying colors. There are two distinct varieties of ceramic base dolls in this group. The first version includes a raised molded lettering on the "N.F.L." notation on the base. The second includes a gold NFL shield decal on top of the base instead of the molded raised lettering. Both versions of each team are valued roughly the same. Note that the Vikings were added to this second and third version of the initial NFL Bobbin Heads. Dolls still in original boxes are worth approximately 1.5 times the value of loose pieces.

1 Baltimore Colts	75.00	150.00
2 Chicago Bears	75.00	150.00
3 Cleveland Browns	100.00	200.00
4 Dallas Cowboys	150.00	250.00
5 Detroit Lions	75.00	150.00
6 Green Bay Packers	75.00	150.00
7 Los Angeles Rams	75.00	150.00
8 Minnesota Vikings	100.00	200.00
9 New York Giants	75.00	150.00
10 Philadelphia Eagles	75.00	125.00
11 Pittsburgh Steelers	100.00	200.00
12 San Francisco 49ers	75.00	150.00
13 St.Louis Cardinals	75.00	150.00
14 Washington Redskins	175.00	300.00

1960-61 Bobbin Heads Football NFL Square Base Wood

The statues in this series feature boy-like faces and various colored bases. Each were produced with a wooden base glued onto the figure. Dolls still in original boxes are worth approximately 1.5 times the value of loose pieces.

1 Baltimore Colts	90.00	150.00
2 Chicago Bears	90.00	150.00
3 Cleveland Browns	125.00	200.00
4 Dallas Cowboys	250.00	400.00
5 Detroit Lions	90.00	150.00
6 Green Bay Packers	250.00	400.00
7 Los Angeles Rams	90.00	150.00
8 Minnesota Vikings	90.00	150.00
9 New York Giants	90.00	150.00
10 Philadelphia Eagles	90.00	150.00
11 Philadelphia Eagles '60 Champs	125.00	200.00
12 Pittsburgh Steelers	125.00	200.00
13 San Francisco 49ers	90.00	150.00
14 St.Louis Cardinals	90.00	150.00
15 Washington Redskins	200.00	350.00

1962-64 Bobbin Heads Football NFL Square Base Black Player

These statues are similar to the 1961-62 NFL Square Ceramic Base set, albeit much tougher to find. Note that not all teams were issued in the black player version. Dolls still in original boxes are worth approximately 1.5 times the value of loose pieces.

1 Baltimore Colts	350.00	600.00
2 Chicago Bears	500.00	800.00
3 Cleveland Browns	400.00	750.00
4 Dallas Cowboys	800.00	1,200.00
5 Detroit Lions	400.00	750.00
6 Green Bay Packers	600.00	1,000.00
7 Los Angeles Rams	350.00	600.00
8 Minnesota Vikings	350.00	600.00
9 New York Giants	350.00	600.00
10 Philadelphia Eagles	350.00	600.00
11 Pittsburgh Steelers	400.00	750.00
12 San Francisco 49ers	350.00	600.00
13 St. Louis Cardinals	350.00	600.00
14 Washington Redskins	1,000.00	1,800.00

1962-64 Bobbin Heads Football NFL Toes Up

This set is identified by the distinctive "toes up" pose of the players. These bobbin' heads were issued over a period of years with at least 4-distinct production runs or versions. The first and second groups were produced with a painted base that matches the team colors. A city name decal was affixed to the base and printed in slightly smaller letters than the third and fourth versions. The player can be found holding the football vertically (first version) or horizontally (second version). The third and fourth groups feature the same doll with a gold painted base and a slightly larger print on the city name decal. The doll's face is also slightly different between the first two versions and third and fourth. The player can be found holding the football vertically (third version) or horizontally (fourth version). Dolls still in original boxes are worth approximately 1.5 times the value of loose pieces.

1 Baltimore Colts	150.00	250.00
2 Chicago Bears	150.00	250.00
3 Cleveland Browns	250.00	350.00
4 Dallas Cowboys	400.00	700.00
5 Detroit Lions	150.00	250.00
6 Green Bay Packers	300.00	450.00
7 Los Angeles Rams	150.00	250.00
8 Minnesota Vikings	150.00	300.00
9 New York Giants	150.00	250.00
10 Philadelphia Eagles	150.00	300.00
11 Pittsburgh Steelers	150.00	300.00
12 San Francisco 49ers	150.00	300.00
13 St.Louis Cardinals	150.00	300.00
14 Washington Redskins	400.00	750.00

1965-67 Bobbin Heads: AFL 00 Gold Base

1 Boston Patriots	100.00	175.00
2 Buffalo Bills	125.00	200.00
3 Denver Broncos	100.00	175.00
4 Houston Oilers	100.00	175.00
5 Kansas City Chiefs	100.00	175.00
6 New York Jets	125.00	200.00
7 Oakland Raiders	125.00	200.00
8 San Diego Chargers	100.00	175.00

1965-67 Bobbin Heads: NFL 00 Gold Base

These statues feature a gold painted ceramic base along with the jersey number "00" on the player's shoulders. The manufacturer's sticker was produced in a football shaped design. Dolls still in original boxes are worth approximately 1.5 times the value of loose pieces.

1 Atlanta Falcons	60.00	100.00
2 Baltimore Colts	75.00	125.00
3 Chicago Bears	60.00	100.00
4 Cleveland Browns	125.00	200.00
5 Dallas Cowboys	150.00	250.00
6 Detroit Lions	60.00	100.00
7 Green Bay Packers	75.00	125.00
8 Los Angeles Rams	175.00	300.00
9 Minnesota Vikings	75.00	125.00
10 New Orleans Saints	60.00	100.00
11 New York Giants	60.00	100.00
12 Philadelphia Eagles	90.00	150.00
13 Pittsburgh Steelers	90.00	150.00
14 San Francisco 49ers	125.00	200.00
15 St.Louis Cardinals	60.00	100.00
16 Washington Redskins	150.00	250.00

1965-67 Bobbin Heads: NFL Realistic Face

This set of bobbin' heads feature more realistically sculpted faces than previous issues. They feature a gold painted base and a "00" jersey number on the shoulder. Dolls still in original boxes are worth approximately 1.5 times the value of loose pieces.

1 Atlanta Falcons	150.00	250.00
2 Baltimore Colts	175.00	300.00
3 Chicago Bears	175.00	300.00
4 Cleveland Browns	175.00	300.00
5 Dallas Cowboys	250.00	400.00
6 Detroit Lions	175.00	300.00
7 Green Bay Packers	250.00	400.00
8 Minnesota Vikings	175.00	300.00
9 New Orleans Saints	150.00	250.00
10 New York Giants	175.00	300.00
11 Philadelphia Eagles	150.00	250.00
12 St.Louis Cardinals	150.00	250.00
13 Washington Redskins	350.00	600.00

1965 Bobbin Heads Football AFL Ear Pads

This set of AFL Team Bobbin Heads includes a gold ceramic base with distinctive ear pads on the player's helmet. Dolls still in original boxes are worth approximately 1.5 times the value of loose pieces.

1 Boston Patriots	350.00	500.00
2 Buffalo Bills	400.00	600.00
3 Denver Broncos	500.00	800.00
4 Houston Oilers	350.00	500.00
5 Kansas City Chiefs	400.00	600.00
6 Miami Dolphins	400.00	600.00
7 New York Jets	400.00	600.00
8 Oakland Raiders	500.00	800.00
9 San Diego Chargers	350.00	500.00

1965 Bobbin Heads Football AFL Kissing Pairs

1 Boston Patriots	600.00	1,000.00
2 Buffalo Bills	800.00	1,200.00

1965 Bobbin Heads Football NFL Kissing Pairs

These dolls were issued two to a team, one boy (or team mascot) and one girl in a kissing pose. Prices below reflect that of a pair of dolls for each team. The girl doll can be found with either black or red hair variations on most pieces. She also is most commonly wearing a majorette's hat, but can also be found with a chef's hat variation as well. Dolls still in original boxes are worth approximately 1.5 times the value of loose pieces.

1 Baltimore Colts	250.00	400.00
2 Chicago Bears	200.00	350.00
3 Cleveland Browns	500.00	800.00
4 Dallas Cowboys	300.00	500.00
5 Detroit Lions	200.00	350.00
6 Green Bay Packers	300.00	500.00
7 Los Angeles Rams	200.00	350.00
8 Minnesota Vikings	250.00	400.00
9 New York Giants	250.00	400.00
10 Philadelphia Eagles	200.00	350.00
11 Pittsburgh Steelers	300.00	500.00
12 San Francisco 49ers	300.00	500.00
13 St.Louis Cardinals	200.00	350.00
14 Washington Redskins	500.00	800.00

1968-70 Bobbin Heads: AFL-NFL Merger Series

This series is generally considered the easiest to find of the original ceramic bobbin' head dolls. It was also the last series imported from Japan. Each features a more realistic face than many earlier sets with longer legs and smaller shoes than previous issues. The initial production run included an NFL decal between the feet of the doll. Some were issued later with an AFC decal logo instead. The manufacturer's identification sticker was produced in the shape of an circle. Dolls still in original boxes are worth approximately 1.5 times the value of loose pieces.

1 Atlanta Falcons	50.00	100.00
2 Baltimore Colts AFC	75.00	150.00
3 Baltimore Colts NFL	50.00	100.00
4 Boston Patriots	75.00	150.00
5 Buffalo Bills	100.00	200.00
6 Chicago Bears	50.00	100.00
7 Cincinnati Bengals	50.00	100.00
8 Cleveland Browns AFC	100.00	200.00
9 Cleveland Browns NFL	75.00	150.00
10 Dallas Cowboys	100.00	175.00
11 Denver Broncos	75.00	150.00
12 Detroit Lions	50.00	100.00
13 Green Bay Packers	75.00	125.00
14 Houston Oilers	50.00	100.00
15 Kansas City Chiefs	50.00	100.00
16 Los Angeles Rams	50.00	100.00
17 Miami Dolphins	100.00	200.00
18 Minnesota Vikings	50.00	100.00
19 New England Patriots	50.00	100.00
20 New Orleans Saints	50.00	100.00
21 New York Giants	50.00	100.00
22 New York Jets AFL	75.00	125.00
23 New York Jets NFL	50.00	100.00
24 Oakland Raiders	100.00	175.00
25 Philadelphia Eagles	75.00	150.00
26 Pittsburgh Steelers AFC	100.00	200.00
27 Pittsburgh Steelers NFL	75.00	150.00
28 San Diego Chargers	50.00	100.00
29 San Francisco 49ers	75.00	125.00
30 St.Louis Cardinals	50.00	100.00
31 Washington Redskins	100.00	200.00

1959-63 Hartland Statues Football

The Hartland Plastics Company of Hartland, Wisconsin first released, around 1959, a series of plastic NFL football statues similar to the ones the company had issued for baseball and TV western stars. Hartland produced 5000 Baltimore Colt quarterback figurines of Johnny Unitas -- the only quarterback produced by Hartland. Jon Arnett, the Los Angeles Rams star running back, also had 5000 statues minted and both players sold very well in their respective home markets but seemingly no where else. Therefore Hartland introduced 28 additional football players. At the time there were only 14 teams in the NFL and Hartland made a running back and a lineman each adorned in their respective team colors. They each stand on a green base that has the NFL logo and team named embossed in gold on the front of the base. In total, 5000 of each were manufactured between 1959 and 1963. The football statues were sold in a plain white cardboard box with blue and red ink printing, sketches and logos. The front panel tore away to reveal a cello panel through which one could see the figure. The top flap of the box was then stamped with a black label indicating RUNNINGBACK or LINEMAN. A sheet of uniform numbers and team decals were included inside each box. In 1958 LSU won the NCAA football championship and their star running back, Billy Cannon won the Heisman Trophy in 1959. Hartland used its running back mold and in 1962 created an LSU running back with the purple and gold emblems of the school on each shoulder as well as the orange pants. The university ordered 10,000 figures that were completely sold out by the end of the first semester. The LSU Statue is rarely seen in the hobby. A prototype quarterback from the University of Wisconsin was also produced but rejected and subsequently returned to Hartland from the university. A running back prototype was also sent to Notre Dame for consideration but the university never got back to Hartland and kept the "Fighting Irish" figurine. Prices below reflect that of loose stautes. Statues in clean boxes are worth approximately double the price of a single loose statue.

1 Bears Lineman	125.00	250.00
2 Bears Running Back	175.00	300.00
3 Browns Lineman	200.00	350.00
4 Browns Running Back	200.00	400.00
5 Cardinals Lineman	125.00	250.00
6 Cardinals Running Back	600.00	1,000.00
7 Colts Lineman	350.00	600.00
8 Colts Running Back	200.00	350.00
9 Cowboys Lineman	350.00	600.00
10 Cowboys Running Back	400.00	700.00
11 Eagles Lineman	125.00	250.00
12 Eagles Running Back	150.00	300.00
13 Forty-Niners Lineman	175.00	300.00
14 Forty-Niners Running Back	600.00	1,000.00
15 Giants Lineman	125.00	250.00
16 Giants Running Back	150.00	300.00
17 Lions Lineman	125.00	250.00
18 Lions Running Back	500.00	800.00
19 Packers Lineman	150.00	300.00
20 Packers Running Back	200.00	400.00
21 Rams Lineman	125.00	250.00
22 Rams Rinning Back	150.00	300.00
23 Redskins Lineman	1,000.00	1,500.00
24 Redskins Running Back	400.00	700.00
25 Steelers Lineman	175.00	300.00
26 Steelers Running Back	200.00	350.00
27 Vikings Lineman	125.00	250.00
28 Vikings Running Back	150.00	300.00
29 Jon Arnett	250.00	400.00
30 Johnny Unitas	350.00	600.00
31 LSU Lineman	1,250.00	2,500.00
32 LSU Running Back	1,500.00	3,000.00

1958-62 Kail Football 10-Inch Standing

Each figure in this series features the standing lineman pose and was produced in Japan for Fred Kail Jr. Each figure is wearing a number "00" jersey with a football at his feet, and includes a metal facemask. The bases are often found with the team name decaled on or a local sponsor name or even blank. These statues were also called "Big Joe Jolter." A smaller 5" version of each statue was also produced as well as a 10" bank and a 10" decanter version of each piece.

*BANKS: ADD $25-$50

*DECANTERS: ADD $100-$200

1 Chicago Bears	125.00	250.00
2 Cleveland Browns	125.00	250.00
3 St. Louis Cardinals	125.00	250.00
4 Baltimore Colts	125.00	250.00
5 Dallas Cowboys	400.00	600.00
6 Philadelphia Eagles	125.00	250.00
7 San Francisco 49ers	150.00	300.00
8 New York Giants	125.00	250.00
9 Detroit Lions	125.00	250.00
10 Green Bay Packers	125.00	250.00
11 Los Angeles Rams	125.00	250.00
12 Washington Redskins	500.00	800.00
13 Pittsburgh Steelers	125.00	250.00
14 Minnesota Vikings	125.00	250.00

1958-62 Kail Football 5-Inch Standing

1 Chicago Bears	100.00	200.00
2 Cleveland Browns	100.00	200.00
3 St. Louis Cardinals	100.00	200.00
4 Baltimore Colts	100.00	200.00
5 Dallas Cowboys	300.00	500.00
6 Philadelphia Eagles	100.00	200.00
7 San Francisco 49ers	125.00	250.00
8 New York Giants	100.00	200.00
9 Detroit Lions	100.00	200.00
10 Green Bay Packers	100.00	200.00
11 Los Angeles Rams	100.00	200.00
12 Washington Redskins	250.00	500.00
13 Pittsburgh Steelers	100.00	200.00
14 Minnesota Vikings	100.00	200.00

1958-62 Kail Football Large 3-Point Stance

Each figure in this series features a lineman in a 3-point stance pose with each produced in Japan for Fred Kail Jr. Each figure is wearing a number "00" jersey. The bases are often found with the team name decaled on or a local sponsor name or even blank. These statues were also called "Bruce Bruiser." A smaller version of the stautues was also produced.

1 Chicago Bears	400.00	600.00
2 Cleveland Browns	400.00	600.00
3 St. Louis Cardinals	400.00	600.00
4 Baltimore Colts	400.00	600.00
5 Dallas Cowboys	1,100.00	1,800.00
6 Philadelphia Eagles	400.00	600.00
7 San Francisco 49ers	500.00	800.00
8 New York Giants	400.00	600.00
9 Detroit Lions	400.00	600.00
10 Green Bay Packers	400.00	600.00
11 Los Angeles Rams	400.00	600.00
12 Washington Redskins	1,500.00	2,000.00
13 Pittsburgh Steelers	500.00	800.00
14 Minnesota Vikings	500.00	800.00

1958-62 Kail Football Small 3-Point Stance

1 Chicago Bears	125.00	250.00
2 Cleveland Browns	125.00	250.00
3 St. Louis Cardinals	125.00	250.00
4 Baltimore Colts	125.00	250.00
5 Dallas Cowboys	400.00	600.00
6 Philadelphia Eagles	125.00	250.00
7 San Francisco 49ers	150.00	300.00
8 New York Giants	125.00	250.00
9 Detroit Lions	125.00	250.00
10 Green Bay Packers	125.00	250.00
11 Los Angeles Rams	125.00	250.00
12 Washington Redskins	500.00	800.00
13 Pittsburgh Steelers	125.00	250.00
14 Minnesota Vikings	125.00	250.00

1958-62 Kail Football Ashtrays

1 Chicago Bears	250.00	400.00
2 Cleveland Browns	250.00	400.00
3 St. Louis Cardinals	250.00	400.00
4 Baltimore Colts	250.00	400.00
5 Dallas Cowboys	600.00	1,000.00
6 Philadelphia Eagles	250.00	400.00
7 San Francisco 49ers	250.00	450.00
8 New York Giants	250.00	400.00
9 Detroit Lions	250.00	400.00
10 Green Bay Packers	250.00	400.00
11 Los Angeles Rams	250.00	400.00
12 Washington Redskins	600.00	1,000.00
13 Pittsburgh Steelers	250.00	450.00
14 Minnesota Vikings	250.00	400.00

Hockey Card Price Guide

1956 Adventure R749

The Adventure series produced by Gum Products in 1956, contains a wide variety of subject matter. Cards in the set measure the standard size. The color drawings are printed on a heavy thickness of cardboard and have large white borders. The backs contain the card number, the caption, and a short text. The most expensive cards in the series of 100 are those associated with sports (Louis, Tunney, etc.). In addition, card number 86 (Schmelling) is notorious and sold at a premium price because of the Nazi symbol printed on the card. Although this set is considered by many to be a topical or non-sport set, several boxers are featured (cards 11, 22, 31-35, 41-44, 76-80, 86-90). One of the few cards of Boston-area legend Harry Agannis is in this set. The sports-related cards are in greater demand than the non-sport cards. These cards came in one-card penny packs where were packed 240 to a box.

COMPLETE SET (100) 225.00 450.00
63 Hockey's Hardy Perennials 20.00 40.00
Chuck Rayner
Gordie Howe

1968 Bauer Ads

These oversized cards are approximately 8" x 10" and feature full color fronts, with blank backs. They were issued as premiums with Bauer skates. Since they are unnumbered, they are checklisted below in alphabetical order.

COMPLETE SET (21) 300.00 600.00
1 Andy Bathgate 12.50 25.00
2 Gary Bergman 12.50 25.00
3 Charlie Burns 12.50 25.00
4 Ray Cullen 12.50 25.00
5 Gary Dornhoeffer 12.50 25.00
6 Kent Douglas 12.50 25.00
7 Tim Ecclestone 12.50 25.00
8 Bill Flett 12.50 25.00
9 Ed Giacomin 20.00 40.00
10 Ted Harris 12.50 25.00
11 Paul Henderson 20.00 40.00
12 Ken Hodge 12.50 25.00
13 Harry Howell 12.50 25.00
14 Earl Ingarfield 12.50 25.00
15 Gilles Marotte 12.50 25.00
16 Doug Mohns 12.50 25.00
17 Bobby Orr 75.00 150.00
18 Claude Provost 12.50 25.00
19 Gary Sabourin 12.50 25.00
20 Brian Smith 12.50 25.00
21 Bob Woytowich 12.50 25.00

1971-72 Bazooka

The 1971-72 Bazooka set contains 36 cards. The cards, nearly identical in design to the 1971-72 Topps and O-Pee-Chee hockey cards, were distributed in 12 three-card panels as the bottoms of Bazooka bubble gum boxes. The cards are numbered at the bottom of each obverse. The cards are blank backed and are about 2/3 the size of standard cards. The panels of three are in numerical order, e.g., cards 1-3 are a panel, cards 4-6 form a panel, etc. The prices below refer to cut-apart individual cards; values for panels are 50 percent more than the values below. This is a very scarce set with limited confirmed sales.

COMPLETE SET (36) 4,500.00 9,000.00
1 Phil Esposito 375.00 750.00
2 Frank Mahovlich 200.00 400.00
3 Ed Van Impe 25.00 50.00
4 Bobby Hull 500.00 1,000.00
5 Henri Richard 150.00 300.00
6 Gilbert Perreault 375.00 750.00
7 Alex Delvecchio 125.00 250.00
8 Denis DeJordy 75.00 150.00
9 Ted Harris 30.00 60.00
10 Gilles Villemure 75.00 150.00
11 Dave Keon 150.00 300.00
12 Derek Sanderson 150.00 300.00
13 Orland Kurtenbach 30.00 60.00
14 Bob Nevin 30.00 60.00
15 Yvan Cournoyer 100.00 200.00
16 Andre Boudrias 25.00 50.00
17 Frank St.Marseille 25.00 50.00
18 Norm Ullman 100.00 200.00
19 Garry Unger 40.00 80.00
20 Pierre Bouchard 25.00 50.00
21 Roy Edwards 75.00 150.00
22 Ralph Backstrom 30.00 60.00
23 Guy Trottier 25.00 50.00
24 Serge Bernier 25.00 50.00
25 Bert Marshall 25.00 50.00
26 Wayne Hillman 25.00 50.00
27 Tim Ecclestone 25.00 50.00
28 Walt McKechnie 25.00 50.00
29 Tony Esposito 375.00 750.00
30 Rod Gilbert 100.00 200.00
31 Walt Tkaczuk 30.00 60.00
32 Roger Crozier 75.00 150.00
33 Ken Schinkel 25.00 50.00
34 Ron Ellis 25.00 50.00
35 Stan Mikita 300.00 600.00
36 Bobby Orr 1,800.00 3,000.00

1934-44 Beehive Group I Photos

The 1934-44 Beehive photos are the first of three groups. Production was suspended in 1944 due to wartime priorities. The photos include a facsimile autograph, small script or occasionally block letters. Complete set price is not given due to an ongoing debate over what constitutes a complete set. A number of unconfirmed photos are scattered throughout the Beehive master checklist. If anyone has information to corroborate the existence of any of these cards, please forward it to Beckett Publications.

COMMON PHOTO 7.50 15.00
1 Bobby Bauer 7.50 15.00
2 Red Beattie 12.50 25.00
3 Buzz Boll
(Unconfirmed)
4 Yank Boyd 75.00 150.00
5A Frankie Brimsek 12.50 25.00
(With Net)
5B Frankie Brimsek 15.00 30.00
(Without Net)
8 Dit Clapper 10.00 20.00
9 Roy Conacher 10.00 20.00
10 Bun Cook 10.00 20.00
11 Bill Cowley 10.00 20.00
12 John Crawford 7.50 15.00
13 Woody Dumart 12.50 25.00
14 Don Gallinger 87.50 175.00
15 Ray Getliffe 15.00 30.00
17 Bep Guidolin 50.00 100.00
18 Red Hamill 15.00 30.00
19 Mel Hill 10.00 20.00
24 Pat McReavy 7.50 15.00
25 Alex Motter 15.00 30.00
26 Peggy O'Neil 10.00 20.00
29 Charlie Sands 10.00 20.00
30 Jackie Schmidt 87.50 175.00
31 Milt Schmidt 10.00 20.00
32 Jack Shewchuk 10.00 20.00
33 Eddie Shore 50.00 100.00
35 Tiny Thompson 25.00 50.00
36 Cooney Weiland 10.00 20.00
38 George Allen 12.50 25.00
39 Doug Bentley 15.00 30.00
40 Max Bentley 20.00 40.00
42 Glenn Brydson 62.50 125.00
43 Marty Burke 7.50 15.00
44 Bill Carse 7.50 15.00
45 Bob Carse 7.50 15.00
46 Lorne Chabot 25.00 50.00
47 John Chad 15.00 30.00
49 Les Cunningham 15.00 30.00
50 Cully Dahlstrom 10.00 20.00
53 Leroy Goldsworthy 12.50 25.00
54 Paul Goodman 20.00 40.00
55 Johnny Gottselig 12.50 25.00
56 Philip Hergesheimer 7.50 15.00
58 George(Wingy) Johnston 87.50 175.00
59 Alex Kaleta 15.00 30.00
60 Mike Karakas 15.00 30.00
63 Alex Levinsky 12.50 25.00
64 Sam LoPresti 25.00 50.00
65 Dave Mackay 125.00 250.00
66 Bill MacKenzie
(Unconfirmed)
67 Mush March 7.50 15.00
68 John Mariucci 25.00 50.00
69 Joe Matte 62.50 125.00
70 Red Mitchell UER 87.50 175.00
(Name misspelled
Mitchel)
72 Peter Palangio 40.00 80.00
73 Joe Papike 50.00 100.00
75 Cliff Purpur 87.50 175.00
77 Doc Romnes 25.00 50.00
78 Earl Seibert 10.00 20.00
81 Paul Thompson 15.00 30.00
83 Louis Trudel UER 20.00 40.00
(Name misspelled
Trudell)
84 Audley Tuten 87.50 175.00
85 Art Wiebe 12.50 25.00
86 Sid Abel 15.00 30.00
87 Larry Aurie 7.50 15.00
88 Marty Barry 12.50 25.00
89 Ralph Bowman 12.50 25.00
90 Adam Brown 40.00 80.00
91 Connie Brown 50.00 100.00
92 Jerry Brown 150.00 300.00
93 Mud Bruneteau 10.00 20.00
94 Eddie Bush 125.00 250.00
95 Joe Carveth 7.50 15.00
99 Les Douglas 50.00 100.00
100 Gus Biesebrecht UER 7.50 15.00
(Name misspelled
Geisebrech)
101 Ebbie Goodfellow 10.00 20.00
102 Don Grosso 7.50 15.00
104 Syd Howe 10.00 20.00
105 Bill Jennings 40.00 80.00
106 Jack Keating 15.00 30.00
107 Pete Kelly 10.00 20.00
108 Hec Kilrea 10.00 20.00
109 Ken Kilrea 10.00 20.00
110 Wally Kilrea 10.00 20.00
111 Herb Lewis 10.00 20.00
112 Carl Liscombe 7.50 15.00
114 Douglas McCaig 40.00 80.00
115A Bucko McDonald 50.00 100.00
(Ice photo)
115B Bucko McDonald 50.00 100.00
(Dressing room photo)
116 Pat McReavy 40.00 80.00
118 Johnny Mowers 12.50 25.00
119 Jimmy Orlando 7.50 15.00
120 Gord Pettinger 20.00 40.00
121 John Sherf 20.00 40.00
123 Norm Smith 15.00 30.00
124 John Sorrell 12.50 25.00
125 Jack Stewart 20.00 40.00
128 Carl Voss 50.00 100.00
129 Eddie Wares 12.00 30.00
131 Arch Wilder 12.50 25.00
132 Douglas Young 12.50 25.00
133 Jack Adams 12.50 25.00
134 Marty Barry 200.00 400.00
135 Joe Benoit 10.00 20.00
136 Paul Bibeault 25.00 50.00
137 Toe Blake 15.00 30.00
138 Butch Bouchard 7.50 15.00
139 Claude Bourque 20.00 40.00
140 George Allan Brown 62.50 125.00
141 Walt Buswell 20.00 40.00
143 Murph Chamberlain 25.00 50.00
144 Wilf Cude 15.00 30.00
145 Bunny Dame 25.00 50.00
146 Tony DeMeres UER 7.50 15.00
(Name misspelled
Dremers)
147 Joffre Desilets 10.00 20.00
148 Gordie Drillon 350.00 700.00
149 Polly Drouin 7.50 15.00
151 Johnny Gagnon 7.50 15.00
152 Bert Gardiner 15.00 30.00
153 Ray Getliffe 40.00 80.00
154 Red Goupille 10.00 20.00
155 Tony Graboski 10.00 20.00
157 Paul Haynes 7.50 15.00
158 Gerry Heffernan 75.00 150.00
160 Roger Jenkins 30.00 60.00
161 Aurel Joliat 20.00 40.00
162 Elmer Lach 20.00 40.00
163 Leo Lamoreux UER 62.50 125.00
(Name misspelled
Camoreaux)
164 Pit Lepine 7.50 15.00
165 Rod Lorraine 15.00 30.00
166 Georges Mantha 10.00 20.00
167 Sylvio Mantha 10.00 20.00
169 Armand Mondou 7.50 15.00
170 Howie Morenz 375.00 750.00
171 Pete Morin 75.00 150.00
172 Buddy O'Connor 75.00 150.00
175 Jack Portland 7.50 15.00
176 John Quilty 12.50 25.00
177 Ken Reardon 20.00 40.00
178 Terry Reardon 50.00 100.00
179 Maurice Richard 20.00 40.00
180 Earl Robinson 200.00 400.00
181 Charlie Sands 30.00 60.00
182 Babe Siebert 20.00 40.00
183 Alex Singbush 50.00 100.00
184 Bill Summerhill 87.50 175.00
185 Louis Trudel 40.00 80.00
187 Cy Wentworth 1,500.00 3,000.00
188 Douglas Young 50.00 100.00
189 Bill Beveridge 30.00 60.00
190 Russ Blinco 20.00 40.00
191 Herb Cain 30.00 60.00
192 Gerry Carson UER 87.50 175.00
(Name misspelled
Jerry)
194 Alex Connell 30.00 60.00
195 Tom Cook 20.00 40.00
196 Stewart Evans 15.00 30.00
197 Bob Gracie 50.00 100.00
198 Max Kaminsky 87.50 175.00
199 Bill MacKenzie 62.50 125.00
200 Gus Marker 100.00 200.00
201 Baldy Northcott 30.00 60.00
202 Earl Robinson 25.00 50.00
203 Paul Runge 87.50 175.00
204 Gerry Shannon UER 87.50 175.00
(Name misspelled
Jerry)
206 Des Smith 20.00 40.00
207 Hooley Smith 20.00 40.00
208 Dave Trottier 50.00 100.00
209 Jimmy Ward 20.00 40.00
210 Cy Wentworth 25.00 50.00
211 Viv Allen 30.00 60.00
212 Tom Anderson 20.00 40.00
215 Bill Benson 25.00 50.00
218 Lorne Carr 25.00 50.00
219 Art Chapman 20.00 40.00
222 Red Dutton 25.00 50.00
223 Pat Egan 20.00 40.00
224 Happy Emms 40.00 80.00
225 Wilf Field 20.00 40.00
226 John Gallagher 20.00 40.00
232 Joe Jerwa 25.00 50.00
234 Jim Klein 50.00 100.00
236 Joe Krol 625.00 1,250.00
237 Joe Lamb 40.00 80.00
238 Red Heron 20.00 40.00
241 Hazen McAndrew 750.00 1,500.00
243 Ken Mosdell 200.00 400.00
244 Al Murray 15.00 30.00
245 John O'Flaherty 30.00 60.00
246 Chuck Rayner 100.00 200.00
247 Earl Robertson 25.00 50.00
249 Sweeny Schriner 20.00 40.00
250 Al Shields 50.00 100.00
252 Pete Slobodzian UER 30.00 60.00
(Name misspelled
Slobodian)
255 Nels Stewart 25.00 50.00
256 Fred Thurier 62.50 125.00
257 Harry Watson 112.50 225.00
258 Eddie Wiseman 15.00 30.00
259 Roy Worters 30.00 60.00
260 Ralph Wycherly 30.00 60.00
261 Frank Boucher 20.00 40.00
263 Norm Burns 50.00 100.00
265 Mac Colville 7.50 15.00
266 Neil Colville 10.00 20.00
267 Bill Cook 12.50 25.00
268 Joe Cooper 7.50 15.00
269 Art Coulter 7.50 15.00
270 Gord Davidson 30.00 60.00
271 Cecil Dillon 10.00 20.00
272 Jim Franks 100.00 200.00
273 Red Garrett 75.00 150.00
275 Ott Heller 7.50 15.00
276A Jim Henry 50.00 100.00
(Vertical photo)
276B Jim Henry 30.00 60.00
(Horizontal photo)
277 Bryan Hextall Sr. 15.00 30.00
278 Dutch Hiller 10.00 20.00
279 Ching Johnson 12.50 25.00
280 Bill Juzda 10.00 20.00
281 Butch Keeling 10.00 20.00
282 Davey Kerr 15.00 30.00
283 Bobby Kirk 50.00 100.00
284 Bob Kirkpatrick 50.00 100.00
285 Kilby MacDonald 10.00 20.00
286 Larry Molyneaux 15.00 30.00
287 John Murray Murdoch 20.00 40.00
288 Vic Myles 87.50 175.00
289 Lynn Patrick 10.00 20.00
290 Murray Patrick 7.50 15.00
291 Alf Pike 7.50 15.00
292 Babe Pratt 12.50 25.00
293 Alex Shibicky 7.50 15.00
294 Clint Smith 7.50 15.00
295 Norman Tustin 50.00 100.00
296 Grant Warwick 50.00 100.00
297 Phil Watson 7.50 15.00
298 Syl Apps Sr. 12.50 25.00
299 Murray Armstrong 7.50 15.00
300 Andy Blair 10.00 20.00
301 Buzz Boll 10.00 20.00
302 George Boothman 125.00 250.00
303 Turk Broda 12.50 25.00
304 Lorne Carr 30.00 60.00
305 Murph Chamberlain 7.50 15.00
306 Lex Chisholm 10.00 20.00
307 Jack Church 10.00 20.00
308 Francis Clancy 15.00 30.00
309 Charlie Conacher 12.50 25.00
310 Bob Copp 30.00 60.00
311 Baldy Cotton 10.00 20.00
312 Bob Davidson 7.50 15.00
313 Hap Day 7.50 15.00
314 Ernie Dickens 100.00 200.00
315 Gordie Drillon 7.50 15.00
316 Frank Finnigan 12.50 25.00
317 Jack Forsey 100.00 200.00
318 Jimmy Fowler UER 7.50 15.00
(Name misspelled Jimmie)
319 Bob Goldham 100.00 200.00
320 Hank Goldup 7.50 15.00
321 George Hainsworth 20.00 40.00
322 Reg Hamilton 7.50 15.00
323 Red Heron 10.00 20.00
324 Mel Hill 150.00 300.00
325 Frank Hollett 7.50 15.00
326 Red Horner 10.00 20.00
327 Art Jackson 7.50 15.00
328 Harvey Jackson 7.50 15.00

329 Bingo Kampman 20.00 40.00
330 Reg Kelly 10.00 20.00
331 William Kendall 40.00 80.00
332 Hec Kilrea 25.00 50.00
333 Pete Langelle 10.00 20.00
334 Bucko McDonald 10.00 20.00
335A Norm Mann 12.50 25.00
335B Norm Mann (Name overlaps stick) 87.50 175.00
336 Gus Marker 7.50 15.00
337 Johnny McCreedy 20.00 40.00
338 Jack McLean 50.00 100.00
339 Don Metz 7.50 15.00
340 Nick Metz 7.50 15.00
341 George Parsons 12.50 25.00
342 Bud Poile 87.50 175.00
343 Babe Pratt 125.00 250.00
344 Joe Primeau 12.50 25.00
345 Doc Romnes 25.00 50.00
346 Sweeny Schriner 15.00 30.00
347 Jack Shill 12.50 25.00
348 Wally Stanowski UER (Name misspelled Stanowsky) 7.50 15.00
349 Phil Stein 25.00 50.00
350A Gaye Stewart (Home Sweater) 175.00 350.00
350B Gaye Stewart (Away Sweater) 100.00 200.00
351 Billy Taylor 7.50 15.00
352 Rhys Thompson 200.00 400.00
353 Bill Thoms 7.50 15.00
354 1944-45 Maple Leafs 150.00 300.00
355 1937 Winnipeg Monarchs 75.00 150.00
356 Foster Hewitt 40.00 80.00
357 Wes McKnight 62.50 125.00
358A Allan Cup (Dated on back) 30.00 60.00
358B Allan Cup (Blank Back) 62.50 125.00
359A Lady Byng Trophy (Dated on back) 30.00 60.00
359B Lady Byng Trophy (Blank back) 62.50 125.00
360A Calder Trophy (Dated on back) 30.00 60.00
360B Calder Trophy (Blank back) 62.50 125.00
361A Hart Trophy (Dated on back) 30.00 60.00
361B Hart Trophy (Blank back) 62.50 125.00
362A Memorial Cup (Dated on back) 40.00 80.00
362B Memorial Cup (Blank back) 75.00 150.00
363A Prince of Wales Trophy (Dated on back) 87.50 175.00
363B Prince of Wales Trophy (Blank back) 100.00 200.00
364A Stanley Cup (Dated on back) 30.00 60.00
364B Stanley Cup (Blank back) 50.00 100.00
364C Stanley Cup (Name horizontal) 50.00 100.00
365A Georges Vezina Trophy (Dated on back) 30.00 60.00
365B Georges Vezina Trophy (Blank back) 62.50 125.00

1944-63 Beehive Group II Photos

The 1944-63 Beehive photos are the second of three groups. Issued after World War II, this group generally had new photos and a larger script than was typical of Group I. Facsimile autographs were again featured. There are a number of unconfirmed photos that appeared on the Beehive checklist, among these are the Allan and Memorial Cup trophies in either of their varieties.

1 Bob Armstrong 5.00 10.00
2 Pete Babando 25.00 50.00
3 Ray Barry 25.00 50.00
4 Gus Bodnar 40.00 80.00
5 Leo Boivin 6.00 12.00
6 Frankie Brimsek 12.50 25.00
8 John Bucyk 7.50 15.00
9 Charlie Burns 5.00 10.00
10 Jack Caffery 30.00 60.00
11 Real Chevrefils 5.00 10.00
12A Wayne Connelly 10.00 20.00
12B Wayne Connelly (Name overlaps skate) 30.00 60.00
14 John Crawford 10.00 20.00
15A Dave Creighton (White sweater) 6.00 12.00
15B Dave Creighton (Photo on ice) 30.00 60.00
16 Woody Dumart 12.50 25.00
17 Pat Egan 15.00 30.00
19 Lorne Ferguson 6.00 12.00
20 Fern Flaman 5.00 10.00
21 Bruce Gamble 6.00 12.00
22 Cal Gardner 6.00 12.00
23 Ray Gariepy 10.00 20.00
24 Jack Gelineau 12.50 25.00
25 Jean-Guy Gendron 5.00 10.00
26A Warren Godfrey (A on sweater) 6.00 12.00
26B Warren Godfrey (With puck) 30.00 60.00
26C Warren Godfrey (Without puck) 50.00 100.00
27 Ed Harrison 5.00 10.00
28 Don Head 5.00 10.00
29 Andy Hebenton 7.50 15.00
30 Murray Henderson 7.50 15.00
31 Jim Henry 15.00 30.00
32 Larry Hillman 20.00 40.00
33 Pete Horeck 10.00 20.00
34 Bronco Horvath 5.00 10.00
35 Tom Johnson 6.00 12.00
36 Eddie Johnston 7.50 15.00
38 Joe Klukay 90.00 175.00
39 Edward Kryznowski 6.00 12.00
40 Orland Kurtenbach 20.00 40.00
41 Leo Labine 5.00 10.00
42 Hal Laycoe 5.00 10.00
43 Harry Lumley 7.50 15.00
44 Pentti Lund 500.00 1,000.00
45 Fleming Mackell 5.00 10.00
46 Phil Maloney 10.00 20.00
47 Frank Martin 10.00 20.00
48 Jack McIntyre 10.00 20.00
49 Don McKenney 5.00 10.00
50 Dick Meissner 5.00 10.00
51 Doug Mohns 5.00 10.00
52 Murray Oliver 5.00 10.00
53 Willie O'Ree 7.50 15.00
54A John Peirson 6.00 12.00
54B Johnny Peirson 50.00 100.00
55A Cliff Pennington (Name away from skate) 10.00 20.00
55B Cliff Pennington (Name near skate) 50.00 100.00
56A Bob Perreault (Name away from skate) 12.50 25.00
56B Bob Perreault (Name overlaps skate) 50.00 100.00
57 Jim Peters 10.00 20.00
58 Dean Prentice 6.00 12.00
59 Andre Pronovost 5.00 10.00
60 Bill Quackenbush 10.00 20.00
61 Larry Regan 25.00 50.00
62 Earl Reibel 20.00 40.00
63 Paul Ronty 6.00 12.00
64 Ed Sandford 5.00 10.00
65 Terry Sawchuk 60.00 125.00
66A Norm Defelice ERR (name on front is Don Simmons) 75.00 150.00
66B Norm Defelice COR 5.00 10.00
67 Kenny Smith 6.00 12.00
68A Pat Stapleton (Name away from skate) 10.00 20.00
68B Pat Stapleton (Name near skate) 50.00 100.00
69 Vic Stasiuk 7.50 15.00
70 Red Sullivan 12.50 25.00
71 Jerry Toppazzini 5.00 10.00
72 Zellio Toppazzini 6.00 12.00
73 Grant Warwick 20.00 40.00
74 Tom Williams 5.00 10.00
75 Al Arbour 6.00 12.00
76 Pete Babando 10.00 20.00
77 Earl Balfour 5.00 10.00
78 Murray Balfour 5.00 10.00
79 Jim Bedard 10.00 20.00
80 Doug Bentley 12.50 25.00
81 Gus Bodnar 6.00 12.00
82 Frankie Brimsek 20.00 40.00
83 Adam Brown 10.00 20.00
84 Hank Ciesla 20.00 40.00
85 Jim Conacher 7.50 15.00
86 Pete Conacher 5.00 10.00
87 Roy Conacher 5.00 10.00
88 Joe Conn 40.00 80.00
89 Murray Costello 40.00 80.00
90 Gerry Couture 12.50 25.00
91 Al Dewsbury 6.00 12.00
92 Ernie Dickens 5.00 10.00
93 Jack Evans 5.00 10.00
94 Reggie Fleming 5.00 10.00
95 Lee Fogolin 7.50 15.00
96 Bill Gadsby 5.00 10.00
97 George Gee 6.00 12.00
98 Bob Goldham 12.50 25.00
99 Bep Guidolin 6.00 12.00
100 Glenn Hall 6.00 12.00
101 Murray Hall 15.00 30.00
102 Red Hamill 15.00 30.00
103 Bill Hay 5.00 10.00
104 Jim Henry 15.00 30.00
105 Wayne Hillman 12.50 25.00
107 Bronco Horvath 6.00 12.00
108 Fred Hucul 12.50 25.00
109A Bobby Hull (Jersey 9) 100.00 200.00
109B Bobby Hull (Jersey 16) 15.00 30.00
110 Lou Jankowski 12.50 25.00
111 Forbes Kennedy 25.00 50.00
112 Ted Lindsay 7.50 15.00
113 Ed Litzenberger 5.00 10.00
114 Harry Lumley Goalie 20.00 40.00
115A Len Lunde (Name away from stick) 30.00 60.00
115B Len Lunde (Name overlaps stick) 10.00 20.00
116 Pat Lundy 7.50 15.00
118A Al MacNeil (Name overlaps stick and skate) 20.00 40.00
118B Al MacNeil (Name overlaps stick) 6.00 12.00
119A Chico Maki (Name away from stick) 7.50 15.00
119B Chico Maki (Name overlaps stick) 60.00 125.00
120 Doug McCaig 12.50 25.00
121 Ab McDonald 5.00 10.00
122 Jim McFadden 20.00 40.00
124 Gerry Melnyk UER (Name misspelled Jerry) 5.00 10.00
125 Stan Mikita 6.00 12.00
127 Gus Mortson 5.00 10.00
128 Bill Mosienko 7.50 15.00
129 Ron Murphy 5.00 10.00
130 Ralph Nattrass 12.50 25.00
131 Eric Nesterenko 5.00 10.00
132 Bert Olmstead 12.50 25.00
133 Jim Peters 20.00 40.00
134 Pierre Pilote 5.00 10.00
135 Metro Prystai 6.00 12.00
137 Clare Raglan 15.00 30.00
138A Al Rollins (Vertical photo) 50.00 100.00
138B Al Rollins (Horizontal photo) 15.00 30.00
139 Tod Sloan 5.00 10.00
140 Dollard St. Laurent 5.00 10.00
141 Gaye Stewart 10.00 20.00
142 Jack Stewart 20.00 40.00
143A Bob Turner (Name away from stick) 25.00 50.00
143B Bob Turner (Name overlaps stick) 15.00 30.00
144 Elmer Vasko 5.00 10.00
145 Kenny Wharram 5.00 10.00
146 Larry Wilson 10.00 20.00
147 Howie Young 12.50 25.00
149 Sid Abel 10.00 20.00
150 Al Arbour 20.00 40.00
151 Pete Babando 12.50 25.00
152A Doug Barkley (Stick blade showing) 30.00 60.00
152B Doug Barkley (No blade showing) 10.00 20.00
153 Hank Bassen 6.00 12.00
154 Stephen Black 15.00 30.00
155 Marcel Bonin 7.50 15.00
156 John Bucyk 25.00 50.00
157 John Conacher 100.00 200.00
158 Gerry Couture UER (Name misspelled Jerry) 6.00 12.00
159 Billy Dea 12.50 25.00
160B Alex Delvecchio COR 5.00 10.00
162 Bill Dineen 5.00 10.00
163 Jim Enio 30.00 60.00
164 Alex Faulkner 25.00 50.00
165 Lee Fogolin 6.00 12.00
166 Val Fonteyne 5.00 10.00
167 Bill Gadsby 7.50 15.00
168 Fern Gauthier 20.00 40.00
169 George Gee 7.50 15.00
170 Fred Glover 5.00 10.00
171 Howie Glover 5.00 10.00
172 Warren Godfrey 5.00 10.00
173 Peter Goegan 5.00 10.00
174 Bob Goldham 6.00 12.00
175 Glenn Hall 40.00 80.00
176 Larry Hillman 25.00 50.00
177 Pete Horeck 20.00 40.00
178A Gordie Howe 25.00 50.00
178B Gordie Howe (C on sweater) 40.00 80.00
179 Ron Ingram 20.00 40.00
180 Larry Jeffrey 15.00 30.00
181 Al Johnson 5.00 10.00
182 Red Kelly 5.00 10.00
183 Forbes Kennedy 5.00 10.00
184 Leo Labine 5.00 10.00
185 Tony Leswick 5.00 10.00
186 Ted Lindsay 6.00 12.00
187 Ed Litzenberger 15.00 30.00
188 Harry Lumley 12.50 25.00
189 Len Lunde 5.00 10.00
190 Parker MacDonald 5.00 10.00
191 Bruce MacGregor 5.00 10.00
192 Clare Martin 12.50 25.00
193 Jim McFadden 7.50 15.00
194 Max McNab 12.50 25.00
195 Gerry Melnyk UER (Name misspelled Jerry) 5.00 10.00
196 Don Morrison 12.50 25.00
197 Rod Morrison 25.00 50.00
198 Gerry Odrowski 5.00 10.00
199 Murray Oliver 5.00 10.00
200 Marty Pavelich 5.00 10.00
201 Jim Peters 25.00 50.00
202 Bud Poile 75.00 150.00
203 Andre Pronovost 6.00 12.00
204 Marcel Pronovost 5.00 10.00
205 Metro Prystai 5.00 10.00
206 Bill Quackenbush 25.00 50.00
207 Earl Reibel 5.00 10.00
208 Leo Reise Jr. 6.00 12.00
209A Terry Sawchuk ERR (name misspelled Sawchuck) 20.00 40.00
209B Terry Sawchuk COR (name spelled correctly; different photo) 20.00 40.00
210 Glen Skov 5.00 10.00
211 Floyd Smith 6.00 12.00
212A Vic Stasiuk (Home sweater; full stick showing) 12.50 25.00
212B Vic Stasiuk (Home sweater; partial stick showing) 20.00 40.00
212C Vic Stasiuk (Away sweater) 7.50 15.00
213 Gaye Stewart 15.00 30.00
214 Jack Stewart 15.00 30.00
215 Norm Ullman 5.00 10.00
216 Johnny Wilson 5.00 10.00
217 Benny Woit 5.00 10.00
218 Howie Young 6.00 12.00
219 Larry Zeidel 12.50 25.00
220 Ralph Backstrom 5.00 10.00
221 Dave Balon 5.00 10.00
222 Jean Beliveau 10.00 20.00
223A Red Berenson (White script) 12.50 25.00
223B Red Berenson (Black script) 100.00 200.00
224 Marcel Bonin 5.00 10.00
225 Butch Bouchard 5.00 10.00
226 Tod Campeau 50.00 100.00
227 Joe Carveth 6.00 12.00
228 Murph Chamberlain 25.00 50.00
229 Doc Couture 20.00 40.00
230 Floyd Curry UER (Name misspelled Currie) 5.00 10.00
231 Ian Cushenan 7.50 15.00
232 Lorne Davis 6.00 12.00
233 Eddie Dorohoy 12.50 25.00
234 Gilles Dube 30.00 60.00
235 Bill Durnan 20.00 40.00
236 Norm Dussault 12.50 25.00
237 John Ferguson 6.00 12.00
238 Bob Fillion 7.50 15.00
239 Louie Fontinato 5.00 10.00
240 Dick Gamble 10.00 20.00
241 Bernard Geoffrion 7.50 15.00
242 Phil Goyette 5.00 10.00
243 Leo Gravelle 12.50 25.00
244 John Hanna 30.00 60.00
245 Glen Harmon 10.00 20.00
246 Terry Harper 5.00 10.00
247 Doug Harvey 7.50 15.00
248 Bill Hicke 5.00 10.00
251A Charlie Hodge (White script) 40.00 80.00
251B Charlie Hodge (Black script) 6.00 12.00
252 Tom Johnson 6.00 12.00
253 Vern Kaiser 20.00 40.00
254 Frank King 20.00 40.00
255 Elmer Lach 6.00 12.00
256 Al Langlois 5.00 10.00
257 Jacques Laperriere 5.00 10.00
258 Hal Laycoe 6.00 12.00
259 Jackie Leclair 5.00 10.00
260 Roger Leger 10.00 20.00
261 Ed Litzenberger 12.50 25.00
262 Ross Lowe 20.00 40.00
263 Al MacNeil 5.00 10.00
264 Bud MacPherson 5.00 10.00
265 Cesare Maniago 6.00 12.00
266 Don Marshall 5.00 10.00
267 Paul Masnick 5.00 10.00
268 Eddie Mazur 10.00 20.00
269 John McCormack 6.00 12.00
270 Alvin McDonald 5.00 10.00
271 Calum MacKay 6.00 12.00
272 Gerry McNeil 7.50 15.00
273 Paul Meger 10.00 20.00
274 Dickie Moore 6.00 12.00
275 Kenny Mosdell 10.00 20.00
276 Bert Olmstead 5.00 10.00
277 Gerry Plamondon 10.00 20.00
278 Jacques Plante 20.00 40.00
279 Andre Pronovost 5.00 10.00
280 Claude Provost 5.00 10.00
281 Ken Reardon 12.50 25.00
282 Billy Reay 6.00 12.00
283 Henri Richard 10.00 20.00
284 Maurice Richard 20.00 40.00
285 Rip Riopelle 15.00 30.00
286 George Robertson 50.00 100.00
287 Bobby Rousseau 5.00 10.00
288 Dollard St. Laurent 5.00 10.00
289 Jean-Guy Talbot 5.00 10.00
290A Gilles Tremblay (Dark background) 5.00 10.00
290B Gilles Tremblay (Light background) 100.00 200.00
291A J.C. Tremblay (Dark background) 5.00 10.00
291B J.C. Tremblay (Light background) 100.00 200.00
292 Bob Turner 5.00 10.00
293 Grant Warwick 20.00 40.00
294 Gump Worsley 12.50 25.00
295 Clint Albright 6.00 12.00
296A Dave Balon (Name high on photo) 12.50 25.00
296B Dave Balon (Name low on photo) 5.00 10.00
297A Andy Bathgate (Home sweater) 6.00 12.00
297B Andy Bathgate (Away sweater) 10.00 20.00

298 Max Bentley 25.00 50.00
299 Johnny Bower 25.00 50.00
300 Hy Buller 10.00 20.00
301A Larry Cahan 6.00 12.00
(Home sweater)
301B Larry Cahan 12.50 25.00
(Away sweater)
302 Bob Crystal 15.00 30.00
304 Brian Cullen 5.00 10.00
305 Ian Cushenan 5.00 10.00
306 Billy Dea 15.00 30.00
307 Frank Eddolls 5.00 10.00
308 Pat Egan 20.00 40.00
309A Jack Evans 5.00 10.00
(Name parallel to bottom)
309B Jack Evans 20.00 40.00
(Name printed diagonally)
310 Dunc Fisher 7.50 15.00
311 Louie Fontinato 5.00 10.00
312 Bill Gadsby 5.00 10.00
313 Jean-Guy Gendron 5.00 10.00
314 Rod Gilbert 6.00 12.00
315 Howie Glover 20.00 40.00
317 Phil Goyette 5.00 10.00
318 Aldo Guidolin 25.00 50.00
319 Vic Hadfield 6.00 12.00
320 Ted Hampson 5.00 10.00
321 Doug Harvey 6.00 12.00
322 Andy Hebenton 5.00 10.00
323 Camille Henry 5.00 10.00
324 Wally Hergesheimer 5.00 10.00
325 Ike Hildebrand 15.00 30.00
326 Bronco Horvath 6.00 12.00
327 Harry Howell 5.00 10.00
328A Earl Ingarfield Sr. 5.00 10.00
(Name away from stick)
328B Earl Ingarfield Sr. 12.50 25.00
(Name near stick)
329 Bing Juckes 15.00 30.00
330 Alex Kaleta 7.50 15.00
331 Stephen Kraftcheck 20.00 40.00
332 Eddie Kullman 7.50 15.00
333 Gus Kyle 6.00 12.00
334 Gord Labossiere 25.00 50.00
335 Al Langlois 5.00 10.00
336 Edgar Laprade 7.50 15.00
337 Tony Leswick 6.00 12.00
338 Danny Lewicki 5.00 10.00
339 Pentti Lund 10.00 20.00
340 Don Marshall 12.50 25.00
341 Jack McCartan 6.00 12.00
342 Bill McDonagh 12.50 25.00
343 Don McKenney 10.00 20.00
344 Jackie McLeod 10.00 20.00
345 Nick Mickoski 6.00 12.00
346 Billy Moe 7.50 15.00
348 Ron Murphy 5.00 10.00
349 Buddy O'Connor 7.50 15.00
350 Marcel Paille 50.00 100.00
351 Jacques Plante 50.00 100.00
352 Bud Poile 20.00 40.00
353 Larry Popein 5.00 10.00
354A Dean Prentice 5.00 10.00
(Home sweater)
354B Dean Prentice 7.50 15.00
(Away sweater)
355 Don Raleigh 7.50 15.00
356A Jean Ratelle ERR 25.00 50.00
(Name misspelled John)
356B Jean Ratelle COR 20.00 40.00
357 Chuck Rayner 12.50 25.00
358 Leo Reise Jr. 6.00 12.00
359 Paul Ronty 6.00 12.00
360 Ken Schinkel 5.00 10.00
361 Eddie Shack 15.00 30.00
362 Fred Shero 15.00 30.00
363 Reg Sinclair 20.00 40.00
364 Eddie Slowinski 7.50 15.00
365 Allan Stanley 5.00 10.00
366 Wally Stanowski 6.00 12.00
367 Red Sullivan 5.00 10.00
369 Gump Worsley 5.00 10.00
370 Gary Aldcorn 10.00 20.00
371 Syl Apps Sr. 90.00 175.00
372 Al Arbour 5.00 10.00
373A George Armstrong 6.00 12.00
373B George Armstrong 12.50 25.00
(Dark background)
373C George Armstrong 100.00 200.00
(Light background)
374 Bob Bailey 20.00 40.00
375 Earl Balfour 10.00 20.00
376 Bill Barilko 25.00 50.00
377 Andy Bathgate 25.00 50.00
378 Bob Baun 5.00 10.00
379 Max Bentley 12.50 25.00
380 Jack Bionda 75.00 150.00
381 Garth Boesch 6.00 12.00
382 Leo Boivin 7.50 15.00
383 Hugh Bolton 5.00 10.00
384 Johnny Bower 10.00 20.00
385 Carl Brewer 5.00 10.00
386 Turk Broda 12.50 25.00
387 Larry Cahan 7.50 15.00
388 Ray Ceresino 50.00 100.00
389 Ed Chadwick 6.00 12.00
390 Pete Conacher 50.00 100.00
391 Les Costello 20.00 40.00
392 Dave Creighton 10.00 20.00
393 Barry Cullen 12.50 25.00
394 Brian Cullen 5.00 10.00
395 Robert Dawes 12.50 25.00
396 Kent Douglas 5.00 10.00
397 Dick Duff 5.00 10.00
398 Gary Edmundson 5.00 10.00
399 Gerry Ehman 5.00 10.00
400 Bill Ezinicki 10.00 20.00
401 Fern Flaman 25.00 50.00
402 Cal Gardner 10.00 20.00
403 Ted Hampson 5.00 10.00
404 Gord Hannigan 10.00 20.00
405 Billy Harris 5.00 10.00
406 Bob Hassard 40.00 80.00
407 Larry Hillman 5.00 10.00
408 Tim Horton 12.50 25.00
409 Bronco Horvath 10.00 20.00
410 Ron Hurst 75.00 150.00
411 Gerry James UER 15.00 30.00
(Name misspelled Jerry)
412 Bill Juzda 7.50 15.00
413A Red Kelly 6.00 12.00
(Bare-headed)
413B Red Kelly 15.00 30.00
(Wearing helmet)
414 Ted Kennedy 10.00 20.00
415 Dave Keon 7.50 15.00
416 Joe Klukay 6.00 12.00
417 Stephen Kraftcheck 20.00 40.00
418 Danny Lewicki 12.50 25.00
419 Ed Litzenberger 6.00 12.00
420 Harry Lumley 12.50 25.00
421 Vic Lynn 6.00 12.00
422 Fleming MacKell 7.50 15.00
423 John MacMillan 5.00 10.00
424 Al MacNeil 10.00 20.00
425 Frank Mahovlich 12.50 25.00
426 Phil Maloney 75.00 150.00
427 Cesare Maniago 6.00 12.00
428 Frank Mathers 20.00 40.00
429 John McCormack 30.00 60.00
430 Parker MacDonald 12.50 25.00
431 Don McKenney 20.00 40.00
432 Howie Meeker 7.50 15.00
433 Don Metz 150.00 300.00
434 Nick Metz 100.00 200.00
435 Rudy Migay 5.00 10.00
436 Jim Mikol 5.00 10.00
437 Jim Morrison 5.00 10.00
438 Gus Mortson 6.00 12.00
439 Eric Nesterenko 7.50 15.00
440 Bob Nevin 5.00 10.00
441 Mike Nykoluk 25.00 50.00
442 Bert Olmstead 6.00 12.00
443 Bob Pulford 5.00 10.00
444 Marc Reaume 7.50 15.00
445 Larry Regan 5.00 10.00
446 Dave Reid 75.00 150.00
447 Al Rollins 15.00 30.00
448 Eddie Shack 6.00 15.00
449 Don Simmons 6.00 12.00
450 Tod Sloan 5.00 10.00
451 Sid Smith 5.00 10.00
452 Bob Solinger 30.00 60.00
453A Allan Stanley ERR 6.00 12.00
(Name misspelled Alan; dark background)
453B Allan Stanley COR 12.50 25.00
(Light background)
454 Wally Stanowski 200.00 400.00
455 Ron Stewart 5.00 10.00
456 Harry Taylor 20.00 40.00
457 Jim Thomson 6.00 12.00
458 Ray Timgren 7.50 15.00
459 Harry Watson 6.00 12.00
460 Johnny Wilson 5.00 10.00
461 1962-63 Maple Leafs 200.00 400.00
(Team picture)
462A Lady Byng Trophy 150.00 300.00
(Four white borders)
462B Lady Byng Trophy 60.00 125.00
(White bottom border only)
463A Calder Memorial Trophy 150.00 300.00
(Four white borders)
463B Calder Memorial Trophy 60.00 125.00
(White bottom border only)
464A Hart Trophy 150.00 300.00
(Four white borders)
464B Hart Trophy 60.00 125.00
(White bottom border only)
465A James Norris Memorial Trophy 150.00 300.00
(Four white borders)
465B James Norris Memorial Trophy 60.00 125.00
(White bottom border only)
466A Prince of Wales Trophy 150.00 300.00
(Four white borders)
466B Prince of Wales Trophy 60.00 125.00
(White bottom border only)
467A Art Ross Trophy 150.00 300.00
(Four white borders)
467B Art Ross Trophy 60.00 125.00
(White bottom border only)
468A Stanley Cup 150.00 300.00
(Four white borders)
468B Stanley Cup 60.00 125.00
(White bottom border only)
469A Georges Vezina Trophy 150.00 300.00
(Four white borders)
469B Georges Vezina Trophy 60.00 125.00
(White bottom border only)

1964-67 Beehive Group III Photos

The 1964-67 Beehive photo set is the third of three groups. These photos were issued by St. Lawrence Starch and measure 5 3/8" by 8". The fronts display black-and-white action poses inside a white inner border and a simulated wood-grain outer border. The player's name is displayed on an plaque in the lower wooden border. The backs are blank. A number of unconfirmed photos are part of the Beehive checklist, but have yet to be confirmed.and therefore are not listed below.

1 Murray Balfour 12.50 25.00
2 Leo Boivin 6.00 12.00
3 John Bucyk 7.50 15.00
4 Wayne Connelly 75.00 150.00
5 Bob Dillabough 6.00 12.00
6 Gary Dornhoefer 7.50 15.00
7 Reggie Fleming 6.00 12.00
8 Guy Gendron 60.00 125.00
9 Warren Godfrey 150.00 300.00
10 Ted Green 6.00 12.00
11 Andy Hebenton 90.00 175.00
12 Eddie Johnston 7.50 15.00
13 Tom Johnson 7.50 15.00
14 Forbes Kennedy 10.00 20.00
15 Orland Kurtenbach 20.00 40.00
16 Bobby Leiter 6.00 12.00
17 Parker MacDonald 6.00 12.00
18 Bob McCord 10.00 20.00
19 Ab McDonald 6.00 12.00
20 Murray Oliver 6.00 12.00
21 Bernie Parent 40.00 80.00
22 Cliff Pennington 100.00 225.00
23 Bob Perreault 175.00 350.00
24 Dean Prentice 6.00 12.00
25 Ron Schock UER 6.00 12.00
26 Pat Stapleton 25.00 50.00
27 Ron Stewart 7.50 15.00
28 Ed Westfall 6.00 12.00
29 Tom Williams 6.00 12.00
30 Lou Angotti 6.00 12.00
31 Wally Boyer 6.00 12.00
32 Denis DeJordy 7.50 15.00
33 Dave Dryden 15.00 30.00
34A Phil Esposito 40.00 80.00
34B Phil Esposito 10.00 20.00
35 Glenn Hall ERR 10.00 20.00
36 Murray Hall 100.00 225.00
37 Bill Hay 6.00 12.00
38 Camille Henry 10.00 20.00
39 Wayne Hillman 75.00 150.00
40 Ken Hodge Sr. 7.50 15.00
41A Bobby Hull 100.00 225.00
41B Bobby Hull 200.00 400.00
41C Bobby Hull 15.00 30.00
41D Bobby Hull 15.00 30.00
41E Bobby Hull 200.00 400.00
41F Bobby Hull 15.00 30.00
42 Dennis Hull 6.00 12.00
43 Doug Jarrett 6.00 12.00
44 Len Lunde 6.00 12.00
45 Al MacNeil 6.00 12.00
46A Chico Maki 50.00 100.00
46B Chico Maki 6.00 12.00
47 John McKenzie 15.00 30.00
49 Stan Mikita 10.00 20.00
50 Doug Mohns 6.00 12.00
51A Eric Nesterenko 100.00 225.00
51B Eric Nesterenko 6.00 12.00
52A Pierre Pilote 125.00 250.00
52B Pierre Pilote 7.50 15.00
53 Matt Ravlich 6.00 12.00
55A Fred Stanfield 75.00 150.00
55B Fred Stanfield 50.00 100.00
56 Pat Stapleton 6.00 12.00
57 Bob Turner 125.00 250.00
58 Ed Van Impe 6.00 12.00
59 Elmer Vasko 7.50 15.00
60 Kenny Wharram 6.00 12.00
61 Doug Barkley 6.00 12.00
62 Hank Bassen 7.50 15.00
63A Andy Bathgate 6.00 12.00
63B Andy Bathgate 6.00 12.00
64 Gary Bergman 6.00 12.00
65 Leo Boivin 7.50 15.00
66 Roger Crozier 7.50 15.00
67A Alex Delvecchio 10.00 20.00
67B Alex Delvecchio 150.00 300.00
68 Alex Faulkner 175.00 350.00
69 Val Fonteyne 6.00 12.00
70 Bill Gadsby 6.00 12.00
71 Warren Godfrey 12.50 25.00
72 Pete Goegan 12.50 25.00
73 Murray Hall 6.00 12.00
74 Ted Hampson 6.00 12.00
75 Billy Harris 15.00 30.00
76 Paul Henderson 10.00 20.00
77A Gordie Howe 20.00 40.00
77B Gordie Howe 100.00 225.00
78 Ron Ingram 150.00 300.00
79A Larry Jeffrey 50.00 100.00
79B Larry Jeffrey 30.00 60.00
80A Eddie Joyal 12.50 25.00
80B Eddie Joyal 100.00 225.00
81 Al Langlois 6.00 12.00
82 Ted Lindsay 10.00 20.00
83 Parker MacDonald 6.00 12.00
84A Bruce MacGregor 7.50 15.00
84B Bruce MacGregor 50.00 100.00
85 Pete Mahovlich 6.00 12.00
86 Bert Marshall 6.00 12.00
87 Pit Martin 6.00 12.00
89 Ab McDonald 6.00 12.00
90 Ron Murphy 6.00 12.00
91 Dean Prentice 6.00 12.00
92 Andre Pronovost 10.00 20.00
93 Marcel Pronovost 5.00 10.00
94A Floyd Smith 7.50 15.00
94B Floyd Smith 100.00 225.00
94C Floyd Smith 90.00 175.00
95 Norm Ullman 10.00 20.00
96 Bob Wall 6.00 12.00
97 Ralph Backstrom 6.00 12.00
98 Dave Balon 6.00 12.00
99 Jean Beliveau 12.50 25.00
100 Red Berenson 6.00 12.00
101 Yvan Cournoyer 10.00 20.00
102 Dick Duff 7.50 15.00
103 John Ferguson 6.00 12.00
104 John Hanna 100.00 200.00
105A Terry Harper 6.00 12.00
105B Terry Harper IA 100.00 225.00
106 Ted Harris 6.00 12.00
107 Bill Hicke 7.50 15.00
108 Charlie Hodge 10.00 20.00
109 Jacques Laperriere 6.00 12.00
110A Claude Larose 6.00 12.00
110B Claude Larose 300.00 500.00
111 Claude Provost 6.00 12.00
112 Henri Richard 12.50 25.00
113 Maurice Richard 30.00 60.00
114 Jim Roberts 6.00 12.00
115 Bobby Rousseau 6.00 12.00
116 Jean-Guy Talbot 6.00 12.00
117A Gilles Tremblay 6.00 12.00
117B Gilles Tremblay 50.00 100.00
118 J.C. Tremblay 6.00 12.00
119 Gump Worsley 10.00 20.00
120 Lou Angotti 6.00 12.00
121 Arnie Brown 6.00 12.00
122 Larry Cahan 150.00 300.00
124 Reggie Fleming 6.00 12.00
125 Bernie Geoffrion 10.00 20.00
126 Ed Giacomin 12.50 25.00
127 Rod Gilbert 10.00 20.00
128 Phil Goyette 6.00 12.00
129 Vic Hadfield 7.50 15.00
131 Camille Henry 75.00 150.00
132 Bill Hicke 6.00 12.00
133 Wayne Hillman 6.00 12.00
134 Harry Howell 7.50 15.00
135 Earl Ingarfield Sr. 6.00 12.00
137 Orland Kurtenbach 10.00 20.00
138 Gord Labossiere 75.00 150.00
139 Al MacNeil 6.00 12.00
140 Cesare Maniago 10.00 20.00
141 Don Marshall 6.00 12.00
143 Jim Neilson 6.00 12.00
144 Bob Nevin 6.00 12.00
145 Marcel Paille 20.00 40.00
146 Jacques Plante 40.00 80.00
147 Jean Ratelle 12.50 25.00
148 Rod Seiling 6.00 12.00
151 George Armstrong 10.00 20.00
152 Andy Bathgate 10.00 20.00
153A Bob Baun 60.00 125.00
153B Bob Baun 10.00 20.00
154A Johnny Bower 90.00 175.00
154B Johnny Bower 12.50 25.00
155 Wally Boyer 15.00 30.00
156 John Brenneman 6.00 12.00
157 Carl Brewer 12.50 25.00
158 Turk Broda 15.00 30.00
159 Brian Conacher 6.00 12.00
160 Kent Douglas 6.00 12.00
161 Ron Ellis 6.00 12.00
162 Bruce Gamble 10.00 20.00
163A Billy Harris 50.00 100.00
163B Billy Harris 100.00 225.00
164 Larry Hillman 12.50 25.00
165A Tim Horton 90.00 175.00
165B Tim Horton 15.00 30.00
166 Bronco Horvath 90.00 175.00
167 Larry Jeffrey 15.00 30.00
168 Eddie Joyal 20.00 40.00
169 Red Kelly 10.00 20.00
170 Ted Kennedy 10.00 20.00
171A Dave Keon 75.00 150.00
171B Dave Keon 12.50 25.00
172 Orland Kurtenbach 7.50 20.00
173 Ed Litzenberger 10.00 20.00
174A Frank Mahovlich 90.00 175.00
174B Frank Mahovlich 15.00 30.00
175A Don McKenney 50.00 100.00
175B Don McKenney 10.00 20.00
176 Dickie Moore 10.00 20.00
177 Jim Pappin 6.00 12.00
178A Marcel Pronovost 7.50 15.00
178B Marcel Pronovost 15.00 30.00
180A Bob Pulford 50.00 100.00
180B Bob Pulford 10.00 20.00
181 Terry Sawchuk 15.00 30.00

182 Brit Selby 6.00 12.00
183 Eddie Shack 12.50 25.00
184 Don Simmons 12.50 25.00
185 Allan Stanley 10.00 20.00
186 Pete Stemkowski 6.00 12.00
187A Ron Stewart 90.00 175.00
187B Ron Stewart 30.00 60.00
188 Mike Walton 15.00 30.00
189 Bernie Geoffrion 25.00 50.00
190 Byng Trophy 60.00 125.00
191 Calder Memorial Trophy 60.00 125.00
192 Hart Trophy 60.00 125.00
193 Prince of Wales Trophy 60.00 125.00
194 James Norris Trophy 60.00 125.00
195 Art Ross Trophy 60.00 125.00
196 Stanley Cup 60.00 125.00
197 Vezina Trophy 60.00 125.00

1951 Berk Ross

The 1951 Berk Ross set consists of 72 cards (each measuring approximately 2 1/16" by 2 1/2") with tinted photographs, divided evenly into four series (designated in the checklist as 1, 2, 3 and 4). The cards were marketed in boxes containing two card panels, without gum, and the set includes stars of other sports as well as baseball players. The set is sometimes still found in the original packaging. Intact panels command a premium over the listed prices. The catalog designation for this set is W532-1. In every series the first ten cards are baseball players; the set has a heavy emphasis on Yankees and Phillies players as they were in the World Series the year before. The set includes the first card of Bob Cousy as well as a card of Whitey Ford in his Rookie Card year.

COMPLETE SET (72) 900.00 1,500.00
17-Jan Bill Durnan Hockey 50.00 100.00
18-Jan Bill Quackenbush Hockey 40.00 80.00
16-Feb Jack Stewart Hockey 20.00 40.00
16-Mar Sid Abel Hockey 40.00 80.00

1968-69 Blackhawks Team Issue

This 8-card set measures approximately 4" by 6".

COMPLETE SET (8) 25.00 50.00
1 Dennis Hull 4.00 8.00
2 Doug Jarrett 2.50 5.00
3 Chico Maki 3.00 6.00
4 Gilles Marotte 2.50 5.00
5 Stan Mikita 10.00 20.00
6 Jim Pappin 2.50 5.00
7 Pat Stapleton 2.50 5.00
8 Ken Wharram 3.00 6.00

1970-71 Blackhawks Postcards

This 14-card set measures approximately 4" by 6". T

COMPLETE SET (14) 25.00 50.00
1 Lou Angotti 1.50 3.00
2 Bryan Campbell 1.50 3.00
3 Bobby Hull / Bill Wirtz / Stan Mikita 10.00 20.00
4 Dennis Hull 3.00 6.00
5 Tommy Ivan GM / Billy Reay CO 1.50 3.00
6 Doug Jarrett 1.50 3.00
7 Keith Magnuson 2.50 5.00
8 Pit Martin 1.50 3.00
9 Stan Mikita 5.00 10.00
10 Eric Nesterenko 2.50 5.00
11 Jim Pappin 2.00 4.00
12 Allan Pinder 1.50 3.00
13 Paul Shmyr 1.50 3.00
14 Bill White 2.00 4.00

1979-80 Blackhawks Postcards

COMPLETE SET (22) 12.50 25.00
1 Keith Brown .50 1.00
2 J.P. Bordeleau .50 1.00
3 Ted Bully .50 1.00
4 Alain Daigle .50 1.00
5 Tony Esposito 3.00 6.00
6 Greg Fox .50 1.00
7 Tim Higgins .50 1.00
8 Eddie Johnston CO .40 1.00
9 Reggie Kerr .50 1.00
10 Cliff Koroll .50 1.00
11 Tom Lysiak .50 1.00
12 Keith Magnuson 1.00 2.00
13 John Marks .50 1.00
14 Stan Mikita 4.00 8.00
15 Grant Mulvey 1.00 2.00
16 Bob Murray 1.00 2.00
17 Mike O'Connell .50 1.00
18 Rich Preston .50 1.00
19 Bob Pulford 1.00 2.00
20 Terry Ruskowski .50 1.00
21 Mike Veisor .50 1.00
22 Doug Wilson 2.00 4.00

1980-81 Blackhawks Postcards

These postcard-size cards measure approximately 4" by 6".

COMPLETE SET (16) 12.50 25.00
1 Keith Brown .75 2.00
2 Greg Fox .40 1.00
3 Dave Hutchison .40 1.00
4 Cliff Koroll ACO .40 1.00
5 Keith Magnuson CO .60 1.50
6 Peter Marsh .60 1.50
7 Grant Mulvey .60 1.50
8 Rich Preston .40 1.00
9 Florent Robidoux .40 1.00
10 Terry Ruskowski .60 1.50
11 Denis Savard 2.50 5.00
12 Al Secord .75 2.00
13 Ron Sedlbauer .40 1.00
14 Glen Sharpley .40 1.00
15 Darryl Sutter .75 2.00
16 Miles Zaharko .40 1.00

1980-81 Blackhawks White Border

These 14 blank-backed photos measure approximately 5 1/2" by 8 1/2".

COMPLETE SET (14) 10.00 20.00
1 Murray Bannerman .60 1.50
2 J.P. Bordeleau .40 1.00
3 Keith Brown .75 2.00
4 Tony Esposito 2.50 5.00
5 Greg Fox .40 1.00
6 Tim Higgins .40 1.00
7 Doug Lecuyer .40 1.00
8 John Marks .40 1.00
9 Grant Mulvey .60 1.50
10 Rich Preston .40 1.00
11 Terry Ruskowski .60 1.50
12 Denis Savard 2.50 5.00
13 Darryl Sutter .75 2.00
14 Tim Trimper .40 1.00

1970-71 Blues Postcards

This 20-card set measures approximately 3 1/2" by 5 1/2" and was issued by the team.

COMPLETE SET (20) 20.00 40.00
1 Red Berenson 1.50 3.00
2 Chris Bordeleau 1.00 2.00
3 Craig Cameron 1.00 2.00
4 Tim Ecclestone 1.00 2.00
5 Glenn Hall 5.00 10.00
6 Fran Huck 1.00 2.00
7 Jim Lorentz 1.00 2.00
8 Bill McCreary AGM 1.00 2.00
9 Ab McDonald 1.50 3.00
10 George Morrison 1.00 2.00
11 Noel Picard 1.50 3.00
12 Barclay Plager 2.00 4.00
13 Bill Plager 1.50 3.00
14 Bob Plager 2.00 4.00
15 Jim Roberts 1.00 2.00
16 Gary Sabourin 1.00 2.00
17 Frank St. Marseille 1.50 3.00
18 Bill Sutherland 1.00 2.00
19 Ernie Wakely 1.50 3.00
20 Bob Wall 1.00 2.00

1971-72 Blues Postcards

This 30-card set measures approximately 3 1/2" by 5 1/2".

COMPLETE SET (30) 35.00 70.00
1 Al Arbour CO 2.50 5.00
2 John Arbour 1.00 2.00
3 Curt Bennett 1.00 2.00
4 Chris Bordeleau 1.00 2.00
5 Carl Brewer 1.50 3.00
6 Jacques Caron 1.00 2.00
7 Terry Crisp 2.00 4.00
8 Andre Dupont 1.50 3.00
9 Jack Egers 1.00 2.00
10 Larry Hornung 1.00 2.00
11 Brian Lavender 1.00 2.00
11 Mike Murphy 1.00 2.00
12 G.Marchant/A.McPherson 1.00 2.00
12 Gerry Odrowski 1.00 2.00
13 Bill McCreary AGM .50 1.00
14 Danny O'Shea 1.00 2.00
15 Mike Parizeau 1.00 2.00
16 Noel Picard 1.50 3.00
17 Barclay Plager 2.00 4.00
18 Bill Plager 1.50 3.00
19 Bob Plager 2.00 4.00
20 Phil Roberto 1.50 3.00
21 Gary Sabourin 1.00 2.00
22 Jim Shires 1.00 2.00
23 Frank St. Marseille 1.50 3.00
24 Floyd Thomson 1.00 2.00
25 Garry Unger 2.50 5.00
26 Garry Unger action 2.50 5.00
27 Ernie Wakely 1.50 3.00
28 Tom Woodcock TR 1.00 2.00

1972-73 Blues White Border

Printed on thin white stock, this set of 22 photos measures approximately 6 7/8" by 8 3/4".

COMPLETE SET (22) 30.00 60.00
1 Jacques Caron 1.50 3.00
2 Steve Durbano 2.00 4.00
3 Jack Egers 1.50 3.00
4 Chris Evans 1.50 3.00
5 Jean Hamel 1.50 3.00
6 Fran Huck 1.50 3.00
7 Brent Hughes 1.50 3.00
8 Bob Johnson 2.00 4.00
9 Mike Lampman 1.50 3.00
10 Bob McCord 1.50 3.00
11 Wayne Merrick 2.00 4.00
12 Mike Murphy 1.50 3.00
13 Danny O'Shea 1.50 3.00
14 Barclay Plager 2.50 5.00
15 Bob Plager 2.50 5.00
16 Pierre Plante 1.50 3.00
17 Phil Roberto 2.00 4.00
18 Gary Sabourin 1.50 3.00
19 Wayne Stephenson 2.50 5.00
20 Jean-Guy Talbot CO 1.50 3.00
21 Floyd Thomson 1.50 3.00
22 Garry Unger 2.50 5.00
AC1 Garry Unger 2.50 5.00
AC2 Phil Roberto 2.00 4.00

1973-74 Blues White Border

Printed on thin white stock, this set of 24 photos measures approximately 6 7/8" by 8 3/4". The set is dated by the Glen Sather photo; 1973-74 was his only season with the team.

COMPLETE SET (24) 25.00 50.00
1 Lou Angotti .75 1.50
2 Don Awrey .75 1.50
3 John Davidson 2.50 5.00
4 Ab Demarco .75 1.50
5 Steve Durbano .75 1.50
6 Chris Evans .75 1.50
7 Larry Giroux .75 1.50
8 Jean Hamel .75 1.50
9 Nick Harbaruk .75 1.50
10 J.Bob Kelly 1.00 2.00
11 Mike Lampman .75 1.50
12 Wayne Merrick .75 1.50
13 Barclay Plager 2.00 4.00
14 Bob Plager 2.00 4.00
15 Pierre Plante 1.50 3.00
16 Phil Roberto 2.50 5.00
17 Gary Sabourin .75 1.50
18 Glen Sather 2.00 4.00
19 Wayne Stephenson 2.00 4.00
20 Jean-Guy Talbot CO .75 1.50
21 Floyd Thomson .75 1.50
22 Garry Unger 1.25 2.50
23 Garry Unger action 1.25 2.50
24 Team Photo (1972-73 team) 1.50 3.00

1978-79 Blues Postcards

This 21-postcard set of the St. Louis Blues measures approximately 3 1/2" by 5 1/2".

COMPLETE SET (24) 15.00 30.00
1 Wayne Babych 1.00 2.00
2 Curt Bennett 1.00 2.00
3 Harvey Bennett .50 1.00
4 Red Berenson 1.50 3.00
5 Blue Angels 1.00 2.00
6 Jack Brownschidle 1.00 2.00
7 Mike Crombeen .50 1.00
8 Tony Currie .50 1.00
9 Fanvan .10 .25
10 Bernie Federko 2.00 4.00
11 Barry Gibbs .50 1.00
12 Larry Giroux .50 1.00
13 Inge Hammarstrom 1.00 2.00
14 Neil Labatte .50 1.00
15 Bob Murdoch .50 1.00
16 Phil Myre 1.00 2.00
17 Larry Patey .50 1.00
18 Barclay Plager CO 1.00 2.00
19 Rick Shinske .50 1.00
20 John Smrke .50 1.00
21 Ed Staniowski .50 1.00
22 Bob Stewart .50 1.00
23 Brian Sutter 2.00 4.00
24 Garry Unger 1.50 3.00

1938 Bocnal Tobacco Luminous

Cards measure 1 3/8 x 2 1/2 and feature white design on a black background. They are meant to glow in the dark. Produced for Newgent Cigarettes in London.

19 Field Hockey 15.00 30.00
20 Ice Hockey 25.00 50.00

1938-39 Bruins Garden Magazine Supplement

These large (8 X 10") photos were printed on very thin, sepia-toned stock and inserted in game programs issued at the Boston Gardens. Any additional information would be appreciated.

COMPLETE SET (9) 350.00 700.00
1 Red Beattie 20.00 40.00
2 Walter Galbraith 20.00 40.00
3 Lionel Hitchman 40.00 80.00
4 Joseph Lamb 20.00 40.00
5 Harry Oliver 20.00 40.00
6 Art Ross 75.00 150.00
7 Eddie Shore 125.00 250.00
8 Nels Stewart 40.00 80.00
9 Tiny Thompson 50.00 100.00

1955-56 Bruins Photos

These black and white photos measure approximately 6" x 8" and were distributed in an envelope bearing the Bruins logo.

COMPLETE SET (17) 100.00 200.00
1 Bob Armstrong 5.00 10.00
2 Marcel Bonin 5.00 10.00
3 Leo Boivin 7.50 15.00
4 Real Chevrefils 5.00 10.00
5 Fern Flaman 7.50 15.00
6 Cal Gardner 2.50 5.00
7 Lionel Heinrich 2.50 5.00
8 Leo Labine 7.50 15.00
9 Hal Laycoe 5.00 10.00
10 Fleming Mackell 5.00 10.00
11 Don McKenney 5.00 10.00
12 Doug Mohns 7.50 15.00
13 Bill Quackenbush 7.50 15.00
14 Johnny Peirson 5.00 10.00
15 Terry Sawchuk 25.00 50.00
16 Vic Stasiuk 5.00 10.00
17 Jerry Toppazzini 5.00 10.00
NNO Envelope 10.00 20.00

1957-58 Bruins Photos

This 14-card set measures approximately 6 5/8" by 8 1/8".

COMPLETE SET (20) 100.00 200.00
1 Bob Armstrong 5.00 10.00
2 Jack Bionda 2.50 5.00
3 Leo Boivin 5.00 10.00
4 Johnny Bucyk 25.00 50.00
5 Real Chevrefils 4.00 8.00
6 Fern Flaman 6.00 12.00
7 Jean-Guy Gendron 5.00 10.00
8 Larry Hillman 5.00 10.00
9 Bronco Horvath 6.00 12.00
10 Norm Johnson 6.00 12.00
11 Leo Labine 5.00 10.00
12 Fleming Mackell 4.00 8.00
13 Don McKenney 4.00 8.00
14 Doug Mohns 6.00 12.00
15 Jim Morrison 2.50 5.00
16 Johnny Peirson 2.50 5.00
17 Larry Regan 2.50 5.00
18 Milt Schmidt CO 10.00 20.00
19 Vic Stasiuk 6.00 12.00
20 Jerry Toppazzini 2.50 5.00

1958-59 Bruins Photos

These 6X8 photos were issued by the team.

COMPLETE SET (15) 75.00 150.00
1 Bob Armstrong 5.00 10.00
2 Johnny Bucyk 15.00 30.00
3 Real Chevrefils 5.00 10.00
4 Fern Flaman 6.00 12.00
5 Jean-Guy Gendron 5.00 10.00
6 Larry Hillman 5.00 10.00
7 Leo Labine 5.00 10.00
8 Fleming MacKell 5.00 10.00
9 Don McKenney 5.00 10.00
10 Jim Morrison 5.00 10.00
11 Larry Regan 5.00 10.00
12 Dutch Reibel 5.00 10.00
13 Don Simmons 10.00 20.00
14 Vic Stasiuk 5.00 10.00
15 Jerry Toppazzini 5.00 10.00

1970-71 Bruins Postcards

Cards are standard postcard size and were issued in a binder with perforations.

COMPLETE SET (21) 75.00 150.00
1 Team Photo 2.50 5.00
2 Ed Johnston 2.50 5.00
3 Gerry Cheevers 7.50 15.00
4 Wayne Cashman 2.50 5.00
5 Garnet Bailey 5.00 10.00
6 Don Marcotte 1.50 3.00
7 John Bucyk 5.00 10.00
8 Wayne Carleton 1.50 3.00
9 Reggie Leach 4.00 8.00
10 Ken Hodge 2.50 5.00
11 Ed Westfall 2.00 4.00
12 John McKenzie 2.00 4.00
13 Phil Esposito 10.00 20.00
14 Fred Stanfield 1.50 3.00
15 Derek Sanderson 5.00 10.00
16 Bobby Orr 25.00 50.00
17 Dallas Smith 2.00 4.00
18 Rick Smith 1.50 3.00
19 Ted Green 2.00 4.00
20 Don Awrey 1.50 3.00
21 Tom Johnson CO 2.00 4.00

1970-71 Bruins Team Issue

This set of 18 team-issue photos commemorates the Boston Bruins as 1970 Stanley Cup Champions. The set was issued in two different photo packs of nine photos each. The photos measure approximately 6" by 8".

COMPLETE SET (18) 50.00 100.00
1 Garnet Bailey 5.00 10.00
2 Johnny Bucyk 5.00 10.00
3 Gary Doak 2.00 4.00
4 Phil Esposito 10.00 20.00
5 Ed Johnston 2.50 5.00
6 Don Marcotte 1.50 3.00
7 Derek Sanderson 5.00 10.00
8 Dallas Smith 2.00 4.00
9 Ed Westfall 2.00 4.00
10 Don Awrey 1.50 3.00
11 Wayne Carleton 1.50 3.00
12 Wayne Cashman 2.50 5.00
13 Gerry Cheevers 7.50 15.00
14 Ken Hodge 2.50 5.00
15 John McKenzie 2.00 4.00

16 Bobby Orr	25.00	50.00
17 Rick Smith	1.50	3.00
18 Fred Stanfield	1.50	3.00

1971-72 Bruins Postcards

Originally issued in booklet form, these 20 photo cards measure 3 1/2" by 5 1/2". The cards have perforated tops that allow them to be detached from the yellow booklet, which bears the Bruins logo and crossed hockey sticks on its front.

COMPLETE SET (20)	50.00	100.00
1 Ed Johnston	2.00	4.00
2 Bobby Orr	20.00	40.00
3 Teddy Green	1.50	3.00
4 Phil Esposito	10.00	20.00
5 Ken Hodge	2.00	4.00
6 John Bucyk	4.00	8.00
7 Rick Smith	1.00	2.00
8 Mike Walton	1.50	3.00
9 Wayne Cashman	2.00	4.00
10 Ace Bailey	5.00	10.00
11 Derek Sanderson	4.00	8.00
12 Fred Stanfield	1.00	2.00
13 Ed Westfall	1.50	3.00
14 John McKenzie	1.50	3.00
15 Dallas Smith	1.00	2.00
16 Don Marcotte	1.00	2.00
17 Garry Peters	1.00	2.00
18 Don Awrey	1.00	2.00
19 Reggie Leach	2.00	4.00
20 Gerry Cheevers	5.00	10.00

1932 Bulgaria Zigaretten Sport Photos

142 Field Hockey	5.00	10.00
143 Field Hockey	5.00	10.00
144 Field Hockey	5.00	10.00
148 Ice Hockey	12.50	25.00
149 Dr. B. Watson Canada	10.00	20.00
150 Ice Hockey Goalie	12.50	25.00

1911-12 C55

The C55 Hockey set, probably issued during the 1911-12 season, contains 45 numbered cards. Being one of the early Canadian cigarette cards, the issuer of this set is unknown, although there is speculation that it may have been Imperial Tobacco. These small cards measure approximately 1 1/2" by 2 1/2". The line drawing, color portrait on the front of the card is framed by two hockey sticks. The number of the card appears on both the front and back as does the player's name. The players in the set were members of the NHA: Quebec Bulldogs, Ottawa Senators, Montreal Canadiens, Montreal Wanderers, and Renfrew Millionaires. This set is prized highly by collectors but is the easiest of the three early sets (C55, C56, or C57) to find. The complete set price includes either variety of the Small variation.

COMPLETE SET (45)	7,500.00	15,000.00
1 Paddy Moran	300.00	600.00
2 Joe Hall RC	250.00	500.00
3 Barney Holden	150.00	250.00
4 Joe Malone RC	500.00	1,000.00
5 Ed Oatman RC	150.00	250.00
6 Tom Dunderdale	200.00	350.00
7 Ken Mallen RC	150.00	250.00
8 Jack MacDonald RC	150.00	250.00
9 Fred Lake	150.00	250.00
10 Albert Kerr RC	175.00	300.00
11 Marty Walsh	175.00	300.00
12 Hamby Shore RC	150.00	250.00
13 Alex Currie RC	150.00	250.00
14 Bruce Ridpath	175.00	300.00
15 Bruce Stuart	175.00	300.00
16 Percy Lesueur	175.00	300.00
17 Jack Darragh RC	250.00	400.00
18 Steve Vair RC	150.00	250.00
19 Don Smith RC	150.00	250.00
20 Cyclone Taylor	600.00	1,200.00
21 Bert Lindsay RC	175.00	300.00
22 H.L. Gilmour RC	175.00	300.00
23 Bobby Rowe RC	150.00	250.00
24 Sprague Cleghorn RC	250.00	500.00
25 Odie Cleghorn RC	175.00	300.00
26 Skene Ronan RC	150.00	250.00
27A Walter Smaill RC	350.00	700.00
27B Walter Smaill RC	400.00	800.00
28 Ernest Johnson	250.00	400.00
29 Jack Marshall	175.00	300.00
30 Harry Hyland	175.00	300.00
31 Art Ross	750.00	1,500.00
32 Riley Hern	175.00	300.00
33 Gordon Roberts	250.00	400.00
34 Frank Glass	150.00	250.00
35 Ernest Russell	250.00	400.00
36 James Gardner UER RC	175.00	300.00
37 Art Bernier	150.00	250.00
38 Georges Vezina RC	3,000.00	6,000.00
39 Henri Dallaire RC	175.00	300.00
40 R.(Rocket) Power RC	175.00	300.00
41 Didier Pitre	175.00	300.00
42 Newsy Lalonde	750.00	1,500.00
43 Eugene Payan RC	150.00	250.00
44 George Poulin RC	150.00	250.00
45 Jack Laviolette	250.00	400.00

1910-11 C56

One of the first hockey sets to appear (circa 1910-11), this full-color set of unknown origin (although there is speculation that the issuer was Imperial Tobacco) features 36 cards. The card numbering appears in the upper left part of the front of the card. These small cards measure approximately 1 1/2" by 2 5/8". The player's name and affiliation appear at the bottom within the border. The backs feature the player's name and career affiliations below crossed hockey sticks, a puck and the words "Hockey Series." In 2007, three copies of card number 37 Newsy Lalonde were discovered along with the printing stone that was used to print these cards from 1910. It's not known exactly how many copies were produced, but three is the most common number used.

COMPLETE SET (36)	5,000.00	10,000.00
1 Frank Patrick RC	500.00	800.00
2 Percy Lesueur RC	300.00	500.00
3 Gordon Roberts RC	150.00	300.00
4 Barney Holden RC	100.00	200.00
5 Frank Glass RC	100.00	200.00
6 Edgar Dey RC	100.00	200.00
7 Marty Walsh RC	150.00	300.00
8 Art Ross RC	500.00	1,000.00
9 Angus Campbell RC	125.00	250.00
10 Harry Hyland RC	175.00	350.00
11 Herb Clark RC	75.00	150.00
12 Art Ross RC	500.00	1,000.00
13 Ed Decary RC	75.00	150.00
14 Tom Dunderdale RC	200.00	400.00
15 Cyclone Taylor RC	800.00	1,200.00
16 Joseph Cattarinich RC	100.00	200.00
17 Bruce Stuart RC	175.00	350.00
18 Nick Bawlf RC	75.00	150.00
19 Joseph Jones RC	100.00	200.00
20 Ernest Russell RC	175.00	350.00
21 Jack Laviolette RC	125.00	250.00
22 Riley Hern RC	150.00	300.00
23 Didier Pitre RC	150.00	300.00
24 Skinner Poulin RC	75.00	150.00
25 Art Bernier RC	75.00	150.00
26 Lester Patrick RC	400.00	700.00
27 Fred Lake RC	75.00	150.00
28 Paddy Moran RC	300.00	600.00
29 C.Toms RC	75.00	150.00
30 Ernest Johnson RC	275.00	550.00
31 Horace Gaul RC	75.00	150.00
32 Harold McNamara RC	75.00	150.00
33 Jack Marshall RC	125.00	250.00
34 Bruce Ridpath RC	75.00	150.00
35 Jack Marshall RC	125.00	250.00
36 Newsy Lalonde RC	500.00	1,000.00
37 Newsy Lalonde		

1912-13 C57

This set of 50 black and white cards was produced circa 1912-13. These small cards measure approximately 1 1/2" by 2 5/8". The player's name and affiliation are printed on both the front and back. The card number appears on the back only with the words "Series of 50." Although the origin of the set is unknown, it is safe to assume that the producer who issued the C56 series issued this as well, as the backs of the cards are quite similar. A brief career outline in English is contained on the back. This set is considered to be the toughest to find of the three early hockey sets.

COMPLETE SET (50)	12,000.00	20,000.00
1 Georges Vezina	2,500.00	5,000.00
2 Punch Broadbent RC	350.00	600.00
3 Clint Benedict RC	350.00	600.00
4 A. Atchinson RC	150.00	300.00
5 Tom Dunderdale	200.00	400.00
6 Art Bernier	150.00	300.00
7 Henri Dallaire	150.00	300.00
8 George Poulin	150.00	300.00
9 Eugene Payan	150.00	300.00
10 Steve Vair	150.00	300.00
11 Bobby Rowe	150.00	300.00
12 Don Smith	150.00	300.00
13 Bert Lindsay	150.00	300.00
14 Skene Ronan	150.00	300.00
15 Sprague Cleghorn	350.00	600.00
16 Joe Hall	200.00	400.00
17 Jack MacDonald	150.00	300.00
18 Paddy Moran	300.00	500.00
19 Harry Hyland	150.00	300.00
20 Art Ross	800.00	1,200.00
21 Frank Glass	150.00	300.00
22 Walter Smaill	150.00	300.00
23 Gordon Roberts	150.00	300.00
24 James Gardner	200.00	400.00
25 Ernest Johnson	200.00	400.00
26 Ernie Russell	200.00	400.00
27 Percy Lesueur	300.00	500.00
28 Bruce Ridpath	150.00	300.00
29 Jack Darragh	200.00	400.00
30 Hamby Shore	150.00	300.00
31 Fred Lake	150.00	300.00
32 Alex Currie	150.00	300.00
33 Albert Kerr	150.00	300.00
34 Eddie Gerard RC	200.00	400.00
35 Carl Kendall RC	150.00	300.00
36 Jack Fournier RC	150.00	300.00
37 Goldie Prodgers RC	200.00	400.00
38 Jack Marks RC	150.00	300.00
39 George Broughton RC	150.00	300.00
40 Arthur Boyce RC	150.00	300.00
41 Lester Patrick	500.00	1,000.00
42 Joe Dennison RC	150.00	300.00
43 Cyclone Taylor	700.00	1,200.00
44 Newsy Lalonde	800.00	1,200.00
45 Didier Pitre	150.00	300.00
46 Jack Laviolette	150.00	300.00
47 Ed Oatman	150.00	300.00
48 Joe Malone	500.00	1,000.00
49 Marty Walsh	300.00	600.00
50 Odie Cleghorn	400.00	1,000.00

1912 Imperial Tobacco Lacrosse C61

This set, produced by Imperial Tobacco, features prominent lacrosse stars of the day, but is included in this book because it features several prominent hockey players of the day, including Newsy Lalonde, Jack Laviolette and Clint Benedict.

1 Charlie Querrie	150.00	400.00
2 Dolly Durkin	60.00	150.00
3 Fred Rowntree	60.00	150.00
4 Fred Graydon	60.00	150.00
5 Kid Kinsman	60.00	150.00
6 Al Dade	60.00	150.00
7 Jimmy Hogan	60.00	150.00
8 A. Kenna	60.00	150.00
9 W. O'Kane	60.00	150.00
10 F. Scott	60.00	150.00
11 Newsy Lalonde	500.00	800.00
12 Mickey Ions	100.00	200.00
13 Mag MacGregor	60.00	150.00
14 Dot Phelan	60.00	150.00
15 Spike Griffiths	60.00	150.00
16 Whitey Eastwood	60.00	150.00
17 Red McCarthy	60.00	150.00
18 Jack Shea	60.00	150.00
19 Clint Benedict	250.00	500.00
20 Bobby Pringle	60.00	150.00
21 A. Ranson	60.00	150.00
22 Lawrence Degray	60.00	150.00
23 Francis Cummings	60.00	150.00
24 Fred Degan	60.00	150.00
25 Don Cameron	60.00	150.00
26 James Gifford	60.00	150.00
27 Archie Hall	60.00	150.00
28 W. Turnbull	60.00	150.00
29 Punk Wintermute	60.00	150.00
30 Tom Gifford	60.00	150.00
31 O. Secours	60.00	150.00
32 Dr. Lachapelle	60.00	150.00
33 Joe Cattarinich	100.00	200.00
34 Dare Devil Gauthier	60.00	150.00
35 Jack Laviolette	100.00	200.00
36 George Roberts	60.00	150.00
37 Steve Rochford	60.00	150.00
38 Henry Scott	60.00	150.00
39 J. McIlwane	60.00	150.00
40 Nick Neville	60.00	150.00
41 P.J. Brennan	60.00	150.00
42 Howie McIntyre	60.00	150.00
43 Gus Dillon	60.00	150.00
44 J. Barry	60.00	150.00
45 Johnny Howard	60.00	150.00
46 Eddie Powers	60.00	150.00
47 Art Warwick	60.00	150.00
48 Ernie Menary	60.00	150.00
49 Georgie Kalls	60.00	150.00
50 Fred Stagg	60.00	150.00

1924-25 C144 Champ's Cigarettes

This unnumbered 60-card set was issued during the 1924-25 season by Champ's Cigarettes. There is a brief biography on the card back written in English. The cards are sepia tone and measure approximately 1 1/2" by 2 1/2". Since the cards are unnumbered, they are checklisted in alphabetical order by subject.

COMPLETE SET (60)	10,000.00	20,000.00
1 Jack Adams	150.00	250.00
2 Lloyd Andrews RC	125.00	200.00
3 Clint Benedict	250.00	400.00
4 Louis Berlinquette RC	125.00	200.00
5 Eddie Bouchard	125.00	200.00
6 Billy Boucher	150.00	250.00
7 Bob Boucher RC	125.00	200.00
8 Punch Broadbent	200.00	350.00
9 Billy Burch	200.00	350.00
10 Dutch Cain RC	125.00	200.00
11 Earl Campbell RC	125.00	200.00
12 George Carroll RC	125.00	200.00
13 King Clancy	1,000.00	1,750.00
14 Odie Cleghorn	150.00	250.00
15 Sprague Cleghorn	250.00	400.00
16 Alex Connell RC	250.00	400.00
17 Carson Cooper RC	125.00	200.00
18 Bert Corbeau	150.00	250.00
19 Billy Coutu	125.00	200.00
20 Hap Day RC	250.00	400.00
21 Cy Denneny	200.00	350.00
22 Charlie Dinsmore RC	125.00	200.00
23 Babe Dye	200.00	350.00
24 Frank Finnigan RC	200.00	350.00
25 Vernon Forbes	125.00	200.00
26 Norman Hec Fowler RC	150.00	250.00
27 Red Green	125.00	200.00
28 Shorty Green	200.00	350.00
29 Curly Headley RC	125.00	200.00
30 Jim Herberts RC	125.00	200.00
31 Fred Hitchman RC	125.00	200.00
32 Albert Holway RC	125.00	200.00
33 Stan Jackson	125.00	200.00
34 Aurel Joliat	800.00	1,400.00
35 Louis C. Langlois RC	125.00	200.00
36 Fred Lowrey RC	125.00	200.00
37 Sylvio Mantha	200.00	350.00
38 Albert McCaffrey RC	125.00	200.00
39 Robert McKinnon RC	125.00	200.00
40 Herbie Mitchell RC	125.00	200.00
41 Howie Morenz	2,000.00	3,500.00
42 Dunc Munro RC	150.00	250.00
43 Gerald J.M. Munro RC	125.00	200.00
44 Frank Nighbor	250.00	400.00
45 Reg Noble	200.00	350.00
46 Mickey O'Leary RC	125.00	200.00
47 Goldie Prodgers	125.00	200.00
48 Ken Randall	125.00	200.00
49 George Redding RC	125.00	200.00
50 John Ross Roach	150.00	250.00
51 Mickey Roach	125.00	200.00
52 Sam Rothschild RC	150.00	250.00
53 Werner Schnarr RC	125.00	200.00
54 Ganton Scott RC	125.00	200.00
55 Alf Skinner RC	125.00	200.00
56 Hooley Smith RC	200.00	350.00
57 Chris Speyers RC	125.00	200.00
58 Jesse Spring	125.00	200.00
59 The Stanley Cup	350.00	600.00
60 Georges Vezina	1,200.00	2,000.00

1932 Briggs Chocolate

This set was issued by C.A. Briggs Chocolate company in 1932. The cards feature 31-different sports with each card including an artist's rendering of a sporting event. Although players are not named, it is thought that most were modeled after famous athletes of the time. The cardbacks include a written portion about the sport and an offer from Briggs for free baseball equipment for building a compete set of cards.

2 Hockey	125.00	250.00

1930 Campbell's Soup

Measures approximately 2" x 7" and is black and white. Lower portion of card features a Campbell's slogan. The player pictured is unidentified.

COMPLETE SET (1)	50.00	100.00
NNO Hockey Player	50.00	100.00

1964-65 Canadiens Postcards

This 24-postcard set features the Montreal Canadiens. The standard-size postcards feature action, black and white photography on the front, with the player's autograph stamped on in blue ink. The backs are blank. The set is noteworthy for including collectibles of HOFers Yvan Cournoyer and Rogatien Vachon before their RCs were issued.

COMPLETE SET (24)	100.00	200.00
1 Ralph Backstrom	2.50	5.00
2 Jean Beliveau	12.50	25.00
3 Toe Blake	5.00	10.00
4 Yvan Cournoyer	15.00	30.00
5 Dick Duff	2.50	5.00
6 John Ferguson	5.00	10.00
7 Danny Grant	2.50	5.00
8 Terry Harper	2.50	5.00
9 Ted Harris	2.50	5.00
10 Jacques Laperriere	4.00	8.00
11 Claude Larose	2.50	5.00
12 Jacques Lemaire	10.00	20.00
13 Garry Monahan	2.50	5.00
14 Claude Provost	2.50	5.00
15 Mickey Redmond	10.00	20.00
16 Henri Richard	7.50	15.00
17 Bobby Rousseau	2.50	5.00
18 Serge Savard	5.00	10.00
19 Gilles Tremblay	2.50	5.00
20 J.C. Tremblay	2.50	5.00
21 Carol Vadnais	1.50	3.00
22 Rogatien Vachon	15.00	30.00
23 Bryan Watson	1.50	3.00
24 Gump Worsley	5.00	10.00

1965-66 Canadiens Steinberg Glasses

This set of plastic glasses honoring members of the Montreal Canadiens were issued in the mid 1960's. As they are unnumbered, we are sequencing them in alphabetical order.

COMPLETE SET (12)	75.00	150.00
1 Ralph Backstrom	5.00	10.00
2 Jean Beliveau	15.00	30.00
3 John Ferguson	7.50	15.00
4 Charlie Hodge	7.50	15.00
5 Jacques Laperierre	5.00	10.00
6 Claude Provost	5.00	10.00
7 Henri Richard	10.00	20.00
8 Bob Rousseau	5.00	10.00
9 Jean Guy Talbot	5.00	10.00
10 Gilles Trembley	5.00	10.00
11 J.C. Trembley	6.00	12.00
12 Gump Worsley	10.00	20.00

1966-67 Canadiens IGA

The 1966-67 Canadiens IGA set apparently is comprised of 10 small, postage stamp sized (3/4" by 3/4") cards which likely were part of a larger coupon book. With no attention to date on the card, it has been set by the Gilles Tremblay issue. The cards feature a head shot on a pinkish-red background. If anyone knows of other cards in this set, please forward the information to Beckett Publications.

COMPLETE SET (10)	150.00	300.00

1 J.C. Tremblay 15.00 30.00
2 Ralph Backstrom 15.00 30.00
3 Dick Duff 15.00 30.00
4 Ted Harris 12.50 25.00
5 Claude Larose 12.50 25.00
6 Bobby Rousseau 15.00 30.00
7 Terry Harper 15.00 30.00
8 Gilles Tremblay 12.50 25.00
9 John Ferguson 15.00 30.00
10 Gump Worsley 40.00 80.00

1967-68 Canadiens IGA

The 1967-68 IGA Montreal Canadiens set includes 23 color cards measuring approximately 1 5/8" by 1 7/8". The cards are unnumbered other than by jersey number which is how they are listed below. The cards were part of a game involving numerous prizes. The card backs contain no personal information about the player (only information about the IGA game) and are written in French and English. The set features early cards of Jacques Lemaire and Rogatien Vachon in their Rookie Card year as well as Serge Savard two years prior to his Rookie Card year.

COMPLETE SET (30) 325.00 650.00
1 Gump Worsley 25.00 50.00
2 Jacques Laperriere 15.00 30.00
3 J.C. Tremblay 12.50 25.00
4 Jean Beliveau 40.00 80.00
5 Gilles Tremblay 10.00 20.00
6 Ralph Backstrom 10.00 20.00
8 Dick Duff 12.50 25.00
10 Ted Harris 10.00 20.00
11 Claude Larose 10.00 20.00
12 Yvan Cournoyer 20.00 40.00
14 Claude Provost 10.00 20.00
15 Bobby Rousseau 10.00 20.00
16 Henri Richard 25.00 50.00
17 Carol Vadnais 10.00 20.00
18 Serge Savard 25.00 50.00
19 Terry Harper 12.50 25.00
20 Garry Monahan 10.00 20.00
22 John Ferguson 12.50 25.00
23 Danny Grant 12.50 25.00
24 Mickey Redmond 20.00 40.00
25 Jacques Lemaire 30.00 60.00
30 Rogatien Vachon 40.00 80.00
NNO Toe Blake CO 15.00 30.00

1968-69 Canadiens IGA

The 1968-69 IGA Montreal Canadiens set includes 19 color cards measuring approximately 1 1/4" by 2 1/4". The cards are unnumbered other than by jersey number which is how they are listed below. The cards were part of a game involving numerous prizes. The card backs contain no personal information about the player (only information about the IGA game) and are written in French and English.

COMPLETE SET (30) 300.00 600.00
1 Gump Worsley 30.00 60.00
2 Jacques Laperriere 15.00 30.00
3 J.C. Tremblay 12.50 25.00
4 Jean Beliveau 40.00 80.00
5 Gilles Tremblay 10.00 20.00
6 Ralph Backstrom 12.50 25.00
8 Dick Duff 12.50 25.00
10 Ted Harris 10.00 20.00
12 Yvan Cournoyer 25.00 50.00
14 Claude Provost 10.00 20.00
15 Bobby Rousseau 12.50 25.00
16 Henri Richard 25.00 50.00
18 Serge Savard 20.00 40.00
19 Terry Harper 12.50 25.00
20 Garry Monahan 10.00 20.00
22 John Ferguson 15.00 30.00
24 Mickey Redmond 20.00 40.00
25 Jacques Lemaire 30.00 60.00
30 Rogatien Vachon 30.00 60.00

1968-69 Canadiens Postcards BW

This 20-card set of black and white postcards features full-bleed posed player photos with facsimile autographs in white. This set marks the last year the Canadiens' organization issued black and white postcards. The cards are unnumbered and checklisted below in alphabetical order. Serge Savard appears in this set prior to his Rookie Card year.

COMPLETE SET (20) 40.00 80.00
1 Ralph Backstrom 1.50 3.00
2 Jean Beliveau 7.50 15.00
3 Yvan Cournoyer 4.00 8.00
4 Dick Duff 1.50 3.00
5 John Ferguson 2.50 5.00
6 Terry Harper 1.50 3.00
7 Ted Harris 1.25 2.50
8 Jacques Laperriere 2.00 4.00
9 Jacques Lemaire 5.00 10.00
10 Garry Monahan 1.25 2.50
11 Claude Provost 1.25 2.50
12 Mickey Redmond 4.00 8.00
13 Henri Richard 4.00 8.00
14 Bobby Rousseau 1.50 3.00
15 Claude Ruel CO 1.25 2.50
16 Serge Savard 4.00 8.00
17 Gilles Tremblay 1.25 2.50
18 J.C. Tremblay 1.50 3.00
19 Rogatien Vachon 5.00 10.00
20 Gump Worsley 5.00 10.00

1969-71 Canadiens Postcards Color

This 31-card set of postcards features full-bleed posed color player photos with facsimile autographs in black across the bottom of the pictures. These postcards were also issued without facsimile autographs. For the 1969-70, 1970-71, and 1971-72 seasons, many of the same postcards were issued. The cards are unnumbered and checklisted below in alphabetical order.

COMPLETE SET (31) 50.00 100.00
1 Ralph Backstrom 1.50 3.00
2 Jean Beliveau 6.00 12.00
3 Chris Bordeleau 1.25 2.50
4 Pierre Bouchard 1.25 2.50
5 Guy Charron 1.25 2.50
6 Bill Collins 1.25 2.50
7 Yvan Cournoyer 4.00 8.00
8 John Ferguson 2.00 4.00
9 Terry Harper 1.50 3.00
10 Ted Harris 1.25 2.50
11 Rejean Houle 2.00 4.00
12 Jacques Laperriere 2.00 4.00
13 Guy Lapointe 3.00 6.00
14 Claude Larose 1.25 2.50
15 Jacques Lemaire 4.00 8.00
16 Al MacNeil CO 1.25 2.50
17 Frank Mahovlich 4.00 8.00
18 Peter Mahovlich 3.00 6.00
19 Phil Myre 2.00 4.00
20 Larry Pleau 1.50 3.00
21 Claude Provost 1.50 3.00
22 Mickey Redmond 4.00 8.00
23 Henri Richard 4.00 8.00
24 Phil Roberto 1.25 2.50
25 Jim Roberts 1.25 2.50
26 Bobby Rousseau 1.50 3.00
27 Claude Ruel CO 1.25 2.50
28 Serge Savard 4.00 8.00
29 Marc Tardif 1.50 3.00
30 J.C. Tremblay 1.50 3.00
31 Rogatien Vachon 5.00 10.00

1970-72 Canadiens Pins

This 22-pin set features members of the Montreal Canadiens. Each pin measures approximately 1 3/4" in diameter and has a black and white picture of the player. With the exception of Guy Lafleur, Frank Mahovlich, and Claude Ruel, who are pictured from the waist up, the other pictures are full body shots. The player's name appears below the picture. The pins are made of metal and have a metal clasp on the back. The pins are undated; since Bobby Rousseau's last season with the Canadiens was 1969-70 and 1971-72 was Ken Dryden, Guy Lafleur, and Frank Mahovlich's first season with Montreal, we have assigned 1970-72 to the set, meaning the set was likely issued over a period of years and may, in fact, comprise two distinct sets entirely.

COMPLETE SET (22) 75.00 150.00
1 Jean Beliveau 10.00 20.00
2 Yvan Cournoyer 4.00 8.00
3 Ken Dryden 20.00 40.00
4 John Ferguson 2.50 5.00
5 Terry Harper 2.00 4.00
6 Guy Lafleur 12.50 25.00
7 Jacques Laperriere 2.50 5.00
8 Guy Lapointe 2.50 5.00
9 Jacques Lemaire 4.00 8.00
10 Frank Mahovlich 5.00 10.00
11 Peter Mahovlich 2.50 5.00
12 Henri Richard 5.00 10.00
13 Bobby Rousseau 2.50 5.00
14 Claude Ruel CO 1.50 3.00
15 Serge Savard 2.50 5.00
16 J.C. Tremblay 2.00 4.00
17 Rogatien Vachon 4.00 8.00
18 Ted Harris 2.50 5.00
19 Claude Provost 2.50 5.00
20 Mickey Redmond 3.00 6.00
21 Ralph Backstrom 2.50 5.00
22 Gump Worsley 5.00 10.00

1971-72 Canadiens Postcards

This 25-card set of postcards features full-bleed posed color player photos with facsimile autographs in black across the pictures. For the 1969-70, 1970-71, and 1971-72 seasons, many of the same poses were issued. The cards are unnumbered and checklisted below in alphabetical order. The key cards in the set are Ken Dryden and Guy Lafleur appearing in their Rookie Card year. Also noteworthy is Coach Scotty Bowman's first card.

COMPLETE SET (25) 75.00 150.00
1 Pierre Bouchard .75 1.50
2 Scotty Bowman CO 4.00 8.00
3 Yvan Cournoyer 4.00 8.00
4 Denis DeJordy 1.50 3.00
5 Ken Dryden 20.00 40.00
6 Terry Harper 1.00 2.00
7 Dale Hoganson .75 1.50
8 Rejean Houle 1.00 2.00
9 Guy Lafleur 15.00 30.00
10 Jacques Laperriere 2.00 4.00
11 Guy Lapointe 2.00 4.00
12 Claude Larose .75 1.50
13 Jacques Lemaire 4.00 8.00
14 Frank Mahovlich 4.00 8.00
15 Peter Mahovlich 1.50 3.00
16 Phil Myre 1.50 3.00
17 Larry Pleau 1.00 2.00
18 Henri Richard 4.00 8.00
19 Phil Roberto .75 1.50
20 Jim Roberts .75 1.50
21 Leon Rochefort .75 1.50
22 Serge Savard 2.00 4.00
23 Marc Tardif 1.25 2.50
24 J.C. Tremblay 1.25 2.50
25 Rogatien Vachon 4.00 8.00

1972-73 Canadiens Postcards

This 22-card set features white bordered posed color player photos with pale green backgrounds. A facsimile autograph appears across the picture. The words "Pro Star Promotions, Inc." are printed in the border at the bottom. The Scotty Bowman card is the same as in the 1971-72 set. The cards are unnumbered and checklisted below in alphabetical order. The card of Steve Shutt predates his Rookie Card by two years.

COMPLETE SET (22) 62.50 125.00
1 Chuck Arnason 1.00 2.00
2 Pierre Bouchard 1.50 3.00
3 Scotty Bowman CO 5.00 10.00
4 Yvan Cournoyer 2.50 5.00
5 Ken Dryden 17.50 35.00
6 Rejean Houle 1.50 3.00
7 Guy Lafleur 10.00 20.00
8 Jacques Laperriere 2.00 4.00
9 Guy Lapointe 2.00 4.00
10 Claude Larose 1.00 2.00
11 Chuck Lefley 1.00 2.00
12 Jacques Lemaire 2.50 5.00
13 Frank Mahovlich 2.50 5.00
14 Peter Mahovlich 2.00 4.00
15 Bob Murdoch 1.00 2.00
16 Michel Plasse 2.00 4.00
17 Henri Richard 2.50 5.00
18 Jim Roberts 1.00 2.00
19 Serge Savard 2.00 4.00
20 Steve Shutt 4.00 8.00
21 Marc Tardif 1.50 3.00
22 Murray Wilson 1.00 2.00

1972 Canadiens Great West Life Prints

Cards measure 11" x 14" and were produced by Great West Life Insurance Company. Backs are blank. Cards are unnumbered and checklisted below in alphabetical order.

COMPLETE SET (6) 50.00 100.00
1 Pierre Bouchard 5.00 10.00
2 Yvan Cournoyer 5.00 10.00
3 Ken Dryden 20.00 40.00
4 Pete Mahovlich 5.00 10.00
5 Guy Lafleur 12.50 25.00
6 Steve Shutt 5.00 10.00

1973-74 Canadiens Postcards

This 24-card set features full-bleed color action player photos. The player's name, number and a facsimile autograph are printed on the back. Reportedly distribution problems limited sales to the public. The cards are unnumbered and checklisted below in alphabetical order. The card of Bob Gainey predates his Rookie Card by one year.

COMPLETE SET (24) 40.00 80.00
1 Jean Beliveau (Portrait) 6.00 12.00
2 Pierre Bouchard .75 1.50
3 Scotty Bowman CO 3.00 6.00
4 Yvan Cournoyer 2.50 5.00
5 Bob Gainey 4.00 8.00
6 Dave Gardner .75 1.50
7 Guy Lafleur 5.00 10.00
8 Yvon Lambert .75 1.50
9 Jacques Laperriere 1.25 2.50
10 Guy Lapointe 1.25 2.50
11 Michel Larocque 1.50 3.00
12 Claude Larose SP 2.50 5.00
13 Chuck Lefley .75 1.50
14 Jacques Lemaire 1.50 3.00
15 Frank Mahovlich 2.50 5.00
16 Peter Mahovlich 1.25 2.50
17 Michel Plasse SP 2.50 5.00
18 Henri Richard 2.50 5.00
19 Jim Roberts SP 2.50 5.00
20 Larry Robinson 5.00 10.00
21 Serge Savard 1.25 2.50
22 Steve Shutt 2.50 5.00
23 Wayne Thomas 1.25 2.50
24 Murray Wilson SP 2.50 5.00

1974-75 Canadiens Postcards

This 27-card set features full-bleed color photos of players seated on a bench in the forum. The cards were issued with and without facsimile autographs. Claude Larose (13) and Chuck Lefley (14) went to St. Louis mid-season resulting in limited distribution of their cards. The Mario Tremblay card (25) was issued only without a facsimile autograph. The cards are unnumbered and checklisted below in alphabetical order.

COMPLETE SET (27) 37.50 75.00
1 Pierre Bouchard .75 1.50
2 Scotty Bowman CO 2.00 4.00
3 Rick Chartraw .75 1.50
4 Yvan Cournoyer 2.00 4.00
5 Ken Dryden 6.00 12.00
6 Bob Gainey 4.00 8.00
7 Glenn Goldup .75 1.50
8 Guy Lafleur 4.00 8.00
9 Yvon Lambert .75 1.50
10 Jacques Laperriere 1.00 2.00
11 Guy Lapointe 1.50 3.00
12 Michel Larocque 1.00 2.00
13 Claude Larose SP 1.50 3.00
14 Chuck Lefley SP 1.50 3.00
15 Jacques Lemaire 2.00 4.00
16 Peter Mahovlich 1.00 2.00
17 Henri Richard 2.00 4.00
18 Doug Risebrough 1.00 2.00
19 Jim Roberts SP 1.50 3.00
20 Larry Robinson 4.00 8.00
21 Glen Sather 1.50 3.00
22 Serge Savard 1.00 2.00
23 Steve Shutt 2.00 4.00
24 Wayne Thomas 1.00 2.00
25 Mario Tremblay 1.00 2.00
26 John Van Boxmeer .75 1.50
27 Murray Wilson SP 1.50 3.00

1975-76 Canadiens Postcards

This 20-card set features posed color photos of players on ice. A facsimile autograph appears in a white bottom border. The cards are unnumbered and checklisted below in alphabetical order. The Doug Jarvis card predates his Rookie Card by one year.

COMPLETE SET (20) 25.00 50.00
1 Don Awrey .75 1.50
2 Pierre Bouchard .75 1.50
3 Scotty Bowman CO 2.00 4.00
4 Yvan Cournoyer 2.00 4.00
5 Ken Dryden 6.00 12.00
6 Bob Gainey 2.00 4.00
7 Doug Jarvis 2.00 4.00
8 Guy Lafleur 4.00 8.00
9 Yvon Lambert .75 1.50
10 Guy Lapointe 1.25 2.50
11 Michel Larocque 1.00 2.00
12 Jacques Lemaire 2.00 4.00
13 Peter Mahovlich 1.00 2.00
14 Doug Risebrough .75 1.50
15 Jim Roberts .75 1.50
16 Larry Robinson 3.00 6.00
17 Serge Savard 1.25 2.50
18 Steve Shutt 2.00 4.00
19 Mario Tremblay 1.00 2.00
20 Murray Wilson .75 1.50

1976-77 Canadiens Postcards

This 23-card set features posed color photos of players seated in front of a light blue studio background. A facsimile autograph appears in a white bottom border. The cards are unnumbered and checklisted below in alphabetical order.

COMPLETE SET (23) 25.00 50.00
1 Pierre Bouchard .75 1.50
2 Scotty Bowman CO 2.00 4.00
3 Rick Chartraw .75 1.50
4 Yvan Cournoyer 1.50 3.00
5 Ken Dryden 5.00 10.00
6 Bob Gainey 2.00 4.00
7 Rejean Houle .75 1.50
8 Doug Jarvis 1.00 2.00
9 Guy Lafleur 4.00 8.00
10 Yvon Lambert .75 1.50
11 Guy Lapointe 1.00 2.00
12 Michel Larocque 1.25 2.50
13 Jacques Lemaire 1.50 3.00
14 Peter Mahovlich 1.00 2.00
15 Bill Nyrop .75 1.50
16 Doug Risebrough .75 1.50
17 Jim Roberts .75 1.50
18 Larry Robinson 2.50 5.00
19 Claude Ruel CO .50 1.00
20 Serge Savard 1.00 2.00
21 Steve Shutt 1.50 3.00
22 Mario Tremblay 1.00 2.00
23 Murray Wilson .75 1.50

1977-78 Canadiens Postcards

This 25-card set features posed action color photos of players on the ice. A facsimile autograph appears in a white bottom border. New players were photographed from the shoulders up. Many of the cards are the same as in the 1975-76 set. The cards are unnumbered and checklisted below in alphabetical order.

COMPLETE SET (25) 25.00 50.00
1 Pierre Bouchard .50 1.00
2 Scotty Bowman CO 1.50 3.00
3 Rick Chartraw .50 1.00
4 Yvan Cournoyer 1.50 3.00
5 Ken Dryden 4.50 9.00
6 Brian Engblom .75 1.50
7 Bob Gainey 1.50 3.00
8 Rejean Houle .50 1.00
9 Doug Jarvis .75 1.50
10 Guy Lafleur 3.00 6.00
11 Yvon Lambert .50 1.00
12 Guy Lapointe 1.00 2.00
13 Michel Larocque .75 1.50
14 Pierre Larouche 1.00 2.00
15 Jacques Lemaire 1.25 2.50
16 Gilles Lupien .50 1.00
17 Pierre Mondou .50 1.00
18 Bill Nyrop .50 1.00
19 Doug Risebrough .50 1.00
20 Larry Robinson 2.00 4.00
21 Claude Ruel CO .50 1.00
22 Serge Savard 1.00 2.00
23 Steve Shutt 1.50 3.00
24 Mario Tremblay .75 1.50
25 Murray Wilson .50 1.00

1978-79 Canadiens Postcards

This 26-card set features posed color player photos taken from the shoulders up. All the pictures have a red background except for Ruel and Cournoyer who are shown against blue. A facsimile autograph appears in a white bottom border. The cards are unnumbered and checklisted below in alphabetical order. The key card in the set is Rod Langway, appearing two years before his Rookie Card.

COMPLETE SET (26) 25.00 50.00
1 Scotty Bowman CO 1.50 3.00

2 Rick Chartraw .50 1.00
3 Cam Connor .50 1.00
4 Yvan Cournoyer 1.50 3.00
5 Ken Dryden 4.00 8.00
6 Brian Engblom .50 1.00
7 Bob Gainey 1.50 3.00
8 Rejean Houle .50 1.00
9 Pat Hughes .50 1.00
10 Doug Jarvis .75 1.50
11 Guy Lafleur 3.00 6.00
12 Yvon Lambert .50 1.00
13 Rod Langway 2.00 4.00
14 Guy Lapointe 1.00 2.00
15 Michel Larocque .75 1.50
16 Pierre Larouche 1.00 2.00
17 Jacques Lemaire 1.25 2.50
18 Gilles Lupien .50 1.00
19 Pierre Mondou .50 1.00
20 Mark Napier .50 1.00
21 Doug Risebrough .50 1.00
22 Larry Robinson 2.00 4.00
23 Claude Ruel CO .50 1.00
24 Serge Savard 1.00 2.00
25 Steve Shutt 1.50 3.00
26 Mario Tremblay .50 1.00

1979-80 Canadiens Postcards

This 25-card set features posed color player photos taken from the waist up. All the pictures have a red background except for Ruel who is shown against blue. A facsimile autograph appears in a white bottom border. Several cards are the same as the 1978-79 issue. Bernie Geoffrion's card was not distributed after he resigned as coach on December 12, 1980. Richard Sevigny's card received limited distribution because of late issue. The cards are unnumbered and checklisted below in alphabetical order. The cards measure approximately 3 1/2" by 5 1/2" and the backs are blank.

COMPLETE SET (25) 20.00 40.00
1 Rick Chartraw .50 1.00
2 Normand Dupont .50 1.00
3 Brian Engblom .50 1.00
4 Bob Gainey 1.50 3.00
5 Bernie Geoffrion CO SP 2.50 5.00
6 Danny Geoffrion .50 1.00
7 Denis Herron .75 1.50
8 Rejean Houle .50 1.00
9 Doug Jarvis .50 1.00
10 Guy Lafleur 2.50 5.00
11 Yvon Lambert .50 1.00
12 Rod Langway 1.00 2.00
13 Guy Lapointe 1.00 2.00
14 Michel Larocque .75 1.50
15 Pierre Larouche 1.00 2.00
16 Gilles Lupien .50 1.00
17 Pierre Mondou .50 1.00
18 Mark Napier .75 1.50
19 Doug Risebrough .75 1.50
20 Larry Robinson 1.50 3.00
21 Claude Ruel CO .50 1.00
22 Serge Savard .75 1.50
23 Richard Sevigny SP 2.50 5.00
24 Steve Shutt 1.00 2.00
25 Mario Tremblay .75 1.50

1980-81 Canadiens Postcards

This 26-card set features posed color player photos taken from the waist up against a blue background. A facsimile autograph appears in a white bottom border. The cards are unnumbered and checklisted below in alphabetical order. The cards measure approximately 3 1/2" by 5 1/2" and the backs are blank.

COMPLETE SET (26) 17.50 35.00
1 Keith Acton .60 1.50
2 Bill Baker .40 1.00
3 Rick Chartraw .40 1.00
4 Brian Engblom .40 1.00
5 Bob Gainey .75 2.00
6 Gaston Gingras .40 1.00
7 Denis Herron .75 2.00
8 Rejean Houle .60 1.50
9 Doug Jarvis .40 1.00
10 Guy Lafleur 2.50 5.00
11 Yvon Lambert .40 1.00
12 Rod Langway .60 1.50
13 Guy Lapointe .75 2.00
14 Michel Larocque .75 2.00
15 Pierre Larouche .60 1.50
16 Pierre Mondou .40 1.00
17 Mark Napier .40 1.00
18 Chris Nilan .75 2.00
19 Doug Risebrough .40 1.00
20 Larry Robinson 1.25 3.00
21 Claude Ruel CO .40 1.00
22 Serge Savard .60 1.50
23 Richard Sevigny .40 1.00
24 Steve Shutt .75 2.00
25 Mario Tremblay .60 1.50
26 Doug Wickenheiser .40 1.00

1970-71 Canucks Royal Bank

This 20-card set of Vancouver Canucks was sponsored by Royal Bank, whose company logo appears at the lower left corner on the front. The set is subtitled Royal Bank Leo's Leaders Canucks Player of the Week. The black and white posed player photos measure approximately 5" by 7" and have white borders. The player's signature is inscribed across the bottom of the picture, and the backs are blank. The cards are unnumbered and checklisted below in alphabetical order.

COMPLETE SET (20) 30.00 60.00
1 Andre Boudrias 2.00 4.00
2 Mike Corrigan 1.50 3.00
3 Ray Cullen 2.50 5.00
4 Gary Doak 1.50 3.00
5 George Gardner 1.50 3.00
6 Murray Hall 1.50 3.00
7 Charlie Hodge 4.00 8.00
8 Danny Johnson 1.50 3.00
9 Orland Kurtenbach 2.50 5.00
10 Wayne Maki 1.50 3.00
11 Rosaire Paiement 2.00 4.00
12 Paul Popiel 2.00 4.00
13 Pat Quinn 4.00 8.00
14 Marc Reaume 1.50 3.00
15 Darryl Sly 1.50 3.00
16 Dale Tallon 2.50 5.00
17 Ted Taylor 1.50 3.00
18 Barry Wilkins 1.50 3.00
19 Dunc Wilson 2.50 5.00
20 Jim Wiste 1.50 3.00

1971-72 Canucks Royal Bank

This 20-card set of Vancouver Canucks was sponsored by Royal Bank, whose company logo appears at the lower left corner on the front. The set is subtitled Royal Bank Leo's Leaders Canucks Player of the Week. The black and white posed player photos measure approximately 5" by 7" and have white borders. The player's signature is inscribed across the bottom of the picture, and the backs are blank. The cards are numbered by week of issue. Card number 10 is unknown and may have never been issued.

COMPLETE SET (20) 25.00 50.00
1 Bobby Lalonde 1.00 2.00
2 Mike Corrigan 1.00 2.00
3 Murray Hall 1.00 2.00
4 Jocelyn Guevremont 2.00 4.00
5 Pat Quinn 3.00 6.00
6 Orland Kurtenbach 2.00 4.00
7 Paul Popiel 2.00 4.00
8 Ron Ward 1.00 2.00
9 Rosaire Paiement 1.50 3.00
11 Dale Tallon 2.00 4.00
12 Bobby Schmautz 2.00 4.00
13 Dennis Kearns 1.00 2.00
14 Barry Wilkins 1.00 2.00
15 Dunc Wilson 2.50 5.00
16 Andre Boudrias 2.00 4.00
17 Ted Taylor 1.50 3.00
18 George Gardner 1.00 2.00
19 John Schella 1.00 2.00
20 Wayne Maki 1.50 3.00
21 Gary Doak 1.00 2.00

1972-73 Canucks Nalley's

This six-card set was available on the backs of specially marked Nalley's Triple Pak Potato Chips boxes. The back yellow panel has a 6 3/4" by 5 3/8" (approximately) action shot of a Canuck player beside the goalie and net. One player card is superimposed over the lower left corner of this large action photo. The card is framed by a thin perforated line; if the card were cut out, it would measure about 3" by 3 3/4". The front features a close-up posed color player photo (from the waste up) with white borders. The player's name and position appear in white bottom border. The backs are blank. At the bottom of each back panel are miniature blue-tinted versions of all six player cards. The cards are unnumbered and checklisted below in alphabetical order.

COMPLETE SET (6) 62.50 125.00
1 Andre Boudrias 10.00 20.00
2 George Gardner 10.00 20.00
3 Wayne Maki 12.50 25.00
4 Rosaire Paiement 12.50 25.00
5 Pat Quinn 20.00 40.00
6 Barry Wilkins 10.00 20.00

1972-73 Canucks Royal Bank

This 21-card set of Vancouver Canucks was sponsored by Royal Bank, whose company logo appears at the lower left corner on the front. The set is subtitled Leo's Leaders Canucks Player of the Week. These colorful full body player photos measure approximately 5" by 7" and have white borders. The background of the photos ranges from light blue to royal blue. The player's facsimile signature is inscribed across the bottom of the picture, and the backs are blank. The cards are unnumbered on the front and checklisted below in alphabetical order.

COMPLETE SET (21) 20.00 40.00
1 Dave Balon 1.50 3.00
2 Gregg Boddy 1.00 2.00
3 Larry Bolonchuk 1.00 2.00
4 Andre Boudrias 1.00 2.00
5 Ed Dyck 1.00 2.00
6 Jocelyn Guevremont 1.50 3.00
7 James Hargreaves 1.00 2.00
8 Dennis Kearns 1.00 2.00
9 Orland Kurtenbach 1.50 3.00
10 Bobby Lalonde 1.00 2.00
11 Richard Lemieux 1.00 2.00
12 Don Lever 1.50 3.00
13 Wayne Maki 1.50 3.00
14 Bryan McSheffrey 1.00 2.00
15 Gerry O'Flaherty 1.00 2.00
16 Bobby Schmautz 1.50 3.00
17 Dale Tallon 1.50 3.00
18 Don Tannahill 1.00 2.00
19 Barry Wilkins 1.00 2.00
20 Dunc Wilson 1.50 3.00
21 John Wright 1.00 2.00

1973-74 Canucks Royal Bank

This 21-card set of Vancouver Canucks was sponsored by Royal Bank, whose company logo appears at the lower left corner on the front. The set is subtitled Royal Leaders Canucks Player of the Week. These colorful full body player photos measure approximately 5" by 7" and have white borders. The background of the photos ranges from yellowish green to green. The player's facsimile signature is inscribed across the bottom of the picture, and the backs are blank. The cards are unnumbered on the front and checklisted below in alphabetical order.

COMPLETE SET (21) 20.00 40.00
1 Paulin Bordeleau 1.00 2.00
2 Andre Boudrias 1.00 2.00
3 Jacques Caron 1.00 2.00
4 Bob Dailey 1.00 2.00
5 Dave Dunn 1.00 2.00
6 Jocelyn Guevremont 1.50 3.00
7 Dennis Kearns 1.00 2.00
8 Jerry Korab 1.00 2.00
9 Orland Kurtenbach 2.00 4.00
10 Bobby Lalonde 1.00 2.00
11 Richard Lemieux 1.00 2.00
12 Don Lever 1.50 3.00
13 Bill McCreary 1.00 2.00
14 Bryan McSheffrey 1.00 2.00
15 Gerry O'Flaherty 1.00 2.00
16 Bobby Schmautz 2.00 4.00
17 Gary Smith 2.00 4.00
18 Don Tannahill 1.00 2.00
19 Dennis Ververgaert 1.50 3.00
20 Barry Wilkins 1.00 2.00
21 John Wright 1.00 2.00

1974-75 Canucks Royal Bank

This 20-card set of Vancouver Canucks was sponsored by Royal Bank, whose company logo appears at the lower left corner on the front. The set is subtitled Royal Leaders Player of the Week. These colorful head and shoulders player photos are presented on a white background with a thin black border. The cards measure approximately 5" by 7", have white borders, and are printed on glossy paper. The player's facsimile signature is inscribed across the bottom of the picture, and the backs are blank. The cards are unnumbered on the front and checklisted below in alphabetical order.

COMPLETE SET (20) 20.00 40.00
1 Gregg Boddy 1.00 2.00
2 Paulin Bordeleau 1.50 3.00
3 Andre Boudrias 1.50 3.00
4 Bob Dailey 1.00 2.00
5 Ab DeMarco 1.00 2.00
6 John Gould 1.00 2.00
7 John Grisdale 1.00 2.00
8 Dennis Kearns 1.00 2.00
9 Bobby Lalonde 1.00 2.00
10 Don Lever 1.50 3.00
11 Ken Lockett 1.00 2.00
12 Gerry Meehan 1.50 3.00
13 Garry Monahan 1.00 2.00
14 Chris Oddleifson 1.00 2.00
15 Gerry O'Flaherty 1.00 2.00
16 Tracy Pratt 1.00 2.00
17 Mike Robitaille 1.00 2.00
18 Leon Rochefort 1.00 2.00
19 Gary Smith 1.50 3.00
20 Dennis Ververgaert 1.50 3.00

1975-76 Canucks Royal Bank

This 22-card set of Vancouver Canucks was sponsored by Royal Bank, whose company logo appears at the lower left corner on the front. The set is subtitled Royal Leaders Player of the Week. The cards measure approximately 4 3/4" by 7 1/4" and are printed on glossy paper. The fronts feature a color head and shoulders shot of the player on white background with a thin black border. The player's facsimile autograph appears below the picture. The backs are blank. The cards are unnumbered and we have checklisted them below in alphabetical order.

COMPLETE SET (22) 20.00 40.00
1 Rick Blight 1.00 2.00
2 Gregg Boddy 1.00 2.00
3 Paulin Bordeleau 1.00 2.00
4 Andre Boudrias 1.00 2.00
5 Bob Dailey 1.00 2.00
6 Ab DeMarco 1.00 2.00
7 John Gould 1.00 2.00
8 John Grisdale 1.00 2.00
9 Dennis Kearns 1.00 2.00
10 Bobby Lalonde 1.00 2.00
11 Don Lever 1.50 3.00
12 Ken Lockett 1.00 2.00
13 Garry Monahan 1.00 2.00
14 Bob Murray 1.00 2.00
15 Chris Oddleifson 1.00 2.00
16 Gerry O'Flaherty 1.00 2.00
17 Tracy Pratt 1.00 2.00
18 Mike Robitaille 1.00 2.00
19 Ron Sedlbauer 1.00 2.00
20 Gary Smith 1.50 3.00
21 Harold Snepsts 3.00 6.00
22 Dennis Ververgaert 1.50 3.00

1976-77 Canucks Royal Bank

This 23-card set of Vancouver Canucks was sponsored by Royal Bank, whose company logo appears at the lower left corner on the front. The set is subtitled Royal Leaders Player of the Week. The cards measure approximately 4 3/4" by 7 1/4" and are printed on glossy paper. The fronts feature a color head and shoulders shot of the player on white background with a thin black border. The player's facsimile autograph appears below the picture. The backs are blank. The cards are unnumbered and we have checklisted them below in alphabetical order.

COMPLETE SET (23) 20.00 40.00
1 Rick Blight 1.00 2.00
2 Bob Dailey 1.00 2.00
3 Dave Fortier 1.00 2.00
4 Brad Gassoff 1.00 2.00
5 John Gould 1.00 2.00
6 John Grisdale 1.00 2.00
7 Dennis Kearns 1.00 2.00
8 Bobby Lalonde 1.00 2.00
9 Don Lever 1.50 3.00
10 Cesare Maniago 2.00 4.00
11 Garry Monahan 1.00 2.00
12 Bob Murray 1.00 2.00
13 Chris Oddleifson 1.00 2.00
14 Gerry O'Flaherty 1.00 2.00
15 Curt Ridley 1.00 2.00
16 Mike Robitaille 1.00 2.00
17 Ron Sedlbauer 1.00 2.00
18 Harold Snepsts 2.50 5.00
19 Andy Spruce 1.00 2.00
20 Ralph Stewart 1.00 2.00
21 Dennis Ververgaert 1.50 3.00
22 Mike Walton 1.50 3.00
23 Jim Wiley 1.50 3.00

1977-78 Canucks Canada Dry Cans

This extremely scarce set features the Canucks of the NHL. Each specially-marked regular sized ginger ale can sold in the Vancouver area for a limited time featured a headshot of a player on the back side. Unopened cans sell for a premium of 100 percent.

COMPLETE SET (16) 20.00 40.00
1 Rick Blight 1.00 2.00
2 Brad Gassoff 1.00 2.00
3 Jere Gillis 1.00 2.00
4 Larry Goodenough 1.00 2.00
5 Hilliard Graves 1.00 2.00
6 Dennis Kearns 1.00 2.00
7 Don Lever 1.00 2.00
8 Cesare Maniago 2.50 5.00
9 Jack McIlhargey 1.00 2.00
10 Garry Monahan 1.00 2.00
11 Chris Oddleifson 1.00 2.00
12 Curt Ridley 1.00 2.00
13 Derek Sanderson 2.50 5.00
14 Harold Snepsts 2.00 4.00
15 Mike Walton 1.00 2.00
16 Dennis Ververgaert 1.00 2.00

1977-78 Canucks Royal Bank

This 21-card set of Vancouver Canucks was sponsored by Royal Bank, whose company logo appears at the lower left corner on the front. The set is subtitled Royal Leaders Player of the Week. The cards measure approximately 4 1/4" by 5 1/2" and are printed on thin cardboard stock. The fronts feature a color head and shoulders shot of the player on white background with a thin black border. The player's facsimile autograph appears below the picture. The backs are blank. The cards are unnumbered; they are checklisted below in alphabetical order.

COMPLETE SET (21) 20.00 40.00
1 Rick Blight 1.00 2.00
2 Larry Carriere 1.00 2.00
3 Rob Flockhart 1.00 2.00
4 Brad Gassoff 1.00 2.00
5 Jere Gillis 1.00 2.00
6 Larry Goodenough 1.00 2.00
7 Hilliard Graves 1.00 2.00
8 John Grisdale 1.00 2.00
9 Dennis Kearns 1.00 2.00
10 Don Lever 1.50 3.00
11 Cesare Maniago 2.00 4.00
12 Bob Manno 1.00 2.00
13 Jack McIlhargey 1.00 2.00
14 Garry Monahan 1.00 2.00
15 Chris Oddleifson 1.00 2.00
16 Gerry O'Flaherty 1.00 2.00
17 Curt Ridley 1.50 3.00
18 Ron Sedlbauer 1.00 2.00
19 Harold Snepsts 2.00 4.00
20 Dennis Ververgaert 1.50 3.00
21 Mike Walton 1.00 2.00

1978-79 Canucks Royal Bank

This 23-card set of Vancouver Canucks was sponsored by Royal Bank, whose company logo appears at the upper left corner on the front. The cards measure approximately 4 1/4" by 5 1/2" and are printed on thin cardboard stock. The fronts feature a color head and shoulders shot of the player on white background with a thin blue border. The player's facsimile autograph and the team logo appear above the picture. The backs present biographical and statistical information. The cards are unnumbered; they are checklisted below in alphabetical order.

COMPLETE SET (23) 20.00 40.00
1 Rick Blight .75 1.50
2 Gary Bromley 1.00 2.00
3 Bill Derlago .75 1.50
4 Roland Eriksson .75 1.50
5 Curt Fraser 1.00 2.00
6 Jere Gillis .75 1.50
7 Thomas Gradin 2.00 4.00
8 Hilliard Graves .75 1.50
9 John Grisdale .75 1.50
10 Glen Hanlon 1.25 2.50
11 Randy Holt .75 1.50
12 Dennis Kearns .75 1.50
13 Don Lever 1.00 2.00

14 Lars Lindgren .75 1.50
15 Bob Manno .75 1.50
16 Pit Martin 1.00 2.00
17 Jack McIlhargey .75 1.50
18 Chris Oddleifson .75 1.50
19 Ron Sedlbauer .75 1.50
20 Stan Smyl 2.00 4.00
21 Harold Snepsts 2.00 4.00
22 Dennis Ververgaert 1.00 2.00
23 Lars Zetterstrom .75 1.50

1979-80 Canucks Royal Bank

This 22-card set features posed color player photos from the shoulders up of the Vancouver Canucks. There are actually two different sets with the same value, a team-issued (no reference to Royal Bank) blank back set and a Royal Bank set; the card pictures (and values) are the same in both versions of the set. The sponsor name appears in black print at the card top, with the words "Player of the Week 1979/80" immediately below. The cards measure approximately 4 1/4" by 5 1/2". The front features a color head shot with a blue background and black and white borders. The player's jersey number, facsimile autograph, and team logo appear in the bottom white border. Since this is an unnumbered set, the cards are listed alphabetically. The Royal Bank backs carry biography, career summary, and complete statistical information (season by season, regular schedule, and playoffs).

COMPLETE SET (22) 15.00 30.00
1 Brent Ashton 1.00 2.00
2 Rick Blight .75 1.50
3 Gary Bromley 1.00 2.00
4 Drew Callander .75 1.50
5 Bill Derlago 1.00 2.00
6 Curt Fraser 1.00 2.00
7 Jere Gillis .75 1.50
8 Thomas Gradin 1.50 3.00
9 Glen Hanlon 1.25 2.50
10 John Hughes .75 1.50
11 Dennis Kearns .75 1.50
12 Don Lever 1.00 2.00
13 Lars Lindgren .75 1.50
14 Bob Manno .75 1.50
15 Kevin McCarthy .75 1.50
16 Jack McIlhargey .75 1.50
17 Chris Oddleifson .75 1.50
18 Curt Ridley .75 1.50
19 Ron Sedlbauer .75 1.50
20 Stan Smyl 1.50 3.00
21 Harold Snepsts 1.50 3.00
22 Rick Vaive 1.25 2.50

1980-81 Canucks Silverwood Dairies

This 24-card set of Vancouver Canucks was sponsored by Silverwood Dairies. The cards measure approximately 2 1/2" by 3 1/2" individually but were issued as perforated panels of three. The cards are checklisted below in alphabetical order.

COMPLETE SET (24) 20.00 40.00
1 Brent Ashton .75 2.00
2 Ivan Boldirev .75 2.00
3 Per-Olov Brasar .60 1.50
4 Richard Brodeur 1.50 4.00
5 Gary Bromley .75 2.00
6 Jerry Butler .60 1.50
7 Colin Campbell 1.00 2.50
8 Curt Fraser .75 2.00
9 Thomas Gradin 1.00 2.50
10 Glen Hanlon 1.00 2.50
11 Dennis Kearns .60 1.50
12 Rick Lanz .60 1.50
13 Lars Lindgren .60 1.50
14 Dave Logan .60 1.50
15 Gary Lupul .60 1.50
16 Bob Manno .60 1.50
17 Kevin McCarthy .60 1.50
18 Gerry Minor .60 1.50
19 Kevin Primeau .60 1.50
20 Darcy Rota .60 1.50
21 Stan Smyl 1.25 3.00
22 Harold Snepsts 1.25 3.00
23 Bobby Schmautz .60 1.50
24 Tiger Williams 1.50 4.00

1980-81 Canucks Team Issue

This 22-card set measures approximately 3 3/4" by 4 7/8" and features posed color head and shoulder player photos against a light blue-gray background. The pictures have rounded corners and are enclosed by thick black and thin red border stripes. The player's name, uniform number, position, and the team logo appear in the thicker bottom border. A facsimile autograph runs vertically to the left of the player's head. The backs are blank.

COMPLETE SET (22) 15.00 30.00
1 Brent Ashton .75 2.00
2 Ivan Boldirev .75 2.00
3 Per-Olov Brasar .60 1.50
4 Richard Brodeur 1.50 4.00
5 Gary Bromley .75 2.00
6 Jerry Butler .60 1.50
7 Colin Campbell 1.00 2.50
8 Curt Fraser .75 2.00
9 Thomas Gradin 1.00 2.50
10 Glen Hanlon 1.00 2.50
11 Dennis Kearns .60 1.50
12 Rick Lanz .60 1.50
13 Lars Lindgren .60 1.50
14 Dave Logan .60 1.50
15 Gary Lupul .60 1.50
16 Kevin McCarthy .60 1.50
17 Gerry Minor .60 1.50
18 Darcy Rota .60 1.50
19 Bobby Schmautz .60 1.50
20 Stan Smyl 1.25 3.00
21 Harold Snepsts 1.25 3.00
22 Tiger Williams 1.50 4.00

1974-75 Capitals White Borders

This 25-card set measures approximately 5" by 7" is printed on very thin paper stock. The fronts have black-and-white player portraits with white borders. The player's name and the team logo appear under the photo. The backs are blank. The cards are unnumbered and checklisted below in alphabetical order.

COMPLETE SET (25) 30.00 60.00
1 John Adams 1.00 2.00
2 Jim Anderson CO 1.00 2.00
3 Ron Anderson 1.00 2.00
4 Steve Atkinson 1.00 2.00
5 Michel Belhumeur 2.00 4.00
6 Mike Bloom 1.00 2.00
7 Gord Brooks 1.00 2.00
8 Bruce Cowick 1.00 2.00
9 Denis Dupere 1.00 2.00
10 Jack Egers 1.00 2.00
11 Jim Hrycuik 1.00 2.00
12 Greg Joly 1.50 3.00
13 Dave Kryskow 1.00 2.00
14 Yvon Labre 1.50 3.00
15 Pete Laframboise 1.00 2.00
16 Bill Lesuk 1.00 2.00
17 Ron Low 2.00 4.00
18 Joe Lundrigan 1.00 2.00
19 Mike Marson 1.50 3.00
20 Bill Mikkelson 1.00 2.00
21 Doug Mohns 2.00 4.00
22 Andre Peloffy 1.00 2.00
23 Milt Schmidt GM 2.50 5.00
24 Gord Smith 1.00 2.00
25 Tom Williams 1.50 3.00

1978-79 Capitals Team Issue

This set features the Capitals of the NHL. The oversized cards feature black and white head shots on thin paper stock. It is believed they were issued as a set to fans who requested them by mail.

COMPLETE SET (18) 7.50 15.00
1 Michel Bergeron .75 1.50
2 Greg Carroll .50 1.00
3 Guy Charron .50 1.00
4 Rolf Edberg .50 1.00
5 Rick Green .50 1.00
6 Gordie Lane .50 1.00
7 Mark Lofthouse .50 1.00
8 Jack Lynch .50 1.00
9 Dennis Maruk .75 1.50
10 Paul Mulvey .50 1.00
11 Robert Picard .50 1.00
12 Bill Riley .50 1.00
13 Tom Rowe .50 1.00
14 Bob Sirois .50 1.00
15 Gord Smith .50 1.00
16 Leif Svensson .75 1.50
17 Ryan Walter .50 1.00
18 Bernie Wolf .50 1.00

1979-80 Capitals Team Issue

This set features the Capitals of the NHL. The oversized cards feature black and white head shots on thin paper stock. It is believed they were issued as a set to fans who requested them by mail.

COMPLETE SET (23) 20.00 40.00
1 Pierre Bouchard .50 1.00
2 Guy Charron .50 1.00
3 Rolf Edberg .50 1.00
4 Mike Gartner 12.50 25.00
5 Rick Green .50 1.00
6 Bengt Gustafsson .75 1.50
7 Dennis Hextall .75 1.50
8 Gary Inness .50 1.00
9 Yvon Labre .50 1.00
10 Antero Lehtonen .50 1.00
11 Mark Lofthouse .50 1.00
12 Paul McKinnon .50 1.00
13 Dennis Maruk .75 1.50
14 Paul Mulvey .50 1.00
15 Robert Picard .75 1.50
16 Greg Polis .50 1.00
17 Errol Rausse .50 1.00
18 Tom Rowe .50 1.00
19 Peter Scamurra .50 1.00
20 Bob Surois .50 1.00
21 Wayne Stephenson .50 1.00
22 Leif Svensson .75 1.50
23 Ryan Walter .50 1.00

1949 Carrera Ltd Sports Series

Cards feature blank backs, and come from a multi-sport series of 50 cards. Each card was cutout of a tobacco pack. The Anning single recently was discovered by collector Barry Chreptyk. Based on the numbering, it's possible there may be other hockey players in the set.

44 Les Anning 15.00 40.00
46 Duke Campbell 15.00 40.00

1934-35 CCM Brown Border Photos

These lovely oversized (11 X 9) photos were issued as premiums inside boxes of CCM skates. One such premium was included per box. The photos showed teams of the day and thus are highly prized by today's collectors. They are rarely seen in high grade and when offered, typically bring prices well above those listed below. Since the photos are unnumbered, they are listed below in alphabetical order.

COMPLETE SET (12) 500.00 1,000.00
1 Boston Bruins 50.00 100.00
2 Chicago Blackhawks 50.00 100.00
3 Detroit Red Wings 50.00 100.00
4 Montreal Canadiens 62.50 125.00
5 Montreal Maroons 62.50 125.00
6 New York Americans 62.50 125.00
7 New York Rangers 50.00 100.00
8 Toronto Maple Leafs 50.00 100.00
9 All-Star Game 75.00 150.00
10 Allan Cup Moncton 25.00 50.00
11 Can-Am Providence 30.00 60.00
12 Memorial Cup St. Mike's 25.00 50.00

1935-36 CCM Green Border Photos

Like the previous year's offering, singles from this set were offered as a premium with the purchase of a new pair of CCM skates. This season, however, individual players were offered, along with teams. As they are unnumbered, they are listed below in alphabetical order.

COMPLETE SET (10) 375.00 750.00
1 Boston Cubs (Can-Am champs) 25.00 50.00
2 Boston Bruins 62.50 125.00
3 Halifax (Allan Cup) 25.00 50.00
4 Montreal Maroons 75.00 150.00
5 Toronto Maple Leafs 62.50 125.00
6 Winnipeg (Memorial Cup) 25.00 50.00
7 Frank Boucher 37.50 75.00
8 Lorne Chabot 50.00 100.00
9 Charlie Conacher 50.00 100.00
10 Foster Hewitt 37.50 75.00

1936 Champion Postcards

The set is in the same format as the 1936 Triumph set and was issued in the same manner as the Triumph set, except as an insert in "Boys" magazine published weekly in Great Britain. Three cards were issued in the first week of the promotion in "The Champion" and then one per week in "Boys" magazine. The cards are sepia toned and are postcard size, measuring approximately 3 1/2" by 5 1/2". The set is subtitled "Stars of the Ice Rinks". The cards are unnumbered and hence presented in alphabetical order. The date mentioned below is the issue date as noted on the card back in Canadian style, day/month/year.

COMPLETE SET (10) 875.00 1,750.00
1 Marty Barry 40.00 80.00
Boston Bruins/18/1/36
2 Mush March 40.00 80.00
Chicago Blackhawks/8/2/36
3 Reg(Hooley) Smith 87.50 175.00
Montreal Canadiens/18/1/36
4 Sweeney Schriner/22/2/36 87.50 175.00
5 King Clancy 250.00 500.00
Toronto Maple Leafs/18/1/36
6 Bill Cook 100.00 200.00
New York Rangers/1/2/36
7 Pep Kelly 40.00 80.00
Toronto Maple Leafs/25/1/36
8 Aurel Joliat 225.00 450.00
Montreal Canadiens/15/2/36
9 Charles Conacher 200.00 400.00
Toronto Maple Leafs/29/2/36
10 Bun Cook 100.00 200.00
New York Rangers/7/3/36

1963-65 Chex Photos

The 1963-65 Chex Photos measure approximately 5" by 7". This unnumbered set depicts players from four NHL teams, Chicago Blackhawks, Detroit Red Wings, Toronto Maple Leafs, and Montreal Canadiens. These blank-backed, stiff-cardboard photos are thought to have been issued during the 1963-64 (Canadiens and Maple Leafs) and 1964-65 (Blackhawks, Red Wings, and Canadiens again) seasons. Since these photo cards are unnumbered, they are ordered and numbered below alphabetically according to the player's name. There is rumored to be a Denis DeJordy in this set. The complete set price below includes both varieties of Beliveau and Rousseau.

COMPLETE SET (60) 1,000.00 2,000.00
1 George Armstrong 20.00 40.00
2 Ralph Backstrom 10.00 20.00
3 Dave Balon 7.50 15.00
4 Bob Baun 12.50 25.00
5A Jean Beliveau 50.00 100.00
5B Jean Beliveau 50.00 100.00
6 Red Berenson 10.00 20.00
7 Toe Blake CO 15.00 30.00
8 Johnny Bower 25.00 50.00
9 Alex Delvecchio 20.00 40.00
10 Kent Douglas 7.50 15.00
11 Dick Duff 10.00 20.00
12 Phil Esposito 75.00 150.00
13 John Ferguson 12.50 25.00
14 Bill Gadsby 15.00 30.00
15 Jean Gauthier 7.50 15.00
16 BoomBoom Geoffrion 30.00 60.00
17 Glenn Hall 25.00 50.00
18 Terry Harper 10.00 20.00
19 Billy Harris 7.50 15.00
20 Bill Hay 7.50 15.00
21 Paul Henderson 20.00 40.00
22 Bill Hicke 7.50 15.00
23 Wayne Hillman 7.50 15.00
24 Charlie Hodge 12.50 25.00
25 Tim Horton 50.00 100.00
26 Gordie Howe 112.50 225.00
27 Bobby Hull 100.00 200.00
28 Punch Imlach CO 10.00 20.00
29 Red Kelly 20.00 40.00
30 Dave Keon 30.00 60.00
31 Jacques Laperriere 12.50 25.00
32 Ed Litzenberger 7.50 15.00
33 Parker MacDonald 7.50 15.00
34 Bruce MacGregor 7.50 15.00
35 Frank Mahovlich 30.00 60.00
36 Chico Maki 10.00 20.00
37 Pit Martin 10.00 20.00
38 John MacMillan 7.50 15.00
39 Stan Mikita 30.00 60.00
40 Bob Nevin 7.50 15.00
41 Pierre Pilote 12.50 25.00
42 Marcel Pronovost 15.00 30.00
43 Claude Provost 7.50 15.00
44 Bob Pulford 15.00 30.00
45 Marc Reaume 7.50 15.00
46 Henri Richard 30.00 60.00
47A Bobby Rousseau 10.00 20.00
47B Bob Rousseau 15.00 30.00
48 Eddie Shack 20.00 40.00
49 Don Simmons 10.00 20.00
50 Allan Stanley 15.00 30.00
51 Ron Stewart 7.50 15.00
52 Jean-Guy Talbot 10.00 20.00
53 Gilles Tremblay 7.50 15.00
54 J.C. Tremblay 10.00 20.00
55 Norm Ullman 20.00 40.00
56 Elmer Vasko 7.50 15.00
57 Ken Wharram 10.00 20.00
58 Gump Worsley 25.00 50.00

1972-73 Cleveland Crusaders WHA

This 15-card set measures 8 1/2" x 11" and features a black and white head shot on the front along with a facsimile autograph, and a Cleveland Crusaders color logo in the lower left corner. Featured portraits were done by Charles Linnett. The cards are unnumbered and checklisted below in alphabetical order.

COMPLETE SET (15) 25.00 50.00
1 Ron Buchanan 2.00 4.00
2 Ray Clearwater 2.00 4.00
3 Bob Dillabough 2.00 4.00
4 Grant Erickson 2.00 4.00
5 Ted Hodgson 2.00 4.00
6 Ralph Hopiavouri 2.00 4.00
7 Bill Horton 2.00 4.00
8 Gary Jarrett 2.00 4.00
9 Skip Krake 2.00 4.00
10 Wayne Muloin 2.00 4.00
11 Bill Needham CO 2.00 4.00
12 Rick Pumple 2.50 5.00
13 Paul Shmyr 2.00 4.00
14 Robert Whidden 2.00 4.00
15 Jim Wiste 2.50 5.00

1964-65 Coca-Cola Caps

The 1964-65 Coca-Cola Caps set contains 108 bottle caps measuring approximately 1 1/8" in diameter. The caps feature a black and white picture on the tops, and are unnumbered except for uniform numbers (which is listed to the right of the player's name in the checklist below). These caps were issued with both Coke and Sprite. Because Sprite was sold in lesser quantities than Coke, those caps tend to be harder to find. As such, some dealers charge a slight premium for those caps. There are also rumored to be French variations for both the Coke and the Sprite caps, making a total of four possible ways to put the set together. While no transactions have been reported for these French versions, it's fair to assume that their scarcity alone might earn them a slight premium over the prices listed below. The set numbering below is by teams and numerically within teams as follows: Boston Bruins (1-18), Chicago Blackhawks (19-36), Detroit Red Wings (37-54), Montreal Canadiens (55-72, New York Rangers (73-90), and Toronto Maple Leafs (91-108). A plastic holder (in the shape of a rink) was also available for holding and displaying the caps; the holder is not included in the complete set price below.

COMPLETE SET (108) 375.00 750.00
1 Ed Johnston 1 2.50 5.00
2 Bob McCord 4 1.50 3.00
3 Ted Green 6 2.00 4.00
4 Orland Kurtenbach 7 2.00 4.00
5 Gary Dornhoefer 8 2.00 4.00
6 Johnny Bucyk 9 5.00 10.00
7 Tom Johnson 10 2.00 4.00
8 Tom Williams 11 1.50 3.00
9 Murray Balfour 12 1.50 3.00
10 Forbes Kennedy 14 1.50 3.00
11 Murray Oliver 16 1.50 3.00
12 Dean Prentice 17 2.00 4.00
13 Ed Westfall 18 2.00 4.00
14 Reg Fleming 19 1.50 3.00
15 Leo Boivin 20 2.00 4.00
16 Ab McDonald 21 1.50 3.00
17 Ron Schock 23 1.50 3.00
18 Bob Leiter 24 1.50 3.00
19 Glenn Hall 1 6.00 12.00
20 Doug Mohns 2 2.00 4.00
21 Pierre Pilote 3 2.50 5.00
22 Elmer Vasko 4 1.50 3.00
23 Fred Stanfield 6 1.50 3.00
24 Phil Esposito 7 20.00 40.00
25 Bobby Hull 9 25.00 50.00
26 Bill Hay 11 1.25 2.50
27 John Brenneman 12 1.25 2.50
28 Doug Robinson 14 1.50 3.00
29 Eric Nesterenko 15 2.00 4.00
30 Chico Maki 16 2.00 4.00
31 Ken Wharram 17 1.50 3.00
32 John McKenzie 18 1.50 3.00
33 Al MacNeil 19 1.50 3.00
34 Wayne Hillman 20 1.50 3.00
35 Stan Mikita 21 7.50 15.00
36 Denis DeJordy 30 2.00 4.00
37 Roger Crozier 1 2.50 5.00
38 Albert Langlois 2 1.50 3.00
39 Marcel Pronovost 3 2.00 4.00
40 Bill Gadsby 4 2.00 4.00

41 Doug Barkley 5	1.50	3.00
42 Norm Ullman 7	4.00	8.00
43 Pit Martin 8	2.00	4.00
44 Gordie Howe 9	30.00	60.00
45A Gordie Howe 10	40.00	80.00
45B Alex Delvecchio 10	15.00	30.00
46 Ron Murphy 12	1.50	3.00
47 Larry Jeffrey 14	1.50	3.00
48 Ted Lindsay 15	5.00	10.00
49 Bruce MacGregor 16	1.50	3.00
50 Floyd Smith 17	1.50	3.00
51 Gary Bergman 18	1.50	3.00
52 Paul Henderson 19	3.00	6.00
53 Parker MacDonald 20	1.50	3.00
54 Eddie Joyal 21	1.50	3.00
55 Charlie Hodge 1	2.00	4.00
56 Jacques Laperriere 2	2.00	4.00
57 J.C. Tremblay 3	2.00	4.00
58 Jean Beliveau 4	10.00	20.00
59 Ralph Backstrom 6	2.00	4.00
60 Bill Hicke 8	1.50	3.00
61 Ted Harris 10	1.50	3.00
62 Claude Larose 11	1.50	3.00
63 Yvan Cournoyer 12	7.50	15.00
64 Claude Provost 14	1.50	3.00
65 Bobby Rousseau 15	2.00	4.00
66 Henri Richard 16	6.00	12.00
67 Jean-Guy Talbot 17	2.00	4.00
68 Terry Harper 19	2.00	4.00
69 Dave Balon 20	1.50	3.00
70 Gilles Tremblay 21	1.50	3.00
71 John Ferguson 22	2.50	5.00
72 Jim Roberts 26	1.50	3.00
73 Jacques Plante 1	10.00	20.00
74 Harry Howell 3	2.00	4.00
75 Arnie Brown 4	1.50	3.00
76 Don Johns 6	1.50	3.00
77 Rod Gilbert 7	4.00	8.00
78 Bob Nevin 8	1.50	3.00
79 Dick Duff 9	2.00	4.00
80 Earl Ingarfield 10	1.50	3.00
81 Vic Hadfield 11	2.00	4.00
82 Jim Mikol 12	1.50	3.00
83 Val Fonteyne 14	1.50	3.00
84 Jim Neilson 15	1.50	3.00
85 Rod Seiling 16	1.50	3.00
86 Lou Angotti 17	1.50	3.00
87 Phil Goyette 20	1.50	3.00
88 Camille Henry 21	2.00	4.00
89 Don Marshall 22	2.00	4.00
90 Marcel Paille 23	2.00	4.00
91 Johnny Bower 1	5.00	10.00
92 Carl Brewer 2	2.00	4.00
93 Red Kelly 4	5.00	10.00
94 Tim Horton 7	7.50	15.00
95 George Armstrong 9	4.00	8.00
96 Andy Bathgate 10	4.00	8.00
97 Ron Ellis 11	2.00	4.00
98 Ralph Stewart 12	1.50	3.00
99 Dave Keon 14	4.00	8.00
100 Dickie Moore 16	2.50	5.00
101 Don McKenney 17	1.50	3.00
102 Kent Douglas 19	1.50	3.00
103 Bob Pulford 20	2.50	5.00
104 Bob Baun 21	2.50	5.00
105 Eddie Shack 23	4.00	8.00
106 Terry Sawchuk 24	10.00	20.00
107 Allan Stanley 26	2.50	5.00
108 Frank Mahovlich	6.00	12.00
xx Cap Holder	50.00	100.00
(Plastic Rink		

1965-66 Coca-Cola

This set contains 108 unnumbered black and white cards featuring 18 players from each of the six NHL teams. The cards were issued in perforated team panels of 18 cards. The cards are priced below as perforated cards; the value of unperforated strips is approximately 20-30 percent more than the sum of the individual prices. The cards are approximately 2 3/4" by 3 1/2" and have bi-lingual (French and English) write-ups on the card backs. An album to hold the cards was available from the company on a mail-order basis. It retails in the $50-$75 range in Near Mint. The set numbering below is by teams and numerically within teams as follows: Boston Bruins (1-18), Chicago Blackhawks (19-36), Detroit Red Wings (37-54), Montreal Canadiens (55-72, New York Rangers (73-90), and Toronto Maple Leafs (91-108).

COMPLETE SET (108)	250.00	500.00
1 Gerry Cheevers	15.00	30.00
2 Albert Langlois	.75	1.50
3 Ted Green	1.00	2.00
4 Ron Stewart	.75	1.50
5 Bob Woytowich	.75	1.50
6 Johnny Bucyk	3.00	6.00
7 Tom Williams	.75	1.50
8 Forbes Kennedy	.75	1.50
9 Murray Oliver	.75	1.50
10 Dean Prentice	1.00	2.00
11 Ed Westfall	1.00	2.00
12 Reg Fleming	.75	1.50
13 Leo Boivin	1.50	3.00
14 Parker MacDonald	.75	1.50
15 Bob Dillabough	.75	1.50
16 Barry Ashbee	2.50	5.00
17 Don Awrey	.75	1.50
18 Bernie Parent	15.00	30.00
19 Glenn Hall	5.00	10.00
20 Doug Mohns	1.00	2.00
21 Pierre Pilote	1.50	3.00
22 Elmer Vasko	.75	1.50
23 Matt Ravlich	.75	1.50
24 Fred Stanfield	.75	1.50
25 Phil Esposito	20.00	40.00
26 Bobby Hull	20.00	40.00
27 Dennis Hull	2.50	5.00
28 Bill Hay	1.00	2.00
29 Ken Hodge	1.50	3.00
30 Eric Nesterenko	1.00	2.00
31 Chico Maki	1.00	2.00
32 Ken Wharram	1.00	2.00
33 Al MacNeil	.75	1.50
34 Doug Jarrett	.75	1.50
35 Stan Mikita	6.00	12.00
36 Dave Dryden	1.25	2.50
37 Roger Crozier	1.50	3.00
38 Warren Godfrey	.75	1.50
39 Bert Marshall	.75	1.50
40 Bill Gadsby	1.50	3.00
41 Doug Barkley	.75	1.50
42 Norm Ullman	2.00	4.00
43 Gordie Howe	30.00	60.00
44 Alex Delvecchio	2.50	5.00
45 Val Fonteyne	.75	1.50
46 Ron Murphy	.75	1.50
47 Billy Harris	.75	1.50
48 Bruce MacGregor	.75	1.50
49 Floyd Smith	.75	1.50
50 Paul Henderson	4.00	8.00
51 Andy Bathgate	1.75	3.50
52 Ab McDonald	.75	1.50
53 Gary Bergman	.75	1.50
54 Hank Bassen	1.25	2.50
55 Charlie Hodge	1.50	3.00
56 Jacques Laperriere	1.50	3.00
57 Jean-Claude Tremblay	1.00	2.00
58 Jean Beliveau	7.50	15.00
59 Ralph Backstrom	1.00	2.00
60 Dick Duff	1.25	2.50
61 Ted Harris	1.00	2.00
62 Claude Larose	.75	1.50
63 Yvan Cournoyer	10.00	20.00
64 Claude Provost	1.00	2.00
65 Bobby Rousseau	1.00	2.00
66 Henri Richard	5.00	10.00
67 Jean-Guy Talbot	1.25	2.50
68 Terry Harper	1.00	2.00
69 Gilles Tremblay	.75	1.50
70 John Ferguson	1.25	2.50
71 Jim Roberts	1.00	2.00
72 Gump Worsley	5.00	10.00
73 Ed Giacomin	12.50	25.00
74 Wayne Hillman	.75	1.50
75 Harry Howell	2.00	4.00
76 Arnie Brown	.75	1.50
77 Doug Robinson	.75	1.50
78 Mike McMahon	.75	1.50
79 Rod Gilbert	2.50	5.00
80 Bob Nevin	.75	1.50
81 Earl Ingarfield	.75	1.50
82 Vic Hadfield	1.25	2.50
83 Bill Hicke	.75	1.50
84 John McKenzie	1.00	2.00
85 Jim Neilson	.75	1.50
86 Jean Ratelle	2.50	5.00
87 Phil Goyette	.75	1.50
88 Garry Peters	.75	1.50
89 Don Marshall	.75	1.50
90 Don Simmons	1.25	2.50
91 Johnny Bower	5.00	10.00
92 Marcel Pronovost	2.00	4.00
93 Red Kelly	2.50	5.00
94 Tim Horton	7.50	15.00
95 Ron Ellis	1.00	2.00
96 George Armstrong	2.00	4.00
97 Brit Selby	.75	1.50
98 Pete Stemkowski	.75	1.50
99 Dave Keon	5.00	10.00
100 Mike Walton	1.00	2.00
101 Kent Douglas	.75	1.50
102 Bob Pulford	2.00	4.00
103 Bob Baun	2.00	4.00
104 Eddie Shack	2.50	5.00
105 Orland Kurtenbach	1.00	2.00
106 Allan Stanley	1.50	3.00
107 Frank Mahovlich	5.00	10.00
108 Terry Sawchuk	10.00	20.00
NNO Album	40.00	80.00

1965-66 Coca-Cola Booklets

These four "How To Play" booklets are illustrated with cartoon-like drawings, each measure approximately 4 7/8" by 3 1/2", and are printed on newsprint. Booklets A and B have yellow covers, while booklets C and D have blue covers. The 31-page booklets could be obtained through a mail-in offer. Under bottle caps of Coke or Sprite (marked with a hockey stick) were cork liners bearing the name of the player who wrote a booklet. To receive a booklet, the collector had to send in ten cork liners (with name of the player whose booklet was desired), ten cents, and the correct answer to a trivia question. Issued by Coca-Cola to promote hockey among the school-aged, they are designed in comic book fashion showing correct positions and moves for goalie, forward (both defensive and offensive), and defenseman. They are authored by the hockey players listed below. They are lettered rather than numbered and we have checklisted them below accordingly. The booklets were available in both English and French.

COMPLETE SET (4)	75.00	150.00
A Johnny Bower	25.00	50.00
How To Play		
Goal		
B Dave Keon	25.00	50.00
How To Play		
Forward/Defense		
C Jacques Laperriere	12.50	25.00
How to Play		
Defense		
D Henri Richard	25.00	50.00
How To Play		
Forward/Offense		

1977-78 Coca-Cola

Each of these mini-cards measures approximately 1 3/8" by 1 3/8". The fronts feature a color "mug shot" of the player, with his name given above the picture. Red and blue lines form the borders on the sides of the picture. The year 1978, the city from which the team hails, and the Coke logo appear below the picture. Inside a black border (with rounded corners) the back has basic biographical information. These unnumbered cards are listed alphabetically below.

COMPLETE SET (30)	62.50	300.00
1 Syl Apps	.75	3.00
2 Dave Burrows	.75	3.00
3 Bobby Clarke	6.00	25.00
4 Yvan Cournoyer	2.50	10.00
5 John Davidson	1.50	10.00
6 Marcel Dionne	4.00	15.00
7 Doug Favell	1.25	5.00
8 Rod Gilbert	1.50	10.00
9 Brian Glennie	.75	3.00
10 Butch Goring	.75	3.00
11 Lorne Henning	.75	3.00
12 Cliff Koroll	.75	3.00
13 Guy Lapointe	1.50	5.00
14 Dave Maloney	.75	3.00
15 Pit Martin	.75	3.00
16 Lou Nanne	.75	3.00
17 Bobby Orr	30.00	125.00
18 Brad Park	2.50	10.00
19 Craig Ramsay	.75	3.00
20 Larry Robinson	5.00	20.00
21 Jim Rutherford	1.25	5.00
22 Don Saleski	.75	3.00
23 Steve Shutt	2.50	8.00
24 Darryl Sittler	4.00	20.00
25 Billy Smith	3.00	10.00
26 Bob Stewart	.75	3.00
27 Rogatien Vachon	2.50	10.00
28 Jimmy Watson	.75	3.00
29 Joe Watson	.75	3.00
30 Ed Westfall	.75	3.00

1970-71 Colgate Stamps

The 1970-71 Colgate Stamps set includes 93 small color stamps measuring approximately 1" by 1 1/4". The set was distributed in three sheets of 31. Sheet one featured centers (numbered 1-31) and was available with the giant size of toothpaste, sheet two featured wings (numbered 32-62) and was available with the family size of toothpaste, and sheet three featured goalies and defensemen (numbered 63-93) and was available with king and super size toothpaste. The cards are priced below as individual stamps; the value of a complete sheet would be approximately 20 percent more than the sum of the individual stamp prices. Colgate also issued three calendars so that brushers could stick a stamp on each day for brushing regularly. These calendars retail in the $5-$10 range. The cards were numbered in a star in the upper left corner of the card face.

COMPLETE SET (93)	100.00	200.00
1 Walt McKechnie	.50	1.00
2 Bob Pulford	1.50	3.00
3 Mike Walton	.50	1.00
4 Alex Delvecchio	2.50	5.00
5 Tom Williams	.50	1.00
6 Derek Sanderson	5.00	10.00
7 Garry Unger	1.00	2.00
8 Lou Angotti	.50	1.00
9 Ted Hampson	.50	1.00
10 Phil Goyette	.50	1.00
11 Juha Widing	.50	1.00
12 Norm Ullman	2.00	4.00
13 Garry Monahan	.50	1.00
14 Henri Richard	2.50	5.00
15 Ray Cullen	.50	1.00
16 Danny O'Shea	.50	1.00
17 Marc Tardif	.75	1.50
18 Jude Drouin	.50	1.00
19 Charlie Burns	.50	1.00
20 Gerry Meehan	.75	1.50
21 Ralph Backstrom	.75	1.50
22 Frank St.Marseille	.50	1.00
23 Orland Kurtenbach	.50	1.00
24 Red Berenson	1.00	2.00
25 Jean Ratelle	2.00	4.00
26 Syl Apps	.75	1.50
27 Don Marshall	.50	1.00
28 Gilbert Perreault	5.00	10.00
29 Andre Lacroix	.75	1.50
30 Jacques Lemaire	1.50	3.00
31 Pit Martin	.75	1.50
32 Dennis Hull	.75	1.50
33 Dave Balon	.50	1.00
34 Keith McCreary	.50	1.00
35 Bobby Rousseau	.75	1.50
36 Danny Grant	.75	1.50
37 Brit Selby	.50	1.00
38 Bob Nevin	.50	1.00
39 Rosaire Paiement	.50	1.00
40 Gary Dornhoefer	1.00	2.00
41 Eddie Shack	2.00	4.00
42 Ron Schock	.50	1.00
43 Jim Pappin	.50	1.00
44 Mickey Redmond	1.50	3.00
45 Vic Hadfield	.75	1.50
46 Johnny Bucyk	2.00	4.00
47 Gordie Howe	12.00	30.00
48 Ron Anderson	.50	1.00
49 Gary Jarrett	.50	1.00
50 Jean Pronovost	.75	1.50
51 Simon Nolet	.50	1.00
52 Bill Goldsworthy	.75	1.50
53 Rod Gilbert	2.00	4.00
54 Ron Ellis	.75	1.50
55 Mike Byers	.50	1.00
56 Norm Ferguson	.50	1.00
57 Gary Sabourin	.50	1.00
58 Tim Ecclestone	.50	1.00
59 John McKenzie	.50	1.00
60 Yvan Cournoyer	2.00	4.00
61 Ken Schinkel	.50	1.00
62 Ken Hodge	1.00	2.00
63 Cesare Maniago	1.50	3.00
64 J.C. Tremblay	.75	1.50
65 Gilles Marotte	.50	1.00
66 Bob Baun	1.00	2.00
67 Gerry Desjardins	1.00	2.00
68 Charlie Hodge	1.50	3.00
69 Matt Ravlich	.50	1.00
70 Ed Giacomin	3.00	6.00
71 Gerry Cheevers	4.00	8.00
72 Pat Quinn	.75	1.50
73 Gary Bergman	.50	1.00
74 Serge Savard	1.00	2.00
75 Les Binkley	1.00	2.00
76 Arnie Brown	.50	1.00
77 Pat Stapleton	.50	1.00
78 Ed Van Impe	.50	1.00
79 Jim Dorey	.50	1.00
80 Dave Dryden	1.50	3.00
81 Dale Tallon	.75	1.50
82 Bruce Gamble	1.50	3.00
83 Roger Crozier	1.50	3.00
84 Denis DeJordy	1.50	3.00
85 Rogatien Vachon	2.00	4.00
86 Carol Vadnais	.50	1.00
87 Bobby Orr	20.00	50.00
88 Noel Picard	.50	1.00
89 Gilles Villemure	1.50	3.00
90 Gary Smith	1.50	3.00
91 Doug Favell	1.50	3.00
92 Ernie Wakely	1.50	3.00
93 Bernie Parent	5.00	10.00
NNO Stamp Calendar Sheet	5.00	10.00

1971-72 Colgate Heads

The 16 hockey collectibles in this set measure approximately 1 1/4" in height with a base of 7/8" and are made out of cream-colored or beige plastic. The promotion lasted approximately five months during the winter of 1972. The busts were issued in series of four in the various sizes of Colgate Toothpaste. The player's last name is found only on the back of the base of the head. The Ullmann error is not included in the complete set price below. The heads are unnumbered and checklisted below in alphabetical order.

COMPLETE SET (16)	100.00	200.00
1 Yvon Cournoyer	3.00	8.00
2 Marcel Dionne UER	6.00	15.00
3 Ken Dryden	8.00	20.00
4 Paul Henderson	2.50	6.00
5 Guy Lafleur	8.00	20.00
6 Frank Mahovlich	4.00	10.00
7 Richard Martin SP	15.00	30.00
8 Bobby Orr	20.00	40.00
9 Brad Park SP	20.00	40.00
10 Jacques Plante	6.00	15.00
11 Jean Ratelle	3.00	8.00
12 Derek Sanderson	6.00	15.00
13 Dale Tallon	2.00	5.00
14 Walt Tkaczuk	2.00	4.00
15A Norm Ullman ERR	5.00	12.00
(incorrectly spelled Ullmann		
15B Norm Ullman COR	12.00	30.00
Spelled Ullman		
16 Garry Unger	2.00	5.00

1959 Comet Sweets Olympic Achievements

Celebrating various Olympic events, ceremonies, and their history, this 25-card set was issued by Comet Sweets. The cards are printed on thin cardboard stock and measure 1 7/16" by 2 9/16". Inside white borders, the fronts display water color paintings of various Olympic events. Some cards are horizontally oriented; others are vertically oriented. The set title "Olympic Achievements" appears at the top on the backs, with a discussion of the event below. This set is the first series; the cards are numbered "X to 25."

COMPLETE SET (25)	30.00	60.00
20 Hockey	2.50	5.00

1962-63 Cowan Ceramic Tiles

These unique collectibles featured artistic renditions (by H.M. Cowan) of top NHL players on smallish ceramic tiles. As they were unnumbered, the tiles were checklisted below by the number that appears on their original box.

1 Charlie Burns	75.00	150.00
2 Red Berenson	100.00	200.00
3 Ralph Backstrom	100.00	200.00
4 Larry Cahan	75.00	150.00
5 Bernie Geoffrion	250.00	500.00
6 Phil Goyette	75.00	150.00
7 Doug Harvey	150.00	300.00
8 Bronco Horvath	75.00	150.00
9 Harry Howell	125.00	250.00
10 Andy Hebenton	75.00	150.00
11 Jim Langlois	75.00	150.00
12 Bert Marshall	75.00	150.00
13 Marcel Pronovost	150.00	300.00
14 Henri Richard	350.00	600.00
15 Bobby Rousseau	75.00	150.00

16 Gilles Tremblay	100.00	200.00
17 Jerry Toppazzini	100.00	200.00
18 Gump Worsley	250.00	500.00
19 Dave Balon	75.00	150.00
20 Jean Beliveau	500.00	800.00
21 Claude Provost	125.00	250.00
22 Vic Hadfield	75.00	150.00
23 Jean-Guy Talbot	100.00	200.00
24 Dickie Moore	100.00	200.00
25 Jean Ratelle	75.00	150.00
26 Tom Johnson	100.00	200.00
27 Earl Ingarfield	75.00	150.00
28 Lou Fontinato	100.00	200.00
29 Cesare Maniago	100.00	200.00
30 Ted Hampson	75.00	150.00
31 Muzz Patrick	75.00	150.00
32 Andy Bathgate	100.00	200.00
33 Bill Hicke	75.00	150.00
34 J.C. Tremblay	100.00	200.00

1924-25 Crescent Falcon-Tigers

The 1924-25 Crescent Ice Cream Falcon-Tigers set contains 13 black and white cards measuring approximately 1 9/16" by 2 3/8". The back has the card number (at the top) and two offers: 1) a brick of ice cream to any person bringing to the Crescent Ice Cream plant any 14 Crescent Hockey Pictures bearing consecutive numbers; and 2) a hockey stick to anyone bringing to the ice cream plant three sets of Crescent Hockey Pictures bearing consecutive numbers from 1-14. The complete set price below does not include the unknown card 6, which is believed to have been short printed.

COMPLETE SET (13)	1,200.00	2,400.00
1 Bill Cockburn	112.50	225.00
2 Wally Byron	100.00	200.00
3 Wally Fridfinson	100.00	200.00
4 Murray Murdoch	125.00	250.00
5 Oliver Redpath	100.00	200.00
7 Ward McVey	100.00	200.00
8 Tote Mitchell	100.00	200.00
9 Lorne Carrol	100.00	200.00
10 Tony Wise	100.00	200.00
11 Johnny Myres	100.00	200.00
12 Gordon McKenzie	100.00	200.00
13 Harry Neal	112.50	225.00
14 Blake Watson	112.50	225.00

1923-24 Crescent Selkirks

The 1923-24 Crescent Ice Cream set contains 14 cards measuring approximately 1 9/16" by 2 3/8". The set features the Selkirks hockey club and was produced by Crescent Ice Cream of Winnipeg, Manitoba. The front shows a black and white head and shoulders shot of the player, with the team name written in a crescent over the player's head. At the bottom of the picture, the player's name and position appear in white lettering in a black stripe. The back has the card number (at the top) and two offers: 1) a brick of ice cream to any person bringing to the Crescent Ice Cream plant any 14 Crescent Hockey Pictures bearing consecutive numbers; and 2) a hockey stick to anyone bringing to the ice cream plant three sets of Crescent Hockey Pictures bearing consecutive numbers from 1-14. The complete set price below does not include the unknown card number 6.

COMPLETE SET (13)	600.00	1,200.00
1 Cliff O'Meara	62.50	125.00
2 Leo Benard	50.00	100.00
3 Pete Speirs	50.00	100.00
4 Howard Brandon	50.00	100.00
5 George A. Clark	50.00	100.00
7 Cecil Browne	50.00	100.00
8 Jack Connelly	50.00	100.00
9 Charlie Gardner	100.00	200.00
10 Ward Turvey	50.00	100.00
11 Connie Johanneson	50.00	100.00
12 Frank Woodall	50.00	100.00
13 Harold McMunn	50.00	100.00
14 Connie Neil	62.50	125.00

1924-25 Crescent Selkirks

The 1924-25 Crescent Ice Cream Selkirks set contains 14 black and white cards measuring approximately 1 9/16" by 2 3/8". The back has the card number (at the top) and two offers: 1) a brick of ice cream to any person bringing to the Crescent Ice Cream plant any 14 Crescent Hockey Pictures bearing consecutive numbers; and 2) a hockey stick to anyone bringing to the ice cream plant three sets of Crescent Hockey Pictures bearing consecutive numbers from 1-14.

COMPLETE SET (14)	850.00	1,700.00
1 Howard Brandon	50.00	100.00
2 Jack Hughes	50.00	100.00
3 Tony Baril	50.00	100.00
4 Bill Bowman	50.00	100.00
5 W. Roberts	50.00	100.00
6 Cecil Browne SP	375.00	750.00
7 Errol Gillis	50.00	100.00
8 Selkirks Team On The Ice	100.00	200.00
9 Fred Comfort	50.00	100.00
10 Cliff O'Meara	50.00	100.00
11 Leo Benard	50.00	100.00
12 Pete Speirs	50.00	100.00
13 Peter Meurer	50.00	100.00
14 Bill Borland	50.00	100.00

1935-40 Crown Brand Photos

49 Montreal Maroons 1936-37	30.00	60.00
50 Montreal Canadiens 1936-37	30.00	60.00
51 Baldy Northcott	12.50	25.00
52 Dave Trottier	12.50	25.00
53 Russ Blinco	12.50	25.00
54 Earl Robinson Maroons	12.50	25.00
55 Bob Gracie	12.50	25.00
56 Gus Marker	12.50	25.00
57 Howie Morenz	150.00	250.00
58 Johnny Gagnon	12.50	25.00
59 Wilfred Cude	60.00	100.00
60 Georges Mantha	12.50	25.00
61 Paul Haynes	12.50	25.00
62 Marty Barry	20.00	40.00
63 Peter Kelly	12.50	25.00
64 Dave Kerr	12.50	25.00
65 Roy Worters	12.50	25.00
66 Ace Bailey	20.00	40.00
67 Art Lesieur	15.00	30.00
68 Frank Boucher	15.00	30.00
69 Marty Burke	12.50	25.00
70 Alex Levinsky	12.50	25.00
71 Father Leveque's Maple Leafs	40.00	80.00
72 Father Leveque's Six Stars	40.00	80.00
76 Father Leveque's Canadiens	20.00	40.00
77 Stewart Evans	12.50	25.00
78 Herb Cain	12.50	25.00
79 Carl Voss	20.00	40.00
80 Roger Jenkins	12.50	25.00
81 Jack McGill	12.50	25.00
82 Mush March	15.00	30.00
106 Montreal Maroons 1937-38	40.00	80.00
107 Montreal Canadiens 1937-38	30.00	60.00
108 Toe Blake	40.00	80.00
109 Joffre Desilets	12.50	25.00
110 Babe Siebert	20.00	40.00
111 Frank Clancy	300.00	500.00
112 Aurel Joliat	50.00	100.00
113 Walter Buswell	12.50	25.00
114 Bill MacKenzie	12.50	25.00
115 Pit Lepine	12.50	25.00
116 Cliff Goupille	12.50	25.00
117 Rod Lorrain	12.50	25.00
118 Polly Drouin	12.50	25.00
119 Marvin Wentworth	12.50	25.00
120 Allan Shields	12.50	25.00
121 Jimmy Ward	12.50	25.00
122 Bill Beveridge	12.50	25.00
123 Gerry Shannon	12.50	25.00
124 Des Smith	12.50	25.00
125 Armand Mondou	15.00	30.00
151 Montreal Canadiens 1938-39	40.00	80.00
152 Herb Cain	12.50	25.00
153 Bob Gracie	12.50	25.00
154 Jimmy Ward	12.50	25.00
155 Stew Evans	12.50	25.00
156 Louis Trudel	12.50	25.00
157 Cy Wentworth	12.50	25.00
195 Marty Barry	12.50	25.00
196 Earl Robinson Canadiens	12.50	25.00
197 Ray Getliffe	12.50	25.00
198 Charlie Sands	12.50	25.00
199 Claude Bourque	12.50	25.00
200 Doug Young	12.50	25.00
NNO Montreal Canadiens (1935-36)	40.00	80.00
NNO Montreal Canadiens 1939-40	30.00	60.00
NNO Stanley Cup Champs 1934-35	25.00	50.00
NNO Team Canada 1936	20.00	40.00
NNO Album	25.00	50.00

1970-71 Dad's Cookies

The 1970-71 Dad's Cookies set contains 144 unnumbered color cards. Each card measures approximately 1 7/8" by 5 3/8". Each player is pictured on the front dressed in an "NHL Players" emblazoned jersey. The fronts contain player statistics for the 1969-70 season and for his career. The backs, in both English and French, are the same for all cards. The backs contain an ad for these cards and Dad's Cookies, a special offer for an NHL Players Association decal and a 1969 NHL Players Association copyright line.

COMPLETE SET (144)	100.00	200.00
1 Lou Angotti	.75	2.00
2 Don Awrey	.50	1.00
3 Bob Baun	1.25	3.00
4 Jean Beliveau	6.00	15.00
5 Red Berenson	.75	2.00
6 Gary Bergman	.50	1.00
7 Les Binkley	1.00	2.50
8 Andre Boudrias	.50	1.00
9 Wally Boyer	.50	1.00
10 Arnie Brown	.50	1.00
11 Johnny Bucyk	1.50	4.00
12 Charlie Burns	.50	1.00
13 Larry Cahan	.50	1.00
14 Gerry Cheevers	2.50	6.00
15 Bobby Clarke	5.00	12.00
16 Wayne Connelly	.50	1.00
17 Yvan Cournoyer	1.50	4.00
18 Roger Crozier	1.00	2.50
19 Ray Cullen	.50	1.00
20 Denis DeJordy	1.00	2.50
21 Alex Delvecchio	1.50	4.00
22 Bob Dillabough	.50	1.00
23 Gary Doak	.50	1.00
24 Gary Dornhoefer	1.00	2.50
25 Dick Duff	.75	2.00
26 Tim Ecclestone	.50	1.00
27 Roy Edwards	1.00	2.50
28 Gerry Ehman	.50	1.00
29 Ron Ellis	.75	2.00
30 Phil Esposito	5.00	12.00
31 Tony Esposito	5.00	12.00
32 Doug Favell	1.00	2.50
33 John Ferguson	.75	2.00
34 Norm Ferguson	.50	1.00
35 Reg Fleming	.50	1.00
36 Bill Flett	.50	1.00
37 Bruce Gamble	1.00	2.50
38 Jean-Guy Gendron	.50	1.00
39 Ed Giacomin	2.00	5.00
40 Rod Gilbert	1.50	4.00
41 Bill Goldsworthy	.75	2.00
42 Phil Goyette	.50	1.00
43 Danny Grant	.75	2.00
44 Ted Green	.75	2.00
45 Vic Hadfield	.75	2.00
46 Al Hamilton	.50	1.00
47 Ted Hampson	.50	1.00
48 Terry Harper	.75	2.00
49 Ted Harris	.50	1.00
50 Paul Henderson	2.50	6.00
51 Bryan Hextall	.50	1.00
52 Bill Hicke	.50	1.00
53 Larry Hillman	.50	1.00
54 Wayne Hillman	.50	1.00
55 Charlie Hodge	1.25	3.00
56 Ken Hodge	.75	2.00
57 Gordie Howe	10.00	25.00
58 Harry Howell	1.00	2.50
59 Bobby Hull	8.00	20.00
60 Dennis Hull	.75	2.00
61 Earl Ingarfield	.50	1.00
62 Doug Jarrett	.50	1.00
63 Gary Jarrett	.50	1.00
64 Ed Johnston	1.00	2.50
65 Dave Keon	1.50	4.00
66 Skip Krake	.50	1.00
67 Orland Kurtenbach	.75	2.00
68 Andre Lacroix	.75	2.00
69 Jacques Laperriere	1.25	3.00
70 Jacques Lemaire	1.50	4.00
71 Rick Ley	.50	1.00
72 Bruce MacGregor	.50	1.00
73 Keith Magnuson	.75	2.00
74 Frank Mahovlich	2.00	5.00
75 Chico Maki	.50	1.00
76 Gilles Marotte	.50	1.00
77 Bert Marshall	.50	1.00
78 Don Marshall	.50	1.00
79 Pit Martin	.75	2.00
80 Keith McCreary	.50	1.00
81 Ab McDonald	.50	1.00
82 Jim McKenny	.75	2.00
83 John McKenzie	.75	2.00
84 Mike McMahon	.50	1.00
85 Larry Mickey	.50	1.00
86 Stan Mikita	2.50	6.00
87 Doug Mohns	.50	1.00
88 Wayne Muloin	.50	1.00
89 Jim Neilson	.50	1.00
90 Bob Nevin	.50	1.00
91 Murray Oliver	.50	1.00
92 Bobby Orr	20.00	40.00
93 Danny O'Shea	.50	1.00
94 Rosaire Paiement	.50	1.00
95 Bernie Parent	2.50	6.00
96 Jean-Paul Parise	.50	1.00
97 Brad Park	4.00	10.00
98 Mike Pelyk	.50	1.00
99 Gilbert Perreault	2.00	5.00
100 Noel Picard	.50	1.00
101 Barclay Plager	.75	2.00
102 Jacques Plante	6.00	15.00
103 Tracy Pratt	.50	1.00
104 Dean Prentice	.50	1.00
105 Jean Pronovost	.75	2.00
106 Bob Pulford	.75	2.00
107 Pat Quinn	1.00	2.50
108 Jean Ratelle	1.00	2.50
109 Matt Ravlich	.50	1.00
110 Mickey Redmond	1.00	2.50
111 Henri Richard	2.50	6.00
112 Jim Roberts	.50	1.00
113 Dale Rolfe	.50	1.00
114 Bobby Rousseau	.50	1.00
115 Gary Sabourin	.50	1.00
116 Derek Sanderson	2.50	6.00
117 Glen Sather	1.50	4.00
118 Serge Savard	1.00	2.50
119 Ken Schinkel	.50	1.00
120 Rod Seiling	.50	1.00
121 Brit Selby	.50	1.00
122 Eddie Shack	1.50	4.00
123 Floyd Smith	.50	1.00
124 Fred Stanfield	.50	1.00
125 Pat Stapleton	.60	1.50
126 Frank St.Marseille	.50	1.00
127 Dale Tallon	.60	1.50
128 Walt Tkaczuk	.50	1.00
129 J.C. Tremblay	.50	1.00
130 Norm Ullman	.75	2.00
131 Garry Unger	.75	2.00
132 Rogatien Vachon	2.00	5.00
133 Carol Vadnais	.50	1.00
134 Ed Van Impe	.50	1.00
135 Bob Wall	.50	1.00
136 Mike Walton	.50	1.00
137 Bryan Watson	.50	1.00
138 Joe Watson	.50	1.00
139 Tom Webster	.50	1.00
140 Juha Widing	1.00	2.50
141 Tom Williams	.50	1.00
142 Jim Wiste	.50	1.00
143 Gump Worsley	2.50	6.00
144 Bob Woytowich	.75	2.00

1934-35 Diamond Matchbooks Silver

Covers from this first hockey matchbook issue generally feature color action shots with a silver background and green and black vertical bars on the cover's left side. "The Diamond Match Co., NYC" imprint appears on a double line below the striker. These matchbooks usually were issued in twin-packs through cigar and drug stores of the day. Complete matchbooks carry a 50 percent premium over the prices listed below.

COMPLETE SET (60)	1,500.00	2,400.00
1 Taffy Abel	15.00	25.00
2 Marty Barry	15.00	25.00
3 Red Beattie	15.00	25.00
4 Frank Boucher	25.00	40.00
5 Doug Brennan	15.00	25.00
6 Bill Brydge	15.00	25.00
7 Eddie Burke	35.00	50.00
8 Marty Burke	15.00	25.00
9 Gerald Carson	15.00	25.00
10 Lorne Chabot	35.00	50.00
11 Art Chapman	15.00	25.00
12 Dit Clapper	50.00	80.00
13 Lionel Conacher	50.00	80.00
14 Red Conn	15.00	25.00
15 Bill Cook	35.00	50.00
16 Bun Cook	35.00	50.00
17 Thomas Cook	18.00	30.00
18 Rosario Lolo Couture	15.00	25.00
19 Bob Davie	15.00	25.00
20 Cecil Dillon	15.00	25.00
21 Duke Dutkowski	15.00	25.00
22 Red Dutton	25.00	40.00
23 Johnny Gagnon	15.00	25.00
24 Chuck Gardiner	35.00	50.00
25 Johnny Gottselig	15.00	25.00
26 Robert Gracie	15.00	25.00
27 Lloyd Gross	15.00	25.00
28 Ott Heller	15.00	25.00
29 Normie Himes	15.00	25.00
30 Lionel Hitchman	35.00	50.00
31 Red Jackson	15.00	25.00
32 Roger Jenkins	15.00	25.00
33 Aurel Joliat	50.00	80.00
34 Butch Keeling	15.00	25.00
35 William Kendall	15.00	25.00
36 Jim Klein	15.00	25.00
37 Joe Lamb	15.00	25.00
38 Wildor Larochelle	18.00	30.00
39 Pit Lepine	15.00	25.00
40 Jack Leswick	15.00	25.00
41 Georges Mantha	35.00	50.00
42 Sylvio Mantha	35.00	50.00
43 Mush March	18.00	30.00
44 Ronnie Martin	15.00	25.00
45 Rabbitt McVeigh	15.00	25.00
46 Howie Morenz	200.00	350.00
47 Murray Murdoch	15.00	25.00
48 Harold Oliver	25.00	40.00
49 George Patterson	15.00	25.00
50 Hal Picketts	15.00	25.00
51 Victor Ripley	15.00	25.00
52 Doc Romnes	15.00	25.00
53 Johnny Sheppard	15.00	25.00
54 Eddie Shore	75.00	125.00
55 Art Somers	15.00	25.00
56 Chris Speyers	15.00	25.00
57 Nelson Stewart	35.00	50.00
58 Tiny Thompson	50.00	80.00
59 Louis Trudel	15.00	25.00
60 Roy Worters	35.00	50.00

1935-36 Diamond Matchbooks Tan 1

The reverse of these tan-colored covers feature a brief player history with the player's name and team affiliation or position appearing at the top. "The Diamond Match Co., NYC" imprint appears below the striker on a single line. Complete matchbooks carry a 50 percent premium over the prices below. A matchbook of Joe Starke is reported to exist, but we cannot officially confirm that at this point in time.

COMPLETE SET (69)	1,100.00	1,800.00
1 Andy Aitkenhead	15.00	25.00
2 Vern Ayres	15.00	25.00
3 Bill Beveridge	18.00	30.00
4 Ralph Bowman	15.00	25.00
5 Bill Brydge	15.00	25.00
6 Glenn Brydson	15.00	25.00
7 Eddie Burke	18.00	30.00
8 Marty Burke	15.00	25.00
9 Lorne Carr	15.00	25.00
10 Gerald Carson	15.00	25.00
11 Lorne Chabot	25.00	40.00
12 Art Chapman	15.00	25.00
13 Red Conn	15.00	25.00
14 Bert Connoly	15.00	25.00
15 Bun Cook	25.00	40.00
16 Tommy Cook	15.00	25.00
17 Art Coulter	15.00	25.00
18 Lolo Couture	15.00	25.00
19 Bill Cowley	18.00	30.00
20 Wilf Cude	18.00	30.00
21 Red Dutton	18.00	30.00
22 Frank Finnigan	15.00	25.00
23 Irv Frew	15.00	25.00
24 LeRoy Goldsworthy	15.00	25.00
25 Johnny Gottselig	15.00	25.00
26 Bob Gracie	15.00	25.00
27 Ott Heller	15.00	25.00
28 Normie Himes	15.00	25.00
29 Syd Howe	25.00	40.00
30 Roger Jenkins	15.00	25.00
31 Ching Johnson	30.00	50.00
32 Aurel Joliat	35.00	60.00
33 Max Kaminsky	15.00	25.00
34 Butch Keeling	15.00	25.00
35 Bill Kendall	15.00	25.00
36 Lloyd Klein	15.00	25.00
37 Joe Lamb	15.00	25.00
38 Wildor Larochelle	15.00	25.00
39 Pit Lepine	15.00	25.00
40 Norman Locking	15.00	25.00

41 Georges Mantha 25.00 40.00
42 Sylvio Mantha 25.00 40.00
43 Mush March 15.00 25.00
44 Charlie Mason 15.00 25.00
45 Donnie McFadyen 15.00 25.00
46 Jack McGill 15.00 25.00
47 Rabbit McVeigh 15.00 25.00
48 Armand Mondou 15.00 25.00
49 Howie Morenz 180.00 300.00
50 Murray Murdoch 15.00 25.00
51 Al Murray 15.00 25.00
52 Harry Oliver 25.00 40.00
53 Jean Pusie 15.00 25.00
54 Paul Marcel Raymond 15.00 25.00
55 Jack Riley 15.00 25.00
56 Vic Ripley 15.00 25.00
57 Desse Roche 15.00 25.00
58 Earl Roche 15.00 25.00
59 Doc Romnes 15.00 25.00
60 Sweeney Schriner 30.00 50.00
61 Earl Seibert 25.00 40.00
62 Gerald Shannon 15.00 25.00
63 Alex Smith 15.00 25.00
64 Joe Starke 15.00 25.00
65 Nels Stewart 30.00 50.00
66 Paul Thompson 15.00 25.00
67 Louis Trudel 15.00 25.00
68 Carl Voss 15.00 25.00
69 Art Wiebe 15.00 25.00
70 Roy Worters 25.00 40.00

1935-36 Diamond Matchbooks Tan 2

The Type 2 covers are similar to the Type 1 tan-bordered set except that the player's position or team affiliation information has been omitted from the reverse side. "The Diamond Match Co., NYC" imprint appears in a single line. As complete matchbooks are fairly scarce, they carry a premium of 50 percent over the prices below.

COMPLETE SET (63) 1,100.00 1,800.00
1 Tommy Anderson 15.00 25.00
2 Vern Ayres 15.00 25.00
3 Frank Boucher 25.00 40.00
4 Frank Boucher 25.00 40.00
5 Bill Brydge 15.00 25.00
6 Marty Burke 15.00 25.00
7 Lorne Carr 15.00 25.00
8 Lorne Chabot 25.00 40.00
9 Art Chapman 15.00 25.00
10 Bert Connolly 15.00 25.00
11 Bill Cook 25.00 40.00
12 Bill Cook 25.00 40.00
13 Bun Cook 25.00 40.00
14 Tommy Cook 15.00 25.00
15 Art Coulter 15.00 25.00
16 Lolo Couture 15.00 25.00
17 Wilf Cude 25.00 40.00
18 Cecil Dillon 15.00 25.00
19 Cecil Dillon 15.00 25.00
20 Red Dutton 25.00 40.00
21 Happy Emms 25.00 40.00
22 Irv Frew 15.00 25.00
23 Johnny Gagnon 15.00 25.00
24 Leroy Goldsworthy 15.00 25.00
25 Johnny Gottselig 15.00 25.00
26 Paul Haynes 15.00 25.00
27 Ott Heller 15.00 25.00
28 Irving Jaffee 15.00 25.00
29 Joe Jerwa 15.00 25.00
30 Ching Johnson 25.00 40.00
31 Aurel Joliat 30.00 50.00
32 Butch Keeling 15.00 25.00
33 William Kendall 15.00 25.00
34 Davey Kerr 25.00 40.00
35 Lloyd Klein 15.00 25.00
36 Wildor Larochelle 15.00 25.00
37 Pit Lepine 15.00 25.00
38 Arthur Lesieur 15.00 25.00
39 Alex Levinsky 15.00 25.00
40 Alex Levinsky 15.00 25.00
41 Norm Locking 15.00 25.00
42 Georges Mantha 25.00 40.00
43 Sylvio Mantha 25.00 40.00
44 Mush Marsh 15.00 25.00
45 Charlie Mason 15.00 25.00
46 Donnie McFadyen 15.00 25.00
47 Jack McGill 15.00 25.00
48 Armand Mondou 15.00 25.00
49 Howie Morenz 180.00 300.00
50 Murray Murdoch 15.00 25.00
51 Al Murray 15.00 25.00
52 Harry Oliver 25.00 40.00
53 Eddie Ouellette 15.00 25.00
54 Lynn Patrick 25.00 40.00
55 Lynn Patrick 25.00 40.00
56 Paul Runge 15.00 25.00
57 Sweeney Schriner 25.00 40.00
58 Art Somers 15.00 25.00
59 Harold Starr 15.00 25.00
60 Nels Stewart 30.00 50.00
61 Paul Thompson 15.00 25.00
62 Louis Trudel 15.00 25.00
63 Carl Voss 15.00 25.00
64 Art Wiebe 25.00 40.00
65 Roy Worters 25.00 40.00

1935-36 Diamond Matchbooks Tan 3

The Type 3 matchbook covers are almost identical to the Type 2 covers except that the manufacturer's imprint "Made In The USA/The Diamond Match Co. NYC" is a double line designation. Complete matchbooks are rarely scarce and carry a 50 percent premium over the prices below.

COMPLETE SET (60) 950.00 1,600.00
1 Tommy Anderson 15.00 25.00
2 Vern Ayres 15.00 25.00
3 Frank Boucher 18.00 30.00
4 Bill Brydge 15.00 25.00
5 Marty Burke 15.00 25.00
6 Walter Buswell 15.00 25.00
7 Lorne Carr 15.00 25.00
8 Lorne Chabot 25.00 40.00
9 Art Chapman 15.00 25.00
10 Bert Connolly 15.00 25.00
11 Bill Cook 25.00 40.00
12 Bun Cook 25.00 40.00
13 Tommy Cook 18.00 30.00
14 Art Coulter 15.00 25.00
15 Lolo Couture 15.00 25.00
16 Wilf Cude 18.00 30.00
17 Cecil Dillon 15.00 25.00
18 Red Dutton 18.00 30.00
19 Happy Emms 18.00 30.00
20 Irvin Frew 15.00 25.00
21 Johnny Gagnon 15.00 25.00
22 Leroy Goldsworthy 15.00 25.00
23 Johnny Gottselig 15.00 25.00
24 Paul Haynes 15.00 25.00
25 Ott Heller 15.00 25.00
26 Joe Jerwa 15.00 25.00
27 Ching Johnson 25.00 40.00
28 Aurel Joliat 30.00 50.00
29 Mike Karakas 18.00 30.00
30 Butch Keeling 15.00 25.00
31 Dave Kerr 18.00 30.00
32 Lloyd Klein 15.00 25.00
33 Wildor Larochelle 18.00 30.00
34 Pit Lepine 15.00 25.00
35 Arthur Lesieur 15.00 25.00
36 Alex Levinsky 18.00 30.00
37 Norman Locking 15.00 25.00
38 George Mantha 25.00 40.00
39 Sylvio Mantha 25.00 40.00
40 Mush March 18.00 30.00
41 Charlie Mason 15.00 25.00
42 Charlie Mason 15.00 25.00
43 Donnie McFadyen 15.00 25.00
44 Jack McGill 15.00 25.00
45 Armand Mondou 15.00 25.00
46 Howie Morenz 180.00 300.00
47 Murray Murdoch 15.00 25.00
48 Al Murray 15.00 25.00
49 Harry Oliver 25.00 40.00
50 Eddie Ouellette 15.00 25.00
51 Lynn Patrick 25.00 40.00
52 Paul Runge 15.00 25.00
53 Sweeney Schriner 25.00 40.00
54 Harold Starr 15.00 25.00
55 Nels Stewart 30.00 50.00
56 Paul Thompson 15.00 25.00
57 Louis Trudel 15.00 25.00
58 Carl Voss 18.00 30.00
59 Art Wiebe 18.00 30.00
60 Roy Worters 18.00 30.00

1935-36 Diamond Matchbooks Tan 4

This tan-bordered issue is comprised only of Chicago Blackhawks players. The set is similar to Type 1 in that the player's team name appears between the player's name and bio on the reverse. The "Made in USA/The Diamond Match Co., NYC" imprint appears on two lines. Complete matchbooks carry a 50 percent premium.

COMPLETE SET (15) 180.00 300.00
1 Andy Blair 15.00 25.00
2 Glenn Brydson 15.00 25.00
3 Marty Burke 15.00 25.00
4 Tommy Cook 18.00 30.00
5 Johnny Gottselig 15.00 25.00
6 Harold Jackson 15.00 25.00
7 Mike Karakas 18.00 30.00
8 Wildor Larochelle 18.00 30.00
9 Alex Levinsky 18.00 30.00
10 Clem Loughlin 15.00 25.00
11 Mush March 18.00 30.00
12 Earl Seibert 25.00 40.00
13 Paul Thompson 15.00 25.00
14 Louis Trudel 15.00 25.00
15 Art Wiebe 18.00 30.00

1935-36 Diamond Matchbooks Tan 5

This tan-bordered set features only players from the Chicago Blackhawks. This is the hardest match cover issue to distinguish. The difference is that the team name is not featured between the player's name and his bio on the reverse. Complete matchbooks carry a 50 percent premium over the prices below.

COMPLETE SET (14) 125.00 200.00
1 Glenn Brydson 15.00 25.00
2 Marty Burke 15.00 25.00
3 Tommy Cook 15.00 25.00
4 Cully Dahlstrom 15.00 25.00
5 Johnny Gottselig 15.00 25.00
6 Vic Heyliger 15.00 25.00
7 Mike Karakas 15.00 25.00
8 Alex Levinsky 15.00 25.00
9 Mush March 15.00 25.00
10 Earl Seibert 15.00 25.00
11 William J. Stewart 15.00 25.00
12 Paul Thompson 15.00 25.00
13 Louis Trudel 15.00 25.00
14 Art Wiebe 15.00 25.00

1937 Diamond Matchbooks Tan 6

This 14-matchbook set is actually a reissue of the Type 5 Blackhawks set, and was released one year later. The only difference between the two series is that the reissued matchbooks have black match tips while the Type 5 issue has tan match tips. Complete matchbooks carry a 50 percent premium over the prices listed below.

COMPLETE SET (14) 150.00 250.00
1 Glenn Brydson 15.00 25.00
2 Martin A. Burke 15.00 25.00
3 Tom Cook 15.00 25.00
4 Cully Dahlstrom 15.00 25.00
5 Johnny Gottselig 15.00 25.00
6 Vic Heyliger 15.00 25.00
7 Mike Karakas 15.00 25.00
8 Alex Levinsky 15.00 25.00
9 Mush March 15.00 25.00
10 Earl Seibert 18.00 30.00
11 William J. Stewart 15.00 25.00
12 Paul Thompson 15.00 25.00
13 Louis Trudel 15.00 25.00
14 Art Wiebe 15.00 25.00

1972-83 Dimanche/Derniere Heure

The blank-backed photo sheets in this multi-sport set measure approximately 8 1/2" by 11" and feature white-bordered color sports star photos from Dimanche Derniere Heure, a Montreal newspaper. The player's name, position and biographical information appear within the lower white margin. All text is in French. A white vinyl album was available for storing the photo sheets. Printed on the album's spine are the words, "Mes Vedettes du Sport" (My Stars of Sport).The photos are unnumbered and are checklisted below in alphabetical order according to sport or team as follows: Montreal Expos baseball players (1-117; National League baseball players (118-130); Montreal Canadiens hockey players (131-177); wrestlers (178-202); prize fighters (203-204); auto racing drivers (205-208); women's golf (209); Patof the circus clown (210); and CFL (211-278).

134 Chuck Arnason 1.25 2.50
135 Jean Beliveau VP 2.00 4.00
136 Pierre Bouchard (Action) 1.25 2.50
137 Pierre Bouchard (Posed) 1.25 2.50
138 Scotty Bowman CO 2.00 4.00
139 Yvan Cournoyer (Action) 2.00 4.00
140 Yvan Cournoyer (Posed) 2.00 4.00
141 Ken Dryden 5.00 10.00
142 Bob Gainey 2.00 4.00
143 Dale Hoganson 1.25 2.50
144 Rejean Houle 1.50 3.00
145 Guy Lafleur (Action) 5.00 10.00
146 Guy Lafleur (Posed) 5.00 10.00
147 Yvon Lambert 1.50 3.00
148 Jacques Laperriere (Action) 2.00 4.00
149 Jacques Laperriere (Posed) 2.00 4.00
150 Guy Lapointe (Action) 2.00 4.00
151 Guy Lapointe (Posed) 2.00 4.00
152 Michel Larocque 2.00 4.00
153 Claude Larose (Action) 1.50 3.00
154 Claude Larose (Posed) 1.50 3.00
155 Chuck Lefley (Action) 1.25 2.50
156 Chuck Lefley (Posed) 1.25 2.50
157 Jacques Lemaire (Action) 2.00 4.00
158 Jacques Lemaire (Posed) 2.00 4.00
159 Frank Mahovlich (Action) 3.00 6.00
160 Frank Mahovlich (Posed) 3.00 6.00
161 Pete Mahovlich (Action) 1.50 3.00
162 Pete Mahovlich (Posed) 1.50 3.00
163 Bob J. Murdoch 1.25 2.50
164 Michel Plasse (Action) 2.00 4.00
165 Michel Plasse (Posed) 2.00 4.00
166 Henri Richard (Action) 3.00 6.00
167 Henri Richard (Posed) 3.00 6.00
168 Jim Roberts (Action) 1.50 3.00
169 Jim Roberts (Posed) 1.50 3.00
170 Larry Robinson (Action) 3.00 6.00
171 Larry Robinson (Posed) 3.00 6.00
172 Serge Savard (Action) 2.00 4.00
173 Serge Savard (Posed) 2.00 4.00
174 Steve Shutt (Action) 2.00 4.00
175 Steve Shutt (Posed) 2.00 4.00
176 Marc Tardif 1.50 3.00
177 Wayne Thomas (Action) 1.50 3.00
178 Wayne Thomas (Posed) 1.50 3.00
179 Murray Wilson (Action) 1.25 2.50
180 Murray Wilson (Posed) 1.25 2.50

1925 Dominion Chocolates V31

13 Granite Club HK Olympic Champs 125.00 200.00
28 North Ontario Team HK 125.00 200.00
35 Peterborough Team HK 125.00 200.00
49 Owen Sound Jrs. HK 125.00 200.00
55 E.J. Collett HK 125.00 200.00
56 Hughie J. Fox HK 125.00 200.00
57 Dunc Munro HK 125.00 200.00
58 M.Rutherford HK 125.00 200.00
59 Beattie Ramsay HK 125.00 200.00
60 Bert McCaffrey HK 125.00 200.00
61 Soo Greyhounds HK 125.00 200.00
68 J.P. Aggatts HK 125.00 200.00
69 Hooley Smith HK 200.00 350.00
70 Jack Cameron HK 125.00 200.00
81 William Fraser HK 125.00 200.00
82 Vernon Forbes HK 125.00 200.00
83 Shorty Green HK 175.00 300.00
84 Red Green HK 125.00 200.00
86 Jack Langtry HK 125.00 200.00
89 Billy Coutu HK 125.00 200.00
92 Jack Hughes HK 125.00 200.00
95 Edouard Lalonde HK 250.00 500.00
101 Bill Brydge HK 125.00 200.00
103 Cecil Browne HK 125.00 200.00
106 Red Porter HK 125.00 200.00
112 North Bay Team HK 125.00 200.00
113 Ross Somerville HK 125.00 200.00
114 Harry Watson HK 175.00 300.00
117 Odie Cleghorn HK UER 125.00 200.00
First Name Spelled Ogie
118 Lionel Conacher HK 250.00 500.00
119 Aurel Joliat HK 400.00 800.00
120 Georges Vezina HK 750.00 1,500.00

1964-67 Eaton's Sports Adviser

Issued between 1964 and 1967, these cards were used as promotional material by Eaton's of Canada.

NNO Gordie Howe action 10.00 25.00
NNO Gordie Howe All-Star uniform 10.00 25.00
NNO Gordie Howe standing 10.00 25.00

1935 Edwards, Ringer and Bigg Sports Games in Many Lands

Made as a multi-sport set in Britain, these cards measure approximately 1 1/2 x 2 1/2. Cards are black and white with text on back.

3 Ice Hockey-Canada 30.00 60.00
3 Ice Hockey-Canada 22.50 45.00
same as above, but with Imperial Tobacco

1962-63 El Producto Discs

The six discs in this set measured approximately 3" in diameter. They were issued as a strip of six connected in a fragile manner and were in full color. The discs were unnumbered and checklisted below in alphabetical order. The set in unperforated form is valued 25 percent greater than the value below.

COMPLETE SET (6) 150.00 300.00
1 Jean Beliveau 30.00 60.00
2 Glenn Hall 25.00 50.00
3 Gordie Howe 75.00 150.00
4 Dave Keon 30.00 60.00
5 Frank Mahovlich 25.00 50.00
6 Henri Richard 25.00 50.00

1967-73 Equitable Sports Hall of Fame

This set consists of copies of art work found over a number of years in many national magazines, especially "Sports Illustrated," honoring sports heroes that Equitable Life Assurance Society selected to be in its very own Sports Hall of Fame. The cards consists of charcoal-type drawings on white backgrounds by artists, George Loh and Robert Riger, and measure approximately 11" by 7 3/4". The unnumbered cards have been assigned numbers below using a sport prefix (BB- baseball, BK- basketball, FB- football, HK- hockey, OT-other).

COMPLETE SET (95) 250.00 500.00
HK1 Phil Esposito 3.00 6.00
HK2 Bernie Geoffrion 3.00 6.00
HK3 Gordie Howe 5.00 10.00
HK4 Ching Johnson 2.00 4.00
HK5 Stan Mikita 3.00 6.00
HK6 Maurice Richard 4.00 8.00

1969-73 Equitable Sports Hall of Fame

Little is known about these miniature prints beyond the confirmed checklist. Additional information can be forwarded to hockeymag@beckett.com.

COMPLETE SET (6) 62.50 125.00
1 Phil Esposito 10.00 20.00
2 Bernie Geoffrion 10.00 20.00
3 Gordie Howe 25.00 50.00
4 Ching Johnson 7.50 15.00
5 Stan Mikita 10.00 20.00
6 Maurice Richard 12.50 25.00

1970-71 Esso Power Players

The 1970-71 Esso Power Players set included 252 color stamps measuring approximately 1 1/2" by 2". The stamps were issued in six-stamp sheets and given away free with a minimum purchase of $3 of Esso gasoline. There were 18 stamps for each of the 14 teams then in the NHL. The stamps were unnumbered except for jersey (uniform) number. The set was issued with an album, which could be found in either a soft or hard bound version. The hard cover album supposedly had extra pages with additional players. The stamps and albums were available in both French and English language versions. The set was numbered below numerically within each team as follows: Montreal Canadiens (1-18), Toronto Maple Leafs (19-36), Vancouver Canucks (37-54), Boston Bruins (55-72), Buffalo Sabres (73-90), California Golden Seals (91-108), Chicago Blackhawks (109-126), Detroit Red Wings (127-144), Los Angeles Kings (145-162), Minnesota North Stars (163-180), New York Rangers (181-198), Philadelphia Flyers (199-216), Pittsburgh Penguins (217-234), and St. Louis Blues (235-252). Supposedly there were 59 stamps which are tougher to find than the others. The short-printed stamps were apparently those players who were pre-printed into the soft-cover album and hence not included in the first stamp printing.

COMPLETE SET (252)	125.00	250.00
1 Rogatien Vachon 1	1.50	3.00
2 Jacques Laperriere 2	.38	.75
3 J.C. Tremblay 3	.25	.50
4 Jean Beliveau 4	4.00	8.00
5 Guy Lapointe 5	.50	1.00
6 Fran Huck 6	.20	.40
7 Bill Collins 10	.20	.40
8 Marc Tardif 11	.25	.50
9 Yvan Cournoyer 12	.75	1.50
10 Claude Larose 15	.20	.40
11 Henri Richard 16	2.00	4.00
12 Serge Savard 18	.38	.75
13 Terry Harper 19	.25	.50
14 Pete Mahovlich 20	.38	.75
15 John Ferguson 22	.50	1.00
16 Mickey Redmond 24	.63	1.25
17 Jacques Lemaire 25	.63	1.25
18 Phil Myre 30	.38	.75
19 Jacques Plante 1	4.00	8.00
20 Rick Ley 2	.25	.50
21 Mike Pelyk 4	.20	.40
22 Ron Ellis 6	.25	.50
23 Jim Dorey 8	.20	.40
24 Norm Ullman 9	1.00	2.00
25 Guy Trottier 11	.20	.40
26 Jim Harrison 12	.20	.40
27 Dave Keon 14	1.00	2.00
28 Mike Walton 16	.25	.50
29 Jim McKenny 18	.20	.40
30 Paul Henderson 19	.50	1.00
31 Garry Monahan 20 SP	.50	1.00
32 Bob Baun 21	.38	.75
33 Bill MacMillan 23	.20	.40
34 Brian Glennie 24	.20	.40
35 Darryl Sittler 27	5.00	10.00
36 Bruce Gamble 30	.50	1.00
37 Charlie Hodge 1	.63	1.25
38 Gary Doak 2	.20	.40
39 Pat Quinn 3	.38	.75
40 Barry Wilkins 4	.20	.40
41 Darryl Sly 5 SP	.50	1.00
42 Marc Reaume 6	.20	.40
43 Andre Boudrias 7	.20	.40
44 Danny Johnson 8	.20	.40
45 Ray Cullen 10 SP	.50	1.00
46 Wayne Maki 11	.20	.40
47 Mike Corrigan 12	.20	.40
48 Rosaire Paiement 15	.20	.40
49 Paul Popiel 18 SP	.38	.75
50 Dale Tallon 19	.25	.50
51 Murray Hall 23 SP	.50	1.00
52 Len Lunde 24	.20	.40
53 Orland Kurtenbach 25	.25	.50
54 Dunc Wilson 30 SP	.50	1.00
55 Ed Johnston 1	.50	1.00
56 Bobby Orr 4	12.50	25.00
57 Ted Green 6	.25	.50
58 Phil Esposito 7	2.50	5.00
59 Ken Hodge 8	.38	.75
60 Johnny Bucyk 9	1.00	2.00
61 Rick Smith 10 SP	.50	1.00
62 Wayne Carleton 11 SP	.50	1.00
63 Wayne Cashman 12 SP	.75	1.50
64 Garnet Bailey 14	.20	.40
65 Derek Sanderson 16	2.00	4.00
66 Fred Stanfield 17 SP	.50	1.00
67 Ed Westfall 18	.25	.50
68 John McKenzie 19	.20	.40
69 Dallas Smith 20	.20	.40
70 Don Marcotte 21	.20	.40
71 Don Awrey 26 SP	.50	1.00
72 Gerry Cheevers 30	1.50	3.00
73 Roger Crozier 1	.75	1.50
74 Jim Watson 2	.25	.50
75 Tracy Pratt 3	.20	.40
76 Doug Barrie 5 SP	.50	1.00
77 Al Hamilton 6	.25	.50
78 Cliff Schmautz 7 SP	.50	1.00
79 Reg Fleming 9	.20	.40
80 Phil Goyette 10	.20	.40
81 Gilbert Perreault 11	2.50	5.00
82 Skip Krake 12	.20	.40
83 Gerry Meehan 15	.25	.50
84 Ron Anderson 16	.20	.40
85 Floyd Smith 17 SP	.50	1.00
86 Steve Atkinson 19	.20	.40
87 Paul Andrea 21 SP	.50	1.00
88 Don Marshall 22	.20	.40
89 Eddie Shack 23 SP	1.50	3.00
90 Larry Keenan 26	.20	.40
91 Gary Smith 1	.50	1.00
92 Doug Roberts 2	.20	.40
93 Harry Howell 3	.63	1.25
94 Wayne Muloin 4	.20	.40
95 Carol Vadnais 5	.20	.40
96 Dick Mattiussi 6	.20	.40
97 Earl Ingarfield 7	.20	.40
98 Gerry Ehman 8	.20	.40
99 Bill Hicke 9	.20	.40
100 Ted Hampson 10	.20	.40
101 Gary Jarrett 12	.20	.40
102 Joe Hardy 14 SP	.50	1.00
103 Tony Featherstone 16 SP	.50	1.00
104 Gary Croteau 18	.20	.40
105 Ernie Hicke 20 SP	.50	1.00
106 Ron Stackhouse 21	.20	.40
107 Dennis Hextall 22 SP	.75	1.50
108 Bob Sneddon 30 SP	.50	1.00
109 Gerry Desjardins 1 SP	.75	1.50
110 Bill White 2	.25	.50
111 Keith Magnuson 3	.25	.50
112 Doug Jarrett 4 SP	.50	1.00
113 Lou Angotti 6	.20	.40
114 Pit Martin 7	.25	.50
115 Jim Pappin 8	.20	.40
116 Bobby Hull 9	5.00	10.00
117 Dennis Hull 10 SP	1.00	2.00
118 Doug Mohns 11	.25	.50
119 Pat Stapleton 12	.25	.50
120 Bryan Campbell 14 SP	.50	1.00
121 Eric Nesterenko 15	.25	.50
122 Chico Maki 16	.25	.50
123 Gerry Pinder 18	.25	.50
124 Cliff Koroll 20	.20	.40
125 Stan Mikita 21	3.00	6.00
126 Tony Esposito 35	3.00	6.00
127 Jim Rutherford 1 SP	1.00	2.00
128 Gary Bergman 2	.25	.50
129 Dale Rolfe 3	.20	.40
130 Larry Brown 4 SP	.50	1.00
131 Serge Lajeunesse 5	.20	.40
132 Garry Unger 7	.38	.75
133 Tom Webster 8	.25	.50
134 Gordie Howe 9	7.50	15.00
135 Alex Delvecchio 10	1.00	2.00
136 Don Luce 11 SP	.50	1.00
137 Bruce MacGregor 12	.20	.40
138 Nick Libett 14	.25	.50
139 Al Karlander 15	.20	.40
140 Ron Harris 16	.20	.40
141 Wayne Connelly 17 SP	.50	1.00
142 Billy Dea 21 SP	.50	1.00
143 Frank Mahovlich 27	2.00	4.00
144 Roy Edwards 30	.38	.75
145 Jack Norris 1	.20	.40
146 Dale Hoganson 2	.20	.40
147 Larry Cahan 3	.20	.40
148 Gilles Marotte 4 SP	.50	1.00
149 Noel Price 5 SP	.50	1.00
150 Paul Curtis 6 SP	.50	1.00
151 Ross Lonsberry 8	.20	.40
152 Gord Labossiere 9	.20	.40
153 Doug Robinson 11 SP	.50	1.00
154 Larry Mickey 12	.20	.40
155 Juha Widing 15	.20	.40
156 Eddie Joyal 16	.20	.40
157 Bill Flett 17	.20	.40
158 Bob Berry 18	.25	.50
159 Bob Pulford 20	.38	.75
160 Matt Ravlich 21	.20	.40
161 Mike Byers 24 SP	.50	1.00
162 Denis DeJordy 30	.50	1.00
163 Gump Worsley 1	2.00	4.00
164 Barry Gibbs 2 SP	.50	1.00
165 Fred Barrett 3	.20	.40
166 Ted Harris 4	.20	.40
167 Danny O'Shea 7	.20	.40
168 Bill Goldsworthy 8	.25	.50
169 Charlie Burns 9	.20	.40
170 Murray Oliver 10	.20	.40
171 Jean-Paul Parise 11	.25	.50
172 Tom Williams 12 SP	.50	1.00
173 Bobby Rousseau 15	.25	.50
174 Buster Harvey 18 SP	.50	1.00
175 Tom Reid 20 SP	.50	1.00
176 Danny Grant 21	.25	.50
177 Walt McKechnie 22	.20	.40
178 Lou Nanne 23	.25	.50
179 Danny Lawson 24 SP	.50	1.00
180 Cesare Maniago 30	.50	1.00
181 Ed Giacomin 1	1.50	3.00
182 Brad Park 2	3.00	8.00
183 Tim Horton 3	2.50	5.00
184 Arnie Brown 4	.20	.40
185 Rod Gilbert 7	.75	1.50
186 Bob Nevin 8	.20	.40
187 Bill Fairbairn 10 SP	.50	1.00
188 Vic Hadfield 11	.25	.50
189 Ron Stewart 12	.20	.40
190 Jim Neilson 15	.25	.50
191 Rod Seiling 16 SP	.50	1.00
192 Dave Balon 17 SP	.50	1.00
193 Walt Tkaczuk 18	.25	.50
194 Jean Ratelle 19	.75	1.50
195 Jack Egers 20	.20	.40
196 Pete Stemkowski 21 SP	.50	1.00
197 Ted Irvine 27	.20	.40
198 Gilles Villemure 30	.50	1.00
199 Doug Favell 1	.75	1.50
200 Ed Van Impe 2	.20	.40
201 Larry Hillman 3	.20	.40
202 Barry Ashbee 4	.38	.75
203 Wayne Hillman 6 SP	.50	1.00
204 Andre Lacroix 7	.25	.50
205 Lew Morrison 8	.20	.40
206 Bob Kelly 9 SP	.50	1.00
207 Jean-Guy Gendron 11	.20	.40
208 Gary Dornhoefer 12	.38	.75
209 Joe Watson 14	.20	.40
210 Garry Peters 15 SP	.50	1.00
211 Bobby Clarke 16	5.00	10.00
212 Earl Heiskala 19 SP	.50	1.00
213 Jim Johnson 20	.20	.40
214 Serge Bernier 21	.20	.40
215 Larry Hale 23 SP	.50	1.00
216 Bernie Parent 30	2.50	5.00
217 Al Smith 1	.38	.75
218 Duane Rupp 2	.20	.40
219 Bob Woytowich 3	.20	.40
220 Bob Blackburn 4	.20	.40
221 Bryan Watson 5 SP	.50	1.00
222 Dunc McCallum 6	.25	.50
223 Bryan Hextall 7	.25	.50
224 Andy Bathgate 9 SP	1.25	2.50
225 Keith McCreary 10 SP	.50	1.00
226 Nick Harbaruk 11	.20	.40
227 Ken Schinkel 12	.20	.40
228 Glen Sather 16 SP	1.25	2.50
229 Ron Schock 17	.20	.40
230 Wally Boyer 18	.20	.40
231 Jean Pronovost 19	.25	.50
232 Dean Prentice 20	.25	.50
233 Jim Morrison 27	.20	.40
234 Les Binkley 30 SP	.75	1.50
235 Glenn Hall 1	2.00	4.00
236 Bob Wall 2	.20	.40
237 Noel Picard 4	.20	.40
238 Bob Plager 5	.25	.50
239 Jim Roberts 6	.25	.50
240 Red Berenson 7	.25	.50
241 Barclay Plager 8	.25	.50
242 Frank St.Marseille 9	.20	.40
243 George Morrison 10 SP	.50	1.00
244 Gary Sabourin 11	.20	.40
245 Terry Crisp 12 SP	1.00	2.00
246 Tim Ecclestone 14	.20	.40
247 Bill McCreary 15	.20	.40
248 Brit Selby 18 SP	.50	1.00
249 Jim Lorentz 19 SP	.50	1.00
250 Ab McDonald 20	.20	.40
251 Chris Bordeleau 21 SP	.50	1.00
252 Ernie Wakely 31	.50	1.00
xx Soft Cover Album	7.50	15.00
xx Hard Cover Album	25.00	50.00

1948-52 Exhibits Canadian

These cards measured approximately 3 1/4" by 5 1/4" and were issued on heavy cardboard stock. The cards showed full-bleed photos with the player's name burned in toward the bottom. The hockey exhibit cards were generally considered more scarce than their baseball exhibit counterparts. Since the cards were unnumbered, the set is arranged below alphabetically within teams as follows: Montreal (1-27), Toronto (28-42), Detroit (43-46), Boston (47-48), Chicago (49-50), and New York (51). The set closes with an Action subset (52-65).

COMPLETE SET (65)	750.00	1,500.00
1 Reggie Abbott	6.00	12.00
2 Jean Beliveau	37.50	75.00
3 Jean Beliveau	50.00	100.00
4 Toe Blake	20.00	40.00
5 Butch Bouchard	10.00	20.00
6 Bob Fillion	6.00	12.00
7 Dick Gamble	7.50	15.00
8 Bernie Geoffrion	25.00	50.00
9 Doug Harvey	20.00	40.00
10 Tom Johnson	10.00	20.00
11 Elmer Lach	20.00	40.00
12 Hal Laycoe	6.00	12.00
13 Jacques Locas	6.00	12.00
14 Bud McPherson	6.00	12.00
15 Paul Maznick	6.00	12.00
16 Gerry McNeil	20.00	40.00
17 Paul Meger	6.00	12.00
18 Dickie Moore	20.00	40.00
19 Ken Mosdell	6.00	12.00
20 Bert Olmstead	10.00	20.00
21 Ken Reardon	12.50	25.00
22 Billy Reay	7.50	15.00
23 Maurice Richard	50.00	100.00
24 Maurice Richard	50.00	100.00
25 Dollard St.Laurent	7.50	15.00
26 Grant Warwick	6.00	12.00
27 Floyd Curry	7.50	15.00
28 Bill Barilko	20.00	40.00
29 Turk Broda	20.00	40.00
30 Cal Gardner	10.00	20.00
31 Bill Juzda	6.00	12.00
32 Ted Kennedy	20.00	40.00
33 Joe Klukay	6.00	12.00
34 Fleming Mackell	6.00	12.00
35 Howie Meeker	15.00	30.00
36 Gus Mortson	6.00	12.00
37 Al Rollins	12.50	25.00
38 Sid Smith	7.50	15.00
39 Tod Sloan	6.00	12.00
40 Ray Timgren	6.00	12.00
41 Jim Thomson	6.00	12.00
42 Max Bentley	12.50	25.00
43 Sid Abel	10.00	20.00
44 Gordie Howe	62.50	125.00
45 Ted Lindsay	25.00	50.00
46 Harry Lumley	20.00	40.00
47 Jack Gelineau	6.00	12.00
48 Paul Ronty	6.00	12.00
49 Doug Bentley	12.50	25.00
50 Roy Conacher	7.50	15.00
51 Chuck Rayner	12.50	25.00
52 Boston vs. Montreal	10.00	20.00
53 Detroit vs. New York	30.00	60.00
54 Montreal vs. Toronto	30.00	60.00
55 New York vs. Montreal	30.00	60.00
56 New York vs. Montreal	10.00	20.00
57 Montreal vs. Boston	10.00	20.00
58 Detroit vs. Montreal	10.00	20.00
59 Chicago vs. Montreal	10.00	20.00
60 New York vs. Montreal	25.00	50.00
61 Chicago vs. Montreal	15.00	30.00
62 Detroit vs. Montreal	20.00	40.00
63 Detroit vs. Montreal	10.00	20.00
64 Toronto vs. Montreal	10.00	20.00
65 Chicago vs. Montreal	10.00	20.00

1972-73 Flames Postcards

This 20-card set of the Atlanta Flames measured 3 1/2" by 5 1/2". The fronts featured color action player photos with a white border. The player's autograph was across the bottom of the photo. The backs were blank. The cards were unnumbered and checklisted below in alphabetical order.

COMPLETE SET (20)	30.00	60.00
1 Curt Bennett	1.00	2.00
2 Dan Bouchard	2.50	5.00
3 Rey Comeau	1.00	2.00
4 BoomBoom Geoffrion CO	5.00	10.00
5 Bob Leiter	1.00	2.00
6 Kerry Ketter	1.00	2.00
7 Billy MacMillan	1.00	2.00
8 Randy Manery	1.00	2.00
9 Keith McCreary	1.00	2.00
10 Lew Morrison	1.00	2.00
11 Phil Myre	3.00	6.00
12 Bob Paradise	1.00	2.00
13 Noel Picard	1.00	2.00
14 Bill Plager	1.50	3.00
15 Noel Price	1.50	3.00
16 Pat Quinn	2.50	5.00
17 Jacques Richard	1.50	3.00
18 Leon Rochefort	1.00	2.00
19 Larry Romanchych	1.00	2.00
20 John Stewart	1.00	2.00

1978-79 Flames Majik Market

This 20 card set was issued during the 1978-79 season and features members of the Atlanta Flames. The front had an action shot as well as a facsimile autograph. The back had the player's name, uniform number and some personal statistics. At the bottom, sponsors "Coca-Cola Bottling" and radio station WTLA are credited. Pat Ribble, who was traded during the season, was the most difficult card to obtain and is listed as an SP. We have checklisted this set by the uniform number.

COMPLETE SET (20)	15.00	30.00
1 Rejean Lemelin	1.50	3.00
2 Greg Fox	.50	1.00
3 Pat Ribble SP	5.00	10.00
5 Brad Marsh	2.00	4.00
6 Ken Houston	.50	1.00
7 Bobby LaLonde	.50	1.00
8 David Shand	.50	1.00
9 Jean Pronovost	.75	1.50
10 Bill Clement	1.50	3.00
11 Bob MacMillan	.50	1.00
12 Tom Lysiak	1.00	2.00
15 Rod Seiling	.50	1.00
16 Guy Chouinard	1.00	2.00
17 Don Red Laurence	.50	1.00
19 Ed Kea	.50	1.00
20 Bob Murdoch	.75	1.50
24 Harold Phillipoff	.50	1.00
25 Willi Plett	1.00	2.00
27 Eric Vail	1.00	2.00
30 Daniel Bouchard	1.50	3.00

1979-80 Flames Postcards

This 20-card set was sponsored by the Atlanta Coca-Cola Bottling Company, Winn Dixie, and radio station WLTA-100. The set was in the postcard format, with each card measuring approximately 3 1/2" by 5 1/2". The fronts featured full-bleed color action shots; a facsimile autograph was inscribed across the lower portion of the pictures. The backs carried the player's name, uniform number, biography, and sponsor logos. The cards were unnumbered and checklisted below according to jersey number.

COMPLETE SET (20)	15.00	30.00
1 Jim Craig	2.50	5.00
2 Curt Bennett	.50	1.00
3 Phil Russell	.50	1.00
4 Pekka Rautakallio	.50	1.00
5 Brad Marsh	2.50	5.00
6 Ken Houston	.50	1.00
7 Garry Unger	1.50	3.00
8 David Shand	.50	1.00
9 Jean Pronovost	.75	1.50
10 Bill Clement	2.00	4.00
11 Bob MacMillan	.50	1.00
12 Don Lever	.50	1.00
14 Kent Nilsson	2.50	5.00
16 Guy Chouinard	1.00	2.00
20 Bob Murdoch	.75	1.50
23 Paul Reinhardt	.75	1.50
25 Willi Plett	1.25	2.50
27 Eric Vail	.75	1.50
30 Dan Bouchard	1.50	3.00
31 Pat Riggin	1.25	2.50

1979-80 Flames Team Issue

Cards measured 3 3/4 x 5 1/4 and featured black and white action photos on the front along with a facsimile signature. Backs were blank. Cards were unnumbered and checklisted below in alphabetical order.

COMPLETE SET (22)	20.00	40.00

1 Curt Bennett	.50	1.00
2 Ivan Boldirev	.50	1.00
3 Dan Bouchard	1.50	3.00
4 Guy Chouinard	1.00	2.00
5 Bill Clement	1.50	3.00
6 Jim Craig	2.00	4.00
7 Ken Houston	.50	1.00
8 Brad Marsh	1.50	3.00
9 Bob MacMillan	.50	1.00
10 Al MacNeil	.50	1.00
11 Bob Murdoch	.75	1.50
12 Kent Nilsson	2.00	4.00
13 Willi Plett	1.00	2.00
14 Jean Pronovost	.75	1.50
15 Pekka Rautakallio	.50	1.00
16 Paul Reinhart	.75	1.50
17 Pat Riggin	1.00	2.00
18 Darcy Rota	.50	1.00
19 Phil Russell	.50	1.00
20 David Shand	.50	1.00
21 Garry Unger	1.25	2.50
22 Eric Vail	1.00	2.00

1980-81 Flames Postcards

This 24-postcard set measured approximately 3 3/4" by 5". The fronts featured borderless posed color player photos. The backs were blank. The cards were unnumbered and checklisted below in alphabetical order.

COMPLETE SET (24)	20.00	40.00
1 Daniel Bouchard	1.25	3.00
2 Guy Chouinard	.75	2.00
3 Bill Clement	.75	2.00
4 Denis Cyr	.40	1.00
5 Randy Holt	.40	1.00
6 Ken Houston	.40	1.00
7 Rejean Lemelin	2.50	5.00
8 Kevin Lavallee	.40	1.00
9 Don Lever	.40	1.00
10 Bob MacMillan	.40	1.00
11 Bob Murdoch	.40	1.00
12 Brad Marsh	1.00	2.50
13 Kent Nilsson	1.50	4.00
14 Willi Plett	.60	1.50
15 Jim Peplinski	1.00	2.50
16 Pekka Rautakallio	.75	2.00
17 Paul Reinhart	1.00	2.50
18 Pat Riggin	.75	2.00
19 Phil Russell	.40	1.00
20 Brad Smith	.40	1.00
21 Jay Soleway	.40	1.00
22 Eric Vail	.60	1.50
23 Bert Wilson	.40	1.00
24 Team Photo	.60	1.50

1970-71 Flyers Postcards

This 12-card, team-issued set measured 3 1/2" by 5 1/2" and was in the postcard format. The fronts featured full-bleed color photos, with the players posed on ice at the skating rink. A facsimile autograph was inscribed across the bottom. The white backs carried player information and team logo across the top. The cards were unnumbered and checklisted below in alphabetical order.

COMPLETE SET (12)	20.00	40.00
1 Barry Ashbee	3.00	6.00
2 Gary Dornhoefer	3.00	6.00
3 Warren Elliott	1.00	2.00
Frank Leurs		
4 Doug Favell	3.00	6.00
5 Earl Heiskala	1.50	3.00
6 Larry Hillman	2.50	5.00
7 Andre Lacroix	2.50	5.00
8 Lew Morrison	1.50	3.00
9 Simon Nolet	2.00	4.00
10 Garry Peters	1.50	3.00
11 Vic Stasiuk CO	1.50	3.00
12 George Swarbrick	1.50	3.00

1972 Flyers Mighty Milk

These seven panels, which were issued on the sides of half gallon cartons of Mighty Milk, featured members of the Philadelphia Flyers. After cutting, the panels measured approximately 3 5/8" by 7 1/2". All lettering and the portrait itself were in blue. Inside a frame with rounded corners, each panel displayed a portrait of the player and a player profile. The words "Philadelphia Hockey Star" and the player's name appeared above the frame, while an advertisement for Mighty Milk and another for TV Channel 29 appeared immediately below. The backs were blank. The panels were unnumbered and checklisted below in alphabetical order.

COMPLETE SET (8)	87.50	175.00
1 Serge Bernier	7.50	15.00
2 Bobby Clarke	40.00	80.00
3 Gary Dornhoefer	10.00	20.00
4 Doug Favell	15.00	30.00
5 Jean-Guy Gendron	7.50	15.00
6 Bob Kelly		
7 Bill Lesuk	7.50	15.00
8 Ed Van Impe	10.00	20.00

1973-74 Flyers Linnett

These oversize cards were produce by Charles Linnett Studios. Cards were done in black and white and featured a facsimile signature. Original price per piece was only 50 cents. Cards measure 8 1/2 x 11. They were unnumbered and checklisted below in alphabetical order.

COMPLETE SET (1-18)	40.00	80.00
1 Barry Ashbee	1.50	3.00
2 Bill Barber	5.00	10.00
3 Tom Bladon	1.50	3.00
4 Bob Clarke	5.00	10.00
5 Bill Clement	3.00	6.00
6 Terry Crisp	2.50	5.00
7 Bill Flett	2.00	4.00
8 Bob Kelly	1.50	3.00
9 Orest Kindrachuk	1.50	3.00
10 Ross Lonsberry	1.50	3.00
11 Rick Macleish	2.00	4.00
12 Simon Nolet	2.00	4.00
13 Bernard Parent	5.00	10.00
14 Don Saleski	1.50	3.00
15 Dave Schultz	3.00	6.00
16 Ed Van Impe	1.50	3.00
17 Jimmy Watson	2.00	4.00
18 Joe Watson	2.00	4.00

1936 Frank Coffey Olympics

Produced for the 1936 Berlin Olympics, each card features a full color front along with biographical information on the back.

NNO Ice Hockey	15.00	30.00
NNO Field Hockey	15.00	30.00

1971-72 Frito-Lay

This ten-card set featured members of the Toronto Maple Leafs and Montreal Canadiens. Since the cards were unnumbered, they had been listed below in alphabetical order within team, Montreal (1-5) and Toronto (6-10). The cards were paper thin, each measuring approximately 1 1/2" by 2".

COMPLETE SET (10)	50.00	100.00
1 Yvan Cournoyer	4.00	8.00
2 Ken Dryden	25.00	50.00
3 Frank Mahovlich	5.00	10.00
4 Henri Richard	5.00	10.00
5 J.C. Tremblay	2.00	4.00
6 Bobby Baun	2.00	4.00
7 Ron Ellis	2.00	4.00
8 Paul Henderson	3.00	6.00
9 Jacques Plante	10.00	20.00
10 Norm Ullman	3.00	6.00

1967-68 General Mills

Little is known about this recently catalogued five-card set, save for it measured approximately 2 5/16" by 2 13/16" and featured color player photos in a white border. It appeared the cards were cut-outs from boxes of General Mills cereal, as a full box back picturing Harry Howell with a checklist listing these cards was known to exist. Further information would be appreciated. The backs are blank. The cards are unnumbered and checklisted below in alphabetical order.

COMPLETE SET (5)	500.00	1,000.00
1 Jean Beliveau	75.00	150.00
2 Gordie Howe	150.00	300.00
3 Harry Howell	40.00	80.00
4 Stan Mikita	62.50	125.00
5 Bobby Orr	250.00	500.00

1914 Happy Christmas Postcard

Full color postcard that measures 3 1/2 x 5 1/2. Front featured a young lady with a hockey stick and the words Happy Christmas in the lower right-hand corner. Small print on card back said Series 259 F.

NNO Happy Christmas	10.00	20.00

1975-76 HCA Steel City Vacuum

Little is known about this set beyond the checklist. The set has the same look as the Hamilton Fincups set produced that same season.

COMPLETE SET (22)	5.00	10.00
1 Mike Buchko	.25	.50
2 Pino Caterini	.25	.50
3 Rich Chittley	.25	.50
4 S. Hutchings	.25	.50
5 Jim Italiano	.25	.50
6 Scott Kyle	.25	.50
7 Stan Malecki	.25	.50
8 Mike McHugh	.25	.50
9 Jeff Ninham	.25	.50
10 Brad Roberts	.25	.50
11 Chris Roberts	.25	.50
12 Bruce Shipley	.25	.50
13 G. Stevenson	.25	.50
14 Keith Taylor	.25	.50
15 Mark Tonaj	.25	.50
16 F. Warwick	.25	.50
17 Pat Windsor	.25	.50
18 Bill Zenette	.25	.50
19 Fred LeBlanc PR	.13	.25
20 John Taylor VP	.13	.25
21 Management	.13	.25
22 Ange Savelli CO	.50	1.00

1975-76 Heroes Stand-Ups

These 31 "Hockey Heroes Autographed Pin-up/Stand-Up Sportrophies" featured NHL players from five different teams. The stand-ups came in two different sizes. The Bruins and Flyers stand-ups were approximately 15 1/2" by 8/3/4", while the Islanders stand-ups were approximately 13 1/2" by 7 1/2" and were issued three to a strip. The stand-ups were made of laminated cardboard, and the yellow frame is decorated with red stars. Each stand-up featured a color action shot of the player. A facsimile autograph was inscribed across the bottom of the stand-up. The stand-ups were unnumbered and checklisted below alphabetically according to and within teams as follows: Boston Bruins (1-7), Montreal Canadiens (8-13), New York Islanders (14-19), Philadelphia Flyers (20-25), and Toronto Maple Leafs (26-31).

COMPLETE SET (31)	125.00	250.00
1 Gerry Cheevers	6.00	12.00
2 Terry O'Reilly	3.00	6.00
3 Bobby Orr	25.00	50.00
4 Brad Park	4.00	8.00
5 Jean Ratelle	4.00	8.00
6 Andre Savard	2.50	5.00
7 Gregg Sheppard	2.50	5.00
8 Yvan Cournoyer	4.00	8.00
9 Guy Lafleur	10.00	20.00
10 Jacques Lemaire	4.00	8.00
11 Peter Mahovlich	2.50	5.00
12 Doug Risebrough	2.50	5.00
13 Larry Robinson	6.00	12.00
14 Billy Harris	2.50	5.00
15 Gerry Hart	2.50	5.00
16 Denis Potvin	6.00	12.00
17 Glenn Resch	4.00	8.00
18 Bryan Trottier	6.00	12.00
19 Ed Westfall	2.50	5.00
20 Bill Barber	4.00	8.00
21 Bobby Clarke	6.00	12.00
22 Reggie Leach	2.50	5.00
23 Rick MacLeish	2.50	5.00
24 Bernie Parent	6.00	12.00
25 Dave Schultz	4.00	8.00
26 Lanny McDonald	4.00	8.00
27 Borje Salming	3.00	6.00
28 Darryl Sittler	4.00	8.00
29 Wayne Thomas	3.00	6.00
30 Errol Thompson	2.50	5.00
31 Tiger Williams	4.00	8.00

1924-25 Holland Creameries

The 1924-25 Holland Creameries set contained ten black and white cards measuring approximately 1 1/2" by 3". The front had a black and white head and shoulders shot of the player, in an oval-shaped black frame on white card stock. The words Holland Hockey Competition- appeared above the picture, with the player's name and position below. The cards were numbered in the lower left corner on the front. The horizontally formatted card back had an offer to exchange one complete collection of ten players for either a brick of ice cream or three Holland Banquets. Supposedly the difficult card in the set was Connie Neil, marked as SP in the checklist below.

COMPLETE SET (10)	1,000.00	1,500.00
1 Wally Fridfinson	60.00	150.00
2 Harold McMunn	60.00	150.00
3 Art Somers	60.00	150.00
4 Frank Woodall	60.00	150.00
5 Frank Frederickson	125.00	300.00
6 Bobby Benson	60.00	150.00
7 Harry Neal	60.00	150.00
8 Wally Byron	60.00	150.00
9 Connie Neil SP	300.00	500.00
10 J. Austman	60.00	150.00

1975-76 Houston Aeros WHA

Little was known about this rare WHA issue. The checklist was confirmed and as the cards are unnumbered, they are listed below in alphabetical order. Any additional information can be forwarded to hockeymag@beckett.com.

COMPLETE SET (19)	40.00	80.00
1 Ron Grahame	2.00	4.00
2 Larry Hale	1.00	2.00
3 Murray Hall	1.50	3.00
4 Gordie Howe	15.00	30.00
5 Mark Howe	5.00	10.00
6 Marty Howe	4.00	8.00
7 Andre Hinse	1.00	2.00
8 Frank Hughes	1.00	2.00
9 Glen Irwin	1.00	2.00
10 Gord Labossiere	1.50	3.00
11 Don Larway	1.00	2.00
12 Larry Lund	1.50	3.00
13 Paul Popeil	1.50	3.00
14 Rich Preston	1.50	3.00
15 Terry Ruskowski	1.50	3.00
16 Wayne Rutledge	2.00	4.00
17 John Schella	1.00	2.00
18 Ted Taylor	1.00	2.00
19 John Tonelli	5.00	10.00

1927 Imperial Tobacco

This card was black and white and measured approximately 1 1/2 x 2 1/2.

NNO Montreal Victorias	25.00	50.00

1929 Imperial Tobacco

This card is black and white and measures approximately 2 1/2 x 3.

NNO Ice Hockey	20.00	40.00

1979-80 Islanders Transparencies

These standard postcard size cards featured black and white posed photos on a thin, transparent paper stock. Cards were unnumbered and checklisted below alphabetically.

COMPLETE SET (22)	20.00	40.00
1 Mike Bossy	7.50	15.00
2 Bob Bourne	.38	.75
3 Clark Gillies	.38	.75
4 Billy Harris	.38	.75
5 Lerne Henning	.38	.75
6 Anders Kallur	.38	.75
7 Mike Kaszycki	.38	.75
8 Dave Langevin	.38	.75
9 Dave Lewis	.38	.75
10 Bob Lorimer	.38	.75
11 Wayne Merrick	.38	.75
12 Bob Nystrom	1.00	2.00
13 Stefan Persson	.38	.75
14 Denis Potvin	1.00	2.00
15 Jean Potvin	.38	.75
16 Garry Howatt	.38	.75
17 Glenn Resch	2.50	5.00
18 Bill Smith	2.50	5.00
19 Steven Tambellini	.38	.75
20 John Tonelli	.75	1.50
21 Bryan Trottier	2.00	4.00
22 Header Card	.30	.60

1935 J.A. Pattreiouex Sporting Events and Stars

31 Ice Hockey
Ice Skating
89 G.A. Johnson
Ice Hockey

1978-79 Jets Postcards

This 23-postcard set measured approximately 3 1/2" by 5 1/2". The fronts featured posed-on-ice borderless color player photos with a facsimile player autograph near the bottom. The backs had a postcard format and carried the player's name and a brief biography. The postcards were unnumbered and checklisted below in alphabetical order.

COMPLETE SET (23)	12.50	25.00
1 Mike Amodeo	.38	.75
2 Scott Campbell	.38	.75
3 Kim Clackson	.50	1.00
4 Joe Daley	1.00	2.00
5 John Gray	.38	.75
6 Ted Green	1.00	2.00
7 Robert Guindon	.38	.75
8 Glenn Hicks	.38	.75
9 Larry Hillman	.38	.75
10 Bill Lesuk	.50	1.00
11 Willy Lindstrom	.75	1.50
12 Barry Long	.38	.75
13 Morris Lukowich	.75	1.50
14 Paul MacKinnon	.38	.75
15 Markus Mattsson	.75	1.50
16 Lyle Moffat	.38	.75
17 Kent Nilsson	2.50	5.00
18 Rich Preston	.50	1.00
19 Terry Ruskowski	1.25	2.50
20 Lars-Erik Sjoberg	1.25	2.50
21 Peter Sullivan	.38	.75
22 Paul Terbenche	.38	.75
23 Steve West	.38	.75

1979-80 Jets Postcards

These 28 postcards measured approximately 3 1/2" by 5 1/2" and featured posed-on-ice color player photos on their borderless fronts. A facsimile player autograph rested near the bottom. The backs had a postcard format and carried the player's name and brief biography. The postcards were unnumbered and checklisted below in alphabetical order.

COMPLETE SET (28)	12.50	25.00
1 Mike Amodeo	.38	.75
2 Al Cameron	.38	.75
3 Scott Campbell	.38	.75
4 Wayne Dillon	.38	.75
5 Jude Drouin	.38	.75
6 John Ferguson GM	.50	1.00
7 Hilliard Graves	.38	.75
8 Pierre Hamel	.38	.75
9 Dave Hoyda	.38	.75
10 Bobby Hull	4.00	8.00
11 Bill Lesuk	.38	.75
12 Willy Lindstrom	.75	1.50
13 Morris Lukowich	.75	1.50
14 Jimmy Mann	.75	1.50
15 Peter Marsh	.50	1.00
16 Gord McTavish	.38	.75
17 Tom McVie CO	.38	.75
18 Barry Melrose	1.50	3.00
19 Lyle Moffat	.38	.75
20 Craig Norwich	.38	.75
21 Lars-Erik Sjoberg	1.25	2.50
22 Gary Smith	.50	1.00
23 Gordon Smith	.38	.75
24 Lorne Stamler	.38	.75
25 Peter Sullivan	.38	.75
26 Bill Sutherland ACO	.25	.50
27 Ron Wilson	.50	1.00
28 Title Card	.25	.50

1980-81 Jets Postcards

This 23-card set of the Winnipeg Jets measured approximately 3 1/2" by 5 1/2". The fronts featured borderless black-and-white action player photos. A facsimile autograph rounded out the front. The backs were blank. The cards were unnumbered and checklisted below in alphabetical order.

COMPLETE SET (24)	10.00	20.00
1 David Babych	1.00	2.50
2 Al Cameron	.40	1.00
3 Scott Campbell	.40	1.00
4 Dave Chartier	.40	1.00
5 Dave Christian	.40	1.00
6 Jude Drouin	.40	1.00
7 Norm Dupont	.40	1.00
8 Dan Geoffrion	.40	1.00
9 Pierre Hamel	.40	1.00
10 Barry Legge	.40	1.00
11 Willy Lindstrom	.60	1.50
12 Barry Long	.60	1.50
13 Morris Lukowich	.40	1.00
14 Kris Manery	.40	1.00
15 Jimmy Mann	.60	1.50
16 Moe Mantha	.60	1.50
17 Markus Mattsson	.60	1.50
18 Richard Mulhern	.40	1.00
19 Doug Smail	.60	1.50

20 Don Spring	.40	1.00
21 Anders Steen	.40	1.00
22 Pete Sullivan	.40	1.00
23 Tim Trimper	.40	1.00
24 Ron Wilson	.60	1.50

1972 Kellogg's Iron-On Transfers

These six iron-on transfers each measured approximately 6 1/2" by 10". Each transfer consisted of a cartoon drawing of the player's body with an oversized head. The puck was comically portrayed with human characteristics (face, arms, and legs). A facsimile player autograph appeared below the drawing. At the bottom were instructions in English and French for applying the iron-on to clothing; these were to be cut off before application. These iron-on transfers were unnumbered and checklisted below in alphabetical order.

COMPLETE SET (6)	150.00	300.00
1 Ron Ellis	12.50	25.00
2 Phil Esposito	37.50	75.00
3 Rod Gilbert	20.00	40.00
4 Bobby Hull	62.50	125.00
5 Frank Mahovlich	20.00	40.00
6 Stan Mikita	25.00	50.00

1980-81 Kings Card Night

The cards in this 14-card set were in color and are standard size. The set was produced during the 1980-81 season by All-Star Cards Ltd. for the Los Angeles Kings at the request of owner Jerry Buss. Reportedly 5000 sets were produced, virtually all of which were given away at the Kings' "Card Night." The fronts featured color "mug shots" of the players; the backs provided career highlights and brief biographical information.

COMPLETE SET (14)	10.00	20.00
1 Marcel Dionne	4.00	8.00
2 Glenn Goldup	.30	.75
3 Doug Halward	.30	.75
4 Billy Harris	.40	1.00
5 Steve Jensen	.40	1.00
6 Jerry Korab	.30	.75
7 Mario Lessard	.60	1.50
8 Dave Lewis	.40	1.00
9 Mike Murphy	.30	.75
10 Rob Palmer	.30	.75
11 Charlie Simmer	.75	2.00
12 Dave Taylor	1.25	3.00
13 Garry Unger	.60	1.50
14 Jay Wells	.40	1.00

1948 Kellogg's All Wheat Sport Tips Series 1

17 Hockey: Shooting	3.00	8.00

1948 Kellogg's All Wheat Sport Tips Series 2

1 Hockey: Body Shift	3.00	8.00
2 Hockey: Poke Check	3.00	8.00
3 Hockey: Hook Check	3.00	8.00
4 Hockey:	3.00	8.00
5 Hockey: Board Trick	3.00	8.00
6 Hockey: Shoulder Feint	3.00	8.00
16 Hockey: Defensive Position	3.00	8.00
17 Hockey: Fake Pass	3.00	8.00

1979-80 Lakers/Kings Alta-Dena

This eight-card set was sponsored by Alta-Dena Dairy, and its logo adorns the bottom of both sides of the card. The cards measure approximately 2 3/4" by 4" and feature color action player photos on the fronts. While the sides of the picture have no borders, green and red-orange stripes border the picture on its top and bottom. The player's name appears in black lettering in the top red-orange stripe. The team logo appears in the bottom red-orange stripe. The back has an offer for youngsters 14-and-under, who could present the complete eight-card set in the souvenir folder to the Forum Box Office and receive a half-price discount on certain tickets to any one of the Lakers and Kings games listed on the reverse of the card. The cards are unnumbered and are checklisted below in alphabetical order. This small set features Los Angeles Kings and Los Angeles Lakers as they were both owned by Jerry Buss. Cards 1-4 are Los Angeles Lakers (NBA) and Cards 5-8 are Los Angeles Kings (NHL). The set must have been planned and produced in the late summer of 1979 since Adrian Dantley was traded to Utah for Spencer Haywood on September 13

COMPLETE SET (8)	10.00	20.00
5 Marcel Dionne	3.00	6.00
6 Butch Goring	.50	1.00
7 Mike Murphy	.50	1.00
8 Dave Taylor	1.50	3.00

1927-28 La Patrie

The 1927-28 La Patrie set contained 21 notebook paper-sized (approximately 8 1/2" by 11") photos. The front had a sepia-toned posed photo of the player, enframed by a thin black border. The words "La Patrie" appeared above the picture, with the player's name below it. The photo number and year appeared at the lower right corner of the picture. A patterned border completed the front. The back was blank. Reports indicate a folder may have been issued to hold the photos.

COMPLETE SET (21)	1,250.00	2,500.00
1 Sylvio Mantha	50.00	100.00
2 Art Gagne	30.00	60.00
3 Leo Lafrance	30.00	60.00
4 Aurel Joliat	150.00	300.00
5 Pit Lepine	40.00	80.00
6 Gizzy Hart	30.00	60.00
7 Wildor Larochelle	40.00	80.00
8 Georges Hainsworth	100.00	200.00
9 Herb Gardiner	40.00	80.00
10 Albert Leduc	40.00	80.00
11 Marty Burke	40.00	80.00
12 Charlie Langlois	30.00	60.00
13 Leonard Gaudreault	30.00	60.00
14 Howie Morenz	350.00	700.00
15 Cecil M. Hart	40.00	80.00
16 Leo Dandurand	30.00	60.00
17 Newsy Lalonde	150.00	300.00
18 Didier Pitre	30.00	60.00
19 Jack Laviolette	50.00	100.00
20 Georges Patterson	30.00	60.00
21 Georges Vezina	250.00	500.00

1927-28 La Presse Photos

1 Howie Morenz	200.00	300.00
2 Aurel Joliat	125.00	200.00
3 Sylvio Mantha	50.00	100.00
4 Pit Lepine	50.00	100.00
5 George Hainsworth	125.00	200.00
6 Art Gagne	50.00	100.00
7 Herb Gardiner	50.00	100.00
8 Art Gagne	50.00	100.00
9 Herb Gardiner	50.00	100.00
10 Albert Leduc	50.00	100.00
11 Wildor Larochelle	50.00	100.00
12 Leonard Gaudreault	50.00	100.00
13 Gizzy Hart	50.00	100.00
14 Charlie Langlois	50.00	100.00
15 Georges Vezina	200.00	300.00
16 Cattarinich	60.00	150.00
Hart		
Dandurand		
Letourneau		
17 Eddie Shore	150.00	250.00
18 Lionel Conacher	125.00	200.00
19 Red Porter	50.00	100.00
20 George Patterson	50.00	100.00

1928-29 La Presse Photos

These oversized (10 X16) photos were issued over the course of the 1928-29 season as a premium with the Montreal newspaper, La Presse. They featured color posed images on the front. Because they had standard newspaper coverage on the back, some hobbyists do not consider them true collectibles. However, recent sales information suggests there is significant interest in these pieces. Because of their age and the natural deterioration of newsprint, it is rare to find these in high grade. As they are unnumbered, they are listed below in alphabetical order.

COMPLETE SET (14)	400.00	800.00
1 Clint Benedict	50.00	100.00
2 Frank Boucher	37.50	75.00
3 George Boucher	37.50	75.00
4 Lucien Brunet	10.00	20.00
5 Marty Burke	37.50	75.00
6 Bun Cook	50.00	100.00
7 Hap Day	37.50	75.00
8 Red Dutton	37.50	75.00
9 Georges Mantha	50.00	100.00
10 Armand Mondou	37.50	75.00
11 Bill Phillips	37.50	75.00
12 Babe Siebert	50.00	100.00
13 Nels Stewart	62.50	125.00
14 Jimmy Ward	37.50	75.00

1964 Lamberts Sports and Games

Card measures approximately 1 1/2" x 3 1/2" and featured full color fronts. Came from a series of 25 cards given as a premium for Lambert tea of Norwich, England.

20 Ice Hockey	10.00	20.00

1971-72 Letraset Action Replays

This set of 24 Hockey Action Replays was issued in Canada by Letraset. Printed on thin paper stock, each replay measured approximately 5 1/4" by 6 1/4" and was folded in the center. All replays had a common front consisting of a color photo of a face-off between Danny O'Shea of the Hawks and Jean Ratelle of the Rangers. On the reverse side, a "Know Your Signals" series illustrated arm signals used by hockey referees. The inside unfolded to display a 5" by 4 1/2" color drawings of NHL action shots. Immediately above was a description of the play plus slots for photos of the players involved in the action. The center photos and some of the players needed to complete the play were missing and supplied on a separate run-on transfer sheet. The action scene could be completed by rubbing the players on the transfer sheet onto the action scene. The replays were numbered in the white panel that presents the referee arm signals, and checklisted below accordingly.

COMPLETE SET (24)	100.00	200.00
1 Rogatien Vachon	5.00	10.00
Dave Keon		
Gilles Marotte		
2 Ken Dryden	10.00	20.00
Chico Maki		
Jacques Laperriere		
3 Gary Dornhoefer	4.00	8.00
Roger Crozier		
Tracy Pratt		
4 Walt Tkaczuk	4.00	8.00
Gump Worsley		
Vic Hadfield		
5 Dallas Smith	17.50	35.00
Bobby Orr		
Walt McKechnie		
6 Ab McDonald	4.00	8.00
Gary Sabourin		
Garry Unger		
7 Jim Rutherford	4.00	8.00
Orland Kurtenbach		
Bob Woytovich		
8 Gerry Cheevers	6.00	12.00
Frank Mahovlich		
Don Awrey		
9 Tim Ecclestone	5.00	10.00
Bob Baun		
Jacques Plante		
10 Stan Mikita	6.00	12.00
Ed Giacomin		
Jim Pappin		
11 Doug Favell	4.00	8.00
Danny Grant		
Ed Van Impe		
12 Ernie Wakely	4.00	8.00
Barclay Plager		
Gary Croteau		
13 Bryan Hextall	5.00	10.00
Tony Esposito		
Pat Stapleton		
14 Jean Ratelle	5.00	10.00
Rod Gilbert		
Jim Roberts		
15 Jacques Lemaire	6.00	12.00
Henri Richard		
Yvan Cournoyer		
16 George Gardiner	4.00	8.00
Dennis Hull		
Lou Angotti		
17 Ed Johnston	17.50	35.00
Norm Ullman		
Bobby Orr		
18 Gilles Meloche	4.00	8.00
Wayne Carleton		
Dick Redmond		
19 Al Smith	4.00	8.00
Gary Bergman		
Stan Gilbertson		
20 Dunc Wilson	4.00	8.00
Brad Park		
Dale Tallon		
21 Jude Drouin	4.00	8.00
Doug Favell		
Barry Ashbee		
22 Ron Ellis	10.00	20.00
Ken Dryden		
Paul Henderson		
23 Gary Edwards	4.00	8.00
Jean Pronovost		
Ron Shock		
24 Cesare Maniago	4.00	8.00
Chris Bordeleau		
Ted Harris		

1980 Liberty Matchbooks

This yellow matchbook was part of a multi-sport set, featuring athletes from all the major leagues and Olympics.

NNO Ray Bourque	10.00	20.00

1974-75 Lipton Soup

The 1974-75 Lipton Soup NHL set contained 50 color cards measuring approximately 2 1/4" by 3 1/4". The set was issued in two-card panels on the back of Lipton Soup packages. The backs featured statistics in French and English. Both varieties of Salming were included in the complete set below.

COMPLETE SET (51)	175.00	350.00
1 Norm Ullman	4.00	8.00
2 Gilbert Perreault	4.00	8.00
3 Darryl Sittler	6.00	12.00
4 Jean-Paul Parise	2.00	4.00
5 Garry Unger	2.00	4.00
6 Ron Ellis	2.50	5.00
7 Rogatien Vachon	5.00	10.00
8 Bobby Orr	50.00	100.00
9 Wayne Cashman	2.50	5.00
10 Brad Park	3.00	6.00
11 Serge Savard	2.50	5.00
12 Walt Tkaczuk	2.00	4.00
13 Yvan Cournoyer	4.00	8.00
14 Andre Boudrias	1.50	3.00
15 Gary Smith	2.50	5.00
16 Guy Lapointe	2.00	4.00
17 Dennis Hull	2.50	5.00
18 Bernie Parent	5.00	10.00
19 Ken Dryden	25.00	50.00
20 Rick MacLeish	2.50	5.00
21 Bobby Clarke	7.50	15.00
22 Dale Tallon	2.00	4.00
23 Jim McKenny	1.50	3.00
24 Rene Robert	2.50	5.00
25 Red Berenson	2.00	4.00
26 Ed Giacomin	5.00	10.00
27 Cesare Maniago	3.00	6.00
28 Ken Hodge	2.50	5.00
29 Gregg Sheppard	1.50	3.00
30 Dave Schultz	5.00	10.00
31 Bill Barber	4.00	8.00
32 Henry Boucha	2.00	4.00
33 Richard Martin	2.50	5.00
34 Steve Vickers	2.00	4.00
35 Billy Harris	1.50	3.00
36 Jim Pappin	1.50	3.00
37 Pit Martin	1.50	3.00
38 Jacques Lemaire	4.00	8.00
39 Peter Mahovlich	2.50	5.00
40 Rod Gilbert	4.00	8.00
41A Borje Salming (Horizontal pose)	6.00	12.00
41B Borje Salming (Vertical pose)	6.00	12.00
42 Pete Stemkowski	1.50	3.00
43 Ron Schock	1.50	3.00
44 Dan Bouchard	3.00	6.00
45 Tony Esposito	6.00	12.00
46 Craig Patrick	2.00	4.00
47 Ed Westfall	1.50	3.00
48 Jocelyn Guevremont	1.50	3.00
49 Syl Apps	2.00	4.00
50 Dave Keon	4.00	8.00

1972-73 Los Angeles Sharks WHA

This 19-card standard-size set featured on the front black and white posed player photos, surrounded by a white border. The player's name was given in black lettering below the picture. The backs read "The Original Los Angeles Sharks, 1972-73" and had the Sharks' logo in the center.

COMPLETE SET (19)	20.00	40.00
1 Mike Byers	1.25	2.50
2 Bart Crashley	2.00	4.00
3 George Gardner	1.25	2.50
4 Russ Gillow	1.25	2.50
5 Tom Gilmore	1.25	2.50
6 Earl Heiskala	1.25	2.50
7 J.P. LeBlanc	1.50	3.00
8 Ralph McSweyn	1.25	2.50
9 Ted McCaskill	1.25	2.50
10 Jim Niekamp	1.25	2.50
11 Gerry Odrowski	1.50	3.00
12 Tom Serviss	1.25	2.50
13 Peter Slater	1.25	2.50
14 Steve Sutherland	1.25	2.50
15 Joe Szura	1.50	3.00
16 Gary Veneruzzo	1.25	2.50
17 Jim Watson	1.25	2.50
18 Alton White	1.25	2.50
19 Bill Young	1.25	2.50

1973-74 Mac's Milk

The 1973-74 Mac's Milk set contained 30 unnumbered discs measuring approximately 3" in diameter. These round discs were actually cloth stickers with a peel-off back. They were unnumbered and featured popular players in the National Hockey League. There was no identifying mark anywhere on the discs identifying the sponsor as Mac's Milk. They are checklisted below in alphabetical order by player's name.

COMPLETE SET (30)	75.00	150.00
1 Gary Bergman	1.50	3.00
2 Johnny Bucyk	2.50	5.00
3 Wayne Cashman	2.00	4.00
4 Bobby Clarke	7.50	15.00
5 Yvan Cournoyer	3.00	6.00
6 Ron Ellis	1.50	3.00
7 Rod Gilbert	2.50	5.00
8 Brian Glennie	1.50	3.00
9 Paul Henderson	2.50	5.00
10 Ed Johnston	2.50	5.00
11 Rick Kehoe	1.50	3.00
12 Orland Kurtenbach	1.50	3.00
13 Guy Lapointe	2.50	5.00
14 Jacques Lemaire	2.50	5.00
15 Frank Mahovlich	5.00	10.00
16 Pete Mahovlich	2.50	5.00
17 Richard Martin	2.00	4.00
18 Jim McKenny	1.50	3.00
19 Bobby Orr	20.00	40.00
20 Jean-Paul Parise	1.50	3.00
21 Brad Park	4.00	8.00
22 Jacques Plante	7.50	15.00
23 Jean Ratelle	2.50	5.00
24 Mickey Redmond	2.50	5.00
25 Serge Savard	2.50	5.00
26 Darryl Sittler	5.00	10.00
27 Pat Stapleton	1.50	3.00
28 Dale Tallon	1.50	3.00
29 Norm Ullman	2.50	5.00
30 Bill White	2.00	4.00

1963-64 Maple Leafs Team Issue

This 22-card set of postcards measured approximately 3 1/2" by 5 1/2" and featured black and white action and posed player photos with white borders. The old Toronto Maple Leafs logo was in the bottom right corner. The player's name and position appeared at the bottom. The backs were blank. The cards were unnumbered and checklisted below in alphabetical order.

COMPLETE SET (22)	62.50	125.00
1 Bob Baun (Posed)	2.50	5.00
2 Bob Baun (Posed in white uniform& position not listed)	2.50	5.00
3 Carl Brewer (White uniform)	2.50	5.00
4 Carl Brewer (Dark uniform)	2.50	5.00
5 Kent Douglas	1.50	3.00
6 Dick Duff	2.00	4.00
7 Ron Ellis	2.00	4.00
8 Billy Harris (Portrait)	1.50	3.00
9 Billy Harris (Action)	1.50	3.00
10 Larry Hillman	1.50	3.00
11 Red Kelly	4.00	8.00
12 Dave Keon (No number)	7.50	15.00
13 Dave Keon (Number 14)	7.50	15.00
14 Frank Mahovlich (Dark uniform)	7.50	15.00
15 Frank Mahovlich (Dark uniform with added line NHL All-Star)	7.50	15.00
16 Don McKenney	1.50	3.00
17 Dickie Moore	4.00	8.00
18 Bob Nevin	2.00	4.00
19 Bert Olmstead	2.50	5.00

20 Eddie Shack	5.00	10.00
21 Don Simmons	2.00	4.00
22 Allan Stanley	3.00	6.00

1965-66 Maple Leafs White Border

This 17-card set of postcards measured approximately 3 1/2" by 5 1/2" and featured black and white portrait and full length photos with white borders. The Toronto Maple Leafs logo was printed in both bottom corners. A facsimile autograph appeared at the bottom between the logos. The backs were blank. The cards were unnumbered and checklisted below in alphabetical order.

COMPLETE SET (17)	30.00	60.00
1 George Armstrong	4.00	8.00
2 Bob Baun	2.00	4.00
3 Johnny Bower	4.00	8.00
4 John Brenneman	1.50	3.00
5 Brian Conacher	1.50	3.00
6 Ron Ellis (Portrait)	2.00	4.00
7 Ron Ellis (Full length; name in print)	2.00	4.00
8 Larry Hillman	1.50	3.00
9 Larry Jeffrey	1.50	3.00
10 Bruce Gamble	2.00	4.00
11 Red Kelly	4.00	8.00
12 Dave Keon	5.00	10.00
13 Orland Kurtenbach	2.00	4.00
14 Jim Pappin	1.50	3.00
15 Marcel Pronovost	3.00	6.00
16 Eddie Shack	4.00	8.00
17 Allan Stanley	3.00	6.00

1966-67 Maple Leafs Hockey Talks

Distributed by Esso, this set of 10 albums was a popular premium among Maple Leafs fans. Set consisted of ten records inside colorful paper sleeves. Each set was also housed in a large blue Esso Hockey Talks envelope.

COMPLETE SET (10)	300.00	600.00
1 George Armstrong	30.00	60.00
2 Johnny Bower	40.00	80.00
3 Dave Keon	30.00	60.00
4 Frank Mahovlich	30.00	60.00
5 Tim Horton	30.00	60.00
6 Bob Pulford	40.00	80.00
7 Brit Selby	25.00	50.00
8 Eddie Shack	30.00	60.00
9 Ron Ellis	30.00	60.00
10 Punch Imlach	30.00	60.00
NNO Hockey Caravan Envelope	15.00	30.00

1968-69 Maple Leafs White Border

This 11-card set of postcards measured approximately 3 1/2" by 5 1/2" and featured black and white player photos with white borders. The Pelyk and Smith cards were portraits while the other cards have posed action shots. The Maple Leafs logo was at the bottom left corner. A facsimile autograph appeared at the bottom. The backs were blank. The cards were unnumbered and checklisted below in alphabetical order.

COMPLETE SET (11)	20.00	40.00
1 Johnny Bower	4.00	8.00
2 Jim Dorey	1.50	3.00
3 Paul Henderson	2.00	4.00
4 Tim Horton	5.00	10.00
5 Rick Ley	1.50	3.00
6 Murray Oliver	1.50	3.00
7 Mike Pelyk	1.50	3.00
8 Pierre Pilote	3.00	6.00
9 Darryl Sly	1.50	3.00
10 Floyd Smith	1.50	3.00
11 Bill Sutherland	1.50	3.00

1969-70 Maple Leafs White Border Glossy

This 40-card set of postcards measured approximately 3 1/2" by 5 1/2" and features glossy black and white player photos (posed action or portraits) with white borders. The Maple Leafs logo is printed in black in the bottom left corner. The player's name appears at the bottom in block letters. The backs are blank. The cards are unnumbered and checklisted below in alphabetical order.

COMPLETE SET (40)	75.00	150.00
1 George Armstrong	3.00	6.00
2 Johnny Bower	4.00	8.00
3 Wayne Carleton	1.00	2.00
4 King Clancy	3.00	6.00
5 Terry Clancy	1.00	2.00
6 Brian Conacher	1.00	2.00
7 Marv Edwards	1.50	3.00
8 Ron Ellis (Number 6)	1.50	3.00
9 Ron Ellis (Number 8)	1.50	3.00
10 Ron Ellis (No number)	1.50	3.00
11 Bruce Gamble (Front view)	1.50	3.00
12 Bruce Gamble (Side view)	1.50	3.00
13 Brian Glennie (Portrait)	1.50	3.00
14 Brian Glennie (Full length)	1.50	3.00
15 Jim Harrison	1.00	2.00
16 Larry Hillman	1.00	2.00
17 Tim Horton	5.00	10.00
18 Dave Keon (A on sweater)	3.00	6.00
19 Dave Keon (C on sweater)	3.00	6.00
20 Rick Ley	1.50	3.00
21 Frank Mahovlich	5.00	10.00
22 Jim McKenny	1.00	2.00
23 Larry Mickey	1.00	2.00
24 Murray Oliver	1.00	2.00
25 Jim Pappin	1.00	2.00
26 Mike Pelyk	1.00	2.00
27 Marcel Pronovost	2.00	4.00
28 Bob Pulford (Number on gloves)	2.50	5.00
29 Bob Pulford (No number on gloves)	2.50	5.00
30 Pat Quinn	2.00	4.00
31 Brit Selby	1.00	2.00
32 Al Smith	1.00	2.00
33 Floyd Smith	1.00	2.00
34 Allan Stanley	2.50	5.00
35 Norm Ullman	2.50	5.00
36 Mike Walton (Stick touching border)	1.50	3.00
37 Mike Walton (Stick away from border)	1.50	3.00
38 Ron Ward	1.00	2.00
39 Team Photo 1966-67	3.00	6.00
40 Punch Imlach and King Clancy	3.00	6.00

1969-70 Maple Leafs White Border Matte

This six-card set of postcards measures approximately 3 1/2" by 5 1/2" and featured matte black and white player photos with white borders. The Toronto Maple Leafs logo was printed in black in the bottom left corner. The player's name appeared at the bottom in block letters. The backs were blank. The cards were unnumbered and checklisted below in alphabetical order.

COMPLETE SET (6)	10.00	20.00
1 Brian Glennie	1.50	3.00
2 Dave Keon	4.00	8.00
3 Bill MacMillan	1.25	2.50
4 Larry McIntyre	1.25	2.50
5 Brian Spencer	2.50	5.00
6 Norm Ullman	3.00	6.00

1970-71 Maple Leafs Postcards

This 15-card set measured approximately 3 1/2" by 5 1/2" and featured matte black and white player photos with white borders. The Maple Leafs logo was printed in the bottom left corner. The player's name appeared in block letters, and a facsimile autograph was printed in black. The backs were blank. The cards were unnumbered and checklisted below in alphabetical order. Key card in the set was Darryl Sittler appearing in his Rookie Card year.

COMPLETE SET (15)	25.00	50.00
1 Jim Dorey	1.00	2.00
2 Ron Ellis	1.50	3.00
3 Bruce Gamble	1.50	3.00
4 Jim Harrison	1.00	2.00
5 Paul Henderson	1.50	3.00
6 Rick Ley	1.25	2.50
7 Bob Liddington	1.00	2.00
8 Jim McKenny	1.00	2.00
9 Garry Monahan	1.00	2.00
10 Mike Pelyk	1.00	2.00
11 Jacques Plante	6.00	12.00
12 Brad Selwood	1.00	2.00
13 Darryl Sittler	12.50	25.00
14 Guy Trottier	1.00	2.00
15 Mike Walton	1.50	3.00

1971-72 Maple Leafs Postcards

This 21-card set measured approximately 3 1/2" by 5 1/2" and featured posed color player photos with black backgrounds. (The sweaters had lace-style neck.) The cards featured a facsimile autograph. The backs are blank. The cards were unnumbered and checklisted below in alphabetical order.

COMPLETE SET (21)	25.00	50.00
1 Bob Baun	1.50	3.00
2 Jim Dorey	1.00	2.00
3 Denis Dupere	1.00	2.00
4 Ron Ellis	1.50	3.00
5 Brian Glennie	1.00	2.00
6 Jim Harrison	1.00	2.00
7 Paul Henderson	1.50	3.00
8 Dave Keon	2.50	5.00
9 Rick Ley	1.00	2.00
10 Billy MacMillan	1.00	2.00
11 Don Marshall	1.00	2.00
12 Jim McKenny	1.00	2.00
13 Garry Monahan	1.00	2.00
14 Bernie Parent	4.00	8.00
15 Mike Pelyk	1.00	2.00
16 Jacques Plante	4.00	8.00
17 Brad Selwood	1.00	2.00
18 Darryl Sittler	5.00	10.00
19 Brian Spencer	1.50	3.00
20 Guy Trottier	1.00	2.00
21 Norm Ullman	2.00	4.00

1972-73 Maple Leafs Postcards

This 30-card set measured approximately 3 1/2" by 5 1/2" and featured posed color player photos with a black background. The players were pictured wearing "V-neck" sweaters. The cards featured a facsimile autograph. The backs were blank. The cards were unnumbered and checklisted below in alphabetical order.

COMPLETE SET (30)	40.00	80.00
1 Bob Baun	1.25	2.50
2 Terry Clancy	.75	1.50
3 Denis Dupere	.75	1.50
4 Ron Ellis (Dark print)	1.25	2.50
5 Ron Ellis (Light print)	1.25	2.50
6 George Ferguson	.75	1.50
7 Brian Glennie (Autograph touches stick)	.75	1.50
8 Brian Glennie (Autograph away from stick)	.75	1.50
9 John Grisdale	.75	1.50
10 Paul Henderson (Light print)	1.25	2.50
11 Paul Henderson (Dark print)	1.25	2.50
12 Pierre Jarry	.75	1.50
13 Rick Kehoe	1.25	2.50
14 Dave Keon (Autograph touches skate)	2.50	5.00
15 Dave Keon (Autograph away from skate)	2.50	5.00
16 Ron Low	1.25	2.50
17 Joe Lundrigan	.75	1.50
18 Larry McIntyre	.75	1.50
19 Jim McKenny (Blue tinge)	.75	1.50
20 Jim McKenny (Red tinge)	.75	1.50
21 Garry Monahan	.75	1.50
22 Randy Osburn	.75	1.50
23 Mike Pelyk	.75	1.50
24 Jacques Plante (Autograph through tape)	5.00	10.00
25 Jacques Plante (Autograph under tape)	5.00	10.00
26 Darryl Sittler (Autograph over stick)	5.00	10.00
27 Darryl Sittler (Autograph away from stick)	5.00	10.00
28 Errol Thompson	.75	1.50
29 Norm Ullman (Best Wishes above blueline)	2.00	4.00
30 Norm Ullman (Best Wishes across blueline)	2.00	4.00

1973-74 Maple Leafs Postcards

This 29-card set measured approximately 3 1/2" by 5 1/2" and featured posed color player photos with a blue-green background. The cards featured a facsimile autograph. The backs were blank. The cards were unnumbered and checklisted below in alphabetical order. The key card in the set was Lanny McDonald, whose card predated his Rookie Card.

COMPLETE SET (29)	45.00	90.00
1 Johnny Bower	2.50	5.00
2 Willie Brossart	.75	1.50
3 Denis Dupere	.75	1.50
4 Ron Ellis	1.25	2.50
5 Doug Favell (Standing)	1.50	3.00
6 Doug Favell (Bending)	1.50	3.00
7 Brian Glennie	.75	1.50
8 Jim Gregory	.75	1.50
9 Inge Hammarstrom	.75	1.50
10 Paul Henderson	1.25	2.50
11 Eddie Johnston	1.50	3.00
12 Rick Kehoe (Same as 1972-73 set)	1.50	3.00
13 Rick Kehoe (Bending)	1.50	3.00
14 Rick Kehoe (Standing)	1.50	3.00
15 Red Kelly	3.00	6.00
16 Dave Keon	3.00	6.00
17 Lanny McDonald	6.00	12.00
18 Jim McKenny	.75	1.50
19 Garry Monahan	.75	1.50
20 Bob Neely	.75	1.50
21 Mike Pelyk	.75	1.50
22 Borje Salming	4.00	8.00
23 Eddie Shack	3.00	6.00
24 Darryl Sittler (Bending)	3.00	6.00
25 Darryl Sittler (Standing)	3.00	6.00
26 Errol Thompson	.75	1.50
27 Ian Turnbull	.75	1.50
28 Norm Ullman	1.75	3.50
29 Dunc Wilson	1.25	2.50

1974-75 Maple Leafs Postcards

This 27-card set measured approximately 3 1/2" by 5 1/2" and featured posed color player photos with a pale-blue background and a "Venetian blind" effect. The cards featured facsimile autographs. The backs were blank. The cards were unnumbered and are checklisted below in alphabetical order.

COMPLETE SET (27)	25.00	50.00
1 Claire Alexander	.75	1.50
2 Dave Dunn	.75	1.50
3 Ron Ellis	1.00	2.00
4 George Ferguson (Bending)	.75	1.50
5 George Ferguson (Standing)	.75	1.50
6 Bill Flett (Front view)	.75	1.50
7 Bill Flett (Side view)	.75	1.50
8 Brian Glennie	.75	1.50
9 Inge Hammarstrom	.75	1.50
10 Dave Keon (Bending)	2.00	4.00
11 Dave Keon (Standing)	2.00	4.00
12 Lanny McDonald	3.00	6.00
13 Jim McKenny	.75	1.50
14 Gord McRae	.75	1.50
15 Lyle Moffat	.75	1.50
16 Bob Neely	.75	1.50
17 Gary Sabourin	.75	1.50
18 Borje Salming	2.00	4.00
19 Rod Seiling	.75	1.50
20 Eddie Shack	2.00	4.00
21 Darryl Sittler	2.00	4.00
22 Blaine Stoughton	1.00	2.00
23 Errol Thompson	.75	1.50
24 Ian Turnbull	1.00	2.00
25 Norm Ullman	1.50	3.00
26 Tiger Williams	2.00	4.00
27 Dunc Wilson	1.00	2.00

1975-76 Maple Leafs Postcards

This 30-card set of postcards measured approximately 3 1/2" by 5 1/2" and featured posed color photos of players in blue uniforms. The Maple Leafs logo, the player's name, and number appeared in a white panel at the bottom. A facsimile autograph was inscribed across the picture. The backs had player information. The cards were unnumbered and are checklisted below in alphabetical order.

COMPLETE SET (30)	25.00	50.00
1 Claire Alexander	.75	1.50
2 Don Ashby (Bending)	.75	1.50
3 Don Ashby (Standing)	.75	1.50
4 Pat Boutette	.75	1.50
5 Dave Dunn	.75	1.50
6 Doug Favell	1.00	2.00
7 George Ferguson	.75	1.50
8 Brian Glennie	.75	1.50
9 Inge Hammarstrom (Bending)	.75	1.50
10 Inge Hammarstrom (Standing)	.75	1.50
11 Greg Hubick	.75	1.50
12 Lanny McDonald	2.50	5.00
13 Jim McKenny	.75	1.50
14 Gord McRae	.75	1.50
15 Bob Neely	.75	1.50
16 Borje Salming (Side view)	2.00	4.00
17 Borje Salming (Front view)	2.00	4.00
18 Rod Seiling	.75	1.50
19 Darryl Sittler (Bending)	2.00	4.00
20 Darryl Sittler (Standing)	2.50	5.00
21 Blaine Stoughton	1.00	2.00
22 Wayne Thomas (Crouching)	1.25	2.50
23 Wayne Thomas (Standing)	1.25	2.50
24 Errol Thompson	.75	1.50
25 Ian Turnbull (Bending)	1.00	2.00
26 Ian Turnbull (Standing)	1.00	2.00
27 Stan Weir	.75	1.50
28 Tiger Williams Bending	1.25	2.50
29 Tiger Williams Standing	1.25	2.50
30 Maple Leaf Gardens (Painting)	1.00	2.00

1976-77 Maple Leafs Postcards

This 24-card set in the postcard format measured approximately 3 1/2" by 5 1/2" and featured posed color photos of players in blue uniforms. A white panel at the bottom contained the Maple Leafs logo in each corner, the player's name, and uniform number. A facsimile autograph was inscribed across the picture. The cards were unnumbered and checklisted below in alphabetical order. Key card in the set was Randy Carlyle appearing prior to his Rookie Card year.

COMPLETE SET (24)	20.00	40.00
1 Claire Alexander	.63	1.25
2 Don Ashby	.63	1.25
3 Pat Boutette	.63	1.25
4 Randy Carlyle	1.50	3.00
5 George Ferguson	.63	1.25
6 Scott Garland	.63	1.25
7 Brian Glennie	.63	1.25
8 Inge Hammarstrom	.63	1.25
9 Lanny McDonald	2.00	4.00
10 Jim McKenny	.63	1.25
11 Gord McRae	.63	1.25
12 Bob Neely	.63	1.25
13 Mike Palmateer	2.00	4.00
14 Mike Pelyk	.63	1.25
15 Borje Salming	1.50	3.00
16 Darryl Sittler	2.00	4.00
17 Wayne Thomas	1.00	2.00
18 Errol Thompson	.63	1.25
19 Ian Turnbull	.75	1.50
20 Ian Turnbull	.75	1.50
21 Jack Valiquette	.63	1.25
22 Kurt Walker	.63	1.25
23 Stan Weir	.63	1.25
24 Tiger Williams	2.00	4.00

1977-78 Maple Leafs Postcards

This 19-card set measures approximately 3 1/2" by 5 1/2" and featured posed color photos of players in white uniforms. At the bottom were the Toronto Maple Leafs logo in each corner, the player's uniform number, and the player's name in blue print. The backs were blank. The cards were unnumbered and checklisted below in alphabetical order.

COMPLETE SET (19)	12.50	25.00
1 Pat Boutette	.50	1.00
2 Randy Carlyle	1.00	2.00
3 Ron Ellis	.75	1.50
4 George Ferguson	.50	1.00
5 Brian Glennie	.50	1.00
6 Inge Hammarstrom	.50	1.00
7 Trevor Johansen	.50	1.00
8 Jimmy Jones	.50	1.00
9 Lanny McDonald	2.00	4.00
10 Jim McKenny	.50	1.00
11 Gord McRae	.50	1.00
12 Mike Palmateer	1.50	3.00
13 Borje Salming	1.50	3.00
14 Darryl Sittler	2.00	4.00
15 Errol Thompson	.50	1.00
16 Ian Turnbull	.50	1.00
17 Jack Valiquette	.50	1.00
18 Kurt Walker	.50	1.00
19 Tiger Williams	1.50	3.00

1978-79 Maple Leafs Postcards

This 25-card set in the postcard format measured approximately 3 1/2" by 5 1/2" and featured posed color player photos. At the bottom were the Toronto Maple Leafs logo in each corner, the player's uniform number in the logo at the bottom right, and the player's name in blue print. The cards were unnumbered and checklisted below in alphabetical order.

COMPLETE SET (25)	15.00	30.00
1 John Anderson	.75	1.50
2 Bruce Boudreau	1.50	4.00
3 Pat Boutette	.50	1.00
4 Pat Boutette	.50	1.00
5 Dave Burrows	.50	1.00
6 Jerry Butler	.50	1.00
7 Ron Ellis	.75	1.50
8 Paul Harrison	.50	1.00
9 Dave Hutchison	.50	1.00
10 Trevor Johansen	.50	1.00
11 Jimmy Jones	.50	1.00
12 Dan Maloney	.75	1.50
13 Lanny McDonald	2.00	4.00
14 Walt McKechnie	.50	1.00
15 Garry Monahan	.50	1.00
16 Roger Neilson	1.00	2.00
17 Mike Palmateer	1.25	2.50
18 Borje Salming	1.25	2.50
19 Darryl Sittler	2.00	4.00
20 Lorne Stamler	.50	1.00
21 Ian Turnbull	.50	1.00
22 Tiger Williams	1.25	2.50
23 Ron Wilson	.50	1.00
24 H.Ballard/K.Clancy	1.00	2.00
25 Team Photo	1.25	2.50

1979-80 Maple Leafs Postcards

This 34-card set in the postcard format measured approximately 3 1/2" by 5 1/2" and featured posed color photos of players in blue uniforms. The Toronto Maple Leafs logo was in each bottom corner. A blue panel across the bottom contained the player's name in white print. The player's uniform number was printed in the logo at the bottom right. Most of the pictures had a light blue tint and are taken against a studio background. These cards also featured facsimile autographs on the lower portion of the picture. The backs were printed with a light blue postcard design and carry the player's name and position. The cards were unnumbered and checklisted below in alphabetical order.

COMPLETE SET (34)	20.00	40.00
1 John Anderson	.50	1.00
2 Harold Ballard	.75	1.50
3 Laurie Boschman	.50	1.00
4 Pat Boutette	.38	.75
5 Carl Brewer	.75	1.50
6 Dave Burrows	.38	.75
7 Jerry Butler	.38	.75
8 Jiri Crha	.75	1.50
9 Ron Ellis	.50	1.00
10 Paul Gardner	.38	.75
11 Paul Harrison	.38	.75
12 Greg Hotham	.38	.75
13 Dave Hutchison	.38	.75
14 Punch Imlach CO	1.00	2.00
15 Jimmy Jones	.38	.75
16 Mark Kirton	.38	.75
17 Dan Maloney	.38	.75
18 Terry Martin	.50	1.00
19 Lanny McDonald	2.00	4.00
20 Walt McKechnie	.38	.75
21 Mike Palmateer	1.00	2.00
22 Mike Palmateer (Autograph at different angle)	1.00	2.00
23 Joel Quenneville	.50	1.00
24 Rocky Saganiuk	.38	.75
25 Borje Salming (Autograph touches blue panel)	1.25	2.50
26 Borje Salming (Autograph away from blue panel)	1.25	2.50
27 Darryl Sittler (Autograph closer to blue panel)	2.00	4.00
28 Darryl Sittler	2.00	4.00
29 Floyd Smith	.38	.75
30 Bob Stephenson (Action shot taken at rink; borderless; no facsimile autograph; black print on back)	.50	1.00
31 Ian Turnbull	.38	.75
32 Tiger Williams	1.00	2.00
33 Ron Wilson	.38	.75
34 Faceoff with Cardinal	.63	1.25

1980-81 Maple Leafs Postcards

This 28-card set measured approximately 3 1/2" by 5 1/2" and featured horizontally oriented color player photos on the left half of the card. The right half displayed player information, blue logos, and a facsimile autograph printed in sky blue along with the team logo and a maple leaf carrying the player's jersey number. The backs were blank. The cards were unnumbered and checklisted below in alphabetical order.

COMPLETE SET (28)	12.50	25.00
1 John Anderson	.40	1.00
2 Harold Ballard	.60	1.50
3 Laurie Boschman (Portrait)	.40	1.00
4 Laurie Boschman (Action)	.40	1.00
5 Johnny Bower	1.25	3.00
6 King Clancy	.75	2.00
7 Jiri Crha	.60	1.50
8 Joe Crozier CO	.30	.75
9 Bill Derlago	.40	1.00
10 Dick Duff	.40	1.00
11 Vitezslav Duris	.30	.75
12 Dave Farrish	.30	.75
13 Stewart Gavin	.40	1.00
14 Paul Harrison	.30	.75
15 Pat Hickey	.30	.75
16 Mark Kirton	.30	.75
17 Terry Martin	.30	.75
18 Gerry McNamara	.30	.75
19 Wilf Paiement	.40	1.00
20 Robert Picard	.30	.75
21 Curt Ridley	.30	.75
22 Rocky Saganiuk	.30	.75
23 Borje Salming	.75	2.00
24 Dave Shand	.30	.75
25 Darryl Sittler (Portrait)	1.50	4.00
26 Darryl Sittler (Action)	1.50	4.00
27 Ian Turnbull	.30	.75
28 Rick Vaive	.60	1.50

1971 Mattel Mini-Records

This set was designed to be played on a special Mattel mini-record player, which is not included in the complete set price. Each black plastic disc, approximately 2 1/2" in diameter, features a recording on one side and a color drawing of the player on the other. The picture appears on a paper disk that is glued onto the smooth unrecorded side of the mini-record. On the recorded side, the player's name and the set's subtitle appear in arcs stamped in the central portion of the mini-record. The hand-engraved player's name appears again along with a production number, copyright symbol, and the Mattel name and year of production in the ring between the central portion of the record and the grooves. The ivory discs are the ones which are double sided and are considered to be tougher than the black discs. They were also known as "Mattel Show 'N Tell". The discs are unnumbered and checklisted below in alphabetical order according to sport

COMPLETE SET (18)	200.00	400.00
HK1 Yvan Cournoyer	5.00	10.00
HK2 Tony Esposito	6.00	12.00
HK3 Phil Esposito	7.50	15.00
HK4 Ed Giacomin	5.00	10.00
HK5 Gordie Howe	20.00	40.00
HK6 Frank Mahovlich	6.00	12.00
HK7 Bobby Orr	25.00	50.00
HK8 Jacques Plante	12.50	25.00

1906 McGill Men at Hockey Postcard

Standard sized postcard featured a photo of unknown men playing ice hockey. Back featured U.P.S. Montreal Series No 402.

NNO McGill Men at Hockey Montreal	60.00	120.00

1972-73 Minnesota Fighting Saints Postcards WHA

These borderless postcards featured action photos on the front, along with player name and biographical information. They were issued as promotional giveaways at autograph signings and to by-mail requesters.

COMPLETE SET (25)	35.00	70.00
1 Mike Antonovich	2.00	4.00
2 John Arbour	1.50	3.00
3 Terry Ball	1.50	3.00
4 Keith Christiansen	1.50	3.00
5 Wayne Connelly	2.50	5.00
6 Mike Curran	1.50	3.00
7 Craig Falkman	1.50	3.00
8 Ted Hampson	2.00	4.00
9 Jimmy Johnson	1.50	3.00
10 Bill Klatt	1.50	3.00
11 George Konik	1.50	3.00
12 Leonard Lilyholm	1.50	3.00
13 Bob MacMillan	1.50	3.00
14 Jack McCartan	2.50	5.00
15 Mike McMahon	1.50	3.00
16 George Morrison	1.50	3.00
17 Dick Paradise	1.50	3.00
18 Mel Pearson	1.50	3.00
19 Terry Ryan	1.50	3.00
20 Blaine Rydman	1.50	3.00
21 Frank Sanders	1.50	3.00
22 Glen Sonmor CO	1.50	3.00
23 Fred Speck	1.50	3.00
24 Bill Young	1.50	3.00
25 Carl Wetzel	1.50	3.00

1974-75 Minnesota Fighting Saints WHA

These cards set measure 3 1/2" x 5 1/2" and featured borderless color action photos on the front. Backs featured a head shot and statistics, along with the players position. The Saints logo could be found in black along the top of card back. Several cards are as yet unconfirmed.

1 Mike Antonovich	2.00	4.00
2 John Arbour	1.50	3.00
3 Terry Ball (unconfirmed)		
4 Bob Boyd (unconfirmed)		
5 Ron Busniuk	1.50	3.00
6 Wayne Connelly	2.00	4.00
7 Mike Curran	1.50	3.00
8 Gord Gallant	2.00	4.00
9 Gary Gambucci	1.50	3.00
10 John Garrett	5.00	10.00
11 Ted Hampson	2.00	4.00
12 Murray Heatley	1.50	3.00
13 Fran Huck	1.50	3.00
14 Jim Johnson	1.50	3.00
15 Jack McCartan (unconfirmed)		
16 Mike McMahon	1.50	3.00
17 George Morrison (unconfirmed)		
18 Harry Neale (unconfirmed)		
19 Danny O'Shea (unconfirmed)		
20 Rich Smith	1.50	3.00
21 Glen Sonmor (unconfirmed)		
22 Don Tannahill (unconfirmed)		
23 Mike Walton	2.50	5.00

1910 Murad College Silks S21

Each of these silks was issued by Murad Cigarettes around 1910 with a college emblem and an artist's rendering of a generic athlete on the front. The backs are blank. Each of the S21 silks measures roughly 5" by 7" and there was a smaller version created (roughly 3 1/2" by 5 1/2") of each and cataloged as S22.

*SMALLER S22: .3X TO .8X LARGER S21

1HK Army (West Point) hockey	30.00	60.00
2HK Brown hockey	30.00	60.00
3HK California hockey	30.00	60.00
4HK Chicago hockey	30.00	60.00
5HK Colorado hockey	30.00	60.00
6HK Columbia hockey	30.00	60.00
7HK Cornell hockey	30.00	60.00
8HK Dartmouth hockey	30.00	60.00
9HK Georgetown hockey	30.00	60.00
10HK Harvard hockey	30.00	60.00
11HK Illinois hockey	30.00	60.00
12HK Michigan hockey	30.00	60.00
13HK Minnesota hockey	30.00	60.00
14HK Missouri hockey	30.00	60.00
15HK Navy (Annapolis) hockey	30.00	60.00
16HK Ohio State hockey	30.00	60.00
17HK Pennsylvania hockey	30.00	60.00
18HK Purdue hockey	30.00	60.00
19HK Stanford hockey	30.00	60.00
20HK Stanford hockey	30.00	60.00
21HK Syracuse hockey	30.00	60.00
22HK Texas hockey	30.00	60.00
23HK Wisconsin hockey	30.00	60.00
24HK Yale hockey	30.00	60.00

1911 Murad College Series T51

These colorful cigarette cards featured several colleges and a variety of sports and recreations of the day and were issued in packs of Murad Cigarettes. The cards measure approximately 2" by 3". Two variations of each of the first 50 cards were produced; one variation says "College Series" on back, the other, "2nd Series". The drawings on cards of the 2nd Series are slightly different from those of the College Series. There are 6 different series of 25 in the College Series and they are listed here in the order that they appear on the checklist on the cardbacks. There is also a larger version (5" x 8") that was available for the first 25 cards as a premium (catalog designation T6) offer that could be obtained in exchange for 15 Murad cigarette coupons; the offers expired June 30, 1911.

*2ND SERIES: .4X TO 1X COLLEGE SERIES

18 Rochester Ice Hockey	25.00	50.00

1911 Murad College Series Premiums T6

18 Rochester Ice Hockey	250.00	400.00

1974 Nabisco Sugar Daddy

This set of 25 tiny (approximately 1 1/16" by 2 3/4") cards features athletes from a variety of popular pro sports. One card was included in specially marked Sugar Daddy and Sugar Mama candy bars. The cards were designed to be placed on a 18" by 24" poster, which could only be obtained through a mail-in offer direct from Nabisco. The set is referred to as "Pro Faces" as the cards show an enlarged head photo with a small caricature body. Cards 1-10 are football players, cards 11-16 and 22 are hockey players, and cards 17-21 and 23-25 are basketball players. Each card was produced in two printings. The first printing has a copyright date of 1973 printed on the backs (although the cards are thought to have been released in early 1974) and the second printing is missing a copyright date altogether.

COMPLETE SET (25)	75.00	150.00
11 Phil Esposito	4.00	8.00
12 Dennis Hull	1.50	4.00
13 Reg Fleming	1.50	4.00
14 Garry Unger	1.50	4.00
15 Derek Sanderson	2.50	5.00
16 Jerry Korab	1.50	4.00
22 Mickey Redmond	1.50	4.00

1975 Nabisco Sugar Daddy

This set of 25 tiny (approximately 1 1/16" by 2 3/4") cards features athletes from a variety of popular pro sports. One card was included in specially marked Sugar Daddy and Sugar Mama candy bars. The cards were designed to be placed on a 18" by 24" poster, which could only be obtained through a mail-in offer direct from Nabisco. The set is referred to as "Sugar Daddy All-Stars". As with the set of the previous year, the cards show an enlarged head photo with a small caricature body with a flag background of stars and stripes. This set is referred on the back as Series No. 2 and has a red, white, and blue background behind the picture on the front of the card. Cards 1-10 are pro football players and the remainder are pro basketball (17-21, 23-25) and hockey (11-16, 22) players.

COMPLETE SET (25)	75.00	150.00
11 Phil Esposito	4.00	8.00
12 Dennis Hull	1.50	4.00
13 Brad Park	2.00	5.00
14 Tom Lysiak	1.50	4.00
15 Bernie Parent	2.00	5.00
16 Mickey Redmond	1.50	4.00
22 Don Awrey	1.50	4.00

1976 Nabisco Sugar Daddy 1

This set of 25 tiny (approximately 1 1/16" by 2 3/4") cards features action scenes from a variety of popular sports from around the world. One card was included in specially marked Sugar Daddy and Sugar Mama candy bars. The set is referred to as "Sugar Daddy Sports World - Series 1" on the backs of the cards. The cards are in color with a relatively wide white border around the front of the cards.

COMPLETE SET (25)	40.00	80.00
1 Hockey	5.00	10.00

1976 Nabisco Sugar Daddy 2

This set of 25 tiny (approximately 1 1/16" by 2 3/4") cards features action scenes from a variety of popular sports from around the world. One card was included in specially marked Sugar Daddy and Sugar Mama candy bars. The set is referred to as "Sugar Daddy Sports World - Series 2" on the backs of the cards. The cards are in color with a relatively wide white border around the front of the cards.

COMPLETE SET (25)	40.00	80.00
11 Hockey	5.00	10.00

1974 New York News This Day in Sports

These cards are newspaper clippings of drawings by Hollreiser and are accompanied by textual description highlighting a player's unique sports feat. Cards are approximately 2" X 4 1/4". These are multisport cards and aranged in chronological order.

COMPLETE SET	50.00	120.00
34 Bobby Orr Nov. 15, 1973	2.00	4.00

1974-75 NHL Action Stamps

This set of NHL Action Stamps was distributed throughout North America in large grocery chains such as Loblaw's, IGA, A and P, and Acme. Some of these small stickers (or stamps) mentioned the particular grocery store on back; others had blank backs. A strip of eight player stamps was given out with a grocery purchase. The stamps measured approximately 1 5/8" by 2 1/8". These unnumbered stamps were ordered below alphabetically by teams as follows, Atlanta Flames (1-18), Boston Bruins (19-36), Buffalo Sabres (37-54), California Golden Seals (55-72), Chicago Blackhawks (73-90), Detroit Red Wings (91-108), Los Angeles Kings (109-126), Minnesota North Stars (127-144), Montreal Canadiens (145-162), New York Islanders (163-180), New York Rangers (181-198), Philadelphia Flyers (199-216), Pittsburgh Penguins (217-234), St. Louis Blues (235-252), Toronto Maple Leafs (253-270), Vancouver Canucks (271-288), Kansas City Scouts (289-306), and Washington Capitals (307-324). An album was available for this set which included 20 stamps in the back. Some of the stamps (29, 57, 94, and 164) were only available in the album. Intact strips would be valued at 50 to 75 percent more than the sum of the respective player prices listed below.

COMPLETE SET (324)	100.00	200.00
1 Eric Vail	.25	.50
2 Jerry Byers	.18	.35
3 Rey Comeau	.18	.35
4 Curt Bennett	.18	.35
5 Bob Murray	.18	.35
6 Don Bouchard	.50	1.00
7 Pat Quinn	.50	1.00
8 Larry Romanchych	.18	.35
9 Randy Manery	.18	.35
10 Phil Myre	.50	1.00
11 Buster Harvey	.18	.35
12 Keith McCreary	.18	.35
13 Jean Lemieux	.18	.35
14 Arnie Brown	.18	.35

15 Bob Leiter .18 .35
16 Jacques Richard .25 .50
17 Noel Price .18 .35
18 Tom Lysiak .38 .75
19 Bobby Orr 10.00 20.00
20 Al Sims .25 .50
21 Don Marcotte .18 .35
22 Terry O'Reilly .50 1.00
23 Carol Vadnais .18 .35
24 Gilles Gilbert .75 1.50
25 Bobby Schmautz .25 .50
26 Phil Esposito 2.50 5.00
27 Walt McKechnie .25 .50
28 Ken Hodge .38 .75
29 Dave Forbes .18 .35
30 Wayne Cashman .38 .75
31 Johnny Bucyk .75 1.50
32 Ross Brooks .25 .50
33 Dallas Smith .18 .35
34 Darryl Edestrand .18 .35
35 Gregg Sheppard .18 .35
36 Andre Savard .25 .50
37 Jim Schoenfeld .38 .75
38 Brian Spencer .38 .75
39 Rick Dudley .25 .50
40 Craig Ramsay .18 .35
41 Gary Bromley .38 .75
42 Lee Fogolin .18 .35
43 Jerry Korab .18 .35
44 Larry Mickey .18 .35
45 Roger Crozier .50 1.00
46 Larry Carriere .18 .35
47 Norm Gratton .18 .35
48 Jim Lorentz .18 .35
49 Rene Robert .38 .75
50 Gilbert Perreault 2.00 4.00
(74/75 season on back)
51 Mike Robitaille .18 .35
52 Don Luce .18 .35
53 Richard Martin .38 .75
54 Gerry Meehan .25 .50
55 Bruce Affleck .18 .35
56 Wayne King .18 .35
57 Joseph Johnston .18 .35
58 Ron Huston .18 .35
59 Dave Hrechkosy .18 .35
60 Stan Gilbertson .18 .35
61 Mike Christie .18 .35
62 Larry Wright .18 .35
63 Stan Weir .18 .35
64 Larry Patey .18 .35
65 Al MacAdam .25 .50
66 Ted McAneeley .18 .35
67 Jim Neilson .18 .35
68 Rick Hampton .18 .35
69 Len Frig .18 .35
70 Gilles Meloche .38 .75
71 Robert Stewart .18 .35
72 Craig Patrick .38 .75
73 Dennis Hull .38 .75
74 Dale Tallon .25 .50
75 Bill White .25 .50
76 Jim Pappin .18 .35
77 Cliff Koroll .18 .35
78 Tony Esposito 2.50 5.00
79 Doug Jarrett .18 .35
80 John Marks .18 .35
81 Stan Mikita 2.00 4.00
82 Darcy Rota .18 .35
83 J.P. Bordeleau .18 .35
84 Ivan Boldirev .18 .35
85 Germaine Gagnon UER .18 .35
86 Dick Redmond .18 .35
87 Pit Martin .18 .35
88 Keith Magnuson .25 .50
89 Phil Russell .18 .35
90 Chico Maki .25 .50
91 Jean Hamel .18 .35
92 Nick Libett .25 .50
93 Hank Nowak .18 .35
94 Guy Charron .25 .50
95 Bryan Watson .18 .35
96 Nelson Pyatt .18 .35
97 Billy Lochead .18 .35
98 Danny Grant .25 .50
99 Bill Hogaboam .18 .35
100 Jim Rutherford .50 1.00
101 Doug Grant .18 .35
102 Pierre Jarry .18 .35
103 Doug Roberts .18 .35
104 Red Berenson .38 .75
105 Marcel Dionne 1.75 3.50
106 Mickey Redmond .75 1.50
107 Jack Lynch .18 .35
108 Thommie Bergman .18 .35
109 Mike Corrigan .18 .35
110 Frank St.Marseille .18 .35
111 Gene Carr .18 .35
112 Neil Komadoski .18 .35
113 Gary Edwards .38 .75
114 Sheldon Kannegiesser .18 .35
115 Bob Murdoch .18 .35
116 Rogatien Vachon 1.25 3.00
117 Dave Hutchinson .18 .35
118 Tom Williams .18 .35
119 Butch Goring .38 .75
120 Bob Berry .25 .50
121 Dan Maloney .25 .50
122 Mike Murphy .18 .35
123 Juha Widing .25 .50
124 Don Kozak .18 .35
125 Bob Nevin .18 .35
126 Terry Harper .25 .50
127 Bill Goldsworthy .38 .75
128 Dennis O'Brien .18 .35
129 Dennis Hextall .25 .50
130 Murray Oliver .18 .35
131 Lou Nanne .25 .50
132 Fred Stanfield .18 .35
133 Jean-Paul Parise .25 .50
134 Tom Reid .18 .35
135 Fred Barrett .18 .35
136 Gary Bergman .18 .35
137 Barry Gibbs .18 .35
138 Cesare Maniago .50 1.00
139 Jude Drouin .18 .35
140 Blake Dunlop .18 .35
141 Henry Boucha .25 .50
142 Fern Rivard .18 .35
143 Chris Ahrens .18 .35
144 Don Martineau .18 .35
145 Jacques Lemaire .75 1.50
146 Peter Mahovlich .38 .75
147 Yvon Lambert .18 .35
148 Yvan Cournoyer 1.25 2.50
149 Michel Larocque .38 .75
150 Guy Lapointe .50 1.00
151 Steve Shutt 1.50 3.00
152 Guy Lafleur 3.50 7.00
153 Larry Robinson 1.00 2.00
154 Jacques Laperriere .38 .75
155 Chuck Lefley .18 .35
156 Henri Richard 1.25 2.50
157 Claude Larose .18 .35
158 Ken Dryden 6.00 12.00
159 Pierre Bouchard .18 .35
160 Murray Wilson .18 .35
161 Jim Roberts .25 .50
162 Serge Savard .50 1.00
163 Clark Gillies 1.25 2.50
164 Garry Howatt .18 .35
165 Ernie Hicke .18 .35
166 Craig Cameron .18 .35
167 Ralph Stewart .18 .35
168 Lorne Henning .18 .35
169 Glenn Resch .50 1.00
170 Bill MacMillan .18 .35
171 Doug Rombough .18 .35
172 Jean Potvin .18 .35
173 Gerry Hart .18 .35
174 Bert Marshall .18 .35
175 Billy Harris .18 .35
176 Bob Nystrom .38 .75
177 Dave Lewis .18 .35
178 Billy Smith 1.00 2.00
179 Denis Potvin 4.00 8.00
180 Ed Westfall .25 .50
181 Jerry Butler .18 .35
182 Bobby Rousseau .25 .50
183 Ron Harris .18 .35
184 Bill Fairbairn .18 .35
185 Derek Sanderson 1.50 3.00
186 Jean Ratelle 1.00 2.00
187 Greg Polis .18 .35
188 Rod Gilbert 1.00 2.00
189 Ed Giacomin 1.00 2.00
190 Rod Seiling .18 .35
191 Dale Rolfe .18 .35
192 Walt Tkaczuk .25 .50
193 Pete Stemkowski .25 .50
194 Gilles Villemure .38 .75
195 Ted Irvine .18 .35
196 Brad Park 1.00 2.00
197 Gilles Marotte .25 .50
198 Steve Vickers .25 .50
199 Ross Lonsberry .18 .35
200 Bob Kelly .25 .50
201 Reggie Leach .38 .75
202 Bernie Parent 1.75 3.50
203 Terry Crisp .38 .75
204 Bill Clement .50 1.00
205 Bill Barber .50 1.00
206 Dave Schultz .50 1.00
207 Ed Van Impe .18 .35
208 Jimmy Watson .25 .50
209 Tom Bladon .18 .35
210 Rick MacLeish .38 .75
211 Andre Dupont .25 .50
212 Orest Kindrachuk .25 .50
213 Gary Dornhoefer .38 .75
214 Joe Watson .25 .50
215 Don Saleski .18 .35
216 Bobby Clarke 3.00 6.00
217 Jean Pronovost .38 .75
218 Ab DeMarco .18 .35
219 Wayne Bianchin .18 .35
220 Dave Burrows .18 .35
221 Ron Lalonde .18 .35
222 Syl Apps .38 .75
223 Bob Kelly .18 .35
224 Chuck Arnason .18 .35
225 Steve Durbano .18 .35
226 Ron Schock .18 .35
227 Bob Paradise .18 .35
228 Ron Stackhouse .18 .35
229 Lowell MacDonald .25 .50
230 Bob Johnson .18 .35
231 Rick Kehoe .38 .75
232 Nelson Debenedet .18 .35
233 Vic Hadfield .25 .50
234 Denis Herron .50 1.00
235 Phil Roberto .18 .35
236 Floyd Thomson .18 .35
237 Don Awrey .18 .35
238 Rick Wilson .18 .35
239 John Davidson 1.50 3.00
240 Pierre Plante .18 .35
241 Barclay Plager .38 .75
242 Larry Giroux .18 .35
243 Bob Gassoff .38 .75
244 Dave Gardner .18 .35
245 Brian Ogilvie .18 .35
246 Ed Johnston .50 1.00
247 Bob Plager .25 .50
248 Wayne Merrick .18 .35
249 Larry Sacharuk .18 .35
250 Bill Collins .18 .35
251 Garnet Bailey .18 .35
252 Garry Unger .38 .75
253 Gary Sabourin .18 .35
254 Willie Brossart .18 .35
255 Tim Ecclestone .18 .35
256 Dave Keon .75 1.50
257 Darryl Sittler 1.50 3.00
258 Inge Hammarstrom .18 .35
259 Ian Turnbull .25 .50
260 Jim McKenny .18 .35
261 Norm Ullman .75 1.50
262 Doug Favell .50 1.00
263 Bob Neely .18 .35
264 Lanny McDonald 1.50 3.00
265 Dunc Wilson .38 .75
266 Errol Thompson .18 .35
267 Brian Glennie .18 .35
268 Bill Flett .18 .35
269 Borje Salming .75 1.50
270 Ron Ellis .25 .50
271 Dave Dunn .18 .35
272 Chris Oddleifson .18 .35
273 Barry Wilkins .18 .35
274 Gary Smith .38 .75
275 Dennis Ververgaert .18 .35
276 Jocelyn Guevremont .18 .35
277 Andre Boudrias .25 .50
278 John Gould .18 .35
279 Jim Wiley .18 .35
280 Bob Dailey .18 .35
281 Tracy Pratt .18 .35
282 Ken Lockett .18 .35
283 Paulin Bordeleau .18 .35
284 Gerry O'Flaherty .18 .35
285 Bryan McSheffrey .18 .35
286 Gregg Boddy .18 .35
287 Don Lever .25 .50
288 Dennis Kearns .18 .35
289 Robin Burns .18 .35
290 Gary Coalter .18 .35
291 John Wright .18 .35
292 Peter McDuffe .38 .75
293 Simon Nolet .18 .35
294 Ted Snell .18 .35
295 Gary Croteau .18 .35
296 Lynn Powis .18 .35
297 Dave Hudson .18 .35
298 Richard Lemieux .18 .35
299 Bryan Lefley .18 .35
300 Doug Horbul .18 .35
301 Brent Hughes .18 .35
302 Ed Gilbert .18 .35
303 Michel Plasse .38 .75
304 Dennis Patterson .18 .35
305 Randy Rota .18 .35
306 Chris Evans .18 .35
307 Bill Mikkelson .18 .35
308 Ron Low .50 1.00
309 Doug Mohns .25 .50
310 Joe Lundrigan .18 .35
311 Steve Atkinson .18 .35
312 Ron Anderson .18 .35
313 Mike Marson .38 .75
314 Lew Morrison .18 .35
315 Jack Egers .18 .35
316 Gordy Brooks .18 .35
317 Pete Laframboise .18 .35
318 Mike Bloom .18 .35
319 Bob Collyard .18 .35
320 Dave Kryskow .18 .35
321 Greg Joly .18 .35
322 Jim Hrycuik .18 .35
323 Bob Gryp .18 .35
324 Larry Fullan .18 .35
NNO Album 10.00 20.00

1974-75 NHL Action Stamps Update

A group of 43 previously uncatalogued NHL Action (Loblaw's) stamps had been reported. Thirty-six of these stamps are recropped or airbrushed versions of original stamps listing the player's new team. The remaining seven were completely new stamps to replace nine originals dropped from the set. The discrepancy between the seven added and the nine dropped stamps had led some to speculate that there were at least two other stamps in the set, all the more so since two teams (Islanders and Vancouver) have one less player than all the other teams. These stamps were grouped alphabetically within teams and checklisted below alphabetically according to teams as follows: Atlanta Flames (1), Boston Bruins (2), Buffalo Sabres (3-5), California Golden Seals (6-8), Detroit Red Wings (9-13), Kansas City Scouts (14-16), Minnesota North Stars (17-21), Montreal Canadiens (22-23), New York Islanders (24-25), New York Rangers (26), Pittsburgh Penguins (27-29), St. Louis Blues (30-34), Toronto Maple Leafs (35-37), Vancouver Canucks (38-40), and Washington Capitals (41-43).

COMPLETE SET (43) 25.00 50.00
1 Barry Gibbs .50 1.00
2 Henry Nowak .50 1.00
3 Jocelyn Guevremont .50 1.00
4 Bryan McSheffrey .50 1.00
5 Fred Stanfield .50 1.00
6 Dave Gardner .50 1.00
7 Morris Mott NEW .50 1.00
8 Gary Simmons NEW 2.00 4.00
9 Gary Bergman .75 1.50
10 Dave Kryskow .50 1.00
11 Walt McKechnie .50 1.00
12 Phil Roberto .50 1.00
13 Ted Snell .50 1.00
14 Guy Charron .75 1.50
15 Jean-Guy Lagace NEW .50 1.00
16 Denis Herron 2.00 4.00
17 Craig Cameron .50 1.00
18 John Flesch NEW .50 1.00
19 Norm Gratton .50 1.00
20 Ernie Hicke .50 1.00
21 Doug Rombough .50 1.00
22 Don Awrey .50 1.00
23 Wayne Thomas NEW 2.00 4.00
24 Jude Drouin .50 1.00
25 Jean Paul Parise .50 1.00
26 Rick Middleton NEW 2.50 5.00
27 Lew Morrison .50 1.00
28 Michel Plasse 2.00 4.00
29 Barry Wilkins .50 1.00
30 Red Berenson .75 1.50
31 Chris Evans .50 1.00
32 Claude Larose .50 1.00
33 Chuck Lefley .50 1.00
34 Craig Patrick .75 1.50
35 Dave Dunn .50 1.00
36 George Ferguson NEW .50 1.00
37 Rod Seiling .50 1.00
38 Ab Demarco .50 1.00
39 Gerry Meehan .50 1.00
40 Mike Robitaille .50 1.00
41 Willie Brossart .50 1.00
42 Ron Lalonde .50 1.00
43 Jack Lynch .50 1.00

1972-73 Nordiques Postcards

This standard size postcard featured color photos surrounded by a white border. Card fronts featured a facsimile autograph and were issued by Pro Star Promotions. Backs were blank. The postcards were unnumbered and checklisted below in alphabetical order.

COMPLETE SET (22) 20.00 40.00
1 Michel Archambeault 1.00 2.00
2 Serge Aubry 1.00 2.00
3 Yves Bergeron 1.00 2.00
4 Jacques Blain 1.00 2.00
5 Alain Caron 1.00 2.00
6 Ken Desjardine 1.00 2.00
7 Maurice Filion 1.00 2.00
8 Andre Gaudette 1.00 2.00
9 Jean-Guy Gendron 1.00 2.00
10 Rejean Giroux 1.00 2.00
11 Frank Golembrosky 1.00 2.00
12 Robert Guindon 1.00 2.00
13 Pierre Guite 1.00 2.00
14 Francois Lacombe 1.00 2.00
15 Paul Larose 1.00 2.00
16 Jacques Lemelin 1.00 2.00
17 Michel Parizeau 1.00 2.00
18 Jean Payette 1.00 2.00
19 Michel Rouleau 1.00 2.00
20 Pierre Roy 1.00 2.00
21 J.C. Tremblay 1.50 3.00
NNO Header Card .50 1.00

1973-74 Nordiques Team Issue

This 21-card team issue set featured the 1973-74 Quebec Nordiques of the World Hockey Association. The oversized cards measured approximately 3 1/2" by 5 1/2". The fronts featured glossy color posed photos with white borders. The team and WHA logos were superimposed in the upper corners of the picture. A facsimile autograph was inscribed across the bottom of the picture. The backs were blank. The cards were unnumbered and checklisted below in alphabetical order.

COMPLETE SET (21) 25.00 50.00
1 Mike Archambault 1.25 2.50
2 Serge Aubry 1.25 2.50
3 Yves Bergeron 1.25 2.50
4 Jacques Blain 1.25 2.50
5 Richard Brodeur 4.00 8.00
6 Alain Caron 1.25 2.50
7 Ken Desjardine 1.25 2.50
8 Maurice Filion 1.25 2.50
9 Andre Gaudette 1.25 2.50
10 Jean-Guy Gendron 1.50 3.00
11 Rejean Giroux 1.25 2.50
12 Frank Golembrosky 1.25 2.50
13 Bob Guindon 1.25 2.50
14 Pierre Guite 1.25 2.50
15 Frank Lacombe 1.25 2.50
16 Paul Larose 1.25 2.50
17 Michel Parizeau 1.25 2.50
18 Jean Payette 1.25 2.50
19 Michel Rouleau 1.25 2.50
20 Pierre Roy 1.25 2.50
21 J.C. Tremblay 2.50 5.00

1976 Nordiques Marie Antoinette

This 14-card set measured approximately 8" by 10 1/2" and featured on the fronts color player portraits of the Quebec Nordiques by the artist Claude Laroche. The player's name was printed in black in the lower right with the card logo on the left. The backs were blank. The cards were unnumbered and checklisted below in alphabetical order.

COMPLETE SET (14) 30.00 60.00

1 Paul Baxter	2.00	4.00
2 Serge Bernier	2.00	4.00
3 Paulin Bordeleau	2.00	4.00
4 Andre Boudrias	2.50	5.00
5 Curt Brackenbury	2.00	4.00
6 Richard Brodeur	4.00	8.00
7 Real Cloutier	3.00	6.00
8 Charles Constantin	2.00	4.00
9 Bob Fitchner	2.00	4.00
10 Richard Grenier	2.00	4.00
11 Marc Tardif	3.00	6.00
12 Jean-Claude Tremblay	3.00	6.00
13 Steve Sutherland	2.00	4.00
14 Wally Weir	2.00	4.00

1976-77 Nordiques Postcards

These 20 postcards measured approximately 3 1/2" by 5 1/2" and featured posed-on-ice color player photos on their borderless fronts. A facsimile player autograph rested near the bottom. The backs carried the player's name, uniform number, brief biography, and Nordiques team logo at the upper left. Places for stamp and address appeared on the right. All text is in French. The postcards are unnumbered and checklisted below in alphabetical order.

COMPLETE SET (20)	15.00	30.00
1 Serge Aubry	.75	1.50
2 Paul Baxter	1.00	2.00
3 Jean Bernier	.75	1.50
4 Serge Bernier	1.50	3.00
5 Christian Bordeleau	.75	1.50
6 Paulin Bordeleau	1.00	2.00
7 Andre Boudrias	1.00	2.00
8 Curt Brackenbury	.75	1.50
9 Richard Brodeur	2.00	4.00
10 Real Cloutier	1.50	3.00
11 Charles Constantin	.75	1.50
12 Jim Dorey	1.00	2.00
13 Robert Fitchner	.75	1.50
14 Richard Grenier	.75	1.50
15 Francois Lacombe	.75	1.50
16 Pierre Roy	.75	1.50
17 Steve Sutherland	.75	1.50
18 Marc Tardif	1.50	3.00
19 J.C. Tremblay	1.50	3.00
20 Wally Weir	.75	1.50

1980-81 Nordiques Postcards

Printed in Canada, this 24-card set measured approximately 3" by 5 1/2" and featured members of the 1980-81 Quebec Nordiques. The fronts had borderless, posed color player photos. The backs were in postcard format with a short player biography both in French and in English. The text on some cards was printed in royal blue and on other cards in turquoise. The cards were unnumbered and checklisted below in alphabetical order.

COMPLETE SET (29)	20.00	40.00
1 Michel Bergeron	.40	1.00
2 Serge Bernier	.75	2.00
3 Daniel Bouchard	.40	1.00
4 Ron Chipperfield	.40	1.00
5 Kim Clackson	.60	1.50
6 Real Cloutier	.75	2.00
7 Alain Cote	.60	1.50
8 Michel Dion	.60	1.50
9 Andre Dupont	.60	1.50
10 Robbie Ftorek	.75	2.00
11 Michel Goulet	2.50	5.00
12 Ron Grahame	.40	1.00
13 Jamie Hislop	.40	1.00
14 Dale Hoganson	.40	1.00
15 Dale Hunter	2.50	5.00
16 Pierre Lacroix	.40	1.00
17 Garry Lariviere	.40	1.00
18 Richard Leduc	.40	1.00
19 Lee Norwood	.60	1.50
20 John Paddock	.60	1.50
21 Dave Pichette	.40	1.00
22 Michel Plasse	.75	2.00
23 Jacques Richard	.60	1.50
24 Normand Rochefort	.40	1.00
25 Anton Stastny	.75	2.00
26 Peter Stastny	4.00	8.00
27 Marc Tardif	.75	2.00
28 Wally Weir	.40	1.00
29 John Wensink	.60	1.50

1970-71 North Stars Postcards

This 10-card set measured 3 1/2" by 5 1/2" and was stapled together in a booklet with the team name and logo above two hockey sticks on a pale green background. The fronts featured posed, color player photos. The backs carried the player's name, biographical information and career highlights printed in blue on a white background. The cards were unnumbered and checklisted below in alphabetical order.

COMPLETE SET (10)	17.50	35.00
1 Barry Gibbs	1.00	2.00
2 Bill Goldsworthy	2.50	5.00
3 Danny Grant	2.00	4.00
4 Ted Harris	1.00	2.00
5 Cesare Maniago	3.00	6.00
6 Jean Paul Parise	1.50	3.00
7 Tom Reid	1.00	2.00
8 Bobby Rousseau	1.00	2.00
9 Tom Williams	1.00	2.00
10 Lorne Worsley	5.00	10.00

1972-73 North Stars Glossy Photos

These 20 blank-backed approximately 8" by 10" glossy white-bordered black-and-white photo sheets featured a suited-up posed player photo on the right and, on the left, a posed player head shot. Below the head shot appeared the player's name and the Minnesota North Stars name and logo. The photos were unnumbered and checklisted below in alphabetical order.

COMPLETE SET (20)	10.00	20.00
1 Fred Barrett	.50	1.00
2 Charlie Burns	.50	1.00
3 Jude Drouin	.50	1.00
4 Barry Gibbs	.50	1.00
5 Bill Goldsworthy	1.25	2.50
6 Danny Grant	.75	1.50
7 Ted Harris	.50	1.00
8 Fred(Buster) Harvey	.50	1.00
9 Dennis Hextall	.75	1.50
10 Cesare Maniago	1.00	2.00
11 Doug Mohns	.75	1.50
12 Lou Nanne	.75	1.50
13 Bob Nevin	.50	1.00
14 Dennis O'Brien	.50	1.00
15 Murray Oliver	.50	1.00
16 J.P. Parise	.50	1.00
17 Dean Prentice	.75	1.50
18 Tom Reid	.50	1.00
19 Gump Worsley	2.50	5.00
20 W.Blair/J.Gordon	.50	1.00

1973-74 North Stars Action Posters

These 14 x 20 color action posters were distributed by Mr. Steak restaurants in the Minneapolis area. They were distributed one every two weeks for twenty weeks.

COMPLETE SET (10)	10.00	20.00
1 Henry Boucha	1.00	2.00
2 Jude Drouin	1.00	2.00
3 Barry Gibbs	1.00	2.00
4 Bill Goldsworthy	1.50	3.00
5 Dennis Hextall	1.00	2.00
6 Cesare Maniago	1.50	3.00
7 Lou Nanne	1.50	3.00
8 Dennis O'Brien	1.00	2.00
9 J.P. Parise	1.50	3.00
10 Tom Reid	1.00	2.00

1973-74 North Stars Postcards

These postcard sized cards featured black and white posed photos on the front, and were blank backed. Cards were unnumbered and checklisted below alphabetically.

COMPLETE SET (20)	10.00	20.00
1 Fred Barrett	.38	.75
2 Gary Bergman	.38	.75
3 Jude Drouin	.38	.75
4 Tony Featherstone	.38	.75
5 Barry Gibbs	.38	.75
6 Bill Goldsworthy	.63	1.25
7 Danny Grant	.38	.75
8 Buster Harvey	.38	.75
9 Dennis Hextall	.50	1.00
10 Parker MacDonald	.38	.75
11 Cesare Maniago	.50	1.00
12 Lou Nanne	.50	1.00
13 Rod Norrish	.38	.75
14 Dennis O'Brien	.38	.75
15 Murray Oliver	.38	.75
16 Jean-Paul Parise	.38	.75
17 Dean Prentice	.50	1.00
18 Tom Reid	.38	.75
19 Fred Stanfield	.63	1.25
20 Lorne Worsley	1.50	3.00

1978-79 North Stars Cloverleaf Dairy

This ten-panel set of Minnesota North Stars was issued on the side of half gallon milk cartons as part of a sweepstakes. The picture and text were printed in either red or purple. The panels measured approximately 3 3/4" by 7 5/8", with two players per panel. The North Stars' logo, the team name, year, and panel number appeared at the top of each panel. Each panel featured a "mug shot" and brief biographical information on two players. A North Stars question was included at the bottom of each panel. There were ten questions in all: one per panel, and a tenth question on the final entry panel, which also included a list of all ten questions and gave complete entry information. The unnumbered panel described the sweepstakes promotion and lists the prizes.

COMPLETE SET (11)	60.00	120.00
1 Gilles Meloche Gary Sargent	7.50	15.00
2 Fred Barrett and Per-Olov Brasar	6.00	12.00
3 Jean-Paul Parise and Greg Smith	6.00	12.00
4 Al MacAdam and Kent-Erik Andersson	6.00	12.00
5 Gary Edwards and Bobby Smith	12.50	25.00
6 Mike Polich and Brad Maxwell	6.00	12.00
7 Steve Payne and Glen Sharpley	6.00	12.00
8 Tim Young and Kris Manery	6.00	12.00
9 Ron Zanussi and Tom Younghans	6.00	12.00
10 Final Entry Panel	6.00	12.00
NNO Sweepstakes Promotion	2.50	5.00

1979-80 North Stars Postcards

This 21-card set measured approximately 3 1/2" by 5 1/2" and featured the 1979-80 Minnesota North Stars. The fronts had borderless black-and-white player action photos. The backs had a postcard format and carry the player's name, position, short biography, and the team logo. The cards were unnumbered and checklisted below in alphabetical order.

COMPLETE SET (21)	10.00	20.00
1 Kent-Erik Andersson	.38	.75
2 Fred Barrett	.38	.75
3 Gary Edwards	.75	1.50
4 Mike Fidler	.38	.75
5 Craig Hartsburg	1.00	2.00
6 Al MacAdam	.50	1.00
7 Kris Manery	.38	.75
8 Brad Maxwell	.38	.75
9 Tom McCarthy	.50	1.00
10 Gilles Meloche	1.00	2.00
11 Steve Payne	.50	1.00
12 Mike Polich	.38	.75
13 Gary Sargent	.50	1.00
14 Glen Sharpley	.38	.75
15 Paul Shmyr	.38	.75
16 Bobby Smith	1.50	3.00
17 Greg Smith	.38	.75
18 Glen Sonmor CO	.38	.75
19 Tim Young	.50	1.00
20 Tom Younghans	.38	.75
21 Ron Zanussi	.38	.75

1980-81 North Stars Postcards

This 24-card set measured approximately 3 1/2" by 5 1/2" and featured the 1980-81 Minnesota North Stars. The fronts had borderless color posed player photos with facsimile autographs across the bottom. The backs had a postcard format and carry a short player biography and the team logo in green print. The cards were unnumbered and checklisted below in alphabetical order.

COMPLETE SET (24)	8.00	20.00
1 Kent-Erik Andersson	.30	.75
2 Fred Barrett	.30	.75
3 Don Beaupre	1.00	2.50
4 Jack Carlson	1.00	2.50
5 Steve Christoff	.40	1.00
6 Mike Eaves	.30	.75
7 Gary Edwards	.60	1.50
8 Curt Giles	.40	1.00
9 Craig Hartsburg	.75	2.00
10 Al MacAdam	.40	1.00
11 Brad Maxwell	.30	.75
12 Tom McCarthy	.30	.75
13 Gilles Meloche	.60	1.50
14 Murray Oliver ACO	.30	.75
J.P. Parise ACO Glen Sonmor CO		
15 Steve Payne	.30	.75
16 Mike Polich	.30	.75
17 Gary Sargent	.40	1.00
18 Glen Sharpley	.30	.75
19 Paul Shmyr	.30	.75
20 Bobby Smith	1.00	2.50
21 Greg Smith	.30	.75
22 Tim Young	.30	.75
23 Tom Younghans	.30	.75
24 Ron Zanussi	.30	.75

1979-80 Oilers Postcards

Measuring approximately 3 1/2" by 5 1/4", this 24-card set featured borderless posed-on-ice photos of the Edmonton Oilers on the fronts. The postcard format had each of the horizontal backs bisected by a vertical line, with the player's name, position, and biography on the left side, and the team logo on the right. The cards were unnumbered and checklisted below in alphabetical order. Early cards of Wayne Gretzky, Kevin Lowe, and Mark Messier were featured in this set. The complete set price includes both Mio variations.

COMPLETE SET (24)	50.00	100.00
1 Brett Callighen	.50	1.00
2 Colin Campbell	1.00	2.00
3 Ron Chipperfield	.50	1.00
4 Cam Connor	.50	1.00
5 Peter Driscoll	.50	1.00
6 Dave Dryden	1.00	2.00
7 Bill Flett	.50	1.00
8 Lee Fogolin	.50	1.00
9 Wayne Gretzky	30.00	60.00
10 Al Hamilton	.50	1.00
11 Doug Hicks	.50	1.00
12 Dave Hunter	.50	1.00
13 Kevin Lowe	2.00	4.00
14 Dave Lumley	.50	1.00
15 Blair MacDonald	.50	1.00
16 Kari Makkonen	.50	1.00
17 Mark Messier	12.50	25.00
18A Ed Mio ERR	1.00	2.00
18B Ed Mio COR	1.00	2.00
19 Pat Price	.50	1.00
20 Dave Semenko	1.00	2.00
21 Bobby Schmautz	.50	1.00
22 Risto Siltanen	.75	1.50
23 Stan Weir	.50	1.00

1980-81 Oilers Zellers

1 Wayne Gretzky	500.00	1,000.00
2 Dave Lumley	5.00	10.00
3 Blair MacDonald	5.00	10.00

1932-33 O'Keefe Maple Leafs

This 20-card set was issued by O'Keefe's Beverages and featured the Toronto Maple Leafs, 1931-32 Stanley Cup Champions. Each was designed for use as a coaster. The shape of each card is an eight-pointed star, which measures approximately 5" from one point across to its opposite. Inside a blue border, the front had a black and blue ink portrait or drawing of the player, which was surrounded by cartoons and captions presenting player information. The backs read "O'Keefe's Big 4" and "Each a Leader in its Class." The coasters were numbered on the front near the top and are checklisted below accordingly. Card numbers 13 and 15 are unknown, although many collectors believe it likely that the NNO Doraty and Thoms cards were slated to fill those slots.

COMPLETE SET (20)	6,000.00	12,000.00
1 Lorne Chabot	250.00	600.00
2 Red Horner	250.00	600.00
3 Alex Levinsky	200.00	500.00
4 Hap Day	200.00	500.00
5 Andy Blair	200.00	500.00
6 Ace Bailey	500.00	1,200.00
7 King Clancy	500.00	1,200.00
8 Harold Cotton	250.00	600.00
9 Charlie Conacher	400.00	1,000.00
10 Joe Primeau	400.00	1,000.00
11 Harvey Jackson	400.00	1,000.00
12 Frank Finnigan	200.00	500.00
14 Bob Gracie	200.00	500.00
16 Harold Darragh	200.00	500.00
17 Benny Grant	200.00	500.00
18 Fred Robertson	200.00	500.00
19 Conn Smythe	400.00	1,000.00
20 Dick Irvin	300.00	800.00
NNO Ken Doraty	250.00	600.00
NNO Bill Thoms	250.00	600.00

1933-34 O-Pee-Chee V304A

This first of five O-Pee-Chee 1930's hockey card issues featured a black and white photo of the player portrayed on a colored field of stars. The cards in the set were approximately 2 5/16" by 3 9/16". The player's name appeared in a rectangle at the bottom of the front of the card. Four possible color background fields existed, red, blue, orange and green. The cards were numbered on the back, and a short biography in both English and French is also contained on the back. The catalog designation for this set is V304A. The existence of an album designed to store the cards has been confirmed. It is valued at approximately $250.

COMPLETE SET (48)	9,000.00	15,000.00
WRAPPER (1-CENT)	175.00	350.00
1 Danny Cox RC	150.00	250.00
2 Joe Lamb RC	60.00	100.00
3 Eddie Shore RC	900.00	1,500.00
4 Ken Doraty RC	60.00	100.00
5 Fred Hitchman	60.00	100.00
6 Nels Stewart RC	500.00	800.00
7 Walter Galbraith RC	60.00	100.00
8 Dit Clapper RC	400.00	600.00
9 Harry Oliver RC	200.00	400.00
10 Red Horner RC	175.00	300.00
11 Alex Levinsky RC	90.00	150.00
12 Joe Primeau RC	400.00	600.00
13 Ace Bailey RC	300.00	500.00
14 George Patterson RC	60.00	100.00
15 George Hainsworth RC	250.00	400.00
16 Ott Heller RC	60.00	100.00
17 Art Somers RC	60.00	100.00
18 Lorne Chabot RC	250.00	400.00
19 Johnny Gagnon RC	90.00	150.00
20 Pit Lepine RC	60.00	100.00
21 Wildor Larochelle RC	90.00	150.00
22 Georges Mantha RC	90.00	150.00
23 Howie Morenz	1,200.00	2,500.00
24 Syd Howe RC	200.00	350.00
25 Frank Finnigan	90.00	150.00
26 Bill Touhey RC	90.00	150.00
27 Cooney Weiland RC	200.00	400.00
28 Leo Bourgeault RC	60.00	100.00
29 Normie Himes RC	90.00	150.00
30 Johnny Sheppard RC	60.00	100.00
31 King Clancy	600.00	1,000.00
32 Hap Day	150.00	250.00
33 Harvey Jackson RC	300.00	500.00
34 Charlie Conacher RC	600.00	1,000.00
35 Harold Cotton RC	125.00	200.00
36 Butch Keeling RC	60.00	100.00
37 Murray Murdoch RC	60.00	100.00
38 Bill Cook UER RC	150.00	250.00
39 Ivan Johnson RC	300.00	600.00
40 Happy Emms RC	90.00	150.00
41 Bert McInenly RC	60.00	100.00
42 John Sorrell RC	90.00	150.00
43 Bill Phillips RC	60.00	100.00
44 Charley McVeigh RC	60.00	100.00
45 Roy Worters RC	250.00	400.00
46 Albert Leduc RC	100.00	200.00
47 Nick Wasnie RC	60.00	100.00
48 Armand Mondou RC	125.00	200.00

1933-34 O-Pee-Chee V304B

The second O-Pee-Chee hockey series of the 1930's contained 24 cards and continues the numbering sequence of the Series A cards. The format was exactly the same as the cards of Series A. The cards in the set measureed approximately 2 5/16" by 3 9/16". The catalog designation for this set is V304B.

COMPLETE SET (24)	3,000.00	5,000.00
WRAPPER (1-CENT)	175.00	350.00

49 Babe Siebert RC	250.00	400.00
50 Aurel Joliat	500.00	800.00
51 Larry Aurie RC	175.00	300.00
52 Ebbie Goodfellow RC	150.00	300.00
53 John Roach	125.00	200.00
54 Bill Beveridge RC	125.00	200.00
55 Earl Robinson RC	90.00	150.00
56 Jimmy Ward RC	90.00	150.00
57 Archie Wilcox RC	90.00	150.00
58 Lorne Duguid RC	90.00	150.00
59 Dave Kerr RC	125.00	200.00
60 Baldy Northcott RC	100.00	200.00
61 Marvin Wentworth RC	125.00	200.00
62 Dave Trottier RC	100.00	200.00
63 Wally Kilrea RC	90.00	150.00
64 Glen Brydson RC	125.00	200.00
65 Vernon Ayres RC	90.00	150.00
66 Bob Gracie RC	90.00	150.00
67 Vic Ripley RC	90.00	150.00
68 Tiny Thompson RC	300.00	500.00
69 Alex Smith RC	90.00	150.00
70 Andy Blair RC	90.00	150.00
71 Cecil Dillon RC	90.00	150.00
72 Bun Cook RC	250.00	400.00

1935-36 O-Pee-Chee V304C

While Series C in the O-Pee-Chee 1930's hockey card set continued the numbering sequence of the previous two years, this 24-card set differed significantly in both format and size. The cards in this set measured approximately 2 3/8" by 2 7/8". Each black and white photo portraying the player on the front could be found on four possible color fields, green, orange, maroon, or yellow. The field consisted of a star in the center and cartooned hockey players flanking the center of the card. The backs contained the player's name, the card number, and biographical data in both English and French. The catalog designation for this set is V304C.

COMPLETE SET (24)	2,500.00	4,000.00
WRAPPER (1-CENT)	175.00	350.00
73 Wilfred Cude RC	175.00	300.00
74 Jack McGill RC	75.00	125.00
75 Russ Blinco RC	75.00	125.00
76 Hooley Smith	150.00	250.00
77 Herb Cain RC	90.00	150.00
78 Gus Marker RC	75.00	125.00
79 Lynn Patrick RC	175.00	300.00
80 Johnny Gottselig	75.00	125.00
81 Marty Barry	125.00	200.00
82 Sylvio Mantha	150.00	250.00
83 Flash Hollett RC	90.00	150.00
84 Nick Metz RC	75.00	125.00
85 Bill Thoms	75.00	125.00
86 Hec Kilrea	75.00	125.00
87 Pep Kelly RC	75.00	125.00
88 Art Jackson RC	75.00	125.00
89 Allan Shields RC	75.00	125.00
90 Buzz Boll	75.00	125.00
91 Jean Pusie RC	75.00	125.00
92 Roger Jenkins RC	75.00	125.00
93 Arthur Coulter RC	90.00	150.00
94 Art Chapman	75.00	125.00
95 Paul Haynes	75.00	125.00
96 Leroy Goldsworthy RC	150.00	250.00

1936-37 O-Pee-Chee V304D

The most significant difference between Series D cards and cards from the previous three O-Pee-Chee sets was the fact that these cards are die-cut and could be folded to give a stand-up figure, like the 1934-36 Batter-Up baseball cards. The cards were in black and white with no colored background field. The cards in the set measured approximately 2 3/8" by 2 15/16". As these cards are difficult to find without the backs missing, this set was the most valuable of the 1930's O-Pee-Chee sets. The backs contained the card number and biographical data in English and French. The player's name was given on the front of the card only. The catalog designation for this set is V304D.

COMPLETE SET (36)	9,000.00	15,000.00
WRAPPER (1-CENT)	175.00	350.00
97 Turk Broda RC	700.00	1,200.00
98 Sweeney Schriner RC	250.00	400.00
99 Jack Shill RC	100.00	150.00
100 Bob Davidson RC	125.00	200.00
101 Syl Apps RC	500.00	800.00
102 Lionel Conacher	400.00	600.00
103 Jimmy Fowler RC	125.00	200.00
104 Al Murray RC	100.00	150.00
105 Neil Colville RC	175.00	300.00
106 Paul Runge RC	100.00	150.00
107 Mike Karakas RC	125.00	200.00
108 John Gallagher RC	100.00	150.00
109 Alex Shibicky RC	150.00	250.00
110 Herb Cain	150.00	250.00
111 Bill McKenzie	100.00	150.00
112 Harold Jackson	100.00	150.00
113 Art Wiebe RC	100.00	150.00
114 Joffre Desilets RC	100.00	150.00
115 Earl Robinson	100.00	150.00
116 Cy Wentworth	150.00	250.00
117 Ebbie Goodfellow	125.00	200.00
118 Eddie Shore	1,200.00	1,800.00
119 Buzz Boll	100.00	150.00
120 Wilfred Cude	125.00	200.00
121 Howie Morenz	1,400.00	2,200.00
122 Red Horner	250.00	400.00
123 Charlie Conacher	500.00	800.00
124 Busher Jackson	300.00	500.00
125 King Clancy	600.00	1,000.00
126 Dave Trottier	100.00	150.00
127 Russ Blinco	100.00	150.00
128 Lynn Patrick	300.00	500.00
129 Aurel Joliat	500.00	800.00
130 Baldy Northcott	100.00	150.00
131 Larry Aurie	100.00	150.00
132 Hooley Smith	250.00	400.00

1937-38 O-Pee-Chee V304E

Series E cards continued the numerical series of the 1930's O-Pee-Chee sets and featured a black and white photo of the player within a serrated, colored (blue or purple) frame. A facsimile autograph and a cartooned hockey player appeared on the front in the same color as the frame. The cards in the set measured approximately 2 3/8" by 2 7/8". The backs contained the card number, the player's name, and biographical data in both English and French. The catalog designation for this set is V304E.

COMPLETE SET (48)	4,000.00	7,500.00
WRAPPER (1-CENT)	150.00	300.00
133 Turk Broda	400.00	600.00
134 Red Horner	125.00	200.00
135 Jimmy Fowler	60.00	100.00
136 Bob Davidson	60.00	100.00
137 Reg. Hamilton RC	60.00	100.00
138 Charlie Conacher	300.00	500.00
139 Busher Jackson	175.00	300.00
140 Buzz Boll	60.00	100.00
141 Syl Apps	250.00	400.00
142 Gordie Drillon RC	175.00	300.00
143 Bill Thoms	60.00	100.00
144 Nick Metz	60.00	100.00
145 Pep Kelly	60.00	100.00
146 Murray Armstrong RC	60.00	100.00
147 Murph Chamberlain RC	60.00	100.00
148 Des Smith RC	60.00	100.00
149 Wilfred Cude	90.00	150.00
150 Babe Siebert	125.00	200.00
151 Bill MacKenzie	60.00	100.00
152 Aurel Joliat	300.00	500.00
153 Georges Mantha	60.00	100.00
154 Johnny Gagnon	60.00	100.00
155 Paul Haynes	60.00	100.00
156 Joffre Desilets	60.00	100.00
157 George Allen Brown RC	60.00	100.00
158 Paul Drouin RC	60.00	100.00
159 Pit Lepine	60.00	100.00
160 Toe Blake RC	500.00	800.00
161 Bill Beveridge	90.00	150.00
162 Allan Shields	60.00	100.00
163 Cy Wentworth	125.00	200.00
164 Stew Evans RC	60.00	100.00
165 Earl Robinson	60.00	100.00
166 Baldy Northcott	90.00	150.00
167 Paul Runge	60.00	100.00
168 Dave Trottier	60.00	100.00
169 Russ Blinco	60.00	100.00
170 Jimmy Ward	60.00	100.00
171 Bob Gracie	60.00	100.00
172 Herb Cain	125.00	200.00
173 Gus Marker	60.00	100.00
174 Walter Buswell RC	60.00	100.00
175 Carl Voss RC	125.00	200.00
176 Rod Lorraine RC	60.00	100.00
177 Armand Mondou	60.00	100.00
178 Cliff Goupille RC	60.00	100.00
179 Jerry Shannon RC	60.00	100.00
180 Tom Cook RC	125.00	200.00

1939-40 O-Pee-Chee V301-1

This O-Pee-Chee set of 100 large cards was apparently issued during the 1939-40 season. The catalog designation for this set is V301-1. The cards are black and white and measured approximately 5" by 7". The card backs were blank. The cards were numbered on the front in the lower right corner. Cards in the set were identified on the front by name, team, and position. These cards were premiums and were issued one per cello pack.

COMPLETE SET (100)	4,000.00	7,000.00
1 Reg Hamilton	35.00	60.00
2 Turk Broda	175.00	300.00
3 Bingo Kampman RC	25.00	50.00
4 Gordie Drillon	50.00	80.00
5 Bob Davidson	25.00	50.00
6 Syl Apps	125.00	200.00
7 Pete Langelle RC	25.00	50.00
8 Don Metz RC	25.00	50.00
9 Pep Kelly	25.00	50.00
10 Red Horner	60.00	100.00
11 Wally Stanowsky RC	25.00	50.00
12 Murph Chamberlain	25.00	50.00
13 Bucko MacDonald	25.00	50.00
14 Sweeney Schriner	60.00	100.00
15 Billy Taylor RC	25.00	50.00
16 Gus Marker	25.00	50.00
17 Hooley Smith	60.00	100.00
18 Art Chapman	25.00	50.00
19 Murray Armstrong	25.00	50.00
20 Busher Jackson	90.00	150.00
21 Buzz Boll	25.00	50.00
22 Cliff(Red) Goupille	25.00	50.00
23 Rod Lorraine	25.00	50.00
24 Paul Drouin	25.00	50.00
25 Johnny Gagnon	25.00	50.00
26 Georges Mantha	25.00	50.00
27 Armand Mondou	25.00	50.00
28 Claude Bourque RC	25.00	50.00
29 Ray Getliffe RC	25.00	50.00
30 Cy Wentworth	50.00	80.00
31 Paul Haynes	25.00	50.00
32 Walter Buswell	25.00	50.00
33 Ott Heller	25.00	50.00
34 Arthur Coulter	35.00	60.00
35 Clint Smith RC	60.00	100.00
36 Lynn Patrick	60.00	100.00
37 Dave Kerr	50.00	80.00
38 Murray Patrick RC	25.00	50.00
39 Neil Colville	60.00	100.00
40 Jack Portland RC	25.00	50.00
41 Flash Hollett	25.00	50.00
42 Herb Cain	50.00	80.00
43 Mud Bruneteau	25.00	50.00
44 Joffre DeSilets	25.00	50.00
45 Mush March	25.00	50.00
46 Cully Dahlstrom RC	25.00	50.00
47 Mike Karakas	35.00	60.00
48 Bill Thoms	25.00	50.00
49 Art Wiebe	25.00	50.00
50 Johnny Gottselig	25.00	50.00
51 Nick Metz	25.00	50.00
52 Jack Church RC	25.00	50.00
53 Bob Heron RC	25.00	50.00
54 Hank Goldup RC	25.00	50.00
55 Jimmy Fowler	25.00	50.00
56 Charlie Sands	25.00	50.00
57 Marty Barry	35.00	60.00
58 Doug Young	25.00	50.00
59 Charlie Conacher	150.00	250.00
60 John Sorrell	25.00	50.00
61 Tommy Anderson RC	25.00	50.00
62 Lorne Carr	25.00	50.00
63 Earl Robertson RC	35.00	60.00
64 Wilfy Field RC	25.00	50.00
65 Jimmy Orlando RC	25.00	50.00
66 Ebbie Goodfellow	35.00	60.00
67 Jack Keating RC	25.00	50.00
68 Sid Abel RC	250.00	400.00
69 Gus Giesebrecht RC	25.00	50.00
70 Don Deacon RC	25.00	50.00
71 Hec Kilrea	25.00	50.00
72 Syd Howe	60.00	100.00
73 Eddie Wares RC	25.00	50.00
74 Carl Liscombe RC	25.00	50.00
75 Tiny Thompson	90.00	150.00
76 Earl Seibert RC	25.00	50.00
77 Des Smith RC	25.00	50.00
78 Les Cunningham RC	25.00	50.00
79 George Allen RC	25.00	50.00
80 Bill Carse RC	25.00	50.00
81 Bill McKenzie	25.00	50.00
82 Ab DeMarco RC	25.00	50.00
83 Phil Watson	30.00	50.00
84 Alf Pike RC	25.00	50.00
85 Babe Pratt RC	50.00	80.00
86 Bryan Hextall Sr. RC	50.00	80.00
87 Kilby MacDonald RC	25.00	50.00
88 Alex Shibicky	25.00	50.00
89 Dutch Hiller RC	25.00	50.00
90 Mac Colville	25.00	50.00
91 Roy Conacher RC	60.00	100.00
92 Cooney Weiland	60.00	100.00
93 Art Jackson	25.00	50.00
94 Woody Dumart RC	75.00	150.00
95 Dit Clapper	125.00	200.00
96 Mel Hill RC	25.00	50.00
97 Frank Brimsek RC	150.00	300.00
98 Bill Cowley RC	75.00	150.00
99 Bobby Bauer RC	50.00	100.00
100 Eddie Shore	400.00	600.00

1940-41 O-Pee-Chee V301-2

This O-Pee-Chee set was continuously numbered from the 1939-40 O-Pee-Chee set. These large cards were apparently issued during the 1940-41 season. The catalog designation for this set is V301-2. The cards were sepia and measure approximately 5" by 7". The second series numbers were somewhat larger than the numbers used for the first series. The card backs were blank. The cards were numbered on the front in the lower right corner. Cards in the set were identified on the front by name, team, and position. These cards were premiums and were issued one per cello pack.

COMPLETE SET (50)	3,000.00	5,000.00
101 Toe Blake	175.00	300.00
102 Charlie Sands	30.00	50.00
103 Wally Stanowski	30.00	50.00
104 Jack Adams	30.00	50.00
105 Johnny Mowers RC	50.00	80.00
106 Johnny Quilty RC	30.00	50.00
107 Billy Taylor	30.00	50.00
108 Turk Broda	175.00	300.00
109 Bingo Kampman	30.00	50.00
110 Gordie Drillon	75.00	125.00
111 Don Metz	30.00	50.00
112 Paul Haynes	30.00	50.00
113 Gus Marker	30.00	50.00
114 Alex Singbush RC	30.00	50.00
115 Alex Motter RC	30.00	50.00
116 Ken Reardon RC	90.00	150.00
117 Pete Langelle	30.00	50.00
118 Syl Apps	125.00	200.00
119 Reg. Hamilton	30.00	50.00
120 Cliff(Red) Goupille	30.00	50.00
121 Joe Benoit RC	30.00	50.00
122 Sweeney Schriner	75.00	125.00
123 Joe Carveth RC	30.00	50.00
124 Jack Stewart RC	75.00	125.00
125 Elmer Lach RC	125.00	200.00
126 Jack Schewchuk RC	50.00	80.00
127 Norman Larson RC	50.00	80.00
128 Don Grosso RC	50.00	80.00
129 Lester Douglas RC	50.00	80.00
130 Turk Broda	250.00	400.00
131 Max Bentley RC	175.00	300.00
132 Milt Schmidt RC	250.00	400.00
133 Nick Metz	50.00	80.00
134 Jack Crawford RC	50.00	80.00
135 Bill Benson RC	50.00	80.00
136 Lynn Patrick	90.00	150.00
137 Cully Dahlstrom	50.00	80.00
138 Mud Bruneteau	50.00	80.00
139 Dave Kerr	90.00	150.00
140 Bob(Red) Heron	50.00	80.00
141 Nick Metz	50.00	80.00
142 Ott Heller	50.00	80.00
143 Phil Hergesheimer RC	50.00	80.00
144 Tony Demers RC	50.00	80.00
145 Archie Wilder RC	50.00	80.00
146 Syl Apps	150.00	250.00
147 Ray Getliffe	50.00	80.00
148 Lex Chisholm RC	50.00	80.00
149 Eddie Wiseman RC	50.00	80.00
150 Paul Goodman RC	60.00	120.00

1968-69 O-Pee-Chee

The 1968-69 O-Pee-Chee set contained 216 standard-size color cards. Included are players from the six expansion teams: Philadelphia, Pittsburgh, St. Louis, Minnesota, Los Angeles and Oakland. The cards were originally sold in five-cent wax packs. The horizontally oriented fronts featured the player in the foreground with an artistically rendered hockey scene in the background. The bilingual backs were printed in red and black ink. The player's 1967-68 and career statistics, a short biography, and a cartoon-illustrated fact about the player were included on the back. The cards were printed in Canada and were issued by O-Pee-Chee, even though the Topps Gum copyright is found on the reverse. For the most part, the cards were grouped by teams. However, numerous cards are updated to reflect off-season transactions. The O-Pee-Chee set featured many different poses from the corresponding Topps cards. Card No. 193 can be found either numbered or unnumbered. Rookie Cards in this set included Bernie Parent, Mickey Redmond, Gary Smith and Garry Unger.

COMPLETE SET (216)	1,500.00	2,500.00
1 Doug Harvey	25.00	60.00
2 Bobby Orr	200.00	400.00
3 Don Awrey UER	5.00	8.00
4 Ted Green	6.00	10.00
5 Johnny Bucyk	9.00	15.00
6 Derek Sanderson	25.00	50.00
7 Phil Esposito	25.00	40.00
8 Ken Hodge	6.00	10.00
9 John McKenzie	6.00	10.00
10 Fred Stanfield	5.00	8.00
11 Tom Williams	5.00	8.00
12 Denis DeJordy	6.00	10.00
13 Doug Jarrett	5.00	8.00
14 Gilles Marotte	5.00	8.00
15 Pat Stapleton	6.00	10.00
16 Bobby Hull	50.00	75.00
17 Chico Maki	5.00	8.00
18 Pit Martin	6.00	10.00
19 Doug Mohns	5.00	8.00
20 John Ferguson	6.00	10.00
21 Jim Pappin	5.00	8.00
22 Ken Wharram	5.00	8.00
23 Roger Crozier	6.00	10.00
24 Bob Baun	6.00	10.00
25 Gary Bergman	5.00	8.00
26 Kent Douglas	5.00	8.00
27 Ron Harris RC	5.00	8.00
28 Alex Delvecchio	9.00	15.00
29 Gordie Howe	60.00	100.00
30 Bruce MacGregor	5.00	8.00
31 Frank Mahovlich	12.00	20.00
32 Dean Prentice	5.00	8.00
33 Pete Stemkowski	5.00	8.00
34 Terry Sawchuk	30.00	50.00
35 Larry Cahan	5.00	8.00
36 Real Lemieux RC	5.00	8.00

Card	Low	High
37 Bill White RC	7.00	12.00
38 Gord Labossiere RC	5.00	8.00
39 Ted Irvine RC	5.00	8.00
40 Eddie Joyal	5.00	8.00
41 Dale Rolfe RC	5.00	8.00
42 Lowell MacDonald RC	7.00	12.00
43 Skip Krake UER	5.00	8.00
44 Terry Gray	5.00	8.00
45 Cesare Maniago	6.00	10.00
46 Mike McMahon	5.00	8.00
47 Wayne Hillman	5.00	8.00
48 Larry Hillman	5.00	8.00
49 Bob Woytowich	5.00	8.00
50 Wayne Connelly	5.00	8.00
51 Claude Larose	5.00	8.00
52 Danny Grant UER	10.00	20.00
John Vanderburg pictured		
53 Andre Boudrias RC	5.00	8.00
54 Ray Cullen RC	6.00	10.00
55 Parker MacDonald	5.00	8.00
56 Gump Worsley	9.00	15.00
57 Terry Harper	5.00	8.00
58 Jacques Laperriere	6.00	10.00
59 J.C. Tremblay	6.00	10.00
60 Ralph Backstrom	6.00	10.00
61 Checklist 1	125.00	200.00
62 Yvan Cournoyer	12.00	20.00
63 Jacques Lemaire	15.00	25.00
64 Mickey Redmond RC	40.00	70.00
65 Bobby Rousseau	5.00	8.00
66 Gilles Tremblay	5.00	8.00
67 Ed Giacomin	12.00	20.00
68 Arnie Brown	5.00	8.00
69 Harry Howell	6.00	10.00
70 Al Hamilton RC	5.00	8.00
71 Rod Seiling	5.00	8.00
72 Rod Gilbert	7.00	12.00
73 Phil Goyette	5.00	8.00
74 Larry Jeffrey	5.00	8.00
75 Don Marshall	5.00	8.00
76 Bob Nevin	6.00	10.00
77 Jean Ratelle	7.00	12.00
78 Charlie Hodge	6.00	10.00
79 Bert Marshall	5.00	8.00
80 Billy Harris	5.00	8.00
81 Carol Vadnais	6.00	10.00
82 Howie Young	5.00	8.00
83 John Brenneman RC	5.00	8.00
84 Gerry Ehman	5.00	8.00
85 Ted Hampson	5.00	8.00
86 Bill Hicke	5.00	8.00
87 Gary Jarrett	5.00	8.00
88 Doug Roberts	5.00	8.00
89 Bernie Parent RC	100.00	250.00
90 Joe Watson	5.00	8.00
91 Ed Van Impe	5.00	8.00
92 Larry Zeidel	5.00	8.00
93 John Miszuk RC	5.00	8.00
94 Gary Dornhoefer	6.00	10.00
95 Leon Rochefort RC	5.00	8.00
96 Brit Selby	5.00	8.00
97 Forbes Kennedy	5.00	8.00
98 Ed Hoekstra RC	5.00	8.00
99 Garry Peters	5.00	8.00
100 Les Binkley RC	10.00	20.00
101 Leo Boivin	6.00	10.00
102 Earl Ingarfield	5.00	8.00
103 Lou Angotti	5.00	8.00
104 Andy Bathgate	7.00	12.00
105 Wally Boyer	5.00	8.00
106 Ken Schinkel	5.00	8.00
107 Ab McDonald	5.00	8.00
108 Charlie Burns	5.00	8.00
109 Val Fonteyne	5.00	8.00
110 Noel Price	5.00	8.00
111 Glenn Hall	12.00	20.00
112 Bob Plager RC	12.50	25.00
113 Jim Roberts	5.00	8.00
114 Red Berenson	6.00	10.00
115 Larry Keenan	5.00	8.00
116 Camille Henry	5.00	8.00
117 Gary Sabourin RC	5.00	8.00
118 Ron Schock	5.00	8.00
119 Gary Veneruzzo RC	5.00	8.00
120 Gerry Melnyk	5.00	8.00
121 Checklist 2	150.00	250.00
122 Johnny Bower	9.00	15.00
123 Tim Horton	15.00	25.00
124 Pierre Pilote	7.00	12.00
125 Marcel Pronovost	6.00	10.00
126 Ron Ellis	6.00	10.00
127 Paul Henderson	6.00	10.00
128 Al Arbour	6.00	10.00
129 Bob Pulford	6.00	10.00
130 Floyd Smith	5.00	8.00
131 Norm Ullman	7.00	12.00
132 Mike Walton	6.00	10.00
133 Ed Johnston DP	6.00	10.00
134 Glen Sather	9.00	15.00
135 Ed Westfall DP	6.00	10.00
136 Dallas Smith DP	5.00	8.00
137 Eddie Shack DP	7.00	12.00
138 Gary Doak DP	5.00	8.00
139 Ron Murphy DP	5.00	8.00
140 Gerry Cheevers DP	12.00	20.00
141 Bob Falkenberg RC	5.00	8.00
142 Garry Unger DP RC	18.00	30.00
143 Peter Mahovlich DP	6.00	10.00
144 Roy Edwards	6.00	10.00
145 Gary Bauman DP RC	5.00	8.00
146 Bob McCord DP	5.00	8.00
147 Elmer Vasko DP	5.00	8.00
148 Bill Goldsworthy RC	7.00	12.00
149 Jean-Paul Parise RC	7.00	12.00
150 Dave Dryden	6.00	10.00
151 Howie Young DP	5.00	8.00
152 Matt Ravlich DP	5.00	8.00
153 Dennis Hull DP	6.00	10.00
154 Eric Nesterenko DP	6.00	10.00
155 Stan Mikita DP	18.00	30.00
156 Bob Wall DP	5.00	8.00
157 Dave Amadio RC	5.00	8.00
158 Howie Hughes DP RC	5.00	8.00
159 Bill Flett RC	7.00	12.00
160 Doug Robinson	5.00	8.00
161 Dick Duff DP	6.00	10.00
162 Ted Harris DP	5.00	8.00
163 Claude Provost DP	5.00	8.00
164 Rogatien Vachon DP	25.00	40.00
165 Henri Richard DP	12.00	20.00
166 Jean Beliveau DP	20.00	40.00
167 Reg Fleming DP	5.00	8.00
168 Ron Stewart DP	5.00	8.00
169 Dave Balon	5.00	8.00
170 Orland Kurtenbach DP	5.00	8.00
171 Vic Hadfield DP	6.00	10.00
172 Jim Neilson DP	5.00	8.00
173 Bryan Watson DP	5.00	8.00
174 George Swarbrick DP RC	5.00	8.00
175 Joe Szura RC	5.00	8.00
176 Gary Smith RC	10.00	20.00
177 Barclay Plager UER DP RC	9.00	15.00
178 Tim Ecclestone DP RC	5.00	8.00
179 Jean-Guy Talbot DP	6.00	10.00
180 Ab McDonald DP	5.00	8.00
181 Jacques Plante DP	25.00	60.00
182 Bill McCreary RC	5.00	8.00
183 Allan Stanley DP	7.00	12.00
184 Andre Lacroix RC	7.00	12.00
185 Jean-Guy Gendron DP	5.00	8.00
186 Jim Johnson RC	5.00	8.00
187 Simon Nolet RC	7.00	12.00
188 Joe Daley DP RC	7.00	12.00
189 John Arbour DP RC	5.00	8.00
190 Billy Dea DP	5.00	8.00
191 Bob Dillabough DP	5.00	8.00
192 Bob Woytowich DP	5.00	8.00
193 Keith McCreary RC	5.00	8.00
194 Murray Oliver DP	5.00	8.00
195 Larry Mickey RC	5.00	8.00
196 Bill Sutherland DP RC	5.00	8.00
197 Bruce Gamble DP	6.00	10.00
198 Dave Keon DP	9.00	15.00
199 Gump Worsley AS1	7.00	12.00
200 Bobby Orr AS1	90.00	150.00
201 Tim Horton AS1	8.00	15.00
202 Stan Mikita AS1	9.00	15.00
203 Gordie Howe AS1	40.00	60.00
204 Bobby Hull AS1	30.00	50.00
205 Ed Giacomin AS2	9.00	15.00
206 J.C. Tremblay AS2	6.00	10.00
207 Jim Neilson AS2	5.00	8.00
208 Phil Esposito AS2	15.00	25.00
209 Rod Gilbert AS2	6.00	10.00
210 Johnny Bucyk AS2	6.00	10.00
211 Stan Mikita Triple	9.00	15.00
212 Worsley/Vachon Vezina	25.00	40.00
213 D.Sanderson Calder	25.00	50.00
214 B.Orr Norris	90.00	150.00
215 G.Hall Smythe	7.00	12.00
216 C.Provost Masterson	7.50	15.00

1968-69 O-Pee-Chee Puck Stickers

This set consisted of 22 numbered (on the front), full-color stickers measuring 2 1/2" by 3 1/2". The card backs were blank and contained an adhesive. These stickers were printed in Canada and were inserted one per pack in 1968-69 O-Pee-Chee regular issue hockey packs. The pucks were perforated so that they could be punched out. This was obviously not recommended. Sticker card 22 is a special card honoring Gordie Howe's 700th goal.

Card	Low	High
COMPLETE SET (22)	250.00	500.00
1 Stan Mikita	10.00	25.00
2 Frank Mahovlich	10.00	25.00
3 Bobby Hull	25.00	50.00
4 Bobby Orr	125.00	250.00
5 Phil Esposito	15.00	30.00
6 Gump Worsley	10.00	20.00
7 Jean Beliveau	15.00	30.00
8 Elmer Vasko	7.50	15.00
9 Rod Gilbert	10.00	20.00
10 Roger Crozier	10.00	20.00
11 Lou Angotti	7.50	15.00
12 Charlie Hodge	7.50	15.00
13 Glenn Hall	10.00	25.00
14 Doug Harvey	10.00	25.00
15 Jacques Plante	25.00	50.00
16 Allan Stanley	7.50	15.00
17 Johnny Bower	15.00	30.00
18 Tim Horton	15.00	30.00
19 Dave Keon	15.00	40.00
20 Terry Sawchuk	25.00	50.00
21 Henri Richard	10.00	25.00
22 Gordie Howe Special	30.00	60.00

1969-70 O-Pee-Chee

The 1969-70 O-Pee-Chee set contained 231 standard-size cards issued in two series of 132 and 99. The cards were issued in ten-cent wax packs. Bilingual backs contain 1968-69 and career statistics, a short biography and a cartoon-illustrated fact about the player. The cards were printed in Canada with the Topps Gum Company copyright appearing on the reverse. Many player poses in this set were different from the corresponding player poses of the Topps set of this year. Card 193, Gordie Howe "Mr. Hockey" existed with or without the card number. Stamps inserted in wax packs could be placed on the back of the corresponding player's regular-issue cards in a space provided. A card with a stamp on the back was considered to be of less value than one without the stamp. Rookie Cards include Tony Esposito and Serge Savard.

Card	Low	High
COMPLETE SET (231)	1,200.00	2,000.00
1 Gump Worsley	20.00	35.00
2 Ted Harris	4.00	6.00
3 Jacques Laperriere	5.00	8.00
4 Serge Savard RC	90.00	150.00
5 J.C. Tremblay	5.00	8.00
6 Yvan Cournoyer	6.00	10.00
7 John Ferguson	5.00	8.00
8 Jacques Lemaire	6.00	10.00
9 Bobby Rousseau	4.00	6.00
10 Jean Beliveau	15.00	25.00
11 Dick Duff	5.00	8.00
12 Glenn Hall	7.00	12.00
13 Bob Plager	4.00	6.00
14 Ron Anderson RC	4.00	6.00
15 Jean-Guy Talbot	5.00	8.00
16 Andre Boudrias	4.00	6.00
17 Camille Henry	4.00	6.00
18 Ab McDonald	4.00	6.00
19 Gary Sabourin	4.00	6.00
20 Red Berenson	4.00	6.00
21 Phil Goyette	4.00	6.00
22 Gerry Cheevers	9.00	15.00
23 Ted Green	4.00	6.00
24 Bobby Orr	125.00	250.00
25 Dallas Smith	4.00	6.00
26 Johnny Bucyk	8.00	12.00
27 Ken Hodge	5.00	8.00
28 John McKenzie	5.00	8.00
29 Ed Westfall	5.00	8.00
30 Phil Esposito	18.00	30.00
31 Checklist 2	100.00	150.00
32 Fred Stanfield	4.00	6.00
33 Ed Giacomin	9.00	15.00
34 Arnie Brown	4.00	6.00
35 Jim Neilson	4.00	6.00
36 Rod Seiling	4.00	6.00
37 Rod Gilbert	6.00	10.00
38 Vic Hadfield	5.00	8.00
39 Don Marshall	4.00	6.00
40 Bob Nevin	4.00	6.00
41 Ron Stewart	4.00	6.00
42 Jean Ratelle	6.00	10.00
43 Walt Tkaczuk RC	6.00	10.00
44 Bruce Gamble	5.00	8.00
45 Jim Dorey RC	4.00	6.00
46 Ron Ellis	5.00	8.00
47 Paul Henderson	5.00	8.00
48 Brit Selby	4.00	6.00
49 Floyd Smith	4.00	6.00
50 Mike Walton	5.00	8.00
51 Dave Keon	6.00	10.00
52 Murray Oliver	4.00	6.00
53 Bob Pulford	5.00	8.00
54 Norm Ullman	6.00	10.00
55 Roger Crozier	5.00	8.00
56 Roy Edwards	5.00	8.00
57 Bob Baun	5.00	8.00
58 Gary Bergman	4.00	6.00
59 Carl Brewer	5.00	8.00
60 Wayne Connelly	4.00	6.00
61 Gordie Howe	60.00	120.00
62 Frank Mahovlich	7.50	15.00
63 Bruce MacGregor	4.00	6.00
64 Ron Harris	4.00	6.00
65 Pete Stemkowski	4.00	6.00
66 Denis DeJordy	5.00	8.00
67 Doug Jarrett	4.00	6.00
68 Gilles Marotte	4.00	6.00
69 Pat Stapleton	5.00	8.00
70 Bobby Hull	40.00	80.00
71 Dennis Hull	5.00	8.00
72 Doug Mohns	4.00	6.00
73 Howie Menard RC	4.00	6.00
74 Ken Wharram	4.00	6.00
75 Pit Martin	5.00	8.00
76 Stan Mikita	12.00	20.00
77 Charlie Hodge	5.00	8.00
78 Gary Smith	5.00	8.00
79 Harry Howell	5.00	8.00
80 Bert Marshall	4.00	6.00
81 Doug Roberts	4.00	6.00
82 Carol Vadnais	5.00	8.00
83 Gerry Ehman	4.00	6.00
84 Brian Perry RC	4.00	6.00
85 Gary Jarrett	4.00	6.00
86 Ted Hampson	4.00	6.00
87 Earl Ingarfield	4.00	6.00
88 Doug Favell RC	9.00	15.00
89 Bernie Parent	25.00	40.00
90 Larry Hillman	4.00	6.00
91 Wayne Hillman	4.00	6.00
92 Ed Van Impe	4.00	6.00
93 Joe Watson	4.00	6.00
94 Gary Dornhoefer	5.00	8.00
95 Reg Fleming	4.00	6.00
96 Ralph McSweyn RC	4.00	6.00
97 Jim Johnson	4.00	6.00
98 Andre Lacroix	5.00	8.00
99 Gerry Desjardins RC	7.00	12.00
100 Dale Rolfe	4.00	6.00
101 Bill White	4.00	6.00
102 Bill Flett	4.00	6.00
103 Ted Irvine	4.00	6.00
104 Ross Lonsberry	4.00	6.00
105 Leon Rochefort	4.00	6.00
106 Bryan Campbell RC	4.00	6.00
107 Dennis Hextall RC	6.00	10.00
108 Eddie Joyal	4.00	6.00
109 Gord Labossiere	4.00	6.00
110 Les Binkley	5.00	8.00
111 Tracy Pratt RC	4.00	6.00
112 Bryan Watson	4.00	6.00
113 Bob Blackburn RC	4.00	6.00
114 Keith McCreary	4.00	6.00
115 Dean Prentice	4.00	6.00
116 Glen Sather	5.00	8.00
117 Ken Schinkel	4.00	6.00
118 Wally Boyer	4.00	6.00
119 Val Fonteyne	4.00	6.00
120 Ron Schock	4.00	6.00
121 Cesare Maniago	5.00	8.00
122 Leo Boivin	5.00	8.00
123 Bob McCord	4.00	6.00
124 John Miszuk	4.00	6.00
125 Danny Grant	5.00	8.00
126 Bill Collins RC	4.00	6.00
127 Jean-Paul Parise	5.00	8.00
128 Tom Williams	4.00	6.00
129 Charlie Burns	4.00	6.00
130 Ray Cullen	4.00	6.00
131 Danny O'Shea RC	5.00	8.00
132 Checklist 1	150.00	250.00
133 Jim Pappin	4.00	6.00
134 Lou Angotti	4.00	6.00
135 Terry Cafery RC	5.00	8.00
136 Eric Nesterenko	5.00	8.00
137 Chico Maki	5.00	8.00
138 Tony Esposito RC	75.00	150.00
139 Eddie Shack	6.00	10.00
140 Bob Wall	4.00	6.00
141 Skip Krake	5.00	8.00
142 Howie Hughes	4.00	6.00
143 Jimmy Peters RC	5.00	8.00
144 Brent Hughes RC	5.00	8.00
145 Bill Hicke	4.00	6.00
146 Norm Ferguson RC	5.00	8.00
147 Dick Mattiussi RC	5.00	8.00
148 Mike Laughton RC	5.00	8.00
149 Gene Ubriaco RC	5.00	8.00
150 Bob Dillabough	4.00	6.00
151 Bob Woytowich	4.00	6.00
152 Joe Daley	5.00	8.00
153 Duane Rupp	4.00	6.00
154 Bryan Hextall RC	6.00	10.00
155 Jean Pronovost RC	6.00	10.00
156 Jim Morrison	4.00	6.00
157 Alex Delvecchio	8.00	12.00
158 Paul Popiel	4.00	6.00
159 Garry Unger	6.00	10.00
160 Garry Monahan	4.00	6.00
161 Matt Ravlich	4.00	6.00
162 Nick Libett RC	6.00	10.00
163 Henri Richard	7.00	12.00
164 Terry Harper	5.00	8.00
165 Rogatien Vachon	10.00	20.00
166 Ralph Backstrom	5.00	8.00
167 Claude Provost	5.00	8.00
168 Gilles Tremblay	5.00	8.00
169 Jean-Guy Gendron	5.00	8.00
170 Earl Heiskala RC	5.00	8.00
171 Garry Peters	4.00	6.00
172 Bill Sutherland	4.00	6.00
173 Dick Cherry RC	5.00	8.00
174 Jim Roberts	5.00	8.00
175 Noel Picard RC	5.00	8.00
176 Barclay Plager	5.00	8.00
177 Frank St. Marseille RC	5.00	8.00
178 Al Arbour	5.00	8.00
179 Tim Ecclestone	4.00	6.00
180 Jacques Plante	25.00	40.00
181 Bill McCreary	4.00	6.00
182 Tim Horton	12.00	20.00
183 Rick Ley RC	6.00	10.00
184 Wayne Carleton	4.00	6.00
185 Marv Edwards RC	6.00	10.00
186 Pat Quinn RC	9.00	15.00
187 Johnny Bower	7.00	12.00
188 Orland Kurtenbach	5.00	8.00
189 Terry Sawchuk UER	25.00	40.00
190 Real Lemieux	4.00	6.00
191 Dave Balon	4.00	6.00
192 Al Hamilton	4.00	6.00
193A G.Howe Mr. HK ERR	90.00	150.00
193B G.Howe Mr. HK COR	100.00	175.00
194 Claude Larose	4.00	6.00
195 Bill Goldsworthy	5.00	8.00
196 Bob Barlow RC	4.00	6.00
197 Ken Broderick RC	5.00	8.00

198 Lou Nanne RC	6.00	10.00
199 Tom Polonic RC	5.00	8.00
200 Ed Johnston	5.00	8.00
201 Derek Sanderson	15.00	25.00
202 Gary Doak	4.00	6.00
203 Don Awrey	4.00	6.00
204 Ron Murphy	4.00	6.00
205A P.Esposito Double ERR	15.00	25.00
205B P.Esposito Double COR	12.00	20.00
206 Alex Delvecchio Byng	4.00	6.00
207 J.Plante/G.Hall Vezina	30.00	50.00
208 Danny Grant Calder	4.00	6.00
209 Bobby Orr Norris	50.00	100.00
210 Serge Savard Smythe	4.00	6.00
211 Glenn Hall AS	9.00	15.00
212 Bobby Orr AS	50.00	100.00
213 Tim Horton AS	12.00	20.00
214 Phil Esposito AS	12.00	20.00
215 Gordie Howe AS	30.00	50.00
216 Bobby Hull AS	20.00	35.00
217 Ed Giacomin AS	7.00	12.00
218 Ted Green AS	4.00	6.00
219 Ted Harris AS	4.00	6.00
220 Jean Beliveau AS	20.00	35.00
221 Yvan Cournoyer AS	4.00	6.00
222 Frank Mahovlich AS	7.50	15.00
223 Art Ross Trophy	5.00	8.00
224 Hart Trophy	5.00	8.00
225 Lady Byng Trophy	5.00	8.00
226 Vezina Trophy	6.00	10.00
227 Calder Trophy	5.00	8.00
228 James Norris Trophy	5.00	8.00
229 Conn Smythe Trophy	5.00	8.00
230 Prince of Wales	5.00	8.00
231 The Stanley Cup	25.00	60.00

1969-70 O-Pee-Chee Four-in-One

The 1969-70 O-Pee-Chee Four-in-One set contained 18 four-player adhesive-backed color cards. The cards were standard size, 2 1/2" by 3 1/2", whereas the individual mini-cards were approximately 1" by 1 1/2". These small cards could be separated and then stuck in a small team album/booklet that was also available that year from O-Pee-Chee. This set was distributed as an insert with the second series of regular 1969-70 O-Pee-Chee cards. Cards that had been separated into the mini-cards have very little value. The cards were unnumbered and so they are checklisted below alphabetically by the (upper left corner) player's name.

COMPLETE SET (18)	600.00	1,000.00
1 Baun/Schink/Hort/Parent	30.00	60.00
2 Bink/Hodge/Flem/Laper	30.00	60.00
3 Courn/Neil/Sabo/Misz	30.00	60.00
4 Gamb/Vadn/Mahov/Hillman	30.00	60.00
5 Giac/Beliv/Joyal/Boivin	30.00	60.00
6 Goye/Jarret/Green/Hicke	30.00	60.00
7 Hamp/Brewer/DeJordy/Roche	30.00	60.00
8 Hodge/Quinn/Sand/Rupp	30.00	60.00
9 Ingfld/Robrts/Wors/Hull	50.00	100.00
10 Lacro/Wall/Savard/Croz	30.00	60.00
11 Mani/Orr/Keon/Gendron	150.00	300.00
12 McCr/Larose/Gilb/Cheev	30.00	60.00
13 Mikita/Arbo/Seili/Schock	30.00	60.00
14 Mohn/Woyt/Howe/Desj	75.00	150.00
15 Nev/Plante/Walt/Cullen	30.00	60.00
16 Pulf/Rich/Beren/Shack	40.00	80.00
17 Stapl/Grant/Marsh/Ratel	30.00	60.00
18 VanImp/Rolf/Delv/Espo	30.00	60.00

1969-70 O-Pee-Chee Stamps

The 1969-70 O-Pee-Chee Stamps set contained 26 black and white stamps measuring approximately 1 1/2" by 1 1/4". The stamps were distributed with the first series of regular 1969-70 O-Pee-Chee hockey cards and may also have been available in some of the Topps wax packs of that year as well. The stamps were unnumbered and hence are checklisted below alphabetically for convenience. OPC intended for the stamps to be stuck on the blank space provided on the backs of the corresponding regular card; collectors are strongly encouraged NOT to follow that procedure. The stamps were produced as pairs; intact pairs are now valued at 1.5 to 2 times the sum of the individual player prices listed below.

COMPLETE SET (26)	125.00	250.00
1 Jean Beliveau	7.50	15.00
2 Red Berenson	4.00	8.00
3 Les Binkley	5.00	10.00
4 Yvan Cournoyer	6.00	12.00
5 Ray Cullen	4.00	8.00
6 Gerry Desjardins	5.00	10.00
7 Phil Esposito	7.50	15.00
8 Ed Giacomin	6.00	12.00
9 Rod Gilbert	6.00	12.00
10 Danny Grant	4.00	8.00
11 Glenn Hall	7.50	15.00
12 Ted Hampson	4.00	8.00
13 Ken Hodge	4.00	8.00
14 Gordie Howe	20.00	40.00
15 Bobby Hull	15.00	30.00
16 Eddie Joyal	4.00	8.00
17 Dave Keon	7.50	15.00
18 Andre Lacroix	4.00	8.00
19 Frank Mahovlich	6.00	12.00
20 Keith McCreary	4.00	8.00
21 Stan Mikita	7.50	15.00
22 Bobby Orr	25.00	60.00
23 Bernie Parent	7.50	15.00
24 Jean Ratelle	5.00	10.00
25 Norm Ullman	5.00	10.00
26 Carol Vadnais	4.00	8.00

1970-71 O-Pee-Chee

The 1970-71 O-Pee-Chee set contained 264 standard-size cards. Players from expansion Buffalo and Vancouver are included. Bilingual backs featured a short biography as well as the player's 1969-70 and career statistics. The cards were printed in Canada, and the O-Pee-Chee copyright, and not the Topps, appeared on the back for the first time. Many player poses were different from the Topps set of this year. Cards were grouped by teams. However, there are a number of cards that had updated team names reflecting off-season trades. Card no. 231 is a special memorial to Terry Sawchuk, who passed away in 1970. Card nos. 111, Brit Selby, and 175 Mickey Redmond, could be found with or without a line of text acknowledging trades. Rookie Cards included Wayne Cashman, Bobby Clarke, Brad Park, Guy Lapointe, Gilbert Perreault, and Darryl Sittler.

COMPLETE SET (264)	1,200.00	2,000.00
1 Gerry Cheevers	10.00	25.00
2 Johnny Bucyk	2.50	6.00
3 Bobby Orr	150.00	250.00
4 Don Awrey	1.50	4.00
5 Fred Stanfield	1.50	4.00
6 John McKenzie	2.50	6.00
7 Wayne Cashman RC	8.00	20.00
8 Ken Hodge	2.50	6.00
9 Wayne Carleton	1.50	4.00
10 Garnet Bailey RC	2.50	6.00
11 Phil Esposito	10.00	25.00
12 Lou Angotti	1.50	4.00
13 Jim Pappin	1.50	4.00
14 Dennis Hull	2.50	6.00
15 Bobby Hull	25.00	50.00
16 Doug Mohns	1.50	4.00
17 Pat Stapleton	2.50	6.00
18 Pit Martin	2.50	6.00
19 Eric Nesterenko	2.50	6.00
20 Stan Mikita	8.00	20.00
21 Roy Edwards	2.50	6.00
22 Frank Mahovlich	5.00	12.00
23 Ron Harris	1.50	4.00
24 Checklist 1	100.00	200.00
25 Pete Stemkowski	1.50	4.00
26 Garry Unger	1.50	4.00
27 Bruce MacGregor	1.50	4.00
28 Larry Jeffrey	1.50	4.00
29 Gordie Howe	40.00	80.00
30 Billy Dea	1.50	4.00
31 Denis DeJordy	2.50	6.00
32 Matt Ravlich	1.50	4.00
33 Dave Amadio	1.50	4.00
34 Gilles Marotte	1.50	4.00
35 Eddie Shack	5.00	12.00
36 Bob Pulford	2.50	6.00
37 Ross Lonsberry	2.50	6.00
38 Gord Labossiere	1.50	4.00
39 Eddie Joyal	1.50	4.00
40 Gump Worsley	5.00	12.00
41 Bob McCord	1.50	4.00
42 Leo Boivin	2.50	6.00
43 Tom Reid RC	1.50	4.00
44 Charlie Burns	1.50	4.00
45 Bob Barlow	1.50	4.00
46 Bill Goldsworthy	2.50	6.00
47 Danny Grant	2.50	6.00
48 Norm Beaudin RC	1.50	4.00
49 Rogatien Vachon	5.00	12.00
50 Yvan Cournoyer	5.00	12.00
51 Serge Savard	5.00	12.00
52 Jacques Laperriere	2.50	6.00
53 Terry Harper	1.50	4.00
54 Ralph Backstrom	2.50	6.00
55 Jean Beliveau	5.00	12.00
56 Claude Larose	1.50	4.00
57 Jacques Lemaire	5.00	12.00
58 Peter Mahovlich	4.00	10.00
59 Tim Horton	6.00	15.00
60 Bob Nevin	1.50	4.00
61 Dave Balon	1.50	4.00
62 Vic Hadfield	2.50	6.00
63 Rod Gilbert	5.00	12.00
64 Ron Stewart	1.50	4.00
65 Ted Irvine	1.50	4.00
66 Arnie Brown	1.50	4.00
67 Brad Park RC	20.00	40.00
68 Ed Giacomin	5.00	12.00
69 Gary Smith	2.50	6.00
70 Carol Vadnais	2.50	6.00
71 Doug Roberts	1.50	4.00
72 Harry Howell	2.50	6.00
73 Joe Szura	1.50	4.00
74 Mike Laughton	1.50	4.00
75 Gary Jarrett	1.50	4.00
76 Bill Hicke	1.50	4.00
77 Paul Andrea RC	1.50	4.00
78 Bernie Parent	10.00	25.00
79 Joe Watson	1.50	4.00
80 Ed Van Impe	1.50	4.00
81 Larry Hillman	1.50	4.00
82 George Swarbrick	1.50	4.00
83 Bill Sutherland	1.50	4.00
84 Andre Lacroix	2.50	6.00
85 Gary Dornhoefer	2.50	6.00
86 Jean-Guy Gendron	1.50	4.00
87 Al Smith RC	2.50	6.00
88 Bob Woytowich	1.50	4.00
89 Duane Rupp	1.50	4.00
90 Jim Morrison	1.50	4.00
91 Ron Schock	1.50	4.00
92 Ken Schinkel	1.50	4.00
93 Keith McCreary	1.50	4.00
94 Bryan Hextall	2.50	6.00
95 Wayne Hicks RC	1.50	4.00
96 Gary Sabourin	1.50	4.00
97 Ernie Wakely RC	2.50	6.00
98 Bob Wall	1.50	4.00
99 Barclay Plager	2.50	6.00
100 Jean-Guy Talbot	1.50	4.00
101 Gary Veneruzzo	1.50	4.00
102 Tim Ecclestone	1.50	4.00
103 Red Berenson	2.50	6.00
104 Larry Keenan	1.50	4.00
105 Bruce Gamble	2.50	6.00
106 Jim Dorey	1.50	4.00
107 Mike Pelyk RC	1.50	4.00
108 Rick Ley	1.50	4.00
109 Mike Walton	1.50	4.00
110 Norm Ullman	5.00	12.00
111A Brit Selby no trade	1.50	4.00
111B Brit Selby trade	8.00	20.00
112 Garry Monahan	1.50	4.00
113 George Armstrong	5.00	12.00
114 Gary Doak	1.50	4.00
115 Darryl Sly RC	1.50	4.00
116 Wayne Maki	1.50	4.00
117 Orland Kurtenbach	1.50	4.00
118 Murray Hall	1.50	4.00
119 Marc Reaume	1.50	4.00
120 Pat Quinn	5.00	12.00
121 Andre Boudrias	1.50	4.00
122 Paul Popiel	1.50	4.00
123 Paul Terbenche	1.50	4.00
124 Howie Menard	1.50	4.00
125 Gerry Meehan RC	2.50	6.00
126 Skip Krake	1.50	4.00
127 Phil Goyette	1.50	4.00
128 Reg Fleming	1.50	4.00
129 Don Marshall	2.50	6.00
130 Bill Inglis RC	1.50	4.00
131 Gilbert Perreault RC	100.00	200.00
132 Checklist 2	100.00	200.00
133 Ed Johnston	2.50	6.00
134 Ted Green	2.50	6.00
135 Rick Smith RC	1.50	4.00
136 Derek Sanderson	8.00	20.00
137 Dallas Smith	1.50	4.00
138 Don Marcotte RC	2.50	6.00
139 Ed Westfall	2.50	6.00
140 Floyd Smith	1.50	4.00
141 Randy Wyrozub RC	1.50	4.00
142 Cliff Schmautz RC	1.50	4.00
143 Mike McMahon	1.50	4.00
144 Jim Watson	1.50	4.00
145 Roger Crozier	2.50	6.00
146 Tracy Pratt	1.50	4.00
147 Cliff Koroll RC	2.50	6.00
148 Gerry Pinder RC	2.50	6.00
149 Chico Maki	1.50	4.00
150 Doug Jarrett	1.50	4.00
151 Keith Magnuson RC	5.00	12.00
152 Gerry Desjardins	2.50	6.00
153 Tony Esposito	25.00	50.00
154 Gary Bergman	1.50	4.00
155 Tom Webster RC	2.50	6.00
156 Dale Rolfe	1.50	4.00
157 Alex Delvecchio	5.00	12.00
158 Nick Libett	1.50	4.00
159 Wayne Connelly	1.50	4.00
160 Mike Byers RC	1.50	4.00
161 Bill Flett	1.50	4.00
162 Larry Mickey	1.50	4.00
163 Noel Price	1.50	4.00
164 Larry Cahan	1.50	4.00
165 Jack Norris RC	2.50	6.00
166 Ted Harris	1.50	4.00
167 Murray Oliver	1.50	4.00
168 Jean-Paul Parise	2.50	6.00
169 Tom Williams	1.50	4.00
170 Bobby Rousseau	1.50	4.00
171 Jude Drouin RC	2.50	6.00
172 Walt McKechnie RC	2.50	6.00
173 Cesare Maniago	2.50	6.00
174 Rejean Houle RC	5.00	12.00
175A Mickey Redmond trade	2.50	6.00
175B Mickey Redmond no trade	6.00	15.00
176 Henri Richard	6.00	15.00
177 Guy Lapointe RC	8.00	20.00
178 J.C. Tremblay	2.50	6.00
179 Marc Tardif RC	5.00	12.00
180 Walt Tkaczuk	2.50	6.00
181 Jean Ratelle	5.00	12.00
182 Pete Stemkowski	1.50	4.00
183 Gilles Villemure	2.50	6.00
184 Rod Seiling	1.50	4.00
185 Jim Neilson	1.50	4.00
186 Dennis Hextall	2.50	6.00
187 Gerry Ehman	1.50	4.00
188 Bert Marshall	1.50	4.00
189 Gary Croteau RC	1.50	4.00
190 Ted Hampson	1.50	4.00
191 Earl Ingarfield	1.50	4.00
192 Dick Mattiussi	1.50	4.00
193 Earl Heiskala	1.50	4.00
194 Simon Nolet	1.50	4.00
195 Bobby Clarke RC	60.00	120.00
196 Garry Peters	1.50	4.00
197 Lew Morrison RC	1.50	4.00
198 Wayne Hillman	1.50	4.00
199 Doug Favell	5.00	12.00
200 Les Binkley	2.50	6.00
201 Dean Prentice	1.50	4.00
202 Jean Pronovost	2.50	6.00
203 Wally Boyer	1.50	4.00
204 Bryan Watson	1.50	4.00
205 Glen Sather	2.50	6.00
206 Lowell MacDonald	1.50	4.00
207 Andy Bathgate	2.50	6.00
208 Val Fonteyne	1.50	4.00
209 Jim Lorentz RC	1.50	4.00
210 Glenn Hall	5.00	12.00
211 Bob Plager	2.50	6.00
212 Noel Picard	1.50	4.00
213 Jim Roberts	2.50	6.00
214 Frank St.Marseille	1.50	4.00
215 Ab McDonald	1.50	4.00
216 Brian Glennie RC	1.50	4.00
217 Paul Henderson	3.00	8.00
218 Darryl Sittler RC	50.00	125.00
219 Dave Keon	5.00	12.00
220 Jim Harrison RC	1.50	4.00
221 Ron Ellis	2.50	6.00
222 Jacques Plante	10.00	25.00
223 Bob Baun	2.50	6.00
224 George Gardner RC	1.50	4.00
225 Dale Tallon RC	2.50	6.00
226 Rosaire Paiement RC	1.50	4.00
227 Mike Corrigan RC	1.50	4.00
228 Ray Cullen	1.50	4.00
229 Charlie Hodge	2.50	6.00
230 Len Lunde	1.50	4.00
231 Terry Sawchuk Mem	30.00	60.00
232 Bruins Team Champs	5.00	12.00
233 Espo/Cashman/Hodge	10.00	25.00
234 Tony Esposito AS1	10.00	25.00
235 Bobby Hull AS1	10.00	25.00
236 Bobby Orr AS1	30.00	60.00
237 Phil Esposito AS1	6.00	15.00
238 Gordie Howe AS1	20.00	40.00
239 Brad Park AS1	6.00	15.00
240 Stan Mikita AS2	5.00	12.00
241 John McKenzie AS2	1.50	4.00
242 Frank Mahovlich AS2	2.50	6.00
243 Carl Brewer AS2	1.50	4.00
244 Ed Giacomin AS2	2.50	6.00
245 Jacques Laperriere AS2	1.50	4.00
246 Bobby Orr Hart	30.00	60.00
247 Tony Esposito Calder	10.00	25.00
248A B.Orr Norris Howe	30.00	60.00
248B B.Orr Norris no Howe	30.00	60.00
249 Bobby Orr Ross	30.00	60.00
250 Tony Esposito Vezina	10.00	25.00
251 Phil Goyette Lady Byng	1.50	4.00
252 Bobby Orr Smythe	30.00	60.00
253 Pit Martin Bill Masterton Trophy	1.50	4.00
254 Stanley Cup Trophy	6.00	15.00
255 Wales Trophy	2.50	6.00
256 Conn Smythe Trophy	2.50	6.00
257 James Norris Trophy	2.50	6.00
258 Calder Trophy	2.50	6.00
259 Vezina Trophy	2.50	6.00
260 Lady Byng Trophy	2.50	6.00
261 Hart Trophy	2.50	6.00
262 Art Ross Trophy	2.50	6.00
263 Clarence Campbell Bowl	2.50	6.00
264 John Ferguson	5.00	12.00

1970-71 O-Pee-Chee Deckle

This set consisted of 48 numbered black and white deckle edge cards measuring approximately 2 1/8" by 3 1/8". The set was issued as an insert with the second series regular issue of the same year. The set was printed in Canada.

COMPLETE SET (48)	200.00	400.00
1 Pat Quinn	2.00	5.00
2 Eddie Shack	3.00	6.00
3 Eddie Joyal	2.00	5.00
4 Bobby Orr	40.00	80.00
5 Derek Sanderson	6.00	12.00
6 Phil Esposito	7.50	15.00
7 Fred Stanfield	2.00	5.00
8 Bob Woytowich	2.00	5.00
9 Ron Schock	2.00	5.00
10 Les Binkley	3.00	6.00
11 Roger Crozier	3.00	6.00
12 Reg Fleming	2.00	5.00
13 Charlie Burns	2.00	5.00
14 Bobby Rousseau	2.00	5.00
15 Leo Boivin	2.00	5.00
16 Garry Unger	2.00	5.00
17 Frank Mahovlich	5.00	10.00
18 Gordie Howe	25.00	50.00
19 Jacques Lemaire	3.00	8.00
20 Jacques Laperriere	2.00	5.00
21 Jean Beliveau	10.00	20.00
22 Rogatien Vachon	4.00	10.00
23 Yvan Cournoyer	3.00	8.00
24 Henri Richard	6.00	12.00
25 Red Berenson	2.00	5.00
26 Frank St.Marseille	2.00	5.00
27 Glenn Hall	5.00	10.00
28 Gary Sabourin	2.00	5.00
29 Doug Mohns	2.00	5.00
30 Bobby Hull	20.00	40.00
31 Ray Cullen	2.00	5.00
32 Tony Esposito	10.00	20.00
33 Gary Dornhoefer	2.00	5.00
34 Ed Van Impe	2.00	5.00
35 Doug Favell	3.00	6.00
36 Carol Vadnais	2.00	5.00
37 Harry Howell	2.00	5.00
38 Bill Hicke	2.00	5.00
39 Rod Gilbert	3.00	6.00

40 Jean Ratelle	3.00	6.00
41 Walt Tkaczuk	3.00	6.00
42 Ed Giacomin	4.00	8.00
43 Brad Park	6.00	15.00
44 Bruce Gamble	3.00	6.00
45 Orland Kurtenbach	2.00	5.00
46 Ron Ellis	2.00	6.00
47 Dave Keon	5.00	10.00
48 Norm Ullman	3.00	6.00

1971-72 O-Pee-Chee

The 1971-72 O-Pee-Chee set contained 264 standard-size cards. The unopened wax packs consisted of eight cards plus a piece of bubble gum. Player photos were framed in an oval. Bilingual backs featured a short biography, year-by-year statistics and a cartoon-illustrated fact about the player. Rookie Cards in this set included Marcel Dionne, Ken Dryden, Butch Goring, Guy Lafleur, Reggie Leach, Richard Martin, and Rick MacLeish.

COMPLETE SET (264)	900.00	1,500.00
1 Paul Popiel	3.00	8.00
2 Pierre Bouchard RC	2.00	5.00
3 Don Awrey	1.50	4.00
4 Paul Curtis RC	1.50	4.00
5 Guy Trottier RC	1.50	4.00
6 Paul Shmyr RC	1.50	4.00
7 Fred Stanfield	1.50	4.00
8 Mike Robitaille RC	1.50	4.00
9 Vic Hadfield	2.00	5.00
10 Jim Harrison	1.50	4.00
11 Bill White	1.50	4.00
12 Andre Boudrias	1.50	4.00
13 Gary Sabourin	1.50	4.00
14 Arnie Brown	1.50	4.00
15 Yvan Cournoyer	3.00	8.00
16 Bryan Hextall	2.00	5.00
17 Gary Croteau	1.50	4.00
18 Gilles Villemure	2.00	5.00
19 Serge Bernier RC	2.00	5.00
20 Phil Esposito	8.00	20.00
21 Tom Reid	1.50	4.00
22 Doug Barrie RC	1.50	4.00
23 Eddie Joyal	1.50	4.00
24 Dunc Wilson RC	3.00	8.00
25 Pat Stapleton	2.00	5.00
26 Garry Unger	2.00	5.00
27 Al Smith	2.00	5.00
28 Bob Woytowich	1.50	4.00
29 Marc Tardif	2.00	5.00
30 Norm Ullman	3.00	8.00
31 Tom Williams	1.50	4.00
32 Ted Harris	1.50	4.00
33 Andre Lacroix	2.00	5.00
34 Mike Byers	1.50	4.00
35 Johnny Bucyk	3.00	8.00
36 Roger Crozier	2.00	5.00
37 Alex Delvecchio	4.00	10.00
38 Frank St.Marseille	1.50	4.00
39 Pit Martin	2.00	5.00
40 Brad Park	6.00	15.00
41 Greg Polis RC	1.50	4.00
42 Orland Kurtenbach	1.50	4.00
43 Jim McKenny RC	1.50	4.00
44 Bob Nevin	1.50	4.00
45 Ken Dryden RC	200.00	300.00
46 Carol Vadnais	2.00	5.00
47 Bill Flett	1.50	4.00
48 Jim Johnson	1.50	4.00
49 Al Hamilton	1.50	4.00
50 Bobby Hull	15.00	40.00
51 Chris Bordeleau RC	1.50	4.00
52 Tim Ecclestone	1.50	4.00
53 Rod Seiling	1.50	4.00
54 Gerry Cheevers	4.00	10.00
55 Bill Goldsworthy	2.00	5.00
56 Ron Schock	1.50	4.00
57 Jim Dorey	1.50	4.00
58 Wayne Maki	1.50	4.00
59 Terry Harper	1.50	4.00
60 Gilbert Perreault	10.00	25.00
61 Ernie Hicke RC	1.50	4.00
62 Wayne Hillman	1.50	4.00
63 Denis DeJordy	2.00	5.00
64 Ken Schinkel	1.50	4.00
65 Derek Sanderson	5.00	12.00
66 Barclay Plager	2.00	5.00
67 Paul Henderson	2.00	5.00
68 Jude Drouin	1.50	4.00
69 Keith Magnuson	2.00	5.00
70 Ron Harris	1.50	4.00
71 Jacques Lemaire	3.00	8.00
72 Doug Favell	2.00	5.00
73 Bert Marshall	1.50	4.00
74 Ted Irvine	1.50	4.00
75 Walt Tkaczuk	2.00	5.00
76 Bob Berry RC	3.00	8.00
77 Syl Apps RC	3.00	8.00
78 Tom Webster	2.00	5.00
79 Danny Grant	2.00	5.00
80 Dave Keon	3.00	8.00
81 Ernie Wakely	2.00	5.00
82 John McKenzie	2.00	5.00
83 Ron Stackhouse RC	1.50	4.00
84 Peter Mahovlich	2.00	5.00
85 Dennis Hull	2.00	5.00
86 Juha Widing RC	1.50	4.00
87 Gary Doak	1.50	4.00
88 Phil Goyette	1.50	4.00
89 Lew Morrison	1.50	4.00
90 Ab DeMarco RC	1.50	4.00
91 Red Berenson	2.00	5.00
92 Mike Pelyk	1.50	4.00
93 Gary Jarrett	1.50	4.00
94 Bob Pulford	2.00	5.00
95 Dan Johnson RC	1.50	4.00
96 Eddie Shack	3.00	8.00
97 Jean Ratelle	3.00	8.00
98 Jim Pappin	1.50	4.00
99 Roy Edwards	2.00	5.00
100 Bobby Orr	50.00	100.00
101 Ted Hampson	1.50	4.00
102 Mickey Redmond	3.00	8.00
103 Bob Plager	3.00	8.00
104 Barry Ashbee RC	2.00	5.00
105 Frank Mahovlich	4.00	10.00
106 Dick Redmond RC	1.50	4.00
107 Tracy Pratt	1.50	4.00
108 Ralph Backstrom	2.00	5.00
109 Murray Hall	1.50	4.00
110 Tony Esposito	15.00	40.00
111 Checklist Card	300.00	500.00
112 Jim Neilson	1.50	4.00
113 Ron Ellis	2.00	5.00
114 Bobby Clarke	30.00	60.00
115 Ken Hodge	2.00	5.00
116 Jim Roberts	2.00	5.00
117 Cesare Maniago	2.00	5.00
118 Jean Pronovost	2.00	5.00
119 Gary Bergman	1.50	4.00
120 Henri Richard	4.00	10.00
121 Ross Lonsberry	1.50	4.00
122 Pat Quinn	2.00	5.00
123 Rod Gilbert	3.00	8.00
124 Walt McKechnie	2.00	5.00
125 Stan Mikita	6.00	15.00
126 Ed Van Impe	1.50	4.00
127 Terry Crisp RC	4.00	10.00
128 Fred Barrett RC	1.50	4.00
129 Wayne Cashman	3.00	8.00
130 J.C. Tremblay	2.00	5.00
131 Bernie Parent	8.00	20.00
132 Bryan Watson	2.00	5.00
133 Marcel Dionne RC	75.00	150.00
134 Ab McDonald	2.00	5.00
135 Leon Rochefort	2.00	5.00
136 Serge Lajeunesse RC	2.00	5.00
137 Joe Daley	2.50	6.00
138 Brian Conacher	2.00	5.00
139 Bill Collins	2.00	5.00
140 Nick Libett	2.00	5.00
141 Bill Sutherland	2.00	5.00
142 Bill Hicke	2.00	5.00
143 Serge Savard	4.00	10.00
144 Jacques Laperriere	2.50	6.00
145 Guy Lapointe	2.50	6.00
146 Claude Larose UER	2.00	5.00
147 Rejean Houle	2.50	6.00
148 Guy Lafleur UER RC	100.00	200.00
149 Dale Hoganson RC	2.00	5.00
150 Al McDonough RC	2.00	5.00
151 Gilles Marotte	2.00	5.00
152 Butch Goring RC	4.00	10.00
153 Harry Howell	2.50	6.00
154 Real Lemieux	2.00	5.00
155 Gary Edwards RC	2.50	6.00
156 Rogatien Vachon	4.00	10.00
157 Mike Corrigan	2.00	5.00
158 Floyd Smith	2.00	5.00
159 Dave Dryden	2.50	6.00
160 Gerry Meehan	2.50	6.00
161 Richard Martin RC	8.00	20.00
162 Steve Atkinson RC	2.00	5.00
163 Ron Anderson	2.00	5.00
164 Dick Duff	2.50	6.00
165 Jim Watson	2.00	5.00
166 Don Luce RC	2.00	5.00
167 Larry Mickey	2.00	5.00
168 Larry Hillman	2.00	5.00
169 Ed Westfall	2.50	6.00
170 Dallas Smith	2.00	5.00
171 Mike Walton	2.00	5.00
172 Ed Johnston	2.50	6.00
173 Ted Green	2.50	6.00
174 Rick Smith	2.00	5.00
175 Reggie Leach RC	8.00	20.00
176 Don Marcotte	2.00	5.00
177 Bobby Sheehan RC	2.00	5.00
178 Wayne Carleton	2.00	5.00
179 Norm Ferguson	2.00	5.00
180 Don O'Donoghue RC	2.00	5.00
181 Gary Kurt RC	2.50	6.00
182 Joey Johnston RC	2.00	5.00
183 Stan Gilbertson RC	2.00	5.00
184 Craig Patrick RC	4.00	10.00
185 Gerry Pinder	2.00	5.00
186 Tim Horton	5.00	12.00
187 Darryl Edestrand RC	2.00	5.00
188 Keith McCreary	2.00	5.00
189 Val Fonteyne	2.00	5.00
190 S.Kannegiesser RC	2.00	5.00
191 Nick Harbaruk RC	2.00	5.00
192 Les Binkley	2.50	6.00
193 Darryl Sittler	15.00	40.00
194 Rick Ley	2.00	5.00
195 Jacques Plante	12.00	30.00
196 Bob Baun	2.50	6.00
197 Brian Glennie	2.00	5.00
198 Brian Spencer RC	4.00	10.00
199 Don Marshall	2.50	6.00
200 Denis Dupere RC	2.00	5.00
201 Bruce Gamble	2.50	6.00
202 Gary Dornhoefer	2.00	5.00
203 Bob Kelly RC	2.50	6.00
204 Jean-Guy Gendron	2.00	5.00
205 Brent Hughes	2.00	5.00
206 Simon Nolet	2.00	5.00
207 Rick MacLeish RC	8.00	20.00
208 Doug Jarrett	2.00	5.00
209 Cliff Koroll	2.00	5.00
210 Chico Maki	2.00	5.00
211 Danny O'Shea	2.00	5.00
212 Lou Angotti	2.00	5.00
213 Eric Nesterenko	2.50	6.00
214 Bryan Campbell	2.00	5.00
215 Bill Fairbairn RC	2.00	5.00
216 Bruce MacGregor	2.00	5.00
217 Pete Stemkowski	2.00	5.00
218 Bobby Rousseau	2.00	5.00
219 Dale Rolfe	2.00	5.00
220 Ed Giacomin	4.00	10.00
221 Glen Sather	2.50	6.00
222 Carl Brewer	2.50	6.00
223 George Morrison RC	2.00	5.00
224 Noel Picard	2.00	5.00
225 Peter McDuffe RC	2.50	6.00
226 Brit Selby	2.00	5.00
227 Jim Lorentz	2.00	5.00
228 Phil Roberto RC	2.00	5.00
229 Dave Balon	2.00	5.00
230 Barry Wilkins RC	2.00	5.00
231 Dennis Kearns RC	2.00	5.00
232 Jocelyn Guevremont RC	2.50	6.00
233 Rosaire Paiement	2.00	5.00
234 Dale Tallon	2.00	5.00
235 George Gardner	2.00	5.00
236 Ron Stewart	2.00	5.00
237 Wayne Connelly	2.00	5.00
238 Charlie Burns	2.00	5.00
239 Murray Oliver	2.00	5.00
240 Lou Nanne	2.50	6.00
241 Gump Worsley	4.00	10.00
242 Doug Mohns	2.00	5.00
243 Jean-Paul Parise	2.00	5.00
244 Dennis Hextall	2.50	6.00
245 Bobby Orr Double	20.00	50.00
246 Gilbert Perreault Calder	6.00	15.00
247 Phil Esposito Ross	4.00	10.00
248 Giacmn/Ville Vezina	2.50	6.00
249 Johnny Bucyk Byng	2.50	6.00
250 Ed Giacomin AS1	2.50	6.00
251 Bobby Orr AS1	20.00	50.00
252 J.C. Tremblay AS1	2.50	6.00
253 Phil Esposito AS1 UER	5.00	12.00
254 Ken Hodge AS1	2.50	6.00
255 Johnny Bucyk AS1	2.50	6.00
256 Jacques Plante AS2 UER	6.00	15.00
257 Brad Park AS2	2.50	6.00
258 Pat Stapleton AS2	2.50	6.00
259 Dave Keon AS2	3.00	8.00
260 Yvan Cournoyer AS2	2.50	6.00
261 Bobby Hull AS2	10.00	25.00
262 Gordie Howe Retires	50.00	100.00
263 Jean Beliveau Retires	30.00	60.00
264 Checklist Card	100.00	175.00

1971-72 O-Pee-Chee/Topps Booklets

This set consisted of 24 colorful comic booklets (eight pages in format) each measuring 2 1/2" by 3 1/2". The booklets were included as an insert with the regular issue of the same year and gave a mini-biography of the player. These booklets were also put out by Topps and were printed in the United States. They could be found in either French or English language versions. The booklets were numbered on the fronts with a complete set checklist on the backs. The prices below are valid as well for the 1971-72 Topps version of these booklets although the English version is probably a little easier to find.

COMPLETE SET (24)	50.00	125.00
1 Bobby Hull	6.00	15.00
2 Phil Esposito	3.00	6.00
3 Dale Tallon	1.25	3.00
4 Jacques Plante	4.00	8.00
5 Roger Crozier	1.25	3.00
6 Henri Richard	1.25	3.00
7 Ed Giacomin	2.50	5.00
8 Gilbert Perreault	3.00	6.00
9 Greg Polis	1.25	3.00
10 Bobby Clarke	5.00	10.00
11 Danny Grant	1.25	3.00
12 Alex Delvecchio	1.25	3.00
13 Tony Esposito	3.00	6.00
14 Garry Unger	1.25	3.00
15 Frank St.Marseille	1.25	3.00
16 Dave Keon	2.50	5.00
17 Ken Dryden	8.00	20.00
18 Rod Gilbert	1.25	3.00
19 Juha Widing	1.25	3.00
20 Orland Kurtenbach	1.25	3.00
21 Jude Drouin	1.25	3.00
22 Gary Smith	1.25	3.00
23 Gordie Howe	8.00	20.00
24 Bobby Orr	10.00	25.00

1971-72 O-Pee-Chee Posters

The 1971-72 O-Pee-Chee Posters set contained 24 color pictures measuring approximately 10" by 18". They were originally issued (as a separate issue) in folded form, two to a wax pack. Attached pairs are still sometimes found; these pairs are valued at 25 percent greater than the sum of the individual players included in the pair. The current scarcity of these posters suggests that they may have been a test issue. These posters are numbered and blank backed.

COMPLETE SET (24)	600.00	1,000.00
1 Bobby Orr	125.00	250.00
2 Bob Pulford	10.00	20.00
3 Dave Keon	15.00	30.00
4 Yvan Cournoyer	15.00	30.00
5 Dale Tallon	10.00	20.00
6 Richard Martin	7.50	15.00
7 Rod Gilbert	15.00	30.00
8 Tony Esposito	20.00	40.00
9 Bobby Hull	25.00	50.00
10 Red Berenson	7.50	15.00
11 Norm Ullman	8.00	20.00
12 Orland Kurtenbach	7.50	15.00
13 Guy Lafleur	50.00	100.00
14 Gilbert Perreault	20.00	40.00
15 Jacques Plante	25.00	50.00
16 Bruce Gamble	10.00	25.00
17 Walt McKechnie	7.50	15.00
18 Tim Horton	25.00	50.00
19 Jean Ratelle	15.00	30.00
20 Garry Unger	7.50	15.00
21 Phil Esposito	25.00	50.00
22 Ken Dryden	75.00	150.00
23 Gump Worsley	15.00	30.00
24 Montreal Canadiens	20.00	40.00

1972-73 O-Pee-Chee

The 1972-73 O-Pee-Chee set featured 340 standard-size cards that were printed in Canada. The set featured players from the expansion New York Islanders and Atlanta Flames. Unopened packs consisted of eight cards plus a bubble-gum piece. Tan borders on the front included the team name on the left-hand side. Bilingual backs featured a year-by-year record of the player's career, a short biography and a cartoon-illustrated fact about the player. There were a number of In-Action (IA) cards of popular players distributed throughout the set. Card number 208 was never issued. The last series (290-341), which was printed in lesser quantities, featured players from the newly formed World Hockey Association. Based upon uncut sheets that are known and observed, there were apparently 22 double-printed cards in the first series (1-110) and 22 known double-printed cards in the second series (111-209). These cards were identified by DP in the checklist below.

COMPLETE SET (340)	900.00	1,500.00
1 Johnny Bucyk DP	3.00	8.00
2 Rene Robert RC	2.00	5.00
3 Gary Croteau	1.00	2.50
4 Pat Stapleton	1.00	2.50
5 Ron Harris	1.00	2.50
6 Checklist 1	20.00	50.00
7 Playoff Game 1	1.00	2.50
8 Marcel Dionne	10.00	25.00
9 Bob Berry	1.00	2.50
10 Lou Nanne	1.00	2.50
11 Marc Tardif	1.00	2.50
12 Jean Ratelle	1.50	4.00
13 Craig Cameron RC	1.00	2.50
14 Bobby Clarke	12.00	30.00
15 Jim Rutherford RC	4.00	10.00
16 Andre Dupont RC	1.50	4.00
17 Mike Pelyk	1.00	2.50
18 Dunc Wilson	1.00	2.50
19 Checklist 2	20.00	50.00
20 Playoff Game 2	1.00	2.50
21 Dallas Smith	1.00	2.50
22 Gerry Meehan	1.00	2.50
23 Rick Smith UER	1.00	2.50
24 Pit Martin	1.00	2.50
25 Keith McCreary	1.00	2.50
26 Alex Delvecchio	1.50	4.00
27 Gilles Marotte	1.00	2.50
28 Gump Worsley	1.50	4.00
29 Yvan Cournoyer	1.50	4.00
30 Playoff Game 3	1.00	2.50
31 Vic Hadfield	1.00	2.50
32 Tom Miller RC	1.00	2.50
33 Ed Van Impe	1.00	2.50
34 Greg Polis	1.00	2.50
35 Barclay Plager	1.00	2.50
36 Ron Ellis	1.00	2.50
37 Jocelyn Guevremont	1.00	2.50
38 Playoff Game 4	1.00	2.50
39 Carol Vadnais	1.00	2.50
40 Steve Atkinson	1.00	2.50
41 Ivan Boldirev RC	2.50	6.00
42 Jim Pappin	1.00	2.50
43 Phil Myre RC	3.00	8.00
44 Yvan Cournoyer IA	1.25	3.00
45 Nick Libett	1.00	2.50
46 Juha Widing	1.00	2.50
47 Jude Drouin	1.00	2.50
48A Jean Ratelle IA Def	1.50	4.00
48B Jean Ratelle IA Cent	1.25	3.00
49 Ken Hodge	1.00	2.50
50 Roger Crozier	1.00	2.50
51 Reggie Leach	1.50	4.00
52 Dennis Hull	1.00	2.50
53 Larry Hale RC	1.00	2.50
54 Playoff Game 5	1.00	2.50
55 Tim Ecclestone	1.00	2.50
56 Butch Goring	1.25	3.00
57 Danny Grant	1.00	2.50
58 Bobby Orr IA	15.00	40.00
59 Guy Lafleur	25.00	60.00
60 Jim Neilson	1.00	2.50
61 Brian Spencer	1.00	2.50
62 Joe Watson	1.00	2.50
63 Playoff Game 6	1.00	2.50

64 Jean Pronovost 1.00 2.50
65 Frank St.Marseille 1.00 2.50
66 Bob Baun 1.00 2.50
67 Paul Popiel 1.00 2.50
68 Wayne Cashman 1.00 2.50
69 Tracy Pratt 1.00 2.50
70 Stan Gilbertson 1.00 2.50
71 Keith Magnuson 1.00 2.50
72 Ernie Hicke 1.00 2.50
73 Gary Doak 1.00 2.50
74 Mike Corrigan 1.00 2.50
75 Doug Mohns 1.00 2.50
76 Phil Esposito IA 3.00 8.00
77 Jacques Lemaire 1.50 4.00
78 Pete Stemkowski 1.00 2.50
79 Bill Mikkelson RC 1.00 2.50
80 Rick Foley RC 1.00 2.50
81 Ron Schock 1.00 2.50
82 Phil Roberto 1.00 2.50
83 Jim McKenny 1.00 2.50
84 Wayne Maki 1.00 2.50
85A Brad Park IA Cent 3.00 8.00
85B Brad Park IA Def 2.00 5.00
86 Guy Lapointe 1.25 3.00
87 Bill Fairbairn 1.00 2.50
88 Terry Crisp 1.00 2.50
89 Doug Favell 1.00 2.50
90 Bryan Watson 1.00 2.50
91 Gary Sabourin 1.00 2.50
92 Jacques Plante 8.00 20.00
93 Andre Boudrias 1.00 2.50
94 Mike Walton 1.00 2.50
95 Don Luce 1.00 2.50
96 Joey Johnston 1.00 2.50
97 Doug Jarrett 1.00 2.50
98 Bill MacMillan RC 1.00 2.50
99 Mickey Redmond 1.25 3.00
100 Rogatien Vachon UER 1.50 4.00
101 Barry Gibbs RC 1.00 2.50
102 Frank Mahovlich DP 1.50 4.00
103 Bruce MacGregor 1.00 2.50
104 Ed Westfall 1.00 2.50
105 Rick MacLeish 2.00 5.00
106 Nick Harbaruk 1.00 2.50
107 Jack Egers RC 1.00 2.50
108 Dave Keon 1.50 4.00
109 Barry Wilkins 1.00 2.50
110 Walt Tkaczuk 1.00 2.50
111 Phil Esposito 6.00 15.00
112 Gilles Meloche RC 3.00 8.00
113 Gary Edwards 1.25 3.00
114 Brad Park 4.00 10.00
115 Syl Apps DP 1.25 3.00
116 Jim Lorentz 1.25 3.00
117 Gary Smith 1.25 3.00
118 Ted Harris 1.25 3.00
119 Gerry Desjardins DP .60 1.50
120 Garry Unger 1.25 3.00
121 Dale Tallon 1.25 3.00
122 Bill Plager RC 1.50 4.00
123 Red Berenson DP .60 1.50
124 Peter Mahovlich DP 1.25 3.00
125 Simon Nolet 1.25 3.00
126 Paul Henderson 1.25 3.00
127 Hart Trophy Winners 1.25 3.00
128 Frank Mahovlich IA 1.25 3.00
129 Bobby Orr 40.00 80.00
130 Bert Marshall 1.25 3.00
131 Ralph Backstrom 1.25 3.00
132 Gilles Villemure 1.25 3.00
133 Dave Burrows RC 1.25 3.00
134 Calder Trophy Winners 1.25 3.00
135 Dallas Smith IA 1.25 3.00
136 Gilbert Perreault DP 5.00 12.00
137 Tony Esposito DP 8.00 20.00
138 Cesare Maniago DP .60 1.50
139 Gerry Hart RC 1.25 3.00
140 Jacques Caron RC 1.50 4.00
141 Orland Kurtenbach 1.25 3.00
142 Norris Trophy Winners 1.25 3.00
143 Lew Morrison 1.25 3.00
144 Arnie Brown 1.25 3.00
145 Ken Dryden DP 20.00 40.00
146 Gary Dornhoefer 1.25 3.00
147 Norm Ullman 2.00 5.00
148 Art Ross Trophy 1.25 3.00
149 Orland Kurtenbach IA 1.25 3.00
150 Fred Stanfield 1.25 3.00
151 Dick Redmond DP .60 1.50
152 Serge Bernier 1.25 3.00
153 Rod Gilbert 2.00 5.00
154 Duane Rupp 1.25 3.00
155 Vezina Trophy Winners 1.25 3.00
156 Stan Mikita IA 2.00 5.00
157 Richard Martin DP 2.00 5.00
158 Bill White DP .60 1.50
159 Bill Goldsworthy DP .60 1.50
160 Jack Lynch RC 1.25 3.00
161 Bob Plager DP .60 1.50
162 Dave Balon UER 1.25 3.00
163 Noel Price 1.25 3.00
164 Gary Bergman DP .60 1.50
165 Pierre Bouchard 1.25 3.00
166 Ross Lonsberry 1.25 3.00
167 Denis Dupere 1.25 3.00
168 Byng Trophy Winners DP .60 1.50
169 Ken Hodge 1.25 3.00
170 Don Awrey DP .60 1.50
171 Marshall Johnston DP RC .60 1.50
172 Terry Harper 1.25 3.00
173 Ed Giacomin 2.00 5.00
174 Bryan Hextall DP .60 1.50
175 Conn Smythe Trophy Winners 1.25 3.00
176 Larry Hillman 1.25 3.00
177 Stan Mikita DP 3.00 8.00
178 Charlie Burns 1.25 3.00
179 Brian Marchinko 1.25 3.00
180 Noel Picard DP .60 1.50
181 Bobby Schmautz RC 1.50 4.00
182 Richard Martin IA UER 1.50 4.00
183 Pat Quinn 1.25 3.00
184 Denis DeJordy UER 1.25 3.00
185 Serge Savard 2.00 5.00
186 Eddie Shack 1.50 4.00
187 Bill Flett 1.25 3.00
188 Darryl Sittler 8.00 20.00
189 Gump Worsley IA 1.50 4.00
190 Checklist 2 25.00 60.00
191 Garnet Bailey DP .60 1.50
192 Walt McKechnie 1.25 3.00
193 Harry Howell 1.25 3.00
194 Rod Seiling 1.25 3.00
195 Darryl Edestrand 1.25 3.00
196 Tony Esposito IA 3.00 8.00
197 Tim Horton 3.00 8.00
198 Chico Maki DP .60 1.50
199 Jean-Paul Parise 1.25 3.00
200 Germaine Gagnon UER RC 1.25 3.00
201 Danny O'Shea 1.25 3.00
202 Richard Lemieux RC 1.25 3.00
203 Dan Bouchard RC 4.00 10.00
204 Leon Rochefort 1.25 3.00
205 Jacques Laperriere 1.50 4.00
206 Barry Ashbee 1.25 3.00
207 Garry Monahan 1.25 3.00
209 Dave Keon IA 2.00 5.00
210 Rejean Houle 2.00 5.00
211 Dave Hudson RC 1.50 4.00
212 Ted Irvine 1.50 4.00
213 Don Saleski RC 2.00 5.00
214 Lowell MacDonald 1.50 4.00
215 Mike Murphy RC 2.50 6.00
216 Brian Glennie 1.50 4.00
217 Bobby Lalonde RC 1.50 4.00
218 Bob Leiter 1.50 4.00
219 Don Marcotte 1.50 4.00
220 Jim Schoenfeld RC 5.00 12.00
221 Craig Patrick 1.50 4.00
222 Cliff Koroll 1.50 4.00
223 Guy Charron RC 2.00 5.00
224 Jim Peters 1.50 4.00
225 Dennis Hextall 1.50 4.00
226 Tony Esposito AS1 6.00 15.00
227 Orr/Park AS1 15.00 40.00
228 Bobby Hull AS1 12.00 30.00
229 Rod Gilbert AS1 1.50 4.00
230 Phil Esposito AS1 4.00 10.00
231 Claude Larose UER 1.50 4.00
232 Jim Mair RC 1.50 4.00
233 Bobby Rousseau 1.50 4.00
234 Brent Hughes 1.50 4.00
235 Al McDonough 1.50 4.00
236 Chris Evans RC 1.50 4.00
237 Pierre Jarry RC 1.50 4.00
238 Don Tannahill RC 1.50 4.00
239 Rey Comeau RC 1.50 4.00
240 Gregg Sheppard UER RC 1.50 4.00
241 Dave Dryden 1.50 4.00
242 Ted McAneeley RC 1.50 4.00
243 Lou Angotti 1.50 4.00
244 Len Fontaine RC 1.50 4.00
245 Bill Lesuk RC 1.50 4.00
246 Fred Harvey RC 1.50 4.00
247 Ken Dryden AS2 12.00 30.00
248 Bill White AS2 1.50 4.00
249 Pat Stapleton AS2 1.50 4.00
250 Ratel/Cour/Hadfld LL 2.50 6.00
251 Henri Richard 2.50 6.00
252 Bryan Lefley RC 1.50 4.00
253 Stanley Cup Trophy 6.00 15.00
254 Steve Vickers RC 3.00 8.00
255 Wayne Hillman 1.50 4.00
256 Ken Schinkel UER 1.50 4.00
257 Kevin O'Shea RC 1.50 4.00
258 Ron Low RC 6.00 15.00
259 Don Lever RC 10.00 25.00
260 Randy Manery RC 1.50 4.00
261 Ed Johnston 2.00 5.00
262 Craig Ramsay RC 3.00 8.00
263 Pete Laframboise RC 1.50 4.00
264 Dan Maloney RC 2.50 6.00
265 Bill Collins 1.50 4.00
266 Paul Curtis 1.50 4.00
267 Bob Nevin 1.50 4.00
268 Watson/Magnuson LL 2.00 5.00
269 Jim Roberts 1.50 4.00
270 Brian Lavender RC 1.50 4.00
271 Dale Rolfe 1.50 4.00
272 Espo/Hadf/B.Hull LL 8.00 20.00
273 Michel Belhumeur RC 3.00 8.00
274 Eddie Shack 2.50 6.00
275 Wayne Stephenson RC UER 4.00 10.00
276 Bruins SC Winner 6.00 15.00
277 Rick Kehoe RC 3.00 8.00
278 Gerry O'Flaherty RC 1.50 4.00
279 Jacques Richard RC 2.00 5.00
280 Espo/Orr/Ratelle LL 10.00 25.00
281 Nick Beverley RC 3.00 8.00
282 Larry Carriere RC 1.50 4.00
283 Orr/Espo/Ratelle LL 10.00 25.00
284 Rick Smith IA 2.00 5.00
285 Jerry Korab RC 2.50 6.00
286 Espo/Villem/Worsley LL 5.00 12.00
287 Ron Stackhouse 1.50 4.00
288 Barry Long RC 2.00 5.00
289 Dean Prentice 2.00 5.00
290 Norm Beaudin 3.00 8.00
291 Mike Amodeo RC 3.00 8.00
292 Jim Harrison 3.00 8.00
293 J.C. Tremblay 3.00 8.00
294 Murray Hall 3.00 8.00
295 Bart Crashley 3.00 8.00
296 Wayne Connelly 3.00 8.00
297 Bobby Sheehan 3.00 8.00
298 Ron Anderson 3.00 8.00
299 Chris Bordeleau 3.00 8.00
300 Les Binkley 3.00 8.00
301 Ron Walters 3.00 8.00
302 Jean-Guy Gendron 3.00 8.00
303 Gord Labossiere 3.00 8.00
304 Gerry Odrowski 3.00 8.00
305 Mike McMahon 3.00 8.00
306 Gary Kurt 3.00 8.00
307 Larry Cahan 3.00 8.00
308 Wally Boyer 3.00 8.00
309 Bob Charlebois RC 3.00 8.00
310 Bob Falkenberg 3.00 8.00
311 Jean Payette RC 3.00 8.00
312 Ted Taylor 3.00 8.00
313 Joe Szura 3.00 8.00
314 George Morrison 3.00 8.00
315 Wayne Rivers 3.00 8.00
316 Reg Fleming 4.00 10.00
317 Larry Hornung RC 3.00 8.00
318 Ron Climie RC 3.00 8.00
319 Val Fonteyne 3.00 8.00
320 Michel Archambault RC 3.00 8.00
321 Ab McDonald 3.00 8.00
322 Bob Leduc RC 3.00 8.00
323 Bob Wall 3.00 8.00
324 Alain Caron RC 3.00 8.00
325 Bob Woytowich 3.00 8.00
326 Guy Trottier 3.00 8.00
327 Bill Hicke 3.00 8.00
328 Guy Dufour RC 3.00 8.00
329 Wayne Rutledge RC 4.00 10.00
330 Gary Veneruzzo 3.00 8.00
331 Fred Speck RC 3.00 8.00
332 Ron Ward RC 3.00 8.00
333 Rosaire Paiement 3.00 8.00
334A Checklist 3 ERR 40.00 80.00
334B Checklist 3 COR 25.00 60.00
335 Michel Parizeau RC 3.00 8.00
336 Bobby Hull 25.00 60.00
337 Wayne Carleton 3.00 8.00
338 John McKenzie 4.00 10.00
339 Jim Dorey 3.00 8.00
340 Gerry Cheevers 12.00 30.00
341 Gerry Pinder 8.00 20.00

1972-73 O-Pee-Chee Player Crests

This set consisted of 22 full-color cardboard stickers measuring 2 1/2" by 3 1/2". The set was issued as an insert with the regular issue of the same year in with the first series wax packs. Cards were numbered on the front and have a blank adhesive back. Although the cards were designed so that the crest could be popped out, this is strongly discouraged. These stickers were printed in Canada.

COMPLETE SET (22) 100.00 200.00
1 Pat Quinn 3.00 10.00
2 Phil Esposito 8.00 20.00
3 Bobby Orr 30.00 80.00
4 Richard Martin 2.50 6.00
5 Stan Mikita 4.00 10.00
6 Bill White 2.50 6.00
7 Red Berenson 2.50 6.00
8 Gary Bergman 2.50 6.00
9 Gary Edwards 2.50 6.00
10 Bill Goldsworthy 2.50 6.00
11 Jacques Laperriere 2.50 6.00
12 Ken Dryden 20.00 40.00
13 Ed Westfall 2.50 6.00
14 Walt Tkaczuk 2.50 6.00
15 Brad Park 5.00 12.00
16 Doug Favell 5.00 12.00
17 Eddie Shack 5.00 10.00
18 Jacques Caron 2.50 6.00
19 Paul Henderson 4.00 10.00
20 Jim Harrison 2.50 6.00
21 Dale Tallon 2.50 6.00
22 Orland Kurtenbach 2.50 6.00

1972-73 O-Pee-Chee Team Canada

This attractive set consisted of 28 unnumbered color cards measuring 2 1/2" by 3 1/2". The 28 players are those who represented Team Canada against Russia in the 1972 Summit Series. Only the players' heads were shown surrounded by a border of maple leaves with a Canadian and Russian flag in each corner. The card back provided a summary of that player's performance in the eight-game series. The set was issued as an insert with the second series of the 1972-73 O-Pee-Chee regular issue. Backs were written in both French and English. The cards were printed in Canada.

COMPLETE SET (28) 150.00 300.00
1 Don Awrey 3.00 8.00
2 Red Berenson 3.00 8.00
3 Gary Bergman 3.00 8.00
4 Wayne Cashman 4.00 10.00
5 Bobby Clarke 12.50 25.00
6 Yvan Cournoyer 7.50 15.00
7 Ken Dryden 25.00 50.00
8 Ron Ellis 5.00 12.00
9 Phil Esposito 12.50 25.00
10 Tony Esposito 15.00 30.00
11 Rod Gilbert 5.00 12.00
12 Bill Goldsworthy 3.00 8.00
13 Vic Hadfield 3.00 8.00
14 Paul Henderson 15.00 30.00
15 Dennis Hull 3.00 8.00
16 Guy Lapointe 3.00 8.00
17 Frank Mahovlich 7.50 15.00
18 Pete Mahovlich 3.00 8.00
19 Stan Mikita 10.00 20.00
20 Jean-Paul Parise 3.00 8.00
21 Brad Park 5.00 12.00
22 Gilbert Perreault 3.00 8.00
23 Jean Ratelle 5.00 12.00
24 Mickey Redmond 5.00 12.00
25 Serge Savard 4.00 10.00
26 Rod Seiling 3.00 8.00
27 Pat Stapleton 3.00 8.00
28 Bill White 3.00 8.00

1972-73 O-Pee-Chee Team Logos

This set of 30 team logo pushouts included logos for the 15 NHL established teams as well as the two new NHL teams, the 12 WHA teams, and the WHA League emblem. The cards were die-cut and adhesive backed. They were inserted in with the third series of the 1972-73 O-Pee-Chee wax packs. The expansion and WHA emblems were more difficult to find and are listed as SP in the checklist below. These inserts were standard size, 2 1/2" by 3 1/2". These team logos cards were distinguished by their lack of instructions on the front.

ONE PER SER. 3 OPC PACK
1 NHL Logo 10.00 25.00
2 Atlanta Flames SP 100.00 200.00
3 Boston Bruins 5.00 12.00
4 Buffalo Sabres 5.00 12.00
5 California Seals 10.00 25.00
6 Chicago Blackhawks 5.00 12.00
7 Detroit Red Wings 5.00 12.00
8 Los Angeles Kings 5.00 12.00
9 Minnesota North Stars 6.00 15.00
10 Montreal Canadiens 5.00 12.00
11 New York Islanders SP 60.00 120.00
12 New York Rangers 6.00 15.00
13 Philadelphia Flyers 5.00 12.00
14 Pittsburgh Penguins 6.00 15.00
15 St. Louis Blues 5.00 12.00
16 Toronto Maple Leafs 5.00 12.00
17 Vancouver Canucks 8.00 20.00
18 WHA Logo SP 30.00 60.00
19 Chicago Cougars SP 30.00 60.00
20 Cleveland Crusaders SP 40.00 80.00
21 Edmonton Oilers SP 40.00 80.00
22 Houston Aeros SP 40.00 80.00
23 Los Angeles Sharks SP 30.00 60.00
24 Minnesota Fighting Saints SP 50.00 100.00
25 New England Whalers SP 40.00 80.00
26 New York Raiders SP 30.00 60.00
27 Ottawa Nationals SP 40.00 80.00
28 Phila. Blazers SP 40.00 80.00
29 Quebec Nordiques SP 30.00 60.00
30 Winnipeg Jets SP 50.00 100.00

1973-74 O-Pee-Chee

The 1973-74 O-Pee-Chee NHL set featured 264 standard-size cards. The cards measured 2 1/2" by 3 1/2". The border color on the fronts differed from the Topps set. Cards 1-198 had a red border and cards 199-264 had a green border. Topps cards were a mix of blue and green. Bilingual backs contained 1972-73 and career statistics, a short biography and a cartoon-illustrated fact about the player. Team cards (92-107) contained team and player records on the back. The cards were printed in Canada on both cream or gray card stock. Rookie Cards in this set included Bill Barber, Terry O'Reilly, Larry Robinson, Dave Schultz, and Billy Smith.

COMPLETE SET (264) 300.00 500.00
1 Alex Delvecchio 2.50 5.00
2 Gilles Meloche 1.25 3.00
3 Phil Roberto 1.25 3.00
4 Orland Kurtenbach 1.00 2.50
5 Gilles Marotte 1.00 2.50
6 Stan Mikita 4.00 8.00
7 Paul Henderson 1.25 3.00
8 Gregg Sheppard 1.00 2.50
9 Rod Seiling 1.00 2.50
10 Red Berenson 1.25 3.00
11 Jean Pronovost 1.25 3.00
12 Dick Redmond 1.00 2.50
13 Keith McCreary 1.00 2.50
14 Bryan Watson 1.00 2.50
15 Garry Unger 1.25 3.00
16 Neil Komadoski RC 1.00 2.50

17 Marcel Dionne 6.00 15.00
18 Ernie Hicke 1.00 2.50
19 Andre Boudrias 1.00 2.50
20 Bill Flett 1.00 2.50
21 Marshall Johnston 1.00 2.50
22 Gerry Meehan 1.00 2.50
23 Ed Johnston 1.25 3.00
24 Serge Savard 2.50 5.00
25 Walt Tkaczuk 1.25 3.00
26 Ken Hodge 1.25 3.00
27 Norm Ullman 2.50 5.00
28 Cliff Koroll 1.00 2.50
29 Rey Comeau 1.00 2.50
30 Bobby Orr 25.00 50.00
31 Wayne Stephenson 1.25 3.00
32 Dan Maloney 1.25 3.00
33 Henry Boucha RC 2.50 5.00
34 Gerry Hart 1.00 2.50
35 Bobby Schmautz 1.00 2.50
36 Ross Lonsberry 1.00 2.50
37 Ted McAneeley 1.00 2.50
38 Don Luce 1.00 2.50
39 Jim McKenny 1.00 2.50
40 Jacques Laperriere 1.25 3.00
41 Bill Fairbairn 1.00 2.50
42 Craig Cameron 1.00 2.50
43 Bryan Hextall 1.00 2.50
44 Chuck Lefley RC 1.00 2.50
45 Dan Bouchard 1.25 3.00
46 Jean-Paul Parise 1.00 2.50
47 Barclay Plager 1.25 3.00
48 Mike Corrigan 1.00 2.50
49 Nick Libett 1.00 2.50
50 Bobby Clarke 10.00 20.00
51 Bert Marshall 1.00 2.50
52 Craig Patrick 1.25 3.00
53 Richard Lemieux 1.00 2.50
54 Tracy Pratt 1.00 2.50
55 Ron Ellis 1.25 3.00
56 Jacques Lemaire 2.50 5.00
57 Steve Vickers 1.25 3.00
58 Carol Vadnais 1.00 2.50
59 Jim Rutherford 1.25 3.00
60 Rick Kehoe 1.25 3.00
61 Pat Quinn 1.25 3.00
62 Bill Goldsworthy 1.25 3.00
63 Dave Dryden 1.25 3.00
64 Rogatien Vachon 2.50 6.00
65 Gary Bergman 1.00 2.50
66 Bernie Parent 6.00 10.00
67 Ed Westfall 1.25 3.00
68 Ivan Boldirev 1.25 3.00
69 Don Tannahill 1.00 2.50
70 Gilbert Perreault 7.00 12.00
71 Mike Pelyk 1.00 2.50
72 Guy Lafleur 15.00 25.00
73 Pit Martin 1.25 3.00
74 Gilles Gilbert RC 5.00 8.00
75 Jim Lorentz 1.00 2.50
76 Syl Apps 1.25 3.00
77 Phil Myre 1.25 3.00
78 Bill White 1.00 2.50
79 Jack Egers 1.00 2.50
80 Terry Harper 1.00 2.50
81 Bill Barber RC 12.00 20.00
82 Roy Edwards 1.25 3.00
83 Brian Spencer 1.25 3.00
84 Reggie Leach 1.25 3.00
85 Wayne Cashman 1.25 3.00
86 Jim Schoenfeld 2.50 5.00
87 Henri Richard 2.50 5.00
88 Dennis O'Brien RC 1.00 2.50
89 Al McDonough 1.00 2.50
90 Tony Esposito 6.00 12.00
91 Joe Watson 1.00 2.50
92 Flames Team 2.50 5.00
93 Bruins Team 2.50 5.00
94 Sabres Team 2.50 5.00
95 Golden Seals Team 2.50 5.00
96 Blackhawks Team 2.50 5.00
97 Red Wings Team 2.50 5.00
98 Kings Team 2.50 5.00
99 North Stars Team 2.50 5.00
100 Canadiens Team 4.00 8.00
101 Islanders Team 2.50 5.00
102 Rangers Team 2.50 5.00
103 Flyers Team 2.50 5.00
104 Penguins Team 2.50 5.00
105 Blues Team 2.50 5.00
106 Maple Leafs Team 4.00 8.00
107 Canucks Team 2.50 5.00
108 Vic Hadfield 1.25 3.00
109 Tom Reid 1.00 2.50
110 Hilliard Graves RC 1.00 2.50
111 Don Lever 1.25 3.00
112 Jim Pappin 1.00 2.50
113 Andre Dupont 1.00 2.50
114 Guy Lapointe 1.25 3.00
115 Dennis Hextall 1.00 2.50
116 Checklist 1 20.00 40.00
117 Bob Leiter 1.00 2.50
118 Ab DeMarco 1.00 2.50
119 Gilles Villemure 1.25 3.00
120 Phil Esposito 5.00 10.00
121 Mike Robitaille 1.00 2.50
122 Real Lemieux 1.00 2.50
123 Jim Neilson 1.00 2.50
124 Steve Durbano RC 1.25 3.00
125 Jude Drouin 1.00 2.50
126 Gary Smith 1.25 3.00
127 Cesare Maniago 1.25 3.00
128 Lowell MacDonald 1.00 2.50
129 Checklist 2 20.00 40.00
130 Billy Harris RC 1.25 3.00
131 Randy Manery 1.00 2.50
132 Darryl Sittler 7.50 15.00
133 P.Espo/MacLeish LL 2.50 5.00
134 P.Espo/B.Clarke LL 2.50 5.00
135 P.Espo/B.Clarke LL 2.50 5.00
136 K.Dryden/T.Espo LL 6.00 10.00
137 Schultz/Schnfeld LL 2.50 5.00
138 P.Espo/MacLeish LL 2.50 5.00
139 Rene Robert 1.25 3.00
140 Dave Burrows 1.00 2.50
141 Jean Ratelle 2.50 5.00
142 Billy Smith RC 25.00 50.00
143 Jocelyn Guevremont 1.00 2.50
144 Tim Ecclestone 1.00 2.50
145 Frank Mahovlich 2.50 5.00
146 Rick MacLeish 2.50 5.00
147 Johnny Bucyk 2.50 5.00
148 Bob Plager 1.25 3.00
149 Curt Bennett RC 1.00 2.50
150 Dave Keon 2.50 5.00
151 Keith Magnuson 1.25 3.00
152 Walt McKechnie 1.00 2.50
153 Roger Crozier 1.25 3.00
154 Ted Harris 1.00 2.50
155 Butch Goring 1.25 3.00
156 Rod Gilbert 2.50 5.00
157 Yvan Cournoyer 2.50 5.00
158 Doug Favell 1.25 3.00
159 Juha Widing 1.00 2.50
160 Ed Giacomin 2.50 5.00
161 Germaine Gagnon UER 1.00 2.50
162 Dennis Kearns 1.00 2.50
163 Bill Collins 1.00 2.50
164 Peter Mahovlich 1.25 3.00
165 Brad Park 3.00 6.00
166 Dave Schultz RC 7.50 15.00
167 Dallas Smith 1.00 2.50
168 Gary Sabourin 1.00 2.50
169 Jacques Richard 1.00 2.50
170 Brian Glennie 1.00 2.50
171 Dennis Hull 1.25 3.00
172 Joey Johnston 1.00 2.50
173 Richard Martin 2.50 5.00
174 Barry Gibbs 1.00 2.50
175 Bob Berry 1.00 2.50
176 Greg Polis 1.00 2.50
177 Dale Rolfe 1.00 2.50
178 Gerry Desjardins 1.25 3.00
179 Bobby Lalonde 1.00 2.50
180 Mickey Redmond 1.25 3.00
181 Jim Roberts 1.00 2.50
182 Gary Dornhoefer 1.25 3.00
183 Derek Sanderson 2.50 5.00
184 Brent Hughes 1.00 2.50
185 Larry Romanchych RC 1.00 2.50
186 Pierre Jarry 1.00 2.50
187 Doug Jarrett 1.00 2.50
188 Bob Stewart RC 1.25 3.00
189 Tim Horton 4.00 8.00
190 Fred Harvey 1.00 2.50
191 Series A/Cand/Sabr .75 2.00
192 Series B/Flyrs/Stars .75 2.00
193 Series C/Hwks/Blues .75 2.00
194 Series D/Rngr/Bruins .75 2.00
195 Series E/Cndn/Flyr .75 2.00
196 Series F/Blckh/Rngr .75 2.00
197 Series G/Cndn/Hawk .75 2.00
198 Canadiens Champs 2.50 5.00
199 Gary Edwards 1.25 3.00
200 Ron Schock 1.00 2.50
201 Bruce MacGregor 1.00 2.50
202 Bob Nystrom RC 3.00 6.00
203 Jerry Korab 1.00 2.50
204 Thommie Bergman RC 1.00 2.50
205 Bill Lesuk 1.00 2.50
206 Ed Van Impe 1.00 2.50
207 Doug Roberts 1.00 2.50
208 Chris Evans 1.00 2.50
209 Lynn Powis RC 1.00 2.50
210 Denis Dupere 1.00 2.50
211 Dale Tallon 1.00 2.50
212 Stan Gilbertson 1.00 2.50
213 Craig Ramsay 1.25 3.00
214 Danny Grant 1.25 3.00
215 Doug Volmar RC 1.00 2.50
216 Darryl Edestrand 1.00 2.50
217 Pete Stemkowski 1.00 2.50
218 Lorne Henning RC 1.25 3.00
219 Bryan McSheffrey RC 1.00 2.50
220 Guy Charron 1.25 3.00
221 Wayne Thomas RC 2.50 5.00
222 Simon Nolet 1.00 2.50
223 Fred O'Donnell RC 1.00 2.50
224 Lou Angotti 1.00 2.50
225 Arnie Brown 1.00 2.50
226 Garry Monahan 1.00 2.50
227 Chico Maki 1.00 2.50
228 Gary Croteau 1.00 2.50
229 Paul Terbenche 1.00 2.50
230 Gump Worsley 3.00 6.00
231 Jim Peters 1.00 2.50
232 Jack Lynch 1.00 2.50
233 Bobby Rousseau 1.00 2.50
234 Dave Hudson 1.00 2.50
235 Gregg Boddy RC 1.00 2.50
236 Ron Stackhouse 1.00 2.50
237 Larry Robinson RC 40.00 80.00
238 Bobby Taylor RC 2.50 5.00
239 Nick Beverley 1.00 2.50
240 Don Awrey 1.00 2.50
241 Doug Mohns 1.00 2.50
242 Eddie Shack 2.50 5.00
243 Phil Russell RC 2.50 5.00
244 Pete Laframboise 1.00 2.50
245 Steve Atkinson 1.00 2.50
246 Lou Nanne 1.25 3.00
247 Yvon Labre RC 1.25 3.00
248 Ted Irvine 1.00 2.50
249 Tom Miller 1.00 2.50
250 Gerry O'Flaherty 1.00 2.50
251 Larry Johnston RC 1.00 2.50
252 Michel Plasse RC 2.50 5.00
253 Bob Kelly 1.00 2.50
254 Terry O'Reilly RC 10.00 20.00
255 Pierre Plante RC 1.00 2.50
256 Noel Price 1.00 2.50
257 Dunc Wilson 1.25 3.00
258 J.P. Bordeleau RC 1.25 3.00
259 Terry Murray RC 1.25 3.00
260 Larry Carriere 1.00 2.50
261 Pierre Bouchard 1.25 3.00
262 Frank St.Marseille 1.00 2.50
263 Checklist 3 20.00 40.00
264 Fred Barrett 1.25 3.00

1973-74 O-Pee-Chee Rings

The 1973-74 O-Pee-Chee Rings set contained 17 standard-size cards, featuring the NHL league and team logos. The fronts have a push-out cardboard ring and instructions in English and French. The rings are yellow-colored and feature a NHL team logo in the team's colors. The cards are numbered on the front and the backs are blank.

COMPLETE SET (17) 75.00 175.00
1 Vancouver Canucks 3.00 8.00
2 Montreal Canadiens 5.00 12.00
3 Toronto Maple Leafs 3.00 8.00
4 NHL Logo 3.00 8.00
5 Minnesota North Stars 3.00 8.00
6 New York Rangers 3.00 8.00
7 California Seals 8.00 20.00
8 Pittsburgh Penguins 5.00 12.00
9 Philadelphia Flyers 3.00 8.00
10 Chicago Blackhawks 3.00 8.00
11 Boston Bruins 3.00 8.00
12 Los Angeles Kings 3.00 8.00
13 Detroit Red Wings 3.00 8.00
14 St. Louis Blues 3.00 8.00
15 Buffalo Sabres 3.00 8.00
16 Atlanta Flames 8.00 20.00
17 New York Islanders 3.00 8.00

1973-74 O-Pee-Chee Team Logos

The 1973-74 O-Pee-Chee Team Logos set contains 17 unnumbered, standard-size color stickers, featuring the NHL league and team logos. The cards were die-cut and adhesive backed. After the NHL logo, they were ordered below alphabetically by team city/location. This set was distinguished from the similar set of the previous year by the presence of written instructions on the fronts.

COMPLETE SET (17) 25.00 60.00
1 NHL Logo 2.00 5.00
2 Atlanta Flames 6.00 15.00
3 Boston Bruins 3.00 6.00
4 Buffalo Sabres 2.00 5.00
5 California Seals 5.00 10.00
6 Chicago Blackhawks 2.00 5.00
7 Detroit Red Wings 3.00 6.00
8 Los Angeles Kings 2.00 5.00
9 Minnesota North Stars 3.00 6.00
10 Montreal Canadiens 3.00 6.00
11 New York Islanders 5.00 10.00
12 New York Rangers 2.00 5.00
13 Philadelphia Flyers 2.00 5.00
14 Pittsburgh Penguins 3.00 6.00
15 St. Louis Blues 2.00 5.00
16 Toronto Maple Leafs 3.00 6.00
17 Vancouver Canucks 2.00 5.00

1973-74 O-Pee-Chee WHA Posters

Players featured in this set are from the World Hockey Association (WHA). The set consisted of 20 large posters each measuring approximately 7 1/2" by 13 3/4" and was a separate issue in wax packs. The packs contained two posters and gum; gum stains are frequently seen. Posters were numbered on the front and were issued folded. As a result, folded copies are accepted as being in near mint condition. The posters are blank backed.

COMPLETE SET (20) 50.00 100.00
1 Al Smith 2.50 5.00
2 J.C. Tremblay 2.50 5.00
3 Guy Dufour 1.50 3.00
4 Pat Stapleton 2.50 5.00
5 Rosaire Paiement 1.50 3.00
6 Gerry Cheevers 5.00 10.00
7 Gerry Pinder 2.00 4.00
8 Wayne Carleton 1.50 3.00
9 Bob Leduc 1.50 3.00
10 Andre Lacroix 2.50 5.00
11 Jim Harrison 1.50 3.00
12 Ron Climie 1.50 3.00
13 Gordie Howe 12.50 25.00
14 The Howe Family 12.50 25.00
15 Mike Walton 2.00 4.00
16 Bobby Hull 10.00 20.00
17 Chris Bordeleau 1.50 3.00
18 Claude St.Sauveur 1.50 3.00
19 Bryan Campbell 1.50 3.00
20 Marc Tardif 2.50 5.00

1974-75 O-Pee-Chee

CANADIENS
GUY LAFLEUR

The 1974-75 O-Pee-Chee NHL set contained 396 standard-size cards. The first 264 cards are identical to those of Topps in terms of numbering and photos. Wax packs consisted of eight cards plus a piece of bubble gum. Bilingual backs featured the player's 1973-74 and career statistics, a short biography and a cartoon-illustrated fact about the player. The first six cards in the set (1-6) featured league leaders of the previous season. The set included players from the expansion Washington Capitals and Kansas City Scouts (presently New Jersey Devils). The set marked the return of coach cards, including Rookie Cards of Don Cherry and Scotty Bowman.

COMPLETE SET (396) 300.00 500.00
1 P.Espo/Gldswrthy LL 2.50 5.00
2 B.Orr/D.Hextall LL 9.00 15.00
3 P.Espo/B.Clarke LL 3.00 6.00
4 Favell/B.Parent LL .75 2.00
5 Watson/D.Schulz LL .75 2.00
6 Redmond/MacLsh LL .75 2.00
7 Gary Bromley RC 1.00 2.50
8 Bill Barber 3.00 6.00
9 Emile Francis CO .75 2.00
10 Gilles Gilbert 1.00 2.50
11 John Davidson RC 10.00 15.00
12 Ron Ellis 1.00 2.50
13 Syl Apps .75 2.00
14 Richard/Lysiak TL .75 2.00
15 Dan Bouchard 1.00 2.50
16 Ivan Boldirev 1.00 2.50
17 Gary Coalter RC .75 2.00
18 Bob Berry .75 2.00
19 Red Berenson 1.00 2.50
20 Stan Mikita 3.00 6.00
21 Fred Shero CO RC 4.00 8.00
22 Gary Smith 1.00 2.50
23 Bill Mikkelson .75 2.00
24 Jacques Lemaire UER 1.50 3.00
25 Gilbert Perreault 4.00 8.00
26 Cesare Maniago 1.00 2.50
27 Bobby Schmautz .75 2.00
28 Espo/Orr/Bucyk TL 9.00 15.00
29 Steve Vickers 1.00 2.50
30 Lowell MacDonald UER .75 2.00
31 Fred Stanfield .75 2.00
32 Ed Westfall 1.00 2.50
33 Curt Bennett .75 2.00
34 Bep Guidolin CO .75 2.00
35 Cliff Koroll .75 2.00
36 Gary Croteau .75 2.00
37 Mike Corrigan .75 2.00
38 Henry Boucha .75 2.00
39 Ron Low 1.00 2.50
40 Darryl Sittler 6.00 10.00
41 Tracy Pratt .75 2.00
42 Martin/Robert TL .75 2.00
43 Larry Carriere .75 2.00
44 Gary Dornhoefer .75 2.00
45 Denis Herron RC 2.50 5.00
46 Doug Favell 1.00 2.50
47 Dave Gardner RC .75 2.00
48 Morris Mott RC .75 2.00
49 Marc Boileau CO .75 2.00
50 Brad Park 2.50 5.00
51 Bob Leiter .75 2.00
52 Tom Reid .75 2.00
53 Serge Savard 1.50 3.00
54 Checklist 1-132 UER 18.00 30.00
55 Terry Harper .75 2.00
56 Seals Leaders .75 2.00
57 Guy Charron 1.00 2.50
58 Pit Martin .75 2.00
59 Chris Evans .75 2.00
60 Bernie Parent 3.00 6.00
61 Jim Lorentz .75 2.00
62 Dave Kryskow RC .75 2.00
63 Lou Angotti CO .75 2.00
64 Bill Flett .75 2.00
65 Vic Hadfield 1.00 2.50
66 Wayne Merrick RC .75 2.00
67 Andre Dupont .75 2.00
68 Tom Lysiak RC 1.50 3.00
69 Pappin/Mikita/Bord TL 1.00 2.50
70 Guy Lapointe 1.00 2.50
71 Gerry O'Flaherty .75 2.00
72 Marcel Dionne 6.00 10.00
73 Butch Deadmarsh RC .75 2.00
74 Butch Goring 1.00 2.50
75 Keith Magnuson .75 2.00
76 Red Kelly CO .75 2.00
77 Pete Stemkowski .75 2.00
78 Jim Roberts .75 2.00
79 Don Luce .75 2.00
80 Don Awrey .75 2.00
81 Rick Kehoe 1.00 2.50
82 Billy Smith 6.00 10.00
83 Jean-Paul Parise .75 2.00
84 Rdmnd/Dnne/Hoga TL 1.00 2.50
85 Ed Van Impe .75 2.00
86 Randy Manery .75 2.00
87 Barclay Plager 1.00 2.50
88 Inge Hammarstrom RC .75 2.00
89 Ab DeMarco .75 2.00
90 Bill White .75 2.00
91 Al Arbour CO 1.50 3.00
92 Bob Stewart .75 2.00
93 Jack Egers .75 2.00
94 Don Lever 1.00 2.50

95 Reggie Leach 1.00 2.50
96 Dennis O'Brien .75 2.00
97 Peter Mahovlich 1.00 2.50
98 Grng/St.Mrsle/Kzk TL .75 2.00
99 Gerry Meehan .75 2.00
100 Bobby Orr 25.00 50.00
101 Jean Potvin RC .75 2.00
102 Rod Seiling .75 2.00
103 Keith McCreary .75 2.00
104 Phil Maloney CO RC .75 2.00
105 Denis Dupere .75 2.00
106 Steve Durbano .75 2.00
107 Bob Plager UER 1.00 2.50
108 Chris Oddleifson RC .75 2.00
109 Jim Neilson .75 2.00
110 Jean Pronovost 1.00 2.50
111 Don Kozak RC .75 2.00
112 Gldswrthy/Hxtall TL .75 2.00
113 Jim Pappin .75 2.00
114 Richard Lemieux .75 2.00
115 Dennis Hextall .75 2.00
116 Bill Hogaboam RC .75 2.00
117 Vrgrt/Schmt/Boud TL .75 2.00
118 Jimmy Anderson CO .75 2.00
119 Walt Tkaczuk 1.00 2.50
120 Mickey Redmond 1.00 2.50
121 Jim Schoenfeld 1.00 2.50
122 Jocelyn Guevremont .75 2.00
123 Bob Nystrom 1.00 2.50
124 Cour/F.Mahov/Lrse TL 1.50 3.00
125 Lew Morrison .75 2.00
126 Terry Murray 1.00 2.50
127 Richard Martin AS .75 2.00
128 Ken Hodge AS .75 2.00
129 Phil Esposito AS 2.00 4.00
130 Bobby Orr AS 12.00 20.00
131 Brad Park AS 1.00 2.50
132 Gilles Gilbert AS .75 2.00
133 Lowell MacDonald AS .75 2.00
134 Bill Goldsworthy AS .75 2.00
135 Bobby Clarke AS 3.00 6.00
136 Bill White AS .75 2.00
137 Dave Burrows AS .75 2.00
138 Bernie Parent AS 1.50 3.00
139 Jacques Richard .75 2.00
140 Yvan Cournoyer 1.50 3.00
141 R.Gilbert/B.Park TL 1.50 3.00
142 Rene Robert 1.00 2.50
143 J. Bob Kelly RC .75 2.00
144 Ross Lonsberry .75 2.00
145 Jean Ratelle 1.50 3.00
146 Dallas Smith .75 2.00
147 Bernie Geoffrion CO 2.00 4.00
148 Ted McAneeley .75 2.00
149 Pierre Plante .75 2.00
150 Dennis Hull 1.00 2.50
151 Dave Keon 1.50 3.00
152 Dave Dunn RC .75 2.00
153 Michel Belhumeur 1.00 2.50
154 Clarke/D.Schultz TL 2.00 4.00
155 Ken Dryden 15.00 25.00
156 John Wright RC .75 2.00
157 Larry Romanchych .75 2.00
158 Ralph Stewart RC .75 2.00
159 Mike Robitaille .75 2.00
160 Ed Giacomin 2.00 4.00
161 Don Cherry CO RC 30.00 60.00
162 Checklist 133-264 18.00 30.00
163 Rick MacLeish 1.00 2.50
164 Greg Polis .75 2.00
165 Carol Vadnais .75 2.00
166 Pete Laframboise .75 2.00
167 Ron Schock .75 2.00
168 Lanny McDonald RC 15.00 25.00
169 Scouts Emblem 1.00 2.50
170 Tony Esposito 4.00 8.00
171 Pierre Jarry .75 2.00
172 Dan Maloney 1.00 2.50
173 Peter McDuffe 1.00 2.50
174 Danny Grant 1.00 2.50
175 John Stewart RC .75 2.00
176 Floyd Smith CO .75 2.00
177 Bert Marshall .75 2.00
178 Chuck Lefley UER .75 2.00
179 Gilles Villemure 1.00 2.50
180 Borje Salming RC 15.00 30.00
181 Doug Mohns .75 2.00
182 Barry Wilkins .75 2.00
183 MacDonald/Apps TL .75 2.00
184 Gregg Sheppard .75 2.00
185 Joey Johnston .75 2.00
186 Dick Redmond .75 2.00
187 Simon Nolet .75 2.00
188 Ron Stackhouse .75 2.00
189 Marshall Johnston .75 2.00
190 Richard Martin 1.00 2.50
191 Andre Boudrias .75 2.00
192 Steve Atkinson .75 2.00
193 Nick Libett .75 2.00
194 Bob Murdoch Kings RC .75 2.00
195 Denis Potvin RC 30.00 50.00
196 Dave Schultz 2.00 4.00
197 Unger/Plante TL .75 2.00
198 Jim McKenny .75 2.00
199 Gerry Hart .75 2.00
200 Phil Esposito 3.00 6.00
201 Rod Gilbert 1.50 3.00
202 Jacques Laperriere 1.00 2.50
203 Barry Gibbs .75 2.00
204 Billy Reay CO 1.00 2.50
205 Gilles Meloche 1.00 2.50
206 Wayne Cashman 1.00 2.50
207 Dennis Ververgaert RC .75 2.00
208 Phil Roberto .75 2.00
209 Quarter Finals .75 2.00
210 Quarter Finals .75 2.00
211 Quarter Finals .75 2.00
212 Quarter Finals .75 2.00
213 Semi-Finals .75 2.00
214 Semi-Finals .75 2.00
215 Stanley Cup Finals .75 2.00
216 Flyers Champions 1.00 2.50
217 Joe Watson .75 2.00
218 Wayne Stephenson 1.00 2.50
219 Sittlr/Ullmn/Hend TL 1.00 2.50
220 Bill Goldsworthy 1.00 2.50
221 Don Marcotte .75 2.00
222 Alex Delvecchio CO .75 2.00
223 Stan Gilbertson .75 2.00
224 Mike Murphy .75 2.00
225 Jim Rutherford 1.00 2.50
226 Phil Russell .75 2.00
227 Lynn Powis .75 2.00
228 Billy Harris .75 2.00
229 Bob Pulford CO 1.00 2.50
230 Ken Hodge 1.00 2.50
231 Bill Fairbairn .75 2.00
232 Guy Lafleur 7.50 15.00
233 Harr/Stw/Ptvn TL UER 2.00 4.00
234 Fred Barrett .75 2.00
235 Rogatien Vachon 2.00 5.00
236 Norm Ullman 1.50 3.00
237 Garry Unger 1.00 2.50
238 Jack Gordon CO RC .75 2.00
239 Johnny Bucyk 1.50 3.00
240 Bob Dailey RC .75 2.00
241 Dave Burrows .75 2.00
242 Len Frig RC .75 2.00
243 Henri Richard Mstrsn 1.00 2.50
244 Phil Esposito Hart 2.00 4.00
245 Johnny Bucyk Byng 1.00 2.50
246 Phil Esposito Ross 2.00 4.00
247 Wales Trophy .75 2.00
248 Bobby Orr Norris 12.00 20.00
249 Bernie Parent Vezina 1.00 2.50
250 Philadelphia Flyers SC 2.00 5.00
251 Bernie Parent Smythe 1.00 2.50
252 Denis Potvin Calder 6.00 10.00
253 Campbell Trophy .75 2.00
254 Pierre Bouchard .75 2.00
255 Jude Drouin .75 2.00
256 Capitals Emblem 1.00 2.50
257 Michel Plasse 1.00 2.50
258 Juha Widing .75 2.00
259 Bryan Watson .75 2.00
260 Bobby Clarke UER 7.00 12.00
261 Scotty Bowman CO RC 30.00 60.00
262 Craig Patrick 1.00 2.50
263 Craig Cameron .75 2.00
264 Ted Irvine .75 2.00
265 Ed Johnston 1.00 2.50
266 Dave Forbes RC .75 2.00
267 Red Wings Team CL 2.00 4.00
268 Rick Dudley RC 1.00 2.50
269 Darcy Rota RC 1.00 2.50
270 Phil Myre 1.00 2.50
271 Larry Brown RC .75 2.00
272 Bob Neely RC .75 2.00
273 Jerry Byers RC .75 2.00
274 Penguins Team CL 2.00 4.00
275 Glenn Goldup RC .75 2.00
276 Ron Harris .75 2.00
277 Joe Lundrigan RC .75 2.00
278 Mike Christie RC .75 2.00
279 Doug Rombough RC .75 2.00
280 Larry Robinson 12.00 20.00
281 Blues Team CL 2.00 4.00
282 John Marks RC .75 2.00
283 Don Saleski 1.00 2.50
284 Rick Wilson RC .75 2.00
285 Andre Savard RC .75 2.00
286 Pat Quinn 1.00 2.50
287 Kings Team CL 2.00 4.00
288 Norm Gratton .75 2.00
289 Ian Turnbull RC 1.00 2.50
290 Derek Sanderson 2.00 4.00
291 Murray Oliver .75 2.00
292 Wilf Paiement RC 1.50 3.00
293 Nelson Debenedet RC .75 2.00
294 Greg Joly RC .75 2.00
295 Terry O'Reilly 2.00 4.00
296 Rey Comeau .75 2.00
297 Michel Larocque RC 2.50 5.00
298 Floyd Thomson RC .75 2.00
299 Jean-Guy Lagace RC .75 2.00
300 Flyers Team CL 2.00 4.00
301 Al MacAdam RC 1.50 3.00
302 George Ferguson RC .75 2.00
303 Jimmy Watson RC 1.50 3.00
304 Rick Middleton RC 12.00 20.00
305 Craig Ramsay UER .75 2.00
306 Hilliard Graves .75 2.00
307 Islanders Team CL 2.00 4.00
308 Blake Dunlop RC .75 2.00
309 J.P. Bordeleau .75 2.00
310 Brian Glennie .75 2.00
311 Checklist 265-396 UER 18.00 30.00
312 Doug Roberts .75 2.00
313 Darryl Edestrand .75 2.00
314 Ron Anderson .75 2.00
315 Blackhawks Team CL 2.00 4.00
316 Steve Shutt RC 15.00 30.00
317 Doug Horbul RC .75 2.00
318 Billy Lochead RC .75 2.00
319 Fred Harvey .75 2.00
320 Gene Carr RC .75 2.00
321 Henri Richard 1.50 3.00
322 Canucks Team CL 2.00 4.00
323 Tim Ecclestone .75 2.00
324 Dave Lewis RC .75 2.00
325 Lou Nanne 1.00 2.50
326 Bobby Rousseau .75 2.00
327 Dunc Wilson 1.00 2.50
328 Brian Spencer .75 2.00
329 Rick Hampton RC .75 2.00
330 Canadiens Team CL UER 2.00 4.00
331 Jack Lynch .75 2.00
332 Garnet Bailey .75 2.00
333 Al Sims RC .75 2.00
334 Orest Kindrachuk RC 1.00 2.50
335 Dave Hudson .75 2.00
336 Bob Murray RC 1.00 2.50
337 Sabres Team CL 2.00 4.00
338 Sheldon Kannegiesser .75 2.00
339 Bill MacMillan .75 2.00
340 Paulin Bordeleau RC .75 2.00
341 Dale Rolfe .75 2.00
342 Yvon Lambert RC 1.00 2.50
343 Bob Paradise RC .75 2.00
344 Germaine Gagnon UER .75 2.00
345 Yvon Labre .75 2.00
346 Chris Ahrens RC .75 2.00
347 Doug Grant RC .75 2.00
348 Blaine Stoughton RC 2.00 4.00
349 Gregg Boddy .75 2.00
350 Bruins Team CL 2.00 4.00
351 Doug Jarrett .75 2.00
352 Terry Crisp 1.00 2.50
353 Glenn Resch UER RC 12.00 20.00
354 Jerry Korab .75 2.00
355 Stan Weir RC .75 2.00
356 Noel Price .75 2.00
357 Bill Clement RC 9.00 15.00
358 Neil Komadoski .75 2.00
359 Murray Wilson RC .75 2.00
360 Dale Tallon UER .75 2.00
361 Gary Doak .75 2.00
362 Randy Rota RC .75 2.00
363 North Stars Team CL 2.00 4.00
364 Bill Collins .75 2.00
365 Thommie Bergman UER .75 2.00
366 Dennis Kearns .75 2.00
367 Lorne Henning .75 2.00
368 Gary Sabourin .75 2.00
369 Mike Bloom RC .75 2.00
370 Rangers Team CL 2.00 4.00
371 Gary Simmons RC 2.50 5.00
372 Dwight Bialowas RC .75 2.00
373 Gilles Marotte .75 2.00
374 Frank St.Marseille .75 2.00
375 Garry Howatt RC .75 2.00
376 Ross Brooks RC 1.00 2.50
377 Flames Team CL 2.00 4.00
378 Bob Nevin .75 2.00
379 Lyle Moffat RC .75 2.00
380 Bob Kelly .75 2.00
381 John Gould RC .75 2.00
382 Dave Fortier RC .75 2.00
383 Jean Hamel RC .75 2.00
384 Bert Wilson RC .75 2.00
385 Chuck Arnason RC .75 2.00
386 Bruce Cowick RC .75 2.00
387 Ernie Hicke .75 2.00
388 Bob Gainey RC 18.00 30.00
389 Vic Venasky RC .75 2.00
390 Maple Leafs Team CL 2.00 4.00
391 Eric Vail RC 1.00 2.50
392 Bobby Lalonde .75 2.00
393 Jerry Butler RC .75 2.00
394 Tom Williams .75 2.00
395 Chico Maki .75 2.00
396 Tom Bladon RC 2.00 4.00

1974-75 O-Pee-Chee WHA

The 1974-75 O-Pee-Chee WHA set consisted of 66 color standard-size cards. The cards were originally sold in eight-card ten-cent wax packs. Bilingual backs featured a short biography, the player's 1973-74 and career WHA statistics as well as a cartoon-illustrated hockey fact or interpretation of a referee's signal. Rookie Cards in this set included Anders Hedberg and Ulf Nilsson, although some collectors and dealers considered the Howe Family card to be the Rookie Card for Mark and Marty Howe.

COMPLETE SET (66) 75.00 200.00
1 Gord/Mark/Marty Howe 40.00 75.00
2 Bruce MacGregor 1.50 3.00
3 Wayne Dillon RC 1.50 3.00
4 Ulf Nilsson RC 7.00 12.00
5 Serge Bernier 2.00 4.00
6 Bryan Campbell 1.50 3.00
7 Rosaire Paiement 1.50 3.00
8 Tom Webster 2.00 4.00
9 Gerry Pinder 1.50 3.00
10 Mike Walton 1.50 3.00
11 Norm Beaudin 1.50 3.00
12 Bob Whitlock RC 1.50 3.00
13 Wayne Rivers 1.50 3.00
14 Gerry Odrowski 1.50 3.00
15 Ron Climie 1.50 3.00
16 Tom Simpson RC 1.50 3.00
17 Anders Hedberg RC 7.00 12.00
18 J.C. Tremblay 1.50 3.00
19 Mike Pelyk 1.50 3.00
20 Dave Dryden 2.00 4.00
21 Ron Ward 1.50 3.00
22 Larry Lund RC 1.50 3.00
23 Ron Buchanan RC 1.50 3.00
24 Pat Hickey RC 2.00 4.00
25 Danny Lawson RC 2.00 4.00
26 Bob Guindon RC 1.50 3.00
27 Gene Peacosh RC 1.50 3.00
28 Fran Huck 1.50 3.00
29 Al Hamilton 1.50 3.00
30 Gerry Cheevers 7.50 15.00
31 Heikki Riihiranta RC 2.00 4.00
32 Don Burgess RC 1.50 3.00
33 John French RC 1.50 3.00
34 Jim Wiste RC 1.50 3.00
35 Pat Stapleton 4.00 8.00
36 J.P. LeBlanc RC 1.50 3.00
37 Mike Antonovich RC 1.50 3.00
38 Joe Daley 2.00 4.00
39 Ross Perkins RC 1.50 3.00
40 Frank Mahovlich 7.00 12.00
41 Rejean Houle 1.50 3.00
42 Ron Chipperfield RC 3.00 6.00
43 Marc Tardif 1.50 3.00
44 Murray Keogan RC 1.50 3.00
45 Wayne Carleton 1.50 3.00
46 Andre Gaudette RC 1.50 3.00
47 Ralph Backstrom 2.00 4.00
48 Don McLeod RC 2.00 4.00
49 Vaclav Nedomansky RC 3.00 6.00
50 Bobby Hull 20.00 35.00
51 Rusty Patenaude RC 1.50 3.00
52 Michel Parizeau 1.50 3.00
53 Checklist 20.00 40.00
54 Wayne Connelly 2.00 4.00
55 Gary Veneruzzo 1.50 3.00
56 Dennis Sobchuk RC 2.00 4.00
57 Paul Henderson 2.00 4.00
58 Andy Brown RC 3.00 6.00
59 Paul Popiel 1.50 3.00
60 Andre Lacroix 2.00 4.00
61 Gary Jarrett 1.50 3.00
62 Claude St.Sauveur RC 1.50 3.00
63 Real Cloutier RC 3.00 6.00
64 Jacques Plante 20.00 35.00
65 Gilles Gratton RC 4.00 8.00
66 Lars-Erik Sjoberg RC 4.00 8.00

1975-76 O-Pee-Chee

The 1975-76 O-Pee-Chee NHL set consisted of 396 color standard-size cards. The cards were originally sold in ten-cent wax packs. The first 330 cards had identical fronts (except perhaps for a short traded line) to the Topps set of this year. Number 395 was not issued; however, the set contained two of number 267, which are checklist cards. Team cards (81-98) had a team checklist on the back. Bilingual backs contained year-by-year and career statistics, a short biography and a cartoon-illustrated NHL fact or interpretation of a referee's signal.

COMPLETE SET (396) 200.00 400.00
1 Stanley Cup Finals 1.50 3.00
2 Semi-Finals .40 1.25
3 Semi-Finals .40 1.25
4 Quarter Finals .40 1.25
5 Quarter Finals .40 1.25
6 Quarter Finals .40 1.25
7 Quarter Finals .40 1.25
8 Curt Bennett .40 1.25
9 Johnny Bucyk 1.00 2.50
10 Gilbert Perreault 3.00 6.00
11 Darryl Edestrand .40 1.25
12 Ivan Boldirev .40 1.25
13 Nick Libett .40 1.25
14 Jim McElmury RC .40 1.25
15 Frank St.Marseille .40 1.25
16 Blake Dunlop .40 1.25
17 Yvon Lambert .60 1.50
18 Gerry Hart .40 1.25
19 Steve Vickers .40 1.25
20 Rick MacLeish .60 1.50
21A Bob Paradise NoTR .40 1.25
21B Bob Paradise TR .60 1.50
22 Red Berenson .60 1.50
23 Lanny McDonald 4.00 7.00
24 Mike Robitaille .40 1.25
25 Ron Low .60 1.50
26A Bryan Hextall NoTR .40 1.25
26B Bryan Hextall TR .40 1.25
27A Carol Vadnais NoTR .40 1.25
27B Carol Vadnais TR .40 1.25
28 Jim Lorentz .40 1.25
29 Gary Simmons .60 1.50
30 Stan Mikita 2.50 5.00
31 Bryan Watson .40 1.25
32 Guy Charron .40 1.25
33 Bob Murdoch .40 1.25
34 Norm Gratton .40 1.25
35 Ken Dryden 12.00 20.00
36 Jean Potvin .40 1.25

37 Rick Middleton	2.50	5.00
38 Ed Van Impe	.40	1.25
39 Rick Kehoe	.60	1.50
40 Garry Unger	.60	1.50
41 Ian Turnbull	.60	1.50
42 Dennis Ververgaert	.40	1.25
43 Mike Marson RC	.60	1.50
44 Randy Manery	.40	1.25
45 Gilles Gilbert	.60	1.50
46 Rene Robert	.60	1.50
47 Bob Stewart	.40	1.25
48 Pit Martin	.40	1.25
49 Danny Grant	.60	1.50
50 Peter Mahovlich	.60	1.50
51 Dennis Patterson RC	.40	1.25
52 Mike Murphy	.40	1.25
53 Dennis O'Brien	.40	1.25
54 Garry Howatt	.40	1.25
55 Ed Giacomin	1.00	2.50
56 Andre Dupont	.40	1.25
57 Chuck Arnason	.40	1.25
58 Bob Gassoff RC	.40	1.25
59 Ron Ellis	.60	1.50
60 Andre Boudrias	.40	1.25
61 Yvon Labre	.40	1.25
62 Hilliard Graves	.40	1.25
63 Wayne Cashman	.60	1.50
64 Danny Gare RC	1.50	3.00
65 Rick Hampton	.40	1.25
66 Darcy Rota	.40	1.25
67 Bill Hogaboam	.40	1.25
68 Denis Herron	.60	1.50
69 Sheldon Kannegiesser	.40	1.25
70 Yvan Cournoyer	1.00	2.50
71 Ernie Hicke	.40	1.25
72 Bert Marshall	.40	1.25
73 Derek Sanderson	2.00	4.00
74 Tom Bladon	.40	1.25
75 Ron Schock	.40	1.25
76 Larry Sacharuk RC	.40	1.25
77 George Ferguson	.40	1.25
78 Ab DeMarco	.40	1.25
79 Tom Williams	.40	1.25
80 Phil Roberto	.40	1.25
81 Bruins Team	2.00	4.00
82 Seals Team	2.00	4.00
83 Sabres Team	2.00	4.00
84 Blackhawks Team	2.00	4.00
85 Flames Team	2.00	4.00
86 Kings Team	2.00	4.00
87 Red Wings Team	2.00	4.00
88 Scouts Team	2.00	4.00
89 North Stars Team	2.00	4.00
90 Canadiens Team	2.00	4.00
91 Maple Leafs Team	2.00	4.00
92 Islanders Team	2.00	4.00
93 Penguins Team	2.00	4.00
94 Rangers Team	2.00	4.00
95 Flyers Team	2.00	4.00
96 Blues Team	2.00	4.00
97 Canucks Team	2.00	4.00
98 Capitals Team	2.00	4.00
99 Checklist 1-110	8.00	15.00
100 Bobby Orr	20.00	30.00
101 Germain Gagnon UER	.40	1.25
102 Phil Russell	.40	1.25
103 Billy Lochead	.40	1.25
104 Robin Burns RC	.40	1.25
105 Gary Edwards	.60	1.50
106 Dwight Bialowas	.40	1.25
107 Doug Risebrough UER RC	2.00	4.00
108 Dave Lewis	.40	1.25
109 Bill Fairbairn	.40	1.25
110 Ross Lonsberry	.40	1.25
111 Ron Stackhouse	.40	1.25
112 Claude Larose	.40	1.25
113 Don Luce	.40	1.25
114 Errol Thompson RC	.60	1.50
115 Gary Smith	.60	1.50
116 Jack Lynch	.40	1.25
117 Jacques Richard	.40	1.25
118 Dallas Smith	.40	1.25
119 Dave Gardner	.40	1.25
120 Mickey Redmond	.60	1.50
121 John Marks	.40	1.25
122 Dave Hudson	.40	1.25
123 Bob Nevin	.40	1.25
124 Fred Barrett	.40	1.25
125 Gerry Desjardins	.60	1.50
126 Guy Lafleur UER	9.00	15.00
127 Jean-Paul Parise	.40	1.25
128 Walt Tkaczuk	.60	1.50
129 Gary Dornhoefer	.60	1.50
130 Syl Apps	.40	1.25
131 Bob Plager	.60	1.50
132 Stan Weir	.40	1.25
133 Tracy Pratt	.40	1.25
134 Jack Egers	.40	1.25
135 Eric Vail	.40	1.25
136 Al Sims	.40	1.25
137 Larry Patey RC	.40	1.25
138 Jim Schoenfeld	.60	1.50
139 Cliff Koroll	.40	1.25
140 Marcel Dionne	3.00	8.00
141 Jean-Guy Lagace	.40	1.25
142 Juha Widing	.40	1.25
143 Lou Nanne	.60	1.50
144 Serge Savard	1.00	2.50
145 Glenn Resch	2.50	5.00
146 Ron Greschner RC	1.50	3.00
147 Dave Schultz	1.00	2.50
148 Barry Wilkins	.40	1.25
149 Floyd Thomson	.40	1.25
150 Darryl Sittler	4.00	8.00
151 Paulin Bordeleau	.40	1.25
152 Ron Lalonde RC	.40	1.25
153 Larry Romanchych	.40	1.25
154 Larry Carriere	.40	1.25
155 Andre Savard	.40	1.25
156 Dave Hrechkosy RC	.40	1.25
157 Bill White	.40	1.25
158 Dave Kryskow	.40	1.25
159 Denis Dupere	.40	1.25
160 Rogatien Vachon	1.50	4.00
161 Doug Rombough	.40	1.25
162 Murray Wilson	.40	1.25
163 Bob Bourne RC	1.50	3.00
164 Gilles Marotte	.40	1.25
165 Vic Hadfield	.60	1.50
166 Reggie Leach	.60	1.50
167 Jerry Butler	.40	1.25
168 Inge Hammarstrom	.40	1.25
169 Chris Oddleifson	.40	1.25
170 Greg Joly	.40	1.25
171 Checklist 111-220	8.00	15.00
172 Pat Quinn	.60	1.50
173 Dave Forbes	.40	1.25
174 Len Frig	.40	1.25
175 Richard Martin	.60	1.50
176 Keith Magnuson	.40	1.25
177 Dan Maloney	.40	1.25
178 Craig Patrick	.60	1.50
179 Tom Williams	.40	1.25
180 Bill Goldsworthy	.60	1.50
181 Steve Shutt	2.50	5.00
182 Ralph Stewart	.40	1.25
183 John Davidson	2.50	5.00
184 Bob Kelly	.40	1.25
185 Ed Johnston	.60	1.50
186 Dave Burrows	.40	1.25
187 Dave Dunn	.40	1.25
188 Dennis Kearns	.40	1.25
189 Bill Clement	2.50	5.00
190 Gilles Meloche	.60	1.50
191 Bob Leiter	.40	1.25
192 Jerry Korab	.40	1.25
193 Joey Johnston	.40	1.25
194 Walt McKechnie	.40	1.25
195 Wilf Paiement	.60	1.50
196 Bob Berry	.40	1.25
197 Dean Talafous RC	.40	1.25
198 Guy Lapointe	.60	1.50
199 Clark Gillies RC	6.00	12.00
200A Phil Esposito NoTR	4.00	8.00
200B Phil Esposito TR	2.50	5.00
201 Greg Polis	.40	1.25
202 Jimmy Watson	.60	1.50
203 Gord McRae RC	.60	1.50
204 Lowell MacDonald	.40	1.25
205 Barclay Plager	.60	1.50
206 Don Lever	.40	1.25
207 Bill Mikkelson	.40	1.25
208 Espo/Lafleur/Martin LL	2.50	5.00
209 Clarke/Orr/P.Mahv LL	4.00	8.00
210 Orr/Espo/Dionne LL	4.00	8.00
211 Schltz/Dupnt/Rssll LL	2.00	4.00
212 Espo/Martin/Grant LL	1.50	3.00
213 Parnt/Vach/Drydn LL	4.00	8.00
214 Barry Gibbs	.40	1.25
215 Ken Hodge	.60	1.50
216 Jocelyn Guevremont	.40	1.25
217 Warren Williams RC	.40	1.25
218 Dick Redmond	.40	1.25
219 Jim Rutherford	.60	1.50
220 Simon Nolet	.40	1.25
221 Butch Goring	.60	1.50
222 Glen Sather	.60	1.50
223 Mario Tremblay UER RC	2.50	5.00
224 Jude Drouin	.40	1.25
225 Rod Gilbert	1.00	2.50
226 Bill Barber	2.00	4.00
227 Gary Inness RC	.60	1.50
228 Wayne Merrick	.40	1.25
229 Rod Seiling	.40	1.25
230 Tom Lysiak	.60	1.50
231 Bob Dailey	.40	1.25
232 Michel Belhumeur	.60	1.50
233 Bill Hajt RC	.40	1.25
234 Jim Pappin	.40	1.25
235 Gregg Sheppard	.40	1.25
236A Gary Bergman NoTR	.40	1.25
236B Gary Bergman TR	.40	1.25
237 Randy Rota	.40	1.25
238 Neil Komadoski	.40	1.25
239 Craig Cameron	.40	1.25
240 Tony Esposito	3.00	6.00
241 Larry Robinson	7.00	12.00
242 Billy Harris	.40	1.25
243A Jean Ratelle NoTR	1.50	3.00
243B Jean Ratelle TR	1.00	2.50
244 Ted Irvine UER	.40	1.25
245 Bob Neely	.40	1.25
246 Bobby Lalonde	.40	1.25
247 Ron Jones RC	.40	1.25
248 Rey Comeau	.40	1.25
249 Michel Plasse	.60	1.50
250 Bobby Clarke	5.00	10.00
251 Bobby Schmautz	.40	1.25
252 Peter McNab RC	2.00	4.00
253 Al MacAdam	.40	1.25
254 Dennis Hull	.60	1.50
255 Terry Harper	.40	1.25
256 Peter McDuffe	.60	1.50
257 Jean Hamel	.40	1.25
258 Jacques Lemaire	1.00	2.50
259 Bob Nystrom	.60	1.50
260A Brad Park NoTR	2.00	4.00
260B Brad Park TR	1.50	3.00
261 Cesare Maniago	.60	1.50
262 Don Saleski	.40	1.25
263 J. Bob Kelly	.40	1.25
264 Bob Hess RC	.40	1.25
265 Blaine Stoughton	.60	1.50
266 John Gould	.40	1.25
267A Checklist 221-330	8.00	15.00
267B Checklist 331-396	8.00	15.00
268 Dan Bouchard	.60	1.50
269 Don Marcotte	.40	1.25
270 Jim Neilson	.40	1.25
271 Craig Ramsay	.40	1.25
272 Grant Mulvey RC	.60	1.50
273 Larry Giroux RC	.40	1.25
274 Real Lemieux	.40	1.25
275 Denis Potvin	7.00	12.00
276 Don Kozak	.40	1.25
277 Tom Reid	.40	1.25
278 Bob Gainey	4.00	7.00
279 Nick Beverley	.40	1.25
280 Jean Pronovost	.60	1.50
281 Joe Watson	.40	1.25
282 Chuck Lefley	.40	1.25
283 Borje Salming	4.00	8.00
284 Garnet Bailey	.40	1.25
285 Gregg Boddy	.40	1.25
286 Bobby Clarke AS1	2.50	5.00
287 Denis Potvin AS1	2.50	5.00
288 Bobby Orr AS1	9.00	15.00
289 Richard Martin AS1	.60	1.50
290 Guy Lafleur AS1	3.00	6.00
291 Bernie Parent AS1	1.00	2.50
292 Phil Esposito AS2	2.00	4.00
293 Guy Lapointe AS2	1.00	2.50
294 Borje Salming AS2	2.00	4.00
295 Steve Vickers AS2	.60	1.50
296 Rene Robert AS2	.60	1.50
297 Rogatien Vachon AS2	1.00	2.50
298 Buster Harvey RC	.40	1.25
299 Gary Sabourin	.40	1.25
300 Bernie Parent	2.00	4.00
301 Terry O'Reilly	1.00	2.50
302 Ed Westfall	.60	1.50
303 Pete Stemkowski	.40	1.25
304 Pierre Bouchard	.40	1.25
305 Pierre Larouche RC	4.00	8.00
306 Lee Fogolin RC	.60	1.50
307 Gerry O'Flaherty	.40	1.25
308 Phil Myre	.60	1.50
309 Pierre Plante	.40	1.25
310 Dennis Hextall	.40	1.25
311 Jim McKenny	.40	1.25
312 Vic Venasky	.40	1.25
313 Vail/Lysiak TL	.40	1.25
314 P.Espo/Orr/Bucyk TL	9.00	15.00
315 R.Martin/R.Robert TL	.60	1.50
316 Hrchsy/Ptey/Weir TL	.40	1.25
317 S.Mikita/J.Pappin TL	1.00	2.50
318 D.Grant/M.Dionne TL	1.00	2.50
319 Nolet/Prnni/Charn TL	.40	1.25
320 Nevin/Wdng/Brry TL	.40	1.25
321 Gldswrthy/Hextall TL	.40	1.25
322 Lafleur/P.Mahov TL	1.50	3.00
323 Nystrm/Potvin/Gill TL	1.00	2.50
324 Vick/Gilbert/Ratle TL	1.00	2.50
325 R.Leach/B.Clarke TL	1.00	2.50
326 Pronovost/Schock TL	.40	1.25
327 G.Unger/Sacharuk TL	.60	1.50
328 Darryl Sittler TL	1.00	2.50
329 Lever/Boudrias TL	.40	1.25
330 Williams/Bailey TL	.40	1.25
331 Noel Price	.40	1.25
332 Fred Stanfield	.40	1.25
333 Doug Jarrett	.40	1.25
334 Gary Coalter	.40	1.25
335 Murray Oliver	.40	1.25
336 Dave Fortier	.40	1.25
337 Terry Crisp UER	.40	1.25
338 Bert Wilson	.40	1.25
339 John Grisdale RC	.40	1.25
340 Ken Broderick	.60	1.50
341 Frank Spring RC	.40	1.25
342 Mike Korney RC	.40	1.25
343 Gene Carr	.40	1.25
344 Don Awrey	.40	1.25
345 Pat Hickey	.40	1.25
346 Colin Campbell RC	1.00	2.50
347 Wayne Thomas	.60	1.50
348 Bob Gryp RC	.40	1.25
349 Bill Flett	.40	1.25
350 Roger Crozier	.60	1.50
351 Dale Tallon	.40	1.25
352 Larry Johnston	.40	1.25
353 John Flesch RC	.40	1.25
354 Lorne Henning	.40	1.25
355 Wayne Stephenson	.60	1.50
356 Rick Wilson	.40	1.25
357 Garry Monahan	.40	1.25
358 Gary Doak	.40	1.25
359A Pierre Jarry NoTR	.40	1.25
359B Pierre Jarry TR	.40	1.25
360 George Pesut RC	.40	1.25
361 Mike Corrigan	.40	1.25
362 Michel Larocque	1.00	2.50
363 Wayne Dillon	.40	1.25
364 Pete Laframboise	.40	1.25
365 Brian Glennie	.40	1.25
366 Mike Christie	.40	1.25
367 Jean Lemieux RC	.40	1.25
368 Gary Bromley	.60	1.50
369 J.P. Bordeleau	.40	1.25
370 Ed Gilbert RC	.40	1.25
371 Chris Ahrens	.40	1.25
372 Billy Smith	3.00	6.00
373 Larry Goodenough RC	.40	1.25
374 Leon Rochefort	.40	1.25
375 Doug Gibson RC	.40	1.25
376 Mike Bloom	.40	1.25
377 Larry Brown	.40	1.25
378 Jim Roberts	.40	1.25
379 Gilles Villemure	.60	1.50
380 Dennis Owchar RC	.40	1.25
381 Doug Favell	.60	1.50
382 Stan Gilbertson UER	.40	1.25
383 Ed Kea RC	.40	1.25
384 Brian Spencer	.40	1.25
385 Mike Veisor RC	.60	1.50
386 Bob Murray	.40	1.25
387 Andre St.Laurent RC	.40	1.25
388 Rick Chartraw RC	.60	1.50
389 Orest Kindrachuk	.40	1.25
390 Dave Hutchinson RC	.60	1.50
391 Glenn Goldup	.40	1.25
392 Jerry Holland RC	.40	1.25
393 Peter Sturgeon RC	.40	1.25
394 Alain Daigle RC	.40	1.25
396 Harold Snepsts RC	12.00	20.00

1975-76 O-Pee-Chee WHA

The 1975-76 O-Pee-Chee WHA set consisted of 132 color cards. Printed in Canada, the cards measured 2 1/2" by 3 1/2". Bilingual backs featured 1974-75 and career WHA statistics as well as a short biography.

COMPLETE SET (132)	250.00	400.00
1 Bobby Hull	25.00	50.00
2 Dale Hoganson	2.50	5.00
3 Serge Aubry	3.00	6.00
4 Ron Chipperfield	2.00	4.00
5 Paul Shmyr	2.00	4.00
6 Perry Miller RC	2.00	4.00
7 Mark Howe RC	20.00	50.00
8 Mike Rogers RC	3.00	6.00
9 Bryon Baltimore	2.00	4.00
10 Andre Lacroix	2.50	5.00
11 Nick Harbaruk	2.00	4.00
12 John Garrett RC	6.00	12.00
13 Lou Nistico RC	2.00	4.00
14 Rick Ley	2.00	4.00
15 Veli-Pekka Ketola RC	4.00	8.00
16 Real Cloutier	2.50	5.00
17 Pierre Guite RC	2.00	4.00
18 Duane Rupp	2.00	4.00
19 Robbie Ftorek RC	7.50	15.00
20 Gerry Cheevers	7.50	15.00
21 John Schella RC	2.00	4.00
22 Bruce MacGregor	2.00	4.00
23 Ralph Backstrom	2.50	5.00
24 Gene Peacosh	2.00	4.00
25 Pierre Roy	2.00	4.00
26 Mike Walton	3.00	6.00
27 Vaclav Nedomansky	2.50	5.00
28 Christer Abrahamsson RC	6.00	10.00
29 Thommie Bergman	2.00	4.00
30 Marc Tardif	2.00	4.00
31 Bryan Campbell	2.00	4.00
32 Don McLeod	2.50	5.00
33 Al McDonough	2.00	4.00
34 Jacques Plante	20.00	35.00
35 Andre Hinse RC	2.00	4.00
36 Eddie Joyal	2.00	4.00
37 Ken Baird RC	2.00	4.00
38 Wayne Rivers	2.00	4.00
39 Ron Buchanan	2.00	4.00
40 Anders Hedberg	3.00	6.00
41 Rick Smith	2.00	4.00
42 Paul Henderson	2.50	5.00
43 Wayne Carleton	2.50	5.00
44 Richard Brodeur RC	7.00	12.00
45 John Hughes RC	2.00	4.00
46 Larry Israelson RC	2.00	4.00
47 Jim Harrison	2.00	4.00
48 Cam Connor RC	2.00	4.00
49 Al Hamilton	2.00	4.00
50 Ron Grahame RC	3.00	6.00
51 Frank Rochon RC	2.00	4.00
52 Ron Climie	2.00	4.00
53 Murray Heatley RC	2.00	4.00
54 John Arbour	2.00	4.00
55 Jim Shaw RC	2.50	5.00
56 Larry Pleau RC	3.00	6.00
57 Ted Green	3.00	6.00
58 Rick Dudley	2.00	4.00
59 Butch Deadmarsh	2.00	4.00
60 Serge Bernier	3.00	6.00
61 Ron Grahame AS	2.00	4.00
62 J.C. Tremblay AS	2.00	4.00
63 Kevin Morrison AS	2.00	4.00
64 Andre Lacroix AS	2.00	4.00
65 Bobby Hull AS	12.00	20.00
66 Gordie Howe AS	18.00	30.00
67 Gerry Cheevers AS	4.00	8.00
68 Poul Popiel AS	2.00	4.00
69 Barry Long AS	2.00	4.00

70 Serge Bernier AS 2.00 4.00
71 Marc Tardif AS 2.00 4.00
72 Anders Hedberg AS 2.00 4.00
73 Ron Ward 2.00 4.00
74 Michel Cormier RC 2.00 4.00
75 Marty Howe RC 3.00 6.00
76 Rusty Patenaude 2.00 4.00
77 John McKenzie 2.50 5.00
78 Mark Napier RC 3.00 6.00
79 Henry Boucha 2.00 4.00
80 Kevin Morrison RC 2.00 4.00
81 Tom Simpson 2.00 4.00
82 Brad Selwood RC 3.00 6.00
83 Ulf Nilsson 3.00 6.00
84 Rejean Houle 2.50 5.00
85 Normand Lapointe RC UER 2.00 4.00
86 Danny Lawson 2.50 5.00
87 Gary Jarrett 2.00 4.00
88 Al McLeod RC 2.00 4.00
89 Gord Labossiere 2.00 4.00
90 Barry Long 2.50 5.00
91 Rick Morris RC 2.00 4.00
92 Norm Ferguson 2.00 4.00
93 Bob Whitlock 2.00 4.00
94 Jim Dorey 2.00 4.00
95 Tom Webster 2.50 5.00
96 Gordie Gallant 2.00 4.00
97 Dave Keon 3.00 6.00
98 Ron Plumb RC 2.50 5.00
99 Rick Jodzio RC 2.00 4.00
100 Gordie Howe 30.00 50.00
101 Joe Daley 3.00 6.00
102 Wayne Muloin RC 2.00 4.00
103 Gavin Kirk RC 2.00 4.00
104 Dave Dryden 2.50 5.00
105 Bob Liddington RC 2.00 4.00
106 Rosaire Paiement 2.00 4.00
107 John Sheridan 4.00 8.00
108 Nick Fotiu RC 6.00 12.00
109 Lars-Erik Sjoberg 2.00 4.00
110 Frank Mahovlich 3.00 6.00
111 Mike Antonovich 2.00 4.00
112 Paul Terbenche 2.00 4.00
113 Rich Leduc RC 2.00 4.00
114 Jack Norris 2.50 5.00
115 Dennis Sobchuk 2.00 4.00
116 Chris Bordeleau 2.00 4.00
117 Doug Barrie 2.00 4.00
118 Hugh Harris RC 2.00 4.00
119 Cam Newton RC 2.50 5.00
120 Poul Popiel 2.00 4.00
121 Fran Huck 2.00 4.00
122 Tony Featherstone 2.00 4.00
123 Bob Woytowich 2.00 4.00
124 Claude St.Sauveur 2.00 4.00
125 Heikki Riihiranta 2.50 5.00
126 Gary Kurt 2.50 5.00
127 Thommy Abrahamsson RC 3.00 5.00
128 Danny Gruen RC 2.00 4.00
129 Jacques Locas RC 2.00 4.00
130 J.C. Tremblay 2.50 5.00
131 Checklist Card 25.00 50.00
132 Ernie Wakely 4.00 8.00

1976-77 O-Pee-Chee

The 1976-77 O-Pee-Chee NHL set consisted of 396 color standard-size cards. Printed in Canada, the cards contained both the O-Pee-Chee and the NHL Players Association copyright. The wax packs issued contained eight cards in ten-cent packs along with a bubble-gum slab. Several Record Breaker (RB) cards featured achievements from the previous season. Team cards (132-149) had a team checklist on the back. Bilingual backs contained the player's statistics from the 1975-76 season, career numbers, a short biography and a cartoon-illustrated fact about the player. Cards that featured California players in the 1976-77 Topps set had been updated in this set to show them with the Cleveland Barons. One of those was card 176 Gary Simmons. There are reportedly three variations of the Simmons card. In addition to the basic card, one version had "Team transferred to Colorado" on front. This is an error in itself because the Barons disbanded with players going to Minnesota. The other version had the text shaded or airbrushed out. Information on values and scarcities is not known at this time. Rookie Cards included Bryan Trottier and Dave "Tiger" Williams.

COMPLETE SET (396) 150.00 300.00
1 Leach/Lafleur/Larou LL 1.50 3.00
2 Clarke/Lafleur/Perr LL 1.50 3.00
3 Lafleur/Clarke/Perr LL 1.50 3.00
4 Durbno/Watsn/Schltz LL .40 1.00
5 Espo/Lafleur/Potvin LL 1.50 3.00
6 Dryden/Resch/Laroc LL 2.50 5.00
7 Gary Doak .40 1.00
8 Jacques Richard .40 1.00
9 Wayne Dillon .40 1.00
10 Bernie Parent .75 2.00
11 Ed Westfall .40 1.00
12 Dick Redmond .40 1.00
13 Bryan Hextall .40 1.00
14 Jean Pronovost .40 1.00
15 Peter Mahovlich .60 1.50
16 Danny Grant .40 1.00
17 Phil Myre .40 1.00
18 Wayne Merrick .40 1.00
19 Steve Durbano .40 1.00
20 Derek Sanderson .75 2.00
21 Mike Murphy .40 1.00
22 Borje Salming 2.50 5.00
23 Mike Walton .40 1.00
24 Randy Manery .40 1.00
25 Ken Hodge .40 1.00
26 Mel Bridgman RC 1.00 2.50
27 Jerry Korab .40 1.00
28 Gilles Gratton .40 1.00
29 Andre St.Laurent .40 1.00
30 Yvan Cournoyer .75 2.00
31 Phil Russell .40 1.00
32 Dennis Hextall .40 1.00
33 Lowell MacDonald .40 1.00
34 Dennis O'Brien .40 1.00
35 Gerry Meehan .40 1.00
36 Gilles Meloche .60 1.50
37 Wilf Paiement .40 1.00
38 Bob MacMillan RC .75 2.00
39 Ian Turnbull .40 1.00
40 Rogatien Vachon 1.00 2.50
41 Nick Beverley .40 1.00
42 Rene Robert .60 1.50
43 Andre Savard .40 1.00
44 Bob Gainey 2.00 4.00
45 Joe Watson .40 1.00
46 Billy Smith 2.50 5.00
47 Darcy Rota .40 1.00
48 Rick Lapointe RC .40 1.00
49 Pierre Jarry .40 1.00
50 Syl Apps .40 1.00
51 Eric Vail .40 1.00
52 Greg Joly .40 1.00
53 Don Lever .40 1.00
54 Bob Murdoch Seals .40 1.00
55 Denis Herron .40 1.00
56 Mike Bloom .40 1.00
57 Bill Fairbairn .40 1.00
58 Fred Stanfield .40 1.00
59 Steve Shutt .75 2.00
60 Brad Park .75 2.00
61 Gilles Villemure .40 1.00
62 Bert Marshall .40 1.00
63 Chuck Lefley .40 1.00
64 Simon Nolet .40 1.00
65 Reggie Leach RB .40 1.00
66 Darryl Sittler RB .75 2.00
67 Bryan Trottier RB 5.00 10.00
68 Garry Unger RB .40 1.00
69 Ron Low .40 1.00
70 Bobby Clarke 3.00 6.00
71 Michel Bergeron RC .40 1.00
72 Ron Stackhouse .40 1.00
73 Bill Hogaboam .40 1.00
74 Bob Murdoch Kings .40 1.00
75 Steve Vickers .40 1.00
76 Pit Martin .40 1.00
77 Gerry Hart .40 1.00
78 Craig Ramsay .40 1.00
79 Michel Larocque .40 1.00
80 Jean Ratelle .75 2.00
81 Don Saleski .40 1.00
82 Bill Clement .75 2.00
83 Dave Burrows .40 1.00
84 Wayne Thomas .40 1.00
85 John Gould .40 1.00
86 Dennis Maruk RC 1.50 3.00
87 Ernie Hicke .40 1.00
88 Jim Rutherford .40 1.00
89 Dale Tallon .40 1.00
90 Rod Gilbert .75 2.00
91 Marcel Dionne 3.00 6.00
92 Chuck Arnason .40 1.00
93 Jean Potvin .40 1.00
94 Don Luce .40 1.00
95 Johnny Bucyk .75 2.00
96 Larry Goodenough .40 1.00
97 Mario Tremblay .60 1.50
98 Nelson Pyatt RC .40 1.00
99 Brian Glennie .40 1.00
100 Tony Esposito 2.00 4.00
101 Dan Maloney .40 1.00
102 Dunc Wilson .40 1.00
103 Dean Talafous .40 1.00
104 Ed Staniowski RC .60 1.50
105 Dallas Smith .40 1.00
106 Jude Drouin .40 1.00
107 Pat Hickey .40 1.00
108 Jocelyn Guevremont .40 1.00
109 Doug Risebrough .75 2.00
110 Reggie Leach .60 1.50
111 Dan Bouchard .60 1.50
112 Chris Oddleifson .40 1.00
113 Rick Hampton .40 1.00
114 John Marks .40 1.00
115 Bryan Trottier RC 25.00 60.00
116 Checklist 1-132 6.00 10.00
117 Greg Polis .40 1.00
118 Peter McNab .75 2.00
119 Jim Roberts Mont .40 1.00
120 Gerry Cheevers 1.50 3.00
121 Rick MacLeish .60 1.50
122 Billy Lochead .40 1.00
123 Tom Reid .40 1.00
124 Rick Kehoe .40 1.00
125 Keith Magnuson .40 1.00
126 Clark Gillies .75 2.00
127 Rick Middleton .75 2.00
128 Bill Hajt .40 1.00
129 Jacques Lemaire .75 2.00
130 Terry O'Reilly .75 2.00
131 Andre Dupont .40 1.00
132 Flames Team 1.50 3.00
133 Bruins Team 1.50 3.00
134 Sabres Team 1.50 3.00
135 Seals Team 1.50 3.00
136 Blackhawks Team 1.50 3.00
137 Red Wings Team 1.50 3.00
138 Scouts Team 1.50 3.00
139 Kings Team 1.50 3.00
140 North Stars Team 1.50 3.00
141 Canadiens Team 1.50 3.00
142 Islanders Team 1.50 3.00
143 Rangers Team 1.50 3.00
144 Flyers Team 1.50 3.00
145 Penguins Team 1.50 3.00
146 Blues Team 1.50 3.00
147 Maple Leafs Team 1.50 3.00
148 Canucks Team 1.50 3.00
149 Capitals Team 1.50 3.00
150 Dave Schultz .75 2.00
151 Larry Robinson 3.00 6.00
152 Al Smith .60 1.50
153 Bob Nystrom .60 1.50
154 Ron Greschner .40 1.00
155 Gregg Sheppard .40 1.00
156 Alain Daigle .40 1.00
157 Ed Van Impe .40 1.00
158 Tim Young RC .60 1.50
159 Bryan Lefley .40 1.00
160 Ed Giacomin .75 2.00
161 Yvon Labre .40 1.00
162 Jim Lorentz .40 1.00
163 Guy Lafleur 7.00 12.00
164 Tom Bladon .40 1.00
165 Wayne Cashman .60 1.50
166 Pete Stemkowski .40 1.00
167 Grant Mulvey .40 1.00
168 Yves Belanger RC .60 1.50
169 Bill Goldsworthy .60 1.50
170 Denis Potvin 3.00 6.00
171 Nick Libett .40 1.00
172 Michel Plasse .40 1.00
173 Lou Nanne .40 1.00
174 Tom Lysiak .40 1.00
175 Dennis Ververgaert .40 1.00
176 Gary Simmons .60 1.50
177 Pierre Bouchard .40 1.00
178 Bill Barber .75 2.00
179 Darryl Edestrand .40 1.00
180 Gilbert Perreault 1.50 3.00
181 Dave Maloney RC .75 2.00
182 Jean-Paul Parise .40 1.00
183 Jim Harrison .40 1.00
184 Pete Lopresti RC .60 1.50
185 Don Kozak .40 1.00
186 Guy Charron .40 1.00
187 Stan Gilbertson .40 1.00
188 Bill Nyrop RC .60 1.50
189 Bobby Schmautz .40 1.00
190 Wayne Stephenson .40 1.00
191 Brian Spencer .40 1.00
192 Gilles Marotte .40 1.00
193 Lorne Henning .40 1.00
194 Bob Neely .40 1.00
195 Dennis Hull .40 1.00
196 Walt McKechnie .40 1.00
197 Curt Ridley RC .60 1.50
198 Dwight Bialowas .40 1.00
199 Pierre Larouche .75 2.00
200 Ken Dryden 10.00 20.00
201 Ross Lonsberry .40 1.00
202 Curt Bennett .40 1.00
203 Hartland Monahan RC .40 1.00
204 John Davidson 1.50 3.00
205 Serge Savard .75 2.00
206 Garry Howatt .40 1.00
207 Darryl Sittler 2.50 5.00
208 J.P. Bordeleau .40 1.00
209 Henry Boucha .40 1.00
210 Richard Martin .60 1.50
211 Vic Venasky .40 1.00
212 Buster Harvey .40 1.00
213 Bobby Orr 20.00 50.00
214 Martin/Perreault/Robert 2.00 4.00
215 Barber/Clarke/Leach 2.00 4.00
216 Gillies/Trottier/Harris 2.50 5.00
217 Gainey/Jarvis/Roberts 1.00 2.50
218 Bicentennial Line .40 1.00
219 Bob Kelly .40 1.00
220 Walt Tkaczuk .40 1.00
221 Dave Lewis .40 1.00
222 Danny Gare .75 2.00
223 Guy Lapointe .60 1.50
224 Hank Nowak RC .40 1.00
225 Stan Mikita 2.00 4.00
226 Vic Hadfield .40 1.00
227 Bernie Wolfe RC .60 1.50
228 Bryan Watson .40 1.00
229 Ralph Stewart .40 1.00
230 Gerry Desjardins .60 1.50
231 John Bednarski RC .40 1.00
232 Yvon Lambert .40 1.00
233 Orest Kindrachuk .40 1.00
234 Don Marcotte .40 1.00
235 Bill White .40 1.00
236 Red Berenson .40 1.00
237 Al MacAdam .40 1.00
238 Rick Blight RC .40 1.00
239 Butch Goring .60 1.50
240 Cesare Maniago .60 1.50
241 Jim Schoenfeld .60 1.50
242 Cliff Koroll .40 1.00
243 Scott Garland RC .40 1.00
244 Rick Chartraw .40 1.00
245 Phil Esposito 2.00 4.00
246 Dave Forbes .40 1.00
247 Jimmy Watson .40 1.00
248 Ron Schock .40 1.00
249 Fred Barrett .40 1.00
250 Glenn Resch 1.50 3.00
251 Ivan Boldirev .40 1.00
252 Billy Harris .40 1.00
253 Lee Fogolin .40 1.00
254 Murray Wilson .40 1.00
255 Gilles Gilbert .60 1.50
256 Gary Dornhoefer .60 1.50
257 Carol Vadnais .40 1.00
258 Checklist 133-264 6.00 10.00
259 Errol Thompson .40 1.00
260 Garry Unger .60 1.50
261 J. Bob Kelly .40 1.00
262 Terry Harper .40 1.00
263 Blake Dunlop .40 1.00
264 Canadiens Champs 1.25 2.50
265 Richard Mulhern RC .40 1.00
266 Gary Sabourin .40 1.00
267 Bill McKenzie UER RC .40 1.00
268 Mike Corrigan .40 1.00
269 Rick Smith .40 1.00
270 Stan Weir .40 1.00
271 Ron Sedlbauer RC .40 1.00
272 Jean Lemieux .40 1.00
273 Hilliard Graves .40 1.00
274 Dave Gardner .40 1.00
275 Tracy Pratt .40 1.00
276 Frank St.Marseille .40 1.00
277 Bob Hess .40 1.00
278 Bobby Lalonde .40 1.00
279 Tony White RC .40 1.00
280 Rod Seiling .40 1.00
281 Larry Romanchych .40 1.00
282 Ralph Klassen RC .40 1.00
283 Gary Croteau .40 1.00
284 Neil Komadoski .40 1.00
285 Ed Johnston .40 1.00
286 George Ferguson .40 1.00
287 Gerry O'Flaherty .40 1.00
288 Jack Lynch .40 1.00
289 Pat Quinn .60 1.50
290 Gene Carr .40 1.00
291 Bob Stewart .40 1.00
292 Doug Favell .60 1.50
293 Rick Wilson .40 1.00
294 Jack Valiquette RC .40 1.00
295 Garry Monahan .40 1.00
296 Michel Belhumeur .40 1.00
297 Larry Carriere .40 1.00
298 Fred Ahern RC .40 1.00
299 Dave Hudson .40 1.00
300 Bob Berry .40 1.00
301 Bob Gassoff .40 1.00
302 Jim McKenny .40 1.00
303 Gord Smith RC .40 1.00
304 Garnet Bailey .40 1.00
305 Bruce Affleck RC .40 1.00
306 Doug Halward RC .40 1.00
307 Lew Morrison .40 1.00
308 Bob Sauve RC 1.50 3.00
309 Bob Murray RC 1.25 3.00
310 Claude Larose .40 1.00
311 Don Awrey .40 1.00
312 Bill MacMillan .40 1.00
313 Doug Jarvis RC 1.50 4.00
314 Dennis Owchar .40 1.00
315 Jerry Holland .40 1.00
316 Guy Chouinard RC .75 2.00
317 Gary Smith .60 1.50
318 Pat Price RC .40 1.00
319 Tom Williams .40 1.00
320 Larry Patey .40 1.00
321 Claire Alexander .40 1.00
322 Larry Bolonchuk RC .40 1.00
323 Bob Sirois RC .40 1.00
324 Joe Zanussi RC .40 1.00
325 Joey Johnston .40 1.00
326 J.P. LeBlanc .40 1.00
327 Craig Cameron .40 1.00
328 Dave Fortier .40 1.00
329 Ed Gilbert .60 1.50
330 John Van Boxmeer RC .60 1.50
331 Gary Inness .60 1.50
332 Bill Flett .40 1.00
333 Mike Christie .40 1.00
334 Denis Dupere .40 1.00
335 Sheldon Kannegiesser .40 1.00
336 Jerry Butler .40 1.00
337 Gord McRae .40 1.00
338 Dennis Kearns .40 1.00
339 Ron Lalonde .40 1.00
340 Jean Hamel .40 1.00
341 Barry Gibbs .40 1.00
342 Mike Pelyk .40 1.00
343 Rey Comeau .40 1.00
344 Jim Neilson .40 1.00
345 Phil Roberto .40 1.00
346 Dave Hutchinson .40 1.00
347 Ted Irvine .40 1.00
348 Lanny McDonald 2.00 5.00
349 Jim Moxey RC .40 1.00
350 Bob Dailey .40 1.00
351 Tim Ecclestone .40 1.00
352 Len Frig .40 1.00
353 Randy Rota .40 1.00
354 Juha Widing .40 1.00

Card	Low	High
355 Larry Brown	.40	1.00
356 Floyd Thomson	.40	1.00
357 Richard Nantais RC	.40	1.00
358 Inge Hammarstrom	.40	1.00
359 Mike Robitaille	.40	1.00
360 Rejean Houle	.40	1.00
361 Ed Kea	.40	1.00
362 Bob Girard RC	.40	1.00
363 Bob Murray Vancv	.40	1.00
364 Dave Hrechkosy	.40	1.00
365 Gary Edwards	.40	1.00
366 Harold Snepsts	2.00	4.00
367 Pat Boutette RC	.75	2.00
368 Bob Paradise	.40	1.00
369 Bob Plager	.60	1.50
370 Tim Jacobs RC	.40	1.00
371 Pierre Plante	.40	1.00
372 Colin Campbell	.60	1.50
373 Tiger Williams RC	12.50	25.00
374 Ab DeMarco	.40	1.00
375 Mike Lampman RC	.40	1.00
376 Mark Heaslip RC	.40	1.00
377 Checklist Card	6.00	10.00
378 Bert Wilson	.40	1.00
379 Bntt/Lysk/Qnn/St.S TL	.40	1.00
380 Gre/Perrlt/Mrtin TL	.40	1.00
381 Bucyk/Ratle/O'Rei TL	1.25	2.50
382 Mrtn/Tln/Rsll/Kroll TL	.40	1.00
383 Seals/McAd/Mrdch TL	.40	1.00
384 Charron/Durbano TL	.40	1.00
385 Brgrn/McKch/Wtsn TL	.40	1.00
386 Dione/Htch/Corrig TL	.40	1.00
387 Hoga/Yng/O'Brien TL	.40	1.00
388 Laflr/P.Mahv/Rise TL	1.50	3.00
389 Gillies/Potvin/How TL	1.25	2.50
390 Gilbert/Vick/Espo TL	1.25	2.50
391 Leach/Clrke/Brbr TL	1.25	2.50
392 Lrch/Apps/Schck TL	.40	1.00
393 Lefly/Ungr/Gssf TL	.40	1.00
394 Thmpsn/Sittlr/Will TL	.40	1.00
395 Vgrt/Odl/Krns/Snpst TL	.40	1.00
396 Pyatt/Mhn/Lbr/Whte TL	.40	1.00

1976-77 O-Pee-Chee WHA

The 1976-77 O-Pee-Chee WHA set consisted of 132 color cards featuring WHA players. Cards were 2 1/2" by 3 1/2". The cards were originally sold in ten-cent wax packs. The backs, in both French and English, told a short biography of the player and career statistics. The cards were printed in Canada. Cards 1-6 featured the league leaders from the previous season in various statistical categories. The backs of cards 62-65, 67, and 71 formed a puzzle of Gordie Howe. A puzzle of Bobby Hull was derived from the backs of cards 61, 66, 68-70 and 72. These cards (61-72) comprised the All-Star subset.

Card	Low	High
COMPLETE SET (132)	100.00	200.00
1 Tardif/Clout/Nedom LL	2.00	4.00
2 Tardif/Trembl/Nils LL	1.50	3.00
3 Tardif/B.Hull/Nils LL	4.00	8.00
4 Penalties Leaders	1.00	2.00
5 Tardif/B.Hull/Nils LL	4.00	8.00
6 Goals Against Avg. Leaders	1.00	2.00
7 Barry Long	.60	1.50
8 Danny Lawson	.60	1.50
9 Ulf Nilsson	1.25	3.00
10 Kevin Morrison	.60	1.50
11 Gerry Pinder	.60	1.50
12 Richard Brodeur	3.00	5.00
13 Robbie Ftorek	4.00	8.00
14 Tom Webster	.75	2.00
15 Marty Howe	1.25	3.00
16 Bryan Campbell	.60	1.50
17 Rick Dudley	.60	1.50
18 Jim Turkiewicz RC	.60	1.50
19 Rusty Patenaude	.60	1.50
20 Joe Daley	.75	2.00
21 Gary Veneruzzo	.60	1.50
22 Chris Evans	.60	1.50
23 Mike Antonovich	.60	1.50
24 Jim Dorey	.60	1.50
25 John Gray RC	.60	1.50
26 Larry Pleau	.60	1.50
27 Poul Popiel	.60	1.50
28 Renald Leclerc RC	.60	1.50
29 Dennis Sobchuk	.60	1.50
30 Lars-Erik Sjoberg	.60	1.50
31 Wayne Wood RC	.75	2.00
32 Ron Chipperfield	.60	1.50
33 Tim Sheehy RC	.60	1.50
34 Brent Hughes	.60	1.50
35 Ron Ward	.60	1.50
36 Ron Huston RC	.60	1.50
37 Rosaire Paiement	.60	1.50
38 Terry Ruskowski RC	3.00	5.00
39 Hugh Harris	.60	1.50
40 J.C. Tremblay	.60	1.50
41 Rich Leduc	.60	1.50
42 Peter Sullivan RC	.60	1.50
43 Jerry Rollins RC	.60	1.50
44 Ken Broderick	.75	2.00
45 Peter Driscoll RC	.60	1.50
46 Joe Noris RC	.60	1.50
47 Al McLeod	.60	1.50
48 Bruce Landon RC	.75	2.00
49 Chris Bordeleau	.60	1.50
50 Gordie Howe	20.00	40.00
51 Thommie Bergman	.60	1.50
52 Dave Keon	1.25	3.00
53 Butch Deadmarsh	.60	1.50
54 Bryan Maxwell	.60	1.50
55 John Garrett	.75	2.00
56 Glen Sather	.75	2.00
57 John Miszuk	.60	1.50
58 Heikki Riihiranta	.75	2.00
59 Richard Grenier RC	.60	1.50
60 Gene Peacosh	.60	1.50
61 Joe Daley AS	1.00	2.00
62 J.C. Tremblay AS	1.00	2.00
63 Lars-Erik Sjoberg AS	1.00	2.00
64 Vaclav Nedomansky AS	1.00	2.00
65 Bobby Hull AS	10.00	20.00
66 Anders Hedberg AS	1.00	2.00
67 Chris Abrahamsson AS	1.00	2.00
68 Kevin Morrison AS	1.00	2.00
69 Paul Shmyr AS	1.00	2.00
70 Andre Lacroix AS	1.00	2.00
71 Gene Peacosh AS	1.00	2.00
72 Gordie Howe AS	15.00	25.00
73 Bob Nevin	.60	1.50
74 Richard Lemieux	.60	1.50
75 Mike Ford RC	.60	1.50
76 Real Cloutier	.75	2.00
77 Al McDonough	.60	1.50
78 Del Hall RC	.60	1.50
79 Thommy Abrahamsson	.60	1.50
80 Andre Lacroix	.75	2.00
81 Frank Hughes RC	.60	1.50
82 Reg Thomas RC	.60	1.50
83 Dave Inkpen RC	.60	1.50
84 Paul Henderson	1.25	3.00
85 Dave Dryden	.75	2.00
86 Lynn Powis	.60	1.50
87 Andre Boudrias	.60	1.50
88 Veli-Pekka Ketola	.75	2.00
89 Cam Connor	.60	1.50
90 Claude St.Sauveur	.60	1.50
91 Garry Swain RC	.60	1.50
92 Ernie Wakely	.75	2.00
93 Blair MacDonald RC	.75	2.00
94 Ron Plumb	.60	1.50
95 Mark Howe	7.00	12.00
96 Peter Marrin RC	1.25	3.00
97 Al Hamilton	.75	2.00
98 Paulin Bordeleau	.60	1.50
99 Gavin Kirk	.60	1.50
100 Bobby Hull	15.00	30.00
101 Rick Ley	.60	1.50
102 Gary Kurt	.75	2.00
103 John McKenzie	.75	2.00
104 Al Karlander RC	.60	1.50
105 John French	.60	1.50
106 John Hughes	.60	1.50
107 Ron Grahame	.75	2.00
108 Mark Napier	.75	2.00
109 Serge Bernier	.75	2.00
110 Christer Abrahamsson	.75	2.00
111 Frank Mahovlich	3.50	6.00
112 Ted Green	.75	2.00
113 Rick Jodzio	.60	1.50
114 Michel Dion RC	3.00	6.00
115 Rich Preston RC	.75	2.00
116 Pekka Rautakallio RC	3.00	6.00
117 Checklist Card	12.00	30.00
118 Marc Tardif	.75	2.00
119 Doug Barrie	.60	1.50
120 Vaclav Nedomansky	.75	2.00
121 Bill Lesuk	.60	1.50
122 Wayne Connelly	.60	1.50
123 Pierre Guite	.60	1.50
124 Ralph Backstrom	.75	2.00
125 Anders Hedberg	1.25	3.00
126 Norm Ullman	1.25	3.00
127 Steve Sutherland RC	.60	1.50
128 John Schella	.60	1.50
129 Don McLeod	.75	2.00
130 Canadian Finals	1.50	4.00
131 U.S. Finals	1.50	4.00
132 World Trophy Final	6.00	15.00

1977-78 O-Pee-Chee

The 1977-78 O-Pee-Chee NHL set consisted of 396 color standard-size cards. Unopened packs consisted of 12 cards plus a bubble-gum stick. Cards 203 and 255 featured different players than corresponding Topps cards. Bilingual backs contained yearly statistics and a cartoon-illustrated fact about the player. Cards 322-339 had a team logo on the front with team records on the back. Rookie Cards included Mike Milbury, Mike Palmateer and Paul Holmgren. The Rick Bourbonnais card (312) actually depicted Bernie Federko, predating his Rookie Card by one year.

Card	Low	High
COMPLETE SET (396)	75.00	150.00
1 Shutt/Lafleur/Dionne LL	1.50	3.00
2 Lafleur/Dionne/Sal/ LL	1.00	2.00
3 Lafleur/Dionne/Shutt LL	1.25	2.50
4 Wills/Polnch/Gassoff LL	.30	.75
5 McDonald/Espo/Will LL	.40	1.00
6 Laroc/Dryden/Resch LL	2.00	4.00
7 Perr/Shutt/Lafleur LL	1.25	2.50
8 Dryden/Vach/Parent LL	2.50	5.00
9 Brian Spencer	.25	.60
10 Denis Potvin AS2	2.00	4.00
11 Nick Fotiu	.40	1.00
12 Bob Murray	.25	.60
13 Pete Lopresti	.30	.75
14 J. Bob Kelly	.25	.60
15 Rick MacLeish	.30	.75
16 Terry Harper	.25	.60
17 Willi Plett RC	1.50	3.00
18 Peter McNab	.30	.75
19 Wayne Thomas	.30	.75
20 Pierre Bouchard	.25	.60
21 Dennis Maruk	.40	1.00
22 Mike Murphy	.25	.60
23 Cesare Maniago	.30	.75
24 Paul Gardner RC	.40	1.00
25 Rod Gilbert	.40	1.00
26 Orest Kindrachuk	.25	.60
27 Bill Hajt	.25	.60
28 John Davidson	.75	1.50
29 Jean-Paul Parise	.25	.60
30 Larry Robinson AS1	2.50	5.00
31 Yvon Labre	.25	.60
32 Walt McKechnie	.25	.60
33 Rick Kehoe	.30	.75
34 Randy Holt RC	.25	.60
35 Garry Unger	.30	.75
36 Lou Nanne	.25	.60
37 Dan Bouchard	.30	.75
38 Darryl Sittler	1.50	3.00
39 Bob Murdoch	.25	.60
40 Jean Ratelle	.40	1.00
41 Dave Maloney	.25	.60
42 Danny Gare	.30	.75
43 Jimmy Watson	.25	.60
44 Tom Williams	.25	.60
45 Serge Savard	.40	1.00
46 Derek Sanderson	1.00	2.00
47 John Marks	.25	.60
48 Al Cameron RC	.25	.60
49 Dean Talafous	.25	.60
50 Glenn Resch	1.00	2.00
51 Ron Schock	.25	.60
52 Gary Croteau	.25	.60
53 Gerry Meehan	.25	.60
54 Ed Staniowski	.25	.60
55 Phil Esposito UER	1.50	3.00
56 Dennis Ververgaert	.25	.60
57 Rick Wilson	.25	.60
58 Jim Lorentz	.25	.60
59 Bobby Schmautz	.25	.60
60 Guy Lapointe AS2	.30	.75
61 Ivan Boldirev	.25	.60
62 Bob Nystrom	.25	.60
63 Rick Hampton	.25	.60
64 Jack Valiquette	.25	.60
65 Bernie Parent	1.25	2.50
66 Dave Burrows	.25	.60
67 Butch Goring	.30	.75
68A Checklist 1-132 ERR	4.00	8.00
68B Checklist 1-132 COR	4.00	8.00
69 Murray Wilson	.25	.60
70 Ed Giacomin	.75	1.50
71 Flames Team	.75	2.00
72 Bruins Team	.75	2.00
73 Sabres Team	.75	2.00
74 Blackhawks Team	.75	2.00
75 Barons Team	.75	2.00
76 Rockies Team	.75	2.00
77 Red Wings Team	.75	2.00
78 Kings Team	.75	2.00
79 North Stars Team	.75	2.00
80 Canadiens Team	.75	2.00
81 Islanders Team	.75	2.00
82 Rangers Team	.75	2.00
83 Flyers Team	.75	2.00
84 Penguins Team	.75	2.00
85 Blues Team	.75	2.00
86 Maple Leafs Team	.75	2.00
87 Canucks Team	.75	2.00
88 Capitals Team	.75	2.00
89 Keith Magnuson	.25	.60
90 Walt Tkaczuk	.30	.75
91 Bill Nyrop	.25	.60
92 Michel Plasse	.30	.75
93 Bob Bourne	.30	.75
94 Lee Fogolin	.25	.60
95 Gregg Sheppard	.25	.60
96 Hartland Monahan	.25	.60
97 Curt Bennett	.25	.60
98 Bob Dailey	.25	.60
99 Bill Goldsworthy	.30	.75
100 Ken Dryden AS1	7.50	15.00
101 Grant Mulvey	.25	.60
102 Pierre Larouche	.40	1.00
103 Nick Libett	.25	.60
104 Rick Smith	.25	.60
105 Bryan Trottier	8.00	20.00
106 Pierre Jarry	.25	.60
107 Red Berenson	.30	.75
108 Jim Schoenfeld	.30	.75
109 Gilles Meloche	.30	.75
110 Lanny McDonald AS2	1.25	2.50
111 Don Lever	.25	.60
112 Greg Polis	.25	.60
113 Gary Sargent RC	.25	.60
114 Earl Anderson RC	.25	.60
115 Bobby Clarke	2.50	5.00
116 Dave Lewis	.25	.60
117 Darcy Rota	.25	.60
118 Andre Savard	.25	.60
119 Denis Herron	.30	.75
120 Steve Shutt AS1	1.00	2.00
121 Mel Bridgman	.25	.60
122 Buster Harvey	.25	.60
123 Roland Eriksson RC	.25	.60
124 Dale Tallon	.25	.60
125 Gilles Gilbert	.30	.75
126 Billy Harris	.25	.60
127 Tom Lysiak	.30	.75
128 Jerry Korab	.25	.60
129 Bob Gainey	1.25	2.50
130 Wilf Paiement	.30	.75
131 Tom Bladon	.25	.60
132 Ernie Hicke	.25	.60
133 J.P. LeBlanc	.25	.60
134 Mike Milbury RC	4.00	8.00
135 Pit Martin	.25	.60
136 Steve Vickers	.25	.60
137 Don Awrey	.25	.60
138 Bernie Wolfe	.30	.75
139 Doug Jarvis	.30	.75
140 Borje Salming AS1	1.50	3.00
141 Bob MacMillan	.25	.60
142 Wayne Stephenson	.30	.75
143 Dave Forbes	.25	.60
144 Jean Potvin	.25	.60
145 Guy Charron	.25	.60
146 Cliff Koroll	.25	.60
147 Danny Grant	.30	.75
148 Bill Hogaboam	.25	.60
149 Al MacAdam	.25	.60
150 Gerry Desjardins	.30	.75
151 Yvon Lambert	.25	.60
152 Rick Lapointe	.25	.60
153 Ed Westfall	.30	.75
154 Carol Vadnais	.25	.60
155 Johnny Bucyk	.40	1.00
156 J.P. Bordeleau	.25	.60
157 Ron Stackhouse	.25	.60
158 Glen Sharpley RC	.25	.60
159 Michel Bergeron	.25	.60
160 Rogatien Vachon AS2	.75	2.00
161 Fred Stanfield	.25	.60
162 Gerry Hart	.25	.60
163 Mario Tremblay	.30	.75
164 Andre Dupont	.25	.60
165 Don Marcotte	.25	.60
166 Wayne Dillon	.25	.60
167 Claude Larose	.25	.60
168 Eric Vail	.25	.60
169 Tom Edur RC	.25	.60
170 Tony Esposito	1.50	3.00
171 Andre St.Laurent	.25	.60
172 Dan Maloney	.25	.60
173 Dennis O'Brien	.25	.60
174 Blair Chapman RC	.25	.60
175 Dennis Kearns	.25	.60
176 Wayne Merrick	.25	.60
177 Michel Larocque	.30	.75
178 Bob Kelly	.25	.60
179 Dave Farrish RC	.25	.60
180 Richard Martin AS2	.30	.75
181 Gary Doak	.25	.60
182 Jude Drouin	.25	.60
183 Barry Dean RC	.25	.60
184 Gary Smith	.30	.75
185 Reggie Leach	.30	.75
186 Ian Turnbull	.30	.75
187 Vic Venasky	.25	.60
188 Wayne Bianchin RC	.25	.60
189 Doug Risebrough	.30	.75
190 Brad Park	1.00	2.50
191 Craig Ramsay	.25	.60
192 Ken Hodge	.30	.75
193 Phil Myre	.30	.75
194 Garry Howatt	.25	.60
195 Stan Mikita	1.50	3.00
196 Garnet Bailey	.25	.60
197 Dennis Hextall	.25	.60
198 Nick Beverley	.25	.60
199 Larry Patey	.25	.60
200 Guy Lafleur AS1	6.00	10.00
201 Don Edwards RC	2.00	4.00
202 Gary Dornhoefer	.30	.75
203 Bob Paradise	.25	.60
204 Alex Pirus RC	.25	.60
205 Peter Mahovlich	.30	.75
206 Bert Marshall	.25	.60
207 Gilles Gratton	.30	.75
208 Alain Daigle	.25	.60
209 Chris Oddleifson	.25	.60
210 Gilbert Perreault AS2	1.25	2.50
211 Mike Palmateer RC	4.00	8.00
212 Billy Lochead	.25	.60
213 Dick Redmond	.25	.60
214 Guy Lafleur RB	1.25	2.50
215 Ian Turnbull RB	.25	.60
216 Guy Lafleur RB	1.25	2.50
217 Steve Shutt RB	.30	.75
218 Guy Lafleur RB	1.25	2.50
219 Lorne Henning	.25	.60
220 Terry O'Reilly	.30	.75
221 Pat Hickey	.25	.60
222 Rene Robert	.30	.75
223 Tim Young	.25	.60
224 Dunc Wilson	.30	.75
225 Dennis Hull	.30	.75
226 Rod Seiling	.25	.60
227 Bill Barber	.40	1.00
228 Dennis Polonich RC	.25	.60
229 Billy Smith	1.25	2.50
230 Yvan Cournoyer	.40	1.00

231 Don Luce	.25	.60
232 Mike McEwen RC	.25	.60
233 Don Saleski	.25	.60
234 Wayne Cashman	.30	.75
235 Phil Russell	.25	.60
236 Mike Corrigan	.25	.60
237 Guy Chouinard	.30	.75
238 Steve Jensen RC	.25	.60
239 Jim Rutherford	.30	.75
240 Marcel Dionne AS1	2.00	4.00
241 Rejean Houle	.25	.60
242 Jocelyn Guevremont	.25	.60
243 Jim Harrison	.25	.60
244 Don Murdoch RC	.40	1.00
245 Rick Green RC	.40	1.00
246 Rick Middleton	1.00	2.00
247 Joe Watson	.25	.60
248 Syl Apps	.25	.60
249 Checklist 133-264	4.00	8.00
250 Clark Gillies	.30	.75
251 Bobby Orr	15.00	25.00
252 Nelson Pyatt	.25	.60
253 Gary McAdam RC	.25	.60
254 Jacques Lemaire	.40	1.00
255 Bob Girard	.25	.60
256 Ron Greschner	.30	.75
257 Ross Lonsberry	.25	.60
258 Dave Gardner	.25	.60
259 Rick Blight	.25	.60
260 Gerry Cheevers	1.00	2.00
261 Jean Pronovost	.30	.75
262 Cup Semi-Finals	.25	.60
263 Cup Semi-Finals	.25	.60
264 Canadiens Champs	.40	1.00
265 Rick Bowness RC	.75	2.00
266 George Ferguson	.25	.60
267 Mike Kitchen RC	.25	.60
268 Bob Berry	.25	.60
269 Greg Smith RC	.25	.60
270 Stan Jonathan RC	1.00	3.00
271 Dwight Bialowas	.25	.60
272 Pete Stemkowski	.25	.60
273 Greg Joly	.25	.60
274 Ken Houston RC	.25	.60
275 Brian Glennie	.25	.60
276 Ed Johnston	.30	.75
277 John Grisdale	.25	.60
278 Craig Patrick	.30	.75
279 Ken Breitenbach RC	.25	.60
280 Fred Ahern	.25	.60
281 Jim Roberts	.25	.60
282 Harvey Bennett RC	.25	.60
283 Ab DeMarco	.25	.60
284 Pat Boutette	.25	.60
285 Bob Plager	.30	.75
286 Hilliard Graves	.25	.60
287 Gordie Lane RC	.25	.60
288 Ron Andruff RC	.25	.60
289 Larry Brown	.25	.60
290 Mike Fidler RC	.25	.60
291 Fred Barrett	.25	.60
292 Bill Clement	.30	.75
293 Errol Thompson	.25	.60
294 Doug Grant	.30	.75
295 Harold Snepsts	1.00	2.00
296 Rick Bragnalo RC	.25	.60
297 Bryan Lefley	.25	.60
298 Gene Carr	.25	.60
299 Bob Stewart	.25	.60
300 Lew Morrison	.25	.60
301 Ed Kea	.25	.60
302 Scott Garland	.25	.60
303 Bill Fairbairn	.25	.60
304 Larry Carriere	.25	.60
305 Ron Low	.30	.75
306 Tom Reid	.25	.60
307 Paul Holmgren RC	2.50	5.00
308 Pat Price	.25	.60
309 Kirk Bowman RC	.25	.60
310 Bobby Simpson RC	.25	.60
311 Ron Ellis	.30	.75
312 Rick Bourbonnais RC UER	.60	1.50
313 Bobby Lalonde	.25	.60
314 Tony White	.25	.60
315 John Van Boxmeer	.30	.75
316 Don Kozak	.25	.60
317 Jim Neilson	.25	.60
318 Terry Martin RC	.25	.60
319 Barry Gibbs	.25	.60
320 Inge Hammarstrom	.25	.60
321 Darryl Edestrand	.25	.60
322 Flames Logo	.75	2.00
323 Bruins Logo	.75	2.00
324 Sabres Logo	.75	2.00
325 Blackhawks Logo	.75	2.00
326 Barons Logo	.75	2.00
327 Rockies Logo	.75	2.00
328 Red Wings Logo	.75	2.00
329 Kings Logo	.75	2.00
330 North Stars Logo	.75	2.00
331 Canadiens Logo	.75	2.00
332 Islanders Logo	.75	2.00
333 Rangers Logo	.75	2.00
334 Flyers Logo	.75	2.00
335 Penguins Logo	.75	2.00
336 Blues Logo	.75	2.00
337 Maple Leafs Logo	.75	2.00
338 Canucks Logo	.75	2.00
339 Capitals Logo	.75	2.00
340 Chuck Lefley	.25	.60
341 Garry Monahan	.25	.60
342 Bryan Watson	.25	.60
343 Dave Hudson	.25	.60
344 Neil Komadoski	.25	.60
345 Gary Edwards	.30	.75
346 Rey Comeau	.25	.60
347 Bob Neely	.25	.60
348 Jean Hamel	.25	.60
349 Jerry Butler	.25	.60
350 Mike Walton	.25	.60
351 Bob Sirois	.25	.60
352 Jim McElmury	.25	.60
353 Dave Schultz	.30	.75
354 Doug Palazzari RC	.25	.60
355 David Shand RC	.25	.60
356 Stan Weir	.25	.60
357 Mike Christie	.25	.60
358 Floyd Thomson	.25	.60
359 Larry Goodenough	.25	.60
360 Bill Riley RC	.25	.60
361 Doug Hicks RC	.25	.60
362 Dan Newman RC	.25	.60
363 Rick Chartraw	.25	.60
364 Tim Ecclestone	.25	.60
365 Don Ashby RC	.25	.60
366 Jacques Richard	.25	.60
367 Yves Belanger	.25	.60
368 Ron Sedlbauer	.25	.60
369 Jack Lynch UER	.25	.60
370 Doug Favell	.30	.75
371 Bob Murdoch	.25	.60
372 Ralph Klassen	.25	.60
373 Richard Mulhern	.25	.60
374 Jim McKenny	.25	.60
375 Mike Bloom	.25	.60
376 Bruce Affleck	.25	.60
377 Gerry O'Flaherty	.25	.60
378 Ron Lalonde	.25	.60
379 Chuck Arnason	.25	.60
380 Dave Hutchinson	.25	.60
381A Checklist ERR	4.00	8.00
381B Checklist COR	4.00	8.00
382 John Gould	.25	.60
383 Tiger Williams	2.00	4.00
384 Len Frig	.25	.60
385 Pierre Plante	.25	.60
386 Ralph Stewart	.25	.60
387 Gord Smith	.25	.60
388 Denis Dupere	.25	.60
389 Randy Manery	.25	.60
390 Lowell MacDonald	.25	.60
391 Dennis Owchar	.25	.60
392 Jim Roberts RC	.25	.60
393 Mike Veisor	.30	.75
394 Bob Hess	.25	.60
395 Curt Ridley	.25	.60
396 Mike Lampman	.40	1.00

1977-78 O-Pee-Chee WHA

The 1977-78 O-Pee-Chee WHA set consistedof 66 color standard-size cards. Printed in Canada, the cards were originally sold in 15-cent wax packs containing 12 cards and gum. Bilingual backs featured player statistics and a short biography. Card number 1 featured Gordie Howe's 1000th career goal. There were no key Rookie Cards in this set. This was the final WHA set. The league disbanded following the 1978-79 season with the four surviving teams (Edmonton, New England/Hartford, Quebec and Winnipeg) merging with the NHL.

COMPLETE SET (66)	35.00	70.00
1 Gordie Howe	15.00	30.00
2 Jean Bernier RC	.30	.75
3 Anders Hedberg	.75	2.00
4 Ken Broderick	.60	1.50
5 Joe Noris	.30	.75
6 Blaine Stoughton	.60	1.50
7 Claude St.Sauveur	.30	.75
8 Real Cloutier	.60	1.50
9 Joe Daley	.60	1.50
10 Ron Chipperfield	.30	.75
11 Wayne Rutledge	.60	1.50
12 Mark Napier	.60	1.50
13 Rich Leduc	.30	.75
14 Don McLeod	.60	1.50
15 Ulf Nilsson	.75	2.00
16 Blair MacDonald	.30	.75
17 Mike Rogers	.60	1.50
18 Gary Inness	.60	1.50
19 Larry Lund	.30	.75
20 Marc Tardif	.60	1.50
21 Lars-Erik Sjoberg	.60	1.50
22 Bryan Campbell	.30	.75
23 John Garrett	.60	1.50
24 Ron Plumb	.30	.75
25 Mark Howe	3.00	6.00
26 Garry Lariviere RC	.30	.75
27 Peter Sullivan	.30	.75
28 Dave Dryden	.60	1.50
29 Reg Thomas	.30	.75
30 Andre Lacroix	.60	1.50
31 Paul Henderson	1.25	3.00
32 Paulin Bordeleau	.30	.75
33 Juha Widing	.60	1.50
34 Mike Antonovich	.30	.75
35 Robbie Ftorek	.60	1.50
36 Rosaire Paiement	.30	.75
37 Terry Ruskowski	.60	1.50
38 Richard Brodeur	1.75	3.00
39 Willy Lindstrom RC	1.00	2.50
40 Al Hamilton	.30	.75
41 John McKenzie	.60	1.50
42 Wayne Wood	.60	1.50
43 Claude Larose	.30	.75
44 J.C. Tremblay	.30	.75
45 Gary Bromley	.60	1.50
46 Ken Baird	.30	.75
47 Bobby Sheehan	.30	.75
48 Don Larway RC	.30	.75
49 Al Smith	.60	1.50
50 Bobby Hull	10.00	20.00
51 Peter Marrin	.30	.75
52 Norm Ferguson	.30	.75
53 Dennis Sobchuk	.30	.75
54 Norm Dube RC	.30	.75
55 Tom Webster	.30	.75
56 Jim Park RC	.60	1.50
57 Dan Labraaten RC	.75	2.00
58 Checklist Card	6.00	10.00
59 Paul Shmyr	.30	.75
60 Serge Bernier	.60	1.50
61 Frank Mahovlich	2.00	4.00
62 Michel Dion	.60	1.50
63 Poul Popiel	.30	.75
64 Lyle Moffat	.30	.75
65 Marty Howe	.60	1.50
66 Don Burgess	.75	2.00

1978-79 O-Pee-Chee

The 1978-79 O-Pee-Chee set consisted of 396 standard-size cards. Bilingual backs featured the card number (pictured in a hockey skate), year-by-year player statistics, a short biography and a facsimile autograph. Unlike Topps, All-Star designations did not appear on the front of cards of those players named to the All-Star team. An All-Star subset (325-336) served to recognize these players. Card number 300 honored Bobby Orr's retirement early in the season.

COMPLETE SET (396)	100.00	200.00
1 Mike Bossy HL	6.00	12.00
2 Phil Esposito HL	.75	1.50
3 Guy Lafleur HL	.75	1.50
4 Darryl Sittler HL	.30	.75
5 Garry Unger HL	.20	.50
6 Gary Edwards	.20	.50
7 Rick Blight	.15	.40
8 Larry Patey	.15	.40
9 Craig Ramsay	.15	.40
10 Bryan Trottier	5.00	10.00
11 Don Murdoch	.15	.40
12 Phil Russell	.15	.40
13 Doug Jarvis	.20	.50
14 Gene Carr	.15	.40
15 Bernie Parent	1.00	2.00
16 Perry Miller	.15	.40
17 Kent-Erik Andersson RC	.20	.50
18 Gregg Sheppard	.15	.40
19 Dennis Owchar	.15	.40
20 Rogatien Vachon	.40	1.00
21 Dan Maloney	.15	.40
22 Guy Charron	.15	.40
23 Dick Redmond	.15	.40
24 Checklist 1-132	2.50	5.00
25 Anders Hedberg	.20	.50
26 Mel Bridgman	.15	.40
27 Lee Fogolin	.15	.40
28 Gilles Meloche	.20	.50
29 Garry Howatt	.15	.40
30 Darryl Sittler	1.25	2.50
31 Curt Bennett	.15	.40
32 Andre St.Laurent	.15	.40
33 Blair Chapman	.15	.40
34 Keith Magnuson	.15	.40
35 Pierre Larouche	.20	.50
36 Michel Plasse	.20	.50
37 Gary Sargent	.15	.40
38 Mike Walton	.15	.40
39 Robert Picard RC	.20	.50
40 Terry O'Reilly	.20	.50
41 Dave Farrish	.15	.40
42 Gary McAdam	.15	.40
43 Joe Watson	.15	.40
44 Yves Belanger	.20	.50
45 Steve Jensen	.15	.40
46 Bob Stewart	.15	.40
47 Darcy Rota	.15	.40
48 Dennis Hextall	.15	.40
49 Bert Marshall	.15	.40
50 Ken Dryden	6.00	12.00
51 Peter Mahovlich	.20	.50
52 Dennis Ververgaert	.15	.40
53 Inge Hammarstrom	.15	.40
54 Doug Favell	.20	.50
55 Steve Vickers	.15	.40
56 Syl Apps	.15	.40
57 Errol Thompson	.15	.40
58 Don Luce	.15	.40
59 Mike Milbury	.30	.75
60 Yvan Cournoyer	.30	.75
61 Kirk Bowman	.15	.40
62 Billy Smith	.75	1.50
63 Lafleur/Bossy/Shutt LL	2.50	5.00
64 Trott/Lafleur/Sitt LL	1.25	2.50
65 Lafleur/Trott/Sitt LL	1.25	2.50
66 Schltz/Will/Polnich LL	.30	.75
67 Bossy/Espo/Shutt LL	2.00	4.00
68 Dryden/Parent/Gilb LL	2.00	4.00
69 Lafleur/Barber/Sitt LL	1.00	2.00
70 Parent/Dryden/Espo LL	2.50	5.00
71 Bob Kelly	.15	.40
72 Ron Stackhouse	.15	.40
73 Wayne Dillon	.15	.40
74 Jim Rutherford	.20	.50
75 Stan Mikita	1.25	2.50
76 Bob Gainey	.75	1.50
77 Gerry Hart	.15	.40
78 Lanny McDonald	.75	1.50
79 Brad Park	.75	1.50
80 Richard Martin	.20	.50
81 Bernie Wolfe	.20	.50
82 Bob MacMillan	.15	.40
83 Brad Maxwell RC	.15	.40
84 Mike Fidler	.15	.40
85 Carol Vadnais	.15	.40
86 Don Lever	.15	.40
87 Phil Myre	.20	.50
88 Paul Gardner	.15	.40
89 Bob Murray	.15	.40
90 Guy Lafleur	4.00	7.00
91 Bob Murdoch	.15	.40
92 Ron Ellis	.20	.50
93 Jude Drouin	.15	.40
94 Jocelyn Guevremont	.15	.40
95 Gilles Gilbert	.20	.50
96 Bob Sirois	.15	.40
97 Tom Lysiak	.20	.50
98 Andre Dupont	.15	.40
99 Per-Olov Brasar RC	.15	.40
100 Phil Esposito	1.50	3.00
101 J.P. Bordeleau	.15	.40
102 Pierre Mondou RC	.40	1.00
103 Wayne Bianchin	.15	.40
104 Dennis O'Brien	.15	.40
105 Glenn Resch	.30	.75
106 Dennis Polonich	.15	.40
107 Kris Manery RC	.15	.40
108 Bill Hajt	.15	.40
109 Jere Gillis RC	.15	.40
110 Garry Unger	.20	.50
111 Nick Beverley	.15	.40
112 Pat Hickey	.15	.40
113 Rick Middleton	.30	.75
114 Orest Kindrachuk	.15	.40
115 Mike Bossy RC	50.00	100.00
116 Pierre Bouchard	.15	.40
117 Alain Daigle	.15	.40
118 Terry Martin	.15	.40
119 Tom Edur	.15	.40
120 Marcel Dionne	1.50	3.00
121 Barry Beck RC	1.25	2.50
122 Billy Lochead	.15	.40
123 Paul Harrison RC	.20	.50
124 Wayne Cashman	.20	.50
125 Rick MacLeish	.20	.50
126 Bob Bourne	.20	.50
127 Ian Turnbull	.15	.40
128 Gerry Meehan	.15	.40
129 Eric Vail	.15	.40
130 Gilbert Perreault	.30	.75
131 Bob Dailey	.15	.40
132 Dale McCourt RC	.30	.75
133 John Wensink RC	.50	1.25
134 Bill Nyrop	.15	.40
135 Ivan Boldirev	.15	.40
136 Lucien DeBlois RC	.15	.40
137 Brian Spencer	.15	.40
138 Tim Young	.15	.40
139 Ron Sedlbauer	.15	.40
140 Gerry Cheevers	.75	1.50
141 Dennis Maruk	.20	.50
142 Barry Dean	.15	.40
143 Bernie Federko RC	5.00	10.00
144 Stefan Persson RC	.20	.50
145 Wilf Paiement	.20	.50
146 Dale Tallon	.15	.40
147 Yvon Lambert	.15	.40
148 Greg Joly	.15	.40
149 Dean Talafous	.15	.40
150 Don Edwards	.20	.50
151 Butch Goring	.20	.50
152 Tom Bladon	.15	.40
153 Bob Nystrom	.15	.40
154 Ron Greschner	.20	.50
155 Jean Ratelle	.30	.75
156 Russ Anderson RC	.15	.40
157 John Marks	.15	.40
158 Michel Larocque	.20	.50
159 Paul Woods RC	.30	.75
160 Mike Palmateer	.20	.50
161 Jim Lorentz	.15	.40
162 Dave Lewis	.15	.40
163 Harvey Bennett	.15	.40
164 Rick Smith	.15	.40
165 Reggie Leach	.20	.50
166 Wayne Thomas	.20	.50
167 Dave Forbes	.15	.40
168 Doug Wilson RC	6.00	12.00
169 Dan Bouchard	.20	.50
170 Steve Shutt	.30	.75
171 Mike Kaszycki RC	.15	.40
172 Denis Herron	.20	.50
173 Rick Bowness	.20	.50
174 Rick Hampton	.15	.40
175 Glen Sharpley	.15	.40

Card	Low	High
176 Bill Barber	.30	.75
177 Ron Duguay RC	4.00	8.00
178 Jim Schoenfeld	.20	.50
179 Pierre Plante	.15	.40
180 Jacques Lemaire	.30	.75
181 Stan Jonathan	.15	.40
182 Billy Harris	.15	.40
183 Chris Oddleifson	.15	.40
184 Jean Pronovost	.20	.50
185 Fred Barrett	.15	.40
186 Ross Lonsberry	.15	.40
187 Mike McEwen	.15	.40
188 Rene Robert	.20	.50
189 J. Bob Kelly	.15	.40
190 Serge Savard	.30	.75
191 Dennis Kearns	.15	.40
192 Flames Team	.40	1.00
193 Bruins Team	.40	1.00
194 Sabres Team	.40	1.00
195 Blackhawks Team	.40	1.00
196 Rockies Team	.40	1.00
197 Red Wings Team	.40	1.00
198 Kings Team	.40	1.00
199 North Stars Team	.40	1.00
200 Canadiens Team	.40	1.00
201 Islanders Team	.40	1.00
202 Rangers Team	.40	1.00
203 Flyers Team	.40	1.00
204 Penguins Team	.40	1.00
205 Blues Team	.40	1.00
206 Maple Leafs Team	.40	1.00
207 Canucks Team	.40	1.00
208 Capitals Team	.40	1.00
209 Danny Gare	.20	.50
210 Larry Robinson	1.25	2.50
211 John Davidson	.30	.75
212 Peter McNab	.20	.50
213 Rick Kehoe	.20	.50
214 Terry Harper	.15	.40
215 Bobby Clarke	1.50	3.00
216 Bryan Maxwell UER	.15	.40
217 Ted Bulley RC	.15	.40
218 Red Berenson	.20	.50
219 Ron Grahame	.20	.50
220 Clark Gillies	.20	.50
221 Dave Maloney	.15	.40
222 Derek Smith RC	.15	.40
223 Wayne Stephenson	.20	.50
224 John Van Boxmeer	.15	.40
225 Dave Schultz	.20	.50
226 Reed Larson RC	.50	1.25
227 Rejean Houle	.15	.40
228 Doug Hicks	.15	.40
229 Mike Murphy	.15	.40
230 Pete Lopresti	.20	.50
231 Jerry Korab	.15	.40
232 Ed Westfall	.20	.50
233 Greg Malone RC	.30	.75
234 Paul Holmgren	.20	.50
235 Walt Tkaczuk	.20	.50
236 Don Marcotte	.15	.40
237 Ron Low	.20	.50
238 Rick Chartraw	.15	.40
239 Cliff Koroll	.15	.40
240 Borje Salming	1.00	2.00
241 Roland Eriksson	.15	.40
242 Ric Seiling RC	.15	.40
243 Jim Bedard RC	.30	.75
244 Peter Lee RC	.20	.50
245 Denis Potvin	1.25	2.50
246 Greg Polis	.15	.40
247 Jimmy Watson	.15	.40
248 Bobby Schmautz	.15	.40
249 Doug Risebrough	.20	.50
250 Tony Esposito	1.25	2.50
251 Nick Libett	.15	.40
252 Ron Zanussi RC	.15	.40
253 Andre Savard	.15	.40
254 Dave Burrows	.15	.40
255 Ulf Nilsson	.30	.75
256 Richard Mulhern	.15	.40
257 Don Saleski	.15	.40
258 Wayne Merrick	.15	.40
259 Checklist 133-264	2.50	5.00
260 Guy Lapointe	.20	.50
261 Grant Mulvey	.15	.40
262 Stanley Cup Semifinals	.30	.75
263 Stanley Cup Semifinals	.30	.75
264 Stanley Cup Finals	.30	.75
265 Bob Sauve	.20	.50
266 Randy Manery	.15	.40
267 Bill Fairbairn	.15	.40
268 Garry Monahan	.15	.40
269 Colin Campbell	.20	.50
270 Dan Newman	.15	.40
271 Dwight Foster RC	.15	.40
272 Larry Carriere	.15	.40
273 Michel Bergeron	.15	.40
274 Scott Garland	.15	.40
275 Bill McKenzie	.20	.50
276 Garnet Bailey	.15	.40
277 Ed Kea	.15	.40
278 Dave Gardner	.15	.40
279 Bruce Affleck	.15	.40
280 Bruce Boudreau RC	.75	2.00
281 Jean Hamel	.15	.40
282 Kurt Walker RC	.15	.40
283 Denis Dupere	.15	.40
284 Gordie Lane	.15	.40
285 Bobby Lalonde	.15	.40
286 Pit Martin	.15	.40
287 Jean Potvin	.15	.40
288 Jimmy Jones RC	.15	.40
289 Dave Hutchinson	.15	.40
290 Pete Stemkowski	.15	.40
291 Mike Christie	.15	.40
292 Bill Riley	.15	.40
293 Rey Comeau	.15	.40
294 Jack McIlhargey RC	.20	.50
295 Tom Younghans RC	.15	.40
296 Mario Faubert RC	.15	.40
297 Checklist 265-396	2.50	5.00
298 Rob Palmer RC	.15	.40
299 Dave Hudson	.15	.40
300 Bobby Orr	25.00	40.00
301 Lorne Stamler RC	.15	.40
302 Curt Ridley	.15	.40
303 Greg Smith	.15	.40
304 Jerry Butler	.15	.40
305 Gary Doak	.15	.40
306 Danny Grant	.20	.50
307 Mark Suzor RC	.15	.40
308 Rick Bragnalo	.15	.40
309 John Gould	.15	.40
310 Sheldon Kannegiesser	.15	.40
311 Bobby Sheehan	.15	.40
312 Randy Carlyle RC	3.00	6.00
313 Lorne Henning	.15	.40
314 Tom Williams	.15	.40
315 Ron Andruff	.15	.40
316 Bryan Watson	.15	.40
317 Willi Plett	.15	.40
318 John Grisdale	.15	.40
319 Brian Sutter RC	4.00	8.00
320 Trevor Johansen RC	.15	.40
321 Vic Venasky	.15	.40
322 Rick Lapointe	.15	.40
323 Ron Delorme RC	.20	.50
324 Yvon Labre	.15	.40
325 Bryan Trottier AS UER	2.00	4.00
326 Guy Lafleur AS	1.25	2.50
327 Clark Gillies AS	.20	.50
328 Borje Salming AS	.20	.50
329 Larry Robinson AS	.30	.75
330 Ken Dryden AS	2.50	5.00
331 Darryl Sittler AS	.30	.75
332 Terry O'Reilly AS	.30	.75
333 Steve Shutt AS	.20	.50
334 Denis Potvin AS	.30	.75
335 Serge Savard AS	.20	.50
336 Don Edwards AS	.30	.75
337 Glenn Goldup	.15	.40
338 Mike Kitchen	.15	.40
339 Bob Girard	.15	.40
340 Guy Chouinard	.20	.50
341 Randy Holt	.15	.40
342 Jim Roberts	.15	.40
343 Dave Logan RC	.15	.40
344 Walt McKechnie	.15	.40
345 Brian Glennie	.15	.40
346 Ralph Klassen	.15	.40
347 Gord Smith	.15	.40
348 Ken Houston	.15	.40
349 Bob Manno RC	.15	.40
350 Jean-Paul Parise	.15	.40
351 Don Ashby	.15	.40
352 Fred Stanfield	.15	.40
353 Dave Taylor RC	18.00	30.00
354 Nelson Pyatt	.15	.40
355 Blair Stewart RC	.15	.40
356 David Shand	.15	.40
357 Hilliard Graves	.15	.40
358 Bob Hess	.15	.40
359 Tiger Williams	.75	1.50
360 Larry Wright RC	.15	.40
361 Larry Brown	.15	.40
362 Gary Croteau	.15	.40
363 Rick Green	.20	.50
364 Bill Clement	.20	.50
365 Gerry O'Flaherty	.15	.40
366 John Baby RC	.15	.40
367 Nick Fotiu	.20	.50
368 Pat Price	.15	.40
369 Bert Wilson	.15	.40
370 Bryan Lefley	.15	.40
371 Ron Lalonde	.15	.40
372 Bobby Simpson	.15	.40
373 Doug Grant	.20	.50
374 Pat Boutette	.15	.40
375 Bob Paradise	.15	.40
376 Mario Tremblay	.20	.50
377 Darryl Edestrand	.15	.40
378 Andy Spruce RC	.15	.40
379 Jack Brownschidle RC	.15	.40
380 Harold Snepsts	.30	.75
381 Al MacAdam	.15	.40
382 Neil Komadoski	.15	.40
383 Don Awrey	.15	.40
384 Ron Schock	.15	.40
385 Gary Simmons	.20	.50
386 Fred Ahern	.15	.40
387 Larry Bolonchuk	.15	.40
388 Brad Gassoff RC	.15	.40
389 Chuck Arnason	.15	.40
390 Barry Gibbs	.15	.40
391 Jack Valiquette	.15	.40
392 Doug Halward	.15	.40
393 Hartland Monahan	.15	.40
394 Rod Seiling	.15	.40
395 George Ferguson	.15	.40
396 Al Cameron	.30	.75

1979-80 O-Pee-Chee

The 1979-80 O-Pee-Chee set consisted of 396 standard-size cards. Cards 81, 82, 141, 163, and 263 differed from that of the corresponding Topps issue. Wax packs had 14 cards plus a bubble-gum piece. The fronts featured distinctive blue borders (that are prone to chipping), while bilingual backs featured 1978-79 and career stats, a short biography and a cartoon-illustrated fact about the player. Team cards (#244-261) had checklist backs. The Rookie Card of Wayne Gretzky (No. 18) had been illegally reprinted. Most of the reprints were discovered and then destroyed or clearly marked as reprints. However some still exist in the market. The reprint is difficult to distinguish from the real card, hence, collectors and dealers should be careful.

Card	Low	High
COMPLETE SET (396)	700.00	1,400.00
1 Bossy/Dionne/Lafleur LL	2.50	5.00
2 Trott/Lafleur/Dionne LL	1.50	3.00
3 Trott/Dionne/Lafleur LL	1.50	4.00
4 Williams/Holt/Schultz LL	.60	1.50
5 Bossy/Dionne/Gardner LL	1.50	4.00
6 Dryden/Resch/Parent LL	2.50	6.00
7 Lafleur/Bossy/Trott/ LL	2.00	4.00
8 Dryden/Espo/Parent LL	2.50	6.00
9 Greg Malone	.30	.75
10 Rick Middleton	.60	1.50
11 Greg Smith	.30	.75
12 Rene Robert	.40	1.00
13 Doug Risebrough	.40	1.00
14 Bob Kelly	.30	.75
15 Walt Tkaczuk	.40	1.00
16 John Marks	.30	.75
17 Willie Huber RC	.30	.75
18 Wayne Gretzky UER RC	500.00	800.00
19 Ron Sedlbauer	.30	.75
20 Glenn Resch AS2	.60	1.50
21 Blair Chapman	.30	.75
22 Ron Zanussi	.30	.75
23 Brad Park	.60	1.50
24 Yvon Lambert	.30	.75
25 Andre Savard	.30	.75
26 Jimmy Watson	.30	.75
27 Hal Philipoff RC	.30	.75
28 Dan Bouchard	.40	1.00
29 Bob Sirois	.30	.75
30 Ulf Nilsson	.40	1.00
31 Mike Murphy	.30	.75
32 Stefan Persson	.30	.75
33 Garry Unger	.40	1.00
34 Rejean Houle	.30	.75
35 Barry Beck	.40	1.00
36 Tim Young	.30	.75
37 Rick Dudley	.30	.75
38 Wayne Stephenson	.40	1.00
39 Peter McNab	.40	1.00
40 Borje Salming AS2	.60	1.50
41 Tom Lysiak	.30	.75
42 Don Maloney RC	.75	2.00
43 Mike Rogers	.40	1.00
44 Dave Lewis	.30	.75
45 Peter Lee	.30	.75
46 Marty Howe	.60	1.50
47 Serge Bernier	.30	.75
48 Paul Woods	.30	.75
49 Bob Sauve	.40	1.00
50 Larry Robinson AS1	1.00	2.50
51 Tom Gorence RC	.30	.75
52 Gary Sargent	.30	.75
53 Thomas Gradin RC	.75	2.00
54 Dean Talafous	.30	.75
55 Bob Murray	.30	.75
56 Bob Bourne	.40	1.00
57 Larry Patey	.30	.75
58 Ross Lonsberry	.30	.75
59 Rick Smith UER	.30	.75
60 Guy Chouinard	.40	1.00
61 Danny Gare	.40	1.00
62 Jim Bedard	.40	1.00
63 Dale McCourt UER	.40	1.00
64 Steve Payne RC	.30	.75
65 Pat Hughes RC	.30	.75
66 Mike McEwen	.30	.75
67 Reg Kerr RC	.30	.75
68 Walt McKechnie	.30	.75
69 Michel Plasse	.40	1.00
70 Denis Potvin AS1	.75	2.00
71 Dave Dryden	.60	1.50
72 Gary McAdam	.30	.75
73 Andre St.Laurent	.30	.75
74 Jerry Korab	.30	.75
75 Rick MacLeish	.60	1.50
76 Dennis Kearns	.30	.75
77 Jean Pronovost	.40	1.00
78 Ron Greschner	.40	1.00
79 Wayne Cashman	.60	1.50
80 Tony Esposito	1.00	2.50
81 Jets Logo CL	6.00	15.00
82 Oilers Logo CL	20.00	50.00
83 Stanley Cup Finals	2.50	6.00
84 Brian Sutter	1.00	2.50
85 Gerry Cheevers	.60	1.50
86 Pat Hickey	.30	.75
87 Mike Kaszycki	.30	.75
88 Grant Mulvey	.30	.75
89 Derek Smith	.30	.75
90 Steve Shutt	.60	1.50
91 Robert Picard	.30	.75
92 Dan Labraaten	.30	.75
93 Glen Sharpley	.30	.75
94 Denis Herron	.40	1.00
95 Reggie Leach	.60	1.50
96 John Van Boxmeer	.30	.75
97 Tiger Williams	.60	1.50
98 Butch Goring	.40	1.00
99 Don Marcotte	.30	.75
100 Bryan Trottier AS1	2.00	4.00
101 Serge Savard AS2	.60	1.50
102 Cliff Koroll	.30	.75
103 Gary Smith	.40	1.00
104 Al MacAdam	.30	.75
105 Don Edwards	.40	1.00
106 Errol Thompson	.30	.75
107 Andre Lacroix	.40	1.00
108 Marc Tardif	.40	1.00
109 Rick Kehoe	.40	1.00
110 John Davidson	.60	1.50
111 Behn Wilson RC	.40	1.00
112 Doug Jarvis	.40	1.00
113 Tom Rowe RC	.30	.75
114 Mike Milbury	.60	1.50
115 Billy Harris	.30	.75
116 Greg Fox RC	.30	.75
117 Curt Fraser RC	.40	1.00
118 Jean-Paul Parise	.30	.75
119 Ric Seiling	.30	.75
120 Darryl Sittler	.60	1.50
121 Rick Lapointe	.30	.75
122 Jim Rutherford	.40	1.00
123 Mario Tremblay	.60	1.50
124 Randy Carlyle	.60	1.50
125 Bobby Clarke	1.25	3.00
126 Wayne Thomas	.40	1.00
127 Ivan Boldirev	.30	.75
128 Ted Bulley	.30	.75
129 Dick Redmond	.30	.75
130 Clark Gillies AS1	.60	1.50
131 Checklist 1-132	20.00	40.00
132 Vaclav Nedomansky	.30	.75
133 Richard Mulhern	.30	.75
134 Dave Schultz	.60	1.50
135 Guy Lapointe	.40	1.00
136 Gilles Meloche	.60	1.50
137 Randy Pierce RC	.30	.75
138 Cam Connor	.30	.75
139 George Ferguson	.30	.75
140 Bill Barber	.60	1.50
141 Terry Ruskowski UER	.40	1.00
142 Wayne Babych RC	.60	1.50
143 Phil Russell	.30	.75
144 Bobby Schmautz	.30	.75
145 Carol Vadnais	.30	.75
146 John Tonelli RC	3.00	8.00
147 Peter Marsh RC	.30	.75
148 Thommie Bergman	.30	.75
149 Richard Martin	.60	1.50
150 Ken Dryden AS1	8.00	20.00
151 Kris Manery	.30	.75
152 Guy Charron	.30	.75
153 Lanny McDonald	.75	2.00
154 Ron Stackhouse	.30	.75
155 Stan Mikita	1.25	3.00
156 Paul Holmgren	.30	.75
157 Perry Miller	.30	.75
158 Gary Croteau	.30	.75
159 Dave Maloney	.30	.75
160 Marcel Dionne AS2	1.50	3.00
161 Mike Bossy RB	2.00	4.00
162 Don Maloney RB	.30	.75
163 Whalers Logo CL	6.00	15.00
164 Brad Park RB	.30	.75
165 Bryan Trottier RB	.60	1.50
166 Al Hill RC	.30	.75
167 Gary Bromley UER	.40	1.00
168 Don Murdoch	.30	.75
169 Wayne Merrick	.30	.75
170 Bob Gainey	.60	1.50
171 Jim Schoenfeld	.60	1.50
172 Gregg Sheppard	.30	.75
173 Dan Bolduc RC	.30	.75
174 Blake Dunlop	.30	.75
175 Gordie Howe	10.00	25.00
176 Richard Brodeur	.60	1.50
177 Tom Younghans	.30	.75
178 Andre Dupont	.30	.75
179 Ed Johnstone RC	.40	1.00
180 Gilbert Perreault	.60	1.50
181 Bob Lorimer RC	.30	.75
182 John Wensink	.30	.75
183 Lee Fogolin	.30	.75
184 Greg Carroll RC	.30	.75
185 Bobby Hull	10.00	25.00
186 Harold Snepsts	.30	.75
187 Peter Mahovlich	.40	1.00
188 Eric Vail	.30	.75
189 Phil Myre	.40	1.00
190 Wilf Paiement	.40	1.00
191 Charlie Simmer RC	3.00	8.00
192 Per-Olov Brasar	.30	.75
193 Lorne Henning	.30	.75
194 Don Luce	.30	.75
195 Steve Vickers	.30	.75
196 Bob Miller RC	.30	.75
197 Mike Palmateer	.40	1.00
198 Nick Libett	.30	.75
199 Pat Ribble RC	.30	.75
200 Guy Lafleur AS1	4.00	10.00
201 Mel Bridgman	.40	1.00
202 Morris Lukowich RC	.40	1.00
203 Don Lever	.30	.75
204 Tom Bladon	.30	.75

205 Garry Howatt .30 .75
206 Bobby Smith RC 4.00 10.00
207 Craig Ramsay .40 1.00
208 Ron Duguay .60 1.50
209 Gilles Gilbert .40 1.00
210 Bob MacMillan .30 .75
211 Pierre Mondou .30 .75
212 J.P. Bordeleau .30 .75
213 Reed Larson .40 1.00
214 Dennis Ververgaert .30 .75
215 Bernie Federko 2.50 5.00
216 Mark Howe 1.50 4.00
217 Bob Nystrom .30 .75
218 Orest Kindrachuk .30 .75
219 Mike Fidler .30 .75
220 Phil Esposito .75 2.00
221 Bill Hajt .30 .75
222 Mark Napier .40 1.00
223 Dennis Maruk .40 1.00
224 Dennis Polonich .30 .75
225 Jean Ratelle .60 1.50
226 Bob Dailey .30 .75
227 Alain Daigle .30 .75
228 Ian Turnbull .30 .75
229 Jack Valiquette .30 .75
230 Mike Bossy AS2 10.00 20.00
231 Brad Maxwell .30 .75
232 Dave Taylor 2.00 5.00
233 Pierre Larouche .60 1.50
234 Rod Schutt RC .30 .75
235 Rogatien Vachon .60 1.50
236 Ryan Walter RC .75 2.00
237 Checklist 133-264 UER 20.00 50.00
238 Terry O'Reilly .60 1.50
239 Real Cloutier .40 1.00
240 Anders Hedberg .40 1.00
241 Ken Linseman RC 2.00 5.00
242 Billy Smith .60 1.50
243 Rick Chartraw .30 .75
244 Flames Team 1.50 4.00
245 Bruins Team 1.50 4.00
246 Sabres Team 1.50 4.00
247 Blackhawks Team 1.50 4.00
248 Rockies Team 1.50 4.00
249 Red Wings Team 1.50 4.00
250 Kings Team 1.50 4.00
251 North Stars Team 1.50 4.00
252 Canadiens Team 5.00 12.00
253 Islanders Team 2.00 5.00
254 Rangers Team 1.50 4.00
255 Flyers Team 1.50 4.00
256 Penguins Team 1.50 4.00
257 Blues Team 1.50 4.00
258 Maple Leafs Team 2.00 5.00
259 Canucks Team 2.00 5.00
260 Capitals Team 1.50 4.00
261 Nordiques Team 6.00 15.00
262 Jean Hamel .30 .75
263 Stan Jonathan .30 .75
264 Russ Anderson .30 .75
265 Gordie Roberts RC .40 1.00
266 Bill Flett .30 .75
267 Robbie Ftorek .40 1.00
268 Mike Amodeo .30 .75
269 Vic Venasky .30 .75
270 Bob Manno .30 .75
271 Dan Maloney .30 .75
272 Al Sims .30 .75
273 Greg Polis .30 .75
274 Doug Favell .60 1.50
275 Pierre Plante .30 .75
276 Bob Murdoch .30 .75
277 Lyle Moffat .30 .75
278 Jack Brownschidle .30 .75
279 Dave Keon .60 1.50
280 Darryl Edestrand .30 .75
281 Greg Millen RC 2.00 4.00
282 John Gould .30 .75
283 Rich Leduc .30 .75
284 Ron Delorme .30 .75
285 Gord Smith .30 .75
286 Nick Fotiu .40 1.00
287 Kevin McCarthy RC .40 1.00
288 Jimmy Jones .30 .75
289 Pierre Bouchard .30 .75
290 Wayne Bianchin .30 .75
291 Garry Lariviere .30 .75
292 Steve Jensen .30 .75
293 John Garrett .40 1.00
294 Hilliard Graves .30 .75
295 Bill Clement .40 1.00
296 Michel Larocque .60 1.50
297 Bob Stewart .30 .75
298 Doug Patey RC .30 .75
299 Dave Farrish .30 .75
300 Al Smith .40 1.00
301 Billy Lochead .30 .75
302 Dave Hutchinson .30 .75
303 Bill Riley .30 .75
304 Barry Gibbs .30 .75
305 Chris Oddleifson .30 .75
306 J. Bob Kelly UER .30 .75
307 Al Hangsleben RC .30 .75
308 Curt Brackenbury RC .30 .75
309 Rick Green .40 1.00
310 Ken Houston .30 .75
311 Greg Joly .30 .75
312 Bill Lesuk .30 .75
313 Bill Stewart RC .30 .75
314 Rick Ley .30 .75
315 Brett Callighen RC .30 .75
316 Michel Dion .40 1.00
317 Randy Manery .30 .75
318 Barry Dean .30 .75
319 Pat Boutette .30 .75
320 Mark Heaslip .30 .75
321 Dave Inkpen .30 .75
322 Jere Gillis .30 .75
323 Larry Brown .30 .75
324 Alain Cote RC .30 .75
325 Gordie Lane .30 .75
326 Bobby Lalonde .30 .75
327 Ed Staniowski .30 .75
328 Ron Plumb .30 .75
329 Jude Drouin .30 .75
330 Rick Hampton .30 .75
331 Stan Weir .30 .75
332 Blair Stewart .30 .75
333 Mike Polich RC .30 .75
334 Jean Potvin .30 .75
335 Jordy Douglas RC .30 .75
336 Joel Quenneville RC .40 1.00
337 Glen Hanlon RC 1.25 3.00
338 Dave Hoyda RC .30 .75
339 Colin Campbell .40 1.00
340 John Smrke .30 .75
341 Brian Glennie .30 .75
342 Don Kozak .30 .75
343 Yvon Labre .30 .75
344 Curt Bennett .30 .75
345 Mike Christie .30 .75
346 Checklist 265-396 20.00 40.00
347 Pat Price .30 .75
348 Ron Low .40 1.00
349 Mike Antonovich .30 .75
350 Roland Eriksson .30 .75
351 Bob Murdoch .30 .75
352 Rob Palmer .30 .75
353 Brad Gassoff .30 .75
354 Bruce Boudreau .30 .75
355 Al Hamilton .30 .75
356 Blaine Stoughton .40 1.00
357 John Baby .30 .75
358 Gary Inness .40 1.00
359 Wayne Dillon .30 .75
360 Darcy Rota .30 .75
361 Brian Engblom RC .60 1.50
362 Bill Hogaboam .30 .75
363 Dave Debol RC .30 .75
364 Pete Lopresti .40 1.00
365 Gerry Hart .30 .75
366 Syl Apps .30 .75
367 Jack McIlhargey .30 .75
368 Willy Lindstrom .30 .75
369 Don Laurence RC .30 .75
370 Chuck Luksa RC .30 .75
371 Dave Semenko RC 4.00 10.00
372 Paul Baxter RC .40 1.00
373 Ron Ellis .40 1.00
374 Leif Svensson RC .30 .75
375 Dennis O'Brien .30 .75
376 Glenn Goldup .30 .75
377 Terry Richardson .30 .75
378 Peter Sullivan .30 .75
379 Doug Hicks .30 .75
380 Jamie Hislop RC .30 .75
381 Jocelyn Guevremont .30 .75
382 Willi Plett .40 1.00
383 Larry Goodenough .30 .75
384 Jim Warner RC .30 .75
385 Rey Comeau .30 .75
386 Barry Melrose RC 5.00 10.00
387 Dave Hunter RC .60 1.50
388 Wally Weir RC .30 .75
389 Mario Lessard RC .60 1.50
390 Ed Kea .30 .75
391 Bob Stephenson RC .30 .75
392 Dennis Hextall .30 .75
393 Jerry Butler .30 .75
394 David Shand .30 .75
395 Rick Blight .30 .75
396 Lars-Erik Sjoberg 1.00 3.00

1980-81 O-Pee-Chee

Card fronts of this 396-card standard-size set contained the player's name and position (bilingual text) in a hockey puck on the lower right of the front. Unlike the Topps set of this year, the puck was not issued with a black scratch-off covering. The team name was listed to the left of the puck. The cards were originally sold in 10-card 20-cent wax packs. Bilingual backs featured a short list of career milestones, 1979-80 season and career statistics along with short trivia comments. Members of the U.S. Olympic hockey team (USA in checklist below) were honored with the USA hockey emblem on the card front. Beware when purchasing the cards of Ray Bourque and Mark Messier as they have been counterfeited.

COMPLETE SET (396) 150.00 300.00
1 Philadelphia Flyers RB .60 1.50
2 Ray Bourque RB 5.00 12.00
3 Wayne Gretzky RB 8.00 20.00
4 Charlie Simmer RB .60 1.50
5 Billy Smith RB .40 1.00
6 Jean Ratelle .40 1.00
7 Dave Maloney .30 .75
8 Phil Myre .40 1.00
9 Ken Morrow OLY RC 1.25 3.00
10 Guy Lafleur 1.25 3.00
11 Bill Derlago RC .30 .75
12 Doug Wilson .60 1.50
13 Craig Ramsay .25 .60
14 Pat Boutette .25 .60
15 Eric Vail .25 .60
16 Mike Foligno TL .75 2.00
17 Bobby Smith .75 2.00
18 Rick Kehoe .30 .75
19 Joel Quenneville .25 .60
20 Marcel Dionne .75 2.00
21 Kevin McCarthy .25 .60
22 Jim Craig OLY RC 3.00 8.00
23 Steve Vickers .25 .60
24 Ken Linseman .40 1.00
25 Mike Bossy 3.00 8.00
26 Serge Savard .50 1.25
27 Grant Mulvey TL .30 .75
28 Pat Hickey .25 .60
29 Peter Sullivan .25 .60
30 Blaine Stoughton .30 .75
31 Mike Liut RC 6.00 15.00
32 Blair MacDonald .25 .60
33 Rick Green .25 .60
34 Al MacAdam .30 .75
35 Robbie Ftorek .25 .60
36 Dick Redmond .25 .60
37 Ron Duguay .30 .75
38 Danny Gare TL .30 .75
39 Brian Propp RC 3.00 8.00
40 Bryan Trottier 1.00 2.50
41 Rich Preston .25 .60
42 Pierre Mondou .25 .60
43 Reed Larson .25 .60
44 George Ferguson .25 .60
45 Guy Chouinard .40 1.00
46 Billy Harris .25 .60
47 Gilles Meloche .40 1.00
48 Blair Chapman .25 .60
49 Mike Gartner TL 2.50 6.00
50 Darryl Sittler .50 1.25
51 Richard Martin .40 1.00
52 Ivan Boldirev .25 .60
53 Craig Norwich RC .25 .60
54 Dennis Polonich .25 .60
55 Bobby Clarke .60 1.50
56 Terry O'Reilly .40 1.00
57 Carol Vadnais .25 .60
58 Bob Gainey .50 1.25
59 Blaine Stoughton TL .30 .75
60 Billy Smith .40 1.00
61 Mike O'Connell RC .60 1.50
62 Lanny McDonald .50 1.25
63 Lee Fogolin .25 .60
64 Rocky Saganiuk RC .25 .60
65 Rolf Edberg RC .25 .60
66 Paul Shmyr .25 .60
67 Michel Goulet RC 5.00 12.00
68 Dan Bouchard .40 1.00
69 Mark Johnson OLY RC .50 1.25
70 Reggie Leach .30 .75
71 Bernie Federko TL .75 2.00
72 Peter Mahovlich .40 1.00
73 Anders Hedberg .40 1.00
74 Brad Park .30 .75
75 Clark Gillies .40 1.00
76 Doug Jarvis .25 .60
77 John Garrett .40 1.00
78 Dave Hutchinson .25 .60
79 John Anderson RC .50 1.25
80 Gilbert Perreault .40 1.00
81 Marcel Dionne AS1 .75 2.00
82 Guy Lafleur AS1 1.25 3.00
83 Charlie Simmer AS1 .60 1.50
84 Larry Robinson AS1 .50 1.25
85 Borje Salming AS1 .30 .75
86 Tony Esposito AS1 .60 1.50
87 Wayne Gretzky AS2 10.00 25.00
88 Danny Gare AS2 .30 .75
89 Steve Shutt AS2 .30 .75
90 Barry Beck AS2 .30 .75
91 Mark Howe AS2 .60 1.50
92 Don Edwards AS2 .30 .75
93 Tom McCarthy RC .25 .60
94 P.McNab/R.Middleton TL .40 1.00
95 Mike Palmateer .40 1.00
96 Jim Schoenfeld .40 1.00
97 Jordy Douglas .25 .60
98 Keith Brown RC .30 .75
99 Dennis Ververgaert .25 .60
100 Phil Esposito .60 1.50
101 Jack Brownschidle .25 .60
102 Bob Nystrom .25 .60
103 Steve Christoff OLY RC .40 1.00
104 Rob Palmer .25 .60
105 Tiger Williams .30 .75
106 Kent Nilsson TL .30 .75
107 Morris Lukowich .40 1.00
108 Jack Valiquette .25 .60
109 Richie Dunn RC .25 .60
110 Rogatien Vachon .50 1.25
111 Mark Napier .25 .60
112 Gordie Roberts .25 .60
113 Stan Jonathan .25 .60
114 Brett Callighen .25 .60
115 Rick MacLeish .40 1.00
116 Ulf Nilsson .40 1.00
117 Rick Kehoe TL .30 .75
118 Dan Maloney .25 .60
119 Terry Ruskowski .25 .60
120 Denis Potvin .50 1.25
121 Wayne Stephenson .40 1.00
122 Rich Leduc .25 .60
123 Checklist 1-132 3.00 8.00
124 Don Lever .25 .60
125 Jim Rutherford .40 1.00
126 Ray Allison RC .25 .60
127 Mike Ramsey OLY RC 1.25 3.00
128 Stan Smyl TL .60 1.50
129 Al Secord RC 3.00 8.00
130 Denis Herron .40 1.00
131 Bob Dailey .25 .60
132 Dean Talafous .25 .60
133 Ian Turnbull .25 .60
134 Ron Sedlbauer .25 .60
135 Tom Bladon .25 .60
136 Bernie Federko 1.50 4.00
137 Dave Taylor 1.50 4.00
138 Bob Lorimer .25 .60
139 A.MacAdam/S.Payne TL .30 .75
140 Ray Bourque RC 25.00 60.00
141 Glen Hanlon .40 1.00
142 Willy Lindstrom .25 .60
143 Mike Rogers .25 .60
144 Tony McKegney RC .30 .75
145 Behn Wilson .25 .60
146 Lucien DeBlois .25 .60
147 Dave Burrows .25 .60
148 Paul Woods .25 .60
149 Phil Esposito TL .60 1.50
150 Tony Esposito .60 1.50
151 Pierre Larouche .40 1.00
152 Brad Maxwell .25 .60
153 Stan Weir .25 .60
154 Ryan Walter .25 .60
155 Dale Hoganson .25 .60
156 Anders Kallur RC .25 .60
157 Paul Reinhart RC .75 2.00
158 Greg Millen .40 1.00
159 Ric Seiling .25 .60
160 Mark Howe .60 1.50
161 Goals Leaders .60 1.50
162 Gretzky/Dionne/Lafleur LL 8.00 20.00
163 Dionne/Gretzky/Lafleur LL 12.00 30.00
164 Penalty Minutes LL .40 1.00
165 Sim/Dnne/Gre/Shtt/Stlr LL .75 2.00
166 Goals Against Avg. LL .40 1.00
167 Game-Winning Goals LL .30 .75
168 Espo/Chvrs/Sve/Vach LL .60 1.50
169 Perry Turnbull RC .25 .60
170 Barry Beck .30 .75
171 Charlie Simmer TL .60 1.50
172 Paul Holmgren .40 1.00
173 Willie Huber .25 .60
174 Tim Young .25 .60
175 Gilles Gilbert .40 1.00
176 Dave Christian OLY RC 1.25 3.00
177 Lars Lindgren RC .25 .60
178 Real Cloutier .30 .75
179 Laurie Boschman RC .30 .75
180 Steve Shutt .30 .75
181 Bob Murray .25 .60
182 Wayne Gretzky TL 8.00 20.00
183 John Van Boxmeer .25 .60
184 Nick Fotiu .40 1.00
185 Mike McEwen .25 .60
186 Greg Malone .25 .60
187 Mike Foligno RC 2.00 5.00
188 Dave Langevin RC .25 .60
189 Mel Bridgman .25 .60
190 John Davidson .40 1.00
191 Mike Milbury .40 1.00
192 Ron Zanussi .25 .60
193 Darryl Sittler TL .50 1.25
194 John Marks .25 .60
195 Mike Gartner RC 8.00 20.00
196 Dave Lewis .25 .60
197 Kent Nilsson RC 2.50 6.00
198 Rick Ley .25 .60
199 Derek Smith .25 .60
200 Bill Barber .40 1.00
201 Guy Lapointe .40 1.00
202 Vaclav Nedomansky .25 .60
203 Don Murdoch .25 .60
204 Mike Bossy TL 1.25 3.00
205 Pierre Hamel RC .40 1.00
206 Mike Eaves RC .25 .60
207 Doug Halward .25 .60
208 Stan Smyl RC .60 1.50
209 Mike Zuke RC .25 .60
210 Borje Salming .30 .75
211 Walt Tkaczuk .40 1.00
212 Grant Mulvey .30 .75
213 Rob Ramage RC 3.00 8.00
214 Tom Rowe .25 .60
215 Don Edwards .30 .75
216 G.Lafleur/P.Larouche TL 1.00 3.00
217 Dan Labraaten .25 .60
218 Glen Sharpley .25 .60
219 Stefan Persson .25 .60
220 Peter McNab .30 .75
221 Doug Hicks .25 .60
222 Bengt Gustafsson RC .25 .60
223 Michel Dion .40 1.00
224 Jimmy Watson .25 .60
225 Wilf Paiement .25 .60
226 Phil Russell .25 .60
227 Morris Lukowich TL .40 1.00
228 Ron Stackhouse .25 .60
229 Ted Bulley .25 .60
230 Larry Robinson .50 1.25
231 Don Maloney .25 .60
232 Rob McClanahan OLY RC .30 .75
233 Al Sims .25 .60

234 Errol Thompson .25 .60
235 Glenn Resch .40 1.00
236 Bob Miller .25 .60
237 Gary Sargent .25 .60
238 Real Cloutier TL .30 .75
239 Rene Robert .50 1.25
240 Charlie Simmer .60 1.50
241 Thomas Gradin .25 .60
242 Rick Vaive RC 6.00 15.00
243 Ron Wilson RC .25 .60
244 Brian Sutter .75 2.00
245 Dale McCourt .25 .60
246 Yvon Lambert .25 .60
247 Tom Lysiak .25 .60
248 Ron Greschner .25 .60
249 Reggie Leach TL .30 .75
250 Wayne Gretzky 25.00 60.00
251 Rick Middleton .40 1.00
252 Al Smith .40 1.00
253 Fred Barrett .25 .60
254 Butch Goring .40 1.00
255 Robert Picard .25 .60
256 Marc Tardif .25 .60
257 Checklist 133-264 3.00 6.00
258 Barry Long .25 .60
259 Rene Robert TL .50 1.25
260 Danny Gare .30 .75
261 Rejean Houle .25 .60
262 Islanders/Sabres .30 .75
263 Flyers/North Stars .30 .75
264 Stanley Cup Finals .50 1.25
265 Bobby Lalonde .25 .60
266 Bob Sauve .40 1.00
267 Bob MacMillan .25 .60
268 Greg Fox .25 .60
269 Hardy Astrom RC .50 1.25
270 Greg Joly .25 .60
271 Dave Lumley RC .25 .60
272 Dave Keon .40 1.00
273 Garry Unger .40 1.00
274 Steve Payne .25 .60
275 Doug Risebrough .25 .60
276 Bob Bourne .25 .60
277 Ed Johnstone .25 .60
278 Peter Lee .25 .60
279 Pete Peeters RC 2.50 6.00
280 Ron Chipperfield .25 .60
281 Wayne Babych .40 1.00
282 David Shand .25 .60
283 Jere Gillis .25 .60
284 Dennis Maruk .40 1.00
285 Jude Drouin .25 .60
286 Mike Murphy .25 .60
287 Curt Fraser .25 .60
288 Gary McAdam .25 .60
289 Mark Messier UER RC 30.00 80.00
290 Vic Venasky .25 .60
291 Per-Olov Brasar .25 .60
292 Orest Kindrachuk .25 .60
293 Dave Hunter .25 .60
294 Steve Jensen .25 .60
295 Chris Oddleifson .25 .60
296 Larry Playfair RC .25 .60
297 Mario Tremblay .25 .60
298 Gilles Lupien RC .25 .60
299 Pat Price .25 .60
300 Jerry Korab .25 .60
301 Darcy Rota .25 .60
302 Don Luce .25 .60
303 Ken Houston .25 .60
304 Brian Engblom .25 .60
305 John Tonelli .75 2.00
306 Doug Sulliman RC .25 .60
307 Rod Schutt .25 .60
308 Norm Barnes RC .25 .60
309 Serge Bernier .25 .60
310 Larry Patey .25 .60
311 Dave Farrish .25 .60
312 Harold Snepsts .40 1.00
313 Bob Sirois .25 .60
314 Peter Marsh .25 .60
315 Risto Siltanen RC .25 .60
316 Andre St.Laurent .25 .60
317 Craig Hartsburg RC 2.50 6.00
318 Wayne Cashman .40 1.00
319 Lindy Ruff RC 2.50 6.00
320 Willi Plett .40 1.00
321 Ron Delorme .25 .60
322 Gaston Gingras RC .25 .60
323 Gordie Lane .25 .60
324 Doug Soetaert RC .40 1.00
325 Gregg Sheppard .25 .60
326 Mike Busniuk RC .25 .60
327 Jamie Hislop .25 .60
328 Ed Staniowski .25 .60
329 Ron Ellis .40 1.00
330 Gary Bromley UER .40 1.00
331 Mark Lofthouse RC .25 .60
332 Dave Hoyda .25 .60
333 Ron Low .25 .60
334 Barry Gibbs .25 .60
335 Gary Edwards 1.25 3.00
336 Don Marcotte .25 .60
337 Bill Hajt .25 .60
338 Brad Marsh RC 2.00 5.00
339 J.P. Bordeleau .25 .60
340 Randy Pierce .25 .60
341 Eddie Mio RC .50 1.25
342 Randy Manery .25 .60
343 Tom Younghans .25 .60
344 Rod Langway RC 3.00 8.00
345 Wayne Merrick .25 .60
346 Steve Baker RC .40 1.00
347 Pat Hughes .25 .60
348 Al Hill .25 .60
349 Gerry Hart .25 .60
350 Richard Mulhern .25 .60
351 Jerry Butler .25 .60
352 Guy Charron .25 .60
353 Jimmy Mann RC .40 1.00
354 Brad McCrimmon RC 2.00 5.00
355 Rick Dudley .25 .60
356 Pekka Rautakallio .25 .60
357 Tim Trimper RC .25 .60
358 Mike Christie .25 .60
359 John Ogrodnick RC 2.00 5.00
360 Dave Semenko 1.50 4.00
361 Mike Veisor .40 1.00
362 Syl Apps .25 .60
363 Mike Polich .25 .60
364 Rick Chartraw .25 .60
365 Steve Tambellini RC .40 1.00
366 Ed Hospodar RC .25 .60
367 Randy Carlyle .40 1.00
368 Tom Gorence .25 .60
369 Pierre Plante .25 .60
370 Blake Dunlop .25 .60
371 Mike Kaszycki .25 .60
372 Rick Blight .25 .60
373 Pierre Bouchard .25 .60
374 Gary Doak .25 .60
375 Andre Savard .25 .60
376 Bill Clement .40 1.00
377 Reg Kerr .25 .60
378 Walt McKechnie .25 .60
379 George Lyle RC .25 .60
380 Colin Campbell .25 .60
381 Dave Debol .25 .60
382 Glenn Goldup .25 .60
383 Kent-Erik Andersson .25 .60
384 Tony Currie RC .25 .60
385 Richard Sevigny RC 3.00 8.00
386 Garry Howatt .25 .60
387 Cam Connor .25 .60
388 Ross Lonsberry .25 .60
389 Frank Bathe RC .25 .60
390 John Wensink .25 .60
391 Paul Harrison .40 1.00
392 Dennis Kearns .25 .60
393 Pat Ribble .25 .60
394 Markus Mattsson RC .40 1.00
395 Chuck Lefley .25 .60
396 Checklist 265-396 4.00 10.00

1980-81 O-Pee-Chee Super

These large (approximately 5" by 7") full-color photos were numbered on the back. They were made of thicker cardboard stock and issued as a separate release rather than as an insert. A mail-in offer card was issued in late print run packs of 1981-82 O-Pee-Chee that could be exchanged for one of the cards.

COMPLETE SET (24) 20.00 40.00
1 Brad Park 1.00 2.50
2 Gilbert Perreault .60 1.50
3 Kent Nilsson .40 1.00
4 Tony Esposito .75 2.00
5 Lanny McDonald .60 1.50
6 Pete Mahovlich .30 .75
7 Wayne Gretzky 6.00 15.00
8 Marcel Dionne 1.00 2.50
9 Bob Gainey 1.25 3.00
10 Guy Lafleur 2.50 6.00
11 Larry Robinson .75 2.00
12 Mike Bossy 3.00 6.00
13 Denis Potvin .60 1.50
14 Phil Esposito 1.25 3.00
15 Anders Hedberg .30 .75
16 Bobby Clarke 1.25 3.00
17 Marc Tardif .20 .50
18 Bernie Federko .60 1.50
19 Borje Salming .40 1.00
20 Darryl Sittler .75 2.00
21 Ian Turnbull .20 .50
22 Glen Hanlon .25 .60
23 Mike Palmateer .60 1.50
24 Morris Lukowich .20 .50

1976 Old Timers

This 18-card set of indeterminate origin measures approximately 2 1/2" by 3 5/8" and features black-and-white player photos in a white border. Members of the Red Wings, Maple Leafs and Blackhawks are pictured. The backs are blank. The cards are unnumbered and checklisted below in alphabetical order.

COMPLETE SET (18) 30.00 60.00
1 Gerry Abel 1.25 2.50
2 Sid Abel 4.00 8.00
3 Doug Barkley 1.25 2.50
4 Joe Carveth 1.25 2.50
5 Billy Dea 1.25 2.50
6 Alex Delvecchio 7.50 15.00
7 Bill Gadsby 1.25 2.50
8 Hal Jackson 1.25 2.50
9 Joe Klukay 1.25 2.50
10 Ted Lindsay 7.50 15.00
11 Jim Orlando 1.25 2.50
12 Marty Pavlich 1.25 2.50
13 Jim Peters 1.25 2.50
14 Marcel Pronovost 1.25 2.50
15 Marc Reaume 1.25 2.50
16 Leo Reise Jr. 1.25 2.50
17 Glen Skov 1.25 2.50
18 Jack Stewart 1.25 2.50

1979 Panini Stickers

This "global" hockey set was produced by Figurine Panini and printed in Italy. Each sticker measures approximately 1 15/16" by 2 3/4". The set also has an album available.

COMPLETE SET (400) 30.00 80.00
1 Goal Disallowed .20 .40
2 Butt-Ending .10 .20
3 Slow Whistle .10 .20
4 Hooking .10 .20
5 Charging .10 .20
6 Misconduct Penalty .10 .20
7 Holding .10 .20
8 High-Sticking .10 .20
9 Tripping .10 .20
10 Cross-Checking .10 .20
11 Elbowing .10 .20
12 Icing (I) .10 .20
13 Icing (II) .10 .20
14 Boarding .10 .20
15 Kneeing .10 .20
16 Slashing .10 .20
17 Excessive Roughness .10 .20
18 Spearing .10 .20
19 Interference .10 .20
20 Poster .10 .20
21 Czech.-USSR 6-4 .25 .50
22 Czech.-USSR 6-4 .25 .50
23 USSR-Czech. 3-1 .25 .50
24 USSR-Czech. 3-1 .25 .50
25 USSR-Czech. 3-1 .25 .50
26 USSR-Czech. 3-1 .25 .50
27 Can-Sweden 3-2 .25 .50
28 Can-Sweden 3-2 .25 .50
29 USSR-Canada 5-1 .38 .75
30 USSR-Canada 5-1 .38 .75
31 Czech.-Canada 3-2 .25 .50
32 Czech.-Canada 3-2 .25 .50
33 USSR-Sweden 7-1 .25 .50
34 USSR-Sweden 7-1 .25 .50
35 USA-Finland 4-3 .25 .50
36 USA-Finland 4-3 .25 .50
37 Finland-DDR 7-2 .10 .20
38 DDR-BRD 0-0 .10 .20
39 DDR-BRD 0-0 .10 .20
40 Czechoslovakia .10 .20
41 Poland .10 .20
42 USSR .63 1.25
43 USA .63 1.25
44 Canada 2.50 5.00
45 Deutschland-BRD .10 .20
46 Finland .10 .20
47 Sweden .25 .50
48 Canada Team Picture (upper left) .50 1.00
49 Canada Team Picture (upper right) .50 1.00
50 Canada Team Picture (lower left) .50 1.00
51 Canada Team Picture (lower right) .50 1.00
52 Denis Herron 1.00 2.00
53 Dan Bouchard 1.00 2.00
54 Rick Hampton .25 .50
55 Robert Picard .25 .50
56 Brad Maxwell .25 .50
57 David Shand .25 .50
58 Dennis Kearns .25 .50
59 Tom Lysiak .50 1.00
60 Dennis Maruk 1.00 2.00
61 Marcel Dionne 3.00 6.00
62 Guy Charron .50 1.00
63 Glen Sharpley .25 .50
64 Jean Pronovost .50 1.00
65 Don Lever .25 .50
66 Bob MacMillan .38 .75
67 Wilf Paiement .50 1.00
68 Pat Hickey .38 .75
69 Mike Murphy .25 .50
70 Czechoslovakia Team Picture (upper left) .25 .50
71 Czechoslovakia Team Picture (upper right) .25 .50
72 Czechoslovakia Team Picture (lower left) .25 .50
73 Czechoslovakia Team Picture (lower right) .25 .50
74 Jiri Holecek .38 .75
75 Jiri Crha .50 1.00
76 Jiri Bubla .38 .75
77 Milan Kajki .10 .20
78 Miroslav Dvorak .25 .50
79 Milan Chalupa .25 .50
80 Frantisek Kaberle .20 .40
81 Jan Zajicek .10 .20
82 Jiri Novak .10 .20
83 Ivan Hlinka .30 .75
84 Peter Stastny 5.00 10.00
85 Milan Novy .25 .50
86 Vladimir Martinec .10 .20
87 Jaroslav Pouzar .25 .50
88 Pavel Richter .10 .20
89 Bohuslav Ebermann .10 .20
90 Marian Stastny .50 1.00
91 Frantisek Cernick .20 .40
92 FDR Team Picture (upper left) .10 .20
93 FDR Team Picture (upper right) .10 .20
94 FDR Team Picture (lower left) .10 .20
95 FDR Team Picture (lower right) .10 .20
96 Erich Weishaupt .10 .20
97 Bernhard Engelbrecht .10 .20
98 Ignaz Berndaner .10 .20
99 Robert Murray .10 .20
100 Udo Kiessling .25 .50
101 Klaus Auhuber .10 .20
102 Horst Kretschmer .10 .20
103 Erich Kuhnhackl .25 .50
104 Martin Wild .10 .20
105 Lorenz Funk, Sr .10 .20
106 M. Hinterstocker .10 .20
107 Alois Schloder .10 .20
108 Rainer Philipp .10 .20
109 H. Hinterstocker .10 .20
110 Franz Reindl .10 .20
111 Walter Koberle .25 .50
112 Johann Zach .10 .20
113 Marcus Kuhl .10 .20
114 Poland Team Picture (upper left) .10 .20
115 Poland Team Picture (upper right) .10 .20
116 Poland Team Picture (lower left) .10 .20
117 Poland Team Picture (lower right) .10 .20
118 Henryk Wojtynek .10 .20
119 T. Slowakiewicz .10 .20
120 Henryk Janiszewski .10 .20
121 Henryk Gruth .10 .20
122 Andr. Slowakiewicz .10 .20
123 Andrzej Eskrzycki .10 .20
124 Jerzy Potz .25 .50
125 Marek Marcinczak .10 .20
126 Jozef Batkiewicz .10 .20
127 Stefan Chowaniec .10 .20
128 Andrzej Malysiak .10 .20
129 Walenty Zietara .10 .20
130 Henryk Pytel .10 .20
131 Mieczyslaw Jaskierski .10 .20
132 Andrezei Zabawa .10 .20
133 Tadeusz Oboj .10 .20
134 Jan Piecko .10 .20
135 Leszek Tokarz .10 .20
136 USSR Team Picture (upper left) .38 .75
137 USSR Team Picture (upper right) .38 .75
138 USSR Team Picture (lower left) .38 .75
139 USSR Team Picture (lower right) .38 .75
140 Vladislav Tretiak 5.00 10.00
141 Slava Fetisov 4.00 8.00
142 Vladimir Lutchenko .50 1.00
143 Vasilij Pervukhin .38 .75
144 Valeri Vasiliev 1.00 2.00
145 Gennady Tsygankov .50 1.00
146 Juri Fedorov .20 .40
147 Vladimir Petrov 2.00 4.00
148 Vladimir Golikov .20 .40
149 Victor Zhluktov .25 .50
150 Boris Mikhailov 2.00 4.00
151 Valeri Kharlamov 3.00 6.00
152 Helmut Balderis .50 1.00
153 Sergej Kapustin .38 .75
154 Alexander Golikov .20 .40
155 Alexander Maltsev 2.00 4.00
156 Yuri Lebedev .38 .75
157 Sergei Makarov 2.50 5.00
158 Finland Team Picture (upper left) .10 .20
159 Finland Team Picture (upper right) .10 .20
160 Finland Team Picture (lower left) .10 .20
161 Finland Team Picture (lower right) .10 .20
162 Urpo Ylonen .25 .50
163 Antero Kivela .10 .20
164 Pekka Rautakallio .50 1.00
165 Timo Nummelin .10 .20
166 Risto Siltanen .50 1.00
167 Pekka Marjamaki .10 .20
168 Tapio Levo .20 .40
169 Lasse Litma .10 .20
170 Esa Peltonen .10 .20
171 Martti Jarkko .10 .20
172 Matti Hagman .25 .50
173 Seppo Repo .20 .40
174 Pertti Korvulahti .10 .20
175 Seppo Ahokainen .10 .20
176 Juhani Tamminen .20 .40
177 Jukka Porvari .10 .20
178 Mikko Leinonen .38 .75
179 Matti Rautiainen .10 .20
180 Sweden Team Picture (upper left) .25 .50
181 Sweden Team Picture (upper right) .25 .50
182 Sweden Team Picture (lower left) .25 .50
183 Sweden Team Picture (lower right) .25 .50
184 Goran Hogasta .20 .40
185 Hardy Astrom 1.00 2.00

186 Stig Ostling	.20	.40
187 Ulf Weinstock	.10	.20
188 Mats Waltin	.10	.20
189 Stig Salming	.25	.50
190 Lars Zetterstrom	.10	.20
191 Lars Lindgren	.25	.50
192 Leif Holmgren	.10	.20
193 Roland Ericksson	.10	.20
194 Rolf Edberg	.10	.20
195 Per-Olov Brasar	.25	.50
196 Mats Ahlberg	.10	.20
197 Bengt Lundholm	.25	.50
198 Lars Gunnar Lundberg	.10	.20
199 Nils-Olov Olsson	.10	.20
200 Kent-Erik Anderson	.38	.75
201 Thomas Gradin	.75	1.50
202 USA Team Picture	.38	.75
(upper left)		
203 USA Team Picture	.38	.75
(upper right)		
204 USA Team Picture	.38	.75
(lower left)		
205 USA Team Picture	.38	.75
(lower right)		
206 Peter Lopresti	.38	.75
207 Jim Warden	.25	.50
208 Dick Lamby	.25	.50
209 Craig Norwich	.25	.50
210 Glen Patrick	.25	.50
211 Patrick Westrum	.25	.50
212 Don Jackson	.25	.50
213 Mark Johnson	.50	1.00
214 Curt Bennett	.25	.50
215 Dave Debol	.25	.50
216 Bob Collyard	.25	.50
217 Mike Fidler	.25	.50
218 Tom Younghans	.25	.50
219 Harvey Bennett	.25	.50
220 Steve Jensen	.38	.75
221 Jim Warner	.25	.50
222 Mike Eaves	.50	1.00
223 William Gilligan	.25	.50
224 Poster	.25	.50
225 Poland-Rom. 8-6	.10	.20
226 Poland-Rom. 8-6	.10	.20
227 Poland-Rom. 8-6	.10	.20
228 Poland-Rom. 8-6	.10	.20
229 Poland-Hun. 7-2	.10	.20
230 Poland-Hun. 7-2	.10	.20
231 Japan-Yug. 6-1	.10	.20
232 Japan-Yug. 6-1	.10	.20
233 Italy-Yug. 6-1	.10	.20
234 Italy-Yug. 6-1	.10	.20
235 Romania-Italy 5-5	.10	.20
236 Romania-Italy 5-5	.10	.20
237 Poland	.10	.20
238 Poland	.10	.20
239 Deutschland-DDR	.10	.20
240 Hungary	.10	.20
241 Netherland	.10	.20
242 Romania	.10	.20
243 Switzerland	.10	.20
244 Japan	.10	.20
245 Norway	.10	.20
246 Austria	.10	.20
247 DDR	.10	.20
248 DDR	.10	.20
249 Herzig	.10	.20
Kraske		
250 Simon	.10	.20
Peters		
251 Frenzel	.10	.20
Lempio		
252 Fengler	.10	.20
Slapke		
253 Patschinski	.10	.20
Bielas 1		
254 Peters	.10	.20
Scholz		
255 Bogelsack	.10	.20
Stasche		
256 Switzerland	.10	.20
257 Switzerland	.10	.20
258 Grubauer	.10	.20
Anken		
259 Zenhausern	.10	.20
Meyer		
260 Kolliker	.10	.20
Locher		
261 Mattli	.10	.20
Conte		
262 Holzer	.10	.20
Dellsberger		
263 Horisberger	.10	.20
Rossetti		
264 Berger	.10	.20
Schmid		
265 Hungary	.10	.20
266 Hungary	.10	.20
267 Balagh	.10	.20
Farkas		
268 Kovacs	.10	.20
Hajzer		
269 Flora	.10	.20
Kereszty		
270 Palla	.10	.20
Meszoly		
271 Menyhart	.10	.20
Havran		
272 Poth	.10	.20
Muhr		
273 Buzas	.10	.20
Pek		
274 Netherlands	.10	.20
275 Netherlands	.10	.20
276 Van Bilsen	.10	.20
Krikke		
277 Van Soldt	.10	.20
Peternousek		
278 Kolijn	.10	.20
Van Den		
Broek		
279 Van Wieren	.10	.20
Toren		
280 Van Onlangs	.10	.20
Schaffer		
281 Janssen	.10	.20
Van Der Griendt		
282 De Heer	.10	.20
Koopmans		
283 Japan	.10	.20
284 Japan	.10	.20
285 Iwamoto	.10	.20
Misaw		
286 Ito	.10	.20
Tonozaki		
287 Hori	.10	.20
Nakayama		
288 Tanaka	.10	.20
Kyoya		
289 Kawamura	.10	.20
Hoshino		
290 Misawa	.10	.20
Sakurai		
291 Honma	.10	.20
Hanzawa		
292 Norway	.10	.20
293 Norway	.10	.20
294 Walberg	.10	.20
Goldstein		
295 Martinsen	.10	.20
Molberg		
296 Nilsen	.10	.20
Erevik		
297 Lien	.10	.20
Roymark		
298 Eriksen	.10	.20
Ovstedal		
299 Johansen	.10	.20
Haraldsen		
300 Stethereng	.10	.20
Throrkildsen		
301 Austria	.10	.20
302 Austria	.10	.20
303 Schilcherl	.10	.20
Prohaska		
304 Hyytaienen	.10	.20
Russ		
305 Staribacher	.10	.20
Schneider		
306 Kotnauer	.10	.20
Pok		
307 Sadjina	.10	.20
Konig		
308 Mortl	.10	.20
Pepeunig		
309 Schilchner	.10	.20
Haiszan		
310 Romania	.10	.20
311 Romania	.10	.20
312 Hutan	.10	.20
Netedu		
313 Antal	.10	.20
Gall		
314 Lustinian	.10	.20
Lonita		
315 Hutanu	.10	.20
Halauca		
316 Tureanu	.10	.20
Axinte		
317 Nagy	.10	.20
Costea		
318 Nistor	.10	.20
Olenici		
319 Poster	.10	.20
320 Den.-Net 3-3	.10	.20
321 Den.-Net 3-3	.10	.20
322 Net.-Spain 19-0	.10	.20
323 Net.-Spain 19-0	.10	.20
324 Aus.-Den 7-4	.10	.20
325 Aus.-Den 7-4	.10	.20
326 Net.-Bul. 8-0	.10	.20
327 China-Den. 3-2	.10	.20
328 China-France 8-4	.10	.20
329 Bulgaria	.10	.20
330 France	.10	.20
331 Italy	.10	.20
332 Yugoslavia	.10	.20
333 Belgium	.10	.20
334 China	.10	.20
335 Denmark	.10	.20
336 Spain	.10	.20
337 Belgium	.10	.20
338 Belgium	.10	.20
339 Smeets	.10	.20
Lauwers		
340 Adriaensen	.10	.20
Zwikel		
341 Cuvelier	.10	.20
Sarazin		
342 Vermeulen	.10	.20
Voskertian		
343 Verschraegen	.10	.20
Arnould		
344 Lejeune	.10	.20
Langh		
345 Bulgaria	.10	.20
346 Bulgaria	.10	.20
347 Iliev	.10	.20
Lazarov		
348 Iliev	.10	.20
Krastinov		
349 Hristov	.10	.20
Petrov		
350 Atanasov	.10	.20
Nenov		
351 Todorov	.10	.20
Stoilov		
352 Guerasimov	.10	.20
Batchvarov		
353 China	.10	.20
354 China	.10	.20
355 Ting Wen	.10	.20
Yung Ke		
356 Ke	.10	.20
Shao Tang		
357 Ta Chun	.10	.20
Ung Sheng		
358 Hsi Kiang	.10	.20
Chang Shun		
359 Cheng Hsin	.10	.20
Te Hsi		
360 Shu Ching	.10	.20
Sheng Wen		
361 Denmark	.10	.20
362 Denmark	.10	.20
363 Hansen	.10	.20
Holten		
Moller		
364 Andersen	.10	.20
Pedersen		
365 Henriksen	.10	.20
Hviid		
366 Nielsen	.10	.20
Thomsen		
367 Nielsen	.10	.20
Kahl		
368 Jensen	.10	.20
Gjerding		
369 Spain	.10	.20
370 Spain	.10	.20
371 Estrada	.10	.20
Lizarraga		
372 Gonzalez	.10	.20
Munitiz		
373 Marin	.10	.20
Aguado		
374 Raventos	.10	.20
Encinas		
375 Capillas	.10	.20
Sarazirar		
376 Labayen	.10	.20
Plaza		
377 France	.10	.20
378 France	.10	.20
379 Maric	.10	.20
Del Monaco		
380 Oprandi	.10	.20
Combe		
381 Allard	.10	.20
Le Blond		
382 Vassieux	.10	.20
Rey		
383 Galiay	.10	.20
Le Blond		
384 Vinard	.10	.20
Smaniotto		
385 Italy	.10	.20
386 Italy	.10	.20
387 Tigliani	.10	.20
Gasser		
388 Kostner	.10	.20
Pasqualotto		
389 Lacedelli	.10	.20
Polloni		
390 Insam	.10	.20
De Toni		
391 Strohmaier	.10	.20
Kasslatter		
392 De Marchi	.10	.20
Pugliese		
393 Yugoslavia	.10	.20
394 Yugoslavia	.10	.20
395 Zbontar	.10	.20
Scap		
396 Kumar	.10	.20
Kosir		
397 Kavec	.10	.20
Smolej		
398 Kafner	.10	.20
Lepsa		
399 Poljansek	.10	.20
Kosir		
400 Klemenc	.10	.20
Jan		
xx Sticker Album	10.00	20.00

1943-48 Parade Sportive

These blank-backed photo sheets of sports figures from the Montreal area around 1945 measure approximately 5" by 8 1/4". They were issued to promote a couple of Montreal radio stations that used to broadcast interviews with some of the pictured athletes. The sheets feature white-bordered black-and-white player photos, some of them crudely retouched. The player's name appears in the bottom white margin and also as a facsimile autograph across the photo. The sheets are unnumbered and are checklisted below in alphabetical order within sport as follows: hockey (1-75), baseball (76-95) and various other sports (96-101). Additions to this checklist are appreciated. Many players are known to appear with two different poses. Since the values are the same for both poses, we have put a (2) next to the players name but have placed a value on only one of the photos.

COMPLETE SET	1,250.00	2,500.00
1 George Allen	12.50	25.00
2 Aldege(Bazz) Bastien	12.50	25.00
3 Bobby Bauer	25.00	50.00
Milt Schmidt		
Woody Dumart		
4 Joe Benoit	12.50	25.00
5 Paul Bibeault	12.50	25.00
6 Emile(Butch) Bouchard (2)	20.00	40.00
7 Butch Bouchard	20.00	40.00
Leo Lamoureux		
Bill Durnan		
8 Toe Blake	25.00	50.00
9 Lionel Bouvrette (2)	12.50	25.00
10 Frank Brimsek	20.00	40.00
11 Turk Broda (2)	25.00	50.00
12 Eddie Bruneteau	12.50	25.00
13 Modere Bruneteau (2)	12.50	25.00
14 Jean Claude Campeau	12.50	25.00
15 J.P. Campeau	12.50	25.00
16 Bob Carse	12.50	25.00
17 Joe Carveth	20.00	40.00
18 Denys Casavant (2)	12.50	25.00
19 Murph Chamberlain	12.50	25.00
20 Bill Cowley	12.50	25.00
21 Floyd Curry	12.50	25.00
22 Tony Demers (2)	12.50	25.00
23 Connie Dion	12.50	25.00
24 Bill Durnan (2)	20.00	40.00
25 Normand Dussault (2)	12.50	25.00
26 Frank Eddolls	12.50	25.00
27 Johnny Gagnon	12.50	25.00
28 Bob Fillion (2)	12.50	25.00
29 Johnny Gagnon	12.50	25.00
Aurel Joliat		
Howie Morenz		
30 Armand Gaudreault (2)	12.50	25.00
31 Fernand Gauthier (2)	12.50	25.00
32 Fernand Gauthier	12.50	25.00
Buddy O'Connor		
Dutch Hiller		
33 Jean-Paul Gladu (2)	12.50	25.00
34 Leo Gravelle	12.50	25.00
35 Glen Harmon (2)	12.50	25.00
36 Doug Harvey	20.00	40.00
37 Jerry Heffernan	12.50	25.00
Buddy O'Connor		
Pete Morin		
38 (Sugar) Jim Henry	15.00	30.00
39 Dutch Hiller (2)	12.50	25.00
40 Rosario Joanette	12.50	25.00
41 Michael Karakas (2)	12.50	25.00
42 Elmer Lach	25.00	50.00
43 Ernest Laforce	12.50	25.00
44 Leo Lamoureux	12.50	25.00
45 Edgar Laprade	12.50	25.00
46 Hal Laycoe	12.50	25.00
47 Roger Leger	12.50	25.00
48 Jacques Locas (2)	12.50	25.00
49 Harry Lumley	20.00	40.00
50 Fernand Mageau	12.50	25.00
51 Georges Mantha (2)	12.50	25.00
52 Jean Marois	12.50	25.00
53 Mike McMahon	12.50	25.00
54 Gerry McNeil	12.50	25.00
55 Pierre(Pete) Morin	12.50	25.00
56 Ken Mosdell	12.50	25.00
57 Bill Mosienko	20.00	40.00
Max Bentley		
Doug Bentley		
58 Buddy O'Connor	12.50	25.00
59 Gerry Plamondon	12.50	25.00
60 Robert(Bob) Pepin	12.50	25.00
61 Jimmy Peters	12.50	25.00
62 Jerry Plamondon	12.50	25.00
63 Paul Raymond	12.50	25.00
64 Billy Reay	15.00	30.00
65 John Quilty	12.50	25.00
66 Kenny Reardon	15.00	30.00
67 Maurice Richard (2)	37.50	75.00
68 Maurice Richard	25.00	50.00
Elmer Lach		
Toe Blake		
69 Howie(Rip) Riopelle	12.50	25.00
70 Gaye Stewart	12.50	25.00
71 Phil Watson	15.00	30.00
72 Montreal Canadiens	12.50	25.00
Team Photo 1943-44		
73 Montreal Canadiens	12.50	25.00
{Team Photo 1944-45		
74 Montreal Canadiens	12.50	25.00
{Team Photo 1945-46		
75 Montreal Canadiens	12.50	25.00
{Team Photo 1946-47		

1951-52 Parkhurst

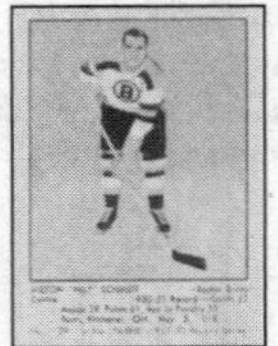

The 1951-52 Parkhurst set contains 105 small cards in crude color. Cards are 1 3/4" by 2 1/2". The player's name, team, card number, and 1950-51 statistics all appear on the front of the card. The backs of the cards are blank. Unopened wax packs, though rarely seen, consist of five cards. The cards feature players from each of the six NHL teams. The set numbering is basically according to teams, i.e., Montreal Canadiens (1-18), Boston Bruins (19-35), Chicago Blackhawks (36-51 and 53), Detroit Red Wings (54-69), Toronto Maple Leafs (70-88), and New York Rangers (89-105). Card #52 features a photo of one of the most famous goals in hockey history as Bill Barilko scored the Stanley Cup winning goal and then went flying into the air. The set features the first cards of hockey greats Gordie Howe and Maurice Richard. Please be alert when purchasing cards of Maurice Richard, Gordie Howe and Terry Sawchuk as counterfeits are known to exist of these players.

COMPLETE SET (105)	6,000.00	12,000.00
1 Elmer Lach	350.00	500.00
2 Paul Meger RC	40.00	60.00
3 Butch Bouchard RC	75.00	200.00
4 Maurice Richard RC	1,200.00	1,800.00
5 Bert Olmstead RC	75.00	125.00
6 Bud MacPherson RC	40.00	60.00
7 Tom Johnson RC	75.00	125.00
8 Paul Masnick RC	40.00	60.00
9 Calum Mackay RC	40.00	60.00
10 Doug Harvey RC	400.00	600.00
11 Ken Mosdell RC	50.00	80.00
12 Floyd Curry RC	50.00	80.00
13 Billy Reay RC	50.00	80.00
14 Bernie Geoffrion RC	400.00	600.00
15 Gerry McNeil RC	175.00	300.00
16 Dick Gamble RC	50.00	80.00
17 Gerry Couture RC	40.00	60.00
18 Ross Robert Lowe RC	40.00	60.00
19 Jim Henry RC	90.00	150.00
20 Victor Ivan Lynn RC	40.00	60.00
21 Walter Kyle RC	40.00	60.00
22 Ed Sandford RC	40.00	60.00
23 John Henderson RC	40.00	60.00
24 Dunc Fisher RC	40.00	60.00
25 Hal Laycoe RC	50.00	80.00
26 Bill Quackenbush RC	75.00	125.00
27 George Sullivan RC	50.00	80.00
28 Woody Dumart	60.00	100.00
29 Milt Schmidt	100.00	150.00
30 Adam Brown RC	40.00	60.00
31 Pentti Lund RC	50.00	80.00
32 Ray Barry RC	40.00	60.00
33 Ed Kryznowski UER RC	40.00	60.00
34 Johnny Peirson RC	50.00	80.00
35 Lorne Ferguson RC	40.00	60.00
36 Clare Raglan RC	40.00	60.00
37 Bill Gadsby RC	75.00	125.00
38 Al Dewsbury RC	40.00	60.00
39 George Clare Martin RC	40.00	60.00
40 Gus Bodnar RC	50.00	80.00
41 Jim Peters RC	40.00	60.00
42 Bep Guidolin RC	50.00	80.00
43 George Gee RC	40.00	60.00
44 Jim McFadden RC	40.00	60.00
45 Fred Hucul RC	40.00	60.00
46 Lee Fogolin RC	40.00	60.00
47 Harry Lumley RC	100.00	175.00
48 Doug Bentley RC	75.00	125.00
49 Bill Mosienko RC	75.00	125.00
50 Roy Conacher	50.00	80.00
51 Pete Babando RC	40.00	60.00
52 B.Barilko/G.McNeil IA	250.00	500.00
53 Jack Stewart	50.00	80.00
54 Marty Pavelich RC	40.00	60.00
55 Red Kelly RC	200.00	300.00
56 Ted Lindsay RC	200.00	300.00
57 Glen Skov RC	40.00	60.00
58 Benny Woit RC	40.00	60.00
59 Tony Leswick RC	50.00	80.00
60 Fred Glover RC	40.00	60.00
61 Terry Sawchuk RC	800.00	1,200.00
62 Vic Stasiuk RC	50.00	80.00
63 Alex Delvecchio RC	300.00	500.00
64 Sid Abel	60.00	100.00
65 Metro Prystai RC	40.00	60.00
66 Gordie Howe RC	2,000.00	3,000.00
67 Bob Goldham RC	40.00	60.00
68 Marcel Pronovost RC	60.00	125.00
69 Leo Reise Jr. RC	40.00	60.00
70 Harry Watson RC	60.00	125.00
71 Danny Lewicki RC	40.00	60.00
72 Howie Meeker RC	90.00	150.00
73 Gus Mortson RC	50.00	80.00
74 Joe Klukay RC	40.00	60.00
75 Turk Broda	125.00	200.00
76 Al Rollins RC	75.00	150.00
77 Bill Juzda RC	40.00	60.00
78 Ray Timgren RC	40.00	60.00
79 Hugh Bolton RC	40.00	60.00
80 Fern Flaman RC	75.00	125.00
81 Max Bentley	60.00	100.00
82 Jim Thomson RC	40.00	60.00
83 Fleming Mackell RC	50.00	80.00
84 Sid Smith RC	75.00	125.00
85 Cal Gardner RC	50.00	80.00
86 Teeder Kennedy RC	175.00	275.00
87 Tod Sloan RC	50.00	80.00
88 Bob Solinger RC	40.00	60.00
89 Frank Eddolls RC	40.00	60.00
90 Jack Evans RC	60.00	100.00
91 Hy Buller RC	40.00	60.00
92 Steve Kraftcheck RC	40.00	60.00
93 Don Raleigh RC	40.00	60.00
94 Allan Stanley RC	90.00	150.00
95 Paul Ronty RC	40.00	60.00
96 Edgar Laprade RC	60.00	100.00
97 Nick Mickoski RC	40.00	60.00
98 Jack McLeod RC	40.00	60.00
99 Gaye Stewart RC	40.00	60.00
100 Wally Hergesheimer RC	50.00	80.00
101 Ed Kullman RC	40.00	60.00
102 Ed Slowinski RC	40.00	60.00
103 Reg Sinclair RC	40.00	60.00
104 Chuck Rayner RC	75.00	125.00
105 Jim Conacher RC	100.00	200.00

1952-53 Parkhurst

The 1952-53 Parkhurst set contains 105 color, line-drawing cards. Cards are approximately 1 15/16" by 2 15/16". The obverse contains a facsimile autograph of the player pictured while the backs contain a short biography in English and 1951-52 statistics. The backs also contain the card number and a special album (for holding a set of cards) offer. The cards feature players from each of the Original Six NHL teams. The set numbering is roughly according to teams, i.e., Montreal Canadiens (1-15, 52, 93), Boston Bruins (68-85), Chicago Blackhawks (16-17, 26-27, 29-33, 35-41, 55-56), Detroit Red Wings (53, 60-67, 86-92, 104), Toronto Maple Leafs (28, 34, 42-48, 50-51, 54, 58-59, 94-96, 105), and New York Rangers (18-25, 49, 57, 97-103). The key Rookie Cards in this set are George Armstrong, Tim Horton, and Dickie Moore.

COMPLETE SET (105)	4,500.00	7,000.00
1 Maurice Richard	800.00	1,200.00
2 Billy Reay	25.00	40.00
3 Boom Boom Geoffrion UER	150.00	250.00
4 Paul Meger	18.00	30.00
5 Dick Gamble	25.00	40.00
6 Elmer Lach	50.00	80.00
7 Floyd Curry	25.00	40.00
8 Ken Mosdell	25.00	40.00
9 Tom Johnson	25.00	40.00
10 Dickie Moore RC	150.00	250.00
11 Bud MacPherson	18.00	30.00
12 Gerry McNeil	60.00	100.00
13 Butch Bouchard	25.00	40.00
14 Doug Harvey	150.00	250.00
15 John McCormack RC	18.00	30.00
16 Pete Babando	18.00	30.00
17 Al Dewsbury	18.00	30.00
18 Ed Kullman	18.00	30.00
19 Ed Slowinski	18.00	30.00
20 Wally Hergesheimer	25.00	40.00
21 Allan Stanley	50.00	80.00
22 Chuck Rayner	40.00	60.00
23 Steve Kraftcheck	18.00	30.00
24 Paul Ronty	18.00	30.00
25 Gaye Stewart	18.00	30.00
26 Fred Hucul	18.00	30.00
27 Bill Mosienko	30.00	50.00
28 Jim Morrison RC	18.00	30.00
29 Ed Kryznowski	18.00	30.00
30 Cal Gardner	25.00	40.00
31 Al Rollins	40.00	60.00
32 Enio Sclisizzi RC	18.00	30.00
33 Pete Conacher RC	25.00	40.00
34 Leo Boivin RC	40.00	60.00
35 Jim Peters	18.00	30.00
36 George Gee	18.00	30.00
37 Gus Bodnar	25.00	40.00
38 Jim McFadden	18.00	30.00
39 Gus Mortson	25.00	40.00
40 Fred Glover	18.00	30.00
41 Gerry Couture	18.00	30.00
42 Howie Meeker	50.00	80.00
43 Jim Thomson	18.00	30.00
44 Teeder Kennedy	60.00	100.00
45 Sid Smith	25.00	40.00
46 Harry Watson	30.00	50.00
47 Fern Flaman	25.00	40.00
48 Tod Sloan	25.00	40.00
49 Leo Reise Jr.	18.00	30.00
50 Bob Solinger	18.00	30.00
51 George Armstrong RC	150.00	250.00
52 Dollard St.Laurent RC	25.00	40.00
53 Alex Delvecchio	90.00	150.00
54 Gord Hannigan RC	18.00	30.00
55 Lee Fogolin	18.00	30.00
56 Bill Gadsby	30.00	50.00
57 Herb Dickenson RC	18.00	30.00
58 Tim Horton RC	500.00	700.00
59 Harry Lumley	60.00	100.00
60 Metro Prystai	18.00	30.00
61 Marcel Pronovost	25.00	40.00
62 Benny Woit	18.00	30.00
63 Glen Skov	18.00	30.00
64 Bob Goldham	18.00	30.00
65 Tony Leswick	18.00	30.00
66 Marty Pavelich	18.00	30.00
67 Red Kelly	90.00	150.00
68 Bill Quackenbush	30.00	50.00
69 Ed Sandford	18.00	30.00
70 Milt Schmidt	40.00	60.00
71 Hal Laycoe	25.00	40.00
72 Woody Dumart	25.00	40.00
73 Zellio Toppazzini RC	18.00	30.00
74 Jim Henry	25.00	40.00
75 Joe Klukay	18.00	30.00
76 Dave Creighton RC	25.00	40.00
77 Jack McIntyre RC	18.00	30.00
78 Johnny Peirson	18.00	30.00
79 George Sullivan	25.00	40.00
80 Real Chevrefils RC	25.00	40.00
81 Leo Labine RC	30.00	50.00
82 Fleming Mackell	25.00	40.00
83 Pentti Lund	18.00	30.00
84 Bob Armstrong RC	18.00	30.00
85 Warren Godfrey RC	18.00	30.00
86 Terry Sawchuk	300.00	500.00
87 Ted Lindsay	90.00	150.00
88 Gordie Howe	600.00	1,000.00
89 Johnny Wilson RC	25.00	40.00
90 Vic Stasiuk	25.00	40.00
91 Larry Zeidel RC	18.00	30.00
92 Larry Wilson RC	18.00	30.00
93 Bert Olmstead	25.00	40.00
94 Ron Stewart RC	25.00	40.00
95 Max Bentley	30.00	50.00
96 Rudy Migay RC	18.00	30.00
97 Jack Stoddard RC	18.00	30.00
98 Hy Buller	18.00	30.00
99 Don Raleigh UER	18.00	30.00
100 Edgar Laprade	25.00	40.00
101 Nick Mickoski	18.00	30.00
102 Jack McLeod UER (Robert on back)	18.00	30.00
103 Jim Conacher	25.00	40.00
104 Reg Sinclair	18.00	30.00
105 Bob Hassard RC	75.00	125.00

1953-54 Parkhurst

The 1953-54 Parkhurst set contains 100 cards in full color. Cards measure approximately 2 1/2" by 3 5/8". The cards were sold in five-cent wax packs each containing four cards and gum. The size of the card increased from the previous year, and the picture and color show marked improvement. A facsimile autograph of the player is found on the front. The backs contain the card number, 1952-53 statistics, a short biography, and an album offer. The back data is presented in both English and French. The cards feature players from each of the six NHL teams. The set numbering is basically according to teams, i.e., Toronto Maple Leafs (1-17), Montreal Canadiens (18-35), Detroit Red Wings (36-52), New York Rangers (53-68), Chicago Blackhawks (69-84), and Boston Bruins (85-100). The key Rookie Cards in this set are Al Arbour, Andy Bathgate, Jean Beliveau, Harry Howell, and Gump Worsley.

COMPLETE SET (100)	3,000.00	4,500.00
1 Harry Lumley	175.00	300.00
2 Sid Smith	20.00	40.00
3 Gord Hannigan	20.00	40.00
4 Bob Hassard	20.00	40.00
5 Tod Sloan	20.00	40.00
6 Leo Boivin	20.00	40.00
7 Teeder Kennedy	40.00	80.00
8 Jim Thomson	20.00	40.00
9 Ron Stewart	20.00	40.00
10 Eric Nesterenko RC	40.00	80.00
11 George Armstrong	60.00	100.00
12 Harry Watson	30.00	60.00
13 Tim Horton	175.00	300.00
14 Fern Flaman	25.00	50.00
15 Jim Morrison	20.00	40.00
16 Bob Solinger	20.00	40.00
17 Rudy Migay	20.00	40.00
18 Dick Gamble	20.00	40.00
19 Bert Olmstead	25.00	50.00
20 Eddie Mazur RC	20.00	40.00
21 Paul Meger	20.00	40.00
22 Bud MacPherson	20.00	40.00
23 Dollard St.Laurent	20.00	40.00
24 Maurice Richard	300.00	500.00
25 Gerry McNeil	50.00	80.00
26 Doug Harvey	125.00	200.00
27 Jean Beliveau RC	600.00	1,000.00
28 Dickie Moore UER	75.00	125.00
29 Bernie Geoffrion	125.00	200.00
30 E.Lach/M.Richard	125.00	200.00
31 Elmer Lach	40.00	80.00
32 Butch Bouchard	25.00	50.00
33 Ken Mosdell	20.00	40.00
34 John McCormack	20.00	40.00
35 Floyd Curry	20.00	40.00
36 Earl Reibel RC	20.00	40.00
37 Bill Dineen UER RC	40.00	80.00
38 Al Arbour RC UER	60.00	100.00
39 Vic Stasiuk	20.00	40.00
40 Red Kelly	60.00	100.00
41 Marcel Pronovost	25.00	50.00
42 Metro Prystai	20.00	40.00
43 Tony Leswick	20.00	40.00
44 Marty Pavelich	20.00	40.00
45 Benny Woit	20.00	40.00
46 Terry Sawchuk	200.00	350.00
47 Alex Delvecchio	60.00	100.00
48 Glen Skov	20.00	40.00
49 Bob Goldham	20.00	40.00
50 Gordie Howe	500.00	800.00
51 Johnny Wilson	20.00	40.00
52 Ted Lindsay	60.00	100.00
53 Gump Worsley RC	275.00	400.00
54 Jack Evans	20.00	40.00
55 Max Bentley	30.00	60.00
56 Andy Bathgate RC	90.00	150.00
57 Harry Howell RC	90.00	150.00
58 Hy Buller	20.00	40.00
59 Chuck Rayner	25.00	50.00
60 Jack Stoddard	20.00	40.00
61 Ed Kullman	25.00	50.00
62 Nick Mickoski	20.00	40.00
63 Paul Ronty	20.00	40.00
64 Allan Stanley	30.00	60.00
65 Leo Reise Jr.	20.00	40.00
66 Aldo Guidolin RC	20.00	40.00
67 Wally Hergesheimer	20.00	40.00
68 Don Raleigh	20.00	40.00
69 Jim Peters	20.00	40.00
70 Pete Conacher	20.00	40.00
71 Fred Hucul	20.00	40.00
72 Lee Fogolin	20.00	40.00
73 Larry Zeidel	20.00	40.00
74 Larry Wilson	20.00	40.00
75 Gus Bodnar	20.00	40.00
76 Bill Gadsby	30.00	60.00
77 Jim McFadden	20.00	40.00
78 Al Dewsbury	20.00	40.00
79 Clare Raglan	20.00	40.00
80 Bill Mosienko	30.00	60.00
81 Gus Mortson	20.00	40.00
82 Al Rollins	25.00	50.00
83 George Gee	20.00	40.00
84 Gerry Couture	20.00	40.00
85 Dave Creighton	20.00	40.00
86 Jim Henry	25.00	50.00
87 Hal Laycoe	20.00	40.00
88 Johnny Peirson UER	25.00	50.00
89 Real Chevrefils	20.00	40.00
90 Ed Sandford	20.00	40.00
91A Fleming Mackell No Bio	25.00	50.00
91B Fleming Mackell Full Bio	250.00	400.00
92 Milt Schmidt	40.00	80.00
93 Leo Labine	20.00	40.00
94 Joe Klukay	20.00	40.00
95 Warren Godfrey	20.00	40.00
96 Woody Dumart	25.00	50.00
97 Frank Martin RC	20.00	40.00
98 Jerry Toppazzini RC	25.00	50.00
99 Cal Gardner	20.00	40.00
100 Bill Quackenbush	75.00	150.00

1954-55 Parkhurst

The 1954-55 Parkhurst set contains 100 cards in full color with both the card number and a facsimile autograph on the fronts. Cards in the set measure approximately 2 1/2" by 3 5/8". Unopened wax packs consisted of four cards. The backs, in both English and French, contain 1953-54 statistics, a short player biography, and an album offer (contained only on cards 1-88). Cards 1-88 feature players from each of the six NHL teams and the remaining cards are action scenes. Cards 1-88 were available with either a stat or a premium back. The cards with the statistics on the back are generally more desirable. The player/set numbering is basically according to teams, i.e., Montreal Canadiens (1-15), Toronto Maple Leafs (16-32), Detroit Red Wings (33-48), Boston Bruins (49-64), New York Rangers (65-76), and Chicago Blackhawks (77-88), and All-Star selections from the previous season are noted discreetly on the card front by a red star (first team selection) or blue star (second team). The key Rookie Card in this set is Johnny Bower, although there are several Action Scene cards featuring Jacques Plante in the year before his regular Rookie Card.

COMPLETE SET (100)	2,500.00	4,000.00
*1-88 PREMIUM BACK: SAME VALUE		
1 Gerry McNeil	75.00	150.00
2 Dickie Moore	50.00	80.00
3 Jean Beliveau	200.00	300.00
4 Eddie Mazur	15.00	25.00
5 Bert Olmstead	18.00	30.00
6 Butch Bouchard	25.00	40.00
7 Maurice Richard	275.00	400.00
8 Bernie Geoffrion	75.00	125.00
9 John McCormack	15.00	25.00
10 Tom Johnson	18.00	30.00
11 Calum Mackay	18.00	30.00
12 Ken Mosdell	18.00	30.00
13 Paul Masnick	18.00	30.00
14 Doug Harvey	75.00	125.00
15 Floyd Curry	15.00	25.00
16 Harry Lumley	25.00	40.00
17 Harry Watson	25.00	40.00
18 Jim Morrison	18.00	30.00
19 Eric Nesterenko	18.00	30.00
20 Fern Flaman	18.00	30.00
21 Rudy Migay	15.00	25.00
22 Sid Smith	15.00	25.00
23 Ron Stewart	18.00	30.00
24 George Armstrong	50.00	80.00
25 Earl Balfour RC	18.00	30.00
26 Leo Boivin	15.00	25.00
27 Gord Hannigan	18.00	30.00
28 Bob Bailey RC	18.00	30.00
29 Teeder Kennedy	30.00	50.00
30 Tod Sloan	15.00	25.00
31 Tim Horton	150.00	250.00
32 Jim Thomson	18.00	30.00
33 Terry Sawchuk	150.00	250.00
34 Marcel Pronovost	18.00	30.00

35 Metro Prystai	15.00	25.00
36 Alex Delvecchio	50.00	80.00
37 Earl Reibel	15.00	25.00
38 Benny Woit	15.00	25.00
39 Bob Goldham	15.00	25.00
40 Glen Skov	18.00	30.00
41 Gordie Howe	400.00	600.00
42 Red Kelly	50.00	80.00
43 Marty Pavelich	15.00	25.00
44 Johnny Wilson	15.00	25.00
45 Tony Leswick	15.00	25.00
46 Ted Lindsay	50.00	80.00
47 Keith Allen RC	18.00	30.00
48 Bill Dineen	15.00	25.00
49 Jim Henry	25.00	40.00
50 Fleming Mackell	18.00	30.00
51 Bill Quackenbush	25.00	40.00
52 Hal Laycoe	15.00	25.00
53 Cal Gardner	15.00	25.00
54 Joe Klukay	15.00	25.00
55 Bob Armstrong	15.00	25.00
56 Warren Godfrey	18.00	30.00
57 Doug Mohns RC	25.00	40.00
58 Dave Creighton	30.00	50.00
59 Milt Schmidt	30.00	50.00
60 Johnny Peirson	15.00	25.00
61 Leo Labine	18.00	30.00
62 Gus Bodnar	15.00	25.00
63 Real Chevrefils	15.00	25.00
64 Ed Sandford	18.00	30.00
65 Johnny Bower UER RC	300.00	500.00
66 Paul Ronty	15.00	25.00
67 Leo Reise Jr.	15.00	25.00
68 Don Raleigh	18.00	30.00
69 Bob Chrystal RC	15.00	25.00
70 Harry Howell	35.00	60.00
71 Wally Hergesheimer	15.00	25.00
72 Jack Evans	15.00	25.00
73 Camille Henry RC	18.00	30.00
74 Dean Prentice RC	25.00	40.00
75 Nick Mickoski	15.00	25.00
76 Ron Murphy RC	15.00	25.00
77 Al Rollins	25.00	40.00
78 Al Dewsbury	15.00	25.00
79 Lou Jankowski RC	15.00	25.00
80 George Gee	15.00	25.00
81 Gus Mortson	15.00	25.00
82 Fred Saskamoose RC	75.00	125.00
83 Ike Hildebrand RC	15.00	25.00
84 Lee Fogolin	15.00	25.00
85 Larry Wilson	15.00	25.00
86 Pete Conacher	15.00	25.00
87 Bill Gadsby	25.00	40.00
88 Jack McIntyre	15.00	25.00
89 Floyd Curry	15.00	25.00
90 Alex Delvecchio	18.00	30.00
91 R.Kelly/H.Lumley	25.00	40.00
92 Lumley/Howe/Stewart	60.00	100.00
93 H.Lumley/R.Murphy	15.00	25.00
94 P.Meger/J.Morrison	15.00	25.00
95 D.Harvey/E.Nesterenko	30.00	50.00
96 T.Sawchuk/T.Kennedy	60.00	100.00
97 Plante/B.Bouchard/Reibel	60.00	100.00
98 J.Plante/Harvey/Sloan	60.00	100.00
99 J.Plante/T.Kennedy	60.00	100.00
100 T.Sawchuk/B.Geoffrion	125.00	200.00

1955-56 Parkhurst

The 1955-56 Parkhurst set contains 79 cards in full color with the number and team insignia on the fronts. Cards in the set measure approximately 2 1/2" by 3 9/16". The set features players from Montreal and Toronto as well as Old-Time Greats. The Old-Time Great selections are numbers 21-32 and 55-66. The backs, printed in red ink, in both English and French, contain 1954-55 statistics, a short biography, a "Do You Know" information section, and an album offer. The key Rookie Card in this set is Jacques Plante. The same 79 cards can also be found with Quaker Oats backs, i.e., green printing on back. The Quaker Oats version is much tougher to locate. Reportedly, cards #1, 33 and 37 are extremely difficult to acquire in the Quaker Oats version, and can often sell for much more than the suggested multipliers.

COMPLETE SET (79)	2,800.00	5,000.00
1 Harry Lumley	200.00	300.00
2 Sid Smith	15.00	30.00
3A Tim Horton COR	150.00	250.00
3B Tim Horton ERR		
4 George Armstrong	50.00	80.00
5 Ron Stewart	15.00	30.00
6 Joe Klukay	12.00	20.00
7 Marc Reaume RC	12.00	20.00
8 Jim Morrison	12.00	20.00
9 Parker MacDonald RC	12.00	20.00
10 Tod Sloan	12.00	20.00
11 Jim Thomson	12.00	20.00
12 Rudy Migay	12.00	20.00
13 Brian Cullen RC	15.00	30.00
14 Hugh Bolton	12.00	20.00
15 Eric Nesterenko	15.00	30.00
16 Larry Cahan RC	12.00	20.00
17 Willie Marshall RC	12.00	20.00
18 Dick Duff RC	50.00	100.00
19 Jack Caffery RC	12.00	20.00
20 Billy Harris RC	15.00	30.00
21 Lorne Chabot OTG	15.00	30.00
22 Harvey Jackson OTG	30.00	50.00
23 Turk Broda OTG	60.00	100.00
24 Joe Primeau OTG	25.00	40.00
25 Gordie Drillon OTG	15.00	30.00
26 Chuck Conacher OTG	25.00	40.00
27 Sweeney Schriner OTG	15.00	30.00
28 Syl Apps OTG	25.00	40.00
29 Teeder Kennedy OTG	30.00	50.00
30 Ace Bailey OTG	40.00	60.00
31 Babe Pratt OTG	15.00	30.00
32 Harold Cotton OTG	15.00	30.00
33 King Clancy CO	60.00	100.00
34 Hap Day	15.00	30.00
35 Don Marshall RC	30.00	50.00
36 Jackie LeClair RC	15.00	30.00
37 Maurice Richard	275.00	400.00
38 Dickie Moore	50.00	80.00
39 Ken Mosdell	15.00	30.00
40 Floyd Curry	12.00	20.00
41 Calum Mackay	12.00	20.00
42 Bert Olmstead	15.00	30.00
43 Bernie Geoffrion	75.00	125.00
44 Jean Beliveau	250.00	350.00
45 Doug Harvey	75.00	125.00
46 Butch Bouchard	15.00	30.00
47 Bud MacPherson	12.00	20.00
48 Dollard St.Laurent	12.00	20.00
49 Tom Johnson	15.00	30.00
50 Jacques Plante RC	800.00	1,200.00
51 Paul Meger	12.00	20.00
52 Gerry McNeil	25.00	40.00
53 Jean-Guy Talbot RC	15.00	30.00
54 Bob Turner RC	12.00	20.00
55 Newsy Lalonde OTG	40.00	60.00
56 Georges Vezina OTG	75.00	125.00
57 Howie Morenz OTG	60.00	100.00
58 Aurel Joliat OTG	40.00	60.00
59 George Hainsworth OTG	60.00	100.00
60 Sylvio Mantha OTG	15.00	30.00
61 Battleship Leduc OTG	15.00	30.00
62 Babe Siebert OTG UER	25.00	40.00
63 Bill Durnan OTG RC	40.00	60.00
64 Ken Reardon OTG	40.00	60.00
65 Johnny Gagnon OTG	15.00	30.00
66 Billy Reay OTG	15.00	30.00
67 Toe Blake CO	30.00	50.00
68 Frank Selke MG	18.00	30.00
69 Hugh Beats Hodge	18.00	30.00
70 Lumley Stops BoomBoom	40.00	60.00
71 J.Plante Is Protected	50.00	80.00
72 Rocket Roars Through	50.00	80.00
73 Richard Tests Lumley	50.00	80.00
74 Beliveau Bats Puck	40.00	60.00
75 Nesterenko/Smith/Plante	50.00	80.00
76 Curry/Lumley/Morrison	15.00	30.00
77 Sloan/MacD/Harvey/Beliv	50.00	80.00
78 Montreal Forum	150.00	300.00
79 Maple Leaf Gardens	150.00	300.00

1955-56 Parkhurst Quaker Oats

1 Harry Lumley	400.00	700.00
2 Sid Smith	20.00	60.00
3 Tim Horton	350.00	600.00
4 George Armstrong	75.00	200.00
5 Ron Stewart	15.00	40.00
6 Joe Klukay	15.00	40.00
7 Marc Reaume RC	15.00	40.00
8 Jim Morrison	15.00	40.00
9 Parker MacDonald RC	15.00	40.00
10 Tod Sloan	20.00	60.00
11 Jim Thomson	15.00	40.00
12 Rudy Migay	15.00	40.00
13 Brian Cullen RC	30.00	80.00
14 Hugh Bolton	15.00	40.00
15 Eric Nesterenko	20.00	60.00
16 Larry Cahan RC	20.00	60.00
17 Willie Marshall RC	15.00	40.00
18 Dick Duff RC	150.00	300.00
19 Jack Caffery RC	15.00	40.00
20 Billy Harris RC	30.00	80.00
21 Lorne Chabot OTG	40.00	100.00
22 Harvey Jackson OTG	60.00	150.00
23 Turk Broda OTG	150.00	300.00
24 Joe Primeau OTG	30.00	80.00
25 Gordie Drillon OTG	30.00	80.00
26 Chuck Conacher OTG	30.00	80.00
27 Sweeney Schriner OTG	30.00	80.00
28 Syl Apps OTG	30.00	80.00
29 Teeder Kennedy OTG	40.00	100.00
30 Ace Bailey OTG	50.00	125.00
31 Babe Pratt OTG	20.00	60.00
32 Harold Cotton OTG	20.00	60.00
33 King Clancy CO	75.00	200.00
34 Hap Day	30.00	80.00
35 Don Marshall RC	40.00	100.00
36 Jackie LeClair RC	20.00	60.00
37 Maurice Richard	500.00	750.00
38 Dickie Moore	60.00	150.00
39 Ken Mosdell	20.00	60.00
40 Floyd Curry	20.00	60.00
41 Calum Mackay	15.00	40.00
42 Bert Olmstead	20.00	60.00
43 Boom Boom Geoffrion	125.00	250.00
44 Jean Beliveau	400.00	700.00
45 Doug Harvey	125.00	250.00
46 Butch Bouchard	20.00	60.00
47 Bud MacPherson	15.00	40.00
48 Dollard St.Laurent	20.00	60.00
49 Tom Johnson	30.00	80.00
50 Jacques Plante RC	2,000.00	3,500.00
51 Paul Meger	20.00	60.00
52 Gerry McNeil	40.00	100.00
53 Jean-Guy Talbot RC	30.00	80.00
54 Bob Turner RC	15.00	40.00
55 Newsy Lalonde OTG	50.00	125.00
56 Georges Vezina OTG	150.00	300.00
57 Howie Morenz OTG	150.00	300.00
58 Aurel Joliat OTG	50.00	125.00
59 George Hainsworth OTG	125.00	250.00
60 Sylvio Mantha OTG	20.00	60.00
61 Battleship Leduc OTG	20.00	60.00
62 Babe Siebert OTG UER (Misspelled Seibert on both sides	30.00	80.00
63 Bill Durnan OTG RC	50.00	125.00
64 Ken Reardon OTG	50.00	125.00
65 Johnny Gagnon OTG	20.00	60.00
66 Billy Reay OTG	20.00	60.00
67 Toe Blake CO	40.00	100.00
68 Frank Selke MG	20.00	60.00
69 Hugh Beats Hodge	20.00	60.00
70 Lum Stops BoomBoom	50.00	125.00
71 J.Plante Is Protected	75.00	200.00
72 Rocket Roars Through	75.00	200.00
73 Richard Tests Lumley	75.00	200.00
74 Beliveau Bats Puck	60.00	150.00
75 Nester Smith Plante	75.00	200.00
76 Curry Lumley Morrison	30.00	80.00
77 Sloan MacDonald Harvey Beliveau	60.00	150.00
78 Montreal Forum	500.00	750.00
79 Maple Leaf Gardens	500.00	750.00

1957-58 Parkhurst

The 1957-58 Parkhurst set contains 50 color cards featuring Montreal and Toronto players. Cards are approximately 2 7/16" by 3 5/8". There are card numbers 1 to 25 for Montreal (M prefix in checklist) and card numbers 1 to 25 for Toronto (T prefix in checklist). The cards are numbered on the fronts and the backs feature resumes in both French and English. The card number, the player's name, and his position appear in a red rectangle on the front. The backs are printed in blue ink. The key Rookie Cards in this set are Frank Mahovlich and Henri Richard. There was no Parkhurst hockey set in 1956-57 reportedly due to market re-evaluation.

COMPLETE SET (50)	2,000.00	3,500.00
M1 Doug Harvey	150.00	275.00
M2 Bernie Geoffrion	80.00	150.00
M3 Jean Beliveau	200.00	300.00
M4 Henri Richard RC	400.00	600.00
M5 Maurice Richard	300.00	400.00
M6 Tom Johnson	15.00	25.00
M7 Andre Pronovost RC	20.00	40.00
M8 Don Marshall	12.00	20.00
M9 Jean-Guy Talbot	12.00	20.00
M10 Dollard St.Laurent	12.00	20.00
M11 Phil Goyette RC	25.00	40.00
M12 Claude Provost RC	25.00	40.00
M13 Bob Turner	12.00	20.00
M14 Dickie Moore	35.00	60.00
M15 Jacques Plante	250.00	400.00
M16 Toe Blake CO	25.00	40.00
M17 Charlie Hodge RC	50.00	80.00
M18 Marcel Bonin	15.00	25.00
M19 Bert Olmstead	15.00	25.00
M20 Floyd Curry	12.00	20.00
M21 Len Broderick IA RC	25.00	40.00
M22 Brian Cullen scores	12.00	20.00
M23 Broderick/Harvey IA	25.00	40.00
M24 Geoffrion/Chadwick IA	30.00	50.00
M25 Olmstead/Chadwick IA	20.00	40.00
T1 George Armstrong	60.00	100.00
T2 Ed Chadwick RC	100.00	175.00
T3 Dick Duff	15.00	25.00
T4 Bob Pulford RC	90.00	150.00
T5 Tod Sloan	18.00	30.00
T6 Rudy Migay	12.00	20.00
T7 Ron Stewart	12.00	20.00
T8 Gerry James RC	15.00	25.00
T9 Brian Cullen	12.00	20.00
T10 Sid Smith	12.00	20.00
T11 Jim Morrison	12.00	20.00
T12 Marc Reaume	12.00	20.00
T13 Hugh Bolton	12.00	20.00
T14 Pete Conacher		
T15 Billy Harris	12.00	20.00
T16 Mike Nykoluk RC		
T17 Frank Mahovlich RC	300.00	500.00
T18 Ken Girard RC		
T19 Al MacNeil RC		
T20 Bob Baun RC	60.00	100.00
T21 Barry Cullen RC		
T22 Tim Horton	100.00	175.00
T23 Gary Collins RC		
T24 Gary Aldcorn RC	12.00	20.00
T25 Billy Reay CO	18.00	30.00

1958-59 Parkhurst

The 1958-59 Parkhurst set contains 50 color cards of Montreal and Toronto players. Cards are approximately 2 7/16" by 3 5/8". In contrast to the 1957-58 Parkhurst set, the cards, numbered on the fronts, are numbered continuously from 1 to 50. Resumes on the backs of the cards are in both French and English. The player's name and the team logo appears in a yellow rectangle at the bottom on the front. The number, position, and (usually) a hockey stick appear on the front at the upper left. The backs are printed in black ink. The key Rookie Card in this set is Ralph Backstrom.

COMPLETE SET (50)	1,200.00	1,800.00
1 Bob Pulford IA	30.00	50.00
2 Henri Richard	125.00	200.00
3 Andre Pronovost	10.00	15.00
4 Billy Harris	12.00	20.00
5 Albert Langlois RC	10.00	15.00
6 Noel Price RC	10.00	15.00
7 G.Armstrong/Johnson IA	15.00	25.00
8 Dickie Moore	25.00	40.00
9 Toe Blake CO	15.00	25.00
10 Tom Johnson	12.00	20.00
11 J.Plante/G.Armstrong	35.00	50.00
12 Ed Chadwick	25.00	40.00
13 Bob Nevin RC	15.00	25.00
14 Ron Stewart	12.00	18.00
15 Bob Baun	25.00	40.00
16 Ralph Backstrom RC	30.00	50.00
17 Charlie Hodge	25.00	40.00
18 Gary Aldcorn	10.00	15.00
19 Willie Marshall	10.00	15.00
20 Marc Reaume	10.00	15.00
21 Jacques Plante IA	40.00	60.00
22 Jacques Plante	200.00	300.00
23 Allan Stanley UER	15.00	25.00
24 Ian Cushenan RC	12.00	18.00
25 Billy Reay CO	12.00	18.00
26 Jacques Plante IA	40.00	60.00
27 Bert Olmstead	12.00	18.00
28 Bernie Geoffrion	50.00	80.00
29 Dick Duff	12.00	18.00
30 Ab McDonald RC	10.00	15.00
31 Barry Cullen	10.00	15.00
32 Marcel Bonin	10.00	15.00
33 Frank Mahovlich	125.00	200.00
34 Jean Beliveau	125.00	200.00
35 Jacques Plante IA	40.00	60.00
36 Brian Cullen Shoots	12.00	18.00
37 Steve Kraftcheck	10.00	15.00
38 Maurice Richard	200.00	300.00
39 Jacques Plante IA	40.00	60.00
40 Bob Turner	10.00	15.00
41 Jean-Guy Talbot	12.00	18.00
42 Tim Horton	75.00	125.00
43 Claude Provost	12.00	18.00
44 Don Marshall	12.00	18.00
45 Bob Pulford	15.00	25.00
46 Johnny Bower UER	90.00	150.00
47 Phil Goyette	12.00	18.00
48 George Armstrong	25.00	40.00
49 Doug Harvey	50.00	80.00
50 Brian Cullen	20.00	40.00

1959-60 Parkhurst

The 1959-60 Parkhurst set contains 50 color cards of Montreal and Toronto players. Cards are approximately 2 7/16" by 3 5/8". The cards are numbered on the fronts. The backs, which contain 1958-59 statistics, a short biography, and a Hockey Gum contest ad, are written in both French and English. The key Rookie Cards in this set are Carl Brewer and Punch Imlach.

COMPLETE SET (50)	700.00	1,400.00
1 Canadiens On Guard Jacques Plante Tom Johnson Phil Goyette	75.00	150.00
2 Maurice Richard	150.00	300.00
3 Carl Brewer RC	40.00	80.00
4 Phil Goyette	12.00	30.00
5 Ed Chadwick	15.00	40.00
6 Jean Beliveau	75.00	150.00
7 George Armstrong	15.00	40.00
8 Doug Harvey	40.00	80.00
9 Billy Harris	12.00	30.00
10 Tom Johnson	12.00	30.00
11 Marc Reaume	12.00	30.00
12 Marcel Bonin	12.00	30.00
13 Johnny Wilson	12.00	30.00
14 Dickie Moore	20.00	50.00
15 Punch Imlach CO RC	20.00	50.00
16 Charlie Hodge	15.00	40.00
17 Larry Regan	12.00	30.00
18 Claude Provost	12.00	30.00
19 Gerry Ehman RC	12.00	30.00
20 Ab McDonald	12.00	30.00
21 Bob Baun	12.00	30.00
22 Ken Reardon VP	12.00	30.00
23 Tim Horton	65.00	120.00

Card	Low	High
24 Frank Mahovlich	75.00	150.00
25 Johnny Bower IA	20.00	50.00
26 Ron Stewart	12.00	30.00
27 Toe Blake CO	12.00	30.00
28 Bob Pulford	12.00	30.00
29 Ralph Backstrom	12.00	30.00
30 Action Around the Net	15.00	40.00
31 Bill Hicke RC	15.00	40.00
32 Johnny Bower	60.00	120.00
33 Bernie Geoffrion	40.00	80.00
34 Ted Hampson RC	12.00	30.00
35 Andre Pronovost	12.00	30.00
36 Stafford Smythe CHC	12.00	30.00
37 Don Marshall	12.00	30.00
38 Dick Duff	12.00	30.00
39 Henri Richard	75.00	150.00
40 Bert Olmstead	12.00	30.00
41 Jacques Plante	125.00	250.00
42 Noel Price	12.00	30.00
43 Bob Turner	12.00	30.00
44 Allan Stanley	20.00	50.00
45 Albert Langlois	12.00	30.00
46 Officials Intervene	12.00	30.00
47 Frank Selke MD	12.00	30.00
48 Gary Edmundson RC	12.00	30.00
49 Jean-Guy Talbot	12.00	30.00
50 King Clancy AGM	50.00	100.00

1960-61 Parkhurst

The 1960-61 Parkhurst set of 61 color cards, numbered on the fronts, contains players from Montreal, Toronto, and Detroit. The numbering of the players in the set is basically by teams, i.e., Toronto Maple Leafs (1-19), Detroit Red Wings (20-37), and Montreal Canadiens (38-55). Cards in the set are 2 7/16" by 3 5/8". The backs, in both French and English, are printed in blue ink and contain NHL lifetime records, vital statistics, and biographical data of the player. This set contains the last card of Maurice "Rocket" Richard. The key Rookie Card in this set is John McKenzie.

Card	Low	High
COMPLETE SET (61)	1,100.00	1,700.00
1 Tim Horton	75.00	150.00
2 Frank Mahovlich	50.00	100.00
3 Johnny Bower	40.00	80.00
4 Bert Olmstead	8.00	20.00
5 Gary Edmundson	6.00	15.00
6 Ron Stewart	6.00	15.00
7 Gerry James	6.00	15.00
8 Gerry Ehman	6.00	15.00
9 Red Kelly	15.00	30.00
10 Dave Creighton	6.00	15.00
11 Bob Baun	8.00	20.00
12 Dick Duff	8.00	20.00
13 Larry Regan	6.00	15.00
14 Johnny Wilson	6.00	15.00
15 Billy Harris	6.00	15.00
16 Allan Stanley	12.00	25.00
17 George Armstrong	12.00	25.00
18 Carl Brewer	8.00	20.00
19 Bob Pulford	8.00	20.00
20 Gordie Howe	200.00	350.00
21 Val Fonteyne RC	6.00	15.00
22 Murray Oliver RC	12.00	25.00
23 Sid Abel CO	12.00	25.00
24 Jack McIntyre	6.00	15.00
25 Marc Reaume	6.00	15.00
26 Norm Ullman	20.00	50.00
27 Brian Smith RC	6.00	15.00
28 Gerry Melnyk UER RC	6.00	15.00
29 Marcel Pronovost	8.00	20.00
30 Warren Godfrey	6.00	15.00
31 Terry Sawchuk	75.00	150.00
32 Barry Cullen	6.00	15.00
33 Gary Aldcorn	6.00	15.00
34 Pete Goegan	6.00	15.00
35 Len Lunde	6.00	15.00
36 Alex Delvecchio	15.00	30.00
37 John McKenzie RC	12.00	25.00
38 Dickie Moore	12.00	25.00
39 Albert Langlois	6.00	15.00
40 Bill Hicke	6.00	15.00
41 Ralph Backstrom	6.00	15.00
42 Don Marshall	6.00	15.00
43 Bob Turner	6.00	15.00
44 Tom Johnson	8.00	20.00
45 Maurice Richard	100.00	200.00
46 Bernie Geoffrion	20.00	50.00
47 Henri Richard	50.00	100.00
48 Doug Harvey	20.00	50.00
49 Jean Beliveau	50.00	100.00
50 Phil Goyette	6.00	15.00
51 Marcel Bonin	6.00	15.00
52 Jean-Guy Talbot	8.00	20.00
53 Jacques Plante	125.00	200.00
54 Claude Provost	6.00	15.00
55 Andre Pronovost	6.00	15.00
56 Hicke/McDonald/Backstrom	12.00	25.00
57 Marsh/H.Richard/Moore	20.00	50.00
58 Provost/Pronovost/Goyette	12.00	25.00
59 Boom/Marshall/Beliveau	40.00	80.00
60 Ab McDonald	6.00	15.00
61 Jim Morrison	50.00	100.00

1961-62 Parkhurst

The 1961-62 Parkhurst set contains 51 cards in full color, numbered on the fronts. Cards are 2 7/16" by 3 5/8". The backs contain 1960-61 statistics and a cartoon; the punch line for which could be seen by rubbing the card with a coin. The cards contain players from Montreal, Toronto, and Detroit. The numbering of the players in the set is basically by teams, i.e., Toronto Maple Leafs (1-18), Detroit Red Wings (19-34), and Montreal Canadiens (35-51). The backs are in both French and English. The key Rookie Card in this set is Dave Keon.

Card	Low	High
COMPLETE SET (51)	1,000.00	1,600.00
1 Tim Horton	100.00	200.00
2 Frank Mahovlich	40.00	80.00
3 Johnny Bower	30.00	60.00
4 Bert Olmstead	10.00	20.00
5 Dave Keon RC	250.00	400.00
6 Ron Stewart	10.00	20.00
7 Eddie Shack	50.00	100.00
8 Bob Pulford	10.00	20.00
9 Red Kelly	12.00	25.00
10 Bob Nevin	10.00	20.00
11 Bob Baun	10.00	20.00
12 Dick Duff	10.00	20.00
13 Larry Keenan RC	7.50	15.00
14 Larry Hillman	10.00	20.00
15 Billy Harris	7.50	15.00
16 Allan Stanley	12.00	25.00
17 George Armstrong	12.00	25.00
18 Carl Brewer	10.00	20.00
19 Howie Glover RC	7.50	15.00
20 Gordie Howe	150.00	250.00
21 Val Fonteyne	7.50	15.00
22 Al Johnson RC	7.50	15.00
23 Pete Goegan	7.50	15.00
24 Len Lunde	7.50	15.00
25 Alex Delvecchio	12.00	25.00
26 Norm Ullman	20.00	40.00
27 Bill Gadsby	7.50	15.00
28 Ed Litzenberger	7.50	15.00
29 Marcel Pronovost	10.00	20.00
30 Warren Godfrey	7.50	15.00
31 Terry Sawchuk	75.00	125.00
32 Vic Stasiuk	7.50	15.00
33 Leo Labine	7.50	15.00
34 John McKenzie	12.00	25.00
35 Bernie Geoffrion	25.00	50.00
36 Dickie Moore	12.00	25.00
37 Albert Langlois	7.50	15.00
38 Bill Hicke	7.50	15.00
39 Ralph Backstrom	10.00	20.00
40 Don Marshall	10.00	20.00
41 Bob Turner	7.50	15.00
42 Tom Johnson	10.00	20.00
43 Henri Richard	40.00	80.00
44 Wayne Connelly RC	12.00	25.00
45 Jean Beliveau	40.00	80.00
46 Phil Goyette	7.50	15.00
47 Marcel Bonin	7.50	15.00
48 Jean-Guy Talbot	10.00	20.00
49 Jacques Plante	100.00	175.00
50 Claude Provost	10.00	20.00
51 Andre Pronovost UER	20.00	40.00

1962-63 Parkhurst

The 1962-63 Parkhurst set contains 55 cards in full color, with the card number and, on some cards, a facsimile autograph on the front. There is also one unnumbered checklist which is part of the complete set price. An unnumbered game or tally card, which is also referred to as the "Zip" card, is not part of the set. Both of these are considered rather difficult to obtain. Cards are approximately 2 7/16" by 3 5/8". The backs, in both French and English, contain player lifetime statistics and player vital statistics in paragraph form. There are several different styles or designs within this set depending on card number, e.g., some cards have a giant puck as background for their photo on the front. Other cards have the player's team logo as background. The numbering of the players in the set is basically by teams, i.e., Toronto Maple Leafs (1-18), Detroit Red Wings (19-36), and Montreal Canadiens (37-54). The notable Rookie Cards in this set are Bobby Rousseau, Gilles Tremblay, and J.C.Tremblay.

Card	Low	High
COMPLETE SET (55)	1,200.00	2,000.00
1 Billy Harris	25.00	40.00
2 Dick Duff	9.00	15.00
3 Bob Baun	9.00	15.00
4 Frank Mahovlich	50.00	80.00
5 Red Kelly	18.00	30.00
6 Ron Stewart	7.00	12.00
7 Tim Horton	60.00	100.00
8 Carl Brewer	9.00	15.00
9 Allan Stanley	10.00	20.00
10 Bob Nevin	9.00	15.00
11 Bob Pulford	9.00	15.00
12 Ed Litzenberger	7.00	12.00
13 George Armstrong	10.00	20.00
14 Eddie Shack	35.00	60.00
15 Dave Keon	60.00	100.00
16 Johnny Bower	30.00	50.00
17 Larry Hillman	9.00	15.00
18 Frank Mahovlich	40.00	70.00
19 Hank Bassen RC	9.00	15.00
20 Gerry Odrowski RC	7.00	12.00
21 Norm Ullman	18.00	30.00
22 Vic Stasiuk	7.00	12.00
23 Bruce MacGregor RC	7.00	12.00
24 Claude Laforge	7.00	12.00
25 Bill Gadsby	7.00	12.00
26 Leo Labine	7.00	12.00
27 Val Fonteyne	7.00	12.00
28 Howie Glover	7.00	12.00
29 Marc Boileau RC	7.00	12.00
30 Gordie Howe	150.00	250.00
31 Gordie Howe	150.00	250.00
32 Alex Delvecchio	15.00	25.00
33 Marcel Pronovost	9.00	15.00
34 Sid Abel CO	9.00	15.00
35 Len Lunde	7.00	12.00
36 Warren Godfrey	7.00	12.00
37 Phil Goyette	7.00	12.00
38 Henri Richard	50.00	80.00
39 Jean Beliveau	50.00	80.00
40 Bill Hicke	7.00	12.00
41 Claude Provost	7.00	12.00
42 Dickie Moore	10.00	20.00
43 Don Marshall	9.00	15.00
44 Ralph Backstrom	9.00	15.00
45 Marcel Bonin	7.00	12.00
46 Gilles Tremblay RC	20.00	40.00
47 Bobby Rousseau RC	15.00	25.00
48 Bernie Geoffrion	25.00	40.00
49 Jacques Plante	75.00	125.00
50 Tom Johnson	9.00	15.00
51 Jean-Guy Talbot	9.00	15.00
52 Lou Fontinato	9.00	15.00
53 Bernie Geoffrion	25.00	40.00
54 J.C.Tremblay RC	40.00	60.00
NNO Zip Entry Game Card	125.00	250.00
NNO Checklist Card	250.00	400.00

1963-64 Parkhurst

The 1963-64 Parkhurst set contains 99 color cards. The cards measure approximately 2 7/16" by 3 5/8". The fronts of the cards feature the player with a varying background depending upon whether the player is on Detroit (American flag), Toronto (Canadian Red Ensign), or Montreal (multi-color striped background). The numbering of the players in the set is basically by teams, i.e., Toronto Maple Leafs (1-20 and 61-79), Detroit Red Wings (41-60), and Montreal Canadiens (21-40 and 80-99). The backs, in both French and English, contain the card number, player lifetime NHL statistics, player biography, and a Stanley Cup replica offer. The set includes two different cards of each Montreal and Toronto player and only one of each Detroit player (with the following exceptions, numbers 15, 20, and 75 (single card Maple Leafs). Each Toronto player's double is obtained by adding 60, e.g., 1 and 61, 2 and 62, 3 and 63, etc., are the same player. Each Montreal player's double is obtained by adding 59, e.g., 21 and 80, 22 and 81, 23 and 82, etc., are the same player. The key Rookie Cards in the set are Red Berenson, Alex Faulkner, John Ferguson, Jacques Laperriere, and Cesare Maniago. Maniago is the last card in the set and is not often found in top condition.

Card	Low	High
COMPLETE SET (99)	1,500.00	2,500.00
1 Allan Stanley	25.00	40.00
2 Don Simmons	9.00	15.00
3 Red Kelly	12.00	25.00
4 Dick Duff	9.00	15.00
5 Johnny Bower	30.00	50.00
6 Ed Litzenberger	7.00	12.00
7 Kent Douglas RC	7.00	12.00
8 Carl Brewer	9.00	15.00
9 Eddie Shack	40.00	80.00
10 Bob Nevin	9.00	15.00
11 Billy Harris	7.00	12.00
12 Bob Pulford	9.00	15.00
13 George Armstrong	10.00	20.00
14 Ron Stewart	7.00	12.00
15 John McMillan RC	7.00	12.00
16 Tim Horton	50.00	100.00
17 Frank Mahovlich	40.00	60.00
18 Bob Baun	9.00	15.00
19 Punch Imlach ACO/GM	12.00	25.00
20 King Clancy ACO	18.00	30.00
21 Gilles Tremblay	9.00	15.00
22 Jean-Guy Talbot	9.00	15.00
23 Henri Richard	40.00	60.00
24 Ralph Backstrom	9.00	15.00
25 Bill Hicke	7.00	12.00
26 Red Berenson RC	25.00	40.00
27 Jacques Laperriere RC	30.00	50.00
28 Jean Gauthier RC	7.00	12.00
29 Bernie Geoffrion	25.00	40.00
30 Jean Beliveau	45.00	80.00
31 J.C.Tremblay	9.00	15.00
32 Terry Harper RC	18.00	30.00
33 John Ferguson RC	50.00	80.00
34 Toe Blake CO	12.00	25.00
35 Bobby Rousseau	9.00	15.00
36 Claude Provost	7.00	12.00
37 Marc Reaume	7.00	12.00
38 Dave Balon	7.00	12.00
39 Gump Worsley	25.00	40.00
40 Cesare Maniago RC	25.00	50.00
41 Bruce MacGregor	7.00	12.00
42 Alex Faulkner RC	90.00	150.00
43 Pete Goegan	7.00	12.00
44 Parker MacDonald	7.00	12.00
45 Andre Pronovost	7.00	12.00
46 Marcel Pronovost	9.00	15.00
47 Bob Dillabough RC	7.00	12.00
48 Larry Jeffrey RC	7.00	12.00
49 Ian Cushenan	7.00	12.00
50 Alex Delvecchio	12.00	25.00
51 Hank Ciesla	7.00	12.00
52 Norm Ullman	18.00	30.00
53 Terry Sawchuk	70.00	110.00
54 Ron Ingram RC	7.00	12.00
55 Gordie Howe	300.00	450.00
56 Billy McNeil	7.00	12.00
57 Floyd Smith RC	7.00	12.00
58 Vic Stasiuk	7.00	12.00
59 Bill Gadsby	7.00	12.00
60 Doug Barkley RC	7.00	12.00
61 Allan Stanley	10.00	20.00
62 Don Simmons	9.00	15.00
63 Red Kelly	12.00	25.00
64 Dick Duff	9.00	15.00
65 Johnny Bower	30.00	50.00
66 Ed Litzenberger	7.00	12.00
67 Kent Douglas	7.00	12.00
68 Carl Brewer	9.00	15.00
69 Eddie Shack	30.00	50.00
70 Bob Nevin	9.00	15.00
71 Billy Harris	7.00	12.00
72 Bob Pulford	9.00	15.00
73 George Armstrong	10.00	20.00
74 Ron Stewart	7.00	12.00
75 Dave Keon	50.00	80.00
76 Tim Horton	50.00	80.00
77 Frank Mahovlich	40.00	60.00
78 Bob Baun	9.00	15.00
79 Punch Imlach ACO/GM	12.00	25.00
80 Gilles Tremblay	9.00	15.00
81 Jean-Guy Talbot	7.00	12.00
82 Henri Richard	40.00	60.00
83 Ralph Backstrom	9.00	15.00
84 Bill Hicke	7.00	12.00
85 Red Berenson RC	25.00	40.00
86 Jacques Laperriere RC	25.00	40.00
87 Jean Gauthier RC	7.00	12.00
88 Bernie Geoffrion	25.00	40.00
89 Jean Beliveau	50.00	80.00
90 J.C.Tremblay	9.00	15.00
91 Terry Harper RC	20.00	30.00
92 John Ferguson RC	50.00	80.00
93 Toe Blake CO	12.00	25.00
94 Bobby Rousseau	9.00	15.00
95 Claude Provost	7.00	12.00
96 Marc Reaume	7.00	12.00
97 Dave Balon	7.00	12.00
98 Gump Worsley	25.00	40.00
99 Cesare Maniago RC	100.00	175.00

1971-72 Penguins Postcards

This 22-card set (measuring approximately 3 1/2" by 5 1/2") features full-bleed posed action color player photos. The cards originally came bound together in a flip book, but had perforations at the card top to allow them to be removed. The backs carry the player's name and biography in blue print on a white background. Only the Red Kelly card has a career summary on its back. The cards are unnumbered and checklisted below in alphabetical order. The set is dated by the inclusion of Roy Edwards, whose only season with the Penguins was 1971-72.

Card	Low	High
COMPLETE SET (22)	20.00	40.00
1 Syl Apps	1.25	2.50
2 Les Binkley	1.25	2.50
3 Dave Burrows	1.00	2.00
4 Darryl Edestrand	.75	1.50
5 Roy Edwards	1.00	2.00
6 Val Fonteyne	.75	1.50
7 Nick Harbaruk	.75	1.50
8 Bryan Hextall	2.00	4.00
9 Sheldon Kannegiesser	.75	1.50
10 Red Kelly CO	2.00	4.00
11 Bob Leiter	.75	1.50
12 Keith McCreary	.75	1.50
13 Joe Noris	.75	1.50
14 Greg Polis	.75	1.50
15 Jean Pronovost	2.00	4.00
16 Rene Robert	1.25	2.50
17 Jim Rutherford	1.25	2.50
18 Ken Schinkel	.75	1.50
19 Ron Schock	1.00	2.00
20 Bryan Watson	1.00	2.00
21 Bob Woytowich	.75	1.50
22 Title Card	.75	1.50

1974-75 Penguins Postcards

This 22-card set features full-bleed black and white action pictures by photographer Paul Salva. The player's autograph is inscribed across the bottom of the picture. The cards are in the postcard format and measure approximately 3 1/2" by 5 1/2". The horizontal backs are blank. The cards are unnumbered and checklisted below in alphabetical order. The set is dated by the fact that Nelson Debenedet was only with the Penguins during the 1974-75 season. Pierre Larouche appears in this set prior to his Rookie Card appearance.

Card	Low	High
COMPLETE SET (22)	15.00	30.00
1 Syl Apps	1.25	2.50
2 Chuck Arnason	.75	1.50
3 Dave Burrows	1.00	2.00
4 Colin Campbell	1.25	2.50
5 Nelson Debenedet	.75	1.50
6 Steve Durbano	.75	1.50
7 Vic Hadfield	1.00	2.00
8 Gary Inness	1.00	2.00
9 Bob(B.J.) Johnson	.75	1.50
10 Rick Kehoe	1.25	2.50
11 Bob Kelly	.75	1.50
12 Jean-Guy Lagace	.75	1.50
13 Ron Lalonde	.75	1.50
14 Pierre Larouche	2.50	5.00
15 Lowell MacDonald	1.00	2.00
16 Dennis Owchar	.75	1.50
17 Bob Paradise	.75	1.50
18 Kelly Pratt	.75	1.50

19 Jean Pronovost	1.00	2.00
20 Ron Schock	1.00	2.00
21 Ron Stackhouse	1.00	2.00
22 Barry Williams	.75	1.50

1977-78 Penguins Puck Bucks

This 18-card set of Pittsburgh Penguins was sponsored by McDonald's restaurants, whose company logo appears at the top of the card face. The cards measure approximately 1 15/16" by 3 1/2" and are perforated so that the bottom tab (measuring 1 15/16" by 1") may be removed. The front of the top portion features a color head shot of the player, with a white border on a mustard-colored background. The back of the top portion has "Hockey Talk," in which a hockey term is explained. The front side of the tab portion shows a hockey puck on an orange background. Its back states that the "puck bucks" are coupons worth 1.00 toward the purchase of any 7.50 Penguins game ticket. These coupons had to be redeemed no later than December 31, 1977.

COMPLETE SET (18)	12.50	25.00
1 Denis Herron	1.50	3.00
3 Ron Stackhouse	1.00	2.00
4 Dave Burrows	.75	1.50
6 Colin Campbell	1.25	2.50
7 Russ Anderson	.75	1.50
9 Blair Chapman	.75	1.50
10 Pierre Larouche	1.50	3.00
12 Greg Malone	1.00	2.00
14 Wayne Bianchin	.75	1.50
17 Rick Kehoe	1.50	3.00
18 Lowell MacDonald	1.00	2.00
19 Jean Pronovost	1.25	2.50
23 Jim Hamilton	.75	1.50
25 Dennis Owchar	.75	1.50
26 Syl Apps	1.00	2.00
27 Mike Corrigan	.75	1.50
29 Dunc Wilson	1.00	2.00
NNO Johnny Wilson CO	.50	1.00

1980-81 Pepsi-Cola Caps

This set of 140 bottle caps features 20 players from each of the seven Canadian hockey teams. The bottle caps are written in French and English. There are two sizes of caps depending on whether the cap was from a small or large bottle. The top of the cap displays the Pepsi logo in the familiar red, white, and blue. The sides of the cap were done in blue and white lettering on a pink background. On the inside of the cap is a "black and aluminum" head shot of the player, with his name and the city (from which the team hails) below. We have checklisted the caps in alphabetical order of the teams as follows: Calgary Flames (1-20), Edmonton Oilers (21-40), Montreal Canadiens (41-60), Quebec Nordiques (61-80), Toronto Maple Leafs (81-100), Vancouver Canucks (101-120), and Winnipeg Jets (121-140). Also the players' names have been alphabetized within their teams. Also available through a mail-in offer -- in either English or French -- was a white plastic circular display plaque (approximately 24" by 24") for the caps. The French version sometimes sells for a slight premium. There also are reports that two different size variations exist: a 10 ounce and a 26 ounce size. There does not appear to be a premium on either size cap at this time.

COMPLETE SET (140)	100.00	200.00
1 Dan Bouchard	.75	2.00
2 Guy Chouinard	.75	2.00
3 Bill Clement	.75	2.00
4 Randy Holt	.60	1.50
5 Ken Houston	.60	1.50
6 Kevin Lavallee	.60	1.50
7 Don Lever	.60	1.50
8 Bob MacMillan	.60	1.50
9 Brad Marsh	1.00	2.50
10 Bob Murdoch	.60	1.50
11 Kent Nilsson	.75	2.00
12 Willi Plett	.75	2.00
13 Jim Peplinski	.75	2.00
14 Pekka Rautakallio	.60	1.50
15 Paul Reinhart	.75	2.00
16 Pat Riggin	.75	2.00
17 Phil Russell	.60	1.50
18 Brad Smith	.60	1.50
19 Eric Vail	.60	1.50
20 Bert Wilson	.60	1.50
21 Glenn Anderson	1.50	4.00
22 Curt Brackenbury	.60	1.50
23 Brett Callighen	.60	1.50
24 Paul Coffey	7.50	15.00
25 Lee Fogolin	.60	1.50
26 Matti Hagman	.60	1.50
27 John Hughes	.60	1.50
28 Dave Hunter	.60	1.50
29 Jari Kurri	4.00	8.00
30 Ron Low	.75	2.00
31 Kevin Lowe	1.00	2.50
32 Dave Lumley	.60	1.50
33 Blair MacDonald	.60	1.50
34 Mark Messier	12.50	25.00
35 Ed Mio	.75	2.00
36 Don Murdoch	.60	1.50
37 Pat Price	.60	1.50
38 Dave Semenko	.75	2.00
39 Risto Siltanen	.60	1.50
40 Stan Weir	.60	1.50
41 Keith Acton	.60	1.50
42 Brian Engblom	.60	1.50
43 Bob Gainey	1.25	3.00
44 Gaston Gingras	.60	1.50
45 Denis Herron	.75	2.00
46 Rejean Houle	.60	1.50
47 Doug Jarvis	.60	1.50
48 Yvon Lambert	.60	1.50
49 Rod Langway	1.25	3.00
50 Guy Lapointe	.75	2.00
51 Pierre Larouche	1.00	2.50
52 Pierre Mondou	.60	1.50
53 Mark Napier	.75	2.00
54 Chris Nilan	1.00	2.50
55 Doug Risebrough	.60	1.50
56 Larry Robinson	1.50	4.00
57 Serge Savard	.75	2.00
58 Steve Shutt	1.25	3.00
59 Mario Tremblay	.75	2.00
60 Doug Wickenheiser	.60	1.50
61 Serge Bernier	.60	1.50
62 Kim Clackson	.75	2.00
63 Real Cloutier	.60	1.50
64 Andre Dupont	.60	1.50
65 Robbie Ftorek	.75	2.00
66 Michel Goulet	2.50	5.00
67 Jamie Hislop	.60	1.50
68 Dale Hoganson	.60	1.50
69 Dale Hunter	1.50	4.00
70 Pierre Lacroix	.60	1.50
71 Garry Lariviere	.60	1.50
72 Rich Leduc	.60	1.50
73 John Paddock	.75	2.00
74 Michel Plasse	.75	2.00
75 Jacques Richard	.60	1.50
76 Anton Stastny	.75	2.00
77 Peter Stastny	3.00	6.00
78 Mark Tardif	.75	2.00
79 Wally Weir	.60	1.50
80 John Wensink	.75	2.00
81 John Anderson	.60	1.50
82 Laurie Boschman	.60	1.50
83 Jiri Crha	.75	2.00
84 Bill Derlago	.60	1.50
85 Vitezslav Duris	.60	1.50
86 Ron Ellis	.75	2.00
87 Dave Farrish	.60	1.50
88 Stewart Gavin	.75	2.00
89 Pat Hickey	.60	1.50
90 Dan Maloney	.75	2.00
91 Terry Martin	.60	1.50
92 Barry Melrose	.75	2.00
93 Wilf Paiement	.75	2.00
94 Robert Picard	.60	1.50
95 Jim Rutherford	1.00	2.50
96 Rocky Saganiuk	.60	1.50
97 Borje Salming	1.25	3.00
98 David Shand	.60	1.50
99 Ian Turnbull	.75	2.00
100 Rick Vaive	1.00	2.50
101 Brent Ashton	.60	1.50
102 Ivan Boldirev	.60	1.50
103 Per-Olov Brasar	.60	1.50
104 Richard Brodeur	1.00	2.50
105 Jerry Butler	.60	1.50
106 Colin Campbell	.75	2.00
107 Curt Fraser	.60	1.50
108 Thomas Gradin	.75	2.00
109 Dennis Kearns	.60	1.50
110 Rick Lanz	.60	1.50
111 Lars Lindgren	.60	1.50
112 Dave Logan	.60	1.50
113 Mario Marois	.60	1.50
114 Kevin McCarthy	.60	1.50
115 Gerald Minor	.60	1.50
116 Darcy Rota	.60	1.50
117 Bobby Schmautz	.60	1.50
118 Stan Smyl	.75	2.00
119 Harold Snepsts	1.00	2.50
120 Tiger Williams	1.00	2.50
121 Dave Babych	.75	2.00
122 Al Cameron	.60	1.50
123 Scott Campbell	.60	1.50
124 Dave Christian	.75	2.00
125 Jude Drouin	.60	1.50
126 Norm Dupont	.60	1.50
127 Dan Geoffrion	.60	1.50
128 Pierre Hamel	.60	1.50
129 Barry Legge	.60	1.50
130 Willy Lindstrom	.60	1.50
131 Barry Long	.60	1.50
132 Kris Manery	.60	1.50
133 Jimmy Mann	.75	2.00
134 Moe Mantha	.60	1.50
135 Markus Mattsson	.75	2.00
136 Doug Smail	.75	2.00
137 Don Spring	.60	1.50
138 Anders Steen	.60	1.50
139 Peter Sullivan	.60	1.50
140 Ron Wilson	.60	1.50
NNO Plastic Circular Display	40.00	80.00

1972-73 Philadelphia Blazers

These postcard-like issues feature the short-lived Blazers of the WHA. While we have confirmed just three cards, it is believed that many more exist. The cards are unnumbered and checklisted below in alphabetical order.

COMPLETE SET (3)	15.00	30.00
1 Danny Lawson	5.00	10.00
2 Bernie Parent	10.00	20.00
3 Ron Plumb	5.00	10.00

1974-75 Phoenix Roadrunners WHA Pins

These pins feature color head shots and measure 3 1/2" in diameter. Player name and team name are featured in a black rectangle at the bottom of the pin. Pins are checklisted below in alphabetical order.

COMPLETE SET (9)	20.00	40.00
1 Bob Barlow	2.00	4.00
2 Cam Connor	2.00	4.00
3 Michel Cormier	2.00	4.00
4 Robbie Ftorek	6.00	12.00
5 Dave Gorman	2.00	4.00
6 John Hughes	2.00	4.00
7 Murray Koegan	2.00	4.00
8 Dennis Sobchuk	2.00	4.00
9 Howie Young	2.00	4.00

1975-76 Phoenix Roadrunners WHA

This 22-card set features players of the WHA Phoenix Roadrunners. The cards measure approximately 3" by 4" and the backs are blank. The front features a poor quality black and white head-and-shoulders shot of the player with a white border. The cards are numbered by the uniform number on the front and we have checklisted them below accordingly. The player's position and weight are also given.

COMPLETE SET (22)	25.00	50.00
1 Serge Beaudoin	1.00	2.00
2 Jim Boyd	1.00	2.00
3 Jim Clarke	1.00	2.00
4 Cam Connors	1.00	2.00
5 Michel Cormier	1.00	2.00
6 Barry Dean	1.00	2.00
7 Robbie Ftorek	7.50	15.00
8 Dave Gorman	1.50	3.00
9 John Gray	1.00	2.00
10 Del Hall	1.00	2.00
11 Ron Huston	1.00	2.00
12 Murray Keogan	1.00	2.00
13 Gary Kurt	1.00	2.00
14 Garry Lariviere	1.00	2.00
15 Al McLeod	1.00	2.00
16 Peter McNamee	1.00	2.00
17 John Migneault	1.00	2.00
18 Lauri Mononen	1.00	2.00
19 Jim Niekamp	1.00	2.00
20 Jack Norris	1.00	2.00
21 Pekka Rautakallio	2.00	4.00
22 Ron Serafini	1.00	2.00

1976-77 Phoenix Roadrunners WHA

This 18-card set features players of the WHA Phoenix Roadrunners. Each card measures approximately 3 3/8" by 4 5/16". The front features a black and white head shot of the player, enframed by an aqua blue border on white card stock. The top and bottom inner borders are curved, creating space for the basic biographical information as well as the team and league logos that surround the picture. The backs are blank. The cards are unnumbered and we have checklisted them below in alphabetical order.

COMPLETE SET (18)	25.00	50.00
1 Serge Beaudoin	1.00	2.00
2 Michel Cormier	1.00	2.00
3 Robbie Ftorek	7.50	15.00
4 Del Hall	1.00	2.00
5 Clay Hebenton	1.00	2.00
6 Andre Hinse	1.00	2.00
7 Mike Hobin	1.00	2.00
8 Frank Hughes	1.00	2.00
9 Ron Huston	1.00	2.00
10 Gary Kurt	1.00	2.00
11 Garry Lariviere	1.00	2.00
12 Bob Liddington	1.00	2.00
13 Lauri Mononen	1.00	2.00
14 Jim Niekamp	1.00	2.00
15 Pekka Rautakallio	2.00	4.00
16 Seppo Repo	2.00	4.00
17 Jerry Rollins	1.00	2.00
18 Juhani Tamminen	2.00	4.00

1975-76 Popsicle

This 18-card set presents the teams of the NHL. The cards measure approximately 3 3/8" by 2 1/8" and are printed in the "credit card format", only slightly thinner than an actual credit card. The front has the NHL logo in the upper left hand corner, and the city and team names in the black bar across the top. A colorful team logo appears on the left side of the card face, while a color action shot of the teams' players appears on the right side. The back provides a brief history of the team. The set was issued in two versions (English and bilingual). We have checklisted the cards below in alphabetical order of the team nicknames.

COMPLETE SET (18)	15.00	30.00
1 Chicago Blackhawks	1.50	3.00
2 St. Louis Blues	1.00	2.00
3 Boston Bruins	1.50	3.00
4 Montreal Canadiens	1.50	3.00
5 Vancouver Canucks	1.00	2.00
6 Washington Capitals	1.00	2.00
7 Atlanta Flames	1.50	3.00
8 Philadelphia Flyers	1.00	2.00
9 California Golden Seals	1.50	3.00
10 New York Islanders	1.00	2.00
11 Los Angeles Kings	1.00	2.00
12 Toronto Maple Leafs	1.50	3.00
13 Minnesota North Stars	1.00	2.00
14 Pittsburgh Penguins	1.00	2.00
15 New York Rangers	1.50	3.00
16 Detroit Red Wings	1.50	3.00
17 Buffalo Sabres	1.00	2.00
18 Kansas City Scouts	1.50	3.00

1976-77 Popsicle

This 18-card set presents the teams of the NHL. The cards measure approximately 3 3/8" by 2 1/8" and are printed in the "credit card format", only slightly thinner than an actual credit card. The front has the NHL logo in the upper left hand corner, and the city and team names in the black bar across the top. A colorful team logo appears on the left side of the card face, while a color action shot of the teams' players appears on the right side. The back provides a brief history of the team. The set was issued in two versions (English and bilingual); a bilingual membership card is known to exist. We have checklisted the cards below in alphabetical order of the team nicknames.

COMPLETE SET (19)	20.00	40.00
1 Cleveland Barons	1.50	3.00
2 Chicago Blackhawks	1.50	3.00
3 St. Louis Blues	1.00	2.00
4 Boston Bruins	1.50	3.00
5 Montreal Canadiens	1.50	3.00
6 Vancouver Canucks	1.00	2.00
7 Washington Capitals	1.00	2.00
8 Atlanta Flames	1.50	3.00
9 Philadelphia Flyers	1.00	2.00
10 New York Islanders	1.00	2.00
11 Los Angeles Kings	1.00	2.00
12 Toronto Maple Leafs	1.50	3.00
13 Minnesota North Stars	1.00	2.00
14 Pittsburgh Penguins	1.00	2.00
15 New York Rangers	1.50	3.00
16 Detroit Red Wings	1.50	3.00
17 Colorado Rockies	1.50	3.00
18 Buffalo Sabres	1.00	2.00
19 Membership Card	1.50	3.00

1966-67 Post Cereal Box Backs

These three box backs seem to vary from the 1967-68 set, so we have listed them seperately. The backs picture Pulford and Hall in All-Star uniforms and Worsely in his Canadiens uniform with a notation that Montreal won the Stanley Cup in 1965-66. A "hockey tip" was printed below the pictures in both English and French, though often the picture was cut from the box without the writing underneath.

1 Gump Worsley	15.00	40.00
2 Bob Pulford	15.00	40.00
3 Glenn Hall	15.00	40.00

1967-68 Post Cereal Box Backs

These photo premiums were issued on the back of Post cereal boxes. They measure approximately 6 1/2 by 7 1/2 and are blank backed. They are unnumbered and so are listed below in alphabetical order.

COMPLETE SET (13)		
1 Gordie Howe {net in background	25.00	50.00
2 Gordie Howe {no net	25.00	50.00
3 Harry Howell {passing	10.00	20.00
4 Harry Howell {kneeling	10.00	20.00
5 Jacques Laperriere {net in background	10.00	20.00
6 Jacques Laperriere {no net	10.00	20.00
7 Stan Mikita {red jersey	15.00	30.00
8 Stan Mikita {white jersey	15.00	30.00
9 Bobby Orr {posed	25.00	50.00
10 Bobby Orr {in action	25.00	50.00
11 Henri Richard {with puck	12.50	25.00
12 Henri Richard {no puck	12.50	25.00
13 Checklist	25.00	50.00

1967-68 Post Flip Books

This 1967-68 Post set consists of 12 flip books. They display a Montreal player on one side of the page and a Toronto player on the other side. In the listing below, the Montreal player is listed first.

COMPLETE SET (12)	100.00	200.00
1 Gump Worsley Johnny Bower	15.00	30.00
2 Rogatien Vachon Johnny Bower	17.50	35.00
3 J.C. Tremblay Tim Horton	12.50	25.00
4 Jacques Laperriere Marcel Pronovost	7.50	15.00
5 Henri Richard Frank Mahovlich	12.50	25.00
6 Dick Duff Dave Keon	10.00	20.00
7 Jean Beliveau Jim Pappin	15.00	30.00
8 Jean Beliveau Ron Ellis	15.00	30.00
9 Gilles Tremblay George Armstrong	10.00	20.00
10 J.C. Tremblay Pete Stemkowski	5.00	10.00
11 Ralph Backstrom Bob Pulford	7.50	15.00
12 Bobby Rousseau Wayne Hillman	5.00	10.00

1968-69 Post Marbles

This set of 30 marbles was issued by Post Cereal in Canada and features players of the Montreal Canadiens (MC) and the Toronto Maple Leafs (TML). Also produced was an attractive game board which is rather difficult to find and not included in the complete set price below.

COMPLETE SET (30)	250.00	500.00
1 Ralph Backstrom MC	4.00	8.00
2 Jean Beliveau MC	20.00	40.00
3 Johnny Bower TML	7.50	15.00
4 Wayne Carleton TML	4.00	8.00
5 Yvan Cournoyer MC	10.00	20.00
6 Ron Ellis TML	4.00	8.00
7 John Ferguson MC	4.00	8.00
8 Bruce Gamble TML	4.00	8.00

9 Terry Harper MC 4.00 8.00
10 Ted Harris MC 4.00 8.00
11 Paul Henderson TML 5.00 10.00
12 Tim Horton TML 20.00 40.00
13 Dave Keon TML 12.50 25.00
14 Jacques Laperriere MC 5.00 10.00
15 Jacques Lemaire MC 12.50 25.00
16 Murray Oliver TML 4.00 8.00
17 Mike Pelyk TML 4.00 8.00
18 Pierre Pilote TML 5.00 10.00
19 Marcel Pronovost TML 5.00 10.00
20 Bob Pulford TML 5.00 10.00
21 Henri Richard MC 10.00 20.00
22 Bobby Rousseau MC 4.00 8.00
23 Serge Savard MC 5.00 10.00
24 Floyd Smith TML 4.00 8.00
25 Gilles Tremblay MC 4.00 8.00
26 J.C. Tremblay MC 4.00 8.00
27 Norm Ullman TML 5.00 10.00
28 Rogatien Vachon MC 15.00 30.00
29 Mike Walton TML 4.00 8.00
30 Gump Worsley MC 10.00 20.00
xx Game Board 87.50 175.00

1970-71 Post Shooters

This set of 16 shooters was intended to be used with the hockey game that Post had advertised as a premium. The shooter consists of a plastic figure with a colorful adhesive decal sheet, with stickers that could be applied to the shooter for identification. All players come with home and away, i.e., red or blue shoulders. The figures measure approximately 3 1/2" by 4 1/2". Players are featured in their NHLPA uniform. They are unnumbered and hence are listed below in alphabetical order.

COMPLETE SET (16) 150.00 300.00
1 Johnny Bucyk 7.50 15.00
2 Ron Ellis 5.00 10.00
3 Ed Giacomin 10.00 20.00
4 Paul Henderson 7.50 15.00
5 Ken Hodge 6.25 12.50
6 Dennis Hull 6.25 12.50
7 Orland Kurtenbach 5.00 10.00
8 Jacques Laperriere 6.25 12.50
9 Jacques Lemaire 7.50 15.00
10 Frank Mahovlich 7.50 15.00
11 Peter Mahovlich 6.25 12.50
12 Bobby Orr 50.00 100.00
13 Jacques Plante 20.00 40.00
14 Jean Ratelle 7.50 15.00
15 Dale Tallon 5.00 10.00
16 J.C. Tremblay 6.25 12.50

1972-73 Post Action Transfers

These 12 cards feature two players on each transfer. Each card depicts an important facet of the game. We are listing the players first and then the English title of the card afterwards.

COMPLETE SET (12) 125.00 250.00
1 Garry Unger 30.00 60.00
Bobby Orr
Defense
2 Red Berenson 7.50 15.00
Dale Tallon
In the Corner
3 Gary Dornhoeffer 7.50 15.00
Wayne Cashman
Face Off
4 Jim McKenny 10.00 20.00
Ed Giacomin
Power Save
5 Pat Quinn 7.50 15.00
Keith Magnuson
Power Play Goal
6 Paul Shmyr 7.50 15.00
Rod Seiling
Break Away
7 Danny Grant 10.00 20.00
Jacques Plante
Slap Shot
8 Syl Apps Jr. 10.00 20.00
Serge Savard
Rebound
9 Gump Worsley 12.50 25.00
Gary Bergman
Wrist Shot
10 Roger Crozier 10.00 20.00
Ed Westfall
Last Minute
11 Dennis Hull 7.50 15.00
Orland Kurtenbach
Goalmouth Scramble
12 Rogatien Vachon 15.00 30.00
Yvan Cournoyer
Chest Save

1938-39 Quaker Oats Photos

This 30-card set of Toronto Maple Leafs and Montreal Canadiens was sponsored by Quaker Oats. The photos were obtainable by mail with the redemption of proofs of purchase. These oversized cards (approximately 6 1/4" by 7 3/8") are unnumbered and hence are listed below alphabetically. Facsimile autographs are printed in white on the fronts of these blank-backed cards.

COMPLETE SET (30) 750.00 1,500.00
1 Syl Apps 62.50 125.00
2 Toe Blake 125.00 250.00
3 Buzz Boll 25.00 50.00
4 Turk Broda 87.50 175.00
5 Walter Buswell 25.00 50.00
6 Herb Cain 30.00 60.00
7 Murph Chamberlain 25.00 50.00
8 Wilf Cude 30.00 60.00
9 Bob Davidson 25.00 50.00
10 Gordie Drillon 50.00 100.00
11 Paul Drouin 25.00 50.00
12 Stew Evans 25.00 50.00
13 James Fowler 25.00 50.00
14 Johnny Gagnon 25.00 50.00
15 Robert Gracie 25.00 50.00
16 Reg Hamilton 25.00 50.00
17 Paul Haynes 25.00 50.00
18 Foster Hewitt 50.00 100.00
19 Red Horner 50.00 100.00
20 Harvey(Busher) Jackson 75.00 125.00
21 Bingo Kampman 25.00 50.00
22 Pep Kelly 25.00 50.00
23 Rod Lorrain 25.00 50.00
24 George Mantha 25.00 50.00
25 Nick Metz 25.00 50.00
26 George Parsons 25.00 50.00
27 Babe Siebert 50.00 100.00
28 Bill Thoms 25.00 50.00
29 James Ward 25.00 50.00
30 Cy Wentworth 30.00 60.00

1945-54 Quaker Oats Photos

Quaker Oats of Canada continued its tradition of redeeming proofs of purchase for photos of Montreal Canadiens and Toronto Maple Leafs in this nine-year series. Many players are featured in multiple versions, as their photos were updated over the years. The photos themselves are black and white with a thin white border and measure 8" X 10". Because of the numerous variations and the potential for more to be unearthed, no complete set price is listed below. Currently, 113 players are featured on 200 different photos. Anyone with information regarding other photos or variations is encouraged to contact Beckett Publications. The photos are blank-backed and unnumbered and are listed below in alphabetical order within their team (Toronto first, then Montreal).

1A Syl Apps/Home Still, CJS Apps auto. 15.00 30.00
1B Syl Apps/Home Still, Syl Apps auto. 12.50 25.00
1C Syl Apps/Away With Stanley Cup 75.00 150.00
2 George Armstrong/Home Action 12.50 25.00
3 Doug Baldwin/Home Still 50.00 100.00
4A Bill Barilko/Home Action
auto. 1/4-inch from border 12.50 25.00
4B Bill Barilko/Home Action
auto. 3/4-inch from border 12.50 25.00
4C Bill Barilko/Away Action 12.50 25.00
5 Baz Bastien/Home Still 62.50 125.00
6 Gordon Bell/Home Still 62.50 125.00
7A Max Bentley/Home Still 10.00 20.00
7B Max Bentley/Home Dressing Room 75.00 150.00
7C Max Bentley/Away Action 10.00 20.00
8 Gus Bodnar/Home Still 20.00 40.00
9A Garth Boesch/Home Still,
closed B in auto. 7.50 15.00
9B Garth Boesch/Home Still, open B in auto. 7.50 15.00
9C Garth Boesch/Away Action 50.00 100.00
10 Hugh Bolton/Home Action 6.00 12.00
11 Leo Boivin/Home Action 15.00 30.00
12A Turk Broda/Away Splits, W.E. auto. 25.00 50.00
12B Turk Broda/Away Splits, Turk auto. 20.00 40.00
12C Turk Broda/Away Action 20.00 40.00
13 Lorne Carr/Home Still 15.00 30.00
14 Les Costello/Home Still 15.00 30.00
15 Bob Davidson/Home Still 12.50 25.00
16A Bill Ezinicki/cropped
William auto., blue tint 10.00 20.00
16B Bill Ezinicki/entire William auto. 6.00 12.00
16C Bill Ezinicki/Home Still, Bill auto. 6.00 12.00
16D Bill Ezinicki/Away Action 6.00 12.00
17 Fernie Flaman/Home Action 7.50 15.00
18A Cal Gardner/Home Still 6.00 12.00
18B Cal Gardner/Away Action 6.00 12.00
19A Bob Goldham/sweeping G in auto. 6.00 12.00
19B Bob Goldham/normal G, entire blade 6.00 12.00
19C Bob Goldham/normal G, blade cropped 75.00 150.00
20 Gord Hannigan/Home Action 15.00 30.00
21 Bob Hassard/Away Action 25.00 50.00
22 Mel Hill/Home Still 40.00 80.00
23 Tim Horton/Home Action 50.00 100.00
24A Bill Judza/Home Still 6.00 12.00
24B Bill Judza/Away Action 6.00 12.00
25A Ted Kennedy/Home Still, blade in corner 25.00 50.00
25B Ted Kennedy/Home Still 25.00 50.00
25C Ted Kennedy/Home Still 50.00 100.00
25D Ted Kennedy/Home Still, C on jersey 10.00 20.00
25E Ted Kennedy/Home With Stanley Cup 87.50 175.00
25F Ted Kennedy/Away Action 10.00 20.00
26A Joe Klukay/Home Still 6.00 12.00
26B Joe Klukay/Away Action 6.00 12.00
27 Danny Lewicki/Home Action 7.50 15.00
28 Harry Lumley/Home Action 30.00 60.00
29A Vic Lynn/Home Still/head
3/8-inch from border 6.00 12.00
29B Vic Lynn/Home Still/head
1/8-inch from border 15.00 30.00
29C Vic Lynn/Away Action 6.00 12.00
30A Fleming Mackell/Home Still 6.00 12.00
30B Fleming Mackell/Away Action 7.50 15.00
31 Phil Maloney/Home Action 40.00 80.00
32 Frank Mathers/Home Still 20.00 40.00
33 Frank McCool/Home Still 62.50 125.00
34 John McCormick/Away Action 15.00 30.00
35A Howie Meeker/Home Still, large image 10.00 20.00
35B Howie Meeker/Home Still, small image 10.00 20.00
35C Howie Meeker/Away Action 10.00 20.00
36A Don Metz/Home, posed to right 6.00 12.00
36B Don Metz/Home, center pose, b&w tint 12.50 25.00
36C Don Metz/Home, center pose, blue tint 40.00 80.00
37A Nick Metz/Home Still, original stick 6.00 12.00
37B Nick Metz/Home Still 12.50 25.00
37C Nick Metz/Home Still 25.00 50.00
38 Rudy Migay/Home Action 30.00 60.00
39 Elwyn Morris/Home Still 40.00 80.00
40 Jim Morrison/Home Action 6.00 12.00
41A Gus Mortson/Home Still 6.00 12.00
41B Gus Mortson/Away Action 6.00 12.00
42 Eric Nesterenko/Home Action 40.00 80.00
43 Bud Poile/Home Still 15.00 30.00
44 Babe Pratt/Home Still 50.00 100.00
45 Al Rollins/Home Action 12.50 25.00
46 Dave Schriner/Home Still 30.00 60.00
47A Tod Sloan/Home Still 12.50 25.00
47B Tod Sloan/Home Action 6.00 12.00
48A Sid Smith/Home Still 12.50 25.00
48B Sid Smith/Away Action 6.00 12.00
49 Bob Solinger 15.00 30.00
50A Wally Stanowski/Home Still,
entire blade 12.50 25.00
50B Wally Stanowski/Home
Still, blade cropped 6.00 12.00
51A Gaye Stewart/Home Still 50.00 100.00
51B Gaye Stewart/Home Still, blue tint 6.00 12.00
52 Ron Stewart/Home Action 50.00 100.00
53 Harry Taylor/Home Still 7.50 15.00
54 Billy Taylor/Home Still 25.00 50.00
55 Cy Thomas/Home Still 25.00 50.00
56A Jim Thomson/Home Still, stick cropped 30.00 60.00
56B Jim Thomson/Home Still
stick touching border 6.00 12.00
56C Jim Thomson/Home Still
stick away from border 30.00 60.00
56D Jim Thomson/Away Action 6.00 12.00
57A Ray Timgren/Home Still 7.50 15.00
57B Ray Timgren/Away Action 6.00 12.00
58A Harry Watson/Home Still, tape on stick 6.00 12.00
58B Harry Watson/Home
Still, no tape visible 6.00 12.00
58C Harry Watson/Away Action 6.00 12.00
59 1947-49 Toronto Team Picture 30.00 60.00
60A Leafs Attack McNeil 87.50 175.00
60B Gardner attacks Harvey 100.00 200.00
60C Rollins, Judza stop Curry 100.00 200.00
60D McNeil Saves on Gardner 100.00 200.00
61 George Allen/Home Still 6.00 12.00
62 Jean Beliveau/Home Action 87.50 175.00
63 Joe Benoit/Home Still 10.00 20.00
64A Toe Blake/Hector Toe Blake auto. 75.00 150.00
64B Toe Blake/Toe Blake auto. above skates 10.00 20.00
64C Toe Blake/Toe Blake auto. below skate 10.00 20.00
65A Butch Bouchard/Home Still, entire skate 6.00 12.00
65B Butch Bouchard/Home
Still, skate cropped 6.00 12.00
65C Butch Bouchard/Home Action 7.50 15.00
66 Todd Campeau/Home Still 6.00 12.00
67 Bob Carse/Home Still 6.00 12.00
68 Joe Carveth/Home Portrait 6.00 12.00
69A Murph Chamberlain/facing
sideways, entire skates 10.00 20.00
69B Murph Chamberlain/Home Still 10.00 20.00
69C Murph Chamberlain/Home
Still, facing forward 15.00 30.00
70 Gerry Couture/Away Action 6.00 12.00
71A Floyd Curry/Home Still 62.50 125.00
71B Floyd Curry/Home Action 6.00 12.00
72 Ed Dorohoy/Home Action 6.00 12.00
73A Bill Durnan/Home Still
stick handle cropped 12.50 25.00
73B Bill Durnan/Home Still 25.00 50.00
73C Bill Durnan/Home Still 87.50 175.00
73D Bill Durnan/Home Action 15.00 30.00
74A Norm Dussault/Home Portrait 6.00 12.00
74B Norm Dussault/Home Action 15.00 30.00
75 Frank Eddolls/Home Still 10.00 20.00
76A Bob Fillion/Home Still/small image 25.00 50.00
76B Bob Fillion/Home Still 6.00 12.00
76C Bob Fillion/Home Still/test 12.50 25.00
76D Bob Fillion/Home
Action{teststesttees/testst 6.00 12.00
77 Dick Gamble/Away Action 10.00 20.00
78 Bernie Geoffrion/Home Action 15.00 30.00
79A Leo Gravelle/Home Still 6.00 12.00
79B Leo Gravelle/Away Still 25.00 50.00
79C Leo Gravelle/Home Action 6.00 12.00
80A Glen Harmon/Home Still, entire puck 6.00 12.00
80B Glen Harmon/Home Still, no puck 6.00 12.00
80C Glen Harmon/Home Action 12.50 25.00
81A Doug Harvey/Home Still 12.50 25.00
81B Doug Harvey/Home Action 10.00 20.00
82 Dutch Hiller/Home Still 10.00 20.00
83 Bert Hirschfield/Home Action
Testtestestsetstset 10.00 20.00
84 Tom Johnson/Home Action
sdfsdfsdfsdfsdfsdfsdf 10.00 20.00
85 Vern Kaiser/Home Action 10.00 20.00
86A Elmer Lach/Home Still, stick in corner 10.00 20.00
86B Elmer Lach/Home Still, stick cropped 10.00 20.00
86C Elmer Lach/Home Still
stick 1/2-inch up from corner 40.00 80.00
86D Elmer Lach/Home Action 10.00 20.00
87A Leo Lamoureaux/Home
Still, entire blade 12.50 25.00
87B Leo Lamoureaux/Home
Still, blade cropped 10.00 20.00
88A Hal Laycoe/Home Portrait 50.00 100.00
88B Hal Laycoe/Home Action 6.00 12.00
89A Roger Leger/Home Still
light background 6.00 12.00
89B Roger Leger/Home Still
dark background 6.00 12.00
89C Roger Leger/Home Action 25.00 50.00
90 Jacques Locas/Home Still 10.00 20.00
91 Ross Lowe/Away Action 10.00 20.00
92 Callum MacKay/Home Action 6.00 12.00
93 Murdo MacKay/Home Portrait 6.00 12.00
94 James MacPherson/Home Action 6.00 12.00
95 Paul Masnick/Home Action 6.00 12.00
96A John McCormick/Home Action, vertical 50.00 100.00
96B John McCormick/Home
Action, horizontal 30.00 60.00
97 Mike McMahon/Home Still 50.00 100.00
98 Gerry McNeil/Home Action 12.50 25.00
99 Paul Meger/Home Action 7.50 15.00
100 Dickie Moore/Home Action 15.00 30.00
101A Ken Mosdell/Home Still, small image 6.00 12.00
101B Ken Mosdell/Home Still,
large image/auto. croppe 25.00 50.00
101C Ken Mosdell/Home Still,
large image/auto. not cr 25.00 50.00
101D Ken Mosdell/Home Action 6.00 12.00
102A Buddy O'Connor/Home
Still, entire blade 20.00 40.00
102B Buddy O'Connor/Home
Still, blade cropped 10.00 20.00
103 Bert Olmstead/Home Action 12.50 25.00
104A Jim Peters/Home Still, large image 6.00 12.00
104B Jim Peters/Home Still, small image 6.00 12.00
105 Gerry Plamondon/Home Action 7.50 15.00
106 Johnny Quilty/Home Portrait 7.50 15.00
107A Ken Reardon/Home Still, large image 10.00 20.00
107B Ken Reardon/Home Still, small image 15.00 30.00
107C Kenny Reardon/Home Action 10.00 20.00
108A Billy Reay/Home Still, large
image/stick touchin 6.00 12.00
108B Billy Reay/Home Still,
large image/stick away fr 6.00 12.00
108C Billy Reay/Home Still, small image 62.50 125.00
108D Billy Reay/Home Action 6.00 12.00
109A Maurice Richard/Home,
screen background 150.00 300.00
109B Maurice Richard/Home,
large image/auto. cropped 15.00 30.00
109C Maurice Richard/Home,
large image/entire auto. 15.00 30.00
109D Maurice Richard/Home Action 30.00 60.00
110A Howie Riopelle/Home Still 10.00 20.00
110B Howie Riopelle/Home Action 10.00 20.00
111 George Robertson/Home Action 20.00 40.00
112 Dollard St. Laurent/Home Action 30.00 60.00
113 Grant Warwick/Home Action 40.00 80.00

1972-73 Whalers New England WHA

This 17-photo card set measures 3 3/4" by 5". The fronts feature black-and-white posed player photographs. The backs are blank. The cards are unnumbered and checklisted below in alphabetical order.

COMPLETE SET (15) 20.00 40.00
1 Mike Byers 1.00 2.00
2 Terry Caffery 1.00 2.00
3 John Cunniff 1.50 3.00
4 John Danby 1.00 2.00
5 Jim Dorey 1.50 3.00
6 Tom Earl 1.00 2.00
7 John French 1.00 2.00
8 Ted Green 2.50 5.00
9 Ric Jordan 1.00 2.00
10 Bruce Landon 1.00 2.00
11 Rick Ley 2.50 5.00
12 Larry Pleau 2.00 4.00
13 Brad Selwood 1.00 2.00
14 Tim Sheehy 1.00 2.00
15 Al Smith 2.50 5.00
16 Tom Webster 2.50 5.00
17 Tom Williams 2.00 4.00

1973-74 Quaker Oats WHA

This set of 50 cards features players of the World Hockey Association. The cards were issued in strips (panels) of five in Quaker Oats products. The cards measure approximately 2 1/4" by 3 1/4" and are numbered on the back. The information on the card backs is written in English and French. The value of unseparated panels would be approximately 20 percent greater than the sum of the individual values listed below.

COMPLETE SET (50) 137.50 275.00
1 Jim Wiste 2.50 5.00
2 Al Smith 3.00 6.00
3 Rosaire Paiement 2.50 5.00
4 Ted Hampson 2.00 4.00
5 Gavin Kirk 2.00 4.00
6 Andre Lacroix 3.00 6.00
7 John Schella 2.00 4.00
8 Gerry Cheevers 10.00 20.00
9 Norm Beaudin 2.00 4.00
10 Jim Harrison 2.00 4.00
11 Gerry Pinder 2.50 5.00
12 Bob Sicinski 2.00 4.00
13 Bryan Campbell 2.00 4.00
14 Murray Hall 2.00 4.00
15 Chris Bordeleau 2.50 5.00
16 Al Hamilton 3.00 6.00
17 Jimmy McLeod 2.00 4.00
18 Larry Pleau 2.50 5.00
19 Larry Lund 2.00 4.00
20 Bobby Sheehan 2.50 5.00
21 Jan Popiel 2.00 4.00
22 Andre Gaudette 2.00 4.00
23 Bob Charlebois 2.00 4.00
24 Gene Peacosh 2.00 4.00
25 Rick Ley 2.50 5.00
26 Larry Hornung 2.00 4.00
27 Gary Jarrett 2.00 4.00
28 Ted Taylor 2.00 4.00
29 Pete Donnelly 2.00 4.00
30 J.C. Tremblay 3.00 6.00
31 Jim Cardiff 2.00 4.00
32 Gary Veneruzzo 2.00 4.00

33 John French	2.00	4.00
34 Ron Ward	2.50	5.00
35 Wayne Connelly	2.50	5.00
36 Ron Buchanan	2.00	4.00
37 Ken Block	2.00	4.00
38 Alain Caron	2.00	4.00
39 Brit Selby	2.50	5.00
40 Guy Trottier	2.00	4.00
41 Ernie Wakely	3.00	6.00
42 J.P. LeBlanc	2.00	4.00
43 Michel Parizeau	2.00	4.00
44 Wayne Rivers	2.00	4.00
45 Reg Fleming	2.50	5.00
46 Don Herriman	2.00	4.00
47 Jim Dorey	2.00	4.00
48 Danny Lawson	3.00	6.00
49 Dick Paradise	2.00	4.00
50 Bobby Hull	30.00	60.00

1954 Quaker Sports Oddities

This 27-card set features strange moments in sports and was issued as an insert inside Quaker Puffed Rice cereal boxes. Fronts of the cards are drawings depicting the person or the event. In a stripe at the top of the card face appear the words "Sports Oddities." Two colorful drawings fill the remaining space: the left half is a portrait, while the right half is action-oriented. A variety of sports are included. The cards measure approximately 2 1/4" by 3 1/2" and have rounded corners. The last line on the back of each card declares, "It's Odd but True." A person could also buy the complete set for fifteen cents and two box tops from Quaker Puffed Wheat or Quaker Rice. If a collector did send in their material to Quaker Oats the set came back in a specially marked box with the cards in cellophane wrapping. Sets in original wrapping are valued at 1.25x to 1.5X the high column listings in our checklist.

COMPLETE SET (27)	125.00	250.00
10 Chicago Blackhawks	7.50	15.00

1950 R423

Many numbers of these small and unattractive cards may be yet unknown for this issue of the early 1950s. The cards are printed on thin stock and measure 5/8" by 3/4"; sometimes they are found as a long horizontal strip of 13 cards connected by a perforation. Complete strips intact are worth 50 percent more than the sum of the individual players on the strip. The cards were available with a variety of back colors, red, green, blue, or purple, with the red and blue being the rarest of the varieties. The cards on the strip are in no apparent order, numerically or alphabetically. The producer's numbering of the cards in the set is very close to alphabetical order. Cards are so small they are sometimes lost. These strips were premiums or prizes in one-cent bubblegum machines; they were folded accordion style and held together by a small metal clip.

1 Taffy Abel	12.50	25.00
2 George Allen	10.00	20.00
3 Syl Apps	12.50	25.00
4 Pete Backor	10.00	20.00
5 Baz Bastien	10.00	20.00
6 Bobby Bauer	10.00	20.00
7 Gordie Bell	10.00	20.00
8 Lin Bend	10.00	20.00
9 Paul Bibeault	10.00	20.00
10 Garth Boesch	10.00	20.00
11 Butch Bouchard	12.50	25.00
12 Frank Boucher	12.50	25.00
13 Adam Brown	10.00	20.00
14 Hal Brown	10.00	20.00
15 Mud Bruneteau	10.00	20.00
16 Frank Bull	10.00	20.00
17 Scotty Cameron	10.00	20.00
18 Joe Carveth	10.00	20.00
19 Murph Chamberlain	10.00	20.00
20 Dit Clapper	12.50	25.00
21 Mac Colville	10.00	20.00
22 Lionel Conacher	15.00	30.00
23 Bun Cook	10.00	20.00
24 Ernie Dickens	10.00	20.00
25 Cecil Dillon	10.00	20.00
26 Connie Dion	10.00	20.00
27 Gordie Drillon	10.00	20.00
28 Bill Ezinicki	10.00	20.00
29 Wilfy Field	10.00	20.00
30 Bob Fillion	10.00	20.00
31 Chuck Gardiner	10.00	20.00
32 George Gee	10.00	20.00
33 Gus Giesebrecht	10.00	20.00
34 Bob Goldham	10.00	20.00
35 Dutch Hiller	10.00	20.00
36 Dick Irvin	10.00	20.00
37 Aurel Joliat	12.50	25.00
38 Alex Kaleta	10.00	20.00
39 Mike Karakas	10.00	20.00
40 Ted Kennedy	15.00	30.00
41 Dave Kerr	12.50	25.00
42 Roger Leger	10.00	20.00
43 Carl Liscombe	10.00	20.00
44 Vic Lynn	10.00	20.00
45 Kilby MacDonald	10.00	20.00
46 Bucko McDonald	10.00	20.00
47 Howie Morenz	20.00	35.00
48 Gus Mortson	10.00	20.00
49 Ken Mosdell	10.00	20.00
50 Frank Nighbor	12.50	25.00
51 Lynn Patrick	12.50	25.00
52 Billy Reay	10.00	20.00
53 Leo Reise	10.00	20.00
54 Earl Babe Seibert	12.50	25.00
55 Clint Smith	10.00	20.00
56 Wally Stanowski	10.00	20.00
57 Gaye Stewart	10.00	20.00
58 Tiny Thompson	15.00	30.00
59 Roy Worters	12.50	25.00

1970-71 Red Wings Volpe Marathon Oil

This 11-card (artistic) portrait set of Detroit Red Wings was part of a (Pro Star Portraits) promotion by Marathon Oil. The cards measure approximately 7 1/2" by 14"; the bottom portion, which measures 7 1/2" by 4 1/16", was a tear-off postcard in the form of a credit card application. The front features a full color portrait by Nicholas Volpe, with a facsimile autograph of the player inscribed across the bottom of the painting. The back included an offer for other sports memorabilia on the upper portion.

COMPLETE SET (11)	40.00	80.00
1 Gary Bergman	2.50	5.00
2 Wayne Connelly	2.00	4.00
3 Alex Delvecchio	5.00	10.00
4 Roy Edwards	2.50	5.00
5 Gordie Howe	25.00	50.00
6 Bruce MacGregor	2.00	4.00
7 Frank Mahovlich	6.00	12.00
8 Dale Rolfe	2.00	4.00
9 Jim Rutherford	3.00	6.00
10 Garry Unger	2.50	5.00
11 Tom Webster	2.50	5.00

1971 Red Wings Citgo Tumblers

These tumblers were available at Citgo gas stations and measure approximately 8" high. Tumblers feature color head shots, a facsimile autograph, and a color artwork action shot. They are made by Cinemac Inc, and feature a copyright of 1971.

COMPLETE SET	100.00	200.00
1 Wayne Connelly	12.50	25.00
2 Alex Delvecchio	20.00	40.00
3 Don Edwards	10.00	20.00
4 Garry Unger	10.00	20.00
5 Gordie Howe	37.50	75.00
6 Frank Mahovlich	15.00	30.00

1973-74 Red Wings Team Issue

Cards measure 8 3/4" x 10 3/4". Fronts feature color photos, and backs are blank. Cards are unnumbered and checklisted below in alphabetical order.

COMPLETE SET (18)	50.00	100.00
1 Ace Bailey	2.50	5.00
2 Red Berenson	4.00	8.00
3 Gary Bergman	2.50	5.00
4 Thommie Bergman	4.00	8.00
5 Guy Charron	2.50	5.00
6 Bill Collins	2.50	5.00
7 Denis Dejordy	4.00	8.00
8 Alex Delvecchio	7.50	15.00
9 Marcel Dionne	7.50	15.00
10 Gary Doak	2.50	5.00
11 Tim Ecclestone	2.50	5.00
12 Larry Johnston	2.50	5.00
13 Al Karlander	2.50	5.00
14 Brian Lavender	2.50	5.00
15 Nick Libett	2.50	5.00
16 Ken Murphy	2.50	5.00
17 Mickey Redmond	7.50	15.00
18 Ron Stackhouse	2.50	5.00

1973-75 Red Wings McCarthy Postcards

Measuring approximately 3 1/4" by 5 1/2", these postcards display color posed action shots on their fronts. The backs are blank. Since there is no Marcel Dionne or Alex Delvecchio (the latter played 11 games in 1973-74 before coaching), it is doubtful that this is a complete set. The date is established by two players: Brent Hughes (1973-74 was his only season with the Red Wings) and Tom Mellor (1974-75). The cards are unnumbered and checklisted below in alphabetical order. The photos and cards were produced by noted photographer J.D. McCarthy.

COMPLETE SET (15)	12.50	25.00
1 Garnet Bailey	1.00	2.00
2 Thommie Bergman	1.00	2.00
3 Henry Boucha	1.25	2.50
4 Guy Charron	1.00	2.00
5 Bill Collins	1.00	2.00
6 Doug Grant	1.00	2.00
7 Ted Harris	1.00	2.00
8 Bill Hogaboam	1.00	2.00
9 Brent Hughes	1.00	2.00
10 Pierre Jarry	1.00	2.00
11 Larry Johnston	1.00	2.00
12 Nick Libett	1.00	2.00
13 Tom Mellor	1.00	2.00
14 Doug Roberts	1.00	2.00
15 Ron Stackhouse	1.00	2.00

1979 Red Wings Postcards

This set features borderless color fronts and was issued by the Red Wings during the 1979 season.

COMPLETE SET (18)	7.50	15.00
1 Thommie Bergman	.38	.75
2 Dan Bolduc	.38	.75
3 Mike Foligno	.38	.75
4 Jean Hamel	.38	.75
5 Glen Hicks	.38	.75
6 Greg Joly	.38	.75
7 Willie Huber	.38	.75
8 Jim Korn	.38	.75
9 Dan Labraaten	.38	.75
10 Barry Long	.38	.75
11 Reed Larson	.38	.75
12 Dale McCourt	.38	.75
13 Vaclav Nedomansky	.38	.75
14 Jim Rutherford	.38	.75
15 Dennis Polonich	.38	.75
16 Errol Thompson	.38	.75
17 Rogie Vachon	.38	.75
18 Paul Woods	.38	.75

1932 Reemstma Olympia

This colorful set was produced by Reemstma for the 1932 winter Olympics. Cards measure approximately 6 3/4 by 4 3/4 and are in full color. Backs are in German. Smaller versions of the cards also exist and are in black and white.

188 Dutch hockey player	10.00	20.00
191 USA vs. Canada	25.00	50.00

1936 Reemstma Olympia

This group of cards may or may not make up a complete set of Reemstma Olympia. These undersized issues picture international hockey players and matches from the early 1930s. It is believed they were issued as some sort of premium -- perhaps with cigarettes -- and it's likely that they were issued in Germany.

30 Team Canada { 6 3/4 x 4 3/4	20.00	40.00
31 Ice Hockey Spectators	20.00	40.00
32 Hockey Action Photo	20.00	40.00
33 Goalie making sliding save	20.00	40.00
34 Hockey Action Photo	20.00	40.00
35 Hockey Action Photo Canada player in crease	20.00	40.00
36 Team Canada Photo	20.00	40.00
37 Team USA Photo	20.00	40.00
38 Gustav Jaenecke	20.00	40.00
39 Teiji Homna Japan Goalie	20.00	40.00
40 Clearing the Ice	20.00	40.00

1976-77 Rockies Puck Bucks

This 20-card set measures approximately 2 9/16" by 2 1/8" (after perforation) and features members of the then-expansion Colorado Rockies team. The set was issued in the Greater Denver area as part of a regional promotion for the Rockies. The cards feature a horizontal format on the front which has the player's photo. The cards were issued two to a panel (they could be separated, but then one couldn't compete in contest). Left side and right side in the rules refers to the two different cards that were joined: an action scene on the left side and a posed head shot in a circle on the right side). If the same player appeared in the action scene and in the circle, and if the ticket values and the color bars below both pictures matched, the contestant became an instant winner of two Colorado Rockies' hockey tickets, whose value is shown in the color bar. One could also save all player pictures until one had the same player appearing in the action scene and in the circle both with matching ticket values and matching color bars. The color bars at the bottom appeared in four different colors (yellow, blue, green, or orange). The cards feature either a "Play Puck Bucks" logo on the back, which also features a skeletal-like picture of a player, or a rules definition. Winners had to claim prizes by February 20, 1977. Since there is no numerical designation for the cards, they are checklisted alphabetically below.

COMPLETE SET (20)	37.50	75.00
1 Ron Andruff	2.00	4.00
2 Chuck Arnason	2.00	4.00
3 Henry Boucha	2.50	5.00
4 Colin Campbell	3.00	6.00
5 Gary Croteau	2.00	4.00
6 Guy Delparte	2.00	4.00
7 Steve Durbano	2.50	5.00
8 Tom Edur	2.00	4.00
9 Doug Favell	3.00	6.00
10 Dave Hudson	2.00	4.00
11 Bryan Lefley	2.00	4.00
12 Roger Lemelin	2.00	4.00
13 Simon Nolet	2.00	4.00
14 Wilf Paiement	2.50	5.00
15 Michel Plasse	3.00	6.00
16 Tracy Pratt	2.00	4.00
17 Nelson Pyatt	2.00	4.00
18 Phil Roberto	2.00	4.00
19 Sean Shanahan	2.00	4.00
20 Larry Skinner	2.00	4.00

1979-80 Rockies Team Issue

This 23-card set of the Colorado Rockies measures approximately 4" by 6". The fronts feature black-and-white action player photos. The backs are blank. The cards are unnumbered and checklisted below in alphabetical order.

COMPLETE SET (23)	20.00	40.00
1 Hardy Astrom	1.50	3.00
2 Doug Berry	.75	1.50
3 Nick Beverley	1.00	2.00
4 Mike Christie	.75	1.50
5 Gary Croteau	1.00	2.00
6 Lucien Deblois	1.00	2.00
7 Ron Delorme	.75	1.50
8 Mike Gillis	.75	1.50
9 Trevor Johansen	.75	1.50
10 Mike Kitchen	.75	1.50
11 Lanny McDonald	2.50	5.00
12 Mike McEwen	.75	1.50
13 Bill McKenzie	.75	1.50
14 Kevin Morrison	.75	1.50
15 Bill Oleschuk	.75	1.50
16 Randy Pierce	.75	1.50
17 Michel Plasse	1.50	3.00
18 Joel Quenneville	1.00	2.00
19 Rob Ramage	2.50	5.00
20 Rene Robert	1.00	2.00
21 Don Saleski	1.00	2.00
22 Barry Smith	1.00	2.00
23 Jack Valiquette	.75	1.50

1930 Rogers Peet

The Rogers Peet Department Store in New York released this set in early 1930. The cards were given out four at time to employees at the store for enrolling boys in Ropeco (the store's magazine club). Employees who completed the set, and pasted them in the album designed to house the cards, were eligible to win prizes. The blankbacked cards measure roughly 1 3/4" by 2 1/2" and feature a black and white photo of the famous athlete with his name and card number below the picture. Additions to this list are appreciated.

10 Lionel Conacher HK	62.50	125.00
22 Frank Boucher HK	50.00	75.00
29 Ching Johnson HK	62.50	125.00
42 Bill Burch HK	35.00	50.00

1952 Royal Desserts

The 1952 Royal Desserts Hockey set contains eight cards. The cards measure approximately 2 5/8" by 3 1/4". The set is cataloged as F219-2. The cards formed the backs of Royal Desserts packages of the period; consequently many cards are found with uneven edges stemming from the method of cutting the cards off the box. Each card has its number and the statement "Royal Stars of Hockey" in a red rectangle at the top. The blue tinted picture also features a facsimile autograph of the player. An album was presumably available as it is advertised on the card. The exact year (or years) of issue of these cards is not verified at this time.

COMPLETE SET (8)	6,500.00	13,000.00
1 Tony Leswick	300.00	750.00
2 Chuck Rayner	400.00	800.00
3 Edgar Laprade	300.00	750.00
4 Sid Abel	600.00	1,200.00
5 Ted Lindsay	600.00	1,200.00
6 Leo Reise Jr.	300.00	750.00
7 Red Kelly	600.00	1,200.00
8 Gordie Howe	3,000.00	6,000.00

1971-72 Sabres Postcards

These standard-sized postcards feature borderless color photos. The backs feature player name, position, uniform number, and biographical information. These postcards were issued in bound form, with perforated top edges so as to be separated if necessary. The postcards are numbered in a long code format (for example, Punch Imlach is 82269-C). For space reasons, the 822 prefix and -C suffix have been deleted in the checklist below. Thanks to collector Edward Morse for updating the information seen below.

COMPLETE SET (22)	15.00	30.00
69 Punch Imlach CO	1.25	3.00
70 Roger Crozier	1.50	4.00
71 Jim Watson	.75	2.00
72 Mike Robitaille	.75	2.00
73 Tracy Pratt	.75	2.00
74 Doug Barrie	.75	2.00
75 Al Hamilton	.75	2.00
76 Richard Martin	1.50	4.00
77 Dick Duff	.75	2.00
78 Danny Lawson	.75	2.00
79 Phil Goyette	.75	2.00
80 Gil Perreault	3.00	6.00
81 Rod Zaine	.75	2.00
82 Gerry Meehan	.75	2.00
83 Ron Anderson	.75	2.00
84 Floyd Smith	.75	2.00
85 Kevin O'Shea	.75	2.00
86 Steve Atkinson	.75	2.00
87 Don Luce	.75	2.00
88 Ray McKay	.75	2.00
89 Eddie Shack	1.25	3.00
90 Dave Dryden	1.25	3.00

1972-73 Sabres Pepsi Pinback Buttons

These smallish buttons were apparently given away with the purchase of Pepsi products in the Buffalo area. The photos are black and white and feature early heroes of the Sabres history.

COMPLETE SET (9)	25.00	50.00
1 Roger Crozier	2.50	5.00
2 Don Luce	2.00	4.00
3 Rick Martin (action)	2.50	5.00
4 Rick Martin (head)	2.50	5.00
5 Gilbert Perreault (action)	5.00	10.00
6 Gilbert Perreault (head)	5.00	10.00
7 Gilbert Perreault (action)	2.50	5.00
8 Jim Schoenfeld	2.50	5.00
9 French Connection	5.00	10.00

1972-73 Sabres Postcards

This set of color postcards was issued by the team in response to autograph requests. It is not known whether they were actually sold in set form at any point, but given the difficulty in completing a set, it seems unlikely.

COMPLETE SET (20)	30.00	60.00
1 Steve Atkinson	1.00	2.00
2 Larry Carriere	1.00	2.00
3 Roger Crozier	4.00	8.00
4 Butch Deadmarsh	1.00	2.00
5 Dave Dryden	1.50	3.00
6 Larry Hillman	1.00	2.00
7 Tim Horton	5.00	10.00
8 Jim Lorentz	1.00	2.00
9 Don Luce	1.50	3.00
10 Richard Martin	3.00	6.00
11 Gerry Meehan	1.50	3.00
12 Larry Mickey	1.00	2.00
13 Gilbert Perreault	5.00	10.00
14 Tracy Pratt	1.50	3.00
15 Craig Ramsay	1.50	3.00
16 Rene Robert	1.50	3.00
17 Mike Robitaille	1.00	2.00
18 Jim Schoenfeld	3.00	6.00
19 Paul Terbenche	1.00	2.00
20 Randy Wyrozub	1.00	2.00

1973-74 Sabres Bells

This set of four photos of Buffalo Sabres players was sponsored by Bells Markets. The photos measure approximately 3 15/16" by 5 1/2" and were sold for 10 cents each. The front has a color action photo. These blank-backed cards are unnumbered and listed alphabetically in the checklist below. The team card was issued and cost 50 cents apiece.

COMPLETE SET (4) 15.00 30.00
1 Roger Crozier 4.00 8.00
2 Jim Lorentz 2.50 5.00
3 Richard Martin 4.00 8.00
4 Gilbert Perreault 6.00 12.00
5 Team Photo

1973-74 Sabres Postcards

This 13-card set was published by Robert B. Shaver of Kenmore, New York. The cards are in the postcard format and measure approximately 3 1/2" by 5 1/2". The fronts feature a black-and-white action shot with white borders. The backs carry the player's name, position, and team name at the upper left and are divided in the middle. The set is dated by the inclusion of Joe Norris, who played with the Sabres only during the 1973-74 season. The cards are unnumbered and checklisted below in alphabetical order.

COMPLETE SET (13) 20.00 40.00
1 Roger Crozier 2.00 4.00
2 Dave Dryden 2.00 4.00
3 Tim Horton 5.00 10.00
4 Jim Lorentz 1.00 2.00
5 Don Luce 1.25 2.50
6 Rick Martin 2.00 4.00
7 Gerry Meehan 1.50 3.00
8 Larry Mickey 1.00 2.00
9 Joe Noris 1.00 2.00
10 Gilbert Perreault 4.00 8.00
11 Mike Robitaille 1.00 2.00
12 Jim Schoenfeld 2.00 4.00
13 Paul Terbenche 1.00 2.00

1974-75 Sabres Postcards

This set of color postcards was issued by the team in response to autograph requests. It is not known whether they were actually sold in set form at any point, but given the difficulty in completing a set, it seems unlikely.

COMPLETE SET (21) 30.00 60.00
1 Gary Bromley 2.00 4.00
2 Larry Carriere 1.00 2.00
3 Roger Crozier 4.00 8.00
4 Rick Dudley 2.00 4.00
5 Rocky Farr 1.00 2.00
6 Lee Fogolin 2.00 4.00
7 Danny Gare 2.00 4.00
8 Norm Gratton 1.00 2.00
9 Jocelyn Guevremont 1.00 2.00
10 Bill Hajt 1.00 2.00
11 Jerry Korab 2.00 4.00
12 Jim Lorentz 1.00 2.00
13 Don Luce 1.25 2.50
14 Richard Martin 2.00 4.00
15 Peter McNab 1.25 2.50
16 Larry Mickey 1.00 2.00
17 Gilbert Perreault 4.00 8.00
18 Craig Ramsay 1.50 3.00
19 Rene Robert 1.50 3.00
20 Jim Schoenfeld 2.00 4.00
21 Brian Spencer 2.50 5.00

1975-76 Sabres Linnett

Produced by Linnett Studios, this 12-card set featured Buffalos Sabres players ftom the 1975-76 season.

COMPLETE SET (12) 15.00 30.00
1 Roger Crozier 2.00 4.00
2 Gerry Desjardins 1.50 3.00
3 Dave Dryden 1.50 3.00
4 Jim Lorentz 1.00 2.00
5 Don Luce 1.25 2.50
6 Richard Martin 2.00 4.00
7 Peter McNab 1.25 2.50
8 Gerry Meehan 1.00 2.00
9 Gilbert Perreault 4.00 8.00
10 Rene Robert 1.50 3.00
11 Jim Schoenfeld 2.00 4.00
12 Fred Stanfield 1.50 3.00

1976-77 Sabres Glasses

Glasses feature a black and white portrait of the player. Glasses were available at Your Host restaurants.

COMPLETE SET (4) 12.50 25.00
1 Jerry Korab 3.00 6.00
2 Rick Martin 3.00 6.00
3 Gilbert Perreault 3.00 6.00
4 Jim Schoenfeld 3.00 6.00

1979-80 Sabres Bells

This set of nine photos of Buffalo Sabres players was sponsored by Bells Markets. The photos measure approximately 7 5/8" by 10". The front has a color action photo, with the player's name and team name in the white border at the lower right hand corner. The back is printed in blue and has the Sabres' logo, a head shot of the player, biographical information, and career statistics.

COMPLETE SET (9) 10.00 20.00
1 Don Edwards 2.00 4.00
2 Danny Gare 1.25 2.50
3 Jerry Korab 1.00 2.00
4 Richard Martin 2.00 4.00
5 Tony McKegney 1.25 2.50
6 Craig Ramsay 1.00 2.00
7 Bob Sauve 2.00 4.00
8 Jim Schoenfeld 1.50 3.00
9 John Van Boxmeer 1.00 2.00

1979-80 Sabres Milk Panels

This set of four confirmed panels feature singles that are approximately 3 1/2 by 1 1/2. The top portion features a blue-toned head shot, while the bottom includes player bio information. The backs are blank.

COMPLETE SET (4) 3.00 6.00
1 Don Edwards .50 1.00
2 Ric Seiling .50 1.00
3 Jerry Korab .50 1.00
4 Gil Perreault .50 1.00

1980-81 Sabres Milk Panels

This set of Buffalo Sabres was issued on the side of half gallon milk cartons. After cutting, the panels measure approximately 3 3/4" by 7 1/2", with two players per panel. The picture and text of the player panels are printed in red; the set can also be found in blue print. The top of the panel reads "Kids, Collect a Complete Set of Buffalo Sabres Players". Arranged alongside each other, the panel features for each player a head shot, biographical information, and player profile. The panels are subtly dated and numbered below the photo area in the following way, Perreault/Seiling is M325-80-4H (M325 is the product code, the number 80 gives the last two digits of the year, and 4 is the card number perhaps also indicating release week).

COMPLETE SET (2) 15.00 30.00
4 Gilbert Perreault 10.00 20.00
Ric Seiling
8 Bob Sauve 6.00 12.00
Richard Martin

1974-75 San Diego Mariners WHA

Sponsored by Dean's Photo Service Inc., this set of seven photos measured approximately 5 3/8" by 8 1/2" and featured black-and-white action pictures against a white background on thin paper stock. The player's name appeared in the white margin below the photo along with the team and sponsor logos. The backs featured biographical information, career highlights, and statistics. The cards came in a light blue paper "picture pack" with the team and sponsor logos and game dates suggested for acquiring autographs. The cards were unnumbered and checklisted below in alphabetical order. This set may be incomplete; additions to the checklist would be welcome.

COMPLETE SET (7) 20.00 40.00
1 Andre Lacroix 5.00 10.00
2 Mike Laughton 2.50 5.00
3 Brian Morenz 2.50 5.00
4 Kevin Morrison 2.50 5.00
5 Gene Peacosh 2.50 5.00
6 Ron Plumb 4.00 8.00
7 Craig Reichmuth 2.50 5.00

1976-77 San Diego Mariners WHA

These cards measure 5" x 8" and were issued in two sheets of seven players each. Card fronts feature black and white photos with a white border. Backs feature player statistics. Cards are unnumbered and checklisted below alphabetically. Prices below are for individual cards.

COMPLETE SET (14) 20.00 40.00
1 Kevin Devine 1.25 2.50
2 Bob Dobek 1.25 2.50
3 Norm Ferguson 1.25 2.50
4 Brent Hughes 1.25 2.50
5 Randy Legge 1.25 2.50
6 Ken Lockett 1.25 2.50
7 Kevin Morrison 1.25 2.50
8 Joe Norris 1.25 2.50
9 Gerry Pinder 2.00 4.00
10 Brad Rhiness 1.25 2.50
11 Wayne Rivers 2.00 4.00
12 Paul Shmyr 1.50 3.00
13 Gary Veneruzzo 1.50 3.00
14 Ernie Wakely 2.50 5.00

1932 Sanella Margarine

The cards in this set measure approximately 2 3/4" by 4 1/8" and feature color images of famous athletes printed on thin stock. The cards were created in Germany and originally designed to be pasted into an album called "Handbook of Sports." The Ruth, and possibly the other cards in the set, was created in four versions with slight differences being found on the cardbacks.

2 Ice Hockey 25.00 50.00

1970-71 Sargent Promotions Stamps

This set consists of 224 total stamps, 16 for each NHL team. Individual stamps measure approximately 2" by 2 1/2". The set could be put into a album featuring Bobby Orr on the cover. Stamp fronts feature a full-color head shot of the player, player's name, and team. The stamp number is located in the upper left corner. The 1970-71 set features one-time appearances in Eddie Sargent Promotions sets by Hall of Famers Gordie Howe, Jean Beliveau, Andy Bathgate. The set also features first appearances of Gil Perreault, Brad Park, and Bobby Clarke. The three have Rookie Cards in both Topps and O-Pee-Chee for the same year.

COMPLETE SET (224) 325.00 650.00
1 Bobby Orr 62.50 125.00
2 Don Awrey .50 1.00
3 Derek Sanderson 5.00 10.00
4 Ted Green .63 1.25
5 Eddie Johnston 1.25 2.50
6 Wayne Carleton .50 1.00
7 Ed Westfall .75 1.50
8 Johnny Bucyk 2.50 5.00
9 John McKenzie .50 1.00
10 Ken Hodge 1.00 2.00
11 Rick Smith .50 1.00
12 Fred Stanfield .50 1.00
13 Garnet Bailey .50 1.00
14 Phil Esposito 10.00 20.00
15 Gerry Cheevers 5.00 10.00
16 Dallas Smith .50 1.00
17 Joe Daley 1.00 2.00
18 Ron Anderson .50 1.00
19 Tracy Pratt .50 1.00
20 Gerry Meehan .75 1.50
21 Reg Fleming .50 1.00
22 Al Hamilton .63 1.25
23 Gil Perreault 12.50 25.00
24 Skip Krake .50 1.00
25 Kevin O'Shea .50 1.00
26 Roger Crozier 1.50 3.00
27 Bill Inglis .50 1.00
28 Mike McMahon .50 1.00
29 Cliff Schmautz .50 1.00
30 Floyd Smith .50 1.00
31 Randy Wyrozub .50 1.00
32 Jim Watson .50 1.00
33 Tony Esposito 15.00 30.00
34 Doug Jarrett .50 1.00
35 Keith Magnuson .63 1.25
36 Dennis Hull 1.00 2.00
37 Cliff Koroll .50 1.00
38 Eric Nesterenko .75 1.50
39 Pit Martin .63 1.25
40 Lou Angotti .50 1.00
41 Jim Pappin .63 1.25
42 Gerry Pinder .63 1.25
43 Bobby Hull 25.00 50.00
44 Pat Stapleton .63 1.25
45 Gerry Desjardins 1.00 2.00
46 Chico Maki .63 1.25
47 Doug Mohns .63 1.25
48 Stan Mikita 10.00 20.00
49 Gary Bergman .63 1.25
50 Pete Stemkowski .63 1.25
51 Bruce MacGregor .50 1.00
52 Ron Harris .50 1.00
53 Billy Dea .50 1.00
54 Wayne Connelly .50 1.00
55 Dale Rolfe .50 1.00
56 Gordie Howe 40.00 80.00
57 Tom Webster .63 1.25
58 Al Karlander .50 1.00
59 Alex Delvecchio 2.50 5.00
60 Nick Libett .63 1.25
61 Garry Unger 1.00 2.00
62 Roy Edwards 1.00 2.00
63 Frank Mahovlich 5.00 10.00
64 Bob Baun 1.25 2.50
65 Dick Duff 1.00 2.00
66 Ross Lonsberry .50 1.00
67 Ed Joyal .50 1.00
68 Dale Hoganson .50 1.00
69 Eddie Shack 2.50 5.00
70 Real Lemieux .50 1.00
71 Matt Ravlich .50 1.00
72 Bob Pulford 1.50 3.00
73 Denis DeJordy 1.25 2.50
74 Larry Mickey .50 1.00
75 Bill Flett .50 1.00
76 Juha Widing .75 1.50
77 Jim Peters .63 1.25
78 Gilles Marotte .63 1.25
79 Larry Cahan .50 1.00
80 Howie Hughes .50 1.00
81 Cesare Maniago 1.25 2.50
82 Ted Harris .50 1.00
83 Tom Williams .50 1.00
84 Gump Worsley 5.00 10.00
85 Tom Reid .50 1.00
86 Murray Oliver .50 1.00
87 Charlie Burns .50 1.00
88 Jude Drouin .50 1.00
89 Walt McKechnie .50 1.00
90 Danny O'Shea .50 1.00
91 Barry Gibbs .50 1.00
92 Danny Grant .63 1.25
93 Bob Barlow .50 1.00
94 J.P. Parise .63 1.25
95 Bill Goldsworthy .75 1.50
96 Bobby Rousseau .63 1.25
97 Jacques Laperriere 1.00 2.00
98 Henri Richard 5.00 10.00
99 J.C. Tremblay .75 1.50
100 Rogie Vachon 4.00 8.00
101 Claude Larose .50 1.00
102 Pete Mahovlich .75 1.50
103 Jacques Lemaire 4.00 8.00
104 Bill Collins .50 1.00
105 Guy Lapointe 1.50 3.00
106 Mickey Redmond 2.50 5.00
107 Larry Pleau .63 1.25
108 Jean Beliveau 12.50 25.00
109 Yvan Cournoyer 4.00 8.00
110 Serge Savard 4.00 8.00
111 Terry Harper .63 1.25
112 Phil Myre 1.00 2.00
113 Syl Apps .63 1.25
114 Ted Irvine .50 1.00
115 Ed Giacomin 5.00 10.00
116 Arnie Brown .50 1.00
117 Walt Tkaczuk .63 1.25
118 Jean Ratelle 2.50 5.00
119 Dave Balon .50 1.00
120 Ron Stewart .50 1.00
121 Jim Neilson .50 1.00
122 Rod Gilbert 2.50 5.00
123 Bill Fairbairn .50 1.00
124 Brad Park 10.00 20.00
125 Tim Horton 7.50 15.00
126 Vic Hadfield .75 1.50
127 Bob Nevin .50 1.00
128 Rod Seiling .50 1.00
129 Gary Smith 1.25 2.50
130 Carol Vadnais .50 1.00
131 Bert Marshall .50 1.00
132 Earl Ingarfield .50 1.00
133 Dennis Hextall .63 1.25
134 Harry Howell 1.50 3.00
135 Wayne Muloin .50 1.00
136 Mike Laughton .50 1.00
137 Ted Hampson .50 1.00
138 Doug Roberts .50 1.00
139 Dick Mattiussi .50 1.00
140 Gary Jarrett .50 1.00
141 Gary Croteau .50 1.00
142 Norm Ferguson .50 1.00
143 Bill Hicke .50 1.00
144 Gerry Ehman .50 1.00
145 Ralph McSweyn .50 1.00
146 Bernie Parent 7.50 15.00
147 Brent Hughes .50 1.00
148 Bobby Clarke 20.00 40.00
149 Gary Dornhoefer .63 1.25
150 Simon Nolet .50 1.00
151 Garry Peters .50 1.00
152 Doug Favell 1.25 2.50
153 Jim Johnson .50 1.00
154 Andre Lacroix .75 1.50
155 Larry Hale .50 1.00
156 Joe Watson .50 1.00
157 Jean-Guy Gendron .50 1.00
158 Larry Hillman .50 1.00
159 Ed Van Impe .50 1.00
160 Wayne Hillman .50 1.00
161 Al Smith 1.00 2.00
162 Jean Pronovost .63 1.25
163 Bob Woytowich .50 1.00
164 Bryan Watson .63 1.25
165 Dean Prentice .75 1.50
166 Duane Rupp .50 1.00
167 Glen Sather 1.00 2.00
168 Keith McCreary .50 1.00
169 Jim Morrison .50 1.00
170 Ron Schock .50 1.00
171 Wally Boyer .50 1.00
172 Nick Harbaruk .50 1.00
173 Andy Bathgate 2.50 5.00
174 Ken Schinkel .50 1.00
175 Les Binkley 1.00 2.00
176 Val Fonteyne .50 1.00
177 Red Berenson .75 1.50
178 Ab McDonald .50 1.00
179 Jim Roberts .50 1.00
180 Frank St. Marseille .50 1.00
181 Ernie Wakely 1.25 2.50
182 Terry Crisp .63 1.25
183 Bob Plager .75 1.50
184 Barclay Plager .75 1.50
185 Chris Bordeleau .50 1.00
186 Gary Sabourin .50 1.00
187 Bill Plager .63 1.25
188 Tim Ecclestone .50 1.00
189 Jean-Guy Talbot .75 1.50
190 Noel Picard .50 1.00
191 Bob Wall .50 1.00
192 Jim Lorentz .50 1.00
193 Bruce Gamble 1.50 3.00
194 Jim Harrison .50 1.00
195 Paul Henderson 1.50 3.00
196 Brian Glennie .50 1.00
197 Jim Dorey .50 1.00
198 Rick Ley .63 1.25
199 Jacques Plante 12.50 25.00
200 Ron Ellis .75 1.50
201 Jim McKenny .50 1.00
202 Brit Selby .50 1.00
203 Mike Pelyk .50 1.00
204 Norm Ullman 2.50 5.00
205 Bill MacMillan .50 1.00
206 Mike Walton .63 1.25
207 Garry Monahan .50 1.00
208 Dave Keon 2.50 5.00
209 Pat Quinn 1.00 2.00
210 Wayne Maki .50 1.00
211 Charlie Hodge 1.25 2.50
212 Orland Kurtenbach .63 1.25
213 Paul Popiel .63 1.25
214 Dan Johnson .50 1.00
215 Dale Tallon .63 1.25
216 Ray Cullen .63 1.25
217 Bob Dillabough .50 1.00
218 Gary Doak .50 1.00
219 Andre Boudrias .75 1.50
220 Rosaire Paiement .63 1.25
221 Darryl Sly .50 1.00
222 George Gardner .50 1.00
223 Jim Wiste .50 1.00
224 Murray Hall .50 1.00
NNO Stamp Album 17.50 35.00
(Bobby Orr on cover)

1971-72 Sargent Promotions Stamps

Issued by Eddie Sargent Promotions in a series of 16 ten-cent sheets of 14 NHL players each, this 224-stamp set featured posed color photos of players in their NHLPA jerseys. The pictures are framed on their tops and sides in different color borders with the players' names and teams appearing along the bottom. Each sheet measured approximately 7 7/8" by 10" and was divided into four rows, with four 2" by 2 1/2" stamps per row. Two of these 16 sections gave the series number (e.g., Series 1), resulting in a total of 14 players per sheet. The sections are perforated and the backs are blank. There was a stamp album (approximately 9 1/2" by 13") which featured information on the team history and individual players. The stamps are numbered in the upper left corner and they are grouped into 14 teams of 16 players each as follows: Boston Bruins (1-16), Buffalo Sabres (17-32), Chicago Blackhawks (33-48), Detroit Red Wings (49-64), Los Angeles Kings (65-80), Minnesota North Stars (81-96), Montreal Canadiens (97-112), New York Rangers (113-128), California Golden Seals (129-144), Philadelphia Flyers (145-160), Pittsburgh Penguins (161-176), St. Louis Blues (177-192), Toronto Maple Leafs (193-208), and Vancouver Canucks (209-224).

COMPLETE SET (224) 225.00 450.00
1 Fred Stanfield .50 1.00
2 Ed Westfall .75 1.50
3 John McKenzie .50 1.00
4 Derek Sanderson 4.00 8.00
5 Rick Smith .50 1.00
6 Teddy Green .63 1.25
7 Phil Esposito 7.50 15.00
8 Ken Hodge 1.00 2.00
9 Johnny Bucyk 4.00 8.00
10 Bobby Orr 50.00 100.00
11 Dallas Smith .50 1.00
12 Mike Walton .63 1.25
13 Don Awrey .50 1.00
14 Unknown .50 1.00
15 Eddie Johnston 1.00 2.00
16 Gerry Cheevers 4.00 8.00
17 Gerry Meehan .75 1.50
18 Ron Anderson .50 1.00
19 Gilbert Perreault 6.00 12.00
20 Eddie Shack 2.00 4.00
21 Jim Watson .50 1.00
22 Kevin O'Shea .50 1.00
23 Al Hamilton .50 1.00
24 Dick Duff .75 1.50
25 Tracy Pratt .50 1.00
26 Don Luce .50 1.00
27 Roger Crozier 1.00 2.00
28 Doug Barrie .50 1.00
29 Mike Robitaille .50 1.00
30 Phil Goyette .50 1.00
31 Larry Keenan .50 1.00
32 Dave Dryden 1.00 2.00
33 Stan Mikita 6.00 12.00
34 Bobby Hull 20.00 40.00
35 Cliff Koroll .50 1.00
36 Chico Maki .63 1.25
37 Danny O'Shea .50 1.00
38 Lou Angotti .50 1.00
39 Andre Lacroix .63 1.25
40 Jim Pappin .50 1.00
41 Doug Jarrett .50 1.00
42 Pit Martin .63 1.25
43 Gary Smith 1.00 2.00
44 Tony Esposito 7.50 15.00
45 Pat Stapleton .50 1.00
46 Dennis Hull 1.00 2.00
47 Bill White .50 1.00
48 Keith Magnuson .63 1.25
49 Bill Collins .50 1.00
50 Bob Wall .50 1.00
51 Red Berenson .75 1.50
52 Mickey Redmond 1.50 3.00
53 Nick Libett .50 1.00
54 Gary Bergman .63 1.25
55 Alex Delvecchio 2.50 5.00
56 Tim Ecclestone .50 1.00
57 Arnie Brown .50 1.00
58 Ron Harris .50 1.00
59 Ab McDonald .50 1.00
60 Guy Charron .63 1.25
61 Al Smith 1.00 2.00
62 Joe Daley 1.00 2.00
63 Leon Rochefort .50 1.00
64 Ron Stackhouse .50 1.00
65A Larry Johnston .75 1.50
65B Juha Widing .50 1.00
66 Bob Pulford 1.00 2.00
67 Bill Flett .50 1.00
68 Rogie Vachon 2.50 5.00
69 Ross Lonsberry .50 1.00
70 Gilles Marotte .50 1.00
71 Harry Howell 1.00 2.00
72 Real Lemieux .50 1.00
73 Butch Goring .50 1.00
74 Ed Joyal .50 1.00
75 Larry Hillman .50 1.00
76 Lucien Grenier .50 1.00
77 Paul Curtis .50 1.00
78 Unknown .50 1.00
79 Unknown .50 1.00
80 Unknown .50 1.00
81 Jude Drouin .50 1.00
82 Tom Reid .50 1.00
83 J.P. Parise .63 1.25
84 Doug Mohns .63 1.25
85 Danny Grant .63 1.25
86 Bill Goldsworthy .75 1.50
87 Charlie Burns .50 1.00
88 Murray Oliver .50 1.00
89 Dean Prentice .75 1.50
90 Bob Nevin .63 1.25
91 Ted Harris .63 1.25
92 Cesare Maniago 1.00 2.00
93 Lou Nanne .63 1.25
94 Ted Hampton .50 1.00
95 Barry Gibbs .50 1.00
96 Gump Worsley 4.00 8.00
97 J.C. Tremblay .75 1.50
98 Guy Lapointe 1.00 2.00
99 Pete Mahovlich .75 1.50
100 Larry Pleau .63 1.25
101 Phil Myre 1.00 2.00
102 Yvan Cournoyer 2.50 5.00
103 Henri Richard 5.00 10.00
104 Frank Mahovlich 5.00 10.00
105 Jacques Lemaire 2.00 4.00
106 Claude Larose .50 1.00
107 Terry Harper .63 1.25
108 Jacques Laperriere 1.00 2.00
109 Phil Roberto .50 1.00
110 Serge Savard 2.00 4.00
111 Marc Tardif .63 1.25
112 Pierre Bouchard .63 1.25
113 Rod Gilbert 2.50 5.00
114 Jean Ratelle 2.50 5.00
115 Pete Stemkowski .50 1.00
116 Brad Park 4.00 8.00
117 Bobby Rousseau .50 1.00
118 Dale Rolfe .50 1.00
119 Rod Seiling .50 1.00
120 Walt Tkaczuk .50 1.00
121 Vic Hadfield .63 1.25
122 Jim Neilson .50 1.00
123 Bill Fairbairn .50 1.00
124 Bruce MacGregor .50 1.00
125 Dave Balon .50 1.00
126 Ted Irvine .50 1.00
127 Gilles Villemure 1.00 2.00
128 Ed Giacomin 4.00 8.00
129 Walt McKechnie .50 1.00
130 Tom Williams .50 1.00
131 Wayne Carleton .63 1.25
132 Gerry Pinder .50 1.00
133 Gary Croteau .50 1.00
134 Bert Marshall .50 1.00
135 Tom Webster .50 1.00
136 Norm Ferguson .50 1.00
137 Carol Vadnais .50 1.00
138 Gary Jarrett .50 1.00
139 Ernie Hicke .50 1.00
140 Paul Shmyr .50 1.00
141 Marshall Johnston .50 1.00
142 Don O'Donoghue .50 1.00
143 Joey Johnston .50 1.00
144 Dick Redmond .50 1.00
145 Simon Nolet .50 1.00
146 Wayne Hillman .50 1.00
147 Brent Hughes .50 1.00
148 Jim Johnson .50 1.00
149 Larry Mickey .50 1.00
150 Ed Van Impe .50 1.00
151 Gary Dornhoefer .63 1.25
152 Bobby Clarke 12.50 25.00
153 Jean-Guy Gendron .50 1.00
154 Larry Hale .50 1.00
155 Serge Bernier .50 1.00
156 Doug Favell 1.00 2.00
157 Bob Kelly .50 1.00
158 Joe Watson .50 1.00
159 Larry Brown .50 1.00
160 Bruce Gamble 1.00 2.00
161 Syl Apps .63 1.25
162 Ken Schinkel .50 1.00
163 Val Fonteyne .50 1.00
164 Bryan Watson .75 1.50
165 Bob Woytowich .50 1.00
166 Les Binkley 1.00 2.00
167 Roy Edwards 1.00 2.00
168 Jean Pronovost .63 1.25
169 Tim Horton 6.00 12.00
170 Ron Schock .50 1.00
171 Nick Harbaruk .50 1.00
172 Greg Polis .50 1.00
173 Bryan Hextall .63 1.25
174 Keith McCreary .50 1.00
175 Bill Hicke .50 1.00
176 Jim Rutherford 1.00 2.00
177 Gary Sabourin .50 1.00
178 Garry Unger 1.00 2.00
179 Terry Crisp .63 1.25
180 Noel Picard .50 1.00
181 Jim Roberts .50 1.00
182 Barclay Plager .75 1.50
183 Brit Selby .50 1.00
184 Frank St. Marseille .50 1.00
185 Ernie Wakely 1.00 2.00
186 Wayne Connelly .50 1.00
187 Chris Bordeleau .75 1.50
188 Bill Sutherland .50 1.00
189 Bob Plager .75 1.50
190 Bill Plager .63 1.25
191 George Morrison .50 1.00
192 Jim Lorentz .50 1.00
193 Norm Ullman 2.50 5.00
194 Jim McKenny .50 1.00
195 Rick Ley .50 1.00
196 Bob Baun 1.00 2.00
197 Mike Pelyk .50 1.00
198 Bill MacMillan .50 1.00
199 Garry Monahan .50 1.00
200 Paul Henderson 1.50 3.00
201 Jim Dorey .50 1.00
202 Jim Harrison .50 1.00
203 Ron Ellis .75 1.50
204 Darryl Sittler 3.00 6.00
205 Bernie Parent 2.50 5.00
206 Dave Keon 2.50 5.00
207 Brad Selwood .50 1.00
208 Don Marshall .50 1.00
209 Dale Tallon .63 1.25
210 Dan Johnson .50 1.00
211 Murray Hall .50 1.00
212 Paul Popiel .63 1.25
213 George Gardner .50 1.00
214 Gary Doak .50 1.00
215 Andre Boudrias .63 1.25
216 Orland Kurtenbach .63 1.25
217 Wayne Maki .50 1.00
218 Rosaire Paiement .63 1.25
219 Pat Quinn 1.00 2.00
220 Fred Speck .50 1.00
221 Barry Wilkins .50 1.00
222 Dunc Wilson 1.00 2.00
223 Ted Taylor .50 1.00
224 Mike Corrigan .50 1.00
NNO Stamp Album 12.50 25.00
(Bobby Orr on cover)

1972-73 Sargent Promotions Stamps

During the 1972-73 hockey season, Eddie Sargent Promotions produced a set of 224 stamps. They were issued in cello packages in a series of 16 sheets and, at that time, sold for ten cents per sheet with one sheet being available each week of the promotion. Each sheet measures approximately 7 7/8" by 10" and was divided into four rows, with four 2" by 2 1/2" sections per row. Since two of the 16 sections gave the series number (e.g., Series 1), color photos of fourteen NHL players were featured in each series. The set features 224 players from sixteen NHL teams. The pictures were numbered in the upper left hand corner and are checklisted below accordingly. The pictures are framed on their top and sides in different color borders, with the player's name and the team's city name given below. There are two sticker albums (approximately 11 1/4" by 12") available for the set, both of which are bilingual. After a general introduction, the album is divided into team sections, with two pages devoted to each team. A brief history of each team is presented, followed by 14 numbered sticker slots. Biographical information and career summary appear below each stamp slot on the page itself. The typically found album has Bobby Orr on the cover. Another album is the more difficult Paul Henderson Team Canada cover. The toughest of the three is the Richard Martin cover. The stamps are numbered on the front and checklisted below alphabetically according to teams as follows: Atlanta Flames (1-14), Boston Bruins (15-28), Buffalo Sabres (29-42), California Seals (43-56), Chicago Blackhawks (57-70), Detroit Red Wings (71-84), Los Angeles Kings (85-98), Minnesota North Stars (99-112), Montreal Canadiens (113-126), New York Islanders (127-140), New York Rangers (141-154), Philadelphia Flyers (155-168), Pittsburgh Penguins (169-182), St. Louis Blues (183-196), Toronto Maple Leafs (197-210), and Vancouver Canucks (211-224).

COMPLETE SET (224) 112.50 225.00
1 Lucien Grenier .25 .50
2 Phil Myre .50 1.00
3 Ernie Hicke .25 .50
4 Keith McCreary .25 .50
5 Bill MacMillan .25 .50
6 Pat Quinn .50 1.00
7 Bill Plager .38 .75
8 Noel Price .25 .50
9 Bob Leiter .25 .50
10 Randy Manery .25 .50
11 Bob Paradise .25 .50
12 Larry Romanchych .25 .50
13 Lew Morrison .25 .50
14 Dan Bouchard .50 1.00
15 Fred Stanfield .25 .50
16 Johnny Bucyk 1.50 3.00
17 Bobby Orr 20.00 40.00
18 Wayne Cashman .38 .75
19 Dallas Smith .25 .50
20 Ed Johnston .75 1.50
21 Phil Esposito 5.00 10.00
22 Ken Hodge .50 1.00
23 Don Awrey .25 .50
24 Mike Walton .25 .50
25 Carol Vadnais .25 .50
26 Doug Roberts .25 .50
27 Don Marcotte .25 .50
28 Garnet Bailey .25 .50
29 Gerry Meehan .25 .50
30 Tracy Pratt .25 .50
31 Gilbert Perreault 2.00 4.00
32 Roger Crozier 1.00 2.00
33 Don Luce .25 .50
34 Dave Dryden .50 1.00
35 Richard Martin .50 1.00
36 Jim Lorentz .25 .50
37 Tim Horton 4.00 8.00
38 Craig Ramsay .25 .50
39 Larry Hillman .25 .50
40 Steve Atkinson .25 .50
41 Jim Schoenfeld .38 .75
42 Rene Robert .38 .75
43 Walt McKechnie .25 .50
44 Marshall Johnston .25 .50
45 Joey Johnston .25 .50
46 Dick Redmond .25 .50
47 Bert Marshall .25 .50
48 Gary Croteau .25 .50
49 Marv Edwards .50 1.00
50 Gilles Meloche .50 1.00
51 Ivan Boldirev .25 .50
52 Stan Gilbertson .25 .50
53 Peter Laframboise .25 .50
54 Reggie Leach .50 1.00
55 Craig Patrick .50 1.00
56 Bob Stewart .25 .50
57 Keith Magnuson .38 .75
58 Doug Jarrett .25 .50
59 Cliff Koroll .25 .50
60 Chico Maki .25 .50
61 Gary Smith .50 1.00
62 Bill White .25 .50
63 Stan Mikita 3.00 6.00
64 Jim Pappin .25 .50
65 Lou Angotti .25 .50
66 Tony Esposito 4.00 8.00
67 Dennis Hull .50 1.00
68 Pit Martin .25 .50
69 Pat Stapleton .25 .50
70 Dan Maloney .25 .50
71 Bill Collins .25 .50
72 Arnie Brown .25 .50
73 Red Berenson .38 .75
74 Mickey Redmond 1.00 2.00
75 Nick Libett .25 .50
76 Alex Delvecchio 1.25 2.50
77 Ron Stackhouse .25 .50
78 Tim Ecclestone .25 .50
79 Gary Bergman .25 .50
80 Guy Charron .25 .50
81 Leon Rochefort .25 .50
82 Larry Johnston .25 .50
83 Andy Brown .25 .50
84 Henry Boucha .38 .75
85 Paul Curtis .25 .50
86 Jim Stanfield .25 .50
87 Rogatien Vachon 1.50 3.00
88 Ralph Backstrom .38 .75
89 Gilles Marotte .25 .50
90 Harry Howell .75 1.50
91 Real Lemieux .25 .50
92 Butch Goring .38 .75
93 Juha Widing .25 .50
94 Mike Corrigan .25 .50
95 Larry Brown .25 .50
96 Terry Harper .38 .75
97 Serge Bernier .25 .50
98 Bob Berry .25 .50
99 Tom Reid .25 .50
100 Jude Drouin .25 .50
101 Jean-Paul Parise .38 .75
102 Doug Mohns .38 .75
103 Danny Grant .38 .75
104 Bill Goldsworthy .50 1.00
105 Gump Worsley 2.50 5.00
106 Charlie Burns .25 .50
107 Murray Oliver .25 .50
108 Barry Gibbs .25 .50
109 Ted Harris .25 .50
110 Cesare Maniago 1.00 2.00
111 Lou Nanne .38 .75
112 Bob Nevin .25 .50
113 Guy Lapointe .75 1.50
114 Peter Mahovlich .38 .75
115 Jacques Lemaire 1.00 2.00
116 Pierre Bouchard .25 .50
117 Yvan Cournoyer 1.25 2.50
118 Marc Tardif .25 .50
119 Henri Richard 2.50 5.00
120 Frank Mahovlich 2.50 5.00
121 Jacques Laperriere .75 1.50
122 Claude Larose .25 .50
123 Serge Savard 1.00 2.00
124 Ken Dryden 10.00 20.00
125 Rejean Houle .38 .75
126 Jim Roberts .25 .50
127 Ed Westfall .38 .75
128 Terry Crisp .38 .75
129 Gerry Desjardins .50 1.00
130 Denis DeJordy .75 1.50
131 Billy Harris .25 .50
132 Brian Spencer .50 1.00
133 Germaine Gagnon UER .25 .50
134 David Hedson .25 .50
135 Lorne Henning .25 .50
136 Brian Marchinko .25 .50
137 Tom Miller .25 .50
138 Gerry Hart .25 .50
139 Bryan Lefley .25 .50
140 James Mair .25 .50
141 Rod Gilbert 1.25 2.50
142 Jean Ratelle 1.25 2.50
143 Pete Stemkowski .25 .50
144 Brad Park 1.50 3.00
145 Bobby Rousseau .25 .50
146 Dale Rolfe .25 .50
147 Ed Giacomin 1.50 3.00
148 Rod Seiling .25 .50
149 Walt Tkaczuk .25 .50
150 Bill Fairbairn .25 .50
151 Vic Hadfield .38 .75
152 Ted Irvine .25 .50
153 Bruce MacGregor .25 .50
154 Jim Neilson .25 .50
155 Brent Hughes .25 .50
156 Wayne Hillman .25 .50
157 Doug Favell .75 1.50
158 Simon Nolet .25 .50
159 Joe Watson .25 .50
160 Ed Van Impe .25 .50
161 Gary Dornhoefer .38 .75
162 Bobby Clarke 5.00 10.00
163 Bob Kelly .25 .50
164 Bill Flett .25 .50
165 Rick Foley .25 .50
166 Ross Lonsberry .25 .50
167 Rick MacLeish .50 1.00
168 Bill Clement .50 1.00
169 Syl Apps .38 .75
170 Ken Schinkel .25 .50
171 Nick Harbaruk .25 .50
172 Bryan Watson .38 .75
173 Bryan Hextall .38 .75
174 Roy Edwards .50 1.00
175 Jim Rutherford .75 1.50

176 Jean Pronovost	.38	.75
177 Rick Kessell	.25	.50
178 Greg Polis	.25	.50
179 Ron Schock	.25	.50
180 Duane Rupp	.25	.50
181 Darryl Edestrand	.25	.50
182 Dave Burrows	.25	.50
183 Gary Sabourin	.25	.50
184 Garry Unger	.50	1.00
185 Noel Picard	.25	.50
186 Bob Plager	.38	.75
187 Barclay Plager	.38	.75
188 Frank St. Marseille	.25	.50
189 Danny O'Shea	.25	.50
190 Kevin O'Shea	.25	.50
191 Wayne Stephenson	.50	1.00
192 Chris Evans	.25	.50
193 Jacques Caron	.25	.50
194 Andre Dupont	.25	.50
195 Mike Murphy	.25	.50
196 Jack Egers	.25	.50
197 Norm Ullman	1.25	2.50
198 Jim McKenny	.25	.50
199 Bob Baun	.50	1.00
200 Mike Pelyk	.25	.50
201 Ron Ellis	.38	.75
202 Garry Monahan	.25	.50
203 Paul Henderson	1.00	2.00
204 Darryl Sittler	1.75	3.50
205 Brian Glennie	.25	.50
206 Dave Keon	1.25	2.50
207 Jacques Plante	5.00	10.00
208 Pierre Jarry	.25	.50
209 Rick Kehoe	.38	.75
210 Denis Dupere	.25	.50
211 Dale Tallon	.38	.75
212 Murray Hall	.25	.50
213 Dunc Wilson	.50	1.00
214 Andre Boudrias	.38	.75
215 Orland Kurtenbach	.38	.75
216 Wayne Maki	.25	.50
217 Barry Wilkins	.25	.50
218 Richard Lemieux	.25	.50
219 Bobby Schmautz	.25	.50
220 Dave Balon	.25	.50
221 Robert Lalonde	.25	.50
222 Jocelyn Guevremont	.25	.50
223 Gregg Boddy	.25	.50
224 Dennis Kearns	.25	.50
NNO1 Stamp Album (Paul Hende	17.50	35.00
NNO2 Stamp Album Richard Martin	25.00	50.00
NNO3 Stamp Album (Bobby Orr	10.00	20.00

1967-68 Seals Team Issue

Produced as a first year team issue of the expansion Oakland Seals, this 19-piece set features 8x10 individual player cards on thin cardboard stock. They are not numbered and are listed below in alphabetical order.

1 Bobby Baun	10.00	20.00
2 Ron Boehm	2.00	4.00
3 Wally Boyer	3.00	6.00
4 Charlie Burns	4.00	8.00
5 Larry Cahan	2.00	4.00
6 Alain Caron	2.00	4.00
7 Terry Clancy	2.00	4.00
8 Kent Douglas	4.00	8.00
9 Gerry Ehman	3.00	6.00
10 Autry Erickson	3.00	6.00
11 Billy Harris	3.00	6.00
12 Ron Harris	3.00	6.00
13 Bill Hicke	3.00	6.00
14 Charlie Hodge	7.50	15.00
15 Mike Laughton	2.00	4.00
16 Bob Lemieux	2.00	4.00
17 Gary Smith	6.00	12.00
18 George Swarbrick	3.00	6.00
19 Joe Szura	3.00	6.00

1972-73 7-Eleven Slurpee Cups WHA

This 20-cup set features a color head shot and facsimile autograph on the front, and a 7-11 logo, team logo, players name, and biographical information on the back. Cups are unnumbered and checklisted below alphabetically.

COMPLETE SET (20)	125.00	250.00
1 Norm Beaudin	5.00	10.00
2 Chris Bordeleau	5.00	10.00
3 Carl Brewer	5.00	10.00
4 Wayne Carleton	6.00	12.00
5 Gerry Cheevers	12.50	25.00
6 Wayne Connelly	7.50	15.00
7 Jean-Guy Gendron	5.00	10.00
8 Ted Green	5.00	10.00
9 Al Hamilton	5.00	10.00
10 Jim Harrison	5.00	10.00
11 Bobby Hull	25.00	50.00
12 Andre Lacroix	6.00	12.00
13 Danny Lawson	5.00	10.00
14 John McKenzie	5.00	10.00
15 Jim Mcleod	5.00	10.00
16 Jack Norris	5.00	10.00
17 John Schella	5.00	10.00
18 J.C. Tremblay	7.50	15.00
19 Ron Ward	5.00	10.00
20 Jim Watson	5.00	10.00

1960-61 Shirriff Coins

This set of 120 coins (each measuring approximately 1 3/8" in diameter) features players from all six NHL teams. These plastic coins are in color and numbered on the front. The coins are checklisted below according to teams as follows: Toronto Maple Leafs (1-20), Montreal Canadiens (21-40), Detroit Red Wings (41-60), Chicago Blackhawks (61-80), New York Rangers (81-100), and Boston Bruins (101-120). The set was also issued on a limited basis as a factory set in a black presentation box.

COMPLETE SET (120)	250.00	500.00
1 Johnny Bower	5.00	10.00
2 Dick Duff	2.50	5.00
3 Carl Brewer	2.50	5.00
4 Red Kelly	5.00	10.00
5 Tim Horton	7.50	15.00
6 Allan Stanley	2.50	5.00
7 Bob Baun	2.50	5.00
8 Billy Harris	1.50	3.00
9 George Armstrong	3.00	6.00
10 Ron Stewart	1.50	3.00
11 Bert Olmstead	2.50	5.00
12 Frank Mahovlich	7.50	15.00
13 Bob Pulford	2.50	5.00
14 Gary Edmundson	1.50	3.00
15 Johnny Wilson	1.50	3.00
16 Larry Regan	1.50	3.00
17 Gerry James	2.00	4.00
18 Rudy Migay	1.50	3.00
19 Gerry Ehman	1.50	3.00
20 Punch Imlach CO	2.00	4.00
21 Jacques Plante	12.50	25.00
22 Dickie Moore	3.00	6.00
23 Don Marshall	1.50	3.00
24 Albert Langlois	1.50	3.00
25 Tom Johnson	2.50	5.00
26 Doug Harvey	5.00	10.00
27 Phil Goyette	1.50	3.00
28 Boom Boom Geoffrion	6.00	12.00
29 Marcel Bonin	1.50	3.00
30 Jean Beliveau	10.00	20.00
31 Ralph Backstrom	2.00	4.00
32 Andre Pronovost	1.50	3.00
33 Claude Provost	2.00	4.00
34 Henri Richard	7.50	15.00
35 Jean-Guy Talbot	2.00	4.00
36 J.C. Tremblay	2.00	4.00
37 Bob Turner	1.50	3.00
38 Bill Hicke	1.50	3.00
39 Charlie Hodge	4.00	8.00
40 Toe Blake CO	2.50	5.00
41 Terry Sawchuk	10.00	20.00
42 Gordie Howe	25.00	50.00
43 John McKenzie	1.50	3.00
44 Alex Delvecchio	5.00	10.00
45 Norm Ullman	3.00	6.00
46 Jack McIntyre	1.50	3.00
47 Barry Cullen	2.00	4.00
48 Val Fonteyne	1.50	3.00
49 Warren Godfrey	1.50	3.00
50 Pete Goegan	1.50	3.00
51 Gerry Melnyk	1.50	3.00
52 Marc Reaume	1.50	3.00
53 Gary Aldcorn	1.50	3.00
54 Len Lunde	1.50	3.00
55 Murray Oliver	1.50	3.00
56 Marcel Pronovost	2.50	5.00
57 Howie Glover	1.50	3.00
58 Gerry Odrowski	1.50	3.00
59 Parker MacDonald	1.50	3.00
60 Sid Abel CO	2.50	5.00
61 Glenn Hall	6.00	12.00
62 Ed Litzenberger	2.00	4.00
63 Bobby Hull	20.00	40.00
64 Tod Sloan	1.50	3.00
65 Murray Balfour	1.50	3.00
66 Pierre Pilote	2.50	5.00
67 Al Arbour	2.50	5.00
68 Earl Balfour	1.50	3.00
69 Eric Nesterenko	2.00	4.00
70 Ken Wharram	2.50	5.00
71 Stan Mikita	12.50	25.00
72 Ab McDonald	1.50	3.00
73 Elmer Vasko	2.00	4.00
74 Dollard St.Laurent	2.00	4.00
75 Ron Murphy	1.50	3.00
76 Jack Evans	1.50	3.00
77 Bill Hay	1.50	3.00
78 Reg Fleming	2.00	4.00
79 Cecil Hoekstra	1.50	3.00
80 Tommy Ivan CO	2.00	4.00
81 Jack McCartan	4.00	8.00
82 Red Sullivan	1.50	3.00
83 Camille Henry	2.00	4.00
84 Larry Popein	1.50	3.00
85 John Hanna	1.50	3.00
86 Harry Howell	2.50	5.00
87 Eddie Shack	5.00	10.00
88 Irv Spencer	1.50	3.00
89 Andy Bathgate	3.00	6.00
90 Bill Gadsby	2.50	5.00
91 Andy Hebenton	1.50	3.00
92 Earl Ingarfield	1.50	3.00
93 Don Johns	1.50	3.00
94 Dave Balon	1.50	3.00
95 Jim Morrison	1.50	3.00
96 Ken Schinkel	1.50	3.00
97 Lou Fontinato	1.50	3.00
98 Ted Hampson	1.50	3.00
99 Brian Cullen	2.00	4.00
100 Alf Pike CO	1.50	3.00
101 Don Simmons	2.50	5.00
102 Fern Flaman	2.50	5.00
103 Vic Stasiuk	2.00	4.00
104 Johnny Bucyk	5.00	10.00
105 Bronco Horvath	2.00	4.00
106 Doug Mohns	4.00	8.00
107 Leo Boivin	2.50	5.00
108 Don McKenney	1.50	3.00
109 Jean-Guy Gendron	1.50	3.00
110 Jerry Toppazzini	1.50	3.00
111 Dick Meissner	1.50	3.00
112 Autry Erickson	1.50	3.00
113 Jim Bartlett	1.50	3.00
114 Orval Tessier	2.00	4.00
115 Billy Carter	1.50	3.00
116 Dallas Smith	2.00	4.00
117 Leo Labine	1.50	3.00
118 Bob Armstrong	1.50	3.00
119 Bruce Gamble	2.50	5.00
120 Milt Schmidt CO	3.00	6.00

1961-62 Shirriff/Salada Coins

This set of 120 coins (each measuring approximately 1 3/8" in diameter) features players of the NHL, all six teams. These plastic coins are in color and numbered on the front. The coins are numbered according to teams as follows: Boston Bruins (1-20), Chicago Blackhawks (21-40), Toronto Maple Leafs (41-60), Detroit Red Wings (61-80), New York Rangers (81-100), and Montreal Canadiens (101-120). The coins were also produced in identical fashion for Salada with a Salada imprint; the Salada version has the same values as listed below. This was the only year of Shirriff coins where collectors could obtain plastic shields for displaying their collection. These shields are not considered part of the complete set.

COMPLETE SET (120)	200.00	400.00
1 Cliff Pennington	1.25	2.50
2 Dallas Smith	2.00	4.00
3 Andre Pronovost	1.25	2.50
4 Charlie Burns	1.25	2.50
5 Leo Boivin	2.50	5.00
6 Don McKenney	1.25	2.50
7 Johnny Bucyk	4.00	8.00
8 Murray Oliver	1.25	2.50
9 Jerry Toppazzini	1.25	2.50
10 Doug Mohns	2.00	4.00
11 Don Head	2.00	4.00
12 Bob Armstrong	1.25	2.50
13 Pat Stapleton	2.00	4.00
14 Orland Kurtenbach	2.00	4.00
15 Dick Meissner	1.25	2.50
16 Ted Green	2.00	4.00
17 Tom Williams	1.25	2.50
18 Autry Erickson	1.25	2.50
19 Phil Watson CO	2.50	5.00
20 Ed Chadwick	2.50	5.00
21 Wayne Hillman	5.00	10.00
22 Stan Mikita	6.00	12.00
23 Eric Nesterenko	2.00	4.00
24 Reg Fleming	1.25	2.50
25 Bobby Hull	12.50	25.00
26 Elmer Vasko	1.25	2.50
27 Pierre Pilote	2.50	5.00
28 Chico Maki	2.00	4.00
29 Glenn Hall	5.00	10.00
30 Murray Balfour	1.25	2.50
31 Bronco Horvath	1.50	3.00
32 Ken Wharram	2.00	4.00
33 Ab McDonald	1.25	2.50
34 Bill Hay	1.25	2.50
35 Dollard St.Laurent	2.00	4.00
36 Ron Murphy	1.25	2.50
37 Bob Turner	1.25	2.50
38 Gerry Melnyk	1.25	2.50
39 Jack Evans	1.25	2.50
40 Rudy Pilous CO	2.50	5.00
41 Johnny Bower	5.00	10.00
42 Allan Stanley	3.00	6.00
43 Frank Mahovlich	5.00	10.00
44 Tim Horton	7.50	15.00
45 Carl Brewer	2.00	4.00
46 Bob Pulford	2.50	5.00
47 Bob Nevin	2.00	4.00
48 Eddie Shack	4.00	8.00
49 Red Kelly	4.00	8.00
50 Bob Baun	2.00	4.00
51 George Armstrong	3.00	6.00
52 Bert Olmstead	2.50	5.00
53 Dick Duff	2.00	4.00
54 Billy Harris	2.00	4.00
55 Larry Keenan	1.25	2.50
56 Johnny MacMillan	1.25	2.50
57 Punch Imlach CO	2.00	4.00
58 Dave Keon	7.50	15.00
59 Larry Hillman	1.25	2.50
60 Al Arbour	2.50	5.00
61 Sid Abel CO	2.50	5.00
62 Warren Godfrey	1.25	2.50
63 Vic Stasiuk	1.25	2.50
64 Leo Labine	1.25	2.50
65 Howie Glover	1.25	2.50
66 Gordie Howe	20.00	40.00
67 Val Fonteyne	1.25	2.50
68 Marcel Pronovost	2.50	5.00
69 Parker MacDonald	1.25	2.50
70 Alex Delvecchio	4.00	8.00
71 Ed Litzenberger	1.25	2.50
72 Al Johnson	1.25	2.50
73 Bruce MacGregor	1.25	2.50
74 Howie Young	1.25	2.50
75 Pete Goegan	1.25	2.50
76 Norm Ullman	3.00	6.00
77 Terry Sawchuk	12.50	25.00
78 Gerry Odrowski	1.25	2.50
79 Bill Gadsby	2.50	5.00
80 Hank Bassen	2.00	4.00
81 Doug Harvey	4.00	8.00
82 Earl Ingarfield	1.25	2.50
83 Pat Hannigan	1.25	2.50
84 Dean Prentice	2.00	4.00
85 Gump Worsley	5.00	10.00
86 Irv Spencer	1.25	2.50
87 Camille Henry	2.00	4.00
88 Andy Bathgate	3.00	6.00
89 Harry Howell	2.50	5.00
90 Andy Hebenton	1.25	2.50
91 Red Sullivan	1.25	2.50
92 Ted Hampson	1.25	2.50
93 Jean-Guy Gendron	1.25	2.50
94 Albert Langlois	1.25	2.50
95 Larry Cahan	1.25	2.50
96 Bob Cunningham	1.25	2.50
97 Vic Hadfield	2.00	4.00
98 Jean Ratelle	5.00	10.00
99 Ken Schinkel	1.25	2.50
100 Johnny Wilson	1.25	2.50
101 Toe Blake CO	2.50	5.00
102 Jean Beliveau	10.00	20.00
103 Don Marshall	1.25	2.50
104 Boom Boom Geoffrion	6.00	12.00
105 Claude Provost	2.00	4.00
106 Tom Johnson	2.50	5.00
107 Dickie Moore	4.00	8.00
108 Bill Hicke	1.25	2.50
109 Jean-Guy Talbot	2.00	4.00
110 Henri Richard	5.00	10.00
111 Lou Fontinato	1.50	3.00
112 Gilles Tremblay	1.25	2.50
113 Jacques Plante	10.00	20.00
114 Ralph Backstrom	2.00	4.00
115 Marcel Bonin	1.25	2.50
116 Phil Goyette	1.25	2.50
117 Bobby Rousseau	2.00	4.00
118 J.C. Tremblay	2.00	4.00
119 Al MacNeil	1.25	2.50
120 Jean Gauthier	1.25	2.50
S1 Boston Bruins Shield	30.00	60.00
S2 Chicago Blackhawks Shield	30.00	60.00
S3 Detroit Red Wings Shield	30.00	60.00
S4 Montreal Canadiens Shield	30.00	60.00
S5 New York Rangers Shield	30.00	60.00
S6 Toronto Maple Leafs Shield	30.00	60.00

1962-63 Shirriff Coins

This set of 60 coins (each measuring approximately 1 1/2" in diameter) features 12 All-Stars, six Trophy winners, and players from Montreal (20) and Toronto (22). The four American teams in the NHL were not included in this set except where they appeared as All-Stars or Trophy winners. These metal coins are in color and numbered on the front. The backs are written in French and English.

COMPLETE SET (60)	200.00	400.00
1 Johnny Bower	5.00	10.00
2 Allan Stanley	4.00	8.00
3 Frank Mahovlich	10.00	20.00
4 Tim Horton	10.00	20.00
5 Carl Brewer	2.50	5.00
6 Bob Pulford	4.00	8.00
7 Bob Nevin	2.50	5.00
8 Eddie Shack	4.00	8.00
9 Red Kelly	4.00	8.00
10 George Armstrong	4.00	8.00
11 Bert Olmstead	3.00	6.00
12 Dick Duff	2.50	5.00
13 Billy Harris	2.00	4.00
14 Johnny MacMillan	2.00	4.00
15 Punch Imlach CO	2.50	5.00
16 Dave Keon	7.50	15.00
17 Larry Hillman	2.00	4.00
18 Ed Litzenberger	2.00	4.00
19 Bob Baun	3.00	6.00
20 Al Arbour	4.00	8.00
21 Ron Stewart	2.00	4.00
22 Don Simmons	3.00	6.00
23 Lou Fontinato	2.00	4.00
24 Gilles Tremblay	2.00	4.00
25 Jacques Plante	12.50	25.00
26 Ralph Backstrom	2.50	5.00
27 Marcel Bonin	2.00	4.00
28 Phil Goyette	2.00	4.00
29 Bobby Rousseau	2.50	5.00
30 J.C. Tremblay	2.50	5.00
31 Toe Blake CO	4.00	8.00
32 Jean Beliveau	10.00	20.00
33 Don Marshall	2.00	4.00
34 Boom Boom Geoffrion	6.00	12.00
35 Claude Provost	2.50	5.00
36 Tom Johnson	3.00	6.00
37 Dickie Moore	5.00	10.00
38 Bill Hicke	2.00	4.00
39 Jean-Guy Talbot	2.50	5.00
40 Al MacNeil	2.50	5.00
41 Henri Richard	7.50	15.00
42 Red Berenson	2.50	5.00
43 Jacques Plante AS	12.50	25.00
44 Jean-Guy Talbot AS	2.50	5.00
45 Doug Harvey AS	5.00	10.00
46 Stan Mikita AS	5.00	10.00
47 Bobby Hull AS	12.50	25.00
48 Andy Bathgate AS	4.00	8.00
49 Glenn Hall AS	5.00	10.00
50 Pierre Pilote AS	4.00	8.00
51 Carl Brewer AS	2.50	5.00
52 Dave Keon AS	7.50	15.00
53 Frank Mahovlich AS	7.50	15.00

54 Gordie Howe AS	20.00	40.00
55 Dave Keon Byng	7.50	15.00
56 Bobby Rousseau Calder	2.50	5.00
57 Bobby Hull Ross	12.50	25.00
58 Jacques Plante Vezina	12.50	25.00
59 Jacques Plante Hart	12.50	25.00
60 Doug Harvey Norris	5.00	10.00

1968-69 Shirriff Coins

This set of 176 coins (each measuring approximately 1 3/8" in diameter) features players from all of the teams in the NHL. These plastic coins are in color and numbered on the front. However the coins are numbered by Shirriff within each team and not for the whole set. The correspondence between the actual coin numbers and the numbers assigned below should be apparent. For those few situations where two coins from the same team have the same number, that number is listed in the checklist below next to the name. The coins are checklisted below according to teams as follows: Boston Bruins (1-16), Chicago Blackhawks (17-33), Detroit Red Wings (34-49), Los Angeles Kings (50-61), Minnesota North Stars (62-74), Montreal Canadiens (75-92), New York Rangers (93-108), Oakland Seals (109-121), Philadelphia Flyers (122-134), Pittsburgh Penguins (135-146), St. Louis Blues (147-158), and Toronto Maple Leafs (159-176). Some of the coins are quite challenging to find. It seems the higher numbers within each team and the coins from the players on the expansion teams are more difficult to find; these are marked by SP in the list below.

1 Eddie Shack	8.00	20.00
2 Ed Westfall	8.00	20.00
3 Don Awrey	10.00	25.00
4 Gerry Cheevers	10.00	25.00
5 Bobby Orr	80.00	150.00
6 Johnny Bucyk	10.00	25.00
7 Derek Sanderson	10.00	25.00
8 Phil Esposito	15.00	40.00
9 Fred Stanfield	12.00	30.00
10 Ken Hodge	12.00	30.00
11 John McKenzie	10.00	25.00
12 Ted Green	12.00	30.00
13 Dallas Smith SP	60.00	150.00
14 Gary Doak SP	60.00	150.00
15 Glen Sather SP	60.00	150.00
16 Tom Williams SP	80.00	150.00
17 Bobby Hull	20.00	50.00
18 Pat Stapleton	12.00	30.00
19 Wayne Maki	10.00	25.00
20 Denis DeJordy	10.00	25.00
21 Ken Wharram	10.00	25.00
22 Pit Martin	10.00	25.00
23 Chico Maki	5.00	12.00
24 Doug Mohns	8.00	20.00
25 Stan Mikita	10.00	25.00
26 Doug Jarrett	15.00	40.00
27 Dennis Hull 11 SP	40.00	100.00
28 Dennis Hull 11	30.00	80.00
29 Matt Ravlich	10.00	25.00
30 Dave Dryden SP	40.00	100.00
31 Eric Nesterenko SP	60.00	150.00
32 Gilles Marotte SP	60.00	150.00
33 Jim Pappin SP	60.00	150.00
34 Gary Bergman	10.00	25.00
35 Roger Crozier	10.00	25.00
36 Peter Mahovlich	10.00	25.00
37 Alex Delvecchio	10.00	25.00
38 Dean Prentice	10.00	25.00
39 Kent Douglas	12.00	30.00
40 Roy Edwards	10.00	25.00
41 Bruce MacGregor	12.00	30.00
42 Garry Unger	10.00	25.00
43 Pete Stemkowski	8.00	20.00
44 Gordie Howe	30.00	80.00
45 Frank Mahovlich	8.00	20.00
46 Bob Baun SP	150.00	250.00
47 Brian Conacher SP	40.00	100.00
48 Jim Watson SP	200.00	300.00
49 Nick Libett SP	50.00	125.00
50 Real Lemieux	8.00	20.00
20 Ted Irvine	8.00	20.00
52 Bob Wall	5.00	12.00
53 Bill White	8.00	20.00
54 Gord Labossiere	8.00	20.00
55 Eddie Joyal	8.00	20.00
56 Lowell MacDonald	8.00	20.00
57 Bill Flett	8.00	20.00
58 Wayne Rutledge	8.00	20.00
59 Dave Amadio	10.00	25.00
60 Skip Krake SP	30.00	80.00
61 Doug Robinson SP	25.00	60.00
62 Wayne Connelly	8.00	20.00
63 Bob Woytowich	8.00	20.00
64 Andre Boudrias	8.00	20.00
65 Bill Goldsworthy	8.00	20.00
66 Cesare Maniago	8.00	20.00
67 Milan Marcetta	8.00	20.00
68 Bill Collins SP 7	40.00	100.00
69 Claude Larose SP 7	40.00	100.00
70 Parker MacDonald	6.00	15.00
71 Ray Cullen	6.00	15.00
72 Mike McMahon	8.00	20.00
73 Bob McCord SP	25.00	60.00
74 Larry Hillman SP	30.00	80.00
75 Gump Worsley	8.00	20.00
76 Rogatien Vachon	8.00	20.00
77 Ted Harris	10.00	25.00
78 Jacques Laperriere	8.00	20.00
79 J.C. Tremblay	10.00	25.00
80 Jean Beliveau	20.00	50.00
81 Gilles Tremblay	10.00	25.00
82 Ralph Backstrom	8.00	20.00
83 Bobby Rousseau	8.00	20.00
84 John Ferguson	8.00	20.00
85 Dick Duff	8.00	20.00
86 Terry Harper	8.00	20.00
87 Yvan Cournoyer	10.00	25.00
88 Jacques Lemaire	8.00	20.00
89 Henri Richard	8.00	20.00
90 Claude Provost SP	50.00	125.00
91 Serge Savard SP	80.00	150.00
92 Mickey Redmond SP	80.00	150.00
93 Rod Seiling	8.00	20.00
94 Jean Ratelle	8.00	20.00
95 Ed Giacomin	12.00	30.00
96 Reg Fleming	8.00	20.00
97 Phil Goyette	8.00	20.00
98 Arnie Brown	8.00	20.00
99 Don Marshall	5.00	12.00
100 Orland Kurtenbach	8.00	20.00
101 Bob Nevin	10.00	25.00
102 Rod Gilbert	8.00	20.00
103 Harry Howell	8.00	20.00
104 Jim Neilson	12.00	30.00
105 Vic Hadfield SP	150.00	400.00
106 Larry Jeffrey SP	200.00	350.00
107 Dave Balon SP	80.00	150.00
108 Ron Stewart SP	300.00	400.00
109 Gerry Ehman	12.00	30.00
110 John Brenneman	15.00	40.00
111 Ted Hampson	25.00	60.00
112 Billy Harris	20.00	50.00
113 George Swarbrick SP 5	50.00	100.00
114 Carol Vadnais SP 5	900.00	1,500.00
115 Gary Smith	12.00	30.00
116 Charlie Hodge	12.00	30.00
117 Bert Marshall	6.00	15.00
118 Bill Hicke	12.00	30.00
119 Tracy Pratt	10.00	25.00
120 Gary Jarrett SP	800.00	1,200.00
121 Howie Young SP	800.00	1,200.00
122 Bernie Parent	15.00	40.00
123 John Miszuk	8.00	20.00
124 Ed Hoekstra SP 3	50.00	100.00
125 Allan Stanley SP 3	60.00	150.00
126 Gary Dornhoefer	8.00	20.00
127 Doug Favell	10.00	25.00
128 Andre Lacroix	10.00	25.00
129 Brit Selby	6.00	15.00
130 Don Blackburn	8.00	20.00
131 Leon Rochefort	15.00	40.00
132 Forbes Kennedy	15.00	40.00
133 Claude Laforge SP	150.00	250.00
134 Pat Hannigan SP	50.00	125.00
135 Ken Schinkel	8.00	20.00
136 Earl Ingarfield	8.00	20.00
137 Val Fonteyne	8.00	20.00
138 Noel Price	10.00	25.00
139 Andy Bathgate	10.00	25.00
140 Les Binkley	12.00	30.00
141 Leo Boivin	12.00	30.00
142 Paul Andrea	6.00	15.00
143 Dunc McCallum	12.00	30.00
144 Keith McCreary	8.00	20.00
145 Lou Angotti SP	100.00	250.00
146 Wally Boyer SP	150.00	250.00
147 Ron Schock	10.00	25.00
148 Bob Plager	10.00	25.00
149 Al Arbour	6.00	15.00
150 Red Berenson	8.00	20.00
151 Glenn Hall	10.00	25.00
152 Jim Roberts	6.00	15.00
153 Noel Picard	8.00	20.00
154 Barclay Plager	8.00	20.00
155 Larry Keenan	8.00	20.00
156 Terry Crisp	10.00	25.00
157 Gary Sabourin SP	60.00	150.00
158 Ab McDonald SP	60.00	150.00
159 George Armstrong	10.00	25.00
160 Wayne Carleton	10.00	25.00
161 Paul Henderson	30.00	80.00
162 Bob Pulford	8.00	20.00
163 Mike Walton	6.00	15.00
164 Johnny Bower	10.00	25.00
165 Ron Ellis	10.00	25.00
166 Mike Pelyk	10.00	25.00
167 Murray Oliver	8.00	20.00
168 Norm Ullman	8.00	20.00
169 Dave Keon	25.00	60.00
170 Floyd Smith	10.00	25.00
171 Marcel Pronovost	10.00	25.00
172 Tim Horton	30.00	80.00
173 Bruce Gamble	20.00	50.00
174 Jim McKenny SP	80.00	150.00
175 Mike Byers SP	60.00	150.00
176 Pierre Pilote SP	80.00	150.00

1935 Sporting Events and Stars

Cards measure approximately 2" x 3". Cards feature black and white fronts, along with informative backs. Set features 96 cards and was issued by various cigarette makers including Senior Service, Junior Member, and Illingworth's.

31 Ice Hockey	20.00	40.00

1933 Sport Kings

The cards in this 48-card set measure 2 3/8" by 2 7/8". The 1933 Sport Kings set, issued by the Goudey Gum Company, contains cards for the most famous athletic heroes of the times. No less than 18 different sports are represented in the set. The baseball cards of Cobb, Hubbell, and Ruth, and the football cards of Rockne, Grange and Thorpe command premium prices. The cards were issued in one-card penny packs which came 100 packs to a box along with a piece of gum. The catalog designation for this set is R338.

COMPLETE SET	10,000.00	16,000.00
19 Eddie Shore Hockey	400.00	800.00
24 Howie Morenz HK	600.00	1,000.00
29 Ace Bailey HK	250.00	400.00
30 Ivan Ching Johnson HK	250.00	400.00

1977-79 Sportscaster Series 1

COMPLETE SET (24)	17.50	35.00
102 Bobby Orr	2.50	5.00

1977-79 Sportscaster Series 2

COMPLETE SET (24)	30.00	60.00
206 Gordie Howe	5.00	10.00
213 The Stanley Cup	1.00	2.00

1977-79 Sportscaster Series 3

COMPLETE SET (24)	15.00	30.00
319 Phil and Tony	1.00	2.00

1977-79 Sportscaster Series 5

COMPLETE SET (24)	12.50	25.00
509 The USA vs. Czechoslovakia	.75	1.50
520 Bobby Hull	2.50	5.00

1977-79 Sportscaster Series 6

COMPLETE SET (24)	12.50	25.00
607 Gump Worsley	1.00	2.00

1977-79 Sportscaster Series 7

COMPLETE SET (24)	15.00	30.00
708 USSR	1.00	2.00
717 Brad Park	1.00	2.00

1977-79 Sportscaster Series 10

COMPLETE SET (24)	17.50	35.00
1014 Jean Beliveau	1.50	3.00

1977-79 Sportscaster Series 11

COMPLETE SET (25)	20.00	40.00
1119 Hat Trick	.50	1.00

1977-79 Sportscaster Series 12

COMPLETE SET (24)	12.50	25.00
1215 World Championship	.75	1.50
1222 Stan Mikita	1.25	2.50

1977-79 Sportscaster Series 14

COMPLETE SET (24)	17.50	35.00
1423 Ken Dryden	2.00	4.00

1977-79 Sportscaster Series 15

COMPLETE SET (24)	12.50	25.00
1513 Yvan Cournoyer	1.25	2.50

1977-79 Sportscaster Series 17

COMPLETE SET (24)	10.00	20.00
1709 Denis Potvin	2.00	4.00

1977-79 Sportscaster Series 18

COMPLETE SET (24)	12.50	25.00
1823 Garry Unger	.50	1.00

1977-79 Sportscaster Series 19

COMPLETE SET (24)	25.00	50.00
1915 World Championship	1.00	2.00

1977-79 Sportscaster Series 21

COMPLETE SET (24)	15.00	30.00
2112 The Equipment	.25	.50

1977-79 Sportscaster Series 27

COMPLETE SET (24)	12.50	25.00
2724 National Hockey	1.50	3.00

1977-79 Sportscaster Series 29

COMPLETE SET (24)	17.50	35.00
2908 The Power Play	1.00	2.00

1977-79 Sportscaster Series 31

COMPLETE SET (24)	12.50	25.00
3103 Penalty Killing	1.25	2.50

1977-79 Sportscaster Series 33

COMPLETE SET (24)	10.00	20.00
3303 Lines in the Ice	.75	1.50

1977-79 Sportscaster Series 35

COMPLETE SET (24)	15.00	30.00
3503 The Spengler Cup	.25	.50

1977-79 Sportscaster Series 38

COMPLETE SET (24)	20.00	40.00
3807 The Seven Professional Trophies	1.50	3.00

1977-79 Sportscaster Series 43

COMPLETE SET (24)	12.50	25.00
4304 Major and Minor	.75	1.50
4306 Rogie Vachon	1.00	2.00

1977-79 Sportscaster Series 44

COMPLETE SET (24)	12.50	25.00
4403 Jaroslav Jirik	.50	1.00
4420 Gerry Cheevers	1.00	2.00

1977-79 Sportscaster Series 45

Card number 11 is not in our checklist. Any information on this missing card is greatly appreciated.

COMPLETE SET (24)	20.00	40.00
4513 Steve Shutt	1.00	2.00

1977-79 Sportscaster Series 46

COMPLETE SET (24)	12.50	25.00
4614 In the Corners	.75	1.50
4621 Bryan Trottier	1.50	3.00

1977-79 Sportscaster Series 47

COMPLETE SET (24)	17.50	35.00
4716 Trio Grande	4.00	8.00
4718 Darryl Sittler	1.50	3.00

1977-79 Sportscaster Series 50

COMPLETE SET (24)	15.00	30.00
5003 Sticks	2.00	4.00
5004 Facemasks	2.00	4.00

1977-79 Sportscaster Series 51

COMPLETE SET (24)	20.00	40.00
5101 Czechoslovakia 1977	.75	1.50
5118 Guy Lafleur	1.50	3.00

1977-79 Sportscaster Series 55

COMPLETE SET (24)	12.50	25.00
5514 Jiri and Jaroslav	1.00	2.00
5523 World Hockey Assoc.	4.00	8.00

1977-79 Sportscaster Series 56

COMPLETE SET (24)	37.50	75.00
5605 Montreal Forum	2.50	5.00

1977-79 Sportscaster Series 60

COMPLETE SET (24)	37.50	75.00
6012 Bobby Clarke	4.00	8.00

1977-79 Sportscaster Series 61

COMPLETE SET (24)	50.00	100.00
6103 Lingo	2.50	5.00

1977-79 Sportscaster Series 62

COMPLETE SET (24)	40.00	80.00
6217 Lester Patrick	2.50	5.00

1977-79 Sportscaster Series 63

COMPLETE SET (24)	30.00	60.00
6309 The Howe Family	6.00	12.00

1977-79 Sportscaster Series 64

COMPLETE SET (24)	25.00	50.00
6416 Sudden Death	2.50	5.00

1977-79 Sportscaster Series 67

COMPLETE SET (24)	40.00	80.00
6721 Bill Chadwick	2.50	5.00

1977-79 Sportscaster Series 70

COMPLETE SET (24)	30.00	60.00
7006 Hall of Fame	2.00	4.00

1977-79 Sportscaster Series 71

COMPLETE SET (24)	40.00	80.00
7104 The Abrahamsson	2.00	4.00
7112 Anders Hedberg	2.50	5.00

1977-79 Sportscaster Series 73

COMPLETE SET (24)	40.00	80.00
7301 USSR vs. NHL	4.00	8.00
7311 Czechoslavakia 1976	2.50	5.00

1977-79 Sportscaster Series 74

COMPLETE SET (24)	200.00	400.00
7417 The 1978 WCH	2.00	4.00
7424 Vaclav Nedomansky	2.50	5.00

1977-79 Sportscaster Series 76

COMPLETE SET (24)	30.00	60.00
7603 NCAA Hockey	2.50	5.00

1977-79 Sportscaster Series 77

COMPLETE SET (24)	150.00	300.00
7710 Wayne Gretzky	125.00	250.00
7724 Expansion	2.00	4.00

1977-79 Sportscaster Series 78

COMPLETE SET (24)	150.00	300.00
7804 Real Cloutier	1.50	3.00

1977-79 Sportscaster Series 80

COMPLETE SET (24)	62.50	125.00
8018 John Davidson	3.00	6.00

1977-79 Sportscaster Series 81

COMPLETE SET (24)	62.50	125.00
8119 Jacques Lemaire	5.00	10.00

1977-79 Sportscaster Series 82

COMPLETE SET (24)	50.00	100.00
8205 Scotty Bowman	7.50	15.00
8223 Dave Dryden	2.50	5.00

1977-79 Sportscaster Series 102

COMPLETE SET (24)	75.00	150.00
10214 Charlamov Petrov	4.00	8.00

1977-79 Sportscaster Series 103

COMPLETE SET (24)	87.50	175.00
10308 Alexander Yakushev	4.00	8.00

1975-76 Stingers Kahn's

This set of 14 photos was issued on wrappers of Kahn's Wieners and Beef Franks and features players of the Cincinnati Stingers of the WHA. The wrappers are approximately 2 11/16" wide and 11 5/8" long. The wiener wrappers are predominantly yellow and carry a 2" by 1 1/4" black-and-white posed photo of the player with a facsimile autograph inscribed across the picture. The beef frank wrappers are identical in design but predominantly red in color. The wrappers are unnumbered and checklisted below in alphabetical order.

COMPLETE SET (14)	62.50	125.00
1 Serge Aubry	5.00	10.00
2 Bryan Campbell	5.00	10.00
3 Rick Dudley	7.50	15.00
4 Pierre Guite	5.00	10.00
5 John Hughes	5.00	10.00
6 Claude Larose	6.00	12.00
7 Jacques Locas UER	5.00	10.00

8 Bernie MacNeil	5.00	10.00
9 Mike Pelyk	5.00	10.00
10 Ron Plumb	5.00	10.00
11 Dave Smedsmo	5.00	10.00
12 Dennis Sobchuk	5.00	10.00
13 Gene Sobchuk	5.00	10.00
14 Gary Veneruzzo	5.00	10.00

1976-77 Stingers Kahn's

This set of six photos was issued on wrappers of Kahn's Wieners and features players of the Cincinnati Stingers of the WHA. The wrappers are approximately 2 11/16" wide and 11 5/8" long. On a predominantly yellow wrapper with red lettering, a 2" by 1 1/4" black and white player action photo appears, with a facsimile autograph inscribed across the picture. The wrappers are unnumbered and checklisted below in alphabetical order. This set is distinguished from the previous year by the fact that these card photo poses (for the players in both sets) appear to be taken in an action sequence compared to the posed photographs taken the previous year.

COMPLETE SET (6)	62.50	125.00
1 Rick Dudley	15.00	30.00
2 Dave Inkpen	12.50	25.00
3 John Hughes	10.00	20.00
4 Claude Larose	12.50	25.00
5 Jacques Locas	10.00	20.00
6 Ron Plumb	10.00	20.00
7 Dennis Sobchuk	10.00	20.00

1980 Superstar Matchbook

These collector issued matchbooks were issued in the New England area in 1980 and featured superstars from all sports but with an emphasis on players who made their fame in New England. Since these are unnumbered, we have sequenced them in alphabetical order.

COMPLETE SET	30.00	60.00
3 Ray Bourque	4.00	8.00
5 Gordie Howe	3.00	6.00
7 Guy LaFleur	2.00	4.00
9 Bobby Orr	5.00	10.00

1910-11 Sweet Caporal Postcards

These black-and-white photo postcards apparently were used by the artists working on the C55 cards of the next year, 1911-12. Printed by the British American Tobacco Co. in England, these cards were distributed by Imperial Tobacco of Canada. One card was reportedly packed in each 50-cigarette tin of Sweet Caporal cigarettes. The backs show the postcard design. The cards are checklisted below according to teams as follows: Quebec Bulldogs (1-8), Ottawa Senators (10-17), Renfrew Millionaires (18-26), Montreal Wanderers (27-36), and Montreal Canadiens (37-45).

COMPLETE SET (45)	9,000.00	18,000.00
1 Paddy Moran	250.00	500.00
2 Joe Hall	175.00	350.00
3 Barney Holden	100.00	200.00
4 Joe Malone	500.00	1,000.00
5 Ed Oatman	100.00	200.00
6 Tom Dunderdale	175.00	350.00
7 Ken Mallen	100.00	200.00
8 Jack MacDonald	100.00	200.00
9 Fred Lake	100.00	200.00
10 Albert Kerr	100.00	200.00
11 Marty Walsh	175.00	350.00
12 Hamby Shore	100.00	200.00
13 Alex Currie	100.00	200.00
14 Bruce Ridpath	100.00	200.00
15 Bruce Stuart	175.00	350.00
16 Percy Lesueur	175.00	350.00
17 Jack Darragh	175.00	350.00
18 Steve Vair	100.00	200.00
19 Don Smith	100.00	200.00
20 Cyclone Taylor	600.00	1,200.00
21 Bert Lindsay	125.00	250.00
22 H.L. Gilmour	175.00	350.00
23 Bobby Rowe	100.00	200.00
24 Sprague Cleghorn	300.00	600.00
25 Odie Cleghorn	125.00	250.00
26 Skein Ronan	100.00	200.00
27 Walter Smaill	125.00	250.00
28 Ernest Johnson	200.00	400.00
29 Jack Marshall	175.00	350.00
30 Harry Hyland	175.00	350.00
31 Art Ross	600.00	1,200.00
32 Riley Hern	175.00	350.00
33 Gordon Roberts	175.00	350.00
34 Frank Glass	100.00	200.00
35 Ernest Russell	200.00	400.00
36 James Gardner	175.00	350.00
37 Art Bernier	100.00	200.00
38 Georges Vezina	2,000.00	4,000.00
39 Henri Dallaire	100.00	200.00
40 R.(Rocket) Power	100.00	200.00
41 Didier Pitre	175.00	350.00
42 Newsy Lalonde	600.00	1,200.00
43 Eugene Payan	100.00	200.00
44 George Poulin	100.00	200.00
45 Jack Laviolette	200.00	400.00

1934-35 Sweet Caporal

This colorful set of 48 large (approximately 6 3/4" by 10 1/2") pictures were actually inserts in Montreal Forum programs during Canadiens and Maroons home games during the 1934-35 season. Apparently a different photo was inserted each game. Players in the checklist below are identified as part of the following teams, Montreal Canadiens (MC), Montreal Maroons (MM), Boston Bruins (BB), Chicago Blackhawks (CBH), Detroit Red Wings (DRW), New York Rangers (NYR), and Toronto Maple Leafs (TML). Card backs contain player biography and an ad for Sweet Caporal Cigarettes, both in French. The cards are unnumbered.

COMPLETE SET (48)	2,500.00	5,000.00
1 Gerald Carson MC	25.00	50.00
2 Nels Crutchfield MC	25.00	50.00
3 Wilfrid Cude MC	30.00	60.00
4 Roger Jenkins MC	25.00	50.00
5 Aurel Joliat MC	175.00	350.00
6 Joe Lamb MC	25.00	50.00
7 Wildor Larochelle MC	25.00	50.00
8 Pete Lepine MC	25.00	50.00
9 Georges Mantha MC	25.00	50.00
10 Sylvio Mantha MC	50.00	100.00
11 Jack McGill MC	25.00	50.00
12 Armand Mondou MC	25.00	50.00
13 Paul Marcel Raymond MC	25.00	50.00
14 Jack Riley MC	25.00	50.00
15 Russ Blinco MM	25.00	50.00
16 Herb Cain MM	40.00	80.00
17 Lionel Conacher MM	125.00	250.00
18 Alex Connell MM	62.50	125.00
19 Stewart Evans MM	25.00	50.00
20 Norman Gainor MM	25.00	50.00
21 Paul Haynes MM	25.00	50.00
22 Gus Marker MM	25.00	50.00
23 Baldy Northcott MM	30.00	60.00
24 Earl Robinson MM	25.00	50.00
25 Hooley Smith MM	50.00	100.00
26 Dave Trottier MM	25.00	50.00
27 Jimmy Ward MM	25.00	50.00
28 Cy Wentworth MM	30.00	60.00
29 Eddie Shore BB	250.00	500.00
30 Babe Siebert BB	62.50	125.00
31 Nels Stewart BB	75.00	150.00
32 Tiny Thompson BB	75.00	150.00
33 Lorne Chabot CBH	50.00	100.00
34 Mush March CBH	25.00	50.00
35 Howie Morenz CBH	400.00	800.00
36 Larry Aurie DRW	25.00	50.00
37 Ebbie Goodfellow DRW	50.00	100.00
38 Herbie Lewis DRW	25.00	50.00
39 Ralph Weiland DRW	50.00	100.00
40 Bill Cook NYR	50.00	100.00
41 Bun Cook NYR	50.00	100.00
42 Ivan(Ching) Johnson NYR	67.50	135.00
43 Dave Kerr NYR	40.00	80.00
44 King Clancy	200.00	400.00
45 Charlie Conacher TML	200.00	400.00
46 Red Horner TML	62.50	125.00
47 Busher Jackson TML	75.00	150.00
48 Joe Primeau TML	100.00	200.00

1935 TCTA

This card measures approximately 3 1/2" x 5 1/2" and was printed in black and white.

NNO Maple Leaf Arena	25.00	50.00

1974 Team Canada L'Equipe WHA

This 24-photo set measures approximately 4 1/8" by 7 1/2" and features posed, glossy, black-and-white player photos on thin stock. The pictures are attached to red poster board. The player's name and two Team Canada L'Equipe logos appear in the white margin at the bottom. The backs are blank. The cards are unnumbered and checklisted below in alphabetical order.

COMPLETE SET (24)	25.00	50.00
1 Ralph Backstrom	1.00	2.00
2 Serge Bernier	.75	1.50
3 Gerry Cheevers	5.00	10.00
4 Al Hamilton	1.00	2.00
5 Billy Harris CO	.50	1.00
6 Jim Harrison	.75	1.50
7 Ben Hatskin OWN	.75	1.50
8 Paul Henderson	2.00	4.00
9 Rejean Houle	1.00	2.00
10 Mark Howe	4.00	8.00
11 Marty Howe	1.00	2.00
12 Bill Hunter	.50	1.00
13 Gordon W. Juckes	.50	1.00
14 Rick Ley	1.00	2.00
15 Frank Mahovlich	4.00	8.00
16 John McKenzie	1.00	2.00
17 Don McLeod	.75	1.50
18 Rick Noonan	.75	1.50
19 Brad Selwood	.75	1.50
20 Rick Smith	.75	1.50
21 Pat Stapleton	1.00	2.00
22 Marc Tardif	1.00	2.00
23 Mike Walton	1.00	2.00
24 Tom Webster	1.00	2.00

1954-55 Topps

Topps introduced its first hockey set in 1954-55. The issue includes 60 cards of players on the four American (Boston, Chicago, Detroit and New York) teams. Cards measure approximately 2 5/8" by 3 3/4". Color fronts feature the player on a white background with facsimile autograph and team logo. The player's name, team name and position appear in bottom borders that are in team colors. The backs, printed in red and blue, contain player biographies, 1953-54 statistics and a hockey fact section. The cards were printed in the USA. Rookie Cards include Camille Henry and Doug Mohns. An early and very popular card of Gordie Howe is the main attraction in this set.

COMPLETE SET (60)	3,000.00	4,500.00
1 Dick Gamble	75.00	150.00
2 Bob Chrystal RC	20.00	40.00
3 Harry Howell	50.00	100.00
4 Johnny Wilson	20.00	40.00
5 Red Kelly	75.00	150.00
6 Real Chevrefils	20.00	40.00
7 Bob Armstrong	20.00	40.00
8 Gordie Howe	1,200.00	1,800.00
9 Benny Woit	20.00	40.00
10 Gump Worsley	125.00	200.00
11 Andy Bathgate	50.00	100.00
12 Bucky Hollingworth RC	20.00	40.00
13 Ray Timgren	20.00	40.00
14 Jack Evans	20.00	40.00
15 Paul Ronty	20.00	40.00
16 Glen Skov	20.00	40.00
17 Gus Mortson	20.00	40.00
18 Doug Mohns RC	75.00	125.00
19 Leo Labine	25.00	60.00
20 Bill Gadsby	40.00	80.00
21 Jerry Toppazzini	25.00	60.00
22 Wally Hergesheimer	20.00	40.00
23 Danny Lewicki	20.00	40.00
24 Metro Prystai	20.00	40.00
25 Fern Flaman	25.00	60.00
26 Al Rollins	40.00	80.00
27 Marcel Pronovost	40.00	80.00
28 Lou Jankowski	20.00	40.00
29 Nick Mickoski	20.00	40.00
30 Frank Martin	20.00	40.00
31 Lorne Ferguson	20.00	40.00
32 Camille Henry RC	40.00	80.00
33 Pete Conacher	25.00	60.00
34 Marty Pavelich	20.00	40.00
35 Don McKenney RC	40.00	80.00
36 Fleming Mackell	25.00	60.00
37 Jim Henry	40.00	80.00
38 Hal Laycoe	20.00	40.00
39 Alex Delvecchio	75.00	150.00
40 Larry Wilson	20.00	40.00
41 Allan Stanley	50.00	100.00
42 George Sullivan	20.00	40.00
43 Jack McIntyre	20.00	40.00
44 Ivan Irwin RC	20.00	40.00
45 Tony Leswick	20.00	40.00
46 Bob Goldham	20.00	40.00
47 Cal Gardner	25.00	60.00
48 Ed Sandford	20.00	40.00
49 Bill Quackenbush	40.00	80.00
50 Warren Godfrey	20.00	40.00
51 Ted Lindsay	75.00	150.00
52 Earl Reibel	25.00	60.00
53 Don Raleigh	20.00	40.00
54 Bill Mosienko	40.00	80.00
55 Larry Popein RC	25.00	60.00
56 Edgar Laprade	25.00	60.00
57 Bill Dineen	25.00	60.00
58 Terry Sawchuk	400.00	700.00
59 Marcel Bonin RC	25.00	50.00
60 Milt Schmidt	150.00	250.00

1957-58 Topps

After a two year hiatus, Topps returned to producing hockey cards for 1957-58. Reportedly, Topps spent the interim evaluating the hockey card market. Cards in this 66-card set were reduced to measure the standard 2 1/2" by 3 1/2". The players in this set are from the four U.S. based teams. The cards are in team order: Boston 1-18, Chicago 19-33, Detroit 34-50 and New York 51-66. Bilingual backs feature 1956-57 statistics, a short player biography and a cartoon question and answer section. Rookie Cards in this include Johnny Bucyk, Glenn Hall, Pierre Pilote, and Norm Ullman.

COMPLETE SET (66)	1,500.00	3,000.00
1 Real Chevrefils	30.00	50.00
2 Jack Bionda RC	15.00	25.00
3 Bob Armstrong	12.00	20.00
4 Fern Flaman	15.00	25.00
5 Jerry Toppazzini	12.00	20.00
6 Larry Regan RC	12.00	20.00
7 Bronco Horvath RC	18.00	30.00
8 Jack Caffery	12.00	20.00
9 Leo Labine	15.00	25.00
10 Johnny Bucyk RC	175.00	300.00
11 Vic Stasiuk	12.00	20.00
12 Doug Mohns	15.00	25.00
13 Don McKenney	12.00	20.00
14 Don Simmons RC	15.00	25.00
15 Allan Stanley	18.00	30.00
16 Fleming Mackell	15.00	25.00
17 Larry Hillman RC	15.00	25.00
18 Leo Boivin	15.00	25.00
19 Bob Bailey	12.00	20.00
20 Glenn Hall RC	250.00	400.00
21 Ted Lindsay	40.00	80.00
22 Pierre Pilote RC	60.00	100.00
23 Jim Thomson	12.00	20.00
24 Eric Nesterenko	15.00	25.00
25 Gus Mortson	12.00	20.00
26 Ed Litzenberger RC	18.00	30.00
27 Elmer Vasko RC	18.00	30.00
28 Jack McIntyre	12.00	20.00
29 Ron Murphy	12.00	20.00
30 Glen Skov	12.00	20.00
31 Hec Lalande RC	12.00	20.00
32 Nick Mickoski	12.00	20.00
33 Wally Hergesheimer	12.00	20.00
34 Alex Delvecchio	30.00	50.00
35 Terry Sawchuk UER	150.00	250.00
36 Guyle Fielder RC	15.00	25.00
37 Tom McCarthy	12.00	20.00
38 Al Arbour	25.00	40.00
39 Billy Dea RC	12.00	20.00
40 Lorne Ferguson	12.00	20.00
41 Warren Godfrey	12.00	20.00
42 Gordie Howe	300.00	500.00
43 Marcel Pronovost	15.00	25.00
44 Bill McNeil RC	12.00	20.00
45 Earl Reibel	12.00	20.00
46 Norm Ullman RC	150.00	250.00
47 Johnny Wilson	12.00	20.00
48 Red Kelly	30.00	50.00
49 Bill Dineen	15.00	25.00
50 Forbes Kennedy RC	15.00	25.00
51 Harry Howell	25.00	40.00
52 Jean-Guy Gendron RC	15.00	25.00
53 Gump Worsley	60.00	100.00
54 Larry Popein	12.00	20.00
55 Jack Evans	12.00	20.00
56 George Sullivan	12.00	20.00
57 Gerry Foley RC	12.00	20.00
58 Andy Hebenton RC	15.00	25.00
59 Larry Cahan	12.00	20.00
60 Andy Bathgate	25.00	40.00
61 Danny Lewicki	12.00	20.00
62 Dean Prentice	15.00	25.00
63 Camille Henry	15.00	25.00
64 Lou Fontinato RC	25.00	40.00
65 Bill Gadsby	18.00	30.00
66 Dave Creighton	30.00	50.00

1958-59 Topps

The 1958-59 Topps set contains 66 color standard-size cards of players from the four U.S. based teams. Bilingual backs feature 1957-58 statistics, player biographies and a cartoon information section on the player. The set features the Rookie Card of Bobby Hull. Due to being the last card and subject to wear, as well as being chronically off-center, the Hull card is quite scarce in top grades. Other Rookie Cards include Eddie Shack and Ken Wharram.

COMPLETE SET (66)	3,000.00	4,500.00
1 Bob Armstrong	25.00	40.00
2 Terry Sawchuk	100.00	175.00
3 Glen Skov	10.00	20.00
4 Leo Labine	12.50	25.00
5 Dollard St.Laurent	10.00	20.00
6 Danny Lewicki	10.00	20.00
7 John Hanna RC	10.00	20.00
8 Gordie Howe UER	250.00	400.00
9 Vic Stasiuk	10.00	20.00
10 Larry Regan	10.00	20.00
11 Forbes Kennedy	10.00	20.00
12 Elmer Vasko	12.50	25.00
13 Glenn Hall	90.00	150.00
14 Ken Wharram RC	12.50	25.00
15 Len Lunde RC	10.00	20.00
16 Ed Litzenberger	12.50	25.00
17 Norm Johnson RC	10.00	20.00
18 Earl Ingarfield RC	10.00	20.00
19 Les Colwill RC	10.00	20.00
20 Leo Boivin	12.50	25.00
21 Andy Bathgate	25.00	40.00
22 Johnny Wilson	10.00	20.00
23 Larry Cahan	10.00	20.00
24 Marcel Pronovost	12.50	25.00
25 Larry Hillman	12.50	25.00
26 Jim Bartlett RC	10.00	20.00
27 Nick Mickoski	10.00	20.00
28 Larry Popein	10.00	20.00
29 Fleming Mackell	12.50	25.00
30 Eddie Shack RC	150.00	250.00
31 Jack Evans	10.00	20.00
32 Dean Prentice	12.50	25.00
33 Claude Laforge RC	10.00	20.00
34 Bill Gadsby	18.00	30.00
35 Bronco Horvath	12.50	25.00
36 Pierre Pilote	30.00	50.00
37 Earl Balfour	10.00	20.00
38 Gus Mortson	10.00	20.00
39 Gump Worsley	50.00	80.00
40 Johnny Bucyk	75.00	125.00
41 Lou Fontinato	12.50	25.00
42 Tod Sloan	10.00	20.00
43 Charlie Burns RC	10.00	20.00
44 Don Simmons	12.50	25.00
45 Jerry Toppazzini	10.00	20.00
46 Andy Hebenton	10.00	20.00
47 Pete Goegan RC	10.00	20.00
48 George Sullivan	10.00	20.00
49 Hank Ciesla RC	10.00	20.00
50 Doug Mohns	10.00	20.00
51 Jean-Guy Gendron	10.00	20.00
52 Alex Delvecchio	25.00	40.00
53 Eric Nesterenko	12.50	25.00
54 Camille Henry	12.50	25.00
55 Lorne Ferguson	10.00	20.00
56 Fern Flaman	12.50	25.00
57 Earl Reibel	10.00	20.00
58 Warren Godfrey	10.00	20.00
59 Ron Murphy	10.00	20.00
60 Harry Howell	18.00	30.00
61 Red Kelly	25.00	40.00
62 Don McKenney	10.00	20.00
63 Ted Lindsay	25.00	40.00
64 Al Arbour	12.50	25.00
65 Norm Ullman	60.00	100.00
66 Bobby Hull RC	2,200.00	3,000.00

1959-60 Topps

The 1959-60 Topps set contains 66 color standard-size cards of players from the four U.S. based teams. The fronts have the player's name and position at the bottom with team name and logo at the top. Bilingual backs feature 1958-59 statistics, a short biography and a cartoon question section.

COMPLETE SET (66)	1,200.00	2,000.00
1 Eric Nesterenko	30.00	50.00
2 Pierre Pilote	25.00	40.00

3 Elmer Vasko	15.00	25.00
4 Peter Goegan	10.00	20.00
5 Lou Fontinato	15.00	25.00
6 Ted Lindsay	25.00	40.00
7 Leo Labine	15.00	25.00
8 Alex Delvecchio	25.00	40.00
9 Don McKenney UER	10.00	20.00
10 Earl Ingarfield	10.00	20.00
11 Don Simmons	15.00	25.00
12 Glen Skov	10.00	20.00
13 Tod Sloan	10.00	20.00
14 Vic Stasiuk	10.00	20.00
15 Gump Worsley	35.00	60.00
16 Andy Hebenton	15.00	25.00
17 Dean Prentice	15.00	25.00
18 Pronovost/Bartlett IA	15.00	25.00
19 Fleming Mackell	15.00	25.00
20 Harry Howell	15.00	25.00
21 Larry Popein	10.00	20.00
22 Len Lunde	10.00	20.00
23 Johnny Bucyk	35.00	60.00
24 Jean-Guy Gendron	10.00	20.00
25 Barry Cullen	10.00	20.00
26 Leo Boivin	15.00	25.00
27 Warren Godfrey	10.00	20.00
28 G.Hall/C.Henry IA	25.00	40.00
29 Fern Flaman	15.00	25.00
30 Jack Evans	10.00	20.00
31 John Hanna	10.00	20.00
32 Glenn Hall	60.00	100.00
33 Murray Balfour RC	15.00	25.00
34 Andy Bathgate	25.00	40.00
35 Al Arbour	15.00	25.00
36 Jim Morrison	10.00	20.00
37 Nick Mickoski	10.00	20.00
38 Jerry Toppazzini	10.00	20.00
39 Bob Armstrong	10.00	20.00
40 Charlie Burns UER	10.00	20.00
41 Bill McNeil	10.00	20.00
42 Terry Sawchuk	90.00	150.00
43 Dollard St.Laurent	10.00	20.00
44 Marcel Pronovost	15.00	25.00
45 Norm Ullman	35.00	60.00
46 Camille Henry	15.00	25.00
47 Bobby Hull	400.00	600.00
48 G.Howe/J.Evans IA	50.00	80.00
49 Lou Marcon RC	10.00	20.00
50 Earl Balfour	10.00	20.00
51 Jim Bartlett	10.00	20.00
52 Forbes Kennedy	10.00	20.00
53 N.Mickoski/J.Hanna IA	10.00	20.00
54 G.Worsley/H.Howell IA	25.00	40.00
55 Brian Cullen	10.00	20.00
56 Bronco Horvath	15.00	25.00
57 Eddie Shack	60.00	100.00
58 Doug Mohns	15.00	25.00
59 George Sullivan	10.00	20.00
60 P.Pilote/F.Mackell IA	10.00	20.00
61 Ed Litzenberger	10.00	20.00
62 Bill Gadsby	18.00	30.00
63 Gordie Howe	250.00	400.00
64 Claude Laforge	10.00	20.00
65 Red Kelly	25.00	40.00
66 Ron Murphy	30.00	50.00

1960-61 Topps

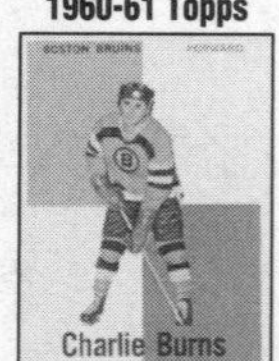

The 1960-61 Topps set contains 66 color standard-size cards featuring players from Boston (1-20), Chicago (23-42) and New York (45-63). In addition to player and team names, the typical card front features color patterns according to the player's team. The backs are bilingual and have 1959-60 statistics and a cartoon trivia quiz. Cards titled "All-Time Greats" are an attractive feature to this set and include the likes of Georges Vezina and Eddie Shore. The All-Time Great players are indicated by ATG in the checklist below. Stan Mikita's Rookie Card is part of this set. The existence of an album issued by Topps to store this set has recently been confirmed. It is valued at approximately $150.

COMPLETE SET (66)	1,100.00	1,800.00
1 Lester Patrick ATG	40.00	80.00
2 Paddy Moran ATG	10.00	20.00
3 Joe Malone ATG	15.00	30.00
4 Ernest Johnson	7.50	15.00
5 Nels Stewart ATG	15.00	30.00
6 Bill Hay RC	10.00	20.00
7 Eddie Shack	40.00	80.00
8 Cy Denneny ATG	7.50	15.00
9 Jim Morrison	6.00	12.00
10 Bill Cook ATG	7.50	15.00
11 Johnny Bucyk	25.00	50.00
12 Murray Balfour	6.00	12.00
13 Leo Labine	6.00	12.00
14 Stan Mikita RC	250.00	400.00
15 George Hay ATG RC	7.50	15.00
16 Red Dutton ATG	7.50	15.00
17 Dickie Boon ATG RC	6.00	12.00
18 George Sullivan	6.00	12.00
19 Georges Vezina ATG	30.00	60.00
20 Eddie Shore ATG	30.00	60.00
21 Ed Litzenberger	6.00	12.00
22 Bill Gadsby	10.00	20.00
23 Elmer Vasko	6.00	12.00
24 Charlie Burns	6.00	12.00
25 Glenn Hall	40.00	80.00
26 Dit Clapper ATG	15.00	30.00
27 Art Ross ATG	25.00	50.00
28 Jerry Toppazzini	6.00	12.00
29 Frank Boucher ATG	7.50	15.00
30 Jack Evans	6.00	12.00
31 Jean-Guy Gendron	6.00	12.00
32 Chuck Gardiner ATG	12.50	25.00
33 Ab McDonald	6.00	20.00
34 Frank Fredrickson ATG RC	7.50	15.00
35 Frank Nighbor ATG	12.50	25.00
36 Gump Worsley	30.00	60.00
37 Dean Prentice	7.50	15.00
38 Hugh Lehman ATG RC	7.50	15.00
39 Jack McCartan RC	15.00	30.00
40 Don McKenney UER	6.00	12.00
(Misspelled McKenny		
on card front		
41 Ron Murphy	6.00	12.00
42 Andy Hebenton	6.00	12.00
43 Don Simmons	7.50	15.00
44 Herb Gardiner ATG	7.50	15.00
45 Andy Bathgate	12.50	25.00
46 Cyclone Taylor ATG	15.00	40.00
47 King Clancy ATG	25.00	50.00
48 Newsy Lalonde ATG	15.00	30.00
49 Harry Howell	7.50	15.00
50 Ken Schinkel RC	6.00	12.00
51 Tod Sloan	6.00	12.00
52 Doug Mohns	7.50	15.00
53 Camille Henry	7.50	15.00
54 Bronco Horvath	6.00	12.00
55 Tiny Thompson ATG	20.00	40.00
56 Bob Armstrong	6.00	12.00
57 Fern Flaman	7.50	15.00
58 Bobby Hull	250.00	400.00
59 Howie Morenz ATG	30.00	60.00
60 Dick Irvin ATG RC	15.00	30.00
61 Lou Fontinato	6.00	12.00
62 Leo Boivin	7.50	15.00
63 Moose Goheen ATG RC	7.50	15.00
64 Al Arbour	7.50	15.00
65 Pierre Pilote	15.00	30.00
66 Vic Stasiuk	15.00	30.00

1961-62 Topps Stamps

There are 52 stamps in this scarce set. They were issued as pairs as an insert in 1961-62 Topps Hockey regular issue card packs. The players in the set are either members of the Boston Bruins (BB), Chicago Blackhawks (CBH), New York Rangers (NYR), or All-Time Greats (ATG). The stamps are unnumbered, so they are listed below alphabetically.

COMPLETE SET (52)	900.00	1,500.00
*PANELS: .6X TO 1.5X SUM OF SINGLE STAMPS		
1 Murray Balfour	15.00	30.00
2 Andy Bathgate	15.00	30.00
3 Leo Boivin	12.50	25.00
4 Dickie Boon	15.00	30.00
5 Frank Boucher	20.00	40.00
6 Johnny Bucyk	20.00	40.00
7 Charlie Burns	10.00	20.00
8 King Clancy	20.00	50.00
9 Dit Clapper	15.00	30.00
10 Sprague Cleghorn	20.00	40.00
11 Alex Connell	15.00	30.00
12 Bill Cook	15.00	30.00
13 Cy Denneny	15.00	30.00
14 Jack Evans	10.00	20.00
15 Frank Frederickson	15.00	30.00
16 Chuck Gardiner	15.00	30.00
17 Herb Gardiner	15.00	30.00
18 Eddie Gerard	15.00	30.00
19 Moose Goheen	15.00	30.00
20 Glenn Hall	25.00	50.00
21 Doug Harvey	20.00	40.00
22 Bill Hay	15.00	30.00
23 George Hay	15.00	30.00
24 Andy Hebenton	10.00	20.00
25 Camille Henry	12.50	25.00
26 Bronco Horvath	10.00	20.00
27 Harry Howell	12.50	25.00
28 Bobby Hull	75.00	150.00
29 Dick Irvin	15.00	30.00
30 Ernest Johnson	15.00	30.00
31 Newsy Lalonde	20.00	40.00
32 Albert Langlois	15.00	30.00
33 Hugh Lehman	15.00	30.00
34 Joe Malone	20.00	40.00
35 Don McKenney	10.00	20.00
36 Stan Mikita	50.00	100.00
37 Doug Mohns	10.00	20.00
38 Paddy Moran	15.00	30.00
39 Howie Morenz	30.00	60.00
40 Ron Murphy	15.00	30.00
41 Frank Nighbor	25.00	50.00
42 Murray Oliver	10.00	20.00
43 Pierre Pilote	15.00	30.00
44 Dean Prentice	10.00	20.00
45 Andre Pronovost	10.00	20.00
46 Art Ross	25.00	50.00
47 Dallas Smith	10.00	20.00
48 Nels Stewart	15.00	30.00
49 Cyclone Taylor	15.00	30.00
50 Elmer Vasko	10.00	20.00
51 Georges Vezina	40.00	80.00
52 Gump Worsley	20.00	40.00

1961-62 Topps

The 1961-62 Topps set contains 66 color standard-size cards featuring players from Boston, Chicago and New York. The card numbering in this set is basically by team order, e.g., Boston Bruins (1-22), Chicago Blackhawks (23-44), and New York Rangers (45-65). Bilingual backs contain 1960-61 statistics and brief career highlights. For the first time, Topps cards were printed in Canada. Rookie Cards include New York Ranger stars Rod Gilbert and Jean Ratelle. The set marks the debut of team and checklist cards within Topps hockey card sets.

COMPLETE SET (66)	750.00	1,500.00
1 Phil Watson CO	15.00	25.00
2 Ted Green RC	25.00	40.00
3 Earl Balfour	7.00	12.00
4 Dallas Smith RC	15.00	25.00
5 Andre Pronovost UER	7.00	12.00
(Misspelled Provonost		
on card back		
6 Dick Meissner RC	7.00	12.00
7 Leo Boivin	9.00	15.00
8 Johnny Bucyk	25.00	40.00
9 Jerry Toppazzini	7.00	12.00
10 Doug Mohns	9.00	15.00
11 Charlie Burns	7.00	12.00
12 Don McKenney	7.00	12.00
13 Bob Armstrong	7.00	12.00
14 Murray Oliver	7.00	12.00
15 Orland Kurtenbach RC	15.00	25.00
16 Terry Gray RC	7.00	12.00
17 Don Head RC	9.00	15.00
18 Pat Stapleton RC	15.00	25.00
19 Cliff Pennington RC	7.00	12.00
20 Bruins Team Picture	25.00	40.00
21 E.Balfour/F.Flaman IA	8.00	14.00
22 A.Bathgate/G.Hall IA	15.00	25.00
23 Rudy Pilous CO RC	9.00	15.00
24 Pierre Pilote	15.00	25.00
25 Elmer Vasko	7.00	12.00
26 Reg Fleming RC	9.00	15.00
27 Ab McDonald	7.00	12.00
28 Eric Nesterenko	9.00	15.00
29 Bobby Hull	150.00	300.00
30 Ken Wharram	9.00	15.00
31 Dollard St.Laurent	7.00	12.00
32 Glenn Hall	40.00	60.00
33 Murray Balfour	7.00	12.00
34 Ron Murphy	7.00	12.00
35 Bill Hay	9.00	15.00
36 Stan Mikita	100.00	150.00
37 Denis DeJordy RC	25.00	40.00
38 Wayne Hillman RC	9.00	15.00
39 Rino Robazzo RC	7.00	12.00
40 Bronco Horvath	7.00	12.00
41 Bob Turner	7.00	12.00
42 Blackhawks Team Picture	25.00	40.00
43 Ken Wharram IA	9.00	15.00
44 St.Laurent/G.Hall IA	15.00	25.00
45 Doug Harvey CO	25.00	40.00
46 Junior Langlois	7.00	12.00
47 Irv Spencer RC	7.00	12.00
48 George Sullivan	7.00	12.00
49 Earl Ingarfield	7.00	12.00
50 Gump Worsley	25.00	40.00
51 Harry Howell	9.00	15.00
52 Larry Cahan	7.00	12.00
53 Andy Bathgate	12.00	20.00
54 Dean Prentice	9.00	15.00
55 Andy Hebenton	7.00	12.00
56 Camille Henry	9.00	15.00
57 Jean-Guy Gendron	7.00	12.00
58 Pat Hannigan RC	7.00	12.00
59 Ted Hampson	7.00	12.00
60 Jean Ratelle RC	75.00	150.00
61 Al Lebrun RC	7.00	12.00
62 Rod Gilbert RC	75.00	150.00
63 Rangers Team Picture	25.00	40.00
64 D.Meissner/G.Worsley IA	12.00	20.00
65 Gump Worsley IA	12.00	20.00
66 Checklist Card	175.00	300.00

1962-63 Topps

The 1962-63 Topps set contains 66 color standard-size cards featuring players from Boston, Chicago, and New York. The card numbering in this set is by team order, e.g., Boston Bruins (1-22), Chicago Blackhawks (23-43), and New York Rangers (45-65). Included within the numbering sequence are team cards. Bilingual backs feature 1961-62 statistics and career highlights. The cards were printed in Canada. Rookie Cards include Vic Hadfield, Chico Maki, and Jim "The Chief" Neilson.

COMPLETE SET (66)	800.00	1,300.00
1 Phil Watson CO	15.00	25.00
2 Bob Perreault RC	10.00	20.00
3 Bruce Gamble RC	20.00	40.00
4 Warren Godfrey	7.00	12.00
5 Leo Boivin	9.00	15.00
6 Doug Mohns	9.00	15.00
7 Ted Green	9.00	15.00
8 Pat Stapleton	9.00	15.00
9 Dallas Smith	9.00	15.00
10 Don McKenney	7.00	12.00
11 Johnny Bucyk	18.00	30.00
12 Murray Oliver	7.00	12.00
13 Jerry Toppazzini	7.00	12.00
14 Cliff Pennington	7.00	12.00
15 Charlie Burns	7.00	12.00
16 Jean-Guy Gendron	7.00	12.00
17 Irv Spencer	7.00	12.00
18 Wayne Connelly	7.00	12.00
19 Andre Pronovost	7.00	12.00
20 Terry Gray	7.00	12.00
21 Tom Williams RC	9.00	15.00
22 Bruins Team	25.00	40.00
23 Rudy Pilous CO	7.00	12.00
24 Glenn Hall	35.00	50.00
25 Denis DeJordy	9.00	15.00
26 Jack Evans	7.00	12.00
27 Elmer Vasko	7.00	12.00
28 Pierre Pilote	12.00	20.00
29 Bob Turner	7.00	12.00
30 Dollard St.Laurent	7.00	12.00
31 Wayne Hillman	9.00	15.00
32 Al McNeil	7.00	12.00
33 Bobby Hull	175.00	300.00
34 Stan Mikita	60.00	125.00
35 Bill Hay	9.00	15.00
36 Murray Balfour	7.00	12.00
37 Chico Maki RC	12.00	20.00
38 Ab McDonald	7.00	12.00
39 Ken Wharram	9.00	15.00
40 Ron Murphy	6.00	12.00
41 Eric Nesterenko	8.00	12.00
42 Reg Fleming	9.00	15.00
43 Murray Hall RC	7.00	12.00
44 Blackhawks Team	25.00	40.00
45 Gump Worsley	25.00	40.00
46 Harry Howell	7.00	12.00
47 Albert Langlois	7.00	12.00
48 Larry Cahan	7.00	12.00
49 Jim Neilson RC	12.00	20.00
50 Al Lebrun	7.00	12.00
51 Earl Ingarfield	7.00	12.00
52 Andy Bathgate	12.00	20.00
53 Dean Prentice	9.00	15.00
54 Andy Hebenton	7.00	12.00
55 Ted Hampson	7.00	12.00
56 Dave Balon RC	7.00	12.00
57 Bert Olmstead	9.00	15.00
58 Jean Ratelle	30.00	50.00
59 Rod Gilbert	30.00	50.00
60 Vic Hadfield RC	30.00	50.00
61 Frank Paice TR RC	7.00	12.00
62 Camille Henry	9.00	15.00
63 Bronco Horvath	7.00	12.00
64 Pat Hannigan	7.00	12.00
65 Rangers Team	25.00	40.00
66 Checklist Card	150.00	250.00

1962-63 Topps Hockey Bucks

These "bucks" are actually inserts printed to look like Canadian currency on thin paper stock. They were distributed as an inserted folded in one buck per wax pack. Since these bucks are unnumbered, they are ordered below in alphabetical order by player's name. The bucks are approximately 4 1/16" by 1 11/16"; there is no information on the backs, just a green-patterned design.

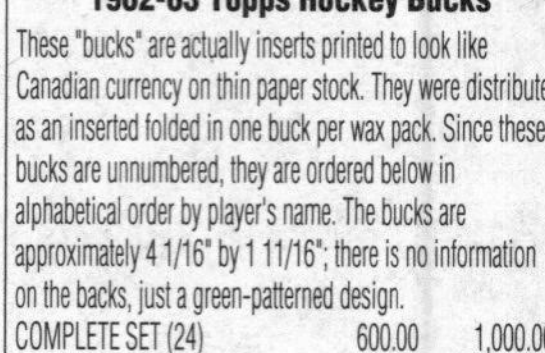

COMPLETE SET (24)	600.00	1,000.00
1 Dave Balon	20.00	40.00
2 Andy Bathgate	20.00	40.00
3 Leo Boivin	20.00	40.00
4 Johnny Bucyk	25.00	50.00
5 Reg Fleming	20.00	40.00
6 Warren Godfrey	20.00	40.00
7 Ted Green	20.00	40.00
8 Glenn Hall	40.00	80.00
9 Bill Hay	25.00	50.00
10 Andy Hebenton	20.00	40.00
11 Harry Howell	20.00	40.00
12 Bobby Hull	100.00	200.00
13 Earl Ingarfield	20.00	40.00
14 Albert Langlois	20.00	40.00
15 Ab McDonald	20.00	40.00
16 Don McKenney	20.00	40.00
17 Stan Mikita	50.00	100.00
18 Doug Mohns	20.00	40.00
19 Murray Oliver	20.00	40.00
20 Pierre Pilote	25.00	50.00
21 Dean Prentice	20.00	40.00
22 Jerry Toppazzini	20.00	40.00
23 Elmer Vasko	20.00	40.00
24 Gump Worsley	40.00	80.00

1963-64 Topps

The 1963-64 Topps standard-size set contains 66 color cards featuring players and team cards from Boston (1-21), Chicago (22-43) and New York (44-65). Bilingual backs contain 1962-63 statistics and a short player biography. A question section, the answer for which could be obtained by rubbing the edge of a coin over a blank space under the question, also appears on the card backs. The cards were printed in Canada. The notable Rookie Cards in this set are Ed Johnston, Gilles Villemure, and Ed Westfall. Jacques Plante makes his first appearance in a Topps set.

COMPLETE SET (66)	700.00	1,000.00
1 Milt Schmidt CO	15.00	25.00
2 Ed Johnston RC	25.00	50.00
3 Doug Mohns	8.00	12.00
4 Tom Johnson	8.00	12.00
5 Leo Boivin	8.00	12.00
6 Bob McCord RC	6.00	10.00
7 Ted Green	8.00	12.00
8 Ed Westfall RC	18.00	30.00
9 Charlie Burns	6.00	10.00
10 Murray Oliver	8.00	12.00
11 Johnny Bucyk	15.00	25.00
12 Tom Williams	8.00	12.00
13 Dean Prentice	8.00	12.00
14 Bob Leiter RC	6.00	10.00
15 Andy Hebenton	6.00	10.00
16 Jean-Guy Gendron	6.00	10.00
17 Wayne Rivers RC	6.00	10.00
18 Jerry Toppazzini	6.00	10.00
19 Forbes Kennedy	6.00	10.00
20 Orland Kurtenbach	8.00	12.00
21 Bruins Team	25.00	40.00
22 Billy Reay CO	8.00	12.00
23 Glenn Hall	25.00	40.00
24 Denis DeJordy	8.00	12.00
25 Pierre Pilote	10.00	15.00
26 Elmer Vasko	6.00	10.00
27 Wayne Hillman	8.00	12.00
28 Al McNeil	6.00	10.00
29 Howie Young RC	6.00	10.00
30 Ed Van Impe RC	10.00	15.00
31 R.Fleming/G.Howe	10.00	15.00
32 Bob Turner	6.00	10.00
33 Bobby Hull	150.00	250.00
34 Bill Hay	8.00	12.00
35 Murray Balfour	6.00	10.00
36 Stan Mikita	60.00	100.00
37 Ab McDonald	6.00	10.00
38 Ken Wharram	8.00	12.00
39 Eric Nesterenko	8.00	12.00
40 Ron Murphy	6.00	10.00
41 Chico Maki	6.00	10.00
42 John McKenzie	10.00	15.00
43 Blackhawks Team	25.00	40.00
44 George Sullivan	6.00	10.00
45 Jacques Plante	75.00	125.00
46 Gilles Villemure RC	18.00	30.00
47 Doug Harvey	18.00	30.00
48 Harry Howell	8.00	12.00
49 Albert Langlois	6.00	10.00
50 Jim Neilson	8.00	12.00
51 Larry Cahan	6.00	10.00
52 Andy Bathgate	10.00	15.00
53 Don McKenney	6.00	10.00
54 Vic Hadfield	10.00	15.00
55 Earl Ingarfield	6.00	10.00
56 Camille Henry	6.00	10.00
57 Rod Gilbert	18.00	30.00
58 P.Goyette/G.Howe	10.00	15.00
59 Don Marshall	8.00	12.00
60 Dick Meissner	6.00	10.00
61 Val Fonteyne	6.00	10.00
62 Ken Schinkel	6.00	10.00
63 Jean Ratelle	18.00	30.00
64 Don Johns RC	6.00	10.00
65 Rangers Team	25.00	40.00
66 Checklist Card	125.00	200.00

1964-65 Topps

The 1964-65 Topps hockey set features 110 color cards of players from all six NHL teams. The size of the card is larger than in previous years at 2 1/2" by 4 11/16". Colorful fronts contain a solid player background with team name at the top and player name and position at the bottom. Bilingual backs have 1963-64 statistics, a brief player bio and a cartoon section featuring a fact about the player. The cards were printed in Canada. Eleven of the card numbers in each series appear to have been short printed based upon configurations found on uncut sheets. They are designated SP below. Rookie Cards include single prints of Gary Dornhoefer and Marcel Paille found in the last series. Other Rookie Cards include Roger Crozier, Jim Pappin, Pit Martin, Rod Seiling and Lou Angotti.

COMPLETE SET (110)	4,000.00	6,000.00
1 Pit Martin RC	60.00	125.00
2 Gilles Tremblay	12.00	20.00
3 Terry Harper	15.00	25.00
4 John Ferguson	30.00	50.00
5 Elmer Vasko	12.00	20.00
6 Terry Sawchuk UER	65.00	100.00
7 Bill Hay	15.00	25.00
8 Gary Bergman SP RC	18.00	30.00
9 Doug Barkley	12.00	20.00
10 Bob McCord	12.00	20.00
11 Parker MacDonald	12.00	20.00
12 Glenn Hall	35.00	60.00
13 Albert Langlois	12.00	20.00
14 Camille Henry SP	18.00	30.00
15 Norm Ullman	18.00	30.00
16 Ab McDonald	12.00	20.00
17 Charlie Hodge	12.00	20.00
18 Orland Kurtenbach	12.00	20.00
19 Dean Prentice	12.00	20.00
20 Bobby Hull SP	200.00	350.00
21 Ed Johnston	15.00	25.00
22 Denis DeJordy	12.00	20.00
23 Claude Provost	12.00	20.00
24 Rod Gilbert	30.00	50.00
25 Doug Mohns	12.00	20.00
26 Al McNeil	12.00	20.00
27 Billy Harris SP	15.00	25.00
28 Ken Wharram SP	15.00	25.00
29 George Sullivan	12.00	20.00
30 John McKenzie	12.00	20.00
31 Stan Mikita	65.00	100.00
32 Ted Green SP	15.00	25.00
33 Jean Beliveau SP	75.00	150.00
34 Arnie Brown RC	12.00	20.00
35 Reg Fleming	12.00	20.00
36 Jim Mikol RC	12.00	20.00
37 Dave Balon	12.00	20.00
38 Billy Reay CO	12.00	20.00
39 Marcel Pronovost SP	18.00	30.00
40 Johnny Bower	35.00	60.00
41 Wayne Hillman	12.00	20.00
42 Floyd Smith	12.00	20.00
43 Toe Blake CO	18.00	30.00
44 Red Kelly	18.00	30.00
45 Punch Imlach CO	15.00	25.00
46 Dick Duff	15.00	25.00
47 Roger Crozier RC	35.00	60.00
48 Henri Richard SP	75.00	125.00
49 Larry Jeffrey	12.00	20.00
50 Leo Boivin	12.00	20.00
51 Ed Westfall SP	15.00	25.00
52 Jean-Guy Talbot	12.00	20.00
53 Jacques Laperriere	15.00	25.00
54 1st Checklist	175.00	300.00
55 2nd Checklist SP	300.00	500.00
56 Ron Murphy	35.00	60.00
57 Bob Baun	35.00	60.00
58 Tom Williams SP	75.00	150.00
59 Pierre Pilote SP	150.00	250.00
60 Bob Pulford	35.00	60.00
61 Red Berenson	25.00	50.00
62 Vic Hadfield	35.00	60.00
63 Bob Leiter	25.00	50.00
64 Jim Pappin RC	35.00	60.00
65 Earl Ingarfield	35.00	60.00
66 Lou Angotti RC	35.00	60.00
67 Rod Seiling RC	25.00	50.00
68 Jacques Plante	100.00	175.00
69 George Armstrong UER	40.00	100.00
70 Milt Schmidt CO	25.00	50.00
71 Eddie Shack	60.00	100.00
72 Gary Dornhoefer SP RC	100.00	200.00
73 Chico Maki SP	100.00	200.00
74 Gilles Villemure SP	100.00	200.00
75 Carl Brewer	35.00	60.00
76 Bruce MacGregor	35.00	60.00
77 Bob Nevin	35.00	60.00
78 Ralph Backstrom	35.00	60.00
79 Murray Oliver	35.00	60.00
80 Bobby Rousseau SP	75.00	150.00
81 Don McKenney	35.00	60.00
82 Ted Lindsay	50.00	80.00
83 Harry Howell	35.00	60.00
84 Doug Robinson RC	35.00	60.00
85 Frank Mahovlich	75.00	125.00
86 Andy Bathgate	50.00	80.00
87 Phil Goyette	35.00	60.00
88 J.C. Tremblay	35.00	60.00
89 Gordie Howe	250.00	400.00
90 Murray Balfour	35.00	60.00
91 Eric Nesterenko SP	75.00	150.00
92 Marcel Paille SP RC	150.00	250.00
93 Sid Abel CO	35.00	60.00
94 Dave Keon	60.00	100.00
95 Alex Delvecchio	50.00	80.00
96 Bill Gadsby	35.00	60.00
97 Don Marshall	25.00	50.00
98 Bill Hicke SP	75.00	150.00
99 Ron Stewart	35.00	60.00
100 Johnny Bucyk	50.00	80.00
101 Tom Johnson	35.00	60.00
102 Tim Horton	80.00	150.00
103 Jim Neilson	25.00	50.00
104 Allan Stanley	35.00	60.00
105 Tim Horton AS SP	200.00	350.00
106 Stan Mikita AS SP	175.00	300.00
107 Bobby Hull AS	125.00	200.00
108 Ken Wharram AS	35.00	60.00
109 Pierre Pilote AS	40.00	80.00
110 Glenn Hall AS	90.00	150.00

1965-66 Topps

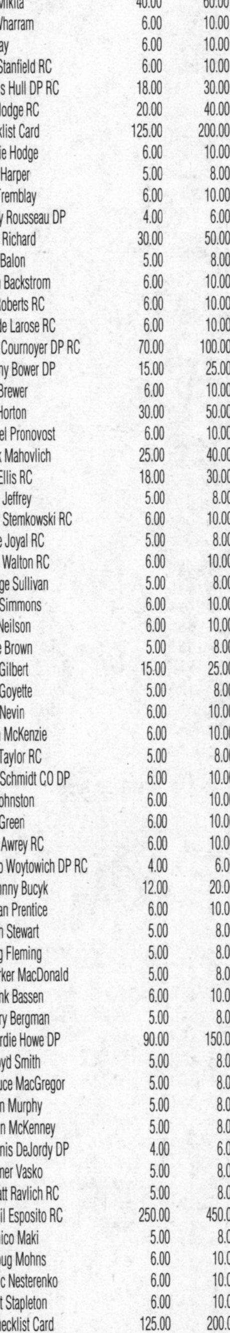

The 1965-66 Topps set contains 128 standard-size cards. Bilingual backs contain 1964-65 statistics, a short biography and a scratch-off question section. The cards were printed in Canada. The cards are grouped by team: Montreal (1-10, 67-76), Toronto (11-20, 77-86), New York (21-30, 87-95), Boston (31-40, 96-105), Detroit (41-53, 106-112) and Chicago (54-65, 113-120). Cards 122-128 are quite scarce and considered single prints. The seven cards were not included on checklist card 121. Rookie Cards include Gerry Cheevers, Yvan Cournoyer, Phil Esposito, Ed Giacomin, Paul Henderson, Ken Hodge and Dennis Hull. Eleven cards in the set were double printed including Cournoyer's Rookie Card.

COMPLETE SET (128)	1,700.00	2,700.00
1 Toe Blake CO	35.00	60.00
2 Gump Worsley	18.00	40.00
3 Jacques Laperriere	6.00	10.00
4 Jean-Guy Talbot	5.00	8.00
5 Ted Harris RC	5.00	8.00
6 Jean Beliveau	35.00	60.00
7 Dick Duff	6.00	10.00
8 Claude Provost DP	4.00	6.00
9 Red Berenson	6.00	10.00
10 John Ferguson	6.00	10.00
11 Punch Imlach CO	6.00	10.00
12 Terry Sawchuk	45.00	75.00
13 Bob Baun	6.00	10.00
14 Kent Douglas	5.00	8.00
15 Red Kelly	12.00	20.00
16 Jim Pappin	6.00	10.00
17 Dave Keon	30.00	50.00
18 Bob Pulford	6.00	10.00
19 George Armstrong	9.00	15.00
20 Orland Kurtenbach	5.00	8.00
21 Ed Giacomin RC	90.00	150.00
22 Harry Howell	6.00	10.00
23 Rod Seiling	5.00	8.00
24 Mike McMahon RC	5.00	8.00
25 Jean Ratelle	15.00	25.00
26 Doug Robinson	5.00	8.00
27 Vic Hadfield	6.00	10.00
28 Garry Peters UER RC	5.00	8.00
29 Don Marshall	6.00	10.00
30 Bill Hicke	5.00	8.00
31 Gerry Cheevers RC	125.00	200.00
32 Leo Boivin	6.00	10.00
33 Albert Langlois	5.00	8.00
34 Murray Oliver DP	4.00	6.00
35 Tom Williams	5.00	8.00
36 Ron Schock RC	5.00	8.00
37 Ed Westfall	6.00	10.00
38 Gary Dornhoefer	6.00	10.00
39 Bob Dillabough	5.00	8.00
40 Paul Popiel RC	5.00	8.00
41 Sid Abel CO	6.00	10.00
42 Roger Crozier	6.00	10.00
43 Doug Barkley	5.00	8.00
44 Bill Gadsby	5.00	8.00
45 Bryan Watson RC	9.00	15.00
46 Bob McCord	5.00	8.00
47 Alex Delvecchio	9.00	15.00
48 Andy Bathgate	9.00	15.00
49 Norm Ullman	9.00	15.00
50 Ab McDonald	5.00	8.00
51 Paul Henderson RC	30.00	50.00
52 Pit Martin	6.00	10.00
53 Billy Harris DP	4.00	6.00
54 Billy Reay CO	6.00	10.00
55 Glenn Hall	18.00	40.00
56 Pierre Pilote	9.00	15.00
57 Al McNeil	5.00	8.00
58 Camille Henry	5.00	8.00
59 Bobby Hull	125.00	200.00
60 Stan Mikita	40.00	60.00
61 Ken Wharram	6.00	10.00
62 Bill Hay	6.00	10.00
63 Fred Stanfield RC	6.00	10.00
64 Dennis Hull DP RC	18.00	30.00
65 Ken Hodge RC	20.00	40.00
66 Checklist Card	125.00	200.00
67 Charlie Hodge	6.00	10.00
68 Terry Harper	5.00	8.00
69 J.C. Tremblay	6.00	10.00
70 Bobby Rousseau DP	4.00	6.00
71 Henri Richard	30.00	50.00
72 Dave Balon	5.00	8.00
73 Ralph Backstrom	6.00	10.00
74 Jim Roberts RC	6.00	10.00
75 Claude Larose RC	6.00	10.00
76 Yvan Cournoyer DP RC	70.00	100.00
77 Johnny Bower DP	15.00	25.00
78 Carl Brewer	6.00	10.00
79 Tim Horton	30.00	50.00
80 Marcel Pronovost	6.00	10.00
81 Frank Mahovlich	25.00	40.00
82 Ron Ellis RC	18.00	30.00
83 Larry Jeffrey	5.00	8.00
84 Peter Stemkowski RC	6.00	10.00
85 Eddie Joyal RC	5.00	8.00
86 Mike Walton RC	6.00	10.00
87 George Sullivan	5.00	8.00
88 Don Simmons	6.00	10.00
89 Jim Neilson	6.00	10.00
90 Arnie Brown	5.00	8.00
91 Rod Gilbert	15.00	25.00
92 Phil Goyette	5.00	8.00
93 Bob Nevin	6.00	10.00
94 John McKenzie	6.00	10.00
95 Ted Taylor RC	5.00	8.00
96 Milt Schmidt CO DP	6.00	10.00
97 Ed Johnston	6.00	10.00
98 Ted Green	6.00	10.00
99 Don Awrey RC	6.00	10.00
100 Bob Woytowich DP RC	4.00	6.00
101 Johnny Bucyk	12.00	20.00
102 Dean Prentice	6.00	10.00
103 Ron Stewart	5.00	8.00
104 Reg Fleming	5.00	8.00
105 Parker MacDonald	5.00	8.00
106 Hank Bassen	6.00	10.00
107 Gary Bergman	5.00	8.00
108 Gordie Howe DP	90.00	150.00
109 Floyd Smith	5.00	8.00
110 Bruce MacGregor	5.00	8.00
111 Ron Murphy	5.00	8.00
112 Don McKenney	5.00	8.00
113 Denis DeJordy DP	4.00	6.00
114 Elmer Vasko	5.00	8.00
115 Matt Ravlich RC	5.00	8.00
116 Phil Esposito RC	250.00	450.00
117 Chico Maki	5.00	8.00
118 Doug Mohns	6.00	10.00
119 Eric Nesterenko	6.00	10.00
120 Pat Stapleton	6.00	10.00
121 Checklist Card	125.00	200.00
122 Gordie Howe 600 SP	250.00	400.00
123 Toronto Maple Leafs SP	50.00	80.00
124 Chicago Blackhawks SP	50.00	80.00
125 Detroit Red Wings SP	50.00	80.00
126 Montreal Canadiens SP	50.00	80.00
127 New York Rangers SP	50.00	80.00
128 Boston Bruins SP	125.00	200.00

1966-67 Topps

At 132 standard-size cards, the 1966-67 issue was the largest Topps set to date. The front features a distinctive wood grain border with a television screen look. Bilingual backs feature a short biography, 1965-66 and career statistics. The cards are grouped by team: Montreal (1-10/67-75), Toronto (11-20/76-84), New York (21-30/85-93), Boston (31-41/94-101), Detroit (42-52/102-109) and Chicago (53-64/110-117). The cards were printed in Canada. The key card in the set is Bobby Orr's Rookie Card. Other Rookie Cards include Emile Francis, Harry Sinden and Peter Mahovlich. The backs of card numbers 127-132 form a puzzle of Bobby Orr.

COMPLETE SET (132)	2,800.00	4,500.00
1 Toe Blake CO	30.00	80.00
2 Gump Worsley	12.00	20.00
3 Jean-Guy Talbot	6.00	10.00
4 Gilles Tremblay	6.00	10.00
5 J.C. Tremblay	7.00	12.00
6 Jim Roberts	7.00	12.00
7 Bobby Rousseau	6.00	10.00
8 Henri Richard	20.00	35.00
9 Claude Provost	6.00	10.00
10 Claude Larose	7.00	12.00
11 Punch Imlach CO	7.00	12.00
12 Johnny Bower	15.00	25.00
13 Terry Sawchuk	35.00	60.00
14 Mike Walton	7.00	12.00
15 Pete Stemkowski	6.00	10.00
16 Allan Stanley	7.00	12.00
17 Eddie Shack	18.00	30.00
18 Brit Selby RC	7.00	12.00
19 Bob Pulford	7.00	12.00
20 Marcel Pronovost	7.00	12.00
21 Emile Francis CO RC	12.00	20.00
22 Rod Seiling	6.00	10.00
23 Ed Giacomin	30.00	50.00
24 Don Marshall	7.00	12.00
25 Orland Kurtenbach	6.00	10.00
26 Rod Gilbert	12.00	20.00
27 Bob Nevin	7.00	12.00
28 Phil Goyette	6.00	10.00
29 Jean Ratelle	12.00	20.00
30 Earl Ingarfield	6.00	10.00
31 Harry Sinden CO RC	25.00	40.00
32 Ed Westfall	7.00	12.00
33 Joe Watson RC	7.00	12.00
34 Bob Woytowich	6.00	10.00
35 Bobby Orr RC	2,000.00	3,500.00
36 Gilles Marotte RC	7.00	12.00
37 Ted Green	7.00	12.00
38 Tom Williams	6.00	10.00
39 Johnny Bucyk	12.00	20.00
40 Wayne Connelly	6.00	10.00
41 Pit Martin	7.00	12.00
42 Sid Abel CO	6.00	10.00
43 Roger Crozier	7.00	12.00
44 Andy Bathgate	7.00	12.00
45 Dean Prentice	6.00	10.00
46 Paul Henderson	9.00	15.00
47 Gary Bergman	6.00	10.00
48 Bryan Watson	7.00	12.00
49 Bob Wall RC	6.00	10.00
50 Leo Boivin	7.00	12.00
51 Bert Marshall RC	6.00	10.00
52 Norm Ullman	9.00	15.00
53 Billy Reay CO	7.00	12.00
54 Glenn Hall	15.00	25.00
55 Wally Boyer RC	6.00	10.00
56 Fred Stanfield	6.00	10.00
57 Pat Stapleton	7.00	12.00
58 Matt Ravlich	6.00	10.00
59 Pierre Pilote	7.00	12.00
60 Eric Nesterenko	7.00	12.00
61 Doug Mohns	7.00	12.00
62 Stan Mikita	30.00	50.00
63 Phil Esposito	75.00	125.00
64 Bobby Hull LL	50.00	75.00
65 C.Hodge/G.Worsley	15.00	25.00
66 Checklist Card	200.00	400.00
67 Jacques Laperriere	7.00	12.00

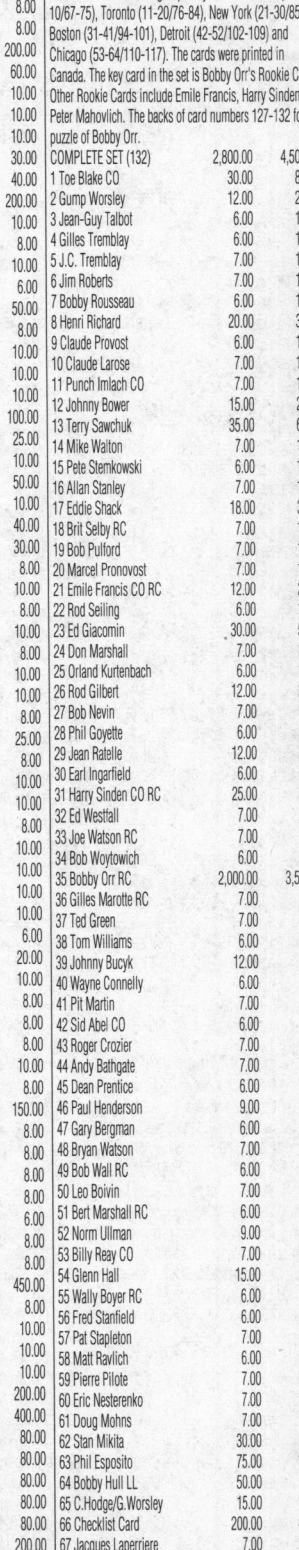

68 Terry Harper 6.00 10.00
69 Ted Harris 6.00 10.00
70 John Ferguson 7.00 12.00
71 Dick Duff 7.00 12.00
72 Yvan Cournoyer 30.00 50.00
73 Jean Beliveau 30.00 50.00
74 Dave Balon 6.00 10.00
75 Ralph Backstrom 7.00 12.00
76 Jim Pappin 6.00 10.00
77 Frank Mahovlich 25.00 40.00
78 Dave Keon 18.00 30.00
79 Red Kelly 12.00 20.00
80 Tim Horton 25.00 40.00
81 Ron Ellis 7.00 12.00
82 Kent Douglas 6.00 10.00
83 Bob Baun 7.00 12.00
84 George Armstrong 9.00 15.00
85 Bernie Geoffrion 15.00 25.00
86 Vic Hadfield 7.00 12.00
87 Wayne Hillman 6.00 10.00
88 Jim Neilson 6.00 10.00
89 Al McNeil 6.00 10.00
90 Arnie Brown 6.00 10.00
91 Harry Howell 7.00 12.00
92 Red Berenson 7.00 12.00
93 Reg Fleming 6.00 10.00
94 Ron Stewart 6.00 10.00
95 Murray Oliver 6.00 10.00
96 Ron Murphy 6.00 10.00
97 John McKenzie 7.00 12.00
98 Bob Dillabough 6.00 10.00
99 Ed Johnston 7.00 12.00
100 Ron Schock 6.00 10.00
101 Dallas Smith 6.00 10.00
102 Alex Delvecchio 12.00 20.00
103 Peter Mahovlich RC 18.00 30.00
104 Bruce MacGregor 6.00 10.00
105 Murray Hall 6.00 10.00
106 Floyd Smith 6.00 10.00
107 Hank Bassen 7.00 12.00
108 Val Fonteyne 6.00 10.00
109 Gordie Howe 125.00 200.00
110 Chico Maki 6.00 10.00
111 Doug Jarrett RC 6.00 10.00
112 Bobby Hull 90.00 150.00
113 Dennis Hull 7.00 12.00
114 Ken Hodge 9.00 15.00
115 Denis DeJordy 7.00 12.00
116 Lou Angotti 6.00 10.00
117 Ken Wharram 6.00 10.00
118 Montreal Canadiens 15.00 25.00
119 Detroit Red Wings 15.00 25.00
120 Checklist Card 200.00 400.00
121 Gordie Howe AS 60.00 100.00
122 Jacques Laperriere AS 7.00 12.00
123 Pierre Pilote AS 7.00 12.00
124 Stan Mikita AS 20.00 40.00
125 Bobby Hull AS 50.00 80.00
126 Glenn Hall AS 15.00 30.00
127 Jean Beliveau AS 15.00 30.00
128 Allan Stanley AS 7.00 12.00
129 Pat Stapleton AS 7.00 12.00
130 Gump Worsley AS 15.00 30.00
131 Frank Mahovlich AS 15.00 30.00
132 Bobby Rousseau AS 15.00 30.00

1966-67 Topps USA Test

This 66-card standard-size set was apparently a test issue with limited distribution solely in America as it is quite scarce. The cards feature the same format as the 1966-67 Topps regular hockey cards. The primary difference is that the card backs in this scarce issue are only printed in English, i.e., no French. The card numbering has some similarities to the regular issue, e.g., Bobby Orr is number 35 in both sets, however there are also many differences from the regular Topps Canadian version which was mass produced. The wood grain border on the front of the cards is slightly lighter than that of the regular issue.

COMPLETE SET (66) 8,000.00 12,000.00
1 Dennis Hull 50.00 80.00
2 Gump Worsley 70.00 120.00
3 Dallas Smith 25.00 50.00
4 Gilles Tremblay 25.00 50.00
5 J.C. Tremblay 25.00 50.00
6 Ralph Backstrom 25.00 50.00
7 Bobby Rousseau 25.00 50.00
8 Henri Richard 125.00 200.00
9 Claude Provost 25.00 50.00
10 Red Berenson 25.00 50.00
11 Punch Imlach CO 25.00 50.00
12 Johnny Bower 70.00 120.00
13 Yvan Cournoyer 90.00 150.00
14 Mike Walton 25.00 50.00
15 Pete Stemkowski 25.00 50.00
16 Allan Stanley 40.00 70.00
17 George Armstrong 40.00 70.00
18 Harry Howell 35.00 60.00
19 Vic Hadfield 25.00 50.00
20 Marcel Pronovost 35.00 60.00
21 Pete Mahovlich 35.00 60.00
22 Rod Seiling 25.00 50.00
23 Gordie Howe 500.00 800.00
24 Don Marshall 25.00 50.00
25 Orland Kurtenbach 25.00 50.00
26 Rod Gilbert 50.00 80.00
27 Bob Nevin 25.00 50.00
28 Phil Goyette 25.00 50.00
29 Jean Ratelle 60.00 100.00
30 Dave Keon 90.00 150.00
31 Jean Beliveau 175.00 300.00
32 Ed Westfall 25.00 50.00
33 Ron Murphy 25.00 50.00
34 Wayne Hillman 25.00 50.00
35 Bobby Orr 5,000.00 8,000.00
36 Boom Boom Geoffrion 90.00 150.00
37 Ted Green 25.00 50.00
38 Tom Williams 25.00 50.00
39 Johnny Bucyk 50.00 80.00
40 Bobby Hull 350.00 600.00
41 Ted Harris 25.00 50.00
42 Red Kelly 50.00 80.00
43 Roger Crozier 35.00 60.00
44 Ken Wharram 25.00 50.00
45 Dean Prentice 25.00 50.00
46 Paul Henderson 50.00 80.00
47 Gary Bergman 25.00 50.00
48 Arnie Brown 25.00 50.00
49 Jim Pappin 25.00 50.00
50 Denis DeJordy 35.00 60.00
51 Frank Mahovlich 75.00 125.00
52 Norm Ullman 50.00 80.00
53 Chico Maki 25.00 50.00
54 Reg Fleming 25.00 50.00
55 Jim Neilson 25.00 50.00
56 Bruce MacGregor 25.00 50.00
57 Pat Stapleton 25.00 50.00
58 Matt Ravlich 25.00 50.00
59 Pierre Pilote 40.00 70.00
60 Eric Nesterenko 25.00 50.00
61 Doug Mohns 25.00 50.00
62 Stan Mikita 175.00 300.00
63 Alex Delvecchio 60.00 100.00
64 Ed Johnston 35.00 60.00
65 John Ferguson 35.00 60.00
66 John McKenzie 50.00 80.00

1967-68 Topps

The 1967-68 Topps set features 132 standard-size cards. Players on the six expansion teams (Los Angeles, Minnesota, Oakland, Philadelphia, Pittsburgh, and St. Louis) were not included until 1968-69. Bilingual backs feature a short biography, 1966-67 and career records. The backs are identical in format to the 1966-67 cards. The cards are grouped by team: Montreal (1-10/67-75), Toronto (11-20/76-83), New York (21-31/84-91), Boston (32-42/92-100), Detroit (43-52/101-108) and Chicago (53-63/109-117). The cards were printed in Canada. Rookie Cards include Jacques Lemaire, Derek Sanderson, Glen Sather, and Rogatien Vachon.

COMPLETE SET (132) 2,000.00 3,000.00
1 Gump Worsley 25.00 40.00
2 Dick Duff 6.00 10.00
3 Jacques Lemaire RC 40.00 80.00
4 Claude Larose 6.00 10.00
5 Gilles Tremblay 5.00 8.00
6 Terry Harper 5.00 8.00
7 Jacques Laperriere 6.00 10.00
8 Garry Monahan RC 5.00 8.00
9 Carol Vadnais RC 6.00 10.00
10 Ted Harris 5.00 8.00
11 Dave Keon 12.00 20.00
12 Pete Stemkowski 5.00 8.00
13 Allan Stanley 6.00 10.00
14 Ron Ellis 6.00 10.00
15 Mike Walton 6.00 10.00
16 Tim Horton 20.00 35.00
17 Brian Conacher RC 5.00 8.00
18 Bruce Gamble 6.00 10.00
19 Bob Pulford 6.00 10.00
20 Duane Rupp RC 5.00 8.00
21 Larry Jeffrey 5.00 8.00
22 Wayne Hillman 5.00 8.00
23 Don Marshall 6.00 10.00
24 Red Berenson 6.00 10.00
25 Phil Goyette 5.00 8.00
26 Camille Henry 5.00 8.00
27 Rod Seiling 5.00 8.00
28 Bob Nevin 6.00 10.00
29 Bernie Geoffrion 15.00 30.00
30 Reg Fleming 5.00 8.00
31 Jean Ratelle 9.00 15.00
32 Phil Esposito 40.00 75.00
33 Derek Sanderson RC 75.00 125.00
34 Eddie Shack 15.00 25.00
35 Ross Lonsberry RC 6.00 10.00
36 Fred Stanfield 5.00 8.00
37 Don Awrey UER 5.00 8.00
38 Glen Sather RC 18.00 30.00
39 John McKenzie 6.00 10.00
40 Tom Williams 5.00 8.00
41 Dallas Smith 5.00 8.00
42 Johnny Bucyk 12.00 20.00
43 Gordie Howe 90.00 150.00
44 Gary Jarrett RC 5.00 8.00
45 Dean Prentice 5.00 8.00
46 Bert Marshall 5.00 8.00
47 Gary Bergman 5.00 8.00
48 Roger Crozier 6.00 10.00
49 Howie Young 5.00 8.00
50 Doug Roberts RC 5.00 8.00
51 Alex Delvecchio 12.00 20.00
52 Floyd Smith 5.00 8.00
53 Doug Shelton RC 5.00 8.00
54 Gerry Goyer RC 5.00 8.00
55 Wayne Maki RC 5.00 8.00
56 Dennis Hull 6.00 10.00
57 Dave Dryden RC 9.00 15.00
58 Paul Terbenche RC 5.00 8.00
59 Gilles Marotte 5.00 8.00
60 Eric Nesterenko 6.00 10.00
61 Pat Stapleton 6.00 10.00
62 Pierre Pilote 6.00 10.00
63 Doug Mohns 5.00 8.00
64 Stan Mikita Triple 18.00 30.00
65 G.Hall/D.DeJordy 12.00 20.00
66 Checklist Card 150.00 250.00
67 Ralph Backstrom 6.00 10.00
68 Bobby Rousseau 5.00 8.00
69 John Ferguson 6.00 10.00
70 Yvan Cournoyer 18.00 30.00
71 Claude Provost 5.00 8.00
72 Henri Richard 15.00 25.00
73 J.C. Tremblay 6.00 10.00
74 Jean Beliveau 25.00 40.00
75 Rogatien Vachon RC 30.00 80.00
76 Johnny Bower 12.00 20.00
77 Wayne Carleton RC 5.00 8.00
78 Jim Pappin 5.00 8.00
79 Frank Mahovlich 15.00 25.00
80 Larry Hillman 5.00 8.00
81 Marcel Pronovost 6.00 10.00
82 Murray Oliver 5.00 8.00
83 George Armstrong 9.00 15.00
84 Harry Howell 6.00 10.00
85 Ed Giacomin 18.00 30.00
86 Gilles Villemure 6.00 10.00
87 Orland Kurtenbach 5.00 8.00
88 Vic Hadfield 6.00 10.00
89 Arnie Brown 5.00 8.00
90 Rod Gilbert 9.00 15.00
91 Jim Neilson 5.00 8.00
92 Bobby Orr 400.00 600.00
93 Skip Krake UER RC 5.00 8.00
94 Ted Green 6.00 10.00
95 Ed Westfall 6.00 10.00
96 Ed Johnston 6.00 10.00
97 Gary Doak RC 6.00 10.00
98 Ken Hodge 6.00 10.00
99 Gerry Cheevers 30.00 50.00
100 Ron Murphy 5.00 8.00
101 Norm Ullman 9.00 15.00
102 Bruce MacGregor 5.00 8.00
103 Paul Henderson 6.00 10.00
104 Jean-Guy Talbot 5.00 8.00
105 Bart Crashley RC 5.00 8.00
106 Roy Edwards RC 6.00 10.00
107 Jim Watson RC 5.00 8.00
108 Ted Hampson 5.00 8.00
109 Bill Orban RC 5.00 8.00
110 Geoffrey Powis RC 5.00 8.00
111 Chico Maki 5.00 8.00
112 Doug Jarrett 5.00 8.00
113 Bobby Hull 75.00 125.00
114 Stan Mikita 25.00 40.00
115 Denis DeJordy 6.00 10.00
116 Pit Martin 6.00 10.00
117 Ken Wharram 5.00 8.00
118 Bobby Orr Calder 150.00 300.00
119 Harry Howell Norris 5.00 8.00
120 Checklist Card 150.00 250.00
121 Harry Howell AS 5.00 8.00
122 Pierre Pilote AS 5.00 8.00
123 Ed Giacomin AS 9.00 15.00
124 Bobby Hull AS 50.00 80.00
125 Ken Wharram AS 5.00 8.00
126 Stan Mikita AS 15.00 25.00
127 Tim Horton AS 12.00 20.00
128 Bobby Orr AS 200.00 400.00
129 Glenn Hall AS 12.00 20.00
130 Don Marshall AS 5.00 8.00
131 Gordie Howe AS 60.00 100.00
132 Norm Ullman AS 12.00 20.00

1968-69 Topps

The 1968-69 Topps set consists of 132 standard-size cards featuring all 12 teams including the first cards of players from the six expansion teams. The fronts feature a horizontal format with the player in the foreground and an artistically rendered hockey scene in the background. The backs include a short biography, 1967-68 and career statistics as well as a cartoon-illustrated fact about the player. The cards are grouped by team: Boston (1-11), Chicago (12-22), Detroit (23-33), Los Angeles (34-44), Minnesota (45-55), Montreal (56-66), New York (67-77), Oakland (78-88), Philadelphia (89-99), Pittsburgh (100-110), St. Louis (111-120) and Toronto (122-132). With O-Pee-Chee printing cards for the Canadian market, text on back is English only. For the first time since 1960-61, Topps cards were printed in the U.S. The only Rookie Card of consequence is Bernie Parent.

COMPLETE SET (132) 450.00 750.00
1 Gerry Cheevers 12.00 20.00
2 Bobby Orr 150.00 250.00
3 Don Awrey UER 2.00 4.00
4 Ted Green 2.50 5.00
5 Johnny Bucyk 3.50 7.00
6 Derek Sanderson 15.00 25.00
7 Phil Esposito 18.00 30.00
8 Ken Hodge 2.50 5.00
9 John McKenzie 2.50 5.00
10 Fred Stanfield 2.00 4.00
11 Tom Williams 2.00 4.00
12 Denis DeJordy 2.50 5.00
13 Doug Jarrett 2.00 4.00
14 Gilles Marotte 2.00 4.00
15 Pat Stapleton 2.50 5.00
16 Bobby Hull 35.00 50.00
17 Chico Maki 2.00 4.00
18 Pit Martin 2.50 5.00
19 Doug Mohns 2.00 4.00
20 Stan Mikita 12.00 20.00
21 Jim Pappin 2.00 4.00
22 Ken Wharram 2.00 4.00
23 Roger Crozier 2.50 5.00
24 Bob Baun 2.50 5.00
25 Gary Bergman 2.00 4.00
26 Kent Douglas 2.00 4.00
27 Ron Harris 2.00 4.00
28 Alex Delvecchio 3.50 7.00
29 Gordie Howe 45.00 75.00
30 Bruce MacGregor 2.00 4.00
31 Frank Mahovlich 7.00 12.00
32 Dean Prentice 2.00 4.00
33 Pete Stemkowski 2.00 4.00
34 Terry Sawchuk 25.00 40.00
35 Larry Cahan 2.00 4.00
36 Real Lemieux RC 2.00 4.00
37 Bill White RC 3.00 6.00
38 Gord Labossiere 2.00 4.00
39 Ted Irvine 2.00 4.00
40 Eddie Joyal 2.00 4.00
41 Dale Rolfe RC 2.00 4.00
42 Lowell MacDonald RC 3.00 6.00
43 Skip Krake UER 2.00 4.00
44 Terry Gray 2.00 4.00
45 Cesare Maniago 2.50 5.00
46 Mike McMahon 2.00 4.00
47 Wayne Hillman 2.00 4.00
48 Larry Hillman 2.00 4.00
49 Bob Woytowich 2.00 4.00
50 Wayne Connelly 2.00 4.00
51 Claude Larose 2.00 4.00
52 Danny Grant UER 5.00 10.00
John Vanderburg pictured
53 Andre Boudrias 2.00 4.00
54 Ray Cullen RC 2.00 4.00
55 Parker MacDonald 2.00 4.00
56 Gump Worsley 6.00 10.00
57 Terry Harper 2.00 4.00
58 Jacques Laperriere 2.50 5.00
59 J.C. Tremblay 2.50 5.00
60 Ralph Backstrom 2.50 5.00
61 Jean Beliveau 9.00 15.00
62 Yvan Cournoyer 7.00 12.00
63 Jacques Lemaire 9.00 15.00
64 Henri Richard 7.00 12.00
65 Bobby Rousseau 2.00 4.00
66 Gilles Tremblay 2.00 4.00
67 Ed Giacomin 7.00 12.00
68 Arnie Brown 2.00 4.00
69 Harry Howell 2.50 5.00
70 Jim Neilson 2.00 4.00
71 Rod Seiling 2.00 4.00
72 Rod Gilbert 3.50 7.00
73 Phil Goyette 2.00 4.00
74 Vic Hadfield 2.50 5.00
75 Don Marshall 2.50 5.00
76 Bob Nevin 2.50 5.00
77 Jean Ratelle 3.50 7.00
78 Charlie Hodge 2.50 5.00
79 Bert Marshall 2.00 4.00
80 Billy Harris 2.00 4.00
81 Carol Vadnais 2.50 5.00
82 Howie Young 2.00 4.00
83 John Brenneman RC 2.00 4.00
84 Gerry Ehman 2.00 4.00
85 Ted Hampson 2.00 4.00
86 Bill Hicke 2.00 4.00
87 Gary Jarrett 2.00 4.00
88 Doug Roberts 2.00 4.00
89 Bernie Parent RC 40.00 60.00
90 Joe Watson 2.00 4.00
91 Ed Van Impe 2.00 4.00
92 Larry Zeidel 2.00 4.00
93 John Miszuk RC 2.00 4.00
94 Gary Dornhoefer 2.00 4.00
95 Leon Rochefort RC 2.00 4.00
96 Brit Selby 2.00 4.00
97 Forbes Kennedy 2.00 4.00
98 Ed Hoekstra 2.00 4.00
99 Garry Peters 2.00 4.00
100 Les Binkley RC 5.00 10.00
101 Leo Boivin 2.50 5.00
102 Earl Ingarfield 2.00 4.00
103 Lou Angotti 2.00 4.00
104 Andy Bathgate 3.00 6.00
105 Wally Boyer 2.00 4.00
106 Ken Schinkel 2.00 4.00
107 Ab McDonald 2.00 4.00
108 Charlie Burns 2.00 4.00
109 Val Fonteyne 2.00 4.00
110 Noel Price 2.00 4.00
111 Glenn Hall 6.00 10.00
112 Bob Plager RC 6.00 12.00
113 Jim Roberts 2.50 5.00
114 Red Berenson 2.00 4.00
115 Larry Keenan 2.00 4.00
116 Camille Henry 2.00 4.00
117 Gary Sabourin RC 2.00 4.00
118 Ron Schock 2.00 4.00
119 Gary Veneruzzo RC 2.00 4.00
120 Gerry Melnyk 2.00 4.00
121 Checklist Card 60.00 100.00
122 Johnny Bower 6.00 10.00
123 Tim Horton 8.00 15.00
124 Pierre Pilote 3.00 6.00
125 Marcel Pronovost 2.50 5.00
126 Ron Ellis 2.50 5.00
127 Paul Henderson 2.50 5.00
128 Dave Keon 4.00 7.00
129 Bob Pulford 2.50 5.00
130 Floyd Smith 2.00 4.00

131 Norm Ullman 3.00 6.00
132 Mike Walton 3.00 6.00

1969-70 Topps

The 1969-70 Topps set consists of 132 standard-size cards. The backs contain 1968-69 and career statistics, a short biography and a cartoon-illustrated fact about the player. Those players in this set who were also included in the insert set of stamps have a place on the card back for placing that player's stamp. This is not recommended as it would be considered a means of defacing the card and lowering its grade. The cards are grouped by team: Montreal (1-11), St. Louis (12-21), Boston (22-32), New York (33-43), Toronto (44-54), Detroit (55-65), Chicago (66-76), Oakland (77-87), Philadelphia (88-98), Los Angeles (99-109), Pittsburgh (110-120) and Minnesota (121-131). The only notable Rookie Card in the set is Serge Savard.

COMPLETE SET (132) 400.00 600.00
1 Gump Worsley 8.00 15.00
2 Ted Harris 1.50 3.00
3 Jacques Laperriere 2.00 4.00
4 Serge Savard RC 12.50 25.00
5 80 2.00 4.00
6 Yvan Cournoyer 2.50 5.00
7 John Ferguson 2.00 4.00
8 Jacques Lemaire 2.50 5.00
9 Bobby Rousseau 1.50 3.00
10 Jean Beliveau 7.00 12.00
11 Henri Richard 5.00 8.00
12 Glenn Hall 5.00 8.00
13 Bob Plager 1.50 3.00
14 Jim Roberts 1.50 3.00
15 Jean-Guy Talbot 2.00 4.00
16 Andre Boudrias 1.50 3.00
17 Camille Henry 1.50 3.00
18 Ab McDonald 1.50 3.00
19 Gary Sabourin 1.50 3.00
20 Red Berenson 1.50 3.00
21 Phil Goyette 1.50 3.00
22 Gerry Cheevers 6.00 10.00
23 Ted Green 1.50 3.00
24 Bobby Orr 75.00 125.00
25 Dallas Smith 1.50 3.00
26 Johnny Bucyk 3.00 6.00
27 Ken Hodge 2.00 4.00
28 John McKenzie 2.00 4.00
29 Ed Westfall 2.00 4.00
30 Phil Esposito 12.00 20.00
31 Derek Sanderson 9.00 15.00
32 Fred Stanfield 1.50 3.00
33 Ed Giacomin 6.00 10.00
34 Arnie Brown 1.50 3.00
35 Jim Neilson 1.50 3.00
36 Rod Seiling 1.50 3.00
37 Rod Gilbert 2.50 5.00
38 Vic Hadfield 2.00 4.00
39 Don Marshall 1.50 3.00
40 Bob Nevin 1.50 3.00
41 Ron Stewart 1.50 3.00
42 Jean Ratelle 2.50 5.00
43 Walt Tkaczuk RC 2.50 5.00
44 Bruce Gamble 2.00 4.00
45 Tim Horton 7.00 12.00
46 Ron Ellis 2.00 4.00
47 Paul Henderson 2.00 4.00
48 Brit Selby 1.50 3.00
49 Floyd Smith 1.50 3.00
50 Mike Walton 2.00 4.00
51 Dave Keon 2.50 5.00
52 Murray Oliver 1.50 3.00
53 Bob Pulford 2.00 4.00
54 Norm Ullman 2.50 5.00
55 Roger Crozier 2.00 4.00
56 Roy Edwards 2.00 4.00
57 Bob Baun 2.00 4.00
58 Gary Bergman 1.50 3.00
59 Carl Brewer 2.00 4.00
60 Wayne Connelly 1.50 3.00
61 Gordie Howe 30.00 50.00
62 Frank Mahovlich 5.00 8.00
63 Bruce MacGregor 1.50 3.00
64 Alex Delvecchio 3.00 6.00
65 Pete Stemkowski 1.50 3.00
66 Denis DeJordy 2.00 4.00
67 Doug Jarrett 1.50 3.00
68 Gilles Marotte 1.50 3.00
69 Pat Stapleton 2.00 4.00
70 Bobby Hull 25.00 40.00
71 Dennis Hull 2.00 4.00
72 Doug Mohns 1.50 3.00
73 Jim Pappin 1.50 3.00
74 Ken Wharram 1.50 3.00
75 Pit Martin 2.00 4.00
76 Stan Mikita 7.00 12.00
77 Charlie Hodge 2.00 4.00
78 Gary Smith 2.00 4.00
79 Harry Howell 2.00 4.00
80 Bert Marshall 1.50 3.00
81 Doug Roberts 1.50 3.00
82 Carol Vadnais 2.00 4.00
83 Gerry Ehman 1.50 3.00
84 Bill Hicke 1.50 3.00
85 Gary Jarrett 1.50 3.00
86 Ted Hampson 1.50 3.00
87 Earl Ingarfield 1.50 3.00
88 Doug Favell RC 5.00 10.00
89 Bernie Parent 10.00 20.00
90 Larry Hillman 1.50 3.00
91 Wayne Hillman 1.50 3.00
92 Ed Van Impe 1.50 3.00
93 Joe Watson 1.50 3.00
94 Gary Dornhoefer 2.00 4.00
95 Reg Fleming 1.50 3.00
96 Jean-Guy Gendron 1.50 3.00
97 Jim Johnson 1.50 3.00
98 Andre Lacroix 2.00 4.00
99 Gerry Desjardins RC 5.00 8.00
100 Dale Rolfe 1.50 3.00
101 Bill White 1.50 3.00
102 Bill Flett 1.50 3.00
103 Ted Irvine 1.50 3.00
104 Ross Lonsberry 1.50 3.00
105 Leon Rochefort 1.50 3.00
106 Eddie Shack 2.50 5.00
107 Dennis Hextall RC 2.50 5.00
108 Eddie Joyal 1.50 3.00
109 Gord Labossiere 1.50 3.00
110 Les Binkley 2.00 4.00
111 Tracy Pratt 1.50 3.00
112 Bryan Watson 1.50 3.00
113 Bob Woytowich 1.50 3.00
114 Keith McCreary 1.50 3.00
115 Dean Prentice 1.50 3.00
116 Glen Sather 2.00 4.00
117 Ken Schinkel 1.50 3.00
118 Wally Boyer 1.50 3.00
119 Val Fonteyne 1.50 3.00
120 Ron Schock 1.50 3.00
121 Cesare Maniago 2.00 4.00
122 Leo Boivin 2.00 4.00
123 Bob McCord 1.50 3.00
124 John Miszuk 1.50 3.00
125 Danny Grant UER 2.00 4.00
John Vanderburg pictured
126 Claude Larose 1.50 3.00
127 Jean-Paul Parise 2.00 4.00
128 Tom Williams 1.50 3.00
129 Charlie Burns 1.50 3.00
130 Ray Cullen 1.50 3.00
131 Danny O'Shea RC 1.50 3.00
132 Checklist Card 35.00 60.00

1970-71 Topps

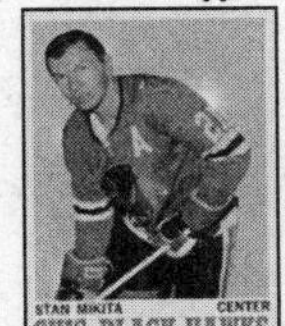

The 1970-71 Topps set consists of 132 standard-size cards. Card fronts have solid player backgrounds that differ in color according to team. The player's name, team and position are at the bottom. The backs feature the player's 1969-70 and career statistics as well as a short biography. Players from the expansion Buffalo Sabres and Vancouver Canucks are included. For the most part, cards are grouped by team. However, team names on front are updated on some cards to reflect transactions that occurred late in the off-season. Rookie Cards include Wayne Cashman, Brad Park and Gilbert Perreault.

COMPLETE SET (132) 300.00 400.00
1 Gerry Cheevers 6.00 15.00
2 Johnny Bucyk 2.00 5.00
3 Bobby Orr 30.00 75.00
4 Don Awrey .75 1.50
5 Fred Stanfield .75 1.50
6 John McKenzie 1.00 2.50
7 Wayne Cashman RC 4.00 8.00
8 Ken Hodge 1.00 2.50
9 Wayne Carleton .75 1.50
10 Garnet Bailey RC 1.00 2.00
11 Phil Esposito 10.00 20.00
12 Lou Angotti .75 1.50
13 Jim Pappin .75 1.50
14 Dennis Hull 1.00 2.50
15 Bobby Hull 20.00 40.00
16 Doug Mohns .75 1.50
17 Pat Stapleton 1.00 2.50
18 Pit Martin 1.00 2.50
19 Eric Nesterenko 1.00 2.50
20 Stan Mikita 6.00 12.00
21 Roy Edwards 1.00 2.50
22 Frank Mahovlich 2.50 6.00
23 Ron Harris .75 1.50
24 Bob Baun 1.00 2.50
25 Pete Stemkowski .75 1.50
26 Garry Unger 1.00 2.50
27 Bruce MacGregor .75 1.50
28 Larry Jeffrey .75 1.50
29 Gordie Howe 25.00 50.00
30 Billy Dea .75 1.50
31 Denis DeJordy 1.00 2.50
32 Matt Ravlich .75 1.50
33 Dave Amadio .75 1.50
34 Gilles Marotte .75 1.50
35 Eddie Shack 1.50 4.00
36 Bob Pulford 1.00 2.50
37 Ross Lonsberry 1.00 2.50
38 Gord Labossiere .75 1.50
39 Eddie Joyal .75 1.50
40 Gump Worsley 1.50 4.00
41 Bob McCord .75 1.50
42 Leo Boivin 1.00 2.50
43 Tom Reid RC .75 1.50
44 Charlie Burns .75 1.50
45 Bob Barlow .75 1.50
46 Bill Goldsworthy 1.00 2.50
47 Danny Grant 1.00 2.50
48 Norm Beaudin RC .75 1.50
49 Rogatien Vachon 3.00 8.00
50 Yvan Cournoyer 1.50 4.00
51 Serge Savard 1.50 4.00
52 Jacques Laperriere 1.00 2.50
53 Terry Harper .75 1.50
54 Ralph Backstrom 1.00 2.50
55 Jean Beliveau 5.00 10.00
56 Claude Larose UER .75 1.50
57 Jacques Lemaire 1.50 4.00
58 Peter Mahovlich 1.00 2.50
59 Tim Horton 6.00 10.00
60 Bob Nevin .75 1.50
61 Dave Balon .75 1.50
62 Vic Hadfield 1.00 2.50
63 Rod Gilbert 1.50 4.00
64 Ron Stewart .75 1.50
65 Ted Irvine .75 1.50
66 Arnie Brown .75 1.50
67 Brad Park RC 12.50 25.00
68 Ed Giacomin 1.50 4.00
69 Gary Smith 1.00 2.50
70 Carol Vadnais 1.00 2.50
71 Doug Roberts .75 1.50
72 Harry Howell 1.00 2.50
73 Joe Szura .75 1.50
74 Mike Laughton .75 1.50
75 Gary Jarrett .75 1.50
76 Bill Hicke .75 1.50
77 Paul Andrea RC .75 1.50
78 Bernie Parent 9.00 15.00
79 Joe Watson .75 1.50
80 Ed Van Impe .75 1.50
81 Larry Hillman .75 1.50
82 George Swarbrick .75 1.50
83 Bill Sutherland .75 1.50
84 Andre Lacroix 1.00 2.50
85 Gary Dornhoefer 1.00 2.50
86 Jean-Guy Gendron .75 1.50
87 Al Smith RC 1.00 2.50
88 Bob Woytowich .75 1.50
89 Duane Rupp .75 1.50
90 Jim Morrison .75 1.50
91 Ron Schock .75 1.50
92 Ken Schinkel .75 1.50
93 Keith McCreary .75 1.50
94 Bryan Hextall 1.00 2.50
95 Wayne Hicks RC .75 1.50
96 Gary Sabourin .75 1.50
97 Ernie Wakely RC 1.00 2.50
98 Bob Wall .75 1.50
99 Barclay Plager 1.00 2.50
100 Jean-Guy Talbot .75 1.50
101 Gary Veneruzzo .75 1.50
102 Tim Ecclestone .75 1.50
103 Red Berenson 1.00 2.50
104 Larry Keenan .75 1.50
105 Bruce Gamble 1.00 2.50
106 Jim Dorey .75 1.50
107 Mike Pelyk RC .75 1.50
108 Rick Ley .75 1.50
109 Mike Walton .75 1.50
110 Norm Ullman 1.50 4.00
111 Brit Selby .75 1.50
112 Garry Monahan .75 1.50
113 George Armstrong 1.50 4.00
114 Gary Doak .75 1.50
115 Darryl Sly RC .75 1.50
116 Wayne Maki .75 1.50
117 Orland Kurtenbach .75 1.50
118 Murray Hall .75 1.50
119 Marc Reaume .75 1.50
120 Pat Quinn 3.00 5.00
121 Andre Boudrias .75 1.50
122 Paul Popiel .75 1.50
123 Paul Terbenche .75 1.50
124 Howie Menard .75 1.50
125 Gerry Meehan RC 1.50 4.00
126 Skip Krake .75 1.50
127 Phil Goyette .75 1.50
128 Reg Fleming .75 1.50
129 Don Marshall 1.00 2.50
130 Bill Inglis RC .75 1.50
131 Gilbert Perreault RC 20.00 40.00
132 Checklist Card 30.00 60.00

1970-71 Topps/OPC Sticker Stamps

This set consists of 33 unnumbered, full-color sticker stamps measuring 2 1/2" by 3 1/2". The backs are blank. The checklist below is ordered alphabetically for convenience. The sticker cards were issued as an insert in the regular issue wax packs of the 1970-71 Topps hockey as well as in first series wax packs of 1970-71 O-Pee-Chee.

COMPLETE SET (33) 300.00 450.00
1 Jean Beliveau 15.00 30.00
2 Red Berenson 6.00 12.00
3 Wayne Carleton 6.00 12.00
4 Tim Ecclestone 6.00 12.00
5 Ron Ellis 6.00 12.00
6 Phil Esposito 15.00 30.00
7 Tony Esposito 15.00 40.00
8 Bill Flett 6.00 12.00
9 Ed Giacomin 10.00 20.00
10 Rod Gilbert 10.00 20.00
11 Danny Grant 6.00 12.00
12 Bill Hicke 6.00 12.00
13 Gordie Howe 20.00 50.00
14 Bobby Hull 15.00 40.00
15 Earl Ingarfield 6.00 12.00
16 Eddie Joyal 6.00 12.00
17 Dave Keon 15.00 30.00
18 Andre Lacroix 6.00 12.00
19 Jacques Laperriere 6.00 12.00
20 Jacques Lemaire 10.00 20.00
21 Frank Mahovlich 10.00 20.00
22 Keith McCreary 6.00 12.00
23 Stan Mikita 10.00 20.00
24 Bobby Orr 40.00 100.00
25 Jean-Paul Parise 6.00 12.00
26 Jean Ratelle 7.50 20.00
27 Derek Sanderson 12.50 25.00
28 Frank St.Marseille 6.00 12.00
29 Ron Schock 6.00 12.00
30 Garry Unger 6.00 12.00
31 Carol Vadnais 6.00 12.00
32 Ed Van Impe 6.00 12.00
33 Bob Woytowich 6.00 12.00

1971-72 Topps

The 1971-72 Topps set consists of 132 standard-size cards. For the first time, Topps included the player's NHL year-by-year career record on back. A short player biography and a cartoon-illustrated fact about the player also appear on back. A League Leaders (1-6) subset is exclusive to the Topps set of this year. The only noteworthy Rookie Card is of Ken Dryden. An additional key card in the set is Gordie Howe (70). Howe does not have a basic card in the 1971-72 O-Pee-Chee set.

COMPLETE SET (132) 200.00 350.00
1 Espo/Bucyk/B.Hull LL 12.00 30.00
2 Orr/Espo/Bucyk LL 12.00 30.00
3 Espo/Orr/Bucyk LL 6.00 15.00
4 Espo/EJ/Cheev/Giaco LL 4.00 10.00
5 Giaco/Espo/Maniago LL 2.50 6.00
6 Plante/Giaco/T.Espo LL 5.00 12.00
7 Fred Stanfield .60 1.50
8 Mike Robitaille RC .60 1.50
9 Vic Hadfield .75 2.00
10 Jacques Plante 6.00 15.00
11 Bill White .60 1.50
12 Andre Boudrias .60 1.50
13 Jim Lorentz .60 1.50
14 Arnie Brown .60 1.50
15 Yvan Cournoyer 1.25 3.00
16 Bryan Hextall .75 2.00
17 Gary Croteau .60 1.50
18 Gilles Villemure .75 2.00
19 Serge Bernier RC .75 2.00
20 Phil Esposito 5.00 12.00
21 Charlie Burns .60 1.50
22 Doug Barrie RC .60 1.50
23 Eddie Joyal .60 1.50
24 Rosaire Paiement .60 1.50
25 Pat Stapleton .75 2.00
26 Garry Unger .75 2.00
27 Al Smith .75 2.00
28 Bob Woytowich .60 1.50
29 Marc Tardif .75 2.00
30 Norm Ullman 1.25 3.00
31 Tom Williams .60 1.50
32 Ted Harris .60 1.50
33 Andre Lacroix .75 2.00
34 Mike Byers .60 1.50
35 Johnny Bucyk 1.50 4.00
36 Roger Crozier .75 2.00
37 Alex Delvecchio 1.25 3.00
38 Frank St.Marseille .60 1.50
39 Pit Martin .75 2.00
40 Brad Park 4.00 10.00
41 Greg Polis RC .60 1.50
42 Orland Kurtenbach .60 1.50
43 Jim McKenny RC .60 1.50
44 Bob Nevin .60 1.50
45 Ken Dryden RC 75.00 125.00
46 Carol Vadnais .75 2.00
47 Bill Flett .60 1.50
48 Jim Johnson .60 1.50
49 Al Hamilton .60 1.50
50 Bobby Hull 25.00 40.00
51 Chris Bordeleau RC .60 1.50
52 Tim Ecclestone .60 1.50
53 Rod Seiling .60 1.50
54 Gerry Cheevers 2.50 6.00
55 Bill Goldsworthy .75 2.00
56 Ron Schock .60 1.50
57 Jim Dorey .60 1.50
58 Wayne Maki .60 1.50
59 Terry Harper .60 1.50
60 Gilbert Perreault 6.00 15.00
61 Ernie Hicke RC .60 1.50
62 Wayne Hillman .60 1.50
63 Denis DeJordy .75 2.00
64 Ken Schinkel .60 1.50
65 Derek Sanderson 2.50 6.00
66 Barclay Plager .75 2.00
67 Paul Henderson .75 2.00
68 Jude Drouin .60 1.50
69 Keith Magnuson .75 2.00
70 Gordie Howe 30.00 60.00

Card	Low	High
71 Jacques Lemaire	1.25	3.00
72 Doug Favell	.75	2.00
73 Bert Marshall	.60	1.50
74 Gerry Meehan	.75	2.00
75 Walt Tkaczuk	.75	2.00
76 Bob Berry RC	1.25	3.00
77 Syl Apps RC	1.25	3.00
78 Tom Webster	.75	2.00
79 Danny Grant	.75	2.00
80 Dave Keon	1.25	3.00
81 Ernie Wakely	.75	2.00
82 John McKenzie	.75	2.00
83 Doug Roberts	.60	1.50
84 Peter Mahovlich	.75	2.00
85 Dennis Hull	.75	2.00
86 Juha Widing RC	.60	1.50
87 Gary Doak	.60	1.50
88 Phil Goyette	.60	1.50
89 Gary Dornhoefer	.75	2.00
90 Ed Giacomin	1.25	3.00
91 Red Berenson	.75	2.00
92 Mike Pelyk	.60	1.50
93 Gary Jarrett	.60	1.50
94 Bob Pulford	.75	2.00
95 Dale Tallon	.75	2.00
96 Eddie Shack	1.25	3.00
97 Jean Ratelle	1.25	3.00
98 Jim Pappin	.60	1.50
99 Roy Edwards	.75	2.00
100 Bobby Orr	25.00	50.00
101 Ted Hampson	.60	1.50
102 Mickey Redmond	1.25	3.00
103 Bob Plager	.75	2.00
104 Bruce Gamble	.75	2.00
105 Frank Mahovlich	1.50	4.00
106 Tony Featherstone RC	.60	1.50
107 Tracy Pratt	.60	1.50
108 Ralph Backstrom	.75	2.00
109 Murray Hall	.60	1.50
110 Tony Esposito	8.00	20.00
111 Checklist Card	30.00	60.00
112 Jim Neilson	.60	1.50
113 Ron Ellis	.75	2.00
114 Bobby Clarke	12.00	30.00
115 Ken Hodge	.75	2.00
116 Jim Roberts	.75	2.00
117 Cesare Maniago	.75	2.00
118 Jean Pronovost	.75	2.00
119 Gary Bergman	.60	1.50
120 Henri Richard	1.50	4.00
121 Ross Lonsberry	.60	1.50
122 Pat Quinn	.75	2.00
123 Rod Gilbert	1.25	3.00
124 Gary Smith	.75	2.00
125 Stan Mikita	4.00	10.00
126 Ed Van Impe	.60	1.50
127 Wayne Connelly	.60	1.50
128 Dennis Hextall	.75	2.00
129 Wayne Cashman	1.25	3.00
130 J.C. Tremblay	.75	2.00
131 Bernie Parent	1.50	4.00
132 Dunc McCallum RC	2.50	6.00

1972-73 Topps

The 1972-73 production marked Topps' largest set to date at 176 standard-size cards. Expansion plays a part in the increase as the Atlanta Flames and New York Islanders join the league. Tan borders include team name down the left side. A tan colored bar that crosses the bottom portion of the player photo includes the player's name and team logo. The back contains the year-by-year NHL career record of the player, a short biography and a cartoon illustrated fact about the player. The key cards in the set are the first Topps cards of Marcel Dionne and Guy Lafleur. The set was printed on two sheets of 132 cards creating 88 double-printed cards. The double prints are noted in the checklist below by DP. Topps gives collectors a look at the various NHL hardware in the Trophy subset (170-176).

Card	Low	High
COMPLETE SET (176)	200.00	400.00
1 Bruins Team DP	3.00	6.00
2 Playoff Game 1	.40	1.00
3 Playoff Game 2	.40	1.00
4 Playoff Game 3	.40	1.00
5 Playoff Game 4 DP	.25	.50
6 Playoff Game 5 DP	.40	1.00
7 Playoff Game 6 DP	.25	.50
8 Stanley Cup Trophy	2.50	5.00
9 Ed Van Impe DP	.25	.50
10 Yvan Cournoyer DP	.60	1.50
11 Syl Apps DP	.60	1.50
12 Bill Plager RC	.60	1.50
13 Ed Johnston DP	.25	.50
14 Walt Tkaczuk	.50	1.25
15 Dale Tallon DP	.25	.50
16 Gerry Meehan	.50	1.25
17 Reggie Leach	1.50	3.00
18 Marcel Dionne DP	5.00	10.00
19 Andre Dupont RC	.60	1.50
20 Tony Esposito	6.00	12.00
21 Bob Berry DP	.25	.50
22 Craig Cameron	.40	1.00
23 Ted Harris	.40	1.00
24 Jacques Plante	6.00	12.00
25 Jacques Lemaire DP	.60	1.50
26 Simon Nolet DP	.25	.50
27 Keith McCreary DP	.25	.50
28 Duane Rupp	.40	1.00
29 Wayne Cashman	.60	1.50
30 Brad Park	3.00	6.00
31 Roger Crozier	.50	1.25
32 Wayne Maki	.40	1.00
33 Tim Ecclestone	.40	1.00
34 Rick Smith	.40	1.00
35 Garry Unger DP	.25	.50
36 Serge Bernier DP	.25	.50
37 Brian Glennie	.40	1.00
38 Gerry Desjardins DP	.25	.50
39 Danny Grant	.50	1.25
40 Bill White DP	.25	.50
41 Gary Dornhoefer DP	.25	.50
42 Peter Mahovlich	.50	1.25
43 Greg Polis DP	.25	.50
44 Larry Hale DP RC	.25	.50
45 Dallas Smith	.40	1.00
46 Orland Kurtenbach DP	.25	.50
47 Steve Atkinson	.40	1.00
48 Joey Johnston DP	.25	.50
49 Gary Bergman	.40	1.00
50 Jean Ratelle	.60	1.50
51 Rogatien Vachon DP	.60	1.50
52 Phil Roberto DP	.25	.50
53 Brian Spencer DP	.25	.50
54 Jim McKenny DP	.25	.50
55 Gump Worsley	.60	1.50
56 Stan Mikita DP	2.50	5.00
57 Guy Lapointe	.50	1.25
58 Lew Morrison DP	.25	.50
59 Ron Schock DP	.25	.50
60 Johnny Bucyk	1.25	2.50
61 Espo/Hadf/B.Hull LL	6.00	10.00
62 Orr/Espo/Ratelle LL DP	6.00	12.00
63 Espo/Orr/Ratelle LL DP	6.00	12.00
64 Espo/Villem/Worsley LL	3.00	6.00
65 Wtsn/Magn/Dorn LL	.40	1.00
66 Jim Neilson	.40	1.00
67 Nick Libett DP	.25	.50
68 Jim Lorentz	.40	1.00
69 Gilles Meloche RC	3.00	6.00
70 Pat Stapleton	.50	1.25
71 Frank St.Marseille DP	.25	.50
72 Butch Goring	.50	1.25
73 Paul Henderson DP	.25	.50
74 Doug Favell	.50	1.25
75 Jocelyn Guevremont DP	.25	.50
76 Tom Miller RC	.40	1.00
77 Bill MacMillan RC	.40	1.00
78 Doug Mohns	.40	1.00
79 Guy Lafleur DP	10.00	20.00
80 Rod Gilbert DP	.60	1.50
81 Gary Doak	.40	1.00
82 Dave Burrows DP RC	.25	.50
83 Gary Croteau	.40	1.00
84 Tracy Pratt DP	.25	.50
85 Carol Vadnais DP	.25	.50
86 Jacques Caron DP RC	.40	1.00
87 Keith Magnuson	.75	2.00
88 Dave Keon	.60	1.50
89 Mike Corrigan	.40	1.00
90 Bobby Clarke	8.00	15.00
91 Dunc Wilson DP	.25	.50
92 Gerry Hart RC	.40	1.00
93 Lou Nanne	.50	1.25
94 Checklist 1-176 DP	15.00	25.00
95 Red Berenson DP	.25	.50
96 Bob Plager	.50	1.25
97 Jim Rutherford RC	3.00	6.00
98 Rick Foley DP RC	.25	.50
99 Pit Martin DP	.25	.50
100 Bobby Orr DP	20.00	50.00
101 Stan Gilbertson	.40	1.00
102 Barry Wilkins	.40	1.00
103 Terry Crisp DP	.25	.50
104 Cesare Maniago DP	.25	.50
105 Marc Tardif	.40	1.00
106 Don Luce DP	.25	.50
107 Mike Pelyk	.40	1.00
108 Juha Widing DP	.25	.50
109 Phil Myre DP RC	1.50	3.00
110 Vic Hadfield	.50	1.25
111 Arnie Brown DP	.25	.50
112 Ross Lonsberry DP	.25	.50
113 Dick Redmond	.40	1.00
114 Gary Smith	.50	1.25
115 Bill Goldsworthy	.50	1.25
116 Bryan Watson	.40	1.00
117 Dave Balon DP	.25	.50
118 Bill Mikkelson DP RC	.25	.50
119 Terry Harper DP	.25	.50
120 Gilbert Perreault DP	3.00	6.00
121 Tony Esposito AS1	3.00	6.00
122 Bobby Orr AS1	12.00	20.00
123 Brad Park AS1	1.50	3.00
124 Phil Esposito AS1	2.50	5.00
125 Rod Gilbert AS1	.40	1.00
126 Bobby Hull AS1	9.00	15.00
127 Ken Dryden AS2 DP	8.00	20.00
128 Bill White AS2 DP	.25	.50
129 Pat Stapleton AS2 DP	.25	.50
130 Jean Ratelle AS2 DP	.60	1.50
131 Yvan Cournoyer AS2 DP	.60	1.50
132 Vic Hadfield AS2 DP	.25	.50
133 Ralph Backstrom DP	.25	.50
134 Bob Baun DP	.25	.50
135 Fred Stanfield DP	.25	.50
136 Barclay Plager DP	.25	.50
137 Gilles Villemure	.50	1.25
138 Ron Harris DP	.25	.50
139 Bill Flett DP	.25	.50
140 Frank Mahovlich	2.00	4.00
141 Alex Delvecchio DP	.60	1.50
142 Paul Popiel	.40	1.00
143 Jean Pronovost DP	.25	.50
144 Denis DeJordy DP	.25	.50
145 Richard Martin DP	1.50	3.00
146 Ivan Boldirev RC	.60	1.50
147 Jack Egers RC	.40	1.00
148 Jim Pappin	.40	1.00
149 Rod Seiling	.40	1.00
150 Phil Esposito	5.00	10.00
151 Gary Edwards	.50	1.25
152 Ron Ellis DP	.25	.50
153 Jude Drouin	.40	1.00
154 Ernie Hicke DP	.25	.50
155 Mickey Redmond	.60	1.50
156 Joe Watson DP	.25	.50
157 Bryan Hextall	.40	1.00
158 Andre Boudrias	.40	1.00
159 Ed Westfall	.50	1.25
160 Ken Dryden	18.00	30.00
161 Rene Robert DP RC	1.00	2.50
162 Bert Marshall DP	.25	.50
163 Gary Sabourin	.40	1.00
164 Dennis Hull	.50	1.25
165 Ed Giacomin DP	.60	1.50
166 Ken Hodge	.50	1.25
167 Gilles Marotte DP	.25	.50
168 Norm Ullman DP	.60	1.50
169 Barry Gibbs RC	.40	1.00
170 Art Ross Trophy	.60	1.50
171 Hart Memorial Trophy	.60	1.50
172 James Norris Trophy	.60	1.50
173 Vezina Trophy DP	.60	1.50
174 Calder Trophy DP	.60	1.50
175 Lady Byng Trophy DP	.60	1.50
176 Conn Smythe Trophy DP	.60	1.50

1973-74 Topps

Once again increasing in size, the 1973-74 Topps set consists of 198 standard-size cards. The fronts of the cards have distinct colored borders including blue and green. This differs from O-Pee-Chee which used red borders for cards 1-198. The backs contain the player's 1972-73 season record, career numbers, a short biography and a cartoon-illustrated fact about the player. Team cards (92-107) give team and player records on the back. Since the set was printed on two 132-card sheets, there are 66 double-printed cards. These double prints are noted in the checklist below by DP. Rookie Cards include Bill Barber, Billy Smith and Dave Schultz. Ken Dryden (10) is only in the Topps set.

Card	Low	High
COMPLETE SET (198)	125.00	200.00
1 P.Espo/MacLeish LL	1.25	3.00
2 P.Espo/B.Clarke LL	1.25	3.00
3 P.Espo/B.Clarke LL	1.25	3.00
4 K.Dryden/T.Espo LL	2.50	6.00
5 D.Schultz/Schoenfeld LL	1.25	3.00
6 P.Espo/MacLeish LL	1.25	3.00
7 Paul Henderson DP	.20	.50
8 Gregg Sheppard DP UER	.20	.50
9 Rod Seiling DP	.20	.50
10 Ken Dryden	25.00	40.00
11 Jean Pronovost DP	.20	.50
12 Dick Redmond	.30	.75
13 Keith McCreary DP	.20	.50
14 Ted Harris DP	.20	.50
15 Garry Unger	.40	1.00
16 Neil Komadoski RC	.30	.75
17 Marcel Dionne	6.00	10.00
18 Ernie Hicke DP	.20	.50
19 Andre Boudrias	.30	.75
20 Bill Flett	.30	.75
21 Marshall Johnston	.30	.75
22 Gerry Meehan	.30	.75
23 Ed Johnston DP	.20	.50
24 Serge Savard	.50	1.25
25 Walt Tkaczuk	.40	1.00
26 Johnny Bucyk	.75	2.00
27 Dave Burrows	.30	.75
28 Cliff Koroll	.30	.75
29 Rey Comeau DP	.20	.50
30 Barry Gibbs	.30	.75
31 Wayne Stephenson	.40	1.00
32 Dan Maloney DP	.20	.50
33 Henry Boucha DP	.30	.75
34 Gerry Hart	.30	.75
35 Bobby Schmautz	.30	.75
36 Ross Lonsberry DP	.20	.50
37 Ted McAneeley	.30	.75
38 Don Luce DP	.20	.50
39 Jim McKenny DP	.20	.50
40 Frank Mahovlich	.50	1.25
41 Bill Fairbairn	.30	.75
42 Dallas Smith	.30	.75
43 Bryan Hextall	.30	.75
44 Keith Magnuson	.40	1.00
45 Dan Bouchard	.40	1.00
46 Jean-Paul Parise DP	.20	.50
47 Barclay Plager	.40	1.00
48 Mike Corrigan	.30	.75
49 Nick Libett DP	.20	.50
50 Bobby Clarke	7.00	12.00
51 Bert Marshall DP	.20	.50
52 Craig Patrick	.40	1.00
53 Richard Lemieux	.30	.75
54 Tracy Pratt DP	.20	.50
55 Ron Ellis DP	.20	.50
56 Jacques Lemaire	.50	1.25
57 Steve Vickers DP	.20	.50
58 Carol Vadnais	.30	.75
59 Jim Rutherford DP	.20	.50
60 Dennis Hull	.40	1.00
61 Pat Quinn DP	.20	.50
62 Bill Goldsworthy DP	.30	.75
63 Fran Huck RC	.30	.75
64 Rogatien Vachon DP	.40	1.00
65 Gary Bergman DP	.20	.50
66 Bernie Parent	.50	1.25
67 Ed Westfall	.40	1.00
68 Ivan Boldirev	.40	1.00
69 Don Tannahill DP	.20	.50
70 Gilbert Perreault DP	3.00	6.00
71 Mike Pelyk DP	.20	.50
72 Guy Lafleur DP	7.50	15.00
73 Jean Ratelle	.50	1.25
74 Gilles Gilbert DP RC	2.00	4.00
75 Greg Polis	.30	.75
76 Doug Jarrett DP	.20	.50
77 Phil Myre DP	.20	.50
78 Fred Harvey DP	.20	.50
79 Jack Egers	.30	.75
80 Terry Harper	.30	.75
81 Bill Barber RC	6.00	10.00
82 Roy Edwards DP	.20	.50
83 Brian Spencer	.40	1.00
84 Reggie Leach DP	.30	.75
85 Dave Keon	.50	1.25
86 Jim Schoenfeld	.75	2.00
87 Henri Richard DP	.40	1.00
88 Rod Gilbert DP	.40	1.00
89 Don Marcotte DP	.20	.50
90 Tony Esposito	3.00	6.00
91 Joe Watson	.30	.75
92 Flames Team	.75	1.50
93 Bruins Team	.75	1.50
94 Sabres Team DP	.75	1.50
95 Golden Seals Team DP	.75	1.50
96 Blackhawks Team	.75	1.50
97 Red Wings Team DP	.75	1.50
98 Kings Team DP	.75	1.50
99 North Stars Team	.75	1.50
100 Canadiens Team	.75	1.50
101 Islanders Teams	.75	1.50
102 Rangers Team DP	.75	1.50
103 Flyers Team DP	.75	1.50
104 Penguins Team	.75	1.50
105 Blues Team	.75	1.50
106 Maple Leafs Team	.75	1.50
107 Canucks Team	.75	1.50
108 Roger Crozier DP	.20	.50
109 Tom Reid	.30	.75
110 Hilliard Graves RC	.30	.75
111 Don Lever	.40	1.00
112 Jim Pappin	.30	.75
113 Ron Schock DP	.20	.50
114 Gerry Desjardins	.40	1.00
115 Yvan Cournoyer DP	.30	.75
116 Checklist Card	12.00	20.00
117 Bob Leiter	.30	.75
118 Ab DeMarco	.30	.75
119 Doug Favell	.40	1.00
120 Phil Esposito	3.00	6.00
121 Mike Robitaille	.30	.75
122 Real Lemieux	.30	.75
123 Jim Neilson	.30	.75
124 Tim Ecclestone DP	.20	.50
125 Jude Drouin	.30	.75
126 Gary Smith DP	.20	.50
127 Walt McKechnie	.30	.75
128 Lowell MacDonald	.30	.75
129 Dale Tallon DP	.20	.50
130 Billy Harris RC	.40	1.00
131 Randy Manery DP	.20	.50
132 Darryl Sittler DP	3.00	6.00
133 Ken Hodge	.40	1.00
134 Bob Plager	.40	1.00
135 Rick MacLeish	.75	2.00
136 Dennis Hextall	.30	.75
137 Jacques Laperriere DP	.30	.75
138 Butch Goring	.40	1.00
139 Rene Robert	.40	1.00
140 Ed Giacomin	.50	1.25
141 Alex Delvecchio DP	.30	.75
142 Jocelyn Guevremont	.30	.75
143 Joey Johnston	.30	.75
144 Bryan Watson DP	.20	.50
145 Stan Mikita	3.00	5.00
146 Cesare Maniago	.40	1.00
147 Craig Cameron	.30	.75
148 Norm Ullman DP	.30	.75
149 Dave Schultz RC	6.00	12.00
150 Bobby Orr	18.00	30.00
151 Phil Roberto	.30	.75
152 Curt Bennett RC	.30	.75
153 Gilles Villemure DP	.20	.50
154 Chuck Lefley RC	.30	.75
155 Richard Martin	1.00	2.50
156 Juha Widing	.30	.75
157 Orland Kurtenbach	.30	.75

Card	Low	High
158 Bill Collins DP	.20	.50
159 Bob Stewart RC	.30	.75
160 Syl Apps	.40	1.00
161 Danny Grant	.40	1.00
162 Billy Smith RC	15.00	25.00
163 Brian Glennie	.30	.75
164 Pit Martin DP	.20	.50
165 Brad Park	2.00	4.00
166 Wayne Cashman DP	.30	.75
167 Gary Dornhoefer	.30	.75
168 Steve Durbano RC	.30	.75
169 Jacques Richard	.30	.75
170 Guy Lapointe	.40	1.00
171 Jim Lorentz	.30	.75
172 Bob Berry DP	.20	.50
173 Dennis Kearns	.30	.75
174 Red Berenson	.40	1.00
175 Gilles Meloche DP	.20	.50
176 Al McDonough	.30	.75
177 Dennis O'Brien RC	.30	.75
178 Germaine Gagnon UER DP	.20	.50
179 Rick Kehoe DP	.20	.50
180 Bill White	.30	.75
181 Vic Hadfield DP	.20	.50
182 Derek Sanderson	1.50	3.00
183 Andre Dupont DP	.20	.50
184 Gary Sabourin	.30	.75
185 Larry Romanchych RC	.30	.75
186 Peter Mahovlich	.40	1.00
187 Dave Dryden	.40	1.00
188 Gilles Marotte	.30	.75
189 Bobby Lalonde	.30	.75
190 Mickey Redmond	.40	1.00
191 Series A	.30	.75
192 Series B	.30	.75
193 Series C	.30	.75
194 Series D	.30	.75
195 Series E	.30	.75
196 Series F	.30	.75
197 Series G	.30	.75
198 Canadiens Champs	1.00	2.50

1973-74 Topps Team Stickers

Card	Low	High
COMPLETE SET (22)	50.00	100.00
1 Atlanta Flames/Sabres	2.00	5.00
2 Boston Bruins/Penguins	2.00	5.00
3 Boston Bruins/Rangers	2.00	5.00
4 Buffalo Sabres/Islanders	2.00	5.00
5 California Golden Seals/Blues	2.00	5.00
6 Chicago Blackhawks/Flames	2.00	5.00
7 Detroit Red Wings/Golden Seals	2.00	5.00
8 Detroit Red Wings/North Stars	2.00	5.00
9 Los Angeles Kings/Maple Leafs	2.00	5.00
10 Minnesota North Stars/Canadiens	2.00	5.00
11 Montreal Canadiens/Maple Leafs	2.00	5.00
12 Montreal Canadiens/Red Wings	2.00	5.00
13 New York Islanders/Bruins	2.00	5.00
14 New York Rangers/Black Hawks	2.00	5.00
15 New York Rangers/Canucks	2.00	5.00
16 Philadelphia Flyers/Red Wings	2.00	5.00
17 Pittsburgh Penguins/Black Hawks	2.00	5.00
18 St. Louis Blues/Canadiens	2.00	5.00
19 Toronto Maple Leafs/Bruins	2.00	5.00
20 Toronto Maple Leafs/Flyers	2.00	5.00
21 Vancouver Canucks/Rangers	2.00	5.00
22 NHL Logo/Kings	2.00	5.00

1974-75 Topps

Topps produced a set of 264 standard-size cards for 1974-75. Design of card fronts offers a hockey stick down the left side. The team name, player name and team logo appear at the bottom in a border that features one of the team colors. The backs feature the player's 1973-74 and career statistics, a short biography and a cartoon-illustrated fact about the player. Players from the 1974-75 expansion Washington Capitals and Kansas City Scouts (presently New Jersey Devils) appear in this set. The set marks the return of coach cards, including Don Cherry and Scotty Bowman.

Card	Low	High
COMPLETE SET (264)	125.00	200.00
1 P.Espo/Goldsworthy LL	1.50	3.00
2 B.Orr/D.Hextall LL	3.00	5.00
3 P.Espo/B.Clarke LL	2.00	4.00
4 D.Favell/B.Parent LL	.60	1.50
5 B.Watson/D.Schultz LL	.25	.60
6 M.Redmond/R.Mac LL	.25	.60
7 Gary Bromley RC	.30	.75
8 Bill Barber	2.00	4.00
9 Emile Francis CO	.25	.60
10 Gilles Gilbert	.60	1.50
11 John Davidson RC	4.00	8.00
12 Ron Ellis	.40	1.00
13 Syl Apps	.25	.60
14 Richard/Lysiak/McCreary TL	.25	.60
15 Dan Bouchard	.30	.75
16 Ivan Boldirev	.30	.75
17 Gary Coalter RC	.25	.60
18 Bob Berry	.25	.60
19 Red Berenson	.30	.75
20 Stan Mikita	2.00	4.00
21 Fred Shero CO RC	1.25	2.50
22 Gary Smith	.30	.75
23 Bill Mikkelson	.25	.60
24 Jacques Lemaire UER	.60	1.50
25 Gilbert Perreault	2.00	4.00
26 Cesare Maniago	.30	.75
27 Bobby Schmautz	.25	.60
28 Espo/Orr/Bucyk TL	4.00	8.00
29 Steve Vickers	.30	.75
30 Lowell MacDonald	.25	.60
31 Fred Stanfield	.25	.60
32 Ed Westfall	.30	.75
33 Curt Bennett	.25	.60
34 Bep Guidolin CO	.25	.60
35 Cliff Koroll	.25	.60
36 Gary Croteau	.25	.60
37 Mike Corrigan	.25	.60
38 Henry Boucha	.25	.60
39 Ron Low	.30	.75
40 Darryl Sittler	2.50	5.00
41 Tracy Pratt	.25	.60
42 R.Martin/R.Robert TL	.25	.60
43 Larry Carriere	.25	.60
44 Gary Dornhoefer	.30	.75
45 Denis Herron RC	1.25	2.50
46 Doug Favell	.30	.75
47 Dave Gardner RC	.25	.60
48 Morris Mott RC	.25	.60
49 Marc Boileau CO	.25	.60
50 Brad Park	1.50	3.00
51 Bob Leiter	.25	.60
52 Tom Reid	.25	.60
53 Serge Savard	.60	1.50
54 Checklist 1-132 UER	7.00	12.00
55 Terry Harper	.25	.60
56 Johnston/McKechnie TL	.25	.60
57 Guy Charron	.25	.60
58 Pit Martin	.25	.60
59 Chris Evans	.25	.60
60 Bernie Parent	.60	1.50
61 Jim Lorentz	.25	.60
62 Dave Kryskow RC	.25	.60
63 Lou Angotti CO	.25	.60
64 Bill Flett	.25	.60
65 Vic Hadfield	.30	.75
66 Wayne Merrick RC	.25	.60
67 Andre Dupont	.25	.60
68 Tom Lysiak RC	.60	1.50
69 Pappin/Mikita/Bord TL	.25	.60
70 Guy Lapointe	.30	.75
71 Gerry O'Flaherty	.25	.60
72 Marcel Dionne	3.00	6.00
73 Butch Deadmarsh RC	.50	1.25
74 Butch Goring	.30	.75
75 Keith Magnuson	.25	.60
76 Red Kelly CO	.25	.60
77 Pete Stemkowski	.25	.60
78 Jim Roberts	.25	.60
79 Don Luce	.25	.60
80 Don Awrey	.25	.60
81 Rick Kehoe	.30	.75
82 Billy Smith	3.00	6.00
83 Jean-Paul Parise	.25	.60
84 Redmond/Dionne/Hog TL	.25	.60
85 Ed Van Impe	.25	.60
86 Randy Manery	.25	.60
87 Barclay Plager	.30	.75
88 Inge Hammarstrom RC	.25	.60
89 Ab DeMarco	.25	.60
90 Bill White	.25	.60
91 Al Arbour CO	.60	1.50
92 Bob Stewart	.25	.60
93 Jack Egers	.25	.60
94 Don Lever	.25	.60
95 Reggie Leach	.30	.75
96 Dennis O'Brien	.25	.60
97 Peter Mahovlich	.30	.75
98 Goring/St.Marseille/Kozak TL	.25	.60
99 Gerry Meehan	.25	.60
100 Bobby Orr	15.00	30.00
101 Jean Potvin RC	.25	.60
102 Rod Seiling	.25	.60
103 Keith McCreary	.25	.60
104 Phil Maloney CO RC	.25	.60
105 Denis Dupere	.25	.60
106 Steve Durbano	.25	.60
107 Bob Plager UER	.30	.75
108 Chris Oddleifson RC	.25	.60
109 Jim Neilson	.25	.60
110 Jean Pronovost	.30	.75
111 Don Kozak RC	.25	.60
112 Goldsworthy/Grant/Hex	.30	.75
113 Jim Pappin	.25	.60
114 Richard Lemieux	.25	.60
115 Dennis Hextall	.25	.60
116 Bill Hogaboam	.25	.60
117 Canucks Leaders	.25	.60
118 Jimmy Anderson CO	.25	.60
119 Walt Tkaczuk	.30	.75
120 Mickey Redmond	.30	.75
121 Jim Schoenfeld	.60	1.50
122 Jocelyn Guevremont	.25	.60
123 Bob Nystrom	.60	1.50
124 Cour/F.Mahov/Larose TL	1.00	2.00
125 Lew Morrison	.25	.60
126 Terry Murray	.30	.75
127 Richard Martin AS	.30	.75
128 Ken Hodge AS	.25	.60
129 Phil Esposito AS	1.25	2.50
130 Bobby Orr AS	7.00	12.00
131 Brad Park AS	.75	2.00
132 Gilles Gilbert AS	.25	.60
133 Lowell MacDonald AS	.25	.60
134 Bill Goldsworthy AS	.25	.60
135 Bobby Clarke AS	2.00	4.00
136 Bill White AS	.25	.60
137 Dave Burrows AS	.25	.60
138 Bernie Parent AS	.60	1.50
139 Jacques Richard	.25	.60
140 Yvan Cournoyer	.60	1.50
141 R.Gilbert/B.Park TL	.60	1.50
142 Rene Robert	.30	.75
143 J. Bob Kelly RC	.25	.60
144 Ross Lonsberry	.25	.60
145 Jean Ratelle	.60	1.50
146 Dallas Smith	.25	.60
147 Bernie Geoffrion CO	1.25	2.50
148 Ted McAneeley	.25	.60
149 Pierre Plante	.25	.60
150 Dennis Hull	.30	.75
151 Dave Keon	.60	1.50
152 Dave Dunn RC	.25	.60
153 Michel Belhumeur	.30	.75
154 B.Clarke/D.Schultz TL	1.00	2.00
155 Ken Dryden	7.50	15.00
156 John Wright RC	.25	.60
157 Larry Romanchych	.25	.60
158 Ralph Stewart	.25	.60
159 Mike Robitaille	.25	.60
160 Ed Giacomin	1.00	2.00
161 Don Cherry CO RC	15.00	25.00
162 Checklist 133-264	7.00	12.00
163 Rick MacLeish	.60	1.50
164 Greg Polis	.25	.60
165 Carol Vadnais	.25	.60
166 Pete Laframboise	.25	.60
167 Ron Schock	.25	.60
168 Lanny McDonald RC	6.00	12.00
169 Scouts Emblem	.40	1.00
170 Tony Esposito	2.50	5.00
171 Pierre Jarry	.25	.60
172 Dan Maloney	.30	.75
173 Peter McDuffe	.30	.75
174 Danny Grant	.30	.75
175 John Stewart	.25	.60
176 Floyd Smith CO	.25	.60
177 Bert Marshall	.25	.60
178 Chuck Lefley UER	.25	.60
179 Gilles Villemure	.30	.75
180 Borje Salming RC	6.00	12.00
181 Doug Mohns	.25	.60
182 Barry Wilkins	.25	.60
183 L.MacDonald/S.Apps TL	.30	.75
184 Gregg Sheppard	.25	.60
185 Joey Johnston	.25	.60
186 Dick Redmond	.25	.60
187 Simon Nolet	.25	.60
188 Ron Stackhouse	.25	.60
189 Marshall Johnston	.25	.60
190 Richard Martin	.60	1.50
191 Andre Boudrias	.25	.60
192 Steve Atkinson	.25	.60
193 Nick Libett	.25	.60
194 Bob Murdoch RC	.30	.75
195 Denis Potvin RC	15.00	25.00
196 Dave Schultz	1.00	2.00
197 G.Unger/P.Plante TL	.25	.60
198 Jim McKenny	.25	.60
199 Gerry Hart	.25	.60
200 Phil Esposito	2.00	4.00
201 Rod Gilbert	.60	1.50
202 Jacques Laperriere	.30	.75
203 Barry Gibbs	.25	.60
204 Billy Reay CO	.30	.75
205 Gilles Meloche	.30	.75
206 Wayne Cashman	.30	.75
207 Dennis Ververgaert RC	.25	.60
208 Phil Roberto	.25	.60
209 Quarter Finals	.35	.75
210 Quarter Finals	.35	.75
211 Quarter Finals	.35	.75
212 Quarter Finals	.35	.75
213 Stanley Cup Semifinals	.35	.75
214 Stanley Cup Semifinals	.35	.75
215 Stanley Cup Finals	.35	.75
216 Flyers Champions	.60	1.50
217 Joe Watson	.25	.60
218 Wayne Stephenson	.30	.75
219 Sittler/Ullman/Hend TL	.60	1.50
220 Bill Goldsworthy	.30	.75
221 Don Marcotte	.25	.60
222 Alex Delvecchio CO	.25	.60
223 Stan Gilbertson	.25	.60
224 Mike Murphy	.25	.60
225 Jim Rutherford	.30	.75
226 Phil Russell	.25	.60
227 Lynn Powis	.25	.60
228 Billy Harris	.25	.60
229 Bob Pulford CO	.30	.75
230 Ken Hodge	.30	.75
231 Bill Fairbairn	.25	.60
232 Guy Lafleur	7.00	12.00
233 Harris/Stew/Potvin TL	1.25	2.50
234 Fred Barrett	.25	.60
235 Rogatien Vachon	.75	2.00
236 Norm Ullman	.60	1.50
237 Garry Unger	.30	.75
238 Jack Gordon CO RC	.25	.60
239 Johnny Bucyk	.60	1.50
240 Bob Dailey RC	.25	.60
241 Dave Burrows	.25	.60
242 Len Frig RC	.25	.60
243 Henri Richard Masterson	.60	1.50
244 Phil Esposito Hart	1.25	2.50
245 Johnny Bucyk Byng	.40	1.00
246 Phil Esposito Ross	1.25	2.50
247 Prince of Wales Trophy	.30	.75
248 Bobby Orr Norris	7.00	12.00
249 Bernie Parent Vezina	.60	1.50
250 Stanley Cup	.40	1.00
251 Bernie Parent Smythe	.60	1.50
252 Denis Potvin Calder	3.00	6.00
253 Flyers Campbell Trophy	.30	.75
254 Pierre Bouchard	.25	.60
255 Jude Drouin	.25	.60
256 Capitals Emblem	.40	1.00
257 Michel Plasse	.30	.75
258 Juha Widing	.25	.60
259 Bryan Watson	.25	.60
260 Bobby Clarke	4.00	8.00
261 Scotty Bowman CO RC	15.00	25.00
262 Craig Patrick	.30	.75
263 Craig Cameron	.25	.60
264 Ted Irvine	.60	1.50

1974-75 Topps Team Cloth Stickers

Card	Low	High
COMPLETE SET (24)	40.00	80.00
1 Atlanta Flames/Canadiens	1.50	4.00
2 Atlanta Flames/Penguins	1.50	4.00
3 Boston Bruins/Flames	1.50	4.00
4 Boston Bruins/Maple Leafs	1.50	4.00
5 Buffalo Sabres/Canucks	1.50	4.00
6 California Golden Seals Canadiens	1.50	4.00
7 Chicago Blackhawks/Bruins	1.50	4.00
8 Detroit Red Wings/Blues	1.50	4.00
9 Kansas City Scouts/Bruins	1.50	4.00
10 Los Angeles Kings/Black Hawks	1.50	4.00
11 Minnesota North Stars/Black Hawks	1.50	4.00
12 Montreal Canadiens/Flyers	1.50	4.00
13 Montreal Canadiens/Rangers	1.50	4.00
14 New York Islanders/North Stars	1.50	4.00
15 New York Rangers/Capitals	1.50	4.00
16 New York Rangers/Golden Seals	1.50	4.00
17 Philadelphia Flyers/Kings	1.50	4.00
18 Pittsburgh Penguins/Flames	1.50	4.00
19 St. Louis Blues/Islanders	1.50	4.00
20 Toronto Maple Leafs/Rangers	1.50	4.00
21 Toronto Maple Leafs/Red Wings	1.50	4.00
22 Vancouver Canucks/Sabres	1.50	4.00
23 Washington Capitals/Scouts	1.50	4.00
24 NHL Logo/Flyers	1.50	4.00
PUZ1 NHL Crest UL	.40	1.00
PUZ2 NHL Crest UCL	.40	1.00
PUZ3 NHL Crest UCR	.40	1.00
PUZ4 NHL Crest UR	.40	1.00
PUZ5 NHL Crest ML	.40	1.00
PUZ6 NHL Crest MCL	.40	1.00
PUZ7 NHL Crest MCR	.40	1.00
PUZ8 NHL Crest MR	.40	1.00
PUZ9 NHL Crest LL	.40	1.00
PUZ10 NHL Crest LCL	.40	1.00
PUZ11 NHL Crest LCR	.40	1.00
PUZ12 NHL Crest LR	.40	1.00

1975-76 Topps

At 330 standard-size cards, the 1975-76 Topps set stands as the company's largest until 1990-91. Fronts feature team name at top and player name at the bottom. The player's position appears in a puck at the bottom. The backs contain year-by-year and NHL career records, a short biography and a cartoon-illustrated hockey fact or referee's signal with interpretation. For the first time, team cards (81-98) with team checklist on back appear in a Topps set.

Card	Low	High
COMPLETE SET (330)	75.00	150.00
1 Stanley Cup Finals	.60	1.50
2 Semi-Finals	.20	.50
3 Semi-Finals	.20	.50
4 Quarter Finals	.20	.50
5 Quarter Finals	.20	.50
6 Quarter Finals	.20	.50
7 Quarter Finals	.20	.50
8 Curt Bennett	.20	.50
9 Johnny Bucyk	.50	1.25
10 Gilbert Perreault	1.25	3.00
11 Darryl Edestrand	.20	.50
12 Ivan Boldirev	.20	.50
13 Nick Libett	.20	.50
14 Jim McElmury RC	.20	.50
15 Frank St.Marseille	.20	.50
16 Blake Dunlop	.20	.50
17 Yvon Lambert	.30	.75
18 Gerry Hart	.20	.50
19 Steve Vickers	.20	.50
20 Rick MacLeish	.30	.75
21 Bob Paradise	.20	.50
22 Red Berenson	.30	.75
23 Lanny McDonald	1.50	4.00
24 Mike Robitaille	.20	.50
25 Ron Low	.30	.75
26 Bryan Hextall	.20	.50
27 Carol Vadnais	.20	.50
28 Jim Lorentz	.20	.50
29 Gary Simmons	.30	.75
30 Stan Mikita	1.25	3.00
31 Bryan Watson	.20	.50
32 Guy Charron	.20	.50
33 Bob Murdoch	.20	.50
34 Norm Gratton	.20	.50
35 Ken Dryden	9.00	15.00
36 Jean Potvin	.20	.50
37 Rick Middleton	1.50	3.00
38 Ed Van Impe	.20	.50
39 Rick Kehoe	.30	.75
40 Garry Unger	.30	.75
41 Ian Turnbull	.30	.75
42 Dennis Ververgaert	.20	.50
43 Mike Marson RC	.20	.50
44 Randy Manery	.20	.50
45 Gilles Gilbert	.30	.75
46 Rene Robert	.30	.75
47 Bob Stewart	.20	.50

1975-76 Topps

48 Pit Martin .20 .50
49 Danny Grant .30 .75
50 Peter Mahovlich .30 .75
51 Dennis Patterson RC .20 .50
52 Mike Murphy .20 .50
53 Dennis O'Brien .20 .50
54 Garry Howatt .20 .50
55 Ed Giacomin .60 1.50
56 Andre Dupont .20 .50
57 Chuck Arnason .20 .50
58 Bob Gassoff RC .20 .50
59 Ron Ellis .30 .75
60 Andre Boudrias .20 .50
61 Yvon Labre .20 .50
62 Hilliard Graves .20 .50
63 Wayne Cashman .30 .75
64 Danny Gare RC 1.00 2.00
65 Rick Hampton .20 .50
66 Darcy Rota .20 .50
67 Bill Hogaboam .20 .50
68 Denis Herron .30 .75
69 Sheldon Kannegiesser .20 .50
70 Yvan Cournoyer UER .50 1.25
71 Ernie Hicke .20 .50
72 Bert Marshall .20 .50
73 Derek Sanderson .75 2.00
74 Tom Bladon .30 .75
75 Ron Schock .20 .50
76 Larry Sacharuk RC .20 .50
77 George Ferguson .20 .50
78 Ab DeMarco .20 .50
79 Tom Williams .20 .50
80 Phil Roberto .20 .50
81 Bruins Team CL 1.00 2.50
82 Seals Team CL 1.00 2.50
83 Sabres Team CL UER 1.00 2.50
84 Blackhawks CL UER 1.00 2.50
85 Flames Team CL 1.00 2.50
86 Kings Team CL 1.00 2.50
87 Red Wings Team CL 1.00 2.50
88 Scouts Team CL UER 1.00 2.50
89 North Stars Team CL 1.00 2.50
90 Canadiens Team CL 1.00 2.50
91 Maple Leafs Team CL 1.00 2.50
92 Islanders Team CL 1.00 2.50
93 Penguins Team CL 1.00 2.50
94 Rangers Team CL 1.00 2.50
95 Flyers Team CL UER 1.00 2.50
96 Blues Team CL 1.00 2.50
97 Canucks Team CL 1.00 2.50
98 Capitals Team CL 1.00 2.50
99 Checklist 1-110 6.00 10.00
100 Bobby Orr 12.00 20.00
101 Germaine Gagnon UER .20 .50
102 Phil Russell .20 .50
103 Billy Lochead .20 .50
104 Robin Burns .20 .50
105 Gary Edwards .30 .75
106 Dwight Bialowas .20 .50
107 D. Risebrough UER RC 1.25 2.50
108 Dave Lewis .20 .50
109 Bill Fairbairn .20 .50
110 Ross Lonsberry .20 .50
111 Ron Stackhouse .20 .50
112 Claude Larose .20 .50
113 Don Luce .20 .50
114 Errol Thompson RC .30 .75
115 Gary Smith .30 .75
116 Jack Lynch .20 .50
117 Jacques Richard .20 .50
118 Dallas Smith .20 .50
119 Dave Gardner .20 .50
120 Mickey Redmond .30 .75
121 John Marks .20 .50
122 Dave Hudson .20 .50
123 Bob Nevin .20 .50
124 Fred Barrett .20 .50
125 Gerry Desjardins .30 .75
126 Guy Lafleur UER 4.00 10.00
127 Jean-Paul Parise .20 .50
128 Walt Tkaczuk .30 .75
129 Gary Dornhoefer .30 .75
130 Syl Apps .20 .50
131 Bob Plager .30 .75
132 Stan Weir .20 .50
133 Tracy Pratt .20 .50
134 Jack Egers .20 .50
135 Eric Vail .20 .50
136 Al Sims .20 .50
137 Larry Patey .20 .50
138 Jim Schoenfeld .30 .75
139 Cliff Koroll .20 .50
140 Marcel Dionne 1.50 4.00
141 Jean-Guy Lagace .20 .50
142 Juha Widing .20 .50
143 Lou Nanne .30 .75
144 Serge Savard .50 1.25
145 Glenn Resch 1.25 3.00
146 Ron Greschner RC 1.00 2.00
147 Dave Schultz .30 .75
148 Barry Wilkins .20 .50
149 Floyd Thomson .20 .50
150 Darryl Sittler .50 1.25
151 Paulin Bordeleau .20 .50
152 Ron Lalonde RC .20 .50
153 Larry Romanchych .20 .50
154 Larry Carriere .20 .50
155 Andre Savard .20 .50
156 Dave Hrechkosy RC .20 .50
157 Bill White .20 .50
158 Dave Kryskow .20 .50
159 Denis Dupere .20 .50
160 Rogatien Vachon .60 1.50
161 Doug Rombough .20 .50
162 Murray Wilson .20 .50
163 Bob Bourne RC 1.00 2.00
164 Gilles Marotte .20 .50
165 Vic Hadfield .30 .75
166 Reggie Leach .30 .75
167 Jerry Butler .20 .50
168 Inge Hammarstrom .20 .50
169 Chris Oddleifson .20 .50
170 Greg Joly .20 .50
171 Checklist 111-220 6.00 10.00
172 Pat Quinn .30 .75
173 Dave Forbes .20 .50
174 Len Frig .20 .50
175 Richard Martin .30 .75
176 Keith Magnuson .20 .50
177 Dan Maloney .20 .50
178 Craig Patrick .30 .75
179 Tom Williams .20 .50
180 Bill Goldsworthy .30 .75
181 Steve Shutt .50 1.25
182 Ralph Stewart .20 .50
183 John Davidson 1.25 3.00
184 Bob Kelly .20 .50
185 Ed Johnston .30 .75
186 Dave Burrows .20 .50
187 Dave Dunn .20 .50
188 Dennis Kearns .20 .50
189 Bill Clement 1.25 3.00
190 Gilles Meloche .30 .75
191 Bob Leiter .20 .50
192 Jerry Korab .20 .50
193 Joey Johnston .20 .50
194 Walt McKechnie .20 .50
195 Wilf Paiement .20 .50
196 Bob Berry .20 .50
197 Dean Talafous RC .20 .50
198 Guy Lapointe .30 .75
199 Clark Gillies RC 2.00 4.00
200 Phil Esposito 1.25 3.00
201 Greg Polis .20 .50
202 Jimmy Watson .30 .75
203 Gord McRae RC .30 .75
204 Lowell MacDonald .20 .50
205 Barclay Plager .30 .75
206 Don Lever .20 .50
207 Bill Mikkelson .20 .50
208 Espo/Lafleur/Martin LL 1.25 3.00
209 Clarke/Orr/P.Mahov LL 1.50 4.00
210 Orr/Espo/Dionne LL 2.00 5.00
211 Schultz/Dupont/Rusl LL .20 .50
212 Espo/Martin/Grant LL .60 1.50
213 Parent/Vach/Dryden LL 2.00 5.00
214 Barry Gibbs .20 .50
215 Ken Hodge .30 .75
216 Jocelyn Guevremont .20 .50
217 Warren Williams RC .20 .50
218 Dick Redmond .20 .50
219 Jim Rutherford .30 .75
220 Simon Nolet .20 .50
221 Butch Goring .30 .75
222 Glen Sather .30 .75
223 Mario Tremblay RC 1.50 3.00
224 Jude Drouin .20 .50
225 Rod Gilbert .50 1.25
226 Bill Barber .50 1.25
227 Gary Inness RC .30 .75
228 Wayne Merrick .20 .50
229 Rod Seiling .20 .50
230 Tom Lysiak .30 .75
231 Bob Dailey .20 .50
232 Michel Belhumeur .30 .75
233 Bill Hajt RC .20 .50
234 Jim Pappin .20 .50
235 Gregg Sheppard .20 .50
236 Gary Bergman .20 .50
237 Randy Rota .20 .50
238 Neil Komadoski .20 .50
239 Craig Cameron .20 .50
240 Tony Esposito 1.25 3.00
241 Larry Robinson 2.50 6.00
242 Billy Harris .20 .50
243 Jean Ratelle .50 1.25
244 Ted Irvine UER .20 .50
245 Bob Neely .20 .50
246 Bobby Lalonde .20 .50
247 Ron Jones RC .20 .50
248 Rey Comeau .20 .50
249 Michel Plasse .30 .75
250 Bobby Clarke 2.50 6.00
251 Bobby Schmautz .20 .50
252 Peter McNab RC 1.25 2.50
253 Al MacAdam .20 .50
254 Dennis Hull .30 .75
255 Terry Harper .20 .50
256 Peter McDuffe .30 .75
257 Jean Hamel .20 .50
258 Jacques Lemaire .50 1.25
259 Bob Nystrom .30 .75
260 Brad Park .75 2.00
261 Cesare Maniago .30 .75
262 Don Saleski .20 .50
263 J. Bob Kelly .20 .50
264 Bob Hess RC .20 .50
265 Blaine Stoughton .30 .75
266 John Gould .20 .50
267 Checklist 221-330 6.00 10.00
268 Dan Bouchard .30 .75
269 Don Marcotte .20 .50
270 Jim Neilson .20 .50
271 Craig Ramsay .20 .50
272 Grant Mulvey RC .30 .75
273 Larry Giroux RC .20 .50
274 Real Lemieux .20 .50
275 Denis Potvin 2.50 6.00
276 Don Kozak .20 .50
277 Tom Reid .20 .50
278 Bob Gainey 1.50 4.00
279 Nick Beverley .20 .50
280 Jean Pronovost .30 .75
281 Joe Watson .20 .50
282 Chuck Lefley .20 .50
283 Borje Salming 2.00 5.00
284 Garnet Bailey .20 .50
285 Gregg Boddy .20 .50
286 Bobby Clarke AS1 1.25 3.00
287 Denis Potvin AS1 1.25 3.00
288 Bobby Orr AS1 6.00 10.00
289 Richard Martin AS1 .20 .50
290 Guy Lafleur AS1 1.50 4.00
291 Bernie Parent AS1 .50 1.25
292 Phil Esposito AS2 .75 2.00
293 Guy Lapointe AS2 .20 .50
294 Borje Salming AS2 1.00 2.50
295 Steve Vickers AS2 .20 .50
296 Rene Robert AS2 .20 .50
297 Rogatien Vachon AS2 .60 1.50
298 Buster Harvey RC .20 .50
299 Gary Sabourin .20 .50
300 Bernie Parent .50 1.25
301 Terry O'Reilly .30 .75
302 Ed Westfall .30 .75
303 Pete Stemkowski .20 .50
304 Pierre Bouchard .20 .50
305 Pierre Larouche RC 2.00 4.00
306 Lee Fogolin RC .30 .75
307 Gerry O'Flaherty .20 .50
308 Phil Myre .30 .75
309 Pierre Plante .20 .50
310 Dennis Hextall .20 .50
311 Jim McKenny .20 .50
312 Vic Venasky .20 .50
313 Flames Leaders .20 .50
314 Espo/Orr/Bucyk TL 2.00 5.00
315 Sabres Leaders .20 .50
316 Seals Leaders .20 .50
317 S.Mikita/J.Pappin TL .20 .50
318 D.Grant/M.Dionne TL .20 .50
319 Scouts Leaders .20 .50
320 Kings Leaders .20 .50
321 North Stars Leaders .20 .50
322 Lafleur/P.Mahov TL .60 1.50
323 Nystrom/Potvin/Gill TL .60 1.50
324 Vick/Gilbert/Ratelle TL .20 .50
325 R.Leach/B.Clarke TL .20 .50
326 Penguins Leaders .20 .50
327 Blues Leaders .20 .50
328 Darryl Sittler TL .60 1.50
329 Canucks Leaders .20 .50
330 Capitals Leaders .20 .50

1976-77 Topps

The 1976-77 Topps set contains 264 color standard-size cards. The fronts contain team name and logo at the top with player name and position at the bottom. The backs feature 1975-76 and career statistics, career highlights and a cartoon-illustrated fact. The first cards of Colorado Rockies (formerly Kansas City) players appear this year. Rookie Cards in this set include Bryan Trottier and Dennis Maruk.

COMPLETE SET (264) 100.00 200.00
1 Leach/Lafleur/Larou LL .75 2.00
2 Clarke/Lafleur/Perr/ LL .75 2.00
3 Lafleur/Clarke/Perr LL .75 2.00
4 Durbno/Watsn/Schultz LL .20 .50
5 Espo/Lafleur/Potvin LL .75 2.00
6 Dryden/Resch/Laroc LL 1.25 3.00
7 Gary Doak .20 .50
8 Jacques Richard .20 .50
9 Wayne Dillon .20 .50
10 Bernie Parent .75 2.00
11 Ed Westfall .25 .60
12 Dick Redmond .20 .50
13 Bryan Hextall .20 .50
14 Jean Pronovost .25 .60
15 Peter Mahovlich .25 .60
16 Danny Grant .20 .50
17 Phil Myre .25 .60
18 Wayne Merrick .20 .50
19 Steve Durbano .20 .50
20 Derek Sanderson .60 1.50
21 Mike Murphy .20 .50
22 Borje Salming 1.00 2.50
23 Mike Walton .20 .50
24 Randy Manery .20 .50
25 Ken Hodge .25 .60
26 Mel Bridgman RC .40 1.00
27 Jerry Korab .20 .50
28 Gilles Gratton .25 .60
29 Andre St.Laurent .20 .50
30 Yvan Cournoyer .40 1.00
31 Phil Russell .20 .50
32 Dennis Hextall .20 .50
33 Lowell MacDonald .20 .50
34 Dennis O'Brien .20 .50
35 Gerry Meehan .20 .50
36 Gilles Meloche .25 .60
37 Wilf Paiement .25 .60
38 Bob MacMillan RC .40 1.00
39 Ian Turnbull .25 .60
40 Rogatien Vachon .50 1.25
41 Nick Beverley .20 .50
42 Rene Robert .25 .60
43 Andre Savard .20 .50
44 Bob Gainey 1.00 2.50
45 Joe Watson .20 .50
46 Billy Smith 1.00 2.50
47 Darcy Rota .20 .50
48 Rick Lapointe RC .20 .50
49 Pierre Jarry .20 .50
50 Syl Apps .50 1.25
51 Eric Vail .20 .50
52 Greg Joly .20 .50
53 Don Lever .20 .50
54 Bob Murdoch Seals .20 .50
55 Denis Herron .25 .60
56 Mike Bloom .20 .50
57 Bill Fairbairn .20 .50
58 Fred Stanfield .20 .50
59 Steve Shutt .75 2.00
60 Brad Park .60 1.50
61 Gilles Villemure .25 .60
62 Bert Marshall .20 .50
63 Chuck Lefley .20 .50
64 Simon Nolet .20 .50
65 Reggie Leach RB .25 .60
66 Darryl Sittler RB .40 1.00
67 Bryan Trottier RB 3.00 8.00
68 Garry Unger RB .25 .60
69 Ron Low .25 .60
70 Bobby Clarke 1.50 4.00
71 Michel Bergeron RC .20 .50
72 Ron Stackhouse .20 .50
73 Bill Hogaboam .20 .50
74 Bob Murdoch Kings .20 .50
75 Steve Vickers .20 .50
76 Pit Martin .20 .50
77 Gerry Hart .20 .50
78 Craig Ramsay .20 .50
79 Michel Larocque .25 .60
80 Jean Ratelle .40 1.00
81 Don Saleski .20 .50
82 Bill Clement .40 1.00
83 Dave Burrows .20 .50
84 Wayne Thomas .25 .60
85 John Gould .20 .50
86 Dennis Maruk RC 1.00 2.00
87 Ernie Hicke .20 .50
88 Jim Rutherford .25 .60
89 Dale Tallon .20 .50
90 Rod Gilbert .40 1.00
91 Marcel Dionne 1.25 3.00
92 Chuck Arnason .20 .50
93 Jean Potvin .20 .50
94 Don Luce .20 .50
95 Johnny Bucyk .40 1.00
96 Larry Goodenough .20 .50
97 Mario Tremblay .25 .60
98 Nelson Pyatt RC .20 .50
99 Brian Glennie .20 .50
100 Tony Esposito .75 2.00
101 Dan Maloney .20 .50
102 Barry Wilkins .20 .50
103 Dean Talafous .20 .50
104 Ed Staniowski RC .20 .50
105 Dallas Smith .20 .50
106 Jude Drouin .20 .50
107 Pat Hickey .20 .50
108 Jocelyn Guevremont .20 .50
109 Doug Risebrough .40 1.00
110 Reggie Leach .25 .60
111 Dan Bouchard .25 .60
112 Chris Oddleifson .20 .50
113 Rick Hampton .20 .50
114 John Marks .20 .50
115 Bryan Trottier RC 20.00 35.00
116 Checklist 1-132 3.00 6.00
117 Greg Polis .20 .50
118 Peter McNab .40 1.00
119 Jim Roberts .20 .50
120 Gerry Cheevers .75 2.00
121 Rick MacLeish .25 .60
122 Billy Lochead .20 .50
123 Tom Reid .20 .50
124 Rick Kehoe .25 .60
125 Keith Magnuson .20 .50
126 Clark Gillies .40 1.00
127 Rick Middleton .75 2.00
128 Bill Hajt .20 .50
129 Jacques Lemaire .40 1.00
130 Terry O'Reilly .40 1.00
131 Andre Dupont .20 .50
132 Flames Team CL .75 2.00
133 Bruins Team CL .75 2.00
134 Sabres Team CL .75 2.00
135 Seals Team CL .75 2.00
136 Blackhawks Team CL .75 2.00
137 Red Wings Team CL .75 2.00
138 Scouts Team CL .75 2.00
139 Kings Team CL .75 2.00
140 North Stars Team CL .75 2.00
141 Canadiens Team CL .75 2.00
142 Islanders Team CL .75 2.00
143 Rangers Team CL .75 2.00
144 Flyers Team CL .75 2.00
145 Penguins Team CL .75 2.00
146 Blues Team CL .75 2.00
147 Maple Leafs Team CL .75 2.00
148 Canucks Team CL .75 2.00
149 Capitals Team CL .75 2.00
150 Dave Schultz .60 1.50
151 Larry Robinson 1.50 4.00
152 Al Smith .25 .60
153 Bob Nystrom .25 .60
154 Ron Greschner UER .20 .50
155 Gregg Sheppard .20 .50
156 Alain Daigle .20 .50
157 Ed Van Impe .20 .50

158 Tim Young RC .25 .60
159 Gary Bergman .20 .50
160 Ed Giacomin .60 1.50
161 Yvon Labre .20 .50
162 Jim Lorentz .20 .50
163 Guy Lafleur 2.50 6.00
164 Tom Bladon .25 .60
165 Wayne Cashman .25 .60
166 Pete Stemkowski .20 .50
167 Grant Mulvey .20 .50
168 Yves Belanger RC .25 .60
169 Bill Goldsworthy .25 .60
170 Denis Potvin 1.50 4.00
171 Nick Libett .20 .50
172 Michel Plasse .25 .60
173 Lou Nanne .20 .50
174 Tom Lysiak .25 .60
175 Dennis Ververgaert .20 .50
176 Gary Simmons .25 .60
177 Pierre Bouchard .20 .50
178 Bill Barber .60 1.50
179 Darryl Edestrand .20 .50
180 Gilbert Perreault .75 2.00
181 Dave Maloney RC .40 1.00
182 Jean-Paul Parise .20 .50
183 Bobby Sheehan .20 .50
184 Pete Lopresti RC .25 .60
185 Don Kozak .20 .50
186 Guy Charron .20 .50
187 Stan Gilbertson .20 .50
188 Bill Nyrop RC .20 .50
189 Bobby Schmautz .20 .50
190 Wayne Stephenson .25 .60
191 Brian Spencer .20 .50
192 Gilles Marotte .20 .50
193 Lorne Henning .20 .50
194 Bob Neely .20 .50
195 Dennis Hull .25 .60
196 Walt McKechnie .20 .50
197 Curt Ridley RC .20 .50
198 Dwight Bialowas .20 .50
199 Pierre Larouche .40 1.00
200 Ken Dryden 6.00 12.00
201 Ross Lonsberry .20 .50
202 Curt Bennett .20 .50
203 Hartland Monahan RC .20 .50
204 John Davidson .75 2.00
205 Serge Savard .40 1.00
206 Garry Howatt .20 .50
207 Darryl Sittler 1.25 3.00
208 J.P. Bordeleau .20 .50
209 Henry Boucha .20 .50
210 Richard Martin .25 .60
211 Vic Venasky .20 .50
212 Buster Harvey .20 .50
213 Bobby Orr 10.00 20.00
214 Martin/Perrlt/Robert .75 2.00
215 Barber/Clarke/Leach 1.00 2.50
216 Gillies/Trottier/Harris 1.50 4.00
217 Gainey/Jarvis/Roberts .40 1.00
218 MacDon/Apps/Pronvst .25 .60
219 Bob Kelly .20 .50
220 Walt Tkaczuk .25 .60
221 Dave Lewis .20 .50
222 Danny Gare .40 1.00
223 Guy Lapointe .25 .60
224 Hank Nowak RC .20 .50
225 Stan Mikita 1.00 2.50
226 Vic Hadfield .25 .60
227 Bernie Wolfe RC .25 .60
228 Bryan Watson .20 .50
229 Ralph Stewart .20 .50
230 Gerry Desjardins .25 .60
231 John Bednarski RC .20 .50
232 Yvon Lambert .20 .50
233 Orest Kindrachuk .20 .50
234 Don Marcotte .20 .50
235 Bill White .20 .50
236 Red Berenson .25 .60
237 Al MacAdam .20 .50
238 Rick Blight RC .20 .50
239 Butch Goring .25 .60
240 Cesare Maniago .25 .60
241 Jim Schoenfeld .25 .60
242 Cliff Koroll .20 .50
243 Mickey Redmond .25 .60
244 Rick Chartraw .20 .50
245 Phil Esposito 1.00 2.50
246 Dave Forbes .20 .50
247 Jimmy Watson .20 .50
248 Ron Schock .20 .50
249 Fred Barrett .20 .50
250 Glenn Resch .75 2.00
251 Ivan Boldirev .20 .50
252 Billy Harris .20 .50
253 Lee Fogolin .20 .50
254 Murray Wilson .20 .50
255 Gilles Gilbert .25 .60
256 Gary Dornhoefer .25 .60
257 Carol Vadnais .20 .50
258 Checklist 133-264 3.00 6.00
259 Errol Thompson .20 .50
260 Garry Unger .25 .60
261 J. Bob Kelly .20 .50
262 Terry Harper .20 .50
263 Blake Dunlop .20 .50
264 Canadiens Champs .60 1.50

1976-77 Topps Glossy Inserts

This 22-card insert set was issued with the 1976-77 Topps hockey card set but not with the O-Pee-Chee hockey cards unlike the glossy insert produced "jointly" by Topps and O-Pee-Chee the next year. This set is very similar to (but much more difficult to find than) the glossy insert set of the following year. The cards were printed in the United States. These rounded-corner cards are approximately 2 1/4" by 3 1/4".

COMPLETE SET (22) 40.00 80.00
1 Bobby Clarke 2.00 4.00
2 Brad Park 1.25 2.50
3 Tony Esposito 1.50 3.00
4 Marcel Dionne 2.00 4.00
5 Ken Dryden 7.50 15.00
6 Glenn Resch 1.00 2.00
7 Phil Esposito 2.50 5.00
8 Darryl Sittler 1.50 3.00
9 Gilbert Perreault 1.00 2.00
10 Denis Potvin 2.00 4.00
11 Guy Lafleur 4.00 8.00
12 Bill Barber 1.00 2.00
13 Syl Apps .50 1.00
14 Johnny Bucyk 1.00 2.00
15 Bryan Trottier 7.50 15.00
16 Dennis Hull .50 1.00
17 Guy Lapointe .75 1.50
18 Rod Gilbert 1.25 2.50
19 Richard Martin .75 1.50
20 Bobby Orr 12.50 25.00
21 Reggie Leach .75 1.50
22 Jean Ratelle 1.25 2.50

1977-78 Topps

The 1977-78 Topps set consists of 264 standard-size cards. Cards 203 (Stan Gilbertson) and 255 (Bill Fairbairn) differ from those of O-Pee-Chee. Card fronts have team name and logo, player name and position at the bottom. Yearly statistics including minor league numbers are featured on the back along with a short biography and a cartoon-illustrated fact about the player. After the initial print run, Topps changed the photos on card numbers 131, 138, 149 and 152. Two of the changes (138 and 149) were necessary corrections. Rookie Cards include Mike Milbury and Mike Palmateer.

COMPLETE SET (264) 45.00 90.00
1 Shutt/Lafleur/Dionne LL 1.00 2.50
2 Lafleur/Dionne/Sal LL .60 1.50
3 Lafleur/Dionne/Shutt LL .75 2.00
4 Williams/Polnch/Gasff LL .15 .40
5 McDonald/Espo/Will LL .30 .75
6 Laroc/Dryden/Resch LL 1.00 2.50
7 Perr/Shutt/Lafleur LL .60 1.50
8 Dryden/Vach/Parent LL 1.25 3.00
9 Brian Spencer .10 .25
10 Denis Potvin AS2 .30 .75
11 Nick Fotiu .30 .75
12 Bob Murray .10 .25
13 Pete Lopresti .15 .40
14 J. Bob Kelly .10 .25
15 Rick MacLeish .30 .75
16 Terry Harper .10 .25
17 Willi Plett RC .30 .75
18 Peter McNab .15 .40
19 Wayne Thomas .15 .40
20 Pierre Bouchard .10 .25
21 Dennis Maruk .30 .75
22 Mike Murphy .10 .25
23 Cesare Maniago .15 .40
24 Paul Gardner RC .30 .75
25 Rod Gilbert .30 .75
26 Orest Kindrachuk .10 .25
27 Bill Hajt .10 .25
28 John Davidson .30 .75
29 Jean-Paul Parise .10 .25
30 Larry Robinson AS1 1.25 3.00
31 Yvon Labre .10 .25
32 Walt McKechnie .10 .25
33 Rick Kehoe .15 .40
34 Randy Holt RC .10 .25
35 Garry Unger .15 .40
36 Lou Nanne .10 .25
37 Dan Bouchard .15 .40
38 Darryl Sittler .75 2.00
39 Bob Murdoch .10 .25
40 Jean Ratelle .30 .75
41 Dave Maloney .10 .25
42 Danny Gare .30 .75
43 Jimmy Watson .10 .25
44 Tom Williams .10 .25
45 Serge Savard .30 .75
46 Derek Sanderson .30 .75
47 John Marks .10 .25
48 Al Cameron RC .10 .25
49 Dean Talafous .10 .25
50 Glenn Resch .30 .75
51 Ron Schock .10 .25
52 Gary Croteau .10 .25
53 Gerry Meehan .10 .25
54 Ed Staniowski .10 .25
55 Phil Esposito .75 2.00
56 Dennis Ververgaert .10 .25
57 Rick Wilson .10 .25
58 Jim Lorentz .10 .25
59 Bobby Schmautz .10 .25
60 Guy Lapointe AS2 .15 .40
61 Ivan Boldirev .10 .25
62 Bob Nystrom .10 .25
63 Rick Hampton .10 .25
64 Jack Valiquette .10 .25
65 Bernie Parent .60 1.50
66 Dave Burrows .10 .25
67 Butch Goring .15 .40
68 Checklist 1-132 2.00 4.00
69 Murray Wilson .10 .25
70 Ed Giacomin .30 .75
71 Flames Team CL .50 1.25
72 Bruins Team CL .50 1.25
73 Sabres Team CL .50 1.25
74 Blackhawks Team CL .50 1.25
75 Barons Team CL .50 1.25
76 Rockies Team CL .50 1.25
77 Red Wings Team CL .50 1.25
78 Kings Team CL .50 1.25
79 North Stars Team CL .50 1.25
80 Canadiens Team CL .50 1.25
81 Islanders Team CL .50 1.25
82 Rangers Team CL .50 1.25
83 Flyers Team CL .50 1.25
84 Penguins Team CL .50 1.25
85 Blues Team CL .50 1.25
86 Maple Leafs Team CL .50 1.25
87 Canucks Team CL .50 1.25
88 Capitals Team CL .50 1.25
89 Keith Magnuson .10 .25
90 Walt Tkaczuk .15 .40
91 Bill Nyrop .10 .25
92 Michel Plasse .15 .40
93 Bob Bourne .15 .40
94 Lee Fogolin .10 .25
95 Gregg Sheppard .10 .25
96 Hartland Monahan .10 .25
97 Curt Bennett .10 .25
98 Bob Dailey .10 .25
99 Bill Goldsworthy .15 .40
100 Ken Dryden AS1 3.00 8.00
101 Grant Mulvey .10 .25
102 Pierre Larouche .30 .75
103 Nick Libett .10 .25
104 Rick Smith .10 .25
105 Bryan Trottier 4.00 10.00
106 Pierre Jarry .10 .25
107 Red Berenson .15 .40
108 Jim Schoenfeld .15 .40
109 Gilles Meloche .15 .40
110 Lanny McDonald AS2 .60 1.50
111 Don Lever .10 .25
112 Greg Polis .10 .25
113 Gary Sargent RC .10 .25
114 Earl Anderson RC .10 .25
115 Bobby Clarke 1.25 3.00
116 Dave Lewis .10 .25
117 Darcy Rota .10 .25
118 Andre Savard .10 .25
119 Denis Herron .15 .40
120 Steve Shutt AS1 .30 .75
121 Mel Bridgman .10 .25
122 Buster Harvey .10 .25
123 Roland Eriksson RC .10 .25
124 Dale Tallon .10 .25
125 Gilles Gilbert .15 .40
126 Billy Harris .10 .25
127 Tom Lysiak .15 .40
128 Jerry Korab .10 .25
129 Bob Gainey .60 1.50
130 Wilf Paiement .15 .40
131A Tom Bladon Standing 1.00 2.00
131B Tom Bladon Skating .10 .25
132 Ernie Hicke .10 .25
133 J.P. LeBlanc .10 .25
134 Mike Milbury RC 2.50 5.00
135 Pit Martin .10 .25
136 Steve Vickers .10 .25
137 Don Awrey .10 .25
138A Bernie Wolfe MacAdam 1.00 2.00
138B Bernie Wolfe COR .10 .25
139 Doug Jarvis .30 .75
140 Borje Salming AS1 .60 1.50
141 Bob MacMillan .10 .25
142 Wayne Stephenson .15 .40
143 Dave Forbes .10 .25
144 Jean Potvin .10 .25
145 Guy Charron .10 .25
146 Cliff Koroll .10 .25
147 Danny Grant .15 .40
148 Bill Hogaboam UER .10 .25
149A Al MacAdam ERR Wolfe 1.00 2.00
149B Al MacAdam COR .10 .25
150 Gerry Desjardins .15 .40
151 Yvon Lambert .10 .25
152A Rick Lapointe ERR 2.00 5.00
152B Rick Lapointe COR .10 .25
153 Ed Westfall .15 .40
154 Carol Vadnais .10 .25
155 Johnny Bucyk .30 .75
156 J.P. Bordeleau .10 .25
157 Ron Stackhouse .10 .25
158 Glen Sharpley RC .10 .25
159 Michel Bergeron .10 .25
160 Rogatien Vachon AS2 .30 .75
161 Fred Stanfield .10 .25
162 Gerry Hart .10 .25
163 Mario Tremblay .15 .40
164 Andre Dupont .10 .25
165 Don Marcotte .10 .25
166 Wayne Dillon .10 .25
167 Claude Larose .10 .25
168 Eric Vail .10 .25
169 Tom Edur .10 .25
170 Tony Esposito .60 1.50
171 Andre St.Laurent .10 .25
172 Dan Maloney .10 .25
173 Dennis O'Brien .10 .25
174 Blair Chapman RC .10 .25
175 Dennis Kearns .10 .25
176 Wayne Merrick .10 .25
177 Michel Larocque .15 .40
178 Bob Kelly .10 .25
179 Dave Farrish RC .10 .25
180 Richard Martin AS2 .30 .75
181 Gary Doak .10 .25
182 Jude Drouin .10 .25
183 Barry Dean RC .10 .25
184 Gary Smith .15 .40
185 Reggie Leach .30 .75
186 Ian Turnbull .15 .40
187 Vic Venasky .10 .25
188 Wayne Bianchin RC .10 .25
189 Doug Risebrough .15 .40
190 Brad Park .30 .75
191 Craig Ramsay .10 .25
192 Ken Hodge .15 .40
193 Phil Myre .15 .40
194 Garry Howatt .10 .25
195 Stan Mikita .75 2.00
196 Garnet Bailey .10 .25
197 Dennis Hextall .10 .25
198 Nick Beverley .10 .25
199 Larry Paley .10 .25
200 Guy Lafleur AS1 2.00 5.00
201 Don Edwards RC 1.00 2.50
202 Gary Dornhoefer .15 .40
203 Stan Gilbertson .10 .25
204 Alex Pirus RC .10 .25
205 Peter Mahovlich .15 .40
206 Bert Marshall .10 .25
207 Gilles Gratton .15 .40
208 Alain Daigle .10 .25
209 Chris Oddleifson .10 .25
210 Gilbert Perreault AS2 .60 1.50
211 Mike Palmateer RC 2.50 5.00
212 Billy Lochead .10 .25
213 Dick Redmond .10 .25
214 Guy Lafleur RB .60 1.50
215 Ian Turnbull RB .10 .25
216 Guy Lafleur RB .60 1.50
217 Steve Shutt RB .30 .75
218 Guy Lafleur RB .60 1.50
219 Lorne Henning .10 .25
220 Terry O'Reilly .30 .75
221 Pat Hickey .10 .25
222 Rene Robert .15 .40
223 Tim Young .10 .25
224 Dunc Wilson .15 .40
225 Dennis Hull .15 .40
226 Rod Seiling .10 .25
227 Bill Barber .30 .75
228 Dennis Polonich RC .10 .25
229 Billy Smith .60 1.50
230 Yvan Cournoyer .30 .75
231 Don Luce .10 .25
232 Mike McEwen RC .10 .25
233 Don Saleski .10 .25
234 Wayne Cashman .30 .75
235 Phil Russell .10 .25
236 Mike Corrigan .10 .25
237 Guy Chouinard .15 .40
238 Steve Jensen RC .10 .25
239 Jim Rutherford .15 .40
240 Marcel Dionne AS1 1.25 2.50
241 Rejean Houle .10 .25
242 Jocelyn Guevremont .10 .25
243 Jim Harrison .10 .25
244 Don Murdoch RC .30 .75
245 Rick Green RC .30 .75
246 Rick Middleton .30 .75
247 Joe Watson .10 .25
248 Syl Apps .10 .25
249 Checklist 133-264 2.00 4.00
250 Clark Gillies .30 .75
251 Bobby Orr 9.00 15.00
252 Nelson Pyatt .10 .25
253 Gary McAdam RC .10 .25
254 Jacques Lemaire .30 .75
255 Bill Fairbairn .10 .25
256 Ron Greschner .15 .40
257 Ross Lonsberry .10 .25
258 Dave Gardner .10 .25
259 Rick Blight .10 .25
260 Gerry Cheevers .30 .75
261 Jean Pronovost .15 .40
262 Mon/NYI Semi-Finals .15 .40
263 Bruins Semi-Finals .15 .40
264 Canadiens Champs .30 .75

1977-78 Topps/O-Pee-Chee Glossy

This set of 22 numbered cards was issued with either square or round corners as an insert with both the Topps and O-Pee-Chee hockey cards of 1977-78. Cards were numbered on the back and measure 2 1/4" by 3 1/4". They are essentially the same as the O-Pee-Chee insert issue of the same year. The O-Pee-Chee inserts have the same card numbers and pictures, same values, but different copyright lines on the reverses. The cards are priced below for the round cornered version; the square cornered cards are worth approximately 10 percent more than the prices below.

COMPLETE SET (22)	7.50	15.00
1 Wayne Cashman	.20	.40
2 Gerry Cheevers	.75	1.50
3 Bobby Clarke	.75	1.50
4 Marcel Dionne	.75	1.50
5 Ken Dryden	2.00	4.00
6 Clark Gillies	.20	.40
7 Guy Lafleur	1.25	2.50
8 Reggie Leach	.18	.35
9 Rick MacLeish	.25	.50
10 Dave Maloney	.13	.25
11 Richard Martin	.20	.40
12 Don Murdoch	.13	.25
13 Brad Park	.38	.75
14 Gilbert Perreault	.50	1.00
15 Denis Potvin	.75	1.50
16 Jean Ratelle	.38	.75
17 Glenn Resch	.38	.75
18 Larry Robinson	.75	1.50
19 Steve Shutt	.38	.75
20 Darryl Sittler	.63	1.25
21 Rogatien Vachon	.38	.75
22 Tim Young	.13	.25

1978-79 Topps

The 1978-79 Topps set consists of 264 standard-size cards. Card fronts have team name, logo and player position in the top left corner. The player's name is within the top border. A short biography, yearly statistics including minor leagues and a facsimile autograph are included on the back.

COMPLETE SET (264)	40.00	80.00
1 Mike Bossy HL	4.00	8.00
2 Phil Esposito HL	.40	1.00
3 Guy Lafleur HL	.40	1.00
4 Darryl Sittler HL	.25	.60
5 Garry Unger HL	.08	.25
6 Gary Edwards	.15	.40
7 Rick Blight	.08	.25
8 Larry Patey	.08	.25
9 Craig Ramsay	.08	.25
10 Bryan Trottier AS1	2.00	5.00
11 Don Murdoch	.08	.25
12 Phil Russell	.08	.25
13 Doug Jarvis	.15	.40
14 Gene Carr	.08	.25
15 Bernie Parent	.40	1.00
16 Perry Miller	.08	.25
17 Kent-Erik Andersson RC	.15	.40
18 Gregg Sheppard	.08	.25
19 Dennis Owchar	.08	.25
20 Rogatien Vachon	.25	.60
21 Dan Maloney	.08	.25
22 Guy Charron	.08	.25
23 Dick Redmond	.08	.25
24 Checklist 1-132	1.00	2.50
25 Anders Hedberg	.15	.40
26 Mel Bridgman	.15	.40
27 Lee Fogolin	.08	.25
28 Gilles Meloche	.15	.40
29 Garry Howatt	.08	.25
30 Darryl Sittler AS2	.60	1.50
31 Curt Bennett	.08	.25
32 Andre St.Laurent	.08	.25
33 Blair Chapman	.08	.25
34 Keith Magnuson	.08	.25
35 Pierre Larouche	.25	.60
36 Michel Plasse	.15	.40
37 Gary Sargent	.08	.25
38 Mike Walton	.08	.25
39 Robert Picard RC	.15	.40
40 Terry O'Reilly AS2	.15	.40
41 Dave Farrish	.08	.25
42 Gary McAdam	.08	.25
43 Joe Watson	.08	.25
44 Yves Belanger	.15	.40
45 Steve Jensen	.08	.25
46 Bob Stewart	.08	.25
47 Darcy Rota	.08	.25
48 Dennis Hextall	.08	.25
49 Bert Marshall	.08	.25
50 Ken Dryden AS1	2.50	6.00
51 Peter Mahovlich	.15	.40
52 Dennis Ververgaert	.08	.25
53 Inge Hammarstrom	.08	.25
54 Doug Favell	.15	.40
55 Steve Vickers	.08	.25
56 Syl Apps	.08	.25
57 Errol Thompson	.08	.25
58 Don Luce	.08	.25
59 Mike Milbury	.25	.60
60 Yvan Cournoyer	.25	.60
61 Kirk Bowman	.08	.25
62 Billy Smith	.25	.60
63 Lafleur/Bossy/Shutt LL	1.50	4.00
64 Trott/Lafleur/Sitt LL	.60	1.50
65 Lafleur/Trott/Sitt LL	.60	1.50
66 Schltz/Wil/Polnich LL	.10	.30
67 Bossy/Espo/Shutt LL	1.00	2.50
68 Dryden/Parent/Gilb LL	1.00	2.50
69 Lafleur/Barber/Sitt LL	.50	1.25
70 Parent/Dryden/Espo LL	1.00	2.50
71 Bob Kelly	.08	.25
72 Ron Stackhouse	.08	.25
73 Wayne Dillon	.08	.25
74 Jim Rutherford	.15	.40
75 Stan Mikita	.60	1.50
76 Bob Gainey	.40	1.00
77 Gerry Hart	.08	.25
78 Lanny McDonald	.40	1.00
79 Brad Park	.40	1.00
80 Richard Martin	.25	.60
81 Bernie Wolfe	.15	.40
82 Bob MacMillan	.08	.25
83 Brad Maxwell RC	.08	.25
84 Mike Fidler	.08	.25
85 Carol Vadnais	.08	.25
86 Don Lever	.08	.25
87 Phil Myre	.15	.40
88 Paul Gardner	.08	.25
89 Bob Murray	.08	.25
90 Guy Lafleur AS1	1.50	4.00
91 Bob Murdoch	.08	.25
92 Ron Ellis	.15	.40
93 Jude Drouin	.08	.25
94 Jocelyn Guevremont	.08	.25
95 Gilles Gilbert	.15	.40
96 Bob Sirois	.08	.25
97 Tom Lysiak	.15	.40
98 Andre Dupont	.08	.25
99 Per-Olov Brasar RC	.08	.25
100 Phil Esposito	.75	2.00
101 J.P. Bordeleau	.08	.25
102 Pierre Mondou RC	.40	1.00
103 Wayne Bianchin	.08	.25
104 Dennis O'Brien	.08	.25
105 Glenn Resch	.25	.60
106 Dennis Polonich	.08	.25
107 Kris Manery RC	.08	.25
108 Bill Hajt	.08	.25
109 Jere Gillis RC	.08	.25
110 Garry Unger	.15	.40
111 Nick Beverley	.08	.25
112 Pat Hickey	.08	.25
113 Rick Middleton	.25	.60
114 Orest Kindrachuk	.08	.25
115 Mike Bossy RC	20.00	40.00
116 Pierre Bouchard	.08	.25
117 Alain Daigle	.08	.25
118 Terry Martin	.08	.25
119 Tom Edur	.08	.25
120 Marcel Dionne	.75	2.00
121 Barry Beck RC	.50	1.25
122 Billy Lochead	.08	.25
123 Paul Harrison	.15	.40
124 Wayne Cashman	.25	.60
125 Rick MacLeish	.25	.60
126 Bob Bourne	.15	.40
127 Ian Turnbull	.08	.25
128 Gerry Meehan	.08	.25
129 Eric Vail	.08	.25
130 Gilbert Perreault	.25	.60
131 Bob Dailey	.08	.25
132 Dale McCourt RC	.40	1.00
133 John Wensink RC	.50	1.25
134 Bill Nyrop	.08	.25
135 Ivan Boldirev	.08	.25
136 Lucien DeBlois RC	.08	.25
137 Brian Spencer	.08	.25
138 Tim Young	.08	.25
139 Ron Sedlbauer	.08	.25
140 Gerry Cheevers	.40	1.00
141 Dennis Maruk	.15	.40
142 Barry Dean	.08	.25
143 Bernie Federko RC	3.00	6.00
144 Stefan Persson RC	.15	.40
145 Wilf Paiement	.15	.40
146 Dale Tallon	.08	.25
147 Yvon Lambert	.08	.25
148 Greg Joly	.08	.25
149 Dean Talafous	.08	.25
150 Don Edwards AS2	.08	.25
151 Butch Goring	.15	.40
152 Tom Bladon	.08	.25
153 Bob Nystrom	.08	.25
154 Ron Greschner	.15	.40
155 Jean Ratelle	.25	.60
156 Russ Anderson RC	.08	.25
157 John Marks	.08	.25
158 Michel Larocque	.15	.40
159 Paul Woods RC	.15	.40
160 Mike Palmateer	.15	.40
161 Jim Lorentz	.08	.25
162 Dave Lewis	.08	.25
163 Harvey Bennett	.08	.25
164 Rick Smith	.08	.25
165 Reggie Leach	.25	.60
166 Wayne Thomas	.15	.40
167 Dave Forbes	.08	.25
168 Doug Wilson RC	4.00	8.00
169 Dan Bouchard	.15	.40
170 Steve Shutt AS2	.25	.60
171 Mike Kaszycki RC	.08	.25
172 Denis Herron	.15	.40
173 Rick Bowness	.15	.40
174 Rick Hampton	.08	.25
175 Glen Sharpley	.08	.25
176 Bill Barber	.25	.60
177 Ron Duguay RC	1.25	3.00
178 Jim Schoenfeld	.15	.40
179 Pierre Plante	.08	.25
180 Jacques Lemaire	.25	.60
181 Stan Jonathan	.08	.25
182 Billy Harris	.08	.25
183 Chris Oddleifson	.08	.25
184 Jean Pronovost	.15	.40
185 Fred Barrett	.08	.25
186 Ross Lonsberry	.08	.25
187 Mike McEwen	.08	.25
188 Rene Robert	.15	.40
189 J. Bob Kelly	.08	.25
190 Serge Savard AS2	.15	.40
191 Dennis Kearns	.08	.25
192 Flames Team CL	.20	.50
193 Bruins Team CL	.20	.50
194 Sabres Team CL	.20	.50
195 Blackhawks Team CL	.20	.50
196 Rockies Team CL	.20	.50
197 Red Wings Team CL	.20	.50
198 Kings Team CL	.20	.50
199 North Stars Team CL	.20	.50
200 Canadiens Team CL	.20	.50
201 Islanders Team CL	.20	.50
202 Rangers Team CL	.20	.50
203 Flyers Team CL	.20	.50
204 Penguins Team CL	.20	.50
205 Blues Team CL	.20	.50
206 Maple Leafs Team CL	.20	.50
207 Canucks Team CL	.20	.50
208 Capitals Team CL	.20	.50
209 Danny Gare	.15	.40
210 Larry Robinson AS1	.60	1.50
211 John Davidson	.25	.60
212 Peter McNab	.15	.40
213 Rick Kehoe	.15	.40
214 Terry Harper	.08	.25
215 Bobby Clarke	.75	2.00
216 Bryan Maxwell UER	.08	.25
217 Ted Bulley	.08	.25
218 Red Berenson	.15	.40
219 Ron Grahame	.15	.40
220 Clark Gillies AS1	.15	.40
221 Dave Maloney	.08	.25
222 Derek Smith RC	.08	.25
223 Wayne Stephenson	.15	.40
224 John Van Boxmeer	.08	.25
225 Dave Schultz	.15	.40
226 Reed Larson RC	.40	1.00
227 Rejean Houle	.08	.25
228 Doug Hicks	.08	.25
229 Mike Murphy	.08	.25
230 Pete Lopresti	.15	.40
231 Jerry Korab	.08	.25
232 Ed Westfall	.15	.40
233 Greg Malone RC	.15	.40
234 Paul Holmgren	.25	.60
235 Walt Tkaczuk	.15	.40
236 Don Marcotte	.08	.25
237 Ron Low	.15	.40
238 Rick Chartraw	.08	.25
239 Cliff Koroll	.08	.25
240 Borje Salming AS1	.40	1.00
241 Roland Eriksson	.08	.25
242 Ric Seiling RC	.08	.25
243 Jim Bedard RC	.20	.50
244 Peter Lee RC	.15	.40
245 Denis Potvin AS2	.60	1.50
246 Greg Polis	.08	.25
247 Jimmy Watson	.08	.25
248 Bobby Schmautz	.08	.25
249 Doug Risebrough	.15	.40
250 Tony Esposito	.50	1.25
251 Nick Libett	.08	.25
252 Ron Zanussi RC	.08	.25
253 Andre Savard	.08	.25
254 Dave Burrows	.08	.25
255 Ulf Nilsson	.25	.60
256 Richard Mulhern	.08	.25
257 Don Saleski	.08	.25
258 Wayne Merrick	.08	.25
259 Checklist 133-264	1.00	2.50
260 Guy Lapointe	.15	.40
261 Grant Mulvey	.08	.25
262 Stanley Cup: Semis	.10	.30
263 Stanley Cup: Semis	.10	.30
264 Stanley Cup Finals	.40	1.00

1978-79 Topps Team Stickers

This set of 22 team inserts measures the standard size. Each insert consists of two stickers: a team logo and a second sticker consisting of three mini-stickers. The mini-stickers picture hockey equipment (mask, stick(s), or puck), a hockey word (center, defense, goal!, goalie, score! or wing), and a number between zero and nine. The backs are blank and the fronts carry a 1978 copyright date.

COMPLETE SET (17)	7.50	15.00
1 Atlanta Flames	.75	1.50
2A Boston Bruins/Puck	.75	1.50
2B Boston Bruins/Stick	.75	2.00
3 Buffalo Sabres	.50	1.00
4 Chicago Blackhawks	.75	1.50
5 Colorado Rockies	.75	1.50
6 Detroit Red Wings	.75	1.50
7 Los Angeles Kings	.50	1.00
8 Minnesota North Stars	.50	1.00
9A Montreal Canadiens/Goalie	.75	1.50
9B Montreal Canadiens/Puck	.75	2.00
10A New York Islanders/Center	.50	1.00
10B New York Islanders/Goal!	.50	1.00
11A New York Rangers/Goalie	.75	1.50
11B New York Rangers/Sticks	.75	1.50
12A Philadelphia Flyers/Goalie	.50	1.00
12B Philadelphia Flyers/Sticks	.50	1.00
13 Pittsburgh Penguins	.50	1.00
14 St. Louis Blues	.50	1.00
15 Toronto Maple Leafs	.75	1.50
16 Vancouver Canucks	.50	1.00
17 Washington Capitals	.50	1.00

1979-80 Topps

The 1979-80 Topps set consists of 264 standard-size cards. Card numbers 81 and 82 (Stanley Cup Playoffs), 163 (Ulf Nilsson RB) and 261 (NHL Entries) differ from those of O-Pee-Chee. Unopened packs consist of ten cards plus a piece of bubble gum. The fronts contain a blue border that is prone to chipping. The player's name, team and position are at the top with team logo at the bottom. Career and 1978-79 statistics, short biography and a cartoon-illustrated fact about the player appear on the back. Included in this set are players from the four remaining WHA franchises that were absorbed by the NHL. The franchises are the Edmonton Oilers, Hartford Whalers, Quebec Nordiques and Winnipeg Jets. The set features the Rookie Card of Wayne Gretzky and the last cards of a Hall of Fame crop including Gordie Howe, Bobby Hull, Ken Dryden and Stan Mikita.

COMPLETE SET (264)	400.00	600.00
1 Bossy/Dionne/Lafleur LL	1.50	4.00
2 Trott/Lafleur/Dionne LL	.75	2.00
3 Trott/Dionne/Lafleur LL	1.00	2.50
4 Williams/Holt/Schultz LL	.25	.60
5 Bossy/Dionne/Gardner LL	1.00	2.50
6 Dryden/Resch/Parent LL	1.25	3.00
7 Lafleur/Bossy/Trott/ LL	1.00	2.50
8A Dryden/Espo/Par LL ERR	3.00	8.00
8B Dryden/Espo/Par LL COR	1.50	4.00
9 Greg Malone	.15	.40
10 Rick Middleton	.25	.60
11 Greg Smith	.15	.40
12 Rene Robert	.25	.60
13 Doug Risebrough	.25	.60
14 Bob Kelly	.15	.40
15 Walt Tkaczuk	.25	.60
16 John Marks	.15	.40
17 Willie Huber RC	.15	.40
18 Wayne Gretzky RC	350.00	550.00
19 Ron Sedlbauer	.15	.40
20 Glenn Resch AS2	.25	.60
21 Blair Chapman	.15	.40
22 Ron Zanussi	.15	.40
23 Brad Park	.40	1.00
24 Yvon Lambert	.15	.40
25 Andre Savard	.15	.40
26 Jimmy Watson	.15	.40
27 Hal Philipoff RC	.15	.40
28 Dan Bouchard	.25	.60
29 Bob Sirois	.15	.40
30 Ulf Nilsson	.25	.60
31 Mike Murphy	.15	.40
32 Stefan Persson	.15	.40
33 Garry Unger	.25	.60
34 Rejean Houle	.15	.40
35 Barry Beck	.25	.60
36 Tim Young	.15	.40
37 Rick Dudley	.15	.40
38 Wayne Stephenson	.25	.60
39 Peter McNab	.25	.60
40 Borje Salming AS2	.25	.60
41 Tom Lysiak	.15	.40
42 Don Maloney RC	.50	1.25
43 Mike Rogers	.25	.60
44 Dave Lewis	.15	.40
45 Peter Lee	.15	.40
46 Marty Howe	.40	1.00
47 Serge Bernier	.15	.40
48 Paul Woods	.15	.40
49 Bob Sauve	.25	.60
50 Larry Robinson AS1	.60	1.50
51 Tom Gorence RC	.25	.60
52 Gary Sargent	.15	.40
53 Thomas Gradin RC	.50	1.25
54 Dean Talafous	.15	.40
55 Bob Murray	.15	.40
56 Bob Bourne	.25	.60
57 Larry Patey	.15	.40
58 Ross Lonsberry	.15	.40
59 Rick Smith	.15	.40
60 Guy Chouinard	.25	.60
61 Danny Gare	.25	.60
62 Jim Bedard	.25	.60
63 Dale McCourt	.15	.40
64 Steve Payne RC	.40	1.00
65 Pat Hughes RC	.15	.40
66 Mike McEwen	.15	.40
67 Reg Kerr RC	.25	.60
68 Walt McKechnie	.15	.40
69 Michel Plasse	.25	.60
70 Denis Potvin AS1	.40	1.00
71 Dave Dryden	.25	.60
72 Gary McAdam	.15	.40
73 Andre St.Laurent	.15	.40
74 Jerry Korab	.15	.40
75 Rick MacLeish	.40	1.00

Card	Low	High
76 Dennis Kearns	.15	.40
77 Jean Pronovost	.25	.60
78 Ron Greschner	.25	.60
79 Wayne Cashman	.40	1.00
80 Tony Esposito	.40	1.00
81 Cup Semi-Finals	.25	.60
82 Cup Semi-Finals	.25	.60
83 Stanley Cup Finals	.60	1.50
84 Brian Sutter	.75	2.00
85 Gerry Cheevers	.40	1.00
86 Pat Hickey	.15	.40
87 Mike Kaszycki	.15	.40
88 Grant Mulvey	.15	.40
89 Derek Smith	.15	.40
90 Steve Shutt	.40	1.00
91 Robert Picard	.15	.40
92 Dan Labraaten	.15	.40
93 Glen Sharpley	.15	.40
94 Denis Herron	.25	.60
95 Reggie Leach	.40	1.00
96 John Van Boxmeer	.15	.40
97 Tiger Williams	.40	1.00
98 Butch Goring	.25	.60
99 Don Marcotte	.15	.40
100 Bryan Trottier AS1	1.00	2.50
101 Serge Savard AS2	.40	1.00
102 Cliff Koroll	.15	.40
103 Gary Smith	.25	.60
104 Al MacAdam	.15	.40
105 Don Edwards	.25	.60
106 Errol Thompson	.15	.40
107 Andre Lacroix	.25	.60
108 Marc Tardif	.25	.60
109 Rick Kehoe	.25	.60
110 John Davidson	.25	.60
111 Behn Wilson RC	.25	.60
112 Doug Jarvis	.25	.60
113 Tom Rowe RC	.15	.40
114 Mike Milbury	.25	.60
115 Billy Harris	.15	.40
116 Greg Fox RC	.15	.40
117 Curt Fraser RC	.25	.60
118 Jean-Paul Parise	.15	.40
119 Ric Seiling	.15	.40
120 Darryl Sittler	.40	1.00
121 Rick Lapointe	.15	.40
122 Jim Rutherford	.25	.60
123 Mario Tremblay	.25	.60
124 Randy Carlyle	.40	1.00
125 Bobby Clarke	.60	1.50
126 Wayne Thomas	.25	.60
127 Ivan Boldirev	.15	.40
128 Ted Bulley	.15	.40
129 Dick Redmond	.15	.40
130 Clark Gillies AS1	.25	.60
131 Checklist 1-132	5.00	12.00
132 Vaclav Nedomansky	.15	.40
133 Richard Mulhern	.15	.40
134 Dave Schultz	.40	1.00
135 Guy Lapointe	.25	.60
136 Gilles Meloche	.25	.60
137 Randy Pierce RC	.15	.40
138 Cam Connor	.15	.40
139 George Ferguson	.15	.40
140 Bill Barber	.40	1.00
141 Mike Walton	.25	.60
142 Wayne Babych RC	.40	1.00
143 Phil Russell	.15	.40
144 Bobby Schmautz	.15	.40
145 Carol Vadnais	.15	.40
146 John Tonelli RC	2.00	5.00
147 Peter Marsh RC	.25	.60
148 Thommie Bergman	.15	.40
149 Richard Martin	.40	1.00
150 Ken Dryden AS1	2.50	6.00
151 Kris Manery	.15	.40
152 Guy Charron	.15	.40
153 Lanny McDonald	.40	1.00
154 Ron Stackhouse	.15	.40
155 Stan Mikita	.60	1.50
156 Paul Holmgren	.25	.60
157 Perry Miller	.15	.40
158 Gary Croteau	.15	.40
159 Dave Maloney	.15	.40
160 Marcel Dionne AS2	.75	2.00
161 Mike Bossy RB	1.00	2.50
162 Don Maloney RB	.15	.40
163 Ulf Nilsson RB	.25	.60
164 Brad Park RB	.15	.40
165 Bryan Trottier RB	.40	1.00
166 Al Hill RC	.15	.40
167 Gary Bromley	.25	.60
168 Don Murdoch	.15	.40
169 Wayne Merrick	.15	.40
170 Bob Gainey	.40	1.00
171 Jim Schoenfeld	.25	.60
172 Gregg Sheppard	.15	.40
173 Dan Bolduc RC	.15	.40
174 Blake Dunlop	.15	.40
175 Gordie Howe	8.00	20.00
176 Richard Brodeur	.40	1.00
177 Tom Younghans	.15	.40
178 Andre Dupont	.15	.40
179 Ed Johnstone RC	.25	.60
180 Gilbert Perreault	.40	1.00
181 Bob Lorimer RC	.15	.40
182 John Wensink	.15	.40
183 Lee Fogolin	.15	.40
184 Greg Carroll RC	.15	.40
185 Bobby Hull	6.00	15.00
186 Harold Snepsts	.15	.40
187 Peter Mahovlich	.25	.60
188 Eric Vail	.15	.40
189 Phil Myre	.25	.60
190 Wilf Paiement	.25	.60
191 Charlie Simmer RC	2.00	5.00
192 Per-Olov Brasar	.15	.40
193 Lorne Henning	.15	.40
194 Don Luce	.15	.40
195 Steve Vickers	.15	.40
196 Bob Miller RC	.15	.40
197 Mike Palmateer	.40	1.00
198 Nick Libett	.15	.40
199 Pat Ribble RC	.15	.40
200 Guy Lafleur AS1	1.50	4.00
201 Mel Bridgman	.25	.60
202 Morris Lukowich RC	.25	.60
203 Don Lever	.15	.40
204 Tom Bladon	.15	.40
205 Garry Howatt	.15	.40
206 Bobby Smith RC	2.00	4.00
207 Craig Ramsay	.25	.60
208 Ron Duguay	.25	.60
209 Gilles Gilbert	.40	1.00
210 Bob MacMillan	.15	.40
211 Pierre Mondou	.15	.40
212 J.P. Bordeleau	.15	.40
213 Reed Larson	.25	.60
214 Dennis Ververgaert	.15	.40
215 Bernie Federko	.75	2.00
216 Mark Howe	.75	2.00
217 Bob Nystrom	.15	.40
218 Orest Kindrachuk	.15	.40
219 Mike Fidler	.15	.40
220 Phil Esposito	.50	1.25
221 Bill Hajt	.15	.40
222 Mark Napier	.25	.60
223 Dennis Maruk	.25	.60
224 Dennis Polonich	.15	.40
225 Jean Ratelle	.25	.60
226 Bob Dailey	.15	.40
227 Alain Daigle	.15	.40
228 Ian Turnbull	.15	.40
229 Jack Valiquette	.15	.40
230 Mike Bossy AS2	5.00	10.00
231 Brad Maxwell	.15	.40
232 Dave Taylor	1.50	4.00
233 Pierre Larouche	.40	1.00
234 Rod Schutt RC	.15	.40
235 Rogatien Vachon	.40	1.00
236 Ryan Walter RC	.40	1.00
237 Checklist 133-264	5.00	12.00
238 Terry O'Reilly	.40	1.00
239 Real Cloutier	.25	.60
240 Anders Hedberg	.25	.60
241 Ken Linseman RC	1.00	2.50
242 Billy Smith	.40	1.00
243 Rick Chartraw	.15	.40
244 Flames Team	.60	1.50
245 Bruins Team	.60	1.50
246 Sabres Team	.60	1.50
247 Blackhawks Team	.60	1.50
248 Rockies Team	.60	1.50
249 Red Wings Team	.60	1.50
250 Kings Team	.60	1.50
251 North Stars Team	.60	1.50
252 Canadiens Team	1.25	3.00
253 Islanders Team	.75	2.00
254 Rangers Team	.60	1.50
255 Flyers Team	.60	1.50
256 Penguins Team	.60	1.50
257 Blues Team	.60	1.50
258 Maple Leafs Team	.75	2.00
259 Canucks Team	.75	2.00
260 Capitals Team	.60	1.50
261 New NHL Entries CL	7.00	15.00
262 Jean Hamel	.15	.40
263 Stan Jonathan	.15	.40
264 Russ Anderson	.60	1.50

1979-80 Topps Team Stickers

This set of team sticker inserts measures the standard size, 2 1/2" by 3 1/2". They were issued one per wax pack and carry a 1979 copyright date. Each team insert consists of two stickers on one card: a team logo and a second sticker that is subdivided into three mini-stickers. The three mini-stickers picture a hockey icon (stick, goalie, puck, etc.), a hockey word (goal, wing, score, defense), and a one-digit number. Many were essentially a re-issue of a 1978-79 sticker with a different copyright date. The horizontally oriented back has an offer for personalized trading cards which expired 12/31/80.

Card	Low	High
COMPLETE SET (22)	10.00	20.00
1 Atlanta Flames	.60	1.50
2 Boston Bruins	.60	1.50
3 Buffalo Sabres	.50	1.25
4 Chicago Blackhawks	.60	1.50
5 Colorado Rockies	.60	1.50
6 Detroit Red Wings	.60	1.50
7 Edmonton Oilers	.60	1.50
8 Hartford Whalers	.50	1.25
9 Los Angeles Kings	.50	1.25
10 Minnesota North Stars	.50	1.25
11A Montreal Canadiens goalie	.60	1.50
11B Montreal Canadiens score	.60	1.50
12 New York Islanders	.50	1.25
13 New York Rangers	.60	1.50
14 Philadelphia Flyers	.50	1.25
15 Pittsburgh Penguins UER	.60	1.50
16 Quebec Nordiques	.60	1.50
17 St. Louis Blues	.50	1.25
18 Toronto Maple Leafs	.60	1.50
19 Vancouver Canucks	.50	1.25
20 Washington Capitals	.50	1.25
21 Winnipeg Jets	.50	1.25

1980-81 Topps

The 1980-81 Topps set features 264 standard-size cards. The fronts contain a puck (black ink) at the bottom right which can be scratched-off to reveal the player's name. Yearly statistics including minor leagues, a short biography and a cartoon-illustrated hockey fact are included on the back. Members of the U.S. Olympic team are designated by USA.

Card	Low	High
COMPLETE SET (264)	100.00	200.00
*SCRATCHED: .20X to .40X		
1 Flyers RB	.30	.75
2 Ray Bourque RB	4.00	10.00
3 Wayne Gretzky RB	6.00	15.00
4 Charlie Simmer RB	.30	.75
5 Billy Smith RB	.20	.50
6 Jean Ratelle	.20	.50
7 Dave Maloney	.15	.40
8 Phil Myre	.20	.50
9 Ken Morrow OLY RC	.60	1.50
10 Guy Lafleur	.60	1.50
11 Bill Derlago RC	.15	.40
12 Doug Wilson	.30	.75
13 Craig Ramsay	.12	.30
14 Pat Boutette	.12	.30
15 Eric Vail	.12	.30
16 Mike Foligno TL	.40	1.00
17 Bobby Smith	.40	1.00
18 Rick Kehoe	.15	.40
19 Joel Quenneville	.12	.30
20 Marcel Dionne	.40	1.00
21 Kevin McCarthy	.12	.30
22 Jim Craig OLY RC	4.00	10.00
23 Steve Vickers	.12	.30
24 Ken Linseman	.20	.50
25 Mike Bossy	1.25	3.00
26 Serge Savard	.25	.60
27 Grant Mulvey TL	.15	.40
28 Pat Hickey	.12	.30
29 Peter Sullivan	.12	.30
30 Blaine Stoughton	.15	.40
31 Mike Liut RC	2.00	5.00
32 Blair MacDonald	.12	.30
33 Rick Green	.12	.30
34 Al MacAdam	.15	.40
35 Robbie Ftorek	.12	.30
36 Dick Redmond	.12	.30
37 Ron Duguay	.15	.40
38 Danny Gare TL	.15	.40
39 Brian Propp RC	2.00	5.00
40 Bryan Trottier	.50	1.25
41 Rich Preston	.12	.30
42 Pierre Mondou	.12	.30
43 Reed Larson	.12	.30
44 George Ferguson	.12	.30
45 Guy Chouinard	.20	.50
46 Billy Harris	.12	.30
47 Gilles Meloche	.20	.50
48 Blair Chapman	.12	.30
49 Mike Gartner TL	1.50	4.00
50 Darryl Sittler	.25	.60
51 Richard Martin	.20	.50
52 Ivan Boldirev	.12	.30
53 Craig Norwich RC	.12	.30
54 Dennis Polonich	.12	.30
55 Bobby Clarke	.60	1.50
56 Terry O'Reilly	.20	.50
57 Carol Vadnais	.12	.30
58 Bob Gainey	.25	.60
59 Blaine Stoughton TL	.15	.40
60 Billy Smith	.20	.50
61 Mike O'Connell RC	.30	.75
62 Lanny McDonald	.25	.60
63 Lee Fogolin	.12	.30
64 Rocky Saganiuk RC	.12	.30
65 Rolf Edberg RC	.12	.30
66 Paul Shmyr	.12	.30
67 Michel Goulet RC	4.00	10.00
68 Dan Bouchard	.20	.50
69 Mark Johnson OLY RC	.60	1.50
70 Reggie Leach	.15	.40
71 Bernie Federko TL	.40	1.00
72 Peter Mahovlich	.20	.50
73 Anders Hedberg	.20	.50
74 Brad Park	.15	.40
75 Clark Gillies	.20	.50
76 Doug Jarvis	.12	.30
77 John Garrett	.20	.50
78 Dave Hutchinson	.12	.30
79 John Anderson RC	.25	.60
80 Gilbert Perreault	.20	.50
81 Marcel Dionne AS1	.40	1.00
82 Guy Lafleur AS1	.60	1.50
83 Charlie Simmer AS1	.30	.75
84 Larry Robinson AS1	.25	.60
85 Borje Salming AS1	.15	.40
86 Tony Esposito AS1	.30	.75
87 Wayne Gretzky AS2	8.00	20.00
88 Danny Gare AS2	.15	.40
89 Steve Shutt AS2	.15	.40
90 Barry Beck AS2	.15	.40
91 Mark Howe AS2	.30	.75
92 Don Edwards AS2	.15	.40
93 Tom McCarthy RC	.12	.30
94 P.McNab/R.Middleton TL	.20	.50
95 Mike Palmateer	.20	.50
96 Jim Schoenfeld	.20	.50
97 Jordy Douglas	.12	.30
98 Keith Brown RC	.15	.40
99 Dennis Ververgaert	.12	.30
100 Phil Esposito	.30	.75
101 Jack Brownschidle	.12	.30
102 Bob Nystrom	.12	.30
103 Steve Christoff OLY RC	.20	.50
104 Rob Palmer	.12	.30
105 Tiger Williams	.15	.40
106 Kent Nilsson TL	.15	.40
107 Morris Lukowich	.20	.50
108 Jack Valiquette	.12	.30
109 Richie Dunn RC	.12	.30
110 Rogatien Vachon	.25	.60
111 Mark Napier	.12	.30
112 Gordie Roberts	.12	.30
113 Stan Jonathan	.12	.30
114 Brett Callighen	.12	.30
115 Rick MacLeish	.20	.50
116 Ulf Nilsson	.20	.50
117 Rick Kehoe TL	.15	.40
118 Dan Maloney	.12	.30
119 Terry Ruskowski	.12	.30
120 Denis Potvin	.50	1.25
121 Wayne Stephenson	.20	.50
122 Rich Leduc	.12	.30
123 Checklist 1-132	1.50	4.00
124 Don Lever	.12	.30
125 Jim Rutherford	.20	.50
126 Ray Allison RC	.12	.30
127 Mike Ramsey OLY RC	1.00	2.50
128 Stan Smyl TL	.30	.75
129 Al Secord RC	1.00	2.50
130 Denis Herron	.20	.50
131 Bob Dailey	.12	.30
132 Dean Talafous	.12	.30
133 Ian Turnbull	.12	.30
134 Ron Sedlbauer	.12	.30
135 Tom Bladon	.12	.30
136 Bernie Federko	.60	1.50
137 Dave Taylor	.75	2.00
138 Bob Lorimer	.12	.30
139 MacAdam/Payne TL	.15	.40
140 Ray Bourque RC	15.00	40.00
141 Glen Hanlon	.20	.50
142 Willy Lindstrom	.12	.30
143 Mike Rogers	.12	.30
144 Tony McKegney RC	.15	.40
145 Behn Wilson	.12	.30
146 Lucien DeBlois	.12	.30
147 Dave Burrows	.12	.30
148 Paul Woods	.12	.30
149 Phil Esposito TL	.30	.75
150 Tony Esposito	.60	1.50
151 Pierre Larouche	.20	.50
152 Brad Maxwell	.12	.30
153 Stan Weir	.12	.30
154 Ryan Walter	.12	.30
155 Dale Hoganson	.12	.30
156 Anders Kallur RC	.12	.30
157 Paul Reinhart RC	.40	1.00
158 Greg Millen	.20	.50
159 Ric Seiling	.12	.30
160 Mark Howe	.60	1.50
161 Goals Leaders	.30	.75
Danny Gare (1)		
Charlie Simmer (1)		
Blaine Stoughton (1)		
162 Gretz/Dio/Laf LL	5.00	12.00
163 Gretz/Dio/Laf LL	4.00	10.00
164 Penalty Minutes	.20	.50
Leaders		
Jimmy Mann (1)		
Dave (Tiger) Williams (2)		
Paul Holmgren (3)		
165 Power Play Goals	.40	1.00
Leaders		
Charlie Simmer (1)		
Marcel Dionne (2)		
Danny Gare (2)		
Steve Shutt (2)		
Darryl Sittler (2)		
166 Goals Against Average	.20	.50
Leaders		
Bob Sauve (1)		
Denis Herron (2)		
Don Edwards (3)		
167 Game-Winning Goals	.15	.40
Leaders		
Danny Gare (1)		
Peter McNab (2)		
Blaine Stoughton (2)		
168 Espo/Chee/Gar/McN	.30	.75
169 Perry Turnbull RC	.12	.30
170 Barry Beck	.15	.40
171 Charlie Simmer TL	.30	.75
172 Paul Holmgren	.20	.50
173 Willie Huber	.12	.30
174 Tim Young	.12	.30
175 Gilles Gilbert	.20	.50
176 Dave Christian OLY RC	.75	2.00
177 Lars Lindgren RC	.12	.30
178 Real Cloutier	.15	.40
179 Laurie Boschman RC	.15	.40
180 Steve Shutt	.15	.40
181 Bob Murray	.12	.30
182 Wayne Gretzky TL	6.00	12.00

183 John Van Boxmeer .12 .30
184 Nick Fotiu .20 .50
185 Mike McEwen .12 .30
186 Greg Malone .12 .30
187 Mike Foligno RC 1.25 3.00
188 Dave Langevin RC .12 .30
189 Mel Bridgman .12 .30
190 John Davidson .20 .50
191 Mike Milbury .20 .50
192 Ron Zanussi .12 .30
193 Darryl Sittler TL .25 .60
194 John Marks .12 .30
195 Mike Gartner RC 6.00 15.00
196 Dave Lewis .12 .30
197 Kent Nilsson RC 1.00 2.50
198 Rick Ley .12 .30
199 Derek Smith .12 .30
200 Bill Barber .20 .50
201 Guy Lapointe .20 .50
202 Vaclav Nedomansky .12 .30
203 Don Murdoch .12 .30
204 Mike Bossy TL .60 1.50
205 Pierre Hamel RC .20 .50
206 Mike Eaves RC .12 .30
207 Doug Halward .12 .30
208 Stan Smyl RC .50 1.25
209 Mike Zuke RC .12 .30
210 Borje Salming .15 .40
211 Walt Tkaczuk .20 .50
212 Grant Mulvey .15 .40
213 Rob Ramage RC .40 1.00
214 Tom Rowe .12 .30
215 Don Edwards .15 .40
216 G.Lafleur/P.Larouche TL .60 1.50
217 Dan Labraaten .12 .30
218 Glen Sharpley .12 .30
219 Stefan Persson .12 .30
220 Peter McNab .15 .40
221 Doug Hicks .12 .30
222 Bengt Gustafsson RC .12 .30
223 Michel Dion .20 .50
224 Jimmy Watson .12 .30
225 Wilf Paiement .12 .30
226 Phil Russell .12 .30
227 Morris Lukowich TL .20 .50
228 Ron Stackhouse .12 .30
229 Ted Bulley .12 .30
230 Larry Robinson .25 .60
231 Don Maloney .12 .30
232 Rob McClanahan OLY RC .15 .40
233 Al Sims .12 .30
234 Errol Thompson .12 .30
235 Glenn Resch .20 .50
236 Bob Miller .12 .30
237 Gary Sargent .12 .30
238 Real Cloutier TL .15 .40
239 Rene Robert .25 .60
240 Charlie Simmer .60 1.50
241 Thomas Gradin .12 .30
242 Rick Vaive RC 1.25 3.00
243 Ron Wilson RC .12 .30
244 Brian Sutter .40 1.00
245 Dale McCourt .12 .30
246 Yvon Lambert .12 .30
247 Tom Lysiak .12 .30
248 Ron Greschner .12 .30
249 Reggie Leach TL .15 .40
250 Wayne Gretzky 20.00 50.00
251 Rick Middleton .20 .50
252 Al Smith .20 .50
253 Fred Barrett .12 .30
254 Butch Goring .20 .50
255 Robert Picard .12 .30
256 Marc Tardif .12 .30
257 Checklist 133-264 1.50 4.00
258 Barry Long .12 .30
259 Rene Robert TL .25 .60
260 Danny Gare .15 .40
261 Rejean Houle .12 .30
262 Stanley Cup Semifinals .15 .40
263 Stanley Cup Semifinals .15 .40
264 Stanley Cup Finals .50 1.25

1980-81 Topps Team Posters

The 1980-81 Topps pin-up posters were issued as folded inserts (approximately 5" by 7" horizontal) to the 1980-81 Topps regular hockey issue. These 16 numbered posters are in full color with a white border on very thin stock. The posters feature posed shots (on ice) of the entire 1979-80 hockey team. The name of the team is indicated in large letters to the left of the hockey puck, which contains the designation 1979-80 Season. Fold lines or creases are natural and do not detract from the condition of the poster. For some reason the Edmonton Oilers, Quebec Nordiques, and Winnipeg Jets were not included in this set.

COMPLETE SET (16) 12.50 25.00
1 New York Islanders .60 1.50
2 New York Rangers .75 2.00
3 Philadelphia Flyers .60 1.50
4 Boston Bruins 1.00 2.50
5 Whalers w/Howe 1.50 4.00
6 Buffalo Sabres .60 1.50
7 Chicago Blackhawks 1.00 2.50
8 Detroit Red Wings 1.00 2.50
9 Minn. North Stars .75 2.00
10 Toronto Maple Leafs 1.00 2.50
11 Montreal Canadiens 1.00 2.50
12 Colorado Rockies 1.00 2.50
13 Los Angeles Kings 1.25 3.00
14 Vancouver Canucks .60 1.50
15 St. Louis Blues .60 1.50
16 Washington Capitals .60 1.50

1956 Topps Hocus Focus

The 1956 Topps Hocus Focus set is very similar in size and design to the 1948 Topps Magic Photos set. It contains at least 96 small (approximately 7/8" by 1 5/8") individual cards featuring a variety of sports and non-sport subjects. They were printed with both a series card number (by subject matter) on the back as well as a card number reflecting the entire set. The fronts were developed, much like a photograph, from a blank appearance by using moisture and sunlight. Due to varying degrees of photographic sensitivity, the clarity of these cards ranges from fully developed to poorly developed. A premium album holding 126-cards was also issued leading to the theory that there are actually 126 different cards. A few High Series (#97-126) cards have been discovered and cataloged below although a full 126-card checklist is yet unknown. The cards do reference the set name "Hocus Focus" on the backs unlike the 1948 Magic Photos. Finally, a slightly smaller version (roughly 7/8" by 1 7/16") of some of the cards has also been found, but a full checklist is not known.

61 Hockey 15.00 30.00

1948 Topps Magic Photos

The 1948 Topps Magic Photos set contains 252 small (approximately 7/8" by 1 7/16") individual cards featuring sport and non-sport subjects. They were issued in 19 lettered series with cards numbered within each series. The fronts were developed, much like a photograph, from a "blank" appearance by using moisture and sunlight. Due to varying degrees of photographic sensitivity, the clarity of these cards ranges from fully developed to poorly developed. This set contains Topps' first baseball cards. A premium album holding 126-cards was also issued. The set is sometimes confused with Topps' 1956 Hocus-Focus set, although the cards in this set are slightly smaller than those in the Hocus-Focus set. The checklist below is presented by series. Poorly developed cards are considered in lesser condition and hence have lesser value. The catalog designation for this set is R714-27. Each type of card subject has a letter prefix as follows: Boxing Champions (A), All-American Basketball (B), All-American Football (C), Wrestling Champions (D), Track and Field Champions (E), Stars of Stage and Screen (F), American Dogs (G), General Sports (H), Movie Stars (J), Baseball Hall of Fame (K), Aviation Pioneers (L), Famous Landmarks (M), American Inventors (N), American Military Leaders (O), American Explorers (P), Basketball Thrills (Q), Football Thrills (R), Figures of the Wild West (S), and General Sports (T).

COMPLETE SET (252) 3,000.00 5,000.00
T3 Ice Hockey 15.00 30.00

1963-64 Toronto Star

This set of 42 photos was distributed one per week with the Toronto Star and was also available as a complete set directly. The photos measure approximately 4 3/4" by 6 3/4" and are entitled, "Hockey Stars in Action." There is a short write-up on the back of each photo. The player's team is identified in the checklist below, Boston Bruins (BB), Chicago Blackhawks (CBH), Detroit Red Wings (DRW), Montreal Canadiens (MC), New York Rangers (NYR), and Toronto Maple Leafs (TML). Since the photos are unnumbered, they are listed below in alphabetical order.

COMPLETE SET (42) 150.00 300.00
1 George Armstrong TML 4.00 8.00
2 Andy Bathgate NYR 4.00 8.00
3 Bob Baun TML 2.50 5.00
4 Jean Beliveau MC 7.50 15.00
5 Leo Boivin BB 2.50 5.00
6 Johnny Bower TML 5.00 10.00
7 Carl Brewer TML 2.50 5.00
8 Johnny Bucyk BB 4.00 8.00
9 Alex Delvecchio DRW 5.00 10.00
10 Kent Douglas TML 2.00 4.00
11 Dick Duff TML 2.50 5.00
12 Bill Gadsby DRW 3.00 6.00
13 Jean-Guy Gendron BB 2.00 4.00
14 BoomBoom Geoffrion MC 7.50 15.00
15 Glenn Hall CBH 6.00 12.00
16 Doug Harvey NYR 5.00 10.00
17 Bill Hay CBH 2.50 5.00
18 Camille Henry NYR 2.50 5.00
19 Tim Horton TML 7.50 15.00
20 Gordie Howe DRW 25.00 50.00
21 Bobby Hull CBH 15.00 30.00
22 Red Kelly TML 5.00 10.00
23 Dave Keon TML 7.50 15.00
24 Parker MacDonald DRW 2.00 4.00
25 Frank Mahovlich TML 7.50 15.00
26 Stan Mikita CBH 7.50 15.00
27 Dickie Moore MC 5.00 10.00
28 Eric Nesterenko CBH 2.50 5.00
29 Marcel Pronovost DRW 2.50 5.00
30 Claude Provost MC 2.50 5.00
31 Bob Pulford TML 3.00 6.00
32 Henri Richard MC 7.50 15.00
33 Terry Sawchuk DRW 10.00 20.00
34 Eddie Shack TML 5.00 10.00
35 Allan Stanley TML 3.00 6.00
36 Ron Stewart TML 2.00 4.00
37 Jean-Guy Talbot MC 2.50 5.00
38 Gilles Tremblay MC 2.00 4.00
39 J.C. Tremblay MC 2.50 5.00
40 Norm Ullman DRW 4.00 8.00
41 Elmer Vasko CBH 2.00 4.00
42 Ken Wharram CBH 2.50 5.00

1964-65 Toronto Star

This set of 48 photos was distributed one per week with the Toronto Star and was also available as a complete set directly. The direct complete sets also included a booklet and glossy photo of Dave Keon in the mail-away package. These blank-backed photos measure approximately 4 1/8" by 5 1/8". The player's team is identified in the checklist below, Boston Bruins (BB), Chicago Blackhawks (CBH), Detroit Red Wings (DRW), Montreal Canadiens (MC), New York Rangers (NYR), and Toronto Maple Leafs (TML). Since the photos are unnumbered, they are listed below in alphabetical order. There was an album (actually a folder) available for each team to slot in cards. However when the cards were placed in the album it rendered the card's caption unreadable as only the action photo was visible.

COMPLETE SET (48) 150.00 300.00
1 Dave Balon MC 2.00 4.00
2 Andy Bathgate TML 4.00 8.00
3 Bob Baun TML 3.00 6.00
4 Jean Beliveau MC 7.50 15.00
5 Red Berenson MC 2.50 5.00
6 Leo Boivin BB 3.00 6.00
7 Carl Brewer TML 2.50 5.00
8 Alex Delvecchio DRW 4.00 8.00
9 Rod Gilbert NYR 4.00 8.00
10 Ted Green BB 2.50 5.00
11 Glenn Hall CBH 5.00 10.00
12 Billy Harris TML 2.00 4.00
13 Bill Hay CBH 2.00 4.00
14 Paul Henderson DRW 3.00 6.00
15 Wayne Hillman CBH 2.00 4.00
16 Charlie Hodge MC 3.00 6.00
17 Tim Horton TML 7.50 15.00
18 Gordie Howe DRW 20.00 40.00
19 Harry Howell NYR 3.00 6.00
20 Bobby Hull CBH 12.50 25.00
21 Larry Jeffrey DRW 2.00 4.00
22 Tom Johnson BB 3.00 6.00
23 Forbes Kennedy BB 2.00 4.00
24 Dave Keon TML 6.00 12.00
25 Orland Kurtenbach BB 2.50 5.00
26 Jacques Laperriere MC 2.50 5.00
27 Parker MacDonald DRW 2.00 4.00
28 Al MacNeil CBH 2.00 4.00
29 Frank Mahovlich TML 6.00 12.00
30 Chico Maki CBH 2.00 4.00
31 Don McKenney TML 2.00 4.00
32 John McKenzie CBH 2.50 5.00
33 Stan Mikita CBH 6.00 12.00
34 Jim Neilson NYR 2.00 4.00
35 Jim Pappin TML 2.00 4.00
36 Pierre Pilote CBH 3.00 6.00
37 Jacques Plante NYR 10.00 20.00
38 Marcel Pronovost DRW 3.00 6.00
39 Claude Provost MC 2.50 5.00
40 Bob Pulford TML 3.00 6.00
41 Henri Richard MC 6.00 12.00
42 Wayne Rivers BB 2.00 4.00
43 Floyd Smith DRW 2.00 4.00
44 Allan Stanley TML 4.00 8.00
45 Ron Stewart TML 2.00 4.00
46 J.C. Tremblay MC 2.50 5.00
47 Norm Ullman DRW 4.00 8.00
48 Elmer Vasko CBH 2.00 4.00
xx Album 12.50 25.00
Folder

1971-72 Toronto Sun

This set of 294 photo cards with two punch holes has never been very popular with collectors. The photos are quite fragile, printed on thin paper, and measure approximately 5" by 7". The checklist below is in team order as follows: Boston Bruins (1-21), Buffalo Sabres (22-41), California Golden Seals (42-61), Chicago Blackhawks (62-82), Detroit Red Wings (83-103), Los Angeles Kings (104-124), Minnesota North Stars (125-145), Montreal Canadiens (146-166), New York Rangers (167-186), Philadelphia Flyers (187-208), Pittsburgh Penguins (209-230), St. Louis Blues (231-252), Toronto Maple Leafs (253-274), and Vancouver Canucks (275-294). The cards were intended to fit in a two-ring binder specially made to hold the cards. Also included was and introduction photo, with text by Scott Young.

COMPLETE SET (294) 300.00 600.00
1 Boston Bruins 1.50 3.00
2 Don Awrey .50 1.00
3 Garnet Bailey .50 1.00
4 Ivan Boldirev .50 1.00
5 Johnny Bucyk 3.00 6.00
6 Wayne Cashman .75 1.50
7 Gerry Cheevers 4.00 8.00
8 Phil Esposito 10.00 20.00
9 Ted Green .75 1.50
10 Ken Hodge .75 1.50
11 Ed Johnston 1.50 3.00
12 Reggie Leach 1.50 3.00
13 Don Marcotte .50 1.00
14 John McKenzie .50 1.00
15 Bobby Orr 30.00 60.00
16 Derek Sanderson 4.00 8.00
17 Dallas Smith .50 1.00
18 Richard Allan Smith .50 1.00
19 Fred Stanfield .50 1.00
20 Mike Walton .75 1.50
21 Ed Westfall .75 1.50
22 Buffalo Sabres 1.00 2.00
23 Doug Barrie .50 1.00
24 Roger Crozier 2.00 4.00
25 Dave Dryden 1.00 2.00
26 Dick Duff .75 1.50
27 Phil Goyette .50 1.00
28 Al Hamilton .50 1.00
29 Larry Keenan .50 1.00
30 Danny Lawson .50 1.00
31 Don Luce .50 1.00
32 Richard Martin 1.00 2.00
33 Ray McKay .50 1.00
34 Gerry Meehan .75 1.50
35 Kevin O'Shea .50 1.00
36 Gilbert Perreault 4.00 8.00
37 Tracy Pratt .50 1.00
38 Mike Robitaille .50 1.00
39 Eddie Shack 2.00 4.00
40 Jim Watson .50 1.00
41 Rod Zaine .50 1.00
42 California Seals 1.50 3.00
43 Wayne Carleton .50 1.00
44 Lyle Carter .50 1.00
45 Gary Croteau .50 1.00
46 Norm Ferguson .50 1.00
47 Stan Gilbertson .50 1.00
48 Ernie Hicke .50 1.00
49 Gary Jarrett 1.00 2.00
50 Joey Johnston .50 1.00
51 Marshall Johnston .50 1.00
52 Bert Marshall .50 1.00
53 Walt McKechnie .50 1.00
54 Don O'Donoghue .50 1.00
55 Gerry Pinder .75 1.50
56 Dick Redmond .50 1.00
57 Robert Sheehan .50 1.00
58 Paul Shmyr .50 1.00
59 Ron Stackhouse SP 6.00 12.00
60 Carol Vadnais .50 1.00
61 Tom Williams .50 1.00
62 Chicago Blackhawks 1.50 3.00
63 Lou Angotti .50 1.00
64 Bryan Campbell .50 1.00
65 Tony Esposito 10.00 20.00
66 Bobby Hull 15.00 30.00
67 Dennis Hull 1.00 2.00
68 Doug Jarrett .50 1.00
69 Jerry Korab .50 1.00
70 Cliff Koroll .50 1.00
71 Darryl Maggs .50 1.00
72 Keith Magnuson .75 1.50
73 Chico Maki .75 1.50
74 Dan Maloney .50 1.00
75 Pit Martin .75 1.50
76 Stan Mikita 6.00 12.00
77 Eric Nesterenko .50 1.00
78 Danny O'Shea .50 1.00
79 Jim Pappin .50 1.00
80 Gary Smith 1.00 2.00
81 Pat Stapleton .50 1.00
82 Bill White .50 1.00
83 Detroit Red Wings 1.50 3.00
84 Red Berenson .75 1.50
85 Gary Bergman .75 1.50
86 Arnie Brown .50 1.00
87 Guy Charron .50 1.00
88 Bill Collins .50 1.00
89 Brian Conacher .50 1.00
90 Joe Daley 1.50 3.00
91 Alex Delvecchio 3.00 6.00
92 Marcel Dionne 7.50 15.00
93 Tim Ecclestone .50 1.00
94 Ron Harris .50 1.00
95 Gerry Hart .50 1.00
96 Gordie Howe 25.00 50.00
97 Al Karlander .50 1.00
98 Nick Libett .75 1.50
99 Ab McDonald .50 1.00
100 James Niekamp .50 1.00
101 Mickey Redmond 2.00 4.00
102 Leon Rochefort .50 1.00
103 Al Smith .75 1.50
104 Los Angeles Kings 1.00 2.00
105 Ralph Backstrom .75 1.50
106 Bob Berry .75 1.50
107 Mike Byers .50 1.00
108 Larry Cahan .50 1.00
109 Paul Curtis .50 1.00
110 Denis DeJordy 1.50 3.00
111 Gary Edwards 1.00 2.00
112 Bill Flett .50 1.00
113 Butch Goring .75 1.50
114 Lucien Grenier .50 1.00
115 Larry Hillman .50 1.00
116 Dale Hoganson .50 1.00
117 Harry Howell 1.50 3.00
118 Eddie Joyal .50 1.00
119 Real Lemieux .50 1.00
120 Ross Lonsberry .50 1.00
121 Al McDonough .50 1.00
122 Jean Potvin .50 1.00
123 Bob Pulford 1.50 3.00
124 Juha Widing .75 1.50
125 Minnesota North Stars 1.00 2.00
126 Fred Barrett .50 1.00
127 Charlie Burns .50 1.00
128 Jude Drouin .50 1.00
129 Barry Gibbs .50 1.00
130 Gilles Gilbert 2.00 4.00
131 Bill Goldsworthy 1.00 2.00
132 Danny Grant .75 1.50
133 Ted Hampson .50 1.00
134 Ted Harris .50 1.00
135 Fred Harvey .50 1.00
136 Cesare Maniago 2.00 4.00
137 Doug Mohns .75 1.50
138 Lou Nanne .75 1.50
139 Bob Nevin .75 1.50
140 Dennis O'Brien .50 1.00
141 Murray Oliver .50 1.00
142 Jean-Paul Parise .75 1.50
143 Dean Prentice .75 1.50
144 Tom Reid .50 1.00
145 Gump Worsley 3.00 6.00
146 Montreal Canadiens 1.50 3.00
147 Pierre Bouchard .50 1.00
148 Yvan Cournoyer 3.00 6.00

Card	Low	High
149 Ken Dryden	25.00	50.00
150 Terry Harper	.75	1.50
151 Rejean Houle	.75	1.50
152 Guy Lafleur	15.00	30.00
153 Jacques Laperriere	1.00	2.00
154 Guy Lapointe	1.50	3.00
155 Claude Larose	.50	1.00
156 Jacques Lemaire	2.00	4.00
157 Frank Mahovlich	6.00	12.00
158 Pete Mahovlich	.75	1.50
159 Phil Myre	1.50	3.00
160 Larry Pleau	.75	1.50
161 Henri Richard	6.00	12.00
162 Phil Roberto	.50	1.00
163 Serge Savard	1.50	3.00
164 Marc Tardif	.75	1.50
165 J.C. Tremblay	.75	1.50
166 Rogatien Vachon	3.00	6.00
167 New York Rangers	1.50	3.00
168 Dave Balon	.50	1.00
169 Ab DeMarco	.50	1.00
170 Jack Egers	.50	1.00
171 Bill Fairbairn	.50	1.00
172 Ed Giacomin	4.00	8.00
173 Rod Gilbert	2.00	4.00
174 Vic Hadfield	.75	1.50
175 Ted Irvine	.50	1.00
176 Bruce MacGregor	.50	1.00
177 Jim Neilson	.50	1.00
178 Brad Park	3.00	6.00
179 Jean Ratelle	2.00	4.00
180 Dale Rolfe	.50	1.00
181 Bobby Rousseau	.75	1.50
182 Glen Sather	1.50	3.00
183 Rod Seiling	.50	1.00
184 Pete Stemkowski	.75	1.50
185 Walt Tkaczuk	.75	1.50
186 Gilles Villemure	1.50	3.00
187 Philadelphia Flyers	1.50	3.00
188 Barry Ashbee	1.00	2.00
189 Serge Bernier	.50	1.00
190 Larry Brown	.50	1.00
191 Bobby Clarke	10.00	20.00
192 Gary Dornhoefer	.75	1.50
193 Doug Favell	1.50	3.00
194 Bruce Gamble	2.00	4.00
195 Jean-Guy Gendron	.50	1.00
196 Larry Hale	.50	1.00
197 Wayne Hillman	.50	1.00
198 Brent Hughes	.50	1.00
199 Jim Johnson	.50	1.00
200 Bob Kelly	.50	1.00
201 Andre Lacroix	.75	1.50
202 Bill Lesuk	.50	1.00
203 Rick MacLeish	1.00	2.00
204 Larry Mickey	.50	1.00
205 Simon Nolet	.50	1.00
206 Pierre Plante	.50	1.00
207 Ed Van Impe	.50	1.00
208 Joe Watson	.50	1.00
209 Pittsburgh Penguins	1.00	2.00
210 Syl Apps	.75	1.50
211 Les Binkley	1.50	3.00
212 Wally Boyer	.50	1.00
213 Darryl Edestrand	.50	1.00
214 Roy Edwards	1.50	3.00
215 Nick Harbaruk	.50	1.00
216 Bryan Hextall	.75	1.50
217 Bill Hicke	.50	1.00
218 Tim Horton	5.00	10.00
219 Sheldon Kannegiesser	.50	1.00
220 Bob Leiter	.50	1.00
221 Keith McCreary	.50	1.00
222 Joe Noris	.50	1.00
223 Greg Polis	.50	1.00
224 Jean Pronovost	.75	1.50
225 Rene Robert	.75	1.50
226 Duane Rupp	.50	1.00
227 Ken Schinkel	.50	1.00
228 Ron Schock	.50	1.00
229 Bryan Watson	.75	1.50
230 Bob Woytowich	.50	1.00
231 St. Louis Blues	1.00	2.00
232 Al Arbour	1.50	3.00
233 John Arbour	.50	1.00
234 Chris Bordeleau	.50	1.00
235 Carl Brewer	.75	1.50
236 Gene Carr	.50	1.00
237 Wayne Connelly	.50	1.00
238 Terry Crisp	.75	1.50
239 Jim Lorentz	.50	1.00
240 Peter McDuffe	1.00	2.00
241 George Morrison	.50	1.00
242 Michel Parizeau	.50	1.00
243 Noel Picard	.50	1.00
244 Barclay Plager	.75	1.50
245 Bob Plager	.75	1.50
246 Jim Roberts	.50	1.00
247 Gary Sabourin	.50	1.00
248 Jim Shires	.50	1.00
249 Frank St.Marseille	.50	1.00
250 Bill Sutherland	.50	1.00
251 Garry Unger	1.00	2.00
252 Ernie Wakely	1.50	3.00
253 Toronto Maple Leafs	1.50	3.00
254 Bob Baun	.75	1.50
255 Jim Dorey	.50	1.00
256 Denis Dupere	.50	1.00
257 Ron Ellis	.75	1.50
258 Brian Glennie	.50	1.00
259 Jim Harrison	.50	1.00
260 Paul Henderson	1.00	2.00
261 Dave Keon	3.00	6.00
262 Rick Ley	.50	1.00
263 Billy MacMillan	.50	1.00
264 Don Marshall	.50	1.00
265 Jim McKenny	.50	1.00
266 Garry Monahan	.50	1.00
267 Bernie Parent	6.00	12.00
268 Mike Pelyk	.50	1.00
269 Jacques Plante	10.00	20.00
270 Brad Selwood	.50	1.00
271 Darryl Sittler	6.00	12.00
272 Brian Spencer	1.00	2.00
273 Guy Trottier	.50	1.00
274 Norm Ullman	2.50	5.00
275 Vancouver Canucks	1.00	2.00
276 Andre Boudrias	.50	1.00
277 George Gardiner	.50	1.00
278 Jocelyn Guevremont	.75	1.50
279 Murray Hall	.50	1.00
280 Danny Johnson	.50	1.00
281 Dennis Kearns	.50	1.00
282 Orland Kurtenbach	.75	1.50
283 Bobby Lalonde	.50	1.00
284 Wayne Maki	.50	1.00
285 Rosaire Paiement	.75	1.50
286 Paul Popiel	.50	1.00
287 Pat Quinn	1.00	2.00
288 John Schella	.50	1.00
289 Bobby Schmautz	.75	1.50
290 Fred Speck	.50	1.00
291 Dale Tallon	.75	1.50
292 Ron Ward	.50	1.00
293 Barry Wilkins	.50	1.00
294 Dunc Wilson	1.50	3.00
xx Binder	12.50	25.00
NNO Introduction Card	2.00	4.00

1972 Tower Hockey Instructions Booklets

Sponsored by Towers and Donimart stores, we have very little information about these oddball hockey instruction booklets.

Card	Low	High
1 Skating Skills	10.00	20.00

1936 Triumph Postcards

This eleven-card set was issued as a supplement to The Triumph (a newspaper). The cards measure approximately 3 1/2" by 5 1/2" and are in the postcard format. The borderless fronts feature full-length black and white posed action shots. The player's name and team name appear in the lower left corner. The back carries the typical postcard design with each player's name and biographical information in the upper corner. Different dates appear on the back of the cards, which represent the date each card was distributed. The cards were issued three the first week with The Triumph, then one per week thereafter. The cards are unnumbered and checklisted below in alphabetical order. The date mentioned below is the issue date as noted on the card back in Canadian style, day/month/year.

Card	Low	High
COMPLETE SET (11)	650.00	1,300.00
1 Lionel Conacher/22/2/36	125.00	250.00
2 Harvey Jackson	125.00	250.00
Toronto Maple Leafs/18/1/36		
3 Ivan Johnson	62.50	125.00
New York Rangers/8/2/36		
4 Herbie Lewis/7/3/36	40.00	80.00
5 Sylvio Mantha	62.50	125.00
Montreal Canadiens/18/1/36		
6 Nick Metz	40.00	80.00
Toronto Maple Leafs/15/2/36		
7 Baldy Northcott	45.00	90.00
Montreal Maroons/1/2/36		
8 Eddie Shore	250.00	500.00
Boston Bruins/25/1/36		
9 Paul Thompson	40.00	80.00
Chicago Blackhawks/29/2/36		
10 Roy Worters	62.50	125.00
New York Americans/18/1/36		
11 Charley Conacher	40.00	80.00

1961-62 Union Oil WHL

This 12-drawing set features players from the Los Angeles Blades (1-8) and the San Francisco Seals (9-12) of the Western Hockey League. The black-and-white drawings by artist Sam Patrick measure approximately 6" by 8" and are printed on textured white paper. The back of each drawing carries the player's career highlights and biographical information. The Union Oil name and logo at the bottom round out the backs. The cards are unnumbered and listed below alphabetically within teams. Reportedly only eight cards were issued to the public, making four of the cards extremely scarce.

Card	Low	High
COMPLETE SET (12)	50.00	100.00
1 Jack Bownass	3.00	6.00
2 Ed Diachuk	3.00	6.00
3 Leo LaBine	5.00	10.00
4 Willie O'Ree	20.00	40.00
5 Bruce Carmichael	3.00	6.00
6 Gordon Haworth	4.00	8.00
7 Fleming Mackell	5.00	10.00
8 Robert Solinger	3.00	6.00
9 Gary Edmundson	3.00	6.00
10 Al Nicholson	3.00	6.00
11 Orland Kurtenbach	7.50	15.00
12 Tom Thurlby	3.00	6.00

1980 USA Olympic Team Mini Pics

Cards measure 1 3/4" x 2 3/4". Card fronts feature a black and white photo, players name, and position. Card backs feature card number and the words MINI PICS and 1980 GOLD MEDAL WINNERS.

Card	Low	High
COMPLETE SET (15)	25.00	50.00
1 Jim Craig	5.00	10.00
2 Mike Eruzione	5.00	10.00
3 John Harrington	.75	2.00
4 Mark Johnson	1.25	3.00
5 Rob McClanahan	.75	2.00
6 Jack O'Callahan	.75	2.00
7 Phil Verchota	.75	2.00
8 Bob Suter	.75	2.00
9 Eric Strobel	.75	2.00
10 Dave Silk	.75	2.00
11 Mike Ramsey	1.25	3.00
12 Marty Pavelich	.75	2.00
13 Steve Christoff	1.25	3.00
14 Dave Christian	1.25	3.00
15 Herb Brooks CO	2.50	5.00
NNO Score Card	2.50	5.00

1980 USSR Olympic Team Mini Pics

Cards measure 1 3/4" x 2 3/4". Card fronts feature a black and white photo, players name, and position. Card backs feature card number and the words MINI PICS.

Card	Low	High
COMPLETE SET (10)	17.50	35.00
1 Juri Fedorov	.75	2.00
2 Irek Gimayev	.75	2.00
3 Alexander Golikov	.75	2.00
4 Sergei Kapustin	.75	2.00
5 V.Kovin	.75	2.00
6 Boris Mikhailov	2.50	5.00
7 V.Myshkin	2.50	5.00
8 Vladimir Petrov	2.50	5.00
9 Vladislav Tretiak	5.00	10.00
10 Valeri Vasilijev	2.50	5.00

1924-26 V128-1 Paulin's Candy

This 70-card set was issued during the 1923-24 season and featured players from the WCHL. The horizontal back explains how to obtain either a hockey stick or a box of Paulin's chocolates by collecting and sending in the complete Famous Hockey Players set. The cards were to be returned to the collector with the hockey stick or chocolates. The cards are in black and white and measure approximately 1 3/8" by 2 3/4".

Card	Low	High
COMPLETE SET (70)	4,500.00	9,000.00
1 Bill Borland	75.00	150.00
2 Pete Speirs	50.00	100.00
3 Jack Hughes	50.00	100.00
4 Errol Gillis	50.00	100.00
5 Cecil Browne	50.00	100.00
6 W. Roberts	50.00	100.00
7 Howard Brandon	50.00	100.00
8 Fred Comfort	50.00	100.00
9 Cliff O'Meara	50.00	100.00
10 Leo Benard	50.00	100.00
11 Lloyd Harvey	50.00	100.00
12 Bobby Connors	50.00	100.00
13 Daddy Dalman	50.00	100.00
14 Dub Mackie	50.00	100.00
15 Lorne Chabot	150.00	300.00
16 Phat Wilson	75.00	125.00
17 Wilf L'Heureux	50.00	100.00
18 Danny Cox	50.00	100.00
19 Bill Brydge	50.00	100.00
20 Alex Gray	50.00	100.00
21 Albert Pudas	50.00	100.00
22 Jack Irwin	50.00	100.00
23 Puss Traub	50.00	100.00
24 Red McCusker	75.00	125.00
25 Jack Asseltine	75.00	125.00
26 Duke Dutkowski	50.00	100.00
27 Charley McVeigh	50.00	100.00
28 George Hay	125.00	250.00
29 Amby Moran	50.00	100.00
30 Barney Stanley	150.00	300.00
31 Art Gagne	50.00	100.00
32 Louis Berlinquette	50.00	100.00
33 P.C. Stevens	50.00	100.00
34 W.D. Elmer	50.00	100.00
35 Bill Cook	200.00	350.00
36 Leo Reise	50.00	100.00
37 Curly Headley	125.00	250.00
38 Newsy Lalonde	350.00	600.00
39 George Hainsworth	350.00	600.00
40 Laurie Scott	50.00	100.00
41 Joe Simpson	200.00	350.00
42 Bob Trapp	50.00	100.00
43 Joe McCormick	50.00	100.00
44 Ty Arbour	50.00	100.00
45 Duke Keats	75.00	125.00
46 Hal Winkler	50.00	100.00
47 Johnny Sheppard	50.00	100.00
48 Crutchy Morrison	50.00	100.00
49 Spunk Sparrow	50.00	100.00
50 Percy McGregor	50.00	100.00
51 Harry Tuckwell	50.00	100.00
52 Chubby Scott	50.00	100.00
53 Scotty Fraser	50.00	100.00
54 Bob Davis	50.00	100.00
55 Clucker White	50.00	100.00
56 Bob Armstrong	50.00	100.00
57 Doc Longtry	50.00	100.00
58 Darb Sommers	50.00	100.00
59 Frank Hacquoil	50.00	100.00
60 Stan Evans	50.00	100.00
61 Ed Oatman	50.00	100.00
62 Red Dutton	250.00	400.00
63 Herb Gardiner	125.00	250.00
64 Bernie Morris	50.00	100.00
65 Bobbie Benson	50.00	100.00
66 Ernie Anderson	50.00	100.00
67 Cully Wilson	50.00	100.00
68 Charlie Reid	75.00	125.00
69 Harry Oliver	125.00	250.00
70 Rusty Crawford	100.00	200.00

1928-29 V128-2 Paulin's Candy

This scarce set of 90 black and white cards was produced and distributed in Western Canada and features Western Canadian teams and players. The cards are numbered on the back and measure approximately 1 3/8" by 2 5/8". The card back details an offer (expiring June 1st, 1929) of a hockey stick prize (or box of chocolates for girls) if someone could bring in a complete set of 90 cards. Players on the Calgary Jimmies are not explicitly identified on the card so they are listed below without a specific player name.

Card	Low	High
COMPLETE SET (90)	2,750.00	5,500.00
1 Univ. of Man. Girls	50.00	100.00
Hockey Team		
2 Elgin Hockey Team	40.00	80.00
3 Brandon Schools	40.00	80.00
Boy Champions		
4 Port Arthur Hockey	40.00	80.00
Team		
5 Enderby Hockey Team	40.00	80.00
6 Humboldt High School	40.00	80.00
Team		
7 Regina Collegiate	40.00	80.00
Hockey Team		
8 Weyburn Beavers	40.00	80.00
9 Moose Jaw College	50.00	100.00
Junior Hockey Team		
10 M.A.C. Junior Hockey	40.00	80.00
11 Vermillion Agri-cultural School	40.00	80.00
12 Rovers& Cranbrook	40.00	80.00
B.C.		
13 Empire School&	40.00	80.00
Moose Jaw		
14 Arts Senior Hockey	40.00	80.00
15 Juvenile Varsity	40.00	80.00
Hockey		
16 St. Peter's College	40.00	80.00
Hockey		
17 Arts Girls Hockey	50.00	100.00
18 Swan River Hockey Team	40.00	80.00
19 U.M.S.U. Junior	40.00	80.00
Hockey Team		
20 Campion College	50.00	100.00
Hockey Team		
21 Drinkwater Hockey Team	40.00	80.00
22 Elks Hockey Team	40.00	80.00
Biggar, Saskatchewan		
23 South Calgary High	40.00	80.00
School		
24 Meota Hockey	40.00	80.00
25 Chartered Accountants	50.00	100.00
26 Nutana Collegiate	40.00	80.00
Hockey Team		
27 MacLeod Hockey Team	50.00	100.00
28 Arts Junior Hockey	40.00	80.00
29 Fort William Juniors	40.00	80.00
30 Swan Lake Hockey Team	40.00	80.00
31 Dauphin Hockey Team	40.00	80.00
32 Mount Royal Hockey	40.00	80.00
Team		
33 Port Arthur W. End	40.00	80.00
Junior Hockey		
34 Hanna Hockey Club	40.00	80.00
35 Vermillion Junior	40.00	80.00
Hockey		
36 Smithers Hockey Team	40.00	80.00
37 Lloydminster High	40.00	80.00
School		
38 Winnipeg Rangers	50.00	100.00
39 Delisle Intermediate	40.00	80.00
Hockey		
40 Moose Jaw College	40.00	80.00
Senior Hockey		
41 Art Bonneyman	25.00	50.00
42 Jimmy Graham	25.00	50.00
43 Pat O'Hunter	25.00	50.00
44 Leo Moret	25.00	50.00
45 Blondie McLennen	25.00	50.00
46 Red Beattie	40.00	80.00
47 Frank Peters	40.00	80.00
48 Lloyd McIntyre	25.00	50.00
49 Art Somers	40.00	80.00
50 Ikey Morrison	25.00	50.00
51 Calgary Jimmies	25.00	50.00
52 Don Cummings	25.00	50.00
53 Calgary Jimmies	25.00	50.00
54 P. Gerlitz	25.00	50.00
55 A. Kay	25.00	50.00
56 Paul Runge	40.00	80.00
57 J. Gerlitz	25.00	50.00
58 H. Gerlitz	25.00	50.00
59 C. Biles	25.00	50.00
60 Jimmy Evans	25.00	50.00
61 Ira Stuart	25.00	50.00
62 Berg Irving	50.00	100.00
63 Cecil Browne	40.00	80.00
64 Nick Wasnie	40.00	80.00
65 Gordon Teal	40.00	80.00
66 Jack Hughes	40.00	80.00
67 D. Yeatman	40.00	80.00
68 Connie Johanneson	25.00	50.00
69 S. Walters	25.00	50.00
70 Harold McMunn	40.00	80.00

71 Smokey Harris	25.00	50.00
72 Calgary Jimmies	25.00	50.00
73 Bernie Morris	25.00	50.00
74 J. Fowler	40.00	80.00
75 Calgary Jimmies	25.00	50.00
76 Pete Spiers	25.00	50.00
77 Bill Borland	40.00	80.00
78 Cliff O'Meara	40.00	80.00
79 F. Porteous	40.00	80.00
80 W. Brooks	40.00	80.00
81 Everett McGowan	25.00	50.00
82 Calgary Jimmies	25.00	50.00
83 George Dame	25.00	50.00
84 Calgary Jimmies	25.00	50.00
85 Calgary Jimmies	25.00	50.00
86 Calgary Jimmies	25.00	50.00
87 Norman Hec Fowler	40.00	80.00
88 Jimmy Hoyle	25.00	50.00
89 Charlie Gardiner	75.00	150.00
90 Calgary Jimmies	40.00	80.00

1933-34 V129

This 50-card set was issued anonymously during the 1933-34 season. Recent research may link the cards' distribution to British Consul Cigarettes. This has yet to be confirmed. The cards are sepia toned and measure approximately 1 5/8" by 2 7/8". The cards are numbered on the back with the capsule biography both in French and in English. Card number 39 is now known to exist but is quite scarce as it was the card that the company (allegedly) short-printed in order to make it difficult to complete the set. The short-printed Oliver card is not included in the complete set price below.

COMPLETE SET (49)	7,500.00	15,000.00
1 Red Horner RC	250.00	500.00
2 Hap Day	175.00	350.00
3 Ace Bailey RC	250.00	500.00
4 Buzz Boll RC	75.00	150.00
5 Charlie Conacher RC	500.00	1,000.00
6 Busher Jackson RC	250.00	500.00
7 Joe Primeau RC	250.00	500.00
8 King Clancy	500.00	1,000.00
9 Alex Levinsky RC	100.00	200.00
10 Bill Thoms RC	75.00	150.00
11 Andy Blair RC	75.00	150.00
12 Harold Cotton RC	100.00	200.00
13 George Hainsworth	250.00	500.00
14 Ken Doraty RC	75.00	150.00
15 Fred Robertson RC	75.00	150.00
16 Charlie Sands RC	75.00	150.00
17 Hec Kilrea RC	75.00	150.00
18 John Roach	100.00	200.00
19 Larry Aurie RC	75.00	150.00
20 Ebbie Goodfellow RC	150.00	300.00
21 Normie Himes RC	100.00	200.00
22 Bill Brydge RC	75.00	150.00
23 Red Dutton RC	150.00	300.00
24 Cooney Weiland RC	200.00	400.00
25 Bill Beveridge RC	100.00	200.00
26 Frank Finnigan	100.00	200.00
27 Albert Leduc RC	100.00	200.00
28 Babe Siebert RC	200.00	400.00
29 Murray Murdoch RC	75.00	150.00
30 Butch Keeling RC	75.00	150.00
31 Bill Cook RC	150.00	300.00
32 Cecil Dillon RC	75.00	150.00
33 Ivan Johnson RC	200.00	400.00
34 Ott Heller RC	100.00	200.00
35 Red Beattie RC	75.00	150.00
36 Dit Clapper	300.00	600.00
37 Eddie Shore RC	1,000.00	2,000.00
38 Marty Barry RC	150.00	300.00
39 Harry Oliver SP RC	7,500.00	15,000.00
40 Bob Gracie RC	75.00	150.00
41 Howie Morenz	1,500.00	3,000.00
42 Pit Lepine RC	75.00	150.00
43 Johnny Gagnon RC	75.00	150.00
44 Armand Mondou RC	75.00	150.00
45 Lorne Chabot RC	150.00	300.00
46 Bun Cook RC	150.00	300.00
47 Alex Smith RC	75.00	150.00
48 Danny Cox RC	75.00	150.00
49 Baldy Northcott RC UER	100.00	200.00
50 Paul Thompson RC	100.00	200.00

1924-25 V130 Maple Crispette

This 30-card set was issued during the 1924-25 season in the Montreal area. The cards are in black and white and measure approximately 1 3/8" by 2 3/8". There was a prize offer detailed on the reverse of every card offering a pair of hockey skates for a complete set of the cards. Card number 15 Cleghorn apparently was the "impossible" card that prevented most collectors of that day from ever getting the skates and it is considered one of the scarcest pre-war hockey cards. Since market sales data is too thin on the card we have not priced it below, but the very occassional reported sale is well over $10,000. The cards are numbered on the front in the lower right hand corner. The set is considered complete without the short-printed Cleghorn.

COMPLETE SET (29)	4,000.00	8,000.00
1 Dunc Munro RC	100.00	200.00
2 Clint Benedict	200.00	400.00
3 Norman Hec Fowler RC	100.00	200.00
4 Curly Headley RC	75.00	150.00
5 Alf Skinner RC	75.00	150.00
6 Lloyd Cook RC	150.00	300.00
7 Smokey Harris RC	75.00	150.00
8 Jim Herberts RC	75.00	150.00
9 Carson Cooper RC	75.00	150.00
10 Red Green	75.00	150.00
11 Billy Boucher	75.00	150.00
12 Howie Morenz	1,000.00	2,000.00
13 Georges Vezina	700.00	1,400.00
14 Aurel Joliat	400.00	800.00
15 Sprague Cleghorn SP	6,000.00	12,000.00
16 Dutch Cain RC	75.00	150.00
17 Charlie Dinsmore RC	75.00	150.00
18 Punch Broadbent	150.00	300.00
19 Sam Rothschild RC	125.00	200.00
20 George Carroll RC	75.00	150.00
21 Billy Burch	150.00	300.00
22 Shorty Green	150.00	300.00
23 Mickey Roach	75.00	150.00
24 Ken Randall	75.00	150.00
25 Vernon Forbes	100.00	200.00
26 Charlie Langlois RC	75.00	150.00
27 Newsy Lalonde	300.00	600.00
28 Fred Lowrey RC	75.00	150.00
29 Ganton Scott RC	75.00	150.00
30 Louis Berlinquette RC (spelled Berlinguette on front)	100.00	200.00

1923-24 V145-1

This relatively unattractive 40-card set is printed in sepia tone. The cards measure approximately 2" by 3 1/4". The cards have blank backs. The cards are numbered on the front in the lower left corner. The player's name, team, and National Hockey League are at the bottom of each card. The issuer of the set is not indicated in any way on the card, although speculation suggests it was William Patterson, Ltd, a Canadian confectioner. This set is easily confused with the other V145 set. Except for the tint and size differences and the different card name/number correspondence, these sets are essentially the same. Thankfully the only player with the same number in both sets is number 3 King Clancy. The Bert Corbeau card (#25) is extremely difficult to find in any condition, as it most likely was short printed. It is not included in the complete set price below.

COMPLETE SET (39)	6,000.00	12,000.00
1 Eddie Gerard	125.00	250.00
2 Frank Nighbor RC	175.00	350.00
3 King Clancy RC	900.00	1,800.00
4 Jack Darragh	100.00	200.00
5 Harry Helman RC	50.00	100.00
6 George Boucher RC	100.00	200.00
7 Clint Benedict	150.00	300.00
8 Lionel Hitchman RC	100.00	200.00
9 Punch Broadbent	125.00	250.00
10 Cy Denneny RC	200.00	400.00
11 Sprague Cleghorn	150.00	300.00
12 Sylvio Mantha RC	125.00	250.00
13 Joe Malone	200.00	400.00
14 Aurel Joliat RC	650.00	1,300.00
15 Howie Morenz RC	1,500.00	3,000.00
16 Billy Boucher RC	60.00	125.00
17 Billy Coutu RC	60.00	125.00
18 Odie Cleghorn	60.00	125.00
19 Georges Vezina	750.00	1,500.00
20 Amos Arbour RC	50.00	100.00
21 Lloyd Andrews RC	50.00	100.00
22 Red Stuart RC	60.00	125.00
23 Cecil Dye RC	150.00	300.00
24 Jack Adams RC	200.00	400.00
25 Bert Corbeau RC SP	10,000.00	20,000.00
26 Reg Noble RC	150.00	300.00
27 Stan Jackson RC	50.00	100.00
28 John Roach RC	60.00	125.00
29 Vernon Forbes RC	60.00	125.00
30 Shorty Green RC	100.00	200.00
31 Red Green RC	50.00	100.00
32 Goldie Prodgers	50.00	100.00
33 Leo Reise RC	50.00	100.00
34 Ken Randall RC	50.00	100.00
35 Billy Burch RC	100.00	200.00
36 Jesse Spring RC	50.00	100.00
37 Eddie Bouchard RC	50.00	100.00
38 Mickey Roach RC	50.00	100.00
39 Chas. Fraser RC	50.00	100.00
40 Corbett Denneny RC	100.00	200.00

1924-25 V145-2

This 60-card set was issued anonymously during the 1924-25 season. The cards have a green-black tint and measure approximately 1 3/4" by 3 1/4". Cards are numbered in the lower left corner and have a blank back. The player's name, team, and National Hockey League are at the bottom of each card. The issuer of the set is not indicated in any way on the card, although speculation points to William Patterson, Ltd., a Canadian confectioner. This set is easily confused with the other V145 set. Except for the tint and size differences and the different card name/number correspondence, these sets are essentially the same. Thankfully the only player with the same number in both sets is number 3 King Clancy.

COMPLETE SET (60)	6,000.00	12,000.00
1 Joe Ironstone RC	250.00	500.00
2 George Boucher	100.00	200.00
3 King Clancy	750.00	1,500.00
4 Lionel Hitchman	75.00	150.00
5 Hooley Smith RC	125.00	250.00
6 Frank Nighbor	100.00	200.00
7 Cy Denneny	125.00	250.00
8 Spiff Campbell RC	50.00	100.00
9 Frank Finnigan RC	75.00	150.00
10 Alex Connell RC	125.00	250.00
11 Vernon Forbes	60.00	125.00
12 Ken Randall	50.00	100.00
13 Billy Burch	100.00	200.00
14 Shorty Green	100.00	200.00
15 Red Green	50.00	100.00
16 Alex McKinnon RC	50.00	100.00
17 Charlie Langlois RC	50.00	100.00
18 Mickey Roach	50.00	100.00
19 Eddie Bouchard	50.00	100.00
20 Jesse Spring	50.00	100.00
21 Carson Cooper RC	50.00	100.00
22 Smokey Harris RC	50.00	100.00
23 Curly Headley RC	50.00	100.00
24 Lloyd Cook UER RC (Bill on front)	200.00	400.00
25 Jim Herberts RC	50.00	100.00
26 Werner Schnarr RC	50.00	100.00
27 Alf Skinner RC	50.00	100.00
28 George Redding RC	50.00	100.00
29 Herbie Mitchell RC	50.00	100.00
30 Norman Hec Fowler RC	60.00	125.00
31 Red Stuart	50.00	100.00
32 Clint Benedict	100.00	200.00
33 Gerald Munro RC	50.00	100.00
34 Dunc Munro RC	60.00	125.00
35 Dutch Cain RC	50.00	100.00
36 Fred Lowrey RC	50.00	100.00
37 Sam Rothschild RC	75.00	135.00
38 Ganton Scott RC	50.00	100.00
39 Punch Broadbent	125.00	250.00
40 Charlie Dinsmore RC	50.00	100.00
41 Louis Berlinquette RC	50.00	100.00
42 George Carroll RC	50.00	100.00
43 Georges Vezina	600.00	1,200.00
44 Billy Coutu	50.00	100.00
45 Odie Cleghorn	60.00	125.00
46 Billy Boucher	75.00	150.00
47 Howie Morenz	1,000.00	2,000.00
48 Aurel Joliat	500.00	1,000.00
49 Sprague Cleghorn	125.00	250.00
50 Billy Mantha RC	75.00	150.00
51 Reg Noble	100.00	200.00
52 John Roach	60.00	125.00
53 Jack Adams	125.00	250.00
54 Cecil Dye	100.00	200.00
55 Reg Reid RC	50.00	100.00
56 Albert Holway RC	50.00	100.00
57 Bert McCaffery RC	50.00	100.00
58 Bert Corbeau	100.00	200.00
59 Lloyd Andrews RC	50.00	100.00
60 Stan Jackson	75.00	150.00

1933-34 V252 Canadian Gum

This unnumbered set of 50 cards was designated V252 by the American Card Catalog. Cards are black and white pictures with a red border. Backs are written in both French and English. Cards measure approximately 2 1/2" by 3 1/4" including a 3/4" tab at the bottom describing a premium (contest) offer and containing one large letter. When enough of these letters were saved so that the collector could spell out the names of five NHL teams, they could be redeemed for a free home hockey game according to the details given on the card backs. The cards are checklisted in alphabetical order.

COMPLETE SET (50)	4,500.00	9,000.00
1 Clarence Abel RC	100.00	200.00
2 Larry Aurie RC	90.00	150.00
3 Ace Bailey RC	200.00	400.00
4 Helge Bostrom RC	50.00	100.00
5 Bill Brydge RC	50.00	100.00
6 Glyn Brydson RC	50.00	100.00
7 Marty Burke RC	50.00	100.00
8 Gerald Carson RC	75.00	125.00
9 Lorne Chabot RC	200.00	400.00
10 King Clancy	450.00	800.00
11 Dit Clapper RC	200.00	400.00
12 Charlie Conacher RC	400.00	750.00
13 Lionel Conacher RC	200.00	400.00
14 Alex Connell	100.00	175.00
15 Bun Cook RC	100.00	175.00
16 Danny Cox RC	50.00	100.00
17 Hap Day	100.00	200.00
18 Cecil Dillon RC	50.00	100.00
19 Lorne Duguid RC	75.00	125.00
20 Duke Dutkowski RC	50.00	100.00
21 Red Dutton RC	100.00	175.00
22 Happy Emms RC	75.00	125.00
23 Frank Finnigan	75.00	125.00
24 Chuck Gardiner RC	100.00	175.00
25 Ebbie Goodfellow RC	100.00	175.00
26 Johnny Gottselig RC	75.00	125.00
27 Bob Gracie RC	50.00	100.00
28 George Hainsworth	200.00	400.00
29 Ott Heller RC	50.00	100.00
30 Normie Himes RC	75.00	125.00
31 Red Horner RC	150.00	300.00
32 Busher Jackson RC	200.00	400.00
33 Walter Jackson RC	50.00	100.00
34 Aurel Joliat	400.00	750.00
35 Dave Kerr RC	75.00	125.00
36 Pit Lepine RC	50.00	100.00
37 Georges Mantha RC	50.00	100.00
38 Howie Morenz	1,000.00	2,000.00
39 Murray Murdoch RC	50.00	100.00
40 Baldy Northcott RC	75.00	125.00
41 John Roach	90.00	150.00
42 Johnny Sheppard	50.00	100.00
43 Babe Siebert RC	125.00	250.00
44 Alex Smith RC	50.00	100.00
45 John Sorrell RC	90.00	150.00
46 Nelson Stewart RC	200.00	400.00
47 Dave Trottier RC	50.00	100.00
48 Bill Touhey RC	50.00	100.00
49 Jimmy Ward RC	50.00	100.00
50 Nick Wasnie RC	50.00	100.00

1933-34 V288 Hamilton Gum

This skip-numbered set of 21 cards was designated V288 by the American Card Catalog. Cards are black and white pictures with a beige, blue, green, or orange background. Backs are written in both French and English. Cards measure approximately 2 3/8" by 2 3/4".

COMPLETE SET (21)	3,000.00	6,000.00
1 Nick Wasnie	62.50	125.00
2 Joe Primeau	200.00	400.00
3 Marty Burke	50.00	100.00
7 Bill Thoms	50.00	100.00
8 Howie Morenz	1,000.00	2,000.00
9 Andy Blair	50.00	100.00
11 Ace Bailey	175.00	350.00
14 Wildor Larochelle	50.00	100.00
17 King Clancy	400.00	800.00
18 Sylvio Mantha	87.50	175.00
21 Red Horner	150.00	300.00
23 Pit Lepine	50.00	100.00
27 Aurel Joliat	400.00	800.00
29 Harvey(Busher) Jackson	175.00	350.00
30 Lorne Chabot	100.00	200.00
33 Hap Day	100.00	200.00
36 Alex Levinsky	62.50	125.00
39 Harold Cotton	75.00	150.00
42 Ebbie Goodfellow	87.50	175.00
44 Larry Aurie	50.00	100.00
49 Charlie Conacher	400.00	800.00

1937-38 V356 World Wide Gum

These greenish-gray cards feature the player's name and card number on the front and the card number, the player's name, his position and biographical data (in both English and French) on the back. Cards are approximately 2 3/8" by 2 7/8". Although the backs of the cards state that the cards were printed in Canada, no mention of the issuer, World Wide Gum, is apparent anywhere on the card.

COMPLETE SET (135)	11,000.00	22,000.00
1 Charlie Conacher	500.00	1,000.00
2 Jimmy Ward	50.00	100.00
3 Babe Siebert	175.00	350.00
4 Marty Barry	100.00	200.00
5 Eddie Shore	750.00	1,500.00
6 Paul Thompson	50.00	100.00
7 Roy Worters	150.00	300.00
8 Red Horner	100.00	200.00
9 Wilfred Cude	75.00	150.00
10 Lionel Conacher	175.00	350.00
11 Ebbie Goodfellow	125.00	250.00
12 Tiny Thompson	150.00	300.00
13 Mush March RC	60.00	125.00
14 Red Dutton	100.00	200.00
15 Butch Keeling	50.00	100.00
16 Frank Boucher RC	100.00	200.00
17 Tommy Gorman RC	50.00	100.00
18 Howie Morenz	1,250.00	2,500.00
19 Marvin Wentworth	75.00	150.00
20 Hooley Smith	100.00	200.00
21 Ivan Johnson RC	150.00	300.00
22 Baldy Northcott	75.00	150.00
23 Syl Apps	400.00	800.00
24 Hec Kilrea	50.00	100.00
25 John Sorrell	50.00	100.00
26 Lorne Carr RC	50.00	100.00
27 Charlie Sands	50.00	100.00
28 Nick Metz	50.00	100.00
29 King Clancy	500.00	1,000.00
30 Russ Blinco	50.00	100.00
31 Pete Martin RC	50.00	100.00
32 Walter Buswell RC	50.00	100.00
33 Paul Haynes	50.00	100.00
34 Wildor Larochelle	60.00	125.00
35 Harold Cotton	60.00	125.00
36 Dit Clapper	200.00	400.00
37 Joe Lamb	50.00	100.00
38 Bob Gracie	50.00	100.00
39 Jack Shill	50.00	100.00
40 Buzz Boll	50.00	100.00
41 John Gallagher	50.00	100.00
42 Art Chapman	50.00	100.00
43 Tom Cook RC	50.00	100.00
44 Bill MacKenzie	50.00	100.00
45 Georges Mantha	50.00	100.00
46 Herb Cain	60.00	125.00
47 Mud Bruneteau RC	75.00	150.00
48 Bob Davidson	50.00	100.00
49 Doug Young RC	50.00	100.00
50 Paul Drouin RC	50.00	100.00
51 Busher Jackson	200.00	400.00
52 Hap Day	150.00	300.00
53 Dave Kerr	100.00	200.00
54 Al Murray	50.00	100.00
55 Johnny Gottselig	60.00	125.00
56 Andy Blair	50.00	100.00
57 Lynn Patrick	200.00	400.00
58 Sweeney Schriner	125.00	250.00
59 Happy Emms	60.00	125.00
60 Allan Shields	50.00	100.00
61 Alex Levinsky	60.00	125.00
62 Flash Hollett	50.00	100.00
63 Peggy O'Neil RC	50.00	100.00
64 Herbie Lewis RC	100.00	200.00
65 Aurel Joliat	400.00	800.00

66 Carl Voss RC 100.00 200.00
67 Stewart Evans 50.00 100.00
68 Bun Cook 125.00 250.00
69 Cooney Weiland 125.00 250.00
70 Dave Trottier 50.00 100.00
71 Louis Trudel RC 50.00 100.00
72 Marty Burke 50.00 100.00
73 Leroy Goldsworthy 50.00 100.00
74 Normie Smith RC 50.00 100.00
75 Syd Howe 150.00 300.00
76 Gordon Pettinger RC 50.00 100.00
77 Jack McGill 50.00 100.00
78 Pit Lepine 50.00 100.00
79 Sammy McManus RC 50.00 100.00
80 Phil Watson RC 75.00 150.00
81 Paul Runge 50.00 100.00
82 Bill Beveridge 60.00 125.00
83 Johnny Gagnon 50.00 100.00
84 Bucko MacDonald RC 60.00 125.00
85 Earl Robinson 50.00 100.00
86 Pep Kelly 50.00 100.00
87 Ott Heller 50.00 100.00
88 Murray Murdoch 50.00 100.00
89 Mac Colville RC 50.00 100.00
90 Alex Shibicky 75.00 150.00
91 Neil Colville 125.00 250.00
92 Normie Himes 60.00 125.00
93 Charley McVeigh 50.00 100.00
94 Lester Patrick 200.00 400.00
95 Connie Smythe 200.00 400.00
96 Art Ross 200.00 400.00
97 Cecil M.Hart RC 125.00 250.00
98 Dutch Gainor RC 50.00 100.00
99 Jack Adams 150.00 300.00
100 Howie Morenz Jr. 150.00 300.00
101 Buster Mundy RC 50.00 100.00
102 Johnny Wing RC 50.00 100.00
103 Morris Croghan RC 50.00 100.00
104 Pete Jotkus RC 50.00 100.00
105 Doug MacQuisten RC 50.00 100.00
106 Lester Brennan RC 50.00 100.00
107 Jack O'Connell RC 50.00 100.00
108 Ray Malenfant RC 50.00 100.00
109 Ken Murray RC 50.00 100.00
110 Frank Stangle RC 50.00 100.00
111 Dave Neville RC 50.00 100.00
112 Claude Burke RC 50.00 100.00
113 Herman Murray RC 50.00 100.00
114 Buddy O'Connor RC 125.00 250.00
115 Albert Perreault RC 50.00 100.00
116 Johnny Taugher RC 50.00 100.00
117 Rene Boudreau RC 50.00 100.00
118 Kenny McKinnon RC 50.00 100.00
119 Alex Bolduc RC 50.00 100.00
120 Jimmy Keiller RC 50.00 100.00
121 Lloyd McIntyre RC 50.00 100.00
122 Emile Fortin RC 50.00 100.00
123 Mike Karakas 60.00 125.00
124 Art Wiebe 50.00 100.00
125 Louis St. Denis RC 50.00 100.00
126 Stan Pratt RC 50.00 100.00
127 Jules Cholette RC 50.00 100.00
128 Jimmy Muir RC 50.00 100.00
129 Pete Morin RC 50.00 100.00
130 Jimmy Heffernan RC 50.00 100.00
131 Morris Bastien RC 50.00 100.00
132 Tuffy Griffiths RC 50.00 100.00
133 Johnny Mahaffey RC 50.00 100.00
134 Trueman Donnelly RC 50.00 100.00
135 Bill Stewart RC 75.00 150.00

1933-34 V357 Ice Kings

This interesting and attractive set of 72 cards features black and white photos on the front, upon which the head of the player portrayed has been tinted in flesh tones. The cards measure approximately 2 3/8" by 2 7/8". The player's name appears on the front of the card. The card number, position, team and player's name is listed on the back as are brief biographies in both French and English. Most cards also appear in a second version with the resumes in English only. Printed in Canada and issued by World Wide Gum, the catalog designation for this set is V357.

COMP.SET (72) 9,000.00 15,000.00
*ENGLISH ONLY BACK: .5X TO 1X
1 Dit Clapper RC 350.00 600.00
2 Bill Brydge RC 50.00 100.00
3 Aurel Joliat UER 500.00 800.00
4 Andy Blair 50.00 100.00
5 Earl Robinson RC 50.00 100.00
6 Paul Haynes RC 50.00 100.00
7 Ronnie Martin RC 50.00 100.00
8 Babe Siebert RC 175.00 300.00
9 Archie Wilcox RC 50.00 100.00
10 Hap Day 150.00 250.00
11 Roy Worters RC 200.00 350.00
12 Nels Stewart RC 350.00 600.00
13 King Clancy 600.00 1,000.00
14 Marty Burke RC 125.00 200.00
15 Cecil Dillon RC 50.00 100.00
16 Red Horner RC 175.00 300.00
17 Armand Mondou RC 50.00 100.00
18 Paul Raymond RC 50.00 100.00
19 Dave Kerr RC 75.00 125.00
20 Butch Keeling RC 50.00 100.00
21 Johnny Gagnon RC 50.00 100.00
22 Ace Bailey RC 300.00 500.00
23 Harry Oliver RC 150.00 250.00
24 Gerald Carson RC 50.00 100.00
25 Red Dutton RC 150.00 250.00
26 Georges Mantha RC 50.00 100.00
27 Marty Barry RC 150.00 250.00
28 Wildor Larochelle RC 75.00 125.00
29 Red Beattie RC 50.00 100.00
30 Bill Cook RC 150.00 250.00
31 Hooley Smith 150.00 250.00
32 Art Chapman RC 50.00 100.00
33 Harold Cotton RC 125.00 200.00
34 Lionel Hitchman 125.00 200.00
35 George Patterson RC 50.00 100.00
36 Howie Morenz 1,200.00 2,000.00
37 Jimmy Ward RC 50.00 100.00
38 Charley McVeigh RC 75.00 125.00
39 Glen Brydson RC 75.00 125.00
40 Joe Primeau RC 300.00 500.00
41 Joe Lamb RC 90.00 150.00
42 Sylvio Mantha 125.00 200.00
43 Cy Wentworth RC 75.00 125.00
44 Normie Himes RC 75.00 125.00
45 Doug Brennan RC 50.00 100.00
46 Pit Lepine RC 50.00 100.00
47 Alex Levinsky RC 75.00 125.00
48 Baldy Northcott RC 75.00 125.00
49 Ken Doraty RC 75.00 125.00
50 Bill Thoms RC 75.00 125.00
51 Vernon Ayres RC 75.00 125.00
52 Lorne Duguid RC 75.00 125.00
53 Wally Kilrea RC 75.00 125.00
54 Vic Ripley RC 75.00 125.00
55 Happy Emms RC 75.00 125.00
56 Duke Dutkowski RC 75.00 125.00
57 Tiny Thompson RC 300.00 500.00
58 Charlie Sands RC 75.00 125.00
59 Larry Aurie RC 75.00 125.00
60 Bill Beveridge RC 75.00 125.00
61 Bill McKenzie RC 75.00 125.00
62 Earl Roche RC 75.00 125.00
63 Bob Gracie RC 75.00 125.00
64 Hec Kilrea RC 75.00 125.00
65 Cooney Weiland RC 250.00 400.00
66 Bun Cook RC 200.00 350.00
67 John Roach 90.00 150.00
68 Murray Murdoch RC 75.00 125.00
69 Danny Cox RC 75.00 125.00
70 Desse Roche RC 75.00 125.00
71 Lorne Chabot RC 250.00 400.00
72 Syd Howe RC 250.00 400.00

1933-34 V357-2 Ice Kings Premiums

These six black-and-white large cards are actually premiums. The cards measure approximately 7" by 9". The cards are unnumbered and rather difficult to find now.

COMPLETE SET (6) 2,000.00 4,000.00
1 King Clancy 500.00 1,000.00
2 Hap Day 175.00 350.00
3 Aurel Joliat 400.00 800.00
4 Howie Morenz 1,000.00 2,000.00
5 Allan Shields 87.50 175.00
6 Reginald Smith 125.00 250.00

1927 Werner and Mertz Field Hockey

Cards measure approximately 2 1/2 x 4 1/2 and feature full color drawings of field hockey action shots. Produced in Germany by Werner & Mertz Aktiengesellschaft, Mainz.

COMPLETE SET (6) 62.50 125.00
1 Womens Field Hockey 12.50 25.00
2 Womens Field Hockey 12.50 25.00
3 Mens Field Hockey 12.50 25.00
Scrum at midfield
4 Mens Field Hockey 12.50 25.00
Chasing the ball
5 Mens Field Hockey 12.50 25.00
Pileup
6 Mens Field Hockey 12.50 25.00
Goalie action shot

1940 Wheaties M4

This set is referred to as the "Champs in the USA" The cards measure about 6" 8 1'4" and are numbered. The drawing portion (inside the dotted lines) measures approximately 6" X 6". There is a Baseball player on each card and they are joined by football players, football coaches, race car drivers, airline pilots, a circus clown, ice skater, hockey star and golfers. Each athlete appears in what looks like a stamp with a serrated edge. The stamps appear one above the other with a brief block of copy describing his or her achievements. There appears to have been three printings, resulting in some variation panels. The full panels tell the cereal buyer to look for either 27, 39, or 63 champ stamps. The first nine panels apparently were printed more than once, since all the unknown variations occur with those numbers.

COMPLETE SET (20) 400.00 800.00
1A R. Ruffing/B. Feller 40.00 80.00
1B R. Ruffing/L. Durocher 30.00 50.00

1962 Wheaties Great Moments in Canadian Sports

This 25 card set, which measure approximately 3 1/2" by 2 1/2" was issued in Canada one per cereal box. The fronts have a color drawing of an important event in Canadian sport history while the backs have a description in both English and French as to what the significance of the event was.

COMPLETE SET (25)
1 Bill Barilko 2.00 5.00
Scores winning goal in 1951 Stanley
7 Frank Mahovlich/1st Maple Leaf 40 goal scorer 3.00 8.00
12 Maurice Richard/1960 Stanley Cup 3.00 8.00
16 Bernie Geoffrion/1961 50th goal 3.00 8.00
22 Lionel Conacher 2.50 6.00
Hockey

1924 Willard's Chocolates Sports Champions V122

43 Harry Watson 125.00 250.00
45 Ernie Collett RC 75.00 150.00
47 Hooley Smith 125.00 250.00
52 Dunc Munro RC 100.00 200.00

1960-61 Wonder Bread Labels

Similar to Wonder Bread Premium Photos, these are the actual labels that were wrapped around the Wonder Bread packages. Little is known about them, and few are confirmed to exist, so no prices have been established.

1 Gordie Howe
2 Bobby Hull
3 Dave Keon
4 Maurice Richard

1960-61 Wonder Bread Premium Photos

Produced and issued in Canada, the 1960-61 Wonder Bread set features four hockey stars. This set of premium photos measure approximately 5" by 7" and are unnumbered. There were actually two sets produced: Bread Labels and Premium Photos. The bread labels are valued at 50 to 100 percent of the values listed below. Reportedly the premium photo was inside the bread package and there was also a small picture of the player on the end of the bread wrapper. Keon's photo is noteworthy for preceding his RC by one year.

COMPLETE SET (4) 300.00 600.00
1 Gordie Howe 150.00 300.00
2 Bobby Hull 100.00 200.00
3 Dave Keon 40.00 80.00
4 Maurice Richard 100.00 200.00

1960-61 York Photos

This set of 37 photos is very difficult to put together. These unnumbered photos measure approximately 5" by 7" and feature members of the Montreal Canadiens (MC) and Toronto Maple Leafs (TML). The checklist below is ordered alphabetically. These large black and white cards were supposedly available from York Peanut Butter as a mail-in premium in return for two proofs of purchase; unfortunately there are no identifying marking on the photo that indicate the producer or the year of issue. The photos are action shots with a facsimile autograph of the player on the photo. The cards were apparently issued very late in the 1960-61 season since the set includes Eddie Shack as a Maple Leaf (he was acquired by Toronto from the Rangers during the 1960-61 season), Gilles Tremblay (his first NHL season was 1960-61 with the Canadiens), and several players (Jean-Guy Gendron, Larry Regan, Bob Turner) who were with other teams for the 1961-62 season.

COMPLETE SET (37) 1,200.00 2,400.00
1 George Armstrong TML 30.00 60.00
2 Ralph Backstrom MC 25.00 50.00
3 Bob Baun TML 30.00 60.00
4 Jean Beliveau MC 87.50 175.00
5 Marcel Bonin MC 17.50 35.00
6 Johnny Bower TML 62.50 125.00
7 Carl Brewer TML 25.00 50.00
8 Dick Duff TML 25.00 50.00
9 Jean-Guy Gendron MC 17.50 35.00
10 Boom Boom Geoffrion MC 62.50 125.00
11 Phil Goyette MC 17.50 35.00
12 Billy Harris TML 17.50 35.00
13 Doug Harvey MC 50.00 100.00
14 Bill Hicke MC 17.50 35.00
15 Larry Hillman TML 17.50 35.00
16 Charlie Hodge MC 25.00 50.00
17 Tim Horton TML 87.50 175.00
18 Tom Johnson MC 25.00 50.00
19 Red Kelly TML 30.00 60.00
20 Dave Keon TML 62.50 125.00
21 Albert Langlois MC 17.50 35.00
22 Frank Mahovlich TML 62.50 125.00
23 Don Marshall MC 25.00 50.00
24 Dickie Moore MC 30.00 60.00
25 Bob Nevin TML 17.50 35.00
26 Bert Olmstead TML 30.00 60.00
27 Jacques Plante MC 175.00 350.00
28 Claude Provost MC 25.00 50.00
29 Bob Pulford TML 30.00 60.00
30 Larry Regan TML 17.50 35.00
31 Henri Richard MC 62.50 125.00
32 Eddie Shack TML 50.00 100.00
33 Allan Stanley TML 30.00 60.00
34 Ron Stewart TML 17.50 35.00
35 Jean-Guy Talbot MC 25.00 50.00
36 Gilles Tremblay MC 25.00 50.00
37 Bob Turner MC 17.50 35.00

1961-62 York Yellow Backs

This set of 42 octagonal cards was issued by York Peanut Butter. The cards are numbered on the backs at the top. An album was originally available as a send-in offer or at certain food stores for 25 cents. The cards measure approximately 2 1/2" in diameter. The set can be dated as a 1961-62 set by referring to the career totals given on the back of each player's cards. The card backs were written in both French and English. The set is considered complete without the album.

COMPLETE SET (42) 300.00 600.00
1 Bob Baun 7.50 15.00
2 Dick Duff 6.00 12.00
3 Frank Mahovlich 12.50 25.00
4 Gilles Tremblay 5.00 10.00
5 Dickie Moore 7.50 15.00
6 Don Marshall 5.00 10.00
7 Tim Horton 15.00 30.00
8 Johnny Bower 10.00 20.00
9 Allan Stanley 7.50 15.00
10 Jean Beliveau 20.00 40.00
11 Tom Johnson 7.50 15.00
12 Jean-Guy Talbot 6.00 12.00
13 Carl Brewer 5.00 10.00
14 Bob Pulford 7.50 15.00
15 Billy Harris 5.00 10.00
16 Bill Hicke 5.00 10.00
17 Claude Provost 6.00 12.00
18 Henri Richard 12.50 25.00
19 Bert Olmstead 7.50 15.00
20 Ron Stewart 5.00 10.00
21 Red Kelly 7.50 15.00
22 Toe Blake CO 7.50 15.00
23 Jacques Plante 25.00 50.00
24 Ralph Backstrom 6.00 12.00
25 Eddie Shack 10.00 20.00
26 Bob Nevin 5.00 10.00
27 Dave Keon 20.00 40.00
28 Boom Boom Geoffrion 10.00 20.00
29 Marcel Bonin 5.00 10.00
30 Phil Goyette 5.00 10.00
31 Larry Hillman 5.00 10.00
32 Larry Keenan 5.00 10.00
33 Al Arbour 7.50 15.00
34 J.C. Tremblay 6.00 12.00
35 Bobby Rousseau 5.00 10.00
36 Al McNeil 5.00 10.00
37 George Armstrong 7.50 15.00
38 Punch Imlach CO 6.00 12.00
39 King Clancy 10.00 20.00
40 Lou Fontinato 5.00 10.00
41 Cesare Maniago 7.50 15.00
42 Jean Gauthier 5.00 10.00
xx Album 20.00 40.00

1962-63 York Iron-On Transfers

These iron-on transfers are very difficult to find. They measure approximately 2 1/4" by 4 1/4". There is some dispute with regard to the year of issue but the 1962-63 season seems to be a likely date based on the careers of the players included in the set. These transfers are numbered at the bottom.

COMPLETE SET (36) 900.00 1,800.00
1 Johnny Bower 25.00 50.00
2 Jacques Plante 75.00 150.00
3 Tim Horton 50.00 100.00
4 Jean-Guy Talbot 15.00 30.00
5 Carl Brewer 15.00 30.00
6 J.C. Tremblay 15.00 30.00
7 Dick Duff 15.00 30.00
8 Jean Beliveau 50.00 100.00
9 Dave Keon 25.00 50.00
10 Henri Richard 40.00 80.00
11 Frank Mahovlich 40.00 80.00
12 BoomBoom Geoffrion 25.00 50.00
13 Kent Douglas 12.50 25.00
14 Claude Provost 15.00 30.00
15 Bob Pulford 15.00 30.00
16 Ralph Backstrom 15.00 30.00
17 George Armstrong 20.00 40.00
18 Bobby Rousseau 12.50 25.00
19 Gordie Howe 125.00 250.00
20 Red Kelly 20.00 40.00
21 Alex Delvecchio 20.00 40.00
22 Dickie Moore 20.00 40.00
23 Marcel Pronovost 15.00 30.00
24 Doug Barkley 12.50 25.00
25 Terry Sawchuk 50.00 100.00
26 Billy Harris 12.50 25.00
27 Parker MacDonald 12.50 25.00
28 Don Marshall 12.50 25.00
29 Norm Ullman 25.00 50.00
30A Andre Pronovost 12.50 25.00
30B Vic Stasiuk 12.50 25.00
31 Bill Gadsby 15.00 30.00
32 Eddie Shack 25.00 50.00
33 Larry Jeffrey 12.50 25.00
34 Gilles Tremblay 12.50 25.00
35 Howie Young 12.50 25.00
36 Bruce MacGregor 12.50 25.00

1963-64 York White Backs

This set of 54 octagonal cards was issued with York Peanut Butter and York Salted Nuts. The cards are numbered on the backs at the top. The cards measure approximately 2 1/2" in diameter. The set can be dated as a 1963-64 set by referring to the career totals given on the back of each player's cards. The card backs were written in both French and English. An album was originally available for holding the set; the set is considered complete without the album.

COMPLETE SET (54) 375.00 750.00
1 Tim Horton 20.00 40.00
2 Johnny Bower 12.50 25.00
3 Ron Stewart 7.50 15.00
4 Eddie Shack 12.50 25.00
5 Frank Mahovlich 15.00 30.00
6 Dave Keon 15.00 30.00
7 Bob Baun 7.50 15.00
8 Bob Nevin 7.50 15.00
9 Dick Duff 7.50 15.00
10 Billy Harris 7.50 15.00
11 Larry Hillman 7.50 15.00
12 Red Kelly 10.00 20.00
13 Kent Douglas 7.50 15.00
14 Allan Stanley 7.50 15.00
15 Don Simmons 7.50 15.00
16 George Armstrong 10.00 20.00
17 Carl Brewer 7.50 15.00

18 Bob Pulford	7.50	15.00
19 Henri Richard	15.00	30.00
20 BoomBoom Geoffrion	12.50	25.00
21 Gilles Tremblay	7.50	15.00
22 Gump Worsley	12.50	25.00
23 Jean-Guy Talbot	7.50	15.00
24 J.C. Tremblay	7.50	15.00
25 Bobby Rousseau	7.50	15.00
26 Jean Beliveau	20.00	40.00
27 Ralph Backstrom	7.50	15.00
28 Claude Provost	7.50	15.00
29 Jean Gauthier	7.50	15.00
30 Bill Hicke	7.50	15.00
31 Terry Harper	7.50	15.00
32 Marc Reaume	7.50	15.00
33 Dave Balon	7.50	15.00
34 Jacques Laperriere	10.00	20.00
35 John Ferguson	10.00	20.00
36 Red Berenson	7.50	15.00
37 Terry Sawchuk	25.00	50.00
38 Marcel Pronovost	7.50	15.00
39 Bill Gadsby	10.00	20.00
40 Parker MacDonald	7.50	15.00
41 Larry Jeffrey	7.50	15.00
42 Floyd Smith	7.50	15.00
43 Andre Pronovost	7.50	15.00
44 Art Stratton	7.50	15.00
45 Gordie Howe	50.00	100.00
46 Doug Barkley	7.50	15.00
47 Norm Ullman	10.00	20.00
48 Eddie Joyal	7.50	15.00
49 Alex Faulkner	15.00	30.00
50 Alex Delvecchio	10.00	20.00
51 Bruce MacGregor	7.50	15.00
52 Ted Hampson	7.50	15.00
53 Pete Goegan	7.50	15.00
54 Ron Ingram	7.50	15.00
xx Album	20.00	40.00

1967-68 York Action Octagons

This 36-card set was issued by York Peanut Butter. Only cards 13-36 are numbered. The twelve unnumbered cards have been assigned the numbers 1-12 based on alphabetizing the names of the first player listed on each card. Each card shows an action scene involving two or three players. Uniform numbers are also given on the cards. The card backs give the details of a send-in contest ending June 30, 1968. Collecting four cards spelling "YORK" entitled one to receive a Bobby Hull Hockey Game. These octagonal cards measure approximately 2 7/8" in diameter. The card backs were written in both French and English.

COMPLETE SET (36)	300.00	600.00
1 Brian Conacher 22	7.50	15.00
Allan Stanley 26		
Leon Rochefor		
2 Terry Harper 19	10.00	20.00
Gump Worsley 30		
Mike Walton 16		
3 Tim Horton 7	20.00	40.00
George Armstrong 10		
Jean Beliveau 4		
4 Dave Keon 14	10.00	20.00
George Armstrong 10		
Claude Provost 14		
5 Jacques Laperriere 2	10.00	20.00
Rogatien Vachon 29		
Bob Pulford 20		
6 Bob Pulford 20	6.00	12.00
Brian Conacher 22		
Claude Provost 14		
7 Bob Pulford 20	6.00	12.00
Jim Pappin 18		
Terry Harper 19		
8 Pete Stemkowski 12	6.00	12.00
Jim Pappin 18		
Harris 10		
9 J.C. Tremblay 3	7.50	15.00
Rogatien Vachon 29		
Pete Stemkowski 12		
10 Rogatien Vachon 29	10.00	20.00
Ralph Backstrom 6		
Bob Pulford 20		
11 Rogatien Vachon 29	10.00	20.00
Jacques Laperriere 2		
Mike Walton 16		
12 Mike Walton 16	6.00	12.00
Pete Stemkowski 12		
J.C. Tremblay 3		
13 Dave Keon 14	7.50	15.00
Mike Walton 16		
J.C. Tremblay 3		
14 Pete Stemkowski 12	5.00	10.00
Ralph Backstrom 6		
15 Rogatien Vachon 29	7.50	15.00
Bob Pulford 20		
16 Johnny Bower 1	7.50	15.00
Ron Ellis 8		
John Ferguson 22		
17 Ron Ellis 8	7.50	15.00
Gump Worsley 30		
18 Gump Worsley 30	12.50	25.00
Jacques Laperriere 2		
Frank Mahovlich 27		
19 J.C. Tremblay 3	7.50	15.00
Dave Keon 14		
20 Claude Provost 14	10.00	20.00
Frank Mahovlich 27		
21 John Ferguson 22	10.00	20.00
Tim Horton 7		
22 Gump Worsley 30	7.50	15.00
Ron Ellis 8		
23 Johnny Bower 1	10.00	20.00
Mike Walton 16		
Jean Beliveau 4		
24 J.C. Tremblay 3	7.50	15.00
Gump Worsley 30		
Bob Pulford 20		
25 Tim Horton 7	15.00	30.00
Johnny Bower 1		
Jean Beliveau 4		
26 Allan Stanley 26	7.50	15.00
Johnny Bower 1		
Dick Duff 8		
27 Ralph Backstrom 6	7.50	15.00
Johnny Bower 1		
28 Yvan Cournoyer 12	20.00	40.00
Jean Beliveau 4		
Frank Mahovlich 27		
29 Johnny Bower 1	10.00	20.00
Larry Hillman 2		
Yvan Cournoyer 12		
30 Johnny Bower 1	10.00	20.00
Yvan Cournoyer 12		
31 Tim Horton 7	10.00	20.00
Rogatien Vachon 29		
32 Jim Pappin 18	7.50	15.00
Bob Pulford 20		
Rogatien Vachon 29		
33 Terry Harper 19	5.00	10.00
Bobby Rousseau 15		
Pronovost 3		
34 Johnny Bower 1	6.00	12.00
Pronovost 3		
Ralph Backstrom 6		
35 Frank Mahovlich 27	12.50	25.00
Gump Worsley 30		
36 Claude Provost 14	6.00	12.00
Johnny Bower 1		

1956 Austrian Platnik and Shone

This single comes from an Austrian-issued multi-sport series. The cards are oversized and feature black and white fronts with blue and white backs, highlighted by the Olympic rings.

NNO Ice Hockey	12.50	25.00

1937 British Sporting Personalities

Card features black and white front with biographical information on back.

37 Joe Beaton	10.00	20.00

1966 Finnish Jaakiekkosarja

This early Finnish set is presented for checklisting purposes only. We have no confirmed sales info and thus the set is unpriced.

COMPLETE SET (220)
1 Jukka Haapala
2 Simo Saimo
3 Hannu Torma
4 Jukka Savunen
5 Tenho Lotila
6 Tapani Koskimaki
7 Matti Saurio
8 Risto Kaitala
9 Raimo Tiainen
10 Esa Isaksson
11 Pentti Rautalin
12 Heikko Stenvall
13 Teppo Rastio
14 Jorma Vehmanen
15 Raimo Kilpio
16 Veikko Ukkonen
17 Lauri Lehtonen
18 Heikki Veravainen
19 Pentti Riitahaara
20 Pekka Kuusisto
21 Tapio Rautalammi
22 Raimo Tuli
23 Matti Paivinen
24 Matti Harju
25 Kari Sillanpaa
26 Matti Keinonen
27 Pekka Lahti
28 Johannes Karttunen
29 Sakari Isomaki
30 Samu Leikko
31 Tapani Suominen
32 Esa Vesslin
33 Pekka Jalava
34 Pertti Makela
35 Juha Rantasila
36 Jukka Haanpaa
37 Teuvo Helenius
38 Anto Virtanen
39 Kimmo Nokikuru
40 Jaakko Honkanen
41 Seppo Nystrom
42 Tuomo Pirskainen
43 Matti Jansson
44 Alpo Suhonen
45 Matti Varpela
46 Kaj Matalamaki
47 Antti Heikkila
48 Jaakko Jaskari
49 Jouko Ojansuu
50 Mikko Myllyniemi
51 Veli-Pekka Ketola
52 Matti Salmi
53 Pentti Vihanto
54 Hannu Luojola
55 Seppo Parikka
56 Martti Salonen
57 Risto Forss
58 Hannu Niittoaho
59 Kari Johansson
60 Henry Leppa
61 Jarmo Rantanen
62 Kari Torkkel
63 Seppo Vikstrom
64 Veijo Saarinen
65 Pekka Lahtela
66 Risto Vainio
67 Reijo Paksal
68 Erkan Nasib
69 Matti Breilin
70 Voitto Soini
71 Urpo Ylonen
72 Rauno Heinonen
73 Heikki Heino
74 Lasse Killi
75 Ilkka Mesikammen
76 Timo Nummelin
77 Pertti Kuismanen
78 Juhani Wahlsten
79 Rauli Ottila
80 Pertti Karelius
81 Teuvo Andelmin
82 Kari Varjanen
83 Kalevi Leppanen
84 Juhani Iso-Eskeli
85 Hannu Koivunen
86 Yrjo Hakala
87 Kari Ruontimo
88 Raimo Lohko
89 Markku Eiskonen
90 Hannu Lemander
91 Timo Vaatamoinen
92 Pekka Moisio
93 Martti Makia
94 Risto Heinvirta
95 Taisto Jahma
96 Veikko Makia
97 Raimo Helppolainen
98 Lalli Partinen
99 Keijo Sinkkonen
100 Antti Ravi
101 Martti Sinkkonen
102 Heikki Juselius
103 Timo Rantala
104 Heikki Mikkola
105 Jaakko Siren
106 Matti Korhonen
107 Erkki Mononen
108 Pertti Valkonen
109 Ilpo Koskela
110 Bengt Wilenius
111 Hannu Lindberg
112 Kristen Bertell
113 Veikko Kuusisto
114 Tapio Majaniemi
115 Leo Vankka
116 Pentti Harju
117 Ari Myllymaki
118 Matti Koskinen
119 Pentti Andersson
120 Pertti Heikkinen
121 Pekka Peltoniemi
122 Jouko Jarvinen
123 Matti Vartiainen
124 Esko Reijonen
125 Erkki Rasanen
126 Timo Viskari
127 Raimo Turkulainen
128 Paavo Tirkkonen
129 Orvo Paatero
130 Juhani Leirivaara
131 Jyrki Turunen
132 Timo Tuomainen
133 Pentti Karkkainen
134 Jussi Piuhola
135 Pentti Pihlapuro
136 Pentti Pennanen
137 Esa Viskari
138 Timo Luostarinen
139 Seppo Iivonen
140 Risto Alho
141 Esko Kiuru
142 Jaakko Hovinheimo
143 Jaakko Koikkalainen
144 Juhani Sodervik
145 Seppo Makinen
146 Teuvo Peltola
147 Antti Alenius
148 Kalevi Numminen
149 Esko Kaonpaa
150 Lauri Salomaa
151 Risto Pirttiaho
152 Antti Leppanen
153 Kari Makinen
154 Jorma Oksala
155 Pekka Marjamaki
156 Jouni Seistamo
157 Pertti Ansakorpi
158 Erkki Jarkko
159 Juhani Peltola
160 Erkki Mannikko
161 Keijo Mannisto
162 Matti Peltonen
163 Hannu Heikkonen
164 Pentti Hyytiainen
165 Antti Virtanen
166 Seppo Nurmi
167 Matti Reunamaki
168 Mikko Raikkonen
169 Esko Rantanen
170 Eero Holopainen
171 Juhani Ruohonen
172 Veikko Savolainen
173 Heikki Sivonen
174 Markku Pulli
175 Pekka Uitus
176 Heikki Keinonen
177 Jorma Saarikorpi
178 Rauno Lehtio
179 Kalevi Toivonen
180 Jorma Vilen
181 Pentti Kuusinen
182 Olavi Haapalainen
183 Seppo Nikkila
184 Jorma Suokko
185 Heino Pulli
186 Risto Lehtio
187 Pekka Lehtolainen
188 Timo Hirsimaki
189 Kari Palo-Oja
190 Pekka Leimu
191 Ali Saadetin
192 Erkki Jarvinen
193 Markku Hakanen
194 Jorma Kallio
195 Vaino Kolkka
196 Timo Saari
197 Jorma Peltonen
198 Pentti Pynnonen
199 Pentti Uotila
200 Timo Lahtinen
201 Juhani Lahtinen
202 Reijo Hakanen
203 Lasse Oksanen
204 Juhani Aromaki
205 Jukka Alkula
206 Pekka Olkkonen
207 Tapani Salo
208 Vesa Kartsalo
209 Antti Komsi
210 Asko Sallamaa
211 Juhani Tarkiainen
212 Antero Hakala
213 Ulf Slotte
214 Raimo Savolainen
215 Matias Savolainen
216 Risto Savolainen
217 Keijo Makinen
218 Tapio Makinen
219 Ossi Peltoniemi
220 Matti Valikangas

1971-72 Finnish Suomi Stickers

COMPLETE SET (384)	200.00	400.00
1 Vitaly Davydov	.30	.75
2 Anatoli Firsov	2.00	5.00
3 Valeri Kharlamov	6.00	15.00
4 Viktor Konovalenko	.30	.75
5 Viktor Kuzkin	.30	.75
6 Yuri Liapkin	.40	1.00
7 Vladimir Lutchenko	.30	.75
8 Alexander Maltsev	2.00	5.00
9 Alexander Martiniuk	.40	1.00
10 Boris Mikhailov	2.00	5.00
11 Evgeni Mishakov	.30	.75
12 Vladimir Petrov	2.00	5.00
13 Alexander Ragulin	.75	2.00
14 Igor Romishevski	.30	.75
15 Vladimir Shadrin	.40	1.00
16 Viatjeslav Starshinov	.40	1.00
17 Vladislav Tretiak	10.00	20.00
18 Gennady Tsygankov	.40	1.00
19 Vladimir Vikulov	.40	1.00
20 Evgeni Zimin	.40	1.00
21 Bedrich Brunschk	.20	.50
22 Jiri Bubla	.75	2.00
23 Josef Cerny	.30	.75
24 Richard Farda	.20	.50
25 Jan Havel	.20	.50
26 Ivan Hnlicka	.20	.50
27 Jiri Holecek	.40	1.00
28 Jiri Holik	.30	.75
29 Josef Horesovsky	.20	.50
30 Jiri Kochta	.20	.50
31 Oldrich Machac	.20	.50
32 Vladimir Martinec	.30	.75
33 Vaclav Nedomansky	.75	2.00
34 Eduard Novak	.20	.50
35 Frantisek Panchartek	.20	.50
36 Frantisek Pospisil	.30	.75
37 Marcel Sakac	.20	.50
38 Bohuslav Stastny	.40	1.00
39 Jan Suchy	.30	.75
40 Christer Abrahamsson	.75	2.00
41 Thommy Abrahamsson	.40	1.00
42 Thommie Bergman	1.25	3.00
43 Arne Carlsson	.20	.50
44 Inge Hammarstrom	4.00	10.00
45 Anders Hedberg	3.00	8.00
46 Leif Holmqvist	.75	2.00
47 Stig-Goran Johansson	.40	1.00
48 Stefan Karlsson	.20	.50
49 Hans Lindberg	.20	.50
50 Tord Lundstrom	.20	.50
51 William Lofqvist	.40	1.00
52 Kjell-Rune Milton	.20	.50
53 Lars-Goran Nilsson	.20	.50
54 Bert-Ola Nordlander	.40	1.00
55 Hakan Nygren	.20	.50
56 Bjorn Palmqvist	.20	.50
57 Hakan Pettersson	.20	.50
58 Ulf Sterner	.20	.50
59 Lennart Svedberg	.40	1.00
60 Hakan Wickberg	.20	.50
61 Esa Isaksson	.20	.50

Card	Low	High
62 Heikki Jarn	.20	.50
63 Veli-Pekka Ketola	.75	2.00
64 Ilpo Koskela	.20	.50
65 Seppo Lindstrom	.20	.50
66 Harri Linnonmaa	.20	.50
67 Hannu Luojola	.20	.50
68 Pekka Mononen	.20	.50
69 Erkki Mononen	.20	.50
70 Lauri Mononen	.20	.50
71 Matti Murto	.40	1.00
72 Lasse Oksanen	.20	.50
73 Esa Peltonen	.20	.50
74 Seppo Repo	.20	.50
75 Tommi Salmelainen	.20	.50
76 Juhani Tamminen	.20	.50
77 Jorma Valtonen	.40	1.00
78 Jorma Vehmanen	.20	.50
79 Urpo Ylonen	.40	1.00
80 Jouko Oystila	.20	.50
81 Tapio Flinck	.20	.50
82 Antti Heikkila	.20	.50
83 Reijo Heinonen	.20	.50
84 Jaakko Honkanen	.20	.50
85 Veli-Pekka Ketola	.75	2.00
86 Raimo Kilpio	.20	.50
87 Tapio Koskinen	.20	.50
88 Kaj Matalamaki	.20	.50
89 Pertti Makela	.20	.50
90 Pekka Rautakallio	.20	.50
91 Markku Riihimaki	.20	.50
92 Matti Salmi	.20	.50
93 Jorma Valtonen	.40	1.00
94 Anto Virtanen	.20	.50
95 Erkki Vakiparta	.20	.50
96 Pertti Ahokas	.20	.50
97 Pertti Arvaja	.20	.50
98 Olli Hietanen	.20	.50
99 Pentti Hiiros	.20	.50
100 Eero Holopainen	.20	.50
101 Kari Kinnunen	.20	.50
102 Ilpo Koskela	.20	.50
103 Timo Kyntola	.20	.50
104 Henry Leppa	.20	.50
105 Erkki Mononen	.20	.50
106 Pertti Nurmi	.20	.50
107 Timo Relas	.20	.50
108 Timo Sutinen	.20	.50
109 Timo Turunen	.20	.50
110 Jouko Oystila	.20	.50
111 Juhani Bostrom	.20	.50
112 Kimmo Heino	.20	.50
113 Esa Isaksson	.20	.50
114 Juhani Jylha	.20	.50
115 Heikki Jarn	.20	.50
116 Mauri Kaukorari	.20	.50
117 Vaino Kolkka	.20	.50
118 Harri Linnonmaa	.20	.50
119 Jaakko Marttinen	.20	.50
120 Matti Murto	.40	1.00
121 Lalli Partinen	.20	.50
122 Juha Rantasila	.20	.50
123 Heikki Riihiranta	.20	.50
124 Jorma Rikala	.20	.50
125 Tommi Salmelainen	.20	.50
126 Jorma Thusberg	.20	.50
127 Matti Vaisanen	.20	.50
128 Jukka Alkula	.20	.50
129 Pertti Ansakorpi	.20	.50
130 Keijo Jarvinen	.20	.50
131 Pertti Koivulahti	.20	.50
132 Ilpo Kuisma	.20	.50
134 Antti Leppanen	.20	.50
135 Pekka Marjamaki	.20	.50
136 Mikko Mynttien	.20	.50
137 Pekka Makinen	.20	.50
138 Seppo Makinen	.20	.50
139 Keijo Mannisto	.20	.50
140 Antti Perttula	.20	.50
141 Tuomo Rautiainen	.20	.50
142 Juhani Saarelainen	.20	.50
143 Jorma Saarikorpi	.20	.50
144 Risto Seesvuori	.20	.50
145 Jorma Siitarinen	.20	.50
146 Raimo Suoniemi	.20	.50
147 Juhani Aaltonen	.20	.50
148 Matti Ahvenharju	.20	.50
149 Hannu Auvinen	.20	.50
150 Jorma Borgstrom	.20	.50
151 Martti Immonen	.20	.50
152 Matti Keinonen	.20	.50
153 Seppo Laakkio	.20	.50
154 Timo Lahtinen	.20	.50
155 Esa Peltonen	.20	.50
156 Keijo Puhakka	.20	.50
157 Antti Ravi	.20	.50
158 Timo Saari	.20	.50
159 Esa Siren	.20	.50
160 Erkki Suni	.20	.50
161 Seppo Suoraniemi	.20	.50
162 Juhani Tamminen	.20	.50
163 Jorma Vehmanen	.20	.50
164 Stig Wetzell	.20	.50
165 Olli Viilma	.20	.50
166 Leo Aikas	.20	.50
167 Sakari Ahlberg	.20	.50
168 Seppo Ahokainen	.20	.50
169 Jorma Aro	.20	.50
170 Esko Eriksson	.20	.50
171 Marku Hakanen	.20	.50
172 Matti Hakanen	.20	.50
173 Reijo Hakanen	.20	.50
174 Martti Helle	.20	.50
175 Timo Hirsimaki	.20	.50
176 Jorma Kallio	.20	.50
177 Esko Kaonpaa	.20	.50
178 Pentti Koskela	.20	.50
179 Pekka Kuusisto	.20	.50
180 Pekka Leimu	.20	.50
181 Jukka Mattila	.20	.50
182 Lasse Oksanen	.20	.50
183 Kari Palooja	.20	.50
184 Jorma Peltonen	.40	1.00
185 Tuomo Sillman	.20	.50
186 Jaakko Siren	.20	.50
187 Veikkoi Suominen	.20	.50
188 Matti Jakonen	.20	.50
189 Kari Johansson	.20	.50
190 Arto Kaunonen	.20	.50
191 Timo Kokkonen	.20	.50
192 Reijo Leppanen	.20	.50
193 Seppo Lindstrom	.20	.50
194 Hannu Luojola	.20	.50
195 Hannu Niittoaho	.20	.50
196 Reijo Paksal	.20	.50
197 Seppo Parikka	.20	.50
198 Jarmo Rantanen	.20	.50
199 Veijo Saarinen	.20	.50
200 Martti Salonen	.20	.50
201 Voitto Soini	.20	.50
202 Kari Torkkel	.20	.50
203 Risto Vainio	.20	.50
204 Pentti Vihanto	.20	.50
205 Seppo Wikstrom	.20	.50
206 Urpo Ylonen	.40	1.00
207 Hannu Haapalainen	.20	.50
208 Jukka-Pekka Jarvenpaa	.20	.50
209 Timo Jarvinen	.20	.50
210 Heikki Keinonen	.20	.50
211 Heimo Keinonen	.20	.50
212 Rauno Lehtio	.20	.50
213 Markku Moisio	.20	.50
214 Seppo Nurmi	.20	.50
215 Esko Rantanen	.20	.50
216 Juhani Ruohonen	.20	.50
217 Mikkp Raikkonen	.20	.50
218 Lauri Salomaa	.20	.50
219 Veikko Savolainen	.20	.50
220 Leo Seppanen	.20	.50
221 Pekka Uitus	.20	.50
222 Jorma Vilen	.20	.50
223 Tapio Virhimo	.20	.50
224 Kauko Fomin	.20	.50
225 Heikki Hurme	.20	.50
226 Eero Juntunen	.20	.50
227 Lauri Jamsen	.20	.50
228 Lasse Kiili	.20	.50
229 Hannu Koivunen	.20	.50
230 Jarmo Koivunen	.20	.50
231 Pekka Lahtela	.20	.50
232 Ilkka Mesikammen	.20	.50
233 Timo Nummelin	.20	.50
234 Rauli Ottila	.20	.50
235 Matti Rautee	.20	.50
236 Pekka Rautee	.20	.50
237 Jari Rosberg	.20	.50
238 Jouni Samuli	.20	.50
239 Harry Silver	.20	.50
240 Rauli Tammelin	.20	.50
241 Bengt Wilenius	.20	.50
242 Mikko Erholm	.20	.50
243 Veikko Ihalainen	.20	.50
244 Heikki Kauhanen	.20	.50
245 Tapani Koskimaki	.20	.50
246 Antti Laine	.20	.50
247 Arto Laine	.20	.50
248 Timo Lehtorinne	.20	.50
249 Hannu Lunden	.20	.50
250 Teppo Rastio	.20	.50
251 Pentti Rautalin	.20	.50
252 Kai Rosvall	.20	.50
253 Ilkka Saarikko	.20	.50
254 Jari Sarronlahti	.20	.50
255 Matti Saurio	.20	.50
256 Hannu Siivonen	.20	.50
257 Erkki Sundelin	.20	.50
258 Simo Suoknuuti	.20	.50
259 Martti Haapala	.20	.50
260 Yrjo Hakulinen	.20	.50
261 Pentti Hirvonen	.20	.50
262 Antero Honkanen	.20	.50
263 Pekka Lavkainen	.20	.50
264 Pentti Lavkainen	.20	.50
265 Pertti Martikainen	.20	.50
266 Pentti Martikainen	.20	.50
267 Seppo Nevalainen	.20	.50
268 Tapio Pohtinen	.20	.50
269 Kari Puustinen	.20	.50
270 Markku Rouhiainen	.20	.50
271 Jarmo Sahlmann	.20	.50
272 Seppo Saros	.20	.50
273 Juha Silvennoinen	.20	.50
274 Unto Turpeinen	.20	.50
275 Kari Viitakahti	.20	.50
276 Erkki Airaksinen	.20	.50
277 Kauko Alkunen	.20	.50
278 Jarmo Gummerus	.20	.50
279 Bjorn Herbert	.20	.50
280 Jarmo Jaakkola	.20	.50
281 Hannu Kapanen	.20	.50
282 Matti Koskinen	.20	.50
283 Martti Kuokkanen	.20	.50
284 Juhani Laine	.20	.50
285 Heikki Leppik	.20	.50
286 Juhani Langstrom	.20	.50
287 Osmo Lotjonen	.20	.50
288 Lauri Mononen	.20	.50
289 Christer Nordblad	.20	.50
290 Juha Poikolainen	.20	.50
291 Kimmo Rantanen	.20	.50
292 Seppo Repo	.20	.50
293 Ilpo Ruokosalmi	.20	.50
294 Arto Siisala	.20	.50
295 Bo Sjostedt	.20	.50
296 Pentti Viitanen	.20	.50
297 Pekka Arbelius	.40	1.00
298 Olli Engvist	.20	.50
299 Hannu Hiltunen	.20	.50
300 Paavo Holopainen	.20	.50
301 Juha Huikari	.20	.50
302 Ari Jalonen	.20	.50
303 Kari Jalonen	.20	.50
304 Ari Kaikkonen	.20	.50
305 Ari Kalmokoski	.20	.50
306 Arto Lehtinen	.20	.50
307 Markku Narhi	.20	.50
308 Ilkka Okkonen	.20	.50
309 Matti Perhonma	.20	.50
310 Juha-Pekka Porvari	.20	.50
311 Arto Ruotanen	.20	.50
312 Reijo Ruotsalainen	.20	.50
313 Matti Ruutti	.20	.50
314 Pertti Raisanen	.20	.50
315 Ari Timosaari	.20	.50
316 Janne Oro	.20	.50
317 Anssi Eronen	.20	.50
318 Seppo Hirvonen	.20	.50
319 Jari Hannu Hamalainen	.20	.50
320 Jari Pekka Hamalainen	.20	.50
321 Timo Harkonen	.40	1.00
322 Jouko Ikonen	.20	.50
323 Lasse Kaiponen	.20	.50
324 Jyri Kemppinen	.20	.50
325 Jouni Kostiainen	.20	.50
326 Kai Kulhoranta	.20	.50
327 Olli Lemola	.20	.50
328 Jari Lopponen	.20	.50
329 Pasi Makkonen	.20	.50
330 Vesa Massinen	.20	.50
331 Timo Minkkila	.20	.50
332 Petri Pellinen	.20	.50
333 Juhan Rasanen	.20	.50
334 Pasi Sallinen	.20	.50
335 Kauko Tamminen	.20	.50
336 Olli Teijonmaa	.20	.50
337 Ismo Tolvanen	.20	.50
338 Timo Vaahtoluoto	.20	.50
339 Kari Heikkila	.20	.50
340 Pekka Helander	.20	.50
341 Jari Hirsimaki	.20	.50
342 Jari Huotari	.20	.50
343 Ilkka Huura	.20	.50
344 Tero Juojarvi	.20	.50
345 Jari Jarvinen	.20	.50
346 Mika Laine	.20	.50
347 Marko Lepaus	.20	.50
348 Pertti Lundberg	.20	.50
349 Tino Minetti	.20	.50
350 Jarom Partanen	.20	.50
351 Olli-Pekka Perala	.20	.50
352 Ari Ruuska	.20	.50
353 Kai Saario	.20	.50
354 Olli-Pekka Turunen	.20	.50
355 Veli-Matti Uusimaa	.20	.50
356 Mauri Viita	.20	.50
357 Timo Virtanen	.20	.50
358 Jarmo Viteli	.20	.50
359 Petri Viteli	.20	.50
360 Ari Havukainen	.20	.50
361 Ismo Heinonen	.20	.50
362 Riku Hoyden	.20	.50
363 Jari Jokinen	.20	.50
364 Timo Joutsenvuori	.20	.50
365 Jyrki Jantti	.20	.50
366 Kimmo Jantti	.20	.50
367 Toni Ketola	.20	.50
368 Juha Korhonen	.20	.50
369 Ari Laine	.20	.50
370 Kari Lainio	.20	.50
371 Juha Makinen	.20	.50
372 Reima Numminen	.20	.50
373 Mika Pirila	.20	.50
374 Kai Pulli	.20	.50
375 Tero Tommila	.20	.50
376 Harri Tuohimaa	.20	.50
377 Pasi Tuohimaa	.20	.50
378 Ari Veijalainen	.20	.50
379 Jean Beliveau	10.00	25.00
380 Phil Esposito	15.00	40.00
381 Tony Esposito	15.00	40.00
382 Gordie Howe	30.00	60.00
383 Bobby Hull	15.00	40.00
384 Bobby Orr	50.00	100.00

1972-73 Finnish Jaakiekko

Card	Low	High
COMPLETE SET (360)	100.00	200.00
1 Vladimir Bednar	.40	1.00
2 Jiri Bubla	.40	1.00
3 Vladimir Dzurilla	1.25	3.00
4 Richard Farda	.20	.50
5 Julius Haas	.20	.50
6 Ivan Hlinka	.75	2.00
7 Jiri Holecek	.75	2.00
8 Jaroslav Holik	.40	1.00
9 Jiri Holik	.40	1.00
10 Josef Horesovsky	.20	.50
11 Jan Klapac	.20	.50
12 Jiri Kochta	.20	.50
13 Milan Kuzela	.20	.50
14 Oldrich Machac	.20	.50
15 Vladimir Martinec	.20	.50
16 Vaclav Nedomansky	2.00	5.00
17 Josef Palecek	.20	.50
18 Frantisek Pospisil	.20	.50
19 Bohuslav Stastny	.20	.50
20 Rudolf Tajcnar	.20	.50
21 Vjatsjeslav Anisin	.40	1.00
22 Juri Blinov	.40	1.00
23 Aleksandr Gusev	.75	2.00
24 Valeri Kharlamov	6.00	15.00
25 Aleksandr Yakushev	4.00	10.00
26 Viktor Kuzkin	.40	1.00
27 Vladimir Lutshenko	.40	1.00
28 Aleksandr Maltsev	2.00	5.00
29 Boris Mikhailov	2.00	5.00
30 Jevgeni Mishakov	.75	2.00
31 Vladimir Petrov	2.00	5.00
32 Aleksandr Ragulin	.75	2.00
33 Igor Romishevski	.40	1.00
34 Vladimir Shadrin	.75	2.00
35 Vladimir Shepovalov	.40	1.00
36 Vjatsjeslav Soloduhin	.40	1.00
37 Vladislav Tretjak	8.00	20.00
38 Gennadi Tsigankov	.40	1.00
39 Valeri Vasiljev	2.00	5.00
40 Vladimir Vikulov	.40	1.00
41 Christer Abrahamsson	1.25	3.00
42 Tommy Abrahamsson	1.25	3.00
43 Thommie Bergman	2.00	5.00
44 Inge Hammarstrom	3.00	8.00
45 Anders Hedberg	3.00	8.00
46 Leif Holmqvist	.75	2.00
47 Bjorn Johansson	.20	.50
48 Stig-Goran Johansson	.40	1.00
49 Stefan Karlsson	.20	.50
50 Stig Larsson	.20	.50
51 Mats Lind	.20	.50
52 Tord Lundstrom	.20	.50
53 Lars-Goran Johansson	.20	.50
54 Bjorn Palmqvist	.20	.50
55 Hakan Pettersson	.20	.50
56 Borje Salming	8.00	20.00
57 Lars-Erik Sjoberg	1.25	3.00
58 Carl Sundqvist	.20	.50
59 Hakan Wickberg	.20	.50
60 Stig Ostling	.20	.50
61 Seppo Ahokainen	.20	.50
62 Matti Keinonen	.20	.50
63 Veli-Pekka Ketola	1.25	3.00
64 Harri Linnonmaa	.20	.50
65 Pekka Marjamaki	.20	.50
66 Lauri Mononen	.20	.50
67 Matti Murto	.20	.50
68 Timo Nummelin	.20	.50
69 Lasse Oksanen	.20	.50
70 Esa Peltonen	.20	.50
71 Juha Rantasila	.20	.50
72 Pekka Rautakallio	1.25	3.00
73 Seppo Repo	.20	.50
74 Heikki Riihiranta	.20	.50
75 Juhani Tamminen	.40	1.00
76 Timo Turunen	.20	.50
77 Pertti Valkeapaa	.20	.50
78 Jorma Valtonen	.20	.50
79 Stig Wetzell	.20	.50
80 Jouko Oystila	.20	.50
81 Juhani Bostrom	.20	.50
82 Kimmo Heino	.20	.50
83 Penti Karlsson	.20	.50
84 Mauri Kaukokari	.20	.50
85 Jarmo Koivunen	.20	.50
86 Heikki Kojola	.20	.50
87 Vaino Kolkka	.20	.50
88 Harri Linnonmaa	.20	.50
89 Jaakko Marttinen	.20	.50
90 Matti Murto	.20	.50
91 Lalli Partinen	.20	.50
92 Juha Rantasila	.20	.50
93 Heikki Riihiranta	.20	.50
94 Jorma Rikala	.20	.50
95 Henry Saleva	.20	.50
96 Tommi Salmelainen	.20	.50
97 Jorma Thusberg	.20	.50
98 Jorma Virtanen	.20	.50
99 Matti Vaisanen	.20	.50
100 Juhani Aaltonen	.20	.50
101 Jorma Immonen	.20	.50
102 Martti Immonen	.20	.50
103 Heikki Jarn	.20	.50
104 Matti Keinonen	.20	.50
105 Seppo Laakkio	.20	.50
106 Timo Lahtinen	.20	.50
107 Esa Peltonen	.20	.50
108 Keijo Puhakka	.20	.50
109 Seppo Railio	.20	.50
110 Antti Ravi	.20	.50
111 Timo Saari	.20	.50
112 Esa Siren	.20	.50
113 Seppo Suoraniemi	.20	.50
114 Juhani Tamminen	.20	.50
115 Jorma Vehmanen	.20	.50
116 Stig Wetzell	.20	.50
117 Leo Aikas	.20	.50
118 Sakari Ahlberg	.20	.50
119 Seppo Ahokainen	.20	.50
120 Jorma Aro	.20	.50
121 Esko Eriksson	.20	.50
122 Markku Hakanen	.20	.50
123 Timo Hirsimaki	.20	.50
124 Jorma Kallio	.20	.50
125 Esko Kaonpaa	.20	.50

Card	Low	High
126 Pentti Koskela	.20	.50
127 Pekka Kuusisto	.20	.50
128 Pekka Leimu	.20	.50
129 Len Lunde	.20	.50
130 Jukka Mattila	.20	.50
131 Lasse Oksanen	.20	.50
132 Hannu Palmu	.20	.50
133 Kari Palo-oja	.20	.50
134 Jorma Peltonen	.20	.50
135 Tuomo Sillman	.20	.50
136 Veikko Suominen	.20	.50
137 Pertti Ahokass	.20	.50
138 Pertti Arvaja	.20	.50
139 Christer Bergenheim	.20	.50
140 Jorma Borgstrom	.20	.50
141 Olli Hietanen	.20	.50
142 Pentti Hiiros	.20	.50
143 Eero Holopainen	.20	.50
144 Kari Kinnunen	.20	.50
145 Keijo Koivunen	.20	.50
146 Ilpo Koskela	.20	.50
147 Timo Kyntola	.20	.50
148 Henry Leppa	.20	.50
149 Erkki Mononen	.20	.50
150 Pertti Nurmi	.20	.50
151 Tero Raty	.20	.50
152 Timo Sutinen	.20	.50
153 Timo Turunen	.20	.50
154 Jouko Oystila	.20	.50
155 Hannu Haapalainen	.20	.50
156 Olavi Haapalainen	.20	.50
157 Jukka-Pekka Jarvenpaa	.20	.50
158 Heimo Keinonen	.20	.50
159 Markku Moisio	.20	.50
160 Heikki Nurmi	.20	.50
161 Seppo Nurmi	.20	.50
162 Oiva Oijennus	.20	.50
163 Reino Pulkkinen	.20	.50
164 Esko Rantanen	.20	.50
165 Juhani Ruohonen	.20	.50
166 Mikko Raikkonen	.20	.50
167 Lauri Salomaa	.20	.50
168 Leo Seppanen	.20	.50
169 Pekka Uitus	.20	.50
170 Jorma Vilen	.20	.50
171 Tapio Virhimo	.20	.50
172 Leo Haakana	.20	.50
173 Seppo Hyvonen	.20	.50
174 Heikki Juselius	.20	.50
175 Hannu Lemander	.20	.50
176 Kyosti Lahde	.20	.50
177 Ari Mikkola	.20	.50
178 Martti Makia	.20	.50
179 Martti Narinen	.20	.50
180 Pekka Nieminen	.20	.50
181 Teijo Rasanen	.20	.50
182 Timo Sartiala	.20	.50
183 Pekka Sartjarvi	.20	.50
184 Keijo Sinkkonen	.20	.50
185 Martti Sinkkonen	.20	.50
186 Arto Summanen	.20	.50
187 Erkki Suni	.20	.50
188 Seppo Urpalainen	.20	.50
189 Matti Vaatamoinen	.20	.50
190 Timo Vaatamoinen	.20	.50
191 Jukka Alkula	.20	.50
192 Pertti Ansakorpi	.20	.50
193 Keijo Jarvinen	.20	.50
194 Pertti Koivulahti	.20	.50
195 Ilpo Kuisma	.20	.50
196 Vesa Lehtoranta	.20	.50
197 Antti Leppanen	.20	.50
198 Pekka Marjamaki	.20	.50
199 Mikko Mynttinen	.20	.50
200 Pekka Makinen	.20	.50
201 Seppo Makinen	.20	.50
202 Antti Perttula	.20	.50
203 Tuomo Rautiainen	.20	.50
204 Jorma Saarikorpi	.20	.50
205 Jorma Siitarinen	.20	.50
206 Raimo Suoniemi	.20	.50
207 Pertti Valkeapaa	.20	.50
208 Kari Horkko	.20	.50
209 Eero Juntunen	.20	.50
210 Lauri Jamsen	.20	.50
211 Kari Kauppila	.20	.50
212 Lasse Kiili	.20	.50
213 Olli Kokkonen	.20	.50
214 Pekka Lahtela	.20	.50
215 Robert Lamoureux	.20	.50
216 Ilkka Mesikammen	.20	.50
217 Timo Nummelin	.20	.50
218 Rauli Ottila	.20	.50
219 Matti Rautee	.20	.50
220 Pekka Rautee	.20	.50
221 Jari Rosberg	.20	.50
222 Jouni Samuli	.20	.50
223 Harri Silver	.20	.50
224 Rauli Tammelin	.20	.50
225 Bengt Wilenius	.20	.50
226 Pertti Hasanen	.20	.50
227 Kari Johansson	.20	.50
228 Arto Kaunonen	.20	.50
229 Timo Kokkonen	.20	.50
230 Reijo Leppanen	.20	.50
231 Seppo Lindstrom	.20	.50
232 Hannu Luojola	.20	.50
233 Hannu Niittoaho	.20	.50
234 Reijo Paksal	.20	.50
235 Seppo Parikka	.20	.50
236 Jarmo Rantanen	.20	.50
237 Kari Salonen	.20	.50
238 Tapani Sura	.20	.50
239 Kari Torkkel	.20	.50
240 Risto Vainio	.20	.50
241 Pentti Vihanto	.20	.50
242 Seppo Wikstrom	.20	.50
243 Urpo Ylonen	.20	.50
244 Tapio Flinck	.20	.50
245 Antti Heikkila	.20	.50
246 Reijo Heinonen	.20	.50
247 Jaakko Honkanen	.20	.50
248 Veli-Pekka Ketola	1.25	3.00
249 Raimo Kilpio	.20	.50
250 Tapio Koskinen	.20	.50
251 Jarkko Levonen	.20	.50
252 Kaj Matalamaki	.20	.50
253 Pertti Makela	.20	.50
254 Hannu Pulkkinen	.20	.50
255 Pekka Rautakallio	1.25	3.00
256 Markku Riihimaki	.20	.50
257 Matti Salmi	.20	.50
258 Jorma Valtonen	.20	.50
259 Anto Virtanen	.20	.50
260 Erkki Vakiparta	.20	.50
261 Martti Jarkko	.20	.50
262 Torsti Jarvenpaa	.20	.50
263 Tapio Kallio	.20	.50
264 Jussi Kiansten	.20	.50
265 Kimmo Korpela	.20	.50
266 Jarmo Kuisma	.20	.50
267 Antero Lehtonen	.20	.50
268 Mikko Leinonen	.20	.50
269 Tuomas Leinonen	.20	.50
270 Lasse Litma	.20	.50
271 Seppo Makinen	.20	.50
272 Heikki Niemi	.20	.50
273 Reijo Narvanen	.20	.50
274 Kalevi Paakkonen	.20	.50
275 Reijo Rossi	.20	.50
276 Seppo Sevon	.20	.50
277 Jorma Siren	.20	.50
278 Risto Sirkkola	.20	.50
279 Risto Hevonkorpi	.20	.50
280 Veijo Hukkanen	.20	.50
281 Timo Hytti	.20	.50
282 Kalle Impola	.20	.50
283 Pertti Jarvenpaa	.20	.50
284 Rauno Jarvinen	.20	.50
285 Antti Kaivola	.20	.50
286 Jorma Karvonen	.20	.50
287 Pekka Karvonen	.20	.50
288 Seppo Kettunen	.20	.50
289 Kari Niemi	.20	.50
290 Timo Niiniviita	.20	.50
291 Jari Nurminen	.20	.50
292 Pentti Poussu	.20	.50
293 Matti Rautiainen	.20	.50
294 Vesa Ronkainen	.20	.50
295 Mauri Salminen	.20	.50
296 Kari Silius	.20	.50
297 Kimo Turtiainen	.20	.50
298 Juha Wikman	.20	.50
299 Juha-Pekka Aho	.20	.50
300 Matti Estola	.20	.50
301 Markku Heinonen	.20	.50
302 Mauri Heinonen	.20	.50
303 Jukka Hirsimaki	.20	.50
304 Jarmo Huhtala	.20	.50
305 Harri Huotari	.20	.50
306 Kari Jarvinen	.20	.50
307 Jari Kaarela	.20	.50
308 Kai Lehto	.20	.50
309 Jari Leppanen	.20	.50
310 Jarmo Lilius	.20	.50
311 Markus Matsson	.20	.50
312 Jari Niinimaki	.20	.50
313 Hannu Oksanen	.20	.50
314 Sakari Pehu	.20	.50
315 Mika Rajala	.20	.50
316 Risto Siltanen	.20	.50
317 Jarmo Siro	.20	.50
318 Jukka Siro	.20	.50
319 Jari Uusikartano	.20	.50
320 Seppo Vartiainen	.20	.50
321 Mika Weissman	.20	.50
322 Seppo Aro	.20	.50
323 Jari Huotari	.20	.50
324 Ilkka Huura	.20	.50
325 Jari Hytti	.20	.50
326 Jarmo Jamalainen	.20	.50
327 Jari Jokinen	.20	.50
328 Tero Juojarvi	.20	.50
329 Jari Jarvinen	.20	.50
330 Lauri Kosonen	.20	.50
331 Aki Laakso	.20	.50
332 Ismo Laine	.20	.50
333 Matti Lisko	.20	.50
334 Dale Lunde	.20	.50
335 Markku Pirkkalanniemi	.20	.50
336 Rauno Saarnio	.20	.50
337 Jukka Silander	.20	.50
338 Olli-Pekka Turunen	.20	.50
339 Mauri Unkila	.20	.50
340 Jarmo Viteli	.20	.50
341 Jukka Ahonen	.20	.50
342 Jari Hallila	.20	.50
343 Jari Helle	.20	.50
344 Jari Hirsimaki	.20	.50
345 Petri Jokinen	.20	.50
346 Kari Jarvinen	.20	.50
347 Arto Laine	.20	.50
348 Ari Leinonen	.20	.50
349 Jukka Oksanen	.20	.50
350 Sten Pakarinen	.20	.50
351 Jyrki Seppa	.20	.50
352 Jari Simola	.20	.50
353 Olli Sarkilahti	.20	.50
354 Kari-Pekka Tarko	.20	.50
355 Timo Toivonen	.20	.50
356 Veli-Matti Uusimaa	.20	.50
357 Risto Viljanen	.20	.50
358 Timo Virtanen	.20	.50
359 Teppo Valimaki	.20	.50
360 Juha Yrjola	.20	.50

1972 Finnish Hellas

This vintage Finnish set appears to feature players who appeared in the previous World Championships.

Card	Low	High
COMPLETE SET (99)	50.00	125.00
1 Seppo Ahokainen	.20	.50
2 Veli-Pekka Ketola	.60	1.50
3 Henry Leppa	.20	.50
4 Harri Linnonmaa	.20	.50
5 Pekka Marjamaki	.20	.50
6 Lauri Mononen	.20	.50
7 Matti Murto	.20	.50
8 Timo Nummelin	.20	.50
9 Lasse Oksanen	.20	.50
10 Esa Peltonen	.20	.50
11 Pekka Rautakallio	.60	1.50
12 Seppo Repo	.20	.50
13 Heikki Riihiranta	.40	1.00
14 Tommi Salmelainen	.20	.50
15 Leo Seppanen	.20	.50
16 Juhani Tamminen	.40	1.00
17 Timo Turunen	.20	.50
18 Pertti Valkeapaa	.20	.50
19 Jorma Valtonen	.40	1.00
20 Jouko Oystila	.20	.50
21 Timo Saari	.20	.50
22 Seppo Suoraniemi	.20	.50
23 Leif Holmqvist	.40	1.00
24 Thommy Abrahamsson	.40	1.00
25 Thommie Bergman	.75	2.00
26 Stig Ostling	.40	1.00
27 Lars Sjoberg	.75	2.00
28 Carl Sundquist	.20	.50
29 Bjorn Johansson	.20	.50
30 Tord Lundstrom	.20	.50
31 Stig-Goran Johansson	.20	.50
32 Stefan Karlsson	.20	.50
33 Lars-Goran Nilsson	.20	.50
34 Stig Larsson	.20	.50
35 Mats Lindh	.20	.50
36 Bjorn Palmqvist	.20	.50
37 Inge Hammarstrom	4.00	10.00
38 Anders Hedberg	2.00	5.00
39 Kurt Larsson	.20	.50
40 Hakan Pettersson	.20	.50
41 Hakan Wickberg	.20	.50
42 Borje Salming	6.00	15.00
43 Franz Funk	.20	.50
44 Otto Schneitberger	.20	.50
45 Josef Volk	.20	.50
46 Rudolph Thanner	.20	.50
47 Paul Langner	.20	.50
48 Harald Kadow	.20	.50
49 Anton Pohl	.20	.50
50 Karl-Heinz Egger	2.00	5.00
51 Lorenz Funk	.20	.50
52 Alois Schloder	.20	.50
53 Gustav Hanig	.20	.50
54 Philips Reiner	.20	.50
55 Bernd Kuhn	.20	.50
56 Johan Eimansberger	.20	.50
57 Rainer Makatsch	.20	.50
58 Michael Eibl	.20	.50
59 Hans Schichti	.20	.50
60 Anrton Hoffher	.20	.50
61 Valdimir Lutchenko	.40	1.00
62 Aleksandr Gusev	.30	.75
63 Vladimir Lutchenko	.40	1.00
64 Viktor Kuzkin	.20	.50
65 Aleksandr Ragulin	.40	1.00
66 Igor Romishevski	.20	.50
67 Gennadi Tsigankov	.40	1.00
68 Valeri Vasiliev	.40	1.00
69 Yuri Blinov	.20	.50
70 Alexander Maltsev	2.00	5.00
71 Evgeny Mishakov	.30	.75
72 Boris Mikhailov	2.00	5.00
73 Vjatseslav Anisin	.30	.75
74 Alexander Yakushev	2.00	5.00
75 Vladimir Petrov	1.25	3.00
76 Valeri Kharlamov	4.00	10.00
77 Vladimir Vikulov	.30	.75
78 Vladimir Shadrin	.30	.75
79 Vladislav Tretiak	6.00	15.00
80 Vladimir Dzurilla	.60	1.50
81 Jiri Holecek	.40	1.00
82 Josef Horesovsky	.20	.50
83 Oldrich Machac	.20	.50
84 Jaroslav Holik	.30	.75
85 Rudolf Tajcnar	.20	.50
86 Frantisek Pospisil	.30	.75
87 Jiri Kochta	.20	.50
88 Jan Klapac	.20	.50
89 Vladimir Martinec	.20	.50
90 Richard Farda	.30	.75
91 Bohuslav Stastny	.30	.75
92 Vaclav Nedomansky	.60	1.50
93 Julius Haas	.20	.50
94 Josef Palecek	.20	.50
95 Jiri Bubla	.40	1.00
96 Milan Kuzela	.20	.50
97 Vladimir Bednar	.20	.50
98 Jiri Holik	.40	1.00
99 Ivan Hlinka	.30	.75

1972 Finnish Panda Toronto

Card	Low	High
COMPLETE SET (118)	50.00	100.00
1 Juhani Bostrom	.40	1.00
2 Gary Engberg	.40	1.00
3 Kimmo Heino	.40	1.00
4 Mauri Kaukokari	.40	1.00
5 Vaino Kolkka	.40	1.00
6 Harri Linnonmaa	.40	1.00
7 Jaakko Marttinen	.40	1.00
8 Matti Murto	.40	1.00
9 Lalli Partinen	.40	1.00
10 Juha Rantasila	.40	1.00
11 Heikki Riihiranta	.40	1.00
12 Jorma Rikala	.40	1.00
13 Tommi Salmelainen	.40	1.00
14 Jorma Thusberg	.40	1.00
15 Jorma Virtanen	.40	1.00
16 Matti Vaisanen	.40	1.00
17 Sakari Ahlberg	.40	1.00
18 Jorma Aro	.40	1.00
19 Esko Eriksson	.40	1.00
20 Markku Hakanen	.40	1.00
21 Matti Hakanen	.40	1.00
22 Reijo Hakanen	.40	1.00
23 Timo Hirsimaki	.40	1.00
24 Jorma Kallio	.40	1.00
25 Esko Kaonpaa	.40	1.00
26 Pentti Koskela	.40	1.00
27 Pekka Kuusisto	.40	1.00
28 Pekka Leimu	.40	1.00
29 Lasse Oksanen	.40	1.00
30 Kari Palo-oja	.40	1.00
31 Jorma Peltonen	.40	1.00
32 Veikko Suominen	.40	1.00
33 Tapio Flinck	.40	1.00
34 Pentti Hakamaki	.40	1.00
35 Antti Heikkila	.40	1.00
36 Reijo Heinonen	.40	1.00
37 Jaakko Honkanen	.40	1.00
38 Veli-Pekka Ketola	.40	1.00
39 Raimo Kilpio	.40	1.00
40 Tapio Koskinen	.40	1.00
41 Kaj Matalamaki	.40	1.00
42 Pekka Rautakallio	.40	1.00
43 Matti Salmi	.40	1.00
44 Kari-Pekka Toivonen	.40	1.00
45 Jorma Valtonen	.40	1.00
46 Anto Virtanen	.40	1.00
47 Erkki Vakiparta	.40	1.00
48 Vitaly Davydov	.75	2.00
49 Anatoly Firsov	.75	2.00
50 Valeri Kharlamov	8.00	20.00
51 Victor Konovalenko	.75	2.00
52 Victor Kuzkin	.75	2.00
53 Yuri Liapkin	.75	2.00
54 Vladimir Lutchenko	.75	2.00
55 Alexander Maltsev	2.00	5.00
56 Alexander Martyniuk	.75	2.00
57 Boris Mikhailov	2.00	5.00
58 Aleksander Ragulin	.75	2.00
59 Igor Romishevskyi	.75	2.00
60 Vladimir Shadrin	.75	2.00
61 Viacheslav Starshinov	.75	2.00
62 Vladislav Tretiak	8.00	20.00
63 Evgenyi Zimin	.75	2.00
64 Christer Abrahamsson	.75	2.00
65 Tommy Abrahamsson	.75	2.00
66 Arne Carlsson	.40	1.00
67 Inge Hammarstrom	2.00	5.00
68 Leif Holmqvist	.75	2.00
69 Stig-Goran Johansson	.40	1.00
70 Stefan Karlsson	.40	1.00
71 Hans Lindberg	.40	1.00
72 Tord Lundstrom	.40	1.00
73 Lars-Goran Nilsson	.40	1.00
74 Bert-Ola Nordlander	.40	1.00
75 Hakan Nygren	.40	1.00
76 Bjorn Palmqvist	.40	1.00
77 Ulf Sterner	.40	1.00
78 Lennart Svedberg	.40	1.00
79 Hakan Wickberg	.40	1.00
80 Josef Cerny	.40	1.00
81 Richard Farda	.40	1.00
82 Ivan Hlinka	.40	1.00
83 Jiri Holecek	.40	1.00
84 Jiri Holik	.40	1.00
85 Josef Horesovsky	.40	1.00
86 Milan Kuzela	.40	1.00
87 Oldrich Machac	.40	1.00
88 Vladimir Martinec	.40	1.00
89 Vladimir Nadrchal	.40	1.00
90 Vaclav Nedomansky	1.50	4.00
91 Frantisek Panchartek	.40	1.00
92 Frantisek Pospisil	.40	1.00
93 Marcel Sakac	.40	1.00
94 Bohuslav Stastny	.40	1.00
95 Rudolf Tajcnar	.40	1.00
96 Esa Isaksson	.40	1.00
97 Heikki Jarn	.40	1.00
98 Veli-Pekka Ketola	1.50	4.00
99 Ilpo Koskela	.40	1.00
100 Seppo Lindstrom	.40	1.00
101 Harri Linnonmaa	.40	1.00
102 Pekka Marjamaki	.40	1.00
103 Erkki Mononen	.40	1.00
104 Lauri Mononen		1.00
105 Matti Murto	.40	1.00
106 Lasse Oksanen	.40	1.00
107 Esa Peltonen	.40	1.00
108 Seppo Repo	.40	1.00

109 Tommi Salmelainen	.40	1.00
110 Jorma Valtonen	.40	1.00
111 Urpo Ylonen	.40	1.00
112 Jouko Oystila	.40	1.00
113 Sovjet - Finland	.40	1.00
114 Sverige - Tjeckoslovakien	.40	1.00
115 Finland - Svergie	.40	1.00
116 Tjeckoslovakien - Sovjet	.40	1.00
117 USA - Sovjet	.40	1.00
118 Hockey Sticks	.40	1.00

1972 Finnish Semic World Championship

Printed in Italy by Semic Press, the 233 cards comprising this set measure 1 7/8" by 2 1/2" and feature posed color player photos on their white-bordered fronts.

1973-74 Finnish Jaakiekko

COMPLETE SET (325)	125.00	250.00
1 Vjatsjeslav Anisin	.75	2.00
2 Aleksandr Bodunov	.75	2.00
3 Aleksandr Gusev	.75	2.00
4 Valeri Kharlamov	6.00	15.00
5 Aleksandr Yakushev	2.00	5.00
6 Juri Lebedev	.75	2.00
7 Juri Liapkin	.75	2.00
8 Vladimir Lutshenko	.75	2.00
9 Aleksandr Maltsev	2.00	5.00
10 Aleksandr Martiniuk	.75	2.00
11 Boris Mikhailov	2.00	5.00
12 Jevgeni Paladiev	.75	2.00
13 Vladimir Petrov	2.00	5.00
14 Aleksandr Ragulin	.75	2.00
15 Vladimir Shadrin	.75	2.00
16 Aleksandr Sidelnikov	.75	2.00
17 Vladislav Tretiak	8.00	20.00
18 Gennadi Tsigankov	.75	2.00
19 Valeri Vasiljev	2.00	5.00
20 Vladimir Vikulov	.75	2.00
21 Aleksandr Voltshkov	.75	2.00
22 Christer Abrahamsson	1.25	3.00
23 Thommy Abrahamsson	1.25	3.00
24 Roland Bond	.40	1.00
25 Arne Carlsson	.40	1.00
26 Inge Hammarstrom	2.00	5.00
27 Anders Hedberg	2.00	5.00
28 Bjorn Johansson	.40	1.00
29 Stefan Karlsson	.40	1.00
30 Curt Larsson	.40	1.00
31 Tord Lundstrom	.40	1.00
32 William Lofqvist	.40	1.00
33 Ulf Nilsson	2.00	5.00
34 Borje Salming	6.00	15.00
35 Lars-Erik Sjoberg	1.25	3.00
36 Ulf Sterner	.40	1.00
37 Karl-Johan Sundqvist	.40	1.00
38 Dan Soderstrom	.40	1.00
39 Hakan Wickberg	.40	1.00
40 Kjell-Arne Wickstrom	.40	1.00
41 Dick Yderstrom	.40	1.00
42 Mats Ahlberg	.40	1.00
43 Peter Adamik	.40	1.00
44 Jiri Bubla	.40	1.00
45 Jiri Crha	1.25	3.00
46 Richard Farda	.40	1.00
47 Ivan Hlinka	.75	2.00
48 Jiri Holecek	.75	2.00
49 Jaroslav Holik	.40	1.00
50 Jiri Holik	.40	1.00
51 Josef Horesovsky	.40	1.00
52 Jan Klapac	.40	1.00
53 Jiri Kochta	.40	1.00
54 Milan Kuzela	.40	1.00
55 Oldrich Machac	.40	1.00
56 Vladimir Martinec	.40	1.00
57 Vaclav Nedomansky	1.25	3.00
58 Jiri Novak	.40	1.00
59 Josef Palecek	.40	1.00
60 Frantisek Pospisil	.40	1.00
61 Bohuslav Stastny	.40	1.00
62 Karel Vohralik	.40	1.00
63 Seppo Ahokainen	.40	1.00
64 Matti Keinonen	.40	1.00
65 Veli-Pekka Ketola	1.25	3.00
66 Ilpo Koskela	.40	1.00
67 Ilpo Kuisma	.40	1.00
68 Pekka Kuusisto	.40	1.00
69 Henry Leppa	.40	1.00
70 Antti Leppanen	.40	1.00
71 Seppo Lindstrom	.40	1.00
72 Lauri Mononen	.40	1.00
73 Timo Nummelin	.40	1.00
74 Lalli Partinen	.40	1.00
75 Esa Peltonen	.40	1.00
76 Pekka Rautakallio	1.25	3.00
77 Seppo Repo	.40	1.00
78 Heikki Riihiranta	.40	1.00
79 Timo Sutinen	.40	1.00
80 Juhani Tamminen	.40	1.00
81 Timo Turunen	.40	1.00
82 Jorma Valtonen	.40	1.00
83 Jorma Vehmanen	.40	1.00
84 Jouko Oystila	.40	1.00
85 Josef Batkiewicz	.40	1.00
86 Krzysztof Bialynicki	.40	1.00
87 Stefan Chowaniec	.40	1.00
88 Ludwik Czachovski	.40	1.00
89 Andrzej Czczepaniec	.40	1.00
90 Stanislav Fryzlewicz	.40	1.00
91 Robert Goralczyk	.40	1.00
92 Mieczyslaw Jaskierski	.40	1.00
93 Tadeusz Kacik	.40	1.00
94 Adam Kopczynski	.40	1.00
95 Valery Kosyl	.40	1.00
96 Tadeusz Obloj	.40	1.00
97 Jerzy Potz	.40	1.00
98 Andrzej Slowakiewicz	.40	1.00
99 Josef Slowakiewicz	.40	1.00
100 Jan Szeja	.40	1.00
101 Leszek Tokarz	.40	1.00
102 Wieslav Tokarz	.40	1.00
103 Henryk Vojtynek	.40	1.00
104 Walenty Zietara	.40	1.00
105 Pertti Arvaja	.40	1.00
106 Olli J. Hietanen	.40	1.00
107 Olli T. Hietanen	.40	1.00
108 Pentti Hiiros	.40	1.00
109 Eero Holopainen	.40	1.00
110 Kari Kinnunen	.40	1.00
111 Ilpo Koskela	.40	1.00
112 Timo Kyntola	.40	1.00
113 Henry Leppa	.40	1.00
114 Jan Lindberg	.40	1.00
115 Lauri Mononen	.40	1.00
116 Mika Rajala	.40	1.00
117 Pertti Nurmi	.40	1.00
118 Jyrki Seivo	.40	1.00
119 Jorma Siitarinen	.40	1.00
120 Seppo Suoraniemi	.40	1.00
121 Timo Sutinen	.40	1.00
122 Timo Turunen	.40	1.00
123 Jorma Valtonen	.40	1.00
124 Seppo Vartiainen	.40	1.00
125 Jouko Oystila	.40	1.00
126 Juhani Bostrom	.40	1.00
127 Matti Hagman	1.25	3.00
128 Kimmo Heino	.40	1.00
129 Jorma Immonen	.40	1.00
130 Pentti Karlsson	.40	1.00
131 Mauri Kaukokari	.40	1.00
132 Jarmo Koivunen	.40	1.00
133 Vaino Kolkka	.40	1.00
134 Harri Linnonmaa	.40	1.00
135 Jaakko Marttinen	.40	1.00
136 Matti Murto	.40	1.00
137 Lalli Partinen	.40	1.00
138 Esa Peltonen	.40	1.00
139 Juha Rantasila	.40	1.00
140 Heikki Riihiranta	.40	1.00
141 Jorma Rikala	.40	1.00
142 Tommi Salmelainen	.40	1.00
143 Henry Saleva	.40	1.00
144 Juhani Tamminen	.75	2.00
145 Jorma Thusberg	.40	1.00
146 Jorma Virtanen	.40	1.00
147 Matti Vaisanen	.40	1.00
148 Stig Wetzell	.40	1.00
149 Jukka Alkula	.40	1.00
150 Pertti Ansakorpi	.40	1.00
151 Hannu Haapalainen	.40	1.00
152 Martti Jarkko	.40	1.00
153 Keijo Jarvinen	.40	1.00
154 Pertti Koivulahti	.40	1.00
155 Ilpo Kuisma	.40	1.00
156 Antero Lehtonen	.40	1.00
157 Antti Leppanen	.40	1.00
158 Lasse Litma	.40	1.00
159 Pekka Marjamaki	.40	1.00
160 Mikko Myntinen	.40	1.00
161 Pekka Makinen	.40	1.00
162 Seppo I. Makinen	.40	1.00
163 Seppo S. Makinen	.40	1.00
164 Keijo Mannisto	.40	1.00
165 Antti Perttula	.40	1.00
166 Tuomo Rautiainen	.40	1.00
167 Jorma Saarikorpi	.40	1.00
168 Juha Silvennoinen	.40	1.00
169 Jorma Siren	.40	1.00
170 Raimo Suoniemi	.40	1.00
171 Pertti Valkeapaa	.40	1.00
172 Sakari Ahlberg	.40	1.00
173 Seppo Ahokainen	.40	1.00
174 Jorma Aro	.40	1.00
175 Esko Eriksson	.40	1.00
176 Markku Hakanen	.40	1.00
177 Reijo Hakanen	.40	1.00
178 Martti Helle	.40	1.00
179 Erkki Jarvinen	.40	1.00
180 Jorma Kallio	.40	1.00
181 Erkki Kesalainen	.40	1.00
182 Pekka Kuusisto	.40	1.00
183 Pekka Leimu	.40	1.00
184 Jukka Mattila	.40	1.00
185 Esko Makinen	.40	1.00
186 Lassse Oksanen	.40	1.00
187 Kari Palo-oja	.40	1.00
188 Jorma Peltonen	.40	1.00
189 Pekka Rampa	.40	1.00
190 Heikki Salminen	.40	1.00
191 Tuomo Sillman	.40	1.00
192 Veikko Suominen	.40	1.00
193 Tapio Virhimo	.40	1.00
194 Juhani Aaltonen	.40	1.00
195 Bjorn Herbert	.40	1.00
196 Hannu Kapanen	.40	1.00
197 Matti Keinonen	.40	1.00
198 Lasse Kiili	.40	1.00
199 Matti Koskinen	.40	1.00
200 Martti Kuokkanen	.40	1.00
201 Urpo Kuukauppi	.40	1.00
202 Seppo Laakkio	.40	1.00
203 Timo Lahtinen	.40	1.00
204 Juhani Laine	.40	1.00
205 Heikki Leppik	.40	1.00
206 Osmo Lotjonen	.40	1.00
207 Kyosti Majava	.40	1.00
208 Keijo Puhakka	.40	1.00
209 Antti Ravi	.40	1.00
210 Seppo Repo	.40	1.00
211 Timo Saari	.40	1.00
212 Arto Siissala	.40	1.00
213 Jorma Vehmanen	.40	1.00
214 Pentti Viitanen	.40	1.00
215 Leo Aikas	.40	1.00
216 Raine Heinonen	.40	1.00
217 Vladimir Jursinov	.40	1.00
218 Jukka-Pekka Jarvenpaa	.40	1.00
219 Pertti Jarvenpaa	.40	1.00
220 Heimo Keinonen	.40	1.00
221 Seppo Kettunen	.40	1.00
222 Veikko Kirveskoski	.40	1.00
223 Reijo Laksola	.40	1.00
224 Raimo Majapuro	.40	1.00
225 Markku Moisio	.40	1.00
226 Heikki Nurmi	.40	1.00
227 Seppo Nurmi	.40	1.00
228 Oiva Oijennus	.40	1.00
229 Esko Rantanen	.40	1.00
230 Matti Rautiainen	.40	1.00
231 Juhani Ruohonen	.40	1.00
232 Mikko Raikkonen	.40	1.00
233 Lauri Salomaa	.40	1.00
234 Veikko Savolainen	.40	1.00
235 Leo Seppanen	.40	1.00
236 Veikko Seppanen	.40	1.00
237 Pekka Uitus	.40	1.00
238 Kari Viitalahti	.40	1.00
239 Jorma Vilen	.40	1.00
240 Asko Ahonen	.40	1.00
241 Tapio Flinck	.40	1.00
242 Matti Hakanen	.40	1.00
243 Antti Heikkila	.40	1.00
244 Reijo Heinonen	.40	1.00
245 Jaakko Honkanen	.40	1.00
246 Jari Kaski	.40	1.00
247 Veli-Pekka Ketola	.40	1.00
248 Raimo Kilpio	.40	1.00
249 Tapio Koskinen	.40	1.00
250 Jarkko Levonen	.40	1.00
251 Kaj Matalamaki	.40	1.00
252 Pertti Makela	.40	1.00
253 Jaakko Niemi	.40	1.00
254 Hannu Pulkkinen	.40	1.00
255 Pekka Rautakallio	.40	1.00
256 Markku Riihimaki	.40	1.00
257 Anto Virtanen	.40	1.00
258 Erkki Vakiparta	.40	1.00
259 Pertti Hasanen	.40	1.00
260 Rainer Holmroos	.40	1.00
261 Kari Johansson	.40	1.00
262 Arto Kaunonen	.40	1.00
263 Timo Kokkonen	.40	1.00
264 Reijo Leppanen	.40	1.00
265 Seppo Lindstrom	.40	1.00
266 Hannu Luojola	.40	1.00
267 Hannu Niittoaho	.40	1.00
268 Reijo Paksal	.40	1.00
269 Seppo Parikka	.40	1.00
270 Jarmo Rantanen	.40	1.00
271 Kari Hyokki	.40	1.00
272 Kari Salonen	.40	1.00
273 Tapani Sura	.40	1.00
274 Kari Torkkel	.40	1.00
275 Risto Vainio	.40	1.00
276 Pentti Vihanto	.40	1.00
277 Urpo Ylonen	.40	1.00
278 Lars Elffolk	.40	1.00
279 Kari Horkko	.40	1.00
280 Hannu Jortikka	.40	1.00
281 Eero Juntunen	.40	1.00
282 Lauri Jamsen	.40	1.00
283 Jari Kapanen	.40	1.00
284 Jari Kauppila	.40	1.00
285 Matti Kauppila	.40	1.00
286 Jukka Koskilahti	.40	1.00
287 Jukka Koivu	.40	1.00
288 Ilkka Laaksonen	.40	1.00
289 Robert Lamoureux	.40	1.00
290 Hannu Lunden	.40	1.00
291 Ilkka Mesikammen	.40	1.00
292 Timo Nummelin	.40	1.00
293 Timo Nurminen	.40	1.00
294 Rauli Ottila	.40	1.00
295 Matti Rautee	.40	1.00
296 Pekka Rautee	.40	1.00
297 Jari Rosberg	.40	1.00
298 Tarmo Saarni	.40	1.00
299 Asko Salminen	.40	1.00
300 Jouni Samuli	.40	1.00
301 Rauli Tammelin	.40	1.00
302 Veijo Wahlsten	.40	1.00
303 Bengt Wilenius	.40	1.00
304 Denis Bavaudin	.40	1.00
305 Mikko Erholm	.40	1.00
306 Matti Forss	.40	1.00
307 Esa Hakkarainen	.40	1.00
308 Veikko Ihalainen	.40	1.00
309 Esa Isaksson	.40	1.00
310 Juhani Jylha	.40	1.00
311 Heikki Kauhanen	.40	1.00
312 Jari Laiho	.40	1.00
313 Arto Laine	.40	1.00
314 Jouni Peltonen	.40	1.00
315 Jouni Rinne	.40	1.00
316 Kai Rosvall	.40	1.00
317 Seppo Santala	.40	1.00
318 Jari Sarronlahti	.40	1.00
319 Matti Saurio	.40	1.00
320 Ari Sjoman	.40	1.00
321 Erkki Sundelin	.40	1.00
322 Ismo Villa	.40	1.00
323 Mikko Ylaja	.40	1.00
324 Veijo Ylanen	.40	1.00
NNO Album	25.00	50.00

1974 Finnish Jenkki

COMPLETE SET (120)	50.00	100.00
1 Sakari Ahlberg	.30	.75
2 Seppo Ahokainen	.30	.75
3 Jukka Alkula	.30	.75
4 Jorma Aro	.30	.75
5 Hannu Haapalainen	.30	.75
6 Veli-Pekka Ketola	1.25	3.00
7 Tapio Koskinen	.30	.75
8 Henry Leppa	.30	.75
9 Antti Leppanen	.30	.75
10 Reijo Leppanen	.30	.75
11 Pekka Marjamaki	.30	.75
12 Matti Murto	.30	.75
13 Esa Peltonen	.30	.75
14 Pekka Rautakallio	1.25	3.00
15 Leo Seppanen	.30	.75
16 Juha Silvennoinen	.30	.75
17 Raimo Suoniemi	.30	.75
18 Seppo Suoraniemi	.30	.75
19 Timo Sutinen	.30	.75
20 Juhani Tamminen	.75	2.00
21 Pertti Valkeapaa	.30	.75
22 Christer Abrahamsson	1.25	3.00
23 Thommie Bergman	1.25	3.00
24 Roland Bond	.30	.75
25 Anders Hedberg	2.00	5.00
26 Bjorn Johansson	.30	.75
27 Stefan Karlsson	.30	.75
28 Mats Lind	.30	.75
29 Tord Lundstrom	.30	.75
30 William Lofqvist	.30	.75
31 Ulf Nilsson	2.00	5.00
32 Bjorn Palmqvist	.30	.75
33 Hakan Pettersson	.30	.75
34 Lars-Erik Sjoberg	.75	2.00
35 Ulf Sterner	.30	.75
36 Karl-Johan Sundqvist	.30	.75
37 Hakan Wickberg	.30	.75
38 Kjell-Arne Wickstrom	.30	.75
39 Dick Yderstrom	.30	.75
40 Mats Ahlberg	.30	.75
41 Stig Ostling	.30	.75
42 Vjatseslav Anisin	.40	1.00
43 Aleksandr Bodunov	.40	1.00
44 Aleksandr Gusev	.40	1.00
45 Valeri Kharlamov	6.00	15.00
46 Aleksandr Yakushev	2.00	5.00
47 Juri Liapkin	.40	1.00
48 Vladimir Lutshenko	.40	1.00
49 Aleksandr Maltsev	2.00	5.00
50 Aleksandr Martiniuk	.40	1.00
51 Boris Mikhailov	2.00	5.00
52 Jevgeni Paladiev	.40	1.00
53 Vladimir Petrov	2.00	5.00
54 Aleksandr Ragulin	.40	1.00
55 Vladimir Shadrin	.40	1.00
56 Aleksandr Sidelnikov	.40	1.00
57 Vladislav Tretiak	6.00	15.00
58 Gennadi Tsigankov	.40	1.00
59 Valeri Vasiljev	2.00	5.00
60 Vladimir Vikulov	.40	1.00
61 Aleksandr Voltshkov	.40	1.00
62 Julij Blinov	.40	1.00
63 Vladimir Sepovalov	.40	1.00
64 Josef Horesovsky	.30	.75
65 Peter Adamik	.30	.75
66 Vladimir Bednar	.30	.75
67 Jiri Bubla	.75	2.00
68 Richard Farda	.30	.75
69 Julius Haas	.30	.75
70 Ivan Hlinka	.75	2.00
71 Jiri Holecek	.75	2.00
72 Jaroslav Holik	.30	.75
73 Jiri Holik	.30	.75
74 Jan Klapac	.30	.75
75 Jiri Kochta	.30	.75
76 Milan Kuzela	.30	.75
77 Oldrich Machac	.30	.75
78 Vladimir Martinec	.30	.75
79 Vaclav Nedomansky	1.50	4.00
80 Josef Palecek	.30	.75
81 Frantisek Pospisil	.30	.75
82 Bohuslav Stastny	.30	.75
83 Rudolf Tajcnar	.30	.75
84 Karl Vohralik	.30	.75
85 Jerzy Potz	.30	.75
86 Andrzej Slowakiewicz	.30	.75
87 Josef Slowakiewicz	.30	.75
88 Leszek Tokarz	.30	.75
89 Wieslav Tokarz	.30	.75
90 Henryk Vojtynek	.30	.75
91 Walenty Zietara	.30	.75
92 Josef Batkiewicz	.30	.75
93 Stefan Chowaniec	.30	.75
94 Ludvik Czachovski	.30	.75
95 Andrzej Czczepaniec	.30	.75
96 Robert Goralczyk	.30	.75
97 Mieczyslaw Jaskierski	.30	.75
98 Tadeusz Kacik	.30	.75
99 Adam Kopczynski	.30	.75
100 Valery Kosyl	.30	.75
101 Tadeusz Obloj	.30	.75
102 Joachim Stasche	.30	.75
103 Roland Peters	.30	.75

Card	Low	High
104 Dietmar Peters	.30	.75
105 Bernd Karrenbauer	.30	.75
106 Peter Prusa	.30	.75
107 Rainer Patschinski	.30	.75
108 Hartmut Nickel	.30	.75
109 Dieter Dewitz	.30	.75
110 Harald Felber	.30	.75
111 Joachim Hurbanek	.30	.75
112 Wolfgang Fischer	.30	.75
113 Frank Braun	.30	.75
114 Dieter Huschto	.30	.75
115 Ruediger Hoack	.30	.75
116 Dieter Simon	.30	.75
117 Hartwig Schur	.30	.75
118 Jochen Philip	.30	.75
119 Rolf Bielas	.30	.75
120 Peter Slapke	.30	.75

1974 Finnish Typotor

Card	Low	High
COMPLETE SET (120)	30.00	80.00
1 Matti Murto	.40	1.00
2 Esa Peltonen	.20	.50
3 Juha Rantasila	.40	1.00
4 Heikki Riihiranta	.75	2.00
5 Juhani Tamminen	.75	2.00
6 Jorma Virtanen	.40	1.00
7 Seppo Ahokainen	.40	1.00
8 Jorma Kallio	.20	.50
9 Ari Kankaanpera	.20	.50
10 Lasse Oksanen	.20	.50
11 Jorma Peltonen	.40	1.00
12 Tapio Virhimo	.20	.50
13 Ilpo Kokela	.20	.50
14 Henry Leppa	.20	.50
15 Seppo Suoraniemi	.20	.50
16 Timo Sutinen	.20	.50
17 Timo Turunen	.20	.50
18 Jorma Valtonen	.40	1.00
19 Mikko Erholm	.20	.50
20 Esa Isaksson	.20	.50
21 Juhani Jylha	.20	.50
22 Tapani Koskimaki	.20	.50
23 Hannu Siivonen	.20	.50
24 Jorma Vehmanen	.40	1.00
25 Jukka Alkula	.20	.50
26 Hannu Haapalainen	.20	.50
27 Martti Jarkko	.20	.50
28 Antti Leppannen	.20	.50
29 Pekka Marjamaki	.20	.50
30 Raimo Suoniemi	.20	.50
31 Lasse Kiili	.20	.50
32 Timo Nummelin	.20	.50
33 Matti Rautee	.20	.50
34 Pekka Rautee	.20	.50
35 Seppo Repo	.20	.50
36 Jouko Oystila	.20	.50
37 Kari Johansson	.20	.50
38 Reijo Leppanen	.20	.50
39 Seppo Lindstrom	.20	.50
40 Hannu Niittoaho	.20	.50
41 Pentti Vihanto	.20	.50
42 Urpo Ylonen	.20	.50
43 Antti Heikkila	.20	.50
44 Reijo Heinonen	.20	.50
45 Veli-Pekka Ketola	.60	1.50
46 Raimo Kilpio	.20	.50
47 Tapio Koskinen	.20	.50
48 Pekka Rautakallio	.75	2.00
49 Seppo Ahokainen	.20	.50
50 Henry Leppa	.20	.50
51 Antti Leppanen	.20	.50
52 Pekka Marjamaki	.20	.50
53 Matti Murto	.20	.50
54 Esa Peltonen	.20	.50
55 Heikki Riihiranta	.40	1.00
56 Timo Sutinen	.20	.50
57 Juhani Tamminen	.75	2.00
58 Rolf Bielas	.20	.50
59 Joachim Hurbanek	.20	.50
60 Reinhard Karger	.20	.50
61 Hartmut Nickel	.20	.50
62 Rudiger Noack	.20	.50
63 Helmut Novy	.20	.50
64 Dietmar Peters	.20	.50
65 Peter Prusa	.20	.50
66 Peter Slapke	.20	.50
67 Vakeri Kharlamov	4.00	10.00
68 Alexander Yakushev	1.50	4.00
69 Alexander Maltsev	1.50	4.00
70 Boris Mikhailov	1.50	4.00
71 Vladimir Petrov	1.50	4.00
72 Vladimir Shadrin	.40	1.00
73 Vladislav Tretiak	6.00	15.00
74 Gennady Tsygankov	.40	1.00
75 Valeri Vasilijev	1.25	3.00
76 Per-Erik Ingier	.20	.50
77 Morten Johansen	.20	.50
78 Hakan Lundenes	.20	.50
79 N. Nilsen	.20	.50
80 Morten Sethereng	.20	.50
81 T. Skar	.20	.50
82 J-E. Solberg	.20	.50
83 K. Thorkildsen	.20	.50
84 T. Troymark	.20	.50
85 J. Borovicz	.20	.50
86 L. Czachovski	.20	.50
87 Michael Jaskierski	.20	.50
88 Tadeusz Kacik	.20	.50
89 Adam Kopczynski	.20	.50
90 Tadeusz Obtoj	.20	.50
91 Jan Szeja	.20	.50
92 Leszek Tokarz	.20	.50
93 Walenty Zietara	.20	.50
94 Christer Abrahamsson	.50	1.50
95 Tommy Abrahamsson	.75	2.00
96 Anders Hedberg	1.50	4.00
97 Stefan Karlsson	.20	.50
98 Kjell-Rune Milton	.20	.50
99 Ulf Nilsson	1.50	4.00
100 Bjorn Palmqvist	.20	.50
101 Dan Soderstrom	.20	.50
102 Mats Ahlberg	.30	.75
103 Guy Dubois	.40	1.00
104 C. Friedrich	.20	.50
105 Charly Henzen	.20	.50
106 Ueli Hofmann	.20	.50
107 Mirco Horisberger	.20	.50
108 M. Lindenmann	.20	.50
109 Alfio Molina	.20	.50
110 Tony Neininger	.20	.50
111 U. Williman	.20	.50
112 Richard Farda	.20	.50
113 Ivan Hlinka	.40	1.00
114 Jiri Holecek	.40	1.00
115 Jiri Holik	.40	1.00
116 Josef Horesovsky	.20	.50
117 Jiri Kochta	.20	.50
118 Oldrich Machac	.20	.50
119 Vladimir Martinec	.20	.50
120 Bohuslav Stastny	.30	.75

1978-79 Finnish SM-Liiga

This set features the top players from Finland's elite league. These odd-sized cards measure 2 X 2 3/8. The set is noteworthy for including the first known card of Hall of Famer Jari Kurri. It is believed the cards were issued in pack form, but that cannot be ascertained at this point.

Card	Low	High
COMPLETE SET (240)	50.00	125.00
1 Hannu Kamppuri	.40	1.00
2 Pekka Rautakallio	.75	2.00
3 Timo Nummelin	.20	.50
4 Pertti Valkeapaa	.20	.50
5 Risto Siltanen	.40	1.00
6 Hannu Haapalainen	.20	.50
7 Markku Kiimalainen	.20	.50
8 Tapio Levo	.40	1.00
9 Lasse Litma	.20	.50
10 Reijo Ruotsalainen	.75	2.00
11 Jukka Porvari	.20	.50
12 Matti Rautiainen	.20	.50
13 Veli-Pekka Ketola	.75	2.00
14 Antero Lehtonen	.20	.50
15 Martti Jarkko	.20	.50
16 Juhani Tamminen	.75	2.00
17 Pertti Koivulahti	.20	.50
18 Kari Makkonen	.20	.50
19 Antero Kivela	.20	.50
20 Veli-Matti Ruisma	.20	.50
21 Stig Wetzell	.20	.50
22 Kyosti Majava	.20	.50
23 Seppo Pakelo	.20	.50
24 Reijo Laksola	.20	.50
25 Heikki Riihiranta	.20	.50
26 Raimo Hirvonen	.20	.50
27 Jorma Immonen	.20	.50
28 Terry Ball	.20	.50
29 Pertti Lehtonen	.20	.50
30 Jaakko Marttinen	.20	.50
31 Esa Peltonen	.40	1.00
32 Lauri Mononen	.40	1.00
33 Tommi Salmelainen	.20	.50
34 Hannu Kapanen	.20	.50
35 Matti Forss	.20	.50
36 Harri Linnonmaa	.20	.50
37 Matti Murto	.20	.50
38 Juhani Bostrom	.20	.50
39 Matti Hagman	.40	1.00
40 Ilkka Sinisalo	.75	2.00
41 Tomi Taimio	.20	.50
42 Ari Lahteenmaki	.20	.50
43 Tapio Virhimo	.20	.50
44 Jukka Airaksinen	.20	.50
45 Hannu Helander	.20	.50
46 Jorma Aro	.20	.50
47 Jouko Urvikko	.20	.50
48 Hannu Pulkkinen	.20	.50
49 Olli Pennanen	.20	.50
50 Ari Kankaanpera	.20	.50
51 Risto Siltanen	.40	1.00
52 Jari Jarvinen	.20	.50
53 Sakari Ahlberg	.20	.50
54 Keijo Kivela	.20	.50
55 Lasse Oksanen	.20	.50
56 Risto Kankaanpera	.20	.50
57 Kari Jarvinen	.20	.50
58 Pekka Orimus	.20	.50
59 Jarmo Huhtala	.20	.50
60 Hannu Oksanen	.20	.50
61 Jari Viitala	.20	.50
62 Veikko Suominen	.20	.50
63 Antti Heikkila	.20	.50
64 Seppo Hiitela	.20	.50
65 Hannu Kamppuri	.40	1.00
66 Patrik Wainio	.20	.50
67 Timo Blomqvist	.40	1.00
68 Ilmo Uotila	.20	.50
69 Pertti Savolainen	.20	.50
70 Jussi Lepisto	.20	.50
71 Jorma Piisinen	.20	.50
72 Robert Barnes	.20	.50
73 Ari Makinen	.20	.50
74 David Conte	.40	1.00
75 Juha Jyrkkio	.20	.50
76 Jari Kurri	20.00	40.00
77 Matti Heikkila	.20	.50
78 Henry Leppa	.20	.50
79 Pekka Kaski	.20	.50
80 Jari Kapanen	.20	.50
81 Ari Mikkola	.20	.50
82 Vesa Rajaniemi	.20	.50
83 Ari Blomqvist	.20	.50
84 Erkki Korhonen	.20	.50
85 Rainer Risku	.20	.50
86 Henry Saleva	.20	.50
87 Leo Seppanen	.20	.50
88 Rauli Sohlman	.20	.50
89 Juhani Ruohonen	.20	.50
90 Tuomo Martin	.20	.50
91 Reijo Mansikka	.20	.50
92 Reino Pulkkinen	.20	.50
93 Mauri Kultakuusi	.20	.50
94 Kari Saarikko	.20	.50
95 Kari Viitalahti	.20	.50
96 Barry Salovaara	.20	.50
97 Auvo Vaananen	.20	.50
98 Pauli Pyykko	.20	.50
99 Ari Jortikka	.20	.50
100 Jukka-Pekka Jarvenpaa	.20	.50
101 Seppo Sevon	.20	.50
102 Pekka Koskela	.20	.50
103 Arto Jokinen	.20	.50
104 Timo Niinivirta	.20	.50
105 Matti Rautiainen	.20	.50
106 Pertti Jarvenpaa	.20	.50
107 Reima Pullinen	.20	.50
108 Jukka-Pekka Vuorinen	.20	.50
109 Petteri Kanerva	.20	.50
110 Kalevi Rantanen	.20	.50
111 Jorma Virtanen	.20	.50
112 Matti Kaario	.20	.50
113 Frank Neal	.20	.50
114 Eero Mantere	.20	.50
115 Harri Nyman	.20	.50
116 Olli Saarinen	.20	.50
117 Jari Saarela	.20	.50
118 Pasi Virta	.20	.50
119 Dave Chalk	.20	.50
120 Hannu Koskinen	.20	.50
121 Harri Toivonen	.20	.50
122 Jarmo Makitalo	.20	.50
123 Kari Makitalo	.20	.50
124 Olavi Niemenranta	.20	.50
125 Pekka Laine	.20	.50
126 Markku Hakulinen	.20	.50
127 Pekka Nissinen	.20	.50
128 Yrjo Hakulinen	.20	.50
129 Timo Heino	.20	.50
130 Hannu Savolainen	.20	.50
131 Ari Hellgren	.20	.50
132 Matti Saikkonen	.20	.50
133 Ilpo Kukkola	.20	.50
134 Pentti Karlsson	.20	.50
135 Pekka Karjala	.20	.50
136 Juha Tuohimaa	.20	.50
137 Pekka Makinen	.20	.50
138 Reijo Ruotsalainen	.75	2.00
139 Seppo Tenhunen	.20	.50
140 Hannu Jalonen	.20	.50
141 Jari Virtanen	.20	.50
142 Juha Huikuri	.20	.50
143 Veikko Torkkeli	.20	.50
144 Markku Kiimalainen	.20	.50
145 Kalevi Hongisto	.20	.50
146 Eero Vartiainen	.20	.50
147 Jouko Kamarainen	.20	.50
148 Kai Suikkanen	.20	.50
149 Ilkka Alatalo	.20	.50
150 Markku Perkkio	.20	.50
151 Jorma Torkkeli	.20	.50
152 Kari Jalonen	.20	.50
153 Hannu Siivonen	.20	.50
154 Kari Kaupinsalo	.20	.50
155 Teppo Mattsson	.20	.50
156 Esa Hakkarainen	.20	.50
157 Jouni Peltonen	.20	.50
158 Timo Peltonen	.20	.50
159 Hannu Luojola	.20	.50
160 Tapani Koskimaki	.20	.50
161 Tuomo Jormakka	.20	.50
162 Mika Rajala	.20	.50
163 Pekka Santanen	.20	.50
164 Jorma Vehmanen	.20	.50
165 Olli Tuominen	.20	.50
166 Hannu Kemppainen	.20	.50
167 Ismo Villa	.20	.50
168 Matti Tynkkynen	.20	.50
169 Jouni Rinne	.20	.50
170 Jari Rastio	.20	.50
171 Harri Tuohimaa	.20	.50
172 Jari Laiho	.20	.50
173 Juhani Wallenius	.20	.50
174 Pekka Strander	.20	.50
175 Pertti Hasanen	.20	.50
176 Petri Karjalainen	.20	.50
177 Jorma Kallio	.20	.50
178 Pekka Marjamaki	.20	.50
179 Hannu Haapalainen	.20	.50
180 Pertti Valkeapaa	.20	.50
181 Lasse Litma	.20	.50
182 Jukka Hirsimaki	.20	.50
183 Oiva Oijennus	.20	.50
184 Jukka Aikula	.20	.50
185 Timo Susi	.20	.50
186 Jukka Porvari	.20	.50
187 Erkki Lehtonen	.20	.50
188 Antero Lehtonen	.20	.50
189 Juha Solvennoinen	.20	.50
190 Pertti Koivulahti	.20	.50
191 Keijo Mannisto	.20	.50
192 Jorma Sevon	.20	.50
193 Martti Jarkko	.20	.50
194 Jari Lindgren	.20	.50
195 Tapio Kallio	.20	.50
196 Tero Kapynen	.20	.50
197 Urpo Ylonen	.20	.50
198 Jorma Valtonen	.20	.50
199 Harri Kari	.20	.50
200 Hannu Jortikka	.20	.50
201 Timo Nummelin	.20	.50
202 Seppo Suoraniemi	.20	.50
203 Ilkka Mesikammen	.20	.50
204 Pertti Ahokas	.20	.50
205 Hannu Niitoaho	.20	.50
206 Arto Kaunonen	.20	.50
207 Pekka Rautee	.20	.50
208 Juhani Tamminen	.20	.50
209 Timo Viljanen	.20	.50
210 Kari Kauppila	.20	.50
211 Bengt Willenius	.20	.50
212 Reijo Leppanen	.20	.50
213 Rauli Tammelin	.20	.50
214 Jukka Koskilahti	.20	.50
215 Markku Haapaniemi	.20	.50
216 Kari Horkko	.20	.50
217 Kalevi Aho	.20	.50
218 Hakan Hjerpe	.20	.50
219 Antero Kivela	.20	.50
220 Pertti Lehti	.20	.50
221 Antti Heikkila	.20	.50
222 Tapio Flinck	.20	.50
223 Pekka Rautakallio	.75	2.00
224 Jaakko Niemi	.20	.50
225 Tapio Levo	.40	1.00
226 Jyrki Levonen	.20	.50
227 Harry Nikander	.20	.50
228 Arto Javanainen	.20	.50
229 Pekka Makela	.20	.50
230 Tapio Koskinen	.20	.50
231 Pekka Stenfors	.20	.50
232 Ari Peltola	.20	.50
233 Veli-Pekka Ketola	.75	2.00
234 Erkki Vakiparta	.20	.50
235 Rauli Levonen	.20	.50
236 Martti Nenonen	.20	.50
237 Jouni Makitalo	.20	.50
238 Veli-Matti Ruisma	.20	.50
239 Tauno Makela	.20	.50
240 Kari Makkonen	.20	.50

1936 German Jaszmatzi

Full color card from the Deutscher Sports series of Germany. Thin paper stock, with back in German.

Card	Low	High
208 Ice Hockey	15.00	30.00

1969-70 Russian National Team Postcards

Card	Low	High
COMPLETE SET (27)	75.00	150.00
1 Viktor Zinger	1.50	4.00
2 Vitali Davydov	1.50	4.00
3 Vladimir Lutchenko	1.50	4.00
4 Viktor Kuzkin	1.50	4.00
5 Alexander Ragulin	4.00	10.00
6 Igor Romishevski	1.50	4.00
7 Boris Mikhailov	6.00	15.00
8 Viacheslav Starshinov	1.50	4.00
9 Evgeny Zimin	1.50	4.00
10 Alexander Maltsev	6.00	15.00
11 Anatoli Firsov	4.00	10.00
12 Evgeny Paladiev	1.50	4.00
13 Alexander Yakushev	6.00	15.00
14 Vladimir Petrov	6.00	15.00
15 Valeri Kharlamov	10.00	25.00
16 Evgeny Mishakov	1.50	4.00
17 Vladimir Vikulov	1.50	4.00
18 Vladimir Yursinov	1.50	4.00
19 Viktor Pushkov	1.50	4.00
20 Arkady Chernishev	1.50	4.00
21 Anatoli Tarasov	4.00	10.00
22 USSR vs Sweden	.75	2.00
23 USSR vs Sweden	.75	2.00
24 USSR vs Sweden	.75	2.00
25 USSR vs Finland, Sweden	.75	2.00
26 USSR vs Canada, Sweden	1.50	4.00
27 Team Photo	1.50	4.00

1970-71 Russian National Team Postcards

This set measures 3 1/2" by 5 3/4". The horizontal fronts feature a color head shot and a preprint blue ink autograph on the left, and a black and white action photo on the right. The backs look like standard postcards. A protective sleeve featuring Russia in action against Sweden is usually found with the set.

Card	Low	High
COMPLETE SET (20)	100.00	150.00
1 Viktor Konovalenko	2.00	5.00
2 Vitali Davydov	2.00	5.00
3 Vladimir Lutchenko	2.00	5.00
4 Valeri Nikitin	2.00	5.00
5 Alexander Ragulin	4.00	10.00
6 Igor Romishevski	2.00	5.00
7 Evgeni Paladiev	2.00	5.00
8 Viacheslav Starshinov	2.00	5.00
9 Viktor Polupanov	2.00	5.00
10 Alexander Maltsev	6.00	15.00
11 Anatoli Firsov	6.00	15.00
12 Evgeni Mishakov	2.00	5.00
13 Boris Mikhailov	6.00	15.00
14 Valeri Vasiliev	4.00	10.00
15 Alexander Yakushev	6.00	15.00
16 Vladimir Petrov	6.00	15.00

17 Valeri Kharlamov 10.00 25.00
18 Vladimir Vikulov 2.00 5.00
19 Vladimir Shadrin 2.00 5.00
20 Vladislav Tretiak 10.00 25.00

1973-74 Russian National Team

This set comes in a commemorative folder and features "cards" that are 4 1/16 by 5 3/4.

COMPLETE SET (25) 60.00 125.00
1 Team Photo 1.50 4.00
2 Vladislav Tretiak 8.00 20.00
3 Alexander Sidelnikov 1.50 4.00
4 Alexander Gusev 1.50 4.00
5 Valeri Vasiliev 3.00 8.00
6 Boris Mikhailov 3.00 8.00
7 Vladimir Petrov 3.00 8.00
8 Valeri Kharlamov 6.00 15.00
9 Kharlamov, Petrov, Mikhailov 4.00 10.00
10 Vladimir Lutchenko 1.50 4.00
11 Gennady Tsygankov 1.50 4.00
12 Alexander Ragulin 1.50 4.00
13 Alexander Volchkov 1.50 4.00
14 Viacheslav Anisin 1.50 4.00
15 Yuri Lebedev 1.50 4.00
16 Alexander Bodunov 1.50 4.00
17 Alexander Martinyuk 1.50 4.00
18 Vladimir Shadrin 1.50 4.00
19 Alexander Yakushev 3.00 8.00
20 Alexander Maltsev 3.00 8.00
21 Evgeny Paladiev 1.50 4.00
22 Yuri Liapkin 1.50 4.00
23 Bobrov .75 2.00
Kulagin CO
24 Boris Mikhailov 3.00 8.00
25 Viktor Kuzkin 1.50 4.00

1974 Russian National Team

Unusually sized (8.25 X 3.5) postcard-type collectibles feature members of the powerful CCCP club. Often found in a folder.

COMPLETE SET (25) 50.00 100.00
1 Vyacheslav Anisin 1.50 4.00
2 Vsevolod Bobrov CO 1.50 4.00
3 Alexander Bodunov 1.50 4.00
4 Alexander Gusev 1.50 4.00
5 Sergei Kapustin 1.50 4.00
6 Valeri Kharlamov 5.00 12.00
7 Boris Kulagin CO 1.50 4.00
8 Viktor Kuzkin 1.50 4.00
9 Yuri Lebedev 1.50 4.00
10 Yuri Liapkin 1.50 4.00
11 Vladimir Lutchenko 1.50 4.00
12 Alexander Maltsev 3.00 8.00
13 Boris Mikhailov 3.00 8.00
14 Boris Mikhailov 3.00 8.00
15 Vladimir Petrov 3.00 8.00
16 Vladimir Repneev 1.50 4.00
17 Vladimir Shadrin 1.50 4.00
18 Yuri Shatalov 1.50 4.00
19 Alexander Sidelnikov 1.50 4.00
20 Vladislav Tretiak 6.00 15.00
21 Gennady Tsygankov 1.50 4.00
22 Valeri Vasiliev 3.00 8.00
23 Alexander Yakushev 3.00 8.00
24 USSR .40 1.00
25 USSR .40 1.00

1979 Russian National Team

This set features the Soviet National Team. The cards measure 8 1/4 by 5 7/8 and were issued in a folder.

COMPLETE SET (24) 37.50 100.00
1 Team Photo .50 1.00
2 Viktor Tikhonov CO 1.00 2.00
3 Vladimir Yursinov CO .50 2.00
4 Vladislav Tretiak 5.00 15.00
5 Alexander Pashkov 1.50 3.00
6 Vladimir Lutchenko 1.00 3.00
7 Valeri Vasiliev 1.00 5.00
8 Gennady Tsygankov 1.00 3.00
9 Yuri Fedorov 1.00 2.00
10 Slava Fetisov 5.00 15.00
11 Zinetula Bilyaletinov 2.50 5.00
12 Vasili Pervukhin 1.00 3.00
13 Boris Mikhailov 2.50 8.00
14 Vladimir Petrov 2.50 8.00
15 Valeri Kharlamov 5.00 15.00
16 Alexander Maltsev 2.50 8.00
17 Sergei Kapustin 1.00 3.00
18 Yuri Lebedev 1.00 2.00
19 Viktor Zhluktov 1.00 3.00
20 Helmut Balderis 1.50 5.00
21 Alexander Golikov 1.00 2.00
22 Sergei Makarov 4.00 15.00
23 Vladimir Golikov 1.00 2.00
24 Team Photo .50 1.00

1932-33 Swedish Marabou

This multi-sport Swedish issue is believed to contain just six hockey players. The singles are very small, measuring about 1/2" by 1". It is believed that two versions of the set exist, one with white borders and another without. The fronts feature a photo, while the backs have the player's name, history, and the set name, Marabou-Sportserie. If anyone knows of other hockey players in this set, please contact us at hockeymag@beckett.com

Hockey players in set (6)
4 C. Abrahamsson
146 Herman Carlsson
147 Folke Wohlin
148 Carl-Erik Furst
149 Bertil Linde
150 Olof Johansson

1964 Swedish Coralli ISHockey

These tiny cards (1 7/8" by 1 1/4") feature players from the Swedish national team, Tre Kroner, as well as many club teams. The cards apparently were distributed as premiums in chocolate bars. According to reports, such sets existed in Sweden as far back as 1955. The card fronts have a posed player photo, name and card number. The backs offer a brief biography in Swedish. An album to hold these cards is believed to exist; this, however, has not been confirmed.

COMPLETE SET (165) 150.00 300.00
1 Sven Johansson 1.50 3.00
2 Ove Malmberg 1.00 2.00
3 Bjorn Larsson 1.00 2.00
4 Ulf Sterner 1.00 2.00
5 Bertil Karlsson 1.00 2.00
6 Leif Holmqvist 5.00 10.00
7 Uno Ohrlund 1.00 2.00
8 Mats Lonn 1.00 2.00
9 Bjorn Palmqvist 1.00 2.00
10 Nils Johansson 1.00 2.00
11 Ander Andersson 1.00 2.00
12 Lennart Haggroth 2.00 4.00
13 Hans Svedberg 1.00 2.00
14 Ronald Pettersson 1.00 2.00
15 Lars Eric Lundvall 1.00 2.00
16 Gert Blome 1.00 2.00
17 Bo Englund 1.00 2.00
18 Folke Bengtsson 1.00 2.00
19 Nils Nilsson 1.00 2.00
20 Lennart Johansson 1.00 2.00
21 Lennart Svedberg 2.50 5.00
22 Lars Ake Sivertsson 1.00 2.00
23 Hakan Wickberg 1.00 2.00
24 Tord Lundstrom 1.00 2.00
25 Ove Andersson 1.00 2.00
26 Bert Ola Nordlander 1.50 3.00
27 Jan Erik Nilsson 1.00 2.00
28 Eilert Maatta 1.00 2.00
29 Roland Stoltz 1.00 2.00
30 Kurt Thulin 1.00 2.00
31 Ove Andersson 1.00 2.00
32 Ingemar Johansson 1.00 2.00
33 Rune Lind 1.00 2.00
34 Bert-Ola Nordlander 1.50 3.00
35 Hans Eriksson 1.00 2.00
36 Antik Johansson 1.00 2.00
37 Bo Hansson 1.00 2.00
38 Jan Back 1.00 2.00
39 Lennart Soderberg 1.00 2.00
40 Benny Soderling 1.00 2.00
41 Anders Parmstrom 1.00 2.00
42 Lennart Selinder 1.00 2.00
43 Bjorn Larsson 1.00 2.00
44 Jorma Salmi 1.00 2.00
45 Berndt Arvidsson 1.00 2.00
46 P.A. Karlstrom 1.00 2.00
47 Lars Erik Sjoberg 5.00 10.00
48 Vilgot Larsson 1.00 2.00
49 Gunnar Andersson 1.00 2.00
50 Roland Bond 1.00 2.00
51 Goran Lysen 1.00 2.00
52 Bosse Englund 1.00 2.00
53 Stig Pavels 1.00 2.00
54 Bengt Bornstrom 1.00 2.00
55 Nisse Nilsson 1.00 2.00
56 Lennart Lange 1.00 2.00
57 Des Moroney 1.00 2.00
58 Folke Bengtsson 1.00 2.00
59 Olle Sjogren 1.00 2.00
60 Knut Knutsson 1.00 2.00
61 Kjell Svensson 1.00 2.00
62 Rickard Eagerlund 2.50 5.00
63 Arne Loong 1.00 2.00
64 Stig Carlsson 1.00 2.00
65 Lars Hagg 1.00 2.00
66 Olle Stenar 1.00 2.00
67 Einar Granath 1.00 2.00
68 Leif Andersson 1.00 2.00
69 Hans Soderstrom 1.00 2.00
70 Kalle Lilja 1.00 2.00
71 Soren Maatta 1.00 2.00
72 Sven Bystrom 1.00 2.00
73 Hans Karlsson 1.00 2.00
74 Stig Goran Johansson 1.50 3.00
75 Jan Allinger 1.00 2.00
76 Kjell Larsson 1.00 2.00
77 Hakan Wickberg 1.00 2.00
78 Tord Lundstrom 1.00 2.00
79 Lennart Svedberg 2.50 5.00
80 Jan Erik Lyck 1.00 2.00
81 Hans Eriksson 1.00 2.00
82 Kjell Jonsson 1.00 2.00
83 Lars Hedenstrom 1.00 2.00
84 Lars Ake Sivertsson 1.00 2.00
85 Lennart Johansson 1.00 2.00
86 Hans Sjoberg 1.00 2.00
87 Hans Dahllof 1.00 2.00
88 Leif Jansson 1.00 2.00
89 Lars Byling 1.00 2.00
90 Bertil Lindstrom 1.00 2.00
91 Arne Eriksson 1.00 2.00
92 Gert Blomer 1.00 2.00
93 Kjell Adrian 1.00 2.00
94 Jan Olsen 1.00 2.00
95 Benny Karlsson 1.00 2.00
96 Tommy Carlsson 1.00 2.00
97 Ulf Sterner 1.00 2.00
98 Kjell-Ove Gustafsson 1.00 2.00
99 Lars Erik Lundvall 1.00 2.00
100 Kjell-Ronny Pettersson 1.00 2.00
101 Ronald Pettersson 1.00 2.00
102 Kjell Jonsson 1.00 2.00
103 Gote Hansson 1.00 2.00
104 Rolf Eklof 1.00 2.00
105 Eine Olsson 1.00 2.00
106 Hans-Erik Fernstrom 1.00 2.00
107 Leif Holmkvist 1.00 2.00
108 Bo Zetterberg 1.00 2.00
109 Ake Zattlin 1.00 2.00
110 Bengt-Olov Andreasson 1.00 2.00
111 Borje Mohlander 1.00 2.00
112 Sture Sundin 1.00 2.00
113 Bertil Karlsson 1.00 2.00
114 Lars Molander 1.00 2.00
115 Benno Persson 1.00 2.00
116 Gert Nystrom 1.00 2.00
117 Sune Bohlin 1.00 2.00
118 Olle Westlund 1.00 2.00
119 Goran Wallin 1.00 2.00
120 Ingemar Persson 1.00 2.00
121 Tommy Bjorkman 1.00 2.00
122 Eddie Wingren 1.00 2.00
123 Lars Bjorn 1.00 2.00
124 Roland Stoltz 1.00 2.00
125 Sven Johansson 1.50 3.00
126 Leif Skold 1.00 2.00
127 Hans Mild 1.00 2.00
128 Kurt Thulin 1.00 2.00
129 Ake Rydberg 1.00 2.00
130 Ove Malmberg 1.00 2.00
131 Lars Lundqvist 1.00 2.00
132 Kurt Svensson 1.00 2.00
133 Gosta Westerlund 1.00 2.00
134 Lars Andersson 1.00 2.00
135 Ulf Rydin 1.00 2.00
136 Lennart Haggroth 2.00 4.00
137 Jan Hedberg 1.00 2.00
138 Karl Soren Hedlund 1.00 2.00
139 Hans Svedberg 1.00 2.00
140 Sture Hoverberg 1.00 2.00
141 Anders Ronnblom 1.00 2.00
142 Ulf Eriksson 1.00 2.00
143 Anders Andersson 1.00 2.00
144 Henrik Hedlund 1.00 2.00
145 Per Lundstrom 1.00 2.00
146 Hakan Nygren 1.00 2.00
147 Bo Berglund, Sr 2.00 4.00
148 Lars Ake Warning 1.00 2.00
149 Sven-Olov Johansson 1.00 2.00
150 Ove Stenlund 1.00 2.00
151 Ivar Larsson 1.00 2.00
152 Nils Johansson 1.00 2.00
153 Sten Olsen 1.00 2.00
154 Lars Gidlund 1.00 2.00
155 Tor Haarstad 1.00 2.00
156 K-O Barrefjord 1.00 2.00
157 Bjorn Palmqvist 1.00 2.00
158 Soren Lindstrom 1.00 2.00
159 Henna Svensson 1.00 2.00
160 Lars Hagstrom 1.00 2.00
161 Ake Eklof 1.00 2.00
162 Ulf Lundstrom 1.00 2.00
163 Ronny Nordstrom 1.00 2.00
164 Paul Stahl 1.00 2.00
165 Kenneth Sahlen 1.50 3.00

1965 Swedish Coralli ISHockey

These tiny (1 7/8" by 1 1/4") feature players from the Swedish National Team, Tre Kroner, as well as many club teams. The cards apparently were issued as premiums with chocolate bars. The card fronts have a posed player photo, name and card number. The backs offer a brief biography in Swedish.

COMPLETE SET (214) 125.00 300.00
1 Sven Johansson 1.25 3.00
2 Ove Malmberg .75 2.00
3 Bjorn Larsson .75 2.00
4 Ulf Sterner .75 2.00
5 Bertil Karlsson 1.00 3.00
6 Leif Holmqvist 4.00 8.00
7 Uno Ohrlund .75 2.00
8 Mats Lonn .75 2.00
9 Bjorn Palmqvist .75 2.00
10 Nils Johansson .75 2.00
11 Anders Andersson .75 2.00
12 Lennart Haggroth 1.50 4.00
13 Hans Svedberg .75 2.00
14 Ronald Pettersson .75 2.00
15 Lars Eric Lundvall .75 2.00
16 Gert Blome .75 2.00
17 Bo Englund .75 2.00
18 Folke Bengtsson .75 2.00
19 Nils Nilsson .75 2.00
20 Lennart Johansson .75 2.00
21 Lennart Svedberg 1.75 4.00
22 Lars Ake Sivertsson .75 2.00
23 Hakan Wickberg .75 2.00
24 Tord Lundstrom .75 2.00
25 Ove Andersson .75 2.00
26 Bert Ola Nordlander 1.25 3.00
27 Jan Erik Nilsson .75 2.00
28 Eilert Maatta .75 2.00
29 Roland Stoltz .75 2.00
30 Kurt Thulin .75 2.00
31 Leif Holmquist 4.00 8.00
32 Ingemar Johansson 1.00 3.00
33 Rune Lind .75 2.00
34 Bert-Ola Nordlander 1.25 3.00
35 Hans Eriksson .75 2.00
36 Antik Johansson .75 2.00
37 Bo Hansson .75 2.00
38 Hans-Ake Carlsson .75 2.00
39 Lennart Soderberg .75 2.00
40 Benny Soderling .75 2.00
41 Anders Parmstrom .75 2.00
42 Lennart Selinder .75 2.00
43 Bjorn Larsson .75 2.00
44 Ove Hedberg .75 2.00
45 Berndt Arvidsson .75 2.00
46 P.A. Carlstrom .75 2.00
47 Lars Erik Sjoberg 4.00 8.00
48 Kjell Fhinn .75 2.00
49 Gunnar Andersson .75 2.00
50 Roland Bond .75 2.00
51 Goran Lysen .75 2.00
52 Bosse Englund .75 2.00
53 Stig Pavels .75 2.00
54 Bengt Bornstrom .75 2.00
55 Nisse Nilsson .75 2.00
56 Lennart Lange .75 2.00
57 Tommy Abrahamsson 4.00 8.00
58 Folke Bengtsson .75 2.00
59 Olle Sjogren .75 2.00
60 Knut Knutsson .75 2.00
61 Kjell Svensson .75 2.00
62 Rickard Eagerlund 1.75 4.00
63 Eilert Maatta .75 2.00
64 Stig Carlsson .75 2.00
65 Lars Hagg .75 2.00
66 Olle Stenar .75 2.00
67 Einar Andersson .75 2.00
68 Leif Andersson .75 2.00
69 Percy Lind .75 2.00
70 Gunnar Tallberg .75 2.00
71 Soren Maatta .75 2.00
72 Sven Bystrom .75 2.00
73 Hans Carlsson .75 2.00
74 Stig Goran Johansson 1.25 3.00
75 Thomas Warming .75 2.00
76 Kjell Larsson .75 2.00
77 Hakan Wickberg .75 2.00
78 Tord Lundstrom .75 2.00
79 Lennart Svedberg 2.00 4.00
80 Jan Erik Lyck .75 2.00
81 Stefan Carlsson .75 2.00
82 Kjell Jonsson .75 2.00
83 Lars Hedenstrom .75 2.00
84 Lars Ake Sivertsson .75 2.00
85 Lennart Johansson .75 2.00
86 Hans Sjoberg .75 2.00
87 Hans Dahllof .75 2.00
88 Hans Lindberg .75 2.00
89 Lars Bylund .75 2.00
90 Sten Edqvist .75 2.00
91 Arne Ericsson .75 2.00
92 Gert Blomer .75 2.00
93 Kjell Adrian .75 2.00
94 Jan Olsen .75 2.00
95 Berny Karlsson .75 2.00
96 Jorma Salmi .75 2.00
97 Ulf Sterner .75 2.00
98 Kjell-Ove Gustafsson .75 2.00
99 Lars Erik Lundvall .75 2.00
100 Kjell-Ronny Pettersson 1.00 3.00
101 Ronald Pettersson .75 2.00
102 Kjell Jonsson .75 2.00
103 Gote Hansson .75 2.00
104 Ove Sterner .75 2.00
105 Eine Olsson .75 2.00
106 Hans-Erik Fernstrom .75 2.00
107 Per-Olov Hardin .75 2.00
108 Bo Zetterberg .75 2.00
109 Ake Zettlin .75 2.00
110 Bengt-Olov Andreasson .75 2.00
111 Borje Molander .75 2.00
112 Sture Sundin .75 2.00
113 Bertil Karlsson 1.00 3.00
114 Lars Molander .75 2.00
115 Benno Persson .75 2.00
116 Rolf Larsson .75 2.00
117 Ronny Francis .75 2.00
118 Olle Westlund .75 2.00
119 Goran Wallin .75 2.00
120 Ingemar Persson .75 2.00
121 Tommy Bjorkman .75 2.00
122 Eddie Wingren .75 2.00
123 Lars Bjorn .75 2.00
124 Roland Stoltz .75 2.00
125 Sven Johansson 1.25 3.00
126 Arne Loong .75 2.00
127 Hans Mild .75 2.00
127 Per Lundstrom .75 2.00
128 Kurt Thulin .75 2.00
129 Ake Rydberg .75 2.00
130 Ove Malmberg .75 2.00
131 Lars Lundqvist .75 2.00
132 Kurt Svensson .75 2.00
133 Gosta Westerlund .75 2.00
134 Lars Andersson .75 2.00
135 Ulf Rydin .75 2.00
136 Lennart Haggroth 1.50 4.00
137 Jan Hedberg .75 2.00
138 Anders Carlberg .75 2.00
139 Hans Svedberg .75 2.00
140 Sture Holverberg .75 2.00
141 Anders Ronnblom .75 2.00
142 Ulf Eriksson .75 2.00
143 Anders Andersson .75 2.00
144 Henrik Hedlund .75 2.00
145 Roger Boman .75 2.00
146 Bo Astrom .75 2.00
147 Bo Berglund 1.50 3.00
148 Lars Ake Warning .75 2.00
149 Sven-Olov Johansson .75 2.00
150 Ove Stenlund .75 2.00
151 Ivar Larsson .75 2.00
152 Nicke Johansson .75 2.00

153 Sten Olsen .75 2.00
154 Lars Gidlund .75 2.00
155 Tor Haarstad .75 2.00
156 Hakan Nygren .75 2.00
157 Bjorn Palmqvist .75 2.00
158 Soren Lindstrom .75 2.00
159 Henry Svensson .75 2.00
160 Lars Hagstrom .75 2.00
161 Ake Eklof .75 2.00
162 Ulf Lundstrom .75 2.00
163 Ronny Nordstrom .75 2.00
164 Paul Stahl .75 2.00
165 Kenneth Sahlen 1.25 3.00
166 Anders Hedlund .75 2.00
167 Ingemar Caris .75 2.00
168 Arne Carlsson .75 2.00
169 Gote Bostrom .75 2.00
170 Roger Olsson .75 2.00
171 Ole Jacobson .75 2.00
172 Curt Edenvik .75 2.00
173 Goran Svensson .75 2.00
174 Eje Lindstrom .75 2.00
175 Curt Larsson 2.50 5.00
176 Gunnar Backman .75 2.00
177 Anders Nordin .75 2.00
178 Ulf Torstensson .75 2.00
179 Kent Lindgren .75 2.00
180 Kent Sjalin .75 2.00
181 Lars Goran Nilsson .75 2.00
182 Heimo Klockare .75 2.00
183 Lars Sattare .75 2.00
184 Lars-Ake Lundell .75 2.00
185 Kjell Savstrom .75 2.00
186 Carl-Goran Oberg .75 2.00
187 Bjorn Larsson .75 2.00
188 Leif Eriksson .75 2.00
189 Dag Olsson .75 2.00
190 Lars Lohman .75 2.00
191 unknown .75 2.00
192 unknown .75 2.00
193 unknown .75 2.00
194 unknown .75 2.00
195 unknown .75 2.00
196 unknown .75 2.00
197 unknown .75 2.00
198 unknown .75 2.00
199 unknown .75 2.00
200 Hans Aleblad .75 2.00
201 Karl Soren Hedlund .75 2.00
202 Clarence Carlsson .75 2.00
203 Bjorn Johansson .75 2.00
204 Kent Persson .75 2.00
205 Goran Thelin .75 2.00
206 Leif Ohrlund .75 2.00
207 Mats Davidsson .75 2.00
208 Leif Artursson .75 2.00
209 Karl Gunnar Backman .75 2.00
210 Hans Mellinger .75 2.00
211 Hans Inge Lund .75 2.00
212 Kent Jansson .75 2.00
213 Anders Ronnkvist .75 2.00
214 Bo Olofsson .75 2.00

1967-68 Swedish Hockey

This 300-card set features the skaters from the Swedish first and second division teams from the 1967-68 season, as well as the national team, Tre Kronor. The cards measure 2" by 3 1/8" and feature posed color photos on the front. The national team cards have the words Tre Kronor and the three crown logo across the top. The backs have the card number, player stats and an invitation to purchase a collectors album, all in Swedish. The album for the set includes numerous pages of text and photos about Swedish hockey, and is valued at $35. Although short on widely recognizable names, the set does include early -- if not first -- cards of Inge Hammarstrom and Christer Abrahamsson.

COMPLETE SET (300) 62.50 150.00
1 Christer Abrahamsson 2.00 4.00
2 Tommy Abrahamsson 1.00 2.00
3 Folke Bengtsson .25 1.00
4 Arne Carlsson .25 1.00
5 Bengt-Ake Gustavsson .25 1.00
6 Anders Hagstrom .25 1.00
7 Inge Hammarstrom 2.50 5.00
8 Leif Henriksson .25 1.00
9 Leif Holmqvist 1.00 2.00
10 Per-Arne Hubinette .25 1.00
11 Mats Hysing .25 1.00
12 Nils Johansson .25 1.00
13 Stig-Goran Johansson .25 1.00
14 Hans Lindberg .25 1.00
15 Tord Lundstrom .25 1.00
16 Lars-Goran Nilsson .25 1.00
17 Anders Nordin .25 1.00
18 Bert-Ola Nordlander .25 1.00
19 Roger Olsson .25 1.00
20 Bjorn Palmquist .25 1.00
21 Kjell Sundstrom .25 1.00
22 Lennart Svedberg .50 2.00
23 Hakan Wickberg .25 1.00
24 Carl-Goran Oberg .25 1.00
25 Lasse Ohman .25 1.00
26 Curt Edenvik .25 1.00
27 Hans Eriksson .25 1.00
28 Rolf Hallgren .25 1.00
29 Bo Hansson .25 1.00
30 Ove Hedberg .25 1.00
31 Kjell Hedman .50 2.00
32 Leif Holmqvist 1.00 2.00
33 Anders Johansson .25 1.00
34 Bengt Larsson .25 1.00
35 Bjorn Larsson .25 1.00
36 Rune Lindh .25 1.00
37 Borje Molander .25 1.00
38 Kjell Nilsson .25 1.00
39 Bert-Ola Nordlander .25 1.00
40 Anders Parmstrom .25 1.00
41 Lennart Sellinder .25 1.00
42 Kjell Savstrom .25 1.00
43 Lars Bylund .25 1.00
44 Hans Dahllof .50 2.00
45 Lennart Gustafsson .25 1.00
46 Lars Hedenstrom .25 1.00
47 Lennart Johansson .25 1.00
48 Kjell Johnsson .25 1.00
49 Stefan Karlsson .25 1.00
50 Nisse Larsson .25 1.00
51 Lennart Lind .25 1.00
52 Hans Lindberg .25 1.00
53 Tord Lundstrom .25 1.00
54 Jan-Erik Lyck .25 1.00
55 Lars-Goran Nilsson .25 1.00
56 Anders Sahlin .50 2.00
57 Lars-Ake Sivertsson .25 1.00
58 Hans Sjoberg .25 1.00
59 Hakan Wickberg .25 1.00
60 Tommy Bjorkman .50 2.00
61 Lasse Bjorn .25 1.00
62 Thomas Carlsson .25 1.00
63 Roland Einarsson .50 2.00
64 Kjell Keijser .25 1.00
65 Stig Larsson .25 1.00
66 Kent Lindgren .25 1.00
67 Tommie Lindgren .25 1.00
68 Lars-Ake Lundell .25 1.00
69 Per Lundstrom .25 1.00
70 Bjorn Palmquist .25 1.00
71 Ulf Rydin .25 1.00
72 Lars-Eric Sjoberg 2.00 4.00
73 Lars Starck .25 1.00
74 Roland Stoltz .25 1.00
75 Henry Svensson .25 1.00
76 Kurt Thulin .25 1.00
77 Gosta Westerlund .25 1.00
78 Eddie Wingren .25 1.00
79 Carl-Goran Oberg .25 1.00
80 Anders Andersson .25 1.00
81 Hasse Andersson .25 1.00
82 Hakan Andersson .25 1.00
83 Anders Asplund .25 1.00
84 Hans Bergqvist .25 1.00
85 Hans Bostrom .25 1.00
86 Kjell Eriksson .50 2.00
87 Conny Evensson .50 2.00
88 Bjorn Fagerlund .50 2.00
89 Ingemar Magnusson .25 1.00
90 Hans-Ake Nilsson .25 1.00
91 Rune Nilsson .25 1.00
92 Kent Olsson .25 1.00
93 Lars Stalberg .25 1.00
94 Christer Sundquist .25 1.00
95 Christer Abrahamsson 2.00 4.00
96 Tommy Abrahamsson 1.00 2.00
97 Bosse Andersson .25 1.00
98 Gunnar Andersson .25 1.00
99 Lars Andersson .25 1.00
100 Folke Bengtsson .25 1.00
101 Roland Bond .25 1.00
102 Kjell Fihnn .25 1.00
103 Jan-Olof Kroon .25 1.00
104 Lennart Lange .25 1.00
105 Sture Leksell .50 2.00
106 Goran Lysen .25 1.00
107 Ulf Martensson .25 1.00
108 Nisse Nilsson .25 1.00
109 Dag Ohlsson .25 1.00
110 Olle Sjogren .25 1.00
111 Ake Sunesson .25 1.00
112 Dan Soderstrom .50 2.00
113 Goran Winge .25 1.00
114 Mats Ahlberg .25 1.00
115 Olle Ost .25 1.00
116 Gunnar Backman .50 2.00
117 Lage Edin .25 1.00
118 Ake Eklof .25 1.00
119 Torbjorn Hubinette .25 1.00
120 Nils Johansson .25 1.00
121 Ulf Kroon .25 1.00
122 Ivar Larsson .50 2.00
123 Christer Nilsson .25 1.00
124 Anders Nordin .25 1.00
125 Hakan Nygren .25 1.00
126 Sten Olsen .25 1.00
127 Paul Stahl .25 1.00
128 Gunnar Safsten .25 1.00
129 Ulf Torstensson .25 1.00
130 Ulf Wigren .25 1.00
131 Lars Ohman .25 1.00
132 Tore Ohman .25 1.00
133 Bengt Andersson .25 1.00
134 Nils Carlsson .25 1.00
135 Kjell Eklind .25 1.00
136 Allan Fernstrom .25 1.00
137 Bengt Gustavsson .25 1.00
138 Bengt-Ake Gustavsson .50 2.00
139 Gote Hansson .25 1.00
140 Per-Arne Hubinette .25 1.00
141 Sven-Ake Jakobsson .25 1.00
142 Goran Johansson .50 2.00
143 Mats Lind .25 1.00
144 Mats Lonn .25 1.00
145 Ulf Nises .25 1.00
146 Bo Olsson .25 1.00
147 Lennart Svedberg .50 2.00
148 Evert Tysk .25 1.00
149 Stig Ostling .25 1.00
150 Ulf Berglund .25 1.00
151 Clarence Carlsson .25 1.00
152 Arne Ekenberg .25 1.00
153 Kenneth Ekman .25 1.00
154 Tom Haugh .50 2.00
155 Rolf Joelsson .25 1.00
156 Bjorn Johanesson .25 1.00
157 Arne Johansson .25 1.00
158 Bengt-Goran Karlsson .25 1.00
159 Kjell Larsson .25 1.00
160 Lasse Larsson .25 1.00
161 Barry Murman .25 1.00
162 Klas Goran Nilsson .25 1.00
163 Rolf Norell .25 1.00
164 Lennart Skordaker .25 1.00
165 Ulf Sterner .50 2.00
166 Arne Wickstrom .25 1.00
167 Bengt-Olov Andreasson .50 2.00
168 Leif Eriksson .25 1.00
169 Ove Evaldson .25 1.00
170 Hans-Erik Fernstrom .25 1.00
171 Kenneth Hillgren .25 1.00
172 Per-Olof Hardin .25 1.00
173 Bertil Karlsson .25 1.00
174 Torsten Karlsson .25 1.00
175 Rolf Larsson .25 1.00
176 William Lofqvist 1.00 2.00
177 Lars Mollander .25 1.00
178 Gert Nystrom .25 1.00
179 Olle Westlund .25 1.00
180 Bo Zetterberg .25 1.00
181 Leif Andersson .25 1.00
182 Borje Burlin .25 1.00
183 Hans Carlsson .25 1.00
184 Stig Carlsson .25 1.00
185 Einar Granath .25 1.00
186 Kjell-Ake Hedstrom .25 1.00
187 Mats Hysing .25 1.00
188 Stig-Goran Johansson .25 1.00
189 Curt Larsson 1.25 2.50
190 Eilert Maatta .25 1.00
191 Soren Maatta .25 1.00
192 Nils-Olof Schilstrom .25 1.00
193 Jan Schullstrom .25 1.00
194 Kjell Svensson .50 2.00
195 Gunnar Tallberg .25 1.00
196 Dick Yderstrom .25 1.00
197 Sten Andersson .50 2.00
198 Lars Arne Bergkvist .25 1.00
199 Anders Edstrom .25 1.00
200 Lars Bertil Eriksson .25 1.00
201 Charles Gustavsson .25 1.00
202 Ake Johansson .25 1.00
203 Lars Karestal .25 1.00
204 Rolf Karlsson .25 1.00
205 Erik Lindahl .25 1.00
206 Freddy Lindfors .50 2.00
207 Lennart Lindkvist .25 1.00
208 Kjell Rune Milton .25 1.00
209 Olle Nilsater .25 1.00
210 Birger Nordlund .25 1.00
211 Inge Tornlund .25 1.00
212 Jan Roger Oberg .25 1.00
213 Kjell Sture Oberg .25 1.00
214 Tommy Andersson .25 1.00
215 Soren Bostrom .25 1.00
216 Anders Bryner .25 1.00
217 Anders Claesson .50 2.00
218 Svante Granholm .25 1.00
219 Inge Hammarstrom 2.50 5.00
220 Borje Holmstrom .25 1.00
221 Jan Johansson .25 1.00
222 Antero Jonasson .25 1.00
223 Ove Jonsson .25 1.00
224 Lennart Lind .50 2.00
225 Jan-Erik Nilsson .25 1.00
226 Kurt Olofsson .25 1.00
227 Gosta Sjokvist .25 1.00
228 Jan Stolpe .25 1.00
229 Kjell Westerlund .25 1.00
230 Olle Ahman .25 1.00
231 Jan-Ivar Bergqvist .25 1.00
232 Lars-Ake Brannlund .50 2.00
233 Hans Bohlmark .25 1.00
234 Jan Christiansson .25 1.00
235 Bengt Eriksson .25 1.00
236 Arne Grenemo .25 1.00
237 Lars-Olof Henriksson .25 1.00
238 Kurt Jakobsson .25 1.00
239 Leif Jakobsson .25 1.00
240 Lars-Goran Johansson .25 1.00
241 Kimo Kivela .25 1.00
242 Borje Maatta .25 1.00
243 Anders Rapp .25 1.00
244 Tommy Sahlsten .25 1.00
245 Stig-Olof Zetterbrg .25 1.00
246 Lennart Abrahamsson .25 1.00
247 John Andersson .25 1.00
248 Ove Andersson .50 2.00
249 Kjell-olov Barrefjord .25 1.00
250 Ulf Barrefjord .25 1.00
251 Kent Bjork .25 1.00
252 Lars Dahlgren .25 1.00
253 Karl-Ove Eriksson .25 1.00
254 Osten Folkesson .25 1.00
255 Anders Hagstrom .25 1.00
256 Eric Jarvholm .25 1.00
257 Ulf Larsson .25 1.00
258 Bengt Lovgren .25 1.00
259 Roger Nilsson .25 1.00
260 Bengt Persson .50 2.00
261 Kjell Sundstrom .25 1.00
262 Roger Osterlund .25 1.00
263 Hans Aleblad .50 2.00
264 Ake Bolander .25 1.00
265 Karl-Gunnar Backman .25 1.00
266 Mats Davidsson .25 1.00
267 Bosse Englund .25 1.00
268 Tommy Eriksson .25 1.00
269 Karl-Soren Hedlund .25 1.00
270 Don Hughes .25 1.00
271 Krister Lindgren .25 1.00
272 Hans Mellinger .25 1.00
273 Des Moroney .25 1.00
274 Bo Olofsson .25 1.00
275 Hakan Olsson .25 1.00
276 Kent Persson .25 1.00
277 Ove Stenlund .25 1.00
278 Goran Thelin .25 1.00
279 Ove Thelin .25 1.00
280 Leif Ohrlund .25 1.00
281 Uno Ohrlund .25 1.00
282 Jan Ostling .25 1.00
283 Gert Blome .25 1.00
284 Ingemar Caris .50 2.00
285 Arne Carlsson .25 1.00
286 Kjell-Ove Gustafsson .25 1.00
287 Henric Hedlund .25 1.00
288 Leif Henriksson .25 1.00
289 Kjell Jonsson .25 1.00
290 Berny Karlsson .25 1.00
291 Goran Lindberg .25 1.00
292 Bernt Lundqvist .25 1.00
293 Lars Eric Lundvall .25 1.00
294 Carl-Fredrik Montan .25 1.00
295 Eine Ohlsson .50 2.00
296 Jan Olsen .25 1.00
297 Roger Olsson .25 1.00
298 Kjell-Ronnie Pettersson .50 2.00
299 Ronald Pettersson .25 1.00
300 Roland Sarnholm .25 1.00

1969-70 Swedish Hockey

This 384-card set was released in Sweden by Williams Forlags AB to commemorate the players and nations competing in the World Championships, as well as club teams from Sweden. The cards measured 1 7/8" by 2 1/2" and featured a small portrait on the front, along with team name and emblem. The backs gave the player's name, vital stats (in Swedish) and sticker number. Early (first?) appearances by many legends make this set notable: look for Valeri Kharlamov, Alexander Yakushev and Ulf Nilsson. An album was available which not only housed the set, but offered stories, photos and stats to wrap up the previous season. This album is valued at $50.

COMPLETE SET (384) 200.00 400.00
1 Valerij Charlamov 7.50 15.00
2 Vitalij Davydov .75 1.50
3 Anatolij Firsov 3.00 6.00
4 Alexander Jakusjev 5.00 10.00
5 Vladimir Jursinov 1.00 2.00
6 Victor Kuzkin .38 .75
7 Vladimir Lutjenko 1.00 2.00
8 Alexander Maltsev 5.00 10.00
9 Boris Michailov 5.00 10.00
10 Jevgenij Misjakov 1.50 3.00
11 Vladimir Petrov 5.00 10.00
12 Jevgenij Poladjev .38 .75
13 Victor Putjkov .50 1.00
14 Alexander Ragulin 1.50 3.00
15 Igor Romisjevskij .38 .75
16 Vjatjeslav Starsjinov 1.25 2.50
17 Vladimir Vikulov .75 1.50
18 Jevgenij Zimin .75 1.50
19 Victor Zinger .50 1.00
20 Josef Augusta .38 .75
21 Vladimir Bednar .38 .75
22 Josef Cerny .50 1.00
23 Vladimir Dzurilla 5.00 10.00
24 Richard Farda .38 .75
25 Josef Golonka .75 1.50
26 Jan Havel .38 .75
27 Jaroslav Holik .75 1.50
28 Jiri Holik .50 1.00
29 Josef Horesovsky .38 .75
30 Jan Hrbaty .38 .75
31 Jaroslav Jirik .38 .75
32 Jan Klapac .38 .75
33 Miroslav Lacky .75 1.50
34 Oldrich Machac .38 .75
35 Vaclav Nedomansky 2.50 5.00
36 Frantisek Pospisil 1.00 2.00
37 Frantisek Sevcik .50 1.00
38 Jan Suchy .50 1.00
39 Ake Carlsson .38 .75
40 Curt Edenvik .38 .75
41 Hans Eriksson .38 .75
42 Bo Hansson .38 .75
43 Ove Hedberg .38 .75
44 Kjell Hedman .75 1.50
45 Leif Holmqvist 1.50 3.00
46 Anders Johansson .38 .75
47 Bjorn Larsson .38 .75
48 Borje Molander .38 .75
49 Ulf Nilsson 10.00 20.00
50 Bert-Ola Nordlander .50 1.00
51 Bo Olofsson .38 .75
52 Anders Parmstrom .38 .75
53 Lennart Selinder .38 .75
54 Hans Stromberg .38 .75
55 Kjell Savstrom .38 .75
56 Lars-Ake Warning .38 .75
57 Lars Bylund .38 .75
58 Inge Hammarstrom 2.50 5.00

59 Hans Dahllof .75 1.50
60 Lars Hedenstrom .38 .75
61 Kjell Johnsson .38 .75
62 Lennart Johansson .38 .75
63 Bertil Karlsson .38 .75
64 Stefan Karlsson .38 .75
65 Lennart Lind .38 .75
66 Hans Lindberg .38 .75
67 Tord Lundstrom .38 .75
68 Jan-Erik Lyck .38 .75
69 William Lovqvist 1.00 2.00
70 Lars-Goran Nilsson .38 .75
71 Stig Salming .50 1.00
72 Lars-Ake Sivertsson .38 .75
73 Lars-Goran Tano .38 .75
74 Hakan Wickberg .38 .75
75 Rolf Berglund .38 .75
76 Lars Alserydh .75 1.50
77 Tage Blom .38 .75
78 Alf Granstrom .38 .75
79 Lennart Haggroth .75 1.50
80 Bertil Karlsson .38 .75
81 Sven-Bertil Lindstrom .38 .75
82 Anders Lundberg .38 .75
83 Goran Lundmark .75 1.50
84 Sven-Erik Lundqvist .38 .75
85 Hans Lundstrom .38 .75
86 Kjell Lang .38 .75
87 Borje Lofstedt .38 .75
88 Olle Nilsson .38 .75
89 Jan-Olof Nordin .38 .75
90 Kjell Rehnstrom .38 .75
91 Peder Rehnstrom .38 .75
92 Leif Tjernstrom .38 .75
93 Kjell-Arne Wikstrom .38 .75
94 Anders Andren .38 .75
95 Thomas Carlsson .38 .75
96 Roland Einarsson 1.00 2.00
97 Lars Granlund .38 .75
98 Stig Larsson .38 .75
99 Lars-Ake Lundell .38 .75
100 Per Lundstrom .38 .75
101 Bjorn Palmquist .38 .75
102 Ulf Rydin .38 .75
103 Christer Sehlstedt .75 1.50
104 Lars Starck .38 .75
105 Roland Stoltz .38 .75
106 Billy Sundstrom .38 .75
107 Henry Svensson .38 .75
108 Ove Svensson .38 .75
109 Ulf Torstensson .38 .75
110 Christer Abrahamsson 2.50 5.00
111 Tommy Abrahamsson 1.00 2.00
112 Gunnar Andersson .38 .75
113 Folke Bengtsson .38 .75
114 Kjell Brus .38 .75
115 Ake Danielsson .38 .75
116 Bo Englund .38 .75
117 Lennart Gustavsson .38 .75
118 Hans Jax .38 .75
119 Jan-Olov Kroon .38 .75
120 Roger Lindqvist .38 .75
121 Gunnar Mars .75 1.50
122 Ulf Martensson .38 .75
123 Nisse Nilsson .38 .75
124 Lars-Erik Sjoberg 2.50 5.00
125 Olle Sjogren .38 .75
126 Dan Soderstrom .38 .75
127 Mats Ahlberg .38 .75
128 Gunnar Backman 1.00 2.00
129 Ulf Croon .38 .75
130 Lage Edin .38 .75
131 Ake Eklof .38 .75
132 Anders Hedberg 10.00 20.00
133 Torbjorn Hubinette .38 .75
134 Nils Johansson .38 .75
135 Ivar Larsson 1.00 2.00
136 Christer Nilsson .38 .75
137 Lennart Norberg .38 .75
138 Anders Nordin .38 .75
139 Hakan Nygren .38 .75
140 Sten Olsen .38 .75
141 Anders Schahlin .38 .75
142 Gunnar Satsten .38 .75
143 Ulf Wigren .38 .75
144 Lars Ohman .38 .75
145 Tore Ohman .38 .75
146 Nils Carlsson .38 .75
147 Kjell Eklund .38 .75
148 Bengt Gustavsson .38 .75
149 Bengt-Ake Gustavsson 1.00 2.00
150 Gote Hansson .38 .75
151 Hans Hansson .38 .75
152 Per-Arne Hubinette .38 .75
153 Sven-Ake Jakobsson .38 .75
154 Goran Johansson .75 1.50
155 Mats Lind .38 .75
156 Mats Lonn .38 .75
157 Borje Marcus .38 .75
158 Lars Mjoberg .38 .75
159 Ulf Nises .38 .75
160 Bo Olsson .38 .75
161 Erling Sundblad .38 .75
162 Lennart Svedberg 1.00 2.00
163 Evert Tysk .38 .75
164 Stig Ostling .38 .75
165 Magnus Andersson .38 .75
166 Erling Bergmark .38 .75
167 Kenneth Hellman .38 .75
168 Bjorn Johansson .38 .75
169 Ulf Johansson .38 .75
170 Berny Karlsson .38 .75
171 Nils-Erik Karlsson .38 .75
172 Rolf Larsson .38 .75
173 Tore Larsson .38 .75
174 Roland Lestander .75 1.50
175 Lennart Lindgren .38 .75
176 Finn Lundstrom .38 .75
177 Kenneth Manberg .38 .75
178 Lars Molander .38 .75
179 Lennart Rudby .38 .75
180 Sven-Ake Rudby .38 .75
181 Curt Svensson .38 .75
182 Sverker Torstensson .38 .75
183 Gunnar Backman 1.00 2.00
184 Arne Carlsson .38 .75
185 Leif Henriksson .38 .75
186 Leif Holmqvist 1.50 3.00
187 Mats Hysing .38 .75
188 Nils Johansson .38 .75
189 Stig-Goran Johansson .75 1.50
190 Stefan Karlsson .38 .75
191 Tord Lundstrom .38 .75
192 Kjell-Rune Milton .38 .75
193 Lars-Goran Nilsson .38 .75
194 Bert-Ola Nordlander .50 1.00
195 Hakan Nygren .38 .75
196 Roger Olsson .38 .75
197 Bjorn Palmquist .38 .75
198 Lars-Erik Sjoberg 2.00 4.00
199 Ulf Sterner .38 .75
200 Lennart Svedberg .75 1.50
201 Dick Yderstrom .38 .75
202 Lennart Abrahamsson .38 .75
203 Anders Bengtsson .75 1.50
204 Agne Bylund .38 .75
205 Jan Edlund .38 .75
206 Goran Hedberg .38 .75
207 Christer Johansson .38 .75
208 Rolf Jager .38 .75
209 Per-Erik Kall .38 .75
210 Anders Norberg .38 .75
211 Janne Petterson .75 1.50
212 Bo Sjostrom .38 .75
213 Dick Sjostrom .38 .75
214 Lasse Sjostrom .38 .75
215 Ulf Stecksen .38 .75
216 Lennart Strohm .38 .75
217 Kurt Tillander .38 .75
218 Roger Osterlund .38 .75
219 Hans-Ake Andersson .38 .75
220 Hans Bejbom .38 .75
221 Carl-Axel Berglund .38 .75
222 Goran Borell .38 .75
223 Bjarne Brostrom .38 .75
224 Per Backman .38 .75
225 Kennet Calen .38 .75
226 Lennart Carlsson .38 .75
227 Mats Davidasson .38 .75
228 Curt Ferding .38 .75
229 Lars-Olof Granstrom .38 .75
230 Rolf Hansson .38 .75
231 Rune Holmgren .38 .75
232 Rune Norrstrom .38 .75
233 Bert-Ake Olsson .38 .75
234 Olle Olsson .38 .75
235 Jan Svedman .38 .75
236 Walter Winsth .38 .75
237 Goran Akerlund .38 .75
238 Borje Burlin .38 .75
239 Hans Carlsson .38 .75
240 Stig Carlsson .38 .75
241 Gunnar Granberg .38 .75
242 Allan Helenefors .38 .75
243 Mats Hysing .38 .75
244 Bertil Jacobsson .38 .75
245 Stig-Goran Johansson .75 1.50
246 Curt Larsson 1.25 2.50
247 Eilert Maatta .38 .75
248 Soren Maatta .38 .75
249 Tommy Bergman .38 .75
250 Nils-Olof Schilstrom .38 .75
251 Jan Schullstrom .38 .75
252 Kjell Svensson .75 1.50
253 Gunnar Tallberg .38 .75
254 Borje Ulweback .38 .75
255 Dick Yderstrom .38 .75
256 Tommy Andersson .38 .75
257 Bulla Berggren .38 .75
258 Anders Bryner .38 .75
259 Anders Claesson .75 1.50
260 Jan Johansson .38 .75
261 Ove Jonsson .38 .75
262 Lennart Lind .38 .75
263 Arne Lundstrom .38 .75
264 Ake Lundstrom .38 .75
265 Jan-Erik Nilsson .38 .75
266 Lennart Norberg .38 .75
267 Sten-Olov Olsson .38 .75
268 Hakan Pettersson .38 .75
269 Stefan Pettersson .38 .75
270 Gosta Sjokvist .38 .75
271 Jan Stolpe .38 .75
272 Ake Soderberg .38 .75
273 Kjell Westerlund .38 .75
274 Olle Ahman .38 .75
275 Krister Andersson .75 1.50
276 Bert Danielsson .38 .75
277 Gert Danielsson .38 .75
278 Bengt Eriksson .38 .75
279 Lars-Anders Gustavsson .38 .75
280 Curt Jacobsson .38 .75
281 Leif Jacobsson .38 .75
282 Lars-Erik Jakobsson .38 .75
283 Lars-Goran Johansson .38 .75
284 Des Moroney .38 .75
285 Borje Maatta .38 .75
286 Lars-Ake Nordin .38 .75
287 Kenneth Pedersen .38 .75
288 Anders Rapp .38 .75
289 Benny Runesson .38 .75
290 Jonny Ryman .38 .75
291 Ake Ryman .38 .75
292 Goran Ahstrom .75 1.50
293 John Andersson .38 .75
294 Kjell-Olov Barrefjord .38 .75
295 Ulf Barrefjord .38 .75
296 Kent Bjork .38 .75
297 Lars Dahlgren .38 .75
298 Karl-Olof Eriksson .38 .75
299 Osten Folkesson .38 .75
300 Anders Hagstrom .38 .75
301 Eric Jarvholm .38 .75
302 Ulf Larsson .38 .75
303 Bo Leong .75 1.50
304 Bengt Lofgren .38 .75
305 Roger Nilsson .38 .75
306 Bengt Persson .75 1.50
307 Ulf Stromsoe .38 .75
308 Kjell Sundstrom .38 .75
309 Leif Andersson .38 .75
310 Bernt Augustsson .38 .75
311 Kjell Augustsson .38 .75
312 Tommy Eriksson 1.00 2.00
313 Lars-Olof Feltendahl .38 .75
314 Karl-Soren Hedlund .38 .75
315 Penti Hyytiainen .38 .75
316 Arne Johansson .38 .75
317 Bengt-Goran Karlsson .38 .75
318 Curt Lundmark 1.00 2.00
319 Hakan Olsson .75 1.50
320 Kent Persson .38 .75
321 Ove Stenlund .38 .75
322 Goran Thelin .38 .75
323 Ove Thelin .38 .75
324 Bo Astrom .38 .75
325 Hasse Mellinger .38 .75
326 Uno Ohrlund .38 .75
327 Jan Ostling .38 .75
328 Kjell Andersson .38 .75
329 Ronny Andersson 1.00 2.00
330 Gert Blome .38 .75
331 Ingemar Caris 1.00 2.00
332 Arne Carlsson .38 .75
333 Svante Granholm .38 .75
334 Henric Hedlund .38 .75
335 Leif Henriksson .38 .75
336 Anders Johansson .38 .75
337 Kjell Jonsson .38 .75
338 Bjorn Lindberg .38 .75
339 Goran Lindberg .38 .75
340 Carl-Fredrik Montan .38 .75
341 Leif Nilsson .38 .75
342 Kurt Olofsson .38 .75
343 Jan Olsen .38 .75
344 Roger Olsson .38 .75
345 Kjell-Ronnie Petterson .38 .75
346 Ulf Sterner .38 .75
347 Rickie Bayes 1.25 2.50
348 Gary Begg .75 1.50
349 Roger Bourbonnais 1.00 2.00
350 Jack Bownass 1.00 2.00
351 Terry Caffery 1.25 2.50
352 Steve Carlyle 1.25 2.50
353 Ab Demarco 1.50 3.00
354 Ted Hargreaves 1.00 2.00
355 Bill Heindl 1.25 2.50
356 Fran Huck .75 1.50
357 Steve King 1.25 2.50
358 Chuck Lefley 2.00 4.00
359 Morris Mott 1.25 2.50
360 Terry O'Malley 1.00 2.00
361 Kevin O'Shea 1.25 2.50
362 Gerry Pinder 2.00 4.00
363 Steve Rexe 1.50 3.00
364 Ken Stephenson 1.25 2.50
365 Wayne Stephenson 5.00 10.00
366 Matti Harju .38 .75
367 Esa Isaksson .38 .75
368 Kari Johansson .38 .75
369 Juhani Jylha .38 .75
370 Matti Keinonen .38 .75
371 Veli-Pekka Ketola 1.50 3.00
372 Lasse Kiili .75 1.50
373 Ilpo Koskela .38 .75
374 Pekka Leimu .38 .75
375 Seppo Lindstrom .38 .75
376 Pekka Marjamaki .38 .75
377 Lauri Mononen .38 .75
378 Lasse Oksanen .38 .75
379 Lalli Partanen .38 .75
380 Esa Peltonen .38 .75
381 Jorma Peltonen .38 .75
382 Juhani Rantasila .38 .75
383 Juhani Wahlsten .38 .75
384 Urpo Ylonen 1.25 2.50

1970-71 Swedish Mastar Serien

This 200-card set was released in Sweden to commemorate the 1970 World Championships held in Bern and Geneva, Switzerland. The cards in the set are inconsistent in their appearance. Cards 1-50 measure approximately 2 3/4" by 3 3/4". Cards 51-100 are 3" by 4". Cards 101-200 are 3" by 3 3/4". All feature color action photos on the front, but only the first and third groupings have numbers on the front. Cards 51-100 were not numbered on the cards but only in the collector's album. The cards were distributed in 5-card, clear plastic packages. The key cards in the set are two of HOFer Ken Dryden as a member of Team Canada. The cards precede his RC by two years. An album was available to store the cards; it is valued at $30.

COMPLETE SET (200) 175.00 350.00
1 Vladimir Dzurila 4.00 8.00
2 Jozef Golonka .50 1.00
3 Jiri Holik .38 .75
4 Vaclav Nedomansky 1.25 2.50
5 Vaclav Nedomansky 1.25 2.50
6 Jaroslav Holik .50 1.00
7 Jozef Golonka .50 1.00
8 Vaclav Nedomansky 1.25 2.50
9 Vladimir Bednar .25 .50
10 Jan Havel .25 .50
11 Jan Hrbaty .25 .50
12 Jan Suchy .38 .75
13 Lasse Oksanen .25 .50
14 Urpo Ylonen .50 1.00
15 Michael Curran .75 1.50
16 Gary Begg .50 1.00
17 Carl Lackey .50 1.00
18 Terry O'Malley .75 1.50
19 Gary Gamuicci .50 1.00
20 Seppo Lindstrom .25 .50
21 Lucenko .75 1.50
Misjakov
Davidov
22 Victor Putjkov .38 .75
23 Alexandr Ragulin 1.00 2.00
24 Gerry Pinder 1.25 2.50
25 Fran Huck .50 1.00
26 Ken Dryden 50.00 100.00
27 Viktor Zinger .38 .75
28 Vladimir Petrov 2.50 5.00
29 Igor Romisjevsky .50 1.00
Viktor Zinger
30 Valerij Charlamov 5.00 10.00
31 Alexandr Ragulin 1.00 2.00
32 Ab Demarco 1.00 2.00
33 Morris Mott .75 1.50
34 Fran Huck .50 1.00
35 Vjatjeslav Starsinov .75 1.50
36 Lars-Goran Nilsson .50 1.00
37 Stig-Goran Stisse Johansson .50 1.00
38 Leif Honken Holmqvist 1.00 2.00
39 Hakan Nygren .25 .50
40 Tord Lundstrom .25 .50
41 Ulf Sterner .25 .50
42 Lars-Erik Sjoberg 1.50 3.00
43 Kjell-Rune Milton .25 .50
44 Leif Honken Holmqvist 1.00 2.00
45 Stefan Lill-Prosten Karlsson .25 .50
46 Lennart Lill-Strimma Svedberg .50 1.00
47 Tord Lundstrom .25 .50
48 Ulf Sterner .25 .50
49 Tord Lundstrom .25 .50
50 Lennart Lill-Strimma Svedberg .50 1.00
51 Sverige (12 st) .25 .50
52 Bert-Ola Nordlander .38 .75
53 Leif Honken Holmqvist 1.00 2.00
54 Lars-Erik Sjoberg 1.50 3.00
55 Lars-Erik Sjoberg 1.50 3.00
56 Nils Nicke Johansson .25 .50
57 Ulf Sterner .25 .50
58 Ulf Sterner .25 .50
Leif Blixten Henriksson
59 Tord Lundstrom .25 .50
60 Mats Hysing .25 .50
Nils Johansson
61 Lars-Goran Nilsson .25 .50
62 Hakan Nygren .25 .50
63 USSR vs. Team Canada 1.25 2.50
Gerry Pinder
Anatolij Firsov
Alexandre Jakusjev
Alexandr Ragulin
Igor Romisjevsky
Stephenson
Ken Dryden
Bill Heindl
Vitalij Misjakov
64 Evgenij Misjakov .50 1.00
65 Vjatjeslav Starsinov .75 1.50
66 Alexandr Ragulin 1.00 2.00
67 Alexandr Maltsev 2.50 5.00
68 Anatolij Firsov 2.00 4.00
69 Vladimir Lucenko .75 1.50
70 Vladimir Petrov 2.50 5.00
71 Vladimir Petrov 2.50 5.00
72 Vjatjeslav Starsinov .75 1.50
73 Vladimir Vikulov .50 1.00
74 Vitaly Davidov .50 1.00
75 Evgenij Zimin .38 .75
76 Vladimir Bednar 1.25 2.50
Vladimir Dzurila
77 Jan Suchy .38 .75
78 Jaroslav Holik .50 1.00
79 Josef Horesovsky .50 1.00
80 Jozef Golonka .50 1.00
81 Richard Farda .25 .50
82 Frantisek Pospisil .50 1.00
Oldrich Machac
83 Ilop Koskela .25 .50
84 Juhani Jylha .25 .50
85 Esa Peltonen .25 .50
86 Lasse Oksanen .25 .50
87 Juhani Wahlsten .25 .50
88 Juha Rantasila .25 .50
89 Bob Paradise .50 1.00
90 Bob Paradise .50 1.00
91 Tim Sheehy .50 1.00
92 Michael Curran .75 1.50

93 Ken Dryden 50.00 100.00
94 Morris Mott .75 1.50
95 Fran Huck .50 1.00
96 unknown .25 .50
97 unknown .25 .50
98 unknown .25 .50
99 unknown .25 .50
100 unknown .25 .50
101 Arne Carlsson .25 .50
102 Nils Nicke Johansson .25 .50
103 Leif Holmqvist 1.00 2.00
104 Leif Henriksson .25 .50
105 Lennart Svedberg .50 1.00
106 Hakan Wickberg .25 .50
107 Gennar Backman .25 .50
108 Roger Olsson .25 .50
109 Kjell-Rune Milton .25 .50
110 Mats Hysing .25 .50
111 Lars-Erik Sjoberg 1.50 3.00
112 Anders Hedberg 5.00 10.00
113 Bjorn Palmqvist .25 .50
114 Tord Lundstrom .25 .50
115 Ulf Sterner .25 .50
116 Stig-Goran Johansson .50 1.00
117 Lars-Goran Nilsson .25 .50
118 Stefan Karlsson .25 .50
119 Anders Nordin .25 .50
120 Hans Virus Lindberg .25 .50
121 Davidov .50 1.00
Starshinov
Polupanov
Jakushev
Maltsev
Firsov
122 Vitaly Davidov .50 1.00
123 Alexandr Jakusjev 2.50 5.00
Valtonen O. Rantasila
124 Alexandr Maltsev 2.50 5.00
125 Valerij Charlamov 5.00 10.00
126 Alexandr Ragulin 1.00 2.00
127 Igor Romisjevskij .25 .50
128 Boris Michailov 2.50 5.00
129 Vyatcheslav Starsinov .50 1.00
Victor Polupanov
Alexander Ragulin
Vladimir Lucenko
130 Victor Konovalenko .25 .50
131 Jakusjev 2.00 4.00
Vitalij Davidov
Boris Michailov
Vladislav Tretiak
Alexander Maltsev
Evgenji Paladjev
132 Vladimir Lucenko 1.50 3.00
Vladimir Petrov
Anatoli Firsov
Valerij Nikitin
Igor Romishevski
Vikulov
Alexander Yakushev
133 Alexandr Maltsev 2.50 5.00
134 Valerij Nikitin .25 .50
135 Vladimir Vikulov .50 1.00
136 Vjatjeslav Starsinov .75 1.50
137 Evgenij Paladjev .25 .50
138 Vladimir Shapovalov .25 .50
139 Anatolij Firsov 2.00 4.00
140 Victor Polupanov .25 .50
141 Jaroslav Jirik .25 .50
142 Miroslav Lacky .50 1.00
143 Jan Suchy .38 .75
144 Lubomir Ujvary .25 .50
145 Vladimir Bednar .25 .50
146 Richard Farda .25 .50
147 Josef Cernyh .38 .75
148 Vaclav Nedomansky 1.25 2.50
149 Jaroslav Holik .75 1.50
150 Jiri Holik .38 .75
151 Julius Haas .38 .75
Vladislav Martinec
152 Vaclav Nedomansky 1.25 2.50
153 Josef Horesovsky .25 .50
154 Oldrich Machac .25 .50
155 Tommy Abrahamsson .50 1.00
Jiri Kochta
156 Vladimir Dzurila 2.00 4.00
Jan Suchy
Vladimir Bednar
157 Jorma Valtonen .50 1.00
158 Veli-Pekka Ketola 1.00 2.00
159 Matti Murto .25 .50
Lauri Mononen
160 Heikki Riihiranta .50 1.00
161 Pekka Leimu .25 .50
162 Lasse Oksanen .25 .50
163 Jorma Valtonen .25 .50
Vaino Kolkka
Pekka Marjamaki
164 Urpo Ylonen .50 1.00
165 Matti Keinonen .25 .50
166 Juha Rantasila .75 1.50
Anatolij Firsov
167 Jorma Vehmanen .25 .50
168 Matti Murto .25 .50
169 Peter Slapke .25 .50
170 Claus Hirche .25 .50
171 Frank Braun .25 .50
172 Rolf Bielas .25 .50
173 Kargar .25 .50
Hiller
Ziesche
Braun
174 Beilas .25 .50
Braun
Hirche
Kolbe
175 Wilfried Rohrbach .25 .50
Hartmut Nickel
176 Plotka .25 .50
Karrenbauer
Rohrbach
Patschinski
177 John Mayasich .25 .50
{James Branch
178 Larry Skime .50 1.00
179 Paul Coppo .50 1.00
180 Larry Pleau .50 1.00
181 Bruce Riutta .50 1.00
Ron Nasland
John Lothrop
182 Jerry Lackey .50 1.00
183 Bob Paradise .75 1.50
Michael Curran
Carl Lackey
184 Paul Coppo .50 1.00
Peter Markle
185 Roger Bourbonnais .75 1.50
186 Ted Hargreaves .75 1.50
187 Fran Huck .50 1.00
188 Wayne Stephenson 2.50 5.00
189 Morris Mott .75 1.50
190 Gerry Pinder 1.25 2.50
191 Gary Begg .50 1.00
192 Ken Dryden 50.00 100.00
Blank Back
193 Felix Goralczyk .25 .50
194 Andrzej Tkacz .25 .50
195 Jan Modzelewski .25 .50
196 Marian Kajzerek .25 .50
197 Josef Stefaniak .25 .50
198 Walery Kosyl .25 .50
199 Jan Modzelewski .25 .50
200 Pajerski .25 .50
Goralczyk
Chachowski
Polen

1970-71 Swedish Hockey

This set of 384-cards was issued by Williams Forlags AB and printed by Panini in Italy. The cards, which measure approximately 2 1/2" by 1 3/4", feature teams from the Swedish first and second divisions, as well as national team members from Tre Kroner, Russia, Czechoslovakia, Finland and East Germany. The card fronts feature a small player portrait along with the team emblem. The backs give player name, a brief bio and card number. The set includes many well known international stars, most prominently the first appearance of HOFer Borje Salming. An album to house the stickers was available as well; it also included text and photos to give a brief history of the teams involved. It is valued at approximately $40. Note: Spellings are as they appear on the cards and, in the case of Russian players, are not necessarily the spellings typically used for these players.

COMPLETE SET (384) 200.00 400.00
1 Leif (Honken) Holmqvist 1.25 2.50
2 Kjell Hedman .75 1.50
3 Lars Danielsson .38 .75
4 Ake Fagerstrom .38 .75
5 Per-Arne Hubinette .38 .75
6 Hakan Lindgren .38 .75
7 Bert-Ola Nordlander .50 1.00
8 Rolf (Rattan) Edberg .38 .75
9 Bo Hansson .38 .75
10 Jan-Olov Kroon .38 .75
11 Ulf Nilsson 5.00 10.00
12 Bosse Olofsson .38 .75
13 Lennart Selinder .38 .75
14 Hans Stromberg .38 .75
15 Kjell Savstrom .38 .75
16 Lars-Ake Warning .38 .75
17 Lars-Goran Nilsson .75 1.50
Alexander Yakushev
18 William Lofqvist .75 1.50
19 Hans Dahllof .75 1.50
20 Lars Bylund .38 .75
21 Lars Hedenstrom .38 .75
22 Kjell Johnsson .38 .75
23 Borje Salming 12.50 25.00
24 Stig Salming .38 .75
25 Stig Ostling .38 .75
26 Inge Hammarstrom 2.50 5.00
27 Lennart Johansson .38 .75
28 Stefan Karlsson .38 .75
29 Lennart Lind .38 .75
30 Hans (Virus) Lindberg .38 .75
31 Tord Lundstrom .38 .75
32 Jan-Erik Lyck .38 .75
33 Lars-Goran Nilsson .38 .75
34 Lars-Ake Sivertsson .38 .75
35 Hakan Wickberg .38 .75
36 puzzle .38 .75
37 puzzle .38 .75
38 puzzle .38 .75
39 puzzle .38 .75
40 puzzle .38 .75
41 puzzle .38 .75
42 puzzle .50 .75
43 puzzle .50 .75
44 puzzle .38 .75
45 puzzle .38 .75
46 puzzle .50 .75
47 puzzle .50 .75
48 Roland Einarsson .75 1.50
49 Ake Eklof .38 .75
50 Christer Ahlstrand .38 .75
51 Thomas Carlsson .38 .75
52 Anders Rylin .38 .75
53 Billy Sundstrom .38 .75
54 Folke Bengtsson .38 .75
55 Stig Larsson .38 .75
56 Lars-Ake Lundell .38 .75
57 Per Lundstrom .38 .75
58 Bjorn Palmqvist .38 .75
59 Ulf Rydin .38 .75
60 Ove Svensson .38 .75
61 Jan Zabrodsky .38 .75
62 Leif Holmqvist PUZ 1.00 2.00
63 Leif Holmqvist PUZ 1.00 2.00
64 Leif Holmqvist PUZ 1.00 2.00
65 Leif Holmqvist PUZ 1.00 2.00
66 Christer Abrahamsson 1.50 3.00
67 Christer Sterner .75 1.50
68 Thommy Abrahamsson .75 1.50
69 Karl-Gustaf Alander .38 .75
70 Gunnar Andersson .38 .75
71 Roland Bond .38 .75
72 Ake Danielsson .38 .75
73 Per-Olov Brasar 1.50 3.00
74 Kjell Brus .38 .75
75 Hans Jax .38 .75
76 Dan Labraaten 1.50 3.00
77 Roger Lindqvist .38 .75
78 Ulf Martensson .38 .75
79 Olle Sjogren .38 .75
80 Ingemar Snis .38 .75
81 Dan Soderstrom .38 .75
82 Mats Ahlberg .38 .75
83 Gunnar Backman .75 1.50
84 Ivar Larsson .75 1.50
85 Lage Edin .38 .75
86 Kjell-Rune Milton .38 .75
87 Ulf Torstensson .38 .75
88 Ulf Wigren .38 .75
89 Ulf Croon .38 .75
90 Hakan Dahllof .38 .75
91 Anders Hedberg 5.00 10.00
92 Torbjorn Hubinette .38 .75
93 Christer Nilsson .38 .75
94 Lennart Norberg .38 .75
95 Anders Nordin .38 .75
96 Hakan Nygren .38 .75
97 Per-Olof Uusitalo .38 .75
98 Lars Ohman .38 .75
99 Tore Ohman .38 .75
100 V. Dzurilla PUZ .75 1.50
101 V. Dzurilla PUZ .75 1.50
102 V. Dzurilla PUZ .75 1.50
103 V. Dzurilla PUZ .75 1.50
104 V. Dzurilla PUZ .75 1.50
105 V. Dzurilla PUZ .75 1.50
106 V. Dzurilla PUZ .75 1.50
107 V. Dzurilla PUZ .75 1.50
108 V. Dzurilla PUZ .75 1.50
109 V. Dzurilla PUZ .75 1.50
110 V. Dzurilla PUZ .75 1.50
111 V. Dzurilla PUZ .75 1.50
112 Bengt-Ake Gustavsson .75 1.50
113 Lars Gustavsson .75 1.50
114 Tommy Andersson .38 .75
115 Hans-Olov Ernlund .38 .75
116 Lars Mjoberg .38 .75
117 Gote Hansson .38 .75
118 L. Svedberg PUZ .50 1.00
119 B. Mikhailov PUZ 1.50 3.00
120 L. Holmqvist PUZ 1.00 2.00
121 Hans Hansson .38 .75
122 Sven-Ake Jakobsson .38 .75
123 Mats Lind .38 .75
124 Mats Lonn .38 .75
125 Borje Marcus .38 .75
126 Ulf Nises .38 .75
127 Borje Skoog .38 .75
128 Erling Sundblad .38 .75
129 Kent Sundkvist .38 .75
130 Curt Larsson 1.00 2.00
131 Torbjorn Hellsing .75 1.50
132 Tommie Bergman 2.00 4.00
133 Arne Carlsson .38 .75
134 Allan Helenefors .38 .75
135 Eilert Maatta .38 .75
136 Jan Schullstrom .38 .75
137 Hans Carlsson .38 .75
138 Tommy Carlsson .38 .75
139 Gunnar Granberg .38 .75
140 Mats Hysing .38 .75
141 Bertil Jacobsson .38 .75
142 Stig-Goran Johansson .38 .75
143 Soren Maatta .38 .75
144 Nils-Olov Schilstrom .38 .75
145 Dick Yderstrom .38 .75
146 Carl-Goran Oberg .38 .75
147 Lennart Svedberg .50 1.00
148 Anders Claesson .75 1.50
149 Kent Othberg .75 1.50
150 Jan Johansson .38 .75
151 Jan-Erik Nilsson .38 .75
152 Stefan Pettersson .38 .75
153 Lennart Svedberg .75 1.50
154 Bo Berggren .38 .75
155 Arne Lundstrom .38 .75
156 Finn Lundstrom .38 .75
157 I. Romisjevskij PUZ .38 .75
158 I. Romisjevskij PUZ .50 1.00
159 Ake Lundstrom .38 .75
160 V. Tretiak PUZ 4.00 8.00
161 V. Tretiak PUZ 4.00 8.00
162 Lennart Norberg .38 .75
163 Hakan Pettersson .38 .75
164 Ake Soderberg .50 1.00
165 Olle Ahman .38 .75
166 puzzle .38 .75
167 puzzle .38 .75
168 puzzle .38 .75
169 puzzle .38 .75
170 puzzle .38 .75
171 puzzle .38 .75
172 puzzle .38 .75
173 puzzle .38 .75
174 puzzle .38 .75
175 puzzle .38 .75
176 puzzle .38 .75
177 puzzle .38 .75
178 Christer Andersson .75 1.50
179 Goran Astrom .75 1.50
180 Kenneth Ekman .38 .75
181 Lars Erik Jakobsson .38 .75
182 Des Moroney .38 .75
183 Borje Maatta .38 .75
184 Kenneth Pedersen .38 .75
185 Anders Rapp .38 .75
186 Sven Crabo .38 .75
187 Lars Anders Gustavsson .38 .75
188 Kurt Jacobsson .38 .75
189 Leif Jacobsson .38 .75
190 Lars Goran Johansson .38 .75
191 Bernt Karlsson .38 .75
192 Benny Runesson .38 .75
193 Jonny Ryman .38 .75
194 Ake Ryman .38 .75
195 Christer Grahn .75 1.50
196 Ronny Sandstrom .38 .75
197 John Andersson .38 .75
198 Karl-Olof Eriksson .38 .75
199 Anders Hagstrom .38 .75
200 Rolf Jager .38 .75
201 Erik Jarvholm .38 .75
202 Lars Nordin .38 .75
203 Ulf Barrefjord .38 .75
204 Lars Dahlgren .38 .75
205 Ulf Ingvarsson .38 .75
206 Ulf Larsson .38 .75
207 Jan Lundqvist .38 .75
208 Ulf Lundstrom .38 .75
209 Bengt Lovgren .38 .75
210 Lars SJostrom .38 .75
211 Kjell Sundstrom .38 .75
212 Ulf Stromsoe .38 .75
213 Hakan Olsson .75 1.50
214 Leif Andersson .38 .75
215 Tommy Eriksson .75 1.50
216 Karl-Soren Hedlund .38 .75
217 Curt Lundmark .75 1.50
218 Ove Nystrom .38 .75
219 Gote Gustavsson .38 .75
220 Hans Hjelm .38 .75
221 Pennti Hyytiainen .38 .75
222 Arne Johansson .38 .75
223 Bengt-Goran Karlsson .38 .75
224 Kent Persson .38 .75
225 Ove Stenlund .38 .75
226 Goran Thelin .38 .75
227 Ove Thelin .38 .75
228 Bo Astrom .38 .75
229 Jan Ostling .38 .75
230 V. Tretiak action 10.00 20.00
231 V. Konovalenko PUZ .38 .75
232 V. Konovalenko PUZ .38 .75
233 V. Konovalenko PUZ .38 .75
234 V. Konovalenko PUZ .38 .75
235 V. Konovalenko PUZ .38 .75
236 V. Konovalenko PUZ .38 .75
237 V. Konovalenko PUZ .38 .75
238 V. Konovalenko PUZ .38 .75
239 V. Konovalenko PUZ .38 .75
240 V. Konovalenko PUZ .38 .75
241 V. Konovalenko PUZ .38 .75
242 V. Konovalenko PUZ .38 .75
243 Ingemar Caris .75 1.50
244 Ronny Andersson .75 1.50
245 Gert Blome .38 .75
246 Anders Johansson .38 .75
247 Goran Lindberg .38 .75
248 Jan Olsen .38 .75
249 Lars-Erik Sjoberg 2.00 4.00
250 Kjell Andersson .38 .75
251 Svante Granholm .38 .75
252 Henrik Hedlund .38 .75
253 Leif Henriksson .38 .75
254 Bjorn Lindberg .38 .75
255 Billy Lindstrom .38 .75
256 Carl-Fredrik Montan .38 .75
257 Leif Nilsson .38 .75
258 Kurt Olofsson .38 .75
259 Roger Olsson .38 .75
260 Kjell-Ronnie Pettersson .38 .75
261 Soviet team PUZ .38 .75
262 Soviet team PUZ .38 .75
263 Soviet team PUZ .38 .75
264 Soviet team PUZ .38 .75
265 Soviet team PUZ .38 .75
266 Soviet team PUZ .38 .75
267 Soviet team PUZ .38 .75
268 Soviet team PUZ .38 .75
269 Soviet team PUZ .38 .75
270 Soviet team PUZ .38 .75
271 Soviet team PUZ .38 .75
272 Soviet team PUZ .38 .75
273 Leif Holmqvist 1.00 2.00
274 Gunnar Backman .75 1.50
275 Christer Abrahamsson 1.50 3.00

276 Thommy Abrahamsson .75 1.50
277 Arne Carlsson .38 .75
278 Nils Johansson .38 .75
279 Ljell-Rune Milton .38 .75
280 Lars-Erik Sjoberg 2.00 4.00
281 Lennart Svedberg .75 1.50
282 Anders Hedberg 5.00 10.00
283 Stig-Goran Johansson .38 .75
284 Stefan Karlsson .38 .75
285 Hans Lindberg .38 .75
286 Tord Lundstrom .38 .75
287 Lars-Goran Nilsson .38 .75
288 Anders Nordin .38 .75
289 Roger Olsson .38 .75
290 Bjorn Palmqvist .38 .75
291 Ulf Sterner .38 .75
292 Hakan Wickberg .38 .75
293 Urpo Ylonen 1.00 2.00
294 Jorma Valtonen .75 1.50
295 Ilpo Koskela .38 .75
296 Seppo Lindstrom .38 .75
297 Pekka Marjamaki .38 .75
298 Lalli Partinen .38 .75
299 Juha Rantasila .38 .75
300 Heikki Riihiranta 1.00 2.00
301 Pekka Keimu .38 .75
302 Matti Keinonen .38 .75
303 Veli-Pekka Ketola 1.50 3.00
304 Vaino Kolkka .38 .75
305 Harri Linnonmaa .38 .75
306 Lauri Mononen .38 .75
307 Matti Murto .75 1.50
308 Lasse Oksanen .38 .75
309 Esa Peltonen .38 .75
310 Jorma Peltonen .38 .75
311 Juhani Tamminen .75 1.50
312 Jorma Vehmanen .38 .75
313 Viktor Konovalenko .75 1.50
314 Vladislav Tretjak 20.00 40.00
315 Vitalij Davidov .75 1.50
316 Vladimir Lutjenko .75 1.50
317 Jevgenij Paladjev .38 .75
318 Alexander Ragulin 1.50 3.00
319 Igor Romisjevski .50 1.00
320 Valerij Vasiljev 2.50 5.00
321 Valerij Nikitin .50 1.00
322 Valerij Charlamov 7.50 15.00
323 Anatolij Firsov 4.00 8.00
324 Alexander Jakusjev 4.00 8.00
325 Alexander Maltsev 4.00 8.00
326 Boris Michailov 4.00 8.00
327 Jevgenij Misjakov 1.25 2.50
328 Vladimir Petrov 2.50 5.00
329 Viktor Polupanov .38 .75
330 Vladimir Sjadrin 1.50 3.00
331 Vjatjeslav Starsinov 1.25 2.50
332 Vladimir Vikulov .50 1.00
333 puzzle .38 .75
334 puzzle .38 .75
335 puzzle .38 .75
336 puzzle .38 .75
337 puzzle .38 .75
338 puzzle .38 .75
339 puzzle .38 .75
340 puzzle .38 .75
341 puzzle .38 .75
342 puzzle .38 .75
343 puzzle .38 .75
344 puzzle .38 .75
345 Vladimir Dzurilla 2.50 5.00
346 Miroslav Lacky .75 1.50
347 Vladimir Bednar .38 .75
348 Josef Horesovsky .38 .75
349 Oldrich Machac .38 .75
350 Frantisek Pospisil .75 1.50
351 Jan Suchy .50 1.00
352 Lubomir Ujvary .38 .75
353 Josef Cerny .50 1.00
354 Richard Farda .38 .75
355 Julius Haas .38 .75
356 Ivan Hlinka .75 1.50
357 Jaroslav Holik .50 1.00
358 Jiri Holik .50 1.00
359 Jan Hrbaty .38 .75
360 Jiri Kochta .38 .75
361 Vladislav Martinec .38 .75
362 Vaclav Nedomansky 1.50 3.00
363 Stanislav Pryl .38 .75
364 Frantisek Sevcik .38 .75
365 Klaus Hirche .75 1.50
366 Diter Purschel .75 1.50
367 Frank Braun .38 .75
368 Dieter Dewitz .38 .75
369 Bernd Karrenbauer .38 .75
370 Helmut Novy .38 .75
371 Dietmar Peters .38 .75
372 Wolfgang Plotka .38 .75
373 Peter Slapke .38 .75
374 Rolf Bielas .38 .75
375 Lothar Fuchs .38 .75
376 Bernd Hiller .38 .75
377 Reinhard Karger .38 .75
378 Hartmut Nickel .38 .75
379 Rudiger Noack .38 .75
380 Rainer Patschinski .38 .75
381 Peter Prusa .38 .75
382 Wilfried Rohrbach .38 .75
383 Dieter Rohl .38 .75
384 Joachim Ziesche .38 .75

1971-72 Swedish Hockey

This set of 400 cards was printed by Panini and released in Sweden by Williams Forlags AB. The cards-- which measure approximately 2 1/2" by 1 3/4" -- feature players from Sweden's top league, as well as from several national teams and NHL clubs. The fronts offer a simple player portrait; the backs contain sticker number and a brief player bio in Swedish. An album to house the set can be found; it is valued approximately at $40. Key stars in this loaded set include Bobby Orr, Gordie Howe and Vladislav Tretiak. NOTE: Spellings used are those found on the sticker. In the case of the Russian players, these spellings may differ from those in common usage.

COMPLETE SET (400) 225.00 450.00
1 Christer Abrahamsson 1.00 2.00
2 Leif (Honken) Holmqvist .50 1.00
3 William (Loken) Lofqvist .50 1.00
4 Thommy Abrahamsson .50 1.00
5 Gunnar Andersson .25 .50
6 Thommie Bergman 1.50 3.00
7 Arne Carlsson .25 .50
8 Kjell-Rune Milton .25 .50
9 Bert-Ola Nordlander .50 1.00
10 Lennart Svedberg .50 1.00
11 Lars-Erik Sjoberg 1.00 2.00
12 Stig Ostling .25 .50
13 Inge Hammarstrom 1.50 10.00
14 Anders Hedberg 4.00 8.00
15 Stig-Goran Johansson .50 1.00
16 Stefan Karlsson .25 .50
17 Dan Labraaten 1.00 2.00
18 Hans (Virus) Lindberg .25 .50
19 Tord Lundstrom .25 .50
20 Lars-Goran Nilsson .25 .50
21 Hakan Nygren .25 .50
22 Bjorn Palmqvist .25 .50
23 Hakan Pettersson .25 .50
24 Ulf Sterner .25 .50
25 Hakan Wickberg .25 .50
26 Viktor Konovalenko .30 .75
27 Vladislav Tretjak 10.00 20.00
28 Gennadij Cigannkov .30 .75
29 Vitali Davidov .30 .75
30 Victor Kuskin .25 .50
31 Vladimir Lutjenko .30 .75
32 Alexander Ragulin 1.00 2.00
33 Igor Romisjevskij .30 .75
34 Valerij Kharlamov 5.00 15.00
35 Anatolij Firsov 2.50 5.00
36 Alexander Maltsev 2.50 5.00
37 Boris Michailov 2.50 5.00
38 Jevgenij Misjakov 1.00 2.00
39 Vladimir Petrov 2.50 5.00
40 Vjatjeslav Starshinov .50 1.00
41 Vladimir Vikulov .30 .75
42 Evgenij Zimin .50 1.00
43 Jiri Holecek .50 1.00
44 Josef Horesovsky .25 .50
45 Oldrich Machac .25 .50
46 Frantisek Panchartek .25 .50
47 Frantisek Pospisil .30 .75
48 Jan Suchy .30 .75
49 Josef Cerny .30 .75
50 Richard Farda .25 .50
51 Jan Havel .25 .50
52 Ivan Hlinka .50 1.00
53 Jiri Holik .30 .75
54 Jiri Kochta .25 .50
55 Vladimir Martinec .30 .75
56 Vaclav Nedomansky 1.00 2.00
57 Eduard Novak .25 .50
58 Bohuslav Stastny .50 1.00
59 Jorma Valtonen .50 1.00
60 Urpo Ylonen .50 1.00
61 Ilpo Koskela .25 .50
62 Seppo Lindstrom .25 .50
63 Hannu Luojola .25 .50
64 Pekka Marjamaki .25 .50
65 Esa Isaksson .25 .50
66 Veli-Pekka Ketola 1.00 2.00
67 Harri Linnonmaa .25 .50
68 Erkki Mononen .25 .50
69 Lauri Mononen .25 .50
70 Matti Murto .50 1.00
71 Lasse Oksanen .25 .50
72 Esa Peltonen .25 .50
73 Juhanni Tamminen .50 1.00
74 Jorma Vehmanen .25 .50
75 Leif (Honken) Holmqvist .50 1.00
76 Bert Jattne .50 1.00
77 Lars Danielsson .25 .50
78 Ake Fagerstrom .25 .50
79 Per-Arne (Hybbe) Hubinette .25 .50
80 Hakan (Flamman) Lindgren .25 .50
81 Bert-Ola Nordlander .50 1.00
82 Lennart (Petter) Pettersson .25 .50
83 Rolf (Rattan) Edberg .25 .50
84 Bo Hansson .25 .50
85 Jan-Olov Kroon .25 .50
86 Gunnar (Gurra) Lindkvist .25 .50
87 Christer Lundberg .25 .50
88 Ulf (Projsarn) Nilsson 4.00 8.00
89 Bo Olofsson .25 .50
90 Jan Olsson .25 .50
91 Lennart (Sillen) Selinder .25 .50
92 Soren Sjogren .25 .50
93 Hans (Strumpan) Stromberg .25 .50
94 Jan Ostling .25 .50
95 Kjell Helling .50 1.00
96 William (Loken) Lofqvist .50 1.00
97 Lars (Bylle) Bylund .25 .50
98 Kjell (Kulan) Johnsson .25 .50
99 Par Malmstrom .25 .50
100 Borje Salming 5.00 10.00
101 Stig Salming .25 .50
102 Stig Ostling .25 .50
103 Inge Hammarstrom 1.50 10.00
104 Lennart Johansson .25 .50
105 Stefan Karlsson .25 .50
106 Lennart (Huppa) Lind .25 .50
107 Hans (Virus) Lindberg .25 .50
108 Tord Lundstrom .25 .50
109 Jan-Erik Lyck .25 .50
110 Lars-Goran Nilsson .25 .50
111 Leif Olsson .25 .50
112 Lars-Ake (Sivert) Sivertsson .25 .50
113 Hakan Wickberg .25 .50
114 Lars Oberg .25 .50
115 Roland Einarsson .50 1.00
116 Peder Nilsson .50 1.00
117 Kent Olsson .50 1.00
118 Thomas Carlsson .25 .50
119 Lars-Ake Lundell .25 .50
120 Jorgen Palm .25 .50
121 Anders Rylin .25 .50
122 Billy Sundstrom .25 .50
123 Kent Soderlund .25 .50
124 Folke (Totte) Bengtsson .25 .50
125 Ake Eklof .25 .50
126 Stig Larsson .25 .50
127 Sven-Bertil Lindstrom .25 .50
128 Thomas Palm .25 .50
129 Bjorn Palmqvist .25 .50
130 Ulf Rydin .25 .50
131 Ove Svensson .25 .50
132 Per-Allan Wikstrom .25 .50
133 Anders Andren .25 .50
134 Per Lundstrom .25 .50
135 Lennart Andersson .50 1.00
136 Kent Bodin .50 1.00
137 Bjorn Fagerlund .50 1.00
138 Ake Carlsson .25 .50
139 Nils (Nicke) Johansson .25 .50
140 Lars-Goran Nilsson .25 .50
141 Kent Olsson .50 1.00
142 Hans-Ake Rosendahl .25 .50
143 Karl-Johan Sundqvist .25 .50
144 Benny Andersson .25 .50
145 Hasse Andersson .25 .50
146 Kent-Erik Andersson .25 .50
147 Berndt Augustsson .25 .50
148 Kjell Augustsson .25 .50
149 Per-Ole Backman .25 .50
150 Conny Evensson .50 1.00
151 Sten Johansson .25 .50
152 Leif Labraaten .25 .50
153 Sven-Ove (Nutte) Olsson .25 .50
154 Ulf Sterner .25 .50
155 Christer Abrahamsson 1.00 2.00
156 Krister Sterner .50 1.00
157 Thommy Abrahamsson .50 1.00
158 Karl-Gustaf Alander .25 .50
159 Gunnar Andersson .25 .50
160 Roland Bond .25 .50
161 Ake Danielsson .25 .50
162 Ulf Weinstock .25 .50
163 Per-Olov Brasar 1.00 2.00
164 Kjell Brus .25 .50
165 Hans (Jacken) Jax .25 .50
166 Dan Labraaten 1.00 2.00
167 Roger (Stoarn) Lindqvist .25 .50
168 Ulf (Marten) Martensson .25 .50
169 Stig Nordin .25 .50
170 Olle (Mapa) Sjogren .25 .50
171 Ingemar Snis .25 .50
172 Dan Soderstrom .25 .50
173 Bo Theander .30 .75
174 Mats (Matta) Ahlberg .25 .50
175 Gunnar (Backis) Backman .25 .50
176 Ivar Larsson .50 1.00
177 Sture Andersson .25 .50
178 Lage Edin .25 .50
179 Kjell-Rune (Mille) Milton .25 .50
180 Per-Olof Uusitalo .25 .50
181 Ulf Wigren .25 .50
182 Hakan Dahlof .25 .50
183 Anders Hedberg 4.00 8.00
184 Torbjorn Hubinette .25 .50
185 Assar Lundgren .25 .50
186 Per Lundqvist .25 .50
187 Christer Nilsson .25 .50
188 Kenneth Nordenberg .25 .50
189 Anders (Ante) Nordin .25 .50
190 Hakan Nygren .25 .50
191 Ulf Thors .25 .50
192 Ulf Torstensson .25 .50
193 Lars Ohman .25 .50
194 Tore Ohman .25 .50
195 Tony Esposito 17.50 35.00
196 Bobby Orr 50.00 100.00
197 Jean Beliveau 12.50 35.00
198 Gordie Howe 40.00 75.00
199 Phil Esposito 12.50 35.00
200 Bobby Hull 20.00 40.00
201 Bengt-Ake Gustavsson .50 1.00
202 Lars Gustavsson .50 1.00
203 Tommy Andersson .25 .50
204 Hans-Olov Ernlund .25 .50
205 Tord Johansson .25 .50
206 Lars Mjoberg .25 .50
207 Per-Erik (Plattis) Olsson .25 .50
208 Tord Svensson .25 .50
209 Jan (Bambis) Danielsson .25 .50
210 Tommy Eriksson .50 1.00
211 Gote Hansson .25 .50
212 Hans Hansson .25 .50
213 Sven-Ake (Saja) Jacobsson .25 .50
214 Mats (Tuppen) Lonn .25 .50
215 Borje Marcus .25 .50
216 Lars Munther .25 .50
217 Ulf Nises .25 .50
218 Anders Rosen .25 .50
219 Borje Skogs .25 .50
220 Kent Sundkvist .25 .50
221 Mikael Collin .50 1.00
222 Bjorn Jansson .50 1.00
223 Curt Larsson .50 1.00
224 Tommie Bergman 1.50 3.00
225 Arne Carlsson .25 .50
226 Christer Karlsson .25 .50
227 Eilert (Garvis) Maatta .25 .50
228 Jan Schullstrom .25 .50
229 Borje (Poppen) Burlin .25 .50
230 Hans Carlsson .25 .50
231 Tommy Carlsson .25 .50
232 Mats Hysing .25 .50
233 Bertil Jacobsson .25 .50
234 Stig-Goran Johansson .50 1.00
235 Dan Landegren .25 .50
236 Kjell Landstrom .25 .50
237 Soren Maatta .25 .50
238 Nils-Olov Schilstrom .25 .50
239 Dick Yderstrom .25 .50
240 Carl Goran (Lillstoveln) Oberg .25 .50
241 Anders Claesson .50 1.00
242 Kent Othberg .50 1.00
243 Jan Johansson .25 .50
244 Jan-Erik (Biffen) Nilsson .25 .50
245 Stefan Pettersson .25 .50
246 Tord Salomonsson .25 .50
247 Lennart Svedberg .50 1.00
248 Bo (Bulla) Berggren .25 .50
249 Bjorn Broman .25 .50
250 Lennart Broman .25 .50
251 Ove Larsson .25 .50
252 Rolf Larsson .25 .50
253 Orjan Lindstrom .25 .50
254 Arne Lundstrom .25 .50
255 Fhinn Lundstrom .25 .50
256 Ake Lundstrom .25 .50
257 Lennart Norberg .25 .50
258 Hakan Pettersson .25 .50
259 Ake (Taget) Soderberg .25 .50
260 Olle Ahman .25 .50
261 Christer Andersson .50 1.00
262 Bengt Gustavsson .25 .50
263 Goran (Klasse) Astrom .25 .50
264 Anders Brostrom .25 .50
265 Kenneth Ekman .25 .50
266 Soren Gunnarsson .25 .50
267 Lars-Erik Jacobsson .25 .50
268 Des Moroney .25 .50
269 Borje Maatta .25 .50
270 Tommy Pettersson .25 .50
271 Bengt Alm .25 .50
272 Sven Crabo .25 .50
273 Bengt (Benken) Eriksson .25 .50
274 Kurt Jakobsson .25 .50
275 Leif (Tvilling) Jakobsson .25 .50
276 Lars-Goran Johansson .25 .50
277 Bert (Berra) Karlsson .25 .50
278 Benny (Nacka) Runesson .25 .50
279 Ake Ryman .25 .50
280 Jan Roger (Joje) Strand .25 .50
281 Christer (Slim) Grahn .30 .75
282 Ronny (Centis) Sandstrom .25 .50
283 John Andersson .25 .50
284 Karl-Olov (Kalle) Eriksson .25 .50
285 Anders (Hagge) Hagstrom .25 .50
286 Ulf (Ingo) Ingvarsson .25 .50
287 Rolf Jager .25 .50
288 Erik (Jarvis) Jarvholm .25 .50
289 Bo Westling .25 .50
290 Ulf (Lill-Barre) Barrefjord .25 .50
291 Kent Bjork .25 .50
292 Lars (Dallas) Dahlgren .25 .50
293 Ulf (Pygge) Larsson .25 .50
294 Jan Lundqvist .25 .50
295 Ulf Lundstrom .25 .50
296 Bengt (Lovet) Lovgren .25 .50
297 Leif Martensson .25 .50
298 Lars-Ake (Nollan) Nordin .25 .50
299 Lars Sjostrom .25 .50
300 Kjell Sundstrom .25 .50
301 Ronny Andersson .50 1.00
302 Ingemar (Sparris) Caris .50 1.00
303 Anders (Johan) Johansson .25 .50
304 Hakan (Norsen) Norstrom .25 .50
305 Jan Olsen .25 .50
306 Lars-Erik Sjoberg .50 1.00
307 Bengt (Bengan) Sjoholm .25 .50
308 Kjell Andersson .25 .50
309 Svante Granholm .25 .50
310 Kjell-Ove Gustavsson .25 .50
311 Henrik (Tosse) Hedlund .25 .50
312 Leif (Blixten) Henriksson .25 .50
313 Lars-Erik Johansson .25 .50
314 Bjorn (Nalle) Lindberg .25 .50
315 Evert Lindstrom .25 .50
316 Willy Lindstrom 1.00 2.00
317 Leif (Nisse) Nilsson .25 .50
318 Kurt (Kulle) Olofsson .25 .50
319 Roger (Viking) Olsson .25 .50
320 Kjell-Ronnie Pettersson .25 .50
321 Kenneth Holmstedt .50 1.00
322 Lars-Erik Larsson .25 .50
323 Lennart (Sly) Eriksson .25 .50
324 Lennart Gustavsson .25 .50
325 Jan-Ake Karlsson .25 .50
326 Rolf Karlsson .25 .50

327 Bengt Lundberg .25 .50
328 Anders Thelander .25 .50
329 Kent Bengtsson .25 .50
330 Gunnar Backman .50 1.00
331 Stefan Canderyd .25 .50
332 Curt Edenvik .25 .50
333 Per Edenvik .25 .50
334 Weine Gullberg .25 .50
335 Nils-Arne Hedqvist .25 .50
336 Bengt-Ake Karlsson .25 .50
337 Christer Kihlstrom .25 .50
338 Stig-Olof (Bullen) Persson .25 .50
339 Christer Sjoberg .25 .50
340 Roddy Skyllqvist .25 .50
341 Lars Blomqvist .50 1.00
342 Bjorn Forsberg .50 1.00
343 Anders Hedlund .25 .50
344 Lennart Johansson .25 .50
345 Martin Kruger .25 .50
346 Harry Namd .25 .50
347 Lennart Strohm .25 .50
348 Peter Bejemark .25 .50
349 Bertil Bond .25 .50
350 Nils Carlsson .25 .50
351 Ulf Pilo .25 .50
352 Claes-Ove Fjallby .25 .50
353 Lars Granlund .25 .50
354 Kjell Keijser .25 .50
355 Lennart Lange .25 .50
356 Bo Mellbin .25 .50
357 Lars Starck .25 .50
358 Leif Svensson .25 .50
359 Kjell Ahlen .25 .50
360 Henry (Henna) Svensson .25 .50
361 Sven-Allan Ellstrom .50 1.00
362 Tommy Eriksson .50 1.00
363 Walter Winsth .50 1.00
364 Hans-Ake Andersson .25 .50
365 Jan Andersson .25 .50
366 Hans Bejbom .25 .50
367 Goran Borell .25 .50
368 Bo Schilstrom .25 .50
369 Bjarne Brostrom .25 .50
370 Kenneth Calen .25 .50
371 Lennart Carlsson .25 .50
372 Mats Davidsson .25 .50
373 Rolf Hansson .25 .50
374 Rune Norrstrom .25 .50
375 Gunther Rauch .25 .50
376 Jan Vestberg .25 .50
377 Bengt Wistling .25 .50
378 Kent Zetterberg .25 .50
379 Goran Akerlund .25 .50
380 Uno (Garvis) Ohrlund .25 .50
381 Goran Hogosta .60 1.50
382 Juha Raninen .50 1.00
383 Bert Backman .25 .50
384 Christer Collin .25 .50
385 Dag Olsson .25 .50
386 Bjorn Resare .25 .50
387 Lars Thoreus .25 .50
388 Stig Andersson .25 .50
389 Borje Engblom .25 .50
390 Christer Englund .25 .50
391 Bo Eriksson .25 .50
392 Mats Eriksson .25 .50
393 Roland Eriksson .25 .50
394 Olle Henriksson .25 .50
395 Yngve Hindrikes .25 .50
396 Kjell Jansson .25 .50
397 Jan Johansson .25 .50
398 Jan Karlsson .25 .50
399 Agne Norberg .25 .50
400 Christian Reuthie .25 .50

1972 Swedish Semic World Championship

Printed in Italy by Semic Press, the 233 cards comprising this set measure 1 7/8" by 2 1/2" and feature posed color player photos on their white-bordered fronts. The white back carries the player's name and text in Swedish. The cards are numbered on the back and arranged by national teams as follows: Soviet Union (1-20), Czechoslovakia (21-41), Sweden (42-70), Finland (71-92), Germany (93-117), United States (118-137), France (138-162), and Canada (163-233).

COMPLETE SET (233) 200.00 400.00
1 Viktor Konovalenko .38 .75
2 Vitalij Davydov .38 .75
3 Vladimir Lutjenko .38 .75
4 Viktor Kuskin .38 .75
5 Alexander Ragulin .75 3.00
6 Igor Romitjevskij .38 .75
7 Gennadij Tsigankov .38 .75
8 Vjatsjeslav Starsjinov .75 1.50
9 Evgenij Zimin .50 1.00
10 Alexander Maltsev 2.50 5.00
11 Anatolij Firsov 1.25 2.00
12 Evgenij Misjakov .38 .75
13 Boris Michailov 2.00 4.00
14 Juri Ljapkin .50 1.00
15 Alexander Martinyk .38 .75
16 Vladimir Petrov 2.00 4.00
17 Valeri Kharlamov 5.00 10.00
18 Vladimir Vikulov .38 .75
19 Vladimir Sjadrin .50 1.00
20 Vladislav Tretiak 10.00 20.00
21 Marcel Sakac .25 .50
22 Jiri Holecek .50 1.00
23 Josef Horesovsky .25 .50
24 Oldrich Machac .25 .50
25 Rudolf Tajcnar .25 .50
26 Frantisek Panchartek .25 .50
27 Frantisek Pospisil .38 .75
28 Jiri Kochta .25 .50
29 Jan Havel .25 .50
30 Vladimir Martinec .25 .50
31 Richard Farda .25 .50
32 Bohuslav Stastny .38 .75
33 Vaclav Nedomansky .75 1.50
34 Josef Cerny .25 .50
35 Bedrich Brunchk .25 .50
36 Jan Suchy .25 .50
37 Eduard Novak .25 .50
38 Jiri Bubla .75 1.50
39 Jiri Holik .38 .75
40 Ivan Hlinka 1.00 2.00
41 Vladimir Bednar .25 .50
42 Leif Holmqvist .50 1.00
43 Christer Abrahamsson 1.00 2.00
44 Christer Andersson .50 1.00
45 Lars-Erik Sjoberg .75 1.50
46 Lennart Svedberg .50 1.00
47 Stig-Goran Johansson .25 .50
48 Bert-Ola Nordlander .25 .50
49 Thommy Abrahamsson .50 1.00
50 Arne Carlsson .25 .50
51 Stefan Karlsson .25 .50
52 Hakan Wickberg .25 .50
53 Hakan Nygren .25 .50
54 Lars-Goran Nilsson .25 .50
55 Thommie Bergman 1.00 2.00
56 Ulf Sterner .38 .75
57 Hans Lindberg .25 .50
58 Tord Lundstrom .25 .50
59 Gunnar Andersson .25 .50
60 Bjorn Palmqvist .25 .50
61 Inge Hammarstrom 1.00 2.00
62 Kjell-Rune Milton .25 .50
63 Kjell Brus .25 .50
64 Kenneth Ekman .25 .50
65 Bengt-Goran Karlsson .25 .50
66 Hakan Pettersson .25 .50
67 Dan Labraaten .75 1.50
68 Dan Soderstrom .25 .50
69 Anders Hedberg 2.50 5.00
70 Ake Soderberg .25 .50
71 Urpo Ylonen .25 .50
72 Ilpo Koskela .25 .50
73 Seppo Lindstrom .25 .50
74 Hannu Luojola .25 .50
75 Pekka Marjamaki .25 .50
76 Jouko Oystila .25 .50
77 Heikki Jarn .25 .50
78 Esa Isaksson .25 .50
79 Veli-Pekka Ketola .75 1.50
80 Harri Linnonmaa .25 .50
81 Erkki Mononen .25 .50
82 Lauri Mononen .25 .50
83 Matti Murto .25 .50
84 Lasse Oksanen .25 .50
85 Esa Peltonen .25 .50
86 Seppo Repo .25 .50
87 Tommi Salmelainen .25 .50
88 Juhani Tamminen .25 .50
89 Jorma Vehmanen .25 .50
90 Jorma Valtonen .38 .75
91 Matti Keinonen .25 .50
92 Juha Rantasila .25 .50
93 Toni Kehle .25 .50
94 Josef Schramm .25 .50
95 Walter Stadler .25 .50
96 Josef Volk .25 .50
97 Hans Schichtl .25 .50
98 Erwin Riedmeier .25 .50
99 Werner Modes .25 .50
100 Johann Eimannsberger .25 .50
101 Karlheinz Egger .25 .50
102 Lorenz Funk, Sr. .25 .50
103 Klaus Ego .25 .50
104 Anton Hofherr .25 .50
105 Otto Schneitberger .25 .50
106 Heinz Weisenbach .25 .50
107 Alois Schloder .25 .50
108 Gustav Hanig .25 .50
109 Rainer Philipp .25 .50
110 Bernd Kuhn .25 .50
111 Paul Langner .25 .50
112 Franz Hofherr .25 .50
113 Reinhold Bauer .25 .50
114 Johann Rotkirch .25 .50
115 Walter Koberle .25 .50
116 Rainer Makatsch .25 .50
117 Carl Wetzel .38 .75
118 Mike Curran .38 .75
119 Jim McElmury .38 .75
120 Bruce Riutta .38 .75
121 Tom Mellor .38 .75
122 Don Ross .38 .75
123 Gary Gambucci .38 .75
124 Keith Christiansen .38 .75
125 Len Lilyholm .38 .75
126 Henry Boucha .75 3.00
127 Craig Falkman .38 .75
128 Tim Sheehy .38 .75
129 Kevin Ahearn .38 1.00
130 Craig Patrick 1.00 2.00
131 Pete Fichuk .38 1.00
132 George Konik .38 1.00
133 Dick McGlynn .38 1.00
134 Dick Toomey .38 1.00
135 Paul Schilling .38 1.00
136 Bob Lindberg .38 1.00
137 Dick Tomasoni .38 1.00
138 Nando Mathieu .25 .50
139 Francis Reinhard .25 .50
140 Gaston Furrer .25 .50
141 Bruno Wittwer .25 .50
142 Andre Berra .25 .50
143 Hans Keller .25 .50
144 Peter Luthi .25 .50
145 Peter Aeschlimann .25 .50
146 Werner Kuenzi .25 .50
147 Tony Neininger .25 .50
148 Jacques Pousaz .25 .50
149 Roger Chappot .25 .50
150 Charly Henzen .25 .50
151 Paul Probst .25 .50
152 Guy Dubois .25 .50
153 Rene Sgualdo .25 .50
154 Rene Hueguenin .25 .50
155 Gaston Pelletier .25 .50
156 Beat Kaufmann .25 .50
157 Alfio Molina .25 .50
158 Gerald Rigolet .25 .50
159 Harald Jones .25 .50
160 Gilbert Mathieu .25 .50
161 Michel Turler .25 .50
162 Reto Taillens .25 .50
163 Norm Ullman 1.50 5.00
164 Dave Keon 2.50 10.00
165 Roger Crozier 2.50 5.00
166 Ron Ellis 1.50 5.00
167 Paul Henderson 2.50 10.00
168 Jim Dorey .50 1.00
169 Jacques Plante 15.00 30.00
170 Jean-Guy Gendron .50 1.00
171 Gary Smith 1.50 3.00
172 Dennis Hextall .50 2.00
173 Norm Ferguson .50 1.00
174 Simon Nolet .50 1.00
175 Bernie Parent 5.00 10.00
176 Ted Hampson .50 1.00
177 Earl Ingarfield .50 1.00
178 Larry Hillman .50 2.00
179 Gary Dornhoefer 1.00 3.00
180 Gary Croteau .50 1.00
181 Carol Vadnais .50 2.00
182 Jim Roberts .50 2.00
183 Red Berenson 1.50 5.00
184 Phil Esposito 12.50 25.00
185 John McKenzie 1.00 3.00
186 Barclay Plager 1.00 3.00
187 Glenn Hall 7.50 15.00
188 Gerry Cheevers 7.50 15.00
189 Jim McKenny .50 1.00
190 Gordie Howe 25.00 50.00
191 Garry Unger 1.00 3.00
192 Roy Edwards 1.50 5.00
193 Alex Delvecchio 2.50 5.00
194 Brad Park 2.50 10.00
195 Frank Mahovlich 5.00 10.00
196 Phil Goyette .50 1.00
197 Don Marshall .50 1.00
198 Henri Richard 5.00 10.00
199 Claude Larose .50 1.00
200 Bobby Rousseau .50 1.00
201 Lorne Worsley 5.00 10.00
202 Gilles Marotte .75 1.50
203 Bob Pulford 1.50 5.00
204 Yvan Cournoyer 2.50 5.00
205 Eddie Joyal .50 1.00
206 Ross Lonsberry .50 1.00
207 Jean Beliveau 10.00 20.00
208 Jacques Lemaire 2.50 5.00
209 Orland Kurtenbach .75 1.50
210 Andre Boudrias .50 1.00
211 Jim Neilson .50 2.00
212 Walter Tkaczuk 1.00 3.00
213 Ed Giacomin 5.00 10.00
214 Jean Ratelle 2.50 5.00
215 Les Binkley 1.50 5.00
216 Jean Pronovost .50 1.00
217 Bryan Watson .50 2.00
218 Dean Prentice .50 1.00
219 Jean-Paul Parise 1.00 3.00
220 Bill Goldsworthy .75 3.00
221 Wayne Maki .50 2.00
222 Dale Tallon .75 3.00
223 Bobby Orr 37.50 75.00
224 Pit Martin .50 2.00
225 Jacques Laperriere 1.50 3.00
226 Bill Flett .50 2.00
227 Stan Mikita 7.50 15.00
228 Bobby Hull 15.00 30.00
229 Larry Pleau .50 2.00
230 Keith Magnuson 1.00 2.00
231 Tony Esposito 7.50 15.00
232 Rogatien Vachon 4.00 10.00
233 Mickey Redmond 7.50 15.00

1972-73 Swedish Stickers

This 300-sticker set was issued in Sweden by Williams Forlags AB for the 1972-73 season. While the majority of the set is taken up by players from the Swedish Elitserien, there also are stickers featuring stars from Russia, Czechoslovakia, Finland and the NHL. Key stickers include pre-NHL appearances from Anders Hedberg, Borje Salming and Ulf Nilsson. NHL stars such as Bobby Orr, Ken Dryden and Bobby Hull also are featured, along with Soviet greats such as Tretiak and Kharlamov. The card fronts feature a posed color photo, while the backs have the sticker number and player information in Swedish. A book to hold the stickers was available at the time for 3.5 kroner, or about fifty cents. It is filled with stories about the teams, league schedules and photos, along with spaces for the stickers. It is valued now at $25. The prices below are for unused stickers; because it was the habit then to put them in the album, relatively few remain in their original state.

COMPLETE SET (300) 150.00 300.00
1 Christer Abrahamsson 1.00 2.00
2 Leif Holmqvist .50 1.00
3 Tommy Abrahamsson .50 1.00
4 Thommie Bergman 1.00 2.00
5 Bjorn Johansson .25 .50
6 Kjell-Rune Milton .25 .50
7 Borje Salming 5.00 10.00
8 Lars-Erik Sjoberg 1.00 2.00
9 Karl-Johan Sundqvist .25 .50
10 Stig Ostling .25 .50
11 Inge Hammarstrom 1.00 2.00
12 Anders Hedberg 2.50 5.00
13 Stig-Goran Johansson .25 .50
14 Stefan Karlsson .25 .50
15 Hans Lindberg .25 .50
16 Mats Lindh .25 .50
17 Tord Lundstrom .25 .50
18 Lars-Goran Nilsson .25 .50
19 Bjorn Palmqvist .25 .50
20 Hakan Wickberg .25 .50
21 Jiri Holecek .50 1.00
22 Josef Horesovsky .25 .50
23 Frantisek Pospisil .38 .75
24 Jaroslav Holik .25 .50
25 Jiri Holik .38 .75
26 Vaclav Nedomansky 1.00 2.00
27 Vladislav Tretiak 10.00 20.00
28 Gennadi Tsigankov .38 .75
29 Igor Romisjevskij .38 .75
30 Valeri Kharlamov 5.00 10.00
31 Alexander Maltsev 2.50 5.00
32 Vladimir Vikulov .38 .75
33 Jorma Valtonen .38 .75
34 Pekka Marjamaki .25 .50
35 Matti Keinonen .25 .50
36 Veli-Pekka Ketola 1.00 2.00
37 Lauri Mononen .25 .50
38 Lasse Oksanen .25 .50
39 Krister Sterner .50 1.00
40 Sten-Ake Bark .25 .50
41 Jan-Erik Silfverberg .25 .50
42 Steffan Andersson .25 .50
43 Roland Eriksson .25 .50
44 Gunnar Johansson .25 .50
45 Jiri Holecek .50 1.00
46 Thommie Bergman 1.00 2.00
47 Josef Horesovsky .25 .50
48 Vladimir Vikulov .38 .75
49 Alexander Maltsev 2.50 5.00
50 Valeri Kharlamov 5.00 10.00
51 Leif Holmqvist .50 1.00
52 Lars Danielsson .25 .50
53 Ake Fagerstrom .25 .50
54 Per-Arne Hubinette .25 .50
55 Hakan Lindgren .25 .50
56 Bert-Ola Nordlander .25 .50
57 Bo Olofsson .25 .50
58 Soren Sjogren .25 .50
59 Jan Olsson .25 .50
60 Lennart Selinder .25 .50
61 Jan Olof Kroon .25 .50
62 Rolf Edberg .25 .50
63 Ulf Nilsson 2.50 5.00
64 Leif Holmgren .25 .50
65 Jan Ostling .25 .50
66 Christer Grahn .50 1.00
67 Karl-Olov Grahn .50 1.00
68 Anders Hagstrom .25 .50
69 Erik Jarvholm .25 .50
70 Bo Westling .25 .50
71 Ulf Ingvarsson .25 .50
72 Bengt Lovgren .25 .50
73 Kjell Sundstrom .25 .50
74 Kent Bjork .25 .50
75 Ulf Lundstrom .25 .50
76 Mats Lundmark .25 .50
77 Ulf Barrefjord .25 .50
78 Lars Dahlgren .25 .50
79 Olle Nilsson .25 .50
80 Roger Nilsson .25 .50
81 Willie Lofqvist .50 1.00
82 Jan-Erik Silfverberg .25 .50
83 Kjell Johnsson .25 .50
84 Jan-Olof Svensson .25 .50
85 Stig Salming .25 .50
86 Borje Salming 5.00 10.00
87 Stig Ostling .25 .50
88 Tord Lundstrom .25 .50
89 Inge Hammarstrom 1.00 2.00
90 Lars-Goran Nilsson .25 .50
91 Hans Lindberg .25 .50
92 Hakan Wickberg .25 .50
93 Jan-Erik Lyck .25 .50
94 Stefan Karlsson .25 .50
95 Lars Oberg .25 .50
96 Roland Einarsson .50 1.00
97 Billy Sundstrom .25 .50
98 Anders Rylin .25 .50
99 Tomas Carlsson .25 .50
100 Ulf Ojerklint .25 .50
101 L-A Gustavsson .50 1.00
102 Jorgen Palm .25 .50
103 Lars-Ake Lundell .25 .50
104 Ake Eklof .25 .50
105 Bengt-Ake Karlsson .25 .50
106 Bjorn Palmqvist .25 .50
107 Per-Allan Wickstrom .25 .50
108 Sven-Bertil Lindstrom .25 .50
109 Totte Bengtsson .25 .50
110 Stig Larsson .25 .50
111 Ken Dryden 20.00 40.00

112 Jacques Laperriere 1.50 3.00
113 Bobby Orr 37.50 75.00
114 Brad Park 2.50 5.00
115 Phil Esposito 10.00 20.00
116 Rod Gilbert 2.50 5.00
117 Vic Hadfield 1.50 3.00
118 Bobby Hull 15.00 30.00
119 Frank Mahovlich 5.00 10.00
120 Jean Ratelle 2.50 5.00
121 Lennart Andersson .50 1.00
122 Karl-Johan Sundqvist .25 .50
123 Nicke Johansson .25 .50
124 Lars-Goran Nilsson .25 .50
125 Ake Carlsson .25 .50
126 Hans-Ake Rosendahl .25 .50
127 Sten-Ake Bark .25 .50
128 Par Backman .25 .50
129 Leif Labraaten .25 .50
130 Berndt Augustsson .25 .50
131 Uffe Sterner .25 .50
132 Benny Andersson .25 .50
133 Conny Evensson .50 1.00
134 Kjell Augustsson .25 .50
135 Hans Andersson .25 .50
136 Kenneth Holmstedt .50 1.00
137 Lennart Gustavsson .25 .50
138 Lennart Eriksson .25 .50
139 Rolf Carlsson .25 .50
140 Bengt Lundberg .25 .50
141 Jan-Ake Karlsson .25 .50
142 Curt Edenvik .25 .50
143 Per Edenvik .25 .50
144 Weine Gullberg .25 .50
145 Gunnar Backman .50 1.00
146 Roddy Skyllqvist .25 .50
147 Stefan Canderyd .25 .50
148 Christer Kihlstrom .25 .50
149 Nils-Arne Hedqvist .25 .50
150 Stig-Olof Persson .25 .50
151 Christer Abrahamsson 1.00 2.00
152 Thommy Abrahamsson .50 1.00
153 Roland Bond .25 .50
154 Gunnar Andersson .25 .50
155 Ulf Weinstock .25 .50
156 Ake Danielsson .25 .50
157 Peter Gudmundsson .25 .50
158 Olle Sjogren .25 .50
159 Hans Jax .25 .50
160 Mats Ahlberg .25 .50
161 Dan Labraaten 1.00 2.00
162 Ulf Martensson .25 .50
163 Kjell Brus .25 .50
164 Dan Soderstrom .25 .50
165 Per Olof Brasar 1.00 2.00
166 Ivar Larsson .50 1.00
167 Sture Andersson .25 .50
168 Lage Edin .25 .50
169 Kjell Rune Milton .25 .50
170 Ulf Wigren .25 .50
171 Hakan Dahllof .25 .50
172 Anders Hedberg 2.50 5.00
173 Assar Lundgren .25 .50
174 Christer Nilsson .25 .50
175 Anders Nordin .25 .50
176 Hakan Nygren .25 .50
177 Ulf Thors .25 .50
178 Ulf Torstensson .25 .50
179 Lasse Ohman .25 .50
180 Tore Ohman .25 .50
181 Bengt Ake Gustafsson .38 .75
182 Tommy Andersson .25 .50
183 Hans-Olof Ernlund .25 .50
184 Tord Johansson .25 .50
185 Tord Svensson .25 .50
186 Jan Danielsson .25 .50
187 Tommy Eriksson .50 1.00
188 Gote Hansson .25 .50
189 Hans Hansson .25 .50
190 Sven-Ake Jacobsson .25 .50
191 Mats Lonn .25 .50
192 Lars Mjoberg .25 .50
193 Lars Munther .25 .50
194 Ulf Nises .25 .50
195 Borje Skogs .25 .50
196 Roland Lestander .25 .50
197 Bosse Andersson .25 .50
198 Hakan Dahlin .25 .50
199 Martin Johansson .25 .50
200 Anders Lindberg .25 .50
201 Lars-Fredrik Nystrom .25 .50
202 Hans Gunnar Skarin .25 .50
203 Jerry Aberg .25 .50
204 Anders Almqvist .25 .50
205 Christer Johansson .25 .50
206 Per Johansson .25 .50
207 Martin Karlsson .25 .50
208 Lars-Gunnar Lundberg .25 .50
209 Hardy Nilsson .25 .50
210 Kjell-Arne Wikstrom .25 .50
211 Mikael Collin .50 1.00
212 Curt Larsson .50 1.00
213 Arne Carlsson .25 .50
214 Bjorn Johansson .25 .50
215 Nils-Olov Schilstrom .25 .50
216 Jan Schullstrom .25 .50
217 Borje Burlin .25 .50
218 Hans Carlsson .25 .50
219 Mats Hysing .25 .50
220 Bertil Jacobsson .25 .50
221 Stisse Johansson .25 .50
222 Dan Landegren .25 .50
223 Kjell Landstrom .25 .50
224 Dick Yderstrom .25 .50
225 Carl-Goran Oberg .25 .50
226 Christer Sehlstedt .25 .50
227 Tommie Lindgren .25 .50
228 Jan-Erik Nilsson .25 .50
229 Stefan Pettersson .25 .50
230 Tord Nansen .25 .50
231 Bo Berggren .25 .50
232 Bjorn Broman .25 .50
233 Ove Larsson .25 .50
234 Kent Lindgren .25 .50
235 Orjan Lindstrom .25 .50
236 Lennart Norberg .25 .50
237 Arne Lundstrom .25 .50
238 Hakan Pettersson .25 .50
239 Ake Soderberg .25 .50
240 Olle Ahman .25 .50
241 Christer Andersson 1.00 2.00
242 Anders Brostrom .25 .50
243 Kenneth Ekman .25 .50
244 Soren Gunnarsson .25 .50
245 Borje Maatta .25 .50
246 Tommy Pettersson .25 .50
247 Kurt Jakobsson .25 .50
248 Leif Jakobsson .25 .50
249 Lars-Goran Johansson .25 .50
250 Bengt-Goran Karlsson .25 .50
251 Berndt Karlsson .25 .50
252 Tadeusz Niedomyst .25 .50
253 Benny Runesson .25 .50
254 Ake Ryman .25 .50
255 Jan-Roger Strand .25 .50
256 Goran Hogosta .50 1.00
257 Bert Backman .25 .50
258 Christer Collin .25 .50
259 Bo Eriksson .25 .50
260 Hakan Norstrom .25 .50
261 Lars Thoreus .25 .50
262 Stig Andersson .25 .50
263 Mats Eriksson .25 .50
264 Roland Eriksson .25 .50
265 Kjell Fhinn .25 .50
266 Olle Henriksson .25 .50
267 Yngve Hindrikes .25 .50
268 Jan Karlsson .25 .50
269 Kjell Jansson .25 .50
270 Ingemar Snis .25 .50
271 Christer Stahl .25 .50
272 Leif Andersson .25 .50
273 Tommy Eriksson .50 1.00
274 Christer Holmstrom .25 .50
275 Curt Lundmark 1.00 2.00
276 Dennis Pettersson .25 .50
277 Ove Thelin .25 .50
278 Bo Wahlberg .25 .50
279 Gote Gustavsson .25 .50
280 Christer Lindgren .25 .50
281 Kent Persson .25 .50
282 Par Marts .25 .50
283 Ove Stenlund .25 .50
284 Bo Olsson .25 .50
285 Bo Astrom .25 .50
286 Ronny Andersson .50 1.00
287 Roger Bergman .25 .50
288 Thommie Bergman 1.00 2.00
289 Anders Johansson .25 .50
290 Jan Olsen .25 .50
291 Lars Erik Sjoberg 1.00 2.00
292 Kjell Andersson .25 .50
293 Svante Granholm .25 .50
294 Henrik Hedlund .25 .50
295 Leif Henriksson .25 .50
296 Mats Lindh .25 .50
297 Evert Lindstrom .25 .50
298 Willy Lindstrom 1.00 2.00
299 Roger Olsson .25 .50
300 Kjell-Ronnie Pettersson .25 .50

1973-74 Swedish Stickers

This 243-sticker set was produced in Sweden by Williams Forlags AB. It features players from the top Swedish league, as well as several Russian teams. The set includes such legendary figures as Valeri Kharlamov, Vladislav Tretiak and a rare card of notorious head coach Vselvolod Bobrov. The fronts feature a color player photo, while the backs have sticker number and information in Swedish. There was an album available to store the set; it currently retails for around $20.

COMPLETE SET (243) 100.00 175.00
1 Christer Abrahamsson 1.00 2.00
2 William Lofqvist .50 1.00
3 Arne Karlsson .25 .50
4 Lars-Erik Sjoberg 1.00 2.00
5 Bjorn Johansson .25 .50
6 Thommy Abrahamsson .50 1.00
7 Borje Salming 5.00 10.00
8 Karl Johan Sundqvist .25 .50
9 Ulf Sterner .25 .50
10 Ulf Nilsson 2.50 5.00
11 Kjell-Arne Wickstrom .25 .50
12 Inge Hammarstrom 2.50 5.00
13 Hakan Wickberg .25 .50
14 Tord Lundstrom .25 .50
15 Dan Soderstrom .25 .50
16 Mats Ahlberg .50 1.00
17 Anders Hedberg 2.50 5.00
18 Dick Yderstrom .30 .75
19 Stefan Karlsson .25 .50
20 Roland Bond .25 .50
21 Kjell-Rune Milton .25 .50
22 Willy Lindstrom .75 1.50
23 Kurt Carlsson .30 .75
24 Mats Walltin .25 .50
25 Roland Eriksson .25 .50
26 Martin Karlsson .25 .50
27 Jiri Holecek .50 1.00
28 Josef Horesovsky .25 .50
29 Oldrich Machac .25 .50
30 Vladimir Martinec .50 1.00
31 Vaclav Nedomansky .75 1.50
32 Jiri Kochta .25 .50
33 Jorma Waltonen .50 1.00
34 Heikki Riihiranta .50 1.00
35 Lauri Mononen .25 .50
36 Timo Turunen .25 .50
37 Matti Keinonen .25 .50
38 Seppo Repo .25 .50
39 Christer Abrahamsson .75 1.50
40 Lars Stenvall .25 .50
41 Per Karlsson .25 .50
42 Roland Bond .25 .50
43 Thommy Abrahamsson .50 1.00
44 Ulf Weinstock .25 .50
45 Gunnar Andersson .25 .50
46 Hans Eriksson .25 .50
47 Peter Gudmundsson .25 .50
48 Mats Ahlberg .50 1.00
49 Per-Olov Brasar .75 1.50
50 Roger Lindqvist .25 .50
51 Dan Soderstrom .25 .50
52 Ulf Martensson .25 .50
53 Kjell Brus .25 .50
54 Hans Jax .25 .50
55 Dan Labraaten .75 1.50
56 Nils-Olov Olsson .25 .50
57 Stig Nordin .25 .50
58 Bo Theander .25 .50
59 Curt Larsson .50 1.00
60 Mikael Collin .50 1.00
61 Arne Carlsson .25 .50
62 Leif Svensson .25 .50
63 Sverker Torstensson .25 .50
64 Bjorn Johansson .25 .50
65 Stisse Johansson .25 .50
66 Carl-Goran Oberg .25 .50
67 Mats Hysing .25 .50
68 Mats Walltin .25 .50
69 Hans Carlsson .25 .50
70 Nils-Olov Schilstrom .25 .50
71 Kjell-Arne Wickstrom .25 .50
72 Jan Schullstrom .25 .50
73 Borje Burlin .25 .50
74 Dick Yderstrom .30 .75
75 Dan Landegren .25 .50
76 Kjell Landstrom .25 .50
77 Vladislav Tretjak 10.00 20.00
78 Alexander Sidelnikov 1.00 2.00
79 Alexander Ragulin 1.25 2.50
80 Vladimir Luttjenko 1.00 2.00
81 Gennadij Tsygankov .75 1.50
82 Alexander Gusev .50 1.00
83 Jevgenij Poladiev .30 .75
84 Jurij Liapkin .75 1.50
85 Valerij Vasiljev 1.50 3.00
86 Boris Michailov 2.50 5.00
87 Valeri Kharlamov 5.00 10.00
88 Vladimir Petrov 2.50 5.00
89 Alexander Maltsev 2.50 5.00
90 Vladimir Sjadrin 1.25 2.50
91 Alexander Yakusjev 2.50 5.00
92 Alexander Martynjuk .30 .75
93 Vjateslav Anissin .50 1.00
94 Jurij Lebedev 1.00 2.00
95 Alexander Bodunov .50 1.00
96 Alexander Volchkov 1.00 2.00
97 Vsevolod Bobrov 2.00 4.00
98 Konstantin Loktev .25 .50
99 Anatolij Firsov 1.50 3.00
100 Viktor Kuzkin .50 1.00
101 Jurij Blochin .25 .50
102 Vladimir Vikulov .50 1.00
103 Jurij Blinov .50 1.00
104 Jevgenij Misjakov 1.00 2.00
105 Vladimir Trunov .25 .50
106 Sergej Glazov .25 .50
107 Vladimir Popov .75 1.50
108 Viktor Zinger .50 1.00
109 Viktor Krivolapov .30 .75
110 Jevgenij Kazatjkin .25 .50
111 Viktor Korotkov .75 1.50
112 Valentin Markov .25 .50
113 Alexander Sapjolkin .25 .50
114 Leonid Borzov .25 .50
115 Gennadij Krylov .25 .50
116 Konstantin Klimov .25 .50
117 Jevgenij Zimin .50 1.00
118 Vladimir Gurejev .25 .50
119 Viktor Jaroslavtsev .25 .50
120 Alexander Pasjkov .30 .75
121 Vladimir Polupanov .50 1.00
122 Vitalij Davydov .75 1.50
123 Michail Alexeenko .25 .50
124 Alexander Filippov .50 1.00
125 Valerij Nazarov .25 .50
126 Vladimir Orlov .25 .50
127 Stanislav Sjtjegolev .25 .50
128 Anatolij Bjelonozjkin .25 .50
129 Vladimir Devjatov .25 .50
130 Jevgenij Kotlov .25 .50
131 Anatolij Motovilov .25 .50
132 Jurij Reps .25 .50
133 Igor Samotjernov .25 .50
134 Alexander Sevidov .25 .50
135 Viktor Sjilov .25 .50
136 Jurij Tjitjurin .30 .75
137 Sune Odling .25 .50
138 Lars-Erik Sjoberg 1.00 2.00
139 Bengt Sjoholm .25 .50
140 Leif Henriksson .25 .50
141 Henric Hedlund .25 .50
142 Roger Olsson .25 .50
143 Kjell-Rune Milton .25 .50
144 Kjell-Ronnie Pettersson .25 .50
145 Svante Granholm .25 .50
146 Kjell Andersson .25 .50
147 Lars-Erik Esbjorn .25 .50
148 Bjorn Lindberg .25 .50
149 Willy Lindstrom .75 1.50
150 Evert Lindstrom .25 .50
151 Lars-Erik Johansson .25 .50
152 Krister Sterner .30 .75
153 Mats Lindh .25 .50
154 Roger Bergman .25 .50
155 Willie Lofqvist .50 1.00
156 Jan Olov Svensson .25 .50
157 Jan Erik Silfverberg .25 .50
158 Stig Ostling .50 1.00
159 Kjell Johansson .25 .50
160 Borje Salming 5.00 10.00
161 Stig Salming .50 1.00
162 Tord Lundstrom .25 .50
163 Hakan Wickberg .25 .50
164 Inge Hammarstrom 2.50 5.00
165 Lars Goran Nilsson .25 .50
166 Jan Erik Lyck .25 .50
167 Stefan Karlsson .25 .50
168 Lennart Lind .50 1.00
169 Hans Ake Persson .25 .50
170 Lars Oberg .25 .50
171 Lars Erik Eriksson .25 .50
172 Bjorn Fagerlund .30 .75
173 Nicke Johansson .25 .50
174 Lars Goran Nilsson .25 .50
175 Hans Erik Jansson .25 .50
176 Per Backman .25 .50
177 Jorgen Palm .25 .50
178 Conny Evensson .30 .75
179 Ulf Sterner .25 .50
180 Sven Ake Rudby .25 .50
181 Lennart Andersson .30 .75
182 Kent Erik Andersson .25 .50
183 Hans Ake Rosendahl .25 .50
184 Karl Johan Sundqvist .25 .50
185 Hasse Andersson .25 .50
186 Benny Andersson .25 .50
187 Gunnar Johansson .25 .50
188 Sten Ake Bark .25 .50
189 Lasse Zetterstrom .25 .50
190 Leif Holmqvist .50 1.00
191 Bert Jattne .50 1.00
192 Lars Danielsson .50 1.00
193 Hakan Lindgren .25 .50
194 Ake Fagerstrom .25 .50
195 Bert-Ola Nordlander .30 .75
196 Leif Holmgren .25 .50
197 Soren Sjogren .25 .50
198 Hans Lindberg .25 .50
199 Jan-Olov Kroon .25 .50
200 Rolf Edberg .25 .50
201 Lennart Selinder .50 1.00
202 Ulf Nilsson 2.50 5.00
203 Jan Olsson .25 .50
204 Jan Ostling .25 .50
205 Christer Lundberg .25 .50
206 Christer Englund .25 .50
207 Bo Olofsson .25 .50
208 Roland Einarsson .50 1.00
209 Ake Danielsson .25 .50
210 Billy Sundstrom .25 .50
211 Thomas Carlsson .25 .50
212 Stig Larsson .25 .50
213 Lars Ake Gustavsson .50 1.00
214 Bjorn Palmqvist .25 .50
215 Anders Hedberg 2.50 5.00
216 Anders Rylin .25 .50
217 Sven Bertil Lindstrom .25 .50
218 Kjell Nilsson .25 .50
219 Claes Goran Wallin .25 .50
220 Ake Eklof .25 .50
221 Peder Nilsson .30 .75
222 Lars Ake Lundell .25 .50
223 Bengt Ake Karlsson .25 .50
224 Ove Svensson .25 .50
225 Soren Johansson .25 .50
226 Christer Sehlstedt .30 .75
227 Lage Edin .25 .50
228 Tommy Andersson .25 .50
229 Janerik Nilsson .25 .50
230 Tommie Lindgren .25 .50
231 Bo Bergman .25 .50
232 Lennart Norberg .25 .50
233 Olle Ahman .25 .50
234 Arne Lundstrom .30 .75
235 Kent Lindgren .25 .50
236 Orjan Lindstrom .25 .50
237 Kent Othberg .30 .75
238 Finn Lundstrom .25 .50
239 Ake Soderberg .25 .50
240 Jan Kock .25 .50
241 Ove Larsson .25 .50
242 Hakan Pettersson .25 .50
243 Stefan Pettersson .25 .50

1974 Swedish Semic World Championship Stickers

This 100-sticker set featuring World Championship players was produced by Semic of Sweden. The stickers measure approximately 2" by 3", and were designed to be placed on one of four team-specific posters. The cards were issued in sheets of two.

COMPLETE SET (100)	40.00	80.00
1 Christer Abrahamsson	.75	1.50
2 William Lofqvist	.50	1.00
3 Arne Carlsson	.25	.50
4 Lars-Erik Sjoberg	1.00	2.00
5 Bjorn Johansson	.25	.50
6 Tommy Abrahamsson	.50	1.00
7 Karl-Johan Sundqvist	.25	.50
8 Ulf Nilsson	2.00	4.00
9 Hakan Wickberg	.25	.50
10 Dan Soderstrom	.25	.50
11 Mats Ahlberg	.30	.75
12 Anders Hedberg	2.00	4.00
13 Dick Yderstrom	.25	.50
14 Stefan Karlsson	.25	.50
15 Roland Bond	.25	.50
16 Kjell-Rune Milton	.25	.50
17 Willy Lindstrom	.50	1.00
18 Mats Waltin	.25	.50
19 Lars-Goran Nilsson	.25	.50
20 Bjorn Palmquist	.25	.50
21 Stig-Goran Johansson	.25	.50
22 Bo Berggren	.25	.50
23 Dan Labraaten	.75	1.50
24 Curt Larsson	.30	.75
25 Mats Lindh	.25	.50
26 Vladislav Tretiak	7.50	15.00
27 Alexander Ragulin	.50	1.00
28 Vladimir Luttjenko	.50	1.00
29 Gennadij Tsygankov	.50	1.00
30 Alexander Gusev	.50	1.00
31 Jevgenij Poladiev	.25	.50
32 Jurij Ljapkin	.50	1.00
33 Boris Michailov	2.00	4.00
34 Valeri Kharlamov	3.00	10.00
35 Vladimir Petrov	2.00	3.00
36 Alexander Maltsev	2.00	4.00
37 Vladimir Sjadrin	.30	.75
38 Alexander Yakusjev	2.00	4.00
39 Alexander Martynjuk	.30	.75
40 Jurij Lebedev	.75	1.50
41 Alexander Bodunov	.50	1.00
42 Anatolij Firsov	.75	1.50
43 Vitalij Davydov	.30	.75
44 Vjateslav Starsjinov	.30	.75
45 Viktor Kuzkin	.25	.50
46 Igor Romitjevskij	.25	.50
47 Jevgenij Zimin	.30	.75
48 Jevgenij Misjakov	.50	1.00
49 Vladimir Vikulov	.30	.75
50 Viktor Konovalenko	.50	1.00
51 Jiri Holecek	.50	1.00
52 Frantisek Pospisil	.30	.75
53 Jiri Bubla	.50	1.00
54 Josef Horesovsky	.25	.50
55 Oldrich Machac	.25	.50
56 Vladimir Martinec	.25	.50
57 Vaclav Nedomansky	.75	1.50
58 Jiri Kochta	.25	.50
59 Milan Novy	.50	1.00
60 Jaroslav Holik	.30	.75
61 Jiri Holik	.50	1.00
62 Jiri Klapac	.25	.50
63 Richard Farda	.30	.75
64 Bohuslav Stastny	.30	.75
65 Jiri Novak	.25	.50
66 Ivan Hlinka	.30	.75
67 Jan Suchy	.30	.75
68 Vladimir Bednar	.25	.50
69 Rudolf Tajcnar	.25	.50
70 Josef Cerny	.25	.50
71 Jan Havel	.30	.75
72 Marcel Sakac	.25	.50
73 Frantisek Pancharek	.25	.50
74 Bedrich Brunchk	.25	.50
75 Edvard Novak	.25	.50
76 Jorma Valtonen	.50	1.00
77 Seppo Lindstrom	.25	.50
78 Pekka Marjamaki	.25	.50
79 Pekka Rautakallio	.75	1.50
80 Heikki Riihiranta	.50	1.00
81 Seppo Suoraniemi	.25	.50
82 Jouko Oystila	.25	.50
83 Veli-Pekka Ketola	.75	1.50
84 Henry Leppa	.25	.50
85 Harri Linnonmaa	.25	.50
86 Matti Murto	.25	.50
87 Lasse Oksanen	.25	.50
88 Esa Peltonen	.25	.50
89 Seppo Repo	.25	.50
90 Raimo Suoniemi	.25	.50
91 Timo Sutinen	.25	.50
92 Juhani Tamminen	.50	1.00
93 Leo Seppanen	.25	.50
94 Hannu Haapalainen	.25	.50
95 Pertti Valkeapaa	.25	.50
96 Sakari Ahlberg	.25	.50
97 Antti Leppanen	.25	.50
98 Kalevi Numminen	.25	.50
99 Lauri Mononen	.25	.50
100 Ilpo Koskela	.30	.75
NNO Ulf Nilsson poster		
NNO Valeri Kharlamov poster		
NNO Vaclav Nedomansky poster		
NNO Timo Sutinen poster		

1974-75 Swedish Stickers

This set of 324 stickers commemorates the competitors on the 1974-75 World Championship, along with players from club teams across Europe. The stickers -- which measure approximately 3" by 2" -- feature action photography on the front, with player name and card number along the bottom. The backs have the set logo, a reprise of the card number and encouragement in Swedish to build the entire set. The last six cards were recently identified by Swedish collector Per Vedin.

COMPLETE SET (324)	100.00	175.00
1 Vladislav Tretiak	7.50	15.00
2 Gennadij Tsigannkov	.50	1.00
3 Valerij Vasiljev	1.50	3.00
4 Alexander Gusev	.50	1.00
5 Valeri Kharlamov	3.00	10.00
6 Vladimir Petrov	2.00	4.00
7 Boris Michailov	2.00	4.00
8 Alexander Maltsev	2.00	4.00
9 Alexander Yakusjev	2.00	4.00
10 Jiri Chra	1.50	3.00
11 Jiri Bubla	.50	1.00
12 Milan Kuzela	.25	.50
13 Oldrich Machac	.25	.50
14 Ivan Hlinka	.50	1.00
15 Vaclav Nedomansky	.75	1.50
16 Boshulav Stastny	.75	1.50
17 Vladimir Martinec	.25	.50
18 Richard Farda	.25	.50
19 Curt Larsson	.30	.75
20 Lars-Erik Sjoberg	1.00	2.00
21 Thommy Abrahamsson	.50	1.00
22 Kjell-Rune Milton	.25	.50
23 Anders Hedberg	2.00	4.00
24 Mats Ahlberg	.30	.75
25 Dan Soderstrom	.25	.50
26 Ulf Nilsson	2.00	4.00
27 Per-Olof Brassar	.75	1.50
28 Stig Wetzell	.25	.50
29 Juha Rantasila	.25	.50
30 Heikki Riihiranta	.50	1.00
31 Timo Saari	.25	.50
32 Seppo Repo	.25	.50
33 Esa Peltonen	.25	.50
34 Juhani Tamminen	.50	1.00
35 Matti Murto	.25	.50
36 Harri Linnonmaa	.25	.50
37 Gennadij Lapsjenkov	.50	1.00
38 Pjotr Zjulin	.25	.50
39 Vladimir Merinov	.25	.50
40 Sergej Tyznych	1.00	2.00
41 Valerij Kostin	.25	.50
42 Valerij Nikitin	.50	1.00
43 Sergej Gusev	.50	1.00
44 Valentin Kozin	.25	.50
45 Viktor Liksiutkin	.25	.50
46 Alexander Golikov	.50	1.00
47 Viktor Zhluktov	.50	1.00
48 Anatolij Frolov	.75	1.50
49 Vladimir Golikov	1.00	2.00
50 Nikolaj Epstein	.25	.50
51 Alexander Kasjajev	.25	.50
52 Alexander Sidelnikov	1.00	2.00
53 Valerij Kuzmin	.50	1.00
54 Viktor Kuznetsov	.50	1.00
55 Jurij Terechin	.30	.75
56 Jurij Tjitjurin	.30	.75
57 Jurij Sjatavalov	.30	.75
58 Vjatjeslav Anissin	.30	.75
59 Alexander Bodunov	.50	1.00
60 Jurij Lebedev	.75	1.50
61 Igor Dmitriev	2.00	4.00
62 Konstantin Klimov	.30	.75
63 Sergej Kapustin	.30	.75
64 Vladimir Repnjov	.30	.75
65 Jevgenij Kucharzj	.30	.75
66 Boris Kulagin	1.00	2.00
67 Viktor Afonin	.25	.50
68 Juris Liberts	.30	.75
69 Igor Kobzev	.30	.75
70 Valerij Odintsov	.30	.75
71 Vjatjeslav Nazarov	.50	1.00
72 Andris Hendelis	.30	.75
73 Alexander Sokolovskij	.30	.75
74 Michail Denisov	.30	.75
75 Helmut Balderis	2.00	4.00
76 Vladimir Sorokin	.25	.50
77 Vladimir Sernjajev	.25	.50
78 Viktor Veriznikov	.25	.50
79 Vladimir Markov	.25	.50
80 Viktor Tichonov	2.50	5.00
81 Edgar Rosenberg	.25	.50
82 Alexander Kotomkin	.25	.50
83 Vladimir Astafjev	.50	1.00
84 Alexander Kulikov	.25	.50
85 Sergej Mosjkarov	.25	.50
86 Vjatjeslav Usjmakov	.25	.50
87 Jurij Fjodorov	.50	1.00
88 Victor Dobrochotov	.25	.50
89 Vitalij Krajov	.25	.50
90 Alexej Masjin	.25	.50
91 Vladimir Orlov	.25	.50
92 Vladimir Smagin	.25	.50
93 Alexander Usov	.25	.50
94 Alexander Fedotov	.50	1.00
95 Alexander Prilepskij	.25	.50
96 Alexander Rogov	.25	.50
97 Seppo Ahokainen	.25	.50
98 Lasse Oksanen	.25	.50
99 Jorma Peltonen	.50	1.00
100 Henry Leppa	.25	.50
101 Seppo Suoraniemi	.25	.50
102 Timi Sutinen	.25	.50
103 Jorma Valtonen	.50	1.00
104 Antti Leppanen	.25	.50
105 Pekka Marjamaki	.25	.50
106 Juoko Oystila	.25	.50
107 Seppo Lindstrom	.25	.50
108 Veli-Pekka Ketola	.75	1.50
109 Jiri Holecek	.50	1.00
110 Jiri Kochta	.25	.50
111 Josef Horesovsky	.25	.50
112 Jaroslav Sima	.25	.50
113 Frantisek Vorlicek	.25	.50
114 Vladimir Kostka	.25	.50
115 Jaroslav Holik	.30	.75
116 Jiri Holik	.50	1.00
117 Jan Suchy	.30	.75
118 Josef Augusta,	.25	.50
119 Miroslav Dvorak	.50	1.00
120 Jan Hrbaty	.25	.50
121 AIK	.25	.50
122 If Bjorkloven	.25	.50
123 Brynas IF	.25	.50
124 Djurgardens IF	.25	.50
125 Farjestads BK	.25	.50
126 IF Karlskoga	.25	.50
127 Leksands IF	.25	.50
128 MoDo AIK	.25	.50
129 Mora IK	.25	.50
130 Skelleftea AIK	.25	.50
131 Sodertalje SK	.25	.50
132 Timra IK	.25	.50
133 Tingsryds AIF	.25	.50
134 V. Frolunda IF	.25	.50
135 Vasteras IK	.25	.50
136 Orebro IK	.25	.50
137 Christer Abrahamsson	.75	1.50
138 Christer Andersson	.25	.50
139 Mikael Collin	.50	1.00
140 Bjorn Fagerlund	.25	.50
141 Christer Grahn	.50	1.00
142 Kenneth Holmstedt	.25	.50
143 Goran Hogosta	.50	1.00
144 Bert Jattne	.25	.50
145 Curt Larsson	.30	.75
146 Ivar Larsson	.25	.50
147 Wille Lofqvist	.50	1.00
148 Peder Nilsson	.25	.50
149 Christer Sehlstedt	.25	.50
150 Krister Sterner	.30	.75
151 Christer Stahl	.25	.50
152 Sune Odling	.25	.50
153 Thommy Abrahamsson	.50	1.00
154 Gunnar Andersson	.25	.50
155 Jan Andersson	.25	.50
156 Leif Andersson	.25	.50
157 Sture Andersson	.25	.50
158 Tommy Andersson	.25	.50
159 Sten Ake Bark	.25	.50
160 Roger Bergman	.25	.50
161 Roland Bond	.25	.50
162 Arne Carlsson	.25	.50
163 Thomas Carlsson	.25	.50
164 Lasse Danielsson	.25	.50
165 Ake Danielsson	.25	.50
166 Kenneth Ekman	.25	.50
167 Lars Erik Esbjors	.25	.50
168 Soren Gunnarsson	.25	.50
169 Mats Hysing	.25	.50
170 Bjorn Johansson	.25	.50
171 Martin Johansson	.25	.50
172 Jan Kock	.25	.50
173 Hakan Lindgren	.25	.50
174 Larsake Lundell	.25	.50
175 Mats Lundmark	.25	.50
176 Kjell-Rune Milton	.25	.50
177 Jan Erik Nilsson	.25	.50
178 Lars Goran Nilsson	.25	.50
179 Hakan Nygren	.25	.50
180 Jan Olsson	.25	.50
181 Jorgen Palm	.25	.50
182 Dennis Pettersson	.25	.50
183 Stefan Pettersson	.25	.50
184 Anders Rylin	.25	.50
185 Stig Salming	.30	.75
186 Nils-Olof Schilstrom	.25	.50
187 Jan Erik Silfverberg	.25	.50
188 Lars Erik Sjoberg	1.50	3.00
189 Karl-Johan Sundqvist	.25	.50
190 Jan-Olof Svensson	.25	.50
191 Leif Svensson	.25	.50
192 Tord Svensson	.25	.50
193 Sverker Torstensson	.25	.50
194 Mats Walltin	.25	.50
195 Ulf Weinstock	.25	.50
196 Jan Ove Wiberg	.25	.50
197 Lars Zetterstrom	.25	.50
198 Stig Ostling	.30	.75
199 Hans Andersson	.25	.50
200 Kent-Erik Andersson	.25	.50
201 Kjell Andersson	.25	.50
202 Ulf Barrefjord	.25	.50
203 Kent Bengtsson	.25	.50
204 Bo Berggren	.25	.50
205 Kjell Brus	.25	.50
206 Per-Olof Brasar	.75	1.50
207 Borje Burlin	.25	.50
208 Per Backman	.25	.50
209 Stefan Canderyd	.25	.50
210 Hans Carlsson	.25	.50
211 Hakan Dahlov	.25	.50
212 Rolf Edberg	.25	.50
213 Ake Eklof	.25	.50
214 Roland Eriksson	.25	.50
215 Conny Evensson	.50	1.00
216 Svante Granholm	.25	.50
217 Peter Gudmundsson	.25	.50
218 Hans Hansson	.25	.50
219 Anders Hedberg	2.00	4.00
220 Henric Hedlund	.25	.50
221 Nils Arne Hedqvist	.25	.50
222 Leif Henriksson	.25	.50
223 Leif Holmgren	.25	.50
224 Sven-Ake Jacobsson	.25	.50
225 Hans Jax	.25	.50
226 Christer Johansson	.25	.50
227 Gunnar Johansson	.25	.50
228 Lars Erik Johansson	.25	.50
229 Stig-Goran Johansson	.25	.50
230 Soren Johansson	.25	.50
231 Bengt Goran Karlsson	.25	.50
232 Bengt-Ake Karlsson	.25	.50
233 Martin Karlsson	.25	.50
234 Stefan Karlsson	.25	.50
235 Jan-Olov Kroon	.25	.50
236 Dan Labraaten	.75	1.50
237 Dan Landegren	.25	.50
238 Kjell Landstrom	.25	.50
239 Ove Larsson	.25	.50
240 Stig Larsson	.25	.50
241 Hans Lindberg	.25	.50
242 Mats Lindh	.25	.50
243 Willy Lindstrom	.50	1.00
244 Orjan Lindstrom	.25	.50
245 Christer Lundberg	.25	.50
246 Lars-Gunnar Lundberg	.25	.50
247 Per Lundqvist	.25	.50
248 Arne Lundstrom	.50	1.00
249 Fhinn Lundstrom	.25	.50
250 Bengt Lovgren	.25	.50
251 Ulf Martensson	.25	.50
252 Par Marts	.25	.50
253 Tadeusz Niedomysl	.25	.50
254 Hardy Nilsson	.25	.50
255 Lars Goran Nilsson	.25	.50
256 Ulf Nilsson	2.00	4.00
257 Anders Nordin	.25	.50
258 Nils-Olof Olsson	.25	.50
259 Bjorn Palmqvist	.25	.50
260 Kent Persson	.25	.50
261 Hakan Pettersson	.25	.50
262 Sven-Ake Rudby	.25	.50
263 Benny Runesson	.25	.50
264 Jan Roger Strand	.25	.50
265 Ake Soderberg	.50	1.00
266 Dan Soderstrom	.25	.50
267 Ulf Torstensson	.25	.50
268 Claes Goran Wallin	.25	.50
269 Hakan Wickberg	.25	.50
270 Kjell Arne Wickstrom	.25	.50
271 Per Allan Wickstrom	.25	.50
272 Dick Yderstrom	.25	.50
273 Mats Ahlberg	.30	.75
274 Olle Ahman	.25	.50
275 Lars Oberg	.25	.50
276 Jan Ostling	.25	.50
277 Akning	.25	.50
278 Akning	.25	.50
279 Akning	.25	.50
280 Skott	.25	.50
281 Skott	.25	.50
282 Skott	.25	.50
283 Puckforing	.25	.50
284 Tekning	.25	.50
285 Malvaktsspel	.50	1.00
286 Malvaktsspel	.50	1.00
287 Forsvarsspel	.25	.50
288 Forsvarsspel	.25	.50
289 Forsvarsspel	.25	.50
290 Forsvarsspel	.25	.50
291 Forsvarsspel	.25	.50
292 Forsvarsspel	.25	.50
293 Forsvarsspel	.25	.50
294 Forsvarsspel	.25	.50
295 Forsvarsspel	.25	.50
296 Forsvarsspel	.25	.50
297 Forsvarsspel	.25	.50
298 Forsvarsspel	.25	.50
299 Forsvarsspel	.25	.50
300 Forsvarsspel	.25	.50
301 Forsvarsspel	.25	.50
302 Forsvarsspel	.25	.50
303 Anfallsspel	.25	.50
304 Anfallsspel	.25	.50
305 Anfallsspel	.25	.50
306 Anfallsspel	.25	.50
307 Anfallsspel	.25	.50
308 Anfallsspel	.25	.50
309 Anfallsspel	.25	.50
310 Anfallsspel	.25	.50
311 Anfallsspel	.25	.50
312 Anfallsspel	.25	.50
313 Inge Hammarstrom	1.00	2.00
314 Borje Salming	3.00	6.00
315 Thommie Bergman	1.25	2.50
316 Leif Holmqvist	.50	1.00
317 Ulf Sterner	.25	.50
318 Tord Lundstrom	.25	.50
319 Tre Kroner puzzle	.25	.50
320 Tre Kroner puzzle	.25	.50
321 Tre Kroner puzzle	.25	.50
322 Tre Kroner puzzle	.25	.50
323 Tre Kroner puzzle	.25	.50
324 Tre Kroner puzzle	.25	.50

1954 UK A and BC Chewing Gum

The cards listed below were part of a multi-sport set issued in England, possibly with packs of A and BC Chewing Gum. They feature b&w headshots and blank backs. The players appear to be from an early English league. It's quite possible that other hockey players were featured. If you can address

this checklist, please contact us at hockeymag@beckett.com.
COMPLETE SET (?)
35 Chick Zamick 8.00 20.00
36 Cliff Ryan 8.00 20.00
37 Sonny Rost 8.00 20.00
38 Malcolm Davidson 8.00 20.00
39 Ray Gariepy 12.00 30.00
40 George Beach 8.00 20.00
41 Lefty Wilmot 8.00 20.00
74 Bill Johnson 8.00 20.00
75 Joe Shack 8.00 20.00
76 Tony Licari 8.00 20.00

1951-52 Bas Du Fleuve

This set features top players from the Quebec Senior League. The cards are similar in size to the Parkhurst set that was released this season. The key card in the set pictures Denis Brodeur.

COMPLETE SET (58) 350.00 700.00
1 Gordon Poirier 12.50 25.00
2 Denis Brodeur 25.00 50.00
3 Conrad Poitras 7.50 15.00
4 Clement Tremblay 7.50 15.00
5 Raymond Leduc 7.50 15.00
6 Jacques Armstrong 7.50 15.00
7 Joe Schmidt 7.50 15.00
8 Gilles Laroche 7.50 15.00
9 Frank Pearce 7.50 15.00
10 Wayne Stephenson 7.50 15.00
11 Guy Lapointe 7.50 15.00
12 Guy Delisle 7.50 15.00
13 Ossie Carnegie 10.00 20.00
14 Gilbert Girouard 7.50 15.00
15 Jean-Paul Vandal 7.50 15.00
16 Guy Lalonde 7.50 15.00
17 Roland Bilodeau 7.50 15.00
18 Gaetan Laliberte 7.50 15.00
19 Maurice Benoit 7.50 15.00
20 Thomas McDougall 7.50 15.00
21 Roger Guay 7.50 15.00
22 Bob Brault 7.50 15.00
23 Edouard Theberge 7.50 15.00
24 Paul Lessard 7.50 15.00
25 Lucien Gilbert 7.50 15.00
26 Real Lafreniere 7.50 15.00
27 Ronald Limoges 7.50 15.00
28 Roger Ste. Marie 7.50 15.00
29 Arthur Leyte 7.50 15.00
30 Magella Laforest 7.50 15.00
31 Bill Leblanc 7.50 15.00
32 Pius Gaudet 7.50 15.00
33 Jean-Roch Bellavance 7.50 15.00
34 Gerard Lachance 7.50 15.00
35 Marcel St. Pierre 7.50 15.00
36 Pierre Brillant 7.50 15.00
37 Paul Provost 7.50 15.00
38 Maurice Lamirande 7.50 15.00
39 Roger Hayfield 7.50 15.00
40 Normand Bellavance 7.50 15.00
41 Marcel Houde 7.50 15.00
42 Dan Janelle 7.50 15.00
43 Roland Rossignol 7.50 15.00
44 Roger Gagne 7.50 15.00
45 Jacques Monette 7.50 15.00
46 Bernie Bernaquez 7.50 15.00
47 Paul Gagnon 7.50 15.00
48 Jean-Marie Fillion 7.50 15.00
49 Bert Scullion 7.50 15.00
50 Don Bellringer 7.50 15.00
51 Frank Cote 7.50 15.00
52 Eddy Bolan 7.50 15.00
53 Maurice Parr 7.50 15.00
54 Many McIntyre 7.50 15.00
55 Roger Jodoin 7.50 15.00
56 Mario Senecal 7.50 15.00
57 Denis Fillion 7.50 15.00
58 Marcel Fillion 12.50 25.00

1952-53 Bas Du Fleuve

This set features players from the Quebec Senior League. The cards are similar in size to the 1951-52 Parkhurst set. Noteworthy players include Denis Brodeur (father of Martin and former Canadian Olympic goalie) and Marcel Paille.

COMPLETE SET (65) 400.00 800.00
1 Roger Gagner 12.50 25.00
2 Martial Pruneau 7.50 15.00
3 Fernand Gladu 7.50 15.00
4 Joseph Lacoursiere 7.50 15.00
5 Maurice Lamirande 7.50 15.00
6 Denis Smith 7.50 15.00
7 Real Jacques 7.50 15.00
8 Roland Landry 7.50 15.00
9 Dan Janelle 7.50 15.00
10 Pete Gaudette 7.50 15.00
11 Normand Bellavance 7.50 15.00
12 Roger Hayfield 7.50 15.00
13 Bill LeBlanc 7.50 15.00
14 Victor Corbin 7.50 15.00
15 Gerard Lachance 7.50 15.00
16 Guy Labrie 7.50 15.00
17 Denis Brodeur 15.00 30.00
18 Gerard Paquin 7.50 15.00
19 Irene St. Hilaire 10.00 20.00
20 Guy Gervais 7.50 15.00
21 Marcel Benoit 7.50 15.00
22 Roger Dumas 7.50 15.00
23 Gaston Gervais 7.50 15.00
24 Maurice St. Jean 7.50 15.00
25 Frank Pearce 7.50 15.00
26 Fernand Bernaquez 7.50 15.00
27 Henri-Paul Gagnon 7.50 15.00
28 Jean-Jacques Pichette 7.50 15.00
29 Jim Hayes 7.50 15.00
30 Fernand Rancourt 7.50 15.00
31 Nils Tremblay 7.50 15.00
32 Clement Tremblay 7.50 15.00
33 Jacques Lalancette 7.50 15.00
34 Marcel Fillion 10.00 20.00
35 Jacques Monette 7.50 15.00
36 Frank Cote 7.50 15.00
37 Bernie Lemonde 7.50 15.00
38 Guildor Levesque 7.50 15.00
39 Hector Legris 7.50 15.00
40 Jacques Gagnon 7.50 15.00
41 Donat Deschesnes 7.50 15.00
42 Bertrand LePage 7.50 15.00
43 Paul Lavoie 7.50 15.00
44 Denis Fillion 7.50 15.00
45 Floyd Crawford 12.50 25.00
46 Paul Duchesne 7.50 15.00
47 Rene Pronovost 7.50 15.00
48 Roger Jodoin 7.50 15.00
49 Mario Senecal 7.50 15.00
50 Garry Plamondon 12.50 25.00
51 Marcel Paille 7.50 15.00
52 Rene Pepin 7.50 15.00
53 Gilles Desrosiers 7.50 15.00
54 Edgard Gendron 7.50 15.00
55 Ronald Limoges 7.50 15.00
56 Roland Bilodeau 7.50 15.00
57 Leon Bouchard 7.50 15.00
58 Bob Leger 7.50 15.00
59 Conrad L'Heureux 7.50 15.00
60 Raymond Leduc 7.50 15.00
61 Bob Brault 7.50 15.00
62 Roger Ste. Marie 7.50 15.00
63 Real Lafreniere 7.50 15.00
64 Lucien Gilbert 7.50 15.00
65 Louis Desrosiers 12.50 25.00

1951-52 Buffalo Bison

This set features the Bison of the AHL. Little is known about this set, but it is believed to be oversized and distributed in set form by the team.

COMPLETE SET (19) 50.00 100.00
1 Team Photo 5.00 10.00
2 Don Ashbee 5.00 10.00
3 Frankie Christy 2.50 5.00
4 Gerry Couture 4.00 8.00
5 Lou Crowdis 2.50 5.00
6 Harry Dick 2.50 5.00
7 Lloyd Finkbeiner 2.50 5.00
8 Ab Demarco 5.00 10.00
9 Leroy Goldsworthy 2.50 5.00
10 Les Hickey 5.00 10.00
11 Vern Kaiser 2.50 5.00
12 Sam Lavitt 2.50 5.00
13 Stan Long 2.50 5.00
14 Cal Mackay 5.00 10.00
15 Ed Mazur 2.50 5.00
16 Sid McNabney 2.50 5.00
17 George Pargeter 2.50 5.00
18 Gordie Pennell 2.50 5.00
19 Grant Warwick 2.50 5.00

1951-52 Cleveland Barons

This set was issued as a photo pack. The cards are printed on thin card stock, and measure 9 X 6 inches. The last card, Joe Lund, may be from the previous year's set, as he did not play for Cleveland in 1951-52.

COMPLETE SET (20) 75.00 150.00
1 Bun Cook CO 5.00 10.00
2 Fred Shero 10.00 20.00
3 Ed Reigle 3.00 6.00
4 Ike Hildebrand 3.00 6.00
5 Eddie Olson 3.00 6.00
6 Jerry Reid 3.00 6.00
7 Fred Thurier 3.00 6.00
8 Steve Wochy 3.00 6.00
9 Joe Carveth 4.00 8.00
10 Tom Williams 5.00 10.00
11 Johnny Bower 25.00 50.00
12 Jack Gordon 4.00 8.00
13 Ken Schultz 3.00 6.00
14 Fern Perreault 3.00 6.00
15 Ray Ceresino 3.00 6.00
16 Bob Bailey 3.00 6.00
17 Bob Chrystal 4.00 8.00
18 Phil Samis 3.00 6.00
19 Paul Gladu 3.00 6.00
20 Joe Lund 3.00 6.00

1960-61 Cleveland Barons

This 19-card set of oversized cards measures approximately 6 3/4" by 5 3/8". The set commemorates the Cleveland Barons 1959-60 season which ended with the team in fourth place after elimination in the Calder Cup Playoffs. The white-bordered fronts display action, black-and-white player photos. A facsimile autograph is printed near the bottom of the photo on all the cards except the team photo card. The backs are blank. Since the cards are unnumbered, they are checklisted below alphabetically.

COMPLETE SET (19) 60.00 120.00
1 Ron Attwell 3.00 6.00
2 Les Binkley 5.00 10.00
3 Bill Dineen 4.00 8.00
4 John Ferguson 10.00 20.00
5 Cal Gardner 4.00 8.00
6 Fred Glover 4.00 8.00
7 Jack Gordon 4.00 8.00
8 Aldo Guidolin 4.00 8.00
9 Greg Hicks 3.00 6.00
10 Wayne Larkin 3.00 6.00
11 Moe Mantha 4.00 8.00
12 Gil Mayer 3.00 6.00
13 Eddie Mazur 3.00 6.00
14 Jim Mikol 3.00 6.00
15 Bill Needham 3.00 6.00
16 Cal Stearns 3.00 6.00
17 Bill Sutherland 4.00 8.00
18 Tom Williams 4.00 8.00
19 Team Photo 5.00 10.00

1966-67 Columbus Checkers

This 16-card set measures 4 x 7 1/4" and features a black and white photo on the front along with players name at the bottom. Backs are blank. Cards are unnumbered and checklisted below alphabetically.

COMPLETE SET (16) 35.00 70.00
1 John Bailey 2.50 5.00
2 Moe Bartoli 2.50 5.00
3 Kerry Bond 2.50 5.00
4 Andre Daoust 2.50 5.00
5 Bert Fizzell 2.50 5.00
6 Marcel Goudreau 2.50 5.00
7 Jim Graham 2.50 5.00
8 Paul Jackson 2.50 5.00
9 Ken Laidlaw 2.50 5.00
10 Noel Lirette 2.50 5.00
11 Gary Longman 2.50 5.00
12 Garry Macmillan 2.50 5.00
13 Gary Mork 2.50 5.00
14 Matt Thorpe 2.50 5.00
15 Jack Turner 2.50 5.00
16 Alton White 2.50 5.00

1967-68 Columbus Checkers

Little is known about this early team-issued photo set from the Checkers of the IHL. It is believed they were issued as a promotional item in response to mailed-in requests from fans. Any further information can be forwarded to hockeymag@beckett.com.

COMPLETE SET (16) 37.50 75.00
1 Team Photo 2.50 5.00
2 Moe Bartoli 2.50 10.00
3 Bill Bond 2.50 5.00
4 Serge Boudreault 2.50 5.00
5 Gord Dibley 2.50 10.00
6 Bert Fizzell 2.50 5.00
7 Chuck Kelly 2.50 5.00
8 Ken Saunders 2.50 5.00
9 Nelson Leclair 2.50 5.00
10 Real Paquette 2.50 5.00
11 Dick Proceviat 2.50 5.00
12 Hartley Estabrooks 2.50 5.00
13 Ken Sutyla 2.50 5.00
14 Nelson Tremblay 2.50 5.00
15 Jack Turner 2.50 5.00
16 Al White 2.50 5.00

1977-78 Granby Vics

This odd-sized (3 1/2 X7") black and white set features the Granby Vics of the LMJHQ. The card fronts are in a horizontal format, with the left half of the card containing a player photo, and the right featuring a player bio and an ad from a local business. The backs are blank and the cards are unnumbered. They are presented below alphabetically.

COMPLETE SET (20) 17.50 35.00
1 Mario Beauregard 1.00 2.00
2 Luc Breton 1.00 2.00
3 Daniel Caron 1.50 3.00
4 Mario Casavant 1.00 2.00
5 Marc Courtemanche 1.00 2.00
6 Yves Courtemanche 1.00 2.00
7 Sylvain d'Amour 1.00 2.00
8 Rene Delorme 1.00 2.00
9 Denis Dumas Jr. 1.00 2.00
10 Pierre Grondin 1.00 2.00
11 Andre Hebert 1.00 2.00
12 Marcel Lachance 1.00 2.00
13 Andre Lemieux 1.00 2.00
14 Pierre Lepage 1.00 2.00
15 Daniel Menard 1.00 2.00
16 Jacques Pomerleau 1.00 2.00
17 Mario Roy 1.00 2.00
18 Alain Tetrault 1.00 2.00
19 Paul Thibert 1.00 2.00
20 Luc Turgeon 1.00 2.00

1975-76 Hamilton Fincups

This 18-card standard-size set features sepia-tone player portraits. The player's name and position are printed in the lower border, which is also sepia-tone. The team name is superimposed over the picture at the bottom center. The backs are blank and grayish in color. The cards are unnumbered and checklisted below in alphabetical order.

COMPLETE SET (18) 15.00 30.00
1 Jack Anderson .75 1.50
2 Mike Clarke .75 1.50
3 Greg Clause .75 1.50
4 Joe Contini .75 1.50
5 Mike Fedorko .75 1.50
6 Paul Foley .75 1.50
7 Greg Hickey .75 1.50
8 Tony Horvath .75 1.50
9 Mike Keating .75 1.50
10 Archie King .75 1.50
11 Ted Long .75 1.50
12 Dale McCourt 2.50 5.00
13 Dave Norris .75 1.50
14 Greg Redquest .75 1.50
15 Glen Richardson .75 1.50
16 Ron Roscoe .75 1.50
17 Ric Seiling 1.25 2.50
18 Danny Shearer .75 1.50

1961-62 Hamilton Red Wings

This oversized set features members of the top farm team of the Red Wings. They were sold as a set by the team.

COMPLETE SET (21) 37.50 75.00
1 Bud Blom 1.50 3.00
2 Eddie Bush 2.00 4.00
3 Bob Dean 1.50 3.00
4 John Gofton 1.50 3.00
5 Bob Hamilton 1.50 3.00
6 Bob Hamilton 1.50 3.00
7 Ron Harris 2.00 4.00
8 Earl Heiskala 2.00 4.00
9 Paul Henderson 7.50 15.00
10 Roger Lafreniere 1.50 3.00
11 Lowell Macdonald 4.00 8.00
12 Pit Martin 5.00 10.00
13 Jim Mclellan 1.50 3.00
14 Harvey Meisenheimer 1.50 3.00
15 Howie Menard 1.50 3.00
16 Wayne Rivers 4.00 8.00
17 Jim Peters 2.00 4.00
18 Bob Wall 1.50 3.00
19 Jack Wildfong 1.50 3.00
20 Terry Urkewicz 1.50 3.00
21 Larry Zilliotto 1.50 3.00

1971-72 Johnstown Jets Acme

This set features the Jets of the EHL. The oversized cards measure 3.5" x 5 " and feature black and white photos. The cards are blank backed and unnumbered, and so are listed below in alphabetical order.

COMPLETE SET (16) 40.00 80.00
1 Dave Birch 2.00 5.00
2 Vern Campigatto 2.00 5.00
3 Len Cunning 2.00 5.00
4 Guy Delparte 2.00 5.00
5 Wynne Dempster 2.00 5.00
6 Ron Docken 2.00 5.00
7 Galen Head 2.00 5.00
8 Eddie Kachur 2.00 5.00
9 Reg Kent(Taschuk) 2.00 5.00
10 Jerry MacDonald 2.00 5.00
11 Gene Peacosh 2.50 6.00
12 Dick Roberge 2.00 5.00
13 Jim Trewin 2.00 5.00
14 Brian Vescio 2.00 5.00
15 Bob Vroman 2.50 6.00
16 Gary Wood 2.00 5.00

1972-73 Johnstown Jets

This set features the Jets of the EHL. The cards reportedly were included as a premium in game day programs and measure an oversized 3 1/2 by 5 inches. The photos on the front are black and white, while the backs are blank.

COMPLETE SET (18) 50.00 100.00
1 Ron Docken 2.50 6.00
2 Brian Coughlin 2.00 5.00
3 Tony McCarthy 2.00 5.00
4 Tom Steeves 2.00 5.00
5 Kevin Collins 2.00 5.00
6 Jerry MacDonald 2.00 5.00
7 Wynne Dempster 2.00 5.00
8 Ted Lanyon 2.00 5.00
9 Brian Vescio 2.00 5.00
10 Denis Erickson 2.50 6.00
11 Vern Campigatto 2.00 5.00
12 Gary Wood 2.00 5.00
13 Dave Birch 2.00 5.00
14 Galen Head 2.50 6.00
15 Reg Kent(Taschuk) 2.00 5.00
16 Tom McVie 2.50 6.00
17 Bill McEwan 2.00 5.00
18 Doug Anderson 2.00 5.00

1952-53 Juniors Blue Tint

The 1952-53 Junior set contains 182 cards measuring approximately 2" by 3". The cards have a blue tint and are numbered on the back. It is not known at this time who sponsored this set. Key cards in this set are "Pre-Rookie Cards" of Al Arbour, Don Cherry, Charlie Hodge, John Muckler, Henri Richard, and Harry Sinden.

COMPLETE SET (182) 1,250.00 2,500.00
1 Dennis Riggin 8.00 20.00
2 Joe Zorica 5.00 10.00
3 Larry Hillman 10.00 25.00
4 Edward(Ted) Reid 5.00 10.00
5 Al Arbour 35.00 75.00
6 Marlin McAlendin 5.00 10.00
7 Ross Graham 5.00 10.00
8 Cumming Burton 5.00 10.00
9 Ed Palamar 5.00 10.00
10 Elmer Skov 6.00 15.00
11 Eddie Louttit 5.00 10.00
12 Gerry Price 5.00 10.00
13 Lou Dietrich 5.00 10.00
14 Gaston Marcotte 5.00 10.00
15 Bob Brown 5.00 10.00
16 Archie Burton 5.00 10.00
17 Marv Edwards 15.00 40.00
18 Norman Defelice 6.00 15.00
19 Pete Kamula 5.00 10.00
20 Charles Marshall 5.00 10.00
21 Alex Leslie 5.00 10.00
22 Minpy Roberts 5.00 10.00
23 Danny Poliziani 5.00 10.00
24 Allen Kellogg 5.00 10.00
25 Brian Cullen 15.00 40.00
26 Ken Schinkel 6.00 15.00
27 W. Hass 5.00 10.00

Card	Low	High
28 Don Nash	5.00	10.00
29 Robert Maxwell	5.00	10.00
30 Eddie Mateka	5.00	10.00
31 Joe Kastelic	5.00	10.00
32 Hank Ciesla	6.00	15.00
33 Hugh Barlow	5.00	10.00
34 Claude Roy	5.00	10.00
35 Jean-Guy Gamache	5.00	10.00
36 Leon Michelin	5.00	10.00
37 Gerard Bergeron	5.00	10.00
38 Herve Lalonde	5.00	10.00
39 J.M. Cossette	5.00	10.00
40 Jean-Guy Gendron	10.00	25.00
41 Gamill Bedard	5.00	10.00
42 Alfred Soucy	5.00	10.00
43 Jean Leclerc	5.00	10.00
44 Raymond St.Cyr	6.00	15.00
45 Lester Lahaye	5.00	10.00
46 Yvan Houle	5.00	10.00
47 Louis Desrosiers	5.00	10.00
48 Douglas Lessor	5.00	10.00
49 Irvin Scott	5.00	10.00
50 Danny Blair	5.00	10.00
51 Jim Connelly	6.00	15.00
52 William Chalmers	5.00	10.00
53 Frank Bettiol	5.00	10.00
54 James Holmes	5.00	10.00
55 Birley Dimme	5.00	10.00
56 Donald Beattie	5.00	10.00
57 Terrance Chattington	5.00	10.00
58 Bruce Wallace	5.00	10.00
59 William McCreary	6.00	15.00
60 Fred Brady	5.00	10.00
61 Ronald Murphy	6.00	15.00
62 Lavi Purola	5.00	10.00
63 George Whyte	5.00	10.00
64 Marcel Paille	25.00	50.00
65 Maurice Collins	5.00	10.00
66 Gerard(Butch) Houle	6.00	15.00
67 Gilles Laperriere	5.00	10.00
68 Robert Chevalier	5.00	10.00
69 Bertrand Lepage	5.00	10.00
70 Michel Labadie	5.00	10.00
71 Gabriel Alain	5.00	10.00
72 Jean-Jacques Pichette	6.00	15.00
73A Camille Henry (Citadelles)	12.00	30.00
73B Camille Henry (New York	100.00	200.00
74 Jean-Guy Gignac	5.00	10.00
75 Leo Amadio	6.00	15.00
76 Gilles Thibault	6.00	15.00
77 Gaston Pelletier	6.00	15.00
78 Adolph Kukulowicz	6.00	15.00
79 Roland Leclerc	5.00	10.00
80 Phil Watson CO	20.00	40.00
81 Raymond Cyr	6.00	15.00
82 Jacques Marcotte	5.00	10.00
83 Floyd Hillman	6.00	15.00
84 Bob Attersley	5.00	10.00
85 Harry Sinden	35.00	75.00
86 Stan Parker	5.00	10.00
87 Bob Mader	5.00	10.00
88 Roger Maisonneuve	5.00	10.00
89 Phil Chapman	5.00	10.00
90 Don McIntosh	5.00	10.00
91 Jack Armstrong	5.00	10.00
92 Carlo Montemurro	5.00	10.00
93 Ken Courtney	5.00	10.00
94 Bill Stewart	6.00	15.00
95 Gerald Casey	5.00	10.00
96 Fred Etcher	5.00	10.00
97 Orrin Carver	5.00	10.00
98 Ralph Willis	5.00	10.00
99 Kenneth Robertson	5.00	10.00
100 Don Cherry	175.00	350.00
101 Fred Pletsch	5.00	10.00
102 Larry Thibault	5.00	10.00
103 James Robertson	5.00	10.00
104 Orval Tessier	10.00	25.00
105 Jack Higgins	5.00	10.00
106 Robert White	5.00	10.00
107 Doug Mohns	15.00	40.00
108 William Sexton	5.00	10.00
109 John Martan	5.00	10.00
110 Tony Poeta	6.00	15.00
111 Don McKenney	10.00	25.00
112 Bill Harrington	5.00	10.00
113 Allen Peal	5.00	10.00
114 John Ford	5.00	10.00
115 Kenneth Collins	6.00	15.00
116 Marc Boileau	6.00	15.00
117 Doug Vaughan	5.00	10.00
118 Gilles Boisvert	5.00	10.00
119 Buddy Horne	5.00	10.00
120 Graham Joyce	5.00	10.00
121 Gary Collins	5.00	10.00
122 Roy Greenan	5.00	10.00
123 Beryl Klynck	5.00	10.00
124 Grieg Hicks	5.00	10.00
125 Jack Novak	5.00	10.00
126 Ken Tennant	5.00	10.00
127 Glen Cressman	5.00	10.00
128 Curly Davies	5.00	10.00
129 Charlie Hodge	37.50	75.00
130 Bob McCord	6.00	15.00
131 Gordie Hollinworth	5.00	10.00
132 Ronald Pilon	5.00	10.00
133 Brian Mackay	5.00	10.00
134 Yvon Chasle	5.00	10.00
135 Denis Boucher	6.00	15.00
136 Claude Boileau	5.00	10.00
137 Claude Vinet	5.00	10.00
138 Claude Provost	20.00	40.00
139 Henri Richard	150.00	300.00
140 Les Lilley	5.00	10.00
141 Phil Goyette	15.00	40.00
142 Guy Rousseau	5.00	10.00
143 Paul Knox	5.00	10.00
144 Bill Lee	5.00	10.00
145 Ted Topazzini	6.00	15.00
146 Marc Reaume	6.00	15.00
147 Bill Dineen	15.00	40.00
148 Ed Plata	5.00	10.00
149 Noel Price	6.00	15.00
150 Mike Ratchford	5.00	10.00
151 Jim Logan	5.00	10.00
152 Art Clune	5.00	10.00
153 Jerry MacNamara	5.00	10.00
154 Jack Caffery	6.00	15.00
155 Les Duff	5.00	10.00
156 Murray Costello	6.00	15.00
157 Ed Chadwick	40.00	80.00
158 Mike Desilets	5.00	10.00
159 Ross Watson	5.00	10.00
160 Roger Landry	5.00	10.00
161 Terry O'Connor	5.00	10.00
162 Ovila Gagnon	5.00	10.00
163 Dave Broadbelt	5.00	10.00
164 Sandy Monrisson	5.00	10.00
165 John MacGillvray	5.00	10.00
166 Claude Beaupre	5.00	10.00
167 Eddie Eustache	5.00	10.00
168 Stan Rodek	5.00	10.00
169 Maurice Mantha	6.00	15.00
170 Hector Lalande	8.00	20.00
171 Bob Wilson	5.00	10.00
172 Frank Bonello	5.00	10.00
173 Peter Kowalchuch	5.00	10.00
174 Les Binkley	25.00	50.00
175 John Muckler	20.00	40.00
176 Ken Wharram	15.00	40.00
177 John Sleaver	5.00	10.00
178 Ralph Markarian	5.00	10.00
179 Ken McMeekin	5.00	10.00
180 Ron Boomer	5.00	10.00
181 Kenneth (Red) Crawford	5.00	10.00
182 Jim McBurney	8.00	20.00

1977-78 Kalamazoo Wings

These standard size cards, sponsored by ISB bank, feature black and white photos with a white border. Backs feature players name, position, and card number.

Card	Low	High
COMPLETE (15)	15.00	30.00
1 George Klsons	1.00	2.00
2 Ron Wilson	1.00	2.00
3 Bob Lemieux	1.00	2.00
4 Len Ircandia	1.00	2.00
5 Ron Kennedy	1.00	2.00
6 Daniel Poulin	1.00	2.00
7 Terry Evans	1.00	2.00
8 Yvon Douris	1.00	2.00
9 Tom Milani	1.00	2.00
10 Mike Wanchuk	1.00	2.00
11 Steve Lee	1.00	2.00
12 Yves Guilmette	1.00	2.00
13 Al Genovy	1.00	2.00
15 Jim Baxter	1.00	2.00
18 Alvin White	1.00	2.00

1951-52 Laval Dairy Lac St. Jean

The 1951-52 Laval Dairy Lac St. Jean set includes 59 green-and-white tinted cards measuring approximately 1 3/4" by 2 1/2". The backs are blank. The cards are numbered on the front.

Card	Low	High
COMPLETE SET (59)	750.00	1,500.00
1 Eddy Daoust	25.00	50.00
2 Guy Gareau	20.00	40.00
3 Gilles Desrosiers	20.00	40.00
4 Robert Desbiens	20.00	40.00
5 James Hayes	20.00	40.00
6 Paul Gagnon	20.00	40.00
7 Gerry Perreault	20.00	40.00
8 Marcel Dufour	20.00	40.00
9 Armand Bourdon	20.00	40.00
10 Jean-Marc Pichette	25.00	50.00
11 Gerry Gagnon	20.00	40.00
12 Jules Racette	20.00	40.00
13 Real Marcotte	20.00	40.00
14 Gerry Theberge	20.00	40.00
15 Rene Harvey	20.00	40.00
16 Joseph Lacoursiere	20.00	40.00
17 Fernand Benaquez	20.00	40.00
18 Andre Boisvert	20.00	40.00
19 Claude Chretien	20.00	40.00
20 Norbert Clark	20.00	40.00
21 Sylvio Lambert	20.00	40.00
22 Lucien Roy	20.00	40.00
23 Gerard Audet	20.00	40.00
24 Jacques Lalancette	20.00	40.00
25 Maurice St.Jean	20.00	40.00
26 Camille Lupien	20.00	40.00
27 Rodrigue Pelchat	20.00	40.00
28 Conrad L'Heureux	20.00	40.00
29 Paul Tremblay	20.00	40.00
30 Robert Vincent	20.00	40.00
31 Charles Lamirande	20.00	40.00
32 Leon Gaudreault	20.00	40.00
33 Maurice Thiffault	20.00	40.00
34 Marc-Aurele Tremblay	20.00	40.00
35 Rene Pronovost	20.00	40.00
36 Victor Corbin	20.00	40.00
37 Tiny Tamminen	25.00	50.00
38 Guildor Levesque	20.00	40.00
39 Gaston Lamirande	20.00	40.00
40 Guy Gervais	20.00	40.00
41 Rayner Makila	25.00	50.00
42 Jules Tremblay	20.00	40.00
43 Roland Girard	20.00	40.00
44 Germain Bergeron	20.00	40.00
45 Paul Duchesne	20.00	40.00
46 Roger Beaudoin	20.00	40.00
47 Georges Archibal	20.00	40.00
48 Claude Basque	20.00	40.00
49 Roger Sarda	20.00	40.00
50 Edgard Gendron	20.00	40.00
51 Gaston Labossiere	20.00	40.00
52 Roland Clantara	20.00	40.00
53 Florian Gravel	20.00	40.00
54 Jean-Guy Thompson	20.00	40.00
55 Yvan Forton	20.00	40.00
56 Yves Laporte	20.00	40.00
57 Claude Germain	20.00	40.00
58 Gerry Brunet	20.00	40.00
59 Maurice Courteau	25.00	50.00

1951-52 Laval Dairy QSHL

The 1951-52 Laval Dairy QSHL set includes 109 black and white blank-back cards measuring approximately 1 3/4" by 2 1/2". These cards were issued in the province of Quebec and the Ottawa region. The cards are numbered and dated on the front. Key cards in this set are "Pre-Rookie Cards" of Jean Beliveau and Jacques Plante. The card numbering is organized by team as follows: Aces de Quebec (1-18 and 37), Chicoutimi (19-36), Sherbrooke (38-51), Shawinigan Falls (52-67), Valleyfield (68-84), Royals de Montreal (85-100), and Ottawa (101-109).

Card	Low	High
COMPLETE SET (109)	1,000.00	2,000.00
1 Jean Beliveau	375.00	750.00
2 Jean Marois	5.00	10.00
3 Joe Crozier	12.50	25.00
4 Jack Gelineau	5.00	10.00
5 Murdo McKay	6.00	12.00
6 Arthur Leyte	5.00	10.00
7 Bill LeBlanc	5.00	10.00
8 Robert Hayes	5.00	10.00
9 Yogi Kraiger	6.00	12.00
10 Frank King	5.00	10.00
11 Ludger Tremblay	6.00	12.00
12 Jackie Leclair	20.00	40.00
13 Martial Pruneau	5.00	10.00
14 Armand Gaudreault	5.00	10.00
15 Marcel Bonin	20.00	40.00
16 Herbie Carnegie	37.50	75.00
17 Claude Robert	5.00	10.00
18 Phil Renaud	5.00	10.00
19 Roland Hebert	5.00	10.00
20 Donat Duschene	5.00	10.00
21 Jacques Gagnon	5.00	10.00
22 Normand Dussault	6.00	12.00
23 Stan Smrke	10.00	20.00
24 Louis Smrke	6.00	12.00
25 Floyd Crawford	5.00	10.00
26 Germain Leger	5.00	10.00
27 Delphis Franche	5.00	10.00
28 Dick Wray	5.00	10.00
29 Guildor Levesque	7.50	15.00
30 Georges Roy	5.00	10.00
31 J.P. Lamirande	5.00	10.00
32 Gerard Glaude	5.00	10.00
33 Marcel Pelletier	10.00	20.00
34 Pete Tkachuck	5.00	10.00
35 Sherman White	5.00	10.00
36 Jimmy Moore	5.00	10.00
37 Punch Imlach	50.00	100.00
38 Alex Sandalax	5.00	10.00
39 William Kyle	5.00	10.00
40 Kenneth Biggs	5.00	10.00
41 Peter Wright	5.00	10.00
42 Rene Pepin	5.00	10.00
43 Tod Campeau	6.00	12.00
44 John Smith	5.00	10.00
45 Thomas McDougall	5.00	10.00
46 Jos. Lepine	5.00	10.00
47 Guy Labrie	5.00	10.00
48 Roger Bessette	5.00	10.00
49 Yvan Dugre	6.00	12.00
50 James Planche	5.00	10.00
51 Nils Tremblay	5.00	10.00
52 Bill MacDonagh	5.00	10.00
53 Georges Ouellet	5.00	10.00
54 Billy Arcand	5.00	10.00
55 Johnny Mahaffy	6.00	12.00
56 Bucky Buchanan	10.00	20.00
57 Al Miller	5.00	10.00
58 Don Penniston	5.00	10.00
59 Spike Laliberte	5.00	10.00
60 Ernie Oakley	5.00	10.00
61 Jack Bownass	5.00	10.00
62 Ted Hodgson	5.00	10.00
63 Lyall Wiseman	5.00	10.00
64 Erwin Grosse	5.00	10.00
65 Mel Read	5.00	10.00
66 Lloyd Henchberger	5.00	10.00
67 Jack Taylor	5.00	10.00
68 Marcel Bessette	5.00	10.00
69 Jack Schmidt	5.00	10.00
70 Paul Saindon	5.00	10.00
71 J.P. Bisaillon	5.00	10.00
72 Eddie Redmond	5.00	10.00
73 Larry Kwong	10.00	20.00
74 Andre Corriveau	5.00	10.00
75 Kitoute Joanette	5.00	10.00
76 Toe Blake	75.00	150.00
77 Georges Bougie	5.00	10.00
78 Jack Irvine	5.00	10.00
79 Paul Larivee	5.00	10.00
80 Paul Leclerc	5.00	10.00
81 Bertrand Bourassa	5.00	10.00
82 Jacques Deslauriers	5.00	10.00
83 Bingo Ernst	5.00	10.00
84 Gaston Gervais	5.00	10.00
85 Gerry Plamondon	6.00	12.00
86 Glen Harmon	5.00	10.00
87 Bob Friday	5.00	10.00
88 Rolland Rousseau	5.00	10.00
89 Billy Goold	5.00	10.00
90 Lloyd Finkbeiner	5.00	10.00
91 Cliff Malone	5.00	10.00
92 Jacques Plante	375.00	750.00
93 Gerard Desaulniers	6.00	12.00
94 Arthur Rose	5.00	10.00
95 Jacques Locas	5.00	10.00
96 Walter Clune	5.00	10.00
97 Louis Denis	5.00	10.00
98 Fernand Perreault	5.00	10.00
99 Douglas McNeil	6.00	12.00
100 Les Douglas	5.00	10.00
101 Howard Riopelle	10.00	20.00
102 Vic Grigg	5.00	10.00
103 Bobby Roberts	5.00	10.00
104 Legs Fraser	5.00	10.00
105 Butch Stahan	5.00	10.00
106 Fritz Frazer	5.00	10.00
107 Bill Robinson	5.00	10.00
108 Eddie Emberg	5.00	10.00
109 Leo Gravelle	12.50	25.00

1951-52 Laval Dairy Subset

The 1951-52 Laval Dairy Subset includes 66 skip-numbered black and white blank-back cards measuring approximately 1 3/4" by 2 1/2". Apparently, this set was intended to update the QSHL set and was issued after the QSHL set perhaps even as late as the 1952-53 season. The card numbering is organized by team as follows: Aces de Quebec (7-15 and 117), Chicoutimi (25-38), Sherbrooke (39-57), Shawinigan Falls (59-67, 89-90, 94-95, 115, 118, and 120), Valleyfield (68-84 and 116), Royals de Montreal (85-86, 92-93, and 96-97), and Ottawa (98-114, 119, and 121).

Card	Low	High
COMPLETE SET (66)	750.00	1,500.00
4 Jack Gelineau SP	25.00	50.00
7 Al Miller	10.00	20.00
8 Walter Pawlyshyn	10.00	20.00
9 Yogi Kraiger SP	25.00	50.00
10 Al Baccari	10.00	20.00
12 Denis Smith	10.00	20.00
13 Pierre Brillant	10.00	20.00
14 Frank Mario	10.00	20.00
15 Danny Nixon	10.00	20.00
25 Leon Bouchard	10.00	20.00
26 Pete Taillefer	10.00	20.00
29 Bucky Buchanan	12.50	25.00
36 Marius Groleau	10.00	20.00
38 Fernand Perreault	10.00	20.00
39 Robert Drainville	10.00	20.00
40 Ronnie Matthews	10.00	20.00
44 Roger Roberge	10.00	20.00
46 Pete Wywrot	10.00	20.00
50 Gilles Dube	10.00	20.00
51 Nils Tremblay SP	25.00	50.00
52 Bob Pepin	10.00	20.00
53 Dewar Thompson	10.00	20.00
55 Irene St.Hilaire	10.00	20.00
56 Martial Pruneau	10.00	20.00
57 Jacques Locas	10.00	20.00
59 Nelson Podolsky	10.00	20.00
60 Bert Giesebrecht	10.00	20.00
61 Steve Brklaicich	10.00	20.00
65 Jack Hamilton	10.00	20.00
66 Dave Gatherum	10.00	20.00
67 Jean-Marie Plante	10.00	20.00
68 Gordie Haworth	12.50	25.00
69 Jack Schmidt SP	25.00	50.00
70 Bruce Cline	12.50	25.00
72 Phil Vitale	10.00	20.00
81 Carl Smelle	10.00	20.00
84 Tom Smelle	10.00	20.00
85 Gerry Plamondon	12.50	25.00
86 Glen Harmon	10.00	20.00
89 Frank Bathgate	10.00	20.00
90 Bernie Lemonde	10.00	20.00
92 Jacques Plante	375.00	750.00
93 Gerard Desaulniers	10.00	20.00
94 J.C. Lebrun	10.00	20.00
95 Bob Leger	10.00	20.00
96 Walter Clune	10.00	20.00
97 Louis Denis	10.00	20.00
98 Jackie Leclair	15.00	30.00
99 John Arundel	10.00	20.00
100 Les Douglas	10.00	20.00
103 Bobby Robertson	10.00	20.00
104 Ray Fredericks	10.00	20.00
106 Emile Dagenais	10.00	20.00
108 Al Kuntz	10.00	20.00
110 Red Johnson	10.00	20.00
111 John O'Flaherty	10.00	20.00
112 Jack Giesebrecht	12.50	25.00
113 Bill Richardson	10.00	20.00
114 Bep Guidolin	20.00	40.00
115 Roger Bedard	10.00	20.00
116 Renald Lacroix	10.00	20.00
117 Gordie Hudson	10.00	20.00
118 Dick Wray	10.00	20.00
119 Ronnie Hurst	10.00	20.00
120 Eddie Joss	10.00	20.00
121 Lyall Wiseman	10.00	20.00

1979-80 Montreal Juniors

This oversized set (approximately 4X6) features black and white images.

1 Jeff Barratt 2.00 5.00
2 Andre Begin 2.00 5.00
3 Dennis Champagne 2.00 5.00
4 Denis Cyr 2.00 5.00
5 Ghyslain Cyr 2.00 5.00
6 Roland Diotte 2.00 5.00
7 Pierre Dubois 2.00 5.00
8 Sylvain Gagne 2.00 5.00
9 Guy Jacob 2.00 5.00
10 Mike Krushelnyski 2.00 5.00
11 Ron Lapointe 2.00 6.00
12 Richard Lavallee 2.00 5.00
13 Daniel Laxton 2.00 5.00
14 Francois Laxton 2.00 5.00
15 Francois Lecompte 2.00 5.00
16 Eikke Leime 2.00 5.00
17 Pierre Martin 2.00 5.00
18 Bill Mulcahey 2.00 5.00
19 Gates Orlando 2.00 5.00
20 Patrice Pare 2.00 5.00
21 Mario Patry 2.00 5.00
22 Fabian Pavlin 2.00 5.00
23 Roger Poitras 2.00 5.00
24 Constant Prindolo 2.00 5.00
25 Denis Savard 5.00 10.00
26 Eric Taylor 2.00 5.00
27 Denis Tremblay 2.50 6.00
28 J.J. Vezina 2.00 5.00
29 Taras Zytynsky 2.00 5.00

1955-56 Montreal Royals

This set features the Royals, Montreal's top farm team. Cards measure 5 1/4" x 4 1/2" and were issued by Hygrade Franks. Card fronts are black and white and card backs feature an ad for Hygrade Franks that encourages purchasers to collect all six cards.

COMPLETE SET (6) 50.00 350.00
1 Walter Cline 6.00 50.00
2 Andre Corriveau 6.00 50.00
3 Jacques Deslauriers 6.00 50.00
4 Cec Hoekstra 10.00 60.00
5 Gerry McNeil 20.00 100.00
6 Guy Rousseau 10.00 60.00

1976-77 Nova Scotia Voyageurs

Set was sponsored by Farmers Twin Cities Co-op Dairy Ltd. Cards measure 4"x 6". Cards are listed below in alphabetical order.

COMPLETE SET (?)
1 Bruce Baker
2 Mike Busniuk
3 Jim Cahoon
4 Cliff Cox
5 Dave Elenbaas
6 Brian Engblom
7 Don Howse
8 Pat Hughes
9 Peter Lee
10 Chuck Luksa
11 Gilles Lupien
12 Al MacNeil CO
13 Gord McTavish
14 Pierre Mondou
15 Hal Phillipoff
16 Mike Polich
17 Rod Schutt
18 Ed Walsh
19 Ron Wilson
20 Paul Woods

1977-78 Nova Scotia Voyageurs

Sponsored by the Farmers Twin Cities Co-op Dairy Ltd., this 24-card set measures approximately 3 1/4" by 6" and features the Nova Scotia Voyageurs of the American Hockey League. The fronts feature posed action player photos bordered in white. In the top border appears "Nova Scotia Voyageurs 1977-78," while the player's name, facsimile autograph, sponsor name and logo, and team logo are printed below the picture. The backs are blank. The cards are unnumbered and checklisted below in alphabetical order.

COMPLETE SET (24) 15.00 30.00
1 Bruce Baker .50 1.00
2 Maurice Barrette .50 1.00
3 Barry Borrett .50 1.00
4 Tim Burke .50 1.00
5 Jim Cahoon .50 1.00
6 Norm Dupont .75 1.50
7 Greg Fox .75 1.50
8 Mike Hobin .50 1.00
9 Bob Holland .50 1.00
10 Don Howse .50 1.00
11 Pat Hughes 1.00 2.00
12 Chuck Luksa .50 1.00
13 Dave Lumley 1.00 2.00
14 Al MacNeil CO .75 1.50
15 Gord McTavish .50 1.00
16 Rick Meagher 1.50 3.00
17 Mike Polich .50 1.00
18 Moe Robinson .50 1.00
19 Gaeton Rochette .50 1.00
20 Pierre Roy .50 1.00
21 Frank St.Marseille 1.00 2.00
22 Derrick St.Marseille TR .25 .50
23 Rod Schutt .50 1.00
24 Ron Wilson 1.00 2.00

1980-81 Oshawa Generals

This 25-card P.L.A.Y. (Police, Laws and Youth) set measures approximately 2 5/8" by 4 1/8" and features color posed action player photos and is bordered by white borders accented by a thin red line. The player's name, position, and team are superimposed in white letters on the picture.

COMPLETE SET (25) 62.50 125.00
1 Generals Logo .40 1.00
2 Ray Flaherty .40 1.00
3 Craig Kitchener .40 1.00
4 Dan Revell .40 1.00
5 Bob Kucheran .40 1.00
6 Pat Poulin .40 1.00
7 Dave Andreychuk 7.50 15.00
8 Barry Tabobondung .40 1.00
9 Steve Konroyd 1.25 3.00
10 Paul Edwards .40 1.00
11 Dale Degray 1.25 3.00
12 Joe Cirella 1.25 3.00
13 Norm Schmidt .40 1.00
14 Markus Lehto .60 1.50
15 Mitch Lamoureux .60 1.50
16 Tony Tanti 1.50 4.00
17 Bill Laforge .40 1.00
18 Greg Gravel .40 1.00
19 Mike Lekun .40 1.00
20 Chris Smith .40 1.00
21 Peter Sidorkiewicz 1.50 4.00
22 Greg Stefan 1.50 4.00
23 Tom McCarthy 1.50 4.00
24 Rick Lanz 1.50 4.00
25 Bobby Orr 40.00 80.00

1936-37 Providence Reds

Printed on thin card stock, this 10-card set measures approximately 2 1/4" by 3 1/2". The fronts feature black-and-white player photos bordered in white. The player's name and position are printed beneath the picture, along with the statement "A New 'Reds' Picture Every Amateur Hockey Night". Unlike the other nine cards, the name of the player on card 10 is not printed beneath his picture. From his facsimile autograph on the picture, his first name may be "Jacques," but his last name remains unidentified. The backs are blank. The cards are unnumbered and checklisted below in alphabetical order.

COMPLETE SET (10) 200.00 400.00
1 Bobby Bauer 37.50 75.00
2 Paddy Byrne 12.50 25.00
3 Woody Dumart 37.50 75.00
4 Jackie Keating 12.50 25.00
5 Art Lesieur 12.50 25.00
6 Bert McInenly 12.50 25.00
7 Gus Rivers 12.50 25.00
8 Milt Schmidt 75.00 150.00
9 Jerry Shannon 12.50 25.00
10 Player Unidentified 12.50 25.00

1956-57 Quebec Aces

The set was also issued on a limited basis as a factory set in a black presentation box. This 15-card set measures approximately 5" by 7" and features black-and-white posed action player photos with a white border. The player's name is inscribed across the lower portion of the photo. On a white background, the backs carry the sponsor (Maurice Pollack Limitee) and team logos. The cards are unnumbered and checklisted below in alphabetical order.

COMPLETE SET (16) 75.00 150.00
1 Gene Achtynichuk 3.00 6.00
2 Bob Beckett 6.00 12.00
3 Marcel Bonin 7.50 15.00
4 Joe Crozier 10.00 20.00
5 Jacque Gagne 3.00 6.00
6 Dick Garnelle 3.00 6.00
7 Floyd Hillman 6.00 12.00
8 Jean Paul Lamonde 3.00 6.00
9 Jean-Marie Loisette 3.00 6.00
10 Brent MacNab 3.00 6.00
11 Al Millar 3.00 6.00
12 Willie O'Ree 15.00 30.00
13 Nick Tabuchie 3.00 6.00
14 Skip Teal 3.00 6.00
15 Orval Tessier 7.50 15.00
16 Judges Tremblay 5.00 10.00

1962-63 Quebec Aces

This 21-card set features the Quebec Aces of the Quebec Senior Hockey League. The cards measure approximately 3 1/2" by 5 1/2" and have black and white posed action photos with white borders. The player's name is printed in black at the bottom. The backs are blank. The cards are unnumbered and checklisted below in alphabetical order. The existence of a corrected version of the Bill Dineen card recently has been confirmed. The set is considered complete with either version.

COMPLETE SET (21) 50.00 100.00
1 Ronald Attwell 2.00 4.00
2 Serge Aubry 3.00 6.00
3 Guy Black 2.00 4.00
4 Skippy Burchell 2.00 4.00
5 Jean Marie Cossette 2.00 4.00
6 Robert Courcy 2.00 4.00
7A Bill Dineen UER 6.00 12.00
(Misspelled Dinenn
7B Bill Dineen COR 7.50 15.00
8 Terry Gray 5.00 10.00
9 Reggie Grigg 2.00 4.00
10 John Hanna 2.00 4.00
11 Michel Harvey 2.00 4.00
12 Charlie Hodge 12.50 25.00
13 Ed Hoekstra 3.00 6.00
14 Michel Labadie 2.00 4.00
15 Claude Labrosse 2.00 4.00
16 Danny Lewicki 4.00 8.00
17 Frank Martin 2.00 4.00
18 Jim Morrison 3.00 6.00
19 Guy Rousseau 2.00 4.00
20 Dollard St. Laurent 5.00 10.00
21 Bill Sutherland 3.00 6.00

1963-64 Quebec Aces

This 23-card set features the Quebec Aces of the Quebec Senior Hockey League. The cards measure approximately 3 1/2" by 5 1/2" and have black and white posed action photos with white borders. The player's name is printed in black at the bottom. The backs are blank. The cards are unnumbered and checklisted below in alphabetical order.

COMPLETE SET (23) 75.00 150.00
1 Gilles Banville 1.50 3.00
2 Don Blackburn 1.50 3.00
3 Skippy Burchell 1.50 3.00
4 Billy Carter 1.50 3.00
5 Floyd Curry CO 5.00 10.00
6 Bill Dineen 5.00 10.00
7 Wayne Freitag 1.50 3.00
8 Jean Gauthier 1.50 3.00
9 Terry Gray 2.50 5.00
10 John Hanna 1.50 3.00
11 Doug Harvey 15.00 30.00
12 Wayne Hicks 1.50 3.00
13 Charlie Hodge 7.50 15.00
14 Charlie Hodge 7.50 15.00
15 Ed Hoekstra 2.50 5.00
16 Frank Martin 1.50 3.00
17 Rene LaCasse 1.50 3.00
18 Cleland Mortson 1.50 3.00
19 Gerry O'Drowski 2.50 5.00
20 Rino Robazzo 2.50 5.00
21 Leon Rochefort 1.50 3.00
22 Cliff Pennington 2.50 5.00
23 Lorne Worsley 17.50 35.00

1964-65 Quebec Aces

This 19-card set features the Quebec Aces of the Quebec Senior Hockey League. The cards measure approximately 3 1/2" by 5 1/2". The fronts have posed black-and-white player photos with white borders. The player's name is printed in black at the bottom. The backs are blank. The cards are unnumbered and checklisted below in alphabetical order.

COMPLETE SET (19) 62.50 125.00
1 Gilles Banville 1.50 3.00
2 Red Berenson 5.00 10.00
3 Don Blackburn 1.50 3.00
4 Jean Guy Gendron 4.00 8.00
5 Bernard Geoffrion 15.00 30.00
6 Terry Gray 4.00 8.00
7 John Hanna 1.50 3.00
8 Doug Harvey 12.50 25.00
9 Wayne Hicks 1.50 3.00
10 Edward Hoekstra 2.50 5.00
11 Rene Lacasse 1.50 3.00
12 Raymond Larose 1.50 3.00
13 Jimmy Morrison 2.50 5.00
14 Cleland Mortson 1.50 3.00
15 Leon Rochefort 4.00 8.00
16 Guy Rousseau 1.50 3.00
17 Bill Sutherland 2.00 4.00
18 Brian Watson 2.00 4.00
19 Lorne Worsley 12.50 25.00

1965-66 Quebec Aces

This 19-card set measures 3 1/2" by 5 1/2". The fronts feature white-bordered posed action shots. The player's name is printed in the wider white border at the bottom. The backs are blank. The cards are unnumbered and checklisted below in alphabetical order.

COMPLETE SET (19) 37.50 75.00
1 Gilles Banville 1.50 3.00
2 Gary Bauman 1.50 3.00
3 Don Blackburn 1.50 3.00
4 Jean-Guy Gendron 2.50 5.00
5 Bernard Geoffrion CO 12.50 25.00
6 Terry Gray 2.50 5.00
7 John Hanna 1.50 3.00
8 Wayne Hicks 1.50 3.00
9 Ed Hoekstra 2.50 5.00
10 Don Johns 1.50 3.00
11 Gordon Labossiere 2.50 5.00
12 Yvon Lacoste 1.50 3.00
13 Jimmy Morrison 2.50 5.00
14 Cleland Mortson 1.50 3.00
15 Simon Nolet 4.00 8.00
16 Noel Price 2.50 5.00
17 Rino Robazzo 2.50 5.00
18 Leon Rochefort 2.50 5.00
19 Bill Sutherland 2.00 4.00

1950 Quebec Citadelles

These 20 blank-backed photos of the Quebec Citadelles measure 4" by 6" and feature cream-bordered sepia tones of the suited-up players posed on the ice. The players' facsimile autographs appear near the bottom of the pictures. The photos are unnumbered and checklisted below in alphabetical order. These photos were sent as a complete set by the team via postal envelopes. Blue-tinted variations of these cards exist. More difficult to locate, they command a premium of up to two times. This set includes the earliest known card-like element of all-time great, Jean Beliveau.

COMPLETE SET (20) 200.00 400.00
1 Neil Amadio 5.00 10.00
2 Jean Beliveau 125.00 250.00
3 Georges Bergeron CO 4.00 8.00
4 Bruce Cline 6.00 12.00
5 Norm Diviney 4.00 8.00
6 Guy Gervais 4.00 8.00
7 Bernard Guay 4.00 8.00
8 Gord Haworth 5.00 10.00
9 Camille Henry 12.50 25.00
10 Gordie Hudson 4.00 8.00
11 Claude Larochelle 6.00 12.00
12 Bernie Lemonde 4.00 8.00
13 Paul-Emile Legault 4.00 8.00
14 Copper Leyte 4.00 8.00
15 Rainer Makila 5.00 10.00
16 Marcel Paille 12.50 25.00
17 Jean-Marie Plante 4.00 8.00
18 Claude Senechal 4.00 8.00
19 Jean Tremblay 12.50 25.00
20 Alphonses Gagnon CO 4.00 8.00

1980-81 Quebec Remparts

This 22-card set measures approximately 2" by 3" and features posed color player photos. The cards were issued as part of a contest. The pictures are full-bleed except for a white bottom border that contains the team logo, player's name, and jersey number. The backs are blank. The collector who obtained the entire set and turned it in became eligible to enter a contest in which the grand prize was a trip to Disney World. The cards are unnumbered and checklisted below in alphabetical order.

COMPLETE SET (22) 10.00 20.00
1 Marc Bertrand .30 .75
2 Jacques Chouinard .30 .75
3 Roger Cote .30 .75
4 Gaston Drapeau CO .20 .50
5 Claude Drouin .30 .75
6 Gaetan Duchesne .75 2.00
7 Scott Fraser .40 1.00
8 Jean-Marc Lanthier .40 1.00
9 Jean Paul Lariviere .30 .75
10 Andre Larocque .30 .75
11 Roberto Lavoie .30 .75
12 Marc Lemay .30 .75
13 Stephane Lessard .30 .75
14 Paul Levesque .30 .75
15 Richard Linteau .30 .75
16 Patrice Masse .30 .75
17 David Pretty .30 .75
18 Guy Riel .30 .75
19 Daniel Rioux .30 .75
20 Roberto Romano .75 2.00
21 Michel Therrien .75 2.00
22 Gilles Tremblay .60 1.50

1910 Richmond College Silks S23

These colorful silks were issued around 1910 by Richmond Straight Cut Cigarettes. Each measures roughly 4" by 5 1/2" and are often called "College Flag, Seal, Song, and Yell" due to the content found on each one. More importantly to most sports collectors is the image found in the lower right hand bottom corner. A few feature a mainstream sports' subject such as a generic player or piece of equipment, while most include a realistic image of the school's mascot or image of the founder or the school's namesake.

10 Cornell HK Stick 60.00 120.00

1963-64 Rochester Americans

Printed on thin paper stock, this set of twenty photos, was issued in two series and measures approximately 4" by 6". This set features borderless black-and-white posed or action shots of the AHL (American Hockey League) Amerks. The white back carries the player's name, age, height, weight, and statistics from previous years in the minors. The cards are unnumbered and checklisted below in alphabetical order.

COMPLETE SET (20) 100.00 200.00
1 Lou Angotti 4.00 8.00
2 Al Arbour 10.00 20.00
3 Norm Armstrong 2.50 5.00
4 Ed Babiuk 2.50 5.00
5 Wally Boyer 4.00 8.00
6 Arnie Brown 4.00 8.00
7 Gerry Cheevers UER 25.00 50.00
8 Don Cherry 30.00 60.00
9 Mike Corbett 2.50 5.00
10 Joe Crozier CO 2.50 5.00
11 Jack Curran TR 2.50 5.00
12 Les Duff 2.50 5.00
13 Gerry Ehman 2.50 5.00
14 Dick Gamble 4.00 8.00
15 Larry Hillman 2.50 5.00
16 Bronco Horvath 7.50 15.00
17 Eddie Lawson 2.50 5.00
18 Jim Pappin 4.00 8.00
19 Darryl Sly 2.50 5.00
20 Stan Smrke 3.00 6.00

1971-72 Rochester Americans

Cards measure 5" x 7" and feature black and white glossy photos on the front, along with a facsimile autograph. Backs are blank. Cards are unnumbered and checklisted below alphabetically.

COMPLETE SET (18) 30.00 80.00
1 Red Armstrong 2.00 5.00
2 Guy Burrowes 2.00 5.00
3 Gaye Cooley 2.00 5.00
4 Bob Craig 2.00 5.00
5 Bob Ellett 2.00 5.00
6 Ron Fogal 2.00 5.00
7 Rod Graham 2.00 5.00
8 Dave Hrechkosy 2.50 6.00
9 Herman Karp 2.00 5.00
10 Bob Kelly 4.00 10.00
11 Larry McKillop 2.00 5.00
12 Bob Malcolm 2.00 5.00
13 Barry Merrell 2.00 5.00

14 Wayne Morusyk	2.00	5.00
15 Rick Pagnutti	2.00	5.00
16 Gerry Sillers	2.00	5.00
17 Gene Sobchuk	2.00	5.00
18 Lynn Zimmerman	2.00	5.00

1977-78 Rochester Americans

These cards feature black and white front photos with a facsimile autograph. Front also features players name, position, biographical information, and statistics. Cards are unnumbered and checklisted below in alphabetical order.

COMPLETE SET (24)	12.50	25.00
1 Team Photo	.50	1.00
2 Duane Rupp	.75	1.50
3 Nate Angelo TR	.25	.50
4 Earl Anderson	.75	1.50
5 Bill Bennett	.50	1.00
6 Daryl Drader	.50	1.00
7 Rene Drolet	.50	1.00
8 Rene Drolet	.50	1.00
9 Darryl Edestrand	.75	1.50
10 Ron Garwasiuk	.50	1.00
11 Rod Graham	.50	1.00
12 Rod Graham	.50	1.00
13 Doug Halward	.75	1.50
14 Bjorn Johansson	.50	1.00
15 Steve Langdon	.50	1.00
16 Ray Maluta	.50	1.00
17 Brian McGregor	.50	1.00
18 Clayton Pachal	.50	1.00
19 Dave Parro	.75	1.50
20 Jim Pettie	.50	1.00
21 Sean Shanahan	.50	1.00
22 Al Sims	1.00	2.00
23 Barry Smith	.75	1.50

1979-80 Rochester Americans

These cards are oversized, measuring 8-by-10.5 inches. They are blank backed and unnumbered. The set was sponsored by Wendy's.

1 Mike Boland	2.00	5.00
2 Mike Breen	2.00	5.00
3 Paul Crowley	2.00	5.00
4 Daryl Drader	2.00	5.00
5 Ron Garwasiuk	2.00	5.00
6 Chris Halyk	2.00	5.00
7 Bill Inglis CO	1.50	4.00
8 Randy Ireland	2.00	5.00
9 Joe Kowal	2.00	5.00
10 Normand Lefebvre	2.00	5.00
11 Bob Mongrain	2.00	5.00
12 Wayne Ramsey	2.00	5.00
13 Jacques Richard	3.00	8.00
14 Geordie Robertson	2.00	5.00
15 Andre Savard	3.00	10.00
16 Ron Schock	3.00	8.00
17 Dave Schultz	12.00	30.00
18 Barry Smith	2.00	5.00
19 Bill Stewart	2.00	5.00
20 Richard Suwek	2.00	5.00
21 Mark Toffolo	2.00	5.00
22 Jim Turkiewicz	2.00	5.00
23 Ed Walsh	2.00	5.00
24 Jim Walsh	2.00	5.00

1976-77 Saginaw Gears

This set features black and white player photos on slightly oversized stock. It's possible that the checklist is not complete. If you have additional information, please forward it to hockeymag@beckett.com.

COMPLETE SET (13)	17.50	35.00
1 Rick Chinnink	1.50	3.00
2 Marcel Comeau	1.50	3.00
3 Michel DeGuise	1.50	3.00
4 Marc Gaudreault	1.50	3.00
5 Greg Hotham	1.50	3.00
6 Stu Irving	1.50	3.00
7 Kevin Kemp	1.50	3.00
8 Mario Lessard	1.50	3.00
9 Gord Malinoski	1.50	3.00
10 Mike Ruest	1.50	3.00
11 D'Arcy Ryan	1.50	3.00
12 Dave Westner	1.50	3.00
13 Wayne Zuk	1.50	3.00

1978-79 Saginaw Gears

This 20-card set features black-and-white posed player photos. The team name and year appear in the top white border with the player's name printed in the bottom border. The player's position is listed on a puck at the bottom left of the photo. The backs are blank. The cards are unnumbered and checklisted below in alphabetical order. This set was the subject of a number of fierce bidding wars over the past two years, leading to a tremendous value increase in this edition.

COMPLETE SET (20)	175.00	300.00
1 Wren Blair	6.00	15.00
2 Marcel Comeau	6.00	15.00
3 Dennis Desrosiers	6.00	15.00
4 Jon Fontas	6.00	15.00
5 Bob Froese	12.50	25.00
6 Gunnar Garrett TR	4.00	10.00
7 Bob Gladney	6.00	15.00
8 Warren Holmes	6.00	15.00
9 Stu Irving	6.00	15.00
10 Larry Hopkins	6.00	15.00
11 Scott Jessee	6.00	15.00
12 Lynn Jorgenson	6.00	15.00
13 Doug Keans	12.50	25.00
14 Claude Larochelle	7.50	15.00
15 Paul McIntosh	6.00	15.00
16 Don Perry	6.00	15.00
17 Greg Steel	6.00	15.00
18 Mark Suzor	6.00	15.00
19 Mark Toffolo	6.00	15.00
20 Dave Westner	6.00	15.00

1980-81 Sault Ste. Marie Greyhounds

Sponsored by Blue Bird Bakery Limited and Coke, this 25-card set captures the 1980-81 Soo Greyhounds of the OHL. The cards measure approximately 2 1/2" by 4" and feature posed, color player photos. Of interest to collectors are the first cards of current NHL stars John Vanbiesbrouck and Ron Francis.

COMPLETE SET (25)	37.50	75.00
1 Ken Porteous	.30	.75
2 Brian Petterle	.30	.75
3 Gord Dineen	.40	1.00
4 Tony Cella	.30	.75
5 Doug Shedden	.60	1.50
6 Terry Tait	.30	.75
7 Greyhounds Logo	.20	.50
8 Steve Smith	.30	.75
9 Huey Larkin	.30	.75
10 Steve Gatzos	.30	.75
11 Tim Zwijack	.30	.75
12 Vic Morin	.30	.75
13 John Vanbiesbrouck	12.50	25.00
14 Ron Francis	12.50	25.00
15 Tony Butorac	.30	.75
16 John Goodwin	.30	.75
17 Ron Handy	.30	.75
18 Jim Pavese	.40	1.00
19 Sault Ste. Marie Police Logo	.20	.50
20 Rick Morocco	.30	.75
21 Ken Latta	.30	.75
22 Kirk Rueter	.30	.75
23 OMJHL Logo	.20	.50
24 Terry Crisp	1.00	2.50
25 Marc D'Amour	.75	2.00

1969-70 Seattle Totems

This set features the Totems of the old WHL. A White Front Stores exclusive at stores in Aurora, Tacoma, Burien, and Bellevue, this set of 20 team photos measures approximately 8" by 10". Printed on thin paper, the front features a posed color player photo with a studio background. The pictures have white borders, and the player's signature is inscribed in the lower right corner. In black print on white, the backs present biography and statistics from the past season.

COMPLETE SET (20)	60.00	150.00
1 Don Head	8.00	20.00
2 Chuck Holmes	3.00	8.00
3 Bob Courcy	3.00	8.00
4 Marc Boileau	3.00	8.00
5 Gerry Leonard	3.00	8.00
6 Art Stratton	3.00	8.00
7 Gary Kilpatrick	3.00	8.00
8 Don Ward	3.00	8.00
9 Jack Michie	3.00	8.00
10 Ronald Ingram	3.00	8.00
11 John Hanna	3.00	8.00
12 Ray Larose	3.00	8.00
13 Jack Dale	3.00	8.00
14 Tom McVie	3.00	8.00
15 Gerry Meehan	6.00	15.00
16 Chris Worthy	3.00	8.00
17 Bobby Schmautz	8.00	20.00
18 Dwight Carruthers	3.00	8.00
19 Patrick Dunn TR	.75	2.00
20 Bill MacFarland CO	.75	2.00

1974-75 Sioux City Musketeers

This 20-card set is printed on yellow stock. According to the producer, the cards were intended to be standard size but actually came out a little larger. The fronts feature bordered, posed player photos that have a dark green tint to them. In dark green lettering, the team name is printed above the picture while the player's name is printed below it. The cards are unnumbered and checklisted below in alphabetical order. Reportedly only 250 sets were made and they were originally sold at home games for $2.50.

COMPLETE SET (20)	50.00	100.00
1 Steve Boyle	2.50	5.00
2 Dave Davies	2.50	5.00
3 Steve Desloges	2.50	5.00
4 Greg Gilbert	2.50	5.00
5 Barry Head	2.50	5.00
6 Steve Heathwood	2.50	5.00
7 Dave Kartio	2.50	5.00
8 Ralph Kloiber	2.50	5.00
9 Pete Maxwell	2.50	5.00
10 Randy McDonald	2.50	5.00
11 Terry Mulroy	2.50	5.00
12 Sam Nelligan	2.50	5.00
13 Julian Nixon	2.50	5.00
14 Mike Noel	2.50	5.00
15 Jim Peck	2.50	5.00
16 Bogdan Podwysocki	2.50	5.00
17 John Saville P/CO	2.50	5.00
18 Alex Shibicky Jr.	5.00	10.00
19 Bob Thomerson	2.50	5.00
20 Jim White	5.00	10.00

1957-58 St. Catharines Tee Pees Murray's Chips

This set features the Tee Pees of the old OHA. The set features players who were in the Chicago Blackhawks farm system. The set is also known as the Murray's Potato Chips set, due to that name appearing on top of these undersized, black and white issues. The cards apparently were distributed in conjunction with the purchase of a bag of chips. The checklist is known to be incomplete, so no set price is listed. While the cards are numbered, we have yet to be able to confirm the numbering for all of the card so we have listed them alphabetically below with the card's number listed after the player's name.

1 Bob Corupe 18	25.00	50.00
2 Don Cosburn	25.00	50.00
3 Roy Edwards 1	40.00	80.00
4 Don Grosso 17	25.00	50.00
5 Ed Hoekstra	30.00	60.00
6 Chico Maki 16	40.00	80.00
7 John McKenzie	50.00	100.00
8 Stan Mikita	200.00	400.00
9 Matt Ravlich	30.00	60.00

1952-53 St. Lawrence Sales

This 108-card black and white set put out by St. Lawrence Sales Agency featured members of the QSHL. The card backs are written in French. The cards measure approximately 1 15/16" by 2 15/16" and are numbered on the back. The key cards in the set are those of future (at that time) NHL greats Jean Beliveau and Jacques Plante. The complete set price includes both versions of card number 17.

COMPLETE SET (108)	700.00	1,400.00
1 Jacques Plante	175.00	350.00
2 Glen Harmon	5.00	10.00
3 Jimmy Moore	5.00	10.00
4 Gerard Desaulniers	5.00	10.00
5 Les Douglas	5.00	10.00
6 Fred Burchell	6.00	12.00
7 Ed Litzenberger	7.50	15.00
8 Rollie Rousseau	5.00	10.00
9 Roger Leger	5.00	10.00
10 Phil Samis	5.00	10.00
11 Paul Masnick	6.00	12.00
12 Walter Clune	5.00	10.00
13 Louis Denis	5.00	10.00
14 Gerry Plamondon	6.00	12.00
15 Cliff Malone	5.00	10.00
16 Pete Morin	6.00	12.00
17A Jack Schmidt	6.00	12.00
17B Aldo Guidolin	10.00	20.00
18 Paul Leclerc	5.00	10.00
19 Larry Kwong	6.00	12.00
20 Rosario Joanette	5.00	10.00
21 Tom Smelle	5.00	10.00
22 Gordie Haworth	6.00	12.00
23 Bruce Cline	6.00	12.00
24 Andre Corriveau	5.00	10.00
25 Jacques Deslauriers	5.00	10.00
26 Bingo Ernst	5.00	10.00
27 Jacques Chartrand	5.00	10.00
28 Phil Vitale	5.00	10.00
29 Renald Lacroix	5.00	10.00
30 J.P. Bisaillon	5.00	10.00
31 Jack Irvine	5.00	10.00
32 Georges Bougie	5.00	10.00
33 Paul Larivee	5.00	10.00
34 Carl Smelle	5.00	10.00
35 Walter Pawlyschyn	5.00	10.00
36 Jean Marois	5.00	10.00
37 Jack Gelineau	5.00	10.00
38 Danny Nixon	5.00	10.00
39 Jean Beliveau	200.00	400.00
40 Phil Renaud	5.00	10.00
41 Leon Bouchard	5.00	10.00
42 Dennis Smith	5.00	10.00
43 Joe Crozier	7.50	15.00
44 Al Bacari	5.00	10.00
45 Murdo MacKay	6.00	12.00
46 Gordie Hudson	5.00	10.00
47 Claude Robert	5.00	10.00
48 Yogi Kraiger	6.00	12.00
49 Ludger Tremblay	6.00	12.00
50 Pierre Brillant	5.00	10.00
51 Frank Mario	5.00	10.00
52 Copper Leyth	5.00	10.00
53 Herbie Carnegie	20.00	50.00
54 Punch Imlach	20.00	40.00
55 Howard Riopelle	5.00	10.00
56 Ken Laufman	5.00	10.00
57 Jackie Leclair	7.50	15.00
58 Bill Robinson	5.00	10.00
59 George Ford	5.00	10.00
60 Bill Johnson	5.00	10.00
61 Leo Gravelle	5.00	10.00
62 Jack Giesebrecht	5.00	10.00
63 John Arundel	5.00	10.00
64 Vic Gregg	5.00	10.00
65 Bep Guidolin	7.50	15.00
66 Al Kuntz	5.00	10.00
67 Emile Dagenais	5.00	10.00
68 Bill Richardson	5.00	10.00
69 Bob Robertson	5.00	10.00
70 Ray Fredericks	5.00	10.00
71 James O'Flaherty	5.00	10.00
72 Butch Stahan	5.00	10.00
73 Roger Roberge	5.00	10.00
74 Guy Labrie	5.00	10.00
75 Gilles Dube	5.00	10.00
76 Pete Wywrot	5.00	10.00
77 Tod Campeau	6.00	12.00
78 Roger Bessette	5.00	10.00
79 Martial Pruneau	5.00	10.00
80 Nils Tremblay	5.00	10.00
81 Jacques Locas	5.00	10.00
82 Rene Pepin	5.00	10.00
83 Bob Pepin	5.00	10.00
84 Tom McDougall	5.00	10.00
85 Peter Wright	5.00	10.00
86 Ronnie Matthews	5.00	10.00
87 Irene St-Hilaire	5.00	10.00
88 Dewar Thompson	5.00	10.00
89 Bob Dainville	5.00	10.00
90 Marcel Pelletier	5.00	10.00
91 Delphis Franche	5.00	10.00
92 Georges Roy	5.00	10.00
93 Andy McCallum	5.00	10.00
94 Lou Smrke	5.00	10.00
95 J.P. Lamirande	5.00	10.00
96 Normand Dussault	5.00	10.00
97 Stan Smrke	6.00	12.00
98 Jack Bownass	5.00	10.00
99 Billy Arcand	5.00	10.00
100 Lyall Wiseman	5.00	10.00
101 Jack Hamilton	5.00	10.00
102 Bob Leger	5.00	10.00
103 Larry Regan	6.00	12.00
104 Erwin Grosse	5.00	10.00
105 Roger Bedard	5.00	10.00
106 Ted Hodgson	5.00	10.00
107 Dave Gatherum	7.50	15.00

1962-63 Sudbury Wolves

These 22 blank-backed cards measure approximately 4" by 6" and feature white-bordered, posed black-and-white studio head shots of Wolves players (Eastern Professional Hockey League). The player's name and position appear above the team name within the broad white bottom border. The imprint, "Crown Life Hockey School," rounds out the card at the bottom. The cards are unnumbered and checklisted below in alphabetical order.

COMPLETE SET (22)	40.00	100.00
1 Paul Andrea	2.50	5.00
2 Norm Armstrong	1.50	3.00
3 Ed Babiuk	2.00	5.00
4 Hub Beaudry ANN	.75	1.50
5 Vern Buffey REF	1.50	3.00
6 Murph Chamberlain CO	1.50	3.00
7 Gerry Cheevers UER	20.00	50.00
8 Wally Chevrier	1.50	3.00
9 Marc Dufour	2.00	4.00
10 Edgar Ehrenverth	1.50	3.00
11 Bill Friday REF	2.50	5.00
12 Jim Johnson	1.50	3.00
13 Chico Kozurok TR	.75	1.50
14 Gord Labossiere	2.00	4.00
15 Dunc McCallum	4.00	8.00
16 Dave McComb	1.50	3.00
17 Hugh McLean REF	1.50	3.00
18 Mike McMahon	1.50	3.00
19 Dave Richardson	1.50	3.00
20 Joe Spence ANN	.75	1.50
21 Ted Taylor	1.50	3.00
22 Bob Woytowich	4.00	8.00

1966-67 Tulsa Oilers

Little is known about this set featuring the Oilers of the old CHL beyond the confirmed checklist. The cards were oversized black and white images and likely were issued in photo-pack form. Any additional information can be forwarded to hockeymag@beckett.com.

COMPLETE SET (12)	25.00	50.00
1 Ken Campbell	1.50	3.00
2 Andrew Champagne	1.50	3.00
3 Doug Dunville	1.50	3.00
4 Bill Flett	5.00	10.00
5 Nick Harbaruk	1.50	3.00
6 Lowell MacDonald	5.00	10.00
7 Jim McKenny	2.50	5.00
8 Al Millar	1.50	3.00
9 Marc Reaume	2.00	4.00
10 Harry Shaw	1.50	3.00
11 Gary Venneruzzo	2.50	5.00
12 Ron Ward	2.00	4.00

1973-74 Vancouver Blazers

This set features the Blazers of the WHA. The cards are actually oversized black and white photos and were issued as a promotional item by the team. The Archambault and Cardiff cards were recently confirmed by collector M.R. LaFleche. No pricing information is available for these singles at this time.

COMPLETE SET (21)	25.00	50.00
1 Jim Adair	1.50	3.00
2 Yves Archambault	1.50	3.00
3 Don Burgess	2.00	4.00
4 Bryan Campbell	2.00	4.00
5 Colin Campbell	2.50	6.00
6 Jim Cardiff	1.50	3.00
7 Mike Chernoff	1.50	3.00
8 Peter Donnelly	1.50	3.00
9 George Gardner	1.50	3.00
10 Sam Gellard	1.50	3.00
11 Ed Hatoum	1.50	3.00
12 Dave Hutchison	2.00	4.00
13 Danny Lawton	1.50	3.00
14 Ralph MacSweyn	1.50	3.00
15 Denis Meloche	1.50	3.00
16 John Migneault	1.50	3.00
17 Murray Myers	1.50	3.00
18 Michel Plante	1.50	3.00
19 Ron Plumb	2.00	4.00
20 Claude St. Sauveur	1.50	3.00
21 Irv Spencer	2.00	4.00